CASSELL'S FRENCH DICTIONARY

Cassell's

French – English
English – French

Dictionary

Dictionnaire

Français – Anglais
Anglais – Français

Completely revised by

DENIS GIRARD
Agrégé de l'Université

With the assistance of

GASTON DULONG, L. ès L.
Professeur Agrégé, Faculté des Lettres, Université Laval, Quebec

OLIVER VAN OSS, M.A. (Oxon.)
Formerly Headmaster of Charterhouse School
Late Lower Master, Eton College

CHARLES GUINNESS, B.A. (Oxon.)
Assistant Master, Eton College

MACMILLAN PUBLISHING COMPANY
New York

Macmillan Publishing Company
866 Third Avenue, New York, N.Y. 10022.

Library of Congress Cataloging in Publication Data
Main entry under title:
Cassell's French dictionary.
Editions for 1920-1960 published under title:
Cassell's French-English, English-French dictionary.
Reprint of the ed. published by Funk & Wagnalls, New York.
Bibliography: p.
1. French language—Dictionaries—English.
2. English language—Dictionaries—French.
I. Girard, Denis.   II. Title: Cassell's French dictionary.
PC2640.C3   1977   443′.21   77-7669
I.S.B.N. 0-02-522610-x (standard) 13th Printing
I.S.B.N. 0-02-522620-7 (thumb-indexed) 13th Printing

Macmillan books are available at special discounts
for bulk purchases for sales promotions, premiums,
fund-raising, or educational use. Special editions
or book excerpts can also be created to specification.
For details, contact:

Special Sales Director
Macmillan Publishing Company
866 Third Avenue
New York, New York 10022

Printed in the United States of America

CONTENTS

PAGE

BIBLIOGRAPHY   vi

PREFACE   vii

PRÉFACE SUR LES CANADIANISMES   ix

ADVICE TO THE USER   x

AVIS AU LECTEUR   xi

KEY TO PRONUNCIATION   xiv

LIST OF ABBREVIATIONS   xvi

PART I: FRENCH-ENGLISH DICTIONARY   1

PART II: ENGLISH-FRENCH DICTIONARY   1

CONVERSION TABLES FOR WEIGHTS AND MEASURES   636

FRENCH IRREGULAR VERBS   638

ENGLISH IRREGULAR VERBS   649

COMMON FRENCH ABBREVIATIONS   652

COMMON ENGLISH ABBREVIATIONS   654

BIBLIOGRAPHY

ENGLISH DICTIONARIES

Shorter Oxford English Dictionary. Oxford, Clarendon Press, 3rd edition 1956.
New International Dictionary of the English Language (N. Webster). London, Bell, 1934.
Chambers's Encyclopaedia. London, G. Newnes Ltd., 1955 (15 vols.).
Encyclopaedia Britannica. London, Encyclopaedia Britannica Co., 1958 (24 vols.).
Cassell's New English Dictionary. London, Cassell & Co. Ltd., 1956.

FRENCH DICTIONARIES

Nouveau Larousse Universel. Paris, Larousse, 1948-9 (2 vols.).
Petit Larousse. Paris, Larousse, 1960.
Dictionnaire Usuel Quillet-Flammarion. Paris, Quillet-Flammarion, 1956.
Dictionnaire de l'Académie Française. Paris, Hachette, 8th edition 1932–5 (2 vols.).
Dictionnaire de la Langue Française (Robert). Paris, Presses Universitaires de France, 1953.

BILINGUAL DICTIONARIES

Harrap's Standard French and English Dictionary. London, Harrap, 1939.
Supplement to Harrap's Standard French and English Dictionary. London, Harrap, 1950.
Aviation, English-French—Français-Anglais (Fontanet). Paris, Didier, 1945.
Vocabulaire Français-Anglais et Anglais-Français de Termes et Locutions Juridiques (J. Jéraute). Paris, Librairie Générale de Droit et de Jurisprudence, 1953.
Vocabulaire du Cinéma. London, Western European Union, 1958.
French-English Science Dictionary (L. de Vries). London, McGraw-Hill, 1951.

PHONETICS

An English Pronouncing Dictionary (Daniel Jones). London, Dent, 11th edition 1957.

PREFACE

CASSELL'S FRENCH DICTIONARY goes back to the 1880's but major revisions were made in 1905, 1910, 1920 and 1951 to keep it up to date. The 1920 edition was basically the work of Dr. E. A. Baker, who did a great deal to take the dust off the old dictionary and modernize it. The present reviser is deeply indebted to him and has benefited greatly from the results of his labours.

Yet dictionaries date very quickly, and perhaps even more so bilingual ones, so that, although it was revised again in 1951 by Prof. Manchon, the publishers felt that the time had come for a complete revision of the present work. The purpose was, on the one hand, to insert new terms which had come to life over the years in both languages, following the tremendous technical and scientific development of our times (for instance, under *air*, no less than sixteen new compound words have been entered in the English-French section), or political, geographical or other changes and, on the other hand, to cut out the dead wood that inevitably amasses in a dictionary as it grows old.

This looked like a rather limited ambition, but when one undertakes a work of this kind one soon finds out that it is a far greater task than one had supposed. The 'dead wood' was exemplified not only by archaic words of interest to philologists alone; it was also, and even principally, to be found among the examples given, which all too often referred to a pre-motorcar era when most vehicles were horse-drawn (the number of phrases referring to horses and stage-coaches was incredible, although the word 'horse-drawn' did not appear!) Of course, care had to be taken in the work of deletion: obsolete words have been kept when they were considered useful for understanding the works of important writers of the seventeenth and eighteenth centuries.

In the same way it was not only new words that needed to be inserted (an average of half a dozen per page) but a larger number of phrases showing the different uses of the same word. These examples were already one of the great qualities of CASSELL'S FRENCH DICTIONARY, but I have tried to make them more comprehensive (the average number of new examples is seven per page throughout the dictionary).

A special effort had also to be made to give more clarity to the dictionary, and this was far from easy as one could not undertake, and did not wish, to alter the general pattern.

Finally, one took advantage of this new edition to correct the mistakes or misprints that inevitably crop up in a work of this kind. The new dictionary will probably not be entirely free of such blemishes but the reviser hopes that they have been reduced to a minimum.

These therefore have been the four aims of the reviser: inserting new words and examples, cutting out obsolete items, except those held indispensable to the ordinary reader, rectifying errors and making the dictionary clearer. To what extent these aims have been realized it is for the user to judge.

Any work of this kind implies a certain amount of personal choice as one cannot include everything. A dictionary of this size cannot aim at giving the experts in various fields—art, commerce, law, the different sciences—all the technical terms they may need in both languages. Yet it must give adequate help to the reader of a general book or article on these subjects as well as to the reader of a major literary work of the last three centuries. In making his choice the reviser has also had in mind the user who is concerned not only with reading texts in, but also wants to speak, the other language. That is why a great number of familiar, colloquial and even slang words and phrases have been inserted. American English has not been forgotten in the English-French section, although there again one could not hope to give a complete list of these special words. French-Canadian terms have been added in both sections, thanks to the valuable collaboration of Prof. Dulong.

Such a vast enterprise could hardly be carried out by a single person and I wish to thank most sincerely all those, English and French, who have helped me in one way or another through certain sections of the dictionary: Mr. A. J. Brewster, Mr. J. H. Douglas, Mr. S. John, Madame Le Gal-Taylor, M. H. Thomas and Mrs. B. C. Tupling. The help I have received from Mr. Van Oss and Mr. Guinness is quite invaluable. This new edition owes a great deal to these two experts, who have given me the benefit of their great experience as linguists and teachers of French.

I should be very ungrateful if I did not also record my debt towards the publishers and more particularly towards Dr. S. H. Steinberg, who has patiently and wisely advised me throughout these long years of arduous work.

D. G.

PRÉFACE SUR LES CANADIANISMES

La responsabilité de fournir des canadianismes à la nouvelle édition du Cassell's comportait certaines difficultés.

S'agissait-il d'incorporer des milliers de mots ou d'expressions dialectales ou patoises qu'une enquête permet de relever dans le milieu canadien-français? Non, car ces mots et ces expressions n'ont leur place que dans les glossaires.

S'agissait-il d'incorporer les anglicismes plus ou moins nombreux qui corrompent le français canadien, surtout dans certaines classes de la société, anglicismes que les enseignants s'efforcent de faire disparaître? Non, c'eût été faire trop d'honneur à des éléments sentis et considérés comme des fautes ou des barbarismes.

Seuls ont été retenus les mots (substantifs, adjectifs ou verbes) que j'appellerai canadianismes de vocabulaire. Ce sont des mots concernant des réalités proprement canadiennes, pour lesquels le français commun, né sous un autre climat et d'autres latitudes, n'a pas d'équivalent. Ces canadianismes ont trait surtout à l'hiver, à la faune, à la flore, aux modes de vie, aux habitudes. Autant de domaines pour lesquels les francophones du Canada ont dû créer ou adapter. Encore fallait-il que ces mots fussent d'un usage assez fréquent pour mériter de figurer dans un dictionnaire du genre du Cassell's.

J'ose croire que cette modeste tentative sera de quelque utilité à l'usager canadien du Cassell's.

G. D.

ADVICE TO THE USER

Grouping of Words

In both sections of the dictionary alphabetical order has been adhered to as far as possible. However, in the English-French portion especially, it has often been found more convenient and logical to group compound and derivative words immediately after the key-word; this is particularly true when the key-word gives rise to a large number of hyphenated compounds. The user should, however, have no difficulty in finding the word he requires.

Numbering of Identical Words

Words which are spelt alike but which differ in origin or pronunciation are numbered separately for the sake of clarity.

Punctuation

When several translations are given for one word it can generally be assumed that those which are separated by commas will have much the same meaning; semi-colons are used where there is a clear difference in meaning or usage.

Words or translations marked with an asterisk (*) are obsolete.

Pronunciation

The phonetic transcription is given in square brackets immediately after the key-word and alternative pronunciations have been given where necessary. The mark ′ precedes the syllable which carries the stress. It has not always been thought necessary to indicate the pronunciation of compound or derivative words; if, however, it cannot easily be deduced from that of the key-word, it is given in full or in part.

The symbols of the International Phonetic Association have been used throughout the dictionary, and the reader who is unfamiliar with these should refer to the Key to Pronunciation.

Daniel Jones' *English Pronouncing Dictionary* has usually been followed in the English-French section.

Examples, Phrases, etc.

Examples are generally listed in the alphabetical order of the first letter of the whole phrase and not of the main word. In longer articles they may be grouped according to the various meanings of the key-word as given at the beginning of the entry, following the order of these meanings.

Accents

For the benefit of the English user, accents on capital letters have been retained. It should be remembered that, with the exception of É, which is fairly common, they are not usually written or printed in French.

AVIS AU LECTEUR

Ordre des mots

Dans les deux parties du dictionnaire on s'est attaché à suivre le plus possible l'ordre alphabétique. Cependant, dans la section anglais-français, en particulier, on a souvent jugé plus pratique et plus logique de grouper les composés et les dérivés dans un même paragraphe, à la suite du mot principal; il en est ainsi toutes les fois que ce mot est à l'origine d'un grand nombre de composés avec trait d'union. Le lecteur ne doit pourtant avoir aucune difficulté à trouver le mot qu'il cherche.

Mots identiques

Les mots qui ont la même orthographe, mais une racine ou une prononciation différente, sont numérotés séparément, par souci de clarté.

Ponctuation

Quand plusieurs traductions sont données pour un même mot, celles qui ne sont séparées que par des virgules ont, en règle générale, des sens à peu près identiques; le point-virgule est utilisé pour indiquer des différences très nettes de sens ou d'emploi.

Les mots ou les traductions précédés d'un astérisque (*) sont désuets.

Prononciation

La transcription phonétique est donnée, entre crochets, immédiatement après le mot principal. Lorsqu'il y a d'autres prononciations admises pour un même mot, elles sont également indiquées. L'accent (') précède la syllabe qui porte l'accent tonique. On n'a pas jugé nécessaire, en principe, de donner la prononciation des composés ou des dérivés. Elle est indiquée cependant, intégralement ou partiellement, quand elle ne peut être facilement déduite de la prononciation du mot principal.

Les signes de l'Association Internationale de Phonétique sont utilisés dans les deux parties du dictionnaire et le lecteur qui n'est pas familiarisé avec ces signes devra se reporter à la Table de Prononciation.

Pour la section anglais-français, on a suivi le dictionnaire de M. Daniel Jones, *An English Pronouncing Dictionary*.

Exemples d'emploi, expressions, etc.

Les exemples sont en principe groupés dans l'ordre alphabétique de la première lettre de toute l'expression et non du mot principal. Dans les articles particulièrement longs, ils peuvent se trouver rassemblés autour des différents sens du mot principal et suivant l'ordre des différentes traductions indiquées en tête de paragraphe.

Accents

Pour aider le lecteur de langue anglaise, on a conservé les accents sur les lettres majuscules. Il faut noter qu'à part l'É, dont l'usage est assez fréquent, ils sont généralement omis dans les textes français imprimés ou manuscrits.

xi

Proper Names

These will now be found in their alphabetical places in the main body of the dictionary. The old table has been suppressed.

Grammatical Information

It is assumed that the user will have a reasonable knowledge of the basic grammar of the two languages. For example, when a French noun merely adds -s for its plural it has not been thought necessary to indicate this. The following remarks should, however, be of assistance:

(1) *Parts of Speech.* These are indicated by an abbreviation in italics (*adv.*, *v.t.*, *a.*, etc.). The List of Abbreviations will give the meanings of these. It has not been felt necessary to indicate the nature of proper names.

(2) *Genders.* In the French-English section most French nouns are classed as *n.m.* for the masculine or *n.f.* for the feminine gender; *n.* denotes a noun that may be masculine or feminine according to context. In the English-French section the gender of French nouns is shown by the abbreviations *m.* and *f.* In a list of nouns the gender is not given after each one, and the user should therefore refer forward to the next gender mentioned. For example, under **inquiry** he will find: 'Demande, investigation, recherche, *f.*' and he will know from this that all these three nouns are feminine.

(3) *Plurals and Feminines.* The plurals and feminines of certain nouns and adjectives are given in brackets in abbreviated form. For example the entry **cheval** (*pl.* -aux) means that the full plural word is **chevaux**. Similarly, **admirateur** (*fem.* -trice) indicates that the feminine form is **admiratrice**.

(4) *Irregular Verbs.* The abbreviation *irr.* after a French verb refers the user to the List of Irregular Verbs.

The past tense and past participle of English irregular verbs are added in brackets. If the user is in doubt, he should refer to the List of English Irregular Verbs.

Tables and Keys

(1) *Key to Pronunciation.* The symbols of the International Phonetic Association have been used; ɹ has been discarded and oə replaced by ɔ: in conformity with modern usage. The key has been made clearer by listing separately all the symbols used in each language, in the order generally adopted by phoneticians.

(2) *Irregular Verbs.* French irregular verbs are given in one alphabetical list, as this is simpler for the user. A list of English irregular verbs has been added for the first time.

(3) *The List of Abbreviations* has been enlarged by the addition of abbreviations such as *Av.*, *Cine.*, *Tel.* and simplified.

(4) *The Tables of French and English Weights and Measures* have been simplified, completed and made clearer. French Canadian measures are included for the first time.

(5) *Common French and English Abbreviations.* A useful innovation is the list of equivalents of common French and English abbreviations.

Noms propres

Ils ont été incorporés dans le dictionnaire à leur place alphabétique normale. L'ancienne table des noms propres a été supprimée.

Indications grammaticales

Le lecteur est considéré comme ayant une connaissance suffisante de la grammaire de base des deux langues. Par exemple, quand un nom français forme son pluriel en « s », il n'a pas paru nécessaire de l'indiquer. Les remarques suivantes pourront cependant s'avérer utiles:

(1) *Nature des mots*. La nature du mot est indiquée par une abréviation en italiques (*adv., v.t., a.* etc.). La *liste des abréviations* en donne la signification. Il n'a pas paru utile d'indiquer la nature des noms propres.

(2) *Genre*. Dans la section français-anglais la plupart des noms français sont classés comme masculins (abréviation *n.m.*) ou féminins (abréviation *n.f.*); l'abréviation *n.* désigne ceux qui demandent soit le masculin soit le féminin selon le contexte. De même, dans la section anglais-français le genre des noms français est représenté par l'abréviation *m.* ou *f.* Quand plusieurs noms se suivent, le genre n'est pas indiqué après chacun d'eux: le lecteur doit se reporter à la première abréviation qui suit et considérer que tous les noms précédents ont le même genre. Par exemple, au mot **inquiry** il trouvera: « Demande, investigation, recherche, *f.* » et en déduira que ces trois noms sont féminins.

(3) *Pluriel et féminin*. Le pluriel ou le féminin de certains noms et adjectifs est donné entre parenthèses, en abrégé. Par exemple, **cheval** (*pl.* -**aux**) signifie que le pluriel est **chevaux**. De même, **admirateur** (*fem.* -**trice**) indique que la forme du féminin est **admiratrice**.

(4) *Verbes irréguliers*. L'abréviation *irr.* après un verbe français renvoie le lecteur à la *liste des verbes irréguliers*.

Le prétérit et le participe passé des verbes irréguliers anglais sont donnés entre parenthèses. Si le lecteur a des doutes, il peut consulter la *liste des verbes irréguliers anglais*.

Tables

(1) *Table de prononciation*. On a utilisé les signes de l'Association Internationale de Phonétique. Le signe ɹ a été supprimé et le signe oə remplacé par ɔ: selon l'usage courant. Pour plus de clarté, la table donne la liste de tous les symboles utilisés dans l'une et l'autre langue, suivant la classification phonétique généralement admise.

(2) *Verbes irréguliers*. Les verbes irréguliers français sont rassemblés dans une seule liste, pour faciliter les recherches. Une liste de verbes irréguliers anglais est également donnée pour la première fois.

(3) *La liste des abréviations* a été complétée par l'addition d'abréviations comme: *Av., Cine., Tel.* et simplifiée.

(4) *Les tables des mesures françaises et anglaises* ont été simplifiées, complétées et rendues plus claires. Des mesures du Canada français ont été ajoutées.

(5) *Abréviations courantes françaises et anglaises*. Cette liste est donnée pour la première fois et l'abréviation équivalente en français ou en anglais est souvent donnée entre parenthèses.

KEY TO PRONUNCIATION

(See also Advice to User, p. xii)

VOWELS

FRENCH (1)

i   as in cri [kri], difficile [difi'sil]
i: ,,   ,,   dire [di:r], finir [fi'ni:r]
e   ,,   ,,   thé [te], mélodie [melɔ'di]
e: ,,   ,,   zée [ze:]
ɛ   ,,   ,,   réel [re'ɛl], gel [ʒɛl]
ɛ: ,,   ,,   bête [bɛ:t], dentaire [dɑ̃'tɛ:r]
a   ,,   ,,   patte [pat], apparat [apa'ra]
a: ,,   ,,   tard [ta:r], barbare [bar'ba:r]
ɑ   ,,   ,,   passé [pɑ'se], tailler [tɑ'je]
ɑ: ,,   ,,   gaz [gɑ:z], pâte [pɑ:t]
ɔ   ,,   ,,   coter [kɔ'te], voler [vɔ'le]
ɔ: ,,   ,,   fort [fɔ:r], porc [pɔ:r]
o   ,,   ,,   côté [ko'te], gros [gro], tôt [to]
o: ,,   ,,   dôme [do:m], rôle [ro:l]
u   ,,   ,,   tout [tu], tourner [tur'ne]
u: ,,   ,,   bourre [bu:r], tous [tu:s]
y   ,,   ,,   rue [ry], salut [sa'ly]
y: ,,   ,,   littérature [litera'ty:r]
ø   ,,   ,,   neveu [nə'vø], rocheux [rɔ'ʃø]
ø: ,,   ,,   ouvreuse [u'vrø:z]
œ   ,,   ,,   feuilleton [fœj'tɔ̃]
œ: ,,   ,,   faveur [fa'vœ:r]
ə   ,,   ,,   premier [prə'mje]

ENGLISH (1)

i: as in seat [si:t]
i   ,,   ,,   finish ['finiʃ], physic ['fizik]
e   ,,   ,,   neck [nek], stead [sted]
æ   ,,   ,,   man [mæn], malefactor ['mælifæktə]
ɑ: ,,   ,,   father ['fɑ:ðə], task [tɑ:sk]
ɔ   ,,   ,,   block [blɔk], waddle [wɔdl]
ɔ: ,,   ,,   shawl [ʃɔ:l], tortoise ['tɔ:təs]
o   ,,   ,,   domain [do'mein]
u   ,,   ,,   good [gud], July [dʒu'lai]
u: ,,   ,,   moon [mu:n], tooth [tu:θ]
ʌ   ,,   ,,   cut [kʌt], somewhere ['sʌmwɛə]
ə: ,,   ,,   search [sə:tʃ], surgeon ['sə:dʒən]
ə   ,,   ,,   cathedral [kə'θi:drəl], never ['nevə]

NASAL VOWELS

ɛ̃   as in faim [fɛ̃], vingt [vɛ̃]
ɛ̃:   ,,   ,,   feindre [fɛ̃:dr], poindre [pwɛ̃:dr]
ɑ̃   ,,   ,,   ensemencement [ɑ̃səmɑ̃s'mɑ̃]
ɑ̃:   ,,   ,,   défendre [de'fɑ̃:dr]
ɔ̃   ,,   ,,   bonbon [bɔ̃'bɔ̃]
ɔ̃:   ,,   ,,   contre [kɔ̃:tr], trompe [trɔ̃:p]
œ̃   ,,   ,,   défunt [de'fœ̃], un [œ̃]
œ̃:   ,,   ,,   humble [œ̃:bl]

DIPHTHONGS

ei   as in great [greit]
ou   ,,   ,,   show [ʃou]
ai   ,,   ,,   high [hai]
au   ,,   ,,   crowd [kraud]
ɔi   ,,   ,,   boy [bɔi]
iə   ,,   ,,   steer [stiə]
ɛə   ,,   ,,   hair [hɛə]
uə   ,,   ,,   moor [muə]

CONSONANTS

FRENCH (1)	ENGLISH (1)
p as in pain [pɛ̃], papier [pa'pje]	p as in paper ['peipə]
b „ „ bonbon [bɔ̃'bɔ̃]	b „ „ ball [bɔːl]
t „ „ tâter [tɑ'te], thé [te]	t „ „ tea [tiː], train [trein]
d „ „ dinde [dɛ̃ːd]	d „ „ deed [diːd]
k „ „ coquelicot [kokli'ko]	k „ „ cake [keik]
g „ „ dégager [dega'ʒe]	g „ „ game [geim]
m „ „ maman [ma'mɑ̃], même [mɛːm]	m „ „ mammoth ['mæməθ]
n „ „ nonne [nɔn]	n „ „ nose [nouz], nanny ['næni]
	ŋ „ „ bring [briŋ], finger ['fiŋgə]
ɲ „ „ agneau [a'ɲo], soigner [swa'ɲe]	
f „ „ fanfare [fɑ̃'faːr]	f „ „ fair [fɛə], far [fɑː]
v „ „ vivre [viːvr]	v „ „ vine [vain]
	θ „ „ thin [θin], bath [bɑːθ]
	ð „ „ thine [ðain], bathe [beið]
s „ „ sucre [sykr]	s „ „ since [sins]
z „ „ raser [rɑ'ze]	z „ „ busy ['bizi]
l „ „ lit [li], valise [va'liːz]	l „ „ land [lænd], hill [hil] (2)
ʃ „ „ charme [ʃarm]	ʃ „ „ shield [ʃiːld], sugar ['ʃuge]
ʒ „ „ engager [ɑ̃ga'ʒe]	ʒ „ „ vision ['viʒən]
r „ „ arrière [a'rjɛːr]	r „ „ rat [ræt], train [trein]
	h „ „ here [hiə], horse [hɔːs]
	x „ „ coronach ['kɔrənæx], ugh [uːx]

SEMI-CONSONANTS

j „ „ rien [rjɛ̃]	j „ „ yellow ['jelou], yes [jes]
w „ „ ouate [wat], oui [wi]	w „ „ wall [wɔːl]
ɥ „ „ huile [ɥil]	

(1) When the same symbol is used in both languages, one should remember that it generally represents a different sound in each language (cp. D. Jones: *An outline of English phonetics* and P. Fouché: *Traité de prononciation française*).

(2) At the end of a syllable the 'l' sound is 'dark'.

′ denotes that the stress is on the following syllable—**physician** [fi'ziʃən].

: denotes that the preceding vowel is long—**zebra** ['ziːbrə].

˜ placed over a vowel-symbol shows that the vowel has a nasal sound— **tantôt** [tɑ̃'to].

LIST OF ABBREVIATIONS

a.	adjective	*Fenc.*	Fencing	*pej.*	pejorative
abbr.	abbreviation	*Feud.*	Feudal	*perf.*	perfect
Acous.	Acoustics	*fig.*	figuratively	*pers.*	person, personal
adv.	adverb	*Fin.*	Financial	*Pharm.*	Pharmacy
adv. phr.	adverbial phrase	*foll.*	the following	*Phil.*	Philosophy
Agric.	Agriculture	*Fort.*	Fortification	*Philol.*	Philology
Alch.	Alchemy	*Fr.*	French	*Phon.*	Phonetics
Alg.	Algebra	*freq.*	frequentative	*Phot.*	Photography
Am.	American	*Ftb.*	Football	*phr.*	phrase
Anat.	Anatomy	*fut.*	future	*Phys.*	Physics
anc.	ancient	*Gard.*	Gardening	*Physiol.*	Physiology
Ant.	Antiquities	*Geog.*	Geography	*pl.*	plural
Arch.	Architecture	*Geol.*	Geology	*poet.*	poetical
Archaeol.	Archaeology	*Geom.*	Geometry	*Polit.*	Politics
Arith.	Arithmetic	*Ger.*	German	*pop.*	popular
art.	article	*Gr.*	Greek	*poss.*	possessive
Artill.	Artillery	*Gram.*	Grammar	*p.p.*	past participle
Astrol.	Astrology	*Gym.*	Gymnastics	*prec.*	the preceding
Astron.	Astronomy	*Her.*	Heraldry	*pred.*	predicate
Austral.	Australian usage	*Hist.*	History	*pref.*	prefix
aux.	auxiliary	*Horol.*	Horology	*prep.*	preposition
Av.	Aviation	*Hort.*	Horticulture	*prep. phr.*	prepositive phrase
Bibl.	Bible, biblical	*Hunt.*	Hunting	*pres.*	present
Bibliog.	Bibliography	*Hydr.*	Hydrostatics	*pres. p.*	present participle
Biol.	Biology	*i.*	intransitive	*pret.*	preterite
Bookb.	Bookbinding	*Ichth.*	Ichthyology	*Print.*	Printing
Bot.	Botany	*imit.*	imitative	*pron.*	pronoun
Box.	Boxing	*impers.*	impersonal	*pronun.*	pronunciation
Bret.	Breton	*incorr.*	incorrectly	*prop.*	proper, properly
Build.	Building	*Ind.*	Industry	*Pros.*	Prosody
(C)	Canadian usage	*indec.*	indecent	*Prov.*	Provençal
c.	circa, about	*indef.*	indefinite	*prov.*	provincial
Carp.	Carpentry	*indic.*	indicative	*Psych.*	Psychology
cent.	century	*inf.*	infinitive	*Pyro.*	Pyrotechnics
Ch.	Church	*int.*	interjection	*r.*	reflexive; reciprocal
Chem.	Chemistry	*inter.*	interrogative	*Rad.*	Radio
Cine.	Cinema	*inv.*	invariable	*Rail.*	Railway
Civ. Eng.	Civil Engineering	*iron.*	ironical	*R.-C.*	Roman Catholic
Cloth.	Clothing	*irr.*	irregular (see table of	*rel.*	relative
Coin.	Coinage		Irregular Verbs, pp.	*Relig.*	Religion
collect.	collective		638–648)	*rhet.*	rhetoric
colloq.	colloquially	*It.*	Italian	*Rom.*	Roman
comb.	combination	*Journ.*	Journalism	*Row.*	Rowing
comb. form	combining form	*L.*	Latin	*Sc.*	Scottish
Comm.	Commerce	*Law*	Law, jurisprudence	*Scand.*	Scandinavian
comp.	comparative	*Lit.*	Literature	*sch.*	schools
Conch.	Conchology	*Log.*	Logic	*Sci.*	Science
cond.	conditional	*m.*	masculine	*Sculp.*	Sculpture
conj.	conjunction	*Mach.*	Machinery	*S. Fr.*	South of France
contr.	contraction	*Manuf.*	Manufacturing	*sing.*	singular
Cook.	Cookery	*Math.*	Mathematics	*Sp.*	Spanish
corr.	corruption	*Mech.*	Mechanics	*Spt.*	Sports
Cost.	Costume	*Med.*	Medicine	*St. Exch.*	Stock Exchange
cp.	compare	*Metal.*	Metallurgy	*subj.*	subjunctive
Cryst.	Crystallography	*Metaph.*	Metaphysics	*subs.*	substantivally
Cycl.	Cycling	*Meteor.*	Meteorology	*suf.*	suffix
dem.	demonstrative	*Mil.*	Military	*superl.*	superlative
Dent.	Dentistry	*Min.*	Mineralogy	*Surg.*	Surgery
dial.	dialect	*mod.*	modern	*t.*	transitive
dim.	diminutive	*Motor.*	Motoring	*Tech.*	Technical
Dress.	Dressmaking	*Mount.*	Mountaineering	*Tel.*	Television
Eccles.	Ecclesiastical	*Mus.*	Music	*Teleg.*	Telegraphy
Econ.	Economics	*Myth.*	Mythology	*Teleph.*	Telephone
Egypt.	Egyptology	*n.*	noun	*Ten.*	Tennis
Elec.	Electricity	*N. A.*	North America	*Tex.*	Textiles
emphat.	emphatic	*Naut.*	Nautical	*Theat.*	Theatrical
Eng.	Engineering	*neg.*	negative	*Theol.*	Theological
Engl.	English	*nom.*	nominative	*Therap.*	Therapeutics
Engr.	Engraving	*Norm.*	Norman	*Trig.*	Trigonometry
Ent.	Entomology	*Num.*	Numismatics	*Univ.*	University
Epis.	Episcopalian	*onom.*	onomatopoeic	*U.S.*	United States
esp.	especially	*Opt.*	Optics	*usu.*	usually
etym.	etymology	*orig.*	origin, originally	*v.*	verb
euph.	euphemistic	*Orn.*	Ornithology	*Vet.*	Veterinary
exc.	except	*Paint.*	Painting	*v.i.*	intransitive verb
ext.	extension	*Pal.*	Palaeontology	*v.r.*	reflexive or reciprocal
f.	feminine	*Parl.*	Parliamentary		verb
fam.	familiarly	*part.*	participle, participial	*v.t.*	transitive verb
facet.	facetiously	*pass.*	passive	*vulg.*	vulgar
fem.	feminine	*Path.*	Pathology	*Zool.*	Zoology

xvi

CASSELL'S
FRENCH-ENGLISH DICTIONARY

A

A, a [ɑ], *n.m.* In French *a* has two sounds: (1) as in *part*, shown in this dictionary by 'a'; (2) as in *pas*, shown by 'ɑ'. *Il ne sait ni A ni B*, he is a perfect ignoramus.

a [a], *3rd sing. indic.* [AVOIR].

à [a], *prep.* [*see also* AU, AUX]. To, at, in, into, on, by, for, from, with, indicating (1) the indirect object of the verb, as in *parler à un ami*, to speak to a friend; (2) the direction in space, as in *aller à Paris*, to go to Paris; (3) the position of a thing, or the place where an action takes place, as in *il demeure à Paris*, he lives in Paris; (4) the time, moment, or period of an event, as in *à l'aube*, at daybreak; (5) the direction in time, as in *à demain!* see you tomorrow! (6) possession, as in *cette montre est à mon frère*, this watch is my brother's; (7) manner, method, instrument, measure, as in *s'habiller à la française*, to dress after the French fashion; *vendre du vin à la bouteille*, to sell wine by the bottle; (8) description, kind, species, as in *un homme à barbe blanche*, a man with a white beard; (9) adjective denoting use, as in *une tasse à thé*, a tea-cup; (10) between or about, when between two numerals, as in *un homme de quarante à cinquante ans*, a man between forty and fifty. (*N.B.* When speaking of things which cannot themselves be divided, *ou* is used in place of *à*, as *quatre ou cinq personnes*, four or five persons.) (11) Before an infinitive, *à* indicates the sense of an adjective, or purpose, intention, etc., or of a noun or verb, as in *facile à savoir*, easy to ascertain.

abaissable [abɛ'sabl], *a.* That can be lowered.

abaisse [a'bɛːs], *n.f.* Undercrust of pastry, piece of rolled paste.

abaissé, *p.p.* (*fem.* **abaissée**) [ABAISSER].

abaisse-langue [abes'lɑ̃ːg], *n.m.* (*Surg.*) An instrument for pushing down the tongue.

abaissement [abes'mɑ̃], *n.m.* Lowering, falling, abatement, depression; humiliation, abasement; (*Surg.*) couching. *L'abaissement des eaux*, the abatement of the waters; *opération de la cataracte par abaissement*, couching.

abaisser [abe'se], *v.t.* To let down, to let fall, to lower; to diminish, to reduce; (*fig.*) to bring low, to humble, to depress; (*Math.*) to reduce, to bring down; (*Geom.*) to drop (a perpendicular); (*Surg.*) to couch; to lower (a wall); to roll out (paste); to lop off (a branch). *Abaisser une cataracte*, to couch a cataract; *abaisser un pont-levis*, to let down a drawbridge; *abaisser une voile*, to lower a sail; *Dieu abaisse les superbes*, God humbles the proud. **s'abaisser,** *v.r.* To sink, to subside, to decrease, to abate, to decline; to humble oneself, to stoop, to cringe. *S'abaisser à le prier*, to stoop to entreat him.

abaisseur [abe'sœːr], *n.m.* (*Anat.*) Depressor. *Les muscles abaisseurs*, the muscles that depress.

abajoue [aba'ʒu], *n.f.* (*Zool.*) Cheek-pouch; (*fig.*) full and pendulous cheek.

abalourdir [abalur'diːr], *v.t.* To make dull or stupid. **abalourdissement,** *n.m.* Rendering dull or stupid; dullness, stupidity.

abandon [abɑ̃'dɔ̃], *n.m.* Relinquishment, surrender, cession; abandonment, the state of being forsaken, forlornness, destitution; ease, lack of restraint. *À l'abandon*, at random, in confusion, at sixes and sevens, (*Naut.*) adrift; *laisser ses enfants à l'abandon*, to neglect one's children; *se livrer avec abandon à*, to indulge in; *un champ qui est à l'abandon*, a field left to run wild.

abandonnable [abɑ̃dɔ'nabl], *a.* That may be abandoned. **abandonnataire** [abɑ̃dɔna'tɛːr], *n.* Releasee. **abandonnateur** [abɑ̃dɔna'tœːr], *n.* (*fem.* **abandonnatrice**) Releasor.

abandonné [abɑ̃dɔ'ne], *a.* (*fem.* **abandonnée**) Abandoned, forsaken, given over; lost to decency, shameless, graceless, profligate. *Un malade abandonné*, a patient given up. *Un objet abandonné*, derelict.

abandonnement [abɑ̃dɔn'mɑ̃], *n.m.* Abandonment; the act of forsaking, desertion; the state of being forsaken; surrender of one's effects; (*fig.*) dissoluteness, profligacy.

abandonnément [abɑ̃dɔne'mɑ̃], *adv.* Freely, unreservedly.

abandonner [abɑ̃dɔ'ne], *v.t.* To give up, to hand over, to surrender; to renounce; to forsake, to desert, to abandon; to leave, to quit; to neglect. *Abandonner la partie*, to throw in one's hand; *abandonner une cause*, to give up a cause; *abandonner une corde*, to let go a rope; *abandonner ses prétentions*, to renounce one's claims; *il abandonna le pays*, he left the district; *mes forces m'abandonnent*, my strength is failing me. **s'abandonner,** *v.r.* To give oneself up, to addict oneself (*à*), to give way (*à*); to indulge (*à*); to commit oneself (*à*); to neglect oneself; to be careless, to be unconstrained in manners, to throw off all restraint. *S'abandonner à la colère, au plaisir, au hasard*, to give way to anger, to indulge in pleasure, to trust to luck. **abandonneur** [abɑ̃dɔ'nœːr], *n.* (*fem.* **-euse**) One who abandons.—*a.* That abandons.

abaque [a'bak], *n.m.* (*Arch.*) Abacus, the slab forming the uppermost part of the capital of a column; (*Arith.*) abacus or counting-machine [BOULIER; COMPTEUR].

*abas [*see* ABAT].

abasourdir [abazur'diːr], *v.t.* To stun, to dumbfound; (*fig.*) to astound. **abasourdissant** [abazurdi'sɑ̃], *a.* (*fem.* **abasourdissante**) Astounding, overwhelming.

abasourdissement [abazurdis'mɑ̃], *n.m.* Stupefaction, consternation.

*abat [a'ba], *n.m.* Killing, knocking down; (also ***abas**) a sudden downpour, a heavy shower; (*pl.* **abats** or **abatis**) [*see* ABATTIS].

abatage [ABATTAGE].

abâtardi [abɑtar'di], *a.* (*fem.* **abâtardie**) Degenerate, corrupt, debased. *Un homme abâtardi*, a degenerate man.

abâtardir [abɑtar'diːr], *v.t.* To render degenerate; to debase, to corrupt, to spoil, to mar. **s'abâtardir**, *v.r.* To degenerate.

abâtardissement [abɑtardis'mã], *n.m.* Degeneracy.

abatée [aba'te], *n.f.* (*Naut.*) Falling back, falling off to leeward; swoop (of a plane).

*****abat-faim** [aba'fɛ̃], *n.m.* (*pl. inv.*) Large joint, substantial dish.

abat-foin [aba'fwɛ̃], *n.m.* (*pl. inv.*) Trap-door above a stable-rack for putting fodder through.

abatis (1) [ABAT].

abatis (2) [ABATTIS].

abat-jour [aba'ʒuːr], *n.m.* (*pl. inv.*) A sloping window for transmitting light from above, a skylight; a lamp-shade, a reflector for shading a lamp; a shade for the eyes.

abat-son [aba'sɔ̃], *n.m.* (*pl.* **abat-son** or **abat-sons**) A series of sloping louvres in the window of a bell-tower for directing the sound downwards.

abattable [aba'tabl], *a.* That may be overturned, defeated, or demolished.

abattage [aba'taːʒ], *n.m.* Cutting down, felling (of trees), slaughtering (of animals); heeling over, careening (a ship for repairs); (*fam.*) a scolding, a wigging; (*Theat.*) dash, brilliancy (of an actor).

abattant [aba'tã], *n.m.* Flap (of a counter, etc.).

abattée [aba'te], *n.f.* [ABATÉE].

abattement [abat'mã], *n.m.* Weakening; prostration; dejection, despondency, low spirits; (*Fin.*)=[RÉDUCTION] abatement. *Jeter dans l'abattement*, to deject; *tomber dans l'abattement*, to become low-spirited; *abattement à la base*, earned-income allowance.

abatteur [aba'tœːr], *n.m.* One who fells (trees, etc.), a slaughterer. *C'est un grand abatteur de quilles*, he is a great braggart; *un abatteur de besogne*, a hard worker.

abattis [aba'ti], *n.m.* Things or materials thrown down such as houses, walls, trees; slaughtered animals, game, etc.; the killing of game; giblets (of poultry); (*Fort.*) a barricade of felled trees, etc.; (*pop.*) arms, legs, hands, feet. *Tu peux numéroter tes abattis*, now be ready for a sound thrashing; *abattis en ragoût*, stewed giblets.

abattoir [aba'twaːr], *n.m.* Slaughter-house; (*fam.*) great bloodshed, butchery.

abattre [a'batr], *v.t.* To throw, hurl or put down; to knock, beat, or batter down; to pull down; to fell, to cut or hew down; to kill, to slaughter; to let fall, to lower; to couch (a cataract); to overthrow, to destroy, to demolish; to dishearten, to unman; to discourage, to cast down, to depress; to humble. *Abattre de la besogne*, to get through a lot of work; *abattre les cuirs*, to skin dead animals; *abattre son jeu*, to lay one's cards on the table; *abattre un mât*, to lower a mast; *abattre un vaisseau pour le caréner*, to careen a ship; *abattre l'orgueil de quelqu'un*, to humble somebody's pride; *la moindre chose l'abat*, the least thing unmans him; *le vent abattra le blé*, the wind will beat the corn down; *un vaisseau dur à abattre*, a ship hard

to swing round.—*v.i.* (*Naut.*) To fall off to leeward, to fall aback. **s'abattre**, *v.r.* To throw oneself down, to fall, to tumble down; to stoop; to abate; to be cast down or dejected; to break down (of horses); to burst (of a storm); to pounce upon. *La chaleur s'abat*, the heat is abating; *le vent s'abat*, the wind is dropping. **abattu** [aba'ty], *a.* (*fem.* **abattue**) Cast down, depressed, dejected; humbled, crestfallen. *À bride abattue*, hell for leather; *je me sens tout abattu*, I am quite out of sorts; *un visage abattu*, a woebegone countenance, a crestfallen face.

abatture [aba'tyːr], *n.f.* The act of felling or pulling down (nuts etc.); (*pl.*) the foil or traces left by a stag.

abat-vent [aba'vã], *n.m. inv.* Louvre-boards (of a window); wind-cowl (of a chimney).

abat-voix [aba'vwa], *n.m. inv.* Sounding-board (of a pulpit).

abbatial [aba'sjal], *a.* (*fem.* **abbatiale**) Abbatial, pertaining to an abbey, abbot, etc.

abbaye [abe'ji], *n.f.* Monastery, abbey; *the benefice or revenues of an abbot or abbess; the buildings of a monastery.

abbé [a'be], *n.m.* Abbot, abbé; (*pop.*) any ecclesiastic. *Monsieur l'abbé*, your Reverence. *L'abbé Martin*, Father Martin.

abbesse [a'bɛs], *n.f.* Abbess.

A.B.C. [abe'se], *n.m.* The alphabet, an A B C book; a primer, a spelling-book; (*fig.*) the elements or rudiments (of an art, science, etc.). *Être l'A.B.C. de*, to be the very beginning or elements of.

abcéder [apse'de], *v.i.* To turn into an abscess, to gather.

abcès [ap'sɛ], *n.m.* Abscess, gathering. *Abcès aux gencives*, gumboil; *vider l'abcès*, to drain the abscess, (*fig.*) to solve a difficult problem.

Abdère [ab'dɛːr], *f.* Abdera.

Abdias [ab'djas], *m.* Obadiah.

abdicataire [abdika'tɛːr], *n.* One who abdicates.—*a.* That has abdicated. **abdication** [abdika'sjɔ̃], *n.f.* Abdication; renunciation (of property etc.); surrender (of authority).

abdiquer [abdi'ke], *v.t.* To abdicate, to resign, to renounce.

abdomen [abdɔ'mɛn], *n.m.* Abdomen. **abdominal** [abdɔmi'nal], *a.* (*fem.* **abdominale**) Abdominal.

abducteur [abdyk'tœːr], *n.m.* (*Anat.*) Abductor.—*a.* (*Anat.*) Abducent. **abduction** [abdyk'sjɔ̃], *n.f.* Abduction.

abécédaire [abese'dɛːr], *a.* Alphabetical. *Ordre abécédaire*, alphabetical order.—*n.m.* Spelling-book; an elementary reading-book; a primer.

abecquer [abɛ'ke], *v.t.* To feed (a bird). **abecquement** [abɛk'mã], *n.m.* Feeding (of birds).

abeille [a'bɛːj], *n.f.* Bee. *Abeille domestique*, hive bee; *abeille mère*, queen bee; *abeille ouvrière*, worker bee; *nid d'abeilles*, honeycomb; *serviette nid d'abeilles*, honeycomb towel. **abeiller** [abɛ'je], *a.* (*fem.* **abeillère**) Pertaining to bees.

aberrant [abɛ'rã], *a.* (*fem.* **aberrante**). Aberrant. **aberration** [abɛra'sjɔ̃], *n.f.* Deviation from the normal or the correct course; (*Astron., Opt., etc.*) aberration; (*fig.*) error of judgment or taste. *Dans un moment d'aberration*, in a moment of absence of mind.

abêtir [abɛ'tir], *v.t.* To render stupid; to dull, to blunt.—*v.i.* To become dull or stupid. **s'abêtir,** *v.r.* To grow stupid. **abêtissement** [abɛtis'mã], *n.m.* Stultification; besotting process.

abhorrer [abɔ're], *v.t.* To abhor, to hate, to loathe; to execrate.

abiétinées [abjeti'ne], *n.f. pl.* (*Bot.*) Abietineae.

abîme [a'biːm], *n.m.* An abyss, the deep, a chasm, a depth; hell; (*fig.*) the extreme, the utmost degree; an unfathomable depth (of mystery, knowledge, etc.).

abîmé [abi'me], *a.* (*fem.* **-ée**) Swallowed up, engulfed; destroyed, ruined; damaged, spoiled. *Abîmé de dettes*, over head and ears in debt; *un fruit abîmé par la pluie*, a fruit spoilt by the rain.

abîmer [abi'me], *v.t.* *To engulf, to swallow up; to overwhelm, to sink, to ruin; to spoil, to damage, to injure. **s'abîmer,** *v.r.* To fall into ruin, to be ruined, to collapse; to be spoiled; to be overcome. *S'abîmer dans le désespoir*, to be sunk in despair.

abject [ab'ʒɛkt], *a.* (*fem.* **abjecte**) Abject, base, vile, despicable. **abjectement** [abʒɛktə'mã], *adv.* Abjectly. **abjection** [abʒɛk'sjɔ̃], *n.f.* Abasement, humiliation; vileness, baseness.

abjuration [abʒyrɑ'sjɔ̃], *n.f.* Solemn renunciation, abjuration. *Faire abjuration*, to abjure. **abjuratoire,** *a.* Abjuratory. *Acte abjuratoire*, act of abjuration.

abjurer [abʒy're], *v.t.* To abjure, to renounce; to give up, to forswear, to abandon.

ablatif [abla'tif], *a.* (*fem.* **ablative**) Ablative. —*n.m.* The ablative case.

ablation [ablɑ'sjɔ̃], *n.f.* (*Surg.*) Ablation, removal (of a part).

able [abl], *n.m.* The bleak; any small freshwater fish of this family [ABLETTE].

ableret [ablə'rɛ], *n.m.* A net for small fish.

ablette [a'blɛt], *n.f.* The bleak [ABLE].

abluer [ably'e], *v.t.* To revive old writing or take out stains in paper or parchment by washing with gall-nut.

ablution [ably'sjɔ̃], *n.f.* Ablution, washing, purification. *Faire ses ablutions*, to wash, to perform one's ablutions.

abnégation [abnegɑ'sjɔ̃], *n.f.* Abnegation, renunciation, sacrifice, self-denial. *Faire abnégation de soi*, to sacrifice oneself.

aboi [a'bwa], *n.m.* A (dog's) bark, barking, baying; (*pl.*) bay, baying (of hounds); (*fig.*) a desperate condition. *Aux abois*, at bay, (*fig.*) in a fix, on his last legs, hard-pressed; *mettre aux abois*, to reduce to extremities.

aboiement [abwa'mã], *n.m.* The faculty or act of barking; barking, baying. *Pousser un aboiement*, to bark, to give tongue.

(C) aboiteau [abwa'to], *n.m.* (*pl.* **aboiteaux**) Sluice; ice-pack; shelter.

abolir [abɔ'liːr], *v.t.* To abolish, to repeal, to annul, to suppress. **abolition** [abɔli'sjɔ̃], *n.f.* Abolition, repeal. **abolitionnisme** [abɔlisjɔ'nism], *n.m.* Abolitionism. **abolitionniste,** *n.m.* Abolitionist.

abominable [abɔmi'nabl], *a.* Abominable, execrable; heinous. **abominablement,** *adv.* Abominably.

abomination [abɔminɑ'sjɔ̃], *n.f.* Abomination, detestation, horror. *Avoir en abomina-*

tion, to hold in detestation; *c'est une abomination*, it's a wretched thing.

abominer [abɔmi'ne], *v.t.* To abominate, to detest.

abondamment [abɔ̃da'mã], *adv.* Abundantly.

abondance [abɔ̃'dãːs], *n.f.* A great quantity, abundance, plenty; ample resources, opulence, affluence; richness (of language). *Corne d'abondance*, horn of plenty, cornucopia; *écrire* or *parler d'abondance*, to write or to speak extempore, off the cuff; *nager dans l'abondance*, to wallow in wealth; *parler avec abondance*, to have the gift of the gab.

abondant [abɔ̃'dã], *a.* (*fem.* **-ante**) Abundant, plentiful, copious; exuberant; effusive, voluble.

abonder [abɔ̃'de], *v.i.* To abound, to be plentiful, to be in great quantity; (*Law*) to be superfluous. *Abonder dans le sens de quelqu'un*, to support somebody's views strongly; *ce qui abonde ne vicie pas*, (*Law*) that which is superfluous does not impair the validity (of an act, procedure, etc.).

abonné [abɔ'ne], *n.m.* (*fem.* **abonnée**) Subscriber (to periodicals, theatres, etc.); season-ticket holder; consumer (of water, gas, electricity). **abonnement** [abɔn'mã], *n.m.* Subscription (to periodicals, theatres, etc.); agreement; season-ticket. *Carte d'abonnement*, season-ticket; *prendre, souscrire un abonnement à un journal*, to subscribe to a newspaper; *les abonnements sont suspendus pour ce soir* (of places of amusement), season-tickets not available this evening.

abonner [abɔ'ne], *v.t.* To subscribe for or to. **s'abonner,** *v.r.* To become a subscriber; to take up a subscription. *On s'abonne à*, subscriptions are received at; *on s'abonnait avec les curés pour les dîmes*, people compounded with the vicars for the tithes.

abonnir [abɔ'niːr], *v.t.* To better, to mend, to improve (wine).—*v.i.* To become good. **s'abonnir,** *v.r.* To mend, to grow better. **abonnissement,** *n.m.* Improvement.

abord [a'bɔːr], *n.m.* Landing; arrival; access, approach, meeting, manner of receiving (someone); onset, attack; (*pl.*) approaches, surroundings. *Avoir l'abord facile*, to be easy of access; *d'abord*, at first, at first sight; *tout d'abord, au premier abord, de prime abord, dès l'abord*, at first, from the very first.

abordable [abɔr'dabl], *a.* Accessible, easily approached, affable. *D'un prix abordable*, at a reasonable price.

abordage [abɔr'daːʒ], *n.m.* (*Naut.*) Boarding; fouling, colliding. *Aller* or *sauter à l'abordage*, to board or grapple a ship.

abordé, *p.p.* (*fem.* **abordée** (1)) [ABORDER].

abordée (2) [abɔr'de], *n.f.* The act of meeting, accosting, beginning, etc. *A l'abordée*, on accosting, on meeting.

aborder [abɔr'de], *v.i.* To arrive; to land. —*v.t.* To arrive at, to come to, to come up with; to approach, to accost; to enter upon (a subject etc.); to attack (the enemy); to grapple (a vessel) in order to board; to run foul of (a ship). *Aborder par accident*, to run foul of; *il m'a abordé dans la rue*, he accosted me in the street. **s'aborder,** *v.r.* To come together in order to converse, to accost each other; to run foul of each other.

abordeur, *a.* That approaches, accosts,

boards, etc.—*n.m.* One who accosts; boarding vessel.

aborigène [abɔri'ʒeːn], *a.* Native, original. —*n.m.* Aboriginal. *Les Aborigènes*, aborigines.

abornement [abɔrnə'mã], *n.m.* The laying out of boundaries, delimitation.

aborner [abɔr'ne], *v.t.* To mark out, to delimit.

abortif [abɔr'tif], *a.* (*fem.* **abortive**) Abortive; premature; liable to cause abortion.—*n.m* A substance used to produce abortion.

abot [a'bo], *n.m.* A clog or hobble (for a horse).

abouchement [abuʃ'mã], *n.m.* Interview, conference, parley; (*Anat.*) anastomosis, inosculation. **aboucher**, *v.t.* To bring (things) together; to put (tubes etc.) end to end; to bring (persons) together. **s'aboucher**, *v.r.* To have an interview, to confer (with); to get in touch (with).

abouler [abu'le], *v.t.* (*pop.*) To give, to shell out. **s'abouler**, *v.r.* To turn up, to arrive, to pop in.

aboulie [abu'liː], *n.f.* Lack of will, abulia. **aboulique**, *a.* Who has no will.

about [a'bu], *n.m.* (*Carp.*) The butt-end of a piece of wood. **aboutage**, *n.m.* (*Naut.*) Bending (of two cables). **abouté**, *p.p.* (*fem.* **aboutée**) [ABOUTER]. **aboutement**, *n.m.* Abutment; placing or fitting end to end.

abouter, *v.t.* To join end to end.

aboutir [abu'tiːr], *v.i.* To end at or in, to result (*à*); to lead or tend (*à*); (*Surg.*) to come to a head (conjugated with *être* or *avoir*), to burst; to come to; to tend to; to end in. *N'aboutir à rien*, to come to nothing; to end in smoke; *ce champ aboutit à un marais*, this field borders upon a fen; *faire aboutir un abcès*, to bring an abscess to a head. **aboutissant**, *a.* (*fem.* **aboutissante**) Bordering upon, abutting on, ending in.— *n.m.pl.* The adjacent parts (of an estate); the relations, circumstances, surroundings, or particulars (of an affair). *Connaître les tenants et aboutissants d'une affaire*, to know the ins and outs of a matter. **aboutissement**, *n.m.* Result, issue; (*Tailoring*) a piece for eking out; (*Surg.*) gathering (of an abscess), coming to a head.

aboyant [abwa'jã], *a.* (*fem.* **aboyante**) Barking.

aboyer [abwa'je], *v.i.* To bark, to bay, to yelp; (*fig.*) to pursue (*après*) pertinaciously, to dun. *Aboyer à la lune*, to complain uselessly; *le renard aboie après tout le monde*, the fox barks at everybody. **aboyeur** *n.m.* Barker, snarler; (*Hunt.*) a hound that stands yelping without attacking the stag; (*Orn.*) greenshank; (*fig.*) dun, tout, hawker. *Ce journaliste n'est qu'un aboyeur*, this journalist is nothing but a snarling critic.

abracadabra [abrakada'bra], *n.m.* Abracadabra (magic word). **abracadabrant**, *a.* Stupendous, amazing, stunning.

Abraham [abra'am], *m.* Abraham.

abraquer [abra'ke] or **embraquer** [ãbra'ke], *v.t.* (*Naut.*) To pull taut, to take in the slack.

abrasif [abra'zif], *n.m.* A substance used for grinding or polishing (*e.g.* sand, emery, etc.), abrasive, abradant. **abrasion** [abra'zjõ], *n.f.* (*Med.*) Abrasion, excoriation.

abrégé [abre'ʒe], *a.* (*fem.* **abrégée**) Short, summary.—*n.m.* Abridgment, résumé, précis, abstract, summary. *En abrégé*, in a few words, briefly; *réduire en abrégé*, to epitomize.—*n.pl.* Trackers (of an organ). **abrégement**, *n.m.* Abridging, abridgment.

abréger, *v.t.* To abridge, to shorten, to epitomize; to abbreviate, to cut down. *Pour abréger*, to be brief, to cut a long story short.

abreuvage [abrœ'vaːʒ] or **abreuvement** [abrœv'mã], *n.m.* Watering, soaking, steaming. **abreuver**, *v.t.* To water (animals), to give drink to, to make (animals) drink; to water (the ground etc.), to wet, to soak, to drench, to fill, to saturate; (*fig.*) to overwhelm (*de*). **s'abreuver**, *v.r.* To drink, to be watered (of animals); to season, to drink plentifully, to be steeped (*de*). *S'abreuver de douleur*, to be filled with grief, to drain sorrow to the dregs; *un cœur abreuvé de fiel*, a heart steeped in gall.

abreuvoir [abrœ'vwaːr], *n.m.* Watering-place, horse-pond; drinking-trough.

abréviateur [abrevja'tœːr], *n.m.* (*fem.* **abréviatrice**) Abbreviator, abridger. **abréviatif**, *a.* (*fem.* **abréviative**) Abbreviatory, abridging. **abréviation**, *n.f.* Abbreviation, contraction, shortening. **abréviativement**, *adv.* Briefly, by abbreviation.

abri [a'bri], *n.m.* Shelter, cover, refuge, dug-out. *Être sous l'abri d'un bois*, to be sheltered by a wood; *sans abri*, homeless; *être à l'abri du vent*, to be sheltered from the wind; *mettre à l'abri*, to shelter; *à l'abri du besoin*, safe from want.

abricot [abri'ko] *n.m.* Apricot. **abricotier**, *n.m.* Apricot-tree. **abricotin**, *n.m.* Early apricot; apricot-plum.

abriter [abri'te], *v.t.* To shelter, to shield, to screen, to shade, to protect; (*Naut.*) to take another's wind, to blanket. **s'abriter**, *v.r.* To take refuge.

abrivent [abri'vã], *n.m.* Shelter; sentry-box; (*Gard.*) matting, screen.

abrogatif [abrɔga'tif], *a.* (*fem.* **abrogative**) Intended to abrogate or repeal.

abrogation [abrɔga'sjõ], *n.f.* Abrogation, repeal, annulment. **abrogative** [ABROGATIF]. **abrogeable** [abrɔ'ʒabl], *a.* Repealable. **abroger**, *v.t.* To abrogate, to repeal, to annul. **s'abroger**, *v.r.* To fall into disuse, to grow obsolete, to lapse.

abrouti [abru'ti], *a.* (*fem.* **abroutie**) Nipped, browsed. **abroutissement**, *n.m.* Damage done (to young trees etc.) by cattle browsing.

abrupt [a'brypt], *a.* (*fem.* **abrupte**) Abrupt, steep, sheer; (*fig.*) blunt, rugged, rough (of style etc.). **abruptement**, *adv.* Abruptly.

abruti [abry'ti], *a.* (*fem.* **-ie**) Brutalized, stupid, sodden with drink.—*n.* A brutalized or stupid person.

abrutir [abry'tiːr], *v.t.* To stupefy, to besot, to brutalize. **s'abrutir**, *v.r.* To become brutalized, stupid, or besotted. **abrutissant**, *a.* (*fem.* **abrutissante**) Brutalizing, stupefying. **abrutissement**, *n.m.* The act of brutalizing; brutishness, degradation. **abrutisseur**, *a.* (*fem.* **abrutisseuse**) Brutalizing. —*n. m.* or *f.* One who or that which brutalizes.

Abruzzes [a'bryːz], **les**, The Abruzzi.

Absalon [absa'lõ], *m.* Absalom.

abscisse [ap′sis], *n.f.* (*Geom.*) Abscissa, **abscission**, *n.f.* (*Surg.*) Cutting off, abscission.

abscons [aps′kɔ̃:s], *a.* (*fem.* -se) Hidden, abstruse, mysterious.

absence [ap′sɑ̃:s], *n.f.* Absence; want, lack. *Absence d'esprit*, absence of mind; *avoir des absences*, to be often absent-minded.

absent [ap′sɑ̃], *a.* (*fem.* **absente**) Absent, away from home; missing, wanting; wandering, woolgathering.—*n.m.* One absent, absentee. *Les absents ont toujours tort*, the absent are always in the wrong. **absentéisme**, *n.m.* Absenteeism. **absentéiste**, *a.* Pertaining to or approving of absenteeism. —*n.m.* or *f.* One who approves of or practises absenteeism. **s'absenter**, *v.r.* To absent oneself, to be away; to play truant.

absidal [apsi′dal], *a.* (*fem.* **absidale**, *pl.* **absidaux**) Apsidal. **abside**, *n.f.* Apse.

absidiole [apsi′djɔl], *n.f.* Small apse.

absinthe [ap′sɛ̃:t], *n.f.* Absinth; wormwood; **absinthé**, *a.* (*fem.* **absinthée**) Mixed or tempered with absinth. **absinther**, *v.t.* To mix with absinth. **s'absinther**, *v.r.* (*pop.*) To drink absinth, *esp.* to excess. **absinthine**, *n.f.* The bitter principle of absinth. **absinthisme**, *n.m.* A morbid condition caused by excessive drinking of absinth. **absinthique**, *a.* Absinthic; excessively addicted to absinth-drinking, or suffering from the effects of this.

absolu [apsɔ′ly], *a.* (*fem.* **absolue**) Absolute, existing independently; despotic, arbitrary; unlimited, unrestricted; imperious, peremptory, positive; (*Gram.*) absolute, not relative; (*Chem.*) pure.—*n.m.* The Absolute. **absolument**, *adv.* Absolutely; arbitrarily, peremptorily; entirely, completely, fully; (*Gram.*) without a complement. *Il refusa absolument*, he gave a flat denial.

absolution [apsɔly′sjɔ̃], *n.f.* Absolution, acquittal; forgiveness, remission.

absolutisme [apsɔly′tism], *n.m.* Absolutism.

absolutiste, *n.* and *a.* Absolutist.

absolutoire [apsɔly′twa:r], *a.* Absolving; implying or involving absolution.

absorbable [apsɔr′babl], *a.* Absorbable. **absorbant**, *a.* (*fem.* **absorbante**) Absorptive, absorbent; engrossing.—*n.m.* An absorbent. **absorbé**, *p.p.* (*fem.* **absorbée**) [ABSORBER]. ***absorbement**, *n.m.* Absorption.

absorber [apsɔr′be], *v.t.* To absorb, to drink up, to imbibe; to consume, to eat or drink; to take up, to cause to disappear; (*fig.*) to occupy completely, to engross. **s'absorber**, *v.r.* To be absorbed; (*fig.*) to be entirely taken up with (*dans*). *S'absorber dans la méditation*, to be absorbed in thought. **absorption** [apsɔrp′sjɔ̃], *n.f.* Absorption.

absoudre [ap′sudr], *v.t. irr.* (*pres.p.* **absolvant**, *p.p.* **absous**, *fem.* **absoute**) To absolve, to acquit; to exonerate, to forgive, to pardon, to excuse. **absoute**, *n.f.* General absolution (on Holy Thursday); (in the Roman Catholic burial service) the last prayer.

abstème [aps′tɛ:m], *a.* Abstemious.

abstenir (s') [apstə′ni:r], *v.r. irr.* (*conjugated like* TENIR) To abstain (from voting); to refrain, to forbear, to forgo. *S'abstenir de vin*, to abstain from wine.

abstention [apstɑ̃′sjɔ̃], *n.f.* Abstention. **abstentionnisme**, *n.m.* The practice of abstaining from voting (in elections). **abstentionniste**, *n.m.* Non-voter.

abstergent [apstɛr′ʒɑ̃], *a.* (*fem.* **abstergente**) (*Med.*) Cleansing, abstergent.—*n.m.* An abstergent.

absterger, *v.t.* To absterge, to cleanse.

abstersif [apstɛr′sif], *a.* (*fem.* **abstersive**) (*Med.*) Abstersive, cleansing. **abstersion**, *n.f.* Abstersion, cleansing.

abstinence [apsti′nɑ̃:s], *n.f.* Abstinence; temperance, sobriety; (*pl.*) fasts, fasting. **abstinent**, *a.* (*fem.* **abstinente**) Abstemious, sober.

abstracteur [apstrak′tœ:r], *n.m.* One given to abstractions, a subtle reasoner. **abstractif**, *a.* (*fem.* **abstractive**) Abstractive.

abstraction [apstrak′sjɔ̃], *n.f.* Abstraction; the faculty of abstraction; an abstract question or idea; (*fig., pl.*) vague, indefinite ideas. *Par abstraction*, abstractedly; *abstraction faite de*, setting aside; exclusive of. **abstractive** [ABSTRACTIF]. **abstractivement**, *adv.* Abstractly, separately.

abstraire [aps′trɛ:r], *v.t. irr.* (*pres.p.* **abstrayant**, *p.p.* **abstrait** (1), *fem.* **abstraite**, *conjugated like* TRAIRE) To abstract, to consider in the abstract; to separate, to isolate. **abstrait** (2), *a.* (*fem.* **abstraite**) Abstract, abstruse; abstracted, absent-minded. **abstraitement**, *adv.* Abstractedly; separately; in the abstract.

abstrus [aps′try], *a.* (*fem.* **abstruse**) Abstruse, intricate, difficult; obscure, recondite.

absurde [ap′syrd], *a.* Absurd, nonsensical, stupid, silly, irrational, preposterous. *Raisonner par l'absurde*, to prove by reductio ad absurdum. **absurdement**, *adv.* Absurdly, nonsensically.

absurdité, *n.f.* Absurdity, nonsense, unreasonableness, preposterousness, foolishness.

abus [a′by], *n.m.* Abuse, evil usage or custom; grievance; misuse (of power, confidence, words, etc.); error. *Réformer* or *corriger les abus*, to redress grievances; *appel comme d'abus*, (*Law*) appeal by writ of error; *abus de confiance*, breach of trust; *abus de pouvoir*, act of a civil servant who overrides his commission.

abuser [aby′ze], *v.t.* To deceive, to lead astray, to delude, to seduce.—*v.i.* To misuse, to make ill use (*de*); to take advantage (*de*); to indulge too freely. *Vous abusez de ma patience*, you take advantage of my patience. **s'abuser**, *v.r.* To mistake, to be mistaken, to deceive oneself. **abuseur**, *n.m.* Deceiver, impostor; seducer.

abusif [aby′zif], *a.* (*fem.* **abusive**) Irregular, improper, contrary to rule or usage; excessive. **abusivement**, *adv.* Irregularly, improperly.

abuter [aby′te], *v.i.* (*Quoits*) To throw nearest the mark for the right of having the first go; (*Shipbuilding*) to abut, to fit exactly (of wood).

abyssal [abi′sal], *a.* (*fem.* -ale) Unfathomable.

abysse [a′bis], *n.m.* Abyss, unfathomable gulf or depth.

Abyssinie [abisi′ni], *f.* Abyssinia.

acabit [aka′bi], *n.m.* Quality (of fruits, vegetables); character, nature, stamp (of persons). *Ce sont des gens du même acabit*, they are all tarred with the same brush, all of the same kidney.

acacia [aka'sja], *n.m.* (*Bot.*) Acacia.

académicien [akademi'sjɛ̃], *n.m.* Academician.

académie [akade'mi], *n.f.* Academy, society of learned men, *esp.* the Académie française; an educational district of the University of France headed by a *recteur*; Plato's Academy; a school (of dancing, fencing, riding, etc.); (*fig.*) the pupils attending this; (*Paint.*) a nude figure drawn or painted from a model.

académique [akade'mik], *a.* Proper, appropriate, or belonging to an academy, academic(al). *Ordre des palmes académiques*, a distinction granted by the French Ministry of Education. **académiquement,** *adv.* Academically.

académisme [akade'mizm], *n.m.* Narrow observance of academic traditions.

Acadie [aka'di], *f.* Acadia.

acagnarder [akaɲar'de], *v.t.* To make lazy. **s'acagnarder,** *v.r.* To drift into an idle, slothful life.

acajou [aka'ʒu], *n.m.* Mahogany. *Noix d'acajou*, cashew nut; *pomme d'acajou*, cashew apple.

acanthe [a'kɑ̃:t], *n.f.* Acanthus, bear's breech.

acanthoptère [akɑ̃tɔp'tɛ:r], *n.m.* An acanthopterygian, one of an order of fishes having spiny fins.

acare [a'ka:r] or **acarus** [aka'ry:s], *n.m.* Acarus, itch-mite.

acariâtre [aka'rjɑ:tr], *a.* Contrary, crabbed, cross-grained, quarrelsome, shrewish.

acariâtreté, *n.f.* Crabbedness, peevishness, shrewishness.

acaride [aka'rid] or **acarien** [aka'rjɛ̃], *n.m.* Acaridan; arachnid, mite. *Les acarides*, the acaridae.

acarpe [a'karp], *a.* (*Bot.*) Acarpous, barren.

acarus [ACARE].

acatalectique [akatalɛk'tik], *a.* Acatalectic, (verse) complete in its syllables.

acatalepsie [akatalɛp'si], *n.f.* (*Phil.*) Acatalepsy, incomprehensibleness; (*Path.*) a nervous malady with symptoms the opposite to those of catalepsy.

acataleptique [akatalɛp'tik], *a.* Acataleptic.

acatène [aka'tɛ:n], *a.* Chainless.—*n.f.* A chainless bicycle.

acaule [a'ko:l], *a.* (*Bot.*) Acaulous, stemless.

accablant [akɑ'blɑ̃], *a.* (*fem.* **accablante**) Oppressive, insupportable, grievous, overwhelming, crushing. *Des preuves accablantes*, overwhelming evidence. **accablement,** *n.m.* Prostration, oppression, extreme discouragement or dejection.

accabler [akɑ'ble], *v.t.* To crush, to overpower, to overcome; (*fig.*) to weigh down, to overload, to overburden, to overwhelm. *Accabler de bienfaits*, to overwhelm with favours.

accalmie [akal'mi], *n.f.* (*Naut.*) Lull.

accalminé [akalmi'ne], *a.* (*Naut.*) Becalmed.

accaparant [akapa'rɑ̃], *a.* (*fem.* **accaparante**) Engrossing. *Une occupation accaparante*, an all-absorbing activity.

accaparement [akapar'mɑ̃], *n.m.* Monopoly, monopolizing, forestalling.

accaparer [akapa're], *v.t.* To monopolize, to hoard, to engross, to corner, to forestall;

(*fig.*) to secure for oneself at the expense of others. *Accaparer l'attention*, to attract all the attention. **accapareur,** *n.m.* (*fem.* **accapareuse**) Monopolist, monopolizer, hoarder.

accastillage [akasti'ja:ʒ], *n.m.* The upper works of a ship, topsides; *the forecastle and poop. *accastiller,** *v.t.* To provide (a ship) with these.

accéder [akse'de], *v.i.* To arrive, to reach, to have access; to accede, to comply with. *Accéder au vœu de quelqu'un*, to comply with somebody's wish.

accélérateur (1) [akselera'tœ:r], *a.* (*fem.* **accélératrice**) Accelerative, with increasing speed. **accélérateur** (2), *n.m.* (*Elec., Mech., Phot., etc.*) Accelerator. (*fam.*) *Appuyer sur l'accélérateur*, to tread on the gas.

accélération, *n.f.* Acceleration.

accéléré [aksele're], *a.* (*fem.* **-ée**) Accelerated; (*Cine.*) speeded-up. *Pas accéléré*, quick march.—*n.m.* (*Cine.*) Time-lapse.

accélérer [aksele're], *v.t.* To accelerate, to quicken, to hasten, to press, to dispatch.

accent [ak'sɑ̃], *n.m.* Pitch, accent, stress, tone, pronunciation; expression (of the voice); tone or intensity (of a picture). *Accent aigu, circonflexe, grave,* (*Gram.*) acute, circumflex, grave accent; *accent nasillard*, twang; *accent très fortement prononcé*, broad accent; *sans accent*, unaccented. *Mettre l'accent sur*, to emphasize.

accenteur [aksɑ̃'tœr], *n.m.* (*Orn.*) Accentor. *Accenteur moucheté*, hedge-sparrow.

accentuable [aksɑ̃'tɥabl], *a.* That may be accented.

accentuation [aksɑ̃tɥa'sjɔ̃], *n.f.* Accentuation, stressing.

accentuer [aksɑ̃'tɥe], *v.t.* To accent, to accentuate, to stress; to lay emphasis upon.

acceptabilité [aksəptabili'te], *n.f.* Acceptability. **acceptable** [aksəp'tabl], *a.* Acceptable, worth accepting. **acceptant,** *a.* (*fem.* **acceptante**) Acceptant.—*n.m.* Acceptant, one who accepts. **acceptation,** *n.f.* Acceptance; acceptation.

accepter [aksɛp'te], *v.t.* To accept, to agree to, to welcome (what is offered or proposed). **accepteur,** *n.m.* (*Comm.*) Acceptor, drawee (of a bill etc.). **acception,** *n.f.* Respect, regard, sense, meaning, acceptation; preference. *Ne faire acception de personne*, to favour no one in particular; *dans toute l'acception du terme*, in the full meaning of the word.

accès [ak'sɛ], *n.m.* Access, opportunity of approach, admittance; attack, fit, paroxysm. *Accès de fièvre*, attack of fever; *par accès*, by fits and starts. **accessibilité,** *n.f.* Accessibility. **accessible,** *a.* Accessible, approachable; within reach; open to (compassion etc.). **accession,** *n.f.* Accession; adhesion, union (of a country, province, etc. to another); (*Law*) an owner's right to an accessory of his property.

accessit [akse'sit], *n.m.* Award of merit, honourable mention; 'proxime accessit'.

accessoire [aksɛ'swa:r], *a.* Accessory, additional, subordinate, adventitious.—*n.m.* An accessory; (*pl.*) (*Theat.*) property. *Accessoires de toilette*, toilet requisites. **accessoirement,**

adv. Accessorily. **accessoiriste,** *n.m.*
Property-man; (*Cine.*) props man.
accident [aksi′dã], *n.m.* Accident, fortuitous
incident; casualty, mishap, mischance;
unevenness, irregularity, undulation (in the
ground); (*Mus., Paint.*) accidental; (*Gram.*)
accidence, variation; (*Phil.*) that which is
accidental, as opposed to substance. *Par
accident,* accidentally; *accident mortel,* fatality;
accident d'auto, car accident; *accident d'avion,*
air crash.
accidenté [aksidã′te], *a.* (*fem.* **accidentée**)
Varied, unequal (of style etc.); rough, uneven, broken, hilly (of ground); chequered
(of life, career, etc.).—*n.m.* One injured by
an accident. **accidentel,** *a.* (*fem.* **accidentelle**) Accidental, adventitious, fortuitous,
unexpected. *Signe accidentel,* (*Mus.*) any
sign (sharp, flat, etc.) not in the signature.
accidentellement, *adv.* Accidentally,
casually, by chance. **accidenter,** *v.t.* To
make irregular or uneven; to diversify, to
chequer, to make picturesque.
accise [ak′si:z], *n.f.* (*Law*). Inland duty,
excise. *Préposé à l'accise,* exciseman.
acclamateur [aklɑmɑ′tœ:r], *n.m.* (*fem.* **accla-
matrice**) Applauder, shouter, cheerer.
acclamatif, *a.* (*fem.* **-ive**) Acclamatory.
acclamation, *n.f.* Acclamation, cheering.
Saluer par des acclamations, to cheer.
acclamer [aklɑ′me], *v.t.* To acclaim, to
applaud, to cheer; to welcome or announce
enthusiastically.
acclimatable [aklima′tabl], *a.* That may be
acclimatized. **acclimatation,** *n.f.* Acclimatization. *Jardin d'acclimatation,* zoo. **acclimatement,** *n.m.* The state of being
acclimatized.
acclimater [aklima′te], *v.t.* To acclimatize,
to introduce or accustom to a new climate.
s'acclimater, *v.r.* To become acclimatized.
acclimateur, *n.m.* One who acclimatizes.
accoinçon [akwɛ̃′sɔ̃], *n.m.* A timber for
maintaining the shape of a roof; a hip-
rafter.
accointance [akwɛ̃′tã:s], *n.f.* (*Used generally in
pl. and in a bad sense.*) Intimacy, familiarity.
Avoir des accointances (*avec*), to have dealings
(with). **accointer,** *v.t.* To make acquainted.
*****s'accointer,** *v.r.* To become intimately
acquainted (*avec*); to have dealings with (for
an evil purpose).
accolade [akɔ′lad], *n.f.* Embrace; kiss;
accolade (in knighting); (*Mus., Print., etc.*)
brace, double curved bracket. *Accolade
brisée,* (*Print.*) half-brace; *donner l'accolade
à,* to embrace (in conferring the Légion
d'honneur), to dub a knight; *recevoir l'accolade,* to be made a knight. **accolader,** *v.t.*
To bracket. **s'accolader,** *v.r.* To embrace
mutually.
accolage [akɔ′la:ʒ], *n.m.* Tying or nailing up
(branches etc.). **accolé,** *a.* (*fem.* **accolée**)
United, joined together; (*Her.*) together (of
figures put side by side or touching each
other). **accolement,** *n.m.* Joining, uniting.
accoler [akɔ′le], *v.t.* To embrace (by putting
the arms round the neck of); to tie up, to
fasten, to place against; (*fig.*) to couple, to
join together, to bracket. **s'accoler,** *v.r.* To
cling to, (*fig.*) to take up with. *Il s'est accolé
avec cette femme,* he has taken up with that

woman. **accolure,** *n.f.* (*Agric.*) A tie, **a**
band (of straw, osier, etc.); a bundle; (*Bookb.*)
a band; (*Naut.*) raft of floated timber.
accombant [akɔ̃′bã], *a.* (*fem.* **accombante**)
(*Bot.*) Lying on another part (of plants),
accumbent.
accommodable [akɔmɔ′dabl], *a.* That may
be arranged; adjustable. **accommodage,**
n.m. Preparation or dressing (of meat).
accommodant, *a.* (*fem.* **accommodante**)
Accommodating, easy-going, courteous. **accommodation,** *n.f.* Accommodation.
accommodement, *n.m.* Accommodation,
arrangement, composition; settlement, reconciliation, compromise. *En venir à un
accommodement,* to come to terms.
accommoder [akɔmɔ′de], *v.t.* To adapt, to
accommodate, to fit, to adjust; to reconcile,
to conciliate; to dress, to trim; to cook, to
do up; to suit, to be convenient. *Ceci
vous accommodera-t-il?* will this suit you?
s'accommoder, *v.r.* To agree, to come to
terms; to accommodate oneself, to adapt
oneself (*à*); to put up with (*de*). *S'accommoder à son siècle,* to move with the times;
s'accommoder à tout, to make the best of
everything; *s'accommoder partout,* to make
oneself at home everywhere; *s'accommoder
de tout,* to put up with anything.
accompagnateur [akɔ̃paɲa′tœ:r], *n.m.* (*fem.*
accompagnatrice) Accompanist (with instrument or voice); conductor (of a tour).
accompagné, *a.* (*fem.* **accompagnée**)
Accompanied (by a person, letter, etc.);
(*Her.*) accompanied (by other bearings).
accompagnement, *n.m.* Accompanying;
attendance, retinue; an accompaniment, an
accessory; (*Mus.*) instrumental accompaniment. *Accompagnement à grand orchestre,* full
accompaniment; *accompagnement d'harmonie,*
accompaniment for wind instruments.
accompagner [akɔ̃pa′ɲe], *v.t.* To accompany,
to attend on; to go with, to escort; to add
to, to back up (an appeal etc.); (*Mus.*) to
accompany instrumentally. *Accompagner
ses remontrances de menaces,* to accompany
one's remonstrances with threats; *j'ai eu
l'honneur de l'accompagner chez elle,* I had
the honour of seeing her home. **s'accompagner,** *v.r.* To be accompanied, to take
with one; to accompany oneself (on an
instrument). *Il s'accompagne lui-même à la
guitare,* he plays his own accompaniment on
the guitar.
accompli [akɔ̃′pli], *a.* (*fem.* **-ie**) Accomplished, performed, fulfilled; complete,
faultless, perfect, out and out. *Une beauté
accomplie,* a perfect beauty, out and out; *une
maîtresse de maison accomplie,* a perfect housewife; *il a vingt ans accomplis,* he has completed his twentieth year; *s'incliner devant le
fait accompli,* to admit the fact.
accomplir [akɔ̃′pli:r], *v.t.* To fulfil, to effect,
to perform; to realize, to carry out. *Accomplir
son devoir,* to do one's duty. **accomplissement,** *n.m.* Accomplishment, fulfilment,
realization.
accon, acconier [ACON etc.].
accorage [akɔ′ra:ʒ], *n.m.* Propping, shoring-
up, staying.
accord [a′kɔ:r], *n.m.* Accord, concurrence,
unanimity, harmony; agreement, bargain,

convention, settlement; (*Gram.*) concordance, agreement; (*Mus.*) chord. *Être d'accord*, to agree, to be agreed; *d'accord*, granted, agreed; *d'un commun accord*, by common consent; *mettre d'accord*, to reconcile; *tomber d'accord*, to come to an agreement; (*Gram.*) *les règles d'accord*, the concords; (*Mus.*) *accord parfait*, common chord; *faux accord*, discord; *être d'accord*, to be in tune; *tenir l'accord*, to keep in tune. **accordable**, *a.* That may be accorded; reconcilable; (*Mus.*) tunable.

accordage or **accordement**, *n.m.* Tuning (of a musical instrument).

accordailles [akɔr'dɑːj], *n.f.* (*used only in pl.*) Betrothal; party given on signing the marriage contract.

accordant [akɔr'dɑ̃], *a.* (*fem.* **accordante**) Accordant, harmonious.

accordé [akɔr'de], *n.m.* (*fem.* **accordée**) Fiancé, fiancée (after the marriage contract is signed). *Les accordés*, the bride and bridegroom.

accordéon [akɔrde'ɔ̃], *n.m.* Accordion. **accordéoniste**, *n.m.* or *f.* Accordionist.

accorder [akɔr'de], *v.t.* To bring into harmony or accord, to make agree, to reconcile; to concede, to grant, to admit, to avow; (*Gram.*) to put in agreement; (*Mus.*) to tune, to harmonize; to bestow (hand in marriage). *Accordez vos flûtes*, settle it between you. **s'accorder**, *v.r.* To agree, to concur, to be in good understanding; to correspond, to square; to suit, to be suited. *S'accorder sur le prix*, to agree upon the price; *il ne s'accorde pas avec lui-même*, he is inconsistent with himself; *le verbe s'accorde avec le sujet*, the verb agrees with the subject.

accordeur [akɔr'dœːr], *a.* That accords.—*n.m.* Tuner (of musical instruments). *Clef d'accordeur*, tuning-hammer. **accordoir**, *n.m.* Tuning-hammer, or -key, or -cone.

accore [a'kɔːr], *a.* Abrupt, sheer, vertical (of a coast).—*n.m.* (*Naut.*) Shore, prop, stay. **accorer**, *v.t.* (*Naut.*) To shore up, to prop, to stay.

accorné [akɔr'ne], *a.* (*Her.*) Horned, with horns of a different colour from the body.

accort [a'kɔːr], *a.* (*fem.* **accorte**) Gracious, courteous, sprightly; trim. *accortise, *n.f.* Courtesy, complaisance, affability; winning disposition.

accostable [akɔs'tabl], *a.* Easy of access, approachable. **accostage**, *n.m.* The act of accosting, approaching, or drawing alongside. **accoste**, *int.* and *n.f.* (*Naut.*) Come aboard! or ashore! (order to the crew of a rowing-boat).

accosté [akɔs'te], *p.p.* (*fem.* **accostée**) Accosted.—*a.* (*Her.*) Bordered or having at the side (of bars, bands, etc. having other bearings arranged in a parallel direction).

accoster [akɔs'te], *v.t.* To accost, to go up to; (*Naut.*) to come alongside. *Ils s'accostèrent*, they stopped and spoke to each other.

accotement [akɔt'mɑ̃], *n.m.* (*Civ. Eng.*) Space between a highway and the ditch, a house and the gutter, a rail and the edge of the ballast; sideway, footpath.

accoter [akɔ'te], *v.t.* To prop up, to support, to stay. **s'accoter**, *v.r.* To lean (*contre*).

accotoir, *n.m.* Prop, support, leaning-post; (*Naut.*) stay, shore.

accouardir [akwar'diːr], *v.t.* To make a coward. **s'accouardir**, *v.r.* To turn coward.

accouchée [aku'ʃe], *n.f.* A woman in childbed, a woman who has just had a child.

accouchement, *n.m.* Child-bed, delivery, confinement. *Faire un accouchement*, to deliver a woman (of a child); *accouchement avant terme*, premature delivery; *accouchement sans douleur*, painless childbirth; *centre d'accouchement*, maternity centre. **accoucher** [aku'ʃe], *v.i.* To lie in, to be brought to bed, to be delivered; (*fig.*) to bring to light. *Accoucher avant terme*, to miscarry; *accouchez donc!* (*colloq.*) come, out with it!—*v.t.* To deliver (a woman).

accoucheur, *n.m.* Man-midwife, accoucheur. **accoucheuse**, *n.f.* Midwife.

accoudement [akud'mɑ̃], *n.m.* The act of leaning (on). **s'accouder**, *v.r.* To lean on one's elbow. **accoudoir**, *n.m.* Elbow-rest; (*Arch.*) rail, balustrade.

accouer [a'kwe], *v.t.* To tie (horse's) head to tail, for marching in file.

accouple [a'kupl], *n.f.* Leash (for tying dogs in couples). **accouplement**, *n.m.* Coupling; pairing; gathering together in couples, accouplement; copulation; (*Elec.*) joining two or more generators, accumulators, etc. (*Mech.*) *Bielle d'accouplement*, cross-bar, tie-rod.

accoupler [aku'ple], *v.t.* To couple; to join together in pairs; (*Elec.*) to connect, to group (batteries etc.); to copulate, to cause to copulate. *Accoupler des bœufs*, to yoke oxen. **s'accoupler**, *v.r.* To couple, to form a pair; to copulate.

accourci [akur'si], *n.m.* Abridgement (of a book).

accourcir [akur'siːr], *v.t.* To shorten, to abridge, to curtail. **s'accourcir**, *v.r.* To become shorter, to decrease. **accourcissement**, *n.m.* Shortening, diminution.

accourir [aku'riːr], *v.i. irr.* (*pres.p.* **accourant**, *p.p.* **accouru**, *conjugated like* COURIR, *with avoir or être according to the sense*) To run up to, to hasten, to flock, to rush up to.

accours, *1st pres. ind.* [ACCOURIR].

accourt, *3rd sing. ind.*, **accouru**, *p.p.*, **accourus**, *1st past def.* [ACCOURIR].

accoutrement [akutrə'mɑ̃], *n.m.* Garb, dress *esp.* as an object of ridicule. **accoutrer** [aku'tre], *v.t.* To rig out, to dress. **s'accoutrer**, *v.r.* To dress absurdly, to rig oneself out. **accoutreur**, *n.m.* (*fem.* **accoutreuse**) (*Gold-wire-drawing*) Person that cleans out the holes in the plate.

accoutumance [akuty'mɑ̃ːs], *n.f.* Habit, custom, wont, usage. **accoutumé**, *a.* (*fem.* **-ée**) Ordinary, accustomed, habitual. *À l'accoutumée*, usually; *comme à l'accoutumée*, as usual.

accoutumer [akuty'me], *v.t.* To accustom, to habituate, to inure.—*v.i.* (*only in compound tenses*) To use, to be wont. **s'accoutumer**, *v.r.* To be accustomed, to be used (*à*).

accouvage [aku'vaːʒ], *n.m.* Hatching, *esp.* by artificial means, incubation. **accouver**, *v.t.* To set (a hen etc.).—*v.i.* To sit, to hatch.

accréditation [akredita'sjɔ̃], *n.f.* Accreditation, accrediting (of an ambassador).

accréditer [akredi'te], *v.t.* To give credit, standing, or sanction to; to authorize; to accredit (an ambassador etc.); to give vogue to, to confirm, to spread (rumours etc.). **s'accréditer**, *v.r.* To gain credit or reputation; to ingratiate oneself; to spread (of rumours etc.). **accréditeur**, *n.m.* Guarantor, surety. **accréditif**, *n.m.* A letter of credit.

accrescent [akrɛ'sɑ̃], *a.* (*fem.* **accrescente**) (*Bot.*) Accrescent.

accroc [a'kro], *n.m.* Impediment, hitch, hindrance; rent, tear; (*fig.*) stain (on one's character). *Faire un accroc à,* to tear.

accrochage [akrɔ'ʃaːʒ], *n.m.* Hanging, hooking, hitching; catching, retarding, stopping; running foul, grazing (vehicles); (*Mil.*) brief engagement, scrimmage. **accroche-cœur,** *n.m. inv.* A little curl flattened down on the temple, kiss-curl. *En accroche-cœur,* curled up, twisted. **accrochement,** *n.m.* Hooking, catching (in something). **accroche-plat,** *n.m. inv.* A plate-hanger.

accrocher [akrɔ'ʃe], *v.t.* To hang upon a hook; to hook, to catch, to hitch, to catch and tear; (*fig.*) to check, to retard, to delay; to get hold of; to pick up (a wireless station), to tune in to; (*slang*) to pawn. *Accrocher sa montre,* to pawn (or pop) one's watch; (*Mil.*) *se laisser accrocher,* to be compelled to make a stand. **s'accrocher,** *v.r.* To catch in; to be caught or hooked (*par*); to lay hold of, to cling (*à*); (*fig.*) to importune.

accrocheur [akrɔ'ʃœːr], *n.* (*fem.* **accrocheuse**) One who hooks, hangs, seizes, etc.

accroire [a'krwaːr], *v.t. irr.* (used only in the infinitive after *faire*) To believe. *En faire accroire à quelqu'un,* to impose upon someone; *s'en faire accroire,* to be self-conceited, to think too much of oneself.

accroissement [akrwas'mɑ̃], *n.m.* Increase, growth, enlargement, extension, development. (*Fin.*) *Taux d'accroissement,* increment per cent.

accroître [a'krwaːtr], *v.t. irr.* (*pres.p.* **accroissant,** *p.p.* **accru,** conjugated like CROÎTRE). To increase, to augment, to enlarge, to amplify; to heighten. **s'accroître,** *v.r.* To increase, to grow; to be augmented or advanced, to improve.

accroupetonner (s') [akruptɔ'ne] [s'ACCROUPIR].

accroupi [akru'pi], *a.* Crouched, crouching, cowering, squatting.

accroupir (s') [akru'piːr], *v.r.* To sit down upon the hams or heels, to squat, to crouch.

accroupissement, *n.m.* Cowering, squatting, crouching.

accru [a'kry], *n.m.* (*Gard.*) Sucker, scion.—*p.p.* (*fem.* **accrue** (1)) [ACCROÎTRE].

accrue (2) [a'kry], *n.f.* Increase of land through the retreat of waters; encroachment of a forest on adjoining land.

accu [a'ky], *n.m.* Abbr. of *accumulateur.* (*fam.*) *Mes accus sont à plat,* my battery is flat.

accueil [a'kœːj], *n.m.* Reception, welcome, greeting; honouring (of bills etc.). *Faire accueil à,* to receive kindly; *faire bon accueil à une traite,* to meet a bill.

accueillant [akœ'jɑ̃], *a.* (*fem.* **accueillante**) Welcoming; graciously affable.

accueillir [akœ'jiːr], *v.t. irr.* (*pres.p.* **accueillant,** *p.p.* **accueilli,** conjugated like CUEILLIR) To receive (well or ill); to receive graciously, to welcome; to entertain; to happen to, to assail; to honour (a bill etc.). *Être bien accueilli,* to be received with a hearty welcome.

*accul [a'kyl], *n.m.* Blind alley; hole, lair (of fox); breeching (of a cannon). *À l'accul,* at bay, cornered.

acculer [aky'le], *v.t.* To drive into a corner; to put in a fix, to bring to a standstill.—*v.i.* (*Naut.*) To be down at the stern. **s'acculer,** *v.r.* To set one's back against something.

accumulateur [akymyla'tœːr], *a.* (*fem.* **accumulatrice**) That accumulates; storing, heaping up, hoarding up.—*n.* An accumulator (person or thing); storage cell or battery. **accumulation,** *n.f.* Accumulation; an accumulation, a mass, a pile.

accumuler [akymy'le], *v.t.* To accumulate, to pile up, to amass. *Accumuler crime sur crime,* to heap crime upon crime. **s'accumuler,** *v.r.* To accumulate, to increase.

accusable [aky'zabl], *a.* Accusable, chargeable. **accusateur,** *a.* (*fem.* **accusatrice**) That accuses, accusing, accusatory.—*n.* Accuser, denouncer, arraigner. *Accusateur public,* public prosecutor.

accusatif [akyza'tif], *a.* (*fem.* **accusative**) (*Gram.*) Accusative.—*n.m.* Accusative case. *À l'accusatif,* in the accusative.

accusation [akyza'sjɔ̃], *n.f.* Accusation, indictment, charge; (*fig.*) prosecution. *Acte d'accusation,* bill of indictment; *chef d'accusation,* count of indictment; *mise en accusation,* arraignment; *intenter une accusation,* to prefer an indictment; *mettre en accusation,* to impeach, indict; *prononcer la mise en accusation,* to find a true bill. **accusatoire,** *a.* Accusatory.

accusé [aky'ze], *n.m.* (*fem.* **accusée**) The accused, prisoner, defendant, culprit. *Accusé de réception,* acknowledgment of a letter, receipt.

accuser [aky'ze], *v.t.* To impute, to charge with; to reproach, to blame; to indict, to impeach, to prosecute; to reveal, to indicate, to show (one's age etc.). *Accuser les muscles,* (*Paint.*) to show up the muscles (under the skin); *accuser réception d'une lettre,* to acknowledge the receipt of a letter. **s'accuser,** *v.r.* To admit, to avow, to confess.

acéphale [ase'fal], *a.* Acephalous, headless.—*n.* One or that which is acephalous. **acéphalie,** *n.f.* Absence of a head.

acer [a'sɛːr], *n.m.* Maple.

acérage [ase'raːʒ], *n.m.* (*Metal.*) Steeling, overlaying with steel.

acérain [ase'rɛ̃], *a.* (*fem.* **acéraine**) Like or pertaining to steel, steely.

acerbe [a'sɛrb], *a.* Sour, harsh, sharp, astringent; (*fig.*) bitter, acrimonious, mordant. **acerbité,** *n.f.* Acerbity, harshness; (*fig.*) bitterness, severity.

acère [a'sɛːr], *a.* (*Ent.*) Hornless, without feelers or tentacles.—*n.m.* Such an insect.

acéré [ase're], *a.* (*fem.* **acérée**) Steely, steeled; sharp, keen; (*fig.*) mordant, trenchant, acute. **acérer,** *v.t.* To steel; to acerate; to sharpen, to render biting, incisive, or mordant. **acérure,** *n.f.* Piece of steel for welding to tool or weapon.

(*C*) **acéricole** [aseri′kɔl], *a.* (*Bot.*) Aceric.

acescence [ase′sã:s], *n.f.* Acescence, acidifying. **acescent,** *a.* (*fem.* **acescente**) Turning acid or sour, acescent.

acétabule [aseta′byl], *n.m.* (*Anat.*) Acetabulum.

acétamide [aseta′mid], *n.m.* (*Chem.*) Acetamide.

acétate [ase′tat], *n.m.* (*Chem.*) Acetate.

acéteux [ase′tø], *a.* (*fem.* **acéteuse**) Acetous, sour, tasting like vinegar. **acétification,** *n.f.* Acetification. **acétifier,** *v.t.* To acetify. **acétimètre** or **acétomètre,** *n.m.* Acetimeter. **acétique,** *a.* Acetic. **acétol,** *n.m.* (*Pharm.*) Vinegar prepared by distillation for medical purposes. **acétomel,** *n.m.* Syrup of vinegar and honey. **acétone,** *n.f.* Acetone. **acétonémie,** *n.f.* Acetonaemia. **acétosité,** *n.f.* The state of being acetous. **acétonurie,** *n.f.* Acetonuria.

acétoselle, *n.f.* Wood-sorrel.

acétylène [aseti′lɛːn], *n.m.* Acetylene. *Lampe à acétylène,* acetylene lamp.

Achaïe [aka′i], *f.* Achaea.

achalandage [aʃalã′da:ʒ], *n.m.* Custom, customers, connexion; drawing custom; the goodwill (of a shop).

achalandé, *a.* (*fem.* **achalandée**) Having plenty of custom. *Boutique bien achalandée,* a well-frequented shop, one driving a good trade. **achalander,** *v.t.* To get custom, to attract customers, to draw trade; (*fig.*) to bring into vogue.

Achantis [aʃã′ti], **l',** *m.* Ashanti.

acharné [aʃar′ne], *a.* Fleshed, fierce, tenacious, implacable; stubborn, obstinate, intense. *Un combat acharné,* a desperate fight; *une haine acharnée,* an implacable hatred; *un travail acharné,* strenuous work. **acharnement,** *n.m.* Tenacity; rancour, animosity, fury; stubbornness, obstinacy, desperation. *Avec acharnement,* unmercifully, furiously; *c'est de l'acharnement,* this is rank fury, a real passion for work.

acharner [aʃar′ne], *v.t.* To flesh; to set on, to excite, to madden; to embitter, to envenom. **s'acharner,** *v.r.* To be intent, bent, or obstinately set upon; to set one's heart upon, to persist in; to be infuriated or implacable. *Il s'acharne à l'étude,* he slaves at his work; *le mauvais sort ne cessa de s'acharner après lui,* ill-luck never ceased to pursue him relentlessly; *s'acharner contre quelqu'un,* to be implacable towards someone.

achat [a′ʃa], *n.m.* Purchasing, buying; purchase. *Faire des achats,* to go shopping; *pouvoir d'achat,* purchasing power; *prix d'achat,* purchase price.

ache [aʃ]. *n.f.* (*Bot.*) Smallage, wild celery.

achée [a′ʃe], *n.f.* (*Angling*) Worms, gentles, etc., used for bait.

acheminement [aʃmin′mã], *n.m.* Progress, advance, conveying. *L'acheminement des marchandises,* the dispatching of goods.

acheminer [aʃmi′ne], *v.t.* To put in the way, to send on (towards a place or object); to train (a horse) to go straight forward. **s'acheminer,** *v.r.* To set out (*pour*), to make one's way towards; to begin one's journey; to proceed towards; to get on.

Achéron [ake′rɔ̃], **l',** *m.* The Acheron.

achetable [aʃ′tabl], *a.* Purchasable.

acheter [aʃ′te], *v.t.* To buy, to purchase; (*fig.*) to bribe. *Acheter cher* or *bon marché,* to buy dear or cheap; *acheter d'occasion,* to buy second-hand; *acheter en bloc,* to buy in the lump; *acheter chat en poche,* to buy a pig in a poke. **s'acheter,** *v.r.* To be bought; to be for sale, to be venal. **acheteur,** *n.m.* (*fem.* **acheteuse**) Buyer, purchaser.

achevage [aʃ′va:ʒ], *n.m.* Completion, finishing; finish (of a work of art).

achevaler [aʃva′le], *v.t.* To be astride of (said of an army occupying both sides of a river, railway, etc.), to straddle.

achevé [aʃ′ve], *a.* (*fem.* **achevée**) Finished, accomplished, perfect, exquisite; absolute, downright, consummate, arrant. *Beauté achevée,* a perfect beauty; *sot achevé,* downright ass; *d'un ridicule achevé,* perfectly ridiculous. **achèvement** [aʃɛv′mã], *n.m.* Completion, conclusion.

achever [aʃ′ve], *v.t.* To finish, to terminate, to put the finishing touch to; to complete, to achieve; to consummate, to perfect; (*fig.*) to do for completely, to ruin, to kill. *Achevez de boire votre vin,* drink up your wine; *achevez!* out with it! *il n'acheva pas,* he said no more.

achevoir [aʃəv′wa:r], *n.m.* Tool or shop for finishing or giving the final touches.

(*C*) **achigan** [aʃi′gã], *n.m.* Black bass.

Achille [a′ʃil], *m.* Achilles.

achillée [aki′le], *n.f.* Milfoil, yarrow; (*Bot.*) any of the genus of plants containing these.

achoppement [aʃɔp′mã], *n.m.* Obstacle, impediment; unforeseen difficulty, embarrassment. *Pierre d'achoppement,* stumbling-block. **achopper,** *v.i.,* and **s'achopper,** *v.r.* To stumble, to knock against anything; (*fig.*) to come to grief, to fail.

achorion [ako′rjɔ̃], *n.m.* Fungoid growth on the heads of infants.

achromatine [akrɔma′tin], *n.f.* Achromatine.

achromatique [akrɔma′tik], *a.* Achromatic. **achromatisation,** *n.f.* The act of achromatizing. **achromatiser,** *v.t.* To achromatize, to make achromatic. **achromatisme,** *n.m.* Achromatism. **achromatopsie,** *n.f.* Achromatopsy; colour-blindness. **achrème,** *a.* Achromous, colourless.

achromie [akrɔ′mi], *n.f.* Insufficient pigmentation of the skin.

aciculaire [asiky′lɛːr], *a.* (*Min.*) Acicular; (*Bot.*) needle-shaped, sharp-pointed.

acide [a′sid], *a.* Acid, sour, tart, sharp.—*n.m.* Acid. **acidifère,** *a.* Producing acids. **acidifiable,** *a.* Acidifiable. **acidifiant,** *a.* (*fem.* **acidifiante**) Acidifying, tending to acidify.—*n.m.* An agent that acidifies. **acidification,** *n.f.* Acidification. **acidifier** [asidi′fje], *v.t.* To acidify. **s'acidifier,** *v.r.* To become acidified. **acidimètre,** *n.m.* Instrument for measuring the strength of acids. **acidimétrie,** *n.f.* Acidimetry. **acidité,** *n.f.* Acidity, sourness, sharpness, tartness.

acidose, *n.f.* (*Med.*) Acidosis.

acidule, *a.* Subacid, acidulous. **acidulé,** *a.* (*fem.* **acidulée**) Acidulated. *Bonbons acidulés,* acid drops. **aciduler,** *v.t.* To acidulate.

acier [a′sje], *n.m.* Steel. *Acier chromé,* chrome steel; *acier coulé* or *fondu,* cast steel; *acier* poule or *de cémentation*, blister steel; *acier doux*, mild steel; *acier inoxydable*, stainless steel; *acier trempé*, tempered steel. **aciération**, *n.f.* Steeling, plating with steel. **aciérer**, *v.t.* To convert into steel, to cover with steel; to acierate. **s'aciérer**, *v.r.* To steel oneself.

aciéreux, *a.* (*fem.* **-euse**) Steely, like steel.

aciérie, *n.f.* Steel factory, steelworks.

acine [a'sin] or **acinus** [asi'ny:s], *n.m.* (*Anat.*) Acinus. **acineux** [asinø], *a.* (*fem.* **acineuse**) Aciniform, acinose, acinous.

acinèse [asi'nɛːz], *n.f.* (*Med.*) Akinesia.

aclinique [akli'nik], *a.* Aclinic.

acné [ak'ne], *n.f.* (*Med.*) Acne.

acolyte [akɔ'lit], *n.m.* (*Eccles.*) Acolyte; (*fig.*) assistant, confederate, associate, accomplice.

acompte [a'kɔ̃:t], *n.m.* Instalment, partial payment.

acon or **accon** [a'kɔ̃], *n.m.* A small lighter, a punt. **aconier** or **acconier**, *n.m.* A lighterman.

aconit [akɔ'nit], *n.m.* Aconite. *Aconit napel*, monk's-hood; *aconit tue-loup*, wolf's-bane; *aconit tue-chien*, dog's-bane. **aconitine**, *n.f.* (*Chem.*) Aconitine.

acoquinant [akɔki'nɑ̃], *a.* (*fem.* **acoquinante**) Alluring, engaging, captivating; degrading (companion).

acoquiner [akɔki'ne], *v.t.* *To debauch; to make fond, to allure, to bewitch, to captivate. **s'acoquiner**, *v.r.* (*fam.*) To be bewitched, to be greatly attached to, to cotton to, to become degraded. *Il s'acoquine auprès de cette femme*, he degrades himself with that woman.

acore [a'kɔ:r], *n.m.* (*Bot.*) Sweet rush.

Açores [a'sɔ:r], **les**, *f.pl.* The Azores.

à-côté [ako'te], *n.m.* Aside; *pl.* (*fem.*) little extras. *Il a quelques à-côtés*, he earns some extra money *or* some money on the side.

acotylédone [akɔtile'dɔn] or **acotylédoné** (*fem.* **-ée**), *a.* (*Bot.*) Acotyledonous.

à-coup [a'ku], *n.m.* Jerk, jolt; sudden stop. *Procéder par à-coups*, to proceed by fits and starts; *sans à-coups*, smoothly.

acousticien [akusti'sjɛ̃], *n.* (*fem.* **acousticienne**) Acoustician.

acoustique (1) [akus'tik], *a.* Acoustic. *Cornet acoustique*, ear-trumpet; *tuyau acoustique*, speaking-tube; *voûte acoustique*, whispering gallery. **acoustique** (2), *n.f.* Acoustics.

acquéreur [ake'rœ:r], *n.m.* (*fem.* **acquéreuse**) Buyer, purchaser. *Se rendre acquéreur de*, to purchase.

acquérir [ake'ri:r], *v.t. irr.* (*pres.p.* **acquérant**, *p.p.* **acquis**) To purchase, to buy, to get; to earn, to win, to gain; to acquire, to obtain. *Être acquis à*, (of things) to belong by right to, (of persons) to be completely devoted to. **s'acquérir**, *v.r.* To get or win for oneself; to be acquired, obtained, or purchased; (*Law*) to accrue.

acquêt [a'kɛ], *n.m.* (*Law*) An acquisition; the common property of two married people, acquest. *Communauté réduite aux acquêts*, marriage settlement through which only acquests accrue to the community.

acquiescement [akjɛs'mɑ̃], *n.m.* Acquiescence, compliance, consent, willingness.

acquiescer [akjɛ'se], *v.i.* To acquiesce, to agree, to assent, to yield, to comply.

acquis [a'ki], *a.* (*fem.* **acquise**) Acquired, secured; devoted (*à*). *Fait acquis*, established fact; *droits acquis*, vested rights; *tenir pour acquis*, to take for granted.—*n.m.* Acquirements, attainments, experience.

acquisitif [akizi'tif], *a.* (*fem.* **acquisitive**) Acquisitive. **acquisition** [akizi'sjɔ̃], *n.f.* Acquisition, acquiring, attaining, acquirement, attainment; purchase, conquest. *Contrat d'acquisition*, deed of purchase. **acquisivité**, *n.f.* Acquisitiveness.

acquit [a'ki], *n.m.* Receipt, discharge, release, acquittance; (*Billiards*) break (i.e. start). *Par acquit de conscience*, as a matter of duty; *par manière d'acquit*, for mere form's sake, negligently; *pour acquit* (on bills), received, paid; *donner acquit de*, to give a receipt for.

acquit-à-caution [akiako'sjɔ̃], *n.m.* (*pl.* **acquits-à-caution**) (*Customs*) Permit (for goods to be forwarded, duty being paid on delivery); excise bond, custom-house bond.

acquittable [aki'tabl], *a.* Payable; worthy of acquittal.

acquittement [akit'mɑ̃], *n.m.* Payment, quittance; (*Law*) acquittal.

acquitter [aki'te], *v.t.* To pay; to discharge, to pay off (a dependant). **s'acquitter**, *v.r* To fulfil, to perform; to pay off one's debts, to be quits (in gambling); to acquit oneself (well or ill).

acre [akr], *n.f.* Acre.

âcre [ɑːkr], *a.* Sour, sharp, tart, acrid; (*fig.*) bitter, pungent, caustic. **âcrement**, *adv.* Tartly, sourly; (*fig.*) acridly, sharply. **âcreté**, *n.f.* Sourness, acridity, sharpness, tartness, acrimony.

acrimonie [akrimɔ'ni], *n.f.* Bitterness, sharpness, keenness, acrimony. **acrimonieusement**, *adv.* Acrimoniously. **acrimonieux**, *a.* (*fem.* **acrimonieuse**) Pungent, acrimonious, ill-natured, sharp.

acrobate [akrɔ'bat], *n.* Acrobat, rope-dancer. **acrobatie**, *n.f.* Acrobatics; (*Av.*) stunt. **acrobatique**, *a.* Acrobatic. **acrobatisme**, *n.m.* Acrobatics.

acrocéphale [akrɔse'fal], *a.* Having a pointed head; acrocephalic, acrocephalous.—*n.* A person with such a head. **acrocéphalie**, *n.f.* The quality of having such a head.

acronyque [akrɔ'nik], *a.* (*Astron.*) Acronychal.

acropole [akrɔ'pɔl], *n.f.* Acropolis.

acrostiche [akrɔs'tiʃ], *a.* and *n.m.* Acrostic.

acrotère [akrɔ'tɛ:r], *n.m.* (*Arch.*) Acroterium, ornamental summit (of a pediment).

acte [akt], *n.m.* Action, deed; (*Law*) deed, indenture, instrument; document, charter; (*Theat.*) act; (*pl.*) records, public registers, rolls, transactions, proceedings. *Acte d'accusation*, bill of indictment; *acte de naissance*, birth certificate; *acte faux*, forged deed; *donner acte de*, to deliver an official certificate of; *expédition d'un acte*, copy of a deed; *faire acte de présence*, to put in an appearance, to mark in; *prendre acte*, to make a note of, to put down; *rédiger un acte*, to draw up a document.

acteur [ak'tœ:r], *n.m.* (*fem.* **actrice**) Actor; actress; player.

actif [ak'tif], *a.* (*fem.* **active**) Active, busy, energetic, assiduous; nimble, brisk, agile; engaged (in work, operation, etc.); actual;

[11]

(*Gram. etc.*) active.—*n.m.* (*Gram.*) Active voice; assets, credit balance. *Dettes actives*, assets; (*fig.*) *mettre à l'actif de quelqu'un*, to credit someone (with something); *armée active*, regular army.

actinie [akti'ni], *n.f.* (*Zool.*) Actinia, sea-anemone.

actinique [akti'nik], *a.* Actinic. **actinisme**, *n.m.* Actinism. **actinographe,** *n.m.* Actinograph. **actinomètre,** *n.m.* Actinometer.

actinium [akti'njɔm], *n.m.* (*Chem.*) Actinium.

action [ak'sjɔ̃], *n.f.* Action, operation, work; activity, motion; deed, feat, performance; fight, engagement, battle; (*Law*) action, law-suit; (*Theat.*) gesture; (*Lit.*) subject, action, plot; (*Comm.*) share, stock. *En action*, in motion; *entrer en action*, to come into force, to begin operations; *hors d'action*, (*Mech.*) out of gear; *mettre en action*, to carry out. *Action d'éclat*, feat of arms. *Action de grâces*, thanksgiving. (*Law*) *Intenter une action à quelqu'un*, to bring an action against someone. (*St. Exch.*) *Action ordinaire*, common stock; *action gratuite*, bonus share; *action au porteur*, bearer certificate; *hausse* or *baisse des actions*, rise or fall of shares; *promesse d'action*, scrip; *titre d'une action*, document of a share.

actionnable [aksjɔ'nabl], *a.* (*Law*) Actionable.

actionnaire [aksjɔ'nɛːr], *n.m.* Shareholder.

actionnariat [aksjɔna'rja], *n.m.* Shareholding. *Actionnariat ouvrier*, industrial co-partnership.

actionner [aksjɔ'ne], *v.t.* To bring an action against, to sue at law; to bestir, to rouse up, to set going; to operate, to run, to drive. *Actionné à la main*, hand-operated. **s'actionner,** *v.r.* To bestir oneself.

activant, *pres.p.* [ACTIVER].

activement [aktiv'mɑ̃], *adv.* Actively, vigorously.

activer [akti've], *v.t.* To press, to accelerate, to forward, to expedite, to stir up (a fire, people). (*fam.*) *Activez!* Hurry up!

activisme, *n.m.* (*Polit.*) Militancy, activism.

activiste, *n.m.* Activist.

activité, *n.* Activity, full swing; nimbleness, alacrity, promptitude, dispatch. *En activité*, in active service; *en pleine activité*, in full swing; *volcan en activité*, active volcano; *marché sans activité*, dull market.

actrice [ACTEUR].

actuaire [ak'tɥɛːr], *n.m.* Actuary.

actualisation [aktɥaliza'sjɔ̃], *n.f.* Actualization; realization. **actualiser,** *v.t.* To bring up to date. **s'actualiser,** *v.r.* To become real.

actualité [aktɥali'te], *n.f.* Actuality; event of the moment, present interest. *Une question d'actualité*, a topical question. (*Cinema*) *Les actualités*, the newsreel.

actuel [ak'tɥɛl], *a.* (*fem.* **actuelle**) Present, of the present time; (*Theol.*) actual. *À l'heure actuelle*, nowadays; *le gouvernement actuel*, the present government; *péché actuel*, personal (as opposed to original) sin; *grâce actuelle*, divine help given to resist temptation etc. (as opposed to natural grace). **actuellement,** *adv.* Now, at the present time.

acuité [akɥi'te], *n.f.* Sharpness, acuteness, keenness. *Acuité visuelle*, keenness of sight.

aculé [aky'le], *a.* (*fem.* **aculée**) (*Zool.*)

Aculeate. **aculéiforme,** *a.* (*Bot.*) Aculeiform.

acuminé [akymi'ne], *a.* (*fem.* **acuminée**) (*Bot.* and *Med.*) Acuminate.

acuponcture [akypɔ̃k'tyːr], *n.f.* Acupuncture.

acutangle [aky'tɑ̃ːgl] or **acutangulaire,** *a.* Acute-angled (of triangles etc.).

acutesse [aky'tɛs], *n.f.* Acuteness, sharpness.

adage [a'daːʒ], *n.m.* Adage, proverb, saying.

Adam [a'dɑ̃], *m.* Adam.

adamantin [adamɑ̃'tɛ̃], *a.* (*fem.* **adamantine**) Adamantine.

adaptable [adap'tabl], *a.* Adaptable. **adaptateur,** *n.m.* adapter, converter. **adaptation,** *n.f.* Adaptation.

adapter [adap'te], *v.t.* To adapt, to adjust, to apply (*à*); to fit, to make suitable. **s'adapter,** *v.r.* To fit, to suit, to adapt oneself (to). *Il sait s'adapter*, he knows how to make the best of things.

additif [adi'tif], *a.* (*fem.* **additive**) Additive. —*n.m.* additional clause.

addition [adi'sjɔ̃], *n.f.* Adding up, addition; that which is added, an addition; bill, reckoning, (*Am.*) check. *Addition composée*, compound addition; *garçon, l'addition!* waiter, bill, please! **additionnel,** *a.* (*fem.* **additionnelle**) Additional. **additionner,** *v.t.* To add up; to increase with (*de*). *Sirop additionné d'eau*, (*Chem.*) diluted syrup.

adducteur [adyk'tœːr], *a.m.* (*Anat.*) Adducent. —*n.m.* Adductor. **adduction,** *n.f.* Adduction. *Adduction d'eau*, water supply.

Adélaïde [adela'id], *f.* Adelaide.

Adèle [a'dɛl], *f.* Adela.

adénite [ade'nit], *n.f.* Adenitis, inflammation of the glands. **adénoïde** [adenɔ'id], *a.* Adenoid. **adénopathie,** *n.f.* Disease of the glands.

adénome [ade'noːm], *n.m.* Adenoma, glandular tumour.

adent [a'dɑ̃], *n.m.* Dovetail, tenon. **adenter,** *v.t.* To dovetail, to join with mortise and tenon.

adepte [a'dɛpt], *n.m.* Adept, initiate, follower.

adéquat [ade'kwa], *a.* (*fem.* **adéquate**) Adequate; (*Phil.*) equal in content; appropriate.

adextré [adɛks'tre], *a.* (*Her.*) Dexterwise.

adhérence [ade'rɑ̃ːs], *n.f.* Adhesion, adherence; (*fig.*) attachment. **adhérent,** *a.* (*fem.* **-ente**) Adherent.—*n.m.* Adherent, follower, partisan. **adhérer,** *v.i.* To adhere, to cling; (*fig.*) to hold (*à*), to cleave (to a sect etc.). *Adhérer à un parti*, to join a party.

adhésif [ade'zif], *a.* (*fem.* **-ive**) Adhesive.— *n.m.* (*Phot.*) Dry-mounting tissue. **adhésion,** *n.f.* Adhesion, adherence, union; approval, approbation, compliance; joining (a party).

adhésivité, *n.f.* Adhesiveness.

adiabatique [adjaba'tik], *a.* Adiabatic. **adiabatisme,** *n.m.* The state of being adiabatic (of gases).

adiante [a'djɑ̃ːt], *n.m.* (*Bot.*) Adiantum. *Adiante capillaire*, maidenhair fern.

adieu [a'djø], *int.* Adieu, good-bye, farewell. —*n.m.* Farewell, parting, leave. *Dire adieu à*, to give up, to renounce; *faire ses adieux à*, to take leave of, to say good-bye to; *sans adieu*, without saying good-bye; *baiser d'adieu*, parting kiss.

à-Dieu vat! [adjɔvat], *int.* Now it is done. We must trust God. (*Naut.*) About ship!

adipeux [adi'pø], *a.* (*fem.* **adipeuse**) Adipose, fat. **adipocire,** *n.f.* Adipocere. **adiposité,** *n.f.* Adipose or fatty condition.

adjacence [adʒa'sɑːs], *n.f.* Adjacency.

adjacent [adʒa'sɑ̃], *a.* (*fem.* **adjacente**) Adjacent, bordering upon, contiguous.

adjectif [adʒɛk'tif], *a.* (*fem.* **adjective**) (*Gram.*) Adjectival.—*n.m.* Adjective. **adjectivement,** *adv.* Adjectively.

adjoignant, etc., *pres.p.*, *etc.* [ADJOINDRE].

adjoindre [ad'ʒwɛ̃ːdr], *v.t.* (*pres.p.* **adjoignant,** *p.p.* **adjoint**) To adjoin, to associate, to add as an assistant. **s'adjoindre,** *v.r.* To join as a partner or associate; to take on as.

adjoint [ad'ʒwɛ̃], *a.* (*fem.* **adjointe**) Adjunct, associate, assistant.—*n.m.* Associate, assistant, deputy. *Adjoint au maire,* deputy-mayor.

adjonction [adʒɔ̃k'sjɔ̃], *n.f.* Adjunction.

adjudant [adʒy'dɑ̃], *n.m.* Company sergeant-major; warrant-officer. *Adjudant-major,* adjutant; (*Am.*) first sergeant; *adjudant-chef,* master sergeant.

adjudicataire [adʒydika'tɛːr], *a.* and *n.* Contracting party; successful tenderer, highest bidder.

adjudicateur [adʒydika'tœːr], *n.m.* (*fem.* **adjudicatrice**) Awarder; auctioneer. **adjudicatif,** *a.* (*fem.* **adjudicative**) (*Law*) Adjudging. **adjudication,** *n.f.* Auction; knocking down; adjudication.

adjuger [adʒy'ʒe], *v.t.* To adjudge, to adjudicate, to knock down (to the highest bidder); to award. *Adjugé!* (at auctions) gone! **s'adjuger,** *v.r.* To appropriate.

adjuration [adʒyra'sjɔ̃], *n.f.* Adjuration, imprecation. **adjurer,** *v.t.* To adjure, to conjure; to call upon, to beseech.

adjuteur [adʒy'tœːr], *n.m.* Coadjutor, assistant.

adjuvant [adʒy'vɑ̃], *a.* (*fem.* **adjuvante**) (*Med.*) Adjuvant.—*n.m.* An adjuvant substance.

admettre [ad'mɛtr], *v.t. irr.* (*p.p.* **admis**) To admit, to let in; to concede, to allow, to acknowledge, to own; to admit of (delay etc.).

administrateur [administra'tœːr], *n.m.* (*fem.* **administratrice**) Manager, director; administrator, administratrix, trustee (of an estate). *Administrateur de biens,* curator; guardian (of the poor). **administratif,** *a.* (*fem.* **administrative**) Administrative. **administration,** *n.f.* Administration, management, direction, government; (*collect.*) the management, the administration. *Administration des sacrements,* the act of administering the sacraments; *conseil d'administration,* board of directors; (*fam.*) *il est dans l'administration,* he is a civil servant. **administrativement,** *adv.* Administratively.

administré [adminis'tre], *n.m.* (*fem.* **administrée**) Person under one's administration or jurisdiction.

administrer [adminis'tre], *v.t.* To manage, to govern, to direct; to administer, to dispense; (*Law*) to produce. *Administrer des preuves,* to produce proofs; (*fam.*) *administrer une bonne râclée,* to give a good hiding.

admirable [admi'rabl], *a.* Admirable; wonderful. **admirablement,** *adv.* Admirably; wonderfully.

admirateur [admira'tœːr], *n.m.* (*fem.* **admira-**

trice) Admirer, praiser. **admiratif** [admira'tif], *a.* (*fem.* **admirative**) Admiring, wondering. *D'un air admiratif,* with a wondering look. **admiration,** *n.f.* Admiration. *Être saisi d'admiration,* to be struck with admiration.

admirer [admi're], *v.t.* To admire; *to wonder at.

admis [ad'mi], *p.p.* [ADMETTRE] (*fem.* **admise**). **admissibilité** [admisibili'te], *n.f.* Admissibility. **admissible,** *a.* Admittable, admissible.—*n.* One who has passed the written part of an examination. **admission,** *n.f.* Admission, admittance. *Concours d'admission,* competitive entrance examination; *soupape d'admission,* inlet valve.

admixtion [admiks'tjɔ̃], *n.f.* Admixture.

admonestation [admɔnɛsta'sjɔ̃], *n.f.* Admonishment, admonition. **admonester,** *v.t.* To reprimand, to admonish.

admoniteur [admɔni'tœːr], *n.m.* (*fem.* **admonitrice**) Admonisher. **admonitif,** *a.* (*fem.* **admonitive**) Admonitory. **admonition,** *n.f.* (*Chiefly R.-C. Ch.*) Admonition, advice, reprimand.

adné [ad'ne], *a.* (*fem.* **adnée**) (*Bot.*) Adnate.

adolescence [adɔlɛ'sɑ̃ːs], *n.f.* Adolescence.

adolescent, *a.* (*fem.* **adolescente**) Adolescent. —*n.* An adolescent, a youth, a teenager.

Adolphe [a'dɔlf], *m.* Adolphus.

*adonc, adoncques, or **adonques** [a'dɔ̃ːk], *adv.* Then.

Adonis [adɔ'niːs], *n.m.* Adonis, beau; (*Bot.*) adonis, pheasant's-eye. **s'adoniser,** *v.t.* To bedizen oneself.

adonné [adɔ'ne], *a.* (*fem.* **-ée**) Given to, addicted, devoted. **s'adonner,** *v.r.* To give, to devote, to addict oneself. *S'adonner à la boisson,* to take to drink.

*adonques [ADONC].

adoptable [adɔp'tabl], *a.* That may be adopted. **adoptant,** *n.m.* Adopter. **adopté,** *a.* (*fem.* **-ée**) Adoptive son, daughter, heir, etc.

adopter [adɔp'te], *v.t.* To adopt; to embrace, to espouse; to pass, to carry (a bill). **adoptif,** *a.* (*fem.* **adoptive**) Adoptive, by adoption. *Enfant adoptif,* adoptive child; *père adoptif,* foster-father. **adoption,** *n.f.* Adoption.

adorable [adɔ'rabl], *a.* Adorable, charming, delightful, exquisite. **adorablement,** *adv.* Adorably, delightfully.

adorateur [adɔra'tœːr], *n.m.* (*fem.* **adoratrice**) Adorer, worshipper. **adoratif,** *a.* (*fem.* **adorative**) Adoring, worshipping, reverential. **adoration,** *n.f.* Adoration, worship; admiration, respect, reverence. (*fig.*) *Il est en adoration devant elle,* he worships her.

adorer [adɔ're], *v.t.* To adore, to worship.

ados [a'do], *n.m.* (*Gard.*) Sheltered bed looking south, warm border (against a wall).

adossé [ado'se], *a.* (*fem.* **adossée**) With one's back against; (*Her.*) addorsed. **adossement,** *n.m.* Position back to back.

adosser [ado'se], *v.t.* To set or lean with the back against; to put back to back. **s'adosser,** *v.r.* To lean the back (*à, contre*); to be backed (by). *S'adosser à un mur,* to lean up against a wall.

adouber [adu'be], *v.t.* (*Chess*) To adjust (a piece) without moving it; to dub (a knight); (*Naut.*) to mend, to repair.

adoucir [adu'si:r], *v.t.* To soften, to sweeten; to mitigate, to alleviate, to smooth. **s'adoucir**, *v.r.* To grow mild, or soft; (of weather) to get milder. **adoucissage**, *n.m.* Softening (of metals etc.); smoothing or polishing (of metals, glass, etc.). **adoucissant**, *a.* (*fem.* **adoucissante**) Softening, soothing, emollient.—*n.m.* Emollient. **adoucissement**, *n.m.* Softening, sweetening; assuaging, appeasing; ease, mitigation, alleviation; consolation. **adoucisseur**, *n.m.* (*fem.* **adoucisseuse**) Glass-polisher.

adragant [adra'gɑ̃], *a.* and *n.* (*fem.* **adragante**) (Gum) tragacanth.

adrénaline [adrena'lin], *n.f.* Adrenalin.

adresse [a'drɛs], *n.f.* Address; a memorial, a document addressed to an assembly or person in authority; skill, dexterity, cleverness. *À l'adresse de*, directed to; *tour d'adresse*, legerdemain.

adresser [adre'se], *v.t.* To direct, to address; to turn, to direct (one's steps etc.). *Adresser la parole à*, to speak to; *lettre mal adressée*, misdirected letter. **s'adresser**, *v.r.* To be directed; to speak, to address oneself, to make application, to appeal (*à*). *Ceci s'adresse à vous*, this applies to you; *s'adresser ici*, apply within; *vous vous adressez mal*, you mistake your man.

Adriatique [adria'tik], **l'**, *f.* The Adriatic.

Adrien [adri'ɛ̃], *m.* Adrian.

Adrienne [adri'ɛn], *f.* Adriana.

adroit [a'drwa], *a.* (*fem.* **adroite**) Ingenious, clever, skilful; artful. **adroitement**, *adv.* skilfully, artfully, cleverly.

adulateur [adyla'tœːr], *a.* (*fem.* **adulatrice**) Flattering, adulatory, *n.* Adulator, flatterer, sycophant. **adulatif**, *a.* (*fem.* **adulative**) Flattering, adulatory. **adulation**, *n.f.* Adulation, flattery, sycophancy. **adulatoire**, *a.* Adulatory. **aduler**, *v.t.* To flatter, to fawn upon, to cringe to.

adulte [a'dylt], *a.* Adult, grown-up.—*n.* Adult.

adultérant [adylte'rɑ̃], *a.* and *n.* (*fem.* **adultérante**) Adulterant. **adultérateur**, *n.m.* Adulterator. **adultération**, *n.f.* (*Comm.*, *Pharm.*, *etc.*) Adulteration; (*Law*) falsification (of money, documents, etc.).

adultère [adyl'tɛːr], *a.* Adulterous. *Femme adultère*, adulteress.—*n.* Adulterer, adulteress.—*n.m.* adultery. *Commettre un adultère*, to commit adultery. **adultérer**, *v.t.* (*Pharm.*) To adulterate; (*Law*) to falsify (money); (*fig.*) to corrupt, to pervert, to falsify. **adultérin**, *a.* (*fem.* **adultérine**) Adulterine.

*****aduste** [a'dyst], *a.* (*Path.*) Adust, burnt, scorched, sunburnt. **adustion**, *n.f.* (*Med.*) Cauterization.

advenir [advə'niːr], *v.i. irr.* (*Conjugated like* VENIR; *used only in inf. and 3rd pers.*) To occur, to happen, to befall. *Advienne que pourra*, happen what may; *il advint que*, it came to pass that; *qu'est-il advenu de lui?* what has befallen him?

adventice [advɑ̃'tis], *a.* Adventitious.

adventif [advɑ̃'tif], *a.* (*fem.* **adventive**) (*Bot.*) Adventitious, casual; (*Law*) casual (said of property acquired by a woman after marriage).

adverbe [ad'vɛrb], *n.m.* Adverb. **adverbial**, *a.* (*fem.* **adverbiale**) Adverbial. **adverbialement**, *adv.* Adverbially.

adversaire [adver'sɛːr], *n.m.* Adversary, opponent.

adversatif [adversa'tif], *a.* (*fem.* **adversative**) (*Gram.*) Adversative.

adverse [ad'vers], *a.* Adverse, opposite; contrary, calamitous. *Avocat adverse*, counsel on the opposite side; *partie adverse*, opposing party. *La fortune adverse*, adversity; bad luck. **adversité**, *n.f.* Adversity, misfortune. *Vivre dans l'adversité*, to live in straitened circumstances.

adviendra, *3rd fut.*, **advienne**, *pres. subj.*, **advint**, *past def.* [ADVENIR].

adynamie [adina'mi], *n.f.* (*Path.*) Adynamia, debility, prostration. **adynamique**, *a.* Adynamic, weak, debile.

aède [a'ɛd], *n.m.* (*Gk. Ant.*) An epic poet, a bard.

aérage [ae'raːʒ], *n.m.* Ventilation, airing. *Puits d'aérage*, air-shaft. **aérateur**, *n.m.* Ventilator. **aération**, *n.f.* Ventilation, airing.

aéré [ae're], *p.p.* Ventilated.—*a.* Airy.

aérer [ae're], *v.t.* To ventilate, to air, to renew the air of; (*Chem.*) to aerate.

aérien [ae'rjɛ̃], *a.* (*fem.* **aérienne**) Aerial; living or occurring in the air, celestial; (*fig.*) light, airy. *Base aérienne*, air-base; *fil aérien*, overhead wire; *ligne aérienne*, airline; *pont aérien*, air-lift; *raid aérien*, air-raid.

aérifère [aeri'fɛːr], *a.* Air-conducting. **aérification**, *n.f.* Gasification. **aérifier** or **aériser**, *v.t.* To gasify. **aériforme**, *a.* Aeriform.

aéro-club [aerɔ'klœb], *n.m.* (*pl.* **aéro-clubs**) Flying-club.

aérodrome [aerɔ'droːm], *n.m.* Aerodrome, airfield.

aérodynamique [aerɔdina'mik], *a.* Aerodynamic, streamlined.—*n.f.* Aerodynamics.

aérogare [aero'gar], *n.f.* Air-station, air-terminal.

aérographe [aerɔ'graf], *n.m.* Aerograph. **aérographie**, *n.f.* Aerography.

aérolithe [aerɔ'lit], *n.m.* Aerolite. **aérolithique**, *a.* Aerolitic.

aérologie [aerɔlɔ'ʒi], *n.f.* Aerology.

aéromètre [aerɔ'mɛtr], *n.m.* Aerometer, air-poise.

aéronaute [aerɔ'noːt], *n.m.* Aeronaut. **aéronautique**, *a.* Aeronautic.—*n.f.* Aeronautics, aerial navigation.

aéronef [aerɔ'nɛf], *n.m.* Air-ship.

aérophagie [aerɔfa'ʒi], *n.f.* Aerophagia.

aéroplane [aerɔ'plan], *n.m.* Aeroplane.

aéroport [aero'pɔr], *n.m.* Airport.

aéroporté [aerɔpɔr'te], *a.* (*fem.* **-ée**) Airborne (troops).

aérosphère [aerɔ'sfɛːr], *n.f.* The mass of air surrounding the globe, atmosphere.

aérostat [aerɔ'sta], *n.m.* Aerostat, air-balloon. **aérostation**, *n.f.* Aerostation, air-navigation. **aérostatique**, *a.* Aerostatic.—*n.m.* Aerostatics.

aérostier [ae'rɔstje], *n.m.* Aeronaut, one directing an aerostat.

aérothérapie [aerɔtera'pi], *n.f.* Aerotherapy.

aétite [ae'tit], *n.f.* (*Min.*) Eagle-stone.

affabilité [afabili'te], *n.f.* Affability, kindness, courtesy. **affable**, *a.* Affable, courteous.

affabulation [afabyla'sjɔ̃], *n.f.* The moral of a fable; plot (of a novel etc.).

affadir [afa′diːr], *v.t.* To make unsavoury or insipid; (*fig.*) to make flat or dull. *Affadir le cœur*, to disgust. **s'affadir,** *v.r.* To become insipid. **affadissant,** *a.* (*fem.* **affadissante**) Cloying, insipid. **affadissement,** *n.m.* Insipidity, nausea, sickliness.

affaiblir [afɛ′bliːr], *v.t.* To enfeeble, to weaken; to lessen. **s'affaiblir,** *v.r.* To grow weak; to abate. **affaiblissant,** *a.* (*fem.* **affaiblissante**) Weakening, enfeebling. **affaiblissement,** *n.m.* Weakening; allaying, abatement. **affaiblisseur,** *a.* (*fem.* **affaiblisseuse**) Reducing (bath or solution). —*n.m.* (*Phot.*) Reducer.

affainéantir (s') [afeneã′tiːr], *v.r.* To grow idle, lazy, or slothful; to get into lazy habits.

affaire [a′fɛːr], *n.f.* Affair, business, concern, matter; trouble, scrape; lawsuit; transaction, bargain. *Affaire de cœur*, love affair; *affaire d'honneur*, duel; *c'est mon affaire*, it is my own concern; *j'en fais mon affaire*, I take that upon myself; *mêlez-vous de vos affaires!* mind your own business! *C'est une sale affaire*, it's a nasty affair; *être hors d'affaire*, to be out of danger; *se tirer d'affaire*, to get out of a difficulty. *Cela ne fait rien à l'affaire*, that does not affect the matter; *faire l'affaire de quelqu'un*, to suit someone's purpose; *c'est l'affaire d'un instant*, it won't take a minute; *c'est toute une affaire*, it's no light matter; *la belle affaire!* pooh! is that all? *Affaire civile*, cause; *affaire criminelle*, criminal case; *être impliqué dans une affaire*, to be involved in a lawsuit; *perdre une affaire*, to lose a lawsuit. *Cabinet d'affaires*, general agency; *c'est une affaire faite*, that's settled; *être dans les affaires*, to be in business; *faire de bonnes affaires*, to thrive, to succeed in business; *homme d'affaires*, business man, legal adviser. *Avoir affaire à*, to have to deal with; *avoir affaire avec*, to have dealings with; *faire affaire avec quelqu'un*, to make a bargain with somebody; *son affaire est faite*, he is done for.

affairé [afɛ′re], *a.* (*fem.* **affairée**) Busy. **affairement,** *n.m.* Hurry, bustle, ado.

affaissement [afɛs′mã], *n.m.* Depression, subsidence, giving way, collapse.

affaisser [afɛ′se], *v.t.* To cause to sink, to weigh down, to press down; to bear down, to overwhelm. **s'affaisser,** *v.r.* To sink, to subside; to give way; to be bent down (by age), to collapse.

affaitage [afɛ′taːʒ] or **affaitement** [afɛt′mã], *n.m.* The training of hawks; dressing of skins, hides, etc. **affaiter,** *v.t.* To train (hawks); to dress (leather).

affalement [afal′mã], *n.m.* (*colloq.*) Discouragement, depression.

affaler [afa′le], *v.t.* (*Naut.*) To haul down (a rope); to drive ashore. *Affale!* lower away. **s'affaler,** *v.r.* To slide down; to be driven ashore; (*colloq.*) to drop, to flop into.

affamé [afa′me], *a.* (*fem.* **affamée**) Famished, hungry, starving; greedy, craving. *Être affamé de*, to be greedy of or eager for.—*n.* One who is greedy or starving; one who is greedy or eager for something.

affamer [afa′me], *v.t.* To starve, to famish, to deprive of food.

affameur [afa′mœːr], *n.m.* Starver.

affangissements [afãʒis′mã], *n.m.* (*used only in pl.*) Shoal; mud-bank (in a river).

arfectable [afɛk′tabl], *a.* Affectible; that may be mortgaged. **affectant,** *a.* (*fem.* **affectante**) That affects. **affectation,** *n.f.* Appropriation, destination, or attribution (to a certain object); simulation, show, pretence, affectation; preference; distinction; (*Law*) mortgage, charge. *Affectation spéciale*, assignment to a reserved occupation; (*Mil.*) *recevoir une affectation*, to be posted.

affecté [afɛk′te], *a.* (*fem.* **affectée**) Affected, assumed, simulated, put on; attributed, destined (to a certain object); (*Path.*) affected (by a disease etc.); (*Mil.*) posted to.

affecter [afɛk′te], *v.t.* To affect, to make frequent or habitual use of, to have a predilection for; to assume (a certain shape etc.); to feign, to pretend; to set apart, to earmark, to destine, to appropriate (to a certain object); to move, to touch, to impress emotionally. **s'affecter,** *v.r.* To be affected.

affectif [afɛk′tif], *a.* (*fem.* **affective**) Affective.

affection [afɛk′sjɔ̃], *n.f.* Affection, love, attachment; (*Med.*) affection, ailment. *Marques d'affection*, tokens of affection; *porter de l'affection à quelqu'un*, to be fond of someone; *prendre quelqu'un en affection*, to become attached to someone.

affectionné [afɛksjɔ′ne], *a.* (*fem.* **affectionnée**) Affectionate, loving, attached, loved, liked.

affectionner [afɛksjɔ′ne], *v.t.* To love, to be fond of, to like. *****s'affectionner,** *v.r.* To attach oneself to, to delight in, to take a fancy to.

affective [AFFECTIF].

affectivité [afɛktivi′te], *n.f.* Affectivity.

affectueusement [afɛktɥøz′mã], *adv.* Affectionately, fondly. **affectueux,** *a.* (*fem.* **affectueuse**) Affectionate, tender, warmhearted.

affenage [afə′naːʒ], *n.m.* The act of foddering. **affener,** *v.t.* To give fodder to, to pasture (animals). **affenoir,** *n.m.* [ABAT-FOIN].

afférent [afe′rã], *a.* (*fem.* **-ente**) Reverting; relating to; assignable to; accruing to; (*Anat.*) afferent, conducting inwards. *Portion afférente à*, portion accruing to.

affermable [afɛr′mabl], *a.* Farmable, rentable. **affermage,** *n.m.* Farming, renting. **affermataire,** *n.* Tenant farmer. **affermateur,** *n.m.* (*fem.* **affermatrice**) Lessor.

affermer [afɛr′me], *v.t.* To farm or let out by lease; to take a lease of, to rent.

affermir [afɛr′miːr], *v.t.* To strengthen, to make firm; to confirm, to establish, to consolidate. **s'affermir,** *v.r.* To become strong, firm, or fast; to become established. **affermissement,** *n.m.* Strengthening, consolidation, establishment; support, prop, stay.

affété [afe′te], *a.* (*fem.* **-ée**) Affected, prim, finical; canting, mincing, pretty-pretty. *Mine affétée*, affected looks. **afféterie,** *n.f.* Affectation, mannerisms, primness.

affichage [afi′ʃaːʒ], *n.m.* Bill-sticking, placarding.

affiche [a′fiʃ], *n.f.* Placard, bill, poster, (*Am.*) billboard. *Affiche électorale*, election poster; *affiche de théâtre*, play-bill; *homme affiche*, sandwich-man; *poser une affiche*, to post up a placard; to stick a bill; (*Theat.*) *tenir l'affiche depuis un an*, to have been running for a year.

afficher [afiˈʃe], *v.t.* To post up; to publish, to divulge, to proclaim; to make a show of, to parade. *Défense d'afficher*, stick no bills; billposting prohibited; *afficher son savoir*, to show off. **s'afficher,** *v.r.* To set up (for); to attract public notice. *Cette femme s'affiche, this woman seeks notoriety; il s'affiche avec elle*, he goes about with her openly. **afficheur,** *n.m.* Bill-sticker.

affidavit [afidaˈvit], *n.m.* Affidavit.

affidé [afiˈde], *a.* (*fem.* **affidée**) Trusty, trustworthy, in the know.—*n.m.* Confederate, confidential agent; spy.

affilage [afiˈlaːʒ] or **affilement** [afilˈmɑ̃], *n.m.* Whetting, sharpening, setting. **affilé,** *a.* (*fem.* **affilée**) Sharp; nimble, glib (of the tongue). **affiler,** *v.t.* To sharpen, to set, to put an edge on. **affilerie,** *n.f.* Grinding shop. **affileur,** *n.m.* Sharpening, knife-grinder.

affilée (d') (*adv. phr.*) At a stretch. *Trois heures d'affilée*, three hours at a stretch.

affiliation [afiljaˈsjɔ̃] *n.f.* Affiliation (to a society, company, plot, etc.). **affilié,** *a.* (*fem.* **affiliée**) Affiliated, admitted a member or associate.—*n.* Affiliated member, associate, confederate. **affilier,** *v.t.* To admit, to affiliate, to receive. **s'affilier,** *v.r.* To become admitted or affiliated, to join.

affiloir [afiˈlwaːr], *n.m.* Hone, oilstone, steel, strop. **affiloire,** *n.f.* Whetstone.

affinage [afiˈnaːʒ] or **affinement** [afinˈmɑ̃], *n.m.* Refining, fining (of metals, sugar, etc.); heckling (of hemp), maturing (of a wine), ripening (of a cheese). **affiner,** *v.t.* To fine, to refine; *to deceive, to cheat. **s'affiner,** *v.r.* To be refined, to be fined; to become finer, wittier, etc. (of the mind). **affinerie,** *n.f.* Metal refinery. **affineur,** *n.m.* Metal refiner.

affinité [afiniˈte], *n.f.* Affinity, relationship.

affinoir [afiˈnwaːr], *n.m.* Carding-brush.

affiquet [afiˈkɛ], *n.m.* Knitting-sheath; (*pl.*) gewgaws, trinkets.

affirmatif [afirmaˈtif], *a.* (*fem.* **affirmative**) Affirmative, asserting. **affirmation,** *n.f.* Affirmation, assertion; (*Log.*) predication. (*Law*) *Affirmation de créances*, proof of indebtedness. **affirmative,** *n.f.* Affirmative statement, answer, etc.; asseveration. *Répondre par l'affirmative*, to answer in the affirmative. **affirmativement,** *adv.* Affirmatively. **affirmer,** *v.t.* To affirm, to assert, to vouch, to declare; to confirm by or on oath; (*Log.*) to predicate. **s'affirmer,** *v.r.* To grow stronger, to assert oneself.

affistoler [afistɔˈle], *v.t.* (*fam.*)=[AFISTOLER].

affixe [aˈfiks], *n.m.* Affix.

affleurement [aflœrˈmɑ̃], *n.m.* Levelling, making flush; (*Mining*) outcrop.

affleurer [aflœˈre], *v.t.* To make even, to level; (*Arch.*) to make flush; (*Shipbuilding*) to fit accurately.—*v.i.* To be level, to be flush (with); (*Mining*) to crop out.

afflictif [aflikˈtif], *a.* (*fem.* **-ive**) (*Law*) Affecting the person, corporal (of punishments).

affliction [aflikˈsjɔ̃], *n.f.* Affliction, trouble, distress; trial, vexation.

affligé [afliˈʒe], *a.* (*fem.* **affligée**) Afflicted, grieved, distressed; (*iron.*) burdened. *Affligé d'un gros héritage*, burdened with a great heritage; *affligé d'une maladie*, labouring

under a disease.—*n.m.* (*pl.*) *Consoler les affligés*, to comfort the afflicted. **affligeant,** *a.* (*fem.* **affligeante**) Afflicting, afflictive, distressing, sad.

affliger [afliˈʒe], *v.t.* To afflict, to trouble, to distress, to grieve, to vex, to torment; to mortify, to chasten. **s'affliger,** *v.r.* To grieve, to be afflicted, troubled, or cast down; to take something to heart.

afflouage [afluˈaːʒ], *n.m.* (*Naut.*) Refloating (of a ship). **afflouer,** *v.t.* To refloat.

affluence [aflyˈɑ̃s], *n.f.* Affluence, abundance, concourse, crowd. *Heures d'affluence*, rush hours. **affluent,** *a.* (*fem.* **affluente**) Falling into, running into (of rivers).—*n.m.* Tributary.

affluer, *v.i.* To fall, to run, to flow into (as a tributary) (*dans*); to abound; to come in great quantity (*à, vers*).

afflux [aˈfly], *n.m.* Afflux.

affolant [afɔˈlɑ̃], *a.* (*fem.* **-ante**) Distracting. **affolé,** *a.* (*fem.* **-ée**) Distracted, panic-stricken, *infatuated; (*Mech.*) disconnected, defective (propeller, magnetic needle). **affolement,** *n.m.* Distraction, panic.

affoler [afɔˈle], *v.t.* To distract; to infatuate; to bewitch; to madden, to drive crazy. **s'affoler,** *v.r.* To fall into a panic, to stampede. *S'affoler de*, to become infatuated with.

afforestage [afɔresˈtaːʒ], *n.m.* Right of cutting firewood, estovers.

afforestation [afɔrestaˈsjɔ̃], *n.f.* Afforestation. **afforester,** *v.t.* To grant the right of cutting firewood.

affouage [aˈfwaːʒ], *n.m.* The communal right of cutting wood. **affouagement,** *n.m.* The exercise of this right. **affouager,** *a.* (*fem.* **affouagère**) Pertaining to the cutting of wood. **affouager,** *v.t.* To make a list of those entitled to *affouage*; to determine the woods to be cut. **affouagiste,** *n.m.* One entitled to *affouage*.

affouillable [afuˈjabl], *a.* Subject or liable to undermining. **affouillement,** *n.m.* Undermining, washing away.

affouiller [afuˈje], *v.t.* To undermine, to wash away.

affouragement or **affourragement** [afuraʒˈmɑ̃], *n.m.* Foraging, foddering. **affourager** or **affourrager,** *v.t.* To fodder, to give fodder to.

affourche [aˈfurʃ], *n.f.* (*Naut.*) Anchor and cable for mooring; mooring with two anchors at an angle. *Ancre d'affourche*, small bow-anchor.

affourcher [afurˈʃe], *v.t.* (*Naut.*) To moor with two anchors placed at an angle; to seat astride; (*Carp.*) to join a tongue and groove. —*v.i.* or **s'affourcher,** *v.r.* (*Naut.*) To ride with two anchors set at an angle.

affranchi [afrɑ̃ˈʃi], *a.* (*fem.* **-ie**) Set free, freed.—*n.* Freedman; freedwoman; (*pop.*) unscrupulous, knowing, hardened (fellow).

affranchir [afrɑ̃ˈʃiːr], *v.t.* To free, to set free, to enfranchise; to absolve, to exempt; to frank (a letter), to stamp. **s'affranchir,** *v.r.* To rid oneself of, to free oneself, to shake off, to break away from.

affranchissement, *n.m.* Enfranchisement, manumission; exemption, discharge; deliverance; payment of postage (of a letter);

prepayment of carriage (of a parcel); emancipation (of mind). **affranchisseur**, *n.m.* Emancipator, liberator, deliverer; castrator, gelder.

affres [a:fr], *n.f.* (*used only in pl.*) Dread, horror, agony. *Les affres de la mort*, the pangs of death, death-throes.

affrètement [afrɛt'mã], *n.m.* Chartering, freighting. **affréter**, *v.t.* (*Naut.*) To charter, to freight (a vessel). **affréteur**, *n.m.* Charterer, freighter.

affreusement [afrøz'mã], *adv.* Frightfully, horribly, dreadfully.

affreux [a'frø], *a.* (*fem.* **affreuse**) Frightful, hideous, shocking, repulsive, horrible, fearful, atrocious, ghastly.

affriander [afriã'de], *v.t.* To make attractive or enticing; to allure, to entice, to tempt.

affricher [afri'ʃe], *v.t.* To leave fallow.

affriolant [afriɔ'lã], *a.* (*fem.* **affriolante**) Appetizing, alluring.

affrioler [afriɔ'le], *v.t.* To allure, to entice, to attract as with a bait.

affriquée [afri'ke:], *n.f.* Affricate or fricative (consonant).

affront [a'frɔ̃], *n.m.* Affront, outrage, insult; inglorious defeat; disgrace. *Essuyer un affront*, to receive a snub; *recevoir un affront sanglant*, to receive an outrageous affront; *boire or avaler un affront*, to swallow an affront. **affrontable**, *a.* That can be faced.

affronté [afrɔ̃'te] *a.* (*fem.* **affrontée**) (*Her.*) Confronting each other, face to face. **affrontement**, *n.m.* The act of putting face to face, confrontation, open defiance.

affronter [afrɔ̃'te], *v.t.* To put face to face, on a level; to face, to confront, to brave; to attack boldly; *to cheat or take in impudently. *affronteur, *n.m.* (*fem.* **affronteuse**) An impudent person; a deceiver, a cheat.

affruiter [afrɥi'te], *v.t.* To plant with fruit-trees.—*v.i.* To bear or supply fruit. **s'affruiter**, *v.r.* To come into fruit.

affublement [afyblə'mã], *n.m.* Grotesque make-up or rig-out (of dress).

affubler [afy'ble], *v.t.* To dress up, to rig out (grotesquely). **s'affubler**, *v.r.* To dress up ridiculously. *S'affubler d'un manteau*, to muffle oneself up in a cloak.

affusion [afy'zjɔ̃] *n.f.* (*Med.*) Affusion.

affût [a'fy], *n.m.* Stand or place for lying in wait, watch; gun-carriage. *Être à l'affût*, to be upon the watch, to lie in wait; *affût à éclipse*, disappearing carriage. **affûtage**, *n.m.* The mounting of a piece of ordnance; a set of tools, sharpening (of tools). **affûter** [afy'te], *v.t.* *To mount (a gun); *to put in a hiding-place; to grind, to sharpen. **affûteur**, *n.m.* Sharpener, setter, grinder; one lying in wait for game, stalker. **affûteuse**, *n.f.* Sharpening machine.

affutiau [afy'tjo], *n.m.* (*pop.*) Trifle, bauble, knick-knack.

afin [a'fɛ̃], *conj.* To, in order (that), so that. **afin de** (*with inf.*). **afin que** (*with subj.*).

afistolement [afistɔl'mã], *n.m.* (*colloq.*) Dressing up sprucely. **afistoler** *v.t.* To dress up sprucely, to adorn. **s'afistoler**, *v.r.* To dress sprucely, to doll oneself up.

africain [afri'kɛ̃], *a.* (*fem.* **africaine**) African.— *n.* Africain (*fem.* **Africaine**) An African.

Afrique [a'frik], *f.* Africa.

afrite [a'frit], *n.m.* (*Myth.*) Afreet.

agaçant [aga'sã], *a.* (*fem.* **agaçante**) Irritating, worrying, provoking, provocative, alluring, enticing.

agace or **agasse** [a'gas], *n.f.* Magpie.

agacement [agas'mã], *n.m.* Irritation, setting on edge. *Agacement des nerfs*, irritation of the nerves.

agacer [aga'se], *v.t.* To worry, to irritate, to set on edge; to excite, to provoke; to entice, to allure. *Avoir les dents agacées*, to have one's teeth on edge. **agacerie**, *n.f.* Allurement, coquetry, enticement. *Faire des agaceries à quelqu'un*, to set one's cap at someone, to lead someone on.

agaillardir [agajar'di:r], *v.t.* To cheer up.

agalacte [aga'lakt], *a.* Wanting in milk (of a woman).—*n.* A milkless woman. **agalactie** or **agalaxie**, *n.f.* Absence of milk (in a woman nursing a child).

agame [a'gam], *a.* (*Bot.*) Agamous.

agami [aga'mi], *n.m.* Agami, trumpeter (S. Am. bird).

aganter [agã'te], *v.t.* (*Naut.*) To overhaul, to catch, to seize (a ship or ropes).

agape [a'gap], *n.f.* Agape, love-feast; (*pl.*) revelling with friends.

agapètes [aga'pɛt], *n. m.* or *f.* (*used only in pl.*) (*Eccles. Ant.*) Monks or virgins in the primitive Church serving in celibate communities of persons of the opposite sex, agapetae.

agaric [aga'rik], *n.m.* (*Bot.*) Agaric. *Agaric champêtre*, field agaric.

agassin [aga'sɛ̃], *n.m.* The unproductive lowest shoot on a grape-vine.

agate [a'gat], *n.f.* Agate. (*C*) (*Print.*) Agate, ruby. *Bille d'agate*, glass marble. **agaté**, *a.* (*fem.* **agatée**) Containing agate.

Agathe [a'gat], *f.* Agatha.

agatifier [agati'fje], *v.t.* To turn into agate. **s'agatifier**, *v.r.* To turn into agate.

agave [a'ga:v] or **agavé** [aga've], *n.m.* (*Bot.*) Agave, American aloe.

age [a:ʒ], *n.m.* Plough-beam.

âge [ɑ:ʒ], *n.m.* Age, years, time from birth; period, epoch, era; (*pl.*) the ages, time. *Bas âge*, infancy; *jeune âge*, childhood; *moyen âge*, Middle Ages; *âge moyen*, middle age; *âge mûr*, mature age; *âge viril*, manhood; *âge de raison*, age of discretion; *d'âge en âge*, from age to age, from generation to generation; *doyen d'âge*, the oldest, senior; *d'un certain âge*, elderly; *entre deux âges*, of uncertain age; *être d'âge à*, to be old enough to; *être bien pour son âge*, to wear well, to bear one's years well; *fleur de l'âge*, prime of life; *paraître son âge, porter son âge*, to look one's age; *quel âge avez-vous?* how old are you?

âgé [ɑ'ʒe], *a.* (*fem.* **âgée**) Aged (so many years); old, elderly. *Âgé de vingt ans*, twenty years old; *un peu âgé*, somewhat elderly.

agence [a'ʒã:s], *n.f.* Agency, bureau, branch office. *Agence immobilière*, estate agency; *agence de placement*, employment bureau; *agence de renseignements*, inquiry agency; *agence de voyages*, travel agency.

agencement [aʒãs'mã], *n.m.* Arrangement, grouping, ordering; (*Arch.*) composition, layout.

agencer [aʒã'se], *v.t.* To arrange, to dispose, to fit up, to group, to adorn.

agenda [aʒɛ̃'da], *n.m.*   Note-book; diary; engagement-book.

agénésie [aʒene'zi], *n.f.*   (*Path.*) Impotence, sterility. **agénésique,** *a.* Impotent, sterile.

agenouillement [aʒnuj'mã], *n.m.* Act of kneeling.

agenouiller [aʒnu'je], *v.t.*   To make kneel down, to bring to his knees. **s'agenouiller** *v.r.* To kneel down, to fall on one's knees; (*fig.*) to bow down (*devant*). **agenouilloir,** *n.m.* Hassock.

agent [a'ʒã], *n.m.* (*fem.* **agente**) Agent; deputy; instrument; middleman; broker. *Agent comptable,* accountant; *agent d'affaires,* agent, man of business; *agent de change,* stock-broker; *agent électoral,* canvasser; *agent de liaison,* liaison officer; *agent de police,* policeman; *agent monétaire,* circulating medium; *agent voyer,* road surveyor.

Agésilas [aʒezi'la:s], *m.* Agesilaus.

agglomérant [aglome'rã], *n.m.*   Binding material (for road).

agglomérat [aglome'ra], *n.m.* (*Geol.*) Conglomerate. **agglomération** [aglomera'sjɔ̃] *n.f.* Agglomeration, built-up area. **aggloméré,** *n.m.* Compressed fuel, briquette.

agglomérer [aglome're], *v.t.* To agglomerate, to mass together, to pile up, to assemble.

agglutinant [aglyti'nã], *a.* (*fem.* **agglutinante**) Agglutinant, adhesive.—*n.m.* (*Philol.*) An agglutinative language. **agglutinateur,** *a.* (*fem.* **agglutinatrice**) Agglutinative. **agglutination,** *n.f.* Agglutination.

agglutiner [aglyti'ne], *v.t.* To agglutinate, to bind, to cake. **s'agglutiner,** *v.r.* To agglutinate, to unite, to cohere; to heal over (wound).

aggravant [agra'vã], *a.* (*fem.* **aggravante**) (*Law*) Aggravating, making more heinous.

aggravation, *n.f.*   Aggravation, additional penalty. *Aggravation de peine,* increase of punishment.

aggrave [a'gra:v], *n.f.* (*Canon Law*) Anathema after the admonitions, with threat of excommunication.

aggraver [agra've], *v.t.* To aggravate, to make worse. **s'aggraver,** *v.r.* To worsen (illness, situation).

agile [a'ʒil], *a.* Agile, nimble. **agilement,** *adv.* Nimbly, with agility.

agilité, *n.f.* Agility, nimbleness, lightness.

agio [a'ʒjo], *n.m.* Agio, premium; profit on money-changing; stock-jobbing, speculation.

agiotage [aʒjɔ'ta:ʒ], *n.m.* Speculation on the rise and fall of public funds, stock-jobbing. *Faire l'agiotage,* to deal in stocks.

agioter, *v.i.* To be a stock-jobber; to speculate or gamble in the funds, to job. **agioteur** *a.* (*fem.* **agioteuse**) That operates or speculates thus.—*n.* A speculator, a jobber.

agir [a'ʒi:r], *v.i.* To act, to do; to operate, to produce a result; to have an effect (*sur*); to negotiate, to manage a business; to sue, to prosecute, to proceed (*contre*); to behave. *Bien agir,* to do right; *mal agir,* to do wrong; *faire agir,* to set going, to bring to bear upon; *agir de concert avec quelqu'un,* to go hand in hand with someone; *il agit en ami,* he acts like a friend; *c'est mal agir,* that is behaving ill. **s'agir,** *v.r.* (*impers.*) To be in question, to be the matter. *Il s'agit,* the question is; *de quoi s'agit-il?* what is it

about? *il s'agit de votre vie,* your life is at stake.

agissant [aʒi'sã], *a.* Active, stirring, busy; efficacious, effective, effectual. **agissement,** *n.m.* (*usu. in pl.*) Conduct, doings, deeds, proceedings. **agitable,** *a.* That may be debated or discussed. **agitant,** *a.* (*fem.* **agitante**) Agitating, exciting, stirring.

agitateur [aʒita'tœ:r], *n.m.* Agitator, stirring rod. **agitation,** *n.f.* Agitation; disturbance, tossing, shaking, tumult; trouble, emotion, uneasiness, restlessness.

agité [aʒi'te], *a.* (*fem.* **agitée**) Restless (sleep), rough (sea), fretful (child).

agiter [aʒi'te], *v.t.* To agitate, to put in motion, to shake, to stir; to disturb, to trouble, to disquiet; to excite, to perturb, to debate, to discuss, to dispute. *Agiter un drapeau,* to wave a flag; *agiter la queue,* to wag one's tail (dog), to whisk one's tail (horse). **s'agiter** *v.r.* To be agitated or in movement; to get rough; to be restless, disturbed, uneasy; to toss, to wave, to flutter; to be debated. *S'agiter dans l'eau,* to flounder about in the water; *s'agiter dans son sommeil,* to toss in one's sleep.

Aglaé [agla'e], *f.* Aglaia.

aglobulie [aglɔby'li], *n.f.* Lack of red globules.

agnat [ag'na], *n.m.* (*Rom. Ant.*) Agnate. **agnation,** *n.f.* Agnation. **agnatique,** *a.* Agnatic.

agneau [a'ɲo], *n.m.* (*fem.* **agnelle**) Lamb, ewe lamb. *Doux comme un agneau,* as gentle as a lamb.

agnelage [aɲə'la:ʒ] or **agnèlement,** *n.m.* Lambing; lambing-time. **agneler,** *v.i.* To lamb, to yean. **agnelet,** *n.m.* *Lambkin, yeanling. **agnelin,** *n.m.* Lambskin dressed with the wool on.

agnelle [AGNEAU].

Agnès [a'ɲɛ:s], *f.* Agnes.

agnès [a'ɲɛ:s], *n.f.* A raw young girl, ingénue.

agnosticisme [agnɔsti'sism], *n.m.* Agnosticism. **agnosticiste** or **agnostique,** *a.* and *n.* Agnostic.

agnus-Dei [ag'ny:sdei], *n.m.* (*R.-C. Ch.*) A wax Agnus Dei; the prayer beginning with the words *Agnus Dei.*

agnus-castus [agnyskas'ty:s], *n.m.* The shrub Agnus Castus, chaste-tree.

agonie [agɔ'ni], *n.f.* Agony, the pangs of death; (*fig.*) trouble, anguish, torture. *Être à l'agonie,* to be at the point of death.

agonir [agɔ'ni:r], *v.t.* To insult grossly, to pull to pieces, to load with abuse.

agonisant [agɔni'zã], *a.* (*fem.* **-ante**) Dying, in a dying condition.—*n.* A dying person. **agoniser,** *v.i.* To be at the point of death.

agonistique [agɔnis'tik], *a.* Agonistic, pertaining to the Greek athletic games.

agonothète [agɔnɔ'tɛt], *n.m.* (*Gr. Ant.*) President of the athletic games.

agoraphobie [agɔrafɔ'bi], *n.f.* Agoraphobia.

agouti [agu'ti], *n.m.* Agouti.

agrafe [a'graf], *n.f.* Fastener, clasp, clip, staple (for papers); (*Arch.*) cramp-iron; a sculptured ornament like an *agrafe*; (*Surg.*) agraffe. *Agrafe et porte,* hook and eye. **agrafer,** *v.t.* To hook, to clasp, to fasten with a clasp; to staple; to buttonhole, (*slang*) to nab, to take hold of. **agrafeuse** [agra'fø:z], *n.f.* Stapler.

agraire [a'grɛːr], *a.* Agrarian.
agrandir [agrɑ̃'diːr], *v.t.* To make greater, to enlarge, to augment; to widen; to exaggerate; to promote, to advance; (*fig.*) to elevate. *Agrandir une photo,* to enlarge a photograph; *ce costume vous agrandit,* this suit makes you look taller; *agrandir ses prétentions,* to raise one's pretensions; *la lecture agrandit l'âme,* reading ennobles the soul. **s'agrandir,** *v.r.* To become greater, larger; to increase one's possessions, etc.
agrandissement, *n.m.* Enlargement, increase; aggrandizement, elevation. (*Phot.*) *Faire un agrandissement,* to make an enlargement.
agrandisseur *a.* (*Phot.*) Used for enlarging. —*n.m.* An enlarger.
agraphie [agra'fi], *n.f.* Agraphia.
agrarianisme [agrɑrja'nism], *n.m.* Agrarianism. **agrariat,** *n.m.* Distribution of land under a system of agrarianism. **agrarien,** *a.* (*fem.* **agrarienne**) Agrarian.—*n.* An advocate of agrarianism; (*n.m. pl.*) great protectionist landowners (in Prussia).
agréable [agre'abl], *a.* Agreeable, pleasing, pleasant, acceptable, grateful. *Agréable au goût,* palatable; **avoir pour agréable,* to allow, think fit; *pour vous être agréable,* to oblige you; *joindre l'utile à l'agréable,* to combine the pleasant with the useful; *faire l'agréable auprès d'une femme,* to be attentive to a lady. **agréablement,** *adv.* Agreeably, pleasantly.
agréé [agre'e], *n.m.* Solicitor; attorney, counsel (in commercial tribunals).
agréer [agre'e], *v.t.* To accept, to approve, to allow, to receive kindly.—*v.i.* To please, to be agreeable. *Cela vous agrée-t-il?* does that suit you? *veuillez agréer mes salutations,* yours truly.
agrégat [agre'ga], *n.m.* Aggregate, a composite mass. **agrégatif,** *a.* (*fem.* **agrégative**) Aggregative.—*n.* (*School slang*) A candidate for *agrégation.*
agrégation [agregɑ'sjɔ̃], *n.f.* (*Phys.*) Aggregation, aggregate; (=*Concours d'agrégation*), competitive examination for admission on the teaching staff of State secondary schools or of faculties of law, medicine, pharmacy.
agrégé [agre'ʒe], *n.m.* or *a. Professeur agrégé,* one who has passed the *agrégation.*
agréger [agre'ʒe], *v.t.* To admit into a society, to incorporate; (*Phys.*) to aggregate.
agrément [agre'mɑ̃], *n.m.* Consent, approbation; pleasure, charm, gracefulness; amenity; (*pl.*) ornaments, embellishments, amenities (of life). *Arts d'agrément,* accomplishments; *notes d'agrément,* (*Mus.*) grace-notes; *voyage d'agrément,* pleasure trip. **agrémenter,** *v.t.* To set off, to ornament, to adorn.
agréner [agre'ne], *v.t.* To pump water out of (a small boat).
agrès [a'grɛ], *n.m.* (*used only in pl.*) Rigging (of a ship etc.); apparatus, gear (of a gymnasium etc.).
agresseur [agre'sœːr], *n.m.* Aggressor. **agressif,** *a.* (*fem.* **agressive**) Aggressive. **agression,** *n.f.* Aggression. **agressivité,** *n.f.* Aggressiveness.
agreste [a'grɛst], *a.* Rustic; countrified (manners). **agrestement,** *adv.* Rustically.
agréyeur [agre'jœːr], *n.m.* Wire-drawer.
agricole [agri'kɔl], *a.* Agricultural.
agriculteur, *n.m.* Agriculturist, husbandman,

farmer. **agriculture,** *n.f.* Agriculture, husbandry, tillage.
agriffer [agri'fe], *v.t.* To claw; to clutch, to grip. **s'agriffer,** *v.r.* To claw (at).
Agrigente [agri'ʒɑ̃ːt], *m.* Agrigentum.
agrion [a'grjɔ̃], *n.m.* Dragon-fly.
agripaume [agri'poːm], *n.f.* (*Bot.*) Mother wort, *Leonurus cardiaca.*
agripper [agri'pe], *v.t.* To grip, to snatch. **s'agripper,** *v.r.* To cling (to).
Agrippine [agri'pin], *f.* Agrippina.
agronome [agrɔ'nɔm], *n.m.* Agronomist, agriculturist. *Ingénieur agronome,* agricultural engineer. **agronomie,** *n.f.* Agronomy. **agronomique,** *a.* Agronomic. *Institut Agronomique,* agricultural college in Paris.
agropyre [agro'piːr], *n.f.* A variety of couch grass.
agrostide [agrɔs'tid], **agrostis** [agrɔs'tis], *n.f.* Agrostis, couch-grass.
agroupement [agrup'mɑ̃], *n.m.* Grouping.
agrouper, *v.t.* To group. **s'agrouper,** *v.r.* To form a group or groups.
agrumes [a'grym], *n.m. pl.* Citrus fruit.
aguerri [age'ri], *a.* (*fem.* **aguerrie**) Inured to war; disciplined. *Soldats mal aguerris,* raw soldiers.
aguerrir [age'riːr], *v.t.* To train or inure to the hardships of war; to accustom, to inure (to hardships etc.). **s'aguerrir,** *v.r.* To inure, or accustom oneself (to hardships, abstinence, etc.), to be inured. **aguerrissement,** *n.m.* Inuring to war, hardening.
aguets [a'gɛ], *n.m.* (*used only in pl.*) Watch, look-out. *Être aux aguets,* to be on the watch; *se tenir aux aguets,* to be on the watch, to be on the look-out.
agui [a'gi], *n.m.* (*Naut.*) Bowline knot.
aguichant [agi'ʃɑ̃], *a.* (*fem.* **aguichante**) Seductive, saucy.
aguicher [agi'ʃe], *v.t.* (*fam.*) To entice, to allure.
ah [ɑ], *int.* Ah! oh! *Ah çà,* now then! *ah! c'est un grand malheur!* oh, it's most unfortunate.
ahan [a'hɑ̃], *n.m.* Great effort or exertion. *Suer d'ahan,* to toil and moil. ***ahaner,** *v.i.* To be exhausted (in doing something), to pant.
*aheurtement [aœrtə'mɑ̃], *n.m.* Stubbornness, obstinacy. **s'aheurter** [aœr'te], *v.r.* To be obstinately bent upon a thing, to stick to it, to persist in. *S'aheurter à une opinion,* to be wedded to an opinion.
ahi [AÏE].
ahuri [ay'ri], *a.* (*fem.* **ahurie**) Bewildered, perplexed, flurried. *Tout ahuri,* flabbergasted.
ahurir [ay'riːr], *v.t.* To bewilder, to strike all of a heap, to flurry, to stupefy. **ahurissant,** *a.* (*fem.* **ahurissante**) Flabbergasting.
ahurissement, *n.m.* Bewilderment, confusion, perplexity.
aï [a'i], *n.m.* The sloth.
aiche or **èche** [ɛʃ], *n.m.* Bait (for fishing). **aicher,** *v.t.* To bait (a hook etc.).
aidant [ɛ'dɑ̃], *a.* (*fem.* **aidante**) Helpful.
aide [ɛːd], *n.f.* Help, relief, assistance; succour, support, protection, rescue; relief (of the poor etc.); helper, female assistant, a help; (*n.m.*) a male assistant; (*n.f. pl.*) aids, subsidies, benevolences levied for State

purposes under the old monarchy; (*Horse-manship*) means employed in controlling a horse, aids; chapel of ease. *Aide chirurgien* (*pl. aides chirurgiens*), assistant-surgeon; *aide de camp* (*pl. aides de camp*), aide-de-camp; *aide de cuisine* (*pl. aides de cuisine*), under-cook; *à l'aide!* help! *à l'aide de*, with the help of; *Dieu vous soit en aide!* God help you! *venir en aide à*, to lend assistance to.

aide-mémoire, *n.m. inv.* Précis; memorandum.

aider [ɛ'de], *v.t.* To aid, to help, to relieve, to assist, to succour; to abet; to conduce to, to further. *Aide-toi, le ciel t'aidera*, God helps those who help themselves; *Dieu aidant*, with God's help! *aider à descendre, à surmonter*, or *à relever*, to help down, over, *or* up.—*v.i.* To be helpful, to be of assistance (*à*). *Aider à la lettre*, to complete the sense, to twist the meaning; *aider au succès*, to contribute to the success. **s'aider,** *v.r.* To make use (*de*); to avail oneself. *On s'aide de ce qu'on a*, people make use of what they have.

aïe [aj], *int.* Oh! oh dear!

aïeul [a'jœl], *n.m.* (*fem.* **aïeule,** *pl.* **aïeuls, aïeules**) Grandfather, grandsire; grandmother, grandam; (*pl.* **aïeux**) forebears, ancestors.

aigail [AUGUAIL].

aigle [ɛ:gl], *n.m.* Eagle; (*fig.*) a clever or brilliant person, a genius; reading-desk, lectern (with effigy of an eagle); (*Astron.*) Aquila.—*n.f.* She-eagle; (*Her.*) eagle (standard). *À vol d'aigle*, eagle-winged; *aux yeux d'aigle*, eagle-eyed; *grand aigle*, double-elephant paper (40 × 26¾ in.).

aiglefin [ɛglə'fɛ̃], *n.m.* Haddock.

aiglette [ɛ'glɛt], *n.f.* (*Her.*) Eaglet.

aiglon [ɛ'glɔ̃], *n.m.* (*fem.* **-onne**) Eaglet, young eagle.

aigre [ɛgr], *a.* Sour, tart; (*fig.*) harsh, bitter, shrill. *Paroles aigres*, sharp words; *voix aigre*, harsh, shrill voice.—*n.m.* Sourness, mustiness. *Cela sent l'aigre*, that smells sour. **aigre-doux,** *a.* (*fem.* **aigre-douce**) Sourish, bitter-sweet.

aigrefin [ɛgrə'fɛ̃], *n.m.* Sharper, swindler, adventurer; haddock [AIGLEFIN].

aigrelet [ɛgrə'lɛ], *a.* (*fem.* **aigrelette**) Sourish.

aigrement [ɛgrə'mã], *adv.* Acrimoniously, sourly, bitterly, roughly, harshly.

aigremoine [ɛgrə'mwan], *n.f.* (*Bot.*) Agrimony.

aigremore [ɛgrə'mɔːr], *n.m.* Powdered charcoal (used in fireworks).

aigret [ɛ'grɛ], *a.* (*fem.* **aigrette** (1)) Sourish.

aigrette (2) [ɛ'grɛt], *n.f.* Aigrette, tuft or plume (of feathers, diamonds, etc.); horn (of the owl); crest (of the peacock); egret tufted heron; (*Bot.*) tuft, crest. **aigretté,** *a.* (*fem.* **aigrettée**) (*Bot. etc.*) Tufted, crested.

aigreur [ɛ'grœːr], *n.f.* Sourness, sharpness, tartness; (*fig.*) harshness, bitterness, surliness, animosity, spite; (*Med.*, *used only in pl.*) acidity of stomach, heartburn, water-brash; (*fig.*) harsh words.

aigri [ɛ'gri], *a.* (*fem.* **-ie**) Embittered (person).

aigrir [ɛ'griːr], *v.t.* To make sour or sharp, to sour; (*fig.*) to irritate, to embitter, to make worse, to incense, to make ill-humoured. *Sa disgrâce lui a aigri l'esprit*, his disgrace has soured his temper.—*v.i.* To

turn sour. **s'aigrir,** *v.r.* To turn sour; (*fig.*) to grow worse, to be exasperated, to be irritated. *Son mal s'aigrit*, his disease gets worse. **aigrissement,** *n.m.* Souring, embittering.

aigu [e'gy], *a.* (*fem.* **aiguë**) Pointed, sharp, keen, acute; (*fig.*) shrill, piercing. *Accent aigu*, acute accent; *angle aigu*, acute angle; *douleur aiguë*, acute pain; *son aigu*, sharp, shrill sound.

aiguade [ɛ'gad], *n.f.* (*Naut.*) Fresh water; *watering-place. Faire aiguade*, to take in fresh water.

aiguail *or* **aigail** [ɛ'ga:j], *n.m.* (*Hunt.*) Dew, dewdrops (on the scent).

aiguayer [ɛgɛ'je], *v.t.* To bathe, to wash; to water (a horse); to rinse (clothes).

aiguë [AIGU].

aigue-marine [ɛgma'rin], *n.f.* (*pl.* **aigues-marines**) Aquamarine.

aiguière [ɛ'gjɛːr], *n.f.* Ewer. **aiguiérée,** *n.f.* A ewer-full.

aiguillage [egɥi'ja:ʒ], *n.m.* (*Rail.*) Switching, shunting; *pl.* switch.

aiguillat [egɥi'ja], *n.m.* Dog-fish.

aiguille [e'gɥi:j], *n.f.* Needle; index, pointer, hand (of a dial, watch, etc.); spire (steeple); point (of an obelisk, peak, etc.); rock pinnacle or needle-shaped peak; needle-shaped fish (of various species); (*pl.*, *Rail.*) switch. *Aiguille aimantée*, magnetic needle; *aiguille à repriser*, darning-needle; *aiguille à tricoter*, knitting-needle; *aiguille de mer*, garfish; *aiguilles* (*à contrepoids*), (*Rail.*) self-acting switch; *aiguille d'emballeur*, packing-needle; *de fil en aiguille*, one thing leading to another; *disputer sur des pointes d'aiguille*, to quarrel about straws; *enfiler une aiguille*, to thread a needle; *ouvrage à l'aiguille*, needlework; *trou d'une aiguille*, eye of a needle.

aiguillée, *n.f.* Needleful.

aiguiller [egɥi'je], *v.t.* (*Rail.*) To shunt; (*fig.*) to switch (on to), to orient.

aiguillerie [egɥij'ri], *n.f.* Needle-making; needle-manufactory; needle-trade.

aiguilletage [egɥij'ta:ʒ], *n.m.* Tagging; (*Naut.*) tying, lashing.

aiguilleter [egɥij'te], *v.t.* To tip (laces etc.); (*Naut.*) to lash, to tie. **aiguilletier** *or* **aiguillettier,** *n.m.* (*fem.* **-ière**) Tip-maker, tagger.

aiguillette [egɥi'jɛt], *n.f.* Aglet, point; (*Mil.*) ornamental shoulder-knot; a long thin slice (of fowl); (*Naut.*) knittle, tricing-line, lanyard; (*Bot.*) lady's comb. *Le ferret de l'aiguillette*, the tip of a point *or* ribbon.

aiguilleur [egɥi'jœːr], *n.m.* (*Rail.*) Pointsman, (*Am.*) switchman.

aiguillier [egɥi'je], *n.m.* (*fem.* **aiguillière**) Needle-maker; garfish net.

aiguillon [egɥi'jɔ̃], *n.m.* Goad, sting; (*fig.*) spur, incentive; (*Bot.*) prickle. *Briser l'aiguillon de*, to take the sting out of. **aiguillonnant,** *a.* (*fem.* **aiguillonnante**) Goading, inciting, stimulating. **aiguillonnement,** *n.m.* Goading; incitement. **aiguillonner,** *v.t.* To goad, to prick; (*fig.*) to incite, to spur on; to stimulate.

aiguillot [egɥi'jo], *n.m.* (*Naut.*) Pintle.

aiguisage [egi'za:ʒ] *or* **aiguisement,** *n.m.* Whetting, sharpening. , **aiguisé,** *a.* (*fem.* **aiguisée**) Whetted, sharpened; (*Her.*)

pointed at the ends. *Une croix aiguisée,* (*Her.*) a pointed cross.

aiguiser [egi′ze], *v.t.* To whet, to sharpen, to set an edge on; to point; (*fig.*) to make keen, acid, piquant, etc.; to excite, to stimulate. *Aiguiser l'appétit,* to sharpen the appetite; *aiguiser une épigramme,* to give point to an epigram; *aiguiser ses couteaux,* to prepare for battle; *meule à aiguiser,* grindstone; *pierre à aiguiser,* whetstone. **aiguiserie** *n.f.* A place where tools, instruments, weapons, etc., are sharpened. **aiguiseur,** *n.m.* Knife-grinder, sharpener. **aiguisoir,** *n.m.* Sharpening-tool, whetstone.

ail [a:j], *n.m.* (*pl.* **aulx** [o:] *l ot.* **ails**) Garlic. *Une tête d'ail,* a bulb of garlic; *une gousse d'ail,* a clove of garlic.

ailante [e′lã:t], *n.m.* (*Bot.*) Ailantus.

aile [εl], *n.f.* Wing; brim (of a hat); flipper (of a penguin); blade (of a propeller); fluke (of an anchor); vane, sail (of a windmill); flank or wing (of an army, building, etc.); wing, mudguard (of a car). *Aile de moulin,* windsail; *à tire d'aile,* swiftly; *avoir des ailes,* to be fast moving, to be elated; *battre de l'aile,* to flutter; (*fig.*) to be ill at ease, to be embarrassed; *couper le bout de l'aile,* to pinion; *d'un coup d'aile,* at a single flight; *en avoir dans l'aile,* to be hard hit; *être sur l'aile,* to be on the wing; *ne battre plus que d'une aile,* to be on one's last legs; *rogner les ailes à quelqu'un,* to clip a person's wings; *sous l'aile maternelle,* under the maternal wing; *tirer une plume de l'aile de quelqu'un,* to get something out of someone; *voler de ses propres ailes,* to stand on one's own legs; *vouloir voler sans avoir des ailes,* to try to run before one can walk. **ailé,** *a.* (*fem.* **ailée**) Winged.

aileron [εl′rɔ̃], *n.m.* Pinion (of a bird); aileron, balancing flap (of an airplane); bilge-keel (of boat), fin (of some fish); float-board (of a water-wheel); (*Arch.*) scroll; (*slang*) arm.

ailette [ε′let], *n.f.* Small wing; vane (of a torpedo etc.); (*Motor.*) rib, fin, flange, gill. *Ailette de refroidissement,* cooling rib; *radiateur à ailettes,* ribbed radiator; *vis à ailettes,* thumb-screw.

ailier [ε′lje], *n.m.* (*Ftb.*) Wing forward, wing-three-quarter.

aillade [a′jad], *n.f.* Garlic sauce.

ailleurs [a′jœ:r], *adv.* Elsewhere, somewhere else. *D'ailleurs,* besides, moreover, in addition to which, in other respects.

ailloli or **aïoli** [ajɔ′li], *n.m.* Sort of mayonnaise made with pounded garlic.

aimable [ε′mabl], *a.* Kind, amiable, obliging. **aimablement,** *adv.* Amiably, kindly.

aimant [ε′mã], *a.* (*fem.* **-ante**) Loving, affectionate—*n.m.* Magnet; (*fig.*) attractiveness. *Aimant en fer à cheval,* horseshoe magnet; *pierre d'aimant,* loadstone.

aimantation, *n.f.* Magnetization. **aimanter,** *v.t.* To magnetize.

Aimée [ε′me], *f.* Amy.

aimer [ε′me], *v.t.* To love, to be fond of, to be in love with; to like. *Aimer à l'idolâtrie,* to idolize; *aimer mieux,* to prefer, to like better; have rather; *aimez qu'on vous conseille et non pas qu'on vous loue,* love to be advised, not to be praised; *aime à monter à cheval,* he delights in riding; *il aime sa personne,* he loves his own dear self; *j'aime à croire que,* I

would rather think that; *qui aime bien châtie bien,* spare the rod and spoil the child; *qui m'aime me suive!* let whoso loves me follow me! *se faire aimer,* to endear oneself (to). **s'aimer,** *v.r.* To love oneself, to be vain.

aine (1) [ε:n], *n.f.* Groin.

aine (2) [ε:n], *n.f.* Herring-stick; leather band on an organ-bellows.

aîné [e′ne], *a.* (*fem.* **aînée**) Eldest, elder, senior.—*n.* The eldest son or daughter.

aînesse, *n.f.* Seniority, priority by age, primogeniture. *Droit d'aînesse,* birthright.

ainsi [ε̃′si], *adv.* Thus, so, in this or that manner. *Ainsi de suite, ainsi du reste,* and so forth; *ainsi soit-il,* so be it; *ainsi va le monde,* so the world goes; *il en est ainsi des autres passions,* thus it is with the other passions; *je suis ainsi fait,* that's my temper; *le monde est ainsi,* such is the world; *pour ainsi dire,* so to speak, as it were; *s'il en est ainsi,* if such is the case. *Ainsi que,* in the same way (as), at the same time (as); *cela s'est passé ainsi que je vous l'ai dit,* that happened in the way I told you.

air (1) [ε:r], *n.m.* Air; wind; (*Chem. etc.*) gas; (*pl.*) atmosphere. *Air comprimé,* compressed air; *chambre à air,* inner tube; *courant d'air,* draught; *en plein air,* in the open air; *être en l'air,* to be in a flutter, all upside down; (*Mil.*) unsupported; *faire des châteaux en l'air,* to build castles in the air; *il ne fait point d'air,* there is not the least breath of wind; *mettre tout en l'air,* to put everything in a muddle; *parler en l'air,* to talk wildly; *paroles en l'air,* empty, idle words; *prendre l'air,* to take an airing, to take a walk; *prise d'air,* air-scoop; (*Av.*) *trou d'air,* air-lock; *vivre de l'air du temps,* to live on air; (*slang*) *se donner de l'air,* to escape, to pop off; *fiche en l'air,* to throw away.

air (2) [ε:r], *n.m.* Mien, look, expression, air, manner, appearance. *Air abattu,* downcast look; *air chagrin,* sorrowful look; *air éveillé,* sharp look; *air farouche,* forbidding look; *les gens du bel air,* gentlefolks, fashionable people; *un air de famille,* a family likeness; *un faux air de ressemblance,* a slight resemblance; *avoir l'air,* to look; *avoir grand air,* to look fine; *avoir l'air comme il faut,* to look respectable; (*fam.*) *cela en a tout l'air,* it looks like it; *avoir un drôle d'air,* to look odd; *se donner des airs,* to put on airs.

air (3) [ε:r], *n.m.* (*Mus.*) Tune. *Air à boire,* drinking song.

airage [ε′ra:3], *n.m.* (*Mining*) Ventilation-gallery; angle of mill-sails.

airain [ε′rɛ̃], *n.m.* *Bronze; (*poet.*) cannon, bell. (*fig.*) *Avoir un cœur d'airain,* to have a heart of stone; *avoir un front d'airain,* to be brazen-faced; *un homme d'airain,* a man of iron.

aire [ε:r], *n.f.* Area, space; threshing-floor; eyrie; (*Naut.*) direction (of the wind). (*Bot.*) aira, fescue. *L'aire d'un triangle,* (*Geom.*) the area or inside of a triangle; *une aire de vent,* (*Naut.*) point of the compass; *aire d'atterrissage,* (*Av.*) landing area, apron.

airée [ε′re], *n.f.* The lot of wheat or other grain placed at one time on a threshing-floor; batch of dough.

airelle [ε′rεl], *n.f.* Whortleberry, bilberry; (*Am.*) huckleberry.

airer [ɛ′re], *v.i.* To make its eyrie or nest (of a bird of prey).

ais [ɛ], *n.m.* Board, plank; stave (of a barrel).

aisance [ɛ′zɑ̃:s], *n.f.* Ease, facility; easiness, affluence; competency; (*Mach.*) play, freedom; the comforts or conveniences of life. *Avoir de l'aisance dans les manières*, to have an easy manner; *être dans l'aisance*, to be comfortably off; (*pl.*) *cabinet* (or *lieu*) *d'aisances*, public convenience; *fosse d'aisances*, cesspool.

aise [ɛ:z], *n.f.* Ease, comfort, convenience; (*pl.*) comforts, comfortable circumstances. *Aimer ses aises*, to love one's ease; *à l'aise*, at ease, comfortable; *elle ne se sent pas d'aise*, she is beside herself for joy; *être à son aise*, to be well off; *mettre quelqu'un à son aise*, to put at ease, to reassure someone; *n'en prendre qu'à son aise*, to do just as one likes, to take it easy; *se pâmer d'aise*, to be overjoyed; *se sentir mal à l'aise*, to feel uncomfortable; *vous en parlez bien à votre aise*, it is easy for you to say so.—*a.* Glad, well pleased. *Je suis bien aise de vous voir*, I am very glad to see you.

aisé [ɛ′ze], *a.* (*fem.* **aisée**) Easy; convenient, comfortable; in easy circumstances. *Cela est aisé à dire*, it is an easy thing to say; *des souliers aisés*, comfortable shoes; *il est fort aisé*, he is a well-to-do man; *un air aisé*, an easy manner. **aisément**, *adv.* Easily, readily, freely; comfortably.

aisseau [ɛ′so], *n.m.* or **aissante**, *n.f.* (*Carp.*) Shingle, wooden tile.

aisselier [ɛs′lje], *n.m.* (*Carp.*) Tie-beam, brace, strut.

aisselière [AISSETTE].

aisselle [ɛ′sɛl], *n.f.* Armpit; (*Bot.*) axil.

aissette [ɛ′sɛt], *n.f.* or **aisceau**, *n.m.* Adze (of a cooper); hooked hammer (of a tiler).

aîtres [ɛtr], *n.m.* *Parvis*, churchyard. (*pl.*) *Connaître les aîtres*, to know the ins and outs.

Aix-la-Chapelle [ɛkslaʃa′pɛl], *f.* Aachen.

ajointer [aʒwɛ̃′te], *v.t.* To join on to, to fit.

ajonc [a′ʒɔ̃], *n.m.* Furze, gorse.

ajour [a′ʒu:r], *n.m.* (*Sculp.*) Opening, hole, aperture, orifice, open-work. **ajouré**, *a.* (*fem.* **ajourée**) Pierced, perforated. **ajourer**, *v.t.* To pierce, to perforate.

ajourné [aʒur′ne], *a.* (*fem.* **ajournée**) and *n.* (Conscript) who has been put back; (candidate) who passed the written part, but not the oral.

ajournement [aʒurnə′mɑ̃], *n.m.* Adjournment, postponement; (*Law*) summons.

ajourner [aʒur′ne], *v.t.* To adjourn; to put off, to defer; (*Law*) to summon (for a specified day). *Ajourner sine die*, to shelve.

ajout [AJOUTAGE].

ajoutable [aʒu′tabl], *a.* That may be added or joined on (to). **ajoutage** or **ajoutoir** *n.m.* Piece joined on, addition.

ajouté [aʒu′te], *p.p.* (*fem.* **-ée**) Added.—*n.m.* Addition or addendum (to a book, MS., etc.).

ajouter [aʒu′te], *v.t.* To add, to join, to subjoin, to supply, to interpolate. *Ce passage a été ajouté à ce livre*, this passage is an interpolation; *ajouter foi à quelque chose*, to give credit to a thing. **s'ajouter**, *v.r.* To be joined, to attach oneself.

ajoutoir [AJOUTAGE].

ajust [a′ʒy], *n.m.* (*Naut.*) or *nœud d'ajust*, or *nœud de vache*, carrick bend.

ajustage [aʒys′ta:ʒ], *n.m.* Adjustment, giving the legal weight to a coin; fitting or adjusting. *Atelier d'ajustage*, fitting shop.

ajusté, *a.* (*fem.* **ajustée**) Close-fitting (clothes).

ajustement, *n.m.* Adjustment, adjusting, arranging, fitting, settlement; laying out; agreement; attire, garb, apparel. *L'ajustement d'un poids*, the adjusting of a weight.

ajuster [aʒys′te], *v.t.* To adjust, to regulate, to square, to fit, to adapt (one thing to another), to make tally; to take aim at; to set in order; (*Mus.*) to tune, to accord; to trim, to bedeck; to conciliate; to settle or arrange (a dispute). *Ajuster un lièvre*, to take aim at a hare; *ajuster de nouveau*, to recompose; *ajuster ses cheveux*, to put one's hair in order; *ajuster un différend*, to settle a difference; *ajuster des passages d'un livre*, to adapt (or collate) passages of a book. **s'ajuster**, *v.r.* To accommodate oneself, to be adapted; to get oneself ready; to dress, to deck oneself out.

ajusteur [aʒys′tœ:r], *n.m.* Fitter, sizer; weigher (at the mint); (*C*) (*Insurance*) average adjustor. **ajustoir**, *n.m.* Assay-scales. **ajusture**, *n.f.* Fitting (of a horseshoe).

ajut [AJUST].

ajutage [aʒy′ta:ʒ] or **ajutoir**, *n.m.* Adjutage, a tube or pipe (used in water-works); nozzle (of engines).

alacrité [alakri′te], *n.f.* Alacrity, cheerful briskness.

Aladin [ala′dɛ̃], *m.* Aladdin.

Alain [a′lɛ̃], *m.* Allen.

alaise [ALÈZE].

alambic [alɑ̃′bik], *n.m.* Alembic, still. *Passer par l'alambic*, to distil, (*fig.*) to investigate carefully. **alambiquage**, *n.m.* Refinement, excessive subtlety. **alambiqué** [alɑ̃mbi′ke], *a.* (*fem.* **alambiquée**) Far-fetched, over-refined, fine-spun. **alambiquer**, *v.t.* To distil, to refine; (*fig.*) to refine too much upon. *S'alambiquer l'esprit sur quelque chose*, to rack one's brains about something. **alambiqueur**, *n.m.* (*fem.* **alambiqueuse**) One with an over-subtle or far-fetched style.

alandier [alɑ̃′dje], *n.m.* (*Ceramics*) Hearth of a hovel.

alangui [alɑ̃′gi:], *a.* (*fem.* **alanguie**) Languid, downcast.

alanguir [alɑ̃′gi:r], *v.t.* To enfeeble, to make languid. **s'alanguir**, *v.r.* To languish, to flag, to become languid.

alanguissement, *n.m.* Languor.

alarguer [alar′ge], *v.i.* (*Naut.*) To bear off, to sheer off, to put to sea.

alarmant [alar′mɑ̃], *a.* (*fem.* **alarmante**) Alarming, startling.

alarme [a′larm], *n.f.* Alarm, affright, sudden fear, uneasiness. *Sonner l'alarme, donner l'alarme*, to sound, to give the alarm; *cloche d'alarme*, alarm-bell; *donner des alarmes*, to cause uneasiness to; *signal d'alarme*, alarm signal; *tenir en alarme*, to keep in constant fear; *tirer la sonnette d'alarme*, to pull the alarm-cord. **alarmer** [alar′me], *v.t.* To alarm, to raise an alarm to; to startle, to render anxious or frightened. **s'alarmer**, *v.r.* To take alarm, to be alarmed. *Ne vous alarmez point*, don't worry.

alarmiste, *a.* and *n.* Alarmist.

alaterne [ala'tɛrn], *n.m.* Species of buckthorn, *Rhamnus alaternus.*
Albanie [alba'ni:], *f.* Albania.
albâtre [al'bɑːtr], *n.m.* Alabaster; (*fig.*) whiteness. *D'albâtre,* of alabaster, snowy white. **albâtrier**, *n.* One working or dealing in alabaster.
albatros [alba'troːs], *n.m.* Albatross.
Albe [alb], *m.* Alba, Alva.
alberge [al'bɛrʒ], *n.f.* Clingstone peach or apricot. **albergier**, *n.m.* Tree bearing this.
Albigeois [albi'ʒwa], *n.m.* (*used only in pl.*) Albigenses, religious sect that arose at Albi at the end of the 11th century.
albinisme [albi'nism], *n.m.* Albinism. **albinos** [albi'noːs], *n. and a.* Albino.
Albion [al'bjɔ̃], *n.f.* (*Poet.*) Albion (England). *La perfide Albion,* perfidious Albion.
albite [al'bit], *n.f.* Albite.
albran [HALBRAN].
albugo [alby'go], *n.m.* (*Path.*) Albugo, a white spot in the tissue of the cornea. **albuginé**, *a* (*fem.* **albuginée**) White (of tissues etc.). **albugineux**, *a.* (*fem.* **-euse**) Whitish.
album [al'bɔm], *n.m.* Album, scrap-book, sketch-book.
albumen [alby'mɛn], *n.m.* (*Bot.*) Albumen. **albumine**, *n.f.* Albumine. **albuminé** (*fem.* **albuminée**) or **albumineux** (*fem.* **albumineuse**), *a.* Albuminous. **albuminoïde**, *a. and n.m.* Albuminoid. **albuminose**, *n.f.* Albuminose. **albuminurie**, *n.f.* (*Path.*) Albuminuria. **albuminurique**, *a.* Suffering from albuminuria.—*n.* A person suffering from this.
alcade [al'kad], *n.m.* (*Sp. Law*) Alcalde.
alcaïque [alka'ik], *a.* Alcaic (verse).
alcalescence [alkale'sɑ̃:s], *n.f.* Alkalescence. **alcalescent**, *a.* (*fem.* **alcalescente**) Alkalescent.
alcali [alka'li], *n.m.* Alkali. (*fam.*) *Alcali volatil,* ammonia. **alcalifiant**, *a.* (*fem.* **alcalifiante**) That alkalifies. **alcalimètre**, *n.m.* Alcalimeter. **alcalimétrie**, *n.f.* Alkalimetry. **alcalin**, *a.* (*fem.* **alcaline**) Alkaline. **alcalinité**, *n.f.* Alkalinity. **alcalisation**, *n.f.* Alkalization. **alcaliser** or **alcaliniser**, *v.t.* To alkalize, to alkalify.
alcarazas [alkara'zɑ:s], *n.m.* A pitcher of porous earthenware used as a water-cooler.
alcée [al'se], *n.f.* (*Bot.*) Hollyhock.
alchimie [alʃi'mi], *n.f.* Alchemy.
alchimique [alʃi'mik], *a.* Alchemical.
alchimiste, *n.m.* Alchemist.
Alcibiade [alsi'bjad], *m.* Alcibiades.
alcool [al'kɔl], *n.m.* Alcohol; spirit(s). *Alcool à brûler, alcool dénaturé,* methylated spirit; *vins et alcools,* wines and spirits. **alcoolat**, *n.m.* (*Pharm.*) Aromatized spirit. **alcoolate**, *n.m.* (*Chem.*) Alcoholate. **alcoolique**, *a.* Alcoholic. **alcoolisable**, *a.* That may be alcoholized. **alcoolisation**, *n.f.* Alcoholization. **alcooliser**, *v.t.* To alcoholize. **s'alcooliser**, *v.r.* To become alcoholized; (*colloq.*) to drink too much. **alcoolisme**, *n.m.* Alcoholism. **alcoolomètre** or **alcoomètre**, *n.m.* Alcoholometer. **alcoolométrie** or **alcoométrie**, *n.f.* Alcoholometry.
Alcoran [CORAN].
alcôve [al'koːv], *n.f.* Alcove, recess. *Secrets d'alcôve,* marital intimacies.

alcôviste, *n.m.* (*Lit.*) A wit who paid court to the 17th-century *précieuses.*
alcyon [al'sjɔ̃], *n.m.* Halcyon; (*Zool.*) alcyonarian. **alcyonnaire** or **alcyonien** (1), *n.m.* (*Zool.*) Alcyonarian. **alcyonien** (2), *a.* (*fem.* **alcyonienne**) Halcyon, peaceful.
Alde [ald], *m.* Aldus. **aldin** [al'dɛ̃], *n.m.* (*fem.* **-ine**) Aldine (edition).
ale [e:l], *n.f.* Ale.
aléa [ale'a], *n.m.* Chance, hazard. **aléatoire**, *a.* Hazardous, uncertain; (*Law*) depending on contingencies, aleatory. **aléatoirement**, *adv.* Uncertainly.
alène [a'lɛn], *n.f.* Awl. *Feuilles en alène,* acuminate leaves. **alénier**, *n.m.* Maker of or dealer in awls.
alénois [ale'nwa], *a.* Of Orleans. *Cresson alénois,* common garden cress.
alentour or **à l'entour** [alɑ̃'tu:r], *adv.* About, around, round about. *À l'entour du troupeau,* around the flock; *les bois d'alentour,* the surrounding woods. **alentours**, *n.m.* (*used only in pl.*) Environs, neighbourhood; *persons around one, associates, familiars.
Aléoutiennes [aleu'sjɛn], **les**, *f.pl.* The Aleutian Islands.
Alep [a'lɛp], *m.* Aleppo.
alépine [ale'pin], *n.f.* (*Tex.*) Bombazine.
alérion [ale'rjɔ̃], *n.m.* (*Her.*) Eaglet represented without beak or feet.
alerte [a'lɛrt], *a.* Alert, vigilant, watchful; active, lively, agile, sprightly, brisk.—*n.f.* Alarm, warning. *Alerte aérienne,* air-raid warning; *en alerte,* on the alert; *donner l'alerte au camp,* to rouse the camp; *fin d'alerte,* (*Mil.*) 'all clear'.—*int.* Quick! up! look out! beware! **alerter**, *v.t.* To give the alarm to, to warn.
alésage [ale'za:ʒ], *n.m.* Boring, drilling.
alèse [ALÈZE].
aléser [ale'ze], *v.t.* To smooth or enlarge the bore of (a tube, gun, etc.). *Aléser un canon,* to bore a cannon. **aléseuse**, *n.f.* Boring-machine. **alésoir**, *n.m.* Borer, boring tool.
alester [ales'te] or **alestir** [ales'ti:r], *v.t.* (*Naut.*) To lighten or disencumber (a vessel).
alésure [ale'zy:r], *n.f.* Metal turnings or filings.
alevin [al'vɛ̃], *n.m.* Fry, young fish. **alevinage**, *n.m.* Breeding young fish; stocking (water) with young fish. **aleviner**, *v.t.* To stock with fry. **alevinier**, *n.m.*, or **alevinière**, *n.f.* Breeding-pond.
Alexandre [alek'sɑ̃:dr], *m.* Alexander.
Alexandrie [aleksɑ̃'dri], *f.* Alexandria.
alexandrin [aleksɑ̃'drɛ̃], *a.* (*fem.* **alexandrine**) (*Pros.*) Alexandrine.—*n.m.* An Alexandrine.
alezan [al'zɑ̃], *a.* (*fem.* **alezane**) Chestnut (of a horse).—*n.* Chestnut horse.
alèze or **alèse** [a'lɛ:z], *n.f.* Draw-sheet (placed under a sick person); wooden lining (of a scabbard).
alfa [al'fa], *n.m.* Esparto-grass.
***alfange** [al'fɑ̃:ʒ], *n.f.* Moorish scimitar.
alfénide [alfe'nid], *n.f.* Britannia metal.
algarade [alga'rad], *n.f.* Insult, affront, rating, blowing up; attack.
algaroth [alga'rɔt], *n.m.* (*Med.*) Oxychloride of antimony used as a purgative or emetic.
algazelle [alga'zɛl], *n.f.* White African gazelle.
algèbre [al'ʒɛbr], *n.f.* Algebra. *C'est de*

l'algèbre pour lui, it is Greek to him. **algébrique,** *a.* Algebraical. **algébriquement,** *adv.* Algebraically. **algébriste,** *n.m.* Algebraist.

Alger [al'ʒe], *m.* Algiers.

Algérie [alʒe'ri], *f.* Algeria.

algérien [alʒe'rjɛ̃], *a.* (*fem.* **-ienne**) *n.* (**Algérien, -ienne**) Algerian.

algide [al'ʒid], *a.* (*Path.*) Cold, algid.

algidité [alʒidi'te], *n.f.* Algidity.

algie [al'ʒi:], *n.f.* Ache.

algorithme [algɔ'ritm], *n.m.* Algorithm.

alguazil [algwa'zil], *n.m.* Alguazil, Spanish policeman.

algue [alg], *n.f.* Sea-weed, alga.

alibi [ali'bi], *n.m.* (*Law*) Alibi.

alibile [ali'bil], *a.* (*Med.*) Nutritive.

aliboron [alibɔ'rɔ̃], *n.m.* Jackass, a stupid, self-conceited fellow. *Maître aliboron*, a donkey; (*fig.*) an ignoramus.

aliboufier [alibu'fje], *n.m.* Storax, a fragrant resin.

alicante [ali'kɑ̃t], *n.m.* A sweet wine from Alicante.

alidade [ali'dad], *n.f.* Alidad, needle, the index of a quadrant, sextant, etc.

aliénabilité [aljenabili'te], *n.f.* Alienability. **aliénable,** *a.* Alienable, transferable.

aliénataire, *n.m.* (*Law*) Alienee. **aliénateur,** *n.m.* (*fem.* **-trice**) Alienator.

aliénation, *n.f.* (*Law*) Conveyance of property to another, alienation; (*fig.*) alienation, mental derangement; estrangement, aversion. *Aliénation mentale* or *d'esprit*, mental derangement.

aliéné [alje'ne], *a.* (*fem.* **-ée**) Lunatic, mad.—*n.* A lunatic. *Asile* (or *hospice* or *maison*) *d'aliénés*, lunatic asylum, madhouse.

aliéner [alje'ne], *v.t.* To alienate, to give away (property), to transfer, to part with, to make over; to estrange, to make hostile; to derange (the mind). *Aliéner sa liberté*, to give up one's freedom; *cette maladie lui a aliéné l'esprit*, this disease has deranged his mind. **s'aliéner,** *v.r.* To become estranged (from). *Il s'est aliéné leur sympathie*, he has lost their sympathy.

aliéniste [alje'nist], *n.m.* Alienist.

alifère [ali'fɛ:r], *a.* (*Ent.*) Aliferous, wing-bearing. **aliforme,** *a.* Aliform, wing-shaped.

alignée [ali'ɲe], *n.f.* Line, row. **alignement,** *n.m.* Alignment, laying out in line; line determining the direction; (*Mil.*) dressing; (*Print.*) ranging. *Cette maison sort de l'alignement*, that house stands out of the row; *rentrer dans l'alignement*, to fall into line; *prendre l'alignement*, to trace the line of; *à droite alignement!* right dress! *rectifier l'alignement*, to correct the dressing.

aligner [ali'ɲe], *v.t.* To align, to lay out in line, to put in a straight line; (*Mil.*) to dress; (*Print.*) to range. *Aligner des troupes*, to form troops in a line; *aligner ses phrases*, to square one's sentences; *aligner un compte*, (*Comm.*) to balance an account. **s'aligner,** *v.r.* (*Mil.*) To dress; (*colloq.*) to have a set-to, to fight a duel.

aliment [ali'mɑ̃], *n.m.* Aliment, food, nourishment, nutriment; (*Law, pl.*) alimony, maintenance, allowance. **alimentaire,** *a.* Alimental, alimentary. *Carte alimentaire*, ration

book; *pension alimentaire*, alimony, maintenance; *régime alimentaire*, diet; *pâtes alimentaires*, farinaceous foods (such as macaroni, semolina, etc.); (*Mech.*) *pompe alimentaire*, feed-pump, donkey engine. **alimentateur,** *a.* (*fem.* **alimentatrice**) Alimentary. **alimentation,** *n.f.* Alimentation; nourishment, feeding, provisionment; feed (of motors etc.). *Câble d'alimentation*, feeder; *rayon d'alimentation*, food department.

alimenter [alimɑ̃'te], *v.t.* To feed, to nourish; to maintain; to supply, to provision; to fuel, to keep up. *Le marché ne fournit pas de quoi alimenter la ville*, the market does not furnish enough to supply the town. **s'alimenter,** *v.r.* (*Med.*) To eat.

alimenteux, *a.* (*fem.* **alimenteuse**) Nutritive.

alinéa [aline'a], *n.m.* Indented line; new paragraph.

aliquante [ali'kɑ̃t], *a.f.* (*Math.*) Aliquant (part).

aliquote [ali'kɔt], *a.f.* and *n.f.* (*Math.*) Aliquot.

alise or **alize** [a'li:z], *n.f.* Sorb-apple, fruit of the service-tree.

alisé [ALIZÉ].

alisier or **alizier** [ali'zje], *n.m.* Service-tree.

alisme [a'lism], *n.m.* Water-plantain.

alitement [alit'mɑ̃], *n.m.* Confinement to bed, retirement to bed. **aliter,** *v.t.* To confine to bed. *Être alité*, to be bedridden. **s'aliter,** *v.r.* To take to one's bed.

alizari [aliza'ri], *n.m.* Madder-root. **alizarine,** *n.f.* (*Chem.*) Alizarin, madder dye.

alizé or **alisé** [ali'ze], *a.* (*fem.* **-ée**) Soft (said of the trade-winds). *Vents alizés*, trade-winds.—*n.m.* Trade-wind. **alizéen,** *a.* (*fem.* **-enne**) Pertaining to the trade-winds.

alizier [ALISIER].

alkali, etc. [ALCALI].

alkékenge [alke'kɑ̃:z], *n.m.* Winter-cherry.

alkermès [alkɛr'mɛːs], *n.m.* Alkermes; extract of kermes; liqueur or confection coloured with kermes.

Alkoran [CORAN].

Allah [a'la], *m.* Allah.

allaise [a'lɛ:z], *n.f.* Sand-bank (in a river).

allaitant [ale'tɑ̃], *a.* (*fem.* **allaitante**) Suckling, nursing, feeding, with one's milk. **allaitement,** *n.m.* Lactation, nursing, suckling. *Allaitement artificiel*, bottle feeding. **allaiter,** *v.t.* To suckle, to nurse.

allant [a'lɑ̃], *a.* (*fem.* **allante**) *Stirring, bustling, gadding.—*n.* *Goer (used only in the phrase *allants et venants*, goers and comers, passers-by); briskness. *Il a de l'allant*, he has plenty of go, of initiative.

alléchant [ale'ʃɑ̃], *a.* (*fem.* **alléchante**) Alluring, enticing, seductive. **allèchement,** *n.m.* Allurement, enticement, seduction, attraction. **allécher,** *v.t.* To allure, to entice, to attract.

allée [a'le], *n.f.* Passage, drive, alley, avenue, walk, (*pl.*) goings. *Une allée couverte*, a shady walk; *faire des allées et venues*, to go to and fro.

allégation [alega'sjɔ̃], *n.f.* Allegation, assertion.

allège [a'lɛ:ʒ], *n.f.* Lighter, hopper; (*Arch.*) window basement, sill of window. *Frais d'allège*, (*Comm.*) lighterage.

allégeable [ale'ʒabl], *a.* That may be lightened or alleviated. **allégeage,** *n.m.* Alleviation, lightening.

allégeance [ale'ʒɑ̃:s], *n.f.* Alleviation, relief; allegiance. *Serment d'allégeance,* oath of allegiance. **allégement,** *n.m.* Alleviation, relief; reduction (of weight, labour, etc.).

alléger [ale'ʒe], *v.t.* To ease, to unburden, to lighten; to unload (a boat); to alleviate, to relieve, to assuage (pain or grief).

Alléghanys [alega'ni], **les Monts,** *m.pl.* The Alleghanies.

allégir [ale'ʒi:r], *v.t.* To reduce the size, volume, etc., of; to fine down.

allégorie [alegɔ'ri], *n.f.* Allegory. *Par allégorie,* allegorically. **allégorique,** *a.* Allegorical. **allégoriquement,** *adv.* Allegorically. **allégoriser,** *v.t.* To allegorize. **allégoriseur,** *n.m.* One who allegorizes. **allégoriste,** *n.m.* Allegorist.

allègre [al'lɛgr], *a.* Lively, nimble, sprightly, jolly, cheerful. **allègrement,** *adv.* Briskly, joyfully, merrily, joyously. **allégresse,** *n.f.* Gaiety, joy, mirth, cheerfulness, sprightliness. *Cris d'allégresse,* shouts of joy, huzzas.

alléguer [alle'ge], *v.t.* To allege, to advance, to urge; (*Law*) to quote, to adduce, to cite, to plead.

alléluia [allely'ja], *n.m.* Hallelujah; (*Bot.*) wood-sorrel.

allemand [al'mɑ̃], *a.* (*fem.* **allemande**) German. *Une querelle d'allemand,* a groundless quarrel.—*n.* (**Allemand, -ande**) A German.—*n.m.* the German language.

allemande, *n.f.* A dance in double or triple time; the music for this; a sauce made of flour, butter, white meal, and yolk of egg.

Allemagne [al'maɲ], *f.* Germany.

aller (1) [a'le], *v.i. irr.* (*pres.p.* **allant,** *p.p.* **allé**) To go, to go on, to proceed, to progress (well, ill, etc.); to be (in good or ill health); to act (in a certain way); to suit, to be adapted, to fit (well or ill); to be on the point of. *Aller à cheval,* to go on horseback, to ride; *aller à pied,* to go on foot; *aller au pas,* to go at a walking pace; *aller bon train,* to go on at a good round pace; *aller çà et là,* to roam about; *aller à la chasse,* to go shooting; *aller se promener,* to go out for a walk; *aller en voiture,* to drive, to go by car; *aller et venir,* to go up and down; *je ne ferai qu'aller et venir,* I won't be a minute; *aller croissant,* to go on increasing; *aller de pair,* to be on a par; *aller de mal en pis,* to go from bad to worse; *cela va tout seul,* it is plain sailing; *cet enfant ira loin,* this child will go far; *aller son petit bonhomme de chemin,* to jog along; *comment allez-vous?* how are you? *je vais bien,* I am well; (*fam.*) *ça va!* all right! *il n'y va pas par quatre chemins,* he does not beat about the bush; *il n'y va pas de main morte,* he goes at it in dead earnest; *cet habit vous va mal,* this coat does not fit you; *ces deux couleurs vont bien ensemble,* these two colours are well matched; *cette coiffure ne vous va pas,* this hair style does not suit you; *il va le faire,* he is going to do it. (Other gallicisms) *Allons!* come on! *allons donc!* surely not! *cela va sans dire,* it stands to reason; *il y va de sa vie,* his life is at stake; *va pour du vin!* (*colloq.*) well, let's have some wine! *Se laisser aller,* to yield, to give way, to abandon oneself to

a thing; *se laisser aller à la douleur,* to give way to one's grief; *se laisser aller à la tentation,* to yield to temptation. **s'en aller,** *v.r.* To go away, to run away; to vanish, to disappear; to die, to wear out. *Il s'en va,* he is dying; *je m'en allai,* I went away; *je m'en vais vous dire,* I'll tell you what; *tout s'en est allé en fumée,* all come to nothing; *va-t'en! allez-vous-en!* go away, be off with you!

aller (2) [a'le], *n.m.* Going, course, run; (*Naut.*) outward voyage. *Aller et retour,* voyage out and in; *billet d'aller et retour,* return ticket; *au pis aller,* at the worst; *c'est un pis aller,* it is a makeshift.

allergie [alɛr'ʒi], *n.f.* Allergy. **allergique,** *a.* Allergic.

alleu [a'lø], *n.m.* Allodium. *Franc alleu (pl. francs alleus),* a freehold.

alliable [a'ljabl], *a.* That may be mingled or combined (with).

alliacé [alja'se], *a.* (*fem.* **alliacée**) (*Bot.*) Alliaceous.

alliage [a'lja:ʒ], *n.m.* Alloy, mixture; (*fig.*) impure mixture or combination; (*Arith.*) alligation. *Sans alliage,* pure, without alloy.

alliaire [a lje:r], *n.f.* (*Bot.*) Alliaria, sauce-alone.

alliance [a'ljɑ̃:s], *n.f.* Alliance, marriage; union, league, coalition, confederacy; compact, covenant; combination (of words etc.); mixture, blending; wedding-ring.

allié [a'lje], *a.* (*fem.* **alliée**) Allied; related (by marriage); akin, kindred.—*n.* Ally; connexion (by marriage).

allier (1) [a'lje], *v.t.* To mix; to combine; to join, to unite, to ally, to marry; to reconcile. *Allier l'or avec l'argent,* to alloy gold with silver. **s'allier,** *v.r.* To be incorporated or mixed; to become allied, to join forces (*avec*); to combine (of metals).

allier (2) [a'lje] or **hallier,** *n.m.* Partridge-net.

alligator [aliga'tɔ:r], *n.m.* Alligator.

allitération [alitera'sjɔ̃], *n.f.* Alliteration.

allo [a'lo], *int.* (*Teleph.*) Hullo!

allocataire [alɔka'tɛ:r], *n.* Recipient of an allowance.

allocation [alɔkɑ'sjɔ̃], *n.f.* Allocation, allowance; amount allocated or allowed. *Allocation de chômage,* dole, unemployment benefit. *Allocations familiales,* family allowances.

allocution [alɔky'sjɔ̃], *n.f.* Allocution, short address, speech.

allodial [alɔ'djal], *a.* (*fem.* **-ale,** *pl.* **-aux**) Allodial, freehold.—*n.m. pl.* Allodial lands.

allogène [alɔ'ʒɛn], *n.* and *a.* Allogeneous.

allonge [a'lɔ̃:ʒ], *n.f.* Eking-piece; leaf (of a table); fly-leaf, addendum; rider (of a document); (*Naut.*) futtock. *Allonge de boucher,* meat-hook.

allongé [alɔ̃'ʒe], *a.* (*fem.* **allongée**) Lengthened, elongated, out-stretched; downcast, long (of face). **allongement,** *n.m.* Lengthening, elongation, protraction.

allonger [alɔ̃'ʒe], *v.t.* To lengthen, to elongate, to piece or eke out; to stretch; to drag out, to protract; (*Fenc.* etc.) to fetch, deal, or strike (a blow). (*colloq.*) *Allonger une gifle à quelqu'un,* to slap somebody's face; *allonger le pas,* to step out; *allonger le tir,* to lengthen the range. **s'allonger,** *v.r.* To stretch out, to grow longer; to stretch, to lie down at full length. (*colloq.*) *S'allonger un bon repas,* to treat oneself to a good meal.

allons! [ALLER (1)].

allonyme [allɔ'nim], *a.* Allonymous.—*n.* Allonym.

allopathe [allɔ'pat], *n.m.* Allopathist. *a.* Allopathic (remedy). **allopathie,** *n.f.* Allopathy. **allopathique,** *a.* Allopathic.

allotir [alɔ'tiːr], *v.t.* To allot. **allotissement,** *n.m.* Allotment.

allotropie [allɔtrɔ'pi], *n.f.* Allotropy. **allotropique,** *a.* Allotropic. **allotropisme,** *n.m.* Allotropism.

allouer [a'lwe], *v.t.* To allow, to grant, to accord; to allocate.

alluchon [aly'ʃɔ̃], *n.m.* Cog, tooth (of a wheel).

allumage [aly'maːʒ], *n.m.* Lighting, kindling; ignition. *Un raté d'allumage,* misfire; *mettre l'allumage,* to switch on; *mettre de l'avance à l'allumage,* to advance the spark; *panne d'allumage,* failure of the ignition.

allumé [aly'me], *a.* (*fem.* **allumée**) Lighted, ignited; (*Her.*) having flames of a distinct colour; (*colloq.*) excited, drunk, lit-up.

allume-feu [alym'fø], *n.m. inv.* Firewood, firelighter, tinder, kindling.

allume-gaz [alym'gaːz], *n.m. inv.* Gas-lighter.

allumer [aly'me], *v.t.* To light; to kindle, to set on fire; (*fig.*) to inflame, to incite, to stir up. *Allumer la lampe,* to turn on the light. **s'allumer,** *v.r.* To light, to kindle, to take fire; to blaze, to sparkle, to glare; to flare up, to break out. *Ce bois a bien de la peine à s'allumer,* this wood won't light.

allumette [aly'mɛt], *n.f.* Match. *Allumette chimique,* lucifer-match; *allumette bougie,* wax vesta; *allumette tison,* fusee; *allumette suédoise,* safety match. **allumettier,** *n.m.* (*fem.* **-ière**) Maker or vendor of matches.

allumeur [aly'mœːr], *n.m.* (*fem.* **allumeuse**) Lighter; (*slang*) decoy; puffer (at cheap-jack auctions); (*Motor*) igniter, primer. *Allumeur de réverbères,* lamp-lighter.—*n.f.* a vamp.

allumoir [aly'mwaːr], *n.m.* Automatic device for lighting (gas, tobacco-pipes, etc.); gas-lighter, electric igniter.

allure [a'lyːr], *n.f.* Carriage, gait, pace, way of walking; demeanour; aspect, look; speed; (*Naut.*) trim, direction (of a vessel in regard to the wind); (*pl.*) ways (of a person). *À vive allure,* at a smart pace; *à toute allure,* at full speed; (*fam.*) *avoir de l'allure,* to look grand; *cette affaire prend une mauvaise allure,* that affair is taking an ugly turn; *je le reconnais à son allure,* I know him by his gait.

allusif [aly'zif], *a.* (*fem.* **allusive**) Allusive. **allusion,** *n.f.* Allusion, hint, innuendo. *Faire allusion à quelque chose,* to allude to something; *faire une allusion peu voilée,* to give a broad hint; (*fam.*) *saisir l'allusion,* to take the hint.

alluvial [aly'vjal], *a.* (*fem.* **alluviale,** *pl.* **alluviaux**), **alluvien,** *a.* (*fem.* **alluvienne**) Alluvial. **alluvion,** *n.f.* Alluvium; alluvion. **alluvionnaire,** *a.* Produced by alluvion. **alluvionnement,** *n.m.* Removal by alluvion; production of alluvion.

almageste [alma'ʒɛst], *n.m.* Almagest.

almanach [alma'na], *n.m.* Almanac, calendar.

almée [al'me], *n.f.* Almah; almeh.

aloès [alɔ'ɛːs], *n.m.* Aloe; aloes. **aloétine,** *n.f.* Purified juice of aloes. **aloétique,** *a.* Aloetic.

aloi [a'lwa], *n.m.* The statutory degree of purity of gold and silver; (*fig.*) standard (good or bad), quality, kind (of persons etc.). *Argent de bon aloi,* good money; *de bon aloi,* genuine, sterling (also *fig.*); *homme de bas aloi,* a cad.

alopécie [alɔpe'si], *n.f.* Alopecia; baldness; fox's evil.

alors [a'lɔːr], *adv.* Then, at that time; in that case, in such a case. *D'alors,* of that time; *alors que,* while, whereas; *jusqu'alors,* up to then, till that moment; *alors même que,* even though.

alose [a'loːz], *n.f.* Shad. **alosier,** *n.m.* or **alosière,** *n.f.* Shad-net.

alouate [a'lwat], *n.m.* Howling-monkey.

alouette [a'lwɛt], *n.f.* Lark. *Alouette de mer,* sandpiper; *alouette des champs,* skylark, *alouette huppée,* tufted lark; *alouette lulu,* wood-lark; *il attend que les alouettes lui tombent toutes rôties dans le bec,* he expects a fortune to drop into his mouth; *pied d'alouette,* larkspur.

alourdir [alur'diːr], *v.t.* To make heavy, dull, or stupid. *Je suis tout alourdi de sommeil,* I feel quite drowsy. **s'alourdir,** *v.r.* To grow heavy, dull. **alourdissant,** *a.* (*fem.* **alourdissante**) Oppressive. **alourdissement,** *n.m.* Heaviness, dullness.

aloyage [alwa'jaːʒ], *n.m.* Alloying, mixture; pewterer's alloy.

aloyau [alwa'jo], *n.m.* Sirloin.

*****aloyer** [alwa'je], *v.t.* To give (gold or silver) the legal degree of purity; to alloy (tin).

alpaca [alpa'ka] or **alpaga,** *n.m.* Alpaca.

alpage [al'paːʒ], *n.m.* Mountain pasture-land.

alpenstock [alpɛn'stɔk], *n.m.* Alpenstock.

Alpes [alp], **les,** *f.pl.* The Alps.

alpestre [al'pɛstr], *a.* Alpine (scenery, flora).

alpha [al'fa], *n.m.* Alpha; (*fig.*) beginning. *L'alpha et l'oméga,* the beginning and the end.

alphabet [alfa'bɛ], *n.m.* Alphabet, spelling-book. **alphabétique,** *a.* Alphabetical. *Par ordre alphabétique,* or **alphabétiquement,** *adv.* Alphabetically.

Alphonse [al'fɔ̃s], *m.* Alfonso.

*****alphonse** [al'fɔ̃ːs], *n.m.* (*slang*) Pimp, ponce.

alpin [al'pɛ̃], *a.* (*fem.* **-ine**) Alpine (club, etc.). **alpinisme,** *n.m.* Mountaineering. **alpiniste,** *n.m.* Alpinist, mountaineer.

alpique [al'pik], *a.* Pertaining to the Alps.

alpiste [al'pist], *n.m.* Alpist, canary-grass.

Alsace [al'zas], **l',** *f.* Alsace.

alsacien [alza'sjɛ̃], *a.* (*fem.* **alsacienne**) Alsatian.—*n.* (**Alsacien,** *fem.* **Alsacienne**) Inhabitant of Alsace.

alsine [al'sin], *n.f.* Chickweed [MORGELINE].

altaïque [alta'ik], *a.* Altaic, Ural-Altaic.

altérabilité [alterabili'te], *n.f.* Alterability. **altérable,** *a.* Alterable.

altérant (1) [alte'rã], *a.* (*fem.* **-ante**) and *n.m.* (*Med.*) Alterative.

altérant (2) [alte'rã], *a.* (*fem.* **-ante**) Exciting thirst.

altérateur [altera'tœːr], *n.m.* (*fem.* **altératrice**) Debaser, adulterator of coinage, etc.

altératif [altera'tif], *a.* (*fem.* **altérative**) (*Med.*) Alterative. **altération,** *n.f.* Deterioration; falsification, adulteration, debasing (of money, etc); weakening, impairing; *alteration, change, modification; (*Mus.*) change of tone indicated by an accidental sign placed before a note. *L'altération de sa voix,* the faltering of his voice.

altercation [altɛrkɑ'sjɔ̃], *n.f.* Altercation, wrangle, dispute, quarrel.

altérer [alte're], *v.t.* To alter for the worse; to impair, to adulterate, to corrupt, to pervert, to debase, to falsify; to disturb, to trouble, to upset; to make thirsty. *Altérer la viande,* to taint meat; *altérer le caractère,* to spoil the temper; *altérer l'amitié,* to weaken friendship; *altérer la monnaie,* to debase coin; *cette sauce aux anchois m'a fort altéré,* that anchovy sauce has made me very thirsty; *le soleil altère les couleurs,* the sun makes colours fade. **s'altérer,** *v.r.* To be impaired, to degenerate. *Le vin s'altère à l'air,* wine spoils when exposed to the air; *sa santé commence à s'altérer,* his health is beginning to fail.

alternance [altɛr'nɑ̃:s], *n.f.* Alternation, rotation. **alternant,** *a.* (*fem.* **-ante**) Alternating, rotating (as crops). **alternat,** *n.m.* Rotation (of crops etc.). **alternateur,** *n.m.* (*Elec.*) Alternator. **alternatif,** *a.* (*fem.* **-tive** (1)) Alternate, alternating, alternative. (*Elec.*) *Courant alternatif,* alternating current. **alternation,** *n.f.* Alternation, succession.

alternative (2), *n.f.* Alternation; choice, option (between two possible actions). **alternativement,** *adv.* Alternately, by turns.

alterne [al'tɛrn], *a.* (*Geom.*) Alternate (of angles); (*Bot.*) alternate.

alterné [altɛr'ne], *a.* (*fem.* **-ée**) (*Her.*) Alternate (of similar patterns on a shield etc.).

alterner [altɛr'ne], *v.i.* To alternate, to succeed each other alternately.—*v.t.* To grow (crops) in rotation.

altesse [al'tɛs], *n.f.* Highness. *Son Altesse Royale,* his or her royal highness.

althée [al'te:], *n.f.* (*Bot.*) Althaea.

altier [al'tje], *a.* (*fem.* **altière** [al'tjɛr]) Haughty, proud, arrogant, lordly, lofty. *Mine altière,* haughty look.

altimètre [alti'mɛtr], *n.m.* Altimeter.

altise [al'ti:z], *n.f.* Flea-beetle.

altiste [al'tist], *n.m.* Singer or performer of alto part.

altitude [alti'tyd], *n.f.* Altitude. *À 1,000 mètres d'altitude,* 3,000 feet high; (*Av.*) *prendre de l'altitude,* to climb; *vol à haute altitude,* altitude flight.

alto [al'to], *n.m.* Alto; tenor violin; tenor saxhorn.

altruisme [altry'ism], *n.m.* Altruism. **altruiste,** *a.* Altruistic.—*n.* Altruist.

alucite [aly'sit], *n.f.* Plume-moth; corn-moth. **alucité,** *a.* (*fem.* **alucitée**) Containing dead bodies of these (of bread, flour, etc.).

alude [a'lyd] or **alute,** *n.f.* Coloured sheepskin, basil (for binding).

*aludel [aly'dɛl], *n.m.* (*Chem.*) Aludel.

*alumelle [aly'mɛl], *n.f.* Long, thin knife or sword-blade.

aluminage [alymi'na:ʒ], *n.m.* Alumination.

aluminaire [alymi'nɛ:r], *a.* Containing alum.

aluminate [alymi'nat], *n.m.* (*Chem.*) Salt of aluminium, aluminate.

alumine [aly'min], *n.f.* Alumina, oxide of aluminium. **aluminer,** *v.t.* To aluminate.

alumine [aly'min], *n.f.* Alumina, oxide of aluminium. **aluminer,** *v.t.* To aluminate,

to aluminize. **aluminerie,** *n.f.* Place where alumina is made or sold. **alumineux,** *a.* (*fem.* **alumineuse**) Aluminous.

aluminium [alymi'njɔm], *n.m.* Aluminium.

aluminothermie, *n.f.* Thermit welding.

alun [a'lœ̃], *n.m.* Alum. **alunage,** *n.m.* (*Dyeing*) Steeping in alum; (*Phot.*) hardening (negatives etc.) in an alum-bath. **alunation,** *n.f.* Production of alum. **aluner,** *v.t.* (*Dyeing*) To steep in alum-water; (*Phot.*) to harden in an alum-bath. **alunerie,** *n.f.* Alum-works. **aluneux,** *a.* (*fem.* **aluneuse**) Aluminous, containing alum. **alunier,** *n.m.* Alum-maker. **alunière,** *n.f.* Alum-pit or mine, alum-works. **alunifère,** *a.* (*Geol.*) Containing alum (of rocks). **alunite,** *n.f.* Alunite.

alute [ALUDE].

alvéolaire [alveɔ'lɛ:r], *a.* Alveolar.

alvéole [alve'ɔl], *n.m.* Alveolus, cell (in a honey-comb); socket (of a tooth). *Alvéoles pulmonaires,* air-cells. **alvéolé,** *a.* (*fem.* **alvéolée**) Alveolate.

alvin [al'vɛ̃], *a.* (*fem.* **alvine**) (*Med.*) Alvine, pertaining to the belly or intestines.

alysson [ali'sɔ̃], *n.m.* or **alysse,** *n.f.* Alyssum, madwort.

amabilité [amabili'te], *n.f.* Amiability, affability, kindness. *Auriez-vous l'amabilité de,* would you be so kind as to.

*amadis [ama'di:s], *n.m.* A tight sleeve buttoning at the wrist.

amadou [ama'du], *n.m.* Amadou, (German) tinder; touchwood.

amadouer [ama'dwe], *v.t.* To coax, to wheedle to cajole, to flatter, to gain over.

amadouvier [amadu'vje], *n.m.* Tinder-agaric.

amaigrir [amɛ'gri:r], *v.t.* To make lean, meagre, or thin; to emaciate; to reduce, to lessen (in bulk etc.); to impoverish; to drain or exhaust (soil etc.); (*Arch.*) to reduce the thickness of.—*v.i.* To fall away, to grow lean or thin; (*Arch.*) to shrink. **s'amaigrir,** *v.r.* To grow thin, to fall away. **amaigrissant,** *a.* (*fem.* **amaigrissante**) Causing emaciation. *Régime amaigrissant,* slimming diet.

amaigrissement, *n.m.* Emaciation, wasting away, falling away; growing thin.

amalgamation [amalgamɑ'sjɔ̃], *n.f.* Amalgamation.

amalgame [amal'gam], *n.m.* Amalgam; (*fig.*) medley, heterogeneous mixture.

amalgamer [amalga'me], *v.t.* To amalgamate, to combine, to blend. **s'amalgamer,** *v.r.* To amalgamate, to blend, to combine.

amande [a'mɑ̃:d], *n.f.* Almond; kernel. *Amande amère, douce,* bitter, sweet, almond; *amandes lissées,* sugar-plums; *amandes à la praline,* burnt almonds; *huile d'amandes douces,* sweet almond oil; *yeux en amande,* almond-shaped eyes. **amandé,** *a.* (*fem.* **amandée**) Containing almond-juice.—*n.m.* Almond milk.

amandier, *n.m.* Almond-tree.

amanite [ama'nit], *n.f.* Amanite.

amant [a'mɑ̃], *n.m.* (*fem.* **amante**) Lover, suitor; sweetheart, mistress; gallant, paramour; votary, passionate admirer. *Amant de cœur,* fancy man.

amarante [ama'rɑ̃:t], *n.f.* Amaranth. *Amarante crête de coq,* cock's-comb; *amarante élégante,* prince's feather; *bois d'amarante*, violet wood.

amareilleur [amarɛ'jœːr], *n.m.* Worker on an oyster-bed.

amarescent [amarɛ'sã], *a.* (*fem.* **amarescente**) Bitterish.

amarinage [amari'naːʒ], *n.m.* (*Naut.*) Manning (a prize). **amariner,** *v.t.* To man (a prize); to inure (a crew etc.) to sea. **s'amariner,** *v.r.* To become used to the sea.

amarrage [ama'raːʒ], *n.m.* (*Naut.*) Mooring; anchorage; lashing. *Ligne d'amarrage*, mooring-line, lashing.

amarre [a'maːr], *n.f.* (*Naut.*) Cable, rope, hawser. *Amarre de fond*, ground-tackle; *rompre ses amarres*, to break adrift. **amarrer,** *v.t.* To moor, to belay, to make fast.

amaryllis [amari'lis], *n.f.* Amaryllis, lily-asphodel.

amas [a'mɑ], *n.m.* Mass, heap, pile, accumulation. *Un amas de peuple*, a great mob. **amassement,** *n.m.* The act of amassing, accumulating, etc. **amasser,** *v.t.* To accumulate, to heap up, to amass; to hoard; to collect, to get together. **s'amasser,** *v.r.* To gather, to get together, to accumulate, to be collected, to crowd, to assemble.

amassette [ama'sɛt], *n.f.* A small palette-knife.

amasseur [ama'sœːr], *n.m.* (*fem.* **amasseuse**) Hoarder. *Amasseur d'écus*, miser.

*****amatelotage** [amatlɔ'taːʒ], *n.m.* (*Naut.*) Classifying sailors by twos for duty. *****amateloter,** *v.t.* (*Naut.*) To class (a crew) by twos.

amateur [ama'tœːr], *n.m.* Amateur; devotee, votary; connoisseur. *Amateur des beaux-arts*, lover of the fine arts; *être amateur de*, to be fond of; *cinéma, théâtre amateur*, amateur cinema, theatricals; *travailler en amateur*, to work as a dilettante.

amatir [ama'tiːr], *v.t.* To mat; to deaden (gold).

amativité [amativi'te], *n.f.* Amativeness.

amaurose [amɔ'roːz], *n.f.* (*Med.*) Amaurosis. **amaurotique,** *a.* Amaurotic.—*n.* An amaurotic person.

amazone [ama'zoːn], *n.f.* Amazon, a woman warrior, a courageous or manlike woman; a horse-woman; a riding-habit. *Habit d'amazone*, riding-habit; *monter en amazone*, to ride side-saddle.

ambages [ã'baːʒ], *n.f.* (*used only in pl.*) Circumlocution, roundabout expression, equivocation. *Sans ambages*, straight out.

ambassade [ãba'sad], *n.f.* Embassy, ambassador's staff; deputation; mission, errand. **ambassadeur,** *n.m.* Ambassador; (*fig.*) envoy, messenger. **ambassadrice,** *n.f.* Ambassadress; (*fig.*) female messenger.

ambe [ãːb], *n.m.* Two numbers taken or coming together at a lottery; at lotto, two numbers placed on the same horizontal line.

ambesas [ãbe'zaːs], *n.m.* Ambs-ace, two aces thrown together at tric-trac (called also *beset* or *besas*).

ambiance [ã'bjãːs], *n.f.* Surroundings, environment; atmosphere. **ambiant,** *a.* (*fem.* **-ante**) Ambient, surrounding, environing.

ambidextre [ãbi'dɛkstr], *a.* Ambidextrous.—*n.* Ambidexter.

ambigu [ãbi'gy], *a.* (*fem.* **ambiguë**) Ambiguous, equivocal; uncertain, dark, obscure.—

n.m. *****Cold collation (with everything served up together); a game of cards somewhat resembling whist; (*fig.*) heterogeneous mixture, medley, olio. **ambiguïté,** *n.f.* Ambiguity. *Parler sans ambiguïté*, to speak plainly. **ambigument,** *adv.* Ambiguously.

ambitieusement [ãbisjɔz'mã], *adv.* Ambitiously.

ambitieux [ãbi'sjø], *a.* (*fem.* **ambitieuse**) Ambitious; pretentious, far-fetched (of style etc.).—*n.* Ambitious person.

ambition [ãbi'sjɔ̃], *n.f.* Ambition. **ambitionner,** *v.t.* To desire earnestly; to be ambitious of, to aspire to.

ambivalence [ãbiva'lãs], *n.f.* Ambivalence. **ambivalent,** *a.* (*fem.* **ambivalente**) Ambivalent.

amble [ãːbl], *n.m.* Amble. *Aller l'amble*, to amble. **ambler,** *v.i.* To amble, to pace.

ambleur, *a.* (*fem.* **ambleuse**) Ambling, pacing.

amblyope [ã'bliɔp], *a.* Amblyopic, weak-sighted.—*n.* Weak-sighted person. **amblyopie,** *n.f.* Amblyopia.

*****ambon** [ã'bɔ̃], *n.m.* Ambo.

ambre [ãːbr], *n.m.* Amber. *Ambre gris*, ambergris; *il est fin comme l'ambre*, he is a shrewd fellow. **ambré,** *a.* (*fem.* **ambrée**) Having perfume of ambergris; amber-coloured. **ambréine,** *n.f.* (*Chem.*) Ambrein.

ambrer, *v.t.* To perfume with amber.

ambrette [ã'brɛt], *n.f.* Amber-seed; musk-seed.

ambroisie [ãbrwa'zi], *n.f.* Ambrosia; an exquisite dish, dainty, or repast. *D'ambroisie*, ambrosial, fragrant, delicious. **ambrosiaque,** *a.* Ambrosial (of perfume).

ambrosien [ãbro'zjɛ̃], *a.* (*fem.* **ambrosienne**) Ambrosian (of chants).

ambulacre [ãby'lakr], *n.m.* (*Zool.*) Ambulacrum; (*Hort.*) a piece of ground planted with regular rows of trees.

ambulance [ãby'lãːs], *n.f.* Ambulance, field-hospital; peripatetic clerkship. *Chirurgien d'ambulance*, field-surgeon. **ambulancier,** *n.m.* (*fem.* **-ière**) Ambulance-man, stretcher-bearer, nurse.

ambulant [ãby'lã], *a.* Ambulant, ambulatory, itinerant, peripatetic; travelling (of a railway post-office). *Comédiens ambulants*, strolling players; *marchand ambulant*, itinerant dealer; *mener une vie ambulante*, to be nomadic, to be on the tramp. **ambulation,** *n.f.* Ambulation. **ambulatoire,** *a.* Ambulatory; (*Law*) movable.—*n.m.* Ambulatory.

âme [aːm], *n.f.* (1) Soul, spirit; sentiment, sensibility; (*fig.*) inhabitant, person (on a lost ship etc.); core, pith, heart (of a thing etc.) *Âme bien née*, a person of excellent disposition; *avoir la mort dans l'âme*, to be grieved to death; *corps et âme*, body and soul; *je le souhaite de toute mon âme*, I wish it with all my soul; *Dieu veuille avoir son âme!* God rest his soul! *errer comme une âme en peine*, to roam like a soul in torment; *rendre l'âme*, to give up the ghost; *être tout âme*, to be all feeling, to be excessively sensitive; *grandeur d'âme*, magnanimity; (*fig.*) *il est l'âme damnée du ministre*, he is the minister's tool; *il fut l'âme du complot*, he was the moving spirit in the conspiracy; *il n'y a pas âme qui vive ici*, there is not a living soul here; *il y a mille âmes sur ce navire,* there are a thousand people on board that ship; *une bonne âme, (iron.)* a good-natured soul. (2) Sounding-board (of a violin etc.); bore (of gun).

améliorable [ameljɔ'rabl], *a.* Improvable. **améliorant,** *a. (fem.* **améliorante)** Ameliorating. **améliorateur,** *a. (fem.* **amélioratrice)** Ameliorative. **amélioration,** *n.f.* Amelioration, improvement; *(pl.)* repairs, embellishments, decorations (of a house etc.).

améliorer, *v.t.* To ameliorate, to improve, to better. **s'améliorer,** *v.r.* To get better, to ameliorate, to mend, to improve.

amen [a'mɛn], *int.* and *n.m.* Amen. *(fig.) Dire amen à tout,* to agree to everything.

*amenage [am'na:ʒ], *n.m.* Transport, carriage.

aménagement [amenaʒ'mã], *n.m.* Arrangement; disposition (of a house etc.); management (of a forest). *Aménagements financiers,* taxation adjustments. **aménager,** *v.t.* To dispose, arrange, lay out; to harness; to regulate the felling of (a wood or forest). *Aménager un arbre,* to cut up a tree; *aménager une maison,* to lay out the inside of a house; *aménager la voie (ferrée),* to grade the track. **aménagiste,** *n.m.* One skilled in managing a forest.

amendable [amã'dabl], *a.* Improvable, mendable.

amende [a'mã:d], *n.f.* Fine, penalty, forfeit, compensation, reparation. *Faire amende honorable,* to make a full apology; *mettre* or *condamner à l'amende,* to fine.

amendement [amãd'mã], *n.m.* Amendment; improvement. *Amendement d'une terre,* improvement, manuring of a piece of ground; *la loi a été votée sans amendement, (Parl.)* the bill passed without amendment. **amender,** *v.t.* To amend, to better. *Amender une terre,* to manure a field, to improve. **s'amender,** *v.r.* To mend, to grow better, to reform.

amène [a'mɛ:n], *a.* Agreeable, pleasant (site).

amenée [am'ne:], *n.f.* Introduction, bringing-in, conveyance. *Conduit d'amenée,* supply-pipe.

amener [am'ne], *v.t.* To lead (hither), to bring; to introduce; to bring about; to occasion, to lead to; *(Naut.)* to haul down, to lower, to strike (colours, sails, etc.). *Amener des maladies,* to bring on diseases; *amener une mode,* to bring in a fashion; *amener quelqu'un à faire une chose,* to induce someone to do a thing; *(Mil.) amener l'avant-train,* to limber up; *amener son pavillon,* to strike one's flag; *cette remarque est bien amenée,* that observation is cleverly introduced, well to the point; *je l'ai amené où je voulais,* I brought him to do what I wanted; *n'amenez jamais la conversation sur la politique,* never introduce politics into conversation; *mandat d'amener,* warrant. **s'amener,** *v.r. (colloq.)* To come along, to turn up.

aménité, *n.f.* Amenity, pleasantness, affability; grace, urbanity; *(pl.)* compliments (often ironic).

aménorrhée [amenɔ're], *n.f. (Path.)* Amenorrhoea.

amentacé [amãta'se], *a. (fem.* **-ée)** *(Bot.)* Amentaceous.—*n.f.pl.* Amentaceous plants.

amenuisement [amenɥiz'mã], *n.m.* Thinning down, growing smaller.

amenuiser [amənɥi'ze], *v.t.* To make thinner, smaller. **s'amenuiser,** *v.r.* To grow thinner, smaller.

amer [a'mɛ:r], *a. (fem.* **amère)** Bitter, harsh; grievous; biting, galling. *Avoir la bouche amère,* to have a bitter taste in the mouth; *des plaintes amères,* bitter complaints; *rendre amer,* to embitter.—*n.m.* (1) Something bitter; gall; bitterness; *(pl.)* bitters. (2) *(Naut.)* Any landmark or leading mark.

amèrement, *adv.* Bitterly, grievously.

américain [ameri'kɛ̃], *a. (fem.* **américaine** (1)) American. *(colloq.) Avoir l'œil* (or *le coup d'œil) américain,* to be quick to spot the right thing or person.—*n.* **(Américain, -aine)** American.

*américaine (2) [ameri'kɛ:n], *n.f.* A phaeton with two interchangeable seats (one hooded).

américaniser [amerikani'ze], *v.t.* To Americanize. **s'américaniser,** *v.r.* To become Americanized.

américanisme, *n.m.* Americanism.

Amérique [ame'rik], *f.* America.

amérir or **amerrir** [ame'rir] *(Av.). v.i.* To alight on the water. **amerrissage,** *n.m.* Alighting (on the water).

amertume [amer'tym], *n.f.* Bitterness, grief; gall, venom.

améthyste [ame'tist], *n.f.* Amethyst.

ameublement [amœblə'mã], *n.m.* Furnishing, suite of furniture.

ameublir [amœ'bli:r], *v.t. (Law)* To turn (real estate) into personalty; *(Agric.)* to make (soil) more broken up or lighter. **ameublissement,** *n.m. (Law)* Conversion into personalty; *(Agric.)* loosening, mellowing.

ameulonner [amœlɔ'ne], *v.t.* To stack (hay, corn, etc.).

ameutement [amœt'mã], *n.m.* Forming a pack (of hounds); gathering of a mob.

ameuter [amœ'te], *v.t.* To put dogs into a pack; *(fig.)* to stir up, to rouse, to excite.

ami [a'mi], *n.m. (fem.* **amie)** Friend; well-wisher, partisan, favourer, patron, lover. *Ami de cœur,* bosom friend; **ami de cour,* a superficial or false friend; *ami d'enfance,* old playmate; *bonne amie,* sweetheart; *c'est un de mes vieux amis,* he is an old pal of mine; *chambre d'ami,* spare room; *être ami de,* to be the companion of, to be partial to; *les bons comptes font les bons amis,* short reckonings make long friends; **m'amie* (for *mon amie)! my dear,* my love, darling! *mon ami!* my dear! *se faire des amis,* to make friends.—*a.* Friendly; sympathetic, favourable, kindly-disposed; kind, propitious. *Vents amis,* favouring winds.

amiable [a'mjabl], *a.* Friendly, courteous; amicable, conciliatory. *Terminer un différend à l'amiable,* to settle a quarrel amicably; *vente à l'amiable,* sale by private contract. **amiablement,** *adv.* Amicably.

amiante [a'mjã:t], *n.m.* Asbestos, amianthus. **amiantin,** *a. (fem.* **amiantine)** Of asbestos. (C) **amiantose** [amjã'to:z], *n.f. (Med.)* Amiantosis.

amibe [a'mib], *n.f.* Amoeba. **amibiase,** *n.f.*

Amoebiasis. **amibien,** *a.* (*fem.* **-ienne**) Amoebic.
amical [ami'kal], *a.* (*fem.* **amicale,** *pl.* **amicaux**) Amicable, friendly.—(*pop.*) *n.f.* Association (professional etc.). **amicalement,** *adv.* Amicably, in a friendly manner
amict [a'mi], *n.m.* Amice.
amide [a'mid], *n.f.* (*Chem.*) Amide.
amidon [ami'dɔ̃], *n.m.* Starch. **amidonnage,** *n.m.* Starching. **amidonner,** *v.t.* To starch. **amidonnerie,** *n.f.* Starch-works. **amidonnier,** *n.m.* (*fem.* **-ière**) Starch-maker.
amincir [amɛ̃'siːr], *v.t.* To make thinner, to reduce the thickness of. **s'amincir,** *v.r.* To become thinner. **amincissement,** *n.m.* Thinning.
amine [a'min], *n.f.* (*Chem.*) Amine.
amiral [ami'ral], *n.m.* (*pl.* **aux**) Admiral. *Contre-amiral,* rear-admiral; *grand amiral,* high-admiral; *vice-amiral,* vice-admiral; *vaisseau amiral,* flagship. **amiralat,** *n.m.* Admiralship. **amirale,** *n.f.* Admiral's wife.
Amirauté [amiro'te], **Îles de l',** *f.* Admiralty Islands.
amirauté, *n.f.* Admiralship; admiralty.
amissibilité [amisibili'te], *n.f.* (*Theol.* and *Law*) Amissibility. **amissible,** *a.* Amissible.
amission, *n.f.* Amission.
amitié [ami'tje], *n.f.* Friendship, affection; favour, kindness; (*pl.*) kind regards, compliments, attentions. *Faites-lui mes amitiés,* remember me kindly to him; *faites-moi l'amitié de lui en parler,* do me the kindness to mention it to him; *mes amitiés à tout le monde,* love to all; *par amitié,* out of friendship; *prendre quelqu'un en amitié,* to take a liking to someone; *se lier d'amitié avec,* to become intimate with; *vivre en amitié avec,* to be on friendly terms with.
ammocète [amɔ'sɛːt], *n.m.* (*Ichth.*) Ammocete; larval lamprey.
ammoniac [amɔ'njak], *a.* (*fem.* **-iaque** (1)) Ammoniac. *Gaz ammoniac,* ammonia; *sel ammoniac,* sal ammoniac; *gomme ammoniaque,* gum ammoniac. **ammoniacal,** *a.* (*fem.* **-ale,** *pl.* **-aux**) Ammoniacal. **ammoniacé,** *a.* (*fem.* **-ée**) Ammoniated.
ammoniaque (1) [AMMONIAC] (2), *n.f.* Ammonia; (*pop.*) solution of ammonia.
ammonite [amɔ'nit], *n.f.* Ammonite.
ammonium [amɔ'njɔm], *n.m.* (*Chem.*) Ammonium.
ammophile [amɔ'fil], *n.m.* (*Ent.*) Digger.
amnésie [amne'zi], *n.f.* Amnesia. **amnésique,** *a.* and *n.* Amnesic.
amnistiable [amnis'tjabl], *a.* That may or should receive an amnesty.
amnistie [amnis'ti], *n.f.* Amnesty, pardon. **amnistié,** *n.m.* (*fem.* **-ée**) Person pardoned by amnesty. **amnistier,** *v.t.* To amnesty.
amnios [am'njos], *n.m.* (*Obstetrics*). Amnion. **amniotique,** *a.* Amniotic.
amocher [amɔ'ʃe], *v.t.* (*slang*) To damage, to put out of order. *Il s'est fait amocher,* he's been knocked about.
***amodiataire** [amɔdja'tɛːr], *n.m.* Lessee (of land for farming etc.). ***amodiateur,** *n.m.* (*fem.* **amodiatrice**) Lessor of land for farming, etc. ***amodiation,** *n.f.* Leasing, letting out to farm. ***amodier,** *v.t.* To let or farm out an estate.
amoindrir [amwɛ̃'driːr], *v.t.* To lessen, to

decrease, to diminish. **s'amoindrir,** *v.r.* To grow less. **amoindrissement,** *n.m.* Lessening, decrease, abatement, diminution.
amollir [amɔ'liːr], *v.t.* To soften; (*fig.*) to mollify; to enervate, to unman, to enfeeble. **s'amollir,** *v.r.* To soften, to grow soft; to grow effeminate or weak. **amollissant,** *a.* (*fem.* **amollissante**) Softening; enervating; mollifying. **amollissement,** *n.m.* Softening, enervation, effeminacy.
amonceler [amɔ̃s'le], *v.t.* To heap up, to lay in a heap; (*fig.*) to accumulate, to amass. **s'amonceler,** *v.r.* To gather; to accumulate, to drift together. *Les nuages s'amoncellent,* the clouds are gathering.
amoncellement, *n.m.* Accumulation; mass, heap, pile.
amont [a'mɔ̃], *n.m.* Upstream water (used chiefly in *en amont,* up-stream, up-river). *Aller en amont,* to go up; *en amont du pont,* above bridge; *vent d'amont,* (*Naut.*) easterly wind, land-breeze.
amoral [amɔ'ral], *a.* (*fem.* **amorale,** *pl.* **amoraux**) Unmoral, amoral. **amoralisme,** *n.m.* Amoral doctrine [AMORALITÉ].
amoralité, *n.f.* The quality or state of being amoral.
amorçage [amɔr'saːʒ], *n.m.* Priming (of pumps, motors, guns, etc.); baiting (of hook, of pool).
amorce [a'mɔrs], *n.f.* Bait; (*fig.*) attraction, allurement, enticement, charm; (*guns etc.*) priming, percussion-cap; priming (for a pump; (*fig.*) beginning. *Sans brûler une amorce,* without firing a shot. **amorcer,** *v.t.* To bait; (*fig.*) to allure, to entice, to decoy; (*Hydraulics*) to fetch, to prime; (*Artill.*) to cap (a shell). *Amorcer des pourparlers,* to initiate negotiations. **amorceur,** *n.m.* (*fem.* **amorceuse**) One who baits, primes, etc.
amorçoir [amɔr'swaːr], *n.m.* Auger, centre punch.
amorphe [a'mɔrf], *a.* Amorphous. **amorphie,** *n.f.* Amorphism.
amortir [amɔr'tiːr], *v.t.* To deaden, to allay, to moderate; to weaken, to render less violent, to break (a fall, shock, etc.); to make (meat etc.) more tender; to redeem, to pay off; to cool (passions); to amortize; (*Paint.*) to flatten. *Amortir des dettes,* to pay off debts; *amortir un coup* or *le bruit,* to deaden a blow *or* the sound; *amortir une pension,* to redeem a pension. **s'amortir,** *v.r.* To be deadened; to be paid off, to be bought up. **amortissable,** *a.* Redeemable.
amortissement, *n.m.* Redemption, buying up; liquidation; amortization, extinction (of a debt etc.); deadening (of a blow etc.), abatement; (*Arch.*) the uppermost part of a building, top, finial. *Caisse d'amortissement,* sinking-fund office; *fonds d'amortissement,* sinking-fund.
amortisseur, *n.m.* Shock absorber.
amouiller [amu'je], *a.* (Cow) about to calf.
amouille [a'muːj], *n.f.* (*prov.*) Beestings.
amour [a'muːr], *n.m.* (*usu. fem. in pl.*) Love, affection, passion; the object of love or passion, flame, fancy. *Amour de soi,* self-love; *avec amour,* lovingly, carefully; *avoir de l'amour pour,* to be in love with; *froides mains, chaudes amours,* cold hand, warm heart; *l'Amour,* (*Myth.*) Eros, Cupid; *les amours,*

(*Myth.*) the Loves; *pour l'amour de Dieu*, for God's sake; *quel amour d'enfant!* what a love of a child! *se marier par amour*, to marry for love; *ses premières amours*, his first love; (*fam.*) *faire l'amour avec*, to have sexual intercourse with.

*amouracher [amura'ʃe], *v.t.* To inspire with a foolish passion. **s'amouracher**, *v.r.* To be smitten with, to become enamoured (*de*).

amourette [amu'rɛt], *n.f.* A passing amour, a love-affair; (*pop.*) quaking-grass, campion, and other plants; (*pl.*) spinal marrow (of sheep or calves). *Amourettes de veau*, calf's marrow.

amoureusement [amurøz'mã], *adv.* Amorously, lovingly; tenderly, softly.

amoureux [amu'rø], *a.* (*fem.* **amoureuse**) Loving, in love, smitten, enamoured (*de*); amorous, showing love or tenderness. *Il est amoureux de cette femme*, he is in love with that woman; *pinceau amoureux*, (*Paint.*) soft, delicate touch; *regards amoureux*, amorous looks.—*n.* Lover, sweetheart; fiancé or fiancée. (*Theat.*) *Jouer les amoureux*, to play the parts of lovers.

amour-propre [amur'prɔpr], *n.m.* Self-respect; vanity, conceit.

amovibilité [amɔvibili'te], *n.f.* Removability, liability to removal; precariousness of tenure. **amovible**, *a.* Removable, revocable, amovable. *Jante amovible*, detachable rim.

ampère [ã'pɛːr], *n.m.* (*Elec.*) Ampere. **ampère-heure**, *n.m.* Ampere-hour. **ampèremètre**, *n.m.* Amperemeter.

amphibie [ãfi'bi], *a.* Amphibious.—*n.m.* Amphibian; (*fig.*) double-dealer, jack-of-all-trades. **amphibiens**, *n.m. pl.* (*Zool.*) Amphibia.

amphibologie [ãfibɔlɔ'ʒi], *n.f.* Amphibology, ambiguity. **amphibologique**, *a.* Amphibological, ambiguous. **amphibologiquement**, *adv.* Ambiguously.

amphibraque [ãfi'brak], *n.m.* (*Pros.*) Amphibrach.

amphictyon [ãfik'tjɔ̃], *n.m.* (*Gr. Ant.*) Amphictyon. **amphictyonie**, *n.f.* Amphictyony. **amphictyonique**, *a.* Amphictyonic.

amphigame [ãfi'gam], *a.* Amphigamous.

amphigouri [ãfigu'ri], *n.m.* Amphigouri, amphigory; rigmarole, gibberish. **amphigourique**, *a.* Amphigoric, nonsensical. **amphigouriquement**, *adv.* Nonsensically.

amphioxus [ãfiɔk'syːs], *n.m.* (*Ichth.*) Amphioxus, lancelet.

amphisbène [ãfiz'bɛːn], *n.m.* (*Zool. and Her.*) Amphisbaena.

amphisciens [ãfi'sjɛ̃], *n.m.* (*used only in pl.*) Amphiscians.

amphithéâtral [ãfitea'tral], *a.* (*fem.* **-ale**, *pl.* **-aux**) Amphitheatrical.

amphithéâtre [ãfite'aːtr], *n.m.* Amphitheatre; the whole body of occupants of this; the gallery in a theatre rising above the boxes and facing the stage; lecture-room. *En amphithéâtre*, in semi-circular tiers.

Amphitrite [ãfi'trit], *n.f.* (*Myth.*) Amphitrite; (*poet.*) the sea.

Amphitryon [ãfitri'ɔ̃], *n.m.* Amphitryon; host, entertainer.

amphore [ã'fɔːr], *n.f.* Amphora. **amphorique**, *a.* (*Med.*) Amphoric.

ample [ã:pl], *a.* Ample, full; large, vast,

spacious; copious, abundant, profuse. **amplement**, *adv.* Amply, fully; largely, plentifully. **ampleur**, *n.f.* Width, fullness (of clothes); abundance, profusion; elevation, dignity (of style etc.); volume (of voice). *Prendre de l'ampleur*, to grow buxom (of a woman), to develop prosperously (trade, business).

ampliatif [ãplia'tif], *a.* (*fem.* **ampliative**) Additional, amplifying. **ampliation**, *n.f.* Distention (of the chest etc.); duplicate (of a receipt etc.). *Pour ampliation*, (*Law*) true copy.

amplifiant [ãpli'fjã], *a.* (*fem.* **amplifiante**) Magnifying (of a lens etc.), amplifying.

amplificateur [ãplifika'tœːr], *a.* (*fem.* **amplificatrice**) Magnifying, amplifying.—*n.m.* (*Phot.*) enlarger; (*Rad. Tel.*) amplifier, intensifier. *Amplificateur à haute fréquence*, high-frequency amplifier. **amplificatif**, *a.* (*fem.* **amplificative**) Magnifying, enlarging, amplifying. **amplification**, *n.f.* Amplification; magnification, enlargement; (*fig.*) exaggeration. **amplificative** [AMPLIFICATIF]. **amplifier**, *v.t.* To amplify, to develop, to enlarge or expatiate upon; (*Opt.*) to enlarge, to magnify; (*fig.*) to exaggerate.

amplitude [ãpli'tyd], *n.f.* Extent, amplitude; degree of amplitude (of an arc, trajectory, etc.); angular extent (of oscillations of a pendulum etc.).

ampoule [ã'pul], *n.f.* Ampulla; phial; blister, swelling; (*Elec.*) bulb; (*Med.*) ampoule. *Faire venir des ampoules*, to raise blisters; *la sainte ampoule*, the holy phial. **ampoulé**, *a.* (*fem.* **ampoulée**) Bombastic, turgid. *Un style ampoulé*, high-flown style.

ampullacé [ãpyla'se], *a.* (*fem.* **ampullacée**) (*Nat. Hist.*) Ampullaceous, bottle- or ampulla-shaped.

amputation [ãpyta'sjɔ̃], *n.f.* Amputation; (*fig.*) curtailment, pruning (of an article for the press etc.). *Faire une amputation*, to perform an amputation. **amputé**, *a.* (*fem.* **amputée**) Who has had a limb amputated. —*n.* One who has had a limb amputated. **amputer**, *v.t.* To amputate, to cut off; to cause (a person) to undergo amputation.

amuissement [amɥis'mã], *n.m.* Progressive disappearance of a sound. **s'amuir**, *v.r.* (of a sound) To become mute.

amulette [amy'lɛt], *n.f.* Amulet, charm.

amunitionnement [amynisjɔnmã], *n.m.* Provisionment.

amunitionner [amynisjɔ'ne], *v.t.* To supply (with munitions etc.), to provision.

amure [a'myːr], *n.f.* (*Naut.*) Tack, clew-line (of sail). *Changer d'amures*, to bring about; *grande amure*, main-tack; *première amure de misaine*, fore-tack; *point d'amure*, weather-tack. **amurer**, *v.t.* To haul or bring aboard the tack of a sail.

*amusable [amy'zabl], *a.* Capable of being amused, amusable. **amusant**, *a.* (*fem.* **amusante**) Amusing, diverting, entertaining.

amuse-gueule [amyz'gœl], *n.m.* (*pl.* **amuse-gueules**) Cocktail snacks.

amusement, *n.m.* Amusement, entertainment, diversion; fooling, trifling. *Faire quelque chose par amusement*, to do something for fun.

[31]

amuser [amy′ze], *v.t.* To amuse, to divert, to entertain; to fool, to beguile, to dupe; to detain, to delay. *Amuser l'ennemi*, to deceive the enemy; *amuser le tapis*, to talk the time away. **s'amuser**, *v.r.* To amuse oneself, to divert oneself; to trifle; to have a good time. *S'amuser de quelqu'un*, to make fun of someone; *ne vous amusez pas en chemin*, don't loiter on the way; *amusez-vous bien!* enjoy yourselves, have a good time.
amusette [amy′zɛt], *n.f.* A petty amusement. *Ce n'est pas une amusette pour moi*, it is no child's play for me. **amuseur**, *n.m.* (*fem.* **amuseuse**) Amuser, entertainer. *****amusoire**, *n.f.* Something to amuse, toy, trifle.
amygdale [ami′dal], *n.f.* (*Anat.*) Tonsil. **amygdalin**, *a.* (*fem.* **amygdaline**) Composed partly of almonds. **amygdaline**, *n.f.* Amygdaline. **amygdalite**, *n.f.* (*Path.*) Tonsillitis. **amygdaloïde**, *a.* (*Geol.*) Amygdaloid, almond-shaped (rock).
amylacé [amila′se], *a.* (*fem.* **amylacée**) (*Chem.*) Amylaceous, resembling starch.
amyle [a′mil], *n.m.* Amyl. **amyloïde**, *a.* and *n.f.* Amyloid.
an [ɑ̃], *n.m.* Year; (*pl.*) years, time, age. *Au bout d'un an*, twelve months after that; *bon an, mal an*, one year with another; *bout de l'an* or *service du bout de l'an*, year's end Mass (for the dead); *elle a quinze ans*, she is fifteen; (*fam.*) *je m'en moque comme de l'an quarante*, I don't care two straws about it; *en l'an de grâce 1960*, in the year of grace *1960*; *le jour de l'an*, New Year's day; *l'outrage des ans*, the ravages of time; *tous les deux ans*, every other year; *une fois* or *deux fois l'an*, once or twice a year.
ana [a′na], *n.m. inv.* Ana, a collection of sayings, etc.—*adv.* (*Med.*) By equal quantities.
anabaptisme [anaba′tism], *n.m.* Anabaptism. **anabaptiste**, *n.m.* Anabaptist.
anacarde [ana′kard], *n.m.* Anacard, cashewnut. **anacardier**, *n.m.* Cashew-tree.
anachorète [anakɔ′rɛt], *n.m.* Anchorite, hermit. **anachorétique**, *a.* Anchoretic. **anachorétisme**, *n.m.* The anchoretic life; devotion to this.
anachronique [anakrɔ′nik], *a.* Anachronic, anachronistic. **anachronisme**, *n.m.* Anachronism.
anacoluthe [anakɔ′lyt], *n.f.* (*Gram.*) Anacoluthon.
anacréontique [anakreɔ̃′tik], *a.* Anacreontic, bacchic, convivial. **anacréontisme**, *n.m.* Cultivation of the anacreontic style.
anacrouse [ana′kruz], *n.f.* Anacrusis.
anaérobie [anaero′bi], *n.m.* Anaerobe.
anaéroïde [ANÉROÏDE].
anagallis [anaga′lis], *n.m.* (*Bot.*) Red pimpernel.
anagénèse [anaʒe′nɛːz], *n.f.* (*Physiol.*) Anagenesis.
anaglyphe [ana′glif], or **anaglypte**, *n.m.* Anaglyph. **anaglyptique**, *a.* Anaglyphic, anaglyptic.
anagnoste [anag′nɔst], *n.m.* (*Rom. Ant.*) Anagnost.
anagogie [anagɔ′ʒi], *n.f.* Anagogy. **anagogique**, *a.* Anagogical. **anagogiste**, *n.m.* An anagogical interpreter (of the Scriptures etc.).
anagrammatique [anagrama′tik], *a.* Ana-

grammatical. **anagrammatiste**, *n.m.* Anagrammatist. **anagramme**, *n.f.* Anagram.
anagyre [ana′ʒiːr] or **anagyris**, *n.m.* (*Bot.*) Bean-trefoil.
anal [a′nal], *a.* (*fem.* **-ale**, *pl.* **-aux**) Anal.
analectes [ana′lɛkt], *n.m.* (*used only in pl.*) Analects, analecta.
analgésie [analʒe′zi], or **analgie**, *n.f.* (*Med.*) Analgesia. **analgésique** or **analgique**, *a.* and *n.m.* Analgesic.
analogie [analɔ′ʒi], *n.f.* Analogy. **analogique**, *a.* Analogous, analogical. **analogiquement**, *adv.* Analogically, by analogy. **analogisme**, *n.m.* Reasoning by analogy. **analogue**, *a.* Analogous, similar.
analphabète [analfa′bɛt], *a.* and *n.* Illiterate. **analphabétisme**, *n.m.* Illiteracy .
analysable [anali′zabl], *a.* Analysable.
analyse [ana′liːʒ], *n.f.* Analysis; outline, précis, abstract (of a book etc.); (*Gram.*) parsing, analysis; (*Phil.*) reasoning from the complex to the simple. *Analyse chimique*, analysis; *analyse du sang*, blood count; (*Gram.*) *analyse grammaticale*, parsing; *analyse logique*, analysis; *analyse infinitésimale*, integral calculus; *analyse transcendentale*, differential calculus; *en dernière analyse*, after complete examination, to sum up, the upshot of it is; *faire l'analyse de l'eau*, to analyse water. **analyser**, *v.t.* To analyse. *Analyser une fleur*, to dissect a flower; *analyser une phrase*, to parse a sentence. **analyseur**, *n.m.* Analyst; (*Opt.*) analyser. **analyste**, *n.m.* Analyser, analyst, esp. one skilled in mathematical analysis. **analytique**, *a.* Analytic, analytical. **analytiquement**, *adv.* Analytically.
anamnèse [anam′nez], *n.f.* Anamnesis.
anamorphose [anamɔr′foːz], *n.f.* Anamorphosis. **anamorphotique**, *a.* Producing or characterized by anamorphosis.
ananas [ana′na], *n.m.* Pineapple. *Champ d'ananas*, pinery.
anandraire [anɑ̃′drɛr], **anandre** [a′nɑ̃dr], *a.* (*Bot.*) Anandrous.
anapeste [ana′pest], *n.m.* (*Pros.*) Anapaest. **anapestique**, *a.* Anapaestic.
anaphore [ana′fɔːr], *n.f.* (*Rhet.*) Anaphora. **anaphorisme**, *n.m.* Excessive use of this.
anaphrodisiaque [anafrɔdi′zjak], *a.* and *n.* (*Pharm.*) Anaphrodisiac.
anaplastie [anaplas′ti], *n.f.* (*Surg.*) Anaplasty.
anarchie [anar′ʃi], *n.f.* Anarchy; (*fig.*) disorder, confusion. **anarchique**, *a.* Anarchical. **anarchiquement**, *adv.* Anarchically. **anarchiser**, *v.t.* To anarchize. **anarchisme**, *n.m.* Anarchism. **anarchiste**, *a.* Anarchic.—*n.* An anarchist.
Anastase [anas′taːz], *m.* Anastasius.
Anastasie [anasta′ziː], *f.* (*fam.*) D.O.R.A. (the censorship).
anastomose [anastɔ′moːz], *n.f.* (*Physiol.*) Anastomosis. **s'anastomoser**, *v.r.* To anastomose.
anastrophe [anas′trɔf], *n.f.* (*Gram.*) Anastrophe.
anathématique [anatema′tik], *a.* Anathematic.
anathématisation [anatematizɑ′sjɔ̃], *n.f.* Anathematization. **anathématiser**, *v.t.* To anathematize, to denounce.
anathème [ana′tɛːm], *n.m.* Anathema, sentence of reprobation or excommunication,

ban, curse; person accursed. *Frapper d'anathème,* to anathematize.—*a.* Anathematized.
anatife [ana'tif], *n.m.* (*Zool.*) Barnacle.
anatocisme [anatɔ'sism], *n.m.* Anatocism.
anatomie [anatɔ'mi], *n.f.* Anatomy, study (of a body etc.) by means of dissection; dissection; methodical analysis (of a book etc.); plaster-cast of a dissected body or part of a body; (*fam.*) body, figure. *Elle a une belle anatomie,* she has a fine figure; *anatomie comparée,* comparative anatomy; *pièce d'anatomie,* anatomical figure. **anatomique,** *a.* Anatomical. **anatomiquement,** *adv.* Anatomically. **anatomiser,** *v.t.* To anatomize, to dissect. *Anatomiser un livre,* to analyse a book. **anatomiste,** *n.* Anatomist.
anaux [ANAL].
ancestral [ɑ̃sɛs'tral], *a.* (*fem.* -**trale,** *pl.* -**traux**) Ancestral.
ancêtre [ɑ̃'sɛ:tr], *n.* Ancestor, ancestress. *n.m. pl.* Ancestors, forefathers.
anche [ɑ̃:ʃ], *n.f.* Reed or tongue (of an oboe or other wind instrument). *Anche simple,* single reed (of a clarinet); *anche double,* double reed (of an oboe); *jeu d'anches,* reed-stop (of an organ). **ancher,** *v.t.* To furnish (an instrument) with a reed or reeds.
anchois [ɑ̃'ʃwa], *n.m.* Anchovy. *Beurre d'anchois,* anchovy paste; *poire d'anchois,* anchovy pear.
ancien [ɑ̃'sjɛ̃], *a.* (*fem.* **ancienne**) Ancient, old; bygone, former, late, ex-; antique. *L'Ancien Testament,* the Old Testament; *un ancien élève,* an old boy; *un ancien ministre,* an ex-minister; *un ancien combattant,* an ex-Serviceman; *des meubles anciens,* antique furniture.—*n.m.* A senior; an ancient; (*Eccles.*) an elder; (*Mil.*) a veteran; (*pl.*) the ancients; our forefathers. *C'est mon ancien,* he is my senior; *les ouvrages des anciens,* the works of the ancients. **anciennement,** *adv.* Anciently, formerly; of yore; in former times. **ancienneté,** *n.f.* Antiquity; seniority. *De toute ancienneté,* from the earliest times; *à l'ancienneté,* by seniority.
ancillaire [ɑ̃sil'lɛ:r], *a.* Ancillary.
ancolie [ɑ̃kɔ'li], *n.f.* (*Bot.*) Columbine.
Ancône [ɑ̃'ko:n], *f.* Ancona.
anconé [ɑ̃kɔ'ne], *n.m.* (*Anat.*) Ancon; extensor of the forearm.—*a.* Pertaining to this or the elbow.
ancrage [ɑ̃'kra:ʒ], *n.m.* Anchorage. *Droits d'ancrage,* anchorage dues.
ancre [ɑ̃:kr], *n.f.* (1) Anchor. *Ancre de miséricorde* (or *de salut*), sheet anchor, (*fig.*) last resource; *ancre de rechange,* spare anchor; *brider l'ancre,* to shoe the anchor; *chasser sur ses ancres,* to drag one's anchors; *être à l'ancre,* to ride at anchor; *fatiguer à l'ancre,* to ride hard; *gouverner sur son ancre,* to steer the ship to her anchor; *jeter* or *mouiller l'ancre,* to cast anchor; *jeter sa dernière ancre,* (*fig.*) to make a last effort; *l'ancre d'affourche,* the small bower anchor; *la seconde ancre,* the best bower anchor; *lever l'ancre,* to weigh anchor; *maîtresse ancre,* the sheet anchor; *mettre l'ancre à poste,* to stow the anchor; *ne pas fatiguer à l'ancre,* to ride easy. (2) Cramp-iron, tie-plate (of a wall). (3) Anchor (of a clock). *Montre à ancre,* lever-watch.

ancré [ɑ̃'kre], *a.* (*fem.* **ancrée**) Anchored; (*fig.*) firmly fixed or established; (*Her.*) curved anchorwise at the ends (of saltires, crosses etc.).
ancrer [ɑ̃'kre], *v.i.* To anchor, to come to an anchor.—*v.t.* To anchor; (*fig.*) to fix or establish firmly. **s'ancrer,** *v.r.* To establish oneself, to get a footing (in a place), to take deep root (in). *Cette passion s'est ancrée en lui,* this passion is rooted in his heart.
ancrure [ɑ̃'kry:r], *n.f.* Crease (in cloth); (*Arch.*) iron prop.
andabate [ɑ̃da'bat], *n.m.* (*Rom. Ant.*) Gladiator who fought blindfolded on horseback.
andain [ɑ̃'dɛ̃], *n.m.* Swath.
andalou [ɑ̃da'lu], *a.* (*fem.* -**ouse**) Andalusian.
Andalousie [ɑ̃dalu'zi], *f.* Andalusia.
Andes [ɑ̃:d], **les,** *f.* The Andes.
Andorre [ɑ̃'dɔ:r], *m.* Andorra.
andouille [ɑ̃'du:j], *n.f.* Pork sausage (made of chitterlings); (*pop.*) imbecile, duffer. *Cela s'en est allé en brouet d'andouille,* it all ended in smoke.
andouiller [ɑ̃du'je], *n.m.* Tine (of antler). *Maître andouiller,* brow antler.
andouillette [ɑ̃du'jɛt], *n.f.* Small pork sausage.
André [ɑ̃'dre], *m.* Andrew.
andrinople [ɑ̃dri'nɔpl], *a.* A cheap cotton fabric, usually coloured Turkey red.
androgyne [ɑ̃drɔ'ʒin], *a.* Androgynous, hermaphrodite.—*n.m.* An androgyne.
Andromède [ɑ̃drɔ'mɛd], *n.f.* Andromeda; (*Bot.*) stagger bush.
androphobe [ɑ̃drɔ'fɔb], *a.* Hating or avoiding the male sex. **androphobie,** *n.f.* Antipathy to the male sex.
androsème [ɑ̃dro'sɛm], *n.m.* (*Bot.*) Tutsan, St. John's wort.
âne [ɑ:n], *n.m.* Ass, donkey; blockhead, stupid, ignorant or foolish person, idiot; bench-vice. *C'est un âne bâté,* he is an arrant fool; *conte de Peau d'âne,* a fairy tale for children; *coq-à-l'âne,* cock-and-bull story; *en dos d'âne,* with a shelving ridge or hog's back [see also DOS]; *faute d'un point, Martin perdit son âne,* spoiling the ship for a ha'p'orth of tar; *il ne sera jamais qu'un âne,* he will be an ass as long as he lives; *on ne saurait faire boire un âne qui n'a pas soif,* you may take a horse to water, but you can't make him drink; *oreilles d'âne* or *bonnet d'âne,* fool's cap; *pont aux ânes,* pons asinorum; *tête d'âne,* bullhead, miller's-thumb; *têtu comme un âne,* as stubborn as a mule.
anéantir [aneɑ̃'ti:r], *v.t.* To annihilate, to destroy utterly, to abolish; (*fig.*) to overwhelm, to prostrate, to dumbfound; to tire out, to knock up. **s'anéantir,** *v.r.* To be annihilated, (*Eccles.*) to come to nothing.; to humble or abase oneself.
anéantissement, *n.m.* Annihilation; destruction, ruin, overthrow; humiliation, prostration; dejection, depression.
anecdote [anɛg'dɔt], *n.f.* Anecdote. **anecdotier,** *n.m.* (*fem.* **anecdotière**) Teller of anecdotes. **anecdotique,** *a.* Anecdotic. *Recueil anecdotique,* collection of anecdotes.
ânée [ɑ'ne], *n.f.* Donkey-load.
anémiant [ane'mjɑ̃], *a.* (*Med.*) Weakening.
anémie [ane'mi], *n.f.* Anaemia. **anémier,** *v.t.* To render anaemic. **anémique,** *a.* Anaemic.

anémographe [anemɔ'graf], *n.m.* Anemograph.

anémomètre [anemɔ'mɛtr], *n.m.* Anemometer. **anémométrie,** *n.f.* Anemometry.

anémone [ane'mɔn], *n.f.* Anemone, windflower. (*Zool.*) *Anémone de mer,* sea-anemone.

anémoscope [anemɔs'kɔp], *n.m.* Wind-vane, anemoscope.

ânerie [ɑn'ri], *n.f.* Stupidity; gross ignorance; a gross blunder. *Dire des âneries,* to talk nonsense.

anéroïde [anerɔ'id], *a.* Aneroid.—*n.m.* An aneroid barometer.

ânesse [ɑ'nɛs], *n.f.* She-ass. *Lait d'ânesse,* ass's milk.

anesthésie [anɛste'zi], *n.f.* (*Med.*) Anaesthesia. **anesthésier,** *v.t.* To anaesthetize. **anesthésique,** *a.* and *n.m.* Anaesthetic. **anesthésiste,** *n.m.* Anaesthetist.

aneth [a'nɛt], *n.m.* (*Bot.*) Anet, dill, fennel.

anévrismal [anevris'mal], *a.* (*fem.* **anévrismale,** *pl.* **anévrismaux**) Aneurismal. **anévrisme,** *n.m.* Aneurism. *Rupture d'anévrisme,* breaking of a blood-vessel.

anfractueux [ɑ̃fraktɥø], *a.* (*fem.* **anfractueuse**) Anfractuous, winding, sinuous, craggy. **anfractuosité,** *n.f.* Anfractuosity, cragginess, twist, jagged (*or* rugged) outlines.

angarie [ɑ̃ga'ri], *n.f.* (*Naval Law*) Angary.

ange [ɑ̃:ʒ], *n.m.* Angel; (*fig.*) a benign, adorable, or beloved person. *Ange bouffi,* a chubby child; *ange déchu,* fallen angel; *ange de mer,* angel-fish, monk-fish; *ange gardien,* guardian angel; *belle comme un ange,* beautiful as an angel; *être aux anges,* to be in raptures; *faiseuse d'anges,* abortionist; *le saut de l'ange,* swallow dive; *lit d'ange,* angel bed; *mon ange,* my love, my dear; *parler aux anges,* to talk to oneself; *rire aux anges,* to have an ecstatic smile.

Angèle [ɑ̃'ʒɛl], *f.* Angela.

angélique (1) [ɑ̃ʒe'lik], *n.f.* (*Bot.*) Angelica.

angélique (2) [ɑ̃ʒe'lik], *a.* Angelic, angelical. *La salutation angélique,* the Hail Mary. **angéliquement,** *adv.* Angelically.

angélolâtrie, *n.f.* Angelolatry.

angelot [ɑ̃ʒ'lo], *n.m.* Old French gold coin (with a figure of St. Michael); cheese made in the *Pays d'Ange,* Normandy; monk-fish.

angélus [ɑ̃ʒe'ly:s], *n.m.* Angelus; ave-bell. *Sonner l'angélus,* to toll the angelus.

angevin [ɑ̃ʒə'vɛ̃], *a.* (*fem.* **angevine**) Of Anjou, native of Anjou.

angine [ɑ̃'ʒin], *n.f.* Angina, quinsy. *Angine couenneuse,* diphtheria; *angine de poitrine,* angina pectoris. **angineux,** *a.* (*fem.* **angineuse**) Anginous.

angiographie [ɑ̃ʒjɔgra'fi], *n.f.* (*Physiol.*) Angiography. **angiologie,** *n.f.* Angiology.

angiosperme [ɑ̃ʒjɔs'pɛrm], *a.* (*Bot.*) Angiospermous. *n.f. pl.* Angiosperms.

anglais [ɑ̃'glɛ], *a.* (*fem.* **-aise**) English; British.—*n.m.* English language. **Anglais** (*fem.* **-aise**) Englishman, English girl or woman; (*pl.*) the English.—*n.f.* Italian hand.— *pl.* (hairdressing) ringlets. *S'en aller* or *filer à l'anglaise,* to slip away, to take French leave.

anglaisage [ɑ̃glɛ'za:ʒ], *n.f.* Docking (a horse's tail). **anglaiser,** *v.t.* To dock (a horse's tail).

angle [ɑ̃:gl], *n.m.* Angle, corner; (*Arch.*) quoin. *A angles saillants,* sharp-cornered; *à*

angle droit, rectangular; *angle aigu,* acute angle; *angle droit,* right angle; *angle plat,* straight angle; *angle rectiligne,* rectilinear angle; *angle rentrant* or *saillant,* re-entrant or salient angle; *voir le problème sous un autre angle,* to see the problem from a different angle. **angler,** *v.t.* To give angular form to; to mould the angles precisely.

anglet [ɑ̃'glɛ], *n.m.* (*Arch.*) Right-angled hollow, indenture, or channel.

Angleterre [ɑ̃glə'tɛ:r], *f.* England.

anglican [ɑ̃gli'kɑ̃], *a.* (*fem.* **anglicane**) Anglican. *L'Église anglicane,* the Anglican Church.—*n.* Anglican, member of the Church of England. **anglicanisme,** *n.f.* Anglicanism.

angliche [ɑ̃'gliʃ], (*pop.*) for *anglais.*

angliciser [ɑ̃glisi'ze], *v.t.* To anglicize. **s'angliciser,** *v.r.* To become anglicized or English. **anglicisme,** *n.m.* Anglicism. **anglicisant** or **angliciste,** *a.* and *n.* Student of English.

anglomane, *a.* and *n.* Anglomaniac. **anglomanie,** *n.f.* Anglomania.

anglo-normand, *a.* and *n.* (*fem.* **anglo-normande**) Anglo-Norman. *Les Îles anglo-normandes,* the Channel Islands.

anglophile, *a.* Anglophil.

anglophobe, *a.* and *n.* Anglophobe. **anglophobie,** *n.f.* Anglophobia.

anglo-saxon, *a.* (*fem.* **anglo-saxonne**) Anglo-Saxon.

angoisse [ɑ̃'gwas], *n.f.* Anguish, agony, great distress; (*Med.*) angor, anguish. *Poire d'angoisse,* pear-shaped gag; (*fig.*) *avaler des poires d'angoisse,* to eat humble pie; *les angoisses de la mort,* the pangs of death. **angoisser,** *v.t.* To distress, to afflict.

angon [ɑ̃'gɔ̃], *n.m.* (*Frankish Ant.*) Hooked javelin; fishing-hook (for crayfish etc.).

angora [ɑ̃gɔ'ra], *a.* Angora.—*n.m.* Angora cat.

anguiforme [ɑ̃gi'fɔrm], *a.* Serpent-shaped, anguine.

anguillade [ɑ̃gi'jad], *n.f.* Lash, stroke, or cut (with an eel-skin, knotted handkerchief, etc.).

anguille [ɑ̃'gi:j], *n.f.* Eel; (*Naut.*) in *pl.,* launching ways, slips. *Anguille de haie,* grass-snake; *anguille de mer,* conger; *écorcher l'anguille par la queue,* to begin a thing at the wrong end; *il y a anguille sous roche,* there is more in it than meets the eye; *nœud d'anguille,* running bowline; (*C*) *anguille de roche,* butter-fish, sand-eel.

anguiller [ɑ̃gi'je], *n.m.* (1) *usual in pl.* (*Naut.*) Limbers, (2) limber-passage.

anguillère or **anguillière** [ɑ̃gi'jɛ:r], *n.f.* Eel-pond.

anguillule [ɑ̃gi'jyl], *n.f.* (*Zool.*) Anguillule, eel-worm. *Anguillule du blé,* wheat worm.

angulaire [ɑ̃gy'lɛ:r], *a.* Angular. *'Distance angulaire,* angular distance (of a star etc.); *pierre angulaire,* corner-stone; (*fig.*) foundation, basis. **angulairement,** *adv.* Angularly. **angulé,** *a.* (*fem.* **angulée**) Angular, angulate. **anguleux,** *a.* (*fem.* **anguleuse**) Angulous, bony, rugged.

angusticlave [ɑ̃gysti'kla:v], *n.m.* (*Rom. Ant.*) A narrow purple stripe bordering the tunic of Roman knights etc.; a tunic bordered with this.

angustifolié [ɑ̃gystifɔ'lje], *a.* (*fem.* **angustifoliée**) (*Bot.*) Angustifoliate.

angusture [ãgys'ty:r], *n.f.* (*Pharm.*) Angostura.

anhélation [anela'sjɔ̃], *n.f.* (*Med.*) Anhelation, difficult respiration; panting. **anhéler,** *v.i.* To breathe with difficulty, to puff, to pant; (*Glass-making*) to blow (the furnace).

anhéleux [ane'lø], *a.* (*fem.* -euse) Gasping, panting, anhelous. ,

anhydre [a'nidr], *a.* (*Chem.*) Anhydrous. **anhydride,** *n.m.* Anhydride. *Anhydride carbonique,* carbon dioxide; *anhydride sulfureux,* sulphur dioxide; *anhydride sulfurique,* sulphur trioxide. **anhydrite,** *n.f.* Anhydrite.

anicroche [ani'krɔʃ], *n.f.* Slight obstacle, hitch, impediment, difficulty.

ânier [a'nje], *n.m.* (*fem.* **ânière**) Ass-driver.

anil [a'nil], *n.m.* (*Bot.*) Anil, indigo. **aniline,** *n.f.* Aniline.

anille [a'ni:j], *n.f.* Mill-rind; (*Bot.*) tendril. **anillée,** *a.* (*Her.*) Moline.

animadversion [animadvɛr'sjɔ̃], *n.f.* Animadversion, reproof, reprimand, censure.

animal [ani'mal], *n.m.* (*pl.* **animaux**) Animal; beast, brute. *Société protectrice des animaux,* R.S.P.C.A. *Ah! l'animal!* what a beast!—*a.* (*fem.* **animale**). Animal; sensual, carnal. *Chaleur animale,* animal heat; *règne animal,* the animal kingdom.

animalesque [anima'lɛsk], *a.* Animal.

animalcule [animal'kyl], *n.m.* Animalcule.

animalier [anima'lje], *n.m.* Animal-painter. —*a.* Of animals (applied to painters etc.).

animalisation [animaliza'sjɔ̃], *n.f.* Animalization. **animaliser,** *v.t.* To animalize, to convert (food) into animal substance. **s'animaliser,** *v.r.* To become animalized.

animalisme [anima'lizm], *n.m.* Animalism.

animalité [animali'te], *n.f.* Animality.

animateur [anima'tœr], *a.* (*fem.* -trice) Animating.—*n.* Animator, quickener. *Animateur de théâtre,* theatrical promoter.

animation, *n.f.* Animation, vitality, life; liveliness, sprightliness, vivacity; excitement, irritation.

animé, *a.* (*fem.* -ée) Animated; spirited, gay, sprightly. (*St. Exch.*) *Marché animé,* brisk market; *rue animée,* busy street.

animer [ani'me], *v.t.* To animate, to give life to, to quicken; to arouse, to excite, to urge on, to embolden; to enliven, to give force or vivacity to (style etc.). *Animer au combat,* to excite to combat; *animer d'ardeur,* to fill with ardour; *animer la conversation,* to enliven the conversation; *animer le teint,* to heighten the complexion. **s'animer,** *v.r.* To become animated or lively; to cheer up; to chafe, to be angry. *La dispute s'anime,* the dispute is getting angrier.

animisme [ani'mism], *n.m.* Animism. **animiste,** *a.* Animistic.—*n.* Animist.

animosité [animozi'te], *n.f.* Animosity, hatred, animus, spite, rancour; warmth, excess of emotion (in a discussion etc.). *Il a de l'animosité contre moi,* he has a grudge against me.

anis [a'ni], *n.m.* Anise, aniseed. *Anis de Verdun,* candied aniseed; *anis de la Chine* or *étoilé,* Chinese anise-tree; *graine d'anis,* aniseed. **aniser,** *v.t.* To flavour with aniseed. **anisette,** *n.f.* Anisette, aniseedcordial.

ankylose [ãki'lo:z], *n.f.* (*Path.*) Anchylosis,

stiffness in the joints. **ankylosé,** *a.* (*fem.* -ée). Affected with anchylosis. **ankyloser,** *v.t.* To produce anchylosis in. **s'ankyloser,** *v.r.* To become anchylosed, stiff (of the limbs etc.).

ankylostome [ãkilɔ'stom], *n.m.* Hookworm.

annal [a'nal], *a.* (*fem.* **annale,** *pl. not used in m.*) Valid for one year only. **annales,** *n.f.* (*used only in pl.*) Annals, public records. **annaliste,** *n.m.* Annalist. **annalité,** *n.f.* The state or quality of lasting for a year.

annate [a'nat], *n.f.* Annates, the first year's income of a living, first-fruits.

anneau [a'no], *n.m.* (*pl.* **anneaux**) Ring; link (of a chain); key-ring; ringlet (of hair); fold, convolution (of a serpent etc.); (*Bot.*) annulus; (*Zool.*) segment of a body, somite.— *pl.* (*Gym.*) the rings. *L'anneau de Saturne,* Saturn's ring; *l'anneau pastoral,* the episcopal ring; *l'anneau du pêcheur,* the Pope's signetring.

année [a'ne], *n.f.* Year, period of twelve months. *Année bissextile,* leap-year; *année scolaire,* school year; *année solaire,* solar year; *d'année en année,* from year to year; *d'un bout de l'année à l'autre,* all the year round; *l'année qui vient* or *l'année prochaine,* next year; *payer à l'année,* to pay by the year; *il est dans sa quarantième année,* he is in his fortieth year; *les belles années,* the prime of life; *une bonne année,* a plentiful year; *souhaiter la bonne année,* to wish a happy New Year; *une année dans l'autre,* one year with another; *années de service,* years of activity (of a civil servant).

année-lumière [anely'mjɛːr], *n.f.* (*pl.* **années-lumière**) Light-year.

annelé [an'le], *a.* (*fem.* **annelée**) Having or arranged in rings, ringed; (*Zool.*) annulated. —*n.m. pl.* (*Zool.*) The annulosa.

anneler [an'le], *v.t.* To curl or arrange the hair in locks or ringlets. **annelet,** *n.m.* Ringlet, a small ring; (*Arch.*) annulet.

annélide, *n.m.* (*Zool.*) Annelid, one of the Annelida.

annexe [a'nɛks], *a.* Appended, attached, annexed.—*n.f.* Annex; appendant, appendage; appendix, schedule, rider; chapel of ease. *Annexe d'une terre,* dependence of an estate. **annexer,** *v.t.* To annex, to join, to attach. **annexion,** *n.f.* Annexation. **annexionisme** or **annexionnisme,** *n.m.* The principle of annexing small States to large neighbouring States. **annexionniste,** *a.* and *n.* Annexationist.

annihilable [anii'labl], *a.* That may be annihilated; (*Law*) annullable. **annihilation,** *n.f.* Annihilation, extinction, destruction; (*Law*) annulment. **annihilationisme** or **annihilationnisme,** *n.m.* (*Theol.*) Annihilationism.

annihiler, *v.t.* To annihilate, to destroy; (*Law*) to cancel, to annul. **s'annihiler,** *v.r.* To be annihilated or abolished.

anniversaire [anivɛr'sɛːr], *a.* and *n.m.* Anniversary. *L'anniversaire de sa naissance, son anniversaire,* his (or her) birthday.

annonce [a'nɔ̃:s], *n.f.* Announcement, notification; indication, sign, mark; advertisement; (*Cards*) declaration. *Annonces de mariages,* announcements of marriages; *faire insérer une annonce,* to put an advertisement in the papers; *annonce de spectacle*, play-bill; *annonces lumineuses*, illuminated signs.

annoncer [anɔ̃'se], *v.t.* To announce, to give notice of, to give out; to advertise; to announce (a visitor), to usher or show in; to proclaim, to make manifest; to augur, to foretell; *to preach, to declare; (*Cards*) to declare. *Cela ne nous annonce rien de bon*, that bodes us no good; *faites-vous annoncer*, send in your name. **s'annoncer**, *v.r.* To present oneself; to manifest itself. *S'annoncer bien*, to be promising; *s'annoncer mal*, not to be promising, to begin badly. **annonceur**, *n.m.* *The actor who gives out the next play; advertiser. (*C*) (*Rad.*) Speaker.

annonciateur [anɔ̃sja'tœːr] *a.* (*fem.* **-trice**) Forerunner.—*n.* Announcer.

annonciation [anɔ̃sja'sjɔ̃], *n.f.* Annunciation; Lady-day (March 25).

annoncier [anɔ̃'sje], *n.m.* Publicity manager.

annotateur [anɔta'tœːr], *n.m.* (*fem.* **annotatrice**) Annotator (of a book etc.).

annotation [anɔta'sjɔ̃], *n.f.* Annotation; inventory of goods attached or distrained.

annoter, *v.t.* To annotate, to make notes on (a text etc.).

annuaire [a'nɥɛːr], *n.m.* Annual, year-book. *L'Annuaire de l'Armée*, the Army list; *l'Annuaire des Téléphones*, the Telephone Directory.

annualité [anɥali'te], *n.f.* The quality or state of being annual.

annuel [a'nɥɛl], *a.* (*fem.* **annuelle**) Annual, yearly, lasting a year or recurring every year. —*n.m.* A mass celebrated every day for a year for a deceased person. **annuellement,** *adv.* Annually, yearly.

annuitaire [anɥi'tɛːr], *a.* Discharged by means of an annuity (of a debt etc.).

annuité [anɥi'te], *n.f.* Annuity. *Les annuités d'une dette*, the yearly instalments of a debt.

annulable [any'labl], *a.* Revocable, defeasible.

annulaire [any'lɛːr], *a.* Annular, ring-shaped; suitable or proper for a ring. *Le doigt annulaire* (or *l'annulaire, n.m.*), the ring-finger, the third finger.

annulatif [anyla'tif], *a.* (*fem.* **annulative**) Annulling, quashing. **annulation,** *n.f.* Annulment, cancellation, repeal, abolition. **annulement,** *n.m.* Annulling, cancelling. (*Naut.*) *Signal d'annulement*, annulling signal; (*Law*) *arrêt d'annulement*, annulment of judgment. **annuler,** *v.t.* To annul, to rescind, to cancel, to abolish, to set aside, to make void.

anobie [anɔ'bi], *n.m.* (*Ent.*) Anobium.

anobli [anɔ'bli], *a.* (*fem.* **anoblie**) Ennobled. —*n.m.* Newly created nobleman.

anoblir [anɔ'bliːr], *v.t.* To ennoble, to raise to the rank of the nobility. **anoblissement,** *n.m.* Ennoblement. *Lettres d'anoblissement*, patent of nobility.

anode [a'nɔd], *n.f.* (*Elec.*) Anode, positive pole.

anodin [anɔ'dɛ̃], *a.* (*fem.* **anodine**) (*Med.*) Anodyne, soothing, assuaging pain; (*fig.*) harmless, mild, inoffensive, insignificant (of verses etc.). *Remèdes anodins*, anodynes.

anodique [anɔ'dik], *a.* (*Elec.*) Anodic, anodal.

anomal [anɔ'mal], *a.* (*fem.* **anomale**, *pl.* **anomaux**) (*Gram.*) Anomalous, irregular abnormal, exceptional. **anomalie,** *n.f.*

Anomaly, irregularity; (*Anat.*) abnormality, monstrosity. **anomalistique,** *a.* (*Astron.*) *Année anomalistique*, anomalistic year.

ânon [ɑ'nɔ̃], *n.m.* Ass's foal, young ass; (*fig.*) a silly child, a little fool.

ânonnement [ɑnɔn'mɑ̃], *n.m.* Faltering, mumbling way of reading a text. **ânonner,** *v.t.* To mumble and blunder through (a lesson etc.).—*v.i.* To read in a faltering way.

anonymat [anɔni'ma], *n.m.* Anonymity. *Garder l'anonymat*, to remain anonymous.

anonyme [anɔ'nim], *a.* Anonymous, nameless.—*n.* Anonymous person. *Société anonyme*, joint-stock company; *sous l'anonyme*, anonymously. **anonymement,** *adv.* Anonymously.

anophèle [anɔ'fɛl], *n.m.* (*Ent.*) Anopheles.

anorak [anɔ'rak], *n.m.* Anorak.

anordie [anɔr'di], *n.f.* A fresh breeze from the north. **anordir,** *v.i.* To veer to northward.

anorexie [anɔrɛ'ksi], *n.f.* Loss of appetite, anorexia.

anormal [anɔr'mal], *a.* (*fem.* **anormale**, *pl.* **anormaux**). Abnormal, irregular, mentally deficient. **anormalement,** *adv.* Abnormally.

anosmie [anɔs'mi], *n.f.* Anosmia, loss of the sense of smell.

anoure [a'nuːr], *a.* Anourous, tailless.—*n.m.pl.* (*Zool.*) Anoura.

anse [ɑːs], *n.f.* Handle (of a pot, basket, etc.); dolphin-handle (of a gun); little bay, creek, cove. *Faire danser l'anse du panier*, (of a servant) to make a market penny; *faire le panier à deux anses*, to walk with a lady on each arm; *faire le pot à deux anses*, to set one's arms a-kimbo; (*Arch.*) *voûte en anse de panier*, three-centered arch.

ansérin [ɑse'rɛ̃], *a.* (*fem.* **ansérine** (1)) (*Med.*) Anserine, goose-like (of the skin). **ansérine** (2), *n.f.* (*pop.*) Goosefoot (applied to the chenopod and other plants).

ansière [ɑ̃'sjɛːr], *n.f.* Fishing-net for small coves etc.

anspect [ɑs'pɛk], *n.m.* (*Naut.*) Handspike, crow-bar.

antagonique [ɑtagɔ'nik], *a.* Antagonistic.

antagonisme [ɑtagɔ'nism], *n.m.* Antagonism. **antagoniste,** *a.* Antagonistic, in opposition. —*n.m.* Antagonist, adversary, opponent; competitor, rival; (*Anat.*) a counteracting muscle, an antagonist.

***antan** [ɑ'tɑ̃], *n.m.* Yesteryear. *Les neiges d'antan*, the snows of yesteryear.

antanaclase [ɑtana'klɑːz], *n.f.* (*rhet.*) Antanaclasis.

antarctique [ɑtark'tik], *a.* Antarctic.

ante [ɑːt], *n.f.* Movable handle of a brush; *pl.* (*Arch.*) antae.

antebois [ɑt'bwa] or **antébois** [ɑte'bwa] or **antibois,** *n.m.* Rail on floor to prevent furniture touching wall, chair-rail.

antécédemment [ɑteseda'mɑ̃], *adv.* Antecedently, previously. **antécédence,** *n.f.* Antecedence. **antécédent,** *a.* (*fem.* **antécédente**) Antecedent, preceding, foregoing, previous.—*n.m.* Precedent; (*Gram.*) antecedent. *Avoir de bons antécédents*, to be known for a person of good character.

***antécesseur** [ɑtese'sœːr], *n.m.* A professor of civil law.

antéchrist [ãte'krist], *n.m.* Antichrist.
antédiluvien [ãtedily'vjẽ], *a.* (*fem.* **antédiluvienne**) Antediluvian.
Antée [ã'te], *m.* Antaeus.
antéfixe [ãte'fiks], *n.f.* (*Arch.*) An ornament (in terracotta etc.) for a frieze, roof, etc., antefix.
antenais [ãtə'nɛ] or **antenois** (*fem.* **-aise,** **-oise**), *a.* and *n.* Lamb or foal from 13 to 23 months old; tegg, colt.
antennaire [ãte'nɛːr], *a.* (*Ent.*) Antennary. —*n.f.* (*Bot.*) Member of a genus of dioecious composites containing the cat's-foot or mountain cudweed.
antenne [ã'tɛn], *n.f.* Yard-arm, especially a lateen sail-yard; (*Rad. Tel.*) aerial; (*Ent.*) antenna, (*pl.*) antennae.
antennule [ãte'nyl], *n.f.* Small antenna.
anténuptial [ãtenyp'sjal], *a.* (*fem.* **anténuptiale,** *pl.* **anténuptiaux**) Antenuptial.
antépénultième [ãtepenyl'tjɛm], *a.* Antepenultimate.—*n.f.* Antepenult.
antérieur [ãte'rjœːr], *a.* (*fem.* **antérieure**) Anterior, earlier, antecedent, previous, former; fore, frontal. *La partie antérieure de la tête*, the forepart of the head; (*Gram.*) *futur antérieur*, future perfect. **antérieurement,** *adv.* Previously, before. **antériorité,** *n.f.* Anteriority, priority, precedence. (*Law*) *Droit d'antériorité*, right of priority.
anthélie [ãte'li], *n.f.* (*Meteor.*) Anthelion, mock-sun, fog-bow.
anthélix [ãte'liks], *n.m.* (*Anat.*) Antihelix.
anthelminthique [ãtɛlmẽ'tik], *a.* (*Med.*) Vermifuge.—*n.m.* Anthelmintic.
anthère [ã'tɛːr], *n.f.* (*Bot.*) Anther. **anthéridie,** *n.f.* Antheridium. **anthérifère,** *a.* Antheriferous.
anthologie [ãtɔlɔ'ʒi], *n.f.* Anthology. **anthologique,** *a.* Anthological.
anthracite [ãtra'sit], *n.m.* Anthracite. **anthraciteux,** *a.* (*fem.* **-euse**) Anthracitic, anthracitous.
anthrax [ã'traks], *n.m.* (*Med.*) Anthrax.
anthropocentrique, *a.* Anthropocentric.
anthropographie [ãtrɔpɔgra'fi], *n.f.* Anthropography. **anthropoïde,** *a.* (*Zool.*) Anthropoid, resembling man.—*n.m.* An anthropoid.
anthropologie [ãtrɔpɔlɔ'ʒi], *n.f.* Anthropology. **anthropologique,** *a.* Anthropological. **anthropologiste** or **anthropologue,** *n.* Anthropologist.
anthropométrie [ãtrɔpɔme'tri], *n.f.* Anthropometry. **anthropométrique,** *a.* Pertaining to anthropometry. *Service anthropométrique*, the branch of the Criminal Investigation Department dealing with measurements of individuals.
anthropomorphe [ãtrɔpɔ'mɔrf], *a.* Anthropomorphous. **anthropomorphisme,** *n.m.* Anthropomorphism. **anthropomorphiste** or **anthropomorphite,** *n.m.* Anthropomorphist.
anthropophage [ãtrɔpɔ'faːʒ], *a.* Anthropophagous.—*n.* A cannibal, a man-eater. **anthropophagie,** *n.f.* Anthropophagy.
anthropopithèque [ãtrɔpɔpi'tɛk], *n.m.* (*Zool.*) Pithecanthrope, a fossil anthropoid found in Java.
anthyllide [ãti'lid], *n.f.* (*Bot.*) Anthyllis. *Anthyllide vulnéraire*, kidney-vetch, lady's fingers.

anti-, *pref.* Anti-, against; ante-, before.
antiadministratif [ãtiadministra'tif], *a.* (*fem.* **antiadministrative**) Contrary to administrative usages, rules, etc.
anti-aérien [ãtiae'rjẽ], *a.* (*fem.* **-ienne**) Anti-aircraft.
antialcoolique [ãtialkɔ'lik], *a.* Anti-alcohol, teetotal. **antialcoolisme,** *n.m.* Teetotalism.
antibiotique [ãtibiɔ'tik], *a.* and *n.m.* Antibiotic.
antibois [ANTEBOIS].
anti-brouillard [ãtibru'jaːr], *n.m.* (*Motor.*) Fog-light.
anti-buée [ãti'bye], *a.* (*Motor.*) Demisting.—*n.m.* Demister.
anticancéreux [ãtikãse'rø], *a.* (*fem.* **-euse**) (*Med.*) Tending to prevent cancer. *Sérum anticancéreux*, cancer-serum.
anticatarrhal [ãtikata'ral], *a.* (*fem.* **-ale,** *pl.* **-aux**) Anticatarrhal.
antichambre [ãti'ʃãːbr], *n.f.* (formerly *m.*) Antechamber, anteroom. *Propos d'antichambre*, servant's gossip; *faire antichambre*, to dance attendance; *pilier d'antichambre*, hanger-on (of a minister).
anti-char [ãti'ʃaːr], *a.* Anti-tank. *Un appareil anti-char*, an anti-tank appliance.
anticholérique [ãtikɔle'rik], *a.* and *n.m.* (*Med.*) Anticholeric.
antichrèse [ãti'krɛːz], *n.f.* (*Law*) Mortgage of revenues of a property in payment of a debt.
antichrétien [ãtikre'tjẽ], *a.* and *n.* (*fem.* **-ienne**) Antichristian.
antichristianisme, *n.m.* Antichristianism.
anticipant [ãtisi'pã], *a.* (*fem.* **anticipante**) (*Med.*) Anticipant (of periodic symptoms).
anticipation [ãtisipɑ'sjɔ̃], *n.f.* Anticipation; encroachment, trespass; (*Mus.*) a note in anticipation of a harmony coming later. *Par anticipation*, in advance, beforehand. **anticipé,** *a.* (*fem.* **anticipée**) Done or occurring in advance. *Connaissance anticipée*, foreknowledge; *joie anticipée*, foretaste of joy; *une vieillesse anticipée*, a premature old age. **anticiper** [ãtisi'pe], *v.t.* To anticipate, to take up or be beforehand, to forestall.—*v.i.* To encroach or trespass (*sur*). *Anticiper sur les droits de quelqu'un*, to encroach upon another's rights; *anticiper sur ses revenus*, to spend one's income in advance.
anticivique [ãtisi'vik], *a.* Anticivic. **anticivisme,** *n.m.* Anticivism. **anticlérical,** *a.* (*fem.* **-ale,** *pl.* **-aux**) Anticlerical. **anticléricalisme,** *n.m.* Anticlericalism.
anticlimax [ãtikli'maks], *n.m.* Anticlimax.
anticlinal [ãtikli'nal], *a.* (*fem.* **-ale,** *pl.* **-aux**) (*Geol.*) Anticlinal.—*n.m.* Anticlinal, an anticline.
anticommunisme [ãtikɔmy'nizm], *n.m.* Anti-communism.
anticonceptionnel [ãtikɔ̃sɛpsjɔ'nɛl], *a.* (*fem.* **-elle**) Contraceptive.
anticonstitutionnel [ãtikɔ̃stitysjɔ'nɛl], *a.* (*fem.* **anticonstitutionnelle**) Anticonstitutional. **anticonstitutionnellement,** *adv.* (the longest French word). Anticonstitutionally.
anticorps [ãti'kɔːr], *n.m.* (*Med.*) Anti-body.
anticyclone [ãtisi'klɔːn], *n.m.* (*Meteor.*) Anticyclone. **anticyclonal, anticyclonique,** *a.* Anticyclonic.

antidate [ăti'dat], *n.f.* Antedate. **antidater,** *v.t.* To antedate.

antidérapant [ătidera'pã], *a.* (*fem.* **antidérapante**) Non-skidding (of appliances used on cycle and motor tyres). *Pneu antidérapant,* non-skid tyre.

antidote [ăti'dɔt], *n.m.* Antidote, counterpoison; (*fig.*) cure, preservative.

anti-éblouissant [ătieblui'sã], *a.* (*Motor.*) Antidazzling.

antienne [ă'tjɛn], *n.f.* Antiphon; anthem; (*fig.*) story. *Chanter toujours la même antienne,* to harp upon the same string.

antiépileptique [ătiepilɛp'tik], *a.* (*Med.*) Counteracting epilepsy.—*n.m.* A medicine that does this.

antiesclavagisme [ătiɛsklava'ʒism], *n.m.* Anti-slavery. **antiesclavagiste,** *a.* Anti-slavery.—*n.* Abolitionist.

antiévangélique [ătievãʒe'lik], *a.* Contrary to the Gospel.

antifasciste [ătifa'ʃist], *a.* and *n.* Anti-fascist.

antifébrile [FÉBRIFUGE].

antigel [ăti'ʒɛl], *n.m. inv.* Anti-freeze.

Antigone [ăti'gɔn], *m.* Antigonus.—*f.* Antigone.

antigoutteux [ătigu'tø], *a.* (*fem.* **-euse**) Tending to prevent or cure gout.—*n.m.* A medicine etc. that does this.

antigouvernemental [ătiguvernmã'tal], *a.* (*fem.* **-ale,** *pl.* **-aux**) Opposed to the Government.

antigréviste [ătigre'vist], *a.* Anti-strike.—*n.* Anti-striker.

antigrippal [ătigri'pal] *a.* Anti-flu.

antihalo [ătia'lo], *n.m.* (*Phot.*) A substance for backing plates and preventing halation.

antihumain [ătiy'mɛ̃], *a.* (*fem.* **-aine**) Opposed to principles of humanity.

antihygiénique [ătiiʒje'nik], *a.* Contrary to hygienic principles.

antijuif [ăti'ʒyif], (*fem.* **-ive**) [ANTI-SÉMITE].

antilibéral [ătilibe'ral], *a.* (*fem.* **-ale,** *pl.* **-aux**) Contrary to Liberal principles (in politics etc.).

Antilles [ă'ti:j], **les,** *f.pl.* The West Indies. *Les Grandes Antilles,* the Greater Antilles; *les Petites Antilles,* the Lesser Antilles; *la mer des Antilles,* the Caribbean Sea.

antilogie [ătilɔ'ʒi], *n.f.* Antilogy. **antilogique** [ătilɔ'ʒik], *a.* Contrary to logic.

antilope [ăti'lɔp], *n.f.* Antelope.

antimilitarisme [ătimilita'rizm], *n.m.* Opposition to militarism etc. **antimilitariste,** *a.* Opposing or agitating against national military service.—*n.* An opponent of or agitator against this; a pacifist.

anti-mite [ăti'mit], *a.* Moth-proof.

antimoine [ăti'mwan], *n.m.* Antimony.

antimonarchique [ătimɔnar'ʃik], *a.* Anti-monarchical. **antimonarchiste,** *a.* Anti-monarchical.—*n.* Antimonarchist.

antimonial [ătimɔ'njal], *a.* (*fem.* **-ale,** *pl.* **-aux**) Antimonial. **antimoniate,** *n.m.* Antimoniate. **antimonié,** *a.* (*fem.* **-ée**) Antimonic. **antimonieux,** *a.* (*fem.* **-euse**) Antimonious.

antinational [ătinasjɔ'nal], *a.* (*fem.* **-ale,** *pl.* **-aux**) Antinational.

antinomie [ătinɔ'mi], *n.f.* Antinomy. **antinomique,** *a.* Antinomic.

Antioche [ă'tjɔʃ], *f.* Antioch.

antipape [ăti'pap], *n.m.* Anti-pope. **antipapisme,** *n.m.* Opposition to the Pope; state of the Church under an anti-pope. **antipapiste,** *a.* Antipapal.—*n.* Antipapist.

antiparalytique [ătiparali'tik], *a.* (*Med.*) Counteracting paralysis.

antiparasite [ătipara'zit], *n.m.* Suppressor.

antiparlementaire [ătiparləmã'te:r], *a.* Unparliamentary.

antipathie [ătipa'ti], *n.f.* Antipathy, aversion. **antipathique,** *a.* Antipathetic. *Il m'est très antipathique,* I have a great aversion to him.

antipatriote [ătipatri'ɔt], *n.* Antipatriot. **antipatriotique,** *a.* Antipatriotic, unpatriotic. **antipatriotisme,** *n.m.* Sentiment or doctrines contrary to patriotism.

antipestilentiel [ătipestilã'sjɛl, *a.* (*fem.* **antipestilentielle**) Antipestilential.

antiphlogistique [ătiflɔʒis'tik], *a.* (*Med.*) Antiphlogistic.—*n.m.* An antiphlogistic.

antiphonaire [ătifɔ'nɛ:r], *n.m.* Antiphonal.

antiphrase [ăti'fra:z], *n.f.* (*Rhet.*) Antiphrasis, irony.

antipodal [ătipɔ'dal], *a.* (*fem.* **antipodale,** *pl.* **antipodaux**) Antipodal, antipodean.

antipode, *n.m.* The region of the globe diametrically opposite; (*fig.*) the very opposite (of anything). *Être aux antipodes,* to be miles away.

antipoétique [ătipɔe'tik], *a.* Contrary to poetry.

antipopulaire, *a.* Contrary to the interest of the people.

antiprogressiste, *a.* Contrary to progress.—*n.* One who is opposed to progress.

antiprohibitionniste, *a.* Opposed to prohibitive tariffs.—*n.* One who opposes prohibitive tariffs.

antiprotectionniste, *a.* and *n.* Opposed to protection.

antiputride [ătipy'trid], *a.* Antiseptic.—*n.m.* An antiseptic.

antipyrétique, *a.* (*Med.*) Antipyretic, febrifuge.

antipyrine, *n.f.* (*Pharm.*) Antipyrin.

antiquaille [ăti'ka:j], *n.f.* *A worthless antique, an antiquity; old stuff, junk; (*fig.*) *Ce n'est qu'une antiquaille,* she is but an antiquated coquette, *or* he is an old fogey.

antiquaire [ăti'kɛ:r], *n.m.* Antiquary, antiquarian, antique-dealer.

antique [ă'tik], *a.* Antique, ancient; old-fashioned.—*n.f.* Antique, ancient work of art. *À l'antique,* in the old style; *dessiner d'après l'antique,* to draw from antique models.

antiquité, *n.f.* Antiquity, ancientness; old times; piece of antiquity; (*pl.*) antiquities. *De toute antiquité,* from the remotest times; *les héros de l'antiquité,* the heroes of former ages; *magasin d'antiquités,* old curiosity shop.

antirationalisme [ătiraʃjɔna'lism], *n.m.* Doctrine opposed to rationalism.

antireligieux, *a.* (*fem.* **-ieuse**) Antireligious.

antirépublicain, *a.* (*fem.* **-aine**) Antirepublican.

antirévolutionnaire, *a.* and *n.* Antirevolutionary.

antirouille [ăti'ru:j], *n.m.* Rust preventive.

antirrhine [ăti'rin], *n.f.* (*Bot.*) Antirrhinum, snapdragon.

antiscien [ăti'sjɛ̃], *a.* (*fem.* **-enne**) Antiscian.—*n.pl.* Antiscii.

antiscorbutique [ãtiskɔrby'tik], *a.* and *n.m.* (*Med.*) Antiscorbutic.

antiscrofuleux, *a.* (*fem.* **-euse**) (*Med.*) Antiscrophulous.

antisémite [ãtise'mit], *n.* Anti-Semite. **antisémitique**, *a.* Contrary or hostile to the Jews. **antisémitisme**, *n.m.* Anti-Semitism.

antisepsie [ãtisɛp'si], *n.f.* Antisepsis.

antiseptique [ãtisɛp'tik], *a.* and *n.m.* (*Med.*) Antiseptic. **antiseptiser**, *v.t.* To render antiseptic.

antisocial [ãtisɔ'sjal], *a.* (*fem.* **-ale**, *pl.* **-aux**) Antisocial. **antisocialiste**, *a.* and *n.* Antisocialist.

antispasmodique [ãtispazmɔ'dik], *a.* (*Med.*) Antispasmodic.

antisportif [ãtispɔr'tif], *a.* Unsportsmanlike; opposed to sports.

antistrophe [ãtis'trɔf], *n.f.* Antistrophe.

antisyphilitique [ãtisifili'tik], *a.* (*Med.*) Antisyphilitic.

antitétanique [ãtiteta'nic], *a.* and *n.* (*Med.*) Antitetanic.

antithèse [ãti'tɛːz], *n.f.* Antithesis. **antithétique**, *a.* Antithetic.

antitoxine [ãtitɔk'sin], *n.f.* (*Med.*) Antitoxin. **antitoxique**, *a.* Antitoxic.

antitrinitaire [ãtitrini'tɛːr], *n.m.* Anti-trinitarian.

antituberculeux [ãtitybɛrky'lø], *a.* (*fem.* **antituberculeuse**) (*Med.*) Preventing or counteracting tuberculosis. *Centre antituberculeux*, tuberculosis centre.

antivariolique [ãtivarjo'lik], *a.* (*Med.*) Antivariolous.

antivénéneux [ãtivene'nø], *a.* (*fem.* **-euse**) Antidotal.

antivénérien [ãtivene'rjɛ̃], *a.* (*fem.* **-ienne**) (*Med.*) Antivenereal.

anti-vol [ãti'vɔl], *a. inv.* Anti-theft.—*n.m.* Theft-proof device.

antivivisection (ãtivivisɛk'sjɔ̃), *n.f.* Antivivisection.

Antoine [ã'twɑn], *m.* Antony. *Marc-Antoine*, Mark Antony.

antoit (ã'twa), *n.m.* (*Naut.*) Wring-bolt.

antonomase (ãtɔnɔ'maːz), *n.f.* (*Rhet.*) Antonomasia.

antonyme [ãtɔ'nim], *n.m.* (*Rhet.*) Antonym. **antonymie**, *n.f.* Antonymy.

antre [ã:tr], *n.m.* Den, lair; cavern, antre; (*fig.*) den (of swindlers or rogues, etc.). *L'antre du lion*, the lion's den, a risky place.

anuiter (s') [anɥi'te], *v.r.* To be benighted, to stay too late (on the road etc.).

anurèse [ANURIE].

anurie [any'ri], *n.f.* (*Med.*) Anury.

anus [a'nyːs], *n.m.* Anus.

Anvers [ã'vɛr], *m.* Antwerp.

anxiété [ãksje'te], *n.f.* Anxiety; uneasiness; (*Med.*) pain in the heart. **anxieusement**, *adv.* Anxiously. **anxieux**, *a.* (*fem.* **anxieuse**) Anxious, uneasy, restless.

aoriste [ao'rist], *n.m.* (*Gram.*) Aorist.

aorte [a'ɔrt], *n.f.* (*Anat.*) Aorta. **aortique**, *a.* Aortic. **aortite**, *n.f.* (*Path.*) Disease of the aorta.

Aoste [a'ɔst], *f.* Aosta.

août [u], *n.m.* August; (*fig.*) harvest. *Faire l'août*, to harvest, to get in the corn; *la mi-août*, the middle of August. **aoûtage**,

n.m. Harvest tax; harvesting, harvest time. **aoûtat** [TROMBIDION]. **aoûté**, *a.* (*fem.* **aoûtée**) Ripened by the heat of August. **aoûtement**, *n.m.* Ripening (of crops for harvest). **aoûter**, *v.t.* and *i.* To ripen. **s'aoûter**, *v.r.* To ripen (in August). **aoûteron**, *n.m.* Reaper, harvester, hired as a journeyman for the harvest. **aoûteur**, *n.m.* Harvester.

apache [a'paʃ], *n.m.* Ruffian of the Paris streets, hooligan.

apaisement [apɛz'mã], *n.m.* Appeasement; abatement, lull.

apaiser [apɛ'ze], *v.t.* To pacify, to calm, to appease; to lull, to still, to quiet; to abate, to allay, to mitigate, to alleviate (pain, sorrow, etc.); to stay (hunger); to quench (thirst). *Apaiser les flots*, to calm the waves; *apaiser un enfant qui crie*, to quiet a crying child; *apaiser une révolte*, to put down a rebellion. **s'apaiser**, *v.r.* To be appeased, assuaged, etc.; to sober down; to grow quiet; to abate, to subside. *L'orage s'est apaisé*, the storm has subsided; *sa colère s'est apaisée*, his anger has died down.

Apalaches [apa'laʃ], *m.pl.* Appalachians. (*C*) **apalachien** [apala'ʃjɛ̃], *a.* (*fem.* **apalachienne**) Appalachian.

apalachine [apala'ʃin], *n.f.* Holly growing in the Appalachian mountains (N. America).

apanage [apa'naːʒ], *n.m.* Apanage; (*fig.*) lot. *Les infirmités sont l'apanage de la nature humaine*, infirmities are the lot of human nature. **apanager** (1), *v.t.* To settle an apanage upon, to endow. ***apanager** (2), *a.* (*fem.* **apanagère**) Bestowed as an apanage. **apanagiste**, *a.* Having an apanage.—*n.m.* One who has an apanage.

apapelardir (s') [apaplar'diːr], *v.r.* To become hypocritical *or* sanctimonious.

aparté [apar'te], *n.m.* An aside, words spoken aside by an actor; a private remark or reflexion. *En aparté*, aside.

apathie [apa'ti], *n.f.* Apathy, indolence, listlessness; want of feeling, insensibility. **apathique**, *a.* Apathetic, listless. **apathiquement**, *adv.* Apathetically.

apatride [apa'trid], *a.* Stateless.—*n.* Stateless person. **apatridie**, *n.f.* Statelessness.

Apennins [apɛ'nɛ̃], **les**, *m.pl.* The Apennines.

apepsie [apɛp'si], *n.f.* (*Path.*) Apepsy, indigestion. **apeptique**, *a.* Dyspeptic.

aperceptible [apɛrsɛp'tibl], *a.* (*Phil.*) That can be perceived. **aperceptif**, *a.* (*fem.* **-ive**) Having the faculty of apperception. **aperception**, *n.f.* Apperception, clear perception.

apercevable [apɛrsə'vabl], *a.* Perceivable, perceptible.

apercevoir [apɛrsə'vwaːr], *v.t.* (*pres. p.* **apercevant**, *p.p.* **aperçu**) To catch sight of; to perceive, to understand, to comprehend. **s'apercevoir**, *v.r.* To catch sight of oneself; (*de quelque chose*) to remark, to notice, to be aware of; to find out, to discover; to be visible. *Ne pas s'apercevoir de quelque chose*, to overlook, not to notice something; *le phare s'aperçoit de loin*, the lighthouse can be seen from a distance.

aperçu [apɛr'sy], *n.m.* Rapid view, glance or survey; rough estimate or summary; judgment, insight. (*Naut.*) *Signal d'aperçu*, answering pennant.

apéritif [aperi'tif], *a.* (*fem.* **apéritive**) Aperient, appetizing.—*n.m.* (*Med.*) An aperient, a laxative; an appetizer, an aperitif.
apéro, *n.m.* (*colloq.*) = APÉRITIF.
apesanteur [apəzɑ̃'tœ:r], *n.f.* Weightlessness.
apétale [ape'tal], *a.* (*Bot.*) Apetalous.
*****apetissement** [aptis'mɑ̃], *n.m.* Diminution.
*****apetisser,** *v.t.*ˈ To diminish, to make smaller. **s'apetisser,** *v.r.* To grow smaller.
à peu près [apø'prɛ], *n.m.* Approximation, approach; a word roughly standing for another.—*adv.* Nearly, about.
apeuré [apø're], *a.* Frightened, scared.
apex [a'pɛks], *n.m.* Apex.
aphasie [afa'zi], *n.f.* (*Path.*) Aphasia. **aphasique,** *a.* Aphasic—*n.m.* Aphasiac.
aphélie [afe'li], *n.m.* (*Astron.*) Aphelion.
aphérèse [afe'rɛ:z], *n.f.* (*Gram.*) Aphaeresis.
aphidé [afi'de] or **aphidien,** *n.m.* (*Ent.*) Aphis, aphidian, greenfly.
aphone [a'fɔn], *a.* Suffering from aphonia, voiceless. **aphonie,** *n.f.* Aphony, loss of voice.
aphorisme [afɔ'rism], *n.m.* Aphorism. **aphoristique,** *a.* Aphoristic.
aphrodisiaque [afrɔdi'zjak], *a.* and *n.m.* Aphrodisiac.
aphte [aft], *n.m.* Aphtha; (*pl.*) thrush, aphthae. **aphteux,** *a.* (*fem.* **aphteuse**) Aphthous. *Fièvre aphteuse,* foot-and-mouth disease.
aphylle [a'fil], *a.* (*Bot.*) Aphyllous, leafless.
api [a'pi], *n.m.* (*Bot.*) *Pomme d'api,* lady-apple. *Avoir un visage de pomme d'api,* to have cheeks like rosy apples.
à-pic [a'pik], *n.m.* Steep hill, cliff.
apicole [api'kɔl], *a.* Apiarian. **apiculteur,** *n.m.* Bee-keeper. **apiculture,** *n.f.* Apiculture, bee-keeping.
apiquage [api'ka:ʒ], *n.m.* (*Naut.*) Peaking (the yards). **apiquer,** *v.t.* To peak (a yard).
apitoiement [apitwa'mɑ̃], *n.m.* Pity, compassion. **apitoyant,** *a.* (*fem.* **-ante**) Piteous, exciting pity.
apitoyer [apitwa'je], *v.t.* To move to pity, to soften. **s'apitoyer,** *v.r.* To pity. *Elle s'est apitoyée sur votre sort,* she felt sorry for you.
aplaigner [aplɛ'ɲe] or **aplaner** [apla'ne], *v.t.* (*Textiles*) To teazle (cloth). **aplaigneur** or **aplaneur** (*fem.* **-euse**), *n.* Teazler.
aplaner etc. [APLAIGNER].
aplanétique [aplane'tik], *a.* (*Opt.*) Aplanatic.
aplaneur etc. [APLAIGNEUR].
aplanir [apla'ni:r], *v.t.* To smooth, to level, to make even; (*fig.*) to level down or remove (obstacles, difficulties, etc.). *Aplanir le chemin,* to level the road; *aplanir les difficultés,* to smooth away difficulties. **s'aplanir,** *v.r.* To grow easy, smooth, etc. **aplanissement,** *n.m.* Smoothing, levelling, making even; smoothness, evenness. **aplanisseur,** *n.m.* (*fem.* **-euse**) One who smooths, levels, etc.
aplat [a'pla], *n.m.* Flat tint.
aplatir [apla'ti:r], *v.t.* To flatten, to beat flat; (*fig.*) to vanquish, to silence, to floor. **s'aplatir,** *v.r.* To become flat, to be flattened; (*fig.*) to crouch, to cringe. **aplatissement** or **aplatissage,** *n.m.* Flattening, flatness; (*fig.*) humiliation. **aplatisseur,** *n.m.* (*Agric.*) A machine for crushing grain for fodder. **aplatissoir,** *n.m.*, or **aplatissoire,** *n.f.* Hammer or flatting roller for flattening metal.

aplomb [a'plɔ̃], *n.m.* Perpendicularity to the horizon; equilibrium; (*fig.*) assurance, self-command, self-possession, steadiness, coolness; impudence, cheek. *Ce mur tient bien son aplomb,* this wall keeps plumb very well; *cette ligne tombe d'aplomb,* that line falls plumb; *d'aplomb,* perpendicularly, upright; *être d'aplomb,* to stand plumb, upright, steady; (*fig.*) to feel all right; *je ne me sens pas bien d'aplomb,* I feel out of sorts; *les aplombs d'un cheval,* poise of a horse's legs in relation to the ground.
apnée [ap'ne], *n.f.* (*Med.*) Apnoea, suspension of breathing.
apocalypse [apɔka:'lips], *n.f.* Apocalypse, the Book of Revelation; (*fig.*) an obscure allegory etc. *C'est un vrai style d'apocalypse,* it is an utterly obscure style; *cheval de l'Apocalypse,* (*pop.*) sorry jade. **apocalyptique,** *a.* Apocalyptic, obscure.
apocarpé [apɔkar'pe], *a.* (*fem.* **apocarpée**) (*Bot.*) Apocarpous.
apocope [apɔ'kɔp], *n.f.* (*Gram.*) Apocope; **apocopé,** *a.* (*fem.* **apocopée**) Elided. .
apocryphe [apɔ'krif], *a.* Apocryphal, spurious. *n.m. pl. Les Apocryphes,* the Apocrypha,
apocyn [apɔ'sɛ̃], *n.m.* (*Bot.*) Dog bane, apocynum.
apode [a'pɔd], *a.* (*Zool.*) Apodal, footless; (*Ichth.*) without ventral fins.—*n.m.* Apod.
apodictique [apɔdik'tik], *a.* Apodictic, incontestably demonstrated.
apodie [apɔ'di], *n.f.* (*Zool.*) Absence of feet.
apodose [apɔ'do:z], *n.f.* (*Gram. etc.*) Apodosis.
apogée [apɔ'ʒe], *n.m.* Apogee; (*fig.*) acme, height, zenith. *La lune est à son apogée,* the moon is at her apogee.
apographe [apɔ'graf], *n.m.* Transcript, copy (of an original writing).—*a.* Copied or transcribed from an original.
Apollon [apɔ'lɔ̃], *m.* Apollo.
apologétique [apɔlɔʒe'tik], *a.* By way of apology, apologetic, exculpatory.—*n.f.* Apologetics.
apologie [apɔlɔ'ʒi], *n.f.* Apology, vindication, justification. *Faire l'apologie,* to vindicate, to justify. **apologique,** *a.* Apologetic. **apologiste,** *n.m.* Apologist.
apologue [apɔ'lɔg], *n.m.* Apologue, fable.
aponévrose [apɔne'vro:z], *n.f.* (*Anat.*) Aponeurosis. **aponévrotique,** *a.* Aponeurotic.
apophtegme [apɔf'tɛgm], *n.m.* Apophthegm.
apophyge [apɔ'fiʒ], *n.f.* (*Arch.*) The concave curve in a column where it joins the base.
apophyse [apɔ'fi:z], *n.f.* (*Anat., Zool., Bot., etc.*). Process or protuberance (on a bone etc.).
apoplectique [apɔplɛk'tik], *a.* and *n.* Apoplectic.
apoplexie [apɔplɛk'si], *n.f.* Apoplexy. *Apoplexie foudroyante,* instantaneously fatal apoplexy; *attaque d'apoplexie,* (apoplectic) stroke; *être frappé d'apoplexie,* to have an apoplectic fit, to have a stroke.
aposiopèse [apɔsjo'pɛz], *n.f.* Aposiopesis, a stopping short for rhetorical effort.
apostase [APOSTÈME].
apostasie [apɔsta'zi], *n.f.* Apostasy. **apostasier,** *v.i.* To apostatize. **apostat,** *a.* and *n.m.* Apostate.
apostème [apɔ'stɛ:m] or *****apostume,** *n.m.* (*Path.*) An external suppurating tumour, a boil.

aposter [apɔs'te], *v.t.* To place in ambush, to station, to set (spies, assassins, etc.).

apostille [apɔs'ti:j], *n.f.* Marginal note, postscript, footnote; recommendatory note (to urge or back a petition). **apostiller,** *v.t.* To add a postscript or a marginal recommendation. *Il a apostillé ma demande,* he has backed my application with his recommendation.

apostolat [apɔstɔ'la], *n.m.* Apostolate, apostleship; (*fig.*) propagation of a doctrine etc.

apostolique, *a.* Apostolic; papal. *Nonce apostolique,* the papal nuncio. **apostoliquement,** *adv.* Apostolically.

apostrophe [apɔs'trɔf], *n.f.* (*Rhet. and Gram.*) Apostrophe; address; (*fig.*) a reprimand, attack. **apostropher,** *v.t.* To apostrophize, to address; (*fig.*) to reprimand, to fly at.

***apostume** [APOSTÊME].

apothécie [apɔte'si] or **apothèce,** *n.f.* (*Bot.*) Apothecium, shield (of lichen).

apothéose [apɔte'o:z], *n.f.* Apotheosis, deification. **apothéoser,** *v.t.* To apotheosize, to deify.

apothicaire [apɔti'kɛ:r], *n.m.* Apothecary. *Un mémoire d'apothicaire,* an exorbitant bill.

apôtre [a'po:tr], *n.m.* Apostle; (*fig.*) advocate, leader or preacher of a cause. *Faire le bon apôtre,* to pretend to be well-intentioned.

apozème [apɔ'zɛ:m], *n.m.* (*Med.*) Decoction.

apparaître [apa'rɛ:tr], *v.i.* irr. (*pres.p.* **apparaissant,** *p.p.* **apparu,** *conjugated like* CONNAÎTRE) To appear, to become visible; to be evident or manifest; *to seem.

apparat [apa'ra], *n.m.* Pomp, show, ostentation, parade. *Un discours d'apparat,* a set speech; *dîner d'apparat,* a banquet.

apparaux [apa'ro], *n.m.* (*used only in pl.*) (*Naut.*) Gear, tackle, outfit, etc.

appareil [apa'rɛ:j], *n.m.* Formal preparation, pomp, display; appearance, show; apparatus, appliances, machinery, paraphernalia; (*Arch.*) structural disposition of stones etc. (in a building, especially arches, vaults, domes, etc.); (*Surg.*) dressing; (*Anat.*) assemblage of organs engaged in a certain function. *Appareil (photographique),* camera; *appareil de cinéma,* cine-camera; *appareil instantané,* snapshot camera; *appareil critique,* critical apparatus; *appareil de pêche,* fishing tackle. *Qui est à l'appareil?* Who is speaking? *lever l'appareil,* to take off the dressing; *mettre le premier appareil,* to give a wound its first dressing; *une assise de haut appareil,* a layer of large stones.

appareillage [apareɛ'ja:z], *n.m.* Installation; (*Naut.*) act of getting under sail, weighing.

appareillement [apareɛj'mã], *n.m.* Coupling, yoking; pairing (for breeding). *L'appareillement des bœufs,* the yoking of oxen.

appareiller [apareɛ'je], *v.t.* To install equipment; to match; to pair, to couple (animals); (*Arch.*) to mark (stones) as they are to be dressed.—*v.i.* To get under way, to weigh anchor. **s'appareiller,** *v.r.* To pair (of birds).

appareilleur [apareɛ'jœ:r], *n.m.* (*Building*) Workman who marks stones as they are to be dressed. *Appareilleur à gaz,* gas-fitter.

apparement [apara'mã], *adv.* Apparently.

apparence [apa'rã:s], *n.f.* Appearance, look, semblance, likelihood, probability. *En*

apparence, seemingly, apparently, outwardly; *sauver les apparences,* to keep up appearances; *selon toute apparence,* in all probability, to all appearances. **apparent,** *a.* (*fem.* **apparente**) Visible, prominent; *specious.

apparentage [aparã'ta:ʒ], *n.m.* Alliance, connexion.

apparenté [aparã'te], *a.* (*fem.* **-ée**) Related. *Bien apparenté,* well connected.

apparentement [aparã'tmã], *n.m.* Political alliance.

apparenter [aparã'te], *v.t.* To ally, to connect by marriage. **s'apparenter,** *v.r.* To ally oneself (by marriage).

appariement or **appariment** [apari'mã], *n.m.* Pairing, matching; coupling, mating. *Appariement d'écoles,* school consolidation. **apparier,** *v.t.* To assort by pairs, to pair (birds etc.), to match (horses, gloves, etc.). **s'apparier,** *v.r.* To couple, to pair.

appariteur [apari'tœ:r], *n.m.* Apparitor; usher, (*Univ.*) beadle.

apparition [apari'sjɔ̃], *n.f.* Apparition, sudden appearance, advent; a short stay or sojourn; phantom, ghost. *Apparition d'anges,* a vision of angels.

apparoir [apa'rwa:r], *v.i.*(*Law, used only in inf. and 3rd sing. pres.*) To appear, to be evident. *Comme il appert,* as it appears; *faire apparoir,* to show.

appartement [aparta'mã], *n.m.* A suite of rooms, a flat. *Appartement meublé,* furnished apartments or flat; *pièce (d'un appartement),* room, apartment.

appartenances [apartə'nã:s], *n.f.* (*used in pl.*) Appurtenances. **appartenant,** *a.* (*fem.* **appartenante**) Belonging, appertaining; *pres.p.* [*see foll.*].

appartenir [apartə'ni:r], *v.i.* irr. (*pres.p.* **appartenant,** *p.p.* **appartenu**) To belong, to appertain; to relate, to pertain, to concern; to behoove,to be the right, privilege, duty, etc. of (*à*). *Il appartient,* (*v.impers.*) it becomes; it is meet or fit; it is the duty of, it behooves,it concerns. *Ainsi qu'il appartiendra,* as it shall seem fit; *à tous ceux qu'il appartiendra,* to whom it may concern. **s'appartenir,** *v.r.* To be master of one's own actions, to be free.

appartenu, *p.p.* (*fem.* **appartenue**) [*see prec.*].

apparu, *p.p.* (*fem.* **apparue**) [APPARAÎTRE].

appas [a'pɑ], *n.m.* *pl.* Feminine charms, attractions.

appât [a'pɑ], *n.m.* Bait; lure, allurement, enticement; attraction. *C'est un trop vieux poisson pour mordre à l'appât,* he is too downy a bird to swallow that. **appâter,** *v.t.* To attract with a bait, to allure; to fatten (fowls etc.).

appauvrir [apo'vri:r], *v.t.* To impoverish. **s'appauvrir,** *v.r.* To grow poor, to become impoverished. **appauvrissement,** *n.m.* Impoverishment.

appeau [a'po], *n.m.* Bird-call; decoy-bird.

appel [a'pɛl], *n.m.* Appeal, call, summons; (*Mil.*) roll-call, muster, the assembly (sounded on the drum); summoning of conscripts to the colours; (*Law*) appeal to a higher court; (*Fin.*) call (on shareholders). *Appel nominal,* (*Parl.*) call of the House; *appel d'air,* intake of air; *battre or sonner l'appel* (*Mil.*), to sound the fall-in;

faire *l'appel*, to call the roll; *manquer à l'appel*, to be absent from roll-call; *répondre à l'appel*, to answer to one's name; *interjeter appel*, to lodge an appeal; *faire un appel de fonds*, to make a call (for money); *jugement sans appel*, final judgment.

appelable [a′plabl], *a.* (*Law*) Appealable. **appelant**, *a.* (*fem.* **-ante**) (*Law*) Appellant; (*Fowling*) decoy-bird.

appelé [ap′le], *a.* (*fem.* **appelée**) Called up.— *n.m.* A soldier called up for service. *Beaucoup d'appelés et peu d'élus*, many are called but few are chosen.

appeler [ap′le], *v.t. irr.* To call, to name in order to bring, to send for; to call over; to call up, to call together; to summon, to cite, to invoke, to call upon, to invite; to name, to term, to give a name to; to lure (birds) by imitating their call; to challenge, to defy. *Appeler au téléphone*, to ring up; *appeler en duel*, to call out; *appeler les choses par leur nom*, to call, a spade a spade; *appeler un médecin*, to call in a physician; *comment appelez-vous cela?* what do you call that? *voilà ce que j'appelle pleuvoir*, that is rain with a vengeance.—*v.i.* To appeal (to a higher court). *J'en appelle à votre honneur*, I appeal to your honour. **s'appeler**, *v.r.* To be called, to call oneself. *Comment s'appelle cet homme-là?* what is that man's name?

appeleur [a′plœːr], *n.m.* Decoy-bird.

appellatif [apela′tif], *a.* (*fem.* **appellative**) (*Gram.*) Appellative. **appellation**, *n.f.* *Appealing, calling; denunciation, appellation; mode of calling over (the letters of the alphabet); trade name. *Appellation contrôlée*, registered trade-name.

appendice [apɛ̃′dis], *n.m.* Appendix, appendage, addition, supplementary part. *L'appendice vermiculaire*, the vermiform appendix.

appendicite, *n.f.* (*Path.*) Appendicitis. **appendiculaire**, *a.* (*Nat. Hist.*) Like an appendix. **appendicule**, *n.m.* A small appendix.

appendre [a′pɑ̃ːdr], *v.t.* To hang up, to suspend, to attach. **appension**, *n.f.* (*Surg.*) Suspension of a limb by means of a sling.

appentis [apɑ̃′ti], *n.m.* Shed, penthouse, lean-to.

appert [APPAROIR].

appesantir [apəzɑ̃′tiːr], *v.t.* To make heavy, to weigh down; to render less active or agile; (*fig.*) to make dull. *Appesantir le joug*, to make the yoke (or tyranny) heavier; *Dieu a appesanti sa main sur ce peuple*, the hand of God fell heavily upon that people. **s'appesantir**, *v.r.* To grow heavy and dull, to be weighed down, to lie heavy; to dwell upon, to expatiate (*sur*). **appesantissement**, *n.m* Heaviness, dullness.

appétence [ape′tɑ̃ːs], *n.f.* Appetency, longing, covetousness, craving.

***appéter** [ape′te], *v.t.* To desire, to crave for, to covet. **appétissant**, *a.* (*fem.* **appétissante**) Desirable, appetizing, tempting; dainty, delicious.

appétit [ape′ti], *n.m.* Appetite, desire, sensuous craving (*usu. in pl.*); appetite (for food), hunger; (*fig.*) inclination, taste, stomach. *Appétit de cheval*, ravenous appetite; *bon appétit!* I wish you a good appetite; *de bon appétit*, heartily; *être sans* appétit, to have no appetite; *l'appétit vient en mangeant*, the more one has the more one wants; *pain dérobé réveille l'appétit*, stolen joys are sweet.

applaudir [aplo′diːr], *v.t.* To clap the hands, to applaud; to praise, to commend, to approve.—*v.i.* To clap the hands, to applaud (*à*). *Je vous applaudis de vous être conduit si prudemment*, I commend you for having acted so prudently. **s'applaudir**, *v.r.* To boast, to glory (in a thing); to congratulate oneself (*de*), to rejoice (*de*). *Il s'applaudit lui-même*, he admires himself. **applaudissement**, *n.m.* (usually *pl.*) Applause, public praise, eulogy; cheering. *Applaudissements prolongés*, great cheering; *salve d'applaudissements*, round of applause or cheering. **applaudisseur**, *n.m.* One who applauds, *esp.* for pay.

applicabilité [aplikabili′te], *n.f.* Applicability, appositeness. **applicable**, *a.* Applicable, apposite, relevant, suitable.

applicage [apli′kaːʒ], *n.m.* Application, applying (of an ornament etc.).

application [aplika′sjɔ̃], *n.f.* Application, applying, laying or fixing (something on); employment (of a sum of money); infliction (of a penalty); attention, care, diligence, sedulousness; appliqué lace; application (of a proverb etc.); adaptation (of a method etc.); practical application (as opposed to theory). *Application d'Angleterre*, Honiton lace; *avec application*, sedulously; *bras d'application*, bracket; *d'application*, practical, feasible; *dentelle d'application*, lace having the decoration sewn to the foundation; *école d'application*, school of (military, naval) instruction; *sans application déterminée*, unappropriated.

applique [a′plik], *n.f.* Ornamental accessories, decoration, trimmings; a candelabrum or bracket fixed to a wall.

appliqué [apli′ke], *a.* (*fem.* **-ée**) Studious. *Sciences appliquées*, applied sciences.

appliquer [apli′ke], *v.t.* To apply (*à*), to lay or fasten on; to hit the mark; to give, to bestow; to apply (one's mind); to adapt, to employ, to use for a practical purpose; to inflict, to impose (a penalty etc.). *Appliquer des ventouses*, (*Surg.*) to cup; *appliquer mal à propos*, to misapply; *appliquer un soufflet*, to give a slap or box on the ear. **s'appliquer**, *v.r.* To apply oneself, to work hard.

appliqueuse [apli′køz], *n.f.* Woman who does appliqué work, on lace or tulle.

appoggiature or **appoggiatura** [apɔʒja′tyːr], *n.f.* (*Mus.*) Appoggiatura.

appoint [a′pwɛ̃], *n.m.* Money paying off an account, balance, change, odd money completing a sum. *Faire l'appoint*, to pay the difference; to make up the even money.

appointage [apwɛ̃′taːʒ], *n.m.* Making pointed.

appointements [apwɛ̃′mɑ̃], *n.m.* (*pl.*) Fixed salary (of employee); emoluments; (*Eccles.*) stipend.—*Toucher ses appointements*, to draw one's salary.

appointé [apwɛ̃′te], *a.* (*fem.* **-ée**) Receiving a salary; (*Her.*) converging towards a point. *Commis appointé*, salaried clerk.

appointer (1) [apwɛ̃′te], *v.t.* To give a salary to; *(*Law*) to arrange or settle (a difference etc.).

appointer (2) [apwɛ̃'te], *v.t.* To sharpen to a point, to point.

appointeur [apwɛ̃'tœːr], *n.* and *a.* (*fem.* **-euse**) Who points or sharpens.

appointir [apwɛ̃'tiːr], *v.t.* To sharpen, to point.

appontement [apɔ̃t'mã], *n.m.* (*Naut.*) Bridge-like structure for loading vessels; (wooden) wharf or pier, landing-stage.

apport [a'pɔːr], *n.m.* Property brought by a husband or wife into the common stock; a shareholder's contribution to the assets of a company; alluvial deposits.

apporter [apɔr'te], *v.t.* To bring; to furnish, to supply; to bring to bear, to employ (trouble, pains, etc.); to cause, to produce, to bring about; to cite, to allege, to adduce; to announce, to communicate (news etc.). *Apporter de bonnes raisons,* to adduce good reasons; *apporter de la précaution,* to use precaution; *apporter des soins à,* to bestow care upon; *graines apportées par le vent,* seeds borne on the wind.

apposer [apo'ze], *v.t.* To set, to put, to affix; to insert (a clause etc.). *Apposer sa signature,* to sign.

apposition, *n.f.* Setting, putting, affixture; (*Gram.*) apposition. *Faire l'apposition des scellés,* to affix the seals.

appréciable [apre'sjabl], *a.* Appreciable, perceptible. **appréciateur,** *a.* (*fem.* **-trice**) One who appreciates; valuer, appraiser, rater. **appréciatif,** *a.* (*fem.* **-ive**) Appreciative, denoting the value of. *État or devis appréciatif,* estimate; (*Theol.*) discerning. **appréciation,** *n.f.* Appreciation, valuation, estimation; rise in value.

apprécier [apre'sje], *v.t.* To value, to estimate, to appraise, to judge; to appreciate, to esteem.

appréhender [apreã'de], *v.t.* To arrest, to apprehend; to be apprehensive of, to fear. *Appréhender au corps,* to arrest; *j'appréhende qu'il n'en soit ainsi,* I am afraid it will be so; *j'appréhende qu'il n'en soit pas ainsi,* I am afraid that it may not turn out so. **appréhensible,** *a.* Apprehensible, comprehensible.

appréhensif, *a.* (*fem.* **-ive**) Apprehensive, anxious, timid. **appréhension,** *n.f.* Apprehension, fear, dread; perception, comprehension. *Avoir des appréhensions,* to be full of apprehension.

apprenant, *pres.p.* [see *foll.*].

apprendre [a'prãːdr], *v.t. irr.* (*conjugated like* PRENDRE) To learn, to acquire (science etc.), to study; to hear of, to be informed of; to acquire (a habit etc.), to give information, to inform; to teach, to impart knowledge of (a subject). *Apprendre à quelqu'un l'art de se taire,* to teach one to keep silent; *apprendre par cœur,* to learn by heart; *faire apprendre un métier à un enfant,* to put a child to a trade; *il m'a appris l'algèbre,* he taught me algebra; *je l'ai appris de bonne part,* I have it from good authority; *je lui apprendrai qui je suis,* I will let him know who I am; *ça lui apprendra,* it serves him right. **s'apprendre,** *v.r.* To teach oneself; to be learned, to be conveyed (of news etc.). *Les malheurs s'apprennent vite,* ill news flies fast. **appris,** *a.* (*fem.* **-ise**) *Bien appris, mal appris,* well bred, ill bred; *c'est un mal appris,* he is a boor.

apprenti [aprã'ti], *a.* (*fem.* **apprentie**) Apprenticed, articled.—*n.* Apprentice; (*fig.*) novice, tyro. **apprentissage,** *n.m.* Apprenticeship; trial, experiment. *Brevet d'apprentissage,* apprentice's indenture; *être en apprentissage,* to be an apprentice; *faire son apprentissage,* to serve one's apprenticeship; *mettre en apprentissage,* to apprentice, to article; *sortir d'apprentissage,* to finish one's time.

apprêt [a'prɛ], *n.m.* Preparation; cooking, dressing (of food); manner of preparing cloth, silk, lace, etc.; the substance used in this process; (*Paint.*) the preparation applied to a surface before painting; (*fig.*) affectation (of style, language, etc.); (*pl.*) preparations. *Faire de grands apprêts,* to make great preparations; *sans apprêt,* unstudied (of style). **apprêtage,** *n.m.* Dressing, application of the preliminary preparation to cloth, silk, etc. **apprêté,** *a.* (*fem.* **apprêtée**) Studied, affected, stiff. *Des manières apprêtées,* affected manners.

apprêter [aprɛ'te], *v.t.* To prepare, to get ready; to dress, to cook; to apply the *apprêts* [see *prec.*] to. *Apprêter un chapeau,* to trim a hat.—*v.i. Apprêter à dîner,* to prepare dinner. **s'apprêter,** *v.r.* To prepare oneself, to get ready, to prepare for oneself. *S'apprêter de grands embarras,* to bring trouble on oneself.

apprêteur, *a.* and *n.* (*fem.* **-euse**) Dresser, finisher.—*n.f.* Hat-trimmer.

appris, *p.p.* (*fem.* **apprise**) [APPRENDRE].

apprivoisable [aprivwa'zabl], *a.* Tamable. **apprivoisement,** *n.m.* Taming.

apprivoisé [aprivwa'ze], *a.* (*fem.* **-ée**) Tame.

apprivoiser [aprivwa'ze], *v.t.* To tame (animals); to win (people) over, to make tractable. **s'apprivoiser,** *v.r.* To become familiar or accustomed; to grow tame (of animals); to become sociable, to lose one's shyness (of persons). **apprivoiseur,** *a.* (*fem.* **apprivoiseuse**) That tames.—*n.* A tamer.

approbateur [aprɔba'tœːr], *a.* (*fem.* **-trice**) That approves.—*n.* Approver, applauder. **approbatif,** *a.* (*fem.* **-tive**) Approbatory. *Geste approbatif,* nod of approbation. **approbation,** *n.f.* Approbation, consent, approval. *Incliner la tête en signe d'approbation,* to nod assent. **approbativement,** *adv.* Approvingly, with approbation.

approchable [aprɔ'ʃabl], *a.* Approachable, easy of access. **approchant** (1), *a.* (*fem.* **approchante**) Like, much the same, not very different, something like, approximate, bordering on. **approchant** (2), *prep.* *About, approximately. Il est approchant de midi,* it is nearly twelve o'clock.

approche [a'prɔʃ], *n.f.* Approach, act of approaching, coming, advance, nearness, proximity; (*pl.*) approaches, access; (*Print.*) space, closing up. *Travaux d'approche,* work of demolition and entrenchment by which besiegers advance, trench-work.

approché [aprɔ'ʃe], *a.* (*fem.* **-ée**) Approximate (figure).

approcher [aprɔ'ʃe], *v.t.* To bring, put, or draw near or nearer; to come near or nearer; to approach, come near to (someone). *Approchez la table du feu,* draw the table near the fire.—*v.i.* To approach, to draw near, to come near, to be something like, to be nearly. *Approcher du but*, to come near the mark; *ceci n'en approche pas*, this does not come near it; *il me fit approcher de lui*, he made me come near him. **s'approcher**, *v.r.* To approach, to advance. *Approchez-vous du feu*, draw near the fire.

approfondir [aprɔfɔ̃'diːr], *v.t.* To deepen, to make deeper; to examine thoroughly, to investigate, to fathom. *Approfondir une question*, to go to the heart of the matter; *étude approfondie*, thorough study. **s'approfondir**, *v.r.* To become deeper. **approfondissement**, *n.m.* Deepening; fathoming; thorough investigation or research.

appropriable [aprɔpri'abl], *a.* Assumable. **appropriation**, *n.f.* Adaptation, assimilation; appropriation.

approprié [aprɔpri'e], *a.* (*fem.* **-ée**) Suitable. **approprier** [aprɔpri'e], *v.t.* To make appropriate, to accommodate, to adapt; to clean, to make neat, to tidy, etc.; to put in a proper condition; to make suitable, to suit, to fit (style to subject etc.). *Approprier son langage aux circonstances*, to adapt one's language to circumstances; *approprier une chambre*, to make a room tidy. **s'approprier** (1), *v.r.* To appropriate a thing to oneself. **s'approprier** (2), *v.r.* To conform, to adapt oneself.

approuver [apru've], *v.t.* To sanction, to consent to, to ratify, to authorize; to approve, to approve of; to pass (accounts). *Approuvé l'écriture ci-dessus*, examined and found correct; *lu et approuvé*, read and approved.

approvisionnement [aprɔvizjɔn'mã], *n.m.* Victualling supply; (*Am.*) provisions, stock. *Vaisseau d'approvisionnement*, victualling-ship. **approvisionner**, *v.t.* To supply with necessaries, to victual, to stock; to charge a rifle magazine. **s'approvisionner**, *v.r.* To supply oneself; to lay in supplies. **approvisionneur**, *n.m.* (*fem.* **-euse**) Caterer, purveyor.

approximatif [aprɔksima'tif], *a.* (*fem.* **-ive**) Approximate. **approximation**, *n.f.* Approximation, rough estimate, conjecture. **approximativement**, *adv.* Approximately, at a rough guess.

appui [a'pɥi], *n.m.* Support, prop, stay; any kind of mechanical support, as buttress, rail, handrail, sill (of windows); (*Mech.*) fulcrum; (*fig.*) corroboration, help, succour; (*Gram.*) stress. *À hauteur d'appui*, breast-high; *à l'appui de*, in support of, in confirmation of; *ce cheval a l'appui bon*, that horse is soft-mouthed; *il est l'appui des malheureux*, he is the support of the unfortunate; *point d'appui*, point of support, prop, fulcrum, base; *sans appui*, helpless, friendless. **appui-main**, *n.m.* (*pl.* **appuis-main**) Painter's maulstick or hand-rest. **appui-tête**, *n.m.* (*pl.* **appuis-tête**) Head-rest.

appuyer [apɥi'je], *v.t. irr.* To hold up by means of a prop, stay, or other support, to support; to lean (something against a wall etc.); (*fig.*) to second, to back up, to uphold, to stand by, to reinforce.—*v.i.* To weigh upon, to lay stress (*sur*); (*fig.*) to insist. *Appuyer les chiens*, to urge on the hounds; *appuyer à droite*, to bear to the right; *appuyer sur un mot*, to lay a stress on a word; *appuyer sur un passage*, to dwell upon a passage; *appuyer*

une maison contre un coteau, to build a house against a hill; *il m'a promis d'appuyer mon placet*, he has promised to back my petition; *son droit est appuyé sur de bons titres*, his claim is founded on just grounds. **s'appuyer**, *v.r.* To lean, to rest, to recline (*sur*); to rely upon, to depend (*sur*); to lay stress or a stress on, to dwell (*sur*). *Appuyez-vous sur moi*, lean upon me; *s'appuyer sur un roseau*, (*fig.*) to trust to a broken reed.

âpre [ɑːpr], *a.* Hard, rough, harsh, rugged; sharp, tart, sour; bitter, biting, bleak, raw; grating (of sound); (*fig.*) austere, rigid, severe; peevish, crabbed; violent, eager (in pursuit of something). *Âpre à la curée*, out for the kill (of animals); (*fig.*) on the make (of persons); *âpre à se venger*, eager for revenge; *âpre au gain*, greedy of gain; *âpre au jeu*, eager for play (a born gambler); *chemin âpre et raboteux*, rough, rugged way. **âprement**, *adv.* Harshly, roughly; peevishly, crabbedly; violently, eagerly.

après [a'prɛ], *prep.* After, behind (in time, order, etc.); next to; in pursuit of. *Après coup*, when a thing is done, too late; *après lui, il faut tirer l'échelle*, no one can come after him; *après quoi*, after or upon which; *après tout*, after all; *il est toujours après moi*, he is always after me (always teasing, persecuting, scolding me); *sa maison vient après la vôtre*, his house is next to yours; *tout le monde crie après lui*, everybody cries out against him; *d'après*, after, from, according to, following; *paysage d'après Poussin*, landscape after Poussin; *peindre d'après nature*, to paint from nature; *d'après ma montre il est 6 heures*, by my watch it is six.—*adv.* Afterwards, later. *Et après?* (*ellipt.*) what next, what then? so what?—*conj. Après que*, after, when; *après que je l'eus vu*, when I had seen him; *après que vous aurez fini*, after you have done.

après-demain [apred'mɛ̃], *adv.* The day after tomorrow. **après-dîner**, *n.m.* (*pl.* **après-dîners**) After dinner. **après-guerre** [aprɛ'gɛr], *n.m.* The post-war period or conditions. **après-midi**, *n.m.* or *f. inv.* Afternoon.

âpreté [aprɑ'te], *n.f.* Harshness, tartness, sharpness; roughness, ruggedness; (*fig.*) acrimony, asperity; eagerness; keenness. *Âpreté à l'argent*, lust for gold.

à-propos [aprɔ'po], *n.m.* Aptness, suitability.

apside [ap'sid], *n.f.* (*Arch.*) Apse; (*Astron.*) apsis.

apte [apt], *a.* Apt, fit, proper, suitable. *Peu apte*, unfit; unsuitable; (boy) poorly gifted mentally.

aptère [ap'tɛːr], *a.* Apterous, wingless. **aptéryx**, *n.m.* Apteryx; kiwi.

aptitude [apti'tyd], *n.f.* Aptitude, natural disposition or capacity (for); (*Law*) capacity (to receive a legacy etc.). *Avoir de l'aptitude pour*, to have a genius or turn for; *certificat d'aptitude*, teacher's certificate.

apurement [apyr'mã], *n.m.* Verification or audit (of accounts). **apurer**, *v.t.* To verify, to audit.

apyre [a'piːr], *a.* Unalterable by fire, infusible, fireproof, incombustible.

apyrétique [apire'tik], *a.* Apyretic. **apyrexie**, *n.f.* Apyrexy.

aquafortiste [akwafɔr'tist], *n.* Etcher.

aquaplane [akwa'plan], *n.f.* Surf-board. *Faire de l'aquaplane*, to go surf-riding.

aquarelle [akwa'rɛl], *n.f.* Painting in water-colours, aquarelle. **aquarelliste**, *n.m.* Painter in water-colours.

aquarium [akwa'rjɔm], *n.m.* Aquarium.

aquatile [akwa'til], *a.* (*Bot.*) Aquatic.

aqua-tinta [akwatɛ̃'ta] or **aquatinte**, *n.f.* Aquatint. **aqua-tintiste** or **aquatintiste**, *n.* An engraver of aquatint.

aquatique [akwa'tik], *a.* Aquatic.

aqueduc [akə'dyk], *n.m.* Aqueduct, conduit; (*Anat.*) duct.

aqueux [a'kø], *a.* (*fem.* **-euse**) Aqueous, watery.

aquicole [akyi'kɔl], *a.* Pertaining to *aquiculture*; aquatic. **aquiculteur**, *n.m.* One practising *aquiculture*. **aquiculture**, *n.f.* Water-culture, or the culture of aquatic plants and animals.

aquifère [akyi'fɛːr], *a.* (*Geol.*) Aquiferous.

aquilin [aki'lɛ̃], *a.* (*fem.* **aquiline**) Aquiline, curved, hooked, Roman (of noses etc.).

aquilon [aki'lɔ̃], *n.m.* North wind, northerly gale, cold blast.

aquitanien [akita'njɛ̃], *n.m.* (*Geol.*) A stage of the Tertiary period strongly displayed in Aquitaine.

aquosité [akɔzi'te], *n.f.* Aquosity.

ara [a'ra], *n.m.* (*Orn.*) Ara, macaw.

araba [ara'ba], *n.f.* A small two-wheeled Algerian cart.

arabe [a'rab], *a.* Arabic, Arabian.—*n.m.* Arabic (language).—*n.* (**Arabe**) Arab, Arabian; (*17th-century usage*) miser, screw, usurer.

arabesque, *a.* Arabesque, Arabian.—*n.f.* Arabesque.

arabette [ara'bet], *n.f.* (*Bot.*) Araby, wall-cress.

Arabie [ara'bi], *f.* Arabia. *Arabie Séoudite* Saudi Arabia.

arabique, *a.* Arabic. *Le golfe arabique*, the Arabian gulf; *gomme arabique*, gum arabic.

arabisant, *n.m.* (*fem.* **-ante**) Arabic scholar, arabist.

arable [a'rabl], *a.* Arable, tillable.

arachide [ara'ʃid], *n.f.* Pea-nut, ground-nut.

arachnéen [arakne'ɛ̃], *a.* (*fem.* **arachnéenne**) Arachnidean, pertaining to spiders.

arachnide, *n.m.* (*Zool.*) Arachnid.

arachnoïde [araknɔ'id], *n.f.* (*Anat.*) The arachnoid (membrane). **arachnoïdien** [araknɔi'djɛ̃], *a.* (*fem.* **-ienne**) (*Anat.*) Arachnoïd; (*Bot.*) cobweb-like, filamentous.

arack or **arac** [a'rak], *n.m.* Arrack.

araignée [are'ɲe], *n.f.* Spider; a spider-like object, implement, part, etc., a branched grapnel used for recovering buckets from wells, a form of net (for fish or for birds); spider-well; (*Mil.*) a series of branching galleries in a mine; (*Naut.*) crowfoot. *Araignée de mer*, spider crab; *j'en ai horreur comme d'une araignée*, (*colloq.*) I hate it as I do sin; *ôter les araignées*, to sweep the cobwebs away; *pattes d'araignée*, spider's legs, scrawling handwriting; *toile d'araignée*, cobweb, spider-work; (*colloq.*) *avoir une araignée dans le plafond*, to be cracked, to have a screw loose.

araire [a'rɛːr], *n.m.* Swing-plough.

araméen [arame'ɛ̃], *a.* (*fem.* **araméenne**) Aramaean.

aramon [ara'mɔ̃], *n.m.* Cheap red wine.

aranéeux [arane'ø], *a.* (*fem.* **aranéeuse**) Cob-webby. **aranéiforme**, *a.* Araneiform, spider-like.

arasement [araz'mã], *n.m.* Levelling, making even. **araser**, *v.t.* To level (a wall, a building, etc.); to saw off, to make even.

arases [a'raz], *n.f. pl.* (*Build.*) Stones put in to make the courses level, also called *pierres d'arases*.

aratoire [ara'twaːr], *a.* Pertaining to farming. *Instruments aratoires*, implements of husbandry.

araucaria [aroka'rja], *n.m.* (*Bot.*) Araucaria, monkey-puzzle.

arbalète [arba'lɛt], *n.f.* Arbalest, cross-bow; a trap (for dormice etc.). *Arbalète à jalet*, a stone-bow; *attelage en arbalète*, unicorn team; *cheval en arbalète*, the front horse of a unicorn team.

arbalétée, *n.f.* Cross-bow-shot (distance).

arbalétrier, *n.m.* Cross-bowman; (*Carp.*) principal rafters of a roof; strut (of mine); (*Orn.*) (black) swift. **arbalétrière** or **arbalétière**, *n.f.* Loophole (for cross-bows).

arbicot [arbi'ko] or **arbi**, *n.m.* (*pop.*) Arab, Algerian.

arbitrage [arbi'traːʒ], *n.m.* Arbitration; (*Banking*) arbitrage.

arbitraire [arbi'trɛːr], *a.* Arbitrary; absolute, despotic.—*n.m.* Arbitrariness. **arbitrairement**, *adv.* Arbitrarily; despotically.

arbitral [arbi'tral], *a.* (*fem.* **arbitrale**, *pl.* **arbitraux**) By arbitration; composed of arbitrators (of a tribunal etc.). **arbitralement**, *adv.* By arbitration.

arbitre [ar'bitr], *n.m.* Arbitrator, umpire, referee; arbiter, disposer. *Libre* or *franc arbitre*, free will; (*Ftb.*) *arbitre de touche*, linesman. **arbitrer**, *v.t.* To arbitrate, to judge, to settle (a dispute etc.), to referee or umpire (a match).

arborer [arbɔ're], *v.t.* To put up, to hoist, to unfurl (a flag or as a flag); (*fig.*) to put on. *Arborer l'étendard de la révolte*, to raise the standard of rebellion; *arborer un pavillon*, to hoist a flag; (*colloq.*) *arborer une cravate voyante*, to sport a loud necktie.

arborescence [arbɔrɛ'sãːs], *n.f.* Arborescence.

arborescent, *a.* (*fem.* **-ente**) Arborescent.

arboricole [arbɔri'kɔl], *a.* (*Zool.*) Living in trees.

arboriculteur [arbɔrikyl'tœːr], *n.m.* Arboriculturist. **arboriculture**, *n.f.* Arboriculture.

arborisation [arbɔriza'sjɔ̃], *n.f.* Arborization.

arborisé, *a.* (*fem.* **-ée**) Having tree-like markings. *Pierres arborisées*, arborized stones.

arboriser [arbɔri'ze], *v.t.* To cultivate trees.

arboriste [ARBORICULTEUR].

arbouse [ar'buːz], *n.f.* Arbutus-berry.

arbousier, *n.m.* Strawberry-tree, *Arbutus unedo*.

arbre [arbr], *n.m.* Tree; (*fig.*) anything resembling this (as a genealogical tree); (*Mach.*) arbor, shaft, spindle, axle-tree; (*Naut.*) mast. *Arbre de plein vent*, standard; *arbre en buisson*, bush; *arbre en espalier*, wall-tree; *arbre fruitier*, fruit-tree; *arbre vert*, evergreen; *entre l'arbre et l'écorce il ne faut pas mettre le doigt*, leave family quarrels severely alone; *grimper sur un arbre*, to climb a tree; *faire monter quelqu'un à l'arbre*, to pull someone's leg; *faire l'arbre fourchu*, to walk on one's hands; *se tenir au gros de l'arbre*, to side with the majority; *l'arbre ne tombe pas du premier coup*, Rome was not built in a day; *tel arbre tel fruit*, a tree is known by its fruits; *l'arbre de la Croix*, the Rood; *arbre de Noël*, Christmas-tree; *arbre de vie*, the tree of life; *arbre généalogique*, genealogical tree. (*Motor.*) *Arbre moteur*, mainshaft; *arbre coudé*, crankshaft; *arbre à cames*, camshaft. (*Naut.*) *Arbre de mestre*, mainmast.

arbreux [ar′brø], *a.* (*fem.* **-euse**) Tree-clad.

arbrisseau [arbri′so], *n.m.* Shrubby tree.

arbuste [ar′byst], *n.m.* Bush, shrub.

arc [ark], *n.m.* Bow, long-bow; (*Arch.*) arch; (*Geom., Phys.*, etc.) arc. *Tir à l'arc*, archery; *à portée d'arc*, within bow-shot; *avoir plusieurs cordes à son arc*, to have more than one string to one's bow; *bander un arc* or *tirer de l'arc*, to draw the bow; *corde de l'arc*, bow-string; *débander* or *détendre l'arc*, to unbend the bow; (*fig.*) to relax one's mind. *Arc en ogive*, pointed arch; *arc de triomphe*, triumphal arch; *arc-doubleau* (*pl. arcs-doubleaux*), principal rib or arch of a vault; *arc en plein cintre*, semi-circular arch; *lampe à arc*, arc lamp.

arcade [ar′kad], *n.f.* Arch-shaped opening; (*pl.*) arcade; (*Anat.*) a part shaped in an arc.

Arcadie [arka′di], *f.* Arcadia.

arcanes [ar′kan], *n.m. pl.* Secrets, mysteries.

arcanne [ar′kan], *n.f.* Diluted red chalk for marking on wood, ruddle.

arcanseur [arkɑ̃′sœr], *n.m.* Pinch-bar.

arcanson [arkɑ̃′sɔ̃], *n.m.* Colophony, a dark resin obtained from turpentine.

arcasse [ar′kas], *n.f.* (*Naut.*) Stern-frame of a wooden ship. *Arcasse d'une poulie*, pulley block.

arcature [arka′ty:r], *n.f.* (*Arch.*) Ornamental arcade or blind arcade.

arc-boutant [arbu′tɑ̃], *n.m.* (*pl.* **arcs-boutants**) (*fig.*) Buttress, arched flying buttress; supporter, pillar.

arc-bouter, *v.t.* To strengthen by a flying buttress; (*fig.*) to support, to buttress. **s'arc-bouter**, *v.r.* To stand or hold oneself firmly, to lean; to set oneself against something.

arc-doubleau [ardu′blo], *n.m.* (*pl.* **arcs-doubleaux**) Groin (of a vault).

arceau [ar′so], *n.m.* Curved part of a vault or arch; anything shaped like an arch; (*Sculp.*) trefoil ornament; (croquet) hoop.

arc-en-ciel [arkɑ̃′sjɛl], *n.m.* (*pl.* **arcs-en-ciel**) Rainbow.

archaïque [arka′ik], *a.* Archaic. **archaïsme**, *n.m.* Archaism, obsolete word, etc. **archaïste**, *n.* Archaist.

archal [ar′ʃal], *n.m.* Brass (used only in *fil d'archal*, brass wire).

archange [ar′kɑ̃:ʒ], *n.m.* Archangel. **archangélique**, *a.* Archangelical.

arche (1) [arʃ], *n.f.* Arch (of a bridge).

arche (2) [arʃ], *n.f.* Ark. *C'est l'arche sainte*, (*fig.*) it is forbidden ground; *l'arche d'alliance*, the Ark of the Covenant; *l'arche de Noé*, Noah's ark; *l'arche du Seigneur*, the ark of the Lord.

archée [ar′ʃe], *n.m.* (*Anc. Physiol.*) Principle of life; (*Alchemy*) the central fire.—*n.f.* Bow-shot (distance).

archelet [arʃə′lɛ], *n.m.* Drill-bow (used by watch-makers etc.).

archéologie [arkeɔlɔ′ʒi], *n.f.* Archaeology.

archéologique, *a.* Archaeological.

archéologue, *n.m.* Archaeologist.

archer [ar′ʃe], *n.m.* Archer, bowman; officer, constable. *Le petit archer*, Cupid.

archère [ARCHIÈRE].

archet [ar′ʃe], *n.m.* Bow used in playing the violin etc., fiddle-stick; arched framework over a cradle, bed, etc.; drill-bow.

archétype [arke′tip], *n.m.* Archetype, prototype; original standard of money, weights, or measures.

archevêché [arʃəvɛ′ʃe], *n.m.* Archbishopric; archiepiscopal diocese; archbishop's residence. **archevêque**, *n.m.* Archbishop.

archi- [ar′ʃi or ar′ki], *pref.* Arch-, archi-, chief, principal, first, original, as *archidiacre, archiduc*, etc.; extremely, as *archiriche*, etc.

archichancelier [arʃiʃɑ̃sə′lje], *n.m.* Chief or grand chancellor.

archichapelain [arʃiʃa′plɛ̃], *n.m.* (*Fr. Hist*) Principal chaplain; head of the Chapel Royal.

archiconfrérie [arʃikɔ̃fre′ri], *n.f.* Title of certain religious or charitable societies.

archidiaconat [arʃidjakɔ′na], *n.m.* Archdeaconry (the office). **archidiaconé**, *n.m.* Archdeaconry.

archidiacre, *n.m.* Archdeacon.

(*C*) **archidiocèse** [arʃidjɔ′sɛ:z], *n.m.* Archbishopric, archdiocese.

archiduc [arʃi′dyk], *n.m.* Archduke. **archiducal**, *a.* (*fem.* **-ale**, *pl.* **-aux**) Archducal.

archiduché, *n.m.* Archdukedom, archduchy. **archiduchesse**, *n.f.* Archduchess.

archiépiscopal [arkiepiskɔ′pal], *a.* (*fem.* **-ale**, *pl.* **-aux**) Archiepiscopal. **archiépiscopat**, *n.m.* Archiepiscopate.

archière [ar′ʃjɛ:r], *n.f.* Loophole.

archiluth [arʃi′lyt], *n.m.* (*Mus.*) An ancient musical instrument larger than a lute.

archimandritat [arʃimɑ̃dri′ta], *n.m.* The office of an archimandrite. **archimandrite**, *n.m.* Archimandrite.

Archimède [arʃi′mɛd], *m.* Archimedes.

archipel [arʃi′pɛl], *n.m.* Archipelago.

archipompe [arʃi′pɔ̃:p], *n.f.* (*Naut.*) Pump-well.

archipresbytéral [arʃiprɛzbite′ral], *a.* (*fem.* **-ale**, *pl.* **-aux**) Appertaining to an arch-priest. **archipresbytérat**, *n.m.* Office or jurisdiction of an arch-priest.

archiprêtre [arʃi′prɛ:tr], *n.m.* Arch-priest.

architecte [arʃi′tɛkt], *n.m.* Architect. *Architecte paysagiste*, landscape-gardener.

architectonique, *a.* Architectonical, architectural.—*n.m.* Architecture; (*Phil.*) architectonics.

architectural, *a.* (*fem.* **-ale**, *pl.* **-aux**) Architectural. **architecture**, *n.f.* Architecture.

architrave [arʃi′tra:v], *n.f.* (*Arch.*) Architrave. **architravé**, *a.* (*fem.* **architravée**) Furnished with an architrave.—*n.f.* Architrave, cornice.

archives [ar′ʃi:v], *n.f.* (*used only in pl.*) Archives; State, civic, or family records; record-office, muniment-room. *Exemplaire des archives*, file copy.

archiviste, *n.m.* Archivist, keeper of records, registrar; filing clerk.

archivolte [arʃi'vɔlt], *n.f.* (*Arch.*) Arcnivolt.

archontat [arkɔ̃'ta], *n.m.* Archonship.

archonte, *n.m.* Archon.

arçon [ar'sɔ̃], *n.m.* Saddle-bow; bow-shaped tool used by hat-makers etc. *Être ferme sur les arçons*, to have a firm seat, (*fig.*) to be true to one's principles; *perdre* or *vider les arçons*, to be thrown from one's horse, (*fig.*) to be disconcerted or embarrassed, to lose one's presence of mind; *pistolets d'arçon*, horse-pistols. **arçonner**, *v.t.* To card or dress (wool etc.) with an *arçon*.

arcot [ar'ko], *n.m.* Dross, slag.

arctique [ark'tik], *a.* Arctic.

arcure [ar'ky:r], *n.f.* (*Hort.*) Arching (of vines or fruit-trees to restrain growth).

ardélion [arde'ljɔ̃], *n.m.* A busybody, meddler.

ardemment [arda'mã], *adv.* Ardently.

ardent [ar'dã], *a.* (*fem.* **ardente**) Burning, hot, fiery, scorching; (*fig.*) violent, intense; ardent, vehement, fervent, earnest, energetic, active; red, reddish (of hair). *Charbons ardents*, live coals; *buisson ardent*, the burning bush; *verre ardent*, burning-glass; *chapelle ardente*, mortuary chapel; *prière ardente*, fervent prayer; *cheval ardent*, a spirited horse; *ardent à l'étude*, keen on one's studies.

ardeur [ar'dœ:r], *n.f.* Intense heat, ardency; ardour, intense activity, fervour, earnestness, strenuousness. *Avec ardeur*, spiritedly; *cheval plein d'ardeur*, high-mettled horse.

*ardez [ar'de] (*Molière*) [REGARDEZ, *see* REGARDER].

ardillon [ardi'jɔ̃], *n.m.* Tongue (of a buckle); barb (of a hook).

ardoise [ar'dwa:z], *n.f.* Slate; (*colloq.*) score, account. *Carrière d'ardoise*, slate-quarry; *couvreur en ardoise*, slater; *crayon d'ardoise*, slate-pencil. **ardoisé**, *a.* (*fem.* **ardoisée**) Slate-coloured. **ardoiser**, *v.t.* To cover (a roof) with slates; to make slate-coloured. **ardoiserie**, *n.f.* Slate-trade. **ardoisier** (1), *n.m.* Owner of or workman in a slate-quarry. **ardoisier** (2) (*fem.* **ardoisière** (1)) or **ardoiseux** (*fem.* **ardoiseuse**), *a.* Slaty. **ardoisière** (2), *n.f.* Slate-quarry.

ardu [ar'dy], *a.* (*fem.* **ardue**) Steep, abrupt; (*fig.*) arduous, difficult.

arduité, *n.f.* Arduousness.

are [a:r], *n.m.* Square of ten metres.

aréage [are'a:ʒ], *n.m.* Surveying.

arec [a'rek] or **aréquier** [are'kje], *n.m.* Areca. *Noix d'arec*, areca-nut.

(C) aréna [are'na], *n.f.* Arena; skating-rink.

arénacé [arena'se], *a.* (*fem.* **arénacée**) Arenaceous, sandy.

arénaire [are'ne:r], *a.* (*Bot.*) Growing or living in sand.—*n.f.* Sandwort, one of the arenaria.

arène [a'rɛ:n], *n.f.* (*poet.*) Sand; arena; (*fig.*) cock-pit, battle-ground, theatre, scene; (*pl.*) the ancient Roman amphitheatres.

*aréner [are'ne], *v.i.*, or **s'aréner**, *v.r.* To sink, to subside (of a building).

arénicole [areni'kɔl], *a.* (*Zool.*) Living in sandy places.—*n.f.* Sand-worm.

arénière [are'nje:r], *n.f.* Sand-pit.

aréolaire [areɔ'le:r], *a.* Areolar.

aréolation, *n.f.* Areolation.

aréole [are'ɔl], *n.f.* (*Anat.*) Areola. **aréolé**, *a.* (*fem.* **aréolée**) Areolate.

aréomètre [areɔ'metr], *n.m.* Areometer, hydrometer. **aréométrie**, *n.f.* Areometry.

aréopage [areɔ'pa:ʒ], *n.m.* Areopagus.

aréopagite, *n.m.* Areopagite.

aréquier [AREC].

arête [a'rɛ:t], *n.f.* Fish-bone; awn or beard of wheat etc.; (*Arch.*) arris; (*Naut.*) quoin; (*Geom.*) line of intersection of two surfaces; corner; (*Geog. etc.*) ridge, arête. *Arête de poisson*, (*Arch.*) herring-bone work; *à vive arête*, (*Carp.*) sharp-edged; *arête du nez*, bridge of the nose.

arêtier [are'tje], *n.m.* Rafter (forming the hip of a roof). *Arêtier avant*, leading edge (of the wing of a plane).

arêtière [are'tje:r], *n.f.* Layer of mortar on the rafters; hip-tile.

arganier [arga'nje], *n.m.* Argan-tree.

argémone [arʒe'mɔn], *n.f.* Thorny Mexican poppy.

argent [ar'ʒã], *n.m.* Silver; silver money; money, cash; (*fig.*) wealth, riches; (*Her.*) argent. *À pomme d'argent*, silver-headed; *argent amati*, dull silver; *argent blanc* or *argent d'Allemagne*, German silver; *argent doré*, silver-gilt; *vif-argent*, quick-silver; *vaisselle d'argent*, silver plate. *Argent comptant*, ready money; *argent dormant*, money lying idle; *argent en caisse*, cash in hand, money put by; *argent monnayé*, coined money; *argent mort*, money paying no interest; *avoir le temps et l'argent*, to have all one can wish for; *bourreau d'argent*, spend-thrift; *c'est de l'argent en barre*, it is as safe as the Bank of England; *coûter un argent fou*, to cost a pretty penny; *en avoir pour son argent*, to have one's money's worth; *être brouillé avec l'argent comptant*, never to have any ready money; *faire argent de tout*, to turn everything into money; *faire rentrer de l'argent*, to call in money; *jeter son argent par la fenêtre*, to throw one's money away; *manger son argent*, to squander one's fortune; *placer de l'argent*, to invest money; *point d'argent, point de Suisse*, no pay, no piper; nothing for nothing; nothing without paying; *prendre quelque chose pour argent comptant*, (*fig.*) to take something for gospel; *rapporter de l'argent*, to bring in money; *toucher de l'argent*, to draw money; *trouver de l'argent*, to raise money; *y aller bon jeu, bon argent*, to be above-board, to act frankly; *au croissant d'argent*, (*Her.*) argent-horned. **argentage** [ARGENTURE].

argentan [arʒã'tã], *n.m.* German silver; nickel silver.

argentation [arʒãta'sjɔ̃], *n.f.* Coloration of anatomical details with nitrate of silver.

argenté [arʒã'te], *a.* (*fem.* **argentée**) Plated, silvered over; silvery.

argenter [arʒã'te], *v.t.* To silver over, to plate; to give the appearance of silver to.

argenterie [arʒã'tri], *n.f.* Plate, silver-plate.

argenteur, *n.m.* Plater, silverer.

*argentier [arʒã'tje], *n.m.* (*Fr. Hist.*) Minister of Finance; treasurer; silversmith.

argentifère [arʒãti'fɛ:r], *a.* Argentiferous.

argentin [arʒã'tɛ̃], *a.* (*fem.* **argentine** (1)) Silvery, argentine tint; silver-toned ringing. —*n.* and *a.* Argentinian.

argentine (2) [arʒɑ̃'tin], *n.f.* Silver-weed, tansy; (*Zool.*) argentine; silver-fish.

Argentine [arʒɑ̃'tin], *f.* Argentina.

argenture [arʒɑ̃'ty:r], *n.f.* or **argentage** [arʒɑ̃'taʒ], *n.m.* Silvering, deposit of silver (on metal etc.); silver-plating.

argilacé [arʒila'se], *a.* (*fem.* **argilacée**) Clayey, argillaceous.

argile [ar'ʒil], *n.f.* Clay, potter's clay, argil. *Argile à porcelaine*, China-clay; *argile réfractaire*, fire-clay. **argileux** [arʒi'lø], *a.* (*fem.* **-euse**) Clayey, clayish. **argilière**, *n.f.* Clay-pit. **argilifère**, *a.* Argilliferous. **argilolithe**, *n.m.* Clay-stone.

argon [ar'gɔ̃], *n.m.* (*Chem.*) Argon.

argonaute [argɔ'no:t], *n.m.* Argonaut, nautilus.

argot [ar'go], *n.m.* Slang, cant.

argoter [argɔ'te], *v.t.* To cut the stub of (a dead branch etc.).

argotier [argɔ'tje], *a.* (*fem.* **argotière**) Using slang. **argotique**, *a.* Slangy.

argoulet [argu'lɛ], *n.m.* (*Fr. Hist.*) Mounted archer (16th century).

argousin [argu'zɛ̃], *n.m.* Convict-warder; (*slang*) policeman, bobby.

argue [arg], *n.f.* (*Tech.*) Drawplate, machine for wire-drawing. **arguer** (1) [ar'gɥe], *v.t.* To wire-draw.

arguer (2) [ar'gɥe], *v.t.* To infer, to deduce, to argue.

argument [argy'mɑ̃], *n.m.* Argument, reasoning; proof, evidence, summary, thesis (of a book etc.); theme, subject. *Argument dans les règles*, argument in due form.

argumentateur, *n.m.* (*fem.* **-trice**) An habitual arguer or disputer.

argumentation, *n.f.* Argumentation, reasoning.

argumenter, *v.i.* To argue; to moot.—*v.t.* To argue (with etc.). **argumenteur**, *n.m.* Arguer.

argus [ar'gy:s], *n.m.* (*Myth.*) Argus; (*Ent. and Orn.*) argus.

argutie [argy'si], *n.f.* Quibble, subtlety, cavil. **argutieux**, *a.* (*fem.* **-ieuse**) Quibbling, cavilling.

argyrol [arʒi'rɔl], *n.m.* Argyrol.

aria [a'rja], *n.m.* (*Mus.*) Aria; (*pop.*) nuisance; fuss, bother.

arianisme [arja'nism], *n.m.* Arianism.

aride [a'rid], *a.* Arid, dry; sterile; (*fig.*) uninteresting, jejune (of style etc.). *Une terre aride*, a barren ground. **aridité**, *n.f.* Aridity, dryness, barrenness, sterility.

arien [a'rjɛ̃], *a.* (*fem.* **arienne**) Arian.—*n.* (**Arien**, *fem.* **Arienne**) Arian.

ariette [a'rjɛt], *n.f.* (*Mus.*) Arietta, light melody.

arille [a'rij], *n.m.* (*Bot.*) Aril. **arillé**, *a.* (*fem.* **arillée**) Arillate, arilled.

Arioste [ar'jɔst], *m.* Ariosto.

ariser [ARRISER].

aristarque [aris'tark], *n.m.* Aristarch, hypercritic.

aristé [aris'te], *a.* (*fem.* **-ée**) (*Bot.*) Aristate.

aristo [aris'to], *n.m.* (*pop.*) A swell, a toff.

aristocrate [aristɔ'krat], *a.* Aristocratic.—*n.* Aristocrat. **aristocratie**, *n.f.* Aristocracy. **aristocratique**, *a.* Aristocratic. **aristocratiquement**, *adv.* Aristocratically. **aristocratiser**, *v.t.* To make aristocratic.

aristoloche [aristɔ'lɔʃ], *n.f.* (*Bot.*) Birthwort. *Aristoloche serpentaire*, Virginia snake-root.

Aristophane [aristɔ'fan], *m.* Aristophanes.

Aristote [aris'tɔt], *m.* Aristotle.

aristotélicien [aristɔteli'sjɛ̃], *a.* (*fem.* **-ienne**) Aristotelian.—*n.* Follower of Aristotle. **aristotélique**, *a.* Aristotelian. **aristotéliser**, *v.i.* To be a follower of Aristotle; to adhere to or teach his philosophy. **aristotélisme**, *n.m.* Aristotelianism.

arithméticien [aritmeti'sjɛ̃], *n.m.* (*fem.* **-ienne**) Arithmetician. **arithmétique**, *n.f.* Arithmetic.—*a.* Arithmetical. *Rapport arithmétique*, arithmetical ratio. **arithmétiquement**, *adv.* Arithmetically. **arithmologie**, *n.m.* The general science of numbers or quantities. **arithmomètre**, *n.m.* Arithmometer, calculating-machine.

arlequin [arlə'kɛ̃], *n.m.* Harlequin; (*fig.*) a turn-coat, a weathercock; (*pop.*) remains of a meal, broken meal. *Habit d'arlequin*, patchwork, motley; medley, miscellany; *manteau d'arlequin*, sides and top of proscenium. **arlequinade**, *n.f.* Harlequinade; (*fig.*) buffoonery; a ridiculous or silly effusion.

armadille (1) [arma'di:j], *n.f.* (*Span. Hist.*) A fleet employed by the Spaniards to keep foreign ships from trading with America.

*armadille (2) [arma'di:j], *n.m.* (*Zool.*) Armadillo; wood-louse.

armagnac [armɑ'ɲak], *n.m.* Brandy (made in the county of Armagnac, S. of France).

armateur [arma'tœ:r], *n.m.* Shipowner; captain of a privateer; a privateer.

armature [arma'ty:r], *n.f.* Armature, iron braces, stays, sheathing, casing, gear, etc.; truss-frame; (*Mus.*) key signature.

arme [arm], *n.f.* Arm, weapon; branch or arm (of the service); (*Her.*) armorial bearings. *Armes à feu*, fire-arms; *armes portatives*, small arms; *arme de trait*, missile weapon; *arme blanche*, cold steel; *assaut d'armes*, assault at arms; *aux armes!* to arms! *en venir aux armes*, to resort to war; *faire* or *tirer des armes*, to fence; *faire passer par les armes*, to shoot, to put to the sword; *faire ses premières armes*, to make one's first campaign; *fournir des armes contre soi*, to provide a rod for one's own back; *né pour les armes*, born a soldier; *pas d'armes*, passage of arms; *passer l'arme à gauche*, (*slang*) to die, to kick the bucket; *place d'armes*, a place in a town etc. where soldiers are drilled, a fortress; *porter les armes*, to serve as a soldier; *prendre les armes*, to take up arms; *prise d'armes*, parade under arms; *rendre* or *déposer les armes*, to lay down one's arms; *cheval d'armes*, charger; *suspension d'armes*, cessation of hostilities; *une salle d'armes*, a fencing-school, armoury; *un fait d'armes*, a warlike feat or exploit; *un maître d'armes*, a fencing-master.

armé [ar'me], *a.* (*fem.* **armée**) Armed, equipped; (*Her.*) armed (with claws, horns, teeth, etc.). *À main armée*, by force of arms; *armé de toutes pièces*, armed from top to toe; *béton armé*, reinforced concrete; *obus armé*, (*Artill.*) fused shell; *verre armé*, wired glass.

armée [ar'me], *n.f.* Army; forces, troops, host; (*fig.*) a body or organization (of officials etc.). *Armée de mer et de terre*, sea and land forces; *armée de l'air*, air-force; *armée permanente*, standing army; *corps d'armée*, army corps; *fournisseur de l'armée*, army contractor; *l'Armée du Salut*, the Salvation Army.

armeline [armə'lin], *n.f.* Ermine (skin).

armement [armə'mã], *n.m.* Arming, raising of forces, warlike preparations; armament, equipment; (*Am.*) ordnance.

Arménie [arme'ni], *f.* Armenia.

arménien [arme'njɛ̃], *a.* (*fem.* **-ienne**) Armenian.—*n.m.* The Armenian language. —*n.* (**Arménien, -ienne**) Armenian.

armer [ar'me], *v.t.* To equip, to furnish with an armament; to raise (men) as soldiers; to put an armature on; (*Artill.*) to load, to mount (guns etc.); to cock (a gun etc.); (*fig.*) to fortify; to strengthen; (*Mus.*) to give key signature to. *Armer en course*, to fit out as a privateer; *armer en guerre*, to fit out (a merchantman) as a warship; *armer une poutre de bandes de fer*, to strengthen a beam with iron bands. **s'armer**, *v.r.* To arm oneself, to take arms; to fortify, protect, or secure oneself (against something). *S'armer de tout son courage*, to summon up all one's courage.

armeria [arme'rja], *n.f.* (*Bot.*) Sea-thrift.

*armet [ar'mɛ], *n.m.* Headpiece of troopers, 15th century.

armillaire [armi'lɛːr], *a.* (*Astron.*) Armillary. *Sphère armillaire*, armillary sphere.

armille [ar'mi:j], *n.f.* (*Ant.*) Bracelet, armlet; (*Anc. Astron.*) armilla; (*Arch.*) annulet (of the Doric capital).

armillé, *a.* (*fem.* **-ée**) Furnished with an annulet.

armistice [armis'tis], *n.m.* Armistice.

armoire [ar'mwa:r], *n.f.* Closet, cupboard; clothes-press, wardrobe. *Armoire à glace*, (mirror) wardrobe. (*Mil.*, *slang*) The pack.

armoiries [armwa'ri], *n.f.* (*used only in pl.*) Arms, armorial bearings, armory.

armoise [ar'mwa:z], *n.f.* Artemisia, wormwood; [ARMOISIN]. *Armoise commune*, mugwort.

armoisin [armwa'zɛ̃], *n.m.* Sarcenet (silk fabric).

armon [ar'mɔ̃], *n.m.* Futchel (of a coach).

armorial [armɔ'rjal], *a.* (*fem.* **-iale**, *pl.* **-iaux**) Armorial, pertaining to heraldry.— *n.m.* An armorial, a book of heraldry.

armoricain [armɔri'kɛ̃], *a.* (*fem.* **-aine**) Armorican (of Brittany).

armorier [armɔ'rje], *v.t.* To put or paint a coat of arms upon, to blazon.

Armorique [armɔ'rik], *f.* Armorica.

armoriste [armɔ'rist], *n.m.* Armorist, heraldic engraver.

armure [ar'my:r], *n.f.* Armour, arms and armour, casing, wrapper; armature (of a magnet etc.); pole-piece (of dynamo); (*Agric.*) tree-guard; cradle (of a scythe); (*Naut.*) fish (of a mast, yard, etc.); (*fig.*) defence, protection. *Armure de la clef*, (*Mus.*) key signature; *armure de tête*, headpiece; *revêtir son armure*, to buckle on one's armour. **armurerie**, *n.f.* Armoury; manufacture of arms; arms factory. **armurier**, *n.m.* Armourer, gunsmith, *Armurier d'aviation*, aviation ordnance man.

arnica [arni'ka], *n.m.* (*Bot.*) Arnica.

arolle [a'rɔl], *n.f.* Arrolla pine.

aromate [arɔ'mat], *n.m.* An aromatic.

aromatique, *a.* Aromatic, fragrant, spicy.

aromatiquement, *adv.* In a fragrant way.

aromatisation, *n.f.* Aromatization. **aromatiser,** *v.t.* To aromatize, to perfume, to flavour.

arome, *n.m.* Aroma, perfume, scent.

aronde [a'rɔ̃:d], *n.f.* *Swallow; (*Carp.*) dovetail, tenon. *Assembler à queue d'aronde*, to dovetail.

arondelle [arɔ̃'dɛl], *n.f.* A line with hooks.

arpège [ar'pɛ:ʒ], *n.m.* Arpeggio. **arpégement,** *n.m.* Performance of arpeggios. **arpéger,** *v.i.* To play arpeggios.

arpent [ar'pã], *n.m.* Acre (French; about one and a half English acres). **arpentage,** *n.m.* Land-measuring; a survey or measurement.

arpenter, *v.t.* *To measure in *arpents*; to survey, to measure (land); (*fig.*) to stride up and down. **arpenteur,** *n.m.* Land-surveyor.

arpenteuse [arpã'tø:z], *n.f.* Span-worm.

arpète [ar'pɛt], *n.f.* (*slang*) Milliner's apprentice, errand boy (or girl).

arpion [ar'pjɔ̃], *n.m.* (*slang*) Foot, trotter.

arpon [ar'pɔ̃], *n.m.* Rip-saw, cross-cut saw.

arqué [ar'ke], *a.* (*fem.* **arquée**) Bent, curved, arched (of horses).

arquebusade [arkəby'zad], *n.f.* Arquebusade.

arquebuse [arkə'by:z], *n.f.* Arquebus; a very strong liqueur. **arquebuser,** *v.t.* To shoot or kill with an arquebus. **arquebuserie,** *n.f.* Musketry, shooting with the arquebus; arquebus-factory; gunsmithery. **arquebusier,** *n.m.* Arquebusier; gunsmith, armourer.

arquer [ar'ke], *v.t.* To bend, to curve, to arch.—*v.i.* To bend, to be curved or arched. **s'arquer,** *v.r.* To become bent.

arrachage [ara'ʃa:ʒ], *n.m.* Pulling up of vegetables, roots, etc. **arraché,** *a.* (*fem.* **arrachée**) Rooted up; (*fig.*) separated, torn away; (*Her.*) having the roots displayed.

arrache-clou, *n.m.* Nail-drawer. **arrachement,** *n.m.* Tearing up or away, pulling or rooting up or out; drawing, extraction; (*Build.*) toothing.

arrache-pied (d') [daraʃ'pje], *adv. phr.* Without interruption. *Travailler d'arrache-pied*, to work with a will.

arracher [ara'ʃe], *v.t.* To pull or tear away, up, or out; to extract, to uproot, to grub up; (*fig.*) to wrest, to wring, to obtain by force or with difficulty; to extort; to detach, to remove (by an effort or with difficulty); to distract (from business etc.). *Arracher des mauvaises herbes*, to grub up weeds; *arracher une dent*, to pull out a tooth; *arracher un secret à quelqu'un*, to get a secret out of someone. **s'arracher,** *v.r.* To tear oneself away, to get away, to break away. *On se l'arrache*, (*colloq.*) he or she is all the rage; *s'arracher au sommeil*, to shake off sleep; *s'arracher les cheveux*, to tear one's hair; *s'arracher les yeux*, to quarrel or wrangle violently.

arrache-racine or **arrache-racines** [araʃra'sin], *n.m.* Hoe for extracting roots; spud.

arracheur [ara'ʃœ'r], *n.m.* (*fem.* **arracheuse**) Drawer. *Arracheur de cors*, corn-cutter; *arracheur de dents*, forceps; *mentir comme un arracheur de dents*, to lie unblushingly or like an epitaph.—*n.f.* (*Hat-making*) Picker. *Arracheuse de pommes de terre*, potato-plough.

*arrachis [ara'ʃi], *n.m.* Wood where trees have been rooted up.

arrachoir [ara'ʃwaːr], *n.m.* Grubbing plough.

arrageois [ara'ʒwa], *a.* and *n.m.* Inhabitant of Arras.

arraisonnement [arɛzɔn'mã], *n.m.* Inspection of a ship, esp. for sanitary reasons.

arraisonner [arɛzɔn'ne], *v.t.* (*Naut.*) To hail (a ship); to stop and examine her.

arraisonneur [arɛzɔ'nœr], *a.* Hailing (ship).

arrangeable [arã'ʒabl], *a.* Reparable.

arrangeant [arã'ʒã], *a.* (*fem.* **arrangeante**) Accommodating, easy to deal with or get on with.

arrangement [arãʒ'mã], *n.m.* Arrangement, disposition, adjustment, setting in order; order, scheme, plan, method, mode; agreement, settlement; composition; (*pl.*) terms; measures; (*Math.*) permutations. *Entrer en arrangement*, to compound; *j'ai pris des arrangements avec eux pour le paiement*, I have come to terms with them respecting payment.

arranger [arã'ʒe], *v.t.* To arrange, to put in order; to settle, to compromise, to compose (a difference etc.); to manage, to regulate; to make suitable, to suit; (*Mus.*) to set, arrange; (*colloq.*) to ill-treat; to fit up (a house); to trim up, to dress out. *Arranger quelque chose*, to contrive something; *arranger ses affaires*, to settle one's affairs; *arranger un ardin*, to do up a garden; *arrangez tout cela*, set all those things in order; *cela m'arrange*, that suits me; *comme vous voilà arrangé!* what a sight you look! *il l'a arrangé de la belle manière*, he let him have it, he gave him a good dressing down. **s'arranger**, *v.r.* To put oneself to rights; to prepare oneself, to make arrangements (*pour*); to come to an agreement, to compound; to be satisfied, to make shift, to put up (*de*). *Arrangez-vous*, do as best you can; that is your look-out; *cela s'arrangera*, that will be all right; *il s'est très bien arrangé*, he has made his house very comfortable; *qu'il s'arrange comme il voudra*, let him do as he likes.

arrangeur [arã'ʒœːr], *n.m.* (*fem.* **arrangeuse**) One who arranges, adapter.

arrentement [arãt'mã], *n.m.* Renting; letting out. *Tenir par arrentement*, to rent.

arrenter [arã'te], *v.t.* To rent; to let out.

arrérager [arera'ʒe], *v.i.* To get in arrears (of a debt etc.). **arrérages**, *n.m.* (used only in *pl.*) Arrears. *Coupon d'arrérages de rentes*, dividend warrant; *laisser courir ses arrérages*, to let one's arrears run on.

arrestation [arɛstɑ'sjɔ̃], *n.f.* Arrest, apprehension; custody. *Être en état d'arrestation*, to be in custody; *mettre quelqu'un en arrestation*, to arrest someone.

arrêt [a'rɛ], *n.m.* Stoppage, stop, check, pause, halt; suspension, cessation, interruption; (*Law*) decision, award, judgment; arrest, apprehension, attachment (of persons or goods); (*Mach.*) rest, stop, catch, stay; (*Horol.*) stop-work; sentence; (*fig.*) decree; (*pl.*) state of arrest, imprisonment. *Arrêt fixe*, all cars stop here; *arrêt facultatif*, request stop; *arrêt de mort*, sentence of death; (*spt.*) *arrêt de volée*, fair catch; *arrêt par défaut*, judgment

by default; *arrêts forcés* or *simples*, (*Mil.*) close *or* open arrest; *aux arrêts*, (*Mil.*) under arrest; *chien d'arrêt*, setter, pointer; *coup d'arrêt*, counter; *cran d'arrêt*, safety-catch; *en arrêt*, at rest (of a lance); at a dead set (of a dog); *faire arrêt sur des marchandises*, to attach or seize goods; *lever les arrêts*, (*Mil.*) to release from arrest; *maison d'arrêt*, jail, lock-up; *mandat d'arrêt*, warrant; *mettre aux arrêts*, (*Mil.*) to put under arrest; *mettre la lance en arrêt*, to couch the lance; *prononcer un arrêt*, to pronounce judgment, to pass sentence; *robinet d'arrêt*, stop-cock; *sans arrêt*, non-stop; *temps d'arrêt*, pause, stoppage, intermission; (*spt.*) *un bel arrêt*, a good tackle.

arrêté (1) [arɛ'te], *a.* (*fem.* **arrêtée**) Stopped, decreed, agreed upon, resolved; arrested; fastened; (*Her.*) represented as standing immovable on their four legs (of figures of animals). *Avoir des idées arrêtées*, to have fixed ideas; *dessein arrêté*, settled design; *départ arrêté*, standing start.

arrêté (2) [arɛ'te], *n.m.* Departmental minute, order, decree, decision. *Arrêté de compte*, final settlement of an account; *arrêté ministériel*, order in council; *prendre un arrêté*, to pass a decree.

arrête-bœuf [arɛt'bœf], *n.m. inv.* Cammock, rest-harrow, *Ononis repens*.

arrêter [arɛ'te], *v.t.* To check, to stop the movement of, to throw out of gear; to delay, to detain, to hinder, to impede, to hold up; to settle (an account); (*Shooting*) to set, to point at; (*Sewing*) to fasten (a stitch); (*Paint.*) to fix the colours or general lines of (a picture etc.). *Arrêter ses yeux sur*, to fix one's eyes upon; *arrêter un courrier*, to delay a courier; *arrêter un domestique, une chambre*, to engage a servant, a room; *arrêter un marché*, to conclude a bargain; *arrêter un moteur*, to switch off an engine; *arrêter un point en cousant*, to fasten off (a stitch); *qu'a-t-on arrêté dans cette réunion?* what was decided at that meeting? *rien ne l'arrête*, he sticks at nothing; *ses créanciers l'ont fait arrêter*, his creditors have had him arrested. —*v.i.* To stop, to stand still, to cease, to leave off (doing, speaking, etc.); to stay, to remain (*dans*); to stop, to bait (horses); to insist (*sur*); to point, to set (of dogs). **s'arrêter**, *v.r.* To stop, to pause; to remain, to loiter; to lag, to give over, to leave off; to be concluded, determined, or resolved (of bargains etc.); to resolve upon; to dwell (upon), to insist (*sur*). *Il ne faut pas s'arrêter à ce qu'il dit*, one must not pay serious attention to what he says; *il s'arrête, la mémoire lui manque*, he hesitates, his memory fails him; *ma montre s'est arrêtée*, my watch has stopped; *vous vous arrêtez à des riens*, you stick at trifles.

arrêtoir [arɛ'twaːr], *n.m.* Stop, catch; pawl.

arrhes [aːr], *n.f. pl.* Earnest (money), deposit.

arrière (1) [a'rjɛːr], *adv.* Behind (of time and place); backward; (*Naut.*) aft, abaft. *Avoir vent arrière*, to have the wind astern; *droit arrière*, right abaft; *faire marche (or machine) arrière*, to back; (*Motor.*) *feux arrière*, rear lights; *siège arrière*, (motor-cycle) pillion-seat.—*int.* Away! avaunt! back!—*n.m.* Back part, rear; (*Naut.*) stern (of a vessel);

(*Mil.*) home front; (*Ftb.*) back. *Jouer arrière*, to play back; *arrière droit*, right back; *en arrière!* back! *en arrière*, backward; behindhand, in arrears; (*Naut.*) astern, abaft; *en arrière de*, behind; *se ranger de l'arrière*, (*Naut.*) to veer; *surveillant de l'arrière*, (*Naut.*) afterguard; *tomber de l'arrière*, to fall astern; *voyager en arrière*, to travel with one's back to the engine.—*n.m. pl.* Lines of communication.

arriéré [arjɛ're], . *a.* (*fem.* **arriérée**) In arrears; behindhand, backward, poorly developed.—*n.m.* Arrears. *Il a beaucoup d'arriéré dans sa correspondance*, he is very much behindhand in his correspondence; *liquider l'arriéré*, to pay up arrears.

[In *pl.* of all the following compounds *arrière* is *inv.* The *n.* has its regular *pl.*]

arrière-ban [arjɛr'bɑ̃], *n.m.* General levy; a general body or assemblage.

arrière-bec [arjɛr'bɛk], *n.m.* Starling pointing downstream (of a bridge-pier).

arrière-bouche [arjɛr'buʃ], *n.f.* Back part of the mouth, pharynx, posterior fauces.

arrière-boutique [arjɛrbu'tik], *n.f.* Room at the back of a shop.

arrière-chœur [arjɛr'kœːr], *n.m.* A choir stationed behind the altar.

arrière-corps [arjɛr'kɔːr], *n.m.* Part of a building at the back; recess.

arrière-cour [arjɛr'kuːr], *n.f.* Court at the rear, back-yard.

arrière-cousin [arjɛrku'zɛ̃], *n.m.* (*fem.* **arrière-cousine**, *pl.* **arrière-cousins** or **-cousines**) Distant cousin, one several times removed.

arrière-cuisine [arjɛrkɥi'zin], *n.f.* Back-kitchen, scullery.

arrière-faix [arjɛr'fɛ], *n.m.* After-birth, placenta; secundines.

arrière-fief [arjɛr'fjɛf], *n.m.* Sub-fief.

arrière-fleur [arjɛr'flœːr], *n.f.* Second efflorescence.

arrière-garde [arjɛr'gard], *n.f.* Rear-guard.

arrière-gorge [arjɛr'gɔrʒ], *n.f.* Opening of the throat, part of the pharynx behind the tonsils.

arrière-goût [arjɛr'gu], *n.m.* After-taste.

arrière-grand-mère [arjɛrgrɑ̃'mɛːr], *n.f.* (*pl.* **arrière-grand-mères**) Great-grandmother. **arrière-grands-parents**, *n.m.pl. inv.* Great-grand-parents. **arrière-grand-père**, *n.m.* (*pl.* **arrière-grands-pères**) Great-grand-father.

arrière-main [arjɛr'mɛ̃], *n.f.* Back of the hand; (*Tennis etc.*) backhand-stroke.—*n.m.* Hindquarters (of a horse).

arrière-neveu [arjɛrnə'vø], *n.m.* Grand-nephew. *Les arrière-neveux*, descendants, posterity. **arrière-nièce**, *n.f.* Grand-niece.

arrière-pays [arjɛr'pei], *n.m. inv.* Hinterland.

arrière-pensée [arjɛrpɑ̃'se], *n.f.* Mental reservation, hidden motive, underlying design.

arrière-petite-fille [arjɛrpətit'fiːj], *n.f.* (*pl.* **arrière-petites-filles**) Great-granddaughter **arrière-petit-fils**, *n.m.* (*pl.* **arrière-petits-fils**) Great-grandson. **arrière-petits-enfants**, *n.m. pl.* Great-grandchildren.

arrière-plan [arjɛr'plɑ̃], *n.m.* (*Paint.*, *Cine.*) Background.

arrière-point [arjɛr'pwɛ̃], *n.m.* Back-stitch.

arrière-port [arjɛr'pɔːr], *n.m.* Inner harbour, inner part of a harbour.

arriérer [arje're], *v.t.* To defer, to put off, to leave in arrears. **s'arriérer**, *v.r.* To stay behind, to be in arrears.

arrière-saison [arjɛrsɛ'zɔ̃], *n.f.* The end of autumn; (*fig.*) the last part of any period. *L'arrière-saison de la vie*, the evening of life, old age.

arrière-train [arjɛr'trɛ̃], *n.m.* The part of a vehicle supported by the back wheels; hind-quarters (of an animal).

arrière-vassal [arjɛrva'sal], *n.m.* Vassal to a lord who is vassal to another lord.

arrière-voussure [arjɛrvu'syːr], *n.f.* (*Arch.*) Arch constructed behind a door, window, etc., rear-arch, rear-vault.

arrimage [ari'maːʒ], *n.m.* (*Naut.*) Stowage, trim of the hold.

arrimer [ari'me], *v.t.* (*Naut.*) To stow (cargo etc.); to trim (the hold etc.).

arrimeur, *n.m.* Stower, stevedore.

arriser or **ariser** [ari'ze], *v.t.* (*Naut.*) To take in sail during a squall, to reef.

arrivage [ari'vaːʒ], *n.m.* Arrival (of ships, merchandise, etc.).

arrivant, *n.m.* (*fem.* **-ante**) Arrival, comer.

arrivée, *n.f.* Arrival, moment of landing, coming, etc., advent. *A l'arrivée de*, on the arrival of; *dès son arrivée*, immediately after his arrival; *jours d'arrivée*, mail days; *ligne d'arrivée*, finishing line; *tuyau d'arrivée*, delivery pipe.

arriver [ari've], *v.i.* (*conjugated with* ÊTRE) To arrive, to come; to arrive at, to attain, to get to, to reach (*à*); to make one's way, to succeed; to happen, to occur, to take place; (*Naut.*) to bear away, to bear down, to veer. *Arriver à l'âge de*, to attain the age of; *arriver à ses fins* or *à son but*, to compass one's ends; *arriver comme mars en Carême*, to come like clockwork; *arriver comme marée en Carême*, to come in the nick of time; *cela ne m'arrivera plus*, I will never do so again; *il arrivait à grands pas*, he was approaching with rapid strides; *il lui est arrivé de dire*, he happened to say; *la nuit arriva*, night came on; *le navire arrive de ce côté*, the ship is bearing down this way; *quoi qu'il arrive*, come what may; *un accident lui est arrivé*, he has met with an accident; *un malheur n'arrive jamais seul*, misfortunes never come singly.

arrivisme [ari'vism], *n.m.* Pushfulness, un-scrupulous ambition.

arriviste, *n.m.* Careerist, unscrupulous fellow.

arroche [a'rɔʃ], *n.f.* Orache, mountain spinach.

arrogamment [arɔga'mɑ̃], *adv.* Arrogantly, haughtily, insolently.

arrogance [arɔ'gɑ̃ːs], *n.f.* Arrogance, haughti-ness, superciliousness. **arrogant**, *a.* (*fem.* **arrogante**) Arrogant, haughty, supercilious, overbearing.

arroger (s') [arɔ'ʒe], *v.r.* To arrogate to one-self, to assume or claim presumptuously.

*arroi [a'rwa], *n.m.* Array (chiefly in *être en mauvais arroi*, to be in a sad plight).

arrondi [arɔ̃'di], *a.* (*fem.* **-ie**) Rounded.—*n.m.* Curve (of shoulder, face, etc.).

arrondir [arɔ̃'diːr], *v.t.* To make round; to

give a curved shape to, to round off; (*fig.*) to enlarge, to extend; (*rhet.*) to round (a period); (*Paint.*) to round off; (*Naut.*) to double (a cape). *Arrondir ses biens*, to increase one's estate; *arrondir une île*, (*Naut.*) to sail round an island; *arrondir une période*, to round a period; *arrondir une somme*, to make a round sum; *une phrase bien arrondie*, a well-turned sentence; *un visage arrondi*, a full face. **s'arrondir,** *v.r.* To grow or become round; to increase one's estate. **arrondissage** [arɔ̃di'sa:ʒ], *n.m.* Rounding, making round. **arrondissement** [arɔ̃dis'mɑ̃], *n.m.* Rounding, making round; roundness; a division of a (French) department; (in Paris) one of the 20 wards.
arrosable [aro'zabl], *a.* That can be watered, irrigated.
arrosage [aro'za:ʒ], or **arrosement**, *n.m.* Watering, sprinkling, irrigation.
arroser [aro'ze], *v.t.* To water, to wet, to sprinkle, to irrigate (land); to soak, to moisten; to flow through (of a river); to bathe (with tears); (*Cook.*) to baste; (*colloq.*) to distribute money, to pay all round, to bribe; (*Mil.*) to shell or bomb. *Arroser des créanciers*, to pay one's creditors a trifle; *arroser un repas de vin*, to wash down a meal with wine; *arrosez ces gens-là*, keep in with those people (by giving them trifling presents); *arroser (ses galons, sa nomination)*, to celebrate. **arroseur,** *n.m.* (*fem.* **arroseuse**) A person who waters, sprinkles, etc.; waterer.—*n.f.* A watering-machine.
arrosoir [aro'zwa:r], *n.m.* Watering-can.
arrugie [ary'ʒi], *n.f.* (*Mining*) Drain, sough.
arsenal [arsə'nal], *n.m.* Arsenal. *Arsenal maritime*, naval dockyard.
arséniate [arse'njat], *n.m.* (*Chem.*) A salt of arsenic acid. **arsenic,** *n.m.* Arsenic. **arsenical,** *a.* (*fem.* **arsenicale,** *pl.* **arsenicaux**) Arsenical.—*n.m. pl.* Arsenical compounds. **arsénicisme,** *n.m.* Arsenical intoxication. **arsénié,** *a.* (*fem.* **arséniée**) Containing arsenic. **arsénieux,** *a.* (*fem.* **arsénieuse**) Arsenious. **arsénique,** *a.* Arsenic. **arsénite,** *n.m.* A salt of arsenious acid. **arséniure,** *n.m.* A compound of arsenic with another metal, arsenide.
*arsin [ar'sɛ̃], *a.* Used only in *Bois arsin*, wood damaged by fire.
arsouille [ar'su:j], *a.* and *n.* Blackguard, low cad.
art [a:r], *n.m.* Art; skill, dexterity, artifice; human work or agency, as opposed to nature. *Arts d'agrément*, accomplishments (music, dancing, etc.); *il a l'art de réussir dans tout ce qu'il entreprend*, he has the art of succeeding in all his undertakings; *l'art perfectionne la nature*, art improves nature; *les arts libéraux*, the liberal arts; *les beaux-arts*, the fine arts; *ouvrage d'art*, work of art.
Artémise [arte'mi:z], *f.* Artemisia.
artère [ar'tɛ:r], *n.f.* Artery; (*fig.*) thoroughfare (in a town). *Piquer une artère*, to open an artery. **artérialisation,** *n.f.* Arterialization. **artérialiser,** *v.t.* To arterialize. **artériel,** *a.* (*fem.* **-ielle**) Arterial. *Tension artérielle*, blood-pressure. **artérieux,** *a.* (*fem.* **-ieuse**) Pertaining to an artery or the arteries. **artériole,** *n.f.* Small artery.

artériopathie, *n.f.* Disease of the arteries. **artériosclérose,** *n.f.* Arteriosclerosis. **artériotomie,** *n.f.* Arteriotomy. **artérite,** *n.f.* Arteritis.
artésien [arte'zjɛ̃], *a.* (*fem.* **artésienne**) Artesian. *Puits artésien*, artesian well.—*n.* (**Artésien,** *fem.* **Artésienne**) An inhabitant or native of Artois.
arthralgie [artral'ʒi], *n.f.* Pain in the joints, arthralgia. **arthralgique,** *a.* Arthralgic.
arthrite [ar'trit], *n.f.* Arthritis. **arthritique,** *a.* Arthritic. **arthritisme,** *n.m.* Arthritism.
arthrodie [artrɔ'di], *n.f.* (*Anat.*) Arthrodia.
arthrologie [artrɔlɔ'ʒi], *n.f.* Arthrology.
arthropodie, *n.f.* Disease of the joints.
arthrotomie, *n.f.* Operation of cutting into an articulation, arthrotomy.
artichaut [arti'ʃo], *n.m.* Globe artichoke; (*pl.*) spikes on a fence, gate, etc. *Artichaut des toits*, house-leek.
artichautière, *n.f.* Artichoke-bed.
article [ar'tikl], *n.m.* Article (in all English senses); (*Ent., Bot.*) part between two joints or articulations; clause, provisions (of a treaty etc.); item; commodity; *pl.* goods. *À l'article de la mort*, at the point of death; *article de fond*, leading article; *article de Paris*, a speciality of Parisian fashion, manufacture, etc.; *ce n'est pas un article de foi*, it is not worthy of credit; *faire l'article*, to puff one's goods; *nous reviendrons sur cet article*, we shall come back to this subject.
articulaire [artiky'lɛːr], *a.* Articular.
articulation [artikyla'sjɔ̃], *n.f.* Articulation, pronunciation; (*Bot., Anat.*) joint, articulation; (*Law*) enumeration of facts.
articulé, *a.* (*fem.* **-ée**) Articulate, clear, distinct; jointed, articulated. *D'une manière articulée*, articulately, distinctly.—*n.m. pl.* (*Zool.*) The Articulata.
articuler [artiky'le], *v.t.* To articulate, to put together by the joints; to pronounce distinctly; (*Law*) to enumerate (alleged facts) article by article. **s'articuler,** *v.r.* To be connected by joints.
articulet [artiky'le], *n.m.* (*colloq.*) A little article.
artifice [arti'fis], *n.m.* Artifice, contrivance, expedient; dodge, trick, stratagem; craft, ruse. *Un feu d'artifice*, fireworks, pyrotechnics; (*fig.*) an (empty) display (of eloquence etc.).
artificiel [artifi'sjɛl], *a.* (*fem.* **-ielle**) Artificial; fictitious, spurious. *Dents artificielles*, false teeth. **artificiellement,** *adv.* Artificially.
artificier [artifi'sje], *n.m.* Firework-maker, pyrotechnist; artificer.
artificieusement [artifisjøz'mɑ̃], *adv.* Cunningly, craftily, artfully, slyly. **artificieux,** *a.* (*fem.* **artificieuse**) Artful, cunning.
artillerie [artij'ri], *n.f.* Artillery, ordnance; (*fig.*) powers, forces (used for defence or attack). *Artillerie d'assaut*, armoured corps; *artillerie de campagne*, field artillery; *artillerie de position*, fortress artillery; *artillerie de siège*, battering or siege artillery; *artillerie légère*, light artillery; *artillerie montée*, horse artillery; *grosse artillerie*, heavy artillery; *une pièce d'artillerie*, a piece of ordnance; *train d'artillerie*, train of artillery.
artilleur, *n.m.* Artilleryman, gunner.

artimon [arti'mɔ̃], *n.m.* Mizen-mast; mizen-sail, mizen. *Hune d'artimon*, mizen-top; *mât d'artimon*, mizen-mast.
artiodactyle [artjɔdak'til], *n.m.* (*Zool.*) Artiodactyl; (*pl.* **artiodactyles**) the Artiodactyla.
artisan [arti'zɑ̃], *n.m.* Artisan, handicrafts-man, operative, mechanic; (*fig.*) author, architect, contriver, maker. **artisanal**, *a.* (*fem.* **-ale**, *pl.* **-aux**) Relating to a craft. **artisanat**, *n.m.* The social class of handi-craftsmen.
artison [arti'zɔ̃], *n.m.* The wood-fretter moth; the clothes-moth.
artiste [ar'tist], *n.* Artist; player, performer. —*a.* Artistic (of persons). **artistement**, *adv.* In an artistic manner; skilfully, artistically.
artistique, *a.* Artistic, pertaining to art. **artistiquement**, *adv.* Artistically.
arum [a'rɔm], *n.m.* Arum, cuckoo-pint.
aruspice [arys'pis], *n.m.* Aruspex, diviner.
aryen [a'rjɛ̃], *a.* (*fem.* **aryenne**) Aryan.
aryténoïde [aritenɔ'id], *a.* (*Anat.*) Cone or pitcher-shaped (two cartilages of the larynx).
arythmie [arit'miː], *n.f.* Arrhythmia (of heart).
arzel [ar'zɛl], *n.m.* Horse with white hind legs and forehead.
as (1) [ɑːs], *n.m.* Ace (at cards, dice); as (Roman coin and weight). *As de carreau*, ace of diamonds; (*fig.*) infantry knapsack; *as de pique*, (*colloq.*) the rump, (in poultry) the parson's nose; *il est fichu comme l'as de pique*, he is a shabby fellow, or misbegotten; *n'avoir plus d'as dans son jeu*, to be done for, to be stumped; *l'as blanc* (*domino*), one blank; (*fig.*) *être un as*, to be a first-rater (at flying, games, etc.); (*Row.*) *un as*, a sculling skiff; *ramer à l'as*, to pull stroke.
as (2) [AVOIR].
asaret [aza'rɛ], *n.m.* (*Bot.*) Azarum [NARD].
asbeste [az'bɛst], *n.m.* Asbestos.
ascaride [aska'rid] or **ascaris**, *n.m.* (*Zool.*) One of the ascarides. **ascaridé**, *n.m.* Any of the family of nematode worms comprising these.
ascendance [asɑ̃'dɑːs], *n.f.* Ascent, ancestry.
ascendant [asɑ̃'dɑ̃], *n.m.* Ascendant; ascen-dency, influence. *Avoir de l'ascendant sur*, to have influence over; (*pl.*) ancestors, as opposed to descendants. *Ascendants et descendants*, ancestors and descendants.—*a.* (*fem.* **ascendante**) Ascending, ascendant; going upward, rising, progressing.
ascenseur [asɑ̃'sœːr], *n.m.* Lift, (*Am.*) elevator, hoist.
ascension [asɑ̃'sjɔ̃], *n.f.* Ascent, climbing, rising; upstroke (of machinery); (*Astron.*) ascension; (*Jour de*) *l'Ascension*, Ascension Day. **ascensionnel**, *a.* (*fem.* **-elle**) Ascen-sional. *Vitesse ascensionnelle*, vertical speed.
ascensionniste or **ascensioniste**, *n.* Climber; balloonist.
ascète [a'sɛt], *n.* Ascetic. **ascétique**, *a.* Ascetic, rigid, severe.—*n.f.* Ascetic doctrine. **ascétiser**, *v.t.* To make ascetic. **s'ascé-tiser**, *v.r.* To become ascetic. **ascétisme**, *n.m.* Asceticism.
ascidie [asi'di], *n.f.* An ascidian.
ascite [a'sit], *n.f.* (*Path.*) Common dropsy. **ascitique**, *a.* Dropsical.—*n.* A dropsical person.
asclépiade (1) [askle'pjad], *a.* (*Pros.*) Ascle-piadic.—*n.m.* Asclepiad.

asclépiade (2) [askle'pjad], *n.f.*, or **asclépias**, *n.m.* (*Bot.*) Asclepiad, swallow-wort.
asepsie [asɛp'si], *n.f.* (*Med.*) Aseptic princi-ples, treatment, etc.; asepsis. **aseptique**, *a.* and *n.* Aseptic. **aseptisation**, *n.f.* Removal of all septic matter. **aseptiser**, *v.t.* To render aseptic.
asexué [asɛk'sɥe] or **asexuel**, *a.* (*fem.* **asexuée** or **asexuelle**) Asexual.
asiatique [azja'tik], *a.* Asiatic; (*fig.*) effemi-nate; ornate, rhetorical (of style). *Grippe asiatique*, Asian flu.—*n.* (*Asiatique*) A native of Asia.
Asie [a'zi], *f.* Asia. *Asie Mineure*, Asia Minor.
asile (1) [a'zil], *n.m.* Asylum, place of refuge, sanctuary, retreat, home (for the aged etc.); (*fig.*) protection, refuge. *Asile de nuit*, night shelter; *donner asile à*, to shelter; *droit d'asile*, right of sanctuary; *le dernier asile*, the grave; *asile d'aliénés*, mental home, mental hospital; *sans asile*, shelterless, homeless; *servir d'asile*, to shelter.
asile (2) [a'zil], *n.m.* Asilus, robber-fly.
asine [a'zin], *a.f.* Asinine, of the ass.
Asmodée [asmɔ'de], *m.* Asmodeus.
asparagus [aspara'gys], *n.m.* Asparagus-fern.
Aspasie [aspa'zi], *f.* Aspasia.
aspe [asp] or **asple**, *n.m.* Winder for silk from cocoons of silk-worms.
aspect [as'pɛ], *n.m.* Aspect, view, look; countenance; phase, bearing; manner of observing, considering, etc., point of view.
asperge [as'pɛrʒ], *n.f.* Asparagus (head of). *Botte d'asperges*, bundle of asparagus; (*colloq.*) *elle est comme une asperge*, she is a tall, gawky girl.
aspergement [aspɛrʒə'mɑ̃], *n.m.* Sprink-ling.
asperger [aspɛr'ʒe], *v.t.* To sprinkle, to be-sprinkle.
aspergerie [aspɛrʒə'ri] or **aspergière**, *n.f.* Asparagus-bed.
aspergès [aspɛr'ʒɛs], *n.m.* (*R.-C. Ch.*) Aspergillum, holy-water sprinkler; asperges, time of sprinkling. *Je suis arrivé à l'aspergès*, I entered (the church) as the priest was sprinkling (the people with holy water).
aspergille [aspɛr'ʒiːj], *n.f.*, **aspergillus**, *n.m.* (*Biol.*) Aspergillus, white fungus on jam.
aspérité [asperi'te], *n.f.* Roughness, harsh-ness; unevenness, ruggedness; (*fig.*) asperity, roughness.
asperme [a'spɛrm], *a.* (*Bot.*) Aspermous.
aspermie, *n.f.* (*Bot.*) Absence of seeds.
aspersion [aspɛr'sjɔ̃], *n.f.* Aspersion, sprink-ling. **aspersoir**, *n.m.* Holy-water sprinkler; rose (of a watering-pot).
aspérule [aspe'ryl], *n.f.* (*Bot.*) Wood-ruff.
asphaltage [asfal'taːʒ], *n.m.* Asphalting; asphalt.
asphalte [as'falt], *n.m.* Bitumen, asphalt. **asphalter**, *v.t.* To asphalt.
asphodèle [asfɔ'dɛl], *n.m.* Asphodel.
asphyxiant [asfik'sjɑ̃], *a.* (*fem.* **asphyxiante**) Asphyxiating, suffocating. *Gaz asphyxiant*, poison-gas.
asphyxie [asfik'si], *n.f.* (*Med.*) Asphyxia, suffocation, suspended animation. **asphyxié**, *a.* (*fem.* **-ée**) Asphyxiated.—*n.* A person in a state of asphyxia. **asphyxier**, *v.t.* To asphyxiate, to suffocate. *Le gaz les*

asphyxia, the gas suffocated them. **s'as-phyxier**, *v.r.* To commit suicide by suffocation.

aspic (1) [as'pik], *n.m.* Asp, viper. *Langue d'aspic*, a viper's tongue, (*fig.*) backbiter.

aspic (2) [as'pik], *n.m.* (*Bot.*) Spike-lavender; (*Cook.*) cold meat or fish, with jelly.

aspidistra [aspidis'tra], *n.m.* Aspidistra.

aspirail [aspi'ra:j], *n.m.* (*pl.* **aspiraux**) Air-hole (in a stove, oven, etc.).

aspirant (1) [aspi'rã], *a.* (*fem.* **aspirante** (1)) Suction, sucking (of pumps). *Pompe aspirante*, suction-pump.

aspirant (2) [aspi'rã], *n.m.* (*fem.* **aspirante** (2)) Aspirant, candidate, suitor; young officer; (*Navy*) midshipman; (*Av.*) apprentice pilot-officer.

aspirateur [aspira'tœ:r], *a.* (*fem.* **-trice**) Aspirating.—*n.m.* Ventilator; suction-pump, exhauster; vacuum cleaner. **aspiratif**, *a.* (*fem.* **-ive**) Aspirate, aspirated.

aspiration [aspira'sjɔ̃], *n.f.* Aspiration (of the letter *h* etc.); inhaling, inspiration; (of pumps) exhaustion, suction; (*fig.*) yearning, aspiration (towards goodness etc.); (*Motor.*) suction, intake. *Tuyau d'aspiration*, exhaust-pipe; *clapet d'aspiration*, intake valve.

aspiratoire, *a.* Concerned with aspiration.

aspiratrice [ASPIRATEUR].

aspiré (aspi're), *a.* (*fem.* **aspirée**) Aspirate. (or rather) fricative.—*n.f.* Such a letter.

aspirer [aspi're], *v.t.* To inspire, to inhale; to draw in, to suck in; (*Gram.*) to aspirate; (*Hydr.*) to exhaust.—*v.i.* To aspire, to aim at. *Aspirer aux honneurs*, to aspire after honours.

aspirine [aspi'rin], *n.f.* Aspirin.

assa-foetida [asafeti'da], *n.f.* Asafoetida.

assagir [asa'ʒi:r], *v.t.* To make wiser, to impart wisdom to. **s'assagir**, *v.r.* To become wise.

assagissement, *n.m.* Making or becoming wise.

assaillant [asa'jã], *a.* (*fem.* **assaillante**) Attacking, aggressive.—*n.m.* Aggressor, assailant, besieger.

assaillir [asa'ji:r], *v.t. irr.* To assault, to assail, to attack suddenly; to worry, to molest, to beset.

assainir [asɛ'ni:r], *v.t.* To render healthy; (*fig.*) to cleanse, to purify morally, etc. **s'assainir**, *v.r.* To become healthy.

assainissement, *n.m.* Purification, sanitation, salubrity.

assaisonnant [asɛzɔ'nã], *a.* (*fem.* **-ante**) Seasoning, savoury (of plants, herbs, etc.).

assaisonnement [asɛzɔn'mã], *n.m.* Seasoning or dressing food; condiment, seasoning, dressing.

assaisonner [asɛzɔ'ne], *v.t.* To season, to dress, to give a relish to; to make palatable, to give a zest to.

assassin [asa'sɛ̃], *a.* (*fem.* **assassine**) Killing, murderous; (*fig.*) provocative, killing. *Œillade assassine*, bewitching glance.—*n.f.* A (black silk) patch formerly worn in a provocative manner by women.—*n.m.* Assassin, murderer; ruffian. *À l'assassin!* murder! *crier à l'assassin*, to cry murder.

assassinant, *a.* (*fem.* **-ante**) Exceedingly tiresome, boring; killing, murdering. **assassinat**, *n.m.* Assassination, wilful murder, homicide.

assassiner, *v.t.* To assassinate, to murder; (*fig.*) to bore, tease, or importune (someone) to death; (*colloq.*) to deteriorate, to ruin.

assaut [a'so], *n.m.* Assault, onset, attack; fencing-match, assault-at-arms. *Colonne d'assaut*, storming-party; *donner l'assaut à une place*, to storm a place; *emporter une ville d'assaut*, to carry a town by storm; *faire assaut d'esprit*, to make a trial of wit.

***assauvagir** [asova'ʒi:r], *v.i.* **s'assauvagir**, *v.r.* To become wild (animal, land).

assavoir [asa'vwa:r], *v.* (*only used in the inf.*). *Faire assavoir que*, to inform.

asseau [a'so], *n.m.* Salter's or cooper's hammer.

assèchement [asɛʃ'mã], *n.m.* Drying up, drainage, the state of being dried up or drained dry. **assécher**, *v.t.* To drain (a mine etc.); to empty and dry up (a pond etc.).—*v.i.* To become dry, to be drained.

assemblage [asã'bla:ʒ], *n.m.* Assemblage, collection, union, combination; (*Print.*) gathering; (*Carp.*) joint, bond, scarf. *Assemblage à queue d'aronde*, dovetailed joint; *assemblage à tenon et mortaise*, mortise and tenon joint; *chaîne d'assemblage*, assembly line.

assemblé [asã'ble], *n.m.* (*Dancing*) A step in which the two feet are brought together.

assemblée [asã'ble], *n.f.* Assembly, meeting, company, party; convocation, congregation (of churches); meet (of hunters); (*Mil.*) the assembly (drum-beat). *L'assemblée se tient*, the meeting is being held; *se réunir en assemblée publique*, to meet in public assembly; *L'Assemblée Nationale*, the French National Assembly.

assembler [asã'ble], *v.t.* To assemble, to convoke, to call together; to collect, to gather; to bring, put, or lay together; (*Print.*) to gather; (*Carp.*) to trim, to scarf. **s'assembler** *v.r.* To assemble, to meet, to congregate. *Qui se ressemble s'assemble*, birds of a feather flock together.

assembleur [asã'blœ:r], *n.m.* (*fem.* **-euse**) One who brings (people or things) together, collector; (*Print.*) gatherer.

asséner [ase'ne], *v.t.* To strike or deal (a blow). *Il lui asséna un coup de poing*, he struck a blow with his fist.

assentiment [asãti'mã], *n.m.* Assent, agreement.

asseoir [a'swa:r], *v.t. irr.* To seat, to put on a seat, to set, to place, to fix, to establish; to pitch (a camp etc.). *Asseoir les fondements d'une maison*, to lay the foundations of a house; *asseoir un camp*, to pitch a camp; *asseoir une opinion*, to ground an opinion; *asseoir une rente*, to settle an annuity. **s'asseoir**, *v.r.* To sit, to sit down, to take a seat, to settle, to perch. *Asseyez-vous*, sit down.

Asser [a'sɛ:r], *m.* Asher.

assermenté [asɛrmã'te], *a.* (*fem.* **-ée**) Sworn in, attested. (*Hist.*) *Prêtre assermenté*, priest who has accepted the constitution; *prêtre non assermenté*, non-juror; *traducteur assermenté*, sworn translator. **assermenter**, *v.t.* To swear in, to administer the oath to.

assertif [asɛr'tif], *a.* (*fem.* **assertive**) Assertive.

assertion, *n.f.* Assertion, affirmation.

asservir [asɛr'vi:r], *v.t.* To enslave, to reduce

to servitude; to bring under subjection, to master, to subdue, to conquer. **s'asservir,** *v.r.* To obey, to submit (*à*). **asservissable,** *a.* That can be enslaved or subdued.

asservissant, *a.* (*fem.* **-ante**) Enslaving, subjecting, coercive. **asservissement,** *n.m.* Bondage, servitude, slavery, subjection. **asservisseur,** *n.m.* (*fem.* **-euse**) Enslaver, subduer.

assesseur [asɛ'sœːr], *n.m.* Assessor (assistant judge). **assessoral** or **assessorial,** *a.* (*fem.* **-ale** or **-iale,** *pl.* **-aux** or **-iaux**) Pertaining to assessorship. **assessorat** or **assessoriat,** *n.m.* Assessorship.

assez [a'se], *adv.* Enough, sufficiently; tolerably, passably. *Assez et plus qu'il n'en faut,* enough and to spare; *assez volontiers* or *d'assez bon cœur,* readily enough; *cela est assez bien,* that is pretty well; *cela est assez de mon goût,* I like it well enough; *cela paraît assez vraisemblable,* that appears likely enough; *c'est assez* or *en voilà assez,* enough, that will do; *c'est assez loin,* it is rather far; *cette femme est assez jolie,* this woman is rather pretty; *j'en ai assez,* I have had enough of it, I am sick of it; *on ne saurait avoir trop de soin de sa santé,* one cannot take too much care of one's health; *suis-je assez malheureux!* could I be more unfortunate!

assibilation [asibila'sjɔ̃], *n.f.* Sibilation of a letter not usually sibilated (as *t* in *suprématie*). **assibiler,** *v.t.* To sibilate.

assidu [asi'dy], *a.* (*fem.* **assidue**) Assiduous, diligent, attentive; punctual; regular, constant. **assiduité,** *n.f.* Assiduity, application, diligence, attention. **assidûment,** *adv.* Assiduously, sedulously, diligently, constantly, steadily, punctually.

assiégé [asje'ʒe], *a.* (*fem.* **-ée**) Besieged; importuned, dunned (by creditors).—*n.* Les assiégés *firent une sortie,* the besieged made a sally.

assiégeant, *a.* (*fem.* **-eante**) Besieging.—*n.* Besieger.

assiéger [asje'ʒe], *v.t.* To besiege, to lay siege to; to surround; to beset, to dun, to importune.

assiette [a'sjɛt], *n.f.* Attitude or posture (in sitting etc.), pose, situation, bearing, basis; seat (in the saddle); position, site; tone, state, disposition (of the mind etc.); a plate; a plateful (of something). *Assiette d'un bâtiment,* foundation of a building; *assiette d'un vaisseau,* trim of a ship; *assiette de l'impôt,* tax base; *assiette d'une rente,* assignment of an annuity; *faire l'assiette de,* to assess; *il n'a pas d'assiette,* he is shaky in the saddle; (*fig.*) *il n'est pas dans son assiette,* he is out of sorts, ill at ease. *Assiette anglaise,* cold buffet; *assiette à soupe,* soup-plate; *assiette d'argent,* silver plate; (*fig.*) *avoir l'assiette au beurre,* to have a nice fat job; *casseur d'assiettes,* swaggerer; *pique-assiette,* sponger, parasite.

assiettée, *n.f.* Plateful.

assignable [asi'ɲabl], *a.* Assignable.

assignat [asi'ɲa], *n.m.* Assignat (French paper money, 1789–97).

assignation [asiɲa'sjɔ̃], *n.f.* Assignment (of a fund etc. in payment), order to pay such sum, transfer; summons, subpoena, writ; appointment, rendezvous, assignation;

(*Comm.*) appointment. *Faire une assignation de,* to make an assignment of; *manquer à l'assignation,* to break an appointment; *signifier une assignation à quelqu'un,* to serve a writ upon someone.

assigner [asi'ɲe], *v.t.* To assign (property in payment of a debt etc.); to cite, to summon, to subpoena; to appoint, to fix (a rendezvous etc.). *Obtenir permission d'assigner quelqu'un,* to take out a writ against someone.

assimilable, *a.* Assimilable.

assimilateur, *a.* (*fem.* **-trice**) Assimilatory.

assimilation, *n.f.* Assimilation.

assimiler [asimi'le], *v.t.* To cause to resemble, to make like; to liken, to compare, to assimilate. *Être assimilé à un fonctionnaire,* to be ranked with civil servants; *s'assimiler à quelqu'un,* to compare onself to someone.

assis [a'si], *a.* (*fem.* **assise** (1)) Seated; situated; established. *Restez assis,* keep your seat; *voter par assis et levé,* to give one's vote by rising or by remaining seated.

assise (2) [a'siːz], *n.f.* A course (of stones etc.), foundation, basis; (*Geol.*) a layer characterized by a distinctive fauna or flora, stratum; (*Mining*) measure (of coal); (*pl.*) session of a criminal court, assizes. *Cet homme tient ses assises dans la maison,* this man is the oracle of the house; *cour d'assises,* Assize Court; *tenir les assises,* to hold the assizes.

Assise [a'siːz], *f.* Assisi.

assistance [asi'stɑ̃ːs], *n.f.* Audience, company, bystanders; congregation (in a church); *attendance, presence, assistance, help, aid; relief, comfort. *Assistance publique,* the poorlaw administration; *obtenir l'assistance judiciaire,* to be allowed to sue *in forma pauperis.*

assistant [asis'tɑ̃], *a.* (*fem.* **assistante**) Assisting, helping (applied especially to a priest assisting the celebrant at the altar).—*n.m.* Assistant (priest, teacher, etc.); person present, bystander, witness, etc. *Assistant(e) social(e),* social welfare worker; *il prit tous les assistants à témoin,* he took all present to witness.—*n.f.* (*R.-C. Ch.*) The deputy of an abbess.

assisté [asis'te], *a.* (*fem.* **-ée**) Receiving public assistance. *Enfant assisté,* foundling. —*n.* A person in receipt of relief.

assister [asis'te], *v.i.* To be at, to be present (*à*), to look on, to be a witness (*à*).—*v.t.* To assist, to help, to succour. *Assister les pauvres,* to relieve the poor; *assister ses amis de son crédit,* to use one's interest in favour of one's friends; *Dieu vous assiste!* God be with you!

associable [asɔ'sjabl], *a.* Associable.

association [asɔsja'sjɔ̃], *n.f.* Association; union; partnership, fellowship, society, order; (*Med.*) combination of different medicaments in one preparation. *Association d'idées,* association of ideas; *association de secours mutuels,* friendly society; *association illégale,* conspiracy; *contrat d'association,* deed of partnership; *faire association avec quelqu'un,* to enter into partnership with someone.

associationnisme, *n.m.* (*Psych.*) Associationism. **associationniste,** *a.* Relating to associationism.—*n.* Associationist.

associé [asɔ'sje], *a.* (*fem.* **-ée**) Associated, admitted (as a member).—*n.* Associate, fellow, member, partner. *Associé bailleur de fonds* or *commanditaire*, sleeping partner; *associé gérant*, managing partner; *associé principal*, senior partner.

associer [asɔ'sje], *v.t.* To associate, to take into partnership etc.; to divide or share something with someone; to link together, to connect (ideas etc.). **s'associer,** *v.r.* To enter into partnership, to associate oneself, to combine (with).

assoiffé [aswa'fe], *a.* (*fem.* **assoiffée**) Thirsty, athirst; eager (for).

assolement [asɔl'mɑ̃], *n.m.* (*Agric.*) Rotation (of crops).

assoler, *v.t.* To vary or rotate (crops).

assombrir [asɔ̃'briːr], *v.t.* To darken, to make gloomy, to throw a gloom over, to cloud. **s'assombrir,** *v.r.* To become dark or gloomy; to darken (of the brow).

assombrissement, *n.m.* Darkening, gloom.

assommant [asɔ'mɑ̃], *a.* (*fem.* **-ante**) Wearisome, tiresome, etc., boring. *Cet homme est assommant,* this man is a great bore.

assommer [asɔ'me], *v.t.* To beat to death, to knock on the head; to beat unmercifully; to overpower; to overwhelm, to stun; (*fig.*) to bore, to importune, to oppress. *Assommer à coups de bâton,* to beat to death with a stick; *assommer un bœuf,* to fell an ox; *la chaleur m'assomme,* the heat overpowers me.

assommeur, *n.m.* (*fem.* **-euse**) One who kills, bores, etc.; slaughterer, feller (of oxen etc.).

assommoir [asɔm'waːr], *n.m.* An instrument for felling, pole-axe; loaded bludgeon, lifepreserver, etc.; fall-trap; *low tavern, drinking den. *Coup d'assommoir,* overpowering blow.

assomptif [asɔ̃p'tif], *a.* (*fem.* **-ive**) (*Phil.*) Assumptive. **assomption,** *n.f.* Assumption; (*Eccl.*) Assumption of the Holy Virgin (Aug. 15).

assonance [asɔ'nɑ̃ːs], *n.f.* Assonance.

assonant, *a.* (*fem.* **-ante**) Assonant.

assorti [asɔr'ti], *a.* (*fem.* **assortie**) Assorted, matched, paired, suitable. *Il n'y a point de marchand mieux assorti,* no shopkeeper is better stocked; *mal assorti,* ill matched; *un mariage bien assorti,* a very suitable match.

assortiment [asɔrti'mɑ̃], *n.m.* Suitability, match; assortment, set, collection (of things that match). *Livres d'assortiment,* books on sale (as opposed to *livres de fonds*).

assortir [asɔr'tiːr], *v.t.* To assort, to match, to pair; to stock, to furnish (with things that go together or match). *Assortir des couleurs,* to match colours; *assortir une boutique,* to stock a shop.—*v.i.* To match, to suit, to go well together. **s'assortir,** *v.r.* To match, to agree, to be suitable, to go well together.

assortissant, *a.* (*fem.* **-ante**) Suitable, matching, going well (with something else).

*****assoter** [asɔ'te], *v.t.* To befool, to infatuate, to besot. **s'assoter,** *v.r.* To be foolishly fond (*de*).

assouchement [asuʃ'mɑ̃], *n.m.* (*Arch.*) Stone forming the base of the triangle in a pediment.

assoupi [asu'pi], *a.* (*fem.* **-ie**) Dozing; dormant (volcano).

assoupir [asu'piːr], *v.t.* To make drowsy, sleepy, heavy, or dull; (*fig.*) to assuage, to

allay, to deaden; *to suppress, to stifle, to hush up. **s'assoupir,** *v.r.* To grow drowsy, sleepy, dull, or heavy; to doze; (*fig.*) to be assuaged, to be appeased, to be stilled.

assoupissant, *a.* (*fem.* **-ante**) Making drowsy or sleepy, soporiferous. *Discours assoupissant,* speech that sends one to sleep.

assoupissement, *n.m.* Drowsiness, sleepiness, heaviness; (*fig.*) carelessness, sloth, negligence, supineness. (*Med.*) Coma.

assouplir [asu'pliːr], *v.t.* To make supple, flexible, or tractable; to break in (a horse). *Assouplir une étoffe,* to make a stuff soft. **s'assouplir,** *v.r.* To become supple, tractable, or manageable. **assouplissement,** *n.m.* Suppleness, tractability, docility. *Exercices d'assouplissement,* physical exercises.

assourdir [asur'diːr], *v.t.* To deafen, to stun; to muffle (a bell, an oar); (*Paint.*) to subdue (colours etc.), to darken, to deaden.

assourdissant, *a.* (*fem.* **-ante**) Deafening.

assourdissement, *n.m.* Deafening, muffling, deadening; a deafening noise; temporary deafness.

assouvir [asu'viːr], *v.t.* To glut, to satiate, to surfeit; to gratify; to cloy. *Assouvir sa faim,* to satiate one's hunger; *assouvir ses passions,* to gratify one's passions. **s'assouvir,** *v.r.* To be satiated, gratified, or cloyed.

assouvissement, *n.m.* Glutting, satiating; slaking.

Assuérus [asye'ryːs], *m.* Ahasuerus.

assujettir [asyʒe'tiːr], *v.t.* To subdue, to bring under subjection, to subjugate; to compel, to oblige; to fix, to fasten. *Assujettir ses passions,* to master one's passions. **s'assujettir,** *v.r.* To subject oneself, to submit. *S'assujettir à quelque chose,* to tie oneself down to a thing.

assujettissant, *a.* (*fem.* **-ante**), *a.* Binding, constraining, fettering, restrictive. **assujettissement,** *n.m.* Subjection, subjugation, enthralment; obligation, fixing.

assumer [asy'me], *v.t.* To take upon oneself, to assume.

assurable [asy'rabl], *a.* Insurable.

assurance [asy'rɑ̃ːs], *n.f.* Confidence, security, assurance; certainty, conviction; warrant, pledge, formal engagement; insurance, underwriting; (*fig.*) boldness, hardihood. *Agréez l'assurance de mon dévouement,* believe me yours truly; *assurance automobile,* motor insurance; *assurance au tiers,* third party insurance; *assurance contre les accidents du travail,* employer's liability insurance; *assurance contre l'incendie,* fire insurance; *assurance maritime,* marine insurance; *assurance sur la vie,* life insurance; *assurance sur risques ordinaires,* ordinary insurance; *Assurances Sociales (les),* social insurance, Social Security Scheme; *assurance vieillesse,* old-age pension scheme; *bureau d'assurance,* insurance office; *courtier d'assurance,* insurance broker; *donnez-moi des assurances,* give me a security; *police d'assurance,* insurance policy; *prime d'assurance,* premium. *Il met son assurance en Dieu,* he puts his trust in God; *il parle avec assurance,* he speaks boldly.

assuré [asy're], *a.* Assured, confident; sure, secure, positive, certain; trusty; insured. *Sa perte est assurée,* his ruin is infallible; *une retraite assurée,* an insured retirement.

—*n.* Person insured. **assurément,** *adv.*
Assuredly, confidently; surely, undoubtedly;
certainly. *Assurément non,* certainly not; *oui
assurément,* yes, most definitely.
assurer [asy′re], *v.t.* To make firm, solid, or
stable; to fix securely, to fasten, to steady;
(*Naut.* and *Mount.*) to belay; to assure, to
guarantee, to secure; to engage; to insure;
to underwrite; to assert, to affirm, to warrant,
to vouch for; to inspire with confidence.
Assurer pour l'aller, (of ships) to insure out;
assurer pour le retour, to insure home; *assurer
une maison contre l'incendie,* to insure a house
against fire; *il a assuré son argent,* he has
made sure of his money. **s'assurer,** *v.r.*
To make sure of, to ascertain; to be confident of; to be convinced. *S'assurer de quelqu'un,* to secure someone, to engage him;
s'assurer d'un poste, to make sure of a position.
assureur [asy′rœ:r], *n.m.* Underwriter, insurer, assurer.
Assyrie [asi′ri], *f.* Assyria.
assyrien [asi′rjɛ̃], *a.* (*fem.* **assyrienne**)
Assyrian. **assyriologie,** *n.f.* Assyriology.
assyriologue, *n.m.* Assyriologist.
astatique [asta′tik], *n.* (*Phys.*) Astatic.
aster [as′tɛ:r], *n.m.* (*Bot.*) Aster, starwort.
astérie [aste′ri], *n.f.* Starfish; (*Zool.*) *asteria,
star-stone.
astérisme [aste′rism], *n.m.* Asterism, constellation. **astérisque,** *n.m.* Asterisk.
astéroïde [astero′id], *n.m.* Asteroid.
asthénie [aste′ni], *n.f.* (*Path.*) Asthenia,
debility. **asthénique,** *a.* Asthenic.
asthmatique [asma′tik], *a.* Asthmatical.
asthme, *n.m.* [asm]. Asthma.
astic [as′tik], *n.m.* Piece of horse's bone used
as a polisher by shoemakers; a wooden
polisher used by soldiers for leather garments.
asticot [asti′ko], *n.m.* Gentle; maggot; (*pop.*)
quel drôle d'asticot! what a queer fellow!
asticoter [astiko′te], *v.t.* (*colloq.*) To tease, to
worry. *Il est toujours à m'asticoter,* he is
always plaguing me.
astigmate [astig′mat], *a.* Astigmatic. **astigmatisme,** *n.m.* Astigmatism. **astigmo-
mètre,** *n.m.* Astigmometer.
astiquage [asti′ka:ʒ], *n.m.* The act of polishing
or furbishing.
astiquer [asti′ke], *v.t.* To polish, to furbish,
to glaze. **s'astiquer,** *v.r.* (*colloq.*) To polish
oneself up, to tidy up.
astome [as′tɔm], *a.* Astomatous.
astracan or **astrakan** [astra′kɑ̃], *n.m.* Astrakhan, Persian lamb (fur).
astragale [astra′gal], *n.m.* (*Arch.*) Astragal;
(*Anat.*) astragalus, ankle-bone; (*Bot.*) astragalus, milk-vetch.
astrakan [ASTRACAN].
astral [as′tral], *a.* (*fem.* **-ale,** *pl.* **-aux**) Astral.
astre [astr], *n.m.* Star; (*fig.*) celebrity, luminary. *Astres errants,* wandering stars; *cette
femme est belle comme un astre,* this woman
is a paragon of beauty; *jusqu'aux astres,*
(praising etc.) to the skies.
astrée [as′tre], *n.f.* (*Zool.*) A genus of madre-
pores, astraea.
Astrée [as′tre], *f.* Astraea.
astreindre [as′trɛ̃:dr], *v.t. irr.* (*pres.p.* **astrei-
gnant,** *p.p.* **astreint;** *conjug. like* CRAINDRE)
To oblige, compel, subject. **s'astreindre,**

v.r. To confine oneself, to tie oneself
down (*d*).
astreinte [as′trɛ̃t], *n.f.* (*Law*) Compulsion;
fine for delay in the performance of a contract.
astringence [astrɛ̃′ʒɑ̃:s], *n.f.* Astringency.
astringent, *a.* (*fem.* **-ente**) and *n.m.* Astringent.
astrodynamique [astrɔdina′mik], *n.f.* Astro-
dynamics.
astroïde [as′trɔid], *a.* Star-shaped.
astrolabe [astrɔ′lab], *n.m.* (*Astron.*) Astrolabe.
astrolâtre [astrɔ′lɑtr], *n.m.* Star-worshipper.
astrolâtrie, *n.f.* Astrolatry.
astrologie [astrɔlɔ′ʒi], *n.f.* Astrology. **astrologique,** *a.* Astrological. **astrologiquement,** *adv.* Astrologically. **astrologue,**
n.m. Astrologer.
astronaute [astrɔ′nɔ:t], *n.m.* Astronaut.
astronautique, *n.f.* Astronautics.
astronome [astrɔ′nɔm], *n.m.* Astronomer.
astronomie, *n.f.* Astronomy. **astronomique,**
a. Astronomical, astronomic.
astrophysique, *a.* Astrophysical.—*n.f.* Astro-
physics.
astrostatique, *n.f.* Astrostatics.
astuce [as′tys], *n.f.* Craft, guile, cunning.
astucieuse [ASTUCIEUX]. **astucieusement,**
adv. Craftily, cunningly. **astucieux,** *a.*
(*fem.* **astucieuse**) Crafty, wily.
Asturies [asty′ri], **les,** *f.pl.* The Asturias.
asymétrie [asime′tri], *n.f.* Asymmetry.
asymétrique, *a.* Asymmetrical.
asymptote [asɛ̃p′tɔt], *n.f.* (*Geom.*) Asymptote.
asymptotique, *a.* Asymptotic, asymptotical.
asynchrone [asɛ̃′krɔn], *a.* Asynchronous.
asynchronisme, *n.m.* Asynchronism.
asyndète [asɛ̃′dɛt], *n.f.* (*Rhet.*) Asyndeton.
Atalante [ata′lɑ̃:t], *f.* Atalanta.
ataraxie [atarak′si], *n.f.* Ataraxia, perfect
quietude.
atavique [ata′vik], *a.* Atavistic.
atavisme [ata′vism], *n.m.* Atavism.
ataxie [ata′ksi], *n.f.* Ataxy. *Ataxie locomotrice,*
locomotor ataxy.
atèle [a′tɛl], *n.m.* (*Zool.*) Spider-monkey.
atelier [atə′lje], *n.m.* Workshop, studio,
atelier; (*collect.*) those working in a particular
atelier, a gang of workmen etc.; (*fig.*) the
followers of an artist; (*Freemasonry*) lodge,
lodge-meeting. *Chef d'atelier,* head-foreman,
overseer; *jour d'atelier,* the best light (for a
statue, picture, etc.); *tout l'atelier m'a quitté,*
all my workmen have left me.
atermoiement [atɛrmwa′mã], *n.m.* Composition (with creditors etc.) for delay of payment; (*fig.*) delay, evasion, shift.
atermoyer [atɛrmwa′je], *v.t.* To put off, to
delay (a payment).—*v.i.* (*fig.*) To put off, to
make shifts. **s'atermoyer,** *v.r.* To compound with one's creditors.
Athanase [ata′na:z], *m.* Athanasius.
athanasien [atana′sjɛ̃], *a.* (*fem.* **-ienne**)
Athanasian. *Le symbole de saint Athanase,* the
Athanasian creed.
athée [a′te], *a.* Atheistic.—*n.* Atheist. **athéisme,** *n.m.* Atheism. **athéiste,** *a.* Atheistic.
athéistique, *a.* Atheistic.
athénée [ate′ne], *n.m.* Athenaeum.
Athènes [a′tɛːn], *f.* Athens.
athénien [ate′njɛ̃], *a.* and *n.* (*fem.* **athénienne**)
Athenian.

athérine [ate'rin], *n.f.* (*Ichth.*) Atherine, sand-smelt.
athermal [ater'mal], *a.* (*fem.* -ale, *pl.* -aux) Not thermal (of cold mineral springs).
athermane [ater'man] or **athermique,** *a.* Athermanous.
athéromateux [aterɔma'tø], *a.* (*fem.* -euse) (*Path.*) Pertaining to *athérome* [*see foll.*].—*n.* A person suffering from this.
athérome [ate'rɔm], *n.m.* (*Path.*) An encysted tumour.
athlète [a'tlɛt], *n.m.* Athlete; strongly built man. **athlétique,** *a.* Athletic.—*n.f.* Athletics. **athlétiquement,** *adv.* Athletically. **athlétisme,** *n.m.* Athleticism; athletics.
atlante [a'tlɑ̃:t], *n.m.* (*Arch.*) Atlantes, Telamones (*pl.*)
Atlantide [atlɑ̃'tid], *f.* Atlantis.
atlantique [atlɑ̃'tik], *a.* Atlantic.—*n.m.* **L'Atlantique,** The Atlantic (ocean).
atlas [a'tlɑ:s], *n.m.* Atlas, volume of plates attached to a work; (*Anat.*) atlas.
atmolyse [atmɔ'li:z], *n.f.* (*Phys.*) Atmolysis.
atmosphère [atmɔs'fɛ:r], *n.f.* Atmosphere.
atmosphérique, *a.* Atmospheric, atmospherical. *Pression atmosphérique,* atmospheric pressure.
(*C*) **atoca** [atɔ'ka], *n.m.* Cranberry.
atoll [a'tɔl], *n.m.* Atoll.
atome [a'tom], *n.m.* Atom, corpuscle; (*fig.*) a particle, a little bit or fragment (of anything). **atomicité,** *n.f.* (*Chem.*) Atomicity, valency. **atomique,** *a.* Atomic, atomical. *Bombe atomique,* atom, atomic bomb; *énergie atomique,* atomic energy; *Commissariat à l'énergie atomique,* Atomic Energy Authority; *pile atomique,* atomic pile. **atomiser,** *v.t.* To pulverize. **atomiseur,** *n.m.* Pulverizer.
atomisme, *n.m.* Atomism, doctrine of atoms. **atomiste,** *n.m.* Atomist. **atomistique,** *a.* Atomical; (*Chem.*) atomism. *Théorie atomistique,* atomic theory.
atonal (*fem.* -ale), *a.* (*Mus.*) Atonal. **atonalité,** *n.f.* Atonality.
atone [a'tɔn], *a.* Atonic, debilitated, dull; lack-lustre, expressionless (of eyes); (*Gram.*) atonic, not accentuated. **atonie,** *n.f.* Atony, debility. **atonique,** *a.* Atonic.
atours [a'tu:r], *n.m.* (*used only in pl.*) Woman's attire, dress, ornament. *Dame d'atours,* lady of the bedchamber; *être dans ses plus beaux atours,* to be dressed in all one's finery.
atout [a'tu], *n.m.* A trump; trump-card; (*fig.*) chance, opportunity; (*colloq.*) stinging blow. *Avoir tous les atouts en main,* to have every chance; *jouer atout,* to play trumps.
atoxique [atɔk'sik], *a.* Non-poisonous.
atrabilaire [atrabi'lɛ:r], *a.* Atrabilious, splenetic, morose, peevish.
âtre [ɑ:tr], *n.m.* Hearth; fire-place. *Au coin de l'âtre,* in the chimney-corner.
Atrée [a'tre], *m.* Atreus.
atroce [a'trɔs], *a.* Atrocious, cruel, excruciating; heinous, odious, dreadful. **atrocement,** *adv.* Atrociously, cruelly, outrageously. **atrocité,** *n.f.* Atrociousness, heinousness; atrocity, cruelty.
atrophie [atrɔ'fi], *n.f.* (*Path.*) Atrophy. **atrophié,** *a.* (*fem.* **atrophiée**) Atrophied, wasted, withered, stunted. **atrophier,** *v.t.* To cause to waste or wither. **s'atrophier,** *v.r.* To waste away. **atrophique,** *a.* Atrophic.

atropine [atrɔ'pin], *n.f.* (*Chem.*) Atropine.
atropisme, *n.m.* Atropism.
attabler [ata'ble], *v.t.* To set at table. **s'attabler,** *v.r.* To sit down to or take one's place at table.
attachant [ata'ʃɑ̃], *a.* (*fem.* -ante) Engaging, winning, attractive.
attache [a'taʃ], *n.f.* That which ties or links, bond, cord, leash, strap, etc.; (*Anat.*) the place where a muscle is attached; place or part where the foot or hand is joined to the limbs; (*fig.*) attachment, strong affection or sentiment for. *Attache métallique,* paper-fastener; *avoir les attaches fines,* to have delicate joints; *être à l'attache,* to be always slaving; *mettre un chien à l'attache,* to tie a dog up; *port d'attache,* (*Naut.*) port of departure and arrival of a boat or liner, home port; *prendre des chevaux à l'attache,* to take in horses; *vivre sans attache,* to live free.
attaché [ata'ʃe], *n.m.* Attaché (of an embassy).
attachement [ataʃ'mɑ̃], *n.m.* Attachment; affection, liaison; eagerness, constant application, zeal; (*pl.*) architect's memoranda of work done. *Attachement à l'étude,* fondness for study.
attacher [ata'ʃe], *v.t.* To fasten, to tie, to attach, to fix, etc., especially by means of a cord, strap, etc.; (*fig.*) to apply, to affix, to attribute; to connect, to associate; to engage, to bind, to endear, to interest, to occupy. *Attacher avec une courroie,* to strap; *attacher avec un crochet,* to hook; *attacher avec une épingle,* to pin; *attacher du prix à quelque chose,* to set a value upon something; *attacher le grelot,* to bell the cat; *c'est ce qui m'attache à vous,* this is what binds me to you.—*v.i.* To catch (macaroni, potatoes) when baking.
s'attacher, *v.r.* To take hold, to attach or fasten oneself; to cling, to cleave, to stick, to adhere; to be attached, to have an affection for; to interest oneself in, to apply oneself to. *Ils s'attachèrent l'un à l'autre,* they became attached to each other; *je m'attachai à lui plaire, mais en vain,* I used all my efforts to please him but in vain; *la poix s'attache aux doigts,* pitch sticks to the fingers; *s'attacher à remplir son devoir,* to strive to fulfil one's duty; *s'attacher aux pas de,* to follow everywhere.
attaquable [ata'kabl], *a.* Assailable, that may be attacked; of doubtful validity.
attaquant, *n.m.* Assailant.
attaque [a'tak], *n.f.* Attack, assault, aggression, hold-up (of a vehicle); fit, stroke. *Être d'attaque,* to be fit and plucky; *y aller d'attaque,* to go at it tooth and nail; *une attaque par les gaz,* a gas attack; *une attaque de nerfs,* a nervous attack, a fit of hysterics.
attaquer [ata'ke], *v.t.* To attack, to assail, to assault, to fall or set upon; to take hold of, to seize suddenly (of illness etc.); to impugn, to criticize, to censure; to contest the validity of (a document); to begin upon (a dish), to open (a subject); (*Row.*) to jump on to it. *Attaquer en justice,* to sue for; *il attaque bien la corde,* (*Mus.*) he plays with great 'attaque'; *il attaque bien la note,* he strikes the note well; *l'attaquer sur sa naissance,* to reproach him with his birth.
s'attaquer, *v.r.* To encounter, to make or conduct an attack (*à*); to attack each other,

to tackle. *Il s'est attaqué à son maître*, he has encountered one who is more than his match.

attaqueur, *n.m.* Attacker, leader of the attack.

attardé [atar'de], *a.* (*fem.* **-ée**) Late, behindhand; mentally retarded (child).

attarder [atar'de], *v.t.* To make late, to delay. **s'attarder**, *v.r.* To be belated, to loiter, to linger.

atteindre [a'tɛ̃:dr], *v.t. irr.* (*pres.p.* **atteignant**, *p.p.* **atteint**; *conjugated like* CRAINDRE) To touch from a distance, to reach, to hit, to attain; to arrive at, to attain to; to overtake, to come up to. *Atteindre l'âge de*, to attain the age of; *atteindre l'ennemi*, to come up with the enemy; *atteindre son maître*, to equal one's master; *ce danger ne saurait m'atteindre*, this danger cannot affect me; *être atteint de*, to be suffering from; *il a beau courir, je l'atteindrai*, it is in vain for him to run, I shall overtake him; *la balle l'atteignit au front*, the ball struck him on the forehead; *nous atteindrons le village avant la nuit*, we shall reach the village before night.—*v.i.* To reach with difficulty, to attain (*à*). *Atteindre à la perfection*, to attain to perfection; *atteindre au but*, to hit the mark; *il n'atteint pas à votre niveau*, he is not up to your standard; *je ne saurais y atteindre*, I could not rise to it.

atteint [a'tɛ̃], *a.* (*fem.* **atteinte** (1)) Hit, struck; attacked, seized, affected; reached. *Atteint par la limite d'âge*, who has reached the age limit, on the retired list; *atteint d'une maladie grave*, suffering from a serious disease.

atteinte (2) [a'tɛ̃:t], *n.f.* Reach, blow, stroke, touch; attack, fit, seizure (of disease); injury, damage, harm, wrong. *Je suis hors de ses atteintes*, I am out of his reach; *les atteintes du froid*, the ill effects of cold; *porter atteinte à*, to injure, to impair, to commit an offence against; *porter atteinte aux droits de*, to infringe the rights of; *sa santé n'a jamais reçu d'atteinte*, his health has never been impaired; *une légère atteinte de goutte*, a slight attack of the gout.

attelable [at'labl], *a.* Fit for harness.

attelage [at'la:ʒ], *n.m.* Harnessing, yoking; team, yoke, set, pair; carriage, horses; (*Rail.*) coupling. *Chaîne d'attelage*, coupling-chain; *attelage à quatre*, four-in-hand.

atteler [at'le], *v.t.* To put horses etc. (to); to harness, yoke, etc. (to); (*fig.*) to subjugate, to drag at one's heels. *C'est une charrette mal attelée*, they are an ill-assorted couple. (*Mil.*) *Attelez!* hook-in! **s'atteler**, *v.r.* To settle down to (*à*); (*fig.*) to associate, apply, or make (oneself) subservient, to hitch one's waggon to.

attelle [a'tɛl], *n.f.* Hames; (*Surg.*) splint.

attenant [at'nã], *a.* (*fem.* **attenante**) Contiguous, adjoining, next door to, close by (*à*).

attendre [a'tã:dr], *v.t.* To await, to wait for, to stay for; to look forward to, to expect; to look for, to count upon, to attend, to be in store for. *Attendez!* wait a minute! *attendez jusqu'à demain*, wait till tomorrow; *attendez-moi sous l'orme*, you may wait for me till doomsday; *attendons encore un peu*, let us wait a little longer; *attendre la mort*, to await death; *c'est là où je l'attends*, there I shall have him; *je l'attends à tout moment*, I expect him any minute; *je suis las d'attendre*, I am

tired of waiting; *le dîner nous attend*, dinner is waiting for us; *qu'il attende*, let him wait; *tout vient à point à qui sait attendre*, everything comes to him who waits; *une question n'attendait pas l'autre*, question followed question; *voilà le sort qui vous attend*, this is the fate in store for you.—*v.i.* To put off, to delay (*de*). *En attendant*, in the meantime, meanwhile, till then; *en attendant mieux*, until something better turns up; *en attendant que*, (*with subj.*) till, until; *jouons en attendant qu'il vienne*, let us play till he comes; *se faire attendre*, to keep people waiting. **s'attendre**, *v.r.* To rely upon, to count upon, to trust (*à*); to expect, to look forward (*à*). *Il ne faut pas s'attendre à cela*, we must not rely upon that; *je m'y attendais*, I expected as much; *je ne m'attendais pas à cela*, I did not expect that.

attendrir [atã'dri:r], *v.t.* To make tender, to soften; to touch, to move, to affect, to mollify. *Cela attendrit la viande*, that makes meat tender; *ses larmes m'ont attendri*, his tears have softened my heart. **s'attendrir** *v.r.* To grow tender; to be moved, to melt, to pity, to relent. *S'attendrir sur le sort de quelqu'un*, to pity the fate of someone.

attendrissant, *a.* (*fem.* **-ante**) Moving, affecting, touching. **attendrissement**, *n.m.* Compassion, pity; tears, sensibility; tenderness.

attendu [atã'dy], *prep.* Considering, on account of, in consideration of. *Attendu que*, seeing that, as, whereas, since.—*n.m. pl.* *les attendus* (of a judgment), the reasons adduced.

attenir [at'ni:r], *v.i.* To adjoin, to be contiguous (*à*); to be related.

attentat [atã'ta], *n.m.* Attempt at crime; crime, attempt; outrage, infringement, violation. *Attentat à la pudeur*, outrage on decency; *attentat contre la vie de*, attempt upon the life of; *attentat contre les lois*, outrage upon the laws.

attentatoire, *a.* Hostile, outrageous, prejudicial.

attente [a'tã:t], *n.f.* Waiting, awaiting, expectation; hope. *Dans l'attente de vous lire*, (*Comm.*) awaiting the favour of a reply; *ligature d'attente*, (*Surg.*) temporary ligature; *pierre d'attente*, (*Build.*) toothing; (*fig.*) stepping-stone; *remplir* or *tromper l'attente*, to come up to or deceive expectation; *salle d'attente*, waiting-room.

attenter [atã'te], *v.i.* To make a criminal attempt. *Attenter à la vie de quelqu'un*, to make an attempt upon someone's life; *attenter à ses jours*, to attempt suicide; *attenter contre la liberté publique*, to make an attack on public liberty.

attentif [atã'tif], *a.* (*fem.* **attentive**) Attentive, heedful, considerate. *Être attentif à*, to look after, to see to.

attention [atã'sjɔ̃], *n.f.* Attention, notice; heed, care, vigilance; regard, respect, consideration. *Attention!* look out! stand by! *attention au commandement!* (*Mil.*) attention! *attention aux travaux*, danger, road up; *avec attention*, attentively; *cela mérite attention*, that deserves notice; *faire attention à*, to mind; *faire une chose avec attention*, to do a thing with care; *faites donc attention*, mind what you say or do; *faute d'attention*, inadvertently; *force d'attention*, intentness; *il a eu l'attention de m'avertir*, he was good enough to warn me; *il a pour moi de grandes attentions*, he has a great regard for me; *manque d'attention*, heedlessness; *n'y faites pas attention!* do not mind it! *prêtez-y attention*, pay attention to it; *sans attention*, reckless; *s'attirer l'attention du public*, to attract the notice of the public.

attentionné [atɑ̃sjɔ'ne], *a.* (*fem.* **attentionnée**) Attentive, considerate.

attentisme [atɑ̃'tism], *n.m.* Wait-and-see policy. **attentiste**, *a.* and *n.* In favour of a wait-and-see policy.

attentivement [atɑ̃tiv'mɑ̃], *adv.* Attentively, carefully.

atténuant [ate'nɥɑ̃], *a.* (*fem.* **atténuante**) Mitigating; (*Law*) palliating, extenuating. —*n.m.* (*Med.*) An attenuant medicine or application.

atténuation [atenɥa'sjɔ̃], *n.f.* Attenuation, extenuation, mitigation, palliation.

atténué [ate'nɥe], *a.* (*fem.* **-ée**) Attenuated, wasted, emaciated; palliated; (*Bot.*) tapering.

atténuer [ate'nɥe], *v.t.* To make smaller, thinner, feebler, etc.; to attenuate; to extenuate, to mitigate, to underrate, to tame (a charge). *Atténuer un crime*, to palliate a crime; *atténuer une chute*, to break a fall.

atterrage [ate'ra:ʒ], *n.m.* (*Naut.*) Landing, landfall, making land.

atterrant [ate'rɑ̃], *a.* (*fem.* **atterrante**) Astounding, startling, overwhelming.

atterrement [ater'mɑ̃], *n.m.* Overthrow; prostration, amazement.

atterré [ate're], *a.* (*fem.* **-ée**) Horror-stricken, dumbfounded.

atterrer [ate're], *v.t.* *To throw or strike down; to overwhelm; to astound.

atterrir [ate'ri:r], *v.i.* To land, to make land.

atterrissage, *n.m.* Landing, making land. *Atterrissage forcé*, forced landing; *pont d'atterrissage*, landing-deck (of aircraft carrier); *terrain d'atterrissage*, landing-ground.

atterrissement [ateris'mɑ̃], *n.m.* Alluvion, accretion, alluvium.

attestation [atɛsta'sjɔ̃], *n.f.* Attestation, evidence; certificate, voucher, testimonial. *Attestation sous serment*, affidavit.

attester [atɛs'te], *v.t.* To attest, to certify, to avouch, to witness, to testify; to call to witness. *J'en atteste le ciel*, I call heaven to witness; *j'en atteste les dieux*, witness, ye gods!

atticisme [ati'sism], *n.m.* Atticism. **atticiste**, *n.m.* Atticist.

attiédir [atje'di:r], *v.t.* To cool, to make lukewarm, to abate, to mitigate the ardour of; to warm. *Le temps attiédira leur zèle*, time will cool their ardour. **s'attiédir**, *v.r.* To grow cool or lukewarm; to cool off.

attiédissement, *n.m.* Lukewarmness, coolness; abatement.

attier [a'tje], *n.m.* (*Bot.*) Sweet-sop.

attifage [ati'fa:ʒ] or **attifement**, *n.m.* Get-up, rig-out.

attifer [ati'fe] (*always in a bad sense*), *v.t.* To dress up, to bedizen. **s'attifer**, *v.r.* To dress or rig oneself out.

attiger [ati'ʒe], *v.i.* (*slang*) To exaggerate; to hit. *Se faire attiger*, to be hit, to catch it.

attignole [ati'ɲɔl], *n.f.* Cheap sausage-cake; faggot, rissole.

Attique [a'tik], *f.* Attica.

attique [a'tik], *a.* Attic; (*fig.*) witty, urbane. *Sel attique*, Attic salt.—*n.m.* (*Arch.*) Attic.

attiquement, *adv.* After the Attic style; in the Attic dialect.

attirable [ati'rabl], *a.* Attractable (by the magnet etc.).

attirail [ati'ra:j], *n.m.* (*collect.*) Apparatus, implements, utensils, gear, furniture, tackle; baggage, train, equipage, paraphernalia; show, pomp. *L'attirail d'une cuisine*, kitchen apparatus and utensils; *l'attirail d'une imprimerie*, the materials and implements of a printing office.

attirance [ati'rɑ̃:s], *n.f.* Attraction (*vers*).

attirant [ati'rɑ̃:], *a.* (*fem.* **attirante**) Attractive, alluring, enticing, engaging.

attirer [ati're], *v.t.* To attract, to draw; to win or gain over, to lure, to wheedle, to entice; to inspire; to occasion, to bring with it. *Attirer l'ennemi dans une embuscade*, to draw the enemy into an ambush; *attirer les yeux* ou *les regards de tout le monde*, to attract the eyes of all the world; *l'aimant attire le fer*, the magnet attracts iron; *un malheur en attire un autre*, misfortunes never come singly. **s'attirer**, *v.r.* To draw to or down upon one, to bring upon one; to incur, to win. *S'attirer des affaires*, to get oneself into scrapes; *s'attirer l'attention du public*, to attract the notice of the public.

attisage [ati'za:ʒ], or **attisement**, *n.m.* The act of stirring up, poking (a fire), fanning the flame, etc.

(*C*) **attisée** [ati'ze], *n.f.* Good-fire; armful (of stove-wood).

attiser [ati'ze], *v.t.* To make or stir up (a fire); to poke; (*fig.*) to incense, to stir up. *Attiser le feu*, (*fig.*) to fan the flame, to envenom. **attiseur**, *n.m.* (*fem.* **attiseuse**) One who stirs up or pokes the fire; (*fig.*) who stirs up hatred or discontent.

attisoir or **attisonnoir**, *n.m.* Poker (especially in foundries); fire-rake.

attitré [ati'tre], *a.* (*fem.* **attitrée**) Recognized, appointed, regular, ordinary; hired. *Juges attitrés*, appointed judges; *marchand attitré*, the shopkeeper one usually deals with; *témoins attitrés*, hired witnesses.

attitude [ati'tyd], *n.f.* Attitude; (*Paint.*) posture; (*fig.*) attitude of mind etc.

attouchement [atuʃ'mɑ̃], *n.m.* Touch, contact.

attracteur [atrak'tœ:r], *a.* (*fem.* **-trice**) Attractile.

attractif, *a.* (*fem.* **-ive**) Attractive.

attraction, *n.f.* Attraction; (*pl.*) attractions, cabaret show.

attractivement, *adv.* Attractively.

attractivité [atraktivi'te], *n.f.* (*Phys.*) Attractivity.

attrait [a'trɛ], *n.m.* Allurement, attraction, charm; inclination, bent; (*pl.*) attractions, charms; bait. *La beauté est un puissant attrait*, beauty is a powerful charm.

attrapade (atra'pad], *n.f.* (*colloq.*) Set-to, quarrel.

attrape [a'trap], *n.f.* Trap, gin; (*fig.*) ruse, deceptiveness; trick, take-in, sell, hoax; (*Naut.*) hawser.

attrape-lourdaud [ATTRAPE-NIGAUD].

attrape-mouche or **attrape-mouches** [atrap'muʃ], *n.m. inv.* (*Bot.*) Venus's fly-trap; fly-catcher.

attrape-niais [ATTRAPE-NIGAUD].

attrape-nigaud [atrapni'go], *n.m.* (*pl.* **attrape-nigauds**) Booby-trap.

attraper [atra'pe], *v.t.* To catch; to entrap, to ensnare; to take in, to cheat, to trick, to bamboozle; to imitate, to catch the manner of; (*fam.*) to scold, to rate; to hit; to seize; to reach, to hit off; to overtake, to catch up; to get accidentally (a cold etc.). *Attrape!* take that! it serves you right; *attrapé!* caught! *Attraper un renard dans un piège*, to catch a fox in a trap; *il en a attrapé de plus fins que vous*, he has taken in people more cunning than you; *attraper le sens d'un auteur*, to grasp the meaning of an author; *je vais l'attraper*, I shall catch it; *la pierre l'a attrapé à la tempe*, the stone hit him on the temple; *attraper quelqu'un sur le fait*, to catch someone in the act; *attraper un caractère*, to hit off a character; *attraper un rhume*, to catch a cold; *se faire attraper*, to be dropped on; to get a wigging; to catch it; to be taken in. **s'attraper**, *v.r.* To hit (against); to be caught (in); to get hold of, to attack; to seize, to cling to, to stick (*à*); (of a horse) to overreach.

attrapeur [atra'pœːr], *n.m.* (*fem.* **attrapeuse**) Deceiver, cheat, trickster.

attrapoire [atra'pwaːr], *n.f.* Trap, pitfall, snare; (*fig.*) wile, trick.

attrayant [atrɛ'jɑ̃], *a.* (*fem.* **attrayante**) Attractive, winning, engaging, charming.

attribuable [atri'bɥabl], *a.* Attributable, referable, due to.

attribuer [atri'bɥe], *v.t.* To assign, to confer; to attribute, to ascribe, to impute (a thing to someone). *Attribuer des privilèges à une charge*, to attach privileges to an office; *dessin attribué à Ingres*, a reputed Ingres drawing. **s'attribuer**, *v.r.* To assume, to take upon oneself, to arrogate to oneself, to claim. *Il s'attribue de grands droits*, he claims extensive rights.

attribut [atri'by], *n.m.* Attribute, peculiar property, prerogative; special symbol or emblem; (*Log.*) that which may be predicated; (*Gram.*) predicate.

attributaire, *n.* (*Law*) assign.

attributif, *a.* (*fem.* **-ive**) (*Gram.*) Attributive; predicative; (*Law*) conferring a right, attributive.

attribution, *n.f.* Attribution, conferment, awarding (of a grant); (*usu. in pl.*) privilege, prerogative (of a person); province, department, jurisdiction; (*Law*) cognizance, competence. *Lettres d'attribution*, patents conferring power (to act).

attristant [atris'tɑ̃], *a.* (*fem.* **-ante**) Saddening, sorrowful, melancholy, grievous.

attrister [atris'te], *v.t.* To grieve, to sadden, to trouble, to cast down, to throw a gloom over. *Cette nouvelle l'attriste*, that piece of news grieves him. **s'attrister**, *v.r.* To be sad, to become sorrowful.

attrition [atri'sjɔ̃], *n.f.* Attrition, friction; (*Theol.*) attrition.

attroupement [atrup'mɑ̃], *n.m.* Riotous assemblage, mob. *Loi contre les attroupements*, Riot Act.

attrouper [atru'pe], *v.t.* To assemble, to gather together in troops or a mob. *Il attroupa toute la canaille*, he gathered all the rabble together. **s'attrouper**, *v.r.* To flock together, to gather in crowds. *Défense de s'attrouper*, no meetings allowed.

au [o], *contraction of* À LE, to the. *Céder au torrent*, to give way to the torrent; *sauce au vin*, wine-sauce.

aubade [o'bad], *n.f.* Aubade, dawn song; (*iron.*) row, hot reception.

aubage [o'baːʒ], *n.m.* Thin boards for panelling.

aubaine [o'bɛn], *n.f.* (*Law*) Escheat, escheatage; windfall, piece of good luck.

aube (1) [oːb], *n.f.* The dawn; alb (priest's vestment). *L'aube du jour*, the break of day.

aube (2) [oːb], *n.f.* Float-board, float; paddle-board (of steamers). *Aube mobile*, feathering paddle; *aubes de moulin*, flat boards of a mill; *roue à aubes*, paddle-wheel.

aubépine [obe'pin], *n.f.* Hawthorn, whitethorn, may.

aubère [o'bɛːr], *a.* (*Horse*) Red roan.

auberge [o'bɛrʒ], *n.f.* Inn, public-house, tavern. *Auberge de (la) jeunesse*, youth hostel.

aubergine [obɛr'ʒin], *n.f.* Aubergine, egg-plant.

aubergiste [obɛr'ʒist], *n.m.* Innkeeper, publican, landlord, host.

auberon [o'brɔ̃], *n.m.* Catch (of a lock).

aubier [o'bje], *n.m.* Sap-wood, alburnum.

aubifoin [obi'fwɛ̃], *n.m.* (*fam.*) Cornflower.

*aubin [o'bɛ̃], *n.m.* A sort of canter or Canterbury gallop, the horse galloping with his fore-legs and trotting with the hind-legs.

aubiner, *v.i.* To canter thus.

aubour [o'buːr], *n.m.* Laburnum; guelder-rose.

aucun [o'kœ̃], *a. and pron.* (*fem.* **aucune**) None, no one, not one; not any; anyone; any. *Aucun ne le dira*, no one will say so; *de tous ceux qui se disaient mes amis aucun m'a-t-il secouru?* did any of all those who called themselves my friends assist me? *il n'a pris aucune disposition*, he has made no arrangements; *il n'y a aucun de ses sujets qui ne mourût pour lui*, there is not one of his subjects who would not die for him; *je doute qu'aucun de vous le fasse*, I doubt whether any of you will do it; *je ne connais aucun de vos juges*, I know none of your judges; *je vous le cède sans bénéfice aucun*, I let you have it without any profit whatever; *sans aucun frais*, without any expense.

aucunement [okyn'mɑ̃], *adv.* In no wise, not at all, not in the least; at all. *Aucunement, Monsieur*, not in the least, Sir.

audace [o'das], *n.f.* Audacity, daring, boldness; impudence, insolence. *Avec audace*, insolently; *payer d'audace*, to brazen it out.

audacieusement, *adv.* Audaciously, daringly, boldly; rashly; impudently. **audacieux**, *a.* (*fem.* **audacieuse**) Audacious, bold, daring; impudent, insolent, presumptuous. *Entreprise audacieuse*, bold enterprise; *projet audacieux*, daring project.

au deçà, au dedans, au dehors, au delà [DEÇÀ, DEDANS, DEHORS, DELÀ].

au-dessous [od'su], *prep.* Below.

au-dessus [od'sy], *prep.* Above.

au-devant [od'vɑ̃], *prep.* Towards. *Aller au-devant d'un danger*, to anticipate danger.

audibilité [odibili'te], *n.f.* Audibility.

audible [o'dibl], *a.* Audible.

audience [o'djã:s], *n.f.* Audience, hearing etc.; reception, hearing (by a sovereign etc.); sitting, session, court, tribunal; auditory. *Audience à huis clos*, a sitting with closed doors, a case heard in camera; *audience publique*, open court; *donner audience*, to give audience; *en pleine audience*, in open court; *jour d'audience*, court day; *l'audience est levée*, the sitting is over; *l'audience est reprise*, the case is resumed; *on le mit hors de l'audience*, he was turned out of court; *ouvrir l'audience*, to open the court; *tenir l'audience*, (of a judge) to sit, to preside.

audiencier, *a.* and *n.m.* (*Huissier*) audiencier, crier of a court.

audiomètre [odjo'mɛtr], or **audimètre**, *n.m.* Audiometer.

audion [o'djɔ̃], *n.m.* Vacuum-tube, audion.

audiophone [odjo'fo:n] or **audiphone**, *n.m.* Audiphone.

audio-visuel [odjovi'zɥel], *a.* Audio-visual. *Moyens audio-visuels*, audio-visual aids.

audit [o'di]. To the said . . .

auditeur [odi'tœ:r], *n.m.* (*fem.* **auditrice**) Hearer, listener; auditor (of accounts). *a.* Acting as auditor. *Les auditeurs*, the audience; *conseiller auditeur*, counsellor acting as referee.

auditif [odi'tif], *a.* (*fem.* **auditive**) Auditory. *Conduit auditif externe*, cavity of the ear.

audition [odi'sjɔ̃], *n.f.* Hearing; (*Law*) hearing (of a case etc.); audition (of a singer etc.). *L'audition des témoins*, the hearing of witnesses; *une audition musicale*, a wireless concert. **auditionner**, *v.t.* To audition.

auditoire [odi'twa:r], *n.m.* Auditory; congregation (in a church), audience (in a theatre etc.).

auditorat [odito'ra], *n.m.* Auditorship (in the *Conseil d'État* or *Cour des Comptes*).

auditrice [AUDITEUR].

Audomarois [odoma'rwa], *n.m.* Inhabitant of St. Omer.

auge [o:ʒ], *n.f.* Trough (for drinking etc.); a plasterer's hod; bucket (of a water-mill); (*Elec.*) cell. *Auge à goudron*, (*Naut.*) tar-bucket; *auge d'écurie*, manger.

augée [o'ʒe], *n.f.* Troughful, hodful.

auget [o'ʒɛ], *n.m.* Small trough; seed-box, drawer (of a birdcage); spout (of a mill-hopper); bucket (of a water-wheel); trough (in a magazine-rifle).

augette [o'ʒɛt], *n.f.* A small trough; (mason's) hod, etc.

Augias [oʒi'a:s], *m.* Augeas.

augment [og'mã], *n.m.* (*Gram.*) Augment; (*Law*) jointure, dowry.

augmentable, *a.* That may be augmented.

augmentateur [ogmãta'tœ:r], *n.m.* (*fem.* **-trice**) Augmenter, esp. one who makes additions to a literary work.

augmentatif [ogmãta'tif], *a.* (*fem.* **-ive**) (*Gram.*) Augmentative.—*n.m.* An augmentative syllable.

augmentation [ogmãta'sjɔ̃], *n.f.* Augmentation, increase, enlargement, addition, rise (in salary).

augmentatrice [AUGMENTATEUR].

augmenter [ogmã'te], *v.t.* To augment, to increase; to enlarge; to raise the salary of. *Augmenter le prix*, to raise the price; *il a augmenté sa maison*, he has enlarged his house; *je vais augmenter mon commis*, I am about to increase my clerk's salary.—*v.i.* To augment, to increase, to grow, to rise (in price), to multiply. *Le sucre a augmenté de prix*, sugar has risen in price. **s'augmenter**, *v.r.* To increase, to enlarge, to better, to improve.

augural [ogy'ral], *a.* (*fem.* **-ale**, *pl.* **-aux**) Augural. **augurat**, *n.m.* The office or dignity of an augur.

augure [o'gy:r], *n.m.* Augur, soothsayer; augury, omen, sign. *De mauvais augure*, ominous, portentous, ill-boding; *funeste augure*, ill-boding omen; *un bon* or *mauvais augure*, a good or bad omen.

augurer [ogy're], *v.t.* To augur; (*fig.*) to conjecture, to surmise. *Je n'en augure rien de bon*, I foresee no good result; I feel pessimistic about it.

Auguste [o'gyst], *m.* Augustus.

auguste [o'gyst], *a.* August, majestic.

augustin [ogys'tɛ̃], *n.m.* (*fem.* **augustine**) Augustinian or Austin friar, or nun.

aujourd'hui [oʒur'dɥi], *adv.* Today, during this day; nowadays, now, at present. *C'est aujourd'hui jeudi*, today is Thursday; *il y a aujourd'hui huit* or *quinze jours*, it is a week or a fortnight ago; *ce n'est pas d'aujourd'hui que nous nous connaissons*, we are no new acquaintances; *d'aujourd'hui en huit*, this day week; *d'aujourd'hui en quinze*, this day fortnight; *dès aujourd'hui*, from today, henceforth; *la mode d'aujourd'hui*, the present fashion.

Aulide [o'lid], *f.* Aulis.

aulique [o'lik], *a.* *Conseiller aulique*, member of the Aulic Council.

aulnaie [AUNAIE]. **aulne** [AUNE (1)]. **aulnée** [AUNÉE (2)].

auloffée [olɔ'fe], *n.f.* (*Naut.*) Luffing.

aulx, *pl.* [AIL].

*aumailles [o'ma:j], *n.f.* Cattle.

aumône [o'mo:n], *n.f.* Alms, alms-giving; (*fig.*) charity, favour, dole. *Demander l'aumône*, to beg; *être réduit à l'aumône*, to be reduced to beggary; *faire l'aumône*, to give alms; *faites-moi l'aumône d'un regard*, bestow but one look upon me; *qui vit d'aumônes, meurt de faim*, beg and starve.

aumônerie, *n.f.* Almonry, chaplaincy.

aumônier, *n.m.* (*Eccles.*) Almoner, chaplain. *Grand aumônier*, (*Fr. Hist.*) chief almoner to the king; *aumônier militaire*, army chaplain, padre.

aumônière, *n.f.* Alms-purse, small bag.

aumusse [o'mys], *n.f.* Amice.

aunage [o'na:ʒ], *n.m.* Ell-measure; the number of ells in a piece of cloth etc.

aunaie or **aulnaie** [o'nɛ], *n.f.* An alder-plot, grove of alders.

aune (1) or **aulne** [o:n], *n.m.* Alder-tree.

aune (2) [o:n], *n.f.* Ell; (*fig.*) measure, standard. *Acheter à l'aune*, to buy by the ell; *en avoir tout du long de l'aune*, to get it with a vengeance; *il sait ce qu'en vaut l'aune*, he knows it to his cost or by experience; *les hommes ne se mesurent pas à l'aune*, one must not judge of a man's merit by his stature; *mesurer les autres à son aune*, to judge others by one's own standards.

aunée (1) [o'ne], *n.f.* The length of an ell.

aunée (2) or **aulnée** [o′ne], *n.f.* Elecampane, *Inula helenium.*

auner [o′ne], *v.t.* To measure by the ell; (*fig.*) to judge of, to evaluate.

auparavant [opara′vɑ̃], *adv.* Before, formerly, previously. *Longtemps auparavant,* a long time before.

auprès [o′prɛ], *adv.* Near, by, close by. *Auprès de,* near to, close to; in comparison with; in the service of; in the opinion of. *Vivre auprès de ses parents,* to live with one's parents; *ambassadeur auprès de la Reine d'Angleterre,* ambassador to the Queen of England; *elle peut tout auprès de lui,* she can do anything with him; *votre malheur n'est rien auprès du sien,* your distress is nothing to his; *être bien auprès de quelqu'un,* to be in someone's good books; *excusez-le auprès de son père,* excuse him to his father; *il cherche à me nuire auprès de vous,* he endeavours to lower me in your esteem.

auquel, *contraction of* À LEQUEL (*fem.* **à laquelle,** *pl.* **auxquels, auxquelles**).

aurate [o′rat], *n.m.* (*Chem.*) Aurate.

Aurèle [o′rɛl], *m.* Aurelius. *Marc-Aurèle,* Marcus Aurelius.

Aurélien [ore′ljɛ̃], *m.* Aurelian.

auréolaire [oreɔ′lɛ:r], *a.* Like an aureole.

auréole [ore′ɔl], *n.f.* Aureole, halo, nimbus; (*fig.*) glory, prestige. **auréolé,** *a.* (*fem.* **-ée**) Encinctured or crowned with a halo.

auréoler, *v.t.* To crown with a halo.

aureux [o′rø], *a.m.* (*Chem.*) Aurous (oxyde).

auriculaire [oriky′lɛ:r], *a.* Auricular. *Le doigt auriculaire,* the little finger (because it is small enough to enter the ear); *témoin auriculaire,* ear-witness.—*n.m.* The little finger.

auricule [ori′kyl], *n.f.* The lower lobe of the ear, auricle; auricula. **auriculé,** *a.* (*fem.* **-ée**) (*Bot.*) Auriculate, eared.

auriculiste or **auriste,** *n.* Ear specialist.

aurifère [ori′fɛ:r], *a.* Auriferous.

aurification [orifika′sjɔ̃], *n.f.* Stopping teeth with gold.

aurifier, *v.t.* To stop (teeth) with gold.

aurige [o′riʒ], *n.m.* (*Ant.*) The coachman of a chariot; (*Astron.*) the waggoner.

Aurigny [ori′ɲi], *m.* Alderney.

aurique [o′rik], *a.* (*Naut.*) Shoulder-of-mutton shaped.—*n.f.* A sail of this shape. *Voiles auriques,* lateen sails.

auriste [o′rist], *n.m.* Ear specialist.

aurochs [o′rɔks], *n.m.* Aurochs, urus.

aurone [o′rɔn], *n.f.* Southern-wood.

Aurore [o′rɔ:r], *f.* Aurora.

aurore [o′rɔ:r], *n.f.* Dawn, morn, daybreak; (*fig.*) promise, beginning, the East; (*Astron.*) aurora. *À l'aurore,* at daybreak; *aurore boréale,* aurora borealis; *avant l'aurore,* before dawn; *du couchant à l'aurore,* from west to east; *l'aurore aux doigts de rose,* rosy-fingered dawn; *l'aurore commençait à poindre,* day was beginning to dawn; *travail d'aurore amène l'or,* early to bed, and early to rise, makes a man healthy, wealthy, and wise.—*a. inv.* Golden yellow.

auscultation [oskylta′sjɔ̃], *n.f.* (*Med.*) Auscultation.

ausculter, *v.t.* To sound with a stethoscope.

auspice [os′pis], *n.m.* Auspice, omen, presage; (*pl.*) auspices, protection, patronage.

aussi [o′si], *adv.* Also, likewise, too, besides; as; so. *Donnez-m'en aussi,* give me some too; *il est aussi sage que vaillant,* he is as prudent as courageous; *il est aussi sot que son ami,* he is as big a fool as his friend; *vous le voulez, et moi aussi,* you want it and so do I; *je sais cela aussi bien que vous,* I know that as well as you; *aussi peu que,* as little as, not more than. —*conj.* And so, accordingly, therefore, consequently; but then. *Ces dentelles sont belles, aussi coûtent-elles cher,* these laces are fine, but then they are dear; *aussi bien,* as well, for, the more so as; *je n'ai que faire de l'en prier, aussi bien ne m'écouterait-il pas,* it would be in vain for me to entreat him, especially as he would not listen to me; *je ne veux point y aller, aussi bien est-il trop tard,* I won't go there, the more so as it is too late.

aussière [o′sjɛ:r], *n.f.* (*Naut.*) Hawser.

aussitôt [osi′to], *adv.* Immediately, forthwith. *Aussitôt après votre départ,* immediately after your departure; *aussitôt dit, aussitôt fait,* no sooner said than done. *Aussitôt que,* as soon as; *aussitôt qu'il viendra,* as soon as he comes.

auster [os′tɛ:r], *n.m.* Auster, south-wind.

austère [os′tɛ:r], *a.* Austere, severe, stern.

austèrement, *adv.* Austerely, with austerity.

austérité, *n.f.* Austerity; severity, rigorousness; strictness.

austral [os′tral], *a.* (*fem.* **australe,** *pl.* **australs** or **austraux**) Austral, southern.

Australasie [ostrala′zi], *f.* Australasia.

australasien [ostrala′zjɛ̃], *a.* (*fem.* **australasienne**) Australasian.

Australie [ostra′li], *f.* Australia.

australien [ostra′ljɛ̃], *a.* (*fem.* **-ienne**) Australian.

Austrasie [ostra′zi], *f.* Austrasia.

austrasien [ostra′zjɛ̃], *a.* (*fem.* **-ienne**) (*Fr. Hist.*) Austrasian, pertaining to the eastern kingdom of the Franks.

autan [o′tɑ̃], *n.m.* (*poet.*) A strong south wind, storm, or blast. *Braver les autans,* to face the storm.

autant (1) [o′tɑ̃], *adv.* As much, so much, as many, so many, etc. *À charge d'autant,* on a fifty-fifty basis; *autant de têtes autant d'avis,* so many men, so many minds; *il y avait autant d'hommes que de femmes,* there were as many men as women; *une fois autant,* as much again; *je l'ai vendu tout autant,* I sold it for quite as much; *autant dire,* you might as well say; *autant en emporte le vent,* all that is idle talk; *autant l'esclavage me répugne, autant la liberté m'effraie,* liberty alarms me as much as slavery is repugnant to me; *autant ne pas y aller du tout,* might as well not go at all; *cela est fini ou autant vaut,* that is as good as done; *autant voudrait dire que,* you might as well say that . . .; *autant que,* as much as, as many as, as far as, in the same way as; *travaillez autant que vous pouvez,* work as much as you can; *autant que jamais,* as much as ever; *autant que j'en puis juger,* as far as I can conjecture; *ce vase contient autant que l'autre,* this vase contains as much as the other. *D'autant,* in the same proportion; *augmenter d'autant la somme,* to increase the sum in the same proportion; *d'autant mieux* or *d'autant plus,* the more, so much the more; *je l'en aime d'autant mieux,* I love her all the more for it; *je l'estime d'autant plus* *qu'il est pauvre*, I respect him the more because he is poor; *d'autant moins*, the less, so much the less; *il en est d'autant moins à craindre*, he is all the less to be feared; *d'autant que*, seeing that, since, more especially as; *pour autant*, for all that.

autarcie [otar'si], **autarchie** [otar'ʃi], *n.f.* Autarky, autarchy.

autel [o'tel], *n.m.* Altar; (*fig.*) ministry, Church, religious life. *Conduire la fiancée à l'autel*, to give the bride away; *le Sacrement de l'autel*, the host, the holy sacrament, the eucharist; *maître autel*, high altar; *nappe d'autel*, altar cloth; *pierre d'autel*, altar-stone; *qui sert à l'autel doit vivre de l'autel*, every man must live by his profession; *tableau d'autel*, altar-piece; *destiné aux autels*, intended for the Church; *il mérite qu'on lui élève des autels*, he deserves the greatest honours; *le trône et l'autel*, the monarchy and the Church.

auteur [o'tœ:r], *n.m.* Author, creator, maker; writer (of a book etc.); perpetrator; achiever, contriver, framer; composer, sculptor, etc.; informant, authority. *Droit d'auteur*, royalty; *l'auteur d'un procédé*, the inventor of a process; *l'auteur d'un projet*, the originator of a project; *nommez votre auteur*, name your informant or authority; *se faire auteur*, to turn author.

authenticité [otɑ̃tisi'te], *n.f.* Authenticity, genuineness.

authentifier [AUTHENTIQUER].

authentique, *a.* Authenticated, genuine, incontestable, positive. **authentiquement**, *adv.* Authentically.

authentiquer, *v.t.* To authenticate; (*Law*) to make legal and binding.

auto [o'to] [*abbr. for* AUTOMOBILE], *n.f. Faire de l'auto*, to go in for motoring; *j'y suis allé en auto*, I went there by car.

auto-allumage [otoaly'ma:ʒ], *n.m.* Knocking (of a car).

autobiographe [otobio'graf], *n.m.* Autobiographer. **autobiographie**, *n.f.* Autobiography. **autobiographique**, *a.* Autobiographical.

autobus [oto'bys], *n.m.* Bus. *Aller en autobus*, to go by bus.

autocar [oto'kar], *n.m.* Motor-coach.

autochenille [oto'ʃnij], *n.f.* (*reg. trade name*) Caterpillar tractor; half-track vehicle.

autochtone [otɔk'to:n], *a.* Autochthonous. —*n.m.* Autochthon.

autoclave [otɔ'kla:v], *a.* and *n.* Vacuum-pan, sterilizer. *Marmite autoclave*, autoclave, digester; pressure cooker.

autocopie [otɔkɔ'pi], *n.f.* A method of reproducing drawings, writing, etc. **autocopier**, *v.t.* To reproduce or multiply thus. **autocopiste**, *n.m.* Machine used for this purpose (jelly-graph, hectograph), cyclostyle.

autocrate [oto'krat], *n.m.* Autocrat. **autocratie** [otɔkra'si], *n.f.* Autocracy. **autocratique**, *a.* Autocratic. **autocratiquement**, *adv.* Autocratically.

autocritique [otɔkri'tik], *n.f.* Self-criticism.

auto-cuiseur [otɔyki'zœ:r], *n.m.* Pressure-cooker.

autodafé [otoda'fe], *n.m.* Auto-da-fé.

autodidacte [otɔdi'dakt], *n.* A self-taught person.

autodrome [otɔ'dro:m], *n.m.* A race-track for motor-cars.

auto-école [otɔe'kɔl], *n.f.* School of motoring.

autogare [otɔ'ga:r], *n.f.* Bus *or* coach station.

autogène [otɔ'ʒɛ:n], *a.* Autogenous.

autographe [otɔ'graf], *a.* Autographic.—*n.m.* Autograph. **autographie**, *n.f.* Autography. **autographier**, *v.t.* To autograph.

auto-greffe [otɔ'grɛf], *n.f.* (*Surg.*) Autograft.

autogyre [otɔ'ʒi:r], *n.m.* Autogyro.

automate [otɔ'mat], *n.m.* Automaton, robot.

automatique, *a.* Automatic. *Distributeur automatique*, penny-in-the-slot machine.—*n.m. L'Automatique*, automatic telephone. **automatiquement**, *adv.* Automatically.

automatisme, *n.m.* Automatism, purely mechanical movement.

***automédon** [otome'dɔ̃], *n.m.* Charioteer, Jehu; (*iron.*) coachman, driver.

automitrailleuse [otomitra'jø:z], *n.f.* Light armoured car.

automnal [otɔ'nal], *a.* (*fem.* **-ale**, *pl.* **-aux**) Autumnal.

automne [o'tɔn], *n.m.* and *f.* Autumn; (*Am.*) fall (of the year); (*fig.*) the autumn of life.

automobile [otɔmɔ'bil], *a.* Self-moving, self-propelling. *Canot automobile*, motor-boat. —*n.f.* (*Am.*) Automobile, (*Eng.*) motor-car. *Salon de l'automobile*, motor show.

automobilisme, *n.m.* Automobilism, motoring. **automobiliste**, *n.* Motorist.

automoteur [otɔmɔ'tœ:r], *a.* (*fem.* **-trice**) Self-acting, self-moving, self-propelling.

(*C*) **auto-neige** [oto'nɛ:ʒ], *n.f.* Snowmobile.

autonome [otɔ'nɔm], *a.* Autonomous.

autonomie, *n.f.* Autonomy, self-government; cruising range. **autonomiste**, *n.m.* Autonomist.

autonyme [otɔ'nim], *a.* Published under the name of the author (of books etc.).

autophagie [otɔfa'ʒi], *n.f.* Autophagy.

autoplastie [otɔplas'ti], *n.f.* (*Surg.*) Autoplasty, plastic surgery.

auto-portrait [otɔpɔr'trɛ], *n.m.* Self-portrait.

auto-propulsé [otɔprɔpyl'se], *a.* (*fem.* **-ée**) Self-propelled.

auto-propulsion, *n.f.* Self-propulsion.

autopsie [otɔp'si], *n.f.* Autopsy; post-mortem examination. **autopsier**, *v.t.* To make an autopsy.

autorail [otɔ'ra:j], *n.m.* Rail-car.

autorisable [otɔri'zabl], *a.* Authorizable.

autorisation [otɔriza'sjɔ̃], *n.f.* Authorization; authority, warrant; written consent or permission, licence (of a preacher).

autoriser [otɔri'ze], *v.t.* To authorize, to empower, to commission; to license, to warrant, to permit, to sanction. **s'autoriser**, *v.r.* To have, get, or assume authority; to act on the authority (of), to be warranted by (*de*).

autoritaire [otɔri'tɛ:r], *a.* Authoritative, commanding, arbitrary.—*n.* Such a person. **autoritairement**, *adv.* Authoritatively.

autoritarisme, *n.m.* System or principles of authoritative action.

autorité [otɔri'te], *n.f.* Authority, legal or legitimate power; an authority; (*fig.*) control. *Alléguer or apporter des autorités*, to quote or cite authorities; *avoir de l'autorité sur*, to have power over; *d'autorité*, of one's own prerogative; *de pleine autorité*, with full powers; *être en autorité*, to be invested with authority; *faire autorité*, to be an authority; *il l'a fait de son autorité privée*, he did it on his own initiative; *les autorités de la ville*, the authorities of the town.

autoroute [otɔ'rut], *n.f.* Motorway; (*Am.*) speedway.

auto-stop [otɔ'stɔp], *n.m.* Hitch-hiking. *Faire de l'auto-stop*, to hitch-hike.

autostrade [oto'strad], *n.f.* Special road for motor-cars, autostrada, autobahn.

autosuggestion [otɔsygʒɛs'tjɔ̃], *n.f.* Auto-suggestion.

autour (1) [o'tuːr], *adv.* About, round about. *Ici autour*, hereabouts; *il regardait tout autour*, he looked all about; *il ne faut pas confondre autour avec alentour*, don't mistake one thing for something quite different. —*prep. phr. Autour de*, about, round, around; *autour de sa personne*, about his person; *autour de deux millions*, about two millions; *autour du bras*, round the arm; *tourner autour du pot*, to beat about the bush.

autour (2) [o'tuːr], *n.m.* (*Orn.*) Goshawk.

autre (1) [oːtr], *a.* Other; second; another, different, distinct (but of the same kind). *Autre part*, elsewhere; *autres temps, autres mœurs*, manners change with the times; *d'autre part*, besides; *il le regarde comme un autre lui-même*, he looks upon him as a second self; *l'autre jour*, the other day; *nous autres*, the like of us; *nous autres Français, nous mangeons beaucoup de pain*, we French people eat a great deal of bread; *c'est tout autre chose*, that's quite a different matter; *vous autres*, you people, you fellows; *une autre fois*, another time.—*pron. indef.* Another person, someone else; (*pl.*) the others, the rest. *A d'autres* or *adressez vous à d'autres*, tell that to the marines; *à l'envi l'un de l'autre*, in emulation of one another; *à l'un ou à l'autre*, to either; *causer de choses et d'autres*, to talk of various things; *c'est un élève comme un autre*, he is an average pupil; *comme dit l'autre*, as somebody says, as the saying is; *de côté et d'autre*, up and down; *de part et d'autre*, on both sides, on all sides; *de temps à autre*, now and then; *encore un autre*, still another; *entre autres*, among other people or among other things; *il dit d'une façon et il fait d'une autre*, he says one thing and does another; *il en sait bien d'autres*, he knows a trick worth two of that; *il n'en fait point d'autres*, he does nothing else, these are his pranks; *j'en ai vu bien d'autres*, I have outlived worse things than that; *les uns et les autres*, all; *les uns se plaisent à une chose, les autres à une autre*, some delight in one thing and some in another; *l'un dans l'autre* or *l'un portant l'autre*, one with another, on an average; *l'un et l'autre*, both; *l'un l'autre*, one another, each other; *l'un ou l'autre*, either; *l'un vaut l'autre*, they are much of a muchness, one is as bad as the other; *ni l'un ni l'autre*, neither; *ni l'un ni l'autre ne vaut rien*, both are good for nothing; *nul autre n'y aurait consenti*, nobody else would have consented to it; *tout autre l'aurait fait*, anybody else would have done it; *un autre le fera*, somebody else will do it; *aucun autre, nul autre, personne d'autre*, no one else.

autrefois [otrə'fwɑ], *adv.* Formerly, in former times; of old. *D'autrefois*, former, bygone; *des mœurs d'autrefois*, bygone customs.

autrement [otrə'mɑ̃], *adv.* Otherwise, after another manner; else; or else. *C'est un homme qui n'est pas autrement riche*, he is a man who is not over rich; *faisons autrement*, let us go to work another way; *entrez, autrement je fermerai la porte*, come in, or I'll shut the door.

Autriche [o'triʃ], *f.* Austria.

autrichien [otri'ʃjɛ̃], *a.* (*fem.* **-ienne**) Austrian. —*n.* (**Autrichien**, *fem.* **-ienne**) Austrian.

autruche [o'tryʃ], *n.f.* Ostrich. *Avoir un estomac d'autruche*, to have the stomach of an ostrich, to digest anything. **autrucherie**, *n.f.* Ostrich-farm. **autruchon**, *n.m.* Young ostrich.

autrui [o'trɥi], *pron. indef. inv.* Others, other people, one's or our neighbours. *Dépendre d'autrui*, to depend on others; *faire à autrui ce que nous voudrions qu'on nous fît*, to do by others as we would be done by; *le bien d'autrui*, other people's property; *mal d'autrui n'est que songe*, we make light of the ills of others.

auvent [o'vɑ̃], *n.m.* Weather-board, porch roof. *Auvent de capot*, bonnet louvre.

auvergnat [ovɛr'ɲa], *a.* (*fem.* **auvergnate**) Belonging to Auvergne.—*n.* (**Auvergnat**, *fem.* **Auvergnate**) An inhabitant of Auvergne. (In Paris, *see* BOUGNAT.)

auvergne [o'vɛrɲ], *n.f.* Tan-liquor in which skins are macerated [*see* CHIPAGE]. **auvergner**, *v.t.* To put (skins) into this.

auvernat [ovɛr'na], *n.m.* A variety of vine cultivated in Loiret. *Auvernat meunier*, a light red wine.

aux (*pl.* of AU) [ʃ].

auxdits, *pl.* (*fem.* **auxdites**) [AUX DITS].

auxiliaire [oksi'ljɛːr], *a.* Auxiliary, aiding, subsidiary. *Service auxiliaire*, (*Mil.*) the service comprising those, unfit for service under arms, employed as clerks, mechanics, etc., in the corps to which they are attached; *verbe auxiliaire*, auxiliary verb.—*n.* Auxiliary; helper, assistant. **auxiliairement**, *adv.* In an auxiliary or subsidiary way. **auxiliateur**, *a.* (*fem.* **-trice**) Helping, succouring.

auxquels, *pl.* (*fem.* **auxquelles**) [AUQUEL].

avachi [ava'ʃi], *a.* (*fem.* **avachie**) Out of shape, worn out; (*fam.*) flabby, floppy, downcast (of a person). **avachir**, *v.t.* To make flabby, limp, or feeble; (*fig.*) to enervate. **s'avachir**, *v.r.* To flag; to grow fat and flabby; to get out of shape or down at heel. **avachissement**, *n.m.* Flabbiness; lack of energy.

aval (1) [a'val], *n.m.* (*pl.* **avals**) Guarantee, endorsement. *Mettez votre aval au dos de ce billet*, endorse that bill.

aval (2) [a'val], *n.m.* The lower or downward part or direction, down stream. *En aval de*, below; *le vent vient d'aval*, the wind is blowing up stream; *vent d'aval*, westerly wind. **avalage**, *n.m.* Passage (of a boat etc.) down stream; putting (wine etc.) in a cellar.

avalaison [avalɛ'zɔ̃] or **avalasse**, *n.f.* Sudden flood, spate; (*Naut.*) a long-continued wind from the sea.

avalanche [ava'lɑ̃ːʃ], *n.f.* Avalanche; (*fig.*) shower (of words, insults, etc.).

avalant [ava′lɑ̃], *a.* (*fem.* **avalante**) Descending, going down stream.

avalasse [AVALAISON].

avalement [aval′mɑ̃], *n.m.* Descent, lowering, letting down; swallowing.

avaler [ava′le], *v.t.* To swallow, to swallow down; to drink, to toss off, to gulp down; to let down, to lower (things into a cellar etc.); (*Gard.*) to lop; (*fig.*) to endure, to pocket (an affront); to believe. *Avaler des bourdes,* to be credulous; *avaler des couleuvres,* to pocket many affronts; *avaler des yeux,* to devour with one's eyes; *avaler la pilule,* (*fig.*) to swallow the pill; *avaler sa langue,* to keep silent, to die; *avaler un affront,* to swallow an insult; *il ne fait que tordre et avaler,* he gobbles up everything; *elle est dure à avaler,* that is a tall story.—*v.i.* To go down (a river etc. with the stream). **s'avaler,** *v.r.* To flag, to hang down (of a horse's belly etc.); (*fig.*) to be swallowed, to be believed.

avale-tout [aval-tu] or **avale-tout-cru,** *n.m. inv.* (*pop.*) A gross feeder, a glutton.

avaleur [ava′lœːr], *n.m.* (*fem.* **avaleuse**) Swallower, glutton. *Avaleur de gens* or *de charrettes ferrées,* a braggart; *avaleur de pois gris,* a great glutton.

avalies [ava′liː], *n.f. pl.* Pelt-wool.

avaliser [avali′ze], *v.t.* To guarantee, to endorse [see AVAL (1)].

avaloire [ava′lwaːr], *n.f.* Breeching (of a shaft-horse); (*slang*) throat, swallow.

avalure [ava′lyːr], *n.f.* (*Vet.*) Sloughing of the horny part of the hoof.

avance [a′vɑ̃ːs], *n.f.* That which is in front; a part of a building etc. projecting forwards; an advance, a start, distance in advance; payment of money in advance; (*fig., pl.*) attentions, first steps in an acquaintanceship, etc. *À l'avance, en avance, par avance,* beforehand, before one's time, by anticipation; *d'avance,* beforehand; *prévenir d'avance,* to warn beforehand; *payer d'avance,* to pay in advance; *il a quatre lieues d'avance sur moi,* he is four leagues ahead of me; *prendre l'avance,* to take the lead; (*Motor.*) *avance à l'allumage,* ignition advance; *mettre toute l'avance,* to advance the spark fully. *Faire les avances d'une entreprise,* to advance the funds for an enterprise; *faire des avances,* to make advances to.

avancé [avɑ̃′se], *a.* (*fem.* **avancée** (1)) Advanced, forward, early; late (of the hour); over-ripe, tainted, high; liberal, progressive (of opinions etc.); paid in advance; put forward, enunciated. *Je n'en suis pas plus avancé,* I am not a bit the better off for it; *les arbres sont avancés,* the trees are forward; *me voilà bien avancé!* a lot of good that's done me! *un élève fort avancé,* a very brilliant pupil; *un homme avancé en âge,* an elderly man; *un jeune homme fort avancé,* a very forward youth; *viande avancée,* meat which is going bad. **avancée** (2), *n.f.* (*Mil.*) Outpost (before the gate); advance (of the line); (*Mining*) the forward part of a gallery; *en avancée,* (*Arch.*) jutting.

avancement [avɑ̃s′mɑ̃], *n.m.* Advancing; projection; progress, advancement; preferment, promotion, rise; (*Law*) payment in advance (to an heir).

avancer [avɑ̃′se], *v.t.* To move, to bring, to put, or hold forward, to advance; to pay beforehand or in advance; to assert, to bring forward, to urge; to promote, to give promotion to, to advantage, to profit; (*fig.*) to bring nearer, to hasten, to forward; to put on (a clock). *Avancer le dîner,* to put dinner forward; *avancez la table,* push the table forward; *avancer le pied,* to put one's foot forward. *Il lui a avancé de l'argent,* he has advanced him some money. *Pouvez-vous prouver ce que vous avancez?* Can you prove your assertion? *Avancer les intérêts de quelqu'un,* to promote someone's interests; *avancer un ouvrage,* to hurry on a piece of work; *cela a avancé sa mort,* that hastened his death; *faire avancer,* to push, to push on; *on l'a avancé,* he has been promoted.—*v.i.* To advance, to proceed, to keep on; to project, to jut out; to make progress, to thrive, to get on, to gain ground; to go too fast. *Avancer en âge,* to advance in years; *avancez donc!* come along! *cette maison avance trop sur la rue,* that house juts out too much into the street; *faire avancer une voiture,* to call a cab; *plus on se hâte moins on avance,* more haste less speed; *l'horloge avance,* the clock is fast. **s'avancer,** *v.r.* To advance, to go on, to move forward; to get on, to improve; to get promoted, to be successful; to grow old etc.; to project. *Cet ambassadeur s'est trop avancé,* that ambassador has gone too far; *le temps s'avance,* time flies; *s'avancer à cheval,* to ride up; *s'avancer à la voile,* to sail up; *s'avancer en courant,* to run up; *s'avancer en voiture,* to drive up.

avançon [avɑ̃′sɔ̃], *n.m.* Snood or hair leader (of a fishing-line).

avanie [ava′ni], *n.f.* Insult, affront; snub.

avant [a′vɑ̃], *prep.* Before, in advance of (of time and order). *Avant J.-C.,* B.C.; *avant tout,* first of all, before all; *avant toutes choses,* above all things; *j'ai vu cela avant vous,* I saw that before you.—*adv.* Before, previously; forward, in front; farther in advance, in depth, distance, etc. *Avant que,* before; *avant qu'il soit un an,* before a year is over; *avant de partir,* before leaving; *bien avant dans la nuit,* very late at night; *creuser fort avant dans la terre,* to dig very deep in the ground; *la fois d'avant,* the time before; *en avant,* forward! march on! *en avant de,* before, in front of; *mettre en avant,* to bring forward; *n'allez pas si avant,* not so fast; *nous étions bien avant en mer,* we had got a great way out to sea; *plus avant,* farther, deeper. —*n.m.* Front; prow, head, bow (of a ship); (*Ftb.*) forward. *Aller de l'avant,* to forge ahead; *de l'avant à l'arrière,* from stem to stern; *gagner l'avant de,* to get ahead of, to get headway (on a ship).

avantage [avɑ̃′taːʒ], *n.m.* Advantage, benefit, profit, the better, superiority; (*Law*) that which is given (to a legatee etc.) over and above his legal share; (*Naut.*) weather-gauge; (*Horsemanship*) whip-hand; (*Cards etc.*) odds; (*Ten.*) 'vantage. *Avoir l'avantage,* to win, to prevail, to be pleased to; *avoir l'avantage sur,* to have the advantage over; *nos troupes ont eu l'avantage,* our troops have had the best of it; *on lui a fait tous les avantages possibles,* they gave him every possible advantage; *on peut dire ceci à son avantage,* this may be said in his favour; *quel avantage vous en revient-il?* what benefit do you reap from it? *s'habiller à son avantage,* to dress to the best advantage; *tirer avantage de tout,* to turn everything to account; *avantage dedans* or *avantage au service,* (*Ten.*) 'vantage in; *avantage dehors,* 'vantage out; *avantage détruit,* deuce again.

avantager [avɑ̃taˈʒe], *v.t.* To advantage, to give an advantage to; to favour. *La nature l'avait avantagé de beaucoup de qualités précieuses,* nature had endowed him with many inestimable qualities. **s'avantager,** *v.r.* To take advantage.

avantageusement, *adv.* Advantageously, to advantage; usefully, favourably. *Parler avantageusement de quelqu'un,* to speak highly of someone. **avantageux,** *a.* (*fem.* **-euse**) Advantageous, profitable, favourable; conceited, presumptuous; (of dress) becoming. *Conditions avantageuses,* advantageous terms; *un ton avantageux,* a confident, assuming tone. *C'est un homme avantageux,* he is a conceited, vain, or presuming fellow; *coiffure avantageuse,* a becoming way of dressing the hair.—*n.m.* (*colloq.*) A conceited or presumptuous fellow; a coxcomb.

(In pl. of the following compounds *avant* is inv. The *n.* has its regular pl.)

avant-bassin [avɑ̃baˈsɛ̃], *n.m.* Outer-dock.

avant-bec [avɑ̃ˈbɛk], *n.m.* Starling of a bridge, ice-breaker, cutwater.

avant-bras [avɑ̃ˈbra], *n.m. inv.* Forearm.

avant-centre [avɑ̃ˈsɑ̃tr], *n.m.* (*Ftb.*) Centre-forward.

avant-corps [avɑ̃ˈkɔːr], *n.m. inv.* (*Arch.*) Fore-part (of a building).

avant-cour [avɑ̃ˈkuːr], *n.f.* Fore-court.

avant-coureur [avɑ̃kuˈrœːr], *n.m.* Fore-runner, precursor, harbinger.—*a.* Going in front, preceding, presaging. *Signes avant-coureurs,* premonitory signs.

avant-courrier [avɑ̃kuˈrje], *n.m.* (*fem.* **-ière**) A horseman riding ahead of a travelling carriage to order relays of horses. (*fig.*) Herald, forerunner, harbinger.

avant-dernier [avɑ̃dɛrˈnje], *a.* and *n.* (*fem.* **-ière**) The last but one. *L'avant-dernière syllabe,* the penultimate syllable.

avant-garde [avɑ̃ˈgard], *n.f.* Vanguard, van. *Hommes d'avant-garde,* leaders of reform; *romancier d'avant-garde,* advanced novelist.

avant-goût [avɑ̃ˈgu], *n.m.* Foretaste, earnest anticipation.

avant-guerre [avɑ̃ˈgɛr], *n.* The pre-war period.

avant-hier [avɑ̃ˈtjɛːr], *adv.* and *n.m.* The day before yesterday.

avant-main [avɑ̃ˈmɛ̃], *n.m.* Flat of the hand; forehand of a horse; (*Ten.*) forehand stroke; (*Cards*) lead.

avant-pays [avɑ̃peˈi], *n.m.inv.* (*Geol.*) Teutonic foreland.

avant-pied [avɑ̃ˈpje], *n.m.* Vamp, upper leather of a boot; (*vulg.*) instep, metatarsus.

avant-port [avɑ̃ˈpɔːr], *n.m.* Outer harbour, tide-dock.

avant-portail [avɑ̃pɔrˈtaːj], *n.m.* Outer portal.

avant-poste [avɑ̃ˈpɔst], *n.m.* (*Mil.*) Advanced post, outpost; (*fig.*) outer defence.

avant-première [avɑ̃prəˈmjɛːr], *n.f.* Dress rehearsal; (*Cine.*) preview.

avant-projet [avɑ̃prɔˈʒɛ], *n.m.* Rough draft.

avant-propos [avɑ̃prɔˈpo], *n.m. inv.* Preface, preamble, introduction, foreword.

avant-quart [avɑ̃ˈkaːr], *n.m.* Warning strokes (before the hour etc. is struck on a bell).

avant-scène [avɑ̃ˈsɛːn], *n.f.* Front of the stage (between curtain and orchestra); proscenium. *Loge d'avant-scène,* stage-box; (*fig.*) previous events.

avant-toit [avɑ̃ˈtwa], *n.m.* Eaves.

avant-train [avɑ̃ˈtrɛ̃], *n.m.* Fore-carriage, limber; part comprising the wheels (of a plough); fore quarters (of a horse). *Amener les avant-trains,* to limber up (before departing).

avant-veille [avɑ̃ˈvɛːj], *n.f.* Two days before.

avare [aˈvaːr], *a.* Avaricious, miserly, covetous, stingy, close-fisted. *À père avare fils prodigue,* a miserly father has a spendthrift son; *être avare de ses louanges,* to be sparing of praise.—*n.m.* Miser, niggard. **avarement,** *adv.* Stingily.

avariable [avaˈrjabl], *a.* That may spoil or go bad, damageable.

avarice [avaˈris], *n.f.* Avarice, greed, covetousness; niggardliness, stinginess. **avaricieux,** *a.* (*fem.* **avaricieuse**) Avaricious, covetous, stingy. **avaricieusement,** *adv.* Avariciously.

avarie [avaˈri], *n.f.* Damage (to a ship or cargo); deterioration; average; (*euphem.*) syphilis. *Avaries communes,* general average; *avaries simples,* ordinary damage; *causer une avarie,* to damage; *menues avaries,* petty averages; *régler les avaries,* to state the averages; *sans avarie,* without mishap.

avarié [avaˈrje], *a.* (*fem.* **-ée**) Damaged, spoiled, deteriorated; (*euphem.*) affected with syphilis.

avarier, *v.t.* To damage, to spoil. **s'avarier,** *v.r.* To become damaged.

avatar [avaˈtar], *n.m.* Avatar.

à vau-l'eau [avoˈlo], *adv. phr.* With the stream, down stream. *Toutes ses entreprises sont allées à vau-l'eau,* all his undertakings have come to nought or to rack and ruin.

ave [aˈve], *n.m. inv.* Ave. *Ave Maria,* ave Maria; Hail Mary.

avec [aˈvɛk], *prep.* With, at the same time as, along or together with; by means of, by; regarding; against, in spite of. *Avec ça!* (*colloq.*) nonsense! *avec dessein,* designedly; *avec tout cela,* for all that, nevertheless; *d'avec,* away from; *discerner le bien d'avec le mal,* to discern good from evil; *il a pris mon manteau, et s'en est allé avec,* he has taken my cloak, and has gone off with it; *venez avec moi,* come with me; *et avec cela monsieur?* Anything more, sir?

aveinière [avɛˈnjɛːr], *n.f.* Oatfield.

avelanède [avlaˈned], *n.f.* Acorn-cup, valonia.

aveline [aˈvlin], *n.f.* Filbert, Kentish cob. **avelinier,** *n.m.* Filbert-tree, hazel-tree.

aven [aˈvɛ̃], *n.m.* Pot-hole, swallow, chasm, (in mountain limestone).

avénacé [avenaˈse], *a.* (*fem.* **avénacée**) (*Bot.*) Avenaceous.

avenant [avˈnɑ̃], *a.* (*fem.* **avenante**) Personable, prepossessing, comely, pleasing, taking. *Manières avenantes,* prepossessing, engaging manners; *physionomie avenante,* pleasing features.—*adv. phr. À l'avenant*, in keeping with, in the same proportions, of a piece; *et tout à l'avenant*, and all to scale, matching; *le dessert fut à l'avenant du repas*, the dessert was in keeping with the repast.—*n.m.* Additional clause (to an insurance policy); rider (to a verdict); codicil (to a treaty).

avènement [avɛn'mɑ̃], *n.m.* Coming, advent, accession, succession (to a throne etc.). *L'avènement du Messie*, the coming of the Messiah; *l'avènement du roi*, the king's accession to the throne (crown); *l'avènement de la télévision*, the advent of television.

avénière [AVEINIÈRE].

avenir (1) [av'niːr], *n.m.* The future, future ages; posterity; (*fig.*) prospects. *À l'avenir*, in future, henceforth; *cet homme n'a aucun avenir*, that man has no prospects; *j'assure un avenir à mes enfants*, I make provision for my children; *on ne peut répondre de l'avenir*, one cannot answer for the future; *dans l'avenir*, at some future date; *dans un avenir prochain*, in the near future; *un musicien d'avenir*, an up and coming musician.

***avenir** (2) [ADVENIR].

à-venir [av'niːr], *n.m.* (*Law*) Summons to appear (addressed by an attorney to the opposite party).

avent [a'vɑ̃], *n.m.* (*Ch.*) Advent.

Aventin [avɑ̃'tɛ̃], l', *m.* The Aventine.

aventure [avɑ̃'tyːr], *n.f.* Surprising or unexpected event or experience, chance, accident, luck; adventure, daring enterprise, hazardous exploit; love affair or intrigue. *A l'aventure*, at random; *d'aventure* or *par aventure*, by chance, perchance; *dire la bonne aventure*, to tell people's fortunes; *la bonne aventure*, a prophecy of future good luck; *se faire dire la bonne aventure*, to have one's fortune told; *une diseuse de bonne aventure*, a fortune-teller; *grosse aventure*, (*Comm.*) loan at high interest at the risk of total loss of capital in case of shipwreck etc., bottomry; *mal d'aventure*, (*pop.*) whitlow; *tenter l'aventure*, to try one's luck; *une plaisante aventure*, a droll adventure.

aventurer [avɑ̃ty're], *v.t.* To venture to hazard, to risk. **s'aventurer**, *v.r.* To venture, to take one's chance, to take risks. *S'aventurer dans un pays ennemi*, to venture into a hostile country.

aventureux [avɑ̃ty'rø], *a.* (*fem.* **-euse**) Venturesome, adventurous; left to chance. *Projet aventureux*, risky plan. **aventurier**, *n.m.* (*fem.* **-ière**) Adventurer, adventuress.

aventurine [avɑ̃ty'rin], *n.f.* Aventurine.

avenu [av'ny], *a.* (*fem.* **avenue** (1)) Used only in *Acte nul et non avenu*, null and void.

avenue (2) [av'ny], *n.f.* Approach; avenue.

avéré [ave're], *a.* (*fem.* **avérée**) Authenticated, established by evidence.

avérer [ave're], *v.t.* To verify, to confirm, to establish. *S'avérer*, to appear, to be distinctly, to turn out to be, to prove.

averrhoïsme [averɔ'ism], *n.m.* Averroism.

avers [a'vɛːr], *n.m.* Obverse (of coins etc.).

averse [a'vɛrs], *n.f.* Sudden and heavy shower of rain, downpour; (*fig.*) flood (of talk etc.).

aversion [avɛr'sjɔ̃], *n.f.* Aversion, dislike, detestation. *Avoir en aversion*, to dislike; *cet homme est ma bête d'aversion*, that man is my

bugbear, my pet aversion; *prendre quelqu'un en aversion*, to take a dislike to someone.

averti [avɛr'ti], *a.* (*fem.* **avertie**) Warned, informed; wide awake. *Se tenir pour averti*, to be on one's guard, to take it as a warning; *un homme averti en vaut deux*, forewarned is forearmed.

avertir [avɛr'tiːr], *v.t.* To inform, to acquaint with, to give notice, to warn, to admonish (*de*). *Faire avertir de*, to send notice, to give word of.

avertissement [avɛrtis'mɑ̃], *n.m.* Information, notification, advice, warning, caution; (*colloq.*) admonition; notice (to pay etc.). *Avertissement au lecteur*, foreword (of a book).

avertisseur [avɛrti'sœːr], *n.m.* Warner; (*Theat.*) call-boy; call-bell, hooter. *Avertisseur d'incendie*, fire-alarm.

aveu [a'vø], *n.m.* (*Feud. Law*) Acknowledgment or recognition (of a vassal by his lord, or vice versa); admission, avowal, confession; approbation, consent. *De l'aveu de tous*, by common consent; *faire l'aveu de*, to confess; *homme sans aveu*, a vagrant, a vagabond.

aveuglant [avœ'glɑ̃], *a.* (*fem.* **-ante**) Blinding, dazzling; (*fig.*) distracting, misleading.

aveugle [a'vœgl], *a.* Blind, sightless; blinded by passion, etc., deluded. *Aveugle de naissance*, born blind; *aveugle comme une taupe*, as blind as a bat; *changer son cheval borgne contre un aveugle*, to change from bad to worse; *en aveugle*, blindly, ignorantly; *la fortune est aveugle*, fortune is blind. *Obéissance aveugle*, implicit obedience.—*n.* Blind person. *C'est un aveugle qui en conduit un autre*, it is the blind leading the blind; *un aveugle y mordrait*, a blind man would see it.

aveuglement [avœgl'mɑ̃], *n.m.* Blindness; (*fig.*) infatuation, delusion.

aveuglément [avœgle'mɑ̃], *adv.* Blindly, rashly, implicitly.

aveugle-né [avœglə'ne], *a.* and *n.* (*fem.* **aveugle-née**, *pl.* **aveugles-nés** or **-nées**) Blind from birth.

aveugler [avœ'gle], *v.t.* To blind, to make blind; (*fig.*) to dazzle; to delude; (*Naut.*) to fother (a leak). *Aveugler une voie d'eau*, (*Naut.*) to stop a leak; *la passion aveugle l'entendement*, love is blind; *la trop grande lumière aveugle*, too much light dazzles the eyes. **s'aveugler**, *v.r.* To shut one's eyes (to); (*fig.*) to be blinded, to be infatuated.

aveuglette, *n.f.* (Only in the phrase *à l'aveuglette*, blindly.) *Aller à l'aveuglette*, to go groping along, to go blindly or rashly. (*Av.*) *Voler à l'aveuglette*, to fly blind.

aveulir [avœ'liːr], *v.t.* To render weak, to enfeeble, to enervate. *S'aveulir*, to sink into sloth. **aveulissant**, *a.* (*fem.* **aveulissante**) Enfeebling, enervating. **aveulissement**, *n.m.* Enfeeblement, enervation.

aviateur [avja'tœːr], *n.m.* (*fem.* **aviatrice**). Aviator; air-man, air-woman; flyer.

aviation [avja'sjɔ̃], *n.f.* Aviation. *Régiment d'aviation*, air-force regiment; *terrain d'aviation*, flying ground, air-field.

avicule [avi'kyl], *n.f.* (*Zool.*) Genus of Mollusca comprising the pearl-oyster.

aviculteur [avikyl'tœːr], *n.m.* One who raises birds or poultry; bird fancier. **aviculture**, *n.f.* Bird-raising; poultry-farming.

avide [a′vid], *a.* Greedy, voracious, rapacious; eager for, grasping. *Avide de gain,* eager for gain; *un homme avide,* a covetous man.

avidement, *adv.* Greedily, voraciously; eagerly.

avidité, *n.f.* Avidity, greediness; eagerness.

avien [a′vjɛ̃], *a.* (*fem.* **avienne**) Avian.

avilir [avi′liːr], *v.t.* To debase, to depreciate, to disparage; to lower; to degrade, to disgrace. **s'avilir,** *v.r.* To degrade oneself, to stoop to (doing something). **avilissant,** *a.* (*fem.* **-ante**) Debasing, degrading, humiliating. **avilissement,** *n.m.* Debasement, degradation; depreciation, disparagement.

avilisseur, *a.* (*fem.* **-euse**) Debasing, degrading.—*n.* One who debases, disparages, or degrades.

aviné [avi′ne], *a.* (*fem.* **avinée**) Drunk, unsteady (from drink); wine-soaked (of a cask). *C'est un corps aviné,* he is a regular tippler.

aviner, *v.t.* To soak or fill with wine. **s'aviner,** *v.r.* To get drunk.

avion [a′vjɔ̃], *n.m.* Aeroplane, aircraft. *Avion de bombardement,* bomber; *avion de chasse,* fighter; *avion de ligne,* air-liner; *avion de réglage (de tir),* spotter; *avion à réaction,* jet-plane; *avion-fusée,* rocket-plane; *avion-taxi,* charter-plane; *par avion,* by air mail.

avir or **havir** [a′viːr], *v.t.* To burn or brown the outside of (bread, roast meat, etc.); to beat over the edges of (tin-plates etc.) in order to join them up.

aviron [avi′rɔ̃], *n.m.* Oar. *L'aviron* (as a sport), rowing; *cercle de l'aviron,* rowing club; *pratiquer l'aviron,* to go in for rowing; *avirons de pointe,* oars; *avirons de couple* (or *rames*), sculls; *border les avirons,* to ship the oars.

avis [a′vi], *n.m.* Opinion, way of thinking, judgment; vote, motion; advice, counsel; information, notice, warning, caution, intelligence. *À mon avis,* in my opinion; *avis au lecteur,* foreword, (*fig.*) a word to the wise; *avis au public,* notice; *deux avis valent mieux qu'un,* two heads are better than one; *dire son avis,* to say or speak one's mind; *donner à quelqu'un un avis,* to advise someone; *donner un avis assez clair à quelqu'un,* to give a pretty broad hint to someone; *être d'avis,* to be of opinion; *faute d'avis,* for want of advice; *j'ai changé d'avis,* I have altered my mind; *je ne suis pas d'avis d'y aller,* I am not for going there; *je profiterai de l'avis que vous me donnez,* I shall avail myself of the caution you have given me; *lettre d'avis,* advice note; *ne m'écris plus jusqu'à nouvel avis,* write no more till further notice; *on a reçu avis de Paris,* we were advised from Paris; *ouvrir un avis,* to broach an opinion; *suivant l'avis de,* as per advice.

avisé [avi′ze], *a.* (*fem.* **avisée**) Shrewd, clear-sighted, wary, circumspect, prudent. *Il est fort avisé,* he is a very discreet man; *bien avisé,* well-advised; *mal avisé,* ill-advised.

aviser [avi′ze], *v.t.* To perceive, to espy; to inform, to apprise; (*Comm.*) to advise by letter.—*v.i.* To consider, to think (about), to look (to). *Vous y aviserez,* you will see to it. **s'aviser,** *v.r.* To think of, to find (an expedient etc.); to bethink oneself, to be so minded; to venture to do. *Il ne s'avise jamais*

de rien, he thinks of nothing; *il s'avisa de,* he took it into his head to; *il s'avisa d'un bon expédient,* he bethought himself of a good expedient.

aviso [avi′zo], *n.m.* (*Naut.*) Aviso, dispatch-boat, sloop, gunboat.

*****avitaillement** [avitaj′mɑ̃], *n.m.* (*Naut., Mil.*) Victualling; stores. *****avitailler,** *v.t.* To victual, to furnish with stores.

avitaminose [avitami′noːz], *n.f.* (*Med.*) Avitaminosis.

avivage [avi′vaːʒ], *n.m.* Brightening, reviving (of colours).

aviver [avi′ve], *v.t.* To revive, to brighten; to sharpen the edges of, to polish, to burnish; to irritate, to exacerbate (a wound, resentment, etc.); (*Surg.*) to lay bare the healthy parts of (a wound), removing the morbid parts. **s'aviver,** *v.r.* To revive.

avives [a′viːv], *n.f.* (*used only in pl.*) (*Vet.*) Vives.

avivoir [avi′vwaːr], *n.m.* Polisher, burnisher.

avocaillon [avɔka′jɔ̃], *n.m.* A pettifogging lawyer.

avocasser [avɔka′se], *v.i.* To be a pettifogger, to drudge at the bar. **avocasserie,** *n.f.* Pettifoggery, chicanery, quibbling. **avocassier,** *a.* (*fem.* **avocassière**) Pettifogging. —*n.m.* Pettifogger.

avocat (1) [avɔ′ka], *n.m.* (*fem.* **avocate**) Barrister, advocate, counsel; (*fig.*) pleader, intercessor, champion. *Être reçu avocat,* to be called to the Bar; *avocat sous l'orme* or *sans cause,* briefless barrister; *avocat consultant,* chamber counsel; *avocat général,* Solicitor-General; *avocat principal,* leading barrister; *plaider par avocat,* to be represented by counsel; *avocat du diable,* Devil's advocate.

avocat (2) [avɔ′ka], *n.m.* Avocado, alligator pear.

avocatoire [avɔka′twaːr], *a.* Recalling (of letters etc.).—*n.m.* A letter recalling a person.

avocette [avɔ′set], *n.f.* (*Orn.*) Avocet.

avoine [a′vwan], *n.f.* Oats; *Avoine nue,* pilcorn; *balle d'avoine,* chaff; *bouillie d'avoine,* porridge; *farine d'avoine,* oatmeal; *folle avoine,* wild oats; *gruau d'avoine,* groats.

avoir (1) [a′vwaːr], *v.t. irr.* (*pres.p.* **ayant,** *p.p.* **eu**) To have, to possess; to experience, to feel (pain, hunger, etc.); to obtain, to get, to buy, etc.; to be aged (so many years); to have on, to wear; to ail. *Avoir à,* to owe, to be under obligation to (do etc.). *En avoir à* (or *contre*) *quelqu'un,* to have a spite against someone. *Y avoir* (*imp.*), to be. *Avoir dans la main,* to hold in the hollow of one's hand; *avoir beaucoup de son père,* to take after one's father; *avoir faim,* to be hungry; *avoir honte,* to be ashamed; *avoir la parole,* to be entitled to speak, to be in possession of the House; *avoir peur,* to be afraid; *avoir pour agréable,* to regard as an agreeable person, to like; *avoir pour patron,* to have as master; *avoir raison,* to be right; *avoir raison de,* to get the mastery over; *avoir soif,* to be thirsty; *avoir tort,* to be wrong; *c'est une femme comme il n'y en a point,* she has not her like or match; *combien y a-t-il de Paris à Londres?* how far is it from Paris to London? (*fam.*) *en avoir,* to catch it; *j'en ai assez,* I have had enough of it, I am sick of it; *faire avoir,* to procure for; *il a quarante ans,* he is forty; *il avait un habit bleu*, he had on a blue coat; *il ne saurait y avoir de différence*, there can be no difference; *il n'y a pas de quoi*, don't mention it, there is no offence; *il n'y a qu'à parler*, he has only to speak; *il y a de quoi*, there is enough or good reason to; *il y a deux mois que je suis ici*, I have been here two months; *il est arrivé il y a trois semaines*, he arrived three weeks ago; *il y a plus*, nay more; *il y a un an qu'il est mort*, he has been dead a year; *il y a une heure que nous écrivons*, we have been writing for the last hour; *il y en a de noirs*, there are some black ones; *il y en a encore*, there is still some left; *j'ai à vous parler*, I have something to tell you; *qu'avez-vous donc?* what's the matter? *quel âge avez-vous?* how old are you? *qu'est-ce que vous avez?* what ails you? what is the matter with you? *vous avez la main, le dé, la boule*, it is your turn to play (at cards, at dice, at billiards); *vous n'avez qu'à dire*, you need only say the word; *on les aura*, we will have (beat) them; *la pièce a cinq mètres de large*, the room is fifteen feet wide.

avoir (2) [a′vwa:r], *n.m.* Possessions, property, what one is worth; (*Comm.*) credit, credit-side. *Voilà tout mon avoir*, this is all I have. *Doit et avoir*, debit and credit.

avoisinant [avwazi′nɑ̃], *a.* (*fem.* **avoisinante**) Neighbouring, adjoining, close by.

avoisiner, *v.t.* To border upon, to be contiguous to; to neighbour. *Être bien* or *mal avoisiné*, to have good or bad neighbours. ***s'avoisiner**, *v.r.* To approach. *L'hiver s'avoisine*, winter is approaching.

avortement [avɔrtə′mɑ̃], *n.m.* Abortion, miscarriage; failure.

avorter [avɔr′te], *v.t.* To miscarry, to have a miscarriage; to fail to develop, ripen, etc. (of plants, fruits, etc.); to prove abortive, to fail. *Ce dessein avorta*, that plan failed; *faire avorter*, to cause or procure abortion; *faire avorter les desseins de quelqu'un*, to baffle someone's designs.

avorton [avɔr′tɔ̃], *n.m.* Abortion; abortive child; (*fig.*) a paltry, miserable person or thing, a miserable specimen.

avouable [a′vwabl], *a.* Avowable, that may be admitted.

avoué [a′vwe], *n.m.* Attorney, solicitor. *Une étude d'avoué*, a solicitor's office.

avouer [a′vwe], *v.t.* To own, to acknowledge, to confess; to approve; to recognize as one's own, to avow. *Avouer un enfant*, to acknowledge a child; *il a avoué le fait*, he has confessed the deed; *il avoue l'avoir fait*, he confesses to it; *j'avouerai tout ce qu'il fera*, I will approve of all he does; *j'étais, je l'avoue, un peu confus*, I was rather confused, I must admit; *s'avouer vaincu*, to admit defeat. ·

avoyer [avwa′je], *n.m.* The chief magistrate in some Swiss cantons.

avril [a′vril], *n.m.* April. *Le premier avril*, All Fools' Day; *donner un poisson d'avril à quelqu'un*, to make someone an April fool; *recevoir un poisson d'avril*, to be made an April fool.

avrillé, *a.* (*fem.* **-ée**) Sown or planted in April.

avulsif [avyl′sif], *a.* (*fem.* **-ive**) Avulsive.

avulsion [avyl′sjɔ̃], *n.f.* Avulsion, extraction.

avunculaire [avɔ̃ky′lɛːr], *a.* Avuncular.

axe [aks], *n.m.* Axis; axle, axle-tree, spindle, trunnion; (*Bot., Geol., Anat., etc.*) axis; (*fig.*) central support or main axis of a system of ideas etc.; (*Polit.*) the Nazi-Fascist Axis. *Axe de manivelle*, crank-shaft; *axe du piston*, gudgeon-pin; *axe de vis*, screw-arbor; *axe tournant*, axle-tree.

axer, *v.t.* (*Mech.*) To centre; (*fig.*) to guide. *Axer sa vie sur*, to concentrate upon.

axial, *a.* (*fem.* **-ale**) or **axuel** (*fem.* **-elle**) Axial.

axifère, *a.* (*Bot.*) Bearing an axis.

axillaire [aksil′lɛːr], *a.* (*Anat., Bot.*) Axillar, axillary. *Fleurs axillaires*, axillary flowers.

axiomatique [aksjɔma′tik], *a.* Axiomatic.

axiome [ak′sjoːm], *n.m.* Axiom; (*fig.*) an accepted proposition, a truism.

axiomètre [aksjɔ′metr], *n.m.* (*Naut.*) Tell-tale (of the tiller).

axis [ak′sis], *n.m.* (*Anat.*) Axis, the second cervical vertebra; (*Zool.*) a small spotted deer, *Cervus axis*.

axonge [ak′sɔ̃:ʒ], *n.f.* (*Pharm. etc.*) Hog's lard, (*Mil.*) grease (for firearms etc.).

axuel (*fem.* **-elle**) [AXIAL].

ayant, *pres.p.* [AVOIR (1)].

ayant cause [ejɑ̃′koːz], *n.m.* (*pl.* **ayants cause**) (*Law*) Trustee, executor, assign.

ayant droit, *n.m.* (*pl.* **ayants droit**) Beneficiary, rightful claimant.

azalée [aza′le], *n.f.* Azalea.

Azarias [aza′rjɑːs], *m.* Azariah.

azédarac [azeda′rak], *n.m.* Bead-tree.

azerole [az′rɔl], *n.f.* Azarole, Neapolitan medlar. **azerolier**, *n.m.* Azarole-tree.

azimut [azi′myt], *n.m.* (*Astron.*) Azimuth.

azimutal, *a.* (*fem.* **-tale**, *pl.* **-taux**) Azimuthal. —*n.m.* A form of mariner's compass.

Azincourt [azɛ̃′kuːr], *m.* Agincourt.

Azof [a′zɔf], *f.* Azov. *La mer d'Azof*, the Sea of Azov.

azotate [azɔ′tat], *n.m.* Nitrate.

azote [a′zɔt], *n.m.* Nitrogen.—*a.* Nitric. **azoté**, *a.* (*fem.* **-ée**) Nitrogenized.

azoter, *v.t.* To charge with nitrogen; to azotize.

azoteux, *a.* (*fem.* **-euse**) Nitrous.

azotine, *n.f.* Organic matter, especially refuse wool, etc., used for greasing.

azotique, *a.* Nitric. **azotite**, *n.m.* Nitrite.

azoture, *n.m.* Nitride. **azoturie**, *n.f.* (*Path.*) Azoturia. **azoturique**, *a.* Pertaining to this.

aztèque [as′tɛk], *a.* Aztec.—*n.* (*colloq.*) A little thin man; an abortion.

azur [a′zyːr], *n.m.* Azure, blue, sky-colour; washing blue. *Azur de Hollande*, Dutch blue; *ciel d'azur*, a blue sky; *pierre d'azur*, (*pop.*) lapis lazuli; *la Côte d'Azur*, the French Riviera. **azurage**, *n.m.* Blueing. **azuré**, *a.* (*fem.* **-ée**) Azure, sky-coloured. *La voûte azurée*, the azure skies. **azurer**, *v.t.* To stain azure colour, to blue. **azurescent**, *a.* (*fem.* **-ente**) Bluish, tending towards blue. **azurin**, *a.* (*fem.* **-ine**) Pale azure.—*n.f.* A shade of blue; blue roach, azurine. **azurite**, *n.f.* (*Min.*) azurite.

azygos [azi′gɔs], *a.* (*Physiol.*) Azygous.

azyme [a′zim], *a.* Azymous, unleavened (bread).—*n.m.* Azyme, unleavened bread. *Fête des azymes*, feast of unleavened bread.

B

B, b [be], *n.m.* The second letter of the alphabet. **Être marqué au b*, to be either bandy-legged, one-eyed, hunch-backed, or lame (*bancal, borgne, bossu, boiteux*). *Ne parler que par b ou par f*, never to speak without swearing, (*b* for *bougre*, *f* for *foutu*).
baba (1) [ba'ba], *n.m.* A sponge cake, with sultanas, steeped in rum and syrup.
baba (2) [ba'ba], *a.* (*fam.*) Astounded. *En rester baba*, to be dumbfounded, flabbergasted.
Babel [ba'bɛl], *n.f.* Babel; (*fig.*) uproar, disorder. *C'est une vraie tour de Babel*, it is a perfect Babel, uproar, or confusion; *tour de Babel*, tower of Babel.
babélique, *a.* Gigantic, extremely high.
babeurre [ba'bœːr], *n.m.* Buttermilk.
babiche [ba'biʃ], *n.f.* or **babichon** [babi'ʃɔ̃], *n.m.* Lap-dog.
babil [ba'bi], *n.m.* Babble, prattle; chit-chat, tattle; chattering, babbling, etc. (of birds etc.). *Il nous étourdit par son babil*, he bewilders us with his chattering. **babillage** or **babillement**, *n.m.* Prattle, babbling, twaddle; tittle-tattle. **babillard**, *a.* (*fem.* **-arde**) Babbling, prattling, talkative, garrulous; gossiping, tell-tale.—*n.* Chatterer, babbler; tattler, blabber, gossip, tell-tale. **babillement** [BABILLAGE]. **babiller**, *v.i.* To babble, to prattle, to chat; to gossip, to chatter; (*fig.*) to blab, to backbite.
babine [ba'bin] or **babouine** [ba'bwin], *n.f.* The pendulous lip (of certain animals); (*colloq.*) human lips. *Il s'en lèche les babines*, he is smacking his lips over it.
babiole [ba'bjɔl], *n.f.* Bauble, gewgaw, toy; (*fig.*) trifle, a trumpery affair.
babiroussa [babiru'sa], *n.m.* Babiroussa (Malaisian swine).
bâbord [ba'bɔːr], *n.m.* (*Naut.*) Port, *larboard. *Venez sur bâbord!* Port the helm. **les bâbordais**, *n.m. pl.* The port-watch.
babouche [ba'buʃ], *n.f.* Turkish heelless slipper, babouche.
babouin [ba'bwɛ̃], *n.m.* Baboon; (*Med.*) pimple (on the lip); monkey, (*fem.* **babouine**) hussy (of a child).
Babylone [babi'lɔn], *f.* Babylon.
Babylonie [babilɔ'ni], *f.* Babylonia.
babylonien [babilɔ'njɛ̃], *a.* and *n.* (*fem.* **babylonienne**) Babylonian.
babylonisme, *n.m.* Grandiosity; craze for huge (buildings).
bac (1) [bak], *n.m.* Ferry, ferry-boat; vat. (*Elec.*) *Bac d'accumulateurs*, accumulator-jar.
bac (2) abbr. of *baccalauréat*.
bacaliau [baka'ljo], *n.m.* (*Naut.*) Stock-fish.
baccalauréat [bakalɔre'a], *n.m.* Baccalaureate, bachelorship (of arts, science, etc.), school-leaving certificate.
baccara [baka'ra], *n.m.* Baccara.
bacchanal [baka'nal], *n.m.* (*colloq.*) Racket, uproar. *Faire du bacchanal*, to make a racket, to kick up a row. **bacchanale**, *n.f.* (*pl.* **bacchanales**) Bacchanalia; (*colloq.*) noisy drinking-bout, revel, debauch; a wild or boisterous dance; (*Paint.*) a picture of a dance of bacchantes and satyrs.
bacchante [ba'kɑ̃ːt], *n.f.* Bacchante, lewd woman; (*pop.*) moustache.

baccifère [baksi'fɛːr], *a.* (*Bot.*) Bacciferous, berry-producing. **bacciforme**, *a.* Bacciform, berry-shaped.
*bacha [PACHA].
bâche [baːʃ], *n.f.* Tilt (for a carriage, cart, boat, etc.); awning; (*Hort.*) hotbed frame; (*Manuf.*) tank, cistern; (*Naut.*) a pocket-shaped net, a drag-net. *Bâche (goudronnée)*, tarpaulin.
*bachelette [baʃ'lɛt], *n.f.* Maid, lass, damsel.
bachelier [baʃə'lje], *n.* (*fem.* **-ière**) Bachelor (of arts, science, *ès Lettres*, *ès Sciences*); (*Feud.*) knight-bachelor.
bâcher [ba'ʃe], *v.t.* To spread a tilt over, to cover (a cart etc.).
bachi-bouzouck [baʃibu'zuk], *n.m.* Bashi-bazouk.
bachique [ba'ʃik], *a.* Bacchic, jovial, convivial. *Chant bachique*, drinking-song.
bachot [ba'ʃo], *n.m.* Wherry, small ferry-boat; (*Univ. slang*) baccalaureate. *Boîte à bachot*, cramming school. **bachotage**, *n.m.* Cramming. **bachoter**, *v.i.* To cram. **bachoteur**, *n.m.* Ferryman; crammer.
bacile [ba'sil], *n.m.* (*Bot.*) Rea-fennel, samphire.
bacillaire [basi'lɛːr], *a.* (*Min.*) Bacilliform; prismatic; (*Path.*) caused by a bacillus.—*n.f.* (*Bot.*) A genus of marine algae related to the diatoms.
bacille [ba'sil], *n.m.* (*Biol.*) Bacillus. *Porteur de bacilles*, germ-carrier. **bacilliforme**, *a.* Bacilliform. **bacillose** [TUBERCULOSE].
bâclage [bɑ'klaʒ], *n.m.* Closing of a port by means of chains, booms, etc.; line of boats (in a port) for the discharge or loading of cargo; (*fig.*) hasty, scamped work.
bâcle [bɑːkl], *n.f.* A bar for fixing behind a door etc., to secure it.
bâcler [bɑ'kle], *v.t.* To bar, fasten, or secure (a door, window, etc.) with a *bâcle*; to close (a river, harbour, etc.) with booms, chains, etc.; to stop, obstruct, or interrupt (traffic, navigation, etc.); (*fig.*) to do hastily, to polish off, to scamp (work). *Bâcler une besogne*, to do a job quickly and anyhow, to scamp a job.
bactéricide [bakteri'sid], *a.* (*Med.*) Destroying or stopping the multiplication of bacteria.
bactérie [bakte'ri], *n.f.* Bacterium, microbe. **bactérien**, *a.* (*fem.* **-ienne**) Bacterial.
bactériologie, *n.f.* Bacteriology. **bactériologique**, *a.* Bacteriological. *Guerre bactériologique*, germ warfare. **bactériologiste**, **bactériologue**, *n.m.* Bacteriologist.
bactériothérapie, *n.f.* Medical treatment by means of bacteria.
(*C*) **bacul** [ba'ky], *n.m.* Swing-bar, pole (of a coach).
badaud [ba'do], *n.m.* (*fem.* **-aude**) Ninny, booby, star-gazer; lounger, idler, rubberneck. **badaudage**, *n.m.* Star-gazing, lounging, loitering, idling. **badauder**, *v.i.* To go gaping about; to lounge, to saunter, to loiter. **badauderie**, *n.f.* Star-gazing, silliness; lounging, idling, sauntering. **badaudier**, *a.* Given to star-gazing, idling, etc.
Bade [bad], *f.* Baden.
baderne [ba'dɛrn], *n.f.* (*Naut.*) Fender; (*fig.*) old, valueless thing or person. *Une vieille baderne*, a dotard, an old fogy; an old crock.
badiane [ba'djan], *n.f.* or **badenier**, *n.m.* Aniseed-tree.

badigeon [badi'ʒɔ̃], *n.m.* Badigeon, filling-paste; whitewash; distemper; (*facet.*) rouge.
badigeonnage, *n.m.* Filling up with badigeon, making up; daubing; whitewashing; (*facet.*) rouging. **badigeonner,** *v.t.* To fill up (stonework, sculpture, etc.) with badigeon; to whitewash; (*fig.*) to disguise defects with varnish, rouge, etc.; (*Med.*) to anoint with a pharmaceutical preparation; (*Sculpt.*) to fill up; (*Med.*) to paint. **badigeonneur,** *n.m.* One who applies badigeon; whitewasher; (*pej.*) dauber.
badin [ba'dɛ̃], *a.* (*fem.* **-ine**) Waggish, jocular, roguish, droll. *Air badin,* playful air; *il a l'humeur badine,* he is of a sportive humour.—*n.* Wag, joker; buffoon, pantaloon.
badinage [badi'naːʒ], *n.m.* Badinage, raillery, banter; playfulness, jocularity (of style); mere child's-play. *Ce n'est pour lui qu'un badinage,* it is mere child's-play for him; *finissez votre badinage,* have done with your fooling; *il se prête volontiers au badinage,* he has no objection to a little trifling.
badine (1) [BADIN].
badine (2) [ba'din], *n.f.* Switch, light cane, wand; (*pl.*) small tongs.
badiner [badi'ne], *v.i.* To trifle, to dally, to toy; to speak or write banteringly or playfully; to play about in the wind; to flaunt. *En badinant,* in fun, by way of a joke; *il ne badine pas,* he is not joking; *la dentelle est trop tendue, il faut qu'elle badine un peu,* the lace is too tight, it must flutter a little; *on ne badine pas avec l'amour,* love is not to be trifled with.—*v.t.* To banter, to play with.
badinerie, *n.f.* Jesting, foolery, trifling; silliness, childishness.
(*C*) **bâdrant** [bɑ'drɑ̃], *a.* (*fem.* **-ante**) Bothersome.
(*C*) **bâdrer** [bɑ'dre], *v.t.* To annoy, to bother.
baffe [baf] or **baffre** [bafr] or **bâfre** (1) [baːfr], *n.f.* (*pop.*) Blow, cuff (on the head).
bafouer [ba'fwe], *v.t.* To scoff at, to make game of. *Il s'est fait bafouer,* he got scoffed at.
bafouillage [bafu'jaːʒ], *n.f.* Gibberish, rigmarole; spluttering; bad running (of engine).
bafouiller [bafu'je], *v.i.* (*colloq.*) To stammer; to splutter; to miss, to chatter (of engine).
bafouilleur, *n.m.* (*fem.* **-euse**) Stammerer.
bâfre (2) [bɑːfr] or **bâfrée,** *n.f.* (*pop.*) Feasting, junketing, blow-out. **bâfrer,** *v.i.* (*pop.*) To guzzle, to eat greedily, to have a blow-out.
bâfreur [bɑ'frœr], *n.m.* (*fem.* **-euse**) Guzzler, glutton, greedy-guts.
bagage [ba'gaːʒ], *n.m.* Baggage; stock-in-trade (of knowledge). *Bagage littéraire,* literary knowledge, literary productions (of an author); *plier bagage,* to pack up and go; (*pl.*) luggage, (*Am.*) baggage. *Bagages à main,* hand luggage; *bagages accompagnés,* luggage travelling with the passenger; *bagages enregistrés,* registered luggage; *laissez vos bagages à la consigne,* leave your luggage at the cloakroom. (*fig.*) *Elle est partie avec armes et bagages,* she has left nothing behind her.
bagarre [ba'gaːr], *n.f.* Riot; uproar; crush, squabble, scuffle. *Se tirer d'une bagarre,* to get out of a scuffle; *se trouver dans une bagarre,* to get involved in a rough-house.
bagasse [ba'gas], *n.f.* Bagasse, cane-trash;

waste stems of indigo, refuse from olive- or raisin-presses etc.
bagatelle [baga'tɛl], *n.f.* Bauble, trinket, trifle, anything frivolous; a trifling sum, a mere nothing; (*fig.*) a bit of a love-affair, an amourette. *Bagatelles que tout cela,* that is all stuff and nonsense; *il ne s'amuse qu'à des bagatelles,* he trifles away his time in fiddle-faddle; *ne penser qu'à la bagatelle,* to be a one for the girls.
bagnard [ba'ɲar], *n.m.* Convict.
bagne [baɲ], *n.m.* Convict-prison; penal servitude.
bagnole [ba'ɲɔl], *n.f.* A wretched carriage; old motor-car.
bagou, bagout [ba'gu], *n.m.* (*colloq.*) Gab, impudent loquacity.
baguage [ba'gaːʒ], *n.m.* Ringing (of a bird).
bague [bag], *n.f.* Ring; ring band (for birds). *La bague d'un champignon,* the annulus of a mushroom; *bague gravée en cachet,* seal-ring; *course* (or *jeu*) *de bague,* tilting at the ring.
bague-agrafe [baga'graf], *n.f.* (*d'un stylo*) (Fountain-pen) clip.
baguenaude [bag'noːd], *n.f.* Bladder-nut; (*fig.*) nonsense, foolery.
baguenauder [bagno'de], *v.i.* To trifle (time away), to fiddle-faddle.—*v.t.* To banter.
baguenauderie, *n.f.* Bantering, trifling, foolery; frivolous chatter.
baguenaudier (1), *n.m.* Trifler, banterer, buffoon; a game with a ring puzzle.
baguenaudier (2) [bagno'dje], *n.m.* Bladder-nut tree, bastard-senna tree.
baguer [ba'ge], *v.t.* To baste, to tack, to stitch; to decorate or hang with rings; (*Hort.*) to ring (trees); to ring (a bird).
baguette [ba'gɛt], *n.f.* Switch, rod, wand; pointer; clock (of stockings), glove-stretcher; long roll (French bread); (*Arch.*) bead, fillet. *Baguette de fée,* fairy-wand; *baguette de fusée,* stick of a rocket; *baguette de fusil,* ramrod; *baguette d'huissier,* usher's rod; *baguette divinatoire,* diviner's rod; *baguette de peintre,* maulstick; *baguettes de tambour,* drumsticks; *ce cheval obéit à la baguette,* that horse obeys the switch; *coup de baguette,* beat of the drum; *mener à la baguette,* to rule with a rod of iron; *passer par les baguettes,* to run the gauntlet.
bagueur [ba'gœːr], *n.m.* Implement for fixing rings on the tubes of a steam-engine; (*Hort.*) tool for ringing trees.
baguier [ba'gje], *n.m.* Casket for rings, jewels, etc., jewel-box, ring-stand.
bah [ba], *int.* Pooh, pshaw, nonsense, fudge.
bahut [ba'y], *n.m.* Cabinet, trunk, chest with a slightly convex top, press, cupboard; (*sch. slang*) school, lycée. *Bahut à glace,* curio cabinet; *en bahut,* rounded, convex.
bahutier, *n.m.* Maker of trunks, chests, cabinets, etc.
bai [bɛ], *a.* (*fem.* **baie** (1)) Bay. *Bai châtain,* chestnut; *bai clair,* light-bay; *bai doré,* yellow dun; *bai miroité,* dapple-bay; *une jument baie,* a bay mare.
baie (2) [bɛ], *n.f.* Bay; gulf.
baie (3) [bɛ], *n.f.* Berry.
baie (4) [bɛ], *n.f.* (*Arch.*) Bay, opening.
baignade [bɛ'ɲad], *n.f.* Bathing; bathing-place.
baignage [bɛ'ɲaz], *n.m.* Soaking; flooding (of a meadow).

baigner [bɛ'ɲe], *v.t.* To bathe, to give a bath, to dip; (*fig.*) to wash, to water (a coast etc.); to wet, to suffuse. *Des yeux baignés de larmes,* eyes bathed in tears; *être baigné de sueur,* to be in a violent sweat; *faire baigner les chevaux,* to take horses to the water.—*v.i.* To be plunged into; to welter (in blood etc.). *On l'a trouvé baignant dans son sang,* he was found weltering in his own blood. **se baigner,** *v.r.* To bathe, to wash.

baigneur [bɛ'ɲœr], *n.m.* (*fem.* **-euse**) Bather; bathkeeper or attendant, bathing-attendant.

***baigneuse,** *n.f.* Bathing-cap for ladies; bathing-dress.

baignoire [bɛ'ɲwa:r], *n.f.* Bath-tub, bath; (*Theat.*) ground-floor box.

bail [ba:j], *n.m.* (*pl.* **baux**) [bo]. Lease. *Bail à ferme,* lease of land; *bail à long terme,* long lease; *bail à loyer,* lease of houses, furniture, etc.; *louer à bail,* to lease out; *passer un bail,* to draw up a lease; to sign an agreement.

bâillant [ba'jɑ̃], *a.* (*fem.* **-ante**) Yawning, gaping.

***baille** [ba:j], *n.f.* Half tub; bucket; (*Mach.*) feed-tank. *Baille à brai,* tar-pail; *baille de sonde,* bucket (for sounding).

bâillement [baj'mɑ̃], *n.m.* Yawning, yawn.

bailler [ba'je], *v.t.* To give, to deliver. *Bailler à bail,* to let, to lease, to farm out; *vous me la baillez belle,* tell me another!

bâiller [ba'je], *v.i.* To yawn, to gape; to open (of fissures etc.); to be ajar (of doors). *Bâiller de sommeil,* to yawn with drowsiness; *on bâille en voyant bâiller les autres,* yawning is catching.

baillet [ba'jɛ], *a.* Sorrel (horse).

bailleur [ba'jœr], *n.m.* (*fem.* **bailleresse**) One who leases, lessor. *Un bailleur de fonds,* money-lender, sleeping partner; *le bailleur,* (in old French tennis or *paume*) server.

bâilleur [ba'jœr], *n.m.* (*fem.* **bâilleuse**) Yawner; gaper.

bailli [ba'ji], *n.m.* (*Fr. Hist.*) Bailiff. **bailliage,** *n.m.* Jurisdiction or tribunal of a bailiff, bailiwick.

bâillon [ba'jɔ̃], *n.m.* Gag, muzzle. **bâillonnement,** *n.m.* Gagging. **bâillonner,** *v.t.* To stop the mouth of, to gag, to muzzle; (*fig.*) to silence.

bain [bɛ̃], *n.m.* Bath; bathing-tub; (*pl.*) baths, bathing establishment, watering-place, spa, thermal or medicinal springs. *Bain de fixage,* (*Phot.*) fixing-bath; *bain d'eau de mer,* salt-water bath; *bain de pied,* foot-bath; *bain de siège,* hip-bath; *bains de mer,* sea-bathing; *bain de vapeur,* steam-bath; *envoyer au bain,* (*colloq.*) to send away with a flea in his ear; *être dans le bain,* to have a finger in; *se mettre dans le bain,* to put oneself in the mood; *la salle de bain,* the bathroom; *l'ordre du Bain,* the Order of the Bath.

bain-douche [bɛduʃ], *n.m.* Shower-bath.

bain-marie [bɛ̃ma'ri], *n.m.* (*pl.* **bains-marie**) (*Cook.*) Double saucepan for foods that burn easily; boiler (in a kitchen-range etc.).

baïonnette [bajo'nɛt], *n.f.* Bayonet; (*pl.*) infantry, forces. *Baïonnette au canon!* fix bayonets; *charger à la baïonnette,* to charge with fixed bayonets; *croiser la baïonnette,* to cross bayonets; *enlever un poste à la baïonnette,* to carry a post at the point of the

bayonet; *remettez la baïonnette!* unfix bayonets.

baisemain [bɛz'mɛ̃], *n.m.* Kissing (of hands); *(fig.)* compliments.

baisement [bɛz'mɑ̃], *n.m.* (*Eccles.*) Kissing (of the Pope's slipper).

baiser [bɛ'ze], *v.t.* (of strictly literary use, no longer decent in conversation, practically replaced by *embrasser*) To kiss.—*n.m.* Kiss, kissing, salute. *Un gros baiser,* a smack; *un baiser de Judas,* a treacherous kiss.

baisoter, *v.t.* To be always kissing, to peck at.

baissant [bɛ'sɑ̃], *a.* (*fem.* **baissante**) Declining, abating; setting (of the sun etc.).—*n.m.* Abatement, fall (of a flood etc.).

baisse [bɛ:s], *n.f.* Fall, abatement, decline; reduction or fall (of prices etc.); falling off (of credit etc.). *En baisse* (*Comm.*), falling; *jouer à la baisse,* (*St. Exch.*) to bear, to speculate on a fall.

baisser [bɛ'se], *v.t.* To let down, to lower; to reduce the height of; to strike (a flag etc.); to bow (the head etc.). *Baisser la tête,* to hold or hang down one's head; *baisser la visière d'un casque,* to lower the beaver of a helmet; *baisser le rideau,* to drop the curtain; *baisser les yeux,* to cast one's eyes down; *faire baisser les yeux,* to stare out of countenance; *baisser pavillon,* to strike one's flag, to knuckle under to one; *donner tête baissée dans le piège,* to fall headlong into the snare; *elle baissa son voile,* she let down her veil; *il marchait les yeux baissés,* he walked with downcast eyes.—*v.i.* (*conjugated with* ÊTRE *or* AVOIR) To go down; to ebb; to be on the decline or the wane; to flag, to droop; to fail, to diminish. *Ce malade baisse,* the patient is losing strength; *ce vieillard baisse,* this old man is breaking up; *il baisse à vue d'œil,* he is visibly sinking; *le jour baisse,* night is coming on; *ses actions baissent,* there is a fall in his shares, (*fig.*) his stock is falling; *les fonds baissent,* the funds are falling; *sa vue commence à baisser,* his sight begins to fail; *son génie baisse,* his genius is on the decline. —*n.m.* Lowering, fall, setting. **se baisser,** *v.r.* To stoop; to bow down; to be lowered. *Il n'a qu'à se baisser pour en prendre,* he has only to pick and choose.

baissier [bɛ'sje], *n.m.* (*fem.* **-ière** (1)) (*St. Exch.*) Bear, operator for a fall.

baissière (2) [bɛ'sjɛ:r], *n.f.* Wine remaining at the bottom of a cask; (*Agric.*) hollow, puddle.

baisure [bɛ'zy:r], *n.f.* Kissing-crust (of a loaf).

baître [bɛ:tr], *n.m.* (*Orn.*) Grebe.

bajoue [ba'ʒu], *n.f.* Jowl, chap (of pigs etc.).

bajoyer [baʒwa'je], *n.m.* Lateral wall or facing (of a river-bank near a bridge, or a lock etc.).

bakchich [bak'ʃiʃ], *n.m.* (Illegal) tip to an officer, baksheesh.

bakélite [bake'lit], *n.f.* Bakelite.

bal [bal], *n.m.* Ball, dance. *Bal blanc,* a ball for young girls; *bal champêtre,* country ball; *bal costumé* or *paré* or *travesti,* fancy-dress ball; *bal de têtes,* ball where the dancers go wearing grotesque heads; *bal masqué,* masked ball; *carnet de bal,* dance programme; *ouvrir le bal,* to open the ball; *salle de bal,* dance hall; (*fig.*) *donner le bal à quelqu'un,* to make someone dance for it; *mettre le bal en train*, to set things going.

balade [ba'lad], *n.f.* (*pop.*) Walk, ramble, stroll. **balader**, *v.t.* *Balader quelqu'un*, to trot someone round; (*fam.*) *envoyer balader*, to send packing, to chuck up. **se balader**, *v.r.* To stroll about, to ramble about aimlessly.

baladeur, *a.* (*fem.* **baladeuse** (1)) Strolling, sauntering. *Train baladeur*, (*Motor.*) gear for changing speed.—*n.* Stroller, saunterer.

baladeuse (2) [bala'dø:z], *n.f.* Costermonger's barrow; portable lamp; trailer (for cycle or tram).

baladin [bala'dɛ̃], *n.m.* (*fem.* **baladine**) Mountebank; buffoon; straw-mattress, palliasse; (*pej.*) comedian, actor. **baladinage**, *n.m.* Buffoonery, nonsense. **baladiner**, *v.i.* To play the buffoon or fool.

balafre [ba'lɑ:fr], *n.f.* Gash, slash, cut; scar. **balafrer** [bala'fre], *v.t.* To gash, to slash.

balai [ba'le], *n.m.* Broom, besom; (*Elec.*) brush; (*Hawking*) tail (of a bird); (*Hunt.*) end of a dog's tail; the last bus or tram; (*Mil.*) a miss (at target practice). *Balai à laver*, mop; *balai de bruyère*, brushwood besom; *balai de crin*, hair-broom; *balai de jonc*, carpet-broom; *balai de plume*, duster; *donner un coup de balai*, to sweep up, (*fig.*) to clear out (people); *faire balai neuf*, to sweep clean as with a new broom; *il n'est rien tel que balai neuf*, a new broom sweeps clean; *manche à balai*, broom-stick; (*Av. slang*) joystick; (*pop.*) a thin, lanky person; *rôtir le balai*, to play a subordinate part; to lead a fast life.

(*C*) **balai** [ba'le], *n.m.* Cedar.

balais [ba'lɛ], *a.* *Un rubis balais*, a balas ruby.

balalaïka [balalai'ka], *n.f.* Balalaika.

balance [ba'lɑ̃:s], *n.f.* Balance, scales, pair of scales; (*Comm.*) balance (of an account), balance sheet; (*Astron.*) Libra; (*Fishing*) a flat net on an iron ring for catching prawns. *Arrêter une balance*, to agree a balance; *balance du commerce*, balance of trade; *balance romaine*, steelyard; *être en balance*, to be undecided; *faire pencher la balance*, to turn the scale; *mettre en balance*, to balance, (*fig.*) to weigh, to consider carefully the pros and cons of; *ses droits peuvent-ils entrer en balance avec les miens?* can his claims be weighed in the same scale with mine?

balancé [balɑ̃'se], *n.m.* (*Dancing*) Setting to one's partner; (*Box.*) swing.—*a.* (*fam.*) (*homme*) *bien balancé*, well set up.

balancelle [balɑ̃'sɛl], *n.f.* Felucca [*It.*].

balancement [balɑ̃s'mɑ̃], *n.m.* Balancing, poising, rocking, see-saw; (*fig.*) fluctuation, wavering, hesitation.

balancer [balɑ̃'se], *v.t.* To balance, to poise, to hold in equilibrium; to swing to and fro, to rock; (*fig.*) to weigh, to consider; to square (accounts); to counterbalance; to hold undecided; (*colloq.*) to give the sack to, to dismiss, to throw (away). *Balancer la victoire*, to keep victory in doubt; *balancer les avantages et les inconvénients*, to weigh the advantages and disadvantages; *balancer les pertes par le gain*, to balance the loss by the profit; *balancer un compte*, to balance an account; *balancer un javelot*, to poise a javelin; *ses vertus balancent tous ses vices*, his

virtues outweigh all his vices.—*v.i.* To hesitate, to be in suspense, to waver; to fluctuate, to oscillate, to remain undecided. *Il balança s'il accepterait la place qu'on lui offrait*, he hesitated whether to accept the situation offered him; *il n'y a pas à balancer*, there are no two ways about it; *il y a consenti sans balancer*, he consented to it without hesitating. **se balancer**, *v.r.* To swing, to rock; to be counterbalanced, to be made up for. *Un oiseau qui se balance dans l'air*, a bird hovering in the air; (*Naut.*) *se balancer sur ses ancres*, to ride at anchor; (*pop.*) *je m'en balance!* I don't care a fig!

balancerie, *n.f.* Scale-maker's works, scale-making.

balancier [balɑ̃'sje], *n.m.* Maker of weights and scales; pendulum, balance; balancing-pole. *Balancier monétaire*, machine for striking money, coining press; *le balancier d'une horloge*, the pendulum of a clock; *le balancier d'une machine à vapeur*, the beam of a steam-engine; *le balancier d'un tourne-broche*, the flyer of a roasting-jack.

balancine [balɑ̃'sin], *n.f.* (*Naut.*) Lift.

balançoire [balɑ̃'swa:r], *n.f.* See-saw; swing; (*fig.*) a fairy-tale, a fib.

balandre [ba'lɑ̃:dr], *n.f.* A flat canal boat.

balane [ba'lan], *n.m.* Acorn-shell. **balanin** or **balanus**, *n.m.* (*Ent.*) Nut-weevil. **balanophore**, *a.* (*Bot.*) Nuciferous. **balanoïde**, *a.* (*Bot.*) Nuciform. **balanophage**, *a.* (*Zool.*) Nucivorous.

balata [bala'ta], *n.m.* Balata, bully-tree.

balayage [balɛ'ja:ʒ] or **balayement**, *n.m.* Sweeping. (*Naut.*) *Balayage des mines*, mine-sweeping; (*Tel.*) scanning.

balayer [balɛ'je], *v.t.* To sweep, to clean with a broom; (*fig.*) to sweep (of drapery etc.), to sweep away, to scour; (*Tel.*) to scan. *Balayer les mers*, to scour the seas; *le vent balaie la plaine*, the wind sweeps the plain; *sa robe balaie la terre*, her gown sweeps the ground. **balayette**, *n.f.* Small broom, whisk.

balayeur [balɛ'jœr], *n.m.* (*fem.* **-euse**) Sweeper, scavenger.—*n.f.* Sweeping-machine; a strip (of cloth, lace, etc., sewn on the edge of a lady's dress). *Balayeuse mécanique*, mechanical sweeper. **balayures**, *n.f.* (*used only in pl.*) Sweepings. *Balayures de mer*, seaweed washed on shore, sea-wrack.

balbutiant [balby'sjɑ̃], *a.* (*fem.* **balbutiante**) Stuttering, stammering. ***balbutie**, *n.f.*, or **balbutiement**, *n.m.* Stuttering, stammering.

balbutier [balby'sje], *v.i.* To stammer, to stutter; to mumble. *Un enfant qui commence à balbutier*, a child beginning to lisp.—*v.t.* To pronounce indistinctly. *Balbutier un compliment*, to stammer out a compliment; *elle balbutia quelques mots*, she stammered out a few words; *il ne fit que balbutier son rôle*, he did nothing but mumble through his part.

balbutieur, *n.m.* (*fem.* **-ieuse**) Stutterer, stammerer.

balbuzard [balby'za:r], *n.m.* (*Orn.*) Bald buzzard.

balcon [bal'kɔ̃], *n.m.* Balcony. (*Naut.*) *Balcon arrière*, quarter gallery; (*Theat.*) dress-circle.

balconet [balkɔ'nɛ], *n.m.* Strapless brassière.

baldaquin [balda'kɛ̃], *n.m.* Baldachin; canopy; tester (of bed).

Bâle [bɑ:l], *f.* Basel, Basle.

bale or **balle** [bal], *n.f.* Husk, chaff, glume.

Baléares [bale'a:r], **les**, *f.pl.* The Balearic Isles.

baleine [ba'lɛ:n], *n.f.* Whale; whalebone; various parts (as of an umbrella) used similarly. *Barbe de baleine*, whalebone; *blanc de baleine*, spermaceti; *huile de baleine*, whale-oil; *la pêche de la baleine*, the whale fishery. **baleiné**, *a.* (*fem.* **baleinée**) Stiffened with whalebone. *Un corset baleiné*, whalebone stays. **baleineau**, *n.m.* Young whale. **baleinier** (*fem.* **baleinière**) *n.m.* Whaler.—*n.f.* Whale-boat. **baleinoptère**, *n.m.* (*Zool.*) Rorqual.

baleston, *n.m.* [LIVARDE].

balisage [bali'za:ʒ], *n.m.* (*Naut.*) Buoying; a series of buoys; signalling; (*Av.*) ground-lights.

balise (1) [ba'li:z], *n.f.* Sea-mark, buoy, beacon; pole marking the course of a railway, canal, etc.; (*Av.*) ground-light.

balise (2) [ba'li:z], *n.f.* Canna-seed.

balisement [baliz'mã], *n.m.* Buoying.

baliser [bali'ze], *v.t.* To buoy, to mark with beacons, with ground-lights.

baliseur [bali'zœr], *n.m.* Person who sets up or inspects beacons, superintendent of towing-paths; buoying-boat.

balisier [bali'zje], *n.m.* Canna, American reed.

baliste [ba'list], *n.f.* War-machine, ballista; trigger-fish. **balistique**, *a.* Ballistic.—*n.f.* Ballistics.

balivage [bali'va:ʒ], *n.m.* Staddling. **baliveau**, *n.m.* Staddle; sapling.

baliverne [bali'vern], *n.f.* Nonsense, humbug. *Il vous conte des balivernes*, he talks nonsense, tells you cock-and-bull stories. **baliverner**, *v.i.* To talk idly, to twaddle.

balkanique [balka'nik], *a.* Of the Balkans.

ballade [ba'lad], *n.f.* Ballade; ballad.

ballage [ba'la:ʒ], *n.m.* (*Metal.*) Hammering of iron before wire-drawing.

ballant [ba'lã], *a.* (*fem.* **ballante**) Waving, swinging, dangling. *Il va les bras ballants*, he walks with his arms dangling.—*n.m.* Oscillation; slack bight (of plane).

ballast [ba'last], *n.m.* (*Rail.*) Ballast. **ballastage**, *n.m.* Ballasting. **ballaster**, *v.t.* To ballast. **ballastière**, *n.f.* Ballast-hole; ballast-tank (in submarine).

balle (1) [bal], *n.f.* Ball; bullet, shot; bale, pack; (*Print.*) pad formerly used for inking; (*slang*) face, head; franc. (*Ten.*) *Balle!* service! *à vous la balle*, it is your turn; *balle morte*, spent ball or bullet; *balle perdue*, wasted or stray shot, (*fig.*) useless effort; *ça m'a coûté six-cents balles*, it cost me ten bob; *c'est un enfant de la balle*, he is a chip of the old block; *enfants de la balle*, children following the business of their father, (*esp.*) born and bred in the theatre; *fusil chargé à balle*, a musket loaded with ball; *juger la balle*, to foresee the end; *marchandise de balle*, common pack-wares; *porter la balle*, to be a colporteur or pedlar; *prendre la balle à la volée*, to hit the ball before it bounces, to volley; *saisir la balle au bond*, to take the ball at the rebound, (*fig.*) to seize the opportunity, to take time by the forelock; *renvoyer la balle*, to return the ball, (*fig.*) to give tit for tat, to turn the tables on.

balle (2) [BALE].

ballerine [bal'rin], *n.f.* Ballerina, ballet-dancer.

ballet [ba'lɛ], *n.m.* Ballet. *Corps de ballet*, corps de ballet.

ballon [ba'lɔ̃], *n.m.* Hand-ball; football; balloon; child's air-balloon; a convex drinking glass; a convex hill-top; (*Chem.*) balloon-flask. *Ballon d'essai*, small balloon for determining the direction of the wind, (*fig.*) a feeler; *envoyer un ballon d'essai*, to send out a feeler; *ballon dirigeable*, air-ship; *manche ballon*, puff sleeve; *pneu ballon*, balloon-tyre. **ballonné**, *a.* (*fem.* **-ée**) Distended, swollen.

ballonnet, *n.m.* Small balloon.

ballonnement, *n.m.* (*Med.*) Swelling of the abdomen.

ballonner (se), *v.r.* To swell out, to distend.

ballonnier, *n.m.* Maker or vendor of toy balloons.

ballon-sonde, *n.m.* Sounding balloon.

ballot [ba'lo], *n.m.* A small pack (of wares for sale); (*pop.*) a fool, a bumpkin. *Voilà votre ballot*, that's the very thing for you.

ballote [ba'lɔt], *n.f.* (*Bot.*) Black horehound.

ballottade [balɔ'tad], *n.f.* A (horse's) jump in the air with all four legs without kicking.

ballottage [balɔ'ta:ʒ], *n.m.* Shaking up, tossing about; ineffective ballot. *Il y a ballottage*, no candidate has been returned; *scrutin de ballottage*, second ballot.

ballottement [balɔt'mã], *n.m.* Tossing, shaking.

ballotter [balɔ'te], *v.t.* To toss, to toss about; to bandy; to keep in suspense; (*fig.*) to debate. *Ballotter quelqu'un*, to send someone from pillar to post.—*v.i.* To shake, to rattle. *Cette porte ballotte*, that door rattles.

balnéable [balne'abl], *a.* Suitable for baths or a spa. **balnéaire**, *a.* Pertaining to baths etc. *Station balnéaire*, watering-place. **balnéation**, *n.f.* Bathing, especially for medical purposes. **balnéothérapie**, *n.f.* Medical treatment by means of baths or medicinal waters.

baloche [ba'lɔʃ], *n.f.* (*pop.*) Village or town fête, fair.

balourd [ba'lu:r], *a.* (*fem.* **balourde**) Dull, heavy, thick-headed.—*n.* A stupid or dull person, numskull, dunce.

balourdise, *n.f.* Gross blunder; stupidity.

balsamier [balza'mje], or **baumier**, *n.m.* Balsam-tree. **balsamifère**, *a.* Balsamiferous. **balsamine**, *n.f.* Balsamine. **balsamique**, *a.* Balsamic, balsamous. **balsamite**, *n.f.* (*Bot.*) A genus of *Compositae* comprising the costmary.

Balthazar [balta'za:r], *m.* Balthazar, Belshazzar.—*n.m.* (*fam.*) Feast.

Baltique [bal'tik], **la**, *f.* The Baltic (Sea).

baluchon [baly'ʃɔ̃], *n.m.* Slop-pail; (*colloq.*) bundle of cloths. *Faire son baluchon*, to pack up.

balustrade [balys'trad], *n.f.* Balustrade; low railing etc. **balustre**, *n.m.* Baluster, hand-rail. **balustrer**, *v.t.* To rail in, surround, or decorate with balusters.

balzan [bal'zã], *a.* (*fem.* **balzane**) White-footed (of a black or bay horse). **balzane**, *n.f.* White stocking (of a horse).

bambin [bã'bɛ̃], *n.m.* (*fem.* **-ine**) (*colloq.*) Urchin, brat, bantling.

bambochade [bãbɔ'ʃad], *n.f.* Grotesque picture, caricature; (*fig.*) a spree.

bamboche [bã′bɔʃ], *n.f.* A big marionette or puppet; (*fam.*) drinking-bout, spree; young bamboo, bamboo-cane. *Faire bamboche*, to have a spree. **bambocher**, *v.i.* (*fam.*) To go on the spree; to play pranks. **bambocheur**, *n.m.* (*fem.* **-euse**) Libertine, rake; loose, disorderly, or dissipated person.

bambou [bã′bu], *n.m.* Bamboo; bamboo-cane. (*fig.*) *Recevoir le coup de bambou*, to have a sunstroke; to get cracked.

bamboula [bãbu′la], *n.f.* Negro dance.—*n.m.* (*pej.*) a Negro.

ban [bã], *n.m.* Ban, announcement, public order, edict or proclamation; proclamation of outlawry or banishment, proscription; (*Feud. Ant.*) assembly of vassals for military service; (*Mil.*) drum-roll or trumpet-blast before a proclamation to troops; (*fig.*) measured applause. *Ban et arrière ban*, barons and retainers, (*fig.*) all one's supporters; *bans*, (*pl.*) banns (of matrimony); *dispense de bans*, marriage licence; *être au ban*, to be under the ban; *garder son ban*, to submit to a decree of banishment etc.; *mettre au ban*, to banish, (*fig.*) to send to Coventry; *rompre son ban* or *être en rupture de ban*, to break one's ban.

banal [ba′nal], *a.* (*fem.* **-ale**, *pl.* **-aux**) (*Feud. Law*) Banal; (*fig.*) common, commonplace, trite, petty. **banalement**, *adv.* Trivially, vulgarly. **banaliser**, *v.t.* To vulgarize. **banalité**, *n.f.* Vulgarity, banality; a commonplace, a trite expression.

banane [ba′nan], *n.f.* Banana. **bananerie**, *n.f.* Banana-plantation. **bananier**, *n.m.* Banana-tree; ship carrying bananas.

banc [bã], *n.m.* Bench, settle, form; reef, shoal, sand-bank; shoal (of fish); (*Geol.*) layer, bed; dock, bar. *Banc d'essai*, (*Motor.*) test bench; assay office, for hall-marking gold and silver; *banc d'église*, church seat, pew; *banc de nage*, rower's seat, thwart; (*C*) *banc de neige*, heap of snow; *banc de pierre*, layer or bed of stone; *banc des témoins*, witness-bench; *banc d'œuvre*, churchwardens' pew; *banc du roi*, King's Bench; *échouer sur un banc de sable*, to run aground on a sandbank; *être au banc des accusés*, to be in the dock; *il est encore sur les bancs*, he is still at school; *un banc à dossier*, a bench with a back to it; *un banc de corail*, a coral reef; *un banc de gazon*, a turf bank; *un banc de harengs*, a shoal of herrings; *un banc d'huîtres*, an oyster-bed; *le (grand) Banc*, the Banks (of Newfoundland).

bancable or **banquable** [bã′kabl], *a.* Bankable.

bancaire [bã′kɛr], *a.* Pertaining to banking.

bancal [bã′kal], *a.* (*fem.* **bancale**, *pl.* **bancaux**) Bandy-legged.—*n.* A bandy-legged person; (*Mil.*) a curved sabre.

banco [bã′ko] [It.], *a.* Banco (a term used in exchange business to distinguish money of account from ordinary currency). *Faire banco*, (*Gaming*) to break the bank.

bancroche [BANCAL].

bandage [bã′da:ʒ], *n.m.* Application of bandages; bandage; belt; truss; tyre (of wheels); hoop (of guns); outer cover (of a pneumatic tyre). *Bandage herniaire*, truss; *délier un bandage*, to undo a bandage.

bandagiste, *n.m.* Maker of trusses.

bande (1) [bã:d], *n.f.* Band, belt, strip; ribbon; bandage; (*Her.*) bend; (*Arch.*) fascia, string; (*Anat.*) tract. *Bande d'essai* (*Cine.*), test film; *bande de papier*, a slip of paper, wrapper; *bande de fréquences*, (*Rad.*) frequency band; *dans la bande des quarante mètres*, on the forty-metre band; *coller sous bande*, (*Billiards*) to play (an opponent's ball) close to the cushion; (*fig.*) to corner, to put in an awkward position; *donner de la bande*, (*Naut.*) to have a list; *faire bande à part*, to keep apart; *la bande d'un billard*, the cushion of a billiard-table; *la bande d'une selle*, the side-bar of a saddle; *mettre un journal sous bande*, to put a newspaper in a wrapper; *bandes molletières*, puttees.

bande (2) [bã:d], *n.f.* Band, troop, company; gang, crew, set of (brigands etc.); flock, pack; (*fig.*) league, cabal. *Ces oiseaux vont par bandes*, those birds go in flocks; *une bande de voleurs*, a gang of thieves; (*fam.*) *toute la bande*, the whole gang.

bandé [bã′de], *a.* (*fem.* **-ée**) Bandaged, taut, stretched; (*Her.*) ornamented with bends.

bandeau [bã′do], *n.m.* Headband, fillet, frontlet, bandage (for the eyes); (*fig.*) veil, mist; (*Arch.*) string-course. *Avoir un bandeau sur les yeux*, to be blindfolded; *en bandeaux* (of the hair), parted centrally.

bandelette [bã′dlet], *n.f.* Little band, string fillet; (*Surg.*) fascia; (*Arch.*) bandelet.

bander [bã′de], *v.t.* To bind or tie up; to bandage; to tighten, to bend (a bow etc.). *Bander une plaie*, to bind up a wound; *se bander les yeux*, to blindfold oneself.—*v.i.* To be stretched; to be taut or too tight.

bandereau [bã′dro], *n.m.* Trumpet-sling.

banderille [bã′dri:j], *n.f.* Banderilla. **banderillero**, *n.m.* A bull-fighter who plants banderillas in the bull.

banderole [bã′drɔl], *n.f.* Banderole, streamer, pennant; lance. **banderolé**, *a.* (*fem.* **-ée**) Decorated with a banderole.

*bandière [bã′djɛ:r], *n.f.* *Banner, flag. *Front de bandière*, front line of battle; bivouac etc.

bandingue [bã′dɛ̃:g], *n.f.* Guy-rope of a fishing-net.

bandit [bã′di], *n.m.* Brigand, bandit; ruffian, blackguard, scamp. (*fam.*) *Mon bandit de cousin*, my rascally cousin. **banditisme**, *n.m.* State of being infested with bandits; brigandage.

bandolier [bãdɔ′lje], **bandoulier** [bãdu′lje], *n.m.* Bandit, Pyrenean smuggler.

bandoline [bãdɔ′lin], *n.f.* Bandoline (for the hair).

bandoulière [bãdu′lje:r], *n.f.* Shoulder-strap, bandolier. *En bandoulière*, slung across the back; *porter la bandoulière*, to be a game-keeper.

bandure [bã′dy:r], *n.f.* Pitcher-plant.

banian [ba′njã], *n.m.* Banian (Indian merchant, shopkeeper, etc.); banyan-tree.

banjo [bã′ʒo], *n.m.* Banjo; part of a rotary motor.

banlieue [bã′ljø], *n.f.* Suburbs, outskirts (of a town). **banlieusard**, *n.m.* (*fam.*) One who lives in a suburb; commuter.

banne [ban], *n.f.* Hamper, awning, **tilt**, tarpaulin; coal-cart. **banneau**, *n.m.* Small hamper, fruit-basket.

banner [ba′ne], *v.t.* To cover with a tilt.

banneret [ban′re], *n.m.* and *a.* Banneret. *Chevalier banneret*, knight-banneret.

banneton [ban'tɔ̃], *n.m.* Bread-basket; (*Fishing*) creel.

bannette [ba'nɛt], *n.f.* Small basket.

banni [ba'ni], *a.* (*fem.* **bannie**) Banished, outlawed; (*fig.*) banned, forbidden.—*n.* An exile, a proscript.

bannière [ba'njɛːr], *n.f.* Banner, standard, flag; (*fig.*) ensign, colours, party-emblem, etc. *Aller au-devant de quelqu'un avec croix et bannière,* to give someone a handsome reception; (*fam.*) *ce fut la croix et la bannière pour le faire venir,* it was the devil and all to make him come; *se ranger sous la bannière de quelqu'un,* to join someone's party; (*colloq.*) *être en bannière,* to be only in one's shirt.

bannir [ba'niːr], *v.t.* To banish; (*fig.*) to expel, to dismiss; to proscribe, to exclude, to reject. **bannissable,** *a.* Deserving banishment. **bannissement,** *n.m.* Banishment. **bannisseur,** *n.m.* Banisher.

banquable [BANCABLE].

banquais [bɑ̃'kɛ], *a.* Engaged in the Newfoundland fishery (of ships, persons, etc.). —*n.* Newfoundland fisher, banker.

banque [bɑ̃ːk], *n.f.* Bank, banking; (*Print.*) wages, pay-day. *Action de la banque,* bank-stock; *assignation de banque,* bank transfer; *avoir un compte en banque,* to have an account at the bank; *billet de banque de cinq livres,* a five-pound (bank-)note; *carnet de banque,* bank-book; *faire la banque,* to be a banker; *faire sauter la banque,* to break the bank; *jour de banque,* (*pop.*) pay-day; *mandat de la banque,* bank post bill; *mettre à la banque,* to put in the bank; *succursale de banque,* branch bank.

banqueroute [bɑ̃'krut], *n.f.* Bankruptcy; (*fig.*) failure, collapse. *Banqueroute frauduleuse,* fraudulent bankruptcy; *faire banqueroute,* to go bankrupt; *faire banqueroute à l'honneur,* to forfeit one's honour.

banqueroutier, *n.m.* (*fem.* **-ière**) Bankrupt.

banquet [bɑ̃'kɛ], *n.m.* Banquet, feast. **banqueter,** *v.i.* To banquet, to feast. **banqueteur,** *n.m.* (*fem.* **-euse**) Banqueter, feaster.

banquette [bɑ̃'kɛt], *n.f.* Bench; balustrade, sill; outside-seat (of a coach); footway (of a road), towing-path; (*Fort.*) banquette. *Banquette irlandaise,* bank; *banquette de piano,* duet-stool. *Jouer devant les banquettes,* (*Theat.*) to play to empty benches.

banquier [bɑ̃'kje], *a.* (*fem.* **banquière**) Pertaining to a bank or banking.—*n.* Money-agent, banker.

banquise [bɑ̃'kiːz], *n.f.* Ice-floe, ice-pack.

banquiste [bɑ̃'kist], *n.m.* Quack, charlatan.

bantam [bɑ̃'tam], *n.m.* Bantam.

baobab [bao'bab], *n.m.* Baobab.

baptême [ba'tɛːm], *n.m.* Baptism, christening. *Baptême de sang,* bloody initiation; *baptême du feu,* first fighting; *baptême de l'air,* first flight; *extrait de baptême,* certificate of baptism; *le baptême de la ligne* or *des tropiques,* the ceremony of ducking etc. in crossing the line (at sea); *nom de baptême,* Christian name; *recevoir le baptême,* to be baptized.

baptiser [bati'ze], *v.t.* To baptize; (*fig.*) to christen, to give a name or nickname to. *Baptiser des cloches,* to consecrate bells; *baptiser quelqu'un,* to give someone a nickname; *baptiser son vin,* to dilute one's wine;

baptiser un vaisseau, to christen a ship. **baptismal,** *a.* (*fem.* **-ale,** *pl.* **-aux**) Baptismal. *Tenir un enfant sur les fonts baptismaux,* to stand godfather or godmother to a child. **baptisme,** *n.m.* The doctrines of the Baptists. **baptistaire,** *a.* Pertaining to baptism. *Registre baptistaire,* parish register. **baptiste,** *n.m.* Baptist. (*colloq.*) *Tranquille comme Baptiste,* perfectly calm, as cool as a cucumber. **baptistère,** *n.m.* Baptistery.

baquet [ba'kɛ], *n.m.* Tub; (*Av.*) cockpit.

baquetage [bak'taːʒ], *n.m.* Drawing, baling, or removing water with a bucket etc.

baqueter [bak'te], *v.t.* To draw, to scoop, to bale with a bucket etc.

baquettes [ba'kɛt], *n.f.* (*used only in pl.*) Tongs used in wire-drawing.

bar (1) [bar], *n.m.* (*Ichth.*) Bass, sea-dace.

bar (2) [bar], *n.m.* Bar (of a public-house etc.).

bar (3) [BARD].

(*C*) **barachois** [bara'ʃwa], *n.m.* Sand-bar (at the mouth of a river); lagoon.

baragouin [bara'gwɛ̃], *n.m.* Gibberish, jargon, lingo. *Je ne comprends pas son baragouin,* I don't understand his gibberish. **baragouinage,** *n.m.* Talking gibberish, jargon, etc. **baragouiner,** *v.i.* To talk gibberish; to gabble. *Comme ces étrangers baragouinent,* how these foreigners do gabble.—*v.t.* To pronounce or talk thus. *Baragouiner un discours,* to sputter out a speech; *baragouiner une langue,* to murder a language.

barandage [barɑ̃'daːʒ], *n.m.* Fishing with a net stretched right across a stream (an illegal method).

baraque [ba'rak], *n.f.* Hut, shed, shanty; (*fam.*) hovel; booth (at a fair). **baraquement,** *n.m.* (*Mil.*) Hutting. **baraquer,** *v.t.* To hut.—*v.i.* To go into or lodge in huts; to kneel down (of a camel).

baraterie [bara'tri], *n.f.* Barratry.

barattage [bara'taːʒ], *n.m.* Churning. **baratte,** *n.f.* Churn. *Baratte normande,* barrel-churn. **baratter,** *v.t.* To churn. **baratton,** *n.m.* Churn staff.

barbacane [barba'kan], *n.f.* (*Fort.*) Barbican; (*Arch.*) loophole.

Barbade [bar'bad], *f.* Barbados.

barbant [bar'bɑ̃], *a.* (*fem.* **-ante**) (*slang*) Boring.

barbaque [bar'bak], *n.f.* (*slang*) Meat.

barbare [bar'baːr], *a.* Barbarous, barbarian; cruel, inhuman; (*fig.*) uncouth, rude, incorrect, ungrammatical.—*n.m.* (*usu. in pl.*) Barbarians, uncivilized people. **barbarement,** *adv.* Barbarously.

barbarée [barba're], *n.f.* Watercress.

barbaresque [barba'rɛsk], *a.* Of or pertaining to Barbary.

Barbarie [barba'ri], **la,** *f.* Barbary.

barbarie [barba'ri], *n.f.* Barbarity, rudeness, lack of civilization, culture, etc.; (*fig.*) inhumanity, cruelty. *Barbarie de langage* or *de style,* crudeness of language or of style.

barbariser, *v.t.* To barbarize.—*v.i.* To use barbarisms. **barbarisme,** *n.m.* (*Gram.*) Barbarism (abusive use of a foreign word); gross howler.

Barbe [barb], *f.* Barbara.

barbe (1) [barb], *n.f.* Beard; whiskers (of cats, dogs etc.,); bristles, beard (of corn, barley, etc.); wattles (of fowls); barbels (of fish); (*pl.*) lappets of a woman's mob-cap. *Barbe-de-bouc*, goat's beard; *barbe-de-capucin* (*pl. barbes-de-capucin*), a winter salad (uncommon in England) made of the bleached roots of chicory; *barbe grise* or *vieille barbe*, old man, greybeard; *faire la barbe à quelqu'un*, to beard someone; *je le lui dirai à sa barbe*, I'll tell it him to his face; *jeune barbe*, beardless boy; *la barbe d'une plume*, the feather of a quill; *rire dans sa barbe*, to laugh in one's sleeve; *se faire faire la barbe*, to get oneself shaved; *se faire la barbe*, to shave oneself; (*slang*) *la barbe!* enough of it! *quelle barbe!* how boring!

barbe (2) [barb], *n.m.* Barb, barbary horse.

barbeau [bar'bo], *n.m.* Barbel; (*Bot.*) bluebottle, cornflower; (*slang*) pimp.—*a. inv. Bleu barbeau*, a clear blue colour, cornflower blue.

Barbe-Bleue [barbə'blø], *m.* Bluebeard.

barbelé [barbə'le], *a.* Barbed, spiked; (*Bot.*) barbate. (*Fil de fer*) *barbelé*, barbed wire; *flèche barbelée*, barbed arrow.

barber [bar'be], *v.t.* (*slang*) To bore. **se barber**, *v.r.* To get bored.

Barberousse [barbə'rus], *m.* Barbarossa.

barbet [bar'bɛ], *n.m.* (*fem.* **barbette** (1)) Water-spaniel. *Ce barbet va bien à l'eau*, that spaniel takes the water well; *crotté comme un barbet*, very muddy.

barbette (2) [bar'bɛt], *n.f.* A kind of nun's wimple; (*Fort.*) barbette. *Coucher à la barbette*, to sleep on a mattress laid on the floor; *tirer en barbette*, to fire over the parapet.

barbeyer [barbɛ'je], *v.i.* (*conjugated like* GRASSEYER) To shake or flap the sails (of the wind).

barbiche [bar'biʃ] or **barbichette**, *n.f.* Beard growing only on the chin, goatee.

barbichon [barbi'ʃɔ̃], **barbichet**, *n.m.* A small shaggy spaniel.

barbier [bar'bje], *n.m.* Barber.

barbifère [barbi'fɛːr], *a.* Barbate.

***barbifier** [barbi'fje], *v.t.* (*colloq.*) To shave; (*slang*) to bore.

barbillon [barbi'jɔ̃], *n.m.* Little barbel; barb (of an arrow, fish-hook, etc.); wattle (of a fowl, turkey, etc.); barbel (of a fish); (*pl.*) barbules.

barbiturate [barbity'rat], **barbiturique** [barbity'rik], *n.m.* (*Chem.*) Barbiturate.

barbon [bar'bɔ̃], *n.m.* Greybeard, dotard; (*Bot.*) andropogon. *Barbon odorant*, lemon grass; *faire le barbon*, to pose as an old man.

barbot [bar'bo], *n.m.*, **barbote** (1), or **barbotte**, *n.f.* Common eel-pout.

barbotage [barbɔ'taːʒ], *n.m.* Mess, muddle; mash (for horses etc.); (*slang*) stealing.

barbote (1) [BARBOT].

barbote (2) [bar'bɔt], *n.f.* Eel-pout; (*C*) catfish.

barbotement [barbɔt'mɑ̃], *n.m.* Splashing, dabbling, muddling.

barboter [barbɔ'te], *v.i.* To dabble about in mud or water (with the beak, like a duck); to paddle, to flounder about in the mud; (*fig.*) to mumble, to mutter, to splutter.—*v.t.* (*slang*) To steal.

barboteur [barbɔ'tœːr], *n.m.* (*fem.* **barboteuse**) Paddler, dabbler; sloven, muddler;

washing apparatus.—*n.f.* Paddling drawers (of a little child).

barbotière [barbɔ'tjɛːr], *n.f.* Duck-pond; mash-tub or trough.

barbotin [barbɔ'tɛ̃], *n.m.* Chain-pulley.

barbotine [barbɔ'tin], *n.f.* A paste for making porcelain and for fixing the ornamentation, barbotine.

barbotte [BARBOT].

barbouillage [barbu'jaːʒ] or **barbouillis**, *n.m.* Daubing; daub; scrawl; (*fig.*) twaddle.

barbouiller [barbu'je], *v.t.* To soil, to dirty, to blot, to daub, to besmear; to scrawl, to scribble; *to slur, to stammer, to splutter out, to mumble; to muddle; to bungle. *Barbouiller le cœur, l'estomac*, to make sick, to upset; *barbouiller un compliment*, to stammer out a compliment; *barbouiller une feuille*, (*Print.*) to slur a sheet; *barbouiller un plancher*, to daub a floor; *barbouiller un récit*, to make a bungle of a story; *il lui a barbouillé le visage*, he has besmeared his face for him; *il n'écrit pas, il barbouille*, he does not write, he scrawls; *il ne peint pas, il barbouille*, he does not paint, he daubs; *on l'a tout barbouillé d'encre*, they have daubed him all over with ink; *qu'est-ce qu'il barbouille?* what is he mumbling?—*v.i.* To mumble, to speak or pronounce badly. **se barbouiller**, *v.r.* To besmear oneself.

barbouilleur, *n.m.* (*fem.* **-euse**) Dauber, scribbler; mumbler, babbler.

barbouillis [BARBOUILLAGE].

***barbouillon** [barbu'jɔ̃], *a.* (*fem.* **-onne**) Bungling, muddling.—*n.* A muddler.

barbu [bar'by], *a.* (*fem.* **barbue** (1)) Bearded, barbate.

barbue (2) [bar'by], *n.f.* Brill.

barbule [bar'byl], *n.f.* Barbule (of a feather).

barca [bar'ka], *int.* (*Mil. slang*) No, nothing doing! enough!

barcarolle [barka'rɔl], *n.f.* (*Mus.*) Barcarolle.

barcasse [bar'kas], *n.f.* A large barque.

Barcelone [barsə'lɔn], *f.* Barcelona.

barcelonnette [BERCELONNETTE].

bard [baːr], *n.m.* Hand-barrow. **bardage**, *n.m.* Conveying on a hand-barrow.

barda [bar'da], *n.m.* (*Mil. slang*) All the kit.

bardane [bar'dan], *n.f.* Bur, burdock.

barde (1) [bard], *n.m.* Bard.

barde (2) [bard], *n.f.* Bard (iron armour for horses); thin rasher of bacon used for larding poultry etc. **bardé, a.** (*fem.* **bardée** (1)) Barded; covered with a thin slice of bacon, larded. *Chapon bardé*, larded capon; (*fam.*) *être bardé de décorations*, to be covered with decorations; *un cheval bardé et caparaçonné*, a horse barded and caparisoned.

bardeau (1) [bar'do], *n.m.* Shingle (roofing-board); a small raft of floating timber; (*Print.*) font-case.

bardeau (2) [BARDOT].

bardée (2) [bar'de], *n.f.* Hand-barrowful; the slices of bacon with which a fowl etc. is larded.

bardelle [bar'dɛl], *n.f.* Shaft of hand-barrow; pack-saddle.

barder [bar'de], *v.t.* To bard a horse; to remove (stones, wood, etc.) on a hand-barrow; to cover with thin slices of bacon, to lard; (*slang*) (*in third person only or inf.*)

ça barde, ça va barder, things are beginning to hum, are getting hot.
bardeur, *n.m.* One who uses a *bard;* stone-carrier.
bardis [bar'di], *n.m.* (*Naut.*) Shifting board (for stowing grain).
bardit [bar'di], *n.m.* (*Ger. Ant.*) War-song.
bardot or **bardeau** [bar'do], *n.m.* Hinny; pack-mule; (*Print.*) waste paper; *(*fig.*) butt, laughing-stock.
barège [ba'rɛːʒ], *n.m.* Barège, light wool.
barème [ba'rɛːm], *n.m.* Ready-reckoner; scale (of marks, prices, salaries, etc.), schedule.
baréter [bare'te], *v.i. irr.* (*conjugated like* ACCÉLÉRER) [BARRIR].
barette [ba'rɛt], *n.f.* An old French football game, similar to rugby.
barge (1) [barʒ], *n.f.* Barge; square hay-mow.
barge (2) [barʒ], *n.f.* (*Orn.*) Godwit. *Barge rousse,* the bar-tailed godwit.
barguignage [bargi'naːʒ], *n.m.* (*colloq.*) Hesitation, wavering, dilly-dallying.
barguigner [bargi'ɲe], *v.i.* To be irresolute, to waver, to shilly-shally. **barguigneur,** *n.m.* (*fem.* **barguigneuse**) Waverer, dallier.
baricaut, bariquaut, barriquaut [bari'ko], *n.m.* Keg.
barigoule [bari'gul], *n.f. Artichaut à la barigoule,* stuffed artichoke.
baril [ba'ri], *n.m.* Small barrel, cask, keg.
barillage, *n.m.* Barrelling; cooperage; barrels, casks.
barillet [bari'jɛ], *n.m.* Keg, runlet; box or barrel (of a watch); drum (of locks); cylinder (of a revolver); cavity behind the eardrum.
*barilleur [bari'jœːr] or **barillier,** *n.m.* Cooper.
bariolage [barjɔ'laːʒ], *n.m.* Variegation, odd medley of colours, motley; variegating.
bariolé [barjɔ'le], *a.* (*fem.* **-ée**) Gaudy, motley, many-coloured.
barioler [barjɔ'le], *v.t.* To streak with several colours, to variegate, to chequer. **bariolure,** *n.f.* Variegation; discordant mixture of colours; medley, motley.
bariquaut [BARICAUT].
barlong [bar'lõ], *a.* (*fem.* **barlongue**) Having one side longer than the other; lopsided.
barlotière [barlɔ'tjɛːr], *n.f.* Rabbeted sash-bar (of a stained-glass window).
barman [bar'man], *n.m.* (*slang*) Barman.
Barnabé [barna'be], *m.* Barnaby, Barnabas.
barnache [bar'naʃ], *n.f.* Barnacle-goose.
barnabite [barna'bit], *n.m.* (*Ch.*) Barnabite.
barnum [bar'nɔm], *n.m.* Showman.
barologie [barɔlɔ'ʒi], *n.f.* Barology.
baromètre [barɔ'mɛtr], *n.m.* Barometer. *Baromètre à cadran,* wheel-barometer; *baromètre enregistreur,* recording barometer; *le baromètre est au beau,* the barometer is at set fair; *le baromètre descend,* the glass is falling. **barométrique,** *a.* Barometrical.
barométrographe, *n.f.* Self-registering barometer.
baron [ba'rõ], *n.m.* Baron; (*fig.*) a lord (of finance etc.). **baronnage,** *n.m.* Baronage.
baronne, *n.f.* Baroness. **baronnet,** *n.m.* Baronet. *Chevalier baronnet,* knight baronet.
baronnial, *a.* (*fem.* **-iale,** *pl.* **-iaux**) Baronial. **baronnie,** *n.f.* Barony.
baroque [ba'rɔk], *a.* Irregular, grotesque,

odd, singular, baroque.—*n.m.* (*Art*) the baroque.
baroscope [barɔ'skɔp], *n.m.* (*Phys.*) Baroscope.
baroud [ba'rud], *n.m.* (*Arab word*) Fight. **baroudeur,** *n.m.* (*fam.*) Fighter.
baroufe [ba'ruf] or **baroufle** [ba'rufl], *n.m.* (*fam.*) Great noise, scandal.
barque [bark], *n.f.* Bark, boat, small craft. *Barque de pêcheur,* fishing boat; *conduire la barque,* to steer the boat; *il conduit bien sa barque,* he is getting on very well; *il sait bien conduire sa barque,* he knows how to manage his affairs. **barquée,** *n.f.* Boat-load (of goods or stores). **barquerolle,** *n.f.* Small mastless barge. **barquette,** *n.f.* Small craft; light puff-biscuit.
barrage [ba'raːʒ], *n.m.* Barrier; toll-bar; dam, weir, barrage. *Tir de barrage,* (*Mil.*) curtain fire; barrage.
barragiste, *n.m.* Overseer of a dam, weir, etc., weir-keeper.
barre [baːr], *n.f.* Bar (of metal, wood, etc.); dash, cross, stroke (of the pen etc.); bar (of courts of judicature, public assemblies, etc.); (*Naut.*) helm, tiller, bar; (*pl.*) prisoners' base; (*Mus.*) bar; (*Her.*) bend. *Avoir barres sur,* to have the advantage over; *barre d'eau* or *de flot,* bore (tidal wave in a river); (*Her.*) *barre de bâtardise,* bend sinister; *barre de fer,* (*fig.*) an inflexible person; *barre de pied,* (*Row.*) stretcher; *barre de torsion,* (*Motor.*) torsion bar; *barre sous le vent!* (*Naut.*) helm alee! *barre fixe,* horizontal bar; *barres parallèles,* parallel bars; *je ne fais que toucher barres,* I am off again immediately or without stopping; *tenir la barre,* to steer; *tirer la barre,* to close the list.
barré [ba'rɛ], *a.* (*fem.* **-ée**) (*Her.*) Barry, divided into equal bars; (*Dent.*) having divergent prongs (of a molar tooth). '*Rue barrée*', 'no thoroughfare'.
barreau [ba'ro], *n.m.* A small bar (of wood, metal, etc.); bench reserved for barristers; (*fig.*) lawyers, barristers; stretcher (of chairs); rung (of a ladder). *Être reçu* or *admis au barreau,* to be called to the bar; *fréquenter le barreau,* to attend the courts; *rayer du barreau,* to disbar.
barrement [bar'mã], *n.m.* Crossing (of a cheque).
barrer [ba'rɛ], *v.t.* To bar or fence up; to obstruct, to thwart, to cross off, to erase, to cancel. *Barrer quelqu'un* or *barrer le chemin à quelqu'un,* (*fig.*) to throw obstacles in someone's way.—*v.i.* To hold the tiller, to steer. **se barrer,** *v.r.* To stop the way for oneself; (*colloq.*) to scram.
barrette (1) or **barette** [ba'rɛt], *n.f.* Square flat cap, biretta; cardinal's hat.
barrette (2) [ba'rɛt], *n.m.* Axle, pin, bolt, etc. (in watches, jewellery, etc.); bar (of medal). (*Steam-engine*) *Barrette du tiroir,* valve-face; *barrette de cheveux,* hair slide.
barreur [ba'rœːr], *n.m.* Helmsman, coxswain.
barricade [bari'kad], *n.f.* Barricade. (*fig.*) *De l'autre côté de la barricade,* in the opposed party. **barricader,** *v.t.* To barricade, to obstruct. **se barricader,** *v.r.* To barricade oneself (in etc.).
barrière [ba'rjɛːr], *n.f.* Railing, barrier; gateway to a town where octroi is levied; farm

gate; bureaux at frontiers etc. for levying duties; (*fig.*) obstruction, obstacle. *Barrière de passage à niveau*, level-crossing gate.

barriquaut [BARICAUT].

barrique [ba'rik], *n.f.* Large barrel or cask, hogshead; the contents of this (225 litres). *Avoir deux ans de barrique* (of wine), to have been two years in the wood.

barrir [ba'riːr], *v.i.* To trumpet (of elephants).

barrissement or **barrit**, *n.m.* Trumpeting (of elephants).

barrot [ba'ro], *n.m.* (*Naut.*) Cross-bar beam.

barroter [barɔ'te], *v.t.* To load (a vessel) up to beams.

barrotin, *n.m.* Small cross-bar between the beams.

bartavelle [barta'vɛl], *n.f.* Rock partridge.

barye [ba'ri], *n.f.* (*Phys.*) Barye.

baryte [ba'rit], *n.f.* Baryta. **baryté**, *a.* Baryta. *Papier baryté*, baryta paper, chalk-overlay.

baryton [bari'tɔ̃], *n.m.* Baritone. **barytoner**, *v.i.* To sing in a baritone voice.

baryum [ba'rjɔm], *n.m.* Barium.

bas (1) [bɑ], *a.* (*fem.* **basse**) Low; in a low situation; lowered; inferior; (*fig.*), vile, base, abject; sordid; trivial, mean; subdued (of sounds); decadent. *Avoir l'âme basse*, to have a sordid soul; *avoir la vue basse*, to be short-sighted; *avoir le cœur haut et la fortune basse*, to have more spirit than fortune; *avoir l'oreille basse*, to be crestfallen; *bas âge*, early infancy; *bas étage*, lower story; *bas latin*, Low Latin; *basse mer*, low water; *basse naissance*, mean birth; *ce bas monde*, this world here below; *des sentiments bas*, mean sentiments; *faire main basse sur*, to pillage, to plunder, to lay hands upon; *faire prendre à quelqu'un un ton plus bas*, to take someone down a peg; *j'ai acheté cela à bas prix*, I bought that dirt cheap; *la chambre basse*, the House of Commons; *la marée est basse*, it is low water; *le bas bout d'une chose*, the lower end of a thing; *le bas comique*, low comedy; *le bas peuple* the common people, the mob; *le Bas-Rhin*, the Lower Rhine; *les basses cartes*, the small cards; *le bas Empire*, the late Empire (Roman); *les eaux sont basses chez lui*, he is in low funds; *les Pays-Bas*, the Netherlands; *le temps est bas*, it is very cloudy; *parler d'un ton bas*, to speak in a low voice; *un bas-Saxon*, a Lower Saxon; *une basse flatterie*, mean flattery; *une basse-fosse*, a dungeon; *une messe basse*, a low mass, *i.e.* one not sung; *une rivière basse*, a shallow river.—*adv.* Low, down; in a subdued voice, tone, etc. *À bas le tyran!* down with the tyrant! *au plus bas*, at the very lowest; *bien bas*, very low; *chapeaux bas!* hats off! *être à bas*, to be ruined; *être bas percé*, to be in a bad way for money etc.; *ici bas*, here below; *jeter bas*, to throw down; *là-bas*, over there, yonder; *le malade est encore bien bas*, the patient is still very weak; *mettre bas*, to lay down (arms etc.); (of animals) to bring forth, to whelp, to foal, to cub, to lamb, to pup, to kitten; *mettre chapeau bas*, to take off one's hat in salutation; *parler bas*, to speak in a low voice; *rire tout bas*, to laugh to oneself; *tenir bas*, to keep in subjection, to keep under.—*n.m.* The lower part, bottom, or foot (of something); (*fig.*) the

humbler or more lowly situation. *Bas de casse*, (*Print.*) the lower half of the type-case, the small letters or minuscules kept here; *du haut en bas*, from top to bottom; *en bas*, below, downstairs; *être au bas*, to be low (of liquids in casks); *il y a des hauts et des bas dans la vie*, there are ups and downs in life; *le bas de l'escalier*, the foot of the stairs; *le bas du pavé*, the side of the pavement towards the gutter; *le bas du visage*, the lower part of the face; *sa voix est belle dans le bas*, his voice is excellent in the lower register.

bas (2) [bɑ], *n.m.* Stocking. *Bas à côtes* or *à jour*, ribbed or open-worked stocking; *bas-bleu*, bluestocking (literary woman); *bas de laine*, woollen stocking, (*fig.*) a place for hoarding or saving; *bas de soie*, silk stocking; *cela vous va comme un bas de soie*, it fits you like a glove.

basalte [ba'zalt], *n.m.* Basalt. **basaltiforme**, *a.* Basaltiform. **basaltique**, *a.* Basaltic.

basane [ba'zan], *n.f.* Sheepskin, basil.

basané [baza'ne], *a.* (*fem.* **basanée**) Sunburnt, bronzed, swarthy, tawny. **basaner**, *v.t.* To sunburn, to make swarthy.

bas-bleu [*see* BAS (2)].

bas-côté [bakɔ'te], *n.m.* (*Ch.*) Aisle; side, shoulder (of a road).

basculant [basky'lɑ̃], *a.* Rocking. *Wagon basculant*, tip-waggon.

bascule [bas'kyl], *n.f.* A machine or part that rises at one end when the other is pushed down; see-saw; weighing-machine or balance for heavy weights; bascule-bridge; (*fig.*) vacillation, playing up alternately to either side, in politics etc. *Bascule romaine*, platform scales; *chaise à bascule*, rocking-chair; *faire la bascule*, to see-saw; *pont à bascule*, weigh-bridge; *bascule de pont-levis*, counterweight of a drawbridge; *mouvement de bascule*, rocking motion. **basculer**, *v.i.* To see-saw; to rock, to swing; (*fig.*) to vacillate, alternate, etc. **basculeur**, *n.m.* Rocking-lever.

bas-dessus [bad'sy], *n.m.* (*Mus.*) Mezzo-soprano, low treble.

base [bɑːz], *n.f.* Base, foundation; lower part, bottom; basis, fundamental principle, ground work; (*Geom., Chem., etc.*) base; radix (of logarithms); (*Mus.*) fundamental note, tonic. *La base d'une montagne*, the foot of a mountain; *la base d'un système*, the basis of a system; *pécher par la base*, to be fundamentally wrong (of an argument etc.); *traitement de base*, basic salary.

base-ball [bes'bol], *n.m.* Baseball.

baselle [ba'zɛl], *n.f.* (*Bot.*) Malabar nightshade.

baser [ba'ze], *v.t.* To found, to base, to ground (an argument on facts etc.). **se baser**, *v.r.* To be grounded; to depend, to rely.

bas-fond [ba'fɔ̃], *n.m.* (*pl.* **bas-fonds**) Low-lying ground, hollow, bottom; shallow, shallow water; (*fig., pl.*) underworld, dregs (of society).

basicité [bazisi'te], *n.f.* (*Chem.*) Basicity.

basilaire [bazi'lɛːr], *a.* (*Anat.*) Basilar.

basilic [bazi'lik], *n.m.* (*Bot.*) Basil, sweet basil; (*Myth.*) basilisk, cockatrice. *Yeux de basilic*, malevolent or baleful eyes.

basilicon [bazili'kɔ̃], or **basilicum**, *n.m.* Sovereign ointment, basilicon.

basilique (1) [bazi'lik], *n.f.* Basilica.
basilique (2) [bazi'lik], *a.* (*Anat.*) Basilical.
basin [ba'zɛ̃], *n.m.* Bombasine, dimity.
basique [bɑ'zik], *a.* (*Chem.*) Basic.
bas-jointé [bɑʒwɛ̃'te], *a.* (*fem.* **bas-jointée**) (*Vet.*) Having a short and nearly horizontal pastern.
basket-ball [basket'bɔl], *n.m.* Basket-ball.
basketteur, *n.m.* (*fem.* **-euse**) Basket-ball player.
bas-mât [bɑ'mɑ], *n.m.* (*pl.* **bas-mâts**) Lower mast.
basoche [ba'zɔʃ], *n.f.* Formerly an association of the clerks of all the Courts of Justice in Paris; (*colloq.*) the legal fraternity.
basochien, *a.* (*fem.* **basochienne**) Pertaining to this.
basquais [bas'kɛ], *a.* (*fem.* **basquaise**) Basque.
basque (1) [bask], *n.f.* Flap, skirt, tail (of a garment). *Être toujours pendu aux basques de quelqu'un*, to be always after or pestering someone.
basque (2) [bask], *a.* Basque. *Béret basque*, beret; *pelote basque*, pelota.—*n.* (**Basque**) A Basque.—*n.m.* The Basque language. *Tambour de Basque*, a tambourine.
basquine [bas'kin], *n.f.* A richly ornamented petticoat worn by Basque women.
bas-relief [barə'ljɛf], *n.m.* (*pl.* **bas-reliefs**) Bas-relief.
basse (1) [bɑːs], *n.f.* Bass, bass voice, part, instrument, singer, etc., bass-string, saxhorn. *Basse continue*, thorough-bass, continuo; (*fig.*) the burden, the continual subject (of one's conversation).
basse (2) [bɑːs], *n.f.* Shallow, flat, shoal, reef.
basse-contre [bɑs'kɔ̃ːtr], *n.f.* (*pl.* **basses-contre**) (*Mus.*) Contra-bass, lower tenor.
basse-cour [bɑs'kuːr], *n.f.* (*pl.* **basses-cours**) Poultry-yard; the animals living in this.
basse-courier, *n.m.* (*fem.* **basse-courière**) Person in charge of the poultry-yard.
basse-étoffe [bɑs'tɔf], *n.f.* (*pl.* **basses-étoffes**) Alloy of lead and tin.
basse-fosse [bɑs'foːs], *n.f.* (*pl.* **basses-fosses**) Dungeon.
bassement [bɑs'mɑ̃], *adv.* Basely, meanly, vilely. *Il s'exprime bassement*, he expresses himself vulgarly; *penser bassement*, to have ignoble thoughts.
bassesse [bɑ'sɛs], *n.f.* Baseness, lowness (of station etc.); meanness, vileness, servility; a mean or sordid action. *Avec bassesse*, meanly; *faire une bassesse*, to do a base action.
basset [bɑ'sɛ], *n.m.* Basset-hound. *Basset allemand*, dachshund; (*Mus.*) *cor de basset*, tenor clarinet.
basse-taille [bɑs'taːj], *n.f.* (*pl.* **basses-tailles**) (*Mus.*) Baritone; (*Sculp.*) bas-relief.
bassette [bɑ'sɛt], *n.f.* Basset (game at cards).
basse-voile [bɑs'vwal], *n.f.* (*pl.* **basses-voiles**) Lower sail of a ship.
bassin [ba'sɛ̃], *n.m.* Basin; pond, reservoir, dock; (*Anat.*) pelvis. *Bassin à flot, bassin ouvert or darse*, floating-dock; *bassin d'échouage or bassin de radoub*, dry dock; *bassin d'un fleuve*, catchment or drainage-basin of a river; *bassin houiller*, a coal-bed; **cracher au bassin*, (*slang*) to contribute, to fork out; to cough it up; *droit de bassin*, dock-due; *le bassin d'un port*, inner harbour, wet-dock;

mettre (or *faire passer*) *dans le bassin*, to dock (a ship).
bassinage [basi'naːʒ], *n.m.* Sprinkling.
bassine [ba'sin], *n.f.* Deep, wide pan, as a preserving-pan, evaporating-dish etc.; panful. **bassinée**, *n.f.* Panful.
bassinement [basin'mɑ̃], *n.m.* Warming.
bassiner [basi'ne], *v.t.* To warm (a bed etc.); to bathe (with warm lotions), to foment, to steep; to water, to sprinkle (crops etc.); (*colloq.*) to bore, to weary.
bassinet [basi'nɛ], *n.m.* Small basin, pan, bowl; fire-pan (of ancient fire-arms); (*Bot.*) crowfoot; (*Anat.*) calyx; (*Armour*) bassinet. *Cracher au bassinet* or *au bassin* [BASSIN].
bassinoire [basi'nwaːr], *n.f.* Warming-pan; (*pop.*) wearisome person, bore; a big watch, a 'turnip'.
bassiste [ba'sist], *n.m.* Saxhorn-player; 'cellist.
basson [ba'sɔ̃], *n.m.* Bassoon; bassoonist. **bassoniste**, *n.m.* Bassoonist.
baste (1) [bast], *int.* Enough, pooh, rot! Never mind!
baste (2) [bast], *n.m.* Ace of clubs (in ombre).
bastide [bas'tid], *n.f.* (*Provence*) Country-cottage, villa; *block-house (in the Middle Ages).
bastille [bas'tiːj], *n.f.* Bastille, fort; fortified castle; the Bastille. **bastillé**, *a.* (*fem.* **bastillée**) (*Her.*) Having inverted battlements.
bastin [bas'tɛ̃], *n.m.* (*Naut.*) Bass-rope; coir.
bastingage [bastɛ̃'gaːʒ], *n.m.* (*Naut.*) A series of lockers on the bulwarks of warships for stowing hammocks etc., forming a protection against musketry; rails. *Filets de bastingage*, boarding-nets; *s'appuyer au bastingage*, to lean over the rails.
bastion [bas'tjɔ̃], *n.m.* Bastion; (*fig.*) stronghold (of tyranny etc.). **bastionner**, *v.t.* To bastion, to fortify with bastions.
bastonnade [bastɔ'nad], *n.f.* Bastinado.
bastringue [bas'trɛ̃ːg], *n.m.* (*pop.*) Public-house dance; (*slang*) noise; kit (*see* BARDA).
bastringuer, *v.i.* (*pop.*) To dance at low public halls; to make a row.
bastude [bas'tyd] or **battude**, *n.f.* Fishing-net (used in salt lagoons).
bas-ventre [ba'vɑ̃ːtr], *n.m.* (*pl.* **bas-ventres**) Lower part of the belly.
bat [bat], *n.m.* Length (of fish, from eye to tail).
bât [bɑ], *n.m.* Pack-saddle. *Chacun sait où le bât le blesse*, everyone knows where the shoe pinches; *cheval de bât*, pack-horse, (*fig.*) stupid person; *porter le bât*, to do all the dirty work; *porter son bât*, to put up with one's lot, to bear one's cross.
bataclan [bata'klɑ̃], *n.m.* (*fam.*) Paraphernalia. (*Et*) *tout le bataclan*, (*colloq.*) the whole boiling or show.
bataille [ba'taːj], *n.f.* Battle, fight, engagement; (*fig.*) quarrel, dispute, struggle; battle-array; (*Cards*) beggar-my-neighbour. *Bataille rangée*, pitched battle; *champ de bataille*, battle-field; *cheval de bataille*, charger, (*fig.*) one's favourite subject or hobby; *en bataille*, disorderly (hair etc.); *livrer bataille*, to give battle; *livrer bataille pour quelqu'un*, to take up the cudgels for someone; *ranger une armée en bataille*, to draw up an army in battle-array. (*Naut.*) *Mettre une*

vergue en bataille, to rig a derrick with a yard. **batailler**, *v.i.* To give battle; to be at war, to fight; to struggle hard, to strive, to dispute. **batailleur**, *a.* (*fem.* **batailleuse**) Combative, pugnacious, quarrelsome; disputatious.—*n.* A combative or disputatious person.

bataillon [bata'jɔ̃], *n.m.* Battalion; (*fig.*) a host; (*pl.*) troops. *Bataillon carré*, a battalion drawn up in square and presenting four fronts to attack; *chef de bataillon*, major; *bataillon d'Afrique*, punishment battalion stationed in North Africa.

bataillonnaire [batajɔ'nɛr], *n.m.* A man who having been previously imprisoned is compelled to serve in special battalions stationed in North Africa.

bâtard [bɑ'taːr], *a.* Bastard, illegitimate; (*fig.*) degenerate, spurious, mongrel; inclined (of writing). *Chien bâtard*, mongrel; *fruits bâtards*, spurious fruits; *porte bâtarde*, housedoor with one flap.—*n.* Bastard, natural child.

batardeau [batar'do], *n.m.* Coffer-dam.

bâtardise [bɑtar'diːz], *n.f.* Bastardy; (*fig.*) spuriousness.

batave [ba'tav], *a.* Batavian.

batavique [bata'vik], *a.* (only in *larme batavique*, Prince Rupert's drop).

batayole [bata'jɔl] or **bataviole**, *n.f.* (*Naut.*) Stanchion.

bâté [bɑ'te], *a.* (*fem.* **bâtée**). Saddled with a pack. *C'est un âne bâté*, he is an ignorant lout.

bat' d'Af [bat'daf], *n.m.* (*abbr. of*) *bataillon d'Afrique* and *bataillonnaire*.

bateau [ba'to], *n.m.* Boat; (*fam.*) large boot; fastidious practical joke. *Arriver en trois bateaux*, to arrive in great state; *bateau automobile*, motor-boat; *bateau à rames*, rowing-boat; *bateau à vapeur*, steamer, steam-boat; *bateau à voiles*, sailing-boat; *bateau-citerne*, tank steamer; *bateau d'agrément*, pleasure-boat; *bateau-école*, training-ship; *bateau de passage*, ferry-boat; *bateau lavoir*, washerwoman's boat; *bateau mouche*, passenger steamer (Paris and Lyons); *bateau non ponté*, open boat; *bateau pêcheur*, fishing-boat; *bateau-phare*, lightship; *bateau plat*, punt; *bateau pompe*, float; *être du même bateau*, to be of the same class, set, etc.; *porter bateau*, (of rivers) to be navigable; (*fam.*) *monter un bateau (à quelqu'un)*, to hoax, to fool somebody.

batelage [ba'tlaːʒ], *n.m.* Juggling, legerdemain; lighterage charges.

batelée [ba'tle], *n.f.* Boat-load, boatful (of people etc.).

bateler [ba'tle], *v.t.* To carry by boat.—*v.i.* To conjure, to perform tricks of legerdemain.

batelet [ba'tlɛ], *n.m.* Little boat.

bateleur [ba'tlœːr], *n.m.* (*fem.* **-euse**) Juggler, buffoon, mountebank, rope-dancer, etc.

batelier [batə'lje], *n.m.* (*fem.* **batelière**) Boatman, boatwoman, ferryman, ferrywoman.

batellerie [batɛl'ri], *n.f.* (*collect.*) Small craft; transport by river barges.

bâter [bɑ'te], *v.t.* To load with a pack-saddle.

bat-flanc [ba'flɑ̃], *n.m.* (*Mil.*) Swinging bail (between horses); (fixed) partition between beds in a row.

bath [bat], *int.* and *a. inv.* (*slang*) Excellent, capital, ripping.

bathomètre [batɔ'mɛtr] or **bathymètre**, *n.m.* Bathometer.

bathyscaphe [batis'kaf], *n.m.* Bathyscaph.

bâti [bɑ'ti], *n.m.* Framing, structure; basting, tacking (of a garment).

bâtière [bɑ'tjɛːr], *n.f.* Pack-saddle; saddle-backed roof.

batifolage [batifɔ'laːʒ], *n.m.* Romping; cuddling. **batifoler**, *v.i.* To play, to romp; to cuddle. **batifoleur**, *a.* (*fem.* **-euse**) Given to romping, frolicsome.

batik [ba'tik], *n.m.* (*Tex.*) Batik.

bâtiment [bɑti'mɑ̃], *n.m.* Building, structure, edifice; building trade; ship, vessel. *Bâtiment de guerre*, warship; *bâtiment marchand*, merchantman; *il est du bâtiment*, (*colloq.*) he is one of the trade, he is one of us.

bâtir [bɑ'tiːr], *v.t.* To build, to erect, to construct; to baste, to tack (a garment); (*fig.*) to establish, to found. *C'est bâtir en l'air*, it is building castles in the air; *bâtir sur le sable*, to build on sand; *faire bâtir*, to have built, to build; *terrain à bâtir*, building site; (*fam.*) *un gars bien bâti*, a strapping fellow. **bâtissable**, *a.* That may be built upon.

bâtissage [bɑti'saːʒ], *n.m.* Basting.

bâtisse, *n.f.* Masonry; ramshackle house.

bâtisseur, *n.m.* One with a mania for building; jerry-builder. (*fig.*) *Un bâtisseur d'empire*, an empire builder.

batiste [ba'tist], *n.f.* Cambric, batiste. *Batiste de coton*, imitation muslin; *batiste de France*, French muslin; *mouchoir de batiste*, cambric handkerchief.

bâton [bɑ'tɔ̃], *n.m.* Stick, staff, cudgel, cane, walking-stick; truncheon, baton; straight stroke (writing). *Aller à cheval sur un bâton*, to ride on a stick; *bâton à deux bouts*, quarterstaff, (*Her.*) narrow bend two-fifths the ordinary length; *bâton d'agent de police*, truncheon; *bâton de cannelle*, roll of cinnamon; *bâton de cire*, stick of sealing-wax; *bâton de commandement*, staff of command; *bâton de maréchal*, field-marshal's baton; *bâton de pavillon*, flagstaff; *bâton de vieillesse*, one who is a support to a person's old age; *donner des coups de bâton à quelqu'un*, to cudgel someone; *faire mourir sous le bâton*, to beat to death; *faire une chose à bâtons rompus*, to do a thing by fits and starts; *il l'a menacé du bâton*, he threatened to cane him; *mettre des bâtons dans les roues*, (*fig.*) to put a spoke in anyone's wheel; *tour de bâton*, perquisites, pickings, illicit profits; *vie de bâton de chaise*, a life of pleasure and licence.

bâtonnat, *n.m.* The presidentship of the order of French advocates; the duration of his office.

bâtonner, *v.t.* To cudgel, to cane; *to cross out.

bâtonnet, *n.m.* A little stick, tipcat (boy's game); (*Biol.*) rod-bacterium.

bâtonnier, *n.m.* *Staff-bearer; president of the French Bar.

bâtonniste, *n.m.* Cudgel-player.

batracien [batra'sjɛ̃], *n.m.* (*Zool.*) Batrachian.

battable [ba'tabl], *a.* That can be or deserves to be thrashed; that can be beaten. **battage**, *n.m.* Threshing of grain, wool, cotton, piles, etc.; churning; time of one such operation exaggerated publicity. *Faire du battage autour d'un livre*, to boom a book. **battant** (1), *n.m.* Clapper (of a bell); leaf (of a table or door); fly (of a flag). *Battant de crosse*, butt swivel; *porte à deux battants*, double door; *porte ouverte à deux battants*, wide-open gate. **battant** (2), *a.* (*fem.* **battante**) Beating, pelting, falling heavily (of rain etc.); ready for battle (of a ship). *Par une pluie battante*, in pelting rain; *porte battante*, swing-door; *tambour battant*, with beat of drum; *mener tambour battant*, to treat (somebody) severely, to hurry on (a business); *tout battant neuf* (*fem. neuve*), brand-new.

batte [bat], *n.f.* Long wooden staff or beater; beating (of gold or silver). *Batte à beurre*, churn-staff; *batte d'Arlequin*, Harlequin's wand, wooden sword; *batte de blanchisseuse*, washing-board; *batte (de cricket)*, (cricket) bat; *batte de terrassier*, turf-beetle.

battée [ba'te], *n.f.* Jamb of door or window.

battement [bat'mã], *n.m.* Beating; clapping (of hands), stamping (of feet), flapping (of wings); beating, throbbing (of the heart); shuffling (of cards); beat (of a clock etc.); (*Dance*) movement with one leg in the air; interval, wait (between two events, two trains). *Battement d'épée*, (*Fenc.*) act of striking one's adversary's sword or foil.

batte-queue [bat'kø], *n.f.* Water wagtail.

batterand [bat'rã], *n.m.* Stone-breaker's hammer.

batterie [ba'tri], *n.f.* *Fight, scuffle; (*Artill.*, *Elec.*, *Cook.*, *etc.*) battery; lock (of firearms); mode of beating (a drum); *la batterie*, (*Mil.*) the drums and bugles; (*Mus.*) the percussion instruments; (*fig.*) plans, methods, devices (for doing something or defeating someone); (*C*) threshing-floor. *Batterie de cuisine*, complete set of kitchen utensils; *batterie électrique*, electric battery; *batterie flottante*, floating battery (early armoured warship); *batterie tractée*, tractor-drawn battery; *dresser ses batteries*, to prepare for action, to take steps (to achieve, overcome, etc.); *en batterie*, ready to fire.

batteur [ba'tœ:r], *n.m.* (*fem.* **batteuse** (1)) Beater; (*Cricket etc.*) batsman; (*Jazz*) drummer. *Batteur de pavé*, idler, lounger, loafer; *batteur d'or*, gold-beater; *batteur en grange*, (*Agric.*) thresher; *batteurs d'estrade*, cavalry sent out on reconnaissance only, (*fig.*) suspicious vagabonds.

batteuse (2) [ba'tø:z], *n.f.* Threshing-machine.

battitures [bati'ty:r], *n.f.* (*used only in pl.*) Scales struck off metal under the hammer in forging.

battoir [ba'twa:r], *n.m.* Washerwoman's beetle; wooden bat; (*fig.*) a large hand.

battologie [batɔlɔ'ʒi], *n.f.* Tautology. **battologique,** *a.* Tautological.

battre [batr], *v.t. irr.* To strike upon, against, etc.; to beat, to thrash, to whip (a horse etc.); to beat up; to mix; to defeat; to shuffle (cards); to flag (of a sail against a mast). *Battre aux champs*; (*Mil.*) to beat the general salute; *battre des mains*, to clap, to applaud; *battre du beurre*, to churn milk; *battre en grange*, to thresh (corn etc.); *battre en retraite*, (*Mil.*) to beat a retreat; *battre la campagne*, to scour the country, (*fig.*) to talk

nonsense; *battre la mesure*, to beat time; *battre la semelle*, to stamp one's feet (to get them warm); *battre le bois*, to beat the wood for game; *battre le fusil*, to strike a light; *battre le pavé*, to loaf about; *battre le pays*, to scour the country; *battre les cartes*, to shuffle the cards; *battre monnaie*, to coin money, (*fig.*) to raise money; *battre quelqu'un de ses propres armes*, to beat someone at his own game; *battre un noyer*, to thrash a walnut-tree; *la fête battait son plein*, the party was in full swing.—*v.i.* To beat, to knock; to pant, to throb; to be loose (of a horseshoe); to applaud; to sound (of arms etc.); (*slang*) to fib, to sham. *Battre de l'aile*, to flutter; *battre froid à quelqu'un*, to give someone the cold shoulder; *le cœur me bat*, my heart beats; *le fer de ce cheval bat*, the shoe of that horse is loose; *le pouls lui bat fort*, his pulse beats violently. **se battre,** *v.r.* To fight, to combat, to scuffle; to hit oneself (*contre etc.*). *Se battre à qui aura quelque chose*, to scramble for something.

battu [ba'ty], *a.* (*fem.* **battue** (1)) Beaten (of a path, road, etc.); frequented; (*fig.*) trite, commonplace; fatigued, worn (of the eyes).

battue (2) [ba'ty], *n.f.* Battue; beat (of a horse's hoofs).

batture [ba'ty:r], *n.f.* Gold-lacquering; (*C*) sand-bar, gravel or mud deposit (on the inward side of a river bend).

bau [bo], *n.m.* (*pl.* **baux** (1)) (*Naut.*) Beam. *Demi-bau*, half-beam; *faux bau*, orlop-beam; *maître bau*, midship-beam.

baudet [bo'dɛ], *n.m.* Ass; (*fig.*) dolt, donkey; sawyer's trestle.

*baudir [bo'di:r], *v.t.* (*Hawking*) To cheer on the hawk, hounds, etc.

Baudouin [bo'dwɛ̃], *m.* Baldwin.

baudrier [bodri'e], *n.m.* Baldrick, shoulder-belt; cross-belt. *Baudrier de cuir*, leather belt; *le baudrier d'Orion*, Orion's belt.

baudroie [bo'drwa], *n.f.* (*Ichth.*) Angler, fishing frog, lophius.

baudruche [bo'dryʃ], *n.f.* Gold-beater's skin.

bauge [bo:ʒ], *n.f.* Lair of a wild boar; squirrel's nest; (*fig.*) a wretched abode, a den; clay and straw mortar.

baume [bo:m], *n.m.* Balm; balsam; (*fig.*) consolation, healing. *Baume d'acier*, a dentist's forceps; *baume de fier-à-bras*, a universal balsam for wounds; *baume de la Mecque*, balm of Gilead; *baume des jardins*, garden mint; *baume sauvage*, wild mint; *baume tranquille*, infusion of mint in olive-oil used as an embrocation; *fleurer comme baume*, to be in good odour; *je n'ai pas de foi dans son baume*, I have no faith in his plan *or* promises.

baumier, *n.m.* Balm-tree.

bauquière [bo'kjɛ:r], *n.f.* (*Naut.*) Girdle supporting beams.

baux (1) (*pl.*) [BAU].

baux (2) (*pl.*) [BAIL].

bauxite [bo'sit], *n.f.* Bauxite.

bavard [ba'va:r], *a.* (*fem.* **bavarde**) Prating, talkative, loquacious; (*fig.*) blabbing, indiscreet.—*n.* Prater, babbler, chatterer. **bavardage,** *n.m.* Babbling, prattling, garrulity; (*fig.*) twaddle, nonsense. **bavarder,** *v.i.* To babble, to prattle; to blab.

bavarois [bava'rwa], *a.* (*fem.* **-oise** (1))

Bavarian.—*n.* **Bavarois** (*fem.* **-oise**) A Bavarian.

bavaroise (2) [bava'rwa:z], *n.f.* Bavarian cream.

bave [ba:v], *n.f.* Slaver; foam; (*fig.*) slime, venom. **baver,** *v.i.* To slobber, to dribble; (*fig.*) to throw aspersion or calumny (*sur*). (*slang*) *En baver,* *to be flabbergasted; to have a rough time of it. **bavette,** *n.f.* Bib, slabbering-bib; (*Cook.*) low part of a sirloin. (*fam.*) *Tailler des bavettes,* to gossip.

baveuse (1) [ba'vø:z], *n.f.* (*Ichth.*) Tom-pot blenny; gattorugine.

baveux [ba'vø], *a.* (*fem.* **baveuse** (2)) Slavery, slobbering. *Omelette baveuse,* a moist omelet; *caractères baveux,* slurred letters.

Bavière [ba'vjɛ:r], *f.* Bavaria.

bavoché [bavɔ'ʃe], *a.* (*fem.* **-ée**) (*Print.*) Uneven, smeary. **bavocher,** *v.i.* To print unevenly, to smear. **bavocheux,** *a.* (*fem.* **-euse**) Smeary, uneven. **bavochure,** *n.f.* Unevenness, smearing.

bavolet [bavɔ'lɛ], *n.m.* Rustic bonnet; a piece of trimming at the back of a hat; (*Motor.*) valance.

bavure [ba'vy:r], *n.f.* Seam (left by a mould); smudge (of a pen). (*pop.*) *Sans bavure,* perfect.

bayadère [baja'dɛ:r], *n.f.* Bayadere, Indian dancing-girl.

bayart [BARD].

****bayer** [bɛ'je], [baje], *v.i.* To gape. *Bayer après les richesses,* to hanker after riches; *bayer aux corneilles,* to stand gaping in the air.

bazar [ba'za:r], *n.m.* Bazaar; (*pop.*) hovel. (*fam.*) *Mettre tout son bazar dans une malle,* to put all one's belongings in a trunk.

bazarder, *v.t.* (*pop.*) To sell (at low price).

bazooka [bazu'ka], *n.m.* (*Artill.*) Bazooka.

bdellium [bdɛ'ljɔm], *n.m.* Bdellium, gum-resin.

béant [be'ɑ̃], *a.* (*fem.* **béante**) Gaping, yawning, wide open. *Gouffre béant,* open pit, yawning chasm.

béat [be'a], *a.* (*fem.* **béate**) Blessed; devout; sanctimonious; complacent (optimism); blissful (smile). **béatement,** *adv.* Sanctimoniously.

béatifiant [beati'fjɑ̃], *a.* (*fem.* **-ante**) Beatifying. **béatification,** *n.f.* Beatification.

béatifier [beati'fje], *v.t.* To beatify. **béatifique,** *a.* Beatifical, blissful.

béatilles [bea'ti:j], *n.f.* (*used only in pl.*) Titbits; small articles made by nuns.

béatitude [beati'tyd], *n.f.* Beatitude, blessedness.

beau [bo], **bel** (before nouns singular beginning with a vowel or *h* mute), *a.* (*fem.* **belle,** *pl.* **beaux, belles**) Beautiful, fine, handsome, fair; smart, spruce; glorious; lofty, noble; seemly, becoming; (*iron.*) nice, precious. *À beau jeu, beau retour,* one good turn deserves another; *au beau milieu,* in the very middle; *avoir beau jeu,* to have good cards, to have fair play; *bel esprit,* wit, elegance, sprightliness; a person having this; *belle demande!* a fine request to make! *cela n'est pas beau,* that is not nice; *c'est un beau parleur,* he has got the gift of the gab; *Charles le Bel* (of Burgundy), Charles the Fair; *comme vous voilà beau aujourd'hui!* how spruce you are today! *de beaux traits,*

handsome features; *déchirer à belles dents,* to criticize mercilessly, to rend; *donner beau jeu à quelqu'un,* to give someone good cards; (*fam.*) *être dans de beaux draps,* to be in a pretty pickle; *faire un beau coup,* (*iron.*) to make a bad blunder; *il en fait de belles,* he is going on at a fine rate, he is playing fine tricks; *il fait beau,* it is a fine day; *il fait beau se promener aujourd'hui,* it is fine weather for walking today; *il fera beau quand j'y retournerai,* it will be a long time before I go there again; *il ferait beau voir,* it would be a pretty (strange) thing to see; *il l'a échappé belle,* he has had a narrow escape of it; *il m'en a conté de belles sur votre compte,* he abused you right and left to me; *la belle plume fait le bel oiseau,* fine feathers make fine birds; *le beau monde,* the fashionable world; *le beau sexe,* the fair sex; *le bel âge,* youth; *le temps se met au beau,* the weather is clearing up; *mourir de sa belle mort,* to die a natural death; *Philippe le Beau,* (of Spain) Philip the Handsome; *se faire beau,* to make oneself smart; *un beau matin* or *un beau jour,* (*iron.*) one fine day; *un beau teint,* a fine complexion; *un bel âge,* an advanced age; *une belle âme,* a lofty soul; *une belle femme,* a handsome woman; *une belle frayeur,* a pretty fright; *une belle main* or *plume,* beautiful hand-writing.—*adv.* Finely, promisingly; in vain. *Avoir beau dire,* to speak in vain; *avoir beau faire,* to try in vain; *bel et bien,* entirely, quite, altogether; *bel et bon,* all very fine; *de plus belle,* with renewed ardour, worse than ever; *tout beau,* gently, not so fast.—*n.* That which is beautiful, fine, excellent, etc.; beauty. *Le beau idéal,* the ideal of beauty; *en beau,* in a favourable aspect; *faire le beau* or *la belle,* to show oneself off, to strut, (of a dog) to beg; *jouer la belle,* to play the final game of a rubber.—*n.m.* A beau, a man elaborately dressed.—*n.f.* A belle, a handsome woman. *La Belle au bois dormant,* the Sleeping Beauty; *La Belle et la Bête,* Beauty and the Beast.

beaucoup [bo'ku], *adv.* Many, much; a great many, a great deal; considerable. *Avoir beaucoup d'argent,* to have much money; *avoir beaucoup d'enfants,* to have many children; *beaucoup de bruit pour rien,* much ado about nothing; *beaucoup moins,* much less; *beaucoup plus,* much more; *de beaucoup,* by far; *il a beaucoup de patience,* he has a great deal of patience; *il n'est pas à beaucoup près aussi riche qu'un tel,* he is not nearly so rich as so-and-so; *il s'en faut de beaucoup que son ouvrage soit achevé,* his work is very far from being finished; *il s'intéresse beaucoup à votre affaire,* he is deeply interested in your case; *vous l'emportez de beaucoup sur lui,* you are far superior to him.

beau-fils [bo'fis], *n.m.* (*pl.* **beaux-fils**) Step-son. **beau-frère,** *n.m.* (*pl.* **beaux-frères**) Brother-in-law. **beau-père,** *n.m.* (*pl.* **beaux-pères**) Father-in-law; step-father. **beau-petit-fils,** *n.m.* (*pl.* **beaux-petits-fils**) Son of a step-son or step-daughter.

beaupré [bo'pre], *n.m.* (*Naut.*) Bowsprit.

beauté [bo'te], *n.f.* Beauty; fineness, comeliness, elegance, agreeableness, neatness. *Crème de beauté,* face or beauty cream; *conserver sa beauté,* to preserve, to keep up one's beauty; *être dans toute sa beauté*, to be in one's prime or at the height of one's beauty; *grain* or *tache de beauté*, beauty-spot, mole; *soins de beauté*, beauty treatment; *une beauté*, a beautiful woman.

beaux (*pl.*) [BEAU].

beaux-arts [boˈzaːr], *n.m. pl.* Fine arts.

beaux-parents [bopaˈrã], *n.m. pl.* Father-in-law and mother-in-law.

bébé [beˈbe], *n.m.* Baby; baby-doll.

bébête [beˈbɛt], *a.* (*fam.*) Childish, simple, babyish, puerile. *Rire bébête*, giggle.

bec [bɛk], *n.m.* Beak, bill; (*fig.*) mouth; snout (of some fishes); spout (of an ewer, a kettle, etc.); gas-jet, burner; mouthpiece (of musical instrument); nib (pen); (*Naut.*) bill (of anchor). *Avoir bec et ongles*, to have teeth and nails, to defend oneself; *avoir le bec bien effilé* or *avoir bon bec*, to have the gift of the gab; *avoir le bec fin*, to be a gourmet; *avoir le bec gelé*, to be tongue-tied; *claquer du bec*, to have nothing to eat; *clouer le bec à quelqu'un*, to silence someone; *donner des coups de bec*, to peck, (*fig.*) to taunt, to heckle; *percer à coups de bec*, to peck through; (*colloq.*) *ferme ton bec!* shut up! *prise de bec*, dispute; *s'humecter le bec*, to wet one's whistle; *rester le bec dans l'eau*, to be stranded, nonplussed; *tenir quelqu'un le bec dans l'eau*, to keep someone in suspense. *Bec Auer*, incandescent burner; *bec Bunsen*, Bunsen burner; *bec de gaz*, lamp-post; (*pop.*) *tomber sur un bec (de gaz)*, to run against an obstacle.

bécane [beˈkan], *n.f.* (*pop.*) *An old-fashioned shunting-engine; bike.

bécard [beˈkar], *n.m.* An adult pike or salmon.

bécarre [beˈkaːr], *a. and n.m.* (*Mus.*) Natural.

bécasse [beˈkas], *n.f.* Woodcock; (*fam.*) stupid woman. *Brider la bécasse*, to take one in; *c'est une bécasse*, she is a goose. **bécasseau**, *n.m.* Sandpiper. **bécassin**, *n.m.* Jack-snipe. **bécassine**, *n.f.* Snipe.

bécau [beˈko], *n.m.* (*pl.* **bécaux**) Young snipe.

bec-croisé [bɛkkrwɑˈze], *n.m.* (*pl.* **becs-croisés**) (*Orn.*) Crossbill.

bec-d'âne (*pl.* **becs-d'âne**) or **bédane** [beˈdan], *n.m.* Mortise-chisel.

bec-de-cane [bɛkdəˈkan], *n.m.* (*pl.* **becs-de-cane**) Lever handle (of shop door etc.).

bec-de-corbin [bɛkdəkɔrˈbɛ̃], *n.m.* (*pl.* **becs-de-corbin**) Bill-head.

bec-de-grue [bɛkdəˈgry], *n.m.* (*pl.* **becs-de-grue**) (*Bot.*) Crane's-bill, stork's-bill.

bec-de-lièvre [bɛkdəˈljɛːvr], *n.m.* (*pl.* **becs-de-lièvre**) Harelip; harelipped person.

bec-en-ciseaux [bɛkɑ̃siˈzo], *n.m.* (*pl.* **becs-en-ciseaux**) (*Orn.*) Scissor-bill.

becfigue or **bec-figue** [bɛkˈfig], *n.m.* A general name for *Passeres*.

bec-fin [bɛkˈfɛ̃], *n.m.* (*pl.* **becs-fins**) Warbler; pipit.

bêchage [bɛˈʃaːʒ], *n.m.* Digging up.

béchamel [beʃaˈmɛl], *n.f.* Cream-sauce, *béchamel*.

bêchard [bɛˈʃaːr], *n.m.* Double-headed hoe.

bêche [bɛːʃ], *n.f.* Spade.

bêche-de-mer [bɛʃdəˈmɛːr], *n.f.* (*pl.* **bêches-de-mer**) Sea-slug, trepang.

bêcher [bɛˈʃe], *v.t.* To dig; (*fig.*) to speak ill of, to pull to pieces.

bêchette [bɛˈʃɛt], *n.f.*, or **bêchot**, *n.m.* Little spade.

bêcheur [bɛˈʃœːr], *n.m.* (*fem.* **bêcheuse**) Digger; (*fig.*) toiler, plodder; detractor.

bêchoir [bɛˈʃwaːr], *n.m.* Broad hoe.

bécot [beˈko], *n.m.* (*pop.*) Little kiss, peck. **(se) bécoter**, *v.* To kiss.

becqué [bɛˈke], *a.* (*fem.* **-ée** (1)) (*Her.*) Beaked.

becquée (2) or **béquée** [bɛˈke], *n.f.* A billful. *Donner la becquée*, to feed.

becquetance [bɛkˈtɑ̃s], *n.f.* (*slang*) Food, grub.

becqueter or **béqueter** [bɛkˈte], *v.t.* To peck: (*colloq.*) to eat. **se becqueter** or **se béqueter**, *v.r.* To peck one another.

bedaine [bəˈdɛn], *n.f.* (*colloq.*) Paunch. *Remplir* or *farcir sa bedaine*, to stuff one's belly.

bédane [BEC-D'ÂNE].

bedeau [bəˈdo], *n.m.* (*pl.* **-eaux**) Beadle, verger.

bédégar or **bédéguar** [bedeˈgar], *n.m.* Bedeguar, rose-gall.

bedon [bəˈdɔ̃], *n.m.* *Tabret, drum; belly.

bedonnant [bədɔˈnɑ̃], *a.* Stout, pot-bellied.

bedonner, *v.i.* To get stout, to grow pursy.

bédouin [beˈdwɛ̃], *a. and n.* (*fem.* **bédouine**) Bedouin.

bée (1) [be], *n.f.* Mill-leet.

bée (2) [be], *a.* *Only used in* '*bouche bée*', gaping open.

béer [BAYER].

beffroi [beˈfrwɑ], *n.m.* Belfry; alarm-bell.

bégaiement [begɛˈmɑ̃], *n.m.*; **bégayant** [begɛˈjɑ̃], *a.* Stammering, faltering.

bégayer [begɛˈje], *v.i.* To stammer; to lisp.—*v.t.* To stammer out, to stutter, to lisp. **bégayeur**, *n.m.* (*fem.* **-euse**) Stammerer, stutterer.

bégonia [begɔˈnja], *n.m.* Begonia.

bégu [beˈgy], *a.* (*fem.* **béguë**) Still marking its age by its incisors (of a horse over five years old).

bègue [bɛg], *a.* Stammering, stuttering.—*n.* Stammerer, stutterer.

béguètement [begɛtˈmɑ̃], *n.m.* Bleating (of goat). **bégueter**, *v.i.* To bleat (of goat).

bégueule [beˈgœl], *n.f.* Prude.—*a.* Prudish, squeamish, straitlaced. **bégueulerie**, *n.f.* *bégueulisme**, *n.m.* Prudery, prudish airs, squeamishness.

béguin [beˈgɛ̃], *n.m.* Hood, child's cap. *Avoir un béguin pour*, to be sweet on; *c'est mon béguin*, he or she is my darling. **béguinage**, *n.m.* Convent of Beguines; devotion. **béguine**, *n.f.* Beguine (Flemish nun); nun; bigoted person.

bégum [beˈgɔm], *n.f.* Begum.

beige [bɛːʒ], *a.* Natural, undyed (of wool); beige.—*n.f.* Unbleached serge.

beigne [bɛɲ], *n.f.* (*pop.*) Blow, clout.

beignet [beˈɲe], *n.m.* Fritter. *Beignet aux pommes*, apple-fritters.

béjaune [beˈʒoːn], *n.m.* (*Falconry*) Eyas, unfledged hawk, nestling; (*fig.*) ninny, novice, new-comer (in a society); treat given by a new-comer to pay his footing; blunder, silliness, mistake. *Montrer à quelqu'un son béjaune*, to show one his ignorance; *payer son béjaune*, to pay one's footing.

bel [BEAU].

bélandre [beˈlɑ̃ːdr], *n.f.* (*Naut.*) Bilander; canal barge.

bêlant [bɛˈlɑ̃], *a.* (*fem.* **bêlante**) Bleating.

bêlement, *n.m.* Bleating (of sheep).

bélemnite [belɛmˈnit], *n.f.* (*Geol.*) Belemnite.

bêler [bɛˈle], *v.i.* To bleat; (*fig.*) to groan, to moan. *Brebis qui bêle perd sa goulée*, least said soonest mended.—*v.t.* To say or deliver in a silly, plaintive, bleating voice.

belette [bəˈlɛt], *n.f.* Weasel.

Belgique [belˈʒik], *f.* Belgium.

belge [belʒ], *a.* Belgian.—*n.* (**Belge**) A Belgian.

bélier [beˈlje], *n.m.* Ram; battering-ram; armoured warship; Aries (one of the signs of the zodiac). *Bélier hydraulique*, hydraulic ram; *coup de bélier*, hammering (of ram), (*fig.*) violent blow.

bélière [beˈljɛːr], *n.f.* Sheep-bell; clapper-ring (of a bell); watch-ring; shackle (of knife); sword-sling.

béliner [beliˈne], *v.i.* To tup (of ram).

belinogramme [bəlinoˈgram], *n.m.* Tele-photograph.

bélître [beˈlitr], *n.m.* Rascal, cad.

belladone [belaˈdɔn], *n.f.* Belladonna, deadly nightshade.

bellâtre [bɛˈlɑːtr], *a.* Having insipid beauty; beauish, foppish.—*n.m.* Insipid beauty, fop, coxcomb.

belle [BEAU].

belle-dame [bɛlˈdam], *n.f.* (*pl.* **belles-dames**) (*Bot.*) Orache; (*Ent.*) *Atriplex hortensis*, painted-lady (butterfly).

belle-de-jour [bɛldəˈʒuːr], *n.f.* (*pl.* **belles-de-jour**) (*Bot.*) Convolvulus minor.

belle-de-nuit [bɛldəˈnɥi], *n.f.* (*pl.* **belles-de-nuit**) (*Bot.*) Marvel of Peru, night-flowering cereus.

belle-d'onze-heures [bɛldɔ̃ˈzœːr], *n.f.* (*pl.* **belles-d'onze-heures**) (*Bot.*) Star-of-Bethlehem.

belle-d'un-jour [bɛldœ̃ˈʒuːr], *n.f.* (*pl.* **belles-d'un-jour**) (*Bot.*) Yellow day-lily.

belle-famille [bɛlfaˈmiːj], *n.f.* (*pl.* **belles-familles**) Wife's or husband's family, (*fam.*) the in-laws.

belle-fille [bɛlˈfiːj], *n.f.* (*pl.* **belles-filles**) Daughter-in-law; stepdaughter.

belle-maman (*colloq.*) [BELLE-MÈRE].

bellement [bɛlˈmɑ̃], *adv.* Prettily, charmingly, softly, gently, moderately.

belle-mère [bɛlˈmɛːr], *n.f.* (*pl.* **belles-mères**) Mother-in-law; stepmother.

belles-lettres [bɛlˈlɛtr], *n.f.* (*used only in pl.*) Polite literature, belles-lettres.

belle-sœur [bɛlˈsœːr], *n.f.* (*pl.* **belles-sœurs**) Sister-in-law; stepsister.

bellicisme [bɛliˈsism], *n.m.* War-mongering.

belliciste [beliˈsist], *a.* Advocate of war.

belligérance [beliʒeˈrɑ̃ːs], *n.f.* Belligerence, belligerency.

belligérant [beliʒeˈrɑ̃], *a.* and *n.* (*fem.* **belligérante**) Belligerent.

belliqueux [beliˈkø], *a.* (*fem.* **belliqueuse**) War-like, martial; bellicose, quarrelsome.

bellis [bɛˈlis], *n.m.* (*Bot.*) Daisy.

bellissime [beliˈsim], *a.* Extremely fine (*iron.*).

Bellone [bɛlˈlɔn], *f.* Bellona.

bellot [beˈlo], *a.* (*fem.* **-otte**) Pretty, neat [BELLÂTRE].—*n.* (*colloq.*) Pretty dear, darling.

belluaire [bɛlˈlɥɛːr], *n.m.* (*Rom. Ant.*) Wild-beast tamer or keeper.

béloce [beˈlɔs], *n.f.* (*Bot.*) Bullace.

belote [bəˈlɔt], *n.f.* A sort of popular game analogous to nap.

bélouga or **béluga** [belyˈga], *n.m.* (*Zool.*) Beluga.

belvédère [bɛlveˈdɛːr], *n.m.* Turret, terrace, belvedere, gazebo; (*Bot.*) belvedere.

Belzébuth [belzeˈbyt], *m.* Beelzebub.

bémol [beˈmɔl], *a.* and *n.m.* (*Mus.*) Flat.

bémoliser, *v.t.* (*Mus.*) To mark flat or with a flat.

ben [bɛ̃], *n.m.* (*Bot., Pharm.*) Fruit of the East Indian horseradish-tree. *Noix de ben*, ben-nut, oil-nut.

bénarde [beˈnard], *a.* and *n.f.* *Clé bénarde*, pin-key; *serrure bénarde*, lock opening and shutting on both sides.

bénédicité [benedisiˈte], *n.m.* Grace (before meals).

bénédictin [benedikˈtɛ̃], *a.* and *n.m.* (*fem.* **bénédictine**) Benedictine; (*fig.*) an un-relaxing scholar. *Travail de bénédictin*, precise and exacting work.

bénédiction [benedikˈsjɔ̃], *n.f.* Benediction, blessing, consecration; (*fig.*) expression of thanks; general esteem or affection; sanctity. *C'est une bénédiction*, everything is most prosperous, all goes well; *combler de bénédictions*, to heap blessings on; *donner* or *répandre des bénédictions*, to shower down blessings (*sur* or *à*); *en bénédiction*, blessed, held sacred; *la bénédiction d'une église*, the consecration of a church; *maison de bénédiction*, house of piety; *pays de bénédiction*, land of plenty; *quelle bénédiction!* what a blessing!

bénef [beˈnɛf], *abbr.* (*pop.*) [BÉNÉFICE].

bénéfice [beneˈfis], *n.m.* Benefit, gain, profit; privilege, advantage; (*Eccles.*) benefice, living. *À bénéfice*, (*Comm.*) at a premium; *avoir une représentation à bénéfice*, (*Theat.*) to have a benefit; *bénéfice brut*, gross profit; *bénéfice net*, net profit; *bénéfice du doute*, benefit of the doubt; *il faut prendre le bénéfice avec les charges*, we must take it for better or worse; *participation aux bénéfices*, profit-sharing; *sous bénéfice d'inventaire*, provided the assets exceed the liabilities.

bénéficiaire [benefiˈsjɛːr], *a.* Receiving a benefit or benefice; in possession of a benefice. *Héritier bénéficiare*, heir liable to no debts above the value of the assets.—*n.* Beneficiary, recipient; (*Theat.*) person who has a benefit.

bénéficial [benefiˈsjal], *a.* (*fem.* **bénéficiale**) Beneficiary (of ecclesiastical livings).

bénéficier (1) [benefiˈsje], *n.m.* Beneficed clergyman, incumbent.

bénéficier (2) [benefiˈsje], *v.i.* To gain, to profit. *Bénéficier d'un non-lieu*, to be discharged.

bénéfique [beneˈfik], *a.* (*Astrol.*) Benefic.

benêt [bəˈnɛ], *n.m.* Booby, fool, simpleton. —*a.m.* Silly, foolish, simple.

bénévole [beneˈvɔl], *a.* Well-disposed, kindly; unpaid. *Lecteur bénévole*, kind or gentle reader. **bénévolement**, *adv.* Out of good-will; voluntarily, spontaneously.

Bengale [bɛ̃ˈgal], *n.m.* Bengal. *Feu de Bengale*, Bengal light; *le Golfe du Bengale*, the Bay of Bengal.

bengali [bɛ̃gaˈli], *a.* and *n.* Bengali; wax bill.

béni, *p.p.* (*fem.* **bénie**) [BÉNIR, *see also* BÉNIT].

Béni-oui-oui [beniwi'wi], *n.m. inv.* (*fam.*) Yes-man.

bénignement [beniɲ'mɑ], *adv.* Benignly, kindly, graciously.

bénignité [beniɲi'te], *n.f.* Benignity, indulgence, kindness; mildness (of a disease).

bénin [be'nɛ̃], *a.* (*fem.* **bénigne**) Benign, good-natured, indulgent; mild (of attacks of disease, remedies, etc.); favourable, propitious.

bénir [be'niːr], *v.t.* To bless, to hallow, to consecrate; to call down blessings on; to thank, to praise. *Dieu vous bénisse*, God bless you (often said facetiously after a sneeze); *être béni des Dieux*, to be one of the lucky ones.

bénissable [beni'sabl], *a.* Worthy to be blessed. **bénissant**, *a.* (*fem.* **-ante**) That blesses.

bénisseur, *a.* (*iron.*) Soapy, unctuous.

bénit [be'ni], *a.* (*fem.* **-ite**) Hallowed, consecrated. *De l'eau bénite*, holy water; *du pain bénit*, consecrated bread; *eau bénite de cour*, empty promises; (*fam.*) *ça c'est pain bénit*, it serves him right.

bénitier [beni'tje], *n.m.* Holy-water basin; fount, stoup. *Bénitier portatif*, aspersorium; *se démener comme un diable dans un bénitier*, to be violently agitated.

benjamin [bɛ̃ʒa'mɛ̃], *n.m.* (*fem.* **benjamine** (1)) Favourite (especially the youngest child).

benjamine (2) [bɛ̃ʒa'min], *n.f.* (*Naut.*) Main trysail.

benjoin [bɛ̃'ʒwɛ̃], *n.m.* Benjamin, benzoin.

benne [ben], *n.f.* Hamper, basket; (*Mining*) cradle, hopper, bucket, skip. *Benne preneuse*, clam-shell bucket.

benoît [bə'nwa], *a.* (*fem.* **benoîte** (1)) Blessed; sanctimonious.

benoîte (2) [bə'nwat], *n.f.* (*Bot.*) Herb-bennet.

benoîtement [bənwat'mɑ], *adv.* Sanctimoniously.

benzène [bɛ̃'zɛn], *n.m.* (*Chem.*) Benzene.

benzine [bɛ̃'zin], *n.f.* Benzine. **benzoïque**, *a.* Benzoic. **benzol**, *n.m.* Benzol.

Béotie [beɔ'si], *f.* Boeotia.

béotien [beɔ'sjɛ̃], *a.* and *n.* (*fem.* **-ienne**) Boeotian; (*fig.*) boorish and ignorant.—*n.* (*fig.*) a dunce. **béotisme**, *n.m.* Dullness, stupidity.

béquée [BECQUÉE].

béquet [be'kɛ] or **becquet**, *n.m.* (*Print.*) Paste-on (to proof).

béqueter [BECQUETER].

béquillard [beki'jaːr], *a.* (*fem.* **-arde**) (*pop.*) Crippled, going on crutches.—*n.* Cripple.

béquille [be'kiːj], *n.f.* Crutch; (*fig.*) support, help, aid; (*Gard.*) spud; (*Naut.*) shore, prop; (*Av.*) tail-skid.

béquiller [beki'je], *v.i.* To walk on crutches.—*v.t.* (*Gard.*) To dig up (weeds) with a spud; (*Naut.*) to shore up.

béquillon [beki'jɔ̃], *n.m.* Small *béquille*; crutch-handled walking-stick; (*Gard.*) spud.

ber [beːr], *n.m.* (*Naut.*) Cradle.

berbère [ber'beːr], *a.* Berber.—*n.m.* The Berber language.—*n.* (**Berbère**) A Berber.

berbéris [berbe'ris], *n.m.* (*Bot.*) Barberry.

bercail [ber'kaːj], *n.m.* (*only used in the sing.*) Sheepfold, fold.

berce [bers], *n.f.* Cow-parsnip.

berceau [ber'so], *n.m.* Cradle; (*fig.*) infancy; origin, source; (*Hort.*) arbour, bower; (*Arch.*) cylindrical vault; (*Naut.*) cradle. *Faire monter la vigne en berceau*, to train the vine arbour-wise.

bercelonnette [bersəlɔ'net] or **barcelonette**, *n.f.* A light hanging cradle; swing-cot.

bercement [bersə'mɑ], *n.m.* Rocking; lulling.

bercer [ber'se], *v.t.* To rock, to lull asleep; to lull, to soothe; (*fig.*) to delude or flatter with vain hopes. *J'ai été bercé de cela*, I have heard that from my cradle. **se bercer**, *v.r.* To rock. (*fig.*) *Il se berce de vaines espérances*, he deludes himself with vain hopes.

berceuse, *n.f.* A woman who rocks an infant; rocking-chair; cradle that rocks; (*Mus.*) lullaby.

béret [be'rɛ], *n.m.* Beret, tam-o'-shanter (worn by the French Alpine regiments).

bergame [ber'gam], *n.f.* Bergamot tapestry.

bergamote [berga'mɔt], *n.f.* Bergamot orange, bergamot pear. **bergamotier, bergamottier**, *n.m.* Bergamot-tree.

berge (1) [berʒ], *n.f.* Steep bank of a river; side of a canal, ditch, roadway, etc.

berge (2) [berʒ], *n.f.* A narrow boat, barge.

berger [ber'ʒe], *n.m.* (*fem.* **bergère** (1)) Shepherd, shepherdess; swain; (*fig.*) pastor, guardian (of the people etc.). *L'heure du berger*, the favourable moment for a lover; (*Chess*) *le coup du berger*, fool's mate.

bergère (2) [ber'ʒeːr], *n.f.* A large and deep arm-chair.

bergerette [berʒə'ret], *n.f.* Young shepherdess, country lass; (*Orn.*) wagtail.

bergerie [berʒə'ri], *n.f.* Sheepfold, pen; (*Lit.*) (chiefly used in the plural) a pastoral.

bergeronnette [berʒərɔ'net], *n.f.* (*Orn.*) Any of the wagtails. *Bergeronnette des ruisseaux*, grey wagtail; *bergeronnette flavéole*, yellow wagtail.

béribéri [beribe'ri], *n.m.* A tropical disease.

béril [BÉRYL].

berle [berl], *n.f.* Water-parsnip, skirret.

berline [ber'lin], *n.f.* Travelling-coach, Berlin.

*berlingot (1) [berlɛ̃'go], *n.m.* One-seated Berline; (*fig.*) ramshackle carriage.

berlingot (2), *n.m.* Sweet made with caramel.

berloque (*vulg.*) [BRELOQUE].

berlue [ber'ly], *n.f.* Passing dimness of sight. *Avoir la berlue*, to be dim-sighted; (*fig.*) to misjudge.

berme [berm], *n.f.* (*Fort. etc.*) Berm.

Bermudes [ber'myd], **les**, *f.pl.* The Bermudas.

bernacle [ber'nakl], **bernache** or **barnache**, *n.f.* Barnacle-goose; barnacle (shell-fish).

bernardin [bernar'dɛ̃], *n.m.* (*fem.* **bernardine**) Bernardine (monk or nun).

bernard-l'ermite [bernarler'mit], *n.m.* Hermit-crab.

Berne [bern], *f.* Bern.

berne (1) [bern], *n.f.* Tossing in a blanket.

berne (2), *n.f.* (*Naut.*) *Mettre le pavillon en berne*, to fly the flag at half-mast; (*Mil.*) *mettre un drapeau en berne*, to furl and crape a flag (as a sign of mourning).

berner [ber'ne], *v.t.* To toss in a blanket; (*fig.*) to ridicule, to make a fool of, to deride. **berneur**, *n.m.* Mocker, banterer.

bernicle [ber'nikl] or **bernique** (1) [ber'nik],

n.f. (*pop.*) Barnacle (shell-fish); barnacle-goose.

Bernin [bɛr'nɛ̃], *m.* Bernini.

bernique (2) [bɛr'nik], *int.* (*pop.*) No use; not a bit of it, no go. *Je croyais le trouver chez lui, mais bernique!* I thought I should find him in, but the bird had flown!

berquinade [bɛrki'nad], *n.f.* Puerile piece of literature.

bersaglier [bɛrsa'lje], *n.m.* Bersagliere.

berthe [bɛrt], *n.f.* Small pelerine worn over low-necked dress; milk-can.

berthon [bɛr'tɔ̃], *n.m.* A small collapsible boat.

bertillonage [bɛrtijɔ'naʒ], *n.m.* Anthropometry (according to Dr. Bertillon's system).

béryl [be'ril] or **béril**, *n.m.* Beryl.

besace [bə'zas], *n.f.* Beggar's wallet, scrip. *Porter la besace*, to be reduced to beggary.

besacier, *n.m.* One who carries a wallet, a beggar; a tramp.

*besaigre [bə'zɛ:gr], *a.* Sourish, tart (of wine). *Tourner au besaigre*, to turn sour.—*n.m.* Wine turning sour.

besaiguë [bazɛ'gy] or **bisaiguë**, *n.f.* Carpenter's twibill; glazier's hammer.

besant [bə'zɑ̃], *n.m.* (*Ant. and Her.*) Bezant. **besanté**, *a.* Charged with bezants.

besas [bə'zɑ:s] or **beset**, *n.m.* [AMBESAS].

bésef [BEZEF].

besicles [bə'zikl], *n.f.* (*used only in pl.*) (*colloq. and iron.*) Spectacles, barnacles (old-fashioned).

bésigue [be'zig], *n.m.* Bezique (card game).

besogne [bə'zɔɲ], *n.f.* Work, business, labour; job, piece of work; (*fig.*) trouble, difficulty. *Abattre de la besogne*, to get through a lot of work; *aimer besogne faite*, to love work done by others, to hate work; *aller vite en besogne*, to act quickly, not to mince matters; *être accablé de besogne*, to be over head and ears in work; *mettre la main à la besogne*, to set to work; *mourir à la besogne*, to die in harness; *s'endormir sur la besogne*, to be slack about one's work; *tailler de la besogne à quelqu'un*, to cut out work for or give trouble to someone; *une rude besogne*, uphill work; *vous avez fait là de la belle besogne!* you have made a pretty mess of it!

besogner, *v.i.* To work, to labour.—**v.t.* To work at, to spend time and trouble on.

besogneux, *a. and n.* (*fem.* **-euse**) Necessitous, needy (person).

besoin [bə'zwɛ̃], *n.m.* Need, want; necessity; poverty, distress, indigence; occasion, emergency; (*pl.*) natural necessities. *Au besoin*, at a pinch, in case of need; *autant qu'il est besoin*, as much as necessary; *avoir besoin de quelque chose*, to want something; *il est dans le besoin*, he is in distress; *il l'a assisté dans le besoin*, he was a friend to him in his distress; *il n'est pas besoin de*, it is not necessary to; *il n'est pas besoin que*, there is no occasion for; *j'en ai plus besoin que vous*, I want it more than you do; *je n'en ai pas besoin*, I have no occasion for it; *n'avoir besoin de rien*, to want nothing; *c'est dans le besoin que l'on connaît les amis*, a friend in need is a friend indeed; *pour subvenir à ses besoins*, to supply one's wants; *si besoin est*, if need be.

Bessarabie [bɛsara'bi], *f.* Bessarabia.

*besson [bɛ'sɔ̃], *a. and n.* (*fem.* **bessonne**) (*dial.*) Twin. **bessonnerie**, *n.f.* Twinship.

bestiaire [bɛs'tjɛ:r], *n.m.* (*Rom. Ant.*) Gladiator, bestiarius; (*Med. Ant.*) bestiary, fable-book.

bestial [bɛs'tjal], *a.* (*fem.* **bestiale**, *pl.* **bestiaux**) Bestial, brutish. **bestialement**, *adv.* Bestially, brutally, like a beast.

bestialiser, *v.t.* To make bestial. **se bestialiser**, *v.r.* To become brutish.

bestialité, *n.f.* Bestiality.

bestiaux, *pl.* [BÉTAIL].

bestiole [bɛs'tjɔl], *n.f.* ***bestion** [bɛs'tjɔ̃], *n.m.* Little animal.

bêta [be'tɑ], *n.m.* (*fem.* **bêtasse**) A bit of a blockhead, rather a simpleton. *C'est un gros bêta*, he is a simple-minded booby.

bétail [be'ta:j], *n.m.* (*pl.* **bestiaux**) Cattle, livestock. *Gros bétail*, oxen etc.; *menu bétail*, sheep, goats, etc.

bêtasse [BÊTA].

bête [bɛ:t], *n.f.* Animal, beast, brute; fool, blockhead, stupid creature. *Bête à bon Dieu*, lady-bird; *bête à cornes*, horned beast; *bête à laine*, sheep; *bête brute*, brute beast; *bête de somme*, beast of burden; *bête de trait*, carriage animal; *bête farouche*, savage beast; *bête féroce*, carnivorous animal; *bête sauvage*, wild animal; *bêtes fauves*, big game; *c'est ma bête noire*, he, she, or it is my pet aversion; *c'est une maligne bête*, he is a spiteful animal; (*colloq.*) *chercher la petite bête*, to be a fusspot; *être livré aux bêtes*, to be given to the beasts (in martyrdom); (*fig.*) to be handed over to the ignorant critic etc.; *faire la bête*, to play the fool; *la bête*, the animal (in our nature); *morte la bête, mort le venin*, dead men tell no tales; *remonter sur sa bête*, to get on one's legs again; (*colloq.*) *reprendre du poil de la bête*, to regain confidence; *une bonne bête*, a good-natured fool.—*a.* Silly, stupid, nonsensical. *Il est bête à manger du foin*, he is a perfect idiot; *pas si bête*, tell me another!

bétel [be'tɛl], *n.m.* (*Bot.*) Betel.

bêtement [bɛt'mɑ̃], *adv.* Like a fool, foolishly, stupidly.

Béthanie [beta'ni], *f.* Bethany.

Bethléem [bɛtle'ɛm], *f.* Bethlehem.

Bethsabée [bɛtsa'be], *f.* Bathsheba.

bêtifier [beti'fje], **v.t.* To make stupid.—*v.i.* To play the fool, to say silly things.

bêtise [be'ti:z], *n.f.* Silliness, stupidity; tomfoolery, foolish act, suggestion, etc., silly thing, absurdity; a futility. *C'est de la bêtise*, it's all nonsense; *c'est sa bêtise qui l'a perdu*, his stupidity was the ruin of him; *faire des bêtises*, to play pranks; *il a dit une bêtise*, he said a silly thing; *il a fait une bêtise*, he did a stupid thing; *il ne dit que des bêtises*, he talks nothing but nonsense; *quelle bêtise!* what an absurdity! *Bêtises de Cambrai*, a kind of mint lollipop.

bétoine [be'twan], *n.f.* (*Bot.*) Betony. *Bétoine officinale* or *des Vosges*, arnica.

bétoire [be'twa:r], *n.m.* Gully-hole; drain-hole; pot-hole (in limestone).

béton [be'tɔ̃], *n.m.* (*Masonry*) Beton, a kind of concrete. *Béton armé*, reinforced concrete. **bétonnage**, *n.m.* Concrete work. **bétonner**, *v.t.* To build with concrete. **bétonnière**, *n.f.* or **bétonneuse**, *n.f.* Concrete-mixer.

bette (1) [bɛt] or **blette** [blɛt], *n.f.* Beet.

bette (2) [bɛt], *n.f.* (*Naut.*) Barge; small Mediterranean craft.

betterave [be'traːv], *n.f.* Beetroot. *Betterave à sucre*, sugar-beet; *betterave fourragère*, mangel-wurzel. **betteraverie**, *n.f.* Factory for making beet-sugar. **betteravier**, *a.* (*fem.* **betteravière**) Pertaining to the manufacture of beet-sugar.—*n.m.* Grower of beet.

bétyle [be'til], *n.f.* (*Ant.*) Sacred stone regarded as the abode of a god.

*****beuglant** [bø'glã], *n.m.* (*slang*) Low musichall.

beuglement [bøglə'mã], *n.m.* Bellowing, lowing (of cattle).

beugler [bø'gle], *v.i.* To bellow, to low; (*fig.*) to cry loudly, to roar. *Il se mit à beugler*, he began to roar like a bull.—*v.t.* To bellow out (a song).

beurre [bœːr], *n.m.* Butter. *Beurre fondu*, melted butter; *beurre noir*, browned butter; *pot à beurre*, butter-jar; *rondelle de beurre*, pat of butter; (*fig.*) *assiette au beurre*, nice fat job; profit; *compter pour du beurre*, (*fam.*) to count for nothing; *faire son beurre*, to make money, to make nice pickings; *gants beurre frais*, butter-coloured gloves; *mettre du beurre dans les épinards*, to improve the situation; *œil au beurre noir*, (*colloq.*) black eye; *on ne peut manier du beurre qu'on ne s'en graisse les doigts*, you cannot handle money without some sticking to your fingers; *promettre plus de beurre que de pain*, to promise more than one can perform. **beurré**, *n.m.* Butter-pear **beurrée**, *n.f.* Slice of bread and butter. **beurrer**, *v.t.* To butter (bread etc.). **beurrerie**, *n.f.* Butter dairy. **beurrier** (1), *a.* (*fem.* **beurrière**) Pertaining to butter.—*n.* Butter-man, butter-woman. **beurrier** (2), *n.m.* Butter-dish.

beuverie [BUVERIE].

bévue [be'vy], *n.f.* Blunder, oversight, mistake; (*colloq.*) howler. *Faiseur de bévues*, blunderer.

bey [bɛ], *n.m.* Bey. **beylical**, *a.* (*fem.* **-ale**, *pl.* **-aux**) Pertaining to a bey. **beylicat**, *n.m.* Government of a bey. **beylik**, *n.m.* Beylic.

bezef [be'zɛf], *adv.* (*slang*) Much. *Bono bezef*, very good; *y en a pas bezef*, there is not much of it, there is none.

bezet [BESAS].

bézoard [be'zwaːr], *n.m.* Bezoar.

biacide [bia'sid], *a.* and *n.m.* Biacid.

biais [bjɛ], *n.m.* Bias, obliquity, slope; (*fig.*) shift, subterfuge. *Aborder de biais une question*, to approach a question indirectly; *couper (une étoffe) de biais*, to cut on the cross; *en biais*, obliquely; *prendre une affaire du bon biais* or *du mauvais biais*, to go the right or the wrong way to work; *user de biais*, to use subterfuges.—*a.* (*fem.* **-se**) Slanting, sloping, askew; oblique. **biaisement**, *n.m.* Sloping, slanting, shift, evasion. **biaiser**, *v.i.* To be oblique, to go obliquely, to slope, to slant, to lean on one side; to use shifts or evasions. *C'est un homme qui biaise*, he is a shuffler.

biatomique [DIATOMIQUE].

bibasique [biba'zik], *a.* (*Chem.*) Dibasic.

bibasse [bi'bas], *n.f.* Japanese medlar, loquat. **bibassier** or **bibacier**, *n.m.* Tree bearing this.

bibelot [bi'blo], *n.m.* Trinket, knick-knack. **bibelotage**, *n.m.* Collection of *bibelots*; mania for this. **bibeloter**, *v.i.* To collect, buy, or sell *bibelots*; (*fig.*) to spend one's time in trifling occupations. **bibeloteur**, *n.m.* (*fem.* **bibeloteuse**) Lover or collector of knick-knacks.

bibelotier [BIMBELOTIER].

biberon (1) [bi'brɔ̃], *n.m.* (*Med.*) Feeding-cup; feeding bottle (for infants). *Élever un enfant au biberon*, to bring up a child on the bottle.

biberon (2), *a.* (*fem.* **biberonne**) Tippling, bibulous.—*n.* Tippler, toper.

bibi [bibi], *n.m.* *Woman's hat worn about 1830; (*slang*) sometimes used for an old worn hat; (*pop.*) I, myself, number one. *C'est pour bibi*, it's for number one, for little me.

bibine [bi'bin], *n.f.* (*colloq.*) *De la bibine*, bad wine, tasteless beer swipes.

bible [bibl], *n.f.* Bible.

bibliographe [biblio'graf], *n.m.* Bibliographer. **bibliographie**, *n.f.* Bibliography. **bibliographique**, *a.* Bibliographical.

bibliomane [biblio'man], *n.m.* Book-collector. **bibliomanie**, *n.f.* Bibliomania.

bibliophile [biblio'fil], *n.m.* Book-lover. **bibliophilie**, *n.f.* Bibliophilism.

bibliothécaire [bibliote'kɛːr], *n.m.* Librarian. **bibliothèque** [biblio'tɛk], *n.f.* Library; bookcase, book-press. *Bibliothèque de gare*, railway bookstall; *c'est une bibliothèque vivante*, he is a walking dictionary.

biblique [bi'blik], *a.* Biblical.

bicarbonate [bikarbɔ'nat], *n.m.* (*Chem.*) Bicarbonate. **bicarboné**, *a.* (*fem.* **bicarbonée**) Containing two atoms of carbon. *Hydrogène carboné* [ÉTHYLÈNE].

bicarbure, *n.m.* Bicarbide.

bicarré [bika're], *a.* (*fem.* **bicarrée**) (*Alg.*) Biquadratic.

bicéphale [bise'fal], *a.* (*Zool.*) Bicephalous, two-headed.—*n.* A bicephalous animal.

biceps [bi'sɛps], *n.m.* Biceps. (*colloq.*) *Avoir du biceps*, to be muscular.

biche [biʃ], *n.f.* Hind; doe; (*colloq.*) girl, young woman. *À pied de biche*, claw-footed (of furniture); *ma petite biche*, my love; *ventre de biche*, rosy-white like a hind's belly.

bichette, *n.f.* (*fam.*) Little dear, darling.

bicher [bi'ʃe], *v.i.* (*slang*) Used chiefly in *ça biche?* how goes it? *ça ne bichera pas*, they can't get friendly.

bichof or **bischof** [bi'ʃɔf], *n.m.* Hot spiced wine.

bichon [bi'ʃɔ̃], *n.m.* (*fem.* **bichonne**) Lapdog with long, silky hair; (*fam.*) little dear; love.—*n.m.* Velvet pad for smoothing silk hats.

bichonner [biʃɔ'ne], *v.t.* To curl; (*fig.*) to caress. **se bichonner**, *v.r.* To curl one's hair; to make oneself smart.

bichromate [bikrɔ'mat], *n.m.* Bichromate.

bicolore [biko'lɔːr], *a.* Bi-coloured.

biconcave [bikɔ̃'kaːv], *a.* Bi-concave.

biconvexe [bikɔ̃'vɛks], *a.* Bi-convex.

bicoque [bi'kɔk], *n.f.* (*colloq.*) Ramshackle house, shanty.

bicorne [bi'kɔrn], *a.* and *n.m.* Cocked (hat).

bicot [bi'ko], *n.m.* (*fam.*) Kid; (*slang, pej.*) Arab.

bicuspidé [bikyspi'de], *a.* (*fem.* **bicuspidée**) (*Bot.*) Bicuspidate.

[89]

*bicycle [bi′sikl], *n.m.*   Bicycle (of the penny-farthing pattern).

bicyclette [bisi′klɛt], *n.f.*   Bicycle. *Bicyclette de course*, racer; *bicyclette de route*, roadster. *Aller à bicyclette*, to cycle, (*Am.*) to wheel.

bide [bid], *n.m.* (*slang*) Belly, paunch.

bident [bi′dɑ̃], *n.m.*   Two-pronged fork; (*Bot.*) bidens.

bidenté [bidɑ̃′te], *a.* (*fem.* **-ée**) Bidentate.

bidet [bi′dɛ], *n.m.*   Pony, small nag; bidet (bath). *Pousser son bidet*, to go on with one's business, not to be disturbed.

bidoche [bi′dɔʃ], *n.f.*   (*pop.*) Meat, esp. bad meat.

bidon [bi′dɔ̃], *n.m.* Tin, can (*esp.* petrol can); camp-kettle; soldier's water-bottle; (*slang*) belly. *Bidon de secours*, spare can.

bidonnant [bidɔ′nɑ̃], *a.* (*slang*) Very funny.

bidonner (se) [bidɔ′ne] *v.r.* (*slang*) To roar.

bidonville [bidɔ̃′vil], *n.m.*   Tin-pot town (in poor suburbs), shanty-town.

bief [bjef], *n.m.*   Mill-leet; mill-race; reach of a canal (between two locks).

bielle [bjɛl], *n.f.* (*Mach.*) Connecting-rod.

bien (1) [bjɛ̃], *n.m.*   Good; that which is pleasant, useful, or advantageous; benefit, welfare, well-being, blessing; wealth, estate, property; gift, boon, mercy. *Avoir du bien au soleil*, to have landed property; *bien mal acquis*, ill-gotten gains; *bien clair et liquide*, unencumbered estate; *bien engagé* or *hypothéqué*, mortgaged estate; *biens*, goods, chattels; fruits, productions (of the soil etc.); *biens de consommation*, consumer goods; *biens immeubles*, landed property; *biens immobiliers*, real estate, (*Am.*) realty; *cela fait du bien*, that does one good; *cela ne fait ni bien ni mal*, that does neither good nor harm; *dépenser* or *manger son bien*, to dissipate one's fortune; *dire du bien de quelqu'un*, to speak well of someone; *en bien*, favourably, in good part; *en tout bien tout honneur*, with honourable intentions; *grand bien vous fasse*, much good may it do you! *le bien et le mal*, good and evil; *le bien public*, public weal; *le mieux est l'ennemi du bien*, leave well alone; *les biens de la terre*, the good things of the earth; *les gens de bien*, respectable people, gentlefolk; *mener à bien*, to bring to a successful issue; *périr corps et biens*, (of ships) to go down with all hands; *rendre le bien pour le mal*, to return good for evil; *séparation de corps et de biens*, judicial separation (a mensa et toro); *souverain bien*, the highest good (summum bonum); *un homme de bien*, a right-thinking man.

bien (2) [bjɛ̃], *adv.*   Well; rightly, finely; much, very, far, entirely, completely; many, great many, a great deal; about, wellnigh; prosperously, auspiciously, favourably, successfully; well off, on good terms, in favour; certainly, truly, indeed; formerly, clearly, expressly. *Assez bien*, pretty well; *auriez-vous bien l'assurance de le̞ nier?* would you really be bold enough to deny it? *aussi bien*, anyhow, in any case; *bien de*, plenty of, many of; *bien lui a pris de*, it was well for him he did so; *bien mieux*, far better; *bien plus*, besides, further, moreover; *bien que*, although; *bien qu'il le sache, il n'en parle pas*, although he knows it, he says nothing about it; *bien trouvé*, well thought of; *c'est bien*, that's right;

c'est être bien prompt, this is being rather hasty; *cette femme est bien*, that woman is good-looking; *cette jeune personne se tient bien*, that young lady has a good carriage; *eh bien!* well! or well? *fort bien*, very well; *il a été bien battu*, he has been soundly beaten; *il est bien avec*, he is on good terms or in favour with; *il est bien de* or *que*, it is well that; *il est déjà bien loin*, he is a long way off by this time; *il parle bien français*, he speaks French well; *il se conduit bien*, he behaves well; *il se porte bien*, he is well; *ils sont fort bien ensemble*, they are on very good terms; *il y a bien dix lieues d'ici*, it is fully ten leagues from here; *il y avait bien du monde*, there were many people present; *je l'ai bien pensé*, I thought so; *je le savais bien* or *je m'en doutais bien*, I knew as much, I suspected as much; *je le veux bien*, I have no objection; *je me trouve bien de ce nouveau régime*, I am all the better for this new diet; *j'en ai bien assez de tout ce monde*, I am heartily sick of all these people; *je suis très bien ici*, I am quite comfortable here; *je vous l'avais bien dit*, I told you so; *nous voilà bien*, we are in a fine pickle; *on est fort bien ici*, this is very comfortable; *ou bien*, or else; *regardez-moi bien*, look at me steadfastly; *si bien que*, so that; *tant bien que mal*, so-so, after a fashion, as best he might; *tout va bien*, all's well; *voilà bien du bruit pour rien*, what a lot of fuss about nothing! *vous êtes bien bon*, you are too kind.—*int.* (sometimes pron. colloq. bɛ̃) Well!

bien-aimé [bjɛ̃nɛ′me], *a.* (*fem.* **bien-aimée,** *pl.* **bien-aimés**) Beloved, well-beloved.—*n.* Darling, dear.

bien-dire [bjɛ̃′diːr], *n.m.* (*no pl.*)   Fine speaking. *Le bien faire vaut mieux que le bien-dire*, to act well is better than to speak well.

*bien-disant [bjɛ̃di′zɑ̃], *a.* (*fem.* **bien-disante**) Well-spoken.

bien-être [bjɛ̃′nɛːtr], *n.m.* (*no pl.*) Well-being, welfare, comfort, snugness. *Tout le monde cherche son bien-être*, every one looks after his own welfare.

bienfaisance [bjɛ̃fə′zɑ̃ːs], *n.f.*   Beneficence, charity, munificence. *Œuvre de bienfaisance*, charity; *bureau de bienfaisance*, relief committee; *société de bienfaisance*, benevolent society. **bienfaisant,** *a.* (*fem.* **-ante**) Charitable, beneficent, kind, gracious; beneficial, salutary.

bienfait [bjɛ̃′fɛ], *n.m.*   Good turn, kindness, benefit, favour, courtesy. *Combler de bienfaits*, to load with favours; *on oublie plus tôt les bienfaits que les injures*, services are sooner forgotten than injuries; *un bienfait n'est jamais perdu*, a kindness is never lost.

bienfaiteur, *n.m.* (*fem.* **bienfaitrice**) Benefactor, patron.

bien-fondé [bjɛ̃fɔ̃′de], *n.m.*   The ground (of a complaint etc.), cogency.

bien-fonds [bjɛ̃′fɔ̃], *n.m.* (*pl.* **biens-fonds**) Real property (lands and houses).

bienheureux [bjɛ̃nœ′rø], *a.* (*fem.* **bienheureuse**) Happy, fortunate; (*Eccles.*) blessed.—*n.* One of the blessed.

bien-jugé [bjɛ̃ʒy′ʒe], *n.m.* (*Law*) Legally valid decision or sentence.

biennal [biɛ′nal], *a.* (*fem.* **biennale** (1), *pl.*

biennaux) Biennial. **biennale** (2), *n.f.* Two-yearly exhibition or festival.

bienséance [bjɛ̃se'ɑ̃:s], *n.f.* Propriety, decency, decorum, seemliness. *Observer la bienséance* or *les bienséances*, to observe decorum. **bienséant,** *a.* (*fem.* **bienséante**) Decent, becoming, seemly, decorous, fit.

bientôt [bjɛ̃'to], *adv.* Soon, ere long, shortly. *À bientôt!* see you soon! *cela est bientôt dit,* that is sooner said than done.

bienveillance [bjɛ̃vɛ'jɑ̃:s], *n.f.* Benevolence, goodwill, favour, kindness. *Faire quelque chose par bienveillance,* to do something out of sheer kindness. **bienveillant,** *a.* (*fem.* **-ante**) Benevolent, kind, friendly, favourable.

bienvenir [bjɛ̃v'ni:r], *v.i.* To ingratiate oneself (only used in the expression *se faire bienvenir de,* to ingratiate oneself into someone's favour).

bienvenu [bjɛ̃v'ny], *a.* (*fem.* **bienvenue** (1)) Welcome. *Soyez le bienvenu,* you are welcome. **bienvenue** (2), *n.f.* Welcome. *Souhaiter la bienvenue à quelqu'un,* to greet, to welcome someone.

bière (1) [bjɛ:r], *n.f.* Beer. *Bière blonde,* ale; *bière brune,* stout; *bière de Munich,* lager; *débit de bière,* ale-house; *petite bière,* small beer; (*fig.*) *ce n'est pas de la petite bière,* it is no trifle.

bière (2) [bjɛ:r], *n.f.* Coffin. *Mise en bière,* coffining.

bièvre [bjɛvr], *n.m.* *Beaver. (*Orn.*) Harle bièvre,* goosander.

biez [BIEF].

biffage [bi'fa:ʒ], *n.m.,* or **biffure,** *n.f.* Crossing-out, cancelling, erasure.

biffe [bif], *n.f.* Cancelling stamp or mark; (*Mil. slang*) infantry.

biffer [bi'fe], *v.t.* To cancel, to run the pen through, to blot out, to erase.

biffin, *n.m.* Ragman; infantryman.

bifide [bi'fid], *a.* (*Bot.*) Bifid. *Une barbe bifide,* a double-pointed beard.

biflore [bi'flɔ:r], *a.* (*Bot.*) Biflorate.

bifocal [bifɔ'kal], *a.* (*fem.* **-ale,** *pl.* **-aux**) Bifocal. *Lunettes bifocales,* bifocal glasses.

bifolié [bifɔ'lje], *a.* (*fem.* **-ée**) (*Bot.*) Bifoliate.

biforme [bi'fɔrm], *a.* Biform.

bifteck [bif'tɛk], *n.m.* Beefsteak. *Bifteck aux pommes,* steak and chips; *bifteck de cheval,* horse steak; (*pop.*) *gagner son bifteck,* to earn one's bread and butter.

bifurcation [bifyrka'sjɔ̃], *n.f.* Bifurcation (of a road), fork; (of railway) branch, junction.

bifurquer, *v.i.* To bifurcate, to divide into two parts or branches.

bigame [bi'gam], *a.* Bigamous. *n.* Bigamist.

bigamie, *n.f.* Bigamy.

bigarade [biga'rad], *n.f.* Seville orange. **bigaradier,** *n.m.* Seville-orange tree.

bigarré [biga're], *a.* (*fem.* **bigarrée**) Parti-coloured, motley, streaked.

bigarreau [biga'ro], *n.m.* White and red cherry, bigaroon. **bigarreautier,** *n.m.* Bigaroon-tree.

bigarrer [biga're], *v.t.* To chequer, to streak, to variegate. **bigarrure,** *n.f.* Medley, mixture, motley, variegation.

bigéminé [biʒemi'ne], *a.* (*fem.* **-ée**) (*Bot.*) Bigeminate; (*Arch.*) dividing in two pairs of ramifying parts, quadrigeminal.

bigle [bigl], *a.* and *n.* Cock-eyed (person).

bigler, *v.i.* To squint.

bigophone [bigo'fɔn], *n.m.* A grotesque and noisy board-pipe; (*pop.*) telephone.

bigorne [bi'gɔrn], *n.f.* Two-beaked anvil. **bigorneau** [bigɔr'no], *n.m.* Small *bigorne;* winkle. **bigorner** (bigɔr'ne), *v.t.* To round (iron etc.) on a *bigorne.* **se bigorner,** *v.r.* (*pop.*) To scuffle.

bigot [bi'go], *a.* (*fem.* **bigote**) Bigoted.—*n.* Bigot. **bigoterie,** *n.f.* **bigotisme,** *n.m.* Bigotry. *Donner dans la bigoterie,* to be something of a bigot.

bigoudi [bigu'di], *n.m.* Curling pin or roller (for the hair); (hair) curler.

bigre [bigr], *int.* Hang it! bother! confound it!

bigrement, *adv.* Deucedly, awfully.

bigrille [bi'grij], *a. Lampe bigrille,* double-grid valve.

bigue [big], *n.f.* Sheers, sheer-legs; (*Naut.*) mast-crane, derrick.

bihebdomadaire [biɛbdɔma'dɛ:r], *a.* Appearing etc. twice a week, bi-weekly.

bihoreau [biɔ'ro], *n.m.* A small species of heron.

bijon [bi'ʒɔ̃], *n.m.* (*Pharm.*) Pine resin.

bijou [bi'ʒu], *n.m.* Jewel, gem; (*fig.*) a charming little person, thing, etc. *Venez, mon bijou,* come, darling. **bijouterie,** *n.f.* Jewellery. **bijoutier,** *n.m.* (*fem.* **bijoutière**) Jeweller.

bijumeau [biʒy'mo], *a.* Double or biform through abnormality.—*n.m.* A biform monster; (*Anat.*) biceps.

bilabiale [bila'bjal], *a.* and *n.f.* Bilabial (consonant).

bilabié [bila'bje], *a.* (*fem.* **bilabiée**) (*Bot.*) Bilabiate.

bilame [bi'lam], *a.* With two blades.

bilan [bi'lɑ̃], *n.m.* Balance-sheet; schedule of assets and liabilities; (*fig.*) weighing up (of an experience, one's life, etc.). *Déposer son bilan,* to declare oneself insolvent.

bilatéral [bilate'ral], *a.* (*fem.* **bilatérale,** *pl.* **bilatéraux**) Bilateral; (*Law*) reciprocal.

bilboquet [bilbɔ'kɛ], *n.m.* Cup-and-ball (toy); small weighted figure that balances itself; (*Print.*) small-job work; curling-pipe. *C'est un véritable bilboquet,* he is a giddy-headed fellow. **bilboquettiste,** *n.* One who plays or is skilled at cup-and-ball.

bile [bil], *n.f.* Bile, spleen, gall; (*fig.*) anger. *Décharger sa bile,* to vent one's anger; *échauffer la bile à quelqu'un,* to provoke someone's anger; *se faire de la bile,* or (*pop.*) *se biler,* to worry. **bileux,** *a.* (*fem.* **bileuse**) (*pop.*) Easily worried. **biliaire,** *a.* (*Med.*) Biliary. **bilieux,** *a.* (*fem.* **bilieuse**) Bilious; (*fig.*) choleric, passionate, angry. *Au teint bilieux,* bilious looking.—*n.* A morose or choleric person.

bilingue [bi'lɛ̃:g], *a.* Bilingual. **bilinguisme,** *n.m.* Bilingualism.

bilitère [bili'tɛ:r], *a.* Word of two letters, as *la, tu.*

billard [bi'ja:r], *n.m.* Billiards; billiard-table; billiard-room. *Monter sur le billard* (*slang*), to lie on the operating table. **billardier,** *n.m.* Billiard-table maker.

bille [bi:j], *n.f.* Billiard-ball; marble, taw; log, unworked piece of timber, billet; (*colloq.*

head, noddle. *Roulement à billes*, ball-bearings.

billebarrer [bijbɑ're], *v.t.* To streak or chequer with ill-assorted colours.

billebaude [bij'bo:d], *n.f.* Hurly-burly, confusion. *À la billebaude*, in confusion, irregularly; *feu de billebaude*, independent firing.

billet [bi'jɛ], *n.m.* Note, missive; bill, hand-bill; ticket, lottery-ticket; promissory note; billet (for quartering soldiers); written or printed circular announcing a birth, marriage, or death. *Billet de banque*, bank-note, *(Am.)* bank-bill; *billet à ordre*, bill payable to order; *billet au porteur*, bill to bearer; *billet à vue*, bill payable at sight; *billet blanc*, a blank bill; *billet d'aller*, single ticket; *billet d'aller et retour*, return ticket; *billet d'abonnement*, season ticket; *billet circulaire*, tourist ticket; *billet de complaisance*, accommodation bill; *billet de faveur*, complimentary ticket (for a theatre); *billet de logement*, billet; *billet d'entrée*, entrance-ticket; *billet de santé*, bill of health; *billet doux*, love-letter; *billet échu*, bill due; *billet payable à présentation*, bill payable on demand; *billet simple*, IOU; *(slang) je vous fous mon billet que*, you may take my word for it.

billette (1) [bi'jet], *n.f.* Notice to pay toll; receipt given by the *douane*.

billette (2) [bi'jet], *n.f.* Billet (of firewood etc.); *(Arch. and Her.)* billet.

billevesée [bilvə'ze], *n.f.* Idle story, stuff, nonsense, bunkum.

billion [bi'ljɔ̃], *n.m.* (since 1948=1 followed by twelve ciphers), billion, one million million(s); *(Am.)* trillion.

billon (1) [bi'jɔ̃], *n.m.* *Copper money containing a small amount of silver, base coin; *Monnaie de billon*, copper or nickel coinage.

billon (2) [bi'jɔ̃], *n.m.* Ridge thrown up by plough. **billonner**, *v.t.*, *v.i.* To ridge, to rafter.

billot [bi'jo], *n.m.* Block, headsman's block; clog (for animals); stock (of anvil).

bilobé [bilɔ'be], *a. (fem. -ée)* Bilobate.

biloculaire [bilɔky'lɛ:r], *a. (Bot.)* Bilocular.

bimane [bi'man], *a.* Bimanous.—*n.m.* A bimanous animal.

bimarginé [bimarʒi'ne], *a. (fem. bimarginée)* Having a double margin (of shells etc.).

bimbelot [bɛ̃'blo], *n.m.* Plaything, toy, bauble; cheap knick-knack, trinket. **bimbeloterie**, *n.f.* Toy and cheap articles, knick-knack trade. **bimbelotier**, *n.m.* Dealer in such goods.

bimensuel [bimɑ̃'sɥɛl], *a. (fem. bimensuelle)* Twice monthly, fortnightly.

bimestre [bi'mestr], *n.m.* Happening, published, etc., every two months; lasting two months. **bimestriel**, *a. (fem. bimestrielle)* Produced or published every two months.

bimétallique [bimeta'lik], *a.* Bimetallic.

bimétallisme, *n.m.* Bimetallism. **bimétalliste**, *a.* Pertaining to this.—*n.m.* Bimetallist.

bimoteur [bimɔ'tœ:r], *a. and n.* Two-engined (plane).

binage [bi'na:ʒ], *n.m. (Agric.)* Second dressing; *(Eccles.)* saying mass twice on the same day.

binaire [bi'nɛ:r], *a.* Binary.

binard or **binart** [bi'na:r], *n.m.* Four-wheeled trolley for carrying stones.

bine [bin], *n.f.* Hoe.

biner [bi'ne], *v.t. (Agric.)* To dig again; to hoe. —*v.i. (Eccles.)* To say two masses the same day.

binervé [binɛr've], *a. (fem. binervée) (Bot.)* Binervate.

binet [bi'nɛ], *n.m.* Save-all (for using up candle-ends).

binette [bi'net], *n.f.* Hoe; *(colloq.)* face, phiz. *Quelle binette!* what a face!

bineur [bi'nœ:r], *n.m.*, or **bineuse**, *n.f.* Hoer.

biniou [bi'nju], *n.m.* Breton bagpipe.

binoche [bi'nɔʃ], *n.f.* Two-pronged hoe; **binochon**, *n.m.* A small *binoche*.

binocle [bi'nɔkl], *n.m.* Lorgnette, pince-nez, binocle. **binoculaire**, *a.* Binocular.

binoir [BINOT].

binôme [bi'no:m], *n.m. (Alg.)* Binomial.

binot [bi'no], *n.m.* Light plough, cultivator (for working the surface of the soil). **binotage**, *n.m.* Dressing (of the soil) with this. **binoter**, *v.t.* To work (the soil) with a *binot*.

bioculaire [BINOCULAIRE].

biochimie [biɔʃi'mi], *n.f.* Biochemistry.

biodynamique [biɔdina'mik], *n.f.* Biodynamics.

biogénèse [biɔʒe'nɛ:z], *n.f.* Biogenesis. **biogénétique**, *a.* Biogenetic.

biographe [biɔ'graf], *n.m.* Biographer. **biographie**, *n.f.* Biography. **biographique**, *a.* Biographical.

biologie [biɔlɔ'ʒi], *n.f.* Biology. **biologique**, *a.* Biological. **biologiste** or **biologue**, *n.m.* Biologist.

biométrique [biɔme'trik] or **biométrie**, *n.f.* Biometry.

bion [bjɔ̃], *n.m.* Sucker, shoot.

bioxyde [biɔk'sid], *n.m.* Dioxide.

biparti [bipar'ti] or **bipartite**, *a.* Bipartite. *Un accord bipartite*, an agreement between two parties. **bipartition**, *n.f.* Bipartition.

bipède [bi'pɛd], *a.* and *n.* Biped. *Bipède antérieur*, fore limbs of a horse; *bipède postérieur*, hind limbs.

bipenne [bi'pɛn], *a. (Zool.)* Bipennate.

biplace [bi'plas], *n.m.* Two-seater (plane).

biplan [bi'plɑ̃], *n.m.* Biplane.

bipolaire [bipɔ'lɛ:r], *a.* Bipolar.

biquadratique [bikwadra'tik], *a. (Alg.)* Biquadratic (equation).

bique [bik], *n.f.* She-goat; *(colloq.)* nag; jade. **biquet** [bi'kɛ], *n.m.* Kid; assay-scales. **biqueter**, *v.i.* To kid (of a she-goat). **biquette**, *n.f.* Kid; she-kid.

biquotidien [bikɔti'djɛ̃], *a.m. (fem. -ienne)* Happening or issued twice a day.

birbe [birb], *n.m. (colloq.)* Old man. *Un vieux birbe*, an old fogy.

biréacteur [bireak'tœ:r], *n.m.* Two-engined jet-plane.

biréfringence [birefrɛ̃'ʒɑ̃:s], *n.f. (Opt.)* Double-refraction. **biréfringent**, *a. (fem. -ente)* Doubly-refractive.

birème [bi'rɛ:m], *n.f.* Bireme.

biribi [biri'bi], *n.m.* A game of chance played with numbered balls and a board with corresponding numbers; *(slang)* disciplinary companies barracked in Algeria (a sort of military hard labour).

birloir [bir'lwa:r], *n.m.* Window-catch.

Birmanie [birma'ni], *f.* Burma.

bis (1) [bi], *a. (fem. bise* (1)*)* Brown; tawny,

swarthy. *Changer son pain blanc en pain bis*, to change for the worse; *du pain bis*, brown bread.

bis (2) [biːs], *adv.* Twice; encore. *Crier bis*, to encore; *le numéro 9 bis*, number 9a.

bisaïeul [biza'jœl], *n.m.* Great-grandfather.

bisaïeule, *n.f.* Great-grandmother.

bisaille [bi'zaːj], *n.f.* Coarse flour, whole meal; mixture of grey peas and vetches (for feeding poultry).

bisannuel [biza'nɥɛl], *a.* (*fem.* **-elle**) (*Bot.*) Biennial.

bisbille [biz'biːj], *n.f.* Petty quarrel, tiff, bickering.

*****biscaïen** (1) [biska'jɛ̃], *n.m.* Long-barrelled musket; large iron bullet.

*****biscaïen** (2) or **biscayen** [biska'jɛ̃], *a.* and *n.* (*fem.* **biscaïenne** or **biscayenne**) Native of or belonging to Biscay.

Biscaye [bis'kaj], *f.* Biscay. *La Mer* or *Le Golfe de Biscaye*, the Bay of Biscay.

bischof [BICHOF].

biscornu [biskɔr'ny], *a.* (*fem.* **biscornue**) Two-horned; (*fig.*) outlandish, odd, queer.

biscotin [biskɔ'tɛ̃], *n.m.* Small, hard, crisp biscuit. **biscotte,** *n.f.* Rusk.

biscuit [bis'kɥi], *n.m.* Biscuit; pastry made with flour, eggs, and sugar; (*Am.*) cracker; unglazed porcelain. *Biscuit à la cuiller*, sponge-finger; *biscuit de Savoie*, sponge cake; *s'embarquer sans biscuit*, (*prov.*) to go to sea without biscuit, (*fig.*) to undertake something without due precautions. **biscuité,** *a.* Applied to bread baked longer than usual, for the use of soldiers. **biscuiter,** *v.t.* To give porcelain its first firing (before the glaze). **biscuiterie,** *n.f.* Biscuit-factory, biscuit-trade.

bise (1) [BIS (1)].

bise (2) [biːz], *n.f.* Dry and cold north wind; (*colloq.*) kiss.

biseau [bi'zo], *n.m.* Bevel, chamfer; bevelling tool; (*Print.*) side-stick, foot-stick; crust of the slash in a loaf. **biseautage,** *n.m.* Bevelling. **biseauter,** *v.t.* To bevel; to mark (cards) with a view to cheating. *Cartes biseautées*, corner-bent cards. **biseauteur,** *n.m.* (*fem.* **biseauteuse**) One who cheats at cards by this means; beveller. **biseautoir,** *n.m.* Bevelling tool or machine.

biser [bi'ze], *v.i.* To spoil, to turn black, to get brown (of seeds). *v.t.* (*colloq.*) To kiss; to dye (a stuff) over again.

biset [bi'zɛ], *n.m.* Rock-dove.

bisette [bi'zɛt], *n.f.* Footing lace; sea-duck.

bismuth [biz'myt], *n.m.* Bismuth.

bison [bi'zɔ̃], *n.m.* Bison, buffalo.

bisonne [bi'zɔn], *n.f.* Grey cloth used for lining book-binding.

bisquain or **bisquin** [bis'kɛ̃], *n.m.* Sheepskin with the wool on.

bisque [bisk], *n.f.* Soup made of crayfish, chicken or game, fish, etc.; (*colloq.*) ill-humour, spite. **bisquer,** *v.i.* (*colloq.*) To be vexed or riled. *Faire bisquer*, (*colloq.*) to rile.

bisquin [BISQUAIN].

bisquine [bis'kin] or **besquine,** *n.f.* Fishing-smack.

bissac [bi'sak], *n.m.* Double wallet, sack or bag, haversack. *Avoir plus d'un tour dans son bissac*, to know many tricks, to be full of expedients.

bisse [bis], *n.f.* (*Her.*) Serpent erect.

bissecter [bisɛk'te], *v.t.* To bisect. **bissecteur,** *a.* (*fem.* **-trice**) Bisecting.—*n.f.* Bisector. **bissection,** *n.f.* Bisection.

bisser [bi'se], *v.t.* To encore.

bissextile [bisɛks'til], *a.* *Année bissextile*, leap-year.

bissexué [bisɛk'sɥe] (*fem.* **-ée**) or **bissexuel,** *a.* (*fem.* **-elle**) (*Bot.*) Bisexual.

bistoquet [bistɔ'kɛ], *n.m.* The cat in the game of tipcat.

bistorte [bis'tɔrt], *n.f.* (*Bot.*) Bistort, snake-weed.

bistortier [bistɔr'tje], *n.m.* Druggist's pestle.

bistouille [bis'tuj], *n.f.* (*N. dialect*) A blend of hot coffee and (low) alcohol.

bistouri [bistu'ri], *n.m.* Bistoury, lancet.

bistournage [bistur'naːʒ], *n.m.* Castration (of the ox, sheep, etc.) by torsion of the testicular cord.

bistourner [bistur'ne], *v.t.* To twist, to distort; to castrate [*see* BISTOURNAGE].

bistre [bistr], *n.m.* Bistre, sepia.—*a.* Of the colour of bistre; swarthy, dusky, tawny. **bistrer,** *v.t.* To make bistre-coloured. *Teint bistré*, swarthy complexion.

bistro or **bistrot** [bis'tro], *n.m.* (*slang*) Pub.

bisulce or **bisulque** [bi'zylk], *a.* (*Zool.*) Bisulcate, cloven-footed. *n.m.pl.* Ruminants.

bisulfate [bisyl'fat], *n.m.* Bisulphate.

bisulfite [bisyl'fit], *n.m.* Bisulphite, acid sulphite.

bisulfure [bisyl'fyr], *n.m.* Disulphide, bisulphide.

bitord [bi'tɔːr], *n.m.* Spun-yarn.

bitte [bit], *n.f.* (*Naut.*) Bitt. **bitter** (1), *v.t.* To bitt (a cable).

bitter (2) [bi'tɛr], *n.m.* Bitter alcoholic drink.

bitton [bi'tɔ̃], *n.m.* Small bitt, timber-head.

bitture or **biture,** *n.f.* Turn of rope round a bitt, bitter-end. (*slang*) *Prendre une biture*, to get drunk.

bitumage [bity'maːʒ], *n.m.* The act or process of bituming.

bitume [bi'tym], *n.m.* Bitumen. **bitumier,** *n.m.* One who asphalts paths etc. **bitumier,** *v.t.* To bitume; to asphalt. **bitumineux** or **bitumeux,** *a.* Bituminous.

biture [BITTURE].

bivalent [biva'lɑ̃], *a.* Divalent, bivalent.

bivalve [bi'valv], *a.* Bivalvular.—*n.m.* Bivalve. **bivalvulaire,** *a.* Bivalvular.

bivouac [bi'vwak], *n.m.* Bivouac. **bivouaquer,** *v.i.* To bivouac.

bizarre [bi'zaːr], *a.* Queer, strange, whimsical, bizarre. **bizarrement,** *adv.* Oddly, queerly, whimsically. **bizarrerie,** *n.f.* Singularity, oddness; caprice, whim.

bizut or **bizuth** [bi'zy], *n.m.* (*sch. slang*) Freshman.

blackboulage [blakbu'laːʒ], *n.m.* Blackballing. **blackbouler,** *v.t.* To blackball.

black-out [blak'aut], *n.m.* Black-out.

blafard [bla'faːr], *a.* (*fem.* **-arde**) Pale, wan, livid. *Lumière blafarde*, pale or wan light.

blague [blag], *n.f.* Tobacco pouch; (*slang*) chaff, humbug, hoax, fib; trick, practical joke. *Blague à part*, (*fam.*) honestly; *faire une blague à quelqu'un*, to play a trick on someone; *la bonne blague!* what a joke! *sans blague!* you don't say! **blaguer,** *v.i.* To talk chaff, to hoax, to humbug.

blagueur [bla'gœːr], *n.m.* (*fem.* **-euse**) Wag, joker, humbug.

blair [blɛːr], *n.m.* (*slang*) Nose, schnozzle.

blairer, *v.* To bear, to stomach.

blaireau [blɛ'ro], *n.m.* Badger; shaving-brush; badger-hair brush. **blaireauter**, *v.t.* (*colloq.*) To paint with excessive care; to soften or blend with the *blaireau*; to niggle at.

blâmable [blɑ'mabl], *a.* Blameworthy.

blâme [blɑːm], *n.m.* Blame; reproach, disapprobation, reprimand, disciplinary action. *Action digne de blâme*, blameworthy action; *donner le blâme à quelqu'un*, to blame someone; *infliger un blâme à quelqu'un*, to inflict a censure on someone; *rejeter le blâme sur*, to throw the blame on; *tout le blâme en tombe sur lui*, all the blame falls upon him. **blâmer**, *v.t.* To blame, to criticize; to censure, to reprimand. *On ne saurait le blâmer*, he cannot be blamed.

Blanc [blɑ̃], **le Cap**, *m.* Cape Blanco.

blanc [blɑ̃], *a.* (*fem.* **blanche** (2) [blɑ̃ːʃ]) White; hoar, hoary; (*Print.*) open (of type); clean; blank; (*fig.*) without effect. *Arme blanche* [ARME]; *blanc comme neige*, as white as snow; *carte blanche*, carte-blanche; *c'est bonnet blanc et blanc bonnet*, it is six of one and half a dozen of the other; *du linge blanc*, clean linen; *gelée blanche*, hoar frost; *le drapeau blanc*, the Bourbon standard; *guerre blanche*, war without hostilities; (*Parl.*) *livre blanc*, white paper; *mariage blanc*, non consummated marriage; *monnaie blanche*, silver money; *passer une nuit blanche*, to have a sleepless night; *montrer patte blanche*, to show one's credentials; *perte blanche*, leucorrhoea; *rouge soir et blanc matin, c'est la journée du pèlerin*, red sky at night shepherd's delight; *sauce blanche*, white sauce; *se faire blanc de son épée*, to clear oneself in a duel; *vers blancs*, blank verse; *vin blanc*, white wine.—*n.m.* White; blank; white powder for the face; white man; white stuff (muslin etc.); (*Billiards*) chalk. *Blanc de baleine*, spermaceti; *blanc de céruse*, ceruse; *blanc de chaux*, whitewash; *blanc de plomb*, white lead; *blanc d'Espagne*, whiting; *blanc de volaille*, breast of a fowl; *blanc d'œuf*, white of egg; *de but en blanc*, point-blank; *dire tantôt blanc, tantôt noir*, to say first one thing, then another; *en blanc*, left blank; *le blanc*, the target, the mark; *le blanc de l'œil*, the white of the eye; *ligne de blanc*, (*Print.*) white line; *chauffer à blanc*, to bring to white heat, (*fig.*) to heat up (a person); *magasin de blanc*, linen draper's shop; *saigner à blanc*, to bleed white; *tirer à blanc*, to shoot with blank ammunition; *tirage en blanc*, (*Print.*) working the white paper; *tirer en blanc*, (*Print.*) to work the white paper; *pour moi, un petit blanc*, mine is a glass of white wine.

blanc-bec [blɑ̃'bɛk], *n.m.* (*pl.* **blancs-becs**) Beardless youth, youngster; greenhorn; sucker.

blanc-bourgeois [blɑ̃buʀ'ʒwa], *n.m.* Best white flour.

blanchaille [blɑ̃'ʃɑːj], *n.f.* Whitebait.

blanchâtre [blɑ̃'ʃɑːtr], *a.* Whitish.

blanche (1) [blɑ̃ːʃ], *n.f.* (*Mus.*) Minim.

blanche (2) [BLANC].

blanche-queue [blɑ̃ʃ'kø], *n.f.* White-tailed eagle.

blanchet [blɑ̃'ʃɛ], *n.m.* White woollen stuff; piece of swan-skin used as strainer; (*Print.*) blanket.

blancheur [blɑ̃'ʃœːr], *n.f.* Whiteness; cleanliness; light; (*fig.*) purity, innocence.

blanchiment [blɑ̃ʃi'mɑ̃], *n.m.* Whitening, bleaching, blanching, washing. *Le blanchiment de l'argent*, the washing of silver.

blanchir [blɑ̃'ʃiːr], *v.t.* To whiten, to make white; to whitewash; to wash, to bleach, to clean; to blanch; to scald (fruit, greens, etc.); (*fig.*) to exonerate, to exculpate. *Blanchir à neuf*, to clear-starch; *blanchir des toiles*, to bleach linen; *blanchir du linge*, to wash linen; *blanchir un ais*, to plane a board; *blanchir un plafond*, to whitewash a ceiling; *on me blanchit*, they do my laundry for me.—*v.i.* To whiten, to grow white; to foam. *Il commence à blanchir*, he is getting grey; *tête de fou ne blanchit jamais*, a fool's head is never grey. **se blanchir**, *v.r.* To whiten, to wash; to soil oneself with white paint etc.

blanchis or **blanchi** [blɑ̃'ʃi], *n.m.* Blaze (on trees to be felled).

blanchissage [blɑ̃ʃi'saːʒ], *n.m.* Washing; refining (of sugar etc.). *Blanchissage de fin*, fine laundering; *note de blanchissage*, laundry list.

blanchissant [blɑ̃ʃi'sɑ̃], *a.* (*fem.* **-ante**) That whitens or grows white; foaming.

blanchissement [blɑ̃ʃis'mɑ̃], *n.m.* Whitening.

blanchisserie [blɑ̃ʃis'ri], *n.f.* Laundry, washhouse. **blanchisseur**, *n.m.* Laundryman. **blanchisseuse**, *n.f.* Washerwoman; laundress. *Blanchisseuse de fin*, clear-starcher.

blanchoyer [blɑ̃ʃwa'je], *v.i.* To grow whitish.

blanc-manger [blɑ̃mɑ̃'ʒe], *n.m.* (*pl.* **blancs-mangers**) Blancmange.

blanc-poudré [blɑ̃pu'dre], *a.* (*fem.* **blanc-poudrée**) Patched, dappled, or spotted with white.—*n.m.* (*used only in pl.*) Hair white in places.

blanc-seing [blɑ̃'sɛ̃], *n.m.* (*pl.* **blancs-seings**) Signature to a blank (document, cheque, etc.) *Donner blanc-seing*, to give full power.

blandice [blɑ̃'dis], *n.f.* Blandishment.

blanquette [blɑ̃'kɛt], *n.f.* A variety of white grapes; a variety of pear with white skin; ragoût with white sauce; a light, sparkling white wine from S. France. *Blanquette de veau*, veal stewed in white sauce.

blasé [blɑ'ze], *a.* (*fem.* **blasée**) Blasé. **blasement**, *n.m.* State of being blasé.

blaser [blɑ'ze], *v.t.* To blunt, to cloy, to sicken, to surfeit. *Il est blasé sur les plaisirs*, he has lost all sense of enjoyment; *il est blasé sur tout*, he is sick of everything. **se blaser**, *v.r.* To be palled or surfeited; to be tired (of).

blason [blɑ'zɔ̃], *n.m.* Coat of arms; blazon; heraldry, blazonry. *Ternir son blason*, (*fig.*) to blot one's escutcheon. **blasonnement**, *n.m.* Blazoning; interpretation of blazonry. **blasonner**, *v.t.* To blazon; to interpret (coats of arms). **blasonneur**, *a.* (*fem.* **-euse**) That blazons.—*n.* Blazoner.

blasphémateur [blasfema'tœːr], *n.m.* (*fem.* **-trice**) Blasphemer. **blasphématoire**, *a.* Blasphemous.

blasphème [blas'fɛːm], *n.m.* Blasphemy.

blasphémer, *v.t.* and *i.* To blaspheme, to curse.

blaste [blast], *n.m.* (*Bot.*) Part of an embryo that develops on germination.
blastème [blas'tɛːm], *n.m.* Blastema. **blastoderme**, *n.m.* Blastoderm. **blastodermique**, *a.* Blastodermic. **blastogénèse**, *n.f.* Blastogenesis.
***blatier** [bla'tje], *n.m.* Corn-chandler; dealer in corn.
blatte [blat], *n.f.* Cockroach, black-beetle.
blaude [bloːd], *n.f.* (*dial.*) Smock-frock (of peasant).
blavet [bla'vɛ], *n.m.* (*dial.*) A sort of agaric.
blé [ble], *n.m.* Corn, wheat. *Blé barbu*, bearded wheat; *blé de Turquie*, Indian corn, maize; *blé froment*, wheat; *blé noir* or *blé sarrasin*, buckwheat; *du blé en herbe*, corn in the blade; *halle au blé*, corn-exchange; *manger son blé en herbe*, to spend one's money before one has it; *les grands blés*, wheat and rye; *les petits blés*, oats and barley.
blèche or **blaiche** [blɛːʃ], *a.* Weak in character; (*slang*) bad, ugly.
bled [bled], *n.m.* (*N. Afric. word*) (*Mil.*) Waste, rough country where fighting is frequent; the heart of the country, the backwoods. *Vivre dans le bled*, to live in an out-of-the-way place. **blédard**, *n.m.* Officer or soldier who lives in the *bled*.
bleime [blɛːm], *n.f.* Sand-crack, irritation on horse's hoof.
blême [blem], *a.* Sallow, pale; wan; ghastly. **blêmir**, *v.i.* To turn or grow pale. **blêmissement**, *n.m.* Turning pale; paleness.
blende [blɛːd], *n.f.* (*Min.*) Blende, sulphide of zinc.
blennie [blɛ'ni], *n.f.* (*Ichth.*) Blenny.
blennorragie [blɛnɔra'ʒi], *n.f.* Gonorrhoea.
blépharite [blefa'rit], *n.f.* Blepharitis.
blèse [blɛːz], *a.* Given to lisping.—*n.* One who lisps. **blèsement**, *n.m.* Lisping.
bléser [ble'ze], *v.i.* To lisp. **blésité**, *n.f.* Lisping.
blessant [blɛ'sɑ̃], *a.* (*fem.* **blessante**) Wounding, offensive, mortifying.
blessé [blɛ'se], *a.* (*fem.* **blessée**) Wounded; (*fig.*) injured, offended, outraged.
blesser [blɛ'se], *v.t.* To wound, to hurt; to offend, to injure; to wring, to shock, to gall. *Blesser la vue*, to offend the eye; *blesser les convenances*, to offend against propriety; *blesser les oreilles chastes*, to offend chaste ears; *blesser l'honneur de quelqu'un*, to wound someone's honour; *cela me blesse*, that hurts me; *cette phrase blesse l'oreille*, that sentence grates upon the ear; *mes souliers me blessent*, my shoes pinch me. **se blesser**, *v.r.* To hurt oneself; (*fig.*) to take offence.
blessure [blɛ'syːr], *n.f.* Wound, hurt, injury; offence, pang. *Coups et blessures*, assault and battery; *les blessures faites à l'honneur*, the wounds inflicted upon one's honour.
blet [blɛ], *a.* (*fem.* **blette** (1)) Over-ripe, sleepy (of fruit). *Poire blette*, sleepy pear.
blète or **blette** (2) [blɛt], *n.f.* Strawberry-spinach.
blettir [blɛ'tiːr], *v.i.* To become over-ripe or sleepy (of fruit). **blettissement**, *n.m.*, or **blettissure**, *n.f.* Becoming over-ripe or sleepy.
bleu [blø], *a.* (*fem.* **bleue**) Blue, livid, black and blue (as a bruise); (*fig.*) amazed. *Avoir les yeux bleus*, to be blue-eyed; *bas-bleu*, blue-

stocking; *conte bleu*, fairy tale; *cordon bleu*, first-rate cook. *Être dans une colère bleue*, to be in a towering rage; *peur bleue*, blue funk; *j'en suis resté bleu*, I stood flabbergasted.—*n.m.* Blue, blueness; washing-blue; Republican soldier (during the Revolution); conscript, recruit, tyro, greenhorn, novice; (*C*) Conservative, Tory. *Bleu d'azur*, smalt; *bleu de ciel*, sky blue; *bleu de cobalt*, cobalt blue; *bleu de Prusse*, Prussian blue; *petit bleu*, light bluish claret; telegram; *l'affaire sera passée au bleu*, the thing will be concealed; *l'argent a passé au bleu*, the money has vanished; *il n'y a vu que du bleu*, he was unaware of what was going on, he did not cotton on.
bleuâtre [blø'aːtr], *a.* Bluish, somewhat blue.
bleuet, *n.m.* [BLEUET].
bleuir [blø'iːr], *v.t.* To make blue, to blue (in washing).—*v.i.* To become blue. **bleuissage**, *n.m.* Blueing. ***bleuissement**, *n.m.* Turning blue.
bleusaille [blø'zaj], *n.f.* (*Mil.* slang) All the recruits; a rookie.
bleutage [blø'taːʒ], *n.m.* Slight tinge of blue. **bleuté**, *a.* (*fem.* **bleutée**) Tinged with blue, bluish.
bleuter [blø'te], *v.t.* To give a blue tinge to.
blin, [blɛ̃], *n.m.* Paving rammer; (*Naut.*) clamp.
blindage [blɛ̃'daːʒ], *n.m.* Protecting with *blindes*; iron-plating, armour-plating.
blinde [blɛ̃ːd], *n.f.* (*usually in pl.*) (*Fort.*) Piece of timber for supporting fascines etc. in trenches etc.
blindé [blɛ̃'de], *a.* (*fem.* **-ée**) Armoured, screened; (*slang*) drunk. *Lampe blindée*, screened lamp; *train blindé*, armoured train.—*n.m. pl. Les blindés*, the armour.
blinder, *v.t.* To furnish (a trench, mine, etc.) with supports; to armour-plate (a ship, fort, etc.).
blizzard [bli'zaːr], *n.m.* Blizzard.
bloc [blɔk], *n.m.* Block, lump, the whole lot; (*slang*) clink, guard-room, prison, arrest, imprisonment. *Bloc à dessin*, drawing-block; *gonfler à bloc*, to inflate to the maximum; (*fig.*) *être gonflé à bloc*, to be in high spirits, in great form; *faire bloc contre*, to unite against; *hisser un pavillon à bloc*, to hoist a flag to the mast-head.
blocage (1) [blɔ'kaːʒ], *n.m.* Blockading; blocking; block (of traffic); obstruction; (*Fin.*) freezing. *Blocage des prix*, price freeze.
blocage (2) [blɔ'kaːʒ], *n.m.* Rubble (used for building); (*Print.*) turned letter (used in place of those temporarily unavailable).
blocaille [blɔ'kaːj], *n.f.* Rubble-stone; pieces of brick.
blockhaus [blɔ'koːs], *n.m. inv.* Blockhouse; (*Naut.*) conning-tower.
bloc-note(s) [blɔk'nɔt], *n.m.* Writing pad.
blocus [blɔ'kyːs], *n.m. inv.* Blockade. *Le blocus continental*, the (Napoleonic) continental system. *Lever le blocus*, to raise the blockade.
blond [blɔ̃], *a.* (*fem.* **blonde**) Blond, fair, light-complexioned. *Des cheveux blonds*, light hair; *bière blonde*, pale ale.—*n.* Blond ardent, auburn; *blond cendré*, light dull yellow, ash-blond; *blond doré*, golden.—*n.f.* (*C*) Sweetheart. *Courtiser la brune et la blonde*, to make love to a number of women.

blondasse, *a.* Sickly blond, flaxen haired, light but dull in complexion. **blondeur**, *n.f.* Blondness.

blondin [blɔ̃'dɛ̃], *a.* (*fem.* **blondine**) Fair-haired.—*n.* A fair-haired child.—*n.m.* Spark, beau. *Un beau blondin*, a fine young spark.

blondinet [blɔ̃di'nɛ], *n.m.* (*fem.* **blondinette**) Fair-haired child.

blondir [blɔ̃'diːr], *v.i.* To grow blond, fair, yellow, or golden. **se blondir**, *v.r.* To lighten the shade of one's hair. **blondissant**, *a.* (*fem.* **blondissante**) Growing yellow or golden (of corn etc.).

blondoiement [blɔ̃dwa'mɑ̃], *n.m.* Golden hue, yellow tinge. **blondoyer**, *v.i.* To have golden lights, a golden tinge, a golden gleam.

bloquer [blɔ'ke], *v.t.* To block up, to fill up (cavities in walls) with mortar; (*Print.*) to put a turned letter in (the place of one temporarily missing); (*Billiards*) to hole (a ball); (*Mil.*) to blockade, to invest (a fortress); (*Fin.*) to freeze (credit, account, etc.); to stop (a train etc.) by putting on the brakes. **se bloquer**, to jam, to get jammed.

bloquet [blɔ'ke], *n.m.* Bobbin (of lace-maker).

bloquette [blɔ'ket], *n.f.* (*sch.*) Hole in the ground against a wall for playing marbles; the game itself.

bloqueur [blɔ'kœːr], *n.m.* (*fem.* **-euse**) One who blocks, puts on brakes, blockades, etc.

blottir (se) [blɔ'tiːr], *v.r.* To curl up, to snuggle, to huddle; to cower, to crouch.

blouse (1) [bluːz], *n.f.* Smock-frock; tunic; blouse; pinafore; overall.

*blouse (2) [bluːz], *n.f.* Pocket (of a billiard-table).

blouser [blu'ze], *v.t.* *To hole or pocket (at billiards); (*fig.*) to mislead, to cheat.—*v.i.* To puff out like a blouse. *Faire blouser*, to give the swelling shape of a blouse. **se blouser**, *v.r.* To pocket one's own ball; (*fig.*) to blunder; to bark up the wrong tree.

blouson [blu'zɔ̃], *n.m.* Battledress blouse; lumber-jacket, wind-cheater. *Blouson noir*, teddy boy.

bluet [bly'ɛ] or **bleuet** [blœ'ɛ], *n.m.* Blue-bottle, corn-flower; (*C*) blueberry.

bluette [bly'ɛt], *n.f.* Spark, flake of fire; (*fig.*) witty sally; literary trifle, novelette.

bluff [blœf], *n.m.* Bluff. **bluffer**, *v.t.* To bluff.

blutage [bly'taːʒ], *n.m.* Bolting, sifting (of flour). **bluteau, blutoir**, *n.m.* A sort of screen or sieve used in bolting-mill. **bluter**, *v.t.* To bolt, to sift (meal etc.). **bluterie**, *n.f.* Bolting-room; bolting-apparatus. **bluteur**, *n.m.* Workman in bolting-mill.

boa [bɔ'a], *n.m.* Boa (snake); boa (of feathers).

Boadicée [bɔadi'se], *f.* Boadicea, Boudicca.

bobard [bɔ'baːr], *n.m.* (*colloq.*) Lie, tall story.

bobèche [bɔ'bɛʃ], *n.f.* Socket (of a candle-stick); sconce. **bobéchon**, *n.m.* Candlestick or sconce with pointed end (for sticking in walls etc.).

bobinage [bɔbi'naːʒ], *n.m.* Winding (thread etc.) on to bobbins.

bobine [bɔ'bin], *n.f.* Bobbin, spool, reel; (*Cine.*) reel; (*fig.*) a grotesque figure. *Bobine de Ruhmkorff*, Ruhmkorff coil, sparking coil; *bobine d'induction*, induction-coil. **bobiner**, *v.t.* To wind on a bobbin, to spool.

bobinette [bɔbi'nɛt], *n.f.* Wooden latch.

bobineur [bɔbi'nœːr], *n.m.* (*fem.* **bobineuse**)

Winder.—*n.f.* Winding-machine. **bobinoir**, *n.m.* Winding-mechanism, winder.

bobo [bɔ'bo], *n.m.* (*Childish*) Hurt, sore, bump. *Avoir bobo* or *du bobo*, to have a slight pain, sore, etc; *faire bobo*, to hurt.

bocage [bɔ'kaːʒ], *n.m.* Copse, grove, bosket; a wooded region. **bocager**, *a.* (*fem.* **-ère**) Of groves or woodlands; woody, bosky, shady.

bocal [bɔ'kal], *n.m.* (*pl.* **-aux**) Druggist's short-necked bottle; carboy; glass jar, fish-globe.

bocard [bɔ'kaːr], *n.m.* (*Metal.*) Stamper, crushing-mill. **bocardage**, *n.m.* Crushing, pounding, stamping. **bocarder**, *v.t.* To stamp, to pound.

Boccace [bɔ'kas], *m.* Boccaccio.

boche [bɔʃ], *n.m.* (aphaeresis of *Alboche*) (*pej.*) German, Jerry.

bock [bɔk], *n.m.* Bock (beer); enema, douche.

boëtte, boitte [bwet], *n.f.* Bait.

bœuf [bœf], *n.m.* (*pl.* **bœufs** [bø]) Ox; beef; cooked meat; (*fig.*) lout, bumpkin. *Accoupler* or *découpler les bœufs*, to yoke *or* to unyoke oxen; *avoir un bœuf sur la langue*, to be paid to keep one's mouth shut; *du bœuf à la mode*, silverside beef; *gros comme un bœuf*, as big as an ox; *le bœuf gras*, the fatted ox, the prize ox; *mettre la charrue devant les bœufs*, to put the cart before the horse; *travailler comme un bœuf*, to work like a horse; *troupeau de bœufs*, drove of oxen.—*a.* (*slang*) Astounding, terrific, magnificent. *Un succès bœuf*, a tremendous success.

bog [bɔg], *n.m.* A card game similar to Pope Joan.

boghei or **boguet** [bɔ'gɛ], *n.m.* Light gig, buggy.

bogie [bɔ'ʒi] or **boggie** [bɔ'gi], *n.m.* Bogie (truck under locomotive etc.).

bogue [bɔg], *n.f.* Chestnut-bur; shovel for loading slop-cart.

boguet [BOGHEI].

Bohême [bɔ'ɛ:m], **la**, *f.* Bohemia.

bohème [bɔ'ɛ:m], *n.f.* Bohemianism, artistic underworld.—*n.* A Bohemian, person of careless, unconventional habits.—*a.* Bohemian. **bohémien**, *a.* and *n.* (*fem.* **-ienne**) A Bohemian; a gipsy.

boïard [BOYARD].

boire [bwaːr], *v.t. irr.* (*pres.p.* **buvant**, *p.p.* **bu**) To drink; to consume or waste on drink; to absorb; to drink in; to swallow (an insult etc.). *Boire le calice jusqu'à la lie*, to drain the cup to the dregs; *boire un affront*, to pocket an affront; *qui fait la folie, la boit*, as you brew, so you must drink.—*v.i.* To drink (to the health of someone); to tipple; to be drowned; to be puckered (of needle-work). *À boire*, some drink; *boire à la bouteille*, to drink from the bottle; *boire à la ronde*, to empty glasses all round; *boire à la santé de quelqu'un*, to drink someone's health; *boire à longs traits*, to drink long draughts; *boire comme un trou*, to drink like a fish; *boire sec*, to drink (whisky etc.) neat; *boire un coup*, to have a drink; *ce n'est pas la mer à boire*, that's no difficult matter; *ce papier boit*, this paper blots; *c'est un homme qui boit*, he is a drunkard; *le vin est tiré, il faut le boire*, in for a penny, in for a pound; *qui a bu, boira*, once a crook, always a crook.—*n.m.* Drink; drinking. *Le boire et le manger*, food and drink;

(*fig.*) *il en a perdu le boire et le manger*, he is off his head with it.

bois [bwɑ], *n.m.* A wood or forest; wood, timber; wooden part or object, especially a handle, stick, or pole (of a weapon, flag, etc.); horns (of a deer etc.). *Bois blanc*, deal; (*C*) linden, basswood *or* whitewood; *bois d'ébène*, (*colloq.*) black ivory, *i.e.* negroes; *bois de charpente*, timber, straight timber; *bois de chauffage*, firewood; *bois de fer*, ironwood; *bois des îles*, West Indian hardwood; (*C*) *bois de plomb*, leatherwood; (*C*) *bois de poêle*, stove wood, firewood; *bois de rose*, rosewood; *bois de sciage*, sawn timber; (*C*) *bois d'original*, high cranberry; (*C*) *bois dur*, ironwood; (*C*) *bois franc*, hardwood; (*C*) *bois rond*, unhewn timbers; *bois sent-bon*, bog myrtle; *faire du bois*, to get wood; *gravure sur bois*, wood-engraving; *homme des bois*, (*colloq.*) orang-outang; *il est du bois dont on fait les flûtes*, he will chime in with anything; *il ne sait plus de quel bois faire flèche*, he does not know which way to turn or what to be at; *je vais vous faire voir de quel bois je me chauffe!* you'll see what metal I am made of! *la faim chasse le loup du bois*, hunger will break through stone walls; *la lisière d'un bois*, the margin of a wood; *le fil du bois*, the grain of the wood; *on n'est pas de bois*, one is not a plaster saint; *touchons du bois!* touch wood! *trouver porte de bois*, to find no one at home; *un bois de haute futaie*, a wood of lofty trees; *un bois de lit*, bedstead; *un bois taillis*, a copse; *une voie de bois*, a load of wood; *un train de bois*, a float of wood; (*fam.*) *avoir la gueule de bois*, to have a hang-over; (*Av.*) *casser du bois*, to make a forced landing.—*n.m. pl.* (*Mus.*) The woodwind (instruments).

boisage [bwɑ'zaːʒ], *n.m.* Wood-work; timbering (of mines etc.); wainscotting.

(*C*) **bois-brûlé** [bwɑbry'le], *n.m.* Half-breed.

(*C*) **bois-debout** [bwɑ'dbu], *n.m.* Standing timber. *En bois-debout*, land that has never been cleared.

boisé [bwɑ'ze], *a.* Abounding with wood, wooded, well-timbered. *Chambre boisée*, wainscotted room.

boisement [bwaz'mɑ̃], *n.m.* Planting land with trees, plantation, timbering.

boiser [bwɑ'ze], *v.t.* To put woodwork to; to timber (a mine etc.); to wainscot; to plant with woods.

boiserie [bwaz'ri], *n.f.* Wainscot, wainscotting.

boiseur [bwɑ'zœːr], *n.m.* (*Mining*) Timberman.

boisseau [bwɑ'so], *n.m.* Bushel; chimney flue tile. **boisselage**, *n.m.* Corn-measuring. **boisselée**, *n.f.* A bushelful. **boisselier**, *n.m.* Bushel-maker, cooper. **boissellerie**, *n.f.* Cooperage, bushel-making.

boisson [bwɑ'sɔ̃], *n.f.* Drink; beverage; (*fig.*) drinking, drunkenness; (*C*) hard liquor. *Boisson forte*, strong drink, (*Am.*) liquor; *être adonné à la boisson*, to be addicted to drinking; *être pris de boisson*, to be intoxicated.

boîtard [bwɑ'taːr], *n.m.* (*Mech.*) Vertical floorbearing.

boite [bwat], *n.f.* Ripeness, maturity of wine; water passed through marc. **En boite*, matured (of wine).

boîte [bwat], *n.f.* Box; casket, caddy, chest; case (of a watch, rudder, etc.); (*Anat.*) cavity occupied by an organ; (*Pyrotech.*) bomb; (*colloq.*) shanty, poor sort of house; prison, place of slavery, drudgery, etc.; (*slang*) school; (*pop.*) mouth; (*Mil. slang*) guardroom. (*fam.*) *Boîte à bachot*, crammers; *boîte à feu*, stoke-hole; *boîte à lait*, milk-can; *boîte à malice*, jack-in-the-box, (*fig.*) (a person's) stock of mischief; *boîte à musique*, musical box; *boîte à ordures*, dust-bin, (*Am.*) ashcan; *boîte à poudre*, powder box; *boîte à savon*, soap-tray; *boîte à thé*, tea-caddy; *boîte aux lettres*, letter-box; *boîte à vapeur*, steamchest; *boîte de conserves*, tin, can; (*Motor.*) *boîte de vitesses*, gear-box; *boîte de montre*, watch-case; *boîte crânienne*, brain-pan; *boîte de nuit*, night-club; *dans les petites boîtes les bons onguents*, good things are packed in small parcels; *il a l'air de sortir d'une boîte*, he looks as if he had just come out of a bandbox; *mettre en boîte*, to box, to tin, to can, (*fig.*) to pull somebody's leg; (*pop.*) *ta boîte!* shut your big mouth!

boitement [bwat'mɑ̃], *n.m.* Halting, limping.

boiter [bwa'te], *v.i.* To limp, to halt, to walk lame; to be lame; to be halting or lacking (in anything). *Boiter d'un pied*, to walk lame of one foot; *en boitant*, limpingly. **boiterie**, *n.f.* Halting, limping (especially in animals).

boiteux [bwa'tø] *a.* (*fem.* **-euse**) Lame, halt, limping; halting; rickety, gimcrack (furniture). *Le Diable boiteux*, the Devil on two sticks, (*fig.*) a lame person; *attendre le boiteux*, to wait for news to be confirmed; *il ne faut pas clocher devant les boiteux*, you must not remind people of their infirmities; *raisonnement boiteux*, lame reasoning; *vers boiteux*, halting lines.—*n.* Lame man or woman.

boîtier (1) [bwɑ'tje], *n.m.* Surgeon's case of instruments; case (of a watch, an electric-torch).

boîtier (2) [bwɑ'tje], *n.m.* Box- or case-maker.

boitillement [bwatij'mɑ̃], *n.m.* Slight limping. **boitiller**, *v.i.* To hobble slightly.

boit-tout [bwa'tu], *n.m.* (*colloq.*) Wine-glass without a foot; (*fam.*) hard drinker, one who spends all his money in drink; (*dial.*) cesspool.

bol (1) [bɔl], *n.m.* (*Pharm.*) A large pill, bolus; (*Min.*) bole. *Bol d'Arménie*, Armenian bole; *bol alimentaire*, alimentary bolus.

bol (2) [bɔl], *n.m.* Bowl, basin; bowlful; finger-glass.

bolaire [bɔ'lɛːr], *a.* (*Min.*) Clayey, bolar.

bolchevik [bɔlʃe'vik], *n.m.* Bolshevik. **bolchevisme**, *n.m.* Bolshevism.

bolduc [bɔl'dyk], *n.m.* Coloured ribbon or tape for tying up parcels etc.

bolée [bɔ'le], *n.f.* Bowlful.

boléro [bɔle'ro], *n.m.* Bolero (dance and costume).

bolet [bɔ'lɛ], *n.m.* (*Bot.*) Boletus.

bolide [bɔ'lid], *n.m.* Bolide, aerolite. (*fig.*) *Filer comme un bolide*, to dash along.

bolivar [bɔli'vaːr], *n.m.* Tall bell-crowned hat as worn by Bolivar (*c.* 1820); (*fam.*) black tall hat.

Bolivie [bɔli'vi], *f.* Bolivia.

Bologne [bɔ'lɔɲ], *f.* Bologna.

bombance [bɔ̃'bã:s], *n.f.* Feasting, junketing. *Faire bombance*, to feast, to revel.

bombarde [bɔ̃'bard], *n.f.* Bombard, mortar; bomb-vessel; (*Mus.*) bombardon, an organ-stop.

bombardement [bɔ̃bardə'mã], *n.m.* Bombardment, shelling. *Bombardement aérien*, bombing-raid; *bombardement en piqué*, dive-bombing; (*Phys.*) *bombardement électronique*, bombardment of the electrons; (*Av.*) *avion de bombardement*, bomber.

bombarder [bɔ̃bar'de], *v.t.* To bombard, to bomb; (*fig.*) to overwhelm (with confetti, compliments, etc.). *Quartier bombardé*, bombed site; *bombarder de demandes*, to pester with requests; *bombarder quelqu'un président*, to pitchfork someone into a chairmanship.

bombardier [bɔ̃bar'dje], *n.m.* Bombardier; bomb-thrower, bomber.

bombardon [bɔ̃bar'dɔ̃], *n.m.* Bombardon.

bombe [bɔ̃:b], *n.f.* Bomb; confection in form of ball; (*colloq.*) feast. *Bombe atomique*, atom bomb; *bombe à retardement*, time-bomb; *bombe à hydrogène*, H-bomb; *bombe incendiaire*, incendiary bomb; *gare la bombe!* look out for squalls! *la bombe a crevé en l'air*, the bomb has burst in the air; *lâcher des bombes*, to drop bombs; *voûte à l'épreuve des bombes*, bomb-proof vault; *bombe glacée*, ice pudding; (*colloq.*) *faire la bombe*, to be on the razzle.

bombé [bɔ̃'be], *a.* (*fem.* **bombée**) Convex, arched; (*colloq.*) hump-backed. **bombement**, *n.m.* Convexity, swelling, bulge.

bomber [bɔ̃'be], *v.t.* To cause (something) to bulge, jut, swell out, arch, curve, or barrel (of roads), etc. *Bomber le torse*, to throw out one's chest; (*fig.*) to swagger.—*v.i.* To bulge, to jut out. **se bomber**, *v.r.* To bulge, (*slang* and *iron.*) to be deprived. *Tu peux te bomber*, you shall not have it.

bombonne [BONBONNE].

bombyx [bɔ̃'biks], *n.m.* (*Ent.*) Bombyx; silkworm.

bôme [bom], *n.m.* (*Naut.*) Spanker-boom.

bomerie [bɔm'ri], *n.f.* Bottomry.

bon (1) [bɔ̃], *a.* (*fem.* **bonne** (1)) Good; kind, favourable; fine, convenient, advantageous, profitable; proper; safe, solvent; witty, smart; clever, expert; well-executed, cleverly done, etc.; large, considerable, long, broad; easy, good-natured; (*iron.*) simple, credulous; rascally, abominable. *À bon vin point d'enseigne*, good wine needs no bush; *à la bonne heure!* good! well done! that's something like! *attendre une bonne heure*, to wait a full hour; *à quelque chose malheur est bon*, it's an ill wind that blows nobody good; *à quoi bon tant de peine?* what is the use of so much trouble? *avoir un bon rhume*, to have a bad cold; *bon!* good! indeed! *bon à boire*, good to drink; *bon an mal an*, taking one year with another; *bon à prendre*, worth taking; *bon marché*, cheap; *bonne année*, happy new year; *bonne foi*, plain dealing, good faith; *bonne nourriture*, wholesome food; *bon pour le service*, fit for duty; *bon sens*, common sense; *cela ne présage rien de bon*, that doesn't look too good; *c'est bon*, all right, very good; *c'est une bonne personne*, she is a good creature; *c'est une bonne tête*, he has a good head-piece; *de bon cœur*, heartily; *de bonne foi*, sincerely;

de bonne heure, early; *elle est bien bonne!* that's a good one! *en bon état*, sound; *être homme à bonnes fortunes*, to be a lady-killer; *faire bonne chère*, to live well; *faire bonne mine à mauvais jeu*, to put a good face upon matters; *il est encore de bonne heure*, it is still early; *il fait bon dans cette pièce*, this room is nice and warm; *il ne fait pas bon avoir affaire à lui*, it is dangerous to meddle with him; *il y va de bonne foi*, he plays fair and square; *la bonne société*, well-educated people; *les bons comptes font les bons amis*, short reckonings make long friends; *pour de bon*, for good and all; *prendre quelque chose en bonne part*, to take something in good part; *se donner du bon temps*, to divert oneself; *sentir bon*, to have a good smell; *si bon vous semble*, if you think fit; *son compte est bon*, he is in for it; *tenir bon*, to hold out, to stand fast; *tenez bon!* hold tight! *tout de bon*, in earnest; *tout lui est bon*, all is fish that comes to his net; *trouver bon*, to approve; *vous êtes bon vous!* I like you! *vous êtes trop bon*, you are too kind.—*n.m.* That which is good; the best, the fun of a thing; that which is pleasant, advantageous, extraordinary, striking, etc. *Il a cela de bon qu'il ne ment jamais*, he has this good quality, that he never tells a lie; *le bon de l'histoire*, the cream of the story.—*adv.* Well, right, properly. *Tout de bon*, seriously, truly.

bon (2) [bɔ̃], *n.m.* Bond, coupon, order, voucher. *Bon du trésor*, treasury bond; *bon d'essence*, petrol coupon.

bonace [bɔ'nas], *n.f.* Calm, smooth sea; (*fig.*) calm, tranquillity.

bonasse [bɔ'nas], *a.* Simple-minded, easy, credulous; soft, complying. **bonassement**, *adv.* Simply, foolishly. **bonasserie**, *n.f.* Simple-mindedness, simplicity.

bon-bec [bɔ̃'bɛk], *n.m.* (*pl.* **bons-becs**) Chatterbox, gossip, who is never at a loss.

bonbon [bɔ̃'bɔ̃], *n.m.* Sweet; (*Am.*) candy.

bonbonne [bɔ̃'bɔn], *n.f.* Demijohn; carboy.

bonbonnerie [bɔ̃bɔn'ri], *n.f.* Bonbon-trade. **bonbonnière**, *n.f.* Sweetmeat-box; (*fig.*) snug little house or flat.

bon-chrétien [bɔ̃kre'tjɛ̃], *n.m.* (*pl.* **bons-chrétiens**) A variety of pear.

bond [bɔ̃], *n.m.* Bound; leap, jump. *Du premier bond*, immediately; *faire un bond*, to make a bound; (*fig.*) to soar (prices, rents, etc.); *il m'a fait faux bond*, he has given me the slip; *il ne va que par sauts et par bonds*, he only works by fits and starts; *il s'élança d'un bond par-dessus la muraille*, he cleared the wall at a bound; *prendre la balle au bond*, to catch the ball at the bound, to seize time by the forelock; *second bond*, rebound; *de bond ou de volée*, anyhow, by hook or by crook.

bonde [bɔ̃:d], *n.f.* Bung-hole, bung; sluice, flood-gate.

bondé [bɔ̃'de], *a.* (*fem.* **bondée**) Chock-full, packed, crammed. *Train bondé de voyageurs*, train packed with passengers.

bonder [bɔ̃'de], *v.t.* To fill.

bondieusard [bɔ̃djø'za:r], *a.* and *n.m.* (*pop.*) Bigot, sanctimonious person. **bondieuserie**, *n.f.* Bigotry, (*pl.*) religious trappings, etc.

bondir [bɔ̃'di:r], *v.i.* To bound, to rebound, to bounce, to caper, to frisk. *Cela fait bondir le cœur*, that makes one's heart leap;

il bondit de rage, he leaped with rage.
bondissant, *a.* (*fem.* **bondissante**) Bounding, skipping, frisking. **bondissement**, *n.m.* Bounding, skipping, frisking.
bondon [bɔ̃'dɔ̃], *n.m.* Bung; a small cheese of this shape. **bondonner**, *v.t.* To bung, to stop with a bung, to close up. **bondonnière**, *n.f.* Bung-borer.
bondrée [bɔ̃'dre:], *n.f.* Honey-buzzard.
Bône [boːn], *f.* Bona.
bon-henri [bɔnɑ̃'ri], *n.m.* (*Bot.*) Wild spinach.
bonheur [bɔ'nœːr], *n.m.* Happiness, prosperity, welfare; good fortune, good luck, advantage, success, victory. *Au petit bonheur, au petit bonheur la chance*, haphazardly; *avoir le bonheur de*, to have the good fortune to; *avoir du bonheur*, to be lucky; *envier le bonheur d'autrui*, to envy another's prosperity; *être en bonheur*, to be fortunate; *faire le bonheur de quelqu'un*, to delight someone; *jouer de bonheur*, to be in luck's way; *par bonheur*, luckily; *porter bonheur*, to bring good luck.
bonheur-du-jour [bɔnœrdy'ʒuːr], *n.m.* (*pl.* **bonheurs-du-jour**) A small writing-table with drawers.
bonhomie [bɔnɔ'mi], *n.f.* Good nature; simplicity, credulity.
bonhomme [bɔ'nɔm], *n.m.*(*pl.* **bonshommes**) [bɔ'zɔm] Simple, good-natured man; foolish or credulous person; (*fig.*) a rough drawing or effigy of a man. *Aller son petit bonhomme de chemin*, to jog quietly along; *bonhomme de neige*, snowman; *faux bonhomme*, one affecting simplicity, sly fellow; *Jacques Bonhomme*, a typical rustic; *petit bonhomme*, little man (child); *vieux bonhomme*, old fellow, old fogy.
boni [bɔ'ni], *n.m.* Bonus. *Avoir cent livres de boni*, to have one hundred pounds to the good.
boniche [bɔ'niʃ], *n.f.* (*colloq.*) A maidservant.
boniface [bɔni'fas], *a.* and *n.* (*pop.*) Simple, artless.
bonification [bɔnifika'sjɔ̃], *n.f.* Amelioration, improvement (of land); (*Fin.*) allowance, bonus, discount; (*St. Exch.*) backwardation.
bonifier [bɔni'fje], *v.t.* To better, to improve, to ameliorate; to make up, to make good; (*Fin.*) to pay, to transfer. **se bonifier**, *v.r.* To improve, to get better.
boniment [bɔni'mɑ̃], *n.m.* Quack's show, puff; (*fig.*) humbug, claptrap speech. **bonimenter**, *v.i.* To kid, to humbug. **bonimenteur**, *n.m.* Humbug.
bonisseur [bɔni'sœr], *n.m.* (*fam.*) Showman; tout.
bonjour [bɔ̃'ʒuːr], *n.m.* and *int.* Good morning, good afternoon, good day. (*fam.*) *Bien le bonjour à votre frère*, remember me to your brother; *c'est simple comme bonjour*, it's as easy as pie; *je vous souhaite le bonjour*, I wish you good morning.
bonne (1) [BON (1)].
bonne (2) [bɔn], *n.f.* Servant-maid; housemaid. *Bonne d'enfants*, nursery-maid; *bonne à tout faire*, maid-of-all-work, general.
bonne-dame [bɔn'dam], *n.f.* (*pl.* **bonnesdames**) (*Bot.*) Orache [see ARROCHE].
bonne-maman [bɔnmɑ̃'mɑ̃], *n.f.* (*pl.* **bonnesmamans**) (*Childish*) Grandmamma.
bonnement [bɔn'mɑ̃], *adv.* Plainly, simply,

honestly, truly, merely. *Tout bonnement*, quite frankly.
bonnet [bɔ'nɛ], *n.m.* Cap. *Avoir la tête près du bonnet*, to be hot-headed; *bonnet de laine*, woollen cap; *bonnet de nuit*, night-cap; (*fig.*) dull fellow; *bonnet de police*, fatigue cap; *bonnet rouge*, red cap of revolution; *ce sont deux têtes dans un bonnet*, they are hand and glove together; *c'est bonnet blanc et blanc bonnet*, it is six of one and half a dozen of the other; *donner le bonnet*, to confer the doctorate; *gros bonnet*, bigwig, big pot; *jeter son bonnet par-dessus les moulins*, to throw off all restraint, to be reckless; *mettre son bonnet de travers*, to be in ill humour; *opiner du bonnet*, to adopt the opinion of the crowd; *prendre sous son bonnet*, to invent or make up a tale; *triste comme un bonnet de nuit*, as dull as ditch water.
bonneteau [bɔn'to], *n.m.* Three-card trick.
bonneterie [bɔn'tri], *n.f.* Hosiery business; hosiery.
bonneteur [bɔn'tœːr], *n.m.* Card-sharper.
bonnetier [bɔn'tje], *n.m.* (*fem.* **-ière**) Hosier. **bonnetière**, *n.f.* Small wardrobe.
bonnette [bɔ'nɛt], *n.f.* Child's bonnet; (*Fort.*) bonnet; (*Naut.*) studding sail; (*Phot.*) extra lens.
bonniche [bɔ'niʃ], *n.f.* [BONICHE].
bon-papa [bɔ̃pa'pa], *n.m.* (*fam.*) Grandpa, grandad.
bon-prime [bɔ̃'prim], *n.m.* (*Comm.*) Free-gift token.
bonsoir [bɔ̃'swaːr], *n.m.* and *int.* Good evening, good night. *Bonsoir et bonne nuit!* a good night's rest to you! **dire bonsoir à tous*, or *à la compagnie*, to die.
bonté [bɔ̃'te], *n.f.* Goodness, kindness; benevolence, indulgence; good quality (of things). *Abuser de la bonté de quelqu'un*, to take advantage of someone's goodness; *avoir la bonté de*, to be so good as to.—*int. Bonté divine!* good gracious!
bonze [bɔ̃ːz], *n.m.* (*fem.* **bonzesse** or **bonzelle**) Bonze (Buddhist priest); (*colloq.*) a dotard. **bonzerie**, *n.f.* Monastery of bonzes.
bookmaker [bukme'kœr] or **book** [buk], *n.m.* Bookmaker (illegal in France).
boom [bum], *n.m.* (*Fin.*) Boom.
boomerang [bum'rɑ̃g], *n.m.* Boomerang; (*fig.*) (argument) which rounds on its author.
boort or **bort** [bɔrt], *n.m.* Diamond dust.
Booz [bɔ'ɔːz], *m.* Boaz.
boqueteau [bɔk'to], *n.m.* Copse, small wood.
boracique [BORIQUE].
borate [bɔ'rat], *n.m.* Borate. **boraté**, *a.* (*fem.* **-ée**) Borated.
borax [bɔ'raks], *n.m.* Borax.
borborygme [bɔrbɔ'rigm], *n.m.* (*Med.*) Rumbling noise in the intestines.
bord [bɔːr], *n.m.* Edge, margin, brink, brim, border, hem, rim; shore, bank, strand, side; (*Naut.*) broadside, board, tack. *À pleins bords*, full to the brim, copiously, freely; *bord à bord*, edge to edge, (*Naut.*) close alongside; *j'ai son nom sur le bord des lèvres*, I have his name on the tip of my tongue; *le bord d'un chapeau*, the brim of a hat; *le bord d'une robe*, the hem of a gown; *le bord d'une table*, the edge of a table; *le bord d'un précipice*, the brink of a precipice; *le bord du trottoir*, the curb. *Aller au bord de la mer*, to go to the

seaside; *le bord de la mer*, the seashore; *le bord d'une rivière*, the bank of a river; *le bord d'un lac*, the side of a lake. *À bord*, on board, aboard; *bord à quai*, alongside the quay; *courir bord au large*, to stand offshore; *bord à terre*, inshore; *faux bord*, list; *franc bord*, free-board; *livre de bord*, log-book; *papiers de bord*, ship's papers; *par-dessus bord*, overboard; *tourner, changer* or *virer de bord*, to tack about, to veer; *vaisseau de haut bord*, ship of the line. (*fig.*) *Être du bord de quelqu'un* or *être du même bord*, to be in the same boat with someone.

bordage [bɔr'daːʒ], *n.m.* Bordering, hemming, etc.; (*Naut.*) planking, bulwarks.

bordaille [bɔr'daːj], *n.f.* Plank (of a ship's sides).

bordant [bɔr'dɑ̃], *n.m.* (*Naut.*) Foot-rope of a sail.

bordé (1) [bɔr'de], *n.m.* Hem, edging, bordering (of a garment); (*Naut.*) planking.

bordé (2) [bɔr'de], *a.* (*fem.* **bordée** (1)) (*Her.*) Bordered (of bearings with margins ornamented with a particular tincture).

bordeaux [bɔr'do], *n.m.* Bordeaux wine; *bordeaux rouge*, claret.

bordée (2) [bɔr'de], *n.f.* (*Naut.*) Broadside; volley, salvo; stretch, tack; watch. *Courir des bordées*, to tack about; (*slang*) to go from public-house to public-house; *lâcher* or *tirer une bordée*, to fire a broadside, (*fam.*) to go on the spree; *une bordée d'injures*, a shower of abuse; *matelots en bordée*, tars on the spree; (*C*) *une bordée de neige*, a snow-fall.

bordel [bɔr'dɛl], *n.m.* (*vulg.*) Brothel; (*pop.*) any disorderly place.

bordelais [bɔrdə'lɛ], *a.* and *n.* (*fem.* **-aise**) (Native) of Bordeaux.

bordelaise [bɔrdə'lɛːz], *n.f.* Cask of 225-30 litres (for claret); a bottle of 75 centil.

border [bɔr'de], *v.t.* To border, to edge, to hem, to line, to skirt, to bind, to border; to tuck in (bedclothes); (*Naut.*) to haul (the sheets). *Border une allée de rosiers*, to line a walk with rose-trees; *border un enfant dans un lit*, to tuck a child in; *border les côtés d'un vaisseau*, to plank a ship; *border les ponts*, to lay a ship's decks; *border une écoute*, to tally a sheet.

bordereau [bɔrdə'ro], *n.m.* Memorandum, note, schedule, account.

bordier [bɔr'dje], *a.* (*fem.* **bordière**) (*Naut.*) Lop-sided.—*n.m.* Lop-sided ship.

bordigue [bɔr'dig], *n.f.* Crawl (for taking fish).

bordoyer [bɔrdwa'je], *v.t.* irr. (*conjugated like* ABOYER) (*Paint. etc.*) To border, to encircle.

bordure [bɔr'dyːr], *n.f.* Frame, edge, edging; margin, border, kerb; rim. *En bordure*, along, bordering on. **bordurer**, *v.t.* To finish with a border, edge, etc.

bore [bɔːr], *n.m.* (*Chem.*) Boron.

boréal [bɔre'al], *a.*(*fem.* **boréale**, *pl.* **boréaux**) Boreal, northern. **borée**, *n.m.* Boreas, north wind (*poet.*).

Borée [bɔ're], *m.* Boreas.

borgne [bɔrɲ], *a.* One-eyed; dark, obscure, suspicious. *Changer son cheval borgne contre un aveugle*, to change for the worse. *Rue borgne*, blind alley.—*n.* One-eyed person. *Au royaume des aveugles les borgnes sont rois*, among the blind, the one-eyed is king.

borgnesse, *n.f.* (*pop.*) One-eyed woman.

borique [bɔ'rik], *a.* Boric. **boriqué**, *a.* (*fem.* **boriquée**) Containing boric acid.

bornage [bɔr'naːʒ], *n.m.* Settling bounds, fixing limits; boundary; (*Naut.*) coastal navigation.

borne [bɔrn], *n.f.* Landmark; boundary, limit, confine; milestone; stone fixed at the corner of a wall etc. to keep vehicles from striking against this; (*fig.*) the street; (*Elec.*) terminal. *Borne kilométrique,* milestone; *cela passe les bornes*, that is going too far; *être planté là comme une borne*, to stand there like a post; *mettre des bornes à son ambition*, to set bounds to one's ambition; *orateur de borne*, street orator.

borné [bɔr'ne], *a.* (*fem.* **bornée**) Bounded, limited, confined; narrow, mean, hidebound. *Esprit borné*, narrow mind.

borne-fontaine [bɔrnfɔ̃'tɛn], *n.f.* (*pl.* **bornes-fontaines**) Street fountain (like a boundary-post).

borner [bɔr'ne], *v.t.* To set landmarks to; to bound, to limit, to circumscribe, to restrict, to confine. *Borner son ambition*, to limit one's ambition. **se borner**, *v.r.* To restrain oneself; to amount (to). *Il faut se borner à cela*, we must be content with that.

bornoyer [bɔrnwa'je], *v.i.* irr. (*conjug. like* ABOYER) To mark out, to examine with one eye to make sure that it is straight, level, etc. —*v.t.* To stake off.

borraginée [bɔraʒi'ne], *n.f.* (*Bot.*) One of the borage family.

borure [bɔ'ryːr], *n.f.* (*Chem.*) Boride.

*bosco(t) [bɔs'ko], *n.* and *a.* (*fem.* **boscotte** [bɔs'kɔt]) (*pop.*) Hunchback; hunchbacked.

Bosnie [bɔs'ni], *f.* Bosnia.

Bosphore [bɔs'fɔːr], **le**, *m.* The Bosphorus.

bosquet [bɔs'ke], *n.m.* Grove, thicket, arbour.

bossage [bɔ'saːʒ], *n.m.* (*Arch.*) Embossment, boss, bossage.

bosse [bɔs], *n.f.* Hump, hunch; bump, bruise; knob, protuberance, lump, boss; (*Arch.*) embossment; (*Sculp.*) relievo, relief; (*Naut.*) stopper, ring-rope; painter; (*Phrenol.*) bump, aptitude. *Dessiner d'après la bosse*, to draw from the round; *ne rêver que plaies et bosses*, to think of nothing but mischief or fighting; *ouvrage en demi-bosse*, figure in half relief; *ouvrage relevé en bosse*, embossed piece of work; *rouler sa bosse*, (*slang*) to rove about, to see the world; *se payer une bosse (de rire)*, to laugh uproariously; *se donner une bosse*, or *bosser*, (*slang*) to go on the spree.

bosselage [bɔs'laːʒ], *n.m.* Embossing.

bosseler [bɔs'le], *v.t.* To dent; to emboss; (*pop.*) to beat. *Casserole bosselée*, battered saucepan. **bossellement**, *n.m.*, or **bosselure**, *n.f.* Embossment; inequalities (of surface); dent; bruise.

bosselle [bɔ'sɛl], *n.f.* Eel-pot.

bosser [bɔ'se], *v.t.* (*Naut.*) To stopper; (*slang*) to work hard.

bossetier [bɔs'tje], *n.m.* Glass-blower; embosser.

bossette [bɔ'sɛt], *n.f.* Boss (of bit); stud (on the blinkers); blinker; small boss of the trigger.

bossoir [bɔ'swaːr], *n.m.* (*Naut.*) Cat-head; davit, bow-timbers.

bossu [bɔ'sy], *a.* (*fem.* **bossue**) Hunchbacked; deformed, crooked. *Bossu pardevant,* pigeon-breasted.—*n.* Hunch-back. *Rire comme un bossu*, to split one's sides with laughter.

bossuer [bɔ'sɥe], *v.t.* To dent, to batter. **se bossuer**, *v.r.* To get bruised, dented.

boston [bɔs'tɔ̃], *n.m.* Boston (card-game, dance).

(*C*) **Bostonnais** [bɔstɔ'nɛ], *n.m.* An American.

bostonner [bɔstɔ'ne], *v.i.* To play at or dance the boston.

bot [bo], *a.* *Pied bot*, club-foot; club-footed; *main bote*, club-hand.

botanique [bɔta'nik], *n.f.* Botany.—*a.* Botanical. **botaniser**, *v.i.* To botanize. **botaniste**, *n.m.* Botanist.

Bothnie [bɔt'ni], *f.* Bothnia.

botte (1) [bɔt], *n.f.* Wellington boot. *Bottes à genouillère*, or *d'égoutier*, jack-boots; *bottes à l'écuyère*, riding-boots; *bottes à revers*, or *bottes retroussées*, top-boots; *bottes de sept lieues*, seven-league boots; (*C*) *botte sauvage*, mocassin; *décrotter* or *cirer des bottes*, to clean or polish boots; *mettre du foin dans ses bottes*, to feather one's nest; *tige de botte*, leg of a boot; *tirant de botte*, boot-strap; *t'-re-botte*, boot-jack. (*fig.*) *A propos de bottes*, about nothing, irrelevantly; *graisser ses bottes*, to prepare for a journey *or* for death; *sous la botte de l'ennemi*, under the heel of the enemy.

botte (2) [bɔt], *n.f.* Bunch, bundle, truss, bale. (*Mil.*) Sound of the bugle for distributing forage. *Une botte d'asperges*, a bundle of asparagus; *une botte de foin*, a truss of hay.

botte (3) [bɔt], *n.f.* (*Fenc.*) Pass, thrust, lunge. *Parer une botte*, to parry a pass; *porter une botte à quelqu'un*, (*Fenc.*) to make a pass or a lunge at someone; (*fig.*) to play a trick on somebody.

botte (4) [bɔt], *n.f.* (*Ent.*) Fly-weevil.

bottelage [bɔ'tla:ʒ], *n.m.* Tying up in bundles.

botteler, *v.t.* To put up in bundles, to truss (hay).

bottelette [bɔ'tlɛt], *n.f.* Small truss. **botteleur**, *n.m.* (*fem.* **botteleuse** (1)) (*Agric.*) Binder. **botteloir**, *n.m.*, or **botteleuse** (2), *n.f.* Sheaf-binding machine, binder.

botter [bɔ'te], *v.t.* To supply with boots; to put boots on (a person); (*fig.*) to please, to suit; (*colloq.*) to kick, to boot. *Botter le derrière à quelqu'un*, to kick someone's behind; *botter le ballon*, (*Ftb.*) to kick the ball; *ce bottier botte bien* or *mal*, this bootmaker makes boots well *or* badly; *cela me botte*, (*vulg.*) that suits me exactly; *Le Chat Botté*, Puss in Boots. **se botter**, *v.r.* To put one's boots on; to ball (with mud). *Cet homme se botte bien*, this man wears well-made boots.

botterie, *n.f.* Boot-shop, boot-trade. **bottier**, *n.m.* Bootmaker.

bottillon (1) [bɔti'jɔ̃], *n.m.* Small bunch or bundle (of herbs, salads, etc.).

bottillon (2) [bɔti'jɔ̃] [BOTTINE].

bottin [bɔ'tɛ̃], *n.m.* A directory published by the firm of Didot Bottin.

bottine [bɔ'tin], *n.f.* (Ankle) boot.

bouc [buk], *n.m.* He-goat; (*fig.*) repulsive man; goatee (beard). *Bouc émissaire*, scapegoat.

boucan [bu'kã], *n.m.* A place used by the American Indians to smoke-dry their meat; a grill for this purpose; (*fig.*) a great noise; a row. *Faire du boucan*, to make a row; *un boucan de tous les diables*, the devil of a row.

boucanage, *n.m.* Smoke-drying.

(*C*) **boucane** [bu'kan], *n.f.* Smoke.

boucaner, *v.t.* To smoke (meat, hides, etc.). —*v.i.* To be smoke-dried; to hunt wild buffaloes etc. for their hides; (*pop.*) to stink.

boucanier [buka'nje], *n.m.* Buccaneer; freebooter; buccaneer's musket. **boucanier**, *a.* (*fem.* **-ière**) Fit for buccaneers (of manners etc.).

(*C*) **boucanière** [buka'nɛr], *n.f.* Smokehouse (for fish).

boucaro [buka'ro], *n.m.* Red clay used for making porous pottery.

*****boucau** [bu'ko], *n.m.* (*dial.*) Entrance to a harbour.

*****boucaut** [bu'ko], *n.m.* Cask (for dry goods).

bouchage [bu'ʃa:ʒ], *n.m.* Stopping, corking.

bouchain [bu'ʃɛ̃], *n.m.* (*Naut.*) Bilge.

boucharde [bu'ʃard], *n.f.* Bush-hammer; roller for cement work. **boucharder**, *v.t.* (*Masonry*) to roughen.

bouche [buʃ], *n.f.* Mouth; lips; tongue; a person (as consumer of food); voice, words, speech; victuals, eating, living; opening, aperture, outfall (of canals, rivers, etc.); muzzle (of a cannon); plug-hole, fire-plug. *Bouche béante* or *bouche bée*, open-mouthed, gaping; *bouche close!* keep it to yourself, mum's the word; *bouche mauvaise*, mouth sour with bile or infected by the breath etc.; *avoir mauvaise bouche*, to have a bad taste in one's mouth; *cela fait venir l'eau à la bouche*, that makes one's mouth water; *cela rend la bouche amère*, that leaves a bitter taste in the mouth; *de bouche*, by word of mouth; *dépense de bouche*, housekeeping expenses; *faire la bouche en cœur*, to screw up one's mouth, to look captivating; *faire la petite bouche*, to be difficult to please; to be dainty or fastidious; *fermer la bouche à quelqu'un*, to stop someone's mouth; *une fine bouche*, a gourmet; *garder une chose pour la bonne bouche*, to keep a titbit till the last; *il dit tout ce qui lui vient à la bouche*, he says whatever comes into his head; *il y en avait à bouche que veux-tu*, there was enough and to spare; *bouche à feu*, gun; *bouche d'eau*, hydrant; *bouche d'égout*, gully hole; *bouche d'incendie*, fire-plug; *munitions de bouche*, provisions; *que l'imposture ne souille point votre bouche*, let not falsehood sully your lips; *un cheval qui n'a ni bouche ni éperon*, a horse that obeys neither bridle nor spur; *un homme fort en bouche*, a man that out-talks everybody.

bouche-bouteille [buʃbu'tɛ:j], *n.m.* (*usu. in pl.* **bouche-bouteilles**) Corking-machine.

bouché [bu'ʃe], *a.* (*fem.* **bouchée** (1)) Stopped up, plugged, shut; (*fig.*) dull-witted. *Cidre bouché*, bottled cider; *temps bouché*, foul weather; *trompette bouchée*, muted trumpet.

bouchée (2) [bu'ʃe], *n.f.* Mouthful. *Bouchée à la reine*, small patty, vol au vent; *mettre les bouchées doubles*, to eat quickly, (*fig.*) to work with a will; *ne faire qu'une bouchée de quelqu'un*, to settle someone's hash quickly.

boucher (1) [bu'ʃe], *v.t.* To stop, to choke, to shut up; to bar, to obstruct, to intercept. *Boucher la vue d'un voisin*, to obstruct a neighbour's view; *boucher une bouteille*, to cork a bottle; *boucher un tonneau*, to bung a barrel; *boucher un trou*, to stop up a gap, (*colloq.*) to pay a debt; (*pop.*) *ça m'en bouche*

un coin! well I never! *se boucher le nez,* to hold one's nose; *se boucher les oreilles,* to stop one's ears.
boucher (2) [bu'ʃe], *n.m.* Butcher. *Boucher en gros,* carcass-butcher. **bouchère,** *n.f.* A butcher's wife; woman keeping a butcher's shop. **boucherie,** *n.f.* Butcher's shop; butchery; (*fig.*) slaughter, carnage, massacre.
bouche-trou [buʃ'tru], *n.m.* (*pl.* **bouche-trous**) Stopgap.
bouchoir [bu'ʃwaːr], *n.m.* Iron door of an oven or furnace.
bouchon [bu'ʃɔ̃], *n.m.* Stopper, cork, plug, bung; bush (hung up in front of a tavern), hence, a tavern; wisp (of straw etc.); packet (of linen); (*Angling*) float; (*fig.*) inequality; knot etc. (in cloth etc.). *Frotter un cheval avec un bouchon de paille,* to rub down a horse with a wisp of straw; *jeu de bouchon* (*a pop. game*), throwing down the cork (and pennies upon it) with *palets*; *ça c'est plus fort que de jouer au bouchon,* it beats the band; *sentir le bouchon,* to be corked (of a wine); (*Mach.*) *bouchon-fusible,* safety plug.
bouchonnage or **bouchonnement,** *n.m.* Rubbing down (horses). **bouchonner,** *v.t.* To rub down (a horse); to twist, to roll up (linen). **bouchonnier,** *n.m.* One who cuts or sells corks.
bouchot [bu'ʃo], *n.m.* Fishing-hurdles; oyster- or mussel-bed.
bouchure [bu'ʃyːr], *n.f.* Quickset hedge.
boucle [bukl], *n.f.* Buckle; brooch; curl, ringlet, lock (of hair); loop, wind (of a river etc.); (*Arch.*) fillet (on moulding of column), knocker; (*Naut.*) staple, ring, shackle. *Des boucles d'oreilles,* ear-rings; *faites une boucle, pas un nœud,* tie it in a bow, not in a knot; *se serrer la boucle,* (*pop.*) to tighten one's belt; *souliers à boucles,* shoes with buckles. **bouclé,** *a.* (*fem.* **bouclée**) Buckled, curled; (*pop.*) closed. *Cheveux bouclés,* curly hair. **bouclement,** *n.m.* Ringing (of a bull, pig, etc.).
boucler, *v.t.* To buckle; to put a ring to; to curl (hair); to ring (pigs etc.); (*pop.*) to close (a suit-case); (*slang*) to put in irons, to imprison. *Boucler la boucle,* to loop the loop; *boucler le budget,* to make both ends meet; (*slang*) *la boucler,* to shut up.—*v.i.* To buckle, to bulge (of a wall etc.); to curl (of the hair).
se boucler, *v.r.* To curl one's hair; (*pop.*) *se boucler la ceinture,* to tighten one's belt.
bouclerie, *n.f.* Buckle-making, buckle-trade. **boucleteau,** *n.m.* Buckling piece; tug. **bouclette,** *n.f.* Small buckle or ring.
bouclier [bukli'je], *n.m.* Buckler, shield; (*fig.*) defence, protection; lump sucker (fish). *Levée de boucliers,* armed revolt; (*fig.*) public protest.
Bouddha [bu'da], *m.* Buddha.
bouddhique [bu'dik], *a.* Buddhistic.
bouddhisme [bu'dism], *n.m.* Buddhism. **bouddhiste,** *n.* Buddhist.
bouder [bu'de], *v.i.* To sulk, to be sullen, to pout; (*Dominoes*) not to be able to play. *Bouder contre son ventre,* to cut off one's nose to spite one's face; *bouder sur l'avoine,* (of a horse) to be off its feed.—*v.t.* To be sulky with. **se bouder,** *v.r.* To be cool towards each other. **bouderie,** *n.f.* Pouting, sulki-

ness. **boudeur,** *a.* (*fem.* **boudeuse** (1)) Sulky, sullen.—*n.* Person who sulks.
boudeuse (2) [bu'døːz], *n.f.* A settee arranged back to back.
boudin [bu'dɛ̃], *n.m.* Black-pudding; saddle-bag, spring (of a coach); (*Arch.*) torus; (*Mining*) long fuse, sausage; (*Rail.*) flange (of wheel). *Boudin blanc,* white pudding; *ressort à boudin,* cylindrical spring; *s'en aller en eau de boudin,* to come to nothing.
boudinage [budi'naːʒ], *n.m.* (*Spinning*) Slubbing, roving.
boudine [bu'din], *n.f.* (*Glass-making*) Knot; bull's eye.
boudiné [budi'ne], *a.* (*fem.* **boudinée**) Dressed in close-fitting garments, roved; podgy (fingers).
boudiner [budi'ne], *v.t.* (*Spinning*) To rove, to slub. **boudineuse,** *n.f.* Rover, slubber.
boudoir [bu'dwaːr], *n.m.* Boudoir, lady's private room.
boue [bu], *n.f.* Mud, mire, dirt, filth; any deposit of offensive matter; slime, clay; sediment (of ink); (*fig.*) sordidness, abuse, obloquy. *Je n'en fais pas plus de cas que de la boue de mes souliers,* I don't value it more than the dirt on my shoes; *tirer quelqu'un de la boue,* to raise someone from the dunghill; *traîner quelqu'un dans la boue,* to load someone with abuse, to drag someone in the mud; *une âme de boue,* a mean soul.
bouée [bu'e], *n.f.* Buoy. *Bouée à sifflet,* whistling-buoy; *bouée de sauvetage,* life-buoy; *bouée lumineuse,* light-buoy; *bouée sonore,* bell-buoy.
***boueur** [bu'œːr] [BOUEUX (2)].
boueux (1) [bu'ø], *a.* (*fem.* **boueuse**) Muddy, dirty, miry; foul. *Écriture boueuse,* bad writing; *encre boueuse,* thick, clogging ink.
boueux (2), *n.m.* Scavenger, dustman.
bouffant [bu'fɑ̃], *a.* (*fem.* **bouffante** (1)) Puffed (sleeve), baggy (trousers).—*n.m.* Puff (of sleeves). **bouffante** (2), *n.f.* Hoop, farthingale.
bouffarde [bu'fard], *n.f.* (*pop.*) Short, thick pipe. *Téter* or *fumer sa bouffarde,* to have a whiff.
bouffe (1) [buf], *a.* Comic. *Opéra bouffe,* comic opera.—*n.m.pl. Les Bouffes,* the Italian opera (in Paris).
bouffe (2), *n.f.* (*pop.*) Food, grub.
bouffée [bu'fe], *n.f.* Puff, gust, blast, whiff; fit. (*Med.*) *Bouffée de chaleur,* sudden flush; *par bouffées,* by fits and starts.
bouffer [bu'fe], *v.i.* *To swell or puff the cheeks with anger, annoyance, etc.; to be fluffy (hair); (*slang*) to eat, to guzzle; to blue (money). *Bouffer des briques,* (*pop.*) to be starving; *se bouffer le nez,* to fight.
bouffette [bu'fɛt], *n.f.* Bow of ribbon etc.; tassel.
bouffi [bu'fi], *a.* (*fem.* **bouffie**) Puffed up, swollen, inflated. *Ange bouffi,* chubby little angel; *bouffi d'orgueil,* puffed up with pride; *des joues bouffies,* puffed out cheeks.
bouffir [bu'fiːr], *v.t.* To puff up, to swell, to bloat.—*v.i.* To swell. **bouffissure,** *n.f.* Swelling, puffing up; turgidity, bombast.
bouffon [bu'fɔ̃], *n.m.* Buffoon, clown; merry-andrew, jester. *Faire le bouffon,* to play the buffoon; *un mauvais bouffon,* a sorry jester.—*a.* (*fem.* **-onne**) Jocose, facetious,

comical. **bouffonner,** *v.i.* To play the buffoon; to be jocose, full of jests. **bouffonnerie,** *n.f.* Buffoonery, drollery, jesting.

bougainvillée [bugɛ̃vi'le], *n.f.* or **bougainvillier** [bugɛ̃vi'lje], *n.m.* Bougainvillea.

bouge [bu:ʒ], *n.m.* *Little closet; den, dirty hole, hovel; bilge of a cask; bulge (of wall).

bougeoir [bu'ʒwa:r], *n.m.* Flat candlestick, chamber-candlestick; taper-stand.

bougeotte [bu'ʒɔt], *n.f.* Craze for travelling. *Avoir la bougeotte*, to have the fidgets.

bouger [bu'ʒe], *v.i.* To stir, to budge, to fidget. *Il ne bouge pas de cette maison*, he is always at that house.—*v.t.* To move (from one place to another). *Ne bougez pas!* don't move!

*****bougette** [bu'ʒɛt], *n.f.* Pilgrim's wallet, small valise, pouch.

bougie [bu'ʒi], *n.f.* Wax-candle, wax-light; (*Surg.*) bougie; (*Elec.*) candle-power. *Bougie d'allumage*, (*Motor.*) sparking-plug.

bougier [bu'ʒje], *v.t.* To wax (cloth etc.).

bougnat [bu'na], *n.m.* (*colloq.*) A small (and often dirty) retailer of charcoal and wine; Auvergnat.

bougon [bu'gɔ̃], *a.* (*fem.* **-onne**) Grumbling. —*n.* Grumbler. **bougonner,** *v.i.* To grumble.

bougran [bu'grɑ̃], *n.m.* Buckram.

bougre [bugr], *n.m.* (*fem.* **bougresse**) Blackguard, jade; (*pop.*) chap, fellow. *Bon bougre*, good sort of fellow; *mauvais bougre*, nasty fellow, ugly customer; *bougre d'idiot*, you idiot.—*int.* The deuce! **bougrement,** *adv.* Extremely, devilishly.

boui-boui [bwi'bwi], *n.m.* (*pl.* **bouis-bouis**) Low theatre or music-hall; disreputable haunt.

bouif [bwif], *n.m.* (*slang*) Cobbler.

bouillabaisse [buja'bɛs], *n.f.* Provençal fish-soup with saffron etc., *bouillabaisse*; (*fig.*) awful mess.

bouillage [bu'ja:ʒ], *n.m.* Boil, boiling (of clothes). **bouillaison,** *n.f.* Fermentation (of beer, cider, etc.).

bouillant [bu'jɑ̃], *a.* (*fem.* **bouillante**) Boiling, hot, scalding; (*fig.*) fiery, hasty, eager, impetuous. *Bouillant de colère*, boiling with anger; *bouillant d'impatience*, burning with impatience; *jeunesse bouillante*, fiery youth.

bouille [bu:j], *n.f.* Fishing-pole, (*slang*) face. *Avoir une bonne bouille*, to have a pleasing face.

bouiller [bu'je], *v.t.* To stir water with a pole (to attract fish).

bouillerie [buj'ri], *n.f.* Brandy distillery.

bouilleur [bu'jœ:r], *n.m.* Brandy distiller; boiler-tube (of an engine). *Bouilleur de cru*, private distiller of home-made wine or cider.

bouilli [bu'ji], *n.m.* Boiled beef (of which broth has been made). **bouillie,** *n.f.* Pap (for infants); pulp (to make paper etc.); (*Viticulture*) wash for removing moss, mildew, etc., from vines. *Bouillie d'avoine*, porridge; *faire de la bouillie pour les chats*, to perform fruitless labour; (*fig.*) *mettre en bouillie*, to reduce to pulp.

bouillir [bu'ji:r], *v.i. irr.* To boil; (*fig.*) to be in a state of excitement. *v.t.* To boil (milk etc.). *Bouillir à gros bouillons*, to boil fast; *bouillir à petits bouillons*, to boil gently; *cela*

sert à faire bouillir la marmite, that helps to keep the pot boiling; *faire bouillir à demi*, to parboil.

bouilloire [buj'wa:r], *n.f.* Kettle.

bouillon [bu'jɔ̃], *n.m.* Broth, beef-tea, *bouillon*; bubble, ripple; ebullition, transport; puff, flounce (of a lady's dress); puffy part (of a wound, scar, etc.); unsold copies (books, newspapers, etc.). *Boire un bouillon*, to swallow a mouthful (in bathing); to meet with a loss; *bouillon de culture*, culture fluid; *bouillon de légumes*, vegetable soup; *bouillon de poulet*, chicken broth; *bouillon gras*, clear soup; *bouillon d'onze heures*, poisoned drink; *bouillon pointu*, (*colloq.*) clyster; *l'eau sort de la roche à gros bouillons*, the water comes gushing out of the rock.

bouillon-blanc [bujɔ̃'blɑ̃], *n.m.* (*pl.* **bouillons-blancs**) (*Bot.*) Mullein.

bouillonnant [bujɔ'nɑ̃], *a.* (*fem.* **-ante**) Bubbling, gurgling, boiling.

bouillonné [bujɔ'ne], *n.m.* Puff, flounce. **bouillonnement,** *n.m.* Bubbling up, spouting or gushing out; (*fig.*) ebullition, effervescence, agitation. **bouillonner,** *v.i.* To bubble, to froth up, to boil, to boil over; (*fig.*) to be in a state of excitement.—*v.t.* To put puffs into. *Bouillonner une robe*, to put puffs in a dress.

bouillotte [bu'jɔt], *n.f.* Foot-warmer; hot-water bottle; small kettle; game at cards (like *brelan*); (*pop.*) head.

bouillotter [bujɔ'te], *v.i.* To simmer.

boujaron [buʒa'rɔ̃], *n.m.* (*Naut.*) Tot, about half a gill (of rum).

boulage [bu'la:ʒ], *n.m.* Boiling (of linen for bleaching it); crushing (of sugar-beets); padding of bull's horns with balls.

boulaie [bu'le], *n.f.* Birch plantation.

boulange [bu'lɑ̃:ʒ], *n.f.* Bakery, bread-making, selling, etc.

boulanger (1) [bulɑ̃'ʒe], *n.m.* (*fem.* **boulangère**) Baker; baker's wife.—*n.f.* Name of a dance, Paul Jones. **boulanger** (2), *v.t.* To make, knead, or bake (bread). *Du pain bien boulangé*, well-made bread. **boulangerie,** *n.f.* Baking, baker's business; bake-house; baker's shop.

boulangisme [bulɑ̃'ʒism], *n.m.* Political party named after General Boulanger. **boulangiste,** *a.* Pertaining to this.—*n.* An adherent of this.

boulant [bu'lɑ̃], *n.m.* Pouter pigeon.

boule (1) [bul], *n.f.* Ball; bowl; (*pop.*) face, pate, head, noddle, sconce. *Arbre en boule* bushy-topped tree; *boule blanche*, white ball (in balloting), *'very good'* (in an examination); *boule d'eau chaude*, hot-water bottle; *boule de gomme*, bubble gum; *boule de neige*, snowball; (*fig.*) *faire boule de neige*, to grow bigger and bigger; *boule de signaux*, (*pl.*) bowls; *boule rouge*, red ball, *'good'* (in an examination); *il est rond comme une boule*, he is as round as a ball; *jouer aux boules*, to play at bowls; *perdre la boule*, (*slang*) to lose one's head; *se mettre en boule*, (*slang*) to lose one's temper; *un jeu de boules*, a bowling-green; (*Mil. slang*) *boule (de son)*, ration loaf.

boule (2) [BOULLE].

bouleau [bu'lo], *n.m.* Birch, birch-tree.

boule-de-neige [buldə'nɛ:ʒ], *n.f.* (*pl.* **boules-de-neige**) Guelder rose.

bouledogue [bul'dɔg], *n.m.* Bulldog. *Chienne bouledogue*, bull bitch.

bouler [bu'le], *v.i.* To swell, to pout (of pigeons); to roll like a ball. *Envoyer bouler*, to send about one's business.—*v.t.* To stir up (mortar); to pad (a bull's horn). *Bouler les cornes d'un taureau*, to put leather balls on the horns of a bull.

boulet [bu'lɛ], *n.m.* Cannon- or musket-ball; (*Mil.*) punishment of chain and ball (abolished 1857); fetlock-joint (of a horse). *Boulets de charbon*, ovoids; *boulet ramé*, chainshot, bar-shot; *boulet rouge*, red-hot shot; *tirer à boulets rouges sur quelqu'un*, to load someone with abuse; *traîner le boulet*, to drag one's chain and ball, (*fig.*) to lead a wearisome life; *un boulet de canon*, a cannon-ball.

bouleté [bul'te], *a.* Upright on fetlock-joint.

boulette [bu'lɛt], *n.f.* Pellet; forced-meat ball; (*colloq.*) blunder. *Il a fait une boulette*, he has dropped a brick.

bouleux [bu'lø], *n.m.* (*fem.* **bouleuse**) Thickset horse, heavy hack. *Un bon bouleux*, a plodding man, a drudge.—*a.* Hard-working, drudging.

boulevard [bul'va:r], *n.m.* *Bulwark, rampart; boulevard. **boulevarder**, *v.i.* To promenade on or frequent the boulevards. **boulevardier**, *n.m.* (*fem.* **-ière**) Frequenter of the boulevards.—*a.* Pertaining to the boulevards.

bouleversant [bulvɛr'sɑ̃], *a.* (*fem.* **bouleversante**) Overthrowing, upsetting; (*fig.*) confusing, staggering.

bouleversé [bulvɛr'se], *a.* (*fem.* **-ée**) Overthrown; upset, distressed.

bouleversement [bulvɛrsə'mɑ̃], *n.m.* Overthrow, overturning; commotion, confusion, disorder; destruction, ruin.

bouleverser [bulvɛr'se], *v.t.* To overthrow, to throw down; to subvert; (*fig.*) to agitate, to upset; to unsettle, to unhinge, to convulse.

boulier [bu'lje], *n.m.* Form of abacus; (*Fishing*) bag-net; scoring-board (at billiards).

boulimie [buli'mi], *n.f.* (*Med.*) Bulimy, bulimia. **boulimique**, *a.* Bulimic, bulimious.—*n.* A bulimious person.

boulin [bu'lɛ̃], *n.m.* Pigeon-hole in a wall for receiving the end of a scaffold pole; putlog.

boulinage [buli'na:ʒ], *n.m.* (*Naut.*) Sailing close to the wind.

bouline [bu'lin], *n.f.* (*Naut.*) Bowline. *Aller à la bouline*, to sail close to the wind, to tack about; *courir la bouline*, to run the gauntlet. **bouliner**, *v.i.* To sail close to the wind.—*v.t.* To haul to windward.

boulingrin [bulɛ̃'grɛ̃], *n.m.* Bowling-green, grass-plot.

boulinier [buli'nje], *a.* (*fem.* **boulinière**) That sails well to windward.

boulle [bul], *n.m.* Buhl (furniture), used chiefly in *Meuble de boulle*.

bouloir [bu'lwa:r], *n.m.* Mason's implement for stirring lime.

boulomane [bulɔ'man], *n.m.* Bowls player.

boulon [bu'lɔ̃], *n.m.* Bolt, large iron pin.

boulonnage [bulɔ'na:ʒ], *n.m.* Bolting.

boulonnais [bulɔ'nɛ], *a.* and *n.* (*fem.* **boulonnaise**) Belonging to or native of Boulogne.

boulonner [bulɔ'ne], *v.t.* To fasten with iron pins, to bolt; (*slang*) to work hard, to swot. **boulonnerie**, *n.f.* Bolt-factory. **boulon-**

nière, *n.f.* Auger or borer for making boltholes.

boulot [bu'lo], *a.* (*fem.* **boulotte**) Fat, dumpy, squatty.—*n.m.* (*slang*) Work, job. **boulotter**, *v.i.* (*slang*) To jog along, to get on comfortably.—*v.t.* To eat; to blue (money).

boulris [JONQUILLE].

boum [bum], *int.* Bang! boom!

boumerang [BOOMERANG].

bouquer [bu'ke], *v.i.* (*Hunt.*) To come out. *Faire bouquer*, to force (a fox etc.) to come out of his earth, (*fig.*) to force (someone) to yield.

bouquet (1) [bu'kɛ], *n.m.* Bunch (of flowers), nosegay, bouquet; birthday ode, sonnet; birthday present; final display of fireworks; the conclusion, the grand finale; aroma (of wine), perfume. *Bouquet de fusées*, bunch of rockets; *c'est le bouquet!* (*colloq.*) that's the limit, that beats everything! *et maintenant, pour le bouquet!* and now to cap the story! *fleur qui vient en bouquets*, flower that grows in bunches; *réserver une chose pour le bouquet*, to keep a thing for the last; *un bouquet d'arbres*, a cluster or a clump of trees; *un bouquet de pierreries*, a spray of jewels; *un bouquet de plumes*, a plume or a tuft of feathers.

bouquet (2) [bu'kɛ], *n.m.* Scab (of sheep etc.).

bouquet (3) *n.m.* Prawn; hare [*see* BOUQUIN (1)].

bouquetier [buk'tje], *n.f.* Flower-vase. **bouquetière**, *n.f.* Flower-girl.

bouquetin [buk'tɛ̃], *n.m.* Bouquetin, ibex.

bouquin (1) [bu'kɛ̃], *n.m.* (*Zool.*) Old he-goat; old hare; buck-hare or rabbit.

bouquin (2) [bu'kɛ̃], *n.m.* Old book; second-hand book; (*colloq.*) book. **bouquinage**, *n.m.* Book-hunting.

bouquiner (1) [buki'ne], *v.i.* To buck, to couple (of hares).

bouquiner (2) [buki'ne], *v.i.* To hunt after old books; to read. **bouquinerie**, *n.f.* Old-book or second-hand book trade; bibliomania. **bouquineur**, *n.* Lover of old books, book-fancier. **bouquiniste**, *n.m.* Dealer in second-hand books.

bourbe [burb], *n.f.* Mud, mire, slush, sediment. **bourbeux**, *a.* (*fem.* **bourbeuse**) Miry, muddy, sloughy, sloshy. **bourbier**, *n.m.* Slough, puddle, mire; (*fig.*) scrape, mess; infamy, obloquy. *Il s'est mis dans un bourbier*, he has got himself into a scrape.

bourbillon [burbi'jɔ̃], *n.m.* Clot of mud, filth, ink, etc.; core (of an abscess).

bourbouille [bur'buj], *n.f.* (*fam.*) Lichen (a tropical disease); prickly heat.

bourcette [MÂCHE].

bourdaine [bur'dɛn] or **bourgène** [bur'ʒɛn], *n.f.* Black alder (*Rhamnus frangula*).

bourdalou [burda'lu], *n.m.* Hat-band; leather band (of a shako); bed-pan, bed-slipper.

bourde [burd], *n.f.* *Fib, lie, tall story; (*fam.*) bloomer. *Commettre une bourde*, to drop a brick.

bourdillon [burdi'jɔ̃], *n.m.* Stave-wood (for casks).

bourdon (1) [bur'dɔ̃], *n.m.* Pilgrim's staff; (*Print.*) out, omission.

bourdon (2) [bur'dɔ̃], *n.m.* Humble-bee; great bell; (*Organ*) drone. *Faux bourdon*, drone.

bourdonnant [burdɔ'nɑ̃], *a.* (*fem.* **-ante**) Humming, buzzing. **bourdonnement,** *n.m.* Buzz, buzzing; hum, humming; singing in the ear. **bourdonner,** *v.i.* To buzz, to hum; to murmur.—*v.t.* To hum.

bourdonnet [burdɔ'nɛ], *n.m.* (*Surg.*) Pledget, dossil; plug.

bourdonneur [burdɔ'nœːr], *a.* Humming.— *n.m.* Humming-bird, colibri.

bourdonnière [burdɔ'pɛr], *n.f.* (*Apiculture*) Apparatus used for getting rid of drones.

bourg [buːr], *n.m.* Borough, market-town. **bourgade,** *n.f.* Small market-town, village.

bourgène [BOURDAINE].

bourgeois [bur'ʒwa], *n.m.* (*fem.* **bourgeoise**) *Burgess, citizen, townsman; commoner; middle-class person, bourgeois; (*colloq.*) master, mistress. *Être en bourgeois,* (of officers) to be dressed in plain clothes, in mufti; *un bon bourgeois,* a respectable citizen; *petit bourgeois,* lower middle-class.—*a.* Pertaining to the bourgeoisie; middle-class, mediocre; plain, common, ordinary, vulgar, philistine. *Avoir l'air bourgeois* or *les manières bourgeoises,* to be common in one's gait and manners; *caution bourgeoise,* good security; *cuisine bourgeoise,* plain, homely cooking; *famille bourgeoise,* good middle-class family; *pension bourgeoise,* private boarding-house. **bourgeoisement,** *adv.* *Maison à louer bourgeoisement,* to be let as a private residence. **bourgeoisie,** *n.f.* Bourgeoisie, middle-class. *Droit de bourgeoisie,* freedom of a city; *haute bourgeoisie,* upper middle-class.

bourgeon [bur'ʒɔ̃], *n.m.* (*Bot.*) Bud, shoot; pimple. **bourgeonnant,** *a.* (*fem.* **-ante**) Budding. **bourgeonné,** *a.* (*fem.* **-ée**) Budded, pimpled. **bourgeonnement,** *n.m.* Budding, budding-time. **bourgeonner,** *v.i.* To bud, to put forth young shoots; to break out in pimples.

bourgeron [burʒə'rɔ̃], *n.m.* Workman's blouse, smock-frock; (*Mil.*) fatigue jacket.

bourgmestre [burg'mɛstr], *n.m.* Burgomaster.

Bourgogne [bur'gɔɲ], *n.f.* Burgundy.—*n.m.* Burgundy (wine).

bourguignon [burgi'ɲɔ̃], *a.* (*fem.* **-onne**) Burgundian, of Burgundy.—*n.* (**Bourguignon,** *fem.* **-onne**) A native or inhabitant of Burgundy. *Un bourguignon,* Burgundian beef (with wine and onions).

bourguignotte [burgi'ɲɔt], *n.f.* Burgonet (16–17th cent.); trench helmet.

bourlinguer [burlɛ̃'ge], *v.i.* (*Naut.*) To labour, to strain (of a ship against the sea); (*colloq.*) to drudge, to moil.

bourrache [bu'raʃ], *n.f.* Borage.

bourrade [bu'rad], *n.f.* Dog's snapping at a hare; (*fig.*) blow, thrust, buffet; taunt.

bourrage [bu'raːʒ], *n.m.* Tamping, stuffing, wadding; (*sch.*) cramming. (*pop.*) *Bourrage de crâne,* eye-wash; bluff.

bourras [bu'ra], *n.m.* Coarse grey canvas or drugget.

bourrasque [bu'rask], *n.f.* Squall, gust; fit of anger, of ill humour.

bourre [buːr], *n.f.* Hair, fluff (of animals); flock (of wool); floss (of silk); wad (for firearms); kind of down (on bud); (*fig.*) stuff, trash. *Lit de bourre,* flock mattress.

bourreau [bu'ro], *n.m.* Hangman, executioner; tormentor, tyrant, butcher. *Un bourreau des cœurs,* a lady-killer; *un bourreau de travail,* an indefatigable worker. (C) *Bourreau des arbres,* (*Bot.*) Bittersweet (*Celastrus*).

bourrée [bu're], *n.f.* Brushwood, faggot; an Auvergne dance; the air to this.

bourrèlement [burɛl'mɑ̃], *n.m.* Pain, anguish; (*fig.*) mental agony.

bourreler [bur'le], *v.t.* To torment, to torture, to rack, to goad; to place *bourrelets* at (a door etc.).

bourrelet [bur'lɛ], *n.m.* Pad, cushion; bag stuffed with hair etc. for keeping out draughts at windows, doors, etc.; sandbag; padded cap (for children); bulging part round the mouth of a gun, cartridge, etc. *Bourrelets de graisse,* rolls of fat.

bourrelier [burə'lje], *n.m.* Harness-maker. **bourrellerie,** *n.f.* Business of a harness-maker; harness-maker's shop.

bourre-pipe [bur'pip], *n.m.* (*pl.* **bourre-pipes**) Pipe-stopper.

bourrer [bu're], *v.t.* To ram a charge home into (a gun etc.), to tamp; to stuff (a chair etc.); to cram (with food, learning, etc.); (*fig.*) to ill-treat, to thrash; to snap at (of hunting-dogs). *Bourrer de coups,* to give a sound thrashing to. **se bourrer,** *v.r.* To cram oneself; to thrash each other.

bourreur [bu'rœːr], *n.m.* (*fam.*) used in *bourreur de crâne,* one who spreads false rumours.

bourriche [bu'riʃ], *n.f.* Game-basket; basket of game; hamper (of oysters).

bourrichon [buri'ʃɔ̃], *n.m.* (*fam.*) only used in *se monter le bourrichon,* to get excited.

bourricot [buri'ko], *n.m.* Donkey.

bourrin [bu'rɛ̃], *n.m.* (*Mil. slang*) Horse.

bourrique [bu'rik], *n.f.* She-ass; stupid person, dolt, dunce. *Faire tourner en bourrique,* to worry to death, to drive mad.

bourriquet, *n.m.* Ass's colt or small ass; hand-barrow for mortar, stones, etc.; (*Mining*) windlass.

bourroir [bu'rwaːr], *n.m.* Tamping-bar.

bourru [bu'ry], *a.* (*fem.* **bourrue**) Cross, peevish, moody, surly, snappish; unfermented (of wine).

bourse (1) (burs), *n.f.* Purse; (*fig.*) money in this, money; scholarship, grant, bursary; exhibition; hair-bag, bag; rabbit-net; (*Anat.*) bursar; (*Bot.*) capsule of anther. *Avoir toujours la bourse à la main,* to be always dipping into one's purse; *bourse de quête,* offertory bag; *bourse d'entretien,* maintenance grant; *bourse entière,* whole scholarship; *demi-bourse,* half-scholarship; *coupeur de bourse,* cutpurse; *faire bourse à part,* each paying his own expenses; *faire bourse commune,* to share expenses; *la bourse ou la vie!* your money or your life! *loger le diable en sa bourse,* to be penniless; *sans bourse délier,* without putting one's hand into one's pocket.

bourse (2) [burs], *n.f.* Stock Exchange, money market. *Coup de Bourse,* bold speculation; *jouer à la Bourse,* to speculate; *Bourse du Travail,* Labour Exchange.

bourse-à-pasteur [bursapas'tœːr], *n.f.* (*pl.* **bourses-à-pasteur**) (*Bot.*) Shepherd's purse.

boursette [BOURSE-À-PASTEUR].

boursicot or **boursicaut** [bursi'ko], *n.m.*

Small purse; small sum. **boursicoter,** *v.i.* To save a little money; to speculate on a small scale. **boursicoteur** or **boursicotier,** *n.m.* (*fem.* **-euse** or **-ière**) Speculator in a small way.

boursier [bur'sje], *n.m.* (*fem.* **boursière**) Speculator on the Stock Exchange, exchange broker; purse-maker; foundation scholar, exhibitioner.—*a.* Pertaining to the Stock Exchange.

boursiller [bursi'je], *v.i.* To club together.

boursouflage [bursu'fla:ʒ], *n.m.* Bombast.

boursouflé [bursu'fle], *a.* (*fem.* **boursouflée**) Bloated; bombastic, swollen, inflated, turgid.

boursouflement, *n.m.* Bloatedness, puffiness; cockle (of paper); blister (of paint).

boursoufler [bursu'fle], *v.t.* To bloat, to make turgid, to puff up. **boursouflure,** *n.f.* Bloatedness (of face etc.); (*fig.*) turgidity (of style).

bousage [bu'za:ʒ], *n.m.* Fixing-baths (in dyeing); dunging.

bousard [bu'za:r], *n.m.* Deer's dung.

bousculade [busky'lad], *n.m.* Jostling, hustling; scrimmage, rush.

bousculer [busky'le], *v.t.* To turn upside down, to throw into disorder; to jostle, to hustle, to squeeze, to bully. **se bousculer,** *v.r.* To jostle each other.

bouse [bu:z], *n.f.* Dung, especially cow-dung. **bouser,** *v.i.* To dung.—*v.t.* To lay (a threshing-floor etc.) with a mixture of earth and cow-dung; (*Dyeing*) to fix.

bousier [bu'zje] *n.m.* Dung-beetle.

bousillage [buzi'ja:ʒ], *n.m.* Mud-walling; mud-wall; (*fig.*) bungling piece of work. **bousiller,** *v.t.* (*fig.*) To bungle, to botch. —*v.i.* To make mud-walling. *Se faire bousiller,* to be killed. **bousilleur,** *n.m.* (*fem.* **-euse**) Mud-wall builder; (*fig.*) bungler, botcher.

bousin (1) [bu'zɛ̃], *n.m.* (*pop.*) Low tavern, den; (*fig.*) row, shindy, scandal.

bousin (2) [bu'zɛ̃], *n.m.* A poor variety of peat; rotten-stone.

bousingot [buzɛ̃'go], *n.m.* Sailor's glazed hat.

boussole [bu'sɔl], *n.f.* Compass; (*fig.*) guide, direction; (*pop.*) head. *Perdre la boussole,* to be round the bend.

boustifaille [busti'fa:j], *n.f.* (*pop.*) Feed; grub, prog, stuffing.

boustrophédon [bustrɔfe'dɔ̃], *n.m.* Boustrophedon (inscription).

bout [bu], *n.m.* End, extremity, tip, top, point, nipple, muzzle, ferrule; fragment, bit, fagend. *À bout de forces,* at the end of one's tether; *à bout portant,* point-blank; *au jusqu'au bout,* to see a thing through; *à tout bout de champ,* at every turn; *au bout de l'aune faut le drap,* the last straw breaks the camel's back; *au bout du compte,* taking it all in all; *au bout d'une heure de conversation,* after an hour's conversation; *bâton à deux bouts,* quarter-staff; *bout à bout,* one joined to the other; *bout d'aile,* pinion; *bout de femme,* a wisp of a woman; *bout de pied,* footstool; *bout d'homme,* a bit of a man; *bouts de manches,* false sleeves; (*Cine.*) *bout d'assai,* test strip; *bout filtrant,* filter-tip (of a cigarette); *brûler la chandelle par les deux bouts,* to burn the candle at both ends, to be a bad manager; *de bout en bout* or *d'un bout à l'autre,* from beginning to end; *il fait des*

économies de bouts de chandelle, he is penny wise and pound foolish; *joindre les deux bouts,* to make ends meet; *jusqu'au bout des ongles,* to one's finger-tips; *laisser voir le bout de l'oreille,* to reveal one's true character; *le bas bout,* the lower end; *le bout de la langue,* the tip of the tongue; *le bout de la mamelle,* the nipple of the breast; *le bout des doigts,* the finger-tips; *mettre la patience de quelqu'un à bout,* to exhaust someone's patience; *on ne saurait en venir à bout,* this cannot possibly be managed; *patience, nous ne sommes pas au bout,* have patience, we have not done yet; *pousser quelqu'un à bout,* to drive someone to extremities; *rire du bout des dents,* to laugh in a forced manner; *savoir une chose sur le bout des doigts,* to have a thing at one's finger-tips, to know it perfectly; *tenir le haut bout,* to have the upper hand or whip-hand; *un bout de ruban,* a bit of ribbon; *venir à bout de,* to succeed, to get through (something); *voir les choses par le gros bout* or *le petit bout de la lorgnette,* to see things too big or too small, to exaggerate or depreciate the importance of things; (*slang*) *mettre les bouts,* to run away.

boutade [bu'tad], *n.f.* Whim, fit, start, caprice, freak; sally, witticism. *Par boutades,* by fits and starts.

bout-dehors [budə'ɔ:r] or **boute-hors** [but'ɔ:r] *n.m.* (*pl.* **bouts-dehors** or **boute-hors**) (*Naut.*) Boom for studding-sails, outrigger, spinnaker boom. *Jouer au bout-dehors,* to try to oust one another, to play at beggar my neighbour.

boute-en-train [butɑ̃'trɛ̃], *n.m. inv.* One who promotes gaiety in others, merry-maker; stallion kept with mares; bird that makes others sing. *Être le boute-en-train,* to be the life and soul of the company.

boutefeu [but'fø], *n.m.* (*pl.* **-eux**) (*Artill.*) Linstock; incendiary; (*fig.*) fire-brand.

boute-hors [BOUT-DEHORS].

bouteille [bu'tɛ:j], *n.f.* Bottle; bottleful; (*Naut.,* *pl.*) ship's latrines. *Boucher une bouteille,* to cork a bottle; *bouteille d'oxygène,* oxygen cylinder; *c'est la bouteille à l'encre,* it's a mysterious affair; *couleur vert-bouteille,* bottle green; *déboucher une bouteille,* to uncork a bottle; *mise en bouteille,* bottling; *n'avoir rien vu que par le trou d'une bouteille,* to know nothing of the world; (*fam.*) *prendre de la bouteille,* to be past one's best.

bouteiller [BOUTILLIER].

bouteillerie [butɛj'ri], *n.f.* Bottle-works.

bouteillon [butɛ'jɔ̃], *n.m.* (*Mil.*) Dixie.

*bouter (1) [bu'te], *v.t.* To put, to place, to seat; (*Arch.*) to support; (*Mil.*) to drive back.

bouter (2) [bu'te], *v.i.* To become ropy (of wine).

bouterolle [bu'trɔl], *n.f.* Chape (of a scabbard); ward (of a lock or key); fishing net.

bouteroue [bu'tru], *n.f.* Stone put at the corner of a building etc., to prevent damage by wheels.

boute-selle [but'sɛl], *n.m.* (*pl.* **boute-selles**) (*Mil.*) Boot and saddle trumpet call.

*boutillier or **bouteiller** [butɛ'je], *n.m.* Cup-bearer.

boutique [bu'tik], *n.f.* Shop; the merchandise in a shop; shopkeepers (as a class); workshop, atelier; (*collect.*) tools, implements;

(iron.) a low or ill-famed house or haunt; *(Naut.)* well for fish. *Boutique bien fournie,* a well-stocked shop; *cela vient de votre boutique,* that is your doing; *(fig.) fermer boutique,* to pack up; *il a vendu toute sa boutique,* he has left off business or disposed of his business; *toute la boutique,* the whole show, the whole bag of tricks. **boutiquier,** *n.m. (fem.* **boutiquière)** Shopkeeper; *(fig.)* vulgar person.—*a.* Shopkeeping; shoppy.

boutisse [bu'tis], *n.f.* Header, bondstone.

boutoir [bu'twa:r], *n.m.* Currier's, farrier's, or shoemaker's knife; snout of a wild boar. *Coup de boutoir,* rough answer.

bouton [bu'tɔ̃], *n.m.* Bud; pimple; button, stud, knob; sight (of a gun); *(Elec. etc.)* button. *Bouton à queue,* shank button; *bouton de col,* collar-stud; *boutons de manchettes,* cuff-links; *bouton-pression,* press-stud; *le bouton d'une serrure,* the knob or button of a lock; *bouton quadrillé,* roughened thumb piece; *serrer le bouton à quelqu'un,* to keep a tight hand over, to press hard upon someone.

bouton d'argent [butɔ̃dar'ʒɑ̃], *n.m. (pl.* **boutons d'argent)** Sneezewort, small mushroom, and other plants.

bouton d'or [butɔ̃'dɔ:r], *n.m. (pl.* **boutons d'or)** *(Bot.)* Buttercup.

boutonnant [butɔ'nɑ̃], *a.* That buttons up.

boutonné [butɔ'ne], *a. (fem.* **-ée)** Buttoned; pimpled; *(fig.)* reserved; *(Her.)* bottony. *C'est un homme boutonné,* he is very reserved; *fleuret boutonné,* foil with button on the point; *nez boutonné,* nose blotched with red pimples. **boutonnement,** *n.m.* Budding.

boutonner [butɔ'ne], *v.t.* To button; *(Fenc.)* to touch.—*v.i.* To bud; to button up. **se boutonner,** *v.r.* To button one's coat. **boutonnerie,** *n.f.* Button trade or manufacture. **boutonneux,** *a. (fem.* **-euse)** Pimply. **boutonnier,** *n.m. (fem.* **-ière (1))** Button-maker. **boutonnière (2),** *n.f.* Buttonhole; *(Surg.)* incision, *(fig.)* cut, gash.

bout-rimé [buri'me], *n.m. (usu. in pl.* **bouts-rimés)** Verse composed to given rhymes.

bouturage [buty'ra:ʒ], *n.m. (Hort.)* Piping. **bouture,** *n.f.* Slip; cutting. **bouturer,** *v.t.* To pipe.—*v.i.* To put forth suckers.

bouvard [bu'va:r], *n.m. (dial.)* Young bull.

bouveau [bu'vo] or **bouvelet** [buv'lɛ], *n.m.* Young ox.

bouveret or **bouvret** [buv'rɛ], *n.m.* African variety of bullfinch.

bouverie [bu'vri], *n.f.* Cattle-shed, byre.

bouvet [bu'vɛ], *n.m.* Joiner's grooving-plane. **bouvetage,** *n.m.* Grooving and tonguing. **bouveter,** *v.t.* To groove and tongue.

bouvier [bu'vje], *n.m. (fem.* **bouvière)** Cowherd, ox-drover; *(fig.)* churl.

bouvillon [buvi'jɔ̃], *n.m.* Young bullock, steer.

bouvret [BOUVERET].

bouvreuil [bu'vrœːj], *n.m.* Bullfinch.

bovidé [bɔvi'de] or **boviné** [bɔvi'ne], *n.m.* Bovid.

bovin [bɔ'vɛ̃], *a. (fem.* **bovine)** Bovine. *Peste bovine,* cattle plague.

bow-window [bowin'do], *n.m.* Bow-window.

box [bɔks], *n.m. (pl.* **boxes)** Horse-box, loose box; lock-up garage; a cubicle in a dormitory. *Le box des accusés,* the dock.

box-calf [bɔks'kaf], *n.m.* Box-calf.

boxe [bɔks], *n.f.* Boxing. **boxer,** *v.i.* To box, to spar. **boxeur,** *a. (fem.* **boxeuse)** Pertaining to boxing.—*n.* Boxer, prize-fighter.

boy [bɔj], *n.m.* Groom; native servant.

boyard or **boiard** (bɔ'ja:r], *n.m.* Boyar (Russian nobleman).

boyau [bwa'jo], *n.m.* Bowel, gut, catgut; hose-pipe; long and narrow path, passage, etc.; *(Fort.)* communication trench; *(Cycl.)* racing tyre (stuck on rim). *Corde de boyau,* catgut for musical instruments; *rendre tripes et boyaux, (slang)* to be violently sick. **boyauderie,** *n.f.* Manufacture of gut; gut-works. **boyaudier,** *n.m. (fem.* **-ière)** Gut-spinner. —*a.* Pertaining to gut-spinning.

boycottage [bɔjkɔ'ta:ʒ], *n.m.* Boycotting. **boycotter,** *v.t.* To boycott. **boycotteur,** *n.m. (fem.* **boycotteuse)** Boycotter.

boy-scout [bɔj'skut], *n.m.* Boy-scout.

brabançon [brabɑ̃'sɔ̃], *a. (fem.* **-onne)** Brabantine, Belgian.—*n.m.* **(Brabançon,** *fem.* **-onne)** A Brabantine or Belgian. *La Brabançonne,* the Belgian national anthem.

brabant [bra'bɑ̃], *n.m.* Belgian plough.

bracelet [bras'lɛ], *n.m.* Bracelet, armlet, bangle.

bracelet-montre [braslɛ'mɔ̃tr], *n.m. (pl.* **bracelets-montres)** Wrist-watch.

brachial [bra'kjal], *a. (fem.* **brachiale,** *pl.* **brachiaux)** *(Anat.)* Brachial.

brachiopodes [brakjɔ'pɔd], *n.m. (used only in pl.) (Zool.)* Brachiopoda.

brachycéphale [brakise'fal], *a.* and *n.* Brachycephalic. **brachycéphalie,** *n.f.* Brachycephalism.

braconnage [brakɔ'na:ʒ], *n.m.* Poaching. **braconner,** *v.i.* To poach, to steal game. **braconnier,** *n.m. (fem.* **-ière)** Poacher.—*a.* Poaching; pertaining to poaching.

bractéaire [brakte'ɛːr] or **bractéal,** *a. (fem.* **-éale,** *pl.* **-éaux)** *(Bot.)* Bracteal. **bractéate,** *a. (Num.)* Bracteate. **bractée,** *n.f. (Bot.)* Bract. **bractéifère,** *a. (Bot.)* Bracteate. **bractéiforme,** *a.* Of the form of a bract. **bractéole,** *n.f. (Bot.)* Bracteole; *(Tech.)* defective gold-leaf.

brader [bra'de], *v.t.* To sell off private goods on the pavement before one's home at a *braderie.* **braderie,** *n.f.* Annual sale (usually in September) of old personal clothing, furniture, etc., jumble-sale.

bradype [bra'dip], *n.m. (Zool.)* Sloth. **bradypepsie** [bradipɛp'si], *n.f.* Slow digestion.

Bragance [bra'gɑ̃:s], *f.* Braganza.

brague [brag], *n.f.* *Breeches; (Naut.)* tackle for limiting the recoil of a gun.

braguette [bra'gɛt], *n.f.* *(Cost.)* Cod-piece; fly (of trousers).

brahmane [bra'man], **brahme** [bram], **brame, bramin** or **bramine,** *n.m.* Brahmin. **brahmanique,** *a.* Brahminical. **brahmanisme,** *n.m.* Brahminism.

brahme [BRAHMANE].

brai [brɛ], *n.m.* Resin, rosin, pitch.

braie [brɛ], *n.f. (pl.)* Ancient Gaulish breeches or trousers; *baby's clout; (Naut.)* sheeting (round the foot of a mast, etc.). *S'en tirer les braies nettes,* to get off unharmed, to get clear of.

braillard [bra'ja:r], *a. (fem.* **-arde)** Brawling, squalling; obstreperous.—*n.m.* Small speaking-trumpet.

braille

braille [braj], *n.m.* Braille, raised typography (for the blind).—*n.f.* Herring-salting shovel.
braillement [braj'mã], *n.m.* Squalling.
brailler, *v.i.* To bawl, to shout, to be noisy. —*v.t.* To shout or bawl (a song etc); to stow (fish) in salt. brailleur, *a.* and *n.* (*fem.* -euse) [BRAILLARD].
braiment [brɛ'mã], *n.m.* Bray of an ass.
braire [brɛːr], *v.i. irr.* To bray; (*fig.*) to cry, to whine.
braise [brɛːz], *n.f.* Wood-embers, live coals; (*slang*) money. *Être sur la braise*, to be in suspense or anxiety; *il l'a donné chaud comme braise*, he blurted it all out; *passer sur une chose comme chat sur braise*, to walk like a cat on hot bricks; *tomber de la poêle dans la braise*, to fall from the frying-pan into the fire. braiser, *v.t.* To braise. braisier, *n.m.* Brazier. braisière, *n.f.* Braising-pan; extinguisher for charcoal.
bramement [bram'mã], *n.m.* Belling (of deer). bramer, *v.i.* To bell (of deer).
bramin or bramine [BRAHMANE].
bran [brã], *n.m.* Bran; excrement, cack. *Bran de judas*, freckles; *bran de scie*, sawdust.
brancard [brã'kaːr], *n.m.* Stretcher, litter, hand-barrow; shaft (of a cart). brancarder, *v.t.* To carry on a stretcher. brancardier, *n.m.* Stretcher-bearer, ambulance-man.
branchage [brã'ʃaːʒ], *n.m.* (*collect.*) Branches, boughs; ramifications.
branche [brã:ʃ], *n.f.* Branch, bough, limb (of a tree etc.); section, part, division; bifurcation, ramification; tine (of antlers). *Branches gourmandes*, suckers; *être comme l'oiseau sur la branche*, to be unsettled; *jeune branche*, twig; *s'accrocher à toutes les branches*, to try every possible means, whether fair or foul; *sauter de branche en branche*, to go from one thing to another; (*pop. term of endearment*) *ma vieille branche*, dear old chum.
branchement, *n.m.* Branching, ramification. brancher, *v.i.* To branch off.—*v.t.* *To hang (a person etc.) on a branch; to divide into branches, to cause to ramify; (*Elec.*) to connect, to plug in; to tap (a gas or water pipe). branchette, *n.f.*, or branchillon, *n.m.* Twig, little branch.
branche-ursine [brãʃyr'sin] or brancursine, *n.f.* Brank-ursine, acanthus.
branchial [brã'ʃjal], *a.* (*fem.* -iale, *pl.* -iaux) (*Zool.*) Branchial. *Opercule branchial*, gill-cover. branchie [brã'ʃi], *n.f.* (*usu. in pl.*) Fish-gills. branchié, *a.* (*fem.* -ée) Branchiate, branchiferous.
branchillon [BRANCHETTE].
branchiopode [brãʃjɔ'pɔd], *a.* (*Zool.*) Branchiopodous.—*n.m.* (*usu. in pl.*) Branchiopod.
branchu [brã'ʃy], *a.* (*fem.* branchue) Forked, bifurcated, ramifying.
brancursine [BRANCHE-URSINE].
brandade [brã'dad], *n.f.* Ragout (of cod).
brande [brã:d], *n.f.* Heather; heath; a bundle of inflammable material used as a firework.
Brandebourg [brãd'buːr], *m.* Brandenburg.
brandebourgs [brãd'buːr], *n.m. pl.* Frogs (and loops) on a uniform.
*brandevin [brãd'vɛ̃], *n.m.* Brandy distilled from wine.
brandillement [brãdij'mã], *n.m.* Tossing, swinging.
brandiller [brãdi'je], *v.t.* To swing, to shake

bras

to and fro.—*v.i.* To swing, to move to and fro. se brandiller, *v.r.* To swing.
brandir [brã'diːr], *v.t.* To brandish, to flourish. brandissement, *n.m.* Brandishing, flourishing.
brandon [brã'dɔ̃], *n.m.* Torch, fire-brand; (*fig.*) flake of fire, flame; (*Law*) wisp of lighted straw (indicating that the crops in a field are seized). *Brandon de discorde*, apple of discord.
branlant [brã'lã], *a.* (*fem.* branlante) Shaking, loose, tottering.
branle [brã:l], *n.m.* Oscillation, shaking or tossing motion; jog, push, shake; an old-fashioned dance, brawl; (*Naut.*) hammock. *Donner le branle* or *mettre en branle*, to set going; *être en branle*, to be in full swing; *mener le branle*, to lead the dance.
branle-bas [brãl'ba], *n.m. inv.* (*Naut.*) Clearing for action; (*fig.*) commotion, disturbance. *Faire le branle-bas*, to clear the decks.
branlement [brãl'mã], *n.m.* Oscillation, shaking, swing.
branle-queue [brãl'kø], *n.m.* (*pl.* branle-queues) Wagtail; dish-washer.
branler [brã'le], *v.t.* To shake, to wag.—*v.i.* To shake, to stagger, to rock; to stir, to move, to budge; to give way, to waver, to be in jeopardy. *Branler dans le manche*, to fit loosely in the handle; (*fig.*) to be insecure in one's post, to be loose in the saddle.
branloire [brã'lwaːr], *n.f.* Seesaw; (*Am.*) teeter; hanging box (under a wagon).
brante [brã:t], *n.f.* Red-bill pochard.
braquage [bra'kaːʒ], *n.m.* Aiming, levelling (of a gun); steering (of a car). *Rayon de braquage*, turning circle.
braque (1) [brak], *n.m.* French pointer.
braque (2) [brak], *a.* Madcap, hare-brained.
*braquemart [brak'maːr], *n.m.* Cutlass, broad, short sword (14th and 15th cent.).
braquement [brak'mã], *n.m.* Pointing (of ordnance etc.).
braquer [bra'ke], *v.t.* To aim, to level, to point. *Braquer un fusil*, to level a gun; *braquer une lunette*, to point a telescope; *braquer le volant (d'une auto)*, to turn, to deflect the wheel-steering; *braquer les yeux sur un point*, to fix one's eyes on a certain point. se braquer, *v.r.* To pull (of a horse); (*fig.*) to be stubbornly opposed.
bras [bra], *n.m.* Arm; bracket, sconce (of a candelabrum); branch (of a stream etc.); (*fig.*) power, action, valour, work, defence, assistance; (*pl.*) embrace, arms. *À bras-le-corps*, in one's arms, round the waist; *à bras raccourcis*, with tooth and nail; *à force de bras*, by strength of arms; *à pleins bras*, by armfuls; *à tour de bras*, with all one's might; *avoir de grandes affaires sur les bras*, to have great concerns in hand; *avoir le bras long*, to have far-reaching influence; *avoir quelqu'un sur les bras*, to have someone to maintain; *bras dessus bras dessous*, arm-in-arm; *bras de mer*, arm of the sea, sound; *bras mort*, backwater (of a river); *bras d'une vergue*, (*Naut.*) tackle for trimming a yard-arm; *chaise à bras*, arm-chair; *demeurer les bras croisés*, to stand with folded arms doing nothing; *donner le bras à quelqu'un*, to walk arm-in-arm with someone; *en prendre long comme le bras*, to take an ell, to impose upon; *être en bras de chemise*, to be

[108]

in one's shirt sleeves; *être le bras droit de quelqu'un*, (*fig.*) to be someone's right hand; *gros comme le bras*, in a large manner; *il a le bras en écharpe*, he has his arm in a sling; *j'ai sur les bras un puissant ennemi*, I have to do with a powerful enemy; *la perte de son protecteur lui a coupé bras et jambes*, the loss of his protector has paralysed him; *les bras de la mort*, the jaws of death; *les bras m'en sont tombés*, I was struck dumb with surprise; *manquer de bras*, to be short of labour; *moulin à bras*, handmill; *ne vivre que de ses bras*, to live by the labour of one's hands; *recevoir quelqu'un à bras ouverts*, to receive someone with open arms; *se jeter dans les bras de quelqu'un*, to fly to someone for protection; *tendre les bras à quelqu'un*, to offer one's aid to someone.

brasage [brɑ'za:ʒ] or **brasement**, *n.m.* Brazing.

braser [brɑ'ze], *v.t.* To braze.

brasero [brazeˈro], *n.m.* Brazier, charcoal-pan.

brasier [brɑ'zje], *n.m.* Quick clear fire; brazier, furnace; (*fig.*) ardour, fervency.

brasillement [brazijˈmã], *n.m.* Glittering, glancing, sparkling (of the sea).

brasiller [braziˈje], *v.t.* To grill, to broil.—*v.i.* To glitter, to shine (of the sea).

brasque [brask], *n.f.* (*Metal.*) Brasque, lute.

brassage (1) [brɑ'sa:ʒ], *n.m.* Mashing, brewing.

brassage (2) [BRASSEYAGE].

brassard [brɑ'sa:r], *n.m.* Brace (armour); arm-guard; armlet, brassard.

brasse [bras], *n.f.* Fathom, six feet; armful, as much as the two arms can hold; stroke (in swimming). *Brasse française* or *sur le ventre*, breast stroke; *brasse indienne* or *sur le côté*, over-arm side stroke; *brasse sur le dos*, back stroke.

brassée [bra'se], *n.f.* Armful; stroke (in swimming).

brassement [bras'mã], *n.m.* Brewing; mixing.

brasser (1) [bra'se], *v.t.* To mix, to brew, to mash; to stir up (*fig.*); to hatch, to contrive, to plot. *Brasser les dominos*, to shuffle the dominoes; *brasser des affaires*, to handle a lot of business.

brasser (2) [bra'se], *v.t.* (*Naut.*) To brace (the yards). *Brasser au vent*, to round in the weather braces.

brasserie [bras'ri], *n.f.* Brewery; brewing; drinking-saloon, 'pub'. **brasseur**, *n.m.* Brewer. *Brasseur d'affaires*, man with many irons in the fire.

brasseyage [brasɛˈja:ʒ], *n.m.* (*Naut.*) Bracing.

brasseyer [BRASSER (2)].

brassiage [bra'sja:ʒ], *n.m.* (*Naut.*) Sounding.

brassicaire [brasiˈkɛ:r], *a.* Of or pertaining to cabbages.

brassicourt [brasiˈku:r], *a.* Bandy-legged, knee-sprung (of horses).

brassière [bra'sjɛ:r], *n.f.* Shoulder-strap (of a knapsack etc.); breast support; infant's vest; *pl.* leading strings (of infants); (*fig.*) *être en brassières*, to be in leading strings.

brassin [bra'sɛ̃], *n.m.* Brewing-tub; mash-tub; a boiling (quantity boiled or brewed).

brasure [brɑ'zy:r], *n.f.* Place where two pieces of metal are brazed or soldered; seam, joint.

bravache [bra'vaʃ], *n.m.* Bravo, bully, swaggerer, blusterer.—*a.* Blustering, bullying.

***bravacherie**, *n.f.* Bluster, swagger.

bravade [bra'vad], *n.f.* Bravado, boast, bluster.

brave [bra:v], *a.* Brave, courageous, gallant; worthy, honest, good; (*dial.*) smart, fine, spruce. *Brave capitaine*, gallant captain; *c'est un brave garçon*, he is a capital fellow or a brick; *c'est un brave homme*, he is an honest, worthy fellow; *il est brave comme l'épée qu'il porte*, he is as true as steel; *il n'est brave qu'en paroles*, he is only brave as far as words go; *un homme brave*, a brave man.—*n.m.* Brave or courageous man; a good fellow; *bravo, ruffian, bully. *Brave à trois poils*, (*colloq.*) hard fighter; *en brave*, bravely, gallantly; *faire le brave*, to play the bully; *faux brave*, blustering bully; *mon brave*, my good fellow. **bravement**, *adv.* Bravely, stoutly, valiantly, manfully; skilfully, finely.

braver [bra've], *v.t.* To defy, to set at defiance, to dare; to brave, to face, to beard. *Braver la mort*, to face death bravely; *braver les autorités*, to set the authorities at defiance.

bravo [bra'vo], *n.m.* and *int.* (*pl.* **bravos**) Bravo. Hear, hear!

bravoure [bra'vu:r], *n.f.* Bravery, courage, gallantry; (*pl.*) exploits. *Il a fait preuve de bravoure*, he has given proofs of courage; *morceau de bravoure* (*Mus.*), bravura, (*Lit.*) purple patch.

braye [brɛ:], *n.f.* Greasy, plastic earth or clay used for puddling; sling, strap.

brayer (1) [brɛ'je], *n.m.* Truss, strap; sash.

brayer (2) [brɛ'je], *v.t.* (*Naut.*) To pay over (with pitch or tar).

brayette [BRAGUETTE].

break [brɛk], *n.m.* Break (carriage).

brebis [brə'bi], *n.f.* Ewe; (*fig.*) sheep, a mild or meek-natured woman, an innocent girl; one of a pastor's flock; (*pl.*) flock. *À brebis tondue Dieu mesure le vent*, God tempers the wind to the shorn lamb; *brebis comptées, le loup les mange*, the best laid schemes often go wrong; *brebis égarée*, stray sheep; *brebis qui bêle perd sa goulée*, it's the silent sow that sucks the wash; *il ne faut qu'une brebis galeuse pour gâter tout un troupeau*, one scabby sheep will taint a whole flock; *mener paître les brebis*, to lead the sheep to pasture; *qui se fait brebis, le loup le mange*, daub yourself with honey, and you'll never want for flies; *une brebis du bon Dieu*, an inoffensive, uncomplaining person; *une brebis galeuse*, a scabby sheep, (*fig.*) a black sheep; *un repas de brebis*, a meal without drink.

brèche [brɛʃ], *n.f.* Breach, flaw; notch, gap; (*fig.*) wrong, injury; (*Geol.*) breccia. *Battre en brèche*, to batter in, to breach, (*fig.*) to attack (a person, principle, etc.) vehemently; *c'est une brèche à l'honneur*, it is a breach of honour; *faire brèche à un pâté*, to cut open a pie; *monter sur la brèche*, to mount the breach.

brèche-dent [brɛʃ'dã], *a.* That has lost a front tooth or two; gap-toothed.—*n.* (*pl.* **brèche-dents**) Person who has lost a front tooth.

bréchet [bre'ʃɛ], *n.m.* (*Orn.*) Breast-bone.

bredi-breda [brədibrə'da], *adv.* (*colloq.*) Hastily.

bredouillage [brədu′jaːʒ] or **bredouille-**
ment, *n.m.* Stammering, stuttering, sputtering.
bredouille [brə′duːj], *n.f.* (*Trictrac*) Lurch.—
a. inv. Empty-handed. *Jouer bredouille*, to
play lurches; *revenir bredouille*, to return
with an empty bag (of sportsmen); *sortir
bredouille*, to go away as one came.
bredouillement [BREDOUILLAGE].
bredouiller [brədu′je], *v.i.* or *t.* To stammer,
to stutter. **bredouilleur**, *a.* (*fem.* -euse)
Stammering, stuttering.—*n.* Stammerer,
stutterer.
bref [brɛf], *a.* (*fem.* **brève** (1)) Short, brief,
concise, succinct; laconic; brusque. *Avoir
le parler bref*, to be a man of few words;
une réponse brève, a brief reply.—*adv.* In a
few words, in short, in fine, in a word.—
n.m. Brief (Pope's pastoral letter); Church
calendar.
bréhaigne [bre′ɛɲ], *a.f.* Barren, sterile (now
chiefly of animals).
brelan [brə′lɑ̃], *n.m.* Brelan (game at cards);
pair-royal; gaming-house. *Avoir brelan d'as*,
to hold three aces; *tenir brelan*, to keep a
gaming-house.
brêle or **brelle** [brɛːl], *n.f.* Float (of timber).
brêler or **breller** [brɛ′le], *v.t.* To make fast
with ropes (beams, joists, etc.); to lash.
brelique-breloque [brəlikbrə′lɔk], *adv.* At
random; (*colloq.*) higgledy-piggledy; slap-
dash.
breller [BRÊLER].
breloque [brə′lɔk], *n.f.* Trinket, gewgaw,
charm (*especially on a chain*); (*Mil.*) dismiss.
Battre la breloque, to sound the dismiss, or
the 'all clear' after an air attack; (*colloq.*) to
talk at random; (*of a watch*) to keep stopping
and starting.
*breluche [brə′lyʃ], *n.f.* Drugget, linsey-
woolsey.
Brême [brɛːm], *m.* Bremen.
brème [brɛːm], *n.f.* Bream. *Brème de mer*,
sea-bream.
breneux [brə′nø], *a.* (*fem.* **breneuse**) (*pop.*)
Dirty, soiled (with excrement).
Brésil [bre′zil], **le**, *m.* Brazil.
brésil [bre′zil], *n.m.* Brazil-wood (for dyeing).
brésilien [brezi′ljɛ̃], *a.* and *n.* (*fem.* **brési-**
lienne) Brazilian.
brésiller [brezi′je], *v.t.* To break small, to
cut small; to dye with Brazil-wood.—*v.i.* To
fall to powder, to moulder away.
Bretagne [brə′taɲ], *f.* Brittany. **La Grande-**
Bretagne, Great Britain; **la Nouvelle-**
Bretagne, New Britain.
brétailler [breta′je], *v.i.* To fight (on any
provocation); to practise fencing. **brétail-**
leur, *n.m.* Fire-eater, bully.
bretauder [brəto′de], *v.t.* To crop (animals)
badly; to crop the ears of; to castrate.
bretèche [brə′tɛʃ], *n.f.* *(*Fort.*) Brattice; bay-
window.
bretelle [brə′tɛl], *n.f.* Strap; brace; (*pl.*) pair
of braces; (*Am.*) suspenders; (*Rail.*) points;
(rifle) sling. *En avoir jusqu'aux bretelles*, to be
over head and ears in trouble. **bretellerie**,
n.f. Manufacture of braces, garters, etc.
bretesse [BRETÈCHE].
bretessé [brətɛ′se], *a.* (*fem.* **bretessée**) (*Her.*)
Crenellated on each side.
breton [brə′tɔ̃], *a.* (*fem.* **bretonne**) Breton.

n.m. (**Breton**, *fem.* **Bretonne**) A Breton;
(*fam.*) *tête de Breton*, headstrong.
*brette [brɛt], *n.f.* Long sword, rapier.
bretté [brɛ′te], *a.* (*fem.* **brettée**) Notched,
indented, jagged.
bretteler [brɛ′tle], *v.t.* To shape (stones etc.)
with a notched implement. **brettellure**,
n.f. Fine hatching on silver-ware etc.
bretter [brɛ′te], *v.t.* To dent, to notch, to
indent.—*v.i.* (*fig.*) To play the bully or
swashbuckler. **bretteur**, *n.m.* Swashbuckler,
duellist. **bretture**, *n.f.* Notching, denting.
bretzel [brɛt′sɛl], *n.m.* Pretzel.
breuil [brœːj], *n.m.* Enclosed coppice, covert.
breuvage [brœ′vaːʒ], *n.m.* Beverage, drink,
liquor; (*Vet.*) drench.
brève (1) [BREF].
brève (2) [brɛːv], *n.f.* Short syllable; (*Mus.*)
breve.
brevet [brə′vɛ], *n.m.* Warrant, brevet, certificate (school etc.), diploma, licence (of
printers), patent; badge (of boy-scouts);
(*Mil.*) commission. *Brevet d'apprentissage*,
indentures; *brevet d'invention*, letters patent;
brevet d'État Major, Staff College certificate.
brevetable, *a.* Patentable. **breveté**, *a.*
(*fem.* -**ée**) Patented, certificated; (of) officer
who has passed Staff Course, P.S.C.—*n.*
Patentee. **breveter**, *v.t.* To patent; to
license; to certificate.
bréviaire [bre′vjɛːr], *n.m.* Breviary.
brévicaule [brevi′kol], *a.* (*Bot.*) Short-
stemmed.
brévipède [brevi′pɛd], *a.* (*Zool.*) Breviped.
brévirostre, *a.* Brevirostrate.
brévité [brevi′te], *n.f.* Shortness (of syllables).
Briarée [bria′re], *m.* Briareus.
bribe [brib], *n.f.* ***Hunk of bread; (*pl.*) Scraps,
bits; odds and ends.
bric [BROC (2)].
bric-à-brac [brika′brak], *n.m. inv.* Curios,
bric-à-brac; curiosity-shop. *Marchand de
bric-à-brac*, dealer in old pictures, stores,
curios, etc.
bricheton [briʃ′tɔ̃], *n.m.* (*slang*) Bread; food.
brick [brik], *n.m.* Brig.
bricolage [brikɔ′laːʒ], *n.m.* Pottering.
bricole [bri′kɔl], *n.f.* Medieval catapult or
mangonel; breast-collar for a horse; porter's
strap; rebound; (*fig.*) petty job; (*pl.*) toils
for deer. *Coup de bricole* (*Billiards*), shot off
the cushion; *par bricole*, indirectly, unfairly,
by a fluke. **bricoler**, *v.i.* To potter, to do
odds and ends. **bricoleur**, *n.m.* (*fem.*
-**euse**) Potterer, jack-of-all-trades; shuffler.
bricolier [brikɔ′lje], *n.m.* Side horse.
bridable [bri′dabl], *a.* That may be bridled.
bridage, *n.m.* Bridling, curbing, checking.
bride [brid], *n.f.* Bridle, bridle-rein, bridle-
harness; check, curb; string (of a woman's
cap, bonnet, etc.); loop (for a button); iron
tie. *À cheval donné on ne regarde pas à la
bride*, one does not look a gift-horse in the
mouth; *courir à toute bride* or *à bride abattue*,
to run at full speed; *lâcher la bride* (*à*), to
give rein, to give full licence (to); *laisser* or
mettre la bride sur le cou, to give (a horse) his
head, (*fig.*) to let someone have his own way;
lui tenir la bride courte, to ride him on a short
rein; *mettre la bride à un cheval*, to put a
bridle upon a horse; *tenir la bride haute à un
cheval*, to keep a tight rein; *tenir quelqu'un en*

bride, to keep someone within bounds; *tourner bride*, to turn back.

brider [bri'de], *v.t.* To bridle; to restrain, to curb; to truss (a fowl); to tie, to fasten; to check, to repress. *Brider l'ancre*, (*Naut.*) to stow the anchor; *brider ses désirs*, to curb one's desires; *brider son cheval par la queue*, to begin at the wrong end; *mon habit me bride sous les bras*, my coat is too tight under the arms; *yeux bridés*, narrow eyes.

bridge [bridʒ], *n.m.* Bridge (*card game*); bridge (*in dentistry*).

bridger [bri'dʒe], *v.i.* To play bridge.

bridgeur [brid'ʒœr], *n.m.* (*fem.* **bridgeuse**) Bridge-player.

bridon [bri'dɔ̃], *n.m.* Snaffle-bridle.

bridure [bri'dy:r], *n.f.* (*Naut.*) Frapping; (*Cook.*) trussing (of a fowl etc.).

brie [bri], *n.m.* Brie cheese.

brièvement [briɛv'mɑ̃], *adv.* Briefly, succinctly, in short. **brièveté**, *n.f.* Brevity, briefness, conciseness.

brife or **briffe** [brif], *n.f.* (*slang*) (Chunk of) bread.

brifer [bri'fe], *v.t.* To eat greedily, to gobble up.

brifeton [brif'tɔ̃], *n.m.* [BRICHETON].

brigade [bri'gad], *n.f.* Brigade; (*fig.*) troop, squad, gang, body. *Brigade de choc*, crack soldiers, first-class troop; *chef de brigade*, foreman (of workmen); *général de brigade*, brigadier.

brigadier [briga'dje], *n.m.* Corporal (in cavalry, artillery); sergeant (of police); (*Naut.*) bowman. **brigadier-chef**, *n.m.* (*pl.* **brigadiers-chefs**) Lance-sergeant.

brigand [bri'gɑ̃], *n.m.* Brigand, highwayman; (*fig.*) robber, ruffian, thief. **brigandage**, *n.m.* Brigandage, plunder. **brigandeau**, *n.m.* Brigand on a small scale; (*fig.*) cheat, rogue, knave. **brigander**, *v.i.* To rob, to plunder.—*v.t.* To rob, to pillage.

brigantin [brigɑ̃'tɛ̃], *n.m.* Brigantine. **brigantine**, *n.f.* Spanker; small vessel in the Mediterranean.

brignole [bri'ɲɔl], *n.f.* French dried plum.

brigue [brig], *n.f.* Intrigue, underhand manœuvre, cabal, faction. **briguer**, *v.t.* To try to obtain by intrigue etc.; to canvas for, to solicit, to court. **brigueur**, *n.m.* (*fem.* -euse) Intriguer, canvasser.

brillance [bri'jɑ̃s], *n.f.* (*Opt.*) Brilliancy.

brillamment [brija'mɑ̃], *adv.* Brilliantly, in a brilliant manner.

brillant [bri'jɑ̃], *a.* (*fem.* **brillante**) Brilliant, sparkling, glittering, bright, showy; beaming, flourishing, splendid, radiant; robust, blooming (of health). *Affaire brillante*, famous action; *brillants appas* or *charmes brillants*, dazzling charms; *brillant causeur*, fascinating talker; *esprit brillant*, sparkling wit.—*n.m.* Brilliance, splendour, lustre; brilliant (diamond). *Brillant pour les ongles*, nail-polish.

brillanté [brijɑ̃'te], *a.* (*fem.* -ée) Cut into a brilliant.—*n.m.* Diaper, damask; machine-made lace. **brillanter**, *v.t.* To cut into a brilliant; to overload with specious ornament. *Brillanter son style*, (*fig.*) to load one's style with ornament. **brillantine**, *n.f.* Brilliantine (hair-oil); glossy cotton-cloth.

briller [bri'je], *v.i.* To shine, to glitter, to sparkle; to be bright or sparkling; (*fig.*) to

blaze, to dawn, to lighten, to flourish, to gleam, to distinguish oneself, to stand out. *Faire briller quelqu'un*, to bring somebody out; *il a brillé par son absence*, his absence was conspicuous; *tout ce qui brille n'est pas or*, all that glitters is not gold.

brillement [brij'mɑ̃], *n.m.* Brilliance, sparkle.

brilloter or **brillotter** [brijɔ'te], *v.i.* To shine or glitter faintly.

brimade [bri'mad], *n.f.* Ragging, hazing (at school, barracks, etc.); vexation, persecution.

brimbalant [brɛ̃ba'lɑ̃], *a.* (*fem.* **brimbalante**) Swinging, oscillating, dangling.

brimbale [brɛ̃'bal] or **bringuebale**, *n.f.* Brake or handle of a pump.

brimbaler [brɛ̃ba'le] or **bringuebaler** [brɛ̃gba'le], *v.t.* To swing, to ring.—*v.i.* To swing, to tote about; to wobble (of wheel).

brimbelle [brɛ̃'bɛl], *n.f.* [MYRTILLE].

brimborion [brɛ̃bɔ'rjɔ̃], *n.m.* Knick-knack, bauble, gewgaw.

brimer [bri'me], *v.t.* To rag, to bully (freshmen, recruits, etc.).

brin [brɛ̃], *n.m.* Blade, slender stalk, shoot (of corn etc.); thread (of a cord, string, etc.); (*fig.*) sprig; bit, jot. *De brin* or *en brin*, unhewn wood; *il n'y en a pas un brin*, there is none at all; *brin à brin*, *brin par brin*, bit by bit, little by little; *un beau brin de bois*, a fine straight piece of timber; *un beau brin d'homme*, a tall well-set youth; *un beau brin de fille*, fine slip of a girl; *un brin d'air*, a breath of air; (*Rad.*) *brins d'une antenne*, wires of an aerial; *un brin de feu*, a bit of fire; *un brin de fil*, a bit of thread; *un brin de paille*, a straw; *un brin de romarin*, a sprig of rosemary.

***brinde** [brɛ̃:d], *n.f.* Health, toast. *Être dans les brindes*, *être brindezingue*, to be drunk; *porter des brindes*, to drink toasts.

brindille [brɛ̃'di:j], *n.f.* Sprig, twig.

bringé [brɛ̃'ʒe], *a.* Brindled (of oxen).

bringue [brɛ̃:g], *n.f.* Bit, piece; (*fam.*) gawky woman; (*slang*) spree. *En bringues*, in bits; (*fam.*) *une grande bringue*, a tall gawky woman; (*slang*) *faire la bringue*, to go on the spree.

bringuebale [BRIMBALE].

brio [bri'o] [Ital.], *n.m.* (*Mus. etc.*) Dash, spirit, go. *Répondre avec brio*, to answer brilliantly, wittily.

briochain [brio'ʃɛ̃] (*fem.* -aine), *a.* and *n.* (*Geol.*) Native or inhabitant of Saint-Brieuc.

brioché, *a.* (*fem.* -ée) Baked like a brioche. *Pain brioché*, bread baked like a brioche.

brioche [bri'ɔʃ], *n.f.* Brioche; (*fig.*) blunder.

brion (1) [bri'ɔ̃], *n.m.* (*Naut.*) Curved timber joining the stem and the keel; gripe.

brion (2) [BRYON].

briquaillon [brika'jɔ̃], *n.m.* Brickbat.

brique [brik], *n.f.* Brick; (*slang*) one million francs. *Brique anglaise*, bath brick; *brique creuse*, hollow brick, perforated brick; *brique pleine*, solid brick; *brique réfractaire*, fire brick; *brique vernissée*, glazed brick; *couleur brique*, *ton de brique*, reddish brown; (*colloq.*) *manger des briques*, to be starving.

briquer [bri'ke], *v.t.* (*Naut.*) To holystone; (*slang*) to clean, to scrub.

briquet [bri'ke], *n.m.* Steel (for strike-a-light), tinder-box; (cigarette) lighter; *short, curved sword (of infantry); beagle, harrier. *Battre le briquet*, to strike a light, (*fig.*) to bark one's shins; (*Pharm.*) *briquet pneumatique*, fire syringe; *pierre à briquet*, flint.

briquetage [brik'ta:ʒ], *n.m.* Brick-work; imitation brick-work.

briqueter [brik'te], *v.t.* To brick, to pave or line with bricks; to imitate brick-work. **briqueterie,** *n.f.* Brick-field, brick-making. **briqueteur,** *n.m.* Bricklayer. **briquetier,** *n.m.* Brick-maker.

briquette [bri'kɛt], *n.f.* Briquette; compressed slack.

bris [bri], *n.m.* (*Law*) Breaking (of doors, glass, seals, etc.); wreckage, waif.

brisant [bri'zã], *n.m.* Sand-bank, reef, shoal; (*pl.*) breakers.

briscard [BRISQUARD].

brise [bri:z], *n.f.* Breeze; strong wind.

brisé [bri'ze], *a.* (*fem.* **brisée**) Broken to pieces; (*fig.*) harassed, fatigued; folding (of furniture); (*Her.*) rompu, broken. *Chaise brisée*, folding-chair; *ligne brisée*, broken line; *lit brisé*, folding-bed; *porte brisée*, folding-door.

brise-bise [briz'bi:z], *n.m. inv.* Weather-strip (for doors, windows, etc.); short curtain for lower part of window.

brisées [bri'ze], *n.f.* (*used only in pl.*) Boughs cut off to mark the place where an animal lies or has passed, or for marking the limits for cutting down wood. *Aller* or *marcher sur les brisées de quelqu'un*, to poach on someone's preserves; *reprendre* or *revenir sur ses brisées*, to retrace one's steps; *suivre les brisées de quelqu'un*, to follow someone's example; to follow in someone's footsteps.

brise-glace [briz'glas], *n.m.* (*pl.* **brise-glace** or **-glaces**) Starling (of a bridge); ice-beam (of a ship); ice-breaker (ship).

brise-jet [briz'ʒɛ], *n.m. inv.* Anti-splash tap-nozzle.

brise-lames [briz'lam], *n.m. inv.* Breakwater.

brisement [briz'mã], *n.m.* Breaking, dashing (of waves); (*fig.*) trouble, contrition.

brise-mottes [briz'mɔt], *n.m. inv.* (*Agric.*) Clod-breaking machine.

brise-pierre [briz'pjɛ:r], *n.m. inv.* (*Surg.*) Stone-crusher.

briser [bri'ze], *v.t.* To break to pieces, to smash, to break, to shatter; to flaw, to burst, to crack, to bruise; to destroy, to demolish, to overthrow. *Être brisé*, to feel sore all over. —*v.i.* To break; to dash (of waves). *Briser avec quelqu'un*, to break with someone; *briser les fers de quelqu'un*, to set someone free; *brisons là*, let us say no more on the subject, enough! **se briser,** *v.r.* To break, to be dashed to pieces; to come to grief; to fold up (of furniture).

brise-tout [briz'tu], *n.m. inv.* Person that breaks everything; rough, clumsy fellow.

briseur [bri'zœ:r], *n.m.* (*fem.* **-euse**) One who breaks or likes to break anything; iconoclast.

brise-vent [briz'vã], *n.m.* (*pl.* **brise-vent** or **brise-vents**) Wind-screen (for protecting plants).

brisis [bri'zi], *n.m.* (*Arch.*) Break (of a mansard roof).

briska [bris'ka], *n.m.* Britzska (Russian carriage).

brisoir [bri'zwa:r], *n.m.* Brake (for flax).

brisque [brisk], *n.f.* A card game; (*Bezique*) the ace or ten; (*Mil.*) stripe; war service

chevron. **brisquard,** *n.m.* (Old) soldier with many *brisques*; old campaigner.

bristol [bris'tɔl], *n.m.* Bristol board; (*fam.*) visiting card.

brisure [bri'zy:r], *n.f.* Break; folding-point in a piece of joiner's work; small fragment; (*Her.*) rebatement; difference. *Brisures de riz*, broken rice.

britannique [brita'nik], *a.* British, Britannic. **Les Îles Britanniques,** the British Isles.

brize [bri:z], *n.f.* (*Bot.*) [AMOURETTE].

broc (1) [bro], *n.m.* Large jug or quart-pot.

broc (2) [brɔk], *n.f.* *Spit. De bric et de broc,* anyhow, piecemeal; *de broc en bouche,* forthwith, without delay.

brocaille [brɔ'ka:j], *n.f.* Rubble, waste stones; iron scrap.

brocantage [brɔkã'ta:ʒ], *n.m.* Dealing in second-hand goods, broker's business; bartering. **brocante,** *n.f.* Second-hand trade; an article of trifling value. **brocanter,** *v.i.* To deal in second-hand goods; to exchange, to barter. **brocanteur,** *n.m.* (*fem.* -euse) Dealer in second-hand goods, junk-shop owner.

brocard (1) [brɔ'ka:r], *n.m.* Yearling (of roe-deer); pricket.

brocard (2) [brɔ'ka:r], *n.m.* Taunt, jeer, scoff; lampoon, squib; raillery. **brocarder,** *v.t.* To taunt, to jeer at, to ridicule. **brocardeur,** *n.m.* (*fem.* -euse) Scoffer, jeerer.

brocart (1) [brɔ'ka:r], *n.m.* Brocade.

brocart (2) [BROCARD (1)].

brocatelle [brɔka'tɛl], *n.f.* Brocaded dress-stuff of silk, wool, cotton, etc.; many-coloured marble.

brochage [brɔ'ʃa:ʒ], *n.m.* Stitching (of books).

brochant [brɔ'ʃã], *a.* (*fem.* **brochante**) Passing over another piece. *Brochant sur le tout,* (*Her.*) placed above another piece or other pieces and passing from side to side of the shield; (*fig.*) to crown all.

broche [brɔʃ], *n.f.* Spit; spindle; skewer; spigot, peg (of casks etc.); stem or gudgeon (of a lock); knitting-needle; brooch; iron-pin; (*pl.*) tusks (of wild boars). (*Elec.*) Fiche à deux broches, two-pin plug; *faire un tour de broche,* to go and warm oneself at the fire; *mettre la viande à la broche,* to spit the meat.

broché [brɔ'ʃe], *a.* (*fem.* **brochée** (1)) Embossed (of linen); brocaded, figured (of stuffs). *Livre broché,* paper-bound book.—*n.m.* Process of weaving designs on stuff, brocading; result of this; brocaded stuff. *Broché de satin,* brocaded satin.

brochée [brɔ'ʃe], *n.f.* Spitful.

brocher [brɔ'ʃe], *v.t.* To stitch (a book etc.); to figure (stuffs); to emboss (linen); to drive nails (into a horse's foot); (*fig.*) to do things in a hurry, to dispatch. *Et pour brocher sur le tout,* and to cap it all.

brochet [brɔ'ʃe], *n.m.* Pike (fish). *Brochet de mer,* sea-pike.

brocheter [brɔʃ'te], *v.t.* To fix with a skewer; to skewer on to the spit.

brocheton [brɔʃ'tɔ̃], *n.m.* Small pike, pickerel.

brochette [brɔ'ʃɛt], *n.f.* Small spit for fixing meat on the main spit; small spit for cooking kidneys etc.; small spitful or skewerful (of meat etc.); stick for feeding birds. *Élever des oiseaux à la brochette,* to feed birds by hand; *enfant élevé à la brochette,* child brought up with great care; *brochette de décorations*, string of decorations; (*fam.*) *une belle brochette*, a good catch (of a gang caught by the police).

brocheur [brɔ'ʃœːr], *n.m.* (*fem.* **brocheuse**) Stitcher, book-stitcher.

brochoir [brɔ'ʃwaːr], *n.m.* Shoeing-hammer.

brochure [brɔ'ʃyːr], *n.f.* Stitching; booklet, brochure, pamphlet, tract; design stitched on to a fabric, embroidery.

brocoli [brɔkɔ'li], *n.m.* Broccoli.

brodequin [brɔd'kɛ̃], *n.m.* Buskin, half-boot, ankle-boot, laced-boot; (*Ant.*) the boot (form of torture); (*fig.*) the sock, comedy. *Chausser le brodequin*, to act in or write comedies.

broder [brɔ'de], *v.t.* To embroider; to adorn, to embellish (a story etc.).—*v.i.* To amplify, to romance. **broderie**, *n.f.* Embroidery; (*fig.*) embellishment; exaggeration, amplification. **brodeur**, *n.m.* (*fem.* **brodeuse**) Embroiderer. *Brodeur mécanique*, embroidering machine. **brodoir**, *n.m.* Bobbin, frame for lace-making.

broie [brwa], *n.f.* Brake (for hemp).

broiement, **broîment** [brwa'mɑ̃] or **broyage**, *n.m.* Grinding, powdering, pounding, pulverization.

broigne [brɔɲ], *n.f.* Leather coat covered with metallic rings (11th cent.).

bromal [brɔ'mal], *n.m.* Bromal.

bromate [brɔ'mat], *n.m.* Bromate.

brome (1) [brɔːm], *n.m.* Bromine.

brome (2) [brɔːm], *n.m.* Grass of the genus *Bromus*.

bromhydrate [brɔmi'drat], *n.m.* (*Chem.*) Hydrobromide.

bromhydrique [brɔmi'dric], *a.* (*Chem.*) Hydrobromic.

bromique [brɔ'mik], *a.* Bromic.

bromure [brɔ'myːr], *n.m.* Bromide. (*Phot.*) *Papier au bromure*, bromide paper.

*bronchade [brɔ̃'ʃad], *n.f.* Stumbling, tripping (of horses).

bronche [brɔ̃ʃ], *n.f.* (*Anat.*) Bronchus (*pl.* bronchia).

bronchement [brɔ̃ʃ'mɑ̃], *n.m.* Stumbling; flinching.

broncher [brɔ̃'ʃe], *v.i.* To stumble, to trip, to reel, to budge, to move; to falter, to fail, to flinch. *Il n'y a si bon cheval qui ne bronche*, even a good horse sometimes stumbles; (*fig.*) even the cleverest may fail; *sans broncher*, without turning a hair.

bronchial [brɔ̃'ʃjal], *a.* (*fem.* **-iale**, *pl.* **-iaux**) (*Anat.*) Bronchial. **bronchique**, *a.* Bronchial. **bronchite**, *n.f.* (*Path.*) Bronchitis. **bronchitique**, *a.* Bronchitic. **bronchocèle** (brɔ̃kɔ'sɛl], *n.m.* Bronchocele. **bronchopneumonie**, *n.f.* Broncho-pneumonia. **bronchoscopie**, *n.f.* Bronchoscopy.

bronzage [brɔ̃'zaːʒ], *n.f.* Bronzing.

bronze [brɔ̃ːz], *n.m.* Bronze; bronze statue or medal; (*poet.*) cannon. *Un cœur de bronze*, a heart of bronze. **bronzer**, *v.t.* To bronze; to paint bronze colour; to tan (the face etc.). *Bronzé par le soleil*, sunburnt, tanned by the sun; *bronzer un canon de fusil*, to bronze the barrel of a musket. **bronzerie**, *n.f.* Art of bronze sculpture etc. **bronzeur** or **bronzier**, *n.m.* Worker or artist in bronze.

brook [bruk], *n.m.* (*spt.*) Large ditch obstacle in steeple-chase.

broquart [BROCARD].

broqueteur [brɔk'tœːr], *n.m.* (*Agric.*) Loader, pitcher (of sheaves).

broquette [brɔ'kɛt], *n.f.* Tack, carpet-nail.

brossage [brɔ'saːʒ], *n.m.* Brushing.

brosse [brɔs], *n.f.* Brush; painter's brush or pencil; (*fig.*) touch; (*pl.*) brushwood, cover. *Brosse à décrotter*, *brosse en chiendent*, hard brush; *brosse à dents*, tooth-brush; *brosse à habits*, clothes-brush; *brosse à peinture*, paint-scrubber; *cheveux en brosse*, crew-cut hair. **brossée**, *n.f.* (*colloq.*) Brushing; drubbing, thrashing.

brosser [brɔ'se], *v.t.* To brush, to rub or clean with a brush; (*fig.*) to beat, to defeat. **se brosser**, *v.r.* To brush oneself. *Se brosser les cheveux*, to brush one's hair; *se brosser (le ventre)*, to have nothing to eat. **brosserie**, *n.f.* Brushmaking business; brush manufactory. **brosseur**, *n.m.* Brusher; (*Mil.*) an officer's batman. **brossier**, *n.m.* Brush-maker; one who sells brushes.

brou [bru], *n.m.* Husk or peel (of nuts, esp. walnuts). *Brou de noix*, walnut stain, walnut liquor.

brouet [bru'ɛ], *n.m.* Thin broth. *Brouet clair*, clear broth; *brouet noir*, black broth.

brouettage [bruɛ'taːʒ], *n.f.* Conveyance in barrows.

brouette [bru'ɛt], *n.f.* Wheelbarrow; *an old form of bath-chair; (*fam.*) slow local railway. *Quelle brouette!* What a slow train! **brouettée**, *n.f.* Barrow-load. **brouetter**, *v.t.* To wheel in a barrow; *to draw in a bath-chair. **brouetteur**, **brouettier**, *n.m.* Barrowman; bath-chairman.

brouhaha [brua'a], *n.m.* Hubbub, uproar, hurly-burly, din.

brouillage [bru'jaːʒ], *n.m.* (*Rad.*) Atmospherics, jamming. *Station de brouillage*, jamming station.

brouillamini [brujami'ni], *n.m.* (*Pharm.*) Armenian bole; (*fig.*) confusion, disorder.

brouillard [bru'jaːr], *n.m.* Fog, mist, haze; (*Comm.*) waste-book. *Brouillard artificiel*, smoke-screen; *être dans le brouillard*, (*euphem.*) to be fogged, fuddled, or tipsy; *je n'y vois que du brouillard*, I am muddled; *un brouillard épais*, a dense fog; (*Av.*) *brouillard au sol*, ground fog.—*a.* Blotting. *Du papier brouillard*, blotting-paper.

brouillasse [bru'jas], *n.f.* Drizzle, Scotch mist. **brouillasser**, *v.impers.* To drizzle. *Il brouillasse*, it is drizzling.

brouille [bru:j], **brouillerie**, *n.f.* Quarrel, falling-out, misunderstanding, estrangement. *Être en brouille avec*, to be on bad terms with, to disagree with.

brouillé [bru'je], *a.* (*fem.* **-ée**) Scrambled (eggs); blurred; on bad terms; (*Geol.*) jumbled. *Être brouillé avec quelqu'un*, to have fallen out with someone; *roches brouillées*, jumbled rocks.

brouillement [bruj'mɑ̃], *n.m.* Mixing together, jumbling.

brouiller [bru'je], *v.t.* To mix together, to jumble up, to shuffle, to confound; to set at variance, to embroil, to confuse, to puzzle; to blur; (*Rad.*) to jam. **se brouiller**, *v.r.* To be out, to put oneself out; to be confounded, to be in trouble or embarrassment; to fall out (with someone). *Le temps se brouille*, the weather is changing for the worse; *se brouiller avec la justice*, to fall foul of the law.

brouillon [bru'jɔ̃], *a.* (*fem.* **-onne**) Mischief-making; blundering.—*n.m.* Rough draft, rough copy; blunderer, bungler; mar-all, mar-plot. **brouillonner**, *v.t.* To write in a blundering, confused way.

brouir [bru'iːr], *v.t.* To blight, to nip, to parch (of the action of the sun on vegetation). **brouissure**, *n.f.* Blight, scorching.

broussailles [bru'saːj], *n.f.* (*usu. in pl.*) Bushes, brushwood, undergrowth. **broussailler**, *v.t.* To cover or protect with brushwood. **broussailleux**, *a.* (*fem.* **-euse**) Bushy, covered with bushes.

brousse [brus], *n.f.* Brushwood, undergrowth, bush (Australia etc.).

broussin [bru'sɛ̃], *n.m.* Excrescence, gnarl on a tree (used in cabinet-making).

brouter [bru'te], *v.t. and i.* To browse, to graze; to chatter, to thump (brake, tool).

broutilles [bru'tiːj], *n.f.* (*usu. in pl.*) Sprigs, small-wood, chat-wood; (*fig.*) trifles.

brouture [bru'tyːr], *n.f.* or **brout**, *n.m.* Browse (young shoots).

brownien [bro'nɛ̃], *a. Mouvements browniens*, molecular motion.

browning [bro'niŋ], *n.m.* Automatic pistol.

broyage [brwa'jaːʒ], *n.m.* Crushing (of ore), grinding (of colours). (*Ind.*) *Broyage à l'eau*, wet crushing; *broyage à sec*, dry crushing.

broyer [brwa'je], *v.t.* To grind, to pound, to pulverize, to crush, to bruise. *Broyer du noir*, to have a fit of the blues; *broyer l'encre*, (*Print.*) to bray the ink. **broyeur**, *a. and n.m.* (*fem.* **broyeuse**) Grinder, pounder, hemp- or flax-breaker (machine). *Cylindres broyeurs*, crushing rolls; *machine à broyer* or *broyeuse*, breaking or pounding machine.

bru [bry], *n.f.* Daughter-in-law.

bruant [bry'ã], *n.m.* Any bird of the Emberiza family. *Bruant jaune*, yellow hammer; *bruant des roseaux*, reed bunting.

brucelles [bry'sɛl], *n.f. pl.* Tweezers.

brugnon [bry'ɲɔ̃], *n.m.* Nectarine.

bruine [brɥin], *n.f.* Small drizzling rain. **bruinement**, *n.m.* Drizzling. **bruiner**, *v.impers.* To drizzle. **bruineux**, *a.* (*fem.* **-euse**) Drizzly, drizzling.

bruire [brɥiːr], *v.t. irr.* To make a noise; to make a confused sound, to rustle, to rattle; to roar, to sough (of the wind). **bruissant**, *a.* (*fem.* **-ante**) Rustling, rattling; roaring, soughing. **bruissement**, *n.m.* Rustling noise, rattling, roaring, soughing (of the wind).

bruit [brɥi], *n.m.* Noise, din, racket, uproar, commotion; clamour; (*fig.*) tumult, sedition; fame, renown, reputation; report, talk, rumour. (*Rad.*) *Bruit de fond*, background noise; *bruits parasites*, strays; *au bruit des cloches* or *du canon*, at the ringing of the bells or the roar of the guns; *beaucoup de bruit pour rien*, much ado about nothing; *cet évènement fait du bruit*, that affair is causing a stir; *des bruits de guerre*, war rumours; *un bruit sourd*, a muffled sound; *grand bruit, petite besogne*, great cry, little wool; *il n'est bruit que de*, there's no talk but of; *le bruit court (que)*, there is a report (that); *sans bruit*, noiselessly; *un faux bruit*, a false rumour.

bruitage [brɥi'taːʒ], *n.m.* Sound-effects. **bruiter**, *v.i.* To make sound-effects. **bruiteur**, *n.m.* Sound-effects specialist.

brûlable [bry'labl], *a.* Burnable, fit to be burnt. **brûlage**, *n.m.* Burning (of rubbish); singeing (of hair); roasting (of coffee) etc. (*Agric.*) *Brûlage du sol*, sod-burning.

brûlant [bry'lã], *a.* (*fem.* **-ante**) Burning, scorching, hot, torrid; (*fig.*) eager, earnest, ardent.

brûlé [bry'le], *n.m.* Smell of burning; (*C*) burnt part of wood, burnbeat field. *Cela sent le brûlé*, that smells of burning; (*fig.*) that smells of heresy; *un cerveau brûlé*, a dare-devil fellow; *un homme brûlé*, a man of ruined reputation; (*fam.*) *être brûlé*, to have been detected, found out.

brûle-bout or **brûle-bouts** [BRÛLE-TOUT].

brûle-gueule [bryl'gœl], *n.m. inv.* (*colloq.*) Short pipe, cutty.

brûle-parfum [brylpar'fœ̃], *n.m. inv.* Perfume-pan, incense-burner.

brûle-pourpoint, à [brylpur'pwɛ̃], *adv.* (Of shooting) close to; point-blank; (*fig.*) to one's face, in one's teeth.

brûler [bry'le], *v.t.* To burn, to consume by fire; to corrode, to cauterize; to scorch, to scar, to parch, to inflame; to singe (hair). *Brûler de fond en comble*, to burn to the ground; *brûler de l'encens devant quelqu'un*, to flatter someone excessively; *brûler du vin*, to distil wine to make brandy; *brûler la cervelle à quelqu'un*, to blow someone's brains out; *brûler la politesse*, to leave someone abruptly; *brûler le pavé*, to dash along at full tilt, to scorch; *brûler les planches*, to play a part with plenty of go (of actors); *brûler les yeux*, to dazzle the eyes; *brûler ses vaisseaux*, (*fig.*) to burn one's boats; *brûler une étape*, to pass a halting-place without stopping; *brûler les signaux*, to over-run signals; *son style brûle le papier*, his style is full of fire.—*v.i.* To burn, to be on fire, to be very hot, to be scorched; (*fig.*) to be impatient, eager, impassioned, etc. *Brûler d'un feu lent*, to be consumed by degrees; *je brûle de vous revoir*, I am impatient to see you again; *les mains lui brûlent*, his hands burn. **se brûler**, *v.r.* To burn oneself, to be burnt, to scorch. *Se brûler la cervelle*, to blow one's brains out; *se brûler les doigts*, to burn one's fingers; *venir se brûler à la chandelle*, to burn one's wings at the candle.

brûlerie [bryl'ri], *n.f.* Brandy-distillery.

brûle-tout [bryl'tu], *n.m. inv.* Save-all (for candle-ends).

brûleur [bry'lœːr], *n.m.* (*fem.* **brûleuse**) Burner; incendiary, house-burner. *Brûleur à anneau*, ring burner; *brûleur à gaz*, gas-ring, gas-jet.

brûlis [bry'li], *n.m.* Burnt part of a wood; burnbeat field.

brûloir [bry'lwaːr], *n.m.* Coffee-burner or roaster.

brûlot [bry'lo], *n.m.* (*Av.*) Flare; fire-ship; burnt brandy; (*fig.*) firebrand, incendiary; (*C*) kind of gnat or midge.

brûlure [bry'lyːr], *n.f.* Burn, frost nip, scald; smut (on corn).

brumaire [bry'mɛːr], *n.m.* Brumaire (second month of the calendar of the first French Republic, from Oct. 22nd to Nov. 20th).

brumal [bry'mal], *a.* (*fem.* **-ale**, *pl.* **-aux**) Brumal, winterly, wintry. **brumasse** or **brumaille**, *n.f.* (*Naut.*) Fogginess, haze. **brumasser**, *v.impers.* To be slightly foggy. **brume** [brym], *n.f.* Haze, mist; (*fig.*) obscurity, uncertainty. **brumeux**, *a.* (*fem.* **-euse**) Hazy, misty; (*fig.*) sombre, obscure.

brun [brœ̃], *a.* (*fem.* **brune**) Brown, dark, dun, dusky.—*n.m.* The colour brown; dark-complexioned person. *Brun châtain*, chestnut brown; *brun clair*, light brown; *brun foncé*, dun-coloured.—*n.f.* Dusk (of the evening); dark woman, dark girl, brunette. *À la brune*, at evening-tide, at nightfall.

(C) **brunante** [bry'nãt], *n.f.* *À la brunante*, in the dusk of the evening.

brunâtre [bry'nɑ:tr], *a.* Brownish.

brunelle [bry'nel], *n.f.* (*Bot.*) Self-heal.

brunet [bry'ne], *a.* (*fem.* **-ette**) Brownish.—*n.f.* Dark woman, dark girl.

brunir [bry'ni:r], *v.t.* To brown, to make brown, to darken; to burnish. *Brunir l'acier*, to brown steel; *brunir l'or*, to burnish gold.—*v.i.* To turn brown. **se brunir**, *v.r.* To turn dark or brown. **brunissage**, *n.m.* Burnishing. **brunisseur**, *n.m.* (*fem.* **brunisseuse**) Burnisher. **brunissoir**, *n.m.* Burnisher (tool). **brunissure**, *n.f.* Burnishing; burnish, polish; cryptogamic disease of vines; brown rust.

brusque [brysk], *a.* Blunt, abrupt, brusque, rough, uncivil; sudden, unexpected. *Tournant brusque*, sharp turn; *variations brusques de température*, sudden changes of temperature.

brusquement [bryskə'mã], *adv.* Brusquely, bluntly, abruptly; roughly, uncivilly.

brusquer [brys'ke], *v.t.* To be sharp with (someone); to treat in a brusque manner; to offend; (*fig.*) to hasten, to precipitate. *Brusquer la fortune*, to try to get rich quickly; *brusquer l'aventure*, to decide at once; *brusquer une chose*, to precipitate matters; *il brusque tout le monde*, he is abrupt with everybody. **brusquerie**, *n.f.* Brusqueness, abruptness, bluntness; suddenness, hastiness.

brut [bryt], *a.* (*fem.* **brute** (1)) Rough, raw, unhewn, unfashioned, unpolished; uncultured, rude, clownish, awkward; inorganic, senseless, not animate (of nature). *Bête brute*, brute beast; *diamant brut*, rough diamond; *pétrole brut*, crude petroleum; *poids brut*, gross weight; *produit brut*, gross produce, gross returns; *sucre brut*, unrefined sugar; *vin brut*, unadulterated wine.—*adv.* (*Comm.*) Gross (opposed to net).

brutal [bry'tal], *a.* (*fem.* **-ale**, *pl.* **-aux**) Brutal, brutish; surly, bearish, churlish. *Manipulations brutales*, rough handling.—*n.m.* Brute, brutal person. **brutalement**, *adv.* Brutally, brutishly, rudely, churlishly.

brutaliser [brytali'ze], *v.t.* To bully, to use brutally; to make brutal, to brutalize. **brutalité**, *n.f.* Brutality, brutishness; outrageous act or language.

brute (1) [bryt], [BRUT].

brute (2) [bryt], *n.f.* Brute, unreasoning beast; brutal person; boor; ruffian.

Bruxelles [bry'sɛl], *f.* Brussels.

bruyamment [bryja'mã], *adv.* Noisily.

bruyant [bry'ã], *a.* Noisy.

bruyère [bry'jɛ:r], *n.f.* Heath, heather. *Bruyère arborescente*, tree heather, briar-wood; *bruyère cendrée*, Scotch heather; *coq*

de bruyère, grouse, heath-cock; *pipe de bruyère*, briar pipe.

bryon [bri'ɔ̃], *n.m.* Tree-moss.

bryone [bri'ɔn], *n.f.* Bryony.

bryozoaire [briɔzɔ'ɛ:r], *n.m.* (*Zool.*) Bryozoon.

bu, *p.p.* (*fem.* **bue**) [BOIRE].

buanderie [bɥã'dri], *n.f.* Wash-house, laundry.

buandier [bɥã'dje], *n.m.* (*fem.* **buandière**) Bleacher; washerman, washerwoman.

bubale [by'bal], *n.m.* Hartebeest, S. African antelope.

bube [byb], *n.f.* Pimple.

bubon [by'bɔ̃], *n.m.* (*Path.*) Bubo. **bubonique**, *a.* Bubonic.

bucarde [by'kard], *n.f.* (*Conch.*) Cockle.

Bucarest [byka'rest], *m.* Bucharest.

buccal [by'kal], *a.* (*fem.* **-ale**, *pl.* **-aux**) (*Anat.*) Buccal; relating to the mouth.

buccin [byk'sɛ̃], *n.m.* (*Mus. Ant.*) Long trumpet; (*Conch.*) whelk.

buccinateur [byksina'tœ:r], *n.m.* (*Anat.*) Buccinator. (*Ant.*) Trumpeter.

Bucéphale [byse'fal], *n.m.* Bucephalus (Alexander's horse); (*fig.*) charger.

bûche [byʃ], *n.f.* Log; (*fig.*) blockhead, dolt. *Ramasser une bûche*, (*pop.*) to fall down; *tirer une bûche*, (at baccara) to draw a ten or a court card.

bûcher (1) [by'ʃe], *n.m.* Wood-house; funeral-pile, pyre; stake.

bûcher (2) [by'ʃe], *v.t.* To rough-hew (a piece of wood, block of stone, etc.); (C) to wood; (*pop.*) to cram, to study. *Bûcher son français*, to swot at French.—*v.i.* To cram, to swot; to work hard, to drudge. **se bûcher**, *v.r.* (*fam.*) To have a set-to, to fight.

bûcheron [byʃ'rɔ̃], *n.m.* (*fem.* **bûcheronne**) Woodcutter.

bûchette [by'ʃet], *n.f.* Stick of dry wood.

bûcheur [by'ʃœ:r], *n.m.* (*fem.* **bûcheuse**) (*colloq.*) Plodder; (*Am.*) grind; (C) woodcutter.

bucoliaste [bykɔli'ast], *n.m.* Bucolic, writer of bucolics.

bucolique [bykɔ'lik], *a.* Bucolic.—*n.f.* Bucolic verse; *(colloq., pl.)* rubbish, rattletraps.

bucrâne or **bucrane** [by'krɑ:n], *n.m.* (*Arch.*) Ox-skull carved as ornament.

budget [byd'ʒe], *n.m.* Budget. *Le budget de la guerre*, the army estimates; *le budget de la marine*, the naval estimates; *le budget de l'État*, the State budget; *le budget d'un ménage* or *le budget familial*, household budget. **budgétaire**, *a.* Pertaining to the budget. **budgétairement**, *adv.* As regards the budget. **budgéter**, *v.t.* To include in the budget.

buée [bɥe], *n.f.* Steam (on window-panes).

buffet [by'fe], *n.m.* Sideboard; buffet; refreshment-table; refreshment-room, railway restaurant; service (of plate); (*pop.*) stomach, belly. *Buffet d'orgues*, organ-case; *buffet de cuisine*, dresser; *danser devant le buffet*, to have a bare cupboard, to have nothing to eat.

buffetier [byf'tje], *n.m.* (*fem.* **buffetière**) Refreshment-room keeper.

buffle [byfl], *n.m.* Buffalo; buffalo hide; buff-leather. **buffleterie**, *n.f.* Buff belts, straps, etc. (of a soldier). **buffletier**, *n.m.* Workman who makes these. **buffletin**, *n.m.* Young buffalo; *buff jerkin. **bufflon**, *n.m.* Young buffalo. **bufflonne** or **bufflesse**, *n.f.* Cow buffalo.

bugle (1) [bygl], *n.f.* Bugle (plant).
bugle (2) [bygl], *n.m.* Key-bugle.
buglosse [by'glɔs], *n.f.* (*Bot.*) Bugloss.
bugrane [by'gran], *n.f.* (*Bot.*) Rest-harrow; cammock.
buire [bɥiːr], *n.f.* Pitcher-shaped flagon; ewer.
buis [bɥi], *n.m.* Box; box-tree, box-wood; sleeking-tool (for polishing the sides of soles etc.). *Buis bénit*, branch of box blessed in church on Palm-Sunday; *buis piquant*, butcher's-broom. **buissaie** or **buissière**, *n.f.* Grove of box-trees.
buisson [bɥi'sɔ̃], *n.m.* Bush; thicket, brake; tree trained to the shape of a bush. *Buisson ardent*, burning bush, pyracanthus; *trouver buisson creux*, to find the birds flown. **buissonner**, *v.i.* To grow into a bush; (*Hunt.*) to beat the bushes; to hide in the thicket (of deer). **buissonnet**, *n.m.* Little bush. **buissonneux**, *a.* (*fem.* -**euse**) Bushy. **buissonnier**, *a.* (*fem.* -**ière**) Retiring into or lurking in the bushes. *Faire l'école buissonnière*, to play the truant; *lapins buissonniers*, thicket-rabbits.—*n.m.* Shrub or tree trained to the shape of a bush; shrubbery.
bulbe [bylb], *n.m.* Bulb; root (of a hair). **bulbeux**, *a.* (*fem.* -**euse**) Bulbous. **bulbifère**, *a.* (*Bot.*) Bulbiferous. **bulbiforme**, *a.* Bulbiform. **bulbille**, *n.f.* Bulbil.
bulgare [byl'gaːr], *a.* and *n.* Bulgarian.
Bulgarie [bylga'ri], *f.* Bulgaria.
bulime [by'lim], *n.m.* (*Conch.*) Bulimus.
bullaire [by'lɛːr], *n.m.* Collection of papal bulls; a writer who copies papal bulls.
bulle [byl], *n.f.* Bubble, air bubble in a casting; blister; seal attached to a document; the document itself; a papal bull; (*Rom. Ant.*) bulla. *Bulle d'air*, air-bubble; *bulle d'eau*, water-bubble.—*a.* Whity-brown (of paper). *Papier bulle*, whity-brown paper.
bullé [by'le], *a.* (*fem.* -**ée**) Authenticated with a seal; by papal bull.
bulletin [byl'tɛ̃], *n.m.* Bulletin, official report (school etc.); certificate, receipt. *Bulletin d'information*, news bulletin; *bulletin de bagages*, luggage-ticket; *bulletin de santé*, bulletin; *bulletin de vote*, ballot paper; *bulletin météorologique*, weather forecast.
bulleux [by'lø], *a.* (*fem.* -**euse**) Bubbly; blistery.
bulteau [byl'to], *n.m.* Tree trimmed to a round shape.
buplèvre [by'plɛːvr], *n.m.* Hare's-ear.
bupreste [by'prɛst], *n.m.* Buprestis (a beetle).
buraliste [byra'list], *n.m.* and *f.* Clerk (in the Post Office); money-taker, receiver of taxes; tobacconist.
burat [by'ra], *n.m.* Drugget; bunting.
buratin [byra'tɛ̃], *n.m.*, or **buratine**, *n.f.* Poplin.
bure (1) [byːr], *n.f.* Drugget; fustian, rough serge (of monk's dress), baize.
bure (2) [byːr], *n.f.* (*Mining*) Shaft, pit-hole.
bureau [by'ro], *n.m.* (*pl.* **bureaux**) Writing-table, desk; counting-house, office, public office; personnel of this; department (of an administrative body); board, bench (in a court of judicature); committee; court (personages); *drugget. Bureau à rideau*, roll-top desk; *bureau de location* (*Theat.*), box office; *bureau de placement*, registry-office for servants, etc.; *bureau de poste*, post office;

bureau de tabac, tobacconist's shop; *chef de bureau*, head clerk, chief of a department; *Deuxième Bureau*, Intelligence Service, M.I.5; *déposer sur le bureau*, (*Parl.*) to lay upon the table; *le bureau du Sénat*, the officers of the Senate; *payer à bureau ouvert*, (*Comm.*) to pay on demand; *prendre l'air du bureau*, to call in at the office, to see how matters stand.
bureaucrate [byrɔ'krat], *n.m.* (*pej.*) Bureaucrat; clerk in a public office; (*fig.*) red-tapist. **bureaucratie**, *n.f.* Bureaucracy; (*fig.*) red tape. **bureaucratique**, *a.* Bureaucratic; formal. **bureaucratiser**, *v.t.* To organize on bureaucratic lines.
burette [by'rɛt], *n.f.* Cruet; altar cruet; oil-can; (*Chem.*) burette; (*slang*) head.
burgau [byr'go], *n.m.*, or **burgaudine**, *n.f.* Dark green; mother-of-pearl.
burgrave [byr'graːv], *n.m.* Burgrave. **burgraviat**, *n.m.* Dignity of burgrave.
burin [by'rɛ̃], *n.m.* Burin, graver, graving-tool; dentist's drill; (*fig.*) pen. **buriner**, *v.t.* To engrave; to drill (a tooth); (*fig.*) to relate in trenchant terms.—*v.i.* To write like copper-plate; (*pop.*) to swot. **burineur**, *n.m.* Engraver; engraving-apparatus; (*pop.*) indefatigable worker, swot.
burlesque [byr'lɛsk], *a.* Burlesque, ludicrous. *Vers burlesques*, doggerel verses.—*n.m.* Burlesque. **burlesquement**, *adv.* Comically, ludicrously, in a burlesque manner.
burnous [byr'nus], *n.m.* Burnous, hooded Arab cloak.
***buron** [by'rɔ̃], *n.m.* Shepherd's hut.
bus [bys], *n.m.* (*fam.*) Bus.
busaigle [by'zɛːgl], *n.m.* Rough-legged buzzard.
busard [by'zaːr], *n.m.* Buzzard. *Busard cendré*, Montagu's harrier; *busard St Martin*, hen harrier.
busc [bysk], *n.m.* Busk (of stays), whalebone; shoulder (of butt).
buse (1) [byːz], *n.f.* Buzzard; (*fig.*) blockhead. *On ne saurait faire d'une buse un épervier*, one cannot make a silk purse out of a sow's ear.
buse (2) [byːz], *n.f.* Channel, pipe; nozzle; (*Mining*) air-shaft.
buson [by'zɔ̃], *n.m.* Variety of buzzard.
busqué [bys'ke], *a.* Aquiline (nose).
busquer [bys'ke], *v.t.* To put a busk in; to shorten, to draw up (of skirts); to curve, to arch.
busserole [bys'rɔl], *n.f.* Bearberry, berberis.
buste [byst], *n.m.* Bust, head and shoulders. *Portrait en buste*, half-length portrait.
bustier [bys'tje], *n.m.* Strapless brassière.
but [by], *n.m.* Mark; object, end, aim, purpose, design, goal, a winning-post, objective. *Arriver le premier au but*, to be the first to reach the goal; *de but en blanc*, bluntly, without any preamble, point-blank; *le but de ses désirs*, the object of his desires; *se proposer un but*, to have an object in view; *viser au but*, to aim at the mark; (*Ftb.*) *coup au but*, shot at goal; *gardien de but*, goalkeeper; *but sur coup franc*, goal from a free kick; *ligne de but*, goal-line; *marquer un but*, to score.
butane [by tan], *n.m.* Butane.
bute [byt], *n.f.* Farrier's knife.
buté [by'te], *a.* (*fem.* -**ée**) Stubborn, dead set on.

butée [by′te] or **buttée**, *n.f.* (*Arch.*) Abutment, pier (receiving the thrust of a bridge).

buter [by′te], *v.i.* To rest or abut (*contre*); to stumble or hit (*contre*). *Ce cheval bute à chaque pas*, that horse stumbles at every step. —*v.t.* To support, to prop. *Buter un mur,* to prop a wall with a buttress. **se buter**, *v.r.* To be bent on, to stick (*à*).

butin [by′tɛ̃], *n.m.* Booty, spoils, prize, plunder. **butiner**, *v.t.* To pillage, to plunder; to pilfer; to collect, to gather.—*v.i.* To pillage, to plunder; (*fig.*) to pilfer. **butineur**, *a.* (*fem.* **-euse**) Plundering, pilfering; honey-gathering (bee).

butoir [by′twa:r], *n.m.* Buffer, buffer-stop (on railway); stop, catch, tappet.

butome [by′tɔm], *n.f.* (*Bot.*) Butomus, flowering rush.

butor [by′tɔ:r], *n.m.* Bittern; (*fig.*) gross, stupid fellow, churl, lout, booby. **butorderie**, *n.f.* Stupidity, loutishness, churlishness.

buttage [by′ta:ʒ], *n.m.* (*Agric.*) Raising, mounding; (*Hort.*) banking up, earthing up.

butte [byt], *n.f.* Rising ground; knoll, mound, hillock. *La butte Montmartre*, Montmartre hill. *Être en butte à*, to be exposed to.

buttée [BUTÉE].

butter (1) [by′te], *v.t.* To raise in a mound; to earth up. *Butter du céleri*, to earth up celery; *butter un arbre*, to heap up earth round the root of a tree.

butter (2) [BUTER].

butteur [BUTTOIR].

buttoir [by′twa:r], or **butteur**, *n.m.* Ridging-plough.

butyreux [byti′rø], *a.* (*fem.* **-euse**) Butyraceous. **butyrine**, *n.f.* Butyrine. **butyrique**, *a.* Butyric.

buvable [by′vabl], *a.* Drinkable, fit to drink.

buvard [by′va:r], *a.m.* *Papier buvard*, blotting paper.—*n.m.* Blotting-case, blotting-pad, blotter.

buverie [by′vri], *n.f.* Drinking, carousal.

buvetier [byv′tje], *n.m.* (*fem.* **buvetière**) Keeper of a tavern.

buvette [by′vɛt], *n.f.* Refreshment-room (in a railway station); pump-room at spa.

buveur [by′vœ:r], *n.m.* (*fem.* **buveuse**) Drinker; toper. *Buveur d'eau*, teetotaller.

buvoter [byvɔ′te], *v.i.* To sip, to tipple.

byssus [bi′sy:s], *n.m.* Byssus.

Byzance [bi′zɑ̃:s], *f.* Byzantium.

byzantin [bizɑ̃′tɛ̃], *a.* and *n.* (*fem.* **byzantine**) Byzantine.

C

C, c [se], *n.m.* The third letter of the alphabet. *C* has two sounds; before the vowels *a, o, u,* or before a consonant, it is pronounced like *k,* as in *car, cor, curieux, clairon;* marked with a cedilla or before *e, i,* or *y,* it is pronounced like *s,* as in *ciel, cygne, façon.*

c' apocope of *ce,* before forms of the verb *être,* as in *c'est, c'était.*

ça (1) [sa], *pron.* [contraction of *cela*]. *C'est toujours ça,* that is something at any rate; *comme ça,* like that, so; *comment vous portez-vous? comme ci comme ça,* how do you do? only so-so; *donnez-moi ça,* give me that; *rien que ça!* is that all!

çà (2) [sa], *adv.* Here. *Çà et là,* here and there. up and down, to and fro.—*int.* Now. *Çà, voyons!* now, let us see! **or çà, commencez!** come, begin! *Ah ça!* Now then!

cabale [ka′bal], *n.f.* Cabal, faction, intrigue; cabbala. **cabaler**, *v.i.* To cabal, to plot.

cabaleur [kaba′lœ:r], *n.m.* (*fem.* **cabaleuse**) Caballer, intriguer. **cabaliser**, *v.i.* To practise cabbalistic arts. **cabalisme**, *n.m.* Cabbalism. **cabaliste**, *n.m.* Cabbalist. **cabalistique**, *a.* Cabbalistic.

caban [ka′bɑ̃], *n.m.* (*Naut.*) Pea jacket; (hooded) cloak (for rainy weather), oilskins.

cabanage [kaba′na:ʒ], *n.m.* Camping in huts; hutments; (*Naut.*) capsizing.

cabane [ka′ban], *n.f.* Cot, hut, shed, cabin, shanty; central part (of aeroplane). *Cabane à lapins,* rabbit-hutch.

cabaneau [kaba′no], *n.m.* Hut or shelter on shore (for cod-fishers).

cabaner [kaba′ne], *v.t.* To live in a *cabane;* to make foliage shelters for silkworms; (*Naut.*) to capsize.

cabanon [kaba′nɔ̃], *n.m.* Small hut, shed, or cabin; small country-house or lodge (in Provence); prison-cell; padded room.

cabaret [kaba′rɛ], *n.m.* Inferior kind of wine-shop, tavern, pot-house; inn; a small table or tray with tea- or coffee-service, liqueur-service, etc. *Cabaret des murailles,* Venus's navel-wort; *pilier de cabaret,* tavern-haunter, tippler. **cabaretier**, *n.m.* (*fem.* **cabaretière**) Publican, tavern-keeper.

cabas [ka′ba], *n.m.* Flat two-handled basket; frail.

cabasson [kaba′sɔ̃], *n.m.* Old-fashioned bonnet.

cabèche [ka′bɛʃ], *n.f.* (*fam.*) Head.

cabeliau [CABILLAUD].

cabestan [kabes′tɑ̃], *n.m.* Capstan, windlass. *Armer le cabestan,* to man the capstan; *cabestan volant,* crab; *envoyer un homme au cabestan,* to send a man to the capstan (to be punished); *grand cabestan,* main capstan.

cabiai [ka′bje], *n.m.* Capybara.

cabillaud [kabi′jo] or **cabeliau**, *n.m.* Fresh cod.

cabillot [kabi′jo], *n.m.* (*Naut.*) Toggle. *Cabillot de tournage,* belaying pin.

cabine [ka′bin], *n.f.* Cabin. *Cabine d'ascenseur,* lift-car; *cabine de bain,* bathing-hut; (*Av.*) *cabine de pilotage,* cockpit; *cabine téléphonique,* call box.

cabinet [kabi′nɛ], *n.m.* Closet, study; practice (of a professional man); bureau, office (of an attorney, barrister, etc.); Cabinet, Cabinet-council; Government, ministry; a collection deposited in a cabinet or show-case; cabinet, or side-board with cupboards, drawers, etc. *Cabinet d'aisances,* or *les cabinets,* watercloset; *cabinet de lecture,* reading room; *cabinet de toilette,* dressing-room; *c'est un homme de cabinet,* he is not a man of action, or of affairs; *le cabinet d'un ministre,* minister's departmental staff; *chef de cabinet,* principal private secretary.

câblage [kɑ′bla:ʒ], *n.m.* (*Elec.*) Wiring.

câble [kɑ:bl], *n.m.* Cable. *Câble métallique,* wire rope; *câble d'affourche,* small bower-cable; *câble de remorque,* tow-cable, hawser;

filer du câble, (*Naut.*) to pay out cable, (*fig.*) to spin out the time; *maître câble*, sheet-cable. **câblé**, *a.* (*fem.* **câblée**) (*Arch.*) Cabled (of mouldings).—*n.m.* Thick cord.

câbleau or **câblot** [kaˈblo], *n.m.* Rope for towing barges on rivers; painter.

câbler [kaˈble], *v.t.* To twist (threads) into a cord; to make (into) cable; to telegraph by cable.

câblière [kɑbliˈɛːr], *n.f.* Anchor-stone.

câblogramme [kɑblɔˈgram], *n.m.* Cable-gram.

câblot [CÂBLEAU].

cabochard [kabɔˈʃaːr], *a.* and *n.* (*fem.* -**arde**) (*fam.*) Obstinate, pig-headed.

caboche [kaˈbɔʃ], *n.f.* (*colloq.*) Pate, noddle, nob; (*Comm.*) hobnail. *Être une fameuse caboche*, to have a good head; *il a la caboche dure*, he's thick-headed.

cabochon [kabɔˈʃɔ̃], *n.m.* Cabochon (person); fancy brass nail. (*Cycl.*) *Cabochon rouge*, red reflector.

cabosse [kaˈbɔs], *n.f.* (*pop.*) Bruise, bump. **cabosser**, *v.t.* To bump, to bruise. *Chapeau tout cabossé*, battered hat.

cabot (1) [kaˈbo], *n.m.* (*pop.*) Actor; (*slang*) dog; (*Mil. slang*) corporal.

cabot (2) [CHABOT].

cabotage [kabɔˈtaːʒ], *n.m.* Coasting, coasting trade. *Vaisseau de cabotage*, coasting vessel. **caboter**, *v.i.* To coast. **caboteur** or **cabotier**, *n.m.* Coasting vessel.

cabotière [kabɔˈtjɛːr], *n.f.* Long Norman flat boat used on the Seine.

cabotin [kabɔˈtɛ̃], *n.m.* Strolling player; bad actor, mummer. **cabotinage**, *n.m.* Strolling player's life; bad acting; quackery. **cabotiner**, *v.i.* To act badly; (*fig.*) to strut.

Caboul [kaˈbul], *m.* Kabul.

caboulot [kabuˈlo], *n.m.* Compartment in a stable; (*pop.*) pot-house; low pub.

cabre [kɑːbr], *n.f.* (*Naut.*) Shear legs.

cabré [kaˈbre], *a.* (*fem.* **cabrée**) Rearing (of a horse); tail-down (of a plane).

cabrer [kaˈbre], *v.t.* To make (a horse, a plane) rear. **se cabrer**, *v.r.* To prance, to rear; (*fig.*) to revolt, to fly into a passion.

cabri [kaˈbri], *n.m.* Kid.

cabriole [kabriˈɔl], *n.f.* Caper, leap; capriole. *Faire une cabriole*, to come a cropper. **cabrioler**, *v.i.* To caper, to cut capers.

cabriolet [kabriɔˈlɛ], *n.m.* Cabriolet, cab, one-horse chaise; a woman's bonnet of the Directory period; twister (of policeman); small arm-chair.

cabron [kaˈbrɔ̃], *n.m.* Kid-skin; burnishing-tool.

cabrouet [kaˈbrue], *n.m.* Hand-truck.

cabus [kaˈby], *a.m.* Round headed (of cab-bages).

caca [kaˈka], *n.m.* (*Childish*) Excrement; filth, dirt. *Faire caca*, to do number two. *Couleur caca d'oie*, gosling green.

cacaber [kakaˈbe], *v.i.* To call (of partridges).

cacade [kaˈkad], *n.f.* Ridiculous failure; mess.

cacahouète [kakaˈwɛt] or **cacahuète**, *n.f.* Peanut, monkey nut.

cacao [kakaˈo], *n.m.* Cacao, chocolate-nut. **cacaoyer** or **cacaotier**, *n.m.* Cacao-tree. **cacaoyère** or **cacaotière**, *n.f.* Cacao-plantation.

(C') **cacaoui** [kakaˈwi], *n.m.* (*Orn.*) Old squaw.

cacatois [kakaˈtwa] or **cacatoès** [kakatɔˈɛːs], *n.m.* Cockatoo; (*Naut.*) royal mast-top.

cachalot [kaʃaˈlo], *n.m.* Cachalot, spermaceti-whale. **cachalotier**, *a.* (*fem.* **cachalotière**) Pertaining to cachalot-fishing.—*n.* Whaler.

cache [kaʃ], *n.f.* Hiding-place; (*Hunt.*) stake-net.—*n.m.* (*Phot.*) Mask; (*Typ.*) frisket.

caché [kaʃe], *a.* (*fem.* -**ée**) Hidden, concealed. *Jeu caché*, underhand game; *n'avoir rien de caché*, to have no secrets; *ressorts cachés*, hidden springs.

In compound nouns with *cache*, *pl.* is unchanged.

cache-cache [kaʃˈkaʃ], *n.m.* Hide-and-seek.

cache-col [kaʃˈkɔl], *n.m.* Scarf.

cache-corset [kaʃkɔrˈsɛ], *n.m.* Camisole, under-bodice.

cache-cou [CACHE-COL].

cachectique [kaʃekˈtik], *a.* Cachectic.

cache-entrée [kaʃɑ̃ˈtre], *n.m.* Drop (of a key-hole).

cache-éperon [kaʃeˈprɔ̃], *n.m.* Spur-cover.

cache-lumière [kaʃlyˈmjɛːr], *n.m.* Lead vent-cover for cannon.

cachemire [kaʃˈmiːr], *n.m.* Cashmere. **cache-mirette**, *n.f.* Cashmerette.

cache-misère [kaʃmiˈzeːr], *n.m.* Overcoat to hide shabby clothes.

cache-mouchoir [kaʃmuˈʃwaːr], *n.m.* Hide-the-handkerchief (child's game), hunt-the-slipper.

cache-nez [kaʃˈne], *n.m.* Muffler, comforter.

cache-pot [kaʃˈpo], *n.m.* Flower-pot cover, jardinière.

cache-poussière [kaʃpuˈsjɛːr], *n.m.* Dust-coat.

cacher [kaˈʃe], *v.t.* To hide, to conceal; to disguise, to dissimulate, to mask. *Cacher sa vie*, to lead a secluded life; *cacher son jeu*, to mask one's play; *cacher son nom* or *son âge*, to conceal one's name *or* one's age; *cachez votre jeu*, hide your cards. **se cacher**, *v.r.* To hide, to secrete oneself; to lurk. *Se cacher à la justice*, to hide from justice.

cacherie [kaʃˈri], *n.f.* [CACHOTTERIE].

cache-sexe [kaʃˈsɛks], *n.m.* Slip, panties.

cachet [kaˈʃɛ], *n.m.* Seal, stamp, signet, signet-ring; ticket; tablet (of aspirin); fee (of an artist); (*fig.*) character, stamp, mark (of genius etc.). *Cachet de chiffres* or *d'armes*, seal with a cipher *or* with a coat of arms; *cachet volant*, flying seal; **courir le cachet*, to give private lessons; *lettre de cachet*, arbitrary warrant of imprisonment; *son style a un cachet particulier*, his style has a certain stamp or character of its own. **cachetage**, *n.m.* Sealing.

cache-tampon [CACHE-MOUCHOIR].

cacheter [kaʃˈte], *v.t.* To seal, to seal up. *Cire à cacheter*, sealing-wax; *pain à cacheter*, wafer; *vin cacheté*, old (vintage) wine.

cachette [kaˈʃɛt], *n.f.* Hiding-place. *En cachette*, secretly, by stealth.

cachexie [kaʃɛkˈsi], *n.f.* Cachexia.

cachot [kaˈʃo], *n.m.* Dungeon, prison.

cachotter [kaʃɔˈte], *v.t.* To make a mystery of, to conceal. **cachotterie**, *n.f.* Mysterious ways; underhand work. **cachottier**, *a.* (*fem.* -**ière**) Mysterious, sly.—*n.* One who makes a mystery of things.

cachou [ka'ʃu], *n.m.* Cachou; (*Bot.*) catechu.
cacique [ka'sik], *n.m.* Cacique (Indian chief); (*sch.*) candidate received first in a competitive exam.
cacochyme [kakɔ'ʃim], *a.* Of a feeble or disordered constitution, decrepit.
cacodyle [kakɔ'dil], *n.m.* Cacodyl. **cacodylique**, *a.* Cacodylic.
cacographie [kakɔgra'fi], *n.f.* Cacography; bad spelling; bad style.
cacolet [kakɔ'lɛ], *n.m.* Horse- or mule-litter for the transport of wounded.
cacologie [kakɔlɔ'ʒi], *n.f.* Cacology. **cacologique**, *a.* Cacological. **cacologue**, *n.m.* One who uses cacology.
cacophonie [kakɔfɔ'ni], *n.f.* Cacophony. **cacophonique**, *a.* Cacophonous.
cactacée [kakta'se] or **cactée**, *n.f.* One of the *Cactaceae*.
cactier [kak'tje] or **cactus**, *n.m.* Cactus. **cactiforme** or **cactoïde**, *a.* Cactoid, cactaceous.
cacuminal [kakymi'nal], *a.* R *cacuminal*, the American R, pronounced with the point of the tongue folded up backwards.
cadastrage [kadas'tra:ʒ], *n.m.* Registration in a cadastre.
cadastral [kadas'tral], *a.* (*fem.* -ale, *pl.* -aux) Cadastral, referring to the register of lands. **cadastration** [CADASTRAGE].
cadastre [ka'dastr], *n.m.* Cadastre, register of the survey of lands. **cadastrer**, *v.t.* To survey.
cadavéreux [kadave'rø], *a.* (*fem.* -euse) Cadaverous, corpse-like, wan, ghastly. **cadavérique**, *a.* Of or pertaining to a corpse.
cadavre [ka'dɑ:vr], *n.m.* Corpse, dead body; (*iron.*) empty bottle. *C'est un cadavre ambulant*, he is a living skeleton.
cade [kad], *n.m.* Spanish juniper, cade.
cadeau [ka'do], *n.m.* (*pl.* cadeaux) Present, gift. *Faire cadeau de*, to make a present of.
cadédiou [kade'dju] or **cadédis**, *int.* (*Gasc. dial.*) The deuce! faith!
cadenas [kad'na], *n.m.* Padlock; *coffer in which were kept the knife, fork, spoon, etc., used by the king or princes. *Cadenas à secret*, secret padlock; *enfermer sous cadenas*, to padlock. **cadenasser**, *v.t.* To padlock, to shut up under padlock.
cadence [ka'dɑ̃:s], *n.f.* Cadence, fall; rhythm, time (in dancing); *(*Mus.*) trill, quaver, shake, cadence. *Aller en cadence*, to keep time.
cadencer [kadɑ̃'se], *v.t.* To cadence, to give rhythm and cadence to, to harmonize. *Cadencer le pas*, to keep step.—*v.i.* (*Mus.*) To trill, to quaver; (*Mil.*) *marcher au pas cadencé*, to march in step.
cadène [ka'dɛ:n], *n.f.* Chain (for convicts); chain-gang; Oriental carpet.
cadenette [kad'nɛt], *n.f.* Tress (of hair).
cadet [ka'dɛ], *a.* (*fem.* cadette) Younger, junior (of two). *Branche cadette*, younger branch.—*n.* The younger; junior (of two). —*n.m.* Cadet; younger brother; younger son; (*colloq.*) young fellow; *young man, youth. *C'est le cadet de mes soucis*, that is the least of my cares; *il est mon cadet de deux ans*, he is two years my junior.—*n.f.* Younger sister, younger daughter; paving-stone; long billiard-cue.

cadi [ka'di], *n.m.* Cadi (Mahommedan magistrate).
cadichon [kadi'ʃɔ̃], *n.m.* Little cadet.
cadis [ka'di], *n.m.* Light woollen serge; Caddis.
Cadix [ka'diks], *f.* Cadiz.
cadmie [kad'mi], *n.f.* (*Chem.*) Cadmia.
cadmium [kad'mjɔm], *n.m.* Cadmium.
cadogan [CATOGAN].
***cadole** [ka'dɔl], *n.f.* Latch, little bolt.
cadrage [ka'dra:ʒ], *n.m.* (*Phot., Cine.*) Centring.
cadran [ka'drɑ̃], *n.m.* Dial-plate, dial. *Cadran solaire*, sun-dial; *faire le tour du cadran*, to sleep the clock round.
cadrané [kadra'ne], *a.* (*fem.* **cadranée**) Attacked by *cadrannure* (of trees).
cadranier [kadra'nje], *n.m.* (*fem.* **cadranière**) Dialist. **cadrannerie**, *n.f.* Dial-making.
cadrannure [kadra'ny:r], *n.m.* Star-shake (malady of trees).
cadrat [ka'dra], *n.m.* (*Print.*) Quadrat. **cadratin**, *n.m.* (*Print.*) Em quadrat. *Demi cadratin*, en quadrat.
cadrature [kadra'ty:r], *n.f.* The assemblage of parts producing the movement of the hands (of a clock).
cadre [kɑ:dr], *n.m.* Frame, framework, skeleton, outline; container (for removals); section (of bee-hive); plan, design; (*fig.*) limits of an area of space, the space itself; (*Mil.*) the staff (forming the nucleus of a regiment); (*Mil.*) cot, bed-frame.—*n.m. pl. Les cadres*, the higher staff (of an administration or a firm). *Hors cadres*, not on the strength; *avoir pour cadre*, to be bounded by; *être sur le cadre*, (*Naut.*) to be on the sick-list; *servir de cadre à*, to bound, to limit.
cadrer [ka'dre], *v.i.* To agree, to tally, to square (*à* or *avec*).—*v.t.* (*Phot., Cine.*) To centre.
caduc [ka'dyk], *a.* (*fem.* caduque) Decrepit, broken-down, decayed; frail, tumble-down, crazy; lapsed, null, void (of legacies); (*Bot.*) deciduous. *Âge caduc*, decrepit old age; *devenir caduc*, to decay; *legs caduc*, lapsed legacy (barred by limitation); *mal caduc*, falling sickness, epilepsy.
caducée [kady'se], *n.m.* Caduceus, Mercury's wand; tipstaff.
caducité [kadysi'te], *n.f.* Caducity, decrepitude.
cæcal [se'kal], *a.* (*fem.* -ale, *pl.* -aux) Caecal.
cæcum [se'kɔm], *n.m.* (*Anat.*) Caecum.
cæsium or **césium** [se'zjɔm] Caesium.
cafard [ka'fa:r], *a.* (*fem.* cafarde) Hypocritical, sanctimonious.—*n.* Hypocrite, sanctimonious person; humbug; (*sch.*) sneak.—*n.m.* Cockroach; (*fam.*) bitter tedium, the blues. **cafardage** [CAFARDISE]. **cafarder**, *v.i.* To sneak, to tell tales (at school). **cafarderie**, *n.f.* Cant, hypocrisy, sanctimoniousness. **cafardise**, *n.f.* Piece of hypocrisy or cant.
café [ka'fe], *n.m.* Coffee; café, coffee-house; coffee-berry. *Café au lait*, coffee with milk; *café complet*, coffee, milk, rolls and butter; *café-crème*, white coffee; *café chantant*, music-hall; *café en grains*, coffee in beans; *rôtir, moudre, prendre du café*, to roast, grind, drink coffee; *tasse de café*, cup of coffee; *garçon de café*, waiter; *donner un mauvais café à*, to give

somebody a dose of poison.—*a.* Coffee-coloured. **caféier** or **cafier,** *n.m.* Coffee-shrub. **caféière,** *n.f.* Coffee-plantation.
caféine [kafeˈiːn], *n.f.* Caffeine. **caféique,** *a.* (*Chem.*) Caffeic. **caféisme,** *n.m.* (*Med.*) Caffeism.
cafetan or **caftan** [kafˈtɑ̃], *n.m.* Caftan.
cafetier [kafˈtje], *n.m.* (*fem.* **cafetière** (1)) Coffee-house keeper. **cafetière** (2), *n.f.* Coffee-pot, percolator; (*slang*) head.
caffut [kaˈfy], *n.m.* (*pl.*) Cast-iron scraps.
cafiot [kaˈfjo], *n.m.* (*colloq.*) Bad, weak, coffee.
cafouillage [kafuˈjaːʒ], *n.m.* Floundering.
cafouille [kaˈfuj], *n.f.* (*pop.*) Mud, mess.
cafouiller, *v.i.* (*sports*) To be unskilful, to miss the ball, to muddle; (of a team, crew) to be at sixes and sevens; (of a motor) to miss. **cafouilleur,** *n.m.* Duffer.
cafre [kɑːfr], *a.* and *n.* Kafir, Bantu.
Cafrerie [kafrəˈri], **la,** *f.* Kaffraria.
caftan [CAFETAN].
cage [kaːʒ], *n.f.* Cage; coop (for fowls); (*fig.*) prison; (*Build. etc.*) frame, casing; (*C*) log or lumber raft. *La belle cage ne nourrit pas l'oiseau,* fine words butter no parsnips; *mettre un homme en cage,* to put a man in prison *or* under lock and key. **cagée,** *n.f.* Cageful (of birds etc.). **cagette,** *n.f.* Bird-trap; little cage.
cageot [kaˈʒo], *n.m.* Little cage, hamper, crate.
(*C*) **cageur** [kaˈʒœːr], *n.m.* Raftman (driving a cage).
cagibi [kaʒiˈbi], *n.m.* Small hut or room.
cagna [kaˈɲa], *n.f.* (*Mil. slang*) Hut, small covered trench, dug-out.
cagnard [kaˈɲaːr], *a.* (*fem.* **cagnarde**) Indolent, lazy, slothful.—*n.* Lazy-bones, skulker; place for skulking or idling in; awning on board ship. **cagnarder,** *v.i.* To idle, to loaf. **cagnarderie** or **cagnardise,** *n.f.* (*colloq.*) Laziness, slothfulness, skulking.
cagne [kaɲ], *n.f.* Slut; crock (of a horse); (*sch.*) preparatory class to *École normale supérieure.*
cagneux [kaˈɲø], *a.* (*fem.* **-euse**) Knock-kneed, splay-footed.—*n.m.* Pupil in the *cagne.*
cagnot [kaˈɲo], *n.m.* Dog-fish; blue shark.
cagnotte [kaˈɲɔt], *n.f.* Kitty, pool, jack-pot.
cagot [kaˈgo], *a.* (*fem.* **cagotte**) Bigoted, hypocritical.—*n.* Bigot, hypocrite; (*Fr. Hist.*) a party of outcasts in Béarn in the Middle Ages. **cagoterie,** *n.f.* An act or word of hypocrisy or bigotry. **cagotisme,** *n.m.* Hypocrisy, bigotry.
cagoule [kaˈgul], *n.f.* Monk's cloak; penitent's cowl.
cagoulard [kaguˈlar], *n.m.* Member of a secret right-wing political society (1937).
cague [kag], *n.f.* Dutch flat barge; keg (15 litres).
cahier [kaˈje], *n.m.* Stitched paper-book; exercise-book; memorial; quarter of a quire of paper; book (manuscript). *Cahier d'écriture,* copy-book; *cahier des charges,* specifications; *cahier des frais,* bill of costs.
cahin-caha [kaɛ̃kaˈa], *adv.* (*colloq.*) So-so, lamely, poorly, slowly. *Vivre cahin-caha,* to muddle along (through life).
cahot [kaˈo], *n.m.* Jerk, jolt (of a coach etc.); (*fig.*) obstacles, vicissitudes. **cahotage** or **cahotement,** *n.m.* Jolting, jerking. **caho-**

tant, *a.* (*fem.* **-ante**) Rough, jolting. **cahoter,** *v.i.* To jolt, to be jerked about.
cahute [kaˈyt], *n.f.* Hut, crib, hovel; (*Naut.*) small cabin.
caiche [kɛʃ], *n.f.* (*Naut.*) Ketch.
caïd [kaˈid], *n.m.* Arab chief or judge.
caïeu or **cayeu** [kaˈjø], *n.m.* (*Hort.*) Offshoot of a bulb, bulbil, clove.
caillage [kaˈjaːʒ], *n.m.* Curdling, congealing.
caillasse [kaˈjas], *n.f.* Gravelly marl of the Tertiary period; road metal.
caille [kaːj], *n.f.* Quail.—(*C*) *a.* Piebald.
caillé [kaˈje], *n.m.* Curdled milk, curds.—*a.* Curdled.
caillebotis [kajbɔˈti], *n.m.* (*Naut.*) Grating of the hatches; (*Mil.*) duckboards in the trenches.
caillebottage [kajbɔˈtaːʒ], *n.m.* Curdling.
caillebotte [kajˈbɔt], *n.f.* Curds. **se caille-botter,** *v.r.* To curdle.
caille-lait [kajˈlɛ], *n.m. inv.* Rennet. (*Bot.*) [GAILLET].
caillement [kaiˈmɑ̃], *n.m.* Curdling, coagulating.
cailler [kaˈje], *v.t.* To curdle, to clot, to curd. **se cailler,** *v.r.* To coagulate, to turn to curds.
cailletage [kajˈtaːʒ], *n.m.* Gossiping, tittle-tattle.
cailleteau [kajˈto], *n.m.* Young quail.
cailleter [kajˈte], *v.i.* To gossip, to chatter; to flirt.
caillette (1) [kaˈjɛt], *n.f.* Rennet; rennet stomach.
caillette (2) [kaˈjɛt], *n.f.* Petrel; flirt.
caillot [kaˈjo], *n.m.* Clot of blood, coagulum.
caillot-rosat [kajoroˈza], *n.m.* (*pl.* **caillots-rosats**) Rose-water pear.
caillou [kaˈju], *n.m.* (*pl.* **cailloux**) Pebble, small stone, flint, flint-stone; (*fig.*) obstacle, embarrassment; (*pop.*) head. **cailloutage,** *n.m.* Gravelling; ballasting; rough-cast, pebble-work. **caillouté,** *n.m.* Fine stoneware; ornamental pebble-work. **caillouter,** *v.t.* To gravel, to ballast. **caillouteur,** *n.m.* Roadman. **caillouteux,** *a.* (*fem.* **-euse**) Pebbly, flinty. **cailloutis,** *n.m.* Broken stones, gravel; road metal.
caïman [kaiˈmɑ̃], *n.m.* American crocodile, cayman.
Caïn [kaˈɛ̃], *m.* Cain.
Caïphe [kaˈif], *m.* Caiaphas.
caïque or **caïc** [kaˈik], *n.m.* (*Naut.*) Caique.
Caire [kɛːr], **le,** *m.* Cairo.
caire [kɛːr], *n.m.* Coir, coco-nut fibre.
cairn [kɛrn], *n.m.* Cairn, tumulus.
caisse [kɛːs], *n.f.* Chest, case, box, trunk; coffer; till, safe, strong-box; (hence) contents of a cash-box, funds, cash; cashier's office, pay-office, pay-desk; drum; (*Anat.*) drum (of the ear); body or frame (of a vehicle). *Avoir tant d'argent en caisse,* to have so much money in hand; *battre la caisse* or *la grosse caisse,* to beat the (big) drum, (*fig.*) to advertise something noisily, to make a great fuss; *caisse d'amortissement,* sinking fund; *caisse de médicaments,* medicine chest; *caisse d'épargne,* savings-bank; *caisse d'escompte,* discounting bank; *caisse de secours mutuels,* sick-fund; *caisse des pensions,* pension fund; *caisse du tympan,* ear drum; *caisse militaire,* military chest; *faire la caisse,* to make up the

cash account; *faire sa caisse*, to make up one's cash-book; *grosse caisse*, big drum *or* big drummer; *petite caisse*, petty cash; *la caisse du régiment*, the regimental chest; *les caisses de l'État*, the coffers of the State; *livre de caisse*, cash-book; *sauver la caisse*, (*facet.*) to run off with the till; *tenir la caisse*, to keep the cash or cash-account, to act as cashier; *payez à la caisse*, pay at the desk.

caissette [kɛ'sɛt], *n.f.* Small box.

caissier [kɛ'sje], *n.m.* (*fem.* **caissière**) Treasurer, cashier.

caisson [kɛ'sɔ̃], *n.m.* Ammunition-wagon; (*Arch.*) coffer, compartment of ceiling; sunk-panel; (*Naut.*) locker. *Caisson à poudre*, powder-chest; *les caissons des vivres*, the provision-wagons; *plafond en caissons*, coffered ceiling; (*fam.*) *se faire sauter le caisson*, to blow one's brains out.

cajoler [kaʒɔ'le], *v.t.* To cajole, to coax, to wheedle.—*v.i.* (*Naut.*) To drift with the tide.

cajolerie, *n.f.* Cajolery, coaxing, wheedling.

cajoleur, *n.m.* (*fem.* **cajoleuse**) Cajoler, coaxer, wheedler.—*a.* Cajoling etc.

cake [kek], *n.m.* Fruit cake.

cal [kal], *n.m.* Callosity, callus.

Calabre [ka'lɑːbr], *f.* Calabria.

calade [ka'lad], *n.f.* Descent, slope (for training horses to gallop).

calage [ka'laːʒ], *n.m.* Lowering (of sails etc.), propping; wedging (of furniture); (*Tech.*) setting.

calaison [kalɛ'zɔ̃], *n.f.* Load-water line, sea-gauge (on ship).

calament [kala'mɑ̃], *n.m.* Calamint.

calaminage [kalami'naːʒ], *n.m.* (*Motor.*) Carbonizing.

calaminaire [kalami'nɛːr], *a.* Pertaining to calamine.

calamine [kala'min], *n.f.* Calamine; carbon (on plugs of a car etc.).

calamistrer [kalamis'tre], *v.t.* To wave (hair).

calamite [kala'mit], *n.f.* Calamite.

calamité [kalami'te], *n.f.* Calamity, misfortune. **calamiteusement**, *adv.* Calamitously. **calamiteux**, *a.* (*fem.* **calamiteuse**) Calamitous.

calandrage [kalɑ̃'draːʒ], *n.m.* Calendering, hot-pressing, mangling.

calandre [ka'lɑ̃ːdr], *n.f.* Mangle; calender; (*Motor.*) radiator grill; a variety of lark; weevil.

calandrelle [kalɑ̃'drɛl], *n.f.* Short-toed lark.

calandrer [kalɑ̃'dre], *v.t.* To calender, to press, to smooth, to mangle.

calandrette [kalɑ̃'drɛt], *n.f.* Song-thrush.

calandreur [kalɑ̃'drœːr], *n.m.* (*fem.* **calandreuse**) Calenderer; mangler.

calanque [ka'lɑ̃k], *n.f.* Creek, cove (in the Mediterranean).

calao [kala'o], *n.m.* Hornbill.

calcaire [kal'kɛːr], *a.* Calcareous.—*n.m.* Limestone.

calcanéum [kalkane'ɔm], *n.m.* (*Anat.*) Calcaneum, heel-bone.

calcédoine [kalse'dwan], *n.f.* Chalcedony. **calcédonieux**, *a.* (*fem.* **-ieuse**) Chalcedonic.

calcéolaire [kalseɔ'lɛːr], *n.f.* Calceolaria.

calcet [kal'sɛ], *n.m.* (*Naut.*) Mast-head.

calcification [kalsifika'sjɔ̃], *n.f.* Calcification. **calcifier**, *v.t.* To calcify.

calcin [kal'sɛ̃], *n.m.* Scale or fur (on a kettle etc.).

calcinable [kalsi'nabl], *a.* Calcinable. **calcination**, *n.f.* Calcination.

calciner [kalsi'ne], *v.t.* To calcine, to burn. **se calciner**, *v.r.* To calcine.

calcium [kal'sjɔm], *n.m.* Calcium.

calcul [kal'kyl], *n.m.* Calculation; arithmetic; computation, reckoning, counting; (*Math.*) calculus; (*fig.*) estimate, forecast; design, selfish motive; (*Med.*) calculus (stone in the bladder). *Calcul approximatif*, rough calculation; *calcul différentiel*, differential calculus; *cela n'entre pas dans mes calculs*, that does not fit in with my plans; *de calcul fait*, everything included; *il apprend le calcul*, he learns arithmetic; *règle à calcul*, slide rule. **calculable**, *a.* Computable, calculable. **calculateur**, *n.* and *a.* (*fem.* **calculatrice**) Calculator, reckoner; accountant; schemer.

calculer [kalky'le], *v.t.* To calculate, to compute, to reckon, to estimate; to forecast, to contrive, to devise; to determine. *Il calcula bien son élan*, he judged his jump well. *Machine à calculer*, calculating machine, computer.

calculeux [kalky'lø], *a.* (*fem.* **-euse**) Calculous.—*n.* Person affected with calculus.

cale (1) [kal], *n.f.* Hold (of a ship); stocks, slip; ducking, keel-hauling (punishment). *À fond de cale*, at the bottom of the hold; *cale de construction*, stocks; *cale de magasin* or *d'un quai*, slip; *cale sèche*, dry dock; *eau de cale*, bilge-water; *être à fond de cale*, (*colloq.*) to be hard up, to be at the end of one's resources; *passager de cale*, stowaway.

cale (2) [kal], *n.f.* Wedge, block, chock; prop, strut; quoin; shim.

calé [ka'le], *a.* (*fem.* **-ée**) Furnished with a hold; (*pop.*) well off, wealthy; (*sch.*) well read, well informed; (*Motor.*) jammed.

calebasse [kal'bas], *n.f.* Calabash, gourd; (*fig.*) pate, nob, noddle. **calebassier**, *n.m.* Calabash-tree.

calèche [ka'lɛʃ], *n.f.* Calash (carriage or head-gear); barouche, open carriage.

caleçon [kal'sɔ̃], *n.m.* (Men's) drawers, pants. *Caleçon de bain*, bathing trunks.

Calédonie [kaledɔ'ni], *f.* Caledonia.

calédonien [kaledɔ'njɛ̃], *a.* and *n.* (*fem.* **-ienne**) Caledonian.

caléfaction [kalefak'sjɔ̃], *n.f.* Calefaction, heating.

calembour [kalɑ̃'buːr], *n.m.* Pun. **calembourdiste** or **calembourdier**, *n.m.* Punster.

calembredaine [kalɑ̃brə'dɛn], *n.f.* Quibble, subterfuge, foolery, nonsense.

calendaire [kalɑ̃'dɛːr], *n.m.* Church register.

calendes [ka'lɑ̃ːd], *n.f. pl.* (*Ant.*) Calends; convocation of the clergy of a diocese. *Renvoyer aux calendes grecques*, to put off till doomsday.

calendrier [kalɑ̃dri'e], *n.m.* Calendar, almanac. *Nouveau calendrier* or *calendrier grégorien*, the new or the Gregorian calendar; *vieux calendrier*, the old calendar (old style); *calendrier à effeuiller*, block calendar.

calendule [kalɑ̃'dyl], *n.f.* Calendula.

cale-pied [kal'pje], *n.m.* Toe clip.

calepin [kal'pɛ̃], *n.m.* Notebook, memorandum-book, pocket-book.

caler (1) [ka'le], *v.t.* (*Naut.*) To lower, to strike (yards, topmasts, etc.); to draw. *Caler la voile*, to yield, to sing small; *caler les voiles*, to strike sail; *cale tout!* let go amain! *le navire cale cinq mètres*, the ship has a draught of 5 metres.—*v.i.* (*sch.*) To knuckle, to shoot (a marble); (*Motor.*) to stall (the engine).

caler (2) [ka'le], *v.t.* To prop up, to wedge; to steady; to jam. (*Row.*) *Caler l'aviron dans le système*, to keep the button up (against the rigger); (*Mil.*) *caler* (*le sac*), to give it up; *se caler les joues*, or *se les caler* (*pop.*), to stuff, to have a good feed. **se caler,** *v.r.* (*Motor.*) To stall.

caleter [CALTER].

caleur [ka'lœːr], *n.m.* (*pop.*) A shirker.

calfait [kal'fɛ], *n.m.* (*Naut.*) Caulking-iron.

calfat [kal'fa], *n.m.* Caulker. **calfatage,** *n.m.* Caulking. **calfater,** *v.t.* To caulk. **calfateur** [CALFAT].

calfeutrage [kalfø'traːʒ] or **calfeutrement,** *n.m.* Stopping of chinks. **calfeutrer,** *v.t.* To stop up the chinks of, to make air-tight. **se calfeutrer,** *v.r.* To be stopped up (of chinks); to shut oneself up.

calibrage [kali'braːʒ] or **calibrement,** *n.m.* Calibrating, gauging the bore of a gun, etc.

calibre [ka'libr], *n.m.* Calibre, bore (of a gun); size, diameter (of a bullet, body, etc.); instrument for measuring the calibre; (*fig.*) kind, sort, stamp. **calibrer,** *v.t.* To calibrate, to take the calibre of; to give the proper calibre to (bullets etc.) **calibreur,** *n.m.* Machine or apparatus for calibrating.

calice (1) [ka'lis], *n.m.* Chalice, communion-cup; (*fig.*) grief, sacrifice. *Boire* or *avaler le calice*, to swallow the pill; *boire le calice jusqu'à la lie*, to drink the cup to the dregs.

calice (2) [ka'lis], *n.m.* (*Bot.*) Calyx, flower, cup; (*Anat.*) calix. **calicé,** *a.* (*fem.* -ée) Furnished with a calyx.

caliche [ka'liʃ], *n.m.* Chilean nitre.

caliciflore [kalisi'floːr], *a.* (*Bot.*) Calycifloral. **caliciforme,** *a.* Caliciform. **calicinal,** *a.* (*fem.* -ale, *pl.* -aux) Calycinal, calycine.

calicot [kali'ko], *n.m.* Calico; (*slang*) counter-jumper.

caliculaire [kaliky'lɛːr], *a.* (*Bot.*) Calicular. **calicule,** *n.m.* Calicle, caliculus.

califat [kali'fa], *n.m.* Caliphate.

calife [ka'lif], *n.m.* Caliph.

Californie [kalifɔr'ni], *f.* California.

califourchon [kalifur'ʃɔ̃], *n.m.* *À califourchon*, astride, astraddle; *à califourchon sur un banc*, astride a bench.

câlin [kɑ'lɛ̃], *a.* (*fem.* **câline**) Wheedling, winning, coaxing. *Cet homme a l'air câlin*, that man has a wheedling look about him. —*n.* Wheedler, cajoler. *C'est une petite câline*, she is a little wheedler. **câliner,** *v.t.* To fondle, to cajole, to wheedle. **se câliner,** *v.r.* To coddle oneself, to take one's ease. **câlinerie,** *n.f.* Wheedling, cajolery, caressing; caress.

caliorne [kali'ɔrn], *n.f.* (*Naut.*) Solid winding-tackle; main purchase.

calleux [ka'lø], *a.* (*fem.* -euse) Callous, horny.

calligraphe [kali'graf], *n.m.* Calligrapher, good penman. **calligraphie,** *n.f.* Calligraphy, penmanship. **calligraphier,** *v.t.* To write well. **calligraphique,** *a.* Calligraphic.

callipyge [kalli'piːʒ], *a.* Callipygian.

callisthénie [kaliste'ni], *n.f.* Callisthenics.

callosité [kalozi'te], *n.f.* Callosity.

calmande [kal'mãːd], *n.f.* Calamanco.

calmant [kal'mã], *a.* (*fem.* -ante) Calming, soothing, sedative.—*n.m.* (*Med.*) Anodyne, sedative.

calmar [kal'maːr], *n.m.* Sleeve fish, calamary.

calme [kalm], *a.* Tranquil, still, quiet, serene, calm; unruffled, composed, collected, dispassionate.—*n.m.* Calm, stillness, quiet composure. *Calme plat*, (*Naut.*) dead calm. **calmement,** *adv.* Calmly. **calmer,** *v.t.* To still, to quiet, to allay, to soothe.—*v.i.* (*Naut.*) To lull, to become calm. **se calmer,** *v.r.* To become calm, to compose oneself; to blow over, to subside.

calmir [kal'miːr], *v.i.* (*Naut.*) To grow calm, to lull, to abate.

calomel [kalɔ'mɛl], *n.m.* Calomel.

calomniateur [kalɔmnja'tœːr], *a.* (*fem.* -trice) Slanderous.—*n.* Calumniator, slanderer; back-biter.

calomnie [kalɔm'ni], *n.f.* Calumny, slander. **calomnier,** *v.t.* To calumniate, to slander. **calomnieusement,** *adv.* Calumniously, slanderously. **calomnieux,** *a.* (*fem.* -ieuse) Calumnious, slanderous.

calorie [kalɔ'ri], *n.f.* Calorie, unit of heat.

calorifère [kalɔri'fɛːr], *n.m.* Hot-air stove or pipe; central heating.—*a.* Heat-conveying.

calorifiant [kalɔri'fjã], *a.* (*fem.* **calorifiante**) Calorifacient, calorific. **calorification,** *n.f.* Calorification. **calorifique,** *a.* Calorific. **calorifuge,** *a.* Insulating. **calorifuger,** *v.t.* To insulate, lag (pipes). **calorimètre,** *n.m.* Calorimeter. **calorimétrie,** *n.f.* Calorimetry. **calorimétrique,** *a.* Calorimetric.

calorique [kalɔ'rik], *a.* and *n.m.* Caloric, heat.

calorisation [kalɔriza'sjɔ̃], *n.f.* Aluminium plating.

calot [ka'lo], *n.m.* Block of unhewn slate; wedge; (*Mil. slang*) forage cap; (*sch.*) taw, big marble; (*pop.*) (big) eye. *Rouler* or *ribouler des calots*, to stare, to be flabbergasted.

calotin [kalɔ'tɛ̃], *n.m.* (*pop.*) Priest; church-goer.

calotte [ka'lɔt], *n.f.* Skull-cap (esp. that worn by priests); hence, *la calotte*, (*pop.*) the priesthood, body of priests; a small dome; knoll, mound, tumulus, etc.; (*Anat.*) brain-pan; (*Arch.*) calotte; (*colloq.*) box on the ears; (*Mach.*) cap of valve, and other rounded objects, parts, etc. *Donner des calottes à*, to box someone's ears; (*fam.*) *la calotte des cieux*, the vault of heaven; *la calotte rouge d'un cardinal*, the red hat of a cardinal.

calotter [kalɔ'te], *v.t.* To box the ears of.

calottier [kalɔ'tje], *n.m.* Calotte-maker, cap-maker.

caloyer [kalwa'je], *n.m.* Caloyer (Greek monk).

calquage [kal'kaːʒ], *n.m.* Tracing; close copying.

calque [kalk], *n.m.* Tracing; imitation, close copy.—*a. Papier calque*, tracing paper.

calquer [kal'ke], *v.t.* To trace; to copy, to imitate closely. **se calquer** (*sur*), *v.r.* To model oneself (on). **calqueur,** *n.m.* (*fem.* **calqueuse**) A person who traces or copies closely. **calquoir,** *n.m.* Tracing-point.

calter [kal'te], *v.i.* (*slang*) To pop off.

calumet [kaly'mɛ], *n.m.* Pipe, calumet. *Fumer*

le calumet de la paix, to smoke the pipe of peace.
calus [ka'lys], *n.m.* Callus [CAL].
calvados [kalva'dos] or *(fam.)* **calva,** *n.m.* Cider-brandy (made in depart. of Calvados in Normandy).
calvaire [kal've:r], *n.m.* A calvary; *(fig.)* torture, suffering, tribulation.
calvanier [kalva'nje], *n.m. (Agric.)* Labourer engaged for the harvest.
calville [kal'vil], *n.m.* A Norman apple.
calvinien [kalvi'njɛ̃], *a. (fem.* **calvinienne)** Calvinistic.
calvinisme [kalvi'nism], *n.m.* Calvinism. **calviniste,** *a.* Calvinistic.—*n.m.* Calvinist.
calvitie [kalvi'si], *n.f.* Calvity, baldness. *Calvitie des paupières,* loss of the eyelashes.
camaïeu [kama'jø], *n.m. (pl.* **-eux)** Monochrome painting (on porcelain); cameo (brooch etc.); a rather dull play or other artistic work.
camail [ka'ma:j], *n.m. (pl.* **camails)** Covering of mail for the neck and shoulders; hood, capuchin, bishop's purple ornament worn over the rochet; hackles (of poultry).
camaldule [kamal'dyl], *n.* Monk or nun of the Order of St. Romuald.
camarade [kama'rad], *'n.* Comrade, fellow, mate, chum, playmate, fellow-labourer, fellow-servant; one's equal or peer. *Camarade de chambre,* chum; *camarade de classe,* school-fellow; *camarade de collège,* college companion; *camarade de lit,* bed-fellow; *camarade de malheur,* fellow-sufferer; *camarade de voyage,* fellow-traveller; *faire camarade,* to surrender. **camaraderie,** *n.f.* Comradeship, intimacy, close friendship; coterie, clique; party spirit.
camard [ka'ma:r], *a. (fem.* **camarde)** Snub-nosed, flat.—*n.* Snub-nosed person. *La camarde, (pop.)* death.
camarilla [kamaril'la], *n.f.* Camarilla (coterie, junta, etc.).
camarin *(pop.)* [PLONGEON].
cambiste [kã'bist], *n.m.* Cambist.
cambium [kã'bjɔm], *n.m. (Bot.)* Cambium.
Cambodge [kã'bɔdʒ], *m.* Cambodia.
cambouis [kã'bwi], *n.m.* Dirty cart-grease or dirty lubricating oil.
cambrage [kã'bra:ʒ], *n.m.* Cambering, bending.
cambrai [kã'brɛ], *n.m.* Machine-made lace; cambric.
cambré [kã'bre], *a. (fem.* **-ée)** Bent, cambered, having a curved back (of horses etc.); arched, well-set. *Pont de navire cambré,* cambered deck. **cambrement,** *n.m.* Arching, curving.
cambrer [kã'bre], *v.t.* To arch, to bend, to curve. **se cambrer,** *v.r.* To be cambered; to warp; to draw oneself up (by throwing the chest forward).
cambrésine [kãbre'zin], *n.f.* Fine cambric.
cambrien [kãbri'ɛ̃], *a. and n. (fem.* **-ienne)** *(Geol.)* Cambrian.
cambrillon [kãbri'jɔ̃], *n.m.* Stiffener (of a shoe); shank.
cambriolage [kãbriɔ'la:ʒ], *n m.* House-breaking, burglary. **cambrioler,** *v.t.* To break into (a house), to burgle. **cambrioleur,** *n.m.* House-breaker, burglar.
cambrique [kã'brik], *a.* Cambrian, Cymric, Welsh (language).—*n.* (**Cambrique**) Welsh.

cambrouse [kã'brus], *n.f. (vulg.)* Country, fields.
cambrure [kã'bry:r], *n.f.* Bend, flexure, curvature, arch; the arched part in a shoe.
cambuse [kã'by:z], *n.f. (Naut.)* Store-room, canteen; *(pop.)* low tavern, drink-shop; poorly furnished house *or* room. **cambusier,** *n.m. (Naut.)* Steward's mate; store-keeper.
came [kam], *n.f.* Cam, wiper. *Arbre à cames,* cam-shaft.
camée [ka'me], *n.m.* Cameo.
caméléon [kamele'ɔ̃], *n.m.* Chameleon; *(fig.)* turn-coat.
caméléopard [kameleɔ'pa:r], *n.m.* Camelo-pard, giraffe.
camélia [kame'lja], *n.m.* Camellia.
camelot [kam'lo], *n.m.* Camlet; cheap-jack stuff; pedlar, hawker, newsboy. *Les camelots du Roi,* a royalist organization for propaganda. **camelote,** *n.f.* Inferior merchandise, shoddy; *(fig.)* trash. **cameloter,** *v.i.* To make camlet; to make trash; to sell camlet; to sell trash. **camelotier,** *n.m.* Pedlar, seller of trash; bad workman; coarse paper.
camembert [kamã'bɛr], *n.m.* Camembert cheese.
caméra [kame'ra], *n.f.* Ciné camera. **caméraman,** *n.m.* Cameraman.
caméral [kame'ral], *a. (fem.* **-ale,** *pl.* **-aux)** Pertaining to State finance, fiscal.
camérier [kame'rje], *n.m.* Chamberlain (of the Pope etc.).
camérière [CAMÉRISTE (2)].
camériste [kame'rist] or **camérière,** *n.f.* *Maid of honour; lady's maid.
camerlingue [kamer'lɛ̃g], *n.m.* Camerlengo, papal chamberlain.
camion [ka'mjɔ̃], *n.m.* Dray, low wagon, lorry; *(Paint.)* kettle; minute pin. **camionnage,** *n.m.* Carting, carriage (in a dray etc.). **camionner,** *v.t.* To convey on a dray, lorry, truck, etc. **camionnette,** *n.f.* Light motor lorry; van. **camionneur,** *n.m.* Drayman; vanman; haulage contractor.
camisard [kami'za:r], *n.m.* Camisard (French Calvinist).
camisole [kami'zɔl], *n.f.* Woman's morning jacket. *Camisole de force,* strait waistcoat or jacket.
camomille [kamɔ'mi:j], *n.f.* Camomile. *Infusion de camomille,* camomile tea.
camouflage [kamu'fla:ʒ] or **camouflement,** *n.m.* Disguise; camouflage.
camoufle [ka'mufl], *n.f. (pop.)* Candle; lamp.
camoufler [kamu'fle], *v.t.* To disguise; to camouflage. **se camoufler,** *v.r.* To disguise or camouflage oneself.
camouflet [kamu'flɛ], *n.m.* Whiff of smoke (in the face); *(fig.)* affront, snub; *(Mil.)* a gallery constructed to counteract an enemy mine by suffocating its defenders.
camp [kã], *n.m.* Camp; *(fig.)* army; party; *(games)* side. *(C)* Shelter in the woods; country cottage. *Camp d'instruction,* training camp; *camp volant,* camp of scouts etc., camp of gipsies etc.; *être en camp volant,* to be there only for a time; *lever le camp,* to strike camp; *ficher le camp, (colloq.)* to pack off, to clear out.
campagnard [kãpa'ɲa:r], *a. (fem.* **campagnarde)** Rustic, countrified, rural, bucolic,

pastoral.—*n.* Countryman or countrywoman, rustic, peasant; clodhopper, clown. *C'est une campagnarde*, she is a village girl.

campagne [kã'paɲ], *n.f.* The country, the fields, flat country, plain; seat, estate, country-house; campaign; (*Naut.*) cruise. *Battre la campagne*, to scour the country, to wander about, (*fig.*) to be delirious, to blunder, to bungle; *campagne électorale*, canvassing; *en pleine* or *rase campagne*, in the open country; *être à la campagne*, to be in the country; (*Mil.*) *être en campagne*, to be in the field; *faire campagne*, to go to war; *faire une campagne*, to wage a campaign; *gens de la campagne*, peasantry; *habit de campagne*, country dress; *la Campagne de Rome*, the Campagna; *les armées sont en campagne*, the armies have taken the field; *ouvrir la campagne*, to open the campaign; *partie de campagne*, picnic; *pièces de campagne*, field-pieces; *tenir la campagne*, to keep the field, to resist the enemy in the open.

campagnol [kãpa'ɲɔl], *n.m.* Vole, field-mouse.

campane [kã'pan], *n.f.* Ornamental covering with fringe and tassels; (*Arch.*) bell (of a capital); pasque-flower.

Campanie [kãpa'ni], *f.* Campania.

campanile [kãpa'nil], *n.m.* Campanile, bell-tower.

campanule [kãpa'nyl], *n.f.* Campanula, bell-flower, bluebell. *Campanule à feuilles rondes*, hare-bell; *campanule raiponce*, rampion. **campanulé**, *a.* (*fem.* **campanulée**) Campanulate, bell-shaped.

campé [kã'pe], *a.* (*fem.* **campée**) Established, firmly planted, well set up. *Garçon bien campé*, sturdy youth; *bien campé sur ses jambes*, firmly planted on one's legs.

campêche [kã'peʃ], *n.m. Bois de campêche*, campeachy wood, logwood.

campement [kãp'mã], *n.m.* Encamping; encampment; camp party, billeting party.

camper [kã'pe], *v.i.* To live in camp, to encamp, to pitch tents, to live a nomad life. *Faire camper son armée*, to encamp one's army.—*v.t.* To encamp (troops etc.); to place, to seat, to fix, to pose, to put, to clap down. *Camper là quelqu'un*, (*fam.*) to leave someone in the lurch; *camper un personnage*, to give life to a character. **se camper**, *v.r.* To encamp; to plant oneself, to clap oneself down. *Il se campa dans un fauteuil*, he sat himself down in an arm-chair; *se camper devant une glace*, to plant oneself before a mirror.

campeur [kã'pør], *n.m.* (*fem.* **-euse**) Camper.

camphorate [kãfɔ'rat], *n.m.* Camphorate. **camphorique**, *a.* Camphoric.

camphre [kã:fr], *n.m.* Camphor. **camphré**, *a.* (*fem.* **camphrée**) Camphorated. *Huile camphrée*, camphorated oil. **camphrer**, *v.t.* To put camphor into (clothes etc.). **camphrier**, *n.f.* Camphor-tree.

campine [kã'pin], *n.f.* Fine fat pullet.

camping [kã'piŋ], *n.m.* Camping. *Faire du camping*, to go camping.

campos [kã'po], *n.m.* (*fam.*) Leave, holiday, relaxation. *Avoir campos*, to be on holiday; *prendre campos*, to take a holiday.

camus [ka'my], *a.* (*fem.* **camuse**) Flat-nosed, snub-nosed.

Canada [kana'da], **le**, *m.* Canada.

canadien [kana'djɛ̃], *a.* and *n.* (*fem.* **-ienne**) Canadian. *Une canadienne*, a Canadian canoe; a furred tunic; (*Motor.*) station-waggon.

canaille [ka'nɑ:j], *n.f.* Rabble, riffraff, mob, scum of the populace; scoundrel. *Ces canailles de domestiques*, these rascally servants! *hors d'ici, canaille!* begone, you scoundrel! *vile canaille*, miserable scum.—*a.* Low, rascally, villainous. **canaillerie**, *n.f.* Blackguardism; vulgarity.

canal [ka'nal], *n.m.* (*pl.* **canaux**) Canal; conduit, duct, drain; pipe, tube, spout; stream, water-course, race (of water-mills); channel, bed; (*fig.*) road, way, means; strait; (*Arch.*) fluting (of a column). *Canal de dérivation*, lateral drain; *canal de larmier*, (*Arch.*) channel of a coping; *canal d'irrigation*, trench for irrigation; *canal latéral*, canal forming an easy channel beside a river etc.; *canal thoracique*, thoracic duct; *il est le canal de toutes les grâces*, all favours come through him.

canaliculaire [kanaliky'lɛːr], *a.* Forming or developing into a small channel, conduit, duct, etc. **canalicule**, *n.f.* Small channel, conduit, pipe, etc. ***canaliculé**, *a.* (*fem.* **-ée**) (*Bot.*) Channelled, furrowed.

canalisation [kanaliza'sjɔ̃], *n.f.* Canalization; mains. *Canalisation de gaz*, gas mains. **canaliser**, *v.t.* To canalize, to intersect with canals; to install pipes for gas, water, etc.

canamelle [kana'mɛl], *n.f.* Sugar-cane.

canapé [kana'pe], *n.m.* Sofa, couch; (*Cookery*) slice of bread fried in butter; *sur canapé*, on toast.

canapé-lit [kanape'li], *n.m.* Sofa-bed.

canaque [ka'nak], *a.* and *n.* Kanaka.

canard (1) [ka'naːr], *n.m.* Duck; drake; (*fig.*) false news, hoax; bit of sugar dipped in brandy or coffee; (*Mus.*) a harsh false note; (*Mil. slang*) horse; (*pop.*) (*of newspapers*) rag. *Canard chipeau*, gadwall; *canard colvert*, mallard; *canard milouin*, pochard; *canard pilet*, pintail; *canard sauvage*, wild duck; *canard souchet*, shoveller; *canard siffleur*, widgeon; (*C*) *canard branchu*, wood duck.

canard (2), *a.* (*fem.* **-arde**) *Bâtiment canard*, vessel that pitches; *chien canard*, water-spaniel.

canardeau, *n.m.* Young duck.

canarder [kanar'de], *v.t.* To shoot from behind a shelter; to snipe.—*v.i.* To make a noise like a duck's quack (on a musical instrument); (*Naut.*) to pitch heavily.

canardière [kanar'djeːr], *n.f.* Duck-pond; decoy-pond; blind (for wild-duck shooting); duck-gun; (*Mil.*) loop-hole.

canari [kana'ri], *n.m.* Canary (bird).

Canaries [kana'ri], **les Îles**, *f. pl.* The Canary Islands.

canasse [ka'nas], *n.f.* Tea-chest, tobacco-box; variety of tobacco.

canasson [kana'sɔ̃] *n.m.* (*vulg.*) Horse, hack.

canasta [kana'sta], *n.f.* Canasta.

cancan [kã'kã], *n.m.* Tittle-tattle, scandal; French cancan. *Faire des cancans*, to indulge in malicious gossip. **cancaner**, *v.i.* To tattle, to invent stories; **cancanier**, *a.* (*fem.* **-ière**) Addicted to gossip.—*n.* Lover of scandal or tittle-tattle; scandal-monger.

*cancel [kɑ̃'sɛl], *n.m.* Chancel of church. **cancellariat,** *n.m.* Chancellorship.

cancer [kɑ̃'sɛːr], *n.m.* (*Astron., Geol., Med.*) Cancer.

cancéreux [kɑ̃se'rø], *a.* (*fem.* **-euse**) Cancerous. **cancériforme,** *a.* Canceriform.

canche [kɑ̃ːʃ], *n.f.* (*Bot.*) Hair-grass.

cancre [kɑ̃ːkr], *n.m.* Crab; (*fig.*) dunce (at school).

cancrelat or **cancrelas** [kɑ̃krə'la], *n.m.* Cockroach.

candélabre [kɑ̃de'laːbr], *n.m.* Candelabrum, sconce; (*Hort.*) pyramidal fruit-tree; type of cactus.

candelette [kɑ̃'dlɛt], *n.f.* (*Naut.*) Bar ton.

candeur [kɑ̃'dœːr], *n.f.* Frankness, candour; ingenuousness.

candi [kɑ̃'di], *a.m.* Candied. *Fruits candis,* crystallized fruits.—*n.m.* Sugar-candy.

candidat [kɑ̃di'da], *n.m.* Candidate. **candidature,** *n.f.* Candidature. *Poser sa candidature,* to make an application.

candide [kɑ̃'did], *a.* Open, frank; ingenuous. **candidement,** *adv.* Openly, frankly, candidly; ingenuously.

candir [kɑ̃'diːr], *v.i.,* or **se candir,** *v.r.* To candy, to crystallize. **candisation,** *n.f.* Candying.

cane [kan], *n.f.* (Female) duck. (*fam.*) *Faire la cane=caner.*

canefice [CANNEBIÈRE].

canéficier [kane'fis], *n.f.* (*pop.*) Cassia. **canéficier,** *n.m.* Cassia-tree.

canepetière [kanpə'tjɛːr], *n.f.* Lesser bustard.

caner [ka'ne], *v.i.* (*fam.*) To shirk danger, to funk, to show the white feather, to back out.

canetière [kan'tjɛːr], *n.f.* Spooler (woman or machine).

caneton [kan'tɔ̃], *n.m.* Young duck, duckling.

canette [ka'nɛt], *n.f.* Small duck, duckling; teal; (*Her.*) duck without legs; (or **cannette**) a measure for beer; bottle, bottleful; bobbin, spool (inside shuttle).

canevas [kan'va], *n.m.* Canvas; sail-cloth; outline sketch, rough scheme or draft; (*Mus.*) words set to a tune. *Faire le canevas d'une comédie,* to sketch out or compose the skeleton of a play; *tracer son canevas,* to prepare one's ground-work.

cange [kɑ̃ːʒ], *n.f.* Light boat used on the Nile.

cangue [kɑ̃ːg], *n.f.* Cang, pillory (used in China).

cani [ka'ni], *a.m.* (*Naut.*) Unsound, crumbling away.—*n.m.* Rotten wood.

caniche [ka'niʃ], *n.m.* Poodle. **canichon,** *n.m.* Small poodle; duckling.

caniculaire [kaniky'lɛːr], *a.* Canicular. *Les jours caniculaires,* the dog-days. **canicule,** *n.f.* Dog-days; (*Astron.*) dog-star.

canif [ka'nif], *n.m.* Penknife. *Donner des coups de canif dans le contrat,* to commit occasional acts of infidelity to the marriage contract.

canillée [kani'je], *n.f.* Duckweed.

canin [ka'nɛ̃], *a.* Canine. *Avoir une faim canine,* to be ravenously hungry; *dent canine,* canine tooth; *exposition canine,* dog show. —*n.f.* Canine tooth.

canitie [kani'si], *n.f.* Whiteness of the hair.

caniveau [kani'vo], *n.m.* (*Arch.*) Channel-stone, gutter.

canna [BALISIER].

cannage [ka'naːʒ], *n.m.* Cane-work (in chairs etc.).

cannaie [ka'nɛ], *n.f.* Cane-plantation, cane-field.

canne [kan], *n.f.* Cane, reed; walking-stick; long measure; glass-blower's pipe. *Canne à épée* or *canne armée,* sword-stick; *canne à pêche,* fishing-rod; *canne à sucre,* sugar-cane; *canne plombée,* weighted stick; *casser sa canne,* (*colloq.*) to die.

canné [ka'ne], *a.* (*fem.* **cannée**) Cane-bottomed (of chairs etc.).

canneau [GODRON].

canneberge [kan'bɛrʒ], *n.f.* Cranberry.

cannebière or **canebière** (*S.-E. France*) [CHÈNEVIÈRE].

cannelas [kan'la], *n.m.* Candied cinnamon.

cannelé [kan'le], *a.* (*fem.* **cannelée**) Fluted (column); grooved (tyre).—*n.m.* Ribbed silk.

canneler [kan'le], *v.t.* To flute, to channel, to groove.

cannelier [kane'lje], *n.m.* Cinnamon-tree.

cannelle (1) [ka'nɛl], *n.f.* Cinnamon bark, cinnamon. *Cannelle blanche,* canella.

cannelle (2) [ka'nɛl] or **cannette** (1), *n.f.* Spigot, tap.

cannelure [kan'lyːr], *n.f.* Fluting, channelling, grooving; (*Bot.*) deep striation (on the stems of certain plants). *Cannelure à côtes,* fluting with intervals; *cannelure avec rudentures,* fluting enriched with cables; *cannelure à vive arête,* fluting without intervals; *cannelures plates,* square fluting.

canner [ka'ne], *v.t.* To cane (a chair).

canneteuse [CANETEUSE].

cannetière [CANETIÈRE].

cannetille [kan'ti:j], *n.f.* Gold, silver, etc., wire (used in embroidery). **cannetiller,** *v.t.* To trim with gold or silver twist.

cannette (1) [CANNELLE (2)].

cannette (2) [CANETTE].

canneur [ka'nœːr], *n.m.* (*fem.* **-euse**) Chair-caner.

cannibale [kani'bal], *n.m.* Cannibal. **cannibalisme,** *n.m.* Cannibalism; (*fig.*) ferocity.

canoë [kano'e], *n.m.* Canadian canoe. **canoéiste,** *n.m.* Paddler.

canon (1) [ka'nɔ̃], *n.m.* Cannon, gun; barrel (of a gun); cylinder, pipe, tube (of lock); stick (of sulphur); horse's cannon, shin measure of ⅛ pint, small glass. *À canon rayé,* rifled; *canon de dix livres,* ten-pounder; *canon de retraite,* (*Naut.*) stern-chaser, gun at the stern; *canon d'un soufflet,* nozzle-pipe of a pair of bellows; *canon renforcé,* cannon whose breech is thicker than its bore; *chair à canon,* (*iron.*) soldiers, cannon-fodder; *de la poudre à canon,* gunpowder; *enclouer un canon,* to spike a gun; *être à portée de canon,* to be within cannon-shot; *être hors de portée de canon,* to be beyond cannon range; *l'affût d'un canon,* the gun-carriage; *la lumière, la culasse,* or *le recul d'un canon,* touch-hole, breech, or recoil of a cannon; *un coup de canon,* a cannon-shot; *une pièce de canon,* a piece of ordnance; *canon anti-aérien,* anti-aircraft gun.

canon (2) [ka'nɔ̃], *n.m.* (*Eccles., Mus., Print., etc.*) Canon. *Canon des Écritures,* the sacred canon; *école de droit canon,* school of canon law; *le canon de la messe,* the canon of the mass; *les canons d'un concile,* the canons of a council; (*Print.*) *canon enluminé*, illuminated canon; *gros canon*, canon; *petit canon*, two-line English.

cañon [ka'ɲɔ̃], *n.m.* Canyon.

canonial [kanɔ'njal], *a.* (*fem.* **-ale**, *pl.* **-aux**) Canonical. **canonialement**, *adv.* Canonically. **canonicat**, *n.m.* Canonry; (*fig.*) sinecure. **canonicité**, *n.f.* Canonicity. **canonique**, *a.* Canonical. **canoniquement**, *adv.* Canonically. **canonisable**, *a.* Canonizable. **canonisation**, *n.f.* Canonization. **canoniser**, *v.t.* To canonize.

canonnade [kanɔ'nad], *n.f.* Cannonading, cannonade. **canonnage**, *n.m.* Gunnery. **canonner**, *v.t.* To attack with heavy artillery, to cannonade. **se canonner**, *v.r.* To cannonade each other. **canonnerie**, *n.f.* Cannon-foundry, gun-foundry. **canonnier**, *n.m.* Gunner. **canonnière**, *n.f.* *Loop-hole for gun; gunner's tent; drain-hole; pop-gun; gunboat.

canot [ka'no], *n.m.* Small open boat, dinghy; (*C*) Canadian canoe. *Canot automobile*, motor-boat; *canot de sauvetage*, lifeboat. **canotage**, *n.m.* Boating, rowing. (*C*) **canotée**, *n.f.* Canoe-load. **canoter**, *v.i.* To go boating. (*C*) **canoteur**, *n.m.* Paddler. **canotier**, *n.m.* One who paddles a hired boat, who goes for a boating party; straw-hat, boater.

canson [kɑ̃'sɔ̃], *n.m.* Canson (drawing-paper).

cantal [kɑ̃'tal], *n.m.* (*pl.* **cantals**) Sort of cheese made in Auvergne.

cantaloup [kɑ̃ta'lu], *n.m.* Cantaloup melon.

cantate [kɑ̃'tat], *n.f.* (*Mus.*) Cantata.

cantatrice [kɑ̃ta'tris], *n.f.* Cantatrice, (classic) singer.

cantharide [kɑ̃ta'rid], *n.f.* (*Ent.*) Cantharis, Spanish fly; (*Pharm.*, *pl.*) cantharides.

canthère [kɑ̃'tɛːr], *n.m.* (*Ichth.*) Bream.

canthus [kɑ̃'tyːs], *n.m.* (*Anat.*) Canthus.

cantilène [kɑ̃ti'lɛːn], *n.f.* Cantilena, ballad, popular song.

cantine [kɑ̃'tin], *n.f.* Canteen; bottle-case, kit-case; lunch stall (in a school). **cantinier**, *n.m.* (*fem.* **-ière**) Sutler, canteen-keeper.

cantique [kɑ̃'tik], *n.m.* Canticle, hymn. *Le Cantique des cantiques*, the Song of Songs.

canton [kɑ̃'tɔ̃], *n.m.* Canton (district); (*Her.*) canton. (*C*) Township.

cantonade [kɑ̃tɔ'nad], *n.f.* (*Theat.*) Either of the wings. *Parler à la cantonade*, to speak to an actor off the stage; (*fig.*) to speak to empty benches.

cantonal [kɑ̃tɔ'nal], *a.* (*fem.* **-ale**, *pl.* **-aux**) Cantonal.

cantonné [kɑ̃tɔ'ne], *a.* (*fem.* **-ée**) (*Arch.*, Her., *Mil.*) Cantoned. **cantonnement**, *n.m.* (*Mil.*) Cantonment, billet, quarters.

cantonner [kɑ̃tɔ'ne], *v.t.* (*Mil.*) To canton, to billet (troops).—*v.i.* To be cantoned. **se cantonner**, *v.r.* To take up a position, quarters, or abode; to fortify oneself; to shut oneself up. *Se cantonner dans l'indifférence*, to remain unmoved.

cantonnier [kɑ̃tɔ'nje], *n.m.* Road-man; (*Rail.*) roadsman.

cantonnière [kɑ̃tɔ'njɛːr], *n.f.* Valance.

canulant [kany'lɑ̃], *a.* (*fem.* **canulante**) (*fam.*) Boring, tiresome.

canular [kany'lar], *n.m.* Student's joke; tall story.

canule [ka'nyl], *n.f.* Clyster-pipe, injection-tube, douche-tube.

canuler [kany'le], *v.t.* (*colloq.*) To bore, to pester, to worry.

Canut [ka'nyt], *m.* Canute. **Canut le Hardi**, Hardicanute.

canut [ka'ny], *n.m.* (*fem.* **canuse**) Silk-weaver (Lyons).

caouanne or **caouane** [ka'wan], *n.f.* Logger-head (large sea-turtle).

caoutchouc [kau'tʃu], *n.m.* Caoutchouc, (India)-rubber; piece of or object in this; *esp.* mackintosh; (*Bot.*) gum-tree; *pl.* galoshes, (*Am.*) rubbers. *Bottes de caoutchouc*, rubber boots, gum boots, Wellingtons. **caoutchouter**, *v.t.* To cover or treat with caoutchouc, to rubberize. **caoutchouteux** (*fem.* **-euse**), *a.* Rubbery. **caoutchoutier**, *n.m.* (*pop.*) Rubber-plant.

Cap [kap], **le**, *m.* The Cape, Capetown.

cap [kap], *n.m.* Head; bow (of a ship); cape, headland, point, promontory, foreland. *De pied en cap*, from top to toe; *avoir le cap au large*, (*Naut.*) to stand off; *cap à cap*, tête-à-tête; *doubler un cap*, to double a cape; *mettre le cap sur*, to steer for; *où est le cap?* (*Naut.*) how is her head? (*fig.*) *avoir franchi le cap de la cinquantaine*, to be in one's fifties, to have turned fifty.

capable [ka'pabl], *a.* Able, fit, capable; apt; competent, efficient, clever. *C'est un homme capable*, he is a clever man; *faire le capable*, to look as if you were in the know; *il est capable de tout*, he is capable of anything; *il est capable de vous desservir*, he is capable of doing you an ill turn; *prendre l'air capable*, to put on a conceited, bumptious, knowing look.

capacité [kapasi'te], *n.f.* Extent, size, capaciousness; ability; (*Law etc.*) capacity; (*Naut.*) bulk, burden, tonnage. *Manquer de capacité*, to lack ability.

caparaçon [kapara'sɔ̃], *n.m.* Caparison, housings, trappings. **caparaçonner**, *v.t.* To caparison (a horse).

cape [kap], *n.f.* Cape, mantle, or cloak with a hood, riding-hood; (*Naut.*) try-sail. *À la cape!* bring to! *être à la cape*, (*Naut.*) to lie to; *n'avoir que la cape et l'épée*, to be titled but penniless; *rire sous cape*, to laugh up one's sleeve; *roman de cape et d'épée*, swash-buckler romance; *vendre sous cape*, to sell on the sly *or* under the counter.

capéer [kape'e], *v.i.* (*Naut.*) To lie to.

capelan [ka'plɑ̃], *n.m.* Beggarly priest; (*Ichth.*) capelin or caplin.

capeler [ka'ple], *v.t.* (*Naut.*) To rig; to put on.

capelet [ka'plɛ], *n.m.* (*Vet.*) Capped hock.

capeline [ka'plin], *n.f.* Woman's ornamental hat formerly worn in hunting; woman's hood or capote; (armour) iron hat with neck-piece.

capendu [kapɑ̃'dy], *n.m.* A short-shank (apple).

capeyer [CAPÉER].

Capharnaüm [kafarna'ɔm], *m.* Capernaum.

capharnaüm [kafarna'ɔm], *n.m.* Place of confusion; lumber-room.

capillaire [kapi'lɛːr], *a.* Capillary.—*n.m.* Capillary; maiden-hair. **capillarité**, *n.f.* Capillarity, capillary attraction or repulsion.

capilotade [kapilɔ'tad], *n.f.* Hash, ragoût; (*fig.*) thrashing; drubbing, slandering. *Mettre* *quelqu'un en capilotade*, to beat someone black and blue, to slander, to pull someone to pieces.

capion [ka'pjɔ̃], *n.m.* (*Mediterranean*) Stern-post, stern.

capiston [kapi'stɔ̃], *n.m.* (*Mil. slang*) Captain.

capitainat [kapitɛ'na], *n.m.* Captaincy.

capitaine [kapi'tɛn], *n.m.* Captain; (*fig.*) eminent soldier, general, or commander. *Capitaine au long cours*, captain of a trading vessel (going to foreign parts); *capitaine aviateur*, flight lieutenant; *capitaine de cavalerie*, captain of cavalry; *capitaine de pavillon*, flag-captain; *capitaine de port*, harbour-master; *capitaine de vaisseau*, post-captain; *capitaine* (of merchantman), master, skipper; *grade de capitaine*, captaincy.

capitainerie, *n.f.* Office of the harbour-master.

capital [kapi'tal], *a.* (*fem.* **capitale**, *pl.* **capitaux**) Capital, main, chief, principal; involving death. *Les sept péchés capitaux*, the seven deadly sins; *peine capitale*, capital punishment.—*n.m.* Capital, principal, property, funds, stock. *Manger son capital*, to use up one's property; *mettre un capital à fonds perdu*, to sink a capital or sum; *rembourser le capital*, to reimburse the principal; *les capitaux engagés*, the vested interests.—*n.f.* Capital, chief city; capital letter. **capitalement**, *adv.* Capitally. **capitalisable**, *a.* Capitalizable. **capitalisation**, *n.f.* Capitalization. **capitaliser**, *v.t.* To put at compound interest; to add to the capital; to realize, to capitalize.—*v.i.* To save, to lay by. **se capitaliser**, *v.r.* To be capitalized. **capitalisme**, *n.m.* Capitalism. **capitaliste**, *n.m.* Capitalist, moneyed man.

capitan [kapi'tɑ̃], *n.m.* Braggadocio, swaggerer.

capitane [kapi'tan], *n.f.* (*Naut.*) Admiral's galley (also called *galère capitane*).

capitan-pacha [kapitɑ̃pa'ʃa], *n.m.* (*pl.* **capitans-pachas**) Turkish admiral.

capitation [kapita'sjɔ̃], *n.f.* Capitation, poll-tax.

capité [kapi'te], *a.* (*fem.* **capitée**) (*Bot.*) Capitate.

capiteux [kapi'tø], *a.* (*fem.* **capiteuse**) Heady, strong. *Bière capiteuse*, strong beer; *vin capiteux*, heavy wine.

capitole [kapi'tɔl], *n.m.* Capitol (of Rome, of Toulouse and of Washington). **capitolin**, *a.* (*fem.* **-ine**) Capitoline.

capiton [kapi'tɔ̃], *n.m.* Silk-flock used in upholstery; padded section (in upholstering). **capitonnage**, *n.m.* Stuffing, wadding, quilting. **capitonner**, *v.t.* To stuff, to pad, etc.; to tuft (a mattress etc.).

capitoul [kapi'tul], *n.m.* Alderman, town-councillor (at Toulouse). **capitoulat**, *n.m.* The dignity of *capitoul*.

capitulaire [kapity'lɛːr], *a.* Capitular.—*n.m.* Capitulary.

capitulard [kapity'laːr], *n.m.* Partisan for capitulation (in the siege of Paris, 1870); a coward, a scuttler.

capitulation [kapityla'sjɔ̃], *n.f.* Capitulation; surrender; compromise. *Amener à une capitulation*, to bring to terms; *capitulation de conscience*, a compromise with one's conscience.

capitule [kapi'tyl], *n.m.* (*Bot.*) Capitulum.

capitulé [kapity'le], *a.* (*fem.* **-ée**) (*Bot.*) Capitate.

capituler [kapity'le], *v.i.* To capitulate, to compound, to compromise. *Capituler avec sa conscience*, to compound with one's conscience.

caplan [CAPELAN].

capnofuge [kapnɔ'fy:ʒ], *a.* Smoke-preventing.

capoc [ka'pɔk], *n.m.* Kapok.

capon [ka'pɔ̃], *a.* (*fem.* **-onne**) Cowardly.—*n.m.* Mean fellow, sneak, cheat; coward; (*Naut.*) cat. *Bossoir de capon*, cat-head; *poulie de capon*, cat-block. **caponner**, *v.i.* To cheat; to be cowardly, to hang back; to rat.—*v.t.* (*Naut.*) To cat (the anchor).

caponnière [kapɔ'njɛːr], *n.f.* (*Fort.*) Caponiere.

caporal [kapɔ'ral], *n.m.* (*pl.* **caporaux**) Corporal; caporal, sort of 'shag' (tobacco). *Le petit caporal*, Napoleon. **caporal-chef**, *n.m.* (*pl.* **caporaux-chefs**) Lance-sergeant. **caporaliser**, *v.t.* To militarize. **caporalisme**, *n.m.* Militarism of the Prussian type.

capot (1) [ka'po], *n.m.* (*Naut.*) Hood (for protecting ladders etc.); (*Motor.*) bonnet, (*Am.*) hood.

capot (2) [ka'po], *a.* (*fem. unchanged*) Capot (at piquet etc.); flabbergasted. *Être capot*, to have lost all the tricks, (*fig.*) to look foolish, to be baulked; *faire capot*, to capot, to win all the tricks, to beat hollow, (*Naut.*) to capsize, to upset.

capotage [kapɔ'ta:ʒ], *n.m.* Hooding; capsizing.

capote [ka'pɔt], *n.f.* Capote, large cloak with a hood; (soldier's) great-coat; capuchin, hood, mantle; baby's bonnet.

capoter [kapɔ'te], *v.i.* (*Naut. etc.*) To capsize; to turn turtle; (*Motor., Av.*) to overturn, to turn a somersault.—*v.t.* To hood (a carriage).

câpre [kɑ:pr], *n.f.* (*Bot.*) Caper.

capricant [kapri'kɑ̃], *a.* (*fem.* **-ante**) Bounding, unequal (pulse).

caprice [ka'pris], *n.m.* Caprice, whim, humour, freak; fit, flight, sally; (*Mus.*) fantasia. *Composer de caprice*, to compose when the spirit moves or when the fit is on; *les caprices de la fortune*, the fickleness of fortune; *les caprices de la mode*, the caprices or freaks of fashion. **capricieusement**, *adv.* Capriciously, fantastically, whimsically. **capricieux**, *a.* (*fem.* **-euse**) Capricious, whimsical, freakish, skittish.

capricorne [kapri'kɔrn], *n.m.* Capricorn-beetle; (*Astron.*) capricorn.

câprier [kɑpri'e], *n.m.* Caper-bush. **câprière**, *n.f.* Caper-plantation; caper-jar.

caprifiguier [kaprifi'gje], *n.m.* Wild fig-tree.

caprin [ka'prɛ̃], *a.* (*fem.* **caprine**) Caprine.

capripède [kapri'pɛd], *a.* Goat-footed (like a satyr).

capron [ka'prɔ̃] or **caperon**, *n.m.* Hautboy strawberry. **capronier**, *n.m.* Hautboy strawberry-plant.

capselle [kap'sɛl], *n.f.* Shepherd's-purse.

capsulage [kapsy'la:ʒ], *n.m.* Capsuling (of bottles etc.).

capsulaire [kapsy'lɛːr], *a.* Capsular.

capsule [kap'syl], *n.f.* Capsule; pod; percussion-cap (of firearms). **capsuler**, *v.t.* To put a capsule on (a bottle etc.).—*v.i.* To miss fire (of firearms).

captage [kap'ta:ʒ], *n.m.* Collecting and piping (of water). *Surface de captage*, catchment.

captateur [kapta'tœːr], *n.m.* (*fem.* **captatrice**) (*Law*) Inveigler. **captation**, *n.f.* Captation, inveigling; intercepting. **captatoire**, *a.* Inveigling.

capter [kap'te], *v.t.* To obtain by underhand methods; to win by insinuation, bribery, etc.; to collect (water) at the head-springs by means of channels, pipes, etc. *Capter la bienveillance de quelqu'un*, to curry favour with someone; *capter les suffrages*, to win votes unfairly, to get by bribery.

capteur [kap'tœːr], *a.* and *n.m.* Captor (ship).

captieusement [kapsjøz'mã], *adv.* Insidiously, cunningly, deceitfully. **captieux**, *a.* (*fem.* **-ieuse**) Insidious, cunning, specious.

captif [kap'tif], *a.* and *n.* (*fem.* **-ive**) Captive, prisoner.

captivant [kapti'vã], *a.* (*fem.* **-ante**) Captivating; enthralling.

captiver [kapti've], *v.t.* To captivate, to charm, to seduce, to enslave. *Captiver l'attention*, to captivate attention; *la beauté qui le captive*, the beauty that enslaves him.

captivité, *n.f.* Capt'vity, bondage. *Racheter de captivité*, to ransom from captivity.

capture [kap'tyːr], *n.f.* Capture, seizure; prize, booty. **capturer**, *v.t.* To capture; to apprehend, to arrest, to catch.

capuce [ka'pys], *n.m.* Pointed hood or cowl; (of a monk).

capuche [ka'pyʃ], *n.f.* Woman's hood.

capuchon [kapy'ʃɔ̃], *n.m.* Hood, cowl. *Prendre le capuchon*, to become a monk. **capuchonné**, *a.* (*fem.* **-ée**) Cowled; (*Bot.*) hooded (like monk's-hood). **capuchonnement**, *n.m.* Giving the cowl to; putting a hood on. **capuchonner**, *v.t.* To cover (a chimney etc.) with a cowl.

capucin [kapy'sɛ̃], *n.m.* (*fem.* **capucine** (1)) Capuchin friar, capuchin nun; capuchin pigeon; hooded seal. *Barbe de capucin*, a very long beard [*see also* BARBE]; *capucins de cartes*, playing-cards folded lengthwise in the middle for building card-castles etc.; *tomber comme des capucins de cartes*, to tumble over one another.

capucinade [kapysi'nad], *n.f.* Stupid sermon.

capucine (1) [CAPUCIN].

capucine (2) [kapy'sin], *n.f.* Nasturtium; ring or band (of a soldier's musket).

capucinière [kapysi'njɛːr], *n.f.* (*iron.*) Capuchin friary; (*fig.*) a house full of pious or sanctimonious people.

capulet [kapy'lɛ], *n.m.* Pyrenean woman's hood.

caquage [ka'kaːʒ], *n.m.* Barrelling (of herrings).

caque [kak], *n.f.* Keg, barrel. *La caque sent toujours le hareng*, what is bred in the bone will out in the flesh; *serrés comme harengs en caque*, packed like sardines. **caquer**, *v.t.* To barrel (herrings).

caquet [ka'kɛ], *n.m.* Cackle (of geese etc.); tittle-tattle, idle talk, gossip, scandal. *Avoir bien du caquet*, to be a chatterbox; *caquet bon bec*, (*colloq.*) magpie; (*fig.*) prattler; *rabattre* or *rabaisser le caquet à quelqu'un*, to take someone down a peg or two. **caquetage**, *n.m.*, or **caqueterie**, *n.f.* Babbling, prattling; tattling, gossiping.

caqueter [kak'te], *v.i.* To cackle, to babble, to chatter; to gossip. **caqueterie** [CAQUETAGE]. **caqueteur**, *a.* (*fem.* **-euse**) Prattling;

gossiping.—*n.* Prattler, tattler, idle prater, gossip.

caqueur [ka'kœːr], *n.m.* (*fem.* **-euse**) Herring-curer.—*n.m.* Herring-curer's knife.

car [kaːr], *conj.* For, because.—*n.m.* (*fam.*) Coach, long-distance bus.

caraba [kara'ba], *n.m.* Mahogany-oil.

carabas [kara'ba], *n.m.* (1) Obsolete form of heavy carriage (in the Parisian region, 18th cent.) (2) *Le Marquis de Carabas* (in Puss-in-Boots), (*fam.*) a nabob.

carabe [ka'rab], *n.m.* Carabus (beetle).

carabin [kara'bɛ̃], *n.m.* *Horse-soldier armed with a carbine; Italian carabiniere; (*colloq.*) saw-bones, medical student.

carabine [kara'bin], *n.f.* Carbine, rifle. **carabiné** [karabi'ne], *a.* (*fem.* **-ée**) Rifled; (*Naut.*) stiff (of the wind); (*colloq.*) strong, violent. *Rhume carabiné*, jolly bad cold. **carabiner**, *v.t.* To rifle (a gun-barrel).—*v.i.* To skirmish. **carabinier**, *n.m.* Carabinier, rifleman. *Arriver comme les carabiniers*, to arrive too late.

caraco [kara'ko], *n.m.* Woman's loose jacket.

caracole [kara'kɔl], *n.f.* Caracol. *En caracole*, winding. **caracoler**, *v.i.* To caracol, to circle; to gambol.

caractère [karak'tɛːr], *n.m.* Character, letter, type, print; hand-writing; nature, disposition, personality, idiosyncrasy; temper, humour, spirit; stamp, mark, expression; quality; strong personality, firmness. (*Print.*) *Beaux caractères*, fine type; *caractères lisibles*, legible print; *gros, petits caractères*, large, small type. *Avoir* or *montrer du caractère*, to have or to show spirit; *c'est un homme de caractère*, he is a spirited or determined man; *je n'ai pas caractère pour agir dans cette affaire*, I have no authority to act in this manner; *il est sorti de son caractère*, he had an unusual reaction; *le caractère d'un auteur*, the stamp of an author, *ne pas démentir son caractère*, to act up to one's character, *un homme d'un bon caractère*, a good-natured man; *un homme qui a mauvais caractère*, a bad-tempered man.

caractériser [karakteri'ze], *v.t.* To characterize, to describe, to mark, to distinguish.

caractéristique [karakteris'tik], *a.* and *n.f.* Characteristic.

carafe [ka'raf], *n.f.* Carafe, decanter, water-bottle. (*fam.*) *Rester en carafe*, to be left aside, or out of it; to stop short. **carafon**, *n.m.* Small carafe or decanter; the contents of this.

caragne [ka'raɲ], *n.f.* American aromatic resin.

Caraïbe [kara'ib], *n.* Carib. **Les Caraïbes**, *f.pl.* The Caribbean Isles.

carambolage [karãbɔ'laːʒ], *n.m.* (*Billiards*) Cannon; (*pop.*) affray, shindy; (*fig.*) rebound (against). **carambole**, *n.f.* (*Billiards*) The red ball. **caramboler**, *v.i.* (*Billiards*) To cannon. **caramboleur**, *n.m.* Good cannon-player.

carambolier [karãbɔ'lje], *n.m.* Cucumber-tree.

carambouillage [karãbu'jaːʒ], *n.m.* **carambouille** [karã'buj], *n.m.* (*fam.*) Swindling (selling at low price goods obtained on credit).

carambouilleur, *n.m.* Swindler who practises *carambouille*.

caramel [kara'mɛl], *n.m.* Caramel. *Caramel au beurre*, butter-scotch, toffee. **caraméliser**, *v.t.* To convert into caramel; to mix, to flavour with caramel.

carapace [kara'pas], *n.f.* Carapace, turtle-shell.

carapater [karapa'te], *v.i.* (*pop.*) To decamp, to skedaddle.

caraque [ka'rak], *n.f.* Carrack (Portuguese Indiaman).—*a.* Applied to a fine porcelain brought to Europe in carracks.

carat [ka'ra], *n.m.* (*Gold*) Carat; small diamonds sold by weight. *C'est un sot à vingt-quatre carats*, he is a fool of the first water.

caravane [kara'van], *n.f.* Caravan, convoy; caravan (on wheels); (*fig.*) company, concourse, body. *Marcher en caravane*, to walk in a band.

caravanier [karava'nje], *n.m.* Caravaneer. **caravaniste**, *n.* Caravanist. **caravan-sérail**, *n.m.* Caravansary; Eastern inn; (*fig.*) place where foreigners congregate.

caravelle [kara'vɛl], *n.f.* Caravel, carvel.

carbatine [karba'tin], *n.f.* Green hide, skin.

carbonari [*Ital.*] [karbɔna'ri], *n.m. pl.* (*sing.* **carbonaro**) Carbonari. **carbonarisme**, *n.m.* Carbonarism.

carbonate [karbɔ'nat], *n.m.* (*Chem.*) Carbonate. *Carbonate (de soude)*, washing soda; **carbonaté**, *a.* (*fem.* **-ée**) Carbonized.

carbone [kar'bɔn], *n.m.* Carbon. **carboné**, *a.* (*fem.* **-ée**) Carbonaceous, carbonized. **carboneux**, *a.* (*fem.* **-euse**) Carbonaceous. **carbonifère**, *a.* Carboniferous. **carbonique**, *a.* Carbonic. **carbonisation**, *n.f.* Carbonization. **carboniser**, *v.t.* To carbonize. **carboniseuse**, *n.f.* Machine for drying wool.

carbonnade [karbɔ'nad], *n.f.* Meat grilled on charcoal.

carbonyle [karbɔ'nil], *n.m.* Carbonyl.

carburant [karby'rɑ̃], *n.m.* Motor-fuel.

carburateur [karbyra'tœːr], *a.* and *n.* (*fem.* **-trice**) Carburettor. **carburation**, *n.f.* Carburization.

carbure [kar'byːr], *n.m.* (*Chem.*) Carbide. **carburé**, *a.* (*fem.* **-ée**) Carburetted.

carburer [karby're], *v.i.* To carburet; to carburize.

carcailler [karka'je], *v.i.* To call (of quails).

carcajou [karka'ʒu], *n.m.* Carcajou, American badger. (*C*) Wolverine.

carcan [kar'kɑ̃], *n.m.* Iron collar (used in pillory); wood yoke (to prevent animals from crossing hedges); [*see also* PALANCHE]; (*vulg.*) horse, jade; shrew.

carcasse [kar'kas], *n.f.* Carcass, skeleton; (*colloq.*) human body; shell; framework.

carcel [kar'sɛl], *n.m.* Carcel lamp; *light unit (9·5 candles).

carcinomateux [karsinɔma'tø], *a.* (*fem.* **-euse**) Carcinomatous.

carcinome [karsi'nɔm], *n.m.* (*Path.*) Carcinoma. **carcinose**, *n.f.* Carcinosis.

cardage [kar'daːʒ], *n.m.* Carding.

cardamine [karda'min], *n.f.* (*Bot.*) Cardamine (lady's-smock etc.).

cardamome [karda'mɔm], *n.m.* Cardamom.

cardan [kar'dɑ̃], *n.m.* (*Mech.*) Joint permitting movement in any direction, universal joint. *Suspendu à la cardan*, hung on gimbals.

carde [kard], *n.f.* Cardoon; the edible stalk of this; teasel; card (instrument for combing wool or flax); carding-machine.

cardée [kar'de], *n.f.* Quantity carded.

carder [kar'de], *v.t.* To card, to comb (wool etc.) with cards. *Machine à carder*, carding-machine. **se carder**, *v.r.* To be carded.

cardère [kar'dɛːr] or **cardière**, *n.f.* (*Bot.*) Teasel (*Dipsacus silvestris*). *Cardère à foulon*, fuller's teasel.

carderie [kardə'ri], *n.f.* Carding-house; carding-room.

cardeur [kar'dœːr], *n.m.* (*fem.* **cardeuse**) Carder, wool-comber.—*n.f.* Carding-machine.

cardialgie [kardjal'ʒi], *n.f.* Cardialgy, heart-burn. **cardialgique**, *a.* Cardialgic.

cardiaque [kar'diak], *a.* and *n.* Cardiac.—*n.f.* (*Bot.*) Motherwort (*Leonorus cardiaca*).

cardinal (1) [kardi'nal], *a.* (*fem.* **-ale** (1), *pl.* **-aux**) Cardinal, chief, principal.

cardinal (2) [kardi'nal], *n.m.* Cardinal; cardinal-bird. **cardinalat**, *n.m.* Cardinalate, cardinalship.

cardinale (2) [kardi'nal], *n.f.* Cardinal-flower.

cardinalice [kardina'lis], *a.* Pertaining to a cardinal. *Recevoir le chapeau cardinalice*, to be made a cardinal.

cardinaliser [kardinali'ze], *v.t.* (*colloq.*) To raise to the dignity of a cardinal.

cardinaliste, *a.* and *n.* (17th cent.) Partisan of Richelieu or Mazarin.

cardiogramme, *n.m.* Cardiogram.

cardiographe, *n.m.* Cardiograph.

cardiographie, *n.f.* Cardiography.

cardiologie, *n.f.* Cardiology.

cardite [kar'dit], *n.f.* (*Path.*) Carditis.

cardon [kar'dɔ̃], *n.m.* Cardoon, edible thistle.

cardonnette [CHARDONNETTE].

carêmage [karɛ'maːʒ], *n.m.* Lent sowing.

carême [ka'rɛːm], *n.m.* Lent; Lent-sermons; (*fig.*) fast, fasting. *Arriver comme mars en carême*, to be sure to happen, to come like clock-work; *cela vient* or *arrive comme marée en carême*, that comes in the very nick of time; *face de carême*, melancholy face; *faire carême*, to keep Lent; *provisions de carême*, fish and vegetables; *rompre le carême*, to break one's fast (during Lent).

carême-prenant [karɛmprə'nɑ̃], *n.m.* (*pl.* **carêmes-prenants**) Carnival time; Shrove Tuesday; masker, reveller.

carénage [kare'naːʒ], *n.m.* Careenage, careening; fairing.

carence [ka'rɑ̃ːs], *n.f.* (*Law*) Absence of assets, insolvency; (*Med.*) deficiency. *Procès-verbal de carence*, declaration of insolvency.

carène [ka'rɛːn], *n.f.* Bottom (keel and sides up to water-mark). *En carène*, keel-shaped. **caréné**, *a.* (*fem.* **-ée**) (*Bot.*) Carinate; keeled; (*Motor.*) stream-lined. **caréner**, *v.t.* To careen; to stream-line.

caressant [karɛ'sɑ̃], *a.* (*fem.* **caressante**) Caressing, endearing; tender.

caresse [ka'rɛs], *n.f.* Caress, endearment. *Il ne faut pas se fier aux caresses de la fortune*, we must not trust to the smiles of Fortune.

caresser [karɛ'se], *v.t.* To caress, to fondle, to stroke; to make much of, to flatter, to pat. *Caresser l'orgueil de quelqu'un*, to pamper someone's pride; *caresser une chimère*, to cherish a visionary scheme; *ces tableaux sont *très caressés*, these pictures have a peculiar richness of finish.

caret [ka'rɛ], *n.m.* Rope-maker's reel; sea-tortoise, turtle. *Fil de caret*, rope-yarn.

carex [ka'rɛks], *n.m.* (*Bot.*) Carex, sedge.

cargaison [kargɛ'zɔ̃], *n.f.* Cargo, freight.

cargo [kar'go], *n.m.* (*Naut.*) Tramp, cargo-boat, tramp steamer.

cargue, *n.f.* (*Naut.*) Brails. **carguer**, *v.t.* To brail up, to clew up, to take in. *Carguer une voile*, to clew up a sail.

cargueur [kar'gœːr], *n.m.* Reefer.

cari [ka'ri], *n.m.* Curry-powder.

cariatide [karja'tid], *n.f.* Caryatid.

Caribe [CARAÏBE].

caribou [kari'bu], *n.m.* Cariboo, Canadian reindeer.

caricatural [karikaty'ral], *a.* (*fem.* **-ale,** *pl.* **-aux**) Caricatural.

caricature [karika'tyːr], *n.f.* Caricature; (*fam.*) a fright. **caricaturer,** *v.t.* To caricature. **caricaturiste,** *n.* Caricaturist.

carie [ka'ri], *n.f.* (*Path.*) Caries, decay; (*Bot.*) brown rust; rot (of timber). **carier,** *v.t.* To make carious, to rot. *Dent cariée*, decayed tooth. **se carier,** *v.r.* To grow carious; to decay.

carillon [kari'jɔ̃], *n.m.* Carillon; chime, peal; musical bells; (*fig.*) racket, din; noisy up-braiding. *À double* or *à triple carillon*, soundly, lustily; *le carillon des verres*, the jingling of glasses. **carillonné,** *a.* (*fem.* **-ée**) Announced by carillons or peals of bells. *Fête carillonnée*, church solemnity. **carillonnement,** *n.m.* Chiming, jingling. **carillonner,** *v.t.* To announce by carillons.—*v.i.* To chime; to ring the changes; to jingle, to clatter. **carillonneur,** *n.m.* Bell-ringer; change-ringer.

Carinthie [karɛ̃'ti], *f.* Carinthia.

cariopse [CARYOPSE].

carlin (1) [kar'lɛ̃], *n.m.* Old Italian coin.

carlin (2) [kar'lɛ̃], *a.* (*fem.* **carline** (1)) Pug; turned-up (of noses). *Chien carlin*, pug-dog.

carline (2) [kar'lin], *n.f.* Carline (thistle).

carlingue [kar'lɛ̃:g], *n.f.* (*Naut.*) Keelson; (*Av.*) cockpit.

carliste [kar'list], *a.* and *n.* Carlist.

carlovingien [CAROLINGIEN].

carmagnole [karma'ɲɔl], *n.f.* Piedmontese jacket; Carmagnole (revolutionary song and dance).

carme [karm], *n.m.* Carmelite friar, White friar. *Carmes déchaussés*, barefooted Carmelites.

Carmel [kar'mɛl], *n.m.* Carmelite convent. *Entrer au Carmel*, to become a Carmelite nun.

carmélite [karme'lit], *n.f.* Carmelite nun.—*a.* Light brown.

carmin [kar'mɛ̃], *n.m.* and *a.* Carmine.

carminatif [karmina'tif], *a.* (*fem.* **-ive**) (*Med.*) Carminative.—*n.m.* Carminative.

carminé [karmi'ne], *a.* (*fem.* **-ée**) Carmine. **carminer,** *v.t.* To colour or tincture with carmine.

carnage [kar'naːʒ], *n.m.* Carnage, slaughter, butchery.

carnaire [kar'nɛːr], *a.* Flesh-eating (fly).

carnassier [karna'sje], *a.* (*fem.* **-ière** (1)) Carnivorous, flesh-eating.—*n.m.* Feline animal; flesh-eater.

carnassière (2) [karna'sjɛːr], *n.f.* Game-bag.

carnation [karna'sjɔ̃], *n.f.* Complexion, carnation; flesh-tint, flesh-colour.

carnau or **carneau** [kar'no], *n.m.* Flue-hole (in furnaces etc.).

carnaval [karna'val], *n.m.* Carnival; masquerade, festival, rejoicing, merriment; guy. **carnavalesque,** *a.* Pertaining to or fit for a carnival.

carne (1) [karn], *n.f.* Corner, edge (of a table, a stone, etc.).

carne (2) [karn], *n.f.* (*pop.*) Bad meat; old horse; nasty person; bad egg.

carné [kar'ne], *a.* Flesh-coloured; composed of meat. *Œillet carné*, flesh-coloured carnation; *diète carnée, régime carné*, meat diet.

carneau [CARNAU].

carnet [kar'nɛ], *n.m.* Notebook, memorandum-book, log-book. *Carnet de chèques*, cheque-book; *carnet d'échéances*, bill-book; *carnet à souches*, counterfoil book; *carnet de bal*, dance programme.

carnier [CARNASSIÈRE (2)].

carnification [karnifika'sjɔ̃], *n.f.* (*Med.*) Carnification. **se carnifier,** *v.r.* (*Med.*) To carnify.

carnivore [karni'vɔːr], *a.* Carnivorous.—*n.* Carnivore.

carogne [ka'rɔɲ], *n.f.* Hag, jade, impudent slut.

Caroline [karɔ'lin], *f.* Carolina.

carolingien [karɔlɛ̃'ʒjɛ̃], *a.* and *n.* (*fem.* **carolingienne**) Carolingian.

Caron [ka'rɔ̃], *m.* Charon.

***caronade** [karɔ'nad], *n.f.* Carronade.

caroncule [karɔ̃'kyl], *n.f.* Caruncle, wattle. **caronculaire,** *a.* Caruncular. **caronculé,** *a.* (*fem.* **-ée**) Carunculate.

carotide [karɔ'tid], *a.* Carotid.—*n.f.* Carotid. **carotidien,** *a.* (*fem.* **-ienne**) *Canal carotidien*, carotid canal.

carottage [karɔ'taːʒ], *n.m.* (*colloq.*) Falsehood, deceit; (*Mil.*) malingering.

carotte [ka'rɔt], *n.f.* Carrot; (*slang*) fake, ruse, hoax; sign outside a tobacconist's shop. *Carotte de tabac*, plug of tobacco; *jouer la carotte*, (*Ten.*) to play tricky balls; *il a voulu me tirer une carotte*, he tried to diddle me out of my money; (*fam.*) *les carottes sont cuites*, we are done for.—*a.* (*inv.*) Ginger (hair). **carotter,** *v.t.* To cheat, to diddle; (*Mil.*) to malinger. **carotteur** or **carottier,** *n.m.* (*fem.* **-euse** or **-ière**) Cheat, trickster; wangler.

caroube [ka'rub] or **carouge,** *n.f.* Carob. **caroubier,** *n.m.* Carob-tree.

carouge [CAROUBE].

Carpathes [kar'pat], **les,** *m.* The Carpathian mountains.

carpe (1) [karp], *n.f.* Carp (fish). *Faire la carpe pâmée*, to sham fainting; *muet comme une carpe*, dumb as an oyster; *faire des yeux de carpe*, to make sheep's eyes; *faire des saut. de carpe*, flop about.

carpe (2) [karp], *n.m.* (*Anat.*) Wrist.

carpeau [kar'po], *n.m.* Small carp.

carpelle [kar'pɛl], *n.f.* (*Bot.*) Carpel. **carpellien,** *a.* (*fem.* **-ienne**) o **carpellaire.** Carpellary.

carpette [kar'pɛt], *n.f.* (Nailed) rug coverin the floor. *Carpette de foyer*, hearth-rug.

carpien [kar'pjɛ̃], *a.* (*fem.* **carpienne**) (*Anat* Carpal.

carpillon [karpi'jɔ̃], *n.m.* Young carp.

carpophage [karpɔ'faz], *n.m.* and *a.* Fruit-eating.

carquois [kar'kwa], *n.m.* Quiver. *Il a vidé son carquois*, he has shot his bolt.

carrare [ka'raːr], *n.m.* Carrara marble.

carre [kaːr], *n.f.* Breadth or thickness (on the square); crown (of a hat); shape (back and shoulders of a person); *carrure*. *La carre d'un chapeau*, the crown of a hat; *la carre d'un soulier*, the square toe of a shoe; *lame à trois carres*, three-edged sword; *un homme d'une bonne carre*, a broad-shouldered man.

carré (1) [ka're], *a.* (*fem.* **carrée**) Square; well-set, well-knit; plain, straightforward; demy (of paper). *Bataillon carré* [CARRÉ D'INFANTERIE]; *garçon carré*, well set-up or plain-spoken lad; *mètres carrés*, square metres; *nombre carré*, square number; *partie carrée*, party of four (two men and two women); *racine carrée*, square root; *tête carrée*, level head; stubborn man; German.

carré (2) [ka're], *n.m.* Square; landing, floor; printing demy (of paper); (*Gard.*) square, patch, plot. *Carré de mouton*, breast of mutton; *carré des officiers*, ward-room; (*Mil.*) *carré creux, carré d'infanterie*, hollow square; *un carré d'eau*, a square sheet of water; *un carré de laitues*, a lettuce patch.

carreau [ka'ro], *n.m.* (*pl.* **carreaux**) Small square, lozenge; square tile or brick, small flag-stone; flooring; pane (of glass); square cushion, hassock; tailor's goose; diamond (at cards); (*fam.*) monocle; (*Arch.*) stretcher; *square-headed bolt, quarrel; (*Path.*) tubercular affection of the mesentery. *As de carreau*, (*Mil. slang*), the pack; *carreau de mine*, mine-head; *coucher sur le carreau*, to sleep on the floor; *étoffes à carreaux*, checked materials; *le carreau des Halles (à Paris)*, the market (like Covent Garden); *mettre au carreau*, to square up (a drawing etc.) (for enlargement); *mettre cœur sur carreau*, to vomit; *rester sur le carreau*, to be left high and dry; *se garder à carreau*, to be ready for any emergency.

carrée [ka're], *n.f.* (*pop.*) Room, digs.

carrefour [kar'fuːr], *n.m.* Cross-roads, place where four roads meet. *Langage de carrefour*, low, vulgar language, Billingsgate; *les carrefours d'une ville*, the public places of a town; *orateur de carrefour*, stump-orator.

carréger [kare'ʒe], *v.i.* (*S. dial.*) (*conjugated like* ACCÉLÉRER) To sail under heavy canvas; to tack.

carrelage [kar'la:ʒ], *n.m.* Tile-flooring, paving-squares; tile-pavement. **carreler**, *v.t.* To pave (a floor) with square tiles, bricks, stones, etc.; to trace squares upon; to cobble (shoes etc.).

carrelet [kar'lɛ], *n.m.* Plaice; square net; shoemaker's (saddler's etc.) awl; square ruler.

carrelette [kar'lɛt], *n.f.* Flat file.

carreleur [kar'lœːr], *n.m.* Floor-tiler, brick-pavier; tramping cobbler.

carrelure [kar'lyːr], *n.f.* New-soling of shoes.

carrément [kare'mɑ̃], *adv.* Squarely; (*fig.*) bluntly, straightforwardly, downrightly. *Couper carrément*, to cut square; *y aller carrément*, to make no bones about it.

carrer [ka're], *v.t.* To square. **se carrer**,

v.r. To strut, to pose; to loll, to look grand. *Se carrer dans son fauteuil*, to sit in state.

carrick [ka'rik], *n.m.* Box-coat, coachman's cape.

carrier [ka'rje], *n.m.* Quarryman.

carrière (1) [ka'rjɛːr], *n.f.* *Race-ground, course, etc.; career, course; life; orbit, scope, play, vent; profession, vocation, walk in life. *La Carrière*, the diplomatic service; *diplomate de carrière*, professional diplomat; *donner libre carrière à son imagination*, to give free scope to one's imagination; *donner carrière à un cheval*, to give a horse his head; *fournir une longue carrière*, to go a long way; *la carrière ouverte aux talents*, tools to those who can handle them; *le bout de la carrière*, the goal; *nuire à sa carrière*, to injure one's prospects; *parcourir la carrière*, to run over the course; *se donner libre carrière*, to throw off all restraint.

carrière (2) [ka'rjɛːr], *n.f.* Quarry.

carriole [ka'rjɔl], *n.f.* Light covered cart, trap; (*C*) sleigh; (*fig.*) any poor sort of conveyance.

carrossable [karɔ'sabl], *a.* Practicable for vehicles (of roads).

carrosse [ka'rɔs], *n.m.* State-coach, four-wheeled carriage. *Aller en carosse*, to ride in a coach; *carrosse de remise*, livery-coach; *cheval de carrosse*, carriage-horse; (*colloq.*) a big lubberly fellow; *rouler carrosse*, to keep one's carriage, to live in grand style. **carrossée**, *n.f.* Coachful, carriageful. **carrosser**, *v.t.* To convey in a coach; to fit the body of a car. **carrosserie**, *n.f.* Coach-building; body (of motors). **carrossier**, *n.m.* Coach-maker, carriage-builder.

carrousel [karu'zel], *n.m.* Merry-go-round, roundabout; tilting-match; tilt-yard; military tournament.

carroyage [karwa'ja:ʒ], *n.m.* Squaring (of a map).

carrure [ka'ry:r], *n.f.* Breadth of shoulders. *D'une belle carrure*, well built.

cartable [kar'tabl], *n.m.* School-satchel, cardboard; portfolio (for drawing).

cartahu [karta'y], *n.m.* (*Naut.*) Whip; girt-line. *Poulie de cartahu*, single block.

cartayer [karte'je], *v.i.* To avoid ruts (in driving a cart etc.).

carte [kart], *n.f.* Pasteboard; card, playing-card, postcard, visiting-card, etc.; ticket; bill of fare; map, chart. *Avoir carte blanche*, to have full power; *battre les cartes*, to shuffle; *brouiller les cartes*, to sow discord, to make mischief; *carte d'abonnement*, season ticket; (*Am.*) commutation ticket; *carte d'alimentation*, ration card, ration book; *carte de géographie*, map, chart; *carte d'identité*, identity card; *carte marine*, sea-chart; *carte postale*, postcard; *carte postale illustrée*, picture postcard; *cartes préparées*, marked cards; *carte topographique*, topographical chart; *donner les cartes*, to deal; *faire des tours de carte*, to play tricks with cards; *faire la carte d'un pays*, to map out a country; *la carte forcée*, Hobson's choice; *les basses cartes*, the small cards; *perdre la carte*, (*fam.*) to lose one's self-possession; *tirer les cartes*, to tell fortunes (with cards); *un jeu de cartes*, a pack of cards; *jouer aux cartes*, to play at cards; *jouer cartes sur table*, to put one's cards on

the table; (*fig.*) to act frankly, openly; *voir le dessous des cartes*, to be in the know.
cartel (1) [kar'tɛl], *n.m.*   Challenge, defiance; cartel, truce; dial-case; wall clock; frieze-panel, frame, scroll.   *Cartel d'armoiries,* (*Her.*) shield.
cartel (2) [kar'tɛl], *n.m.*   (*Comm.*) Cartel, trust; (*Polit.*) coalition.
carte-lettre [kartə'lɛtr], *n.f.* (*pl.* **cartes-lettres**) Letter-card.
carter [kar'ter], *n.m.*   Gear-case (of bicycle); crank-case (of car).
carterie [kar'tri], *n.f.*   Card-making; card-factory.
carteron [QUARTERON].
cartésianisme [kartezja'nism], *n.m.* Cartesian philosophy.   **cartésien,** *a.* and *n.* (*fem.* **-ienne**) Cartesian.
Carthage [kar'ta:ʒ], *m.* Carthage.
Carthagène [karta'ʒɛ:n], *f.* Cartagena.
carthaginois [kartaʒi'nwa], *a.* and *n.* (*fem.* **-oise**) Carthaginian.
carthame [kar'tam], *n.m.* (*Bot.*) Safflower.
cartilage [karti'la:ʒ], *n.m.* Cartilage, gristle. **cartilagineux,** *a.* (*fem.* **-euse**) Cartilaginous, gristly.
cartographe [kartɔ'graf], *n.m.* Cartographer, map- or chart-maker. **cartographie,** *n.f.* Cartography, map- or chart-making. **cartographique,** *a.* Cartographic.
cartomancie [kartɔmã'si], *n.f.* Cartomancy. **cartomancien,** *n.m.* (*fem.* **-ienne**) Fortune-teller (by cards).
carton [kar'tɔ̃], *n.m.* Cardboard, pasteboard; cardboard box, bandbox, hat-box, etc.; artist's portfolio; (*Paint.*) cartoon; (*Print.*) four-page cancel; miniature target; (*Phot.*) mount. *Carton à chapeau,* hat-box; *carton lissé,* glazed pasteboard; *carton bitumé,* roofing felt; *homme de carton,* nonentity, man of straw; *les cartons de Raphaël,* the cartoons of Raphael; *rester dans les cartons,* to be shelved.
cartonnage, *n.m.* (*Bookb.*) Boarding. **cartonner,** *v.t.*   To bind (a book) in boards; to fit or furnish with cardboard.—*v.i.* (*colloq.*) To play cards. **cartonnerie,** *n.f.* Cardboard manufactory. **cartonneur,** *n.m.* (*fem.* **-euse**) Binder, boarder (of books). **cartonnier,** *n.m.* (*fem.* **-ière**) Cardboard-maker or -seller, cardboard case, portfolio.
carton-pâte [kartɔ̃'pɑ:t], *n.m.* Millboard; *papier-mâché.*
carton-pierre [kartɔ̃'pjɛ:r], *n.m.* Pasteboard for making ornaments.
cartothèque [kartɔ'tɛk], *n.f.* Card-index.
cartouche (1) [kar'tuʃ], *n.m.* Escutcheon, scroll.
cartouche (2) [kar'tuʃ], *n.f.* Cartridge. **cartoucherie,** *n.f.* Cartridge manufactory. **cartouchier,** *n.m.* **cartouchière,** *n.f.* Cartridge-pouch or box. *Cartouchière d'infirmier,* first-aid case.
cartulaire [karty'lɛ:r], *n.m.* Cartulary.
*****carus** [ka'ry:s], *n.m.* Deep coma.
carvelle [kar'vɛl], *n.f.* Square-headed ship-nail.
carvi [kar'vi], *n.m.* Caraway. *Graines de carvi,* caraway-seed.
caryophyllé [kariɔfi'le], *a.* (*fem.* **-ée**) (*Bot.*) Caryophyllaceous.—*n.f. pl.* Caryophyllaceous plants.
caryopse [ka'rjɔps], *n.m.* (*Bot.*) Caryopsis.

cas [kɑ], *n.m.*   Case; instance, circumstance, state of things, conjuncture; (*Law*) cause; (*Gram.*) case. *Au cas où cela serait* or *en cas que cela soit,* in case it should turn out to be; *cas de conscience,* (*R.-C. Ch.*) case left to the individual conscience, a matter of conscience; *ce n'est pas le cas,* that is not so; *c'est bien le cas de le dire,* you may well say so; *c'est le cas de parler,* it is the time to speak out; *c'est le cas ou jamais,* it is now or never; *en cas de besoin,* in case of need; *en ce cas,* in that case, if that is so; *en tel cas* or *en pareil cas,* in such a case; *en tout cas,* at all events, however, nevertheless; *faire peu de cas,* to make light of, to slight; *faire grand cas de quelqu'un,* to have a great esteem for some-one, to value someone highly; *hors le cas,* unless, except; *il n'est pas dans le cas de vous nuire,* he is not in a position to harm you; *le cas échéant,* if such should prove to be the case, in that case; *un cas imprévu,* an unfore-seen case; *un cas pendable,* a hanging matter; *un en cas,* a snack (in case of need); *un tout cas,* a sunshade, a parasol.
casanier [kaza'nje], *n.m.* (*fem.* **-ière**) Domes-tic person.—*a.* Domestic, stay-at-home, home-loving.
casaque [ka'zak], *n.f.*   Mantle with large sleeves; woman's mantle [JUSTAUCORPS]; jockey's jacket; cassock. *Tourner casaque,* to change sides, to rat. **casaquin,** *n.m.* Woman's short gown; (*fam.*) *donner sur le casaquin à quelqu'un,* to thrash someone.
casbah [kas'ba], *n.f.*   Arab fortified palace; (*pop.*) house.
cascade [kas'kad], *n.f.*   Cascade, waterfall; (*fig.*) succession; misbehaviour; (*pl.*) fits and starts; (*Theat.*) gag. *Faire des cascades,* to play the fool; *prendre un rôle à la cascade,* to caricature a part; *une cascade de rires, d'applaudissements,* a round of laughter, of applause. **cascader,** *v.i.*   To fall in cascades; (*fig.*) to play the fool, to lead a fast life; (*Theat.*) to gag. **cascadeur,** *n.m.* (*fem.* **-euse**) Trifler; actor who gags.
*****cascaret** [kaska'rɛ], *n.m.* (*pop.*) Whipper-snapper.
cascarille [kaska'ri:j], *n.f.* (*Bot.*) Cascarilla.
cascatelle [kaska'tɛl], *n.f.* Small cascade.
case [kɑ:z], *n.f.*   Cabin, hut, small house; division, compartment; box (for animals); pigeon-hole; point (backgammon); square (of chess, or draughtboard); (*Naut.*) berth.
caséeux [kaze'ø], *a.* (*fem.* **-euse**) Caseous.
caséifier [kazei'fje], *v.t.*   To turn (milk) into cheese.
caséine [kaze'in], *n.f.* (*Chem.*) Casein. **caséinerie,** *n.f.*   Manufactory where casein is extracted from buttermilk. **caséique** [LACTIQUE].
casemate [kas'mat], *n.f.* (*Fort.*) Casemate. **casemater,** *v.t.* (*Fort.*) To provide with casemates.
caser [kɑ'ze], *v.t.*   To put in order, to put away, to file (documents), to find a place for, to provide for; to marry off. *Le voilà casé,* he is provided for.—*v.i.* (*Backgammon*) To make a point. **se caser,** *v.r.* To take up one's abode, to get settled.
caserel [kaz'rɛl], *n.m.,* or **caserette** [kaz'rɛt], *n.f.* Cheese-mould.
caserne [ka'zɛrn], *n.f.*   Barracks. *Caserne de*

pompiers, fire (-brigade) station. **caserne-ment**, *n.m.* Barracking, quartering in barracks; a system of barracks. **caserner**, *v.t.* To quarter in barracks; to quarter, lodge, etc.—*v.i.* To be in barracks.

casernet [kazɛr'nɛ], *n.m.* (*Naut.*) Entry-book.

casernier [kazɛr'nje], *n.m.* Barrack-warden.

caset [ka'ze], *n.m.* Caddis-worm.

casette [ka'zɛt], *n.f.* *Little house, cottage; (Pottery)* saggar.

caséum [CASÉINE].

casher [ka'ʃɛr], *a.* (*fem.* **-ère**) Kosher (meat, etc., according to Jewish ritual).

casier [ka'zje], *n.m.* Rack, card- or music-stand, set of pigeon-holes, ledger-rack, etc. *Casier à homards*, lobster-pot; *casier judiciaire*, police record.

casilleux [kazi'jø], *a.* (*fem.* **-euse**) Brittle.

casimir [kazi'miːr], *n.m.* Kerseymere, Casimir satinette.

casino [kazi'no], *n.m.* Casino, club.

casoar [kazɔ'aːr], *n.m.* Cassowary; plume of shako (worn by *Saint-Cyriens*, French cadets).

caspien [kas'pjɛ̃], *a.* (*fem.* **caspienne**) Caspian. **Caspienne** [kas'pjen], **la Mer**, *f.* Caspian Sea.

casque [kask], *n.m.* Helmet, head-piece; (*Nat. Hist.*) hood, crest; (*Conch.*) helmet-shell; head-phone (wireless). *Avoir le casque,* (*colloq.*) to have a hangover (after drinking etc.); *casque à mèche*, night-cap; *casque protecteur*, crash helmet.

casqué [kas'ke], *a.* (*fem.* **-ée**) Helmeted.

casquer [kas'ke], *v.i.* (*slang*) To pay up, to shell out.

casquette [kas'kɛt], *n.f.* (vizored) Cap. *Casquette à (trois) ponts*, apache's cap.

cassable [ka'sabl], *a.* Breakable.

cassade [ka'sad], *n.f.* *Fib; bluff (at cards).

cassage [ka'saːʒ], *n.m.* Breakage.

Cassandre [ka'sɑ̃:dr], *m.* Cassander.—*f.* Cassandra.

cassant [ka'sɑ̃], *a.* (*fem.* **-ante**) Brittle; crisp; breakable; short (steel); not bendable or malleable; (*fig.*) abrupt, gruff.

cassation [kasa'sjɔ̃], *n.f.* (*Law*) Cassation, annulment, repeal, quashing; (*Mil. etc.*) reduction to the ranks. *Cour de cassation*, the highest court of appeal in France; *se pourvoir en cassation*, to lodge an appeal.

cassave [ka'sav], *n.f.* (*Bot.*) Cassava.

casse (1) [kaːs], *n.f.* Breakage; breakages; things broken; damage, losses. *Casse nette*, a clean break; *donner la casse à quelqu'un*, to sack somebody; *gare la casse*, look out for squalls; *payer la casse*, to pay the damage.

casse (2) [kaːs], *n.f.* (*Print.*) Case. *Apprendre la casse*, to learn the boxes; *bas de casse*, (*Print.*) lower case; *haut de casse*, upper case.

casse (3) [kaːs], *n.f.* Cassia. *Casse aromatique*, bastard cinnamon [*see* SÉNÉ].

casse (4) [kaːs], *n.f.* Disease affecting the taste and colour of wine.

casse (5) [kaːs], *n.f.* Ladle.

cassé [ka'se], *a.* (*fem.* **-ée**) Broken-down, infirm, crazy; affected with *casse* (of wines).

casseau [ka'so], *n.m.* (*Print.*) Half-case.

casse-bras [kas'bra], *n.m. inv.* (*pop.*) Misfortune, blow.

casse-cou [kas'ku], *n.m. inv.* Death-trap; rough-rider; dare-devil.

casse-croûte [kas'krut], *n.m. inv.* Quick meal, cold spread, snack.

casse-gueule [kas'gœl], *n.m. inv.* (*pop.*) Liquor, raw spirit, etc.

casse-lunette(s) [kasly'nɛt], *n.m.* (*Bot.*) Eyebright.

cassement [kas'mɑ̃], *n.m.* Breaking. *Cassement de tête*, (*fig.*) head-splitting anxiety, worry, etc.

casse-motte or **casse-mottes** [kas'mɔt], *n.m. inv.* (*Agric.*) Clod-breaker.

casse-noisette [kasnwa'zɛt], *n.m.* (*pl.* **casse-noisettes**) Nut-cracker; (*Orn.*) nut-hatch. *Figure de casse-noisette*, face like a nut-cracker (with nose and chin nearly meeting).

casse-noix [kas'nwa], *n.m. inv.* Nut-crackers; (*Orn.*) nut-cracker.

casse-noyau [kasnwa'jo], *n.m.* (*pl.* **casse-noyaux**) (*Orn.*) Hawfinch.

casse-pattes [kas'pat] = CASSE-GUEULE.

casse-pieds [kas'pje], *n.m. inv.* (*pop.*) Bore.

casse-pierre or **casse-pierres** [kas'pjɛːr], *n.m. inv.* Stone-breaker's hammer; stone-breaking machine; (*pop.*) saxifrage.

casse-pipes [kas'pip], *n.m. inv.* Shooting-gallery; (*pop.*) war.

casse-poitrine [CASSE-GUEULE].

casser [ka'se], *v.t.* To break, to shatter, to smash; to cashier (an officer), to reduce to the ranks; to dissolve (Parliament etc.); to annul, to rescind, to quash, to set aside. *Tout cassé de vieillesse*, worn out with old age; *casser aux gages*, to dismiss, to discharge; *casser les vitres*, to break the windows, to run amok; *casser la croûte*, to take a snack; *casser un jugement*, to reverse a judgment; *qui casse les verres les paie* or *il faut payer les pots cassés*, you must pay the damages; *une noce à tout casser*, a rare old jollification; *voix cassée*, broken voice; *vous me cassez la tête*, you bore me to death; (*fam.*) *ça ne casse rien*, it's not up to much.—*v.i.* To break. **se casser**, *v.r.* To break, to snap; to break down. *Se casser la jambe*, to break one's leg; *se casser la tête*, to break one's head, to rack one's brains; *se casser le cou*, to break one's neck.

casserole [kas'rɔl], *n.f.* Saucepan, stewpan, stew; (*pop.*) a big watch, a 'turnip'. **casserolée**, *n.f.* Saucepanful.

casse-tête [kas'tɛːt], *n.m. inv.* Knobkerry, club (used by savages); bludgeon; (*fig.*) din, deafening uproar; tiring or puzzling task; conundrum; heady wine. *Quel casse-tête!* what a din!

cassetin [kas'tɛ̃], *n.m.* (*Print.*) Box.

cassette [ka'set], *n.f.* Casket; money-box, cash-box. *La cassette du roi*, the king's privy purse.

casseur [ka'sœːr], *n.m.* (*fem.* **casseuse**) Breaker, smasher. *Un casseur d'assiettes*, a quarrelsome fellow, blusterer, bully.

cassier (1) [ka'sje], *n.m.* Cassia-tree.

cassier (2) [ka'sje], *n.m.* (*Print.*) Case-rack.

*cassine [ka'sin], *n.f.* Week-end cottage; badly-kept house; (*Mil.*) small blockhouse.

cassis (1) [ka'sis], *n.m.* Black currant; black-currant bush; black-currant wine.

cassis (2) [ka'si], *n.m.* Furrow-drain (across a road, down a hill).

cassolette [kasɔ'lɛt], *n.f.* Perfuming pan.

casson [ka'sɔ̃], *n.m.* Piece of broken glass,

pottery, etc.; rough lump (of sugar). **cassonade**, *n.f.* Moist brown sugar.

cassoulet [kasu'le], *n.m.* Stew made of goose, mutton, pork and beans.

cassure [kɑ'syːr], *n.f.* Break, crack, fracture; broken piece.

castagnette [kasta'nɛt], *n.f.* Castanet.

castagneux [kasta'nø], *n.m.* Dabchick.

caste [kast], *n.f.* Caste.

*****castel** [kas'tɛl], *n.m.* (*S. France*) Castle.

castillan [kasti'jɑ̃], *a.* and *n.* (*fem.* **-ane**) Castilian.

Castille [kas'tiːj], *f.* Castile.

*****castille** [kas'tiːj], *n.f.* Altercation, bickering.

castine [kas'tin], *n.f.* (*Metal.*) Flux.

castor [kas'tɔːr], *n.m.* Beaver; beaver fur; *beaver hat. Castor du Canada*, musquash (fur). **castoréum**, *n.m.* Castoreum. **castorine**, *n.f.* Cloth made of beaver-fur and wool.

castramétation [kastrametɑ'sjɔ̃], *n.f.* Castrametation.

castrat [kas'tra], *n.m.* (*Mus.*) Castrato. **castration**, *n.f.* Castration. *****castrer** [CHÂTRER]. **castreur** [CHÂTREUR].

casualisme [kazɥa'lism], *n.m.* Casualism. **casualité**, *n.f.* Fortuitousness.

casuel [ka'zɥɛl], *a.* (*fem.* **-uelle**) Casual, contingent, fortuitous, accidental.—*n.m.* Perquisites, fees. *Le casuel d'une cure*, surplice fees; (*Gram.*) *flexions casuelles*, case-endings. **casuellement**, *adv.* Casually, by chance, fortuitously.

casuiste [ka'zɥist], *n.m.* Casuist. **casuistique**, *n.f.* Casuistry.

catabolique [katabɔ'lik], *a.* Catabolic. **catabolisme**, *n.m.* Catabolism.

catachrèse [kata'krɛːz], *n.f.* Catachresis.

cataclysme [kata'klism], *n.m.* Cataclysm; (*fig.*) disaster, overthrow. **cataclysmique**, *a.* Cataclysmic.

catacombes [kata'kɔ̃ːb], *n.f. pl.* Catacombs.

catacoustique [katakus'tik], *a.* and *n.f.* Catacoustics.

catadioptre [CATAPHOTE].

catadioptrique [katadjɔp'trik], *a.* Catadioptric.—*n.f.* Catadioptrics.

catafalque [kata'falk], *n.m.* Catafalque.

cataire (1) [ka'tɛːr], *a.* *Frémissement cataire*, (*Med.*) thrill, purring tremor (of the heart).

cataire (2) [ka'tɛːr], *n.f.* (*Bot.*) Catmint; (*Am.*) cat-nip.

catalan [kata'lɑ̃], *a.* and *n.m.* (*fem.* **catalane**) Catalonian.

catalectes [kata'lɛkt], *n.m.* (*used only in pl.*) Catalects. **catalectique**, *a.* Catalectic.

catalepsie [katalɛp'si], *n.f.* Catalepsy. **cataleptique**, *a.* Cataleptic.

Catalogne [kata'lɔɲ], *f.* Catalonia.

catalogue [kata'lɔg], *n.m.* List, enumeration, catalogue. **cataloguement**, *n.m.* Cataloguing. **cataloguer**, *v.t.* To catalogue. **catalogueur**, *n.m.* (*fem.* **-euse**) Cataloguer.

catalpa [katal'pa], *n.m.* (*Bot.*) Catalpa.

catalyse [kata'liːz], *n.f.* (*Chem.*) Catalysis. **catalyseur**, *n.m.* Catalyser. **catalytique**, *a.* Catalytic.

catamaran [katama'rɑ̃], *n.m.* *En catamaran*, (*Naut.*) parallel, paired.

cataphote [kata'fɔt], *n.m.* Cat's eye (reflector).

cataplasme [kata'plasm], *n.m.* Cataplasm, poultice.

catapulte [kata'pylt], *n.f.* Catapult (a war engine). **catapulter**, *v.t.* To catapult.

cataracte [kata'rakt], *n.f.* Cataract, waterfall; (*Path.*) cataract.

catarrhal [kata'ral], *a.* (*fem.* **-ale**, *pl.* **-aux**) Catarrhal. **catarrhe**, *n.m.* Catarrh. *Catarrhe d'été*, hay-fever. **catarrheux**, *a.* (*fem.* **-euse**) Catarrhous.

catastrophe [katas'trɔf], *n.f.* Catastrophe, calamity. **catastrophé**, *a.* (*fem.* **-ée**) (*pop.*) Dismayed, dumbfounded. **catastrophique**, *a.* Catastrophic. **catastrophisme**, *n.m.* (*Geol.*) Catastrophism.

catau [ka'to], *n.f.* Farm or inn wench, slut.

catch [katʃ], *n.m.* Catch-as-catch-can. **catcher**, *v.i.* To play catch-as-catch-can. **catcheur**, *n.m.* Catch-as-catch-can wrestler.

catéchèse [kate'ʃɛːz], *n.f.* (*Eccles. Ant.*) Catechism. **catéchète**, *n.m.* Catechizer. **catéchétique**, *a.* Catechetic.—*n.f.* Catechetics.

catéchisation [kateʃizɑ'sjɔ̃], *n.f.* Catechizing. **catéchiser**, *v.t.* To catechize; (*fig.*) to reason with; to lecture; to coach up. **catéchisme**, *n.m.* Catechism. *Faire le catéchisme à quelqu'un*, to coach someone. **catéchiste**, *n.m.* Catechist.

catéchu [kate'ʃy], *n.m.* Catechu.

catéchuménat [katekyme'na], *n.m.* State of being a catechumen. **catéchumène**, *n.m.* and *f.* Catechumen.

catégorie [kategɔ'ri], *n.f.* Category. **catégorique**, *a.* Categorical, explicit. **catégoriquement**, *adv.* Categorically, to the purpose. **catégorisation**, *n.f.* Classification by categories. **catégoriser**, *v.t.* To class by categories. **catégoriseur**, *n.m.* One who establishes categories.

caténaire [kate'nɛr], *a.* Catenary, chained.

caténation [katenɑ'sjɔ̃], *n.f.* Catenation.

catharsis [katar'sis], *n.f.* (*Med.*) Catharsis; (*fig.*) purgation (of our passions).

cathartique [katar'tik], *a.* and *n.m.* Cathartic, non-drastic purgative, laxative.

cathédral [kate'dral], *a.* (*fem.* **-ale**) Cathedral. **cathédrale**, *n.f.* Cathedral.

Catherine [ka'trin], *n.pr.f.* Catharine. (*fam.*) *Coiffer sainte Catherine*, to reach one's twenty-fifth year without marrying.

catherinette [katri'nɛt], *n.f.* Girl (*esp.* milliner) still unmarried at twenty-five. (*C*) Dwarf raspberry.

cathéter [kate'tɛːr], *n.m.* (*Surg.*) Catheter. **cathétériser**, *v.t.* To sound with this.

cathode [ka'tɔd], *n.f.* Cathode. **cathodique**, *a.* Cathode, cathodic. *Rayons cathodiques*, cathode rays.

catholicisme [katɔli'sism], *n.m.* Catholicism. **catholicité**, *n.f.* Catholicity.

catholicon [katɔli'kɔ̃], *n.m.* Catholicon, a mixture of rhubarb and senna, which was deemed a panacea [*see* SENNA].

catholique [katɔ'lik], *a.* Catholic; moral, orthodox. *Cela n'est pas catholique*, that does not ring true.—*n.* A Catholic. **catholiquement**, *adv.* Catholically.

cati [ka'ti], *n.m.* Gloss, lustre.

*****catiche** [ka'tiʃ], *n.f.* (*Norm. dial.*) Otter's hole or lair.

*****catimini** [katimi'ni], *adv.* *En catimini*, slyly, stealthily.

catin [ka'tɛ̃], *n.f.* Harlot, strumpet, slut.

catir [ka'ti:r], *v.t.* To give a gloss to. *Catir à chaud*, to hot-press; *catir à froid*, to cold-press. **catissage**, *n.m.* Glossing, pressing. **catisseur**, *a.* and *n.* (*fem.* **-euse**) Presser.

catmarin [katma'rɛ̃], *n.m.* (*Zool.*) Red-throated diver.

catogan [katɔ'gɑ̃] or **cadogan**, *n.m.* Knot of hair at back of head (worn in 18th cent.).

Caton [ka'tɔ̃], *m.* Cato.

catoptrique [katɔp'trik], *n.f.* Catoptrics.

Catulle [ka'tyl], *m.* Catullus.

Caucase [ko'ka:z], **le**, *m.* The Caucasus.

caucasien [kɔka'zjɛ̃], *a.* and *n.* (*fem.* **-ienne**) Caucasian.

cauchemar [kɔʃ'ma:r], *n.m.* Nightmare. *C'est mon cauchemar*, that tires me to death. **cauchemardant**, *a.* (*fem.* **-ante**) Boring, fatiguing. **cauchemarder**, *v.t.* (*fam.*) To bore stiff.

cauchois [ko'ʃwa], *a.* (*fem.* **-oise**) Of Caux.—*n.m.* (**Cauchois**, *fem.* **-oise**) A native or inhabitant of *pays de Caux* (N. Normandy).

caudal [ko'dal], *a.* (*fem.* **-ale,** *pl.* **-aux**) Caudal.

caudataire [koda'tɛ:r], *n.m.* Train-bearer; (*fig.*) toady.

caudé [ko'de], *a.* (*fem.* **-ée**) (*Her.*) Tailed; (*Nat. Hist.*) caudate.

caudex [ko'dɛks], *n.m.* Caudex, stem of a tree.

caudicule [kodi'ky:l], *n.f.* (*Bot.*) Caudicle.

caudrette [ko'drɛt], *n.f.* Lobster-net.

caulescent [kolɛ'sɑ̃], *a.* (*fem.* **-ente**) (*Bot.*) Caulescent.

caulicole [koli'kɔl], *a.* (*Bot.*) Living as a parasite on a plant-stem.—*n.f.* (used only in *pl.*) (*Arch.*) Caulices. **caulifère**, *a.* (*Bot.*) Cauliferous. **caulinaire**, *a.* (*Bot.*) Cauline.

cauri, cauris, or **coris** [ko'ri], *n.m.* Cowry.

causal [ko'zal], *a.* (*fem.* **-ale**) Causal. **causaliser**, *v.i.* (*Phil.*) To proceed from effects to causes or from causes to effects by logical deduction. **causalité**, *n.f.* Causality.

causant [ko'zɑ̃], *a.* (*fem.* **-ante**) Chatty, talkative.

causatif [koza'tif], *a.* (*fem.* **-ive**) (*Gram.*) Causative, causal. **causation**, *n.f.* Causation.

cause [ko:z], *n.f.* Cause; grounds; motive; interest; case, trial, suit, action. *À cause de*, for the sake of, on account of, because of, for; *à ces causes*, (*Law*) these reasons moving us thereunto; *avoir gain de cause*, to gain the day; *cause appelée* or *remise*, cause called in court *or* put off; *cause embrouillée* or *douteuse*, intricate *or* doubtful case; *donner gain de cause à*, to decide in favour of; *être condamné sans connaissance de cause*, to be condemned without a hearing; *être hors de cause*, not to be concerned in a law-suit; *être la cause innocente* or *involontaire d'un accident*, to be the harmless *or* involuntary cause of an accident; *il ne le fera pas, et pour cause*, he won't do it, and for a very good reason; *mettre en cause*, to sue; *mettre hors de cause*, to dismiss the parties (to a suit), (*fig.*) to free from blame, to put out of the question; *question hors de cause*, irrelevant question; *parler en connaissance de cause*, to speak from inside information; *pour quelle cause?* for what motive? *prendre fait et cause pour quelqu'un*, to espouse someone's cause, to side with someone; *se mettre en cause*, to come forward; *ses héritiers ou ayants cause*, his heirs or assigns; *un avocat sans cause*, a briefless barrister.

causer (1) [ko'ze], *v.t.* To cause, to be the cause of, to occasion, to give rise to.

causer (2) [ko'ze], *v.i.* To chat, to talk; to prate. *Causer de choses et d'autres*, to talk of one thing and another; *causer de la pluie et du beau temps*, to talk of this and that, to talk of nothing special; *causer littérature* or *voyages*, to talk about literature *or* travels. **causerie**, *n.f.* Talk, chat, gossip; a chatty essay, review, etc. **causette**, *n.f.* Chit-chat, small talk. *Faire la causette*, to have a chat. **causeur**, *a.* (*fem.* **-euse** (1)) Talkative, chatty.—*n.* Talker. **causeuse** (2), *n.f.* Small sofa, settee for two.

causse [ko:s], *n.m.* Calcareous table-land (in S. France).

causticité [kostisi'te], *n.f.* Causticity. **caustification**, *n.f.* Process of rendering caustic. **caustifier**, *v.t.* To render caustic. **caustique**, *a.* Caustic, mordant; biting, cutting, satirical.—*n.m.* Caustic. **caustiquement**, *adv.* Caustically.

***cautèle** [ko'tɛl], *n.f.* Craft, finesse, cunning. **cauteleusement** [kotləz'mɑ̃], *adv.* Craftily, slyly. **cauteleux**, *a.* (*fem.* **-euse**) Cunning, crafty.

cautère [ko'tɛ:r], *n.m.* (*Med.*) Cautery; artificial ulcer, issue. *C'est un cautère sur une jambe de bois*, it is putting a poultice on a wooden leg; *panser un cautère*, to dress a cautery. **cautérisation**, *n.f.* Cauterization. **cautériser**, *v.t.* To cauterize, to sear, to burn.

caution [ko'sjɔ̃], *n.f.* Security, bail, surety, bondsman; (*fig.*) pledge, guarantee. *Admettre une caution*, to grant bail; *donner caution pour*, to stand bail for; *verser une caution*, to pay a deposit. *Un renseignement sujet à caution*, an unreliable information. **cautionnement**, *n.m.* Bail; security. **cautionner**, *v.t.* To stand bail for someone; to stand security for.

cavage [ka'va:ʒ], *n.m.* Cellarage; storage of goods in a cellar; rent of a cellar.

cavalcade [kaval'kad], *n.f.* Procession; cavalcade. **cavalcader**, *v.i.* To ride on horseback in a company or cavalcade. ***cavalcadour**, *n.m.* Equerry, master of the horse (to a prince etc.)

cavale [ka'val], *n.f.* Mare; (*fig.*) big, ungainly woman.

cavaler [kava'le], *v.i.*, or **se cavaler**, *v.r.* (*vulg.*) To run away, to pop off.

cavalerie [kaval'ri], *n.f.* Cavalry; a body of horses (belonging to a company etc.). *Cavalerie légère*, light horse; *cavalerie motorisée*, motorized cavalry.

cavalier [kava'lje], *n.m.* Horseman, rider, trooper; *gentleman*, gallant; (*Dancing*) cavalier, partner; (*C*) lover, sweetheart; (*Chess*) knight; (*Fort.*) cavalier. *Habit de cavalier*, riding-coat; *servir de cavalier à une dame*, to escort a lady.—*a.* (*fem.* **-ière** (1)) Cavalier, brusque, haughty, unceremonious (of manners etc.). *À la cavalière*, in an off-hand manner; *allée cavalière*, ride (in a park); *vue cavalière*, bird's-eye view. **cavalière** (2), *n.f.* Horsewoman riding as a man. **cavalièrement**, *adv.* Cavalierly, bluntly, unceremoniously.

cavatine [kava'tin], *n.f.* Cavatina.

cave (1) [kaːv], *a.* Hollow. *Année cave*, lunar
year (353 days); *mois cave*, lunar month of
29 days; *œil cave*, sunken eye; *veine cave*,
vena cava.
cave (2) [kaːv], *n.f.* Cellar, vault, cellarage;
wine-cellar, wine-vault; wine in a cellar;
*boot (of a coach); case of bottles, cellaret;
(*Cards*) pool. *Cave à liqueurs*, case with
compartments for liqueur-bottles, liqueur-
cabinet; *de la cave au grenier*, from cellar to
garret; *rat de cave*, twisted taper, (*iron.*)
exciseman.
caveau [kaˈvo], *n.m.* Small cellar; sepulchral
vault.
cavecé [kavˈse], *a.* (Said of a horse with head
of distinct colour from that of the body.)
Cheval rouan cavecé de noir, roan horse with
a black head.
caveçon [kavˈsɔ̃], *n.m.* Headstall or curb (for
unruly horses). *Il a besoin de caveçon*, he
wants curbing.
cavée [kaˈve], *n.f.* (*Hunt.*) Sunken track in
a forest.
caver (1) [kaˈve], *v.t.* To hollow, to make
hollow, to scoop out, to dig under; (*fig.*) to
undermine; (*Fenc.*) to lunge. se caver, *v.r.*
To become hollow or sunken.
caver (2) [kaˈve], *v.i.* To play for stakes.
Caver au plus fort, to play deep, to carry
things to extremes.
caverne [kaˈvɛrn], *n.f.* Cavern, cave, hollow;
(*fig.*) retreat, lair, haunt. *L'âge des cavernes*,
the age of the cave-man. caverneux, *a.*
(*fem.* -euse) Cavernous, hollow, sepulchral
(of sounds etc.); (*Anat.*) spongy. *Voix
caverneuse*, hollow voice.
cavet [kaˈvɛ], *n.m.* (*Arch.*) Hollow moulding.
caviar [kaˈvjaːr], *n.m.* Caviare.
caviarder [kavjarˈde], *v.t.*, or *passer au caviar.*
To block-out (a passage in a newspaper).
cavillation [kavilaˈsjɔ̃], *n.f.* Sophistry, cavil.
cavin [kaˈvɛ̃], *n.m.* = CAVÉE.
caviste [kaˈvist], *n.m.* Cellarer, cellarman.
cavité [kaviˈte], *n.f.* Cavity, hollow.
caye [kaːj], *n.f.* (*W. Indies*) Key, coral
island.
cayenne [kaˈjɛn], *n.f.* Sailors' depot; floating-
barracks; cook-house, canteen (for sailors
during the commissioning of their ship).
ce [sə], *dem. a.* (*before vowels* cet, *fem.*
cette, *pl.* ces) This, that, (*pl.*) these, those.
Ce héros, this hero; *ce livre*, this book; *ce
livre-ci*, this book; *ce livre-là*, that book; *ces
livres*, these books; *cet arbre*, this tree; *cet
homme*, this man; *cette femme*, this woman,
ce dernier, the latter. *dem. pron.* It, that
(*sometimes*=he, she, or, *with plural verb*,
they). *C'en est fait*, it is all over, it is done;
c'en est fait de moi, it is all up with me; *ce
sera pour demain*, it will be for tomorrow;
c'est jeudi, it is Thursday; *c'est-à-dire*, that is
to say; *c'était à vous à parler*, it was your turn
to speak; *c'était à vous de parler*, it was your
duty to speak; *et ce, pour cause*, and this for
a good reason; *j'aime votre frère, c'est un
bon ami*, I love your brother, he is a good
friend; *ce sont*, it is (they who), they are;
ce furent eux, ce sera nous, it was they,
etc.; *est-ce lui?* is it he? *est-ce moi?* is it I?
est-ce nous qu'il menace? is it towards us his
threats are directed? *lisez Corneille et Racine,
ce sont de grands poètes*, read Corneille and

Racine, they are great poets; *quand sera-ce?*
when will it be? *quel jour est-ce aujourd'hui?*
what day is it today? *qu'est-ce?* what is that?
qu'est-ce que je vois là-bas? what do I see yonder? *qui est-ce?* who is he? *qui est-ce qui arrive
là?* who is coming there? *qui était-ce?* who
was it? *qui sera-ce?* who will it be? *si c'était à
refaire*, if it were to be done again; *sont-ce
là les dames que vous attendez?* are these the
ladies you expected? *oui, ce sont elles*, yes,
they are; *sont-ce là vos chevaux?* are these
your horses? *oui, ce sont eux*, yes, they are;
sont-ce les Anglais? is it the English? *ce que*,
that which, what; *ce que j'ai vu de beau*, the
fine things I saw; *ce que je vous dis*, what
I tell you; *ce qui réussit est toujours approuvé*,
what meets with success always meets with
approbation; *ce qui se passe*, what happens;
c'est ce que je disais, that is what I said; *faites
ce dont je vous ai parlé*, do what I told you
of; *je ne sais ce que nous deviendrons*, I do not
know what will become of us; *tout ce qu'on
fait de mauvais*, all the mischief that is done;
ce que c'est que de nous! what poor mortals we
are; *ce que je crains, c'est d'être surpris*, what
I fear is to be surprised; *ce qu'il demande,
c'est une pension*, what he asks for is a pension;
ce qu'on vous a dit, ce sont des contes, what
you have been told are mere idle tales; *ces
malheureux ne savent ce que c'est que la vertu*,
these wretches know not what virtue is; *c'est
à qui parlera*, they vie with one another as to
who shall speak; *c'est à vous que je parle*, it is
to you I am speaking; *c'est d'elle que je parle*,
it is of her that I speak; *c'est là que je les
attends*, there I shall have them; *c'est moi
qu'on veut perdre*, I am the man they wish to
ruin; *c'est que*, the fact is that, I must tell
you; *c'est un bonheur que d'avoir échappé*, it is
good luck to have escaped; *sont-ce les richesses
qui vous rendront heureux?* can riches make
you happy? *si ce n'est*, but for, except; *ce
disant*, saying which; *pour ce qui est de . . .*,
as for . . . .
*céans [seˈɑ̃], *adv.* Within, here within, in
this house, at home. *Il dînera céans*, he will
dine at home; *maître de céans*, master of the
house.
ceci [səˈsi], *dem. pron.* This, this thing.
Écoutez bien ceci, listen to this; *que veut dire
ceci?* what does this mean?
Cécile [seˈsil], *f.* Cecilia.
cécité [sesiˈte], *n.f.* Blindness. *Être frappé de
cécité*, to be struck blind.
cédant [seˈdɑ̃], *a.* (*fem.* cédante) That
grants; (*Law*) that assigns, transfers.—*n.*
(*Law*) Grantor, assignor, transferrer.
céder [seˈde], *v.t.* (*conjugated like* ACCÉLÉRER)
To give up, to yield, to surrender, to cede;
to transfer, to sell, to make over. *Céder le
haut du pavé*, to give the wall; *céder le pas à
quelqu'un*, to give precedence to someone.—
v.i. To give way; to submit, to succumb, to
give in. *Céder à ses penchants*, to give way to
one's inclinations; *il faut céder*, we must
submit; *je lui cède en tout*, I give in to him
in everything; *la porte céda*, the door gave
way; *ne le céder à personne*, to yield to no one,
to be second to none. (*Mus.*) *Cédez*, rallen-
tando.
cédille [seˈdiːj], *n.f.* Cedilla.
cédrat [seˈdra], *n.m.* Citron-tree; citron.

cédraterie, *n.f.* Citron-plantation. **cédratier,** *n.m.* Persian variety of citron-tree.
cèdre [se:dr], *n.m.* Cedar.
cédrel, *n.m.,* or **cédrèle** [se'drɛl], *n.f.* Cedrela.
cédrie [se'dri], *n.f.* Cedar-resin.
(*C*) **cédrière** [se'drje:r], *n.f.* Cedar grove or forest.
cédulaire [sedy'lɛ:r], *a.* Pertaining to income-tax schedules. *Impôt cédulaire,* scheduled tax.
cédule [se'dyl], *n.f.* Schedule, memorandum; notice; (*Law*) notification.
cégétiste [seʒe'tist], *n.m.* A member of C.G.T. (*Confédération Générale du Travail.*)
ceindre [sɛ̃:dr], *v.t. irr.* (*conjug. like* CRAINDRE, *pres.p.* **ceignant,** *p.p.* **ceint**) To gird, to encircle, to encompass, to surround, to wreathe; to bind or gird on; to gird up (the loins etc.). *Ceindre le diadème,* to put on or wear the diadem; *ceindre une épée,* to gird on a sword; *une corde lui ceignait les reins,* his loins were girt with a cord. **se ceindre,** *v.r.* To bind round one, to put on (a scarf etc.); to encircle one's brow (with a crown etc.).
ceint (*fem.* **ceinte** (1)), *p.p.* [CEINDRE].
ceinte (2) [sɛ̃:t], *n.f.* (*Naut.*) Girdle (of a ship).
*****ceintrage** [sɛ̃'tra:ʒ], *n.m.* (*Naut.*) Frapping.
ceintre [CINTRE]. *****ceintrer,** *v.t.* To frap, to gird. *Ceintrer un vaisseau,* to frap a ship.
ceinture [sɛ̃'ty:r], *n.f.* Sash, girdle, belt, waist-band, waist-ribbon; waist, middle; enclosure, girdle, zone, circle; (*Arch.*) cincture (of a column). *Bonne renommée vaut mieux que ceinture dorée,* kind hearts are more than coronets; *ceinture cartouchière,* cartridge-belt; *ceinture de sauvetage,* life-belt; *nu jusqu'à la ceinture,* naked to the waist; *chemin de fer de ceinture,* inter-station railway; (in Paris) *la Petite Ceinture,* the inner-circle railway or bus-line; *la Grande Ceinture,* the outer-circle railway; *une ceinture de murailles,* a girdle of walls. (*pop.*) *S'en mettre plein la ceinture,* to stuff oneself; *se serrer la ceinture,* to eat less. **ceinturer,** *v.t.* To girdle, to surround, to embrace; to collar (an opponent). **ceinturier,** *n.m.* Maker or vendor of belts, straps, etc. **ceinturon,** *n.m.* Belt, sword-belt. **ceinturonnier** [CEINTURIER].
ceinture-arrière [sɛ̃tyra'rjɛr], *n.f.* (*Wrestling*) Cross-buttock.
cela [sə'la, sla], *dem. pron.* That, that thing (in opposition to this, of which we are speaking). *Cela est vrai,* that is true; *ce n'est pas cela,* that's not it, that will not do; *c'est cela,* that's it; *c'est cela même,* that's the very thing; *comment cela?* how so? *il est comme cela,* it is his way, it is just like him; *n'est-ce que cela?* is that all? *par cela même,* for that very reason; *pour cela non,* certainly not; *pour cela oui,* most certainly; *qu'est-ce que c'est que cela?* what is that? *In popular speech* cela *becomes* ça. *Pas de ça,* none of that; *comme ci comme ça,* middling; *où ça?* where was that?
céladon [sela'dɔ̃], *n.m. and a.* Sea-green (colour). *Ruban céladon,* sea-green ribbon.— *n.m.* *****Sentimental swain or lover. **céladonique,** *a.* Sentimental, lackadaisical. **céladonisme,** *n.m.* Maudlin sentimentality; philandering.
célan [CÉLERIN].

célation [sela'sjɔ̃], *n.f.* (*Law*) Concealment (of birth).
célébrant [sele'brã], *n.m.* Celebrant (officiating priest at mass). **célébrateur,** *n.m.* Celebrator. **célébration,** *n.f.* Solemn performance, celebration.
célèbre [se'lɛbr], *a.* Celebrated, famous, renowned; eminent, distinguished.
célébrer [sele'bre], *v.t.* To celebrate, to praise, to extol; to solemnize. *Célébrer les louanges de . . . ,* to sing the praises of. . . . **célébrité,** *n.f.* Celebrity.
*****celer** [sə'le], *v.t.* To conceal, to keep close or secret, to secrete. *****se celer,** *v.r.* To conceal oneself, to hide.
céleri [sel'ri], *n.m.* Celery. *Un pied de céleri,* a stick of celery.
célerin [sel'rɛ̃], *n.m.* (*Ichth.*) Pilchard.
céleri-rave [selri'ra:v], *n.m.* Celeriac.
célérité [seleri'te], *n.f.* Celerity, rapidity, dispatch, speed.
céleste [se'lɛst], *a.* Celestial, heavenly, divine. *Bleu céleste,* sky-blue; *la colère céleste,* the wrath of heaven; *la voûte céleste,* the vault of heaven.
célestin [seles'tɛ̃], *n.m.* (*fem.* **célestine** (1)) Celestine (monk or nun).
célestine (2) [seles'tin], *n.f.* (*Min.*) Celestine.
céliaque [CŒLIAQUE].
célibat [seli'ba], *n.m.* Celibacy, single life, unmarried state. **célibataire,** *a.* Single.— *n.m.* Single man, bachelor.—*f.* Spinster.
celle [CELUI].
cellérier [sele'rje], *n.m.* (*fem.* **-ière**) Cellarer.
cellier [se'lje], *n.m.* Cellar, store-room.
cellophane [selo'fan], *n.f.* Cellophane.
cellulaire [sely'lɛ:r], *a.* Cellular. *Voiture cellulaire,* Black Maria.
cellule [se'lyl], *n.f.* Cell. (*Mil.*) Cells. *Cellule photo-électrique,* electric eye. **cellulé,** *a.* (*fem.* **-ée**) Celled, cellulate; imprisoned in a cell. **celluleux,** *a.* (*fem.* **-euse**) Cellular. **cellulite,** *n.f.* Fibrositis. **celluloïd** or **celluloïde,** *n.m.* Celluloid. **cellulose,** *n.f.* Cellulose. **cellulosité,** *n.f.* Cellulosity.
célosie [selo'zi], *n.f.* (*Bot.*) Cock's comb.
celte [sɛlt], *n.m.* Celt. **celtique,** *a.* Celtic.— *n.m.* Celtic language. **celtisant,** *n.m.* (*fem.* **-ante**) or **celtiste,** *n.* Celtologist. **celtophile,** *a. and n.* Celtophil.
celui [sə'lɥi], *dem. pron. m.* (*fem.* **celle,** *pl.* **ceux, celles**) The one, that, those (*sometimes*=he or she). (a) *Followed by* **-ci** or **-là**=this one, that one etc. or the latter *and* the former. (*fem.* **celle-ci, celle-là.** *pl.* **ceux-ci, celles-ci, ceux-là, celles-là**) *Aimez-vous mieux celui-ci?* do you like this best? *celui-ci est meilleur que celui-là,* this is better than that; *celui-là n'est pas si beau,* that one is not so fine. (b) *Followed by a relative pronoun. Quel livre? Celui dont je parlais,* Which book? The one I was talking about. *Celui qui hésite est perdu,* he who hesitates is lost. (c) *Followed by de, du, etc. Mon auto et celle de ma femme,* my car and my wife's.
cément [se'mã], *n.m.* Cement. **cémentation,** *n.f.* (*Metal.*) Cementation. **cémentatoire,** *a.* Cementatory. **cémenter,** *v.t.* To subject (metal) to cementation. **cémenteux,** *a.* (*fem.* **-euse**) Of the nature of cement.

cénacle [se′nakl], *n.m.* (*Ant.*) Guest-chamber (where the Lord's supper was taken); (*fig.*) literary society or coterie.

cendre [sã:dr], *n.f.* Ashes, cinders; dust, ashes (of the dead). *Feu qui couve sous la cendre*, smouldering fire; *la cendre* or *les cendres des morts*, the ashes of the dead; *le Mercredi des Cendres*, Ash-Wednesday; *mettre en cendres*, to lay in ashes; *renaître de ses cendres*, to rise from one's ashes.

cendré [sã′dre], *a.* (*fem.* **cendrée** (1)) Ash-coloured, ashy, ashen. *Gris cendré*, ashy grey, pale grey; *lumière cendrée*, earth-shine (on the moon).

cendrée (2) [sã′dre], *n.f.* Small shot; cinders (for track). *Piste en cendrée*, dirt track, cinder track.

cendrer [sã′dre], *v.t.* To paint ash-grey; to mix or cover with ashes. **cendreux**, *a.* (*fem.* **-euse**) Ashy, full of or covered with ashes. **cendrier** (1), *n.m.* (*fem.* **cendrière** (1))* Vendor of ashes for scouring. **cendrier** (2), *n.m.* Ash-pan, ash-hole, ash-pit; ash-tray. **cendrière** (2), *n.f.* Peat.

cendrillon [sãdri′jɔ̃], *n.f.* Cinderella, drudge; slovenly servant-maid.

cendrure [sã′dry:r], *n.f.* Rough-grain, minute pits or flaws (on the surface of steel).

cène [sɛ:n], *n.f.* The Lord's Supper, Holy Communion.

cenelle [sə′nɛl], *n.f.* Haw, hawthorn-fruit.

cénobite [senɔ′bit], *n.m.* Coenobite. **cénobitique**, *a.* Coenobitic. **cénobitisme**, *n.m.* Coenobitism.

cénotaphe [senɔ′taf], *n.m.* Cenotaph.

cens [sã:s], *n.m.* Census; property qualification (for the franchise); (*Feud. law*) quit-rent.

censé [sã′se], *a.* (*fem.* **censée**) Accounted, deemed, reputed, supposed. *Il est censé être*, he is supposed to be. **censément**, *adv.* By supposition; supposedly, ostensibly.

censeur [sã′sœ:r], *n.m.* Censor; critic; censor of the press, examiner of plays, etc.; proctor (*of Eng. Univ.*); assistant headmaster (in French *Lycées*).

*censitaire [sãsi′tɛr], *n.m.* Copy-holder, one qualified (by amount of his quit-rent) for the franchise. *Électeur censitaire*, qualified voter.

censorial [sãsɔ′rjal], *a.* (*fem.* **-ale**, *pl.* **-aux**) Censorial.

censuel [sã′sɥel], *a.* (*fem.* **-uelle**) Pertaining to quit-rent.

censurable [sãsy′rabl], *a.* Censurable.

censure [sã′sy:r], *n.f.* Censorship; criticism, censure, blame, reproof, vote of censure; audit (of accounts); ecclesiastical censure; board of censors. **censurer**, *v.t.* To find fault with, to blame, to criticize; to censure, to condemn.

cent [sã], *a.* One hundred. *Au vers deux cent*, at the 200th line; *cent un ans*, one hundred and one years; *les Cent Jours*, the Hundred Days (from March 20th to end of June, 1815); *faire les cent pas*, to walk up and down. —*n.m.* A hundred. *Cinq pour cent*, five per cent; *deux cents pesant*, two hundredweight; *je vous le donne en cent*, it's 100 to 1 against your guessing it. [*Cent* takes the sign of the plural if preceded and multiplied, but not followed by a number: *trois cents hommes*, 300 men; *trois cent cinquante hommes*, 350 men.]

centaine [sã′tɛn], *n.f.* A hundred; a hundred or so; thread that ties up a skein.

centaure [sã′tɔ:r], *n.m.* Centaur.

centaurée [sãtɔ′re], *n.f.* (*Bot.*) Centaury. *Centaurée noire*, knap-weed.

centauresse [sãtɔ′rɛs], *n.f.* Centauress.

centenaire [sãt′nɛ:r], *a.* A hundred years old; of a hundred years' standing. —*n.* Centenarian. —*n.m.* Centenary.

centenille [sã′tnij], *n.f.* (*Bot.*) Chaff-weed.

centésimal [sãtezi′mal], *a.* (*fem.* **-ale**, *pl.* **-aux**) Centesimal. **centésimo**, *adv.* For the hundredth time.

centiare [sã′tja:r], *n.m.* The hundredth part of an *are* (1·1960 square yards).

centième [sã′tjɛm], *a.* Hundredth.—*n.m.* The hundredth part. **centièmement**, *adv.* In the hundredth place.

centigrade [sãti′grad], *a.* Centigrade.

centigramme [sãti′gram], *n.m.* Centigram, the hundredth part of a gram (·1543 grain).

centilitre [sãti′litr], *n.m.* Centilitre, the hundredth part of a litre (·61028 cubic in.).

centime [sã′tim], *n.m.* Centime, the hundredth part of a franc.

centimètre [sãti′metr], *n.m.* Centimetre, the hundredth part of a metre (.39371 in.); (*fam.*) tape-measure.

centipède [sãti′pɛd], *n.m.* Centipede.

centon [sã′tɔ̃], *n.m.* Cento. **centoniser**, *v.t.* To compose in centos.

centrage [sã′tra:ʒ], *n.m.* Centering.

central [sã′tral], *a.* (*fem.* **-ale**, *pl.* **-aux**) Central; chief, principal, head.—*n.m. Central téléphonique*, telephone exchange. *pl.* (*colloq.*) *Les centraux*, the students at the École Centrale.—*n.f.* This school. *La centrale*, the central prison (of any Department); *centrale électrique*, electric power station. **centralement**, *adv.* Centrally.

centralisateur [sãtraliza′tœ:r], *a.* (*fem.* **-trice**) Centralizing. **centralisation**, *n.f.* Centralization. **centraliser**, *v.t.* To centralize. **centralisme**, *n.m.* Centralism. **centraliste**, *n.m.* Centralist.

centre [sã:tr], *n.m.* Centre, middle, midst; (*Parl.*) cross-benches, the Centre; (*Mil.*) main body. *Centre de gravité*, centre of gravity; *centre d'aviation*, air station; *chaque chose tend à son centre*, everything converges towards its centre; *le centre gauche*, the Left Centre.

centrer [sã′tre], *v.t.* To centre; to bring to the centre; (*Ftb.*) to centre (the ball). **centreur**, *n.m.* Centering apparatus.

centrifuge [sãtri′fy:ʒ], *a.* Centrifugal. **centrifuger**, *v.t.* To centrifugalize. **centrifugeur**, *n.m.* Centrifugal machine.

centripète [sãtri′pɛt], *a.* Centripetal.

centrisque [sã′trisk], *n.m.* Trumpet-fish.

cent-suisses [sã′sɥis], *n.m. pl.* The hundred Swiss guards of the king of France. *Un cent-suisse*, one of these.

centumvir [sãtɔm′vi:r], *n.m.* Centumvir. **centumviral**, *a.* (*fem.* **-ale**, *pl.* **-aux**) Centumviral.

centuple [sã′typl], *a.* and *n.m.* Centuple, hundredfold. **centuplement**, *adv.* A hundredfold. **centupler**, *v.t.* To multiply a hundredfold, to centuple.

centurie [sãty′ri], *n.f.* (*Rom. Ant.*) Century; (*pl.*) annals divided by centuries.

centurion [săty′rjɔ̃], *n.m.* Centurion.
cep [sep], *n.m.* Vine-stock; frame of a plough; **(pl.)* prisoner's chain. **cépage**, *n.m.* Vineplant. *Les cépages de la Bourgogne,* the vines of Burgundy.
cèpe or **ceps** [sep], *n.m.* Edible boletus.
cépée [se′pe], *n.f.* (*Agric.*) Tuft of shoots from a pollarded stump; copse of one or two years' growth.
cependant [spă′dã], *adv.* In the meantime, meanwhile.—*conj.* Yet, still, however, nevertheless.
céphalalgie [sefalal′ʒi], *n.f.* Cephalalgy, headache. **céphalalgique**, *a.* Cephalalgic. **céphalée**, *n.f.* (*Path.*) Headache. **céphalique**, *a.* Cephalic. **céphalite**, *n.f.* Cephalitis. **céphaloïde**, *a.* Cephaloid. **céphalopode**, *n.m.* (*Zool.*) Cephalopod. **céphalotomie**, *n.f.* Cephalotomy.
cérame [se′ram], *n.m.* Terra-cotta vase.
céramique [sera′mik], *a.* Ceramic.—*n.f.* Ceramics. **céramiste**, *n.m.* Ceramist.
cérasine [sera′sin], *n.f.* Cerasin.
céraste [se′rast], *n.m.* Cerastes, horned viper.
cérat [se′ra], *n.m.* Ointment, salve.
Cerbère [ser′bɛːr], *m.* (*Myth.*) Cerberus; (*fig.*) watch-dog, brutal guardian.
cerce [sers], *n.f.* Hoop, band (used in pottery-making, construction, etc.).
cerceau [ser′so], *n.m.* Hoop, ring; hoop-net; (*Surg.*) cradle; (*pl.*) pinion-feathers. *Faire courir un cerceau,* to trundle a hoop.
cercelle [SARCELLE].
cerclage [ser′klaːʒ], *n.m.* Hooping (of casks etc.); trying (of wheels).
cercle [serkl], *n.m.* Circle, ring; circumference, hoop; barrel, cask; club, club-house. *Cercle polaire arctique* or *antarctique,* Arctic or Antarctic Circle; *cercle vicieux,* vicious circle; *décrire* or *former un cercle,* to describe or form a circle; *un demi-cercle,* a semi-circle; *un quart de cercle,* a quadrant; (*Mech.*) *cercle de contact,* piston ring; *vin en cercle,* wine in the cask. **cerclé**, *a.* (*fem.* **-ée**) Ringed. **cercler**, *v.t.* To bind with hoops, to hoop.
cerclier [ser′klje], *n.m.* Hoop-maker.
cercueil [ser′kœːj], *n.m.* Coffin; (leaden) shell; (*fig.*) the tomb, death. *Descendre au cercueil,* to die; *mettre au cercueil,* to bring to the grave.
céréale [sere′al], *n.f.* Cereal, corn, grain, corn crops. *Commerce des céréales,* corn-trade.—*a.* Cereal. **céréaline**, *n.f.* Cerealin.
cérébelleux [serebɛ′lø], *a.* (*fem.* **-euse**) Cerebellar.
cérébral [sere′bral], *a.* (*fem.* **-ale**, *pl.* **-aux**) Cerebral. *Fièvre cérébrale,* brain fever.—*n.* (*fam.*) Brain-worker, thinker. **cérébrite**, *n.f.* (*Path.*) Cerebritis, inflammation of the brain.
cérébrospinal, *a.* (*fem.* **-ale**, *pl.* **-aux**) Cerebrospinal.
cérémonial [seremɔ′njal], *a.* (*fem.* **-ale**, *pl.* **-aux**) Ceremonial.—*n.m.* (*no pl.*) Ceremonial, formality, etiquette, state, pomp. **cérémonialisme**, *n.m.* Ceremonialism.
cérémonie [seremɔ′ni], *n.f.* Ceremony; pomp; formality, elaborate etiquette; fuss, ado. *En grande cérémonie,* in state; *faire des cérémonies,* to stand upon ceremony; *sans cérémonie,* without ceremony; *sans plus de cérémonie,* forthwith; *visite de cérémonie,*

formal visit. **cérémonieusement**, *adv.* Ceremoniously. **cérémonieux**, *a.* (*fem.* **-euse**) Ceremonious, formal, precise.
Cérès [se′rɛːs], *f.* Ceres.
cerf [sɛːr], *n.m.* Stag, hart, deer. *Cerf commun,* red-deer; *corne de cerf,* hartshorn; *un bois de cerf,* the horns of a stag.
cerfeuil [ser′fœːj], *n.m.* Chervil. *Cerfeuil musqué,* sweet cicely.
cerf-volant [servɔ′lã], *n.m.* (*pl.* **cerfs-volants**) Stag-beetle; kite, paper-kite.
cerisaie [səri′zɛ], *n.f.* Cherry-orchard.
cerise [sə′riːz], *n.f.* Cherry.—*n.m.* Cherry-colour, cerise.—*a.* Cherry-coloured, cerise. **cerisette**, *n.f.* Dried cherry; beverage made with cherries. **cerisier**, *n.m.* Cherry-tree, cherry-wood.—(*C*) *n.f. Cerisier à grappes,* choke-cherry.
cerne [sern], *n.m.* Circle (round eyes, moon, wound, etc.); (*Bot.*) ring (of a tree). **cerné**, *a.* (*fem.* **cernée**) *Des yeux cernés,* eyes with dark circles round them.
cerneau [ser′no], *n.m.* (*pl.* **-eaux**) Green walnut.
cerner [ser′ne], *v.t.* To cut or dig round (a tree), to ring (a tree); to surround, to encompass, to hem in; (*Mil.*) to invest; to take the kernel out of (green walnuts); (*fig.*) to circumvent.
céroplastique [serɔplas′tik], *a.* Ceroplastic.
certain [ser′tɛ], *a.* Certain, sure, positive; undoubted, true; reliable, trustworthy, trusty; appointed, stated, fixed, determined. *À certaines époques de l'année,* at certain periods of the year; *c'est un homme d'un certain mérite,* he is a man of some merit; *d'un certain âge,* not so young; *dans certains cas,* in certain cases; *est-il certain qu'il réussisse?* is it certain that he will succeed? *soyez certain que . . . ,* rest assured that . . . ; *un certain personnage,* a certain personage.—*n.m.* Certainty; a sure thing, price, etc. *Il ne faut pas quitter le certain pour l'incertain,* we must not quit a certainty for an uncertainty. **certainement**, *adv.* Certainly, assuredly, without fail, infallibly; yes, to be sure.
certes, *adv.* Indeed, most certainly.
certificat [sertifi′ka], *n.m.* Certificate; testimonial; diploma; (*fig.*) proof, assurance. *Certificat de vie,* attestation, affidavit of existence; *certificat d'origine,* pedigree. **certificateur**, *n.m.* Certifier, voucher. **certificatif**, *a.* (*fem.* **-ive**) Certifying. **certification**, *n.f.* Certification. **certifier**, *v.t.* To certify, to testify, to vouch for, to attest, to assure, to affirm, to aver. *Certifier une caution,* to guarantee that bail is valid; *certifier véritable,* to witness (a signature).
certitude [serti′tyd], *n.f.* Certitude, certainty; assurance; (*fam.*) dead cert. *Avoir la certitude,* to be certain.
cérulé [sery′le], *a.* (*fem.* **-ée**) or **céruléen** (*fem.* **-éenne**) Cerulean. **cérulescent**, *a.* (*fem.* **-ente**) Turning to azure.
cérumen [sery′mɛn], *n.m.* Cerumen, ear-wax. **cérumineux**, *a.* (*fem.* **-euse**) Ceruminous.
céruse [se′ryːz], *n.f.* Ceruse, white lead. **cérusite**, *n.f.* Cerusite.
cervaison [serve′zɔ̃], *n.f.* Stag (hunting) season.
cerveau [ser′vo], *n.m.* Brain; mind, intellect, intelligence. *Avoir le cerveau creux,* to be

a dreamer; *cerveau brûlé*, hot-headed person; *cerveau vide*, empty-headed person; *être pris du cerveau*, to have a cold in one's head; *rhume de cerveau*, cold in the head; *vous me rompez le cerveau*, you tire me out.

cervelas [sɛrvə'la], *n.m.* Saveloy.

cervelet [sɛrvə'lɛ], *n.m.* Cerebellum.

cervelle [sɛr'vɛl], *n.f.* Brains; mind, intelligence, wit; pith (of palm-trees). *Avoir une cervelle de lièvre*, to be scatter-brained; *cela lui tourne la cervelle*, that turns his head; *se brûler la cervelle*, to blow out one's brains; *se creuser la cervelle*, to rack one's brains.

cervical [sɛrvi'kal], *a.* (*fem.* **-ale**, *pl.* **-aux**) (*Anat.*) Cervical.

cervin [sɛr'vɛ̃], *a.* (*fem.* **-ine**) Cervine. *Le (Mont) Cervin*, the Matterhorn.

cervoise [sɛr'vwaːz], *n.f.* (*Gallic Ant.*) A sort of barley-beer.

ces [CE].

César [se'zaːr], *m.* Caesar.—*n.m.* Caesar, emperor. **césarien**, *a.* (*fem.* **-ienne**) Caesarean, Caesarian.—*n.f.* Caesarean operation. **césarisme**, *n.m.* Caesarism.

césium [CAESIUM].

cessant [sɛ'sã], *a.* (*fem.* **-ante**) Ceasing, suspended. *Toute affaire cessante*, to the suspension of all other business. **cessation**, *n.f.* Cessation, suspension, stoppage. **cesse**, *n.f.* Ceasing, intermission, respite. *Sans cesse*, unceasingly.

cesser [sɛ'se], *v.i.* To cease, to leave off, to discontinue, to stop. *Faire cesser*, to put a stop or an end to; *il ne cesse de pleurer*, he never leaves off crying.—*v.t.* To leave off, to break off. *Cesser ses paiements*, (*Comm.*) to stop payment.

cessibilité [sɛsibili'te], *n.f.* (*Law*) Transferability, assignability. **cessible**, *a.* Transferable, assignable

cession [sɛ'sjɔ̃], *n.f.* Transfer, assignment (of property); relinquishment; surrender. **cessionnaire**, *n.m.* Grantee, assignee, transferee.

c'est-à-dire [sɛta'diːr], *conj. ph.* That is to say, in other words.

ceste [sɛst], *n.m.* (*Ant.*) Cestus.

césure [se'zyːr], *n.f.* Caesura.

cet, cette [CE].

cétacé [seta'se], *a.* (*fem.* **-ée**) Cetaceous.—*n.m.* Cetacean.

cétérac [sete'rak], *n.m.* Ceterach, fingerfern.

cétine [se'tin], *n.f.* Pure spermaceti.

cétoine [se'twan], *n.f.* (*Bot.*) Rose-chafer.

cette [CE]. **ceux** [CELUI].

cévenol [sev'nɔl], *a.* (*fem.* **-ole**) Of or pertaining to the Cévennes.

Ceylan [se'lã], *m.* Ceylon.

chablage [ʃa'blaːʒ], *n.m.* Piloting (of boats on rivers). **chable**, *n.m.* Rope passing through a pulley for lifting a bale etc. **chableau** or **chablot**, *n.m.* Tow-line. **chabler**, *v.t.* To tow (a boat) with a rope; to fasten (a bundle etc.) to a rope. *Chabler les noyers*, to knock down walnuts with a pole. *****chableur**, *n.m.* (*formerly*) Water-bailiff.

chablis (1) [ʃa'bli], *n.m.* Wind-fallen wood, dead-wood.

chablis (2) [ʃa'bli], *n.m.* Chablis (white wine).

chabot [ʃa'bo] or **cabot**, *n.m.* (*Ichth.*) Miller's-thumb, bull-head; chub.

chabotte [ʃa'bɔt], *n.f.* Bronze bed of a steam-hammer.

chabraque [SCHABRAQUE].

chabrol [ʃa'brɔl], *n.m.* (*S. dial.*) Broth with wine. *Faire chabrol*, to mix wine in soup.

chacal [ʃa'kal], *n.m.* Jackal; (*Mil. slang*) zouave.

chacone [ʃa'kɔn] or **chaconne**, *n.f.* Chaconne (dance and tune).

chacun [ʃa'kœ̃], *pron. indef. sing.* (*fem.* **chacune**) Each, each one, every one. *Chacun a sa marotte*, every man has his hobby; *chacun (à) son goût*, every man to his taste; *chacun à son tour*, each in his turn; *chacun de tes désirs*, your every wish; *chacun est maître chez soi*, every man is master in his own house; *chacun le sien*, every one his own; *chacun pour soi et Dieu pour tous*, everyone for himself and God for all; *chacun vit à sa guise*, everyone lives as he likes; *donnez à chacun sa part*, give everyone his share; *ils auront chacun leur part*, each of them will have his share; *ils s'en retournèrent chacun chez eux* or *chacun chez soi*, each of them returned to his own home; *rendre à chacun ce qui lui appartient*, to return everyone his own; *tous les membres ont voté chacun selon ses instructions*, every member voted according to his instructions.

*****chacunière** [ʃaky'njɛːr], *n.f.* One's own house.

chadouf [ʃa'duf], *n.m.* Well-sweep (in Egypt, Tunisia, etc.).

chafaud [ʃa'fo], *n.m.* *****Scaffold; platform for drying codfish.

chafouin [ʃa'fwɛ̃], *a.* (*fem.* **-ouine**) Weasel-faced, mean-looking.

chagrin (1) [ʃa'grɛ̃], *n.m.* Grief, vexation, chagrin, annoyance; regret, sorrow; fretfulness; peevishness. *Mourir de chagrin*, to die of a broken heart.—*a.* (*fem.* **chagrine**) Gloomy, melancholy, sad; fretful, peevish.

chagrin (2) [ʃa'grɛ̃], *n.m.* Shagreen. *Demi-chagrin*, half-bound.

chagrinant [ʃagri'nã], *a.* (*fem.* **-ante**) Vexatious, distressing, sad, provoking.

chagriner (1) [ʃagri'ne], *v.t.* To grieve, to afflict; to cross, to vex, to provoke, to annoy. **se chagriner**, *v.r.* To fret, to grieve, to take on.

chagriner (2) [ʃagri'ne], *v.t.* To make (a skin) into shagreen. **chagrinier**, *n.m.* Shagreen-maker.

chah [SCHAH].

chahut [ʃa'y], *n.m.* *****A high-kicking, vulgar dance (*c.*1840); (*fig.*) row, shindy. **chahutage**, *n.m.* Booing, barracking. **chahuter**, *v.i.* To dance the chahut; to make a row, to kick up a shindy.—*v.t.* To upset, to disorder, to boo, to barrack (a team), to ballyrag (somebody). **chahuteur**, *n.m.* (*fem.* **-euse**) High-kicker; disorderly person; (*sch.*) ragger.

chai or **chais** [ʃɛ], *n.m.* Wine or spirit store (above ground).

chaille [ʃaːj], *n.f.* (*Geol.*) Siliceous concretion. Jurassic flint.

chaînage [ʃɛː'naːʒ], *n.m.* Chain-bond, iron-work (for holding buildings together); (*Surveying*) chaining.

chaîne [ʃɛːn], *n.f.* Chain; shackle, fetters; bonds, bondage, servitude; belting, chain-course (for walls); drag-chain (of canals);

(*Weaving*) warp; surveying-chain, Gunter's chain; (*Dancing*) right and left; (*Naut.*) cable; boom (for closing a harbour); (*fig.*) series, catena, succession, range. *À la chaîne*, chained up; *attacher avec des chaînes*, to chain up; (*Ind.*) *chaîne de montage*, assembly-line; *chaîne de montre*, watch-guard; *chaîne de montagnes*, range of mountains; *chaîne de sûreté*, coupling chain; *charger quelqu'un de chaînes*, to load with fetters; *faire la chaîne*, to form in line, to pass buckets from hand to hand (at a fire); *la chaîne des idées*, the train of thought; *faire une chaîne de mailles*, to cast off a row of stitches (*in knitting*). **chaîner**, *v.t.* (*Surveying*) To measure (land) with the chain. **chaînier** or **chaîniste**, *n.m.* Chainmaker. **chaînette**, *n.f.* Little chain; (*Arch.*) catenary arch. *Point de chaînette*, chainstitch. **chaîneur**, *n.m.* (*Surveying*) Measurer with the chain. **chaînon**, *n.m.* Link.

chaintre [ʃɛ̃:tr], *n.m.* (*Agric.*) Balk, headland.

chair [ʃɛːr], *n.f.* Flesh; meat (opposed to fish, fowl, and vegetable food); (*fig.*) the human body, the flesh; (*Paint., pl.*) naked flesh; pulpy substance of fruit. *Bien en chair*, fleshy, well-fed, well-developed; *chair à canon* [CANON (1)]; *chair à saucisses*, sausage-meat; *chair blanche*, white meat; *chair de poule*, goose-flesh; *chair ferme*, firm flesh; *chair molle*, soft flesh; *chair morte*, dead skin; *chair noire*, game; *chair vive*, quick flesh; *chairs baveuses*, (*Med.*) proud flesh; *convoitises de la chair*, the lusts of the flesh; *couleur de chair*, flesh-colour; *en chair et en os*, in flesh and blood, in person; *chair de sa chair*, one's own flesh and blood; *hacher menu comme chair à pâté*, to make mincemeat of; *j'en ai la chair de poule*, I shudder at the thought, it makes my flesh creep; *la chair d'un poisson*, the fleshy part of a fish; *la résurrection de la chair*, the resurrection of the body; *le Verbe s'est fait chair*, the Word was made flesh; *ni chair ni poisson*, neither fish (flesh) nor fowl, (a man who is) neither one thing nor the other; *pester entre cuir et chair*, to keep one's ill-humour to oneself.

chais [CHAI].

chaire [ʃɛːr], *n.f.* *Seat, chair; pulpit, tribune, professorial chair; professorship; bishop's throne. *Chaire apostolique*, apostolic or papal see; *chaire de droit*, professorship of law; *en pleine chaire*, before the whole congregation; *l'éloquence de la chaire*, pulpit oratory; *monter en chaire*, to mount the pulpit, to preach.

chaise [ʃɛːz], *n.f.* Chair, seat; (*Rail.*) chair; (*Carp. etc.*) timber-work (supporting clock etc.), bracket (for supporting an axle etc.); post-chaise. *Chaise à bascule*, rocking-chair; *chaise à deux chevaux*, chaise and pair; *chaise à dos*, high-backed chair; *chaise à porteurs*, sedan-chair; *chaise brisée*, folding chair; *chaise curule*, curule chair; *chaise de paille*, straw-bottomed chair; *chaise de poste*, post-chaise; *chaise longue*, lounging chair; couch, sofa with only one raised end; *chaise roulante*, Bath chair; *chaise percée*, commode; *chaise de chœur*, choir stall; (*Naut.*) *nœud de chaise*, bowline on a bight. **chaisier**, *n.m.* (*fem.* **-ière**) Chair maker; one who lets chairs (in gardens, in church).

chako [SHAKO].

chaland (1) [ʃaˈlɑ̃], *n.m.* Lighter, barge. **chalandeau**, *n.m.* Lighterman, bargeman.

chaland (2) [ʃaˈlɑ̃], *n.m.* (*fem.* **chalande**) Customer, purchaser, client.

chalaze [kaˈlɑːz], *n.f.* (*Biol.*) Chalaza.

chalcographe [kalkɔˈgraf], *n.m.* Chalcographer, engraver on metal. **chalcographie**, *n.f.* Chalcography; engraving establishment. **chalcographier**, *v.t.* To engrave on metal.

chalcopyrite [kalkɔpiˈrit], *n.f.* Chalcopyrite.

chaldaïque [kaldaˈik], *a.* Chaldaic.

Chaldée [kalˈde], *f.* Chaldea.

chaldéen [kaldeˈɛ̃], *a.* and *n.* (*fem.* **-éenne**) Chaldean.

châle [ʃɑːl], *n.m.* Shawl.

chalet [ʃaˈlɛ], *n.m.* Chalet, Swiss cottage; country cottage (made of wood). *Chalet de nécessité*, public lavatory.

chaleur [ʃaˈlœːr], *n.f.* Heat; warmth, high temperature; warm weather; (*fig.*) glow; passion, eagerness, earnestness, zeal, ardour; (*Phys.*) caloric. *Coup de chaleur*, heat stroke; '*Craint la chaleur*', 'Store in a cool place'; *les grandes chaleurs*, the hot season, the height of summer; *vague de chaleur*, heat wave; *être en chaleur*, to be on heat (of female animals). **chaleureusement**, *adv.* Cordially, warmly, passionately. **chaleureux**, *a.* (*fem.* **-euse**) Warm, animated, cordial.

chalicose [ʃaliˈkoːz], *n.f.* Silicosis.

châlit [ʃaˈli], *n.m.* Bedstead.

***chaloir** [ʃaˈlwaːr], *v. impers.* To matter. *Il ne m'en chaut*, I don't care, it matters not to me; *peu m'en chaut*, it signifies little to me.

chalon [ʃaˈlɔ̃], *n.m.* Drag-net.

chaloupe [ʃaˈlup], *n.f.* Ship's boat, long-boat, launch. *Chaloupe cannonière*, gun-boat. **chalouper**, *v.i.* (*slang*) To walk or dance with a roll.

chaloupier, *n.m.* Sailor in boat's crew.

chalumeau [ʃalyˈmo], *n.m.* Stalk of corn, reed, etc., drinking-straw; flute, pan-pipe, or other musical instrument of the same family; reed-pipe; blow-pipe; blow-lamp; (*C*) spout (fixed on the sugar maple-tree).

chalut [ʃaˈly], *n.m.* Drag-net, trawl. **chalutage**, *n.m.* Trawling. **chaluter**, *v.i.* To trawl. **chalutier**, *a.* (*fem.* **-ière**) Trawling. —*n.m.* Trawler.

chalybé [kaliˈbe], *a.* (*fem.* **-ée**) Chalybeate.

chamade [ʃaˈmad], *n.f.* *Battre la chamade*, to sound a parley, to surrender; (heart) to beat wildly.

chamaillard [ʃamaˈjaːr], *a.* (*fem.* **-arde**) Squabbling, quarrelsome.—*n.* Squabbler, wrangler. **chamaille**, *n.f.* Noisy squabble, wrangle.

chamailler [ʃamaˈje], *v.i.* To bicker, to squabble, to wrangle. **se chamailler**, *v.r.* To squabble, to wrangle. **chamaillerie**, *n.f.* Squabble, quarrel. **chamaillis**, *n.m.* Fray; squabble, wrangle; uproar, din.

chaman or **chamane** [ʃaˈman], *n.m.* Shaman. **chamanisme**, *n.m.* Shamanism.

chamarrage [ʃamaˈraːʒ], *n.m.* Bedizenment.

chamarre [ʃaˈmaːr], *n.f.* *Judge's gown; *lace, embroidery. **chamarrer**, *v.t.* To bedizen, to bedeck. **chamarrure**, *n.f.* Bedizenment.

chambard or **chambart** [ʃɑ̃ˈbaːr], *n.m.* (*pop.*)

Racket, row. **chambardement,** *n.m.* Row, upset. **chambarder,** *v.t.* To upset, to pillage, to sack.

chambellan [ʃãbɛ'lã], *n.m.* Chamberlain. **chambellanie,** *n.f.* Office of chamberlain.

chambertin [ʃãbɛr'tɛ̃], *n.m.* Chambertin, a red Burgundy wine.

chambouler [ʃãbu'le], *v.t.* (*slang*) To upset, to turn topsy-turvy.

chambourin [ʃãbu'rɛ̃], *n.m.* White sand (to make strass).

chambranle [ʃã'brã:l], *n.m.* Door-frame, window-frame. *Chambranle de cheminée,* mantelpiece.

chambre [ʃã:br], *n.f.* Chamber, room; lodging, apartment; Parliament House; Chamber, assembly; tribunal, court (of justice); (*Artill.*) chamber (of gun); (*Naut.*) cabin. *Arrêter* or *louer une chambre,* to hire a room; *chambre à air,* inner tube (bicycle etc.); *chambre à coucher,* bedroom; *chambre à un (deux) lit(s),* single (double) room; *chambre à gaz,* gas-chamber; *chambre à vapeur,* steam-chest; *chambre claire,* camera lucida; *chambre d'ami,* spare bedroom; *chambre d'écluse,* lock; *chambre de commerce,* Chamber of Commerce; *chambre garnie,* furnished apartment; *Chambre haute,* House of Lords; *chambre noire,* camera obscura; *convoquer les Chambres,* to convoke Parliament; *faire une chambre,* to do (clean) a room; *femme de chambre,* chambermaid; *garder la chambre,* to keep one's room; *musique de chambre,* chamber music; *pot de chambre,* chamber (pot); *robe de chambre,* dressing-gown; *chambre d'alimentation,* feed block (of a gun). **chambré,** *a.* (*fem.* **-ée**) Chambered (of fire-arms etc.), provided with a powder-chamber; honeycombed, pitted (of cannon etc.). **chambrée,** *n.f.* Barrack-room; roomful; (*Theat. etc.*) house; takings.

chambrer [ʃã'bre], *v.i.* To lodge or to chum (together).—*v.t.* To keep (someone) confined; to take aside, to lead apart; to bring (wine) from cellar to room temperature. **se chambrer,** *v.r.* To become pitted.

chambrette [ʃã'brɛt], *n.f.* Little room.

***chambrier** [ʃã'bri'e], *n.m.* Chamberlain, steward. **chambrière,** *n.f.* *Chambermaid; long horse-whip; prop (for vehicle).

chameau [ʃa'mo], *n.m.* Camel; (*pop.*) nasty, evil-minded, mischievous person. *Rejeter le moucheron et avaler le chameau,* to strain at the gnat and swallow the camel. **chamelée,** *n.f.* Camel-load. **chamelier,** *n.m.* Camel-driver. **chamelle,** *n.f.* She-camel. **chamelon,** *n.m.* Young camel.

chamite [ka'mit], *n.m.* Hamite. **chamitique,** *a.* Hamitic.

chamois [ʃa'mwɑ], *n.m.* Chamois; chamois leather; chamois colour.—*a.* Chamois-coloured, buff. **chamoisage,** *n.m.* Chamois-dressing. **chamoiser,** *v.t.* To prepare (leather) like chamois. **chamoiserie,** *n.f.* Chamois-leather factory; chamois leather. **chamoiseur,** *n.m.* Chamois- or leather-dresser.

champ (1) [ʃã], *n.m.* Field, piece of ground; fields, open country; scope, range; (*Her.*) field; (*poet.*) country, land, territory; (*fig.*) space, compass. *Aller aux champs,* to go into the country; *à travers champs,* across country; *battre* or *sonner aux champs,* (*Mil.*) to sound

a salute; *champ clos,* lists (for combat); *champ d'aviation,* airfield; *champ de bataille,* battle-field; *champ de courses,* race-course; *champ de repos,* churchyard, God's acre; *champ de tir,* rifle-range; *champ magnétique,* magnetic field; *courir les champs,* to run wild; *donner la clef des champs,* to give (someone) his liberty; *en plein champ,* in the open field; *il est fou à courir les champs,* he is as mad as a March hare; *le champ,* (Racing) the field; *le champ d'honneur,* the field of honour; *le champ est libre,* the coast is clear; *prendre du champ,* to take room; *prendre la clef des champs,* to take to one's heels, to bolt; *sur-le-champ,* at once, immediately.

champ (2) [CHANT (2)].

champagne [ʃã'paɲ], *n.m.* Champagne. *Champagne frappé,* iced champagne; *champagne mousseux,* sparkling champagne; *champagne non mousseux,* still champagne; *fine champagne,* brandy from the champagne near Cognac. **champagniser** [ʃãpaɲi'ze], *v.t.* To make (wine) effervescent like champagne.

champart [ʃã'pa:r], *n.m.* (*Feud. law*) Field-rent paid in kind to the lord.

champbord [ʃã'bɔr], *n.m.* Spoil-bank.

champelure [CHAMPLURE].

champenois [ʃãpə'nwa], *a.* and *n.* (*fem.* **champenoise**) Of Champagne.

champêtre [ʃã'pɛ:tr], *a.* Rural, rustic, sylvan. *Garde champêtre,* village policeman.

champi or **champis** [ʃã'pi], *a.* and *n.* (*fem.* **champisse**) (*dial.*) Foundling.

champignon [ʃãpi'ɲɔ̃], *n.m.* Mushroom, fungus; (*fig.*) waster, thief (in a candle); bonnet- or hat-stand, peg; (*fam.*) accelerator. *Blanc de champignon,* mushroom spawn; *champignon vénéneux,* toadstool; *pousser comme un champignon,* to grow (fast) like a mushroom. (*fam.*) *Appuyer sur le champignon,* to step on the gas. **champignonnière,** *n.f.* Mushroom bed. **champignonniste,** *n.m.* Mushroom-grower.

champion [ʃã'pjɔ̃], *n.m.* (*fem.* **-onne**) Champion. **championnat,** *n.m.* Championship.

champlé [ʃã'ple], *a.* (*fem.* **-ée**) Frost-bitten (of vines).

champlever [ʃãl'vе], *v.i.* To cut out the copper ground (in enamelling).

champlure [ʃã'ply:r], *n.f.* Frost-bite (of a fruit-tree).

champoreau [ʃãpɔ'ro], *n.m.* (*North Africa*) Hot coffee with rum.

chançard [ʃã'sa:r], *a.* and *n.* (*fem.* **-arde**) (*fam.*) Lucky (person).

chance [ʃã:s], *n.f.* *Hazard (at dice etc.); chance; luck, good luck, good fortune; (*pl.*) chances, (*fam.*) odds. *Avoir de la chance,* to be lucky; *courir la chance,* to run the risk; *il n'a pas de chance,* he has no chance; *il n'est chance qui ne retourne,* luck will change; *il y avait toujours la chance que,* it was always on the cards that; *pas de chance,* no luck; *par chance,* by good luck; *porter chance,* to bring luck; *quelle chance!* how lucky! *souhaiter bonne chance à quelqu'un,* to wish someone good luck.

chancelant [ʃãs'lã], *a.* (*fem.* **-ante**) Staggering, tottering; unsettled, unsteady, wavering.

chancelariat [ʃãsəla'rja], *n.m.* Chancellorship.

chanceler [ʃãs'le], *v.i.* To stagger, to totter; to reel, to falter, to waver, to be unsteady.

chancelier [ʃãsəˈlje], *n.m.* Chancellor. *Grand Chancelier*, Lord Chancellor. **chancelière**, *n.f.* Chancellor's wife; foot-muff.

chancellement [ʃãsɛlˈmã], *n.m.* Tottering, unsteadiness.

chancellerie [ʃãsɛlˈri], *n.f.* Chancellor's office, chancellery; chancellor's residence. *Grande Chancellerie*, administration of the Legion of Honour.

chanceux [ʃãˈsø], *a.* (*fem.* **chanceuse**) Lucky, fortunate; risky, uncertain, doubtful (of things).

chanci [ʃãˈsi], *a.* (*fem.* **chancie**) Mouldy.— *n.m.* Dung-heap, sown with fungus spawn.

chancir [ʃãˈsiːr], *v.i.* To grow musty or mouldy. **chancissure**, *n.f.* Mustiness, mouldiness.

chancre [ʃãːkr], *n.m.* Ulcer, tumour; canker; (*fig.*) ruinous vice, defect, etc.; (*Path.*) chancre. **chancreux**, *a.* (*fem.* **-euse**) Ulcerous; cankered; chancrous. **chancroïde**, *n.m.* (*Path.*) Simple chancre.

chandail [ʃãˈdaːj], *n.m.* Jersey, sweater.

chandeleur [ʃãˈdlœːr], *n.f.* Candlemas.

chandelier (1) [ʃãdəˈlje], *n.m.* Candlestick; (*Naut.*) crutch; (*fig.*) screen for a wife's lover. *Chandelier à manche*, flat candlestick; *être placé sur le chandelier*, to occupy a conspicuous position; *mettre la lumière sur le chandelier*, to make known the truth.

chandelier (2) [ʃãdəˈlje], *n.m.* (*fem.* **chandelière**) Tallow-chandler; candle-maker.

chandelle [ʃãˈdɛl], *n.f.* (Tallow) candle; (*fig.*) light; (*Tennis*) lob; (*Build.*) prop; (*fam.*) drop (at the end of the nose). *Aux chandelles*, into the light; *brûler la chandelle par les deux bouts*, to burn the candle at both ends; *c'est une économie de bouts de chandelle*, that is penny wise and pound foolish; *chandelle de glace*, icicle; *chandelle romaine*, Roman candle; *éteindre la chandelle*, to put out the candle; *il vous doit une belle chandelle*, he ought to be very grateful to you, you saved him from a great danger; *le jeu n'en vaut pas la chandelle*, the game is not worth the candle; *moucher la chandelle*, to snuff the candle; *s'en aller comme une chandelle*, to go off like the snuff of a candle; *souffler la chandelle*, to blow out the candle, (*fig.*) to die; *tenir la chandelle*, to hold the candle (to help a love-affair); *travailler à la chandelle*, to work by candle-light; *voir trente-six chandelles*, to see stars. **chandellerie**, *n.f.* Candle-factory; candle-trade.

chanfraindre or **chanfreindre** [CHANFREI-NER].

chanfrein [ʃãˈfrɛ̃], *n.m.* Chamfron (armour) or plume (for a horse's head); blaze (on forehead of a horse); (*Arch. etc.*) chamfer.

chanfreiner, *v.t.* (*Arch.*) To chamfer, to rabbet, to bevel; to arm *or* decorate (a horse) with a chamfron *or* a plume *or* both.

change [ʃãːʒ], *n.m.* Exchange; exchange of money; exchange office; agio; (*Hunt.*) wrong scent. *Agent de change*, stockbroker; *au change de*, at the rate of exchange of; *bureau de change*, exchange office; *change du jour*, current exchange; *change extérieur*, foreign exchange; *commerce de change*, exchange business; *cours du change*, rate of exchange; *donner le change à quelqu'un*, to put someone on the wrong scent; *fausse lettre de change*,

forged bill; *le change est au pair*, the exchange is at par; *lettre de change sur l'étranger*, foreign bill of exchange; *lettres de change*, letters of exchange; *prendre le change*, to be outwitted or misled, to go on the wrong scent; *rendre le change à quelqu'un*, to pay someone back in his own coin; *tirer une lettre de change sur quelqu'un*, to draw a bill on someone.

changeable [ʃãˈʒabl], *a.* That may be changed, changeable; exchangeable. **changeant**, *a.* (*fem.* **changeante**) Changeable, fickle, variable; inconstant, unstable; unsettled (of the weather). **changement**, *n.m.* Change, alteration, variation, mutation; (*Law*) amendment. *Amener un changement*, to bring about a change; *changement à vue*, (*Theat.*) scene-shifting without dropping the curtain; *changement de propriétaire*, under new management; *changement de vitesse*, (*Motor.*) gear; *changement de voie*, (*Rail.*) shunting.

changer [ʃãˈʒe], *v.t.* To change, to exchange; to shift (scenery etc.); to give change for (a piece of money); to alter, to turn, to convert, to transform.—*v.i.* (*conjugated with* ÊTRE *or* AVOIR) To change, to alter. *Changer d'avis*, to alter one's mind; *changer de chemise*, to change one's shirt; *changer de logis* or *de demeure*, to shift one's quarters, to remove; *changer d'habits*, to change clothes; *changer de place*, to change seats; *changer de train*, to change trains; *changer de voie*, (*Rail.*) to shunt. **se changer**, *v.r.* To be changed, to alter, to change; to change one's clothes. **changeur**, *n.m.* (*fem.* **-euse**) Money-changer.

chanlatte [ʃãˈlat], *n.f.* Eavesboard.

chanoine [ʃaˈnwan], *n.m.* Canon. **chanoinesse**, *n.f.* Canoness. **chanoinie**, *n.f.* Canonry, canonship.

chanson [ʃãˈsõ], *n.f.* Song, ballad; (*fig.*) idle story, stuff, trash. *C'est toujours la même chanson*, it is the same thing over and over again, it is always harping on the same string; *chanson de geste*, medieval epic; *chanson de route*, marching song; *chansons que tout cela!* all idle stories! humbug, stuff! *mettre en chanson*, to satirize, to lampoon; *voilà bien une autre chanson*, that is another story altogether. **chansonner**, *v.t.* To lampoon. **chansonnette**, *n.f.* Little song, ditty; comic song. **chansonneur**, *n.m.* Lampooner. **chansonnier**, *n.m.* (*fem.* **-ière**) Song-writer, ballad-writer; singer of satirical songs; song-book.

chant (1) [ʃã], *n.m.* Singing, vocal music; song, lay, ditty; air, tune, melody; poem; canto, book; chant, hymn. *Chant funèbre*, dirge; *le chant du coq*, the crowing of the cock, cock-crow; *maître* or *professeur de chant*, singing-master; *plain chant*, plain-song.

chant (2) [ʃã], *n.m.* Narrow side, edge (of a board etc.). *De* or *sur chant*, edgewise, on edge.

chantable [ʃãˈtabl], *a.* Fit to be sung, worth singing.

chantage [ʃãˈtaːʒ], *n.m.* Extortion of hush-money, blackmailing.

chantant [ʃãˈtã], *a.* (*fem.* **chantante**) That sings; easily sung, easily set to music; musical, harmonious. *Café chantant*, café where concerts take place.

chanteau [ʃɑ̃'to], *n.m.* Hunch (of bread), bit (of stuff etc.), remnant; felloe (of wheel); (*Dress.*) gore; stave (of barrel).

chantepleure [ʃɑ̃t'plœ:r], *n.f.* Funnel with a rose; watering-pot with a long spout; spigot of a barrel; tap of a cask; gulley-hole.

chanter [ʃɑ̃'te], *v.i.* To sing; to speak, read, etc., in a sing-song tone; to chirp, to carol, to warble, to crow. *Cela vous chante-t-il?* How do you like the idea? *c'est comme si vous chantiez*, it is as if you were talking to the wind; *chanter à faire pitié*, to sing wretchedly; *chanter à livre ouvert*, to sing at sight; *chanter faux*, to sing out of tune; *chanter juste, agréablement*, or *passablement*, to sing true, agreeably, or tolerably; *chanter sur tous les tons*, to ring the changes on; *faire chanter quelqu'un*, to blackmail someone; *la cigale chante*, the cicada chirps; *l'alouette chante*, the lark carols; *le coq chante*, the cock crows; *pain à chanter*, wafer; *si ça vous chante*, if you are in the mood for it; *tel chante qui ne rit pas*, the heart may be sad though the face be gay.—*v.t.* To extol, to praise, to celebrate; to sing, to warble. *Chanter la messe*, to sing mass; *chanter victoire*, to crow over a victory; *je lui ai chanté sa gamme*, I gave him a good lecture; *que me chantez-vous là?* what stuff are you telling me now? **se chanter**, *v.r.* To be sung. *Cet air se chante partout*, this tune is heard everywhere.

chanterelle (1) [ʃɑ̃'trɛl], *n.f.* First string of a violin etc.; decoy-bird; musical bottle. *Appuyer trop sur la chanterelle*, to insist too much on the important point.

chanterelle (2) [ʃɑ̃'trɛl], *n.f.* Cantharellus (mushroom).

chanteur [ʃɑ̃'tœ:r], *a.* (*fem.* **chanteuse**) Singing, given to singing; singing (of birds). —*n.* Singer, vocalist; songster (of birds). *Chanteur de charme*, crooner; *chanteur des rues*, ballad-singer; *maître chanteur*, blackmaiier.

chantier [ʃɑ̃'tje], *n.m.* Timber-yard, wood-yard; stone-yard; dock-yard; site; stand-block, block; barrel-horse; (*Naut.*) stocks. (*C*) Shanty, lumber camp. *Chantier de charbon*, coal-yard; *chantier de construction*, ship-building yard; *chantiers de la jeunesse*, youth camps (run by the Vichy government); *l'ouvrage est sur le chantier*, the work is begun or in hand.

chantignole [ʃɑ̃ti'ɲɔl], *n.f.* Wooden block or cleat (nailed on rafters); brick of half-thickness used in chimneys.

chantonné [ʃɑ̃tɔ'ne], *a.* (*fem.* **chantonnée**) Defective (of paper), lumpy.

chantonnement [ʃɑ̃tɔn'mɑ̃], *n.m.* Humming, hum; drawl.

chantonner [ʃɑ̃tɔ'ne], *v.i.* and *t.* To hum.

chantournage [ʃɑ̃tur'na:ʒ], *n.m.* Cutting in profile. **chantournement**, *n.m.* Profile, contour.

chantourner [ʃɑ̃tur'ne], *v.t.* To cut in profile. *Scie à chantourner*, bow saw.

chantre [ʃɑ̃:tr], *n.m.* Singer, *esp.* a chorister; precentor, lay-clerk; (*fig.*) poet, bard, songster, songstress (of birds). *Les chantres des bois*, the feathered songsters. **chantrerie**, *n.f.* Precentorship.

chanvre [ʃɑ̃:vr], *n.m.* Hemp. *Cravate de chanvre*, halter (for hanging). **chanvreux**,

a. (*fem.* **-euse**) Hempen, resembling hemp.

chanvrier, *n.m.* (*fem.* **chanvrière** (1)) Hemp-dresser, dealer in hemp.—*a.* Hemp (of industry etc.).

chanvrière (2) [CHÉNEVIÈRE].

chaos [ka'o], *n.m.* Chaos; (*fig.*) confusion, disorder. **chaotique**, *a.* Chaotic.

chaouch [ʃa'uʃ], *n.m.* (*Arab word*) Servant.

chapardage [ʃapar'da:ʒ], *n.m.* (*slang*) Stealing, scrounging. **chaparder** [ʃapar'de], *v.t.* (*slang*) To steal; to scrounge. **chapardeur**, *a.* (*fem.* **-euse**) Thievish.—*n.* Thief, scrounger.

chape [ʃap], *n.f.* Cope (ecclesiastical vestment); chape; cope (for sculptor's mould); frame (of a pulley); tread (of a tyre); cover (of a dish); inner box (of compass). *Disputer de la chape à l'évêque*, to dispute about what does not concern one. **chapé**, *a.* (*fem.* **-ée**) Coped, wearing a cope.

chapeau [ʃa'po], *n.m.* (*pl.* **chapeaux**) Hat; (*Mech. etc.*) cap; pileus (of a mushroom); (*Print.*) heading; (*Comm.*) primage. *Chapeau à grand bord*, broad-brimmed hat; *chapeau haut de forme*, top-hat; *chapeau à petit bord*, narrow-brimmed hat; *chapeau bas*, hat in hand; *chapeau chinois*, Chinese bells, jingling Johnnie; *chapeau de cardinal*, cardinal's hat; *chapeau de fleurs*, garland of flowers; *chapeau de paille*, straw hat; *chapeau de paille d'Italie*, Leghorn hat; *chapeau de roue*, (*Motor.*) hub cap; *chapeau de velours*, velvet bonnet; *chapeau melon*, bowler hat; *chapeau mou*, felt hat; *chapeaux bas!* hats off! *cordon de chapeau*, hatband; *enfoncer son chapeau*, to pull one's hat over one's eyes, to screw up one's courage; *la carre d'un chapeau*, the crown of a hat; *le bord, la passe*, or *la forme d'un chapeau*, the border, the front, or the shape of a hat; *ôter son chapeau*, to take off one's hat; *perdre la plus belle rose de son chapeau*, to lose one's chief ornament; *recevoir le chapeau*, to be made a cardinal; (*fam.*) *travailler du chapeau*, to talk through one's hat; *un coup de chapeau*, a bow.

chapeauter [ʃapo'te], *v.t.* To fit with a hat. *Femme bien chapeautée*, smartly hatted lady.

chapelain [ʃa'plɛ̃], *n.m.* Chaplain.

chapeler [ʃa'ple], *v.t.* To scrape the crust off (bread).

chapelet [ʃa'plɛ], *n.m.* Rosary, string of beads, beads; prayers recited to this; string (of objects), series; (*Arch. etc.*) chaplet; (*Hydraul.*) chain-pump. *Chapelet de bombes*, stick of bombs; *chapelet d'oignons*, string of onions; *défiler son chapelet*, to say all one has to say; *dire son chapelet*, to tell one's beads.

chapelier [ʃapə'lje], *a.* (*fem.* **chapelière** (1)) Who makes or sells hats.—*n.* Hatter, hat-manufacturer, hat-seller. **chapelière** (2), *n.f.* Saratoga trunk.

chapelle [ʃa'pɛl], *n.f.* Chapel; body of clergy, choristers, etc., serving this; coterie, school (of literature etc.); church plate; living; vault of an oven. *Chapelle ardente*, mortuary chapel; *faire chapelle*, (*Naut.*) to broach to; *maître de chapelle*, precentor; *soupapes en chapelle*, (*Motor.*) side valves; *tenir chapelle*, to attend divine service in state (of the Pope etc.).

chapellenie [ʃapɛl'ni], *n.f.* Chaplaincy.

chapellerie [ʃapɛl'ri], *n.f.* Hat-making; hat trade, shop, or business.

chapelure [ʃa'ply:r], *n.f.* Grated bread-crumbs, raspings.

chaperon [ʃa'prɔ̃], *n.m.* Hood; (*sch.*) professional vestment with shoulder-band; coping of a wall; (*fig.*) chaperon. *Le petit chaperon rouge*, Little Red Riding Hood. **chaperonner**, *v.t.* To cope a wall; to hood (a hawk); (*fig.*) to chaperon (a young girl).

chapier [ʃa'pje], *n.m.* Cope-bearer; precentor or priest with a cope; cope-stand or cup-board; cope-maker, cope-seller.

chapiteau [ʃapi'to], *n.m.* Capital (of column etc.); cornice, crest, top (of a press, mirror, etc.); head (of a still); apron (of a cannon); cap (of a fusee); big top (circus).

chapitral [ʃapi'tral], *a.* (*fem.* **-ale**, *pl.* **-aux**) Pertaining to a chapter (ecclesiastical council).

chapitre [ʃa'pitr], *n.m.* Chapter (of a book, of knights, of a cathedral); chapter (meeting); chapter-house; subject, matter of discourse, head, section, phase. *Aborder un chapitre délicat*, to touch on a risky subject; *avoir voix au chapitre*, to be qualified to express one's views; *en voilà assez sur ce chapitre*, that is quite enough on that score; *passons sur ce chapitre*, let us waive the subject.

chapitrer [ʃapi'tre], *v.t.* To reprimand, to rebuke, to lecture (someone).

chapon [ʃa'pɔ̃], *n.m.* Capon; sop in broth; vine-plant that has not yet borne fruit. *Chapon de Gascogne*, crust of bread rubbed with garlic (which is added to salad); *qui chapon mange chapon lui vient*, money begets money. **chaponnage**, *n.m.* Caponizing. **chaponneau**, *n.m.* Young capon. **chaponner**, *v.t.* To caponize. **chaponnière*, *n.f.* Stew pan (for capons).

chapoter [ʃapɔ'te], *v.t.* To plane (wood).

chapska [ʃap'ska], *n.m.* Lancer's cap.

chaptaliser [ʃaptali'ze], *v.t.* To add sugar to the must before fermentation. **chaptalisation**, *n.f.* The process of adding sugar to the must.

chaque [ʃak], *a.* Each, every. *À chaque jour suffit sa peine*, sufficient for the day is the evil thereof; *chaque pays a ses coutumes*, every country has its customs.

char [ʃa:r], *n.m.* Chariot, carriage, vehicle. *Char d'assaut*, (*Mil.*) tank; *les chars*, the armour; *char de triomphe*, triumphal car; *char funèbre*, hearse.

charabia [ʃara'bja], *n.m.* Auvergne patois; gibberish.

charade [ʃa'rad], *n.f.* Charade.

charançon [ʃarɑ̃'sɔ̃], *n.m.* Weevil. **charançonné**, *a.* (*fem.* **-ée**) (Of corn) weevilled.

charasse [ʃa'ras], *n.f.* Crate for packing china.

charbon [ʃar'bɔ̃], *n.m.* Charcoal; (*pl.*) embers, live coals; (*Agric.*) black rust; (*Path.*) anthrax; (*Chem.*) carbon. *Cave à charbon*, coal-cellar; *charbon ardent*, fire (glowing but not flaming) charcoal, live coals; *charbon de bois*, charcoal; *charbon (de terre)*, coal; *être sur des charbons ardents*, to be on tenterhooks; *manquer de charbon*, to be out of coals; *mine de charbon*, coal-mine; *une voie de charbon*, a sack of charcoal. **charbonnage**, *n.m.* Coal-mining; colliery; (*Naut.*) bunkering. **charbonnaille**, *n.f.* Small coal (in mines and factories). **charbonnée**, *n.f.* Piece of grilled meat; layer of charcoal in a lime-kiln; charcoal-drawing. **charbonner**, *v.t.* To carbonize; to char; to black with coal etc.; to besmut; (*Naut.*) to bunker.—*v.i.* To be carbonized. **se charbonner**, *v.r.* To be charred, to burn black. *Se charbonner le visage*, to black one's face. **charbonnerie**, *n.f.* Coal depôt; the Carbonari. **charbonnette**, *n.f.* Wood for making charcoal. **charbonneux**, *a.* (*fem.* **-euse**) Coaly; affected or infected with anthrax. **charbonnier**, *n.* (*fem.* **charbonnière**) Charcoal-burner; charcoal-seller; coal-man.—*n.m.* Coal-heaver; coal-shed, coal-hole; Carbonaro; coal-fish; (*Naut.*) collier. *La foi du charbonnier*, implicit faith; *charbonnier est maître chez soi*, a man's house is his castle.—*n.f.* Charcoal-kiln; coal-scuttle; (*Orn.*) great tit. *Petite charbonnière*, coal-tit.

charbouille [ʃar'bu:j], *n.f.* Smut (on grain).

charcuter [ʃarky'te], *v.t.* To hack and hew (meat); to hack, to mangle, (of a surgeon) to butcher. **charcuterie**, *n.f.* Pork-butcher's meat; pork-butcher's business or shop. **charcutier**, *n.m.* (*fem.* **charcutière**) Pork-butcher; (*colloq.*) clumsy surgeon, sawbones.

chardon [ʃar'dɔ̃], *n.m.* Thistle; spikes (on a wall or railing); (*fig.*) obstacles, pricks. *Bête à manger du chardon*, as silly as an ass; *chardon à foulon*, teasel; *chardon bénit*, knap-weed; *chardon bleu*, sea holly; *chardon étoilé*, star-thistle; *hérissé comme un chardon*, prickly as a porcupine; *chardon Roland* or *roulant* [PANICAUT].

chardonneret [ʃardɔn'rɛ], *n.m.* Goldfinch.

chardonnet [ʃardɔ'nɛ], *n.m.* Jamb of a sluice-gate.

chardonnette [ʃardɔ'nɛt] or **cardonnette**, *n.f.* Prickly artichoke, cardoon.

chardonnière [ʃardɔ'njɛ:r], *n.f.* Teasel-ground.

Charenton [ʃarɑ̃'tɔ̃], *n.m.* A suburb east of Paris where there is a lunatic asylum; *il est mûr pour Charenton*, now he's ripe for Bedlam.

charge [ʃarʒ], *n.f.* Pack, burden, weight; load, freight, encumbrance; expense, cost, charges; accusation, imputation, indictment; post, place, office, employment; directions, order, command, commission; care, trust, custody; charge, onset; signal to charge; charge (of a gun); (*fig.*) attempt, effort; caricature, pleasantry, joke. *À charge de*, upon condition that or provided that; *à charge de revanche*, provided that I may return the favour; *avoir de hautes charges*, to hold an important office; *cela est à ma charge*, I have to pay for that; *charge d'âmes*, cure of souls; *en avoir sa charge*, to have enough to carry; *enfants à charge*, dependent children; *être à charge à quelqu'un*, to be a burden upon someone; *être à la charge de quelqu'un*, to be employed or supported by a person, to be in a person's charge; *il faut prendre le bénéfice avec les charges*, we must take the good with the bad; *libre de toute charge*, free from all encumbrances; *mettre une batterie en charge*, to put a battery on charge; *navire de charge*, supply-ship; *on a donné trop de charge à ce mur*, this wall has been overloaded; *prendre charge*, to take in cargo; *prendre en charge*, to take under one's responsibility; *revenir à la charge*, to make a new attempt; *se démettre de sa charge*, to resign one's place or office; *sonner la charge*, to sound the charge; *témoin à charge*, witness for the prosecution.

chargé [ʃar'ʒɛ], *a.* (*fem.* **chargée**) Loaded, charged, laden, freighted; overloaded, encumbered, burdened; (*Print.*) foul (of proofs). *Chargé d'humidité*, saturated with moisture; *dés chargés*, loaded dice; *langue chargée*, coated tongue; *le temps est chargé*, the weather is overcast; *lettre chargée*, registered letter; *obus chargé*, live shell; *nuage chargé d'électricité*, thunder cloud.—*n.m.* Agent, minister, envoy. *Chargé d'affaires*, chargé d'affaires; *chargé de cours*, assistant-lecturer, deputy-professor.

*chargeant [ʃar'ʒɑ̃], *a.* (*fem.* **-geante**) Clogging, heavy (on the stomach).

chargement [ʃarʒə'mɑ̃], *n.m.* Cargo, lading, freight, shipment; bill of lading; load, waggon-load, cart-load; registered letter or registration (of a letter); charging (of a battery).

charger [ʃar'ʒe], *v.t.* To load, to charge; to burden, to clog, to overburden, to encumber; to impute, to charge with; to give a thing in charge to, to entrust with; to load (with insults etc.); to register (a letter); to charge (of troops etc.), to fall upon, to make an onset on; to load (a gun); to fill (a pipe etc.); to accuse; to set down to (an account); to enter in, to set down; to lay on; (*Paint. etc.*) to exaggerate, to make ridiculous; (of an actor) to overplay (a part); (*Naut.*) to lay (a ship) on her side. *Charger de coups*, to belabour; *charger l'estomac*, (of food) to lie heavy on the stomach; *charger une lettre*, to register a letter; *charger une chaudière*, to stoke a boiler; *charger un fusil*, to load a gun. **se charger**, *v.r.* To take upon oneself, to undertake; to become responsible for; to become overcast (of the weather); to burden oneself, to saddle oneself with (*de*); to charge each other. **chargeur**, *n.m.* Loader, shipper; stoker, fireman (of a furnace etc.); (*Naut.*) gunner responsible for loading; (*Artill.*) automatic loader; battery-charger; (*Phot. Cine.*) cassette.

chargeure [ʃar'ʒyːr], *n.f.* (*Her.*) Charge.

chariot [ʃa'rjo], *n.m.* Waggon, go-cart; (*Mach.*) truck, trolley; sliding-carriage, cradle, etc.; (*Am.*) freight car. *Chariot d'atterrissage*; undercarriage, landing gear; **chariot de guerre*, war chariot; *le grand chariot*, Charles's wain, Ursa Major; *le petit chariot*, Ursa Minor; *tour à chariot*, turning-lathe.

charioter [ʃarjo'te], *v.t.* To turn on a lathe.

charitable [ʃari'tabl], *a.* Charitable (*envers*). **charitablement**, *adv.* Charitably.

charité [ʃari'te], *n.f.* Charity; benevolence, alms, almsgiving. *Charité bien ordonnée commence par soi-même*, charity begins at home; *dame de charité*, district visitor; *demander la charité*, to beg; *faire la charité*, to give alms; *par pure charité*, out of mere charity; *sœur de charité*, sister of mercy.

charivari [ʃariva'ri], *n.m.* Rough music, mock serenade; hubbub, clatter, noise, uproar. **charivarique**, *a.* Discordant; noisy, uproarious. **charivariser**, *v.t.* To give rough music to; to create an uproar.

charivarieur (*fem.* **-euse**) or **charivariste**, *n.m.* Mock-musician; rioter, roysterer.

charlatan [ʃarla'tɑ̃], *n.m.* (*fem.* **-ane**) Charlatan, mountebank, impostor (especially in medicine), quack. **charlatanerie**, *n.f.* Quackery, charlatanry. **charlatanesque**, *a.* Charlatanic, quackish. **charlatanisme**, *n.m.* Quackery, charlatanism.

charlemagne [ʃarlə'maɲ], *n.m.* *Faire charlemagne*, to leave when winning (at cards).

Charles [ʃarl], *m.* Charles. *Charles le Téméraire*, Charles the Bold; *Charles-Quint*, Charles V (in Germany, I in Spain).

Charlot [ʃar'lo], *m.* Charlie.

charlot [ʃar'lo], *n.m.* (*Orn.*) Curlew; (*pop.*) the public executioner of Paris (18th cent.). (*Orn.*) *Charlot de plage*, purple sand-piper.

charlotte [ʃar'lɔt], *n.f.* Charlotte (pudding); woman's hat trimmed with ribbons and lace.

charmant [ʃar'mɑ̃], *a.* (*fem.* **-ante**) Charming, delightful, pleasing, attractive.

charme (1) [ʃarm], *n.m.* Charm; spell, enchantment; attraction; (*pl.*) charms, beauties (of a person). *Cela vous va comme un charme*, that fits you perfectly, splendidly, to a T; *faire du charme*, to put oneself out to be charming; *se porter comme un charme*, to be in perfect health; *sous le charme*, under the spell.

charme (2) [ʃarm], *n.m.* (*Bot.*) Hornbeam.

charmer [ʃar'me], *v.t.* To charm, to enchant, to bewitch, to fascinate, to captivate, to delight, to beguile, to while away. *Charmer la douleur*, to alleviate or soothe pain; *je suis charmé de vous voir*, I am delighted to see you. **charmeur**, *n.m.* (*fem.* **charmeuse** or ***charmeresse**) Charmer, enchanter; bewitching woman, enchantress. *Charmeur de serpents*, snake charmer.—*n.f.* (*Tex.*) Charmeuse.

charmille [ʃar'miːj], *n.f.* Hedge of young hornbeam; bower, arbour.

charnel [ʃar'nɛl], *a.* (*fem.* **-elle**) Carnal; sensual (person). **charnellement**, *adv.* Carnally.

charnier [ʃar'nje], *n.m.* Charnel-house, ossuary; *larder; (*Naut.*) drinking tank.

charnière [ʃar'njɛːr], *n.f.* Hinge; joint, articulation. (*fam.*) *Nom à charnière*, double-barrelled name. **charnon**, *n.m.* Knuckle of a hinge.

charnu [ʃar'ny], *a.* (*fem.* **charnue**) Fleshy, plump; pulpy (of fruits). ***charnure**, *n.f.* Flesh (the fleshy parts of the body collectively).

charogne [ʃa'rɔɲ], *n.f.* Carrion; (*pop.*) bad, putrid meat; blackguard, dirty beast; slut.

charpentage [ʃarpɑ̃'taːʒ], *n.m.* Carpentry.

charpente [ʃar'pɑ̃ːt], *n.f.* Frame, framework, structure; build (of a person). *Bois de charpente*, timber; *la charpente d'un roman*, the structure of a novel. **charpenté**, *a.* (*fem.* **-ée**) Built, framed, constructed. *Un homme bien charpenté*, a well-built man. **charpenter**, *v.t.* To square (timber); (*fig.*) to frame, to construct. **charpenterie**, *n.f.* Carpentry, carpenter's work or trade; timber-work, timber-yard (of dock-yards). **charpentier**, *n.m.* Carpenter; ship-carpenter, shipwright. **charpentière**, *n.f.* Borer (insect).

charpi [ʃar'pi], *n.m.* Cooper's block.

charpie [ʃar'pi], *n.f.* Lint. *En charpie*, boiled to rags (of meat); *faire de la charpie*, to shred linen.

charquer [ʃar'ke], *v.t.* To desiccate (meat) for preserving.

charrée [ʃa're], *n.f.* Buck-ashes; lye.

charretée [ʃar'te], *n.f.* Cart-load.

charretier [ʃar'tje], *n.m.* (*fem.* **-ière**) Carter, waggoner. *Il n'y a si bon charretier qui ne verse*, it's a good horse that never stumbles; *jurer comme un charretier*, to swear like a trooper.—*a.* Passable for carts etc. *Chemin charretier*, cart-road; *voie charretière*, track (space between the two wheels of a cart), carriage-way.

charretin [ʃar'tɛ̃] or **charreton**, *n.m.* Truck; flat cart.

charrette [ʃa'rɛt], *n.f.* Cart. *Charrette à bras*, hand-cart, barrow; *charrette anglaise*, trap; (*fam.*) *il est la cinquième roue de la charrette*, he counts for nothing. **charretterie**, *n.f.* Cart-shed.

charriable [ʃa'rjabl], *a.* Transportable, carriageable. **charriage**, *n.m.* Cartage; haulage; drifting of ice.

charrier (1) [ʃa'rje], *v.t.* To cart, to convey in a cart; to carry along.—*v.i.* To drift (of ice), to scud (of clouds), (*slang*) to exaggerate, to poke fun at. *La rivière charrie*, the river is filled with drift-ice.

charrier (2) [ʃa'rje], *n.m.* Bucking-cloth.

charrière [ʃa'rjɛːr], *n.f.* Cart-track.

charroi [ʃa'rwa], *n.m.* Cartage, waggonage; (*Mil.*) train, transport.

charron [ʃa'rɔ̃], *n.m.* Wheelwright. **charronnage**, *n.m.* Wheelwright's work. **charronnerie**, *n.f.* Wheelwright's business.

charroyer [ʃarwa'je], *v.t. irr.* (*conjug. like* ABOYER) To cart (heavy things). **charroyeur**, *n.m.* Carter, waggoner, carrier.

charrue [ʃa'ry], *n.f.* Plough. (C) *Charrue à neige*, snow-plough; *cheval de charrue*, plough-horse, cart-horse; (*fig.*) clod-hopper; *mettre la charrue devant les bœufs*, to put the cart before the horse; *passer la charrue sur*, to plough; *tirer la charrue*, to drudge, to have a hard life of it.

charruage [ʃary'aːʒ], *n.m.* Ploughing.

charte [ʃart], *n.f.* Charter. *Charte-partie*, charter-party; *la grande charte*, Magna Charta; *École des chartes* (in Paris), school of palaeography. *La Charte de l'Atlantique*, The Atlantic Charter.

chartil [ʃar'ti], *n.m.* Harvest-waggon; cart-shed, farm-shed, etc.

chartisme [ʃar'tism], *n.m.* Chartism. **chartiste**, *n.m.* (1) Chartist. (2) (former) student of the *École des chartes*.

*****chartre** [ʃartr], *n.f.* Prison. *Tenir quelqu'un en chartre privée*, to detain someone illegally.

chartré [ʃar'tre], *a.* (*fem.* **chartrée**) Chartered, privileged under charter.

chartreuse [ʃar'trøːz], *n.f.* Carthusian monastery or convent; Carthusian nun; isolated country-house or college; chartreuse (liqueur).

chartreux [ʃar'trø], *n.m.* Carthusian friar; cat of a bluish-grey colour.

chartrier [ʃartri'e], *n.m.* Keeper of charters; archives, collection of charters; muniment room.

Charybde [ka'ribd], *n.m.* Charybdis. *Tomber de Charybde en Scylla*, to jump out of the frying-pan into the fire.

chas [ʃɑ], *n.m.* Eye (of a needle); plumb; weaver's starch.

chasme [kasm], *n.m.* Chasm.

chassable [ʃa'sabl], *a.* That may be hunted, runnable (of stags etc.); that may be expelled.

châsse [ʃɑːs], *n.f.* Reliquary, shrine; frame mounting; check (of a balance); *pl.* (*slang*) eyes.

chasse (1) [ʃas], *n.f.* Hunting; the hunt, the chase; a chase, park, or preserve for hunting; game, sport, bag; the hunt (huntsmen, dogs, etc.); pursuit (especially of a ship); room, space; play (of machinery etc.); scour (of water); flush (of a w.c.). *Avoir droit de chasse*, to have the right to hunt or shoot; *bonne chasse!* good sport! *chasse à courre*, hunting; *chasse au lévrier*, coursing; *chasse au tir*, shooting; *chasse au vol* or *chasse aux oiseaux*, fowling; *chasse aux flambeaux*, bat-fowling; *chasse gardée*, game preserve; *donner la chasse à*, to pursue; *peloton de chasse*, (*Mil.*) hard drill as a punishment; *permis de chasse*, shooting-licence; *prendre .·chasse*, (*Naut.*) to sheer off; *un garde-chasse*, a game-keeper.

chasse (2) [ʃas], *n.f.* Tool, of various forms, used (by coopers etc.) for breaking open, breaking, etc.

chassé [ʃa'se], *n.m.* Chassé (a step in dancing).

[In the following compounds **chasse** is *inv.*]

chasse-avant [ʃasa'vɑ̃], *n.m.* Overseer, foreman.

chasse-bondieu [ʃasbɔ̃'djø], *n.m.* Punch to drive a wedge into a log.

chasse-clous, *n.m.* Brad punch, nail drawer.

chasse-cousin(s) [ʃasku'zɛ̃], *n.m.* Paltry dinner, bad wine; cold shoulder, poor reception.

chassé-croisé [ʃasekrwa'ze], *n.m.* (*pl.* **chassés-croisés**) (*Dancing*) A dance step; (*fig.*) a series of moves or changes that end in nothing; a reciprocal change of office or situation. *Faire un chassé-croisé*, to exchange places.

chasse-goupille(s) [ʃasgu'piːj], *n.m.* Steel tool for extracting pins.

chasselas [ʃas'la], *n.m.* Table grapes.

chasse-marée [ʃasma're], *n.m.* Fish-cart; driver of a fish-cart; three-masted coasting-vessel.

chasse-mouches [ʃas'muʃ], *n.m.* A form of fan; fly-swatter; fly-net (for horses).

chasse-neige [ʃas'nɛːʒ], *n.m.* Snow-plough.

chasse-pierre(s) [ʃas'pjɛːr], *n.m.* (*Rail.*) Guard-iron, cow-catcher.

chasse-pointe(s) [ʃas'pwɛ̃t], *n.m.* Punch for driving rivets etc.

*****chassepot** [ʃas'po], *n.m.* Chassepot (breech-loading rifle in use in the French army 1866–74).

chasse-punaise [ʃaspy'nɛːz], *n.f.* (*pl.* **chasse-punaise(s)**) (*pop.*) Bugbane.

chasser [ʃa'se], *v.t.* To hunt; to chase, to pursue; to drive, to drive in (a nail etc.); to expel, to turn out, to drive away, to dispel, to dissipate, to dislodge, to discharge, to dismiss, to banish; to drive forward, to propel. *Chasser la terre*, (*Naut.*)

to reconnoitre or look out for the coast; *chasser le mauvais air*, to ventilate; *chasser un clou*, to drive in a nail; *chasser un domestique*, to dismiss or discharge a servant; *chassez le naturel, il revient au galop*, what's bred in the bone comes out in the flesh; *ne pas chasser deux lièvres à la fois*, not to have too many irons in the fire; *se faire chasser*, to get sent away or dismissed.—*v.i.* To go shooting or hunting; to roll along easily, to slip, to glide along without taking hold, (*Motor.*) to skid; to go, come, or to drive (of clouds, wind, rain, etc.); (*Print.*) to overrun, to drive out; (*fig.*) to take up more room (of characters). *Chasser à courre*, to hunt; *chasser au lièvre*, to course; *chasser au faucon*, to hawk; *chasser au fusil*, to shoot; *chasser de race*, to be a chip of the old block, to run in the blood; *chasser sur les terres d'autrui*, to poach on someone else's preserves; *chasser sur son ancre*, to drag the anchor; *il aime à chasser au plat*, he prefers eating game to shooting it. **se chasser**, *v.r.* To drive one another away, to expel each other; to be hunted. **chasseresse**, *n.f.* Huntress, sportswoman.

chasse-rivet(s) [ʃasri'vɛ], *n.m. inv.* Coppersmith's riveting tool.

chasse-roue(s) [ʃas'ru], *n.m. inv.* Guard-iron for protecting walls etc. from damage by wheels.

chasseur [ʃa'sœːr], *n.* (*fem.* **chasseuse**) Hunter or huntress, sportsman or sportswoman.—*n.m.* Page-boy, buttons; commissionnaire; light infantry soldier; (*Av.*) fighter; [CHASSERESSE]. *Chasseurs à cheval*, (*Mil.*) light cavalry.—*a.* Fond of or given to hunting, chasing, pursuing.

chassie [ʃa'si], *n.f.* Gum on the edge of the eyelids, bleanedness. **chassieux**, *a.* (*fem.* **-ieuse**) Blear-eyed, rheumy-eyed.

châssis [ʃa'si], *n.m.* Case, frame, framework; window-sash; garden-frame; printer's chase; (*Motor.*) chassis, under-frame; (*Theat.*) flat for scenery. *Châssis dormant*, the fixed part of a window-frame; *châssis à guillotine*, sash-window; *châssis de jardin*, garden-frame, glass-frame; *châssis d'imprimerie*, printer's chase; *châssis mobile*, movable sash; *châssis-presse*, (*Phot.*) printing-frame.

chassoir [ʃa'swaːr], *n.m.* Driver (tool).

chaste [ʃast], *a.* Chaste, continent; pure, virtuous; refined, correct (of style). **chastement**, *adv.* Chastely, purely, virtuously. **chasteté**, *n.f.* Chastity, continence, purity.

chasuble [ʃa'zybl], *n.f.* Chasuble. **chasublerie**, *n.f.* Church-vestments, church-furniture. **chasublier**, *n.m.* (*fem.* **-ière**) Church-ornament maker, church-furnisher.

chat [ʃa], *n.m.* (*fem.* **chatte**) Cat; (*colloq.*) puss, pussy-cat; darling, dear little thing; (*Naut.*) cat. *À bon chat bon rat*, set a thief to catch a thief, diamond cut diamond; *appeler un chat un chat*, to call a spade a spade, not to mince matters; *avoir un chat dans la gorge*, to have a frog in one's throat (of singers); *ces gens vivent comme chien et chat*, these people live a cat-and-dog life; *chat à neuf queues*, cat-o'-nine-tails; *chat bon aux souris*, good mouser; *chat échaudé craint l'eau froide*, a burnt child dreads the fire; once bitten, twice shy; *chat en poche*, a pig in a poke; *chat*

marin, cat-fish; *chat musqué*, civet, musk-cat; (*C*) *chat sauvage*, raccoon; *comme un chat sur braise*, like a cat on hot bricks; *herbe aux chats*, cat mint; *il n'y a pas là de quoi fouetter un chat*, it is a mere trifle; *il n'y a pas un chat*, there is not a living soul; *jouer à chat* or *au chat*, to play tag; *la nuit tous les chats sont gris*, all cats are grey in the dark; *le chat parti, les souris dansent*, when the cat is away the mice will play; *le mou est pour les chats*, let each have his own; *mon petit chat* or *ma chatte*, my dear, my darling; *n'éveillez pas le chat qui dort*, let sleeping dogs lie; *non, c'est le chat!* no, it's only the cat (or Mr. Nobody); *nous avons d'autres chats à fouetter*, we have other fish to fry; *petit chat*, kitten; *retomber comme un chat sur ses pattes*, to fall on one's feet; *sabbat de chat* or *musique de chat*, caterwauling; *trou du chat*, (*Naut.*) lubber's hole. *Le Chat Botté*, Puss in Boots.

châtaigne [ʃa'tɛɲ], *n.f.* Chestnut; (*slang*) a smack, a blow. *Châtaigne amère*, horse-chestnut; *châtaigne d'eau*, water-caltrops. **châtaigneraie**, *n.f.* Chestnut-grove. **châtaignier**, *n.m.* Chestnut-tree. **châtain**, *a. inv.* Chestnut, nut-brown, auburn.—*n.m.* Chestnut colour; an auburn- or chestnut-haired man. *Châtain clair*, light auburn.

chataire [CATAIRE (1) and (2)].

chat-cervier [ʃaser'vje], *n.m.* (*pl.* **chats-cerviers**) Lynx.

château [ʃa'to], *n.m.* (*pl.* **châteaux**) Castle, feudal fortress, stronghold; country-seat, mansion, hall, or palace. *Château d'eau*, water-tower; *château de cartes*, house of cards; *château fort*, medieval citadel; *château seigneurial*, baronial hall; *faire des châteaux en Espagne*, to build castles in the air; *la vie de château*, country-house life.

châteaubriant [ʃatobri'ã], *n.m.* Large grilled rump-steak.

châtelain [ʃa'tlɛ̃], *n.m.* (*fem.* **châtelaine**) Lord or lady of a manor, squire or squire's wife.—*n.f.* Chatelaine; key-chain.

châtelé [ʃa'tle], *a.* (*fem.* **-ée**) (*Her.*) Turreted.

***châtelet** [ʃa'tlɛ], *n.m.* Small castle; a former prison or law-court in Paris.

châtellenie [ʃatɛl'ni], *n.f.* Castellany, castle-ward.

chat-huant [ʃa'ɥɑ̃], *n.m.* (*pl.* **chats-huants**) Tawny or wood owl.

châtiable [ʃa'tjabl], *a.* Chastisable, punishable.

châtié [ʃa'tje], *a.* (*fem.* **châtiée**) Polished (of the style of a writer).

châtier [ʃa'tje], *v.t.* To chastise, to punish, to flog; (*fig.*) to correct, to chasten, to purify. *Châtier une pièce de vers*, to polish a piece of poetry; *qui aime bien, châtie bien*, spare the rod and spoil the child.

chatière [ʃa'tjɛːr], *n.f.* Cat's hole (in door etc.).

châtieur [ʃa'tjœːr], *n.m.* Chastiser.

châtiment [ʃati'mã], *n.m.* Chastisement, punishment, castigation; (*fig.*) correction, chastening.

chatoiement or **chatoîment** [ʃatwa'mã], *n.m.* Play of colours, changing lustre (as of shot-silk, opals, etc.).

chaton (1) [ʃa'tɔ̃], *n.m.* Kitten; catkin. **chatonner**, *v.i.* To kitten.

chaton (2) [ʃa'tɔ̃], *n.m.*　Setting of a gem; a stone in a setting. **chatonner**, *v.r.*　To set (a stone).

chatouillant [ʃatu'jɑ̃], *a.* (*fem.* **-ante**) Tickling; (*fig.*) pleasing, flattering. **chatouillement**, *n.m.*　Tickling, titillation.

chatouiller [ʃatu'je], *v.t.*　To tickle, to titillate; (*fig.*) to please, to gratify, to flatter, to excite, to arouse; to touch a horse lightly with the spur. **chatouilleux**, *a.* (*fem.* **-euse**) Ticklish; (*fig.*) susceptible, delicate, touchy.

chatoyant [ʃatwa'jɑ̃], *a.* (*fem.* **-ante**) Shot, glistening (of colours etc.). **chatoyer**, *v.i. irr.* (*conjugated like* ABOYER) To shimmer, to glisten, to play (of colours); (of style) to be florid, colourful.

chat-pard [ʃa'paːr], *n.m.* (*pl.* **chats-pards**) Mountain-cat (Portuguese lynx).

châtré [ʃa'tre], *a.* (*fem.* **-ée**) Emasculate, castrated.—*n.m.* Eunuch. *Voix de châtré*, falsetto voice.

châtrer [ʃa'tre], *v.t.*　To castrate, to geld; to take away the honey and wax from a bee-hive; (*Hort. etc.*) to lop, to prune; (*fig.*) to expurgate, to curtail, to retrench, to mutilate. **châtreur**, *n.m.* (*fem.* **-euse**) Gelder.

chatte [CHAT].

chattée [ʃa'te], *n.f.*　Litter of kittens.

chattemite [ʃat'mit], *n.f.*　Demure-looking person; sycophant. *Faire la chattemite*, to assume smooth voice and gentle manners; (*fam.*) to toady (to).

chattepeleuse [ʃatp'løz], *n.f.* (sometimes **chattepelouse**) Green (or processionary) caterpillar.

chatter [ʃa'te], *v.i.*　To kitten.

chatterie [ʃat'ri], *n.f.*　Playfulness, pretty or coaxing way; wheedling caress; (*pl.*) dainties, titbits.

chat-tigre [ʃa'tigr], *n.m.* (*pl.* **chats-tigres**) Tiger-cat.

chatterton [ʃater'tɔ̃], *n.m.*　Insulating tape.

chaud [ʃo], *a.* (*fem.* **chaude** (1)) Hot, warm, burning, glowing; (*fig.*) ardent, fervent, fervid, animated, lively, brisk; zealous, eager; hasty, hot-headed, passionate; interesting, fresh (of news etc.); (*slang*) too dear. *Jouer à la main chaude*, to play hot cockles; *avoir la main chaude*, to keep on winning (at cards etc.); *avoir la tête chaude*, to be passionate; *fièvre chaude*, violent fever; *mains froides, chaudes amours*, cold hands, warm heart; *il faut battre le fer pendant qu'il est chaud*, strike while the iron is hot, make hay while the sun shines; *l'action fut chaude*, (*Mil.*) the engagement was a warm one; *manger chaud* or *boire chaud*, to eat or drink warm things; *pleurer à chaudes larmes*, to cry bitterly; *tout chaud*, piping hot.—*n.m.* Heat, warmth; a hot-head, a hot-headed person. *Avoir chaud*, to be hot; *cela ne fait ni chaud ni froid*, that is immaterial, that is neither here nor there; *cela ne lui fait ni chaud ni froid*, that is quite indifferent to him; *chaud, chaud!* quick, hurry! *il fait chaud*, it is hot; (*fam.*) *nous avons eu chaud!* we had a narrow escape! *souffrir le chaud et le froid*, to endure heat and cold; *tenir au chaud*, to keep in a warm place.—*adv.* Hot, warm. *Servir chaud*, to serve up hot; *marquer à chaud*, to brand; *opération à chaud*, (*Surg.*)

emergency operation. **chaude** (2), *n.f.*　A brisk fire for heating; (*Metal.*) heat, heating.

chaudeau [ʃo'do], *n.m.*　Egg-flip.

chaudement [ʃod'mɑ̃], *adv.*　Warmly; (*fig.*) quickly, eagerly, fiercely, hotly.

chaud-froid [ʃo'frwa], *n.m.*　Cold jellied chicken or game with mayonnaise.

chaudière [ʃo'djɛːr], *n.f.*　Copper; boiler (of a steam-engine etc.); (*C*) pail. (*C*) *Faire chaudière*, to prepare a meal, to eat (in a forest).

chaudron [ʃo'drɔ̃], *n.m.*　Cauldron. **chaudronnée**, *n.f.*　Cauldronful. **chaudronnerie**, *n.f.*　Coppersmith's or brazier's wares, shop, or business; boiler works. **chaudronnier**, *n.m.* (*fem.* **-ière**) Brazier, coppersmith, tinker.

chauffage [ʃo'faːʒ], *n.m.*　Heating, warming; stoking; fuel, firewood, firing; right of cutting firewood; (*pop.*) cramming. *Chauffage central*, central heating. **chauffe**, *n.f.* Furnace, heater, fire-box; distillation; (*Metal.*) heating. *Chambre de chauffe*, stoke-hole; *surface de chauffe*, heating surface. **chauffe-assiette**, *n.m.* (*pl.* **chauffe-assiettes**) Plate-warmer. **chauffe-bain**, *n.m.* (*pl.* **chauffe-bains**) Geyser. **chauffe-eau**, *n.m. inv.*　Water-heater. **chauffe-linge**, *n.m. inv.*　Clothes-horse, airing cup-board. **chauffe-lit**, *n.m.* (*pl.* **chauffe-lit** or **chauffe-lits**) Bed-warmer. **chauffe-pieds**, *n.m. inv.*　Foot-warmer.

chauffard [ʃo'far], *n.m.*　(*pop.*) Road-hog.

chauffer [ʃo'fe], *v.t.*　To heat, to warm; (*fig.*) to excite, to push on, to urge; (*sch.*) to cram. —*v.i.* To get warm, to grow hot; to be brewing; (*fig.*) to be urgent or pressing; to get up steam (of a steam-engine). *Ça chauffe*, (*colloq.*) things are getting hot; *ce n'est pas pour vous que le four chauffe*, there is nothing for you; *le moteur chauffe*, the engine is running hot. **se chauffer**, *v.r.*　To warm oneself. *Ne pas se chauffer du même bois*, not to be of the same way of thinking; *vous allez voir de quel bois je me chauffe!* you'll see what stuff I'm made of!

chaufferette [ʃo'frɛt], *n.f.*　Foot-warmer; chafing-dish. **chaufferie**, *n.f.*　Stoke-hold.

chauffeur [ʃo'fœːr], *n.m.*　Fireman; (*Motor.*) driver, chauffeur; (*sch.*) crammer. **chauffeuse**, *n.f.* Chauffeuse, paid woman driver; heater, warmer; low chair for the fireside.

***chauffoir** [ʃo'fwaːr], *n.m.*　Warming-room (in a monastery, public building, etc.); warm cloth (for rubbing patient down).

chaufour [ʃo'fuːr], *n.m.*　Lime-kiln. **chaufournerie**, *n.f.*　Lime-burning. **chaufournier**, *n.m.*　Lime-burner, lime-merchant.

chaulage [ʃo'laːʒ], *n.m.*　(*Agric.*) Liming. **chauler**, *v.t.*　To lime (soil); to steep wheat in lime-water previous to sowing it. **chaulier**, *n.m.* Lime-burner.

chaumage [DÉCHAUMAGE].

chaume [ʃoːm], *n.m.*　Stubble; stubble-field; thatch; (*Bot.*) culm, haulm. *Couvreur en chaume*, thatcher; *couvrir de chaume*, to thatch; *être né sous le chaume*, to be born in a cottage; *plein de chaume*, stubbly; **chaumer**, *v.t., v.i.* (*Agric.*) To cut stubble [DÉCHAUMER]. **chaumier**, *n.m.*　Stubble-cutter; thatcher; heap of stubble or straw. **chaumière**, *n.f.*　Thatched house, cottage. **chaumine**, *n.f.* Small thatched cottage, hut.

chaussant [ʃoˈsɑ̃], *a.* (*fem.* **chaussante**) Easy to put on, fitting (leg or foot).

chausse [ʃoːs], *n.f.* Shoulder-band (worn in universities etc.); straining-bag, filter; *(*pl.*) hose (covering the body from waist to foot), breeches, small-clothes. *C'est elle qui porte les chausses*, she is the one who wears the trousers; *tirer ses chausses*, to escape, to scamper away.

chaussée [ʃoˈse], *n.f.* Embankment, dike; causeway; (*Am.*) pavement; raised part of a street or highway; submarine shoal, reef. *Le rez-de-chaussée*, the ground floor.

chausse-pied [ʃosˈpje], *n.m.* (*pl.* **chausse-pieds**) Shoe-horn.

chausser [ʃoˈse], *v.t.* To put (shoes, boots, stockings) on; to shoe, to provide with shoes, boots, stockings, etc.; to make (the shoes etc.) for; to wear (such and such a size of boots etc.); (*colloq.*) to fit, to suit (well, ill, etc.); to get firmly fixed into one's head; (*Hort.*) to earth up (plants, trees). *Bien chaussé*, well-shod; *cet homme n'est pas aisé à chausser*, (*colloq.*) that man is not easily persuaded; *chausser le brodequin*, to put on the sock, to go on the comic stage, to compose or act comedy; *chausser le cothurne*, to put on the buskin, to go on the tragic stage, to write in an inflated style; *chausser les étriers*, to put one's feet in the stirrups; *être chaussé d'une opinion*, to be wedded to an opinion; *les cordonniers sont les plus mal chaussés*, nobody is worse shod than the shoemaker's wife.—*v.i.* To wear shoes (of a certain size). *Chausser du 40*, to take 7 (in shoes). **se chausser**, *v.r.* To put on one's shoes, boots, or stockings; (*fig.*) to become strongly wedded to an opinion. *chaussetier, *n.m.* Hosier.

chausse-trape [ʃosˈtrap], *n.f.* (*pl.* **chausse-trapes**) Snare, trap; (*Bot.*) star-thistle; (*fam.*) ruse.

chaussette [ʃoˈsɛt], *n.f.* Sock; under-stocking; half-hose. *Chaussettes russes*, (*Mil.*) foot-cloth.

chausseur [ʃoˈsœːr], *n.m.* Footwear dealer.

chausson [ʃoˈsɔ̃], *n.m.* Slipper; gym shoe (for rackets, fencing, etc.); bootee (for infants); savate (French method of boxing). *Chausson aux pommes*, apple turnover.

chaussure [ʃoˈsyːr], *n.f.* Foot-wear (shoes, slippers, boots, pumps, etc.). *Il a trouvé chaussure à son pied*, he has found what he wanted, he has met with his match.

chaut [ʃo], *v.impers.* [CHALOIR].

chauve [ʃoːv], *a.* Bald, bald-pated; denuded, hairless, bare (of a mountain etc.).—*n.m.* Bald-pate.

chauve-souris [ʃovsuˈri], *n.f.* (*pl.* **chauves-souris**) Bat, flittermouse.

chauvin [ʃoˈvɛ̃], *n.m.* Jingo, fanatical patriot. —*a.* Chauvinistic, jingoistic. **chauvinisme**, *n.m.* Chauvinism, jingoism. **chauviniste**, *a.* Chauvinistic.

*chauvir** [ʃoˈviːr], *v.i.* To prick up the ears (of horses, asses, mules, etc.).

chaux [ʃo], *n.f.* Lime; limestone. *Blanc* or *lait de chaux*, limewash, whitewash; *chaux éteinte*, slaked lime; *chaux hydraulique*, hydraulic lime; *chaux vive*, quicklime; *blanchir à la chaux, donner un blanc de chaux*, to give a coat of whitewash; *être fait à chaux et à ciment* or *à chaux et à sable*, to be well

and solidly built, (*fig.*) to have a sound constitution; *pierre à chaux*, limestone.

chavirable [ʃaviˈrabl], *a.* (*Naut.*) Cranky, tender.

chavirage [ʃaviˈraːʒ], *n.m.* Capsizing, upsetting.

chavirement [ʃavirˈmɑ̃], *n.m.* Upset, capsize.

chavirer [ʃaviˈre], *v.i.* To capsize, to upset; (*fig.*) to show the whites (of eyes).—*v.t.* To turn upside down, to upset.

chébec [ʃeˈbɛk], *n.m.* (*Naut.*) Xebeck.

chèche [ʃɛʃ], *n.m.* Scarf (worn by French troops in North Africa).

chéchia [ʃeˈʃja], *n.f.* Red tarboosh (as worn by Arabs and French troops in Africa).

cheddite [ʃeˈdit], *n.f.* Cheddite.

chef [ʃɛf], *n.m.* Chief, commander, conductor, master, principal, ringleader, foreman (of a jury); founder (of a dynasty etc.); head-cook, chef; (*Law*) head, count, bill (of indictment etc.); head (of family); *(Anat.*) head; (*Naut.*) end of a cable; (*Med.*) tail of a bandage; (*Her.*) chief (of a shield). *Au premier chef*, in the highest degree; *au second chef*, in the second degree; *chef d'accusation*, count of indictment, charge; *chef d'atelier*, foreman; *chef de bureau*, senior clerk; *chef de cabinet*, principal private secretary; *chef de clinique*, (*Med.*) head surgeon (in teaching hospital); *chef de cuisine*, head cook, chef; *chef d'équipe*, (*spt.*) team leader, captain; *chef de gare*, station master; *chef d'état-major*, chief of staff; *chef d'état major-général*, quartermaster-general; *chef de famille*, head of a house; *chef de file*, leading man (or ship); *chef de musique*, bandmaster; *chef de nage*, (*Naut.*) stroke; *chef d'orchestre*, conductor; *chef de parti*, party leader; *chef de pièce*, (*Naut.*) captain of a gun; *chef de rayon*, head of a department, floorwalker; *chef de service*, head of department; *chef de train*, railway guard; (*Am.*) conductor; *de son chef*, of one's own right or authority; *du chef de sa femme*, in right of his wife; *en chef*, in chief.

chef-d'œuvre [ʃeˈdœːvr], *n.m.* (*pl.* **chefs-d'œuvre**) Chef-d'œuvre, masterpiece.

cheftaine [ʃefˈtɛn], *n.f.* Scout-mistress.

chefferie [ʃefˈri], *n.f.* (*Mil.*) District of an officer of engineers.

chef-lieu [ʃefˈljø], *n.m.* (*pl.* **chefs-lieux**) Chief town, county seat.

chégros [ʃeˈgro], *n.m.* Shoemaker's thread or end, wax-end.

cheik [SCHEIK].

chéiroptère [CHIROPTÈRE].

chelem or **schelem** [ʃlɛm], *n.m. inv.* Slam (at cards). *Faire chelem*, to make a slam; *grand, petit chelem*, grand, little slam.

chélidoine [keliˈdwan], *n.f.* (*Bot.*) Celandine.

chélifère [keliˈfɛr], *n.m.* False scorpion.

chélonée [keloˈne], *n.f.* Chelone, turtle. **chélonien**, *n.m.* Chelonian.

chemin [ʃəˈmɛ̃], *n.m.* Way, road, path, track, route; passage, opening; (*fig.*) means; course; distance. *Aller son petit bonhomme de chemin*, to jog along; *aller toujours son chemin*, to pursue one's point; *à mi-chemin*, half-way; *chemin battu*, beaten track; *chemin couvert*, (*Fort.*) covered way, corridor; *chemin creux*, lane between high banks; *chemin de Croix*, (*Relig.*) the stations of the Cross; *chemin de fer*, railway, (*Am.*) railroad; *chemin *de halage*, tow-path; *chemin détourné*, by-road; *chemin de table*, table runner; *chemin de terre*, cart-track; *chemin de traverse*, side-road; *chemin de velours* or *de fleurs*, the primrose path; *chemin du paradis*, a strait and narrow path; *chemin faisant*, on the way; *chemins vicinaux* or *communaux*, village or local roads; *chemin très passant*, much-frequented thoroughfare; *être en bon chemin*, to be getting on well; *être toujours par voies et par chemins*, to be always gadding about; *faire beaucoup de chemin*, to go a great way or a long distance; *faire du chemin*, to make headway; *faire son chemin*, to thrive; *grand chemin*, highway, high-road; *le chemin du crime*, the highroad to crime; *le chemin des écoliers*, the longest way; *ne pas y aller par quatre chemins*, not to beat about the bush; *passez votre chemin*, go your way; *prendre le bon chemin*, to go the right way; *qui trop se hâte reste en chemin*, slow and sure wins the race; *rebrousser chemin*, to go back; *se mettre en chemin*, to set out on a journey; *suivre le droit chemin*, to live virtuously; *sur mon chemin*, in my path; *tous les chemins mènent à Rome*, there are more ways to heaven than one; all roads lead to Rome.

chemineau [ʃəmi'no], *n.m.* A tramp, a vagabond.

cheminée [ʃəmi'ne], *n.f.* Chimney, flue; smoke-stack, funnel; fire-place; chimney-piece, mantelpiece; nipple (of a percussion-gun); ventilating tube (to drain etc.). *Sous le manteau de la cheminée*, confidentially; *tuyau de cheminée*, chimney-flue.

cheminement [ʃəmin'mã], *n.m.* Walking, trudging along; (*Mil.*) approaches, progress (of siege operations); progress and processes (of thought).

cheminer [ʃəmi'ne], *v.i.* To walk, to tramp; to proceed; (*Mil.*) to approach gradually (towards the enemy's position).

cheminot [ʃəmi'no], *n.m.* Railwayman; plate-layer.

chemise [ʃə'miːz], *n.f.* Shirt, coat (of a mould); wrapper, cover, folder, case; (*Motor* etc.) jacket. *Chemise de nuit*, night-gown, night-shirt; *devant de chemise*, shirt-front; *en bras de chemise*, in shirt-sleeves; *être en chemise*, to have only one's shirt on; *passer une chemise*, to put on a shirt; *vendre jusqu'à sa chemise*, to sell the shirt off one's back. **chemiser**, *v.t.* To coat. **chemiserie**, *n.f.* Shirt-factory or warehouse; shirt-making; shirts. **chemisette**, *n.f.* Short-sleeved shirt (men). **chemisier**, *n.m.* (*fem.* **chemisière**) Shirt-maker or seller; lady's blouse.

chênaie [ʃɛ'nɛ], *n.f.* Oak-plantation, grove of oaks.

chenal [ʃə'nal], *n.m.* Channel, fairway, passage (of harbours etc.); mill-race.

chenapan [ʃəna'pã], *n.m.* Vagabond, good-for-nothing, scamp.

chêne [ʃɛːn], *n.m.* Oak; (*fig.*) a sturdy man. *Chêne vert*, ilex, holm oak. **chêneau**, *n.m.* Young oak. **chêne-liège**, *n.m.* (*pl.* **chênes-lièges**) Cork-tree, cork-oak.

chéneau [ʃe'no], *n.m.* (Eaves) gutter (on roof).

chenet [ʃə'nɛ], *n.m.* Fire-dog.

chènevière [ʃɛn'vjɛːr], *n.f.* Hemp-field. **chènevis**, *n.m.* Hemp-seed. **chènevotte**, *n.f.* Stalk (of hemp); (*Naut.*) junk.

chènevotter [ʃɛnvɔ'te], *v.i.* To send out weak shoots (of vines).

chenil [ʃə'ni], *n.m.* Dog-kennel; kennels; hovel.

chenille [ʃə'niːj], *n.f.* Caterpillar; kind of silk cord, chenille. *Tracteur à chenilles*, (*reg. trade name*) Caterpillar tractor; *laid comme une chenille*, ugly as sin. **chenillère**, *n.f.* Nest of caterpillars.

chenillette [ʃəni'jɛt], *n.f.* (*Mil.*) (*reg. trade name*) Caterpillar; scorpiurus.

chénopode [kenɔ'pɔd], *n.m.* (*Bot.*) Chenopodium; goose-foot.

chenu [ʃə'ny], *a.* (*fem.* **chenue**) Hoary, grey-headed; snow-capped. *Vin chenu*, good old wine.

cheptel [ʃə'tɛl, ʃɛp'tɛl], *n.m.* (*Law*) Lease of cattle; cattle leased out; the live-stock (of a country). *Cheptel mort*, buildings and agricultural implements leased out.

chèque [ʃɛk], *n.m.* Cheque; (*Am.*) check. *Chèque barré*, crossed cheque; *chèque non barré*, open cheque; *chèque sans provision*, bad (or dud) cheque; *carnet de chèques*, cheque-book; *encaisser un chèque*, to pay in a cheque; *toucher un chèque*, to cash a cheque.

chéquard [ʃe'kar], *n.m.* (*fam.*) Bribed politician.

chéquier [ʃe'kje], *n.m.* Cheque-book.

cher [ʃɛːr], *a.* (*fem.* **chère** (1)) Dear, beloved; precious; expensive. *La vie est chère à Paris*, living is dear in Paris; *rendre cher*, to endear. —*adv.* Dear, dearly, expensively. *Acheté* or *payé cher*, dear bought; *faire payer trop cher*, to ask too much for; *ne valoir pas cher*, not to be worth much.

cherché [ʃɛr'ʃe], *a.* (*fem.* **cherchée**) Affected, mannered.

chercher [ʃɛr'ʃe], *v.t.* To seek, to look for, to search for, to hunt for; to try to find; to try to obtain; to go or be directed towards; to endeavour, to try, to attempt; (*fig.*) to try to know or understand; to go to meet, to be on the look out for (trouble etc.). *Aller chercher*, to go and fetch, to go for; *allez me chercher la lettre*, go and bring me the letter; *chercher des yeux*, to look for; (*pop.*) *cela ira chercher dans les vingt mille francs*, this will fetch twenty thousand francs or so; *chercher midi à quatorze heures*, to seek for difficulties where there are none; *chercher noise* or *chercher querelle à*, to pick a quarrel with; *chercher quelqu'un par mer et par terre*, to look for someone high and low; *chercher une aiguille dans une botte de foin*, to look for a needle in a haystack; *cherchez la femme*, you will find a woman at the bottom of it; *chercher la petite bête*, to be over-critical; *envoyer chercher*, to send for; *il cherche un emploi*, he is on the look out for a situation; *je viendrai vous chercher*, I will come for you; *qui cherche, trouve*, he that seeks shall find; *vous l'avez bien cherché!* you asked for it! **se chercher**, *v.r.* To be in quest of each other. **chercheur**, *n.m.* (*fem.* **-euse**) Seeker, searcher, research worker. *Un esprit chercheur*, an inquiring or studious mind.

chère (1) [ʃɛːr] [CHER].

chère (2) [ʃɛːr], *n.f.* *Mien, air, demeanour; *welcome, reception (to one's table); entertainment, fare. *Bonne chère*, good cheer, good living; *faire bonne chère*, to live well; *faire maigre chère*, to live poorly; *homme de* *bonne chère*, a man who likes good living. **chèrement**, *adv.* Dearly, tenderly; dear, at a high price. *Vendre chèrement sa peau, (Mil.)* to die hard.

chéri [ʃeˈri], *a.* (*fem.* **chérie**) Beloved; cherished.—*n.* Darling, dearest.

chérif [ʃeˈrif], *n.m.* Shereef (Arabian prince).

chérir [ʃeˈriːr], *v.t.* To love dearly, to cherish, to be attached to. **chérissable**, *a.* Worthy of love.

chérot [ʃeˈro], *a.* (*pop.*) A bit too expensive.

cherté [ʃɛrˈte], *n.f.* Dearness, high price.

chérubin [ʃeryˈbɛ̃], *n.m.* Cherub. **chérubique**, *a.* Cherubic.

chervis or **chervi** [ʃɛrˈvi], *n.m.* Skirret, water-parsnip; caraway.

chester [ʃɛsˈter], *n.m.* Cheshire cheese.

chétif [ʃeˈtif], *a.* (*fem.* **chétive**) Puny, pitiful, paltry; mean, worthless. **chétivement**, *adv.* Meanly, pitifully, poorly, feebly. **chétiveté**, *n.f.* Puniness, paltriness, stuntedness, meanness.

chevaine [CHEVESNE].

cheval [ʃəˈval], *n.m.* (*pl.* **chevaux**) Horse; nag, steed; (*colloq.*) a powerful man, a brutal man. *Aller à cheval*, to ride; *c'est un vrai cheval à la besogne*, he is a glutton for work; *chair de cheval*, horse-flesh; *changer son cheval borgne contre un aveugle*, to make a bad bargain, to change for the worse; *cheval à bascule*, rocking-horse; *cheval au vert*, horse out at grass; *cheval d'amble*, ambling nag; *cheval d'attelage*, carriage-horse: *cheval de bât*, pack-horse, (*fig.*) drudge, lout; *cheval de bois*, wooden horse, (*Gym.*) vaulting horse; *chevaux de bois*, merry-go-round; *cheval de charrue* or *de labour*, plough-horse; *cheval de course*, race-horse; *cheval de frise*, cheval de frise; *cheval de gauche*, near-side horse; *cheval de louage*, horse for hire, livery horse; *cheval de bataille*, (*fig.*) hobby-horse, fad; *cheval de race* or *de pur sang*, blood-horse; *cheval de retour*, (*fig.*) lag, old offender, (or) ancient beauty; *cheval de selle, de chasse, de trait*, saddle-horse, hunter, draught-horse; *cheval de volée*, leader in a tandem; *cheval entier*, entire horse, stallion; *cheval fondu*, high cockalorum; *cheval hongre*, gelding; *cheval marin*, sea-horse, walrus; *cheval qui a beaucoup d'action*, high stepper; *cheval simulé*, (*Fowling*) stalking-horse; *être à cheval*, to be on horseback (or) to be astride; *être à cheval sur l'étiquette*, to be a stickler for etiquette; *fer à cheval*, horse-shoe; *fièvre de cheval*, violent fever; *il n'est si bon cheval qui ne bronche*, even a good horse may stumble; *l'art de monter à cheval*, horsemanship; *lettre à cheval*, a threatening letter; *monter sur ses grands chevaux*, to ride the high horse; *petit cheval*, nag, pony; *petits chevaux*, game of chance; donkey engine; *remède de cheval*, drastic remedy; *travail de cheval*, hard work.

cheval-arçons [ʃəvalarˈsɔ̃], *n.m.* Gymnastic vaulting-horse.

chevalement [ʃəvalˈmã], *n.m.* (*Build.*) Prop, stay, shore.

chevaler [ʃəvaˈle], *v.t.* To prop, to shore up.

chevaleresque [ʃəvalˈrɛsk], *a.* Chivalrous, knightly. **chevaleresquement**, *adv.* Chivalrously.

chevalerie [ʃəvalˈri], *n.f.* Knighthood, chivalry. *Chevalerie errante*, knight-errantry.

chevalet [ʃəvaˈlɛ], *n.m.* Easel; bridge (of a stringed instrument); horse for scraping hides on etc.; sawing-trestle or horse; buttress, prop, shore; clothes-horse, towel-horse. *Tableau de chevalet*, (*Paint.*) easel-painting.

chevalier (1) [ʃəvaˈlje], *n.m.* Knight; chevalier rider; knight (at chess); redshank. *Chevalier à pieds verts*, greenshank; *chevalier de la Légion d'Honneur*, knight of the Legion of Honour; *chevalier d'industrie*, one who lives by his wits, sharper; *chevalier errant*, knight-errant; *le chevalier de la Triste Figure*, Don Quixote; *se faire le chevalier de quelqu'un*, to stand up for someone. **chevalière**, *n.f.* Knight's lady; signet-ring.

chevalier (2) [ʃəvaˈlje], *n.m.* (*Orn.*) Sandpiper; redshank. *Chevalier arlequin*, spotted redshank; *chevalier gambette*, redshank; *chevalier guignette*, common sandpiper.

chevalin [ʃəvaˈlɛ̃], *a.* (*fem.* **chevaline**) Equine. *Boucherie chevaline*, horse butcher's shop.

cheval-vapeur [ʃəvalvaˈpœːr], *n.m.* (*pl.* **chevaux-vapeur**) Horse-power.

chevauchable [ʃəvoˈʃabl], *a.* Fit for horse-traffic.

chevauchant [ʃəvoˈʃã], *a.* (*fem.* **-ante**) Overlapping; (*Bot.*) equitant. **chevauchée**, *n.f.* Ride, excursion on horseback; circuit; cavalcade. **chevauchement**, *n.m.* Overlap or crossing of parts (tiles, wires); (*Surg.*) displacement of fractured bones. **chevaucher** [ʃəvoˈʃe], *v.i.* To ride on horseback; to be astride; to overlap, to be out of alignment; *v.t.* To ride on (a horse etc.). **chevaucheur**, *n.m.* Rider, horseman. **chevauchure**, *n.f.* Overlapping.

chevau-léger [ʃəvoleˈʒe], *n.m.* Light-horse-man; (*pl.*) light horse, light cavalry.

chevelu [ʃəˈvly], *a.* Hairy, long-haired; (*Bot.*) comose, fibrous. *Comète chevelue*, haired comet; *cuir chevelu*, scalp.—*n.m.* (*Bot.*) beard of the root.

chevelure [ʃəˈvlyːr], *n.f.* Hair, head of hair; fiery tresses; tail, of a comet. *La chevelure de Bérénice*, Berenice's hair (constellation).

chevesne [ʃəˈven], *n.m.* (*Ichth.*) Chub.

chevet [ʃəˈvɛ], *n.m.* Head (of a bed); bolster; pillow; bedside; (*Arch.*) apse with radiating chapels. **C'est son épée de chevet*, he is his trusty councillor, it is always his resource; *lampe, livre, table de chevet*, bed-side lamp, book, table; *veiller au chevet d'un malade*, to watch by someone's bedside.

chevêtre [ʃəˈvɛːtr], *n.m.* (*Carp.*) binding-joist; (*Surg.*) bandage to support the lower jaw.

chevêtrier [ʃəvetriˈe], *n.m.* Joist, beam.

cheveu [ʃəˈvø], *n.m.* (*pl.* **cheveux**) *Un cheveu*, a single hair; crack (in china); *les cheveux*, the hair (of the head); *cela fait dresser les cheveux sur la tête*, that makes one's hair stand on end; *cela ne tenait qu'à un cheveu*, it was a near thing; *cheveux d'ébène*, raven locks; *cheveux épars*, thin, scanty hair; *cheveux postiches*, false hair; *cheveux roux*, sandy hair; *couper un cheveu en quatre*, to split hairs; *en cheveux*, bare-headed (of women); *être à un cheveu de*, (*fam.*) to be within a hair's breadth of; *prendre l'occasion aux cheveux*, to take time by the forelock;

raser les cheveux, to shave the head; se faire des cheveux (blancs), (fam.) to worry, to be bored; se faire couper les cheveux, to have one's hair cut; se prendre aux cheveux, to take each other by the hair, (fig.) to quarrel, to fight; avoir mal aux cheveux, (fam.) to have a bit of a head, a hangover; tiré par les cheveux, far-fetched; tresse de cheveux, plait of hair; cheveux à la garçonne, a boyish crop; cheveux à la Jeanne d'Arc, bobbed hair.

chevillage [ʃəviˈjaːʒ], n.m. Fastening, pegging; bolts, pins, etc. (in a piece of construction).

chevillard [ʃəviˈjaːr], n.m. (slang) Wholesale meat-salesman (he buys carcasses hanging on the peg (cheville) in the abattoir).

cheville [ʃəˈviːj], n.f. Peg, pin, tree-nail, bolt; plug; botch, stopgap; ankle, ankle-bone; (poet. etc.) expletive. Cheville ouvrière, pole-bolt of a coach; (fig.) king-pin, mainspring of a party, affair, etc.; (fam.) être en cheville avec quelqu'un, to be in league with someone; trouver à chaque trou une cheville, to find a peg for every hole; vente à la cheville, sale (of meat) by the carcass; vous ne lui arrivez pas à la cheville, you are a pigmy compared with him.

cheviller [ʃəviˈje], v.t. To pin or fasten with a pin, peg, bolt, etc.; (fig.) to pad out (verses etc.). Des vers chevillés, padded verses; il a l'âme chevillée au corps, he has nine lives.—v.i. To pad.

chevillette [ʃəviˈjɛt], n.f. *Latch (of a door); key or peg (of a bookbinder's sewing-press). **chevilleur**, n.m. One who pegs (books etc.) together. **chevillot**, n.m. (Naut.) Belaying-pin. **chevillure**, n.f. Third branch of a deer's head.

cheviotte [ʃəˈvjɔt], n.f. Cheviot (tweed).

chèvre [ʃɛːvr], n.f. Goat, she-goat; crab, gin; saw-horse; jack; (Astron.) Capella. Prendre la chèvre, to take offence; ménager la chèvre et le chou, to run with the hare and hunt with the hounds; où la chèvre est attachée il faut qu'elle broute, one must cut one's clothes according to the cloth.

chevreau [ʃəˈvro], n.m. Kid (the animal or its skin).

chèvrefeuille [ʃɛvrəˈfœːj], n.m. Honeysuckle, woodbine. Chèvrefeuille des bois or des buissons, fly honeysuckle.

***chèvre-pied** [ʃɛvrəˈpje], a. (pl. chèvre-pieds) (Of satyrs) goat-footed.—n.m. Satyr.

chèvrerie [ʃɛvrəˈri], n.f. Goat-pen.

chevrette [ʃəˈvrɛt], n.f. Small goat; young roe; shrimp, prawn; trivet; small fire-dog.

chevretter [ʃəvrɛˈte], or **chevroter** v.i. To kid (of goats).

chevreuil [ʃəˈvrœːj], n.m. Roe, roe-deer.

chevrier [ʃəvriˈe], n.m. (fem. chevrière) Goat-herd; goat-girl.

chevrillard [ʃəvriˈjaːr], n.m. Fawn of roe-buck.

chevron [ʃəˈvrɔ̃], n.m. Rafter; chevron, stripe (on a soldier's sleeve); (Her.) chevron. **chevronnage**, n.m. Rafters, raftering. **chevronné**, a. (fem. -ée) (Her.) Chevroned; (fam.) experienced. Dents chevronnées, (Mech.) herring-bone teeth (of wheel). **chevronner**, v.t. To rafter; to stripe, to chevron.

chevrotain or **chevrotin** (1) [ʃəvrɔˈtɛ̃], n.m. Chevrotain; musk-deer.

chevrotant [ʃəvrɔˈtɑ̃], a. (fem. -ante) Quavering, tremulous. **chevrotement**, n.m. Tremulous motion, trembling (of the voice etc.).

chevroter (1) [CHEVRETTER].

chevroter (2) [ʃəvrɔˈte], v.i. To sing or speak in a tremulous voice.

chevrotin (1) [CHEVROTAIN].

chevrotin (2) [ʃəvrɔˈtɛ̃], n.m. Fawn of roe-deer; kid (leather).

chevrotine [ʃəvrɔˈtin], n.f. Buck-shot.

chez [ʃe], prep. At, to, in (the house, family, or country of); in, with, among; in the service of, at the time of, in the works of, (on letters) care of. Avoir un chez soi, to have a home of one's own; ce livre se trouve chez tous les libraires, this book is stocked by all booksellers; c'est chez lui une habitude, it is a habit with him; chacun est maître chez soi, every man is master in his own house; chez les auteurs romains, in the Latin authors; chez les Canadiens, among the Canadians; il n'y a pas de petit chez soi, home is home be it ever so humble; j'ai été chez vous, I have been at your house; je viens de chez ma mère, I have come from my mother's.

chiader [ʃjaˈde], v.t. and i. (sch. slang) To grind. **chiadeur**, a. and n. Grind.

chialer [ʃjɑˈle], v.i. (slang) To cry, to snivel.

chiasma [kjasˈma], n.m. (Anat.) Chiasm.

chiasme [kiˈasm], n.m. (Rhet.) Chiasmus.

chiasse [ʃjas], n.f. Dross, scum; dung (of flies); (slang) diarrhoea.

chiasser [ʃjaˈse], v.i. To funk, shrink in fear.

chibouque or **chibouk** [ʃiˈbuk], n.f. Chibouk (Turkish pipe).

chic [ʃik], n.m. Knack, style, chic, touch (in painting etc.); aplomb, ease and elegance. Il a du chic, there is something stylish about him; peint de chic, painted without model. —a. inv. Stylish, smart; (fam.) helpful. Un chic type, a decent sort; ce n'est pas chic, it is not very sporting, it is unfair; les gens chic, the smart set.—adv. Chic alors! Good! excellent!

chicane [ʃiˈkan], n.f. Cavil, evasion, quibble; chicanery, pettifogging, quirks of the law. Chercher chicane à quelqu'un, to pick a trumpery quarrel with someone; gens de chicane, pettifoggers. **chicaner**, v.i. To cavil, to quibble, to use tricks; to wrangle, to quarrel.—v.t. To quarrel or wrangle with. Chicaner le vent, (Naut.) to hug the wind. **chicanerie**, n.f. Chicanery, quibbling, cavilling. **chicaneur**, n.m. (fem. -euse) or **chicanier**, n.m. (fem. -ière) Barrator, caviller, pettifogger.—a. Litigious, cavilling, wrangling.

chiche (1) [ʃiʃ], a. Niggardly, stingy, parsimonious; (fig.) mean, contemptible. Être chiche de ses paroles, to be sparing of one's words.

chiche (2) [ʃiʃ], a. Pois chiches, chick-peas.

chiche (3) [ʃiʃ], int. (fam.) I bet you can't!

chichement [ʃiʃˈmɑ̃], adv. Penuriously, stingily, parsimoniously.

chichi [ʃiˈʃi], n.m. (fam.) Curls of false hair. (fig.) Faire des chichis, to have affected manners, to make a fuss, to make difficulties; to mince (in speaking); gens à chichis, affected, snobbish people.

chicon [ʃiˈkɔ̃], n.m. Cos lettuce.

chicorée [ʃikɔˈre], n.f. (1) Cichorium endiviva,

endive; (2) *Cichorium intybus* or *chicorée sauvage*, or *endive* or *witloof*, chicory, succory.
chicot [ʃi'ko], *n.m.* Stub or stump (of a tree); stump (of teeth). **chicote**, *n.f.* Whip (made of hippopotamus hide).
chicoter [ʃiko'te], *v.i.* (*pop.*) To wrangle, to trifle, to split hairs.
chicotin [ʃiko'tɛ̃], *n.m.* Bitter juice of aloes. *Amer comme chicotin*, as bitter as gall.
chien [ʃjɛ̃], *n.m.* (*fem.* **chienne**) Dog; (*contempt.*) hound, cur; push-cart, mineral-trolley; hammer, cock (of a gun or pistol). *Avoir d'autres chiens à fouetter*, to have other fish to fry; *avoir du chien*, to have pluck, (of a woman) to be attractive (although not beautiful); *bons chiens chassent de race*, like father like son; *c'est Saint-Roch et son chien*, they are like Darby and Joan, they are inseparable; *cette chienne est pleine*, that bitch is with pup; *chien courant*, beagle; *chien d'arrêt*, pointer; *chien d'attache*, watch-dog; *chien de berger*, sheep-dog; *chien de berger alsacien*, Alsatian; *chien de chasse*, sporting dog; *chien de ferme*, house-dog; *chien de mer*, dog-fish; *chien de race*, pedigree dog; *chien de salon* or *d'appartement*, lap-dog; *chien de Terre-neuve*, Newfoundland dog; *chien-loup*, wolf-dog; *chien métis*, half-bred dog, mongrel; *chien qui aboie ne mord pas*, his bark is worse than his bite; *chien savant*, dog trained to perform; *chien terrier*, terrier; *chien turc*, Barbary or Turkish dog; *chien volant*, tailless bat; *coiffure à la chien*, fringe; *donner* or *lâcher les chiens*, to let loose or cast off the dogs; *entre chien et loup*, in the dusk of the evening; *être comme un chien à l'attache*, to work like a galley slave; *être comme le chien du jardinier*, to be a dog in the manger; *être reçu comme un chien dans un jeu de quilles*, to be as welcome as a bull in a china-shop; *faire le chien couchant*, to creep and crouch and truckle; *ils s'accordent comme chien et chat*, they get on like cat and dog; *ils se regardent en chiens de faïence*, they stare menacingly at one another; *jeter sa langue aux chiens*, to give it up (of a riddle); *mener une vie de chien*, to lead a dog's life; *n'être pas bon à jeter aux chiens*, to be worthless; *quel temps de chien!* what miserable weather! *qui m'aime, aime mon chien*, love me, love my dog; *qui veut noyer son chien l'accuse de la rage*, give a dog a bad name and hang him; *rompre les chiens*, to call off the dogs, (*fig.*) to change the conversation; *se donner un mal de chien*, to give oneself a deal of trouble; *une meute de chiens*, a pack of hounds; *un petit* or *jeune chien*, a puppy, a whelp.—*a.* Doggish; harsh, stingy.
chienchien [ʃjɛ̃'ʃjɛ̃], *n.m.* (*fam.*) *Mon p'tit chienchien*, doggie; darling.
chiendent [ʃjɛ̃'dɑ̃], *n.m.* Couch-grass; (*pop.*) obstacle, difficulty, trouble. *Brosse en chiendent*, scrubbing brush.
chienlit [ʃiɑ̃'li], *n.m. inv.* Person who soils his bed; carnival mask; freak, guy.
chiennée [ʃje'ne], *n.f.* A litter of pups.
chienner [ʃje'ne], *v.i.* To whelp, to pup.
chiennerie [ʃjɛn'ri], *n.f.* Nastiness, meanness, trickery; utter shamelessness.
chier [ʃje], *v.i.* (*indecent*) To shit.
chiffe [ʃif], *n.f.* Poor stuff, rag; (*fig.*) weak, spineless person.

chiffon [ʃi'fɔ̃], *n.m.* Rag, scrap, bit; chiffon; frippery. *Parler chiffons*, to talk dress.
chiffonnage, *n.m.* Rumpled drapery, rumpling, crumpling. **chiffonné**, *a.* (*fem.* -ée) Crumpled, rumpled; pretty but irregular (of features). **chiffonner**, *v.t.* To rumple, to crumple, to tumble; (*colloq.*) to ruffle, to tease, to vex.—*v.i.* To be a rag-collector; (*colloq.*) to busy (oneself) with one's toilet and dress. **chiffonnerie**, *n.f.* Rag-pickers, rag-picking, rag-trade; rags; (*colloq.*) trifles. **chiffonnier**, *n.m.* (*fem.* -ière) Rag-picker; chiffonnier (kind of chest of drawers).
chiffrable [ʃi'frabl], *a.* Calculable. **chiffrage** or **chiffrement**, *n.m.* Figuring, figures; estimates, calculation; writing in cipher, coding.
chiffre [ʃifr], *n.m.* Figure, number; total amount, cipher, cryptogram; flourish of letters, monogram. *C'est un zéro en chiffre*, he is a mere cipher; *chiffre d'affaires*, turn-over; *chiffre périodique*, (*Arith.*) figure of the recurring period; *écrire en chiffre*, to write in cipher; *service du chiffre*, coding or cipher department. **chiffrer**, *v.i.* To cipher, to write in cipher.—*v.t.* To calculate, to tot up, to figure; to number (of music); to code. **chiffreur**, *n.m.* (*fem.* -euse) Reckoner, cipherer.
chignard [ʃi'naːr], *n.m.* (*colloq.*) Grumbler; blubberer. **chigner**, *v.i.* To snivel; to be always grumbling.
chignole [ʃi'nɔl], *n.f.* Ratchet drill; (*pop.*) old motor-car, 'bus'.
chignon [ʃi'nɔ̃], *n.m.* Chignon, coil of hair, 'bun'.
chimère [ʃi'mɛːr], *n.f.* Chimera; myth, idle fancy, vain imagination; (*Zool.*) chimera. **chimérique**, *a.* Chimerical, visionary, fantastical. **chimériquement**, *adv.* Chimerically.
chimie [ʃi'mi], *n.f.* Chemistry. *Chimie minérale*, inorganic chemistry. **chimico-**, *comb. form.* Chemico-. **chimico-physique**, *a.* Chemico-physical. **chimiothérapie**, *n.f.* Chemotherapy. **chimique**, *a.* Chemical. *Rayons chimiques*, (*Phot.*) actinic rays. **chimiquement**, *adv.* Chemically. **chimisme**, *n.m.* Chemism. **chimiste**, *n.m.* Chemist.
chimpanzé [ʃɛ̃pɑ̃'ze], *n.m.* Chimpanzee.
chinage [ʃi'naːʒ], *n.m.* Figuring, variegation (of stuffs); (*fam.*) begging, cadging; ragging.
chinchilla [ʃɛ̃ʃil'la], *n.m.* Chinchilla.
Chine [ʃin], **la**, *f.* China.
chiné [ʃi'ne], *a.* (*fem.* **chinée**) Variegated, figured (of stuffs); (*pop.*) *tabac chiné* or *tabac de Chine*, cadged tobacco.—*n.m.* Figuring, speckling, watering.
chiner [ʃi'ne], *v.t.* To colour differently, to water, to figure (stuffs); (*pop.*) to get by begging, to cadge; to pull somebody's leg; to run down. **chineur**, *n.m.* (*fem.* -euse) One who shadows or clouds (material); (*slang*) practical joker.
chinois [ʃi'nwa], *a.* and *n.* (*fem.* **chinoise**) Chinese.—*n.m.* *Un chinois*, a small green orange preserved in brandy. **chinoiserie**, *n.f.* Chinese thing, curio; (*fig.*) trick; red tape, unnecessary complication.
chiot [ʃjo], *n.m.* (*fam.*) Puppy.
chiottes [ʃjɔt], *n.f. pl.* (*pop.*) Latrines.

chiourme [ʃjurm], *n.f.* Convict-gang.
chipage [ʃi'paːʒ], *n.m.* Bating of two skins.
chiper [ʃi'pe], *v.t.* (*Tanning*) To tan (by *chipage*); (*colloq.*) to pilfer, to pinch.
chipette [ʃi'pɛt], *n.f.* Jot, bit, trifle. *Ne valoir pas chipette*, to be worth nothing.
chipeur [ʃi'pœːr], *n.m.* (*fem.* -**euse**) (*colloq.*) Pilferer, scrounger.
chipie [ʃi'pi], *n.f.* (*fam.*) Affected, bad-tempered woman; prude.
chipolata [ʃipɔla'ta], *n.f.* Onion stew; small sausage.
chipotage [ʃipɔ'taːʒ], *n.m.* Dawdling; disputing about trifles, haggling.
chipoter [ʃipɔ'te], *v.i.* To dally, to dawdle; to dispute about trifles, to haggle; to peck at a dish. **chipoterie**, *n.f.* Useless shuffling or chicane. **chipotier**, *n.m.* (*fem.* -**ière**) Trifler, dallier, shuffler.
chique [ʃik], *n.f.* Quid of tobacco; jigger (insect). (*pop.*) *Couper la chique à*, to cut somebody short, to nonplus him.
chiqué [ʃi'ke], *n.* and *a.* (*slang*) *C'est du chiqué*, it's a fake, it's all make-believe, a put-up job. *Faire du chiqué*, to put it on.
chiquement [ʃik'mã], *adv.* Smartly.
chiquenaude [ʃik'noːd], *n.f.* Flick. **chiquenauder**, *v.t.* To flick (with the finger).
chiquer [ʃi'ke], *v.i.* To chew tobacco.
chiquet [ʃi'ke], *n.m.*, or **chiquette** [ʃi'ket], *n.f.* Driblet, bit, shred.
chiqueur [ʃi'kœːr], *n.m.* Chewer of tobacco; pretender.
chirographaire [kirɔgra'fɛːr], *a.* (*Law*) In writing, on note of hand (of a creditor).
chirographe [kirɔ'graf], *n.m.* Chirograph. **chirographie**, *n.f.* Chirography. **chirographique**, *a.* Chirographic. **chiromancie**, *n.f.* Chiromancy, palmistry. **chiromancien**, *n.m.* (*fem.* -**ienne**) Chiromancer, palmist.
chiroptère [kirɔp'tɛːr], *n.m.* (*Zool.*) Cheiropter, bat.
chirurgical [ʃiryrʒi'kal], *a.* (*fem.* -**ale**, *pl.* -**aux**) Surgical. **chirurgicalement**, *adv.* Surgically.
chirurgie [ʃiryr'ʒi], *n.f.* Surgery. **chirurgien**, *n.m.* Surgeon. *Aide-chirurgien* (*pl.* aides-chirurgiens), assistant-surgeon. **chirurgique**, *a.* Surgical.
chiure [ʃjyːr], *n.f.* Fly-speck. *Marqué de chiures de mouches*, fly-blown.
chlamyde [kla'mid], *n.f.* (*Ant.,Bot.*) Chlamys.
chloral [klɔ'ral], *n.m.* Chloral. **chloralisme**, *n.m.* Chloralism.
chlorate [klɔ'rat], *n.m.* Chlorate.
chlore [klɔːr], *n.m.* (*Chem.*) Chlorine. (*Bot.*) *Chlora perfoliata*. **chloré**, *a.* (*fem.* -**ée**) Containing chlorine. **chloreux**, *a.* (*fem.* -**euse**) Chlorous.
chlorhydrate [klɔri'drat], *n.m.* (*Chem.*) Hydrochlorate. **chlorhydrique**, *a.* Hydrochloric.
chlorique [klɔ'rik], *a.* (*Chem.*) Chloric. **chlorite**, *n.f.* Chlorite.
chloroforme [klɔrɔ'fɔrm], *n.m.* Chloroform. **chloroformer**, *v.t.* To chloroform. **chloroformique**, *a.* Pertaining to chloroform. **chloroformisation**, *n.f.* Administration of chloroform.
chloromètre [klɔrɔ'mɛːtr], *n.m.* Chlorometer.

chlorophylle [klɔrɔ'fil], *n.f.* (*Bot.*) Chlorophyll.
chlorose [klɔ'roːz], *n.f.* (*Path.*) Chlorosis, green sickness; (*Bot.*) etiolation. **chlorotique**, *a.* Chlorotic.
chlorure [klɔ'ryːr], *n.m.* (*Chem.*) Chloride. **chlorurer**, *v.t.* To turn into chloride.
choc [ʃɔk], *n.m.* Shock, collision, blow, impact; clash, encounter; conflict, opposition. *Soutenir* or *supporter le choc*, to stand the shock; *troupes de choc*, shock troops.
chochotte [ʃɔ'ʃɔt], *n.f.* (*pop.*) Ducky, dearest.
chocolat [ʃɔkɔ'la], *n.m.* Chocolate. *Bâton de chocolat*, stick of chocolate. *a.* Chocolate-coloured. *Être chocolat*, (*slang*) to be cheated, deceived. **chocolaté**, *a.* (*fem.* -**ée**) Containing chocolate. **chocolaterie**, *n.f.* Chocolate-making or trade; chocolate-factory. **chocolatier**, *n.m.* (*fem.* -**ière** (1)) Chocolate-maker or seller. **chocolatière** (2), *n.f.* Chocolate-pot.
chœur [kœːr], *n.m.* Choir; chancel; (*Ant. and fig.*) chorus. *Chanter en chœur*, to sing in chorus; *enfant de chœur*, choir-boy, chorister.
choir [ʃwaːr], *v.i. irr.* (*p.p.* chu) To fall, to drop. *Laisser choir quelqu'un* (*fig.*), to drop somebody.
choisi [ʃwa'zi], *a.* (*fem.* **choisie**) Choice, select. *Poésies choisies*, selected poems.
choisir [ʃwa'ziːr], *v.t.* To choose (between or among); to make choice of, to single out, to select; to decide, to determine. *Il n'y a point à choisir*, there is no choice left.
choix [ʃwa], *n.m.* Choice, choosing, alternative; a choice, a selection; election, distinction. *Au choix*, all at one price; *avancement au choix*, promotion by selection; *avoir le choix forcé*, to have Hobson's choice; *des hommes de choix*, picked men; *des marchandises de choix*, first-quality articles; *n'avoir que l'embarras du choix*, to have only to choose; *par choix*, from choice; *sans choix*, indifferently.
cholagogue [kɔla'gɔg], *n.m.* and *a.* (*Med.*) Cholagogue. **cholédoque**, *a.* (*Anat.*) *Canal cholédoque*, hepatic duct.
choléra [kɔle'ra], *n.m.* Cholera. *Choléra nostras* or *faux choléra*, cholerine; (*pop.*) *un choléra*, a very disagreeable person or thing. **cholérine**, *n.f.* Cholerine. **cholérique**, *a.* Choleraic.—*n.* Person affected with cholera.
choliambe [kɔli'ãːb], *n.m.* Choliambic verse.
chômable [ʃo'mabl], *a.* (Of days, fêtes, etc.) To be kept as a holiday.
chômage [ʃo'maːʒ], *n.m.* Unemployment, enforced idleness; stoppage. *Le chômage d'un moulin*, the standing still of a mill; *indemnité, allocation de chômage*, unemployment benefit, 'dole'.
chômer [ʃo'me], *v.t.* To cease from work on (a particular day). *C'est un saint qu'on ne chôme pas*, he is a saint whose day no one observes; (*fig.*) he has lost his credit.—*v.i.* To cease work, to be doing nothing; to be at a standstill, to cease; to be short (*de*); (*Agric.*) to lie fallow. *Chômer de quelque chose*, to stand in need of something; *il chôme d'argent*, he is short of money; *il chôme de besogne*, he is short of work.
chômeur [ʃo'mœr], *n.m.* (*fem.* **chômeuse**) Idle worker, unemployed.
chondrine [kɔn'drin], *n.m.* Chondrine.

chondrite, *n.f.* Chondritis. **chondroïde,** *a.* Chondroid.

chope [ʃɔp], *n.f.* Large beer-glass; mug of beer.

choper [ʃɔ'pe], *v.t.* (*vulg.*) To catch, pick up (germ etc.); to arrest, 'pinch'.

chopine [ʃɔ'pin], *n.f.* Half-litre (a measure nearly equal to an English pint). **chopiner,** *v.i.* To tipple. **chopinette,** *n.f.* (*colloq.*) A little *chopine*.

chopper [ʃɔ'pe], *v.i.* To stumble, to trip (*contre*); to blunder.

choquant [ʃɔ'kɑ̃], *a.* (*fem.* **choquante**) Offensive, unpleasant, improper.

choquer [ʃɔ'ke], *v.t.* To shock, to strike or dash against; to displease, to grate upon, to offend, to give offence (to).—*v.i.* To strike glasses; to be offensive, to be shocking. **se choquer,** *v.r.* To take offence; to come into collision with each other.

choral [kɔ'ral], *a.* (*fem.* **-ale**) Choral.—*n.m.* (*pl.* **-als**) Choral(e).—*n.f.* Choral society.

chorée (1) [kɔ're], *n.f.* Chorea, St. Vitus's dance.

chorée (2) [TROCHÉE].

chorège [kɔ'rɛːʒ], *n.m.* (*Ant.*) Choragus. **chorégie,** *n.f.* Choregy. **chorégique,** *a.* Choragic.

chorégraphe [kɔre'graf], *n.m.* Choreographer. **chorégraphie,** *n.f.* Choreography. **chorégraphique,** *adj.* Choreographical.

choriambe [kɔ'rjɑ̃:b], *n.m.* (*Pros.*) Choriamb. **choriambique,** *a.* Choriambic.

chorion [kɔ'rjɔ̃], *n.m.* (*Anat.*) Chorion.

chorique [kɔ'rik], *a.* Choric.

choriste [kɔ'rist], *n.m.* Chorister; (*Theat.*) member of the chorus.

chorographe [kɔrɔ'graf], *n.m.* Chorographer. **chorographie,** *n.f.* Chorography. **chorographique,** *a.* Chorographic.

choroïde [kɔrɔ'id], *a.* and *n.f.* (*Anat.*) Choroid.

chorus [kɔ'ryːs], *n.m.* Chorus. *Faire chorus,* to sing the chorus; (*fig.*) to join in, to chime in, to approve, to agree.

chose [ʃoːz], *n.f.* Thing; matter, business, affair; (*Law*) chattel, property. *Bien des choses chez vous,* kind regards at home; *bien des choses à votre frère,* remember me to your brother; *ce n'est pas grand'chose,* it's no great matter; *c'est quelque chose,* it is something (of some importance); *c'est tout autre chose,* that is quite another thing; *être tout chose,* (*colloq.*) to be out of sorts, to feel queer; *je vois la chose,* I see how the matter stands; *la chose publique,* the commonwealth, State; *Monsieur chose,* Mr. What's-his-name; *ne pas faire les choses à demi,* not to do things by halves; *peu de chose,* a mere trifle or nothing; *quelque chose,* something, something important, anything; *quelque chose de,* something of a; *quelque chose de beau,* something fine; *voilà où en sont les choses,* that's how matters stand. *Choses de flot* or *de la mer,* (*Naut.*) flotsam and jetsam, wreckage. *Chose jugée* (*Law*), a case that has been decided.

chosette [ʃo'zɛt], *n.f.* Little thing.

chott [ʃɔt], *n.m.* Algerian salt lagoon.

chou [ʃu], *n.m.* (*pl.* **choux**) Cabbage, kale; *cole-wort; (*colloq.*) puff-paste; darling, dear; bow, rosette *Aller planter ses choux,* to retire into private life; *c'est bête comme chou,* it's simplicity itself, or it's idiotic; as stupid as an owl; *chou à la crème,* cream puff; *choux de Bruxelles,* Brussels sprouts; *choux brocolis,* broccoli; *chou de chien,* dog's mercury; *chou de Milan,* savoy; *chou frisé,* kale; *chou marin,* sea-kale; *chou palmiste,* palm cabbage; *chou pommé,* white-headed cabbage; *chou vert,* borecole; *choux blancs,* white-hearted cabbages; *être dans les choux,* (spt.) to be nowhere; *faire chou blanc,* to miss, to make a duck (at games); *feuille de chou,* third-rate newspaper; *il en fait ses choux gras,* he feathers his nest with it; *ménager la chèvre et le chou,* to have it both ways; *lui rentrer dans le chou,* (slang) to go for him; *mon petit chou,* my little darling; *pomme de chou,* cabbage-head; *tige* or *trognon de chou,* cabbage-stalk.

chouan [ʃwɑ̃], *n.m.* Chouan, Breton royalist insurgent (in French Revolution). **chouanner,** *v.i.* To carry on a guerrilla warfare (after the manner of the Chouans). **chouannerie,** *n.f.* The party of the Chouans (Vendean royalists); a rising of peasants.

choucas [ʃu'kɑ], *n.m.,* or **chouchette** [ʃu'ʃɛt], *n.f.* Jackdaw.

chouchou [ʃu'ʃu], *n.m.* (*fam.*) *Être le chouchou de quelqu'un,* to be someone's darling.

chouchouter [ʃuʃu'te], *v.t.* (*colloq.*) To pet, to cuddle, to spoil.

choucroute [ʃu'krut], *n.f.* Sauerkraut.

chouette (1) [ʃwɛt], *n.f.* Screech-owl, barn-owl.

chouette (2) [ʃwɛt], *int.* (*pop.*) Fine, marvellous.—*a.* Nice, fine, good of its kind.

chou-fleur [ʃu'flœːr], *n.m.* (*pl.* **choux-fleurs**) Cauliflower.

chou-navet [ʃuna've], *n.m.* (*pl.* **choux-navets**) Rape-colewort.

chouque [ʃuk] or **chouquet** [ʃu'kɛ], *n.m.* (*Naut.*) Block, cap (of mast-head).

chou-rave [ʃu'rav], *n.m.* (*pl.* **choux-raves**) Kohl-rabi, turnip-cabbage.

choyer [ʃwa'je], *v.t.* To take great care of, to be fond of, to pamper, to pet. **se choyer,** *v.r.* To pamper oneself.

chrême [krɛːm], *n.m.* Chrism, holy oil. **chrémeau,** *n.m.* Chrism-cloth.

chrestomathie [krɛstɔma'ti], *n.f.* Anthology.

chrétien [kre'tjɛ̃], *a.* and *n.* (*fem.* **chrétienne**) Christian. **chrétiennement,** *adv.* Like a Christian. **chrétienté,** *n.f.* Christendom.

*chrismal [kris'mal], *n.m.* (*Eccles.*) Chrismatory.

chrisme [krism], *n.m.* Christian symbol (on banners etc.); labarum.

christ [krist], *n.m.* Crucifix; painting or other representation of Christ crucified. **le Christ,** Jesus Christ.

christe-marine [kristma'rin], *n.f.* Samphire, sea-fennel.

christianisation [kristjani'zasjɔ̃], *n.f.* Christianization.

christianiser [kristjani'ze], *v.t.* To Christianize. **christianisme,** *n.m.* Christianity. **christologie,** *n.f.* Christology. **christologique,** *a.* Christological.

Christophe [kris'tɔf], *m.* Christopher.

chromage [kro'maːʒ], *n.m.* Chromium plating.

chromate [krɔ'mat], *n.m.* (*Chem.*) Chromate. **chromater** [CHROMER]. **chromatique,** *n.f.* (*Mus., Paint.*) Chromatics.—*a.* (*Chem. and*

Mus.) Chromatic. **chromatiser**, *v.t.* To make iridescent or chromatic. **chromatoscope**, *n.m.* Chromatoscope. **chromatotrope**, *n.m.* Chromatotrope.
chrome [kro:m], *n.m.* Chromium, chrome. **chromé** [kro:'me], *a.* (*fem.* -ée) Treated with chromium; chromium-plated. *Acier chromé*, chrome-steel. **chromer**, *v.t.* To combine with chromium; to chrome.
chromique [kro'mik], *a.* Chromic. **chromo** [*short for* CHROMOLITHOGRAPHIE]. **chromographe**, *n.m.* Chromograph. **chromolithographe**, *n.m.* Chromolithographer. **chromolithographie**, *n.f.* Chromolithography. **chromolithographique**, *a.* Chromolithographic. **chromosphère**, *n.m.* Chromosphere. **chromotypographie** or **chromotypie**, *n.f.* Chromotypography.
chromosome [kromo'zo:m], *n.m.* Chromosome.
chronicité [kroni'site], *n.f.* (*Med.*) Chronicity.
chronique (1) [kro'nik], *n.f.* Chronicle, history; news-summary, reports. *Chronique scandaleuse*, tittle-tattle, scandalous reports.
chronique (2) [kro'nik], *a.* (*Med.*) Chronic.
chroniquer [kroni'ke], *v.i.* To write chronicles. **chroniqueur**, *n.m.* Chronicler; newswriter, columnist.
chronogramme [krono'gram], *n.m.* Chronogram.
chronographe [krono'graf], *n.m.* Chronographer. **chronographie**, *n.f.* Chronography.
chronologie [kronolo'ʒi], *n.f.* Chronology. **chronologique**, *a.* Chronological. **chronologiquement**, *adv.* Chronologically. **chronologiste**, *n.m.* Chronologer.
chronométrage [kronome'tra:ʒ], *n.m.* Chronometric measurement, timing.
chronomètre [krono'mɛ:tr], *n.m.* Chronometer. **chronométrer**, *v.t.* To time. **chronométreur**, *n.m.* Time-keeper. **chronométrie**, *n.f.* Chronometry. **chronométrique**, *a.* Chronometric. **chronophotographie**, *n.f.* Chronophotography. **chronoscope**, *n.m.* Chronoscope.
chrysalide [kriza'lid], *n.f.* Chrysalis.
chrysanthème [krizã'tɛ:m], *n.m.* Chrysanthemum.
chrysobéril [krizobe'ril], *n.m.* Chrysoberyl.
chrysocale [krizo'kal], or **chrysocalque**, *n.m.* Pinchbeck.
chrysocolle [krizo'kol], *n.f.* Chrysocolla.
chrysolithe [krizo'lit], *n.f.* Chrysolite.
chrysoprase [krizo'pra:z], *n.f.* Chrysoprase.
chu, *p.p.* (*fem.* **chue**) [CHOIR].
chuchotement [ʃyʃot'mã], *n.m.* Whispering, whisper, rustling.
chuchoter [ʃyʃo'te], *v.i., v.t.* To whisper. **chuchoterie**, *n.f.* Whispering. **chuchoteur**, *n.m.* (*fem.* **chuchoteuse**) Whisperer.
chuintant [ʃyɛ̃'tã], *a.* Said of the fricative consonants [ʃ, ʒ].
chuintement [ʃyɛ̃'mã], *n.m.* Hooting (of owls); hissing; pronunciation of [ʃ, ʒ] instead of [s, z].
chuinter [ʃyɛ̃'te], *v.i.* To hoot (of owls); to hiss (of gas); to pronounce [ʃ, ʒ] instead of [s, z].
chut [ʃːt], *int.* and *n.m.* Hush!
chute [ʃyt], *n.f.* Fall, tumble, falling down; collapse, failure, overthrow, ruin, downfall;

catastrophe, disaster. *Chute d'eau*, waterfall, cataract; *chute des reins*, small of the back; *chute d'une voile*, (*Naut.*) depth of a sail; drop (of the principal square sails); *faire une chute (de cheval)*, to have a fall; (*Dress.*) *jeter les chutes*, to throw away the cuttings; *la chute du jour*, the close of day; *la chute du rideau*, the fall of the curtain; *la chute de la monarchie*, the fall of the monarchy.
chuter (1) [ʃy'te], *v.i.* (*fam.*) To fall, to tumble, to fail. *Chuter d'une levée*, (*Cards*) to be one trick down.
chuter (2) [ʃy'te], *v.t.* To cry *chut!* (hush!) to.
chyle [ʃil], *n.m.* Chyle. **chyleux**, *a.* Chylous. **chylifère**, *a.* Chyliferous. **chylification**, *n.f.* Chylification. **chylifier**, *v.t.* To chylify.
chyme [ʃim], *n.m.* Chyme. **chymification**, *n.f.* Chymification. **chymifier**, *v.t.* To chymify.
Chypre [ʃipr], *f.* Cyprus.
ci (1) [si], *adv.* (*contr.* of *ici* (here), with compounds). *Celui-ci est meilleur que celui-là*, this one is better than that; *cet homme-ci*, this man; *ci-après*, hereafter; *ci-contre*, on the other side, opposite; *ci-dessous*, below; *ci-dessus*, above; *ci-devant*, before, formerly, ex-, former; *ci-gît*, here lies; *ci-inclus*, *ci-joint*, subjoined, herewith; *les ci-devant* (*nobles*), the royalists, the aristocracy; *par-ci, par-là*, here and there, off and on; *de-ci de-là*, on all sides, in every direction.
ci (2) [si], *dem. pron.* (*fam.*) *Comme ci, comme ça*, so so.
cible [sibl], *n.f.* Target, mark; (*fig.*) object, aim, purpose.
ciboire [si'bwa:r], *n.m.* Ciborium (sacred vase), pyx. **ciborium**, *n.m.* (*Arch.*) Ciborium (canopy).
ciboule [si'bul], *n.f.* Stone-leek, Welsh onion.
ciboulette [CIVETTE (1)].
ciboulot [sibu'lo], *n.m.* (*vulg.*) Noddle, nut (head).
cicatrice [sika'tris], *n.f.* Scar, seam, mark.
cicatriciel, *a.* (*fem.* -ielle) Cicatricial. **cicatricule**, *n.f.* Cicatricule. **cicatrisable**, *a.* That will cicatrize. **cicatrisant**, *a.* (*fem.* -ante) Cicatrizing. **cicatrisation**, *n.f.* Cicatrization. **cicatriser**, *v.t.* To cicatrize; to close, to heal up; (*fig.*) to calm, to heal. **se cicatriser**, *v.r.* To skin over, to heal up.
cicéro [sise'ro], *n.m.* (*Print.*) Pica. *Cicéro gros œil*, small pica; *cicéro petit œil*, small pica.
cicérole [sise'rol], *n.f.*, or **cicer**, *n.m.* Chicpea.
Cicéron [sise'rõ], *m.* Cicero.
cicérone [sisero'ne], *n.m.* Cicerone, guide.
cicéronien [sisero'njɛ̃], *a.* (*fem.* -ienne) Ciceronian. **ciceroniser**, *v.i.* To imitate the style of Cicero.
cicindèle [sisɛ̃'dɛl], *n.f.* Tiger-beetle.
cicutaire [CIGUË].
ci-dessus, ci-devant, etc. [CI].
cidre [sidr], *n.m.* Cider. **cidrerie**, *n.f.* Cider making; cider-factory.
ciel [sjɛl], *n.m.* (*pl.* **cieux**) The heavens, the firmament, the sky, the atmosphere; heaven, paradise; (*fig.*) the Deity, God; joy, felicity; (*pl.* **ciels**) (*Eccles.*) the canopy which is carried over the host; skies (as portrayed by artists); the roof of a quarry; climate. *À ciel ouvert*, in broad daylight, openly; *aide-toi,*

le ciel t'aidera, heaven helps those who help themselves; *arc-en-ciel* (*pl. arcs-en-ciel*), rainbow; *bleu ciel,* sky-blue; *c'est un coup du ciel,* it is a judgment of heaven; *ciel de lit* (*pl. ciels de lits*), bed-tester; *élever jusqu'au ciel,* to praise to the skies; *être au septième ciel,* to be in the seventh heaven; *être toujours entre ciel et terre,* to be always in the clouds; *grâces au ciel,* thanks be to heaven; *juste ciel!* good heavens! great god! *l'Italie est sous un des plus beaux ciels de l'Europe,* Italy has one of the finest climates in Europe; *remuer ciel et terre,* to leave no stone unturned; *tomber du ciel,* to come suddenly, like a bolt from the blue.

cierge [sjɛrʒ], *n.m.* Taper, church candle, cierge, wax-light; great mullein and other long-stemmed plants. *Cierge du Pérou,* giant cactus; *cierge pascal,* Easter cierge; *cierges d'eau,* water-jets; *droit comme un cierge,* as stiff as a poker; *il lui doit un beau cierge,* he ought to be very grateful to him. **cierger,** *v.t.* To wax (cloth etc.) to stiffen it.

cieux, *pl.* [CIEL].

cigale [si'gal], *n.f.* Cicada. (*Naut.*) Anchor-ring. *Cigale de mer,* shrimp; *cigale de rivière,* water-grasshopper.

cigare [si'ga:r], *n.m.* Cigar.

cigarette [siga'rɛt], *n.f.* Cigarette.

cigarière [siga'rjɛ:r], *n.f.* Woman making cigars.

ci-gît [CI].

cigogne [si'gɔɲ], *n.f.* Stork; (*fam.*) tall, thin woman; handle of a grindstone. *Bec de cigogne,* crane's-bill; *contes de la cigogne,* absurd, improbable stories. **cigogneau,** *n.m.* Young stork.

ciguë [si'gy], *n.f.* Hemlock (plant or poison). *Ciguë vireuse* or *ciguë d'eau,* water-hemlock, cow-bane; (*petite*) *ciguë des jardins,* fool's parsley.

ci-joint [CI].

cil [sil], *n.m.* Eyelash; (*Bot.*) hair, filament.

ciliaire [si'ljɛ:r], *a.* Ciliary.

cilice [si'lis], *n.m.* Cilice, hair-shirt.

cilié [ci'lje], *a.* (*fem.* **ciliée**) (*Bot.*) Ciliated, lashed. **ciliforme,** *a.* Ciliform.

cillement [sij'mɑ̃], *n.m.* Blink, winking.

ciller [si'je], *v.t.* To wink, to blink (the eyes); (*Hawking*) to seel.—*v.i.* To wink, to blink.

cimaise or **cymaise** [si'mɛ:z], *n.f.* Cyma, ogee; dado-rail. *Un tableau placé sur la cimaise,* a picture hung 'on the line'.

cime [sim], *n.f.* Top, summit, peak; (*Bot.*) cyme.

ciment [si'mɑ̃], *n.m.* Cement. *Ciment armé,* reinforced concrete. **cimentaire,** *a.* Pertaining to cement. **cimentation,** *n.f.* Cementation. **cimenter,** *v.t.* To cement; to confirm, to strengthen, to consolidate. **cimentier,** *n.m.* Cement-maker.

cimeterre [sim'tɛ:r], *n.m.* Scimitar.

cimetière [sim'tjɛ:r], *n.m.* Cemetery, church-yard.

cimier [si'mje], *n.m.* Crest (of a helmet); buttock (of beef). *Cimier de cerf* or *de bête fauve,* haunch of venison.

cimmérien [sime'rjɛ̃], *a.* (*fem.* **cimmérienne**) Cimmerian.

cinabre [si'nabr], *n.m.* Cinnabar, vermilion.

cincenelle [sɛ̃s'nɛl] or **cinquenelle,** *n.f.* Tow-line.

cinchonine [sɛ̃kɔ'nin], *n.f.* Cinchonia, cinchonine. **cinchonique,** *a.* Cinchonaceous.

cincle [sɛ̃kl], *n.m.* Water-ouzel, dipper.

ciné [si'ne], *n.m.* (*fam.*) Cinema.

cinéaste [sine'ast], *n.m.* Film producer.

ciné-club [sine'klʌb], *n.m.* (*pl.* **ciné-clubs**) Film club.

cinégraphique [sinegra'fik], *a.* Cinematographic.

cinéma [sine'ma], *n.m.* Cinema; picture-palace. *Aller au cinéma,* to go to the pictures.

cinémascope [sinemas'kɔp], *n.m.* Cinemascope.

cinémathèque [sinema'tɛk], *n.f* Film library.

cinématique [sinema'tik], *a.* Cinematic. **cinématiquement,** *adv.* Cinematically.

cinématographe [sinematɔ'graf], *n.m.* Cinematograph. **cinématographier,** *v.t.* To film. **cinématographique,** *a.* Cinematographic.

cinéraire (1) [sine'rɛ:r], *a.* Cinerary (urn). —*n.m.* Cinerarium.

cinéraire (2) [sine'rɛ:r], *n.m.* or *f.* (*Bot.*) Cineraria.

cinérama [sinera'ma], *n.m.* Cinerama.

cinétique [sine'tik], *n.f.* Kinetics.—*a.* Kinetic, motive (energy). **cinétiquement,** *adv.* Kinetically.

cingalais [sɛ̃ga'lɛ], *a.* (*fem.* **cingalaise**) Cingalese (language and people).

cinglage (1) [sɛ̃'glaːʒ], *n.m.* Sailing, ship's course, run of a ship in twenty-four hours.

cinglage (2) [sɛ̃'glaːʒ], *n.m.* (*Metal.*) Blooming.

cinglant [sɛ̃g'lɑ̃], *a.* (*fem.* **-ante**) Lashing; biting, bitter; (*fig.*) cutting.

cinglé [sɛ̃'gle], *a.* (*fem.* **cinglée**) (*slang*) Cracked, crackers.

cinglement [sɛ̃gl'mɑ̃], *n.m.* Lashing, slashing, cutting; (*fig.*) slashing criticism.

cingler (1) [sɛ̃'gle], *v.i.* To sail before the wind, to scud along.

cingler (2) [sɛ̃'gle], *v.t.* To lash; (*fig.*) to chastize; (*Metal.*) to bloom.

cingleur [sɛ̃'glœːr], *n.m.* (*Metal.*) Lift-hammer; shingler.

cinglon [sɛ̃'glɔ̃], *n.m.* Lash, cut (with whip etc.). **cinglure,** *n.f.* Sting, smart; lashing.

cinname [si'nam] or **cinnamome** [sina'mɔm], *n.m.* Cinnamon. **cinnamique,** *a.* Cinnamomic, cinnamic.

cinq [sɛ̃:k], *a.* Five.—*n.m.* Five.

cinquantaine [sɛ̃kɑ̃'tɛn], *n.f.* About fifty; half a hundred. *Il a passé la cinquantaine,* he is over fifty.

cinquante [sɛ̃'kɑ̃:t], *a.* Fifty. **cinquante-naire,** *a.* and *n.m.* Quinquagenarian.—*n.m.* Fiftieth anniversary, jubilee. **cinquantième,** *a.* Fiftieth.—*n.m.* Fiftieth part.

cinquenelle [CINCENELLE].

cinquième [sɛ̃'kjɛm], *a.* Fifth.—*n.m.* Fifth part; fifth floor.—*n.f.* The fifth form (in French *lycées* and *collèges*); in England the 2nd form. **cinquièmement,** *adv.* Fifthly.

cintrage [sɛ̃'traːʒ], *n.m.* Centering, arching, curving (of arches etc.).

cintre [sɛ̃:tr], *n.m.* Concave, curve of an arch, vault, etc.; truss; coat-hanger; (*Theat.*) highest tier of boxes. *A plein cintre,* semi-circular (of arches); *cette cave est en cintre,* that cellar is built arch-wise. **cintré,** *a.* (*fem.* **cintrée**) Arched, curved, bent.

Manteau cintré, close-fitting coat. **cintrement,** *n.m.* Centering (an arch).

cintrer [sɛ̃'tre], *v.t.* To arch, to build in the form of an arch, to curve.

cipaye [si'pa:j], or **cipahi,** *n.m.* Sepoy.

cipolin [sipɔ'lɛ̃], *n.m.* Cipollino, cipolin marble.

cippe [sip], *n.m.* Cippus (half-column).

cirage [si'ra:ʒ], *n.m.* Waxing; blacking (composition or process); boot-polish. *Être dans le cirage (fam.)*, to be woolly-minded; *noir comme du cirage*, pitch-black.

circassien [sirka'sjɛ̃], *a.* and *n.* (*fem.* **-ienne**) Circassian.

circée [sir'se], *n.f.* (*Bot.*) Enchanter's nightshade.

circinal [sirsi'nal], *a.* (*fem.* **-ale**, *pl.* **-aux**) (*Bot.*) Circinate.

circoncire [sirkɔ̃'si:r], *v.t. irr.* To circumcise. **circoncis,** *a.* (*fem.* **-ise**) Circumcised.— *n.m.* One who is circumcised. **circoncision,** *n.f.* Circumcision.

circonférence [sirkɔ̃fe'rɑ̃:s], *n.f.* Circumference. **circonférentiel,** *a.* (*fem.* **-ielle**) Circumferential.

circonflexe [sirkɔ̃'flɛks], *n.m.* and *a.* Circumflex.

circonlocution [sirkɔ̃lɔky'sjɔ̃], *n.f.* Circumlocution.

circonscription [sirkɔ̃skrip'sjɔ̃], *n.f.* Circumscription, circumscribing; division, district; constituency.

circonscrire [sirkɔ̃'skri:r], *v.t.* To circumscribe, to encircle; to enclose, to limit.

circonspect [sirkɔ̃'spekt -spe] (*fem.* **-specte**) [-spɛkt] Circumspect, wary, discreet, reserved. **circonspection,** *n.f.* Circumspection, wariness, caution. *Avec circonspection*, cautiously.

circonstance [sirkɔ̃'stɑ̃:s], *n.f.* Circumstance; occurrence, event; conjuncture, case. *Circonstance aggravante*, aggravation (of an offence etc.); *circonstances atténuantes*, extenuating circumstances; *circonstances et dépendances*, (*Law*) appurtenances; *dans les circonstances critiques*, on critical occasions, in emergencies; *être à la hauteur des circonstances*, to rise to the occasion; *de circonstance*, required by or adapted to circumstances; *en pareille circonstance*, under such circumstances; *pièce de circonstance*, piece written for the occasion; *sourire de circonstance*, smile put on for the occasion; *suivant les circonstances*, as the case may be. **circonstancié,** *a.* (*fem.* **-iée**) Circumstantial, detailed. **circonstanciel,** *a.* (*fem.* **-ielle**) Circumstantial. **circonstancier,** *v.t.* To state circumstantially, to circumstantiate, to particularize.

circonvallation [sirkɔ̃vala'sjɔ̃], *n.f.* Circumvallation.

circonvenir [sirkɔ̃v'ni:r], *v.t. irr.* (*conjugated like* VENIR) To circumvent, to outwit, to overreach. **circonvention,** *n.f.* Circumvention, fraud. *User de circonvention*, to circumvent. **circonvenu,** *a.* (*fem.* **-ue**) Circumvented; outwitted.

circonvoisin [sirkɔ̃vwa'zɛ̃], *a.* (*fem.* **circonvoisine**) Circumjacent, neighbouring, adjoining.

circonvolution [sirkɔ̃vɔly'sjɔ̃], *n.f.* Circumvolution.

circuit [sir'kɥi], *n.m.* Circuit, circumference; roundabout road, detour; round, lap. (*Elec.*) *Court circuit*, short circuit; *en circuit*, connected, switched on, in circuit.

circulaire [sirky'lɛ:r], *n.f.* A circular.—*a.* Circular, round. *Billet circulaire*, tourist ticket. **circulairement,** *adv.* Circularly.

circulant [sirky'lɑ̃], *a.* (*fem.* **circulante**) Circulating.

circularité [sirkylari'te], *n.f.* Circularity.

circulation [sirkyla'sjɔ̃], *n.f.* Circulation; currency; traffic. *Arrêter la circulation*, to hold up the traffic; *route à grande circulation*, major, main road.

circulatoire [sirkyla'twa:r], *a.* Circulatory, circulating.

circuler [sirky'le], *v.i.* To circulate, to revolve, to move round or about; to pass from hand to hand; to spread, to be current. *Circulez, Messieurs!* move on, please! *faire circuler*, to make people move on.

circumduction [sirkɔmdyk'sjɔ̃], *n.f.* Circumduction.

circumnavigateur [sirkɔmnaviga'tœ:r], *n.m.* Circumnavigator. **circumnavigation,** *n.f.* Circumnavigation.

circumpolaire [sirkɔmpɔ'lɛ:r], *a.* Circumpolar.

cire [si:r], *n.f.* Beeswax; wax; taper. *Cire à cacheter*, sealing-wax. **ciré,** *a.* (*fem.* **cirée**) Waxed, polished. *Toile cirée*, American cloth. —*n.m.* (*Naut.*) (suit of) oilskins. **cirer,** *v.t.* To wax; to black or to polish (boots). **cireur,** *n.m.* (*fem.* **cireuse** (1)) Polisher. *Cireur de bottes*, bootblack; *cireuse électrique*, electric polisher. **cireux,** *a.* (*fem.* **-euse** (2)) Waxy. **cirier,** *a.* (*fem.* **-ière**) Producing wax (of bees etc.).—*n.m.* Wax-chandler; waxworker; candle-berry, wax-tree.—*n.f.* Cell-making bee.

ciron [si'rɔ̃], *n.m.* Mite.

cirque [sirk], *n.m.* Circus; (*Geol.*) cirque.

cirre [si:r], *n.m.* (*Bot.*) Tendril; (*Zool.*) cirrus. **cirreux,** *a.* (*fem.* **cirreuse**) Ending in a cirrus, cirrose.

cirrhose [sir'ro:z], *n.f.* (*Path.*) Cirrhosis.

cirrus [sir'ry:s], *n.m.* Cirrus (curl-cloud).

cirure [si'ry:r], *n.f.* Prepared wax.

cisaille [si'za:j], *n.f.* Clipping or shearings of metals; (*pl.*) shears; wire-cutter; hedge-clipper; (*Bookb.*) guillotine. **cisaillement,** *n.m.* Shearing, clipping (of coins etc.). **cisailler,** *v.t.* To pare, to clip (coins etc.); to cut with shears. *Pneu cisaillé*, nipped tyre.

cisalpin [sizal'pɛ̃], *a.* (*fem.* **-ine**) Cisalpine.

ciseau [si'zo], *n.m.* (*pl.* **ciseaux**) Chisel; (*fig.*) touch or manner (of a sculptor), sculpture; (*pl.*) scissors. *Ciseau à froid*, cold chisel; *ciseau d'orfèvre*, graver; *ciseaux de tailleur*, tailor's shears; *travailler à coups de ciseaux*, to work with scissors and paste.

ciseler [siz'le], *v.t.* To chisel; to work with a chisel, to chase, to emboss, to sculpture. **ciselet,** *n.m.* Small chisel, graver. **ciseleur,** *n.m.* Chaser; carver, sculptor; (*fig.*) delicate worker, writer, etc. **ciselure,** *n.f.* Chasing, sculpture, carving; chased work, carved work.

cisoir [si'zwa:r], *n.m.* Watchmaker's chisel.

cisoires [si'zwa:r], *n.f.* (*used only in pl.*) Big bench-shears (to cut sheet iron).

ciste (1) [sist], *n.f.* (*Gr. Ant.*) Basket.

ciste (2) [sist], *n.m.* Cistus, rock-rose.

cistercien [sistɛr'sjɛ̃], *a.* and *n.* (*fem.* **cistercienne**) Cistercian.

cistophore [sistɔ'fɔr], *n.f.* (*Gr. Ant.*) Canephora, girl carrying basket.

cistre [sistr], *n.m.* Stringed instrument used in 16–17th cent., zither.

citable [si'tabl], *a.* Quotable, citable.

citadelle [sita'dɛl], *n.f.* Citadel; (*fig.*) stronghold, centre.

citadin [sita'dɛ̃], *a.* (*fem.* **citadine**) Of the city.—*n.* Citizen, townsman.

citateur [sita'tœːr], *n.m.* (*fem.* **citatrice**) Habitual quoter; book of quotations.

citation [sita'sjɔ̃], *n.f.* Citation, quotation; summons. *Lancer une citation*, to issue a summons; *se faire délivrer une citation*, to take out a summons; (*Mil.*) *citation (à l'ordre du jour)*, mention in dispatches.

cité [si'te], *n.f.* City; town; ancient centre of a town. *Cités ouvrières*, blocks of workers' flats, housing estate; *droits de cité*, the rights of a citizen, freedom (of a city), citizenship; *la cité sainte*, the heavenly city; *la sainte cité*, Jerusalem; *une cité-jardin*, a garden-city; *une cité universitaire*, students' residential blocks.

citer [si'te], *v.t.* To cite, to quote; to name, to point out (as an instance or example); to summon, to subpoena.

citérieur [site'rjœːr], *a.* (*fem.* **citérieure**) (*Geog.*) Nearer, hithermost.

citerne [si'tɛrn], *n.f.* Cistern, reservoir; (*Naut.*) tanker. *Wagon citerne*, bulk liquid conveyor. **citerneau**, *n.m.* Small cistern or tank.

cithare [si'taːr], *n.f.* Zither.

citoyen [sitwa'jɛ̃], *n.m.* (*fem.* **citoyenne**) Citizen, burgess; (*fig.*) patriot. *Citoyen d'honneur d'une ville*, freeman of a city; *droits de citoyen*, rights of citizenship; *soldat citoyen*, citizen-soldier. **citoyenneté**, *n.f.* Citizenship.

citragon [sitra'gɔ̃], *n.m.* Balm-mint.

citrate [si'trat], *n.m.* Citrate.

citrin [si'trɛ̃], *a.* (*fem.* **citrine**) Citrine, lemon-coloured, pale yellow.

citrique [si'trik], *a.* Citric.

citron [si'trɔ̃], *n.m.* Lemon, citron; (*vulg.*) head.—*a.* Lemon-coloured. **citronnade**, *n.f.* Lemon-squash. **citronnat**, *n.m.* Candied citron-peel; sugar-plum with citron-peel in it. **citronné**, *a.* (*fem.* **-ée**) Lemon-flavoured.

citronnelle [sitrɔ'nɛl], *n.f.* (1) *Verveine des herboristes*, (*Lippia citriodora*) vervain; (2) *Mélisse*, melissa; (3) Barbados water (made of lemon). **citronner**, *v.t.* To flavour with citron. **citronnier**, *n.m.* Citron-tree.

citrouille [si'truːj], *n.f.* Pumpkin, gourd; (*slang*) head; fathead.

cive [siːv], **civette** (1), or **ciboulette**, *n.f.* Chive.

civet [si'vɛ], *n.m.* Wine stew (of venison). *Civet de lièvre*, jugged hare; *mettre en civet*, to jug.

civette (1) [CIVE].

civette (2) [si'vɛt], *n.f.* Civet-cat; civet (odour).

civière [si'vjɛːr], *n.f.* Hand-barrow; stretcher; bier.

civil [si'vil], *a.* (*fem.* **civile**) Civil; private, plain; courteous, polite. *Droit civil*, (*Law*) common law; (*pl.*) civil rights; *guerre civile*,

civil war; *mort civile*, deprivation of civil rights; *partie civile*, public prosecutor; (*Mil.*) *en civil*, in civilian clothes, in mufti.—*n.m.* Civilian. *Dans le civil*, in civilian life.

civilement, *adv.* Civilly; courteously, politely.

civilisable [sivili'zabl], *a.* Civilizable.

civilisateur [siviliza'tœːr], *a.* (*fem.* **civilisatrice**) Civilizing.

civilisation [siviliza'sjɔ̃], *n.f.* Civilization.

civiliser [sivili'ze], *v.t.* To civilize. **se civiliser**, *v.r.* To become civilized.

civiliste [sivi'list], *n.m.* Common lawyer.

civilité [sivili'te], *n.f.* Civility, good manners, politeness, courtesy; (*pl.*) compliment. *Faire des civilités à*, to be civil to; *mes civilités à monsieur votre frère*, my compliments to your brother.

civique [si'vik], *a.* Civic. *Instruction civique*, civics.

civisme [si'vism], *n.m.* Good citizenship.

clabaud [kla'bo], *n.m.* (*Hunt.*) Noisy hound, hound that barks at the wrong time; (*fig.*) bawler, ranter; gossip. **clabaudage**, *n.m.* Barking, baying; (*fig.*) clamour, bawling; spiteful gossip. **clabauder**, *v.i.* To give tongue (falsely); (*fig.*) to clamour, to bawl out. **clabauderie**, *n.f.* [CLABAUDAGE]. **clabaudeur**, *n.m.* (*fem.* **-euse**) Brawler, clamourer, scandalmonger.

cladonie [kladɔ'niː], *n.f.* (*Bot.*) Reindeer moss.

claie [klɛ], *n.f.* Wattle, hurdle; screen (of a sieve), riddle (minerals). *Passer à la claie*, to screen; *traîner sur la claie*, to drag on a hurdle (to execution etc.).

clair [klɛːr], *n.m.* Light, brightness, clearness; (*Paint.*) high light. *Il fait clair de lune*, it is moonlight; *lettre en clair*, letter written in clear (not in cypher); *tirer au clair*, to bottle off, to clarify; *tirer une chose au clair*, to get to the bottom of a thing.—*a.* (*fem.* **claire** (1)) Clear, bright, luminous, light; light-coloured, transparent, limpid, pure, serene, cloudless; thin (of liquids etc.); acute, clear-sighted; distinct; perspicuous; plain, intelligible, obvious, undeniable. *C'est clair comme le jour*, it is as plain as a pike-staff; *couleurs claires*, bright or light colours; *étoffe claire*, thin, flimsy stuff; *il fait très clair*, it is daylight; *lait clair*, whey; *le plus clair de son temps* (*argent etc.*), the greater part, best part, of one's time; *n'être pas clair*, to be obscure; *œuf clair*, wind-egg, unfertilized egg.—*adv.* Clearly, distinctly, plainly. *Ne pas y voir clair*, not to see clearly; (*fig.*) not to understand; not to see through; *parler clair et net*, to speak out plainly, not to mince matters; *sabre au clair*, with drawn sword.

clairçage [klɛr'saːʒ], *n.m.* Decolouring or clarifying (of sugar). **claircer**, *v.t.* To decolour or clarify (sugar).

Claire [klɛːr], *f.* Clara.

claire (2) [klɛːr], *n.f.* Bone-ash; sugar-boiler; clear pool (for oysters).

clairement [klɛr'mã], *adv.* Clearly, plainly, distinctly, evidently, intelligibly.

clairer [CLAIRCER].

clairet [klɛ'rɛ], *a.* (*fem.* **clairette** (1)) Palish, lightish (of wines).—*n.m.* Light-red wine.

clairette (2) [klɛ'rɛt], *n.f.* White grape from the South; sparkling wine made from this; disease of silkworms [*see* MÂCHE].

claire-voie [klɛr'vwɑ], *n.f.* (*pl.* **claires-voies**) Wooden fencing; grating or barred opening (in garden wall), wicket; skylight; clerestory. *Porte à claire-voie*, gate; *caisse à claire-voie*, crate; *semer à claire-voie*, to sow thin.

clairière [klɛ'rjɛːr], *n.f.* Clearing, glade; thin part (in linen).

clair-obscur [klɛrɔps'kyːr], *n.m.* (*pl.* **clairs-obscurs**) Chiaroscuro; light and shade.

clairon [klɛ'rɔ̃], *n.m.* Clarion, bugle; bugler. **claironnant**, *a.* (*fem.* **-ante**) Loud and metallic (of voice). **claironner**, *v.t.* To sound the bugle. *Claironner une nouvelle à tous vents*, to proclaim from the house-tops.

clairsemé [klɛrsə'me], *a.* (*fem.* **clairsemée**) Thin, thinly sown, scattered.

clairvoyance [klɛrvwa'jɑ̃ːs], *n.f.* Sharpness, acuteness, perspicacity, clear-sightedness; clairvoyance. **clairvoyant**, *a.* (*fem.* **clairvoyante**) Clear-sighted, discerning, sharp, acute; clairvoyant.

clamer [klɑ'me], *v.t.* To cry out, to shout. **clameur**, *n.f.* Clamour, outcry.

clampin [klɑ̃'pɛ̃], *a.* (*fem.* **clampine**) Lazy, slow, halting.—*n.* Straggler, slowcoach, lazybones. **clampiner**, *v.i.* To lag, to loiter, to idle.

clampser [klɑ̃'pse], **clamcer**, *v.i.* (*slang*) To die; to kick the bucket.

clan [klɑ̃], *n.m.* Clan; (*fig.*) clique. *Chef de clan*, chieftain of a clan; *membre d'un clan*, clansman.

clandestin [klɑ̃dɛs'tɛ̃], *a.* (*fem.* **-ine**) Clandestine, secret, underhand, underground. **clandestinement**, *adv.* Clandestinely, secretly.

clandestinité [klɑ̃dɛstini'te], *n.f.* Secrecy; underground activity.

clapement etc. [CLAPPEMENT].

clapet [kla'pɛ], *n.m.* Valve, clapper, clack.

clapier [kla'pje], *n.m.* Hutch (for rabbits). *Lapins de clapier* or *clapiers*, tame rabbits.

clapir [kla'piːr], *v.i.* To squeak (of rabbits). **se clapir**, *v.r.* To hide in a hole, to squat, to cower.

clapotage [klapɔ'taːʒ], **clapotement**, or **clapotis**, *n.m.* Rippling, plashing; (*Naut.*) lapping. **clapotant**, *a.* (*fem.* **-ante**) [CLAPOTEUX]. **clapoter**, *v.i.* To plash, to chop. **clapoteux**, *a.* (*fem.* **-euse**) Plashing, choppy, rough.

clappement [klap'mɑ̃], *n.m.* Clacking, smacking, click (of the tongue against the palate). **clapper**, *v.i.* To clack, to smack (of the tongue).

claque (1) [klak], *n.f.* Slap, smack; claque (paid applauders at theatres); (*pl.*) (*C*) clogs, galoshes. *En avoir sa claque*, to have had enough, to be tired of something; *face à claques*, sneering face (one which you would like to slap); *prendre ses cliques et ses claques*, (*colloq.*) to be off bag and baggage.

claque (2) [klak], *n.m.* Opera-hat, crush-hat. *Chapeau à claque*, cocked hat.

claqué [kla'ke], *a.* Vamped (boot); (*fam.*) exhausted, tired out (man, horse); dead.

claquebois [klak'bwɑ], *n.m.* Xylophone.

claquedent [klak'dɑ̃], *n.m.* Poor, half-starved wretch, beggar; pot-house, low tavern or den.

claquement [klak'mɑ̃], *n.m.* Clapping, clap; snapping (of the fingers); cracking (of whips); chattering (of the teeth); slamming (of door).

claquemurer [klakmy're], *v.t.* To immure, to coop up, to confine, to imprison. **se claquemurer**, *v.r.* To shut oneself up.

claquer [kla'ke], *v.i.* To snap, to crack, to clap, to clack; to slam, bang; (*slang*) to die, to pop off. *Claquer des dents*, to chatter (of teeth); *claquer des mains*, to clap; *faire claquer*, to crack (a whip), to snap (one's fingers), to smack (one's tongue); *faire claquer son fouet*, to crack one's whip; (*fig.*) to boast.—*v.t.* To slap, to crack, to slam; (*fig.*) to applaud; (*slang*) to run through (a fortune etc.). **se claquer**, *v.r.* (*fam.*) To overwork oneself. (*spt.*) *Se claquer un muscle*, to have a muscle rupture.

claquet [kla'kɛ], *n.m.* Mill-clapper; clack. *Sa langue va comme un claquet de moulin*, (*fam.*) his (or her) tongue goes like a clack.

claqueter [klak'te], *v.i.* To cackle (of a hen after laying); to cry (of the stork).

claquette [kla'kɛt], *n.f.* Clapper, rattle; musical instrument imitating smacking noise of whip. *Danseur à claquettes*, tap-dancer.

claqueur [kla'kœːr], *n.m.* (*Theat.*) Claquer, hired applauder.

claquoir [CLAQUETTE].

clarification [klarifika'sjɔ̃], *n.f.* Clarification.

clarifier [klari'fje], *v.t.* To clarify; to purify, to fine. **se clarifier**, *v.r.* To clarify, to get clarified, to settle.

clarine [kla'rin], *n.f.* Bell (attached to cattle).

clariné [klari'ne], *a.* (*fem.* **-ée**) (*Her.*) Belled.

clarinette [klari'nɛt], *n.f.* Clarinet; (*Mil. slang*) rifle. **clarinetter**, *v.i.* (*colloq.*) To play on this. **clarinettiste**, *n.* Clarinetist, clarinet-player.

clarté [klar'te], *n.f.* Light, brightness, splendour; limpidity; clearness.

classe [klɑːs], *n.f.* Class, order, rank; kind, tribe; class or form (in a school); classroom; lesson; (*pl.*) school-hours; school-time; (*Naut.*) rating; (*Mil.*) annual contingent. *Aller en classe*, to go to school; *de première classe, de grande classe*, first class, first rate; *en classe*, in school; *faire la classe*, to teach; *faire ses classes*, (*Mil.*) to drill as a recruit; *hautes classes* or *classes supérieures*, upper classes or orders; *la classe dirigeante*, the governing class; *la classe moyenne*, the middle class; *la classe ouvrière*, the working class; *il a fait toutes ses classes*, he has gone through all the forms; *la rentrée des classes*, the beginning of the school year; *les hommes de la classe* or *la classe*, the contingent to be discharged; *la classe 1930*, those who were called up in 1930.

classé [kla'se], *a.* (*fem.* **-ée**) Definitely filed or shelved (case); listed (monument); (*fam.*) sized up (man).

classement [klas'mɑ̃], *n.m.* Classing, classification, filing; results (of a competition).

classer [kla'se], *v.t.* To class, to classify, to sort; (*Naut.*) to enrol; (*fig.*) to reckon or count (among); to file and dispose of (a case); to shelve (a question). *Il s'est classé cinquième*, he has been placed fifth (in a competition).

classeur [kla'sœːr], *n.m.* Portfolio; rack; card-index; file; sorting apparatus for minerals.

classicisme [klasi'sism], *n.m.* Classicism.

classification [klasifika′sjɔ̃], *n.f.* Classification. **classificatoire**, *a.* Classifying.

classifier [klasi′fje], *v.t.* To classify.

classique [kla′sik], *a.* Classic, classical; standard (of authors, books, etc.) recognized, most approved (method); for school use (books). *Études classiques*, classical education; *excuse classique*, traditional excuse.— *n.m.* A classic (author, book, etc.). **classiquement**, *adv.* Classically.

clastique [klas′tik], *a.* Clastic.

claudicant [klodi′kɑ̃], *a.* (*fem.* **-ante**) Lame, limping. **claudication**, *n.f.* Lameness, limping, halting.

clause [klo:z], *n.f.* Clause.

claustral [klos′tral], *a.* (*fem.* **-ale**, *pl.* **-aux**) Claustral; monastic. **claustration**, *n.f.* Claustration, confinement.

claustrer [klos′tre], *v.t.* To cloister, to confine.

claustrophobie [klostrɔfɔ′bi], *n.f.* Claustrophobia.

clavaire [kla′vɛ:r], *n.f.* (*Bot.*) Club-topped mushroom.

clavé [kla′ve], *a.* (*fem.* **-ée**) (*Bot.*) Club-shaped.

claveau (1) [kla′vo], *n.m.* (*Arch.*) Key- or arch-stone.

claveau (2) [CLAVELÉE].

clavecin [klav′sɛ̃], *n.m.* Harpsichord, clavecin. **claveciniste**, *n.* Harpsichord-player.

clavelé [klav′le] or **claveleux**, *a.* (*fem.* **-ée** (1)) or **-euse**, *a.* Affected with sheep-pox. **clavelée** (2), *n.f.*, or **claveau**, *n.m.* Sheep-pox. **claveliser**, *v.t.* To inoculate for the sheep-pox.

clavette [kla′vɛt], *n.f.* (*Tech.*) Peg, pin; key, cotter. *Clavette à tête*, gib key; *clavette dormante*, feather. **claveter**, *v.t.* To key, to cotter.

claviculaire [klaviky′lɛ:r], *a.* Clavicular. **clavicule**, *n.f.* Clavicle, collar-bone. **claviculé**, *a.* (*fem.* **-ée**) Having a collar-bone.

clavier [kla′vje], *n.m.* Clavier, key-board (piano, typewriter), key-frame (of piano, organ, etc.); key-ring.

claviforme [klavi′fɔrm], *a.* Claviform, club-shaped.

clayère [klɛ′jɛ:r], *n.f.* Oyster bed or breeding-ground.

clayon [klɛ′jɔ̃], *n.m.* Wattle; wire-netting for protecting window-glass; stand (for draining cheese). **clayonnage**, *n.m.* Wattling, hedging in (banks etc.). **clayonner**, *v.t.* To wattle, to fence in.

clearing [kli′riŋ], *n.m.* (*Fin.*) Clearing.

clebs [klɛbs], *n.m.* (*slang*) Tyke.

clef or **clé** [kle], *n.f.* Key; plug (of a cock); turn-screw, screw-wrench, spanner; keystone (of arch); (*Mus.*) clef, tuning-key. *Avoir la clef des champs*, to be free to go anywhere; *clé à écrous*, spanner; *clef anglaise*, monkey-wrench; *clef à molette*, adjustable spanner; *clef bénarde*, key with solid shank; *clef d'accordeur*, tuning-hammer; *clef de robinet*, plug of a cock; *clef de sol*, treble clef; *clef de voûte*, keystone of a vault; *fausse clef*, skeleton key; *fermer une porte à clef*, to lock a door; *la clef est sur la porte*, the key is in the door; *mettre la clef sous la porte*, to run away from one's creditors, to bolt; *mettre sous clef*, to lock up; *prendre la clef des champs*, to escape, to

run away; *tenir sous clef*, to keep under lock and key; *un problème clef*, a key problem; *un trousseau de clefs*, a bunch of keys; *un roman à clef*, a novel, the characters of which are real, but the names fictitious.

clématite [klema′tit], *n.f.* (*Bot.*) Clematis.

clémence [kle′mɑ̃:s], *n.f.* Clemency, mercy.

Clément [kle′mɑ̃], *m.* Clement.

clément [kle′mɑ̃], *a.* (*fem.* **-ente**) Clement, merciful, lenient; mild (of the weather).

clémentine [klemɑ̃′tin], *n.f.* Clementine.

clenche [klɑ̃:ʃ] or **clenchette** [klɑ̃′ʃɛt], *n.f.* Catch or latch (of a lock).

Cléopâtre [kleɔ′pɑ:tr], *f.* Cleopatra.

clepsydre [klɛp′sidr], *n.f.* Clepsydra, water-clock.

cleptomane [klɛptɔ′man], *n.m.* and *f.* Kleptomaniac. **cleptomanie**, *n.f.* Kleptomania.

clerc [klɛ:r], *n.m.* Ecclesiastic, clergyman; (*fig.*) scholar, learned person; clerk (in a lawyer's office). *Ce n'est pas un grand clerc*, he is no great scholar; *les plus grands clercs ne sont pas toujours les plus fins*, the most learned are not always the most clever; *pas de clerc*, blunder; *petit clerc*, junior clerk; *principal clerc*, head-clerk.

clergé [klɛr′ʒe], *n.m.* Clergy. ***clergie**, *n.f.* Knowledge, scholarship (as attainments of the clergy). *Bénéfice de clergie*, (*Law*) benefit of clergy.

clérical [kleri′kal], *a.* (*fem.* **-ale**, *pl.* **-aux**) Clerical. **cléricalement**, *adv.* Clerically. **cléricaliser**, *v.t.* To clericalize. **cléricalisme**, *n.m.* Clericalism. **cléricaliste**, *n.m.* Clericalist, pro-clerical. **cléricature**, *n.f.* Clerkship; ministry, Holy orders; body of clergy.

clic-clac [klik′klak], *n.m.* The cracking (of a whip).

clichage [kli′ʃa:ʒ], *n.m.* Stereotyping, stereotype. **cliché**, *n.m.* Stereotype plate, cliché; (*fig.*) stereotyped phrase; (*Phot.*) negative; (*Sculp.*) cast. **clicher**, *v.t.* To stereotype. **clicherie**, *n.f.* Stereotyping workshop. **clicheur**, *n.m.* Stereotyper.

client [kli′ɑ̃], *n.m.* (*fem.* **cliente**) Client (of lawyers etc.); patient (of physicians); customer (of tradesmen). **clientèle**, *n.f.* Clientele; practice (of physicians etc.); connection; custom patrons (of tradesmen); goodwill (of a business).

clifoire [kli′fwa:r], *n.f.* Squirt (toy).

clignement [klin′mɑ̃], *n.m.* Winking, blinking, wink.

cligner [kli′ɲe], *v.t.* and *i.* To look with the eyelids half-shut. *Cligner les yeux*, to blink; *cligner de l'œil*, to wink; *cligner des yeux*, to signify one's assent by winking. **clignotant**, *a.* (*fem.* **-ante**) Winking, blinking.—*n.m.* (*Motor.*) Winker, flashing indicator. **clignotement**, *n.m.* Winking, blinking. **clignoter**, *v.i.* To wink, to blink.

climat [kli′ma], *n.m.* Climate; region, country; (*fig.*) atmosphere. **climatérique** (1) or **climatique**, *a.* Climatic. *Station climat(ér)ique*, health resort. **climatisation**, *n.f.* Air conditioning. **climatiser**, *v.t.* To air-condition.

climatérique (2) [klimate′rik], *a.* and *n.* Climacteric, critical. *La grande climatérique*, the great climacteric. **climatologie**, *n.f.*

Climatology. **climatologique**, *a.* Climatological. **climatothérapie**, *n.f.* Climatotherapy. **climature**, *n.f.* Climature.
clin [klɛ̃] (1), *n.m.* Wink (of an eye). *En un clin d'œil*, in the twinkling of an eye, in an instant; *faire un clin d'œil à quelqu'un*, to wink at someone.
clin [klɛ̃] (2), *n.m.* Lap-joint. *Yole à clins*, clinker-built yawl.
clinfoc [klɛ̃'fɔk], *n.m.* (*Naut.*) Flying jib. *Baïonnette de clinfoc*, flying-jib boom.
clinicien [klini'sjɛ̃], *a.* Clinical.—*n.m.* Clinical physician.
clinique [kli'nik], *a.* Clinical. *Leçons cliniques*, clinical lectures, bedside instruction.—*n.f.* Clinical surgery, medicine, or lectures; clinic, nursing-home.
clinquant [klɛ̃'kɑ̃], *a.* (*fem.* **clinquante**) Showy, gaudy, trumpery.—*n.m.* Tinsel; (*fig.*) glitter, affectation. **clinquanter**, *v.t.* To cover or decorate with clinquant, tinsel, etc.
clip [klip], *n.m.* Clip-fastened jewel.
clipper [kli'pɛr], *n.m.* (*Naut.* and *Av.*) Clipper.
clique [klik], *n.f.* (*Contempt.*) Set, coterie, party, clique; (*pl.*) clogs, galoshes. *Prendre ses cliques et ses claques* [CLAQUE (1)]; (*Mil.*) *la clique*, the band of bugles and drums in an infantry battalion.
cliquet [kli'kɛ], *n.m.* Catch, pawl. *Vilbrequin à cliquet*, ratchet brace.
cliqueter [klik'te], *v.i.* To click, clank, clash, or jingle; (*Motor.*) to knock. **cliquetis**, *n.m.* Clanking, clash, clatter, rattling, jingle, etc.
cliquette [kli'kɛt], *n.f.*, *usual pl.* Bones (a kind of castanets); sinker (of fishing net).
clissage [kli'sa:ʒ], *n.m.* Wickering.
clisse [klis], *n.f.* Wicker mat for draining cheese; basket-work cover for a bottle; [ÉCLISSE]. **clissé**, *a.* (*fem.* **clissée**) Cased in wicker (of bottles). **clisser**, *v.t.* To wicker, to cover with wicker-work etc.
clitoris [klitɔ'ri:s], *n.m.* (*Anat.*) Clitoris.
clivable [kli'vabl], *a.* (*Min.*) Cleavable.
clivage [kli'va:ʒ], *n.m.* (*Min.*) Cleavage; cleaving.
cliver [kli've], *v.t.* To cleave (diamonds etc.). **se cliver**, *v.r.* To split, to be cleft.
cloacal [klɔa'kal], *a.* (*fem.* **-ale**, *pl.* **-aux**) Cloacal.
cloaque [klɔ'ak], *n.m.* Drain, sewer, sink, cesspool; (*fig.*) filthy hole, place, etc. (*Anat.*) cloaca.
clochage [klɔ'ʃa:ʒ], *n.m.* Putting or cultivating plants under bell-glasses.
clochard [klɔ'ʃar], *n.m.* (*slang*) Tramp, vagrant; (*U.S.*) hobo.
cloche [klɔʃ], *n.f.* Bell; dish-cover; blister (on the hands, feet, etc.); (*Cook.*) stew-pan; (*Gard.*) bell-glass, cloche; (*Chem.*, *Phys.*) receiver. *Cloche à fromage*, cheese cover; *cloche à plongeur*, diving-bell; *cloche flottante*, bellbuoy; *déménager à la cloche de bois*, to move surreptitiously. *faire sonner la grosse cloche*, to sound the big bell; *qui n'entend qu'une cloche n'entend qu'un son*, one should hear both sides of a question; *se taper la cloche*, (*pop.*) to get one's bellyful; *un autre son de cloche*, a different version.
clochement [klɔʃ'mɑ̃], *n.m.* Hobbling, halting.
cloche-pied [klɔʃ'pje], *n.m.* Hopping on one leg. *Aller à cloche-pied*, to hop (on one foot).

clocher (1) [klɔ'ʃe], *n.m.* Steeple, belfry; (*fig.*) parish, native place. *Course au clocher*, steeple-chase; point-to-point race; *esprit de clocher*, narrow-mindedness, prejudice, short-sightedness; *il n'a jamais quitté son clocher*, he does not know the world; *intérêts de clocher*, local matters.
clocher (2) [klɔ'ʃe], *v.i.* (*dial.*) To sound like a bell.—*v.t.* (*Gard.*) To cover with a bellglass.
clocher (3) [klɔ'ʃe], *v.i.* To halt, to limp, to hobble; (*fig.*) to go wrong somewhere, to be defective. *Clocher du pied droit*, to limp with the right foot; *il y a quelque chose qui cloche*, there's something wrong somewhere, there's a hitch somewhere; *raisonnement qui cloche*, lame argument.
clocheton [klɔʃ'tɔ̃], *n.m.* Bell-turret.
clochette [klɔ'ʃɛt], *n.f.* Small bell, hand-bell; bell-flower; any campanula or convolvulus.
cloison [klwa'zɔ̃], *n.f.* Partition (of boards or masonry), division, compartment; (*Anat.*, *Bot.*) dividing membrane; (*Naut.*) bulkhead. *Cloison étanche*, watertight compartment.
cloisonnage, cloisonnement, *n.m.* Partition-work, wainscotting. **cloisonné**, *a.* (*fem.* **-ée**) Partitioned, divided into compartments; (*Conch.*) chambered; (*Ceramics*) cloisonné. **cloisonner**, *v.t.* To partition.
cloître [klwa:tr], *n.m.* Cloister; cathedral close; (*fig.*) monastic life. **cloîtré**, *a.* (*fem.* **-ée**) Cloistered (of a person). **cloîtrer**, *v.t.* To shut up in a cloister, to cloister; to immure. **se cloîtrer**, *v.r.* To enter the monastic life. **cloîtrier**, *n.m.* (*fem.* **-ière**) Cloistered monk or nun.
clopin-clopant [klɔpɛ̃klɔ'pɑ̃], *adv.* Limpingly, haltingly, hobbling along.
clopiner [klɔpi'ne], *v.i.* To limp, to halt, to hobble.
cloporte [klɔ'pɔrt], *n.m.* Woodlouse; (*slang*) concierge, door-keeper (a pun on *clôt-porte*).
cloque [klɔk], *n.f.* Blister (on hand, foot, paint, etc.); blight, rust (of plants). **cloqué**, *a.* (*fem.* **-ée**) Blistered; (*Tex.*) goffered. —*n.m.* Goffered material. **cloquer**, *v.i.* To blister (of paint).
clore [klɔ:r], *v.t. irr.* (chiefly used in *p.p.*) To close, to shut, to stop up; to enclose, to fence; to end, to finish, to conclude; to close (accounts, discussions, a session, etc.).—*v.i.* To close, to shut. **se clore**, *v.r.* To close, to be closed; to end.
clos [klo], *a.* (*fem.* **close**) Closed, shut, sealed; finished, completed. *À huis clos*, in camera, with closed doors; *à nuit close*, after nightfall; *bouche close*, mum's the word; *ce sont lettres closes*, it's a secret, it is incomprehensible; *champ clos*, lists, tourney ground; *clos et couvert*, wind-and-water tight; *les yeux clos*, without looking, blindly.—*n.m.* Close; enclosure, field. *Clos de vigne*, vineyard (*esp.* in Burgundy).
closeau [klo'zo], *n.m.* Small garden.
closerie [kloz'ri], *n.f.* Small enclosed farm or garden; a bit of land.
Clotaire [klɔ'tɛ:r], *m.* Clotharius.
Clot(h)ilde [klɔ'tild], *f.* Clotilda.
clôture [klo'ty:r], *n.f.* Enclosure; cloister-wall; seclusion (of nuns etc.); closing, close; (*Parl.* and *Theat.*) closure. *Bris de clôture*, breach of close; *cours*, *prix de clôture*,

(*St. Exch.*) closing price; *demander la clôture,* (*Parl.*) to move the closure (of a debate etc.); *mettre une clôture,* to enclose. (*C*) *Clôture de perches,* rail fence. **clôturer,** *v.t.* To close; (*Parl.*) to closure; (*Comm.*) to wind up, close (business, accounts).

clou [klu], *n.m.* Nail, spike, stud; (*Path.*) carbuncle, boil, nail-sore (of horse); (*fig.*) pawnshop; prison; chief attraction. *Cela ne vaut pas un clou,* that's not worth a straw; *clou à grosse tête,* hobnail; *clou de girofle,* clove; *maigre comme un clou,* thin as a rake; (*fam.*) *mettre une montre au clou,* to pawn a watch; *river son clou à quelqu'un,* to clinch someone's argument; *un clou chasse l'autre,* one idea drives away another. (*pl.*) (*fam.*) *Les clous,* the pedestrian crossing (between studs). **clouage** or **clouement,** *n.m.* Nailing; nail-work. **cloué,** *a.* (*fem.* **clouée**) Nailed, riveted. *Tapis cloué,* fitted carpet.—*n.m. Du cloué,* riveted shoes. **clouer,** *v.t.* To nail; to fix; to rivet; (*fig.*) to detain, to confine, to pin down, to put in a fix. (*fam.*) *Clouer le bec à quelqu'un,* to shut someone up; *être cloué au lit,* to be bedridden; *rester cloué sur place,* to remain rooted to the spot. **clouter,** *v.t.* To adorn with nails, to stud. *Chaussures cloutées,* hobnailed boots; *passage clouté,* pedestrian crossing. **clouterie,** *n.f.* Nail-factory; nail trade. **cloutier,** *n.m.* Nail-maker, nail-dealer. **cloutière,** *n.f.* Anvil for making nails; nail-box. **clouure,** *n.f.* Nailing; nail-hole.

clovisse [klɔ'vis], *n.f.* Winkle; cockle.

clown [klun], *n.m.* Clown, funny-man. **clownerie,** *n.f.,* trick of clown(s), clownery. **clownesque,** *a.* Clownish.

cloyère [klwa'jɛ:r], *n.f.* Oyster-basket; basket of 25 dozen.

club [klʌb, klyb], *n.m.* Club (sporting or political). **clubiste** or **clubman,** *n.m.* Member of a club.

cluniste [kly'nist], *n.m.* Cluniac monk.

cluse [klyz], *n.f.* (*E. dial.* and *Geog.*) A narrow transversal valley cut through a mountain range, esp. in Jura.

clysoir [kli'zwa:r], *n.m.* Clyster-pipe. **clystère,** *n.m.* Clyster, injection, enema.

cnémide [kne'mid], *n.f.* Greave.

coaccusé [koaky'ze], *n.m.* (*fem.* **-ée**) Fellow-prisoner; co-defendant.

coacquéreur [koake'rœ:r], *n.m.* Co-purchaser, joint buyer. **coacquisition,** *n.f.* Joint purchase.

coactif [koak'tif], *a.* (*fem.* **coactive**) Coactive. **coaction,** *n.f.* Coercion, compulsion.

coadjuteur [koadʒy'tœ:r], *n.m.* Coadjutor (of a prelate). **coadjutorerie,** *n.f.* Coadjuter-ship. **coadjutrice,** *n.f.* Coadjutrix (of an abbess etc.).

coadjuvant [koadʒy'vã], *a.* (*fem.* **-ante**) Contributory.

coadministrateur [koadministra'tœ:r], *n.m.* Co-trustee.

coagulant [koagy'lã], *a.* (*fem.* **-ante**) Coagulant. **coagulateur,** *n.m.* (*fem.* **-trice**) Coagulator. **coagulation,** *n.f.* Coagulation. **coaguler,** *v.t.* To coagulate. **se coaguler,** *v.r.* To coagulate.

coalescence [koale'sã:s], *n.f.* Coalescence. **coalescent,** *a.* (*fem.* **-ente**) Coalescent. **coalisé,** *a.* (*fem.* **-ée**) Allied (of powers).

coaliser, *v.t.* To unite in a coalition. **se coaliser,** *v.r.* To coalesce, to league, to unite, to combine. **coalisés,** *n.m.* (*used only in pl.*) Allies. **coalition,** *n.f.* Coalition, union league.

coallié, *a.* (*fem.* **coalliée**) [COALISÉ].

coaltar, coltar [kol'tar], *n.m.* Tar. **coaltarer,** *v.t.* To tar.

coaptation [koapta'siɔ̃], *n.f.* Coaptation; setting of bones.

coassement [koas'mã], *n.m.* Croaking (of frogs). **coasser,** *v.i.* To croak (of frogs).

coassocié [koasɔ'sje], *n.m.* Co-partner.

coauteur [koo'tœ:r], *n.m.* Co-author.

cobalt [kɔ'balt], *n.m.* Cobalt. **cobaltifère,** *a.* Cobaltiferous.

cobaye [kɔ'ba:j], *n.m.* Guinea-pig.

cobra [kɔ'bra], *n.m.* Cobra, hooded-snake.

coca [kɔ'ka], *n.m.* (*Bot.*) Coca.—*n.f.* (*Pharm.*) Coca.

cocagne [kɔ'kaɲ], *n.f. Mât de cocagne,* greasy pole; *pays de cocagne,* land of plenty.

cocaïne [kɔka'in], *n.f.* Cocaine. **cocaïnisme,** *n.m.* Cocainism. **cocaïnomane,** *n.m.* Cocaine addict. **cocaïnomanie,** *n.f.* Cocainomania.

cocarde [kɔ'kard], *n.f.* Cockade; rosette, knot of ribbons, etc. *Avoir sa cocarde,* (*fam.*) to be tipsy; *cocarde tricolore,* three-coloured cockade; *prendre la cocarde,* to enlist. **cocardier,** *a.* (*fem.* **-ière**) Fond of the military cockade, the uniform, etc., jingo.—*n.* Such a person.

cocasse [kɔ'kas], *a.* (*fam.*) Odd, laughable, comical. **cocasserie,** *n.f.* Drollery, farce.

coccinelle [kɔksi'nɛl], *n.f.* Lady-bird.

coccyx [kɔk'sis], *n.m.* (*Anat.*) Coccyx.

coche (1) [kɔʃ], *n.m.* Coach. *C'est la mouche du coche,* he is a busybody; *manquer le coche,* to let slip the opportunity.

coche (2) [kɔʃ], *n.f.* Notch, score, nick, indentation. *Faire une coche,* to notch.

coche (3) [kɔʃ], *n.f.* Sow.

cochenillage [kɔʃni'ja:ʒ], *n.m.* Cochineal bath. **cochenille** [kɔʃ'ni:j], *n.f.* Cochineal. **cocheniller,** *v.t.* To dye with cochineal. **cochenillier,** *n.m.* Cochineal-fig, nopal.

cocher (1) [kɔ'ʃe], *n.m.* Coachman, driver. (*Astron.*) Auriga. *Cocher de fiacre,* cabman.

cocher (2) [kɔ'ʃe], *v.t.* To notch.

cocher (3) [kɔ'ʃe], *v.t.* To tread (of birds).

cochère [kɔ'ʃɛ:r], *a.f.* For carriages. *Porte cochère,* carriage-entrance, gateway.

cochet [kɔ'ʃɛ], *n.m.* Young cock, cockerel.

cochevis [kɔʃ'vi], *n.m.* Tufted or crested lark.

Cochinchine [kɔʃɛ̃'ʃin], *f.* Cochin China.

cochléaria [kɔklea'rja], *n.m.* Cochlearia, scurvy-grass.

cochlée [kɔk'le], *n.f.* (*Anat.*) Cochlea. **cochléiforme,** *a.* Cochleiform.

cochoir [kɔ'ʃwa:r], *n.m.* Cooper's curved axe.

cochon [kɔ'ʃɔ̃], *n.m.* Hog, pig; pork; (*fig.*) dirty, fat, greedy, or beastly person; (*Metal.*) sow, dross. *Amis comme cochons,* as thick as thieves; *cochon de lait,* sucking-pig; *cochon de mer,* porpoise; *cochon d'Inde* or *de Barbarie,* guinea-pig; *fromage de cochon,* brawn; *un tour de cochon,* a dirty trick.—*a.* (*colloq.*) Dirty, filthy, beastly, lewd.

cochonnaille [kɔʃɔ'na:j], *n.f.* (*vulg.*) Dressed pork; sausage-meat. **cochonnée,** *n.f.* Litter (of pigs). **cochonner,** *v.i.* To farrow, to pig.—*v.t.* To do (something) in a slovenly

manner, to botch. **cochonnerie,** *n.f.*
Nastiness, filth; beastliness, beastly action or
language, obscenity; (*fig.*) trash, rubbish.
cochonnet, *n.m.* Young pig; jack (at bowls);
die with twelve sides.
cocker [kɔ'kɛr], *n.m.* Cocker spaniel.
cocktail [kɔk'tɛl], *n.m.* Cocktail; cocktail
party.
coco (1) [ko'ko], *n.m.* Coco-nut; (*colloq.*) chap,
fellow; darling; (*slang*) head; (*childish*) egg.
Lait de coco, coco-nut milk; *quel drôle de
coco!* what a queer chap! *il a le coco un peu
fêlé*, he is a bit cracked; *tapis de coco*, coco-nut
matting.
coco (2) [ko'ko], *n.f.* (*slang*) [COCAÏNE].
cocon [kɔ'kɔ̃], *n.m.* Cocoon. **coconille,** *n.f.*
Twist or yarn of waste silk. **coconnage,**
n.m. Formation of cocoons. **coconner,** *v.i.*
To form a cocoon. **coconnier,** *a.* (*fem.*
coconnière) Pertaining to cocoons.
cocorli [kɔkɔr'li], *n.m.* (*Zool.*) Curlew, sandpiper.
cocorico [kɔkɔri'ko], *n.m.* Cock-a-doodle-doo!
cocotier [kɔkɔ'tje], *n.m.* Coco-nut palm.
cocotte [kɔkɔt], *n.f.* (*childish*) Chicken, hen;
folded paper hen; horse, gee-gee; inflammation of the eyelids; (*Vet.*) foot-and-mouth
disease; loose woman, tart; stew-pan or
casserole. **cocotter,** *v.i.* (*vulg.*) To stink.
cocréancier [kokreɑ̃'sje], *n.m.* (*fem.* **cocréan-
cière**) Joint-creditor.
coction [kɔk'sjɔ̃], *n.f.* Coction, boiling; digestion (of food).
cocu [kɔ'ky], *n.m.* Cuckold, a deceived husband. **cocuage,** *n.m.* Cuckoldom. **cocu-
fier,** *v.t.* To cuckold.
coda [kɔ'da], *n.f.* Coda.
code [kɔd], *n.m.* Code (digest or collection of
laws); law, rule, criterion, standard. *Le code
de la route*, the highway code; *le code
militaire*, the articles of war; military law; (*fam.*) *les
codes*, the anti-dazzle headlamps.
codébiteur [kodebi'tœːr], *n.m.* (*fem.* **codébi-
trice**) Joint-debtor.
codemandeur [kodəmɑ̃'dœːr], *n.m.* (*fem.* **co-
demanderesse**) Co-plaintiff, joint-plaintiff.
coder [kɔ'de], *v.t.* To code (telegram).
codétenteur [kodetɑ̃'tœːr], *n.m.* (*fem.* **codé-
tentrice**) Joint-holder.
codétenu [kodet'ny], *n.m.* (*fem.* **codétenue**)
Fellow-prisoner.
codex [kɔ'dɛks], *n.m.* Pharmacopoeia; codex.
codicillaire [kɔdisi'lɛːr], *a.* Contained in a
codicil.
codicille [kɔdi'sil], *n.m.* Codicil, rider.
codificateur [kɔdifika'tœːr], *n.m.* (*fem.* **codi-
ficatrice** Codifier. **codification,** *n.f.*
Codification, coding; digest (of the law).
codifier [kɔdi'fje], *v.t.* To codify.
codirecteur [kodirɛk'tœr], *n.m.* Joint-manager.
codonataire [kodɔna'tɛːr], *a.* and *n.* Joint-
donee. **codonateur,** *a.* and *n.* (*fem.*
codonatrice) Joint-donor.
cœcum [CAECUM].
coéducation [koedyka'sjɔ̃], *n.f.* Coeducation.
coefficient [kɔefi'sjɑ̃], *n.m.* Coefficient.
cœlacanthe [sela'kɑ̃:t], *n.m.* Coelacanth.
coemption [koɑ̃p'sjɔ̃], *n.f.* Coemption.
coéquation [koekwa'sjɔ̃], *n.f.* Proportional
assessment (of taxes etc.).
coéquipier [koeki'pje], *n.m.* Fellow member
(of a crew, a team, etc.).

coercer [koɛr'se], *v.t.* To coerce. **coerci-
bilité,** *n.f.* Coercibility. **coercible,** *a.*
Coercible. **coercitif,** *a.* (*fem.* -**ive**) Coercive. **coercition,** *n.f.* Coercion.
coéternel [koeter'nɛl], *a.* (*fem.* **coéternelle**)
Coeternal. **coéternité,** *n.f.* Coeternity.
cœur [kœːr], *n.m.* Heart; (*fig.*) bosom, breast,
feelings, mind, soul; courage, spirit, mettle,
pluck; stomach; core, middle, midst, depth;
love, affection, tenderness. *À cœur joie*, to
one's heart's content; *à cœur ouvert*, frankly;
à contre-cœur, against one's will, reluctantly,
against the grain; *affaire de cœur*, love affair;
au cœur de l'été, in the height of summer; *avoir
au cœur dur*, hard-hearted; *avoir à cœur* or
prendre à cœur, to have at heart; *avoir bon
cœur*, to be good-natured; *avoir du cœur*, to
be (a man) of active sympathies, to be plucky,
(*Cards*) to have hearts (in hand); *avoir mal
au cœur*, to feel sick; *avoir le cœur brisé*, to be
broken-hearted; *avoir le cœur gros*, to be
ready to cry, to have a lump in one's throat;
avoir le cœur sur les lèvres, to be open-hearted;
avoir le cœur tendre, to be tender-hearted;
avoir quelque chose sur le cœur, to have something on one's mind; *avoir un cœur d'artichaut*, to be very fickle; *à vous de cœur*,
affectionately yours; *de bon* or *grand cœur*,
heartily, with pleasure, gladly; *de cœur avec
quelqu'un*, with somebody in spirit; *de gaîté
de cœur*, in sheer wantonness; *de tout mon
cœur*, with all my heart; *du fond de son
cœur*, from the bottom of one's heart; *en avoir le
cœur net*, to know the rights of something, to
get to the bottom of it; *faire contre mauvaise
fortune bon cœur*, to put a good face upon
matters; *faire quelque chose de bon* (*mauvais*)
cœur, to do something gladly (unwillingly);
il a le cœur à l'ouvrage, he loves his work; *il
a le cœur bien accroché*, his heart is in the
right place; *il n'a point de cœur*, he has no
spirit; *la paix du cœur*, peace of mind; *le cœur
lui saigne*, his heart bleeds; *le cœur me manqua*, my heart failed me; *loin des yeux, loin du
cœur*, out of sight, out of mind; *mauvaise tête
bon cœur*, foolish but good-hearted; *mettre
du cœur au ventre à quelqu'un*, to put heart
into someone; *mon cœur*, my love, my dearest;
ouvrir son cœur à quelqu'un, to unbosom oneself to someone; *par cœur*, by heart, by rote;
quelque chose qui soulève le cœur, something
sickening, which turns the stomach; *sans
cœur*, heartless; *serrement de cœur*, heart-
pang; *si le cœur vous en dit*, if you feel inclined; *un homme de cœur*, a great-hearted man.
coexistant [koɛgzis'tɑ̃], *a.* (*fem.* **coexistante**)
Coexistent. **coexistence,** *n.f.* Coexistence.
coexister, *v.i.* To coexist.
coffin [kɔ'fɛ̃], *n.m.* Water-box or sheath for
mower's whetstone.
coffrage [kɔ'fra:ʒ], *n.m.* Coffering (in mines);
framing (for concrete).
coffre [kɔfr], *n.m.* Chest, trunk, box; coffer;
(*colloq.*) chest (part of the body); drum (of a
mill); (*Naut.*) mooring-buoy; (*Print.*) coffin.
Avoir du coffre or *le coffre solide*, to be strong-
chested; *coffre à avoine*, corn-bin; *les coffres
de l'État*, the public treasury. **coffre-fort,**
n.m. (*pl.* **coffres-forts**) Strong-box, safe.
coffrer, *v.t.* (*colloq.*) To imprison, to lock
up; to coffer (a shaft). **coffret,** *n.m.* Little
chest, casket, ornamental box

cogérance [koʒe'rã:s], *n.f.* Joint management. **cogérant**, *n.m.* (*fem.* **-ante**) Joint manager (manageress).

cogitation [koʒita'sjɔ̃], *n.f.* Cogitation, reflection.

cognac [ko'ɲak], *n.m.* Cognac brandy.

cognasse [ko'ɲas], *n.f.* Wild quince. **cognassier**, *n.m.* Quince-tree.

cognat [kog'na], *n.m.* (*Law*) Cognate. **cognation**, *n.f.* Cognation.

cogne [koɲ], *n.m.* (*slang*) Policeman, bobby.

cognée [ko'ɲe], *n.f.* Axe, hatchet. *Jeter le manche après la cognée,* to give up in despair; *mettre la cognée à l'arbre,* to lay the axe to the tree, (*fig.*) to begin an overdue reform.

cogner [ko'ɲe], *v.t.* To knock in, to drive in; to thump.—*v.i.* To hit, bump (*contre*), knock (engine). **se cogner**, *v.r.* To knock (against), to hit oneself; (*pop.*) to fight.

cognitif [kogni'tif], *a.* (*fem.* **cognitive**) Cognitive. **cognition**, *n.f.* Cognition.

cognoscibilité [kognosibili'te], *n.f.* Cognoscibility. **cognoscible**, *a.* Cognoscible.

cohabitant [koabi'tã], *a.* (*fem.* **cohabitante**) Cohabiting (with). **cohabitation**, *n.f.* Cohabitation.

cohabiter [koabi'te], *v.i.* To cohabit.

cohérence [koe'rã:s], *n.f.* Coherence. **cohérent**, *a.* (*fem.* **cohérente**) Coherent.

cohériter [koeri'te], *v.i.* To inherit conjointly. **cohéritier**, *n.m.* (*fem.* **cohéritière**) Co-heir, co-heiress.

cohésif [koe'sif], *a.* (*fem.* **cohésive**) Cohesive. **cohésion** [koe'zjɔ̃], *n.f.* Cohesion.

cohobation [koɔba'sjɔ̃], *n.f.* (*Chem.*) Redistillation. **cohober**, *v.t.* To redistil.

cohorte [ko'ort], *n.f.* Cohort; (*poét.*) troop, host; (*colloq.*) crew, gang.

cohue [ko'y], *n.f.* Throng, mob, crush.

coi [kwa], *a.* (*fem.* **coite** (1)) Quiet, calm, still. *Se tenir* or *demeurer coi,* to remain still or quiet, to lie low.

coiffe [kwaf], *n.f.* Coif, cap, hood, head-dress; caul (of infant); skull-cap; lining. *Coiffe blanche,* (*Naut.*) white cap cover; *coiffe de chapeau,* hat-lining; *coiffe de fusée,* fuse-cap; *coiffe d'obus,* shell-cap. **coiffé**, *a.* (*fem.* **coiffée**) With the hair arranged; hatted, covered; (*fig.*) taken with, infatuated (*de*). *Être né coiffé,* to be born with a caul; (*fig.*) to be born with a silver spoon in one's mouth.

coiffer [kwa'fe], *v.t.* To put on the head of; to dress the hair of; (*fig.*) to please, to infatuate; (*colloq.*) to deceive, to take in; to make tipsy; (*Naut.*) to lay back; to cap (bottles). *Cette femme coiffe son mari,* that woman deceives her husband; *coiffer sainte Catherine,* to remain an old maid after 25; *coiffer une bouteille,* to cap a bottle; *être bien coiffé,* to have one's hair well dressed, to have a hat that becomes one; *il est coiffé de cette femme,* he is smitten with that woman [*see* COQUELUCHE].—*v.i.* To dress hair; to become; to suit; (*Naut.*) to be laid aback. **se coiffer**, *v.r.* To wear on one's head (*de*); to dress one's hair; to get intoxicated; to be infatuated (*de*). **coiffeur**, *n.m.* (*fem.* **coiffeuse** (1)) Hairdresser, hair-stylist. **coiffeuse** (2), *n.f.* Lady's dressing-table. **coiffure**, *n.f.* Head-dress, coiffure, style of arranging the hair.

coin [kwɛ̃], *n.m.* Corner, angle made by two plane surfaces, nook; little bit, small piece (of land etc.); wedge (for cleaving timber etc.); corner cupboard or seat; (*Coin. etc.*) stamp; (*fig.*) character, imprint; (*Rail.*) pin; (*Print.*) quoin. *À trois coins,* three-cornered; *au coin du feu,* by the fireside; (*fam.*) *ça m'en bouche un coin!* Well, I never! *coins et recoins,* nooks and corners, cracks and crannies; *enfoncer le coin,* to drive in the wedge; *être marqué au coin,* to bear the stamp of; *frappé au bon coin,* of the right sort, excellent in every way; *il n'a pas bougé du coin du feu,* he has never been from home; *jouer aux quatre coins,* to play puss in the corner; *place de coin,* corner seat; *les quatre coins du monde,* the four quarters of the globe; *regarder du coin de l'œil,* to look at out of the corner of one's eye; *regard en coin,* sidelong glance; *rester dans son coin,* not to mix with other people; *un joli coin,* a beauty spot.

coinçage [kwɛ̃'sa:ʒ], *n.m.* Tightening with a wedge, wedging. **coincement**, *n.m.* Jamming (of a machine). **coincer**, *v.t.* To wedge, to tighten with a wedge; (*slang*) to corner, to arrest, to 'pinch'. **se coincer**, *v.r.* To jam (of machines).

coïncidence [koɛ̃si'dã:s], *n.f.* Coincidence. **coïncident**, *a.* (*fem.* **coïncidente**) Coincident, coinciding (*avec*, with). **coïncider**, *v.i.* To coincide, to be coincident.

coin-coin [kwɛ̃kwɛ̃], *n.m.* Quack (of a duck); toot-toot (of motor horn).

coing [kwɛ̃], *n.m.* Quince.

coïntéressé [koɛ̃tere'se], *a.* (*fem.* **-ée**) Jointly interested.—*n.* Associate, partner having a joint interest with another.

coir [kwa:r], *n.m.* Coir, coco-fibre.

coït [koit], *n.m.* Coition, copulation.

coite (1) [COI].

coite (2) [COUETTE].

cojouissance [koʒwi'sã:s], *n.f.* (*Law*) Joint use.

coke [kok], *n.m.* Coke. **cokéfier**, *v.t.* To coke.

col [kɔl], *n.m.* *Neck of a man etc.; neck (of a bottle, dress, etc.); collar; pass, col, saddle (of mountain); (*Anat.*) cervix (of uterus etc.). *Col de cygne,* swan-neck, goose-neck; *col cassé,* wing collar; *col droit,* stick-up collar; *col rabattu,* turn-down collar; *col montant,* high neck; *col raide, mou,* stiff, soft collar; *faux col,* detachable collar.

colateur [kɔla'tœ:r], *n.m.* Outlet channel.

colature [kɔla'ty:r], *n.f.* (*Pharm.*) Straining, filtering; liquid thus filtered.

colback [kɔl'bak], *n.m.* Busby.

colchique [kɔl'ʃik], *n.m.* (*Bot.*) Meadow-saffron, colchicum.

colcotar [kɔlko'ta:r], *n.m.* (*Chem.*) Colcothar, (jewellers') rouge.

colégataire [kolega'te:r], *n.m.* Co-legatee.

coléoptère [koleop'te:r], *a.* Coleopterous.—*n.m.* Coleopter, beetle.

colère [ko'le:r], *n.f.* Anger, wrath, rage, fury. *Accès de colère,* fit of passion; *être en colère,* to be angry; *se mettre en colère,* to fly into a passion.—*a.* Passionate, hasty, choleric. **coléreux**, *a.* (*fem.* **-euse**) Irascible, peppery. **colérique**, *a.* Choleric, irascible.

coliart [ko'lja:r], *n.m.* Skate (fish).

colibacille [koliba'sil], *n.m.* Colon bacillus. **colibacillose**, *n.f.* (*Med.*) Colon bacillus infection.

colibri [kɔli'bri], *n.m.* Humming-bird.

colicitant [kɔlisi'tã], *n.m.* Co-vendor.

colifichet [kɔlifi'ʃɛ], *n.m.* Trinket, knick-knack; tinsel, finery; bird-cake.

colimaçon [kɔlima'sɔ̃], *n.m.* Snail. *Escalier en colimaçon*, spiral stairs.

colin [kɔ'lɛ̃], *n.m.* Hake; American partridge.

colin-maillard [kɔlɛ̃ma'ja:r], *n.m. inv.* Blindman's-buff; blindman (at blindman's-buff).

colin-tampon [kɔlɛ̃tã'pɔ̃], *n.m.* Drum-beat of the ancient Swiss Guards. *Je m'en moque comme de colin-tampon*, (*fam.*) I do not care a straw about it.

colique [kɔ'lik], *n.f.* Colic, stomach-ache. (*vulg.*) *Avoir la colique*, to be afraid; *colique de miserere*, iliac passion; *colique des peintres* or *colique saturnine*, painter's colic.

colis [kɔ'li], *n.m.* Package, parcel, case, piece of luggage. *Colis postal*, parcel-post packet.

collaborateur [kɔlabɔra'tœ:r], *n.m.* (*fem.* **collaboratrice**) Collaborator; pro-German person (under the Vichy government). **collaboration**, *n.f.* Collaboration. **collaborer**, *v.i.* To collaborate.

collage [kɔ'la:ʒ], *n.m.* Pasting, gluing, sizing (of paper); paper-hanging; clarifying or clearing (wine); (*slang*) cohabiting (without marriage).

collant [kɔ'lã], *a.* (*fem.* **collante**) Sticky; tight, close-fitting. (*fam.*) *Une personne collante*, a regular sticker.—*n.m. pl.* Tights.

collapsus [kɔlap'sy:s], *n.m.* (*Path.*) Collapse.

collatéral [kɔlate'ral], *a.* (*fem.* **-ale**, *pl.* **-aux**) Collateral.—*n.* (*Law*) A collateral.—*n.f.* Aisle (of churches). **collatéralement,** *adv.* Collaterally.

collateur [kɔla'tœ:r], *n.m.* Collator (to a benefice).

collation [kɔla'sjɔ̃], *n.f.* Conferring (of degree, title, etc.); (*Eccl.*) advowson; light meal; comparison (of documents etc.). **collationnement,** *n.m.* Collating, comparing. **collationner,** *v.t.* To collate, to compare. —*v.i.* To have a snack.

colle [kɔl], *n.f.* Paste, gum, mucilage; (*sch.*) question, difficulty, poser; sham, fib, bouncing lie; detention. *Colle de peau*, size; *colle de poisson*, isinglass; *colle forte*, glue; *poser une colle*, (*fam.*) to put a difficult question, a poser.

collecte [kɔ'lɛkt], *n.f.* Collection (of money etc.); collect (prayer). **collecteur,** *n.m.* (*fem.* **-trice**) Collector; tax-gatherer.—*a.* Collecting. *Égout collecteur*, main-sewer. *Poils collecteurs*, (*Bot.*) hairs on stigma receiving pollen.

collectif [kɔlɛk'tif], *a.* (*fem.* **-ive**) Collective.— *n.m.* (*Gram.*) Collective noun. **collection,** *n.f.* Collection; set. **collectionner,** *v.t.* To collect, to make collections of things. **collectionneur,** *n.m.* (*fem.* **-euse**) Collector. **collectivement,** *adv.* Collectively.

collectivisme [kɔlɛkti'vism], *n.m.* Collectivism. **collectiviste,** *n.* Collectivist. **collectivité,** *n.f.* Collectivity, community; common ownership.

collège [kɔ'lɛ:ʒ], *n.m.* College; grammar-school, high-school. *Collège électoral*, body of electors. **collégial,** *a.* (*fem.* **-iale**, *pl.* **-iaux**) Collegial; collegiate.—*n.f. Une collégiale*, a collegiate church. **collégien,** *n.m.* (*fem.* **-ienne**) High-school boy or girl.

collègue [kɔ'lɛg], *n.m.* Colleague.

coller [kɔ'le], *v.t.* To paste, to glue, to size; to stick together; to clear (with isinglass etc.); (*fig.*) to silence, to stump or embarrass; to plough (at exam.); (*slang*) to apply (a blow etc.). *Être collé*, to be close up against the cushion (at billiards); (*sch.*) to be ploughed, to be kept in.—*v.i.* To stick, to adhere; to fit tight (of clothes). *Ce pantalon colle bien*, those trousers fit nicely; (*slang*) *ça colle*, it goes all right. **se coller,** *v.r.* To stick to; (*colloq.*) to stick (in a place); (*slang*) to cohabit (without marriage); to concentrate or fix one's mind (on). *Se coller au mur*, to keep close to the wall.

collerette [kɔl'rɛt], *n.f.* Collarette, collar (for ladies); (*Bot.*) involucrum consisting of one row of sepals, frill on stem of mushroom; flange of pipe.

collet [kɔ'lɛ], *n.m.* Collar (of gown, coat, etc.); cape; band (for the neck); neck (of teeth); scrag or neck (of meat); (*Hunt.*) snare, noose (for birds, rabbits, etc.); flange. *Collet de mouton*, neck of mutton; *collet montant*, stick-up collar; *collet rabattu*, turned-down collar; *prendre* or *saisir quelqu'un au collet*, to collar someone, to seize him by the scruff of the neck; *un collet monté*, a strait-laced, prudish person, prig.

colleter [kɔl'te], *v.t.* To collar, to seize by the neck.—*v.i.* To set snares (for game). **se colleter,** *v.r.* To come to grips (with someone). **colleteur,** *n.m.* Snare-setter.

colleur [kɔ'lœ:r], *n.m.* Gluer, paster, paper-hanger, sizer, bill-sticker; (*school slang*) examiner.

colleuse [kɔ'løz], *n.f.* Machine for sizing cloth etc.

collier [kɔ'lje], *n.m.* Necklace; gold chain (of knightly orders etc.); collar (for dogs, horses, etc.); (*Mach.*) clamp, jubilee clip. *Cheval de collier*, draught-horse; *collier de barbe*, Newgate fringe; *collier de frein*, brake band; *collier de force*, training collar; *collier de misère*, drudgery; *donner un coup de collier* or *donner à plein collier*, to make a strenuous effort; *être franc du collier*, to work well (of a horse), (*fig.*) never to shirk one's work, to be always in earnest; *reprendre le collier*, to get back into harness, resume work.

colliger [kɔli'ʒe], *v.t.* To collect, to make a collection (of extracts).

collimateur [kɔlima'tœ:r], *n.m.* Collimator. **collimation,** *n.f.* Collimation.

colline [kɔ'lin], *n.f.* Hill, hillock. *Le penchant d'une colline*, the slope or declivity of a hill.

collision [kɔli'zjɔ̃], *n.f.* Collision.

collocation [kɔlɔka'sjɔ̃], *n.f.* Classification (of creditors etc.); sum allowed to a creditor in consequence of this.

collodion [kɔlɔ'djɔ̃], *n.m.* Collodion. **collodionné,** *a.* (*fem.* **-ée**) Collodioned.

colloïdal [kɔlɔi'dal], *a.* (*fem.* **-ale**, *pl.* **-aux**) Colloidal. **colloïde,** *n.m.* Colloid.

colloque [kɔ'lɔk], *n.m.* Colloquy, conference.

colloquer [kɔlɔ'ke], *v.t.* (*fam.*) To dispose of, to plant (a person etc. in an unwelcome place); to get rid of, to sell, place, etc. (with someone); to rank or place in order (creditors).

collotypie [kɔlɔti'pi], *n.f.* Collotype.

[167]

collusion [kɔly'zjɔ̃], *n.f.* Collusion. **collu-soire**, *a.* Collusory, collusive.

collutoire [kɔly'twaːr], *n.m.* (*Med.*) Mouthwash; gargle.

collyre [kɔ'liːr], *n.m.* (*Med.*) Eye-wash, eye-salve.

colmatage [kɔlma'taːʒ], *n.m.* (*Agric.*) Warping (of land); filling up (of pot-holes); clogging (pipe, filter). **colmate**, *n.m.* Warp; warped land.

colmater [kɔlma'te], *v.t.* To warp (land); to fill up; to clop.

colocataire [kɔlɔka'tɛːr], *n.f.* Joint tenant.

Colomb [kɔ'lɔ̃], *m.* Columbus.

colombage [kɔlɔ̃'baːʒ], *n.m.* (*Carp.*) Timber framing (for cob-walls); half-timbering.

colombe [kɔ'lɔ̃:b], *n.f.* (*poet.*) Pigeon, dove; (*Carp.*) cooper's large plane. **colombelle**, *n.f.* Young dove. **colombier**, *n.m.* Dovecot, pigeon-house; (*fig.*) paternal home; (*Print.*) pigeon-hole, gap; paper of large format; (*Naut.*) prop or shore. *Grand colombier*, atlas paper. **colombin**, *a.* (*fem.* -ine) Columbine; dove-colour.—*n.m.* (*Min.*) Lead-ore; (*vulg.*) turd.—*n.f.* Pigeon-dung, fowls'-dung.

colombophile [kɔlɔ̃bo'fil], *a.* and *n.* Breeder or fancier of carrier-pigeons.

colon (1) [kɔ'lɔ̃], *n.m.* Colonist, planter; farmer, cultivator; settler; (*Mil. slang*) colonel.

côlon (2) [ko'lɔ̃], *n.m.* (*Anat.*) Colon.

colonel [kɔlɔ'nɛl], *n.m.* Colonel; (*Av.*) group captain. **colonelle**, *n.f.* Colonel's wife.

colonial [kɔlɔ'njal], *a.* (*fem.* -iale, *pl.* -iaux) Colonial.—*n.* A colonial. **colonialisme**, *n.m.* Colonialism. **colonialiste**, *a.* and *n.* In favour of colonialism. **colonie**, *n.f.* Colony, settlement. *Colonie de vacances*, holiday camp. **colonisable**, *a.* Colonizable. **colonisateur**, *a.* (*fem.* -trice) Colonizing.—*n.* Colonizer. **colonisation**, *n.f.* Colonization. **coloniser**, *v.t.* To colonize.

colonnade [kɔlɔ'nad], *n.f.* (*Arch.*) Colonnade.

colonne [kɔ'lɔn], *n.f.* Column, pillar; row or column (of units, tens, etc.); (*fig.*) support, mainstay, tower of strength. *Colonne cannelée*, fluted column; *colonne torse*, wreathed column; *lit à colonnes*, four-poster; *colonne d'eau*, water-spout; *colonne vertébrale*, spinal column, backbone; *les colonnes d'Hercule*, the Pillars of Hercules. **colonnette**, *n.f.* Little column.

colophane [kɔlɔ'fan], *n.f.* Black resin, colophony.

coloquinte [kɔlɔ'kɛ̃:t], *n.f.* Colocynth, bitter apple.

colorable [kɔlɔ'rabl], *a.* Colourable. **colorant**, *a.* (*fem.* -ante) Colouring.—*n.m.* Dye, colouring stuff. **coloration**, *n.f.* Coloration, staining.

coloré [kɔlɔ're], *a.* (*fem.* -ée) Coloured; (*fig.*) highly coloured (of style etc.). *Teint coloré*, ruddy complexion; *vin coloré*, deep-coloured wine.

colorer [kɔlɔ're], *v.t.* To colour, to dye; to varnish (to give a false appearance to). **se colorer**, *v.r.* To colour (of a thing).

coloriage [kɔlɔ'rjaːʒ], *n.m.* (*Paint.*) Colouring. **colorier**, *v.t.* To colour, to stain (a drawing etc.). **colorifique**, *a.* Colorific.

coloris [kɔlɔ'ri], *n.m.* Colouring, art of colouring; colour *or* brilliance (of style etc.). **coloriste** [kɔlɔ'rist], *n.m.* Colourer; colourist, an artist in colour.

colossal [kɔlɔ'sal], *a.* (*fem.* -ale, *pl.* -aux) Colossal, of giant proportions. **colossalement**, *adv.* Colossally.

colosse [kɔ'lɔs], *n.m.* Colossus, giant.

colportage [kɔlpɔr'taːʒ], *n.m.* Hawking, peddling. **colporter**, *v.t.* To hawk about; to retail; to spread. *Colporter une nouvelle*, to retail a piece of news. **colporteur**, *n.m.* Hawker, pedlar; (*fig.*) spreader of news.

coltin [kɔl'tɛ̃], *n.m.* Coalheaver's hat. **coltinage**, *n.m.* Carrying of heavy sacks etc. **coltiner**, *v.t.* To carry heavy loads (on head and back). **coltineur**, *n.m.* Coalheaver, load-porter.

columbaire [kɔlɔ̃'bɛːr] or **columbarium**, *n.m.* Columbarium.

columelle [kɔly'mɛl], *n.f.* (*Bot.* and *Zool.*) Columella.

colza [kɔl'za], *n.m.* Colza, rape, rape-seed.

coma [kɔ'ma], *n.m.* Coma. **comateux**, *a.* (*fem.* -euse) Comatose.

combat [kɔ̃'ba], *n.m.* Combat, fight, battle, contest; struggle; strife; agitation. *Au fort du combat*, in the thick of the fight; *combat à outrance*, fight to the death; *combat égal*, drawn battle; *combat simulé*, sham fight; *combat singulier*, single combat; *être hors de combat*, to be disabled.

combatif [kɔ̃ba'tif], *a.* (*fem.* -ive) Pugnacious. **combativité**, *n.f.* Combativity.

combattable [kɔ̃ba'tabl], *a.* Combatable, disputable. **combattant**, *n.m.* (*fem.* -ante) Combatant; champion; ruff (bird). *Anciens combattants*, ex-service men.

combattre [kɔ̃'batr], *v.t. irr.* To fight, to combat, to wage war against, to strive against. *Combattre une opinion*, to combat an opinion. —*v.i.* To fight, to contend, to vie, to struggle. **se combattre**, *v.r.* To combat; to contend with each other.

combe [kɔ̃:b], *n.f.* Small valley, dale (in Jura).

combien [kɔ̃'bjɛ̃], *adv.* How much, how many; how; how far; how long. *Combien cela vaut-il?* what is that worth? *combien y a-t-il depuis cela?* how long is it since then? *en combien de temps?* in how long? *combien de fois?* how many times? *tous les combien?* every how often?

combinable [kɔ̃bi'nabl], *a.* Combinable.

combinaison [kɔ̃binɛ'zɔ̃], *n.f.* Combination; contrivance, scheme; calculation; overalls.

combinard [kɔ̃bi'nar], *n.m.* (*fam.*) One who knows the ropes, schemer.

combinat [kɔ̃bi'na], *n.m.* Industrial combine (in U.S.S.R.).

combinateur [kɔ̃bina'tœːr], *n.m.* (*fem.* -trice) Combiner, contriver.—*a.* Combining. **combinatoire**, *a.* Combinative.

combine [kɔ̃'bin], *n.f.* (*slang*) Scheme.

combiné [kɔ̃bi'ne], *n.m.* (*Chem.*) Compound; (*Rad.*) radiogram.

combiner [kɔ̃bi'ne], *v.t.* To combine; (*fig.*) to plan, to contrive; to concoct. **se combiner**, *v.r.* To combine, to scheme.

comble [kɔ̃:bl], *n.m.* Heaping up above a full measure, overmeasure; summit, height, top; (*fig.*) highest pitch, zenith, lowest depth, last degree; (*pl.*) roof, roof-timbers. *Au comble* *de*, at the height of; *c'est le comble!* it's the limit! *de fond en comble*, from top to bottom; *il loge sous les combles*, he lives in a garret; *mettre le comble à*, to complete, to crown; *pour comble de gloire*, to complete his glory; *pour comble de malheur*, to crown all; *ruiné de fond en comble*, utterly ruined.—*a.* Full, overflowing, heaped up full to the top. *Salle comble*, house full, packed.

comblement [kɔ̃blə'mã], *n.m.* Filling up, heaping up.

combler [kɔ̃'ble], *v.t.* To heap up, to fill up to the brim; to complete, to fulfil, to gratify; to overwhelm, to load; to make up, to make good (a deficit etc.). *Combler de faveurs*, to load with flowers.

combrière [kɔ̃'brjɛːr], *n.f.* Tunny-net.

combuger [kɔ̃by'ʒe], *v.t.* To rinse out (casks).

comburant [kɔ̃by'rã], *a.* (*fem.* **-ante**) (*Chem.*) Causing burning (of oxygen etc.).—*n.m.* Fuel.

combustibilité [kɔ̃bystibili'te], *n.f.* Combustibility. **combustible**, *a.* Combustible. —*n.m.* Combustible; fuel, firing.

combustion [kɔ̃bys'tjɔ̃], *n.f.* Combustion, conflagration, flame.

comédie [kɔme'di], *n.f.* Comedy; theatre; players, comedians. *Comédie de mœurs*, comedy of manners; *donner la comédie*, to make people laugh, to be a laughing-stock; *jouer la comédie*, to play-act, to put it on; *le sujet, l'intrigue*, or *le dénouement d'une comédie*, the subject, plot, or final solution of a comedy.

comédien [kɔme'djɛ̃], *n.m.* (*fem.* **comédienne**) Comedian, actor, actress, player; (*fig.*) hypocrite, one acting a part. *Comédiens ambulants*, strolling players; *troupe de comédiens*, company of actors.—*a.* (*fig.*) Affected, theatrical.

comédon [kɔme'dɔ̃], *n.m.* (*Med.*) Comedo, blackhead.

comestibilité [kɔmɛstibili'te], *n.f.* Edibility. **comestible** [kɔmɛs'tibl], *a.* Edible, eatable. —*n.m.* Eatable; (*pl.*) eatables.

comète [kɔ'mɛt], *n.f.* Comet. *Vin de la comète*, wine of the year 1811; (*fig.*) fabulously good wine.

comice [kɔ'mis], *n.m.* Meeting; electoral meeting. *Comice agricole*, agricultural show; (*pl., Rom. Ant.*) comitia.

comifère [kɔmi'fɛːr], *a.* (*Bot.*) Comose, criniferous.

comique [kɔ'mik], *a.* Comic; comical, ludicrous, funny. *Acteur comique*, comic actor; *le genre comique*, comedy.—*n.m.* The comic art, comedy; comical part or aspect; comic actor, author, or singer.

comiquement [kɔmik'mã], *adv.* Comically.

comitard [kɔmi'tar], *n.m.* Member of a committee (*always pejorative*).

comité [kɔmi'te], *n.m.* Meeting of a few persons; committee, board. *Comité de lecture*, committee for selecting new plays for performance; *comité d'entreprise*, joint production committee; *comité permanent*, standing committee; *comité secret*, private sitting; *dîner en petit comité*, to have a small dinner-party of intimate friends; *la chambre formée en comité*, a committee of the whole house; *petit comité*, a small party, a select few.

comitial [kɔmi'sjal], *a.* (*fem.* **-iale**, *pl.* **-iaux**)

Pertaining to the *comices* or the comitia. *Mal comitial*, epilepsy.

comma [kɔ'ma], *n.m.* (*pl.* **comma** or **commas**) (*Print.*) Colon; (*Mus.*) comma.

command [kɔ'mã], *n.m. Déclaration de command*, (*Law*) (in an auction sale) declaration made by buyer when acting for a third party.

commandant [kɔmã'dã], *a.* (*fem.* **-ante**) Commanding.—*n.m.* Commander, commanding officer, commandant; major. *Commandant d'armes*, town major; *commandant de place*, governor (of a fortified town); *commandant d'une escadre*, commodore; *commandant en chef*, commander-in-chief.—*n.f.* Major's or commandant's wife.

commande [kɔ'mãːd], *n.f.* Order; (*Mach.*) driving-wheel. *Louanges de commande*, forced praise; *maladie de commande*, feigned sickness; *ouvrage de commande*, work done to order; *sur commande*, to order; *organes* or *leviers de commande*, controls; *moteur de commande*, driving motor.

commandement [kɔmãd'mã], *n.m.* Command, act of commanding; authority, disposal, control; word of command, order; commandment, law, rule, injunction; order to pay. *Commandement à la mer*, sea-going command; *tourelle de commandement*, conning tower.

commander [kɔmã'de], *v.t.* To command, to order; to govern, to control, to have the command of; to give an order for, to bespeak; to overlook. *Cette tour commande la ville*, that tower overlooks the town; *une pièce commande l'autre*, access to one room is had through the other. *En service commandé*, on special duty.—*v.i.* To command, to have authority; to give the word of command. *Commander à la route*, (*Naut.*) to shape a ship's course; *commander à ses passions*, to master one's passions. **se commander**, *v.r.* To control oneself; to be subject (to) or at the disposal (of). *Cela ne se commande pas*, that cannot be had just for the asking; that can't be helped.

commandeur [kɔmã'dœːr], *n.m.* Commander (in orders of knighthood).

commanditaire [kɔmãdi'tɛr], *n.* Sleeping partner.

commandite [kɔmã'dit], *n.f.* Limited partnership; capital invested by sleeping partner. *Société en commandite simple*, Joint Stock Co. Ltd.; *S. en commandite par actions*, Joint Stock Co.

commanditer [kɔmãdi'te], *v.t.* To finance (a commercial undertaking), to become a sleeping partner in.

commando [kɔmã'do], *n.m.* Commando.

comme [kɔm], *adv.* As; like, such as; almost, nearly, as if; how, in what way, to what extent. *C'est tout comme*, it comes to the same thing; *comme ci comme ça*, so so, indifferently; *comme il faut*, in a proper, suitable manner; *comme vous me traitez!* how badly you treat me! *faites comme lui*, do as he does; *il a gagné, Dieu sait comme!* he has won, the Lord knows how! *il est gentil comme tout*, he's as nice as anything; *il est comme mort*, he is almost dead; *vous voyez comme il travaille*, you see how hard he works.—*conj.* As, since, because. *Comme il arrivait*, just as he was arriving.

commémoraison [kɔmemɔrɛ'zɔ̃], *n.f.* (*R.-C. Ch.*) Commemoration, remembrance, mention (of a saint).

commémoratif [kɔmemɔra'tif], *a.* (*fem.* -tive) Commemorative; memorial.

commémoration [kɔmemɔra'sjɔ̃], *n.f.* Commemoration. *La commémoration des morts*, All Souls' Day.

commémorer [kɔmemɔ're], *v.t.* To commemorate, to remember, to recollect.

commençant [kɔmɑ̃'sɑ̃], *n.m.* (*fem.* -ante) Beginner, novice. **commencement**, *n.m.* Beginning, commencement. *Au commencement*, in the beginning, at first.

commencer [kɔmɑ̃'se], *v.t.* To begin, to commence, to set about; to initiate, to impart the first principles to. *Commencer quelqu'un*, to initiate someone; *commencer un cheval*, to begin training a horse.—*v.i.* To commence, to begin. *À moitié fait qui commence bien*, well begun is half done; *cet enfant commence à parler*, this child is beginning to talk; *lorsqu'il commença de parler*, when he started to speak.

commendataire [kɔmɑ̃da'tɛ:r], *a.* (*Eccles.*) Commendatory.

commende [kɔ'mɑ̃:d], *n.f.* (*Eccles.*) Commendam. **commender**, *v.t.* To give in commendam.

commensal [kɔmɑ̃'sal], *n.m.* (*fem.* -ale, *pl.* -aux) Commensal, habitual guest; fellow-boarder, messmate. *Être commensaux*, to be companions at meals; *être commensal d'une maison*, to be a regular visitor in a house.

commensurabilité [kɔmɑ̃syrabili'te], *n.f.* Commensurability. **commensurable**, *a.* Commensurable. **commensuration**, *n.f.* Process of finding commensurate quantities.

comment [kɔ'mɑ̃], *adv.* How, in what manner; why, wherefore. *Comment cela?* how is that? *comment faire?* what is to be done? how can it be helped?—*int.* What! indeed! *Et comment!* and how! *comment! vous voulez le faire!* what! you wish to do it?—*n.m.* Savoir *le pourquoi et le comment*, to know the why and the wherefore.

commentaire [kɔmɑ̃'tɛ:r], *n.m.* Commentary, exposition; (*fig.*) unfavourable comment, or remark. *Point de commentaire!* (*colloq.*) no remarks. **commentateur**, *n.m.* (*fem.* -trice) Commentator, annotator.

commenter [kɔmɑ̃'te], *v.t.* To comment on, to explain, to annotate.—*v.i.* To criticize adversely.

commérage [kɔme'ra:ʒ], *n.m.* Gossiping; gossip, tittle-tattle.

commerçant [kɔmer'sɑ̃], *a.* (*fem.* commerçante) Commercial, mercantile, trading (town, centre, etc.).—*n.m.* Trader, merchant, tradesman, shopkeeper.

commerce [kɔ'mers], *n.m.* Commerce, trade, trading, traffic; intercourse, dealings. *Ministère du commerce*, Board of Trade; *chambre de commerce*, chamber of commerce; *commerce de détail*, retail trade; *commerce en gros*, wholesale trade; *commerce intérieur, extérieur*, home, foreign trade; *être dans le commerce*, to be in business; *fonds de commerce*, business, stock; *il fait un gros commerce*, he is doing a large business; *le commerce va très bien*, business is good; *le haut commerce*, merchants; *le petit commerce*, small tradespeople;

livres de commerce, account-books; *un petit commerce*, a small shop or business; *il est d'un commerce agréable*, he is easy to get on with.

commercer [kɔmer'se], *v.i.* To trade, to deal, to traffic; to hold intercourse (*avec*).

commercial [kɔmer'sjal], *a.* (*fem.* -ale, *pl.* -aux) Commercial. **commercialement**, *adv.* Commercially. **commercialisation**, *n.f.* Commercialization. **commercialiser**, *v.t.* To commercialize. **commercialité**, *n.f.* Negotiability.

commère [kɔ'mɛr], *n.f.* *A godmother was called by the godfather *ma commère*; thence *ma commère* as a fam. term of endearment. *Une commère*, a gossip; *c'est une fine* or *rusée commère*, she is a bold, cunning woman; *la commère (d'une revue)*, the leading lady; *les Joyeuses Commères de Windsor*, the Merry Wives of Windsor; *cet homme est une vraie commère*, that man is a regular gossip.

commettage [kɔme'ta:ʒ], *n.m.* (*Naut.*) Laying of ropes and cables.

commettant [kɔme'tɑ̃], *n.m.* Constituent; employer; principal. *Corps de commettants*, constituents, constituency.

commettre [kɔ'metr], *v.t. irr.* (*p.p.* **commis**, conjugated like METTRE) To commit, to perpetrate; to appoint, to commission, to empower; to commit to someone's charge, to entrust, to confide; (*Naut.*) to lay (rope). **se commettre**, *v.r.* To commit oneself; to expose oneself; to hazard oneself; to be committed.

commination [kɔmina'sjɔ̃], *n.f.* Commination. **comminatoire**, *a.* Comminatory, threatening, denunciatory.

comminuer [kɔmi'nɥe], *v.t.* (*Surg.*) To comminute. **comminutif**, *a.* (*fem.* -ive) Comminutive. **comminution**, *n.f.* Comminution; compound fracture.

commis (1) [kɔ'mi], *n.m.* (*fem.* -ise (1)) Clerk. *Commis de magasin*, shop assistant; *commise*, shop-girl; *commis voyageur*, commercial traveller, bagman; (*U.S.*) drummer; *premier commis*, head clerk.

commis (2) [kɔ'mi], *a.* (*fem.* **commise** (2)) Committed, appointed, entrusted.

commisération [kɔmizera'sjɔ̃], *n.f.* Commiseration, compassion, pity.

commissaire [kɔmi'sɛ:r], *n.m.* Member of a commission; commissioner; manager, steward, trustee; purser (of a vessel); (*Racing*) clerk of course. *Commissaire de police*, superintendent of police; *commissaire des comptes*, auditor; *commissaire de chemin de fer*, railway superintendent.

commissaire-priseur [kɔmiserpri'zœ:r], *n.m.* Official auctioneer or valuer.

commissariat [kɔmisa'rja], *n.m.* Commissaryship, trusteeship; commissary's office; (*Mil., Navy*) commissariat; police station.

commission [kɔmi'sjɔ̃], *n.f.* Commission, trust, charge; errand, message; power, authority; (*Comm.*) percentage; mandate; warrant; committee. *Avoir commission de* or *pour*, to be commissioned or empowered to; *commission d'enquête*, committee of inquiry; *commission d'examens*, board of examiners; *commission rogatoire*, writ of inquiry; *commission consultative*, advisory committee; *en commission*, (*Navy*) in commission; *faire des* commissions, to run errands or to obtain orders; *faire la commission*, to be a commission agent; *maison de commission*, commission agency; *obtenir commission d'un juge*, to obtain a judge's warrant; *renvoyer un projet de loi à une commission*, to commit a bill.

commissionnaire [kɔmisjɔ'nɛːr], *n.m.* Commission agent, commissionnaire; messenger, porter. *Commissionnaire de roulage*, carrier; *petit commissionnaire*, errand-boy.

commissionner [kɔmisjɔ'ne], *v.t.* To empower, to commission; to order (goods).

commissoire [kɔmi'swaːr], *a.* Binding on pain of forfeiture (of clauses etc.).

commissural [kɔmisy'ral], *a.* (*fem.* -ale, *pl.* -aux) Commissural.

commissure [kɔmi'syːr], *n.f.* (*Anat.*) Commissure; corner (of the lips); line of junction.

commodat [kɔmɔ'da], *n.m.* (*Law*) Free loan (to be returned in kind).

commode [kɔ'mɔd], *a.* Convenient, commodious, handy; comfortable, snug, pleasant, agreeable, proper, suitable; easy, good-natured, accommodating; (*iron.*) convenient enough, very simple. *Il n'est pas commode*, he is not accommodating, not easy to get on with; *mari commode*, complaisant husband; *peu* or *pas commode*, inconvenient, uncomfortable, unsuitable.—*n.f.* Chest of drawers, commode. **commodément**, *adv.* Commodiously, conveniently; comfortably, suitably, easily. **commodité**, *n.f.* Convenience, comfort, commodiousness; accommodation; (*pl.*) conveniences, water-closet.

commotion [kɔmo'sjɔ̃], *n.f.* Commotion; shock; concussion. **commotionné**, *a.* (*fem.* -ée) Suffering from concussion.

commuabilité [kɔmɥabili'te], *n.f.* Commutability. **commuable**, *a.* Commutable.

commuer, *v.t.* (*Law*) To commute.

commun [kɔ'mœ̃], *a.* (*fem.* **commune** (1)) Common, general, universal; usual, ordinary; mean, vulgar. *À frais communs*, jointly; *d'une commune voix*, *d'un commun accord*, unanimously; *faire bourse commune*, to have one common stock or purse; *je n'ai rien de commun avec lui*, I have nothing in common with him; *le bien commun*, the common weal; *le droit commun*, common law; *le sens commun*, common sense; *lieux communs*, commonplaces; *maison commune*, town-hall; *nom commun*, common noun; *peu commun*, uncommon, unusual; *une voix commune*, a vulgar voice.—*n.m.* Joint possession, use, etc.; most people, common people, the mob; (*pl.*) privy; domestic offices, outbuildings. *Le commun des mortels*, the generality of men; *vivre en commun*, to live in common.

communal [kɔmy'nal], *a.* (*fem.* -ale, *pl.* -aux) Communal, parochial; common.—*n.m. pl.* (*Biens*) *communaux*, communal property. **communalement**, *adv.* Regarding the commune. **communaliste**, *n.* and *a.* Communalist.

communard, *n.* (*fem.* -arde) Communard, member of the Commune of Paris in 1871.

communautaire [kɔmyno'tɛːr], *a.* Relating to society, etc. *Vie communautaire*, community life.

communauté [kɔmyno'te], *n.f.* Community, society, corporation; communion, religious community. *Communauté de biens*, community of property (between husband and wife). (*Polit.*) *La Communauté*, the (French) Community.

commune (2) [kɔ'myn], *n.f.* Commune (parish, township, in France). (*Hist.*) *La Commune de Paris* [*see* COMMUNARD]; *la Chambre des Communes*, the House of Commons.

communément [kɔmyne'mã], *adv.* Commonly, usually, generally.

communiant [kɔmy'njã], *n.m.* (*fem.* -ante) Communicant. *Premier communiant*, boy partaking of the sacrament for the first time.

communicabilité [kɔmynikabili'te], *n.f.* Communicability. **communicable**, *a.* Communicable. **communicateur**, *n.m.* (*fem.* -trice) Communicator.—*a.* (*Elec.*) Connecting (wire). **communicatif**, *a.* (*fem.* -ive) Communicative, open.

communication [kɔmynika'sjɔ̃], *n.f.* Intercourse, communication; (*Teleph.*) call. *Communication de pièces*, (*Law*) production of documents; *communication locale, à longue distance*, local call, trunk call; *en communication avec*, in communication with; *donnez-moi la communication avec N.*, put me through to N. **communicativement**, *adv.* Communicatively.

communier [kɔmy'nje], *v.i.* To communicate, to receive the sacrament; (*fig.*) to be in intellectual communion.—*v.t.* To administer the communion.

communion [kɔmy'njɔ̃], *n.f.* Communion, fellowship; belief, persuasion, particular faith; Holy Communion, sacrament, Lord's Supper. *Faire sa (première) communion*, to receive the sacrament for the first time.

communiqué [kɔmyni'ke], *n.m.* Official communication, statement, communiqué.

communiquer [kɔmyni'ke], *v.t.* To communicate, to impart; to inform of, to tell, to acquaint.—*v.i.* To be in relation or correspondence (with). **se communiquer**, *v.r.* To be communicative; to communicate with, to spread, to be communicated.

communisant [kɔmyni'zã], *a.* (*fem.* -ante) Communistic.—*n.m. f.* Fellow-traveller.

communisme [kɔmy'nism], *n.m.* Communism. **communiste**, *n.* Communist.

communité [kɔmyni'te], *n.f.* Community (of goods etc.).

commutable *See* COMMUABLE. **commutateur**, *n.m.* (*Elec.*) Commutator, switch. **commutatif**, *a.* (*fem.* -ive) Commutative, of equal exchange. **commutation**, *n.f.* Change; commutation. **commuter** [COMMUER].

compacité [kɔ̃pasi'te], *n.f.* Compactness, density. **compact** [kɔ̃'pakt], *a.* (*fem.* -acte) Compact, dense, serried; (*Phys.*) dense, solid.

compagne [kɔ̃'paɲ], *n.f.* Female companion, consort, .partner, helpmate; playmate; (of animals) mate. *Fidèle compagne*, faithful attendant.

compagnie [kɔ̃pa'ɲi], *n.f.* Society, companionship; party, gathering of persons; fellowship, partnership; (*Comm.*) company, corporation; (*Mil.* and *Theat.*) company, troop. *Aller de compagnie*, to go together; *compagnies de discipline*, corps stationed in Africa to which soldiers are sent as a punishment; (see BIRIBI); *dame* or *demoiselle de compagnie*, lady's companion; *être de bonne* *compagnie*, to be well bred; *fausser compagnie à quelqu'un*, to desert someone, to give someone the slip; *former une compagnie*, to establish a company; *fréquenter la bonne, mauvaise, compagnie*, to keep good, bad, company; *la maison Salmon et Cie*, the firm of Salmon and Co.; *tenir compagnie à quelqu'un*, to keep someone company; *une compagnie de perdrix*, a covey of partridges.

compagnon [kɔ̃paˈɲɔ̃], *n.m.* Companion, fellow, comrade; playmate; mate, partner, fellow-workman; (*Bot.*) campion. *Compagnon d'armes*, companion in arms; *compagnon d'école* or *d'étude*, schoolfellow; *compagnon de jeu*, play-fellow; *compagnon de table*, messmate; *joyeux compagnon*, jolly fellow; *traiter de pair à compagnon*, to be hail-fellow-well-met with.

compagnonnage [kɔ̃paɲɔˈnaːʒ], *n.m.* *Time of service as journeyman after apprenticeship; trade-guild.

comparable [kɔ̃paˈrabl], *a.* Comparable, to be compared. **comparablement,** *adv.* In comparison (with).

comparaison [kɔ̃parɛˈzɔ̃], *n.f.* Comparison; simile, similitude. *Ce n'est qu'un ignorant en comparaison d'un tel*, he is a mere ignoramus in comparison with such a one; *comparaison n'est pas raison*, comparison is not proof; *il n'y a point de comparaison de vous à lui*, there is no comparison between you and him; *par comparaison à* (or *avec) ce que j'ai fait*, in comparison to (or with) what I have done; *sans comparaison*, without or beyond comparison; *infinitely*; *toute comparaison cloche* or *toute comparaison est odieuse*, comparisons are odious.

comparaître [kɔ̃paˈrɛːtr], *v.i. irr.* To appear, to answer a summons (before a tribunal). **comparant,** *a.* (*fem.* **-ante**) Appearing in court. —*n.* Person appearing in court on a summons.

comparateur [kɔ̃paraˈtœːr], *a.* (*fem.* **-trice**) Who likes to compare.—*n.m.* (*Phys.*) Comparator.

comparatif [kɔ̃paraˈtif], *a.* (*fem.* **-ive**) Comparative.—*n.m.* Comparative, comparative degree. **comparatiste,** *n.m.* Comparativist. **comparativement,** *adv.* Comparatively.

comparé [kɔ̃paˈre], *a.* (*fem.* **-ée**) Comparative (law, literature, philology, etc.).

comparer [kɔ̃paˈre], *v.t.* To compare. **se comparer,** *v.r.* To be compared.

*comparoir [COMPARAÎTRE].

comparse [kɔ̃ˈpars], *n.m.* (*Theat.*) Supernumerary; (*fam.*) super, walking-on part; conjuror's stooge; confederate; (*fig.*) a mere nonentity.

compartiment [kɔ̃partiˈmɑ̃], *n.m.* Compartment, division. **compartimentage,** *n.m.* Division into compartments. **compartimenter,** *v.t.* To compart.

comparution [kɔ̃paryˈsjɔ̃], *n.f.* (*Law*) Appearance in court.

compas [kɔ̃ˈpa], *n.m.* Pair of compasses; mariner's compass; (*fig.*) measure, criterion; (*fam.*) legs, step. (*Mil.* and *fam.*) *Allonger le compas*, to quicken the step; *compas à trois branches*, triangular compasses; *compas d'épaisseur*, callipers; *compas de réduction*, proportional compasses; *compas de variation*,

azimuth compass; *faire toutes choses par règle et par compas*, to do everything by rule and compass; *il a le compas dans l'œil*, he has a good eye for distances *or* he has a sure eye.

compassé [kɔ̃paˈse], *a.* (*fem.* **compassée**) Formal, stiff, starchy. *Un homme bien compassé*, a formal man. **compassement,** *n.m.* Compassing; (*fig.*) stiffness, starchiness.

compasser [kɔ̃paˈse], *v.t.* To measure, set out, or divide with compasses; to proportion, to regulate; (*fig.*) to weigh, to consider.

compassion [kɔ̃paˈsjɔ̃], *n.f.* Compassion, pity, mercy. *Avoir de la compassion pour quelqu'un*, to have compassion for someone; *être digne de compassion*, to arouse pity.

compatibilité [kɔ̃patibiliˈte], *n.f.* Compatibility. **compatible,** *a.* Compatible, consistent. *Son humeur n'est pas compatible avec la mienne*, his temper does not agree with mine.

compatir [kɔ̃paˈtiːr], *v.i.* To sympathize, to feel, to bear (with); to agree, to be compatible (with). **compatissant,** *a.* (*fem.* **-ante**) Compassionate, tender, pitying.

compatriote [kɔ̃patriˈɔt], *n.* Compatriot, fellow-countryman, fellow-countrywoman.

compendieusement [kɔ̃pɑ̃djøzˈmɑ̃], *adv.* In brief, compendiously.

compendieux [kɔ̃pɑ̃ˈdjø], *a.* (*fem.* **-euse**) Summarized, concise.

compendium [kɔ̃pɑ̃ˈdjɔm], *n.m.* Summary.

compénétration [kɔ̃penetraˈsjɔ̃], *n.f.* Compenetration.

compensable [kɔ̃pɑ̃ˈsabl], *a.* That may be compensated.

compensateur [kɔ̃pɑ̃saˈtœːr], *a.* (*fem.* **-trice**) (*Horo.*) Compensative, compensating. *Pendule compensateur*, compensating pendulum.—*n.m.* Compensating balance; (*Av.*) balanced surface, trim-tab. *Compensateur magnétique*, magnetic compensator.

compensatif, *a.* (*fem.* **-ive**) Compensative.

compensation [kɔ̃pɑ̃saˈsjɔ̃], *n.f.* Compensation, amends, reparation; set-off, consideration. *Faire compensation*, to compensate, to make amends for; *chambre de compensation*, clearing-house; *caisse de compensation*, equalization fund; *en compensation de*, to offset, in consideration of. *Antenne de compensation*, balancing aerial.

compensatoire, *a.* Compensatory.

compenser [kɔ̃pɑ̃ˈse], *v.t.* To counterbalance, to compensate, to make up for, to make amends for. *Rien ne compense la perte de l'honneur*, nothing can make up for the loss of honour. **se compenser,** *v.r.* To compensate each other; to be balanced, to be set off against.

compère [kɔ̃ˈpɛːr], *n.m.* Godfather (with regard to a godmother see COMMÈRE); (*fig.*) gossip, crony, pal, confederate (in a confidence trick etc.). *Un bon compère*, a good companion or fellow; *un rusé compère*, a sly old fox.

compère-loriot [kɔ̃pɛrlɔˈrjo], *n.m.* (*pl.* **compères-loriots**) Golden oriole (bird); sty (on the eyelid).

compétence [kɔ̃peˈtɑ̃ːs], *n.f.* Competence, right to judge a cause, cognizance; (*fig.*) department, sphere, province; skill, proficiency. *Cela n'est pas de votre compétence*, that is outside your province.

compétent [kɔ̃pe'tã], *a.* (*fem.* **compétente**) Competent, qualified; (*fig.*) suitable, requisite. *C'est un juge compétent*, he is a competent judge. *Vous n'êtes pas compétent pour cela*, you are not fit for that.

compéter [kɔ̃pe'te], *v.i. irr.* (*conjugated like* ACCÉLÉRER) To belong (by right), to be due (*à*); to be within the competence (of a court).

compétiteur [kɔ̃peti'tœːr], *n.m.* (*fem.* **-trice**) Competitor, candidate. **compétitif**, *a.* (*fem.* **-ive**) Competitive. **compétition**, *n.f.* Competition, rivalry.

compilateur [kɔ̃pila'tœːr], *n.* Compiler. **compilation**, *n.f.* Compilation. **compiler**, *v.t.* To compile.

complainte [kɔ̃'plɛ̃ːt], *n.f.* Tragic or plaintive ballad; (*fig.*) lament, lamentation.

complaire [kɔ̃'plɛːr], *v.i. irr.* (*pres.p.* **complaisant**, *p.p.* **complu**) To be pleasing (*à*). **se complaire**, *v.r.* To delight (*dans or à*).

complaisamment [kɔ̃plɛza'mã], *adv.* Complaisantly, obligingly.

complaisance [kɔ̃plɛ'zãːs], *n.f.* Complaisance, willingness, good-nature; complacency. *Abuser de la complaisance de quelqu'un*, to abuse someone's kindness; *avoir de la complaisance or des complaisances pour*, to be very kind to; *faire une chose par complaisance*, to do a thing to oblige. *Il se regarde avec complaisance*, he regards himself complacently. *Effet de complaisance*, (*Comm.*) accommodation bill. **complaisant**, *a.* (*fem.* **-ante**) Affable, civil, obliging, kind.—*n.* Flatterer; go-between.

complanter [kɔ̃plã'te], *v.t.* To plant thickly with trees.

complément [kɔ̃ple'mã], *n.m.* Complement; (*Gram.*) object; rest, remainder; extension (of subject). **complémentaire**, *a.* Complementary, completing, further (details).

complet [kɔ̃'plɛ], *a.* (*fem.* **complète**) Complete, whole, perfect; full, filled. *Œuvres complètes*, complete works; *un habillement complet*, a complete suit of clothes; *un athlète complet*, all-round athlete. *C'est complet!* full up! (bus); (*fig.*) it's the last straw!—*n.m.* Completeness, complement, full number; suit (of clothes). *Au grand complet*, quite full, all present; *être au complet*, to be full; *un complet veston*, lounge suit. **complètement**, *adv.* Completely, entirely, thoroughly. **complétement**, *n.m.* Finishing, completion. **compléter**, *v.t.* To complete, to perfect; to fill up, to make up. **complétif**, *a.* (*fem.* **-ive**) (*Gram.*) Completive.

complexe [kɔ̃'plɛks], *a.* Complex, complicated; (*Gram.*) having two complements, compound.—*n.m. Un complexe d'infériorité*, inferiority complex.

complexion [kɔ̃plɛk'sjɔ̃], *n.f.* Constitution; disposition, humour, temper.

complexité [kɔ̃plɛksi'te], *n.f.* Complexity.

complication [kɔ̃plika'sjɔ̃], *n.f.* Complication, intricacy.

complice [kɔ̃'plis], *a.* Accessory, privy to.—*n.* Accomplice, accessory, a party to; co-respondent (in adultery). **complicité**, *n.f.* Complicity, participation.

complies [kɔ̃'pli], *n.f.* (*used only in pl.*) (*R.-C. Ch.*) Compline.

compliment [kɔ̃pli'mã], *n.m.* Compliment; (*pl.*) compliments, civilities, regards, congratulations. *Faire compliment à quelqu'un*, to compliment someone; *faites-lui mes compliments*, give him or her my regards; *mes compliments chez vous*, remember me to all at home; *compliments de condoléance*, see CONDOLÉANCE; *sans compliment*, really, sincerely. **complimenter**, *v.t.* To compliment, to congratulate. **complimenteur**, *a.* (*fem.* **-euse**) and *n.* Over-complimentary; obsequious.

compliqué [kɔ̃pli'ke], *a.* (*fem.* **-ée**) Complicated, intricate; knotty; subtle, tortuous (of a mind).

compliquer [kɔ̃pli'ke], *v.t.* To render intricate, to complicate, to entangle, to perplex. **se compliquer**, *v.r.* To become complicated.

complot [kɔ̃'plo], *n.m.* Plot, conspiracy. *Le chef du complot*, ringleader. **comploter**, *v.t.* To plot. **comploteur**, *n.m.* Plotter, schemer.

complu [COMPLAIRE].

componction [kɔ̃pɔ̃k'sjɔ̃], *n.f.* Compunction; solemn manners or expression.

componé [kɔ̃pɔ'ne], *a.* (*fem.* **-ée**) (*Her.*) Composed of two tinctures, in alternate squares, in one row; compony.

comportement [kɔ̃pɔrtə'mã], *n.m.* Demeanour, deportment, behaviour. *Psychologie du comportement*, behaviourism.

comporter [kɔ̃pɔr'te], *v.t.* To permit, to allow, to admit of; to call for, require; to comprise, include. *Un système qui comporte de grands inconvénients*, a system involving great disadvantages. **se comporter**, *v.r.* To behave, to demean oneself; to act, to manage. *Il se comportera mieux à l'avenir*, he will behave better in future; *se comporter mal*, to misbehave.

composant [kɔ̃po'zã], *a.* (*fem.* **-ante**) Composing.—*n.m.* (*Chem.*) Component, constituent.—*n.f.* (*Mech.*) One of the component forces producing a resultant. (*Elec.*) *Composante wattée, en phase*, watt component.

composé [kɔ̃po'ze], *a.* (*fem.* **-ée**) Composed, compound; (*Bot.*) composite; (*fig.*) stiff. *Il a l'air composé*, he has an impassive, formal expression; *un mot composé*, a compound word.—*n.m.* Compound.

composer [kɔ̃po'ze], *v.t.* To compose, to compound, to make up; to form, to create; to fashion, to adjust, to regulate. *Composer sa mine*, to adjust one's looks; *composer un numéro*, to dial a number.—*v.i.* To compose music etc.; (*sch.*) to write a composition or an examination paper; to compound, to compromise, to make up; to capitulate. *Il a composé avec ses créanciers*, he has compounded with his creditors. **composeuse**, *n.f.* Type-setting machine.

composite [kɔ̃po'zit], *a.* Composite.—*n.m.* Composite order.

compositeur [kɔ̃pozi'tœːr], *n.m.* (*fem.* **-trice**) Composer (of music); (*Print.*) compositor. *Amiable compositeur*, (*Law*) (friendly) arbitrator.

composition [kɔ̃pozi'sjɔ̃], *n.f.* Composition; chemical composition or combination; adjustment, arrangement, settlement; (*fig.*) disposition, temperament; (*Print.*) composing; (*School etc.*) paper, test, essay. *Entrer en* *composition*, to come to terms (*avec*); *un homme de bonne composition*, an easy, tractable person; *un acteur de composition*, actor capable of playing many parts.

compost [kɔ̃'pɔst], *n.m.* (*Agric.*) Compost.

composter, *v.t.* To compost; to date or obliterate (ticket etc.).

Compostelle [kɔ̃pɔs'tɛl], *f.* Compostella.

composteur [kɔ̃pɔs'tœːr], *n.m.* (*Print.*) Composing-stick; dating and numbering machine.

compote [kɔ̃'pɔt], *n.f.* Stewed fruit, compote. *Compote de pommes*, stewed apple. (*fam.*) *Avoir la tête, les yeux en compote*, to have a bruised face, a pair of black eyes. **compotier**, *n.m.* Fruit-dish.

compound [kɔ̃'pund], *a. Machine compound*, compound engine.

compréhensibilité [kɔ̃preãsibili'te], *n.f.* Comprehensibility. **compréhensible**, *a.* Understandable, intelligible. **compréhensif**, *a.* (*fem.* **compréhensive**) Comprehensive; broadminded, understanding.

compréhension [kɔ̃preã'sjɔ̃], *n.f.* Comprehension; (*fig.*) understanding, intelligence. **compréhensivité**, *n.f.* Comprehensiveness, faculty of comprehending.

comprenant [*see foll.*].

comprendre [kɔ̃'prãːdr], *v.t. irr.* (*pres.p.* **comprenant**, *p.p.* **compris**, *conjugated like* PRENDRE). To include, to comprise, to contain; to understand, to conceive, to realize. *La maison comprend dix pièces*, the house consists of ten rooms; *à ce que je comprends*, by what I understand; *comprendre mal*, to misunderstand; *je ne le comprends pas*, I do not know what to make of him (*or* it); *cela se comprend*, that's understandable.

comprenette [kɔ̃prə'nɛt], *n.f.* (*fam.*) Understanding. *Avoir la comprenette dure*, to be slow in the uptake.

compresse [kɔ̃'prɛːs], *n.f.* (*Surg.*) Compress, pledget. **compresseur**, *a.* Compressive. —*n.m.* Compressor, roller. (*Rouleau*) *compresseur*, steam-roller.

compressibilité [kɔ̃presibili'te], *n.f.* Compressibility. **compressible**, *a.* Compressible. **compressif**, *a.* (*fem.* **-ive**) Compressive, repressive. **compression**, *n.f.* Compression; condensation; (*fig.*) constraint; (*Surg.*) astriction.

comprimable [kɔ̃pri'mabl], *a.* Compressible.

comprimant, *a.* (*fem.* **-ante**) Compressing.

comprimé, *a.* (*fem.* **-ée**) Compressed, condensed; put down, kept under.—*n.m.* (*Pharm.*) Tabloid, tablet.

comprimer [kɔ̃pri'me], *v.t.* To compress, to condense; to repress, to restrain, to curb.

compris [kɔ̃'pri], *a.* (*fem.* **-ise**) Understood; included. *Non compris*, not including, exclusive of, without; *y compris*, inclusive of, including; *tout compris*, inclusive, all found.

compromettant [kɔ̃prɔme'tã], *a.* (*fem.* **-ante**) Compromising; damaging, disreputable.

compromettre [kɔ̃prɔ'mɛtr], *v.t. irr.* (*p.p.* **compromis** (1), *conjugated like* METTRE) To expose, to commit, to compromise, to jeopardize, to impair, to endanger. *Compromettre son autorité*, or *sa dignité*, to impair one's authority *or* character.—*v.i.* To compromise; to consent to a reference, to submit to the decision of arbitrators. **se compro-**

mettre, *v.r.* To compromise oneself; to commit a blunder.

compromis (2) [kɔ̃prɔ'mi], *n.m.* Compromise, mutual agreement. *Mettre en compromis*, to submit to arbitration.

compromission, *n.f.* (*usu. pej.*) Compromise, surrender of principle etc. **compromissoire** *a.* Pronounced by arbiters (of decisions etc.); stipulating arbitration (of clauses etc.).

comptabilité [kɔ̃tabili'te], *n.f.* Accountancy, book-keeping; accountant's department or office. *Il entend bien la comptabilité*, he has a thorough knowledge of accounting.

comptable [kɔ̃'tabl], *a.* Charged with or responsible for accounts; accountable, responsible. *Agent comptable*, accountant; *expert-comptable*, auditor, chartered accountant.—*n. m.* Accountant, book-keeper; (*Naut.*) Purser.

comptant [kɔ̃'tã], *a.m.* (Of money) ready; (of payment) in cash.—*n.m.* Ready money, cash. *Au comptant*, for (prompt) cash; *avoir du comptant*, to be well provided with cash; *payer partie comptant*, to pay so much down; *payer comptant*, to pay cash; *voilà tout mon comptant*, here is all my cash.

compte [kɔ̃ːt], *n.m.* Reckoning, calculation; account, score, statement, report; (*fig.*) profit, advantage, benefit; esteem, value, regard. *À bon compte*, cheap, at small cost; *à ce compte-là*, at that rate, in that case; *à compte* (or *acompte*), on account; *arrêter un compte*, to strike a balance; *au bout du compte*, when all is said and done, after all; *auditeur des comptes*, auditor of the exchequer; *avoir un compte en banque*, to have a banking account; *à votre compte*, according to you; *c'est bien le compte* or *le compte y est*, the account is right; *compte courant*, current or running account; *compte rendu*, report, return, review (of a book etc.); *compte rond*, round, even sum; *la Cour des Comptes*, the Audit Office; *demander son compte*, to ask for one's salary or wages (before throwing up a situation); *demander des comptes à quelqu'un*, to call someone to account; *donner son compte à*, to dismiss *or* cashier; *en fin de compte*, in the end; *erreur n'est pas compte*, errors can always be verified; *être de bon compte*, to be fair in one's dealings, to be exact, (*fig.*) to be sincere, honest, just; *être de compte à demi avec quelqu'un*, to share profits or losses with someone; *faites-en le compte*, add it all up; *il a son compte*, his goose is cooked; *il faut lui rendre compte de tout*, we must account to him for everything; *il n'y a pas trouvé son compte*, he did not find what he expected *or* that it paid; *ils sont bien loin de compte*, they are a long way out; *je prends cela sur mon compte*, I will be responsible for that; *les bons comptes font les bons amis*, short reckonings make long friends; *livre de compte*, account book; *mettre* or *faire entrer en ligne de compte*, to take into account; *mettre sur le compte de*, to lay to the account of, to impute to; *ne tenir ni compte ni mesure*, to leave all at sixes and sevens; *on ne sait à quoi s'en tenir sur son compte*, we do not know what to think of him (*or* it); *pour solde de compte*, in full settlement; *régler son compte*, to settle one's account; *règlement de comptes*, (*fig.*) a settling of scores; *rendre compte*, to give an account; *se rendre compte de*, to get a clear idea of, to realize; *recevoir* *son compte*, to be dismissed; *sur le compte de*, with regard to; *tenir compte de*, to bear in mind, to be grateful for; to make allowance for; *valider un compte*, to verify an account; *vous m'en rendrez compte*, you shall answer for it; (*fam.*) *vous verrez comment je lui règlerai son compte!* you'll see how I'll settle his hash! *compte à rebours*, countdown.

compte-fils [kɔ̃t'fil], *n.m. inv.* Thread counter, weaver's glass.

compte-gouttes [kɔ̃t'gut], *n.m. inv.* (*Med.*) Drop-tube, dropper; filler. (*fig.*) *Au compte-gouttes*, sparingly.

compte-pas [PODOMÈTRE].

compter [kɔ̃'te], *v.t.* To count, to reckon, to calculate, compute; to pay down, to give, to reach, to attain; to include, to comprise; to consider, to deem, to think. *Il compte des rois parmi ses ancêtres*, he has kings among his ancestors; *marcher à pas comptés*, to walk with measured steps; *sans compter*, besides, let alone.—*v.i.* To reckon, to count; to be reckoned, to be counted, to be among the number of; to think, to expect; to intend, to purpose; to have confidence in, to count or rely (*sur*). *À compter de ce jour-là*, reckoning from that day; *compter avec quelqu'un*, to reckon with someone; *comptez là-dessus*, depend upon it; *compter pour beaucoup* or *pour rien*, to go a long way, to go for a good deal, *or* to go for nothing; *comptez que* (with indicative), remember that; *compter sur*, to depend upon, to rely upon, to expect; *je compte le voir demain*, I expect to see him tomorrow; *quand comptez-vous partir?* when do you propose setting out? **se compter**, *v.r.* To be reckoned, included, or taken into account. *Ses fautes ne se comptent pas*, he makes innumerable mistakes.

compteur [kɔ̃'tœːr], *a.* and *n.* (*fem.* **-euse**) That counts; accountant, computer.—*n.m.* Automatic recording-machine; meter. (C) *Compteur de stationnement*, parking meter; *compteur de vitesse*, speedometer.

comptine [kɔ̃'tin], *n.f.* Children's counting rhyme.

comptoir [kɔ̃'twaːr], *n.m.* Counter; cashier's desk; counting-house; branch bank, bank; factory, settlement (in a foreign country). *Dame* or *demoiselle de comptoir*, saleswoman; barmaid; *garçon de comptoir*, barman, bartender.

compulsation [kɔ̃pylsa'sjɔ̃], *n.f.* Examination, checking, inspection (of papers, books, etc.).

compulser [kɔ̃pyl'se], *v.t.* To cause the production of (papers, books, etc.); to go through, inspect, or examine (on a judge's order). **compulsion**, *n.f.* Compulsion. **compulsoire**, *n.m.* Examination of papers etc. on a judge's order.

comput [kɔ̃'pyt], *n.m.* (*Eccles.*) Computation. **computateur**, *n.m.* (*Av.*) Computer; computing scale. **computation**, *n.f.* Computation. **computer**, *v.t.* To compute.

comtal [kɔ̃'tal], *a.* (*fem.* **-ale**, *pl.* **-aux**) Pertaining to an earl or a countess.

comtat [kɔ̃'ta], *n.m.* (*Local*) County (of Avignon or Venaissin).

comte [kɔ̃t], *n.m.* Count; earl. **comté**, *n.m.* County, shire; earldom; (C) electoral circumscription. **comtesse**, *n.f.* Countess.

concassage [kɔ̃ka'saːʒ], *n.m.* Pounding, crushing. **concasser**, *v.t.* To pound, to bruise, to crush. **concasseur**, *n.m.* Bruising- or crushing-mill; steam-roller.

concaténation [kɔ̃katena'sjɔ̃], *n.f.* Concatenation; chain (of syllogisms).

concave [kɔ̃'kaːv], *a.* Concave. **concavité**, *n.f.* Concave; concavity. **concavo-convexe**, *a.* Concavo-convex.

concéder [kɔ̃se'de], *v.t. irr.* (*conjugated like* ACCÉLÉRER) To grant, to concede, to allow; to give up (a point etc.).

concentration [kɔ̃sɑ̃tra'sjɔ̃], *n.f.* Concentration; condensation. *Camp de concentration*, concentration camp. **concentrationnaire**, *a.* Concerning concentration camps.

concentré [kɔ̃sɑ̃'tre], *a.* (*fem.* **-ée**) Concentrated; (*fig.*) close, silent, reserved. *Haine concentrée*, concentrated hatred; *un homme toujours concentré*, a thoughtful, uncommunicative man.—*n.m.* Extract.

concentrer [kɔ̃sɑ̃'tre], *v.t.* To concentrate, to focus; (*fig.*) to dissemble, to repress, to smother (anger etc.). *Concentrer sa fureur*, to contain or hide one's rage. **se concentrer**, *v.r.* To concentrate, to meet in one centre; to retire within oneself.

concentrique [kɔ̃sɑ̃'trik], *a.* Concentric. **concentriquement**, *adv.* Concentrically.

concept [kɔ̃'sɛpt], *n.m.* Concept.

conceptacle [kɔ̃sɛp'takl], *n.m.* (*Bot.*) Conceptacle.

conceptibilité [kɔ̃sɛptibili'te], *n.f.* Conceivability. **conceptible**, *a.* Conceivable. **conceptif**, *a.* (*fem.* **-ive**) Conceptive.

conception [kɔ̃sɛp'sjɔ̃], *n.f.* Conception; apprehension; thought, notion, understanding. *Il a la conception vive, facile*, or *dure*, he is quick, easy, or dull of apprehension. *L'Immaculée Conception*, (R.-C. Ch.) Immaculate Conception; festival celebrating this.

conceptualisme [kɔ̃sɛptɥa'lism], *n.m.* Conceptualism. **conceptualiste**, *n.* and *a.* Conceptualist. **conceptuel**, *a.* (*fem.* **-elle**) Conceptual.

concernant [kɔ̃sɛr'nɑ̃], *prep.* Concerning, relating to, about, in regard to.

concerner [kɔ̃sɛr'ne], *v.t.* To relate (to), to concern, to regard. *En, pour, ce qui concerne . . .* , with regard to; as far as . . . is concerned.

concert [kɔ̃'sɛːr], *n.m.* Harmony; concert; (*fig.*) unanimity, concord. *Agir de concert*, to act in concert; *concert de louanges*, chorus of praise; *concert européen*, European concert or entente; *concert spirituel*, oratorio, sacred music.

concertant [kɔ̃sɛr'tɑ̃], *a.* Singing or performing in a concert; in concert (of a piece of music). *Symphonie concertante*, symphony with brilliant solo part or parts.—*n.* Performer in a concert.

concerté [kɔ̃sɛr'te], *a.* (*fem.* **-ée**) Concerted, united; studied, stiff.

concerter [kɔ̃sɛr'te], *v.t.* To contrive in concert; to concert; to plan, to devise; to compose (one's demeanour etc.).—*v.i.* To play or sing in a concert. **se concerter**, *v.r.* To plan together, to concert, or consult together.

concertiste [kɔ̃sɛr'tist], *n.* Performer (at a concert).

concerto [kɔ̃sɛr'to] (*It.*), *n.m.* Concerto.
concesseur [kɔ̃sɛ'sœːr], *n.m.* Grantor. **concessible**, *a.* That may be conceded. **concessif**, *a.* (*fem.* **-ive**) Concessive. **concession** [kɔ̃sɛ'sjɔ̃], *n.f.* Concession, privilege; grant of land etc., allotment. **concessionnaire**, *a.* Concessionary. *Société concessionnaire*, a society holding a concession.—*n.* Concessionnaire, grantee. *Concessionnaire d'un privilège*, patentee, licenceholder. **concetti** [kɔ̃tʃe'ti] (*It.*), *n.m.* (*used only in pl.*) Witty conceits, elaborate witticism. **concevabilité** [kɔ̃səvabili'te], *n.f.* Conceivability. **concevable**, *a.* Conceivable, imaginable. **concevoir** [kɔ̃sə'vwaːr], *v.t. irr.* (*conjugated like* RECEVOIR) To become pregnant, to conceive; to imagine, to understand; to comprehend; to word, to express. *Cela se conçoit*, that may be conceived, that is natural; *difficile à concevoir*, difficult to comprehend; *elle est hors d'âge de concevoir*, she is past childbearing; *une lettre ainsi conçue*, a letter in these terms.
conche [kɔ̃ːʃ], *n.f.* (*S.W. dialect*) Brine-pit (in salt-marshes).
conchifère [kɔ̃ki'fɛːr], *a.* Conchiferous. **conchoïdal**, *a.* (*fem.* **-ale**, *pl.* **-aux**) Conchoidal. (*Geol.*) *Cassure conchoïdale*, conchoidal fracture. **conchoïde**, *a.* and *n.f.* Conchoid. **conchylien**, *a.* (*fem.* **-ienne**) Shell-bearing (of strata etc.). **conchylifère** [CONCHIFÈRE]. **conchyliologie**, *n.f.* Conchology.
concierge [kɔ̃'sjɛrʒ], *n.* Concierge, houseporter, portress, door-keeper, hall-porter, caretaker. **conciergerie**, *n.f.* Caretaker's lodge; caretaker's post. *La Conciergerie*, a prison in Paris (during French Revolution).
concile [kɔ̃'sil], *n.m.* An assembly of prelates and doctors, council, synod; decrees and decisions of a council; (*fig.*) any assembly, meeting, etc.
conciliable [kɔ̃si'ljabl], *a.* Reconcilable.
conciliabule [kɔ̃silja'byl], *n.m.* Conventicle, cabal, secret meeting. *Conciliabule en plein air*, field conventicle.
conciliaire [kɔ̃si'ljɛːr], *a.* Of or belonging to a council.
conciliant [kɔ̃si'ljã], *a.* (*fem.* **-ante**) Conciliating, reconciling, conciliatory, largeminded. **conciliateur**, *n.* (*fem.* **-trice**) Conciliatory.—*n.* Conciliator, reconciler, appeaser. **conciliation**, *n.f.* Conciliation; reconciliation. *Tribunal de conciliation*, court of conciliation. **conciliatoire**, *a.* Conciliatory.
concilier [kɔ̃si'lje], *v.t.* (*conjugated like* PRIER) To conciliate, to reconcile, to accord; to gain, to win, to procure. **se concilier**, *v.r.* To gain, to win, to attract to oneself. *Se concilier les esprits*, to gain people's goodwill.
concis [kɔ̃'si], *a.* (*fem.* **-ise**) Concise, brief, short. **concision**, *n.f.* Concision, brevity, conciseness.
concitoyen [kɔ̃sitwa'jẽ], *a.* (*fem.* **concitoyenne**) Fellow-citizen, fellow-townsman or townswoman.
conclave [kɔ̃'klaːv], *n.m.* Conclave, assembly of all the cardinals. **conclaviste**, *n.m.* Priest attending cardinal in the conclave.

concluant [kɔ̃kly'ã], *a.* (*fem.* **-ante**) Conclusive, decisive.
conclure [kɔ̃'klyːr], *v.t. irr.* (*p.p.* **conclu**) To conclude, to finish; to infer. *Qu'en voulez-vous conclure?* what do you infer from that? *C'est conclu*, that's settled.—*v.i.* To come to a conclusion; to be conclusive; to think, to judge; to conclude, to finish. *Cette raison ne conclut pas*, this reason proves nothing; *conclure criminellement contre quelqu'un*, to bring someone in guilty. **se conclure**, *v.r.* To conclude, to come to an end. **conclusif**, *a.* (*fem.* **-ive**) Conclusive. **conclusion**, *n.f.* Conclusion, close, end; issue, inference, upshot. *En conclusion*, in short, to conclude.
concombre [kɔ̃'kɔ̃:br], *n.m.* Cucumber.
concomitamment [kɔ̃kɔmita'mã], *adv.* Concomittantly.
concomitance [kɔ̃kɔmi'tãːs], *n.f.* Concomitance. **concomitant**, *a.* (*fem.* **-ante**) Attendant, concomitant, going together.
concordance [kɔ̃kɔr'dãːs], *n.f.* Agreement; accord; (*Gram.*) agreement; (*Bibl. etc.*) concordance. *Concordance des temps*, rules for sequence of tenses (in relative clauses etc.). **concordant**, *a.* (*fem.* **-ante**) Concordant, harmonious. (*Geol.*) *Stratification concordante*, conformable stratification.
concordat [kɔ̃kɔr'da], *n.m.* Concordat, pact, agreement; (*Comm.*) composition, bankrupt's certificate. **concordataire**, *n.m.* Certificated bankrupt.
concorde [kɔ̃'kɔrd], *n.f.* Concord, agreement, harmony; good understanding. *Mettre la concorde entre des ennemis*, to reconcile enemies. **concorder**, *v.i.* To be in accord, to agree, to concur.
concourant (1) [kɔ̃ku'rã], *a.* (*fem.* **concourante**) Concurrent, converging.
concourir [kɔ̃ku'riːr], *v.i. irr.* (*pres.p.* **concourant** (2), *p.p.* **concouru**, *conjug. like* COURIR) To concur, to contribute to; to co-operate; to compete; to converge, to unite. *Ces deux hommes ont concouru pour le prix*, these two men competed for the prize; *être admis à concourir*, to be allowed to compete; *tout concourt à prouver (que)*, everything goes to prove (that); *tout concourt à ma ruine*, all things conspire to my ruin.
concours [kɔ̃'kuːr], *n.m.* Concourse, meeting; concurrence; conjuncture, coincidence; co-operation; competitive examination. *Concours agricole*, cattle show; *concours hippique*, horse-show; *concours général*, annual competitions between all *lycées*; *hors concours*, with no possible rivals; *par un heureux concours de circonstances*, through favourable circumstances; *se présenter au concours*, to compete; *son concours m'a été fort utile*, his co-operation has been very useful to me.
concrescence [kɔ̃krɛ'sãːs], *n.f.* Concrescence, coalescence.
concréfier (se) [kɔ̃kre'fje], *v.r.* To concrete.
concret [kɔ̃'krɛ], *a.* (*fem.* **concrète**) Concrete, solid. *Un cas concret*, a definite example.—*n.m.* (*Log.*) Concrete. **concrétion**, *n.f.* Concretion. **concrétiser**, *v.t.* To put in concrete form (a scheme etc.).
concubinage [kɔ̃kybi'naːʒ], *n.m.* Concubinage. **concubinaire**, *n.m.* One who lives in concubinage. **concubinairement**, *adv.* In concubinage.

concubine [kɔ̃ky'bin], *n.f.* Concubine.
concupiscence [kɔ̃kypi'sã:s], *n.f.* Concupiscence, lust.
concurremment [kɔ̃kyra'mã], *adv.* Concurrently, in concurrence; jointly, together.
concurrence [kɔ̃ky'rã:s], *n.f.* Competition; rivalry, opposition; struggle (for existence etc.). *Concurrence déloyale*, unfair competition. *Faire concurrence à*, to compete with, to oppose; *jusqu'à concurrence de*, to the amount of, to the extent of; *sans concurrence*, unrivalled. **concurrencer**, *v.t.* To rival, to compete with. **concurrent**, *n.m.* (*fem.* -ente) Competitor, rival. **concurrentiel**, *a.* (*fem.* -elle) Competitive, rival.
concussion [kɔ̃ky'sjɔ̃], *n.f.* Extortion, embezzlement, peculation. *User de concussion*, to be guilty of bribery. **concussionnaire**, *a.* Guilty of peculation, of bribery, or extortion.—*n.m.* Extortioner, peculator, embezzler.
condamnable [kɔ̃dɑ'nabl], *a.* Condemnable, blamable, criminal.
condamnation [kɔ̃danɑ'sjɔ̃], *n.f.* Condemnation, judgment, sentence; penalty; (*fig.*) blame, censure, disapproval. *Condamnation par défaut*, judgment by default; *passer condamnation*, to confess oneself in the wrong; *condamnation pour infraction aux règlements*, conviction for an offence against regulations; *subir sa condamnation*, to undergo one's sentence. **condamné**, *a.* (*fem.* -ée) Condemned, convicted. *Condamné à mort*, under sentence of death.—*n.* Convict.
condamner [kɔ̃dɑ'ne], *v.t.* To condemn, to sentence; to convict, to doom, to prove guilty; (*fig.*) to blame, to censure; to prohibit (books etc.); to block up (doors, windows, etc.); to give over (a patient etc.). *Condamner à une amende*, to fine; *condamner d'avance*, to prejudge; *condamner une porte*, to block up a door; *condamner sa porte*, to refuse to see visitors. **se condamner**, *v.r.* To be condemned; to condemn oneself; to compel oneself (to do, read, etc.).
condensabilité [kɔ̃dãsabili'te], *n.f.* Condensability. **condensable**, *a.* Condensable.
condensateur, *n.m.* (*Phys.*) *Condensateur à plateaux*, (*Elec.*) plate condenser. **condensation**, *n.f.* Condensation.
condensé [kɔ̃dã'se], *a.* Condensed. *Lait condensé*, condensed milk, evaporated milk.—*n.m.* Digest.
condenser [kɔ̃dã'se], *v.t.* To condense. *Condenser de nouveau*, to recondense; *machine à condenser*, condensing-engine. **se condenser**, *v.r.* To condense, to be condensed. **condenseur**, *n.m.* Condenser.
condescendance [kɔ̃desã'dã:s], *n.f.* Condescension; compliance. *Acte de condescendance*, act of condescension.
condescendant, *a.* (*fem.* -ante) Condescending, complying. *D'un air condescendant*, with a patronizing air, patronizingly.
condescendre, *v.i.* (*conjugated like* DESCENDRE) To condescend, to yield, to comply.
condiment [kɔ̃di'mã], *n.m.* Condiment, seasoning.
condisciple [kɔ̃di'sipl], *n.m.* Schoolfellow.
condit [kɔ̃'di], *n.m.* Candied fruit (angelica, orange, etc.); electuary.

condition [kɔ̃di'sjɔ̃], *n.f.* Condition, state, rank, station; domestic service; *good rank, quality, genteel station; situation, circumstances; necessary condition; condition on which a sale etc. is made, terms; (*silk manuf.*) drying-room. *À condition* or *sous condition*, on condition, on approval; *à condition que*, on condition, provided that; *améliorer sa condition*, to better one's circumstances; *chacun doit vivre selon sa condition*, everyone ought to live according to his station; *conditions de travail*, working conditions; *en condition*, in service (of servants); *être de basse condition*, to be low born; *être de condition*, to be well born; *ils se sont rendus à des conditions honorables*, they surrendered upon honourable terms; *sans condition*, without proviso; *toutes les conditions ont leurs désagréments*, every condition has its own drawbacks; *vendre sous condition*, to sell on approval. **conditionné**, *a.* (*fem.* -ée) Conditioned (*bien* or *mal*); well-conditioned, sound, downright. **conditionnel**, *a.* (*fem.* -elle) Conditional; (*Law*) provisory.—*n.m.* (*Gram.*) Conditional. **conditionnellement**, *adv.* Conditionally, on condition. **conditionnement**, *n.m.* Drying (of silk); drying-room. **conditionner**, *v.t.* To condition, to manufacture in good condition; to dry (silk); to season (wood).
condoléance [kɔ̃dɔle'ã:s], *n.f.* Condolence. *Faire une visite de condoléance à quelqu'un*, to pay a visit of condolence to someone; to assure him of one's heartfelt sympathy. **condoléant**, *a.* (*fem.* -ante) Condoling.
condominium [kɔ̃dɔmi'njɔm], *n.m.* Condominium. (*e.g.* The New Hebrides.)
condor [kɔ̃'dɔ:r], *n.m.* Condor.
conductance [kɔ̃dyk'tã:s], *n.f.* (*Elec.*) Conductance.
conducteur [kɔ̃dyk'tœ:r], *n.m.* (*fem.* -trice) Conductor, conductress, leader, guide; driver, drover. *Conducteur de chemin de fer, d'omnibus*, etc., guard.—*a.* (*Phys.*) Conducting, transmitting. *Fil conducteur*, conducting-wire, conductor-wire; *poulie conductrice*, driving pulley.
conductibilité [kɔ̃dyktibili'te], *n.f.* Conductibility. **conductible**, *a.* Conductible. **conduction**, *n.f.* (*Phys.*) Conduction; (*Civic Law*) hiring.
conduire [kɔ̃'dɥi:r], *v.t. irr.* (*pres. p.* conduisant, *p.p.* conduit (1)) To conduct, to lead, to guide; to accompany, to escort; to command, to direct; to govern, to sway; to manage, to be at the head of; to convey, to transmit. *Conduire à l'autel*, to give away; *conduire un bâtiment* or *un travail*, to be surveyor of a building, to have the direction of a work; *conduire une expérience*, to carry out an experiment; (*Ind.*) *conduire la chauffe*, to stoke, to attend to the firing; *conduire une affaire*, to manage a business; *conduire un troupeau*, to drive a flock; *conduire les opérations*, to supervise the operation; *conduisez monsieur à sa chambre*, show the gentleman to his room; *difficile à conduire*, hard to manage; *savoir conduire sa barque*, to play one's cards well.—*v.i.* To lead (*à*); to extend; to drive. *Ce chemin conduit à la ville*, this road leads to the town; *l'art de conduire*, the art of driving; *permis de conduire*, driving licence;

elle sait conduire, she can drive. **se conduire,** *v.r.* To conduct or behave oneself; to act; to find one's way. **conduit** (2) [kɔ̃'dɥi], *n.m.* Conduit, duct, passage, tube, canal. *Conduit acoustique,* speaking-pipe; *conduit auditif,* auditory passage; *conduit de distribution,* delivery pipe. **conduite** [kɔ̃'dɥit], *n.f.* Conducting, leading, driving, steering, guidance; management, direction, administration, rule, government, command; conveyance, distribution, channel; scheme, plan, arrangement (of a book etc.); water-pipe conduit; behaviour, demeanour, deportment, dealings; prudence, discretion. *Conduite à gauche, à droite,* left-hand, right-hand driving; *conduite d'échappement,* exhaust-pipe; *conduite régulière,* orderly conduct; *la conduite d'une pièce de théâtre,* the disposition or arrangement of a play; *manquer de conduite,* to misconduct oneself, to be ill-behaved; *se charger de la conduite d'une affaire,* to undertake the management of a business; *une conduite intérieure,* any car of the sedan type (with a top). **condyle** [kɔ̃'dil], *n.m.* (*Anat.*) Condyle. **condylien,** *a.* (*fem.* **condylienne**) Condylar. **condyloïde,** *a.* Condyloid. **cône** [koːn], *n.m.* Cone; pine-cone, strobile. *En cône,* conical; (*Eng.*) *cône de transmission,* cone-pulley, speed-cone; *embrayage à cône,* bevel coupling. (*Geol.*) *Cône d'éboulement,* talus; *cône d'alluvion,* cone delta, alluvial fan. **côné,** *a.* (*fem.* **cônée**) Conical. **confabulation** [kɔ̃fabyla'sjɔ̃], *n.f.* Confabulation, chat. **confection** [kɔ̃fɛk'sjɔ̃], *n.f.* Preparation, making, construction; making out, drawing up; execution, completion; making of ready-made clothes; (*Pharm.*) confection, electuary. *La confection d'un inventaire,* the completing of an inventory; *maison de confection,* dress-making establishment; ready-made shop; *vêtements de confection,* ready-made clothes. **confectionnement,** *n.m.* Making, execution, making up. **confectionner,** *v.t.* To make, to manufacture, to finish. **se confectionner,** *v.r.* To be made. **confectionneur,** *n.m.* (*fem.* **-euse**) Maker, finisher (of wearing apparel), clothier, outfitter. **confédération** [kɔ̃federa'sjɔ̃], *n.f.* Confederation, confederacy. *La Confédération Générale du Travail* or C.G.T., compare AFL-CIO; *Confédération Helvétique,* Swiss Confederation. **confédéré,** *a.* and *n.m.* (*fem.* **-ée**) Confederate, associate, federate. **confédérer,** *v.t. irr.* (*conjugated like* ACCÉLÉRER) To confederate, to unite, to combine. **se confédérer,** *v.r.* To combine, to enter into confederation. **conférence** [kɔ̃fe'rãːs], *n.f.* Conference, public discussion; religious or theological discourse; lecture. *Conférence de presse,* press conference; *le directeur est en conférence,* the manager is having a meeting; *maître de conférences,* lecturer. **conférencier,** *n.m.* (*fem.* **-ière**) Lecturer, speaker in a conference. **conférer** [kɔ̃fe're], *v.t. irr.* (*conjugated like* ACCÉLÉRER) To confer, to bestow, to grant. *Conférer un auteur avec un autre,* to collate two authors.—*v.i.* To consult together, to

confer. *Il dut en conférer avec ses supérieurs,* he had to consult his superiors about it. **conferve** [kɔ̃'fɛrv], *n.f.* Conferva, silk-weed. **confesse** [kɔ̃'fɛs], *n.f.* (*always used with* à *or* de). *Aller à confesse,* to go to confession; *venir de confesse,* to come from confession. **confesser** [kɔ̃fɛ'se], *v.t.* To confess; to acknowledge, to own, to admit; to shrive, to receive the confession of; to proclaim, to avow. *C'est le diable à confesser,* it is a terribly hard thing to do. **se confesser,** *v.r.* To confess one's sins, to confess (to a priest). **confesseur,** *n.m.* Confessor; father confessor. **confession** [kɔ̃fɛ'sjɔ̃], *n.f.* Confession, acknowledgment, avowal. *On lui donnerait le bon Dieu sans confession,* you would trust him (or her) with untold gold. **confessionnal,** *n.m.* Confessional. **confessionnel,** *a.* (*fem.* **-elle**) Confessional. **confessionniste,** *n.m.* Lutheran approving of the Confession of Augsburg. **confetti** [kɔ̃fɛt'ti], *n.m. pl.* Confetti. **confiance** [kɔ̃'fjãːs], *n.f.* Confidence, reliance, trust; assurance, self-conceit. *Avoir confiance en quelqu'un,* to repose confidence in someone; *confiance en soi,* self-confidence; *confiance sans bornes,* unbounded faith; *homme de confiance,* confidential clerk; *inspirer confiance,* to look reliable; *une personne de confiance,* a trustworthy person; *poser la question de confiance,* to ask for a vote of confidence. **confiant,** *a.* (*fem.* **-ante**) Confident, unsuspecting, sanguine; self-conceited. **confidemment** [kɔ̃fida'mã], *adv.* Confidentially. **confidence** [kɔ̃fi'dãːs], *n.f.* Confidence, disclosure; secret. *Être dans la confidence de quelqu'un,* to be in someone's confidence; *faire une confidence à quelqu'un,* to tell a secret to someone, to take someone into one's confidence; *il était dans la confidence,* he was in the secret; *un échange de confidences,* an exchange of secrets. **confident,** *n.m.* (*fem.* **confidente**) Confidant, confidante. **confidentiel,** *a.* (*fem.* **-elle**) Confidential. **confidentiellement,** *adv.* Confidentially. **confier** [kɔ̃'fje], *v.t.* (*conjugated like* PRIER) To confide, to entrust, to commit (*à*); to tell in confidence. *Confier la direction à quelqu'un,* to entrust the management to someone. **se confier,** *v.r.* To be entrusted; to place reliance, to confide; to unbosom oneself (*à*). *Je me confie à vous,* I rely on you; *se confier en ses forces,* to trust to one's own strength. **configuration** [kɔ̃figyra'sjɔ̃], *n.f.* Configuration, form, shape, lay (of the land). **configurer,** *v.t.* To configure, to form, to shape. **confinement** [kɔ̃fin'mã], *n.m.* Confinement; overcrowding. **confiner** [kɔ̃fi'ne], *v.i.* To border upon, to be adjoining. *Un tel courage confine à la folie,* such bravery is little short of madness.—*v.t.* To confine, to imprison. *Air confiné,* stuffy atmosphere. **se confiner,** *v.r.* To confine or to limit oneself; to shut oneself up, to retire. **confins** [kɔ̃'fɛ̃], *n.m.* (*used only in pl.*) Confines, borders. *Aux confins de la terre,* at the ends of the earth. **confire** [kɔ̃'fiːr], *v.t. irr.* (*pres.p.* **confisant,** *p.p.* **confit**) To conserve; to candy, to pickle; to soak, to steep (skins); (*fig.*) to keep, to preserve. *Prendre un air confit,* to assume a saint-like air; *confit en dévotion,* extremely devout; *fruits confits,* comfits. **se confire,** *v.r.* To be preserved; (*fig.*) to be steeped (in piety).

confirmatif [kɔ̃firma'tif], *a.* (*fem.* **-ive**) Confirmative. **confirmation,** *n.f.* Confirmation, ratification, sanction. *Cela a besoin de confirmation,* that requires confirmation; *recevoir la confirmation* (*R.-C. Ch.*), to receive the sacrament of confirmation. **confirmatoire,** *a.* Confirmatory.

confirmé [kɔ̃fir'me], *a.* (*fem.* **-ée**) Confirmed, proven. *Nouvelles non confirmées,* unconfirmed news.—*n.* (*Eccles.*) Confirmand.

confirmer [kɔ̃fir'me], *v.t.* To strengthen, to corroborate; to confirm; to ratify, to sanction; to bear out (evidence); (*Eccles.*) to confirm. *Confirmer quelqu'un,* (*colloq.*) to give someone a slap in the face. **se confirmer,** *v.r.* To be confirmed.

confiscable [kɔ̃fis'kabl], *a.* Confiscable, forfeitable, liable to forfeiture. **confiscateur,** *n.m.* (*fem.* **-trice**) Confiscator. **confiscation,** *n.f.* Confiscation, forfeiture.

confiserie [kɔ̃fiz'ri], *n.f.* Confectionery; confectioner's shop. **confiseur,** *n.m.* (*fem.* **confiseuse**) Confectioner.

confisquer [kɔ̃fis'ke], *v.t.* To confiscate, to forfeit, to impound; to seize.

confit (1), *p.p.* (*fem.* **confite**) [CONFIRE].

confit (2) [kɔ̃'fi], *n.m.* Meat, poultry, etc., preserved in fat; bran-mash (for pigs etc.).

confiteor [kɔ̃fite'ɔːr], *n.m. inv.* Confiteor. *Dire son confiteor,* to express one's repentance.

confiture [kɔ̃fi'tyːr], *n.f.* Preserve, jam. *Confiture d'oranges,* marmalade. **confiturerie,** *n.f.* Manufacture or store of preserves etc.; preserves. **confiturier,** *a.* (*fem.* **-ière**) Making preserves.—*n.* Dealer in preserves etc., confectioner; preserve-maker.

conflagration [kɔ̃flagra'sjɔ̃], *n.f.* Conflagration.

conflit [kɔ̃'fli], *n.m.* Conflict, collision, encounter; contention, strife, contest, rivalry; jar, clash. *Conflit d'intérêts,* clash of interests; *conflits du travail,* trade disputes.

confluence [kɔ̃fly'ãːs], *n.f.* Confluence. **confluent,** *a.* (*fem.* **-ente**) Confluent. *Petite vérole confluente,* confluent small-pox.—*n.m.* Confluence, junction (of rivers); (*Path.*) confluence (of arteries etc.). **confluer,** *v.i.* To meet, to unite (of streams etc.).

confondre [kɔ̃'fɔ̃ːdr], *v.t.* To confound, to confuse; to mix, to mingle; to mistake, to make no distinction between; to identify with; (*fig.*) to amaze, to astound, to abash. *Confondre ses ennemis,* to silence one's enemies. **se confondre,** *v.r.* To mingle, to be lost in; to be confounded, to be abashed. *Se confondre en excuses,* to be over-apologetic.

conformateur [kɔ̃fɔrma'tœːr], *n.m.* Head-measuring appliance used by hatters.

conformation, *n.f.* Conformation, structure.

conforme [kɔ̃'fɔrm], *a.* Conformable; congenial, consonant, consistent. *Pour copie conforme,* certified true copy. **conformé,** *a.* (*fem.* **-ée**) Formed, shaped (*bien* or *mal*). **conformément,** *adv.* Suitably, conformably; according to. *Conformément à vos instructions,* in compliance with your instructions.

conformer [kɔ̃fɔr'me], *v.t.* To give form to;

to cause to conform. **se conformer,** *v.r.* To conform, to comply with, to accommodate oneself (*à*). *Se conformer aux circonstances,* to conform to circumstances; *conformez-vous à ces indications,* follow these indications; *se conformer à la loi,* to observe the law; *se conformer au prix indiqué,* to keep within the price given.

conformisme [kɔ̃fɔr'mism], *n.m.* Conformity, orthodoxy. *Un plat conformisme,* a shallow spirit of imitation, lack of originality. **conformiste,** *n.* (*Engl. Ch.*) Conformist.

conformité [kɔ̃fɔrmi'te], *n.f.* Likeness, agreement, consistency; conformity, analogy, compliance, congeniality. *En conformité,* conformably, in compliance with.

confort [kɔ̃'fɔːr], *n.m.* *Help, succour; comfort, ease, convenience. **confortable,** *a.* *Consolatory; cosy, comfortable.—*n.m.* Comfort, ease. **confortablement,** *adv.* Comfortably.

confraternel [kɔ̃frater'nɛl], *a.* (*fem.* **confraternelle**) Fraternal. **confraternité,** *n.f.* Confraternity, brotherhood, fellowship.

confrère [kɔ̃'frɛːr], *n.m.* Confrère, colleague; fellow-member. **confrérie,** *n.f.* Brotherhood, confraternity.

confrontation [kɔ̃frɔ̃ta'sjɔ̃], *n.f.* Confrontation; comparing, collation (of writings etc.). **confronter,** *v.t.* To confront, to stand face to face; to compare, to collate. *Confronter la copie à l'original,* to compare the copy with the original.

confucianisme [kɔ̃fysja'nizm], *n.m.* Confucianism. **confucianiste,** *a.* and *n.* Confucianist.

confus [kɔ̃'fy], *a.* (*fem.* **confuse**) Confused, mixed, muddled, vague, indistinct, obscure; abashed, crest-fallen. *Bruit confus,* confused rumour; *je suis confus de vous déranger,* I am sorry to disturb you. **confusément,** *adv.* Confusedly, vaguely, dimly.

confusion [kɔ̃fy'zjɔ̃], *n.f.* Confusion, jumble, disorder, disturbance, bewilderment, distraction; embarrassment, shame, blush; misunderstanding. *Couvrir de confusion,* to put to shame; *mettre tout en confusion,* to disturb everything; *confusion mentale,* psychosis, mental disorder, alienation.

conge [kɔ̃ʒ], *n.m.* (*Rom. Ant.*) a Roman measure, about 6 pints, congius; ore-basket.

congé [kɔ̃'ʒe], *n.m.* Leave, permission; leave of absence, furlough, holiday; discharge, dismissal; warning, notice to (quit); congé; permit; (*Mil.*) period of service; discharge from this; furlough; (*Naut.*) pass, clearance; sea-brief; (*Arch.*) concave moulding in column where shaft joins capital, tapered collar. *En congé,* on furlough; *jour de congé,* holiday; *prendre congé,* to take one's leave. *Congé de douane,* clearance. **congéable,** *a.* (*Law*) held under tenancy at will.

congédiable [kɔ̃ʒe'djabl], *a.* Dismissable.

congédiement, *n.m.* Discharging, paying off. *Congédiement massif,* lock-out (of workmen).

congédier [kɔ̃ʒe'dje], *v.t.* (*conjugated like* PRIER) To discharge, to dismiss, to pay off; to disband, to break up.

congelable [kɔ̃ʒ'labl], *a.* Congealable. **congelant,** *a.* Congealing. **congélateur,** *n.m.* Refrigerator, freezing-machine. **congélation,** *n.f.* Congelation; (*Arch.*) rock-work.

Conservation par congélation, cold storage (of food); *point de congélation*, freezing-point. **congeler** [kɔ̃ʒˈle], *v.t.* To congeal, to freeze; to coagulate. **se congeler**, *v.r.* To congeal, to freeze; to coagulate. **congénère** [kɔ̃ʒeˈnɛːr], *a.* Congeneric; of same species; (*Philol.*) cognate.—*n.* Congener. **congénial** [kɔ̃ʒeˈnjal], *a.* (*fem.* **-iale**, *pl.* **-iaux**) Congenial, of the same nature. **congénital** [kɔ̃ʒeniˈtal], *a.* (*fem.* **-ale**, *pl.* **-aux**) Congenital, hereditary. **congère** [kɔ̃ˈʒɛr], *n.f.* Snow-drift. **congestif** [kɔ̃ʒɛsˈtif], *a.* (*fem.* **-ive**) Congestive. **congestion** [kɔ̃ʒɛsˈtjɔ̃], *n.f.* Congestion; accumulation of blood. *Congestion cérébrale*, brain stroke; *congestion pulmonaire*, pneumonia. **congestionné**, *a.* (*fem.* **-tionnée**) Congested; flushed (face); jammed (street). **congestionner**, *v.t.* To congest. **congiaire** [kɔ̃ˈʒjɛːr], *n.m.* (*Rom. Ant.*) Distribution by emperors to people. **conglobation** [kɔ̃glɔbɑˈsjɔ̃], *n.f.* (*Rhet.*) Conglobation. **conglober**, *v.t.* To conglobate, to conglobe. **conglomérat** [kɔ̃glɔmeˈra], *n.m.* (*Geol.*) Conglomerate. *Conglomérat volcanique*, volcanic conglomerate; *conglomérat aurifère*, auriferous banket. **conglomération**, *n.f.* Conglomeration. **conglomérer**, *v.t.* To conglomerate. **conglutinant** [kɔ̃glytiˈnɑ̃], *a.* (*fem.* **-ante**) or **conglutinatif** (*fem.* **-ive**), *a.* Conglutinative. **conglutination**, *n.f.* Conglutination. **conglutiner**, *v.t.* To glue or stick together; to thicken, to conglutinate. **se conglutiner**, *v.r.* To become stuck together. **congratulant** [kɔ̃gratyˈlɑ̃], *a.* (*fem.* **-ante**) Congratulatory. **congratulateur**, *a.* (*fem.* **-trice**) (*usu. iron.*) Congratulatory.—*n.* Congratulator. **congratulation** [kɔ̃gratylaˈsjɔ̃], *n.f.* Congratulation. **congratulatoire**, *a.* Congratulatory. **congratuler**, *v.t.* To congratulate, to felicitate. **congre** [kɔ̃ːgr], *n.m.* Conger, conger-eel. **congréganisme** [kɔ̃gregaˈnism], *n.m.* System, doctrines, etc., of the congregation (under the Restoration). **congréganiste**, *a.* Belonging to a congregation; directed by monks, nuns, etc. (of schools). **congrégation** [kɔ̃gregaˈsjɔ̃], *n.f.* Fraternity, brotherhood, general body (of an order etc.); assembly of such; community. *La congrégation des fidèles*, the whole body of the Church. **congrès** [kɔ̃ˈgrɛ], *n.m.* Congress (United States); general meeting, congress, conference. **congressiste**, *n.m.* Congressman (U.S.); member of a congress. **congru** [kɔ̃ˈgry], *a.* (*fem.* **congrue**) Suitable, consistent, agreeable, congruous, proper. *Portion congrue*, subsistence allowance, bare living; *réduit à la portion congrue*, (*fig.*) on short commons. **congruence**, *n.f.* Congruence. **congruent**, *a.* (*fem.* **-ente**) Congruent. **congruité**, *n.f.* Congruity, consistency, propriety. **congrûment**, *adv.* Congruously, properly. **conicité** [kɔnisiˈte], *n.f.* Conicalness; cone angle; taper (of bullets, wedge). **conifère** [kɔniˈfɛːr], *a.* Coniferous.—*n.m.* Conifer.

coniforme [CONIQUE]. **conique** [kɔˈnik], *a.* Conical.—*n.f. pl.* Conics, conic sections. **conjectural** [kɔ̃ʒɛktyˈral], *a.* (*fem.* **-ale**, *pl.* **-aux**) Conjectural. **conjecturalement**, *adv.* Conjecturally. **conjecture**, *n.f.* Conjecture, surmise, guess. *Par conjecture*, by guess; *se perdre en conjectures*, not to know what to think. **conjecturer**, *v.t.* To conjecture, to guess, to surmise. **conjoindre** [kɔ̃ˈʒwɛ̃ːdr], *v.t. irr.* To conjoin, to unite together; to marry. **conjoint**, *a.* Conjoined, united, joint. *Feuilles conjointes*, (*Bot.*) conjugate leaves; *règle conjointe*, chain-rule.—*n.* Spouse, wedded partner. *Les futurs conjoints*, the bride and bridegroom; *les conjoints*, husband and wife; *l'un des conjoints*, one of the parties. **conjointement**, *adv.* Conjointly, unitedly. *Conjointement à*, jointly with. **conjoncteur** [kɔ̃ʒɔ̃kˈtœːr], *n.m.* (*Elec.*) Circuit-closer, switch key. **conjoncteur-disjoncteur**, *n.m.* Self-closing circuit-breaker. **conjonctif** [kɔ̃ʒɔ̃kˈtif], *a.* (*fem.* **-ive**) Conjunctive.—*n.f.* (*Anat.*) Conjunctiva. **conjonction**, *n.f.* Conjunction; union, connexion; coition. **conjonctionnel**, *a.* (*fem.* **-elle**) Conjunctional. **conjonctival**, *a.* (*fem.* **-ale**, *pl.* **-aux**) (*Anat.*) Pertaining to the conjunctiva. **conjonctive**, *n.f.* [CONJONCTIF]. **conjonctivement**, *adv.* Conjunctively. **conjonctivite**, *n.f.* Inflammation of the conjunctiva. **conjoncture**, *n.f.* Conjuncture, juncture. *Conjoncture favorable*, favourable outlook. **conjugable** [kɔ̃ʒyˈgabl], *a.* (*Gram.*) That can be conjugated. **conjugaison** [kɔ̃ʒygɛˈzɔ̃], *n.f.* Conjugation; (*Biol.*) fusion of two gametes. **conjugal** [kɔ̃ʒyˈgal], *a.* (*fem.* **-ale**, *pl.* **-aux**) Conjugal. **conjugalement**, *adv.* Conjugally. **conjugué** [kɔ̃ʒyˈge], *a.* (*fem.* **-guée**) (*Mech.*) Twin. *Machines conjuguées*, twin engines. **conjuguer** [kɔ̃ʒyˈge], *v.t.* (*Gram.*) To conjugate. *Ils conjuguèrent leurs efforts*, they joined forces. **se conjuguer**, *v.r.* To be conjugated. **conjungo** [kɔ̃ʒɔ̃ˈgo], *n.m.* (Latin formula meaning: "I pronounce you married") (*facet.*) Wedding, marriage; (*Palaeography*) writing without stops or spaces. **conjuration** [kɔ̃ʒyrɑˈsjɔ̃], *n.f.* Conspiracy, plot; conjuration, exorcism, incantation; (*pl.*) entreaties, supplications. **conjuré**, *a.* (*fem.* **-ée**) Confederate, sworn, conspiring; exorcized (of danger etc.).—*n.* Conspirator, plotter. **conjurer** [kɔ̃ʒyˈre], *v.t.* To implore, to adjure; to conspire, to plot; to swear, to conjure up, to raise (evil spirits), to exorcize, to cast off, to ward off, to avert. *Il trouva moyen de conjurer la tempête*, he found a way of warding off the storm.—*v.i.* To conspire. **connaissable** [kɔnɛˈsabl], *a.* Recognizable, easily known. **connaissance** [kɔnɛˈsɑ̃ːs], *n.f.* Knowledge, understanding, learning; acquirements; notion, idea, consciousness (*de*); acquaintance; information, familiarity, intercourse; (*Law*) cognizance; (*Hunt.*) the print of a stag's foot; (*pl.*) attainments, acquirements. *Avoir* *connaissance de*, to be acquainted with, to know; *c'est une connaissance de ma femme*, he is an acquaintance of my wife's; *donner connaissance d'une chose à*, to make a matter known to, to notify; *être en pays de connaissance*, to be among friends; *faire connaissance avec quelqu'un*, to make someone's acquaintance; *il perdit connaissance*, he lost consciousness, he fainted; *la connaissance du bien et du mal*, the knowledge of good and evil; *parler en connaissance de cause*, to speak knowingly; *prendre connaissance d'une cause*, to take cognizance of a case; *ses connaissances sont très bornées*, his knowledge is very limited; *un homme aux vastes connaissances*, a man of wide learning. **connaissant**, *a.* (*fem.* **-ante**) Well acquainted (with).

connaissement [kɔnɛs'mã], *n.m.* (*Naut.*) Bill of lading.

connaisseur [kɔnɛ'sœːr], *a.* (*fem.* **connaisseuse**) Expert, skilled.—*n.* Connoisseur, expert.

connaître [kɔ'nɛːtr], *v.t. irr.* (*pres.p.* **connaissant**, *p.p.* **connu**) To know, to be aware of, to perceive; to understand, to be versed in; to be acquainted with, to have to do with; to experience; to discern, to distinguish, to recognize. *Connaissez-vous cet homme-là?* are you acquainted with that man? *connaître à fond*, to know thoroughly; *connaître le malheur*, to be acquainted with grief; *connaître son affaire*, to know what one is about; *dès qu'il est question d'intérêt, il ne connaît plus personne*, in matters of interest everybody is a stranger to him; *faire connaître*, to make it appear, to reveal, to make known; *il ne connaissait plus de frein*, there were no restraints to his passion etc.; (*colloq.*) *je connais la musique*, you don't deceive me, I see through you; *je le connais de vue*, I know him by sight; *je le ferai connaître*, I will show him up; *je ne connais que cela*, that's all I can say, all I know; *ne connaître ni Dieu ni diable*, to care for neither God nor devil, to be utterly reckless; *ne connaître que son devoir*, to heed nothing but duty; *se faire connaître*, to make oneself or one's qualities, worth, etc., known.—*v.i.* To have or to take cognizance of; to deal with (a matter). **se connaître**, *v.r.* To know oneself; to know each other, to be acquaintances; to be a connoisseur or judge (*en*); (of things) to be known. *Connais-toi toi-même*, know thyself; *il ne se connaît plus*, he is out of his senses; *je m'y connais*, I understand all about it, I am an expert at it; *ne plus se connaître de joie*, to be beside oneself with joy; *se connaître en quelque chose*, to understand something, to be a judge of something.

connecter [kɔnɛk'te], *v.t.* To connect; (*Elec.*) to couple (up), to group.

connectif, *a.* (*fem.* **-ive**) (*Bot.*) Connective.—*n.m.* Connective (of anther).

connétable [kɔnɛ'tabl], *n.m.* High constable. —*n.f.* High constable's wife. *connétablie, n.f.* The court and jurisdiction of the high constable; residence of the high constable.

connexe [kɔ'nɛks], *a.* (*Law*) Connected. **connexion**, *n.f.* Connexion, affinity. (*Elec.*) *Connexion de six lampes*, six-valve system; *connexions compensatrices*, equalizing connexions. **connexité**, *n.f.* Connexion.

connivence [kɔni'vãːs], *n.f.* Connivance. *Être de connivence* (*avec*), to act in complicity (with), to be accomplices. **connivent**, *a.* (*fem.* **connivente**) (*Anat.*, *Bot.*) Connivent.

***conniver** [kɔni've], *v.i.* To connive, to be in collusion with.

connotatif [kɔnota'tif], *a.* (*fem.* **-ive**) Connotative. **connotation**, *n.f.* Connotation.

connu [kɔ'ny], *a.* (*fem.* **connue**) Known, understood; discovered, explored; well-known, celebrated. *Connu!* that's an old story; *en chiffres connus*, in plain figures; *il est connu comme le loup blanc*, he is known by everybody; *il gagne à être connu*, he improves on acquaintance; *universellement connu*, world-famous.—*n.m.* That which is known.

conoïdal [kɔnɔi'dal], *a.* (*fem.* **-ale**, *pl.* **-aux**) Conoidal. **conoïde**, *a.* and *n.m.* Conoid.

conque [kɔ̃ːk], *n.f.* Conch, sea-shell; (*Anat.*) concha (concavity of the ear).

conquérant [kɔ̃ke'rã], *a.* (*fem.* **conquérante**) Conquering; (*colloq.*) killing, spruce.—*n.* Conqueror; (*colloq.*) lady-killer.

conquérir [kɔ̃ke'riːr], *v.t. irr.* (*pres.p.* **conquérant**, *p.p.* **conquis**, *conjugated like* ACQUÉRIR) To conquer, to subdue (a country); (*fig.*) to gain, to obtain, to win over (hearts). *Vous m'avez conquis*, you have persuaded me.

conquêt [kɔ̃'kɛ], *n.m.* (*Law*) Acquisition, acquired property (esp. acquired by two married people).

conquête [kɔ̃'kɛːt], *n.f.* Conquest, acquisition. *Faire la conquête de quelqu'un*, to win over somebody's heart.

conquis [kɔ̃'ki], *p.p.* (*fem.* **-ise**) Conquered, gained. *Se conduire comme en pays conquis*, to behave like a tyrant.

consacrant [kɔ̃sa'krã], *a.* (*fem.* **-ante**) Consecrating, officiating.—*n.m.* Consecrator, officiant.

consacrer [kɔ̃sa'kre], *v.t.* To consecrate, to dedicate, to devote, to hallow, to sanctify; to sanction, to perpetuate; to authorize. *Consacrer son temps à*, to devote one's time to. **se consacrer**, *v.r.* To devote oneself; to become consecrated.

consanguin [kɔ̃sã'gɛ̃], *a.* (*fem.* **-guine**) Related on the father's side; (*horse*) inbred. *Frère consanguin, sœur consanguine*, half-brother, half-sister, on the father's side.—*n.* Relative of this nature. *Les consanguins*, half-brothers and sisters on the father's side. **consanguinité**, *n.f.* Consanguinity (through the father).

consciemment [kɔ̃sja'mã], *adv.* Consciously, knowingly.

conscience [kɔ̃'sjãːs], *n.f.* Consciousness, perception; conscience, conscientiousness, morality, integrity; (*Tech.*) plastron, breastplate; (*Print.*) work paid by the day; the compositors paid by the day. *Avec conscience*, conscientiously; *avoir conscience de*, to be conscious of; *conscience nette*, clear conscience; *conscience professionnelle*, professional reliability, seriousness in one's trade; *cri de la conscience*, qualm of conscience; *en conscience*, conscientiously, truly, candidly, honestly; *être en règle avec sa conscience*, to have confessed one's sins, to be in peace with one's conscience; *il a dit tout ce qu'il avait sur la conscience,* he has opened his mind without reserve; *il a la conscience large,* he is not over scrupulous; *la main sur la conscience,* candidly, sincerely; *liberté de conscience,* freedom of conscience; *manque de conscience,* unscrupulousness; *mettre sur la conscience,* to make oneself responsible for; *objecteur de conscience,* conscientious objector; *par acquit de conscience,* for conscience' sake; *perdre conscience,* to become unconscious, to faint; *remords de conscience,* remorse, sting of conscience; *se faire un cas de conscience d'une chose,* to make a matter of conscience of something; *transiger avec sa conscience,* to compound with one's conscience. **consciencieusement** [kɔ̃sjɑ̃sjøz'mɑ̃], *adv.* Conscientiously. **consciencieux,** *a.* (*fem.* -euse) Conscientious.

conscient [kɔ̃'sjɑ̃], *a.* (*fem.* **consciente**) Conscious (*de*); self-conscious. *Pleinement conscient de,* fully aware of; *un être conscient,* a sentient being.

conscription [kɔ̃skrip'sjɔ̃], *n.f.* Enlistment, enrolling; conscription.

conscrit [kɔ̃'skri] *a.* Conscript. *Père conscrit,* Roman senator.—*n.m.* Conscript; recruit, raw soldier; (*fig.*) freshman, greenhorn.

consécrateur [CONSACRANT].

consécration [kɔ̃sekra'sjɔ̃], *n.f.* Consecration, dedication; ordination; sanction. *La consécration d'un talent,* the public acknowledgment of a talent. *Avoir reçu la consécration du temps,* to be time-hallowed.

consécutif [kɔ̃seky'tif], *a.* (*fem.* -ive) Consecutive, following, ensuing; resulting. *Après des échus consécutifs,* after a series of failures. **consécution,** *n.f.* Sequence; (*Astron.*) period of 28½ days between new moons. **consécutivement,** *adv.* Consecutively.

conseil [kɔ̃'sɛːj], *n.m.* Counsel, advice; resolution, determination; designs; *prudence, wisdom; council, committee, board; (*Law*) barrister consulted in a case, counsel. *Conseil d'administration,* board of directors, directorate; *Conseil d'État,* Council of State; *Conseil de l'Amirauté,* Board of Admiralty; *Conseil de Sécurité (de l'ONU),* (UNO) Security Council; *conseil de famille,* family council (for considering the interests of a minor); *conseil judiciaire,* guardian (of a spendthrift); *conseil de guerre,* court-martial, council of war; *conseil de révision,* board of examiners of recruits (to pronounce them fit or unfit); *conseil des ministres,* cabinet council; *conseil municipal,* town council, corporation; *il ne prend conseil que de sa tête,* he does everything by himself, without consulting anyone; *la nuit porte conseil!* sleep on it! *plus d'un bon conseil,* more than one piece of sound advice; *suivez mon conseil,* take my advice; *tenir conseil,* to hold counsel, to deliberate.

conseillable [kɔ̃sɛ'jabl], *a.* That may be counselled; advisable.

conseiller (1) [kɔ̃sɛ'je], *v.t.* To advise, to counsel; to recommend; to excite to.

conseiller (2) [kɔ̃sɛ'je], *n.m.* (*fem.* -ère) Counsellor, adviser. *Conseiller juridique,* legal adviser; *conseiller municipal,* town councillor.

conseilleur [kɔ̃sɛ'jœːr], *n.m.* (*fem.* -euse) Adviser; (*fig.*) officious person.

consensuel [kɔ̃sɑ̃'sɥel], *a.* (*fem.* -elle) (*Law*) By consent of the parties.

consensus [kɔ̃sɑ̃'syːs], *n.m.* Consent, consensus.

consentant [kɔ̃sɑ̃'tɑ̃], *a.* (*fem.* -ante) Consenting, willing. **consentement,** *n.m.* Consent, assent; approval, acquiescence.

consentir [kɔ̃sɑ̃'tiːr], *v.i. irr.* To consent, to agree, to acquiesce (*à*); to believe, to assent (*que*); (*Naut.*) to spring, to break (of masts). *Qui ne dit mot consent,* silence gives consent.—*v.t.* To authorize.

conséquemment [kɔ̃seka'mɑ̃], *adv.* Consequently, accordingly, in consequence.

conséquence [kɔ̃se'kɑ̃ːs], *n.f.* Consequence, sequel; event, issue, result; inference, conclusion; (*fig.*) moment, importance, weight. *Cela tire à conséquence,* that will be a precedent; *de peu de* or *de la dernière conséquence,* of no or of the greatest consequence; *en conséquence,* accordingly; *en conséquence de vos ordres,* according to your orders; *faire l'homme de conséquence,* to set up for a man of consequence; *prévoir les conséquences d'une démarche,* to foresee the consequences of a measure; *sans conséquence,* of no importance; *tirer une conséquence,* to draw an inference.

conséquent [kɔ̃se'kɑ̃], *a.* (*fem.* -ente) Rational, consistent, coherent; conformable (*à* or *avec*); (*vulg.*) important, big.—*n.m.* (*Log.*, *Math.*) Consequent. *Par conséquent,* consequently, therefore, accordingly.

conservateur [kɔ̃sɛrva'tœːr], *a.* (*fem.* -trice) Preserving, conservative.—*n.* Conservative, Tory.—*n.m.* Conservator, guardian, keeper, curator. *Conservateur des chasses,* ranger; *conservateur des eaux et forêts,* commissioner of woods and forests. **conservatif,** *n.m.* Preservative.—*a.* (*fem.* -ive) Conservative, preservative. **conservation,** *n.f.* Conservation, preservation; Conservatism; guardianship, commissionership; registration (of mortgages etc.).

conservatisme [kɔ̃serva'tism], *n.m.* Conservatism.

conservatoire [kɔ̃sɛrva'twaːr], *a.* Conservative, preservative. (*Law*) *Saisie conservatoire,* distraint.—*n.m. Le Conservatoire* (academy of music and school of elocution); *le Conservatoire des Arts et Métiers,* the School and Museum of Arts and Crafts (both in Paris).

conserve [kɔ̃'sɛrv], *n.f.* Preserve; canned food; (*Pharm.*) conserve; (*Naut.*) consort; (*pl.*) *coloured spectacles. *Naviguer de conserve,* to convoy; *conserves au vinaigre,* pickles; *bœuf de conserve,* corned beef.

conserver [kɔ̃sɛr've], *v.t.* To preserve; to keep; to maintain; (*Naut.*) to convoy. *Ce tableau est bien conservé,* this painting is well preserved; *conserver toute sa tête,* to preserve one's faculties; *être bien conservé,* to bear one's age well, to be hale and hearty. **se conserver,** *v.r.* To be preserved; to preserve oneself; to last, to bear one's age well; to keep (of meat, fruit, etc.). *Son teint s'est bien conservé,* her complexion wears well.

conserverie [kɔ̃sɛrvə'riː], *n.f.* Canning industry.

considérable [kɔ̃side'rabl], *a.* Considerable, notable, eminent, illustrious, important. *Peu considérable,* of little importance. **considérablement,** *adv.* Considerably.

considérant [kɔ̃side'rɑ̃], *n.m.* (usually *plur.*) (*Law*) Preamble, grounds.—*conj. phr.* *Considérant que*, whereas.

considération [kɔ̃siderɑ'sjɔ̃], *n.f.* Consideration, attention; motive, reason, grounds; regard, respect; esteem, importance; (*pl.*) reflections, thoughts, notes. *Agir sans considération*, to act inconsiderately; *cela mérite considération*, that requires consideration; *en considération de*, in consideration of, for the sake of; *il n'a nulle considération dans le monde*, he is held in no esteem whatever; *n'avoir aucune considération pour les gens*, to have no regard for people; *prendre en considération*, to take into account.

considérément [kɔ̃sidere'mɑ̃], *adv.* Considerately, prudently, circumspectly.

considérer [kɔ̃side're], *v.t. irr.* (*conjug. like* ACCÉLÉRER) To consider, to gaze upon, to survey, to look at, to view; to take into consideration, to ponder, to examine, to weigh; to appreciate, to value, to esteem, to respect; to mind, to pay attention to, to heed. *Considérer comme un devoir de*, to consider it a duty to; *considérer comme utile*, to think useful, to deem advisable; *considérer une chose en elle-même*, to look at a thing in itself; *il faut bien considérer les choses avant de s'engager*, you must look before you leap; *tout bien considéré*, all things considered. **se considérer**, *v.r.* To look at or regard oneself; to look at each other; to esteem oneself; to value or judge oneself.

consignataire [kɔ̃siɲa'tɛːr], *n.m.* Trustee, depositary; (*Comm.*) consignee.

consignateur, *n.m.* (*fem.* -trice) (*Comm.*) Consignor, shipper.

consignation [kɔ̃siɲa'sjɔ̃], *n.f.* (*Comm.*) Consignation, deposit, consignment. *Caisse des dépôts et consignations*, State deposit and consignment bank; *en consignation*, on consignment.

consigne [kɔ̃'siɲ], *n.f.* (*Mil.*) Order, password, instructions; (*fig.*) strict command, prohibition, etc.; (*Rail.*) cloak-room (at stations); (*sch.*) gating, keeping in. (*Mil.*) *Consigne au quartier*, confinement to barracks; *consigne à la chambre*, close arrest (of an N.C.O.). *Forcer la consigne*, to infringe orders; *lever la consigne*, to revoke orders; to release from confinement; *manquer à la consigne*, to disregard orders; *marchandises en consigne à la douane*, goods held up at the custom-house.

consigner [kɔ̃si'ɲe], *v.t.* To deposit; to consign; to record, to enter, to register; to order, to instruct; to confine to barracks; to keep in; to refuse admittance to. *Maison consignée à la troupe*, house put out of bounds.

consistance [kɔ̃sis'tɑ̃ːs], *n.f.* Consistency, consistence; firmness, stability; (*fig.*) credit, consideration. *C'est un esprit qui n'a point de consistance*, he is a person of no consistency; *cette nouvelle prend de la consistance*, the news is gaining ground. **consistant**, *a.* (*fem.* -ante) Consisting (*en*); consistent, firm, solid, compact.

consister [kɔ̃sis'te], *v.i.* To consist; to be composed of. *Le tout consiste à savoir*, the main point is to know; *son revenu consiste en rentes*, his revenue consists of property in the funds.

consistoire [kɔ̃sis'twaːr], *n.m.* Consistory. **consistorial**, *a.* (*fem.* -iale, *pl.* -iaux) Consistorial. **consistorialement**, *adv.* In consistory.

consœur [kɔ̃'sœr], *n.f.* (*fem.* of *confrère*) Colleague.

consolable [kɔ̃sɔ'labl], *a.* Consolable. **consolant**, *a.* (*fem.* -ante) Consoling, comforting, consolatory. **consolateur**, *a.* (*fem.* -trice) Consoling, consolatory.—*n.* Comforter, consoler. **consolation**, *n.f.* Consolation, comfort, solace.

console [kɔ̃'sɔl], *n.f.* Console, bracket; hanger, overhung support; console-table.

consoler [kɔ̃sɔ'le], *v.t.* To console, to solace, to comfort. **se consoler**, *v.r.* To solace, to console oneself. *Elle se console vite*, she is quick to forget.

consolidant [kɔ̃sɔli'dɑ̃], *a.* (*fem.* -ante) Consolidating; (*Med.*) healing up.—*n.m.* Consolidating remedy. **consolidation**, *n.f.* Consolidation; stiffening, strengthening; funding (of interest etc.). **consolidé**, *a.* (*fem.* -ée) Funded.—*n.m.* (*Fin.*, used only in *pl.*) Consols. **consolider**, *v.t.* To consolidate; to strengthen, to make durable or permanent; (*Fin.*) to fund; (*Med.*) to heal up. **se consolider**, *v.r.* To consolidate, to grow firm; to take root.

consommable [kɔ̃sɔ'mabl], *a.* Consumable, edible.

consommateur [kɔ̃sɔma'tœːr], *n.m.* Consumer (opposed to producer), eater, drinker, guest (in restaurant etc.); (*Theol.*) perfector.

consommation [kɔ̃sɔma'sjɔ̃], *n.f.* Consumption, using up (of commodities etc.); destruction, waste; consummation, accomplishment, end; food, drinks, refreshments, expense. *Jusqu'à la consommation des siècles*, until the Last Day, until Judgment Day; *payer la consommation*, to pay the expenses or the bill; *pour ma consommation particulière*, for my private use.

consommé [kɔ̃sɔ'me], *a.* (*fem.* -ée) Consumed, used, consummated; consummate, perfect; clever, accomplished.—*n.m.* Clear soup.

consommer [kɔ̃sɔ'me], *v.t.* To consume, to use; (*fig.*) to waste, to destroy; to consummate, to complete, to accomplish.—*v.i.* (*pop.*) To have a drink.

consomptible [kɔ̃sɔ̃p'tibl], *a.* (*Law*) Consumable.

consomption [kɔ̃sɔ̃p'sjɔ̃], *n.f.* Consumption, using up; waste, destruction; (*Path.*) phthisis, decline.

consonance [kɔ̃sɔ'nɑ̃ːs], *n.f.* Consonance; (*fig.*) harmony, concord. **consonant**, *a.* (*fem.* -ante) Consonant. **consonantique**, *a.* Characterized by consonance. **consonantisme**, *n.m.* Consonantal system (of a language). **consonne**, *n.f.* Consonant. **consonner** or **consoner**, *v.i.* To harmonize, to accord; to produce consonance.

consort [kɔ̃'sɔːr], *a.* Consort (of the husband or wife of a sovereign).—*n.m.* (*used only in pl.*) Consorts, confederates; (*Law*) associates, people connected together or having the same interest.

consortium [kɔ̃sɔr'sjɔm], *n.m.* Consortium.
consoude [kɔ̃'sud], *n.f.* (*Bot.*) Comfrey.

conspirateur [kɔ̃spira'tœːr], *n.m.* (*fem.* **-trice**) Conspirator.—*a.* Conspiring, plotting.
conspiration [kɔ̃spira'sjɔ̃], *n.f.* Conspiracy, plot, cabal; (*fig.*) combined effort. *La Conspiration des Poudres,* the Gunpowder Plot.
conspirer [kɔ̃spi're], *v.i.* To conspire, to agree together, to concur, to combine; to plot. *Tout conspire à me ruiner,* everything combines to ruin me.—*v.t.* To plot, to plan secretly, to meditate. *Conspirer la ruine de l'État,* to plot the ruin of the State.
conspuer [kɔ̃s'pɥe], *v.t.* *To spit upon; (*fig.*) to despise, to spurn, to revile; to boo, to barrack.
constamment [kɔ̃sta'mɑ̃], *adv.* With constancy, steadily; continually, constantly.
constance [kɔ̃s'tɑ̃ːs], *n.f.* Constancy, faithfulness, loyalty, steadfastness; perseverance, steadiness, firmness, persistence. **constant,** *a.* (*fem.* **-ante**) Constant, faithful, unshaken, loyal, steadfast; persevering; (*Math.*) unvarying, invariable. *Il est constant que,* it is an established fact that. **constante,** *n.f.* (*Math.*) Constant.
Constantin [kɔ̃stɑ̃'tɛ̃], *m.* Constantine.
Constantine [kɔ̃stɑ̃'tin], *f.* Constantina.
constat [kɔ̃s'sta], *n.m.* (*Law*) Certified report. *Constat d'huissier,* affidavit made by process server.
constatation [kɔ̃stata'sjɔ̃], *n.f.* Authentication; verification; declaration, statement; inquest, findings of an inquiry.
constater [kɔ̃sta'te], *v.t.* To prove, to verify, to establish undeniably; to ascertain, to state, to declare.
constellation [kɔ̃stɛla'sjɔ̃], *n.f.* Constellation. **constellé,** *a.* (*fem.* **-ée**) Constellated; studded; star-like. *Constellé de décorations,* covered with medals. **consteller,** *v.t.* To constellate, to strew, to sow as if with stars, to stud.
consternant [kɔ̃stɛr'nɑ̃], *a.* (*fem.* **-ante**) Overwhelming, alarming.
consternation [kɔ̃stɛrna'sjɔ̃], *n.f.* Consternation, dismay. **consterné,** *a.* (*fem.* **-ée**) Dismayed, struck with consternation, overwhelmed. **consterner,** *v.t.* To strike with consternation, to dismay, to dishearten; to astound, to amaze.
constipant [kɔ̃sti'pɑ̃], *a.* (*fem.* **-ante**) Constipating. **constipation** [kɔ̃stipa'sjɔ̃], *n.f.* Constipation, costiveness. **constipé,** *a.* (*fem.* **-ée**) Costive, constipated. **constiper,** *v.t.* To constipate, to bind. ↻
constituant [kɔ̃sti'tɥɑ̃], *a.* (*fem.* **-ante**) Constituent; (*Law*) constituting an endowment, conferring a power of attorney, etc.; (*Constitutional Law*) drawing upon or authorized to draw up a constitution.—*n.m.* (*Fr. Hist.*) Member of the Constituent Assembly (in 1789).—*n.f.* Constituent Assembly.
constituer [kɔ̃sti'tɥe], *v.t.* To constitute, to be the essence or elements of; to form, to compose, to make; to establish, to organize, to give a constitution to, to incorporate (a society etc.); to appoint, to empower to act as; to settle, to assign (a dowry, annuity, etc.); to give into custody. *Constituer une rente,* to settle an annuity; *constituer un précédent,* to establish a precedent; *qui vous a constitué juge?* who made you judge in

the matter? **se constituer,** *v.r.* To constitute oneself; to form oneself. *Se constituer prisonnier,* to give oneself up.
constitutif, *a.* (*fem.* **-ive**) Constitutive.
constitution [kɔ̃stity'sjɔ̃], *n.f.* Constitution, establishment, polity, settlement (of an annuity etc.); declaration of powers conferred, fundamental principles of the State, appointment; temper, temperament. *Avoir une bonne constitution,* to be bodily fit; *le texte de la constitution,* the written constitution. **constitutionnalité,** *n.f.* Constitutionality. **constitutionnel,** *a.* (*fem.* **-elle**) Constitutional; inherent in, essential. *Maladie constitutionnelle,* organic disease; *le droit constitutionnel,* the constitutional power.—*n.m.* Constitutionalist. **constitutionnellement,** *adv.* Constitutionally.
constricteur [kɔ̃strik'tœːr], *a.* (*Anat.*) Constrictive. *Boa constricteur,* boa constrictor.—*n.m.* Constrictor. **constrictif,** *a.* (*fem.* **-ive**) Constringent.
constriction [kɔ̃strik'sjɔ̃], *n.f.* Constriction, compression; (*Surg. etc.*) astriction.
constringent [kɔ̃strɛ̃'ʒɑ̃], *a.* (*fem.* **-ente**) Constringent.
constructeur [kɔ̃stryk'tœːr], *n.m.* Constructor, builder; shipbuilder, shipwright.
construction [kɔ̃stryk'sjɔ̃], *n.f.* Building, construction; a building, edifice, erection, structure; (*Gram.*) arrangement and connexion of words in a sentence. *En construction,* building, (*Naut.*) on the stocks; *faire de nouvelles constructions,* to erect new buildings; *vaisseau de construction française,* French-built ship.
constructivité [kɔ̃stryktivi'te], *n.f.* Constructiveness.
construire [kɔ̃s'trɥiːr], *v.t.* (*pres.p.* **construisant,** *p.p.* **construit**) To construct, to build, to erect, to frame; to arrange, to put together; (*Gram.*) to construct. *Construire un rectangle,* to construct (draw) a rectangle.
consubstantialité [kɔ̃sypstɑ̃sjali'te], *n.f.* Consubstantiality. **consubstantiation,** *n.f.* Consubstantiation. **consubstantiel,** *a.* (*fem.* **-elle**) Consubstantial.
consul [kɔ̃'syl], *n.m.* Consul. **consulaire,** *n.m.* A man of consular rank.—*a.* Consular. *Personnage consulaire,* ex-consul. **consulairement,** *adv.* Consularly; by consuls. **consulat,** *n.m.* Consulate, consulship. *Consulat général,* consulate-general.
consultant [kɔ̃syl'tɑ̃], *a.* (*fem.* **-ante**) Consulting, advising. *Avocat consultant,* chamber-counsellor; *médecin consultant,* consulting physician.—*n.m.* Consultant, adviser, person consulted; consulting physician. **consultatif,** *a.* (*fem.* **-ive**) Consultative, deliberative. *Avoir voix consultative,* to have the right of discussion without that of voting.
consultation [kɔ̃sylta'sjɔ̃], *n.f.* Consultation; conference; opinion, advice. *Cabinet de consultation,* surgery (of physician), chambers (of lawyer); *salle de consultation* (in hospital), outpatients' department.
consulte [kɔ̃'sylt], *n.f.* (*Switzerland and Italy*) administrative or judicial assembly. *Senatus-consulte,* decree by the Senate.
consulter [kɔ̃syl'te], *v.t.* To consult, to advise with, to take advice of; to refer to.

Consulter son chevet, to consult one's pillow, to think over something at night, *consulter un avocat*, to take counsel's opinion, to advise with a lawyer.—*v.i.* To deliberate, to take counsel; to take counsel together. *Il en veut consulter avec ses amis*, he wishes to confer with his friends about it; *ils consultèrent ensemble*, they laid their heads together. **se consulter**, *v.r.* To consider, to reflect, to deliberate. *La voix de la raison ne se consulte jamais*, the voice of reason is never listened to.

consumable [kɔ̃sy'mabl], *a.* Consumable.

consumant, *a.* (*fem.* **-ante**) Consuming, devouring, burning.

consumer [kɔ̃sy'me], *v.t.* To consume; to destroy, to wear out or wear away, to squander, to waste, to spend. *Cette maladie le consume*, that disease is wearing him out; *consumé de veilles*, worn out with insomnia; *le temps consume toutes choses*, time wears out everything. **se consumer**, *v.r.* To decay, to waste away, to smoulder, to wear out; to ruin oneself; to undermine one's health; to waste one's strength. *Il se consume d'ennui*, he is wasting away with weariness; *se consumer de douleur*, to pine away with grief.

contabescence [kɔ̃tabɛ'sɑ̃:s], *n.f.* Consumption (through reduction of mineral matter in the body); (*Bot.*) abortion (of pollen).

contact [kɔ̃'takt], *n.m.* Contact; touch; connexion, relation; (*fig.*) similarity. *Au contact de*, in contact with; (*Elec.*) *contact à la terre*, earth-connexion, earth-contact; (*Motor.*) *clé de contact*, ignition key; *prendre contact avec quelqu'un*, to get into touch with somebody, to contact; (*Opt.*) *verres de contact*, contact lenses.

contacter [kɔ̃tak'te], *v.t.* To contact, to approach.

contagieux [kɔ̃ta'ʒjø], *a.* (*fem.* **-euse**) Contagious, catching; infectious. **contagion**, *n.f.* Contagion, infection. *Contagion de mœurs*, corruption of manners; *la contagion du vice*, the infection of vice. **contagionner**, *v.t.* To infect. **se contagionner**, *v.r.* To become infected. **contagiosité**, *n.f.* Contagiousness.

contaille [kɔ̃'ta:j], *a.f.* *Soie contaille*, floss-silk.

contamination [kɔ̃tamina'sjɔ̃], *n.f.* Contamination, pollution. **contaminé**, *a.* (*fem.* **-née**) Polluted, contaminated, infected. *Eau contaminée*, polluted water. **contaminer**, *v.t.* To contaminate. **se contaminer**, *v.r.* To be contaminated, to catch a disease.

conte [kɔ̃:t], *n.m.* Story, tale; (*fig.*) falsehood, fib, fairy-tale. *Ce sont des contes*, they are only made-up stories; *c'est un grand faiseur de contes*, he is a great fibber, a great story-teller; *conte de bonne femme*, *conte à dormir debout*, or *conte bleu*, idle, silly story, old wives' tale; *conte en l'air*, improbable story, fiction; *conte fait à plaisir*, made-up story; *contes de fées*, fairy-tales; *il brode un peu le conte*, he exaggerates the story a little (*i.e.* improves upon it); *un vrai conte*, an improbable story; *un conte vrai*, a true story.

contemplateur [kɔ̃tɑ̃pla'tœ:r], *n.m.* (*fem.* **-trice**) Contemplator. **contemplatif**, *a.* (*fem.* **-ive**) Contemplative. **contemplation**, *n.f.* Contemplation, meditation.

contempler [kɔ̃tɑ̃'ple], *v.t.* To contemplate,

to survey, to gaze on.—*v.i.* To contemplate, to meditate, to reflect.

contemporain [kɔ̃tɑ̃pɔ'rɛ̃], *a.* (*fem.* **contemporaine**) Contemporary, contemporaneous (with). *Histoire contemporaine*, modern history.—*n.* Contemporary. **contemporanéité**, *n.f.* Contemporaneity, contemporaneousness.

contempteur [kɔ̃tɑ̃p'tœ:r], *a.* (*fem.* **-trice**) Contemptuous, scornful, insolent, disdainful. —*n.* Contemner, despiser, scorner.

*contemptible, *a.* Contemptible, despicable, mean.

contenance [kɔ̃t'nɑ̃:s], *n.f.* Capacity; cubical content; bulk, volume; extent, area; (*fig.*) countenance, posture, air, bearing; (*Naut.*) burden. *Contenance assurée*, bold look; *contenance d'un wagon*, capacity, tonnage, of a waggon; *contenance étudiée*, studied deportment; *contenance fière*, haughty air; *contenance ridicule*, ridiculous demeanour; *faire bonne contenance*, to show spirit or resolution; *faire perdre contenance*, to put out of countenance; *il n'a point de contenance*, he does not know which way to turn; *ne savoir quelle contenance prendre*, not to know how to look; *perdre contenance*, to be abashed or put out of countenance; *se donner une contenance*, to keep oneself in countenance.

contenant [kɔ̃t'nɑ̃], *a.* Holding, containing.— *n.m.* Holder, container.

contendant [kɔ̃tɑ̃'dɑ̃], *a.* Competing. *Les parties contendantes*, the contending parties, the candidates.—*n.m.* Competitor, rival.

contenir [kɔ̃t'ni:r], *v.t. irr.* (*pres.p.* **-ant**, *p.p.* **contenu**, *conjugated like* TENIR) To contain, to comprise, to hold, to include; to consist of; to confine, to hold in, to keep within, to restrain; to repress, to keep in check, to bridle. *Les gardes avaient peine à contenir la foule*, the guards had difficulty in keeping the crowds in check; *on ne saurait le contenir*, there is no keeping him within bounds. **se contenir**, *v.r.* To keep within bounds, to be moderate; to restrain oneself, to keep one's temper; to control oneself.

content [kɔ̃'tɑ̃], *a.* (*fem.* **-ente**) Content, satisfied; pleased, glad, gratified. *Avoir l'air content*, to look pleased; *être content*, to be willing, to be satisfied; *être content de quelqu'un*, to be pleased with someone; *il est content de sa condition*, he is content with his lot.—*n.m.* Sufficient, fill. *Avoir son content de*, to have one's fill or enough of. **contentement**, *n.m.* Contentment, satisfaction; comfort, pleasure. *Contentement passe richesse*, enough is as good as a feast.

contenter [kɔ̃tɑ̃'te], *v.t.* To content, to satisfy; to please, to gratify, to indulge. *On ne saurait contenter tout le monde*, one cannot please everybody. **se contenter**, *v.r.* To be satisfied, to be content. *Contentez-vous de cela*, be satisfied with that.

contentieusement [kɔ̃tɑ̃sjøz'mɑ̃], *adv.* Contentiously, litigiously. **contentieux**, *a.* (*fem.* **contentieuse**) Contentious, controvertible, disputable; litigious; in litigation, in dispute; quarrelsome. *Esprit contentieux*, quarrelsome fellow.—*n.m.* Debatable matter, affair in litigation, disputed point, claim, etc. *Agent du contentieux*, solicitor; *bureau du contentieux*, office for the settlement of disputed claims, legal department.

contentif [kɔ̃tɑ̃'tif], *a.* (*fem.* **-ive**) (*Surg.*) Retentive, binding (of bandages).

contention [kɔ̃tɑ̃'sjɔ̃], *n.f.* Application, vehemence, intensity, vehement or prolonged effort; contention, contest, debate, strife. *Contention d'esprit*, intense application of mind.

contenu [kɔ̃t'ny], *p.p.* (*fem.* **contenue**) Contained, comprised; (*fig.*) repressed, kept in control.—*n.m.* Contents; enclosure; tenor, terms (of a letter etc.). *Contenu d'un télégramme*, wording of a telegram.

conter [kɔ̃'te], *v.t.* To tell, to relate. *En conter*, to romance, to tell fibs; *en conter à une femme, lui conter des douceurs*, or *lui conter fleurette*, to talk amorous nonsense to a woman; *en conter de belles* or *conter des sornettes*, to tell what is untrue, to humbug, to deceive; *on conte que* . . ., people say that . . .; *s'en laisser conter*, to be too ready to believe.

contestable [kɔ̃tɛs'tabl], *a.* Contestable, debatable, controvertible. **contestablement,** *adv.* Contestably. **contestant,** *a.* (*fem.* **-ante**) Contending (at law).—*n.* Contesting party, litigant. **contestation,** *n.f.* Contestation, contest; dispute, debate; strife, variance, litigation. *En contestation*, at issue, at variance, at odds; *hors de toute contestation*, beyond all dispute. ***conteste,** *n.m.* (only used in) *Sans conteste*, indisputably, beyond contradiction.

contester [kɔ̃tɛs'te], *v.t.* To dispute, to contest; to contend, to debate. *Contester la validité d'un acte*, to challenge the validity of a deed; *il me conteste ma qualité*, he calls my rank in question; *on lui conteste cette terre*, his right to that estate is disputed.—*v.i.* To quarrel; to be contentious.

conteur [kɔ̃'tœːr], *a.* (*fem.* **-euse**) Who tells stories.—*n.* Story-teller, tale-teller, narrator, teller; (*fig.*) romancer, fibber.

contexte [kɔ̃'tɛkst], *n.m.* Context; text (of a deed).

contexture [kɔ̃tɛks'tyːr], *n.f.* Contexture (of the muscles etc.); texture (of stuff); flow (of material fibres); (*fig.*) arrangement, structure.

contigu [kɔ̃ti'gy], *a.* (*fem.* **-uë**) Contiguous, adjoining; (*fig.*) analogous. *Ces deux provinces sont contiguës*, these two provinces border on each other; *mon champ est contigu à la forêt*, my field adjoins the forest. **contiguïté,** *n.f.* Contiguity.

continence [kɔ̃ti'nɑ̃ːs], *n.f.* Continency, chastity. **continent** (1), *a.* Chaste, continent; (*Med.*) continuous, unremitting. *Fièvre continente*, incessant fever.

continent (2) [kɔ̃ti'nɑ̃], *n.m.* Continent, mainland. **continental,** *a.* (*fem.* **-ale**, *pl.* **-aux**) Continental.

contingence [kɔ̃tɛ̃'ʒɑ̃ːs], *n.f.* Contingency, casualty. **contingent,** *a.* (*fem.* **-ente**) Contingent, accidental, casual.—*n.m.* Quota, share, portion; contingent, levy, the soldiers of the same age-group, the call-up.

continu [kɔ̃ti'ny], *a.* (*fem.* **-ue**) Continuous, continual, uninterrupted; unintermitting, incessant. *Basse continue*, (*Mus.*) thoroughbass; (*Text.*) *métier continu*, throstle frame. —*n.m.* (*Phil.*) That which is divisible, matter, body, space. (*Elec.*) *En continu*, by direct current. **continuateur,** *n.m.* (*fem.* **-trice**)

Continuator. continuation, *n.f.* Continuation; (*Law*) continuance. **continuel,** *a.* (*fem.* **-elle**) Continual, uninterrupted, perpetual. **continuellement,** *adv.* Continually, uninterruptedly, perpetually.

continuer [kɔ̃ti'nɥe], *v.t.* To continue, to proceed with; to go on with, to carry on; to lengthen, to prolong, to extend.—*v.i.* To continue, to keep on, not to stop or cease. *Continuez à bien faire, et vous vous en trouverez bien*, be good and you will always be happy; *continuez, je vous prie*, pray go on. **se continuer,** *v.r.* To be continued, to last; to be prolonged.

continuité [kɔ̃tinɥi'te], *n.f.* Continuity; continuance. (*Geom.*) *Continuité d'une courbe*, fixed course of a curve; *solution de continuité*, solution of continuity, break. **continûment,** *adv.* Unremittingly, continuously, without cessation.

contondant [kɔ̃tɔ̃'dɑ̃], *a.* (*fem.* **-ante**) (*Surg.*) Bruising, contusing; blunt (of instruments). **contondre,** *v.t.* To contuse, to bruise.

contorsion [kɔ̃tɔr'sjɔ̃], *n.f.* Contortion, distortion; grimace. *Les contorsions d'un pitre*, the antics of a clown. **contorsionniste,** *n.m.* Contortionist.

contour [kɔ̃'tuːr], *n.m.* Circuit, circumference; contour, outline. (*Av.*) *Contour de l'aile*, wing plan, wing contour. **contourné,** *a.* (*fem.* **-ée**) Distorted, bizarre; (*Her.*) turned towards the left (of figures of animals). *Style contourné*, tortuous, bombastic style. **contournement,** *n.m.* Outlining, tracing; winding, rounding, convolution. *Route de contournement*, by-pass (road).

contourner [kɔ̃tur'ne], *v.t.* To outline, to give the proper contour to; to distort, to twist, to deform; to twine round, to twist round; to turn round, to go or wind round. **se contourner,** *v.r.* To grow crooked, to become bent, twisted, deformed. **contourneuse,** *n.f.* Shaping-machine.

contractant [kɔ̃trak'tɑ̃], *a.* (*fem.* **-ante**) *Partie contractante*, contracting party.—*n.* Stipulator, covenanter. **contracté** [kɔ̃trak'te], *a.* (*fem.* **-ée**) Contracted, shortened. (*Gram.*) *Verbe contracté*, contracted verb.

contracter [kɔ̃trak'te], *v.t.* To contract; to covenant, to stipulate, to bargain, to make a contract concerning; to acquire, to get, to catch. *Contracter de bonnes habitudes*, to acquire good habits. **se contracter,** *v.r.* To contract, to shrink, to straiten; to shorten, to be combined by elision; to be agreed or settled by contract.

contractif, *a.* (*fem.* **-ive**) Contractive. **contractile,** *a.* Contractile. **contraction,** *n.f.* Contraction.

contractuel [kɔ̃trak'tɥel], *a.* (*fem.* **-elle**) Stipulated, agreed upon, done by contract. **contractuellement,** *adv.* By contract.

contracture [kɔ̃trak'tyːr], *n.f.* (*Arch.*) Diminution (in upper part of column); (*Path.*) contraction (of muscle in tetanus etc.), contracture.

contradicteur [kɔ̃tradik'tœːr], *n.m.* Contradictor; (*Law*) adversary, opposer, opponent. **contradiction,** *n.f.* Contradiction, denial; opposition, impediment, obstacle; inconsistency, discrepancy, incompatibility. *Esprit de contradiction*, contrariness.

contradictoire [kɔ̃tradik'twaːr], *a.* Contradictory, inconsistent, conflicting. *Examen contradictoire,* cross-examination; *jugement contradictoire,* judgment after hearing all parties; *réunion politique contradictoire,* political meeting with debate. **contradictoirement,** *adv.* Contradictorily; inconsistently.

contraignable [kɔ̃trɛ'ɲabl], *a.* Compellable, constrainable. *Contraignable par corps,* attachable, liable to arrest. **contraignant,** *a.* (*fem.* **-ante**) Compelling, compulsive; troublesome.

contraindre [kɔ̃'trɛ̃ːdr], *v.t. irr.* (*pres.p.* **contraignant,** *p.p.* **contraint,** *conjugated like* CRAINDRE) To constrain, to compel, to coerce, to oblige by force; to restrain; to squeeze, to cramp, to embarrass; (*Law*) to attach, to arrest for debt. **se contraindre,** *v.r.* To restrain oneself, to refrain, to control oneself.

contraint [kɔ̃'trɛ̃], *a.* (*fem.* **contrainte** (1)) Constrained, forced, affected. *L'air contraint,* with an uneasy, awkward look. **contrainte** (2), *n.f.* Constraint, compulsion, coercion; restraint; uneasiness; (*fig.*) shackles, fetters; (*Mech.*) stress; (*Law*) arrest, imprisonment. *Avec contrainte,* restrainedly; *contrainte par corps,* arrest for debt; *jugement de contrainte par corps,* capias. *Parler sans contrainte,* to speak freely. *Porteur de contrainte,* writ-server.

contraire [kɔ̃'trɛːr], *a.* Contrary, opposite, repugnant, inconsistent; opposed, against, adverse; hurtful, prejudicial, unfavourable. *L'alcool vous est contraire,* liquor is bad for you; *contraire à la nature,* unnatural.—*n.m.* Contrary, opposite, reverse. *Aller au contraire d'une chose* or *d'une personne,* to go or speak against a thing or a person; *au contraire,* on the contrary, on the other hand; *tout au contraire* or *bien au contraire,* quite the contrary, quite the reverse. **contrairement,** *adv.* Contrarily, in opposition.

contralte [CONTRALTO].

contraltiste [kɔ̃tral'tist], *n.* Contralto (singer).

contralto [kɔ̃tral'to], *n.m.* Contralto, countertenor.

contrapontiste [kɔ̃trapɔ̃'tist], *n.m.* Contrapuntist.

contrariant [kɔ̃tra'rjɑ̃], *a.* (*fem.* **-ante**) Thwarting, baffling, contrary, annoying, upsetting.

contrarier [kɔ̃tra'rje], *v.t.* (*conjugated like* PRIER) To thwart, to counteract, to baffle; to oppose, to annoy, to vex; to disappoint. (*Arch.*) to set (bricks) in alternation; to break (joint). *Être contrarié par les vents,* to be wind-bound. *Contrarier les projets de quelqu'un,* to thwart someone's plans. **contrariété,** *n.f.* Contrariety, contradiction; vexation, annoyance; impediment, hindrance, difficulty; disappointment. *Quelle contrariété!* how annoying!

contrastant [kɔ̃tras'tɑ̃], *a.* (*fem.* **-ante**) Contrasting. **contraste,** *n.m.* Contrast, opposition. **contraster,** *v.i.* To be in contrast, to form a contrast.—*v.t.* To put in contrast, to contrast (two things).

contrat [kɔ̃'tra], *n.m.* Contract, deed, instrument, indenture; agreement, bargain. *Contrat de mariage,* contract of marriage;

marriage settlement; *le contrat social,* the supposed compact between freemen constituting the State; *dresser un contrat,* to draw up a deed; *minute d'un contrat,* draft of a deed; *passer un contrat,* to sign and seal a deed; *rupture de contrat,* break of contract; *un contrat en bonne forme,* a contract in due form. *Bridge-contrat,* contract bridge.

contravention [kɔ̃travɑ̃'sjɔ̃], *n.f.* Contravention, minor offence or infraction.

contre [kɔ̃:tr], *prep.* Against, versus, contrary to; close up against, near; in exchange for. *Aller contre vents et marées,* to sail against wind and tide; *ci-contre,* opposite, in the margin; *contre le bon sens,* against common sense; *par contre,* by contrast, on the other hand; *pour et contre,* for and against, pro and con; *se battre contre quelqu'un,* to fight against someone; *se fâcher contre quelqu'un,* to be angry with someone.—*adv.* Against. *Être contre,* to be opposed to something; *tout contre,* close by; *voter contre,* to vote against. —*n.m.* The opposite side of the question; double (*Bridge*). *Le pour et le contre,* the pros and cons; *savoir le pour et le contre,* to know both sides of the question.

contre-accusation [kɔ̃trakyza'sjɔ̃], *n.f.* Counter-accusation.

contre-à-contre, *adv.* (*Naut.*) Alongside.

contre-alizé, *a.* Anti-trade.—*n.m.* Anti-trade wind.

contre-allée, *n.f.* Side-walk, side-alley.

contre-amiral, *n.m.* (*pl.* **contre-amiraux**) Rear-admiral; rear-admiral's flagship.

contre-appel, *n.m.* Second roll-call, check-roll.

contre-approches, *n.f.* (used only in pl.) (*Fort.*) Counter-approaches.

contre-assurance, *n.f.* Counter-assurance.

contre-attaque, *n.f.* (*Mil.*) Counter-attack; (*Fort., pl.*) counterworks.

contre-avions, *a.* Anti-aircraft.

contre-avis, *n.m.* Contrary opinion.

contrebalancer [kɔ̃trəbalɑ̃'se], *v.t.* To counterbalance, to counterpoise.

contrebande [kɔ̃trə'bɑ̃:d], *n.f.* Contraband, smuggling; smuggled goods. *Contrebande de guerre,* contraband of war; *contrebande d'alcools,* (*Am.*) bootlegging; *faire la contrebande,* to smuggle, to deal in smuggled goods. **contrebandier,** *a.* (*fem.* **-ière**) Devoted to contraband.—*n.* Smuggler, gunrunner; smuggling vessel.

contre-bas (en) [kɔ̃trə'ba], *adv.* Downwards.

contrebasse [kɔ̃trə'bɑːs], *n.f.* Double-bass, contra-bass; bass-viol. **contrebassiste** or **contre-bassier,** *n.m.* Double-bass player.

contre-basson, *n.m.* Double bassoon; double-bassoon player.

contre-batterie [kɔ̃trəba'tri], *n.f.* Cross-battery, counter-battery, counter-plot.

contre-biais, *n.m.* (*Weaving*) Crossing in the opposite direction to the principal thread. *À contre-biais,* contrariwise, the wrong way, the other way.

contre-bord (à), *adv.* (*Naut.*) On the opposite tack. *Les deux vaisseaux courent à contre-bord,* the two vessels are running aboard of each other.

contre-boutant or **contre-boutement,** *n.m.* Counterfort, abutment, buttress. **contrebouter,** *v.t.* To buttress; to shore up.

contre-brasser, *v.t.* (*Naut.*) To brace about (the yards), to counterbrace.

contrecarrer, *v.t.* To thwart, to oppose.

contre-caution, *n.f.* (*Law*) Counter-surety.

contre-châssis, *n.m.*   Outer sash, double sash.

contre-clef, *n.f.* (*Arch.*) Second voussoir (from the keystone) in an arch.

contre-cœur, *n.m.* Chimney-back. *À contre-cœur*, reluctantly, against the grain.

contre-coup, *n.m.* Rebound, repercussion, counterblow; (*fig.*) consequence, result, effect. *Par contre-coup*, as a consequence.

contre-courant, *n.m.* Counter-current.

contredanse [kɔ̃trə'dɑ̃ːs], *n.f.* Quadrille (dance or tune).

contre-déclaration [kɔ̃trədeklarɑ'sjɔ̃], *n.f.* Counter-declaration.

contre-dégagement, *n.m.* (*Fenc.*) Double. **contre-dégager,** *v.t.*, *v.i.* (*Fenc.*) To double.

contre-digue, *n.f.* Embankment or dike (for strengthening another).

contredire [kɔ̃trə'diːr], *v.t. irr.* (*conjug. like* MÉDIRE) To contradict, to gainsay; to be inconsistent with; (*Law*) to confute, to disprove, to answer. **se contredire,** *v.r.* To contradict oneself; to contradict one another; to be inconsistent, to be contradictory. **contredisant,** *a.* (*fem.* **-ante**) Contradicting. **contredit,** *n.m.* Contradiction; answer, reply; (*Law*) objection, rejoinder. *On peut dire sans crainte d'être contredit*, it may safely be pronounced; *sans contredit*, incontestably, beyond a doubt.

contrée [kɔ̃'tre], *n.f.* Country, region, district.

contre-écaille [kɔ̃tre'kɑːj], *n.f.* The inside or reverse of a shell.

contre-écarteler, *v.t.* (*Her.*) To quarter (two quarters of a shield already quartered).

contre-échange, *n.m.* Mutual exchange. **contre-échanger,** *v.t.*   To exchange mutually.

contre-écrou, *n.m.* Lock-nut.

contre-enquête, *n.f.* Counter-inquiry.

contre-épaulette, *n.f.* Epaulet without fringe.

contre-épreuve, *n.f.* (*Engraving*) Counter-proof; (*fig.*) spiritless copy, feeble imitation; (*Parl.*) counter-vote or verification. **contre-épreuver,** *v.t.* To take a counter-proof of.

contre-espalier, *n.m.* Espalier facing another (with a walk between).

contre-espionnage, *n.m.* Counter-espionage.

contre-étambot, *n.m.* (*Naut.*) Inner stern-post.

contre-étrave, *n.f.* (*Naut.*) Apron.

contre-expertise, *n.f.*   Counter-valuation, examination, or experiment.

contrefaçon [kɔ̃trəfa'sɔ̃], *n.f.* Counterfeiting, forgery, infringement; counterfeit, spurious copy, edition, etc. **contrefacteur,** *n.m.* Counterfeiter (of coins etc.); forger (of bills etc.); infringer (of patents etc.). **contre-faction,** *n.f.* Counterfeiting, forgery.

contrefaire [kɔ̃trə'fɛːr], *v.t. irr.* (*conjug. like* FAIRE) To counterfeit, to imitate, to copy; to forge; to mimic, to ape; to feign, to, assume the appearance of; to disguise; to pirate (edition). **se contrefaire,** *v.r.* To dissemble, to sham. **contrefaiseur,** *n.m.* (*fem.* **-euse**) Counterfeiter, mimicker, imitator. **contrefait,** *a.* (*fem.* **-aite**) Counterfeit;

deformed. *Un homme tout contrefait*, a deformed man.

contre-fanon [kɔ̃trəfa'nɔ̃], *n.m.* (*Naut.*) Buntline.

contre-fenêtre, *n.f.* Inside sash, shutter.

contre-feu, *n.m.* Fire-back; fire made in a wood to check a conflagration.

contre-fiche, *n.f.* (*Carp.*) Prop, strut.

contre-fil, *n.m.*   The opposite direction. *À contre-fil*, backwards; against the stream; against the grain; the wrong way; *le contre-fil de l'eau*, upstream.

contre-finesse, *n.f.* Counter-trick, counter-cunning; trick for trick.

contre-foc, *n.m.* (*Naut.*) Fore-top stay-sail.

contrefort [kɔ̃trə'fɔːr], *n.m.* Counterfort, buttress; (*Geol.*) lesser chain buttressing a mountain range, spur; stiffener (of boots).

contre-fossé [kɔ̃trəfo'se], *n.m.* (*Fort.*) Advance-fosse.

contre-fracture, *n.f.* (*Surg.*) Counterfracture.

contre-fruit, *n.m.* (*Arch.*) Upward diminution of the thickness of a wall.

contre-fugue, *n.f.* Counter-fugue.

contre-garde, *n.f.* (*Fort.*) A work protecting another.

contre-hacher, *v.t.* (*Engr.*) To cross-hatch. **contre-hachure,** *n.f.* Cross-hatching.

contre-haut (en), *adv.* Upwards.

contre-heurtoir, *n.m.* Plate (of doorknocker).

contre-indication, *n.f.* (*Med.*) Contra-indication. **contre-indiquer,** *v.t.*   To contra-indicate.

contre-interrogatoire, *n.m.* Cross-examination.

contre-jour, *n.m.* (*Phot.*) Low light. *À contre-jour*, against the light.

contre-latte, *n.f.* Lath (laid on rafters).

contre-lettre, *n.f.* (*Law*) Counter-deed, defeasance.

contre-maille, *n.f.* Double-mesh (in a net). **contre-mailler,** *v.t.* To double-mesh.

contremaître [kɔ̃trə'mɛːtr], *n.m.* (*fem.* **contremaîtresse**) Overseer, foreman, forewoman; (*Naut.*) first mate, boatswain's mate.

contremandement [kɔ̃trəmɑ̃d'mɑ̃], *n.m.* Countermand. **contremander,** *v.t.*   To countermand.

contre-manifestant [kɔ̃trəmanifɛs'tɑ̃], *n.m.* Counter-demonstrator. **contre-manifestation,** *n.f.* Counter-demonstration.

contre-manœuvre [kɔ̃trəma'nœːvr], *n.f.* Counter-movement or manœuvre.

contremarche [kɔ̃trə'marʃ], *n.f.* Counter-march; rise (in stairs). **contremarcher,** *v.i.* To countermarch.

contremarée [kɔ̃trəma're], *n.f.* Undertow or counter-tide. *À contre-marée*, against the tide.

contremarque [kɔ̃trə'mark], *n.f.* Counter-mark; (*Theat.*) check ticket. **contremarquer,** *v.t.* To countermark.

contre-mesure [kɔ̃trəmə'zyːr], *n.f.* Counter-measure.

contre-mine [kɔ̃trə'min], *n.f.* Countermine. **contre-miner,** *v.t.* To countermine. **contre-mineur,** *n.m.* Counterminer.

contre-mot, *n.m.* Countersign.

contre-mur, *n.m.* (*Fort.*) Countermure, outer wall. **contre-murer,** *v.t.*   To strengthen with a countermure, to double-wall.

contre-offensive, *n.f.* Counter-attack.
contre-opposition, *n.f.* Minority detaching itself from an opposition (in an assembly).
contre-ordre, *n.m.* Counter-order.
contre-ouverture, *n.f.* Counter-opening; (*Surg.*) opening or incision made opposite a natural opening or a wound.
contre-partie, *n.f.* Counterpart; (*fig.*) the opposite, the contrary; opposite opinion; return match.
contre-pas (à), (*Mil.*) *adv.* Out of step.
contre-passation, *n.f.,* or **contre-passement,** *n.m.* (*Comm.*) Debiting or crediting per contra; transfer. **contre-passer,** *v.t.* To return (a draft) to the order of the drawer; to pass per contra.
contre-pédaler, *v.i.* To back-pedal.
contre-pente, *n.f.* Opposite slope; slope carrying waters the wrong way.
contre-peser, *v.t.* To counter-balance.
contre-pèterie, *n.f.* Spoonerism.
contre-pied, *n.m.* (*Hunt.*) Back-scent; (*fig.*) the reverse way, the contrary. *A contre-pied de,* contrary to, against; *il prend toujours le contre-pied de ce qu'on dit,* he always disagrees with what is said; *les chiens avaient pris le contre-pied,* the dogs had taken the wrong back-scent; *il joue souvent le contre-pied,* he often catches his (or her) opponent on the wrong foot.
contreplacage, *n.m.* Plywood construction.
contre-plainte, *n.f.* (*Law*) Counter-charge.
contre-planche, *n.f.* (*Engr.*) Second plate for bringing the acid into contact with the parts untouched by the first.
contre-plaqué, *a.* and *n.* Laminated, two- (or three-) ply wood.
contrepoids, *n.m.* *inv.* Counter-poise, counter-balance, counterweight; balancing-pole; (*fig.*) equilibrium.
contre-poil, *n.m.* Wrong way of the hair or of the nap. *A contre-poil,* against the grain; *prendre quelqu'un à contre-poil,* to rub someone up the wrong way; *prendre une affaire à contre-poil,* to get hold of the wrong end of the stick.
contre-poinçon, *n.m.* Clincher, die (instrument). **contre-poinçonner,** *v.t.* To stamp with a die.
contrepoint [kɔ̃trə'pwɛ̃], *n.m.* Counterpoint.
contrepointe [kɔ̃trə'pwɛ̃:t], *n.f.* Edged part of back of sabre; fencing in which this is used. **contrepointer,** *v.t.* To stick through and through.
contrepointiste [CONTRAPONTISTE].
contrepoison [kɔ̃trəpwa'zɔ̃], *n.m.* Antidote, counter-poison.
contre-porte, *n.f.* Double-door, baize door (outside another).
contre-poser, *v.t.* To misplace; (*Comm.*) to set down wrong. **contre-position,** *n.f.* Misentry, misplacement.
contre-projet, *n.m.* Counter-plan.
contre-promesse, *n.f.* (*Law*) Bond not to avail oneself of a promise.
contre-proposition, *n.f.* Counter-proposal; reply, retort.
contre-quille, *n.f.* Keelson.
contrer [kɔ̃'tre], *v.t.* (*Bridge*) To double.
contre-rail [kɔ̃trə'raj], *n.m.* Guard- or check-rail.
contre-réforme, *n.f.* Counter-reformation.

contre-ressort, *n.m.* Shock-absorber; counter-spring.
contre-retable, *n.m.* Back of the altar-piece.
contre-révolution, *n.f.* Counter-revolution.
contre-révolutionnaire, *a.* Counter-revolutionary.—*n.* Counter-revolutionist.
contre-ronde, *n.f.* Round performed as a check on previous rounds.
contre-ruse, *n.f.* Counter-ruse.
contre-saison (à), (Flower) produced out of season; ill-timed.
contre-salut, *n.m.* Answer to a salute.
contre-sanglon, *n.m.* Saddlegirth, girth-leather.
contrescarpe [kɔ̃trɛs'karp], *n.f.* Counter-scarp.
contre-sceau [kɔ̃trə'so] or **contre-scel** [kɔ̃trə'sɛl], *n.m.* Counter-seal. **contre-sceller,** *v.t.* To counter-seal.
contreseing [kɔ̃trə'sɛ̃], *n.m.* Counter-signature, countersign.
contresens [kɔ̃trə'sã:s], *n.m.* Contrary sense, contrary meaning; wrong construction, mistranslation; false reading; misunderstanding, absurdity; wrong side (of stuffs). *A contresens,* in a wrong way, on the wrong side. *Employer une étoffe à contresens,* to make up a stuff on the wrong side; *faire un contresens,* to mistranslate, to misinterpret, to misconceive.
contre-signal [kɔ̃trəsi'nal], *n.m.* (*pl.* **-aux**) Counter-signal.
contresignataire [kɔ̃trəsiɲa'te:r], *n.m.* Countersigner. **contresigner,** *v.t.* To countersign.
contre-taille [kɔ̃trə'ta:j], *n.f.* (*Comm.*) Counter-tally; (*Engr.*) cross-line, cross-hatch.
contretemps [kɔ̃trə'tã], *n.m.* (*pl. unchanged*) Untoward accident, disappointment, mischance, mishap; (*Mus.*) syncopation. *A contretemps,* unseasonably, at the wrong time; (*Mus.*) out of time, with syncopation.
contre-terrasse [kɔ̃trəte'ras], *n.f.* Lower terrace.
contre-tirer, *v.t.* To counterdraw, to trace, to take a counterproof of.
contre-torpilleur, *n.m.* Torpedo-boat destroyer, light cruiser.
contre-valeur, *n.f.* (*Fin.*) Exchange value.
contre-vapeur, *n.f.* (*Mech.*) Reversed steam, back-pressure.
contrevenant [kɔ̃trəv'nã], *n.m.* (*fem.* **-ante**) Contravener, infringer, offender, transgressor.
contrevenir [kɔ̃trəv'ni:r], *v.i. irr.* (*conjug. like* VENIR) To contravene, infringe, act contrary to (*à*).
contrevent [kɔ̃trə'vã], *n.m.* Outside window-shutter.
contre-vérité [kɔ̃trəveri'te], *n.f.* Untruth; ironical statement.
contre-visite, *n.f.* Second visit or examination.
contre-voie (à) [kɔ̃trə'vwa:], *adv. phr. Descendre du train à contre-voie,* to get out on the wrong side of the train.
contribuable [kɔ̃tri'bɥabl], *a.* Taxable, rateable.—*n.* Tax-payer, rate-payer. **contribuant,** *n.m.* Contributor.
contribuer [kɔ̃tri'bɥe], *v.i.* To contribute, to pay; (*fig.*) to conduce, to tend, to be accessory (*à*). *Contribuer au succès de,* to contribute to the success of; *il y a contribué,* he has

contributed to it; *on a fait contribuer tout le pays*, the whole country was laid under contribution. **contributaire**, *a.* Contributory. **contributif**, *a.* (*fem.* **-ive**) Contributive.

contribution [kɔ̃triby'sjɔ̃], *n.f.* Contribution; tax, impost; rate, share, part, portion; (*Comm.*) average, average share. *Contribution foncière*, land tax; *contributions directes*, direct or assessed taxes; *contributions indirectes*, indirect taxes or excise; *mettre à contribution*, to lay under contribution, to put in requisition. **contributoire**, *a.* What has to be paid; contributory. *Portion contributoire*, amount to be paid, assessment. **contributoirement**, *adv.* By way of contribution.

contrister [kɔ̃tris'te], *v.t.* To grieve, to vex, to sadden, to pain.

contrit [kɔ̃'tri], *a.* (*fem.* **-ite**) Contrite, penitent; afflicted, grieved. **contrition**, *n.f.* Contrition.

contrôlable [kɔ̃tro'labl], *a.* That may be checked, verified.

contrôle [kɔ̃'troːl], *n.m.* Control-register, register for purposes of verification; registration-duty; verification; roll, list; controller's office; authority; stamp, plate-mark, assay-mark, hall-mark (on gold and silver); stamp-office; (*Theat.*) ticket-checking counter; (*Mil.*) muster-roll; (*fig.*) control, censure, criticism. *Contrôle des changes*, exchange control. *Rayer quelqu'un des contrôles*, to strike someone off the rolls. *Perdre tout contrôle de soi*, to lose all self-control. **contrôlement**, *n.m.* Checking; stamping.

contrôler [kɔ̃tro'le], *v.t.* To register, to put on the rolls; to stamp, to hall-mark; to check, to verify, to examine; to audit; to censure, to criticize. *Contrôler de l'argenterie*, to mark plate. **contrôleur**, *n.m.* (*fem.* **-euse**) Controller, superintendent; (*Taxes, Rail.*) inspector; time-keeper; tallyman; (*Theat.*) check-taker, ticket-collector; (*fig.*) censurer, critic.

contrordre [CONTRE-ORDRE].

controuver [kɔ̃tru've], *v.t.* To forge, to fabricate; to invent, to counterfeit.

controversable [kɔ̃trɔvɛr'sabl], *a.* Controvertible, controversial.

controverse [kɔ̃trɔ'vɛrs], *n.f.* Controversy, discussion, dispute.

controverser [kɔ̃trɔvɛr'se], *v.t.* To ʾdispute, to controvert. **controversiste**, *n.m.* Disputant, controversialist.

contumace [kɔ̃ty'mas], *n.f.* Contumacy, non-appearance or default, contempt of court; obstinacy, perversity. *Condamner par contumace*, to sentence by default; *purger la contumace*, to surrender to the law.—*a.* Contumacious.—*n.* Defaulter, contumacious person.

contumax, *n.* and *a.* [CONTUMACE].

contus [kɔ̃'ty], *a.* (*fem.* **-e**) Bruised contused. **contusion**, *n.f.* Contusion, bruise. **contusionner**, *v.t.* To contuse, to bruise.

convaincant [kɔ̃vɛ̃'kɑ̃], *a.* (*fem.* **-ante**) Convincing.

convaincre [kɔ̃'vɛ̃:kr], *v.t. irr.* (*conjug. like* VAINCRE) To convince; to persuade, to satisfy; to convict (of error etc.). **se convaincre**, *v.r.* To convince or satisfy oneself. **convaincu, a.** (*fem.* **convaincue**)

Convinced, persuaded; sincere, earnest; convicted.

convalescence [kɔ̃valɛ'sɑ̃:s], *n.f.* Convalescence. *En pleine convalescence*, quite convalescent; *congé de convalescence*, sick leave. **convalescent**, *a.* (*fem.* **-ente**) Convalescent.—*n.* Convalescent person.

convallaire [kɔ̃va'lɛ:r], *n.f.* Lily of the valley.

convection [kɔ̃vɛk'sjɔ̃], *n.f.* Convection.

convenable [kɔ̃v'nabl], *a.* Suitable, fit, decent, proper; convenient, expedient; meet, seemly; becoming; fitting. *Juger convenable*, to deem proper; *peu convenable*, unseemly, unfit. **convenablement**, *adv.* Suitably, fitly, becomingly, decently, expediently.

convenance [kɔ̃v'nɑ̃:s], *n.f.* Fitness, propriety; seasonableness (of time); decency, expediency; seemliness, convenience; (*pl.*) propriety, decorum; social conventions. *Avec une convenance parfaite*, with perfect good breeding. *Blesser les convenances*, to offend against propriety; *braver les convenances*, to defy convention; *manquer de convenance envers quelqu'un*, to be guilty of a breach of good manners towards someone. *Mariage de convenance*, marriage of convenience; marriage for money and position.

*****convenant** [kɔ̃v'nɑ̃], *a.* (*fem.* **-ante**) Suitable, fit, proper, expedient.

convenir [kɔv'niːr], *v.i. irr.* (*pres.p.* **convenant**, *p.p.* **convenu**, *conjug. like* VENIR; *takes the auxiliary* AVOIR *when it means* to suit *etc., and* ÊTRE *when it means* to agree *etc.*) To agree, to be in accord; to admit, to own, to acknowledge (*de*); to suit, to fit, to match, to serve one's turn; to be proper (*with dative*); (*impers.*) to become, to be fit, advisable, convenient, or proper. *Cette maison m'a convenu*, that house suited me. *Il convient que vous y alliez*, it is proper you should go there. *J'en conviens*, I admit it. *Nous sommes convenus d'y aller*, we have agreed to go there. **se convenir**, *v.r.* To suit each other, to agree.

conventicule [kɔ̃vɑ̃ti'kyl], *n.m.* Conventicle.

convention [kɔ̃vɑ̃'sjɔ̃], *n.f.* Agreement, pact, covenant, treaty; (social and other) convention, custom; (*pl.*) conditions, articles, clauses (of an agreement). *De convention*, conventional; *je m'en tiens à la convention*, I stand by the agreement. *Membre de la Convention Nationale*, (*Fr. Hist.*) member of the National Convention. **conventionnel**, *a.* (*fem.* **-elle**) Conventional.—*n.m.* (*Fr. Hist.*) Member of the National Convention. **conventionnellement**, *adv.* By agreement.

conventualité [kɔ̃vɑ̃tɥali'te], *n.f.* Monastic life. **conventuel**, *a.* (*fem.* **-elle**) Conventual. *n.* Conventual. **conventuellement**, *adv.* Conventually.

convenu, *p.p.* (*fem.* **convenue**) [CONVENIR]. *a.* Agreed, stipulated; conventional, banal. *Un langage convenu*, banal language.

convergence [kɔ̃vɛr'ʒɑ̃:s], *n.f.* Convergence. **convergent**, *a.* (*fem.* **-ente**) Convergent. **converger**, *v.i.* To tend to one point, to converge.

convers [kɔ̃'vɛ:r], *a.* (*fem.* **converse** (1)) Lay (employed in convent). *Frère convers* or *sœur converse*, lay brother *or* sister.

conversation [kɔ̃vɛrsa'sjɔ̃], *n.f.* Conversation, converse, talk; art of conversation.

Être à la conversation, to be attending to the conversation; *laisser tomber la conversation,* to drop the conversation; *par où entamer la conversation?* how shall we begin the conversation? *s'emparer de la conversation,* to monopolize the conversation; *conversation téléphonique,* telephone call. **conversationniste,** *n.* Conversationalist.
converse (2) [kɔ̃'vɛrs], *n.f.* and *a.* (*Log.*) Converse. *Proposition converse,* converse proposition; (*Math.*) inverted proposition.
converser [kɔ̃vɛr'se], *v.i.* To converse, to talk; to discourse, to commune; (*Mil.*) to wheel about.
conversible [CONVERTIBLE].
conversion [kɔ̃vɛr'sjɔ̃], *n.f.* Conversion; transformation; change of form, character, etc.; transmutation; (*Mil.*) wheeling about. *Faire une conversion,* (*Mil.*) to wheel round. *La conversion des rentes,* the conversion or funding of stock.
converti [kɔ̃vɛr'ti], *n.m.* (*fem.* **convertie**) Convert. **convertibilité,** *n.f.* Convertibility. **convertible,** *a.* Convertible. **convertiblement,** *adv.* Convertibly.
convertir [kɔ̃vɛr'ti:r], *v.t.* To convert, to transform, to change, to turn; to make a convert of; to bring over, to turn. **se convertir,** *v.r.* To be converted, to turn; to be made a convert. **convertissable,** *a.* Convertible. **convertissant,** *a.* (*fem.* -**ante**) Converting. **convertissement,** *n.m.* Conversion. **convertisseur,** *n.m.* (*fem.* -**euse**) Converter; electrical or metallurgical transformer.
convexe [kɔ̃'vɛks], *a.* Convex. **convexité,** *n.f.* Convexity.
conviction [kɔ̃vik'sjɔ̃], *n.f.* Conviction, convincing proof; strong opinion, firmly held tenet. *Agir par conviction,* to act from conviction; *avoir la conviction intime,* to be thoroughly convinced, to be quite sure; (*Law*) *pièce à conviction,* exhibit. **convictionnel,** *a.* (*fem.* -**elle**) Convictive.
convié [kɔ̃'vje], *a.* and *n.* (*fem.* **conviée**) Invited. *Les conviés,* the guests.
convier [kɔ̃'vje], *v.t.* To invite, to bid; to request the company of someone; (*fig.*) to incite, to urge. *Convier à un dîner,* to invite to dinner.
convive [kɔ̃'viv], *n.* Guest; fellow diner. *C'est un bon convive,* he is a good table-companion.
convocable [kɔ̃vɔ'kabl], *a.* Convocable.
convocateur [kɔ̃vɔka'tœr], *n.m.* (*fem.* -**trice**) Convoker, summoner.
convocation [kɔ̃vɔka'sjɔ̃], *n.f.* Convocation; official invitation; summons.
convoi [kɔ̃'vwa], *n.m.* (*Mil.,* *Navy*) Convoy; (*Rail. etc.*) train. *Aller au* or *suivre le convoi,* to attend the funeral; *convoi funèbre,* funeral procession; *en convoi,* (*Navy*) in convoy. **convoiement,** *n.m.* Convoying, convoy.
convoitable [kɔ̃vwa'tabl], *a.* Covetable.
convoiter [kɔ̃vwa'te], *v.t.* To covet, to conceive a violent passion for, to lust after. **convoiteur,** *n.m.* (*fem.* -**euse** (I)) Coveter. **convoitise,** *n.f.* Covetousness; lust.
convoler [kɔ̃vɔ'le], *v.i.* *To marry; to marry again (of a widow). *Convoler en justes noces,* (*fam.*) to marry; *convoler en secondes* or *troisièmes noces,* to marry a second *or* a third time.

convoluté [kɔ̃vɔly'te], *a.* (*fem.* -**ée**) (*Bot.*) Convoluted.
convolution [kɔ̃vɔly'sjɔ̃], *n.f.* Convolution.
convolvulus [kɔ̃vɔlvy'ly:s], *n.m.* (*Bot.*) Convolvulus.
convoquer [kɔ̃vɔ'ke], *v.t.* To convoke, to convene, to call together; to summon (to examination or interview).
convoyer [kɔ̃vwa'je], *v.t.* To convoy, to escort.
convoyeur [kɔ̃vwa'jœːr], *n.m.* (*fem.* -**euse**) Convoying officer; convoy (ship); (*Mech.*) conveyor; elevator.
convulser [kɔ̃vyl'se], *v.t.* To convulse. **se convulser,** *v.r.* To be or become convulsed. **convulsibilité,** *n.f.* Liability to convulsion. **convulsif,** *a.* (*fem.* -**ive**) Convulsive. **convulsion,** *n.f.* Convulsion. *Donner des convulsions,* to throw into convulsions; *tomber en convulsions,* to be seized with convulsions. **convulsionnaire,** *a.* Subject to convulsions.—*n.* Convulsionist. **convulsionner,** *v.t.* (*Med.*) To convulse, to produce convulsions. **convulsivement,** *adv.* Convulsively.
conyse, conise [kɔ'niz], or **conisa,** *n.f.* (*Bot.*) Fleabane.
coobligation [kɔɔbliga'sjɔ̃], *n.f.* Joint obligation. **coobligé,** *n.m.* (*fem.* -**ée**) Co-obligant.
coolie or **coulis** [ku'li], *n.m.* Coolie.
coopérateur [kɔɔpera'tœːr], *n.m.* (*fem.* -**trice**) Co-operator, fellow-labourer, fellow-workman.—*a.* Co-operating. **coopératif,** *a.* (*fem.* -**ive**) Co-operative. **coopération,** *n.f.* Co-operation. **coopératisme,** *n.m.* Co-operative system. **coopérativement,** *adv.* Co-operatively. **coopérer,** *v.i.* To co-operate.
cooptation [kɔɔpta'sjɔ̃], *n.f.* Co-optation, co-option. **coopter,** *v.t.* To co-opt.
coordination [kɔɔrdina'sjɔ̃], *n.f.* Co-ordination. **coordonnant,** *a.* (*fem.* -**ante**) Co-ordinating. **coordonnateur,** *a.* (*fem.* -**trice**) Co-ordinating. **coordonné,** *a.* (*fem.* -**ée**) Co-ordinate.—*n.f. pl.* (*Gram., Geom.*) Co-ordinates. **coordonner,** *v.t.* To co-ordinate.
copahu [kɔpa'y], *n.m.* Copaiba. **copaïer** or **copayer,** *n.m.* Copaiba-tree.
copain [kɔ'pɛ̃], *n.m.* (*colloq.*) Pal, mate, crony.
copal [kɔ'pal], *n.m.* Copal.
copartage [kɔpar'taːʒ], *n.m.* Co-partnership, joint sharing. **copartageant,** *a.* (*fem.* -**ante**) Having a joint share.—*n.* Co-partner, joint partaker. **copartager,** *v.t.* To partake of or share with others.
copayer [COPAÏER].
copeau [kɔ'po], *n.m.* (*pl.* **copeaux**) Shaving, chip (of wood). *Vin de copeaux,* (new) wine clarified with shavings.
Copenhague [kɔpə'nag], *f.* Copenhagen.
copermutant [kɔpɛrmy'tɑ̃], *n.m.* (*fem.* -**ante**) One who exchanges with another, permuter. **copermutation,** *n.f.* The act of exchanging, permutation. **copermuter,** *v.t.* To permute, to exchange.
Copernic [kɔpɛr'nik], *m.* Copernicus. **copernicien** [kɔpɛrni'sjɛ̃], *a.* (*fem.* **copernicienne**) Copernican.
cophte [COPTE].
copie [kɔ'pi], *n.f.* Copy, image, transcript;

imitation, reproduction; (*Print.*) 'copy'; candidate's paper, exercise; carbon copy. *Copie au net*, fair copy; *copie-lettres*, letter-book.

copier, *v.t.* (*conjugated like* PRIER) To copy; to imitate, to reproduce; to mimic, to take off, to ape. *Encre à copier*, copying-ink.

copieusement [kɔpjøz'mã], *adv.* Copiously, abundantly, heartily (of drinking, eating).

copieux [kɔ'pjø], *a.* (*fem.* **-euse**) Copious, plentiful. *Un homme copieux en paroles*, a man of many words.

co-pilote [kopi'lɔt], *n.m.* Second pilot.

copine [kɔ'pin], *n.f.* (*pop.*) *fem.* of *copain*.

copiste [kɔ'pist], *n.m.* Copier, transcriber, copyist; imitator, mimic.

copossesseur [kopɔsɛ'sœːr], *n.m.* Joint owner. **copossession**, *n.f.* Joint ownership.

copra [kɔ'pra], *n.m. Huile de copra*, coco-nut oil.

copreneur [koprə'nœːr], *n.m.* Co-lessee, joint-tenant.

coprolithe or **coprolite** [koprɔ'lit], *n.m.* Coprolite. **coprophage**, *a.* Coprophagous.

copropriétaire [koprɔprie'tɛːr], *n.* Joint-proprietor. **copropriété**, *n.f.* Joint property.

copte [kɔpt] or **cophte**, *a.* Coptic. *La langue copte*, the Coptic language; *un moine copte*, a Coptic monk.—*n.* (**Copte** or **Cophte**) A Copt.

coptée [kɔp'te], *n.f.* (*dial.*) Toll, stroke (of a bell). **copter**, *v.t.* To toll.

copulateur [kɔpyla'tœːr], *a.* Copulatory.

copulatif [kɔpyla'tif], *a.* (*fem.* **-ive**) (*Gram.*) Copulative.—*n.f.* Copulative conjunction. **copulation**, *n.f.* Copulation.

copule [kɔ'pyl], *n.f.* Copula.

coq (1) [kɔk], *n.m.* Gallinaceous bird, especially a cock; cock of other species; weathercock; (*fig.*) vigorous or combative man. *Au chant du coq*, at cock-crow; *coq de bruyère*, grouse; *coq de combat*, game-cock; *coq de bois*, cock of the rock; *coq des jardins*, costmary; *coq d'Inde*, turkey-cock; *coq du village* or *coq de la paroisse*, cock of the walk; *être comme un coq en pâte*, to be in clover; *être rouge comme un coq*, to be as red as a turkey-cock; *fier comme un coq*, all cock-a-hoop; *faire jouter des coqs*, to make cocks fight; *jeune coq*, cockerel; *joute* or *combat de coqs*, cock-fight. *Poids coq*, (*Box.*) bantam weight.

coq (2) [kɔk], *n.m.* (*Naut.*) Ship's cook.

coq-à-l'âne [kɔka'lɑːn], *n.m. inv.* Nonsense, cock-and-bull story; absurd, incoherent skit or parody. *Il fait toujours des coq-à-l'âne*, he is always talking nonsense.

coq-souris [kɔksu'ri], *n.m.* (*Naut.*) Form of studding-sail used on small craft.

coquard [kɔ'kaːr], *n.m.* Old cock; (*fig.*) ridiculous old beau; booby, noodle.

coque [kɔk], *n.f.* Shell (of eggs, walnuts, fruits, snails, etc); cocoon, web, envelope (of chrysalis etc.); cockle-shell (small boat); looped bow; (*Naut.*) hull. *Au sortir de la coque*, as soon as hatched; *des œufs à la coque*, boiled eggs (for 3 minutes only) [*see* MOLLET]. *Je ne donnerais pas une coque de noix de toutes ses promesses*, I would not give a straw for all his promises.

coquebin [kɔk'bɛ̃], *n.m.* (*fam.*) Simpleton, greenhorn.

coquecigrue [kɔksi'gry], *n.f.* (*colloq.*) Idle story, stuff, fiddle-faddle. *À la venue des coquecigrues*, never.

coque-fuselage [kɔkfyz'laʒ], *n.m.* Hull (of flying-boat).

coquelicot [kɔkli'ko], *n.m.* Corn-poppy.

coquelourde [kɔk'lurd], *n.f.* Pasque-flower; rose-campion.

coqueluche [kɔ'klyʃ], *n.f.* *Hood, cowl; (*fig.*) the rage, darling, favourite; (*Med.*) whooping-cough. *Il est la coqueluche des femmes*, he is a great favourite with women (because *elles en sont coiffées*). **coquelucheux**, *a.* (*fem.* **-euse**) Suffering from whooping-cough. **coqueluchon** (*n.m.*). (*Bot.*) Monk's hood.

coquemar [kɔk'maːr], *n.m.* Big kettle.

coquerelle [kɔ'krɛl], *n.f.*, or **coqueret**, *n.m.* Winter cherry; strawberry tomato.

coquerico [kɔkri'ko], *n.m.* Cock-a-doodle-doo.

coquerie [kɔ'kri], *n.f.* (*Naut.*) Cook's galley, caboose.

coqueriquer [kɔkri'ke], *v.i.* To crow.

coqueron [kɔ'krɔ̃], *n.m.* (*Naut.*) Store-room.

coquet [kɔ'kɛ], *a.* (*fem.* **-ette**) Coquettish; stylish, smart, natty, neat. *Une somme assez coquette*, a tidy sum.—*n.* Coquette, flirt; coxcomb, dandy. **coqueter**, *v.i.* To coquet, to flirt.

coquetier [kɔk'tje], *n.m.* Egg-merchant, poulterer; egg-cup. **coquetière**, *n.f.* Egg-boiler.

coquette [COQUET].

coquettement [kɔkɛt'mã], *adv.* Coquettishly, daintily.

coquetterie [kɔkɛ'tri], *n.f.* Coquettishness, coyness, flirtation; affectation (in dress etc.); finicalness. *Être en coquetterie avec*, to try to charm or seduce; *faire des coquetteries à*, to try to please; *une coquetterie de langage*, language used to please.

coquillage [kɔki'jaʒ], *n.m.* Shell-fish; shell; shell-work.

coquillart [kɔki'jaːr], or **coquillard**, *n.m.* Calcareous bed of shells and stones.

coquille [kɔ'kiːj], *n.f.* Shell (of shell-fish, egg, fruits, etc.); (*fig.*) house, dwelling, den; quillon (of a sword); swelling or blister (on bread); (*Cook.*) Dutch oven; pat (of butter); (*Print.*) wrong letter, misprint; thumb (of a latch); foot-board (of coach-box); (*Paper*) post demy, small post; (*Arch.*) soffit of arch of staircase; arch of niche; (*Ornament*) conch. *Coquille de beurre*, pat of butter; *coquille St-Jacques*, scallop; *épée à poignée en coquille*, basket-hilted sword; *rentrer dans sa coquille*, to withdraw into one's shell; *une coquille de noix*, a cockleshell (of a boat). **coquiller**, *v.i.* (Of bread) to swell, to form blisters. **coquillier** (1), *n.m.* Collection of shells; cabinet of shells. **coquillier** (2), *a.* (*fem.* **-ière**) Conchiferous.

coquin [kɔ'kɛ̃], *a.* (*fem.* **coquine**) Roguish; rascally.—*n.m.* Knave, rascal, rogue, scamp. *Tour de coquin*, knavish trick. *n.f.* Slut, hussy, jade. **coquiner**, *v.i.* To play the knave. **coquinerie**, *n.f.* Knavery, rascality, roguery. **coquinet**, *n.m.* Little rascal.

cor (1) [kɔːr], *n.m.* Horn, hunting-horn; horn-player. *À cor et à cri*, with hue and cry, with might and main; *cor anglais*, tenor oboe, cor anglais; *cor des Alpes*, Alpine horn; *cor d'harmonie*, French horn.

cor (2) [kɔːr], *n.m.* Corn (on the foot).

cor (3) [kɔːr], *n.m.* Tine (of antler). *Un dix-cors*, a five-pointer.

corail [kɔ'raːj], *n.m.* (*pl.* **coraux**) Coral. *Des lèvres de corail*, rosy lips.
coraillère [kɔra'jɛːr], *n.f.* Coral-fishing boat. **corailleur**, *n.m.* Coral-fisher; coral-worker; coral-fishing boat.—*a.* Of coral fishing. *Bateau corailleur*, coral-fisher's boat. **corailleux**, *a.* (*fem.* **-euse**) Made of coral. **corallaire**, *a.* Coralliform. **corallien**, *a.* (*fem.* **-enne**) Coralline. **corallifère**, *a.* Coralliferous. **coralliforme**, *a.* Coralliform. **coralligène**, *a.* Coralligenous. **corallin**, *a.* (*fem.* **-ine**) Red like coral, coralline.—*n.f.* (*Zool.*) Coralline.
coran [kɔ'rã], *n.m.* Koran.
coraux, *pl.* [CORAIL].
corbeau [kɔr'bo], *n.m.* (*pl.* **corbeaux**) Crow; raven; (*Arch.*) corbel; (*Naut.*) grappling-iron. (*slang*) Priest; rapacious individual. *Nid de corbeau*, (*Naut.*) crow's-nest.
corbeille [kɔr'bɛːj], *n.f.* Flat, wide basket or pannier; the contents of this; (*Arch.* and *Fort.*) corbeil; (*Hort.*) round or oval flower-bed; (*St. Exch.*) reserved enclosure, stock-brokers' ring; (*Theat.*) dress-circle. *Corbeille à linge*, laundry basket; *corbeille à papier*, waste-paper basket, (*Am.*) waste basket; *corbeille de mariage* or *de noces*, wedding presents (from bridegroom to bride); *une corbeille de fleurs*, a basket of flowers. **corbeillée**, *n.f.* Basketful.
corbillard [kɔrbi'jaːr], *n.m.* Hearse.
corbillat [kɔrbi'ja], *n.m.* Young raven.
corbillon [kɔrbi'jɔ̃], *n.m.* Small basket; crambo (game).
corbillot [CORBILLAT].
corbin [kɔr'bɛ̃], *n.m.* Crow. *À bec de corbin* [BEC-DE-CORBIN], **corbine**, *n.f.* Carrion-crow.
corbleu [kɔr'blœ], *int.* By Jove!
corcelet [CORSELET].
cordage [kɔr'daːʒ], *n.m.* Cord, rope, cordage, rigging; the measuring of wood by the cord. *Cordage de rechange*, spare ropes; *cordage en trois*, rope made with three strands; *vieux cordage*, junk.
cordat [kɔr'da], *n.m.* Packing-cloth, sacking.
corde [kɔrd], *n.f.* Cord, rope; twine, twist; ribbon; bowstring; girdle (worn by monks); string (mus. instrument, racquet); band, line; string-course; (*Mus., Geom., etc.*) chord; tone, note; span (of an arch); thread (of cloth); hanging (death by) gallows; (*Anat.*) ligament; cord (measure for firewood). *Avoir de la corde de pendu*, to have the devil's own luck; *il a plusieurs cordes à son arc*, he has two strings to his bow; *cela est usé jusqu'à la corde*, that is thoroughly hackneyed; *corde à boyau*, catgut; *corde à danser*, dancing-rope; *corde de violon*, fiddle-string; *cordes vocales*, vocal cords; *danseur de corde*, rope-dancer; *échelle de corde*, rope-ladder; *être au bout de sa corde*, to be at the end of one's tether; *filer sa corde*, to go the way of the gallows; *flatter la corde*, to play with delicacy; *friser la corde*, narrowly to escape hanging; *homme de sac et de corde*, criminal. *Instrument à cordes*, stringed instrument; *les cordes*, the strings (of an orchestra); *ne touchez point cette corde-là*, do not harp upon that string. *Son habit montre la corde*, his coat is thread-bare; *tenir la corde*, to be on the inside, to lead (of a race-horse, runner, etc.); *toucher la grosse corde*, to hit the main point; *ça ne*

rentre pas dans mes cordes, it's not in my line. *Une corde de bois*, a cord of cut wood.
cordé (1) [kɔr'de], *a.* (*fem.* **-ée**) Twisted, corded.
cordé (2) [kɔr'de], *a.* (*fem.* **-ée**) Cordate, heart-shaped.
cordeau [kɔr'do], *n.m.* Cord; line; fuse; (*Naut.*) tow-rope. *Au cordeau*, in a straight line; *rue tirée au cordeau*, a perfectly straight street; *cordeau de mesure*, measuring tape.
cordée [kɔr'de], *n.f.* As much as a cord will surround; fishing-line; line of roped mountaineers; cord (of wood).
cordeler [kɔrdə'le], *v.t.* To twist, to twine. **cordelette**, *n.f.* Small cord; string.
Cordélie [kɔrde'li], *f.* Cordelia.
cordelier [kɔrdə'lje], *n.m.* Cordelier, Franciscan friar, Grey Friar. **cordelière**, *n.f.* *Franciscan nun; girdle (of dressing-gown etc.); cordelier's girdle; (*Arch.*) twisted fillet, cable-moulding.
cordelle [kɔr'dɛl], *n.f.* Towline, tow-rope.
corder [kɔr'de], *v.t.* To twist (into cord); to cord; to bind with a cord; to string (racquet). *Corder du bois*, to measure wood by the cord. **se corder**, *v.r.* To be corded; (of plants etc.) to get stringy.
corderie [kɔr'dri], *n.f.* Rope-walk, rope-yard; rope-making; rope-trade; (*Naut.*) boatswain's storeroom.
cordial [kɔr'djal], *a.* (*fem.* **-ale**, *pl.* **-aux**) Cordial, hearty, sincere.—*n.m.* Cordial. **cordialement**, *adv.* Cordially, heartily, sincerely. **cordialité**, *n.f.* Cordiality, heartiness.
cordier [kɔr'dje], *n.m.* Rope-maker; (of violins) tail-piece.
cordiforme [kɔrdi'fɔrm], *a.* Cordiform, heart-shaped.
Cordillères [kɔrdi'jɛːr], **les**, *f. pl.* The Cordilleras.
cordite [kɔr'dit], *n.f.* Cordite.
cordon [kɔr'dɔ̃], *n.m.* Strand (of a rope); twist, string; cord; cordon, ribbon (of an order); border, edging, band, line; edge (of a coin); girdle (worn by monks); check-string (of carriages); (*Arch.*) string-course, cordon; (*C*) ¼ of a cord of wood. *Cordon bleu*, blue-ribbon, first-rate cook. *Cordon de sonnette*, bell-pull; *cordon de souliers*, shoe-string; *cordon de troupes*, cordon of troops; *cordon ombilical*, umbilical cord; *cordon tire-feu*, (*Artill.*) lanyard; *le cordon s'il vous plaît*, open the door, please; *tirer le cordon*, to pull the string, to be a house-porter; *tenir les cordons de la bourse*, to hold the purse-strings; *cordon sanitaire*, isolation.
cordonnage [kɔrdɔ'naːʒ], *n.m.* Milling, edging (of coins).
cordonner [kɔrdɔ'ne], *v.t.* To twist, to twine, to braid; to edge (coins).
cordonnerie [kɔrdɔn'ri], *n.f.* Shoe-making; trade in boots and shoes; cobbler's shop.
cordonnet [kɔrdɔ'nɛ], *n.m.* Twist; braid; milled edge (of coins).
cordonnier [kɔrdɔ'nje], *n.m.* (*fem.* **cordonnière**) Shoe-maker. *Cordonnier pour femmes*, ladies' shoe-maker.
cordouan [kɔrdu'ɑ̃], *a.* Cordova (leather).
Cordoue [kɔr'du], *f.* Cordova.
corédacteur [koredak'tœːr], *n.m.* (*fem.* **-trice**) Co-editor, joint editor.

Corée [kɔ're], **la,** *f.* Korea.

corégence [kore'ʒɑ̃ːs], *n.f.* Co-regency. **corégent,** *n.m.* Co-regent.

coreligionnaire [kɔrliʒjɔ'nɛːr], *n.* Co-religionist.

Corfou [kɔr'fu], *f.* Corfu.

coriace [kɔ'rjas], *a.* Tough, leathery; (*fig.*) close, niggardly. *Un homme coriace,* a close-fisted fellow. **coriacé,** *a.* (*fem.* **coriacée**) Coriaceous. **coriacité,** *n.f.* Coriaceousness.

coriambe [kɔ'rjɑ̃:b], *n.m.* Choriambus.

coriandre [kɔ'rjɑ̃:dr], *n.f.* Coriander.

coricide [kɔri'sid], *n.m.* Corn cure.

corindon [kɔrɛ̃'dɔ̃], *n.m.* Corundum.

Corinne [kɔ'rin], *f.* Corinna.

Corinthe [kɔ'rɛ̃:t], *f.* Corinth.

corinthien [kɔrɛ̃'tjɛ̃], *a.* and *n.* (*fem.* **-ienne**) Corinthian.

corli [kɔr'li], **courlis** or **corlieu,** *n.m.* Curlew.

corme [kɔrm], *n.f.* Service- or sorb-apple. **cormier,** *n.m.* Service-tree, *Sorbus domestica.*

cormoran [kɔrmɔ'rɑ̃], *n.m.* Cormorant.

cornac [kɔr'nak], *n.m.* Elephant-driver, mahout; guide or mentor (to another man).

cornage [kɔr'na:ʒ], *n.m.* Roaring, wheezing (of horses).

cornaline [kɔrna'lin], *n.f.* Cornelian.

cornard [kɔr'na:r], *a.* Roaring, wheezy (of horses); (*fam.*) cuckold.—*n.m.* Cuckold; glass-worker's tool.

corne (1) [kɔrn], *n.f.* Horn, outside rind (of animal's feet etc.); hoof; horny matter; dog's-ear (on books, leaves); point, corner (of a cap etc.). *Bête à cornes,* horned beast; *chapeau à trois cornes,* three-cornered hat; *corne à chaussures,* shoe-horn; *corne d'abondance,* cornucopia, horn of plenty; *corne d'appel,* horn; *coup de corne,* thrust with the horns, (*fig.*) a malicious attack; *faire des cornes à un livre,* to dog's-ear a book; *faire les cornes à quelqu'un,* to mock, or jeer at someone; *faire une corne à une carte de visite,* to turn down the corner of a visiting-card; *les cornes de la lune,* the horns of the moon; *lever les cornes,* to hold up one's head again; *montrer les cornes,* to show one's teeth; *prendre par les cornes,* to take by the horns.

corne (2) [kɔrn], *n.f.* Cornel (berry).

corne de cerf [kɔrndə'sɛr], *n.f.* (*Bot.*) Wart cress, *Senebiera coronopus.*

corné [kɔr'ne], *a.* (*fem.* **cornée**) Corneous, horny.

cornéal [kɔrne'al], *a.* (*fem.* **-ale,** *pl.* **-aux**) Of or pertaining to the cornea.

corneau [kɔr'no], *n.m.* Cross between a mastiff and a hound; *pl.* (*Naut.*) the heads, (crew's W.C.).

cornée [kɔr'ne], *n.f.* Cornea.

cornéenne [kɔrne'ɛn], *n.f.* Horn-stone.

corneillard [CORNILLAS].

cornélien [kɔrne'ljɛ̃], , *adj.* (*fem.* **-enne**) Heroic (word or act), *à la* Corneille.

corneille [kɔr'nɛ:j], *n.f.* Crow. *Bayer aux corneilles,* to stare about vacantly; *corneille chauve,* rook; *corneille grise* or *mantelée,* hooded crow; *corneille de clocher,* jackdaw; *il y va comme une corneille qui abat des noix,* he goes at it tooth and nail.

corneillon [CORNILLAS].

cornement [kɔrnə'mɑ̃], *n.m.* Buzzing in the ears.

cornemuse [kɔrnə'my:z], *n.f.* Bagpipe. *Joueur de cornemuse* or **cornemuseur,** *n.m.* Piper.

corner (1) [kɔr'ne], *v.i.* To blow, wind, or sound a horn; to speak into an ear-trumpet; to tingle (of the ears). *Les oreilles me cornent,* my ears tingle, somebody is talking about me. —*v.t.* To blare out, to blurt out, to trumpet; to turn down, to dog's-ear (a leaf). *Corner quelque chose aux oreilles de quelqu'un,* to din something into someone's ears; *il a corné cela par toute la ville,* he has trumpeted it through the whole town.

corner (2) [kɔr'nɛr], *n.m.* (*Ftb.*) Corner-kick, corner.

cornet [kɔr'nɛ], *n.m.* Horn, hooter; ink-horn; cone; (*Naut.*) case (of a mast). **Cornet à bouquin,* cowherd's horn; *cornet acoustique,* ear trumpet; *cornet à dés,* dice box; *cornet à pistons,* cornet; *cornet à tabac,* packet of tobacco; *cornet de glace,* ice-cone; *cornet de postillon,* post-boy's horn.

corneter, *v.t.* (*Vet.*) To cup (a horse etc.).

cornette [kɔr'nɛt], *n.f.* (Coif) cornet, mob-cap; pennant of cavalry; cornetcy; (*Navy*) broad pendant, commodore's flag.—*n.m.* Officer who carried the *cornette,* ensign (of cavalry).

corneur [kɔr'nœːr], *a.* (*fem.* **-euse**) Wheezing or roaring.—*n.* Broken-winded horse.

corniaud [kɔr'njo], *n.m.* (*pop.*) Nitwit, clot.

corniche [kɔr'niʃ], *n.f.* Cornice; ledge. *Route en corniche,* coast road. (*sch. slang*) Army class (preparing for Saint-Cyr).

cornichon [kɔrni'ʃɔ̃], *n.m.* Gherkin; little horn; (*fig.*) greenhorn, muff, specially a schoolboy.

cornier [kɔr'nje], *a.* (*fem.* **-ière**) At the corner or angle. *Pilastre cornier,* corner-column.—*n.f.* Corner gutter; angle-iron, T-piece; (*Print.*) corner-iron.

corniforme [kɔrni'fɔrm], *a.* Corniform. **cornigère,** *a.* Cornigerous.

cornillas [kɔrni'ja] or **corneillon,** *n.m.* Young crow.

cornique [kɔr'nik], *a.* and *n.* Cornish. *Le cornique,* the Cornish language.

corniste [kɔr'nist], *n.m.* Horn-player.

Cornouaille [kɔr'nwɑ:j], **la,** *f.* Cornwall.

cornouille [kɔr'nu:j], *n.f.* Cornel-berry. **cornouiller,** *n.m.* Cornel-tree. *Cornouiller sanguin,* or *bois purant,* dogwood.

cornu [kɔr'ny], *a.* (*fem.* **cornue** (1)) Horned, angular, cornered; (*fig.*) extravagant, absurd.

cornue (2) [kɔr'ny], *n.f.* Retort; steel converter.

corollaire [kɔrɔ'lɛːr], *n.m.* Corollary.

corollacé [kɔrɔla'se], *a.* (*fem.* **-ée**) Corollaceous.

corolle [kɔ'rɔl], *n.f.* Corolla. **corollé,** *a.* (*fem.* **-ée**) Corollate. **corollifère,** *a.* Bearing a corolla. **corollin,** *a.* (*fem.* **-ine**) Coroline.

coron [kɔ'rɔ̃], *n.m.* Fluff, refuse (of wool etc.); group of miner's dwellings (in N. France and Belgium).

coronaire [kɔrɔ'nɛːr], *a.* (*Anat.*) Coronary.

coronal [kɔrɔ'nal], *a.* (*fem.* **-ale,** *pl.* **-aux**) (*Anat.*) Coronal.

coronille [kɔrɔ'ni:j], *n.f.* (*Bot.*) Coronilla; scorpion-senna.

coronoïde [kɔrɔnɔ'id], *a.* (*Anat.*) Coronoid.

corossol [kɔrɔ'sɔl], *n.m.* Custard-apple. **corossolier,** *n.m.* Anona, custard-apple tree.

corozo [kɔrɔ'zo], *n.m.* Ivory-nut.

corporal [kɔrpɔ'ral], *n.m.* Communion cloth, corporal.

corporatif [kɔrpɔra'tif], *a.* (*fem.* **-ive**) Corporative. **corporation,** *n.f.* Corporation, corporate body, guild.

corporel [kɔrpɔ'rɛl], *a.* (*fem.* **-elle**) Corporal, bodily. **corporellement,** *adv.* Corporally, bodily.

corps [kɔ:r], *n.m.* Matter, substance; thickness, consistence; body, trunk as opposed to limbs etc.; garment or part of garment covering this; corpse; main portion, chief part; collection, set, company; corporation, company; society, commonalty, college; corps, regiment; fellow-creature; barrel (of pump); caudex (of root); (*Print.*) depth, body, of a letter; shell (of house, pulley, etc.). *À bras-le-corps,* by the waist; *à corps perdu,* headlong, desperately; *à son corps défendant,* (*fig.*) reluctantly; *c'est un corps de fer que cet homme,* that man is made of iron; *c'est un pauvre corps,* he is a poor weak fellow; *condamner par corps en paiement de,* to sentence to a fine under pain of imprisonment; *corps à corps,* hand to hand, (*Box.*) in-fight(ing); *corps céleste,* heavenly body, star; *corps d'armée,* army corps; *corps d'armée féminin,* women's army corps, w.a.c.; *corps diplomatique,* diplomatic corps; *le corps enseignant,* the teaching profession, teaching staff; *corps expéditionnaire,* expeditionary force; *corps de bâtiment,* main building; *corps de logis,* detached building; *corps glorieux,* glorified body; *corps mort,* dead body; *corps morts,* (*Naut.*) fixed moorings; *du corps,* bodily; *en corps,* in a body, all together; *esprit de corps,* community spirit; *être séparés de corps et de biens,* to be separated (mensa et toro); *faire corps (avec),* to be intimately united (to); *garde du corps,* life-guard; *il a le diable au corps,* he is like one possessed; *il fait bon marché de son corps,* he makes himself very cheap, he exposes himself unnecessarily to danger; *il faut voir ce que cet homme a dans le corps,* we must see what stuff this man is made of; *ils font corps à part,* they are a separate body; *le corps du clergé,* the body of the clergy; *le corps du délit,* substance of an offence (*corpus delicti*); *le vaisseau a sombré corps et biens,* the vessel foundered with all hands; *n'avoir rien dans le corps,* to have taken no food, to be a person of no pluck; *passer son épée au travers du corps à quelqu'un,* to run someone through the body; *prendre corps,* to take shape; *répondre corps pour corps,* to be personally answerable for; *corps de garde,* a guard-house, round-house; *un corps d'infanterie,* an infantry corps; *un vin qui a du corps,* a full-bodied wine.

corpulence [kɔrpy'lɑ̃:s], *n.f.* Corpulence, corpulency; stoutness. **corpulent,** *a.* (*fem.* **-ente**) Corpulent, stout, burly.

corpusculaire [kɔrpysky'lɛ:r], *a.* Corpuscular. **corpuscule,** *n.m.* Corpuscule, corpuscle.

correct [kɔ'rɛkt], *a.* (*fem.* **-ecte**) Correct, accurate, decent. **correctement,** *adv.* Correctly, accurately. **correcteur,** *n.m.*

(*fem.* **-trice**) Corrector, emendator; (*Print.*) reader. (*Monastic*) *Père correcteur,* superior of a convent. **correctif,** *a.* (*fem.* **-ive**) Corrective.—*n.m.* Corrective.

correction [kɔrɛk'sjɔ̃], *n.f.* Correction, rectification; correctness, accuracy; (*Print.*) reading, correcting, alteration (on a proof etc.); (*fig.*) reprimand, reproof, chastisement, punishment. *Maison de correction,* reformatory; *sauf corrections,* subject to correction. **correctionnel,** *a.* (*fem.* **-elle**) Within the jurisdiction of the *Tribunal de police correctionnelle,* court of petty sessions.

corrélatif [kɔrela'tif], *a.* (*fem.* **-ive**) Correlative.—*n.* Correlative. **corrélation,** *n.f.* Correlation. **corrélativement,** *adv.* Correlatively.

correspondance [kɔrɛspɔ̃'dɑ̃:s], *n.f.* Correspondence, exchange of letters etc.; letters etc.; communication, connexion, relations, intercourse; conformity, harmony; change of trains, connexion. *Être en correspondance avec quelqu'un,* to correspond with someone; *entretenir une correspondance avec quelqu'un,* to keep up a correspondence with someone; *manquer la correspondance,* to miss a connexion; *service de correspondance,* branch-coach service, cross-post.

correspondant [kɔrɛspɔ̃'dɑ̃], *a.* (*fem.* **-ante**) Correspondent, corresponding.—*n.* Correspondent, corresponding member; parents' representative (at boarding-school); pen-friend. (*Comm.*) *Nos correspondants,* our agents.

correspondre [kɔrɛs'pɔ̃:dr], *v.i.* To correspond, to communicate, to be in correspondence (*entre* or *avec*); to agree, to suit, to harmonize (*à* or *avec*.)

corridor [kɔri'dɔ:r], *n.m.* Corridor, gallery, passage. *Cette porte donne sur le corridor,* this door opens out into the gallery or passage.

corrigé [kɔri'ʒe], *n.m.* Corrected (schoolboy's) exercise; fair copy; key (book), crib.

corriger [kɔri'ʒe], *v.t.* To correct, to rectify; to repair, to amend; to reprove, to chide, to chastise. *Corriger des épreuves,* (*Print.*) to correct proofs. **se corriger,** *v.r.* To correct oneself, to amend, to reform. *Elle s'est bien corrigée de cela,* she has quite broken herself of that. **corrigeur,** *n.m.* (*Print.*) Corrector (of mistakes marked by reader).

corrigible, *a.* Corrigible.

corroborant [kɔrɔbɔ'rɑ̃], *a.* (*fem.* **-ante**) Corroborant.—*n.m.* (*Med.*) Corroborant. **corroboratif,** *a.* (*fem.* **-ive**) (*Med.*) Corroborative.—*n.m.* Corroborative. **corroboration,** *n.f.* Corroboration, strengthening. **corroborer,** *v.t.* To strengthen; to corroborate.

corrodant [kɔrɔ'dɑ̃], *a.* (*fem.* **-ante**) Corroding, corrosive.—*n.m.* Corrodent. **corroder,** *v.t.* To corrode.

corroi [kɔ'rwa], *n.m.* Currying (of leather); claying, puddling. **corroierie,** *n.f.* Currier's shop; currying.

corrompre [kɔ'rɔ̃:pr], *v.t. irr.* To corrupt, to infect, to vitiate; to spoil; to taint (meat); (*fig.*) to pervert, to deprave; to falsify (a text etc.); to bribe, to buy over. *Corrompre des témoins,* to bribe witnesses; *corrompre le cuir,* to make leather supple; *les mauvaises compagnies corrompent les bonnes mœurs,* evil

communications corrupt good manners; *se laisser corrompre*, to take a bribe. **se corrompre**, *v.r.* To grow corrupt; to become tainted, to fester. **corrompu**, *a.* Corrupted, unsound; bribed. *Homme corrompu*, debauchee; *mœurs corrompues*, dissolute morals. **corrosif** [kɔro'zif], *a.* and *n.* (*fem.* -ive) Corrosive.
corrosion [kɔro'zjɔ̃], *n.f.* Corrosion. **corrosiveté**, *n.f.* Corrosiveness.
corroyage [kɔrwa'ja:ʒ], *n.m.* Currying (of leather); trimming (of wood), etc.
corroyer [kɔrwa'je], *v.t. irr.* (*conjugated like* ABOYER) To curry (leather); to prepare (clay) for puddling; to puddle. *Corroyer du bois*, to plane wood; *corroyer du fer*, to hammer or weld iron; *corroyer du sable*, to roll sand. **corroyeur**, *n.m.* Currier.
corrugateur [kɔryga'tœːr], *a.* and *n.m.* (*Anat.*) Corrugator. **corrugation**, *n.f.* Corrugation, wrinkling.
corrupteur [kɔryp'tœːr], *a.* (*fem.* -trice) Corrupting, perverting, infectious.—*n.* Corrupter, seducer; briber. **corruptibilité**, *n.f.* Corruptibility. **corruptible**, *a.* Corruptible. **corruptif**, *a.* (*fem.* -ive) Corruptive.
corruption [kɔryp'sjɔ̃], *n.f.* Corruption; putridity, rottenness; (*fig.*) seduction, depravity, defilement; (*Polit.*) bribery.
corruptrice [CORRUPTEUR].
corsage [kɔr'sa:ʒ], *n.m.* *Bust, chest (of the body); corsage, bodice, body (of a dress).
corsaire [kɔr'sɛːr], *n.m.* Privateer, commander of a privateer, corsair, rover; (*fig.*) shark. *À corsaire, corsaire et demi*, set a thief to catch a thief.
Corse [kɔrs], *f.* Corsica. **corse** [kɔrs], *a.* and *n.* (**Corse**) Corsican.
corsé [kɔr'se], *a.* (*fem.* -ée) Rich, full-bodied, having consistency, body, or tone (of wine etc.); (*colloq.*) strong, thick, stout, substantial; (of stories etc.) spicy, racy.
corselet [kɔrsə'lɛ], *n.m.* Corselet.
corser [kɔr'se], *v.t.* To stiffen, to thicken, to complicate. *Les choses se corsent* or *ça se corse*, the plot thickens.
corset [kɔr'sɛ], *n.m.* Corset, stays. **corsetier** *n.m.* (*fem.* -ière) Corset-maker, stays-maker.
cortège [kɔr'tɛːʒ], *n.m.* Train, retinue, suite, attendants, procession.
Cortès [kɔr'tɛːz], *n.f.* (*used only in pl.*) Cortes (Spanish or Portuguese Parliament).
cortical [kɔrti'kal], *a.* (*fem.* -ale, *pl.* -aux) (*Bot., Anat.*) Cortical. **corticifère**, *a.* Corticiferous. **corticiforme**, *a.* Corticiform. **corticine**, *n.f.* Corticin. **cortiqueux**, *a.* (*fem.* -euse) Corticate.
corton [kɔr'tɔ̃], *n.m.* A Burgundy wine.
coruscation [kɔryska'sjɔ̃], *n.f.* Coruscation.
corvéable [kɔrve'abl], *a.* (*Feud.*) Liable to forced labour.—*n.* One liable to forced labour.
corvée [kɔr've], *n.f.* (*Feud.*) Forced or statute labour, villain labour; fatigue duty done by soldiers; fatigue party; call to fatigue duty; (*fig.*) unpleasant job, toil, drudgery. *Être de corvée*, to be on fatigue duty; *quelle corvée!* what a drudgery!
corvette [kɔr'vɛt], *n.f.* Corvette, sloop of war.
corybante [kɔri'bɑ̃ːt], *n.m.* (*Gr. Ant.*) Priest of Cybele. **corybantique**, *a.* Corybantic.
corydale [kɔri'dal], *n.m.* (*Bot.*) Corydalis.

corymbe [kɔ'rɛ̃:b], *n.m.* Corymb. **corymbé**, *a.* (*fem.* -ée) or **corymbeux**, *a.* (*fem.* -euse) Corymbose. **corymbifère**, *a.* Corymbiferous. **corymbiforme**, *a.* Corymbiform.
coryphée [kɔri'fe], *n.m.* Coryphæus; (*Theat.*) leader of ballet or chorus, coryphée; (*fig.*) leader, chief.
coryza [kɔri'za], *n.m.* Coryza, cold in the head.
cosaque [kɔ'zak], *n.m.* Cossack; (*fig.*) fierce or brutal man.—*n.f.* Cossack dance.
cosécante [kɔsɛ'kɑ̃:t], *n.f.* Cosecant.
coseigneur [kɔsɛ'ɲœːr], *n.m.* Joint lord of a manor. **coseigneurie**, *n.f.* Joint lordship.
cosignataire [kɔsiɲa'tɛːr], *a.* Cosignatory.
cosinus [kɔsi'nyːs], *n.m.* Cosine.
cosmétique [kɔsme'tik], *a.* and *n.m.* Cosmetic; mascara (for eyelashes and eyebrows).—*n.f.* Art of using cosmetics.
cosmique [kɔs'mik], *a.* Cosmic. *Rayons cosmiques*, cosmic rays.
cosmogonie [kɔsmɔgɔ'ni], *n.f.* Cosmogony. **cosmogonique**, *a.* Cosmogonic.
cosmographe [kɔsmɔ'graf], *n.m.* Cosmographer. **cosmographie**, *n.f.* Cosmography. **cosmographique**, *a.* Cosmographic.
cosmologie [kɔsmɔlɔ'ʒi], *n.f.* Cosmology. **cosmologique**, *a.* Cosmologic. **cosmologiste** or **cosmologue**, *n.* Cosmologist.
cosmopolite [kɔsmɔpɔ'lit], *n.m.* Cosmopolite.—*a.* Cosmopolitan. **cosmopolitisme**, *n.m.* Cosmopolitanism.
cosmos [kɔs'mos], *n.m.* Cosmos.
cossard [kɔ'sar], *a.* (*fam.*) Lazy.
cosse [kɔs], *n.f.* Pod, shell, husk, rind; (*Naut.*) thimble; (*Elec.*) eyelet. (*slang*) *Avoir la cosse*, to be lazy.
cosser [kɔ'se], *v.t.* To butt (of rams).
cosson [kɔ'sɔ̃], *n.m.* Weevil; new shoot (of a vine).
cossu [kɔ'sy], *a.* (*fem.* **cossue**) *Husked, podded; (*fig.*) substantial, wealthy. *Un homme cossu*, a moneyed man.
costal [kɔs'tal], *a.* (*fem.* -ale, *pl.* -aux) (*Anat.*) Costal.
costaud, costeau [kɔs'to], *n.m.* and *a.* (*slang*) Strong, stalwart, strapping.
costière [kɔs'tjɛːr], *n.f.* (1) (*Theat.*) Groove for the uprights. (2) [CÔTIÈRE].
costume [kɔs'tym], *n.m.* Costume, dress; uniform. **costumé**, *a.* (*fem.* **costumée**) Dressed up. *Bal costumé*, fancy-dress ball. **costumer**, *v.t.* To dress (in a certain style etc.). **se costumer**, *v.r.* To dress oneself up; to dress in fancy dress. **costumier**, *n.m.* (*fem.* -ière) Costumier.
cotable [kɔ'tabl], *a.* (*St. Exch.*) Quotable.
cotangente [kɔtɑ̃'ʒɑ̃:t], *n.f.* Cotangent.
cotation [kɔta'sjɔ̃], *n.f.* (*St. Exch.*) Quotation, quoting.
cote [kɔt], *n.f.* Quota, share, proportion; letter, number, figure (to indicate order etc.); (*St. Exch.*) stock list; quotation of exchanges; (*Comm.*) price-current, price-list; odds on or against (of a horse); (*sch.* and *exam.*) marks, appreciation; press-mark (in a library); *la cote* or *la cote d'amour*, favouritism. *Il a la cote*, he is a great favourite with his superiors. (*Mil.*) *La cote 250*, hill 250. *Faire une cote mal taillée*, to make a rough and ready compromise.
côte [koːt], *n.f.* Rib (of the body, cloth, fruit, etc.); upward slope, hill, acclivity; shore,

sea-coast. *À mi-côte*, half-way up; *bas à côtes*, ribbed stockings; *côte à côte*, side by side; *côte d'aloyau*, wing-rib; *côte de fer*, (*Hist.*) ironside; *course de côte*, hill climb; *être à la côte*, to be in a fix; *fausses côtes*, short ribs; *le long de la côte*, along the hill or the shore; *ranger la côte*, to coast; *raser la côte*, to sail along or to hug the shore; *rompre les côtes à quelqu'un*, to break someone's bones; *se casser une côte*, to break a rib; *se mettre à la côte*, to run aground or ashore; (*fig.*) *être à la côte*, to be on the rocks; *se tenir les côtes de rire*, to shake one's sides with laughter; *vitesse en côte*, speed up-hill.

côté [ko'te], *n.m.* Side; part, quarter, hand, way, direction; face, aspect. *À côté de*, by, near; *c'est son côté faible*, it is his weak side; *d'à côté*, adjoining, next; *dans la chambre à côté*, in the next room; *de côté*, sideways, aslant, askew, obliquely; *de côté et d'autre*, up and down, here and there, on all sides; *de l'autre côté*, on the other side, on the other hand; *de l'autre côté du fleuve*, on the other side of the river; *de mon côté*, for my own part; *de tous côtés*, on all sides; *frapper, passer à côté*, to miss; *être à côté de la question*, to be beside the question; *il a un point de côté*, he has got a stitch in his side; *il est du côté gauche*, he is a natural child; *il se met du côté du plus fort*, he takes the strongest side; *ils sont parents du côté maternel*, they are related on the mother's side; *laisser de côté*, to abandon; *mettre les rieurs de son côté*, to turn the laugh against someone; *mettre une bouteille or un tonneau sur le côté*, to empty a bottle *or* a cask; *mettre une chose de côté*, to lay by or put aside a matter; *par certains côtés*, in some ways; *prendre la vie du bon côté*, to have an optimistic view of life; *regarder de côté*, to look askance at; *s'asseoir à côté de quelqu'un*, to sit down by the side of someone; *se ranger du côté de quelqu'un*, to side with someone; *une vue de côté*, a side-view; *vent de côté*, side-wind.

coté [ko'te], *a.* Marked; classed; backed. *Point coté*, (on a map) trig-point; *cheval bien coté*, well-backed horse; (*personne*) *haut-cotée*, in high esteem.

coteau [ko'to], *n.m.* (*pl.* -**eaux**) Slope; little hill.

côtelé [kot'le], *a.* (*fem.* -**ée**) Ribbed (of cloth).

côtelette [ko'tlɛt], *n.f.* Cutlet, chop; (*pl.*) mutton-chop whiskers. *Côtelette de porc*, pork chop; *côtelette de gigot*, chump chop; *côtelette de veau*, veal cutlet; *côtelette de mouton*, mutton chop.

coter [ko'te], *v.t.* To number; to price, to fix the price of; (*St. Exch.*) to quote. **se coter**, *v.r.* To be quoted, to be priced.

coterie [ko'tri], *n.f.* Coterie, set, circle, clique.

cothurne [ko'tyrn], *n.m.* Buskin. *Chausser le cothurne*, to put on the buskin (play in tragedy); to write tragedies. **cothurné**, *a.* (*fem.* -**ée**) Wearing the buskin.

côtier [ko'tje], *a.* (*fem.* -**ière** (1)) Of, along, or acquainted with the coast, coasting.—*n.m.* Coasting-vessel; extra trace-horse (on a hill).

côtière (2), *n.f.* Side stone in furnace of smithy; each half of mould for lead pipe; (*Hort.*) sloping bed.

cotignac [koti'ɲak], *n.m.* Quince jelly or marmalade. **cotignelle**, *n.f.* Quince wine.

cotillon [koti'jɔ̃], *n.m.* Under-petticoat; cotillion (dance with paper caps etc.) *Il aime le cotillon*, (*fig.*) he is fond of women.

cotillonner, *v.i.* To dance the cotillion.

cotillonneur, *n.m.* (*fem.* -**euse**) Dancer of the cotillion.

cotir [ko'ti:r], *v.t.* To bruise or damage (fruit).

cotisation [kotiza'sjɔ̃], *n.f.* Assessment, quota, share; subscription. **cotiser**, *v.t.* To assess, to rate. **se cotiser**, *v.r.* To club together; to get up a subscription, to subscribe.

cotissure [koti'sy:r], *n.f.* Damage, bruising (of fruit).

coton [ko'tɔ̃], *n.m.* Cotton; fluff; down (of fruit and hair on the face); cotton wool. *Balle de coton*, bale of cotton; *bobine de coton*, reel of cotton; *coton à repriser*, darning cotton; *coton à tricoter*, crochet cotton; *coton brut*, raw cotton; *coton de couleur*, coloured cotton; *coton épluché*, picked cotton; *coton filé*, cotton yard, spun cotton; *coton hydrophile*, absorbent cotton-wool; *coton plat*, darning-cotton; *écheveau de coton*, skein of cotton; *élever dans du coton*, to mollycoddle, to bring up delicately; *il file un mauvais coton*, he is in a bad way, he is going to the dogs; *mettre dans du coton*, to coddle, to nurse, to indulge; *toile de coton*, cotton cloth.

cotonnade [kotɔ'nad], *n.f.* Cotton-cloth, cotton goods.

cotonné [kotɔ'ne], *a.* (*fem.* -**ée**) Covered with or full of cotton; downy; woolly (of hair); wadded, padded.

cotonner [kotɔ'ne], *v.t.* To fill or to stuff with cotton; to pad. **se cotonner**, *v.r.* To be covered with down; to become downy; to become mealy (of vegetables). *Les artichauts or les radis se cotonnent*, artichokes *or* radishes grow pithy or spongy. **cotonnerie**, *n.f.* Cotton-mill. **cotonneux**, *a.* (*fem.* -**euse**) Cottony, downy; spongy, mealy.

cotonnier [kotɔ'nje], *a.* (*fem.* -**ière**) Of or pertaining to cotton.—*n.* Worker in cotton-mill etc.—*n.m.* Cotton-bush. **cotonnine**, *n.f.* Cotton sail-cloth. **coton-poudre**, *n.m.* Gun-cotton.

côtoyer [kotwa'je], *v.t. irr.* (*conjugated like* ABOYER) To go by the side of, to skirt; to coast, to coast along; (*fig.*) to keep close to without reaching.

cotre [ko:tr], *n.m.* Cutter (vessel).

cotret [ko'trɛ], *n.m.* Faggot; stick of this; slat (of arm of windmill). *De l'huile de cotret*, (*fig.*) stirrup-oil, cudgelling; *sec comme un cotret*, as thin as a lath.

cottage [ko'ta:ʒ], *n.m.* Cottage.

cotte (1) [kot], *n.f.* Short petticoat; (engineer's) overalls. *Cotte d'armes*, surcoat worn over armour; *cotte de mailles*, coat of mail.

cotte (2) [kot], *n.m.* (*Ichth.*) Bull-head or father-lasher, or short-spined sea scorpion.

cotuteur [koty'tœ:r], *n.m.* (*fem.* **cotutrice**) Joint-guardian.

cotyle [ko'til], *n.f.* Cotyle.

cotylédon [kotile'dɔ̃], *n.m.* Cotyledon. **cotylédonaire**, *a.* Cotyledonal. **cotylédoné**, *a.* (*fem.* **cotylédonée**) Cotyledonous.

cou [ku] or ***col**, *n.m.* Neck. *Avoir la bride sur le cou*, to have full rein or full liberty of action; *cou de cygne*, swan's neck, (*fig.*) tap or pipe shaped like this; *cou de travers,* wry-neck; *couper le cou à,* to cut the neck of; *jusqu'au cou,* up to the neck, completely, altogether; *lui tordre le cou,* to twist his neck, to kill; *prendre ses jambes à son cou,* to take to one's heels; *rompre le cou à,* to break the neck of; *sauter* or *se jeter au cou de quelqu'un,* to fall on someone's neck; *se casser* or *se rompre le cou,* to break one's neck.

couac [kwak], *n.m.* False note; squawk.

couagga [kwa'ga], *n.m.* Quagga.

couard [kwa:r], *a. (fem.* **-arde)** Coward, cowardly.—*n.* Coward, dastard. **couardise** *n.f.* Cowardice.

couchage [ku'ʃa:ʒ], *n.m.* Act of lying in bed; bed, night's lodging; bedding, beds. *Sac de couchage,* sleeping-bag.

couchant [ku'ʃā], *a. (fem.* **-ante)** Setting; couchant, lying; *(fig.)* fawning. *Faire le chien couchant,* to crawl and cringe; *soleil couchant,* setting sun; *un chien couchant,* a setter—*n.m.* West. *Être à son couchant,* to be declining.

couche [kuʃ], *n.f.* Bed, couch; bedstead; marriage-bed, marriage; confinement, child-bed, lying-in; delivery, birth; swaddling-clothes, nappy, wrapper; layer, stratum, row; *(Min.)* seam; *(Gard.)* hotbed, bed; coat (of varnish or colour); *(fig.)* social stratum, class, rank; *(Play)* stake. *Couche ligneuse,* wood-ring (in a tree); *dans le sens de la couche,* with the strata; *elle est morte en couches,* she died in childbed; *être en* or *faire ses couches,* to be confined, to lie-in, *en avoir une couche, (fam.)* to be stupid; *fausse couche,* miscarriage; *heureuse couche,* good delivery; *la couche nuptiale,* the nuptial bed; *les couches sociales,* the classes of society; *par couches,* in layers; *partager la couche de quelqu'un,* to share someone's bed. **couché,** *a. (fem.* **-ée** (1)) In bed, gone to bed, lying down, recumbent; *(Her.)* couchant. **couchée** (2), *n.f.* Act of lying down; sleeping place; bed; night's lodging.

coucher [ku'ʃe], *v.t.* To put to bed; to lay down; to beat down, to lay low, to lodge (corn etc.); to knock down; to incline, to slope, to slant; to lay on; to write down, to inscribe; to stake. *Coucher par écrit,* to write down; *coucher quelqu'un en joue,* to take aim at someone, to cover someone; *coucher les terres,* to turn ploughed land into meadows.—*v.i.* To sleep, to pass the night, to lie down, to rest. *Coucher à la belle étoile,* to sleep in the open air; *coucher au cabaret,* to sleep at a public-house; *coucher sur la dure,* to sleep upon bare boards or on the ground; (to a dog) *couchez!* lie down! **se coucher,** *v.r.* To go to bed; to lay oneself down, to lie down, to lie flat; to set, to go down. *Allez vous coucher,* go to bed, *(colloq.)* go to blazes! *comme on fait son lit, on se couche,* as you make your bed, so you must lie in it; *il n'est pas encore temps d'aller se coucher,* it is not bed-time yet; *le soleil se couche,* the sun is setting; *se coucher comme les poules,* to go to bed with the sun *(i.e.* very early); *se coucher sur son aviron,* to lie on one's oar.—*n.m.* Going to bed; bed-time; setting (of the sun etc.). *C'est l'heure de son coucher,* it is his bed-time; *le petit coucher (du roi),* couchee.

coucherie [kyʃ'ri], *n.f. (fam.)* Sexual inter-course.

couchette [ku'ʃɛt], *n.f.* Small bed, crib; berth; bunk (on a ship). *Wagon à couchettes,* second-class sleeper.

coucheur [ku'ʃœ:r], *n.m. (fem.* **-euse)** Bed-fellow. *Mauvais coucheur, (fig.)* awkward customer.

couchis [ku'ʃi], *n.m.* Layer of sand on which is laid the pavement of a bridge; lathing of a floor.

couci-couci [kusiku'si] or **couci-couça** *(fam.) adv.* So-so, middling, indifferently.

coucou [ku'ku], *n.m.* Cuckoo; cuckoo-clock; *(Bot.)* cowslip; *one-horse chaise (about 1830); (fam.)* an old engine or aeroplane; *(interj.)* peep-bo!

coude [kud], *n.m.* Elbow; bend, angle; winding, turning, turn; knee (of pipe); elbow (of machinery etc.). *Donner des coups de coude,* to elbow, to nudge; *faire un coude,* to make a turn or bend; *hausser* or *lever le coude,* to drink, to tipple; *jouer des coudes,* to elbow (one's way). **coudé,** *a. (fem.* **coudée** (1)) Bent, elbowed, cranked.

coudée (2), *n.f.* Length of arm from elbow to tip of middle finger, cubit. *Avoir ses coudées franches,* to have elbow room, (lit. and *fig.*) full play, scope, freedom.

cou-de-pied [kud'pje], *n.m. (pl.* **cous-de-pied)** Instep.

couder [ku'de], *v.t.* To bend, to make an elbow in. **se couder,** *v.r.* To elbow, to form an elbow.

coudoiement [kudwa'mā], *n.m.* Elbowing, jostling.

coudoyer [kudwa'je], *v.t.* To elbow, to jostle. **se coudoyer,** *v.r.* To elbow or jostle each other.

coudraie [ku'drɛ], *n.f.* Hazel-copse; filbert-orchard.

*coudre (1) [kudr] [COUDRIER].

coudre (2) [kudr], *v.t. irr. (pres.p.* **cousant,** *p.p.* **cousu)** To sew, to stitch; to sew up, to sew on; *(fig.)* to attach, to connect, to join together, to unite. *Coudre à,* to stitch or sew to; *coudre à grands points,* to take long stitches; *coudre du linge,* to sew linen; *coudre un bouton,* to stitch a button on; *machine à coudre,* sewing-machine.

coudrette [ku'drɛt], *n.f.* Small hazel-copse.

coudrier, *n.m.* Hazel-tree.

couenne [kwan], *n.f.* Scraped pig-skin; crackling (of pork); rind; *(Med.)* buffy coat, birth-mark, mole; *(colloq.)* blockhead, duffer.

couenneux, -euse [kwa'nø], *(Med.)* Buffy (blood). *Angine couenneuse,* diphtheria.

couette [kwɛt] or **coit(t)e,** *n.f.* Feather-bed; sea-gull; (hare's) scut; *(pl.) (Naut.)* (wooden) ways (of a ship in yards).

couffe [kuf], *n.f.,* or **couffin,** *n.m.* Hamper-frail, basket.

couguar [ku'ga:r], *n.m.* Cougar, puma.

couic [kwik], *(onom. fam.) Faire couic,* to squeak, to die; *ne comprendre que couic,* to understand nothing.

couiner [kwi'ne], *v.i.* To squeak (of guinea-pigs, mice, etc.).

coulage [ku'la:ʒ], *n.m.* Flow (of metal in fusion); melting, casting; running out (of liquid); leakage, waste; pilferage.

coulant [ku'lā], *a. (fem.* **-ante)** Flowing, fluent, smooth, natural (of style etc.); *(fig.)* easy, accommodating. *Nœud coulant,* slip

or running knot, noose; *style coulant*, easy, fluent style.—*n.m.* Sliding ring (for a purse, necktie, pincers, umbrella, etc.); slider (in mine-shaft).
coule (1) [kul], *n.f.* (*colloq.*) Waste, leakage; servants' pilferings. (*slang*) *Être à la coule*, to be a smart hand, to be up to snuff (in a bad sense), to know the ropes.
coule (2) [kul], *n.f.* Cowl [CAGOULE].
coulé [ku'le], *n.m.* (*Mus.*) Slur; (*Dance*) slide; (*Billiards*) follow through; (*Metal.*) cast-(ing); (*Swim.*) *faire un coulé*, to dive, slide under water near the surface and get out without any movement of the limbs.
coulée [ku'le], *n.f.* Running-hand (of writing); (*Metal.*) tapping; flow, rush (of a torrent etc.); (*Hunt.*) track, path.   *Trou de coulée*, (*Metal.*) tap-hole.   **coulement**, *n.m.* Running, flow (of liquids).
couler [ku'le], *v.i.* To flow, to run; to glide along; to trickle, to drop, to ooze out, to be spilled; to leak, to run out; to glide away, to fly away, to slip (of time etc.); to flow, to stream, to gush; to proceed, to run, to flow (of verse etc.); to founder (of a ship etc.); (*Founding*) to run through the mould; to gutter; to touch lightly (*sur*); to be shed, to fall off (of leaves etc.); to creep, to steal. *Couler à fond*, to flow, to founder, to sink to the bottom; *couler de source*, to come naturally, from the heart; *couler sur un fait*, to glide or slur over a fact; *faire couler*, to shed; (*fig.*) *cette histoire a fait couler beaucoup d'encre*, there has been much ink spilt about that story; *la chandelle coule*, the candle gutters; *laisser couler les heures*, to let time glide by; *l'encre ne coule pas*, the ink does not run freely; *le nez lui coule*, his nose runs; *les larmes lui coulent des yeux or de ses yeux*, tears are flowing from his eyes; *se laisser couler jusqu'à terre*, to slide down to the ground.—*v.t.* To cast; to strain; to slip (*dans*); to sink, to run down, to cause to founder; to scald or buck (linen); to swamp; (*Mus.*) to slur, to glide over.   *Couler une statue*, to cast a statue; *couler un pas*, to pass smoothly over a step (in dancing); *couler un vaisseau à fond*, to sink a ship; *c'est un homme coulé*, he is done for.   **se couler**, *v.r.* To slip, to creep, to steal, to glide; to be cast (of metals); (*colloq.*) to do for oneself, to be ruined.   *Se la couler douce*, (*slang*) to take it easy.
coulette [ku'let], *n.f.* Spindle for silk and thread spools.
couleur [ku'lœ:r], *n.f.* Colour; colouring-matter, dye, paint; complexion, colouring; (*fig.*) appearance; pretext, excuse; pretence, falsehood, fib; hue; opinion; suit (at cards); (*pl.*) (*Naut.*) colours; *livery.   *Adoucir or amortir les couleurs*, to soften or to deaden the colours; *appliquer les couleurs*, to lay on the colours; *ce rôti a bien pris couleur*, that roast meat is nicely browned; *changer de couleur*, to change colour; *couleur à l'huile*, oil-colour; *couleur de rose*, rose-tinted; *couleur éclatante*, striking colour; *couleur foncée*, dark colour; *couleur locale*, local colour; *couleur tranchante*, glaring colour; *couleur voyante*, showy colour; *couleurs assorties*, colours that blend or go well together; *couleurs passées*, faded colours; *marchand de couleurs*, chandler; *de quelle*

couleur tourne-t-il? what are trumps? *jouer dans la couleur*, (*Cards*) to follow suit; *diversifier, mêler, or assortir les couleurs*, to vary, to blend, *or* to match colours; *haut en couleur*, high-coloured, florid, rubicund; *il l'a trompé sous couleur d'amitié*, he deceived him under a show of friendship; *il m'en a fait voir de toutes les couleurs*, he played me all sorts of tricks; *juger or parler d'une chose comme un aveugle des couleurs*, to judge or talk of a thing without knowledge; *l'affaire prend couleur*, the matter is looking better or is taking shape; *lampes de couleur*, variegated lamps; *hommes de couleur*, coloured men; *linge de couleur*, coloured linen (not white); *mettre en couleur*, to stain (a floor etc.); *pâles couleurs*, (*fam.*) chlorosis, green sickness; *peindre à pleines couleurs*, to paint with a full brush; *prendre couleur*, to look well, to assume a character, (of persons) to declare oneself, to take side openly; *rehausser les couleurs*, to touch up colours; *reprendre couleur*, to be in favour again; *sans couleur*, pale; *sous couleur de*, under the pretext of; *style sans couleur*, colourless style.
couleuvre [ku'lœ:vr], *n.f.* (Grass) snake. (*fig.*) *Faire avaler des couleuvres à quelqu'un*, to heap all sorts of indignities upon someone.
couleuvrée [kulœ'vre], *n.f.* (*Bot.*) *Couleuvrée blanche* [BRYONE]. *Couleuvrée noire* [TAMINIER].
couleuvrin [kulœ'vrɛ̃], *a.* (*fem.* **couleuvrine** (1)) Snakish, snaky, colubrine.
couleuvrine (2) [kulœ'vrin], *n.f.* (*Artill.*) Culverin.
coulinage [kuli'na:ʒ], *n.m.* (*Agric.*) Singeing (of fruit-trees).   **couliner**, *v.t.* To singe (fruit-trees).
coulis [ku'li], *n.m.* Strained juice from meat etc. slowly stewed; grout.   *Vent coulis*, wind that comes through cracks and chinks, an insidious draught.
coulisse [ku'lis], *n.f.* Groove, channel, coulisse; string, running string; (*Theat.*) side-scene, wing; (*fig.*) behind the scenes; (*St. Exch.*) outside brokers.   *Banc à coulisse* (*Row.*), slide; *porte à coulisse*, sliding door; *pied à coulisse*, slide calipers; *être dans la coulisse*, (*fig.*) to pull the strings, to be behind the scene; *faire les yeux en coulisse*, to look sideways, to make sheep's eyes; *propos de coulisses*, green-room talk.   **coulissé**, *a.* (*fem.* **-ée**) Grooved.   **coulisseau**, *n.m.* Small groove; slide-block; (*pl.*) wooden grooves (for bedstead with castors).   **coulisser**, *v.i.* To slide.—*v.t.* (*St. Exch.*) To do business as an outside broker; (*Dress.*) to run up.   **coulissier**, *a.* (*fem.* **-ière**) Pertaining to the coulisse.—*n.m.* Stock-jobber, outside broker; green-room frequenter.
couloir [ku'lwa:r], *n.m.* Passage, corridor, lobby, gangway, exit; skimming-dish, strainer.   *Les couloirs de la Chambre*, the lobby of the House; *wagon-couloir*, corridor-carriage.
couloire [ku'lwa:r], *n.f.* Colander, strainer.
coulpe [kulp], *n.f.* Sin, guilt.   *Je bats ma coulpe*, I confess my sin.
coulure [ku'ly:r], *n.f.* Falling off, dropping off (of grapes or other fruit); running (of metal).
coumarine [kuma'rin], *n.f.* (*Chem.*) Couma-rin.   **coumarou**, *n.m.* Brazilian name for

following. **coumarouna**, *n.m.* Tonka-bean tree.

coup [ku], *n.m.* Blow, stroke, hit, thump, knock, stab, thrust; wound; beat (of a drum, clock, etc.); draught (of liquids); clap (of thunder); (*Artill.*) charge; move (at chess, draughts, etc.); (*Fenc.*) thrust; gust (of wind); throw, cast (at dice); discharge, shot, report (of fire-arms); aim; moment, instant (of time); turn, bout, fling, go; attempt, attack; deed, action; event, result, chance; (*pl.*) beating; (*Archaeol.*) hand-axe (of stone). *À coup perdu*, in vain; *à coup sûr*, certainly, unquestionably; *à deux coups*, double-barrelled (gun); *après coup*, too late, after the event; *asséner un coup*, to deal a blow; *assommer* or *rouer quelqu'un de coups*, to beat someone in a cruel manner; *à tout coup*, every time; *au premier coup d'œil*, at first sight; *avoir le coup d'œil juste*, to have a carpenter's eye; *boire un coup de trop*, to have a drop too much; *boire un grand coup*, to take a long draught; *buvez encore un coup*, have another drink; *buvons un coup ensemble*, let us have a drink together; *c'est comme un coup d'épée dans l'eau*, it is like beating the air; *c'est un coup qui porte*, that is a home-thrust; *cette démarche a porté coup*, this step has taken effect; *coup d'air*, sudden gust of air, breeze or draught; the effect of such; *un coup d'air dans l'œil, dans l'oreille*, sore eye, ear-ache due to a slight chill; *coup dans l'eau*, useless attempt; *coup d'arrêt*, stop hit; *coup d'assommoir*, overwhelming or stunning blow; *coup d'autorité*, act of authority; *coup de baguette*, wave, touch, of the wand; *coup de bâton*, blow with a stick, cudgelling; *coup de bec*, peck, (*fig.*) caustic remark; *coup de chapeau*, salute; *coup d'éclat*, striking act, brilliant exploit; *coup de coude*, nudge; *coup de dents*, bite; *coup d'envoi*, (*Ftb.*) kick-off; *coup d'essai*, first attempt; *coup d'État*, coup d'état; *coup de fleuret*, pass; *coup de foudre*, thunderbolt; *coup de grisou*, firedamp explosion; *coup de Jarnac*, treacherous or unexpected attack; *coup de langue*, slander, backbiting; *coup de main*, (*Mil.*) coup-de-main, surprise, unexpected attack; *coup de maître*, master-stroke; *coup de massue*, blow with a club, stunning blow, thunder-stroke; *coup d'œil*, glance, look; *coup de partance*, (*Naut.*) farewell gun, signal for departure; *coup de plume*, stroke of the pen, literary attack; *coup de poing*, blow with the fist; *coup de sang*, apoplectic fit, congestion of the brain; *coup de soleil*, sunstroke; *coup de téléphone*, telephone call; *coup de temps*, surprise, accident, (*Fenc.*) feint; *coup de tête*, butt; (*fig.*) impulsive act; *coup de théâtre*, dramatic surprise; *coup d'étourdi*, rash act; *coup du ciel*, providential stroke; *coup du sort*, bad luck; *coup imprévu*, unexpected accident; *coup mortel*, death-blow; *coup perdu*, random shot; *coup sur coup*, one after another, without cessation; *détourner le coup*, to ward off the blow; *donner des coups de bâton à quelqu'un*, to cudgel someone; *donner des coups de fouet*, to lash; *donner des coups de pied*, to kick; *donner un coup de chapeau*, to take off one's hat; *donner un coup de collier*, to make a powerful but temporary effort; *donner un coup de main à quelqu'un*, to give someone a

helping hand; *donner un coup d'épaule à quelqu'un*, to help someone; *donner un coup d'épée*, to deal a sword thrust; *donnez-vous un coup de peigne*, comb yourself; *d'un seul coup*, at one blow, at one swoop; *du premier coup*, at the first, at once; *encore un coup*, once more, again, one more blow; *être aux cent coups*, to be at one's wits' end, not to know which way to turn; *faire d'une pierre deux coups*, to kill two birds with one stone; *faire les cent coups*, to play all sorts of tricks, to run riot; *flanquer des coups à quelqu'un*, to give someone a thrashing; *frapper de grands coups*, to resort to decisive measures; *heureux coup*, lucky hit; *il a fait le coup*, he has done the deed; *il a reçu un coup de fusil*, he was wounded by a gunshot, (or, *slang*) he has been overcharged (at the hotel); *jeter un coup d'œil sur*, to glance at; *le coup de grâce*, the coup-de-grâce, the finishing stroke; *cela vaut le coup*, it is worth trying; *manquer son coup*, to miss one's aim, to fail; *par un coup de hasard*, by a mere chance; *petit coup*, pat, (of liquids); *porter un coup*, to deal a blow; *pour le coup*, this time, for once; *sans coup férir*, without striking a blow, without firing a shot; *sous le coup de*, under the influence of (drink, passion, etc.); *sous le coup de la loi*, within the provisions (of law); *sur le coup de midi*, at the stroke of 12 noon; *tirer un coup de feu*, to fire a shot; *tout à coup*, all of a sudden, suddenly; *tout d'un coup*, at once, all at once; *tuer quelqu'un à coups de bâton*, to beat someone to death; *un coup de patte*, a sarcastic remark; *un coup de chance*, a stroke of fortune; *un coup de malheur*, a stroke of misfortune; *un coup de revers*, backstroke, back-hander; *un coup de sifflet*, a whistle; *un coup de vent*, a squall.

coupable [ku'pabl], *a.* Culpable, guilty; at fault; sinful, criminal. *Déclarer quelqu'un coupable*, to bring someone in guilty; *se déclarer coupable* or *non coupable*, to plead guilty *or* not guilty.—*n.* Guilty person, culprit. **coupablement**, *adv.* Culpably, guiltily.

coupage [ku'paːʒ], *n.m.* Cutting; diluting (of wine); blending (of spirits); watering (to weaken a liquid).

coupant [ku'pɑ̃], *a.* (*fem.* **-ante**) Cutting, sharp; (*Geom.*) bisecting.—*n.m.* Edge (of a sword etc.).

coup-de-poing [kud'pwɛ̃], *n.m.* Pocket-pistol; (*Archaeol.*) hand-axe (of flint); *coup de poing américain*, knuckle-duster.

coupe (1) [kup], *n.f.* Cutting, chopping, cutting down, felling (of wood); amount of wood felled; the cut end; a fall of timber; cut (style in clothes etc.); cut (place); profile, shape; cutting (at cards); (*Arch.*) section, plan; (*Pros.*) division, cadence, arrangement of pauses; (*Swimming*) overarm stroke. *À la coupe*, by the cut; *coupe d'un ouvrage*, division of a work into parts; *coupe réglée*, annual cutting; *coupe sombre*, removal of a portion of the trees in a wood, (*fig.*) drastic reduction; *être sous la coupe de quelqu'un*, to play after someone (at cards), (*fig.*) to be in someone's power; *faire sauter la coupe*, to make the pass; *il a la coupe malheureuse*, he is very unlucky at cutting; *la coupe des cheveux*, hair-cutting; *la coupe des pierres*, stone-cutting; *la coupe des vers*, the division of the verse, caesura; *la coupe d'un bois taillis se fait tous les neuf ans*, coppice wood is felled every ninth year; *la coupe et liaison des scènes*, the division and connexion of the scenes; *mettre en coupe*, to mark for cutting; *mettre quelqu'un en coupe réglée*, (*fig.*) to lay someone under regular contribution; *nager à coupe*, to swim arm over arm.

coupe (2) [kup], *n.f.* Cup, goblet, chalice; basin (of a fountain etc.); fount; (*Theol.*) the cup. *Coupe à champagne*, champagne glass; *boire la coupe jusqu'à la lie*, to drink the cup of bitterness to the dregs; *il y a loin de la coupe aux lèvres*, there's many a slip 'twixt the cup and the lip; *une coupe à fruits*, a fruit bowl.

coupé (1) [ku'pe], *a.* (*fem.* **coupée**) Intersected; diluted, mixed with water; (*Her.*) divided into two equal parts; (*fig.*) abrupt, short, laconic. *Du lait coupé*, milk and water; *du vin coupé d'eau*, wine and water; *une balle coupée*, (*Tennis*) cut, chop.

coupé (2) [ku'pe], *n.m.* Coupé (kind of brougham); front part of a French diligence; a dance step.

[In the following compounds *coupe* is inv.]

coupe-bourgeon [kupbur'ʒɔ̃], *n.m.* Vinegrub.

coupe-bourse, *n.m. inv.* Cutpurse.

coupe-cercle, *n.m.* Compasses with a cutting-limb; round punch.

coupe-choux, *n.m.* (*Mil. slang*) Pigsticker.

coupe-cigares, *n.m. inv.* Cigar-cutter.

coupe-circuit, *n.m. inv.* Cut-out circuit-breaker. *Coupe-circuit à fusible*, fuse.

coupe-cors, *n.m. inv.* Corn-cutter.

coupe-coupe or **coupe coupe** [kupkup], *n.m. inv.* Machete.

coupée [ku'pe], *n.f.* (*Naut.*) Gangway; opening in the side of a ship. *Échelle de coupée*, accommodation ladder.

coupe-file, *n.m. inv.* Police pass.

coupe-foin [kup'fwɛ̃], *n.m. inv.* Hay-cutter.

coupe-gazon, *n.m. inv.* Turf-cutter, turfing-iron.

coupe-gorge, *n.m. inv.* Cut-throat place, den, nest of thieves, swindlers, etc.; (*Lansquenet*) the dealer turning up his own card first.

coupe-jarret, *n.m.* Cut-throat, assassin, ruffian.

coupe-légumes, *n.m. inv.* Vegetable-cutter.

coupé-lit [kupe'li], *n.m.* (*pl.* **coupés-lits**) Sleeping compartment.

coupellation [kupɛlla'sjɔ̃], *n.f.* Cupellation, assaying, testing. **coupelle**, *n.f.* Small cup; cupel. *Argent de coupelle*, purest silver; *essai à la coupelle*, cupellation; *mettre à la coupelle*, to submit to cupellation, to put to the test. **coupeller**, *v.t.* To test (metals).

coupe-paille [kup'pɑːj], *n.m. inv.* Chaff-cutter.

coupe-papier, *n.m. inv.* Paper-knife; paper-cutting machine.

coupe-pâte, *n.m. inv.* Dough-knife.

couper [ku'pe], *v.t.* To cut; to cut off, to dock, to lop, to strike off; to cut down; to cut out; to clip, to pare, to cut away; to castrate; to geld; to hinder, to impede; (*Mil.*) to intercept; to amputate; to cut up, to carve; to chop up etc.; to dilute (milk,

wine, with water); to divide, to intersect; to interrupt, to stop, to break; to cross; (*fig.*) to put many pauses into (one's style etc.). *À couper au couteau*, thick enough to cut with a knife; *ça te la coupe*, (*pop.*) that knocks you; *couper bras et jambes à*, (*fig.*) to dumbfound, to paralyse; *couper la bourse à quelqu'un*, to pick someone's pocket; *couper la fièvre*, to stop the fever; *couper la ligne*, (*Mil.*) to break through the line; *couper la parole à quelqu'un*, to interrupt someone; *couper les ponts*, to break all relations; *couper le chemin à quelqu'un*, to stop someone's way; *couper le cours d'une rivière*, to interrupt the course of a river; *couper l'herbe sous le pied*, (*fig.*) to supplant someone, to lay by the heels; *couper le sifflet à quelqu'un*, (*slang*) to cut someone's throat, (*fig.*) to silence someone; *couper le souffle à quelqu'un*, to take someone's breath away; *couper les vivres à*, to cut off supplies from; *couper les vivres à une armée*, to intercept the provisions of an army; *couper menu*, to mince; *couper par tranches*, to slice, to cut into slices; *couper les cheveux en quatre*, to split hairs; *couper un vêtement*, to cut out a garment; *les sanglots lui coupent la voix*, her sobs stifle her utterance; *lui couper les cheveux*, to cut his hair; *ne coupez pas*, hold the line, hold on (telephone); *pour couper court*, to be brief, in short.—*v.i.* To cut (to be sharp); to make an incision; to cut in (at cards); to take a short cut (across fields etc.); to chop. *À qui à couper?* (*at cards*) whose cut is it? *couper avec un atout*, to trump; *couper court à une conversation*, to cut a conversation short; *couper dans le vif*, to cut to the quick, (*fig.*) to take strong measures; *couper par le plus court*, to take the shortest way. (*Mil. slang*) *couper à*, to shun, to keep out of. **se couper**, *v.r.* To cut oneself; to cut each other; to intersect, to cross one another; (*colloq.*) to contradict, to betray oneself; to chafe, to be chafed; to wear out in the folds (of clothes). *Ce cuir s'est coupé*, this leather has burst; *se couper la gorge*, to cut one's throat.

coupe-racines [kupra'sin], *n.m. inv.* Root-cutter.

couperet [ku'prɛ], *n.m.* (Butcher's) chopper; knife (of guillotine).

couperose [ku'proːz], *n.f.* Copperas; (*pop.*) blotched face, roseola. *Couperose blanche*, white vitriol; *couperose bleue*, blue vitriol. **couperosé**, *a.* (*fem.* **-ée**) Blotched. **couperoser**, *v.t.* To blotch (the face).

coupe-sève [kup'sɛːv], *n.m. inv.* Ringing-knife.

coupeur [ku'pœːr], *n.m.* (*fem.* **-euse**) Cutter; (*Lansquenet*) player.—*n.f.* Cutting machine. *Coupeur de bourses*, pickpocket, cutpurse; *coupeur d'oreilles*, assassin, brigand.

(C) **coupe-vent** [kup'vɑ̃], *n.m.* Wind breaker.

couplage [ku'plaːʒ], *n.m.* Coupling; assemblage; connecting.

couple [kupl], *n.f.* Brace, leash, couple (two things of the same kind); brace (of game). *Une couple de bœufs*, a pair of oxen; *une couple de perdrix*, a brace of partridges.—*n.m.* Couple (two beings acting in concert); married couple (husband and wife); pair (of animals, male and female); (*Naut.*) frame, timbers; (*Mech.*) torque. *C'est un couple bien assorti*, they are a well-matched couple; *par* *couples*, in pairs; (*Row.*) *ramer* (or *tirer*) *en couple*, to double-scull. **coupler,** *v.t.* To couple, to link together, to join by couples.

couplet [ku′plɛ], *n.m.* Couplet, verse of two rhyming lines; (*pl.*) verses; song; (*fig.*) tirade, speech; (*Tech.*) hinge.

coupleur [ku′plœːr], *n.m.* (*Elec.*) Make-and-break.

coupoir [ku′pwaːr], *n.m.* Cutter (sharp instrument), large blade or knife.

coupole [ku′pɔl], *n.f.* Cupola; (*Naut.*) revolving gun-turret. *Sous la Coupole*, at the Académie Française.

coupon [ku′pɔ̃], *n.m.* Remnant; coupon; divident-warrant, cheque; (*Comm.*) part (of shares); (*Theat.*) ticket. *Coupon détaché*, ex-dividend, ex-coupon.

coupure [ku′pyːr], *n.f.* Cut, incision, slit, break; piece cut out; suppression (cut in a play etc.); water-trench, drain; (*Banking*) small note; (*Geol.*) fracture. *Coupure de courant*, electricity cut; *coupure de journal*, newspaper cutting.

cour [kuːr], *n.f.* Court (of a prince, of justice, etc.); court of a building, yard; courtyard, (*fig.*) courtship, suit, civilities. *C'est la cour du roi Pétaud*, it is Bedlam broken loose; *cour d'école*, school playground; *cour de ferme*, farm-yard; *cour de derrière*, backyard; *cour d'entrée*, entrance-court, front yard; (*Mil.*) *cour du quartier*, barrack square; *eau bénite de cour*, empty promises; *être bien* or *mal en cour*, to be in or out of favour at court; *être* or *se rendre à la cour*, to be at or go to court; *faire sa* or *la cour à*, to court, to woo, to pay one's addresses to, (*iron.*) to dance attendance on; *faire un doigt de cour*, to show some attention to; *la Cour des Comptes*, the Audit Office; *les gens de cour*, courtiers; *tenir sa cour*, to hold his or her court, to keep state; *un homme de cour*, a courtier.

courade [ku′rad], *n.f.* Breton sardine.

courage [ku′raːʒ], *n.m.* Courage, daring, gallantry; pluck; spirit, mettle; fortitude, greatness of soul; heart, goodwill, cheerfulness. *Avoir du courage*, to be courageous, to be a man; *courage!* or *du courage!* come! take courage! cheer up; *je n'ai pas le courage de refuser*, I have not the heart to refuse; *manquer de courage*, to be wanting in courage; *perdre courage*, to lose heart; *prendre courage*, to take heart, to pluck up courage; *tenir* or *prendre son courage à deux mains*, to summon up one's courage, to come to the sticking-point.

courageusement [kuraʒøz′mɑ̃], *adv.* Courageously, bravely, gallantly, resolutely.

courageux [kura′ʒø], *a.* (*fem.* **-euse**) Courageous, daring, gallant, fearless, spirited, manful; plucky, game.

courailler [kura′je], *v.i.* (*colloq.*) To gad about; to lead a loose life, to philander. **courailleur,** *n.m.* (*fem.* **-euse**) Philanderer.

couramment [kura′mɑ̃], *adv.* Fluently, readily. *Il lit couramment*, he reads fluently.

courant (1) [ku′rɑ̃], *a.* (*fem.* **-ante** (1)) Running, current; present; usual, ordinary, everyday; fair, middling (of goods); lineal (of measures). *Chien courant*, beagle; *compte*

courant, current account; *eau courante*, running water; *écriture courante*, running hand; *le mois courant*, the present month; *le six courant*, the sixth inst.; *le prix courant*, the current price; *main courante*, hand-rail, hand-rope; *monnaie courante*, current coin.

courant (2) [ku′rɑ̃], *n.m.* Stream, current; tide; course, run, march (of time etc.); regular course, routine; present price; present (time). *Courant électrique*, electric current; *courant d'air*, draught; *être au courant des nouvelles*, to know the news of the day; *fin courant*, (*Comm.*) at the end of the present month; *je vous tiendrai au courant*, I'll keep you informed; *le courant des affaires*, the course of affairs; *le courant du marché*, the market price; *le fil du courant*, the direction of the stream; *se mettre au courant de*, to acquaint oneself with; *suivre le courant*, to go with the stream.

courante (2) [ku′rɑ̃ːt], *n.f.* Courant, coranto (old-fashioned dance); running-hand (of writing); (*vulg.*) diarrhoea.

courantille [kurɑ̃′tiːj], *n.f.* Drift-seine (for tunny-fishing).

*courantin [kurɑ̃′tɛ̃], *n.m.* (*fem.* **-ine**) Gadabout; errand boy (or girl); line rocket.

courbage [kur′baːʒ], *n.m.* Bending, curving.

courbaril [kurba′ri], *n.m.* Locust-tree. *Bois de courbaril*, locust-wood.

courbatu [kurba′ty], *a.* (*fem.* **-ue**) Foundered (of horses); knocked up; stiff in the joints; (*Med.*) affected with lumbago. *Je me sens tout courbatu*, I feel stiff and bruised all over. **courbature,** *n.f.* Floundering, lameness; (*Path.*) stiffness in the back and limbs, lumbago. **courbaturer,** *v.t.* To knock up; to make (someone) feel stiff all over.

courbe [kurb], *a.* Curved, bent, crooked.—*n.f.* Curve; (*Naut.* and *Carp.*) knee; (*Vet.*) curb; (*Math.*) graph, graphic curve.

courber [kur′be], *v.t.* To curve, to bend, to warp, to make crooked; to cause to sag, to weigh down. *Courbé de vieillesse*, bent with age; *se tenir courbé*, to stoop.—*v.i.* To bend, to sag, to give way. **se courber,** *v.r.* To bend, to stoop; to bow down; (*fig.*) to humble oneself.

courbet [kur′bɛ], *n.m.* Bill-hook.

courbette [kur′bɛt], *n.f.* Curvet; (*pl.*) bowing and scraping, cringing. *Faire des courbettes*, to bow and scrape, to cringe. **courbetter,** *v.i.* To curvet.

courbure [kur′byːr], *n.f.* Curvature, curve; bend; sagging.

courcailler [kurka′je], *v.i.* To cry like a quail. **courcaillet,** *n.m.* Cry of the quail; quail-pipe.

courçon [COURSON].

coureau [ku′ro], *n.m.* (*pl.* **-eaux**) Strait, channel between rocks, shoals, etc.; yawl.

courette [ku′rɛt], *n.f.* Small yard.

coureur [ku′rœːr], *a.* (*fem.* **-euse**) Good at running, swift.—*n.* Runner, racer; courser, hunter (horse); light porter; running footman, groom; gadder, rover, stroller; rake, libertine; (*Mil.*) skirmisher; scout. *Coureur de dot*, fortune-hunter. *Coureur automobile*, racing driver; *coureur cycliste*, cycling racer; *coureur de vitesse*, sprinter; *coureur de fond*, stayer; *coureur des bois*, trapper.—*n.f.* Streetwalker.

courge [kurʒ], *n.f.* Gourd. *Courge à la moelle,* vegetable marrow, marrow squash.

courgette [kurʒet], *n.f.* Marrow squash.

courir [kuˈriːr], *v.i. irr.* (*pres.p.* **courant,** *p.p.* **couru**) To run; to be in a race; to go quickly, to hasten; to ramble, to gad about, to rove, to run up and down; to flow, to glide; to run on, to pass, to slip away (of time etc.); to extend, to stretch; to be prevalent, to be current, to circulate; (*Naut.*) to sail. *Au temps* or *par le temps qui court,* these days, nowadays; *courir à bride abattue,* to ride full gallop; *courir à l'autre bord,* (*Naut.*) to stand upon the other tack; *courir des bordées,* to tack; *courir après,* to run after; *courir à sa fin,* to draw to an end; *courir à sa perte,* to hasten to one's ruin; *courir au feu,* to run where the fire is; *courir au large,* to stand off; *courir au plus presse,* to do that which is most urgent; *courir aux armes,* to fly to arms; *courir çà et là,* to run about or up and down, (*fig.*) to gad about; *en courant,* in a hurry; *faire courir,* to keep a racing stable; *faire courir des bruits,* to spread reports; *faire courir toute la ville,* to draw the whole of the town; *il me court* (*sur l'haricot*), (*slang*) he bores me, he pesters me; *j'y cours,* I'll go there at once; *la mode qui court,* the prevailing fashion; *l'année qui court,* the present year; *le bruit court qu'il est mort,* there is a report that he is dead.—*v.t.* To run after, to pursue; to traverse, to travel over; to hunt; to frequent; to infest; to expose oneself to, to run (a risk etc.). *Courir la poste,* to do a thing precipitately; *courir la prétentaine, to* gad about; *courir le même lièvre,* to be engaged in the same pursuit; *courir le monde,* to travel; *courir le pays,* to rove, to stroll about; *courir le plat pays* or *la mer,* to be a pirate; *courir les bals* or *les théâtres,* to frequent balls or theatres; *courir les rues,* to run about the streets; *courir même fortune,* to be in the same boat.

courlis [kurˈli] or **courlieu,** *n.m.* Curlew. *Petit courlis,* whimbrel.

couroir [kuˈrwaːr], *n.m.* (*Naut.*) Narrow passage (between cabins).

couronne [kuˈrɔn], *n.f.* Crown, diadem; coronet; wreath; crown (a coin); (*Vet.*) cornet; (*Fort.*) crown work; (of paper) large foolscap. *C'est le plus beau fleuron de sa couronne,* it is the brightest jewel in his crown; *couronne civique,* civic crown; *couronne d'épines,* crown of thorns; *couronne d'une dent,* crown of a tooth; *couronne impériale,* crown imperial (flower); *décerner une couronne,* to award a garland; *discours de la couronne,* speech from the throne; *domaine de la couronne,* Crown lands; *la couronne du martyre,* the crown of martyrdom; *ni fleurs ni couronnes,* no flowers by request; *papier couronne,* large foolscap, crown; *traiter de couronne à couronne,* to treat as from sovereign to sovereign. **couronné,** *a.* (*fem.* **-ée**) Crowned, capped (*avec*); encompassed; rewarded; (*Vet.*) broken-kneed. *Arbre couronné,* tree the top of which is withering; *cheval couronné,* broken-kneed horse.—*n.m.* (*Fort.*) An advanced earthwork thrown out in front of and covering the main line. **couronnement,** *n.m.* Crowning, coronation; completion, consummation;

(*Arch.*) crowning, top, coping (of walls); top-piece, cap (of blocks etc.); (*Naut.*) taffrail of a ship; (*Bot.*) disease causing trees to wither at the top.

couronner [kuroˈne], *v.t.* To crown; to crown monarch; to award a prize etc. to; to honour, to reward (*avec*); to consummate; to wreathe; (*Arch.*) to cap. *Couronner de fleurs,* to crown with flowers. **se couronner,** *v.r.* To begin to wither at the top (of trees); to break a knee (of a horse).

couronnure, *n.f.* Crown (on a stag's head).

courre [kuːr], *v.t.* *(Hunt.)* To run. Only used in *chasse à courre,* hunting, and *laisser courre,* to slip the hounds.

courrier [kuˈrje], *n.m.* Messenger, courier, post-boy; mail, mail-coach, mail-steamer, mail-ship; post; letters, correspondence. *Faire son courrier,* to write one's letters; *jour de courrier,* post-day; *l'heure du courrier,* post-time; *lire* or *dépouiller son courrier,* to read one's letters; *par le courrier de ce jour,* by today's post; *par retour du courrier,* by return (of) post; (*navire*) long-courrier, liner carrying mail.

courriériste [kurieˈrist], *n.m.* Specialized feature writer, columnist.

courroie [kuˈrwa], *n.f.* Strap, thong; driving belt or band. *Courroie de transmission,* driving belt; *lâcher la courroie,* to give in.

courroucer [kuruˈse], *v.t.* To provoke to anger, to incense, to irritate. *Flots courroucés* (*poet.*), angry waves. **se courroucer,** *v.r.* To become angry, to rage.

courroux [kuˈru], *n.m.* Wrath, anger, rage. *Être en courroux,* to be angry.

courroyer etc. [CORROYER].

cours [kuːr], *n.m.* Course, stream, current, flow; movement to and fro (of a piston etc.); lapse, flight, passage; path, track, orbit; length, extent (of a river etc.); career, play, vent, scope; public drive, walk, or promenade; vogue, circulation, currency; credit; series of lectures etc.; treatise; (*pl.*) studies, lessons, classes; (*St. Exch.*) market price, rate; (*Naut.*) voyage, expedition. *Avoir cours* (of coins), to be in circulation; *cours d'eau,* stream, watercourse, canal; *donner cours à,* to give currency to; *donner libre cours à sa fureur,* to give full vent to one's anger; *suivre les cours de droit,* to read law; *faire un cours de,* to give a course of lectures on, to teach, to give lessons in; *la maladie suit son cours,* the disease is taking its course; *le cours du change,* the rate of exchange; *le cours du marché,* the market price; *affaires en cours,* outstanding business; *le cours du soleil est d'orient en occident,* the course of the sun is from east to west; *salle de cours,* lecture-room; *suivre un cours,* to attend a course of lectures; *les cours du soir,* evening classes; *voyage au long cours,* ocean voyage; *capitaine au long cours,* master mariner.

course [kurs], *n.f.* Running, run; course; drive, ride, journey, walk, excursion, trip; career; race; match; raid, incursion; privateering; cruise or expedition; coursing; length of the stroke, travel (of a piece of machinery). *Aller aux courses,* to go to the races; *course au clocher,* point-to-point race; *course d'obstacles,* steeplechase; *course de chars,* chariot-race; *course de chevaux,* horse-race; *course de haies,* hurdle-race; *course à pied,* foot-race; *course d'automobiles,* car race; *faire des courses,* to go on errands, to go shopping; *faire une course à cheval,* to take a ride; *faire une course à pied,* to walk out on foot; *faire une longue course,* to go a long walk, ride, etc.; *garçon de course,* errand boy; *la guerre de course,* privateering; *le monde des courses,* the Turf; *surpasser à la course,* to outrun; *vaisseau armé en course,* ship armed for cruising, privateer; *vélo de course,* racing bicycle; *être en course,* to be out (on business).

coursier [kur′sje], *n.m.* Charger; (*poet.*) steed, courser; (*Naut.*) bow-gun, bow-chaser; mill-race; office messenger.

coursive [kur′siːv], *n.f.* (*Naut.*) Gangway, passage running lengthwise of a vessel, or a dirigible.

courson [kur′sɔ̃], *n.m.* (*Agric.*) Shoot cut down to three or four eyes; branch or shoot left; stake.

court [kuːr], *a.* (*fem.* **courte**) Short; brief; concise, curt, succinct; limited, deficient, scanty; transient, fleeting. *Avoir la vue courte,* to be near-sighted; (*Cine.*) *court métrage,* short film; *prendre le plus court,* to take the shortest way.—*adv.* Short, abruptly. *Couper court à quelqu'un,* to cut someone short; *demeurer court,* to stop short, to forget what one would say; *être à court d'argent,* to be short of money; *s'arrêter tout court,* to stop short; *tenir quelqu'un de court,* to keep someone on a very short leash, in leading-strings; *vous me prenez de court,* you give me short notice; *tourner court,* to turn short; *tout court,* only that, nothing more.

court [kɔrt, kur], *n.m.* Tennis court.

courtage [kur′taːʒ], *n.m.* Business of a broker; brokerage, commission. *Courtage de change,* bill-brokerage; *faire le courtage,* to carry on the business of a broker.

courtaud [kur′to], *a.* (*fem.* **-aude**) Thick-set, dumpy; docked, crop-eared (dogs, horses). *Étriller quelqu'un comme un chien courtaud,* to give someone a good licking.—*n.m.* Short, thick-set person; docked or crop-eared horse.

courtauder, *v.t.* To dock, to crop (horses etc.).

court-bouillon [kurbu′jɔ̃], *n.m.* (*pl.* **courts-bouillons**) A wine sauce to boil fish in. *Court-bouillon de saumon,* dish of salmon prepared in this.

court-circuit [kursir′kɥi], *n.m.* (*pl.* **courts-circuits**) Short-circuit. **court-circuiter**, *v.t.* To short-circuit.

courtement [kurtə′mɑ̃], *adv.* Shortly, briefly.

courtepointe [kurtə′pwɛ̃t], *n.f.* Counterpane, quilt.

courtequeue [kurtə′kø], *a.* Docked (horse or dog).—*n.f.* Short-stemmed cherry.

courtier [kur′tje], *n.m.* (*fem.* **courtière**) Broker, agent. *Courtier d'assurances* or *d'actions,* insurance- or share-broker; *courtier de change,* bill-broker, money-broker; *courtier de mariage,* matrimonial agent; *courtier électoral,* electioneering agent, canvasser; *courtier en librairie,* book canvasser; *courtier maritime,* ship-broker.

courtil [kur′til], *n.m.* *Small garden (adjoining a peasant's cottage); garth.

courtilière [kurti′ljɛːr], *n.f.* Mole-cricket.

courtine [kur′tin], *n.f.* *Curtain; (*Fort.*)

fortified curtain; (*Arch.*) façade flanked by pavilions.

courtisan [kurti′zɑ̃], *n.m.* Courtier; flatterer, fawner. **courtisane**, *n.f.* Courtesan. **courtisanerie**, *n.f.* Court flattery, toadyism; behaviour of or worthy of a courtesan. **courtisanesque**, *a.* Courtier-like.

courtiser [kurti′ze], *v.t.* To court, to pay court to, to make love to; to woo; to flatter.

court-jointé [kurʒwɛ̃′te], *a.* (*fem.* **court-jointée**, *pl.* **court-jointés**) Short-legged (hawk); short-pasterned (horse).

court-monté [kurmɔ̃′te], *a.* (*fem.* **court-montée**, *pl.* **court-montés**) Low-backed (of horses).

courtois [kur′twa], *a.* (*fem.* **-oise**) Courteous, polite, well bred. *Armes courtoises,* blunted weapons. **courtoisement**, *adv.* In a courteous manner, courteously. **courtoisie**, *n.f.* Courtesy, politeness, civility; kindness, good turn.

couru [ku′ry], *a.* (*fem.* **-ue**) Sought after, pursued, frequented; (*fig.*) in demand, popular; certain. *C'est couru,* it is a settled job, a certainty.

couscous [kus′kus], *n.m.* Couscous (Arab dish made of semolina).

cousette [ku′zɛt], *n.f.* (*fam.*) Apprentice or assistant of a dressmaker.

couseur [ku′zœːr], *n.m.* (*fem.* **couseuse**) Sewer, stitcher (of books).

cousin (1) [ku′zɛ̃], *n.m.* (*fem.* **cousine**) Cousin; (*fig.*) friend, crony. *Cousin au troisième degré,* third cousin; *cousin germain,* first cousin, cousin-german; *le roi n'est pas son cousin,* he is very proud; *nous sommes cousins à la mode de Bretagne,* we are distantly connected.

cousin (2) [ku′zɛ̃], *n.m.* Midge (a big mosquito).

cousinage [kuzi′naːʒ], *n.m.* Cousinhood; cousins; relationship, kindred. **cousiner**, *v.t.* To call cousin; to live or act familiarly with; to be related to; to hob-nob.—*v.i.* To sponge, to live on others; to be friends or cronies; to go (well or ill) together. **cousinière**, *n.f.* (*colloq.*) Swarm of cousins or relations.

cousoir [ku′zwaːr], *n.m.* Sewing-press.

coussin [ku′sɛ̃], *n.m.* Cushion, hassock; pad; pillow; (*Surg.*) bolster. *Coussin de mire,* bed of a cannon. **coussiner**, *v.t.* To pad, to cushion. **coussinet**, *n.m.* Small cushion, pad; iron wedge; pillion; (*Surg.*) bolster; (*Arch.*) cushion; (*Rail.*) chair; (*Mach.*) bearing, bush; (*fam.*) whortleberry, cranberry.

cousu [ku′zy], *a.* (*fem.* **-ue**) Sewed, stitched. *Cousu (à la) main,* hand-sewn; (*fig.*) *c'est du cousu main,* it is first class; *cousu à la machine,* machine stitched; *bouche cousue,* mum's the word; *être tout cousu d'argent,* to be rolling in money; *ses finesses sont cousues de fil blanc,* his tricks are very obvious.

coût [ku¹, *n.m.* Costs, charge. *Le coût de la vie,* the cost of living. **coûtant,** *a.m.* Costing. *Prix coûtant,* prime cost. *À prix coûtant,* at cost price.

couteau [ku′to], *n.m.* (*pl.* **-eaux**) Knife; *short sword, hanger, dagger. *Aiguiser ses couteaux,* to prepare for the engagement; *couteau à cran d'arrêt,* clasp-knife with lockback; *couteau à découper,* carving-knife, (*Am.*)

butcher knife; *couteau à ressort*, spring-knife; *couteau pliant* or *couteau de poche*, clasp-knife; *couteau poignard*, dagger-knife; *donner un coup de couteau à quelqu'un*, to stab someone with a knife; *ils sont à couteaux tirés*, they are at daggers drawn; *le couteau sous la gorge*, under threat; *planche à couteaux*, knife-board; *poudre à (nettoyer les) couteaux*, knife-polish; *brouillard à couper au couteau*, pea-soup fog; *figure en lame de couteau*, hatchet face.

coutelas [kut'lɑ], *n.m.* Cutlass; large kitchen-knife; sword-fish.

coutelier [kutə'lje], *n.m.* Cutler. **coutelière,** *n.f.* Knife-case; cutler's wife. **coutellerie,** *n.f.* Cutler's shop or business; cutlery, cutler's ware.

coûter [ku'te], *v.i.* To cost (*cher etc.*); to be expensive; (*fig.*) to be painful, troublesome, mortifying, etc. *Rien ne lui coûte*, he spares no trouble, he sticks at nothing; *tout lui coûte*, everything is an effort to him.—*v.t.* To cost, to cause, to occasion. *Cela lui coûta la vie*, that cost him his (or her) life; *coûte que coûte*, come what may, cost what it will; *il lui en coûte beaucoup de dire cela*, it is very painful to him to say that; *l'argent ne lui coûte rien*, he knows not the value of money; *que coûte-t-il de souhaiter?* what harm is there in wishing? **coûteusement,** *adv.* Expensively. **coûteux,** *a.* (*fem.* **-euse**) Expensive, costly.

coutil [ku'ti], *n.m.* Tick, ticking; (*Tex.*) drill, duck. *Fil de coutil*, drill.

coutissé [kuti'se], *a.* (*fem.* **-ée**) Covered with ticking.

couton [ku'tɔ̃], *n.f.* Pin-feathers (in poultry).

cou-tors [ku'tɔːr], *n.m. inv.* Wry-neck (bird).

coutre [kutr], *n.m.* Plough-share, coulter, axe. **coutrier,** *n.m.* Subsoil-plough.

coutume [ku'tym], *n.f.* Custom, habit, practice, wont, usage. *Avoir coutume de*, to be accustomed to; *comme de coutume*, as usual; *une fois n'est pas coutume*, it is only once in a way. **coutumier,** *a.* (*fem.* **-ière**) Customary, common, ordinary; accustomed, wonted, habitual; (*Feud.*) common. *Droit coutumier*, unwritten law sanctioned by usage; *être coutumier du fait*, to be in the habit of doing something; *pays coutumier*, country governed by common law.—*n.m.* Customary (book of common law). **coutumièrement,** *adv.* Customarily, habitually; according to custom.

couture [ku'tyːr], *n.f.* Sewing, needlework; seamstress's work, business, or wares; seam, suture; cicatrice, scar. *Couture ouverte*, (*Naut.*) open seam; *couture rabattue*, flat seam; (*fig.*) *examiner sous toutes les coutures*, to examine thoroughly; *ils ont été battus à plate couture*, they were beaten hollow. **couturer,** *v.t.* To seam. *Il a le visage couturé*, his face is seamed or scarred. **couturier,** *n.m.* Ladies' tailor; (*Anat.*) sartorius.—*a.* Sartorial. **couturière,** *n.f.* Dressmaker, seamstress, needle-woman; (*pop.*) warbler.

couvage [COUVAISON].

couvain [ku'vɛ̃], *n.m.* Eggs of bees, breeding-cells etc.; honeycomb containing eggs or larvae. **couvaison,** *n.f.* Brooding-time, sitting, incubation.

couvée [ku've], *n.f.* Sitting of eggs; brood, covey; (*fig.*) generation, progeny.

couvent [ku'vɑ̃], *n.m.* Convent, monastery, nunnery; convent school. **couventine,** *n.f.* Nun; convent schoolgirl.

couver [ku've], *v.t.* To sit on, to incubate, to hatch; to brood, to prepare in secret (a plot etc.); to brood over. *Couver de mauvais desseins*, to brew evil designs; *couver quelqu'un des yeux*, to look tenderly at someone, to devour with one's eyes, to gloat over; *couver une maladie*, to be sickening for an illness.—*v.i.* To lie hidden, to lurk; to smoulder.

couvercle [ku'vɛrkl], *n.m.* Cover, lid, cap, shutter. *Il n'y a si méchant pot qui n'ait son couvercle*, no girl is so ugly as not to find a mate.

couvert (1) [ku'vɛːr], *n.m.* Dinner things, breakfast things, cover (plate, spoon, knife, fork); shelter, lodging; cover, wrapper, envelope; covert, shady place, thicket; (*fig.*) pretext, responsibility. *Donner le couvert à quelqu'un*, to shelter someone; *le vivre et le couvert*, board and lodging; *mettre le couvert*, to lay the cloth, to set the table; *ôter le couvert*, to remove the cloth, to clear the table; *table de dix couverts*, table laid for ten; *un couvert de plus*, another place set (at table); *sous le couvert de l'amitié*, under the cloak of friendship. *À couvert*, under cover, sheltered, secure; *être à couvert* (*Fin.*), to have good security; *vendre à couvert* (*St. Exch.*), to sell for delivery.

couvert (2) [ku'vɛːr], *a.* (*fem.* **couverte** (1)) Covered; clad, clothed; having a hat etc. on; loaded (with fruit etc.); cloudy, overcast (of the weather); (*fig.*) hidden, secret, close, concealed; obscure, ambiguous (of words); (*Fort.*) protected (of a battery etc.). *À mots couverts*, in innuendoes; *chemin couvert*, (*Fort.*) covert-way; *couvert de plaies*, covered with sores; *il est toujours bien couvert*, he is always well clothed; *lieu couvert*, shady place; *pays couvert*, woody country; *restez couvert*, keep your hat on; *temps couvert*, cloudy weather. **couverte** (2), *n.f.* Glaze, glazing, enamel (on porcelain); (*Mil. slang*) blanket.

couverture [kuvɛr'tyːr], *n.f.* Covering, cover, wrapper; coverlet, counterpane, quilt, bed-clothes; cover (of a book); removable wrapper for this; roofing; (*fig.*) cloak, blind, pretext; (*Comm.*) guaranty, security. *Couverture chauffante*, electrically heated blanket; *couverture de cheval*, horse-cloth; *couverture de laine*, blanket; *couverture de selle*, saddle-cloth; *couverture de voyage*, travelling-rug; *couverture piquée*, quilt; *lettre de couverture*, covering letter; *sous couverture de*, under the pretext of; *tirer la couverture à soi*, (*colloq.*) to take more than one's share; *troupes de couverture*, covering troops.

couvet [ku'vɛ], *n.m.* Earthenware or copper foot-warmer.

couveuse [ku'vøːz], *n.f.* Broody hen. *Couveuse artificielle*, incubator.

couvi [ku'vi], *a.m.* Addled, rotten (egg).

couvoir [ku'vwaːr], *n.m.* Incubator.

[In the following compounds *couvre* is inv.]

couvre-bouche [kuvrə'buʃ], *n.m.* Leather or canvas covering for mouth of cannon. **couvre-chef,** *n.m.* Headgear, head-dress.

couvre-feu, *n.m.* (*pl. unchanged*) Curfew; curfew-bell; fire-cover, fire-plate. **couvre-lit**, *n.m.* Light bed-cover, coverlet. **couvre-lumière**, *n.m.* Apron (for covering the breech of a cannon). **couvre-nuque**, *n.m.* Part of helmet covering the neck; havelock. **couvre-pied** or **couvre-pieds**, *n.m.* (*pl.* **couvre-pieds**) Foot-coverlet; embroidered quilt, counterpane. **couvre-plat**, *n.m.* Dish-cover. **couvre-théière**, *n.m.* Tea-cosy.

couvreur [kuˈvrœːr], *n.m.* Roofer. *Couvreur en ardoise*, slater; *couvreur en chaume*, thatcher; *convreur en tuiles*, tiler.

couvrir [kuˈvriːr], *v.t. irr.* (*pres.p.* **couvrant**, *p.p.* **couvert**) To cover; to envelop, to wrap up; to spread, to cover (with); to overlay, to overspread; to roof, to tile, to thatch; to heap, to load, to overwhelm; to dress, to clothe; to defend, to shelter, to screen, to protect; to overspread, to overrun, to over-flow; to excuse, to palliate; to compensate, to make up for, to counterbalance, to obliterate; to cloak, to keep secret, to dis-guise; to defray (expenses etc.); (of animals) to couple with, to serve; (*Cards etc.*) to stake upon. *Couvrir de honte*, to cover with shame; *couvrir sa faute*, to palliate one's fault; *couvrir un toit*, to roof; *un bon général doit savoir couvrir sa marche*, a good general should know how to conceal his march. **se couvrir**, *v.r.* To cover oneself, to put on (one's hat), to be covered; to muffle oneself; to defend oneself; to conceal oneself; to get under cover; to be overcast (of the weather); (*Comm.*) to reimburse oneself. *Couvrez-vous*, put your hat on; *le temps se couvre*, the weather is becoming overcast.

covenant [kɔvˈnã], *n.m.* Covenant. **covenantaire**, *n.m.* Covenanter.

covendeur [kovãˈdœːr], *n.m.* Joint-vendor.

cow-boy [koˈbɔi], *n.m.* Cow-boy.

coxal [kɔkˈsal], *a.* (*fem.* **-ale**, *pl.* **-aux**) (*Anat.*) Of the hip, coxal, iliac. **coxalgie**, *n.f.* Coxitis.

coyau [kwaˈjo, kɔˈjo], *n.m.* (*Build.*) Furrings.

coyer [kwaˈje], *n.m.* = COFFIN.

coyote [kɔˈjɔt], *n.m.* Prairie wolf.

crabe [krɑːb], *n.m.* Crab. **crabier**, *n.m.* Crab-eater (bird).

crac [krak], *int.* Cracking noise, crack, pop! *Crac! le voilà parti*, he was off like a shot.

crachat [kraˈʃa], *n.m.* Spittle, expectoration; (*pop.*) star, grand cross. *Maison faite de boue et de crachat*, jerry-built house.

crachement [kraʃˈmã], *n.m.* Spitting.

cracher [kraˈʃe], *v.t.* To spit; (*fig.*) to spit out, to utter explosively, to come out with; (*slang*) to come down with, to fork out (money).—*v.i.* To spit, to splutter (of speech, pens, etc.); to splash; (*Naut.*) to give at the joints; (*Mach. etc.*) to spark, to backfire. (*slang*) *Cracher au bassinet*, to contribute; *cracher au nez* or *au visage de quelqu'un*, to spit in someone's face; *cracher en l'air*, to be hoist with one's own petard; *c'est son père tout craché*, he is the very image *or* the very spit of his father. **cracheur**, *n.m.* (*fem.* **-euse**) Spitter. **crachoir**, *n.m.* Spittoon. *Tenir le crachoir*, to hold the floor.

crachin [kraˈʃɛ̃], *n.m.* (*dial.*) Drizzle. **crachiner**, *v.i.* To mizzle.

crachotement [kraʃotˈmã], *n.m.,* or **crachoterie**, *n.f.* Continual spitting. **crachoter**, *v.i.* To spit often.

Cracovie [krakɔˈvi], *f.* Cracow.

crafe [kraf], *n.f.* Bed of stone in slate-quarry.

crag [krag], *n.m.* (*Geol.*) Crag (shelly sand formation).

craie [krɛ], *n.f.* Chalk. *Marquer avec de la craie*, to chalk.

craignant etc. [CRAINDRE].

craillement [krajˈmã], *n.m.* Cawing (of crows). **crailler**, *v.i.* To caw.

craindre [krɛ̃ːdr], *v.t. irr.* (*pres.p.* **craignant**, *p.p.* **craint**) To fear; to be afraid of, to dread, to stand in awe; to hesitate; to dis-like, to be unable to bear. *À craindre*, to be feared; dangerous; to be avoided; *ces arbres craignent le froid*, these trees cannot stand the cold; *il craint d'être découvert*, he is afraid of being discovered; *il craint que sa femme ne meure*; he fears his wife will die; *je ne crains pas de le dire*, I do not hesitate to say so; *se faire craindre de quelqu'un*, to make oneself respected by someone.

crainte [krɛ̃ːt], *n.f.* Fear, apprehension; dread, awe. *Avec crainte*, fearfully, in terror, in dread; *crainte de* or *de crainte de*, for fear of; *de crainte d'être surpris*, for fear of being surprised; *de crainte que*, for fear that or lest; *de crainte qu'il ne le fasse*, lest he should do it; *retenir quelqu'un par la crainte*, to keep someone in awe; *sans crainte*, fearlessly. **craintif**, *a.* (*fem.* **-ive**) Fearful, apprehensive, timid, timorous, cowardly. **craintivement**, *adv.* Fearfully, timorously.

crambe [krɑːb], or **crambé** [krɑ̃ˈbe], *n.m.* Sea-kale.

craminer [kramiˈne], *v.t.* To stretch and soften (hides) before tanning.

cramoisi [kramwaˈzi], *a.* and *n.m.* (*fem.* **-ie**) Crimson. *Devenir cramoisi*, to flush.

crampe [krɑ̃ːp], *n.f.* Cramp; cramp-iron, crampon. *Crampe d'estomac*, gnawing pain in the stomach; *crampe du tennis*, tennis elbow.

crampon [krɑ̃ˈpɔ̃], *n.m.* Crampon, cramp-iron, grappling-iron; calkin, foot-nail (of horse-shoe); spur, fulcrum (of root); (*fam.*) button holer, burr. *Crampon de fer à cheval*, frost-nail (of a horse-shoe). **cramponné**, *a.* (*fem.* **cramponnée**) (*Her.*) Having half a potence at both ends, cram-ponee; (*Farriery*) with calkins. **cramponner**, *v.t.* To cramp, to fasten with a cramp-iron; to rough-shoe (a horse); (*fam.*) to freeze on to, to stick to importunately. *Cramponner un cheval*, to shoe a horse with frost-nails or calkins. **se cramponner**, *v.r.* To hold fast, to fasten on to something, to cling like grim death to. **cramponnet**, *n.m.* Small cramp, tack; loop, staple of a lock). *Cramponnet de targette*, lock staple.

cran (1) [krɑ̃], *n.m.* Notch; cog; catch, tooth; ridge (of waved hair); (*Print.*) nick; (*colloq.*) pluck. (*Rifle*) *Cran de sûreté*, safety catch; *au cran de sûreté*, at half cock; *au cran d'armé*, at full cock; *baisser* or *monter d'un cran*, to lower *or* raise a peg; *descendre d'un cran*, to come down a peg; (*fam.*) *être à cran*, to be very touchy; *avoir du cran*, to have plenty of pluck, of mettle; *serrer sa ceinture d'un cran*, to tighten one's belt a hole; *huit crans*, eight days in guard-room (or C.B.).

cran (2) [krɑ̃], *n.m.* Horse-radish.
cranage (1) [kra'na:ʒ], *n.m.* Notching, indenting.
cranage (2) [CARÉNAGE].
crâne [krɑ:n], *n.m.* Skull, cranium.—*a.* Bold, plucky. **crânement,** *adv.* Pluckily; in style, famously.
craner [kra'ne], *v.t.* To notch, to indent (a clock wheel).
crâner [krɑ'ne], *v.i.* To swagger, to bluster. **crânerie,** *n.f.* Daring, pluck; swaggering, blustering, swank. **crâneur,** *n.m.* (*fem.* **-euse**) Braggart, swanker.
crangon [krɑ̃'gɔ̃], *n.m.* Shrimp.
crânien [krɑ'njɛ̃], *a.* (*fem.* **-ienne**) (*Anat.*) Cranial. *La boîte crânienne,* the brain-pan.
craniologie etc. [CRANOLOGIE].
craniomètre [krɑnjɔ'mɛtr], *n.m.* Craniometer. **craniométrie,** *n.f.* Craniometry. **craniométrique,** *a.* Craniometrical. **craniotomie,** *n.f.* Craniotomy.
cranologie [krɑnɔlɔ'ʒi] or **craniologie,** *n.f.* Craniology. **cranologique** or **craniologique,** *a.* Craniological. **cranologiste, craniologiste,** or **craniologue,** *n.m.* Craniologist.
cranter [krɑ̃'te], *v.t.* To notch.
crapaud [kra'po], *n.m.* Toad; toad-fish; jumping cracker; flaw in a diamond; infection of a horse's hoof; (*fig.*) ugly person, urchin, brat. *Avaler un crapaud,* to do something repugnant, to swallow an insult; *c'est un vilain crapaud,* he is a hideous fellow; *crapaud de gouvernail,* (*Naut.*) goose-neck; *crapaud de mer,* toad-fish; *crapaud pêcheur,* fishing-frog; *crapaud volant,* goatsucker (bird); *fauteuil crapaud,* low easy chair; *la bave d'un crapaud,* toad-spittle; *laid comme un crapaud,* hideous; *piano crapaud,* baby grand piano. **crapaudière,** *n.f.* Nest of toads; (*fig.*) low, swampy place. **crapaudine,** *n.f.* A toadstone; grating of an escape-pipe; infection of a horse's hoof; wort; socket in which a pivot moves. *À la crapaudine,* cut open and broiled, spatchcocked (of chicken, pigeons, etc.).
crapouillot [krapu'jo], *n.m.* Trench-mortar.
crapule [kra'pyl], *n.f.* Low vulgar debauchery, gluttony, drunkenness; low or debauched people, blackguards. ***crapuler,** *v.i.* To live in vice, to give oneself to low debauchery. **crapuleusement,** *adv.* Dissolutely. **crapuleux,** *a.* (*fem.* **crapuleuse**) Low, debauched, vicious, dissolute. **crapulerie,** *n.f.* (*pop.*) A foul trick.
craquant [kra'kɑ̃], *a.* (*fem.* **-ante**) Cracking, crackling (bread etc.).
craque [krak], *n.f.* Fib, humbug.
craquelage [kra'kla:ʒ], *n.m.* Crackling (china). **craquelé,** *a.* (*fem.* **-ée**) Crackled (of china). **craqueler,** *v.t.* To crackle (china).
craquelin [kra'klɛ̃], *n.m.* Cracknel (biscuit); crackler (crab).
craquelot [kra'klo], *n.m.* Bloater.
craquelure [kra'kly:r], *n.f.* Crack in the enamel etc. (of china).
craquement [krak'mɑ̃], *n.m.* Crack, cracking noise, creaking, snapping (of trees, boughs, etc.).
craquer [kra'ke], *v.i.* To crack, to crackle, to snap, to creak, to crunch; (*fig.*) (*of a scheme etc.*) to be upset or thrown into disorder. *Faire craquer ses doigts,* to make one's

finger-joints crack. **craquerie,** *n.f.* (*fam.*) Boasting, drawing the long bow; story, fib.
craquètement, *n.m.* Crackling; chattering (of the teeth); gabbing (of the stork and other birds). **craqueter,** *v.i.* To crackle, to crepitate; to gabble (of some birds).
craqueur [kra'kœ:r], *n.m.* (*fem.* **-euse**) (*fam.*) Lying, boasting person, bouncer, braggart.
crase [krɑ:z], *n.f.* Crasis.
crassane [kra'san], *n.f.* Bergamot (pear).
crasse (1) [kras], *a.* Gross, thick, coarse, crass. *Une ignorance crasse,* gross or crass ignorance.
crasse (2) [kras], *n.f.* Dirt, filth, squalor; stinginess; dross, slag; (*fam.*) dirty trick. *Crasse de la tête,* dandruff; *la crasse des métaux,* the dross or scale (of metals).
crassement, *n.m.* Fouling (of fire-arms).
crasser, *v.t.* To foul, to dirty (fire-arms etc.). **se crasser,** *v.r.* To become foul (of fire-arms etc.). **crasseux,** *a.* (*fem.* **-euse**) Dirty, filthy, nasty, squalid; sordid, stingy, mean. *Cheveux crasseux,* greasy hair.—*n.* Sloven, slut; niggard, miser, skinflint. *Un crasseux,* a filthy fellow. **crassier,** *n.m.* Slag heap; rubbish dump.
crassule [kra'syl], *n.f.* (*Bot.*) Crassula, houseleek.
cratère [kra'tɛ:r], *n.m.* Crater (mouth of volcano); (Greek or Roman) bowl or cup.
cratériforme, *a.* Crateriform.
cravache [kra'vaʃ], *n.f.* Riding-whip. **cravachée,** *n.f.* Blow or lashing with this.
cravacher, *v.t.* To horsewhip (a person).
cravan [kra'vɑ̃], *n.m.* Barnacle; brent-goose.
*cravate (1) [kra'vat], *n.m.* Croatian horse; light horseman.—*a.* *Cheval cravate,* Croatian horse.
cravate (2) [kra'vat], *n.f.* Cravat, (neck-)tie; (*Wrestling*) an illegitimate form of grip; ruff (of birds); (*Naut.*) thick cable. *Cravate de chanvre* (*fig.*), noose (for hanging a man); *cravate d'un drapeau,* knot or tassel of a flagstaff. **cravater,** *v.t.* To put a cravat or neck-tie on; to go round the neck, to fit. **se cravater,** *v.r.* To put on one's (neck-)tie. **cravatier,** *n.m.* Maker or vendor of neckties.
crave [kra:v], *n.m.* Chough (small crow with scarlet bill and legs).
crawl [krol], *n.m.* Crawl. **crawleur,** *n.m.* Crawl-swimmer.
crayer [krɛ'je], *v.t.* (*conjugated like* BALAYER) To chalk, to mark up etc. with chalk.
crayère, *n.f.* Chalk-pit. **crayeux,** *a.* (*fem.* **-euse**) Chalky.
crayon [krɛ'jɔ̃], *n.m.* Pencil; drawing or portrait in crayon; (*fig.*) manner of drawing, style; sketch, rough draft, outline; marl. *Au crayon,* in pencil; *crayon à bille,* ball-point pen; *crayon de couleur,* coloured pencil; *crayon noir,* blacklead pencil; *dessin aux trois crayons,* drawing or sketch in charcoal, red and white chalks. **crayonnage,** *n.m.* Pencildrawing. **crayonner,** *v.t.* To draw with a pencil; to mark or draw or write upon with a pencil; (*fig.*) to sketch, to trace the outline of, to describe, to delineate. **crayonneur,** *n.m.* (*fem.* **-euse**) (*fam.*) Poor artist. **crayonneux,** *a.* (*fem.* **-euse**) Chalky, cretaceous; like chalk.
créance [kre'ɑ̃:s], *n.f.* Credence, trust, belief;

credit, confidence; money owing; right to a debt, title; (*Hunt.*) command. *Donner créance à une chose*, to give credit to a thing; *lettre de créance*, letter of credit, credentials; *les créances et les dettes de la maison*, due to and by the firm. **créancier**, *n.m.* (*fem.* **créancière**) Creditor. *Créancier hypothécaire*, mortgagee; *créancier importun*, dun.

créateur [krea'tœːr], *n.m.* (*fem.* **-trice**) Creator, maker, author.—*a.* Creative, inventive. *Il a le génie créateur*, he has an inventive genius.

créatine [krea'tin], *n.f.* (*Chem.*) Creatine.

création [krea'sjɔ̃], *n.f.* Creation; the universe, all created things; foundation, establishment. *Une création de chez Dior*, a Dior design.

créature [krea'tyːr], *n.f.* Creature; man, as opposed to God; (*fam.*) creature, a mere thing; dependant, protégé, tool. *C'est une pauvre créature*, he's a poor creature.

crécelle [kre'sɛl], *n.f.* Child's *or* hand rattle. *Voix de crécelle*, harsh voice.

crécerelle [kresˈrɛl], *n.f.* (*Orn.*) Kestrel, *Falco tinnunculus*, windhover.

crèche [krɛːʃ], *n.f.* Manger; crib; (*public*) day nursery (for infants under two years), crèche.

crécy [kre'si], *n.m.* Carrot (orig. from Crécy). *Potage à la Crécy*, soup made with this.

crédence [kre'dãːs], *n.f.* Credence-table; side-board. **crédencier**, *n.m.* *Pantler.

crédibilité [kredibili'te], *n.f.* Credibility.

crédit [kre'di], *n.m.* Credit; trust; authority, influence, esteem, vogue; parliamentary grant. *À crédit*, on credit, on trust, to no purpose, gratuitously, without ground; *acheter à crédit*, to buy on hire purchase; *avoir du crédit*, to have influence; *cela l'a mis en crédit*, that brought him into repute; *crédit est mort*, old trust is dead; *crédit foncier*, loan society (on real estate); *crédit mobilier*, loan society (on personal estate); *crédit municipal*, municipal department providing loans on security; *être en grand crédit*, to be in high repute; *faire crédit, vendre*, or *donner à crédit*, to credit, to give trust, *or* to give credit to; *il a bon crédit*, his credit is good; *lettre de crédit*, letter of credit; *mettre en crédit*, to give credit to; *ouvrir un crédit à quelqu'un*, to open a credit account with someone. **créditer**, *v.t.* To enter to the credit account of; to credit. *Créditer un compte*, to credit an account. **créditeur**, *n.m.* Creditor.—*a.* Credit. *Compte créditeur*, credit account.

credo [kre'do], *n.m.* (*no plural*) Creed, belief. *Credo politique*, political creed.

crédule [kre'dyl], *a.* Credulous. **crédulement**, *adv.* Credulously. **crédulité**, *n.f.* Credulity.

créer [kre'e], *v.t.* To create, to make; to produce, to beget; to invent, to imagine; to appoint; to constitute, to establish. *Créer quelqu'un chevalier*, to knight someone; *créer une rente*, to invest funds for an annuity; *se créer des moyens*, to find means; *se créer des ressources*, to find resources.

crémaillère [krema'jɛːr], *n.f.* Pot-hanger, pot-hook; rack, toothed rack. *Chaise à crémaillère*, chair with adjustable back; *chemin de fer à crémaillère*, rack railway; *engrenage à crémaillère*, rack and pinion; *pendre la crémaillère*, to give a house-warming. **crémaillon**, *n.m.* Small pot-hook.

crémant [kre'mã], *a.* and *n.m.* Very lightly sparkling (of champagne).

crémation [krema'sjɔ̃], *n.f.* Cremation. **crématoire**, *a.* Crematory. *Four crématoire*, cremifying furnace. **crématorium**, *n.m.* (*pl.* **crématoria**) Crematorium.

crème [krɛːm], *n.f.* Cream; custard; sweet liqueur; the best part of a thing, the cream. *Crème de menthe*, peppermint liqueur; *crème de tartre*, cream of tartar; *crème froide*, cold-cream; *crème fouettée*, whipped cream, (*fig.*) flimsy stuff; *fromage à la crème*, cream-cheese. *C'est la crème des hommes*, he's a very fine man.

crémer (1) [kre'me], *v.i. irr.* (*conj. like* ACCÉLÉRER) To cream.—*v.t.* To dye cream colour.

crémer (2) [kre'me], *v.t. irr.* (*conjugated like* ACCÉLÉRER) To cremate.

crémerie [krɛm'ri], *n.f.* Milk-shop, dairy; small (and inexpensive) restaurant.

crémeux, *a.* (*fem.* **-euse**) Creamy.

crémier, *n.m.* (*fem.* **-ière**) Milkman, dairy-man.—*n.f.* Cream-jug.

Crémone [kre'mɔn], *f.* Cremona.

crémone [kre'mɔn], *n.f.* A sort of espagnolette like a casement bolt.

crénage [kre'naːʒ], *n.m.* or **crénerie** [kre'nri], *n.f.* (*Type-founding*) Kerning.

créneau [kre'no], *n.m.* Battlement. *Écrou à créneaux*, castellated nut.

crénelage [kren'laːʒ], *n.m.* Milling, milled edge (on coins), crenellation. **crénelé**, *a.* (*fem.* **-ée**) Battlemented; indented, notched. (*Her.*) embattled; loop-holed; cogged (of wheels); milled (of coins); (*Bot.*) denticulated, crenated. **créneler**, *v.t.* To embattle; to indent, to notch. *Créneler une pièce de monnaie*, to mill a piece of money; *créneler une roue*, to tooth, to cog (a wheel). **crénelure**, *n.f.* Crenellation; notching; (*Anat.*) indentation; (*Bot.*) denticulation, crenature.

créner [kre'ne], *v.t.* (*Type-founding*) To nick, to give a kern to (type).

créole [kre'ɔl], *n.* and *adj.* Creole.

créosote [kreɔ'sɔt], *n.f.* Creosote. **créosoter**, *v.t.* To creosote.

crépage [kre'paːʒ], *n.m.* Glossing (of crape etc.); crisping (of the hair). *Crêpage de chignon*, a row among women.

crêpe (1) [krɛːp], *n.m.* Crape; (*fig.*) veil or hat-band of this; crape-rubber; (*poet.*) pall. *Crêpe crêpé*, crisped crape; *crêpe lisse*, smooth crape; *il porte un crêpe à son chapeau*, he wears a crape hat-band.

crêpe (2) [krɛːp], *n.f.* Pancake.

crêpé [krɛ'pe], *n.m.* Hair-pad, a small tuft of hair worn by women.

crêpelu [kre'ply], *a.* Frizzy (hair). **crêpelure**, *n.f.* Frizziness.

crêper [kre'pe], *v.t.* To crisp, to back-comb. *Cheveux crêpés*, frizzy hair. **se crêper**, *v.r.* To be crisped or frizzy. (*pop.*) *Se crêper le chignon*, to have a set-to (of women).

crépi [kre'pi], *n.m.* Rough-cast, parget.

crépin [SAINT-CRÉPIN].

crépine [kre'pin], *n.f.* Fringe (woven on the top); strainer, rose; omentum, caul (covering the bowels of sheep). **crépiner**, *v.t.* To trim with *crépine*.

crépir [kre'piːr], *v.t.* To parget, to rough-cast, to plaster. *Crépir le crin*, to crisp hair; *crépir le cuir*, to grain leather. **crépissage** or

crépissement, *n.m.* Plastering, pargeting, rough-casting. **crépisseuse,** *n.f.* Machine for graining morocco leather. **crépissure,** *n.m.* Parget, rough-cast; rough-casting.

crépitant [krepi'tɑ̃], *a.* (*fem.* **-ante**) Crepitating; crackling. **crépitation,** *n.f.*, or **crépitement,** *n.m.* Crepitation; crackling. **crépiter,** *v.i.* To crackle; to crepitate.

crépon [kre'pɔ̃], *n.m.* Frizette, hair-pad.

crépu [kre'py], *a.* (*fem.* **crépue**) Crisped, frizzy; woolly. *Ils ont les cheveux crépus,* They have frizzy hair.

crépure [kre'py:r], *n.f.* Crisping; craping.

crépusculaire [krepysky'lɛ:r], *a.* Crepuscular. *Lumière crépusculaire,* twilight; *papillons crépusculaires,* crepuscular lepidoptera.

crépuscule [krepys'kyl], *n.m.* Twilight; dawn; (*fig.*) decline. *Crépuscule du soir,* twilight, dusk.

crèque [krɛk], *n.f.* (*N. dialect*) Sloe. **créquier** *n.m.* Sloe-tree.

crescendo [krɛʃɛ̃'do], *adv.* (*Mus.*) Crescendo.

cressiculture [kresikyl'tyr], *n.f.* Cress-growing.

cresson [krə'sɔ̃], *n.m.* Cress. *Cresson alénois,* garden-cress; *cresson de fontaine,* water-cress; *cresson des prés,* lady's-smock; *cresson doré,* golden saxifrage; *cresson sauvage,* water-plantain; (*pop.*) *ne pas avoir de cresson sur la fontaine,* to be bald. **cressonnière,** *n.f.* Water-cress bed.

Crésus [kre'zy:s], *m.* Croesus.

crésus [kre'zy:s], *n.m. inv.* Very rich man.

crétacé [kreta'se], *a.* (*fem.* **-ée**) Cretaceous, chalky.

Crète [krɛːt], *f.* Crete.

crête [krɛːt], *n.f.* Crest, comb (of a cock or hen); tuft, top-knot; ridge, top, brow; coping. *Baisser la crête,* to be crestfallen; *crête baissée,* crestfallen; *crête de coq,* cock's comb; yellow rattle (plant); *crête d'une grosse vague,* crest of a billow; *crête d'une montagne,* ridge of a mountain; *crête d'un fossé,* bank on the side of a ditch; *lever la crête,* to be conceited, to hold one's head high; *rabaisser la crête à quelqu'un,* to pull someone down a peg.

crêté [krɛ'te], *a.* (*fem.* **-ée**) Crested, tufted.

crête-de-coq [krɛtdə'kɔk], *n.f.* (*pl.* **crêtes-de-coq**) (*Bot.*) Cockscomb, corn-rattle.

crêteler [krɛ'tle], *v.i.* To cackle (of hens).

crételle [kre'tɛl], *n.f.* (*Bot.*) Dog's tail grass.

crétin [kre'tɛ̃], *a.* (*fem.* **-ine**) Cretinous; idiotic.—*n.* Cretin; idiot, dunce. **crétinerie,** *n.f.* Idiotic behaviour; foolishness. **crétiniser,** *v.t.* To make cretinous, to brutalize, to make an idiot of. **crétinisme,** *n.m.* Cretinism.

crétique [kre'tik], *a.* (*Pros.*) Cretic.

crétois [kre'twa], *a.* and *n.* (*fem.* **-oise**) Cretan.

cretonne [krə'tɔn], *n.f.* Cretonne.

cretons [krə'tɔ̃], *n.m.* (*used only in pl.*) Residuum of melted tallow, greaves. *Cretons de lard,* scrapings.

creusage [krø'za:ʒ] or **creusement,** *n.m.* Deepening, hollowing; excavation.

creuser [krø'ze], *v.t.* To hollow, to excavate, to scoop out, to sink a cavity in; to sink, to drive (a well, shaft, etc.); to make hollow or empty. *Creuser l'estomac,* to whet the appetite; *creuser la terre,* to dig the ground;

creuser une question, to examine a question thoroughly; *creuser un fossé,* to dig a ditch; *creuser un puits,* to sink a well.—*v.i.* To dig; to hollow, to grow hollow. *Creuser sous terre,* to dig underground. **se creuser,** *v.r.* To become hollow. *Se creuser la cervelle* or *la tête,* to rack one's brains.

creuset [krø'zɛ], *n.m.* Crucible, melting-pot; (*fig.*) test, trial, ordeal. *Passer par le creuset,* to assay, to refine; *le creuset de la douleur,* the test of grief.

creusoir [krø'zwa:r], *n.m.* Gouging-tool (used by violin-makers).

creux [krø], *a.* (*fem.* **creuse**) Hollow; cavernous; deep; empty; (*fig.*) unsubstantial, airy, chimerical, extravagant. *Avoir les joues creuses,* to have hollow cheeks; *chemin creux,* sunken road; *des yeux creux,* eyes sunk in the head; *esprit creux* or *cerveau creux,* cracked brain, empty head; *heure creuse,* slack time; *il a le ventre creux,* his belly is empty; *pensées creuses,* airy notions; *un fossé creux de trois pieds,* a ditch three feet deep.—*n.m.* Hollow, cavity; pit, hole, chasm; mould, mortar, trough. *Creux de l'aisselle,* armpit; *creux de l'estomac,* pit of the stomach; *creux de la main,* hollow of the hand; *creux d'une voile,* cavity of a sail (which retains the wind); *creux d'un vaisseau,* depth of a ship's hold; *creux planté d'arbres,* dell planted with trees; *creux profond dans une mine,* groove in a mine; *il a un bon creux,* he has a fine bass voice.—*adv.* Hollow. *Sonner creux,* to sound hollow.

crevable [krə'vabl]. That can be punctured.

crevaille [krə'va:j], *n.f.* (*slang*) Guzzling, gormandizing; tuck-in, blow-out.

crevaison [krəve'zɔ̃], *n.f.* Puncture (of a bicycle etc.); (*vulg.*) death.

crevant [krə'vɑ̃], *a.* (*vulg.*) Tiresome; killing (toil etc.); killing (funny).

crevasse [krə'vas], *n.f.* Crevice, rift, crack, chink, crevasse, gap, cranny, flaw; chap (in the hands etc.).

crevasser [krəva'se], *v.t.* To split; to crack; to chap; to make cracks or crevasses in. **se crevasser,** *v.r.* To crack, to split, to gape, to become chapped.

crève [krɛːv], *n.f.* (*pop.*) *Attraper la crève,* to catch one's death.

crevé [krə've], *n.m.* (*Dress.*) Opening, slash (in sleeves). *Petit crevé,* fop, fast young fellow.—*a.* Punctured (tyre); dead (dog); tired out.

crève-cœur [krɛv'kœ:r], *n.m. inv.* Heart-break; heart-breaking thing, heart-sore.

crève-la-faim [krɛvla'fɛ̃], *n.m. inv.* Starveling, down and out.

crever [krə've], *v.t.* To burst, to split, to crack, to break open, to rend; to stave in; to puncture; to pierce (the eyes etc.); to cram (someone) with victuals. *Crever le cœur à quelqu'un,* to break someone's heart; *crever les yeux à quelqu'un,* to put out someone's eyes, (*fig.*) to be under someone's very nose, to be self-evident; *crever un cheval,* to work a horse to death.—*v.i.* To burst; (*pop.*) to die, to perish. *C'est une médecine à faire crever un cheval,* this medicine is enough to kill a horse; *crever de biens,* to wallow in wealth; *crever de faim,* to be dying with hunger; *crever de rire,* to split one's sides with laughing; *crever* *d'orgueil*, to be bursting with pride. **se crever**, *v.r.* To burst; to kill oneself. *Se crever de boire et de manger*, to cram or stuff till one is ready to burst; *se crever de travail*, to kill oneself with work.

crevette [krɑ'vɛt], *n.f.*, or *crevette grise* or *petite crevette*, shrimp; *grosse crevette* or *crevette rouge*, prawn. **crevettière**, *n.f.* Shrimp-net, prawn-net. **crevettine**, *n.f.* Sand-flea.

crève-vessie [krɛvvɛ'si], *n.m. inv.* Apparatus for illustrating atmospheric pressure (by bursting a bladder).

cri [kri], *n.m.* Cry; scream, roar, bawling, howl, yell, shriek, screech, wail, wailing; outcry, clamour. *À cor et à cri*, with hue and cry; *cri aigre, aigu* or *perçant*, scream, shriek, shrill cry; *cri d'armes*, (*Her.*) motto; *cri de guerre*, war-cry; *cri de joie* or *cri d'allégresse*, shouting, huzza, acclamation; *demander à grands cris*, to demand with a loud voice; *je poussai un grand cri*, I shrieked out; *jeter les hauts cris*, to complain or cry out loudly; *jeter un cri, faire des cris* or *pousser un cri*, to utter a cry, to cry out, to raise an outcry, to complain loudly; *le cri du sang* or *de la nature*, the call of the blood; *le dernier cri*, the last word, the utmost refinement (of fashion etc.).

criaillement [kriaj'mɑ̃], *n.m.* Shouting, clamour, wrangling, brawling; scolding. **criailler**, *v.i.* To bawl, to cry, to clamour; to scold, to chide; to brawl; to gabble (of geese). **criaillerie**, *n.f.* Brawling, clamouring, scolding, wrangling. **criailleur**, *n.m.* (*fem.* **-euse**) Brawler, bawler, wrangler; shrew, scold.

criant [kri'ɑ̃], *a.* Crying; (*fig.*) glaring, shocking, howling. *Injustice criante*, crying or glaring injustice.

criard [kri'a:r], *a.* (*fem.* **-arde**) Crying, noisy, clamorous; scolding; (*fig.*) shrill, discordant, crude. *Couleur criarde*, loud colour; *dettes criardes*, pressing or urgent debts; *voix criarde*, shrill voice.—*n.* Bawler, clamourer. —*n.f.* Scold, shrew.

criblage [kri'bla:ʒ], *n.m.* Sifting, screening (of coals etc.).

crible [kribl], *n.m.* Sieve, riddle. *Passer au crible*, to sift; *percé comme un crible*, as full of holes as a sieve, riddled.

cribler [kri'ble], *v.t.* To sift, to riddle; to pierce all over, to riddle (with wounds etc.); (*fig.*) to overwhelm. *Cribler de coups*, to shoot, run, or stab through and through; *criblé de dettes*, over head and ears in debt; *criblé de mitraille*, riddled, peppered with shot. **cribleur**, *n.m.* (*fem.* **cribleuse** (1)) Sifter.—*n.f.* Sifting-machine. **cribleux**, *a.* (*fem.* **cribleuse** (2)) (*Anat.*) Pierced like a sieve, sieve-like. **criblure**, *n.f.* Siftings. **cribreux**, *a.* (*fem.* **cribreuse**) Sieve-like.

cric (1) [kri], *n.m.* Jack, screw-jack, hand-screw; (*pop.*) brandy.

cric (2) [krik], *int.* Crack! rip! bang!

cricket [kri'kɛ], *n.m.* Cricket (game).

cri-cri [kri'kri], *n.m. inv.* (*fam.*) Cricket (insect); chirping.

crid [CRISS].

criée [kri'e], *n.f.* (Public) auction. *Vente à la criée*, sale by auction; *audience des criées*, auction mart.

crier [kri'e], *v.i.* To cry out, to cry; to shout, to halloo, to bawl; to scream, to shriek, to squall, to clamour; to squeak; to call out; to whine, to pule; to complain loudly, to inveigh, to exclaim; to chirp (of grasshoppers and other insects); to creak (of doors etc.). *C'est à qui criera le plus fort*, everyone is trying to shout down everyone else; *crier à l'injustice*, to exclaim against an injustice; *crier à tue-tête* or *comme un perdu*, to cry out or shriek at the top of one's voice; *crier au feu, au meurtre*, or *au voleur*, to cry out fire, murder, *or* stop thief; *crier au scandale*, to inveigh against a scandal; *crier au secours*, to call out for help; *crier aux armes*, to call to arms; *crier aux oreilles de*, to din into (one's) ears; *crier bien fort*, to cry out lustily; *crier famine*, to cry famine; *crier gare*, to cry out beware! take care! *crier miséricorde*, to cry for mercy; *il crie avant qu'on l'écorche*, he cries out before he is hurt.—*v.t.* To cry, to shout; to proclaim, to hawk, to put up for sale; to publish, to announce; to demand loudly. *Crier ses marchandises*, to cry or hawk one's wares. **crieur**, *n.m.* (*fem.* **-euse**) Bawling man or woman, bawler; crier; (*Theat.*) call-boy; auctioneer; hawker. *Crieur public*, town-crier; *crieur de journaux*, newsboy.

crime [krim], *n.m.* Crime, offence. *Crime capital*, capital offence, felony; *crime contre-nature*, unnatural crime; *crime de lèse-majesté*, high treason; *crime d'État*, treason; *crime qualifié*, indictable offence; *endurci dans le crime*, hardened in crime; *être porté au crime*, to be prone to crime; *faire un crime à quelqu'un de*, to censure someone severely (for a trifle).

Crimée [kri'me], **la**, *f.* The Crimea.

criméen [krime'ɛ̃], *a.* and *n.* (*fem.* **criméenne**) Crimean.

criminaliser [kriminali'ze], *v.t.* To remove a cause from a civil to a criminal court. **criminaliste**, *n.m.* Writer on criminal law, **criminalité**, *n.f.* Criminality; crime. **criminatoire**, *a.* Criminatory.

criminel [krimi'nɛl], *a.* (*fem.* **criminelle**) Criminal, unlawful; felonious, guilty. *Chambre criminelle* or *cour criminelle*, criminal court; *juge criminel*, a judge that tries criminal cases.—*n.* Criminal, felon, culprit, offender. —*n.m* Criminal affair; proceedings before a criminal court. *Au criminel*, in a criminal court; *criminel d'État*, State criminal. **criminellement**, *adv.* Criminally, culpably, guiltily.

crin [krɛ̃], *n.m.* Coarse hair (of the mane and tail of the horse and other animals); horse-hair, bristles, fibres, mane. *À tous crins*, with flowing mane and tail, (*fig.*) zealous, indefatigable; *être comme un crin*, to be cantankerous. **crinal**, *a.* (*fem.* **-ale**, *pl.* **-aux**) Hairy, shaggy, mane-like.

crincrin [krɛ̃'krɛ̃], *n.m.* (*fam.*) (Screeching) Fiddle.

crinière [kri'njɛ:r], *n.f.* Mane (of horse, lion, etc.); horse-tail (of a helmet); (*fig., fam.*) abundant and long hair.

crinoline [krinɔ'lin], *n.f.* Crinoline.

criocère [kriɔ'sɛ:r], *n.m.* (*Ent.*) Crioceris (ram's horn).

crique [krik], *n.f.* Creek, cove; flaw, crack (of metal).

criquer [kri'ke], *v.i.* To crack, to chink (of metals); to become brittle (of wool). **se criquer,** *v.r.* (*pop.*) To pop off, to skedaddle.
criquet (1) [kri'kɛ], *n.m.* Locust; (*fig.*) bad horse; (*fam.*) whippersnapper; light wine. **criquet** (2) [CRICKET].
criqueter [krik'te], *v.i.* To make a grating or rasping noise.
criquetis [krik'ti], *n.m.* Sharp sound (produced by burin on copper).
criqûre = CRIQUE (flaw).
crise [kri:z], *n.f.* Crisis, conjuncture, decisive moment; fit, convulsion, attack. *Crise de nerfs,* fit of hysteria; *une crise de foie,* a liver attack; *crise économique,* economic crisis; *une crise se prépare,* a crisis is approaching; *un état de crise,* a critical condition; *la crise (des affaires),* slump.
crispant [kris'pã], *a.* (*fem.* **-ante**) Jarring, irritating.
crispation [krispa'sjõ], *n.f.* Shrivelling, crispation; fidgets. *Donner des crispations à quelqu'un,* to exasperate someone.
crisper [kris'pe], *v.t.* To shrivel, to make shrink; to irritate (the nerves), to give (someone) the fidgets. *Avoir les mains crispées,* to clench one's hands. **se crisper,** *v.r.* To shrivel, to contract.
crispin [kris'pɛ̃], *n.m.* Valet (as in Molière's comedies); short cloak; addition to gauntlets covering wrists (in fencing etc.). *C'est un crispin,* he looks like a valet; *jouer les crispins,* to perform the part of valets.
criss, kriss [kris], *n.m.* Creese (Malay dagger).
crissement [kris'mã], *n.m.* Grating (of teeth; of brakes etc.).
crisser [kri'se], *v.i.* To grate, to squeak.
cristal [kris'tal], *n.m.* (*pl.* **cristaux**) Crystal, fine glass, crystal ware, cut glass; (*fig.*) limpidity. *Cristal de mine,* quartz; *cristal de roche,* rock-crystal; (*poet.*) *le cristal de l'onde,* the limpidity of water. **cristallerie,** *n.f.* Glass-cutting; crystal-manufactory, glass-works. **cristallier,** *n.m.* Glass-cutter; glass-cupboard. **cristallière,** *n.f.* Rock-crystal mine; machine for glass-cutting. **cristallifère,** *a.* Crystalliferous. **cristallin,** *a.* (*fem.* **-ine**) Crystalline; pellucid.—*n.m.* (*Anat.*) Crystalline humour or lens (of the eye); (*Astron.*) crystalline heaven or sphere. **cristallinien,** *a.* (*fem.* **-ienne**) (*Anat.*) Relating to the crystalline. **cristallisable,** *a.* Crystallizable. **cristallisant,** *a.* (*fem.* **-ante**) Crystallizing; determining crystallization. **cristallisation,** *n.f.* Crystallization. **cristalliser,** *v.t.* To crystallize.—*v.i.* To be converted into crystal. *Sucre cristallisé,* granulated sugar. **se cristalliser,** *v.r.* To crystallize; to candy. **cristallisoir,** *n.m.* Crystallizing-pan, crystallizer. **cristallographie,** *n.f.* Crystallography. **cristallographique,** *a.* Crystallographic. **cristalloïde,** *a.* and *n.* Crystalloid. **cristallométrie,** *n.f.* Crystallometry. **cristallotechnie,** *n.f.* Art of producing artificial crystal. **cristallotomie,** *n.f.* The art of cutting crystals.
criste-marine or **cristhme** [CHRISTE-MARINE].
critère [kri'tɛ:r] or **critérium** [krite'rjɔm], *n.m.* Criterion, standard, test; touchstone. *L'évidence est le critérium de la vérité,* evidence is the criterion of truth.

criticisme [kriti'sism], *n.m.* (*Phil.*) Critical philosophy (of Kant). **criticiste,** *a.* Pertaining to this.—*n.* Partisan of this.
critiquable [kriti'kabl], *a.* That may be criticized, censurable, exceptionable. **critiquant,** *a.* (*fem.* **critiquante**) Critical, censorious.
critique [kri'tik], *a.* Critical; censorious, carping; ticklish, momentous, dangerous; critical (in the literary sense). *Étude critique,* critical appreciation; *humeur critique,* censorious temper; *pouls critique,* alarming pulse; *signes critiques,* critical symptoms; *situation critique,* emergency.—*n.m.* Critic; censor, censorious person, carper.—*n.f.* Criticism, science of criticism; review, critique; unfavourable review. *Faire de la critique,* to write criticisms, to be a critic; *faire la critique d'un ouvrage,* to criticize, to review a work; *la critique,* the critics.
critiquer [kriti'ke], *v.t.* To criticize unfavourably; to censure, to find fault with. **critiqueur,** *n.m.* (*fem.* **critiqueuse**) Criticizer, fault-finder, carper.
croassement [kroas'mã], *n.m.* Croak, croaking, cawing (of rooks). **croasser,** *v.i.* To croak, to caw (of crows, rooks, etc.).
croate [krɔ'at], *a.* Croatian.—*n.* (**Croate**) Croat.
Croatie [krɔa'si], *f.* Croatia.
croc (1) [kro], *n.m.* Hook; fang (of dog); tusk (of walrus). *Croc de marinier,* boat-hook; *mettre* or *pendre au croc,* to put or lay on the shelf, to lay by; *moustaches en croc,* handlebar moustache.
croc (2) [krɔk], *int.* Crunch. *Faire croc sous la dent,* to crunch with the teeth.
croc-en-jambe [krɔkã'ʒã:b], *n.m.* (*pl.* **crocs-en-jambe**) Trip. *Donner un croc-en-jambe à quelqu'un,* to trip someone up, to play someone a dirty trick.
croche [krɔʃ], *a.* Crooked, bent; (*fig.*) grasping. *Avoir la main croche,* (*fig.*) to be grasping.—*n.f.* (*Mus.*) Quaver; (*pl.*) smith's tongs. *Double croche,* semi-quaver; *triple croche,* demi-semiquaver.
crocher [krɔ'ʃe], *v.t.* To hook, to catch hold of with a hook; to bend like a hook, to crook. *Crocher l'organeau d'une ancre,* to fish up the anchor by the ring.
crochet [krɔ'ʃɛ], *n.m.* Small hook; knitting-needle, crochet-hook; (*Print.*) square bracket; teeth of certain animals; poison fang of a snake. *Clou à crochet,* tenter-hook; *crochet de chiffonnier,* hooked stick used by rag-gatherers; *crochet à boutons,* button-hook; *crochet de serrurier,* pick lock; *faire du crochet,* to crotchet; *ouvrages au crochet,* crochet-work. (*fig.*) *Vivre aux crochets de quelqu'un,* to live at another person's expense; *faire un crochet,* to make a detour. **crochetable,** *a.* Pickable (of locks). **crochetage,** *n.m.* Lock-picking. **crocheter,** *v.t.* To pick (a lock); to crochet. **crocheteur,** *n.m.* *Porter. *Crocheteur (de serrure),* picklock, housebreaker; *injures de crocheteur,* Billingsgate abuse. **crochetier,** *n.m.* Hook-maker, clasp-maker. **crocheton,** *n.m.* Small hook, crotchet.
crochu [krɔ'ʃy], *a.* (*fem.* **-ue**) Crooked, hooked. *Il a les mains crochues,* he is light-fingered.
crocodile [krɔkɔ'dil], *n.m.* Crocodile; (*Rail.*) automatic stop. *Crocodile d'Amérique,*

alligator; *larmes de crocodile*, crocodile tears. **crocodilien**, *n.m.* Crocodilian.

crocus [krɔ′kyːs], *n.m.* (*Bot.*) Crocus.

croire [krwɑːr], *v.t. irr.* (*pres.p.* **croyant**, *p.p.* **cru**) To believe, to hold true; to have faith in, to place reliance on; to think, to deem, to judge, to be persuaded. *À ce que je crois*, as I believe, to the best of my belief; *à l'en croire* or *s'il faut l'en croire, tout est perdu*, if he is to be believed, all is lost; *croire une chose trop légèrement*, to believe something too easily; *croyez-vous qu'il le fasse?* or *le fera?* do you think he will do it? *faire croire*, to give out, to persuade; *il est à croire qu'il le veut ainsi*, it is to be presumed that he will have it so; *il le croit bonnement*, he quite believes it; *je crois pouvoir le faire*, I think I can do it; *je crois qu'il le fera*, I think he will do it; *je le crois bien*, I really believe it; *je te crois!* not half! *j'en crois à peine mes yeux*, I can hardly believe my eyes; *je n'en crois rien*, I don't believe a word of it; *je ne sais que croire*, I don't know what to think; *n'en croyez rien*, don't you believe it; *s'il faut en croire les apparences*, if appearances are to be trusted.—*v.i.* To believe, to have faith (*à*), to be a believer. *C'est à ne pas y croire*, it is past belief; *croire aux revenants*, to believe in ghosts; *croire en Dieu*, to believe in God; *il ne croit point*, he has no belief; *je crois bien*, I should think so! no wonder! *je crois que oui*, I believe so; *je crois que non*, I believe not. **se croire**, *v.r.* To believe or think oneself, to consider oneself; to be believed, to be credible. *Cela peut se croire*, it is credible; *cet homme se croit habile*, that man thinks himself skilful; *il se croit tout permis*, he thinks he may do anything; *il s'en croit beaucoup*, he thinks a great deal of himself.

croisade [krwɑ′zad], *n.f.* Crusade.

croisé [krwɑ′ze], *a.* (*fem.* **croisée** (1)) Crossed; twilled, double-milled (of cloth); cross (of the breeds of animals). *Avoir les jambes croisées*, to sit cross-legged; *demeurer* or *se tenir les bras croisés*, to sit with folded arms, to do nothing; *feux croisés*, cross-fire; *gilet croisé*, double-breasted waistcoat; *mots croisés*, cross-words; *rimes croisées*, alternate rhymes.—*n.m.* Crusader; twill; crossing (a step in dancing). *Chassé croisé*, (*fig.*) change of places.

croisée (2) [krwɑ′ze], *n.f.* Crossing point; cross (of a sword); breadth (of an anchor); casement window (opening inside); (*fig.*) *Être à la croisée des chemins*, to be at the crossroads *or* at the parting of the ways.

croisement [krwɑz′mã], *n.m.* Act of crossing; crossing (of two roads etc.); meeting; cross-breeding (of animals).

croiser [krwɑ′ze], *v.t.* To cross, to set or lay crosswise; to lay across, to fold across; to cross (breeds of animals); to thwart. *Croiser les bras*, to fold one's arms, (*fig.*) to do nothing; *croiser le chemin de quelqu'un*, to cross someone (in his designs); *je l'ai croisé dans la rue*, I passed him in the street.—*v.i.* To overlap; to cruise. *Croiser sur une côte*, to cruise along a coast. **se croiser**, *v.r.* To cross or pass each other; to be crossed; to lie athwart each other; to interest each other; to thwart one another; to take up the

cross, to engage in a crusade. **croiserie**, *n.f.* Wicker-work.

croisette [krwɑ′zɛt], *n.f.* Small cross; (*Her.*) crosslet; (*Bot.*) [GAILLET]; cross-stone; (*pl.*) (*Naut.*) cross trees.

croiseur [krwɑ′zœːr], *n.m.* Cruiser. *Croiseur auxiliaire*, armed merchant-cruiser.

croisière, *n.f.* Cruise; cruising fleet; (*Rail.*) intersection of two lines. *Vitesse de croisière*, cruising speed.

croisillon [krwɑzi′jɔ̃], *n.m.* Cross-bar; sash-bar.

croissance [krwɑ′sãːs], *n.f.* Growth, increase. *Arrêter dans sa croissance*, to stunt the growth of; *avoir pris toute sa croissance*, to be full-grown; *en pleine croissance*, growing fast.

croissant [krwɑ′sã], *a.* (*fem.* **-ante**) Growing, increasing.—*n.m.* The moon in her increase; crescent; pruning-hook, hedging-bill; crescent roll; the Turkish standard; the Turkish power. *En croissant* or *en forme de croissant*, lunated; *les cornes du croissant*, the horns of the crescent.

croisure [krwɑ′zyːr], *n.f.* Crossing, mill (in stuffs); (*Pros.*) intermixture of crossed rhymes.

croît [krwɑ], *n.m.* Increase (from breeding).

croître [krwɑːtr], *v.i. irr.* (*pres.p.* **croissant**, *p.p.* **crû**) To grow; to increase in size etc.; to grow (of plants etc.); to grow up, to grow tall; to wax (moon); to spring up, to sprout, to shoot; to increase; to lengthen; to swell or swell out, to be swollen. *Croître trop rapidement*, to overgrow; *elle ne fait que croître et embellir*, she grows handsomer every day; *les jours commencent à croître*, the days begin to draw out; *la rivière croît*, the river is rising; *mauvaise herbe croît toujours*, all weeds grow apace.—*v.t.* To cause to grow, to increase.

croix [krwɑ], *n.f.* Cross; the Cross, the Holy Rood, crucifix; (*fig.*) Christianity; (*fig.*) affliction, trouble, tribulation; (*Coin.*) obverse; (*Print.*) obelisk, dagger; (*Her.*) saltire. *Avoir les jambes en croix*, to sit cross-legged; *croix de Lorraine*, cross with two bars; *croix de Malte*, Maltese cross; *croix de Saint André*, St. Andrew's cross, saltire; *croix du Sud* or *croix australe*, Southern Cross; *croix gammée*, swastika; *faire le signe de la croix*, to cross oneself; *grand-croix*, Knight Grand Cross; *gagner la croix de bois*, (*Mil.*) to be killed in action; *il faut faire une croix à la cheminée*, we must make a cross on the chimney, we must chalk that up; *jouer à croix ou pile*, to play at heads or tails, at pitch and toss; *La Croix Rouge*, The Red Cross; *La Croix de Guerre*, French military decoration; *les bras d'une croix*, the arms of a cross; *mettre les vergues en croix*, (*Naut.*) to square the yards; *mettre quelque chose en croix*, to put something crosswise; *on est allé au-devant de lui avec la croix et la bannière*, they went to meet him with cross and banner, or with great ceremony; *porter sa croix*, to bear one's cross; *sainte croix*, Holy Rood.

cromesquis [krɔmes′ki], *n.m.* Kromesky.

cromlech [krɔm′lɛk], *n.m.* (*Archaeol.*) Stone circle.

cromorne [krɔ′mɔrn], *n.m.* (*Mus.*) Cromorne.

crône [kroːn], *n.m.* Crane (on a wharf).

croppetons [CROUPETONS].

croquade [krɔ'kad], *n.f.* Rough sketch.
croquant [krɔ'kã], *a.* (*fem.* **croquante**) Crisp, crackling, short, crunching. *Biscuit croquant,* hard biscuit.—*n.m.* Poor wretch; clodhopper; (*pl.*) name given to French peasants who rebelled under Henri IV.—*n.f.* Crisp almond-cake.
croque-au-sel (à la) [krɔko'sɛl], *adv. phr.* With salt only.
croque-en-bouche [krɔkã'buʃ], *n.m. inv.* Crisp sweetmeat, crisp cake.
croque-lardon [krɔklar'dɔ̃], *n.m. inv.* Lick-spittle, sponger, parasite.
croquement [krɔk'mã], *n.m.* Crackling, crunching.
croque-mitaine [krɔkmi'tɛn], *n.m.* (*pl.* **croque-mitaines**) Bogy-man.
croque-monsieur [krɔkmə'sjø], *n.m. inv.* Sandwich of ham and cheese, grilled and served hot.
croque-mort [krɔk'mɔːr], *n.m.* (*pl.* **croque-morts**) (*fam.*) Undertaker's man, mute.
croque-note [krɔk'nɔt], *n.m.* (*pl.* **croque-notes**) Sorry musician, scraper, strummer.
croquenot or **croqueneau** [krɔk'no], *n.m.* (*slang*) Shoe, boot.
croquer [krɔ'ke], *v.i.* To crackle between the teeth, to make a scrunching noise.—*v.t.* To crunch; to devour, to eat hastily; to make the first sketch or rough draft of, to sketch; (*Mus.*) to slur, to pass over (a note); (*Naut.*) to hook or grapple (something). *Croquer le marmot,* (*fam.*) to dance attendance; *être gentil à croquer,* to be extremely pretty.
croquet [krɔ'kɛ], *n.m.* Crisp biscuit; croquet (game).
croquette [krɔ'kɛt], *n.f.* Croquette.
croqueur [krɔ'kœːr], *n.m.* (*fem.* **-euse**) Devourer, gormandizer, glutton.
croquignole [krɔki'pɔl], *n.f.* Cracknel; fillip; (C) doughnut.
croquignolet [krɔkiɲɔ'lɛ], *a.* (*fem.* **-ette**) (*fam.*) Tiny, dainty, sweet.
croquis [krɔ'ki], *n.m.* First sketch, rough draft, outline. *Cahier de croquis,* sketch-book; *faire un croquis,* to sketch.
crosne [kron], *n.m.* An edible tuber first imported from Japan to Crosne near Paris.
cross [krɔs], *n.m.* (*Box.*) Cross-counter; cross-country run.
crosse [krɔs], *n.f.* Crooked stick, crosier (of bishops); butt-end (of musket etc.); stock; hockey-stick, crosse, golf-club etc.; the recurved part of various tools, instruments, etc. (C) *Jeu de crosse,* lacrosse game; *jouer à la crosse,* to play at lacrosse; *mettre la crosse en l'air,* to surrender. **crossé,** *a.* (*fem.* **crossée**) Crosiered, mitred. *Un abbé crossé et mitré,* a crosiered and mitred abbot; *une abbesse crossée,* a mitred abbess.
crosser [krɔ'se], *v.t.* To strike (a ball etc.) with a crosse, golf club, hockey-stick, etc.; to play lacrosse; (*fam.*) to beat, to scold.
crosseron [krɔs'rɔ̃], *n.m.* The curled end of a crosier.
crossette [krɔ'sɛt], *n.f.* Last year's shoot with heel attached (of a vine etc.), used as a slip or cutting.
crosseur [krɔ'sœr], *n.m.* Hockey-player, lacrosse-player.
crossillon [CROSSERON].

crotale [krɔ'tal], *n.m.* (*Ant.*) Rattle, castanet (of priestesses of Cybele); rattlesnake.
crotalidé, *n.m.* (*Zool.*) Rattlesnake.
crotaphite [krɔta'fit], *a.* (*Anat.*) Of the temporal muscle.—*n.m.* This muscle.
croton [krɔ'tɔ̃], *n.m.* (*Bot.*) Croton.
crotte [krɔt], *n.f.* Dung; dirt, mud, mire. *Une crotte de chocolat,* a chocolate.—*int.* (*pop.*)=ZUT! **crotté,** *a.* (*fem.* **-ée**) Dirty, muddy; (*fig.*) squalid, wretched, sorry. *Crotté comme un barbet,* as dirty as a pig; *crotté jusqu'à l'échine,* with mud up to the eyes, draggle-tailed. **crotter,** *v.t.* To dirty, to bemire; to draggle, to bespatter. **se crotter,** *v.r.* To get dirty, to dirty oneself or one's clothes. **crottin,** *n.m.* Dung (of horses, mules, etc.).
croulant [kru'lã], *a.* (*fem.* **-ante**) Sinking, crumbling; ready to fall, tottering, tumble-down. **croulement,** *n.m.* Sinking, falling in, collapse. **crouler,** *v.i.* To give way, to fall in, to collapse, to break up; to cry (of a woodcock). (*Theat.*) *Il fit crouler la salle,* he brought the house down.—*v.t.* To cause to give way; *(Hunt.)* to wag (said of stags when they are frightened). *Le cerf croule la queue,* the stag wags his tail.
*****croulier** [kru'lje], *a.* (*fem.* **-ière**) Quaggy, swampy, shifting (of land).
croup [krup], *n.m.* (*Path.*) Croup, diphtheria.
croupade [kru'pad], *n.f.* Buck-jump (of horse).
croupal [kru'pal], *a.* (*fem.* **-ale,** *pl.* **-aux**) Pertaining to the croup; laryngitic.
croupe [krup], *n.f.* Croup, crupper, the buttocks (of a horse), rump; top or brow (of a hill); (*Arch.*) small cupola on chevet of a church, hipped roof. *En croupe,* behind; *être, aller,* or *monter en croupe,* to ride behind (the rider), to ride pillion.
croupé [kru'pe], *a.* (*fem.* **-ée**) With a rump or crupper (of a stated kind). *Cheval bien croupé,* horse with a fine crupper. *****à croupetons,** *adv. phr.* Squatting.
croupi [kru'pi], *a.* (*fem.* **-ie**) Stagnant, putrid (of water). *De l'eau croupie,* ditch-water.
croupier [kru'pje], *n.m.* Croupier (at a gaming-table); partner (of a financier etc.).
croupière [kru'pjɛːr], *n.f.* Saddle-tie, crupper; (*Naut.*) stern cable. *Mouiller en croupière,* to cast anchor by the stern; *tailler des croupières à quelqu'un,* (*fig.*) to cut out work for someone, to put obstacles in his way; (*Mil.*) to press hard upon (the enemy).
croupion [kru'pjɔ̃], *n.m.* Rump. *Le Parlement-Croupion,* the Rump (Parliament). *Le croupion (d'une volaille),* the parson's nose.
croupir [kru'piːr], *v.i.* To stagnate, to lie stagnant; to wallow, to be sunk in. *Croupir dans le vice* or *l'oisiveté,* to wallow in sin or in idleness. **croupissant,** *a.* (*fem.* **-ante**) Stagnant, putrescent. *****croupissement,** *n.m.* Stagnation, putrefaction.
croupon [kru'pɔ̃], *n.m.* Square hide, butt.
croustade [krus'tad], *n.f.* Dish prepared with crusts; pasty.
croustillant [krusti'jã], *a.* (*fem.* **-ante**) Crisp, crusty; (*fig.*) spicy. *Histoire croustillante,* smutty story. **croustille,** *n.f.* Little crust; (*fig.*) snack. **croustiller,** *v.i.* To bite, eat, crunch a crust, to munch, to crunch.
croustilleux [krusti'jø], *a.* (*fem.* **-euse**)

Broad, free, spicy. *Des contes croustilleux,* smutty tales.

croûte [krut], *n.f.* Crust; pie-crust; cake (formed on the surface of anything); scab; (*C*) crust (of the snow); (*fig.*) bad painting, daub. (*fam.*) *Casser la croûte,* to have a snack; *la croûte de dessous,* the undercrust; *ne manger que des croûtes,* to fare badly. **croûtelette,** *n.f.* Little crust. **croûter,** *v.t.* (*vulg.*) To eat, to munch. **croûteux,** *a.* (*fem.* -euse) Crusty; scabby. **croûtier,** *n.m.* Dauber, poor painter.

croûton [kru'tɔ̃], *n.m.* Bit of crust, crusty end; sippet; (*fig.*) wretched dauber, drudge. **croûtonner,** *v.i.* To daub, to paint daubs; to munch bread between meals.

croyable [krwa'jabl], *a.* Credible, likely. *Cela n'est pas croyable,* that is not likely.

croyance [krwa'jã:s], *n.f.* Belief; creed, faith, persuasion; conviction, opinion. *Cela passe toute croyance,* that surpasses all belief; *fausse croyance,* misbelief; *la croyance des chrétiens,* the Christian faith; *la croyance des Juifs,* the Jewish creed.

croyant [krwa'jã], *n.m.* (*fem.* -ante) Believer.

cru (1) [kry], *n.m.* Growth; production (esp. of wine); vine-estate, vineyard; soil; (*fig.*) invention, making, fabrication. *Boire du vin de son cru,* to drink wine of one's own growth; *cela n'est pas de son cru,* that is not his own idea; *des fruits d'un bon cru,* fruit of a good soil; *les grands crus de Bourgogne,* famous Burgundy wines; *vin du cru,* wine of the country.

cru (2) [kry], *a.* (*fem.* **crue** (1)) Raw, uncooked; indigestible; unwrought; (*fig.*) crude, coarse, rough, harsh; indecent, smutty, obscene; (*C*) sharp (weather). *À cru,* on the bare skin, next to the skin; *couleur crue,* harsh colour; *cuir cru,* undressed leather; *eau crue,* hard water; *monter à cheval à cru,* to ride a horse bareback; *tout cru,* quite raw; *une lumière crue,* a hard light.

cru (3), *p.p.* [CROIRE].

crû (4), *p.p.* [CROÎTRE].

cruauté [kryo'te], *n.f.* Cruelty, inhumanity; cruel deed. *La cruauté du sort,* the harshness of fate.

cruche [kryʃ], *n.f.* Pitcher, jar, jug; (*colloq.*) blockhead, booby, dolt. *Tant va la cruche à l'eau qu'à la fin elle se casse,* the pitcher that often goes to the well gets broken at last. **cruchée,** *n.f.* Pitcherful, jugful, jarful.

crucherie [kryʃ'ri], *n.f.* (*colloq.*) Stupidity, silliness. *Tu ne dis que des crucheries,* you only talk nonsense. **cruchette** [kry'ʃɛt], *n.f.* Little jug or jar. **cruchon,** *n.m.* Little pitcher; (stone) hot-water bottle.

crucial [kry'sjal], *a.* (*fem.* -iale, *pl.* -iaux) Cross-shaped, crucial; (*fig.*) decisive, crucial. **crucifère** [krysi'fɛr], *a.* (*Bot.*) Cruciferous.— *n.f.* Crucifer.

crucifiement [krysifi'mã], *n.m.* Crucifixion. **crucifier,** *v.t.* To crucify.

crucifix [krysi'fi], *n.m.* Crucifix. **crucifixion,** *n.f.* Crucifixion.

cruciforme [krysi'fɔrm], *a.* Cruciform, cross-shaped, cross-like.

crudité [krydi'te], *n.f.* Crudity, rawness; coarse expression; (*pl.*) raw vegetables or fruit.

crue (1) [CRU (2)].

crue (2) [kry], *n.f.* Growth, increase; rise, swelling (of water etc.); flood, freshet. *Cet arbre a pris toute sa crue,* that tree has attained its full growth; *crue de mer,* surge of the sea; *la crue des eaux,* the rising of the waters; *torrent en crue,* torrent in spate.

cruel [kry'ɛl], *a.* (*fem.* -elle) Cruel, merciless, ruthless; remorseless; bloodthirsty; hard, inflexible; grievous, sad, bitter, painful.—*n.* Cruel person. **cruellement,** *adv.* Cruelly; unmercifully, ruthlessly; grievously, severely. *Cruellement éprouvé,* sorely tried.

crûment [kry'mã], *adv.* Roughly, coarsely; harshly, crudely.

cruor [kry'ɔr], *n.m.* (*Physiol.*) Cruor.

crural [kry'ral], *a.* (*fem.* -ale, *pl.* -aux) (*Anat.*) Crural.

Crusoé [kryzo'e], *m.* Crusoe.

crustacé [krysta'se], *a.* (*fem.* -ée) Crustaceous.—*n.m.* Crustacean; shell-fish.

cryolite or **cryolithe** [krio'lit], *n.f.* Cryolite.

crypte [kript], *n.f.* Crypt.

cryptogame [kriptɔ'gam], *a.* Cryptogamous. —*n.f.* Cryptogam. **cryptogamie,** *n.f.* Cryptogamy.

cryptogramme [kriptɔ'gram], *n.m.* Cryptogram, cipher.

cryptographe [kriptɔ'graf], *n.m.* Cryptographer. **cryptographie,** *n.f.* Cryptography. **cryptographique,** *a.* Cryptographic.

cryptonyme [kriptɔ'nim], *n.m.* Cryptonym.

cubage [ky'ba:ʒ], *n.m.* Cubage, cubature; cubic content.

cubain [ky'bɛ̃], *a.* and *n.* (*fem.* -aine) Cuban.

cubature [kyba'ty:r], *n.f.* Cubature.

cube [kyb], *a.* Cubic.—*n.m.* Cube (shape and measure); (*sch.*) a pupil in his third year (of preparation for a competitive examination).

cubèbe [ky'beb], *n.m.* (*Bot.*) Cubeb.

cuber [ky'be], *v.t.* To cube; to contain in cubic feet etc.

cubilot [kybi'lo], *n.m.* Cupola (furnace).

cubique [ky'bik], *a.* Cubic; cubical. *Racine cubique,* cube root.

cubisme [ky'bism], *n.m.* (*Art*) Cubism. **cubiste,** *n.* and *a.* Cubist.

cubital [kybi'tal], *a.* (*fem.* -ale, *pl.* -aux) (*Anat.*) Cubital.

cuboïde [kybɔ'id], *a.* and *n.m.* Cuboid.

cuculle [ky'kyl], *n.f.* Monk's hood. **cucullaire,** *a.* Cucullate. **cuculliforme,** *a.* Cuculliform.

cucurbitacé [kykyrbita'se], *a.* (*fem.* -ée) (*Bot.*) Cucurbitaceous.—*n.f.* Cucurbitaceous plant (*e.g.* melon). **cucurbite,** *n.f.* (*Chem.*) Cucurbit.

cueillage [kœ'ja:ʒ], *n.m.*, **cueillaison** or **cueille,** *n.f.* Gathering-time, gathering. **cueillette,** *n.f.* Gathering of a crop; harvesting time. (*Naut.*) *Navire chargé en cueillette,* tramp loaded with such cargo as the captain may pick up. **cueilleur,** *n.m.* (*fem.* -euse) Gatherer, picker.

cueillir [kœ'ji:r], *v.t. irr.* (*pres.p.* **cueillant,** *p.p.* **cueilli,** *indic.* **je cueille**) To gather, to cull, to pick, to pluck; to take up, to acquire; (*colloq.*) to seize, to apprehend, to nab; (*Naut.*) to coil. *Cueillir des fleurs,* to pluck flowers; *cueillir des lauriers,* to win laurels. **cueilloir,** *n.m.* Fruit-basket; implement for picking fruit.

cuffat or **cufat** [ky'fa], *n.m.* (*Mining*) Skip, (hoisting) tub or bucket.

cuiller or **cuillère** [kɥi'jɛr], *n.f.* Spoon; scoop etc. *Cuiller à bouche*, or *à soupe*, soup-spoon; *cuiller à café*, tea-spoon; *cuiller à pot*, ladle; *cuiller à dessert*, dessert-spoon; *biscuit à la cuiller*, finger biscuit; *ne pas y aller avec le dos de la cuiller*, to lay it on thick; (*vulg.*) *la cuiller* instead of *la main*. **cuillerée**, *n.f.* Spoonful, ladleful. *Grande cuillerée* or *cuillerée à bouche*, tablespoonful; *petite cuillerée* or *cuillerée à café*, teaspoonful. **cuilleron**, *n.m.* Bowl of a spoon.

cuir [kɥi:r], *n.m.* Hide; dressed hide, dressed skin; leather; strop; (*fig.*) an incorrect liaison. *Cuir à rasoir*, razor-strop; *cuir chevelu*, scalp; *cuir de Russie*, Russian leather; *de cuir*, leathern; *entre cuir et chair*, under the skin, (*fig.*) secretly, privately; *faire des cuirs en parlant*, to make incorrect liaisons; *tanner le cuir à quelqu'un*, to give someone a hiding.

cuirasse [kɥi'ras], *n.f.* Cuirass, breast-plate; armour-plate; shell; (*Ent.*) elytra. *Le défaut de la cuirasse*, the chink in the armour, (*fig.*) vulnerable part. **cuirassé**, *a.* (*fem.* **-ée**) Armed with a cuirass; armour-plated; (*fig.*) ready armed or prepared; hardened; secret, close. *Il est cuirassé*, he is prepared for anything, he is incapable of remorse; *vaisseau cuirassé*, iron-clad ship.—*n.m.* (*Naut.*) Armoured ship; battleship. **cuirassement**, *n.m.* Armour-plating. **cuirasser**, *v.t.* To arm with a cuirass; to armour-plate; (*fig.*) to steel, to harden, to season. **se cuirasser**, *v.r.* To put on a cuirass; to harden or fortify oneself. **cuirassier**, *n.m.* Cuirassier.

cuire [kɥi:r], *v.t. irr.* (*pres.p.* **cuisant**, *p.p.* **cuit**, *conjugated like* CONDUIRE) To cook; to burn (of the sun); to ripen. *Cuire à l'eau*, to boil; *cuire au four*, to bake; *cuire à l'étuvée*, to stew; *cuire à feu doux*, to simmer; *cuire des briques*, to burn bricks.—*v.i.* To cook, to be cooked, to be done; to bake, broil, boil, etc.; to get cooked; to smart, to burn. *Il vous en cuira*, you shall smart for it; *la main me cuit*, my hand smarts; *trop gratter cuit, trop parler nuit*, least said, soonest mended. **se cuire**, *v.r.* To get cooked, to be done.

cuisage [kɥi'za:ʒ], *n.m.* Burning (of charcoal), charring.

cuisant [kɥi'zɑ̃], *a.* Sharp, smarting, piercing, poignant. *Douleur cuisante*, violent pain.

cuiseur [kɥi'zœ:r], *n.m.* Pressure cooker; brick-burner.

cuisine [kɥi'zin], *n.f.* Kitchen; cookery; the cooks; cooked food; fare, living; (*Naut.*) galley; (*fig.*) underhand tricks, subterfuge. *Aide de cuisine*, undercook; *chef de cuisine*, chief cook, chef; *cuisine bourgeoise*, plain cooking, homely fare; *cuisine roulante*, (*Mil.*) field kitchen; *faire la cuisine*, to cook; *fille de cuisine*, kitchen-maid; *la cuisine est bonne*, the cooking is good; *livre de cuisine*, cookery book. **cuisiner**, *v.t., v.i.* To cook; (*fig.*) to interrogate, to pump (a man under remand); to cook the books. **cuisinier**, *n.m.* (*fem.* **-ière**) Cook.—*n.f.* Dutch oven; kitchener (stove).

cuissard [kɥi'sa:r], *n.m.* Cuisse (armour); (*Surg.*) thigh-piece, socket (for amputated limb); (*cyclist's*) seatless trousers.

cuisse [kɥis], *n.f.* Thigh; quarter (of venison);

leg (of poultry). *Se croire issu de la cuisse de Jupiter*, to have an exaggerated opinion of one's own importance.

cuisseau [kɥi'so], *n.m.* Leg (of veal).

cuissière [kɥi'sjɛ:r], *n.f.* Drummer's apron.

cuisson [kɥi'sɔ̃], *n.f.* Cooking (baking, boiling, roasting, etc.); smart (pain). *Pain de cuisson*, home-made bread; *ressentir une cuisson*, to feel a smarting pain.

cuissot [kɥi'so], *n.m.* Haunch (of venison).

cuistance [kɥis'tɑ̃s], *n.f.* (*Mil. slang*) Cookery; cooking. **cuisteau, cuistot**, *n.m.* (*slang*) Cook.

cuistre [kɥistr], *n.m.* *College-scout; (*colloq.*) vulgar, pedantic fellow; cad, tactless fellow. **cuistrerie**, *n.f.* Vulgar pedantry; caddish behaviour.

cuit [kɥi], *a.* (*fem.* **cuite** (1)) Cooked, done (roasted, boiled, baked, etc.); (*fig.*) done for, dished; (*colloq.*) ripe, mature. *Avoir son pain cuit*, (*colloq.*) to be well provided for; *cela est trop cuit*, that is done too much, overdone (of meat); *cuit à point*, done to a turn; *vin cuit*, sweet wine. (*fam.*) *Je suis cuit*, I've 'had it'.

cuite (2) [kɥit], *n.f.* Baking; burning (of bricks etc.); ovenful, kilnful; (*slang*) intoxication. **se cuiter**, *v.r.* (*slang*) To get drunk.

cuivrage [kɥi'vra:ʒ], *n.m.* Coppering; copper-plating.

cuivre [kɥi:vr], *n.m.* Copper; copper money; engraving on copper, copper-plate. *Cuivre battu*, wrought copper; *cuivre jaune*, brass; *cuivre rouge*, copper; *cuivre vierge*, native copper; *faire les cuivres*, to do the brass; (*Mus.*) *les cuivres*, the brass (wind instruments). **cuivré**, *a.* (*fem.* **-ée**) Copper-coloured; (*fig.*) bronzed (complexion), ringing, clear, sonorous. **cuivrer**, *v.t.* To cover with sheet copper; to copper; to give copper-colour to. **cuivrerie**, *n.f.* Copper-works; copper-making; copper wares. **cuivreux**, *a.* (*fem.* **-euse**) Coppery. **cuivrique**, *a.* Cupreous.

cul [ky], *n.m.* (*indec.*) Backside, bum; posterior; bottom (of bottle or bag); end; stern (of ship). *Cul de porc*, (*Naut.*) wall-knot; *cul par-dessus tête*, head over heels; *mettre à cul une carriole, un tonneau*, to tip up a carriole, a barrel; (*Mil.*) *tirer au cul*, to malinger.

culasse [ky'las], *n.f.* Breech (of a cannon, musket, etc.); (*Elec.*) yoke (of electro-magnet); cylinder-head (of car engine etc.) **culasser**, *v.t.* To breech (fire-arms).

cul-blanc [ky'blɑ̃], *n.m.* (*pl.* **culs-blancs**) (*Orn.*) Wheatear.

culbutant [kylby'tɑ̃], *n.m.* Tumbler (pigeon); (*slang*) pair of trousers.

culbute [kyl'byt], *n.f.* Somersault; fall, tumble; (*fig.*) ruin, failure, bankruptcy. *Au bout du fossé la culbute*, look before you leap; *faire la culbute*, to turn a somersault; (*fig.*) to fall into disgrace, to become bankrupt. **culbuter**, *v.t.* To throw over, to upset violently; to overthrow, to do for.—*v.i.* To fall head over heels; to be upset; (*fig.*) to fail (in business). **culbuteur**, *n.m.* Tipper, rocker-arm; tumbling-jack (toy). **culbutis**, *n.m.* Confused heap, jumble.

cul de bouteille [kydbu'tɛj], *n.m.* Bottom of bottle.—*a.* Bottle-green.

cul-de-chaudron [kydʃo'drɔ̃], *n.m.* (*pl.* **culs-de-chaudron**) Hole formed by explosion in mine. **cul-de-jatte**, *n.m.* (*pl.* **culs-de-jatte**) Legless cripple, cripple whose legs are paralysed. **cul-de-lampe**, *n.m.* (*pl.* **culs-de-lampe**) (*Arch.*) Pendant; (*Print.*) tail-piece. **cul-de-sac**, *n.m.* (*pl.* **culs-de-sac**) Blind alley; cul-de-sac; (*fig.*) deadlock.

culée [ky'le], *n.f.* Abutment (of bridges); (*Naut.*) stern-way.

culer [ky'le], *v.i.* To go backwards; to fall astern, to make stern-way; to veer astern (of the wind). *Nager à culer*, to back water.

culeron [kyl'rɔ̃], *n.m.* Crupper-loop.

culière [ky'ljɛːr], *n.f.* Hind girth, crupper (of harness); gutter-stone, kennel-stone.

culinaire [kyli'nɛːr], *a.* Culinary.

culmifère [kylmi'fɛːr], *a.* (*Bot.*) Culmiferous.

culminance [kylmi'nãːs], *n.f.* Culmination, highest point. **culminant**, *a.* (*fem.* **-ante**) Culminating, highest; prominent. **culmination**, *n.f.* Culmination. **culminer**, *v.i.* To culminate.

culot [ky'lo], *n.m.* Bottom (of lamps, crucibles, etc.); residuum, (*fam.*) dottle (in a pipe); metal end (of cartridges, crucibles, etc.). (*slang*) *Avoir du culot*, to have plenty of cheek.

culottage [kylɔ'taːʒ], *n.m.* Colouring, seasoning (of pipes).

culotte [ky'lɔt], *n.f.* Breeches; (*iron.*) trousers; (*pl.*) shorts; tights; woman's knickers; (*Cook.*) rump (of an ox); (*fig.*) heavy loss in gaming. *Culotte bouffante*, knickerbockers; *culotte courte*, knee-breeches; *culotte de course (à pied)*, shorts; *culotte collante*, tights; *culotte de bœuf*, rump of beef; *culotte de cheval*, riding-breeches; *culotte de golf*, plus-fours; *culotte de peau*, leather breeches, (*fig.*) old retired officer; *porter la culotte*, to wear the trousers (of a masterful woman); *prendre une (belle* or *forte) culotte*, to lose heavily (at cards); to get drunk.

culotté [kylɔ'te], *a.* (*Garçon*) *culotté*, saucy, cheeky, plucky (boy); *pipe (bien) culottée*, (well) seasoned pipe; *bouquins culottés*, (old) well-thumbed books.

culotter [kylɔ'te], *v.t.* To breech, to put in breeches; to colour (pipes). **se culotter**, *v.r.* To put on one's breeches; to get coloured (of pipes). **culotteur**, *n.m.* One who colours pipes. *Culotteur de pipes*, hardened pipe-smoker. **culottier**, *n.m.* (*fem.* **-ière**) Breeches-maker.

culpabilité [kylpabili'te], *n.f.* Culpability; guilt.

culte [kylt], *n.m.* Worship, adoration; (*fig.*) cult, religion, creed; veneration, honour, love, respect, enthusiastic admiration. *Rendre une sorte de culte à*, to worship. *Liberté du culte*, freedom of worship.

cul-terreux [kytɛ'rø], *n.m.* Clodhopper.

cultisme [kyl'tism], *n.m.* Cultism.

cultivable [kylti'vabl], *a.* Cultivable, arable.

cultivateur [kyltiva'tœːr], *n.m.* (*fem.* **cultivatrice**) Cultivator, farmer, grower, agriculturist; cultivator (implement).—*a.* Agricultural. **cultivé**, *a.* (*fem.* **-ée**) Cultivated; (of the mind) cultured.

cultiver [kylti've], *v.t.* To cultivate; to till; to improve (the mind); to devote oneself to, to study, to exercise, to practise; to cultivate the acquaintance of.

cultriforme [kyltri'fɔrm], *a.* Cultriform. **cultrirostre**, *a.* Cultrirostral.

cultuel [kyl'tɥɛl], *a.* (*fem.* **-elle**) Pertaining to worship.

cultural [kylty'ral], *a.* (*fem.* **-ale**, *pl.* **-aux**) Cultural (in relation to agriculture).

culture [kyl'tyːr], *n.f.* Culture, cultivation, tillage, husbandry; education, improvement; (*pl.*) cultivated land; rearing, breeding (of fish, oysters). *La petite culture*, farming on a small scale (raising of poultry etc.); *bouillon de culture*, culture fluid; *une culture classique*, a classical education. **culturel**, *a.* (*fem.* **-elle**) Cultural (in relation to intellectual culture).

cumène [ky'mɛn], *n.m.* (*Chem.*) Cumene.

cumin [ky'mɛ̃], *n.m.* Cumin. **cuminique**, *a.* Cumic.

cumul [ky'myl], *n.m.* Plurality of offices or places, pluralism. *Par cumul*, by accumulation. **cumulard**, *n.m.* (*fam.*) Pluralist, twicer. **cumulatif**, *a.* (*fem.* **cumulative**) Accumulative. **cumulativement**, *adv.* By accumulation. **cumuler**, *v.t.* To accumulate; to hold several (offices, salaries, etc.).

cumulus [kymy'lyːs], *n.m.* Cumulus.

cunéaire [kyne'ɛːr], *a.* Cuneate, wedge-shaped. **cunéiforme**, *a.* Cuneiform (of bones or writing).

cunette [ky'nɛt], *n.f.* Channel at bottom of a drain, aqueduct, etc.; (*Fort.*) channel at bottom of moat etc.

cupide [ky'pid], *a.* Covetous, greedy, grasping. **cupidement**, *adv.* Greedily, covetously. **cupidité**, *n.f.* Cupidity, covetousness, greed.

Cupidon [kypi'dɔ̃], *n.m.* (*Myth.*) Cupid, Love. *Vieux cupidon*, old beau.

cuprique [ky'prik], *a.* Cupric. **cuprite**, *n.m.* Cuprite.

cupulaire [kypy'lɛːr], *a.* (*Bot.*) Cup-shaped. **cupule**, *n.f.* Cupule, cup (of acorns). **cupulé**, *a.* (*fem.* **-ée**) Cupulate. **cupulifère**, *a.* Cupuliferous.

curabilité [ky'rabili'te], *n.f.* Curability. **curable**, *a.* Curable.

curaçao [kyra'so], *n.m.* Curaçao (liqueur).

curage [ky'raːʒ] or **curement**, *n.m.* Cleansing, (of harbours, sewers, etc.); water-pepper (plant).

curare [ky'raːr], *n.m.* Curare (arrow-poison). **curarine**, *n.f.* Curarine. **curariser**, *v.t.* To curarize.

curatelle [kyra'tɛl], *n.f.* Guardianship, trusteeship. **curateur**, *n.m.* (*fem.* **curatrice**) Guardian, trustee.

curatif [kyra'tif], *a.* (*fem.* **-ive**) Curative.— *n.m.* Curative agent.

curcuma [kyrky'ma], *n.m.* Curcuma, turmeric.

cure [kyr], *n.f.* *Care, attention; medical treatment, cure, healing; vicarship, rectorship; vicarage, rectory, presbytery. *N'en avoir cure*, to pay no heed to; *faire une cure à Vichy*, to take the waters at Vichy.

curé [ky're], *n.m.* Parish priest; parson, rector, vicar. *C'est Gros Jean qui en remonte à son curé*, he is teaching his grandmother to suck eggs; *monsieur le curé*, your reverence.

cure-dent [kyr'dã], *n.m.* (*pl.* **cure-dents**) Tooth-pick.

curée [ky're], *n.f.* (*Hunt.*) Part of the animal

given to the hounds after a kill, quarry, chase; (*fig.*) prey, booty, spoils. *Être à la curée*, to be in at the death, (*fig.*) to share the spoils; *la curée des places*, the scramble for office; *mettre en curée*, to flesh the hounds, to feed them; *sonner la curée*, to sound the quarry.

curement [CURAGE].

cure-môle [kyr'mo:l], *n.m.* (*pl.* **cure-môles**) Dredging-machine. **cure-ongles,** *n.m. inv.* Nail-file. **cure-oreille,** *n.m.* (*pl.* **cure-oreilles**) Ear-spoon. **cure-pied,** *n.m.* (*pl.* **cure-pieds**) Hoof-pick.

curer [ky're], *v.t.* To cleanse, to clean out (harbours, sewers, etc.); to pick (teeth, ears, etc.). *Se curer les dents*, to pick one's teeth. —*v.i.* To seize the quarry (of hawks etc.).

curetage [kyr'ta3], *n.m.* Scraping, curetting.

curette [ky'rɛt], *n.f.* Scraper, scoop, cleaner.

cureur [ky'rœ:r], *n.m.* Cleanser (of harbours, sewers, etc.).

curial (1) [ky'rjal], *a.* (*fem.* **-iale** (1), *pl.* **-iaux**) Vicarial, rectorial. *Maison curiale*, parsonage.

curial (2) or **curiale** (2) [ky'rjal], *a.* (*Rom. Ant.*) Curial.

curie [ky'ri], *n.f.* (*Rom. Ant.*) Curia.

curieusement [kyrjøz'mã], *adv.* Curiously; inquisitively; carefully, minutely; quaintly.

curieux [ky'rjø], *a.* (*fem.* **curieuse**) Curious; inquisitive, prying; inquiring; careful, nice, dainty, fastidious, fussy; particular; strange, surprising, singular. *Chose assez curieuse*, a rather curious thing; *il est curieux de tableaux*, he is fond of pictures; *je serais curieux de savoir comment*, I should like to know how.—*n.* Interested person; inquisitive person; sight-seer, looker-on; curious thing or fact. *Le curieux de la chose est*, the odd thing about it is.

curiosité [kyrjozi'te], *n.f.* Curiosity; inquisitiveness, prying disposition; curio, rarity; quaintness. *Par curiosité*, out of curiosity.

curiste [ky'rist], *n.m.* Person taking a cure.

curseur [kyr'sœ:r], *n.m.* Slide, index (in mathematical instrument).

cursif [kyr'sif], *a.* (*fem.* **-ive**) Cursive, running; cursory.—*n.f.* Running hand (writing).

cursivement, *adv.* Cursively; cursorily.

curule [ky'ryl], *a.* (*Rom. Ant.*) Curule. *Chaise curule*, curule chair.

curure [ky'ry:r], *n.f.* Dirt, muck (from a drain etc.), sewage.

curvatif [kyrva'tif], *a.* (*fem.* **-ive**) Slightly curved. **curvicaude,** *a.* Curvicaudate. **curvifolié,** *a.* (*fem.* **-ée**) Curvifoliate. **curviligne,** *a.* Curvilinear. **curvirostre,** *a.* Curvirostral, hook-billed.

cuscute [kys'kyt], *n.f.* (*Bot.*) Dodder.

cuspide [kys'pid], *n.f.* (*Bot.*) Cusp. **cuspidé,** *a.* (*fem.* **-ée**) Cuspidate.

cussonné [kysɔ'ne], *a.* (*fem.* **-ée**) Worm-eaten (of wood).

custode (1) [kys'tɔd], *n.f.* Curtain of the high altar; pyx-cover; custodial; arm-rest; curtain. *Sous la custode*, in private.

custode (2) [kys'tɔd], *n.m.* Warden (among monks); custodian, inspector.

cutané [kyta'ne], *a.* (*fem.* **-ée**) Cutaneous.

cuticulaire [kytiky'lɛ:r], *a.* Cuticular.

cuticule [kyti'kyl], *n.f.* Cuticle. **cuticuleux,** *a.* (*fem.* **-euse**) Cuticular.

cuvage [ky'va3], *n.m.,* or **cuvaison,** *n.f.* Fermenting of (wine); room where vats are placed.

cuve [ky:v], *n.f.* Tub, vat (also applied to many other household or industrial containers). *À fond de cuve*, (*fig.*) thoroughly, exhaustively; *cuve de brasseur*, brewing-vat; *cuve à lessive*, wash-tub; *cuve à tanner*, tan-pit. **cuveau,** *n.m.* Small vat, small tub. **cuvée,** *n.f.* Tubful; vatful; (*colloq.*) sort, kind, set. *En voici d'une autre cuvée*, here's one of another sort for you; *première cuvée* or *tête de cuvée*, the first-quality growth of wine.

cuvelage [ky'vla:3] or **cuvellement,** *n.m.* Lining, casing (of mine-shafts); introduction of tubing (in artesian wells). **cuveler,** *v.t.* To line, to case (mine-shafts etc.).

cuver [ky've], *v.i.* To work, to ferment, to settle.—*v.t.* To ferment; (*fam.*) to sleep off the effects of (wine). *Cuver son vin*, to sleep oneself sober.

cuvette [ky'vet], *n.f.* Shallow basin; wash-hand basin; cistern, bulb (of barometers, steam-engines, etc.); cap (of watch); bowl (of compass); pedestal (of a harp); (*Geog.*) basin. *Montre à cuvette*, capped watch.

cuvier [ky'vje], *n.m.* Wash-tub.

cyanamide [sjana'mid], *n.f.* (*Chem.*) Cyanamide.

cyanate [sja'nat], *n.m.* (*Chem.*) Cyanate. **cyanhydrique,** *a.* Hydrocyanic, prussic.

cyanine [sja'nin], *n.f.* (*Chem.*) Cyanine. **cyanique,** *a.* Cyanic. **cyanite,** *n.m.* Cyanite. **cyanogène,** *n.m.* Cyanogen. **cyanomètre,** *n.m.* Cyanometer. **cyanose,** *n.f.* Cyanosis.

cyanure [sja'ny:r], *n.m.* (*Chem.*) Cyanide.

cyathe [sjat], *n.m.* (*Gr. Ant.*) Goblet (to fill the cups).

cybernétique [siberne'tik], *n.f.* Cybernetics.

cyclable [si'klabl], *a.* Fit or reserved for cycling. *Piste cyclable*, cycle track.

cyclamen [sikla'men], *n.m.* Cyclamen, sow-bread.

cycle [sikl], *n.m.* Cycle (of events); a stage in education, *e.g. premier cycle*, first four years in a grammar school; group of epic poems on a common subject, *e.g. le cycle de Charlemagne*; (*colloq.*) bicycle, tricycle, etc. *Cycle solaire*, solar cycle; *cycle à 4 temps* (*d'un moteur*), 4-stroke cycle (of an engine).

cyclique [si'klik], *a.* Cyclical. **cyclisme,** *n.m.* Cycling. **cycliste,** *n.* Cyclist.

cyclographe [siklɔ'graf], *n.m.* Cyclograph.

cycloïdal [siklɔi'dal], *a.* (*fem.* **-ale,** *pl.* **-aux**) Cycloidal. **cycloïde,** *n.f.* Cycloid.

cyclomoteur [siklɔmɔ'tœr], *n.m.* Auto-cycle.

cyclonal [siklɔ'nal], *a.* (*fem.* **-ale,** *pl.* **-aux**) Cyclonic.

cyclone [si'klo:n], *n.m.* Cyclone. **cyclonique,** *a.* Cyclonic.

cyclope [si'klɔp], *n.m.* Cyclops. **cyclopéen,** *a.* (*fem.* **-éenne**) Cyclopean.

cyclotron [siklɔ'trɔ̃], *n.m.* Cyclotron.

cygne [sin], *n.m.* Swan. *Jeune cygne*, cygnet; *le cygne de Cambrai*, Fénelon; *le cygne de Mantoue*, Virgil; *chant de cygne*, swan-song; *en col de cygne*, swan-necked (tap etc.).

cylindrage [silɛ̃'dra:3], *n.m.* Mangling (of linen etc.); rolling (of roads).

cylindre [si'lɛ̃:dr], *n.m.* Cylinder; roller; garden-roller; mangle, calender; (*Organ*) barrel. *Moteur à 4 cylindres*, 4-cylinder engine, *passer au cylindre*, to pass through the mangle. **cylindrée**, *n.f.* Cubic capacity of an engine. **cylindrer**, *v.t.* To calender; to roll. **cylindreur**, *n.m.* (*fem.* **-euse**) One who rolls, calenders, etc. **cylindrique**, *a.* Cylindrical. **cylindroïde**, *a.* Cylindroid.

cymaise [CIMAISE].

cymbalaire [sɛ̃ba'lɛːr], *n.f.* (Ivy-leaved) toad-flax (*Linaria cymbalaria*).

cymbale [sɛ̃'bal], *n.f.* (*Mus.*) Cymbal. **cymbalier**, *n.m.* Cymbal-player.

cyme [sim], *n.f.* (*Bot.*) Cyme.

cymrique [KYMRIQUE].

cynancie [ESQUINANCIE].

cynanque [si'nɑ̃:k] or **synanche**, *n.m.* (*Bot.*) Dog's-bane, cynanchum.

cynégétique [sineʒe'tik], *a.* Relating to hunting and dogs.—*n.f.* The art of hunting with dogs, cynegetics.

cynips [si'nips], *n.m.* Gall-fly.

cynique [si'nik], *a.* Cynical, snarling, snappish; impudent, barefaced, indecent.—*n.m.* Cynic. **cyniquement**, *adv.* Cynically. **cynisme**, *n.m.* Cynicism, cynicalness; impudence, barefacedness, indecency.

cynocéphale [sinɔse'fal], *n.m.* (*Zool.*) Cynocephalus; dog-faced baboon.

cynodon [sinɔ'dɔ̃], *n.m.* (*Bot.*) Dog's-tooth grass, *Cynodon dactylon*.

cynodrome [sinɔ'drɔːm], *n.m.* Greyhound racing track.

cynoglosse [sinɔ'glɔs], *n.f.* Hound's-tongue.

cynorrhodon [sinɔrɔ'dɔ̃], *n.m.* (*Bot.*) Hip.

cynosure [sinɔ'syːr], *n.f.* (*Astron.*) Cynosure; Little Bear; (*Bot.*) dog's tail grass.

cyphose [si'foːz], *n.f.* (*Med.*) Cyphosis.

cyprès [si'prɛ], *n.m.* Cypress, cypress-tree, cypress-wood; (*fig.*) death, grief, mourning. **cyprière**, *n.f.* Cypress-grove.

cyprin [si'prɛ̃], *n.m.* (*Ichth.*) Cyprine. *Cyprin doré*, gold fish.

cypriote [si'priɔt], *n.* and *a.* Cyprian, Cypriot.

cypripède [sipri'pɛd], *n.m.* (*Bot.*) Lady's-slipper.

cyrard [si'rar], *n.m.* (*fam.*) Short for SAINT-CYRIEN.

cyrillien [siri'ljɛ̃] (*fem.* **-ienne**) or **cyrillique**, *a.* Cyrillic. *Alphabet cyrillien*, the Slavonic alphabet (invented in the 9th century by St. Cyril).

cystalgie [sistal'ʒi], *n.f.* Neuralgia of the bladder.

cystique [sis'tik], *a.* (*Anat.*) Cystic. **cystite**, *n.f.* (*Path.*) Cystitis. **cystocèle**, *n.f.* Cystocele; hernia of the bladder.

cytise [si'tiːz], *n.m.* Cytisus. *Cytise aubour*, laburnum.

cytoblaste [sitɔ'blast], *n.m.* Cytoblast.

cytologie [sitɔlɔ'ʒi], *n.f.* (*Biol.*) Cytology.

czar etc. [TZAR].

D

D, d [de], *n.m.* The fourth letter of the alphabet. *Employer le système D*, (*slang*) to wangle.

d', *abbr.* [DE].

da [da], *particle* (used after *oui*, *non*) Truly, indeed. *Oui-da*, yes, indeed.

dab [dab], *n.m.* (*slang*) Father, 'governor', boss.

d'abord [ABORD].

dactyle [dak'til], *n.m.* Dactyl; (*Bot.*) orchard grass. **dactylique**, *a.* Dactylic.

dactylo [dakti'lo], *n.f.* Short for DACTYLO-GRAPHE.

dactylographe [daktilɔ'graf], *n.m.* Typist. **dactylographie**, *n.f.* Typewriting. **dactylographier**, *v.t.* To type(write). **dactylographique**, *a.* Typewritten (report); typewriting (material).

dactyloptère [daktilɔp'tɛːr], *a.* (*Ichth.*) Finger-finned.—*n.m.* Flying-fish.

dada [da'da], *n.m.* (*Childish*) Horse, cock-horse; gee-gee; (*colloq.*) hobby, hobby-horse. *Aller à dada*, to ride a cock-horse; *être sur son dada*, to indulge in one's hobby; *l'école dada* or *dadaïsme*, the Dada school.

dadais [da'dɛ], *n.m.* Booby, clown, ninny.

dagard [DAGUET].

*dagorne [da'gɔrn], *n.f.* One-horned cow.

dague [dag], *n.f.* Dagger, dirk; (*pl.*) first horns (of a two-year-old deer).

daguerréotype [dagerɛɔ'tip], *n.m.* Daguerreo-type. **daguerréotyper**, *v.t.* To daguerreo-type. **daguerréotypie**, *n.f.* Daguerreotypy.

daguet [da'gɛ], *n.m.* (*Hunt.*) Brocket, yearling deer, pricket.

daguette [da'gɛt], *n.f.* Small dagger or dirk.

dahlia [da'lja], *n.m.* Dahlia.

daigner [dɛ'ɲe], *v.i.* To deign, to condescend.

d'ailleurs [AILLEURS].

daim [dɛ̃], *n.m.* Deer, fallow-deer; buck; (*fam.*) mug, idiot. *Chaussures de daim*, buck-skin shoes.

daine [dɛn], *n.f.* Doe.

dais [dɛ], *n.m.* Canopy.

daleau [DALOT].

dallage [da'laːʒ], *n.m.* Paving with flagstones, flagging.

dalle [dal], *n.f.* Flag, flagstone; slab; (*pop.*) mouth, throat. *Avoir la dalle en pente*, to be always thirsty; *se rincer la dalle*, to drink. **daller**, *v.t.* To pave with flagstones, to flag. **dalleur**, *n.m.* Pavior.

dalmate [dal'mat], *a.* and *n.* Dalmatian.

dalmatique [dalma'tik], *n.f.* Dalmatic.

dalot [da'lo], *n.m.* Scupper-hole, scupper. *Dalot de pompe*, pump-dale.

daltonisme [daltɔ'nism], *n.m.* Daltonism, colour-blindness.

dam [dɑ̃], *n.m.* *Hurt, injury; (*Theol.*) damnation. *À son, votre*, or *leur dam*, to his, your, or their injury.

damage [da'maːʒ], *n.m.* Ramming.

damas [da'ma], *n.m.* Damask; damask linen, diaper; damson; Damascus blade, Damascus steel.

damasquinage [damaski'naːʒ], *n.m.*, or **damasquinure**, *n.f.* Damascening.

damasquiner [damaski'ne], *v.t.* To damas-cene. **damasquinerie**, *n.f.* Damascening. **damasquineur**, *n.m.* Damascener. **damasquinure** [DAMASQUINAGE].

damassé [dama'se], *n.m.* Damask linen, damask cloth. **damasser**, *v.t.* To damask. **damasserie**, *n.f.* Damask linen manu-factory. **damasseur**, *n.m.* (*fem.* **damasseuse**) Damask weaver. **damassin**, *n.m.* Figured linen cloth, diaper. **damassure**, *n.f.* Damasking (of linen); damask work.

dame   daube

dame (1) [dam], *n.f.* (Married) lady, dame; rowlock; beetle, rammer; (*Backgammon*) man, piece; (*Draughts*) king; (*Cards* and *Chess*) queen. *Aller à dame*, to make a king (at draughts), to queen a pawn (at chess); *dame d'onze heures* (*Bot.*), Star of Bethlehem; *dame de nage*, rowlock; *dame d'honneur*, maid of honour; *elle fait la dame*, she sets up for a lady; *jeu de dames*, draughts; *jouer aux dames*, to play at draughts; *les dames de la halle*, the market-women; *Notre-Dame*, our Lady; *saluez vos dames*, bow to your partners.

dame (2) [dam], *n.f.* Dam; old-man.

dame (3) [dam], *int. Dame oui!* why, yes! *Dame! c'est juste*, well, you see, it is right!

dame-jeanne [dam'ʒɑːn], *n.f.* (*pl.* **dames-jeannes**) Demijohn, carboy.

damer [dɑ'me], *v.t.* (*Draughts*) To crown (a man); (*Chess*) to queen; to ram (earth etc.) with a beetle. *Damer le pion à quelqu'un*, to outwit someone, to be more than a match for someone.

*dameret [dam'rɛ], *a.* Foppish.—*n.m.* Lady's man, spark, beau.

damier [dɑ'mje], *n.m.* Draught-board; (*Bot.*) fritillary. *En damier*, in check pattern.

damnable [dɑ'nabl], *a.* Damnable. **damnablement**, *adv.* Damnably.

damnation [dɑnɑ'sjɔ̃], *n.f.* Damnation.

damné [dɑ'ne], *a.* and *n.* (*fem.* **damnée**) Damned. *C'est l'âme damnée du ministre*, he is the tool of the minister (does his dirty work for him); (*fam.*) *cette damnée histoire*, this confounded story; *les damnés*, the damned; *souffrir comme un damné*, to suffer horribly.

damner [dɑ'ne], *v.t.* To damn. **se damner**, *v.r.* To damn oneself. *Cet enfant fait damner ses parents*, this child drives his parents mad; *il ferait damner un saint*, he would make a saint swear.

damoiseau [damwa'zo] or **damoisel**, *n.m.* *Squire; fop, spark.

*damoiselle [damwa'zɛl], *n.f.* Young lady of quality; damsel.

dancing [dɑ̃'siŋ], *n.m.* Dancing-hall, palais de dance.

dandin [dɑ̃'dɛ̃], *n.m.* Ninny.

dandinant [dɑ̃di'nɑ̃], *a.* (*fem.* -**ante**) Swinging, rolling.

dandine [dɑ̃'din], *n.m.* Iron-rod (for stirring wine during the fining process).

dandinement [dɑ̃din'mɑ̃], *n.m.* Swinging (of the body); rolling gait.

dandiner [dɑ̃di'ne], *v.i.* To swing (the arms), to dandle (a baby). **se dandiner**, *v.r.* To waddle.

dandy [dɑ̃'di], *n.m.* Dandy. **dandysme**, *n.m.* Dandyism.

danger [dɑ̃'ʒe], *n.m.* Danger, peril, risk, hazard, jeopardy. *Affronter les dangers*, to face dangers; *être en danger de*, to be in danger of; *hors de danger*, out of danger; *pas de danger!* No fear! **dangereusement**, *adv.* Dangerously. **dangereux**, *a.* (*fem.* -**euse**) Dangerous.

danois [da'nwa], *a.* (*fem.* **danoise**) Danish.— *n.m.* (**Danois**, *fem.* **Danoise**) Dane.—*n.m.* Great dane (dog).

dans [dɑ̃], *prep.* In, within; into; with; through, according to; during; out of; about.

Boire dans une tasse, to drink out of a cup; *il fait cela dans le dessein de s'établir*, he does so with the intention of establishing himself; *j'ai beaucoup travaillé dans le temps*, I used to study a good deal in my time; *rester dans la légalité*, to remain within the law; *tomber dans l'oubli*, to sink into oblivion.

dansant [dɑ̃'sɑ̃], *a.* (*fem.* -**ante**) Dancing. *Soirée dansante*, dancing party, evening party.

danse [dɑ̃ːs], *n.f.* Dance; dancing; (*fig.*) beating, hiding. *Aimer la danse*, to like dancing; *danse de Saint-Guy*, St. Vitus's dance; *donner une danse à quelqu'un*, to give someone a drubbing; *entrer en danse*, to join the dance, (*fig.*) to join in; *il a une danse contrainte*, he has a stiff way of dancing; *la danse va commencer*, now we are in for it.

danser [dɑ̃'se], *v.i.* To dance. *Danser en mesure*, to keep time in dancing; *faire danser quelqu'un*, to lead someone a dance; *il ne sait sur quel pied danser*, he does not know which way to turn.—*v.t.* To dance. *Danser un menuet*, to dance a minuet. **se danser**, *v.r.* To be danced. **danseur**, *n.m.* (*fem.* **danseuse**) Dancer, ballet-girl, partner (at a dance). *Danseur de corde*, rope-dancer.

daphné [daf'ne], *n.m.* (*Bot.*) Daphne, laurel.

darce [DARSE].

dard [daːr], *n.m.* Dart; sting; forked tongue (of a snake); pistil. *Le dard d'une abeille*, the sting of a bee. **darder**, *v.t.* To hurl; to spear; to shoot forth, to beam, to dart (beams etc.). *Le soleil darde ses rayons*, the sun darts forth his rays. **dardillon**, *n.m.* Small dart; barb (of a fish-hook).

dare-dare [dar'daːr], *adv.* In great haste, in double-quick time.

dariole [dar'rjɔl], *n.f.* Custard-tart.

darne [darn], *n.f.* Slice (of fish).

darse or **darce** [dars], *n.f.* Wet-dock, inner basin of harbour, esp. in Mediterranean.

dartre [dartr], *n.f.* Slight and dry eruption (of the skin), scurf, etc. *Dartres farineuses*, pityriasis. **dartreux**, *a.* (*fem.* -**euse**) Herpetic, scurfy.—*n.* Person affected with skin disease.

darwinien [darwi'njɛ̃], *a.* (*fem.* **darwinienne**) Darwinian. **darwinisme**, *n.m.* Darwinism, **darwiniste**, *n.* Darwinist.

datation [data'sjɔ̃], *n.f.* Dating.

date [dat], *n.f.* Date. *De longue date*, of long standing, long since; *en date du*, under date of, bearing the date; *je suis le premier en date*, I have the priority; *prendre date*, to count from, (*fig.*) to fix a date. **dater**, *v.t.* To date (a letter etc.).—*v.i.* To date (*de*); to form a period; to reckon. *À dater de*, reckoning from; *dater de loin*, to date far back, to happen long ago.

datif [da'tif], *a.* (*fem.* -**ive**) Dative. *Tutelle dative*, dative guardianship.—*n.m.* (*Gram.*) Dative, dative case.

dation [dɑ'sjɔ̃], *n.f.* (*Law*) Giving. *Dation en paiement*, giving in payment.

datisme [da'tism], *n.m.* Accumulation of synonyms.

datte [dat], *n.f.* Date. (*pop.*) *Des dattes!* No! Nothing doing! **dattier**, *n.m.* Date-tree.

datura [daty'ra], *n.m.* Datura, thorn-apple. **daturine**, *n.f.* Daturine.

daube [doːb], *n.f.* Stew.

dauber [do'be], *v.t.* To cuff, to drub; (*fig.*) to banter, to jeer at; (*Cook.*) to stew, to braise. *Dauber quelqu'un* or *sur quelqu'un*, to go for someone. **daubeur,** *n.m.* (*fem.* -**euse**) Jeerer, banterer, sneerer.

daubière [do'bjɛːr], *n.f.* Stew-pan.

daumont [do'mɔ̃], *n.f. Une daumont,* or *un attelage à la daumont* (or *d'Aumont*), carriage and four with two postillions.

dauphin [do'fɛ̃], *n.m.* Dolphin; dauphin (eldest son of the king of France). **dauphine,** *n.f.* Wife of the dauphin.

dauphinelle [dofi'nɛl], *n.f.* (*Bot.*) Larkspur, delphinium.

daurade [do'rad], *n.f.* Gilt-head (fish).

davantage [davɑ̃'taːʒ], *adv.* More, any more; any longer, any further. *Je n'en dirai pas davantage,* I shall say no more; *je n'en sais pas davantage,* I know nothing more about it; *ne restez pas davantage,* do not stay any longer.

davier [da'vje], *n.m.* Dentist's forceps; cramp; (*Naut.*) fore-roller, davit.

de (1) [də], *prep.* (With *le, la, les, de* becomes *du, de la, des*; before a vowel or silent *h* the *e* is elided, thus *d'*) Of; out of, made of, composed of, from; by; with; between; at, for, on account of; concerning, about. *Avoir besoin d'argent,* to be in want of money; *d'après l'original,* from the original; *de bouche en bouche,* from mouth to mouth; *de ce que,* because; *de chez vous,* from your house; *de mal en pis,* from bad to worse; *de nuit,* by night; *de Paris à Londres,* from Paris to London; *de par le roi,* in the king's name; *de près, de loin,* near, afar; *de vous à moi,* between you and me; *être de,* to be one of (a party etc.); *faire de son mieux,* to do one's best; *il n'y a personne de blessé,* there is no one wounded; *il vient de me le donner,* he has just given it me; *il y eut cent hommes de tués,* there were a hundred men killed; *indigne de vivre,* unworthy to live; *leçons de danse,* dancing lessons; *le désir d'apprendre,* the wish to learn; *les hommes d'à-présent* or *d'aujourd'-hui,* the men of today; *l'un d'entre eux,* one of them; *n'avez-vous point d'enfants?* haven't you any children? *plus d'actes et moins de paroles,* more deeds and fewer words; *quelque chose de bon,* something good; *qu'est-ce que de nous!* what poor creatures we are! *sauter de joie,* to leap for joy; *se moquer de quelqu'un,* to laugh at someone; *signe de tête,* nod; *trait de plume,* stroke of the pen; *un collier de perles,* a pearl necklace; *un coup de bâton,* a blow with a stick; *un coup de fusil,* a shot; *une lame d'épée,* a sword-blade; *un enfant d'un bon naturel,* a good-natured child; *une prise de tabac,* a pinch of snuff; *un plat d'argent,* a silver dish; *vivre de fruits et de légumes,* to live on fruit and vegetables.

de (2) [də]. The nobiliary particle, correctly used only after a Christian name or a title, *e.g., Alfred de Vigny,* or *le comte de Vigny,* or *M. de Vigny*; otherwise *Vigny.*

dé (1) [de], *n.m.* Die (for playing); (*fig.*) throw, hazard; (*Arch.*) quoin, block, dado; (*Coin.*) die. *Avoir le dé,* to be one's turn to play; *à vous le dé,* now it is your turn or your throw; *jouer aux dés,* to play at dice; *les dés sont jetés,* the die is cast. *Tenir le dé dans la conversation,* to monopolize the conversation.

dé (2) [de], *n.m.* Thimble.

déambulatoire [deɑ̃byla'twaːr], *n.m.* (*Arch.*) Ambulatory.

déambuler [deɑ̃by'le], *v.i.* (*fam.*) To stroll along, to walk up and down.

débâchage [debɑ'ʃaːʒ], *n.m.* Uncovering.

débâcher [debɑ'ʃe], *v.t.* To uncover, to untilt.

débâclage [debɑ'klaːʒ], *n.m.* Clearing, opening (of a port etc.).

débâcle [de'bɑːkl], *n.f.* Breaking up (of ice); clearing (of a harbour etc.); (*fig.*) downfall, collapse, disaster. **débâclement** [DÉBÂ-CLAGE]. **débâcler,** *v.i.* To break up (of ice). —*v.t.* To clear (a harbour etc.); to unfasten or unbar (doors etc.). *Débâcler une porte* or *une fenêtre,* to unbar a door *or* window.

débâcleur, *n.m.* Water or port-bailiff.

débagouler [debagu'le], *v.t.* To vomit abuse at, to abuse foully.—*v.i.* (*vulg.*) To spew, to vomit.

déballage [deba'laːʒ], *n.m.* Unpacking; show (of goods for sale at low prices).

déballer [deba'le], *v.t.* To unpack; (*fam.*) to show, to display. **déballeur,** *n.m.* Unpacker; hawker.

débandade [debɑ̃'dad], *n.f.* Rout, stampede; breaking the ranks. *À la débandade,* in confusion, helter-skelter, at sixes and sevens; *mettre tout à débandade,* to put everything in confusion.

débander [debɑ̃'de], *v.t.* To unbind; to loosen. *Débander les yeux à quelqu'un,* to take off the handkerchief tied over someone's eyes. **se débander,** *v.r.* To slacken, to relax; to disband; to leave the ranks, to unbend.

débaptiser [debati'ze], *v.t.* To change the name of.

débarbouillage [debarbu'jaːʒ], *n.m.* Washing, cleansing.

débarbouiller [debarbu'je], *v.t.* To wash, to cleanse. **se débarbouiller,** *v.r.* To wash one's face etc.; (*fig.*) to extricate oneself.

(*C*) **débarbouillette** [debarbu'jɛt], *n.f.* Face cloth.

débarcadère [debarka'dɛːr], *n.m.* Landing, landing-place, wharf; (*Rail.*) station; arrival platform.

débardage [debar'daːʒ], *n.m.* Unloading (of wood etc.).

débarder [debar'de], *v.t.* To unload (wood etc.); to clear (a wood etc.) of the trees felled in it. **débardeur,** *n.m.* Workman who unloads etc.; stevedore, wharf-porter, lighterman, docker.

débarqué [debar'ke], *a.* (*fem.* -**ée**) Disembarked, landing.—*n.* Person landing. *Un nouveau débarqué,* one just come to town, a raw countryman. **débarquement,** *n.m.* Landing, disembarkment (of persons); unloading (of goods).

débarquer [debar'ke], *v.t.* To disembark, to land, to unship; (*fig.*) to dismiss.—*v.i.* To land, to disembark. *Au débarquer,* on landing; *nous débarquâmes en tel endroit,* we went ashore at such a place.

débarras [deba'rɑ], *n.m.* Riddance, disencumbrance. *Bon débarras!* a good riddance! *chambre* or *cabinet de débarras,* lumber-room, box-room.

débarrasser [debara'se], *v.t.* To disencumber, to rid, to free, to disembarrass; to disentangle, to extricate. *Débarrasser* (*la table*), to clear the table; (*fam.*) *débarrasser le plancher*, to clear out. **se débarrasser**, *v.r.* To extricate oneself, to rid oneself of, to shake off; to get clear; to be cleared (of the road, the way, etc.).

débarrer [deba´re], *v.t.* To unbar, to undo the bars of.

débat [de´ba], *n.m.* Dispute, altercation, strife, contest; debate, discussion; (*pl.*) parliamentary debates; (*Law*) pleadings. *Assister aux débats*, to be present at the trial; *vider un débat*, to settle a dispute.

débatelage [debatə´la:ʒ], *n.m.* Unlading (of boats etc.).

débateler [debatə´le], *v.t.* To unlade (boats etc.).

débâter [deba´te], *v.t.* To unsaddle; to take a packsaddle off (a horse etc.).

débâtir [deba´ti:r], *v.t.* To pull down, to demolish; to unbaste, to untack (garments etc.).

débattre [de´batr], *v.t. irr.* (*p.p.* **débattu**; *conjugated like* BATTRE) To debate, to discuss, to argue. **se débattre**, *v.r.* To be argued, to be debated; to struggle, to strive; to flounder, to flutter.

débauche [de´bo:ʃ], *n.f.* Debauch; debauchery; lewdness, dissoluteness.

débauché [debo´ʃe], *n.m.* (*fem.* **-ée**) Debauchee, rake. **débaucher**, *v.t.* To debauch; to corrupt, to seduce; to entice away, to lead astray. **se débaucher**, *v.r.* To become debauched; to go astray; to be led away (from one's occupations etc.). *****débaucheur**, *n.m.* (*fem.* **-euse**) Debaucher, seducer.

débet [de´bɛ], *n.m.* Debit, balance of an account. *Être en débet*, to owe a balance.

*****débiffer** [debi´fe], *v.t.* To disorder, to enfeeble, to put out of sorts. *Être tout débiffé*, to be quite out of sorts; *visage débiffé*, haggard countenance.

débile [de´bil], *a.* Weakly, weak, feeble. *Avoir le cerveau débile*, to be weak in the head; *mémoire débile*, weak memory. **débilement**, *adv.* Feebly, weakly. **débilitant**, *a.* (*fem.* **-ante**) Debilitating, weakening.—*n.m.* Debilitating medicine. **débilité**, *n.f.* Debility, weakness. *Débilité mentale*, mental deficiency. **débiliter**, *v.t.* To debilitate, to enfeeble.

débine [de´bin], *n.f.* (*slang*) Poverty, straits, embarrassment, mess. *Il est tombé dans la débine*, he has fallen into poverty. **débiner**, *v.t.* (*slang*) To abuse, to malign, to slander. **se débiner**, *v.r.* To skedaddle. **débineur**, *n.m.* (*fem.* **-euse**) Slanderer, detractor.

débit [de´bi], *n.m.* Sale; market; retail; retail shop or warehouse; licence to sell; supply; cutting up (of logs); flow (of rivers); intensity (of electric current); (*fig.*) delivery, utterance; (*Book-keeping*) debit, debit side. *Débit de tabac*, tobacconist's shop; *il a un beau débit*, he has a fine delivery; *marchandise de bon débit*, goods that have a ready sale; *porter au débit de quelqu'un*, to debit someone with.

débitage [debi´ta:ʒ], *n.m.* Cutting up (of stones, timber, etc.).

débitant [debi´tã], *n.m.* (*fem.* **-ante**) Retailer, dealer.

débiter [debi´te], *v.t.* To sell; to retail; to supply (gas, electricity, etc.); to yield (of a machine); to debit; to cut up (wood, stone, etc.); (*fig.*) to spread, to report, to utter; to recite, to declaim, to spout. *Débiter des nouvelles*, to spread news; *débiter en gros* or *en détail*, to sell wholesale or by retail; *débiter son rôle*, to recite one's part. **débiteur** (1), *n.m.* (*fem.* **-trice**) Debtor. *Être débiteur de*, to be in debt to.—*a.* Debtor. *Compte débiteur*, debtor's account. **débiteur** (2), *n.m.* (*fem.* **-euse**) Prattler, newsmonger. *C'est une grande débiteuse de mensonges*, she is a regular fibber.

débitter [debi´te], *v.t.* (*Naut.*) To unbitt (a cable).

déblai [de´blɛ], *n.m.* Clearing; excavation; (*pl.*) earth, stones, etc., cleared away, rubbish; (*fig.*) riddance. *Être en déblai*, to have been excavated; *route en déblai*, sunk road; *voie* (*ferrée*) *en déblai*, cutting. **déblayage**, *n.m.* Sweeping away (obstacles). **déblaiement** or **déblayement**, *n.m.* Clearing away, clearance; cutting, excavation, digging.

déblatérer [deblate´re], *v.i. irr.* (*conjug. like* ACCÉLÉRER) To utter violent abuse, to rail (*contre*).

déblayement [DÉBLAIEMENT].

déblayer [deble´je], *v.t.* (*conjugated like* BALAYER) To clear away; to clear; (*fig.*) to sweep away (obstacles etc.).

déblocage [deblɔ´ka:ʒ], *n.m.* (*Print.*) Turning letters, releasing.

déblocquement [deblɔk´mã], *n.m.* Raising the blockade of a port etc.

débloquer [deblɔ´ke], *v.t.* To raise the blockade from; (*Print.*) to turn letters; to unlock (a wheel); to release (goods).

débobinage [debɔbi´na:ʒ], *n.m.* Unwinding.

débobiner [debɔbi´ne], *v.t.* To unwind.

déboire [de´bwa:r], *n.m.* After-taste; (*fig.*) disappointment, vexation.

déboisement [debwaz´mã], *n.m.* Clearing of trees, deforestation. **déboiser**, *v.t.* To clear of trees.

déboîtement [debwat´mã], *n.m.* Dislocation. **déboîter**, *v.t.* To put out of joint, to dislocate; to disjoint, to take to pieces; (*Elec.*) to disconnect, to uncouple.—*v.i.* (*Motor.*) To filter. **se déboîter**, *v.r.* To be dislocated; to be able to be taken to pieces; to get out of joint (knee etc.).

débonder [debɔ̃´de], *v.t.* To take the bung out of; to loosen, to unbind. *Débonder un étang*, to open the sluice of a pond.—*v.i.*, or **se débonder**, *v.r.* To gush, to break out, to burst forth, to escape; to be relaxed (of a person). **débondonnement**, *n.m.* Unbunging. **débondonner**, *v.t.* To take the bung out of.

débonnaire [debɔ´nɛ:r], *a.* Good-natured, compliant, easy-tempered, (*Bibl.*) meek. **débonnairement**, *adv.* Compliantly, easily. **débonnaireté**, *n.f.* Compliance, good-nature.

débord [de´bɔ:r], *n.m.* Flow, overflow; (*Med.*) defluxion; edge (of a coin). **débordé**, *a.* (*fem.* **-ée**) Overflowing (river); overwhelmed (man); outflanked (troops). *Je suis débordé de travail*, I am overwhelmed with work. **débordement**, *n.m.* Overflowing, flood; outbreak, outburst; (*fig.*) dissoluteness, excess, debauchery; (*Path.*) overflow (of bile etc.).

déborder [debɔr'de], *v.i.* To overflow, to run over; to be flooded; to project, to jut out; to untuck (a bed); (*Naut.*) to get clear (*de*), to sheer off (*de*). *Cette maison déborde,* that house juts out; *la doublure déborde,* the lining bags.—*v.t.* To take off the border from; to go beyond, to overtop; to outrun; to leave behind; (*Mil.*) to outflank; (*Naut.*) to cause to sheer off, to fend off; (*fig.*) to pass, to surpass. **se déborder,** *v.r.* To overflow; to run over, to burst forth. **débordoir,** *n.m.* Edging-tool (of a plumber etc.); spoke-shave.

débosseler [debɔs'le], *v.t.* To take the dents out of.

débosser [debɔ'se], *v.t.* (*Naut.*) To take off the stoppers.

débotté or **débotter** (1) [debɔ'te], *n.m.* The moment of taking boots off. (*fig.*) *Au débotté,* at once, immediately upon arrival. **débotter** (2), *v.t.* To pull off boots from. **se débotter,** *v.r.* To pull off one's boots.

débouché [debu'ʃe], *n.m.* Outlet, issue; waterway; (*fig.*) opening (for career or trade), expedient; (*Comm.*) market sale. **débouchage** or **débouchement,** *n.m.* Debouchment, debouchure; uncorking, unstopping; outlet, opening, issue; market sale.

déboucher [debu'ʃe], *v.t.* To open, to clear; to uncork.—*v.i.* To pass out, to emerge; to fall, to empty itself (of rivers); (*Mil.*) to debouch. *Au déboucher du défilé,* on coming out of the defile. **débouchoir,** *n.m.* Implement for uncorking, opening, clearing, etc.; lapidary's tool.

déboucler [debu'kle], *v.t.* To unbuckle; to uncurl.

débouler [debu'le], *v.i.* To roll down (like a ball); to start off suddenly (like a hare).

déboulonnement [debulɔn'mɑ̃] or **déboulonnage** [debulɔ'naːʒ], *n.m.* Unbolting, unriveting. **déboulonner** [debulɔ'ne], *v.t.* To unrivet, unbolt; (*fig.*) to knock somebody off his pedestal. **déboulonneur,** *n.m.* (*fem.* -euse) One who does this.

débouquement [debuk'mɑ̃], *n.m.* (*Naut.*) Narrow passage or channel, strait; disemboguement; emergence from a strait etc. **débouquer,** *v.i.* To emerge from a channel, passage, etc.; to disembogue.

débourbage [debur'baːʒ], *n.m.* (*Metal. etc.*) Cleansing, clearing of mud, etc. *débourber,* *v.t.* To cleanse, to take the mud away from; to take the muddy taste out of (fish etc.); (*fig.*) to get out of a mess. *Débourber une voiture,* to draw a carriage out of the mire.

débourrement [debur'mɑ̃], *n.m.* Bursting of the down of the buds of trees.

débourrer [debu're], *v.t.* To draw the wad or wadding out of (fire-arms); to empty the tobacco out of (a pipe); (*fig.*) to polish (a person). *Débourrer un cheval,* to break in a horse; *débourrer un jeune homme,* to form or polish a young man.

débours [de'buːr] or **déboursé,** *n.m.* Disbursement, outlay, sum laid out. *Il est rentré dans ses débours,* he has recovered his outlay. **déboursement,** *n.m.* Disbursement, outlay, expenditure. **débourser,** *v.t.* To disburse, to expend, to lay out.

debout [də'bu], *adv.* Upright, on end, standing up; standing on one's feet; out of bed, risen; alive, in existence; (*Naut.*) ahead (of the wind). *Allons, debout, il est déjà grand jour,* come, get up, it is broad daylight; *avoir le vent debout,* to have the wind ahead or a head wind; *être debout,* to be up, to be stirring; *il se tient debout,* he is standing up; *un conte à dormir debout,* a wearisome yarn, a rigmarole, a tall story; *un projet qui ne tient pas debout,* a preposterous scheme.—*int.* Up, get up, out of bed!

débouté [debu'te], *n.m.* (*Law*) Dismission, nonsuit.

débouter [debu'te], *v.t.* (*Law*) To dismiss, to reject, to nonsuit. *Il a été débouté de sa demande,* his demand was rejected, he was nonsuited.

déboutonner [debutɔ'ne], *v.t.* To unbutton. **se déboutonner,** *v.r.* To unbutton oneself; (*colloq.*) to unbosom oneself.

débraillé [debrɑ'je], *a.* (*fem.* -ée) Loosely dressed, in disorder. *Tout débraillé,* all untidy.—*n.m.* Disorder, untidiness; (*fig.*) licence. **se débrailler,** *v.r.* To uncover one's breast, to be untidy or disordered.

débrancher [debrɑ̃'ʃe], *v.t.* (*Elec.*) To disconnect.

débrayage [debre'jaːʒ] or **désembrayage,** *n.m.* Disengaging gear (of motors etc.); declutching. **débrayer,** *v.t.* (*conjugated like* BALAYER) To throw out of gear, to disengage, to declutch.—*v.i.* (*pop.*) To give up work, to go out.

débredouiller [debrədu'je], *v.t.,* or **se débredouiller,** *v.r.* (*Backgammon*) To save (oneself) the lurch.

débridement [debrid'mɑ̃], *n.m.* Unbridling; (*Surg.*) relieving constriction by incision; (*fig.*) dispatch, hurry. **débrider,** *v.t., v.i.* To unbridle (horse); to halt; (*Surg.*) to remove constriction by incision. *Sans débrider,* without stopping, at a stretch. *Débrider les yeux à quelqu'un,* to open some one's eyes.

débris [de'bri], *n.m.* (*usu. in pl.*) Remains, wreck, debris; waste; rubbish.

débrochage [debrɔ'ʃaːʒ], *n.m.* Unspitting; unstitching. **débrocher,** *v.t.* To take from the spit; to unstitch.

débrouillard [debru'jaːr], *a.* (*fem.* -arde) (*colloq.*) Smart, quick at getting out of a fix etc.; resourceful, having plenty of gumption. —*n.* Resourceful man or woman.

*débrouillement** [debruj'mɑ̃], *n.m.* Disentangling, unravelling.

débrouiller [debru'je], *v.t.* To disentangle, to unravel; (*fig.*) to clear up, to explain. **se débrouiller,** *v.r.* To be cleared up; to get out of difficulties, to manage.

débroussailler [debrusa'je], *v.t.* To clear of undergrowth.

débrutir [debry'tiːr], *v.t.* To clear the rough off; to rough-polish (gems etc.). **débrutissement,** *n.m.* Rough-polishing.

débucher [deby'ʃe], *v.i.* (*Hunt.*) To start (of an animal); to break cover.—*v.t.* To dislodge, to start.—*n.m.* Start. *Il se trouva au débucher,* he was present at the start.

débusquement [debyskə'mɑ̃], *n.m.* Driving out, dislodging. **débusquer,** *v.t.* To turn out, to oust, to expel; (*Hunt.*) to start, to dislodge.

début [de'by], *n.m.* Lead, first cast or throw; outset, commencement; début, first appearance. *Au début de la guerre*, at the outbreak of the war; *voilà un beau début*, that is a fine beginning. **débutant,** *n.m.* (*fem.* **débutante**) Actor or actress appearing for the first time; beginner, débutant or débutante. **débuter,** *v.i.* To lead, to play first; to begin, to open; to start; to set out; to make one's first appearance or début. *Il a débuté à trente-mille francs par mois*, he started at thirty thousand francs a month; *il a mal débuté dans le monde*, he made a bad beginning in life.—*v.t.* To drive from the jack (at bowls); to lead (at cards).

deçà [də'sa], *prep.* On this side of; short of, well within. *En deçà, au deçà, de deçà*, or *par deçà la rivière*, this side of the river; *en deçà de la vérité*, short of the truth.—*adv.* Here, on this side. *Deçà (et) delà*, here and there, on this side and on that.

décachetable [dekaʃ'tabl], *a.* To be unsealed or opened.

décachetage [dekaʃ'taːʒ], *n.m.* Unsealing, opening.

décacheter [dekaʃ'te], *v.t.* To unseal, to open, to break the seal of.

décadaire [deka'dɛːr], *a.* Decadal.

décade [de'kad], *n.f.* Decade, group of ten; ten days (in republican calendar); ten chapters.

décadenasser [dekadnɑ'se], *v.t.* To unpadlock.

décadence [deka'dɑ̃ːs], *n.f.* Decadence, decline, wane, downfall. **décadent,** *a.* (*fem.* **-ente**) Decadent.—*n.* A decadent. **décadentisme,** *n.m.* Principles, character, etc., of the decadents.

décadi [deka'di], *n.m.* The tenth day of a decade (in the calendar of the first French Republic).

décaèdre [deka'ɛdr], *a.* Decahedral.—*n.m.* Decahedron.

décaféiner [dekafei'ne], *v.t.* To remove the caffeine.

décagonal [dekagɔ'nal], *a.* (*fem.* **-ale,** *pl.* **-aux**) Decagonal (ten-sided).

décagone [deka'gɔn], *n.m.* Decagon.

décagramme [deka'gram], *n.m.* Decagramme, ten grammes.

décaissement [dekɛs'mɑ̃] or **décaissage,** *n.m.* Uncasing, unpacking. **décaisser,** *v.t.* To take out of the box or crate, to unpack; to pay out.

décalage [deka'laːʒ], *n.m.* Unwedging; shifting of the zero; time-lag. **décaler,** *v.t.* To unwedge; to stagger (rivets), to set off; to shift the zero. *Décaler un horaire,* to stagger a time-table.

décalaminage [dekalami'naːʒ], *n.m.* (*Motor.*) Decarbonizing. **décalaminer,** *v.t.* To decarbonize.

décalcifiant [dekalsi'fjɑ̃], *a.* (*fem.* **-ante**) Decalcifying (diet). **décalcification,** *n.f.* Decalcification. **se décalcifier,** *v.r.* To become decalcified.

décalcomanie [dekalkoma'ni], *n.f.* Transfer.

décalitre [deka'litr], *n.m.* Decalitre (2·2 gallons).

décalogue [deka'lɔg], *n.m.* Decalogue.

décalquage, décalcage [dekal'kaːʒ], or **décalque,** *n.m.* Transfer (of a drawing),

counter-tracing. **décalquer,** *v.t.* To transfer (a tracing), to countertrace; (*fig.*) to copy, to imitate.

décalvant [dekal'vɑ̃], *a.* (*fem.* **-ante**) Baldening.

décamètre [deka'mɛtr], *n.m.* Decametre

décamper [dekɑ̃'pe], *v.i.* To decamp; (*fig.*) to pack off, to bolt, to levant.

décanailler [dekanɑ'je], *v.t.* To refine, to purge (a person) of low-class manners, etc.; to make a gentleman of.

décanal [deka'nal], *a.* (*fem.* **-ale,** *pl.* **-aux**) Decanal.

décanat [deka'na], *n.m.* Deanery, deanship.

décaniller [dekani'je], *v.i.* (*slang*) To go away, to clear out.

décantation [dekɑ̃ta'sjɔ̃], *n.f.,* or **décantage,** *n.m.* (*Chem.*) Decantation. **décanter,** *v.t.* To decant, to pour off gently. **décanteur,** *n.m.* Instrument used in decanting.

décapage [deka'paːʒ] or **décapement,** *n.m.* Cleaning, scraping (of metal).

décapelage [dekap'laːʒ] or **décapèlement,** *n.m.* (*Naut.*) Process of unrigging. **décapeler,** *v.t.* To unrig.

décapement [DÉCAPAGE].

décaper (1) [deka'pe], *v.i.* (*Naut.*) To double a cape.

décaper (2) [deka'pe], *v.t.* To clean or scrape (metal). **décapeur,** *n.m.* Scourer; dipper.

décapitation [dekapita'sjɔ̃], *n.f.* Decapitation, beheading. **décapité,** *n.m.* (*fem.* **-ée**) A person beheaded. **décapiter,** *v.t.* To behead, to decapitate.

décapode [deka'pɔd], *n.m.* Decapod.—*a.* Decapod, decapodal.

décapotable [dekapɔ'tabl], *a.* (Car) with folding hood. **décapoter,** *v.t.* To fold the hood (of a car).

décapuchonner [dekapyʃɔ'ne], *v.t.* To take off a hood; to unfrock (a monk).

décarboniser [dekarbɔni'ze], *v.t.* To decarbonize. **décarburant,** *a.* (*fem.* **-ante**) Decarbonizing. **décarburation,** *n.f.* Decarbonization. **décarburer,** *v.t.* To decarburize.

décarcasser (se) [dekarka'se], *v.r.* (*fam.*) To drudge; to toil and moil.

décarrelage [dekar'laːʒ], *n.m.* Unpaving, untiling (of a floor). **décarreler,** *v.t.* To take up the tiles from (a floor), to unpave.

décartonner [dekartɔ'ne], *v.t.* To take off the cardboard cover. *Décartonner un livre,* to strip a book.

décastère [deka'stɛːr], *n.m.* Measure of 10 steres or cubic metres (13·1 cubic yards).

décastyle [deka'stil], *a.* and *n.m.* (*Arch.*) Decastyle.

décasyllabe [dekasi'lab] or **décasyllabique,** *a.* Decasyllabic.

décathlon [dekat'lɔ̃], *n.m.* (*spt.*) Decathlon.

décatir [deka'tiːr], *v.t.* To sponge (woollen cloth) so as to remove the gloss. **décatir (se),** *v.r.* (*fam.*) To lose one's youth or beauty. **décatissage,** *n.m.* Sponging, removing the gloss. **décatisseur,** *n.m.* Sponger, scourer.

decauville [dəko'vil], *n.m.* Narrow gauge railway.

décavage [deka'vaːʒ], *n.m.* Cleaning out (at play); state of being cleaned out. **décavé,** *a.* (*fem.* **-ée**) Cleaned out, ruined, beggared.

décaver, *v.t.* To win the whole of the stakes from, to clean out; (*fig.*) to ruin, to beggar.

décédé [dese'de], *n.m.* (*fem.* -ée) Deceased, person deceased.

décéder [dese'de], *v.i. irr.* (*conjugated like* ACCÉLÉRER; *takes the auxiliary* ÊTRE) To die, to decease.

décelable [desə'labl], *a.* That can be revealed.

décèlement [desel'mɑ̃], *n.m.* Disclosure, exposure, discovery.

déceler [des'le], *v.t. irr.* (*conjug. like* AMENER) To disclose, to reveal, to betray. **se déceler,** *v.r.* To betray oneself. **déceleur,** *n.m.* (*fem.* -euse) Betrayer, revealer.

décembre [de'sɑ̃:br], *n.m.* December.

décemment [desa'mɑ̃], *adv.* In a decent manner, decently.

décemvir [desem'vi:r], *n.m.* Decemvir. **décemviral,** *a.* (*fem.* -ale, *pl.* -aux) Decemviral. **décemvirat,** *n.m.* Decemvirate.

décence [de'sɑ̃:s], *n.f.* Decency, the proprieties.

décennal [desɛ'nal], *a.* (*fem.* -ale, *pl.* -aux) Decennial.

décent [de'sɑ̃], *a.* (*fem.* -ente) Decent, becoming; modest. *Peu décent*, immodest.

décentralisant [desɑ̃trali'zɑ̃], *a.* (*fem.* -ante) Decentralizing. **décentralisateur,** *a.* (*fem.* -trice) Pertaining to decentralization.—*n.* Supporter or advocate of decentralization. **décentralisation,** *n.f.* Decentralization.

décentraliser [desɑ̃trali'ze], *v.t.* To decentralize.

décentration [desɑ̃tra'sjɔ̃], *n.f.*, or **décentrement** [desɑ̃trə'mɑ̃], *n.m.* (*Opt.*) Defective adjustment of lenses with regard to centering, decentering. **décentrer,** *v.t.* To cause this (in optical apparatus), to decentre. *Être décentré* (of a wheel), to be out of true. **décentrer (se),** *v.t.* To get out of true.

déception [desɛp'sjɔ̃], *n.f.* Disappointment; deception, deceit.

décercler [desɛr'kle], *v.t.* To unhoop (barrels).

décernement [desɛrnə'mɑ̃], *n.m.* Awarding.

décerner [desɛr'ne], *v.t.* To decree, to enact; to award, to bestow, to confer (an honour), to issue (a summons etc.). *Décerner un mandat d'amener*, to issue a writ of arrest.

décès [de'sɛ], *n.m.* Decease, demise, death.

décevable [des'vabl], *a.* Deceivable. **décevant,** *a.* (*fem.* -ante) Deceptive; disappointing.

décevoir [desə'vwa:r], *v.t. irr.* (*see* RECEVOIR) To deceive, to mislead, to dupe; to disappoint.

déchaînement [deʃɛn'mɑ̃], *n.m.* Unbridling, bursting (of storm); outburst (of passion); fury, rage, violence; inveighing, invective.

déchaîner [deʃɛ'ne], *v.t.* To unchain, to unbind, to let loose; to give vent to (passion, fury, etc.). **se déchaîner,** *v.r.* To break loose, to burst from one's chains; to burst upon; to run riot, to run wild (of passions etc.).

déchalander [DÉSACHALANDER].

déchalement [deʃal'mɑ̃], *n.m.* Ebbing, ebb; lying dry. **déchaler,** *v.i.* To ebb, to flow down; to lie dry.

déchanter [deʃɑ̃'te], *v.i.* To lower one's key (in singing); (*fig.*) to change one's tone, to

lower one's pretensions, to sing another tune. *Je le ferai déchanter*, I'll make him pipe down.

déchapage [de'ʃa'pa:ʒ], *n.m.* Peeling (of tyres. **déchaper (se),** *v.r.* To peel.

déchaperonner [deʃaprɔ'ne], *v.t.* To unhood (a hawk etc.); to uncope (a wall).

décharge [de'ʃarʒ], *n.f.* Unloading, unlading; relief, exoneration; rebate (on a tax); outlet, discharge (of water etc.); (*Law*) discharge, acquittal, release; (*Arch.*) prop, stay; (*Mil.*) volley, round; output (of accumulator). *Donner décharge de*, to release from, to give a receipt in full for; *entendre les témoins à charge et à décharge*, to hear witnesses for and against; *décharge publique*, dump; *porter en décharge*, to credit with; *témoin à décharge*, witness for the defence. **déchargement,** *n.m.* Unloading, unlading. **déchargeoir,** *n.m.* Place of discharge (of water etc.), outlet, outfall, sluice; roller (of loom).

décharger [deʃar'ʒe], *v.t.* To unload, to unlade; to relieve (of a burden); to empty, to disembogue; to vent, to disburden; to lighten, to diminish (taxes etc.); to discharge, to throw or shoot out; to give a discharge for; to fire (fire-arms); to release, to set free; to dismiss; exonerate, to acquit (*de*). *Décharger sa bile* or *sa colère sur quelqu'un*, to vent one's wrath upon someone; *décharger sa conscience*, to clear one's conscience, to make a clean breast of it; *décharger son cœur*, to open one's heart; *décharger un accusé*, to exculpate or to discharge an accused person; *il a été déchargé de toute accusation*, he was entirely exculpated.—*v.i.* To unload, to unlade; to come off (of ink). **se décharger,** *v.r.* To be unloaded, to discharge (of liquids); to flow into (of rivers); to give vent to; to go off of itself (of a gun); to throw off (the blame etc.), to exonerate oneself; to unburden oneself, to relieve oneself. *Se décharger d'une faute sur quelqu'un*, to shift the blame on to someone. **déchargeur,** *n.m.* Unloader, wharf-porter, heaver, lumper.

décharné [deʃar'ne], *a.* (*fem.* -ée) Fleshless; stripped of flesh; lean, spare, emaciated; (*fig.*) bald, meagre (of style). *Style décharné*, bald style; *visage décharné*, gaunt face. **décharnement,** *n.m.* Leanness; emaciation; baldness (of style). **décharner,** *v.t.* To strip the flesh off; to make lean, to emaciate; (*fig.*) to impoverish (style).

décharpir [deʃar'pi:r], *v.t.* To tear to rags; to tear apart.

déchasser [deʃa'se], *v.i.* (*Dancing*) To chassé to the left (after a chassé to the right).

déchaumage [deʃo'ma:ʒ], *n.m.* (*Agric.*) Digging up the stubble; ploughing up fallow ground. **déchaumer,** *v.t.* To plough up the stubble on; to break up (fallow land). **déchaumeur,** *n.m.*, or **déchaumeuse,** *n.f.* Stubble-plough, scarifier.

déchaussé [deʃo'se], *a.* (*fem.* **déchaussée**) Barefooted. **déchaussement,** *n.m.* Pulling off shoes or stockings; laying bare the root of a plant etc., or the foundations of a building etc.; baring the neck of a tooth.

déchausser [deʃo'se], *v.t.* To pull off shoes and stockings; to lay bare the root, base, foundations, etc. (of trees, buildings, teeth, etc.). **se déchausser,** *v.r.* To take off one's shoes and stockings; to be bared to the root (foundations etc.); to get loose (teeth). **déchaussoir**, *n.m.* Lancet for baring the neck of teeth; implement for working the earth at the foot of plants.

déchaux [DÉCHAUSSÉ].

dèche [dɛʃ], *n.f.* (*slang*) Poverty. *Être dans la dèche*, to be hard up.

déchéance [deʃe'ãːs], *n.f.* Forfeiture; disqualification; fall, disgrace, decadence; dethronement, deposition.

déchet [de'ʃɛ], *n.m.* Loss, waste, offal; (*fig.*) falling off, diminution; (*pl.*) waste products.

décheveler [deʃə'vle], *v.t.* To dishevel [ÉCHEVELER].

déchevêtrer [deʃəvɛ'tre], *v.t.* To take the halter off, to unhalter (a beast of burden).

décheviller [deʃəvi'je], *v.t.* To unpeg, to unpin.

déchiffrable [deʃi'frabl], *a.* Capable of being deciphered, legible. **déchiffrement**, *n.m.* Deciphering; reading or playing at sight.

déchiffrer [deʃi'fre], *v.t.* To decipher, to unravel, to unriddle, to penetrate, to make clear; to read or play at sight. **se déchiffrer**, *v.r.* To be deciphered, to be unravelled. **déchiffreur**, *n.m.* (*fem.* **-euse**) Decipherer; player at sight. *Déchiffreur de radar*, radar scanner.

déchiquetage [deʃik'taːʒ], *n.m.* Slashing, mangling; pinking. **déchiqueté**, *a.* Jagged, indented; (*Bot.*) laciniate. *Feuille déchiquetée*, jagged leaf.

déchiqueter [deʃik'te], *v.t.* To cut, to slash, to hack; to cut into long pieces. **déchiqueteur**, *n.m.* (*fem.* **-euse**) One who does or is fond of doing this. **déchiqueture**, *n.f.* Tear, slash, awkward cut in a piece of cloth etc., with the scissors.

déchirage [deʃi'raːʒ], *n.m.* Ripping up, breaking up (of a ship etc.). *Bois de déchirage*, old ship-timber. **déchirant**, *a.* (*fem.* **-ante**) Heart-rending, harrowing, piercing; excruciating. **déchirement**, *n.m.* Rending, tearing, laceration; (*fig.*, *pl.*) intestine broils, discords. *Déchirement d'entrailles*, excruciating pain in the bowels; *déchirements de cœur*, anguish of heart, heart-break.

déchirer [deʃi're], *v.t.* To tear to pieces, to rend, to lacerate; (*fig.*) to torture, to distress; to revile, to defame. *Déchirer à coups de fouet*, to lash to ribbons; *déchirer l'oreille*, to grate on the ear; *déchirer quelqu'un à belles dents*, to tear someone to pieces; *déchirer son prochain*, to slander one's neighbour; *être déchiré de remords*, to be tortured with remorse. **se déchirer**, *v.r.* To tear, to be torn, to be rent; to vilify, abuse, or defame each other. *Ce papier se déchire très facilement*, this paper tears very easily; *je sentis mon cœur se déchirer*, I felt my heart breaking. **déchireur**, *n.m.* (*fem.* **-euse**) Tearer, render; breaker up (of boats, ships, etc.). **déchirure**, *n.f.* Rent, tear; fissure, cleft.

déchloruré [deklɔry're], *a.* Salt-free (diet).

déchoir [de'ʃwaːr], *v.i. irr.* (*p.p.* **déchu**; with the auxiliary AVOIR or ÊTRE *according as the action or state is expressed*) To decay, to fall off, to decline; to sink, to fall. *Commencer à déchoir*, to begin to fall away; *déchoir de ses espérances*, to be less sanguine in one's hopes; *déchoir de son rang*, to fall

from one's rank; *être déchu d'un droit*, to have forfeited a claim.

déchouement [deʃu'mã], *n.m.* Floating (of a stranded ship). **déchouer**, *v.t.* To get off, to set afloat.

déchristianiser [dekristjani'ze], *v.t.* To dechristianize. **se déchristianiser**, *v.r.* To fall away from Christianity.

déchu [de'ʃy], *a.* (*fem.* **-ue**) Fallen, decayed, sunk. *Ange déchu*, fallen angel.

décidé [desi'de], *a.* (*fem.* **-ée**) Decided, determined, resolved; resolute, confident. *La chose est décidée*, the matter is settled. **décidément**, *adv.* Decidedly, positively; resolutely, firmly; definitely.

décider [desi'de], *v.t.* To decide, to determine, to settle; to induce, to persuade.—*v.i.* To decide, to come to a decision, to make a determination. *Cet événement décida de mon sort*, that event decided my fate; *que le sort décide entre nous*, let fate determine between us. **se décider**, *v.r.* To decide, to determine, to make up one's mind; to be decided, to be settled. *La victoire s'est décidée en faveur de nos armes*, victory favoured our arms; *tout se décidait par intérêt*, everything was decided by interest.

décidu [desi'dy], *a.* (*fem.* **-ue**) (*Bot.*) Deciduous.

décigramme [desi'gram], *n.m.* Decigram (one-tenth of a gramme, 1·54 grains).

décilitre [desi'litr], *n.m.* Decilitre (one-tenth of a litre).

décimal [desi'mal], *a.* (*fem.* **-ale**, *pl.* **-aux**) Decimal. *n.f.* A decimal. **décimalisation**, *n.f.* Decimalization. **décimaliser**, *v.t.* To decimalize.

décimateur [desima'tœːr], *n.m.* Tithe-owner.

décime [de'sim], *n.m.* Tenth part of a franc. —*n.f.* Tithe on ecclesiastical revenues.

décimer [desi'me], *v.t.* (*Rom. Ant.*) To decimate (to punish every tenth soldier); (*fig.*) to destroy, to annihilate.

décimètre [desi'mɛtr], *n.m.* Decimetre (3·937 inches).

décimo [desi'mo], *adv.* Tenthly.

décintrage [desɛ̃'traːʒ] or **décintrement**, *n.m.* (*Arch.*) Removing the centerings (of vaults, arches, etc.). **décintrer**, *v.t.* To remove the centres from.

décirer [desi're], *v.t.* To take the wax off.

décisif [desi'sif], *a.* (*fem.* **-ive**) Decisive, conclusive; positive, peremptory. *C'est un homme décisif*, he is a positive man; *prendre un ton décisif*, to assume a peremptory tone. **décision**, *n.f.* Decision, determination; result, final issue; resolution. *Une décision de droit*, a decision in law. **décisivement**, *adv.* Decisively; peremptorily, positively.

décisoire [desi'zwaːr], *a.* (*Law*) Decisive (oath).

décistère [desi'stɛːr], *n.m.* Tenth of a stere (3·53 cubic feet).

déciviliser [desivili'ze], *v.t.* To decivilize.

déclamateur [deklama'tœːr], *n.m.* Declaimer; (*fig.*) stump-orator, tub-thumper, declamatory writer or speaker. *Ce n'est qu'un déclamateur*, he is a mere ranter.—*a.m.* Declamatory, stilted, bombastic.

déclamation [deklamɑ'sjɔ̃], *n.f.* Declamation, elocution; manner or art of reciting; declamatory style, inflated expression or phraseology. *Déclamation oratoire or théâtrale*, oratorical *or* theatrical elocution; *il s'est livré à des déclamations contre la partie adverse*, he indulged in invective against his adversary; *professeur de déclamation*, teacher of elocution. **déclamatoire**, *a.* Declamatory, high-flown.

déclamer [dekla'me], *v.t., vi.* To declaim; to spout, to mouth.

déclancher [DÉCLENCHER].

déclarant [dekla'rã], *n.m.* (*Law*) Informant, avowant.

déclaratif [deklara'tif], *a.* (*fem.* -ive) Declaratory.

déclaration [deklara'sjɔ̃], *n.f.* Declaration, proclamation; disclosure; notification, announcement; statement. *Déclaration d'amour*, avowal of love; *déclaration de biens*, schedule of assets; *déclaration d'entrée* or *de sortie*, clearance inwards *or* outwards; *déclaration sous serment*, affidavit. **déclaratoire**, *a.* Declaratory.

déclarer [dekla're], *v.t.* To declare, to make known; to proclaim; to certify; to denounce; to find (guilty or not guilty). *Déclarer sa volonté*, to make known one's will; *déclarer un décès*, to notify a death; *déclarer un enfant à la mairie*, to register a child at the town-hall; *ennemi déclaré*, declared or avowed enemy. **se déclarer**, *v.r.* To speak one's mind; to declare oneself or itself; to show oneself or itself. *La petite vérole s'est déclarée*, smallpox has broken out.

déclassé [dekla'se], *a.* (*fem.* -ée) Come down in the world; obsolete (ship).—*n.* One who has come down in the world; one rejected by his own class or sphere. **déclassement**, *n.m.* Loss of social position; (*Rail.*) transfer from one class to another; dismantling (of fortress etc.).

déclasser [dekla'se], *v.t.* To derange or unsettle the classing of; to transfer from one class to another (on trains, boats . . .); to unclass; to strike off the rolls, to dismiss from the service. **déclassifier**, *v.t.* To alter the classification of.

déclencher [deklã'ʃe], *v.t.* To unlatch (a door); to unhook, to detach, to separate (two pieces joined together); to release; to start in motion; (*Mil.*) to launch (an attack). (*Phot.*) *Déclencher l'obturateur*, to release the shutter.

déclic [de'klik], *n.m.* Pawl, click, catch; escapement, trigger, monkey (of a pile-driver).

déclimater [deklima'te], *v.t.* To declimatize.

déclin [de'klɛ̃], *n.m.* Decline; decay; wane (of the moon); ebb; close (of day etc.). *Déclin du jour*, twilight; *l'hiver est à son* or *sur son déclin*, winter is drawing to a close. **déclinable**, *a.* (*Gram.*) Declinable. **déclinaison**, *n.f.* (*Gram.*) Declension; (*Astron., Phys.*) declination. *Déclinaison de la boussole*, variation of the compass. **déclinant**, *a.* (*fem.* -ante) Declining. **déclinateur** [DÉCLINATOIRE]. **déclinatif**, *a.* (*fem.* -ive) Declinable. **déclination**, *n.f.*, *or* **déclinement**, *n.m.* Decadence, decline. **déclinatoire**, *a.* (*Law*) Taking exception, denying jurisdiction.

décliner [dekli'ne], *v.t.* To refuse; (*Gram.*) to decline; (*Law*) to refuse to recognize (the jurisdiction of a court etc.). *Décliner son*

nom, to state one's name; *décliner une juridiction*, to take exception to the jurisdiction of a court of law.—*v.i.* To decline, to deviate, to be on the wane, to fall off; (*Mariner's compass*) to decline from the meridian. *Ce malade décline tous les jours*, the patient is getting worse day by day. **déclinomètre**, *n.m.* Declinometer.

décliquer [dekli'ke], *v.t.* To undo the *déclic* or fastening of (a pile-driver); to release (pawl). **décliquetage**, *n.m.* Undoing the escapement. **décliqueter**, *v.t.* To undo the escapement of (a watch or clock), to uncog, to unclick.

déclive [de'kliːv], *a.* Declivous, sloping.—*n.f.* Slope, inclination. **décliver**, *v.i.* To slope. **déclivité**, *n.f.* Declivity, slope.

déclocher [deklɔ'ʃe], *v.t.* To take away the bell-glasses covering (plants).

décloîtrer [deklwa'tre], *v.t.* To withdraw from a convent, to uncloister; to secularize. **se décloîtrer**, *v.r.* To leave the cloister, to return to the world.

déclore [de'klɔːr], *v.t.* irr. (*conjugated like* CLORE) To unclose, to throw open. **déclos**, *p.p.* (*fem.* **déclose**) Unclosed.

déclouer [deklu'e], *v.t.* To unnail.

décoagulation [dekɔagyla'sjɔ̃], *n.f.* Liquefaction (of coagulated substance). **décoaguler**, *v.t.* To liquefy, to dissolve.

décochement [dekɔʃ'mã], *n.m.* Discharge, shooting (of arrows, shafts, etc.).

décocher [dekɔ'ʃe], *v.t.* To discharge, to dart (arrows etc.); to let fly (insults, epigrams, etc.).

décoction [dekɔk'sjɔ̃], *n.f.* Decoction.

décohéreur [dekɔe'rœːr], *n.m.* (*Teleg.*) Decoherer.

décoiffer [dekwa'fe], *v.t.* To remove or undo the coiffure of, to undress the hair of; (*colloq.*) to take the sealing-wax off (the cork of a bottle). *Décoiffer St-Pierre pour coiffer St-Paul*, to rob Peter to pay Paul. **se décoiffer**, *v.r.* To undo one's head-dress; to take off one's cap.

décoincement [dekwɛ̃s'mã], *n.m.* Unwedging; loosening; (*Rail.*) unkeying. **décoincer**, *v.t.* To unwedge; (*Rail.*) to unkey. **se décoincer**, *v.r.* To get unwedged, loose.

décollage [dekɔ'laːʒ], *n.m.* (*Av.*) Taking off.

décollation [dekɔla'sjɔ̃], *n.m.* Decollation, beheading.

décollement [dekɔl'mã], *n.m.* Ungluing, unpasting; separation, coming off; detachment (of retina).

décoller (1) [dekɔ'le], *v.t.* To unglue, to unpaste; (*Billiards*) to drive off the cushion. —*v.i.* (*Av.*) to take off; (*Cycl.*) to lose touch with the pacer; (*pop.*) to become thinner. **se décoller**, *v.r.* To get unglued, to come off; (*Billiards*) to come off the cushion.

décoller (2) [dekɔ'le], *v.t.* To behead.

décolletage [dekɔl'taːʒ], *n.m.* Lowness in the neck, or letting down (of dresses); baring the neck and shoulders; (*Agric.*) cutting the top of cultivated roots to prevent sprouting.

décolleté [dekɔl'te], *a.* (*fem.* -ée) (*Dress*) Low-necked.—*n.m.* Neck-line (of a dress), décolletage. **décolleter** [dekɔl'te], *v.t.* To uncover the neck, shoulders, etc., of; to cut (a dress) low; (*Agric.*) to cut the tops of (roots) to prevent sprouting; to cut (screw).

Tour à décolleter, screw-cutting lathe. **se décolleter,** *v.r.* To bare one's shoulders; to wear a low dress.

décolorant [dekɔlɔ'rɑ̃], *a.* (*fem.* **-ante**) Bleaching, decolorizing.—*n.m.* Decolorant, bleaching substance.

décoloration [dekɔlɔra'sjɔ̃], *n.f.* Discoloration, bleaching. **décoloré,** *a.* (*fem.* **-ée**) Discoloured, faded; (*fig.*) tame, colourless (of style). **décolorer,** *v.t.* To discolour, to take away the colour of, to change the natural hue of. **se décolorer,** *v.r.* To become discoloured, to fade. *Ces roses se décolorent,* these roses are losing their colour; *se décolorer les cheveux,* to bleach one's hair.

décombres [de'kɔ̃br], *n.m.* (*used only in pl.*) Rubbish, debris, ruins.

décommander [dekɔmɑ̃'de], *v.t.* To countermand; to cancel.

décommettre [dekɔ'mɛtr], *v.t. irr.* (*Naut.*) To unlay (a rope).

décompléter [dekɔ̃ple'te], *v.t. irr.* (*conjugated like* ACCÉLÉRER) To render incomplete.

décomposable [dekɔ̃po'zabl], *a.* Decomposable. **décomposant,** *a.* (*fem.* **-ante**) Decomposing, causing decomposition. **décomposé,** *a.* (*fem.* **-ée**) Decomposed; (*fig.*) discomposed. *Un visage décomposé,* a distorted countenance.

décomposer [dekɔ̃po'ze], *v.t.* To decompose; to split up, to break up; to discompose, to distort. **se décomposer,** *v.r.* To decompose, to become decomposed, to rot, to decay; (*fig.*) to be distorted (of the face etc.).

décomposition, *n.f.* Decomposition, analysis; splitting up; putrefaction; (*fig.*) discomposition of the face etc.).

décompresseur [dekɔ̃prɛ'sœ:r], *n.m.* (*Motor.*) Exhaust-valve, decompressor. **décompression,** *n.f.* Decompression.

décomprimer [dekɔ̃pri'me], *v.t.* To expand (steam, gas, etc.).

décompte [de'kɔ̃:t], *n.m.* Deduction, abatement, discount, allowance; balance, deficit; (*fig.*) drawback; disappointment. *Payer le décompte,* to pay the balance that is owing; *trouver du décompte,* to be disappointed. **décompter,** *v.t.* To deduct, to abate; to make some reduction on; to reckon off.—*v.i.* (*fig.*) To be disappointed, to lose one's illusions.

déconcertant [dekɔ̃sɛr'tɑ̃], *a.* (*fem.* **-ante**) Disconcerting.

déconcerter [dekɔ̃sɛr'te], *v.t.* To disconcert, to put out; to foil, to baffle. **se déconcerter,** *v.r.* To be disconcerted or put out.

*déconfire [dekɔ̃'fi:r], *v.t. irr.* (*p.p.* **déconfit;** *conjugated like* CONFIRE) To discomfit; to do for, to defeat.

déconfiture [dekɔ̃fi'ty:r], *n.f.* Discomfiture; overthrow, break-down; failure, ruin, insolvency. *Tomber en déconfiture,* to go bankrupt.

décongeler [dekɔ̃'ʒle], *v.t. irr.* (*conjug. like* AMENER) To thaw (chilled meat).

décongestionner [dekɔ̃ʒɛstjɔ'ne], *v.t.* To relieve congestion.

déconseiller [dekɔ̃sɛ'je], *v.t.* To dissuade; to advise somebody against.

déconsidération [dekɔ̃sidera'sjɔ̃], *n.f.* Disrepute, disesteem, discredit.

déconsidérer [dekɔ̃side're], *v.t.* To bring into disrepute, to discredit. **se déconsidérer,** *v.r.* To fall into disrepute.

déconsigner [dekɔ̃si'ɲe], *v.t.* To take (luggage) out of the cloakroom; to let free (troops confined to barracks).

décontenance [dekɔ̃t'nɑ̃:s], *n.m.* Lack of self-assurance, embarrassment. **décontenancement,** *n.m.* Mortification, embarrassment. **décontenancer,** *v.t.* To abash, to put out of countenance. **se décontenancer,** *v.r.* To be put out of countenance, to be abashed.

décontracté [dekɔ̃trak'te], *a.* (*fem.* **-ée**) Relaxed. **décontracter,** *v.t.* To relax, to slacken (one's muscles). **se décontracter,** *v.r.* To relax.

déconvenue [dekɔ̃v'ny], *n.f.* Discomfiture; disappointment, set-back.

décor [de'kɔ:r], *n.m.* Decoration, ornamental painting; (*Theat., pl.*) scenery, stage-effects; (*cyclist slang*) *Entrer dans le décor,* to corner, to smash into (a hedge, a wall, etc.); *changement de décor,* scene-shifting; *décor bois,* graining in imitation of wood; *peintre de décors,* scene-painter. **décorateur,** *n.m.* (*fem.* **-trice**) Ornamental painter, decorator; scene-painter. **décoratif,** *a.* (*fem.* **-ive**) Decorative, ornamental.

décoration [dekɔra'sjɔ̃], *n.f.* Decoration, embellishment; insignia, ribbon, star (of an order). *Porter une décoration,* to wear a medal; *remise de décorations,* investiture. **décorativement,** *adv.* Decoratively, in a decorative manner.

décorder [dekɔr'de], *v.t.* To untwist, to untwine (a cord etc.); to untie the rope (of a box, a case, etc.).

décoré [dekɔ're], *a.* (*fem.* **décorée**) Decorated; wearing the insignia of some order or its ribbon in his buttonhole.

décorer [dekɔ're], *v.t.* To decorate, to adorn; to dignify, to set off; to confer the Legion of Honour etc. upon.

décorner [dekɔr'ne], *v.t.* To dishorn. *Décorner un livre,* to undo the dog's-ear of a book; *il fait un vent à décorner les bœufs,* it is blowing great guns.

décortication [dekɔrtika'sjɔ̃], *n.f.* Decortication, stripping off bark. **décortiquer,** *v.t.* To decorticate, to bark, to husk.

décorum [dekɔ'rɔm], *n.m.* Decorum, propriety, decency. *Blesser le décorum,* to offend against the laws of decorum; *pour garder le décorum,* for decency's sake.

découcher [deku'ʃe], *v.i.* To sleep away from home; to stay out all night.

découdre [de'kudr], *v.t. irr.* (*conjugated like* COUDRE (2)) To unsew, to unstitch; to rip up.—*v.i.* (*fam.*) *En découdre,* to fight; *ils veulent en découdre,* they are bent on coming to blows *or* fighting it out. **se découdre,** *v.r.* To come unstitched.

découenner [dekwa'ne], *v.t.* To skin (a pig).

découler [deku'le], *v.i.* To trickle, to flow, to run; to spring, to proceed. *C'est de Dieu que les grâces découlent,* all blessings flow from God; *la sueur découlait de son front,* the sweat was running down his forehead.

découpage [deku'pa:ʒ], *n.m.* Cutting out, carving out. *Découpage à l'emporte-pièce,* punching; (*Cine.*) *découpage technique,* shooting script. **découpe,** *n.f.* Ornamental cut (in cloth etc.). **découpé,** *a.* (*fem.* **-ée**) (*Bot.*) Cut, denticulated.

découper [deku′pe], *v.t.* To cut up; to pink, to slash; to cut out; to punch. *Découper des figures,* to cut out silhouettes; *découper une jupe,* to cut out a skirt; *découper une volaille,* to carve a fowl; *un couteau à découper,* a carving-knife. **se découper,** *v.r.* To stand out, to show up (against). **découpeur,** *n.m.* (*fem.* **-euse**) Carver; pinker, cutter.

découple [de′kupl] or **découpler** (1), *n.m.* (*Hunt.*) Uncoupling, unleashing of dogs.

découplé [deku′ple], *a.* (*fem.* **-ée**) Strapping. *C'est un gaillard bien découplé,* he is a strapping fellow; *une fille bien découplée,* a well set up girl.

découpler (2) [deku′ple], *v.t.* To uncouple, to unleash, to let loose (in pursuit).

découpoir [deku′pwa:r], *n.m.* Punch, stamping-machine, stamping-press. **découpure,** *n.f.* Cutting out, pinking, work cut out; cut paper-work; indentation.

décourageant [dekura′ʒã], *a.* (*fem.* **-ante**) Discouraging, disheartening. **découragement,** *n.m.* Discouragement; despondency. *Tomber dans le découragement,* to become discouraged.

décourager [dekura′ʒe], *v.t.* To discourage, to dishearten, to daunt, to deter. **se décourager,** *v.r.* To be disheartened. *Il y a de quoi se décourager,* it is enough to dishearten one.

découronner [dekurɔ′ne], *v.t.* To discrown; to untop (trees etc.). *Découronner une hauteur,* to sweep the top of a hill (of troops).

décours [de′ku:r], *n.m.* Decrease; wane (of the moon).

décousu [deku′sy], *a.* (*fem.* **-ue**) Unsewn, unstitched; (*fig.*) desultory, loose, disconnected (of style etc.). *Des idées décousues,* disconnected ideas; *style décousu,* rambling style.—*n.m.* Incoherence, inconsistency (of style, etc.). **décousure,** *n.f.* Seam or stitch undone (*Hunt.*) gash (by a wild boar).

découvert [deku′ve:r], *a.* (*fem.* **découverte** (1)) Uncovered; discovered; open, unguarded, unprotected; bare, unwooded, bareheaded, unmasked, undecked (of boats). *À découvert,* in the open, exposed to the fire of the enemy, unprotected, barefaced, (*Comm.*) overdrawn; *une allée découverte,* an open walk; *un pays découvert,* an open country.— *n.m.* (*Comm.*) Uncovered balance, overdraft, deficit. **découverte** (2), *n.f.* Discovery, detection; (*Mil.*) reconnoitring. *À la découverte,* (*Naut.*) on the look out; *aller à la découverte,* to make a reconnaissance; *envoyer à la découverte de,* to send to reconnoitre. **découvreur,** *n.m.* (*fem.* **-euse**) Discoverer.

découvrir [deku′vri:r], *v.t.* (*conjugated like* COUVRIR) To uncover, to expose, to lay bare; to unmask, to unroof, etc.; to discover, to disclose, to find out, to discern, to detect, to begin to perceive. *Cette ville est entièrement découverte,* this town is wholly unprotected; *découvrir le pot aux roses,* to unmask the intrigue; *découvrir les racines d'un arbre,* to lay bare the roots of a tree; *découvrir son jeu,* to show one's hand, to betray oneself; *je lui ai découvert mon cœur,* I opened my heart to him. **se découvrir,** *v.r.* To uncover oneself, to take off one's

hat, to stand bareheaded; to unbosom oneself; to expose oneself; to make oneself known, to betray oneself; to be detected, to be discovered; to lie open or bare; to clear up (of the sky); (*Box.*) to break guard.

décramponner [dekrãpɔ′ne], *v.t.* To unspike. **se décramponner,** *v.r.* To let go one's hold.

décrassage [dekra′sa:ʒ], *n.m.* Scouring, taking off the dirt.

décrasser [dekra′se], *v.t.* To take the dirt off, to clean, to scour; to brush up, to polish; (*fig.*) to make respectable or presentable. *Il faut décrasser ce jeune homme,* that young man needs some polishing. **se décrasser,** *v.r.* To wash, to clean oneself; to become polished, respectable, etc.

décrassoir [dekra′swar], *n.m.* Fine-tooth comb; (*dial.*) coarse towel.

décréditement [dekredit′mã], *n.m.* Discrediting. **décréditer,** *v.t.* To discredit, to bring into discredit or disrepute, to disgrace. **se décréditer,** *v.r.* To sink into discredit, to lose one's credit or reputation.

décrépi [dekre′pi], *a.* (*fem.* **-ie**) Unplastered, dilapidated. **décrépir,** *v.t.* To unplaster. **se décrépir,** *v.r.* To lose its plaster (of a wall etc.); to deteriorate. *décrépissage, *n.m.* Unplastering.

décrépit [dekre′pi], *a.* (*fem.* **décrépite**) Decrepit, broken-down; worn out.

décrépitation [dekrepita′sjɔ̃], *n.f.* Decrepitation, crackling. **décrépiter,** *v.i.* To decrepitate, to crackle.—*v.t.* To calcine (salt etc.) until it no longer crackles.

décrépitude [dekrepi′tyd], *n.f.* Decrepitude.

décret [de′krɛ], *n.m.* Decree, order, enactment; (*Law*) writ, warrant. **décret-loi,** *n.m.* Order in Council.

décrétale [dekre′tal], *n.f.* Decretal.

décréter [dekre′te], *v.t.* (*conjugated like* ACCÉLÉRER) To decree, to order, to enact; (*Law*) to issue a writ or warrant against.

décreusage, décreuser, etc. [DÉCRUER].

décri [de′kri], *n.m.* Official crying down or depreciation (of coinage); (*fig.*) disrepute, discredit.

décrier [dekri′e], *v.t.* (*conjugated like* PRIER) To decry, to run down; (*fig.*) to discredit, to bring into disrepute. **se décrier,** *v.r.* To bring oneself into disrepute; to decry one another.

décrire [de′kri:r], *v.t.* *irr.* (*conjugated like* ÉCRIRE) To describe, to depict. **se décrire,** *v.r.* To be described.

décrocher [dekrɔ′ʃe], *v.t.* To unhook, to take down, to disconnect. (*Mil.*) *Décrocher les avant-trains,* to unlimber (guns). **se décrocher,** *v.r.* To become unhooked; to fall out of step.

décrochez-moi ça [dekrɔʃemwa′sa], *n.m. inv.* (*pop.*) Second-hand suit; hand-me-down shop. *Il s'habille au décrochez-moi ça,* he dresses sloppily.

décroisement [dekrwas′mã], *n.m.* Uncrossing. **décroiser,** *v.t.* To uncross (the legs etc.).

décroissant [dekrwa′sã], *a.* (*fem.* **-ante**) Decreasing, diminishing; subsiding. **décroissement,** *n.m.,* or **décroissance,** *n.f.* Decrease, diminution, wane. **décroît,** *n.m.* Wane (of the moon).

décroître [de′krwa:tr], *v.i. irr.* (*p.p.* **décru;**

conjugated like CROÎTRE) To decrease, to diminish, to wane; to draw in (of days); to come down (in life).

décrottage [dekrɔ'ta:ʒ], *n.m.* Cleaning (of boots, trousers, etc.).

décrotter [dekrɔ'te], *v.t.* To rub the dirt off; to clean; to brush up; (*fig.*) to improve the manners of. **se décrotter,** *v.r.* To clean oneself; to clean one's boots etc. **décrotteur,** *n.m.* (*fem.* **-euse**) Shoe-black. **décrottoir,** *n.m.* A scraper (for shoes). **décrottoire,** *n.f.* Shoe-brush.

décru, *p.p.* [DÉCROÎTRE].

décrue [de'kry], *n.f.* Decrease; fall (of water). *La crue et la décrue de l'eau,* the rise and fall of water.

décruer [dekry'e], **décruser,** or **décreuser,** *v.t.* (*Dyeing*) To scour (silk etc.) in preparation for the dye. **décrueur** or **décruseur,** *n.m.* One who performs this operation. **décrûment, décrurage, décrusage, décreusage,** *n.m.* Scouring.

décrypter [dekrip'te], *v.t.* To decipher.

déçu, *p.p.* (*fem.* **déçue**) [DÉCEVOIR].

décubitus [dekybi'tys], *n.m. Décubitus* (*dorsal* or *latéral*), the recumbent position (on one's back or side).

décuiter (se) [dekɥi'te], *v.r.* (*vulg.*) To sober up.

déculassement [dekylas'mɑ̃], *n.m.* Unbreeching. **déculasser,** *v.t.* To unbreech (a gun).

déculotter [dekylɔ'te], *v.t.* To take off (somebody's) breeches, (a child's) pants; to debag; to clean of accumulated deposits (of a pipe).

décuple [de'kypl], *a.* and *n.m.* Tenfold, decuple. *Il a gagné le décuple de ce qu'il avait avancé,* he has gained ten times as much as he laid out. **décupler,** *v.t.* To increase tenfold.

décurie [deky'ri], *n.f.* (*Rom. Ant.*) Subdivision of the century; a troop of ten soldiers. **décurion,** *n.m.* Decurion.

décurrent [deky'rɑ̃], *a.* (*fem.* **-ente**) (*Bot.*) Decurrent.

décuvage [deky'va:ʒ], *n.m.,* or **décuvaison,** *n.f.* Tunning (of wine). **décuver,** *v.t.* To tun.

dédaigner [dedɛ'ɲe], *v.t.* To disdain, to scorn, to despise; to disregard. **dédaigneusement,** *adv.* Disdainfully, scornfully. **dédaigneux,** *a.* (*fem.* **-euse**) Disdainful, scornful; regardless. *Faire le dédaigneux,* to turn up one's nose.

dédain [de'dɛ̃], *n.m.* Disdain, scorn, disregard. *Prendre en dédain,* to conceive a contempt for; *répondre avec dédain,* to answer scornfully.

dédale [de'dal], *n.m.* Labyrinth, maze; (*pl.*) intricacies.

dedans [dǝ'dɑ̃], *adv.* Within, in, inside; at home. *De dedans,* from within; *donner dedans,* to fall into the trap; *en dedans,* on the inside, within; *être dedans,* to be in for it; *être tout en dedans,* to be uncommunicative, reticent, close; *il est là dedans,* he is in there; *mettre quelqu'un dedans,* to take someone in; (*Mil.*) *fourrer (un homme) dedans,* to put him in clink, in quod; *par dedans,* within, inside; *sa porte était fermée en dedans,* his door was fastened inside; (*fam.*) *se mettre dedans,* to get taken in.—*n.m.* Inside, interior. *Au dedans et au dehors,* at home and abroad; *du dedans au dehors,* from within outwards.

dédicace [dedi'kas], *n.f.* Dedication, consecration (of a church etc.). **dédicacer,** *v.t.* To furnish with a dedication. **dédicateur,** *n.m.* (*fem.* **dédicatrice**) Dedicator. **dédication,** *n.f.* (*Law*) Dedication (of a temple etc.). **dédicatoire,** *a.* Dedicatory.

dédier [de'dje], *v.t.* To dedicate, to consecrate; to devote; to inscribe (a book etc.).

dédire [de'di:r], *v.t. irr.* (*conjugated like* DIRE, *except 2nd pl. ind.* **dédisez,** *imp.* **dédisez**) To disavow, to disown; gainsay, to contradict. **se dédire,** *v.r.* To recant, to unsay what one has said. *Il ne peut s'en dédire,* he cannot back out of it; *se dédire de sa promesse,* to revoke one's promise.

dédit [de'di], *n.m.* Unsaying, renunciation, retraction; forfeit, forfeiture. *Au dédit de,* on the forfeiture of; *avoir son dit et son dédit,* to say yes one day and no the next.

dédommagement [dedɔmaʒ'mɑ̃], *n.m.* Indemnification, reparation; compensation, damages.

dédommager [dedɔma'ʒe], *v.t.* To make amends for, to make good; to compensate, to make up for. **se dédommager,** *v.r.* To indemnify oneself, to recoup oneself.

dédorer [dedɔ're], *v.t.* To ungild. *Noblesse dédorée,* impoverished gentry. **se dédorer,** *v.r.* To lose its gilt (of metal etc.).

dédouanement [dedwan'mɑ̃], *n.m.* (Customs) clearance. **dédouaner** [dedwa'ne], *v.t.* To clear (goods) from the custom house.

dédoublement [dedublǝ'mɑ̃] or **dédoublage,** *n.m.* Dividing into two; unlining; diluting. *Dédoublement de la personnalité,* splitting of the personality.

dédoubler [dedu'ble], *v.t.* To take out the lining of; to divide into two. *Dédoubler une pierre,* to cut a stone into two parts lengthwise; *dédoubler un autocar,* to run a relief coach; *dédoubler un train,* to run an extra train; (*Mil.*) *dédoubler les rangs,* to form single file. **se dédoubler,** *v.r.* To be divided into two.

déductif [dedyk'tif], *a.* (*fem.* **déductive**) Deductive. **déduction,** *n.f.* Deduction, allowance, abatement; inference.

déduire [de'dɥi:r], *v.t. irr.* (*conjugated like* CONDUIRE) To deduct, to subtract; to deduct, to infer.

*déduit [de'dɥi], *n.m.* Amusement, pleasure.

déesse [de'ɛs], *n.f.* Goddess, female deity.

défâcher [defa'ʃe], *v.t.* To pacify. **se défâcher,** *v.r.* To be pacified, to cool down; to cease to be angry. *S'il est fâché, qu'il se défâche,* if he is angry let him cool down again.

défaillance [defa'jɑ̃:s], *n.f.* Fainting fit, swoon, faintness, weakness; failure, exhaustion, decay, extinction (of a family etc.); (*fig.*) error, shortcoming. *Tomber en défaillance,* to fall into a swoon. **défaillant,** *a.* (*fem.* **-ante**) Failing, giving way, falling off; decaying, near extinction, without heirs; weak, feeble; faltering, unsteady; *n.* (*Law*) Defaulter.

défaillir [defa'ji:r], *v.i. irr.* To fail, to default; to decay; to swoon, to faint away. *Je me sentis défaillir,* I felt I was giving way; *ses forces défaillent tous les jours,* his strength is steadily failing.

défaire [de'fɛ:r], *v.t. irr.* (*pres.p.* **défaisant,**

p.p. **défait**; *conjugated like* FAIRE) To undo, to unmake; to unpin, unrip, unknit, etc.; to defeat, to rout; to eclipse, to obscure; to emaciate, to waste; to embarrass, to discompose; to deliver, to rid. *Défaire une malle,* to unpack a trunk; *défaire un marché* or *défaire un mariage,* to annul or break off a bargain *or* a marriage; *défaire un nœud,* to untie or a knot; *défaites-moi de cet importun,* rid me of that troublesome fellow; *sa maladie l'a bien défait,* his illness has made him look worn out. **se défaire,** *v.r.* To rid oneself, to get rid (*de*), to give up, to forsake, to leave off; to come undone, to become loose; to lose strength and quality (of wine). *Défaites-vous de vos préjugés,* shake off your prejudices; *se défaire de sa marchandise,* to sell off one's wares; *se défaire de son ennemi,* to dispatch one's enemy; *se défaire d'un domestique,* to discharge a servant; *se défaire d'une mauvaise habitude,* to break oneself of a bad habit. **défaiseur,** *n.m.* (*fem.* **-euse**) Undoer. **défait,** *a.* (*fem.* **défaite** (1)) Undone, defeated; meagre, lean, wasted; pale, worn out, wan. **défaite** (2), *n.f.* Defeat, overthrow; evasion, shift, sham, pretence, excuse. **Ces marchandises-là sont de bonne défaite,* those goods command a ready sale; *c'est une défaite,* that is a mere evasion.

défaitisme [defɛ'tism], *n.m.* Defeatism. **défaitiste,** *a.* and *n.* Defeatist; scuttler.

défalcation [defalkɑ'sjɔ̃], *n.f.* Deduction; embezzlement. **défalquer,** *v.t.* To take off, to deduct.

défasse etc. [DÉFAIRE].

défatiguer [defati'ge], *v.t.* To refresh.

défaufiler [defofi'le], *v.t.* To untack.

défausser [defo'se], *v.t.* To straighten, to set right, to redress. **se défausser,** *v.r.* (*Cards*) To get rid of useless cards; to discard.

défaut [de'fo], *n.m.* Absence, lack, default; defect, fault, flaw, blemish, shortcoming; (*Law*) non-appearance. *À défaut de,* in default of, in lieu of, instead of, for want of; *le défaut de la cuirasse,* break; (*fig.*) weak point; *cette pièce de porcelaine a un défaut,* there is a flaw in that piece of china; *faire défaut,* to be wanting, to be missing; to default; *il n'y a personne sans défaut,* there is no man but has his faults; *les chiens sont en défaut,* (*Hunt.*) the hounds have lost the scent; *mettre quelqu'un en défaut,* to baffle, to foil, to throw someone off the scent; *trouver quelqu'un en défaut,* to find someone at fault.

défaveur [defa'vœːr], *n.f.* Disfavour, discredit. **défavorable,** *a.* Unfavourable, disadvantageous. **défavorablement,** *adv.* Unfavourably, disadvantageously.

défécation [defekɑ'sjɔ̃], *n.f.* Defecation; (*Pharm.*) clarification.

défectif [defɛk'tif], *a.* (*fem.* **défective**) (*Gram.*) Defective. **défection,** *n.f.* Defection, falling off, disloyalty **défectivité,** *n.f.* (*Gram.*) Defectiveness. **défectueux,** *a.* (*fem.* **-euse**) Defective, imperfect. (*Mil.*) *Tir défectueux,* bad shooting. **défectuosité,** *n.f.* Defect, imperfection, flaw.

défendable [defɑ̃'dabl], *a.* Defensible, tenable.

défendeur [defɑ̃'dœːr], *n.m.* (*fem.* **défenderesse**) Defendant; respondent.

défendre [de'fɑ̃ːdr], *v.t.* (*pres.p.* **défendant,**

p.p. **défendu**) To defend, to protect; to shield, to shelter; to support, to uphold, to vindicate; to forbid, to prohibit. *Défendre sa maison à quelqu'un,* to forbid someone the house; *faire une chose à son corps défendant,* to do a thing reluctantly; *la raison nous défend de faire une injustice,* reason forbids us to do an injustice; *on a défendu le port des armes,* the carrying of arms is prohibited. **se défendre,** *v.r.* To defend oneself, to resist; to excuse oneself (from doing a thing); to clear oneself, to plead one's own cause; to deny; to guard (against); to refrain, to forbear. *Cet accusé a voulu se défendre lui-même,* that prisoner wanted to conduct his own defence; *il ne peut se défendre de tant de reproches,* he cannot clear himself from so many imputations; (*pop.*) *il se défend bien,* he is doing well; *je ne m'en défends pas,* I admit it, I own it; *nous ne pouvons nous défendre de l'aimer,* we cannot help liking him; *se défendre du froid,* to protect oneself from the cold.

défenestration [defənɛstra'sjɔ̃], *n.f.* (*Hist.*) Defenestration.

*défens or **défends** [de'fɑ̃], *n.m.* (*Forestry*) Prohibition of cutting (woods).

défense [de'fɑ̃ːs], *n.f.* Defence, protection, safeguard; resistance; screen, shield, shelter; prohibition, interdiction; apology, vindication, justification, plea; (*Law*) the defence, counsel for the defendant; (*Fort.*, *pl.*) outworks; tusk, fang (of boars); tusk (of elephants); (*Naut.*) fender. *Armé* or *muni de défenses,* tusked, fanged (of boars, elephants, etc.); *arrêt de défense,* decree to suspend the execution of a former decree; *bois en défense,* a wood so far grown that cattle may be let into it without danger to the trees; *cas de légitime défense,* (*Law*) case of self-defence; *défense contre avions,* D.C.A., (*Mil.*) anti-aircraft defence; *cordes de défense,* (*Naut.*) fenders of junk or old cable; *défense de fumer,* no smoking; *défense d'entrer,* no admittance; *être hors de défense,* not to be in a condition to defend oneself; *faire défense,* to forbid, to prohibit; *la place opposa une belle défense,* the fortress offered a splendid resistance; *preuves alléguées pour la défense (d'une cause),* plea; *se mettre en défense,* to stand upon one's defence; *défense passive,* civil defence. **défenseur,** *n.m.* Defender, protector, supporter, vindicator; advocate, defender, counsel. *Un défenseur nommé d'office,* a counsel appointed by the court. **défensif,** *a.* (*fem.* **-ive**) Defensive.—*n.f.* Defensive. *Se tenir sur la défensive,* to stand upon the defensive. **défensivement,** *adv.* Defensively.

déféquer [defe'ke], *v.t. irr.* (*conjugated like* ACCÉLÉRER) To defecate.

déférence [defe'rɑ̃s], *n.f.* Deference, regard, respect.

déférent [defe'rɑ̃], *a.* (*fem.* **-ente**) Deferential, complying. (*Anat.*) *Canal déférent,* deferent.

déférer [defe're], *v.t. irr.* (*conjug. like* ACCÉLÉRER) **To confer, to bestow; to tender, to administer; to accuse, to impeach, to inform against. *Déférer le serment à quelqu'un,* to tender an oath to, to put someone on oath; *déférer quelqu'un au parquet,* to place someone's case in the charge of the Public

Prosecutor's department; *déférer quelqu'un à la justice*, to impeach someone in court.—*v.i.* To defer, to yield, to comply, to condescend. *Déférer à quelqu'un*, to pay deference to someone; *déférer aux sentiments des autres*, to defer to the opinions, feelings of others.

déferler [defer'le], *v.t.* (*Naut.*) To unfurl. —*v.i.* To break into foam (of the sea). *La lame déferle*, the wave bursts into foam.

déferrer [defe're], *v.t.* To unshoe (a horse); to unfetter (a convict). **se déferrer**, *v.r.* To come unshod, to lose a shoe. *Mon lacet se déferre*, the tag is coming off my lace.

défets [de'fɛ], *n.m.* (*pl.*) Waste sheets (of a book).

défeuillaison [defœjɛ'zɔ̃], *n.f.* Defoliation. **défeuiller**, *v.t.* To take the leaves off. *Le vent a défeuillé les arbres*, the wind has stripped the trees. **se défeuiller**, *v.r.* To shed its leaves (of ⁺rees).

défi [de'fi], *n.m.* Defiance, challenge. *Envoyer un défi à quelqu'un*, to send someone a challenge; *je lui ai lancé un défi aux échecs*, I challenged him to a game of chess; *mettre au défi*, to defy; *un cartel de défi*, a written challenge.

défiance [de'fjɑ̃:s], *n.f.* Distrust, mistrust; diffidence, caution. *Avec défiance*, distrustfully; *concevoir de la défiance*, to entertain distrust; *se sentir plein de défiance*, to be full of misgivings; *une sotte défiance le retient*, he is held back by a foolish diffidence. **défiant**, *a.* (*fem.* **défiante**) Distrustful, mistrustful, suspicious.

déficeler [defis'le], *v.t.* To untie; to undo.

déficience [defi'sjɑ̃:s], *n.f.* Deficiency. **déficient** [defi'sjɑ̃], *a.* (*fem.* **déficiente**). Deficient.

déficit [defi'sit], *n.m.* Deficit, deficiency. *Combler le déficit*, to make up the deficit.

défier [de'fje], *v.t.* (*conjugated like* PRIER) To defy, to challenge; to brave, to face, to confront (death etc.); to set at defiance; (*Naut.*) to fend, to dodge. *Défier les dangers*, to face dangers; *défier quelqu'un au jacquet*, to challenge someone at backgammon; *défiez le vent*, (*Naut.*) keep her to; *il ne faut jamais défier un fou*, never challenge a madman; *je vous défie de m'en donner la preuve*, I defy you to give me proof of it.—*v.i.* To be suspicious or wary. **se défier**, *v.r.* To defy or to challenge each other; to distrust, ⁺o be mistrustful, to beware (*de*). *Je me défie de cet homme*, I distrust that man; *se défier de ses forces*, to distrust one's own strength; *se défier de soi-même*, to be diffident.

défiger [defi'ʒe], *v.t.* To liquefy. **se défiger**, *v.r.* To liquefy; (*fig.*) to thaw (of persons).

défigurant [defigy'rɑ̃], *a.* (*fem.* **-ante**) Disfiguring. **défiguration**, *n.f.*, or **défigurement**, *n.m.* Disfigurement, defacement.

défigurer [defigy're], *v.t.* To disfigure, to mar; to distort. *Défigurer la vérité*, to distort the truth; *la petite vérole l'a tout défiguré*, the smallpox has quite disfigured him. **se défigurer**, *v.r.* To disfigure oneself; to become disfigured or deformed.

défilade [defi'lad], *n.f.* Filing off or past, marching past; succession. *Un feu de défilade*, the fire of each ship in turn as she passes by.

défilé [defi'le], *n.m.* Defile, narrow pass,

gorge; (*fig.*) strait, difficulty; (*Mil.*) defiling, filing off or past, marching past. *Un défilé de mannequins*, a mannequin parade. **défilement**, *n.m.* (*Fort.*) Construction of fortifications so as to shelter the defenders, defilading.

défiler [defi'le], *v.t.* To unstring, to unthread; to untwist; (*Fort.*) to defilade. *Défiler son chapelet*, (*fig.*) to say all one has to say (on a subject); *défiler un ouvrage*, (*Fort.*) to defilade a work.—*v.i.* To defile, to file off, to march past; (*Naut.*) to bear away. *Les soldats ne pouvaient défiler que deux par deux*, the soldiers could only march past two by two.—*n.m.* (*Mil.*) Filing off, marching past. **se défiler**, *v.r.* To come unthreaded or unstrung; (*Mil.*) to take cover; (*fam.*) to make off, to slip away.

défilocher. [EFFILOCHER.]

défini [defi'ni], *a.* (*fem.* **définie**) Definite, determined, defined. *Nombre défini*, definite number.

définir [defi'ni:r], *v.t.* To define; to determine, to decide; to explain, to describe. *Définir une personne*, to give an idea of a person. **se définir**, *v.r.* To be defined, to be determined, to become clear. **définissable**, *a.* Definable. **définisseur**, *n.m.* Definer.

définiteur [defini'tœ:r], *n.m.* (*R.-C. Ch.*) Deputy (to the chapter of a religious order).

définitif [defini'tif], *a.* (*fem.* **-ive**) Definitive, final; ultimate, eventual. *En définitive*, definitively, after all; *en définitive, que voulez-vous?* in a word, what do you want?

définition [defini'sjɔ̃], *n.f.* Definition. *Définition de l'image*, (*Tel.*) picture resolution.

définitivement [definitiv'mɑ̃], *adv.* Definitively, positively, decidedly; ultimately, eventually.

défis, 1st *sing. past* [DÉFAIRE].

déflagration [deflagra'sjɔ̃], *n.f.* (*Chem.*) Deflagration.

déflation [defla'sjɔ̃], *n.f.* Deflation.

défléchir [defle'ʃi:r], *v.i.* To turn from or aside, to deflect. *Tir défléchi*, deflected shooting.

déflecteur [deflɛk'tœ:r], *n.m.* (*Motor.*) Ventilating window; deflector.

déflegmation [deflɛgmɑ'sjɔ̃], *n.f.* Process of rectifying alcohol. **déflegmer**, *v.t.* To rectify (alcohol).

défleuraison [DÉFLORAISON.]

défleurir [deflœ'ri:r], *v.i.* To lose its flowers. —*v.t.* To cause (a plant) to lose its flowers; (*fig.*) to take away the bloom of.

déflexion [deflɛk'sjɔ̃], *n.f.* Deviation; (*Gram.*) deflection.

défloraison [deflɔrɛ'zɔ̃] or **défleuraison**, *n.f.* Fall or withering of the blossom.

défloration [deflɔrɑ'sjɔ̃], *n.f.* Defloration.

déflorer [deflɔ're], *v.t.* To deflower, to seduce. *Déflorer un sujet*, to take the freshness off a subject.

défonçage [defɔ̃'sa:ʒ] or⁺ **défoncement**, *n.m.* Staving in (of the head of casks), breaking or smashing in; (*Agric.*) subsoil ploughing, deep trenching.

défoncer [defɔ̃'se], *v.t.* To stave in, to bilge (a cask), to knock in (the head of a cask); to dig deeply, to trench (ground); (*Mil.*) to rout. *Défoncer un chapeau*, to batter in a hat. *Un chemin défoncé*, a road full of holes. **se défoncer**, *v.t.* To give way at the bottom; to break up (of roads); to get cut up.

défonceuse [defɔ̃'søz], *n.f.* Trenching plough.
déforestation [defɔresta'sjɔ̃], *n.f.* Deforestation.
déformable [defɔr'mabl], *a.* That can be put out of shape. **déformant**, *a.* (*fem.* -ante) Distorting (mirror etc.).
déformation [defɔrma'sjɔ̃], *n.f.* Deformation.
déformer [defɔr'me], *v.t.* To put out of shape, to deform, to distort. **se déformer**, *v.r.* To lose its form, to get out of shape. *Sa taille se déforme*, her figure is losing its shape.
défortifier [defɔrti'fje], *v.t.* (*conjugated like* PRIER) To dismantle the fortifications of.
défournage [defur'naːʒ] or **défournement**, *n.m.* Drawing out (of the oven, the kiln).
défourner, *v.t.* To draw out (of an oven or a kiln). *Défourner le pain*, to draw the batch.
défourrer [defu're], *v.t.* To unwrap, to take out of the cover; to thresh (corn); (*Naut.*) to unkeckle.
défrai [de'frɛ], *n.m.* Defraying, settling expenses.
défraîchir [defrɛ'ʃiːr], *v.t.* To tarnish, to take away the brilliancy, gloss, or freshness of. **se défraîchir**, *v.r.* To lose its brilliancy, freshness, etc., to tarnish. *Articles un peu défraîchis*, slightly soiled goods.
défranciser [defrɑ̃si'ze], *v.t.* To unfrenchify.
défrayer [defrɛ'je], *v.t.* (*conjugated like* BALAYER) To defray, to bear the cost of; to amuse, to divert, to entertain. *Défrayer la conversation*, to be the life or the topic of the conversation; *défrayer la chronique*, to be a topic of conversation or a butt for the Press.
défrayeur, *n.m.* (*fem.* -euse) Defrayer.
défriche [de'friʃ], *n.f.*, or **défriché**, *n.m.* Piece of cleared land.
défrichement [defriʃ'mɑ̃] or **défrichage**, *n.m.* Clearing, breaking up (of land for tillage). *Ce défrichement est en plein rapport cette année*, this piece of cleared land is in full bearing this year; *faire le défrichement d'un terrain*, to clear a piece of ground.
défricher [defri'ʃe], *v.t.* To clear, to break up (ground) for tillage; to reclaim. **défricheur**, *n.m.* Clearer; settler.
défriper [defri'pe], *v.t.* To unrumple; to smooth out.
défrisement [defriz'mɑ̃], *n.m.* Uncurling. **défriser**, *v.t.* To uncurl, to put out of curl; (*fam.*) to disappoint, to ruffle. **se défriser**, *v.r.* To come uncurled.
défroncement [defrɔ̃s'mɑ̃], *n.m.* Smoothing out; unfolding. **défroncer**, *v.t.* To undo the gathers, folds, or plaits in; to unknit (the brows).
défroque [de'frɔk], *n.f.* The effects left by a dying monk; hence, old things or effects, cast-off clothes, etc.
défroqué, *a.* and *n.m.* Unfrocked (priest).
défroquer [defrɔ'ke], *v.t.* To unfrock. **se défroquer**, *v.r.* To renounce one's order (of monks).
défruiter [defrɥi'te], *v.t.* To strip of its fruit.
***défubler** [DÉSAFFUBLER].
défunt [de'fœ̃], *a.* (*fem.* **défunte**) Defunct, deceased, late.—*n.* The deceased.
dégagé [dega'ʒe], *a.* Free, easy, unconstrained; flippant, bold, free and easy; slender, graceful. *Chambre dégagée*, room with a private

exit; *d'un air dégagé*, in an off-hand manner; *escalier dégagé*, private stairs; *taille dégagée*, free, easy figure.—*n.* (*Row.*) Recovery.
dégagement [degaʒ'mɑ̃], *n.m.* Disengagement, redemption, release; clearance, disencumberment; liberation, discharge (of gas etc); (*fig.*) unconcern. *Escalier de dégagement*, emergency staircase; *le dégagement d'effets déposés au mont-de-piété*, redeeming of articles at the pawnbroker's; *le dégagement de la poitrine*, easing of the chest; *le dégagement de la voie publique*, clearing of the street; *le dégagement de sa parole*, revocation of a promise etc.; *tuyau de dégagement*, waste-pipe.
dégager [dega'ʒe], *v.t.* To disengage, to extricate, to disentangle, to disembarrass, to disencumber; to deliver, to rescue; (*Fenc.*) to disengage; to release, to emit (fumes etc.); to redeem, to take out of pawn; (*Naut.*) to clear. *Cet habit dégage la taille*, that coat sets off the figure to advantage; *dégager la tête* or *la poitrine*, to ease, relieve, or lighten the head *or* the chest; *dégager le fer*, (*Fenc.*) to disengage; *dégager quelqu'un de sa promesse*, to release someone from his promise; *dégager sa parole*, to keep one's word, (more often) to withdraw one's word; *dégager une porte*, to clear a doorway; *il l'a dégagé de ses ennemis*, he rescued him from his enemies; *je le dégageai de ses liens*, I freed him from his bonds. **se dégager**, *v.r.* To be disengaged, relieved, or liberated (*de*); to extricate, disengage, or disentangle oneself; to break loose, to get away, to become clear; (*Chem.*) to be emitted. *Se dégager d'une promesse*, to be released from a promise.
dégaine [de'gɛːn], *n.f.* (*colloq.*) Awkward gait.
dégainer [degɛ'ne], *v.t.* To unsheathe (one's sword etc.).—***n.m.* Être brave jusqu'au dégainer*, to be brave till it comes to the push.
déganter [degɑ̃'te], *v.t.* To unglove. **se déganter**, *v.r.* To take off one's gloves.
dégarnir [degar'niːr], *v.t.* To untrim, to unfurnish, to strip; to dismantle; to thin (trees, woods, etc.); to unrig; to unman (a ship etc.). *Dégarnir une chambre* or *une maison*, to unfurnish a room *or* a house; *dégarnir un vaisseau de ses agrès*, to strip a vessel of its rigging. **se dégarnir**, *v.r.* To strip oneself (*de*); to empty, to become empty; to grow thin; to lose branches etc.; to get bald; to part with; to wear lighter clothes. *La salle se dégarnit*, the house is getting empty; *il se dégarnit*, his hair is growing thin. **dégarnissage**, *n.m.* Clearing the plaster from a wall. **dégarnissement**, *n.m.* Dismantling etc.
dégât [de'gɑ], *n.m.* Havoc, damage, ravage. *La grêle a fait de grands dégâts*, the hail has caused great havoc.
dégauchir [dego'ʃiːr], *v.t.* To smooth, to plane, to level, to straighten; (*fig.*) to form, to polish. *Dégauchir un jeune homme*, to give polish to a young man. **dégauchissement** or **dégauchissage**, *n.m.* Planing, straightening, levelling, smoothing. **dégauchisseuse**, *n.f.* Planing-machine.
dégazonnage [degazɔ'naːʒ] or **dégazonnement**, *n.m.* Unturfing. **dégazonner**, *v.t.* To unturf.

dégel [de'ʒel], *n.m.* Thaw. *Le vent est au dégel,* the wind will bring on a thaw. **dégèlement,** *n.m.* Thawing (of water-pipes). **dégeler,** *v.t., v.i.* To thaw. **se dégeler,** *v.r.* To thaw; (*fig.*) to come out.

dégelée [de'ʒle], *n.f.* (*fam.*) A shower of blows.

dégénération [deʒenerɑ'sjɔ̃], *n.f.* Degeneration, degeneracy, deterioration.

dégénéré [deʒene're], *a.* and *n.m.* (*fem.* **-ée**) Degenerate.

dégénérer [deʒene're], *v.i. irr.* (*conjug. like* ACCÉLÉRER) To decline, to degenerate, to fall away (*de*); to become worse (of an illness). *Dégénérer de ses ancêtres,* to degenerate from one's ancestors. **dégénérescence,** *n.f.* Degeneracy. **dégénérescent,** *a.* (*fem.* **-ente**) Degenerating.

dégingandé [deʒɛ̃gɑ̃'de], *a.* (*fem.* **-ée**) Ungainly, gawky, awkward in one's gait; clumsy, disjointed, irregular. **dégingander,** *v.t.* To give (gait or attitude) awkwardness, etc. **se dégingander,** *v.r.* To be ungainly, ill-knit, etc.

dégîter [deʒi'te], *v.t.* (*Hunt.*) To dislodge, to start (a hare etc.).

dégivrage [deʒi'vraːʒ], *n.m.* De-icing. **dégivrer,** *v.t.* To de-ice. **dégivreur,** *n.m.* (*Motor., Av.*) De-icer.

déglacer [deglɑ'se], *v.t.* To unglaze (paper); to warm up (a person).

déglingué [deglɛ̃'ge], *a.* (*fem.* **-ée**) (*fam.*) Ramshackle, falling into pieces, out of order.

dégluer [degly'e], *v.t.* To take the bird-lime off; to unglue. **se dégluer,** *v.r.* To get rid of bird-lime; to get unglued or cleared (of the eyes).

déglutir [degly'tiːr], *v.t.* To swallow. **déglutition,** *n.f.* Deglutition, swallowing.

dégobiller [degɔbi'je], *v.t.* (*vulg.*) To bring up, to spew, to vomit.—*v.i.* To puke.

dégoiser [degwa'ze], *v.t., v.i.* (*fam.*) To spout. *En dégoise-t-elle!* how she does rattle on, to be sure! *il a dégoisé tout ce qu'il savait,* he let out all he knew.

dégommage [degɔ'maːʒ], *n.m.* Ungumming. **dégommer,** *v.t.* To wash the gum out of; (*slang*) to turn out of office, to oust, to sack.

dégonder [degɔ̃'de], *v.t.* To unhinge.

dégonflement [degɔ̃flə'mɑ̃], *n.m.* Deflating (of tyre, balloon); collapse; reduction. **dégonfler,** *v.t.* To cause to collapse; to reduce (a swelling); to empty (a balloon). *Mon pneu avant est dégonflé,* my front tyre is down. **se dégonfler,** *v.r.* To go down, to be reduced; to subside, to collapse (of a balloon etc.); (*slang*) to be afraid, not to be so cocksure, to sing small; to make a full confession.

dégorgement [degɔrʒ'mɑ̃], *n.m.* Breaking out, overflow; unstopping; disgorging; outfall, outflow. *Dégorgement d'un tuyau,* cleansing or unstopping of a pipe. **dégorgeoir,** *n.m.* Primer, vent-bit (for guns); outlet, issue, spout; (*Fishing*) disgorger.

dégorger [degɔr'ʒe], *v.t.* To disgorge, to vomit; to unstop, to clear; to cleanse, to scour.—*v.i.* To discharge, to overflow, to empty. *Faire dégorger,* to purge (fish etc.); (*fig.*) to make (someone) stump up. **se dégorger,** *v.r.* To discharge or empty itself or oneself, to get unstopped, to be cleared.

dégoter or **dégotter** [degɔ'te], *v.t.* (*pop.*) To knock down; to oust, to displace, to supplant, to turn out; to get or find by chance. —*v.i.* To look fine.

dégouliner [deguli'ne], *v.i.* (*pop.*) To drip, to trickle; to roll down.

dégoupiller [degupi'je], *v.t.* To unpin (a grenade, mechanical parts, etc.).

dégourdi [degur'di], *a.* (*fem.* **-ie**) Quick, sharp, acute, smart; with the chill off; tepid (of water).—*n.* A shrewd, pert, or forward person. *C'est un dégourdi,* he is a shrewd fellow.

dégourdir [degur'diːr], *v.t.* To revive, to quicken; to take the chill or numbness off; (*fig.*) to sharpen, to render shrewd; to polish. *Dégourdir ses jambes,* to stretch one's limbs; *dégourdir un jeune homme,* to polish a young man; *faire dégourdir de l'eau,* to take the chill off water. **se dégourdir,** *v.r.* To lose numbness, to feel warmer; to get sharper; to brighten up. **dégourdissement,** *n.m.* Removal of numbness; return of circulation; quickening, reviving.

dégoût [de'gu], *n.m.* Disrelish, dislike, distaste; disgust, aversion; chagrin, mortification. *Avoir du dégoût pour la vie,* to be disgusted with life; *il lui a pris du dégoût pour la viande,* he has taken a dislike to meat; *on l'a abreuvé de dégoûts,* they made him swallow many a bitter pill. **dégoûtant,** *a.* (*fem.* **-ante**) Disgusting, distasteful, nauseous; unpleasant, disheartening. **dégoûtation,** *n.f.* (*pop.*) Disgusting person or thing. **dégoûté,** *a.* (*fem.* **-ée**) Fastidious.— *n.* Fastidious person. *Faire le dégoûté,* to be squeamish or fastidious; *il est dégoûté de la vie,* he is disgusted with life; *vous n'êtes pas dégoûté!* you're not at all particular!

dégoûter [degu'te], *v.t.* To disgust; to cause to feel repugnance, aversion, etc., to put out of conceit (with). *Cela est bien fait pour dégoûter quelqu'un du métier,* that is well calculated to disgust someone with the business; **se dégoûter,** *v.r.* To take a disgust, dislike, or distaste (*de*).

dégouttant [degu'tɑ̃], *a.* (*fem.* **dégouttante**) Dripping, falling in drops. **dégouttement,** *n.m.* Drip, falling in drops.

dégoutter [degu'te], *v.i.* To drip, to fall in drops, to trickle; to be dripping. *La sueur lui dégouttait du front,* the perspiration was rolling off his forehead.

dégradant [degra'dɑ̃], *a.* (*fem.* **-ante**) Degrading, debasing.

dégradateur [degrada'tœːr], *n.m.* (*Phot.*) Vignetting shade.

dégradation [degradɑ'sjɔ̃], *n.f.* Degradation; debasement; (*fig.*) damage, defacement; (*Paint.*) gradation of light and shade. (*Law*) *Dégradation nationale* or *civile,* loss of civil rights; *dégradation militaire,* drumming out, dismissal, cashiering.

dégradé [degra'de], *a.* (*fem.* **-ée**) (*Paint.*) Shading off (colours); (*Phot.*) graduated (light-filter).—*n.m.* Gradual range of colours or shades.

dégrader [degra'de], *v.t.* To degrade, to debase; to deface, to damage, to dilapidate; (*Mil.*) to cashier, to dismiss, to drum out; (*Paint.*) to graduate the light and shade of (a picture etc.). *Le temps a dégradé ce monument,* time has defaced that monument. **se**

dégrader, *v.r.* To degrade, debase, or disgrace oneself; to become damaged, defaced, or dilapidated.

dégrafer [degra′fe], *v.t.* To unclasp, to unhook. **se dégrafer**, *v.r.* To become unhooked or unfastened (of garments etc.); to unbutton, unhook, or unfasten one's clothes.

dégraissage [degrɛ′saːʒ], or **dégraissement**, *n.m.* Dry-cleaning (garments); scouring (wool).

dégraisser [degrɛ′se], *v.t.* To remove grease from; to take the fat off; to remove greasy stains from; to impoverish (land); to thin, to beard (wood). *Dégraisser un bouillon*, to skim the fat off broth; *dégraisser un veston*, to clean a man's coat; *les ravines dégraissent les terres*, torrents impoverish land (by carrying off the soil); *terre à dégraisser*, fuller's earth. **dégraisseur**, *n.m.* (*fem.* -euse) Scourer (of wool); dry-cleaner (of clothes etc.). **dégraissoir**, *n.m.* Scraper.

dégras, *n.m.* Dressing of fish-oil and nitric acid (for leather).

dégravoiement [degravwa′mã], *n.m.* Laying bare the foundations of a wall etc. by erosion of water, erosion of gravel etc. **dégravoyer**, *v.t.* To wash clean, to lay bare (of water); to erode or wash away (gravel etc.).

degré [də′gre], *n.m.* Step, stair; stage, grade, degree; point, extent, height, pitch. *À un très haut degré*, to a very great extent; *au suprême degré*, in the highest degree; *cousin au quatrième degré*, a cousin four times removed; *degré alcoolique d'un vin*, alcoholic strength of a wine; *degré de juridiction*, each of the courts to which a cause can be successively submitted; *degré de longitude*, degree of longitude; *enseignement du premier degré*, primary education; *équation du second degré*, quadratic equation; *monter les degrés*, to go up the steps; *par degrés*, gradually.

dégréement [degre′mã] or **dégréage**, *n.m.* (*Naut.*) Unrigging. **dégréer**, *v.t.* To unrig. *Dégréer un mât*, to strip a mast.

dégrèvement [degrɛv′mã], *n.m.* Reduction; abatement, tax allowance, relief; redemption.

dégrever [degrə′ve], *v.t.* To diminish, to reduce (a tax etc.); to relieve (someone of a tax); to disencumber, to free (an estate etc.); to redeem, to pay off (a mortgage).

dégringolade [degrɛ̃gɔ′lad], *n.f.* . (*fam.*) Fall, tumble; (*fig.*) decadence, downfall. **dégringoler**, *v.i.* To tumble down, to topple over; (*fig.*) to go from bad to worse, to go to the dogs.—*v.t.* (*vulg.*) To rush down (stairs).

dégrisement [degriz′mã], *n.m.* (*colloq.*) Sobering, getting sober; (*fig.*) cooling down. **dégriser**, *v.t.* To sober; (*fig.*) to cool down, to bring to one's senses. **se dégriser**, *v.r.* To sober down; (*fig.*) to come to one's senses; to lose one's illusions.

dégrossage [degro′saːʒ], *n.m.* Drawing fine; (*Wire-drawing*) reducing, thinning. **dégrosser**, *v.t.* To reduce, to thin (ingots etc.).

dégrossir [degro′siːr], *v.t.* To rough-hew; (*fig.*) to make a rough sketch of; to clear up, to unravel; to polish, to civilize. *Dégrossir un bloc de marbre*, to chip a block of marble. **dégrossissage** or **dégrossissement**, *n.m.* Rough-hewing; (*Carp.*) dressing, trimming.

dégrossisseur, *n.m.* (*fem.* -euse) One who rough-hews, trims, etc.

déguenillé [degəni′je], *a.* (*fem.* -ée) Tattered, ragged, in rags. *Elle était toute déguenillée*, she was in rags and tatters; *un habit déguenillé*, a ragged coat.—*n.* Tatterdemalion, ragamuffin. *Quelle est cette petite déguenillée?* who is that little girl in rags and tatters?

déguerpir [deger′piːr], *v.i.* To pack off, to move off; to be gone. *Déguerpir au plus vite*, to be gone as fast as possible; *je le ferai bien déguerpir*, I'll make him pack off. **déguerpissement**, *n.m.* Quitting, giving up, abandonment.

dégueuler [degœ′le], *v.t.* (*vulg.*) To spew, to cat. **dégueulade**, *n.f.* Spew. **dégueulasse**, *a.* Disgusting.

déguignonner [deginɔ′ne], *v.t.* To stop the ill luck of, to bring better luck to.

déguisable [degi′zabl], *a.* Disguisable. **déguisement**, *n.m.* Disguise, concealment. *Parlez sans déguisement*, speak openly.

déguiser [degi′ze], *v.t.* To disguise, to cloak; to conceal under false appearances; to dissemble, to misrepresent. *On le déguisa en femme*, they disguised him as a woman. **se déguiser**, *v.r.* To disguise oneself, to put on fancy dress.

dégustateur [degysta′tœːr], *n.m.* (*fem.* **dégustatrice**) Taster (of wines etc.) **dégustation**, *n.f.* Tasting (of wines etc.). **déguster**, *v.t.* To taste; to sip, to savour.

déhaler [dea′le], *v.t.* (*Naut.*) To tow out; to haul off.

déhâler [deɑ′le], *v.t.* To take away sun-burn, freckles, tan, etc., from. **se déhâler**, *v.r.* To clear one's complexion.

déhanché [deɑ̃′ʃe], *a.* (*fem.* -ée) Hipped, having the hips dislocated; (*fig.*) ungainly, having a waddling gait. **déhanchement**, *n.m.* Waddling gait, waddle. **se déhancher**, *v.r.* To sway one's hips, to have a waddling, loose gait.

déharnachement [dearnaʃ′mã], *n.m.* Unharnessing. **déharnacher**, *v.t.* To unharness.

déhiscence [dei′sãːs], *n.f.* (*Bot.*) Dehiscence. **déhiscent**, *a.* (*fem.* -ente) Dehiscent.

dehors [də′ɔːr], *adv.* Out, without, outside; out of doors, abroad; externally; (*Naut.*) at sea, in the offing. *Au dedans et au dehors*, at home and abroad; *au dehors*, outwardly; *de dehors*, from without; *en dehors*, without, outside; *mettre quelqu'un dehors*, to turn someone out.—*n.m.* (*pl. unchanged*) Outside, exterior; (*pl.*) appearances; (*Fort.*) outworks; dependencies, approaches, grounds (of a house). *Sauver les dehors*, to save appearances.

déicide [dei′sid], *a.* and *n.m.* Deicide.

déification [deifika′sjɔ̃], *n.f.* Deification. **déifier**, *v.t.* To deify. **déiforme**, *a.* Deiform. **déisme**, *n.m.* Deism. **déiste**, *a.* Deistic.—*n.* Deist.

déité [dei′te], *n.f.* Deity (god or goddess), divinity.

déjà [de′ʒa], *adv.* Already, before, previously. *Je le lui ai déjà dit*, I have already told him; *vous en avez déjà trop dit*, you have said too much as it is.

déjaler [deʒa′le], *v.t.* (*Naut.*) To unstock (anchor).

déjauger   délicat

déjauger [deʒo'ʒe], *v.t.* To sew (a ship).
déjection [deʒɛk'sjɔ̃], *n.f.* (*Med.*) Dejection, ejection, evacuation.
déjeté [deʒ'te], *a.* (*fem.* **-ée**) Awry, lopsided, off the straight.
déjeter [deʒ'te], *v.t. irr.* (*conjug. like* APPELER) To warp, ᵗo turn awry. **se déjeter,** *v.r.* To warp (of wood etc.); (*Path.*) to deviate. **déjettement,** *n.m.* Warping; deviation.
déjeuner (1) [deʒœ'ne], *n.m. Petit déjeuner,* breakfast; *déjeuner,* lunch, luncheon; *un déjeuner de porcelaine,* a porcelain breakfast-set. *C'est un déjeuner de soleil,* it is too good to last. **déjeuner** (2), *v.i.* To breakfast; to lunch.
déjouer [de'ʒwe], *v.t.* To baffle, to frustrate, to foil; to elude (someone's vigilance); (*Mil.*) to outmanœuvre. *Déjouer un projet,* to baffle a plan.
déjucher [deʒu'ʃe], *v.t.* To unroost.—*v.i.* To come down from the roost. *Je vous ferai bien déjucher de là,* I will make you come down from there.
déjuger (se) [deʒy'ʒe], *v.r.* To reverse one's opinion.
delà [də'la], *prep.* On the other side of; beyond. *Au delà, de delà, par delà,* or *en delà,* beyond, farther on, upwards; *deçà et delà,* right and left, both here and there, both this and that; *l'au-delà,* the hereafter.
délabré [dela'bre], *a.* (*fem.* **délabrée**) Tattered, shabby (garments); tumbledown, ramshackle (house). *Terre délabrée,* land gone to waste; *une santé délabrée,* shattered health; *un estomac délabré,* a disordered stomach; *un navire délabré,* a dismantled vessel. **délabrement,** *n.m.* Decay, dilapidation; shabbiness, raggedness. **délabrer,** *v.t.* To shatter, to ruin, to tear to tatters. **se délabrer,** *v.r.* To fall to tatters or to pieces, to go to ruin or decay. *Tous mes meubles se délabrent,* my furniture is all going to rack and ruin.
délacer [dela'se], *v.t.* To unlace (shoes etc.). **se délacer,** *v.r.* To unlace oneself; to come undone (of shoes, strings, etc.).
délai [de'lɛ], *n.m.* Delay; extension of time, respite, reprieve. *Délai de repentir,* (*Mil.*) time of grace (before an absentee is declared a deserter); *dans un délai de,* within (a given time); *sans délai,* immediately; *user de délais,* to put off, to procrastinate.
délainage [delɛ'naːʒ], *n.m.* Scraping the wool off the hide. **délainer,** *v.t.* To scrape the wool off the hide.
délaissé [delɛ'se], *a.* (*fem.* **-ée**) Abandoned, forlorn, forsaken, friendless. *Des orphelins délaissés,* helpless orphans. **délaissement,** *n.m.* Desertion; destitution, forlornness, helplessness; (*Law*) abandonment to a mortgagee. **délaisser,** *v.t.* To forsake, to abandon; to desert, to leave; to relinquish, to renounce (a right etc.). **se délaisser,** *v.r.* To give up one's property (in favour of another).
délaiter [delɛ'te], *v.t.* To dry (butter).
délardement [delardə'mã], *n.m.* Unlarding; (*Arch.*) splay, slope; bevelling, chamfering. **délarder,** *v.t.* To unlard; (*Arch.*) to splay, to bevel, to chamfer; (*Naut.*) to beard.
délassant [dela'sã], *a.* (*fem.* **-ante**) Refreshing, diverting. **délassement,** *n.m.* Remission of attention or application, relaxation; repose, recreation, diversion.

délasser [dela'se], *v.t.* To refresh, to relax, to divert. *Le sommeil vous délasse,* sleep refreshes you; *un changement d'occupation délasse l'esprit,* a change of occupation relaxes the mind. **se délasser,** *v.r.* To refresh oneself, to rest.
délateur [dela'tœːr], *n.m.* (*fem.* **délatrice**) Informer, accuser. **délation,** *n.f.* Informing.
délatter [dela'te], *v.t.* To unlath.
délavage [dela'vaːʒ], *n.m.* Diluting or washing of colour (in drawing and water-colour painting); soaking. **délaver,** *v.t.* To dilute or wash (colour) in drawing and water-colour painting; to soak into, to wet. **se délaver,** *v.r.* To become soaked, to take up water; to lose colour.
délayable [delɛ'jabl], *a.* Dilutable. **délayage,** *n.m.* Diluting, dilution; verbose style, padding. **délayant,** *a.* (*fem.* **-ante**) Diluent.—*n.m.* Diluent.
délayé [delɛ'je], *a.* Watery; wordy, prolix.
délayer [delɛ'je], *v.t.* (*conjugated like* BALAYER) To dilute; (*fig.*) to spin out.
deleatur [delea'tyːr], *n.m. inv.* (*Print.*) Delete.
délectabilité [delɛktabili'te], *n.f.* Delectability. **délectable,** *a.* Delectable, delightful. **délectation,** *n.f.* Delectation, delight, gratification. **délecter,** *v.t.* To delight. **se délecter,** *v.r.* To take delight. *Se délecter à l'étude,* to delight in study.
délégant [dele'gã], *n.m.* (*fem.* **-ante**) Delegator. **délégataire,** *n.* Delegatee. **délégateur,** *n.m.* (*fem.* **-trice**) One who appoints a proxy. **délégation,** *n.f.* Delegation, assignment; proxy. **délégatoire,** *a.* Delegatory. **délégué,** *n.m.* (*fem.* **déléguée**) Delegate, deputy; proxy. **déléguer,** *v.t.* To delegate, to depute; to assign. *Déléguer son autorité,* to delegate one's authority. **se déléguer,** *v.r.* To be delegated.
délestage [delɛs'taːʒ], *n.m.* Unballasting. **délester,** *v.t.* To unballast. **délesteur,** *n.m.* Ballast-heaver, ballast-lighter.
délétère [dele'tɛːr], *a.* Deleterious.
délibérant [delibe'rã], *a.* (*fem.* **-ante**) Deliberative. **délibératif,** *a.* (*fem.* **-ive**) Deliberative. **délibération,** *n.f.* Deliberation; resolution. *Mettre en délibération,* to bring under deliberation. **délibéré,** *a.* (*fem.* **-ée**) Deliberate, decided, resolute. *De propos délibéré,* with set purpose, designedly; *purposely; marcher d'un pas délibéré,* to walk resolutely.—*n.m.* (*Law*) Deliberation; deliberative judgment. *Affaire en délibéré,* case under consideration. **délibérément,** *adv.* Deliberately, resolutely.
délibérer [delibe're], *v.i. irr.* (*conjug. like* ACCÉLÉRER) To deliberate; to determine, to resolve. *Il en sera délibéré,* it will be taken into consideration; *le jury se retire pour délibérer,* the jury retire to consult together; *il n'y a pas lieu à délibérer,* there is no cause for deliberating.—*v.t.* To deliberate upon.
délicat [deli'ka], *a.* Delicate, dainty, exquisite; nice, fastidious; ticklish, embarrassing; fragile, frail. *Affaire délicate,* ticklish affair, *faire le délicat,* to be fastidious; *il est délicat sur le point d'honneur,* he is very touchy on points of honour; *vous êtes bien délicat,* you are very fastidious.—*n.* Fastidious person.

délicatement, *adv.* Delicately, daintily, tenderly. *Peu délicatement*, indelicately.

délicatesse [delika'tɛs], *n.f.* Delicacy, weakness, fragility; tenderness; daintiness, fastidiousness; refinement, squeamishness; nicety (of language etc.); ticklishness; considerateness; (*pl.*) dainties. *Avoir une grande délicatesse de conscience*, to have a very scrupulous conscience; *ce serait une délicatesse de votre part*, it would be very kind of you; *ils sont en délicatesse*, their relations are slightly strained; *les délicatesses d'une langue*, the niceties of a language.

délice [de'lis], *n.m. in sing. (used chiefly in f.pl.)* Delight, pleasure, happiness. *Faire ses délices d'une chose*, to revel in a thing; *goûter les délices de la vie*, to enjoy the good things of life.

délicieusement [delisjøz'mã], *adv.* Deliciously, delightfully.

délicieux [deli'sjø], *a.* (*fem.* -ieuse) Delicious, delightful; capital. *Cette histoire est délicieuse*, that's a capital story.

délicoter [deliko'te], *v.t.* To slip the halter (of horses etc.).

délictueux [delik'tɥø], *a.* (*fem.* **délictueuse**) Unlawful, felonious.

délié [de'lje], *a.* (*fem.* -ée) Slender, slim, thin, fine; sharp, shrewd, subtle; glib, facile, flowing (of style etc.); untied, loose. *Avoir la langue déliée*, to have the gift of the gab; *avoir l'esprit délié*, to be quick or shrewd. —*n.m.* (*Penmanship*) Thin stroke, upstroke.

délier [de'lje], *v.t.* (*conjugated like* PRIER) To unbind, to untie; to liberate, to release; to absolve. *Délier quelqu'un d'un serment*, to free someone from an oath; *on l'a délié de ses vœux*, he was liberated from his vows. **se délier**, *v.r.* To come untied, to get unfastened, to get loose.

délimitation [delimita'sjɔ̃], *n.f.* Delimitation, fixing of boundaries. **délimiter**, *v.t.* To delimit, to settle the boundaries of.

délinéation [delinea'sjɔ̃], *n.f.* Delineation. **délinéer**, *v.t.* To delineate.

délinquance [delɛ̃'kɑ̃s], *n.f.* Delinquency. **délinquant** [delɛ̃'kɑ̃], *n.m.* (*fem.* -ante) Delinquent, offender, trespasser.—*a. Enfance délinquante*, juvenile offenders.

déliquescence [delike'sɑ̃s], *n.f.* Deliquescence; (*Lit. slang*) general deterioration of style. **déliquescent**, *a.* (*fem.* -ente) Deliquescent. **déliquium**, *n.m.* Deliquium.

délirant [deli'rɑ̃], *a.* (*fem.* -ante) Delirious, frenzied, frantic; rapturous, ecstatic.—*n.* A delirious or ecstatic person. **délire**, *n.m.* Delirium, frenzy, rage, folly. *Avoir le délire*, to rave; *tomber en délire*, to become delirious. **délirer**, *v.i.* To be delirious, to rave, to wander.

delirium tremens, *n.m.* Delirium tremens; (*fam.*) the horrors, the jumps, the D.T.s.

délissage [deli'sa:ʒ], *n.m.* Unrumpling and sorting (of rags, paper, etc.). **délisser**, *v.t.* To unruffle and sort (paper, rags, etc.).

délit (1) [de'li], *n.m.* Misdemeanour, offence. *En flagrant délit*, in the very act.

délit (2) [de'li], *n.m.* Wrong side (of stone, *i.e.* different from the way it was bedded).

délitation [delita'sjɔ̃], *n.f.*, **délitage** or **délitement**, *n.m.* Surbedding (of stones in masonry), exfoliation (of stone).

déliter [deli'te], *v.t.* To surbed (stones). **se déliter**, *v.r.* To break in the grain, to cleave; to scale off (of stones in masonry), to split.

délitescence [delitɛ'sɑ̃:s], *n.f.* Delitescence. **délitescent**, *a.* (*fem.* -ente) Delitescent.

délivrance [deli'vrɑ̃:s], *n.f.* Rescue, deliverance, release; issue (of tickets); delivery (of certificates etc.); accouchement; after-birth. **délivre**, *n.m.* (*Anat.*) After-birth, placenta.

délivrer [deli'vre], *v.t.* To deliver, to release, to set free; to rid of, to rescue; to hand over, to give up; to issue; to accouche; (*Naut.*) to rip off. *Délivrer des marchandises consignées*, to release consigned goods; *délivrer de prison*, to release from prison; *se faire délivrer*, to obtain, to take out. **se délivrer**, *v.r.* To deliver oneself, to free oneself, to shake off, to get rid (*de*). **délivreur**, *n.m.* Deliverer, rescuer; one of the two drums of a cotton-machine.

délogement [delɔʒ'mɑ̃], *n.m.* Removal, change of quarters, departure, decamping.

déloger [delɔ'ʒe], *v.i.* To remove, to go (from one's house etc.), to go away, to march off. *Déloger sans tambour ni trompette*, to march off in silence, to steal away, to decamp quietly.—*v.t.* To turn out (of house etc.), to oust; to drive away; (*Mil.*) to dislodge.

délot [de'lo], *n.m.* Finger- or thumb-stall; (*Naut.*) leather stall on the left little finger of caulkers.

délover [delɔ've], *v.t.* (*Naut.*) To uncoil.

déloyal [delwa'jal], *a.* (*fem.* -ale, *pl.* -aux) Disloyal, false, treacherous, unfair; foul. *Concurrence déloyale*, unfair competition; *coup déloyal*, foul blow. **déloyalement**, *adv.* Disloyally, unfairly.

déloyauté [delwajo'te], *n.f.* Disloyalty, perfidiousness, treachery.

Delphes [dɛlf], *f.* Delphi.

delta [dɛl'ta], *n.m.* Delta.

deltoïde [dɛlto'id], *a.* Deltoid.

déluge [de'ly:ʒ], *n.m.* Deluge, flood. *Un déluge de paroles*, a torrent of words.

déluré [dely're], *a.* (*fem.* -ée) Wide-awake, sharp. **délurer**, *v.t.* To make wide-awake.

délustrer [delys'tre], *v.t.* To take the lustre or gloss from.

délutage [dely'ta:ʒ], *n.m.* Removing the lute (from a vase etc.). **déluter**, *v.t.* To remove the lute from (a vase etc.).

démagnétisation [demaɲetiza'sjɔ̃], *n.f.* Demagnetization. **démagnétiser**, *v.t.* To demagnetize.

démagogie [demagɔ'ʒi], *n.f.* Demagogy. **démagogique**, *a.* Demagogic. **démagogue**, *n.* Demagogue.

démaigrir [demɛ'gri:r], *v.t.* To thin (a board etc.).

démailler [dema'je], *v.t.* To undo the meshes of (a net etc.); to make a run in (a stocking).

démailloter [demajo'te], *v.t.* To unswathe (a baby etc.).

demain [də'mɛ̃], *adv.* Tomorrow. *Demain matin*, tomorrow morning; *demain soir*, tomorrow night.—*n.m.* Tomorrow. *À demain!* see you tomorrow! *avec lui c'est toujours demain*, he is always procrastinating.

démanché [demɑ̃'ʃe], *a.* (*fem.* -ée) Off the handle; (*fig.*) ungainly, loose, disjointed.

—*n.m.* Ungainly fellow; (*Mus.*) [DÉMANCHE-MENT]. **démanchement,** *n.m.* Taking the handle off; (*Mus.*) shifting the hand from the neck (of·a violin etc.) to the body of the instrument. **démancher,** *v.t.* To take off the handle of; (*fig.*) to dislocate, to disjoint. —*v.i.* (*Naut.*) To disembogue. **se déman-cher,** *v.r.* To lose its handle; to go wrong.

demande [də'mã:d], *n.f.* Question, query; demand, request, application, petition; claim, suit, request in marriage; (*Comm.*) order. *À la demande,* to order, as required; *appuyer une demande,* to second a request; *à sotte demande point de réponse,* a silly question needs no answer; *argent payable sur demande,* call money; *avez-vous fait votre demande?* have you asked her (or her parents)? *demande d'augmentation,* wage increase claim; *demande de poste,* application for a job; *demande de renseignements,* inquiry; *demande en divorce,* action for divorce; *demande en mariage,* proposal; *faire sa demande par écrit,* to present one's request in writing; *l'offre et la demande,* supply and demand; *sur sa propre demande,* at his own request.

demander [dəmã'de], *v.t.* To ask, to beg, to request; to sue for, to demand; to desire, to wish; to require, to call for; to need, to want; to inquire for or about; to ask to see; to seek in marriage; (*Comm.*) to order. *Bien* or *très demandé,* in great demand; *cela demande une explication,* that requires an explanation; *demander l'aumône,* to ask for alms; *demander pardon,* to ask forgiveness; *demander son pain,* to beg one's bread; *faire demander,* to send or ask for, to call for; *ne pas demander mieux,* to ask for nothing better, to be only too glad, to be most happy; *n'est-il venu personne me demander?* has nobody called for me? *on demande,* wanted; *on vous demande,* you are wanted; *que demandez-vous?* what do you want? **se demander,** *v.r.* To ask oneself, to wonder. *Je me demande si,* I wonder whether. **de-mandeur,** *a.* (*fem.* -euse) Always asking. —*n.m.* (*fem.* **demanderesse**) Asker, appli-cant; (*Law*) plaintiff.

démangeaison [demãʒe'zõ], *n.f.* Itching; longing. (*fam.*) *Avoir une grande déman-geaison de parler,* to be dying to talk.

démanger, *v.i.* To itch; to long. *La tête me démange,* my head itches. (*fig.*) *La langue lui démange,* he is itching to say it; *les pieds lui démangent,* he longs to go out.

démantèlement [demãtɛl'mã], *n.m.* (*Fort.*) Dismantling. **démanteler,** *v.t.* To dis-mantle (a fort).

démantibuler [demãtiby'le], *v.t.* To break, to dislocate; to put out of order. **se déman-tibuler,** *v.r.* To break. (*fam.*) *Il crie à se démantibuler la mâchoire,* he is yelling fit to burst.

démaquiller [demaki'je], *v.t.* To take off the make-up. **se démaquiller,** *v.r.* To cleanse one's face.

démarcatif [demarka'tif], *a.* (*fem.* **démarca-tive**) Demarcating. **démarcation,** *n.f.* Demarcation. *Ligne de démarcation,* line of demarcation.

démarche [de'marʃ], *n.f.* Gait, walk, bearing; proceeding, measure, step, course. *Démarche noble,* noble bearing; *faire une démarche,* to

take a step; *on observe toutes ses démarches,* all his proceedings are watched. **démar-cheur,** *n.m.* Canvasser.

démarier [dema'rje], *v.t.* (*fam.*) To annul the marriage of; (*Hort.*) to thin out (of seedlings). **se démarier,** *v.r.* To be divorced.

démarquage [demar'ka:ʒ], *n.m.* Unmarking; plagiarism. **démarquer,** *v.t.* To unmark; to plagiarize. **se démarquer,** *v.r.* (*Ftb.*) To elude the vigilance of the opponent.—*v.i.* To lose the mark of its age (of a horse).

démarrage [dema'ra:ʒ], *n.m.* Unmooring; start, spurt. **démarrer,** *v.t.* To unmoor, to cast off; to unfasten, to unlash. *Démarrer un cordage,* to unbend a rope; *démarrer le moteur,* to start the engine.—*v.i.* To leave, to slip her moorings (of a ship); to move, to get away, to start; to spurt.

démarreur [dema'rœr], *n.m.* Self-starter (*Motor.*); (*spt.*) runner who is good at forcing the pace suddenly or spurting.

démasquer [demas'ke], *v.t.* To unmask; to show ‘up. *Démasquer une batterie,* to unmask a battery; (*fig.*) *démasquer ses batteries,* to show one's hand. **se démasquer,** *v.r.* To unmask, to take off one's mask.

démâtage [demɑ'ta:ʒ] or **démâtement,** *n.m.* (*Naut.*) Dismasting. **démâter,** *v.t.* To dismast.—*v.i.* To lose her masts (of a ship).

démêlage [deme'la:ʒ], *n.m.* Combing (of wool); mixing of malt and hot water in brewing; brewing.

démêlé [deme'le], *n.m.* Strife, contest, con-tention, quarrel. *Leur démêlé est fini,* their difference is at an end.

démêler [deme'le], *v.t.* To unravel, to dis-entangle, to separate; to clear up; to distin-guish, to discern; to comb out (hair), to tease (wool). *Démêler le vrai d'avec le faux,* to distinguish truth from falsehood; *je ne veux rien avoir à démêler avec lui,* I will have nothing to do with him. **se démêler,** *v.r.* To be unravelled, to be disentangled; to stand out clear, to be recognized; to comb one's hair.

démêloir [deme'lwa:r], *n.m.* Large-tooth comb. **démêlures,** *n.f. pl.* Combings.

démembrement [demãbrə'mã], *n.m.* Dis-memberment; disruption; breaking up. **démembrer,** *v.t.* To tear limb from limb, to dismember; to divide; to break-up.

déménagement [demenaʒ'mã], *n.m.* (House-hold) removal, removing one's furniture. *Voiture de déménagement,* furniture van, pantechnicon. **déménager,** *v.t.* To remove (one's furniture).—*v.i.* To remove. *Déména-ger à la cloche de bois,* to remove surrepti-tiously;(*fam.*)*il déménage,*he is getting queer. **déménageur,** *n.m.* Furniture-remover.

démence [de'mã:s], *n.f.* Insanity, madness, lunacy. *Tomber en démence,* to become insane.

démener (se) [dem'ne], *v.r. irr.* (*conjug. like* AMENER) To stir, to struggle, to make a great fuss, to strive hard, to give oneself trouble. *Se démener avec vigueur,* to struggle vigorously; *il se démène comme un diable dans un bénitier,* he has got the fidgets; *se démener pour une affaire,* to give oneself a lot of trouble about a matter.

dément [de'mã], *a.* and *n.m.* (*fem.* **-ente**) Mad (person).

démenti [demā'ti], *n.m.* Denial, flat contradiction; disappointment. *Donner un démenti à quelqu'un*, to give someone the lie; *vous en aurez le démenti*, you are doomed to failure.

démentiel [demā'sjɛl], *a.* (*fem.* **-ielle**) Caused by or having the appearance of madness. *Acte démentiel*, act of insanity.

démentir [demā'ti:r], *v.t. irr.* (*conjug. like* MENTIR) To give the lie to, to contradict; to deny; to belie, to refute. *Démentirez-vous votre signature?* will you deny your signature? *démentir sa gloire*, to belie one's fame; *le gouvernement a démenti cette nouvelle*, the government has contradicted that report; *ses actions démentent ses discours*, his actions belie his words. **se démentir**, *v.r.* To contradict oneself; to belie one's reputation etc.; to fall off, to flag, to give way. *Cet ouvrage se dément un peu vers la fin*, this work falls off a little towards the end.

démérite [deme'rit], *n.m.* Demerit, blame. **démériter**, *v.i.* To lose esteem, merit, or favour. *Je n'ai point démérité de vous* or *auprès de vous*, I have done nothing to forfeit your esteem. **démeritoire**, *a.* Demeritorious.

démesure‧ [demə'zy:r], *n.f.* Immoderation, excess. **démesuré**, *a.* (*fem.* **-ée**) Immoderate, inordinate, excessive, enormous. *C'est la preuve d'un orgueil démesuré*, it shows how inordinately proud he is. **démesurément**, *adv.* Immoderately, inordinately, excessively, hugely.

démettre [de'mɛtr], *v.t. irr.* (*conjug. like* METTRE) To put out of joint, to dislocate; to dismiss; (*Law*) to overrule, to nonsuit. **se démettre**, *v.r.* To be put out of joint; to suffer dislocation; to resign (from an appointment). *Il s'est démis le poignet*, he has dislocated his wrist; *se démettre de son emploi*, to resign one's position; *se démettre d'un appel*, (*Law*) to dismiss an appeal.

démeublement [demœblə'mā], *n.m.* Unfurnishing; absence of furniture. **démeubler**, *v.t.* To unfurnish, to strip of furniture.

demeurant [dəmœ'rā], *a.* (*fem.* **-ante**) Dwelling, living.—*n.m.* Remainder.—*adv.* *Au demeurant*, after all, nevertheless.

demeure [də'mœːr], *n.f.* Abode, home, dwelling, lodgings; stay, sojourn; (*Law*) delay. *Changer de demeure*, to change one's lodgings; *la dernière demeure*, the last resting place; *être à demeure*, to be fixed, stationary, or stable; *mettre en demeure*, (*Law*) to summon, to compel, to lay under the necessity (*de*); *péril en la demeure*, danger in delay.

demeurer [dəmœ're], *v.i.* To live, to lodge, to reside; to stop, to stand, to rest; to continue, to remain, to stay. *Où demeurez-vous?* Where do you live? *demeurer d'accord*, to agree; *demeurer en arrière*, to stay behind; *demeurons-en là*, let us leave it at that; *il demeura interdit*, he stood there tongue-tied; *la question demeure indécise*, the matter is still unsettled.

demi [də'mi], *a.* (*fem.* **demie**) Half. *Un demi-pied*, half a foot; *une heure et demie*, an hour and a half; *un pied et demi*, a foot and a half. *adv.* *Ne pas faire les choses à demi*, not to do things by halves.—*n.m.* (*Arith.*) Half; (*Ftb. etc.*) *un demi*, a half-back; *demi-centre*, centre-half; *demi de mêlée*, scrum-half; *demi*

d'ouverture, stand-off half; *deux demis valent un entier*, two halves make a whole; *un demi de bière*, a glass of beer (about ½ litre).—*n.f.* Half; half-hour. *La pendule sonne les demies*, the clock strikes the half-hours.

(*C*) **demiard** [də'mjaːr], *n.m.* A liquid measure (=½ pint).

In the following compounds *demi* is *inv.* The noun has its regular plural, unless otherwise indicated.

demi-bain [dəmi'bɛ̃], *n.m.* Hip-bath.

demi-bas [dəmi'ba], *n.m. inv.* Half-length stocking.

demi-botte, *n.f.* Wellington boot.

demi-cercle, *n.m.* Semicircle. *En demi-cercle*, semicircular.

demi-colonne, *n.f.* (*Arch.*) Semi-column.

demi-deuil, *n.m.* Half-mourning.

demi-dieu, *n.m.* Demigod.

démieller [demjɛ'le], *v.t.* To take the honey from.

demi-finale [dəmifi'nal], *n.f.* (*spt.*) Semi-final.

demi-fleuron, *n.m.* (*Bot.*) Floret (in *Compositae*).

demi-fond, *n.m. inv.* Middle distance (race).

demi-frère, *n.m.* Half-brother.

demi-guêtre, *n.f.* Spat; (*Mil.*) regulation legging.

demi-heure, *n.f.* Half-hour. *Une demi-heure*, half an hour.

demi-jour, *n.m.* Twilight.

demi-journée, *n.f.* Morning or afternoon.

demi-lune, *n.f.* (*Fort.*) Demi-lune, half-moon.

demi-mesure, *n.f.* Half-measure.

demi-mondain, *a.* (*fem.* **demi-mondaine**) Pertaining to the demi-monde. **demi-monde**, *n.m.* Demi-monde.

demi-mort, *a.* (*fem.* **demi-morte**) Half-dead.

demi-mot, *adv. phr.* *Comprendre à demi-mot*, to take the hint.

déminage [demi'naːʒ], *n.m.* Mine clearing. **déminer**, *v.t.* To clear of mines.

demi-pension [dəmipā'sjɔ̃], *n.f.* Half-pension. **demi-pensionnaire**, *n.* Day-boarder.

demi-place, *n.f.* Half-fare.

demi-quart, *n.m.* An eighth of a pound.

demi-queue, *n.m. inv.* Boudoir grand (piano).

demi-reliure, *n.f.* Half-binding.

demi-rond, *n.m.* Currier's knife.

démis, *p.p.* (*fem.* **démise**) [DÉMETTRE].

demi-saison [dəmisɛ'zɔ̃], *n.f.* Autumn or spring.

demi-sang, *n.m. inv.* Half-bred horse.

demi-savant, *n.m.* Superficial scholar; sciolist.

demi-savoir, *n.m.* Superficial knowledge.

demi-sel, *n.m.* Slightly salted cream-cheese.

demi-setier, *n.m.* Quarter of a litre.

demi-sœur, *n.f.* Half-sister.

demi-solde, *n.f.* Half-pay. *Officier en demi-solde* or *demi-solde*, *n.m. inv.*, half-pay officer.

demi-soupir, *n.m.* (*Mus.*) Quaver-rest.

démission [demi'sjɔ̃], *n.f.* Resignation. *Donner sa démission*, to send in one's resignation, to resign. **démissionnaire**, *a.* Who has resigned, thrown up his commission, or vacated his seat.—*n.* Resigner. *Il est démissionnaire*, he has resigned (his position).

démissionner, *v.i.* To resign.

demi-tasse [dəmi'taːs], *n.f.* Half-cup (small cup); half a cup (of coffee etc.).
demi-teinte, *n.f.* Half-tint.
demi-terme, *n.m.* Half a quarter's rent.
demi-ton, *n.m.* (*Mus.*) Half-tone.
demi-tour, *n.m.* Half-turn; (*Mil.*) about turn. *Faire faire demi-tour à des hommes*, to face men about; to send them back; *faire demi-tour*, to turn back.
démiurge [demi'yrʒ], *n.m.* Demiurge. **demi-urgique**, *a.* Demiurgic.
demi-vierge [dəmi'vjɛrʒ], *n.f.* A flirt who just keeps within the limit.
demi-volée, *n.f.* Half-volley.
démobilisation [demɔbiliza'sjɔ̃], *n.f.* Demobilization. **démobiliser**, *v.t.* To demobilize.
démocrate [demɔ'krat], *a.* Democratic.—*n.* Democrat. **démocratie**, *n.f.* Democracy. **démocratique**, *a.* Democratic. **démocratiquement**, *adv.* Democratically. **démocratiser**, *v.t.* To democratize. **se démocratiser**, *v.r.* To become democratized.
démodé [demɔ'de], *a.* (*fem.* -**ée**) Old-fashioned, antiquated. **démoder**, *v.t.* To make out of fashion. **se démoder**, *v.r.* To get out of fashion.
démographe [demɔ'graf], *n.m.* Demographer. **démographie**, *n.f.* Demography. **démographique**, *a.* Demographic.
demoiselle [dəmwa'zɛl], *n.f.* *Young lady (of noble birth), gentlewoman; unmarried lady, spinster, single woman; young girl, maiden, damsel; dragon-fly; paving-beetle, rammer; (*Naut.*) stern bolts. *Demoiselle d'honneur*, maid of honour; bridesmaid; *demoiselle de compagnie*, lady companion; *demoiselle de magasin*, shop-assistant.
démolir [demɔ'liːr], *v.t.* To demolish, to pull down; to knock down; to rip up, to break; to overthrow, to ruin. *Je l'ai démoli*, (*pop.*) I floored him. **démolisseur**, *n.m.* (*fem.* -**euse**) Demolisher, puller-down; house-breaker. **démolition**, *n.f.* Demolition; (*pl.*) old building materials. *Par suite de démolitions*, because of the pulling down of the building.
démon [de'mɔ̃], *n.m.* Demon; divinity; (good or evil) genius; devil, fiend; imp. *Faire le démon*, to play the devil; *quel démon vous agite?* what evil spirit torments you?
*démone, *n.f.* Demoness.
démonétisation [demɔnetiza'sjɔ̃], *n.f.* Demonetization (withdrawal from circulation). **démonétiser**, *v.t.* To demonetize (to withdraw from circulation).
démoniaque [demɔ'njak], *a.* Demoniac, possessed of a devil.—*n.* Demoniac. **démonisme**, *n.m.* Demonism. **démoniste**, *n.* Demonist. **démonographie** or **démonologie**, *n.f.* Demonology.
démonstrateur [demɔ̃stra'tœːr], *n.m.* Demonstrator, lecturer. **démonstratif**, *a.* (*fem.* -**ive**) Demonstrative. **démonstration**, *n.f.* Demonstration, proof; exhibition, show. **démonstrativement**, *adv.* Demonstratively.
démontable [demɔ̃'tabl], *a.* That can be taken to pieces; collapsible (canoe). **démontage**, *n.m.* Taking to pieces.
démonte-pneu [demɔ̃t'pnø], *n.m.* Tyre lever.
démonter [demɔ̃'te], *v.t.* To unhorse, to dismount, to throw or put off his horse; to set (a squadron etc.) on foot; to supersede (the captain of a ship etc.); to take to pieces, to undo; to unship; (*fig.*) to nonplus, to baffle. *Démonter le gouvernail*, to unship the rudder; *mer démontée*, very rough sea. **se démonter**, *v.r.* . . . may be taken to pieces (of machinery); to lose countenance, to be nonplussed or disconcerted; to be getting out of order (of machinery etc.).
démontrable [demɔ̃'trabl], *a.* Demonstrable.
démontrer, *v.t.* To demonstrate, to prove.
démoralisant [demɔrali'zɑ̃], *a.* (*fem.* -**ante**) Demoralizing. **démoralisateur**, *a.* (*fem.* -**trice**) Corrupting, demoralizing. **démoralisation**, *n.f.* Demoralization. **démoraliser**, *v.t.* To demoralize; to corrupt; to dishearten. *Troupes démoralisées*, troops who have lost their morale.
démordre [de'mɔrdr], *v.i. irr.* (*conjug. like* MORDRE) To let go one's hold; to desist, to yield, to give in. *Faire démordre quelqu'un*, to make one change his resolution; *il n'en démordra pas*, he will not abate an inch.
Démosthène [demɔs'tɛːn], *m.* Demosthenes.
démotique [demɔ'tik], *a.* Demotic.
démoucheter [demuʃ'te], *v.t.* To take off the button from (a foil), to uncap it.
démoulage [demu'laːʒ], *n.m.* Taking from the mould. **démouler**, *v.t.* To take from the mould.
démultiplier [demyltipli'e], *v.t.* To gear down.
démunir [demy'niːr], *v.t.* To strip (of ammunition), to leave unprovided. **se démunir**, *v.r.* To deprive oneself, to leave oneself unprovided for.
démurer [demy're], *v.t.* To unwall (a window, door, etc.), to open.
démuseler [demyz'le], *v.t.* To unmuzzle; (*fig.*) to unchain, to let loose.
dénager [dena'ʒe], *v.i.* (*Row.*) To backwater. *Dénage partout!* Back her down, all!
dénantir [denɑ̃'tiːr], *v.t.* To deprive of security. **se dénantir**, *v.r.* To give up one's securities; to part with.
dénatalité [denatali'te], *n.f.* Fall in the birth-rate.
dénationalisation [denasjɔnaliza'sjɔ̃], *n.f.* Denationalization. **dénationaliser**, *v.t.* To denationalize.
dénatter [dena'te], *v.t.* To unplait (hair etc.).
dénaturalisation [denatyraliza'sjɔ̃], *n.f.* Denaturalization. **dénaturaliser**, *v.t.* To denaturalize.
dénaturant [denaty'rɑ̃], *n.m.* A denaturing ingredient.
dénaturation [denatyra'sjɔ̃], *n.f.* Denaturing, perversion, debasement; medication of spirit etc. (with methylene etc.). **dénaturé**, *a.* (*fem.* -**ée**) Unnatural, barbarous, cruel. **dénaturer**, *v.t.* To denature, to alter the nature of; to misrepresent, to pervert, to distort; to disfigure, to disguise; to methylate (alcohol).
dénazification [denazifika'sjɔ̃], *n.f.* Denazification.
dénazifier [denazi'fje], *v.t.* To denazify.
dendrite [dɑ̃'drit], *n.f.* (*Geol.*) Dendrite. **dendritique**, *a.* Dendritic. **dendroïde**, *a.* Dendroid. **dendrologie**, *n.f.* Dendrology. **dendromètre**, *n.m.* Dendrometer.

dénégation [denega'sjɔ̃], *n.f.* Denial, denegation. **dénégatoire**, *a.* Of the nature of denegation.

dengue [dɑ̃:g], *n.f.* Dengue (-fever).

déni [de'ni], *n.m.* Denial, refusal. *Déni de justice*, denial of justice.

déniaisé [denjɛ'ze], *a.* (*fem.* **-ée**) Sharpened, who has had his or her eyes opened; who has lost her innocence. *Jeune homme déniaisé*, lad who knows what's what. **déniaiser**, *v.t.* To sharpen the wits of; to initiate; to seduce. **se déniaiser**, *v.r.* To learn to be sharp, to grow cunning; (*fam.*) to lose one's innocence.

dénicher [deni'ʃe], *v.t.* To take out of the nest; to hunt out, to find out; to rout out, to dislodge. *Dénicher une statue*, to remove a statue from its niche.—*v.i.* To forsake its nest (of a bird); to make off, to run away. *Allons, il faut dénicher*, come, be off with you; *les oiseaux ont déniché*, the birds have flown. **dénicheur**, *n.m.* Bird's-nester.

dénicotiniser [denikɔtini'ze], *v.t.* To take (a great part of) the nicotine out of tobacco.

denier [də'nje], *n.m.* (*Rom. Ant.*) Denarius; (*Fr. Ant.*) denier; penny; farthing, mite; a sum of money, cash; interest; (*pl.*) State revenues. *À beaux deniers comptants*, in hard cash, in ready money; *denier à Dieu*, keymoney; *denier du culte*, church rate; *le denier de la veuve*, the widow's mite; *le denier de Saint-Pierre*, Peter's pence; *les deniers publics*, the public funds.

dénier [de'nje], *v.t.* (*conjugated like* PRIER) To deny, to refuse. **se dénier**, *v.r.* To be denied, to deny oneself.

dénigrant [deni'grɑ̃], *a.* (*fem.* **-ante**) Disparaging. **dénigrement**, *n.m.* Disparagement. **dénigrer**, *v.t.* To disparage; to discredit, to traduce, to vilify. **dénigreur**, *n.m.* (*fem.* **-euse**) Disparager, petty critic.

Denis [də'ni], *m.* Dionysius, Denis, Dennis. **Denis l'ancien**, Dionysius the elder; **Denis le jeune**, Dionysius the younger.

dénitrification [denitrifika'sjɔ̃], *n.f.* Denitrifying. **dénitrifier**, *v.t.* (*conjugated like* PRIER) To denitrify.

déniveler [deni'vle], *v.t. irr.* (*conjugated like* APPELER) To put out of level, to make uneven. **dénivellation**, *n.f.* **dénivellement**, *n.m.* Difference of level; unevenness.

dénombrement [denɔ̃brə'mɑ̃], *n.m.* Enumeration; census, count (of persons or things). **dénombrer**, *v.t.* To number, to enumerate.

dénominateur [denɔmina'tœ:r], *n.m.* (*Arith.*) Denominator. **dénominatif**, *a.* (*fem.* **-ive**) Denominative. **dénomination**, *n.f.* Denomination, designation, name.

dénommer [denɔ'me], *v.t.* To designate; to name.

dénoncer [denɔ̃'se], *v.t.* To denounce, to inform against; to announce, to designate, to indicate; to give notice of, to proclaim, to declare (war etc.). **dénonciateur**, *n.m.* (*fem.* **-trice**) Denunciator, informer, accuser. **dénonciation**, *n.f.* Denunciation, declaration; information.

dénotation [denɔta'sjɔ̃], *n.f.* Denotation. **dénoter**, *v.t.* To denote, to betoken; to mark out.

dénouement or **dénoûment** [denu'mɑ̃], *n.m.* Dénouement, unravelling (esp. of a play etc.).

dénouer, *v.t.* To untie, to loosen; to give elasticity to (the limbs etc. as with exercise); to solve (difficulties etc.); to unravel (the plot of a novel etc.). **se dénouer**, *v.r.* To come untied, to be unravelled; to be solved, to be cleared up. *Sa langue s'est dénouée à la fin*, he has spoken out at last.

dénoyauter [denwajo'te], *v.t.* To stone (fruit).

denrée [dɑ̃'re], *n.f.* Commodity, produce, provisions, articles of food etc. *Denrées alimentaires*, food products, foodstuffs; *denrées de première nécessité*, essential goods.

dense [dɑ̃:s], *a.* Dense, close, thick. (*Mil.*) *En formation dense*, in close order. **densimètre**, *n.m.* Densimeter. **densimétrie**, *n.f.* Densimetry. **densité**, *n.f.* Density, thickness.

dent [dɑ̃], *n.f.* Tooth; fang; notch; cog; prong. *Armé jusqu'aux dents*, armed to the teeth; (*fam.*) *avoir la dent*, to be hungry; *avoir la dent dure*, to be fiercely critical; *avoir les dents longues*, to be very greedy, (*fig.*) to require a big share (of money, etc.); *avoir mal aux dents*, to have a toothache; (*fig.*) *être guéri du mal de dents*, to be dead; *avoir une dent contre quelqu'un*, to have an old grudge against someone; *ce couteau a des dents*, that knife is notched; *c'est vouloir prendre la lune avec les dents*, it is aiming at impossibilities; *cet enfant perce ses dents*, that child is cutting his teeth; *chacun lui donne un coup de dent*, everyone has a fling at him; *coup de dent*, bite, backbiting; *déchirer à belles dents*, to tear to pieces, (*fig.*) to slander savagely; *dents de lait*, first teeth; *dents d'en bas*, lower teeth; *dents d'en haut*, upper teeth; *dents de sagesse*, wisdom teeth; *être sur les dents*, to be tired out or done up; *faire ses dents*, to cut one's teeth; *grincer des dents*, to gnash the teeth; *l'alvéole d'une dent*, the socket of a tooth; *le fruit vert agace les dents*, green fruit sets the teeth on edge; *le mal de dents*, the toothache; *les dents d'une roue*, the cogs of a wheel; *les dents lui claquent*, his teeth chatter; *les dents lui tombent*, he is losing his teeth; *manger du bout des dents*, to eat with no appetite, to play with one's food; *montrer les dents à quelqu'un*, to show one's teeth to someone; *murmurer entre ses dents*, to mutter to oneself; *n'avoir rien à se mettre sous la dent*, not to have a morsel to put in one's mouth; *ne pas desserrer les dents*, not to open one's lips; *parler entre ses dents*, to speak through one's teeth, to mumble; *rire du bout des dents*, to pretend to laugh, to force a laugh; *se curer les dents*, to pick one's teeth; *se laver les dents*, to clean one's teeth; *serrer les dents*, to set the teeth; *une dent qui branle*, a loose tooth; *une vieille sans dent*, a toothless hag.

dentaire [dɑ̃'tɛ:r], *a.* Dental. *L'art dentaire*, dentistry; *une école dentaire*, a dental school. *n.f.* Tooth-wort.

dental [dɑ̃'tal], *a.* (*fem.* **-ale**, *pl.* **-aux**) (*Gram.*) Dental. *n.f.* (*Gram.*) Dental.

dent-de-lion [dɑ̃də'ljɔ̃], *n.m.* (*pl.* **dents-de-lion**) Dandelion. **dent-de-loup**, *n.m.* (*pl.* **dents-de-loup**) Pin, bolt (of a carriage).

denté [dɑ̃'te], *a.* (*fem.* **-ée**) Toothed; (*Bot.*) dentated. *Feuille dentée en scie*, serrated leaf; *roue dentée*, cogged wheel.

dentelaire [dɑ̃'tlɛ:r], *n.f.* (*Bot.*) Leadwort.

dentelé   dépelotonner

dentelé [dɑ̃'tle], *a.* (*fem.* **-ée**) Notched, denticulated, toothed, indented, jagged.—*n.m.* (*Anat.*) Denticulated muscle. **denteler,** *v.t.* To indent, to notch, to tooth, to cog.

dentelle [dɑ̃'tɛl], *n.f.* Lace, lace-work. *Manchettes de dentelle,* lace ruffles; *dentelle à l'aiguille,* point-lace. **dentellerie,** *n.f.* Lace trade. **dentellier,** *a.* (*fem.* **dentellière**) Pertaining to lace.—*n.* Lace-maker.

dentelure [dɑ̃'tly:r], *n.f.* Denticulation, indenting; scallop.

denticule [dɑ̃ti'kyl], *n.m.* Denticle; (*pl.,* *Arch.*) denticles. **denticulé,** *a.* (*fem.* **-ée**) (*Bot.*) Denticulated, indented.

dentier [dɑ̃'tje], *n.m.* Set of teeth (esp. artificial). **dentifrice,** *a.* *Pâte* (or *poudre*) *dentifrice,* toothpaste (or powder); *eau dentifrice,* mouth-wash.—*n.m.* Toothpaste.

dentiste [dɑ̃'tist], *n.m.* Dentist. *Chirurgien dentiste,* dental surgeon. **dentition,** *n.f.* Dentition, cutting of teeth. **denture,** *n.f.* Set of teeth; (*Horol.*) teeth of a wheel.

dénudation [denyda'sjɔ̃], *n.f.* Denudation. **dénuder,** *v.t.* To denude; to lay bare; to strip.

dénuement or **dénûment** [deny'mɑ̃], *n.m.* Destitution, deprivation, penury, want. **dénuer,** *v.t.* To strip, to leave destitute. *Dénué d'esprit,* devoid of wit; *dénué de ressources,* bereft of support; *dénué d'intérêt,* dull. **se dénuer,** *v.r.* To strip oneself; to leave oneself destitute.

déontologie [deɔ̃tɔlɔ'ʒi], *n.f.* Deontology.

dépaillage [depa'ja:ʒ], *n.m.* Unbottoming (of chairs). **dépailler,** *v.t.* To take off the rush (or straw) bottom (of a chair).

dépaler [depa'le], *v.t.* (*Naut.*) *Être dépalé,* to be driven to leeward, to be carried away.

dépannage [depa'na:ʒ], *n.m.* Repairing a broken-down car. *Service de dépannage,* break-down service. **dépanner** [depa'ne], *v.t.* To set going anew (a broken-down car).

dépaqueter [depak'te], *v.t.* To unpack; (*Naut.*) to loosen.

dépareillé [depare'je], *a.* (*fem.* **-ée**) Unmatched, odd. *Articles dépareillés,* oddments; *gants dépareillés,* unmatched gloves; *livres dépareillés,* odd books.

dépareiller [depare'je], *v.t.* To unmatch, to spoil the pair of, to render incomplete.

déparer [depa're], *v.t.* To strip (of ornaments); (*fig.*) to mar, to disfigure, to spoil the beauty of.

déparier [depa'rje], *v.t.* (*conjugated like* PRIER) To take away one (of a pair); to separate (a pair of animals).

déparler [depar'le], *v.i.* (*fam.*) To talk rubbish; (*always neg.*) to stop talking. *Elle ne déparle pas,* she never stops talking (nonsense).

déparquer [depar'ke], *v.t.* To unpen, to let out (cattle); to unbed (oysters).

départ [de'pa:r], *n.m.* Departure, start; setting out; (*Chem.*) parting. *Départ lancé,* (*Cycl.*) flying start; *être sur son* (or *le*) *départ,* to be on the eve of setting out; *faire le départ entre,* to discriminate between; *prix de départ,* upset price; *tertre de départ,* (*golf*) tee.

départager [departa'ʒe], *v.t.* To settle by a casting-vote. *Départager les voix,* to give a casting vote.

département [departə'mɑ̃], *n.m.* Department; line, business (province or business assigned to a particular person). *Cela n'est pas de son département,* that is not in his line, does not lie in his province; *les départements de la France,* the departments of France. **départemental,** *a.* (*fem.* **-ale,** *pl.* **-aux**) Departmental.

départir [depar'ti:r], *v.t.* *irr.* (*conjugated like* SERVIR) To separate; to distribute, to divide, to endow, to bestow. **se départir,** *v.r.* To desist, to give up; to swerve, to deviate. *Il s'est départi de ses droits,* he has desisted from his rights; *sans se départir de son calme,* while keeping his composure; *se départir de son devoir,* to swerve from one's duty.

dépassement [depas'mɑ̃], *n.m.* Overstepping (of credit, etc.); (*Motor.*) overtaking.

dépasser [depa'se], *v.t.* To go beyond, to pass, to get ahead of; to outwalk, outride, outsail, etc.; to exceed, to surpass, to excel; to be higher, taller, etc., than; to draw out, to peep, to show (ribbons etc.). (*fam.*) *Cela me dépasse,* that's beyond me; *cette théorie est dépassée,* that theory is now obsolete; *dépasser ses pouvoirs,* to exceed one's powers; (*Mil.*) *dépasser l'ennemi,* to outmarch the enemy; *dépasser le but,* to overshoot the mark; (*Naut.*) *dépasser une manœuvre,* to unreeve a rope; *dépasser un mât,* to get down a mast; *il me dépasse de trois pouces,* he is taller than I am by three inches; *son jupon dépasse,* her slip is showing.

dépavage [depa'va:ʒ], *n.m.* Unpaving. **dépaver,** *v.t.* To unpave, to take up the pavement of.

dépaysé [depei'ze], *a.* (*fem.* **-ée**) Away from home, out of one's element. *Se trouver dépaysé* (*dans une société*), to feel out of one's own circle. **dépaysement,** *n.m.* Removal from the natural sphere, country, home, etc. **dépayser,** *v.t.* To send away from home; to remove from his natural sphere etc.; to give new habits etc. to; (*fig.*) to bewilder, to put on a wrong scent. **se dépayser,** *v.r.* To leave one's home; to go abroad; to get out of one's element.

dépècement [depɛs'mɑ̃] or **dépeçage,** *n.m.* Cutting up, cutting in pieces, carving, tearing up, dismemberment. **dépecer,** *v.t.* *irr.* (*conjugated like* AMENER) To cut up (a carcass), to carve, to cut in pieces; to dismember. **dépeceur,** *n.m.* (*fem.* **-euse**) Carver, cutter, meat-dresser.

dépêche [de'pɛ:ʃ], *n.f.* Dispatch (letter on affairs of State); communication, esp. a telegram.

dépêcher [depɛ'ʃe], *v.t.* To dispatch, to do quickly, to polish off; to send quickly, to send by messenger; to make away with, to kill.—*v.i.* To dispatch, to send off a courier or messenger. **se dépêcher,** *v.r.* To make haste, to look sharp. *Dépêchez-vous,* hurry up.

dépeigner [depɛ'ne], *v.t.* To ruffle (hair).

dépeindre [de'pɛ̃:dr], *v.t.* *irr.* (*conjugated like* CRAINDRE) To depict, to describe; to portray, to paint.

dépelotonner [deplɔtɔ'ne], *v.t.* To unwind. **se dépelotonner,** *v.r.* To come unwound; to uncurl (of cat).

dépenaillé [depnɑ'je], *a.* (*fem.* -**ée**) Tattered, ragged, in rags; ill-clad, slatternly. **dépenaillement,** *n.m.* Raggedness.
dépendance [depɑ̃'dɑ̃:s], *n.f.* Subordination; dependence; appendage, annex, outhouse, (*pl.*) offices, out-buildings; dependencies. *Être sous la dépendance de quelqu'un,* to be dependent on someone; *tenir quelqu'un dans la dépendance,* to keep someone in a state of dependency; *maison et dépendances,* messuage. **dépendant,** *a.* (*fem.* -**ante**) Dependent.—*adv. phr.* (*Naut.*) *En dépendant,* edging away (or down).
dépendre (1) [de'pɑ̃:dr], *v.t.* To take down; to unhang.
dépendre (2) [de'pɑ̃:dr], *v.i.* To depend, to be dependent; to result; to belong (to); (*Naut.*) to blow (of the wind). *Cela dépend de moi,* that depends on *or* rests with me.
dépens [de'pɑ̃], *n.m.* (*used only in pl.*) Expense, cost; (*fig.*) detriment. *Il a gagné son procès avec dépens,* he gained his lawsuit with costs; *il l'apprendra à ses dépens,* he will have to pay for it; *vivre aux dépens d'autrui,* to live at other people's expense.
dépense [de'pɑ̃:s], *n.f.* Expenditure, outlay, waste, flow, amount (of water, gas, etc.) supplied in a given period; steward's office, pantry; (*pl.*) supplies. *De folles dépenses,* extravagant expenses; *dépense de temps,* waste of time; *dépenses de bouche,* living expenses; *faire de la dépense,* to spend money; *faire la dépense,* to pay the expenses, to do the housekeeping; *ne pas regarder à la dépense,* not to spare expense; *sa dépense excède ses revenus,* his expenditure exceeds his income; *se mettre en dépense,* to spend more than usual; to put oneself out.
dépenser [depɑ̃'se], *v.t.* To spend, to expend, to consume; to waste. *Il aime à dépenser,* he is fond of spending. **se dépenser,** *v.r.* To exert oneself. *Il se dépense trop,* he is wasting his energy. **dépensier,** *a.* (*fem.* -**ière**) Extravagant.—*n.* Extravagant person, spendthrift; bursar, dispenser, storekeeper.
déperdition [deperdi'sjɔ̃], *n.f.* Loss, waste.
dépérir [depe'ri:r], *v.i.* To decay, to decline, to pine away, to wither, to dwindle, to waste away. **dépérissement,** *n.m.* Decay, withering, falling away.
dépersonnaliser [depɛrsɔnali'ze], *v.t.* To depersonalize.
dépêtrer [depɛ'tre], *v.t.* To disentangle, to extricate. **se dépêtrer,** *v.r.* To get clear of.
dépeuplement [depœplə'mɑ̃], *n.m.* Depopulation; thinning (of forests etc.). **dépeupler,** *v.t.* To depopulate; to unstock; to thin; *Dépeupler une forêt,* to thin a forest. **se dépeupler,** *v.r.* To become depopulated, to be unstocked.
déphasage [defa'za:ʒ], *n.m.* (*Elec.*) Phase displacement. **déphasé,** *a.* (*fem.* -**ée**) Out of phase (current).
dépiauter [depjo'te], *v.t.* (*vulg.*) To skin (rabbit).
dépilage (1) [depi'la:ʒ] or **dépilement,** *n.m.* (*Mining*) Removal of timber supports.
dépilage (2) [depi'la:ʒ], *n.m.* Removal of hairs, bristles, etc. (from hides etc.).
dépilatif [depila'tif], *a.* (*fem.* -**ive**) Depilatory. **dépilation,** *n.f.* Depilation. **dépilatoire,**
n.m. Depilatory. **dépiler,** *v.t.* To cause the hair to fall.
dépiquage [depi'ka:ʒ], *n.m.* Threshing or treading out (corn etc.).
dépiquer (1) [depi'ke], *v.t.* To unquilt, to unstitch.
dépiquer (2) [depi'ke], *v.t.* To tread out (corn).
dépistage [depis'ta:ʒ], *n.m.* Tracking down (disease, virus, etc.).
dépister [depis'te], *v.t.* To track down; to hunt out; to dodge; (*fig.*) to throw off the scent.
dépit [de'pi], *n.m.* Spite, grudge; resentment, vexation. *Avoir du dépit,* to be vexed; *écrire en dépit du bon sens,* to write nonsense; *en dépit de,* in spite of, with all; *par dépit,* out of spite; *il pleurait de dépit,* he wept for vexation. **dépiter,** *v.t.* To vex, to spite. **se dépiter,** *v.r.* To be vexed, to fret, to sulk, to get out of temper.
déplacé [depla'se], *a.* (*fem.* **déplacée**) Displaced, misplaced, ill-timed, unbecoming, improper, amiss. *Discours déplacé,* uncalled for speech; *personnes déplacées,* (*Polit.*) displaced persons. **déplacement,** *n.m.* Change of place, removal; displacement; trip. *Déplacement d'un navire,* displacement of a vessel; *frais de déplacement,* travelling expenses.
déplacer [depla'se], *v.t.* To displace, to move; to remove, to change from its or his place, to shift; to misplace; to have a displacement of (of ships etc.). **se déplacer,** *v.r.* To change one's place, to leave one's residence; to be displaced (of things); to travel.
déplaire [de'plɛ:r], *v.i. irr.* (*conjugated like* PLAIRE) To displease, to offend; to be disagreeable, to give offence. *Cela me déplaît,* I don't like this; *n'en déplaise à,* with all due deference to; *ne vous en déplaise,* with your leave, if you don't mind. **se déplaire,** *v.r.* To be displeased, to feel dissatisfied, annoyed, etc.; to displease each other; not to thrive (of animals or plants). *Je ne me déplairais pas ici,* I should not mind living here; *les troupeaux se déplaisent dans cet endroit-là,* the flocks do not thrive in that place. **déplaisant,** *a.* (*fem.* -**ante**) Unpleasant, disagreeable.
déplaisir [deplɛ'zi:r], *n.m.* Displeasure, annoyance; grief, chagrin, trouble.
déplantage [deplɑ̃'ta:ʒ], *n.m.,* or **déplantation,** *n.f.* Displanting. **déplanter,** *v.t.* To displant, to dig or take up (a plant). *Déplanter une ancre,* (*Naut.*) to start an anchor. **déplantoir,** *n.m.* Garden trowel.
déplâtrage [deplɑ'tra:ʒ], *n.m.* Unplastering. **déplâtrer,** *v.t.* To unplaster.
dépliant [depli'ɑ̃], *n.m.* Folding page; folder, prospectus, leaflet.
déplier [depli'e], *v.t.* (*conjugated like* PRIER) To unfold, to open out; to spread out; to lay out, to display (goods). **se déplier,** *v.r.* To come unfolded.
déplissage [depli'sa:ʒ], *n.m.* Unpleating. **déplisser,** *v.t.* To unpleat. **se déplisser,** *v.r.* To come unpleated; to lose its pleats (of a skirt etc.).
déploiement or **déploîment** [deplwa'mɑ̃], *n.m.* Unfolding, display, show; (*Mil.*) deployment.

déplombage [deplɔ̃'baːʒ], *n.m.* Unsealing; unstopping. **déplomber,** *v.t.* To take the custom-house seal off (goods); to unstop (a tooth).

déplorable [deplɔ'rabl], *a.* Deplorable, lamentable, wretched. **déplorablement,** *adv.* Deplorably, lamentably, wretchedly.

déplorer [deplɔ're], *v.t.* (*poet.*) To deplore, to bewail, to lament, to mourn.

déployer [deplwa'je], *v.t. irr.* (*conjugated like* ABOYER) To unfold, to unroll, to unfurl, to spread out, to open; to display, to show; (*Mil.*) to deploy. *À gorge déployée,* at the top of one's voice, lustily, with all one's might; *déployer les voiles,* to spread the sails; *déployer toute son éloquence,* to put forth all one's eloquence; *enseignes déployées,* colours flying; *voguer à voiles déployées,* (*Naut.*) to be under full sail, **se déployer,** *v.r.* To unroll, to display oneself; to be displayed; (*Mil.*) to deploy.

déplumer [deply'me], *v.t.* To take the feathers from, to pluck; (*fig.*) to despoil; to tear the hair from. **se déplumer,** *v.r.* To moult, to shed feathers; to pluck each other's feathers; (*fam.*) to lose one's hair.

dépoétiser [depoeti'ze], *v.t.* To take the poetry out.

dépoitraillé [depwa'traːje], *a.* (*fem.* -ée) With bare breast.

dépolarisation [depɔlariza'sjɔ̃], *n.f.* Depolarization. **dépolariser,** *v.t.* To depolarize.

dépolir [depɔ'liːr], *v.t.* To make the surface (of glass, metal, etc.) dull. *Dépolir du verre,* to frost glass; *le feu dépolit le marbre,* fire takes the polish off marble. **dépolissage** or **dépolissement,** *n.m.* Grinding, roughing (of glass).

déponent [depɔ'nɑ̃], *a.* and *n.m.* (*Gram.*) Deponent.

dépopulateur [depɔpyla'tœːr], *a.* (*fem.* -trice) Depopulating. **dépopulation,** *n.m.* Depopulation.

déport [de'pɔːr], *n.m.* *Self-withdrawal (of a judge); (*Stock Exch.*) backwardation. *Sans déport,* forthwith.

déportation [depɔrta'sjɔ̃], *n.f.* Transportation. **déporté,** *n.m.* (*fem.* -ée) Person sentenced to be transported.

déportements [depɔrtə'mɑ̃], *n.m. pl.* Misconduct, evil-doings.

déporter [depɔr'te], *v.t.* To deport, to transport for life; (*fig.*) to relegate, to set aside; to carry away, to drift. *La voiture fut déportée vers la droite,* the car swerved to the right. **se déporter,** *v.r.* (*Law*) To desist. *Se déporter de ses prétentions,* to withdraw one's claims.

déposant [depo'zɑ̃], *a.* (*fem.* -ante) Giving evidence; depositing.—*n.* Witness; depositor.

déposer [depo'ze], *v.t.* To put down, to lay down; to lay aside; to divest oneself of; to depose; to deposit; to lodge (a complaint etc.). *Ce vin dépose beaucoup de lie,* this wine deposits a good deal of sediment; *déposer son bilan,* to file one's petition (in bankruptcy); *il déposa son fardeau,* he laid down his burden; *marque déposée,* registered trademark; *on le déposa de sa charge,* he was removed from office.—*v.i.* To give evidence; to settle, to leave a sediment.

dépositaire [depozi'teːr], *n.m.* Depositary, trustee; agent. *Dépositaire de journaux,* newsagent.

déposition [depozi'sjɔ̃], *n.f.* Deposition, deposing, evidence. *La déposition porte que,* the evidence says that.

dépositoire [depɔzi'twaːr], *n.m.* Depository, mortuary.

déposséder [depɔse'de], *v.t. irr.* (*conjug. like* ACCÉLÉRER) To dispossess, to oust. **dépossesseur,** *n.m.* Dispossessor. **dépossession,** *n.f.* Dispossession, deprivation.

dépôt [de'po], *n.m.* Depositing, deposit; thing deposited, sediment; depository, warehouse, magazine; (*Mil.*) depot; (*Med.*) tumour, abscess; (*pl.*) deposits, alluvium. *Dépôt de mendicité,* workhouse; *dépôt d'armes,* armoury; *dépôt de marchandises,* warehouse; *dépôt d'essence,* petrol station; *en dépôt,* as a deposit in trust, (*Comm.*) on sale; *faire un dépôt,* to make a deposit; *mandat de dépôt,* writ of imprisonment, committal, mittimus; *placé sous mandat de dépôt,* remanded.

dépotage [depo'taːʒ] or **dépotement,** *n.m.* Unpotting; decanting, drawing off. **dépoter,** *v.t.* To take out of a pot; to decant.

dépotoir [depo'twaːr], *n.m.* Deposit of nightsoil; (*fig.*) sump, dregs.

dépoudrer [depu'dre], *v.t.* To unpowder. **se dépoudrer,** *v.r.* To unpowder one's hair or face.

dépouille [de'puːj], *n.f.* Slough, cast-off skin or hide; skin stripped from an animal etc., spoil; remains, relics, wardrobe (of persons deceased); (*pl.*) crop, harvest; booty, plunder; (*pl.*) spoils, booty. *Dépouille mortelle,* mortal remains; *dépouilles opimes,* spolia opima; *il a laissé sa dépouille à un tel,* he left his wardrobe to So-and-so; *il s'enrichit des dépouilles d'autrui,* he enriches himself with the spoils of others; *la dépouille d'un serpent,* the slough of a serpent; *l'âme quitta sa dépouille mortelle,* the soul forsook its earthly tenement. **dépouillement,** *n.m.* Spoliation, despoiling; privation; scrutiny (of a ballot-box); abstract (of an account). *Au dépouillement du scrutin,* on counting the votes.

dépouiller [depu'je], *v.t.* To strip, to skin; to denude, to lay bare; to unclothe, to disrobe; to rob, to plunder, to despoil; to throw off, to lay aside; to cast off (of insects); to gather, to reap (crops); to inspect, to count up (a ballot-box); to present an abstract (of accounts). *Dépouiller le courrier,* to read one's letters; *dépouiller une anguille,* to skin an eel; (*fig.*) *dépouiller le vieil homme,* to turn over a new leaf. **se dépouiller,** *v.r.* To shed its skin (of insects and animals), to moult; to divest oneself of, to strip oneself of, to throw off.

dépourvoir [depur'vwaːr], *v.t. irr.* (*pres.p.* dépourvoyant, *p.p.* dépourvu; *conjugated like* POURVOIR) To leave unprovided or destitute. **se dépourvoir,** *v.r.* To leave oneself unprovided. *Se dépourvoir d'argent,* to leave oneself without cash. **dépourvu,** *a.* (*fem.* dépourvue) Destitute, unprovided. *Au dépourvu,* unawares; *pris au dépourvu,* caught napping.

dépoussiérage [depusie'raːʒ], *n.m.* Removal

of dust (esp. with a machine). **dépoussiérer**, *v.t.* To remove dust.

dépravation [deprava'sjɔ̃], *n.f.* Vitiation, depravity, depravation; alteration, corruption (of morals, taste, etc.). **dépravé**, *a.* (*fem.* **-ée**) Vitiated, depraved, corrupt, perverted. *Goût dépravé*, depraved taste.—*n.* Depraved person. **dépraver**, *v.t.* To deprave, to corrupt, to pervert. **se dépraver**, *v.r.* To become vitiated, depraved, or corrupted.

déprécatif [depreka'tif], *a.* (*fem.* **-ive**) Deprecative. **déprécation**, *n.f.* Deprecation.

dépréciateur [depresja'tœːr], *n.m.* (*fem.* **dépréciatrice**) Depreciator. **dépréciation**, *n.f.* Depreciation.

déprécier [depre'sje], *v.t.* (*conjugated like* PRIER) To depreciate, to undervalue, to underrate; to belittle, to disparage. **se déprécier**, *v.r.* To depreciate oneself; to fall in value (of things).

déprédateur [depreda'tœːr], *n.m.* (*fem.* **déprédatrice**) Depredator, plunderer. **déprédation**, *n.f.* Plundering, depredation; malversation.

déprendre [de'prɑ̃ːdr], *v.t. irr.* (*conjugated like* PRENDRE) To loosen, to detach, to part. **se déprendre**, *v.r.* To get loose; to detach oneself (*de*).

dépressif [depre'sif], *a.* (*fem.* **-ive**) Depressive. **dépression**, *n.f.* Depression, hollow; (*fig.*) dejection; recession, slump (of business); (*Astron.*) dip.

déprimant [depri'mɑ̃], *a.* (*fem.* **-ante**) (*Med.*) Depressing (climate etc.).

déprimer [depri'me], *v.t.* To press down, to depress; (*fig.*) to discourage.

depuis [də'pɥi], *prep.* Since, for; from, after. *Depuis ce temps-là*, since then; *depuis deux ans*, two years since; *depuis la création du monde*, since the creation of the world; *depuis longtemps*, for a long time; *depuis peu*, lately; *depuis quand?* since when? *Depuis le Rhin jusqu'à l'océan*, from the Rhine to the ocean; (*Comm.*) *costumes depuis dix mille francs*, suits at ten thousand francs and upwards.—*adv.* Since (then), afterwards, since that time. *Je ne l'ai point vu depuis*, I have not seen him since.—*Depuis que*, since; *depuis que vous êtes parti*, since you went away.

dépuratif [depyra'tif], *a. and n.m.* (*fem.* **-ive**) Depurative. **dépuration**, *n.f.* Depuration. **dépuratoire**, *a.* Depuratory. **dépurer**, *v.t.* To depurate.

députation [depyta'sjɔ̃], *n.f.* Deputation; deputy ship; body of deputies (of a department etc.).

député [depy'te], *n.m.* Deputy, delegate; Member of Parliament.

députer [depy'te], *v.t.* To send as representative, to depute.

déraciné [derasi'ne], *n.m.* (*fem.* **-ée**) One torn from his (or her) native country.

déracinement [derasin'mɑ̃], *n.m.* Rooting up, eradication.

déraciner [derasi'ne], *v.t.* To deracinate, to root up; to eradicate, to extirpate. *Déraciner un cor*, to cut out a corn; *déraciner un mal*, to eradicate an evil. **se déraciner**, *v.r.* To be torn up by the roots.

dérader [dera'de], *v.t.* To be driven out to sea.

déraidir [dere'diːr], *v.t.* To unstiffen; to

make pliant, to soften. **se déraidir**, *v.r.* To grow pliant, soft, or supple; to unstarch one's manners.

déraillement [deraj'mɑ̃], *n.m.* Running off the rails, derailment. **dérailler**, *v.i.* To run off the line; (*fig.*) to leave the straight and narrow; to talk nonsense. **dérailleur**, *n.m.* (*Cycl.*) Shifting gear.

déraison [dere'zɔ̃], *n.f.* Unreasonableness, folly, irrationality. **déraisonnable**, *a.* Unreasonable, senseless. **déraisonnablement**, *adv.* Unreasonably, irrationally. **déraisonnement**, *n.m.* Irrational talk, raving. **déraisonner**, *v.i.* To reason falsely, to talk nonsense, to talk irrationally; to rave.

dérangement [derɑ̃ʒ'mɑ̃], *n.m.* Derangement, discomposure; trouble, embarrassment; disorder, disturbance. **déranger**, *v.t.* To derange, to put out of place or order; to discompose; to disconcert; to disturb, to upset; to unsettle, to turn (from the proper course, duty, etc.). *Cela m'a tout dérangé*, that has quite disconcerted me; *estomac dérangé*, disordered stomach; *la moindre chose le dérange*, the least thing in the world unsettles or upsets him; *pardon de vous déranger*, excuse my disturbing you. **se déranger**, *v.r.* To move, to stir; to be deranged, to get out of order; to be unwell; to trouble or disturb oneself, to put oneself out; to misconduct oneself, to lead a disorderly life. *Ne vous dérangez pas, je vous prie*, please don't move; don't bother.

déraper [dera'pe], *v.i.* (*Naut.*) To get atrip (of anchors); to skid, to side-slip (bicycle, car, etc.).

dératé [dera'te], *n.m.* (*fem.* **-ée**) (*Only used in*) *Courir comme un dératé*, to run like a greyhound. **dérater**, *v.t.* To take the spleen out of.

dératiser [derati'ze], *v.t.* To exterminate rats.

derby [dɛr'bi], *n.m.* Derby race.

derechef [dər'ʃef], *adv.* Over again, afresh, anew.

déréglé [dere'gle], *a.* (*fem.* **-ée**) Out of order, loose; out of gear; irregular; (*fig.*) unruly, dissolute. *Appétit déréglé*, immoderate appetite; *imagination déréglée*, disordered imagination; *vie déréglée*, irregular life. **dérèglement**, *n.m.* Irregularity, disorder; dissoluteness, licentiousness. *Vivre dans le dérèglement*, to lead a disorderly life. **dérégler**, *v.t. irr.* (*conjugated like* ACCÉLÉRER) To put out of order, to disorder. **se dérégler**, *v.r.* To get out of order, to be deranged; to lead a disorderly life.

dérelier [derə'lje], *v.t.* To unbind, to remove the binding from (a book).

dérider [deri'de], *v.t.* To unwrinkle, to smooth; to enliven, to brighten, to cheer up. *Il ne s'est pas déridé de la journée*, he was morose all day. **se dérider**, *v.r.* To smooth one's brow; to cheer up.

dérision [deri:'zjɔ̃], *n.f.* Derision, mockery, ridicule. *Par dérision*, out of ridicule; *tourner tout en dérision*, to turn everything into ridicule. **dérisoire**, *a.* Derisive, derisory, mocking. *À des prix dérisoires*, at competitive, ridiculously low, prices.

dérivatif [deriva'tif], *a.* (*fem.* **-ive**) Derivative.- *n.m.* (*Med.*) Derivative, counterirritant.

dérivation [deriva'sjɔ̃], *n.f.* Diversion (of water etc.) from its proper course; (*Elec.*) branching, shunting; (*Med.*) counter-irritant; (*Naut.*) drift, leeway; (*Av.*) windage. (*Elec.*) *Circuit en dérivation*, branch-circuit.

dérive [de'ri:v], *n.f.* (*Naut.*) Drift, leeway, drop-keel; (*Artill.*) allowance for wind; (*Av.*) fin. (*Av.*) *Aile de dérive*, lee-board; *avoir belle dérive*, to have good sea-room; *en* or *à la dérive*, adrift.

dérivé [deri've], *a.* (*fem.* **-ée**) Turned or drifted from the shore.—*n.m.* (*Gram.*) Derivative.—*n.f.* (*Math.*) Derivative.

dériver (1) [deri've], *v.i.* To be turned from its proper course; to come, to proceed (*de*); (*Naut.*) to drift (from the shore), to go adrift, to make leeway.—*v.t.* To turn from its course, to divert; to derive. *Faire dériver*, to derive.

dériver (2) [deri've] or **dériveter** [deriv'te], *v.t.* To unrivet.

dermatite [derma'tit], *n.f.* Dermatitis. **dermatologie**, *n.f.* Dermatology. **dermatologiste**, *n.m.* Dermatologist. **dermatose**, *n.f.* Skin disease, dermatosis.

derme [dɛrm], *n.m.* (*Anat.*) Derm, skin. **dermique**, *a.* Dermic.

dernier [dɛr'nje], *a.* (*fem.* **dernière**) Last, latest; vilest, meanest; utmost, extreme (highest, greatest, etc.); the one just past; youngest (of a family of children). *Arriver au dernier degré*, to get to, reach the highest degree; *avoir le dernier mot*, to have the last word; *cela est du dernier ridicule*, that is ridiculous to a degree; *c'est la dernière lettre qu'il ait écrite*, it is the last letter he wrote; *dans ces derniers jours*, during the last few days; *en dernier lieu*, in the last place; (*Mil.*) *le dernier rang*, the rear rank; *en dernier ressort*, as a last resource; *la dernière mode*, the latest fashion; *mettre la dernière main à quelque chose*, to put the finishing touch to something; *rendre le dernier soupir*, to breathe one's last; *une affaire de la dernière importance*, an affair of the greatest importance.—*n.* The last; the highest, lowest, etc. *Le dernier des hommes*, the vilest of men; *dernier-né* (*pl. derniers-nés*), last-born male child; *jusqu'au dernier*, to the last; *aux derniers les bons morceaux*, last come, best served. **dernièrement**, *adv.* Lately, of late, recently, not long ago.

dérobé [derɔ'be], *a.* (*fem.* **-ée**) Stolen, hidden, secret. *Escalier dérobé*, secret staircase; *porte dérobée*, hidden door. *À la dérobée* (*adv. phr.*), stealthily; *s'en aller à la dérobée*, to steal away, to slip out. **dérober**, *v.t.* To steal, to pilfer, to purloin; to take away, to remove; to conceal, to hide; to protect, to screen, to shelter; to shell (beans). *Dérober quelqu'un à la justice*, to screen someone from justice. **se dérober**, *v.r.* To steal away, to escape, to disappear; to swerve (of horses). *Il s'est dérobé*, he has stolen away; *le vaisseau se déroba bientôt à la vue*, the ship was soon lost to sight; *se dérober à la justice*, to fly from justice.

dérochage [derɔ'ʃa:ʒ], *n.m.* Scouring (of metals) with acid; clearing of rocks. **dérochement**, *n.m.* Clearing of rocks. **dérocher**, *v.t.* To scour (metals) with acid; to clear of rocks.

dérogation [derɔga'sjɔ̃], *n.f.* Derogation. **dérogatoire**, *a.* Derogatory.

déroger [derɔ'ʒe], *v.i.* To derogate; to detract; to condescend, to stoop. *Déroger à la noblesse*, to forfeit one's nobility; *déroger à l'usage établi*, to act contrarily to established custom.

déroidir [DÉRAIDIR].

dérougir [deru'ʒi:r], *v.t.* To take the redness off.

dérouillement [deruj'mã], *n.m.* Loss or removal of rust. **dérouiller**, *v.t.* To remove the rust from; (*fig.*) to polish, to brighten up. **se dérouiller**, *v.r.* To lose its or one's rust; to polish oneself up, to brighten up; to read a subject up again. *L'esprit se dérouille dans le grand monde*, social intercourse rubs the corners off one.

déroulage [derul'a:ʒ], *n.m.* Wood-peeling.

déroulement [derul'mã], *n.m.* Unrolling, unfolding. **dérouler**, *v.t.* To unroll; to spread out, to display; (*Geom.*) to produce (an evolute). **se dérouler**, *v.r.* To unroll, to be unfolded; to spread out, to open to the view; to roll in (of the waves); to develop, to pass along, to take place (of events).

déroutant [deru'tã], *a.* (*fem.* **-ante**) Baffling, confusing.

déroute [de'rut], *n.f.* Rout, overthrow; ruin; disorder, confusion. *En pleine déroute*, in full flight; *mettre quelqu'un en déroute*, to confuse, nonplus, or silence someone; *mettre une armée en déroute*, to rout an army; *ses affaires sont en déroute*, he is in a bad way (financially).

dérouter [deru'te], *v.t.* (*Naut.*) To divert (a ship); to lead astray, to turn out of his course, to set at fault; to embarrass, to disconcert, to perplex; to baffle, to foil. *Je suis tout dérouté*, I am quite at sea. **déroutement**, *n.m.* (Temporary) alteration of course (ship); deviation of route (train).

derrière [dɛ'rjɛ:r], *prep.* Behind, on the other side of. *Laisser loin derrière soi*, to leave far behind one; *regardez derrière vous*, look behind you.—*adv.* Behind, after. *Par derrière*, from behind; *sens devant derrière*, wrong side foremost.—*n.m.* Back, hinder part; posteriors, backside, behind; tail-board (of a cart); rear (of a house); (*Naut.*) stern, poop. *Être logé sur le derrière de l'immeuble*, to lodge at the back of the house; *pattes de derrière*, hind legs; *porte de derrière*, back-door.—*n.m. pl. Les derrières de l'armée*, the rear of the army.

derviche [dɛr'viʃ] or **dervis**, *n.m.* Dervish.

des [*contr. of* DE LES].

dès [dɛ], *prep.* From, since, as early as. *Dès à présent*, from this moment, forthwith, henceforth; *dès demain*, tomorrow, from tomorrow onwards; *dès le berceau*, from the cradle; *dès lors*, from that moment, ever since then; consequently; *dès que*, when, as soon as, since; *dès que je serai arrivé*, as soon as I get there; *dès qu'il parut*, as soon as he appeared; *dès lors que vous acceptez*, seeing that you agree.

désabonnement [dezabɔn'mã], *n.m.* Withdrawal of subscription. **se désabonner**, *v.r.* To withdraw one's subscription (to a magazine).

désabusement [dezabyz'mã], *n.m.* Disabusing, undeceiving. **désabuser**, *v.t.* To

disabuse, to undeceive. **se désabuser,** *v.r.*
To be undeceived, to undeceive oneself.
Désabusez-vous, face the facts !

désaccord [deza'kɔːr], *n.m.* Disagreement,
discord. *Être en désaccord,* to be at variance;
être en désaccord avec soi-même, to be inconsistent with oneself. **désaccorder,** *v.t.* To
untune; (*fig.*) to set at variance. *Être
désaccordé,* to be out of tune (piano etc.). **se
désaccorder,** *v.r.* To get out of tune.

désaccouplement [dezakuplǝ'mã], *n.m.* Uncoupling. **désaccoupler,** *v.t.* To uncouple.
se désaccoupler, *v.r.* To get uncoupled;
to come asunder.

***désaccoutumance** [dezakuty'mãːs], *n.f.*
Breach of habit or custom.

désaccoutumer [dezakuty'me], *v.t.* To disaccustom. **se désaccoutumer,** *v.r.* To
break oneself of, to lose the habit of. *Se
désaccoutumer de faire une chose,* to leave off
doing a thing.

désachalandage [dezaʃalã'daːʒ], *n.m.* Loss
of customers. **désachalander,** *v.t.* To take
away the customers from.

désaffectation [dezafɛkta'sjɔ̃], *n.f.* Secularization; transfer.

désaffecter [dezafɛkte], *v.t.* To secularize (a
church); (*Mil.*) to transfer; to put a
building to another use.

désaffection [dezafɛk'sjɔ̃], *n.f.* Loss of
affection. **désaffectionner,** *v.t.* To cause
(someone) to lose his or her affection, to
disaffect. **se désaffectionner,** *v.r.* To lose
affection.

désaffourcher [dezafur'ʃe], *v.t.* (*Naut.*) To
unmoor or heave up the anchor of.

***désaffubler** [dezafy'ble], *v.t.* To unmuffle.

désagencement [dezaʒãs'mã], *n.m.* Throwing out of gear. **désagencer,** *v.t.* (*conjugated like* AGENCER) To throw out of gear,
to disarrange, to disorder.

désagréable [dezagre'abl], *a.* Disagreeable,
unpleasant; obnoxious, offensive, distasteful.
Cela est désagréable à voir, that is displeasing
to the sight. **désagréablement,** *adv.* Disagreeably, unpleasantly. ***désagréer,** *v.i.*
To be displeasing. *Cela ne me désagrée pas,*
I do not dislike that.

désagrégation [dezagrega'sjɔ̃], *n.f.* Disaggregation. **désagréger,** *v.t.* To disaggregate, to break up, to separate. **se
désagréger,** *v.r.* To become disaggregated,
to break up.

désagrément [dezagre'mã], *n.m.* Disagreeableness, unpleasantness, trouble; annoyance, discomfort.

désaimanter [dezɛmã'te], *v.t.* To demagnetize.

désajustement [dezaʒystǝ'mã], *n.m.* Disarrangement; disorder. **désajuster,** *v.t.* To
derange, to disturb, to put out of order. **se
désajuster,** *v.r.* To become disarranged, to
get out of order. *Sa coiffure s'est désajustée,*
her hair has become disarranged.

désallier [deza'lje], *v.t.* (*conjugated like* PRIER)
To separate or disunite (allies).

désaltérant [dezalte'rã], *a.* (*fem.* **-ante**)
Thirst-quenching. **désaltérer,** *v.t.* To
quench the thirst of, to refresh. **se désaltérer,** *v.r.* To quench one's thirst.

désamorçage [dezamɔr'saːʒ], *n.m.* Unpriming.

désamorcer [dezamɔr'se], *v.t.* To unprime,

to uncap (fire-arms etc.). **se désamorcer,**
v.r. To run down (dynamo); to fail, to run
dry (pump).

désancrer [dezã'kre], *v.i.* To weigh anchor.

***désappareiller** [DÉPAREILLER].

désapparier [dezapa'rje], *v.t.* (*conjugated like*
PRIER) To unpair (birds etc.).

désappointement [dezapwɛt'mã], *n.m.* Disappointment. **désappointer,** *v.t.* To disappoint; to deceive.

désapprendre [deza'prãːdr], *v.t. irr.* (*conjugated like* PRENDRE) To unlearn, to forget.

désapprobateur [dezaprɔba'tœːr], *a.* (*fem.*
désapprobatrice) Disapproving, censuring, carping. *Un geste désapprobateur,* a
gesture of disapprobation.—*n.* Censurer,
fault-finder. **désapprobation,** *n.f.* Disapprobation, disapproval.

désappropriation [dezaprɔpria'sjɔ̃], *n.f.* Renunciation (of property). **désapproprier,** *v.t.*
(*conjugated like* PRIER) To disappropriate. **se
désapproprier,** *v.r.* To renounce (property).

désapprouver [dezapru've], *v.t.* To disapprove of, to blame, to object.

désapprovisionner [dezaprovizjɔ'ne], *v.t.*
(*Mil.*) To remove the cartridges from the
magazine (of a rifle).

désarçonner [dezarsɔ'ne], *v.t.* To unsaddle,
to unhorse; (*fig.*) to baffle, to floor, to
stagger.

désargentage [dezarʒã'taːʒ], *n.m.* **désargentation** or **désargenture,** *n.f.* Unsilvering,
unplating. **désargenter,** *v.t.* To unsilver
(a piece of plate); (*fam.*) to drain of ready
money. *Ces emplettes m'ont désargenté,*
these purchases have emptied my purse.
se désargenter, *v.r.* To lose its plating;
to spend all one's ready money.

désarmement [dezarmǝ'mã], *n.m.* Disarming, disarmament; (*Naut.*) laying up.
désarmer, *v.t.* To disarm, to unarm; (*fig.*)
to appease, to calm; to uncock (a gun);
(*Naut.*) to unship (oars); to lay up, to dismantle (a vessel). *Désarmer la colère de
quelqu'un,* to appease someone's anger;
désarmer un vaisseau, to lay up a ship, to pay
off the officers and crew.—*v.i.* To disarm; to
give up maintaining troops.

désarrimer [dezari'me], *v.t.* To unstow, to
shift (cargo) in the hold.

désarroi [deza'rwa], *n.m.* Disorder, disarray,
confusion.

désarticulation [dezartikyla'sjɔ̃], *n.f.* Disarticulation. **désarticuler,** *v.t.* To disarticulate, to disjoint.

désassemblage [dezasã'blaːʒ] or **désassemblement,** *n.m.* Disjoining. **désassembler,** *v.t.* To take to pieces, to separate.

désassocier [dezasɔ'sje], *v.t.* To disassociate,
to dissociate.

désassortiment [dezasɔrti'mã], *n.m.* Unmatching, ill-assortment; unstocking. **désassortir,** *v.t.* To unmatch, to unsort.

désastre [de'zastr], *n.m.* Disaster. **désastreusement,** *adv.* Disastrously. **désastreux,** *a.* (*fem.* **-euse**) Disastrous,
unfortunate. *C'est désastreux,* it is very sad
indeed.

désavantage [dezavã'taːʒ], *n.m.* Disadvantage; detriment, prejudice; drawback, handicap. *L'affaire a tourné à leur désavantage,* the
business turned out badly for them; *parler*

au désavantage de quelqu'un, to speak disparagingly of someone. **désavantager,** *v.t.* To disadvantage, to handicap. **désavantageusement,** *adv.* Disadvantageously; disparagingly. **désavantageux,** *a.* (*fem.* **-euse**) Disadvantageous; detrimental, prejudicial, unfavourable.

désaveu [deza'vø], *n.m.* (*pl.* **-eux**) Disavowal; denial; retractation, recantation. *Désaveu de paternité*, (*Law*) repudiation of paternity; *il fait le désaveu de cette action*, he disowns that action.

désavouer [deza'vwe], *v.t.* To disown, to disclaim, to disavow; to retract, to recant. *Cette mère a désavoué son enfant*, that mother has disowned her child; *désavouer sa signature*, to repudiate one's signature.

désaxé [deza'kse], *a.* (*fem.* **-ée**) Offset, out of truth (of a wheel, etc.); (*fig.*) out of joint.

désaxer [deza'kse], *v.t.* To set over.

désazoter [dezazɔ'te], *v.t.* To denitrify.

descellement [desɛl'mã], *n.m.* Loosening, unsealing. **desceller,** *v.t.* To unseal; to unfasten, to loosen (masonry etc.). **se desceller,** *v.r.* To become loosened or unsealed.

descendance [desã'dã:s], *n.f.* Descent, lineage. **descendant,** *a.* (*fem.* **-ante**) Descending, going down; belonging to posterity or descendants; (*Mil.*) coming off duty, relieved. *Marée descendante*, out-going tide; *train descendant*, down-train.—*n.* Descendant, offspring, issue.

descendre [de'sã:dr], *v.i.* (*takes the auxiliary* AVOIR *or* ÊTRE *according as it expresses action or condition*) To descend, to go down; to go downstairs; to come, to step, to get down, to alight; to go ashore, to land; to extend downwards, to slope, to incline; to fall, to ebb, to subside. *Descendez vite*, make haste and come down; *descendre dans sa conscience*, to examine one's conscience; *descendre dans un puits*, to go down into a well; *descendre de cheval*, to dismount; *descendre de voiture*, to get out of or alight from a carriage; (*Av.*) *descendre en piqué*, to nose-dive; *descendre en vol plané*, to glide down; *descendre d'une famille illustre*, to be descended from an illustrious family; *faire descendre*, to send, let, or bring down; *il descendit à l'hôtel*, he put up at the hotel; *il descendit me parler*, he came down to speak to me; *il vaut mieux monter que descendre*, it is better to rise than to fall; *la marée descend*, the tide is ebbing; *le baromètre descend*, the glass is falling; *nous descendîmes dans une île*, we landed on an island; *tout le monde descend*, all change.—*v.t.* To take down, bring, or let down; to go or come down (a staircase etc.); to set down (of a cab etc.); to land. *Descendez ce tableau*, take that picture down; *descendre un avion*, to shoot down a plane; *descendre une rivière*, to row down a river; *où vous descendrai-je?* where shall I set you down?

descente [de'sã:t], *n.f.* Descent, going down; taking down; subsidence (of waters etc.); dismounting, alighting, disembarkment; downward slope, declivity; raid, irruption, incursion on a coast; down-pipe, funnel; down-stroke (of a piston etc.); (*pop.*) rupture, hernia. *Descente de lit*, bedside carpet or rug; *descente de bain*, bath-mat; *la justice a*

fait une descente chez lui, the police have raided his house; (*Av.*) *descente en vrille*, a spinning dive.

descripteur [deskrip'tœːr], *n.m.* Describer. **descriptible,** *a.* Describable. **descriptif,** *a.* (*fem.* **-ive**) Descriptive.

description [deskrip'sjɔ̃], *n.f.* Description; picturing; inventory.

déséchouer [DÉCHOUER].

désemballage [dezãbaˈlaːʒ], *n.m.* Unpacking. **désemballer,** *v.t.* To unpack. *On a désemballé les marchandises*, the goods have been unpacked.

désembarquement [dezãbarkəˈmã], *n.m.* Disembarking, landing. **désembarquer,** *v.t.* To disembark, to land; to unship, to unload.

désembellir [dezãbɛˈliːr], *v.t.* To disfigure. —*v.i.* To lose one's or its beauty.

désemboîter [dezãbwaˈte], *v.t.* To dislocate, to put out of the socket. **se désemboîter,** *v.r.* To become disjointed.

désembourber [dezãburˈbe], *v.t.* Tɔ draw out of the mire.

désembrayer [DÉBRAYER].

désemparé [dezãpaˈre], *a.* (*fem.* **-ée**) In distress, helpless.

désemparer [dezãpaˈre], *v.i.* To quit, to go away. *Sans désemparer*, on the spot, at once, without intermission.—*v.t.* (*Naut.*) To disable. *Désemparer un vaisseau*, to disable a ship.

désempeser [dezãpəˈze], *v.t.* To unstarch. **se désempeser,** *v.r.* To become unstarched, to get limp.

désemplir [dezã'pliːr], *v.t.* To make less full, to diminish the contents of, to empty in part. *Désemplir un tonneau*, to empty a cask partly.—*v.i.* To get emptier or less full (used only with negative). *Sa maison ne désemplit point*, his house is always full of company. **se désemplir,** *v.r.* To become less full.

désempoissonner [dezãpwasɔ'ne], *v.t.* To unstock (a pond etc.) of fish.

désenchaîner [dezãʃeˈne], *v.t.* To unchain.

désenchantement [dezãʃãt'mã], *n.m.* Disenchantment. **désenchanter,** *v.t.* To disenchant. **se désenchanter,** *v.r.* To become disenchanted, to lose one's illusions. **désenchanteur,** *a.* (*fem.* **désenchanteresse**) Disenchanting.

désenclaver [dezãklaˈve], *v.t.* To disenclose (land).

désenclouer [dezãkluˈe], *v.t.* *Désenclouer un canon*, to unspike a cannon; *désenclouer un cheval*, to take a nail out of a horse's foot.

désencombrement [dezãkɔ̃brə'mã], *n.m.* Disencumbrance; dispersing. **désencombrer,** *v.t.* To disencumber, to clear (a road etc.).

désenfiler [dezãfiˈle], *v.t.* To unthread, to unstring. **se désenfiler,** *v.r.* To come unthreaded or unstrung.

désenfler [dezã'fle], *v.t.* To reduce the swelling of.—*v.i.* To become less swollen. **se désenfler,** *v.r.* To become less swollen. **désenflure,** *n.f.*, or **désenflement,** *n.m.* Diminution or disappearance of a swelling.

désengager [dezãga'ʒe], *v.t.* To disengage, to release from an engagement.

désengrener [dezãgrə'ne], *v.r. irr.* (*conjug. like* AMENER) To throw out of gear.

désenivrer [dezăni'vre], *v.t.*, *v.i.* To sober, to make sober again. *Il ne désenivre pas,* he is always drunk. **se désenivrer,** *v.r.* To get sober again. *Se désenivrer en dormant,* to sleep it off.

désenlaidir [dezălɛ'di:r], *v.t.* To render less ugly.—*v.i.* To become less ugly.

désennuyer [dezănɥi'je], *v.t.* (*conjugated like* APPUYER) To enliven, to cheer, to divert, to amuse. **se désennuyer,** *v.r.* To find amusement, to divert oneself, to kill time.

désenrayer [dezărɛ'je], *v.t.* (*conjugated like* BALAYER) To unlock or unskid (a wheel etc.).

désenrhumer [dezăry'me], *v.t.* To cure of a cold. **se désenrhumer,** *v.r.* To get rid of a cold.

désenrôlement [dezărol'mã], *n.m.* (*Mil.*) Discharge. **désenrôler,** *v.t.* To discharge.

désenrouer [deză'rwe], *v.t.* To cure of hoarseness. **se désenrouer,** *v.r.* To cure one's hoarseness.

désensabler [dezăsa'ble], *v.t.* To get (a ship etc.) out of the sand.

désensevelir [dezăsə'vli:r], *v.t.* To unshroud. **désensevelissement,** *n.m.* Unshrouding, exhumation, disinterment.

désensorceler [dezăsɔrsə'le], *v.t.* To disenchant. **désensorcellement,** *n.m.* Disenchantment.

désentortiller [dezătɔrti'je], *v.t.* To untwist, to unravel.

désentraver [dezătra've], *v.t.* To untrammel, to unhobble (a horse etc.).

déséquilibre [dezeki'libr], *n.m.* Lack of balance, unbalance. **déséquilibré,** *a.* and *n.m.* (*fem.* **-ée**) Unbalanced (person). **déséquilibrer,** *v.t.* To unbalance.

désert [de'zɛ:r], *a.* (*fem.* **-erte**) Uninhabited, unfrequented, solitary; wild, waste, deserted. —*n.m.* Desert, waste, wilderness; solitary place; (*C*) clearing in a forest. *C'est prêcher dans le désert,* a voice crying in the wilderness.

déserter [dezɛr'te], *v.t.* To desert, to abandon, to forsake; to quit, to leave; (*C*) to clear land, to break up (ground) for tillage.—*v.i.* To desert, to go over to (the enemy). **déserteur,** *n.m.* Deserter. **désertion,** *n.f.* Desertion.

désespérance [dezɛspe'rã:s], *n.f.* Despair. **désespérant,** *a.* (*fem.* **-ante**) Desperate, hopeless, discouraging, disheartening; distressing, provoking. **désespéré,** *a.* (*fem.* **-ée**) Hopeless, desperate; disconsolate, despondent, disheartened.—*n.* Person in despair, madman, madwoman. *Agir en désespéré,* to behave like a madman; *se battre en désespéré,* to fight desperately. **désespérément,** *adv.* Desperately, despairingly, hopelessly.

désespérer [dezɛspe're], *v.i. irr.* (*conjug. like* ACCÉLÉRER) To despair, to despond, to give up all hope. *Désespérer de quelqu'un or de quelque chose,* to despair of someone *or* of something, to give up someone *or* something for lost.—*v.t.* To drive to despair; to dishearten, to dispirit; to distress. **se désespérer,** *v.r.* To be in despair, to despond.

désespoir [dezɛs'pwa:r], *n.m.* Despair, hopelessness, despondency, grief, affliction; act of desperation. *De désespoir,* through despair; *en désespoir de cause,* as a last resource or shift; *être au désespoir,* to be in despair or distress, to be vexed or grieved; *faire le*

désespoir de quelqu'un, to be a source of grief, despair, to someone; *mettre* or *réduire au désespoir,* to drive to despair, to vex extremely; *tomber dans le désespoir,* to sink into despair. *Désespoir des peintres,* (*Bot.*) London pride.

déshabiliter [dezabili'te], *v.t.* To disqualify.

déshabillé [dezabi'je], *n.m.* Deshabille, undress. *En déshabillé,* partly or scantily dressed. **déshabiller,** *v.t.* To undress, to strip; (*fig.*) to expose. **se déshabiller,** *v.r.* To undress oneself.

déshabituer [dezabi'tɥe], *v.t.* To disaccustom, to break off. **se déshabituer,** *v.r.* To lose the habit of; to break oneself of. *Se déshabituer d'une chose,* to leave off doing a thing.

déshérence [deze'rã:s], *n.f.* (*Law*) Escheat. *Droit de déshérence,* right of escheat; *tomber en déshérence,* to escheat.

déshérité [dezeri'te], *a.* (*fem.* **-ée**) Disinherited; poor, desolate (country).—*n.m. pl.* *Les déshérités,* the outcasts of fortune. **déshéritement** [dezerit'mã], *n.m.* Disinheriting. **déshériter,** *v.t.* To disinherit.

déshonnête [dezɔ'nɛ:t], *a.* Immodest, indecent, unseemly. **déshonnêtement,** *adv.* Indecently, immodestly. **déshonnêteté,** *n.f.* Indecency, immodesty, unseemliness.

déshonneur [dezɔ'nœr], *n.m.* Dishonour, disgrace, shame, discredit. *Faire déshonneur à quelqu'un,* to disgrace someone; *il a mis le comble à son déshonneur,* he has put the finishing touch to his dishonour.

déshonorable [dezɔnɔ'rabl], *a.* Dishonourable, disgraceful. **déshonorablement,** *adv.* Dishonourably. **déshonorant,** *a.* (*fem.* **-ante**) Dishonourable, disgraceful, shameful.

déshonorer [dezɔnɔ're], *v.t.* To dishonour, to disgrace, to bring to shame; to seduce, to tarnish; to disparage. **se déshonorer,** *v.r.* To dishonour or disgrace oneself.

déshydrater [dezidra'te], *v.t.* To dehydrate.

desideratum [dezidera'tɔm], *n.m.* (*pl.* **-rata**) Desideratum.

désignatif [deziɲa'tif], *a.* (*fem.* **-ive**) Designative, indicative. **désignation,** *n.f.* Designation, indication; nomination, choice, election.

désigner [desi'ɲe], *v.t.* To designate, to denote, to fix; to appoint, to name, to nominate, to choose, to point out, to call; (*Mil.*) to tell off, to detail.

désillusion [dezily'zjõ], *n.f.* Disillusion. **désillusionnant,** *a.* (*fem.* **-ante**) Disillusioning. **désillusionnement,** *n.m.* Disillusion. **désillusionner,** *v.t.* To undeceive, to disillusion, to disappoint.

désincarné [dezɛ̆kar'ne], *a.* (*fem.* **-ée**) Disincarnate.

désincorporer [dezɛ̆kɔrpɔ're], *v.t.* To disincorporate, to separate, to disembody (troops).

désinence [dezi'nã:s], *n.f.* (*Gram.*) Termination, inflexion, ending.

désinfatuer [dezɛ̆fa'tɥe], *v.t.* To disabuse, to undeceive, to get (someone) over an infatuation. **se désinfatuer,** *v.r.* To cease to be infatuated.

désinfectant [dezɛ̆fɛk'tã], *a.* (*fem.* **-ante**) Disinfecting.—*n.m.* Disinfectant. **désinfecter,** *v.t.* To disinfect, to cleanse, to purify, to decontaminate. **désinfecteur,** *a.* and *n.m.* Disinfecting. **désinfection,** *n.f.* Disinfection.

désintégration [dezε̃tegrɑ'sjɔ̃], *n.f.* Disintegration; fission. **désintégrer,** *v.t.* To disintegrate; to split (atom).

désintéressé [dezε̃terε'se], *a.* (*fem.* -**ée**) Not implicated; disinterested; unselfish, impartial, unbiased. **désintéressement,** *n.m.* Disinterestedness. **désintéressément,** *adv.* Disinterestedly. **désintéresser,** *v.t.* To indemnify, to buy out the interest of. **se désintéresser,** *v.r.* *Se désintéresser d'une chose,* to dissociate oneself from a thing.

désintoxication [dezε̃tɔksikɑ'sjɔ̃], *n.f.* Deintoxication. **désintoxiquer,** *v.t.* To deintoxicate.

désinvestir [desε̃vεs'ti:r], *v.t.* (*Mil.*) To raise the siege of.

désinviter [dezε̃vi'te], *v.t.* To cancel an invitation.

désinvolte [dezε̃'vɔlt], *a.* Free, easy, unconstrained; impertinent, offhand (manner, attitude). **désinvolture,** *n.f.* Casual, easy bearing or gait; unconstraint; casualness, offhandedness.

désir [de'zi:r], *n.m.* Desire, wish, longing; thing desired. *Au gré de ses désirs,* according to his wishes; *brûler du désir de,* to long to do; *désir déréglé,* inordinate desire. **désirable,** *a.* Desirable. **désirer,** *v.t.* To desire, to wish for, to long for, to want. *Cela laisse à désirer,* there is room for improvement; *cet ouvrage ne laisse rien à désirer,* this work is most satisfactory in all respects; *que désirez-vous de moi?* what do you want of me?

désireux, *a.* (*fem.* -**euse**) Desirous, anxious, eager (to).

désistement [dezistə'mɑ̃], *n.m.* Desistance, withdrawal. **se désister,** *v.r.* To desist from, to abandon, to renounce, to withdraw.

desman [dez'mɑ̃], *n.m.* Musk-rat.

désobéir [dezɔbe'i:r], *v.i.* To disobey, to refuse to obey, to be disobedient (*à*), to break (a rule etc.). **désobéissance,** *n.f.* Disobedience, contumacy. **désobéissant,** *a.* (*fem.* -**ante**) Disobedient.

désobligeamment [dezɔbliʒa'mɑ̃], *adv.* Disobligingly; unkindly. **désobligeance,** *n.f.* Disobliging action or disposition, lack of complaisance; unkindness. **désobligeant,** *a.* (*fem.* -**eante**) Disobliging; unkind, uncivil. **désobliger,** *v.t.* To disoblige, to displease.

désobstruant [dezɔpstry'ɑ̃] or **désobstructif,** *a.* (*fem.* -**ante** or -**ive**) and *n.m.* (*Med.*) Deobstruent, aperient. **désobstruer,** *v.t.* To clear from obstructing.

désodorisant [dezɔdori'zɑ̃], *a.* (*fem.* -**ante**) and *n.m.* Deodorant. **désodoriser,** *v.t.* To deodorize.

désœuvré [dezœ'vre], *a.* (*fem.* -**ée**) Unoccupied, idle. *Le temps pèse aux gens désœuvrés,* time hangs heavy on the hands of idle people. **désœuvrement,** *n.m.* Want of occupation, idleness.

désolant [dezɔ'lɑ̃], *a.* (*fem.* -**ante**) Grievous, distressing. **désolation,** *n.f.* Desolation, ruin, destruction; deep affliction, grief. **désolé,** *a.* (*fem.* -**ée**) Afflicted, disconsolate, broken-hearted; very sorry, grieved; dreary, desolate (place). *Je suis désolé, mais il m'est*

impossible de venir, I am very sorry but I cannot possibly come.

désoler [dezɔ'le], *v.t.* To devastate, to desolate, to lay waste; to afflict, to grieve; to annoy, to torment. *Ce retard me désole,* this delay vexes me. *La mort de son ami le désole,* the death of his friend cuts him to the quick. **se désoler,** *v.r.* To grieve, to be disconsolate.

désolidariser [desɔlidari'ze], *v.t.* To break the ties which keep together (a party, friends, etc.).

désoperculer [dezɔperky'le], *v.t.* To uncap (honeycomb).

désopilant [dezɔpi'lɑ̃], *a.* (*fem.* -**ante**) Very funny, side-splitting. *Une bouffonnerie désopilante,* a screaming farce. **désopiler,** *v.t.* (*Med.*) To clear of obstruction; (*fig.*) to cheer up, to enliven. *Cela désopile la rate,* that cheers you up. **se désopiler,** *v.r.* (*fam.*) To be highly amused; to shake with laughter.

désordonné [dezɔrdɔ'ne], *a.* (*fem.* -**ée**) Disorderly; (*fig.*) dissolute, unruly; inordinate, extravagant. *Appétit désordonné,* immoderate appetite.

désordonner [dezɔrdɔ'ne], *v.t.* To disorder, to disturb; to throw into confusion, to trouble. **se désordonner,** *v.r.* To become disordered.

désordre [de'zɔrdr], *n.m.* Disorder, confusion; disorderly life; discomposure, perturbation. —*n.m. pl.* Disturbances, riots. *En désordre,* in disorder; *faire cesser le désordre,* to put an end to the disturbance; *il a l'esprit en désordre,* his mind is confused.

désorganisateur [dezɔrganiza'tœ:r], *a.* (*fem.* -**trice**) Disorganizing.—*n.* Disorganizer. **désorganisation,** *n.f.* Disorganization.

désorganiser [dezɔrgani'ze], *v.t.* To disorganize; to confound, to throw into confusion. **se désorganiser,** *v.r.* To become disorganized.

désorienter [dezɔrjɑ̃'te], *v.t.* To lead astray, to mislead, to bewilder; to put out, to disconcert. *Être désorienté,* to lose one's way or one's bearings, to be out of one's reckoning; *notre guide était tout à fait désorienté,* our guide had lost his bearings.

désormais [dezɔr'mε], *adv.* Henceforth, hereafter, from now on.

désossement [dezɔs'mɑ̃], *n.m.* Boning. **désossé,** *a.* (*fem.* -**ée**) Boneless, flabby. **désosser,** *v.t.* To bone. **se désosser,** *v.r.* To become disjointed, limp, flabby, etc.

désoxydation [dezɔksidɑ'sjɔ̃] or **désoxygénation,** *n.f.* Deoxidation. **désoxyder** or **désoxygéner,** *v.t.* To deoxidate. **se désoxyder,** *v.r.* To become deoxidized.

despote [dεs'pɔt], *n.m.* Despot. **despotique,** *a.* Despotic. **despotiquement,** *adv.* Despotically. **despotisme,** *n.m.* Despotism.

desquamation [dεskwamɑ'sjɔ̃], *n.f.* Desquamation. **desquamer,** *v.t.* To desquamate, to peel (of skin).

desquels (*fem.* **desquelles**) [DE LEQUELS].

dessabler [desɑ'ble], *v.t.* To clear of sand, to take the sand away from.

dessaisir [dese'zi:r], *v.t.* To let go, to disseize, to dispossess. **se dessaisir,** *v.r.* To give up, to part with. **dessaisissement,** *n.m.* Parting with, abandonment.

dessalé [desa'le], *a.* (*fem.* **-ée**) Unsalted, free from salt; (*fam.*) sharp, cunning.—*n.* Sharp, knowing person. *Une fille dessalée*, a girl who knows a thing or two. **dessalement**, *n.m.*, **dessalaison**, *n.f.*, or **dessalage**, *n.m.* Clearing of salt, unsalting. **dessaler**, *v.t.* To remove salt from (meat etc.), to unsalt; (*fig.*) to make sharp, cunning, etc.

dessangler [desɑ̃'gle], *v.t.* To ungirth, to loosen the girth of (a horse etc.).

dessaouler [DESSOULER].

desséchant [dese'ʃɑ̃], *a.* (*fem.* **-ante**) Drying, parching. **dessèchement**, *n.m.* Drying up; dryness; withering; loss of sensitiveness. **dessécher**, *v.t.* To dry up; to parch; (*fig.*) to wither (the heart etc.); to waste, to emaciate. *Des marais desséchés*, drained marshes; *des ossements desséchés*, dried bones. **se dessécher**, *v.r.* To become dry, to dry up; (*fig.*) to wither, to waste away.

dessein [de'sɛ̃], *n.m.* Design, plan, scheme, purpose, view; intention, intent, resolution. *À bon dessein*, with a good intention; *à dessein*, intentionally; *à dessein de*, in order to; *à dessein que*, that, to the end that; *avoir de grands, desseins*, to have great plans; *avoir dessein de*, to intend; *cacher son dessein*, to hide one's purpose; *changer de dessein*, to alter one's mind; *de dessein prémédité*, of set purpose; *former le dessein de*, to plan to; *sans dessein*, undesignedly, unintentionally.

desseller [dese'le], *v.t.* To unsaddle.

dessemeler [desəm'le], *v.t.* To take soles off (boots etc.).

desserrage [dese'ra:ʒ], *n.m.* Loosening, easing. ***desserre**, *n.f.* Undoing, unfastening (one's purse etc.). *Être dur à la desserre*, to be close-fisted. **desserrer**, *v.t.* To loosen, to relax; to ease; (*Print.*) to unlock. *Je n'ai pas desserré les dents*, I never opened my lips, I never said a word. *Desserrer les freins*, to release brakes. **se desserrer**, *v.r.* To become loose, to relax.

dessert (1) [de'sɛ:r], *n.m.* Dessert. *Au dessert*, at dessert.

dessert (2), *3rd sing. indic.* [DESSERVIR].

desserte [de'sɛrt], *n.f.* Leavings, remains (of a meal); small table or sideboard for receiving these; curé's functions, parochial duty; railway service.

dessertir [desɛr'tiːr], *v.t.* To unset (gems).

desservant [desɛr'vɑ̃], *n.m.* Curé, officiating minister (of a parish etc.).

desservir [desɛr'viːr], *v.t. irr.* (*pres.p.* **desservant**, *p.p.* **desservi**; *conjugated like* SERVIR) To take away plates etc. from, to clear (a table), to remove the cloth from; to officiate in a parish etc. (of clergymen); to ply between (of boats, railways, etc.); (*fig.*) to do someone a disservice, a bad turn. *Il vous a desservi auprès du ministre*, he has done you an ill turn with the minister.

dessiccant [desi'kɑ̃], *a.* (*fem.* **-ante**) Desiccant. **dessiccateur**, *n.m.* Desiccating apparatus. **dessiccatif**, *a.* (*fem.* **-ive**) Desiccative.—*n.m.* A desiccative, desiccant. **dessiccation**, *n.f.* Desiccation.

dessiller or **déciller** [desi'je], *v.t.* To open, to undeceive (eyes etc.). *Dessiller les yeux de quelqu'un*, to undeceive someone. **se dessiller**, *v.r.* To become opened (of eyes).

dessin [de'sɛ̃], *n.m.* Drawing; sketch, draft, plan; pattern, design. *Cette étoffe est d'un joli dessin*, this stuff is of a pretty pattern; *dessin à la craie*, chalk drawing; *dessin à main levée*, free-hand drawing; *dessin à la plume*, pen-and-ink sketch; *dessin d'ornement*, decorative design; *dessin au lavis*, wash drawing; *dessin au trait*, outline drawing; *dessin industriel*, machine drawing; *dessin linéaire*, line drawing; *dessin ombré*, shaded drawing; *dessin animé*, (*Cine.*) cartoon. **dessinateur**, *n.m.* (*fem.* **-trice**) Draughtsman; designer, pattern-drawer. **dessiner**, *v.t.* To draw, to sketch, to delineate; to set off, to show off clearly, to indicate; to trace, to lay out. *Dessiner au crayon*, to draw with a pencil; *dessiner de fantaisie*, *d'après nature*, or *d'après la bosse*, to draw from fancy, from nature, or from the cast; *un vêtement qui dessine bien les formes*, a dress that sets off the figure to advantage. *Une figure bien dessinée*, a well-drawn face; *un jardin bien dessiné*, a garden well laid out. **se dessiner**, *v.r.* To be delineated, to be visible, to stand out; to appear, to take shape, to be conspicuous. *Un clocher se dessina dans la brume*, the outline of a steeple became visible through the mist.

dessolement [desɔl'mɑ̃], *n.m.* Change in the rotation of crops. **dessoler** (1), *v.t.* To change the rotation of crops on.

dessoler (2) [desɔ'le], *v.t.* To take the sole off (a horse etc.).

dessouder [desu'de], *v.t.* To unsolder. **se dessouder**, *v.r.* To come unsoldered.

dessouler [desu'le], *v.t.* (*vulg.*) To sober.—*v.i.* To get sober again. *Il ne dessoule pas*, he is never sober. **se dessouler**, *v.r.* To get sober again.

dessous [də'su], *adv.* Under, underneath, below. *Au-dessous*, below, under, beneath; inferior; *ci-dessous*, underneath, below; after, farther on, below; *en dessous*, in the lower part, (looking) downward, underneath; *là-dessous*, under there; *par-dessous*, under, beneath. *Agir en dessous*, to act slyly; *regarder en dessous*, to look furtively at; *servir par en dessous*, (*Ten.*) to serve underhand. —*n.m.* Lower part, under side; secret or hidden side; wrong side, worst; lee, leeward (of the wind); (*pl.*) underclothing (of women); shady side (of a question). *Le dessous d'une assiette*, bottom of a plate; *un dessous de plat*, table-mat; *un dessous de bouteille*, coaster; *avoir le dessous*, to be worsted, to have the worst of it; *le dessous du vent*, leeward; *voir le dessous des cartes*, to be in the secret, to have been behind the scenes; *un dessous de table*, (*fam.*) money paid to seller in excess of legal price; a gratification.—*prep. phr.* *Cet emploi est au-dessous de lui*, that employment is beneath him; *je suis logé au-dessous de lui*, I have a room below him.

dessus [də'sy], *adv.* On, upon, over, above; uppermost. *Au-dessus*, above, overhead; upwards (of numbers etc.); *bras dessus, bras dessous*, arm in arm; *ci-dessus*, above; *voyez ci-dessus*, see above; *en dessus*, on the upper or right side, in the upper part, above, at or on the top, uppermost; *cela est noir en dessus et blanc en dessous*, it is black on the upper side, and white underneath; *il n'est ni dessus* *ni dessous*, neither one thing nor another; *là-dessus*, on that, on or about this subject, upon this head, thereupon, with these words; *passons là-dessus*, let us dismiss the subject; *vous pouvez compter là-dessus*, you may rely upon that; *par-dessus*, above, over, over and above, besides; *il sauta par-dessus*, he jumped over; *sens dessus dessous*, upside down.—*prep. phr. Cela est au-dessus de ses forces*, that is beyond his strength; *cet homme est au-dessus de la calomnie*, this man is out of the reach of slander; *il a des affaires par-dessus les yeux*, he is up to his eyes in work; *ôtez cela de dessus la table*, take that off the table; *par-dessus le marché*, into the bargain; *par-dessus tout*, above all.—*n.m.* Top, upper part, upper side; right side; cover, lid; upper hand, advantage; weather-gauge, the wind; (*Mus.*) treble. *Avoir* or *prendre le dessus*, to gain the ascendancy or the upper hand, to rally (from illness); *dessus de lit*, bedspread; *dessus de marbre*, marble-top; *le dessus de la main*, the back of the hand; *le dessus de la tête*, the crown of the head; *le dessus d'un livre*, the cover of a book; *le dessus du panier*, (*fig.*) the upper crust, the pick of the bunch; *le dessus du vent*, the weather-gauge.

destin [dɛs'tɛ̃], *n.m.* Destiny, doom, fate; life, career. *On ne peut fuir son destin*, no one can escape his destiny; *Zeus lui-même était soumis au Destin*, Zeus himself was subject to Fate.

destinataire [dɛstina'tɛːr], *n.* Addressee; receiver, recipient; (*Comm.*) consignee; payee.

destination [dɛstina'sjɔ̃], *n.f.* Destination; intention, object, end. *À destination de*, addressed to, bound for; *être rendu à destination*, to have come to the end of the journey; *rendre un immeuble à sa destination primitive*, to turn back a building to its original use.

destinée [dɛsti'ne], *n.f.* Fate, destiny, doom. *Finir sa destinée*, to terminate one's career; *remplir ses destinées*, to fulfil one's destiny.

destiner [dɛsti'ne], *v.t.* To fix, to determine, to destine, to purpose; to reserve (for a particular fate etc.). *À qui destine-t-on un si riche présent?* for whom is so rich a present intended? *il était destiné à périr de cette manière*, he was doomed to perish in this way. **se destiner**, *v.r.* To be destined; to intend oneself. *Il se destine au barreau*, he intends to go in for the law.

destituable [dɛsti'tɥabl], *a.* Removable from office; dismissible

destituer [dɛsti'tɥe], *v.t.* To dismiss, to discharge, to remove (from office). **destitution**, *n.f.* Dismissal, removal (from office).

*destrier [dɛstri'e], *n.m.* Steed, charger, war-horse.

destroyer [dɛstrwa'jœːr], *n.m.* (*Navy*) Destroyer.

destructeur [dɛstryk'tœːr], *a.* (*fem.* **-trice**) Destructive, deadly, ruinous, subversive.—*n.* Destroyer; ravager, spoiler. **destructibilité**, *n.f.* Destructibility. **destructif**, *a.* (*fem.* **-ive**) Destructive, destroying. **destruction**, *n.f.* Destruction.

désuet [desɥ'ɛ], *a.* (*fem.* **-ète**) Obsolete, out-of-date. *Usage désuet*, obsolete custom. **désuétude**, *n.f.* Disuse, desuetude. *Tomber en désuétude*, to fall into disuse, to become obsolete (of words).

désunion [dezy'njɔ̃], *n.f.* Disunion; disjunction, disaccord. **désunir**, *v.t.* To disunite, to disjoin, to part, to separate, to cause to fall out. **se désunir**, *v.r.* To disunite, to come asunder; to fall out.

détachage [deta'ʃaːʒ], *n.m.* Cleaning, scouring, removal of spots, stains, etc.

détachant [deta'ʃɑ̃], *n.m.* Cleaner, stain-remover.

détaché [deta'ʃe], *a.* (*fem.* **-ée**) Detached; isolated; indifferent; (*Mus.*) staccato. *Fonctionnaire détaché*, seconded civil servant; *morceaux détachés*, extracts; *prendre un air détaché*, to look unconcerned.

détachement [detaʃ'mɑ̃], *n.m.* Indifference, unconcern; (*Mil.*) detachment, draft, party.

détacher (1) [deta'ʃe], *v.t.* To remove stains, spots, etc.

détacher (2) [deta'ʃe], *v.t.* To detach, to untie, to unfasten; to undo, to separate, to cut off; to deal (a blow); (*Mil.*) to detail; to second; to render conspicuous. *Détacher une agrafe*, to undo a clasp; *détacher une épingle*, to take out a pin. *Détacher un soufflet à quelqu'un*, to give someone a box on the ear. **se détacher**, *v.r.* To come unfastened, to get loose, to come undone; to detach oneself, to disengage oneself; to break away or off, to come off or away; to stand out clearly. *Se détacher d'une femme*, to break off with a woman; *se détacher du jeu*, to leave off gambling.

détail [de'taj], *n.m.* Division into parts, particulars, etc.; retail; complete enumeration, detailed account; detail, small matter, trifle, particular, circumstance. *En détail*, minutely, piecemeal, bit by bit; *je n'ai omis aucun des détails*, I omitted none of the circumstances; *vendre au détail*, to sell by retail. **détaillant**, *a.* (*fem.* **-ante**) Retailer, small dealer. **détaillé**, *a.* (*fem.* **-ée**) Detailed, circumstantial (account, narrative). **détailler**, *v.t.* To cut in pieces, to retail, to sell by retail; to detail, to relate minutely. **se détailler**, *v.r.* To be cut up, to be related minutely; to be related.

détaler [deta'le], *v.i.* (*fam.*) To be off, to decamp, to take oneself off.

détalinguer [detalɛ̃'ge], *v.t.* (*Naut.*) To unbend (a cable).

détaper [deta'pe], *v.t.* (*Artill.*) To take the tampion out of (a gun).

détartrer [detar'tre], *v.t.* To scale (a boiler); to decarbonize (an engine). **détartreur**, *n.m.* Descaling device.

détaxation [detaksa'sjɔ̃], *n.f.* Decontrol (of prices). **détaxe**, *n.f.* Reduction of tax. **détaxer**, *v.t.* To reduce or take off a tax; to decontrol.

détecter [detɛk'te], *v.t.* To detect. **détecteur**, *n.m.* Appliance for detecting fire-damp in coal-mines; (*Elec.*) detector; (*Mil.*) mine detector. **détection**, *n.f.* Detection.

détective [detɛk'tiːv], *n.m.* Detective.

déteindre [de'tɛ̃ːdr], *v.t. irr.* (*pres.p.* **déteignant**, *p.p.* **déteint**; *conjug. like* CRAINDRE) To take the dye or colour out of.—*v.i.* To lose colour, to fade; to come off (of colours). *Cette étoffe déteint beaucoup*, this stuff fades very much. *Déteindre sur quelqu'un*, (*fig.*) to influence someone (*usu. pej.*).

se déteindre, *v.r.* To lose colour, to fade; to come off (of colours).

dételage [de'tla:ʒ], *n.m.* Taking out of harness, unharnessing. **dételer,** *v.t.* To unharness, to unhook, to unyoke; (*fig.*) to give up (a gay life), to ease off.

détendeur [detɑ̃'dœ:r], *n.m.* Pressure-reducer.

détendre [de'tɑ̃:dr], *v.t.* To slacken, to relax, to loosen; to reduce the pressure of; to take down, to unhang. *Détendre son esprit,* to relax one's mind; *détendre un arc,* to unbend a bow. *Détendre une tapisserie,* to take down a set of hangings; *détendre une tente,* to strike a tent. **se détendre,** *v.r.* To slacken, to unbend, to become easier. **détendu,** *a.* (*fem.* **-ue**) Slack; relaxed (mind, atmosphere).

détenir [det'ni:r], *v.t. irr.* (*pres.p.* **détenant,** *p.p.* **détenu;** *conjugated like* TENIR) To detain, to withhold, to keep back; to confine. *Détenir quelqu'un en prison,* to keep someone in prison.

détente [de'tɑ̃:t], *n.f.* Trigger (of a gun etc.); detent, stop (of a clock etc.); expansion, cut-off (of an engine); calm, relaxation, easing. *Presser sur la détente,* to press the trigger; *être dur à la détente,* (*colloq.*) to be close-fisted; to be reluctant; *il y a une sorte de détente dans les esprits,* public tension has slackened somewhat; *machine à détente,* expansion-engine. **détenteur,** *n.* (*fem.* **-trice**) Holder, detainer. **détention,** *n.f.* Detention, detainment, withholding; imprisonment. *Détention illégale,* unlawful possession. **détenu,** *a.* (*fem.* **détenue**) Detained, imprisoned.—*n.* Prisoner.

détergent [deter'ʒɑ̃], *a.* (*fem.* **-ente**) (*Med.*) Detergent.—*n.m.* A detergent. **déterger,** *v.t.* To cleanse, to purify. *Déterger une plaie,* to cleanse a wound.

détérioration [deterjɔra'sjɔ̃], *n.f.* Deterioration; wear and tear, dilapidations. **détériorer,** *v.t.* To dilapidate, to impair, to make worse. **se détériorer,** *v.r.* To deteriorate, to become defaced, debased, or the worse for wear.

déterminabilité [determinabili'te], *n.f.* Determinability. **déterminable,** *a.* Determinable. **déterminant,** *a.* (*fem.* **-ante**) Determinative, decisive, conclusive.—*n.m.* (*Math.*) Determinant. **déterminatif,** *a.* (*fem.* **-ive**) (*Gram.*) Determinative.—*n.m.* Determinative word.

détermination [determina'sjɔ̃], *n.f.* Determination, resolution, decision; resolute character. **déterminé,** *a.* (*fem.* **-ée**) Determined, decided, fixed, resolved on; resolute, firm. *Il est déterminé à tout,* he is ready for anything. *Un sens déterminé,* a definitive meaning.

déterminer [determi'ne], *v.t.* To determine, to settle, to fix; to ascertain; to decide, to resolve; to cause to take a resolution; to fix the meaning of; to lead to, to cause, to bring about. *C'est moi qui l'ai déterminé à cela,* it was I who made him take that resolve; *déterminer les bénéfices,* to apportion the profits. **se déterminer,** *v.r.* To resolve, to determine, to make up one's mind. *Je ne puis me déterminer à rien,* I cannot resolve upon anything. **déterminisme,** *n.m.* (*Phil.*)

Determinism. **déterministe,** *n.* Determinist.

déterré [detɛ're], *n.m.* Person dug up or disinterred. *Avoir l'air d'un déterré,* to look like one risen from the dead; *il a l'air d'un déterré,* he is as pale as a ghost. **déterrer,** *v.t.* To dig up, to disinter, to discover, to unearth, to bring to light, to ferret out. **déterreur,** *n.m.* Hunter out, ferreter.

détersif [deter'sif], *a.* (*fem.* **-ive**) (*Med.*) Detersive, detergent, cleansing.—*n.m.* A detergent.

détestable [detɛs'tabl], *a.* Detestable, hateful, odious; wretchedly bad, wretched. **détestablement,** *adv.* Detestably, abominably. **détestation,** *n.f.* Detestation, abhorrence. **détester,** *v.t.* To detest, to hate, to abhor, to execrate. *Je déteste d'attendre,* I hate to wait.

détirer [deti're], *v.t.* To draw out, to stretch, to wire-draw. *Détirer des cuirs,* to stretch hides; *détirer une étoffe,* to pull out a material.

détisser [deti'se], *v.t.* To unweave.

détitrer [deti'tre], *v.t.* To distitle, to deprive (of a title); to lower the title of coinage, the grade of a liquor.

détonant [detɔ'nɑ̃], *a.* (*fem.* **-ante**) Detonating.—*n.m.* Explosive. **détonateur,** *n.m.* Detonator. **détonation,** *n.f.* Detonation, report. *À détonation,* detonating. **détoner,** *v.i.* To detonate.

détonneler [detɔn'le], *v.t.* To draw from a cask.

détonner [detɔ'ne], *v.i.* To be out of tune, to play or sing out of tune; to be discordant, to jar.

détordre [de'tɔrdr], *v.t.* To untwist; to unwring; to unravel. **se détordre,** *v.r.* To come untwisted.

détors [de'tɔ:r], *a.* (*fem.* **détorse**) Untwisted.

détortiller [detɔrti'je], *v.t.* To untwist; to unravel. **se détortiller,** *v.r.* To become untwisted; to be unravelled.

détoucher [detu'ʃe], *v.t.* (*Naut.*) To get off (a ship that has grounded).—**v.i.* To get afloat again.

détouper [detu'pe], *v.t.* To unstop, to take the bung out of; to clear of brambles.

détour [de'tu:r], *n.m.* Turning, wind, change of direction; roundabout way, circuitous road; (*fig.*) shift, evasion, trick. *Au détour d'un chemin,* at the bend of a road; *être sans détour,* to be sincere, straightforward; *faire un grand détour,* to come a long way round; *quel détour vous avez fait!* what a roundabout way you have come! *User de détours,* to resort to shifts and evasions.

détourné [detur'ne], *a.* (*fem.* **-ée**) Out of the way, retired, unfrequented, sequestered; crooked, indirect, roundabout. *Des chemins détournés,* by-ways. *Voie détournée,* indirect means. **détournement,** *n.m.* Turning away, turning aside; embezzlement, misappropriation. *Détournement de mineur,* (*Law*) abduction or seduction of a minor.

détourner [detur'ne], *v.t.* To change the direction of, to turn away, to turn aside; to lead astray; to divert, to avert, to ward off; to embezzle, to misappropriate; to deter, to dissuade. *Cela me détourne de mes occupations,* that distracts me from my business;

détourner la conversation (*du sujet principal sur une question accessoire*), to draw a red herring across the path. *Détourner la vue*, to turn the eyes away; *détourner un coup*, to avert a blow. *On l'accuse d'avoir détourné ces fonds*, he is accused of having embezzled this sum.—*v.i.* To turn, to turn off. **se détourner**, *v.r.* To turn away, to turn aside, to swerve; to leave, to abandon (*de*). *Se détourner de son devoir*, to swerve from one's duty; *se détourner de son travail*, to leave one's work.

détracteur [detrak'tœːr], *n.m.* (*fem.* **-trice**) Detractor, disparager.—*a.* Detractive, detracting.

détraqué [detra'ke], *n.m.* (*fem.* **-ée**) Person shattered in mind or body.—*a.* Out of order; deranged. **détraquement** [detrak'mã], *n.m.* Breakdown (mechanism, mind, health).

détraquer [detra'ke], *v.t.* To spoil (a horse's) paces, to throw (a horse) out of his paces; (*fig.*) to disorder, to put out of order; to throw into confusion. **se détraquer**, *v.r.* To lose its paces (of a horse); (*fig.*) to get out of order, to be disordered. *Cette montre se détraque*, this watch is out of order; *sa tête se détraque*, his brain is disordered; *il se détraque l'estomac*, he wrecks his digestion.

détrempe [de'trãːp], *n.f.* Distemper, painting in distemper. *Ouvrage en détrempe*, a poor copy of another work. **détremper**, *v.t.* To dilute, to dissolve, to moisten; (*fig.*) to weaken, to enervate. *Détremper de l'acier*, to soften steel; *détremper de la farine avec des œufs*, to beat up flour with eggs; *détremper des couleurs*, to dilute colours; *détremper de la chaux*, to slake lime.

détresse [de'trɛs], *n.f.* Distress, grief, trouble, anguish; straits. *J'eus pitié de sa détresse*, I took compassion on his sorrow; *il est dans la détresse*, he is in financial difficulties.

détresser [detre'se], *v.t.* To unravel; to unplait.

détriment [detri'mã], *n.m.* Detriment, injury, prejudice; (*Nat. Hist.*) debris, remains. *Au détriment de*, to the prejudice of.

détritage [detri'taːʒ], *n.m.* Crushing (of olives). **détriter**, *v.t.* To crush. **détrition**, *n.f.* Detrition. **détritique**, *a.* Detrital. **détritoir**, *n.m.* Crushing-mill.

détritus [detri'tys], *n.m.* Detritus, residue, refuse; offal.

détroit [de'trwa], *n.m.* Strait, channel, sound, narrow firth.

détromper [detrɔ'pe], *v.t.* To undeceive. **se détromper**, *v.r.* To be undeceived.

détrônement [detron'mã], *n.m.* Dethronement. **détrôner**, *v.t.* To dethrone. **détrôneur**, *n.m.* Dethroner.

détrousser [detru'se], *v.t.* To untruss, to untuck, to let down; (*fig.*) to rifle, to rob. *Détrousser les voyageurs*, to plunder travellers. **détrousseur**, *n.m.* (*fem.* **-euse**) Highwayman, robber; (*fam.*) seducer (of women).

détruire [de'trɥiːr], *v.t. irr.* (*pres.p.* **détruisant**, *p.p.* **détruit**; *conjugated like* CONDUIRE) To destroy, to demolish, to ruin; to exterminate, to do away with, to efface, to suppress. *Détruire la santé*, to ruin the health. *Détruire radicalement*, to eradicate. *Détruire une armée*, to overthrow an army; *détruire une ville de fond en comble*, to raze a town to the ground.

se détruire, *v.r.* To fall into ruin or decay; to destroy each other, to neutralize one another; (*pop.*) to destroy oneself, to make away with oneself.

détruisant, détruit [DÉTRUIRE].

dette [dɛt], *n.f.* Debt; obligation, indebtedness. *Contracter* or *faire des dettes*, to contract debts, to run into debt; *dette d'honneur*, debt of honour; *dette hypothécaire*, debt upon mortgage; *dettes passives*, liabilities; *être accablé, perdu*, or *criblé de dettes*, to be up to one's neck in debt, to be riddled with debt; *la dette publique*, the national debt.

deuil [dœ:j], *n.m.* Mourning; grief, sorrow; gloom, mournful aspect; period of mourning; bereavement, mourning clothes, colours, etc.; funeral cortège. *Faire prendre le deuil à*, to put into mourning; *faire son deuil d'une chose*, to resign oneself to the loss of anything; *grand deuil*, deep mourning; *habit de deuil*, mourning; *deuil de veuve*, widow's weeds; *porter le deuil de quelqu'un*, to wear mourning for someone; *le deuil de la nature*, the gloom or sadness of nature; *ongles en deuil*, dirty finger-nails; *personne qui mène le deuil*, chief mourner; *suivre le deuil*, to be one of the mourners; *voiture de deuil*, mourning-coach.

Deutéronome [døterɔ'nɔm], *n.m.* Deuteronomy.

deux [dø], *a.* Two, both; second. *Couper en deux*, to cut in two; *deux à deux*, two by two; *deux avis valent mieux qu'un*, two heads are better than one; *deux fois*, twice; *deux fois autant*, twice as much, twice as many; *en moins de deux*, in a jiffy; (*fam.*) *entre les deux*, so-so; *être entre deux vins*, to be half-seasover; *Henri deux*, Henry the Second; *maintenant à nous deux*, now I am ready for you, now we'll have it out together; *ne faire ni une ni deux*, (*colloq.*) to decide at once; *piquer des deux*, to clap spurs to one's horse; *regarder quelqu'un entre deux yeux*, to stare at someone; *tous deux*, both together; *tous les deux*, both; *tous les deux mois*, every other month; *un mot qui s'écrit avec deux 'l'*, a word which is spelt with double 'l'.—*n.m.* Two; second (of the month); (*Cards, Dice, etc.*) deuce. *Le deux de carreau*, the two of diamonds; *le deux du mois*, the second of the month; (*Ten.*) *à deux*, deuce; *à deux encore*, deuce again; *à deux de jeux*, five all; *on peut faire cela à deux*, two can play at that game. **deuxième**, *a.* Second.—*n.m.* Second floor. **deuxièmement**, *adv.* Secondly.

deux-pièces [dø'pjɛs], *n.m. inv.* (Women's) two-piece suit.

deux-points [dø'pwɛ̃], *n.m. inv.* (*Print.*) Colon.

dévaler [deva'le], *v.t.* To descend, to go or come down; to let down, to lower. *Dévaler du vin à la cave*, to let wine down into the cellar; *dévaler les degrés*, to hurry downstairs.—*v.i.* To descend, to slope; to go or rush down (of streams etc.).

dévaliser [devali'ze], *v.t.* To rifle, to strip, to rob. **dévaliseur**, *n.m.* (*fem.* **-euse**) Thief, burglar.

dévalorisation [devalɔriza'sjɔ̃], *n.f.* Loss in value. **dévaloriser**, *v.t.* To lose in value.

dévaluation [devalɥa'sjɔ̃], *n.f.* Devaluation. **dévaluer**, *v.t.* To devaluate. **dévaluateur**, *a.* (*fem.* **-trice**) *Mesure dévaluatrice*, devaluation measure.

devancer [dəvɑ̃'se], *v.t.* To precede, to go before; to get before, to outrun, to outstrip; to have precedence of; to forestall, to anticipate; to surpass, to outdo. *Devancer l'ennemi*, to forestall the enemy; *devancer l'appel*, to enlist before conscription; *j'allais vous voir, mais vous m'avez devancé*, I was going to see you but you have forestalled me. **devancier, n.m.** (*fem.* **-ière**) Predecessor; (*pl.*) ancestors, forefathers.

devant [də'vɑ̃], *prep.* Before; in front of, over against, opposite to; previous or anterior to. *Il marchait devant moi*, he walked before me; *ils passent par devant chez nous*, they pass our door; *quand il fut devant ses juges*, when he was in the presence of his judges; *regarder devant soi*, to look before one *or* ahead. —*prep. phr. Aller au-devant des désirs de quelqu'un*, to anticipate someone's wishes; *aller au-devant d'une chose*, to prevent something; *aller, venir, or envoyer au-devant de quelqu'un*, to go, come, or send to meet someone, (*fig.*) to meet half-way, to meet, to encounter, to provide for or against, to oppose, to obviate.—*adv.* In front, before, ahead. *Passez devant*, go before; *être blessé par devant*, to receive a wound in front; *sens devant derrière*, hind part foremost. —*n.m.* Front, the forepart. *Devant d'autel*, frontal (of an altar); *devant de cheminée*, firescreen; *devant de chemise*, shirt front; *il est logé sur le devant*, he lodges in the front; *les jambes de devant*, the forelegs. *Prendre le devant or les devants*, to set out before, to get before, to forestall; *un ci-devant*, (*Fr. Hist.*) an ex-noble.

devanture [dəvɑ̃'tyːr], *n.f.* Front(age) (of a building). *Devanture (de magasin)*, shopfront, shop-window.

dévaser [devɑ'ze], *v.t.* To dredge, clear of silt.

dévastateur [devasta'tœːr], *n.m.* (*fem.* **-trice**) Devastator, despoiler, ravager.—*a.* Devastating, destructive. **dévastation, n.f.** Devastation, ravage, havoc. **dévaster, v.t.** To devastate, to lay waste, to desolate, to ravage.

déveine [de'vɛːn], *n.f.* (*fam.*) (Run of) ill-luck. *Quelle déveine!* what ill-luck!

développable [devlɔ'pabl], *a.* Susceptible of development. **développante, a.** and *n.f.* (*Geom.*) Involute.

développement [devlɔp'mɑ̃], *n.m.* Unfolding, opening; development, growth, progress; (*Mil.*) deployment; (*Cycl.*) distance covered in one revolution of the pedals; gear. *Sa bicyclette a un développement de 5 mètres*, his bicycle is geared to 58 inches.

développer [devlɔ'pe], *v.t.* To open, to unwrap, to unfold; to expand, to display, to expound, to elucidate, to explain; to develop; (*Cycle*) to cover (a certain distance) in one revolution of the pedals; to have a gear of. *Développer le plan d'un ouvrage*, to explain the plan of a work; (*Phot.*) *développer une pellicule*, to develop a negative; *développer un système*, to expound a system. **se développer,** *v.r.* To expand, to unfold, to be unfolded or displayed; to be cleared up, to be unravelled; to extend, to spread out, to be stretched out; to develop. *Cet enfant se développe*, that child is growing; *la raison se*

développe, reason is asserting itself; *les bourgeons commencent à se développer*, the buds are beginning to expand.

devenir [dəv'niːr], *v.i. irr.* (*pres.p.* **devenant,** *p.p.* **devenu;** conjugated like VENIR) To become, to grow, to get, to turn into. *Cela commence à devenir fatigant*, that begins to grow tiresome; *ces fruits deviennent rouges en mûrissant*, those fruits turn red when ripening; *faire devenir fou*, to drive one mad; *je ne sais ce qu'il est devenu*, I don't know what has become of him; *je ne sais que devenir*, I don't know which way to turn; *que deviendrai-je?* what will become of me? *qu'est devenu votre frère?* what has become of your brother? *que voulez-vous devenir?* what do you intend to be?—*n.m.* Gradual development (of beings or of things), their ēvolution or process. *Le devenir de l'homme*, the evolution of man.

déventer [devɑ̃'te], *v.t.* (*Naut.*) To take the wind out (of sails); to shiver.

devenu, *p.p.* (*fem.* **devenue**) [DEVENIR].

dévergondage [devɛrgɔ̃'daːʒ], *n.m.* Shamelessness; profligacy, dissoluteness. **dévergondé, a.** (*fem.* **-ée**) Abandoned, shameless; profligate; extravagant. **se dévergonder,** *v.r.* To become dissolute.

déverrouillement [devɛruj'mɑ̃], *n.m.* Unbolting. **déverrouiller, v.t.** To unbolt; (*fig.*) to set free.

devers [də'vɛːr], *prep.* Towards. *Il a les papiers par devers lui*, he is possessed of the papers; *par devers*, in the presence of, in one's possession; *par devers la loi*, in the eyes of the law.

dévers [de'vɛːr], *a.* (*fem.* **déverse**) Inclined, leaning, bending, out of the vertical or of alignment. *Ce mur est dévers*, that wall juts out.—*n.m.* Inclination, bending; warping; discharge, overflow (of water from a canal etc.).

déverser [devɛr'se], *v.i.* To lean, to incline, to jut out; to warp.—*v.t.* To bend, to incline; to throw, to dump; to pour out (water etc.). *Déverser le mépris*, to throw contempt (upon someone); *déverser une pièce de bois*, to bend a piece of wood. **se déverser,** *v.r.* To fall, to empty (of rivers, canals, etc.). **déversoir,** *n.m.* Overflow (of a canal etc.); outfall, overfall; (*fig.*) outlet (for energy).

dévêtir [deve'tiːr], *v.t. irr.* (*pres.p.* **dévêtant,** *p.p.* **dévêtu;** conjugated like VÊTIR) To undress, to strip of clothes; to strip off; (*Law*) to divest. **se dévêtir,** *v.r.* To take off one's clothes, to undress, to strip; to divest oneself. *Se dévêtir d'un héritage*, to give up an inheritance.

déviation [devja'sjɔ̃], *n.f.* Deviation, deflexion; diversion (of a road). *Déviation de la colonne vertébrale*, curvature of the spine. **déviationnisme, n.m.** (*Polit.*) Deviationism. **déviationniste, n.** Deviationist.

dévidage [devi'daːʒ], *n.m.* Winding or reeling off. **dévider, v.t.** To wind off (into skeins etc.); (*fig.*) to explain. *Dévider toute son affaire*, to unfold the whole story. **dévideur, n.m.** (*fem.* **-euse**) Winder, reeler. **dévidoir, n.m.** Reel, skein-winder, spool.

dévier [de'vje], *v.i.* (conjugated like PRIER) To deviate, to turn aside; to swerve; to glance off.—*v.t.* To cause to deviate or swerve. **se dévier,** *v.r.* To deviate, to swerve; to become crooked (of spine). *Se dévier de son chemin*, to deviate from one's road.

devin [də'vɛ̃], *n.m.* (*fem.* **devineresse**) Diviner, augur, soothsayer; fortune-teller. *Serpent devin*, boa-constrictor.

deviner [dəvi'ne], *v.t.* To divine, to foretell, to predict; to guess, to conjecture; to understand, to fathom. *Cela se devine*, it is easily imaginable, you can see it at a glance; *devinez ce que j'ai fait*, guess what I have done; *deviner juste*, to guess correctly; *deviner mal*, to be off the mark; *en devinant*, at a guess. **se deviner,** *v.r.* To understand each other. **devinette,** *n.f.* Poser, riddle, conundrum. **devineur,** *n.m.* (*fem.* **devineuse**) Guesser.

dévirer [devi're], *v.t.* (*Naut.*) To heave back, unwind (the capstan).

devis [də'vi], *n.m.* Estimate; specification, bill of quantities. *Avant de commander un travail, demandez un devis*, before ordering any work, ask for an estimate.

dévisager [deviza'ʒe], *v.t.* To disfigure, to scratch the face of; to stare someone down.

devise [də'viːz], *n.f.* Device, emblem; motto, slogan; (*Fin.*) currency. *Des devises étrangères*, foreign currency; *devise forte*, hard currency.

deviser [dəvi'ze], *v.i.* To talk casually, to chat.

dévissage [devi'saːʒ] or **dévissement,** *n.m.* Unscrewing. **dévisser,** *v.t.* To unscrew. **se dévisser,** *v.r.* To come unscrewed.

dévitaliser [devitali'ze], *v.t.* To kill the nerve (tooth etc.).

dévitrification [devitrifika'sjɔ̃], *n.f.* Devitrification. **dévitrifier,** *v.t.* To devitrify.

dévoiement [devwa'mɑ̃], *n.m.* Looseness, relaxation (of the bowels); (*Arch.*) inclination, slope; (*fig.*) a departure from the normal path.

dévoilement [devwal'mɑ̃], *n.m.* Unveiling, disclosure. **dévoiler,** *v.t.* To unveil, to discover, to reveal, to disclose. **se dévoiler,** *v.t.* To unveil, to be revealed.

dévoîment [DÉVOIEMENT].

devoir (1) [də'vwaːr], *v.t. irr.* (*pres.p.* **devant,** *p.p.* **dû**) (*a*) (*debt*) To owe (money, gratitude); (*b*) (*foll. by inf.*) (*compulsion, duty*) to be obliged to, to be bound to, to have to, must; (*c*) (*future*) to be to; (*d*) (*probability*) must. (*a*) *Devoir une somme d'argent à quelqu'un*, to owe someone a sum of money; *il doit au tiers et au quart*, he owes money right and left; *je lui dois tout*, I owe everything to him. (*b*) *Fais ce que dois, advienne que pourra*, do your duty, come what may; *il ne devrait pas abandonner ses parents*, he ought not to forsake his parents; *nous devons obéir aux lois*, we must obey the laws; *vous auriez dû vous conduire autrement*, you should have behaved otherwise. (*c*) *Dussé-je le regretter plus tard*, were I to regret it later; *il devait mourir*, he was fated to die; *il devait partir ce matin*, he was to have set out this morning; *il doit partir dans quelques jours*, he is to set out in a few days; *je dois parler sur ce sujet*, I am to speak on that subject; *le train doit arriver à deux heures*, the train is due at two. (*d*) *Il a dû quitter Londres ce matin*, he must have left London this morning; *il doit être riche aujourd'hui*, he must be a rich man now;

la campagne doit être belle maintenant, the country must be beautiful now. **se devoir,** *v.r.* To owe oneself; to owe it to oneself. *Cela ne se doit pas*, that is not right, that ought not to be; *on se doit d'être honorable*, a man owes it to himself to be honourable.

devoir (2) [də'vwaːr], *n.m.* Duty; (*sch.*) work set, homework; (*pl.*) respects, compliments. *J'irai lui rendre mes devoirs*, I shall go and pay my respects to him; *les derniers devoirs*, funeral rites. *Manquer à son devoir*, to fail in one's duty; *rentrer dans son devoir*, to return to one's duty; *s'acquitter de son devoir*, to perform one's duty; *se faire un devoir de*, to make a point of; *se mettre en devoir de faire une chose*, to set about doing a thing.

dévoltage [devɔl'taːʒ], *n.m.* (*Elec.*) Reduction of voltage. **dévolter,** *v.t.* To reduce the voltage, to step down (current). **dévolteur,** *n.m.* Reducing transformer.

dévolu [devɔ'ly], *a.* (*Law*) Devolved, vested; fallen (to); escheated. *Terre dévolue à la couronne*, an escheat; *une tâche qui m'est dévolue*, a task which has fallen to me.—*n.m.* Choice, preference; (*Eccles.*) lapse (of right). *J'ai jeté mon dévolu sur cela*, I have fixed my choice upon that; *un bénéfice tombe en dévolu*, a benefice fallen into lapse of right. **dévolution,** *n.f.* Devolution; escheat.

dévonien [devɔ'njɛ̃], *a.* (*fem.* **-ienne**) (*Geol.*) Devonian.

dévorant [devɔ'rɑ̃], *a.* (*fem.* **-ante**) Devouring, ravenous; (*fig.*) consuming, wasting. *Appétit dévorant*, ravenous appetite. *Chaleur dévorante*, wasting heat; *soif dévorante*, burning thirst; *un mal dévorant*, a wasting disease. **dévorateur,** *a.* (*fem.* **-trice**) Devouring.—*n.* Devourer, destroyer.

dévorer [devɔ're], *v.t.* To devour, to eat up greedily; to destroy, to consume; to dissipate, to squander; to gaze at eagerly, to gloat upon; to pore over; to swallow (an insult etc.). *Dévorer un livre*, to devour a book; *dévorer quelqu'un des yeux*, to gaze at someone passionately or greedily; *dévorer sa douleur*, to stifle one's sorrow; *dévorer un affront*, to swallow an affront; *il a dévoré tout son bien*, he has squandered all his fortune; *il est dévoré d'ambition*, he is consumed with ambition; *il dévore les kilomètres*, he eats up the miles. ***dévoreur,** *n.m.* (*fem.* **-euse**) Devourer; glutton. *Dévoreur de livres*, bookworm.

dévot [de'vo], *a.* (*fem.* **dévote**) Devout, pious; sanctimonious; devoted; holy (of books etc.). *Avoir l'air dévot*, to look sanctimonious.—*n.* Devout person, devotee; sanctimonious person, bigot. *Ne vous y fiez pas, c'est un faux dévot*, put no trust in him, he is a hypocrite. **dévotement** or **dévotieusement,** *adv.* Devoutly, piously. **dévotieux,** *a.* (*fem.* **-ieuse**) Ostensibly devout.

dévotion [devo'sjɔ̃], *n.f.* Devotion, piety, disposal, service, command; devoutness; devotedness. *Donner dans la dévotion*, to become a devotee; *faire ses dévotions*, to perform one's devotions; *tout ce qu'il a est à ma dévotion*, all he has is at my disposal.

dévouement or **dévoûment** [devu'mɑ̃], *n.m.* Self-devotion, self-sacrifice, self-immolation; devotion, devotedness, attachment; zeal. **dévouer,** *v.t.* To devote, to offer up, to dedicate, to consecrate; to consign, to give up (to). *Dévouer quelqu'un au mépris*, to consign someone to contempt. *Il lui est entièrement dévoué*, he is entirely devoted, loyal, to him; *votre bien* (or *votre tout*) *dévoué*, yours truly or sincerely. **se dévouer,** *v.r.* To devote oneself; to dedicate oneself; to sacrifice or risk one's life. *Se dévouer à la patrie*, to give up oneself for one's country. **dévoyé** [devwaˈje], *a.* (*fem.* -ée) Stray, gone astray.—*n.* Black sheep. **dévoyer,** *v.t. irr.* (*conjugated like* ABOYER) To corrupt, to lead astray; (*Arch.*) to place obliquely; to cause looseness (of the bowels). **se dévoyer,** *v.r.* (*fig.*) To leave the straight and narrow path, to become corrupted.

déwatté [dewaˈte], *a.* (*Elec.*) Wattless. *Courant déwatté*, wattless current.

dextérité [dɛksteriˈte], *n.f.* Dexterity, adroitness, skill. ***dextre,** *a.* Skilful; (*Her.*) dexter.—*n.f.* The right hand. ***dextrement,** *adv.* Dexterously.

dextrine [dɛksˈtrin], *n.f.* Dextrin.

dextrorsum [dɛkstrɔrˈsɔm], *a.* Dextrorse.— *adv.* Clockwise (direction).

dextrose [dɛksˈtroːz], *n.f.* Dextrose, glucose.

dey [de], *n.m.* Dey.

dia! [dja], *int.* Hoi! (to make horses turn to the left) (*Am.*) Haw! *Il n'entend ni à dia ni à hue*, there is no making him hear reason; *l'un tire à dia et l'autre à hue*, they pull different ways.

diabase [djaˈbaːz], *n.m.* Diabase, green-stone.

diabète [djaˈbɛt], *n.m.* Diabetes. *Diabète sucré*, diabetes mellitus. **diabétique,** *a.* Diabetic.

diable [djaːbl], *n.m.* Devil; wayward child; deuce, dickens; fellow, wretch; jack-in-the-box; machine for carding raw cotton, hair, etc.; luggage-truck; drag. *Allé au diable*, gone to the devil; *au diable!* *au diable soit de*, or *le diable l'emporte*, the devil take it; *c'est au diable vert*, it's miles away, the back of beyond; *cela ne coûte pas le diable*, that is not expensive; *c'est là le diable*, there's the rub; *c'est le diable à confesser*, it is terribly hard to do; *c'est une diable d'affaire*, it is a confounded business; *elle est très diable*, she is a regular tomboy; *faire le diable à quatre*, to play the devil, to kick up a shindy; *faire un bruit de tous les diables*, to make a devil of a din; *habillé à la diable*, dressed anyhow; *il a le diable au corps*, the devil is in him; *il est très diable*, he is full of spirit, of mischief; *le beauté du diable*, youth and freshness; *le diable bat sa femme et marie sa fille*, it rains and shines at the same time; *le diable s'en mêle*, the devil is in it; *quel diable d'homme est-ce là?* what devil of a fellow is this? *tirer le diable par la queue*, to be hard up; *un bon diable*, a good-natured fellow; *un méchant diable*, a mischievous dog; *un pauvre diable*, a poor wretch; *un ragoût à la diable*, an awful concoction; *va t'en au diable*, go to the devil.—*int.* The devil, the deuce, confound it! hang it! *À quoi diable s'amuse-t-il?* what the deuce is he about? *comment diable!* how the devil! *de quoi diable se mêle-t-il?* why on earth doesn't he mind his own business? *que diable avez-vous?* what the devil is the matter with you?—*n.m.* **Diable-de-mer** [BAUDROIE]. (*C*) *Diable des bois*, wolverine.—*adv. phr.*

Méchant en diable, extremely malicious. **diablement,** *adv.* Devilishly. **diablerie,** *n.f.* Devilry, diabolism, witchcraft; mischief (of children). **diablesse,** *n.f.* She-devil; shrew, vixen. *Une pauvre diablesse*, a poor wretch. **diablotin,** *n.m.* Imp, little devil; troublesome imp; (Christmas) cracker; (*Naut.*) stay-sail. **diabolique,** *a.* Diabolical, devilish. **diaboliquement,** *adv.* Diabolically, devilishly.

diabolo [djaboˈlo], *n.m.* Diabolo.

diachylon [djaʃiˈlɔ̃] or **diachylum,** *n.m.* Diachylon.

diacode [djaˈkɔd], *n.m.* Syrup of white poppy heads.

diaconal [djakɔˈnal], *a.* (*fem.* -ale, *pl.* -aux) Diaconal. **diaconat,** *n.m.* Diaconate, deaconry, deacon's orders. **diaconesse,** *n.f.* Deaconess.

diacre [djakr], *n.m.* Deacon.

diacritique [djakriˈtik], *a.* Diacritical.

diadelphe [djaˈdɛlf], *a.* (*Bot.*) Diadelphous.

diadème [djaˈdɛːm], *n.m.* Diadem; coronet.

diadoque [djaˈdɔk], *n.m.* *One of the diadochi; (in Greece) the heir apparent.

diagnose [djagˈnoːz], *n.f.* (Art of) Diagnosis. **diagnostic,** *n.m.* Diagnosis. **diagnostique,** *a.* Diagnostic. **diagnostiquer,** *v.t.* To diagnose.

diagonal [djagɔˈnal], *a.* (*fem.* -ale, *pl.* -aux) Diagonal.—*n.f.* Diagonal; cloth with diagonal rib; twill. **diagonalement,** *adv.* Diagonally.

diagramme [djaˈgram], *n.m.* Diagram.

diagraphe [djaˈgraf], *n.m.* Diagraph.

dialecte, *n.m.* Dialect.

dialectal [djalɛkˈtal], *a.* (*fem.* -ale, *pl.* -aux) Dialect, dialectal.

dialecticien [djalɛktiˈsjɛ̃], *n.m.* Dialectician.

dialectique [djalɛkˈtik], *a.* Dialectical.—*n.f.* Dialectics, logic. *La dialectique marxiste*, Marxist dialectics. **dialectiquement,** *adv.* Dialectically.

dialogique [djalɔˈʒik], *a.* Dialogic.

dialogue [djaˈlɔg], *n.m.* Dialogue, colloquy. **dialoguer,** *v.i.* To converse, to chat.—*v.t.* To write in dialogue form. *Dialoguer un roman*, to turn a novel into a play; *une scène bien dialoguée*, a scene with a good dialogue. **dialoguiste,** *n.m.* (*Cine.*) Dialogue-writer.

dialyse [djaˈliːz], *n.f.* Dialysis. **dialyser,** *v.t.* To dialyse. **dialyseur,** *n.m.* Dialyser.

diamagnétique [djamaɲeˈtik], *a.* Diamagnetic. **diamagnétisme,** *n.m.* Diamagnetism.

diamant [djaˈmɑ̃], *n.m.* Diamond. *Diamant brut*, rough diamond; *diamont taillé*, cut diamond; *diamant de vitrier*, glazier's diamond. **diamantaire,** *a.* Of diamond brilliancy.—**n.m.* Diamond-cutter or seller. **diamanter,** *v.t.* To set with diamonds; to make shine like a diamond; to tinsel, to frost. **diamantifère,** *a.* Diamantiferous.

diamétral [djameˈtral], *a.* (*fem.* -ale, *pl.* -aux) Diametrical. **diamétralement,** *adv.* Diametrically. *Sentiments diamétralement opposés*, sentiments diametrically opposed to each other.

diamètre [djaˈmɛtr], *n.m.* Diameter. *Demi-diamètre*, semi-diameter.

diandre [diˈɑ̃dr] or **diandrique,** *a.* (*Bot.*) Diandrous (having two stamens).

diane [djan], *n.f.* Reveille; (*Naut.*) morning-gun, morning-watch.

diantre [djɑ̃:tr] (*int.*) The deuce! Dash! Blast! *Au diantre soit l'imbécile!* the deuce take the fool! **diantrement,** *adv.* Deucedly, confoundedly.

diapason [djapa'zɔ̃], *n.m.* Diapason, pitch; tuning-fork. *Se mettre au diapason de quelqu'un,* to adapt oneself to someone, to adopt the same tone or opinions.

diapédèse [djape'dɛ:z], *n.f.* (*Path.*) Diapedesis.

diaphane [dja'fan], *a.* Diaphanous, transparent, translucent. **diaphanéité,** *n.f.* Diaphaneity, transparency.

diaphorèse [djafɔ're:z], *n.f.* Perspiration. **diaphorétique,** *a.* Diaphoretic.

diaphragmatique [djafragma'tik], *a.* (*Anat.*) Diaphragmatic. **diaphragme,** *n.m.* Diaphragm, midriff; (*Phot.*) diaphragm stop. **diaphragmer,** *v.t.* (*Phot.*) To stop down (lens). **diaphragmite,** *n.f.* Diaphragmitis.

diapositive [djapozi'ti:v], *n.f.* Transparent positive, transparency, lantern-slide.

diapré [dja'pre], *a.* (*fem.* **diaprée**) Dappled, variegated. **diaprer,** *v.t.* To dapple, to variegate, to mottle. **diaprure,** *n.f.* Variegation, dappling.

diarrhée [dja're], *n.f.* Diarrhoea. **diarrhéique,** *a.* Diarrhoeic.

diarthrose [djar'tro:z], *n.f.* Diarthrosis.

diascopie [djaskɔ'pi], *n.f.* Diascopy.

diastaltique [djastal'tik], *a.* Diastaltic.

diastase [djas'ta:z], *n.f.* (*Chem.*) Enzyme; (*Surg.*) diastasis. **diastasique,** *a.* Diastasic.

diastole [djas'tɔl], *n.f.* Diastole. **diastolique,** *a.* Diastolic.

diathermane [djater'man], *a.* Diathermanous. **diathermanéité,** *n.f.* Diathermancy.

diathèse [dja'tɛ:z], *n.f.* Diathesis, disposition.

diatomée [djatɔ'me:], *n.f. gen. in plur.* Diatoma.

diatonique [djatɔ'nik], *a.* (*Mus.*) Diatonic. **diatoniquement,** *adv.* In a diatonic scale, diatonically.

diatribe [dja'trib], *n.f.* Diatribe, bitter criticism or dissertation.

dichotome [dikɔ'tɔm], *a.* Dichotomous. **dichotomie,** *n.f.* Dichotomy. **dichotomique,** *a.* Dichotomic.

dichroïque [dikrɔ'ik], *a.* Dichroic. **dichroïsme,** *n.m.* Dichroism. **dichromatique,** *a.* Dichromatic.

dicotylédone [dikɔtile'dɔn] or **dicotylédoné,** *a.* (*fem.* **-ée**) (*Bot.*) Dicotyledonous. —*n.f.* Dicotyledon.

dicrote [di'krɔt], *a.* Dicrotic (pulse).

dictame [dik'tam], *n.m.* Dittany; (*fig.*) balm, remedy.

dictamen [dikta'mɛn], *n.m.* Dictate, suggestion (of our conscience).

dictateur [dikta'tœ:r], *n.m.* Dictator. **dictatorial,** *a.* (*fem.* **-iale,** *pl.* **-iaux**) Dictatorial. **dictatorialement,** *adv.* Dictatorially. **dictature,** *n.f.* Dictatorship.

dictée [dik'te], *n.f.* Act of dictating, dictation. *Écrire sous la dictée,* to write from dictation. **dicter,** *v.t.* To dictate; (*fig.*) to suggest, to inspire; to impose.

diction [dik'sjɔ̃], *n.f.* Diction, style; delivery.

dictionnaire [diksjɔ'nɛ:r], *n.m.* Dictionary. *À coups de dictionnaire,* by constant reference to the dictionary; *c'est un dictionnaire vivant,* he is a walking dictionary; *dictionnaire de*

géographie, geographical dictionary, gazetteer.

dicton [dik'tɔ̃], *n.m.* Common saying, saw, proverb, dictum.

didactique [didak'tik], *a.* Didactic.—*n.f.* Didactic art, art of teaching. **didactiquement,** *adv.* Didactically.

didelphe [di'dɛlf], *n.m. usu. in pl.* (*Zool.*) Didelphia, marsupials.

didyme [di'dim], *a.* (*Bot.*) Didymous.

didyname [didi'nam] or **didynamique,** *a.* (*Bot.*) Didynamous.

dièdre [di'ɛdr], *a.* and *n.m.* Dihedral.

diélectrique [djelɛk'trik], *a.* Dielectric, insulating.

diérèse [dje're:z], *n.f.* (*Gram.*) Diaeresis.

dièse [dje:z], *n.m.* (*Mus.*) Sharp. **diésé,** *a.* (*fem.* **diésée**) Marked with a diesis. **diéser,** *v.t.* To mark (a note) with a diesis; to sharpen.

diesel [dje'zɛl], *n.m.* Diesel (engine).

diète (1) [djɛt], *n.f.* Diet (regimen). *Être à la diète,* to be on a low or starvation diet; *faire diète,* to diet oneself, to live moderately.

diète (2) [djɛt], *n.f.* (*Hist.*) Diet.

diététicien [djeteti'sjɛ̃], *n.m.* (*fem.* **-ienne**) Dietician, dietist. **diététique** [djete'tik], *a.* Dietetical.—*n.f.* Dietetics.

dieu [djo], *n.m.* (*pl.* **dieux**) God. (*Int.*) *Dieu! Grand Dieu!* Dear me! My goodness! *Mon Dieu, quelle surprise!* Good heavens, what a surprise! *Mon Dieu, oui!* why, yes! *Dieu merci!* fortunately; *Grâce à Dieu,* thank God; *Dieu le veuille,* God grant it, would to God; *Dieu m'en garde, Dieu m'en préserve,* or *à Dieu ne plaise,* God forbid; *Dieu sait qui, quand, pourquoi* (etc.), Heaven only knows who, when, why (etc.); *Dieu vous bénisse,* God bless you (said to a person who sneezes); *il y a un bon Dieu pour les ivrognes,* there is a providence watching over drunken men; *jurer ses grands dieux,* to swear by all that is holy; *le bon Dieu,* God Almighty, the host, the eucharist; *le dieu des armées,* the Lord of Hosts; *les dieux du paganisme,* the heathen gods; *plaisir des dieux,* pleasure worthy of the gods; *porter le bon Dieu à un malade,* to carry the host to a sick person; *s'il plaît à Dieu, avec l'aide de Dieu,* or *Dieu aidant,* God willing, God helping. (N.B.—*Bon Dieu!* and *nom de Dieu!* are profane (and very vulgar) oaths. All the other int. sentences quoted above are decent.)

diffa [di'fa], *n.f.* A state reception and banquet (Arab).

diffamant [difa'mɑ̃], *a.* (*fem.* **-ante**) Defamatory, libellous, slanderous. **diffamateur,** *n.m.* (*fem.* **-trice**) Defamer, slanderer, calumniator. **diffamation,** *n.f.* Defamation, aspersion, calumny. *Diffamation verbale,* slander. **diffamatoire,** *a.* Defamatory, libellous, slanderous. **diffamer,** *v.t.* To defame, to slander, to libel.

différé [dife're], *a.* (*fem.* **-ée**) Deferred.

différemment [difera'mɑ̃], *adv.* Differently.

différence [dife'rɑ̃:s], *n.f.* Difference, unlikeness, diversity, disproportion, contrast, disparity. *À la différence de,* contrary to; *avec cette différence que,* except that; *différence du tirant d'eau,* difference in the draught of water. **différenciation,** *n.f.* Differentiation. **différencier,** *v.t.* (*conjugated like*

PRIER) To make a difference, to distinguish; (*Math.*) to differentiate.
différend [dife´rɑ̃], *n.m.* Difference, quarrel, dispute; difference (of value). *Avoir un différend avec quelqu'un*, to be at variance with someone; *partager le différend*, to split the difference.
différent [dife´rɑ̃], *a.* (*fem.* **-ente**) Different, dissimilar, unlike; (*pl.*) various, divers, several. *À des degrés différents*, in various degrees. *Différents l'un de l'autre*, unlike.
différentiel [diferɑ̃´sjɛl], *a.* (*fem.* **-ielle**) Differential. *Calcul différentiel*, differential calculus.—*n.m.* (*Motor.*) Differential.—*n.f.* (*Math.*) Differential.
différentier [diferɑ̃´sje], *v.t.* (*conjugated like* PRIER) (*Math.*) To differentiate.
différer [dife´re], *v.t. irr.* (*conjug. like* AC-CÉLÉRER) To defer, to put off, to postpone, to adjourn. *Ce qui est différé n'est pas perdu*, what is put off is not lost.—*v.i.* To defer, to put off, to delay; to differ, to be unlike; to disagree. *Ces couleurs diffèrent de ton*, these colours are different in tone.
difficile [difi´sil], *a.* Difficult; hard, trying, painful; unpleasant; hard to please, particular; hard to understand, unintelligible. *D'accès difficile*, hard to get at. *Faire le difficile*, to be difficult to please; *il est difficile sur les aliments*, he is fastidious (or particular) about his meals. *Temps difficiles*, hard times; *un homme difficile*, a man hard to please.
difficilement, *adv.* With difficulty, with great pains, not easily.
difficulté [difikyl´te], *n.f.* Difficulty; obstacle, hindrance, impediment; cross, rub; objection; misunderstanding, quarrel. *Avoir des difficultés*, to be in trouble; *difficulté de respirer*, shortness of breath; *faire des difficultés*, to raise objections; *faire difficulté de quelque chose*, to scruple about something. *Il y a entre eux quelque difficulté*, there is some tiff between them. *Trancher la difficulté*, to decide peremptorily, to cut the Gordian knot. **difficultueux**, *a.* (*fem.* **-euse**) Prone to raise difficulties; hard to please; captious; (job) fraught with difficulties.
diffluence [difly´ɑ̃:s], *n.f.* Diffluence. **diffluent**, *a.* (*fem.* **-ente**) Diffluent. **diffluer**, *v.i.* To spread diffusely.
difforme [di´form], *a.* Deformed, misshapen. **difformité**, *n.f.* Deformity, malformation; hideousness.
diffracter [difrak´te], *v.t.* To diffract. **diffractif**, *a.* (*fem.* **-ive**) Diffractive. **diffraction**, *n.f.* Diffraction.
diffus [di´fy], *a.* (*fem.* **-use**) Diffuse, prolix, verbose, diffused (light). **diffusément**, *adv.* Diffusely, verbosely, wordily. **diffuser**, *v.t.* To diffuse; (*Rad. Tel.*) to broadcast. **diffuseur**, *n.m.* Diffuser, spray cone; loudspeaker. **diffusif**, *a.* (*fem.* **-ive**) Diffusive. **diffusion**, *n.f.* Diffusion; diffusiveness, wordiness, verbosity; propagation, spread (of knowledge etc.), broadcasting. *Diffusion de style*, prolixity of style.
digamma [diga´ma], *n.m.* Digamma.
digérer [diʒe´re], *v.t. irr.* (*conjug. like* AC-CÉLÉRER) To digest; to ponder, to discuss; to brook, to stomach, to put up with. *Bien digérer*, to master thoroughly. *Digérer de la viande*, to digest meat; *non digéré*, undigested.

Il ne peut digérer cet affront, he cannot swallow that affront.
*digeste [di´ʒɛst], *n.m.* (*Rom. Law*) Digest.
digesteur, *n.m.* (*Chem.*) Digester. **digestibilité**, *n.f.* Digestibility. **digestible**, *a.* Digestible. **digestif**, *a.* (*fem.* **-ive**) Digestive. *Tube digestif*, alimentary canal.—*n.m.* A digestive. **digestion**, *n.f.* Digestion.
digital [diʒi´tal], *a.* (*fem.* **-ale** (1), *pl.* **-aux**) Digital. *Empreinte digitale*, finger-print.—*n.m.* Finger-shaped mushroom.
digitale (2) [diʒi´tal], *n.f.* Foxglove. *Digitale pourprée*, dead-man's finger (flower). **digitaline**, *n.f.* (*Chem.*) Digitaline.
digité [diʒi´te], *a.* (*fem.* **-ée**) (*Bot.*) Digitate, finger-like. **digitiforme**, *a.* Digitaliform. **digitigrade**, *n.m.* (*Zool.*) Digitigrade.
digne [diɲ], *a.* Deserving, meritorious, worthy; dignified, serious; upright. *Cela est digne de lui*, that's just like him; *digne de foi*, deserving of credit; *il était digne d'un meilleur sort*, he deserved a better fate; *un digne homme*, a worthy man. *Un digne magistrat*, an upright magistrate. **dignement**, *adv.* Worthily, deservedly, justly, according to one's deserts; properly, suitably, with dignity. *Il s'acquitte dignement de sa charge*, he performs the duties of his office in a worthy manner.
dignitaire [diɲi´tɛːr], *n.m.* Dignitary.
dignité [diɲi´te], *n.f.* Dignity (function, office); dignity, nobility, seriousness; self-respect. *Il soutient la dignité de son rang*, he maintains the dignity of his station. *Parvenir aux dignités*, to attain to honours. *Un homme sans dignité*, a man lacking in self-respect.
digon [di´gɔ̃], *n.m.* (*Naut.*) Flagstaff, flag-yard; fish-gig.
digramme [di´gram], *n.m.* Digraph.
digraphie [digra´fi], *n.f.* Book-keeping by double entry.
digresser [digrɛ´se], *v.i.* To digress, to depart from the main subject. **digressif**, *a.* (*fem.* **-ive**) Digressive. **digression**, *n.f.* Digression. *Faire des digressions*, to wander away from one's subject. **digressivement**, *adv.* Digressively.
digue [dig], *n.f.* Dike, dam, embankment; (*fig.*) bound, limit; bulwark, security. **diguer**, *v.t.* To dam, to embank.
digyne [di´ʒin], *a.* (*Bot.*) Digynous (having two pistils).
dilacération [dilaserɑ̃´sjɔ̃], *n.f.* Tearing or rending, dilaceration. **dilacérer**, *v.t.* To dilacerate, to tear to pieces.
dilapidateur [dilapida´tœːr], *n.m.* (*fem.* **-trice**) Squanderer.—*a.* Wasteful, extravagant. **dilapidation**, *n.f.* Waste; embezzlement; peculation. **dilapider**, *v.t.* To waste, to squander (a fortune); to embezzle.
dilatabilité [dilatabili´te], *n.f.* Dilatability. **dilatable**, *a.* Dilatable, expansible. **dilatant**, *a.* (*fem.* **-ante**) Dilating.—*n.m.* (*Surg.*) Dilating body, agent, or instrument. **dilatateur**, *a.* (*fem.* **-trice**) Dilating.—*n.m.* (*Surg.*) Dilator. **dilatation**, *n.f.* Dilation, expansion, distension. *La dilatation d'une plaie*, the dilation of a sore. **dilater**, *v.t.* To dilate, to distend, to expand. *La joie dilate le cœur*, joy gladdens the heart. **se dilater**, *v.r.* To dilate, to be dilated, to be distended. **dilatoire**, *a.* (*Law*) Dilatory.

*dilection [dilɛk'sjɔ̃], *n.f.* Pure and tender love.

dilemme [di'lɛm], *n.m.* Dilemma.

dilettante [dilɛ'tãːt], *n.* Dilettante. **dilettantisme,** *n.m.* Dilettantism, amateurism.

diligemment [diliʒa'mã], *adv.* Diligently, promptly; carefully, sedulously.

diligence [dili'ʒãːs], *n.f.* Diligence; dispatch, care, industry, application; stage-coach; (*Law*) suit, proceedings. *À la diligence d'un tel,* (*Law*) at the suit of such a one. *Faire diligence,* to go with speed, to hurry.

diligent [dili'ʒã], *a.* (*fem.* **diligente**) Diligent, assiduous, active, industrious.

dilogie [dilɔ'ʒi], *n.f.* Play with a double plot; (*Log.*) double meaning.

diluer [di'lɥe], *v.t.* To dilute. **dilution,** *n.f.* Dilution.

diluvial [dily'vjal], *a.* (*fem.* **-iale,** *pl.* **-iaux**) Diluvial. **diluvien,** *a.* (*fem.* **diluvienne**) Diluvian. *Une pluie diluvienne,* (*fig.*) an absolute deluge. **diluvium,** *n.m.* Diluvium.

dimanche [di'mãːʃ], *n.m.* Sunday, Sabbath. *Habits des dimanches* or *du dimanche,* Sunday clothes, Sunday best; *le dimanche de Pâques,* Easter Sunday; *tel qui rit vendredi dimanche pleurera,* laugh today and cry tomorrow.

dîme [dim], *n.f.* Tithe; (U.S.) dime, ten cents.

dimension [dimã'sjɔ̃], *n.f.* Dimension, size.

dîmer [di'me], *v.t.* To tithe, to levy tithes upon.—*v.i.* To levy tithe.

diminué [dimin'ɥe], *a.* (*fem.* **-ée**) Diminished; weakened physically or mentally.

diminuer [dimi'nɥe], *v.t.* To diminish, to lessen, to reduce, to curtail; to impair.—*v.i.* To diminish, to decrease, to abate, to fall (in price etc.); to draw in (of days). **diminutif,** *a.* (*fem.* **-ive**) Diminutive.—*n.m.* Diminutive.

diminution, *n.f.* Diminution, reduction, abatement; tapering (of columns). *Diminution de dépenses,* curtailment of expenses.

dimorphe [di'mɔrf], *a.* Dimorphous. **dimorphie.** *n.f.,* or **dimorphisme,** *n.m.* Dimorphism.

dinanderie [dinã'dri], *n.f.* Brass wares. **dinandier,** *n.m.* Maker or vendor of these.

dînatoire [dina'twaːr], *a.* Relating to dinner. *Déjeuner dînatoire,* large lunch equivalent to a dinner.

dinde [dɛ̃ːd], *n.f.* Turkey-hen; turkey; (*fig.*) goose, silly woman.

dindon [dɛ̃'dɔ̃], *n.m.* Turkey-cock; (*fig.*) goose (person). *C'est un dindon,* he is a thorough goose. *Être le dindon de la farce,* to be fooled, to be taken in. **dindonneau,** *n.m.* (*pl.* **-eaux**) Young turkey. **dindonner,** *v.t.* To dupe, to take in. **dindonnier,** *n.m.* (*fem.* **-ière**) Turkey-keeper.

dîné [DÎNER (2)].

dîner (1) [di'ne], *v.i.* To dine, to have dinner. *Dîner de,* to dine off; *dîner par cœur,* to go dinnerless; *prier à dîner,* to invite to dine.

dîner (2) [di'ne], *n.m.* Dinner; dinner-party; that which is had for dinner. *L'heure du dîner,* dinner-time; *donner un (grand) dîner,* to give a dinner-party; *dîner de têtes,* dinner at which guests wear masks or disguise.

dînette [di'nɛt], *n.f.* Child's or doll's dinner; a little dinner or meal. *Faire la dînette,* to play at dinners.

dîneur [di'nœːr], *n.m.* (*fem.* **dîneuse**) Diner; diner-out.

dingue [dɛ̃g], **dingo** [dɛ̃'go], *n.m.* and *a.* (*slang*) Mad, off his nut.

dinguer [dɛ̃'ge], *v.i.* (*vulg.*) Only in *envoyer dinguer quelqu'un* or *quelque chose,* to fling away, to chuck up.

dinornis [dinɔr'nis], *n.m.* (*Pal.*) Dinornis.

dinosaurien, *n.m.* Dinosaurian.

dinotherium, *n.m.* Dinotherium.

diocésain [djɔse'zɛ̃], *a.* (*fem.* **-aine**) Diocesan. —*n.* Inhabitant of a diocese. **diocèse,** *n.m.* Diocese.

diodon [djɔ'dɔ̃], *n.m.* (*Ichth.*) Diodon, globe-fish.

dionée [djɔ'ne], *n.f.* (*Bot.*) Dionaea, catch-fly; a kind of jelly-fish.

dionysiaque [djɔni'zjak], *a.* Dionysiac, of Bacchus. **dionysiaques** or **dionysies,** *n.f. pl.* (*Gr. Ant.*) Dionysian games.

dioptrie [djɔp'tri], *n.f.* Diopter. **dioptrique,** *a.* Dioptric.—*n.f.* Dioptrics.

diorama [djɔra'ma], *n.m.* Diorama. **dioramique,** *a.* Dioramic.

diorite [djɔ'rit], *n.f.* Diorite (greenstone).

diphasé [difa'ze], *a.* (*fem.* **-ée**) (*Elec.*) Two-phase, diphasic.

diphtérie [difte'ri], *n.f.* Diphtheria. **diphtérique,** *a.* Diphtheric. **diphtéroïde,** *a.* Diphtheroid.

diphtongal [diftɔ̃'gal], *a.* (*fem.* **-ale,** *pl.* **-aux**) Diphthongal. **diphtongue,** *n.f.* Diphthong. **diphtonguer,** *v.t.* To sound as a diphthong, diphthongize. **se diphtonguer,** *v.r.* To have the sound of a diphthong.

diplégie [diple'ʒi], *n.f.* Bilateral paralysis, diplegia.

diplex [di'plɛks], *a.* and *n.m.* (*Teleg.*) Diplex.

diplomate [diplɔ'mat], *n.m.* Diplomatist, diplomat.—*a.* Diplomatic. **diplomatie,** *n.f.* Diplomacy; diplomatic service. **diplomatique,** *a.* Diplomatic; tactful. **diplomatiquement,** *adv.* Diplomatically.

diplôme [di'ploːm], *n.m.* Diploma. **diplômé** [diplo:'me], *a.* and *n.m.* (*fem.* **-ée**) Qualified (person). *Être diplômé,* to have qualifications, to be qualified; *une infirmière diplômée,* a certificated nurse.

diplômer, *v.t.* To confer a diploma upon.

diplopie [diplɔ'pi], *n.f.* Double vision, diplopia.

dipode [di'pɔd], *a.* Having two feet or two fins. **dipodie,** *n.f.* (*Pros.*) Dipody.

dipsomane [dipsɔ'man], *n.m.* Dipsomaniac. **dipsomanie,** *n.f.* Dipsomania.

diptère [dip'tɛːr], *a.* Dipteral; (*Ent.*) dipteran. —*n.m.* Dipteran insect; dipteral temple; (*pl.*) Diptera.

diptyque [dip'tik], *n.m.* Diptych.

dire (1) [diːr], *v.t. irr.* (*pres.p.* **disant,** *p.p.* **dit**) To say, to speak; to tell; to recite, to repeat, to declaim; to order, to bid, to instruct; to show; to express; to think, to believe; to predict; to wish. *À ce qu'il dit,* according to him; *à qui le dites-vous?* you're telling me! *à vrai dire,* to tell the truth; *cela en dit long sur son caractère,* that speaks volumes about his character; *cela ne dit rien,* that is hardly to the point; *cela ne me dit rien,* that means nothing to me; *(cela) soit dit en passant,* but that by the way; *cela va sans dire,* that goes without saying, that is a matter of course; *cela vous plaît à dire*, you are pleased to say so; *ce n'est pas à dire que*, it does not follow that; *c'est-à-dire*, that is to say; *c'est beaucoup dire*, that's saying a good deal; *c'est tout dire*, I needn't say more! *dire d'avance*, to say beforehand; *dire des injures à quelqu'un*, to call someone names; *dire du bien* or *du mal de quelqu'un*, to speak well or ill of someone; *dire la bonne aventure à quelqu'un*, to tell someone's fortune; *dire la messe*, to say mass; *dire que* . . . , to think that . . . ; *dire quelque chose à l'oreille*, to whisper something; *dis-je*, said I; *dites donc*, look here, I say; *dites toujours*, let's hear it anyway; *dites votre avis*, give your opinion; *dit-on*, as it is said, as we hear; *est-ce à dire que?* does it follow that? *faire dire à quelqu'un*, to make someone say, to send word to someone; *c'est de la déveine, il n'y a pas à dire*, it's bad luck and no mistake; *je ne sais que dire de tout cela*, I do not know what to think of all that; *je ne vous l'envoie pas dire*, I am not saying it behind your back; *le cœur vous en dit-il?* are you agreeable? *les 'on dit'*, gossip, rumours; *on le dit parti*, he is said to have left; *on dirait que*, one would think that; *pour ainsi dire*, so to speak; *pour tout dire*, in a word; *quand je vous le disais, je vous le disais bien*, or *je vous l'avais bien dit*, didn't I tell you so! or, what did I tell you? *qu'en dites-vous?* what about it? *qui l'aurait dit?* who would have thought it? *comment dirais-je?* how shall I put it? *que veut dire cela?* or *qu'est-ce que cela veut dire?* what is the meaning of that? *qui ne dit mot consent*, silence gives consent; *sans mot dire*, without a word; *se moquer du qu'en dira-t-on*, not to care what people say; *si le cœur vous en dit*, if you feel so minded; *soit dit entre nous*, between ourselves; *tout est dit*, all is over; there's an end of it. **se dire**, *v.r.* To call oneself, to give oneself out as, to be called; to say to oneself; to be said. *Cela ne se dit plus*, that is no longer said; *comment est-ce que cela se dit en français?* how do you say it in French?

dire (2) [diːr], *n.m.* What one says, words, statement; (*Law*) allegation. *Au dire de tout le monde*, according to what everybody says, by all accounts. *À dire d'experts*, at a valuation. *Le dire du défendeur*, the statement of the defendant. *Se fier pour quelque chose au dire des autres* or *d'autrui*, to take something upon trust.

direct [di'rɛkt], *a.* Direct, straight, immediate. *En ligne directe*, in a straight line; by direct descent. *Impôts directs*, direct taxes. *Par train direct*, by express, through train.—*n.m.* (*Box.*) Straight blow. *Un direct du gauche*, a straight left. **directement**, *adv.* Directly, point-blank; expressly, positively; in a straight line. *Aller directement au but*, to go straight to one's goal.

directeur [dirɛk'tœːr], *n.m.* (*fem.* **directrice**) Director, manager, superintendent, head; directress, principal, head mistress. *Directeur de la monnaie*, master of the mint; *directeur général*, general manager. *Directeur de conscience*, spiritual director.—*a.* Directing, controlling (of lines etc.). *Idée directrice*, leading idea. *Roue directrice*, (*Cycl.*) front wheel.

direction [dirɛk'sjɔ̃], *n.f.* Directing, direction; management, control; directorship; director's office; editorial board; instruction; (*Naut.*) bearing, steering; (*Motor.*) steering. *Avoir la direction*, to preside. *Par suite d'une mauvaise direction*, by sheer mismanagement. (*Mil.*) *La direction du tir*, control of fire, gunnery control.

directives [dirɛk'tiːv], *n.f. pl.* (*Mil.*) General directions or rules; (*Polit.*) main lines (of a party's policy), directive(s).

directoire [dirɛk'twaːr], *n.m.* (*Eccles.*) Directory. **directorat**, *n.m.* Directorship, directorate. **directorial**, *a.* (*fem.* -**iale**, *pl.* -**iaux**) Directorial.

dirigeable [diri'ʒabl], *a.* Dirigible.—*n.m.* Dirigible balloon or airship. **dirigeant**, *a.* (*fem.* **dirigeante**) Directing, leading.—*n.* Ruler, leader.

diriger [diri'ʒe], *v.t.* To direct; to control; to conduct, to steer, to manage, to govern; to send, to aim (a weapon etc.). *Diriger des poursuites contre*, to take proceedings against. **se diriger**, *v.r.* To make for, to go (towards); to steer; to conduct, direct, or govern oneself. *Antenne dirigée*, (*Teleg.*) directional aerial. *Monnaie dirigée*, managed or controlled currency.

dirigisme [diri'ʒism], *n.m.* (*Polit.*) State planning or controls.

dirimant [diri'mɑ̃], *a.* (*fem.* -**ante**) (*Canon Law*) Invalidating. *Empêchement dirimant*, an impediment that invalidates a marriage. **dirimer**, *v.t.* To invalidate, to nullify.

discale [dis'kal], *n.f.* (*Comm.*) Loss, tret, tare, shrinkage (of goods in bulk). **discaler**, *v.i.* To tare, to diminish.

discernable [disɛr'nabl], *a.* Discernible. **discernement**, *n.m.* Discernment; discrimination; judgment. *Âge de discernement*, years of discretion *or* of understanding.

discerner [disɛr'ne], *v.t.* To discern; to distinguish, to discriminate. *Discerner le vrai du faux*, to distinguish truth from untruth.

disciple [di'sipl], *n.m.* Disciple, follower.

disciplinable [disipli'nabl], *a.* Disciplinable, tractable. **disciplinaire**, *a.* Disciplinary. *n.m.* Soldier in a disciplinary company [BIRIBI].

discipline [disi'plin], *n.f.* Discipline; education, training; (*sch.*) subject. *Conseil de discipline*, (*sch.*) disciplinary board or committee; *quelle discipline enseignez-vous?* what subject do you teach? **disciplinement**, *n.m.* Disciplining. **discipliner**, *v.t.* To discipline. **se discipliner**, *v.r.* To be disciplined.

discobole [disko'bɔl], *n.m.* (*Ant.*) Discobolus. **discoïde** [disko'id] or **discoïdal**, *a.* (*fem.* -**ale**, *pl.* -**aux**) (*Conch.*) Discoid(al).

discolore [disko'lɔːr], *a.* Two-coloured.

discontinu [diskɔ̃ti'ny], *a.* (*fem.* -**ue**) Discontinuous. **discontinuation**, *n.f.* Discontinuance, discontinuation. **discontinuer**, *v.t.* To discontinue, to interrupt, to suspend.—*v.i.* To discontinue, to cease, to leave off. **discontinuité**, *n.f.* Discontinuity, discontinuance, interruption.

disconvenance [diskɔ̃v'nɑ̃ːs], *n.f.* Incongruity, discrepancy, unsuitableness; dissimilarity, disproportion, inequality.

disconvenir [diskɔ̃v'niːr], *v.i. irr.* (*conjugated like* VENIR) To deny, to disown; to be

incompatible, to disagree, to be unsuitable
(à). *Il ne disconvient pas du fait*, he does not
deny the fact.
discord [dis'kɔːr], *a.* (*Mus.*) Out of tune,
discordant. **discordance**, *n.f.* Discordancy,
dissonance; (*Geol.*) inconformability. **discordant**, *a.* (*fem.* **-ante**) Discordant, dissonant, harsh, out of tune; inharmonious,
incongruous; (*Geol.*) unconformable. **discorde**, *n.f.* Discord, disagreement, disunion, dissension, strife. *Pomme de discorde*,
bone of contention. **discorder**, *v.i.* (*Mus.*)
To be out of tune, to be discordant; to be
in a state of dissension.
discothèque [disko'tɛk], *n.f.* Record library.
discoureur [disku'rœːr], *n.m.* (*fem.* **-euse**)
Talker, chatterer. *Quel ennuyeux discoureur!*
what a long-winded bore!
discourir [disku'rir], *v.i. irr.* (*pres.p.* **dis-
courant**, *p.p.* **discouru**; *conjugated like*
COURIR) To discourse; to descant (*sur*); to
chat, to babble.
discours (1) [dis'kuːr], *n.m.* Discourse;
speech, oration, address; language, words,
diction; treatise. *C'est un bon discours*, it is
a good speech; *discours en l'air*, idle talk;
faire un discours, to make a speech, to deliver
an address, a speech; *perdre le fil de son
discours*, to lose the thread of one's argument.
discours (2), *1st* and *2nd sing. ind.* [DISCOURIR].
discourtois [diskur'twa], *a.* (*fem.* **-oise**)
Discourteous, unmannerly, uncivil. **dis-
courtoisement**, *adv.* Discourteously. **dis-
courtoisie**, *n.f.* Discourtesy, unmannerliness, incivility.
discrédit [diskre'di], *n.m.* Discredit, disrepute; loss of credit. **discréditer**, *v.t.* To
discredit, to bring into discredit.
discret [dis'krɛ], *a.* (*fem.* **-ète**) Discreet,
considerate; cautious, wary, reserved, shy;
secret, close. *Couleurs discrètes*, subdued
colours. **discrètement**, *adv.* Discreetly;
warily, prudently; reservedly.
discrétion [diskre'sjɔ̃], *n.f.* Circumspection,
prudence; discretion; reserve, secrecy. *Agir*
or *parler avec discrétion*, to act or speak
warily; *l'âge de discrétion*, years of discretion;
se rendre à discrétion, to surrender unconditionally. *Pain à discrétion*, bread ad lib. **discrétionnaire**, *a.* Discretionary. **discré-
tionnairement**, *adv.* In a discretionary
manner.
discriminant [diskrimi'nɑ̃], *a.* (*fem.* **-ante**)
Discriminating.—*n.m.* (*Math.*) Discriminant.
discrimination, *n.f.* Discrimination. **discriminer**, *v.t.* To discriminate.
*****disculpation** [diskylpɑ'sjɔ̃], *n.f.* Exculpation.
disculper [diskyl'pe], *v.t.* To exculpate, to
vindicate, to exonerate. **se disculper**, *v.r.*
To exculpate or justify oneself.
discursif [diskyr'sif], *a.* (*fem.* **-ive**) Discursive.
discussion [disky'sjɔ̃], *n.f.* Discussion, debate;
altercation, dispute. *Passer à la discussion
des articles*, (*Engl. Parl.*) to go into committee; (*Fr. Parl.*) to discuss the various
clauses. **discutable**, *a.* Debatable, disputable, contestable. **discuteur**, *n.m.* (*fem.*
-euse). Arguer.
discuter [disky'te], *v.t.* To discuss, to debate,
to argue; to examine, to inquire into, to
scan, to sift. *Discuter les biens d'un débiteur*,

to distrain the goods of a debtor. *Discuter
un point de droit*, to discuss a point of law.
discutailler, *v.i.* (*fam.*) To wrangle about
trifles.
disert [di'zɛːr], *a.* (*fem.* **diserte**) Copious,
fluent, eloquent. **disertement**, *adv.* Copiously, fluently.
disette [di'zet], *n.f.* Scarcity, dearth, want;
poverty, penury.
diseur [di'zœːr], *n.m.* (*fem.* **diseuse**) Sayer,
teller; diseuse. *Diseur de bonne aventure*,
fortune-teller; *diseur de bons mots*, wit;
diseur de nouvelles, newsmonger; *diseur de
riens*, idle talker; *un beau diseur*, a fine talker.
disgrâce [diz'grɑːs], *n.f.* Disfavour; disgrace,
misfortune, reverse; plainness (of features).
disgracié, *a.* (*fem.* **-iée**) Out of favour;
(*fig.*) ill-favoured, deformed. *Disgracié de
la nature*, deformed, disfigured, ill-favoured.
—*n.m.* Deformity, ills (of fortune etc.). **disgracier**, *v.t.* To disgrace, to put out of
favour. **disgracieusement**, *adv.* Awkwardly, ungracefully, uncouthly. **disgracieux**, *a.* (*fem.* **-ieuse**) Awkward,
ungraceful, uncouth, ungracious, disagreeable, unpleasant.
disjoindre [diz'ʒwɛ̃ːdr], *v.t. irr.* (*pres.p.* **disjoi-
gnant**, *p.p.* **disjoint**; *conjugated like* CRAIN-
DRE) To disjoin, to disunite. **se disjoindre**,
v.r. To come apart, to disunite. **disjoint**, *a.*
(*fem.* **-ointe**) Separated, disjointed, discontinuous.
disjoncteur [dizʒɔ̃k'tœːr], *n.m.* (*Elec.*) Circuit
breaker.
disjonctif [dizʒɔ̃k'tif], *a.* (*fem.* **-ive**) Disjunctive.—*n.f.* (*Gram.*) Disjunctive. **disjonction**, *n.f.* Disjunction, separation;
(*Law*) severance of causes.
dislocation [disloka'sjɔ̃], *n.f.* Dislocation,
dismemberment, luxation. *Il y a dislocation*,
the bone is out of joint; *la dislocation d'une
armée*, the breaking up of an army. **dis-
loquement**, *n.m.* Dislocation. **disloquer**,
v.t. To dislocate, to dismember, to disjoint, to put out of joint; to take to pieces
(machines etc.); (*Mil.*) to break up (an
army). **se disloquer**, *v.r.* To dislocate
one's arm etc.; to be taken to pieces; to
come apart, to be broken up, disbanded, etc.
dispache [dis'paʃ], *n.f.* (*Maritime Insurance*)
Assessment; average adjustment. **dis-
pacheur** or **dispatcheur**, *n.m.* Assessor,
average adjuster.
disparaître [dispa're:tr], *v.i. irr.* (*conjugated
like* CONNAÎTRE) To vanish, to disappear; to
get out of the way, to abscond; to die.
disparate [dispa'rat], *a.* Dissimilar, incongruous, unlike, ill-matched.—*n.f.* Incongruity, dissimilarity. **disparité**, *n.f.*
Disparity, dissimilarity.
disparition [dispari'sjɔ̃], *n.f.* Disappearance.
disparu, *p.p.* (*fem.* **disparue**) [DISPARAÎTRE].
—*n.* Missing.
dispendieusement [dispãdjøz'mã], *adv.* Expensively. **dispendieux**, *a.* (*fem.* **-ieuse**)
Expensive, costly.
dispensaire [dispã'sɛːr], *n.m.* Dispensary;
out-patients' department. **dispensateur**,
n.m. (*fem.* **-trice**) Dispenser; bestower,
giver.
dispensation [dispãsɑ'sjɔ̃], *n.f.* Dispensation;
distribution; dispensing.

dispense [dis'pɑ̃:s], *n.f.* Dispensation (from fasting); exemption (from military service). *Dispense d'âge*, waiving of age limit; *dispense de bans*, marriage licence.

dispenser [dispɑ̃'se], *v.t.* To dispense, to bestow, to distribute; to exempt; to dispense (with). *Dispensez-moi de faire cela*, excuse me from doing that. *Le soleil dispense à tous sa lumière*, the sun bestows his light upon all. **se dispenser,** *v.r.* To dispense with; to exempt or excuse oneself (from); to spare oneself.

disperser [dispɛr'se], *v.t.* To disperse, to spread broadcast; to scatter, to dispel, to break up. (*Mil.*) *Ordre dispersé*, extended order; *dispersez-vous!* scatter! **se disperser,** *v.r.* To be dispersed, to break up, to be scattered. **dispersif,** *a.* (*fem.* **dispersive**) Dispersive. **dispersion,** *n.f.* Dispersion, breaking up. (*Mil.*) *La dispersion du tir*, the spread of the shot.

disponibilité [dispɔnibili'te], *n.f.* (*Law*) State of being disposable, disposal (of property); (*Mil.*) state of being unattached. *Être en disponibilité*, (*Mil.*) to be unattached, on half-pay. *Fonds en disponibilité* or *disponibilités*, available funds. *Mise en disponibilité*, release. **disponible,** *a.* Disposable, at one's disposal, available; unoccupied, disengaged, vacant.—*n.m.* That which is available; realizable assets. *Marché du disponible*, spot market.

dispos [dis'po], *a.* (*fem.* **dispose**) Fit and well, in good fettle, nimble, alert; cheerful, hearty.

disposer [dispo'ze], *v.t.* To dispose, to arrange, to lay out, to prepare, to make ready; to incline, to prevail upon; to have at command. *Un homme bien disposé pour quelqu'un*, a man well disposed towards someone.—*v.i.* To dispose (*de*); to prescribe, to ordain, to settle; (*Comm.*) to draw a bill. *Disposez de moi*, make what use you like of me. *Il dispose de grands capitaux*, he has a large capital at his command. *Être disposé à faire quelque chose*, to be prepared, inclined, to do something. *Maintenant, vous pouvez disposer*, now you may go. **se disposer,** *v.r.* To dispose oneself, to be disposed; to get ready, to prepare.

dispositif [dispozi'tif], *n.m.* (*Law*) Recital, purview terms (of an act, decree, etc.); (*Tech.*) apparatus, appliance, device; (*Mil.*) disposition (of troops).

disposition [dispozi'sjɔ̃], *n.f.* Disposition, arrangement; disposal; inclination, frame of mind, propensity; mind, resolution, intention; (*pl.*) preparations, arrangements. *Cela est à votre disposition*, that is at your service. *Disposition testamentaire*, (*Law*) will, bequest. *Être en bonne disposition*, to enjoy good health, to be very fit. *Il a des gens à sa disposition*, he has people at his disposal. *Il a de très bonnes dispositions pour vous*, he is very well disposed towards you. *Les dispositions d'une loi*, the provisions (conditions, clauses) of a law.

disproportion [dispropor'sjɔ̃], *n.f.* Disproportion. **disproportionné,** *a.* (*fem.* **-ée**) Disproportionate, inadequate, unsuitable. **disproportionnel,** *a.* (*fem.* **-elle**) Disproportional.

disputable [dispy'tabl], *a.* Disputable, debatable, doubtful.

disputailler [dispyta'je], *v.i.* (*colloq.*) To wrangle (about trifles), to cavil. **disputaillerie,** *n.f.* Wrangling, squabbling, bickering. **disputailleur,** *n.m.* (*fem.* **-euse**). Caviller, wrangler.

dispute [dis'pyt], *n.f.* Dispute, debate, controversy, contest, wrangle; disputation, discussion; (*pop.*) quarrel. **disputer,** *v.i.* To discuss, to argue, to dispute; to contend, to wrangle. *De quoi dispute-t-on?* what is the matter under discussion? *Disputer sur un point de droit*, to discuss a point of law.—*v.t.* To contend for, to fight for; to dispute, to call in question; (*colloq.*) to quarrel with. *Disputer le passage à quelqu'un*, to oppose someone's passage; (*spt.*) *disputer un match*, to fight a match; *il lui dispute le prix*, he contends with him for the prize. **se disputer,** *v.r.* To dispute, to contend, to quarrel, to wrangle. **disputeur,** *a.* (*fem.* **-euse**) Contentious, quarrelsome.—*n.* Wrangler, disputant.

disqualification [diskalifika'sjɔ̃], *n.f.* Disqualification. **disqualifier,** *v.t.* To disqualify.

disque [disk], *n.m.* Discus, quoit; disk; (*Rail.*) signal-disk; gramophone record. *Disque longue durée* or *microsillon*, long-playing record.

disruptif [disryp'tif], *a.* (*fem.* **-ive**) Disruptive. **disrupteur,** *n.m.* (*Elec.*) Interrupter.

dissecteur [disɛk'tœːr], *n.m.* Dissector. **dissection,** *n.f.* Dissection. *Dissection des nerfs*, neurotomy.

dissemblable [disɑ̃'blabl], *a.* Dissimilar, unlike, different. **dissemblablement,** *adv.* Dissimilarly. **dissemblance,** *n.f.* Dissimilarity, difference. **dissemblant,** *a.* (*fem.* **-ante**) Dissimilar, different.

dissémination [disemina'sjɔ̃], *n.f.* Dissemination; scattering (of seeds etc.). **disséminer,** *v.t.* To disseminate, to scatter.

dissension [disɑ̃'sjɔ̃], *n.f.* Dissension, discord, disunion; strife, feud. **dissentiment,** *n.m.* Dissent, disagreement.

disséquer [dise'ke], *v.t. irr.* (*conjugated like* ACCÉLÉRER) To dissect; to analyse. **disséqueur** [DISSECTEUR].

dissertateur [disɛrta'tœːr], *n.m.* One given to dissertation, speechifying. **dissertation,** *n.f.* Dissertation, treatise; composition, essay (in schools). **disserter,** *v.i.* To dissert, expound one's ideas. *Disserter sur un point d'histoire*, to expatiate on a point of history. **disserteur,** *n.m.* (*fem.* **-euse**) Dissertationist.

dissidence [disi'dɑ̃:s], *n.f.* Dissidence, difference of opinion, dissent. **dissident,** *a.* (*fem.* **-ente**) Dissident, dissentient, dissenting. *Secte dissidente*, nonconformist sect.—*n.* Dissident, dissenter, rebel.

dissimilaire [disimi'lɛːr], *a.* Dissimilar, different, unlike. **dissimilarité,** *n.f.* Dissimilarity. **dissimiler,** *v.t.* To render unlike; (*Phonol.*) to modify a sound under the influence of another. **dissimilitude,** *n.f.* Dissimilitude, difference, unlikeness.

dissimulateur [disimyla'tœːr], *n.m.* (*fem.* **-trice**) Dissembler, hypocrite. **dissimulation,** *n.f.* Dissimulation, dissembling; double-dealing. *User de dissimulation*, to dissemble. **dissimulé,** *a.* (*fem.* **-ée**) Dissembling, double-faced, artful. *Caractère* *dissimulé*, artful disposition; *homme profondément dissimulé*, extremely double-faced man. —*n.* Dissembler, hypocrite. **dissimuler**, *v.t.* To dissemble, to conceal; to keep secret, to hide. *Dissimuler sa haine*, to dissemble one's hatred; *dissimuler une injure*, to take no notice of an insult. **se dissimuler**, *v.r.* To conceal from oneself; to hide from each other; to hide oneself, to pass unnoticed; to be concealed.

dissipateur [disipa'tœːr], *a.* (*fem.* -**trice**) Lavish, wasteful, extravagant.—*n.* Squanderer, spendthrift, prodigal. **dissipation**, *n.f.* Dissipation, waste; idleness, distraction, diversion. *Vivre dans la dissipation*, to lead a dissipated life. **dissipé**, *a.* (*fem.* -**ée**) Dissipated, profligate; fast, loose (person); inattentive, unsteady (schoolboy). **dissiper**, *v.t.* To dissipate, to dispel, to disperse; to scatter, to consume fruitlessly, to waste, to squander; to divert, to entertain. *Dissiper les factions*, to quell factions. *Dissiper son bien*, to squander one's wealth. **se dissiper**, *v.r.* To be dispersed, dispelled, or dissipated; to vanish, to pass away; to be squandered; to be inattentive (in class-room).

dissociable [disɔ'sjabl], *a.* Dissociable.

dissocier, *v.t.* To dissociate.

dissolu [disɔ'ly], *a.* (*fem.* -**ue**) Dissolute, profligate, licentious. **dissolubilité**, *n.f.* Dissolubility. **dissoluble**, *a.* Dissoluble, dissolvable. *****dissolutif**, *a.* (*fem.* -**ive**) Dissolving, solvent.

dissolution [disɔly'sjɔ̃], *n.f.* Dissolution; solution; dissoluteness, licentiousness. *Dissolution de société*, dissolution of partnership; *la dissolution d'un mariage*, the annulling of a marriage.

dissolvant [disɔl'vɑ̃], *a.* (*fem.* -**ante**), and *n.m.* Dissolvent, solutive, solvent. *L'eau est un grand dissolvant*, water is a powerful solvent. *Dissolvant (pour ongles)*, varnish remover.

dissonance [disɔ'nɑ̃ːs], *n.f.* Dissonance, discord. **dissonant**, *a.* (*fem.* -**ante**) Dissonant, discordant, jarring.

dissoudre [di'sudr], *v.t. irr.* (*pres.p.* **dissolvant**, *p.p.* **dissous**; *conjugated like* ABSOUDRE) To dissolve; to break up; to annul; to dissipate, to dispel. *Dissoudre un mariage*, to annul a marriage. **se dissoudre**, *v.r.* To dissolve, to be dissolved, to melt; to break up.

dissous [di'su], *a.* (*fem.* -**oute**) Dissolved; broken up.

dissuader [disɥa'de], *v.t.* To dissuade, to advise to the contrary of. **dissuasif**, *a.* (*fem.* -**ive**) Dissuasive. *****dissuasion**, *n.f.* Dissuasion.

dissyllabe [disi'lab], *a.* (*Gram.*) Dissyllabic. —*n.m.* Dissyllable. **dissyllabique**, *a.* Dissyllabic.

dissymétrie [disime'tri], *n.f.* Asymmetry. **dissymétrique**, *a.* Assymetric(al).

distance [dis'tɑ̃ːs], *n.f.* Distance; interval (of place or time). *À combien de distance*, how far off; *de distance en distance*, from place to place, at different points; *à faible distance*, at short range; (*Opt.*) *distance focale*, focal length; *distance parcourue en un jour*, day's run; *garder ses distances*, *se tenir à distance*, to keep one's distance, to hold aloof; *tenir à distance*, to keep at a distance. **distancer**, *v.t.* To out-distance, to surpass, to outrun,

to outdo. **distant**, *a.* (*fem.* -**ante**) Distant, remote; aloof, stand-offish.

distendre [dis'tɑ̃ːdr], *v.t.* To distend. **distension**, *n.f.* Distension, strain.

distillable [disti'labl], *a.* Distillable. **distillateur**, *n.m.* Distiller. **distillation**, *n.f.* Distillation. **distillatoire**, *a.* Distillatory.

distiller [disti'le], *v.t.* To distil; to discharge, drop, exude, or secrete drop by drop. *Distiller son venin sur quelqu'un*, to vent one's spite upon someone.—*v.i.* To drop, to distil, to drizzle, to trickle. **distillerie**, *n.f.* Distillery, still-house, distilling.

distinct [dis'tɛ̃], *a.* (*fem.* **distincte**) Distinct, different, separate; clear, plain. **distinctement**, *adv.* Distinctly, clearly, plainly. **distinctif**, *a.* (*fem.* **distinctive**) Distinctive, distinguishing, characteristic. *Caractère distinctif* or *marque distinctive*, characteristic. **distinction**, *n.f.* Distinction, discrimination, distinguishing, differentiating; division, difference; eminence, superiority, honours; elegance, refinement, good breeding. *Défaut de distinction*, want of distinction; *des marques de distinction*, marks of distinction. *Faire distinction de l'ami et de l'ennemi*, to distinguish between friend and foe; *par distinction*, for distinction's sake; *sans distinction*, promiscuously, indiscriminately. **distinctivement**, *adv.* Distinctively.

distinguable [distɛ̃'gabl], *a.* Distinguishable.

distingué, *a.* (*fem.* -**ée**) Distinguished, eminent, noted; elegant, well-bred.

distinguer [distɛ̃'ge], *v.t.* To distinguish, to discern, to make out; to discriminate, to separate, to make distinction between; to single out, to honour, to take notice of, to treat with distinction. **se distinguer**, *v.r.* To be noticeable or conspicuous; to gain distinction, to signalize oneself. *Il se distingue par son courage*, he is conspicuous for his bravery.

distinguo [distɛ̃'go], *n.m.* Distinction. *Faire un distinguo*, to make a subtle distinction.

distique [dis'tik], *n.m.* Distich; couplet.—*a.* (*Bot.*) Distichous.

distordre [dis'tɔrdr], *v.t.* To distort; to sprain. **se distordre**, *v.r.* To become distorted. **distorsion**, *n.f.* Distortion; sprain.

distraction [distrak'sjɔ̃], *n.f.* Separation, subtraction; abstraction; absence of mind, heedlessness, inattention; recreation, diversion, change, hobby. *Il est sujet à des distractions*, he is subject to fits of absence of mind. *Par distraction*, inadvertently, by inattention.

distraire [dis'trɛːr], *v.t. irr.* (*p.p.* **distrait**; *conjugated like* TRAIRE) To separate, to subtract; to distract, to disturb, to turn (from); to entertain, to amuse. *Distraire des études*, to distract from study; *la moindre chose le distrait*, the least thing distracts his attention. **se distraire**, *v.r.* To be disturbed, to be diverted (*de*); to amuse oneself, to take relaxation. **distrait**, *a.* (*fem.* -**aite**) Absentminded, inattentive, heedless; distracted, vacant. *Air distrait* or *regards distraits*, absent air, vacant looks; *écouter d'une oreille distraite*, to listen inattentively.—*n.m.* Absentminded man. **distraitement**, *adv.* Absentmindedly, absently. **distrayant**, *a.* (*fem.* -**ante**) Diverting, pleasing, entertaining.

distribuable [distri'bɥabl], *a.* Distributable.
distribuer [distri'bɥe], *v.t.* To distribute, to divide, to deal or portion out; to dispose, to lay out, to arrange; (*Print.*) to distribute; (*Theat.*) to cast, to allot (parts). *Distribuer des aumônes,* to distribute alms; *distribuer un appartement,* to lay out a suite of rooms; *distribuer des rations,* to serve out rations. **distributaire,** *a.* Receiving (a portion).—*n.* Recipient, receiver, sharer. **distributeur,** *a.* (*fem.* **-trice**) Distributing.—*n.* Distributer, bestower, dispenser. *Distributeur des vivres,* (*Naut.*) purser's steward, purser's mate. *Distributeur automatique,* automatic machine, penny-in-the-slot machine. **distributif,** *a.* (*fem.* **-ive**) Distributive. **distribution,** *n.f.* Distribution; division; disposition, arrangement (of rooms etc.); delivery (of letters by post); (*Print.*) distribution (of type); (*Theat.*) casting, cast. *Distribution des prix,* prizegiving; *distribution d'eau,* water supply; *la distribution de cet appartement est commode,* this suite of rooms is conveniently laid out. *Ordre de distribution,* roll of creditors (for dividends).
district [dis'trikt], *n.m.* (Administrative) district; region.
dit [di], *a.* (*fem.* **dite**) Said, spoken, agreed; surnamed, called. *Aussitôt dit, aussitôt fait,* no sooner said than done; *autrement dit,* in other words; *cela dit,* thereupon; *ce qui fut dit fut fait,* he was as good as his word; *se le tenir pour dit,* to learn one's lesson.—*n.m.* Maxim; saying; (*Medieval*) fable, tale. *Avoir son dit et son dédit* [DÉDIT]; *les dits et faits des anciens,* the acts and sayings of the ancients.
dithyrambe [diti'rɑ̃:b], *n.m.* Dithyramb; (*Pros.*) dithyrambic. **dithyrambique,** *a.* Dithyrambic.
dito [di'to], *adv.* (*Comm.*) Ditto, (*abbr.*) do.
dittographie [ditɔgra'fi], *n.f.* Dittography.
diurèse [diy're:z], *n.f.* Diuresis. **diurétique** [diyre'tik], *a.* and *n.m.* Diuretic.
diurnal [djyr'nal], *a.* (*fem.* **-ale**, *pl.* **-aux**) Diurnal.—*n.m.* Diurnal, daily prayer-book. **diurne,** *a.* Diurnal, daily.—*n.m.* Diurnal insect.
divagant [diva'gɑ̃], *a.* (*fem.* **-ante**) Wandering, rambling. **divagateur,** *a.* (*fem.* **-trice**) Desultory, rambling.—*n.* Desultory, rambling speaker. **divagation,** *n.f.* Divagation, wandering, rambling, going astray. *Se perdre dans des divagations,* to lose sight of the question. **divaguer,** *v.i.* To ramble, to wander from the question; to go astray; to stray (of cattle); to be incoherent (in writing or speaking).
divan [di'vɑ̃], *n.m.* Divan; couch.
divarication [divarika'sjɔ̃], *n.f.* Divarication. **divariqué,** *a.* (*fem.* **-ée**) (*Bot.*) Straggling. **divariquer,** *v.i.* To divaricate.
*dive [di:v], *a.f.* Divine. *La dive bouteille,* (*fig.*) rosy Bacchus, the good red wine.
divergence [diver'ʒɑ̃:s], *n.f.* Divergence, divergency; (*fig.*) difference (of opinion etc.); (*Alg.*) opposition. **divergent,** *a.* (*fem.* **-ente**) Divergent; different; (*Bot.*) spreading. **diverger,** *v.i.* To diverge, to branch off, to spread; (*fig.*) to be widely different.
divers [di'vɛːr], *a.* (*fem.* **diverse**) Diverse, multifarious, miscellaneous; changing, vary-

ing; (*pl.*) divers, sundry, several. *Faits divers,* news items; *frais divers,* sundry expenses. **diversement,** *adv.* Diversely, variously, differently. **diversicolore,** *a.* Variegated. **diversifiable,** *a.* Diversifiable. **diversifier,** *v.t.* To diversify, to vary; to variegate. *Diversifier l'entretien,* to give variety to the conversation. **se diversifier,** *v.r.* To be varied or diversified.
diversion [diver'sjɔ̃], *n.f.* Diversion; change, distraction. **diversité,** *n.f.* Diversity, variety, difference.
divertir [diver'tiːr], *v.t.* To amuse, to recreate, to delight, to exhilarate; to divert; to embezzle, to convert to one's own use. *Divertir des fonds,* to misapply funds. **se divertir,** *v.r.* To amuse oneself; to be diverted or amused, to be merry; to make sport (*de*). **divertissant,** *a.* (*fem.* **-ante**) Diverting, entertaining, amusing. **divertissement,** *n.m.* Diversion, pastime, relaxation; recreation, amusement, entertainment; (*Mus.*) light piece of music; (*Theat.*) interlude; (*Law*) embezzlement, misappropriation.
divette [di'vɛt], *n.f.* Musical comedy actress.
dividende [divi'dɑ̃:d], *n.m.* Dividend. *Dividende arriéré,* unclaimed dividend.
divin [di'vɛ̃], *a.* (*fem.* **divine**) Divine, godlike, heaven-born, heavenly; (*fig.*) admirable, exquisite. *L'office divin,* divine service; *le Divin Enfant,* the Holy Child. *Ouvrage divin,* most admirable work.—*n.m.* The divine.
divinateur [divina'tœːr], *a.* (*fem.* **-trice**) Prophetic, divining, foreseeing.—*n.m.* Diviner, seer. **divination,** *n.f.* Divination. *Divination par le feu,* pyromancy. **divinatoire,** *a.* Divinatory, divining.
divinement [divin'mɑ̃], *adv.* Divinely; (*fig.*) admirably, exquisitely. **divinisation,** *n.f.* Divinization. **diviniser,** *v.t.* To deify; to laud to the skies. **divinité,** *n.f.* Divinity, Godhead, deity. *Adorer la divinité,* to worship the Divinity. *C'est une divinité,* that woman is an angel.
divis [di'vi], *a.* (*fem.* **divise**) (*Law*) Divided.—*n.m.* Apportioned estate. *Posséder par divis,* to possess a portion of.
diviser [divi'ze], *v.t.* To divide, to parcel out, to portion out; to disunite, to set at variance. *Diviser le tout en ses parties,* to divide the whole into its parts. **se diviser,** *v.r.* To be divided; to be split into parts; to be disunited, to be at variance. **diviseur,** *n.m.* (*Arith.*) Divisor; divider. *Diviseur commun,* common factor.—*a.* Divisive, dividing. **divisibilité,** *n.f.* Divisibility. **divisible,** *a.* Divisible.
division [divi'zjɔ̃], *n.f.* Division, partition, dividing; (*Mil.*) division. *Être en division,* to be at variance. **divisionnaire,** *a.* Divisional, divisionary. *Monnaie divisionnaire,* small coin; (*Mil.*) *ambulance divisionnaire,* field hospital.—*n.m.* (short for) *général de division.* **divisoire,** *a.* Dividing.
divorce [di'vɔrs], *n.m.* Divorce; (*fig.*) separation, rupture, variance. *Demander le divorce,* to sue for a divorce. *Faire divorce,* to renounce. *Ils sont dans un continuel divorce,* they are always at variance. **divorcer,** *v.i.* To divorce oneself (*de*); to break with. *Elle a divorcé d'avec lui,* she has been divorced from him; *ils sont divorcés,* they have been

divorced. **divorcé**, *a.* and *n.m.* (*fem.* **-ée**) Divorced; a divorced person.

divulgation [divylgɑ'sjɔ̃], *n.f.* Divulgation, divulgence; revelation; publishing. **divulguer**, *v.t.* To divulge, to reveal, to make public. *Se divulguer*, to leak out (secret).

dix [dis], or before a vowel [diz], *a.* Ten; tenth. *Innocent dix*, Innocent the Tenth.— *n.m.* Ten; ten (of hearts etc.). **dix-huit** [di'zɥit], *a.* and *n.m.* Eighteen. **dix-huitième**, *a.* Eighteenth. **dixième**, *a.* Tenth. —*n.m.* Tenth part. **dixièmement**, *adv.* Tenthly. **dix-neuf** [diz'nœf], *a.* and *n.m.* Nineteen; nineteenth. **dix-neuvième**, *a.* and *n.* Nineteenth.—*n.m.* Nineteenth part. **dix-sept** [dis'sɛt], *a.* and *n.m.* Seventeen; seventeenth. **dix-septième**, *a.* and *n.* Seventeenth.—*n.m.* Seventeenth part.

dizain [di'zɛ̃], *n.m.* Strophe or stanza of ten lines; rosary consisting of ten beads; set of ten packs (of cards). **dizaine**, *n.f.* Half a score; ten; about ten.

Djaggernat [dʒagɛr'nat] or **Jaggernath**, *n.m.* Juggernaut.

djinn [dʒin], *n.m.* Jinn(ee).

do [do], *n.m.* (*Mus.*) Do or ut; (the note) C.

dochmiaque [dɔkmi'ak], *a.* Dochmiac.

docile [dɔ'sil], *a.* Docile, tractable, submissive, amenable. **docilement**, *adv.* With docility, submissively. **docilité**, *n.f.* Docility, tractability.

dock [dɔk], *n.m.* Dock, dockyard; warehouse. **docker** [dɔ'kɛːr], *n.m.* Docker.

docte [dɔkt], *a.* Erudite, learned. **doctement**, *adv.* Learnedly; pedantically.

docteur [dɔk'tœːr], *n.* Doctor, savant, scholar. *Docteur en théologie, en droit,* or *en médecine,* doctor of divinity, of law or of medicine; *docteur ès lettres,* D.Litt.; *docteur ès sciences,* doctor of science. *Envoyer chercher le docteur,* to call for a physician. *Le docteur Moore,* Dr. Moore. **doctissime**, *a.* Most learned. **doctoral**, *a.* (*fem.* **-ale**, *pl.* **-aux**) Doctoral. **doctoralement**, *adv.* Doctorally. **doctorat**, *n.m.* Doctorate, doctor's degree. **doctoresse**, *n.f.* Sometimes used for '*femme médecin*'.

doctrinaire [dɔktri'nɛːr], *n.m.* Doctrinaire.— *a.* Stiff, formal, pedantic. **doctrinairement**, *adv.* Stiffly, formally, pedantically. **doctrinarisme**, *n.m.* Political system of the doctrinaires. **doctrinal**, *a.* (*fem.* **-ale**, *pl.* **-aux**) Doctrinal. **doctrinalement**, *adv.* Doctrinally.

doctrine [dɔk'trin], *n.f.* Doctrine.

document [dɔky'mã], *n.m.* Document (title, title-deed, charter, certificate, etc.), *pl.* Documents, records. **documentaire**, *a.* Documentary.—*n.m.* (*Cine.*) Documentary film. **documentation**, *n.f.* Documentation. **documenter**, *v.t.* To give information; to document. *Se documenter,* to gather documentary evidence, historical or social facts. *Ouvrage bien documenté,* a work based on documentary evidence.

dodécaèdre [dɔdeka'ɛdr], *n.m.* Dodecahedron. **dodécaédrique**, *a.* Dodecahedral, twelve-sided. **dodécagonal**, *a.* (*fem.* **-ale**, *pl.* **-aux**) Dodecagonal. **dodécagone**, *n.m.* Dodecagon.

dodelinement [dɔdlin'mã], *n.m.* Wagging, nodding (of head); dandling. **dodeliner**, *v.t.*

To dandle, to rock (a child).—*v.i.* To wag, nod (head).

dodinage [dodi'naːʒ], *n.m.* Oscillation, rocking; shaking up, stirring (of wine etc.). **dodiner**, *v.t.* To rock, to dandle.—*v.i.* To oscillate. **se dodiner**, *v.r.* To rock one's body; to nurse or coddle oneself.

dodo [do'do], *n.m.* (*Infantile*) Bye-bye, (*fig.*) sleep, bed. *Aller au dodo,* to go to bed, to go to sleep; *faire dodo,* to go to bye-byes.

dodu [dɔ'dy], *a.* (*fem.* **dodue**) Plump.

dogaresse [dɔga'rɛs], *n.f.* Wife of a doge.

doge [dɔːʒ], *n.m.* Doge.

dogmatique [dɔgma'tik], *a.* Dogmatic.—*n.f.* Dogmatics. **dogmatiquement**, *adv.* Dogmatically. **dogmatiser**, *v.i.* To dogmatize. —*v.t.* To state, order, etc., dogmatically. **dogmatiseur**, *n.m.* Dogmatizer. **dogmatisme**, *n.m.* Dogmatism. **dogmatiste**, *n.m.* Dogmatist.

dogme [dɔgm], *n.m.* Dogma, tenet.

dogre [dɔgr], *n.m.* Dutch dogger, doggerboat.

dogue [dɔg], *n.m.* Mastiff; (*fig.*) a bull-dog (of a man).

doguer (se) [dɔ'ge], *v.r.* To butt each other (of rams).

doguin [dɔ'gɛ̃], *n.m.* Whelp of mastiff; pug.

doigt [dwa], *n.m.* Finger; digit; (as a measure) finger's breadth, nip, thimbleful. *Avoir sur les doigts,* to be rebuked or chastised; *donner sur les doigts,* to give a rap on the knuckles, to reprimand, to rebuke; *être à deux doigts de sa ruine,* to be upon the brink of ruin; *être comme les deux doigts de la main,* to be hand and glove together, to be inseparable; *il est à deux doigts de la mort,* he is at death's door; *il lui obéit au doigt et à l'œil,* he is at his beck and call; *tu t'es mis le doigt dans l'œil,* you are entirely mistaken; *vous avez mis le doigt dessus,* you have hit the nail on the head; *mon petit doigt me l'a dit,* a little bird told me so; *on le montre du doigt,* he is pointed at (*usu.* with scorn or derision); *savoir quelque chose sur le bout du doigt,* to have a thing at one's finger-tips; *se mordre les doigts de quelque chose,* to repent of a thing; *s'en lécher les doigts,* to lick one's lips, to gloat over something; *il est anglais jusqu'au bout des doigts,* he is every inch an Englishman. *Un doigt de vin,* a thimbleful of wine. *Doigts de pied,* toes.

doigté [dwa'te], *n.m.* (*Mus.*) Fingering, touch; (*fig.*) tact, adroitness. **doigter**, *v.i.* (*Mus.*) To finger. **doigtier**, *n.m.* Finger-stall.

doit [dwa], *n.m.* Debit, debtor side of an account. *Doit et avoir,* (*Comm.*) debtor and creditor; debit and credit.

dol [dɔl], *n.m.* Deceit, fraud.

dolage [dɔ'laːʒ], *n.m.* Planing.

doléances [dɔle'ãːs], *n.f.*, *pl.* Complaint; grievance. *Exprimer* or *présenter ses doléances,* to tell one's griefs, to pour out one's troubles.

dolemment [dɔla'mã], *adv.* Dolefully.

dolent, *a.* (*fem.* **dolente**) Doleful, piteous, plaintive; painful.

doler [dɔ'le], *v.t.* To smooth with the adze; to plane, to pare.

dolichocéphale [dɔlikɔse'fal], *a.* and *n.* Dolichocephalic (man or woman). **dolichocéphalie**, *n.f.* Dolichocephalism.

dolman [dɔl'mã], *n.m.* Dolman, jacket, hussar's pelisse.

dolmen [dɔl'mɛn], *n.m.* Dolmen, table-shaped megalith.

doloir [dɔ'lwaːr], *n.m.* Paring-knife, parer.

doloire, *n.f.* Cooper's adze; mason's axe. *Doloire de guerre*, battle-axe.

dolomie [dɔlɔ'mi] or **dolomite**, *n.f.* Dolomite (marble).

dolosif [dɔlɔ'zif], *a.* (*fem.* **-ive**) Fraudulent.

dom [dɔ̃], *n.m.* Dom (Benedictine title).

domaine [dɔ'mɛːn], *n.m.* Domain, estate, property; realm, province, sphere. *Cela n'est point de mon domaine*, that is not in my province. *Le domaine de la couronne*, the Crown lands; *tomber dans le domaine public*, to become public property, to be out of copyright. **domanial**, *a.* (*fem.* **-iale**, *pl.* **-iaux**) Domainal. *Forêts domaniales*, Crown forests.

dôme [doːm], *n.m.* Dome; canopy, vault; (in Italy) cathedral. *Dôme du palais*, roof of the mouth.

domestication [dɔmɛstikɑ'sjɔ̃], *n.f.* Domestication. **domesticité**, *n.f.* Domesticity; state of being in domestic service; (*collect.*) domestic servants.

domestique [dɔmɛs'tik], *a.* Domestic, homely, home-bred; tame, domesticated.—*n.* Servant, domestic; (*collect.*) body of servants or domestics (of a house); household. *Il a changé tout son domestique*, he has changed all his servants. **domestiquer**, *v.t.* To domesticate, to tame. **se domestiquer**, *v.r.* To become domesticated.

domicile [dɔmi'sil], *n.m.* Domicile, residence. *À domicile*, at one's own house, at home; *domicile civil*, ordinary residence, dwelling; *domicile politique*, political residence; *élire domicile* or *faire élection de domicile*, to choose one's residence, to settle down. **domiciliaire**, *a.* Domiciliary. *Faire une visite domiciliaire chez quelqu'un*, to search someone's house. **domiciliation**, *n.f.* Domiciliation. **domicilié**, *a.* (*fem.* **-ée**) Resident, domiciled. *Il est domicilié à Paris*, he resides in Paris. **se domicilier**, *v.r.* (*conjugated like* PRIER) To settle down, to dwell in a place.

dominance [dɔmi'nɑ̃ːs], *n.f.* Dominance. **dominant**, *a.* Dominant, predominant, prevalent. *Goût dominant*, reigning taste; *idée dominante*, leading idea; *passion dominante*, ruling passion.—*n.f.* (*Mus.*) Dominant, key-note.

dominateur [dɔminɑ'tœːr], *a.* (*fem.* **-trice**) Ruling, governing, dominant, domineering, arrogant.—*n.* Dominator, ruler, tyrant. **domination**, *n.f.* Domination; dominion, rule, sway; (*pl.*) dominions (of angels).

dominer [dɔmi'ne], *v.i.* To rule, to bear rule, to have the mastery, to control; to dominate, to preponderate, to prevail; to domineer, to lord it; to tower, to rise. *Il faut que la raison domine sur les passions*, reason must prevail over the passions. *Sa tête domine au-dessus de la foule*, his head rises above the crowd. —*v.t.* To dominate, to master, to command; to rule, to govern; to prevail over, to domineer over; to rise above, to command a view of. *Le château domine le village*, the castle towers over the village. **se dominer**, *v.r.* To control one's feelings.

Dominicaine [dɔmini'kɛn], **la République**, *f.* The Dominican Republic.

dominicain [dɔmini'kɛ̃], *a.* (*fem.* **-aine**) Dominican.—*n.* Dominican, Dominican friar or nun.

dominical [dɔmini'kal], *a.* (*fem.* **-ale**, *pl.* **-aux**) Dominical. *Lettre dominicale*, dominical letter; *l'oraison dominicale*, the Lord's Prayer; *repos dominical*, Sunday rest.—*n.f.* Sunday sermon (not in Advent or Lent).

dominion [dɔmi'njɔ̃], *n.m.* Dominion.

Dominique [dɔmi'nik], *m.* Dominic.

domino [dɔmi'no], *n.m.* Domino. *En domino*, in a domino. *Faire domino*, to play out, to win. *Jouer aux dominos*, to play at dominoes.

Domitien [dɔmi'sjɛ̃], *m.* Domitian.

dommage [dɔ'maːʒ], *n.m.* Damage, injury, hurt, detriment, loss, harm. *Cela me porte dommage*, that is a loss to me; *c'est dommage*, it is a pity; *dommages et intérêts* or *dommages-intérêts*, (*Law*) damages; *dommages de guerre*, war damage compensation; *causer du dommage*, to do harm. **dommageable**, *a.* Hurtful, prejudicial, injurious.

domptable [dɔ̃'tabl], *a.* Tamable, manageable. **domptage**, *n.m.* Taming.

dompter [dɔ̃'te], *v.t.* To subdue, to subjugate, to master; to tame, to break in. *Dompter des animaux*, to tame animals; *dompter ses passions*, to overcome one's passions; *dompter un cheval*, to break in a horse. **se dompter**, *v.r.* To quell, to overcome one's passions. **dompteur** [dɔ̃'tœːr], *n.m.* (*fem.* **-euse**) Subduer, vanquisher; tamer; breaker-in.

dompte-venin, *n.m. inv.* (*Bot.*) Any species of *Asclepias*, formerly regarded as an antidote to poison; common celandine.

don (1) [dɔ̃], *n.m.* Gift, donation, present; (*fig.*) endowment, aptitude, talent. *Don gratuit*, free gift; *dons de la nature*, natural endowments; *il a le don de plaire*, he has the knack of pleasing; *le don de la parole*, the gift of the gab; *les dons du ciel*, the gifts of heaven.

don (2) [dɔ̃], *n.m.* Don. **doña, dona** [dɔ'ɲa], *n.f.* Donna.

donataire [dɔna'tɛːr], *n.* Donee, receiver. **donateur**, *n.m.* (*fem.* **-trice**) Donor, giver.

donation [dɔna'sjɔ̃], *n.f.* Donation, free gift; deed of gift. *Donations de la couronne*, grants of the Crown. *Faire donation de ses biens*, to make over one's property by deed of gift.

donc [dɔ̃ːk, dɔ̃], *conj.* Then, therefore, accordingly, hence; consequently; of course, to be sure. *Je pense, donc je suis*, I think, therefore I exist. *Qu'ai-je donc fait?* whatever have I done?. *Répondez donc*, answer, I tell you. *Taisez-vous donc!* Do be quiet!

dondaine [FARIDONDAINE].

dondon [dɔ̃'dɔ̃], *n.f.* (*colloq.*) Plump woman or girl.

donjon [dɔ̃'ʒɔ̃], *n.m.* Keep, castle-keep; (*Arch.*) turret (on a roof). **donjonné**, *a.* (*fem.* **-ée**) (*Her.*) Turreted.

don-juanesque [dɔ̃ʒɥa'nɛsk], *a.* Donjuanesque, like a Don Juan. **don-juanisme**, *n.m.* Donjuanism.

donnant [dɔ'nɑ̃], *a.* (*fem.* **-ante**) Open-handed, generous. *Donnant donnant*, give and take, cash down; *il n'est pas donnant*, he is not generous.

donne [dɔn], *n.f.* Deal (at cards). *Nouvelle donne*, new deal.

donnée [dɔ'ne], *n.f.* Given fact, datum; notion, idea; (*Math.*) known quantity; theme of a play, poem, etc.; (*pl.*) data, particulars.

donner [dɔ'ne], *v.t.* To give, to bestow, to present (a person) with, to make a present of; to grant, to confer; to ascribe; to occasion, to produce, to cause; to show, to exhibit; to indicate; to publish, to produce (a play etc.); to inflict, to furnish, to supply; to deal (at cards). *C'est à vous à donner*, it is your turn to deal; *c'est donné!* it's dirt cheap! (*fam.*) *donner du Monsieur à quelqu'un*, to call someone 'Sir'; *donner de la peine*, to trouble; *donner du chagrin*, to vex; *donner en échange*, to give in exchange; *donner faim, soif, chaud, froid, sommeil*, etc., to make hungry, thirsty, hot, cold, sleepy, etc.; *donner gain de cause*, to decide in favour of; *donner la chasse*, to pursue; *donner la vie*, to grant life (to); *donner le bonjour à quelqu'un*, to wish someone good-day; *donner le branle à une affaire*, to set an affair going; *donner le change à quelqu'un*, to take someone in; *donner l'éveil*, to arouse suspicion; *donner le ton*, to set the fashion; *donner rendez-vous*, to make an appointment; *donner sa parole*, to give one's word; *donner sa voix* or *son suffrage*, to give one's vote; *donner tort à quelqu'un*, to blame someone; *donnez-nous à manger*, give us something to eat; *donner un coup de main*, to give a helping hand; *en donner à quelqu'un*, to beat or to maul someone, to take someone in; *je vous le donne en cent*, I'll give you a hundred guesses; *quel âge lui donnez-vous?* how old do you think he is?; *mal donner*, to misdeal.— *v.i.* To give, to give way; to strike, to hit, to stumble (*dans*); to fall, to rush; to be addicted to *or* fond of; to charge, to be engaged, to attack (of troops etc.); to be given; to yield, to bear, to produce; to look, to overlook. *Donner à boire*, to give to drink; *donner à penser à quelqu'un*, to set someone thinking; *donner de la tête contre*, to bump into, to run into; *donner dedans, dans le piège*, or *dans le panneau*, to fall into the trap; *donner or taper dans l'œil*, to fascinate, to dazzle; *donner dans une embuscade*, to fall into an ambuscade; *donner sur les doigts*, to punish; *donner sur les nerfs*, to grate on the nerves; (*Mil.*) *faire donner les blindés*, to attack with the armour; *les blés ont beaucoup donné*, the wheat yielded well; *le soleil donne dans ma chambre*, the sun shines into my room; *mes fenêtres donnent sur la rue*, my windows overlook the street. **se donner**, *v.r.* To be given, to give oneself; to procure; to take place (of battles etc.); to ascribe to oneself; to give oneself out (*pour*); to be addicted (*à*). *Se donner à quelqu'un*, to abandon or devote oneself to someone; *se donner au jeu*, to be addicted to gambling; *se donner des airs*, to give oneself airs; *se donner la peine de*, to take the trouble to; *s'en donner à cœur joie*, to indulge oneself to one's heart's content, to take one's fill of something. **donneur**, *n.m.* (*fem.* **donneuse**) Giver, donor; one fond of giving; dealer (of cards). *Donneur de sang*, blood donor.

don Quichotte [dõki'ʃɔt], *n.m.* (*pl.* **don Quichottes**) Don Quixote, quixotic person; lanky fellow. **don quichottisme**, *n.m.* Quixotism.

dont [dõ], *pron.* Whose, of which, of whom, from whom, etc. *Ce cadeau dont je suis content et dont je vous remercie*, this gift with which I am delighted and for which I thank you; *ce dont il s'agit*, the business in hand; *Dieu dont nous admirons les œuvres*, God whose works we admire; *la famille dont je sors*, the family I come from; *l'affaire dont je vous ai parlé*, the business I spoke to you about.

donzelle [dõ'zɛl], *n.f.* Damsel; wench.

doper [dɔ'pe], *v.t.* (*spt.*) To dope (a horse, an athlete, etc.). **doping** [dɔ'piŋ], *n.m.* Dope; doping.

dorade [dɔ'rad], *n.f.* (*Ichth.*) Dorado coryphene (a dolphin-like fish). *Dorade bilunée*, sea-bream.

dorage [dɔ'raʒ], *n.m.* Gilding (of plate); glazing (of pastry).

doré [dɔ're], *a.* (*fem.* **dorée** (1)) Gilt, gilded, golden, gold-coloured. *Doré sur tranche*, gilt-edged; *jeunesse dorée*, gilded youth; *langue dorée*, winning, deceitful tongue.

dorée (2) [dɔ're], *n.f.* John Dory (fish).

dorénavant [dɔrena'vɑ̃], *adv.* Henceforth, hereafter, from this time forward.

dorer [dɔ're], *v.t.* To gild; to cover with or as with gold or a golden hue; to glaze (pastry). *Dorer la pilule*, to gild the pill. *Dorer un pâté*, to glaze a pie with yolk of egg. **se dorer**, *v.r.* To gild; to assume a golden hue, to become yellow. **doreur**, *n.m.* (*fem.* **doreuse**) Gilder.

dorien [dɔ'rjɛ̃], *a.* and *n.* (*fem.* **dorienne**) Dorian. *Le dorien*, the Doric dialect.

dorine [dɔ'rin], *n.f.* (*Bot.*) Golden saxifrage.

dorique [dɔ'rik], *a.* and *n.m.* Doric.

doris [dɔ'ris], *n.m.* Dory (of cod-fishers).

dorloter [dɔrlɔ'te], *v.t.* To fondle, to pamper, to coddle, to pet. **se dorloter**, *v.r.* To coddle oneself; to indulge oneself.

dorlotine [dɔrlɔ'tin], *n.f.* (a sort of) chaise-longue.

dormant [dɔr'mɑ̃], *a.* (*fem.* **dormante**) Sleeping, asleep; inert, dormant, stagnant; dull (of business), unemployed (of money). *Châssis dormant*, fixed sash. *Eau dormante*, stagnant water; *les sept dormants*, the Seven Sleepers. *Manœuvre dormante*, (*Naut.*) standing part of a tackle.—*n.m.* Fixed frame (of window etc.).

dormeur [dɔr'mœ:r], *n.m.* (*fem.* **dormeuse** (1)) Sleeper; sluggard.—*a.* Sleepy, drowsy, sluggish. **dormeuse** (2), *n.f.* Sort of chaise-longue; stud ear-ring.

dormir [dɔr'mi:r], *v.i. irr.* (*pres.p.* **dormant**, *p.p.* **dormi**) To sleep, to be asleep; to remain or be immovable; to lie still; to lie dormant (of money); to be stagnant (of water); to do nothing. *Un conte à dormir debout*, an old wives' tale, a tall story; *dormir d'un bon sommeil* or *d'un bon somme*, to sleep soundly; *dormir sur les deux oreilles*, to sleep soundly, (*fig.*) to feel perfectly secure; *dormir debout*, to be unable to keep one's eyes open; *il n'y a pire eau que l'eau qui dort*, still waters run deep; *qui dort dîne*, sleeping is as good as eating.—**n.m.* Sleep.

dormitif [dɔrmi'tif], *a.* (*fem.* **-ive**) Soporific, dormitive. *Une potion dormitive*, a sleeping-draught.—*n.m.* A dormitive.

doronic [dɔrɔ'nik], *n.m.* (*Bot.*) Doronicum, leopard's bane.

Dorothée [dɔrɔ'te], *f.* Dorothy.

dorsal [dɔr′sal], *a.* (*fem.* **-ale**, *pl.* **-aux**) Dorsal. *L'épine dorsale*, the spine, the back-bone.—*n.f.* Dorsal fin.—*n.m.* Dorsal. **dorsibranche**, *n.m.* A dorsibranchiate annelid.

dortoir [dɔr′twaːr], *n.m.* Dormitory.

dorure [dɔ′ryːr], *n.f.* Gilding; glazing (of pastry with yolk of egg).

doryphore [dɔri′fɔːr], *n.m.* Colorado beetle; *pl.* (*fam.*) the Germans, 'Jerries' (1940-1944).

dos [do], *n.m. inv.* Back; rear; top, ridge (of a mountain etc.). *Avoir bon dos*, to take the blame, or to shoulder extra burdens, to be able to 'take it'; *avoir quelqu'un sur le dos*, to be saddled with somebody; *j'en ai plein le dos*, I am fed up with it; *il me scie le dos*, he bores me to death; *dos courbé* or *voûté*, bent back; *faire le gros dos*, to arch its back (of a cat), (*fig.*) to put one's back up, to give oneself airs. *Le juge les renvoya dos à dos*, the judge non-suited them both; *se mettre le juge à dos*, to set the judge against one. *Sur le dos*, on the back, on one's back; *tourner le dos*, to turn tail, to take to flight; *tourner le dos à quelqu'un*, to turn one's back on or to desert someone; *passer la main dans le dos à quelqu'un*, to flatter, to wheedle him. *Dos d'âne*, ridge sloping away to each side; *toit en dos d'âne*, saddle-back roof; *pont en dos d'âne*, hump-backed bridge; *route en dos d'âne*, high-crowned road. *Voir au dos*, see overleaf.

dosable [do′zabl], *a.* The quantity, ingredients, etc., of which can be determined, measurable. **dosage**, *n.m.* Dosage; titration; quantity determination.

dose [doːz], *n.f.* Dose; quantity; portion. **doser**, *v.t.* To put the right quantity of (a drug etc.) in a dose, to proportion. **dosimétrique**, *a.* Dosimetric.

dossard [do′sar], *n.m.* (*spt.*) Big number pinned on the back of each racer or player.

dosse [dos], *n.f.* Slab (of timber).

dosseret [do′sre], *n.m.* Backing (of saw); jamb (of door); pier (of chimney, wall).

dossier [do′sje], *n.m.* Back (of a seat, chair, etc.); brief (of a barrister); notes, papers filed together; record (of a person's antecedents etc.), dossier. **dossière**, *n.f.* Back-band, ridge-band (of harness); back-plate (of a cuirass).

dot [dɔt], *n.f.* Marriage portion, dowry. *Coureur de dots*, fortune-hunter; *jeune fille sans dot*, portionless girl; *la dot d'une religieuse*, what a nun pays for being admitted into a nunnery. **dotal**, *a.* (*fem.* **-ale**, *pl.* **-aux**) Of or concerning dowry. **dotation**, *n.f.* Endowment. *Caisse de dotation*, endowment fund. **doter**, *v.t.* To give a dowry to; to endow; to make a grant.

douaire [dwɛːr], *n.m.* (Widow's) dower; jointure, marriage-settlement. *Il lui a assigné dix mille livres de douaire*, he has settled ten thousand pounds upon her. **douairière**, *n.f.* Dowager; (*fam.*) imposing old lady.

douane [dwan], *n.f.* The customs; custom-house; custom-duty, duty. *La visite de la douane*, the customs examination; *droit de douane*, customs duty. **douanier** (1), *n.m.* Customs officer; (*Naut.*) tide-waiter. **douanier** (2), *a.* (*fem.* **douanière**) Relating to the custom-house, of customs. *Union douanière*, Customs union.

douar [dwar], *n.m.* Arab village of tents; rural district (in N. Africa).

doublage [du′blaːʒ], *n.m.* Lining, plating, doubling, sheathing, etc.; (*Print.*) double; (*Cine.*) dubbing.

double [dubl], *a.* Twofold, twice as much, twice as many; double, duplicate; of double strength, quality, etc.; (*fig.*) deceitful, double dealing; downright. *Agent double*, a double agent, spy for both sides; *faire coup double*, to do a right and left; *jouer le double jeu*, to play a double game; *mot à double sens*, ambiguous word; *partie double*, foursome; *valise à double fond*, suit-case with a false bottom.—*n.m.* Double, as much again, as many again, etc.; carbon copy, duplicate, replica, counterpart (of a deed etc.); (*Theat.*) substitute, understudy; (*Ten.*) double. *Jouer quitte ou double*, to play double or quits; *mettre une chose au double*, to double a thing; *facture en double*, invoice in duplicate; *parier double contre simple*, to bet two to one; *plus du double*, more than twice as much.—*adv.* Double. *Voir double*, to see double. **doublé**, *n.m.* Gold- or silver-plated ware; (*Billiards*) cannon off the cushion; (*Hunt.*) right and left (shooting). *Doublé or*, rolled gold.

doubleau [du′blo], *n.m.* (*pl.* **-eaux**) Ceiling-beam (larger than others).

doublement (1) [dublə′mã], *n.m.* Doubling. **doublement** (2), *adv.* Doubly, in a double manner. **doubler**, *v.t.* To double; to double up, to fold in two; to line (clothes etc.); to sheathe (a ship etc.); (*Theat.*) to play as understudy; (*Cine.*) to dub; to repeat a class. *Doubler le pas*, to go faster. *Doubler une voiture*, to overtake a car; (*Naut.*) *doubler un cap*, to round a cape.

doublet [du′blɛ], *n.m.* Doublet.

doubleur [du′blœːr], *n.m.* (*fem.* **-euse**) Doubler, throwster, twister.—*n.f.* Doubling-frame.

doublier [du′blje], *n.m.* Double rack (for sheep).

doublon [du′blɔ̃], *n.m.* Doubloon, Spanish pistole; (*Print.*) double.

doublure [du′blyːr], *n.f.* Lining; (*Theat.*) understudy.

douce [DOUX].

douce-amère [dusa′mɛːr], *n.f.* (*pl.* **douces-amères**) Woody nightshade, bitter-sweet.

douceâtre [du′sɑːtr], *a.* Sweetish, sickly.

doucement [dus′mã], *adv.* Gently, softly, tenderly; slowly, leisurely, quietly; mildly; peaceably, calmly, smoothly, placidly; meekly, patiently; indifferently, not very well, so-so. *Aller tout doucement*, to be so-so; (*colloq.*) *allez-y doucement sur la dépense*, go easy on the expenses.

doucereusement [dusrøz′mã], *adv.* Sweetishly, mawkishly; in a soft-spoken manner. **doucereux**, *a.* (*fem.* **-euse**) Sweetish, mawkish, mealy-mouthed.

doucet [du′se], *a. and n.* (*fem.* **-ette** (1)) Demure, mild, affected (person). *Faire le doucet*, to look demure.—*n.m.* (*Ichth.*) dragonet.

doucette (2) [du′sɛt], *n.f.* Corn salad; Venus's looking-glass.

doucettement [dusɛt′mã], *adv.* (*colloq.*)

Gently, softly, so-so. *Il va tout doucettement,* he's only so-so.

douceur [du'sœːr], *n.f.* Sweetness, mildness, softness; sweet savour, fragrance, etc.; kindness, good-nature; calmness, peacefulness; smoothness; meekness, gentleness; (*pl.*) sweet things, sweets, confectionery, etc.; (*fig.*) sweet sayings or words, gallantries. *Employer la douceur,* to use gentle means; *en douceur,* carefully, gently; *goûter les douceurs de la vie,* to enjoy the charms of life; *plus fait douceur que violence,* kindness does more than harshness; *prendre quelqu'un par la douceur,* to treat someone gently or by gentle means, to appease.

douche [duʃ], *n.f.* Douche, shower-bath. *Douche écossaise,* alternating cold and hot shower-bath; (*fig.*) succession of good and bad news. **doucher,** *v.t.* To give a douche to; to cool off (excitement etc.). **doucheur,** *n.m.* (*fem.* **-euse**) One who administers douches.

doucine [du'sin], *n.f.* (*Arch.*) Cyma; (*Carp.*) moulding-plane.

doucir [du'siːr], *v.t.* To polish (looking-glasses etc.). **doucissage,** *n.m.* Polishing. **doucisseur,** *n.m.* Polisher.

douelle [dwɛl], *n.f.* (*Arch.*) Inside or outside facing of a voussoir; small stave (of a cask).

doué [dwe], *a.* (*fem.* **-ée**) Gifted, endowed with. *Un élève doué,* a bright pupil. **douer,** *v.t.* To endow, to bestow upon.

douille [duːj], *n.f.* Socket; case or shell (of cartridges). *Douille d'embrayage,* clutch casing; *douille de lampe,* lamp-socket, lampholder.

douillet [du'jɛ], *a.* (*fem.* **douillette** (1)) Effeminate, delicate; tender, sensitive; soft, downy.—*n.* Soft, effeminate person. **douillette** (2), *n.f.* Wadded dress, wadded greatcoat (of a priest). **douillettement,** *adv.* Softly, tenderly, delicately, cosily.

douleur [du'lœːr], *n.f.* Pain, suffering, ache, soreness, anguish, pang; grief, sorrow, woe. *Chant plein de douleur,* song full of pathos; *douleur aiguë,* acute pain; *douleur éloignée, douleur vague,* remote pain; *sans douleur,* painlessly. (*pl.*) *Douleurs de l'accouchement,* labour pains. **douloureusement,** *adv.* Painfully, grievously. **douloureux,** *a.* (*fem.* **-euse**) Painful, smarting, sore; grievous, afflicting, sad. *Cri douloureux,* mournful cry. —*n.f.* (*fam.*) *La douloureuse,* the bill.

doute [dut], *n.m.* Doubt, uncertainty, irresolution; suspicion, misgiving, distrust; scepticism; dread, fear. (*Law*) *Bénéfice du doute,* benefit of the doubt; *cela ne fait aucun doute,* there is no doubt about it; *faire naître des doutes,* to give rise to misgivings; *jeter des doutes dans l'esprit,* to fill the mind with distrust; *mettre en doute,* to call in question; *sans doute,* no doubt, doubtless, unquestionably, to be sure; *sans doute que,* no doubt that. **douter,** *v.i.* To doubt, to question, to hesitate; to scruple. *Il doute de tout,* he doubts everything; *je doute que cela soit,* I doubt whether it be so; *je doute qu'il veuille le faire,* I doubt whether he will do it; *je ne doute pas qu'il (ne) le fasse,* I do not doubt that he will do it; *ne doute de rien,* to be over confident, to be too credulous. **se douter,** *v.r.* To suspect, to surmise, to

conjecture; to distrust, to mistrust, to fear. *Je me doutais qu'il viendrait,* I thought he would come; *je m'en doutais bien,* I thought as much; *ne se douter de rien,* to suspect nothing, to be unconscious of what is going on; *pouvais-je me douter qu'il dût venir si tôt?* could I imagine that he was to come so soon? *se douter de quelque chose,* to be on one's guard, to feel suspicious. **douteur,** *a.* (*fem.* **-euse**) Doubting.—*n.* Doubter. **douteusement,** *adv.* Doubtfully. **douteux,** *a.* (*fem.* **-euse**) Doubtful, uncertain; dubious, ambiguous, questionable. *D'une manière douteuse,* doubtfully; *il est douteux qu'il le fasse,* it is doubtful whether he will do it; *un individu douteux,* a shady character.

douvain [du'vɛ̃], *n.m.* Stave-(oak)wood.

douve [duːv], *n.f.* Stave (for casks); trench, ditch, moat; (*Bot.*) spearwort.

Douvres [duːvr], *m.* Dover.

doux [du], *a.* (*fem.* **douce**) Sweet; fragrant; affable, kindly, bland, charming, pleasant; soft, smooth; easy; gentle, mild; peaceful, calm; unfermented; fresh (of water); mellow; ductile, malleable; dulcet. *Douce rêverie,* sweet musing; *eau douce,* fresh water, soft water; *faire les yeux doux,* to cast amorous glances; *il est doux comme un agneau,* he is as gentle as a lamb; *il fait bien doux,* the weather is very mild; *mener une vie douce,* to lead an easy, agreeable life; *poisson d'eau douce,* fresh-water fish; *senteur douce,* sweet smell; *tabac doux,* mild tobacco; *un billet doux* [BILLET]; *un doux sourire,* a gracious smile; *une pente douce,* a gradual slope; *une taille douce,* a copper-plate engraving.—*n.m.* Softness, sweetness, etc.—*adv.* Gently; submissively. *Filer doux,* to knuckle under, to eat humble pie; *tout doux,* softly, gently; *en douce!* (*Row.*) easy! *or* paddle again; (*fam.*) discreetly, on the quiet; (*colloq.*) *filer en douce,* to slip away, to take French leave.

douzaine [du'zɛn], *n.f.* Dozen. *À la douzaine* or *par douzaine,* by the dozen; *c'est un poète à la douzaine,* he is a very ordinary poet; *une demi-douzaine,* half a dozen.

douze [duːz], *a.* Twelve. *Charles Douze,* Charles the Twelfth.—*n.m.* Twelfth. *C'est le douze aujourd'hui,* today is the twelfth; *le douze du mois,* the twelfth instant; *un in-douze,* a duodecimo. **douzième,** *a.* and *n.m.* Twelfth. **douzièmement,** *adv.* Twelfthly, in the twelfth place.

doxologie [dɔksɔlɔ'ʒi], *n.f.* Doxology.

doyen [dwa'jɛ̃], *n.* (*fem.* **doyenne**) Senior, oldest member.—*n.m.* Dean, of chapter, of faculty.—*n.f.* Superior of a convent or chapter. **doyennat,** *n.m.* Deanship (of a faculty). **doyenné,** *n.m.* Seniorship, deanship, deanery; a luscious variety of pear.

dracéna [DRAGONNIER].

drachme [drakm], *n.f.* Drachma; (*Pharm.*) dram.

draconien [drakɔ'njɛ̃], *a.* (*fem.* **-ienne**) Draconian, harsh, severe.

drag [drag], *n.m.* Horse-race, which simulates a hunt; tally-ho coach for ladies following the sham hunt.

dragage [dra'gaːʒ], *n.m.* Dragging (of a river etc.). *Dragage de mines,* mine-sweeping operation, mine-sweeping; *dragage aurifère*, gold-dredging.

dragée [dra'ʒe], *n.f.* Sugar-almond, sugar-plum, bonbon; sugar-coated pill; small shot; (*Mil. slang*) bullet. *Avaler la dragée*, to swallow the pill; *tenir la dragée haute à*, to keep in suspense, to make to pay dearly.

drageoir, *n.m.* Comfit-dish.

drageon [dra'ʒɔ̃], *n.m.* Sucker. **drageonner**, *v.i.* To put forth suckers.

dragon (1) [dra'gɔ̃], *n.m.* Dragon; virago, vixen, termagant; dragoon; (*Astron.*) Draco. *Dragon ailé*, flying dragon; *dragon de vertu*, great prude; *sa femme est un vrai dragon*, his wife is a regular termagant. **dragon** (2), *a.* (*fem.* **dragonne** (1)) Dragonish. *À la dragonne*, in a vixenish or shrewish manner.

dragonnade, *n.f.* Dragonnade, brutal religious persecution. **dragonne** (2), *n.f.* Sword-knot. ***dragonner**, *v.t.* To dragoon; to worry. **dragonnier** or **dracéna**, *n.m.* Dragon-tree, dracaena.

drague [drag], *n.f.* Dredger, dredging-machine; dredge-net; drag, grappling-iron; (*pl.*) grains (of malt). *Drague à godets*, bucket dredger; *drague à vis*, screw dredger; *drague de sapeur*, scraper. **draguer**, *v.t.* To drag, to dredge, to sweep. *Draguer une ancre*, to sweep the bottom for a lost anchor. **dragueur**, *n.m.* Dredger. *Dragueur de mines*, minesweeper.

draille [draj], *n.f.* (*Mil.*) Ridge rope (of tent).

drain [drɛ̃], *n.m.* Drain, drain-pipe; drainage-tube. **drainage**, *n.m.* Drainage.

draine or **drenne** [drɛ:n], *n.f.* Missel-thrush.

drainer [drɛ'ne], *v.t.* To drain. *Drainer toutes les ressources du pays*, to tap, to monopolize, all the country's resources.

draisienne [drɛ'zjɛn], *n.f.* Primitive bicycle, without pedals (about 1816).

dramatique [drama'tik], *a.* Dramatic. *Auteur dramatique*, playwright; *critique dramatique*, theatre critic; *une journée dramatique*, an eventful day.—*n.m.* Drama, dramatic style. **dramatiser**, *v.t.* To dramatize. **dramatiseur**, *n.m.* Dramatizer. **dramaturge**, *n.m.* Dramatist, playwright. **dramaturgie**, *n.f.* Dramaturgy.

drame [dram], *n.m.* Drama.

drap [dra], *n.m.* Cloth; (bed) sheet. *Drap d'or*, cloth of gold; *drap fin*, broadcloth; *drap mortuaire*, pall; *être dans de beaux draps*, to be in a fine mess or pickle; *gros drap*, coarse cloth; *tailler en plein drap*, to have abundant means at command; *une paire de draps blancs*, a pair of clean sheets. **drapage** [DRAPEMENT].

drapeau [dra'po], *n.m.* (*pl.* -eaux) Flag, standard, ensign, streamer, colours; rag. *Drapeau blanc*, the royal standard of France; (*Mil.*) flag of truce; *la garde du drapeau*, colour party; *se ranger sous les drapeaux de*, to serve under; to espouse the cause of; *sous les drapeaux*, on active service.

drapement [drap'mɑ̃], *n.m.* Draping.

draper [dra'pe], *v.t.* To cover with cloth; to hang (a carriage etc.) with black; to arrange or decorate with drapery; (*Paint.*, *Sculp.*) to drape. *Drapé à l'antique*, draped in the antique style. **se draper**, *v.r.* To arrange the folds of one's garments; (*fig.*) to make a show, to parade; to assume an air of importance. *Se draper dans sa dignité*, to wrap

oneself in one's dignity. **draperie**, *n.f.* Drapery; woollen cloths; cloth-trade, cloth-making. **drapier**, *n.m.* (*fem.* **drapière** (1)) Draper, clothier. **drapière** (2), *n.f.* Packing-pin.

drastique [dras'tik], *a.* and *n.m.* (*Med.*) Drastic.

drave (1) [drav] or **drave printanière**, *n.f.* (*Bot.*) *Draba verna*, the smallest of crucifers. (*C*) **drave** (2) [drav], *n.f.* Floating, drive, log-running. **draver**, *v.t.* To float (pulpwood bolts), to drive, to drift. **draveur**, *n.m.* Wood-floater, driver, raftsman, rafter.

drayage [drɛ'ja:ʒ], *n.m.* Fleshing (of hides). **drayer**, *v.t. irr.* (*conjugated like* BALAYER). To flesh (hides). **drayoire**, *n.f.* Fleshing-knife. **drayure**, *n.f.* Fleshing (of hides).

drêche [drɛʃ], *n.f.* Draff; brewer's grains.

dréger [dre'ʒe], *v.t.* To ripple (hemp, flax).

drelin [drɔ'lɛ̃], *n.m.* (*onom.*) Tinkle, jingle. *Drelin-drelin!* ting-a-ling!

drenne [DRAINE].

dressage [drɛ'sa:ʒ], *n.m.* Erection, raising; training (of animals); breaking (of horses); pitching (a tent).

dresser [drɛ'se], *v.t.* To erect, to set up, to construct, to mount, to raise; to straighten, to level; to lay out, to arrange, to adjust; to raise up, to hold upright; to lay (a snare); to pitch a camp, a tent; to trim (a boat); to steer; to make out (accounts); to draw up (a report); to prick up (the ears); to train (animals); to break (a horse); to drill (soldiers). *Dresser la barre du gouvernail*, to right the helm; *dresser la tête*, to raise the head; *dresser l'inventaire*, to take stock; *dresser quelqu'un*, to form someone; *dresser un acte*, *un plan*, to draw up a deed, a plan; *dresser un buffet*, to lay out a sideboard; *dresser un lit*, to put up a bed. **se dresser**, *v.r.* To stand on end (of hair); to stand erect; to rear; to be trained. *Se dresser contre la tyrannie*, to rise up against tyranny. **dresseur**, *n.m.* Trainer (of dogs etc.). **dressoir**, *n.m.* Dresser, sideboard.

dribble [dribl], *n.m.* (*Ftb.*) Dribble, dribbling. **dribbler**, *v.t.* To dribble. **dribbleur**, *n.m.* Dribbler.

drill [drij], *n.m.* Drill, kind of baboon.

drille [dri:j], *n.m.* (1)* Soldier; (used today in) *un joyeux* or *un bon drille*, a jolly fellow, a gay dog; *un pauvre drille*, a poor wretch.—*n.f.* (2) hand-drill, borer. *Une drille à levier*, ratchet-drill. **driller**, *v.t.* To drill, to bore.

*drilles [dri:j], *n.f. pl.* Rags (for paper-making).

drisse [dris], *n.f.* Halyard, yard-rope.

drive [driv], *n.m.* (*Ten.*) Drive.

drogman [drɔg'mɑ̃], *n.m.* Dragoman.

drogue [drɔg], *n.f.* Drug; doctor's stuff, physic; rubbish, stuff; dope, doping. *N'être que de la drogue*, to be nothing but trash, rubbish. **droguer**, *v.t.* To drug, to physic. **se droguer**, *v.r.* To physic or doctor oneself, to dope oneself. **droguerie**, *n.f.* Drug-store; drug-trade, drysaltery. **droguiste**, *n.* Retailer in drugs and chemicals.

droguet [drɔ'gɛ], *n.m.* (*Tex.*) Drugget.

droit (1) [drwa], *a.* (*fem.* **droite**) Straight, right, direct; perpendicular to the horizon, vertical, upright; just, righteous, equitable; sincere, true; right (opposed to left). *En droite ligne*, in a straight line; *il est droit comme* un i, he is as straight as an arrow; *le côté droit*, the right-hand side; *ligne droite*, straight line; *remettre quelqu'un dans le droit chemin*, to put someone in the right way again; *tenir la tête droite*, to hold one's head erect; *un col droit*, a stand-up collar.—*adv.* Straight, straight on, directly; honestly, uprightly. *Aller droit au but*, to go straight to the mark; *allez tout droit*, go straight on; *droit comme ça*, (*Naut.*) right on, steady the helm.—*n.f.* Right hand, right; right side; the right (or Conservative) benches or party; (*Geom.*) straight line. *A droite*, on the right; *à droite et à gauche*, right and left; *prendre la droite* or *tourner à droite*, to turn to the right; (*Mil.*) *à droite par trois!* Form threes, right!

droit (2) [drwa], *n.m.* Right, equity; the law; right (to), claim, title; fee; due (tax), duty, custom-duty. *A bon droit*, with good reason; *aller sur les droits de*, to encroach on the rights of; *à qui de droit*, to those whom it may concern; *de droit et de fait*, de facto and de jure; *de plein droit* or *de droit*, without need of sanction; *donner droit à*, to entitle; *droits d'admission*, entry money; *droit d'aînesse*, primogeniture; *droit d'auteur*, royalty, copyright; *droit de péage*, toll; *droit divin*, divine right; *droits acquis*, vested interests; *droits de port*, port dues; *droits de reproduction*, copyright; *droits de sortie*, export duty; *droits de succession*, estate duties; *faire droit à la demande de quelqu'un*, to accede to someone's request; *faire son droit*, to study law, to read for the bar; *jouir de ses droits*, to enjoy one's rights; *le droit commun*, the common law; *le droit des gens* or *international*, the law of nations; *les droits de l'hospitalité*, the rights of hospitality; *renoncer à ses droits*, to give up one's right; *y avoir droit*, to have a right to.

droitement [drwat'mɑ̃], *adv.* Rightly, justly; sincerely, straightforwardly.

droitier [drwa'tje], *a.* (*fem.* **-ière**) Right-handed.—*n.* Right-handed person.

droiture [drwa'ty:r], *n.f.* Equity, justice; uprightness, integrity, honesty, rectitude. **En droiture*, directly, in a direct manner.

drolatique [drɔla'tik], *a.* Amusing, laughable, facetious.

drôle [dro:l], *a.* Funny, droll, jocose, ludicrous; strange, curious, queer. (*fam.*) *Un drôle de numéro*, a queer fellow, an odd fish; *la drôle de guerre*, the 'phoney' war (1939–40). —*n.* Rogue, rascal, scoundrel. **drôlement**, *adv.* Comically, facetiously, jocosely; (*fam.*) jolly, excessively. **drôlerie**, *n.f.* Drollery; droll thing; buffoonery. **drôlesse**, *n.f.* Jade, hussy.

dromadaire [drɔma'dɛ:r], *n.m.* Dromedary.

drome [drɔm], (1) *n.m.* (*Orn.*) Dromas. [*see also* HÉRON CRABIER].

drome [drɔm], (2) *n.f.* Main beam (of forge-hammer); (*Naut.*) float (of a raft); spare masts and yards. *Drome des embarcations*, place where boats of laid-up ships are kept.

drosère [drɔ'zɛ:r] or **droséra**, *n.m.* (*Bot.*) Sundew.

drosse [drɔs], *n.f.* (*Naut.*) Wheel-rope, tiller-rope.

drosser [drɔ'se], *v.i.* (*Naut.*) To drive or drift.

droussage [dru'sa:ʒ], *n.m.* First process of carding by hand. **drousse** or **droussette**, *n.f.* Card used for this. **drousser**, *v.t.* To

card (wool). **drousseur**, *n.m.* (*fem.* **-euse**) Wool-comber.

dru [dry], *a.* (*fem.* **drue**) Strong, vigorous, sturdy; dense (of rain); brisk, lively, smart; close-planted, thick-set; fledged (of birds).— *adv.* Thick, thickly; briskly, fast, hard. *Les balles tombaient dru comme grêle*, the bullets fell as thick as hail.

druide [dryid], *n.m.* Druid. **druidesse**, *n.f.* Druidess. **druidique**, *a.* Druidical. **druidisme**, *n.m.* Druidism.

drupacé [drypa'se], *a.* (*fem.* **drupacée**) (*Bot.*) Drupaceous. **drupe**, *n.m.* or *f.* Any stone-fruit. **drupéole**, *n.m.* Drupel.

dryade [dri'ad], *n.f.* Dryad; (*Bot.*) dryas.

du [dy], (contraction of DE LE) Of the, from the, by the; some, any.

dû (1) [dy], *n.m.* Due, what is owed, what is owing. *A chacun son dû*, give each man his due.

dû (2), *p.p.* (*fem.* **due**) [DEVOIR].

dualisme [dya'lism], *n.m.* Dualism. **dualiste**, *a.* and *n.* Dualist. **dualité**, *n.f.* Duality.

dubitatif [dybita'tif], *a.* (*fem.* **-ive**) Dubitative. **dubitativement**, *adv.* Dubitatively.

duc [dyk], *n.m.* Duke; horned owl; two-seated barouche. *Grand-duc*, grand-duke; great horned owl, eagle-owl; *petit-duc*, scops (owl). **ducal**, *a.* (*fem.* **-ale**, *pl.* **-aux**) Ducal.

ducat [dy'ka], *n.m.* Ducat. **ducaton**, *n.m.* Ducatoon.

duché [dy'ʃe], *n.m.* Dukedom, duchy.

duchesse [dy'ʃes], *n.f.* Duchess; a luscious autumn variety of pear. *Lit à la duchesse*, a form of four-post canopied bedstead.

ducroire [dy'krwa:r], *n.m.* (*Comm.*) Del credere agent or commission.

ductile [dyk'til], *a.* Ductile, malleable. **ductilité**, *n.f.* Ductility.

dudgeon [dyd'ʒɔ̃], *n.m.* Tube expander. **dudgeonnage**, *n.m.* (*Ind.*) Expanding of tubes.

dudit [DU DIT].

duègne [dɥɛɲ], *n.f.* Duenna, chaperon.

duel (1) [dɥɛl], *n.m.* Duel; struggle. *Provoquer en duel*, to challenge; *se battre en duel*, to fight a duel; *duel d'artillerie*, exchange of fire.

duel (2) [dɥɛl], *a.* (*fem.* **duelle**) (*Gram.*) Dual. —*n.m.* Dual number.

duelliste [dɥe'list], *n.m.* Duellist.

dugong [dy'gɔ̃], *n.m.* Sea-cow.

duite [dɥit], *n.f.* Pick (of weft).

dulcifiant [dylsi'fjɑ̃], *a.* (*fem.* **-iante**) Dulcifying. **dulcification**, *n.f.* Dulcification. **dulcifier**, *v.t.* To dulcify.

Dulcinée [dylsi'ne], *f.* Dulcinea. **dulcinée**, *n.f.* Sweetheart.

dulie [dy'li], *n.f.* (*R.-C. Ch.*) Dulia (worship of angels, saints, etc.).

dûment [dy'mɑ̃], *adv.* Duly, properly, regularly.

dumping [dʌm'piŋ], *n.m.* Dumping, unfair competition.

dundee [dœ̃'di:], *n.m.* (*Naut.*) Ketch.

dune [dyn], *n.f.* Dune, sand-hill. *Dunes littorales*, coast dunes; *dunes mouvantes*, shifting sand-hills.

dunette [dy'nɛt], *n.f.* Poop-deck.

duo [dy'o], *n.m.* Duet.

duodécimal [dyɔdesi'mal], *a.* (*fem.* **-ale**, *pl.* **-aux**) Duodecimal. **duodécimo**, *adv.* Duodecimally, twelfthly.

duodénal [dyɔde'nal], *a.* Duodenal. **duodénum,** *n.m.* Duodenum.

duodi [dyɔ'di], *n.m.* Second day of the decade in the calendar of the first French Republic.

dupe [dyp], *n.f.* Dupe. **duper,** *v.t.* To dupe, to gull, to take in. **duperie,** *n.f.* Dupery, trickery; trick, take-in, sell. **dupeur,** *n.m.* (*fem.* **-euse**) Cheat, trickster.

duplex [dy'plɛks], *n.m.* (*Teleg.*) Duplex system; (*Rad. Tel.*) duplex broadcast. **duplicata,** *n.m.* Duplicate. **duplicateur,** *n.m.* (*Elec.*) Duplicator. **duplicatif,** *a.* (*fem.* **-ive**) Duplicative. **duplication,** *n.f.* Duplication.

duplicité [dyplisi'te], *n.f.* Duplicity, double-dealing, deceit.

*duplique [dy'plik], *n.f.* (*Law*) Surrejoinder.

duquel [DE LEQUEL].

dur [dyːr], *a.* (*fem.* **dure**) Hard; tough; (*fig.*) unyielding, harsh, obdurate, merciless, unkind, unfeeling, hard-hearted; hardy, courageous; austere, painful, laborious; difficult. *Avoir la tête dure,* to be thick-headed; *avoir l'oreille dure,* to be hard of hearing; *dur à cuire,* tough, hard; *il a les traits durs,* his features are hard; *les temps sont durs,* these are hard times; *œuf dur,* hard-boiled egg; *un hiver dur,* a severe winter; *un style dur,* a stiff style.—*n.m.* (*colloq.*) Tough old chap. *Un dur à cuire,* a die-hard. (*Build.*) *En dur,* in concrete, in cement.—*n.m.* Hard ground or floor in *coucher sur la dure.*—*adv.* Hard; firmly. *Travailler dur,* to work hard.

durabilité [dyrabili'te], *n.f.* Durability. **durable,** *a.* Durable, lasting, solid. **durablement,** *adv.*

duralumin [dyraly'mɛ̃], *n.m.* Duralumin.

duramen [dyra'mɛn], *n.m.* Heartwood.

durant [dy'rɑ̃], *prep.* During. *Durant sa vie* or *sa vie durant,* during his lifetime.

dur-bec [dyr'bɛk], *n.m.* (*pl.* **durs-becs**) (*Orn.*) Pine grosbeak, *Pinicola enucleator.*

durcir [dyr'siːr], *v.t.* To harden, to make hard or tough.—*v.i.* To harden, to become hard, to stiffen. **se durcir,** *v.r.* To harden, to grow hard. **durcissement,** *n.m.* Hardening, stiffening, induration.

durée [dy're], *n.f.* Duration, continuance. *Durée de validité d'un billet,* validity of a ticket; *durée d'un bail,* term of a lease; (*Elec.*) *durée d'une lampe,* life of a lamp; *être de longue durée,* to be durable.

durement [dyr'mɑ̃], *adv.* Hard; harshly, sharply, roughly, rigorously.

dure-mère [dyr'mɛːr], *n.f.* (*Anat.*) Dura mater.

durer [dy're], *v.i.* To last, to continue, to remain; to endure, to last a long time; to suffer, to put up with; to wait. *Cela ne peut pas durer,* that is unbearable, that must cease; *le temps lui dure,* time hangs heavy upon him; *ne pouvoir durer en place,* to be unable to sit still; *une étoffe qui dure,* a stuff that wears well.

dureté [dyr'te], *n.f.* Hardness, toughness; harshness, austerity, unkindness; (*pl.*) harsh, offensive words. *Dureté de cœur,* hardheartedness, callousness; *la dureté des lignes,* harshness of contours (in drawing).

durillon [dyri'jɔ̃], *n.m.* Callosity, corn.

dus, dusse, du [DEVOIR].

duumvir [dyɔm'viːr], *n.m.* Duumvir. **duumviral,** *a.* Duumviral. **duumvirat,** *n.m.* Duumvirate.

duvet [dy've], *n.m.* Down; wool, nap, bloom (of peaches etc.); fluff; down mattress or quilt. **duveté,** *a.* (*fem.* **-ée**) Downy (of birds etc.); like down. **duveteux,** *a.* (*fem.* **-euse**) Downy, covered with down; like down.

dyname [di'nam], *n.m.* A unit of work, 1000 kilogrammetres.

dynamique [dina'mik], *a.* Dynamic.—*n.f.* Dynamics. **se dynamiser,** *v.r.* To concentrate oneself, to assume the character of an active force. **dynamisme,** *n.m.* Dynamism. **dynamiste,** *n.m.* Dynamist.

dynamitage [dinami'taːʒ], *n.m.* Blasting, blowing up.

dynamite [dina'mit], *n.f.* Dynamite. **dynamiter,** *v.t.* To dynamite, to blow up. **dynamiterie,** *n.f.* Dynamite-factory. **dynamiteur,** *n.m.* Dynamiter.

dynamo [dina'mo], *n.f.* Dynamo. *Dynamofrein,* brake-dynamo. **dynamographe,** *n.m.* Dynamograph. **dynamomètre,** *n.m.* Dynamometer. *Dynamomètre à cadran,* dial-dynamometer. **dynamométrique,** *a.* Dynamometric.

dynaste [di'nast], *n.m.* Dynast, monarch. **dynastie,** *n.f.* Dynasty. **dynastique,** *a.* Dynastic.

dyne [din], *n.f.* Dyne.

dysenterie [disɑ̃'tri], *n.f.* Dysentery. **dysentériforme,** *a.* Dysentery-like. **dysentérique,** *a.* Dysenteric.

dyspepsie [dispɛp'si], *n.f.* Dyspepsia. **dyspepsique** or **dyspeptique,** *a.* Dyspeptic.

dyspnée [dis'pne], *n.f.* Dyspnoea. **dyspnéique,** *a.* Dyspnoic.

dysurie [dizy'ri], *n.f.* Dysuria. **dysurique,** *a.* Dysuric.

dytique [di'tik], *n.m.* Genus of coleopters, water-beetle.

E

E, e [ə], *n.m.* The fifth letter of the alphabet, connotes three sounds, (1) *e* mute, which is either not sounded at all or sounded very feebly [ə], (2) closed *e* [e], as in *duché, cachez,* (3) open *e* [ɛ], as in *frêle, pelle, succès.*

eau [o], *n.f.* Water; rain, wet; liquor; lake, sea, flood; (*pl.*) waters, mineral or thermal waters; watering-place; stream, river; sweat, perspiration, urine; saliva; tears; juice (of plants etc.); liquid wash; track, wake; lustre, gloss. *À fleur d'eau,* on a level with the water; *aller aux eaux,* to go to a watering-place; *au bord de l'eau,* at the water's edge; *cela fait venir l'eau à la bouche,* that makes one's mouth water; *cela s'en est allé en eau de boudin,* that came to nothing at all; *d'ici là il passera bien de l'eau sous les ponts,* it will be a long time before that happens; *eau bénite* [BÉNITE]; *eau de cuivre,* liquid metal polish; *eau de mer,* sea-water; *eau de source,* spring-water; (*facet.*) *eau de vaisselle,* thin broth; *eau douce* [DOUX]; *eau glacée,* ice water; (*Chem.*) *eau lourde,* heavy water. *eau morte,* still water; *morte eau,* neap tide; *eau oxygénée,* hydrogen peroxide; *eau potable*, drinking water; *eau saumâtre*, brackish water; *eau vive*, running water; *c'est la goutte d'eau qui fait déborder le vase*, it is the last straw that breaks the camel's back; *faire de l'eau*, (*Naut.*) to water, to take in fresh water; *faire eau*, to spring a leak; *faire une pleine eau*, to take a bath in the sea, a river, etc.; *faire venir l'eau au moulin*, to bring grist to the mill; *grandes eaux (de Versailles)*, fountains in full play; *hautes eaux*, high water; *il est tout en eau*, he is in a bath of perspiration; *il n'est pire eau que l'eau qui dort*, still waters run deep; *ils se ressemblent comme deux gouttes d'eau*, they are as like as two peas; (*pop.*) *il tombe de l'eau*, it is raining; *lancer un navire à l'eau*, to launch a ship; *l'eau va toujours au moulin*, money begets money; *les eaux sont basses chez lui*, he is hard up; *maître des eaux et forêts*, ranger of the woods and forests; *mettre de l'eau dans son vin*, to come down a peg or two; *nager entre deux eaux*, to swim under water, (*fig.*) to waver between two parties; *ne sentir que l'eau*, to be insipid; *passer l'eau*, to cross the water; *pêcher en eau trouble*, to fish in troubled waters; *porter de l'eau à la rivière*, to carry coals to Newcastle; *question de l'eau*, ordeal by water; *revenir sur l'eau*, to come above water again; *se noyer dans un verre d'eau*, to come to grief in trifling difficulties; *suer sang et eau*, to make tremendous efforts, to be over-anxious; *tempête dans un verre d'eau*, storm in a tea-cup; *tomber à l'eau*, to fall into water, (*fig.*) to fall through (of a project); *tout va à vau l'eau*, all is going to rack and ruin; *violer les eaux territoriales (d'un pays)*, to infringe on the territorial waters (of a country). *Un diamant de la plus belle eau*, a diamond of the first water. *Une pièce d'eau* or *une nappe d'eau*, a sheet of water, an artificial lake; *un jet d'eau*, a water-spout, a fountain. **eau-de-vie,** *n.f.* (*pl.* **eaux-de-vie**) Brandy. **eau-forte,** *n.f.* Aqua fortis; (*pl.* **eaux-fortes**) etching. **eaux-vannes,** *n.f. pl.* Sewage.

ébahi [eba'i], *a.* (*fem.* **ébahie**) Astonished, stupefied, dumbfounded. **s'ébahir,** *v.r.* To wonder at, to be amazed, to be staggered. **ébahissement,** *n.m.* Amazement, astonishment.

ébarbage [ebar'ba:ʒ] or **ébarbement,** *n.m.* Paring, paring away; (*Engraving*) edging off, scraping. **ébarber,** *v.t.* To pare, to nip burrs from; to edge off, to scrape (engravings etc.); to trim (plants, hedges, etc.). **ébarbeuse,** *n.f.* Machine for doing this. **ébarboir** *n.m.* Parer, scraper. **ébarbure,** *n.f.* Burr (on a casting etc.).

ébats [e'ba], *n.m. pl.* Pastime, sport, gambol, frolic. *Prendre ses ébats*, to disport oneself. **s'ébattre,** *v.r. irr.* (*conjugated like* BATTRE) To sport, to take one's pleasure, to gambol, to frolic.

ébaubi [ebo'bi], *a.* (*fem.* **ébaubie**) (*colloq.*) Amazed, astonished, dumbfounded. **ébaubir,** *v.t.* To astound. **s'ébaubir,** *v.r.* To be astounded. **ébaubissement,** *n.m.* Astonishment, amazement.

ébauchage [ebo'ʃa:ʒ], *n.m.* Sketching, roughing out. **ébauche,** *n.f.* Rough draft, rough shape, or outline. **ébaucher,** *v.t.* To make the first draft of, to draw an outline of, to

sketch; to rough-cast, to rough-hew. **ébaucheur,** *n.m.* Workman employed to rough-hew. **ébauchoir,** *n.m.* (*Sculp.*) Roughing-chisel; (*Carp.*) mortise-chisel.

*****ébaudir** [ebo'di:r], *v.t.* To enliven, to divert. **s'ébaudir,** *v.r.* To frolic, to frisk, to divert oneself. *****ébaudissement,** *n.m.* Jollity, frolicking.

ébène [e'bɛ:n], *n.f.* Ebony, ebony work. *Des cheveux d'ébène*, raven locks; *commerce de bois d'ébène*, (*fam.*) slave-trade. **ébéner,** *v.t. irr.* (*conjug. like* ACCÉLÉRER) To ebonize. **ébénier,** *n.m.* Ebony-tree. **ébéniste,** *n.m.* Cabinet-maker. **ébénisterie,** *n.f.* Cabinet-work.

éberlué [eber'lye], *a.* (*fem.* **-ée**) (*fam.*) Stupefied, flabbergasted. **éberluer,** *v.t.* To astound.

ébiseler [ebi'zle], *v.t.* To chamfer, to bevel.

éblouir [eblu'i:r], *v.t.* To dazzle; (*fig.*) to fascinate, to amaze. *Il veut nous éblouir*, he wants us to admire him; *le soleil nous éblouit*, the sun dazzles us. **s'éblouir,** *v.r.* To be dazzled or fascinated. **éblouissant,** *a.* (*fem.* **éblouissante**) Dazzling, resplendent, amazing. **éblouissement,** *n.m.* Dazzle, dazzlement; state of being dazzled or dazed; (*fig.*) bewilderment, astonishment. *Le chauffeur a eu un éblouissement*, the driver had a black-out.

ébonite [ebo'nit], *n.f.* Ebonite; vulcanite.

éborgnage [ebɔr'ɲa:ʒ], *n.m.* Nipping off of useless buds (on fruit-trees).

*****éborgner** [ebɔr'ɲe], *v.t.* To blind in one eye, to put out (a person's) eye; to nip the buds off (fruit-trees).

ébouage [ebu'a:ʒ], *n.m.* Scavenging. **ébouer,** *v.t.* To scavenge. **éboueur,** *n.m.* (*fem.* **-euse**) Road-sweeper, scavenger.—*n.f.* Road-sweeping machine.

ébouillanter [ebujã'te], *v.t.* To dip in hot water, to scald.

*****ébouillir** [ebu'ji:r], *v.i. irr.* (*conjugated like* BOUILLIR) To boil away.

éboulement [ebul'mã], *n.m.* Falling in, fall; debris; caving in, collapse. *Éboulement de terrain*, landslide. **ébouler,** *v.i.* To fall in, to fall down, to sink.—*v.t.* To cause to fall in etc. **s'ébouler,** *v.r.* To fall in, to fall down, to cave in, to sink, to collapse. **ébouleux,** *a.* (*fem.* **ébouleuse**) Falling in or tending or liable to fall in. **éboulis,** *n.m. inv.* Debris, fallen rocks, etc.

ébouqueter [ÉBOURGEONNER].

ébourgeonnement [ebur30n'mã] or **ébourgeonnage,** *n.m.* (*Hort.*) Nipping of buds, dis-budding. **ébourgeonner,** *v.t.* To nip the buds off. **ébourgeonneur,** *n.m.* Workman thus employed. **ébourgeonnoir,** *n.m.* Nipping-tool.

ébouriffant [eburi'fã], *a.* (*fem.* **-ante**) Fluttering, disturbing, amazing, incredible. *Des nouvelles ébouriffantes*, breathtaking news.

ébouriffé, *a.* (*fem.* **-ée**) Disordered, ruffled, in disorder; (*fig.*) in a flutter. *Elle arriva tout ébouriffée*, she came in with her hair all ruffled; *vous voilà tout ébouriffé*, you are all of a flutter. **ébouriffer,** *v.t.* To ruffle, to disorder; (*fig.*) to startle, to amaze.

ébousiner [ebuzi'ne], *v.t.* To clean the surface of (ashlar etc.).

ébouter [ebu'te], *v.t.* To cut off (the end).

ébraiser [ebrɛ'ze], *v.t.* To remove the embers from (an oven, furnace, etc.).

ébranchage [ebrã'ʃaːʒ] or **ébranchement**, *n.m.* (*Hort.*) Pruning, lopping, trimming.

ébrancher, *v.t.* To prune, to lop, to trim (fruit-trees etc.). **ébranchoir**, *n.m.* Pruning-tool.

ébranlement [ebrãl'mã], *n.m.* Shock, concussion, shaking; (*fig.*) commotion, perturbation, disturbance, trouble. **ébranler**, *v.t.* To shake, to cause to shake, stagger, or totter; to disturb, to unsettle. *Ébranler la résolution de quelqu'un*, to shake someone's resolution; *les vents ont ébranlé cette maison*, the winds have shaken that house. **s'ébranler**, *v.r.* To get under way, to be in motion. *La voiture s'ébranla*, the coach got under way; *quand les deux armées s'ébranlèrent*, when the two armies moved forward.

ébrasement [ebrɑz'mã], *n.m.* (*Arch.*) Splaying. **ébraser**, *v.t.* To splay. **ébrasure**, *n.f.* Splay.

ébréché [ebrɛ'ʃe], *a.* (*fem.* **-ée**) Cracked, damaged.

ébrécher [ebrɛ'ʃe], *v.t. irr.* (*conjug. like* ACCÉLÉRER) To notch, to indent; to break a bit off, to make a gap in; (*fig.*) to impair. *Ses folles dépenses ont ébréché sa fortune*, his extravagant living has made a hole in his fortune. **s'ébrécher**, *v.r.* To be notched; to break off a piece (of one's tooth).

ébriété [ebrie'te], *n.f.* Ebriety, inebriety. *En état d'ébriété*, intoxicated, under the influence of drink.

ébrouage [ebru'aːʒ] or **ébrouissage**, *n.m.* (*Dyeing*) Washing, scouring (before dyeing).

ébrouement [ebru'mã], *n.m.* Snorting.

ébrouer [ebru'e], *v.t.* (*Dyeing*) To wash, to rinse (wool etc.).

s'ébrouer [ebru'e], *v.r.* To snort from fear (of horses); to flutter about in the dust etc. (of birds). *S'ébrouer dans son bain*, to splash about in one's bath.

ébruiter [ebrɥi'te], *v.t.* To make known, to spread about. **s'ébruiter**, *v.r.* To spread, to be noised abroad.

ébuard [e'bɥaːr], *n.m.* Wooden wedge (for splitting logs).

ébullition [ebyli'sjɔ̃], *n.f.* Boiling, ebullition; (*fig.*) effervescence. *Entrer en ébullition*, to come to the boil.

éburné [ebyr'ne] or **éburnéen**, *a.* (*fem.* **-ée** or **-éenne**) Eburnean, ivory-like.

écachement [ekaʃ'mã], *n.m.* Squashing, crumpling, crushing. **écacher**, *v.t.* To crush, to crumple, to squash, to squeeze flat. *Nez écaché*, flat nose.

écaillage [eka'jaːʒ], *n.m.* Scaling; opening (of oysters etc.); chipping (of porcelain etc.); flaking off (of paintings). **écaille**, *n.f.* Scale; plates (of a tortoise-shell etc.); oyster-shell, tortoise-shell. *Des écailles d'huître*, oyster-shells; *écailles de fer*, hammer slag; *peigne d'écaille*, tortoise-shell comb. **écaillé**, *a.* (*fem.* **-ée**) Scaly, covered with scales. **écaillement**, *n.m.* Scaling (of fish etc.). **écailler** (1), *v.t.* To scale; to cover (a dome etc.) with scales or scale-like plates. *Écailler des huîtres*, to open oysters. **s'écailler**, *v.r.* To peel off, to scale, to scale off; to chip off. **écailler** (2), *n.m.* (*fem.* **-ère**) Oyster-man, oyster-woman; one who opens oysters.

écaillette, *n.f.* Small scale. **écailleux**, *a.* (*fem.* **-euse**) Scaly, squamous.

écale [e'kal], *n.f.* Shell, pod (of peas etc.); hull, husk (of walnut); shuck (of chestnut).

écaler, *v.t.* To shell (beans, peas, etc.); to hull, to husk (almonds, nuts, etc.). **s'écaler**, *v.r.* To come out of the shell.

écanguer [ekã'ge], *v.t.* To beat (hemp, flax, etc.), to scutch.

écarlate [ekar'lat], *n.f. and a.* Scarlet; hectic red. *Écarlate de honte*, burning with shame.

écarquillement [ekarkij'mã], *n.m.* (*colloq.*) Opening wide, spreading out (of one's eyes, legs, etc.). **écarquiller**, *v.t.* To open, to spread out, to open wide. **Écarquiller les jambes*, to spread out one's legs; *écarquiller les yeux*, to open one's eyes wide, to strain one's eyes, to stare.

écart (1) [e'kaːr], *n.m.* Stepping aside, step aside, swerving; mistake, fault; deviation, digression; variation, difference; (*Vet.*) strain; setting aside of certain cards (at écarté etc.); cards discarded. *À l'écart*, aside, apart, in solitude, in a lonely place; *ce cheval s'est donné un écart*, that horse has strained itself; *faire le grand écart*, to do the splits; *faire son écart*, to discard; *faire un écart*, to step aside; *faire un écart dans un discours*, to make a digression in a speech; *il fit un écart pour éviter le coup*, he stepped aside to avoid the blow; *il le prit à l'écart*, he took him aside; *il y a un écart entre les deux comptes*, there is a difference between the two accounts; *laisser à l'écart*, to leave aside, to shun, to omit; *l'écart entre les salaires et le coût de la vie*, the margin between salaries and the cost of living; *les écarts de la jeunesse*, the errors of youth; *les écarts de l'imagination*, the flights of the imagination; *mettre à l'écart*, to put by, to set aside; *se mettre* or *se tenir à l'écart*, to keep aloof, to stand aside.

écart (2) [e'kaːr], *n.m.* (*Her.*) Square or quarter (of a shield).

écarté (1) [ekar'te], *n.m.* Écarté (game of cards).

écarté (2) [ekar'te], *a.* (*fem.* **-ée**) Remote, lonely, secluded. *Balle écartée* (cricket), wide (ball).

écartelé [ekartə'le], *a.* (*fem.* **-ée**) (Of mind, heart, etc.) Divided, torn asunder. (*Her.*) Quartered. **écartèlement**, *n.m.* Tearing to pieces, quartering. **écarteler**, *v.t.* To tear to pieces; (*Her.*) to quarter. **écartelure**, *n.f.* (*Her.*) Quartering.

écartement [ekartə'mã], *n.m.* Putting aside; removal; separation, distance apart, spacing; spread. (*Rail.*) *Écartement de la voie*, railway gauge; *écartement des essieux*, wheel-base.

écarter [ekar'te], *v.t.* To separate, to open, to throw wide apart; to set aside; to hold apart, to avert; to cause to deviate; to dispel, to deviate; to spread, to disperse, to scatter; to discard. *Écarter un coup*, to ward off a blow; *écarter une mauvaise pensée*, to dismiss an evil thought.—*v.i.* (*Bull-fighting*) To turn aside. **s'écarter**, *v.r.* To turn aside, to swerve; to deviate; to err, to stray, to ramble; to wander; to make way. *La foule s'écarta*, the crowd made way; *s'écarter de son chemin*, to go out of one's way; *s'écarter de son devoir*, to swerve from one's duty; *s'écarter de son sujet*, to stray from one' subject. **écarteur**, *n.m.* Dodger (of the bull); (*Surg.*) retractor.

ecchymose [εki'moːz], *n.f.* (*Med.*) Ecchymosis.

Ecclésiaste [εkle'zjast], *n.m.* Ecclesiastes.

ecclésiastique [εklezjas'tik], *a.* Ecclesiastic; clerical.—*n.m.* Clergyman, ecclesiastic. **ecclésiastiquement**, *adv.* Ecclesiastically.

écéper or **écepper** [ese'pe], *v.t. irr.* (*conjug. like* ACCÉLÉRER) To break off the old shoots of (a vine etc.).

écervelé [esεrvə'le], *a.* Hare-brained, rash, giddy. *Une tête écervelée*, a madcap.—*n.* Madcap; scatter-brain. *C'est un écervelé*, he is not to be relied upon.

échafaud [eʃa'fo], *n.m.* Scaffold; *platform, stage, stand. **échafaudage**, *n.m.* Scaffolding; (*fig.*) structure. *Un échafaudage de mensonges*, a whole maze of lies. **échafauder**, *v.i.* To erect scaffolding.—*v.t.* To scaffold; to pile up; (*fig.*) to build up, to lay out (a plan, a system, etc.).

échalas [eʃa'la], *n.m.* Vine-prop, vine-stick; hop-pole. *C'est un échalas*, he is as thin as a rake. **échalassage** or **échalassement**, *n.m.* Propping. **échalasser**, *v.t.* To prop (vines etc.).

échalier [eʃa'lje] or **échalis**, *n.m.* Stile (through a hedge); wooden fence.

échalote [eʃa'lɔt], *n.f.* (*Bot.*) Shallot.

échamp [e'ʃɑ̃], *n.m.* Space between two rows of vines.

échampir [RÉCHAMPIR].

échancrer [eʃɑ̃'kre], *v.t.* To make a crescent-shaped cut (in the neck of a shirt etc.); to indent. **échancrure**, *n.f.* Notch, cut, indentation; opening.

échandole [eʃɑ̃'dɔl], *n.f.* Shingle (for roofing).

échange [e'ʃɑ̃ːʒ], *n.m.* Exchange, barter. *Libre échange*, free trade. **échangeabilité**, *n.f.* Exchangeability. **échangeable**, *a.* Exchangeable. **échanger**, *v.t.* To exchange, to barter; to interchange. *Échanger une propriété contre une autre*, to exchange one property for another. **échangeur**, *n.m.* (*fem.* -euse) Changer. **échangiste**, *n.m.* Exchanger. *Libre-échangiste*, free-trader.

échanson [eʃɑ̃'sɔ̃], *n.m.* Cup-bearer. **échansonnerie**, *n.f.* (*collect.*) Cup-bearers of a prince; royal wine-cellars.

échantignole [CHANTIGNOLE].

échantillon [eʃɑ̃ti'jɔ̃], *n.m.* Sample, pattern, specimen; tally; gauge (for weights and measures); (*fig.*) model, type, example; (*Naut.*) scantling. (*On parcels*) '*Échantillon*', post sample. **échantillonnage**, *n.m.* Sampling; gauging. **échantillonner**, *v.t.* To sample; to gauge (weights and measures); to cut samples of.

échanvrer [eʃɑ̃'vre], *v.t.* To separate the wood fibre in (hemp etc.), to hackle. **échanvroir**, *n.m.* Hackle.

*****échappade** [eʃa'pad], *n.f.* (*Engr.*) Slip; (*fig.*) escapade.

échappatoire [eʃapa'twaːr], *n.f.* Shift, subterfuge, loop-hole, evasion. *Chercher des échappatoires*, to try to find means or excuses (to avoid some duty); to hedge.

échappé [eʃa'pe], *a. and n.* (*fem.* **échappée** (1)) *n.* One who has escaped, a runaway; a cross-bred horse. *Un échappé du bagne*, an escaped convict; *un échappé de la maison de*

fous, an escaped madman. **échappée** (2), *n.f.* *Escape; escapade, prank; short space of time, snatch; space for carriages to turn in; space between the stairs and the roof of a staircase; (*Cycl.*) break-away. *Une belle échappée sur la vallée*, a fine view down the valley; *une échappée de beau temps*, a short spell of fine weather. **échappement**, *n.m.* Escape; leakage; (*Horol.*) escapement; space to turn in; exhaust, release. *Échappement à ancre*, anchor- or lever-escapement; *échappement à recul*, recoil-escapement; *échappement à repos*, dead-beat escapement; *soupape d'échappement*, exhaust-valve; *tuyau d'échappement*, exhaust-pipe.

échapper [eʃa'pe], *v.i.* To escape, to make good one's escape, to get away, to get out, to fly; to be overlooked, forgotten, etc. *Cela m'a échappé*, it escaped me (i.e. I did not know of it), I said it inadvertently; *cela m'est échappé*, that has slipped my memory; *échapper à la prison*, to escape imprisonment; *échapper de prison*, to escape from prison; *faire échapper un prisonnier*, to favour a prisoner's escape; *laisser échapper*, to overlook, to pass over, to let pass; *laisser échapper l'occasion*, to let slip an opportunity; *laisser échapper un mot*, to drop a word; *la situation leur échappa*, they lost control of the situation.—*v.t.* To escape, to avoid. *Échapper la côte*, to escape stranding; *l'échapper belle*, to have a narrow escape. **s'échapper**, *v.r.* To get loose; to get away, to escape, to steal away; (*Cycl.*) to break away; to vanish, to disappear; to forget oneself.

écharbot [eʃar'bo], *n.m.* (*Bot.*) Water-caltrop.

écharde [e'ʃard], *n.f.* Prickle (of a thistle etc.); splinter (driven under the nail or skin).

échardonnage [eʃardɔ'naːʒ], *n.m.* Clearing of thistles. **échardonner**, *v.t.* To clear of thistles. **échardonnette**, *n.f.* **échardonnet** or **échardonnoir**, *n.m.* Thistle-hook.

écharner [eʃar'ne], *v.t.* To flesh, pare, or scrape (hides). **écharneuse**, *n.f.* Machine for doing this. **écharnoir**, *n.m.* Fleshing-knife. **écharnure**, *n.f.* Scrapings or parings of hides.

écharpage [ÉCHARPEMENT].

écharpe [e'ʃarp], *n.f.* Scarf, sash; arm-sling. *Avoir le bras en écharpe*, to have one's arm in a sling; *coup d'épée en écharpe*, slanting cut; *en écharpe*, over the shoulder, in a sling, aslant; *le camion prit l'auto en écharpe*, the lorry bumped into the side of the car; *le canon tire en écharpe*, the cannon fires aslant; (*poet.*) *l'écharpe d'Iris*, rainbow. *L'écharpe du Maire*, the Mayor's scarf, the Mayor's badge. **écharpement**, *n.m.* (*Mil.*) Slanting or oblique march; (*Tech.*) slinging or tying a band round (a bale etc.) for hoisting.

écharper [eʃar'pe], *v.t.* To slash, to cut. *Écharper un régiment*, to cut a regiment to pieces; *il lui a écharpé le visage*, he gave him a slash across the face.

écharpiller [eʃarpi'je], *v.t.* To cut to pieces; to hackle (wool, flax, etc.).

échasse [e'ʃaːs], *n.f.* Stilt. *Échasse à manteau noir*, long-legged plover; *échasse d'échafaud*, scaffolding-pole; (*fig.*) *il est monté sur des échasses*, he is walking on stilts, he has very long legs, he is on a high horse.

échassier (1) [eʃa'sje], *n.m.*   Stilt-walker; (*colloq.*) long-legged person.

échassier (2) [eʃa'sje], *n.m.*   Long-legged wading-bird; wader, grallatory bird.

échauboulé [eʃobu'le], *a.* (*fem.* **-ée**) Full of pimples. **échauboulure,** *n.f.*   Pimple, blotch, pustule.

échaudage [eʃo'daːʒ], *n.m.* Whitewash; whitewashing; scalding.

échaudé (1) [eʃo'de], *n.m.* Simnel, cracknel.

échaudé (2) [eʃo'de], *a.* (*fem.* **-ée**) Scalded. *Chat échaudé craint l'eau froide,* a burnt child dreads the fire; *blé échaudé,* wheat with grains containing little flour. **échaudement,** *n.m.* Shrivelling (of wheat).

échauder (1) [eʃo'de], *v.t.* To scald. **s'échauder,** *v.r.*   To burn oneself; to burn one's fingers. *Il s'y est échaudé,* he burnt his fingers in that business; *se faire échauder,* to learn one's lesson; to be fleeced.

échauder (2) [eʃo'de], *v.t.* To steep in limewash; to whitewash.

échaudoir [eʃo'dwaːr], *n.m.* Scalding-house; scalding-tub. **échaudure,** *n.f.* Scald.

échauffaison [eʃofɛ'zɔ̃], *n.f.* (*Path.*) Overheating, eruption, rash. **échauffant,** *a.* (*fem.* **-ante**) Heating, binding (food).

échauffe [e'ʃoːf], *n.f.*   Sweating-room (for hides).

échauffé [eʃo'fe], *n.m.*   Odour (caused by excessive heat). *Sentir l'échauffé,* to have or exhale a hot smell. **échauffée,** *n.f.* First heating operation of salt-makers. **échauffement,** *n.m.*   Heating; over-excitement.

échauffer [eʃo'fe], *v.t.* To warm, to heat, to over-heat; to excite, to inflame, to irritate. *Cela lui échauffe la bile,* that provokes him. **s'échauffer,** *v.r.*   To grow warm, to overheat oneself; to grow angry, to chafe, to fume. *Il s'est échauffé à marcher,* walking has made him warm; *la querelle s'échauffe,* the quarrel is running high; *le jeu s'échauffe,* the game is warming up; *le moteur s'échauffe,* the engine is warming up.

échauffourée [eʃofu're], *n.f.* Rash, headlong, or blundering enterprise; brush, scuffle, affray.

échauffure [eʃo'fyːr], *n.f.* Red rash.

échauguette [eʃo'gɛt], *n.f.* (*Mil.*) Watch-tower.

èche [AICHE].

échéable [eʃe'abl], *a.* Due, payable.

échéance [eʃe'ɑ̃ːs], *n.f.* Falling due (of bill); date (of payment, of maturity); expiration (of tenancy). *À brève échéance,* at a short date, short-dated; *à longue échéance,* at a long date, long-dated; *à six mois d'échéance,* at six months date; *faire face aux échéances,* to meet the bills; *jusqu'à l'échéance,* till due; *payer une lettre de change à l'échéance,* to pay a bill of exchange at maturity; *venir à échéance,* to fall due. **échéancier,** *n.m.* Bill-book.

échéant, *a.* (*fem.* **-ante**) Falling due. *Le cas échéant,* if such should be the case, in that case.

échec [e'ʃɛk], *n.m.*   Check, repulse, defeat, failure, blow, loss. *Faire échec (à),* to check; *être échec et mat,* to be checkmated; *il a essuyé un grand échec,* he has suffered a dreadful blow; *tenir une armée en échec,* to keep an army at bay; *tenir un homme en échec,* to have a man under one's thumb; *voué à l'échec,* bound to fail.

échecs [e'ʃɛk], *n.m. pl.*   Chess; board and set of chess-men; chess-men. *Jouer aux échecs,* to play chess; *joueur d'échecs,* chess-player.

échelette [eʃ'lɛt], *n.f.* Rack (for pack-saddles, carts, etc.); (*Orn.*) tree-creeper. **échelier,** *n.m.* Peg-ladder.

échelle [e'ʃɛl], *n.f.* Ladder; scale; gradation. *À l'échelle de,* on the scale of; *après lui il faut tirer l'échelle,* he has left nothing to be done, you cannot get one better; *échelle à incendie* or *de sauvetage,* fire-escape; (*Mus.*) *échelle chromatique,* chromatic scale; (*Naut.*) *échelle de commandement,* accommodation-ladder; *échelle de corde,* rope-ladder; *échelle de coupée,* gangway-ladder; *échelle de revers,* Jacob's ladder, (*Bot.*) Greek valerian; *échelle de siège,* scaling-ladder; *échelle mobile,* sliding-scale; *échelles du Levant,* seaports in the Levant; *faire la courte échelle,* to give one's back and shoulders to someone to mount by; *l'échelle sociale,* the social hierarchy; *sur une grande* or *petite échelle,* on a large or a small scale.

échelon [eʃ'lɔ̃], *n.m.* Round, rung, step (of a ladder); stepping-stone; degree, grade, gradation; (*Mil.*) echelon. *À l'échelon ministériel,* at ministerial level; *descendre d'un échelon,* to come down a step; *marcher en échelons,* to march in echelon. **échelonner,** *v.t.* To draw up in echelon; to arrange according to gradation. *Échelonner un corps d'infanterie,* to draw up a body of infantry in echelon. *Vacances échelonnées,* staggered holidays. **s'échelonner,** *v.r.* To be graduated; to slope gradually; to be arranged or drawn up in echelon.

écheneau, échenau, écheno [eʃ'no] or **échenal,** *n.m.* (*pl.* **-aux** or **-eaux**) Sand basin (for fused metal) [CHENEAU].

échenillage [eʃni'jaːʒ], *n.m.* Ridding of caterpillars. (*fig.*) *Échenillage d'une traduction,* checking of a translation. **écheniller,** *v.t.*   To rid (plants, trees, etc.) of caterpillars. (*fig.*) *Écheniller un texte,* to examine a text in detail. **échenillage,** *n.m.* Caterpillar-destroyer. **échenilloir,** *n.m.* Instrument used for cutting away branches infested with caterpillars; branch-lopper.

écheno [ÉCHENEAU].

écherra, *fut.* of ÉCHOIR.

écheveau [eʃ'vo], *n.m.* Hank, skein. *Démêler l'écheveau d'une intrigue,* to disentangle the skein of an intrigue.

échevelé [eʃə'vle], *a.* (*fem.* **-ée**) Dishevelled, whose hair hangs loose and disordered; (*fig.*) wild, extravagant. **écheveler,** *v.t.* To dishevel.

échevette [eʃ'vɛt], *n.f.* Small skein (100 metres long).

*****échevin** [eʃ'vɛ̃], *n.m.* Sheriff; alderman. (C) Municipal magistrate. **échevinage,** *n.m.* Shrievalty, sheriffdom; aldermanry. **échevinal,** *a.* (*fem.* **-ale,** *pl.* **-aux**) Pertaining to sheriffs. (C) **échevinat,** *n.m.* The function of a municipal magistrate.

échidné [ekid'ne], *n.m.* (*Zool.*) Echidna.

échiffe [e'ʃif] or **échiffre,** *n.m.*   *****Watch-tower (in wood) on a city-wall; frame-work of a staircase.

échigner [ÉCHINER].

échignole [eʃi'ɲɔl], *n.f.* Bobbin for reeling silk.

échine (1) [eʹʃin], *n.f.* Spine, backbone, chine. *À la longue échine*, long-backed; *crotté jusqu'à l'échine*, all over mud; (*fig.*) *frotter l'échine à quelqu'un*, to give someone a thrashing; *une maigre échine*, a thin, lank person.

échine (2) [eʹʃin], *n.f.* (*Arch.*) Echinus, ovolo.

échinée [eʃiʹne], *n.f.* Griskin, chine-piece (of pork).

échiner [eʃiʹne], *v.t.* *To break the back of; to beat unmercifully; to tire out. **s'échiner**, *v.r.* (*pop.*) To knock oneself up (with work etc.), to work oneself to death.

échinoderme [ekinɔʹdɛrm], *n.m.* Echinoderm.

échinope [ekiʹnɔp] or **échinops**, *n.m.* (*Bot.*) Echinops, globe-thistle.

échiqueté [eʃikʹte], *a.* (*fem.* **-ée**) Chequered.

échiquier [eʃiʹkje], *n.m.* Chess-board; chequer-work, chequer-pattern; exchequer; square net. (*Hist.*) *L'Échiquier*, the Exchequer, the Courts of the Exchequer; *Chancelier de l'Échiquier*, Chancellor of the Exchequer. *En échiquier*, in squares, chequerwise, (*Naut.*) in bow and quarter line; *ouvrage fait en échiquier*, chequer-work.

écho [eʹko], *n.m.* Echo. *Se faire l'écho d'un bruit*, to repeat a rumour. *pl. Échos*, news items; *échos littéraires*, literary news.

échoir [eʹʃwaːr], *v.i. irr.* (*pres.p.* **échéant**, *p.p.* **échu**; *conjugated like* CHOIR) To expire, to fall due, to lapse; to happen, to fall, to befall. *Cela lui est échu en partage*, that fell to his lot; *cette lettre de change est échue*, that bill of exchange is due; *le premier payement doit échoir* or *écherra à Noël*, the first payment falls due at Christmas.

échoppage [eʃɔʹpaːʒ], *n.m.* Engraving with a burin etc.

échoppe (1) [eʹʃɔp], *n.f.* Booth, covered stall. *Une échoppe de savetier*, a cobbler's workshop.

échoppe (2) [eʹʃɔp], *n.f.* Round or flat graver, scooper, burin. **échopper**, *v.t.* To gouge, to work with a burin.

échotier [ekoʹtje], *n.m.* Gossip-writer, columnist.

échouage [eʹʃwaːʒ], *n.m.* (*Naut.*) Stranding, running aground; place where a boat may be beached; beaching-strand. **échouement**, *n.m.* Running aground, stranding; (*fig.*) failure.

échouer [eʹʃwe], *v.i.* To run aground, to be stranded; (*fig.*) to miscarry, to fail, to be disappointed. *Échouer à un examen*, to fail, to be ploughed; *la frégate échoua contre un rocher*, the frigate struck upon a rock.—*v.t.* To strand, to run (a vessel) aground. **s'échouer**, *v.r.* To run aground; to get stranded.

échu, *p.p.* (*fem.* **échue**) [ÉCHOIR].

écimage [esiʹmaːʒ], *n.m.* Topping, pollarding.

écimer [esiʹme], *v.t.* To top (plants etc.), to pollard (trees).

éclaboussement [eklabusʹmɑ̃], *n.m.* Splashing, bespattering. **éclabousser**, *v.t.* To splash, to bespatter. *Il veut éclabousser les voisins*, he wants to dazzle the neighbours with his wealth. **éclaboussure**, *n.f.* Splash, splash of mud.

éclair [eʹklɛːr], *n.m.* Lightning, flash of lightning; flash; variety of chocolate cake. *Éclairs de chaleur*, summer-lightning; *des éclairs de génie*, flashes of inspiration; *faire des éclairs*, to lighten; *il a passé comme un éclair*, he shot by like lightning. **éclairage**, *n.m.* Lighting, illumination. *Circuler sans éclairage*, to drive without the lights on; *éclairage au gaz*, gas-lighting, gas-light; *gaz d'éclairage*, illuminating gas; *éclairage à l'électricité*, electric light; *éclairage de scène*, stage-lighting. **éclairant**, *a.* (*fem.* **-ante**) Lighting, giving light, illuminating.

éclaircie [eklɛrʹsi], *n.f.* Opening, rift (in clouds etc.); fine or clear interval, break, clearing up; glade, vista; (*fig.*) favourable change of affairs.

éclaircir [eklɛrʹsiːr], *v.t.* To make clear or clearer, to clear up, to brighten; to clarify; to make thin or thinner; to throw light on, to elucidate, to illustrate, to explain, to solve. *Cet auteur éclaircit bien des vérités*, that author illustrates many truths; *éclaircir quelqu'un*, to enlighten, instruct, or inform someone; *éclaircir un malentendu*, to clear up a misunderstanding; *il faut l'en éclaircir*, he must be informed of it. **s'éclaircir**, *v.r.* To clear, to become clear, bright, or fine; to grow light; to be solved, to be explained, to be elucidated. *La foule s'éclaircit*, the crowd is thinning out; *le temps s'éclaircit*, the weather is clearing up; *son teint commence à s'éclaircir*, her complexion is becoming clearer. **éclaircissement**, *n.m.* Clearing up, explanation, elucidation, solution; hint, light. *Avoir* or *en venir à un éclaircissement*, to come to an explanation with someone).

éclaire [eʹklɛːr], *n.f.* Celandine. *La grande éclaire*, greater celandine; swallow-wort; *la petite éclaire*, lesser celandine, pile-wort.

éclairé [eklɛʹre], *a.* (*fem.* **-ée**) Lighted; well-lighted; (*fig.*) well-informed; intelligent; enlightened.

éclairer [eklɛʹre], *v.t.* To light, to give light to, to illuminate; to show a light to, to lead, to guide; to enlighten, instruct, to observe, to watch; (*Mil.*) to send out scouts before, to scout out, to reconnoitre.—*v.i.* To sparkle, to shine, to brighten, to glitter. *La lampe éclaire mal*, the lamp gives a dim light. **s'éclairer**, *v.r.* To become enlightened; to instruct or enlighten one another; to light up. *S'éclairer sur une question*, to gather information on a question. **éclaireur**, *n.m.* (*Mil.*) Scout; boy-scout; (*Navy*) advice-ship; (*fig.*) card-sharper's accomplice. *Aller en éclaireur*, to scout; *chef éclaireur*, scout-master.

éclamé [eklaʹme], *a.* (*fem.* **éclamée**) Broken-legged or broken-winged (of birds).

éclampsie [eklɑ̃ʹpsi], *n.f.* Eclampsia.

éclanche [eʹklɑ̃ːʃ], *n.f.* Shoulder of mutton.

éclat [eʹkla], *n.m.* Burst, sudden bursting; crash, clap, peal, sudden uproar; shiver, splinter (of wood, stone, brick, etc.); brightness, refulgence, glare, glitter; lustre, pomp, magnificence; renown, fame; gaudiness (of colours); rumour, scandal. *Action d'éclat*, splendid achievement, brilliant action; *craindre l'éclat*, to be afraid of a scandal; *on ne saurait soutenir l'éclat du soleil*, there is no bearing the glare of the sun; *rire aux éclats*, to roar with laughter; *un éclat d'obus*, a splinter of a shell; *un éclat de pierre*, a fragment of stone; *un éclat de rire*, a burst of laughter; *un grand éclat de voix*, a loud shout;

voler en éclats, to be shivered, to fly into a thousand pieces. **éclatant,** *a.* (*fem.* **-ante**) Bright, sparkling, glittering, brilliant, dazzling; gorgeous, magnificent; signal, striking, obvious, remarkable; piercing, loud, shrill. *Actions éclatantes*, brilliant exploits; *bruit éclatant*, crash; *son éclatant*, shrill sound; *tout éclatant de lumière*, all radiant with light; *vengeance éclatante*, signal vengeance. **éclatement,** *n.m.* Bursting, breaking up, explosion. **éclater,** *v.i.* To split, to shiver, to break into pieces, to burst, to explode; to make a loud and sudden noise, to clap; to cry out, to exclaim, to break out, to blaze out; to shine, to sparkle, to flash; to show, to manifest itself. *Éclater de rire*, to burst out laughing; *éclater en injures*, to burst forth into abuse; *éclater en sanglots*, to burst into sobs; *faire éclater*, to shatter, to splinter; to burst, to cause to explode; to give vent to; to show, to make appear, to prove (innocence etc.); *le tonnerre vient d'éclater*, there has just been a clap of thunder; *l'incendie éclata pendant la nuit*, the fire broke out during the night. **éclateur,** *n.m.* (*Elec.*) Spark-gap. **éclectique** [eklɛk'tik], *a.* and *n.m.* Eclectic; dilettante. **éclectisme,** *n.m.* Eclecticism. **écli** [e'kli], *n.m.* (*Naut.*) Splinter. **éclier** [e'klje], *v.t.* To splinter. **éclipse** [e'klips], *n.f.* Eclipse; (*fig.*) disappearance; absence. (*Naut.*) *Feu à éclipses*, occulting *or* intermittent light. **éclipser,** *v.t.* To eclipse, to occult; (*fig.*) to conceal, to hide; to surpass, to throw into the shade. **s'éclipser,** *v.r.* (*fig.*) To disappear, to vanish. *Il s'éclipsa tout d'un coup*, he suddenly disappeared. *Ne vous éclipsez pas*, don't steal away. **écliptique,** *n.f.* and *a.* Ecliptic. **éclissage** [ekli'sa:ʒ], *n.m.* (*Eng.*) *Plaque d'éclissage*, butt-strap. **éclisse** [e'klis], *n.f.* (*Surg.*) Splint, splinter; cheese-wattle; split-wood, side-piece (of violins, pails, tubs, casks, etc.); (*Rail.*) fish-plate. **éclisser,** *v.t.* (*Surg.*) To splint; to fish (rails). **éclissette,** *n.f.* Small splint. **éclopé** [eklɔ'pe], *a.* (*fem.* **éclopée**) Crippled, halt; footsore, lame, disabled. *Il est tout éclopé*, he is quite lame.—*n.* Cripple. **éclopement,** *n.m.* State of being crippled. **écloper,** *v.t.* To lame, to disable. **éclore** [e'klɔ:r], *v.i. irr.* (*p.p.* **éclos**) To be hatched, to hatch; to open (of eggs); to open, to blossom, to bloom (of flowers); (*fig.*) to break, to dawn, to come to light, to be born, to appear, to show itself. *Faire éclore des oiseaux*, to hatch birds; *les poussins commencent à éclore*, the chickens are beginning to hatch out; *lilas frais éclos*, fresh-blown lilacs; *une conspiration près d'éclore*, a conspiracy ready to break out. **éclosion,** *n.f.* Hatching; (*fig.*) opening, breaking forth, springing up, blooming; manifestation, appearance, advent. *Éclosion artificielle*, hatching in an incubator. **écluse** [e'kly:z], *n.f.* Lock (on canals etc.). *Porte d'écluse*, sluice, flood-gate. *Écluse de moulin*, mill-gate. (*Eng.*) *Écluse à pas*, pound lock; *écluse simple*, flash lock. **éclusée,** *n.f.* Lockful (of water). **écluser,** *v.t.* To lock; to furnish with locks; to take (a boat etc.)

through a lock. **éclusier,** *a.* (*fem.* **-ière**) Pertaining to locks.—*n.m.* Sluice-man, lock-keeper. **écobuage** [ekɔ'bɥa:ʒ], *n.m.* Grubbing and burning of weeds. **écobuer,** *v.t.* To grub (a field etc.) and burn the weeds, to denshire. **écœurant** [ekœ'rã], *a.* (*fem.* **-ante**) Disgusting, nauseating. **écœurement,** *n.m.* Disgust; nausea; dejection. **écœurer,** *v.t.* To disgust, to sicken; (*fig.*) to shock, to deject, to dishearten. **écoinçon** or **écoinson** [ekwɛ̃'sɔ̃], *n.m.* (Wooden) corner-piece or corner-stone in the angle of two walls. **écolage** [ekɔ'la:ʒ], *n.m.* Schooling; school fees. **école** [e'kɔl], *n.f.* School, college; school-house, scholastic philosophy; sect; (*Mil.*) training, course; (*fig.*) manner, doctrine, practice, experience, teaching, discipline. *Camarade d'école*, schoolfellow; *cela sent l'école*, that savours of pedantry. *École Centrale (des Arts et Manufactures)* (in Paris), engineering college; *école de droit, d'équitation, de natation*, law-, riding-, swimming-school; *école maternelle*, infant school; *école normale*, training college; *faire école*, to be at the head of a school or sect, to found a school (of art, literature, etc.); *faire l'école buissonnière*, to play truant; *envoyer à l'école*, to peg; *haute école*, higher horsemanship; *l'école de l'adversité*, the school of misfortune; *les querelles de l'École*, the scholastic arguments; (*Mil.*) *école de compagnie*, company drill; *école de pilotage*, flying school; *l'École de guerre*, the Staff College; *écoles à feu*, target practice. **écolier** [ekɔ'lje], *n.m.* (*fem.* **-ière**) Schoolboy, schoolgirl, pupil, student; (*fig.*) learner, novice, greenhorn, tyro. *Ce n'est qu'un écolier*, he is but a novice; *en écolier*, boylike; *papier écolier non réglé*, plain foolscap paper; *prendre le chemin des écoliers*, to go a roundabout way, to loiter; *tour d'écolier*, schoolboy trick. **écolleter** [ekɔl'te], *v.t.* To round off (a piece of jewellery) on the anvil. **éconduire** [ekɔ̃'dɥi:r], *v.t. irr.* (*conjugated like* CONDUIRE) To show out, to bow out, to dismiss; to put off, to refuse. *Il nous éconduit poliment*, he gives us a polite refusal; *se faire éconduire*, to be shown out, to suffer a rebuke. **économat** [ekɔnɔ'ma], *n.m.* Stewardship, bursarship, bursary; steward's or bursar's office. **économe** [ekɔ'nɔm], *n.* Steward, housekeeper, manager, bursar, treasurer (of colleges, hospitals, etc.).—*a.* Economical, saving, thrifty. *Être économe de louanges*, to be sparing of praise; (*Mil.*) *économe en chef*, chief, commissary steward. **économie** [ekɔnɔ'mi], *n.f.* Economy, good management, husbandry; thrift, saving; retrenchment. *Faire des économies*, to put by money, to save; *il n'y a pas de petites économies*, a penny saved is a penny earned; *l'économie de l'univers*, the scheme of the universe; *l'économie du corps humain*, the harmony of the human body; *l'économie d'un discours*, the arrangement of a speech; *l'économie dirigée*, directed or controlled or planned economy; *économie politique*, political economy, economics. **économique,** *a.*

(*applied to things only*) Economic, economical, cheap. *Fourneau économique*, fuel-saving stove; *ménage économique*, economical housekeeping.—*n.f.* Economics. **économiquement**, *adv.* Economically. *Les économiquement faibles*, the underprivileged. **économiser**, *v.t.*, *v.i.* To economize, to save (up), to spare, to husband. *Économiser ses forces*, to husband one's strength. **économiseur**, *n.m.* Economizer (part of distilling apparatus, for saving fuel). **économiste**, *n.m.* Economist; scholar in economics.

écope [e'kɔp], *n.f.* Scoop, ladle; (*Naut.*) bailer. **écoper**, *v.t.* To ladle, to bail out.—*v.i.* (*colloq.*) To be blamed, to be beaten, to cop it.

écoperche [eko'pɛrʃ], *n.f.* Derrick; upright pole supporting scaffolding.

écorçage [ÉCORCEMENT].

écorce [e'kɔrs], *n.f.* Bark, rind, peel; shell, outside, surface; (*Geol.*) crust (of the earth). *Entre l'arbre et l'écorce il ne faut pas mettre le doigt*, you should not interfere in other people's quarrels; *juger du bois par l'écorce*, to judge by appearances.

écorcement or **écorçage**, *n.m.* Barking or stripping (of trees etc.); peeling. **écorcer**, *v.t.* To bark, to strip (trees etc.), to peel.

écorché [ekɔr'ʃe], *n.m.* (*Paint.*) Écorché, anatomical figure (for the study of the muscles); (*fig.*) oversensitive person. *Crier comme un écorché*, to scream as if flayed alive.

écorchement [ekɔrʃə'mɑ̃], *n.m.* Excoriation, flaying, skinning. **écorcher**, *v.t.* To flay, to skin; to peel off, to graze, to gall, to rub the skin off; to peel, to bark; (*fig.*) to strip, to fleece; to disfigure, to distort. *Cela écorche les oreilles*, that grates on one's ears; *ce procureur écorchait ses clients*, that attorney fleeced his clients; *écorcher le français*, to murder the French language; *il crie avant qu'on ne l'écorche*, he cries before he is hurt. **s'écorcher**, *v.r.* To rub or tear one's skin off, to be galled, to be grazed. **écorcherie**, *n.f.* Knacker's yard. **écorcheur**, *n.m.* (*fem.* **-euse**) Knacker, flayer; (*fig.*) fleecer.

écorchure, *n.f.* Scratch, graze, excoriation, slight wound.

écore [e'kɔːr], *n.f.* Score, register of accounts (of a fishing-boat). **écorer**, *v.t.* To supervise the sale of fish.

écoreur, *n.m.* Supervisor and accountant.

écorner [ekɔr'ne], *v.t.* To break the horn or horns of; to break the corners of, to dog-ear; to curtail, to impair, to diminish; to squander. *Écorner son patrimoine*, to make a hole in one's heritage; (*fig.*) *il fait un vent à écorner un bœuf*, it is blowing great guns.

écornifler [ekɔrni'fle], *v.t.* To sponge upon.

écorniflerie, *n.f.* Sponging, hanging on.

écornifleur, *n.m.* (*fem.* **-euse**) Sponger, scrounger.

écornure [ekɔr'nyːr], *n.f.* Broken-off corner, break at the edges, chip.

écossais [ekɔ'sɛ], *a.* (*fem.* **écossaise**) Scottish, Scotch; plaid (material).—*n.m.* Scots (Scottish language), Scotch; plaid, tartan cloth; (**Écossais**, *fem.* **Écossaise**) Scot, Scotsman, Scotswoman.

Écosse [e'kɔs], *f.* Scotland. *La Nouvelle Écosse*, *f.* Nova Scotia.

écosser [ekɔ'se], *v.t.* To shell, to husk (peas or beans). **écosseur**, *n.m.* (*fem.* **-euse**) Sheller.

écot (1) [e'ko], *n.m.* Share (of a reckoning); bill, reckoning, score. (Usually in the expression: *payer son écot*, to pay one's share.)

écot (2) [e'ko], *n.m.* Stump of a tree, lopwood.

écouer [e'kwe], *v.t.* To dock (dog, horse).

écoufle [e'kufl], *n.m.* Kite (bird or toy).

écoulement [ekul'mɑ̃], *n.m.* Flowing, flow, running, drainage; issue, passage, course, emanation, outlet; (*Comm.*) sale, disposal, export. *L'écoulement de l'eau*, the flow of water; *l'écoulement de nos produits*, the sale of our commodities; *voie d'écoulement*, outlet. **écouler**, *v.t.* To dispose of, to sell. **s'écouler**, *v.r.* To run or flow away, to pass, to glide away, to slip away, to elapse; (*Comm.*) to go off, to be disposed of. *Ces marchandises s'écoulent vite*, these goods are in good demand; *le temps s'écoule*, time passes.

écourgeon [ESCOURGEON].

écourter [ekur'te], *v.t.* To shorten, to dock, to crop; to curtail. *Cheval écourté*, cropped horse; *écourter un chien*, to crop a dog; *écourter un discours*, to abridge a speech; *écourter ses vacances*, to shorten one's holiday.

écoutant [eku'tɑ̃], *a.* (*fem.* **-ante**) Listening, attending. *Avocat écoutant*, briefless barrister. **écoute** (1), *n.f.* Hiding-place for listening. *Écoutes radiophoniques*, *téléphoniques*, radio, telephone, listening-post; *être aux écoutes*, to be on the watch; *être*, *rester*, *à l'écoute*, (*Teleph.*, *Rad.*) to listen in; *poste d'écoute*, listening-post; *service d'écoutes radiotéléphoniques*, news monitoring-board.

écoute (2) [e'kut], *n.f.* (*Naut.*) Sheet, mainsheet. *Entre deux écoutes*, both sheets aft; *nœud d'écoute*, sheet-bend; *point d'écoute*, clew.

écouter [eku'te], *v.t.* To listen to, to hearken to; to overhear; to tap (telephone); to give ear to, to hear; to pay attention to, to mind. *Écoute! écoutez!* listen! look here! *écouter les avis de quelqu'un*, to follow someone's advice; *écouter un discours jusqu'au bout*, to hear a speech out; *il n'écoute personne*, he heeds nobody; *ne l'écoutez pas!* never mind him! *on nous écoute*, we are overheard; *se faire écouter*, to obtain a hearing, to enforce obedience. **s'écouter**, *v.r.* To like the sound of one's own voice; to be over-careful of oneself, to indulge oneself. *Il s'écoute trop*, he nurses himself too much. **écouteur**, *n.m.* (*fem.* **-euse** (1)) Listener, listener-in; (*Teleph.*) receiver; (*Teleg.*) ear-phone. *C'est un écouteur aux portes*, he is an eavesdropper. **écouteux**, *a.* (*fem.* **-euse** (2)) Skittish (horse).

écoutille [eku'tiːj], *n.f.* (*Naut.*) Hatchway.

écouvillon [ekuvi'jɔ̃], *n.m.* Long-handled baker's oven mop; sponge (for gun). **écouvillonnage**, *n.m.* Swabbing, sponging out. **écouvillonner**, *v.t.* To sponge out.

écrabouiller [ekrabu'je], *v.t.* (*fam.*) To squash, to reduce to pulp.

écran [e'krɑ̃], *n.m.* Screen. *Écran de cheminée*, fire-screen; (*Phot.*) *écran de sélection*, colour screen; (*Cine.*) *porter un roman à l'écran*, to film a novel; *vedette de l'écran*, film-star.

écrasant [ekra'zɑ̃], *a.* (*fem.* **-ante**) Crushing; (*fig.*) humiliating, exorbitant, excessive;

overwhelming. **écrasé**, *a.* (*fem.* **-ée**) Crushed, ruined; overwhelmed. *Nez écrasé*, flat nose; *visage écrasé*, flat face.—*n.f.* Caving in (in a mine). **écrasement**, *n.m.* Crushing, bruising; (*fig.*) overwhelming; defeat, collapse.

écrase-purée [e'krɑz pu're], *n.m.* Moulinette, mixer.

écraser [ekrɑ'ze], *v.t.* To crush, to squash, to tread down; to bruise; to weigh down, to overburden, to overwhelm, to ruin, to annihilate. *Écraser d'impôts*, to overburden with taxes; *écraser une balle*, (*Ten.*) to smash (a ball); *écraser ses rivaux*, to crush one's rivals; *être écrasé de travail*, to be overwhelmed with work; *j'ai manqué d'être écrasé*, I was nearly run over. (*vulg.*) *En écraser*, to sleep like a log, to be sound asleep. **écraseur**, *n.m.* (*fem.* **-euse**) Crusher; (*Motor.*) road-hog; roller.

écrémage [ekre'maːʒ], *n.m.* Creaming, skimming (of milk). **écrémer**, *v.t. irr.* (*conjugated like* ACCÉLÉRER) To take the cream off, to skim; (*fig.*) to take the best of. **écrémeuse**, *n.f.* Separator. **écrémoir**, *n.m.*, or **écrémoire**, *n.f.* Skimmer, milk-skimmer.

écrêter [ekrɛ'te], *v.t.* To take the crest off, to knock off the top of (a parapet etc).

écrevisse [ekrə'vis], *n.f.* Crayfish; (*Am.*) crawfish; (*Astron.*) Cancer, the Crab; (*Mil.*) double hoop for raising guns; blacksmith's tongs. *Marcher comme les écrevisses*, to walk backwards; *rouge comme une écrevisse*, as red as a boiled lobster; *une écrevisse de mer*, a sea crawfish, spiny lobster.

écrier (s') [ekri'e], *v.r.* To cry out, to exclaim.

écrille [e'kriːj], *n.f.* Grate (of a fish-pond).

écrin [e'krɛ̃], *n.m.* Casket, jewel-box or case.

écrire [e'kriːr], *v.t. irr.* (*pres.p.* **écrivant**, *p.p.* **écrit**) To write; to mark, to set down, to write down. *Cela était écrit au ciel*, it was written in the stars: *c'était écrit*, it was bound to happen; *comment écrivez-vous ce mot-là?* how do you spell that word? *écrire comme un chat*, to write illegibly; *écrire que*, to write to say that, to state that; *faire écrire*, to get to write; *il est écrit*, it is written, it is determined, fated, etc.; *l'art d'écrire*, the art of writing; *machine à écrire*, typewriter; *papier à écrire*, writing-paper. **s'écrire**, *v.r.* To be written; to be spelled; to write to each other. **écrit**, *n.m.* Writing, something written; agreement, pamphlet, written work. *Mettre en* or *par écrit*, to set down in writing. **écriteau**, *n.m.* Bill (poster); board, signboard. **écritoire**, *n.f.* Writing-desk; inkstand. **écriture**, *n.f.* Writing, hand-writing; scripture; (*pl.*) accounts, papers, documents, correspondence. *Avoir une belle écriture*, to write a good hand; *écriture anglaise*, Italian hand; *commis aux écritures*, copying-clerk; *l'Écriture sainte* or *les Écritures*, the Holy Scriptures, the Bible; *mauvaise écriture*, scrawl. **écrivailler** [ekriva'je], *v.t.* (*colloq.*) To scribble. **écrivaillerie**, *n.f.* Scribbling. **écrivailleur**, *n.m.* (*fem.* **-euse**) Scribbler.

écrivain [ekri'vɛ̃], *n.m.* Writer, author; *scrivener. *Écrivain public*, public scrivener; *femme écrivain*, woman writer, authoress.

écrivassier [ekriva'sje], *n.m.* (*fem.* **-ière**) (*colloq.*) Scribbler.

écrou (1) [e'kru], *n.m.* Female screw; screw-nut. *Écrou à oreilles*, thumb-nut, wing-nut.

écrou (2) [e'kru], *n.m.* Jail-entry. *Livre* or *registre d'écrou*, jail-book; *levée d'écrou*, order of release.

écrouelles [ekru'ɛl], *n.f. pl.* King's evil, scrofula. **écrouelleux**, *a.* (*fem.* **-euse**) Scrofulous.—*n.* Person affected with the king's evil.

écrouer [ekru'e], *v.t.* To enter in the jail-book; to imprison, to lock up, to consign to prison.

écrouir [ekru'iːr], *v.t.* To hard-hammer (metal). **écrouissement** or **écrouissage**, *n.m.* Hammer-hardening.

écroulement [ekrul'mã], *n.m.* Falling in, falling down, collapse; wreck, ruin. **s'écrouler**, *v.r.* To fall in, to fall down, to fall to pieces, to collapse; to perish, to be destroyed. *Cet édifice vint à s'écrouler*, that building fell down; *faire s'écrouler*, to pull or bring down; *la terre s'écroula*, the ground gave way; *un empire écroulé*, an overthrown empire.

écroûtage [ekru'taːʒ], *n.m.* Removing the crust of earth on fallow ground. **écroûter**, *v.t.* To take the crust off (a fallow), to scarify.

écru [e'kry], *a.* (*fem.* **écrue**) Raw, unbleached. *Fil écru, soie écrue*, raw thread, raw silk; *toile écrue*, (brown) holland.

écrues [e'kry], *n.f.* (*used only in pl.*) Wood of new and spontaneous growth.

ectocyste [ɛktɔ'sist], *n.m.* Ectocyst. **ectoderme**, *n.m.* Ectoderm. **ectoplasme**, *n.m.* Ectoplasm.

ectropion [ɛktrɔ'pjɔ̃], *n.m.* (*Path.*) Ectropion (eversion of the eyelids).

écu [e'ky], *n.m.* Shield; crown (an obsolete French coin formerly worth 3 francs); (*fig.*) money, cash; (*Her.*) escutcheon, arms. *Amasser des écus*, to hoard up money. (*Bot.*) *Herbe aux écus*, moneywort. **écuage**, *n.m.* Scutage, land-tax.

écubier [eky'bje], *n.m.* (*Naut.*) Hawse-hole.

écueil [e'kœːj], *n.m.* Reef, rock; (*fig.*) peril, danger, stumbling-block. *Donner sur un écueil*, to strike a rock. (*fig.*) *Le monde est plein d'écueils*, the world is full of dangers.

écuelle [e'kɥɛl], *n.f.* Porringer, bowl, basin. *Manger à la même écuelle*, to eat from the same porringer, (*fig.*) to live in the greatest intimacy. (*Bot.*) *Écuelle d'eau*, water (or marsh) pennywort. **écuellée**, *n.f.* Bowlful.

écuisser [ekɥi'se], *v.t.* To split (the trunk of a tree in felling it).

éculer [eky'le], *v.t.* To tread down at heel. *Des souliers éculés*, down-at-heel shoes.

écumage [eky'maːʒ], *n.m.* Skimming. **écumant**, *a.* (*fem.* **écumante**) Foaming, frothing, seething; (*fig.*) stormy, raging.

écume [e'kym], *n.f.* Foam, froth, sweat; lather; dross, slag; (*fig.*) scum. *Écume de mer*, meerschaum; *jeter de l'écume*, to foam (of a horse etc.); *l'écume de la société*, the dregs of society.

écumer [eky'me], *v.i.* To foam, to froth. *Il écumait de rage*, he was foaming with rage. —*v.t.* To skim the froth off; to scour. *Écumer le pot*, to skim the pot; *écumer la marmite*, to be a sponger; *écumer les mers*, to scour the seas. **écumeur**, *n.m.* (*fem.* **écumeuse** (1))

Skimmer; hanger-on, parasite; pirate. *Écumeur de marmites*, sponger; *écumeur de mer*, pirate, sea-rover. **écumeux**, *a.* (*fem.* **écumeuse** (2)) Frothy, foaming, yeasty. **écumoire**, *n.f.* Skimmer.

écurage [eky'ra:ʒ], *n.m.* Scouring, cleaning. **écurer**, *v.t.* To scour, to cleanse. *Écurer la vaisselle*, to scour dishes.

écureuil [eky'rœ:j], *n.m.* Squirrel.

écureur [eky'rœ:r], *n.m.* (*fem.* **-euse**) Scourer, cleaner, scavenger. *Écureur de puits*, well-cleanser.

écurie [eky'ri], *n.f.* Stable, mews; stud. *Garçon* or *valet d'écurie*, stable-boy, groom, ostler.

écusson [eky'sɔ̃], *n.m.* Escutcheon; shield, coat of arms; escutcheon (plate on a key-hole etc.); (*Hort.*) slip with bud for grafting; (*Mil.*) tab. **écussonnable**, *a.* (*Hort.*) That can be budded. **écussonnage**, *n.m.* (*Hort.*) Budding, grafting. **écussonner**, *v.t.* To decorate or furnish with an escutcheon; (*Hort.*) to bud. **écussonnoir**, *n.m.* Budding-knife.

écuyer [ekɥi'je], *n.m.* Squire; equerry; riding-master; professional rider, circus rider; wall hand-rail (of a staircase). *Écuyer de cirque*, circus rider; *écuyer tranchant*, carver; *grand écuyer*, master of the horse; *il est bon écuyer*, he is a good horseman. **écuyère**, *n.f.* Horse-woman; female equestrian performer. *Monter à l'écuyère*, to ride astride; *bottes à l'écuyère*, top-boots, riding-boots.

eczéma [ɛgze'ma], *n.m.* Eczema. **eczémateux**, *a.* (*fem.* **-euse**) Eczematous.

edelweiss [edɛl'vajs], *n.m.* (*Bot.*) Edelweiss.

édénien [ede'njɛ̃], *a.* (*fem.* **-ienne**). **édénique**, *a.* Paradisiac.

édenté [edɑ̃'te], *a.* (*fem.* **-ée**) Toothless; (*Zool.*) edentate. *Un peigne édenté*, a broken-toothed comb; *vieille édentée*, toothless hag. —*n.* (*Zool.*) Edentate.

édenter [edɑ̃'te], *v.t.* To break the teeth of (combs, saws, etc.); to deprive of teeth. *La vieillesse nous édente*, old age causes us to lose our teeth.

édictal [edik'tal], *a.* (*fem.* **-ale**, *pl.* **-aux**) Edictal. **édicter**, *v.t.* To enact, to decree. *Peines édictées par la loi*, penalties enacted by law.

édicule [edi'kyl], *n.m.* Small building (pavilion, kiosk, conveniences, etc.) in a public place.

édifiant [edi'fjɑ̃], *a.* (*fem.* **-ante**) Edifying.

édificateur [edifika'tœ:r], *n.m.* Builder, constructor. **édification**, *n.f.* Building, erection; (*fig.*) edification.

édifice [edi'fis], *n.m.* Edifice, building, pile; (*fig.*) structure, fabric. **édifier**, *v.t.* To build, to erect, to construct; (*fig.*) to edify, to improve; to instruct, to enlighten; to satisfy. *Il m'a édifié sur son compte*, he told me all about him (often in a bad sense); he gave me the low-down on him.

édile [e'dil], *n.m.* Edile; (*facet.*) town councillor.

édilité, *n.f.* Aedileship; town council.

Édimbourg [edɛ̃'bu:r], *m.* or *f.* Edinburgh.

édit [e'di], *n.m.* Edict.

éditer [edi'te], *v.t.* To publish; to edit. **éditeur**, *n.m.* (*fem.* **éditrice**) Publisher. **édition** [edi'sjɔ̃], *n.f.* Edition; (*fig.*) publica-

tion, reproduction, repetition. *Maison d'édition*, publishing firm. **éditorial**, *a.* (*fem.* **-ale**, *pl.* **-aux**) Editorial.—*n.m.* Leading article, leader. **éditorialiste**, *n.m.* Leader-writer.

Édmond [ɛd'mɔ̃], *m.* Edmund.

Édouard [e'dwa:r], *m.* Edward.

édredon [edrə'dɔ̃], *n.m.* Eider-down; (*Am.*) comforter; large eider-down pillow. *Édredon américain*, eider-down quilt.

éducabilité [edykabili'te], *n.f.* Educability. **éducable**, *a.* Educable. **éducateur**, *a.* (*fem.* **-trice**) Educative, instructing.—*n.* Educator. *Éducateur de vers à soie*, silkworm-breeder. **éducatif**, *a.* (*fem.* **-ive**) Educative, educational.

éducation [edyka'sjɔ̃], *n.f.* Education; training; rearing (of animals); breeding, manners. *Faire l'éducation d'un jeune homme*, to educate a young man; *il n'a point d'éducation*, he has no breeding; *maison d'éducation*, educational establishment, boarding-school.

éducationnel, *a.* (*fem.* **-elle**) (*rare*) Educational.

édulcoration [edylkɔra'sjɔ̃], *n.f.* Edulcoration (sweetening). **édulcorer**, *v.t.* To sweeten.

éduquer [edy'ke], *v.t.* (*colloq.*) To bring up, to educate (children).

éfaufiler [efofi'le], *v.t.* To unravel (textile fabrics).

effaçable [efa'sabl], *a.* Effaceable. **effaçage**, *n.m.* Effacing, erasing. **effacement**, *n.m.* Effacement, obliteration; disappearance; humility, self-effacement.

effacer [efa'se], *v.t.* To efface, to expunge, to erase, to rub out, to blot out, to scrape out, to scratch out, to obliterate; to eclipse, to throw into the shade; to surpass, to outdo. *Effacer les épaules*, to throw back the shoulders; *effacer ses péchés par ses larmes*, to wash out one's sins with one's tears. **s'effacer**, *v.r.* To get obliterated; to wear away; to keep in the background; to draw aside, to give way; (*Fenc.*) to move aside in order to evade one's opponent. *Il s'effaça pour éviter le coup*, he drew aside to avoid the blow. **effaçure**, *n.f.* Erasure, blotting out, obliteration.

effaner [efa'ne], *v.t.* To strip of leaves.

effarant [efa'rɑ̃], *a.* (*fem.* **-ante**) Unbelievable, bewildering.

(*C*) **effardocher** [efardɔ'ʃe], *v.t.* To clear away undergrowth.

effaré [efa're], *a.* (*fem.* **-ée**) Wild, scared, bewildered; surprised, astounded; (*Her.*) salient. *Un visage effaré*, a haggard, scared countenance. **effarement**, *n.m.* Bewilderment, distraction, terror, affright. **effarer**, *v.t.* To frighten, to scare, to flurry; to surprise, to astound. **s'effarer**, *v.r.* To be scared, to take fright; to be surprised or astounded.

effarouchant [efaru'ʃɑ̃], *a.* (*fem.* **-ante**) Startling, disquieting; shocking, annoying. ***effarouchement**, *n.m.* Scare, affright; umbrage. **effaroucher** [efaru'ʃe], *v.t.* To startle, to frighten; to flurry; to amaze; to shock, to give umbrage to. **s'effaroucher**, *v.r.* To be scared, to be startled, to take fright; to take umbrage; to be shocked.

effectif [efɛk'tif], *a.* (*fem.* **-ive**) Actual, real, positive; available.—*n.m.* Effective force (of troops etc.); size (of a class). *Effectifs du temps de paix*, peace establishment. *Le bateau a son effectif au complet*, that ship has her full complement. **effectivement**, *adv.* In effect, actually, indeed, in fact. (*In answer*) that is so.

effectuer [efɛk'tɥe], *v.t.* To effect, to execute, to accomplish, to carry out. *Effectuer une réconciliation*, to bring about a reconciliation; *effectuer une multiplication*, to perform a multiplication. **s'effectuer**, *v.r.* To be accomplished, to take place, to be carried out.

effémination [efemina'sjɔ̃], *n.f.* Effeminacy. **efféminé**, *a.* (*fem* -ée) Effeminate, womanish. **efféminer**, *v.t.* To effeminate, to enervate.

efférent [efe'rɑ̃], *a.* (*fem.* -ente) (*Anat.*) Efferent (vessel, canal, duct).

effervescence [efɛrvɛ'sɑ̃:s], *n.f.* Effervescence; (*fig.*) agitation, excitement, ferment. **effervescent**, *a.* (*fem.* -ente) Effervescent; (*fig.*) excited, excitable, irascible.

effet [e'fɛ], *n.m.* Effect, consequence, result; performance, execution; impression (made by a speech etc.); power (transmitted by machinery etc.); (*Comm.*) bill of exchange, bill; (*pl.*) belongings, clothes; movables, chattels; funds; stocks; (*Billiards*) screw; (*Cricket, Ten.*) break, twist, screw, spin. *À cet effet*, to that end, for that purpose; *à double effet*, double-acting; (*Law*) *à l'effet de*, to the end that, with a view to; *à quel effet?* to what purpose? *à simple effet*, simpleacting (of machines); *ces choses-là font un vilain effet*, those things look bad; *effet à échoir*, running bill; *effet à payer*, bill payable; *effet à recevoir*, bill receivable; (*Billiards*) *effet à revenir*, screw back; *effet de côté*, side screw; *en effet*, in reality, indeed, in fact, quite so; *faire de l'effet*, to make a show; to be effective (of threats, medicine, etc.); *faire honneur à un effet*, to honour a bill; *faire l'effet de*, to look or sound like; *faire les fonds d'un effet*, to provide for a bill; *mettre à l'effet*, to carry into effect; *produire de l'effet*, to make an impression; *souscrire un effet*, to sign a bill.

effeuillage [efœ'ja:ʒ], *n.m.* Stripping off the leaves (of fruit-trees etc.), defoliation. **effeuillaison**, *n.f.* Fall of the leaves. **effeuillement**, *n.m.* Fall of the leaves; leaflessness. **effeuiller**, *v.t.* To strip off leaves, to pick (a flower) to pieces. **s'effeuiller**, *v.r.* To lose or shed its leaves (of a tree, flower, etc.). *Les roses s'effeuillent*, the roses are shedding their petals.

efficace [efi'kas], *a.* Efficacious, effectual, effective. *À portée efficace*, (*Mil.*) at effective range.—* *n.f.* Efficacy. **efficacement**, *adv.* Efficaciously, effectually, efficiently. **efficacité**, *n.f.* Efficacy, effectiveness, efficiency. **efficience**, *n.f.* (*Phil.*) Efficiency. **efficient**, *a.* (*fem.* -ente) Efficient (cause).

effigie [efi'ʒi], *n.f.* Effigy. *Pendre en effigie*, to hang in effigy.

effilage [efi'la:ʒ], *n.m.* Unravelling, unweaving. **effilé**, *a.* Slender, slim; sharp, keen, trenchant. *Avoir la taille effilée*, to have a slender figure; *des doigts effilés*, tapering fingers.—*n.m.* Fringe, border of thread, silk, etc. **effiler**, *v.t.* To unweave, to fray, to unravel, to taper; (*Hunt.*) to tire out (dogs). **s'effiler**, *v.r.* To ravel out, to come un-

ravelled, to taper, to thin out, to become sharp, to fray.

effileur [EFFILOCHEUR].

effiloche [efi'lɔʃ] or **effiloque**, *n.f.* Floss silk, light refuse silk. **effilocher** or **effiloquer**, *v.t.* To ravel out, to undo. **effilocheur**, **effiloqueur**, or **effileur**, *n.m.* (*fem.* -cheuse, -queuse, or -leuse) Person who unravels rags etc. for paper-making.—*n.f.* Machine for doing this.

effilure [efi'ly:r], *n.f.* Unravelled thread.

efflanqué [eflɑ̃'ke], *a.* (*fem.* -ée) Lean, thin, lank, raw-boned (esp. of horses, dogs, etc.); (*fig.*) dry; meagre. *Style efflanqué*, meagre style. **efflanquer**, *v.t.* To make lean, to emaciate.

effleurage [eflœ'ra:ʒ] or **effleurement**, *n.m.* Grazing, skimming the surface, stroking, light massage, etc. **effleurer**, *v.t.* To graze, to skim the surface of, to touch lightly; (*fig.*) to touch upon, to glide over, to dip into.

efflorescence [eflɔrɛ'sɑ̃:s], *n.f.* Efflorescence. **efflorescent**, *a.* (*fem.* -ente) Efflorescent.

effluence [efly'ɑ̃:s], *n.f.* Effluence, emanation. **effluent**, *a.* (*fem.* -ente) Effluent.

effluve [e'fly:v], *n.m.* Effluvium, emanation.

effondrement [efɔ̃drə'mɑ̃], *n.m.* (*Agric.*) Digging deep, trenching; falling in, sinking, collapse, downfall. **effondrer**, *v.t.* To dig deeply, to break up (ground etc.); to break in, open, or through; to overwhelm. *Être effondré (dans la douleur)*, to be prostrate with grief. **s'effondrer**, *v.r.* To fall in, to collapse. **effondrilles**, *n.f. pl.* Grounds, sediment, dregs.

efforcer (s') [efɔr'se], *v.r.* To exert oneself, to strain, to strive, to endeavour.

effort [e'fɔ:r], *n.m.* Effort, exertion, endeavour; stress; (*Med.*) strain, rupture. *Faire effort pour*, to make an effort to; *faire tous ses efforts*, to try one's best, to strive or exert oneself to the utmost; *faire un effort sur soi-même*, to do oneself violence, to strive to overcome one's repugnance; *l'effort de l'eau a rompu cette digue*, the force of the water has broken down that dike; *se donner un effort*, to overstrain oneself, to sprain oneself.

effraction [efrak'sjɔ̃], *n.f.* Breaking into, breaking open, house-breaking. *Vol avec effraction*, burglary.

effraie [e'frɛ], *n.f.* Barn-owl, screech owl.

effranger [efrɑ̃'ʒe], *v.t.* To fray (material) at the edges. **s'effranger**, *v.r.* To become unravelled, to fray at the edges.

effrayant [efrɛ'jɑ̃], *a.* (*fem.* -ante) Frightful, dreadful, appalling, terrific, enormous.

effrayer [efrɛ'je], *v.t. irr.* (*conjugated like* ABOYER) To frighten, to alarm, to terrify, to startle. **s'effrayer**, *v.r.* To be frightened, to be startled, to take fright, to take alarm. *Il s'effraie de peu de chose*, he is easily frightened.

effréné [efre'ne], *a.* (*fem.* -ée) Unbridled, unrestrained, unruly, lawless; wild, frantic. *Passions effrénées*, unbridled passions.

effritement [efrit'mɑ̃], *n.m.* Exhaustion (of land etc.), crumbling into dust. **effriter**, *v.t.* To make sterile, to exhaust (land), to render friable. **s'effriter**, *v.r.* *To become exhausted (of land); to crumble.

effroi [e'frwa], *n.m.* Fright, terror, consternation, dread, dismay. *Porter partout l'effroi*, to carry consternation everywhere.

effronté [efrɔ̃'te], *a.* (*fem.* **-ée**) Shameless, brazen-faced, impudent.—*n.* Such a person. **effrontément**, *adv.* Impudently, boldly, shamelessly. **effronterie**, *n.f.* Effrontery, impudence, shamelessness. *Il a eu l'effronterie de me menacer*, he had the effrontery to threaten me; *il est plein d'effronterie*, he is full of impudence; *payer d'effronterie*, to brazen a thing out.

effroyable [efrwɑ'jabl], *a.* Frightful, dreadful, awful; shocking, hideous, repulsive. *Elle est d'une laideur effroyable*, she is frightfully ugly. **effroyablement**, *adv.* Frightfully, horribly, dreadfully.'

effruiter [efrɥi'te], *v.t.* To strip (trees) of fruit.

effusion [efy'zjɔ̃], *n.f.* Effusion, pouring out, shedding; overflowing. *Avec effusion*, effusively; *effusion de sang*, bloodshed, haemorrhage.

éfourceau [efur'so], *n.m.* (*pl.* **-eaux**) Two-wheeled timber-carriage.

égailler (s') [ega'je], *v.r.* To scatter, to disperse.

égal [e'gal], *a.* (*fem.* **égale**, *pl.* **égaux**) Equal, uniform, like, alike; even, level, smooth; indifferent, all the same. (*fam.*) *C'est égal, si j'avais su*, never mind, if I had only known; *cela m'est égal*, it is all the same to me; *tout lui est égal*, it is all one to him; *une humeur égale*, an even temper.—*n.* Equal. *À l'égal de*, as much as, equal to; *d'égal à égal*, between equals, on equal terms; *sans égal*, matchless.

égalable, *a.* That can be equalled. **également**, *adv.* Equally, alike, impartially, uniformly; also, likewise, too. **égaler**, *v.t.* To equal, to be equal to, to come up to, to match; to make equal; to compare, to liken; *to level, to smooth. **s'égaler**, *v.r.* To equal; to compare oneself (*à*).

égalisation [egaliza'sjɔ̃], *n.f.* Equalization. **égaliser**, *v.t.* To equalize; to make level; to square (accounts etc.). *Égaliser un terrain*, to level a piece of ground; *ils ont égalisé une minute avant la fin du match*, (*Ftb.*) they equalized one minute before the end of the match.

égalitaire [egali'tɛ:r], *a.* Based on equality or on equal rights.—*n.* Equalitarian, egalitarian. **égalité** [egali'te], *n.f.* Equality, parity; evenness, uniformity. *À égalité de mérite*, where there is equality of merit; *égalité d'âme*, equanimity; *sur un pied d'égalité*, on an equal footing.

égard [e'ga:r], *n.m.* Regard, account, consideration, respect; deference, (*pl.*) attentions. *À cet égard*, in this respect, on that account; *à l'égard de*, with regard to; *à tous égards*, in every respect; *avoir des égards pour*, to have consideration for, to pay deference to; *avoir égard*, to pay regard; *avoir égard à quelque chose*, to consider something; *eu égard à*, considering, making allowance for; *par égard pour*, out of regard for; *par égard pour vous*, for your sake.

égaré [ega're], *a.* (*fem.* **-ée**) Wandering, strayed; misguided, misled; mislaid; disordered, distracted, bewildered. *Colis égaré*, miscarried *or* gone astray (parcel); *balle égarée*, stray bullet; *brebis égarées*, lost sheep; *des yeux égarés*, wild eyes.—*n.* A person who has lost the way; (*fig.*) a person gone astray (morally etc.). **égarement**, *n.m.* Straying,

losing one's way; aberration, mistake, error; disorder, ill-conduct; frenzy, bewilderment. *Égarement d'esprit*, mental aberration.

égarer [ega're], *v.t.* To mislead, to misguide; to mislay, to lose; to lead astray, to lead into error; to bewilder; to impair (intellect). **s'égarer**, *v.r.* To lose one's way, to stray; to err, to mistake. *Il s'égara dans la forêt*, he lost himself in the forest.

égayer [ege'je], *v.t. irr.* (*conjugated like* ABOYER) To enliven, to make cheerful, to cheer, to cheer up; (*Hort.*) to prune (trees). *Égayer un appartement*, to make an apartment lighter. **s'égayer**, *v.r.* To brighten up, to be cheerful; to make merry, to amuse oneself. *Nous nous égayâmes à ses dépens*, we made merry at his expense; *il faut vous égayer*, you must cheer up.

Égée [e'ʒe], *m.* Aegeus. **L'Égée**, *f.* The Aegean (Sea).

Égérie [eʒe'ri], *f.* Egeria; female adviser.

égide [e'ʒid], *n.f.* Ægis (shield of Jupiter, of Pallas); shield, buckler. *Il me sert d'égide*, he is my protector, I am under his ægis.

églantier [eglɑ̃'tje], *n.m.* Eglantine, briar, dog-rose (bush). *Églantier odorant*, sweet-briar. **églantine**, *n.f.* Eglantine, dog-rose (flower).

églefin [AIGREFIN].

église [e'gli:z], *n.f.* Church. *Gueux comme un rat d'église*, as poor as a church mouse; *l'Église anglicane*, the Anglican Church; *un homme d'Église*, a churchman, a clergyman.

églogue [e'glɔg], *n.f.* Eclogue.

égocentrique [egosɑ̃'trik], *a.* Egocentric, self-centred. **égocentrisme**, *n.m.* Egocentrism, self-centredness.

égohine [EGOÏNE].

égoïne [egɔ'in], *n.f.* Pilot hand-saw (for jobbing carpenters).

égoïsme [egɔ'ism], *n.m.* Egoism, selfishness. **égoïste**, *a.* Egoistic, selfish.—*n.* Egoist, selfish person. **égoïstement**, *adv.* Egoistically.

égopode [egɔ'pɔd], *n.m.* (*Bot.*) Aegopodium, bishop's weed.

égorgement [egɔrʒə'mɑ̃], *n.m.* Cutting of the throat; slaughter. **égorger**, *v.t.* To cut the throat of, to slaughter, to butcher, to kill; (*fig.*) to ruin, to charge exorbitantly. **égorgeur**, *n.m.* Slaughterer, murderer.

égosiller (s') [egozi'je], *v.r.* To make oneself hoarse (with speaking, singing, etc.); to bawl, to strain one's voice. *Les serins s'égosillaient*, the canaries warbled away merrily.

égotisme [egɔ'tism], *n.m.* Egotism. **égotiste**, *n.* Egotist.—*a.* Egotistic(al).

égout [e'gu], *n.m.* Running or falling of water; sink, drain, sewer; lower edge of roof. *Tuyau d'égout*, drain-pipe; *égout collecteur*, main-sewer; *eaux d'égout*, sewage, sullage; *tout à l'égout*, sewerage. **égoutier**, *n.m.* Sewerman. **égouttage** *or* **égouttement**, *n.m.* Drainage, draining; dripping. **égoutter**, *v.t., v.i.* To drain, to drip. **s'égoutter**, *v.r.* To drip, to drain. **égouttoir**, *n.m.* Drainer (plate-rack etc.). **égoutture**, *n.f.* Drainings, drippings.

égrainer [ÉGRENER].

égrappage [egra'pa:ʒ], *n.m.* Picking (of grapes, currants, etc.) from the bunch. **égrapper**, *v.t.* To pick (grapes, currants, etc.) from the bunch.

égratigner [egrati′ɲe], *v.t.* To scratch. *S'il ne mord pas, il égratigne,* if he does not bite he scratches. **égratignure,** *n.f.* Scratch; slight wound. *Il ne saurait souffrir la moindre égratignure,* he is extremely touchy.

égrenage [egrə′na:ʒ], *n.m.* Picking off (of grapes etc.). **égrener,** *v.t.* (*conjugated like* AMENER) To tell (beads); to unstring (beads etc.); to pick off (grapes etc.) from the bunch. **s'égrener,** *v.r.* To fall from the stalk, to be detached, to drop one by one. **égreneuse,** *n.f.* Corn-shelling machine.

égrillard [egri′ja:r], *a.* Lively, lewd, broad, naughty. *Propos égrillards,* spicy talk.

égrilloir [egri′jwa:r], *n.m.* Weir; grate (to keep fish in a pond).

égrisage [egri′za:ʒ], *n.m.* Grinding (of diamond, marble etc.). **égrisé,** *n.m.,* or **égrisée,** *n.f.* Diamond-dust. **égriser,** *v.t.* To grind, to polish (diamonds etc.).

égrotant [egro′tɑ̃], *n.* and *a.* (*fem.* **-ante**) Sickly, weakly (person).

égrugeoir [egru′ʒwa:r], *n.m.* Mortar, mealer. **égruger,** *v.t.* To pound, to grind in a mortar, to meal. *Égruger du sel,* to pound salt.

*égueulement [egœl′mɑ̃], *n.m.* Breaking or wearing at the mouth of a cannon, vase, etc. **égueuler,** *v.t.* To break off the mouth or neck (of glass and other vessels).

Égypte [e′ʒipt], *f.* Egypt. *Basse-Égypte,* Lower Egypt. *Haute-Égypte,* Upper Egypt.

égyptien [eʒip′sjɛ̃], *a.* (*fem.*-**ienne**) Egyptian.— *n.m.* (**Égyptien,** *fem.* **-ienne**) An Egyptian. —*n.f.* (*Typ.*) Clarendon. **égyptologie,** *n.f.* Egyptology. **égyptologique,** *a.* Egyptological. **égyptologue,** *n.* Egyptologist.

eh [e] *int.* Ah! well! hey! *Eh bien!* well! *eh bien, soit,* well, be it so.

éhanché [DÉHANCHÉ].

éhonté [eɔ̃′te], *a.* (*fem.* **-ée**) Shameless.

éhouper [eu′pe], *v.t.* To lop the top off (a tree).

eider [e′dɛ:r], *n.m.* Eider, eider-duck.

éjaculateur [eʒakyla′tœ:r], *a.* (*fem.* **-trice**) (*Anat.*) Ejaculatory. **éjaculation,** *n.f.* Throwing out with force, discharge; ejaculation (fervent and short prayer). **éjaculatoire,** *a.* Ejaculatory. **éjaculer,** *v.t.* To throw out, to discharge, to ejaculate.

éjecter [eʒɛk′te], *v.t.* To eject. **éjecteur,** *a.* Ejective, ejecting. (*Av.*) *Siège éjecteur,* ejector seat. *Tuyau éjecteur,* discharge pipe. —*n.m.* Ejector (of firearm).

éjouir (s') [RÉJOUIR].

élaboration [elabɔra′sjɔ̃], *n.f.* Elaboration. **élaboré,** *a.* (*fem.* **-ée**) Wrought, laboured; elaborate. **élaborer,** *v.t.* To elaborate, to work out.

élagage [ela′ga:ʒ], *n.m.* (*Hort.*) Lopping; branches lopped off. **élaguer,** *v.t.* To lop, to prune; (*fig.*) to curtail, to cut down, to cut out. *Élaguez ces détails inutiles,* cut out those useless details. **élagueur,** *n.m.* (*Hort.*) Pruner.

élan (1) [e′lɑ̃], *n.m.* Start, spring, bound, rush, sally, flight, glow, burst, transport; dash, enthusiasm; impetus. *D'un seul élan,* at one rush; *l'élan vital,* the vital impulse; *par élans,* by starts; *prendre son élan,*·to get up speed, to take off (for a jump). *Saut sans élan,* standing jump; *saut avec élan,* running jump.

élan (2) [e′lɑ̃], *n.m.* Elk; moose, wapiti (Canada), eland (S. Africa).

élancé [elɑ̃′se], *a.* (*fem.* **élancée**) Slender, slim; straight-built, well-shaped; lank.

élancement, *n.m.* Darting forward; shooting pain, twinge; (*pl.*) transports.

élancer [elɑ̃′se], *v.t.* *To launch, to dart, to hurl; to emit with force or ardour.—*v.i.* To shoot, to twitch (of pain). **s'élancer,** *v.r.* To bound, to shoot or dart forth, to rush, to dash; to surge up, to soar up. *Il s'élança sur l'ennemi,* he rushed upon the enemy; *il s'élança sur son cheval,* he leapt on horseback; *la flèche de la cathédrale s'élance dans le ciel,* the spire of the cathedral soars up to the sky; *mon âme s'élança vers Dieu,* my soul soared up to God; *s'élancer sur quelqu'un,* to spring upon someone.

élaphis [ela′fis], *n.m.* A genus of European colubrine snakes.

élaps [e′laps], *n.m.* Another genus of ophidians; one of them is the Mexican *serpent corail.*

élargir [elar′ʒi:r], *v.t.* To widen, to make wider, to let out, to enlarge; to release, to set at large. *Élargir un compas,* to open a pair of compasses; *élargir un habit,* to let out a coat; *élargir un prisonnier,* to set a prisoner free. **s'élargir,** *v.r.* To widen, to become wider; to stretch; to enlarge one's estate; to set oneself free. **élargissement,** *n.m.* Widening, enlarging; release, discharge (from prison etc.). **élargissure,** *n.f.* Piece let in, gusset.

élasticité [elastisi′te], *n.f.* Elasticity, springiness. **élastique,** *a.* Elastic, springy.—*n.m.* India-rubber; elastic band etc.; (*Anat.*) spring-tissue.

élatère [ela′tɛ:r], *n.m.* (*Ent.*) Elater, click-beetle, skip-jack; (*Bot.*) elater.

élatérion [elate′rjɔ̃], *n.m.* Squirting-cucumber; elaterium.

élatérite [elate′rit], *n.f.* Mineral rubber.

élatine [ela′tin], *n.f.* (*Bot.*) Water-wort.

élavé [ela′ve], *a.* (*fem.* **-ée**) (*Hunt.*) Washed-out, discoloured (of hounds).

élaver [ela′ve], *v.t.* (*Paper-making*) To wash (rags).

Elbe (1) [ɛlb], **l'île d',** *f.* The island of Elba.

Elbe (2) [ɛlb], *f.* The river Elbe.

elbeuf [ɛl′bœf], *n.m.* Woollen cloth made at Elbeuf nr. Rouen.

eldorado [ɛldɔra′do], *n.m.* El Dorado.

éléatique [elea′tik], *a.* and *n.m.* (*Phil.*) Eleatic.

électeur [elɛk′tœ:r], *n.m.* (*fem.* **-trice**) Elector (a German title); *f.* electress; (*Polit.*) elector, voter, constituent. **électif,** *a.* (*fem.* **-ive**) Elective.

élection [elɛk′sjɔ̃], *n.f.* Election, return, polling; choice, appointment. *Aux élections générales,* at the general election; *une élection partielle,* a by-election. *C'est son pays d'élection,* it is his favourite country. **électivement,** *adv.* By election.

électoral, *a.* (*fem.* **-ale,** *pl.* **-aux**) Electoral. *Campagne électorale,* election campaign; *priver du droit électoral,* to disfranchise. **électorat,** *n.m.* Electorate.

Électre [e′lɛktr], *f.* Electra.

électricien [elɛktri′sjɛ̃], *n.m.* Electrician.

électricité [elɛktrisi′te], *n.f.* Electricity. **électrification,** *n.f.* Electrification. **électrifier,**

v.t. To provide with current, to electrify. **électrique,** *a.* Electric. *Conducteur électrique,* electric conductor; *secousse électrique,* electric shock. **électriquement,** *adv.* Electrically. **électrisable,** *a.* Electrifiable. **électrisant,** *a.* (*fem.* -ante) Electrifying. **électrisation,** *n.f.* Electrification. **électriser,** *v.t.* To electrify. *Fil de fer électrisé,* live wire. **s'électriser,** *v.r.* To be electrified, to electrify. **électriseur,** *n.m.* Electrifier; electrifying machine. **électro-aimant,** *n.m.* (*pl.* **électro-aimants**) Electro-magnet. **électrocardiogramme,** *n.m.* Electrocardiogram. **électrochimie,** *n.f.* Electrochemistry. **électrochoc,** *n.m.* Electroshock. *On lui a fait des électrochocs,* he was given shock treatment. **électrocuter,** *v.t.* To electrocute. **électrocution,** *n.f.* Electrocution. **électrode,** *n.f.* Electrode. **électrodynamique,** *n.f.* Electrodynamics; *a.* Electrodynamic. **électrolyse,** *n.f.* Electrolysis. **électrolyser,** *v.t.* To electrolyze. **électrolyte,** *n.m.* Electrolyte. **électromagnétique,** *a.* Electromagnetic. **électromagnétisme,** *n.m.* Electromagnetism. **électrométallurgie,** *n.f.* Electrometallurgy. **électromètre,** *n.m.* Electrometer. **électromoteur,** *a.* (*fem.* **électromotrice**) Electromotive.—*n.m.* Electromotor. **électron,** *n.m.* Electron. **électronégatif,** *a.* (*fem.* **électronégative**) Electronegative. **électronique,** *a.* Electronic. **électrophore,** *n.m.* Electrophorus. **électrophysiologie,** *n.f.* Electro-physiology. **électrophysiologique,** *a.* Electro-physiological. **électropositif,** *a.* (*fem.* -ive) Electropositive. **électroscope,** *n.m.* Electroscope. **électrostatique,** *a.* Electrostatic. **électrothérapeutique,** *a.* Electro-therapeutic.—*n.f.* Electro-therapy. **électrothérapie,** *n.f.* Electro-therapy. **électrothermie,** *n.f.* Thermo-electricity. **électrothermique,** *a.* Thermo-electric. **électrotype,** *n.m.* Electrotype. **électrum,** *n.m.* Electrum.
électuaire [elɛk'tɥɛːr], *n.m.* Electuary.
élégamment [elega'mã], *adv.* Elegantly, stylishly.
élégance [ele'gãs], *n.f.* Elegance, style.
élégant, *a.* (*fem.* -ante) Elegant, fashionable, stylish.—*n.* Gentleman or lady of fashion; swell, exquisite.
élégiaque [ele'ʒjak], *a.* Elegiac.—*n.m.* Elegist.
élégie [ele'ʒi], *n.f.* Elegy.
élégir [ele'ʒiːr], *v.t.* To reduce thickness of (wood, iron, etc.) by mouldings.
élément [ele'mã], *n.m.* Element, component part. *Être dans son élément,* to be quite at home (in anything); *la chasse est son élément,* hunting is his favourite pursuit; (*Mil.*) *des éléments de reconnaissance,* scouting parties; *les quatre éléments,* the elements. **élémentaire,** *a.* Elementary, elemental.
élémi [ele'mi], *n.m.* (*Pharm.*) Elemi (gum).
éléphant [ele'fã], *n.m.* Elephant; (*fam.*) jumbo. *Éléphant de mer,* sea-elephant. **éléphanteau,** *n.m.* (*pl.* -eaux) Young elephant. **éléphantiasis,** *n.f.* Elephantiasis. **éléphantin,** *a.* (*fem.* -ine) Elephantine.
élevage [el'vaːʒ], *n.m.* Breeding, raising, rearing (of cattle); place where this is done, stud, (*Australia*) station.

élévateur [eleva'tœːr], *a.* (*fem.* -trice) Raising, lifting; elevatory.—*n.m.* Elevator, lift, hoist. *Élévateur de tension,* power transformer.
élévation [eleva'sjɔ̃], *n.f.* Elevation, lifting up, raising; rising ground, eminence, height; preferment, promotion; loftiness, exaltation, greatness (of soul); elevation of the host; increase, rise (of prices etc.). *Élévation dans le style,* loftiness of style; *élévation de côté,* side-view (of a building etc.); *il a beaucoup d'élévation,* he is very high-minded; *il lui doit son élévation,* he is indebted to him for his promotion. **élévatoire,** *n.m.* Elevatory. —*a.* Lifting, hoisting. *Usine élévatoire,* waterworks.
élève (1) [e'lɛːv], *n.* Pupil; student, disciple; articled pupil, apprentice; (*Agric.*) animal brought up by a breeder. *Élève maître (m.), maîtresse (f.),* pupil-teacher. **élève** (2), *n.f.* *(Agric.)* Breeding (of stock).
élevé [el've], *a.* (*fem.* -ée) Raised, grand; heroic, eminent, stately, lofty; high (of prices, *etc.*). *C'est un jeune homme bien élevé,* he is a very well-bred young man; *mal élevé,* ill-mannered, ill-bred.
élever [el've], *v.t.* To raise, to lift up; to carry up, to cause to go up; to erect, to set up; to promote, to exalt; to ennoble; to augment, to run up (accounts etc.); to bring up, to rear; to educate, to train up, to foster. *Élever la voix,* to raise one's voice; *élever quelqu'un jusqu'aux nues,* to extol someone to the skies; (*Mil.*) *élever un ouvrage de terre,* to throw up an earthwork; *j'ai eu de la peine à élever ces plantes,* I took some trouble to raise those plants; *élever un nombre à la puissance* n, to raise a number to the power of *n.* **s'élever,** *v.r.* To rise, to ascend; to mount, to go up; to run up; to amount; to be set up, constructed, or elevated; to increase, to augment; to run up (of accounts); to be raised, excited, or started; to burst forth, to break out. *Celui qui s'élève sera abaissé,* he who exalts himself shall be humbled; *il s'éleva une querelle,* a quarrel broke out; *les vagues s'élevèrent hautes et menaçantes,* the waves rolled high and threatening; *une tempête s'éleva,* a storm arose.
éleveur, *n.* (*fem.* -euse (1)) Raiser; cattle-breeder, grazier.
éleveuse (2), *n.f.* Incubator; hen kept for hatching eggs.
*****élevure,** *n.f.* Pimple, blotch.
elfe [ɛlf], *n.m.* Elf, brownie.
élider [eli'de], *v.t.* (*Gram.*) To cut off, to elide. **s'élider,** *v.r.* To be elided, to be cut off or left out. *Cette voyelle s'élide,* that vowel is elided.
Élie [e'li], *m.* Elias, Elijah.
éligibilité [eliʒibili'te], *n.f.* Eligibility.
éligible, *a.* Eligible.
élimer [eli'me], *v.t.* To wear out. **s'élimer,** *v.r.* To wear threadbare (of clothes etc.).
élimination [elimina'sjɔ̃], *n.f.* Elimination. **éliminatoire,** *a.* and *n.f.* (*spt.*) Eliminating (heat); disqualifying. *Épreuve éliminatoire* (*spt.*) eliminating heat; *note éliminatoire* (in an examination), disqualifying mark.
éliminer, *v.t.* To eliminate; to strike out or off, to expel, to dismiss; to discard, to remove, to delete.
élingue [e'lɛ̃ːg], *n.f.* (*Naut.*) Sling. **élinguer.** *v.t.* To sling (for hoisting).

élire [e'liːr], *v.t. irr.* (*pres.p.* **élisant,** *p.p.* **élu;** *conjugated like* LIRE) To elect, to choose; to return, to appoint, to designate. *Élire domicile,* to take up one's abode.

Élisabeth [eliza'bɛt], *f.* Elizabeth. **élisabéthain,** *a.* (*fem.* -aine) Elizabethan.

Élise [e'liːz], *f.* Eliza.

Élisée [eli'ze], *m.* Elisha.

élision [eli'zjɔ̃], *n.f.* Elision.

élite [e'lit], *n.f.* Choice, pick, select few, élite, flower, prime. *D'élite,* choice, picked, select; *l'élite de l'armée,* the pick of the army; *soldats d'élite,* picked troops; *tireur d'élite,* crack shot.

élixir [elik'siːr], *n.m.* Elixir.

elle [ɛl], *pron. 3rd pers., fem. of* LUI (*pl.* **elles**) She, her, it. *Je les lui donne à elle-même,* I give them to her, place them in her own hands; *je les vois, elles et leur frère,* I see them and their brother; *je parle d'elle,* I speak of her; *elle me parle,* she is speaking to me; *je reviens à elle,* I return to her.

ellébore [ɛle'bɔːr], *n.m.* Hellebore. *Ellébore fétide,* setterwort, stinking hellebore, bear's foot; *ellébore noir,* or *rose de Noël,* Christmas rose. **elléborine,** *n.f.* Glucoside extracted from hellebore.

ellipse [ɛ'lips], *n.f.* Ellipse; (*Gram.*) ellipsis. **ellipsoïdal,** *a.* (*fem.* -ale, *pl.* -aux) Ellipsoidal. **ellipsoïde,** *n.m.* Ellipsoid.

ellipticité [eliptisi'te], *n.f.* Ellipticity. **elliptique,** *a.* Elliptical. **elliptiquement,** *adv.* Elliptically.

Elme (Feu Saint-) [føsɛ̃'tɛlm], *n.m.* Corposant, St. Elmo's fire.

élocution [elɔky'sjɔ̃], *n.f.* Elocution.

éloge [e'lɔːʒ], *n.m.* Eulogy, encomium, praise; panegyric. *Digne d'éloge,* praiseworthy; *éloge funèbre,* funeral oration; *faire l'éloge d'un auteur,* to speak in praise of an author; *faire soi-même son éloge,* to blow one's own trumpet. **élogieusement,** *adv.* Eulogistically. **élogieux,** *a.* (*fem.* -ieuse) Laudatory, eulogistic, flattering.

Éloi [e'lwa], *m.* Eloy.

éloigné [elwa'ɲe], *a.* Removed, distant, remote, absent, foreign. *Cause éloignée,* remote cause; *d'une manière éloignée,* distantly; *il est fort éloigné de le croire,* he is far from believing it; *se tenir éloigné,* to keep away, to stand aloof; *temps éloignés,* distant times. **éloignement,** *n.m.* Removal, removing; distance, remoteness; aversion, dislike, antipathy; estrangement, unwillingness. *Il vit dans l'éloignement du monde,* he lives apart from the world.

éloigner [elwa'ɲe], *v.t.* To remove, to put far or farther away; to dismiss; to set aside, to discard, to repudiate; to waive; to banish, to drive away; to put off, to delay, to retard; to alienate, to estrange. *Éloigner les soupçons,* to avert suspicion; *éloigner quelqu'un de,* to indispose someone (towards); *éloigner quelqu'un de son pays,* to send someone away from his country; *éloignez de vous ces mauvaises pensées,* dismiss such evil thoughts. **s'éloigner,** *v.r.* To go away, to remove, to stand aloof, to absent oneself; to withdraw; to ramble, to digress; to swerve, to deviate; to differ (*de*), to dislike; to be estranged or alienated; (*Paint.*) to appear in the distance. *Cette opinion s'éloigne de la mienne,* that opinion differs from mine; *ne vous éloignez pas,* don't go away or too far away; *s'éloigner*

de son sujet, to digress from one's subject; *tous s'éloignaient de lui,* they all shunned, avoided him.

élongation [elɔ̃gɑ'sjɔ̃], *n.f.* Elongation; digression.

élonger [elɔ̃'ʒe], *v.t.* To stretch; (*Naut.*) to sheer off, to lay alongside of; to splice; to skirt (a shore). *Élonger une côte,* to skirt a coast.

élongis [elɔ̃'ʒi], *n.m.* (*Naut.*) Trestle-tree.

éloquemment [elɔka'mɑ̃], *adv.* Eloquently.

éloquence [elɔ'kɑ̃ːs], *n.f.* Eloquence, oratory. *Éloquence de la tribune,* parliamentary eloquence. **éloquent,** *a.* (*fem.* -ente) Eloquent.

élu [e'ly], *a.* (*fem.* **élue**) Elected, chosen, elect; appointed, designated, returned.—*n.m.* *Un élu,* one chosen; *les élus,* the elect. *Le nouvel élu,* the newly elected member.

élucidation [elysidɑ'sjɔ̃], *n.f.* Elucidation. **élucider,** *v.t.* To elucidate, to clear up.

élucubration [elykybrɑ'sjɔ̃], *n.f.* Lucubration. *élucubrer, *v.t.* To lucubrate.

éludable [ely'dabl], *a.* Eludible. **éluder,** *v.t.* To elude, to evade.

élyme [e'lim], *n.m.* (*Bot.*) Lyme grass.

Élysée [eli'ze], *n.m.* Elysium. *L'Élysée,* the residence (in Paris) of the President of the Republic.—*a.* Elysian. *Les Champs Élysées,* the Elysian Fields; famous avenue in Paris. **élyséen,** *a.* (*fem.* -éenne) Elysian.

élytre [e'litr], *n.m.* (*Ent.*) Elytron, wing-sheath; shard.

elzévir [elze'viːr], *n.m.* Elzevir (edition). **elzévirien,** *a.* (*fem.* -ienne) Elzevirian.

émaciation [emasjɑ'sjɔ̃], *n.f.* Emaciation. **émacié,** *a.* (*fem.* -ée) Emaciated. **s'émacier,** *v.r.* To emaciate. **s'émacier,** *v.r.* To become emaciated.

émail [e'maːj], *n.m.* (*pl.* **émaux**) Enamel; (*Her.*) tincture; (*fig.*) lustre, gloss, brilliancy. *Émail de Hollande,* Dutch blue; *peintre en émail,* enameller. **émaillage,** *n.m.* Enamelling. **émailler,** *v.t.* To enamel; (*fig.*) to adorn, to embellish; to bedeck. **émaillerie,** *n.f.* Art of enamelling. **émailleur,** *n.m.* Enameller. **émaillure,** *n.f.* Enamelling.

émanation [emanɑ'sjɔ̃], *n.f.* Emanation.

émancipateur [emɑ̃sipɑ'tœːr], *a.* (*fem.* **émancipatrice**) Emancipatory.—*n.* Emancipator. **émancipation,** *n.f.* Emancipation. **émanciper,** *v.t.* To emancipate. **s'émanciper,** *v.r.* To emancipate oneself; to overstep the mark, to forget oneself. *Vous vous émancipez trop,* you are getting rather too free.

émaner [ema'ne], *v.i.* To emanate.

émargement [emarʒə'mɑ̃], *n.m.* Writing in the margin, marginal note; signature in the margin. **émarger,** *v.t.* To write or sign in the margin, esp. on receipt; hence, to draw one's salary; (*Tech.*) to diminish the margin of (engravings etc.). **émarginé,** *a.* (*fem.* -ée) (*Bot.*) Emarginate.

émasculation [emaskylɑ'sjɔ̃], *n.f.* Emasculation, castration. **émasculer,** *v.t.* To emasculate, to castrate; (*fig.*) to mutilate, to enfeeble.

*****émabouiner** [ãbabwi'ne], *v.t.* To wheedle, to cajole (into doing something).

embâcle [ã'baːkl], *n.m.* Ice-pack (in a river etc.).

emballage [ãba'laːʒ], *n.m.* Packing up, packing; package; (*spt.*) spurt. *Toile d'emballage,* packing-canvas, pack-cloth; *papier d'emballage*, brown paper. **emballement**, *n.m.* Excitement; flying into a temper; burst of enthusiasm. **emballer**, *v.t.* To pack up, to wrap up; (*colloq.*) to pack off, to send away, to bundle off, to arrest, to run somebody in; to tell someone off, to give a dressing-down. *Un cheval emballé*, a runaway horse. **s'emballer**, *v.r.* To bolt, to run off (of a horse etc.); to wrap oneself up; to be carried away (by rage, enthusiasm, etc.), to fly into a temper; to race (of an engine). *Ne vous emballez pas!* Keep cool! **emballeur**, *n.m.* Packer.

embarbouiller [ăbarbu'je], *v.t.* To besmear; (*colloq.*) to confuse, to muddle. **s'embarbouiller**, *v.r.* To get muddled.

embarcadère [ăbarka'dɛːr], *n.m.* Wharf, pier, landing-stage.

embarcation [ăbarka'sjɔ̃], *n.f.* Small boat, craft.

embardée [ăbar'de], *n.f.* Yaw, lurch (of a boat, a car, etc.). *Faire une embardée*, to yaw, to lurch (of boat); to swerve, to skid (of car).

embarder, *v.i.* (*Naut.*) To yaw, to lurch.

embargo [ăbar'go], *n.m.* Embargo. *Lever l'embargo*, to take off the embargo; *mettre un embargo sur*, to lay an embargo on.

embariller [ăbari'je], *v.t.* To barrel, to barrel up.

embarquement [ăbarkə'mã], *n.m.* Embarkation, embarking; shipment. **embarquer**, *v.t.* To embark, to put aboard; to take on board; to ship (water etc.). (*Mil.*) *Embarquer des troupes en avion, en chemin de fer*, to emplane, to entrain troops. (*fam.*) *On l'a embarqué dans une méchante affaire*, he has been drawn into a bad business.—*v.i.* To embark, to go on board. **s'embarquer**, *v.r.* To embark, to go on board; (*fig.*) to embark upon, to launch into.

embarras [ăba'rɑ], *n.m.* (*pl. unchanged*) Encumbrance, hindrance, impediment; difficulty, fuss, distress, straits; (*pl.*) embarrassing circumstances; trouble, embarrassment, nervousness, perplexity; (*Med.*) obstruction, derangement. *Avoir l'embarras du choix*, to have too much to choose from; *être dans l'embarras*, to have a lot of trouble; *cet homme fait bien de l'embarras*, that man makes a great fuss; *embarras de voitures*, traffic block; *embarras gastrique*, bilious attack; *faire des embarras*, to put on airs, to be fussy; *je suis dans l'embarras*, I am at a loss; *vous m'avez tiré d'embarras*, you have helped me out of my difficulty. **embarrassant**, *a.* (*fem.* **-ante**) Embarrassing, puzzling, awkward, perplexing; cumbersome, troublesome.

embarrassé, *a.* (*fem.* **-ée**) Embarrassed, perplexed, obstructed; constrained, out of countenance. *Être embarrassé*, to be at a loss; *être embarrassé de sa personne*, not to know what to do with oneself; *il est embarrassé pour répondre*, he is at a loss for an answer.

embarrasser, *v.t.* To embarrass, to hamper, to encumber, to obstruct; to trouble, to confound, to puzzle, to put at a loss; to inconvenience, to incommode; to entangle, to ensnare. *Cette question l'a embarrassé*, that question puzzled him; *embarrasser une rue*, to obstruct a street; *je crains de vous embarrasser*, I don't want to be in the way.

s'embarrasser, *v.r.* To entangle oneself; to be embarrassed, to be at a loss; to be solicitous about, to concern oneself (with), to get mixed up (with); to hamper oneself. *Il ne s'embarrasse de rien*, nothing ever troubles him; *il s'embarrassa dans son discours*, he got confused, he did not know what he was saying; *sa langue s'embarrasse*, his tongue begins to falter.

*embarrer [ăba're], *v.t.* To put a lever under a load etc. to lift it. **s'embarrer,** *v.r.* To get the leg caught over the partition-bar (of horses).

embase [ă'baːz], *n.f.* Shoulder (of trunnions); flange (of shaft).

embasement [ăbaz'mã], *n.m.* (*Arch.*) Continuous projecting base (of a building).

embastillement [ăbastij'mã], *n.m.* Imprisonment; surrounding with fortifications. **embastiller,** *v.t.* To imprison; to surround with fortifications.

embatage [EMBATTAGE].

embâtage [ăbɑ'taːʒ], *n.m.* Saddling (a beast of burden).

embâter [ăbɑ'te], *v.t.* To put a pack-saddle on, to saddle.

embâtonner [ăbɑtɔ'ne], *v.t.* (*Arch.*) To place reeds in the flutings of (a column).

embattage or **embatage** [ăba'taːʒ], *n.f.* Tyring (of wheels). **embatteur** or **embateur,** *n.m.* Workman who puts the iron tyres on wheels.

embattre or **embatre** [ă'batr], *v.t. irr.* (*conjugated like* BATTRE) To case, to tyre (a wheel).

embauchage [ăbo'ʃaːʒ], *n.m.*, or **embauche,** *n.f.* Hiring, taking on, engaging (of workmen); enlisting, recruiting (soldiers). *Chercher de l'embauche*, to look for work.

embaucher, *v.t.* To hire, to engage, to sign on (workmen); to enlist (soldiers).

embaucheur, *n.m.* (*fem.* **-euse**) Hirer, labour-contractor; recruiter.

embauchoir (1) [ăbo'ʃwaːr], *n.m.* Boot-tree, boot-last.

embauchoir (2) [ăbo'ʃwaːr], *n.m.*, or **embouchoir,** *n.m.* Mouth-piece (of wind instruments); upper band (of rifle).

embaumement [ăbom'mã], *n.m.* Embalming. **embaumer,** *v.t.* To embalm; to perfume or scent with.—*v.i.* To smell sweet. (*fam.*) *Embaumer la rose*, to smell of roses. **embaumeur,** *n.m.* Embalmer.

embecquer [ăbe'ke], *v.t.* To feed (a bird); to bait (a hook).

embéguiner [ăbegi'ne], *v.t.* To muffle up. **s'embéguiner,** *v.r.* To wrap oneself up; (*fig.*) to be infatuated with.

*embelle [ă'bɛl], *n.f.* (*Naut.*) Waist (of a ship).

embellie [ăbe'li], *n.f.* Lull, momentary calm.

embellir [ăbe'liːr], *v.t.* To embellish, to beautify; to adorn, to set off.—*v.i.* To grow handsomer. *Elle ne fait que croître et embellir*, she grows taller and handsomer every day. **s'embellir,** *v.r.* To grow more beautiful; to improve in looks, to grow handsomer; to enhance, improve one's own looks. **embellissant,** *a.* (*fem.* **-ante**) Embellishing, adorning. **embellissement,** *n.m.* Embellishment, adornment; improvement.

emberlificoter [ăberlifiko'te], *v.t.* (*colloq.*) To muddle, to entangle; to inveigle, to entrap.

s'emberlificoter, *v.r.* To get entangled, inveigled, etc.
*emberlucoquer (s') [ăbɛrlykɔ'ke], *v.r.* (*colloq.*) To be taken with, to be wedded to an opinion etc.
*embesogné [ăbəzɔ'ɲe], *a.* (*fem* .-ée) Busy, busily engaged.
embêtant [ăbe'tă], *a.* (*fem.* -ante) (*colloq.*) Boring, annoying. **embêtement,** *n.m.* (*colloq.*) Annoyance, bother; nuisance, bore. **embêter,** *v.t.* To bore, to annoy, to rile, to worry. **s'embêter,** *v.r.* To feel dull or bored.
emblavage [ăbla'va:ʒ], *n.m.* Wheat-sowing. **emblaver,** *v.t.* To sow with wheat etc. **emblavure,** *n.f.* Land sown with wheat etc.
emblée (d') [ă'ble], *adv.* At the first, at the first onset, at the first attempt, directly.
emblématique [ăblema'tik], *a.* Emblematical. **emblématiquement,** *adv.* Emblematically.
emblème [ă'blɛːm], *n.m.* Emblem, symbol, badge, crest; (*fig.*) attribute. *Être l'emblème de,* to be emblematical of.
embobeliner [ăbɔbli'ne], *v.t.* or **embobiner.** To wheedle, get round, coax; hoodwink.
emboire [ă'bwaːr], *v.t. irr.* (*conjugated like* BOIRE) (*Sculp.*) To coat (a mould etc.) with oil or wax.—*n.m.* [*see* EMBU]. **s'emboire,** *v.r.* (*Paint.*) To get dull or flat.
emboîtage [ăbwa'taːʒ], *n.m.* Fitting, inserting (book) into its cover; boards, cover (book). **emboîtement,** *n.m.* Fitting in, jointing, clamping. **emboîter,** *v.t.* To fit in, to encase, to put (book) into its boards; to clamp. *Emboîter le pas,* (*Mil.*) to lock, to march lock-step, (*fig.*) to model oneself closely on. *Tubes emboîtés,* nested tubes. **s'emboîter,** *v.r.* To fit, to fit in; (*fig.*) to model oneself upon. **emboîture,** *n.f.* Socket, clamp; frame, joint, juncture. *Emboîture du moyeu,* axle-box.
embolie [ăbɔ'li], *n.f.* (*Path.*) Embolism, embolus. **embolique,** *a.* Embolic.
embolisme [ăbɔ'lism], *n.m.* Embolism. **embolismique,** *a.* Embolismic.
embonpoint [ăbɔ̃'pwɛ̃], *n.m.* Plumpness, stoutness, obesity. *Prendre de l'embonpoint,* to put on flesh; *perdre son embonpoint,* to lose flesh.
emboquer [ăbɔ'ke], *v.t.* To cram food into (poultry etc.).
embordurer [ăbɔrdy're], *v.t.* To put in a frame, to frame.
embossage [ăbɔ'sa:ʒ], *n.m.* (*Naut.*) Bringing a vessel broadside on. **embosser,** *v.t.* To bring (a vessel) broadside on. **s'embosser,** *v.r.* To be brought thus.
embouche [ă'buʃ], *n.f.* Cattle fattening. *Pré d'embouche* or *embouche, n.m.,* rich meadow or pasture-land.
emboucher [ăbu'ʃe], *v.t.* To put to one's mouth, to sound (wind instruments); to bit (a horse). (*fig.*) *Emboucher la trompette,* to adopt an elevated style. (*colloq.*) *C'est un homme mal embouché,* he is foul-mouthed. **s'emboucher,** *v.r.* *To empty, to discharge (of rivers); (*Naut.*) to enter a narrow passage (of a boat).
embouchoir [EMBAUCHOIR].
embouchure [ăbu'ʃyːr], *n.f.* Embouchure, mouth (of a river, harbour, etc.); mouthpiece (of wind-instruments); opening (of a vessel).

emboudiner [ăbudi'ne], *v.t.* (*Naut.*) To cover (an anchor-ring) with puddening. **emboudinure,** *n.f.* Puddening.
*embouer [ăbu'e], *v.t.* To cover with mud; (*fig.*) to smear, to vilify.
embouquement [ăbuk'mă], *n.m.* (*Naut.*) Entrance to a canal, strait, etc. **embouquer,** *v.i.* To enter a strait etc.
embourber [ăbur'be], *v.t.* To put in the mire, to bemire; (*fig.*) to implicate in a dirty or troublesome affair. **s'embourber,** *v.r.* To stick in the mire; (*fig.*) to be involved (in some trouble); to put one's foot in it.
embourgeoiser (s') [ăburʒwa'ze], *v.t.* To become a *bourgeois,* to rise to the middle-class.
*embourrer [ăbu're], *v.t.* To stuff, to pad.
embourser [ăbur'se], *v.t.* *To put into one's purse; to receive, to pocket (affronts etc.).
embout [ă'bu], *n.m.* Ferrule. **embouter,** *v.t.* To put a ferrule on (a cane etc.).
embouteillage [ăbute'ja:ʒ], *n.m.* Bottling (of wine); bottling up (of a fleet); bottleneck, traffic jam.
embouteiller [ăbuteje], *v.t.* To bottle; to bottle up; to block up.
emboutir [ăbu'tiːr], *v.t.* To beat out (coppersmith's work etc.); to scoop out, to stamp; (*fam.*) to bump into; (*Arch.*) to sheet with metal, to plate. **s'emboutir,** *v.r.* To crash, to cannon into. *Il s'est embouti contre un arbre,* he crashed into a tree.
embranchement [ăbrăʃ'mă], *n.m.* Branching off; branch-road, branch-line, branch-pipe, etc.; junction. **embrancher,** *v.t.* To put together, to join up (several roads, parts, etc.). **s'embrancher,** *v.r.* To join (of a minor road or line joining a major one).
embraquer [ăbra'ke], *v.t.* (*Naut.*) To haul (a rope) taut, to tighten.
embrasement [ăbraz'mă], *n.m.* Conflagration; illumination. **embraser,** *v.t.* To fire, to set on fire; (*fig.*) to inflame; to illuminate. *La guerre a embrasé toute l'Europe,* war has set all Europe ablaze. **s'embraser,** *v.r.* To kindle, to catch fire; to glow, to be aglow, to be inflamed. *Le phosphore s'embrase facilement,* phosphorus easily catches fire.
embrassade [ăbra'sad], *n.f.* Embrace, hug; kissing, kiss.
embrasse [ă'bras], *n.f.* Curtain-loop.
embrassement [ăbras'mă], *n.m.* Embrace, embracing. **embrasser,** *v.t.* To embrace, to clasp; to kiss; (*fig.*) to encompass, to encircle; to comprise, to include; to seize, to avail oneself of, to undertake. *Embrasser la querelle de quelqu'un,* to espouse someone's quarrel; *embrasser une occasion,* to seize or avail oneself of an opportunity; *embrasser une religion,* to embrace a faith; *ils se tenaient embrassés,* they remained locked in each other's arms; *qui trop embrasse, mal étreint,* grasp all, lose all. **s'embrasser,** *v.r.* To embrace or kiss one another; to be embraced, included, or comprised. **embrasseur,** *n.m.* (*fem.* -euse) Embracer, kisser.
embrassure [ăbras'syːr], *n.f.* Band of iron, binder.
embrasure [ăbra'zyːr], *n.f.* Embrasure, window-opening, recess.
embrayage [ăbrɛ'ja:ʒ], *n.m.* Connecting (of wheels etc.); (*Motor*) coupling-gear, clutch. **embrayer,** *v.t., v.i.* To connect up, to throw

into gear, to clutch, to lock; to let in the clutch; (*pop.*) to resume work.

***embrener** [ãbrə'ne], *v.t.* (*conjugated like* AMENER) (*pop.*) To dirty, to soil. *S'embrener dans quelque affaire*, to get mixed up in a dirty piece of business.

embrèvement [ãbrɛv'mã] or **embreuvement** [ãbrœv'mã], *n.m.* (*Carp.*) Mortise, mortise-joint. **embrever** or **embreuver**, *v.t.* To mortise, to joggle.

embrigadement [ãbrigad'mã], *n.m.* Forming into a brigade or brigades, brigading; grouping; enrolment. **embrigader**, *v.t.* To organize in brigades, to enrol, to rope in.

embrocation [ãbrɔka'sjɔ̃], *n.f.* Embrocation.

embrochement [ãbrɔʃ'mã], *n.m.* Spitting (of meat). **embrocher**, *v.t.* To spit, to put upon the spit. *Embrocher quelqu'un*, to run someone through the body.

embroncher [ãbrɔ̃'ʃe], *v.t.* To overlap, to make (tiles etc.) overlap.

embrouillamini [BROUILLAMINI].

embrouillement [ãbruj'mã], *n.m.* Embroiling, entanglement, intricacy, complication, perplexity. **embrouiller**, *v.t.* To embroil, to confuse, to confound, to jumble up; to perplex, to obscure. **s'embrouiller**, *v.r.* To become intricate or entangled; to get confused, fuddled, or muddled. **embrouilleur**, *n.m.* (*fem.* **-euse**) Muddler, blunderer.

embroussaillé [ãbrusa'je], *a.* (*fem.* **-ée**) Covered with brushwood, bushy, matted; tousled (hair); (*fig.*) intricate. **embroussailler**, *v.t.* To cover with brushwood, etc. **s'embroussailler**, *v.r.* To become covered with brushwood etc.

embruiné [ãbrɥi'ne], *a.* (*fem.* **-ée**) Covered with drizzle.

embrumer [ãbry'me], *v.t.* To overcast, to cover with fog or mist. **s'embrumer**, *v.r.* To be covered with fog, etc.; to get misty or hazy; (*fig.*) to grow sombre or gloomy.

embrun [ã'brœ̃], *n.m.* (usually *pl.*) Spray, spindrift.

embrunir [ãbry'ni:r], *v.t.* To brown, to make brown or sombre, to darken.

embryogénie [ãbriɔʒe'ni], *n.f.* Embryogeny. **embryologie**, *n.f.* Embryology. **embryologique**, *a.* Embryological. **embryologiste**, *n.* Embryologist. **embryon**, *n.m.* Embryo; germ; (*fig.*) little bit of a man, dwarf, shrimp. **embryonnaire**, *a.* Embryonic, in embryo.

embu [ã'by], *a.* (*fem.* **embue**) (*Paint.*) Soaked in, dried in; of which the colours are dried in.—*n.m.* Dullness, flatness (of pictures).

embûche [ã'byʃ], *n.f.* Ambush, snare.

***embûcher** [ãby'ʃe], *v.t.* To begin cutting (trees). **s'embûcher**, *v.r.* (*Hunt.*) To return to cover (of a stag).

embuer [ã'bye], *v.t.* To make hazy, to dim. *Ses yeux étaient tout embués de larmes*, her eyes were dim with tears.

embuscade [ãbys'kad], *n.f.* Ambuscade, ambush; lurking-place, snare. *Dresser une embuscade*, to lay an ambush (for); *être, se mettre, se tenir en embuscade*, to lie in wait or in ambush. **embusqué** [ãbys'ke], *n.m.* (*Mil. slang*) Shirker, scrimshanker, soldier not at the front. **embusquer**, *v.t.* To place in ambuscade, post. **s'embusquer**, *v.r.* To lie in wait; to shirk active service.

éméché [eme'ʃe], *a.* (*fam.*) Slightly drunk, lit up.

émender [emã'de], *v.t.* (*Law*) To amend, to correct.

émeraude [em'ro:d], *n.f.* Emerald.

émergence [emɛr'ʒã:s], *n.f.* Emersion, emergence. **émergent**, *a.* (*fem.* **-ente**) Emergent. **émerger**, *v.i.* To emerge, to rise out.

émeri [em'ri], *n.m.* Emery. *Bouché à l'émeri*, with a ground stopper, (*fam.*) stupid; *papier émeri*, emery-paper.

émerillon [emri'jɔ̃], *n.m.* (*Orn.*) Merlin; (*Naut.*) swivel-hook. **émerillonné**, *a.* (*fem.* **-ée**) Brisk, sprightly, lively (as a merlin). **émerillonner**, *v.t.* To brighten, to make lively or brisk.

émeriser [emri'ze], *v.t.* To cover with emery. *Papier émerisé, toile émerisée*, emery-paper, emery-cloth.

émérite [eme'rit], *a.* *Emeritus; practised, perfect, eminent.

émersion [emɛr'sjɔ̃], *n.f.* Emersion.

émerveillement [emɛrvɛj'mã], *n.m.* Wonder, astonishment. **émerveiller**, *v.t.* To astonish, to amaze. **s'émerveiller**, *v.r.* To marvel, to be astonished.

émétique [eme'tik], *a.* and *n.m.* Emetic. **émétiser**, *v.t.* To put an emetic in (a mixture); to treat with emetics.

émetteur [eme'tœr], *a.* and *n.* (*fem.* **émettrice**) (*Teleg., Rad. Tel.*) *Poste émetteur* or *station émettrice*, broadcasting station. **émetteur-récepteur**, *n.m.* Transmitter-receiver, (*fam.*) walkie-talkie.

émettre [e'mɛtr], *v.t. irr.* (*p.p.* **émis**; *conjug. like* METTRE) To emit, to issue, to give out; to put in circulation, to utter, to express, to set forth; (*Rad., Tel.*) to broadcast.

émeu [e'mø], *n.m.* (*Orn.*) Emu.

émeulage [emø'la:ʒ], *n.m.* Grinding (polishing) of mother-of-pearl. **émeuler**, *v.t.* To polish (mother-of-pearl) by grinding; to buff (metal).

émeute [e'mø:t], *n.f.* Riot, disturbance, tumult, rising, outbreak. *Chef d'émeute*, ringleader. **émeuter**, *v.t.* To rouse, to stir up, to excite. **émeutier**, *n.m.* (*fem.* **émeutière**) Rioter.

émiettement [emjɛt'mã], *n.m.* Crumbling. **émietter** [emjɛ'te], *v.t.* To crumble. **s'émietter**, *v.r.* To crumble.

émigrant [emi'grã], *n.m.* (*fem.* **-ante**) Emigrant.—*a.* Emigrating. **émigration**, *n.f.* Emigration, migration. **émigré**, *n.m.* (*fem.* **-ée**) Emigrant; refugee; (*Fr. Hist.*) royalist exile. **émigrer**, *v.i.* To emigrate; to migrate.

Émile [e'mil], *m.* Emile.

Émilie [emi'li], *f.* Emily, Amelia.

émincé [emɛ̃'se], *n.m.* (*Cook.*) Thin slices (of meat). **émincer**, *v.t.* To slice (meat).

éminemment [emina'mã], *adv.* Eminently, in a high degree.

éminence [emi'nã:s], *n.f.* Eminence, elevation, rising ground, height. **éminent**, *a.* (*fem.* **-ente**) Eminent, high, lofty, conspicuous. **éminentissime**, *a.* Most eminent (applied to cardinals).

émir [e'mi:r], *n.m.* Ameer, emir.

émis, émise [e'mi], *p.p.* (*fem.* **émise**) [ÉMETTRE].

émissaire [emi'sɛ:r], *n.m.* Emissary, messenger; overflow pipe, overflow channel.

Bouc émissaire, scapegoat. **émissif,** *a.* (*fem.* **-ive**) Emissive.

émission [emi′sjɔ̃], *n.f.* Emission; issue, uttering, putting into circulation; broadcasting. *Prix d'émission,* issue price. (*Rad., Tel.*) *Nos émissions sont terminées,* we are closing down. **émissionnaire,** *a.* Issuing, uttering. —*n.* Person doing this.

emmagasinage [ămagazi′naːʒ] or **emmagasinement,** *n.m.* Storage, warehousing. **emmagasiner,** *v.t.* To warehouse, to store.

emmaillotement [ămajɔt′mã], *n.m.* Swaddling, swathing. **emmailloter,** *v.t.* To swaddle, to swathe; to bind lightly.

emmanchement [ămãʃ′mã] or **emmanchage,** *n.m.* Hafting, helving (putting a handle on); (*fig.*) joining, jointing, fitting together, managing. **emmancher,** *v.t.* To put a handle to, to haft, to helve; (*fig.*) to set about, to manage. *Affaire mal emmanchée,* ill-managed affair at the start. **s'emmancher,** *v.r.* To fit on a handle; (*fig.*) to start (of an affair).

emmancher [ămã′ʃe], *v.i.* (*Naut.*) To enter a channel (of ships etc.).

emmancheur [ămã′ʃœːr], *n.m.* Handle-maker or fitter. **emmanchure,** *n.f.* Armhole, sleeve-hole.

emmanteler, *v.t.* [ămã′tle] To wrap in a cloak or mantle; (*Fort.*) to enclose in a rampart, fortifications, etc.

emmarchement [ămarʃə′mã], *n.m.* Tread of stair.

emmêlement [ămɛl′mã], *n.m.* Tangle, muddle. **emmêler,** *v.t.* To entangle, to tangle; to complicate (an affair). **s'emmêler,** *v.r.* To get entangled.

emménagement [ămenaʒ′mã], *n.m.* Moving into (a new house), installation; (*pl.*) internal arrangements, accommodation (on shipboard). **emménager,** *v.t.* To move in; to fit out (a ship etc.).—*v.i.* and **s'emménager,** *v.r.* To move in; to settle in.

emmener [ăm′ne], *v.t. irr.* (*conjugated like* AMENER) To take away, to lead away, to fetch away, to convey away. (*Mil.*) *Emmener* (*un prisonnier*) *sous escorte,* to march (a prisoner) off. *Emmenez-le!* off with him; *il l'a emmené dans sa voiture,* he took him away in his car.

emmenotter [ămnɔ′te], *v.t.* To handcuff.

emmerder [ămɛr′de], *v.t.* (Very coarse verb, not in decent use.) Current euphemisms are *embêter, emmieller,* etc. To be a great nuisance, to create trouble; to bore.

emmeuler [ămø′le], *v.t.* To stack (hay etc.).

emmiellé [ămjɛ′le], *a.* Honeyed, sweet, soft. *Paroles emmiellées,* honeyed words. **emmieller,** *v.t.* To honey, to sweeten with or as with honey; euphemism for *emmerder.* **emmiellure,** *n.f.* (*Vet.*) Resolvent plaster.

emmitonner [ămitɔ′ne], *v.t.* To wrap up (warmly); to wheedle, to coax.

emmitoufler [ămitu′fle], *v.t.* To wrap up warmly.

emmortaiser [ămɔrtɛ′ze], *v.t.* To mortise, to set in a mortise.

emmurer [ămy′re], *v.t.* To wall in, to immure.

emmuseler [ămyz′le], *v.t.* To muzzle; (*fig.*) to silence, to gag.

émoi [e′mwa], *n.m.* Emotion, excitement,

anxiety, flutter. *Être en émoi,* to be agitated or in a ferment; *mettre en émoi,* to put in a flutter.

émollient [emɔ′ljã], *a.* (*fem.* **-ente**) Emollient, softening.—*n.m.* Emollient.

émolument [emɔly′mã], *n.m.* Emolument, fee, perquisite; (*pl.*) salary, emoluments. **émolumentaire,** *a.* Emolumentary.

émonctoire [emɔ̃k′twaːr], *n.m.* Emunctory.

émondage [emɔ̃′daːʒ] or **émondement,** *n.m.* Pruning, lopping, trimming. **émonde,** *n.f.* Dung (of birds of prey). **émonder,** *v.t.* To prune, to lop; to blanch (almonds etc.); to clean, to sort out (seeds, grain, etc.). **émondes,** *n.f.* (*used only in pl.*) Branches lopped off; (*fig.*) trash, refuse. **émondeur,** *n.m.* (*fem.* **-euse**) Pruner, trimmer. **émondoir,** *n.m.* Pruning-hook.

émorfiler [emɔrfi′le], *v.t.* To cut off rough edges etc. on (a piece of metal, leather, etc.).

émotif [emo′tif], *a.* (*fem.* **-ive**) Pertaining to emotions, emotive. *Crise émotive,* fit of hysterics; *il est peu émotif,* he does not get easily excited.—*n.* Person who gets easily excited. **émotion,** *n.f.* Emotion; stir, commotion. **émotionnable,** *a.* Emotional. **émotionner,** *v.t.* To excite emotion in, to thrill, to move **s'émotionner,** *v.r.* (*fam.*) To be stirred. **émotivité,** *n.f.* Emotivity, emotiveness.

émottage [emɔ′taːʒ] or **émottement,** *n.m.* Clod-crushing. **émotter,** *v.t.* To break up (soil, a field, etc.). **émottoir,** *n.m.* Roller, clod-breaker.

émoucher [emu′ʃe], *v.t.* To drive flies away from, to clear of flies; (*Fenc.*) to take off the button (of a sword). **s'émoucher,** *v.r.* To whisk away the flies.

émouchet [emu′ʃɛ], *n.m.* Sparrow-hawk, *Accipiter nisus.*

émoucheter [DÉMOUCHETER].

émouchette [emu′ʃɛt], *n.f.* Fly-net (for horses etc.) **émoucheur,** *n.m.* (*fem.* **-euse**) Fly-fanner. **émouchoir,** *n.m.* Fly-whisk.

émoudre [e′mudr], *v.t. irr.* (*pres.p.* **émoulant,** *p.p.* **émoulu,** *conjugated like* MOUDRE) To whet, to grind, to sharpen. *Émoudre des couteaux,* to grind knives. **émoulage,** *n.m.* Knife-grinding. **émouleur,** *n.m.* Knife-grinder. **émoulu,** *a.* (*fem.* **-ue**) Sharpened, sharp. *Combattre à fer émoulu,* to fight with sharp weapons; *il est frais émoulu du collège,* he is fresh from college.

émoussage [emu′saːʒ], *n.m.* (*Agric.*) Removal of moss from trees or soil.

émoussement [emus′mã], *n.m.* Blunting; (*fig.*) dulling, enfeebling, deadening. **émousser** (1), *v.t.* To blunt, to take the edge off; (*fig.*) to dull; to enfeeble, to deaden. *Émousser un rasoir,* to take the edge off a razor. *Un esprit émoussé,* a dull mind; *émousser les sens,* to deaden the senses. **s'émousser,** *v.r.* To get blunt; to become dull, deadened or blunted.

émousser (2) [emu′se], *v.t.* To take the moss off (trees etc.). **émoussoir,** *n.m.* Moss-scraper.

émoustiller [emusti′je], *v.t.* (*colloq.*) To exhilarate, to put into good spirits; (*fam.*) to ginger up; to excite. **s'émoustiller,** *v.r.* To bestir oneself, to look alive, to get jolly, rowdy.

émouvant [emu'vã], *a.* (*fem.* **-ante**) Touching, moving, affecting, stirring.

émouvoir [emu'vwaːr], *v.t. irr.* (*p.p.* **ému**, *conjugated like* MOUVOIR) To move, to touch, to affect, to stir; to excite, to agitate, to rouse. *Émouvoir la bile à quelqu'un*, to incite someone's anger; *il est ému de crainte*, he is moved with fear; *il sait l'art d'émouvoir les passions*, he knows how to stir up the passions. **s'émouvoir**, *v.r.* To be roused, touched, or moved; to be stirred; to be agitated, to take alarm; to be anxious. *Il s'émut à la vue du péril*, he was troubled at the sight of the danger; *il s'émeut d'un rien*, the least thing upsets him.

empaillage [ãpɑ'jaːʒ] or **empaillement**, *n.m.* Bottoming (with straw); stuffing (of animals). **empaillé**, *a.* (*fem.* **-ée**) Stuffed. (*fam.*) *Avoir l'air empaillé*, to be slow, dull-witted. **empailler**, *v.t.* To pack in straw; to straw-bottom; to stuff (birds etc.). *Empailler des ballots*, to pack up bales in straw; *empailler une plante*, to wrap straw round a plant. **empailleur**, *n.m.* (*fem.* **-euse**) Chair-mender; bird- or animal-stuffer.

empalement [ãpal'mã], *n.m.* Impalement. **empaler**, *v.t.* To impale. **s'empaler**, *v.r.* To be impaled; to wound oneself on a spike etc.

***empan** [ã'pã], *n.m.* Span.

empanacher [ãpana'ʃe], *v.t.* To plume, to adorn with or as with a plume; (*colloq.*) to touch up. *Style empanaché*, flowery, ornate style.

empanner [ãpa'ne], *v.t.* (*Naut.*) To bring to. *Être empanné*, to be brought by the lee.

empaquetage [ãpak'taːʒ], *n.m.* Packing, putting into a bundle or bundles. **empaqueter**, *v.t.* To pack up, to make up into a bundle, to do up. **s'empaqueter**, *v.r.* To wrap oneself up. *Il s'empaqueta dans son manteau*, he wrapped himself up in his cloak.

emparer (s') [ãpa're], *v.r.* To possess oneself, to get hold (*de*); to make oneself master (*de*); to seize, to secure; to engross (conversation). *S'emparer du pouvoir*, to seize power.

empatage [EMPATTEMENT].

empâtement [ãpat'mã], *n.m.* Stickiness, clamminess; thickness (of the voice); cramming (of poultry); (*Paint.*) impasto; puffiness, fleshiness. **empâter**, *v.t.* To make clammy or sticky; to cram (fowls); (*Paint.*) to impaste. *Cela m'a empâté les mains*, that has made my fingers sticky. *Lettres empâtées*, (*Print.*) over-inked types. *Langue empâtée*, coated tongue. **empâteur**, *n.m.* (*fem.* **empâteuse**) Fattener (of poultry).

empattement [ãpat'mã] or **empatage**, *n.m.* Footing, foundation, base; flare (of tree); platform (for a crane etc.); (*Naut.*) splicing; (*Motor. etc.*) wheel-base; width (of aeroplane). **empatter**, *v.t.* To join (pieces of wood) by means of tenon, mortise, etc.; to splice (a rope etc.); to support (a crane) by a wooden platform etc.

empaumer [ãpo'me], *v.t.* To receive or strike (a tennis-ball etc.) with the palm of the hand or with a bat; (*fig.*) to get hold of, to grasp, to take possession of; (*fam.*) to cheat, to take someone in. *Empaumer la voie*, (*Hunt.*) to catch the scent. *Empaumer une affaire*, to conduct an affair ably.

empaumure [ãpo'myːr], *n.f.* Palm-piece of a glove; top antlers.

empêchement [ãpɛʃ'mã], *n.m.* Hindrance, obstacle, impediment, obstruction, bar, objection. *Je n'y mets point d'empêchement*, I do not oppose it. **empêcher**, *v.t.* To oppose, to prevent, to put a stop to; to hinder, to obstruct, to impede. *Cela n'empêcha pas qu'il ne le fît*, that did not prevent him from doing it (*i.e.*, he did it all the same); *cela n'empêche pas que* or *il n'empêche que* or *n'empêche que*, and yet, for all that; *cette muraille empêche la vue*, this wall obstructs the view; *être empêché de sa personne*, to be greatly embarrassed; *il m'empêche de travailler*, he hinders me from working; *l'un n'empêche pas l'autre*, the one does not bar the other. **s'empêcher**, *v.r.* (always in the negative). To forbear, to refrain from, to keep from, to abstain. *Il ne saurait s'empêcher de médire*, he cannot help slandering. **empêcheur**, *n.m.* (*fem.* **-euse**) Usually in the (*fam.*) expression: *empêcheur de danser en rond*, spoil-sport.

empeigne [ã'pɛɲ], *n.f.* Upper leather (of shoe).

empellement [ãpɛl'mã], *n.m.* Sluice, dam (of a pond).

empennage [ãpe'naːʒ], *n.m.* Feathering (arrows); tail, stabilizer, rudders (of aeroplanes); fins or vanes (of a bomb). **empennelage** [ãpɛn'laːʒ], *n.m.* Backing (of anchor). **empenneler**, *v.t.* To back (an anchor). **empennelle**, *n.f.* Small anchor. **empenner** [ãpe'ne], *v.t.* To feather (arrows); to fit on (the empennage or the fins).

empenoir [ãpə'nwaːr], *n.m.* Lock-maker's chisel.

empereur [ã'prœːr], *n.m.* Emperor; (*Ent.*) fritillary; (*Orn.*) wren.

emperler [ãpɛr'le], *v.t.* To ornament with pearls or beads; (*poet.*) to cover with dew.

empesage [ãpə'zaːʒ], *n.m.* Starching. **empesé**, *a.* (*fem.* **-ée**) Starched; stiff (of style etc.), formal. **empeser**, *v.t.* To starch; (*fig.*) to stiffen, to give stiffness or formality to. *Empeser un col*, to starch a collar.

empester [ãpɛs'te], *v.t.* To infect, to taint; to cause to stink horribly; (*fig.*) to corrupt.

empêtrer [ãpe'tre], *v.t.* To entangle, to catch, to hamper, to fetter; to embarrass, to worry. *Empêtrer quelqu'un dans une mauvaise affaire*, to involve someone in an unpleasant business. **s'empêtrer**, *v.r.* To become entangled, hampered, or embarrassed; to hamper or worry oneself.

emphase [ã'faːz], *n.f.* Grandiloquence, pomposity; emphasis, stress. **emphatique**, *a.* Bombastic, affected; emphatic.

emphysémateux [ãfizema'tø], *a.* (*fem.* **-euse**) Emphysematous. **emphysème**, *n.m.* Emphysema.

emphytéose [ãfite'oːz], *n.f.* Long lease conferring right of mortgage, feudal holding (eighteen to ninety-nine years). **emphytéote**, *n.m.* Tenant on a long lease. **emphytéotique**, *a.* *Bail emphytéotique*, very long lease; *redevance emphytéotique*, ground-rent.

empiècement [ãpjɛs'mã], *n.m.* Yoke (of blouse).

empierrement [ãpjɛr'mã], *n.m.* Macadamization, ballasting (a road etc.); broken stones for a metalled road. **empierrer,** *v.t.* To stone, to metal (roads etc.).

empiétement [ɑ̃pjet′mɑ̃], *n.m.* Encroaching, encroachment, infringement, trespass. **empiéter,** *v.t.* To encroach upon, to entrench upon, to invade, to trespass upon.—*v.i.* To encroach (*sur*). *Il empiète sur mes droits,* he encroaches upon my rights.

empiffrer [ɑ̃pi′fre], *v.t.* To cram, to stuff; to fatten. **s'empiffrer,** *v.r.* To cram, to guzzle.

empile [ɑ̃′pil], *n.f.* (*Angling*) Gut line, snell.

empilement [ɑ̃pil′mɑ̃], *n.m.* Piling, stacking. **empiler,** *v.t.* To pile up, to stack; (*Angling*) to fasten (a fishing-hook) to the gut; (*slang*) to rob, to swindle. *Empiler des écus,* to make money; *se faire empiler,* (*slang*) to be cheated. **s'empiler,** *v.r.* To be stacked, piled up; to pack into (a confined space). **empileur,** *n.m.* (*fem.* **-euse**) Stacker; (*slang*) robber, swindler.

empire [ɑ̃′pi:r], *n.m.* Nation, state, or country, under an emperor; empire, sovereignty, control, authority, dominion, command, ascendency; (*fig.*) prestige, influence, sway, mastery, dominions. *Bas-empire,* Byzantine Empire; *empire d'Occident, d'Orient,* the Western, the Eastern Empire. *Se disputer l'empire,* to contend for sovereignty. *Traiter quelqu'un avec empire,* to treat one imperiously. *Avoir de l'empire sur soi-même,* to be self-controlled.

empirer [ɑ̃pi′re], *v.t.* To make worse.—*v.i.* To grow worse. *La chose empira,* matters grew worse; *sa maladie empire chaque jour,* his illness gets worse day by day.

empirique [ɑ̃pi′rik], *a.* Empiric, empirical. —*n.m.* Empiric. **empiriquement,** *adv.* Empirically. **empirisme,** *n.m.* Empiricism.

emplacement [ɑ̃plas′mɑ̃], *n.m.* Site, place, situation, ground, piece of ground.

emplanture [ɑ̃plɑ̃′ty:r], *n.f.* (*Naut.*) Step (of a mast); socket (of the wing of an aeroplane).

emplâtre [ɑ̃′plɑ:tr], *n.m.* Plaster, salve, ointment; (*fig.*) palliative; (*colloq.*) helpless, clumsy creature. *C'est un véritable emplâtre,* he is fit for nothing, he has no backbone. *Mettre un emplâtre à,* to put a plaster on.

emplette [ɑ̃′plɛt], *n.f.* Purchase. *Faire emplette de quelque chose,* to purchase something; *faire des emplettes,* to go shopping.

emplir [ɑ̃′pli:r], *v.t.* To fill, to fill up. **s'emplir,** *v.r.* To fill; to be filled. **emplissage** [REMPLISSAGE].

emploi [ɑ̃′plwa], *n.m.* Employ, employment; use, function; occupation, situation, place, post; (*Theat.*) speciality; (*Law*) appropriation. *Chef d'emploi,* chief actor in a particular line; (*Advertising*) *demande, offre, d'emploi,* situation wanted, vacant; *emploi du temps,* time-table; *emploi d'un mot,* usage of a word; *donner de l'emploi,* to give employment; *double emploi,* useless repetition; *faire un bon emploi de son temps,* to make a good use of one's time; *mauvais emploi,* misemployment; *plein emploi,* full employment; *sans emploi,* out of employment. **employable,** *a.* Employable. **employé,** *a.* (*fem.* **-ée**) Employed.—*n.* Person employed, employee, assistant, clerk, servant, etc.

employer [ɑ̃plwaj′e], *v.t. irr.* (*conjugated like* ABOYER) To employ, to use, to make use of; to give employment to, to engage; to spend, to lay out, to invest. *Bien employer son temps,* to employ one's time well; *employer mal,* to misuse; *employer une phrase,* to use a phrase; *je l'ai employé à cela,* I set him to work on that; *employer la force,* to resort to force. **s'employer,** *v.r.* To employ oneself, to exert or busy oneself; to use one's interest; to be used. *S'employer pour quelqu'un,* to use one's interest in someone's favour. *Un mot qui s'emploie rarement,* a word which is rarely used.

employeur, *n.m.* (*fem.* **-euse**) Employer.

emplumer [ɑ̃ply′me], *v.t.* To feather, to fledge. **s'emplumer,** *v.r.* To become fledged.

empocher [ɑ̃pɔ′ʃe], *v.t.* To pocket. *Il empoche tout ce qu'il gagne,* he pockets all his winnings.

empoignade [ɑ̃pɔ′ɲad, ɑ̃pwa-], *n.f.* (*colloq.*) Dispute, row, set-to.

empoignant [ɑ̃pɔ′ɲɑ̃, ɑ̃pwa-], *a.* (*fem.* **-ante**) Thrilling, poignant.

empoignement [ɑ̃pɔɲ′mɑ̃, ɑ̃pwa-], *n.m.* Capture, arrest.

empoigner [ɑ̃pɔ′ɲe, ɑ̃pwa-], *v.t.* To grasp, to seize, to lay hold of; (*colloq.*) to take into custody, to arrest. *Cette scène a empoigné le public,* that scene thrilled (gripped) the public. *Je vous ferai empoigner,* I shall have you arrested. **s'empoigner,** *v.r.* To lay hold of each other, to grapple. *Ils se sont empoignés,* they grappled with each other, they had a set-to.

empointer [ɑ̃pwɛ̃′te], *v.t.* To stitch; to point (pins, needles, etc.). **empointeur,** *n.m.* Pointer (of pins etc.).

empois [ɑ̃′pwa], *n.m.* Starch.

empoisonnant [ɑ̃pwazɔ′nɑ̃], *a.* (*fem.* **-ante**) (*fam.*) Utterly boring; irritating.

empoisonné, *a.* (*fem.* **-ée**) Poisoned, (*fig.*) poisonous, corrupt. **empoisonnement,** *n.m.* Poisoning; (*fig.*) corruption; a nuisance, an awful bore.

empoisonner [ɑ̃pwazɔ′ne], *v.t.* To poison; to put poison into; (*fig.*) to infect; to mar, to corrupt; to embitter, to envenom; to distort, to give a false colour to; (*slang*) to bore to death; to irritate.—*v.i.* To be poisonous, (*fig.*) to be malodorous. *Ces maximes sont capables d'empoisonner la jeunesse,* these maxims are calculated to corrupt the young. **s'empoisonner,** *v.r.* To poison oneself, to take poison; to be poisoned. **empoisonneur,** *a.* (*fem.* **-euse**) Poisoning, poisonous; (*fig.*) corrupting.—*n.* Poisoner; (*fig.*) corrupter; (*colloq.*) wretched cook, restaurant-keeper, etc.

empoisser [POISSER].

empoissonnement [ɑ̃pwasɔn′mɑ̃], *n.m.* Stocking with fish. **empoissonner,** *v.t.* To stock with fish.

emporté [ɑ̃pɔr′te], *a.* (*fem.* **-ée**) Fiery, passionate, hasty, hot-headed; runaway, unmanageable. **emportement,** *n.m.* Transport, fit of passion, outburst (of anger, rage, frenzy, etc.).

emporte-pièce [ɑ̃pɔrtə′pjɛs], *n.m.* Punch (instrument), puncher, cutting-out machine; (*fig.*) sarcastic or trenchant person. *C'est une réponse à l'emporte-pièce,* it is a very cutting answer.

emporter [ãpɔr'te], *v.t.* To carry away, to take away, to convey away; to remove, to cause (stains etc.) to disappear; to carry off, to transport (of emotion etc.); to sweep away, to hurry along; to blow away; to entail, to involve; to gain, to obtain. *Autant en emporte le vent*, gone with the wind; *vain threats, promises*; *cette considération l'emporte sur toutes les autres*, that consideration outweighs every other; *cette maladie l'a emporté*, that illness carried him off; *cette sauce vous emporte la bouche*, that sauce is very hot; *emporter d'assaut*, to carry by storm; *emporter la balance*, to turn the scale; *emporter la pièce*, to strike home, to be cutting; *emporter ses cliques et ses claques*, to pack up bag and baggage; *l'emporter*, to preponderate, to overcome, to outweigh, to surpass; *l'emporter sur*, to prevail over, to get the better of; *le vent a emporté mon chapeau*, the wind has blown my hat off; *que le diable l'emporte!* the devil take him! **s'emporter**, *v.r.* To fly into a passion, to flare up; to declaim or inveigh (*contre*); to bolt (of horses). *S'emporter comme une soupe au lait*, to take fire like gunpowder. *S'emporter contre le vice*, to declaim against vice.

empotage [ãpɔ'ta:ʒ], *n.m.* Potting (of plants etc.). **empoté**, *a.* and *n.m.* (*fem.* **-ée**) (*fam.*) Slow, awkward (fellow). **empoter**, *v.t.* To pot (plants).

empourpré [ãpur'pre], *a.* (*fem.* **-ée**) Crimson.

empourprer [ãpur'pre], *v.t.* To purple, to tinge or colour with red or purple. **s'empourprer**, *v.r.* To turn crimson, to flush; to assume a purple tinge.

empreignant, *pres.p.* [EMPREINDRE].

empreindre [ã'prɛ̃:dr], *v.t. irr.* (*pres.p.* **empreignant**, *p.p.* **empreint**; conjugated like CRAINDRE) To imprint, to stamp, to mark, to impress. **s'empreindre**, *v.r.* To become tinged. **empreinte**, *n.f.* Stamp, print, impression; mark; (*fig.*) impress, characteristic sign. *L'empreinte d'un cachet*, the stamp of a seal; *marqué à l'empreinte de*, bearing the stamp of. *Empreintes digitales*, fingerprints.

empressé [ãprɛ'se], *a.* (*fem.* **-ée**) Eager, earnest; assiduous, officious, gushing. *Des soins empressés*, assiduous attentions; *faire l'empressé*, to be officious; *il paraît fort empressé auprès d'elle*, he appears markedly attentive to her. **empressement**, *n.m.* Alacrity, promptness, eagerness, earnestness; haste, hurry. *Avec empressement*, eagerly, earnestly, industriously; *trop d'empressement*, overforwardness. **s'empresser**, *v.r.* To be eager (to), to be earnest, forward, ardent, etc.; to flock, to crowd, to press (*autour* etc.). *S'empresser de parler*, to hasten to speak; *s'empresser auprès de quelqu'un*, to pay polite attentions to someone.

emprise [ã'pri:z], *n.f.* Expropriation (of land); (*fig.*) ascendancy, hold, control (over a person); (*Her.*) device.

emprisonnement [ãprizɔn'mã], *n.m.* Imprisonment, custody. *Emprisonnement cellulaire*, solitary confinement. **emprisonner**, *v.t.* To imprison, to confine; (*fig.*) to box up.

emprunt [ã'prœ̃], *n.m.* Borrowing; loan. *Argent d'emprunt*, borrowed money; *faire un emprunt*, to contract a loan; *il est toujours aux emprunts*, he is always borrowing; *une beauté d'emprunt*, an artificial beauty. **emprunté**, *a.* (*fem.* **-ée**) Borrowed, factitious; assumed, affected, constrained. *Air emprunté*, embarrassed look; *nom emprunté*, assumed name. **emprunter**, *v.t.* To borrow; to assume; to make use of, to take (path, means of communication). *Emprunter de l'argent à quelqu'un*, to borrow money from or off someone; *ne choisit pas qui emprunte*, beggars cannot be choosers.

emprunteur, *a.* (*fem.* **-euse**) Borrowing, prone to borrow; not original.—*n.* Borrower.

empuantir [ãpɥã'ti:r], *v.t.* To give an ill smell to, to infect. ***s'empuantir**, *v.r.* To stink, to have a bad odour. ***empuantissement**, *n.m.* Stench.

empyème [ãpi'ɛm], *n.m.* (*Path.*) Empyema.

empyrée [ãpi're], *n.m.* The empyrean; (*fig.*) the firmament.—*a.* Empyrean, empyreal.

empyreumatique [ãpirøma'tik], *a.* Empyreumatic. **empyreume**, *n.m.* Empyreuma.

ému [e'my], *a.* (*fem.* **émue**) Moved, touched, affected. *Fort ému*, deeply moved.

émulation [emyla'sjɔ̃], *n.f.* Emulation, rivalry. **émule**, *n.* Rival, competitor.

émulgent [emyl'ʒã], *a.* (*fem.* **-ente**) (*Physiol.*) Emulgent.

émulsif [emyl'sif], *a.* (*fem.* **-ive**) Emulsive. **émulsion**, *n.f.* Emulsion. **émulsionnement**, *n.m.* Emulsification. **émulsionner**, *v.t.* To emulsionize.

émyde [e'mid], *n.f.* Marsh-tortoise.

en (1) [ã], *prep.* In; to; within; into; at; like, in the form of, as; out of, by, through, from; for, on. *Agir en honnête homme*, to act like an honest man. *Aller en France*, to go to France; *changer des livres en francs*, to change pounds into francs; *de mal en pis*, from bad to worse; *de plus en plus*, more and more. *En arrière* [ARRIÈRE]; *en avant* [AVANT]; *en bas* [BAS]; *en cas de*, in case of; *en ce temps-là*, at that time; *en dedans*, within; *en dehors*, without; *en dépit de* [DÉPIT]; *en attendant*, in the meantime; *en guerre*, at war; *en haut*, up, above, upstairs; *en hiver*, in winter; *en nourrice*, out at nurse; *en outre, en plus de*, in addition, what is more; *en paix*, at peace; *en passant*, by the way; *en prière*, at prayer; *en tout temps*, at all times; *en trois jours*, in three days; *être en bonne santé*, to be in good health; *être en tête*, to be at the head; *être en province*, to be in the provinces; *être en robe de chambre*, to be in one's dressing-gown; *en somme*, briefly, in a word; *il l'aborda en souriant*, he came up to her with a smile; *je l'ai mise en pension*, I have sent her to a boarding-school; *mettre en vente*, to put up for sale; *une montre en or*, a gold watch; *tomber en décadence*, to fall into decay; *vivre en roi*, to live like a king; *voir en songe*, to see in a dream; *en congé*, on leave; *en faction*, on guard; *en temps et lieu*, at the right time or place; *en vérité*, really; *en vrac*, loose, in bulk; anyhow; *d'aujourd'hui en huit*, today week.

en (2) [ã], *pron. rel.* (*pl. unchanged*) Of him, of her, of it, its, of them, their; from him, by him, about him, etc.; thence, from thence; some of it, any. *Après cela ils en vinrent aux mains*, after that they came to blows; *avez-vous de l'argent? j'en ai*, have you any money?

I have some; *c'est un bœuf, j'en vois les cornes*, it is an ox, I see its horns; *donnez-m'en*, give me some; *en avoir le cœur net*, to get to the bottom of; *en être à se demander*, to be doubtful about; *en faire à sa tête*, to have one's way; *en voulez-vous?* will you have some? *en vouloir à quelqu'un*, to have a grudge against someone; *il en est aimé*, he is loved by her; *il en est de cela comme de la plupart des choses*, it is with that as with most other things; *il en est fou*, he is madly in love with her; *il en est mort un*, one of them is dead; *il ne sait où il en est*, he does not know how far he has got; *il s'en faut de beaucoup*, you are a long way off; *j'en ai pour cinq minutes*, it will take me five minutes, I'll be five minutes; *j'en suis bien aise*, I am very glad of it; *j'en suis fâché*, I am sorry for it; *j'en suis surpris*, I wonder at it; *parlez-lui-en*, speak to him of it; *qu'en dites-vous?* what do you say to it? *s'en aller*, to go away; *c'en est fait*, it is all over; *ne vous en faites pas!* Don't worry! *s'en retourner*, to return; *voulez-vous en être?* will you join us? *vous en parlez toujours*, you are always speaking of him or of it.

énallage [enal′la:ʒ], *n.f.* (*Gram.*) Enallage.
enamourer [ãnamu′re], *v.t.* To inspire with love. **s'enamourer**, *v.r.* To fall in love; to be enamoured (*de*).
enarbrer [ãnar′bre], *v.t.* To mount on an arbor, axle, etc.
énarthrose [enar′tro:z], *n.f.* Enarthrosis.
encablure [ãka′bly:r], *n.f.* Cable's length, one-tenth of a nautical mile = 185 metres (about 200 yards).
encadrement [ãkɑdrə′mã], *n.m.* Framing, frame; border, margin; (*fig.*) environment. **encadrer**, *v.t.* To frame; to encircle, to surround; to introduce, to insert; (*Mil.*) to straddle, to bracket (objective); to officer (troops). *Faire encadrer un tableau*, to have a picture framed. **s'encadrer**, *v.r.* To be introduced, inserted, or enclosed; to fit in. **encadreur**, *n.m.* Picture-frame maker, framer.
encager [ãka′ʒe], *v.t.* To cage, to put in a cage.
encaissage [ãkɛ′sa:ʒ], *n.m.* Encasing; (*Hort.*) tubbing. **encaissant**, *a.* (*fem.* **-ante**) Encasing, confining, environing. **encaisse**, *n.f.* Cash in hand, cash-balance. *Encaisse métallique*, metallic reserve, bullion; *encaisse or*, gold reserve. **encaissé**, *a.* Encased, embanked with steep banks; sunk, hollow. *Cette rivière est encaissée*, that river flows between high banks. **encaissement**, *n.m.* Packing, packing in cases, putting in boxes, etc.; embankment; bed, base (of a road etc.); collection, paying in (of money). **encaisser**, *v.t.* To encase, to pack, to put in a box etc.; to bank, pay in; to encash, to collect, to receive (money etc.); (*colloq.*) to take a blow. (*colloq.*) *Je ne peux pas l'encaisser*, I can't stand him. **encaisseur**, *n.m.* Cash-collector, cashier.
encan [ã′kã], *n.m.* Public auction. *Mettre à l'encan*, to put up for sale; *vendre à l'encan*, to sell by auction.
encanailler [ãkana′je], *v.t.* To degrade, to lower (by mixing with low company). **s'encanailler**, *v.r.* To keep low company; to lose caste.

encapuchonner [ãkapyʃɔ′ne], *v.t.* To put a cowl on; to cause to enter a monastic order. **s'encapuchonner**, *v.r.* To put on a cowl; to wrap one's head up; to arch the neck (of horses).
encaquement [ãkak′mã], *n.m.* Packing, barrelling (of herrings). **encaquer**, *v.t.* To barrel (herrings); to cram in. **encaqueur**, *n.m.* (*fem.* **-euse**) Herring-packer.
encart [ã′ka:r], *n.m.* (*Print.*) Middle leaves; inset; inserted prospectus, advertisement folder. **encarter**, *v.t.* To insert as an inset; to interleave; to card-index.
encartonnement [ãkartɔn′mã] or **encartonnage**, *n.m.* Pressing or glazing between pasteboards. **encartonner**, *v.t.* To glaze (paper etc.) by pressing thus.
en-cas [ã′kɑ], *n.m. inv.* Anything kept for use in emergency; small umbrella; light meal prepared in case of need.
encaserner [ãkazer′ne], *v.t.* To quarter (soldiers) in barracks.
encasteler (s') [ãkastə′le], *v.r.* (*Vet.*) To be hoof-bound (of horses). **encastelure**, *n.f.* Contraction of the hoof.
encastrement [ãkastra′mã], *n.m.* Fitting, fitting in by means of grooves, notches, etc. **encastrer**, *v.t.* To fit in, to encase, to imbed. **s'encastrer**, *v.r.* To fit in or together, to tail in.
encaustiquage [ãkosti′ka:ʒ], *n.m.* Wax-polishing.
encaustique [ãkos′tik], *a.* Encaustic.—*n.f.* Encaustic, furniture-paste, floor-polish. **encaustiquer**, *v.t.* To coat or polish with this.
encavement [ãkav′mã], *n.m.* Storing (in cellar), cellaring. **encaver**, *v.t.* To put or store in a cellar, to cellar.
enceignant, *pres.p.* [ENCEINDRE].
enceindre [ã′sẽ:dr], *v.t. irr.* (*pres.p.* **enceignant**, *p.p.* **enceint**; *conjugated like* CRAINDRE) To encircle, to encompass, to surround, to enclose. *Enceindre de murailles*, to enclose with walls. **enceinte**, *n.f.* Circuit, circumference, enclosure, precincts; (*Fort.*) enceinte. *Dans cette enceinte*, within these walls; *mur d'enceinte*, surrounding wall.—*a.f.* Pregnant, with child, expectant. *Enceinte de sept mois*, seven months gone.
encellulement [ãselyl′mã], *n.m.* Putting into or confining in a cell or cells. **encelluler**, *v.t.* To put into a cell; to confine or retain in a cell.
encens [ã′sã], *n.m.* Incense, frankincense; (*fig.*) fragrance; eulogy, flattery. *Brûler de l'encens sur les autels*, to burn incense on the altars. *Donner de l'encens à quelqu'un*, to flatter someone. **encensement**, *n.m.* Incensing, censing; (*fig.*) praising, praise, flattery. **encenser**, *v.t.* To incense, to burn incense to; to perfume with or as with incense; (*fig.*) to flatter, to shower praise on; (horse) to toss the head. **encenseur**, *n.m.* (*fem.* **-euse**) Burner of incense; (*fig.*) flatterer. **encensier**, *n.m.* (*Bot.*) Rosemary. **encensoir**, *n.m.* Censer, incenser; (*fig.*) ecclesiastical power; flattery, excessive eulogy. *Donner de l'encensoir par le nez* or *casser le nez à coups d'encensoir*, to flatter fulsomely.
encéphale [ãse′fal], *n.m.* Encephalon (brain). **encéphalique**, *a.* Encephalic. **encéphalite**, *n.f.* Encephalitis, inflammation of the brain.

encerclement [ãsɛrklə'mã], *n.m.* Encircling, (*Polit.*) encirclement. **encercler,** *v.t.* To encircle.

enchaînement [ãʃɛn'mã], *n.m.* Enchainment; linking; concatenation, chain, series, connexion. **enchaîner,** *v.t.* To enchain, to chain up, to bind in chains; (*Theat.*) to take the cue, to follow up; (*Cine.*) to fade in; (*fig.*) to detain, to restrain; to captivate; to link, to connect. **s'enchaîner,** *v.r.* To be connected or linked together; to link oneself. *Tous ces faits s'enchaînent,* all these facts are linked, interdependent. **enchaînure,** *n.f.* Chain-work, interlacing, connexion (of parts in machinery etc.).

enchanté [ãʃã'te], *a.* (*fem.* -**ée**) Enchanted; (*fig.*) charmed, delighted. *La Flûte enchantée,* the Magic Flute.

enchanteler [ãʃã'tle], *v.t.* To pile or arrange (timber) in a yard; to set (casks) on gantries.

enchantement [ãʃãt'mã], *n.m.* Enchantment, sorcery, spell, incantation, magic, witchery; (*fig.*) charm, delight. *Il est dans l'enchantement,* he is delighted. **enchanter,** *v.t.* To enchant, to lay under a spell; (*fig.*) to fascinate, to enrapture, to charm, to gratify. *Je suis enchanté de vous voir,* I am delighted to see you. **enchanteur,** *a.* (*fem.* -**eresse**) Enchanting, entrancing, captivating. *Voix enchanteresse,* enchanting voice.—*n.* Enchanter, enchantress, charmer.

enchaper [ãʃa'pe], *v.t.* To enclose (one cask etc.) in another.

enchaperonner [ãʃaprɔ'ne], *v.t.* To hood (a hawk, infant, head, etc.).

encharner [ãʃar'ne], *v.t.* To put hinges on.

enchâsser [ãʃa'se], *v.t.* To enchase, to enshrine; to insert, to set; to introduce. *Enchâsser un diamant dans de l'or,* to set a diamond in gold. *Enchâsser une citation dans un discours,* to introduce a quotation into a speech. **enchâssure,** *n.f.* Setting, mount; insertion; housing (of axle).

enchatonner [ãʃatɔ'ne], *v.t.* To set, to mount (in a bezel).

enchausser [ãʃo'se], *v.t.* (*Hort.*) To straw, to earth up.

enchaux [ã'ʃo], *n.m.* Lime-wash (for tanning).

enchemiser [ãʃəmi'ze], *v.t.* (*Bookb.*) To put a dust-cover on (books).

enchère [ã'ʃɛːr], *n.f.* Bid (at an auction); auction. *Il est à l'enchère,* it is to be bought by the highest bidder; *mettre aux enchères,* to bring to the hammer, to put up to auction; *mettre* or *porter une enchère,* to bid; *vendre à l'enchère* or *aux enchères,* to sell by auction.

enchérir, *v.t.* To bid for, to outbid, to overbid; to raise (prices etc.).—*v.i.* To rise (in price), to become dearer; (*fig.*) to surpass, to outdo, to go further; to bid, to outbid. *La volaille a enchéri,* poultry has risen in price, has gone up. *Elle enchérit sur la générosité de son frère,* she outdoes her brother in generosity. **enchérissement,** *n.m.* Rise, increase, advance in price. **enchérisseur,** *n.m.* Bidder (at an auction).

enchevalement [ãʃval'mã], *n.m.* Propping or underpinning (of a house, etc.). **enchevaler,** *v.t.* To prop, to underpin.

enchevaucher [ãʃvo'ʃe], *v.t.* To cause (tiles etc.) to overlap each other. **enchevauchure,** *n.f.* Overlap.

enchevêtrement [ãʃvɛtra'mã], *n.m.* Entanglement, confusion. **enchevêtrer,** *v.t.* To halter (a horse etc.); to join or bind together with or as with a halter; to entangle, to complicate, to confuse. **s'enchevêtrer,** *v.r.* To get a foot entangled in the halter (of a horse); to get entangled, confused, or embarrassed. **enchevêtrure,** *n.f.* (*Carp.*) Structure of joists etc. supporting a shaft; (*Vet.*) halter-cast.

enchifrènement [ãʃifrɛn'mã], *n.m.* Blocking of the nose (by a cold in the head), snuffles. **enchifrener,** *v.t. irr.* (*conjug. like* AMENER) To snuff up the nose (of a cold in ʒhe head). *Je suis tout enchifrené,* my nose is all stuffed up. **s'enchifrener,** *v.r.* To get the snuffles.

enchymose [ãki'moːz], *n.f.* Cutaneous hyperaemia; flushing.

encirer [ãsi're], *v.t.* To smear with wax, to wax.

enclave [ã'klaːv], *n.f.* Enclave, piece of enclosed land. **enclavement,** *n.m.,* or **enclavure,** *n.f.* Enclosing, enclosure, enclavement. **enclaver,** *v.t.* To enclose, to hem in, to wedge in, to dovetail.

enclenchement [ãklãʃ'mã], *n.m.* Interlocking, throwing into gear; automatic clutch. **enclencher,** *v.t.* To clench; to throw into gear.

enclin [ã'klɛ̃], *a.* (*fem.* **encline**) Inclined; prone, addicted, apt, given to.

encliquetage [ãklik'taːʒ], *n.m.* Ratchet, catch (on a wheel etc.). **encliqueter,** *v.t.* To cog, to catch, to stop with a catch.

enclitique [ãkli'tik], *n.f.* (*Gram.*) Enclitic.

encloîtrer [CLOÎTRER].

enclore [ã'klɔːr], *v.t. irr.* (*p.p.* **enclos**; *conjugated like* CLORE) To enclose, to fence in, to take in, to shut in. **enclos,** *n.m.* Enclosure, close; paddock; fencing or wall.

enclouage [ãklu'aːʒ], *n.m.* Spiking (of guns). **enclouer,** *v.t.* To prick (animals) in shoeing; *to spike (a gun). **enclouure** [ãklu'yr], *n.f.* Prick (in shoeing etc.).

enclume [ã'klym], *n.f.* Anvil; (*Anat.*) incus. *Billot d'enclume,* anvil-block. *Être entre le marteau et l'enclume,* to be between the devil and the deep sea; *il frappe toujours sur la même enclume,* he is always harping on the same string; *remettre sur l'enclume,* to re-model. **enclumeau** or **enclumot,** *n.m.* Hand-anvil; bench-anvil.

encoche [ã'kɔʃ], *n.f.* Notch (on a key, tally, etc.); nock (of arrow); tommy-hole (of a screw-head); slot. **encocher,** *v.t.* To notch. *Encocher une flèche,* to fit an arrow in the bow.

encoffrer [ãkɔ'fre], *v.t.* To shut in a coffer; *to lay up, to save avariciously; (*fig.*) to shut, to cage.

encoignure [ãkɔ'ɲyːr], *n.f.* Corner, angle (of a street etc.); corner-piece; corner-cupboard.

encollage [ãkɔ'laːʒ], *n.m.* Sizing, gluing, pasting; glue, gum, size. **encoller,** *v.t.* To size, to gum, to glue, to paste.

encolure [ãkɔ'lyːr], *n.f.* Neck and shoulders of a horse; neck-line of a garment; size (of collars); (*fig.*) appearance, look (of a person). *Gagner la course par une encolure,* to win by a neck.

encombrant [ãkɔ̃'brã], *a.* (*fem.* -**ante**) Cumbrous, encumbering, cumbersome.

encombre [ă′kɔ̃br], *n.m.* (now only used after *sans*) Impediment, hindrance, obstacle, accident. **encombrement,** *n.m.* Obstruction, stoppage; crowding, crowd, congestion (of traffic); block (of cars); floor-space occupied by an object. **encombrer,** *v.t.* To obstruct, to encumber, to embarrass; to crowd, to throng.

encontre (à l' . . . **de)** [ală′kɔ̃:tr], *prep. phr.* Against, counter to. *Aller à l'encontre de quelque chose,* to run counter to a thing; to oppose.

encor (*poet.*) [ENCORE].

encorbellement [ăkɔrbɛl′mă], *n.m.* Corbelling, construction by stories projecting one over the other; (*Naut.*) sponson. *Route en encorbellement,* overhanging road. **encorbeller,** *v.t.* To support on corbels.

encordage [ăkɔr′da:ʒ], *n.m.* Cording, tying-up (parcels).

encorder [ăkɔr′de], *v.t.* (*Mount.*) To rope together.

encore [ă′kɔ:r], *adv.* Yet, still, as yet; anew, again, once more; further, moreover, besides; even, but, only. *À sept heures j'attendais encore,* at 'seven o'clock I was still waiting; *encore?* what, again? *encore moins,* still less; *encore mieux,* better still. *Encore si j'étais sûr,* if I were only sure; *encore s'il voulait m'envoyer dire,* if only he would send me word. *Encore une fois je vous dis,* I tell you once more; *hier encore,* only yesterday; *il est encore plus riche que son frère,* he is even richer than his brother; *il n'est encore que sous-officier,* he is only a non-commissioned officer as yet; *il n'est pas encore venu,* he hasn't come yet. *Outre l'argent, on lui donna encore un cheval,* besides the money he had a horse given him; *prenez encore un verre de vin,* have another glass of wine; *quoi encore?* what else? *Non seulement* . . . *mais encore,* not only . . . but also. *Mais encore?* and what then? *J'ai un exemplaire de ce livre, encore est-il incomplet,* I have a copy of the book, though even that is incomplete. *Vous l'aurez demain, et encore!* you will get it tomorrow, if then!

encorné [ăkɔr′ne], *a.* (*fem.* **-ée**) Horned. *Bouc haut encorné,* a high-horned goat; (*fam.*) *mari encorné,* cuckold. **encorner,** *v.t.* To horn, to furnish with horns; to gore, to toss, (*fam.*) to cuckold.

encornet [ăkɔr′nɛ], *n.m.* Calamary, cuttle-fish, squid.

encourageant [ăkura′ʒă], *a.* (*fem.* **-ante**) Encouraging, cheering, inspiriting. **encouragement,** *n.m.* Encouragement, incitement, incentive; countenance, support. **encourager,** *v.t.* To encourage, to foster, to stimulate; to countenance, to support, to be a promoter of. **s'encourager,** *v.r.* To encourage each other, to take courage.

encourir [ăku′ri:r], *v.t. irr.* (*pres.p.* **encourant,** *p.p.* **encouru**; *conjugated like* COURIR) To incur (disgrace, reproach), to draw upon oneself, to fall under. *Encourir le mépris de tout le monde,* to draw general contempt thereupon one one.

encouture [ăku′ty:r], *n.f.* (*Naut.*) Clinker-work. **encouturer,** *v.t.* To dispose (planks etc.) clinker-wise.

encrage [ă′kra:ʒ], *n.m.* (*Print.*) Inking.

encrassement [ăkras′mă], *n.m.* Fouling (of fire-arms etc.). **encrasser,** *v.t.* To make dirty, to dirty, to foul. **s'encrasser,** *v.r.* To get foul, greasy, dirty; to become slovenly.

encre [ă:kr], *n.f.* Ink. *Encre de Chine,* Indian ink; *encre d'imprimerie,* printing-ink; *encre d stylo,* fountain-pen ink; *encre sympathique,* sympathetic *or* invisible ink; *table d'encre,* (*Print.*) ink-table; *tacher d'encre,* to splash with ink. *C'est la bouteille à l'encre,* there's no seeing through that. *Écrire de sa meilleure encre,* to write in one's best style.

encrêper [ăkrɛ′pe], *v.t.* To cover with crape.

encrer [ă′kre], *v.t.* To ink. **encreur,** *a. Ruban encreur,* inking ribbon.—*n.m.* (*Print.*) Inking roller. **encrier,** *n.m.* Ink-stand, ink-pot; (*Print.*) ink-trough.

encroué [ăkru′e], *a.* (*fem.* **-ée**) Entangled in the branches of another (of trees).

encroûtant [ăkru′tă], *a.* (*fem.* **-ante**) Forming a crust; covered with a crust; **encroûté,** *a.* (*fem.* **-ée**) Covered with a crust; (*fig.*) crusted over (with crotchets, prejudices etc.) —*n.* A 'Blimp'.

encroûtement [ăkrut′mă], *n.m.* Crusting over; crust; becoming hide-bound.

encroûter [ăkru′te], *v.t.* To crust; to plaster (walls etc.); (*fig.*) to make stupid, prejudiced, etc. **s'encroûter,** *v.r.* To crust, to get hard; to become dull, stupid, hide-bound.

enculasser [ăkyla′se], *v.t.* To breech (a gun).

encuvage [ăky′va:ʒ] *or* **encuvement,** *n.m.* Tubbing. **encuver,** *v.t.* To put into a vat, to tub.

encyclique [ăsi′klik], *n.f.* Encyclical letter. —*a.* Encyclical.

encyclopédie [ăsiklɔpe′di], *n.f.* Encyclopaedia. **encyclopédique,** *a.* Encyclopaedic. **encyclopédiste,** *n.m.* Encyclopaedist.

endécagone [HENDÉCAGONE].

endémie [ăde′mi], *n.f.* Endemic disease. **endémique,** *a.* Endemic.

endenté [ădă′te], *a.* (*fem.* **-ée**) Indented; toothed, furnished with teeth. *Gens bien endentés,* people with keen appetites. **endenter,** *v.t.* To cog, to tooth; to fit together by means of teeth; to mesh.

endettement [ădɛt′mă], *n.m.* Running into debt. **endetter,** *v.t.* To get (a person) into debt. **s'endetter,** *v.r.* To run into debt.

endeuiller [ădœ′je], *v.t.* To put into mourning; to sadden.

****endêvé** [ădɛ′ve], *a.* Angry; unruly (child). **endêver,** *v.i.* To tease, to rag. *Faire endêver quelqu'un,* to drive someone mad.

endiablé [ădja′ble], *a.* (*fem.* **-ée**) Possessed; (*fig.*) devilish, diabolical, reckless (music, rhythm, etc.), irrepressible. **endiabler,** *v.i.* To be furious. *Faire endiabler,* to torment, to plague to death; to render furious.

endiamanter [ădjamă′te], *v.t.* To adorn, to stud, with or as with diamonds.

endiguement [ădig′mă], *n.m.* Damming, damming up. **endiguer,** *v.t.* To dam in, to dam up, to embank.

endimanchement [ădimăʃ′mă], *n.m.* Dressing in Sunday best or in all one's finery. **s'endimancher,** *v.r.* To put on one's Sunday best.

endive [ă′di:v], *n.f.* (Broad-leaved) chicory. *See also* CHICORÉE.

endivisionner [ădivizj′ɔne], *v.t.* (*Mil.*) To form into divisions.

endocarde [ãdɔ'kard], *n.m.* Endocardium. **endocardiaque**, *a.* Endocardiac. **endocardite**, *n.f.* Endocarditis. **endocarpe**, *n.m.* Endocarp. **endocrâne**, *n.m.* Endocrane.

endocrine, *a.* Endocrine (glands). **endocrinologie**, *n.f.* Endocrinology.

endoctrinement [ãdɔktrin'mã], *n.m.* Indoctrination. **endoctriner**, *v.t.* To indoctrinate, to teach, to give his cue to. **endoctrineur**, *n.m.* One who indoctrinates.

endoderme [ãdɔ'dɛrm], *n.m.* Endoderm.

endogamie, *n.f.* Endogamy.

endogène, *a.* Endogenous.—*n.* Endogen.

endolorir [ãdɔlɔ'riːr], *v.t.* To make sore, tender, or painful; to make (the heart etc.) ache. **s'endolorir**, *v.r.* To become sore. **endolorissement**, *n.m.* Pain, ache, soreness.

endolymphe [ãdɔ'limf], *n.f.* Endolymph.

endométrite, *n.f.* Endometritis.

endommagement [ãdɔmaʒ'mã], *n.m.* Loss, injury, damage. **endommager**, *v.t.* To damage, to injure.

endoparasite [ãdɔpara'zit], *n.m.* Endoparasite.

endoplasme, *n.m.* Endoplasm. **endoplaste**, *n.m* Endoplast.

endoplèvre, *n.f.* Endopleura.

endormant [ãdɔr'mã], *a.* (*fem.* **-ante**) Somniferous, soporific; (*fig.*) boring, sleep-compelling. **endormeur**, *n.m.* (*fem.* **-euse**). One who puts to sleep; (*fig.*) cajoler, sycophant, flatterer; bore, tiresome person. **endormi**, *a.* (*fem.* **-ie**) Asleep, sleeping; sleepy, drowsy, sluggish; benumbed.—*n.* Sleepy person, person asleep; (*fam.*) sleepyhead. *Faire l'endormi*, to sham sleep.

endormir [ãdɔr'miːr], *v.t. irr.* To send to sleep, to rock to sleep; to anaesthetize; to wheedle, to deceive; to benumb; to bore, to weary. *Cela m'a endormi la jambe*, that has made my leg go numb. *On l'a endormi*, he was hoodwinked. *Sa conversation vous endort*, his conversation sends you to sleep. **s'endormir**, *v.r.* To fall asleep, to slumber; (*fig.*) to be lulled into security. *Il s'est endormi sur cette affaire*, he was neglectful about that business; *s'endormir dans le vice*, to be steeped in vice. *S'endormir du sommeil de la tombe*, to sleep the sleep of death.

endos [ã'do] or **endossement**, *n.m.* Endorsement.

endoscope [ãdɔs'kɔp], *n.m.* Endoscope. **endosmose**, *n.f.* Endosmose, endosmosis. **endosmotique**, *a.* Endosmotic. **endosperme**, *n.m.* Endosperm. **endospermé**, *a.* (*fem.* **-ée**) Endospermic.

endossage [ENDOSSURE].

endosse [ã'dos], *n.f.* Trouble, burden, responsibility.

endossement [ENDOS].

endosser [ãdo'se], *v.t.* To put on one's back, to buckle on, to put on; to saddle oneself with (an obligation etc.); to back, to endorse. *Endosser le harnais*, to put on the harness; *endosser l'uniforme*, to don the uniform. *Endosser une lettre de change*, to endorse a bill of exchange. **endosseur**, *n.m.* Endorser. **endossure**, *n.f.*, or **endossage**, *n.m.* Gluing or pasting the back of a book for rebinding.

endothélium [ãdɔte'ljɔm], *n.m.* Endothelium.

endothermique [ãdotɛr'mik], *a.* Endothermal, endothermic.

endroit [ã'drwa], *n.m.* Place, spot, locality; point, side; right side (of a material); part, passage (of a book etc.). *À l'endroit*, right side out. *Endroit faible*, weak point; *endroit sensible*, sensitive point; *étoffe à deux endroits*, reversible material; *il a mal agi à mon endroit*, he has acted ill with regard to me; *par endroits*, here and there.

enduire [ã'dɥiːr], *v.t. irr.* (*conjugated like* CONDUIRE) To do over, to render, to coat, to smear. *Enduire une muraille de plâtre*, to do a wall over with plaster; *l'enduire de ciment*, to render it with cement. **enduisage**, *n.m.* Coating, rendering. **enduit**, *n.m.* Coating, layer, plaster, glaze, varnish, polish.

endurable [ãdy'rabl], *a.* Endurable. **endurance**, *n.f.* Endurance, fortitude; staying power. *Épreuve d'endurance*, reliability test. **endurant**, *a.* (*fem.* **-ante**) Patient, tolerant, meek; enduring. *Peu endurant*, quick-tempered, touchy.

endurci [ãdyr'si], *a.* (*fem.* **-ie**) Hardened, obdurate; inured, callous. *Un cheval endurci aux coups*, a horse inured to blows. *Célibataire endurci*, confirmed bachelor.

endurcir [ãdyr'siːr], *v.t.* To harden, to toughen, to make resistant or enduring; to render obdurate, to indurate, to render callous. *L'avarice avait endurci son cœur*, avarice had hardened his heart. **s'endurcir**, *v.r.* To harden, to grow hard; to be steeled, to become callous. **endurcissement**, *n.m.* Hardening, obduracy; hardness of heart, callousness.

endurer [ãdy're], *v.t.* To endure, to bear, to undergo; to put up with, to stand (used negatively). *Il ne peut endurer les manières de son neveu*, he cannot stand his nephew's behaviour.

énergétique [enɛrʒe'tik], *n.f.* Energetics.—*a.* Energizing.

énergie [enɛr'ʒi], *n.f.* Energy, strength, vigour, power. *L'énergie atomique*, atomic energy, power. **énergique**, *a.* Energetic, vigorous, forcible. *Remède énergique*, powerful, drastic remedy. *Paroles énergiques*, forcible language. **énergiquement**, *adv.* Energetically, vigorously, strenuously.

énergumène [enɛrgy'mɛːn], *n.m.* Energumen, one possessed of a devil; fanatic; ranter.

énervant [enɛr'vã], *a.* (*fem.* **-ante**) Enervating; debilitating, nerve-racking. (*fam.*) *C'est énervant!* It's most annoying, irritating! **énervation**, *n.f.* (*Surg.*) Enervation, excision of nerves; debilitation, prostration. **énervé**, *a.* (*fem.* **-ée**) Nerveless; nervy, fidgety. **énervement**, *n.m.* Nervous tension.

énerver [enɛr've], *v.t.* To enervate, to debilitate; to weaken; to unnerve; (*fam.*) to get on the nerves. **s'énerver**, *v.r.* To become enervated, unnerved; irritable, fidgety.

enfaîteau [ãfɛ'to], *n.m.* (*pl.* **enfaîteaux**) Ridge-tile. **enfaîtement**, *n.m.* Ridge-lead; covering the ridge of a roof with lead etc. **enfaîter**, *v.t.* To cover (a roof-ridge etc.) with lead, ridge-tiles, etc.

enfance [ã'fãːs], *n.f.* Infancy, childhood; boyhood or girlhood; childishness, puerility, dotage; (*fig.*) children; beginning. *Dès ma* *première enfance*, from my infancy; *sortir de l'enfance*, to emerge from childhood. *Tomber en enfance*, to become childish. *Un ami d'enfance*, a childhood friend.

enfant [ãˈfã], *n.* Child, infant, baby; son or daughter; descendant; citizen, native; (*Law*) offspring, issue. *C'est bien l'enfant de son père*, he is a chip of the old block; *c'est un bon enfant*, he is a good fellow; *discours d'enfant*, childish language; *enfant adoptif*, adopted child; *enfant de chœur*, chorister; *enfant gâté*, spoilt child; *enfant terrible*, incorrigible child; *enfant trouvé*, foundling; *en travail d'enfant*, in labour; *faire l'enfant*, to behave like a child; *il n'y a plus d'enfants*, children are all grown up nowadays; *l'enfant à naître*, the child unborn; *l'enfant prodigue*, the prodigal son; *les enfants de France*, the children or grandchildren of the King of France; *les enfants trouvés*, the Foundling Hospital; *petits enfants*, little children; *petits-enfants*, grandchildren; *qu'il est enfant!* what a child he is! *un enfant à la mamelle*, an infant at the breast; *enfant de troupe*, soldier's boy. *Bon enfant*, *a. inv.* Good-natured. (*See also* BALLE.) **enfantement**, *n.m.* Childbirth. **enfanter**, *v.t.* To bring forth, to bear; (*fig.*) to produce, to beget, to bring to light, to give birth to. **enfantillage**, *n.m.* Child's-play, childishness. **enfantin**, *a.* (*fem.* -ine) Infantile, childish.

enfariner [ãfariˈne], *v.t.* To flour, to sprinkle with flour. *Être enfariné de quelque science*, to have a smattering of some science; *être enfariné d'une mauvaise doctrine*, to be infatuated with a bad doctrine. *Il est venu nous dire cela la bouche enfarinée*, (*pop.*) he came to tell us that in his mealy-mouthed way.

enfer [ãˈfɛːr], *n.m.* Hell; infernal or lower regions; (*fig.*) torture, torment, misery; place in a library where books of doubtful character are kept. *Au fond de l'enfer*, in the depths of hell; *les peines de l'enfer*, the torments of hell; *mener un train d'enfer*, to go at a furious pace; *tison d'enfer*, hell-hound; *un bruit d'enfer*, infernal din; *un feu d'enfer*, a roaring fire; *un jeu d'enfer*, ruinous play.

enfermer [ãfɛrˈme], *v.t.* To shut, to shut in, to shut up; to lock up, to imprison, to put away (in an asylum etc.); to enclose, to coop up, to hem in; to hide, to conceal; to comprehend, to comprise. *C'est un homme à enfermer*, that man ought to be locked up; *enfermer à clef*, to keep under lock and key. *Enfermer un parc de murailles*, to wall in a park. **s'enfermer**, *v.r.* To lock oneself in, to seclude oneself. *S'enfermer dans un silence obstiné*, to take refuge in an obstinate silence.

enferrer [ãfɛˈre], *v.t.* To run (someone) through with a sword etc., to pierce, to transfix. **s'enferrer**, *v.r.* To run oneself through with a sword etc.; (*fig.*) to injure oneself; to get into a fix; to give oneself away.

enficeler [ãfisˈle], *v.t.* To tie with string etc.

enfieller [ãfjɛˈle], *v.t.* To make sour, bitter; to embitter.

enfièvrement [ãfjɛvrɔˈmã], *n.m.* Feverishness. **enfiévrer**, *v.t. irr.* (*conjug. like* ACCÉLÉRER) To make feverish; (*fig.*) to inflame, to impassion.

enfilade [ãfiˈlad], *n.f.* Suite (of chambers etc.),

string (of phrases etc.); (*Mil.*) enfilade. *Prendre en enfilade*, to enfilade; *tir d'enfilade*, raking fire.

enfile-aiguilles [ãfileˈgч̃iːj], *n.m. inv.* Needle-threader.

enfiler [ãfiˈle], *v.t.* To thread (a needle etc.); to string (beads etc.); to pierce, to run (someone) through with a sword etc.; to pass through, to go down (a street etc.); (*Mil.*) to enfilade, to rake fore and aft; to dupe; to pull on, slip on (clothes). *Enfiler des perles*, to string pearls, (*fig.*) to lose one's time; *enfiler un discours*, to begin a long-winded speech; *enfiler une aiguille*, to thread a needle. **s'enfiler**, *v.r.* To be threaded; to be run through, to be pierced; to get engaged or involved in. (*Slang*) *S'enfiler un litre*, to drink a bottle. **enfileur**, *n.m.* (*fem.* -euse) Threader (in pin-making etc.). *Enfileur de paroles*, prattler.

enfin [ãˈfɛ̃], *adv.* At last, finally, at length, after all, lastly; in short, in a word.

enflammé [ãflɑˈme], *a.* (*fem.* -ée) On fire, in flames, ignited; kindled, inflamed, excited.

enflammer [ãflɑˈme], *v.t.* To set on fire, to set in a blaze, to kindle; (*fig.*) to inflame, to excite, to incense, to provoke. **s'enflammer**, *v.r.* To take fire, to ignite, to be kindled, to blaze; (*fig.*) to be inflamed, to be incensed. *On vit tout le navire s'enflammer*, they saw the whole ship break into flames.

enflé [ãˈfle], *a.* (*fem.* -ée) Swollen, inflated, puffed up; (*fig.*) bombastic, turgid, high-flown (style etc.).

enflécher [ãfleˈʃe], *v.t. irr.* (*conjugated like* ACCÉLÉRER) (*Naut.*) To put ratlines to (the shrouds). **enfléchure**, *n.f.* Ratlines.

enfler [ãˈfle], *v.t.* To swell out, to puff up, to distend; (*fig.*) to elate, to excite; to inflate, to exaggerate. *Le vent enflait nos voiles*, the wind swelled our sails.—*v.i.* (*Path.*) To swell. **s'enfler**, *v.r.* To swell, to grow turgid; (*fig.*) to be puffed up. *La voile s'enfle*, the sail swells out. *S'enfler d'orgueil*, to be puffed up with pride. **enflure**, *n.f.* Bloatedness, swelling; bombast, turgidity. *Enflure du style*, turgidity of style.

enfoncé [ãfɔ̃ˈse], *a.* (*fem.* -ée) Broken open; sunken; deep, profound; (*pop.*) beaten, done for. *Des yeux enfoncés*, deep-set eyes.

enfoncement [ãfɔ̃sˈmã], *n.m.* Driving in; breaking through, breaking in, bursting open; sinking; nook, bottom, hollow, recess; (*Paint.*) background.

enfoncer [ãfɔ̃ˈse], *v.t.* To thrust, to push in, down, etc., to drive in or down, to sink, to sink to the bottom; to break in, to burst open, to smash in, to blow up; to dish, to get the better of. *Enfoncer son chapeau*, to pull one's hat over one's eyes. *Enfoncer un clou dans la muraille*, to drive a nail into the wall. *Enfoncer une porte ouverte*, (*fig.*) to enunciate a self-evident truth.—*v.i.* To sink, to founder. **s'enfoncer**, *v.r.* To sink, to go deep or far down; to bury oneself; to plunge; (*fig.*) to fail, to make a mess of. *S'enfoncer dans l'étude*, to bury oneself in study; *s'enfoncer dans la débauche*, to plunge into debauchery. *S'enfoncer dans un bois*, to dive into a wood. **enfonceur**, *n.m.* (*iron.*) One who breaks in or through something. **enfonçure**, *n.f.* Cavity, hole, hollow; bottom (of a bedstead etc.); bottom pieces (ot casks etc.).

enforcir [ãfɔr'si:r], *v.t.* To strengthen.—*v.i.* and **s'enforcir**, *v.r.* To gather strength; to grow stronger.

enformer [ãfɔr'me], *v.t.* To fashion; to put on the block, to block (hats).

enfouir [ã'fwi:r], *v.t.* To put or bury in the ground, to cover with earth; (*fig.*) to hide, to keep secret; to waste (one's talents etc.). **s'enfouir**, *v.r.* To bury oneself (in an out-of-the-way place etc.). **enfouissement**, *n.m.* Burying, hiding in the ground. **enfouisseur**, *n.m.* Burier.

enfourcher [ãfur'ʃe], *v.t.* To bestride, to straddle, to mount; to pierce with a pitchfork etc. **enfourchure**, *n.f.* Fork; crotch.

enfournage [ãfur'na:ʒ], **enfournement**, *n.m.* Putting in the oven or kiln.

enfourner [ãfur'ne], *v.t.* To put in the oven or as in the oven; (*fig.*) to set about. *Bien enfourner* or *mal enfourner*, to make a good or a bad beginning. **s'enfourner**, *v.r.* To get into a blind alley, a scrape, etc.

enfranger [ãfrã'ʒe], *v.t.* To fringe, to put a fringe on.

enfreindre [ã'frɛ̃:dr], *v.t. irr.* (*pres.p.* **enfreignant**, *p.p.* **enfreint**; *conjugated like* CRAINDRE) To infringe, to break, to violate. *Enfreindre les lois*, to transgress the laws; *enfreindre un traité*, to break a treaty; *enfreindre un ordre*, to disregard an order.

enfroquer [ãfrɔ'ke], *v.t.* To make (someone) turn monk. **s'enfroquer**, *v.r.* To turn monk.

enfuir (s') [ã'fɥi:r], *v.r. irr.* (*pres.p.* **enfuyant**; *conjugated like* FUIR) To run away, to flee, to escape; to elope; to run out, to leak; to vanish, to be forgotten. *Ils s'étaient enfuis de prison*, they had made their escape from prison. *Le temps s'enfuit*, time slips away.

enfumage [ãfy'ma:ʒ], *n.m.* Filling with smoke; smoking out (vermin etc.). **enfumer**, *v.t.* To smoke, to fill with smoke, to blacken with smoke, to smoke (vermin etc.) out; (*fig.*) to cloud (the brain etc.). **enfumoir**, *n.m.* Smoking-apparatus (for stupefying bees).

enfûtage [ãfy'ta:ʒ], *n.m.* Casking. **enfutailler** or **enfuter**, *v.t.* To cask, to barrel, to tun (wine etc.).

engagé [ãga'ʒe], *a.* (*fem.* **engagée**) Pledged; engaged, enlisted; in action; (*Naut.*) water-logged. *Littérature engagée*, literature taking a stand on contemporary events; *écrivain engagé*, committed writer. *Vaisseau engagé*, water-logged ship.—*n.m.* *Un engagé* (*volontaire*), man who has joined the army before or after the age of compulsory service. (*spt.*) *Il y a quinze engagés dans cette course*, there are fifteen entries for that race. **engageant**, *a.* (*fem.* **-eante**) Engaging, prepossessing, pleasing. *Il a des manières engageantes*, he has winning manners.

engagement [ãgaʒ'mã], *n.m.* Engagement, promise, obligation, commitment; bond, pledging, pawning; mortgage; appointment; (*Mil.*) enlisting; action, fight, scrap; entry (for a sporting event); (*pl.*) liabilities. *Entrer dans un engagement*, to enter into an engagement; *faire face à ses engagements*, to meet one's liabilities; *manquer à un engagement*, to fail to keep an engagement.

engager [ãga'ʒe], *v.t.* To pledge, to pawn; to engage, to promise; to put under an obligation; to invite, to induce, to persuade, to urge; to enlist, to hire; to involve, to entangle; to compel. *Cela ne vous engage à rien*, that binds you to nothing. *Engager le combat*, to begin the action. *Engager quelqu'un dans une mauvaise affaire*, to entangle someone in a bad business. *Engager ses meubles*, to pledge one's furniture. *Engager une clef dans une serrure*, to insert a key in a lock. *Engager (le jeu)*, (*ftb.*) to kick off; (*hockey*) to bully off. **s'engager**, *v.r.* To engage oneself, to undertake an engagement, to take upon oneself (*à*); to stand security, to be bound (*pour*); to enlist, to join the army; to entangle oneself, to get involved; to become fouled (engine), to get out of control. *Le combat ne tarda pas à s'engager*, the battle soon began. *S'engager dans une mauvaise affaire*, to get involved in a bad business. *S'engager dans une rue étroite*, to turn into a narrow street. *S'engager pour un ami*, to stand security for a friend.

engaîner [ãge'ne], *v.t.* To sheathe; to encase, to envelop.

engamer [ãga'me], *v.i.* To swallow the hook (of fish).

engazonner [ãgazɔ'ne], *v.t.* To turf, to cover or edge with turf; to sow grass-seed.

engeance [ã'ʒã:s], *n.f.* Breed; brood, esp. of poultry; (*fig.*) race, kidney, spawn. **Des poules d'une grande engeance*, hens of a large breed. *Quelle engeance!* what a set!

*engeigner [ã:ʒe' ɲe], *v.t.* To deceive, to catch.

engelure [ãʒ'ly:r], *n.f.* Chilblain.

engendrer [ãʒã'dre], *v.t.* To beget, to engender; (*fig.*) to produce, to give rise to, to occasion. *La familiarité engendre le mépris*, familiarity breeds contempt; *ne pas engendrer la mélancolie*, to be of a gay disposition.

engeoler [ENJÔLER].

engerber [ãʒɛr'be], *v.t.* To sheaf, to bind; (*fig.*) to heap up.

engin [ã'ʒɛ̃], *n.m.* Machine, engine; snare, gin, net; tool, instrument. *Engin de levage*, hoist. *Engin téléguidé*, guided missile.

englober [ãglɔ'be], *v.t.* To unite, to put together; (*fig.*) to comprehend, to comprise, to embrace.

engloutir [ãglu'ti:r], *v.t.* To swallow, to devour, to engulf; (*fig.*) to absorb; to dissipate, to squander. **s'engloutir**, *v.r.* To be swallowed up, to be engulfed. **engloutissement**, *n.m.* Engulfing, swallowing up. **engloutisseur**, *n.* (*fem.* **-euse**) Swallower, devourer.

engluement [ãgly'mã], *n.m.* Liming. **engluer**, *v.t.* To lime, to daub with bird-lime; to capture thus; (*fig.*) to take in. **s'engluer**, *v.r.* To be caught, to be limed; (*fig.*) to be taken in.

engobe [ã'gɔb], *n.m.* (*Ceramics*) Slip. **engober**, *v.t.* To decorate with slip.

engommer [ãgɔ'me], *v.t.* To gum; to glaze.

engoncé [ãgɔ̃'se], *a.* (*fem.* **-ée**) Stiff (in one's clothes). *Avoir l'air engoncé*, to look awkward and stiff. **engoncer**, *v.t.* (of clothes) To make look stiff.

engorgement [ãgɔrʒə'mã], *n.m.* Obstruction, stopping up (of a pipe, tube, conduit, etc.);

(*Med.*) congestion; (*Econ.*) glut, overabundance. **engorger**, *v.t.* To obstruct, to block, to choke, to stop up; (*Med.*) to congest. **s'engorger**, *v.r.* To be obstructed or choked up; (*Med.*) to be congested.

engouement [ăgu'mɑ̃], *n.m.* Choking, obstruction, congestion; (*fig.*) infatuation, craze. *On ne saurait le faire revenir de son engouement*, it is impossible to cure him of his infatuation. **engouer**, *v.t.* To obstruct (the throat etc.); (*fig.*) to infatuate. **s'engouer**, *v.r.* To half choke oneself; (*fig.*) to be infatuated. *S'engouer d'une femme*, to be obsessed by a woman.

engouffrement [ăgufrə'mɑ̃], *n.m.* Engulfing, swallowing up; rushing in (of wind). **engouffrer**, *v.t.* To engulf; (*fig.*) to swallow up, to devour. **s'engouffrer**, *v.r.* To be engulfed; to be lost, to be swallowed up; to blow hard, to rush (of the wind in a narrow passage). *Le vent s'engouffre dans la cheminée*, the wind howls down the chimney. *Il s'engouffra dans le hall de la gare*, he disappeared into the station.

engoulevent [ăgul'vɑ̃], *n.m.* Nightjar, goatsucker. *Engoulevent d'Amérique*, nighthawk.

engoûment [ENGOUEMENT].

engourdi [ăgur'di], *a.* (*fem.* **-ie**) Torpid, benumbed, dull. **engourdir**, *v.t.* To benumb, to make torpid; to dull, to make languid, to enervate. *Le froid engourdit les mains*, cold benumbs one's hands. *L'oisiveté engourdit l'esprit*, idleness benumbs the mind. **s'engourdir**, *v.r.* To get benumbed; to become torpid, enervated, or sluggish.

engourdissement, *n.m.* Numbness, torpor, enervation. *Avoir un engourdissement au bras*, to have a numbness in the arm. *Tirer quelqu'un de son engourdissement*, to rouse someone from his torpor.

engrainer [ENGRENER].

engrais [ă'grɛ], *n.m.* Manure, fertilizer; fattening (cattle). *Mettre des bœufs à l'engrais*, to put oxen to fatten. *Engrais chimiques*, fertilizers; *engrais verts*, manure crops. **engraissant**, *a.* (*fem.* **-ante**) Fattening. **engraissement**, *n.m.* Fattening; growing fat. **engraisser**, *v.t.* To fatten, to cram (poultry etc.); to manure; (*fig.*) to enrich.— *v.i.* To grow fat, to become corpulent; (*fig.*) to thrive. **s'engraisser**, *v.r.* To fatten, to grow fat or stout; (*fig.*) to grow rich. *S'engraisser des misères publiques*, to batten on public misfortune. **engraisseur**, *n.m.* Fattener.

engrangement [ăgrăʒə'mɑ̃], *n.m.* Garnering (wheat etc.). **engranger**, *v.t.* To get in, to garner (wheat etc.).

engravement [ăgrav'mɑ̃], *n.m.* Stranding (of a vessel). **engraver**, *v.t.* To run aground, to strand; to cover with sand.—*v.i.* or **s'engraver**, *v.r.* To run aground, to be stranded.

engrêlé [ăgrɛ'le], *a.* (*fem.* **-ée**) (*Her.*) Engrailed. **engrêler**, *v.t.* To engrail; to purl (lace etc.). **engrêlure**, *n.f.* Purl (of lace); (*Her.*) engrailings.

engrenage [ăgrə'na:ʒ], *n.m.* Gear, gearing, cog-wheels etc.; action of these, catching etc.; (*fig.*) mesh, correlation (of circumstances etc.).

engrènement [ăgrɛnə'mɑ̃], *n.m.* Feeding

with corn (threshing-machine etc.), on corn (cattle etc.).

engrener (1) [ăgrə'ne], *v.t. irr.* (*conjug. like* AMENER) To put corn into (the mill-hopper); to feed with corn.

engrener (2) [ăgrə'ne], *v.t. irr.* (*conjug. like* AMENER) To throw into gear, to engage, to connect, to mesh; (*fam.*) to start, to set going. **s'engrener**, *v.r.* To work into each other (of toothed wheels); to be put in gear. *Ces roues s'engrènent bien*, these wheels mesh well. **engrenure**, *n.f.* Engagement of teeth, cogs, etc.; toothing, cogging.

engrosser [ăgro'se], *v.t.* (*vulg.*) To make pregnant, to get with child. **engrossir**, *v.i.* To be with child, to become pregnant.

engrumeler [ăgrym'le], *v.t.* To clot, to coagulate. **s'engrumeler**, *v.r.* To clot.

enguenillé [ăgni'je], *a.* (*fem.* **-ée**) Clothed in tatters.

engueulade [ăgœ'lad], *n.f.* (*vulg.*) Abuse, a slanging match; scolding, a 'telling-off'. **engueuler**, *v.t.* To abuse, to swear at, to tell (someone) off.

enguirlander [ăgirlă'de], *v.t.* To engarland; euphemism, instead of *engueuler*.

enhardir [ăar'di:r], *v.t.* To embolden, to encourage. *Ce succès l'avait enhardi*, that success had emboldened him. **s'enhardir**, *v.r.* To make bold, to grow bold. *Il s'est enhardi à parler en public*, he made bold to speak in public. **enhardissement**, *n.m.* Emboldening; boldness.

enharmonie [ănarmɔ'ni], *n.f.* Enharmonic change. **enharmonique**, *a.* Enharmonic.

*enharnachement [ănarnaʃ'mɑ̃], *n.m.* Harnessing; harness. ***enharnacher**, *v.t.* To harness; (*fig.*) to rig out, to deck out. *Vous voilà plaisamment enharnaché*, you are oddly accoutred.

enherber [ănɛr'be], *v.t.* To put land under grass.

enhuché [ăy'ʃe], *a.* (*Naut.*) High out of water (ship).

énieller [enjɛ'le], *v.t.* To clear (corn etc.) of corn-cockles.

énigmatique [enigma'tik], *a.* Enigmatical. **énigmatiquement**, *adv.* Enigmatically.

énigme [e'nigm], *n.f.* Enigma, riddle. *Mot d'une énigme*, answer to a riddle; *proposer une énigme*, to put a riddle; *vous parlez par énigmes*, you speak in riddles.

enivrant [ăni'vrɑ̃], *a.* (*fem.* **-ante**) Intoxicating, inebriating, heady; (*fig.*) seductive. **enivrement**, *n.m.* Intoxication, elation. **enivrer**, *v.t.* To intoxicate, to inebriate; (*fig.*) to elate. *La bière enivre comme le vin*, beer intoxicates as well as wine. *La prospérité nous enivre*, prosperity elates us. **s'enivrer**, *v.r.* To get intoxicated; (*fig.*) to be elated (*de*). *Il s'est enivré à ce repas*, he got intoxicated at that dinner.

enjabler [ăʒa'ble], *v.t.* To bottom or head (a cask).

enjaler [ăʒa'le], *v.t.* (*Naut.*) To stock (an anchor).

enjambé [ăʒă'be], *a.* (*fem.* **enjambée** (1)) Legged (in a certain way). *Être court enjambé*, to be short-legged. **enjambée** (2), *n.f.* Stride. *Faire de grandes enjambées*, to take long strides. **enjambement**, *n.m.* (*Pros.*) Run-on line, enjambment.

enjamber [ãʒã'be], *v.t.* To stride over; to skip or leap over; to stride; (*fig.*) to encroach upon; (*Pros.*) to make enjambment.
enjarreté [ãʒar'te], *a.* Hobbled (of horses).
enjaveler [ãʒa'vle], *v.t.* To sheaf (corn).
enjeu [ã'ʒø], *n.m.* (*pl.* **-eux**) Stake (*gaming* and *fig.*). *Retirer son enjeu,* to withdraw one's stake, (*colloq.*) to declare off.
enjoindre [ã'ʒwɛ̃:dr], *v.t. irr.* (*pres.p.* **enjoignant,** *p.p.* **enjoint;** *conjugated like* CRAINDRE) To enjoin, to charge, to direct, to prescribe. *Il lui est enjoint de,* he is directed to.
enjôlement [ãʒol'mã], *n.m.* Wheedling, coaxing, inveigling, cajoling. **enjôler,** *v.t.* To coax, to wheedle, to inveigle, to seduce. **enjôleur,** *n.m.* (*fem.* **-euse**) Wheedler, coaxer.
enjolivement [ãʒɔliv'mã], *n.m.* Embellishment, decoration, ornament. **enjoliver,** *v.t.* To embellish, to set off, to beautify. **enjoliveur,** *n.m.* (*fem.* **-euse**) Embellisher. **enjolivure,** *n.f.* (Small) embellishment.
enjoué [ã'ʒwe], *a.* (*fem.* **-ée**) Playful, sprightly, lively, jovial, sportive. *Il a l'humeur enjouée,* he is of a playful disposition; *il écrit d'un style enjoué,* he writes in a sprightly style. **enjouement** or **enjoûment,** *n.m.* Playfulness, sportiveness, sprightliness, liveliness, humour. *Avec enjouement,* playfully.
***enjuponner** [ãʒypɔ'ne], *v.t.* To put into petticoats.
enkysté [ãkis'te], *a.* (*fem.* **-ée**) (*Med.*) Encysted. **s'enkyster,** *v.r.* To become encysted.
enlacement [ãlas'mã], *n.m.* Lacing, interlacing, entwining. **enlacer,** *v.t.* To lace; to entwine, to interlace, to interweave; to clasp, to embrace. *Enlacer dans ses bras,* to clasp in one's arms. **s'enlacer,** *v.r.* To entwine, to be interlaced.
enlaidir [ãlɛ'di:r], *v.t.* To make ugly; to disfigure.—*v.i.* To grow ugly, to be disfigured. **s'enlaidir,** *v.r.* To make oneself ugly. **enlaidissement,** *n.m.* Uglification, disfigurement.
enlevage [ãl'vaʒ], *n.m.* (*Row.*) Spurt.
enlèvement [ãlɛv'mã], *n.m.* Carrying off; removal; rubbing out, wiping off, kidnapping, rape. *Enlèvement de mineure,* abduction. *L'enlèvement des Sabines,* the rape of the Sabines. *L'enlèvement d'une tache,* the removal of a stain. **enlever,** *v.t.* To lift, to raise, to pull up; to carry off, to carry away; to seize and carry away forcibly, to kidnap, to steal; to clear away, to remove, to rub out, to wipe off; to charm, to delight, to transport (with enthusiasm etc.). *Enlever des taches,* to take out stains. *Enlever la peau,* to flay the skin; *enlever tous les prix,* to carry off all the prizes. *Enlever un morceau de musique,* to dash off a piece of music. *Enlever une place,* to carry or capture a town. *Enlevez cela de dessus la table,* take that off the table. *La mort l'a enlevé à la fleur de l'âge,* death carried him off in his prime; *on lui a enlevé sa femme,* his wife has been carried off; *se faire enlever par,* to elope with. **s'enlever,** *v.r.* To rise, to be lifted; to come off, to peel off; to come out; to be snapped up (of goods on sale); to get into a passion.
enlève-taches [ãlɛv'taʃ], *n.m. inv.* Stain remover.
enliasser [ãlja'se], *v.t.* To tie up in a bundle.

enlier [ã'lje], *v.t.* (*conjugated like* PRIER) To bond, to bind (stones) together in building.
enlignement [ãliɲ'mã], *n.m.* Putting in line; alignment. **enligner,** *v.t.* To put in line.
enlisement or ***enlizement** [ãliz'mã], *n.m.* Sinking, swallowing up (in quicksand). **enliser** or ***enlizer,** *v.t.* To engulf. **s'enliser,** *v.r.* To be engulfed or swallowed up; to sink (in moving sand or into ground); (*fig.*) to become bogged down (in routine).
enluminer [ãlymi'ne], *v.t.* To colour; to illuminate; (*fig.*) to flush (the complexion); to overload (one's style). *Visage enluminé,* flushed or red face. **s'enluminer,** *v.r.* To rouge, to paint; to flush. **enlumineur,** *n.m.* (*fem.* **-euse**) Colourer of maps, prints, MSS., etc.; illuminator. **enluminure,** *n.f.* Colouring; illuminating; coloured print; high colour (of the face); tinsel (of style).
ennéagonal [ɛnneagɔ'nal], *a.* (*fem.* **-ale,** *pl.* **-aux**) (*Geom.*) Nine-angled. **ennéagone,** *n.m.* Nonagon. **ennéagyne,** *a.* (*Bot.*) Enneagynous. **ennéandre,** *a.* (*Bot.*) Enneandrous. **ennéandrie,** *n.f.* Enneandria. **ennéapétale,** *a.* Enneapetalous.
enneigé [ãnɛ'ʒe], *a.* (*fem.* **-ée**) Snow-covered. **enneigement,** *n.m.* The fact of being snow-covered. *Bulletin d'enneigement,* snow report.
ennemi [ɛn'mi], *n.m.* (*fem.* **ennemie**) Enemy, foe; (*fig.*) injurious or prejudicial thing. *C'est autant de pris sur l'ennemi,* it is so much gained from the enemy; *ennemi déclaré,* open or avowed enemy; *il n'y a pas de petit ennemi,* every enemy is to be feared; *passer à l'ennemi,* to desert to the enemy, (*fig.*) to betray or desert one's party; *être tué à l'ennemi,* to be killed in action. *Le mieux est l'ennemi du bien,* leave well alone; *l'eau et le feu sont ennemis,* fire and water are opposites.—*a.* Hostile, inimical; contrary, opposite; injurious, adverse, prejudicial. *La fortune ennemie,* adverse fortune. *L'armée ennemie,* the enemy. *Il est ennemi de toute reforme,* he is hostile to any reform.
ennoblir [ãnɔ'bli:r], *v.t.* *To ennoble; (*fig.*) ~o dignify, to exalt. **s'ennoblir,** *v.r.* To be ennobled or exalted. **ennoblissement,** *n. m.* Ennoblement, exaltation.
ennui [ã'nɥi], *n.m.* Ennui, weariness, boredom; tiresome thing, nuisance, vexation; anxiety. *Quel ennui!* what a nuisance! *Mourir d'ennui,* to be bored to death. *Avoir des ennuis d'argent,* to be worried about money. ***ennuyant,** *a.* (*fem.* **-ante**) Annoying, tedious, irksome, tiresome. **ennuyer,** *v.t. irr.* (*conjug. like* ABOYER) To bore, to weary, to be tiresome; to pester; (*fig.*) to annoy, to upset, to vex. *Cela m'ennuie,* that annoys me. **s'ennuyer,** *v.r.* To be bored, to have a bad time of it, to feel dull; to miss. *Il s'ennuie de vous,* he misses you. *Il s'ennuie de Londres,* he is bored with London. **ennuyeusement,** *adv.* Tediously, irksomely. **ennuyeux,** *a.* (*fem.* **-euse**) Tedious, dull, tiresome; annoying, provoking, vexing. —*n.* Tiresome person, bore.
énoncé [enɔ'se], *n.m.* Statement, enunciation, terms (of a mathematical problem etc.), wording (of an act). **énoncer,** *v.t.* To state, to express, to word, to enunciate. **s'énoncer,**

v.r. *To express oneself; to be worded or expressed. **énonciatif,** *a.* (*fem.* **-ive**) Enunciative. **énonciation,** *n.f.* Enunciation, delivery; statement; expression, wording.

enorgueillir [ănɔrgœ'jiːr], *v.t.* To make proud, to elate, to puff up. **s'enorgueillir,** *v.r.* To be or grow proud of, to be puffed up, to be elated or to glory (*de*).

énorme [e'nɔrm], *a.* Enormous, huge, atrocious. **énormément,** *adv.* Enormously, beyond measure. **énormité,** *n.f.* Hugeness, vastness; enormity; blunder, shocking remark.

énouer [e'nwe], *v.t.* To burl, to pick the knots etc. out of (cloth).

enquérir (s') [ăke'riːr], *v.r.irr.* (*pres.p.* **enquérant,** *p.p.* **enquis,** conjugated like ACQUÉRIR) To inquire, to make inquiries. *Il faut s'enquérir de la vérité du fait,* we must inquire into the truth of the matter; *s'enquérir d'un ami,* to inquire after a friend.

enquête [ă'keːt], *n.f.* Inquiry, investigation, examination; commission of inquiry, inquisition, inquest. *Aux fins d'enquête,* for investigation; *enquête en matière criminelle,* criminal investigation; *ordonner une enquête,* to direct an inquiry to be made, to appoint a commission of inquiry. **enquêter,** *v.i.* To inquire into a matter (*sur*), to conduct an inquiry.

enquêteur, *n.m.* (*fem.* **-euse**) Investigator.

enquiquiner [ăkiki'ne], *v.t.* (*pop.*) To bore (somebody) to death; to tease; to pester.

enracinement [ărasin'mă], *n.m.* Rooting, taking root; deep-rootedness. **enraciner,** *v.t.* To root; (*fig.*) to implant. *Des préjugés enracinés,* inveterate prejudices. **s'enraciner** *v.r.* To take root, to become rooted. *Il ne faut pas laisser s'enraciner les maux,* evils must not be allowed to take root.

enragé [ăra'ʒe], *a.* (*fem.* **-ée**) Mad, rabid, enraged; (*fig.*) violent, obstinate, determined, keen, enthusiastic. *Manger de la vache enragée,* to know hard times. *Un chien enragé,* a mad dog. *Un communiste enragé,* a rabid communist.—*n.* Madman, madwoman; desperate person. *Un enragé de bridge,* (*fig.*) a bridge fiend. **enrageant,** *a.* (*fem.* **-ante**) Maddening, vexing. **enrager,** *v.i.* To be mad, to go mad; to be enraged, to fume. *Enrager de faire quelque chose,* to desire madly to do something (*de*). *Faire enrager,* to tease, to madden.

enrayage [ăre'jaʒ], *n.m.* (*Mil.*) Jam (in rifle, gun, etc.); putting spokes to (a wheel).

enrayement or **enraiement** [ărej'mă], *n.m.* Putting on the drag, skidding, locking.

enrayer (1) [ăre'je], *v.t.* (*conjugated like* BALAYER) To put spokes to (a wheel); to skid (a wheel), to put the drag on, to apply the brakes to; (*fig.*) to stop, to keep down, to moderate; to check, to slow up (an attack); to stem (an epidemic); to jam, to stop (a machine-gun etc.).

enrayer (2) [ăre'je], *v.t.* (*Agric.*) To plough the first furrow in; to draw (the furrows).

enrayure (1) [ăre'jyːr], *n.f.* Drag, skid, lockchain.

enrayure (2) [ăre'jyːr], *n.m.* (*Agric.*) First furrow.

enrégimentation [ăreʒimăta'sjɔ̃], *n.f.* Enregimenting. **enrégimenter,** *v.t.* To enregi-

ment, to form into regiments; (*fig.*) to enrol (in a party).

enregistrable [ărəʒis'trabl], *a.* Recordable. **enregistrement,** *n.m.* Registration, recording, entry, enrolment; registry; booking (of luggage); (*Acous.*) recording. *Faire l'enregistrement,* to register. **enregistrer,** *v.t.* To register, to enter in a register, to record, to book (luggage). *Musique enregistrée,* recorded music. **enregistreur,** *n.m.* Registrar; recording machine.—*a.* Self-registering (of thermometers etc.), self-recording.

enrêner [ăre'ne], *v.t.* To rein in, to fix (a horse's head) up by the reins.

enrhumer [ăry'me], *v.t.* To give a cold to (someone). *Être enrhumé du cerveau,* to have a cold in the head. **s'enrhumer,** *v.r.* To catch a cold.

enrichi [ări'ʃi], *a.* (*fem.* **enrichie**) Newly enriched.—*n.* Upstart, parvenu, new rich.

enrichir [ări'ʃiːr], *v.t.* To enrich, to make rich; (*fig.*) to enlarge, to adorn, to embellish. *Enrichir son esprit,* to enrich one's mind. **s'enrichir,** *v.r.* To enrich oneself, to grow rich, to thrive, to make one's pile. *S'enrichir des dépouilles d'autrui,* to thrive on the spoils of others. **enrichissement,** *n.m.* Enrichment; (*fig.*) embellishment, adornment.

enrobage [ărɔ'baːʒ], *n.m.* Coating, wrapping. **enrober,** *v.t.* To wrap, to cover, to coat.

enrochement [ărɔʃ'mă], *n.m.* Foundation of rough masonry under water, stone bedding. **enrocher,** *v.t.* To furnish (a bridge, jetty, quay, etc.) with stone-pack.

enrôlement [ărol'mă], *n.m.* Enrolment; (*Mil.*) enlistment. **enrôler,** *v.t.* To enlist; to enrol. **s'enrôler,** *v.r.* To enrol oneself, to enlist.

enroué [ă'rwe], *a.* (*fem.* **-ée**) Hoarse, husky. **enrouement,** *n.m.* Hoarseness, huskiness. **enrouer,** *v.t.* To make hoarse. **s'enrouer,** *v.r.* To become hoarse or husky.

***enrouiller** [ăru'je], *v.t.* To cover with rust, to make rusty. **s'enrouiller,** *v.r.* To grow rusty.

enroulement [ărul'mă], *n.m.* Rolling up; (*Arch.*) scroll, volute. **enrouler,** *v.t.* To roll, to roll up, to coil. **s'enrouler,** *v.r.* To roll oneself up, to roll up; to twine, to twist round (of plants etc.).

enrubanner [ăryba'ne], *v.t.* To deck out with ribbons. **s'enrubanner,** *v.r.* To beribbon oneself.

ensablement [ăsablə'mă], *n.m.* Sand-bank; ballasting, gravelling; stranding (of a ship); silting up. **ensabler,** *v.t.* To cover with sand; to ballast; to run aground, to strand. **s'ensabler,** *v.r.* To run aground; to sink in sand, to be blocked up with sand, to silt up.

ensachage [ăsa'ʃaːʒ] or **ensachement,** *n.m.* Putting into sacks. **ensacher,** *v.t.* To put in bags or sacks. **ensacheuse,** *n.f.* Baggingmachine.

ensanglanter [ăsăglă'te], *v.t.* To make bloody, to stain with blood.

ensauvager [ăsova'ʒe], *v.t.* To make wild.

enseignable [ăsɛ'nabl], *a.* Teachable. **enseignant,** *a.* (*fem.* **-ante**) Teaching. *Corps enseignant,* body of teachers, teaching profession.—*n.m. pl. Les enseignants,* the teachers.

enseigne [ă'sɛɲ], *n.f.* Sign, signboard; mark, index, token, proof; standard, ensign, flag; (*Nav.*) streamer (flag). *À bonne enseigne,* on sure grounds, on good authority. *À bon vin point d'enseigne,* good wine needs no bush. *À telle enseigne que,* by token, as proof. *Être logé à la même enseigne,* to be in the same boat. *Enseigne lumineuse,* electric sign. *(Mil.) Enseignes déployées,* with colours flying.—*n.m.* (*Navy*) *Ensign officer, standard bearer. *Enseigne de vaisseau,* (*Navy*) sub-lieutenant; (U.S.) ensign.

enseignement [ãsɛɲ'mã], *n.m.* Teaching, education, tuition, lesson, precept; teaching profession. *Enseignement du premier, du second degré,* primary, secondary education; *enseignement public,* education by the State; *il est dans l'enseignement,* he is a teacher.

enseigner, *v.t.* To teach, to instruct; to instruct in; to inform, to direct.

ensellé [ãsɛ'le], *a.* (*fem.* -ée) Saddle-backed (horse). **ensellure,** *n.f.* Curve of the back.

ensemble [ã'sã:bl], *adv.* Together, at the same time. *Ils ne sont pas bien ensemble,* they are not on good terms; *mêler ensemble,* to mix together.—*n.m.* Whole, general effect, mass; uniformity, harmony; two- or three-piece (clothing); suite (furniture). *Dans l'ensemble,* on the whole; *le tout ensemble,* the whole, the general effect; *morceau d'ensemble,* a concerted piece of music, part music; *mouvement d'ensemble,* combined movement; *tout cela forme un assez bel ensemble,* all that forms a fairly harmonious whole; *une vue d'ensemble,* a general view.

ensemblier [ãsãbli'e], *n.m.* Artist, esp. decorative artist, who aims at the unity or general effect.

ensemencement [ãsəmãs'mã], *n.m.* Sowing; (*Med.*) seeding (of vaccine lymph). **ensemencer,** *v.t.* To sow with seed.

enserrer (1) [ãsɛ're], *v.t.* To enclose, to contain; to lock up; to encompass, to hem in. *Enserrer comme dans un étau,* to squeeze as in a vice.

enserrer (2) [ãsɛ're], *v.t.* (*Gard.*) To put into a greenhouse.

ensevelir [ãsə'vli:r], *v.t.* To shroud, to put into a shroud; (*fig.*) to bury; to swallow up, to entomb, to engulf; to absorb. *Ensevelir les morts,* to bury the dead. *Être enseveli dans le chagrin,* to be absorbed in grief. **s'ensevelir,** *v.r.* To bury oneself. **ensevelissement,** *n.m.* Putting in a shroud; burial. **ensevelisseur,** *n.m.* (*fem.* -euse) Layer-out; burying-beetle.

ensiforme [ãsi'fɔrm], *a.* Ensiform, sword-shaped.

ensilage [ãsi'la:ʒ] or **ensilotage,** *n.m.* Ensilage. **ensiler** or **ensiloter,** *v.t.* To ensilage.

ensoleillé [ãsɔlɛ'je], *a.* (*fem.* -ée) Sunny, bathed in sunshine. **ensoleiller,** *v.t.* To light up with sunshine; (*fig.*) to brighten.

ensommeillé [ãsɔmɛ'je], *a.* (*fem.* -ée) Heavy with sleep; (*fig.*) torpid.

ensorcelant [ãsɔrsə'lã], *a.* (*fem.* -ante) Bewitching, enchanting.

ensorceler [ãsɔrsə'le], *v.t.* To bewitch. **ensorceleur,** *n.m.* (*fem.* -euse) Enchanter.—*a.* Bewitching. **ensorcellement,** *n.m.* Bewitchment.

ensoufrer [ãsu'fre], *v.t.* To impregnate with sulphur, to sulphur.

ensouple [ã'supl], *n.f.* Cylinder in a loom.

ensoutaner [ãsuta'ne], *v.t.* To frock, to force to take Holy Orders.

ensuifer [ãsɥi'fe], *v.t.* To cover with tallow.

ensuite [ã'sɥit], *adv.* After, afterwards, then, in the next place; what then? what next? what of that! well! *Ensuite il me dit,* then he told me. *Et ensuite?* what then? *Vous irez là ensuite,* you will go there afterwards.

ensuivre (s') [ã'sɥi:vr], *v.r.* (used only in the 3rd pers. sing. and pl.; p.p. ensuit) To follow, to result, to ensue. *De grands malheurs s'ensuivirent,* great misfortunes resulted from it; *il ne s'ensuit pas que j'aie tort,* it does not follow that I am wrong. *Et tout ce qui s'ensuit,* and all the rest of it.

entablement [ãtablə'mã], *n.m.* (*Arch.*) Entablature.

entacher [ãta'ʃe], *v.t.* To sully, to tarnish; to taint, to blemish, to cast a slur on.

entaillage [ãta:'jaːʒ], *n.m.* Notching, grooving. **entaille,** *n.f.* Notch; jag, cut; gash, slash; groove. **entailler,** *v.t.* To notch, to cut.

entame [ã'tam], *n.f.* First cut, first or outside slice (of a loaf etc.); (*Cards*) opening (of a suit). **entamer,** *v.t.* To make the first cut in; to make an incision in; (*Cards*) to open (a suit); to broach, to begin (a conversation etc.); to break into; to encroach upon; to impair, to injure; to prevail upon, to persuade. *Entamer d'un coup de dent,* to bite into; *entamer la peau,* to break the skin. *Entamer la réputation de quelqu'un,* to injure someone's reputation. *Entamer une matière* or *un sujet,* to broach a subject. *Entamer un pain,* to begin a loaf. *Entamer des pourparlers,* to open negotiations. **entamure,** [ENTAME].

entartrage [ãtar'traːʒ], *n.m.* Furring, scaling. **entartrer (s')** [ãtar'tre], *v.r.* To scale, to become scaled, to become furred.

entassement [ãtas'mã], *n.m.* Accumulation, heap, pile, mass; crowding together. **entasser,** *v.t.* To heap or pile up, to accumulate; to hoard up; to amass; to cram, to crowd, to huddle, to pack together. *Entasser des écus,* to hoard up money. **s'entasser,** *v.r.* To heap up; to crowd together. **entasseur,** *n.m.* (*fem.* -euse) (*colloq.*) Hoarder.

ente [ã:t], *n.f.* Graft, scion; branch bearing a graft.

entendement [ãtãd'mã], *n.m.* Understanding; judgment, sense. (*colloq.*) *Cela passe l'entendement,* this is beyond understanding. **entendeur,** *n.m.* One who understands. *À bon entendeur salut,* a word to the wise is sufficient, or, if the cap fits, wear it.

entendre [ã'tã:dr], *v.t.* To hear; to listen to; to understand; to know; to intend; to mean. *À vous entendre,* according to you; *cet homme n'entend rien aux affaires,* that man knows nothing about business; *chacun fait comme il l'entend,* everybody does as he thinks proper; *donner à entendre,* to intimate, to hint; *entendez-vous?* do you comprehend? *entendons-nous,* let us come to a right understanding; *entendre à demi-mot,* to take the hint. *Entendre la messe* or *entendre les vêpres,* to attend mass or vespers; *entendre les témoins,* to hear the witnesses; *entendre mal,* to be hard of hearing; *entendre raison,* to listen to reason. *Il a fait allusion à votre disgrâce, mais sans y entendre malice,* he alluded to your mishap, but he did not mean any harm. *Il*

entend bien son métier, he knows his trade well; *il entend un peu l'anglais,* he understands a little English; *il ne l'entend pas de cette oreille-là,* he does not agree, he cannot accept it; *il n'entend pas raillerie,* he cannot take a joke; *il n'est pire sourd que celui qui ne veut pas entendre,* none so deaf as those who won't hear; *j'ai entendu dire,* I have heard people say; *j'entends qu'il vienne,* I intend him to come; *laisser à entendre,* to insinuate, to let it be understood (that); *qu'entendez-vous par là?* what do you mean by that?—**v.i.* To approve of, to consent (à). *Ne savoir auquel entendre,* not to know whom to listen to or which to attend to first. **s'entendre,** *v.r.* To hear each other's voices; to hear one's own voice; to be audible, to be heard; to be understood; to understand one another; to act in concert, to have a secret understanding (*avec*); to come to an arrangement, to come to terms (*avec*); to agree with, to be on good terms with; to be skilful in, to be a judge of. *Cela s'entend* or *cela s'entend bien,* let it be understood, of course, to be sure; *il ne s'entend pas mal à cela,* he is pretty well up in that; *il s'entend en musique,* he understands music; *il s'y entend bien,* he is good at it. *Ils s'entendent comme larrons en foire,* they are as thick as thieves; *ils s'entendent pour me nuire,* they have put their heads together to injure me; *je m'entends bien,* I know very well what I mean. *Le bruit est si grand qu'on ne s'entend pas,* there is so much noise that we cannot hear each other speak. *On l'accuse de s'entendre avec l'ennemi,* he is accused of acting in concert with the enemy.
entendu [ãtã:'dy], *a.* (*fem.* **-ue**) Heard; understood; agreed, arranged; intelligent, skilful. *C'est entendu,* that's a bargain, that's settled; *entendu!* all right, agreed! *Bien entendu,* of course. *Faire l'entendu,* to put on a knowing look. *Un homme bien entendu aux affaires,* a man well up in business matters.
enténébré [ãtene'bre], *a.* (*fem.* **-ée**) Gloomy. **enténébrer,** *v.t. irr.* (*conjug. like* ACCÉLÉRER). To plunge in darkness; to wrap in darkness.
entente [ã'tã:t], *n.f.* Meaning; skill, judgment; understanding, agreement. *Entente cordiale,* hearty understanding. *L'entente du coloris,* skill in colouring. *Mots à double entente,* words with a double meaning.
enter [ã'te], *v.t.* To graft upon, to engraft; to adapt, join; to assemble (timbers); to ally (families). *Enter de nouveau,* to regraft; *enter une tête de lion sur un corps de chèvre,* to graft a lion's head on the body of a goat.
entérinement [ãterin'mã], *n.m.* Ratification, confirmation. **entériner,** *v.t.* To ratify, to confirm.
entérique [ãte'rik], *a.* Enteric. **entérite,** *n.f.* Enteritis. **entérocèle,** *n.f.* Enterocele. **entérolithe,** *n.m.* Enterolite. **entérotomie,** *n.f.* Enterotomy.
enterrement [ãtɛr'mã], *n.m.* Burial, interment, funeral. *Avoir une mine d'enterrement,* to look gloomy. **enterrer,** *v.t.* To bury, to inter, to set in the ground; to attend the funeral of; (*fig.*) to survive; to end, to put an end to, to terminate; to sink (money etc.). *Enterrer le carnaval,* to see the carnival out. *Enterrer sa vie de garçon,* to give a bachelor party before one's wedding. *Enterrer une*

affaire, to hush up an affair. *Molière a enterré tous ses devanciers,* Molière threw all his predecessors into the shade. *Une route enterrée,* a sunken road. **s'enterrer,** *v.r.* To bury oneself; (*Mil.*) to dig oneself in (trenches).
en-tête [ã'tɛ:t], *n.m.* (*pl.* **en-têtes**) Heading, head, headline; (U.S.) caption. *En-tête de facture,* bill-head; *papier à en-tête,* headed writing-paper.
entêté [ãtɛ'te], *a.* (*fem.* **-ée**) Stubborn, obstinate, wayward; infatuated. *Entêté comme un âne,* as stubborn as a mule.—*n.* A stubborn person. **entêtement,** *n.m.* Stubbornness, obstinacy; infatuation. *Son entêtement le perdra,* his stubbornness will be his ruin.
entêter [ãtɛ'te], *v.t.* To give a headache to; to make giddy, to intoxicate; to head (pins). *Les louanges nous entêtent,* praises are apt to make us conceited. *Vin qui entête,* heady wine. **s'entêter,** *v.r.* To be stubborn, wayward or obstinate; to be infatuated (*de*); to be bent upon or determined (à).
enthousiasme [ãtu'zjasm], *n.m.* Enthusiasm, rapture, ecstasy. **enthousiasmer,** *v.t.* To render enthusiastic, to enrapture. *Il est enthousiasmé de cette musique,* he is in raptures over that music. **s'enthousiasmer,** *v.r.* To be enthusiastic, to be in raptures (*de*). **enthousiaste,** *a.* Enthusiastic.—*n.* Enthusiast.
enthymème [ãti'mɛ:m], *n.m.* (*Log.*) Enthymeme.
entiché [ãti'ʃe], *a.* (*fem.* **-ée**) Infatuated, wedded to, keen on. **entichement,** *n.m.* Infatuation, addiction.
enticher [ãti'ʃe], *v.t.* To infatuate. *Vous l'avez entiché de ce système,* you have infatuated him with that system. **s'enticher** (*de*), *v.r.* To be infatuated (with).
entier [ã'tje], *a.* (*fem.* **-ière**) Entire, whole, complete; (*Arith.*) integral; total, utter, absolute; (*fig.*) obstinate, positive, self-willed. *Cheval entier,* stallion, entire horse. *Il est très entier,* he is very self-willed or obstinate. *Nombre entier,* (*Arith.*) integer; *pain entier,* whole loaf; *une entière soumission,* complete submission. *Tout entier,* completely.—*n.m.* Entireness, totality; (*Arith.*) integral number. *En (son) entier,* at full length; in full, wholly. **entièrement,** *adv.* Entirely, wholly. *Entièrement ruiné,* utterly ruined.
entité [ãti'te], *n.f.* Entity.
entoilage [ãtwa'la:ʒ], *n.m.* Pasting or mounting on canvas etc.; mounting, canvas, lining; (*Av.*) canvas cover. **entoiler,** *v.t.* To mount upon canvas etc.; to line; to cover with canvas.
entoir [ã'twa:r], *n.m.* (*Hort.*) Grafting-knife.
entôler [ãto'le], *v.t.* (*slang*) To rob, to fleece.
entomologie [ãtomolo'ʒi], *n.f.* Entomology. **entomologique,** *a.* Entomological. **entomologiste,** *n.m.* Entomologist. **entomophage,** *a.* Entomophagous. **entomophile,** *a.* Entomophilous.
entonnage [ãtɔ'na:ʒ], *n.m.,* or **entonnaison,** *n.f.,* or **entonnement,** *n.m.* Tunning, barrelling, casking. **entonner** (1), *v.t.* To tun, to barrel, to put into casks. **s'entonner,** *v.r.* To rush into, to blow down (of the wind). *Le vent s'entonne dans la cheminée,* the wind blows down the chimney.
entonner (2) [ãtɔ'ne], *v.t.* To begin to sing; to strike up; (*poet.*) to celebrate.

entonnoir [ɑ̃tɔ'nwaːr], *n.m.* Funnel; (*pop.*) throat; (*Mil.*) shell hole, crater. *Fleurs en entonnoir,* funnel-shaped flowers.

entophyte [ɑ̃tɔ'fit], *n.m.* Entophyte.

entorse [ɑ̃'tɔrs], *n.f.* Sprain; strain, twist; shock. *Il a donné une entorse à la vérité,* he twisted the truth. *Il s'est donné une entorse au pied,* he has sprained his ankle.

entortillage [ɑ̃tɔrti'jaːʒ], *n.m.,* or **entortillement,** *n.m.* Entanglement, intricacy; winding, twisting, coiling (of a snake); abstruseness, obscurity; subterfuge; circumlocution, equivocation. **entortiller,** *v.t.* To wrap, roll, wind, or coil round; to twist, to distort, to perplex, to entangle; (*colloq.*) to win over, to get the better of. *Entortiller ses pensées,* to express one's thoughts in an obscure manner. (*colloq.*) *Elle l'a entortillé,* she has got round him. **s'entortiller,** *v.r.* To twist or wind oneself round; to twine; to wrap oneself up (*dans*); to be obscure, abstruse, etc.

entour [ɑ̃'tuːr], *n.m.* (*used only in pl. except in the adverbial expression* **à l'entour,** around) Environs, adjacent parts; *persons around one. **entourage,** *n.m.* *Setting, mounting (of jewellery); frame; entourage, advisers, friends, relations, circle, attendants, etc. **entourant,** *a.* (*fem.* -**ante**) (*Bot.*) Enveloping, surrounding the stem. **entourer,** *v.t.* To surround, to encompass, to hem in; to gather round, to be about; (*fig.*) to overwhelm (with attentions etc.). *Entouré d'ennemis,* surrounded with foes. *Entourer quelqu'un de soins,* to lavish attentions upon someone. *Entourer une ville de murailles,* to encompass a town with walls. *Une personne très entourée,* a person with a wide circle of friends. **s'entourer,** *v.r.* To gather or summon round one.

entourloupette [ɑ̃turlu'pɛt], *n.f.* (*pop.*) Dirty trick, swindle, cheat.

entournure [ɑ̃tur'nyːr], *n.f.* Arm-hole, sloping (of sleeves). *Être gêné dans les entournures,* (*fam.*) to be awkward; to feel paralysed.

en-tout-cas [CAS (1)].

entozoaire [ɑ̃tɔzɔ'ɛːr], *n.m.* Entozoon.

entr'accorder (s') [ɑ̃trakɔr'de], *v.r.* To agree together.

entr'accuser (s') [ɑ̃traky'ze], *v.r.* To accuse one another.

entracte [ɑ̃'trakt], *n.m.* (*pl.* **entractes**) Interval (between the acts); interlude. *Dans l'entracte,* between the acts. *Faire de longs entractes,* to have long intervals or waits.

entraide [ɑ̃'trɛd], *n.f.* (*Always sing.*) Mutual aid.

entraider (s') or **entr'aider (s')** [ɑ̃trɛ'de], *v.r.* To help one another.

entrailles [ɑ̃'traːj], *n.f.* (*used only in pl.*) Intestines, entrails, bowels; (*fig.*) feelings, tenderness, heart; pity. *Elle a pour moi des entrailles de mère,* she has a motherly affection for me; *homme sans entrailles,* ruthless man.

entrain [ɑ̃'trɛ̃], *n.m.* Warmth, heartiness; spirit, animation, life, go. *Avec entrain,* briskly, spiritedly.

entraînant [ɑ̃trɛ'nɑ̃], *a.* Captivating, inspiriting, seductive. *Éloquence entraînante,* winning eloquence; *un air entraînant,* a lively tune; *un style entraînant,* a captivating style. **entraînement,** *n.m.* Enthusiasm, rapture; impulse, sway, temptation, allurement,

seduction; (*spt.*) coaching, training, apprenticeship; feed, drive (of machines).

entraîner [ɑ̃trɛ'ne], *v.t.* To draw or drag along; to carry away, to sweep off; to hurry away, to bring, win, or gain over; to entail, to involve; to carry away, to transport; to train. *Entraîner les cœurs,* to win all hearts. *Entraîner quelqu'un dans l'erreur,* to lead someone into error. *La guerre entraîne bien des maux,* war brings with it many evils; *se laisser entraîner,* to allow oneself to be carried away.

entraîneur, *n.m.* Trainer (esp. of horses); pace-maker, pacer (in races); coach (of teams). **entraîneuse,** *n.f.* Dance hostess.

entrait [ɑ̃'trɛ], *n.m.* Tie-beam.

entrant [ɑ̃'trɑ̃], *a.* (*fem.* -**ante**) Ingoing, incoming, entering upon office etc. *Les conseillers entrants,* the newly appointed councillors.—*n.* Person coming in etc. *Les entrants et les sortants,* the incomers and outgoers.

entr'apercevoir [ɑ̃trapɛrsə'vwar], *v.t.* To catch a quick glimpse of.

entr'appeler (s') [ɑ̃tra'ple], *v.r.* To call one another.

entrave [ɑ̃'traːv], *n.f.* Clog, shackle, fetter, hobble; (*fig.*) hindrance, obstacle, impediment. *Entrave à la liberté du travail,* impeding the liberty to work. **entraver,** *v.t.* To shackle, to clog, to trammel; (*fig.*) to fetter, to hinder, to impede, to thwart. *Entraver la circulation,* to hold up the traffic. *Jupe entravée,* hobble-skirt.

entre [ɑ̃ːtr], *prep.* Between, betwixt; among, amongst; into. *Cela soit dit entre nous,* that is between ourselves; *d'entre ses mains,* from out of his hands; *entre autres,* among others; *une personne remarquable entre toutes,* a most remarkable person; *entre chien et loup* [CHIEN]; *entre ciel et terre,* between heaven and earth; *être entre deux vins,* to be half seas over; *entre deux âges,* middle-aged; *nager entre deux eaux,* to swim underwater, (*fig.*) to keep in with both sides; *ils résolurent entre eux,* they resolved among themselves. *Je le remettrai entre vos mains,* I will deliver it into your hands. *Nous dînerons entre nous,* we will dine alone. *Regarder quelqu'un entre les deux yeux,* to look someone straight in the face.

entrebâillé [ɑ̃trəba'je], *a.* (*fem.* -**ée**) Ajar, half-open. **entrebâillement,** *n.m.* Small opening, gap, chink. **entrebâiller,** *v.t.* To half-open, to set ajar. **entrebâilleur,** *n.m.* Door-porter.

entre-bande [ɑ̃trə'bɑ̃ːd], *n.f.* (*pl.* **entrebandes**) Coloured end-selvedge (cloth).

entrechat [ɑ̃trə'ʃa], *n.m.* Caper in dancing, entrechat.

entrechoquement [ɑ̃trəʃɔk'mɑ̃], *n.m.* Clash, collision, conflict. **s'entrechoquer,** *v.r.* To knock, to run, or dash against each other; to interfere with or to thwart each other.

entre-clos [ɑ̃trə'klo], *a.* (*fem.* -**close**) Half-closed; half-drawn.

entr'éclos [ɑ̃tre'klo], *a.* (*fem.* -**ose**) Half-opened (flower).

entrecolonne, *n.f.,* or **entre-colonnement** [ɑ̃trəkɔlɔn'mɑ̃], *n.m.* Intercolumniation.

entrecôte [ɑ̃trə'koːt], *n.f.* Steak cut from between the ribs.

entrecoupé [ɑ̃trəku'pe], *a.* (*fem.* -**ée**) Broken,

interrupted (of words, speech, etc.). **entre-couper**, *v.t.* To intersect; to interrupt; to intersperse (with quotations etc.).

entre-croisement or **entrecroisement** [ãtrəkrwɑz'mã], *n.m.* Intersection, crossing. **entrecroiser**, *v.t.* To intersect. **s'entrecroiser**, *v.r.* To cross one other, to intersect.

entre-déchirer (s') [ãtrədeʃi're], *v.r.* To tear one another to pieces.

entre-détruire (s') [ãtrəde'trɥiːr], *v.r.* To destroy one another.

entre-deux [ãtrə'dø], *n.m.* (*pl.* unchanged) Intermediate space; partition; insertion (of lace etc.); (*Naut.*) waist (between masts); trough (between waves). *L'entre-deux-guerres*, the inter-war period, 1918–39.

entre-dévorer (s') [ãtredevɔ're], *v.r.* To devour each other; to ruin one another.

entrée [ã'tre], *n.f.* Entering, coming in; entry, entrance; mouth, opening, gate, vestibule, inlet; reception; beginning, début, introduction; opening dance; first course, side-dish; admission, free access; entrance-money; town-dues. *À l'entrée de l'hiver*, at the beginning of winter; *entrée en matière*, beginning (speech, essay). *Avoir ses entrées*, to have free admission or access to, to be on the free-list. *Entrée interdite*, no admittance. *Entrée et sortie d'un acteur*, entrance and exit of an actor. *L'entrée d'un port*, the mouth of a harbour. *Droit d'entrée*, admission (fee); *payer les droits d'entrée*, to pay import duties or town-dues. *Tuyau d'entrée*, inlet-pipe.

entrefaites [ãtrə'fɛt], *n.f. pl.* Interval, meantime. *Sur ces entrefaites*, meanwhile; while this was going on.

entrefer [ãtrə'fɛr], *n.m.* (*Elec.*) Air-gap (of electro-magnet etc.).

entrefilet [ãtrəfi'lɛ], *n.m.* A (short) paragraph, note, etc. (in a newspaper).

entre-frapper (s') [ãtrəfra'pe], *v.r.* To strike one another.

entregent [ãtrə'ʒã], *n.m.* Tact, cleverness (in dealing with people). *Avoir de l'entregent*, to have a worldly wisdom, social tact, gumption.

entr'égorger (s') [ãtregɔr'ʒe], *v.r.* To cut one another's throats; to kill one another.

entre-haïr (s') [ãtrəa'iːr], *v.r.* To hate one another.

entre-heurter (s') [ãtrəœr'te], *v.r.* To knock against one another.

entre-jambes [ãtrə'ʒãb], *n.m.* (*inv.* in *pl.*) (*Tailoring*) Crutch. *La longueur d'entre-jambes*, the length from fork to heel.

entrelacement [ãtrəlas'mã], *n.m.* Interlacing, interweaving, wreathing, blending, intertwining. **entrelacer**, *v.t.* To interlace, to intertwine, to interweave, to wreathe. *Des branches entrelacées*, tangled branches. **s'entrelacer**, *v.r.* To entwine, to twist round each other. **entrelacs** [ãtrə'la], *n.m.* Interlaced ribbons etc.; (*Arch.*) ornament composed of interlacing figures.

entrelardé [ãtrəlar'de], *a.* (*fem.* -ée) Interlarded, streaky. **entrelarder**, *v.t.* To lard; to insert between.

entre-ligne [ãtrə'liɲ], *n.m.* (*pl.* entre-lignes) Space between lines, interlineation; (*Print.*) space-line, lead.

entremêlement [ãtrəmɛl'mã], *n.m.* Intermixing, intermingling. **entremêler**, *v.t.* To intermingle, to intermix; to intersperse; to mix up. **s'entremêler**, *v.r.* To intermingle, to intermix; to meddle. *Des nuances qui s'entremêlent*, shades (of colour) which merge into one another.

entremets [ãtrə'mɛ], *n.m. inv.* Side-dish, sweet.

entremetteur [ãtrəmɛ'tœːr], *n.m.* (*fem.* entremetteuse) Go-between, mediator; (*pej.*) procurer, pimp.

entremettre (s') [ãtrə'mɛtr], *v.r. irr.* (*p.p.* entremis) To interpose, to interfere, to meddle. **entremise**, *n.f.* Intervention, interference, mediation; medium, intermediary agency; (*Naut.*) carling. *Par l'entremise de la presse*, through the medium of the press; *par son entremise*, thanks to him.

entre-nœud [ãtrə'nø], *n.m.* (*pl.* entre-nœuds) (*Bot.*) Internode.

entre-nuire (s') [ãtrə'nɥiːr], *v.r. irr.* To hurt each other, to injure each other.

*entrepas [ãtrə'pɑ], *n.m.* (Vicious) ambling pace (of a horse); (U.S.) single foot.

entre-percer (s') [ãtrəper'se], *v.r.* To run each other through, to pierce each other.

entrepont [ãtrə'põ], *n.m.* (*Naut.*) Between decks. *Passagers d'entrepont*, steerage passengers.

entreposage [ãtrəpo'zaːʒ], *n.m.* Warehousing, bonding. **entreposer**, *v.t.* To store, to warehouse; to bond, to put in bond. **entreposeur**, *n.m.* Warehouse-keeper. **entrepositaire**, *n.m.* Bonder; depositor (of goods).

entrepôt [ãtrə'po], *n.m.* Bonded warehouse, store; mart, emporium, depot. *Mettre en entrepôt*, to bond.

entreprenable [ãtrəprə'nabl], *a.* Undertakable. **entreprenant**, *a.* (*fem.* entreprenante) Enterprising, adventurous, pushing; daring, bold, go-ahead.

entreprendre [ãtrə'prãːdr], *v.t. irr.* (*conjugated like* PRENDRE) To undertake, to attempt, to take in hand; to contract for or to; to adventure, to try. *Entreprendre quelqu'un*, to set on someone, to take someone to task.—*v.i.* To encroach, to infringe (*sur*). **entrepreneur**, *n.m.* (*fem.* entrepreneuse) Contractor; master-builder. *Entrepreneur de transports*, forwarding agent; *entrepreneur de maçonnerie*, master-mason; *entrepreneur de pompes funèbres*, undertaker.

entreprise [ãtrə'priːz], *n.f.* Enterprise, undertaking, attempt, venture; contract; concern, firm, business, company; usurpation, encroachment. *Travail à l'entreprise*, work by contract. *Entreprise douteuse*, doubtful venture; *esprit d'entreprise*, enterprising spirit; *il échoue dans ses entreprises*, he fails in his undertakings; *tenter l'entreprise*, to make the attempt; *tenter une entreprise*, to set up an undertaking. *Entreprise sur l'autorité du gouvernement*, attempt upon the authority of the government.

entre-quereller (s') [ãtrəkərə'le], *v.r.* To quarrel with one another.

entrer [ã'tre], *v.i.* (usually with the auxiliary ÊTRE) To enter, to come or go in, to get in, to walk, march, or step in; to be contained, comprised, or included in; to be employed or used in the composition or making of; to pierce, to run into; to enter in a book. *Cela ne m'est jamais entré dans la tête*, that never came into my head; *cela n'entre pas dans le programme*, that is not included in the plan;

cette clef n'entre pas dans la serrure, this key does not fit the lock; *entrer à l'université*, go to, to go up to, a university; *entrer au service de quelqu'un*, to enter someone's service; *entrer bien avant*, to penetrate deeply; *entrer en campagne*, to take the field; *entrer en monde*, to go into society; *entrer dans les intérêts de quelqu'un*, to side with someone; *entrer dans les goûts de*, to be of (someone's) taste; *entrer dans sa vingtième année*, to enter on one's twentieth year; *entrer dans les détails*, to go into details; (*Motor.*) *entrer dans un arbre*, to crash into a tree; *entrer en ébullition*, to begin to boil; *entrer en condition*, to go into domestic service; *entrer en danse*, to begin to dance, (*colloq.*) to begin to act, speak, etc.; *entrer en jeu*, to come into play; *entrer en possession*, to take possession; *entrer en religion*, to become a monk or nun; *entrer en vacances*, to break up; *entrer une seconde fois*, to re-enter; *faire entrer*, to show in, to usher in, to send in; *faire entrer dans la tête de quelqu'un*, to drive into someone's head; *faire entrer un vaisseau dans un bassin*, to dock a ship; *il y entre pour un cinquième*, he has a fifth share in the business; *on n'entre pas ici*, no admittance here; *vous n'entrez pas dans ma pensée*, you mistake my meaning.

entre-rail [ãtrə'rɑːj], *n.m.* (*pl.* **entre-rails**) (*Rail.*) Gauge, distance between the rails.

entre-regarder (s') [ãtrərəgar'de], *v.r.* To look at one another.

entresol [ãtrə'sɔl], *n.m.* Mezzanine, entresol (low rooms between the ground floor and the first floor).

entre-sourcils [ãtrəsur'si], *n.m. inv.* Space between the eyebrows.

entretaille [ãtrə'tɑːj], *n.f.* (*Engr.*) Light stroke, light cut (between two cuts).

entre-tailler (s') [ãtreta'je], *v.r.* To interfere (of horses). ***entretaillure**, *n.f.* (*Vet.*) Injury caused by this.

entre-temps [ãtrə'tã], *n.m. inv.* Interval. *Dans l'entre-temps*, meanwhile.—*adv.* Meanwhile.

entreteneur [ãtrət'nœːr], *n.m.* Keeper (of a mistress).

entretenir [ãtrət'niːr], *v.t. irr.* (*pres. p.* **entretenant**, *p.p.* **entretenu**; *conjugated like* TENIR) To hold together, to keep up, to keep in repair or good order etc.; to maintain, to support, to provide for, to feed; to converse or talk with, to entertain. *Entretenir la paix*, to maintain peace; *entretenir quelqu'un de promesses*, to keep someone quiet with promises; *entretenir le feu*, to make up the fire; *entretenir une route*, to keep a road in good repair. **s'entretenir**, *v.r.* To hold each other together; to be kept up, to be sustained, maintained, or supported; tc maintain, to keep, to support oneself, to subsist, to converse, to talk. *S'entretenir avec quelqu'un*, to talk with someone; *s'entretenir avec soi-même*, to meditate, to reflect; *s'entretenir de quelqu'un*, to speak of someone. **entretenu**, *a.* (*fem.* **-ue**) Kept, maintained. *Femme entretenue*, kept woman; *ondes entretenues*, (*Phys.*) continuous waves.

entretien [ãtrə'tjɛ̃], *n.m.* Maintenance, servicing (of car etc.); upkeep, preservation, care; living, livelihood; conversation, talk, interview, conference; sermon, homily. *Avoir* *un entretien avec quelqu'un*, to have a talk with someone; *faire l'entretien du public*, to be the talk of the town; *frais d'entretien*, cost of maintenance; *un homme d'un agréable entretien*, a man of agreeable conversation.

entretoile [ãtrə'twal], *n.f.* Insertion of lace or open-work.

entretoise [ãtrə'twaːz], *n.f.* Tie-beam, cross-bar, cross-piece; transom. **entretoisement**, *n.m.* Bracing etc. **entretoiser**, *v.t.* To brace, to strut, to tie.

entre-toucher (s') [ãtrətu'ʃe], *v.r.* To touch each other.

entre-tuer (s') [ãtrə'tɥe], *v.r.* To kill each other.

entre-voie [ãtrə'vwa], *n.f.* (*pl.* **entre-voies**) (*Rail.*) Space between the tracks; six-foot way (in England).

entrevoir [ãtrə'vwaːr], *v.t. irr.* (*pres.p.* **entrevoyant**, *p.p.* **entrevu**, *conjugated like* VOIR) To catch a glimpse of, to see imperfectly, to be just able to see; to have an imperfect notion of, to foresee confusedly. *Entrevoir quelqu'un*, to have a glimpse of someone. *J'entrevois de grands obstacles*, I foresee great difficulties. *Laisser entrevoir*, to show a glimpse of, to discover, to disclose.

entrevous [ãtrə'vu], *n.m.* Interval between two beams or girders; case-bay. **entrevouter**, *v.t.* To fill (this) with plaster.

entrevoyant [ãtrəvwa'jã], *pres.p.* **entrevu** [ãtrə'vy], *p.p.* (*fem.* **entrevue** (1)) [ENTREVOIR]. **entrevue** (2), *n.f.* Interview.

entr'obliger (s') [ãtrɔbli'ʒe], *v.r.* To oblige each other.

entropie [ãtrɔ'pi], *n.f.* (*Phys.*) Entropy.

entr'ouvert [ãtru'veːr], *a.* (*fem.* **entr'ouverte**) Partly open, ajar; gaping.

entr'ouvrir [ãtru'vriːr], *v.t. irr.*(*pres.p.* **entr'ouvrant**, *p.p.* **entr'ouvert**) To open a little, to half-open. **s'entr'ouvrir**, *v.r.* To open a little, to be ajar; to gape, to open up.

enturbanné [ãtyrba'ne], *a.* (*fem.* **-ée**) Wearing a turban.

enture [ã'tyːr], *n.f.* (*Gard.*) Incision, cut (for grafting).

énucléation [enyklea'sjɔ̃], *n.f.* Enucleation, stoning (of fruit). **énucléer**, *v.t.* To enucleate; to stone (fruit).

énumérateur [enymera'tœːr], *n.m.* (*fem.* **énumératrice**) Enumerator.

énumératif [enymera'tif], *a.* (*fem.* **-ive**) Enumerative. **énumération**, *n.f.* Enumeration.

énumérer, *v.t. irr.* (*conjug. like* ACCÉLÉRER) To enumerate, to count, to reckon.

envahir [ãva'iːr], *v.t.* To invade, to overrun, to spread over, to overgrow; to encroach upon, to usurp. *Les eaux ont envahi toute la contrée*, the waters have overflowed the whole country. **envahissant**, *a.* (*fem.* **-ante**) Invading, encroaching. **envahissement**, *n.m.* Invasion, overrunning; encroachment, usurpation. **envahisseur**, *n.m.* (*fem.* **-euse**) Invader.—*a.* Invading, encroaching.

envasement [ãvaz'mã], *n.m.* Filling with or enveloping in mud; silting. **envaser**, *v.t.* To fill up or to choke with silt; to thrust into or envelop in mud. **s'envaser**, *v.r.* To stick fast in the mud; to become filled up or choked with silt.

enveillotage [ãvɛjɔ'taːʒ], *n.m.* Putting into cocks. **enveilloter**, *v.t.* To cock (hay etc.)

enveloppant [ãvlɔ'pã], *a.* (*fem.* **-ante**) Enveloping, encircling; (*fig.*) captivating. *Un mouvement enveloppant*, (*Mil.*) an encircling movement. *Charme enveloppant*, captivating charm.

enveloppe [ã'vlɔp], *n.f.* Wrapper, cover, covering; envelope; exterior, outside; appearance; coat, shell, jacket, casing (of cylinders), tunic (of the eye); (*Metal.*) mould; (*Motor.*) outer cover; (*Geom.*) envelope. *Enveloppe gommée*, adhesive envelope; *sous enveloppe*, under cover. *Sous une rude enveloppe*, beneath a rough exterior. **enveloppement**, *n.m.* Enveloping, wrapping up; (*Med.*) pack. **envelopper**, *v.t.* To envelop, to wrap up, to cover, to do up; to beset, to hem in, to surround; to involve, to entangle; to darken, to shroud, to hide, to disguise. *Envelopper l'ennemi*, to hem in the enemy; *envelopper quelque chose de papier*, to wrap something up in paper. **s'envelopper**, *v.r.* To cover or wrap oneself up, to envelop oneself, to involve oneself.

envenimement [ãvnimə'mã], *n.m.* Poisoning; aggravation (of a quarrel). **envenimer**, *v.t.* To poison, to envenom; to irritate, to inflame, to exasperate. *Envenimer une plaie*, to irritate a wound; *envenimer une querelle*, to aggravate a quarrel. **s'envenimer**, *v.r.* To be envenomed; to fester, to rankle. *La discussion s'envenima*, the discussion became bitter.

enverguer [ãvɛr'ge], *v.t.* To bend (a sail etc.) to the yards. **envergure** [ãvɛr'gyːr], *n.f.* Extent (of sail upon the yards); length of a yard; spread (of sail); spread, span (of a bird's wings when extended, of an aeroplane); (*fig.*) breadth or scope of intelligence etc. *De grande envergure*, far-reaching, on a large scale; wide-ranging (of the mind).

envers (1) [ã'vɛːr], *prep.* Towards, to (in respect of). *Je vous défendrai envers et contre tous*, I will defend you against the whole world; *soyez juste envers lui*, be fair to him.

envers (2) [ã'vɛːr], *n.m.* Wrong side, reverse side, back; contrary; ugly or bad side. *À l'envers*, on the wrong side, inside out; *il a l'esprit à l'envers*, he is crack-brained, or beside himself.

envi (à l') [ã'vi], *adv. phr.* In emulation of one another, emulously, vying with each other. *À l'envi l'un de l'autre*, in emulation of each other; *ils travaillent à l'envi l'un de l'autre*, they vie with each other as to who shall work most.

enviable [ã'vjabl], *a.* Enviable, to be envied.

envidage [ãvi'daːʒ], *n.m.* Filling of bobbins etc. **envider**, *v.t.* To fill (bobbins etc.) with thread.

envie [ã'vi], *n.f.* Envy, enviousness; wish, desire, longing, inclination; birth-mark; hangnail. *Avoir envie de parler*, to have a mind to speak; *avoir envie de gâteau*, to want some cake; *avoir envie de dormir*, to feel drowsy; *faire envie*, to be tempting; *digne d'envie*, enviable; *faire envie à quelqu'un*, to make someone envious; *il a une envie au visage*, he has a birth-mark on his face; *il m'en a ôté l'envie*, he has put me out of conceit with it; *il ne fait envie à personne*, no one envies him; *j'ai grande envie d'aller la voir*, I have a great mind to go and see her;

l'envie le dévore, he is consumed with envy; *l'envie lui en est passée*, his longing is over; *mourir d'envie*, to be most anxious (to); *on lui en a donné envie*, they have set him all agog upon it; *passer son envie de quelque chose*, to satisfy one's longing for something; *porter envie à quelqu'un*, to envy someone; *regarder avec envie*, to look longingly; *sécher d'envie*, to pine away with envy.

***envieilli** [ãvjɛ'ji], *a.* (*fem.* **-ie**) Inveterate, long-established, old, of long standing; hardened. *Pécheur envieilli*, hardened sinner. ***envieillir**, *v.t.* To cause to look old.

envier [ã'vje], *v.t.* (*conjugated like* PRIER) To envy, to be envious of; to desire, to long for, to wish for eagerly; to grudge. *Je ne lui envie point sa bonne fortune*, I do not envy him his good fortune; *il est envié de tout le monde*, he is envied by everybody. **envieux**, *a.* and *n.* (*fem.* **-ieuse**) Envious, jealous (person). *Faire des envieux*, to excite envy.

environ [ãvi'rɔ̃], *adv.* About, nearly, thereabouts. *Il y a environ quatre jours*, about four days ago.—***prep.* Near, about.—*n.m. pl.* Environs, vicinity, neighbourhood, surroundings. *Aux environs de Paris*, on the outskirts of Paris. **environnant**, *a.* (*fem.* **-ante**) Surrounding. **environner**, *v.t.* To surround, to stand round; to encompass, to environ, to encircle, to enclose. *L'éclat qui l'environne*, the splendour which surrounds him; *les gardes qui environnaient le prince*, the guards who stood round the prince.

envisager [ãviza'ʒe], *v.t.* To look, to stare in the face, to eye, to face; to consider, to view, to regard, to envisage (a fact etc.). *Envisager de sang froid le péril*, to look danger in the face.

envoi [ã'vwa], *n.m.* Sending (thing sent); packet, parcel, package; goods forwarded, consignment, dispatch, shipment; (*Pros.*) envoy. *Compléter un envoi*, to make up a parcel; *dans mon prochain envoi*, in my next consignment; (*Law*) *envoi en possession*, writ of possession; *faire un envoi*, to send off a parcel or package; *lettre d'envoi*, covering letter, letter of advice; *par l'envoi du 21 avril*, by our consignment of the 21 April; *envoi de renforts*, dispatch of reinforcements; *coup d'envoi*, (*Ftb.*) kick-off.

envoiler (s') [ãvwa'le], *v.r.* To warp, to bend (of metal). **envoilure**, *n.f.* Warping, bending (of metal).

envoisiner [ãvwazi'ne], *v.t.* To surround with neighbours. *Être bien envoisiné*, to have good neighbours.

envol [ã'vɔl], *n.m.* Taking wing (of birds), taking off (of aeroplanes), start. *Piste d'envol*, runway.

envolée [ãvɔ'le], *n.f.* Flight; (*fig.*) élan.

envoler (s') [ãvɔ'le], *v.r.* To fly away, to take wing; to take off, to fly off; (*fig.*) to be carried off (by the wind etc.); (*fig.*) to disappear, to vanish. *L'oiseau s'est envolé*, the bird has flown; (*fam.*) *s'envoler pour le Canada*, to take the plane for Canada.

envoûtement [ãvut'mã], *n.m.* Spell or magical charm. **envoûter**, *v.t.* To prick the wax image of a person in order to injure him magically; hence, to cast a spell on someone. **envoûteur**, *n.m.* (*fem.* **-euse**) Person who casts spells; (*fig.*) charmer.

envoyable [ăvwa'jabl], *a.* Sendable. **envoyé,** *n.m.* (*fem.* **-ée**) Person sent; envoy; deputy, delegate, messenger. *Envoyé spécial* (of a paper), special correspondent.

envoyer [ăvwa'je], *v.t. irr.* To send, to forward, to dispatch, to transmit; to delegate, to send as envoy; to emit. *Envoie!* (*Naut.*) 'bout ship! *envoyer au diable* or *envoyer à tous les diables,* to send to the devil; *envoyer un baiser,* to blow a kiss; *envoyer chercher,* to send for; *envoyer dire,* to send word; *envoyer en prison,* to commit to prison; (*fam.*) *envoyer paître* or *envoyer promener,* to send about one's business, to send away with a flea in his ear; *envoyez-moi un mot,* drop me a line; (*Naut.*) *envoyer* (*les couleurs*), to hoist (colours). **s'envoyer,** *v.r.* To send to each other; to be sent; (*pop.*) to treat oneself to (a good meal etc.); (*vulg.*) to have sexual intercourse with. **envoyeur,** *n.m.* (*fem.* **-euse**) Sender. *Retour à l'envoyeur* (*Post Office*), return to sender.

enzyme [ã'ʒim], *n.f.* Enzyme.

éocène [eɔ'sɛn], *a.* (*Geol.*) Eocene.

éolien [eɔ'ljɛ̃], *a.* and *n.* (*fem.* **éolienne**) Aeolic, Aeolian.

éolipile or **éolipyle** [eɔli'pil], *n.m.* Aeolipile (smoke-driving apparatus); soldering lamp.

éolique [eɔ'lik], *a.* Aeolic.

éolithe [eɔ'lit], *n.m.* Eolith.

éon [e'ɔ̃], *n.m.* Aeon.

épacte [e'pakt], *n.f.* (*Astron.*) Epact.

épagneul [epa'nœl], *n.m.* (*fem.* **-eule**) Spaniel.

épais [e'pɛ], *a.* Thick, dense; stout, thickset, bulky; heavy; (*fig.*) dull, gross, heavy-witted; muddy, turbid. *Avoir la langue épaisse,* to speak thick; *herbe épaisse,* dense grass; *ignorance épaisse,* gross ignorance; *mur épais de deux pieds,* wall two feet thick; *ténèbres épaisses,* thick darkness; *un homme épais,* a blockhead.—*n.m.* Thickness; thick part. *Au plus épais de la mêlée,* in the thick of the fight.—*adv.* Thick, thickly. *Semer épais,* to sow thick. **épaisseur,** *n.f.* Thickness, density; stoutness, bulkiness; coarseness, dullness. **épaissir,** *v.t.* To thicken, to make thicker.—*v.i.* and **s'épaissir,** *v.r.* To become thick, to grow thicker, to grow big or stout; to become heavy or dull. *Sa langue s'épaissit,* his speech is becoming thick. **épaississement,** *n.m.* Thickening.

épamprage [epã'praːʒ], *n.m.* Lopping off; pruning (of a vine). **épamprer,** *v.t.* To lop or prune (a vine).

épanchement [epãʃ'mã], *n.m.* Pouring out, shedding, discharge; (*Med.*) overflow; (*fig.*) outpouring (emotion etc.). **épancher,** *v.t.* To pour out, to shed; to open, to discharge, to vent. *Épancher son cœur,* to open one's heart. **s'épancher,** *v.r.* To be discharged, poured out or effused, to overflow; to open one's heart, to unbosom oneself. **épanchoir,** *n.m.* Outlet, overflow channel.

épandage [epã'daːʒ], *n.m.* Scattering, strewing. *Champ d'épandage,* sewage farm. **épandre,** *v.t.* To scatter, to strew, to throw here and there; to shed (light etc.). *Épandre du fumier,* to spread muck. **s'épandre,** *v.r.* To spread; (*fig.*) to stretch (of a sheet of water etc.).

épanoui [epa'nwi], *a.* (*fem.* **-ie**) In full bloom (of a flower), (*fig.*) beaming. **épanouir,** *v.t.*

To cause to open or expand; (*fig.*) to brighten, to gladden. *Épanouir la rate,* to make merry, to drive away the spleen. **s'épanouir,** *v.r.* To blow, to expand, to open (of flowers); to brighten up (of the face etc.). *Son visage s'épanouit,* his face brightened up. **épanouissement,** *n.m.* Blowing, opening, expansion (of flowers); (*fig.*) brightness, glow, bloom.

épar [e'par], *n.m.* Cross-bar; shaft-bar, transom; slat.

éparcet [epar'sɛ] or **esparcet,** *n.m.,* **éparcette** or **esparcette,** *n.f.* Sainfoin.

épargnant [epar'ɲã], *a.* (*fem.* **-ante**) Sparing, saving, economical, parsimonious.—*n.* *Les petits épargnants,* small investors.

épargne [e'parɲ], *n.f.* Saving, thrift, economy, parsimony. *User d'épargne,* to save, to be saving; *avec épargne,* sparingly; *caisse d'épargne,* savings bank; *il vit de ses épargnes,* he lives on his savings. **épargner,** *v.t.* To save, to lay by; to spare; to husband, to economize. *Épargner son bien,* to save one's wealth; *épargner sur sa toilette,* to save on dress; *ne m'épargnez pas,* do not spare me; *on ne lui épargne pas les encouragements,* they give him plenty of encouragement.

éparpillement [eparpij'mã], *n.m.* Scattering, dispersing, dispersion; scattered state. **éparpiller,** *v.t.* To scatter, to strew about, to spread, to disperse; to fritter away, to squander. *Éparpiller ses troupes,* to scatter one's troops. **s'éparpiller,** *v.r.* To disperse.

épars [e'paːr], *a.* (*fem.* **éparse**) Scattered, dispersed, disseminated, sparse; straggling; dishevelled (of hair).

éparvin [epar'vɛ̃] or **épervin,** *n.m.* Spavin.

épatant [epa'tã], *a.* (*fem.* **-ante**) (*fam.*) Amazing, splendid, ripping. **épate,** *n.f.* Bluff, swank. *Faire de l'épate,* to show off, to cut a dash. **épaté,** *a.* (*fem.* **-ée**) With the foot broken off (of glasses); flat, squat (of noses); amazed, dumbfounded. **épatement,** *n.m.* Flatness (of nose); (*fam.*) amazement.

épater [epa'te], *v.t.* To damage an animal's foot; to flatten; to break the foot off (a glass); (*fam.*) to amaze, to dumbfound, to flabbergast. **s'épater,** *v.r.* To be flabbergasted.

épateur, *n.m.* (*fem.* **-euse**) Swanker, bouncer.

épaulard [epo'laːr], *n.m.* Grampus, orc.

épaule [e'poːl], *n.f.* Shoulder. (*Mil.*) *Arme sur l'épaule!* Slope arms! *avoir les épaules assez larges pour,* to be broad-shouldered or capable enough for; *avoir la tête (enfoncée) dans les épaules,* to be short-necked; *avoir la tête sur les épaules,* to be sensible; *donner un coup d'épaule* or *prêter l'épaule à quelqu'un,* to help someone, to give him a leg-up; *épaule de mouton,* shoulder of mutton; *épaules d'un vaisseau,* bows of a ship; *faire une chose par-dessus l'épaule,* to leave a thing undone or half-done; *hausser les épaules,* to shrug one's shoulders; *l'épaule d'un bastion,* the flank of a bastion; *marcher des épaules,* to slouch; *plier les épaules,* to put up with; *porter sur ses épaules,* (*fig.*) to be saddled with. **épaulée,** *n.f.* Push (with the shoulders); fore-quarter of mutton without the shoulder. *Faire une chose par épaulées,* to do a thing by fits and starts. **épaulement,** *n.m.* Shoulder-piece; shoulder; (*Naut.*) shoulder, bows; (*Fort.*)

epaulement, breast-work. ¯**épauler**, *v.t.* To splay the shoulder (a horse etc.); to cover with an epaulement; (*fig.*) to help, to back (a person); to bring a rifle to the shoulder; to level it (in order to aim). *Bête épaulée*, animal with a sprained shoulder; *épauler des troupes*, to cover troops by means of an epaulement.

épaulette [epo'lɛt], *n.f.* Shoulder-strap, shoulder-piece; epaulet. *Obtenir l'épaulette*, to obtain a commission. **épaulière**, *n.f.* Shoulder-strap; shoulder-plate (armour).

épave [e'pa:v], *n.f.* Wreck; unclaimed object, waif, stray. *Épaves maritimes* or *épaves de mer*, wreckage; *épaves flottantes*, flotsam; *épaves à la côte*, jetsam. (*fig.*) *Cet homme n'est plus qu'une épave*, that man is but a wreck now.—*a.* *(Law)* (animal or thing) strayed, ownerless, unclaimed. *Abeilles épaves*, strayed (swarm of) bees.

épeautre [e'po:tr], *n.m.* (*Bot.*) Spelt.

épée [e'pe], *n.f.* Sword; (*fig.*) brand, steel. *Briser son épée*, to give up the profession of arms; *c'est son épée de chevet*, he is his bosom friend, his constant companion, (*fig.*) it is his favourite theme; *c'est un coup d'épée dans l'eau*, it is beating the air; *épée de mer*, sword-fish; *il est brave comme l'épée qu'il porte*, he is as true as steel; *mettre l'épée à la main*, to draw one's sword; *n'avoir que la cape et l'épée*, to have no other fortune than one's sword; *passer au fil de l'épée*, to put to (the edge of) the sword; *passer l'épée au travers du corps*, to run a man through the body; *presser quelqu'un l'épée dans les reins*, to press someone hard; *rendre son épée*, to surrender; *se battre à l'épée*, to fight with swords; *une bonne épée*, a good swordsman; *un homme d'épée*, a swordsman, a soldier.

épeiche [e'pɛ:ʃ], *n.f.* Witwall, great spotted woodpecker. **épeichette**, *n.f.* Lesser spotted woodpecker.

épéiste [epe'ist], *n.m.* Fencer who uses a sword (not a foil).

épeler [e'ple], *v.t. irr. (conjug. like* AMENER*)* To spell. *Épeler mal*, to misspell; *épelez ce mot*, spell that word. **épellation**, *n.f.* Spelling, naming the letters of a word.

épenthèse [epɑ̃'tɛ:z], *n.f.* (*Gram.*) Epenthesis. **épenthétique**, *a.* Epenthetic.

épépiner [epepi'ne], *v.t.* To take out the pips.

éperdu [epɛr'dy], *a.* (*fem.* **-ue**) Distracted, bewildered, aghast. *Tout éperdu d'amour*, quite distraught with love. **éperdument**, *adv.* Madly, distractedly.

éperlan [epɛr'lɑ̃], *n.m.* (*Ichth.*) Smelt, sparling.

éperon [e'prɔ̃], *n.m.* Spur; (*fig.*) wrinkle, crow's foot; gaffle (of game-cocks); (*Arch.*) buttress, counter-fort; starling, breakwater (of a bridge etc.); (*Naut.*) prow, cutwater, ram. *Chausser les éperons*, to put on spurs; *il a besoin d'éperons*, he wants spurring on. **éperonné**, *a.* (*fem.* **-ée**) Spurred; armed with spurs. *Botté et éperonné*, booted and spurred. **éperonner**, *v.t.* To spur; to arm with spurs; to spur on, to urge forward; (*Naut.*) to ram. **éperonnier**, *n.m.* Spur-maker; Asiatic peacock. **éperonnière**, *n.f.* (*Bot.*) Larkspur.

épervier [epɛr'vje], *n.m.* Sparrow-hawk; cast-net. **épervière** [epɛr'vjɛ:r], *n.f.* (*Bot.*) Hawkweed.

épervin [ÉPARVIN].

épeuré [epø're], *a.* (*fem.* **-ée**) Scared.

éphèbe [e'fɛb], *n.m.* Ephebe.

éphèdre [e'fɛdr], *n.f.* (*Bot.*) Shrubby horse-tail.

éphédrine [efe'drin], *n.f.* (*Pharm.*) Ephedrin.

éphélide [efe'lid], *n.f.* Sunburn, freckle.

éphémère [efe'mɛ:r], *a.* Ephemeral.—*n.m.* Ephemera, may-fly.—*n.f.* (*Bot.*) The genus Tradescantia, containing the spider-worts.

éphéméride, *n.f.* Ephemeris; block calendar. —*n.m. pl.* (*Ent.*) Ephemerides.—*n.f. pl.* Astronomical tables; nautical almanac.

éphod [e'fɔd], *n.m.* (*Jewish Ant.*) Ephod.

éphore [e'fɔːr], *n.m.* (*Greek Ant.*) Ephor.

épi [e'pi], *n.m.* Ear of corn; (*fig.*) cluster (of flowers along a stem etc.); (*Rail.*) system of marshalling tracks; (*Hydr.*) wharf, groin. *Appareil en épi*, herring-bone arrangement of bricks; *en épi*, like an ear of corn (arranged in rows along a stem); *épi bien garni*, well-filled ear; *épi de cheveux*, tuft of hair arranged in the opposite direction to the rest, cow's lick; *épi de diamants*, cluster of diamonds arranged like an ear of corn. **épiage**, *n.m.*, **épiaison** or **épiation**, *n.f.* Earing of (grain).

épiaire [e'pjɛ:r], *n.f.* (*Bot.*) Woundwort; a common name of several Stachys, such as *épiaire dressée, ortie puante, crosne*.

épicarpe [epi'karp], *n.m.* Epicarp.

épice [e'pis], *n.f.* Spice. *(Anc. Law)* Épices des juges, judges' fees, douceur. *Les quatre épices*, all-spice. *Pain d'épice*, gingerbread.

épicé, *a.* (*fem.* **-ée**) Spiced, spicy; hot, seasoned; smutty (story).

épicéa [epise'a], *n.m.* Norway spruce.

épicène [epi'sɛːn], *a.* (*Gram.*) Epicene.

épicentre [epi'sɑ̃tr], *n.m.* Epicentrum.

épicer [epi'se], *v.t.* To spice; to make (a story etc.) spicy. **épicerie**, *n.f.* Spices; grocer's shop, grocery, grocery-business. *Petite épicerie*, chandlery.

épicier [epi'sje], *n.m.* (*fem.* **épicière**) Grocer; (*fig.*) vulgar, commonplace person, philistine.

épicrâne [epi'krɑ:n], *n.m.* Epicranium.

épicuréisme [ÉPICURISME].

épicurien [epiky'rjɛ̃], *a.* (*fem.* **-ienne**) Epicurean, voluptuous, elegantly sensual.—*n.* Epicure. **épicurisme**, *n.m.* Epicureanism, epicurism.

épicycle [epi'sikl], *n.m.* Epicycle. **épicycloïdal**, *a.* (*fem.* **-ale**, *pl.* **-aux**) Epicycloidal. **épicycloïde**, *n.f.* Epicycloid.

épidémie [epide'mi], *n.f.* Epidemic. **épidémiologie**, *n.f.* Epidemiology. **épidémique**, *a.* Epidemic. **épidémiquement**, *adv.* Epidemically.

épiderme [epi'dɛrm], *n.m.* Epidermis, cuticle. *Avoir l'épiderme sensible*, to be touchy. **épidermique**, *a.* Epidermic, epidermal. **épidermoïde**, *a.* Epidermoid.

épidiascope [epidja'skɔp], *n.m.* Epidiascope.

épier (1) [e'pje], *v.i.* (*conjugated like* PRIER) To ear, to form into ears.

épier (2) [e'pje], *v.t.* (*conjugated like* PRIER) To watch; to spy upon; to lie in wait for, to be on the watch for. *Épier l'occasion*, to watch for the chance; *il épie ce que vous faites*, he is a spy upon your actions; *on épie vos démarches*, your every movement is watched. **s'épier**, *v.r.* To watch each other.

épierrage [epjɛ'ra:ʒ] or **épierrement**, *n.m.*

Clearing land of stones. **épierrer**, *v.t.* To clear away stones from (land etc.).

épieu [e'pjø], *n.m.* Boar-spear, hunting-pole.

épigastre [epi'gastr], *n.m.* Epigastrium. **épigastrique**, *a.* Epigastric.

épigénèse [epiʒe'nɛːz], *n.f.* Epigenesis. **épigénésique**, *a.* Epigeneous.

épigénie [epiʒe'ni], *n.f.* (*Min.*) Pseudomorphism.

épiglotte [epi'glɔt], *n.f.* Epiglottis. **épiglottique**, *a.* Epiglottic.

épigrammatique [epigrama'tik], *a.* Epigrammatical. **épigrammatiquement**, *adv.* Epigrammatically. **épigrammatiste**, *n.m.* Epigrammatist. **épigramme**, *n.f.* Epigram.

épigraphe [epi'graf], *n.f.* Epigraph. **épigraphie**, *n.f.* Epigraphy. **épigraphique**, *a.* Epigraphic. **épigraphiste**, *n.m.* Epigraphist.

épigyne [epi'ʒin], *a.* (*Bot.*) Epigynous.—*n.f.* Epigynous part.

épilation [epilɑ'sjɔ̃], *n.f.* Depilation. **épilatoire**, *a.* Depilatory.

épilepsie [epilɛp'si], *n.f.* Epilepsy. *Attaque d'épilepsie*, epileptic fit. **épileptique**, *a.* and *n.* Epileptic. **épileptoïde**, *a.* Epileptoid.

épiler [epi'le], *v.t.* To depilate; to skim (molten pewter). **s'épiler**, *v.r.* To pluck out one's hairs. **épileur**, *n.m.* (*fem.* **épileuse**) Depilator (person).

épillet [epi'jɛ], *n.m.* (*Bot.*) Spikelet.

épilobe [epi'lɔb], *n.m.* (*Bot.*) Epilobium, (name of several willow-herbs, such as) *épilobe hérissé*, great hairy willow-herb, or codlins-and-cream; *épilobe en épis* or *laurier de Saint-Antoine*, rose-bay willow-herb.

épilogue [epi'lɔg], *n.m.* Epilogue. **épiloguer**, *v.i.* To carp, to find fault, to split hairs.—*v.t.* To censure, to criticize. **épilogueur**, *n.m.* (*fem.* **-euse**) Critic, fault-finder, carper.—*a.* Fault-finding.

épiloir [epi'lwaːr], *n.m.* Tweezers.

épinaie [epi'nɛ], *n.f.* Brake, thorny thicket.

épinard [epi'naːr], *n.m.* Spinach; (*pl.*) spinach greens. *Épaulettes à graine d'épinards*, epaulets with large bullions; *mettre du beurre dans les épinards*, to make life more comfortable; *plat d'épinards*, a bad picture, having too much green in it.

épinçage [epɛ̃'saːʒ], *n.m.* (*Gard.*) Disbudding.

épincelage etc. [ÉPINCETAGE].

épincer [epɛ̃'se], *v.t.* (*Gard.*) To disbud; [ÉPINCETER].

épincetage [epɛ̃s'taːʒ], *n.m.* Burling. **épinceter**, *v.t.* To shape (stone) with a paviour's hammer; to burl (cloth). **épinceteur**, *n.m.* (*fem.* **-euse**) Burler. **épincette**, *n.f.* Burling tweezers.

épine [e'pin], *n.f.* Thorn, prickle; thorn-bush; (*fig.*) cross, rub, obstacle, difficulty. (*Anat.*) *Épine dorsale*, spine, backbone; (*Bot.*) *épine blanche*, hawthorn; *épine noire*, blackthorn, sloe. (*fig.*) *Avoir une épine au pied*, to have a thorn in one's side; *être sur des épines*, to be on tenterhooks; *tirer à quelqu'un une épine du pied*, to get someone over a difficulty. **épiner**, *v.t.* To put thorn branches round (trees etc.).

épinette [epi'nɛt], *n.f.* *Spinet; box for fattening poultry; thorn-hook (for fishing); (*Bot.*) spruce. *Épinette rouge*, tamarack; (*C*) *épinette blanche*, white spruce; *épinette noire*, black spruce.

(*C*) **épinettière** [epinɛ'tjɛːr], *n.f.* A grove or forest of tamarack, spruce or fir trees.

épineux [epi'nø], *a.* (*fem.* **-euse**) Thorny, prickly; (*fig.*) irritable, over-particular; knotty, ticklish, intricate. *Question épineuse*, ticklish question.

épine-vinette [epinvi'nɛt], *n.f.* (*pl.* **épines(s)-vinettes**) (*Bot.*) Barberry.

épinglage [epɛ̃'glaːʒ], *n.m.* Pinning. **épingle**, *n.f.* Pin; scarf-pin, breast-pin. *Épingle anglaise*, *épingle de nourrice*, *épingle double*, safety-pin; *à coups d'épingles*, by pin-pricks; *épingle à cheveux*, hairpin; *épingle de bois*, peg; *épingle de cravate*, tie pin; *il est tiré à quatre épingles*, he looks as if he had just stepped out of a bandbox, he is spick and span; *ôter les épingles de*, to unpin; *tirer son épingle du jeu*, to get out of a scrape; *virage en épingle à cheveux*, hairpin bend. **épinglé**, *a.* (*fem.* **-ée**) Pinned; corded, terry.—*n.m.* Terry velvet etc. **épingler**, *v.t.* To pin, to fix, secure, or attach with pins. **épinglerie**, *n.f.* Pin-factory; pinware. **épinglette**, *n.f.* Priming-wire; (*Artill.*) priming-iron; (*Mining*) piercer; (*Mil.*) pricker, badge of first shot. **épinglier**, *n.m.* (*fem.* **épinglière**) Pin-maker; pin-tray.

épinier [epi'nje], *n.m.* (*Hunt.*) Covert, thicket.

épinière [epi'njɛːr], *a.f.* (*Anat.*) Spinal. *Moelle épinière*, spinal marrow.

épinoche [epi'nɔʃ], *n.f.* (*Ichth.*) Stickleback.

Épiphanie [epifa'ni], *n.f.* Epiphany.

épiphénomène [epifenɔ'mɛn], *n.m.* (*Phil.*) Epiphenomenon.

épiphonème [epifɔ'nɛːm], *n.m.* (*Rhet.*) Sententious phrase at the end.

épiphylle [epi'fil], *a.* Epiphyllus.—*n.m.* Epiphyllum.

épiphyse [epi'fiːz], *n.f.* (*Anat.*) Epiphysis.

épiphyte [epi'fit], *n.f.* Epiphyte. **épiphytique**, *a.* Epiphytic.

épiploïque [epiplɔ'ik], *a.* Epiploic. **épiploon**, *n.m.* Epiploon.

épique [e'pik], *a.* Epic, epical.

épirrhize [epi'riz], *a.* Epirhizous.

épiscopal [episkɔ'pal], *a.* (*fem.* **-ale**, *pl.* **-aux**) Episcopal. **épiscopalien**, *a.* and *n.* (*fem.* **-ienne**) Episcopalian (in the U.S.A.). **épiscopat**, *n.m.* Episcopate, episcopacy. **épiscopaux**, *n.m.* (*used only in pl.*) Episcopalians (in Scotland).

épisode [epi'zɔd], *n.m.* Episode. *Film à épisodes*, serial film. **épisodique**, *a.* Episodical, temporary.

épispastique [epispas'tik], *a.* and *n.m.* (*Med.*) Epispastic.

épispermatique [epispɛrma'tik], *a.* (*Bot.*) Epispermic. **épisperme**, *n.m.* Seed-coat, episperm.

épisser [epi'se], *v.t.* To splice. **épissoir**, *n.m.*, or **épissoire**, *n.f.* Marline-spike. **épissure**, *n.f.* Splice.

épistaminal [epistami'nal], *a.* (*fem.* **-ale**, *pl.* **-aux**) Growing on the stamens.

épistémologie [epistemɔlɔ'ʒi], *n.f.* Epistemology.

épistolaire [epistɔ'lɛːr], *a.* Epistolary. **épistolier**, *n.m.* (*fem.* **-ière**) (*colloq.*) Letter-writer. *épistolographe**, *n.m.* Letter-writer of antiquity etc. **épistolographie**, *n.f.* Epistolography. **épistolographique**, *a.* Epistolographic.

épistrophe [epis′trɔf], *n.f.* Epistrophe.
épistyle [epis′til], *n.m.* Epistyle, architrave.
épitaphe [epi′taf], *n.f.* Epitaph.
épithalame [epita′lam], *n.m.* Epithalamium, nuptial song.
épithélial [epite′ljal], *a.* (*fem.* -iale, *pl.* -iaux) Epithelial. **épithélium**, *n.m.* Epithelium.
épithème [epi′tɛːm], *n.m.* Epithem.
épithète [epi′tɛt], *n.f.* Epithet.
épitoge [epi′tɔːʒ], *n.f.* (*Rom. Ant.*) Mantle worn over toga; (*Univ. etc.*) shoulder-knot or band, which takes the place in France of a (graduate's) hood.
épitomé [epito′me], *n.m.* Epitome, abridgment.
épître [e′pitr], *n.f.* Epistle, letter, missive. *Le côté de l'épître*, the right-hand or south side of the altar.
épizootie [epizɔɔ′ti], *n.f.* Murrain; epizooty. **épizootique**, *a.* Epizootic. *Maladie épizootique*, epizootic distemper.
éploré [eplɔ′re], *a.* (*fem.* -ée) In tears, weeping, disconsolate, distressed.
éployé [eplwa′je], *a.* (*fem.* -ée) (*Her.*) Spread (eagle).
épluchage [eply′ʃaːʒ], *n.m.* **épluchement**, *n.m.* Cleaning, picking; peeling (fruit and vegetables). **éplucher**, *v.t.* To pick, to purl; to clean; to peel (fruit etc.); (*fig.*) to sift, to examine minutely. *Éplucher la vie de quelqu'un*, to examine minutely into someone's life; *éplucher un ouvrage*, to pick a work to pieces. (C) **épluchette**, *n.f.* Corn-husking party. **éplucheur**, *n.m.* (*fem.* -euse) Picker; fault-finder, hair-splitter. **épluchoir**, *n.m.* Paring-knife. **épluchures**, *n.f. pl.* Parings, peelings, offal (of meat).
épode [e′pɔd], *n.f.* Epode.
épointé [epwɛ̃′te], *a.* (*fem.* -ée) With a broken thigh (of a dog); hip-shot (of a horse); blunt (pencil, needle).
épointement [epwɛ̃′mã], *n.m.* Bluntness. **épointer**, *v.t.* To break the point off, to blunt. **s'épointer**, *v.r.* To have its point broken off.
éponge [e′pɔ̃ːʒ], *n.f.* Sponge; calkin, heel (of horseshoe); (*Bot.*) bedeguar. *Il boit comme une éponge*, he drinks like a fish; *passer l'éponge sur quelque action*, to say no more about an action; *presser l'éponge*, to squeeze the sponge, to exact too much; *serviette éponge*, Turkish towel. **épongeage**, *n.m.* Sponging. **éponger**, *v.t.* To sponge, to clean with a sponge.
épontille [epɔ̃′tiːj], *n.f.* (*Naut.*) Stanchion, shore, prop. **épontiller**, *v.t.* To prop, to shore.
éponyme [epɔ′nim], *a.* Eponymous.—*n.m.* Eponym. **éponymique**, *a.* Eponymic.
épopée [epɔ′pe], *n.f.* Epopee, epic.
époque [e′pɔk], *n.f.* Epoch, period, era; time, date. *À l'époque de*, at the time of; *dès cette époque*, from that time; *faire époque*, to mark an era; *qui fait époque*, epoch-making.
épouffer (s') [epu′fe], *v.r.* To steal away; to get out of breath (from laughing).
épouillage [epu′jaːʒ], *n.m.* Delousing. **épouiller**, *v.t.* To delouse, to clean of lice.
époumoner [epumɔ′ne], *v.t.* To tire the lungs of, to exhaust. **s'époumoner**, *v.r.* To tire one's lungs, (*fig.*) to shout oneself hoarse.
*****épousailles** [epu′zaːj], *n.f.* (*used only in pl.*) Espousals, nuptials.

épouse [e′puːz], *n.f.* Spouse, bride, wife, consort. **épousée**, *n.f.* Bride. **épouser**, *v.t.* To marry, to take in marriage, to wed; (*fig.*) to embrace, to take up. *Épouser la forme de*, to take the form of. **s'épouser**, *v.r.* To marry, to be married to each other. **épouseur**, *n.m.* (*colloq.*) Marrying man; suitor.
époussetage [epus′taːʒ], *n.m.* Dusting. **épousseter**, *v.t.* To dust, to wipe the dust off, to beat the dust out of; *(colloq.)* to leather, to thrash. *Épousseter quelqu'un*, to dust someone's jacket for him. **époussette**, *n.f.* Dusting-brush; duster.
époustouflant [epustu′flã], *a.* (*fem.* -ante) (*colloq.*) Astounding. **époustoufler**, *v.t.* To astound, to amaze.
épouti [epu′ti], *n.m.* Orts (in cloth); burl (in wool). **époutiage, époutillage**, *n.m.* Picking, cleaning, or burling (cloth). **époutier**, *v.t.* To pick, to burl, to clean (cloth etc.).
épouvantable [epuvã′tabl], *a.* Frightful, dreadful, shocking, horrible, appalling. *À un degré épouvantable*, to a frightful degree. **épouvantablement**, *adv.* Frightfully, dreadfully. **épouvantail**, *n.m.* Scarecrow; (*fig.*) bugbear. *C'est un épouvantail*, she is a perfect scarecrow, a fright.
épouvante [epu′vãːt], *n.f.* Terror, fright. *Frapper d'épouvante*, to dismay, to affright; *l'épouvante les a pris*, they were seized with dismay; *porter l'épouvante*, to spread terror. **épouvanté**, *a.* (*fem.* -ée) Terror-stricken. **épouvanter**, *v.t.* To terrify, to frighten, to appal, to scare. **s'épouvanter**, *v.r.* To be frightened or terrified; to take fright.
époux [e′pu], *n.m.* (*pl. unchanged*) Husband, bridegroom; (*pl.*) married couple, husband and wife. *Futur époux*, intended husband.
épreindre [e′prɛ̃ːdr], *v.t. irr.* (*conjugated like* CRAINDRE) To squeeze out, to press.
épreintes [e′prɛ̃ːt], *n.f. pl.* Tenesmus, straining. (*Hunt.*) spraints.
éprendre (s') [e′prãːdr], *v.r. irr.* (*conjugated like* PRENDRE) To be seized with, to be smitten with, to fall in love (*de*).
épreuve [e′prœːv], *n.f.* Proof, test; ordeal, trial; examination; (*Print.*) proof-sheet, revise; (*Phot.*) print. *À l'épreuve de l'eau, des balles*, or *du feu*, waterproof, bullet-proof, or fire-proof; *à toute épreuve*, trusty, faithful, foolproof; *courage à toute épreuve*, courage proof against everything. *Épreuve judiciaire*, ordeal. (*sch.*) *Épreuves écrites*, written examination; *épreuves orales*; oral test; (*spt.*) *épreuve éliminatoire*, (eliminating) heat. *J'en ai fait l'épreuve*, I have tried it; *mettre à l'épreuve* or *tenter une épreuve sur*, to put to the test; *passer par de rudes épreuves*, to go through hard trials; *prendre à l'épreuve*, to take on trial. *Épreuve avant la lettre*, (*Engr.*) proof before letters; *épreuve chargée*, (*Print.*) foul proof; *épreuve nette*, clean proof; *première épreuve d'auteur*, (*Print.*) reader's proof; *seconde épreuve d'auteur*, (*Print.*) revise; *dernière épreuve de bon à tirer*, press proof; *tirer une épreuve*, to pull a proof.
épris [e′pri], *a.* (*fem.* **éprise**) In love, taken with. *Il en est épris*, he is smitten with her.
éprouvé [epru′ve], *a.* (*fem.* -ée) Tried, tested; well-tried (treatment etc.); sorely tried (soldiers etc.); stricken with misfortune (of a family, country, etc.); impaired (health).

éprouver, *v.t.* To try, to test; to put to the proof; (*fig.*) to feel, to experience, to meet with. *Éprouver des malheurs*, to meet with misfortunes; *éprouver un canon*, to test a cannon; *éprouver une douleur*, to feel a pain. **éprouvette**, *n.f.* Gauge; steam-gauge; test-tube; eprouvette (for testing gunpowder); (*Surg.*) probe.

épucer [epu'se], *v.t.* To clear of fleas.

épuisable [epɥi'zabl], *a.* Exhaustible. **épuisant**, *a.* (*fem.* **-ante**) Exhausting, trying.

épuisement [epɥiz'mã], *n.m.* Exhaustion, draining, draining off; impoverishment, diminution, enervation. *L'épuisement des finances*, the low state of the finances; *tuyau d'épuisement*, exhaust-pipe. **épuiser**, *v.t.* To exhaust, to drain; to use up, to consume; to tire out, to wear out, to wear threadbare. *Énergie épuisée*, spent energy; *épuiser un sujet*, to exhaust a subject; *l'édition est épuisée*, the book is out of print; *terre épuisée*, exhausted ground. **s'épuiser**, *v.r.* To be exhausted, to be worn out; to exhaust oneself, to use up one's strength etc.; to be sold out, to run out of print.

épuisette [epɥi'zɛt], *n.f.* Landing-net; scoop.

épuise-volante [epɥizvɔ'lãt], *n.f.* (*pl.* **épuises-volantes**) Wind-pump.

épurateur [epyra'tœːr], *a.* (*fem.* **-trice**) Purifying.—*n.m.* Purifier. **épuratif**, *a.* (*fem.* **-ive**) Purifying, refining. **épuration**, *n.f.* Purification, purifying, refining, refinement; (*Polit.*) purge. *Épuration du sang*, purifying of the blood. **épuratoire**, *a.* Purifying.

épure [e'pyːr], *n.f.* Draught, working-drawing (of a building etc.).

épurement [epyr'mã], *n.m.* Purifying. *Épurement d'un texte*, expurgation of a text. **épurer**, *v.t.* To purify; to clear, to clarify; to refine, to purge. *Épurer de l'eau bourbeuse*, to clear muddy water; *épurer de l'or*, to refine gold. **s'épurer**, *v.r.* To be purified, to become pure; to grow more refined (of style, language, etc.).

épurge [e'pyrʒ], *n.f.* (*Bot.*) Spurge. *Euphorbia lathyris*.

équanime [ekwa'nim], *a.* Equanimous. **équanimité**, *n.f.* Equanimity.

équarrir [eka'riːr], *v.t.* To square; to cut up a carcass (esp. of horses). **équarrissage**, *n.m.* Squaring; squareness; flaying and cutting up (of horses etc.). *Bois d'équarrissage*, squared timber; *dix pouces d'équarrissage*, ten inches square. **équarrissement**, *n.m.* Squaring. **équarrisseur**, *n.m.* One who squares wood etc.; knacker. **équarrissoir**, *n.m.* Knacker's knife, knacker's yard.

équateur [ekwa'tœːr], *n.m.* Equator.

équation [ekwɑ'sjɔ̃], *n.f.* Equation. *Équation du premier degré*, simple equation; *équation du second degré*, quadratic equation; *poser une équation*, to state an equation; *résoudre une équation*, to solve an equation; *inconnues d'une équation*, unknown quantities of an equation.

équatorial [ekwatɔ'rjal], *a.* (*fem.* **-iale**, *pl.* **-iaux**) Equatorial.—*n.m.* Equatorial (telescope). **équatorialement**, *adv.* Equatorially.

équerre [e'kɛːr], *n.f.* Square, set-square, square rule, knee-piece. *À fausse équerre*, out of square, on the bevel; *courbe à équerre*, (*Naut.*) square knee; *dresser à l'équerre*, to square; *équerre de fer*, iron knee; angle-iron;

être d'équerre, to be at right angles, to be square; *mettre d'équerre*, to true.

équerrer [ekɛ're], *v.t.* To square, to bevel.

équestre [e'kɛstr], *a.* Equestrian.

équiangle [ekɥi'ãːgl], *a.* Equiangular.

équidés [ekɥi'de], *n.m. pl.* Equidae.

équidistant [ekɥidis'tã], *a.* (*fem.* **-ante**) Equidistant.

équilatéral [ekɥilate'ral], *a.* (*fem.* **-ale**, *pl.* **-aux**) Equilateral.

équilibrage [ekili'braːʒ], *n.m.* Counter-balancing.

équilibration [ekilibrɑ'sjɔ̃], *n.f.* Equilibration.

équilibre [eki'libr], *n.m.* Equilibrium, equipoise, poise, balance; (*Hist.*) balance of power. *Faire l'équilibre*, to make things equal; *mettre en équilibre*, to balance; *mettre le budget en équilibre*, to balance the budget; *perdre l'équilibre*, to lose one's balance. **équilibrer**, *v.t.* To equilibrate, to balance, to put in equilibrium. **s'équilibrer**, *v.r.* To be in equilibrium, to balance (of things). **équilibriste**, *n.* Tight-rope walker, acrobat.

équille [e'kiːj], *n.f.* (*Norm. dial.*) Sand-eel.

équin [e'kɛ̃], *a.* (*fem.* **équine**) Equine. *Pied équin*, club foot.

équinoxe [eki'nɔks], *n.m.* Equinox. *Vents d'équinoxe*, equinoctial gales. **équinoxial**, *a.* (*fem.* **-iale**, *pl.* **-iaux**) Equinoctial.

équinter [ekɛ̃'te], *v.t.* To cut (a strap etc.) to a point.

équipage [eki'paːʒ], *n.m.* Equipage, suite; carriage; turn-out, garb, dress; gear, tackle, implements; plight; (*Mil.*) equipment, accoutrements; (*Naut., Av.*) personnel, crew. *Avoir équipage*, to keep one's carriage; *le train des équipages*, the Army Service Corps; *maître d'équipage*, (*Naut.*) boatswain.

équipe [e'kip], *n.f.* Train of boats; set, gang (of workmen etc.); team (of sportsmen), crew (of rowing-boat). *Chef d'équipe*, foreman; *homme d'équipe*, railway workman; (*Cine.*) *équipe de tournage*, film unit.

équipée [eki'pe], *n.f.* Prank, escapade.

équipement [ekip'mã], *n.m.* Outfit, fitting out; equipment; (*Mil.*) *Grand équipement*, accoutrements; *petit équipement*, kit. **équiper**, *v.t.* To equip, to fit out; to furnish, to man. *Équiper une flotte*, to fit out a fleet. **s'équiper**, *v.r.* To fit oneself out; to rig oneself out.

équipier [eki'pje], *n.m.* (*fem.* **-ière**) Any member of an *équipe*.

*****équipollé** [ekipɔ'le], *a.* (*Her.*) Having equal squares (on a shield etc.).

équipollence [ekipɔ'lãːs], *n.f.* Equipollence. **équipollent**, *a.* (*fem.* **-ente**) Equipollent. *****équipoller**, *v.t.* To be equivalent to, to balance.

équipotentiel [ekipɔ'tɑ̃'sjɛl], *a.* (*fem.* **-ielle**) Equipotential.

équisetum [ekise'tɔm], *n.m.* (*Bot.*) Equisetum, horsetail.

équitable [eki'tabl], *a.* Equitable, just, fair. **équitablement**, *adv.* Equitably, justly, fairly. **équitation** [ekitɑ'sjɔ̃], *n.f.* Horsemanship, riding.

équité [eki'te], *n.f.* Equity, fairness.

équivalence [ekiva'lãːs], *n.f.* Equivalence. **équivalent**, *a.* (*fem.* **-ente**) Equivalent; tantamount (to).—*n.m.* Equivalent. **équivaloir**, *v.i. irr.* (*p.p.* **équivalu**; *conjug. like* VALOIR) To be equivalent, to be tantamount (*à*).

équivoque [eki'vɔk], *a.* Equivocal; ambiguous; doubtful, uncertain.—*n.f.* Equivocation, ambiguity; evasion, shuffling. *User d'équivoques,* to equivocate. **équivoquer,** *v.i.* To equivocate, to speak ambiguously, to quibble. **s'équivoquer,** *v.r.* To make a slip, to be mistaken.

érable [e'rabl], *n.m.* Maple, maple-tree. *Érable à sucre,* sugar-maple; *sucre d'érable,* maple-sugar; *(C) eau d'érable,* maple sap; *sirop d'érable,* maple syrup.

(C) érablière [era'bljɛ:r], *n.f.* A forest of maple trees; a factory producing maple syrup and sugar.

éradication [eradika'sjɔ̃], *n.f.* Eradication.

érafler [era'fle], *v.t.* To scratch slightly, to graze. **éraflure,** *n.f.* Slight scratch, graze.

éraillé [erɑ'je], *a.* (*fem.* -ée) Frayed, wrinkled; bloodshot (of the eyes); unravelled (of stuff); raucous, hoarse, husky (of the voice). **éraillement,** *n.m.* Eversion of the eyelids, ectropion; unravelling, unweaving; huskiness, hoarseness.

érailler [erɑ'je], *v.t.* To unravel, to fret (of a rope); to fray, to chafe, to scratch. **s'érailler,** *v.r.* To fray; to chafe; to become bloodshot (of the eyes); to become husky or hoarse (of the voice). *La gaze est sujette à s'érailler,* gauze is apt to fray. **éraillure,** *n.f.* Fret, fraying; scratch.

ère [ɛ:r], *n.f.* Era, epoch. *L'an 940 de notre ère,* in A.D. 940.

érecteur [erɛk'tœ:r], *a.* (*fem.* -trice) (*Anat.*) Erector (of the muscles). **érectile,** *a.* Erectile.

érection [erɛk'sjɔ̃], *n.f.* Erection, erecting; establishment, institution, setting up.

éreintant [erɛ̃'tɑ̃], *a.* (*fem.* -ante) (*fam.*) Very tiring. *Travail éreintant,* exhausting work. **éreinté,** *a.* (*fem.* -ée) Dead beat. **éreintement** or **éreintage,** *n.m.* Breaking the back; thrashing, slating; exhaustion; (*fig.*) slating (in a paper). **éreinter,** *v.t.* To break the back (of); to tire out, to knock up, to do up; to beat unmercifully; (*fig.*) to slate, to cut to pieces, to lash (satire etc.). **s'éreinter,** *v.r.* To break one's back, to tire oneself out, to drudge, to toil and moil. **éreinteur,** *n.m.* (*fem.* -euse) (*colloq.*) A savage critic.

érémitique [eremi'tik], *a.* Eremitic.

érésipèle [ERYSIPÈLE].

éréthisme [ere'tism], *n.m.* Erethism.

erg [ɛrg], *n.m.* Erg (a measure); erg, sand-hill (in the Sahara).

ergastule [ɛrgas'tyl], *n.f.* (*Rom. Ant.*) Slaves' prison.

ergo [ɛr'go], *conj.* Ergo, then, therefore.

ergot [ɛr'go], *n.m.* Spur (of certain birds etc.); ergot (of rye); stub (on fruit-tree); catch, stop (of machine); dew-claw (of mammals). *Ergot de coq,* cock's spur; *être sur ses ergots,* to be stand-offish; *monter* or *se dresser sur ses ergots,* to ride the high horse. **ergotage, ergotement,** *n.m.,* or **ergoterie,** *n.f.* Cavilling, quibbling, quibble. **ergoté,** *a.* (*fem.* -ée) Spurred, having a dew-claw (of a dog); attacked with ergot. *Seigle ergoté,* spurred rye; *un coq bien ergoté,* a well-spurred cock. **ergoter,** *v.i.* (*colloq.*) To cavil, to wrangle. *Il ergote sur tout,* he finds fault with everything. **ergoteur,** *n.m.* (*fem.* -euse) Cavilling.

—n. Caviller, quibbler. **ergotine,** *n.f.* Ergotine. **ergotisme,** *n.m.* **Cavilling, quibble; (*Path.*) ergotism.

éricacées [erika'se], *n.f. pl.* Ericaceous plants.

ériger [eri'ʒe], *v.t.* To erect, to raise, to rear; to set up, to institute; to exalt. **s'ériger,** *v.r.* To set up for, to pose (*en*); to be erected, raised or built. *S'ériger en censeur public,* to set up as a public censor.

érigéron [eriʒe'rɔ̃], *n.m.* (*Bot.*) Erigeron, flea-bane.

érigne [e'riɲ] or **érine,** *n.f.* (*Surg.*) Attollent, levator.

éristique [eris'tik], *a.* Eristic.

erminette [HERMINETTE].

ermitage [ɛrmi'ta:ʒ], *n.m.* Hermitage. **ermite,** *n.m.* Hermit, recluse.

éroder [ero'de], *v.t.* To erode.

érosif, *a.* (*fem.* -ive) Erosive.

érosion, *n.f.* Erosion.

érotique [erɔ'tik], *a.* Erotic. **érotisme,** *n.m.* Eroticism. **érotomanie,** *n.f.* Erotomania, nymphomania.

erpétologie or **herpétologie** [ɛrpetɔlɔ'ʒi], *n.f.* Herpetology (science of reptiles). **erpétologique,** *a.* Herpetologic. **erpétologiste,** *n.m.* Herpetologist.

errant [ɛ'rɑ̃], *a.* (*fem.* -ante) Wandering, roving, errant, rambling, vagrant; erring (person). *Chevalier errant,* knight-errant; *le Juif errant,* the Wandering Jew.—*n.m.* Lost sheep.

errata [ɛra'ta], *n.m. inv.* List of errata.

erratique [ɛra'tik], *a.* Erratic.

erratum [ɛra'tom], *n.m.* (*pl.* **errata**) Erratum.

erre [ɛ:r], *n.f.* Course, way; (head) way (of a ship); (*pl.*) track (of a stag etc.). *Aller à grande erre,* to go very fast; *marcher sur les erres de quelqu'un,* to tread in someone's footsteps.

errements [ɛr'mɑ̃], *n.m.* (*used only in pl.*) Manner, way; vagaries, follies. *Revenir à ses anciens errements,* to relapse into one's bad old ways.

errer [ɛ're], *v.i.* To wander, to stray; to range, to rove, to roam, to ramble; to err, to mistake, to go astray. *Aller errant,* to wander up and down; *errer çà et là,* to ramble, to stroll up and down, to wander to and fro; *errer partout,* to ramble about.

erreur [ɛ'rœ:r], *n.f.* Error, mistake, blunder; fallacy, delusion. *Erreurs de jeunesse,* mistakes of youth; *erreur n'est pas compte,* misreckoning is no payment; *sauf erreur,* errors excepted, unless I am mistaken; *tirer quelqu'un de son erreur,* to convince someone of his error; *tomber dans l'erreur,* to fall into error.

erroné [ɛrɔ'ne], *a.* (*fem.* -ée) Erroneous, mistaken, false. **erronément,** *adv.* Erroneously.

ers [ɛ:r], *n.m.* Genus of leguminous plants comprising the vetches, lentils, etc.

ersatz [ɛr'zats], *n.m. inv.* A (bad) substitute.

erse [ɛrs], *a.* and *n.* Erse (Gaelic, Irish, Scottish).—*n.f.* (*Naut.*) Strop; selvagee.

erseau [ɛr'so], *n.m.* (*Naut.*) Grummet.

érubescence [erybe'sã:s], *n.f.* Erubescence. **érubescent,** *a.* Erubescent, reddening.

éructation [erykta'sjɔ̃], *n.f.* Eructation, belching. **éructer,** *v.t.* To eructate, to belch.

érudit [ery'di], *a.* (*fem.* **érudite**) Erudite, learned.—*n.* Scholar, learned person. **érudition,** *n.f.* Erudition, scholarship.

érugineux [eryʒi'nø], *a.* (*fem.* **-euse**) The colour of verdigris.

éruptif [eryp'tif], *a.* (*fem.* **-ive**) Eruptive. **éruption,** *n.f.* Eruption; (*Med.*) cutting (of teeth); breaking out (of a rash). *Faire éruption,* to erupt.

éryngium [erɛ̃'ʒjɔm], *n.m.*, or **érynge,** *n.f.* (*Bot.*) Eryngium.

érysipélateux [erizipela'tø] or **érésipélateux,** *a.* (*fem.* **-euse**) Erysipelatous. **érysipèle** or **érésipèle,** *n.m.* Erysipelas.

érythème [eri'tɛm], *n.m.* Erythema.

ès [ɛs], (*contraction of* EN (1) LES) In, of. *Saint-Pierre-ès-Liens,* Saint Peter in bonds; *bachelier ès lettres,* bachelor of arts.

esbaudir [ÉBAUDIR].

esbigner (s') [ɛsbi'ɲe], *v.r.* (*pop.*) To make off, to bolt.

esbroufe [ɛz'bruf], *n.f.* (*pop.*) Swank. *Vol à l'esbroufe,* hustling (robbery). **esbroufer,** *v.t.* To impress by swank.

esbroufeur, *n.m.* (*fem.* **-euse**). Braggart; hustler (thief).

escabeau [ɛska'bo], *n.m.* (*pl.* **-eaux**) Stool; step-ladder. **escabelle,** *n.f.* Three-legged stool.

escache [ɛs'kaʃ], *n.f.* Oval bit (for horses).

escadre [ɛs'kadr], *n.f.* (*Naut.*) Squadron; (*Av.*) wing. *Chef d'escadre,* commodore. **escadrille,** *n.f.* Small squadron, flotilla. *Escadrille d'avions,* air squadron, (*by ext.*) a flight of planes.

escadron [ɛska'drɔ̃], *n.m.* Squadron (of horse). *Chef d'escadron,* cavalry major.

escalade [ɛska'lad], *n.f.* Scaling (a wall), escalade. **escalader,** *v.t.* To scale, to climb over.

escale [ɛs'kal], *n.f.* Port of call. *Faire escale à dans un port,* to put into a port, to touch, to call at a port; *vol sans escale,* non-stop flight; *terrain d'escale,* stopping-place.

escalier [ɛska'lje], *n.m.* Staircase, stairs, flight of stairs, steps. *Escalier de commandement,* (*Naut.*) accommodation ladder; *faire des escaliers dans les cheveux de quelqu'un,* to cut someone's hair in a slovenly fashion; *escalier dérobé,* hidden or secret staircase; *escalier roulant,* escalator; *escalier de dégagement,* back stairs; *avoir l'esprit de l'escalier,* to think of the good retort when it is too late.

escalope [ɛska'lɔp], *n.f.* Collop (of veal); steak (of fish).

escamotable [ɛskamɔ'tabl], *a.* Which can be tucked away. (*Av.*) *Train escamotable,* retractable landing-gear.

escamotage [ɛskamɔ'taːʒ], *n.m.* Juggling, sleight of hand, legerdemain; (*fig.*) pinching, filching. **escamote,** *n.f.* Juggler's cork ball. **escamoter,** *v.t.* To juggle away; to pilfer, to make away with; (*Av.*) to retract (the undercarriage). *On lui a escamoté sa bourse,* they relieved him of his purse. **escamoteur,** *n.m.* (*fem.* **-euse**) Juggler, conjurer; fleecer, pilferer, pickpocket.

escampette [ɛskɑ̃'pɛt], *n.f.* (*Used only in*) *Il a pris la poudre d'escampette,* he has bolted.

escapade [ɛska'pad], *n.f.* Escapade, prank, lark. *Faire une escapade,* to have a lark.

escape [ɛs'kap], *n.f.* (*Arch.*) Scape (spring or shaft of a column).

escarbille [ɛskar'biːj], *n.f.* Cinder (of coal); glowing cinder (from a steam train).

escarbot [ɛskar'bo], *n.m.* (*Ent.*) Hister; (*dial.*) dung-beetle; may-bug. *Escarbot doré,* rose chafer.

escarboucle [ɛskar'bukl], *n.f.* Carbuncle (precious stone).

escarcelle [ɛskar'sɛl], *n.f.* (*Mediev. Ant.*) Purse, money-bag (hanging from the belt).

escargot [ɛskar'go], *n.m.* Snail (esp. edible); corkscrew stairs. **escargotière,** *n.f.* Snail-farm.

escarmouche [ɛskar'muʃ], *n.f.* Skirmish; brush; (*fig.*) cavilling, bickering. *Aller à l'escarmouche,* to go out skirmishing. **escarmoucher,** *v.i.* To skirmish; (*fig.*) to cavil, to bicker. **escarmoucheur,** *n.m.* Skirmisher.

escarole [ɛska'rɔl], *n.f.* Endive.

escarpe (1) [ɛs'karp], *n.f.* Scarp, escarp.

escarpe (2) [ɛs'karp], *n.m.* (*slang*) Ruffian, murderous thief.

escarpé [ɛskar'pe], *a.* (*fem.* **-ée**) Scarped, steep, precipitous; (*fig.*) difficult. **escarpement,** *n.m.* Escarpment; steep face or slope.

escarper [ɛskar'pe], *v.t.* To cut (a hill-side etc.) steep; (*Fort.*) to escarp, to counterscarp.

escarpin [ɛskar'pɛ̃], *n.m.* Pump, dancing-shoe.

escarpolette [ɛskarpɔ'lɛt], *n.f.* Swing.

escarre (1) or **esquarre** [ɛs'kaːr], *n.f.* (*Her.*) Compartment of a shield formed by a square enclosing one of the corners.

escarre (2) [ɛs'kaːr] or **eschare,** *n.f.* Scab. **escarrifier** or **escharifier,** *v.t.* To produce a scab.

eschatologie [ɛskatɔlɔ'ʒi], *n.f.* Eschatology. **eschatologique,** *a.* Eschatological.

escient [ɛ'sjɑ̃], *n.m.* (*Used only in*) *À bon escient,* in good earnest, wittingly, knowingly; *à son escient,* to his knowledge.

esclaffer (s') [ɛskla'fe], *v.r.* To laugh noisily, to guffaw.

esclandre [ɛs'klɑ̃ːdr], *n.m.* Scandal, exposure, scene. *Faire de l'esclandre,* to make a scene.

esclavage [ɛskla'vaːʒ], *n.m.* Slavery; bondage, thraldom, subjection. **esclavagiste,** *n.* Supporter of slavery.

esclave [ɛs'klaːv], *n.* Slave, bondman, thrall; drudge. *On est esclave dans cette maison,* one is a regular drudge in that house; *marchand d'esclaves,* slave-trader.—*a.* Slavish. *Être esclave de sa parole,* to stick to one's promise.

escobar [ɛskɔ'baːr], *n.m.* Equivocator, shuffler. **escobarder,** *v.i.* To equivocate, to shuffle. **escobarderie,** *n.f.* Equivocation, shuffling.

escoffier [ɛskɔ'fje], *v.t.* (*slang*) To kill, to murder.

escogriffe [ɛskɔ'grif], *n.m.* (*colloq.*) Tall, lanky, ungainly fellow.

escomptable [ɛskɔ̃'tabl], *a.* Discountable.

escompte [ɛs'kɔ̃ːt], *n.m.* Discount, rebate. *À escompte,* at a discount; *faire l'escompte,* to discount bills; *le taux d'escompte,* the Bank Rate. **escompter,** *v.t.* To discount, to pay cash before date; (*fig.*) to anticipate, to forestall. *Escompter un billet* or *un effet,* to cash a bill. **escompteur,** *n.m.* Discounter.

*****escopette** [ɛskɔ'pɛt], *n.f.* Blunderbuss.

escorte [ɛs'kɔrt], *n.f.* Escort; (*Navy*) convoy; (*fig.*) retinue, train, attendants. *Vaisseau d'escorte*, convoy-ship. **escorter**, *v.t.* To escort; (*fig.*) to accompany, to attend. *Faire escorter*, to send an escort with. **escorteur**, *n.m.* Escort ship.

escot [ɛs'ko], *n.m.* Kind of dark serge (worn chiefly by nuns).

escouade [ɛs'kwad], *n.f.* Squad, small party (of soldiers); gang (of workmen).

escourgeon [ɛskur'ʒɔ̃] or **écourgeon**, *n.m.* Winter-barley.

escrime [ɛs'krim], *n.f.* Fencing. *Salle d'escrime*, fencing-school; *escrime à la baïonnette*, bayonet drill. **escrimer**, *v.i.* To fence; (*fig.*) to have a trial of skill etc. **s'escrimer**, *v.r.* (*colloq.*) To strive; to try. *Il s'escrime toujours, mais rien n'y fait*, he keeps on pegging away but nothing comes of it. **escrimeur**, *n.m.* Fencer.

escroc [ɛs'kro], *n.m.* Sharper, swindler, cheat. **escroquer**, *v.t.* To swindle out of, to get hold of by cheating; to swindle, to cheat. **escroquerie**, *n.f.* Swindling.

esculape [ɛsky'lap], *n.m.* A (clever) physician.

esculent [ɛsky'lɑ̃], *a.* (*fem.* **-ente**) Edible, eatable, esculent.

ésopique [ezɔ'pik], *a.* Aesopic.

ésotérique [ezɔte'rik], *a.* Esoteric. **ésotérisme**, *n.m.* Esoterism.

espace [ɛs'paːs], *n.m.* Space, room; duration, time; (*Mus.*) interval. *Court espace de temps*, short space of time.—*n.f.* (*Print.*) Space. **espacé**, *a.* (*fem.* **-ée**) Far apart. **espacement**, *n.m.* Interval; (*Print.*) spacing. **espacer**, *v.t.* To leave a space between; to separate, to place apart; (*Print.*) to space. **s'espacer**, *v.r.* To become less frequent or numerous.

espadon [ɛspa'dɔ̃], *n.m.* Two-handed sword; swordfish.

espadrille [ɛspa'driːj], *n.f.* Canvas shoe with cord soles.

Espagne [ɛs'paɲ], *f.* Spain.

espagnol [ɛspa'ɲɔl], *a.* (*fem.* **espagnole**) Spanish.—*n.m.* The Spanish language.—*n.m.* (**Espagnol**, *fem.* **Espagnole**) Spaniard.

espagnolette [ɛspaɲɔ'lɛt], *n.f.* Bolt of French window.

espalier [ɛspa'lje], *n.m.* Espalier (tree or wall).

espalmer [ɛspal'me], *v.t.* To grave, to tallow (the bottom of a boat with the palm).

espar [ɛs'paːr], **espart**, or **épart**, *n.m.* (*Naut.*) Spar; (*Mil.*) lever (for big guns).

esparcet [ɛspar'sɛ], **éparcet**, *n.m.*, **esparcette** or **éparcette**, *n.f.* (*Bot.*) Sainfoin.

espèce [ɛs'pɛs], *n.f.* Species; kind, sort, nature; (*Law*) question at issue, case in point; (*pl.*) specie, ready money, hard cash; (*Theol.*) elements. *Espèces sonnantes*, hard cash, cash down; *l'espèce humaine*, mankind; *payer en espèces*, to pay in cash; (*fam.*) *espèce de* (before a noun), *espèce d'idiot*, you silly fool. (*Relig.*) *Communion sous les deux espèces*, communion in both kinds.

espérance [ɛspe'rɑ̃ːs], *n.f.* Hope, trust, expectation. *Répondre à ses espérances*, to answer one's expectations; *se nourrir d'espérance* or *vivre d'espérance*, to live on hope. (*pl.*) *Des espérances*, hopes (of a legacy etc.).

espérantiste [ɛsperɑ̃'tist], *a.* Esperanto.—*n.* Esperantist. **espéranto**, *n.m.* Esperanto.

espérer [ɛspe'rе], *v.t.* To hope, to hope for; to expect; to trust; (*dial.*) to wait for. *Je n'espère plus rien*, I have no further hope.—*v.i.* To hope, to be hopeful; to put one's trust in.

esperluète [ɛspɛrly'ɛt], *n.f.* (*Print.*) Ampersand.

espiègle [ɛs'pjɛgl], *a.* Mischievous, arch, roguish.—*n.* Such a person. **espièglerie**, *n.f.* Frolic, roguish trick, prank.

*espingole [ɛspɛ̃'gɔl], *n.f.* Blunderbuss.

espion [ɛs'pjɔ̃], *n.m.* (*fem.* **espionne**) Spy; window-mirror. **espionnage**, *n.m.* Espionage, spying. **espionner**, *v.t.* To spy, to pry into.

esplanade [ɛspla'nad], *n.f.* Esplanade, parade.

espoir [ɛs'pwaːr], *n.m.* Hope. *Avoir l'espoir de*, to be in hopes of; *mettre son espoir dans*, to set one's hopes on; *sans espoir*, hopeless.

esponton [ɛspɔ̃'tɔ̃], *n.m.* *Spontoon, halfpike; (*Naut.*) boarding-pike.

esprit [ɛs'pri], *n.m.* Spirit, ghost; soul, vital breath, vital principle; mind, sense, understanding, intellect; wit; fancy; humour, disposition, temper, character; meaning; spirits, spirituous liquor; (*Gr. Gram.*) breathing, aspirate. *Avoir de l'esprit*, to be intelligent, to be witty; *avoir l'esprit bien fait*, to be good-tempered; *avoir l'esprit de l'escalier*, to think of a witty retort too late; *avoir l'esprit sain*, to be of sound mind; *croire aux esprits*, to believe in ghosts; *cultiver l'esprit*, to cultivate the mind; *esprits animaux*, animal spirits; *esprit borné*, narrow intellect; *esprit de corps*, devotion to one's society, fraternity, etc., team-spirit, fellow-feeling; *esprit de parti*, party spirit; *esprit dérangé*, disordered mind; *esprit de sel*, spirits of salt; *esprit de suite*, consistency; *esprit d'ordre*, orderliness, management; *esprit follet*, goblin; *esprit malin*, evil spirit, fiend; *faire de l'esprit*, to play the wit; *faire revenir l'esprit à quelqu'un*, to bring someone to his or her senses; *Saint-Esprit* [SAINT]; *les grands esprits se rencontrent*, great minds think alike; *l'esprit de la loi*, the spirit (as opposed to the letter) of the law; *ne pas avoir l'esprit tranquille*, to be uneasy in one's mind; *où avait-il l'esprit?* where were his wits? what was he thinking of? *perdre l'esprit*, to go mad; *présence d'esprit*, presence of mind; *rendre l'esprit*, to give up the ghost; *reprendre ses esprits*, to recover one's senses, to come to; *s'alambiquer l'esprit*, to puzzle one's brains; *tour d'esprit*, turn of mind, bent, disposition; *un bel esprit*, a wit; *un esprit fort*, a free-thinker; *un homme à l'esprit étroit*, a narrow-minded man; *un homme d'esprit*, an amusing, witty man, a wit; *un ouvrage d'esprit*, a work of talent; *venir à l'esprit*, to come into one's mind, to occur to one; *vous n'avez pas saisi l'esprit de cet auteur*, you have not understood the meaning of that author.

esquif [ɛs'kif], *n.m.* (Any) small boat.

esquille [ɛs'kiːj], *n.f.* Splinter (of a bone). **esquilleux**, *a.* (*fem.* **-euse**) Splintering.

esquimau [ɛski'mo], *n.m.* (*pl.* **-aux**) (*fam.*) Choc-ice; child's rompers. **esquimau**, *a.* and *n.* Eskimo.

esquinancie [ɛskinɑ̃'si], *n.f.* Quinsy. (*Bot.*) *Herbe à l'esquinancie*, squinancy wort.

esquine (1) [ɛs'kin], *n.f.* Horse's loins; (*Bot.*) China-root. *Un cheval fort d'esquine*, a horse strong in the loins. **esquine** (2) [SQUINE].

esquintant [ɛskɛ̃'tɑ̃], *a.* (*fem.* **-ante**) (*fam.*) Fagging (work). **esquinter**, *v.t.* (*slang*) To tire out; to smash; to spoil. *Esquinter une auto*, to flog a car.

esquisse [ɛs'kis], *n.f.* Sketch, outline, rough draft or plan. *Cahier d'esquisses*, sketch-book; *l'esquisse d'un poème*, the sketch of a poem. **esquisser**, *v.t.* To sketch, to outline.

esquive [ɛs'kiv], *n.f.* (*spt.*) Dodging. (*Box.*) *Esquive de la tête*, duck. **esquivement**, *n.m.* Avoiding, evading. **esquiver**, *v.t.* To avoid, to elude; to duck; to dodge, to slip aside. **s'esquiver**, *v.r.* To escape, to steal away, to give the slip, to make off.

essai [ɛ'sɛ], *n.m.* Trial; attempt, endeavour; experiment, testing, assaying; sample; (*Rugby*) try; (*Lit.*) essay. *Essai sur la peinture*, essay on painting; *faire l'essai de*, to make a trial of; *faire l'essai de l'or*, to assay gold (see also *banc*); *faire son coup d'essai*, to make one's first attempt; *faites-en l'essai*, try it; *pilote d'essai*, test pilot; *prendre à l'essai*, to take on trial; *marquer deux essais dont un transformé*, to score two tries, one of them converted; *tube à essai*, (*Chem.*) test-tube.

essaim [ɛ'sɛ̃], *n.m.* Swarm; (*fig.*) crowd, host, multitude. **essaimage**, *n.m.* Swarming; swarming-time; hiving off. **essaimer**, *v.i.* To swarm; to hive off.

essanger [ɛsɑ̃'ʒe], *v.t.* To soak (dirty linen etc.).

essarder [ɛsar'de], *v.t.* (*Naut.*) To swab.

essart [ɛ'sa:r] *n.m.* Land that has been cleared.

essartement [ɛsartə'mɑ̃] or **essartage**, *n.m.* Grubbing, clearing (of lands). **essarter**, *v.t.* To clear, to grub.

essaver [ɛsa've], *v.t.* To scoop out (a brook, a ditch, etc.).

essayage [ɛsɛ'ja:ʒ], *n.m.* Trying, proving, testing; trying-on (of clothes). **essayer**, *v.t.* (*conjugated like* BALAYER) To try; to try on; to essay, to attempt, to make a trial of; to assay. *Essayer de l'or*, to assay gold; *essayer une chose*, to try a thing.—*v.i.* To try, to make an attempt, to make a trial (*de*). *Essayer de marcher*, to try to walk; *essayez de le persuader*, try to persuade him. **s'essayer**, *v.r.* To try one's strength or skill, to try one's hand. *Il s'est essayé à peindre*, he has tried his hand at painting. **essayeur**, *n.m.* (*fem.* **-euse**) Assayer; (*cloth*) fitter. **essayiste**, *n.* Essayist.

esse [ɛs], *n.f.* S-shaped object; linch-pin (of the axle-tree of a coach); forelock (of a gun-carriage); S-shaped hole in a violin.

*****esséminer** [ɛsemi'ne], *v.t.* To disperse, to scatter, to disseminate.

essence [ɛ'sɑ̃s], *n.f.* Essence; species (of trees etc.); main point, pith; petrol; (*Am.*) gasoline, gas; attar (of roses). *Par essence*, by its very nature, essentially. *Essence de térébenthine*, oil of turpentine; *poste d'essence*, petrol-pump, filling station.

essénien [ɛse'njɛ̃], *n.m.* Essene. **essénisme**, *n.m.* Essenism.

essente [ɛ'sɑ̃t] or **écente** [e'sɑ̃t], *n.f.* (Roof) shingle; **essenter**, *v.t.* To cover (and protect) a wall with shingle-boards or tiles, or slates.

essentiel [ɛsɑ̃'sjɛl], *a.* (*fem.* **-ielle**) Essential, material.—*n.m.* Essential, essential or main point. *C'est là l'essentiel*, that is the main point. **essentiellement**, *adv.* Essentially, absolutely, above all.

esseret [ɛse'rɛ], *n.m.* Carpenter's long auger.

esseulé [ɛsœ'le], *a.* (*fem.* **-ée**) (*poet.*) Solitary, abandoned. **esseulement**, *n.m.* Solitude.

essieu [ɛ'sjø], *n.m.* (*pl.* **-eux**) Axle-tree; spindle; pin (of a block). *Boîte d'essieu*, axle-box; *écartement des essieux*, wheel base (motor); *essieu moteur*, driving-shaft.

essor [ɛ'sɔ:r], *n.m.* Flight, soaring, soar; (*fig.*) progress, impulse, impetus, life, vigour. *Donner l'essor à*, to give wings to, to give scope to; *l'essor du génie*, the soaring of genius; *prendre son essor*, to take one's flight.

essorage [ɛsɔ'ra:ʒ], *n.m.* Wringing or hanging out of clothes to dry. **essorer**, *v.t.* To hang in the air in order to dry, to wring out (washing). **essoreuse**, *n.f.* Drying-machine, mangle.

essorant, *a.* (*fem.* **-ante**) (*Her.*) Soarant.

essoriller [ɛsɔri'je], *v.t.* To cut the ears (of a dog etc.); to crop the hair of.

essouchement [ɛsuʃ'mɑ̃], *n.m.* Grubbing up (of vines, stumps, etc.). **essoucher**, *v.t.* To grub up.

essoufflement [ɛsuflə'mɑ̃], *n.m.* Panting, breathlessness. **essouffler**, *v.t.* To wind (horses etc.). *Être tout essoufflé*, to be quite out of breath. **s'essouffler**, *v.r.* To be out of breath; to be winded.

essuie-glace [ɛsɥi'glas], *n.m. inv.* Windscreen wiper.

essuie-main or **essuie-mains** [ɛsɥi'mɛ̃], *n.m. inv.* Towel. **essuie-pieds**, *n.m. inv.* Doormat. **essuie-plume** or **essuie-plumes**, *n.m. inv.* Penwiper.

essuyage [ɛsɥi'ja:ʒ], *n.m.* Wiping, drying. **essuyer**, *v.t.* To wipe, to wipe off, to wipe away, to wipe dry, to wipe up; to dry; to sustain, to bear, to endure, to undergo. *Essuyer des affronts*, to endure affronts; *essuyer les larmes de quelqu'un*, to console someone; *essuyer un refus* or *un revers*, to meet with a refusal or a check; *essuyer un coup de feu*, to be shot at; *essuyer le feu (de l'ennemi)*, to come under fire; *essuyer un grain*, to weather a squall. **s'essuyer**, *v.r.* To wipe (dry) one's face, hands, etc. *S'essuyer les mains* or *la figure*, to wipe one's hands or one's face. **essuyeur**, *n.m.* (*fem.* **-euse**) Wiper.

est [ɛst], *n.m.* East. *À l'est* or *vers l'est*, to the east or the eastward; *un vent d'est*, an easterly wind.

estacade [ɛsta'kad], *n.f.* Breakwater; pier or boom made of timbers.

estafette [ɛsta'fɛt], *n.f.* Courier, express messenger; dispatch rider.

estafier [ɛsta'fje], *n.m.* (*fam.*) Tall footman, flunkey, livery servant, lanky Jack; hector, bully.

estafilade [ɛstafi'lad], *n.f.* Cut, gash (in the face etc.); slash, rent (in clothes etc.).

estagnon [ɛsta'ɲɔ̃], *n.m.* Copper or tin container used for exporting oil etc. in S. France.

estaminet [ɛstami'nɛ], *n.m.* (*North. dialect*) Coffee-house or room; tavern; small restaurant or café.

estampage [ɛstɑ̃'pa:ʒ], *n.m.* Stamping (of metal etc.); (*fam.*) fleecing (of the customers).

estampe [ɛs'tɑ̃:p], *n.f.* Print, engraving. *Magasin d'estampes*, print-shop. **estamper**, *v.t.* To stamp, to punch; (*fam.*) to fleece, to rob. **estampeur**, *n.m.* (*fem.* **-euse** (1))

Stamper; (*fam.*) swindler.—*a.* Stamping.
estampeuse (2), *n.f.* Stamping-machine.
estampillage, *n.m.* Stamping, marking.
estampille, *n.f.* Stamp, mark, trade-mark.
estampiller, *v.t.* To stamp, to mark.
estampilleuse, *n.f.* Stamping-machine (for leather etc.).
estarie [ɛstaˈri], *n.f.* (*Naut.*) Lay days.
ester [ɛsˈte], *v.t.* (*only used in infin.*) (*Law*) To appear in court, to plead.
*****esteuble** or **esteule** [ÉTEULE].
esthète [ɛsˈtɛt], *n.m.* Aesthete. **esthétique**, *a.* Aesthetic.—*n.f.* Aesthetics. **esthétiquement**, *adv.* Aesthetically. **esthétisme**, *n.m.* Aestheticism.
Esthonie [ɛstɔˈni], *f.* Estonia.
estimable [ɛstiˈmabl], *a.* Estimable; fairly good. **estimateur**, *n.m.* Appraiser, valuer. **estimatif**, *a.* (*fem.* **estimative**) Estimative. *Devis estimatif*, estimate.
estimation [ɛstimaˈsjɔ̃], *n.f.* Estimation, appraising, valuation, estimate. *Faire une estimation de*, to appraise, to estimate.
estime [ɛsˈtim], *n.f.* Esteem, regard, estimation; (*Naut.*) reckoning. *À l'estime*, by guesswork; *être perdu d'estime et de réputation*, to have lost one's reputation; *tenir en grande estime*, to have a high regard for.
estimer [ɛstiˈme], *v.t.* To estimate, to value, to rate, to assess; to esteem, to regard, to prize; to consider, to deem. *Estimer des meubles*, to value furniture; *estimer trop*, to overrate. **s'estimer**, *v.r.* To esteem oneself; to consider or deem oneself.
estivage (1) [ɛstiˈvaː3], *n.m.* Summering (of cattle) in the mountains.
estivage (2) [ɛstiˈvaː3], *n.m.* (*Naut.*) Packing or stowing (of goods).
estival [ɛstiˈval], *a.* (*fem.* **-ale**, *pl.* **-aux**) Aestival. **estivation**, *n.f.* (*Bot.*) Aestivation; torpor (of cattle etc.).
estivant [ɛstiˈvɑ̃], *n.m.* (*fem.* **-ante**) Summer visitor.
estiver (1) [ɛstiˈve], *v.i.* To summer (in the mountains, of cattle).—*v.t.* To send (cattle) to the mountains for the summer.
estiver (2) [ɛstiˈve], *v.t.* (*Naut.*) To stow, to trim, to press (cargo etc.) down.
estoc [ɛsˈtɔk], *n.m.* Point (of a sword); trunk, stock (of trees etc.). *Couper à blanc estoc*, to cut down to the root; *frapper d'estoc et de taille*, to cut and thrust; to lay about (recklessly); *parler d'estoc et de taille*, to talk at random.
estocade [ɛstɔˈkad], *n.f.* Stoccado, thrust; (*fig.*) unexpected attack.
estomac [ɛstɔˈma], *n.m.* Stomach. *Avoir l'estomac creux*, to feel empty or hungry; *avoir l'estomac dans les talons*, to be famished; *avoir de l'estomac*, to have pluck, or cheek, to be game or strong; *avoir mal à l'estomac*, to have a stomach-ache; *le creux de l'estomac*, the pit of the stomach; *soulever l'estomac*, to turn the stomach.
estomaquer [ɛstɔmaˈke], *v.t.* (*colloq.*) To take the breath away, to astound. *J'en suis estomaqué*, I'm flabbergasted.
estompage [ɛstɔ̃ˈpaː3], *n.m.* (*Drawing*) Stumping. **estompe**, *n.f.* Stump. *Dessin à l'estompe*, stump-drawing. **estomper**, *v.t.* To stump; to shade off, to blur; (*fig.*) to tone down (a narrative etc.).

estoquer [ɛstɔˈke], *v.t.* To thrust at (a bull).
estourbir [ɛsturˈbiːr], *v.t.* (*slang*) To kill, to assassinate.
estrade [ɛsˈtrad], *n.f.* *Road, highway; platform, stand, stage. *Batteurs d'estrade*, scouts; (*colloq.*) tramps; *battre l'estrade*, to scout; to be on the tramp.
estragon [ɛstraˈgɔ̃], *n.m.* (*Bot.*) Tarragon.
*****estramaçon** [ɛstramaˈsɔ̃], *n.m.* Two-edged broad sword.
estran or **estrand** [ɛsˈtrɑ̃], *n.m.* Flat seabeach, strand.
estrapade [ɛstraˈpad], *n.f.* Strappado; gibbet used for this; (*Gym.*) skinning the cat.
estrapader, *v.t.* To give the strappado to; to torture.
estrope [ɛsˈtrɔp], *n.f.* (*Naut.*) Strop. **estroper**, *v.t.* To strop.
estropié [ɛstrɔˈpje], *a.* (*fem.* **-iée**) Crippled, lame, disabled. *Être estropié d'un bras*, to have a crippled arm.—*n.* Cripple.
estropier [ɛstrɔˈpje], *v.t.* To cripple, to maim, to disable; (*fig.*) to mutilate, to distort, to mangle, to murder. *Estropier un mot*, to mispronounce a word; *estropier un rôle*, to murder a part.
estuaire [ɛsˈtɥɛːr], *n.m.* Estuary.
estudiantin [ɛstydjɑ̃ˈtɛ̃], *a.* (*fem.* **-ine**) Of students. *La jeunesse estudiantine*, the students.
esturgeon [ɛstyrˈ3ɔ̃], *n.m.* Sturgeon.
et [e], *conj.* And.—*inter.* Et mes cinquante francs? What about my fifty francs?
établage [etaˈblaːʒ], *n.m.* Putting farm animals in their shed, stabling (horses).
étable [eˈtabl], *n.f.* Shed (for oxen, sheep, goats, etc.); stall; pigsty, sty. **établer**, *v.t.* To put in a shed, to stable (horses).
établi [etaˈbli], *n.m.* Bench (joiner's, tailor's, etc.).
établir [etaˈbliːr], *v.t.* To set, to fix, to erect, to set up; to set up in business; to establish, to institute, to found; to make good, to lay down (statements), to assert; to strike (a balance); to impose (a tax); (*Naut.*) to trim (a sail). *Établir par des exemples*, to prove by examples; *établir sa fille*, to marry off one's daughter; *établir un camp*, to pitch a camp; *établir un devis*, to make out an estimate; *établir un fait*, to state a fact, to make it good. **s'établir**, *v.r.* To establish oneself, to take up one's residence; to settle down, to settle (marry); to set up in business, to set up for oneself. **établissement**, *n.m.* Establishment, establishing, foundation, setting up; fixing, placing, erecting; proving, making out, showing; imposition (of taxes); setting up in business. *Dans l'établissement*, on the premises; *frais de premier établissement*, initial expenses; *l'établissement de ses enfants*, the settlement in life of one's children; *l'établissement d'un fait*, the proving of a fact.
étage [eˈtaːʒ], *n.m.* Story, floor, flight (of stairs); (*fig.*) stage; degree, class, rank; tier; (*Geol., Mining*) layer, stratum. *De bas étage*, of low degree or low birth; *il demeure au troisième étage*, he lives on the third floor; *un immeuble de cinq étages*, a five-storied building. **étager**, *v.t.* To dispose in tiers. **s'étager**, *v.r.* To rise tier upon tier, to rise

gradually one over another. **étagère**, *n.f.* Whatnot, set of shelves.
étai [e'tɛ], *n.m.* Stay, shore, prop, strut; (*fig.*) support. *Étai d'artimon*, mizzen-stay; *étai de misaine*, fore-stay; *étai du grand mât*, main-stay.
étaiement [ÉTAYAGE].
étaim [e'tɛ̃], *n.m.* Fine carded wool.
étain [e'tɛ̃], *n.m.* Tin; pewter. *Collectionneur d'étains*, collector of pewter.
étal [e'tal], *n.m.* (*pl.* **-aux** or **-als**) Butcher's stall, butcher's shop. **étalage**, *n.m.* Laying out, exposure of goods for sale; goods exposed for sale; shop window, frontage; charge for stallage, stall tax; (*fig.*) showing off, ostentatious display, show. *Faire de l'étalage*, to show off; *faire étalage de son esprit*, to parade one's wit; *mettre à l'étalage*, to put on display; *payer l'étalage*, to pay the stall tax; *vol à l'étalage*, shop-lifting. **étalagiste**, *n.m.* Stall-keeper, window-dresser.
étale [e'tal], *a.* Still, slack, dead (of water), settled, steady (of the wind). *Mer étale*, slack water.—*n.m.* The moment when the tide is slack.
étalement [etal'mã], *n.m.* Display, parade, exposure for sale etc; staggering (of holidays).
étaler, *v.t.* To expose for sale; to put in the shop window; to spread out, to show, to display, to parade; to show off; (*Cards*) to lay down one's hand; (*Naut.*) to stem (current); to weather (gale). *Étaler l'erre*, to check the way. **s'étaler**, *v.r.* To stretch oneself out, to sprawl; to show off. *S'étaler sur l'herbe*, to stretch oneself at full length on the grass. **étalier**, *n.m.* (*fem.* **étalière**) Journeyman-butcher.
étalinguer [etalɛ̃'ge], *v.t.* To bend, to clinch (a cable) to the anchor. **étalingure**, *n.f.* Clinch, bend (of a cable) on to the anchor.
étalon (1) [eta'lɔ̃], *n.m.* Stallion. *Étalon de haras*, stud-horse; *étalon rouleur*, travelling sire.
étalon (2) [eta'lɔ̃], *n.m.* Standard (of weights and measures). *Mètre étalon*, standard (official) metre. *L'étalon d'or*, the gold standard. **étalonnage** or **étalonnement**, *n.m.* Standardization; stamping (of weights etc.); gauging. **étalonner**, *v.t.* To standardize, to calibrate, to gauge, to rate (light). *Étalonner les stations*, (*Rad.*), to log the stations. **étalonneur**, *n.m.* Gauger, inspector of weights and measures.
étamage [eta'ma:ʒ], *n.m.* Tinning; quicksilvering (of glass).
étambot [etã'bo], *n.m.* (*Naut.*) Stern-post.
étambrai [etã'brɛ], *n.m.* (*Naut.*) Partner (of a mast etc.).
étamer [eta'me], *v.t.* To tin; to quicksilver. **étameur**, *n.m.* Tinner; silverer (of mirrors). *Étameur ambulant*, tinker.
étamine (1) [eta'min], *n.f.* Thin stuff; sieve, strainer, bolting-cloth; (*Naut.*) bunting. *Il a passé par l'étamine*, he has been strictly examined; *passer par l'étamine*, to sift.
étamine (2) [eta'min], *n.f.* (*Bot.*) Stamen.
étampage [etã'pa:ʒ], *n.m.* Stamping; punching. **étampe**, *n.f.* Die; punch. **étamper**, *v.t.* To punch (horse-shoes etc.); to stamp (sheet metal etc.). **étampeur**, *n.m.* Stamper. **étampure**, *n.f.* Splay or widening of the hole (in a horse-shoe etc.).

étamure [eta'my:r], *n.f.* Tinning; material for tinning.
étance [e'tã:s], *n.f.* Roughly squared timber (for a post, stanchion, etc.).
étanche [e'tã:ʃ], *a.* Water-tight, air-tight, steam-tight, etc. **étanchéité**, *n.f.* (Water-) tightness.
étanchement [etãʃ'mã], *n.m.* Stanching, stopping; quenching; slaking. *L'étanchement du sang*, the stanching of blood.
étancher, *v.t.* To stanch, to stop; to render water-tight; (*fig.*) to slake, to quench. *Étancher la soif*, to quench the thirst; *étancher un vaisseau*, to free a ship of water.
étançon [etã'sɔ̃], *n.m.* Stay, shore; stanchion.
étançonnement, *n.m.* Propping, shoring, etc. **étançonner**, *v.t.* To prop, to underprop, to stay, to shore.
étang [e'tã], *n.m.* Pond, mere, pool.
étant, *pres.p.* [ÊTRE].
étape [e'tap], *n.f.* Halting-place, stage, station; day's march, distance between staging points; *depot, emporium. Brûler l'étape*, to pass through without stopping; *course par étapes*, (*Cycl.*) race by stages; *faire étape dans une ville*, to stop in a town.
étarque [e'tark], *a.* (*Naut.*) Hoisted home (sail). **étarquer**, *v.t.* To hoist home.
état [e'ta], *n.m.* State, case, condition; position, circumstance, plight, predicament; account, statement, return; list, register, inventory, estimate; establishment; calling, profession, station, business; (**État**) State, body politic; (**état**) estate of the realm; (*pl.*) dominions. *Affaires d'État*, State affairs; *avoir* or *tenir un grand état*, to keep a large establishment; *coup d'État*, coup d'État, sudden revolution; *de son état*, by profession, by trade; *en état de*, in a proper condition for or to; *en quelque état que soit l'affaire*, however the matter may stand; *en tout état de cause*, in any case; *état de choses*, state of things; *état de comptes*, statement of accounts; *état néant*, nil return; *états de service*, record of service; *état des lieux*, inventory of fixtures; *état des dépenses*, statement of expenses; *état nominatif*, list of names; *États Généraux*, States General; *état militaire*, military profession; *être* or *se mettre dans tous ses états*, to be very upset; *faire peu d'état de*, to have a poor opinion of; *homme d'État*, statesman; *il est en état de payer*, he is in a position to pay; *les États-Unis d'Amérique*, the United States of America; *un juge ne saurait faire état de ce témoignage*, no judge can admit this evidence; *mettre quelqu'un en état de*, to enable someone to; *mettre hors d'état de*, to put it out of someone's power to; *ministre* or *secrétaire d'État*, minister or secretary of State; *raison d'État*, State policy; *remettre en état*, to set right again; *tenir une chose en état*, to keep a thing ready; *le Tiers État*, third order in the French State (before the Revolution), i.e. the commoners; *état civil*, civil status; *archives de l'état civil*, registrar general's office. **étatique**, *a.* Under State control. **étatiser**, *v.t.* To nationalize (the key industries etc.). **étatisme** [eta'tism], *n.m.* State-socialism, State control (of industries, public services, etc.). **étatiste**, *n.m.* State-socialist.
état-major [etama'ʒɔ:r], *n.m.* (*pl.* **états-majors**)

(*Mil.*) Staff, general staff; headquarters; managerial staff (in industry etc.). *Carte d'état-major*, ordnance survey map.

étau [e'to], *n.m.* (*pl.* **étaux**) Vice. *Être pris or serré comme dans un étau*, to be caught, as it were, in a vice; *les mâchoires de l'étau*, the jaws of the vice.

étaupiner [etopi'ne], *v.t.* To clear (ground) of moles.

étayage [etɛ'jaːʒ], **étayement** [etɛj'mã] or **etaiement** [etɛ'mã], *n.m.* Staying, shoring, bearing up, propping, supporting. **étayer**, *v.t.* To stay, to shore, etc.; to support (a theory etc.).

et caetera [etsete'ra], *adv.* Et cetera.

été [e'te], *n.m.* Summer. *Au milieu or au fort de l'été*, in the middle of summer; *en été*, in summer; *être dans son été*, to be in one's prime; *heure d'été*, summer time; *le semestre d'été*, the summer months; *par un beau jour d'été*, on a fine summer's day; *se mettre en été*, to put one's summer clothes on. (*C*) *Été des Sauvages*, Indian summer.

éteignant, *pres.p.* [ÉTEINDRE].

éteigneur [etɛ'nœːr], *n.m.* (*fem.* **-euse**) Extinguisher (person). **éteignoir**, *n.m.* Extinguisher (for candles); (*fig.*) a dull person, a wet blanket.

éteindre [e'tɛ̃ːdr], *v.t. irr.* (*pres.p.* **éteignant**, *p.p.* **éteint**; *conjug. like* CRAINDRE) To put out, to switch off (electric light), to extinguish; (*fig.*) to slake, to quench; to appease; to soften (colours); to smother (a noise); to exterminate, to destroy, to obliterate; to cancel, to annul, to liquidate (a debt etc.). *Éteignez la lumière*, put out the light; *éteindre de la chaux*, to slake lime; *éteindre la soif*, to quench the thirst; *éteindre le souvenir de*, to obliterate the memory of; *éteindre une couleur*, to soften down a colour; *éteindre une obligation*, to cancel an obligation. **s'éteindre**, *v.r.* To be extinguished, to be put out or quenched; to die away, to die out; to die peacefully; to decrease, to diminish, to become extinct; to be slaked (of lime). *Cette maison va s'éteindre*, that family will soon be extinct; *le feu s'éteint*, the fire is going out. **éteint**, *a.* (*fem.* **-te**) Extinguished; extinct; (*fig.*) dull, lustreless. *Des yeux éteints*, dull eyes; *d'une voix éteinte*, in a scarcely audible voice. ***éteinte**, *n.f.* (*Law*) Extinction. *Adjudication à l'éteinte de chandelle*, adjudication closed with the extinction of a burning candle.

étendage [etã'daːʒ], *n.m.* Lines to hang things to dry upon; drying-room, drying-ground; hanging out to dry.

étendard [etã'daːr], *n.m.* Standard (of cavalry), banner, flag; (*Naut.*) great ensign. *Arborer, déployer, lever or planter un étendard*, to hoist, display, raise, or plant a standard.

étendoir [etã'dwar], *n.m.* Clothes-line; drying-room; (*Print.*) T-shaped instrument formerly used for handling wet sheets.

étendre [e'tãːdr], *v.t.* To extend, to spread out; to stretch, to expand, to distend; to stretch out, to lengthen, to prolong, to draw out, to enlarge; to lay dead, to kill on the spot, to overthrow, to throw down; to wire-draw; to lay on (colours); to dilute. *Étendre du beurre sur du pain*, to spread butter upon bread; *étendre du lait*, to water milk; *étendre*

du linge, to hang out linen; *étendre le bras*, to stretch out one's arm; *étendre les ailes*, to spread one's wings; *étendre son commerce*, to extend one's trade; (*sch. slang*) *se faire étendre*, to be ploughed. **s'étendre**, *v.r.* To stretch oneself out, to lay oneself down; to stretch out, to reach, to extend; to expatiate, to dwell on. *Il s'étendit tout de son long sur l'herbe*, he laid himself at full length upon the grass; *l'armée s'étendit dans la plaine*, the army spread over the plain; *s'étendre au loin*, to spread far and wide; *s'étendre sur un sujet*, to expatiate upon a subject. **étendu**, *a.* (*fem.* **étendue** (1)) Outstretched, outspread, extended; vast, wide, extensive; diluted. *Alcool étendu*, diluted spirit; *c'est un esprit fort étendu*, he is a man of vast intellect; *des connaissances étendues*, extensive knowledge; *il a une voix très étendue*, he has great compass of voice; *la vue est ici fort étendue*, the view here is very extensive. **étendue** (2), *n.f.* Extent, extensiveness; reach, scope, compass, length; (*Phil.*) extension. *Dans toute son étendue*, to the full; *grande étendue de voix*, great compass of voice; *la vaste étendue des mers*, the wide expanse of ocean.

éternel [eter'nɛl], *a.* (*fem.* **-elle**) Eternal, everlasting, endless. *Le Père éternel*, God Almighty; *les neiges éternelles*, perpetual snow.—*n.m.* That which is eternal. *L'Éternel*, God, the Eternal. **éternellement**, *adv.* Eternally. **éterniser**, *v.t.* To eternize, to perpetuate. **s'éterniser**, *v.r.* To be perpetuated, to be rendered eternal; to stop or remain for ever. *La discussion s'éternise*, the discussion is dragging on endlessly. **éternité**, *n.f.* Eternity. *De toute éternité*, from all eternity.

éternuement or **éternûment** [eterny'mã], *n.m.* Sneezing, sneeze. **éternuer**, *v.i.* To sneeze. **éternueur**, *n.m.* (*fem.* **-euse**) Sneezer.

étésien [ete'zjɛ̃], *a.* (*fem.* **étésienne**) Etesian.

étêtage [etɛ'taːʒ] or **étêtement**, *n.m.* Pollarding, topping. **étêter**, *v.t.* To top, to pollard; to take off the heads of (nails, pins, etc.), to pollard (a tree).

éteuble [ÉTEULE].

*éteuf [e'tœf], *n.m.* Ball (at tennis); button on a foil. *Renvoyer l'éteuf*, to send the ball back; (*fig.*) to make a repartee, to get even with someone.

éteule [e'tœl], **esteule**, **éteuble**, or **esteuble**, *n.f.* Stubble.

éthane [e'tan], *n.m.* (*Chem.*) Ethane.

éther [e'teːr], *n.m.* Ether. **éthéré**, *a.* (*fem.* **éthérée**) Ethereal. **éthérification**, *n.f.* Etherification. **éthérifier**, *v.t.* To etherify. **éthérisation**, *n.f.* Etherization. **éthériser**, *v.t.* To etherize. **éthérisme**, *n.m.* Etherism. **éthéromanie**, *n.f.* Etheromania.

Éthiopie [etjɔ'pi], *f.* Ethiopia.

éthiopien [etjɔ'pjɛ̃], *a.* and *n.m.* (*fem.* **-ienne**) Ethiopian.—*n.m.* Ethiopian language. **éthiopique**, *a.* Ethiopic.

éthique [e'tik], *a.* Ethic, ethical.—*n.f.* Ethics, morals.

ethmoïdal [ɛtmɔi'dal], *a.* (*fem.* **-ale**, *pl.* **-aux**) Ethmoidal. *L'os ethmoïdal*, ethmoidal bone. **ethmoïde**, *a.* and *n.m.* Ethmoid.

ethnique [ɛt'nik], *a.* Ethnic, ethnical. **ethnographe**, *n.m.* Ethnographer. **ethnographie**,

n.f. Ethnography. **ethnographique,** *a.*
Ethnographic.
ethnologie [ɛtnɔlɔ'ʒi], *n.f.* Ethnology. **ethnologique,** *a.* Ethnologic. **ethnologique-
ment,** *adv.* Ethnologically. **ethnologue**
or **ethnologiste,** *n.* Ethnologist.
éthologie [etɔlɔ'ʒi], *n.f.* Ethology.
éthyle [e'til], *n.m.* Ethyl. **éthylène,** *n.m.*
(*Chem.*) Ethylene. **éthylique,** *a.* Ethylic.
Alcool éthylique, ordinary alcohol.
étiage [e'tja:ʒ], *n.m.* Low-water mark; (*fig.*)
level.
Étienne [e'tjɛn], *m.* Stephen.
étier [e'tje], *n.m.* Ditch or canal (for conveying
sea-water to a salt-marsh).
etincelant [etɛ̃s'lɑ̃], *a.* (*fem.* -**ante**) Sparkling,
glittering, glistening.
étinceler [etɛ̃s'le], *v.i.* To sparkle, to flash,
to gleam, to glitter; to be brilliant (of wit
etc.). *Cet ouvrage étincelle d'esprit,* that work
sparkles with wit; *les yeux lui étincellent de
colère,* his eyes are flashing with anger.
étincelle, *n.f.* Spark, flash, brilliance. *Il
n'a pas une étincelle de bon sens,* he is utterly
devoid of good sense; *jeter des étincelles,* to
throw out sparks. **étincellement,** *n.m.*
Sparkling, twinkling, scintillation.
étiolement [etjɔl'mɑ̃], *n.m.* Etiolation, sickliness (of plants etc.); chlorosis, paleness, emaciation. **étioler,** *v.t.* To etiolate (plants);
to make pale or emaciated; (*fig.*) to enervate.
s'étioler, *v.r.* To become etiolated (of
plants); (*fig.*) to waste away, to become
enervated.
étiologie [etjɔlɔ'ʒi], *n.f.* Aetiology. **étiolo-
gique,** *a.* Aetiological.
étique [e'tik], *a.* Consumptive; lean, lank,
emaciated.
étiquetage [etik'ta:ʒ], *n.m.* Labelling, ticket-
ing. **étiqueter,** *v.t.* To label, to ticket.
étiqueteur, *n.m.* (*fem.* -**euse**) Ticketer,
labeller.
étiquette [eti'kɛt], *n.f.* Ticket, label, tag;
(*Am.*) sticker; etiquette, ceremonial. *Cela
est contraire à l'étiquette,* that is bad form;
être à cheval sur l'étiquette, to be very strict
on etiquette; *tenir à l'étiquette,* to stand on
ceremony.
étirage [eti'ra:ʒ], *n.m.* Stretching; wire-drawing. **étire,** *n.f.* Stretching-iron (of curriers).
étirer, *v.t.* To stretch; to lengthen, to wire-
draw. **s'étirer,** *v.r.* To stretch one's limbs.
étisie [eti'zi], *n.f.* Consumption.
étoc [ESTOC].
étoffe [e'tɔf], *n.f.* Material; fabric, stuff, cloth;
condition, quality, worth; (*pl.*, *Print.*) the
printer's gross profit. *Étoffe suffisante,*
enough material; *il a de l'étoffe,* he has got
some stuff in him; *il a l'étoffe d'un grand
romancier,* he has the makings of a great
novelist in him. (*C*) *Étoffe du pays,* homespun, coarse woollen cloth. **étoffé,** *a.* (*fem.*
-**ée**) Stuffed full, well-lined; upholstered (of
furniture); rich (of voice); (*fig.*) comfortably
off; stout, full-bodied, substantial. *Discours
bien étoffé,* speech full of capital things;
homme bien étoffé, stout, in good circumstances. **étoffer,** *v.t.* To stuff, to put
enough stuff into, to furnish with materials;
to upholster.
étoile [e'twal], *n.f.* Star; (*fig.*) fate, destiny;
blaze (on horse's head); (*Mil.*) various

decorations; (*Theat.*, *Cine.*, etc.) star; star
(crack) in glass. *À la lumière des étoiles,* by
starlight; *coucher à la belle étoile,* to sleep in
the open air; *étoile de mer,* starfish; *étoile
éclairante,* (*Mil.*) a Very light; *étoile filante,*
shooting star; *étoile polaire,* pole-star; *né sous
une mauvaise étoile,* born under an unlucky
star; *voir des étoiles en plein midi,* to see stars,
to be dazed. **étoilé,** *a.* (*fem.-* **ée**) Starry,
full of stars, studded with stars; star-shaped.
Bouteille étoilée, starred (cracked) bottle; *la
bannière étoilée,* the Star-spangled banner;
la voûte étoilée, the starry vault; **étoile-
ment,** *n.m.* Cracking, starring. **étoiler,** *v.t.*
To star, to stud with stars; to crack. **s'étoiler,**
v.r. To star, to crack.
étole [e'tɔl], *n.f.* Stole.
étonnamment [etɔna'mɑ̃], *adv.* Astonishingly, wonderfully, amazingly. **étonnant,** *a.*
(*fem.* -**ante**) Astonishing, wonderful,
marvellous.
étonnement [etɔn'mɑ̃], *n.m.* Astonishment,
amazement; admiration, wonder; shock,
fissure, crack. *À l'étonnement de tout le
monde,* to everyone's astonishment; *je ne
reviens pas de mon étonnement,* I cannot get
over my astonishment; *tout le monde est dans
l'étonnement,* everybody is amazed. **étonner,**
v.t. To astonish, to amaze, to startle, to
astound; to shock; to cause to shake; to
cause to crack. *Cela m'étonne,* I am surprised; *je suis étonné qu'il ne m'en ait rien dit,*
I wonder he said nothing about it to me.
s'étonner, *v.r.* To be astonished, to wonder;
to become cracked. *Il ne s'étonne de rien,* he
is astonished at nothing.
étouffade [ÉTOUFFÉE].
étouffant [etu'fɑ̃], *a.* (*fem.* **étouffante**) Suffocating, sultry, close. *Chaleur étouffante,*
sweltering heat.
étouffée [etu'fe], *n.f.* Stewing in a closed
vessel; stew made thus.
étouffement [etuf'mɑ̃], *n.m.* Suffocation,
stifling, asphyxiation. **étouffer,** *v.t.* To
suffocate, to choke, to smother; (*fig.*) to
stifle, to suppress, to hush up; to deaden,
to drown (sound etc.); (*Naut.*) to lash up, to
spill (a sail). *Étouffer la voix,* to drown the
voice; *les mauvaises herbes étouffent le blé,*
weeds choke the corn.—*v.i.* To choke, to
suffocate. *Étouffer de rire,* to choke with
laughter; *on étouffe ici,* it is suffocating here.
s'étouffer, *v.i.* To be choking, to be
suffocated; to swelter. **étouffoir,** *n.m.* Extinguisher (for charcoal); damper (of a piano);
(*fig.*) stuffy room.
étoupe [e'tup], *n.f.* Tow, oakum. *Étoupe de
coton,* cotton waste; *étoupe goudronnée* or
noire, tarred oakum; *faire de l'étoupe,* to pick
oakum; *mettre le feu aux étoupes,* to touch off
a gun, *to add fuel to the flame, to fan.
étouper, *v.t.* To stop (with tow or oakum);
to caulk. *S'étouper les oreilles,* to stop one's
ears with cotton-wool. **étoupier,** *n.m.* (*fem.*
-**ière**) Oakum picker.
étoupille [etu'pi:j], *n.f.* Quick-match or tube
for firing gun or firework. **étoupiller,** *v.t.*
To prime (a friction tube).
étoupillon [etupi'jɔ̃], *n.m.* Vent-plug (for
touch-hole of gun).
étourderie [eturda'ri], *n.f.* Heedlessness,
thoughtlessness; thoughtless or giddy act,

blunder. *Il fait toujours des étourderies,* he is always committing some thoughtless act or other; *par étourderie,* thoughtlessly. **étourdi,** *a.* (*fem.* **-ie**) Giddy, thoughtless, heedless.—*n.* Such a person, madcap, romp. *À l'étourdie,* giddily, heedlessly, rashly; *c'est une étourdie,* she is a giddy creature; *jeter à l'étourdie,* to blurt out. **étourdiment,** *adv.* Heedlessly, thoughtlessly. **étourdir,** *v.t.* To stun, to deafen, to daze, to make dizzy or giddy; to din (one's ears etc.); to astound, to stagger; to benumb, to assuage (pain); to parboil (water). *Étourdir de la viande,* to cook meat slightly; *étourdir de l'eau,* to take the chill off the water; *étourdir la grosse faim,* to take the edge off one's appetite. **s'étourdir,** *v.r.* To divert one's thoughts; to try to forget something. *Il s'étourdit sur son chagrin,* he tries to forget his grief. **étourdissant,** *a.* (*fem.* **étourdissante**) Deafening; stunning, staggering, astounding. **étourdissement,** *n.m.* Dizziness, giddiness, vertigo; stupefaction, stupor; shock. *Il a des étourdissements,* he is subject to attacks of giddiness; *le premier étourdissement passé,* when the first shock was over.

étourneau [etur'no], *n.m.* (*pl.* **-eaux**) Starling; (*fig.*) giddy fellow; flea-bitten horse.

étouteau [etu'to], *n.m.* (*pl.* **étouteaux**) Catch, pin (on watch-wheel, bayonet, etc.).

étrange [e'trã:ʒ], *a.* Strange, odd, queer, extraordinary. *C'est une personne bien étrange,* she is a very queer sort of person; *chose étrange!* strange to say!—*n.m.* Strange thing, strangeness. *L'étrange de l'affaire,* the strange thing about it. **étrangement,** *adv.* Strangely, queerly, extraordinarily.

étranger [etrã'ʒe], *a.* (*fem.* **-ère**) Foreign; strange; unknown; irrelevant. *Corps étranger,* extraneous body; *être étranger à,* to be unacquainted with; *ministre des Affaires étrangères,* minister for foreign affairs; *un fait étranger à la cause,* a fact unconnected with, or foreign to, the case; *une langue étrangère,* a foreign language.—*n.* Foreigner, alien; stranger, outsider; foreign parts. *À l'étranger,* abroad.

étrangeté [etrãʒ'te], *n.f.* Strangeness, oddness.

étranglé [etrã'gle], *a.* (*fem.* **-ée**) Compressed, restricted, scanty, too narrow. *Voix étranglée,* choking voice.

étranglement [etrãglə'mã], *n.m.* Strangling; garotting; strangulation, constriction. **étrangler,** *v.t.* To strangle, to throttle, to choke, to stifle; to constrict, to compress, to confine; (*fig.*) to smother, to suppress, to slur over; (*Naut.*) to bowse (a sail). *Cet habit est étranglé,* that coat is too scanty; *étrangler une affaire,* to slur over a business.—*v.i.* To be choked, to be almost choked, to be short of breath. **s'étrangler,** *v.r.* To strangle oneself; to choke; be constricted. **étrangleur,** *n.m.* and *a.* (*fem.* **-euse**) Strangler, garotter. **étrangloir,** *n.m.* (*Naut.*) Trail, bowsing. **étranguillon,** *n.m.* (*Vet.*) Strangles. *Poire d'étranguillon,* choke-pear.

étrape [e'trap] or **étrapoire,** *n.f.* Small sickle (for stubble). **étraper,** *v.t.* To cut (stubble).

étrave [e'tra:v], *n.f.* Stem, stem-post (of ship).

être (1) [ɛ:tr], *v.i. irr.* (*pres.p.* **étant,** *p.p.* **été**; used esp. as copula connecting subject and attribute, and as auxiliary in compound tenses

of passive, reflexive, and some intransitive verbs) To be, to exist; to belong; to stand; to take part (*à*); to be a member (*de*); (in past tenses), to have gone; to lie; to prove to be, to turn out to be. *Ainsi soit-il,* so be it, amen; *cela n'en est pas,* that does not belong to it; *cela n'est pas,* it is not so; *c'en est fait de lui,* it is all over with him; *ce sont eux qui,* it is they who; *c'est à vous à parler,* it is your turn to speak; *c'est à vous de parler,* it is for you to speak; *c'est que,* the fact is; *cette fois ça y est,* now for it! done this time, and no mistake! *comme si de rien n'était,* as if nothing had happened; *en êtes-vous encore là?* do you still believe that? *en être là,* to have come to that; *en être pour sa peine,* to have lost all one's trouble; *en être pour ses frais,* to have lost one's time and money; *en être pour son argent,* to have lost one's money; *être à l'étroit,* to be cramped for room; *être tout à quelque chose,* to be engrossed in something; *être bien avec quelqu'un,* to be on good terms with someone; *être de moitié,* to go halves; *être en bonne santé,* to be in good health; *être mal avec quelqu'un,* to be on bad terms with someone; *être sage,* (of children) to be good; *eh bien, soit!* well, be it so; *il en sera ce qu'il plaira à Dieu,* it will be as God pleases; *il en sera de nous comme des autres,* it will be with us as with the rest; *il est à plaindre,* he is to be pitied; *il est à présumer,* it is to be presumed; *il est de Paris,* he is a native of Paris; *il était une fois,* once upon a time there was . . .; *il n'en est rien,* it is nothing of the sort; *il ne sait où il en est,* he does not know how he stands; *il n'est pas en moi de l'éviter,* it does not depend upon me to avoid it; *je me suis promené,* I went for a walk; *je n'en suis plus,* I cry off; *je n'y suis pour personne,* I am at home to no one; *je n'y suis pour rien,* I have no hand in the matter; *je pense donc je suis,* I think therefore I exist; *je suis à vous dans un moment,* I shall be at your service or with you in a moment; *je suis des vôtres,* I am a member of your party; *je suis tout à vous,* I am entirely at your service; *j'y suis pour un tiers,* I am in for a third share; *madame n'y est pas,* my mistress is not at home; *n'être plus,* to be no more, to be dead; *n'eût été que,* had it not been for; *on ne peut pas être et avoir été,* you can't have your cake and eat it; *quelle date sommes-nous aujourd'hui?* what is the date today *?que sera-ce de?* what will become of? *qu'est-ce que c'est?* what is it? *quoi qu'il en soit,* at all events, be that as it may; *si ce n'est que,* except that; *voilà où nous en sommes,* such is our present situation; *vous y êtes,* you have hit it.

être (2) [ɛ:tr] *n.m.* Being, existence; creature; frame. *L'Être suprême,* the Supreme Being; *un frisson parcourut tout son être,* a shiver went through his whole frame.—*n.m. pl.* Beings, creatures (in *êtres vivants*); [AÎTRES].

étrécir [etre'si:r], *v.t.* To narrow; to take in (clothes etc.). **s'étrécir,** *v.r.* To become more narrow, to contract. **étrécissement,** *n.m.* Tightening, narrowing, contraction. **étrécissure,** *n.f.* Narrowness, tightness.

étreindre [e'trɛ̃:dr], *v.t. irr.* (*pres.p.* **étreignant,** *p.p.* **étreint**; *conjug. like* CRAINDRE) To embrace, clasp, grip. *Qui trop embrasse mal étreint,* grab all lose all. **étreinte,** *n.f.*

Embrace, hug; grip. *De douces étreintes,* sweet embraces.

étrenne [e'trɛn], *n.f.* New Year's gift (*usually in pl.*); gift, present; shopkeeper's first sale each day. *En avoir l'étrenne,* to be the first to have it. **étrenner,** *v.t.* To give a New Year's gift; to handsel; to try or put on for the first time; to buy the first lot from.—*v.i.* To be the first to buy (of shopkeepers etc.).

étrésillon [etrezi'jɔ̃], *n.m.* (*Mining etc.*) Prop, stay, support. **étrésillonner,** *v.t.* To prop.

étrier [etri'e], *n.m.* Stirrup; (*Surg.*) caliper; (*Arch.*) strap. *Coup de l'étrier,* stirrup-cup; *courir à franc étrier,* to ride full speed; *faire perdre les étriers à quelqu'un,* to put someone out of countenance; *il a toujours le pied à l'étrier,* he is always ready to ride or for an emergency; *il est ferme sur ses étriers,* he has a firm seat in the saddle; *tenir l'étrier à,* to help into the saddle; *vider les étriers,* to lose the stirrups, to fall from one's horse, (*fig.*) to be disconcerted. **étrière,** *n.f.* Stirrup-bar.

étrille [e'tri:j], *n.f.* Curry-comb. **étriller,** *v.t.* To curry, to comb (a horse); (*fig.*) to fleece; to give a thrashing to, to drub.

étriper [etri'pe], *v.t.* To gut (an animal). *Aller à étripe-cheval,* to ride a horse at breakneck speed. **s'étriper,** *v.r.* To fray (of a rope).

étriqué [etri'ke], *a.* (*fem.* **-ée**) Scanty, narrow, curtailed. *Habits étriqués,* too tight clothes.

étriquer [etri'ke], *v.t.* To shorten, to curtail, to make too small.

étrive [e'triv], *n.f.* (*Naut.*) Cross, bend (in a rope); throat seizing. **étriver,** *v.t.* To jam, to seize.

étrivière [etri'vjɛːr], *n.f.* Stirrup-leather. *Donner les étrivières à quelqu'un,* to give someone a belting; to thrash him.

étroit [e'trwɑ], *a.* Narrow, tight, strait; limited, confined; (*fig.*) scanty, small; strict, rigorous. *À l'étroit,* narrowly; *esprit étroit,* narrow mind; *être à l'étroit,* to be pinched, to be poor, to be badly off for room; *étroite amitié,* close friendship; *habit étroit,* tight coat; *vivre à l'étroit,* to live economically. **étroitement,** *adv.* Narrowly, tightly, intimately, closely; sparingly. *Étroitement surveillé,* closely watched; *étroitement uni,* closely united. **étroitesse,** *n.f.* Narrowness, straitness; tightness, closeness. *Étroitesse d'esprit,* narrow-mindedness.

étron [e'trɔ̃], *n.m.* (*Vulg.*) Turd.

étronçonner [etrɔ̃sɔ'ne], *v.t.* To cut off the lower branches (of a tree).

étrope [ESTROPE].

Étrurie [etry'ri], *f.* Etruria.

étrusque [e'trysk], *a.* Etruscan.—*n.m.* Etruscan language.—*n.* (**Étrusque**) An Etruscan.

étude [e'tyd], *n.f.* Study; room for study, time of preparation; office, chambers, practice (of attorneys); essay, article, short literary work or survey; (*Mus.* and *Art.*) study. *À l'étude,* (of plans) being considered, under consideration; (of plays) in rehearsal; *cabinet d'étude,* study; *étude de notaire,* notary's office; *programme des études,* curriculum; *il a fait de bonnes études,* he has had a good education; *il a fait ses études,* he has finished his education; *bureau d'études,* research department; *mettre une question à l'étude,* to survey a question.

étudiant [ety'djɑ̃], *n.m.* (*fem.* **-ante**) Student; undergraduate. *Étudiant en droit,* law student.

étudié [ety'dje], *a.* Studied, carefully considered; calculated for effect, affected. *Langage étudié,* affected speech. **étudier,** *v.t.* To study, to learn, to read; to practise (music); to rehearse (a play); to watch, to examine, to observe. *Étudier la nature,* to study nature; *étudier son rôle,* to study one's part.—*v.i.* To study, to learn; to practise (music). **s'étudier,** *v.r.* To make it one's study, to school oneself; to make a point of.

étui [e'tɥi], *n.m.* Case, box, sheath. *Étui à cigarettes,* cigarette case; *étui à ciseaux,* scissor-case; *étui-musette,* (*Mil.*) haversack; *étui de revolver,* holster.

étuve [e'ty:v], *n.f.* Sweating-room, hot-room (in a bath); stove, drying stove, disinfecting-oven; drying room; incubator. **étuvée,** *n.f.* Stew. **étuvement,** *n.m.,* or **étuvage,** *n.m.* (*Med.*) Bathing or fomenting (of a wound etc.). **étuver,** *v.t.* To stew; to dry or heat in a stove; (*Med.*) to bathe, to foment.

étymologie [etimɔlɔ'ʒi], *n.f.* Etymology. **étymologique,** *a.* Etymological. **étymologiquement,** *adv.* Etymologically. **étymologiste,** *n.* Etymologist.

eucalyptus [økalip'ty:s], *n.m. inv.* Eucalyptus, gum-tree.

eucharistie [økaris'ti], *n.f.* Eucharist. **eucharistique,** *a.* Eucharistic.

euclidien [økli'djɛ̃], *a.* (*fem.* **-ienne**) Euclidean.

eucologe or **euchologe** [økɔ'lɔ:ʒ], *n.m.* Euchology, prayer-book.

eudémonisme [ødemɔ'nism], *n.m.* Eudemonism. **eudémoniste,** *n.* Eudemonist. —*a.* Eudemonistic.

eudiomètre [ødjɔ'mɛtr], *n.m.* Eudiometer. **eudiométrie,** *n.f.* Eudiometry. **eudiométrique,** *a.* Eudiometrical.

eufraise [ø'frɛːz], *n.f.* (*Bot.*) Euphrasy, eyebright.

eugénique [øʒe'nik], *n.f.,* or **eugénisme,** *n.m.* Eugenics.

euh [ø], *int.* Aha! oh! hum!

Euménide [øme'nid], *n.f.* (*Gr. Myth.*) Fury.

eunecte [ø'nɛkt], *n.m.* Anaconda.

eunuque [ø'nyk], *n.m.* Eunuch.

eupatoire [øpa'twaːr], *n.f.* Genus of compositous plants comprising many American plants, also the hemp-agrimony.

eupepsie [øpɛp'si], *n.f.* Eupepsia. **eupeptique,** *a.* Eupeptic.

euphémique [øfe'mik], *a.* Euphemistic. **euphémiquement,** *adv.* Euphemistically. **euphémisme,** *n.m.* Euphemism.

euphonie [øfɔ'ni], *n.f.* Euphony. **euphonique,** *a.* Euphonical. **euphoniquement,** *adv.* Euphonically.

euphorbe [ø'fɔrb], *n.m.* *Euphorbia* (a genus of herbaceous plants comprising le petit cyprès, l'épurge). *See also* WARTWORT.

euphorie [øfɔ'riː], *n.f.* Euphoria.

euphraise or **euphraisie** [EUFRAISE].

Euphrate [ø'frat], *l',* *m.* Euphrates.

euphuïsme [øfy'ism], *n.m.* Euphuism.

eurasien [øra'zjɛ̃] (*fem.* **-ienne**), *a.* and *n.* Eurasian.

Euripide [øri'pid], *m.* Euripides.

Europe [ø'rɔp], *f.* (*Myth.*) Europa; (*Geog.*) l', Europe.

européaniser [ørɔpeani'ze], *v.t.* To Europeanize.

européen [ørɔpe'ɛ̃], *a.* and *n.* (*fem.* **-éenne**) European.

eurythmie [ørit'miː], *n.f.* Eurhythmy. **eurythmique,** *a.* Eurhythmic.

eustache [øs'taʃ], *n.m.* Rough clasp-knife, with a wooden handle (made by *Eustache Dubois*).

euthanasie [øtana'zi], *n.f.* Euthanasia.

eux [ø], *pron. pers. m.pl.* They; them. *Entre eux,* between them; *eux-mêmes,* themselves.

évacuant [eva'kɥɑ̃] or **évacuatif,** *a.* (*fem.* **-ante** or **-ive**) Evacuant.—*n.m.* Evacuant.

évacuation [evakɥa'sjɔ̃], *n.f.* Evacuation; ejection. *L'évacuation d'une place,* the evacuation of a fortress or town; *l'évacuation des blessés,* evacuation of the wounded.

évacué [eva'kɥe], *n.m.* (*fem.* **-ée**) Evacuee.

évacuer [eva'kɥe], *v.t.* To evacuate; to throw off, to eject, to clear. *Évacuer la bile,* to get rid of bile; *faites évacuer la salle,* clear the room. **s'évacuer,** *v.r.* To discharge (into).

évadé [eva'de] (*fem.* **-ée**), *a.* and *n.* Escaped; escapee.

évader (s') [eva'de], *v.r.* To make one's escape, to escape; to get away or out of (*de*).

évaluable [eva'lɥabl], *a.* Rateable, appraisable. **évaluateur,** *n.m.* (*fem.* **-trice**) Valuer, appraiser.

évaluation [evalɥa'sjɔ̃], *n.f.* Valuation, estimate. **évaluer,** *v.t.* To value, to estimate, to appreciate.

évanescent [evanɛ'sɑ̃], *a.* (*fem.* **-ente**) Evanescent.

évangélique [evɑ̃ʒe'lik], *a.* Evangelical. **évangéliquement,** *adv.* Evangelically. **évangéliser,** *v.t.* To evangelize, to preach the Gospel to. **évangélisme,** *n.m.* Evangelism. **évangéliste,** *n.m.* Evangelist.

évangile [evɑ̃'ʒil], *n.m.* Gospel. *Côté de l'évangile,* left-hand side of the altar; *il croit cela comme l'évangile,* he takes that for Gospel; *prendre tout pour parole d'évangile,* to take all for Gospel.

évanouir (s') [eva'nwiːr], *v.r.* To faint, to swoon, to lose consciousness; (*fig.*) to vanish, to disappear. *Cette nouvelle l'a fait évanouir,* that news made her swoon; *tous nos espoirs se sont évanouis,* all our hopes have vanished. **évanouissement,** *n.m.* Swoon, fainting fit; disappearance; (*Math.*) cancelling out. *Revenir d'un évanouissement,* to come round from a swoon.

évaporable [evapɔ'rabl], *a.* Evaporable. **évaporateur,** *n.m.* Evaporator. **évaporatif,** *a.* (*fem.* **-ive**) Evaporative. **évaporation,** *n.f.* Evaporation. **évaporatoire,** *a.* Evaporating. **évaporé,** *a.* (*fem.* **-ée**) Frivolous, thoughtless. *Une jeune fille évaporée,* a giddy-brained girl.—*n.* Such a person.

évaporer [evapɔ're], *v.t.* To evaporate; (*fig.*) to exhale, to give vent to, to pour out in words etc. *Évaporer son chagrin,* to give vent to one's grief. **s'évaporer,** *v.r.* To evaporate; (*fig.*) to be exhaled; to get giddy, flighty, or heedless. *Elle commence à s'évaporer,* her conduct is becoming irregular.

évaporimètre, *n.m.* Evaporimeter.

évasé [eva'ze], *a.* (*fem.* **-ée**) Wide, bell-shaped, bell-mouthed; flared (skirt). **évasement,** *n.m.* Width, widening (at the mouth of a vase etc.); (*Arch.*) splay; flare of (a skirt).

évaser [eva'ze], *v.t.* To widen (an opening); (*Arch.*) to splay; to flare (a skirt). **s'évaser,** *v.r.* To be widened; to extend, to spread.

évasif [eva'zif], *a.* (*fem.* **-ive**) Evasive. **évasion,** *n.f.* Escape, flight; evasion; escapism. **évasivement,** *adv.* Evasively.

évasure [eva'zyːr], *n.f.* Widening (of an opening), splay.

évêché [evɛ'ʃe], *n.m.* Bishopric, episcopate, see; bishop's palace.

évection [evɛk'sjɔ̃], *n.f.* (*Astron.*) Evection.

éveil [e'vɛːj], *n.m.* Awakening; warning, hint, alarm. *Donner l'éveil à,* to warn; *en éveil,* on one's guard, on the watch. **éveillé,** *a.* Wide-awake; brisk, lively, sprightly; sharp, smart, intelligent. *C'est un garçon très éveillé,* he is a very bright boy. **éveiller,** *v.t.* To awaken, to rouse; to excite, to enliven. *Éveiller les soupçons,* to arouse suspicion. **s'éveiller,** *v.r.* To awaken, to wake up; to become animated. *Elle s'est éveillée en sursaut,* she awoke with a start. **éveilleur,** *n.m.* (*fem.* **-euse**) Awakener, rouser.

événement [evɛn'mɑ̃], *n.m.* Event, occurrence; issue, result, end; climax. *À tout événement,* at all events, in any emergency; *en cas d'événement,* in cases of emergency.

évent [e'vɑ̃], *n.m.* Open air; vent-hole, air-hole; blow-hole (of cetaceans); (*Artill.*) windage; (*fig.*) flatness, vapidness, deadness. *Avoir la tête à l'évent,* to be thoughtless or hare-brained; *sentir l'évent,* to smell fusty.

éventail [evɑ̃'taːj], *n.m.* (*pl.* **-s**) Fan; fan-light; punkah. *En éventail,* fan-shaped; *fenêtre en éventail,* fan-light; *l'éventail des salaires,* the wage range. **éventailliste,** *n.* Fan-maker; fan-painter; fan-seller.

éventaire [evɑ̃'tɛːr], *n.m.* Flat tray (carried by hawkers on their chests); street stall.

éventé [evɑ̃'te], *a.* (*fem.* **-ée**) Fanned, aired; flat, stale (beer etc.); (*fig.*) giddy, thoughtless. *Un homme éventé,* a giddy, scatter-brained man.

éventer [evɑ̃'te], *v.t.* To fan; to winnow (corn); to air; to injure by exposure to the air; to let (wine etc.) get flat; to discover, to get wind of; to let out (a secret), to divulge; (*Naut.*) to fill (a sail). *Éventer la quille,* to bring the keel out of the water; *éventer la voie,* to scent game (of hounds). **s'éventer,** *v.r.* To fan oneself; to evaporate, to become flat; to be divulged. **éventoir,** *n.m.* Fire-fan.

éventration [evɑ̃tra'sjɔ̃], *n.f.* (*Path.*) Eventration, large ventral hernia; ripping open; disembowelling.

éventrer [evɑ̃'tre], *v.t.* To disembowel, to eviscerate, to gut (fish etc.); to rip up, to break open; to cut open (a pie); (*Naut.*) to split (a sail). **s'éventrer,** *v.r.* To rip one's bowels open; to commit hara-kiri. **éventreur,** *n.m.* Disemboweller, ripper.

éventualité [evɑ̃tɥali'te], *n.f.* Contingency, eventuality. **éventuel,** *a.* (*fem.* **éventuelle**) Contingent, possible, eventual.—*n.m.* An eventuality, a contingency; perquisite, contingent, emolument, capitation-fee. **éventuellement,** *adv.* Possibly; on occasion.

évêque [e'vɛːk], *n.m.* Bishop. *Monseigneur l'évêque*, my Lord Bishop; *pierre d'évêque*, amethyst.

éversif [evɛr'sif], *a.* (*fem.* **-ive**) Subversive. **éversion**, *n.f.* Overthrow.

évertuer (s') [evɛr'tɥe], *v.r.* To strive, to exert or bestir oneself. *Je m'évertue à le faire*, I do all I can to accomplish it.

éviction [evik'sjɔ̃], *n.f.* Eviction, ejectment.

évidage [evi'daːȝ], *n.m.* Scooping out, hollowing. **évidement**, *n.m.* Scooping out; groove, hollow.

évidemment [evida'mɑ̃], *adv.* Evidently, obviously, clearly.—*int.* Of course!

évidence [evi'dɑ̃ːs], *n.f.* Obviousness, plainness, clearness; conspicuousness. *Être en évidence*, to be conspicuous, to be in the limelight; *mettre en évidence*, to make conspicuous, to bring to light; *se rendre à l'évidence*, to recognize the truth of. **évident**, *a.* (*fem.* **-ente**) Evident, plain, clear, obvious. *C'est évident*, that stands to reason.

évider [evi'de], *v.t.* To hollow, to groove, to scoop out; to round, to pink. **évidoir**, *n.m.* Auger, gouge. **évidure**, *n.f.* Groove, hollow.

évier [e'vje], *n.m.* Sink.

évincement [evɛ̃s'mɑ̃], *n.m.* Ousting. **évincer**, *v.t.* To evict, to eject, to oust. *Il a été évincé*, he was turned out.

éviré [evi're], *a.* (*Her.*) Without sex.

éviscération [evisera'sjɔ̃], *n.f.* Evisceration. **éviscérer** [evise're], *v.t.* To eviscerate, disembowel.

évitable [evi'tabl], *a.* Avoidable.

évitage [evi'taːȝ], *n.m.*, or **évitée**, *n.f.* (*Naut.*) Swinging, swinging-room, berth. *Avoir son évitée*, to have a wide berth; *le vaisseau fait son évitée*, the ship is swinging to.

évitement [evit'mɑ̃], *n.m.* (*Rail.*) Siding, shunting. *Gare* or *voie d'évitement*, siding; *route d'évitement*, by-pass road.

éviter [evi'te], *v.t.* To shun, to avoid, to evade; to abstain from, to eschew. *Éviter les mauvaises compagnies*, to shun bad company; *éviter de la tête*, to duck; *éviter les périls*, to avoid dangers; *gens à éviter*, people to steer clear of.—*v.i.* (*Naut.*) To swing. *Éviter à la marée*, to stem the tide; *éviter au vent*, to stem the wind.

évocable [evɔ'kabl], *a.* That may be evoked; (*Law*) removable. **évocateur**, *a.* (*fem.* **-trice**) Evocative. *Un style évocateur*, a vivid, picturesque style.

évocation [evɔka'sjɔ̃], *n.f.* Evocation, raising up; recall, recollection; (*Law*) removal. **évocatoire**, *a.* (*Law*) For removal (from one court to another).

évolué [evɔ'lɥe], *a.* (*fem.* **-ée**) Highly civilized. *Un peuple peu évolué*, a backward people.

évoluer [evɔ'lɥe], *v.i.* (*Mil., Naut.*) To perform evolutions; to evolve; to develop. **évolution**, *n.f.* Evolution. (*Mil.*) *Évolutions tactiques*, tactical exercises. **évolutionnisme**, *n.m.* Evolutionism.

évoquer [evɔ'ke], *v.t.* To evoke, to conjure up (spirit); to call up (from memory etc.); to allude to, to mention; (*Law*) to remove. *Évoquer à un tribunal supérieur*, to remove to a superior court.

évulsif [evyl'sif], *a.* (*fem.* **-ive**) Pulling or tearing out. **évulsion**, *n.f.* Evulsion.

exacerbation [egzasɛrba'sjɔ̃], *n.f.* Exacerbation. **exacerber**, *v.t.* To exacerbate.

exact [eg'zakt], *a.* Exact, accurate, correct; precise, regular, punctual. *Exact à faire tout ce qu'on vous dit*, punctual in doing all you are told; *exacte analyse*, close analysis; *l'heure exacte*, the right time. **exactement**, *adv.* Exactly, accurately; precisely, punctually.

exacteur [egzak'tœːr], *n.m.* Exactor, extorter.

exaction [egzak'sjɔ̃], *n.f.* Exaction, impost, extortion.

exactitude [egzakti'tyd], *n.f.* Exactness, correctness, accuracy, punctuality, precision.

ex aequo [ɛkse'ko], *a. inv. Ils sont ex aequo*, they are of equal merit; *premier prix ex aequo*, first prize divided.

exagératif [egzaȝera'tif], *a.* (*fem.* **-ive**) Exaggerative. **exagération**, *n.f.* Exaggeration, amplification, overrating. **exagéré**, *a.* (*fem.* **-ée**) Exaggerated, excessive. **exagérément**, *adv.* In an exaggerated manner. **exagérer**, *v.t. irr.* (*conjug. like* ACCÉLÉRER) To exaggerate, to magnify.

exaltant [egzal'tɑ̃], *a.* (*fem.* **-ante**) Elating, exciting. **exaltation**, *n.f.* Exaltation; excitement; extolling; (*Med.*) over-excitement. **exalté**, *a.* (*fem.* **-ée**) Exalted, over-excited, heated, feverish.—*n.* Enthusiast, fanatic. **exalter**, *v.t.* To exalt, to extol, to magnify; to excite, to inflame, to over-excite. **s'exalter**, *v.r.* To become excited, to be exalted, inflamed, or elated.

examen [egza'mɛ̃], *n.m.* Examination; survey, inspection, scrutiny; investigation, research. *Après mûr examen*, after thorough examination; *examen de conscience*, self-examination; *faire examen d'un livre*, to examine a book; *libre examen*, free-thought. (*sch.*) *Être reçu (refusé) à un examen*, to pass (fail) an exam; *examen de passage*, entrance exam (to a higher form); *jury d'examen*, board of examiners; *passer un examen*, to sit an exam. **examinateur**, *n.m.* (*fem.* **-trice**) Examiner. **examiner**, *v.t.* To examine, to inspect, to survey; to weigh, to discuss, to investigate, to explore. *Examiner à fond*, to sift thoroughly; *examiner rapidement*, to glance over. **s'examiner**, *v.r.* To examine or search oneself; to examine one's own conscience; to examine or to observe each other attentively.

exanthémateux [egzɑ̃tema'tø], (*fem.* **-euse**) or **exanthématique**, *a.* Suffering or characterized by eruption. **exanthème**, *n.m.* Eruption on the skin.

exarchat [egzar'ka], *n.m.* Exarchate. **exarque**, *n.m.* Exarch.

exaspérant [egzaspe'rɑ̃], *a.* (*fem.* **-ante**) Exasperating, aggravating. **exaspération**, *n.f.* Exasperation, aggravation. **exaspéré**, *a.* (*fem.* **-ée**) Infuriated, incensed. **exaspérer**, *v.t. irr.* (*conjug. like* ACCÉLÉRER) To exasperate, to incense, to inflame; to aggravate (pain etc.). **s'exaspérer**, *v.r.* To become exasperated, enraged, or incensed; to become aggravated (pain etc.).

exaucement [egzos'mɑ̃], *n.m.* Granting, hearing (of prayers). **exaucer**, *v.t.* To hearken to, to grant

excavateur [ɛkskava'tœːr], *n.m.* Excavator, steam-shovel, digging-machine.

excavation [ɛkskava'sjɔ̃], *n.f.* Excavation. **excaver**, *v.t.* To excavate, to hollow out.

excédant [ɛkse'dɑ̃], *a.* (*fem.* -ante) Exceeding, excessive; unfortunate, unbearable. **excédent,** *n.m.* Overplus, surplus, excess. *Excédent de bagages,* excess luggage.

excéder [ɛkse'de], *v.t. irr.* (*conjug. like* ACCÉLÉRER) To exceed, to surpass, to rise above (in level, price, etc.); (*fig.*) to wear out, to tire out. *Excédé de fatigue,* worn out; *il a excédé son pouvoir,* he has exceeded his power; *il était excédé,* he was driven to distraction.

excellemment [ɛksɛla'mɑ̃], *adv.* Excellently, surpassingly.

excellence [ɛksɛ'lɑ̃:s], *n.f.* Excellence, Excellency. *Par excellence,* pre-eminently, above all. *Son Excellence,* His Excellency (of an ambassador or a minister); *Votre Excellence* or *Excellence,* Your Excellency. (*sch.*) *Prix d'excellence,* class-prize. **excellent,** *a.* (*fem.* -ente) Excellent; delightful. **excellentissime,** *a.* Most excellent. **exceller,** *v.i.* To excel, to be eminent, to transcend, to surpass.

excentricité [ɛksɑ̃trisi'te], *n.f.* Eccentricity. **excentrique,** *a.* Eccentric, odd; out of centre; far away.—*n.m.* Eccentric-wheel; eccentric person. **excentriquement,** *adv.* Eccentrically.

excepté [ɛksɛp'te], *prep.* Except, excepting, but. *Excepté que,* except that.

excepter [ɛksɛp'te], *v.t.* To except, to exclude.

exception [ɛksɛp'sjɔ̃], *n.f.* Exception; (*Law*) incidental plea, plea in bar, demurrer. *À cette exception que,* with this exception that; *à l'exception de,* with the exception of; *à une exception près,* with one exception; *c'est l'exception qui confirme la règle,* it is the exception that proves the rule; *mesures d'exception,* exceptional steps; *tous sans exception,* one and all. **exceptionnel,** *a.* (*fem.* -elle) Exceptional. **exceptionnellement,** *adv.* Exceptionally.

excès [ɛk'sɛ], *n.m. inv.* Excess; (*pl.*) riot, outrages, violence. *À l'excès, avec excès,* or *jusqu'à l'excès,* to excess, excessively, immoderately; *faire des excès,* to be guilty of excesses; *se porter à des excès contre,* to commit violence upon; *excès de jeu* or *jeu excessif,* backlash. **excessif,** *a.* (*fem.* -ive) Excessive, exorbitant; intemperate. **excessivement,** *adv.* Excessively, to excess.

exciper [ɛksi'pe], *v.i.* To plead or allege an exception, to put in a plea. *Exciper de sa bonne foi,* to allege one's good faith.

excipient [ɛksi'pjɑ̃], *n.m.* (*Pharm.*) Excipient.

excise [ɛk'si:z], *n.f.* Excise; excise-office.

exciser [ɛksi'ze], *v.t.* To cut out, to excise. **excision,** *n.f.* Excision, cutting out or off.

excitabilité [ɛksitabili'te], *n.f.* Excitability. **excitable,** *a.* Excitable. **excitant,** *a.* (*fem.* -ante) Exciting.—*n.m.* (*Med.*) Excitant. **excitateur,** *n.m.* (*fem.* -trice) Exciter.—*a.* Provocative. **excitatif,** *a.* (*fem.* -ive) Excitative.

excitation [ɛksita'sjɔ̃], *n.f.* Exciting, excitation; excitement. **excitement,** *n.m.* (*Med.*) Excitement, excitation. **exciter,** *v.t.* To excite, to stir up, to rouse; to stimulate, to animate, to quicken; to instigate, to prompt, to spur, to inflame, to irritate. *Exciter un chien contre quelqu'un,* to set a dog at someone. **s'exciter,** *v.r.* To excite oneself, to work oneself up; to animate or encourage each other; to be excited. **exciteur,** *n.m.* (*fem.* -euse) Excitor.

exclamatif [ɛksklama'tif], *a.* (*fem.* -ive) Exclamative; (*Gram.*) of exclamation.

exclamation [ɛksklama'sjɔ̃], *n.f.* Exclamation. *Point d'exclamation,* exclamation mark. **exclamativement,** *adv.* Exclamatively. **s'exclamer,** *v.r.* To exclaim, to cry out; to protest.

exclu [ɛks'kly], *n.m.* (*fem.* **exclue**) Person excluded (from the army etc.).

exclure [ɛks'kly:r], *v.t. irr.* (*p.p.* **exclu;** *conjugated like* CONCLURE) To exclude, to debar, to shut out; to bar; to be incompatible with. *Cela n'est pas exclu,* that is not impossible. **s'exclure,** *v.r.* To exclude each other; to be mutually incompatible. **exclusif,** *a.* (*fem.* -ive) Exclusive; intolerant. **exclusion,** *n.f.* Exclusion.—*pr.phr. À l'exclusion de,* excluding. **exclusivement,** *adv.* Exclusively. **exclusivisme,** *n.m.* Exclusivism. **exclusivité,** *n.f.* Exclusiveness; (*Comm.*) exclusive rights. *Cinéma d'exclusivité,* a cinema with exclusive rights on new films.

excogitation [ɛkskɔʒita'sjɔ̃], *n.f.* Excogitation.

excommunication [ɛkskɔmynika'sjɔ̃], *n.f.* Excommunication. **excommunié,** *a.* (*fem.* -ée) Excommunicated.—*n.* Excommunicated person. **excommunier,** *v.t.* To excommunicate.

excoriation [ɛkskɔrja'sjɔ̃], *n.f.* Excoriation, grazing the skin. **excorier,** *v.t.* To excoriate.

excrément [ɛkskre'mɑ̃], *n.m.* Excrement. *Excrément de la terre,* scum of the earth. **excrémenteux** or **excrémentiel,** *a.* (*fem.* -euse, -ielle) Excrementitious, excremental, excrementitial. **excréter,** *v.t. irr.* (*conjugated like* ACCÉLÉRER) To excrete, to evacuate. **excréteur** (*fem.* -trice), **excrétoire,** *a.* Excretory, excretive. **excrétion,** *n.f.* Excretion.

excroissance [ɛkskrwa'sɑ̃:s], *n.f.* Excrescence (tumour etc.).

excursion [ɛkskyr'sjɔ̃], *n.f.* Excursion, ramble, tour, trip; inroad, raid; (*fig.*) digression. *En excursion,* on an excursion; *faire une excursion en France,* to take a trip to France; *une excursion à pied,* a hike; *une excursion à la campagne,* a ramble in the country, an outing; *être en excursion,* to be on a jaunt. **excursionniste,** *n.* Tripper. **excursus,** *n.m.* Excursus.

excusabilité [ɛkskyzabili'te], *n.f.* Excusability. **excusable,** *a.* Excusable, pardonable, venial.

excuse [ɛks'ky:z], *n.f.* Excuse, (*pl.*) apology; (*Law*) plea. *Faire des excuses,* to apologize; *je vous fais mes excuses,* I beg your pardon. **excuser,** *v.t.* To excuse; to pardon; to serve as an excuse for; to apologize for. *On doit excuser les fautes de la jeunesse,* one must bear with the errors of youth; *se faire excuser,* to decline an invitation; *voulez-vous m'excuser auprès de lui,* will you apologize for me to him. **s'excuser,** *v.r.* To excuse or exculpate oneself; to apologize, to make an apology; to ask to be excused; to decline. *Qui s'excuse, s'accuse,* excuses proceed from a guilty conscience.

exeat [egze'at], *n.m.* Exeat, pass; discharge (from hospital); (*R.-C. Ch.*) leave (to go out of one diocese into another). *Donner à*

quelqu'un son exeat, to send off or dismiss someone, (*fam.*) to sack someone.
exécrable [egze'krabl], *a.* Execrable; abominable, detestable. **exécrablement**, *adv.* Execrably.
exécration [egzekra'sjɔ̃], *n.f.* Execration. *Tout le monde l'a en exécration*, he is held in abhorrence by everybody. **exécratoire,** *a.* Execratory. **exécrer,** *v.t. irr.* (*conjug. like* ACCÉLÉRER) To execrate, to abhor.
exécutable [egzeky'tabl], *a.* Feasible, practicable. **exécutant,** *n.m.* (*fem.* **-ante**) Performer, player (esp. of music).
exécuter [egzeky'te], *v.t.* To execute, to perform, to accomplish; to carry out, to achieve, to fulfil; (*Law*) to distrain; to put to death; (*St. Exch.*) to hammer (a defaulter); (*Journ.*) to tear (a book) to pieces. *Exécuter un arrêt*, to carry out a sentence; *j'exécuterai ce que j'ai promis,* I shall perform what I promised; *les critiques ont exécuté son livre,* the critics have torn his book to pieces. **s'exécuter,** *v.r.* To be performed, to be done, to take place; to yield, to comply, to submit. *Allons, exécutez-vous,* come, do the needful. **exécuteur,** *n.m.* (*fem.* **exécutrice**) Executor, executrix. *Exécuteur (des hautes œuvres*), executioner, hangman, headsman; *exécuteur testamentaire,* executor; *livrer à l'exécuteur,* to deliver over to the executioner. **exécutif,** *a.* (*fem.* **-ive**) Executive.—*n.m.* The executive.
exécution [egzeky'sjɔ̃], *n.f.* Execution, accomplishment, performance, fulfilment; (*St. Exch.*) hammering (of defaulter). *En exécution de,* in pursuance of; *exécution d'un débiteur,* distraint; *l'exécution d'un morceau de musique,* the performance of a piece of music; *mettre à exécution,* to carry out; *mettre des ordres à exécution,* to execute orders; *ordre d'exécution,* death-warrant, warrant for execution; *homme d'exécution,* man of action; (*Mil.*) *peloton d'exécution,* firing squad. **exécutoire,** *a.* (*Law*) Executory; pertaining to a writ of execution.—*n.m.* Writ of execution.
exèdre [eg'zɛdr], *n.m.* Exedra.
exégèse [egze'ʒɛːz], *n.f.* Exegesis. **exégète,** *n.m.* Exegetist. **exégétique,** *a.* Exegetical.
exemplaire [egzā'plɛːr], *a.* Exemplary.—*n.m.* Model, pattern, archetype; copy (of printed books, engravings, etc.), specimen. *J'ai trois exemplaires de ce livre-là,* I have three copies of that book. **exemplairement,** *adv.* Exemplarily, in an exemplary manner.
exemple [eg'zā:pl], *n.m.* Example, pattern, model; precedent, parallel, instance. *À l'exemple de,* in imitation of; *donner le bon exemple,* to set a good example; *faire un exemple de,* to make an example of; *il n'y en a point d'exemple,* there is no precedent for it, there is no example of such a thing; *ne vous réglez pas sur son exemple,* do not follow in his footsteps; *par exemple,* for instance; upon my word! *par exemple, voilà qui est fort!* well now, I like that! *prêcher d'exemple,* to practise what one preaches; *prendre exemple sur quelqu'un,* to be guided by someone; *proposer un exemple,* to offer an example; *sans exemple,* extraordinary, unparalleled.
exempt (1) [eg'zā], *a.* (*fem.* **exempte**) Exempt, exempted, free (from).

exempt (2) [eg'zā], *n.m.* Adjutant. *Exempt de police,* police officer.
exempté [egzā'te], *a. and n.m.* (*fem.* **-ée**) Exempt. (*Mil.*) *Exempté de corvée,* excused from fatigue. **exempter,** *v.t.* To exempt, to free; to dispense, to exonerate. **exemption,** *n.f.* Exemption, immunity; dispensation; *(sch.)* good mark voucher. *Lettre d'exemption des droits de douane,* bill exempting from duty.
exequatur [egzekwa'ty:r], *n.m. inv.* Exequatur.
exerçant [egzɛr'sā], *a.* Practising. *Médecin exerçant,* practising doctor. **exercer,** *v.t.* To exercise, to train up; to drill; to exert; to perform, to practise; to fulfil (an office etc.); to follow, to carry on (a trade or profession); (*fig.*) to try, to prove (one's patience etc.). *Exercer des soldats,* to drill soldiers; *exercer la médecine,* to practise medicine; *exercer la patience de quelqu'un,* to try someone's patience; *j'exerçai toute ma force,* I exerted all my strength; *il exerce une grande influence sur,* he has great influence on. **s'exercer,** *v.r.* To exercise, to practise; to exercise or train oneself; to exert oneself.
exercice [egzɛr'sis], *n.m.* Exercise, practice, use; (*Customs*) inspection; (*Administration*) period (of receipts and expenditure), financial year; (*Mil.*) drill, drilling. *En exercice,* in action, at work; *entrer en exercice,* to commence one's duties; *exercice de piété,* a pious practice; *faire faire l'exercice à des soldats,* to drill or train soldiers; *faire l'exercice,* to exercise, to drill; *l'exercice est clos,* the account for the year is closed; *l'exercice financier suivant,* the next fiscal period; *prendre de l'exercice,* to take exercise; *règlement d'un exercice,* balancing of a budget.
exerciseur [egzɛrsi'zœr], *n.m.* (*Gym.*) Chest expander.
exérèse [egze'rɛːz], *n.f.* (*Surg.*) Extraction, amputation, cutting off.
exergue [eg'zɛrg], *n.m.* Exergue.
exfoliation [ɛksfɔljɔ'sjɔ̃], *n.f.* Exfoliation. **exfolier,** *v.t.,* and **s'exfolier,** *v.r.* To exfoliate.
exhalaison [egzale'zɔ̃], *n.f.* Exhalation, vapour, effluvium. **exhalation,** *n.f.* Exhalation, exhaling.
exhaler [egza'le], *v.t.* To send forth, to exhale; to give forth, to give vent to, to emit. *Ces fleurs exhalent une douce odeur,* these flowers emit a sweet smell; *exhaler sa colère,* to give vent to one's anger. **s'exhaler,** *v.r.* To be emitted, to be exhaled; to give vent to. *S'exhaler en plaintes* or *en menaces,* to give vent to complaints, *or* to threats.
exhaure [eg'zɔr], *n.f.* (*Min.*) Pumping out water.
exhaussement [egzos'mā], *n.m.* Raising up, elevation, erection. **exhausser,** *v.t.* To raise, to make higher.
exhaustif [egzos'tif], *a.* (*fem.* **-ive**) Exhaustive. **exhaustion,** *n.f.* Exhaustion.
exhérédation [egzereda'sjɔ̃], *n.f.* Disinheriting, disinheritance. **exhéréder,** *v.t. irr.* (*conjugated like* ACCÉLÉRER) To disinherit.
exhiber [egzi'be], *v.t.* To exhibit (in a lawcourt); to produce, to show. *Exhiber ses papiers* or *son passeport,* to produce one's papers *or* one's passport. **s'exhiber,** *v.r.* (*pej.*) To show off; (of a woman) to be

improperly dressed. **exhibition**, *n.f.* Exhibition, producing, exhibiting. **exhibitionnisme**, *n.m.* Exhibitionism. **exhibitionniste**, *n.m.* Exhibitionist.

exhilarant [egzila'rɑ̃], *a.* (*fem.* **-ante**) Exhilarating.

exhortatif [egzɔrta'tif], *a.* (*fem.* **-ive**) Exhortative.

exhortation [egzɔrtɑ'sjɔ̃], *n.f.* Exhortation. **exhorter**, *v.t.* To exhort, to encourage.

exhumation [egzymɑ'sjɔ̃], *n.f.* Exhumation, disinterment; unearthing (of something old). **exhumer**, *v.t.* To exhume, to disinter; (*fig.*) to bring to light, to rake up.

exigeant [egzi'ʒɑ̃], *a.* (*fem.* **-eante**) Unreasonable, over-particular, exacting, hard to please.

exigence [egzi'ʒɑ̃s], *n.f.* Unreasonableness; unreasonable claim or demand; exigency, exigence. *Selon l'exigence du cas*, as occasion may require; *se soumettre à toutes les exigences*, to meet all requirements.

exiger [egzi'ʒe], *v.t.* To exact, to require, to demand; to call for, to necessitate. *Exiger des égards*, to enforce respect; *si le besoin l'exige*, if need be. **exigibilité**, *n.f.* Exigibility. **exigible**, *a.* Demandable.

exigu [egzi'gy], *a.* (*fem.* **exiguë**) Very small, exiguous, tiny (house); scanty, slender, slight. **exiguïté**, *n.f.* Scantiness, slenderness, slightness, exiguity.

exil [eg'zil], *n.m.* Exile, banishment. *Envoyer en exil*, to banish. **exilé**, *a.* (*fem.* **-ée**) Exiled.—*n.* Exile. **exiler**, *v.t.* To exile, to banish. **s'exiler**, *v.r.* To exile oneself; to seclude oneself. *Il s'est exilé du monde*, he has withdrawn from the world.

existant [egzis'tɑ̃], *a.* (*fem.* **-ante**) Existing, in being, existent; extant; in force. **existence**, *n.f.* Existence, being, life; subsistence, living; (*pl.*) (*Comm.*) stock on hand. *Existence en magasin*, quantity of commodities in stock. **existentialisme** [egzistɑ̃sja'lism], *n.m.* Existentialism. **existentialiste**, *n.m.* and *a.* Existentialist.

exister [egzis'te], *v.i.* To exist, to be in existence, to live; to be extant. *Cette dette n'existe plus*, this debt is extinct; *les ouvrages qui existent*, the works which are extant.

ex-libris [ɛksli'bris], *n.m. inv.* Book-plate, ex-libris.

exocet [egzɔ'sɛ], *n.m.* Flying-fish.

exode [eg'zɔd], *n.m.* Exodus; exode.

exoderme [ECTODERME].

exogame [egzɔ'gam], *a.* Exogamous. **exogamie**, *n.f.* Exogamy.

exogène [egzɔ'ʒɛn], *a.* (*Bot.*) Exogenous.

exonder (s') [egzɔ̃'de], *v.r.* To dry (of flooded ground).

exonération [egzɔnerɑ'sjɔ̃], *n.f.* Exoneration. **exonérer**, *v.t. irr.* (*conjugated like* ACCÉLÉRER) To exonerate, to discharge, to free from blame, obligation, etc.

exophtalmie [egzɔftal'mi], *n.f.* Exophthalmia. **exophtalmique**, *a.* Exophthalmic.

exorable [egzɔ'rabl], *a.* Lenient, merciful.

exorbitance [egzɔrbi'tɑ̃s], *n.f.* Exorbitance. **exorbitant**, *a.* (*fem.* **-ante**) Exorbitant, unconscionable. **exorbité**, *a.* Out of the orbit. *Des yeux exorbités*, eyes popping out of their sockets.

exorciser [egzɔrsi'ze], *v.t.* To exorcize, to put out (devils etc.). **exorciseur**, *n.m.* Exorcist. **exorcisme**, *n.m.* Exorcism.

exorciste [EXORCISEUR].

exorde [eg'zɔrd], *n.m.* Exordium, beginning (of a speech etc.).

exosmose [egzɔs'moːz], *n.f.* Exosmose, exosmosis. **exosmotique**, *a.* Exosmotic.

exosquelette [egzɔskə'lɛt], *n.m.* Exoskeleton.

exostose [egzɔs'toz], *n.f.* Exostosis.

exotérique [egzɔte'rik], *a.* Exoteric.

exotique [egzɔ'tik], *a.* Exotic; foreign, outlandish. **exotisme**, *n.m.* Exotism, exoticism.

expansibilité [ɛkspɑ̃sibili'te], *n.f.* Expansibility. **expansible**, *a.* Expansible, expansive. **expansif**, *a.* (*fem.* **-ive**) Expansive; (*fig.*) unreserved, open-hearted, overflowing, communicative.

expansion [ɛkspɑ̃'sjɔ̃], *n.f.* Expansion; development; (*fig.*) unreservedness, opening out. *Avoir de l'expansion*, to be open, unreserved, communicative; *avec expansion*, effusively; *expansion économique*, economic expansion.

expatriation [ɛkspatriɑ'sjɔ̃], *n.f.* Expatriation; self-banishment. **expatrier**, *v.t.* To expatriate, to exile, to banish from one's country. **s'expatrier**, *v.r.* To expatriate oneself; to leave one's country.

expectant [ɛkspɛk'tɑ̃], *a.* (*fem.* **-ante**) Expectant. *Candidat expectant*, prospective candidate.

expectatif [ɛkspɛkta'tif], *a.* (*fem.* **expec⁺ative** (1)) Expectative. **expectation**, *n.f.* Expectation; (*Med.*) expectant treatment. **expectative** (2), *n.f.* Expectation, hope, expectancy. *Être dans l'expectative*, to live in hopes.

expectorant [ɛkspɛktɔ'rɑ̃], *a.* and *n.* (*fem.* **-ante**) Expectorant.

expectoration [ɛkspɛktɔrɑ'sjɔ̃], *n.f.* Expectoration; sputa. **expectorer**, *v.t.* To expectorate, to spit.

expédiée [ɛkspe'dje], *n.f.* Running hand (writing).

expédient (1) [ɛkspe'djɑ̃], *a.* (*fem.* **-ente**) Expedient, advisable, fit, meet.

expédient (2) [ɛkspe'djɑ̃], *n.m.* Expedient, device, way; last shift. *En être réduit aux expédients*, to be reduced to expedients *or* to shifts; *homme d'expédients*, man full of expedients *or* man of resource; *son dernier expédient*, one's last shift.

expédier [ɛkspe'dje], *v.t.* To dispatch, to send off, to forward; to do quickly, to knock off, to clear off, to clear (at the custom-house); to draw up (a deed etc.). *Expédier des marchandises*, to forward goods; *expédier des troupes*, to send off troops; *expédier un acte*, to draw up a deed. **expéditeur**, *n.m.* (*fem.* **-trice**) Sender (by post); shipper, consigner. **expéditif**, *a.* (*fem.* **-ive**) Expeditious, quick.

expédition [ɛkspedi'sjɔ̃], *n.f.* Expedition, dispatch; sending, shipment; consignment, thing sent; execution, performance; (*Law*) copy (of a deed etc.); (*Geog.*) expedition. *Faire l'expédition de*, to forward; *homme d'expédition*, business-like man; *bulletin d'expédition*, way-bill; (*fait*) *en double expédition*, in duplicate; (*Polit.*) *expédition des affaires courantes*, taking charge of the normal business; *une expédition de secours*, a rescue party. **expéditionnaire**, *a.* Expeditionary. —*n.m.* Sender, shipper; commission-agent,

copying-clerk, forwarding-clerk. *(Mil.)* *Corps expéditionnaire*, expeditionary force. **expéditive** [EXPÉDITIF]. **expéditivement**, *adv.* Expeditiously.
expérience [ɛkspe´rjɑ̃:s], *n.f.* Experience; trial, experiment, test. *Des expériences de chimie*, experiments in chemistry; *faire une expérience*, to make an experiment; *il n'a pas d'expérience*, he is inexperienced; *parler par expérience*, to speak from experience.
expérimental [ɛksperimɑ̃´tal], *a.* (*fem.* -ale, *pl.* -aux) Experimental. **expérimentalement**, *adv.* Experimentally. **expérimentalisme**, *n.m.* Experimentalism. **expérimentaliste**, *a.* Experimental.—*n.* Experimentalist. **expérimentateur**, *a.* (*fem.* -trice) Experimentative.—*n.* Experimenter. **expérimentation**, *n.f.* Experimentation. **expérimenté**, *a.* (*fem.* -ée) Experienced. **expérimenter**, *v.t.* To experiment, to test; to experience.
expert [ɛks´pɛ:r], *a.* (*fem.* -te) Expert, skilful, well versed in.—*n.m.* Connoisseur; appraiser, valuer, surveyor; expert. *À dire d'experts*, according to expert advice; *(Naut.) expert en avaries*, average adjustor; *expert comptable*, chartered accountant. **expertement**, *adv.* Expertly, skilfully. **expertise**, *n.f.* Survey, valuation, assessment (of specially appointed surveyors); report (of survey), appraisement. *Faire une expertise*, to make a valuation. **expertiser**, *v.t.* To make a survey of; to appraise, to value, to assess.
expiable [ɛks´pjabl], *a.* Expiable. **expiateur**, *a.* (*fem.* -trice) Expiatory.
expiation [ɛkspja´sjɔ̃], *n.f.* Expiation, atonement, satisfaction. *En expiation de*, as an atonement for; *faire expiation de*, to make an atonement for. **expiatoire**, *a.* Expiatory. *Sacrifice expiatoire*, sin-offering.
expier [ɛks´pje], *v.t.* To expiate, to atone, to make reparation for.
expirant [ɛkspi´rɑ̃], *a.* (*fem.* -ante) Expiring, dying. **expirateur**, *a.m.* *(Anat.)* Expiratory (muscle).
expiration [ɛkspira´sjɔ̃], *n.f.* Expiration, breathing out; expiry. **expirer**, *v.t.* To breathe out; exhale.—*v.i.* To expire, to breathe one's last, to die; to die away, to come to an end, to run out. *Mon bail a expiré hier*, my lease was up yesterday.
explétif [ɛksple´tif], *a.* (*fem.* -ive) *(Gram.)* Expletive.—*n.m.* Expletive. **explétivement**, *adv.* By way of expletive.
explicable [ɛkspli´kabl], *a.* Explicable. **explicateur**, *a.* (*fem.* -trice) Explicative.—*n.* Explainer; cicerone, guide. **explicatif**, *a.* (*fem.* -ive) Explicative, explanatory.
explication [ɛksplika´sjɔ̃], *n.f.* Explanation, explication; interpretation, construing; meaning. *Avoir une explication avec*, to have it out with; *cela demande explication*, that requires an explanation; *explication de texte*, literary exercise involving detailed commentary on a passage.
explicite [ɛkspli´sit], *a.* Explicit, clear, express. **explicitement**, *adv.* Explicitly, clearly. **expliciter**, *v.t.* To make explicit.
expliquer [ɛkspli´ke], *v.t.* To explain, to account for, to expound; to interpret, to construe; to make known. *Expliquer une énigme*, to solve a riddle. **s'expliquer**, *v.r.*

To explain oneself; to have an explanation; to be explained, to be accounted for, to be cleared up. **expliqueur**, *n.m.* Explainer.
exploit [ɛks´plwa], *n.m.* Exploit, achievement, feat; *(Law)* writ, process. *Dresser un exploit*, to draw up a writ; *signifier un exploit*, to serve a writ.
exploitabilité [ɛksplwatabili´te], *n.f.* Workableness. **exploitable**, *a.* Workable, that may be turned to account; *(Law)* distrainable. *Cette mine est encore exploitable*, that mine may still be worked. **exploitant**, *n.m.* (*fem.* -ante) Operator (of mines etc.); farmer, grower.—*a.* Process-serving. *Huissier exploitant*, process-server.
exploitation [ɛksplwata´sjɔ̃], *n.f.* Working, improving (of lands etc.); farming estate; cultivation (of woods etc.); employing, using; taking advantage of, exploitation, cheating, sweating system. *En exploitation*, being worked; *exploitation d'un champ*, cultivation of a field; *exploitation rurale*, farming; *matériel d'exploitation*, working-stock; *mettre en exploitation*, to work; *l'exploitation des chemins de fer*, the administrative railway work. **exploiter**, *v.t.* To work, to improve, to cultivate, to use; to make the most of; to exploit, to take (unfair) advantage of, to impose upon. *Cet homme m'a exploité*, that man has taken advantage of me; *exploiter la curiosité publique*, to trade on public curiosity; *exploiter une mine*, to work a mine; *exploiter une place*, to make the most of a situation.— *v.i.* *(Law)* To serve writs. **exploiteur**, *n.m.* (*fem.* -euse) Exploiter, person who takes advantage (of others), who works or uses (others), sweater of labour.
explorable [ɛksplɔ´rabl], *a.* Explorable. **explorateur**, *n.m.* (*fem.* -trice) Explorer.—*a.* Exploratory; exploring.
exploration [ɛksplɔra´sjɔ̃], *n.f.* Exploration. **explorer**, *v.t.* To explore, to search into, to investigate. *Explorer une plaie*, to probe a wound.
exploser [ɛksplo´ze], *v.i.* To explode, to blow up. **exploseur**, *n.m.* Electric exploder. **explosible**, *a.* Explosive. **explosif**, *a.* (*fem.* -ive) Explosive, that explodes.—*n.m.* Explosive, blasting agent. *Explosif nucléaire*, nuclear explosive; *un explosif à haute puissance*, a high explosive.
explosion [ɛksplo´zjɔ̃], *n.f.* Explosion; bursting, blowing up; *(fig.)* outbreak, outburst. *Explosion de colère*, outburst of anger; *faire explosion*, to explode, to burst out, to break out, to burst.
exponentiel [ɛkspɔnɑ̃´sjɛl], *a.* (*fem.* exponentielle (1)) Exponential. **exponentielle** (2), *n.f.* Exponential.
exportable [ɛkspɔr´tabl], *a.* Exportable. **exportateur** [ɛkspɔrta´tœːr], *a.* (*fem.* -trice) Exporting.—*n.* Exporter.
exportation [ɛkspɔrta´sjɔ̃], *n.f.* Exportation, export, export trade. *Prime d'exportation*, bounty, drawback.
exporter [ɛkspɔr´te], *v.t.* To export.
exposant [ɛkspo´zɑ̃], *n.m.* (*fem.* -ante) Exhibitor; *(Law)* petitioner; *(Math.)* exponent, index.
exposé [ɛkspo´ze], *n.m.* Statement, explanation; account, report. *Exposé de motifs*, explanatory statement; *faire un exposé*, to

draw up a statement.—*a.* (*fem.* **-ée**) Exposed, on view; exposed or dangerous (position). *Objet exposé*, exhibit; *une maison bien exposée*, a house with a pleasant aspect.
exposer [ɛkspo'ze], *v.t.* To expose, to expose to view, to show, to exhibit; to lay bare; to state, to set forth, to expound, to explain; to endanger, to render liable to, to lay open to. *Exposer en vente*, to expose for sale; *exposer son point de vue*, to state one's views; *exposer un corps mort sur un lit de parade*, to lay out a dead body in state; *exposer un enfant*, to abandon a child; *exposer un système*, to unfold a system.—*v.i.* To explain; to expound one's views etc.; to exhibit. *Ce peintre n'a pas encore exposé*, that painter has not yet exhibited; *je ne connais personne qui expose mieux*, I know no one who can explain a thing better. **s'exposer**, *v.r.* To expose oneself; to be exposed, to be liable, to lay oneself open, to lie open. *Il s'expose à la risée de tout le monde*, he makes himself the laughing-stock of everybody.
exposition [ɛkspozi'sjɔ̃], *n.f.* Exhibition, show; exposure; lying-in-state (of the dead); situation, aspect; statement, explanation, recital, account; introduction (to a play etc.). *Exposition de fleurs*, flower-show; *exposition internationale*, international exhibition; *faire une fidèle exposition de toutes ses raisons*, to give a faithful account of all one's reasons; *maison dans une exposition agréable*, house with a pleasant aspect.
expositoire [ɛkspozi'twaːr], *a.* Expository.
exprès [ɛks'prɛ], *a.* (*fem.* **expresse**) Express, precise, formal, positive. *La loi est expresse sur ce point*, the law is positive on that point. —*n.m.* Express (messenger).—*adv.* Expressly, purposely, on purpose. *C'est un fait exprès*, it is done on purpose; *elle l'a dit exprès*, she said it on purpose; *il semble fait exprès pour cela*, he seems to be cut out for it. **express** [ɛks'prɛs], *a.* (*Rail.*) Express.—*n.m.* Express train. **expressément**, *adv.* Expressly, positively; clearly, distinctly. *Il est expressément défendu de fumer*, smoking is strictly prohibited.
expressif [ɛksprɛ'sif], *a.* (*fem.* **-ive**) Expressive.
expression [ɛksprɛ'sjɔ̃], *n.f.* Expression; manner of this, expressiveness, terms, diction, style, gesture, utterance; squeezing out (a liquid); (*Math.*) expression. *Au delà de toute expression*, beyond all expression; *expression imaginaire*, (*Alg.*) imaginary expression; *la plus simple expression*, (*Math.*) the lowest terms; *sans expression*, unexpressive. **expressivement**, *adv.* Expressively, with expression.
exprimable [ɛkspri'mabl], *a.* Expressible.
exprimer [ɛkspri'me], *v.t.* To express, to press or squeeze out; to be expressive of; to convey by words, gesture, etc., to utter, to voice, to betoken. *Exprimer le suc d'une plante*, to squeeze the juice out of a plant. **s'exprimer**, *v.r.* To express one's thoughts etc.; to be expressed. *Je m'exprime mal*, I am expressing myself badly, that's not really what I mean.
expropriation [ɛksproprɑ'sjɔ̃], *n.f.* Expropriation, dispossession, compulsory purchase. *Jury d'expropriation*, valuation jury. **exproprier**, *v.t.* To expropriate, to dispossess; to requisition (buildings).

expulser [ɛkspyl'se], *v.t.* To expel, to turn out; to eject, to drive out; to eliminate. *Expulser un locataire*, to evict a tenant. **expulsif** (*fem.* **-ive**), *a.* Expulsive. **expulsion**, *n.f.* Expulsion; (*Law*) ejection; (*Med.*) evacuation.
expurgation [ɛkspyrgɑ'sjɔ̃], *n.f.* Expurgation. **expurgatoire**, *a.* Expurgatory. **expurger**, *v.t.* To expurgate, to bowdlerize (a book).
exquis [ɛks'ki], *a.* (*fem.* **-ise**) Exquisite, nice, refined, delicate, choice, select. *Avoir un goût exquis*, to have exquisite taste; *vin exquis*, delicious wine. **exquisement**, *adv.* Exquisitely. **exquisité**, *n.f.* Exquisiteness.
exsangue [ɛk'sãːg], *a.* Bloodless, anaemic.
exsuccion or **exsuction** [ɛksyk'sjɔ̃], *n.f.* Sucking up or out.
exsudation [ɛksydɑ'sjɔ̃], *n.f.* Exudation, sweat, perspiration; oozing out. **exsuder**, *v.i.* To exude, to perspire; to ooze out.—*v.t.* To exude.
extase [ɛks'taːz], *n.f.* Ecstasy, rapture, transport; (*Med.*) trance. *Tomber en extase*, to be entranced, to fall into ecstasy. **s'extasier**, *v.r.* To be enraptured, to be ravished, to be entranced with admiration, enthusiasm, etc.
extatique [ɛkstatik], *a.* Ecstatic, rapturous.
extemporané [ɛkstãpora'ne], *a.* (*fem.* **-ée**) Extemporaneous, improvised, made offhand; unpremeditated. **extemporanéité**, *n.f.* Extemporaneousness.
extenseur [ɛkstã'sœːr], *a.* and *n.m.* (*Anat.*) Extensor; chest-expander, exerciser. *Extenseur de pantalon*, trouser-press.
extensibilité [ɛkstãsibili'te], *n.f.* Extensibility. **extensible**, *a.* Extensible. **extensif**, *a.* (*fem.* **-ive**) Causing extension; extensive.
extension [ɛkstã'sjɔ̃], *n.f.* Extension, stretching; extent, span; increase, augmentation. *Prendre de l'extension*, to grow, to increase, to spread.
extenso (in) [inɛkstɛ̃'so], *adv. phr.* In full.
exténuant [ɛkste'nɥɑ̃], *a.* (*fem.* **-ante**) Extenuating. **exténuation**, *n.f.* Extenuation, exhaustion, debility. **exténuer**, *v.t.* To extenuate, to enfeeble, to weaken, to debilitate; to attenuate. *Être exténué de fatigue*, to be worn out, dead tired. **s'exténuer**, *v.r.* To wear oneself out.
extérieur [ɛkste'rjœːr], *a.* Exterior, external, outward; foreign.—*n.m.* Exterior; outside appearance; foreign countries, abroad; (*Cine.*) exterior. *A l'intérieur et à l'extérieur*, outside and in; at home and abroad. **extérieurement**, *adv.* Externally, outwardly; (*fig.*) in appearance, superficially. **extériorisation**, *n.f.* Exteriorization. **extérioriser**, *v.t.* To exteriorize. **s'extérioriser**, *v.r.* To express one's inner feelings.
exterminateur [ɛkstermina'tœːr], *a.* (*fem.* **-trice**) Exterminating, destroying.—*n.* Destroyer, exterminator.
extermination [ɛkstermina'sjɔ̃], *n.f.* Extermination. **exterminer**, *v.t.* To exterminate, to destroy, to annihilate. **s'exterminer**, *v.r.* To destroy each other; (*fam.*) to exert oneself to death.
externat [ɛkster'na], *n.m.* Day-school; post of dresser (in hospital).
externe [ɛks'tern], *a.* External, exterior, outer. (*Med.*) *Pour l'usage externe*, not to be

taken.—*n.m.* Day-scholar; non-resident medical student (in hospitals), dresser.

exterritorialité [ɛksteritɔrjali'te], *n.f.* Exterritoriality.

extincteur [ɛkstɛ̃k'tœːr], *a.* (*fem.* **-trice**) Extinguishing (fire).—*n.m.* Fire-extinguisher.

extinction [ɛkstɛ̃k'sjɔ̃], *n.f.* Extinction, destruction, suppression, cessation, abolition; redemption (of annuities); liquidation, settlement (of debts); quelling, suppression (of disturbances); quenching (of thirst); slaking (of lime). *Extinction de voix*, loss of voice; *l'extinction des feux*, (*Mil.*) the lights-out call.

extinguible, *a.* Extinguishable; quenchable.

extirpage [ɛkstir'paːʒ], *n.m.* (*Agric.*) Scarifying. **extirpateur**, *a.* (*fem.* **-trice**) Extirpating.—*n.m.* Extirpator, destroyer; (*Agric.*) weeder, weeding-tool, scarifier.

extirpation [ɛkstirpɑ'sjɔ̃], *n.f.* Extirpation. **extirper**, *v.t.* To extirpate.

extorquer [ɛkstɔr'ke], *v.t.* To extort, to wrest or worm out of. **extorsion**, *n.f.* Extortion.

extra [ɛks'tra], *n.m. inv.* Extra, something extra. *C'était ma fête et nous avons fait un extra* or *un peu d'extra*, it was my birthday, so we had something extra, *or* out of the common.—*a.* Extra (special). *Un vin extra*, perfect, superfine wine.

extrabudgétaire [ɛkstrabydʒe'teːr], *a.* (Of expenses) Not included in the budget.

extra-conjugal [ɛkstrakɔ̃ʒy'gal], *a.* (*fem.* **-ale**, *pl.* **-aux**) Extra-marital. *Plaisirs extra-conjugaux*, illicit pleasures.

extra-courant [ɛkstraku'rɑ̃], *n.m.* Extra-current.

extracteur [ɛkstrak'tœr], *n.m.* Extractor. **extractible**, *a.* Extractible. **extractif**, *a.* (*fem.* **-ive**) Extractive.

extraction [ɛkstrak'sjɔ̃], *n.f.* Extraction; origin, descent, birth. *De basse extraction*, of low birth, of humble parentage; *l'extraction d'une dent*, the drawing of a tooth.

extrader [ɛkstra'de], *v.t.* To extradite. **extradition**, *n.f.* Extradition.

extrados [ɛkstra'do], *n.m. inv.* (*Arch.*) Extrados. **extradosser**, *v.t.* To curve (an arch).

extra-fin [ɛkstra'fɛ̃], *a.* (*fem.* **extra-fine**) Extra-fine, superfine.

extraire [ɛks'trɛːr], *v.t. irr.* (*conjugated like* TRAIRE) To extract, to draw, to take, pull, dig, or put out; to make extracts from.

extrait [ɛks'trɛ], *n.m.* Extract; excerpt, selection; abstract; certificate. *Extrait de naissance, de baptême*, or *de mariage*, certificate of birth, baptism, *or* marriage; *extrait mortuaire*, certificate of death. *Extrait de bœuf*, beef extract.

extrajudiciaire [ɛkstraʒydi'sjɛːr], *a.* Extrajudicial. **extrajudiciairement**, *adv.* Extrajudicially, out of court.

extra-muros [ɛkstramy'roːs], *adv.* Outside the walls (of a city). *Cimetière extra-muros*, suburban cemetery.

extranéité [ɛkstranei'te], *n.f.* (*Law*) Alien status.

extraordinaire [ɛkstraɔrdi'nɛːr], *a.* Extraordinary, unusual, uncommon; odd, queer; prodigious. *Ambassadeur extraordinaire*, Ambassador extraordinary; (*Polit.*) *réunion extraordinaire*, special meeting; *visage extra-ordinaire*, odd face.—*n.m.* Extraordinariness; extraordinary, queer, or uncommon thing.

L'extraordinaire c'est que . . . , the extraordinary part of it is . . . **extraordinairement**, *adv.* Extraordinarily, unusually; oddly, enormously.

extrapolation [ɛkstrapɔla'sjɔ̃], *n.f.* (*Math.*) Extrapolation. **extrapoler**, *v.t.* To extrapolate.

extra-scolaire [ɛkstraskɔ'lɛr], *a.* Out-of-school (activities).

extra-terrestre [ɛkstrate'rɛstr], *a.* Extra-terrestrial.

extravagamment [ɛkstravaga'mɑ̃], *adv.* Extravagantly, unreasonably.

extravagance [ɛkstrava'gɑ̃ːs], *n.f.* Extravagance, extravagant act. *Il a dit mille extravagances*, he said a lot of foolish things; *j'ai pitié de son extravagance*, I pity his folly. **extravagant**, *a.* (*fem.* **-ante**) Extravagant, wild, exorbitant (price, etc.), immoderate.— *n.* Extravagant person, eccentric.

extravaguer, *v.i.* To talk wildly, to rave, to be light-headed.

extravasation [ɛkstravaza'sjɔ̃] or **extravasion**, *n.f.* Extravasation, effusion (of blood etc.). **s'extravaser**, *v.r.* To be extravasated (of blood etc.).

extrême [ɛks'trɛːm], *a.* Extreme, utmost; excessive, outrageous.—*n.m.* Extreme or utmost point. *Il se jette dans les extrêmes*, he runs into extremes; *jusqu'à l'extrême* or *à l'extrême*, to an extreme; *les extrêmes se touchent*, extremes meet. **extrêmement**, *adv.* **extrême-onction**, *n.f.* Extreme unction.

Extrême-Orient [ɛkstremɔ'rjɑ̃], *m.* Far East.

extrémiste [ɛkstre'mist], *n.m.* Extremist, diehard.

extrémité [ɛkstremi'te], *n.f.* Extremity, end; tip, point; last moment, end of life; (*fig.*) verge, border, brink; (*pl.*) extremes, extremities. *À l'extrémité*, to extremity, without resource, dying; *à toute extrémité*, at the worst; *pousser à la dernière extrémité*, to drive to extremities.

extrinsèque [ɛkstrɛ̃'sɛk], *a.* Extrinsic. *Valeur extrinsèque des monnaies*, value assigned to coins independently of their actual weight. **extrinsèquement**, *adv.* Extrinsically.

extrorse [ɛks'trɔrs], *a.* (*Bot.*) Extrorse.

exubérance [ɛgzybe'rɑ̃ːs], *n.f.* Exuberance, luxuriance. **exubérant**, *a.* (*fem.* **-ante**) Exuberant, luxuriant.

exulcérant [ɛgzylse'rɑ̃] or **exulcératif**, *a.* (*fem.* **-ante** or **-ive**) Producing ulcers or exulceration. **exulcération**, *n.f.* Exulceration. **exulcérer**, *v.t.* To exulcerate.

exultation [ɛgzylta'sjɔ̃], *n.f.* Exultation, rapture. **exulter**, *v.i.* To exult.

exutoire [ɛgzy'twaːr], *n.m.* (*Med.*) Issue; (*fig.*) outlet.

ex-voto [ɛksvo'to], *n.m. inv.* Ex-voto, votive offering.

eyra [e'ra], *n.m.* South American cougar.

Ézéchiel [eze'kjɛl], *m.* Ezekiel.

F

F, f [ɛf], *n.m.* The sixth letter of the alphabet. **f.** or **fr.**, franc; **f.** (*Mus.*) *forte*. **ff.**, *fortissimo*.

fa [fa], *n.m.* (*Mus.*) fa; F. *Clef de fa*, bass, bass-clef.

fabagelle [faba'ʒɛl], *n.f.*, or **fabago**, *n.m.* False caper, bean caper.

Fabien [fa'bjɛ̃], *m.* Fabian.

fable [fɑːbl], *n.f.* Fable; story, tale, myth; mythology; (*fig.*) untruth, fiction, invention, falsehood; laughing-stock, byword. *Être la fable de tout le monde*, to be the laughing-stock or byword of everybody. **fabliau** (*pl.* -iaux) or **fableau**, *n.m.* A medieval short story in old French. **fablier**, *n.m.* Book of fables; fabulist.

fabricant [fabri'kɑ̃], *n.m.* Manufacturer, maker.

fabricateur [fabrika'tœːr], *n.m.* (*fem.* -trice) Fabricator, coiner, forger. *Fabricateur de fausse monnaie*, coiner of base money.

fabrication [fabrikɑ'sjɔ̃], *n.f.* Fabrication, manufacture, making; forgery; coining. *La fabrication d'un faux acte*, the forging of a deed.

fabricien [fabri'sjɛ̃], *n.m.* Vestry-man.

fabrique [fa'brik], *n.f.* Building, fabric (esp. of churches); vestry-board; manufactory, factory, works, mill; fabrication; making, make. *Conseil de fabrique*, select vestry; *fabrique de chaussures*, boot-factory; *marque de fabrique*, trade-mark; *prix de fabrique*, cost or manufacturer's price.

fabriquer [fabri'ke], *v.t.* To manufacture, to make, to prepare; to fabricate, to invent, to forge, to coin (money); (*slang*) to cheat, to pinch. **se fabriquer**, *v.r.* To be manufactured; to make for oneself.

fabulation [fabylɑ'sjɔ̃], *n.f.* (*Lit.*) Working out of a plot.

fabuleuse [FABULEUX].

fabuleusement [fabyløz'mɑ̃], *adv.* Fabulously; (*fig.*) incredibly.

fabuleux [faby'lø], *a.* (*fem.* -euse) Fabulous, fictitious; (*fig.*) extraordinary, incredible.

fabuliste [faby'list], *n.m.* Fabulist.

façade [fa'sad], *n.f.* Façade, front, face (of an edifice); (*fig.*) exterior, appearance.

face [fas], *n.f.* Face, visage, countenance; front, façade (of a building); surface; side (of a record); (*fig.*) state, aspect, appearance; posture, turn (of affairs). *A la face de*, in the presence of, at the sight of; *de face*, in front, abreast of, full face; *en face de*, in the face of, opposite, in the presence of; *la maison d'en face*, the house opposite; *face à face*, face to face; *face de carême*, pale face; *face de réprouvé*, sinister-looking countenance; *face de lame*, flat of (sword) blade; *faire face à*, to face, to fulfil, to meet; *faire face à ses engagements*, to meet one's engagements; *faire volte-face*, to face about; *jouer à pile ou face*, to play pitch-and-toss, at heads or tails; *les affaires ont bien changé de face*, things have taken quite another turn; *perdre la face*, to lose face; *sauver la face*, to save face; *une face réjouie*, a jolly face; *vu de face*, seen in front or from the front.

face-à-main [fasa'mɛ̃], *n.m.* (*pl.* **faces-à-main**) Lady's lorgnette.

facétie [fase'si], *n.f.* Facetiousness; jest, joke, witty saying. *Recueil de facéties*, collection of facetiae. **facétieusement**, *adv.* Facetiously. **facétieux**, *a.* (*fem.* -ieuse) Facetious, jocular, humorous.—*n.m.* Facetious literature etc.; jester, joker.

facette [fa'sɛt], *n.f.* Facet, face. *Diamant taillé à facettes*, diamond cut into facets. **facetter**, *v.t.* To cut with facets.

fâcher [fɑ'ʃe], *v.t.* To anger, to offend, to vex, to displease. *Être fâché avec*, to be on bad terms with; *être fâché contre quelqu'un*, to be angry with someone; *il est fâché de vous avoir offensé*, he is sorry he has offended you; *soit dit sans vous fâcher*, with all due deference. **se fâcher**, *v.r.* To get angry, to be offended. *Ne vous fâchez pas*, do not take offence. **fâcherie**, *n.f.* Angry feeling; disagreement, quarrel, vexation. **fâcheusement**, *adv.* Unfortunately, unpleasantly, inopportunely, disagreeably, awkwardly. **fâcheux**, *a.* (*fem.* -euse) Troublesome, vexatious; unfortunate, inopportune; cross, peevish. *C'est un fâcheux personnage*, he is a troublesome personage; *il est fâcheux que vous n'ayez pas été averti à temps*, it is a pity that you were not told in time.—*n.* Troublesome or disagreeable person or thing, pesterer, intruder, bore. *Le fâcheux de l'affaire*, the worst of the matter.

facial [fa'sjal], *a.* (*fem.* -iale, *pl.* -iaux) (*Anat.*) Facial. *Angle facial*, facial angle; *massage facial*, face massage.

faciès [fa'sjɛːs], *n.m. inv.* Aspect of the face, physiognomy; aspect, bearing.

facile [fa'sil], *a.* Easy; facile; free, flowing, fluent; ready, quick; yielding, complying, pliant, weak. *Avoir la parole facile*, to have a fluent tongue, to be a ready speaker; *style facile*, easy, fluent style; *tout cela est plus facile à dire qu'à faire*, all that is easier said than done; *un homme facile*, an easy-going man. **facilement**, *adv.* Easily, readily; yieldingly; fluently. **facilité**, *n.f.* Facility, ease; readiness; fluency; quickness; (*pl.*) facilities, easy terms (for payment). *Il a une grande facilité de parole*, he has great fluency of speech. **faciliter**, *v.t.* To facilitate, to make easy.

façon [fa'sɔ̃], *n.f.* Make, shape, fashion, cut; making, workmanship, labour, work; (*Agric.*) dressing; (*fig.*) way, manner, style, mode; look, appearance, mien; kind, sort, quality; imitation; compliment; affectation; ceremony, fuss, attention, (*pl.*) ceremony, elaborate civilities, fuss; (*Naut.*) runs. *A la façon de*, after the manner of; *avoir bonne façon*, to look well, to be good-looking; *donner à façon*, to put out to make; *ici on travaille à façon*, customers' own materials are made up on the premises; *tailleur à façon*, bespoke tailor; *cela n'a ni mine ni façon*, that has neither grace nor shape; *c'est sa façon de penser*, it is his way of thinking; *de cette façon*, in this manner; *de façon que* or *de telle façon que*, in such a way as, so that; *de quelque façon que ce soit*, anyhow; *de sa façon*, of his own invention; *des vers de ma façon*, verses of my own composition; *à toute façon*, at any rate; *en aucune façon*, by no means; *faire des façons*, to be ceremonious; *la façon d'un habit*, the make or the cut of a coat; *sans façon*, without ceremony.

faconde [fa'kɔ̃ːd], *n.f.* Talkativeness, loquacity; fluency of speech. *Avoir de la faconde*, to have the gift of the gab.

façonné [fasɔ'ne], *a.* (*fem.* -ée) Figured (of stuffs); wrought.—*n.m.* Figured stuff. **façonnement**, **façonnage**, *n.m.*, or **façonnerie**, *n.f.* Fashioning, shaping, making.

façonner [faso'ne], *v.t.* To make, to fashion, to figure, to form; to work, to mould, to cultivate; to accustom, to use (to discipline etc.).

façonnier [faso'nje], *a.* (*fem.* **-ière**) Ceremonious, formal, affected.—*n.* Bespoke tailor.

fac-similaire [faksimi'lɛ:r], *a.* Exactly copied. **fac-similé,** *n.m.* Facsimile. **fac-similer,** *v.t.* To make an exact copy.

factage [fak'ta:ʒ], *n.m.* Porterage, carriage, transport (of goods or parcels); delivery service or company; cost of transport.

facteur [fak'tœ:r], *n.m.* (*fem.* **-trice**) Maker, manufacturer (of musical instruments); agent, merchant's assistant; postman, letter-carrier; railway porter; (*Math., Biol.*) factor. **Facteur aux halles,* public crier of goods at markets; *facteur de pianos,* pianoforte-maker; *facteur d'orgues,* organ-builder.

factice [fak'tis], *a.* Factitious, artificial; unnatural, forced, got up (of words). *Bouteilles, boîtes factices,* dummy bottles, boxes.—*n.* That which is factitious; rubber substitute. **facticement,** *adv.* Factitiously. **facticité,** *n.f.* Factitiousness.

factieux [fak'sjø], *a.* (*fem.* **-ieuse**) Factious, mutinous, seditious.—*n.* Rebel, sedition-monger.

faction [fak'sjɔ̃], *n.f.* Watch, sentry-duty; faction. *Être en faction* or *de faction,* to be on sentry duty; *relever de faction,* to relieve sentry. **factionnaire,** *n.m.* Sentry.

factitif [fakti'tif], *a.* (*fem.* **-ive**) Factitive.

factorerie [faktɔrə'ri], *n.f.* Trading depot, factory (in a colony etc.).

factorielle [faktɔ'rjɛl], *n.f.* (*Alg.*) Factorial.

factotum [faktɔ'tɔm], *n.m.* Factotum, odd-job-man.

factrice [FACTEUR].

factum [fak'tɔm], *n.m.* (*Law*) Printed statement (of a cause); memorial, address, pamphlet.

facturation [faktyrɑ'sjɔ̃], *n.f.* (*Fin.*) Invoicing.

facture (1) [fak'ty:r], *n.f.* Making, make, composition, workmanship (of music, verse, etc.); quality, dimensions (of organ pipes). *Couplet de facture,* couplet showing technical accomplishment; *morceau de facture,* piece of music for display of execution; *poème d'une belle facture,* well written poem.

facture (2) [fak'ty:r], *n.f.* (*Comm.*) Bill (of sale), invoice, bill. *Faire une facture,* to make out an invoice; *livre de factures,* invoice-book; *entête de facture,* bill-head. **facturer,** *v.t.* To invoice. **facturier,** *n.m.* Invoice-book; invoice-clerk.

facule [fa'kyl], *n.f.* (*Astron.*) Facula.

facultatif [fakylta'tif], *a.* (*fem.* **-ive**) Optional, discretionary. *Arrêt facultatif,* request stop. **facultativement,** *adv.* Facultatively.

faculté [fakyl'te], *n.f.* Faculty, ability, power, property, quality; option, privilege, right; (*pl.*) mental faculties. *Facultés intellectuelles,* mind, intellectual faculties; *la Faculté des Lettres,* (*Univ.*) the Faculty of Arts; *la Faculté,* the (medical) Faculty, the Doctors, the medical profession; *les facultés de l'esprit,* the powers of the mind.

fada [fa'da], *a. and n.* (*S. Fr.*) Not all there, simple, touched.

fadaise [fa'dɛ:z], *n.f.* Trifle, stuff, nonsense, twaddle. *Fadaises que tout cela!* tomfoolery!

fadasse [fa'das], *a.* Insipid; (*fig.*) mawkish, sickening; washed-out.

fade [fad], *a.* Insipid, unsavoury, tasteless, dull; (*fig.*) pointless, tame, flat, stale. **fadement,** *adv.* Insipidly, tastelessly; mawkishly.

fadeur [fa'dœr], *n.f.* Insipidity, tastelessness; (*fig.*) pointlessness, tameness.

fading [fe'diŋ], *n.m.* (*Rad.*) Fading effect.

fafiot [fa'fjo], *n.m.* (*Slang*) Banknote.

fagne [faɲ], *n.f.* (*Ardennes*) Heath, peat-moss.

fagot [fa'go], *n.m.* Faggot, bundle of sticks etc.; (*fig.*) uncouth person; (*slang*) former convict, ticket-of-leave man; **(colloq.)* idle tale. *Vin de derrière les fagots,* the best wine (concealed and kept by the vine-grower); *être habillé comme un fagot,* to be dressed in a slovenly manner; *fagot d'épines,* thorny, unapproachable person; *il y a fagots et fagots,* there are men and men, men or things are not all alike; *sentir le fagot,* to be suspected of heresy (alluding to burning at the stake). **fagotage** or **fagotement,** *n.m.* Faggot-making, tying up of faggots; faggot-wood; bad way of dressing.

fagoter [fago'te], *v.t.* To faggot, to tie into faggots; (*fig.*) to jumble together; to dress in a slovenly manner, to dress like a fright. *Comme le voilà fagoté,* how slovenly dressed he is, what a fright he looks; *peut-on fagoter ainsi un enfant?* how can people make such a fright of a child? **se fagoter,** *v.r.* To dress in a slovenly manner, to dress like a fright. *Cette femme semble prendre à tâche de se fagoter,* that woman seems to do her best to make herself a fright. **fagoteur,** *n.m.* (*fem.* **-euse**) Faggot-maker; (*fig.*) bungler, scribbler.

fagotin [fago'tɛ̃], *n.m.* Small faggot; **monkey dressed up (in man's clothes); (*fig.*) clown, merry-andrew.

faiblard [fɛ'bla:r], *a.* (*fem.* **-arde**) (*fam.*) Weakish.

faible [fɛ:bl], *a.* Weak, feeble; deficient, poor, sorry, slender, slight; (*Naut.*) cranky. *Faible de corps et d'esprit,* weak in body and mind; *homme faible,* weak man; *le plus faible est toujours écrasé,* the weakest goes to the wall. —*n.m.* Weak person; weak side, weak part; defect, foible, failing; partiality, weakness (for). *Avoir un faible pour,* to have a partiality for; *je le tiens par son faible,* I have got him by his weak spot. **faiblement,** *adv.* Weakly, feebly; slenderly, poorly. **faiblesse,** *n.f.* Weakness, feebleness; faintness, fainting fit, swoon, deficiency, backwardness, slenderness, thinness, poorness; defect; foible; partiality, weakness. *Il lui a pris une faiblesse,* he or she was seized with a fainting fit; *tomber en faiblesse,* to swoon, to have a fainting fit; *une femme qui a eu une faiblesse,* a woman that has made a slip. *Les faiblesses de la nature humaine,* human weakness. *Faire preuve d'une grande faiblesse envers quelqu'un,* to be very partial to someone. **faiblir,** *v.i.* To become weak, to flag, to give way, to yield, to abate, to relax. **faiblissant,** *a.* (*fem.* **-ante**) Weakening; dwindling (light).

faïence [fa'jɑ̃:s], *n.f.* Crockery, earthenware, faïence, delft-ware. *Faïence anglaise,* cream ware. **faïencé,** *a.* (*fem.* **-ée**) Imitating faïence. **faïencerie,** *n.f.* Crockery or earthenware factory; crockery shop, pottery (shop or factory). **faïencier,** *n.m.* (*fem.* **-ière**) Dealer in or maker of crockery.

faille (1) [fa:j], *n.f.* (*Geol.*) Fault.

faille (2) [fa:j], *n.f.* Flemish silk of coarse grain, faille; mantle etc. of this.

failli (1) [fa′ji], *a.* and *n.* (*fem.* **faillie**) Bankrupt, insolvent.

faillibilité [fajibili′te], *n.f.* Fallibility, liability to err. **faillible,** *a.* Fallible.

faillir [fa′ji:r], *v.i. irr.* (*p.p.* **failli** (2)) To err, to trespass, to transgress; to give way, to yield, to be lacking; to fail; to go bankrupt; to be on the point of, to be wellnigh. **Fille qui a failli,* a girl who has made a slip; *il a failli tomber,* he all but fell; *il s'en faut beaucoup* or *il s'en faut de beaucoup,* very far from it; *j'irai sans faillir,* I will go without fail; *le cœur me faut,* my heart fails me; *les plus doctes sont sujets à faillir,* the most learned are liable to be mistaken; *peu s'en faut,* very nearly; *tant s'en faut,* far from it.

faillite [fa′jit], *n.f.* Bankruptcy, insolvency; failure. *Actif d'une faillite,* assets in a bankruptcy; *déclaration de faillite,* declaration of insolvency; *être acculé à la faillite,* to be on the verge of bankruptcy; *être en faillite,* to be a bankrupt; *faire faillite,* to fail, to become bankrupt.

faim [fɛ̃], *n.f.* Hunger, appetite; famine; (*fig.*) intense desire, longing, thirst. *Apaiser la faim de quelqu'un,* to stay someone's hunger; *avoir faim,* to be hungry; *faim de loup,* rabid hunger; *faire mourir de faim* or *réduire par la faim,* to starve out; *la faim chasse le loup hors du bois,* hunger will break through stone walls; *mourir de faim,* to be starving; *un meurt-de-faim,* a starveling.

faim-valle [fɛ̃′val], *n.f.* Intense hunger; boulimia (in horses).

faîne [fɛ:n], *n.f.* Beechnut; beechmast.

fainéant [fɛne′ɑ̃], *a.* (*fem.* **-ante**) Idle, lazy, slothful, sluggish.—*n.* Sluggard, loiterer, idler. **fainéanter,** *v.i.* (*colloq.*) To be idle, to be indolent, to loaf. **fainéantise,** *n.f.* Idleness, laziness, sloth.

faire (1) [fɛ:r], *v. irr.* (*pres.p.* **faisant,** *p.p.* **fait**) (The most used verb in the language; *faire* not only translates to do, to make, to form, but, followed by a substantive or an infinitive, it can take the place of practically any verb; followed by an adjective or an adverb it forms many current idioms.)

I. *v.t.* To do; to make; to be. *Aussitôt dit, aussitôt fait,* no sooner said than done; *avoir beaucoup à faire* or *avoir fort à faire,* to have a great deal to do; *cela fait mon affaire,* this is exactly what I want; *cela fait beaucoup,* that makes a great difference; *cela fait mes délices,* that is my greatest delight; *cela ne fait rien,* that makes no difference; *cela ne me fait rien,* that is nothing to me; *ce qui est fait est fait,* what is done cannot be undone; *combien cela fait-il?* how much does that come to? *donner fort à faire à quelqu'un,* to give someone a great deal of trouble; *faire accueil à,* to welcome; *faire marcher une machine,* to set a machine going; *faire attention,* to pay attention, to give heed; *faire banqueroute,* to go bankrupt; *faire bâtir,* to have built; *faire bonne chère,* to live well, to eat luxuriously; *faire bonne mine à quelque*

chose, to put a good face on something; *faire cas de,* to value, to have a high opinion of; *faire compassion,* to excite compassion; *faire connaître,* to make known; *faire des bassesses,* to behave meanly; *faire des provisions,* to store goods; *faire des recrues,* to recruit; (*Motor.*) *faire du 50 à l'heure,* to do 50 m.p.h.; *faire réciter une leçon à quelqu'un,* to hear someone say his lesson; *faire don,* to make a donation; *faire du bien* or *du mal,* to do good or harm; *faire eau,* to have sprung a leak, to leak; *faire entendre à quelqu'un,* to give someone to understand; *faire envie,* to create envy; *faire feu,* to fire; *faire force de voiles,* to crowd on all sail; *faire front,* to face; *faire la charité* or *l'aumône,* to give alms or to do good; *faire la cuisine,* to cook; *faire la moisson,* to get in the harvest; *faire la sourde oreille,* to turn a deaf ear; *faire le malade,* to sham illness; *faire le mort,* to sham dead; *faire le roi,* to play the king; *faire le savant,* to set up for a learned man; *faire l'innocent,* to affect innocence; *faire maison nette,* to make a clean sweep of one's servants; *faire mine de* or *faire semblant de,* to feign, to pretend; *faire montre de,* to make a show of; *faire part de,* to inform, to announce; *faire peu de cas de,* to set little store by; *faire pitié,* to excite pity; *faire sa besogne,* to do one's work; *faire savoir,* to inform; *faire ses dents,* to cut one's teeth; *faire son apprentissage,* to serve one's apprenticeship; *faire son chemin,* to get on (in life); *faire son devoir,* to do one's duty; *faire tête,* (*Hunt.*) to stand at bay; *faire tous ses efforts* or *tout son possible,* to do one's utmost; *faire (un) affront à,* to insult; *faire une bonne action,* to do a good deed; *faire une chambre,* to clean a room; *faire une confidence à quelqu'un,* to entrust a secret to someone; *faire une lieue à pied,* to walk a league; *faire une promenade,* to take a walk; *faire une sottise,* to do a foolish thing; *faire un mauvais coup,* to play a dirty trick; *faire un tour de jardin,* to take a turn in the garden; *faire venir,* to send for; *faire voile,* to set sail; *faire voir,* to show; *faites ce que vous voudrez, c'est le moindre de mes soucis,* do your worst, I care not; *faites-le entrer,* show him in; *il faisait semblant de n'en rien savoir,* he pretended to know nothing about it; *il fait bien ses affaires,* he is getting on well; *il le fit mettre à mort,* he had him put to death; *il ne fait que d'arriver,* he has only just arrived; *il ne sait pas faire son métier,* he does not know his job; *je le lui ai fait avoir,* I have procured it for him; *je n'ai que faire de lui,* I am in no way interested in him; *je n'ai rien à faire,* I have nothing to do; *je ne ferai rien de la sorte* or *je n'en ferai rien,* I shall do nothing of the kind; *ne faire cas que de l'argent,* to value nothing but money; *faire qu'un,* to be hand and glove together; *il n'y a rien à y faire,* it cannot be helped; *pour bien faire,* by rights; *que faites-vous aujourd'hui?* what are you going to do today? *que ferez-vous de votre fils?* what do you want your son to do in life? *qu'est-ce que cela fait là?* what is that doing there? *qu'est-ce que cela vous fait?* what is that to you? *que voulez-vous que j'y fasse?* what can I do, how can I help it? *qu'y faire?* what is to be done? *rien n'y faisait,* nothing would do; *se laisser faire,* to make no resistance.

II. *v.i.* To do; to mean, to signify, to look; to fit, to suit; to deal (at cards); to arrange, to manage. *À qui à faire?* whose deal is it? *avoir à faire,* to have work to do; *c'en est fait de,* it is all up with; *en faire à sa guise,* to do as one likes; *faire bien,* to do right; *faire mal,* to do wrong; *faire jeune,* to look young; *faites en sorte que je vous voie,* contrive to let me see you; *faites qu'il soit content,* see that he is satisfied; *il ne fait que de sortir,* he has only just gone out; *il ne fait qu'entrer et sortir,* he does nothing but go out and in; *je viens de faire,* I have just dealt; *l'or fait bien avec le vert,* gold goes well with green. III. *v. impers.* To be. *Il fait beau,* it is fine; *il fait bon ici,* it is nice, comfortable, pleasant here; *il fait chaud,* it is hot; *il fait cher vivre à Londres,* living is dear in London; *il fait froid,* it is cold; *quel temps fait-il?* what sort of weather is it? IV. **se faire,** *v.r.* To be done, to be made; to happen, to become, to turn; to give oneself out as, to pretend to be; to have, make, or get oneself; to be used or inured (*à*), accustom oneself (*à*); to improve, to get better. *Cela ne se fait pas,* that is not done or is not good form; *cela se fait maintenant,* that is the fashion now; *il peut se faire que,* it is possible that; *il pourrait se faire que,* it might happen that; *il se fait plus riche qu'il ne l'est,* he gives himself out as richer than he is; *il se fait tard,* it is getting late; *je me suis fait au bruit de la rue,* I have got accustomed to the noise of the street; *Paris ne s'est pas fait en un jour,* 'Rome was not built in a day'; *quelle idée vous faites-vous de cet homme-là?* what is your idea of that man? *se faire aimer,* to make oneself popular; *se faire à la fatigue,* to inure oneself to fatigue; *se faire des amis,* to make oneself friends; *se faire jour,* to force one's way through; *se faire la main,* to get one's hand in; *se faire mal,* to hurt oneself; *se faire médecin,* to become a doctor; *se faire saigner,* to get oneself bled; *se faire un devoir de,* to make it a duty *or* a point of; *se faire vieux* or *vieille,* to be getting old; *se faire voir,* to show oneself, (*colloq.*) to be swindled; *si cela peut se faire,* if that can be done.

faire (2) [fɛːr], *n.m.* Doing, making; (*Paint. etc.*) execution, manner, style. *Il y a loin du dire au faire,* there is a difference between doing and saying.

faire-part [fer'paːr], *n.m. inv. Un faire-part,* or *une lettre de faire-part* (*de décès, de mariage*), notification of death, wedding-card.

faire-valoir [fɛːrva'lwaːr], *n.m.* (*Fin.*) Turning to account (of one's money); (*Agric.*) cultivation (of land). *Faire-valoir direct,* cultivation by the owner of the land (not by a farmer).

faisable [fə'zabl], *a.* Practicable, feasible.

faisan [fə'zɑ̃], *n.m.* (*fem.* **faisane**) Pheasant. *Coq faisan,* cock-pheasant; *faisan noir* or *de montagne,* heath-cock; *une poule faisane,* a hen-pheasant.

faisances [fɛ'zɑ̃ːs], *n.f.* (*used only in pl.*) Dues (in kind) by a tenant over and above the rent.

faisandé [fəzɑ̃'de], *a.* (*fem.* **-ée**) Gamy, high; (*fam.*) spicy (story).

faisandeau [fəzɑ̃'do], *n.m.* (*pl.* **-eaux**) Young pheasant. **faisander,** *v.t.* To keep (game)

till it is high, to make gamy. **se faisander,** *v.r.* To get high.

faisanderie [fəzɑ̃'dri], *n.f.* Pheasantry. **faisandier,** *n.m.* (*fem.* **-ière**) Pheasant-breeder.

faisane (*fem.*) [FAISAN].

faisant, *pres.p.* [FAIRE (1)].

faisceau [fɛ'so], *n.m.* (*pl.* **-eaux**) Bundle; sheaf (of arrows etc.); stack, pile (of arms etc.); (*fig.*) union, alliance, number; (*Anat.*) fasciculus; (*Opt.*) pencil; (*Elec.*) beam; (*Antiq., pl.*) fasces. *En faisceau,* in a bundle or bundles, (*Arch.*) clustered; *faisceau aimanté,* compound magnet; *faisceau de rayons* or *faisceau lumineux,* (*Opt.*) pencil of rays; *faisceau hertzien,* (*Rad.*) wireless beam; (*Mil.*) *former les faisceaux,* to pile arms.

faiseur [fə'zœːr], *n.m.* (*fem.* **-euse**) Maker; monger, doer; charlatan, quack. *Faiseur d'affaires,* promoter, jobber; *faiseuse d'anges,* abortionist; *faiseur de systèmes,* system-monger; *faiseur de tours,* mountebank; *faiseur de vers,* versifier, poetaster; *les grands diseurs ne sont pas les faiseurs,* great talkers are little doers; *mangez de ce pâté, c'est d'un bon faiseur,* try a piece of this pie, it is made by a first-rate hand.

faisselle [fɛ'sel], *n.f.* (*dial.*) Basket (to drain cheese); table (to press pomace).

fait (1) [fɛ, fɛt], *n.m.* Act, deed; fact, actual event; actuality, reality, case, matter, business, point in business; what suits; exploit, fine action. *Au fait,* incidentally; *c'est un fait à part,* that is another matter; *de fait,* indeed, certainly; *de ce fait,* because of that; *dire à quelqu'un son fait,* to tell someone what you think of him; *être au fait de,* to know all about; *être sûr de son fait,* to be sure of one's facts; *faits et gestes, doings; il est au fait de cette affaire,* he is well acquainted with that affair; *il est de fait que,* it is a fact that; *l'avarice n'est pas son fait,* he is not a miser; *les hauts faits d'un guerrier,* the exploits of a warrior; *par le seul fait,* by the simple fact, ipso facto; *pour en venir au fait,* to come to the point; *prendre fait et cause pour quelqu'un,* to side with someone; *prendre quelqu'un sur le fait,* to catch someone in the very act; *si fait,* yes, yes, indeed; *tout à fait,* entirely, quite; *voies de fait,* violence, assault.

fait (2) [fɛ], *a.* (*fem.* **faite**) Made; done; shaped; fit, qualified; dressed, got up; grown, full grown, grown up; mature, ripe (of cheese). *Ce fromage est fait,* that cheese is ripe; *c'est bien fait,* it serves him (her, you, or them) right; *comme le voilà fait!* what a sight he looks! *il n'est pas fait pour ce métier,* he is not the man for that job; *tout fait,* ready-made, cut and dried; *porter du tout-fait,* to wear ready-made clothes; *une femme bien faite,* a woman with a nice figure; *un homme fait,* a grown-up man.

faîtage [fɛ'taːʒ], *n.m.* Ridge-plate, ridge-piece (of roof), roof-tree.

faîte [fɛːt], *n.m.* Top, pinnacle; ridge, coping (of building); (*fig.*) summit, highest point, zenith, height. *Faîte de cheminée,* chimney-top; *le faîte des grandeurs,* the pinnacle of greatness. **faîteau,** *n.m.* (*pl.* **faîteaux**) Ridge-tile.

faîtière [fɛ'tjɛːr], *n.f.* Ridge-tile.—*a.* Pertaining to the ridge of a roof. *Lucarne faîtière,* skylight.

faits divers [fɛdi'vɛr], *n.m. pl.* News items, news in brief.

fait-tout or **faitout** [fɛ'tu], *n.m. inv.* Stew-pan; casserole.

faix [fɛ], *n.m. inv.* Weight, burden, load. *Plier sous le faix*, to sink under the burden.

fakir [fa'kiːr], *n.m.* Fakir.

falaise [fa'lɛːz], *n.f.* Cliff.

falbala [falba'la], *n.m.* (*usu. in pl.*) Furbelow, flounce, falbala.

falciforme [falsi'fɔrm], *a.* (*Bot.*) Falcate, falciform.

fallacieusement [falasjœz'mã], *adv.* Fallaciously, falsely.

fallacieux [fala'sjø], *a.* (*fem.* -ieuse) Fallacious, deceptive.

falloir [fa'lwaːr], *v. impers. irr.* (*p.p.* **fallu**) To be necessary, to be obligatory, proper, or expedient (should, must); to be needful to, to be wanting or lacking to. *Ce qu'il faut*, what is wanted or necessary; *c'est l'homme qu'il faut*, he is the very man for the place or for the work; *combien vous en faut-il?* how much do you want? *des gens comme il faut*, well-bred people; *faites cela comme il faut*, do that properly; *faut-il le demander?* need you ask? *il aurait fallu s'y prendre ainsi*, you should have gone to work in this way; *il fait ce qu'il faut*, he does what is required; *il fallait venir plus tôt*, you ought to have come sooner; *il fallait voir comme il était content*, you should have seen how pleased he was; *il faudra le satisfaire*, you will have to satisfy him; *il faut le faire*, it must be done; *il faut que je fasse cela*, I must do that; *il me faut de l'argent*, I must have some money; *il me menace d'un procès, c'est ce qu'il faudra voir!* he threatens me with an action, but we shall see about that; *j'en ai plus qu'il ne m'en faut*, I have more than I need; *je ne sais ce qu'il lui faut*, I do not know what he wants; *que lui faut-il pour sa peine?* how much must he have for his trouble? *il s'en fallut de peu que je ne fusse écrasé*, I was near being run over; *il s'en faut de beaucoup*, very far from it; *il s'en faut de beaucoup que la somme y soit*, the sum is far from complete; *il s'en faut de peu qu'il ne soit aussi grand que son frère*, he is nearly as tall as his brother; *peu s'en faut*, very nearly; *peu s'en est fallu qu'il ne mourût*, he very nearly died; *tant s'en faut qu'il consente*, he is very far from consenting.

falot (1) [fa'lo], *n.m.* Large hand-lantern; *esp.* (*Mil.*) guard-house lantern.

falot (2) [fa'lo], *a.* (*fem.* **falote**) *Comical, droll, funny, queer (person); ridiculously insignificant; colourless (style).

falourde [fa'lurd], *n.f.* Large faggot or bundle of firewood.

falque [falk] or **falcade**, *n.f.* (1) Curvet in which a horse throws himself repeatedly on his haunches. (2) [*see* FARGUES]. **falquer**, *v.t.* To make (a horse) do this.

falquet [fal'kɛ], *n.m.* Variety of falcon, hobby.

falsifiable [falsi'fjabl], *a.* Falsifiable. **falsificateur**, *a.* (*fem.* -trice) Falsifying.—*n.* Falsifier; debaser (of money etc.). **falsification**, *n.f.* Falsification; adulteration, debasement.

falsifier [falsi'fje], *v.t.* To falsify; to alter or corrupt (texts etc.); to adulterate (milk, metals); to tamper with.

faluche [fa'lyʃ], *n.f.* Student's beret.

falun [fa'lœ̃], *n.m.* Shell-marl. **faluner**, *v.t.* To manure with shell-marl. **falunière**, *n.f.* Shell-marl pit.

falzar(d) [fal'zar], *n.m.* (*slang*) Trousers, slacks.

famé [fa'me], *a.* (*fem.* -ée) Famed. *Bien famé*, of good repute; *rue mal famée*, street of bad repute.

famélique [fame'lik], *a.* Starving, famishing. *Auteur famélique*, starving author.—*n.* Starveling. *Il a bien l'air d'un famélique*, he certainly looks like a poor starving wretch.

fameusement [famœz'mã], *adv.* (*fam.*) Famously, extremely.

fameux [fa'mø], *a.* (*fem.* -euse) Famous, celebrated; excellent, first-rate, capital; (*iron. adj. before noun*) precious, perfect. *Fameux imbécile*, perfect fool; *la cuisine y est fameuse*, you eat wonderfully well there.

familial [fami'ljal], *a.* (*fem.* -iale, *pl.* -iaux) Pertaining to family. **familiariser**, *v.t.* To accustom to, to familiarize. **se familiariser**, *v.r.* To familiarize oneself (*avec*), to become accustomed; to grow familiar, to adopt a familiar tone (*avec*). **familiarité**, *n.f.* Familiarity, familiar terms, intimacy; (*pl.*) liberties.

familier [fami'lje], *a.* (*fem.* -ière) Familiar, intimate; free, unconstrained; homely, simple, plain; tame.—*n.* Familiar. *C'est un des familiers du prince*, he is one of the prince's set. **familièrement**, *adv.* Familiarly.

famille [fa'miːj], *n.f.* Family, kindred, kin; race, tribe, house, parentage; home; (*fig.*) kind, set. *Affaires de famille*, domestic concerns; *chef de famille*, head of a family; *être chargé de famille*, to have a large family; *fils de famille*, young man of good family; *un air de famille*, a family likeness; *vous dînerez en famille*, you'll dine at home, with my family; *famille de mots*, words having a common stem.

famine [fa'min], *n.f.* Famine, dearth, scarcity. *Crier famine sur un tas de blé*, to plead poverty though rolling in riches; *prendre par la famine*, to starve out, to reduce by famine; *salaire de famine*, starvation wages.

fanage [fa'naːʒ], *n.m.* Tossing or tedding of hay, haymaking; dry leaves of a plant.

fanal [fa'nal], *n.m.* (*pl.* -aux) Signal-light, watch-light, beacon; lantern of a ship.

fanatique [fana'tik], *a.* Fanatical, bigoted.—*n.* Fanatic, bigot, zealot, enthusiast. **fanatiquement**, *adv.* Fanatically. **fanatiser**, *v.t.* To fanaticize. **fanatiseur**, *a.* Fanaticizing.—*n.m.* Fanaticizer. **fanatisme**, *n.m.* Fanaticism.

fanchon [fã'ʃɔ̃], *n.m.* Kerchief (for the head); from *Fanchon*, Fanny, an easy-going girl in folk-song.

fandango [fãdã'go], *n.m.* Fandango.

fane [fan], *n.f.* Haulm (of potatoes); dead leaf; involucre (of flower).

faner [fa'ne], *v.t.* To toss or ted (hay); to cause to fade; to tarnish. **se faner**, *v.r.* To fade, to droop, to wither; to tarnish. *Cette femme commence à se faner*, that woman is beginning to fade, to lose her looks. **faneur**, *n.m.* (*fem.* -euse) Haymaker.—*n.f.* Haymaking machine.

fanfare [fãˈfaːr], *n.f.* Flourish (of trumpets), fanfare; brass band. *Sonner la fanfare*, to strike up a flourish. **fanfariste**, *a.* Belonging to a brass band.—*n.* brass bandsman.

fanfaron [fãfaˈrɔ̃], *a.* (*fem.* **-onne**) Blustering, swaggering, bragging, boasting.—*n.* Blusterer, swaggerer; boaster of vices or virtues he or she does not possess; braggart. *Faire le fanfaron*, to play the braggart. **fanfaronnade**, *n.f.* Bluster, boast, vaunt, brag; boasting. **fanfaronner**, *v.i.* To boast etc. **fanfaronnerie**, *n.f.* Blustering, swaggering etc.

fanfreluche [fãfrəˈlyʃ], *n.f.* Bauble, gewgaw.

fange [fãːʒ], *n.f.* Mire, mud, dirt; vileness, degradation; (*fig.*) insult, calumny. **fangeux**, *a.* (*fem.* **-euse**) Miry, muddy, dirty.

fanion [faˈnjɔ̃], *n.m.* (*Mil.*) Battalion flag.

fanon [faˈnɔ̃], *n.m.* Dewlap (oxen); fetlock (horse); horny strip (in whales); (*Eccles.*) maniple; (*pl.*) pendant (of a bishop's mitre); (*Mil.*) pennon (of lance).

fantaisie [fãtɛˈzi], *n.f.* Imagination; fancy; whim, caprice, crochet, odd fancy; (*Mus.*) fantasia. *Avoir des fantaisies*, to have whims; *bijoux fantaisie* or *de fantaisie*, costume jewellery; *cela est-il à votre fantaisie?* is that to your liking? *il lui a pris la fantaisie d'aller voyager*, he has taken it into his head to travel; *kirsch de fantaisie*, imitation kirschwasser; *par fantaisie*, out of pure whim; *tenue de fantaisie* (*Mil.*), uniform not of service pattern; *tissu fantaisie*, fancy pattern material; *vivre à sa fantaisie*, to live as one likes. **fantaisiste**, *a.* Whimsical, fantastic.—*n.* Whimsical painter, writer, or other artist.

fantasia [fãtaˈzja], *n.f.* Display of Arab horsemen, fantasia.

fantasmagorie [fãtazmagɔˈri], *n.f.* Phantasmagoria, dissolving view. **fantasmagorique**, *a.* Phantasmagorical.

fantasme, *n.m.* [PHANTASME].

fantasque [fãˈtask], *a.* Fantastic, bizarre, whimsical; queer, strange, odd. **fantasquement**, *adv.* Oddly, whimsically.

fantassin [fãtaˈsɛ̃], *n.m.* Foot-soldier; infantryman.

fantastique [fãtasˈtik], *a.* Fantastic, fanciful, chimerical.—*n.m.* The uncanny. **fantastiquement**, *adv.* Fantastically.

fantoche [fãˈtɔʃ], *n.m.* Marionette, puppet. *Gouvernement fantoche*, puppet government.

fantomal [fãtɔˈmal], *a.* (*fem.* **-ale**, *pl.* **-aux**) Spectral, phantom-like. **fantomatique**, *a.* Pertaining to a phantom or phantoms.

fantôme [fãˈtoːm], *n.m.* Phantom, spectre, ghost; (*fig.*) chimera, fancy, empty appearance; very thin person. *Le Vaisseau Fantôme*, the Flying Dutchman.

fanu [faˈny], *a.* (*fem.* **-ue**) (*Bot.*) Haulmy.

faon [fã], *n.m.* Fawn, calf of deer.

faonner [faˈne], *v.i.* To fawn (of deer etc.).

faquin [faˈkɛ̃], *n.m.* Cad, rascal. **faquinerie**, *n.f.* Rascality, rascally meanness.

faquir [FAKIR].

faradique [faraˈdik], *a.* (*Elec.*) Faradaic; pertaining to Faraday or his theories. **faradisation**, *n.f.* Faradization.

faramineux [faramiˈnø], *a.* (*fem.* **-euse**) (*fam.*) Stupendous, colossal.

farandole [farãˈdɔl], *n.f.* Farandole (Provençal dance). **farandoler**, *v.i.* To dance this.

farandoleur, *n.m.* (*fem.* **-euse**) Provençal dancer.

faraud [faˈro], *n.m.* Fop, swell.—*a.* Stuck up, affected. *Un paysan faraud*, a toffed-up bumpkin. **farauder**, *v.i.* To play the swell; to tog up; to swank.

farce [fars], *n.f.* Stuffing, force-meat; farce, piece of low comedy; buffoonery, drollery, tomfoolery; practical joke, waggish trick, prank. *Faire ses farces, to sow one's wild oats; *faire une farce à quelqu'un*, to play someone a trick; *tirez le rideau, la farce est jouée*, ring down the curtain, the farce is ended.—*a.* (*fam.*) Waggish, droll; absurd. *Ça c'est farce*, that's too funny; *c'est un peu trop farce*, there is too much slapstick. **farceur**, *n.m.* (*fem.* **-euse**) Farce-player; droll dog, practical joker; humbug. *Faire le farceur*, to play the fool, to try to be funny.—*a.* Waggish, facetious.

farci, *p.p.* (*fem.* **farcie**) [FARCIR].

farcin [farˈsɛ̃], *n.m.* (*Vet.*) Farcin, farcy. **farcineux**, *a.* (*fem.* **-euse**) Affected with farcy.

farcir [farˈsiːr], *v.t.* To stuff with force-meat etc.; to cram, to fill. **se farcir**, *v.r.* To stuff, to cram, to be filled. **farcissure**, *n.f.* (Act of) stuffing.

fard [faːr], *n.m.* Paint (for the complexion), rouge, make-up; (*fig.*) varnish, disguise. *Sans fard*, plainly, frankly; *se mettre du fard à la figure*, to rouge one's face; (*pop.*) *piquer un fard*, to blush, to lobster. **fardage** (I), *n.m.* Rouging; (*slang*) deception of customers by trading defective goods by means of selected specimens.

fardage (2) [farˈdaːʒ], *n.m.* (*Naut.*) Dunnage.

farde [fard], *n.f.* Bale of Mocha coffee (weighing about 400 pounds).

fardeau [farˈdo], *n.m.* (*pl.* **-eaux**) Burden, load, weight; mash (for brewing); (*Mining*) mass. *Imposer un fardeau à quelqu'un*, to put a burden upon someone; *s'imposer un fardeau*, to take a burden upon oneself.

farder (I) [farˈde], *v.t.* To paint or rouge (the face), to make up; (*fig.*) to varnish, to gloss over, to camouflage. **se farder**, *v.r.* To paint one's face, to make up.

farder (2) [farˈde], *v.i.* *To sink, to give way; (*Naut.*) to fill, to swell out (of sails). *Ce mur commence à farder*, this wall is beginning to sink.

fardier [farˈdje], *n.m.* Trolley, dray (for stones or other heavy loads).

(C) **fardoches** [farˈdɔʃ], *n.f. pl.* Brushwood, brush.

farfadet [farfaˈdɛ], *n.m.* Goblin, elf; leprechaun; (*fig.*) trifler.

farfouiller [farfuˈje], *v.i.* (*fam.*) To rummage. **farfouilleur**, *n.m.* (*fem.* **-euse**) Person who loves to do this.

fargues [farg], *n.f. pl.* Planks above gunwale of boat; wash-boards. **farguer**, *v.t.* To fit (a boat) with such.

faribole [fariˈbɔl], *n.f.* Idle story; trifle; nonsense. (*fam.*) *Tout ça c'est des fariboles*, it is all moonshine.

farigoule [fariˈgul], *n.f.* (*S. Fr.*) Thyme.

faridondaine [faridɔ̃ˈdɛn], **faridondon** [faridɔ̃ˈdɔ̃] (Two nonsensical words used as a burden; *la faridondaine, la faridondon* or *la farira dondaine, la farira dondé*.) Fiddle-dedee.

farinacé [farina′se], *a.* (*fem.* -ée) Farinaceous.
farine [fa′rin], *n.f.* Flour; meal. *Fleur de farine*, (wheaten) flour; *folle farine*, mill-dust; *gens de la même farine*, birds of a feather. **fariner**, *v.t.* To flour, to sprinkle with flour. —*v.i.* To take a flour-like appearance. **farineux** [fari′nø], *a.* (*fem.* -euse) Mealy, farinaceous; white with flour. **farinier**, *n.m.* (*fem.* -ière) Flour-dealer.—*n.f.* Meal-tub, flour-bin.
farlouse [far′luːz], *n.f.*, or *alouette des prés*. Meadow titlark.
farniente [farnjɛn′te], [It.], *n.m. Far niente*, doing nothing, pleasant idleness.
faro [fa′ro], *n.m.* Belgian beer.
faroba [COURBARIL].
farouch or **farouche** (1) [fa′ruʃ], *n.m.* (*Bot.*) Red clover, French clover.
farouche (2) [fa′ruʃ], *a.* Wild; fierce; sullen, unsociable; shy. *Cette femme est bien farouche*, that woman is very shy; *regard farouche*, fierce look. **farouchement**, *adv.* Fiercely.
farrago [fara′go], *n.m.* Farrago.
fart [faːr], *n.m.* Ski wax. **fartage**, *n.m.* Waxing. **farter**, *v.t.* To wax.
fasce [fas], *n.f.* (*Her.*) Fesse. **fascé**, *a.* (*fem.* -ée) Fessy.
fascia [fa′sja], *n.f.* Fascia. **fascial**, *a.* (*fem.* **fasciale**, *pl.* **fasciaux**) Pertaining to or of the nature of this. **fasciation**, *n.f.* (*Bot.*) Fasciation.
fasciculaire [fasiky′lɛːr], *a.* Fascicular. **fasciculation**, *n.f.* Fasciculation.
fascicule [fasi′kyl], *n.m.* Fascicle, small bundle (of plants, herbs, etc.); part or number (of a work). (*Mil.*) *Fascicule de mobilisation*, detachable part of the *livret militaire*, small book of every reservist. *Livre publié par fascicules*, book published in instalments. **fasciculé**, *a.* (*fem.* -ée) (*Bot.*) Fasciculate.
fascié, *a.* (*fem.* -ée) (*Bot.*) Fasciated.
fascinage [fasi′naːʒ], *n.m.* (*Fort.*) Fascine-work; the making of fascines.
fascinant [fasi′nɑ̃], *a.* (*fem.* -ante) Fascinating. **fascinateur**, *a.* (*fem.* -trice) Fascinating.—*n.* Fascinator. **fascination**, *n.f.* Fascination.
fascine [fa′sin], *n.f.* Faggot (of small branches); (*Fort.*) fascine.
fasciner (1) [fasi′ne], *v.t.* To fascinate.
fasciner (2) [fasi′ne], *v.t.* To face or line with fascines.
fascisme [fa′ʃism], *n.m.* Fascism. **fasciste**, *n.m.* and *a.* Fascist.
faséole [faze′ɔl], *n.f.* Horse-bean.
faséyer [FASIER].
*****fashion** [fa′ʃjɔ̃], *n.f.* Fashion, mode; elegant society. *****fashionable**, *a.* Fashionable.—*n.* Fashionable person, beau or belle, swell.
fasier [fa′zje], **faseyer**, or **faséier**, *v.i.* To shiver (of sails).
faste [fast], *a.* Favourable, lucky. *Jours fastes et néfastes*, lucky and unlucky days.—*n.m.* (used only in sing.) Pomp, ostentation, pageantry.
fastes [fast], *n.m.* (used only in pl.) Fasti, annals, records.
fastidieusement [fastidjøz′mɑ̃], *adv.* Tediously, irksomely.
fastidieux [fasti′djø], *a.* (*fem.* -ieuse) Irksome, tedious, wearisome, dull.
fastigié [fasti′ʒje], *a.* (*fem.* -iée) Fastigiate, fastigiated.

fastueusement [fastɥøz′mɑ̃], *adv.* Ostentatiously, pompously; splendidly, gorgeously.
fastueux [fas′tɥø], *a.* (*fem.* -euse) Ostentatious, pompous, showy; sumptuous, stately.
fat [fat], *a.m.* Conceited, vain, foppish.—*n.m.* Fop, coxcomb.
fatal [fa′tal], *a.* Fatal, disastrous; irrevocable, inevitable; mortal, deadly. *Ces remèdes ont été fatals au malade*, those remedies proved fatal to the patient; *la barque fatale*, Charon's boat; *l'heure fatale*, the moment of death; *terme fatal*, (*Comm.*) expiration of days of grace; *une femme fatale*, a vamp. *C'était fatal*, it was bound to happen. **fatalement**, *adv.* Fatally; inevitably. **fataliser**, *v.t.* To fatalize. **fatalisme**, *n.m.* Fatalism. **fataliste**, *n.* Fatalist. **fatalité**, *n.f.* Fatality.
fatidique [fati′dik], *a.* Fatidic. **fatidiquement**, *adv.* Fatidically.
fatigant [fati′gɑ̃], *a.* (*fem.* **fatigante**) Fatiguing, toilsome, tiring, wearisome.
fatigue [fa′tig], *n.f.* Fatigue, tiredness, weariness; hard toil, hardship. *Être mort de fatigue*, to be dead-tired, dead-beat; *habits de fatigue*, working clothes; *tomber de fatigue*, to be dropping with tiredness; *supporter la fatigue*, to stand fatigue; *un homme de fatigue*, a man capable of resisting fatigue. **fatigué**, *a.* (*fem.* -ée) Fatigued, jaded, tired, run down; (*fig.*) worn, used, faded, threadbare. *Des chevaux fatigués*, jaded horses. **fatiguer**, *v.t.* To fatigue; to tire; to weary, to harass; to overwork; to importune; (*Paint.*) to labour. (*fam.*) *Fatiguer la salade*, to keep on mixing or turning over a salad; *la lecture fatigue la vue*, reading tires the sight.—*v.i.* To tire; to be fatiguing; (*Naut.*) to labour. *Fatiguer à l'ancre*, (*Naut.*) to ride hard. **se fatiguer**, *v.r.* To fatigue or tire oneself out, to be jaded; to be tired (*de*).
fatras [fa′trɑ], *n.m.* Jumble, medley, litter confusion; balderdash, rubbish, trash.
fatuité [fatɥi′te], *n.f.* Fatuity, self-conceit, foppishness. *Quelle fatuité!* what a piece of impertinence!
fauber or **faubert** [fo′bɛːr], *n.m.* (*Naut.*) Swab, mop. **fauberter** or **fauberder**, *v.t.* To swab, to mop (the deck).
faubourg [fo′buːr], *n.m.* Faubourg, outskirts, suburb. *Le noble faubourg*, the Faubourg Saint-Germain (the old aristocratic quarter of Paris), hence *le faubourg Saint-Germain*, the old French aristocracy; *les faubourgs*, the working-class population of the faubourgs. **faubourien**, *a.* (*fem.* -ienne) Belonging to the faubourgs, working-class, vulgar.—*n.* Inhabitant of a faubourg.
faucard [fo′kaːr], *n.m.* Long-handled scythe (for cutting down water-weeds). **faucardage** or **faucardement**, *n.m.* Cutting down weeds with this. **faucarder**, *v.t.* To cut down with this.
fauchage [fo′ʃaːʒ], *n.m.* Mowing; (*Mil.*) sweeping fire (of guns). **fauchaison**, *n.f.* Mowing-time. **fauchard**, *n.m.* Double-edged slasher. **fauche**, *n.f.* Mowing; mowing-time. **fauché** (*fem.* -ée), *a.* Mown; (*slang*) broke. *Fauché comme les blés*, stone broke. **fauchée**, *n.f.* Day's mowing. **faucher**, *v.t.* To mow, to cut down, to reap, (*fig.*) to mow down, (*slang*) to guillotine (a man), to pinch (something).—*v.i.* To throw

the forelegs sideways in walking (of a horse). **fauchet,** *n.m.* Hay-rake (in wood); billhook. **fauchette,** *n.f.* Small hedge-knife. **faucheur,** *n.m.* Mower, reaper; field-spider, harvester; (U.S.) daddy-longlegs. [*See* MARINGOUIN]. **faucheuse,** *n.f.* (Mechanical) mower.

faucille [fo'si:j], *n.f.* Sickle, reaping-hook. **faucillon,** *n.m.* Small sickle.

faucon [fo'kɔ̃], *n.m.* Falcon, hawk. *Faucon émerillon,* merlin, (*Am.*) pigeon hawk; *faucon pèlerin,* peregrine falcon. **fauconneau,** *n.m.* (*pl.* **fauconneaux**) Young hawk; *(Artill.)* falconet. **fauconnerie,** *n.f.* Falconry, hawking; falcon house. **fauconnier,** *n.m.* Falconer. *Monter à cheval en fauconnier,* to mount a horse on the offside. **fauconnière,** *n.f.* Hawking-pouch, falconer's bag; saddlebag.

faudra, *3rd sing. fut.* [FALLOIR].

faufil or **faufile** [fo'fil], *n.m.* Basting thread. **faufiler,** *v.t.* To tack, to baste (needlework); (*fig.*) to insinuate, to introduce adroitly. **se faufiler,** *v.r.* To insinuate or intrude oneself, to sneak in; to find a way in; to weave, to nip in and out of crowd; to ingratiate oneself; to curry favour (*auprès*). *Il se faufile partout,* he introduces himself everywhere.

faune (1) [fo:n], *n.m.* (*fem.* **faune** or **faunesse**) Faun. **faune** (2), *n.f.* (*Zool.*) Fauna.

faussaire [fo'sɛ:r], *n.* Forger. *Poursuivre comme faussaire,* to prosecute for forgery.

faussement [fos'mã], *adv.* Falsely, erroneously, wrongfully.

fausser [fo'se], *v.t.* To bend, to twist, to warp; to corrupt, to falsify, to pervert, to violate; to break, to force or strain (a lock, key, etc.); (*Mus.*) to put out of tune. *Fausser compagnie à quelqu'un,* to give someone the slip; *fausser l'esprit de quelqu'un,* to warp, to pervert someone's mind; *fausser une cuirasse,* to dent a cuirass; *roue faussée,* warped wheel. **se fausser,** *v.r.* To bend, to get warped, to get perverted, etc.; (*Mus.*) to get out of tune.

fausset (1) [fo'se], *n.m.* (*Mus.*) Falsetto.

fausset (2) [fo'sɛ] or **fosset,** *n.m.* Faucet, spigot, vent-peg. *Trou de fausset,* venthole.

fausseté [fos'te], *n.f.* Falsity, falsehood; duplicity, insincerity, treachery.

Faust [fo:st], *m.* Faustus, Faust.

faut, *3rd sing. indic. pres.* [FALLOIR, FAILLIR].

faute [fo:t], *n.f.* Want, lack, scarcity, dearth, shortcoming; defect, imperfection; fault, mistake, error. *A faute de,* (*Law*) in default of; *à qui la faute?* whose fault is it? *faire une faute,* to make a mistake; *faute de,* for want of; *faute d'impression,* misprint; *faute d'inattention,* slip; *faute de mieux,* for want of something better; *faute d'orthographe,* spelling mistake; *rejeter la faute sur,* to lay the blame on; *il est mort faute de secours,* he died for want of help; *ne pas se faire faute de,* not to be sparing of; *ne vous en faites pas faute,* do not be sparing; *prendre* or *surprendre quelqu'un en faute,* to catch someone in the act; *relever une faute,* to point out a mistake; *rien ne vous fera faute,* you will want for nothing; *sans faute,* without fail. **fauter,** *v.i.* To go wrong, to be seduced (of a woman).

fauteuil [fo'tœ:j], *n.m.* Arm-chair; chair (speaker's, president's seat). *Fauteuil académique,* seat (in the French Academy); *fauteuil d'orchestre,* orchestra stall; *fauteuil roulant,* bath-chair, wheel-chair; *fauteuil voltaire,* high-backed arm-chair. (*fam.*) *Arriver comme dans un fauteuil,* to win (a race) in a canter; *occuper le fauteuil,* to fill the presidential chair.

fauteur [fo'tœ:r], *n.m.* Abettor, favourer, fomenter. *Être fauteur de,* to abet; *fauteur de troubles, de désordre,* sedition-monger.

fautif [fo'tif], *a.* (*fem.* **-ive**) Faulty, at fault, defective, incorrect; responsible (for mistake). **fautivement,** *adv.* Wrongly.

fauve [fo:v], *a.* Fawn-coloured, fallow, tawny. *Bêtes fauves,* fallow-deer, stag, etc.; wild beasts. *Odeur fauve* or *de fauve,* musky smell.—*n.m.* (*no pl.*) This colour.—*n.m.* Wild animal. *Chasser le fauve,* to hunt wild animals; *les grands fauves,* the greater cats, the big game. *Les Fauves,* group of French painters at the beginning of this century. **fauveau,** *n.m.* (*pl.* **-eaux**) Fawn-coloured ox.

fauvette [fo'vet], *n.f.* Warbler. *Fauvette à tête noire,* blackcap; *fauvette babillarde,* lesser white-throat; *fauvette d'hiver,* dunnock; *fauvette grise* or *grisette,* white throat; *fauvette effarvate,* reed warbler; *petite fauvette* or *fauvette des jardins,* garden-warbler.

fauvisme [fo'vism], *n.m.* A French school of painting (early 20th century, led by Matisse).

faux (1) [fo], *n.f. inv.* Scythe; (*Anat.*) falx.

faux (2) [fo], *a.* (*fem.* **fausse**) False, untrue, erroneous, wrong; spurious, base, counterfeit, forged (coinage); fictitious, sham; insincere, treacherous, deceitful; equivocal; (*Mus.*) out of tune. *Chose fausse,* untruth; *démentir un.faux bruit,* to give the lie to a calumny or false report; *esprit faux,* warped mind; *faire fausse route,* to take the wrong road, to be on the wrong track; *faire un faux mouvement,* to strain a muscle; *faire un faux pas,* to stumble, (*fig.*) to make a slip; *faux bijoux,* paste jewellery; *faux bilan,* fraudulent balance-sheet; *faux brillant,* tinsel; *fausse cartouche,* dummy cartridge; *faux chignon, postiche,* false bun; *fausse couche,* miscarriage; *fausse démarche,* wrong step; *fausse fenêtre,* blank window; *fausse note,* wrong note; *faux renard,* thresher shark; *fausse sortie,* sham sortie; *voix fausse,* voice out of tune.—*n.m.* Falsehood; error; forgery. *Arguer de faux,* to accuse, to tax as false; *commettre un faux,* to commit a forgery; *discerner le vrai d'avec le faux,* to discern truth from falsehood; *être dans le faux,* to be in error; *plaider le faux pour savoir le vrai,* to plead on the wrong side in order to get at the truth; *s'inscrire en faux contre une chose,* to deny the truth of an assertion.—*adv.* Falsely, erroneously, wrongfully; (*Mus.*) out of tune. *A faux,* falsely, unjustly; *cette poutre porte à faux,* that post is out of the perpendicular.

faux-bourdon [fobur'dɔ̃], *n.m.* (*pl.* **faux-bourdons**) Drone.

faux-filet [fofi'lɛ], *n.m.* Sirloin.

faux-fuyant [fofɥi'jã], *n.m.* (*pl.* **faux-fuyants**) *By-path, by-way; subterfuge, evasion.

faux-monnayeur [fomɔne'jœr], *n.m.* Coiner, counterfeiter.

faux-pont [fo′pɔ̃], *n.m.* (*pl.* **faux-ponts**) (*Naut.*) Orlop deck; between-decks.
faverole [FÉVEROLE].
faveur [fa′vœːr], *n.f.* Favour, boon, kindness; privilege, protection, interest, grace; vogue; (narrow) silk ribbon. *À la faveur de,* by favour of, by means of; *à la faveur de la nuit,* under cover of darkness; *en faveur de,* on behalf of, in favour of; *être en faveur,* to be in favour or in vogue; *billet de faveur,* complimentary (free) ticket; *jours de faveur,* days of grace; *mettre en faveur,* to bring into favour or into vogue; *prendre faveur,* to come into favour or into vogue; *prix de faveur,* special price, preferential price.
faveux [fa′vø], *a.* (*fem.* **-euse**) (*Med.*) Covered with yellowish scabs (of scurf). [TEIGNE.]
favorable [favɔ′rabl], *a.* Favourable, propitious, indulgent, benevolent. *Le ciel vous soit favorable!* heaven befriend you! **favorablement,** *adv.* Favourably.
favori [favɔ′ri], *a.* and *n.* (*fem.* **favorite**) Favourite.—*n.m. pl.* Side-whiskers. **favoriser,** *v.t.* To favour, to befriend, to countenance; to aid, to assist, to protect, to promote, to facilitate. **favoritisme,** *n.m.* Favouritism.
fayard [fa′jaːr], *n.m.* Beech.
fayot [fa′jo], *n.m.* (*fam.*) Haricot bean; kidney bean; (*sch. slang*) swot.
***féage** [fe′aːʒ], *n.m.* Feoffment.
féal [fe′al], *a.* (*fem.* **féale,** *pl.* **féaux**) Trusty, faithful.—**n.* Trusty, faithful friend. *À nos amis et féaux,* to our trusty and well-beloved friends.
fébricitant [febrisi′tɑ̃], *a.* (*fem.* **fébricitante**) (*Med.*) Feverish.—*n.* Fever-patient.
fébrifuge [febri′fyːʒ], *a.* Febrifugal, antifebrile.—*n.m.* Febrifuge. **fébrile,** *a.* Febrile, feverish. **fébrilement,** *adv.* Feverishly. **fébrilité,** *n.f.* Feverishness.
fécal [fe′kal], *a.* (*fem.* **fécale,** *pl.* **fécaux**) Faecal. *Matières fécales,* faeces, stool. **fèces,** *n.f. pl.* (*Pharm.*) Sediment; (*Med.*) faeces.
fécial [fe′sjal], *a.* and *n.m.* (*fem.* **féciale,** *pl.* **féciaux**) (*Rom. Ant.*) Fetial.
fécond [fe′kɔ̃], *a.* (*fem.* **-onde**) Fruitful, prolific; copious, abundant, teeming, voluble. *Avoir l'esprit fécond,* to have a fertile imagination; *être fécond en,* to teem with; *mine féconde,* rich mine. **fécondant,** *a.* (*fem.* **-ante**) or **fécondateur,** *a.* (*fem.* **-trice**) Fertilizing, fecundating. **fécondation,** *n.f.* Fecundation, impregnation; fertilization, fructification. **féconder,** *v.t.* To fecundate, to impregnate, to make fruitful, to fertilize. **fécondité,** *n.f.* Fecundity, fruitfulness, fertility.
fécule [fe′kyl], *n.f.* Faecula, starch. **féculence** *n.f.* Feculence. **féculent,** *a.* (*fem.* **-ente**) Feculent.—*n.m.* Starchy food. *Les féculents,* pulse foods; starch foods. **féculerie,** *n.f.* Starch factory.
fédéral [fede′ral], *a.* and *n.m.* (*fem.* **fédérale,** *pl.* **fédéraux**) Federal. **fédéraliser,** *v.t.* To federalize. **fédéralisme,** *n.m.* Federalism. **fédéraliste,** *a.* and *n.* Federalist. **fédératif,** *a.* (*fem.* **-tive**) Federate, federative. **fédération,** *n.f.* Federation, alliance. **fédéré,** *a.* (*fem.* **-ée**) Federate, confederate; amalgamated.—*n.m.* Delegate to the Federation of 1790; Federated National Guard; soldier of the Commune of Paris in 1871.

se fédérer, *v.r. irr.* (*conjug. like* ACCÉLÉRER) To federate, to combine, to band together.
fée [fe], *n.f.* Fairy, fay. *C'est la fée Carabosse,* she's an old hag; *château des fées,* imaginary castle; *comme une fée,* fairy-like; *conte de fées,* fairy-tale; *doigts de fée,* nimble fingers, fingers capable of exquisite (needle)work; *pays des fées,* fairy-land. **féerie,** *n.f.* Enchantment; fairy scene, dramatic piece in which fairies figure; fairy-land. **féerique,** *a.* Fairy-like; enchanting, wonderful, marvellous, magical.
feignant, *pres. p.* [FEINDRE].
feindre [fɛ̃ːdr], *v.t. irr.* (*pres.p.* **feignant,** *p.p.* **feint;** *conjugated like* CRAINDRE) To feign, to simulate, to sham, to pretend; to imagine, to suppose; to dissemble. *Feindre une maladie,* to sham illness.—*v.i.* To feign, to sham; to limp (of a horse). *Il possède l'art de feindre,* he is an adept in the art of dissembling. **feint,** *a.* (*fem.* **feinte**) Feigned, make-believe, pretended, sham. *Amitié feinte,* pretended friendship.—*n.f.* Feint; dodge; pretence, dissimulation; artifice; fiction, invention; slight limp (in horse); (*Print.*) friar. *Il fit une feinte,* (*Fenc.*) he made a feint; *sans feinte,* frankly; *user de feinte,* to dissemble. **feinter,** *v.i.* (*Box.*) To feint.—*v.t.* (*fam.*) To gull, to take in.
feld-maréchal [fɛldmare′ʃal], *n.m.* (*pl.* **feld-maréchaux**) Field-marshal (English and German title).
feldspath [fɛls′pat], *n.m.* Feldspar. **feldspathique,** *a.* Feldspathic.
fêle or **felle** or **fesle** [fɛl], *n.f.* Hollow iron bar for glass-blowing.
fêlé [fɛ′le], *a.* (*fem.* **-ée**) Cracked (of glass); (*fig.*) crack-brained. *C'est un cerveau fêlé,* he is a hare-brained fellow; *les pots fêlés sont ceux qui durent le plus,* threatened men live longest. **fêler,** *v.t.* and **se fêler,** *v.r.* To crack (of glass etc.).
félibre [fe′libr], *n.m.* (*fem.* **-esse**) Modern Provençal writer. **félibrée,** *n.f.* Meeting or banquet of the *félibres.* **félibréen,** *a.* (*fem.* **-éenne**) Pertaining to the *félibres.* **félibrige,** *n.m.* Literary society of Provençal writers (followers of Mistral).
Félicie [feli′si], *f.* Felicia.
félicitation [felisita′sjɔ̃], *n.f.* Felicitation, congratulation. *Lettre de félicitations,* letter of congratulation. **félicité,** *n.f.* Felicity, bliss, happiness. **féliciter,** *v.t.* To congratulate, to felicitate. **se féliciter,** *v.r.* To congratulate oneself, to be pleased or satisfied.
félidé [feli′de], *n.m.* Felid; one of the Felidae (the cat-tribe).
félin [fe′lɛ̃], *a.* and *n.m.* (*fem.* **féline**) Feline. *Les grands félins,* the greater cats.
fellah [fɛl′la], *n.m.* Fellah (Egyptian peasant); (*pl.*) fellaheen.
felle [FÊLE].
félon [fe′lɔ̃], *a.* (*fem.* **félonne**) Disloyal, traitorous.—*n.* Traitor, caitiff. **félonie,** *n.f.* (*Feud.*) Felony, disloyalty to one's lord, treason.
felouque [fə′luk], *n.f.* (*Naut.*) Felucca.
fêlure [fɛ′lyːr], *n.f.* Crack, fissure; (*fig.*) wound, rupture. (*fam.*) *Il a une fêlure,* he is a bit cracked.
femelle [fə′mɛl], *n.f.* Female, she-animal; (*pej.*) woman.—*a.* Female, feminine, she-.

femelot [fəm'lo], *n.m.*, *usu. in pl.* (*Naut.*) Gudgeons.

féminité [femini'te], *n.f.* Femineity, womanliness.

féminin [femi'nɛ̃], *a.* (*fem.* **-ine**) Feminine, female, womanish, womanly, effeminate. *Genre féminin*, feminine gender; *l'éternel féminin*, the eternal feminine, *rime féminine*, rhyme ending in mute syllable; *sexe féminin*, female sex.—*n.m.* (*Gram.*) Feminine. **féminisation**, *n.f.* Feminization. **féminiser**, *v.t.* To feminize, to render effeminate; (*Gram.*) to make feminine. **féminisme**, *n.m.* Feminism. **féministe**, *n.* and *a.* Feminist.

femme [fam], *n.f.* Woman; mature woman, married woman; wife; female attendant; lady. *Adonné au vin et aux femmes*, given to wine and women; *avoir femme*, to have a wife; *bonne femme*, good, obliging woman, old woman, simple, or rustic woman; *chercher femme*, to seek a wife; *cherchez la femme*, there's a woman at the bottom of it; *comme une femme*, womanlike; *de femme*, womanly; *femme de chambre*, parlour-maid, lady's maid; *femme de charge*, housekeeper; *femme de journée* or *femme de ménage*, charwoman; *femme en puissance de mari*, (*Law*) feme covert; *femme célibataire*, feme sole, spinster; *mari et femme*, man and wife; *prendre femme*, to take a wife; *une femme de lettres*, an authoress; *une femme poète*, poetess; *une femme sculpteur*, a woman sculptor; *une femme médecin*, a lady doctor.

femme-agent [fama'ʒɑ̃], *n.f.* Police-woman.

femmelette [fam'let], *n.f.* Silly, weak woman; effeminate man.

femme-soldat [famsɔl'da], *n.f.* Service-woman.

femme-serpent [famsɛr'pɑ̃], *n.f.* Contortionist.

fémoral [femɔ'ral], *a.* (*fem.* **fémorale**, *pl.* **fémoraux**) Femoral.

fémur [fe'myːr], *n.m.* Femur, thigh-bone. *Tête du fémur*, apophysis of the femur.

fenaison [fənɛ'zɔ̃], *n.f.* Hay-time, haymaking.

fendage [fɑ̃'daːʒ], *n.m.* Splitting, cleaving.

*fendant [fɑ̃'dɑ̃], *n.m.* Cut (with sword); hector, brawler, bully. *Faire le fendant*, to play the bully.—*a.* Hectoring, bullying.

fenderie [fɑ̃'dri], *n.f.* Slitting (of iron into rods); slitting-mill. **fendeur**, *n.m.* (*fem.* **fendeuse**) Cleaver, slitter, splitter. *Fendeur de roues*, wheel-cutter. **fendille**, *n.f.* Small crack produced in forging iron. **fendillement**, *n.m.* Cracking, splitting, flawing. **fendiller**, *v.t.* To chink, to crack, to produce small cracks in. **se fendiller**, *v.r.* To be covered with small cracks, to crack, to split.

fendre [fɑ̃ːdr], *v.t.* To cleave, to split, to rive, to slit, to crack, to cut open, to rend, to rip; to break, to burst; to plough (the sea); to elbow one's way through. *C'est à fendre l'âme*, it is heart-breaking; *fendre du bois*, to cleave wood; *fendre la foule*, to break through the crowd; *fendre la tête*, to split the ears (of noise); *fendre le cœur*, to cut to the quick; *fendre les airs*, to cleave the air; *fendre l'oreille à un officier*, to place an officer on the retired list; *un navire qui fend l'eau*, a ship that ploughs the sea. **se fendre**, *v.r.* To burst asunder, to split, to be ready to burst; to rive,

to gape; (*Fenc.*) to lunge; (*fam.*) to fork out.

fendu, *a.* (*fem.* **-ue**) Cleft, split, cloven. *Bien fendu*, long-legged, well shaped for riding; *des yeux bien fendus*, large, well-shaped eyes; *jupe fendue*, divided skirt.

fenestré [FENÊTRÉ].

fenêtrage [fənɛ'traːʒ], *n.m.* Fenestration; (*collect.*) windows, lights (of a house etc.); arrangement of these.

fenêtre [fə'nɛːtr], *n.f.* Window, casement, window-frame; (*Anat.*) fenestra. *Châssis de fenêtre*, window-sash; *condamner une fenêtre*, to block up a window; *fausse fenêtre*, blind window; *fenêtre à battants*, french window; *fenêtre à châssis* or *à guillotine*, sash-window; *fenêtre de projection* (*Cine.*), film gate; *jeter par les fenêtres*, to throw out of the window, to squander (one's money); *regarder par la fenêtre*, to look out of a window; *mettre le nez à la fenêtre*, to thrust one's head out of the window; (*slang*) to be guillotined. **fenêtré**, *a.* (*fem.* **fenêtrée**) Windowed; (*Bot.*) fenestrate; (*Anat.*) fenestrated. **fenêtrelle**, *n.f.* Peep-hole (for inspecting an engine etc.). **fenêtrer**, *v.t.* To put windows in; to make (a plaster etc.) fenestrated.

fenière [FENIL].

fenil [fə'ni], *n.m.* Hayloft.

fennec [fɛ'nɛk], *n.m.* Fennec (Sahara fox).

fenouil [fə'nuːj], *n.m.* Fennel. *Fenouil des Alpes*, baldmoney, spignel; *fenouil bâtard*, dill; *fenouil de mer*, sea-fennel, samphire; *fenouil de porc*, hog's-fennel, milk-wort, sulphur-wort; *fenouil sauvage*, hemlock.

fenouillet, *n.m.* Fennel-scented apple.

fenouillette, *n.f.* Fennel-apple; fennel-brandy.

fente [fɑ̃ːt], *n.f.* Slit, clink, cleft, chap; gap, cranny, crevice.

fenton [fɑ̃'tɔ̃], *n.m.* Iron-cramp, iron-tie.

fenugrec [fəny'grɛk], *n.m.* (*Bot.*) Fenugreek.

féodal [feɔ'dal], *a.* (*fem.* **-ale**, *pl.* **-aux**) Feudal. **féodalement**, *adv.* Feudally. **féodalisation**, *n.f.* Feudalization. **féodaliser**, *v.t.* To feudalize. **féodalisme**, *n.m.* Feudalism. **féodaliste**, *n.* Feudalist. **féodalité**, *n.f.* Feudality, feudal system.

fer (1) [fɛːr], *n.m.* Iron; iron tool, punch, etc.; horseshoe; iron lip, head, point, etc.; (*fig.*) sword, brand, steel; (Golf) club; (*pl.*) irons, chains, fetters; (*pop.*) forceps. *Âge de fer*, iron age; *à tête de fer*, resolute, determined; *battre le fer*, to fence; *battre le fer quand il est chaud*, to strike while the iron is hot; *bois de fer*, iron-wood; *croiser le fer*, to cross swords, to fight a duel; *donner un coup de fer*, to iron up, to press; *employer le fer et le feu*, to use the knife and cautery, to employ drastic means; *être aux fers* or *être dans les fers*, to be fettered, bound, or in chains, to be in captivity; *fer à cheval*, horseshoe; *fer aigre*, brittle iron; *fer à marquer*, branding-iron, marking-iron; *fer à friser*, curling-iron; *fer à repasser*, iron, flat-iron; *fer à souder*, soldering-iron; *fer battu* or *forgé*, wrought iron; *fer de lacet* or *fer d'aiguillette*, tag of a lace; *fer de lance*, lance-head; *fer doux*, soft iron; *fer dur*, hard iron; *fer en barres*, bar-iron; *fil de fer*, (iron) wire; *fer en gueuse*, pig-iron; *le fer d'une pique*, the head of a pike; *le fer et le feu*, fire and the sword; *limaille de fer*, iron filings; *marquer au fer rouge*, to brand; *mettre les fers au feu*, to put the irons into the fire, to fall to work; *petit fer*, bookbinder's punch; *porter le fer et le feu dans*, to ravage with fire and the sword; *tomber les quatre fers en l'air*, to fall upon one's back, to be struck all of a heap.

*fer (2) [fɛːr], *n.m.* *Fer en meubles*, stuffing, padding for furniture.

féra [fe'ra], *n.f.* or **férat**, *n.m.* Sort of mackerel, dace.

fer-blanc [fɛr'blɑ̃], *n.m.* (*pl.* **fers-blancs**) Tin, tin-plate. **ferblanterie**, *n.f.* Tin-ware. **ferblantier**, *n.m.* Tinman.

fer-chaud [fɛr'ʃo], *n.m.* *Cautery; heart-burn, pyrosis.

férial [fe'rjal], *a.* (*fem.* **-iale**, *pl.* **-iaux**) Ferial, (pertaining to weekdays).

férie [fe'ri], *n.f.* (*Rom. Hist.*) Feria; *holiday; (*R.-C.*) weekday. **férié**, *a.* (*fem.* **-iée**) Holiday. *Jour férié*, holiday, general holiday, bank-holiday. **férier**, *v.t.* To hold or celebrate as a holiday.

*férir [fe'riːr], *v.t. irr.* [only used in *infin.* and past participle, **féru**]. To strike. *Sans coup férir*, without striking a blow.

ferlage [fɛr'laːʒ], *n.m.* (*Naut.*) Furling. **ferler**, *v.t.* To furl (sails).

fermage [fɛr'maːʒ], *n.m.* Rent (of a farm). *Refus de payer le fermage*, denial of rent.

fermail [fɛr'maːj], *n.m.* Clasp, buckle.

fermant [fɛr'mɑ̃], *a.* (*fem.* **fermante**) Closing, shutting (with lock and key).

ferme (1) [fɛrm], *a.* Firm, fast; solid, fixed, stable; strong, stout, stiff, steady; unshaken, constant, resolute. *Avoir le poignet ferme*, to have a strong wrist; *de pied ferme*, resolutely, without wavering; *d'un ton ferme*, in a decided tone; *être ferme à cheval*, to have a good seat.—*adv.* Firmly, fast, hard. *Frapper ferme*, to strike hard; *tenir ferme*, to hold fast; to stand fast.—**int.* Courage! cheer up! go it!

ferme (2) [fɛrm], *n.f.* Lease, farming, letting out on lease; farm, farmhouse, farmstead; farming (of taxes). *Donner* or *bailler à ferme*, to let, to farm out; *ferme école*, agricultural school; *ferme générale*, (*Fr. Hist.*) general farmers of the revenue; *monter une ferme*, to stock a farm; *prendre à ferme*, to farm (a piece of land or an estate).

ferme (3) [fɛrm], *n.f.* Framework of beams, trusses, girders, etc., supporting roof; trussed girder, main couple; (*Theat.*) set-piece. *Fermes de remplage*, middle rafters; *ferme triangulaire*, (*Carp.*) truss; *maîtresses fermes*, principal rafters bearing on the girders.

fermé [fɛr'me], *a.* (*fem.* **-ée**) (*Phon.*) Close (vowel); closed; land-locked (bay); exclusive (society, club); insusceptible (heart). *Il est fermé aux beautés de la nature*, he is blind to natural beauties.

fermement [fɛrmə'mɑ̃], *adv.* Firmly, steadily, steadfastly; strongly, stoutly, resolutely.

ferment [fɛr'mɑ̃], *n.m.* Ferment, leaven. **fermentable**, *a.* Fermentable. **fermentatif**, *a.* (*fem.* **-ive**) Fermentative. **fermentation**, *n.f.* Fermentation, working; (*fig.*) ferment. **fermenter**, *v.i.* To ferment, to rise, to work. *La pâte fermente*, the dough is rising. **fermentescible**, *a.* Fermentescible.

fermer [fɛr'me], *v.t.* To shut, to close; to fasten; to shut up; to seal up; to put an end to (a discussion etc.); to enclose. *Fermer boutique*, to shut up shop; *fermer la bouche à quelqu'un*, to stop someone's mouth; *fermer la marche*, (*Mil.*) to bring up the rear; *fermer la porte à clef*, to lock the door; *fermer la porte à double tour*, to double-lock the door; *fermer la porte au nez de quelqu'un*, to shut the door in someone's face; *fermer l'eau, le gaz*, to turn off the water, the gas; *fermer le courant*, to switch off at the main; *fermer l'électricité*, to switch off; *fermer l'oreille aux médisances*, to ignore slander; *fermer les yeux à* or *de quelqu'un*, to close someone's eyes (in death); *fermer les yeux à la lumière*, to shut one's eyes to the truth; *fermer les yeux sur quelque chose*, to wink at something; *fermer un circuit*, to establish a circuit; (*vulg.*) *ferme ta boîte* or *ta gueule!* shut your trap! *ferme-la* or *la ferme!* shut up!—*v.i.* To shut, to be shut. *On ferme!* Closing time; 'Time, gentlemen!' **se fermer**, *v.r.* To shut, to close, to be closed; to bang to, to close down; to lock, to be capable of locking. *Cette plaie se fermera bientôt*, that wound will soon close up.

fermeté [fɛrmə'te], *n.f.* Firmness; steadiness, stability; constancy, courage; vigour, resolution.

fermeture [fɛrmə'tyːr], *n.f.* Closing, shutting; fastening (of a window etc.). *La fermeture de la chasse*, close of the shooting season; *fermeture de culasse*, rifle-bolt; *fermeture à glissière*, *fermeture éclair*, zip fastener.

fermier [fɛr'mje], *n.m.* (*fem.* **fermière**) Tenant-farmer, tenant (of a farm). *Fermier général, farmer-general (of revenues).—*n.f.* Farmer's wife.

fermoir [fɛr'mwaːr], *n.m.* Clasp, snap, catch, fastener.

féroce [fe'rɔs], *a.* Ferocious, fierce, savage. *Bête féroce*, wild beast. **férocement**, *adv.* Ferociously. **férocité**, *n.f.* Ferocity, fierceness.

ferrade [fɛ'rad], *n.f.* (*S. Fr.*) Branding of the bulls; holiday in Provence on that day.

ferrage [fɛ'raːʒ], *n.m.* Fixing iron on, shoeing (of horses etc.).

ferraille [fɛ'raːj], *n.f.* Old iron, scrap-iron. **ferrailler**, *v.i.* To clash swords together (in fencing); to fence clumsily; to fight (with swords); to fight, to draw one's sword; (*fig.*) to squabble, to wrangle.

ferrailleur [fɛra'jœːr], *n.m.* Dealer in old iron, clumsy fencer; regular duellist; (*fig.*) fighter, wrangler.

ferrant [fɛ'rɑ̃], *a.m.* *Maréchal ferrant*, farrier, shoeing-smith.

ferrate [fɛ'rat], *n.m.* (*Chem.*) Ferrate.

ferré [fɛ're], *a.* (*fem.* **-ée**) Bound, shod, etc., with iron; metalled, stoned; ferruginous, chalybeate (of water); (*colloq.*) skilled, versed (*sur*). *Chemin ferré*, metalled road; *eau ferrée*, chalybeate water; *ferré à glace*, rough-shod, (*colloq.*) skilled (*sur*); *voie ferrée*, railway, (*Am.*) railroad; *réseau ferré*, railway system.

ferrement [fɛr'mɑ̃], *n.m.* Putting the iron on (convicts); (*pl.*) iron-work, iron fitting. **ferrer**, *v.t.* To bind, hoop, etc., with iron, to shoe (a horse etc.). *Ferrer à glace*, to rough-shoe; *ferrer la mule*, to make illicit profits; *ferrer une canne*, to put a ferrule on or tip a cane; *ferrer une étoffe*, to mark with an iron stamp; *ferrer un poisson*,

(*Angling*) to strike a fish; *ferrer un cheval*, to shoe a horse; *ferrer un lacet*, to tag a lace. **ferrerie**, *n.f.* Iron-trade; heavy ironwork.

ferret [fɛ'rɛ], *n.m.* Iron rod used by glass-blowers; tag (of a lace); (*Min.*) hard nodule in a stone. *Ferret d'Espagne*, red haematite.

ferreur [fɛ'rœːr], *n.m.* Shoeing-smith; tagger (of laces).

ferricyanure [fɛrisja'nyːr], *n.m.* (*Chem.*) Ferricyanide.

ferrière [fɛ'rjɛːr], *n.f.* Tool-bag (of farriers, locksmiths, etc.).

ferrifère [fɛri'fɛːr], *a.* Ferriferous. **ferrique**, *a.* Ferric.

ferronnerie [fɛrɔn'ri], *n.f.* Iron-foundry; iron-store; ironmongery; wrought iron. **ferronnier**, *n.m.* (*fem.* **-ière**) Ironmonger, iron-worker.—*n.f.* Chain with jewel (worn on lady's head).—*a.* Pertaining to iron-mongery.

ferroviaire [fɛrɔ'vjɛr], *a.* Pertaining to railways. *Le réseau ferroviaire*, the railway system.

ferrugineux [fɛryʒi'nø], *a.* (*fem.* **-euse**) Ferruginous. *Eau ferrugineuse*, chalybeate water.

ferrure [fɛ'ryːr], *n.f.* Iron binding; iron-work; shoeing (of a horse etc.).

ferry-boat [fɛri'bot], *n.m.* Train ferry. *Le ferry-boat de Dunkerque*, the Dunkerque ferry.

*****ferté** [fɛr'te], *n.f.* (*Old French*) Stronghold; (*used in town names, e.g.* la Ferté-Frênel, la Ferté-Macé, etc.).

fertile [fɛr'til], *a.* Fertile, fruitful; teeming, prolific. **fertilement**, *adv.* Fertilely, abundantly. **fertilisable**, *a.* Fertilizable. **fertilisant**, *a.* (*fem.* **-ante**) Fertilizing. **fertilisation**, *n.f.* Fertilization. **fertiliser**, *v.t.* To fertilize, to manure. **fertilité**, *n.f.* Fertility, fruitfulness.

féru [fe'ry], *a.* (*fem.* **férue**) Smitten, struck; stung to the quick. *Féru d'amour*, lovesick. [*See* FÉRIR.]

férule [fe'ryl], *n.f.* Ferula, giant fennel; (*sch.*) cane, ferule, rod; stroke, cut; (*fig.*) severity, discipline.

fervemment [fɛrva'mã], *adv.* Fervently (*rare*).

fervent [fɛr'vã], *a.* (*fem.* **-ente**) Fervent.—*n.* Enthusiast, devotee, fan.

ferveur [fɛr'vœr], *n.f.* Fervour, ardour.

fesse [fɛs], *n.f.* Buttock, rump; (*pl.*) backside, bottom; (*Naut.*) breech or quarters (of wooden vessel).

fessée [fɛ'se], *n.f.* Spanking.

fesse-mathieu [fɛsma'tjø], *n.m.* (*pl.* **fesse-mathieux**) Miser, old hunks, skinflint.

fesser [fɛ'se], *v.t.* To spank, to smack. *Se faire fesser*, to expose oneself to humiliations.

fesseur, *n.m.* (*fem.* **-euse**) Spanker, flogger. **fessier**, *a.* (*fem.* **fessière**) Pertaining to the buttocks.—*n.m.* Buttocks, bottom. **fessu**, *a.* (*fem.* **-ue**) Large-breeched.

festin [fɛs'tɛ̃], *n.m.* Feast, banquet. *Faire festin* or *faire un festin*, to feast, to banquet; *du pain pour tout festin*, bread was the only fare. *****festiner**, *v.t.* To feast, to entertain. —*v.i.* To banquet, to carouse.

festival [fɛsti'val], *n.m.* Festival.

festivité [fɛstivi'te], *n.f.* Festivity.

festoiement [fɛstwa'mã], *n.m.* Feasting, carousing.

feston [fɛs'tɔ̃], *n.m.* Festoon; architectural ornament cut like a festoon; scallop. **festonné**, *a.* (*fem.* **-ée**) Decorated with festoons. **festonner**, *v.t.* To festoon; to cut in festoons, to scallop.

festoyer [fɛstwa'je] or **fétoyer** (*rare*), *v.t. irr.* (*conjug. like* ABOYER) To entertain, to fête, to feast.—*v.i.* To feast, to make good cheer, to carouse.

fêtard [fɛ'taːr], *a.* (*fem.* **fêtarde**) (*fam.*) Festal, pleasure-making.—*n.* Reveller, rollicker.

fête [fɛːt], *n.f.* Holiday, festival; saint's day or feast; parish feast; birthday; fête, entertainment; festivity, merry-making; display (of sports etc.). *Ce n'est pas tous les jours fête*, 'Christmas comes but once a year'; *faire fête à quelqu'un*, to make someone welcome; *faire la fête*, to lead a rollicking life; *fête carillonnée*, high holiday, festival announced by bell-ringing; *fête d'aviation*, air display; *fêtes mobiles*, movable feasts; *fête légale*, bank holiday; *jour de sa fête*, one's saint's day; *se faire une fête de* or *se faire fête de*, to look forward with pleasure to; *souhaiter la fête à quelqu'un*, to wish someone many happy returns; *trouble-fête*, kill-joy, spoilsport; *troubler la fête*, to mar the pleasure (of the company); *la Fête des Morts*, All Souls' Day. **fête-Dieu**, *n.f.* Corpus Christi day. **fêter**, *v.t.* To keep, celebrate, or observe, as a holiday; to entertain, to feast. *Fêter quelqu'un*, to receive someone with open arms, to make someone very welcome.

fétiche [fe'tiʃ], *n.m.* Fetish; mascot. **fétichisme**, *n.m.* Fetichism.

fétide [fe'tid], *a.* Fetid, rank, offensive. **fétidité**, *n.f.* Fetidity, offensive smell.

fêtoyer [FESTOYER].

fétu [fe'ty], *n.m.* Straw; (*fig.*) pin, rap. *Cela ne vaut pas un fétu*, that is not worth a rap.

fétuque [fe'tyk], *n.f.* (*Bot.*) Fescue-grass.

feu (1) [fø], *n.m.* (*pl.* **feux**) Fire; burning, combustion, conflagration; heat; discharge of fire-arms, firing; fire-place, hearth, chimney; set of fire-irons; (*fig.*) family, household; light, signal-light, flare, torch-light; brilliancy, lustre; ardour, flame, passion; vivacity, spirit, animation, mettle. *Activer le feu*, to stir the fire; *aller au feu*, (*Mil.*) to go into action; to be fire-proof (of earthen-ware); *arme à feu*, fire-arm; *avez-vous du feu?* have you got a light? (*pop.*) *avoir le feu au derrière*, to be in a great hurry; *cesser le feu*, to cease fire; *c'est le feu et l'eau*, they are as opposite as fire and water; *condamner au feu*, to condemn to the stake; *couleur de feu*, flame-colour; *coup de feu*, shot, gun-shot wound; *crier 'au feu'*, to cry 'fire!' *dans le feu de la discussion*, in the heat of the moment; *entretenir un feu*, to keep a fire in; *faire du feu*, to make a fire; *faire feu*, to fire; *faire feu sur*, to shoot at; *faire feu des quatre pieds*, to strain every nerve; *faire feu de tout bois*, to make use of every little thing; *faire long feu*, to hang fire, to miscarry; *ne pas faire long feu*, not to last long; *faire mourir quelqu'un à petit feu*, to keep someone on tenterhooks; *feu à éclats*, flashing light; *feu à volonté* (*Mil.*), independent fire; *feu de bivouac*, watch fire; *feu en rafales*, firing in bursts; *feu de paille*, flash in the pan; *feu d'artifice*, fireworks; *feu de joie*, bonfire; *feu d'enfer*, scorching, scathing fire; *feu du ciel*, lightning; *feu follet*, ignis fatuus, will-o'-the-wisp; *feu roulant* (*Mil.*), running fire; *feu tournant*, revolving light; *feux de position*, riding lights (*Naut.*), parking lights (*Motor.*); *garniture de feu*, set of fire-irons; *il n'a jamais vu le feu*, he has never smelt gunpowder; *il n'y a point de fumée sans feu*, there is no smoke without fire; *il y a tant de feux dans ce village*, there are so many homes (so many families) in this village; *j'en mettrais ma main au feu*, I would stake my life upon it; *jeter de l'huile sur le feu*, to add fuel to the flames; *jeter feu et flamme*, to be violently incensed; *jouer avec le feu*, to play with fire; *le feu a pris à la maison*, the house has caught fire; *le feu du génie*, the inspiration of genius; *le feu lui sort par les yeux*, his eyes flash fire; *les feux de l'été*, the heat of summer; *le visage en feu*, with cheeks blazing; *mettre le feu à une chose*, to set a thing on fire; *mettre le feu au four*, to heat the oven; *mettre tout à feu et à sang*, to put everything to fire and the sword; (*fam.*) *n'y voir que du feu*, to be hoodwinked; *prendre feu*, to catch fire, to be incensed; *se jeter dans le feu pour quelqu'un*, to go through fire and water for someone; *se tenir au coin du feu*, to keep in the chimney-corner; *soutenir le feu*, to stand fire.

feu (2) [fø], *a.* (*fem.* **feue**) Late, deceased, defunct. *Feu les princes* or *les feus princes*, the late princes; *la feue reine* or *feu la reine*, the late queen; *le feu roi*, the late king.

feudataire [føda'tɛːr], *a.* and *n.* Feudatory.

feuillage [fø'jaːʒ], *n.m.* Foliage, leaves, leafage, frondescence. **feuillaison**, *n.f.* (*Bot.*) Foliation.

feuillant [fø'jɑ̃], *n.m.* (*fem.* **-ine**) Religious (monk or nun) of the strict order of St. Bernard.—*n.f.* A kind of puff-pastry.

feuillard [fø'jaːr], *n.m.* Branches with foliage (for winter feed); (*Cooperage*) hoop-wood; sheet-metal.

feuille [fœːj], *n.f.* Leaf; sheet (of paper, metal, etc.); print, newspaper, list; account; veneer (cabinet-making); foil (of mirrors); (*pl.*) (*Arch.*) foliation; feathering. *Bonnes feuilles* (*Print.*), advance-proofs; *dur de la feuille*, (*slang*) deaf; *feuille anglaise*, sheet rubber; *feuille d'acanthe*, acanthus leaf; *feuille d'appel*, muster-roll; *feuille de chou*, cabbage-leaf, (*pej.*) bad newspaper, rag; *feuille de papier*, sheet of paper; *feuille de paye*, pay-roll; *feuille de rose*, rose-leaf; *feuille de route*, way-bill, (*Mil.*) marching orders, itinerary; travelling warrant; *feuille de service*, duty roster; *feuille d'étain*, tinfoil; *feuille de vigne*, fig-leaf (on sculpture); *feuille d'impôt*, tax-return sheet; *feuille d'or*, gold leaf; *feuille hebdomadaire*, weekly paper; *feuille morte*, dead leaf; *feuille quotidienne*, daily news-paper; *feuille volante*, loose sheet, fly-sheet; *tourner les feuilles*, to turn over the leaves. **feuillé**, *a.* (*fem.* **feuillée** (1)) Leafy.

***feuillée** (2), *n.f.* Bower, green arbour; (*Paint.*) foliage; *pl.* (*Mil.*) camp latrines.

feuille-morte, *a. inv.* Of a yellow-brown (or dead-leaf) colour.

feuiller [fœ'je], *v.i.* To put on leaves; (*Paint.*) to paint the foliage of (a picture etc.).

feuilleret [fœj'rɛ], *n.m.* Fillister.

feuillet [fœ'jɛ], *n.m.* Leaf (two pages of a book); leaf of veneer; lamina; thin plate; third stomach of ruminants. *Faire une corne à un feuillet*, to turn down a leaf.

feuilletage [fœj'taːʒ], *n.m.* Turning over of leaves; puff-paste, flaky paste.

feuilleter [fœj'te], *v.t.* To turn over; to peruse rapidly, to run over; to make (pastry) flaky. *Gâteau feuilleté*, flaky puff. **feuilletis**, *n.m.* Cleavage line (in slates etc.); the cutting edge of (a diamond).

feuilleton [fœj'tɔ̃], *n.m.* Feuilleton (literary article, story, etc.); serial. **feuilletoniser**, *v.i.* (*colloq.*) To write feuilletons. **feuilletoniste**, *n.* Writer of feuilletons.

feuillette [fœ'jɛt], *n.f.* Half-hogshead cask (containing 135 litres or about 30 gals.); small measure (less than ½ litre) used for liqueurs.

feuillu [fœ'jy], *a.* (*fem.* **-ue**) Leafy, folious.

feuillure [fœ'jyːr], *n.f.* Groove, rabbet (of doors or windows).

***feurre** [fœːr], *n.m.* Straw (for chair-bottoms etc.).

feutier [fø'tje], *n.m.* Fire- or furnace-attendant (in a large building).

feutrable [fø'trabl], *a.* That may be felted. **feutrage** or **feutrement**, *n.m.* Felting.

feutre [føːtr], *n.m.* Felt; felt hat; packing (for a saddle). **feutré**, *a.* (*fem.* **-ée**) Padded. *Marcher à pas feutrés*, to walk very softly; to pad along. **feutrer**, *v.t.* To felt; to pad, to pack. **se feutrer**, *v.r.* To felt, to become matted. *Les lainages mal lavés se feutrent*, woollens felt when not properly washed. **feutrier**, *n.m.* (*fem.* **feutrière**) Felt-maker.

fève [fɛːv], *n.f.* Bean. *Grosse fève* or *fève des marais*, broad bean, berry resembling this; chrysalis. *Donner un pois pour avoir une fève*, to throw a sprat to catch a herring; *rendre fève pour pois*, to give tit for tat; *roi de la fève*, king of twelfth-night; *trouver la fève au gâteau*, to have a lucky find.

féverole [fe'vrɔl] or **faverole**, *n.f.* Horse-bean; dried kidney-bean.

févier [fe'vje], *n.m.*, or *févier trois-épines*, (*Bot.*) Honey-locust, gladitschia.

fèvre [fɛːvr], *n.m.* Boiler-tender (in salt-works); *metal worker.

février [fevri'e], *n.m.* February. *Les Journées de février*, the Revolution of 1848 in Paris.

fez [fɛːz], *n.m. inv.* Fez (Turkish cap).

fi! [fi], *int.* Fie! fie upon you. *Faire fi d'une chose*, to turn up one's nose at something; *fi donc*, fie! for shame.

(C) **fiable** [fjabl], *a.* Trustworthy, loyal.

fiacre [fjakr], *n.m.* Hackney-coach, cab; hack. *Cocher de fiacre*, cabman; *en fiacre*, in a hackney-coach.

fiançailles [fjɑ̃'saːj], *n.f.* (*used only in pl.*) Betrothal, engagement.

fiancé [fjɑ̃'se], *n.m.* (*fem.* **fiancée**) Betrothed (lover), fiancé or fiancée.

fiancer [fjɑ̃'se], *v.t.* To betroth, to affiance. **se fiancer**, *v.r.* To become engaged to each other.

fiasco [fjas'ko], *n.m. inv.* Fiasco, failure. *Faire fiasco*, to fail utterly; *c'est un fiasco complet*, it is a complete wash-out.

fiasque [fjask], *n.f.* Flask, Italian wine-bottle.

fibrane [fi'bran], *n.f.* (*Tex.*) Staple fibre.

fibre [fibr], *n.f.* Fibre, filament; (*fig.*) sensibility, feeling, disposition, aptitude. **fibreux**, *a.* (*fem.* **-euse**) Fibrous, stringy.

fibrillaire [fibri'lɛːr], *a.* Fibrillar, fibrillation. —*n.f.* Fibrillation. **fibrille**, *n.f.* Fibril.
fibrilleux, *a.* (*fem.* **-euse**) Fibrillous.
fibrine [fi'brin], *n.f.* (*Chem.*) Fibrine. **fibrineux**, *a.* (*fem.* **-euse**) Fibrinous.
fibrociment [fibrɔsi'mã], *n.m.* Fibrocement.
fibrome [fi'brom], *n.m.* Fibroma.
fibule [fi'byl], *n.f.* Fibula.
fic [fik], *n.m.* Fig (big wart on horse's frog). *Herbe de fic* [FICAIRE].
ficaire [fi'kɛːr], *n.f.* (*Bot.*) Lesser celandine, figwort, pilewort.
ficeler [fis'le], *v.t. irr.* (*conjug. like* APPELER) To bind or tie up with string; to do up; to dress up. *Comme le voilà ficelé!* what a sight he looks! **ficeleur**, *n.m.* (*fem.* **-euse**) Packer. **ficelier**, *n.m* [FICELLIER].
ficelle [fi'sɛl], *n.f.* String, packthread, twine; (*fig.*) dodge; (*Theat.*) stage-trick; (*Mil.*) *ficelle (de nettoyage)*, pull-through; (*Mil. slang*) stripe. *Montrer la ficelle*, to betray the secret motive; *connaître les ficelles*, to be up to all the tricks (of the trade), to know the ropes.—*a. Il est ficelle*, he's a trickster.
ficellier [fisɛ'lje], *n.m.* String-winder; person, actor who knows all the ropes.
fichaise [fi'ʃɛːz], *n.f.* (*slang*) Trash, rot.
fichant [fi'ʃã], *a.* (*fem.* **-ante**) (*Mil.*) Plunging; (*slang*) annoying. *Feu fichant*, plunging fire.
fiche [fiʃ], *n.f.* Peg, pin (for a hinge etc.); counter (at cards); small card, slip; (*Whist*) booby prize; (*colloq.*) slip of paper, memo. *Fiche de consolation*, bit of comfort; *fiche (de téléphone)*, phone plug; *mettre en fiches*, to card-index.
ficher [fi'ʃe], *v.t.* To drive in, to thrust in, to fasten in; (*fam. instead of* foutre). *Aller se faire fiche*, to go and be hanged; *envoyer faire fiche*, to send to the deuce; *ficher dedans*, (*slang*) to take in, to cheat, to imprison; *ficher le camp*, to decamp, to be off; *ficher quelqu'un à la porte*, to kick someone out; *je t'en fiche!* nothing of the sort! **se ficher**, *v.r.* (*colloq.*) To laugh at, to make game (*de*).
ficheron, *n.m.* Iron pin, bolt. **fichet**, *n.m.* Ivory peg (to mark with at backgammon etc.). **fichoir**, *n.m.* Peg, clothes-peg.
fichier [fi'ʃje], *n.m.* Card-index (cabinet).
fichtre [fiʃtr], *int.* (*colloq.*) (*euphem.* instead of *foutre*). The deuce; the devil; hang it! **fichtrement**, *adv.* Deucedly, a lot.
fichu (1) [fi'ʃy], *n.m.* Small shawl.
fichu (2) [fi'ʃy], *a.* (*fem.* **-ue**) (*euphem.* instead of *foutu*). Bad, poor, sorry, pitiful; (*slang*) done for. *Comme le voilà fichu!* what a sight he looks! *fichu comme l'as de pique*, badly got up, badly dressed; *fichu de*, capable of; *il a l'air mal fichu*, he does not look too good; *je suis fichu*, it is all up with me.
ficiforme [fisi'fɔrm], *a.* Fig-shaped.
ficoïde [fikɔ'id], *n.f.* (*Bot.*) A species of mesembrianthemum; fig-marigold. *Ficoïde comestible*, Hottentot's fig.
fictif [fik'tif], *a.* (*fem.* **fictive**) Supposed, fictitious, imaginary; (*Law*) feigned.
fiction [fik'sjɔ̃], *n.f.* Fiction, figment, fabrication; fable. **fictionnaire**, *a.* Founded on legal fiction.
fictivement [fiktiv'mã], *adv.* Fictitiously.
fidéicommis [fideikɔ'mi], *n.m. inv.* Trust. (*Law*) Fidei-commissum. **fidéicommis-**

saire, *n.m.* Fidei-commissary, feoffee in trust, beneficiary of trust.
fidéjusseur [fideʒy'sœːr], *n.m.* (*Law*) Caution, surety. **fidéjussion**, *n.f.* Caution, security.
fidèle [fi'dɛl], *a.* Faithful, loyal, true; exact, accurate, safe, sure. *Copie fidèle*, exact copy; *mémoire fidèle*, retentive memory; *peu fidèle*, not to be relied upon; *traducteur fidèle*, accurate translator.—*n.* Faithful friend etc.; (*pl.*) believers, worshippers, faithful. *Les fidèles*, the congregation. **fidèlement**, *adv.* Faithfully, truly, loyally; accurately, exactly.
fidélité, *n.f.* Fidelity, faithfulness, loyalty, constancy; integrity; exactness, accuracy; retentiveness (of the memory). *Fidélité éprouvée*, proven loyalty; *prêter serment de fidélité*, to take an oath of fidelity or allegiance.
fiduciaire [fidy'sjɛːr], *a.* Fiduciary, in trust. *Circulation fiduciaire*, paper currency; *monnaie fiduciaire*, paper-money.—*n.m.* Fiduciary, trustee. **fiduciairement**, *adv.* In trust. **fiducie**, *n.f.* (*Law*) Trust. **fiduciel**, *a.* (*fem.* **-ielle**) Fiducial.
fief [fjɛf], *n.m.* Fief, fee, feof. *Franc fief*, freehold.
fieffé [fjɛ'fe], *a.* (*fem.* **fieffée**) Holding or granted in fief; (*colloq.*) arrant, downright, regular. *Fripon fieffé*, arrant knave.
fieffer [fjɛ'fe], *v.t.* To enfeoff, to invest with a fee; to give or grant in fief.
fiel [fjɛl], *n.m.* Gall; (*fig.*) hatred, bitterness, rancour, spleen. *Amer comme fiel*, as bitter as gall; *il a vomi tout son fiel*, he has vented all his spleen; *un homme plein de fiel*, a man full of malice; *fiel de terre*, (*Bot.*) lesser centaury, earth-gall, erythroea. **fielleux**, *a.* (*fem.* **-euse**) Full of gall or spleen; bitter as gall.
fiente [fjɑ̃ːt], *n.f.* Dung, droppings. **fienter**, *v.i.* To void excrement, to dung; to mute (of birds).
fier (1) [fje], *v.t.* (*conjugated like* PRIER) To trust, to confide, to entrust. **se fier**, *v.r.* To trust (*à*), to rely, to depend upon, to put one's trust (*à*). *Bien fol est qui s'y fie*, more fool he who relies upon her (a woman); *fiez-vous-y*, trust it! *je me fie à vous*, I trust to you; *fiez-vous à moi*, leave it to me.
fier (2) [fjɛːr], *a.* (*fem.* **fière**) Proud, imperious, haughty; stuck-up; boastful, vainglorious; high-spirited, lofty; intrepid, bold; (*colloq.*) precious, stunning, famous, fine, capital. *Faire le fier*, to swank; *il est fier comme Artaban*, he is as proud as Lucifer; *j'ai fait un fier déjeuner* or *dîner*, I have had a capital breakfast or I have dined like a lord; *je n'étais pas trop fier*, I felt rather sheepish; *il nous a rendu un fier service*, he has done us a rare service. **fier-à-bras**, *n.m.* (*pl. unchanged*) Fire-eater, hector, braggart. **fièrement**, *adv.* Proudly, arrogantly, haughtily; spiritedly, boldly; (*colloq.*) preciously, finely, famously, soundly. **fiérot**, *a.* (*fam.*) Haughty, foppish. **fierté**, *n.f.* Pride, haughtiness, arrogance; loftiness, high-mindedness; high spirit, boldness; dignity. *Rabaisser* or *rabattre la fierté de quelqu'un*, to humble someone's pride.
fieu or **fieux** [fjə], *n.m.* (*N.W. dial.*) (*fam.*) Son, sonny, (used chiefly as follows) *mon fieu*, my boy; *un bon fieu*, a good chap.

fièvre [fjɛːvr], *n.f.* Fever, feverishness; ague; (*fig.*) restlessness, excitement. *Accès de fièvre*, fit of fever, ague; *avoir la fièvre* or *un peu de fièvre*, to be feverish; *donner la fièvre*, to put into a fever; *fièvre de cheval*, violent fever; *fièvre de lait*, milk fever; *fièvre intermittente*, intermittent fever, ague, paludism; *fièvre lente*, low fever, hectic; *fièvre quarte*, quartan fever; *fièvre tierce*, tertian fever; *sortir de fièvre*, to recover from a fever; *tomber de fièvre en chaud mal*, to fall from the frying-pan into the fire. **fiévreusement**, *adv.* Feverishly. **fiévreux**, *a.* (*fem.* **-euse**) Feverish; liable to fever; causing fever; (*fig.*) excited, restless.—*n.* Fever-patient. *Salle des fiévreux*, fever-ward. **fiévrotte**, *n.f.* (*fam.*) Slight fever.

fifi [fi'fi], *n.m.* (*fem.* **fifille**) [fi'fij] Dear little thing, ducky.

fifre [fifr], *n.m.* Fife; fifer. **fifrer**, *v.i.* To fife.

figaro [figa'ro], *n.m.* Barber; *knavish valet.

figé [fi'ʒe], *a.* (*fem.* **-ée**) Stiff, cold, set (features, smile, etc.).

figement [fiʒ'mɑ̃], *n.m.* Congealment, coagulation, curdling. **figer**, *v.t.* To congeal, to coagulate, to curdle. **se figer**, *v.r.* To congeal, to coagulate, to curd; (*fig.*) to be very cold; to take a very stiff attitude.

fignolage [fiɲɔ'laːʒ], *n.m.* Finicking.

fignoler [fiɲɔ'le], *v.i.* To be finicky, to split hairs.—*v.t.* To do up in style. *Fignoler le travail*, to do one's work meticulously.

figue [fig], *n.f.* Fig. *Faire la figue à*, to treat with contumely, to flout; *mi-figue, mi-raisin*, bitter-sweet, so-so; *figue de Barbarie*, prickly pear; *figue caque*, persimmon. **figuerie**, *n.f.* Fig-garden. **figuier**, *n.m.* Fig-tree, fig-eater (bird). *Feuille de figuier*, fig-leaf; *figuier d'Adam* or *figuier des banians*, banian, baniantree; *figuier d'Inde*, opuntia, Indian fig-tree; *figuier de Pharaon* or *d'Égypte*, sycamore.

figulin [figy'lɛ̃], *a.* (*fem.* **figuline**) Figuline. —*n.f.* Figuline (pot, vase, of earthenware).

figurable [figy'rabl], *a.* Figurable.

figurant [figy'rɑ̃], *n.* (*fem.* **-ante**) (*Theat.*) Figurant, ballet-dancer; walker-on; supernumerary; (*Cine.*) film super.

figuratif [figyra'tif], *a.* (*fem.* **-ive**) Figurative. **figuration**, *n.f.* Figuration. (*Theat.*) Supers, extras. **figurativement**, *adv.* Figuratively.

figure [fi'gyːr], *n.f.* Figure, form, shape; face, countenance, appearance, air; rôle, part, show (in the world); character, personage; symbol, type; (*Cards*) face card; (*Mus.*) figured passage. *À la figure*, to one's face, in one's teeth; *demi-figure*, half-length; *faire bonne figure*, to make a good figure in the world; *faire triste figure*, to have a sorrowful countenance, to cut a poor figure; *figure de proue*, figurehead; *figures de cire*, waxworks; *prendre figure*, to take shape. **figuré**, *a.* (*fem.* **figurée**) Figured; figurative. *Sens figuré*, figurative meaning.—*n.m.* Figurative sense. **figurément**, *adv.* Figuratively. **figurer**, *v.t.* To figure, to represent, to typify, to represent allegorically or by an allegorical sign.—*v.i.* To figure, to appear; (*Theat.*) to be a figurant or supernumerary. (*Mil.*) *Figurer sur les contrôles*, to be on the rolls. **se figurer**, *v.r.* To imagine, fancy, or picture to oneself. *Figurez-vous que . . .*, would you believe

that . . .? *se figure-t-il que . . .?* does he imagine for a moment that . . .?

figurine [figy'rin], *n.f.* Figurine, statuette. **figuriste**, *n.m.* Figurist, moulder of figurines.

fil [fil], *n.m.* Thread; wire; yarn; edge; grain, vein (in stones etc.); (*fig.*) clue, thread (of a plot etc.); nexus, thread (of an argument etc.); course (of a stream etc.); chain, string, series. *À fil fin*, fine-grained (of wood etc.); *à gros fil*, coarse-grained; *aller contre le fil*, to go against the stream or the grain; *aller de droit fil*, to go straightforwardly; *avoir des fils*, to be stringy (of French beans etc.); *de fil en aiguille*, one thing leading to another; *de droit fil*, the way of the grain; *des finesses cousues de fil blanc*, tricks easily found out; *donner du fil à retordre à quelqu'un*, to give no end of trouble to someone; *donner le fil à*, to sharpen, to put an edge on; *donner un coup de fil*, to give a ring; *être au bout du fil*, to be speaking (on the phone); *fil à couper le beurre*, cheese-wire; *fil à coudre*, sewing-thread; *fil à plomb*, plumb-line; *fil de fer*, iron wire; *fil de fer barbelé*, barbed wire; *fil d'Ariane*, Ariadne's thread; *fil de fouet*, whip-cord; *fil de laiton*, brass wire; *fil de la Vierge*, gossamer; *fil d'emballage*, pack-thread; *laine deux fils*, two-ply wool; *passer au fil de l'épée*, to put to the edge of the sword; *ne tenir qu'à un fil*, to hang by a thread; *ôter le fil de*, to take the edge off; *sans fil*, wireless; *suivre le fil de l'eau* or *du courant*, to go with the stream.

filable [fi'labl], *a.* That may be spun. **filage**, *n.m.* Spinning; drawing (of metal).

filaire [fi'lɛːr], *n.f.* Thread-worm, guinea-worm, filaria.

filament [fila'mɑ̃], *n.m.* Filament, thread. **filamenteux**, *a.* (*fem.* **filamenteuse**) Filamentous, thready, stringy.

filandière [filɑ̃'djɛːr], *n.f.* Spinner, spinster. *Les sœurs filandières*, the Fates, the fatal sisters. **filandre**, *n.f.* Gossamer, air-thread; fibre; thread-worm; thread-like vein (in marble etc.). **filandreux**, *a.* (*fem.* **filandreuse**) Fibrous, stringy, thready.

filant [fi'lɑ̃], *a.* (*fem.* **filante**) Flowing; ropy; shooting (of stars).

filanzane [filɑ̃'zan], *n.f.* Carrying-chair (in Madagascar).

filariose [fila'rioz], *n.f.* (*Med.*) Filariasis.

filasse [fi'las], *n.f.* Filasse, harl, tow (of flax, hemp, etc.); oakum (made of ropes). **filassier**, *n.m.* (*fem.* **filassière**) Tow-dresser.

filateur [fila'tœːr], *n.m.* Spinning-mill owner, spinner. **filature**, *n.f.* Spinning-mill; spinning; shadowing (by a detective). *Filature de coton*, cotton-mill.

file [fil], *n.f.* File. *À la file*, one after another; *file creuse*, blank file; *chef de file*, file-leader, fugleman, leader; *en file* or *à la file indienne*, in Indian file; *par file à droite* or *à gauche!* right or left wheel! *prendre la file*, to take one's place or put one's carriage at the end of the line; *ranger par file*, to draw up in file.

filé [fi'le], *n.m.* Thread, spun thread used for weaving; gold, silver, etc., thread twisted around a silk or cotton one.—*a.* (*fem.* **-ée**) Drawn out, sustained, even. *Son filé*, even and sustained note.

fil-en-quatre [filɑ̃'katr], *n.m.* Strong brandy. **filer** [fi'le], *v.t.* To spin; to wiredraw; (*fig.*)

to conduct, to carry on; to spin out (a story etc.); (*Naut.*) to pay out (a rope); to scud (before the wind), to trail, to shadow; (*colloq.*) to follow stealthily, to track, to go at a certain speed; to play out (one's cards). *Filer le parfait amour*, to be all love and sentiment; *filer un mauvais coton*, to be in a bad way (esp. of health); *machine à filer*, spinning-machine.—*v.i.* To rope (of viscous matter); to file off, to march; to go, to shoot (of ships, stars, etc.); to flare (of a lamp etc.); to cut one's stick, to take oneself off. *Allons, filez*, come, make yourself scarce, clear out! *ce sirop file*, this syrup is ropy; *la lampe file*, the lamp is smoking; *du temps que La Reine Berthe filait*, in the good old times; *filer à l'anglaise*, to slip away, to take French leave; *filer doux*, to be all submission, to sing small; *il faut filer*, we must be off; *le temps file*, time is going.

filerie [fi'lri], *n.f.* Hemp-spinning mill; ropewalk; wire-drawing; wire-mill.

filet [fi'le], *n.m.* Slender thread, string; (*Rail.*) rack; filament, fibre; (*Bot., Arch., etc.*) fillet; slender loin (of beef); beading; dash, drop (of water etc.); (*fig.*) streak, gleam; streamlet; runner (of strawberries); (*Anat.*) frenum; string (of the tongue); snafflebridle; (*Print.*) rule; netting, network; birdnet; (*fig.*) snare, stratagem, ambush. *Coup de filet*, cast of a net, haul; *faire tomber dans un filet*, to ensnare; *faiseur de filets*, netmaker; *filet à cheveux*, hair-net; *filet à provisions*, string-bag; *filet d'eau*, a thin stream of water; *filet de soie*, silk net; *filet de voix*, thin voice; *filet d'une vis*, thread of a screw; *prendre au filet*, to catch in a net; *tendre* or *jeter un filet*, to lay a snare; *un filet de vinaigre*, a dash of vinegar. **filetage**, *n.m.* Thread-making (of screws etc.); thread (of screws etc.); bird-netting. **fileter**, *v.i.* To thread (a screw etc.); to draw (wire). **filetier**, *n.m.* Net-maker.

fileur [fi'lœr], *n.m.* (*fem.* **fileuse**) Spinner; wire-drawer.

filial [fi'ljal], *a.* (*fem.* **-iale** (1), *pl.* **-iaux**) Filial.

filiale (2), *n.f.* Subsidiary company, provincial branch. **filialement**, *adv.* Filially. **filialité**, *n.f.* Filiality. **filiation**, *n.f.* Filiation; (*fig.*) connexion, relationship.

filière [fi'ljɛːr], *n.f.* Draw-plate; screw-plate; implement with holes for moulding vermicelli; (*Carp.*) purlin; spinneret (of silkworm etc.); (*fig.*) channel, progression, string, series, ordeal; (*Naut.*) line, manrope. *Passer par la filière*, to go through the regular channel.

filiforme [fili'fɔrm], *a.* Filiform, thread-shaped.

filigrane [fili'gran], *n.m.* Filigree, filigree-work; water-mark (in paper); embossing. **filigraner**, *v.t.* To work in filigree; to emboss. **filigraniste**, *n.m.* Filigree artist.

filin [fi'lɛ̃], *n.m.* (*Naut.*) Rope.

filipendule [filipã'dyl], *n.f.* (*Bot.*) Drop-wort.

fille [fiːj], *n.f.* Female child, daughter; girl, young unmarried woman, spinster; maiden; servant-maid; easy woman, prostitute. *Arrière-petite-fille*, great-granddaughter; *belle-fille*, daughter-in-law, stepdaughter; *jeune fille*, girl; *nom de jeune fille*, maiden name; *fille à marier*, marriageable daughter; *fille de* service, housemaid; *fille du roi*, a king's daughter; *fille-mère*, unmarried mother; *fille publique*, or *fille de joie*, or just *fille*, prostitute; *fille repentie*, Magdalen; *grande fille*, adolescent girl, girl having reached puberty; *petite-fille*, granddaughter; *petite fille*, little girl; *rester fille*, to remain single, to be an old maid; *vieille fille*, old maid, spinster. **fillette**, *n.f.* Little girl; lass, lassie; (*W. Fr.*) half-bottle of wine.

filleul [fi'jœl], *n.m.* (*fem.* **filleule**) Godchild, godson, goddaughter; protégé. *Filleul de guerre*, (war) protégé.

film [film], *n.m.* Film (photo, cinema, etc.); (*Am.*) movie. *Film en couleurs*, colour film; *film fixe*, film strip; *film muet*, silent film; *film parlant*, talking pictures, talkie. **filmer**, *v.t.* To film.

filoche [fi'lɔʃ], *n.f.* Network, tissue of silk or thread. **filocher**, *v.t.* To make this.

filon [fi'lɔ̃], *n.m.* Metallic vein, lode, reef (of gold); (*fig.*) vein, good job; tip. *Ça c'est le filon*, a cushy job, I call it.

filoselle [filɔ'zɛl], *n.f.* Floss-silk, filoselle.

filou [fi'lu], *n.m.* Crook, pickpocket, thief; sharper, cheat, swindler. **filouter**, *v.t.* To pick, to steal, to filch; to cheat, to swindle. **filouterie**, *n.f.* Picking pockets, filching, swindling, cheating; crooked deal.

fils [fis], *n.m.* (*pl. unchanged*) Son, male child; descendant, offspring; (*term of endearment, like* fieu) sonny. *Arrière-petit-fils*, great-grandson; *beau-fils*, step-son, son-in-law; *être bien le fils de son père*, to be a chip of the old block; *fils de famille*, young man of good family; *fils de France*, male children of the kings of France; *fils de ses œuvres*, self-made man; *fils unique*, only son; *il est bon fils*, he is a good *or* an easy-going fellow; *le désir est fils de besoin*, desire is the offspring of need; *petit-fils*, grandson; *un fils à papa*, a young man with expectations.

filtrage [fil'traːʒ], *n.m.* Filtering, straining. **filtrant**, *a.* (*fem.* **-ante**) Filtering, straining. *Bout filtrant*, filter-tip. **filtration**, *n.f.* Filtration, straining, percolation.

filtre (1) [filtr], *n.m.* Filter; filtering-machine. (*Phot. Cine.*) Filter. *Papier filtre*, porous paper, filter-paper; *filtre-presse*, filter-press. *Filtre à café*, percolator; *un filtre*, a cup of filtered coffee.

filtre (2) [PHILTRE].

filtrer [fil'tre], *v.t.* To filter, to strain. (*Teleg.*) *Filtrer un poste émetteur*, to by-pass a station; *pierre à filtrer*, filtering-stone. *v.i.* and **se filtrer**, *v.r.* To filter, to pass through a filter; to percolate, to leach; to seep; to leak out. *Comment ces renseignements ont-ils pu filtrer?* How could the information have leaked out?

filure [fi'lyːr], *n.f.* Texture of a spun fabric.

fimbriaires [fɛ̃bri'ɛːr], *n.m. pl.* A genus of intestinal worms.

fimbrié [fɛ̃bri'e], *a.* (*fem.* **-iée**) (*Bot.*) Fimbriate, fringed.

fin (1) [fɛ̃], *n.f.* End, extremity, conclusion, termination, expiration, close; death; destination; aim, design, object, intention; purpose. *À bonne fin*, for a laudable purpose; *à ces fins* or *à cette fin*, for this or that end; *à la fin*, at last, at length, in the end, in the long run; *aller* or *tendre à ses fins*, to pursue one's point; *à quelle fin?* to what purpose? *à telle fin que de raison,* for any possible emergency; *à toutes fins utiles,* to be used as you think fit; *cheval à toute fin,* horse fitted to ride or drive; *en fin de compte,* to sum up, finally; *être à sa fin,* to be at one's last shift; *faire une belle fin,* to make a good ending, to die peacefully; *faire une fin,* to make an end of it, to make a complete alteration in one's life, to get married; *fin d'alerte,* all clear; *fin de non-recevoir,* (*Law*) estoppel, plea in bar, exception; *mener à bonne fin,* to bring to a successful conclusion; *mettre fin à,* to put an end to; *qui veut la fin veut les moyens,* the end justifies the means; *sans fin,* endless, endlessly; *tirer à sa fin* or *être sur sa fin,* to be drawing to an end.

fin (2) [fɛ̃], *a.* (*fem.* **fine**) Fine, thin, slender; delicate, subtle, nice, refined, polite; acute, shrewd, cunning, sly, sharp, artful; small (of handwriting). *Avoir le nez fin,* to have a good nose, to be far-sighted; *c'est un fin matois,* he is a knowing fellow; *connaissez-vous le fin mot de l'affaire?* Do you know how the story ended up? *des traits fins,* delicate features; *du fin fond,* from the very depths of; *au fin fond de la Chine,* in farthest China; *fines herbes,* small savoury herbs; *il a l'oreille fine,* he has a quick ear; *pierres fines,* gems, precious stones; *plus fin que lui n'est pas bête,* he is as sharp as they make them.—*n.m.* Sharp fellow, cunning dog; gist, main point; real gold etc.; fine linen. *Blanchisseuse de fin,* clear-starcher; *écrire en fin,* to write small; *jouer au plus fin,* to finesse, to vie in cunning; *savoir le fort et le fin de son art,* to know every trick of the trade.—*n.f.* Fine (champagne). *Une fine à l'eau,* brandy and water.—*adv.* Finely; quite, completely. *Être fin prêt,* to be quite ready; *prendre une bille trop fin,* (*Bill.*) to strike a ball too fine.

finage [fi'naːʒ], *n.m.* Bounds, limits (of a *commune, i.e.* parish).

final [fi'nal], *a.* (*fem.* **finale**, *pl.* **finals**) Final, last, ultimate. **finale**, *n.m.* (*Mus.*) Finale. —*n.f.* (*Gram.*) Last syllable or letter (of a word); (*spt.*) final. **finalement**, *adv.* Finally, lastly. **finaliste**, *a.* and *n.* (*spt., Phil.*) Finalist. **finalité**, *n.f.* Finality.

finance [fi'nãːs], *n.f.* *Cash, ready money; (collect.) financiers; (pl.) one's finances, one's ready money; finance; (pl.) public finances, exchequer, treasury. *Ministre des Finances,* Chancellor of the Exchequer. *Projet de loi de finances,* bill of supply. **financement**, *n.m.* Financing. **financer**, *v.t.* To lay out money, to pay; to finance; to back (an enterprise). **financier**, *a.* (*fem.* **-ière**) Pertaining to finance or financiers.—*n.m.* Financier. **financièrement**, *adv.* Financially.

finasser [fina'se], *v.i.* (*colloq.*) To shuffle, to finesse. **finasserie**, *n.f.* Finesse, petty trickery. **finasseur**, *n.m.* (*fem.* **-euse**), or **finassier** (*fem.* **-ière**) Cunning person, artful dodger.

finaud [fi'no], *a.* (*fem.* **finaude**) Sly, artful, cunning.—*n.* Sly, artful person, slyboots.

fine [FIN (2)].

finement [fin'mã], *adv.* Finely, delicately; ingeniously, shrewdly; artfully, slyly; archly.

finesse [fi'nɛs], *n.f.* Fineness, slenderness,

thinness, lightness; delicacy, nicety, sensitiveness; acuteness, shrewdness, ingenuity; finesse, artifice, craftiness, slyness; (*pl.*) subtleties, fine shades. *Entendre finesse à une chose,* to put a malicious or witty interpretation on a thing; *finesse de goût,* delicacy of taste; *user de finesse,* to display cunning.

finet [fi'nɛ], *a.* (*fem.* **finette** (1)) Sly, subtle, cunning.

finette (2) [fi'nɛt], *n.f.* Thin stuff of wool or cotton, flannelette.

fini [fi'ni], *a.* (*fem.* **finie**) Finished, ended, over; concluded, settled; (*fig.*) consummate, arrant. *C'est fini,* all is over; *c'est une affaire finie,* it is a settled thing; *c'est un homme fini,* he is done for.—*n.m.* Finish, high finish, perfection; finite. *Donner le fini à,* to put the finishing touch to; *le fini et l'infini,* the finite and the infinite.

finir [fi'niːr], *v.t.* To finish, to complete; to end, to discontinue, to leave off, to terminate; to be the end or conclusion to.—*v.i.* To end, to terminate, to conclude, to be over; to expire, to run out, to die. *A n'en plus finir,* without end, endless; *as-tu fini!* (*colloq.*) have you done! shut up! *cela n'en finit pas,* there's no end to it; *en finir avec,* to have done with, to end the matter for good and all; *finissez donc!* do be quiet! *il ne finira jamais,* he will never stop; *pour en finir,* to cut a long story short, to have done with it; *voulez-vous finir?* will you be quiet? **finissage**, *n.m.* Finishing touches. **finissant** (*fem.* **-ante**), *a.* Declining, dying. *Le jour finissant,* the dying light (of day); *une société finissante,* a declining society. **finisseur**, *n.m.* (*fem.* **-euse**) Finisher.

finition [fini'sjɔ̃], *n.f.* Finishing.

Finlande [fɛ̃'lɑ̃ːd], *f.* Finland.

finnois [fi'nwa], *a.* (*fem.* **finnoise**) Finnish. —*n.m.* (**Finnois**, *fem.* **Finnoise**) Finn.

finot. [*See* FINAUD.]

fiole [fjɔl], *n.f.* Phial, flask; (*slang*) head, mug.

fion. [fjɔ̃], *n.m.* (*slang*) *Avoir le fion,* to have a knack, style, or chic; *donner le coup de fion,* to give the final touch.

fiord or **fjord** [fjɔr], *n.m.* A (Norwegian) fjord.

fioriture [fjɔri'tyːr], *n.f.* (*usu. in plur.*) Flourishes (to handwriting), grace-notes (to music); (*fig.*) embellishments (of style etc.).

firmament [firma'mã], *n.m.* Firmament, sky.

firman [fir'mã], *n.m.* Firman, sultan's order.

firme [firm], *n.f.* Firm, style of firm.

fisc [fisk], *n.m.* Public treasury, fisc. **fiscal**, *a.* (*fem.* **-ale**, *pl.* **-aux**) Fiscal, financial. *Charges fiscales,* taxes; *timbre fiscal,* Inland Revenue stamp. **fiscalement**, *adv.* Fiscally. **fiscalité**, *n.f.* Fiscal laws or matters.

fissible [fi'sibl], *a.* Fissile (of radio-active materials). **fissile**, *a.* Fissile, cleavable (of schists). **fission**, *n.f.* Fission, splitting (of atom). *Fission de l'atome,* nuclear fission. **fissipare** [fisi'paːr], *a.* Fissiparous. **fissiparité**, *n.f.* Fissiparity; schizogenesis. **fissipède**, *a.* Fissiped. **fissirostre**, *a.m.* Fissirostral.

fissure [fi'syːr], *n.f.* Fissure, crack, rent. **fissurer**, *v.t.* To fissure, to cause cracks. **se fissurer**, *v.r.* To become fissured.

fiston [fis'tɔ̃], *n.m.* (*pop.*) Laddie, chappie, sonny.

fistot [fis'to], *n.m.* (*Naut.*) Naval cadet in his first year.

fistulaire [fisty'lɛːr], *a.* Fistular; fistuliform. **fistule** [fis'tyl], *n.f.* Fistula. **fistuleux,** *a.* (*fem.* **-euse**) Fistulous; fistular.
five-o'clock [faivɔ'klɔk], *n.m.* Afternoon tea.
fixable [fik'sabl], *a.* Fixable. **fixage,** *n.m.* Fixing. **fixateur,** *a.* (*fem.* **-trice**) Fixative.— *n.m.* Fixer, fixing material. **fixatif,** *a.* (*fem.* **-ive**) Fixative.—*n.m.* Fixative (for fusain, pastel, etc.) **fixation,** *n.f.* Fixation, fixing; localization; determination; settlement; rating, assessment. *Abcès de fixation,* derivative abscess, artificial abscess.
fixe [fiks], *a.* Fixed, set, firm, steady, fast; invariable, permanent, settled, stationary; appointed, regular. *À jour fixe,* on stated days; (*Meteor.*) *beau fixe,* set fair; *c'est une idée fixe,* it is an obsession; *prix fixe,* set price; *traitement fixe,* regular salary.—*n.m.* Fixed salary.—*int.* (*Mil.*) Eyes front! Steady! **fixé,** *n.m.* Small oil-painting on glass. **fixement,** *adv.* Fixedly, steadily.
fixer [fik'se], *v.t.* To fix, to fasten, to stick; to settle; to determine, to establish; to rivet the gaze on, to stare at; to attract, to captivate. *Fixer l'attention de quelqu'un,* to attract someone's attention; *fixer les soupçons sur,* to fix suspicion on; *fixer l'ennemi,* to hold the enemy; *fixer quelqu'un,* to stare at someone; *je suis fixé sur son compte,* I have got his measure, I know all about him; (*fam.*) *je ne suis pas (encore) fixé,* I have not made up my mind. **se fixer,** *v.r.* To be fixed, to fasten (à); to settle down, to take one's abode; to settle. *Se fixer sur quelque chose,* to stick to something. **fixibilité,** *n.f.* State of being fixable. **fixité,** *n.f.* Fixity, stability.
fla [fla], *n.m.* Double beat of the drum, slightly with the right, then strongly with the left.
flabellate [flabɛ'lat], *n.m.* (*Zool.*) Flabellate. **flabellé** (*fem.* **-ée**) or **flabelliforme,** *a.* (*Bot.*) Flabelliform, fan-shaped.
flac [flak], *int.* Slap! bang! plop!—*n.m.* Anti-aircraft gunfire.
flaccidité [flaksidi'te], *n.f.* Flaccidity.
flache [flaʃ], *a.* Soft.—*n.f.* Flaw (in timber etc.); hole in the pavement, depression in a road; puddle; cleft, fissure inside rock.
flacherie [fla'ʃri], *n.f.* Disease of silkworms, flaccidity.
flacon [fla'kɔ̃], *n.m.* Case-bottle, bottle; decanter; phial.
fla-fla [fla'fla], *n.m.* (*Painting*) Cheap effect; (*fig.*) show, showing-off. *Faire des fla-flas,* to show off.
flagellant [flaʒɛ'lɑ̃], *n.m.* Flagellant. **flagellate** (*fem.* **-ate**) *a.* (*Zool.*) Flagellate organism. **flagellateur,** *n.m.* Flagellator. **flagellation,** *n.f.* Flagellation, scourging, flogging. **flagellé,** *a.* (*fem.* **-ée**) Flagellate. **flageller,** *v.t.* To flagellate, to scourge, to flog; (*fig.*) to lash with words. **flagelliforme,** *a.* Flagelliform, whip-shaped. **flagellum,** *n.m.* (*Zool. etc.*) Flagellum.
flageoler [flaʒɔ'le], *v.i.* To tremble, to shake (of the legs etc.).
flageolet [flaʒɔ'le], *n.m.* Flageolet (music); (small) green kidney bean.
flagorner [flagɔr'ne], *v.t.* To flatter servilely, to toady. **flagornerie,** *n.f.* Sycophancy, base flattery. **flagorneur,** *n.m.* (*fem.* **-euse**) Sycophant, toady.

flagramment [flagra'mɑ̃], *adv.* (*rare*) Flagrantly. **flagrance,** *n.f.* Flagrancy. **flagrant,** *a.* (*fem.* **-ante**) Flagrant, gross; (*fig.*) evident, obvious. *En flagrant délit,* in the very act, red-handed.
flair [flɛːr], *n.m.* (*Hunt.*) Nose; (*fig.*) perspicacity. *Il a du flair,* he knows how to find out things. **flairer,** *v.t.* To smell, to scent; to detect, to foresee; (*colloq.*) to smell of; to find out. *Flairer la violette,* to smell like a violet; *flairer quelque chose* or *un danger,* to smell a rat. **flaireur,** *n.m.* Smeller; (*fig.*) tracker, smeller-out.
flamand [fla'mɑ̃], *a.* (*fem.* **-ande**) Flemish.— *n.m.* (**Flamand,** *fem.* **Flamande**) Fleming.
flamant [fla'mɑ̃], *n.m.,* or **flamant rose** Flamingo.
flambage [flɑ̃'baːʒ], *n.m.* Singeing. **flambant,** *a.* (*fem.* **-ante**) Blazing, flaming; (*pop.*) smart, flashy.—*n.m.* Flaming coal. (*fam.*) **flambard,** *a.* (*fem.* **-arde**) (*fam.*) Showy, smart, flashy—*n.m.* Flaming coal; (*fam.*) jolly fellow; (*Naut.*) fishing-smack.
flambeau [flɑ̃'bo], *n.m.* (*pl.* **-eaux**) Torch, link; candle, taper; candlestick; (*fig.*) light, luminary; brand, flames. *À la lumière des flambeaux,* by torch-light; *les flambeaux de la nuit,* the stars.
flambée [flɑ̃'be], *n.f.* Blaze. **flamber,** *v.t.* To singe; to fumigate, to disinfect. *Flamber une volaille,* to singe a fowl; (*fam.*) *il est flambé,* he is done for; *mon argent est flambé,* my money is lost.—*v.i.* To blaze, to flame, to flare; to burn. *Faire flamber,* to set fire to.
flamberge [flɑ̃'bɛrʒ], *n.f.* Sword, brand. (*iron.*) *Mettre flamberge au vent,* to draw one's sword.
flamboiement [flɑ̃bwa'mɑ̃], *n.m.* Flaming, flare, blaze. **flamboyant,** *a.* (*fem.* **-ante**) Flaming, blazing; flashing. (*Arch.*) flamboyant. **flamboyer,** *v.i. irr.* (*conjug. like* ABOYER) To flame, blaze, flare; (*fig.*) to flash, glow.
flamine [fla'min], *n.m.* (*Rom. Ant.*) Flamen.
flamingant [flamɛ̃'gɑ̃], *a.* Flemish-speaking.
flamme (1) [flɑːm], *n.f.* Flame, blaze; (*fig.*) flames, fire; glow, lustre; ardour, passion; (*Naut.* and *Mil.*) pennon, pennant. *Ce feu ne fait point de flamme,* that fire does not blaze; *être tout feu, tout flamme,* to be all fire; *jeter des flammes,* to blaze, to flame; *jeter feu et flamme,* to fret and fume; *retour de flamme,* (*Motor.*) backfire; (*Artill.*) back-flash.
flamme (2) [flɑːm], *n.f.* (*Vet.*) Fleam.
flammé, *a.* (*fem.* **-ée**) Flame-shaped. *Grès flammés,* glazed earthenware with flame-shaped spots, tiger-ware.
flammèche [fla'mɛʃ], *n.f.* Flake of fire, spark.
flammer [fla'me], *v.t.* To singe (material).
flammerole [flam'rɔl], *n.f.* (*pop.*) Will-o'-the-wisp.
flammette [fla'mɛt], *n.f.* Little flame; (*Bot.*) clematis; lesser spearwort.
flan [flɑ̃], *n.m.* (Baked) custard tart; flan; disk (blank coin); (*Print.*) flong, paper used for stereotyping-matrix.
flanc [flɑ̃], *n.m.* Flank, side; broadside; (*fig.*) womb, bowels, entrails. *Être sur le flanc,* (*colloq.*) to be laid up; *marche de flanc,* march to right or left; *par le flanc droit!* (*Mil.*) right turn! *prêter le flanc à,* to lay oneself open to; (*fam.*) *se battre les flancs,* to exert

oneself (to no purpose); (*Mil. slang*) *tirer au flanc*, to malinger; *un tire-au-flanc*, a malingerer. **flanc-garde**, *n.m.* Flank guard.

flancher [flɑ̃'ʃe], *v.i.* (*fam.*) To give in; to rat, to jib; (of motor) to stop, to break down.

flanchet [flɑ̃'ʃɛ], *n.m.* Flank (of beef or of cod).

Flandre [flɑ̃:dr], *f.* Flanders.

flandrin [flɑ̃'drɛ̃], *n.m.* (*colloq.*) *Un grand flandrin*, a long, lanky fellow.

flâne [flɑ:n], (*colloq.*) [FLÂNERIE].

flanelle [fla'nɛl], *n.f.* Flannel. *Gilet de flanelle*, flannel under-vest; *pantalon de flanelle blanche* or *grise*, white or grey flannels.

flâner [flɑ'ne], *v.i.* To lounge, to saunter, to stroll, to loaf. **flânerie**, *n.f.* Lounging; lounge; stroll; sauntering; loafing. **flâneur**, *n.m.* (*fem.* **flâneuse**) Lounger, saunterer, loafer.—*n.f.* Long, low folding-chair.

flanquant [flɑ̃'kɑ̃], *a.* (*fem.* **-ante**) (*Fort.*) Flanking. **flanquement**, *n.m.* (*Fort.*) Flanking; (*Mil.*) supporting the flanks.

flanquer (1) [flɑ̃'ke], *v.t.* To flank; (*Mil.*) to defend, to secure, to guard; to set side by side with or at the side of something.

flanquer (2) [flɑ̃'ke], *v.t.* (*colloq.*) To deal (a blow); to throw, to fling, to pitch. *Flanquer à la porte*, to bundle out; *flanquer un soufflet à quelqu'un*, to box someone's ears; *je lui ai flanqué une pile*, I gave him a sound licking. **se flanquer**, *v.r.* *Se flanquer par terre*, to throw oneself down, to tumble down; *se flanquer un coup, une indigestion, etc.*, to give oneself (a blow, a fit of indigestion, etc.).

flanqueur [flɑ̃'kœːr], *n.m.* (*Mil.*) Flanker.

flapi or **flappi** [fla'pi], *a.* (*fam.*) Done up, jaded; fagged out.

flaque [flak], *n.f.* Small pool, puddle.

flaquée [fla'ke], *n.f.* (*colloq.*) Dash (of water), splash sent with some force.

flaquer [fla'ke], *v.t.* To fling, to dash (water etc.).

flash [flaʃ], *n.m.* (*Phot.*) Flash-light; (*Cine.*) flash.

flasque (1) [flask], *a.* Limp, slack, flabby, flaccid.

flasque (2) [flask], *n.m.* Cheek (of a gun-carriage); flake-chock (of anchor).—*n.m. pl.* Flask-boards (of forge-bellows); (*Naut.*) cheeks (of mast), whelps (of capstan).

flasque (3) [flask], *n.f.* Powder-horn.

flatter [fla'te], *v.t.* To stroke, to smooth, to pat, to caress; to flatter; to soothe, to please; to cajole, to deceive. *Elle aime à s'entendre flatter*, she likes to be flattered; *flatter de*, to delude with expectations of; *la musique flatte l'oreille*, music soothes the ear; *le chien flatte son maître*, the dog fawns upon his master; *un portrait flatté*, a flattering likeness. **se flatter**, *v.r.* To flatter oneself; to pride oneself; to hope, to expect. **flatterie**, *n.f.* Flattery, adulation. **flatteur**, *a.* (*fem.* **-euse**) Flattering, complimentary, eulogistic; gratifying, pleasing.—*n.* Flatterer. **flatteusement**, *adv.* Flatteringly.

flatueux [fla'tɥø], *a.* (*fem.* **-euse**) Flatulent, causing flatulence. **flatulence**, *n.f.* Flatulence, wind. **flatulent**, *a.* (*fem.* **-ente**) Flatulent, windy. **flatuosité**, *n.f.* Flatulency.

flavescent [flave'sɑ̃], *a.* (*fem.* **-ente**) Flavescent; golden yellow.

fléau [fle'o], *n.m.* (*pl.* **fléaux**) Flail; (*fig.*) scourge, plague, calamity; wearisome person,

bore; beam (of a balance); iron bar (to fasten folding-gates).

flèche [flɛʃ], *n.f.* Arrow, dart, bolt; shaft, straight barrel, trunk, or stem (of trees, canes, etc.); (*Astron.*) Sagitta; (*Arch.*) slender spire, flèche; (*Backgammon*) point; (*Trig.*) versed sine; (*Av.*) camber (of wing); sag, dip (of cable etc.); (*Naut.*) mât de flèche, topmast. *Cheval de flèche*, head horse; *chevaux attelés en flèche*, horses harnessed tandem; *faire flèche de tout bois*, to leave no stone unturned; *flèche de l'amour*, dart of love; *flèche de lard*, flitch of bacon; *flèche de trajectoire*, highest point of trajectory; *monter en flèche* (of prices etc.), to soar; *tirer une flèche*, to let fly an arrow. **flécher**, *v.i. irr.* (*conjug. like* ACCÉLÉRER) To send up a stem (of sugar-canes). —*v.t.* To shoot at or hit with an arrow. **fléchette**, *n.f.* Small arrow, dart. **fléchière**, *n.f.* (*Arch.* and *Bot.*) Arrow-head.

fléchir [fle'ʃiːr], *v.t.* To bend, to bow; to flex (the arm); (*fig.*) to move, to melt, to touch, to soften, to persuade. *Se laisser fléchir*, to relent, to give in, to consent.—*v.i.* To bend, to bow, to yield, to give way; to sag (cable); to stagger, to waver. **fléchissement**, *n.m.* Bending, giving way. **fléchisseur**, *n.* and *a.m.* (*Anat.*) Flexor.

flegmatique [flegma'tik], *a.* (*Med.*) Phlegmatic; (*fig.*) stolid, sluggish.—*n.* Stolid, phlegmatic person. **flegmatiquement**, *adv.* Phlegmatically.

flegme [flɛgm], *n.m.* Phlegm; (*fig.*) coolness, impassivity, unconcern, slackness.

flegmon [PHLEGMON].

flémard [fle'maːr], *a.* (*fem.* **-arde**) (*fam.*) Slack, lazy.—*n.* Slack fellow, lazy-bones. **flème** or **flemme**, *n.f.* Laziness, sloth, inertia. **flémer**, *v.i. irr.* (*conjug. like* ACCÉLÉRER) or *battre sa flemme*, to be lazy or idle.

fléole [fle'ɔl], *n.f.* (*Bot.*) *Phleum pratense*, cat's-tail grass.

flétan [fle'tɑ̃], *n.m.* *Grand flétan*, halibut; *petit flétan*, or *flet*, flounder.

flétrir (1) [fle'triːr], *v.t.* To wither, to dry up, to cause to fade; (*fig.*) to blight, to blast, to tarnish, to blemish. **se flétrir**, *v.r.* To fade, to wither.

flétrir (2) [fle'triːr], *v.t.* To brand; to dishonour, to stain, to stigmatize. **flétrissant**, *a.* (*fem.* **-ante**) Dishonouring, blighting.

flétrissure (1) [fletri'syːr], *n.f.* Fading, withering.

flétrissure (2) [fletri'syːr], *n.f.* Brand, stigma, blemish, blot, discredit, disgrace.

flette [flɛt], *n.f.* Flat-bottomed boat; punt.

fleur [flœːr], *n.f.* Flower, blossom; bloom (powder); (*fig.*) prime, lustre; choice, best, pick; surface. *À fleur d'eau*, at water level; (*Naut.*) between wind and water; *à fleur de peau*, superficially; *à fleur de terre*, level with the ground; *avoir la fleur d'une chose*, to have the best of a thing; *en pleine fleur*, full-blown, in full bloom; *entrer en fleur*, to flower; to bloom; *être dans la fleur de l'âge*, to be in the prime of life; *fleur de coucou*, lychnis; *fleur de farine*, best flour, whites; *fleur de lis*, fleur-de-lis; (*C*) *fleur de mai*, may-flower; *fleur de soufre*, flowers of sulphur; *fleurs d'arbre*, blossoms of a tree; *semer de fleurs*, to strew with flowers; *yeux à fleur de tête*, prominent or goggle eyes. **fleurage**, *n.m.* Floral pattern (on a carpet etc.); flowers produced by crystallization. **fleuraison** or (*more usually*) **floraison,** *n.f.* Efflorescence, flowering season.

fleurdeliser [flœrdəli'ze], *v.t.* To mark with a fleur-de-lis.

fleuré [flœ're], *a.* (*fem.* **fleurée**) (*Her.*) Flowered, fleury.

fleurer [flœ're], *v.i.* To smell, to exhale. *Cela fleure bon,* that smells nice.

fleuret [flœ'rɛ], *n.m.* Foil; miner's drill; silk ferret.

fleureter [flœr'te], *v.i. irr.* (*conjugated like* APPELER) To make gallant speeches.

fleurette [flœ'rɛt], *n.f.* Little flower, floweret; amorous discourse, gallant speech. *Conter fleurette,* to murmur sweet nothings, to flirt.

fleuri [flœ'ri], *a.* (*fem.* **fleurie**) Flowery; florid. *Écrire d'une manière fleurie,* to write in a florid style; *teint fleuri,* florid complexion.

fleurir [flœ'ri:r], *v.i.* To flower, to blossom; (*fig.*) to thrive, to flourish, to prosper (*in this sense, imperf.* **florissais** etc.). *Cet arbre fleurissait tous les ans deux fois,* this tree blossomed twice every year; *cet auteur florissait sous le règne de,* that author flourished under the reign of; *les arts et les sciences florissaient alors,* arts and sciences flourished then.—*v.t.* To decorate with flowers. **se fleurir,** *v.r.* To adorn oneself with flowers; to take a flower to put in one's coat etc.

fleurissant, *a.* (*fem.* **-ante**) Blossoming, blooming. **fleuriste,** *a.* and *n.* Florist, floriculturist; artificial flower-maker or seller; (*in compound words*) flower. *Jardin fleuriste,* flower-garden.

fleuron [flœ'rɔ̃], *n.m.* Floret (of a composite flower); carved or painted flower; (*fig.*) flower-work; jewel; ornament; (*Print.*) printer's flower; tailpiece. *Le plus beau fleuron de sa couronne,* the brightest jewel in his crown.

fleuronné, *a.* (*fem.* **-ée**) Decorated with fleurons; (*Bot.*) having florets [FLEURÉ].

fleuve [flœ:v], *n.m.* River (falling into the sea), large stream; (*Myth.*) river-god; (*fig.*) course, current, torrent. *Fleuve de la vie,* the current of one's life.

flexibilité [flɛksibili'te], *n.f.* Flexibility, pliancy. **flexible,** *a.* Flexible, pliable, supple. **flexion,** *n.f.* Flexion, bending. **flexionnel,** *a.* (*fem.* **-elle**) Flexional. **flexueux,** *a.* (*fem.* **-euse**) Flexuous. **flexuosité,** *n.f.* Flexuosity. **flexure,** *n.f.* Flexure.

flibot [fli'bo], *n.m.* Dutch flat-bottomed, two-masted boat; flyboat.

flibuste [fli'byst], *n.f.* Filibustering, buccaneering. **flibuster,** *v.i.* To buccaneer, to filibuster, to freeboot—*v.t.* (*colloq.*) To filch, to pinch. **flibusterie,** *n.f.* Filibustering; robbery, theft. **flibustier,** *n.m.* Buccaneer, pirate; freebooter, robber.

flic [flik], *n.m.* (*slang*) Policeman, cop, bobby.

flicflac or **flic flac** [flik'flak], *n.m.* Crack of a whip.

flingot [flɛ̃'go], *n.m.*, or **flingue,** *n.m.* (*slang*) Infantry soldier's rifle; (*pop.*) gun (of any kind).

flirt [flœrt], *a.* and *n.m.* Flirtation; flirt. *Elle est très flirt,* she is a terrible flirt; *un ancien flirt,* an old flame. **flirter,** *v.i.* To flirt. **flirteur,** *n.m.* (*fem.* **flirteuse**) Flirt.

floc [flɔk], *n.m.* Tuft, tassel.—*int.* Flop!

floche [flɔʃ], *a.* Flossy, shaggy; (*Cards*) flush. *Soie floche,* floss-silk.

flocon [flɔ'kɔ̃], *n.m.* Flock or tuft (of silk or wool); flake (of snow); wreath (of smoke). *La neige tombait à gros flocons,* snow fell in great flakes; *flocons d'avoine,* flaked oats; *un flocon de laine,* a flock of wool. **floconneux,** *a.* (*fem.* **-euse**) Flaky.

flonflon [flɔ̃'flɔ̃], *n.m.* *Tol-de-rol, tra-la-la; (*pl.*) blare of a (distant) band.

flopée or **floppée** [flɔ'pe], *n.f.* (*slang*) Large quantity, crowd.

floraison [FLEURAISON].

floral [flɔ'ral], *a.* (*fem.* **-ale,** *pl.* **-aux**) Floral. *Jeux floraux,* floral games (of Toulouse). **floralies,** *n.f.pl.* (International) flower-show.

Flore [flɔ:r], *f.* Flora.—*n.f.* Flora.

floréal [flɔre'al], *n.m.* Floreal (the eighth month of the calendar of the first French republic, from April 20th to May 19th).

florence [flɔ'rɑ̃:s], *n.m.* Sarcenet.—*n.f.* Silk gut (for fishing line).

florencé [flɔrɑ̃'se], *a.* (*fem.* **-ée**) (*Her.*) Flowery.

florentin [flɔrɑ̃'tɛ̃], *a.* (*fem.* **florentine** (1)) Florentine.—*n.m.* (**Florentin,** *fem.* **Florentine** (2), *n.f.* Florentine) A Florentine. **florentine** (2), *n.f.* Florentine (silk stuff).

florer [flɔ're], *v.t.* (*Naut.*) To grease (a ship).

florès [flɔ'rɛ:s], *n.m.* *Faire florès.* To be a success, to be in vogue.

floriculture [flɔrikyl'ty:r], *n.f.* Floriculture.

florifère, *a.* (*Bot.*) Floriferous. **floriforme,** *a.* Floriform.

florilège [flɔri'lɛ:ʒ], *n.m.* Anthology.

florin [flɔ'rɛ̃], *n.m.* Florin. (*Bot.*) *Herbe à mille florins,* lesser centaury.

florir [FLEURIR]. **florissant** [flɔri'sɑ̃], *a.* (*fem.* **-ante**) Prosperous, flourishing.

floriste [flɔ'rist], *n.m.* Florist; flowering plant expert, writer or researcher.

flosculeux [flɔsky'lø], *a.* (*fem.* **flosculeuse**) Floscular, flosculous.

flot [flo], *n.m.* Wave, billow; (*fig.*) surge, tide, flood, flood-tide; crowd, multitude (of persons); (*pl.*) the sea, stream, torrent, immense quantity, float or raft (floating of timber). *À flot perdu,* at the mercy of the current; *à flots,* in streams, in torrents, in crowds; *être à flot,* to be afloat, *bassin à flot,* wet dock; *le bruit des flots,* the roaring of the waves; *les flots de la mer,* the waves of the sea; *mettre un vaisseau à flot,* to set a ship afloat; *se remettre à flot,* to recover one's fortunes; *un flot de paroles,* a stream of words; *un flot d'injures,* a stream of abuse.

flottable [flɔ'tabl], *a.* (River) where rafts of wood may be floated; buoyant (wood). **flottage,** *n.m.* Floating of wood, rafting, floating wood.

flottaison [flɔtɛ'zɔ̃], *n.f.* Floating. *Ligne de flottaison,* water-line or marks; ship's gauge.

flottant [flɔ'tɑ̃], *a.* (*fem.* **-ante**) Floating, waving, flowing; (*fig.*) irresolute, wavering, fluctuating.

flottard [flɔ'tar], *n.m.* (*fam.*) Naval cadet.

flotte (1) [flɔt], *n.f.* Fleet; navy; (*pop.*) rain. **flotte** (2) [flɔt], *n.f.* Cable-buoy; (fishing) float.

flottement [flɔt'mɑ̃], *n.m.* Floating; (*fig.*) wavering, irresolution; (*Mil.*) undulation of troops on the march. **flotter,** *v.i.* To float, to swim; to flutter (of flag); to drift, to be

wafted; to flow, to undulate; to be irresolute, to fluctuate, to waver; (*pop.*) to rain. *Faire flotter du bois*, to float wood.—*v.t.* To float (wood etc.); to float (a cable etc.) on the surface of the water.
flotteur [flɔ'tœːr], *n.m.* Raftsman; fishing-float; cable-buoy; water-gauge.
flottille [flɔ'tiːj], *n.f.* Flotilla.
flou [flu], *a.* (*fem.* **floue**) (Image, figure, landscape, photograph, etc.) not quite distinct, hazy, soft, blurred, muzzy, out of focus.—*n.m.* Softness, haziness (of outlines); (*Dress.*) light dresses; looseness.
flouer [flu'e], *v.t.* (*slang*) To cheat, to diddle, to swindle. **flouerie,** *n.f.* Cheating, swindling. **floueur,** *n.m.* Sharper, cheat, gull-catcher.
flouve [fluːv], *n.f.* (*Bot.*) Flouve odorante, vernal grass.
fluctuant [flyk'tɥɑ̃], *a.* (*fem.* **-ante**) Fluctuating. **fluctuation,** *n.f.* Fluctuation. **fluctuer,** *v.i.* To fluctuate. **fluctueux,** *a.* (*fem.* **-euse**) Fluctuating, agitated, boisterous.
*****fluer** [flɥ'e], *v.i.* To flow (of the tide).
fluet [flɥ'ɛ], *a.* (*fem.* **fluette**) Slender, thin, slim.
flueurs [LEUCORRHÉE].
fluide [flɥ'id], *a.* Fluid (liquid).—*n.m.* Fluid. **fluidement,** *adv.* As a fluid. **fluidifier,** *v.t.* (*conjugated like* PRIER) To fluidify. **fluidité,** *n.f.* Fluidity.
fluor [flɥ'ɔːr], *n.m.* (*Chem.*) Fluorine; (*Min.*) fluor-spar. *Spath fluor,* fluor, fluorspar. **fluorescéine,** *n.f.* Fluorescein. **fluorescence,** *n.f.* Fluorescence. **fluorescent,** *a.* (*fem.* **-ente**) Fluorescent. **fluorhydrique,** *a.* Hydrofluoric. **fluorine,** *n.f.* Fluor, natural fluoride of calcium. **fluorique** [FLUORHYDRIQUE]. **fluoroscope,** *n.m.* Fluoroscope. **fluoroscopie,** *n.f.* Fluoroscopy. **fluorure,** *n.m.* Fluoride.
flûte (1) [flyt], *n.f.* Flute; flute-player, flautist; long French roll; tall glass (for champagne); tapestry-weaver's shuttle; (*pl.,* *colloq.*) spindle shanks, long-legs. *Accordez vos flûtes,* settle it between you; *ajuster ses flûtes,* to tune one's pipes, to prepare one's measures; *ce qui vient de la flûte s'en retourne par le tambour,* lightly come, lightly go; *en bec de flûte,* like the mouthpiece of a flute; *flûte à l'oignon,* reed-pipe; *jeu de flûtes,* (Organ) flute stop; *flûte de pan* or *de chevrier,* Pan pipe, syrinx; *jouer des* or *se tirer des flûtes,* (*colloq.*) to run; *jouer de la flûte,* to play the flute; *petite flûte,* piccolo.—*int.* Botheration!
*****flûte** (2) [flyt], *n.f.* Large, narrow-sterned Dutch cargo-boat (seventeenth century).
flûté [fly'te], *a.* (*fem.* **flûtée**) Soft, fluted, fluty (of a voice). **flûteau,** *n.m.* Child's whistle; water-plantain. **flûter,** *v.i.* To flute, to pipe. **flûtiste,** *n.m.* Flautist, flute-player.
fluvial [fly'vjal], *a.* (*fem.* **-iale,** *pl.* **-iaux**) Fluvial. **fluviatile,** *a.* Fluviatile, fluviatic. **fluviographe** or **fluviomètre,** *n.m.* Fluvio-meter.
flux [fly], *n.m.* Flux, flow, flood, rising. *Flux de sang,* bloody flux; *flux de ventre,* dysentery; *le flux et le reflux,* the ebb and the flow.
fluxion [flyk'sjɔ̃], *n.f.* Inflammation, swelling; (*pl.,* *Math.*) fluxions. *Une fluxion de poitrine,* inflammation of the lungs, pneumonia.

fluxionnaire, *a.* Fluxionary, subject to inflammation; (*Math.*) fluxional.
foc [fɔk], *n.m.* (*Naut.*) Jib, staysail. *Bâton de foc,* jib-boom; *grand foc,* standing-jib; *petit foc,* fore staysail.
focal [fɔ'kal], *a.* (*fem.* **focale,** *pl.* **focaux**) Focal. **focalisation,** *n.f.* Focalization.
foëne [fɔ'en] or **fouëne** [fwen], *n.f.* Eel-spear. **foëner,** *v.t.* To spear (fish).
fœtal [fe'tal], *a.* (*fem.* **-ale,** *pl.* **-aux**) Foetal.
fœtus [fe'tyːs], *n.m. inv.* Foetus.
foi [fwa], *n.f.* Faith, belief, creed; trust; credit; fidelity, faithfulness, loyalty, honour; evidence, proof, testimony; (*Feud.*) fealty. *Agir de bonne foi,* to act in good faith; *ajouter foi à quelque chose,* to give credit to something; *article de foi,* article of faith, Church dogma; *bonne foi,* good faith, honesty, plain-dealing; *de bonne foi,* sincerely, candidly; *en faire foi,* to be a proof of it; *en foi de quoi,* in testimony whereof; *faire foi de,* to prove, to be evidence of; *foi de gentilhomme* or *d'honnête homme,* on the honour of a gentleman; *garder sa foi,* to keep one's word; *ma foi! par ma foi!* or *sur ma foi!* really! to be sure! *manque de foi,* treachery; *manquer à sa foi, trahir sa foi,* to break one's word; *mauvaise foi,* bad faith, dishonesty, falsehood, double-dealing; *n'avoir ni foi ni loi,* to regard neither law nor gospel, to be utterly reckless; *ligne de foi,* axis of gun-sight; *profession de foi,* creed; *un homme de bonne foi,* an honest man; *un homme de peu de foi,* an unbeliever.
foie [fwa], *n.m.* Liver. *Maladie de foie,* liver-complaint; (*slang*) *avoir les foies (blancs),* to be in a (blue) funk.
foin (1) [fwɛ̃], *n.m.* Hay; (of artichokes) choke, heart. *Avoir du foin dans ses bottes,* to be well off; *faire ses foins,* to make profits; *faire du foin,* (*slang*) to kick up a row; *faire les foins,* to make hay; *grenier à foin,* hayloft; *meule de foin,* haystack; *rhume des foins,* hay-fever.
foin (2) [fwɛ̃], *int.* (*only used in*) *foin de (la richesse)* and *faire foin de la (richesse),* not care a fig for (money), to snap one's fingers at it.
foire (1) [fwaːr], *n.f.* Fair (market); fairing; (*fam.*) din, row, noisy and disorderly place. *Champ de foire,* fair-ground, market-place; *ils s'entendent comme larrons en foire,* they are hand in glove together.
foire (2) [fwaːr], *n.f.* (*vulg.*) Diarrhoea. **foirer,** *v.i.* To have diarrhoea; (*fig.*) to show the white feather, to fail, to miscarry. **foireux,** *a.* (*fem.* **foireuse**) Lax, relaxed; having diarrhoea; (*pop.*) funky, miscarried.—*n.* One who has diarrhoea; a funk.
fois [fwa], *n.f. inv.* Time (turn, occasion). *À la fois* or *tout à la fois,* all together, all at once; *à plusieurs fois,* repeatedly; *autant de fois que* or *toutes les fois que,* as often as; *bien des fois,* many a time; *cette fois,* this time, in these circumstances; *combien de fois?* how many times? how often? *deux fois par semaine,* twice a week; *par deux fois,* (emphatically) twice; *plusieurs fois,* several times; *trois fois plus que,* three times as many as; *une autre fois,* another time; *une bonne fois* or *une fois pour toutes,* once for all; *une fois,* once, once upon a time; *une fois autant,* as much again;

une fois n'est pas coutume, once does not constitute a habit; *une fois par an*, once a year; *y regarder à deux fois*, to look twice (before doing anything).—*adv. phr. Des fois* (*pop.*), by chance; *des fois que*, ... if it happens that . . . ; *non, mais des fois!* (an indignant protest) really, that's a bit thick!

foison [fwaˈzɔ̃], *n.f.* Plenty, abundance. (*chiefly used in*) *À foison*, plentifully, abundantly, galore. **foisonnant**, *a.* (*fem.* **-ante**) Abundant. **foisonnement**, *n.m.* Expansion, swarming, multiplying. **foisonner**, *v.i.* To abound, to increase (in volume), to expand (of earth); to multiply, to swarm (of animals etc.).

fol [FOU].

folâtre [fɔˈlɑːtr], *a.* Playful, gay, frolicsome. **folâtrer**, *v.i.* To play, to sport, to frolic, to frisk about; to toy, to sally. **folâtrerie**, *n.f.* Frolic, prank, gambol; dalliance.

foliacé [fɔljaˈse], *a.* (*fem.* **foliacée**) (*Bot.*) Foliaceous. **foliaire**, *a.* Foliar; of leaves. **foliation**, *n.f.* Foliation.

folichon [fɔliˈʃɔ̃], *a.* (*fem.* **folichonne**) (*fam.*) Frolicsome, waggish, wanton (*chiefly used in a negative sentence*). *Ce n'est pas folichon*, it is not very exciting. **folichonner**, *v.i.* To gambol, to play the wag, to be gay.

folie [fɔˈli], *n.f.* Madness, distraction, dementia, lunacy, folly; piece of folly, foolery; extravagance, misguided passion or enthusiasm; jest, mad thing, mania, hobby; *whimsical building, folly. *Aimer à la folie*, to love to distraction; *dire des folies*, to talk wildly; *faire des folies*, to squander money, to behave foolishly; *la folie des grandeurs*, megalomania; *un accès de folie*, a fit of madness.

folié [fɔˈlje], *a.* (*fem.* **foliée**) Foliated.

folio [fɔˈljo], *n.m.* Folio. *Folio recto*, right-hand or odd-numbered page; *folio verso*, left-hand or even-numbered page; *un infolio* (*pl. unchanged*), a folio (book).

foliole [fɔˈljɔl], *n.f.* (*Bot.*) Foliole.

folioter [fɔljɔˈte], *v.t.* To paginate; to number the pages of (a book etc.). **folioteuse**, *n.m.* Numbering-machine.

folklore [fɔlˈklɔːr], *n.m.* Folk-lore. **folklorique**, *a.* Belonging to folk-lore. *Chant folklorique*, folk-song; *danse folklorique*, folk-dance. **folkloriste**, *n.* Folklorist.

folle [FOU].

follement [fɔlˈmɑ̃], *adv.* Madly, foolishly, extravagantly; dotingly, distractedly; (*fam.*) tremendously. *S'amuser follement*, to have a grand time.

follet [fɔˈlɛ], *a.* (*fem.* **follette** (1)) Wanton, playful, frolicsome, waggish; downy (of hair). *Esprit follet*, sprite, elf, hobgoblin. *Feu follet* [FEU (1)]; *poil follet*, down.

follette (2), *n.f.* [ARROCHE].

folliculaire [fɔlikyˈlɛːr], *n.m.* Pamphleteer, penny-a-liner; hack (journalist).

follicule [fɔliˈkyl], *n.m.* Follicle. **folliculeux**, *a.* (*fem.* **-euse**) Folliculous.

fomentateur [fɔmɑ̃taˈtœːr], *a.* (*fem.* **fomentatrice**) Fomenting.—*n.* Fomenter. **fomentation**, *n.f.* Fomentation. **fomenter**, *v.t.* To foment; (*fig.*) to feed, to excite. *Fomenter des troubles*, to excite riots; *fomenter une querelle*, to stir up a quarrel.

fonçage [fɔ̃ˈsaːʒ], *n.m.* Bottoming (of casks etc.); sinking (of wells).

foncé [fɔ̃ˈse], *a.* (*fem.* **foncée**) Dark, deep (of colour). **foncer**, *v.t.* To fit a bottom to (a cask etc.); (*Cook.*) to place dough at the bottom of a cake tin; to sink (wells etc.); to deepen (colours).—*v.i.* To dash, to rush, to charge, to swoop (upon). **se foncer**, *v.r.* (of colour) To deepen.

foncier [fɔ̃ˈsje], *a.* (*fem.* **foncière**) Landed, based on or derived from land; (*fig.*) deep-seated, thorough. *Crédit foncier*, mortgage-loan society, land bank; *impôt foncier*, land-tax; *propriétaire foncier*, landowner; *qualité foncière*, fundamental quality; *rente foncière*, ground-rent.—*n.m.* Land-tax. **foncièrement**, *adv.* Thoroughly, completely, fundamentally.

fonction [fɔ̃kˈsjɔ̃], *n.f.* Function, duty, office; occupation, employment, work. *Dans l'exercice de ses fonctions*, in the performance of his duties; *en fonction*, acting, at work; *en fonction de*, in terms of, dependent of; *entrer en fonction*, to enter upon one's duties; *être fonction de*, to depend on, to be conditional on; *faire fonction de*, to discharge the office of; *faisant fonction de*, acting as; *fonctions publiques*, public offices; *la Fonction Publique*, the Civil Service. **fonctionnaire**, *n.m.* Civil servant, officer, official. **fonctionnel**, *a.* (*fem.* **fonctionnelle**) Functional. **fonctionnement**, *n.m.* Operation, working, action. **fonctionner**, *v.i.* To work, to act, to operate.

fond [fɔ̃], *n.m.* Bottom, lowest part; bed, ground; back part, farther end, extremity, corner; ground-work, foundation, substratum; depth; (*fig.*) centre, heart, essence, gist; basis; seat; subject matter; punt (of a bottle); (*Paint.*) background; (*Theat.*) back-cloth; back-scene; (*Mining*) underground; staying-power, wind (of a horse). *À fond*, thoroughly, fully, to the bottom; *à fond de cale*, in the bottom of the hold, at the end of one's resources; *à fond de train*, at full speed; *article de fond*, leader (in a paper); *au fond*, in the main, at bottom; *cheval de fond*, a horse with good staying-power; *coureur de fond*, stayer; *course de fond*, long-distance race; *ligne de fond*, ground line (*for fishing*), (*Ten.*) base-line; *jeu de fond*, base-line play; *couler à fond*, to sink, to run down, (*fig.*) to ruin completely; *dans le fond*, at bottom, in reality; *de fond en comble*, wholly, from top to bottom; *des arbres occupent le fond du tableau*, trees occupy the background of the picture; *faire fond sur*, (*fig.*) to rely, to depend on; *fin fond*, lowest depth, innermost recesses; *fond de lit*, wooden bottom of bed; *fond de teint*, make-up foundation; *il possède cette science à fond*, he is a thorough master of that science; *il y a vingt brasses de fond*, it is twenty fathoms deep; *le fond d'un bois*, the heart of a forest; *le fond de la coupe*, the dregs of the cup; *fond de cale*, bilge; *le fond d'un miroir*, the back of a looking-glass; *malle à double fond*, trunk with a false or double bottom; *sans fond*, bottomless; *tomber au fond*, to fall to the bottom; *velours à fond d'or*, velvet with a gold ground; *vider le fond de son sac*, to spill the beans.

fondage [fɔ̃ˈdaːʒ], *n.m.* Casting, smelting, melting.

fondamental [fɔ̃damɑ̃'tal], *a.* (*fem.* **fondamentale,** *pl.* **fondamentaux**) Fundamental, essential. *Les trois couleurs fondamentales,* the three primary colours. **fondamentalement,** *adv.* Fundamentally, essentially, radically; at the core.

fondant [fɔ̃'dɑ̃], *a.* (*fem.* **fondante**) Melting, dissolving, juicy, luscious.—*n.m.* Fondant (sweetmeat); flux (for metals); softening (ointment).

fondateur [fɔ̃da'tœːr], *n.m.* (*fem.* **fondatrice**) Founder; promoter. *Parts de fondateur,* founder's shares.—*a.* Who has founded or is founding.

fondation [fɔ̃dɑ'sjɔ̃], *n.f.* Foundation; groundwork; basis; establishment (of a fund etc.); endowment, endowed institution; founding. *La fondation d'une colonie,* the establishment of a colony.

fondé [fɔ̃'de], *a.* (*fem.* **-ée**) Founded, well-founded, authentic, authorized; (*Fin.*) consolidated. *Être fondé à,* to have a right to, to be justified in; *être fondé en droit,* to have a just cause.—*n.m.* Proxy. *Fondé de pouvoir* or *de procuration,* agent acting under power of attorney, legal representative. *Le bien fondé,* the cogency, legitimacy, justice (of a claim, case, accusation, etc).

fondement [fɔ̃d'mɑ̃], *n.m.* Foundation; ground-work, substructure, bed; basis, ground, cause; (*Med.*) fundament. *Ce bruit est sans fondement,* that report is without foundation; *dénué de fondement,* groundless; *jeter les fondements de la paix,* to lay the foundations of peace.

fonder [fɔ̃'de], *v.t.* To lay the foundation of, to found, to establish; to institute, to create, to build; to ground, to base, to establish; to justify; to endow. *Fonder un empire,* to lay the foundation of an empire; *fonder une revue,* to start a review. **se fonder,** *v.r.* To rely or rest (upon), to be based or founded (*sur*). *Se fonder sur l'analogie,* to be based upon analogy.

fonderie [fɔ̃'dri], *n.f.* Foundry; melting-house, smelting-house; founding, smelting, casting. *Fonderie de caractères,* type-foundry. *Fonderie de canons,* gun factory. **fondeur,** *n.m.* Founder, caster, smelter. *Fondeur en caractères,* type-founder.

fondis [fɔ̃'di] or **fontis,** *n.m.* Giving away, sinking, subsidence, settling (of ground).

fondoir [fɔ̃'dwaːr], *n.m.* Melting-house.

fondre [fɔ̃:dr], *v.t.* To melt; to dissolve; to thaw; to smelt; (*Paint.*) to soften; (*fig.*) to blend; to move, to touch; to convert. *Fondre une cloche,* to cast a bell.—*v.i.* To melt, to melt away; to dissolve; to dart, to pounce (*sur*); (of birds) to swoop; to fall away, to vanish; to blow out (of a fuse). *Fondre en larmes,* to burst into tears. *Il fondit sur lui,* he pounced upon him. **se fondre,** *v.r.* To melt; to dissolve; to be cast; to blend, to coalesce; to be merged, to be fused; to diminish, to disappear, to melt away.

fondrière [fɔ̃dri'ɛːr], *n.f.* Bog, quagmire, *esp.* hole in road, pothole; slough; pitfall.

fonds [fɔ̃], *n.m.* (*pl.* unchanged) Land, soil, ground; landed property, estate; funds, stock, capital, principal; (*colloq.*) cash, ready money; business, stock-in-trade, goodwill;

business assets; (*pl.*) funds, stocks, etc. *Acheter des fonds,* to put money in the funds; *biens fonds* [BIENS-FONDS]; *céder son fonds,* to give up one's business; *ce marchand a vendu son fonds,* that tradesman has sold his business and stock-in-trade. *Être en fonds,* to be in cash; *faire rentrer des fonds,* to call in money; *fonds secret,* secret service funds; *fonds social,* company or industrial capital; *manger le fonds et le revenu,* to spend capital and income; *placer de l'argent à fonds perdu,* to sink money in an annuity; *spéculer sur les fonds publics,* to speculate in the public funds; *un fonds inépuisable de science,* an inexhaustible mine of information.

fondu [fɔ̃'dy], *a.* (*fem.* **-ue**) Melted; molten (metals); cast.—*n.m.* (*Paint.*) Mellow tone; (*Cine.*) dissolve.—*n.f.* Dish of melted cheese and eggs.

fonger [fɔ̃'ʒe], *v.i.* To blot (of paper), to soak up.

fongible [fɔ̃'ʒibl], *a.* (*Law*) Fungible.

fongicide [fɔ̃ʒi'sid], *a.* Fungicide. **fongiforme,** *a.* Fungiform. **fongique,** *a.* Fungic.

fongivore, *a.* Fungivorous. **fongoïde,** *a.* Fungoid. **fongosité,** *n.f.* Fungosity.

fongueux, *a.* (*fem.* **-euse**) Fungous.

fongus [fɔ̃'gys], *n.m.* (*Med.*) Fungus.

fontaine [fɔ̃'tɛːn], *n.f.* Fountain, fount, spring; cistern, filter [*see also* WALLACE]. *De l'eau de fontaine,* spring-water. *Il a été à la fontaine de Jouvence,* he has renewed his youth. *Il ne faut jamais dire, 'Fontaine, je ne boirai pas de ton eau,'* we must never say, 'I shall never need that,' 'Such a thing will never happen.'

fontainier [FONTENIER].

fontanelle [fɔ̃ta'nɛl], *n.f.* (*Anat.*) Fontanel, fontanelle.

***fontange** [fɔ̃'tɑ̃ːʒ], *n.f.* Knot or bow of ribbons worn on women's head-dress in the reign of Louis XIV.

fonte [fɔ̃:t], *n.f.* Melting, smelting; cast-iron; casting, cast; thaw, thawing; (*Print.*) fount; (*Paint.*) blending (of colours); holster (of saddles). *Fer de fonte* or *fonte,* cast-iron; *jeter en fonte,* to cast; *pièces de fonte,* castings.

fontenier [fɔ̃tə'nje] or **fontainier,** *n.m.* Fountain-maker, filter-maker; turncock.

fontis [FONDIS].

fonts [fɔ̃], *n.m.* (*used only in pl.*) Font. *Tenir quelqu'un sur les fonts,* to stand godfather or godmother to someone.

football [fut'bɔl], *n.m.* Association Football. **footballeur,** *n.m.* Footballer.

footing [fu'tiŋ], *n.m.* Walking (for training).

for [fɔːr], *n.m.* *Tribunal; today *le for intérieur* means *conscience; en mon (son) for intérieur,* inwardly, in my (his) innermost heart.

forage [fɔ'raːʒ], *n.m.* Boring, drilling; sinking (of well).

forain [fɔ'rɛ̃], *a.* *Foreign, alien, outlandish; non-resident, travelling, itinerant. *Fête foraine,* fun fair; *les forains,* showmen, strolling players, etc.; *marchand forain,* hawker, pedlar. (*Naut.*) *Rade foraine,* open roadstead.

foraminé [fɔrami'ne], *a.* (*fem.* **-ée**) Foraminous, foraminated.

forban [fɔr'bɑ̃], *n.m.* Pirate, corsair, free-booter.

forçage [fɔr'saːʒ], *n.m.* (*Coin.*) Overweight; (*Hort.*) forcing.

forçat [fɔr'sa], *n.m.* *Galley-slave; convict. Un travail de forçat, (fig.)* drudgery, slavery.

force [fɔrs], *n.f.* Strength, might, force, power; authority, command, violence, strong hand, constraint, necessity; vigour, activity, energy, intensity; efficacy; fortitude, resolution; skill, cleverness, proficiency; (*pl.*) troops, forces. *À force de,* by dint of; *à force d'argent,* by virtue of money; *à force de bras,* by strength of arm; *à toute force,* by all means, at all costs; *céder à la force majeure,* to yield to superior force; *dans toute la force du terme,* in every sense of the word; *de force à,* strong enough to, equal to; *de force* or *par force,* forcibly, by force, by forcible means; *de gré ou de force,* whether you like it or no; *de vive force,* by main strength, by storm; *employer la force,* to use force; *être à bout de forces,* to be done up, exhausted; *faire force de rames,* to row with all one's might, to pull hard; *faire force de voiles,* to crowd on all sail; *force d'âme,* courage, fortitude; *force ascensionnelle* (of aeroplane), lifting power; *force d'inertie,* force of inertia; *force est de,* it behoves, it is necessary; *force me fut de,* I was obliged to; *frapper de toute sa force,* to strike with all one's might; *la force de la vérité,* the power of truth; *la force des choses,* the force of circumstances; *la force de l'âge,* the prime of life; *les forces lui manquent,* his strength is failing him; *jambe de force,* strut; *mettre des forces sur pied,* to raise forces; *rassembler ses forces,* to muster one's strength; *tour de force,* a feat requiring considerable strength (physical or mental), a clever feat; *travailler à force,* to work hard.— **adv.* A great deal, plenty of, a great many. *Force gens,* any number of people; *je leur fis force compliments,* I paid them many compliments. **forcé,** *a.* (*fem.* **-ée**) Forced, constrained, compulsory; unnatural, strained, far-fetched, artificial. *C'est forcé,* it is inevitable. *Les travaux forcés,* hard labour. *Une comparaison forcée,* a strained comparison.

forcement [fɔrsə'mã], *n.m.* Forcing, compelling, compulsion.

forcément [fɔrse'mã], *adv.* Forcibly, by force, compulsorily; necessarily, inevitably.

forcené [fɔrsə'ne], *a.* (*fem.* **-ée**) Mad, furious, frantic; passionate, infuriated, enraged.—*n.* Mad person.

forceps [fɔr'seps], *n.m. inv.* Forceps.

forcer [fɔr'se], *v.t.* To force; to compel, to constrain, to oblige; to urge, to impel; to strain; to break open, to break through; to take by force, to storm; to overcome by force; to outrage; to wear out (a horse etc.). *Forcer la nature,* to force or outrage nature. *Forcer le pas,* to quicken one's pace. *Forcer l'admiration,* to compel admiration; *forcer quelqu'un à faire une chose,* to compel someone to do a thing; *forcer sa voix,* to strain one's voice; *forcer un cerf,* to bring a stag to bay; *forcer un cheval,* to override a horse; *forcer la consigne,* (*Mil.*) to break an order; *forcer la note,* to overdo it; *forcer une serrure,* to force a lock.—*v.i.* To make a great effort. *Forcer de voiles,* to crowd on sail; *forcer de vitesse,* to increase speed. **se forcer,** *v.r.* To strain, to over-exert oneself; to do violence to one's feelings.

forcerie [fɔrsə'ri], *n.f.* Forcing-house. *Forcerie de raisins,* vinery.

forces [fɔrs], *n.f. pl.* Shears.

forcet [fɔr'se], *n.m.* Whip-cord, cord (for tying up tobacco etc.).

forcir [fɔr'sir], *v.i.* To grow strong (of a child); to put on flesh.

forclore [fɔr'klɔːr], *v.t. irr.* (*p.p.* **forclos**; conjugated like CLORE; *used only in the pres., inf., and p.p.*) (*Law*) To foreclose, to estop.

forclusion, *n.f.* Foreclosure, estoppage.

forer [fɔ're], *v.t.* To bore, to drill, to perforate, to pierce. **forerie,** *n.f.* Drilling-machine; drilling-shop.

forestier [fɔres'tje], *a.* (*fem.* **-ière**) Pertaining to forests. *École forestière,* school of forestry; *garde forestier,* forester, ranger.—*n.m.* Ranger, keeper, forester.

foret [fɔ'rɛ], *n.m.* Borer, drill. *Foret à hélice,* twist-drill.

forêt [fɔ're], *n.f.* Forest; forest-land, woodland; (*fig.*) a host, a mass, shock (of hair etc.). *Convertir en forêt,* to afforest. *Une forêt de cheveux,* a great shock of hair. *Forêt-Noire,* Black Forest; *forêt vierge,* virgin forest.

foreur [fɔ'rœr], *n.m.* Borer, driller. **foreuse,** *n.f.* machine drill; *foreuse à main,* hand-drill.

forfaire [fɔr'fɛːr], *v.i. irr.* (*used only in inf., p.p. and compound tenses*) To fail (in one's duty); to trespass, to transgress, to be false to. *Il a forfait à l'honneur,* he has been false to honour.—*v.t.* To forfeit (a fief). **forfait** (1) [fɔr'fɛ], *n.m.* Crime, heinous offence, grave transgression. **forfait** (2) *n.m.* Contract (under pain of forfeit). *Entreprendre à forfait,* to contract for; *prix à forfait,* price as per contract. *Déclarer forfait,* to scratch (a horse, a racer) and pay the fine. **forfaitaire,** *a.* Contractual. *Paiement forfaitaire,* payment by contract, lump sum. **forfaitairement,** *adv.* By contract.

forfaiture [fɔrfɛ'tyːr], *n.f.* Forfeiture; breach of duty.

forfanterie [fɔrfã'tri], *n.f.* Romancing, bragging, boasting.

forficule [fɔrfi'kyl], *n.f.* (*Ent.*) Earwig.

forge [fɔrʒ], *n.f.* Forge, smithy, blacksmith's shop; farriery; iron-works. *Forge de campagne,* travelling forge; *grosse forge,* large forge; *maître de forges,* iron-master. **forgeable,** *a.* Forgeable. **forgeage** [fɔr'ʒaːʒ] or **forgement,** *n.m.* Forging. **forger,** *v.t.* To forge, to hammer; (*fig.*) to invent, to fabricate, to contrive, to coin. *Fer forgé,* wrought iron. *Forger des mots,* to coin words; *forger des nouvelles,* to fabricate news.—*v.i.* To overreach (of horses). **se forger,** *v.r.* To imagine, to conjure up, to fancy. **forgerie,** *n.f.* Forging. **forgeron,** *n.m.* Smith, blacksmith. *C'est en forgeant qu'on devient forgeron,* practice makes perfect. **forgeur,** *a.* (*fem.* **-euse**) Who forges.—*n.m.* Forger; (*fig.*) contriver, inventor, fabricator.

forjet [fɔr'ʒɛ], *n.m.* Jutting out (of a wall).

forjeter, *v.i. irr.* (*conjug. like* APPELER) To jut out.—*v.t.* To build so as to make it jut out. **forjeture** [FORJET].

formage [fɔr'maːʒ], *n.m.* Shaping, moulding.

formaliser [fɔrmali'ze], *v.t.* To offend, to shock. **se formaliser,** *v.r.* To take exception or offence (*de*).

formalisme [fɔrma'lism], *n.m.* Formalism.
formaliste, *n.m.* Formalist; quibbler.—*a.*
Formal, precise, ceremonious. *Il est trop
formaliste*, he is too precise. **formalité**, *n.f.*
Formality; form, ceremony; ceremonious-
ness. *Défaut de formalité* or *manque de
formalité*, (*Law*) informality; *sans autre* or
sans plus de formalité, without further
ceremony or ado.
formariage [forma'rjaːʒ], *n.m.* (*Feud. Law*)
Marriage between serfs belonging each to a
different lord.
format [fɔr'ma], *n.m.* Format (size, shape,
etc., of a book).
formateur [forma'tœːr], *a.* (*fem.* **-trice**) Formative, creative.—*n.* Former, creator. **formatif**, *a.* (*fem.* **-ive**) Formative. **formation**, *n.f.* Formation, forming; setting (of
fruit); education, moulding (of character);
(*Geol.*) structure, formation. (*Mil.*) *Formation anti-chars*, anti-tank unit; *formation
sanitaire*, hospital unit.
forme [fɔrm], *n.f.* Form, shape, figure, make,
configuration; usage, etiquette, manners;
formula; mould-frame, block; crown (of a
hat); mould (in paper-making); (*Print.*)
form; seat, stall (in a choir); bed of gravel or
sand (in road-making etc.); (*Vet.*) ring-bone;
(*Naut.*) dock. *Argument en forme*, formal
argument; *avoir les formes un peu rudes*, to be
somewhat rough in manner; *dans les formes*
or *en bonne forme*, in due form, in order; *en
forme*, formally; *en forme d'œuf*, egg-shaped;
être en forme, to be fit and well, in fine fettle;
forme de chapeau, hat-block; *forme de procédure*, procedure; *forme de soulier*, last, boot-
tree; *mettre des souliers en forme*, to put shoes
on the last; *pour la forme*, for form's sake,
as a matter of form; *prendre forme*, to take
shape, to look ship-shape; *sans autre forme
de procès*, without any further formality; *sans
forme*, shapeless; *sous la forme de*, in the
shape of. **formé**, *a.* (*fem.* **-ée**) Formed,
full-grown, mature; set (of fruit); having
reached puberty (of a girl). **formel**, *a.* (*fem.*
-elle) Formal, express, precise, plain,
explicit. **formellement**, *adv.* Formally;
expressly, precisely, strictly.
formène [fɔr'mɛn], *n.m.* Marsh-gas, formene,
methane.
former [fɔr'me], *v.t.* To form, to frame, to
fashion; to compose, to make up; to conceive; to bring up, to train, to educate; to
mould, to season; to constitute. *Former un
jeune homme*, to train up a youth. *Former les
faisceaux*, to pile arms. **se former**, *v.r.* To
form or make for oneself; to be formed; to
be improved (in manners etc.), to assume a
form, to take shape; to resolve oneself or
themselves into (a committee etc.). *Il se
formera avec le temps*, he will become polished
with time. *Se former une idée de quelque chose*,
to form an idea of something.
formicant [fɔrmi'kã], *a.m.* Weak and frequent,
formicant (of the pulse).
formication [FOURMILLEMENT].
formidable [fɔrmi'dabl], *a.* Formidable, fearful; (*fam.*) terrific. **formidablement**, *adv.*
Formidably.
formier [fɔr'mje], *n.m.* Last-maker.
formique [fɔr'mik], *a.* Formic. **formol**, *n.m.*
Formol.

Formose [fɔr'moːz], *f.* Formosa, Taiwan.
formulaire [fɔrmy'lɛːr], *n.m.* Formulary.
formulation, *n.f.* Formulation. ~
formule [fɔr'myl], *n.f.* Formula, form;
model; recipe. *Formule d'algèbre*, algebraic
formula. *Formule de télégramme*, telegraph
form; *remplir une formule*, to fill in a form.
formuler, *v.t.* To formulate, to draw up
in due form; to detail, to state precisely;
(*Med.*) to write a prescription in due form;
(*Alg.*) to reduce to a formula.
fornicateur [fɔrnika'tœːr], *n.m.* (*fem.* **-trice**)
Fornicator. **fornication**, *n.f.* Fornication.
forniquer, *v.i.* To fornicate.
*fors** [fɔːr], *prep.* Except, but (used only in
two sentences). *Tout est perdu, fors l'honneur*,
all is lost, but honour. *Il y a remède à tout,
fors à la mort*, there is a cure for everything,
except death.
forsythie [fɔrsi'ti], *n.f.* (*Bot.*) Forsythia.
fort [fɔːr], *a.* (*fem.* **forte**) Strong, sturdy,
robust, hardy, able-bodied, vigorous; able,
powerful, mighty; energetic; skilful, clever;
large, considerable; plentiful, copious; thick,
stout; strong-smelling, disagreeable (to taste),
over-spiced (food); outrageous, shocking;
severe, hard, painful, difficult; high (wind);
heavy (ground, rain). *À plus forte raison*, so
much the more, all the more reason; *avoir
la tête forte* or *l'esprit fort*, to be strong-
minded; *c'est plus fort que moi*, I cannot help
it, I must speak my mind; *c'est trop fort* or
c'est par trop fort, it is too bad; *colle forte*,
glue; *de plus fort en plus fort*, continually
increasing, going on from strength to
strength; *être fort aux échecs*, to play chess
very well; *être fort en thème*, (*sch.*) to be
clever, a swot; *expression forte*, telling
expression; *forte somme*, large sum; *le plus
fort est fait*, the worst is over; *haleine forte*,
bad breath; *place forte*, stronghold; *la
manière forte*, the strong hand; *se faire fort
de*, to undertake, to feel confident of being
able to; *se porter fort pour quelqu'un*, to
answer for someone; *terre forte*, heavy soil;
trouver plus fort que soi, to meet with more
than one's match; *un esprit fort*, a free-
thinker; *voilà qui est fort*, come! I like that;
(*fam.*) *c'est un peu fort*, that's too much!
celle-là, elle est un peu forte ! well, I call it a
whopping lie!—*n.m.* Strong side, part, etc.;
the best; the thickest part (of a wood);
stronghold, fort; strength, skill; depth, heat,
height; centre, main point. *Au fort de la tempête*, in the height of the storm; *connaître* or
savoir le fort et le faible de, to know the pros
and cons of; *dans le fort de* or *au fort de l'hiver*,
in the depth of winter; *dans le fort du combat*,
in the heat of the fight; *la critique est son fort*,
criticism is his forte; *la raison du plus fort est
toujours la meilleure*, might is right; *le fort
d'une affaire*, the main point of a business; *le
fort portant le faible*, one thing with another,
on an average; *les forts des Halles*, licensed
porters (Paris Market).—*adv.* Very, very
much, highly, extremely, vastly, exceedingly;
hard, forcibly. *Aller fort*, to exaggerate; *avoir
fort à faire pour*, to have some trouble to;
bien fort, very hard or very loud; *crier plus
fort que*, to shout louder than; *de plus en plus
fort*, harder and harder, louder and louder;
fort bien, very well; *fort et ferme*, resolutely,

for all one is worth; *frapper fort*, to strike hard; *il pleut fort*, it is raining fast.
forte [fɔrte], (It.), *adv.* (*pl. unchanged*) (*Mus.*) Forte.
fortement [fɔrtə'mɑ̃], *adv.* Strongly, vigorously, with force; much, exceedingly.
forteresse [fɔrtə'rɛs], *n.f.* Fortress, stronghold.
fortifiant [fɔrti'fjɑ̃], *a.* (*fem.* -iante) Strengthening, fortifying, invigorating, bracing.—*n.m.* (*Med.*) Tonic.
fortification [fɔrtifika'sjɔ̃], *n.f.* Fortification; fort, redoubt.
fortifier [fɔrti'fje], *v.t.* (*conjugated like* PRIER) To strengthen, to invigorate, to brace; to fortify, to defend or surround with fortifications; to corroborate, to confirm. *Le bon vin fortifie l'estomac*, good wine is strengthening. **se fortifier,** *v.r.* To fortify oneself, to grow strong; to be strengthened or confirmed (*dans*); to make oneself proficient, to gain proficiency, to become skilled (*dans*).
fortin [fɔr'tɛ̃], *n.m.* Small fort.
*****fortitude** [fɔrti'tyd], *n.f.* Fortitude.
fortrait [fɔr'trɛ], *a.* Overworked, spent (of horses). *****fortraiture,** *n.f.* Overfatigue (of a horse).
fortuit [fɔr'tɥi], (*fem.* **-te**) Fortuitous, casual. *Cas fortuit*, mere chance, accident. **fortuitement,** *adv.* Fortuitously, casually, by chance.
fortune [fɔr'tyn], *n.f.* Fortune, chance, hazard, risk; success, luck; wealth; (*Myth.*) Fortune. *Artisan de sa fortune*, architect of one's own fortune; *installation de fortune*, makeshift apparatus; *avoir de la fortune*, to be rich; *bonne fortune*, good luck, windfall; *bonnes fortunes*, lucky amorous adventures; *brusquer la fortune*, to tempt fortune; *courir après la fortune*, to hunt after riches; *de fortune*, by good luck, by hazard; *mât de fortune*, jury mast; *pont de fortune*, improvised bridge; *demi-fortune*, one-horse carriage; *faire fortune*, to make a fortune; *fortune de mer*, sea-risks; *homme à bonnes fortunes*, lady-killer, a Don Juan; *il faut faire contre mauvaise fortune bon cœur*, we must put a good face on misfortune; *la fortune du pot*, pot-luck; *la Fortune lui sourit*, Fortune smiles upon him; *manger sa fortune*, to squander one's fortune; *un revers de fortune*, a reverse, set-back. **fortuné,** *a.* (*fem.* **-ée**) Fortunate, lucky; happy; well-to-do, rich.
forum [fɔ'rɔm], *n.m.* Forum; the political arena.
forure [fɔ'ry:r], *n.f.* Bore, hole drilled; pipe (of a key).
fosse [fo:s], *n.f.* Hole in the ground, pit; grave; (*Anat.*) fossa; (*Hort.*) trench; (*Naut.*) boatswain's store-room. *Fosse à chars*, a tank trap; *fosse à purin*, midden; *fosse aux lions*, lion's den; *fosse aux ours*, bear-pit; *fosse commune*, pauper's grave; *fosse d'aisance*, cess-pool; *fosse d'orchestre*, orchestra pit; *fosses nasales*, nasal fossae; *fosse septique*, septic tank. *Avoir un pied dans la fosse*, to have one foot in the grave; *mettre dans la fosse*, to lay in the grave.
fossé [fo'se], *n.m.* Ditch, drain, trench; moat. *Fossé d'irrigation*, water-trench; (*fig.*) *sauter le fossé*, to take the plunge, to cross the Rubicon, to cast the die. **fossette,** *n.f.* Dimple; chuck hole, chuck-farthing (game).

fossile [fɔ'sil], *a.* and *n.m.* Fossil; fossilized (ideas etc.). **fossilifère,** *a.* Fossiliferous.
fossilisation, *n.f.* Fossilization. **fossiliser,** *v.t.* To fossilize. **se fossiliser,** *v.r.* To become fossilized.
fossoyage [foswa'ja:ʒ], *n.m.* Ditching; grave-digging. **fossoyer,** *v.t.* To ditch, to dig a trench round. **fossoyeur,** *a.m.* Fossorial (insect).—*n.m.* Grave-digger; sexton beetle.
fou (1) [fu], *a.* (*before vowels* **fol**, *fem.* **folle**) Mad, crazy, insane, demented; wild, rash, meaningless, foolish, silly, loud; tremendous, excessive. *Devenir fou*, to go mad; *être fou de*, to be mad about, to be passionately fond of; *faire devenir* or *rendre fou*, to drive mad; *fol à lier*, raving mad; (*C*) *folle avoine*, wild rice; *fou de joie*, wild with delight; *fou rire*, uncontrollable laugh; *que vous êtes fou!* how foolish you are! *un fol espoir*, a foolish hope; *un prix fou*, an exorbitant price; *fou de douleur*, frantic with grief; *folle de son corps*, wanton; *un mal de dents fou*, a raging toothache; *un succès fou*, a tremendous success. *Des herbes folles*, rank weeds. *Une poulie folle*, a loose pulley; *une roue folle*, an idle wheel.—*n.* Madman, madwoman; madcap, feather-brain; jester, buffoon, fool; (*Chess*) bishop. *Faire le fou*, to play the fool; *maison de fous*, lunatic-asylum; *plus on est de fous, plus on rit*, the more the merrier.
fou (2) [fu], *n.m.* (*Orn.*) Gannet, booby. *Fou de Bassan*, Solan goose.
fouace [fwas], *n.f.* Hearth-cake.
fouage [fwa:ʒ], *n.m.* (*Feud. Law*) Hearth-tax.
fouailler [fwa'je], *v.t.* To lash, to whip. **fouailleur,** *n.m.* Whipper, lasher; flogger.
foucade [FOUGADE].
fouchtra [fuʃ'tra], *int.* (*dial. of Auvergne*)= *Fichtre!* q.v.
foudre (1) [fudr], *n.f.* Lightning; thunder, thunderbolt; (*fig.*) sudden calamity, blow, etc.; divine anger; (*pl.*) thunders, threats, warnings, fulminations. *Coup de foudre*, clap of thunder, (*fig.*) unexpected blow, love at first sight; *être tué par la foudre*, to be killed by lightning; *lancer ses foudres*, to hurl one's thunders, to anathematize.—*n.m.* (*fig.*) *Un foudre de guerre*, a great captain; *un foudre d'éloquence*, a mighty speaker.
foudre (2) [fudr], *n.m.* Large cask, tun.
foudroiement [fudrwa'mɑ̃], *n.m.* Striking, blasting (by thunder or lightning); (*fig.*) destruction, crushing, overwhelming.
foudroyant [fudrwa'jɑ̃], *a.* (*fem.* **-ante**) Fulminating, thundering, terrible, crushing (news); lightning (disease, progress, etc.).
foudroyer, *v.t. irr.* (*conjug. like* ABOYER) To strike (thunder or lightning); to batter with cannon, mortars, etc., to riddle with shot; (*fig.*) to blast, to crush, to overwhelm, to ruin. *Foudroyer du regard*, to cast a withering glance at.—*v.i.* To thunder or lighten; (*fig.*) to fulminate.
fouée [fwe], *n.f.* Oven-fire; faggot.
fouëne [FOÊNE].
fouet [fwɛ], *n.m.* Whip; thong; lash; whip-cord; whipping, flogging, lashing, slating (criticism); runner (of strawberry-plant etc.); brush (of animal's tail); egg-whisk. *Coup de fouet*, lashing, cut; pain from sudden tearing of muscle of leg; (*fig.*) fillip, stimulus; *donner un coup de fouet à*, to stimulate, give a fillip to;

donner le fouet à quelqu'un, to whip someone; *faire claquer son fouet*, to sound one's own trumpet; *faire claquer un fouet*, to crack a whip; *se faire donner le fouet*, to get whipped; *tir de plein fouet*, direct fire upon a visible object. **fouettage,** *n.m.* Whipping; whisking. **fouettard** [PÈRE]. **fouetté,** *a.* Whipped; streaked (of flowers and fruit). *Crème fouettée*, whipped cream. *Tulipe fouettée*, streaked tulip. **fouettement,** *n.m.* Whipping, flogging; jumping (of gun). **fouette-queue,** *n.m.* (*pl.* **fouette-queues**) Star-lizard. **fouetter,** *v.t.* To whip, to horsewhip, to lash, to scourge, to flog; to beat, to whisk (eggs etc.); to flick; (*fig.*) to stimulate, to rouse, to excite; (*Naut.*) to flap back against the masts (of sails). *Fouette, cocher!* off we go! *il a bien d'autres chats* (or *chiens*) *à fouetter*, he has other fish to fry; *il n'y a pas là de quoi fouetter un chat*, it is a mere trifle.—*v.i.* To beat, patter (of hail, rain, snow). **fouetteur,** *n.m.* (*fem.* **-euse**) Flogger, whipper.—*a.* That whips.

fougade [fu'gad] or **foucade,** *n.f.* Sudden whim, fit, spurt.

fougasse [fu'gas], *n.f.* (*Mil.*) Fougasse (small mine); hearth-cake.

fouger [fu'ʒe], *v.i.* (*Hunt.*) To grub (of boars).

fougeraie [fuʒ'rɛ], *n.f.* Fern-patch, fernery.

fougère [fu'ʒɛːr], *n.f.* Fern. *Fougère aspidie*, shield-fern; *fougère aigle* or *arborescente*, bracken. **fougerole,** *n.f.* Small fern.

fougue [fug], *n.f.* Ardour, impetuosity; fire, spirit, mettle; (*Naut.*) mizzen-top. *Dans la fougue de la colère*, in the heat of passion; *la fougue de la jeunesse*, the impetuosity of youth; *un cheval qui a trop de fougue*, a mettlesome horse. **fougueux,** *a.* (*fem.* **-euse**) Fiery, hot, impetuous, ardent, spirited, passionate, high-mettled. *Cheval fougueux*, spirited horse.

fouille [fuːj], *n.f.* Excavation, digging; (*fam.*) search. *Faire des fouilles*, to make excavations.

fouiller [fu'je], *v.t.* To excavate, to investigate by digging; (*fig.*) to pry into, to rummage, to ransack, to probe to the bottom; to think out (problems etc.); (*Paint., Sculp.*) to sink. *Fouiller quelqu'un*, to search someone. *Fouiller une mine*, to work a mine.—*v.i.* To dig, to search, to make excavations; (*fig.*) to investigate, to rummage, to ransack. *Fouiller dans sa mémoire*, to rack one's brains. **se fouiller,** *v.r.* To search one's pockets, to feel in one's pockets. (*pop.*) *Tu peux te fouiller!* No! Never! **fouilleur,** *n.m.* (*fem.* **fouilleuse**) Excavator, investigator.—*n.f.* subsoil-plough.

fouillis [fu'ji], *n.m.* Medley, jumble, litter, mess; confused mass (of foliage etc.).

fouinard [fwi'nar], *a.* (*fem.* **-arde**) Sly, sneaking.—*n.m.* Nosey Parker.

fouine (1) [fwin], *n.f.* Marten.

fouine (2) [fwin], *n.f.* Pitchfork, fork; fish-spear.

fouiner [fwi'ne], *v.i.* (*colloq.*) To nose about, to ferret; to slink off, to steal off; to rat.

fouineur [fwi'nœr], *a.* and *n.* (*fem.* **-euse**) [FOUINARD].

fouir [fwiːr], *v.t.* To dig; to burrow. **fouissement,** *n.m.* Digging; burrowing. **fouisseur,** *a.* (*fem.* **-euse**) Burrowing (animal).

foulage [fu'laːʒ], *n.m.* Fulling; treading, pressing (of grapes).

foulant [fu'lɑ̃], *a.* (*fem.* **-ante**) Pressing; forcing; (*colloq.*) tiring (in negative sentences). *Pompe foulante*, force-pump.

foulard [fu'laːr], *n.m.* Silk neckerchief; foulard.

foule [ful], *n.f.* Crowd, throng, multitude, concourse; mob, rabble, common herd; fulling (of cloth); migration (of caribou, in Canada). *En foule*, in crowds; *entrer en foule*, to crowd in; *faire foule*, to draw a crowd; *sortir de la foule*, to rise above the common herd; *venir en foule*, to flock, to throng together.

foulée [fu'le], *n.f.* Pile (of skins for fulling); tread (of steps); (*Hunt.*) foiling, slot, track; stride (of a horse); pace (of racers).

fouler [fu'le], *v.t.* To tread, to trample on; to trample down; to press, to crush; to full; (*fig.*) to tread or walk on (one's native soil etc.); to grind down, to oppress; to gall; to sprain (ankle); to twist (wrist); (*Hunt.*) to beat (a wood). *Fouler aux pieds*, to trample under foot. *Fouler du drap*, to full cloth. *Fouler un cheval*, to override a horse.—*v.i.* (*Print.*) To press (of the printing-press on the leaves). **se fouler,** *v.r.* (*colloq.*) To give oneself trouble. *Ne pas se fouler*, to take things easy. *Se fouler le pied*, to sprain one's foot. **foulerie,** *n.f.* Fullery, fulling-mill. **fouleur,** *a.* (*fem.* **-euse**) Fulling.—*n.* Fuller; wine-presser.—*n.f.* Fulling-machine (for hats). **fouloir,** *n.m.* Beater, rammer; tobacco-plug; fulling-mill. **fouloire,** *n.f.* Fulling-board. **foulon,** *n.m.* Fuller. *Moulin à foulon*, fulling-mill; *terre à foulon*, fuller's earth. **foulonnier,** *n.m.* Owner of fulling-mill.

foulque [fulk], *n.f.* Coot.

foulure [fu'lyːr], *n.f.* Sprain, wrench, strain.

four [fuːr], *n.m.* Oven; bakehouse; furnace; kiln; (*slang*) failure, bungle, frost. *Charger le four*, to heat the oven; *des petits fours*, fancy biscuits, small cakes; *être un four*, to be unsuccessful, to fail, (*Theat.*) to be a flop, fiasco; *four à briques*, brick-kiln; *four à chaux*, lime-kiln; *four de campagne*, portable oven; *mettre le pain au four*, to put the batch into the oven; *pièce de four*, baked cake.

fourbe [furb], *a.* Cheating, deceitful, two-faced.—*n.* Cheat, swindler, impostor. **fourberie,** *n.f.* Cheating, knavery, imposture, deceit.

fourbi [fur'bi], *n.m.* (*Mil. slang*) Kit; bother; thing, gadget. *Quel fourbi!* what a bother!

fourbir [fur'biːr], *v.t.* To furbish, to polish, to burnish. **fourbissage** or **fourbissement,** *n.m.* [FOURBISSURE]. **fourbisseur,** *n.m.* Furbisher; sword-cutler.

fourbissure [furbi'syːr], *n.f.* Furbishing, polishing.

fourbu [fur'by], *a.* (*fem.* **-ue**) Foundered, run down (of horses); dead tired (of persons). **fourbure,** *n.f.* Foundering, inflammation of the feet.

fourche [furʃ], *n.f.* Pitchfork, fork, garden-fork. *Faire la fourche*, to fork, to branch off. *Fourche à faner*, hay-fork; *fourche à trois dents*, three-pronged fork; *fourches Caudines*, Caudine forks; *fourches patibulaires*, forked gibbet. *En fourche*, forked. **fourchée,** *n.f.*

Pitchforkful. **fourcher**, *v.i.* To fork; to divide; (*colloq.*) to trip (of the tongue). *Chemin qui fourche*, road that divides; *la langue lui a fourché*, he made a slip of the tongue. **se fourcher**, *v.r.* To fork, to branch off.

fourchet [furˈʃɛ], *n.m.* Two-pronged fork; crotch (of trousers); forking of a tree; (*Vet.*) foot-rot.

fourchetée [furʃˈte], *n.f.* Table-forkful.

fourchette [furˈʃet], *n.f.* Table-fork; prop (for carts etc.); breast-bone (of birds); fork-shaped object of various kinds; bracket (in ranging); (*Mil. slang*) bayonet. *Avoir un bon coup de fourchette*, to have a hearty appetite. (*vulg.*) *Coup de fourchette*, blow in the eyes of one's adversary with the thumb and index-finger outspread. *Déjeuner à la fourchette*, a fork lunch. *Fourchette à découper*, carving-fork. *Fourchette du pied d'un cheval*, the frog of a horse's foot. *La fourchette du père Adam*, the fingers. *Les dents d'une fourchette*, the prongs of a fork.

fourchon [furˈʃɔ̃], *n.m.* Prong (of a fork); fork (of a tree).

fourchu [furˈʃy], *a.* (*fem.* **-ue**) Forked; cloven (of animal's hoofs); furcate. *Avoir le pied fourchu*, to be malevolent or rascally, to show the cloven hoof; *barbe fourchue*, forked beard; *chemin fourchu*, road branching off; *menton fourchu*, cleft chin. **fourchure**, *n.f.* Furcation, fork.

fourgon (1) [furˈgɔ̃], *n.m.* Van, wagon, luggage-van, guard's van; (*Mil.*) (general service) wagon. *Fourgon de munitions*, ammunition wagon.

fourgon (2) [furˈgɔ̃], *n.m.* Poker, fire-iron (for ovens etc.). **fourgonner**, *v.i.* To poke the fire (of an oven); (*colloq.*) to poke, to rummage.

fouriérisme [furjeˈrism], *n.m.* Fourierism.

fourmi [furˈmi], *n.f.* Ant, pismire; emmet. *Fourmi blanche*, white ant, termite. *Avoir des fourmis dans les jambes*, to have pins and needles in one's legs. **fourmilier**, *n.m.* Ant-eater; ant-thrush. **fourmilière**, *n.f.* Ant-hill, ants' nest; (*fig.*) swarm; crowd. **fourmilion**, *n.m.* Ant-lion. **fourmillement**, *n.m.* Tingling, pins and needles; swarming, teeming. **fourmiller**, *v.i.* To swarm, to abound, to be full (*de*); to multiply rapidly; to have pins and needles (in one's limbs etc.).

fournage [furˈnaːʒ], *n.m.* (*Hist.*) Charge for baking (bread) or roasting (joint, turkey, etc.).

fournaise [furˈnɛːz], *n.f.* Furnace; (*fig.*) oven.

fourneau [furˈno], *n.m.* (*pl.* **-eaux**) Stove, cooking-range; furnace; (*Mil.*) chamber (of a mine), mine; (*slang*) a fool, a silly ass. *Fourneau de cuisine*, kitchen-stove; *fourneau électrique*, electric cooker; *fourneau à gaz*, gas cooker. *Haut fourneau*, blast-furnace. *Le fourneau d'une pipe*, the bowl of a pipe.

fournée [furˈne], *n.f.* Batch, baking; ovenful, kilnful (of bricks).

fourni [furˈni], *a.* (*fem.* **-ie**) Provided, supplied, provisioned; (*fig.*) thick, bushy, shaggy. *Magasin bien fourni*, well-stocked store. *Barbe bien fournie*, bushy beard.

fournier [furˈnje], *n.m.* (*fem.* **-ière**) Oven-keeper; parish baker.

fournil [furˈni], *n.m.* Bakehouse.

fourniment [furniˈmɑ̃], *n.m.* (*Mil.*) Equipment.

fournir [furˈniːr], *v.t.* To furnish, to supply, to stock, to provision, to provide, to afford; to guarantee; to make up, to complete (a sum of money); to draw (a bill); (*fig.*) to accomplish, to go over (the whole course). *Fournir des défenses*, to furnish means of defence; *fournir l'armée de vivres*, to supply the army with provisions. *Fournir une longue course*, to accomplish a long course.—*v.i.* To supply provisions; to contribute (*à*); to be sufficient, to suffice; (*Cards*) to play a card of the suit demanded. *Fournir à la dépense*, to bear the expense.

fournissement, *n.m.* Furnishing, supplying; share of capital, share. **fournisseur**, *n.m.* Army contractor; purveyor; tradesman (with whom one regularly deals). *Fournisseur breveté de*, purveyor by appointment to.

fourniture [furniˈtyːr], *n.f.* Furnishing, providing, supplying; supply, provision; equipment (of a tradesman etc.); (*Cook.*) fine herbs (in salad); (*Mus.*) furniture-stop (of organ). *Faire fourniture de*, to supply; *fournitures de bureau*, stationery, sundries; *fournitures pour chapeaux*, hat trimmings.

fourrage [fuˈraːʒ], *n.m.* Fodder, provender; forage; foraging-party; (*Artill.*) wad, wadding. *Envoyer au fourrage*, to send out foraging. **fourrager** (1), *v.i.* To forage; to plunder, to ravage; (*fig.*) to rummage. *Fourrager au vert*, to forage for grass.—*v.t.* To ravage; to rummage; to upset, to disorder (papers etc.). **fourrager** (2), *a.* (*fem.* **fourragère**) (1) Fit for fodder. *Plantes fourragères*, fodder-plants. **fourragère** (2), *n.f.* (*Mil.*) Forage wagon; shoulder lanyard (a collective decoration of certain units). **fourrageur**, *n.m.* Forager; (*fig.*) marauder; rummager. *En fourrageurs*, (cavalry) in extended order. **fourrageux**, *a.* (*fem.* **-euse**) Suitable for fodder.

fourré [fuˈre], *a.* (*fem.* **fourrée**) Thick, furry; lined with fur, thick and warmly lined (of clothing); wooded, braky; (*fig.*) underhand (of a blow etc.). *Bois fourré*, wood full of thickets and briers; *pays fourré*, country full of woods, hedges, etc. *Coup fourré*, (*Fenc.*) blow given and received simultaneously; (*fig.*) underhand trick or thrust. *Langue fourrée*, (*Cook.*) savoury tongue. *Médaille fourrée*, plated medal. *Paix fourrée*, patched-up hollow peace.—*n.m.* Thicket, brake; scraggy bush.

fourreau [fuˈro], *n.m.* Sheath; case; scabbard; cover; tight-fitting dress. *La lame use le fourreau*, the sword wears out the sheath, (*fig.*) the mind is too active for the body.

fourrer [fuˈre], *v.t.* To cover or line with fur; to plate (medals etc.); to cover; to serve (cables, ropes, etc.); (*colloq.*) to thrust, to poke; to cram, to stuff, to shove; *euph.* for *foutre*. *Fourrer quelque chose dans la tête de quelqu'un*, to hammer a thing into someone's head; *fourrer quelqu'un dedans*, to take someone in; *fourrez cela dans l'armoire*, put that away in the cupboard; *il fourre du latin dans ses discours*, he stuffs his speeches with Latin; *il fourre son nez partout*, he pokes his nose everywhere; *il est toujours fourré chez elle*, he is never away from her house. **se fourrer**, *v.r.* To thrust oneself or poke oneself in, to intrude; to wrap oneself up warm, to wear thick clothing or furs. *Il se fourre partout*, he pokes his nose in everywhere; *ne savoir où se fourrer*, not to know where to put oneself, to be very embarrassed; (*pop.*) *on s'en est fourré par dessus les oreilles*, we had a regular gorge (or tuck-in); *se fourrer le doigt dans l'œil*, to get hold of the wrong end of the stick. **fourreur**, *n.m.* Furrier.

fourrier [fu'rje], *n.m.* Quartermaster-sergeant; *officer sent in advance to provide lodgings etc. for an important personage; (*fig.*) precursor, harbinger. *Sergent-fourrier*, assistant to quartermaster-sergeant.

fourrière [fu'rjɛːr], *n.f.* Pound (for strayed animals). *Mettre un cheval en fourrière*, to impound a horse.

fourrure [fu'ryːr], *n.f.* Fur, furred gown; (*Her.*) ermine and vair; (*Naut.*) service junk.

fourvoiement [furvwa'mã], *n.m.* Going astray, wandering; (*fig.*) blunder, mistake, error. **fourvoyer**, *v.t. irr.* (*conjug. like* ABOYER) To lead astray, to mislead; (*fig.*) to baffle, to foil. **se fourvoyer**, *v.r.* To go astray, to stray, to lose one's way; (*fig.*) to go on the wrong scent, to blunder badly.

foutaise [fu'tɛz], *n.f.* (*vulg.*) Nonsense, rubbish.

fouteau [fu'to], *n.m.* (*pl.* **-eaux**) Beech. **foutelaie**, *n.f.* Beech-grove or plantation.

foutre [futr], *v.t.* (*p.p.* **foutu**) *Vulg. and not decent; generally written f. . . .*; *and replaced in decent use by ficher*, or *flanquer*, or *fourrer*. To thrust, to stick; to give, to deal (blows etc.); to do. *Foutre!* the devil! *foutre le camp*, to decamp. *Foutre la paix à quelqu'un*, to leave someone alone. *Qu'est-ce que vous foutez là*, what on earth are you doing there? **se foutre**, *v.r.* To care or trouble nothing; *se foutre de*, not to care a damn for.

foutriquet, *n.m.* (*vulg.*) Little squirt.

fovéole [fɔve'ɔl], *n.f.* (*Bot.*) Foveola. **fovéolé**, *a.* (*fem.* **-ée**) Foveolate, to be pitted.

fox [fɔks], *n.m.* (1) Fox-terrier. (2) Foxtrot.

foyard [HÊTRE].

foyer [fwa'je], *n.m.* Hearth; hearthstone; the fire; fireside; grate, furnace, fire-box (of an engine); (*fig.*) home, family; (*Theat.*) foyer, lobby, green-room; focus, seat, source, nucleus. *Aimer à garder son foyer*, to like to stay at home. *Foyer des acteurs*, greenroom; *foyer du public*, lobby, crush-room. *Le foyer du marin*, seaman's home; *le foyer des étudiants*, students' hostel; *renvoyer dans ses foyers*, (*Mil.*) to dismiss home; *un appareil à foyer fixe*, a fixed-lens camera.

frac [frak], *n.m.* Frock-coat.

fracas [fra'ka], *n.m.* Noise, din, fracas; disturbance, riot; bustle, fuss. *Avec fracas*, with a crash. **fracasser**, *v.t.* To break to pieces, to shatter. **se fracasser**, *v.r.* To crash to pieces.

fraction [frak'sjɔ̃], *n.f.* Breaking; fraction, portion. *Fraction constituée*, (*Mil.*) complete unit. **fractionnaire**, *a.* Fractional. **fractionnement**, *n.m.* Dividing into fractions. *Fractionnement des partis*, (*Polit.*) party splintering. **fractionner**, *v.t.* To divide into fractions.

fracture [frak'tyːr], *n.f.* Breaking (with violence), rupture; (*Surg.*) fracture. **fracturer**, *v.t.* To break, to smash, to force; (*Surg.*) to

fracture. *Réduire une fracture*, to set a fracture. **se fracturer**, *v.r.* To fracture oneself; to be fractured.

fragile [fra'ʒil], *a.* Fragile, brittle; frail, weak; unstable. *Fragile comme du verre*, as brittle as glass. **fragilité**, *n.f.* Fragility, brittleness; frailty, instability.

fragment [frag'mã], *n.m.* Fragment, piece, remnant. **fragmentaire**, *a.* Fragmentary. **fragmentation**, *n.f.* Fragmenting. **fragmenter**, *v.t.* To reduce to fragments.

fragon [fra'gɔ̃], *n.m.*, or *petit houx*, or *houx-frelon*. Butcher's broom, knee-holly.

fragrance [fra'grãːs], *n.f.* Fragrance. **fragrant**, *a.* (*fem.* **-ante**) Fragrant.

frai [frɛ], *n.m.* Fraying, rubbing, wearing; spawn; spawning (of fish); fry (young fish); loss by wear and abrasion (in coins).

fraîche (1) [FRAIS (1)].

fraîche (2) [frɛʃ], *n.f.* The cool of the day; morning *or* evening breeze.

fraîchement [frɛʃ'mã], *adv.* Coolly, freshly, coldly; newly, recently; (*colloq.*) with little warmth or cordiality. **fraîcheur**, *n.f.* Coolness, freshness, coldness, cold; floridness, ruddiness; chill; bloom, lustre; vivacity, brilliancy; (*Naut.*) flaw of wind.

fraîchir [frɛ'ʃiːr], *v.i.* To freshen, to begin to blow fresh; to get cool. *Le vent fraîchit*, it is beginning to blow.

fraie [frɛ], **fraieson** [frɛ'zɔ̃], *n.f.* Spawning time.

frairie [frɛ'ri], *n.f.* *Merry-making; feast, fair; Faire frairie or être de frairie*, to be at a merry-making.

frais (1) [frɛ], *a.* (*fem.* **fraîche**) Cool, coldish; fresh, brisk, lively; recent, new; youthful; blooming, florid, ruddy, hale; sweet, untainted; new-laid (of eggs); (*colloq.*) in a pretty plight. *Des nouvelles fraîches*, fresh news; *des œufs frais*, new-laid eggs; *du pain frais*, new bread; *du saumon frais*, fresh salmon; *eau fraîche*, cold water; *plaie toute fraîche*, raw wound; *temps frais*, cool weather; *un teint frais*, a florid complexion; *vous voilà fraîche!* you are in a nice fix!—*n.m.* Coolness, freshness; a cool spot; (*Naut.*) fresh breeze, half a gale. *Au frais*, in the cool of the evening; *bon frais* or *joli frais*, fresh breeze; *grand frais*, strong breeze; *il fait frais*, it is cool; *mettre du vin au frais*, to cool wine; *prendre le frais*, to go out for an airing.—*adv.* Freshly, newly, recently, just. *Frais éclos*, just hatched, opened; *frais émoulu*, just left (school). *Rasé de frais*, freshly shaved.

frais (2) [frɛ], *n.m.* (*used only in pl.*) Expense, expenses; charge, charges, cost, outlay. *À frais communs*, jointly, at joint expense; *à grands frais*, very expensively; *à peu de frais*, at little cost, cheaply; *en être pour ses frais*, to be out of pocket; *faire des frais*, *se mettre en frais*, to incur expense, to take trouble, to make efforts (to please etc.); *faire les frais de la conversation*, to do most of the talking; *faire ses frais*, to cover one's expenses; *faux frais*, incidental expenses; *les frais d'un procès*, the costs of a lawsuit; *menus frais*, petty expenses; *recommencer sur nouveaux frais*, to begin over again; *sans me mettre en frais de prouver*, without going to the trouble of proving; *frais de représentation*, expense account; *frais généraux*, trade expenses, overheads; *frais scolaires*, school fees; *tous frais faits*, all expenses paid; *sans frais*, free of charge.

fraise (1) [frɛːz], *n.f.* Strawberry; strawberry-mark; ruff; wattle (of turkey); crow (of lamb); (*Fort.*) fraise, countersink; (*Hunt.*) start. *Fraise des bois*, wild strawberry.

fraise (2) [frɛːz], *n.f.* Fraise (tool for enlarging a drill-hole etc.). **fraisement** or **fraisage**, *n.m.* Fraising (a drill-hole etc.).

fraiser [frɛ'ze], *v.t.* To plait, to ruffle; to enlarge (a drill-hole) with a fraise; to countersink; to knead (dough).

fraisette [frɛ'zɛt], *n.f.* Small ruff.

fraisier [frɛ'zje], *n.m.* Strawberry-plant; strawberry grower. *Faux fraisier* [POTENTILLE]. **fraisière**, *n.f.* Strawberry-bed.

fraisil [frɛ'zi], *n.m.* Charcoal-dust or cinders.

framboise [frɑ̃'bwaːz], *n.f.* Raspberry. **framboisé**, *a.* (*fem.* **-ée**) Flavoured with raspberries. **framboiser**, *v.t.* To give a raspberry flavour to. **framboisier**, *n.m.* Raspberry-bush.

framée [fra'me], *n.f.* Frankish javelin.

franc (1) [frɑ̃], *n.m.* Franc (French coin). *Nouveau franc*, new franc (of 1960, worth 100 old francs).

franc (2) [frɑ̃], *a.* (*fem.* **franche**) Free; exempt; frank, ingenuous, honest, sincere; true, thorough, downright; pure, unadulterated; mere; arrant; whole, clear; (*Paint.*) bold; (*Hort.*) on its own stock (of a fruit-tree), ungrafted. *Avoir ses coudées franches*, to have freedom of action; *avoir son franc parler*, to speak one's mind; *cœur franc*, open, ingenuous heart, open-hearted person. *Jouer franc jeu*, to play fair. *Lettres franches de port*, franked letters, letters post-paid or carriage-paid. *Un franc charlatan*, a downright quack; *une franche coquette*, an arrant jilt. *Une situation franche*, a clear or obvious situation. (*Naut.*) *Barre franche*, tiller. *-adv.* Frankly, freely, plainly; openly, sincerely; clean, quite, completely, entirely.

franc (3) [frɑ̃], *a.* (*fem.* **franque**) Frankish.—*n.m.* (**Franc**, *fem.* **Franque**) Frank.

français [frɑ̃'sɛ], *a.* (*fem.* **-aise**) French. *À la française*, in the French fashion; *la langue française*, the French tongue.—*n.m.* (**Français**, *fem.* **-aise**) Frenchman, Frenchwoman. *Le Français*, the Théâtre français.—*n.m.* (**français**) French. *En bon français*, in plain terms; *entendre le français*, to understand French; *parler français*, to speak French, to call a spade a spade; *parler français comme une vache espagnole*, to murder the French language. (Here *vache* for *Basque*.)

franc-bord [frɑ̃'bɔːr], *n.m.* (*Naut.*) Freeboard. *Yole à francs-bords*, carvel-built yawl.

France [frɑ̃ːs], **la**, *f.* France.

franc-fief [frɑ̃'fjɛf], *n.m.* (*pl.* **francs-fiefs**) Fief; fief exempt from homage, frank fee.

franche [FRANC (2)].

franchement [frɑ̃ʃ'mɑ̃], *adv.* Frankly, openly, sincerely; unreservedly, plainly; boldly; really, without hesitation. *J'avoue franchement (que)*, I readily admit (that).

franchir [frɑ̃'ʃiːr], *v.t.* To leap, to jump over; to clear; to pass, to pass over or beyond, to overstep; to overcome, to surmount. *Franchir le mur du son*, (*Av.*) to break the sound barrier. *Franchir le pas* or *le saut*, to take the

leap. *Franchir les bornes du devoir*, to overstep the bounds of duty. *Franchir les montagnes*, to cross the mountains. *Franchir une barrière*, to clear a gate; *franchir le parapet*, (*Mil.*) to go over the top; *il a franchi le fossé*, he has jumped the ditch.—*v.i.* (*Naut.*) To begin to become favourable (of the wind).

franchise [frɑ̃'ʃiːz], *n.f.* Exemption, immunity; freedom (of a city); freedom from taxes, etc.; right of asylum or sanctuary; a place possessing this; (*fig.*) frankness, sincerity, openness, candour; (*Paint.*) boldness, freedom of style. *En franchise de droit*, duty-free. *Franchise postale*, free post. *Franchise du coloris*, (*Paint.*) freedom of colouring. *Parler avec franchise*, to speak frankly.

franchissable [frɑ̃ʃi'sabl], *a.* Passable, capable of being crossed. **franchissement**, *n.m.* Leaping over, crossing.

francisation [frɑ̃siza'sjɔ̃], *n.f.* Gallicizing of foreign word; registration as a French ship.

franciscain [frɑ̃sis'kɛ̃], *a.* and *n.* (*fem.* **-aine**) Franciscan, grey friar, Franciscan nun.

franciser [frɑ̃si'ze], *v.t.* To gallicize; to Frenchify. **se franciser**, *v.r.* To become French or Frenchified.

francisque [frɑ̃'sisk], *n.f.* Frankish battle-axe.

franc-maçon [frɑ̃mɑ'sɔ̃], *n.m.* (*pl.* **francs-maçons**) Freemason. **franc-maçonnerie**, *n.f.* Freemasonry.

franco [frɑ̃'ko], *adv.* Free of charge, free of expense; prepaid. *Envoyer franco*, to send free of charge; *franco de port*, carriage paid.

françois [*see* PÈRE].

François [frɑ̃'swa], *m.* Francis.

Françoise [frɑ̃'swaːz], *f.* Frances.

francolin [frɑ̃kɔ'lɛ̃], *n.m.* Francolin.

francophile [frɑ̃kɔ'fil], *a.* and *n.* Francophile. **francophobe**, *a.* and *n.* Francophobe.

franc-parler [frɑ̃par'le], *n.m.* Frankness or freedom of speech. **franc-quartier**, *n.m.* (*pl.* **francs-quartiers**) (*Her.*) Quarter. **franc-tenancier**, *n.m.* (*pl.* **francs-tenanciers**) Freeholder. **franc-tillac**, *n.m.* (*pl.* **francs-tillacs**) (*Naut.*) Flush-deck; upper deck. **franc-tireur**, *n.m.* Franc-tireur; sniper.

frange [frɑ̃ːʒ], *n.f.* Fringe. **frangé**, *a.* (*fem.* **frangée**) Fringed; (*Bot.*) fimbriate. **franger** (1), *v.t.* To fringe. **frangier** or **franger** (2), *n.m.* (*fem.* **frangière**, **frangère** or **frangeuse**) Fringe-maker.

frangin [frɑ̃'ʒɛ̃], *n.m.* (*fem.* **frangine**) (*vulg.*) Brother, sister.

frangipane [frɑ̃ʒi'pan], *n.f.* Frangipane (almond-cake). **frangipanier**, *n.m.* Red jasmine tree.

franque [FRANC (3)].

franquette [frɑ̃'kɛt], *n.f.* (used only in '*À la bonne franquette*', simply, without fuss).

franquiste [frɑ̃'kist], *n.* Supporter of General Franco.

frappage [fra'paːʒ], *n.m.* Striking, stamping, coining. **frappant**, *a.* (*fem.* **-ante**) Striking, impressive. **frappe**, *n.f.* (*Coin.*) Stamp; minting; (*Typewr.*) touch; (*Print.*) set of matrices. **frappé**, *a.* (*fem.* **-ée**) Struck, surprised, astounded; iced (of liquids etc.); (*fig.*) strong and close (of cloth); powerful, forcible (of verses etc.). *Frappé d'étonnement*, struck with wonder. *Immeuble frappé d'alignement*, building coming under a demolition order. *Vers bien frappés*, spirited verses.—*n.m.* (*Mus.*) Down beat. **frappe-devant** [frapdə'vã], *n.m. inv.* Sledge-hammer. **frappement,** *n.m.* Striking, stamping; clapping (of hands).

frapper [fra'pe], *v.t.* To strike, to slap, to hit; to wound; to make an impression on, to affect, to move; to astonish, to surprise, to frighten; to stamp, to coin; to ice (liquids); (*Naut.*) to fasten, to bend (a rope etc.). *Frapper la terre du pied*, to stamp one's foot upon the ground, to paw the ground (of a horse etc.); *frapper légèrement*, to pat; *frapper au but*, to register a hit; *frapper un coup*, to strike a blow; *frapper vivement*, to rap. *Frapper la monnaie*, to coin money. *Frapper une marchandise d'une taxe*, to levy or impose a tax on an article.—*v.i.* To knock, to rap. *Entendre frapper*, to hear a knock; *frapper à la porte*, to knock at the door; *on frappe*, there is a knock; *entrez sans frapper*, walk straight in; *frapper juste*, to strike home. **se frapper,** *v.r.* To strike oneself; to strike each other; to be impressed, affected, or frightened. **frappeur,** *n.m.* (*fem.* **-euse**) Beater, striker.—*a.* Striking, rapping. *Esprit frappeur*, rapping spirit.

frasque [frask], *n.f.* Prank, escapade.

fraternel [frater'nɛl], *a.* (*fem.* **-elle**) Fraternal, brotherly. **fraternellement,** *adv.* Fraternally. **fraternisation,** *n.f.* Fraternization. **fraterniser,** *v.t.* To fraternize. **fraternité,** *n.f.* Fraternity, brotherhood.

fratricide [fratri'sid], *n.m.* Fratricide.—*a.* Fratricidal.

fraude [fro:d], *n.f.* Fraud, deceit; fraudulency; evasion (of taxes). *En fraude*, fraudulently; *entrer* or *passer en fraude dans*, to smuggle into; *faire une fraude*, to commit a fraud. **frauder,** *v.t.* To defraud.—*v.i.* To smuggle. **fraudeur,** *n.m.* (*fem.* **-euse**) Defrauder, smuggler.—*a.* Fraudulent; smuggling. **frauduleusement,** *adv.* Fraudulently. **frauduleux,** *a.* (*fem.* **-euse**) Fraudulent.

fraxinelle [fraksi'nɛl], *n.f.* False dittany.

frayement [frɛj'mã], *n.m.* Tracing, clearing; galls (of horse).

frayer [frɛ'je], *v.t.* (*conjugated like* BALAYER) To trace out, to open out, to mark out; to make (a way etc.); to rub against, to graze, to brush. *Chemin frayé*, beaten path or track. *Le coup n'a fait que frayer sa botte*, the blow only grazed his boot.—*v.i.* To wear away; to milt, to spawn (of fish); (*fig.*) to frequent, consort with, to have relations (*avec*), to be on good terms (*avec*). *Ces deux hommes ne frayent pas ensemble*, these two men do not get on well together. **se frayer,** *v.r.* To open for oneself; to prepare or carve out (a way) for oneself. *Se frayer un chemin*, to clear a way for oneself. **frayère,** *n.f.* Spawning place or season.

frayeur [frɛ'jœ:r], *n.f.* Fright, terror, dread, fear. *Être saisi de frayeur*, to be seized with terror.

frayoir [frɛj'wa:r], *n.m.* Fraying-place (of deer).

fredaine [frə'dɛn], *n.f.* (*colloq.*) Frolic, prank, freak. *Faire des fredaines*, to sow one's wild oats.

Frédéric [frede'rik], *m.* Frederick.

Frédérique [frede'rik], *f.* Frederica.

fredon [frə'dɔ̃], *n.m.* Song, refrain. **fredonnement,** *n.m.* Humming. **fredonner,** *v.t., v.i.* To hum. **fredonneur,** *a.* (*fem.* **-euse**) Fond of trilling or humming.—*n.* Triller.

frégate [fre'gat], *n.f.* Frigate; frigate bird. (*Navy*) *Capitaine de frégate*, commander.

frein [frɛ̃], *n.m.* Bit, bridle, curb, check; brake, drag, skid (of carriages etc.); (*Artill.*) recoil buffer; (*fig.*) restraint; (*Anat.*) frenum, string ligament. *Il faut mettre un frein à sa cruauté*, his cruelty must be curbed; *mettre un frein à sa langue*, to bridle one's tongue; *ronger son frein*, to champ the bit, (*fig.*) to fret oneself; *serrer le frein*, to put on the brake; *frein sur jante*, rim-brake. **freinage,** *n.m.* Braking. **freiner,** *v.t.* To brake (a vehicle etc.); to curb (production etc.).

frelatage [frəla'ta:ʒ], **frelatement,** *n.m.,* **frelaterie,** or **frelatation,** *n.f.* Adulteration; sophistication. **frelater,** *v.t.* To adulterate, to sophisticate. *Ce vin est frelaté*, this wine is adulterated. *Plaisirs frelatés*, unhealthy or dubious pleasures.

frêle [frɛ:l], *a.* Frail, fragile, weak.

freloche [frə'lɔʃ], *n.f.* Gauze-net, butterfly-net.

frelon [frə'lɔ̃], *n.m.* Hornet.

freluche [frə'lyʃ], *n.f.* Tuft or tassel (of silk); gossamer; (*fig.*) rubbish, frivolous thing.

freluquet [frəly'kɛ], *n.m.* Conceited young man, puppy.

frémir [fre'mi:r], *v.i.* To quiver, to shudder, to tremble; to vibrate, to rustle; to be agitated; to simmer. *Frémir de colère*, to tremble with anger. *J'entendais frémir le feuillage*, I heard the leaves rustling. **frémissant,** *a.* (*fem.* **-ante**) Quivering, trembling. **frémissement,** *n.m.* Quivering, trembling, shuddering; thrill, tremor, vibration; rustling; murmuring (of water); simmering. *Frémissement cataire*, (*Med.*) purring tremor of the heart.

frênaie [frɛ'nɛ], *n.f.* Ash-grove or plantation. **frêne,** *n.m.* Ash, ash-tree.

frénésie [frene'zi], *n.f.* Frenzy, madness. **frénétique,** *a.* Frantic, frenzied.—*n.* Raving, frantic person. **frénétiquement,** *adv.* Frantically.

fréquemment [freka'mã], *adv.* Frequently, often.

fréquence [fre'kã:s], *n.f.* Frequency; quickness (of the pulse etc.). *Fréquence téléphonique*, audio-frequency. *Modulation de fréquence*, (*Rad.*) frequency modulation, very high frequency (V.H.F.). **fréquent,** *a.* (*fem.* **-ente**) Frequent. *Pouls fréquent*, quick pulse. **fréquentatif,** *a.* and *n.* (*fem.* **-ive**) (*Gram.*) Frequentative.

fréquentation [frekãta'sjɔ̃], *n.f.* Frequentation. *Les mauvaises fréquentations*, evil company. **fréquenter,** *v.t.* To frequent, to keep company with; to resort to; to haunt. *Lieu peu fréquenté*, quiet little place.—*v.i.* To frequent, to associate (*chez*); to be a frequent caller at.

frère [frɛ:r], *n.m.* Brother; fellow-member; yoke-fellow, helpmate; friar, monk; (*pop.*) true friend, brick. *Demi-frère*, half-brother; *faux frère*, traitor, hypocrite; *frère aîné*, elder brother; *frère cadet*, younger brother; *frère consanguin*, brother by the father's side; *frère d'armes*, brother in arms; *frère de lait*, foster-brother; *frère utérin*, brother by the mother's side; *frères jumeaux*, twins. *Il est bon frère*, he is a jolly fellow. *Mes très chers frères*, dearly beloved brethren. *C'est un frère*, (*pop.*) he's a true friend, a good sort. **frérot**, *n.m.* (*colloq.*) Little brother.

fresaie [frə'zɛ] [EFFRAIE].

fresque [frɛsk], *n.f.* Fresco. *Peindre à fresque*, to paint in fresco.

fressure [frɛ'syːr], *n.f.* Pluck (of calf, sheep); fry (of.lamb); harslet (of pork); purtenance.

fret [frɛ], *n.m.* Freight, cargo. *Prendre du fret*, to take in freight. **frètement**, *n.m.* Freighting. **fréter**, *v.t. irr.* (*conjugated like* ACCÉLÉRER) To charter; to freight; to equip (a vessel); to hire (a car). **fréteur**, *n.m.* Freighter, charterer.

frétillage [FRÉTILLEMENT].

frétillant [freti'jɑ̃], *a.* (*fem.* -ante) Wriggling, lively; frisky; fidgety. **frétillement**, *n.m.* Wriggling; frisking. **frétiller**, *v.i.* To wriggle, to jump about; to frisk. *Frétiller de joie*, to quiver with joy; *frétiller de la queue*, to wag its tail (of a dog). **frétillon**, *n.m.* Fidgety person.

fretin [frə'tɛ̃], *n.m.* Fry, young fish; (*fig.*) trash, rubbish. *Menu fretin*, small fry.

frettage [frɛ'taːʒ], *n.m.* Hooping, binding; coiling.

frette (1) [frɛt], *n.f.* Iron hoop or band, tyre.

frette (2) [frɛt], *n.f.* (*Arch.*) Fret (interlacing fillets or bands); (*Her.*) bars crossed and interlaced. **fretté, a.** (*fem.*-ée) (*Her.*) Fretty.

fretter [frɛ'te], *v.t.* To hoop, to bind; to coil.

freudien [frø'djɛ̃], *a.* (*fem.* -ienne) Freudian. **freudisme**, *n.m.* Freud(ian)ism.

freux [frø], *n.m.* Rook. *Colonie de freux*, rookery.

friabilité [friabili'te], *n.f.* Friability. **friable**, *a.* Friable, crumbling easily; crisp, short.

friand [fri'ɑ̃], *a.* (*fem.* **friande**) Dainty, nice; partial to, fond (*de*); delicate, appetizing. *Avoir le goût friand*, to have a taste for sweets. *Être friand de*, to be fond of or partial to. *Un morceau friand*, a titbit.—*n.* Dainty person, epicure. **friandise**, *n.f.* Daintiness; epicurism; dainty, titbit.

fric [frik], *n.m.* (*slang*) Money.

fric-frac [frik'frak], *n.m.* (*slang*) Burglary.

fricandeau [frikɑ̃'do], *n.m.* (*pl.* -eaux) Larded meat (or fish) stewed.

fricassée [frika'se], *n.f.* Hash. **fricasser,** *v.t.* To fricassee. **fricasseur**, *n.m.* Bad cook.

fricatif [frika'tif], *a.* (*fem.* -ive) Fricative.— *n.f.* (*fricative*, a fricative consonant (such as s, z, h, f, v, r); *fricative sourde*, hiss; *fricative sonore*, buzz.

friche [friʃ], *n.f.* Waste or fallow land. *Laisser une terre en friche*, to let a piece of ground lie fallow.

frichti (*Mil. slang*) [FRICOT].

fricot [fri'ko], *n.m.* (*colloq.*) Ragout, stew; (*Mil. slang*) food, grub. **fricoter,** *v.i.* To cook.—*v.t.* To squander; to act on the sly; to cook accounts; (*Mil.*) to mike; to scrounge. **fricoteur**, *n.m.* (*fem.* **fricoteuse**) Feaster; fast liver; (*Mil.*) scrounger; shirker.

friction [frik'sjɔ̃], *n.f.* Friction, rubbing; (*Pharm.*) liniment. *Gants à friction*, flesh-gloves. **frictionner,** *v.t.* To rub.

Frigidaire [friʒi'dɛr], *n.m.* Refrigerator (trade mark but often used for *réfrigérateur*).

frigide [fri'ʒid], *a.* Frigid.

frigidité [friʒidi'te], *n.f.* Frigidity.

frigo [fri'go], *n.m.* (*fam.*) Cold store; chilled, or frozen meat.

frigorifier, *v.t.* To chill or freeze (meat etc.).

frigorifique [frigɔri'fik], *a.* Frigorific, chill. *Chambre frigorifique*, cold store. *Industrie frigorifique*, cold storage trade.—*n.m.* Freezer, cold storage.

frigothérapie [frigotera'pi], *n.f.* Frigotherapy.

frileusement [friløz'mɑ̃], *adv.* As though feeling chill; cosily (wrapped). **frileux,** *a.* (*fem.* -euse) Chilly; susceptible of cold.— *n.f.* Head shawl.—*n.m.* Redbreast, robin.

frimaire [fri'mɛːr], *n.m.* Third month of calendar of first French republic (Nov. 21 to Dec. 20).

frimas [fri'mɑ], *n.m.* *Rime, hoar-frost; (*fig.*) frost, winter. *Saison des frimas*, the wintry season.

frime [frim], *n.f.* (*pop.*) Show, pretence, sham. *C'est de la frime*, it's all sham, make-believe, window-dressing.

frimousse [fri'mus], *n.f.* (*pop.*) Pert, roguish little face.

fringale [frɛ̃'gal], *n.f.* (*colloq.*) Sudden pang of hunger. *Avoir la fringale*, to feel hungry all of a sudden.

fringant [frɛ̃'gɑ̃], *a.* (*fem.* -ante) Brisk, nimble, frisky; smart, dapper. *Cheval fringant*, frisky horse.

fringille [frɛ̃'ʒiːj], *n.m.* Finch.

fringuer [frɛ̃'ge], *v.i.* To skip; to prance (of a horse); (*fam.*) to cut a dash. **se fringuer** (*slang*) To dress oneself.

fringues [FRUSQUES].

fripe [frip], *n.f.* Rag, scrap of cloth, etc. **friper,** *v.t.* To crumple, to rumple. **se friper,** *v.r.* To get rumpled, shabby.

friperie, *n.f.* Frippery, rubbish, old clothes, old furniture, etc.; trade in old clothes etc.; junk shop. **fripier**, *n.m.* (*fem.* **fripière**) Dealer in old clothes, furniture, etc.

fripon [fri'pɔ̃], *a.* (*fem.* -onne) Cheating, knavish, rascally.—*n.* Rogue, cheat, swindler, rascal. *Un tour de fripon*, a knavish trick. **friponneau**, *n.m.* Little rogue, rascal, cheat. **friponnerie**, *n.f.* Cheating, roguery, knavery.

fripouille [fri'puːj], *n.f.* (*pop.*) Scoundrel, bad lot.

friquet [fri'kɛ], *n.m.* Tree-sparrow.

frire [friːr], *v.t., v.i. irr.* To fry. *Il n'a plus de quoi frire*, he is quite ruined. *Il n'y a rien à frire*, (*colloq.*) there is nothing to eat, there is nothing to be gained. *Poêle à frire*, frying pan.

frisage [fri'zaːʒ], *n.m.* Curling, frizzing (of hair etc.).

frise (1) [friːz], *n.f.* (*Arch. etc.*) Frieze.

frise (2) [friːz], *n.f.* Frieze (cloth).

frise (3) [friːz] [CHEVAL-DE-FRISE].

friselis [friz'li], *n.m.* (Slight) rustling (of leaves).

friser [fri'ze], *v.t.* To curl, to frizz (hair), to crisp; to graze, to touch lightly; to all but touch, to border upon. *Elle frise la quarantaine*, she is close on forty. *Friser la corde*, to escape hanging narrowly.—*v.i.* To curl; (*Print.*) to slur. **se friser,** *v.r.* To curl, to curl naturally (of hair); to curl one's hair. **frisette**, *n.f.* Small curl. **frisoir**, *n.m.* Curling-iron; part of a frizzing machine for cloth. **frison**, *n.m.* Curl of a frizz; floss (of wool, silk, etc.); rags, scraps of chiffon; wavy lines (of marbled paper); (*Print.*) slur. **frisotter**, *v.t.* To curl lightly.—*v.i.* To be curled, to be frizzy.

frisquet [fris'kɛ], *a.* (*fem.* **frisquette** (1)) (*fam.*) Coldish, chilly.

frisquette (2) [fris'ket], *n.f.* (*Print.*) Frisket.

frisson [fri'sɔ̃], *n.m.* Shiver, cold fit, chilliness; shudder, thrill. *Avoir le frisson*, to have the shivers; *cela donne le frisson*, that makes one shudder. **frissonnant**, *a.* (*fem.* **-ante**) Shuddering, shivering. **frissonnement**, *n.m.* Shivering, shudder; flutter, thrill. **frissonner**, *v.i.* To shiver; to shudder; to feel a thrill; to quake, to tremble.

frisure [fri'zy:r], *n.f.* Crisping; curling, head-dress of curls.

frit [fri], *a.* (*fem.* **frite**) Fried; (*slang*) ruined. *Il est frit*, he is done for.—*n.f. pl. Des frites*, fried potatoes, chips.

fritillaire [friti'lɛːr], *n.f.* (*Bot.*) Fritillary. *Fritillaire méléagride*, snake's head.

fritte [frit], *n.f.* (*Glass-making*) Frit. **fritter**, *v.t.* To frit, to calcinate.

friture [fri'ty:r], *n.f.* Frying; thing fried, fried fish, etc.; dish of fried food; butter, grease, etc., for frying; (*Teleph.*) crackling in the receiver.

frivole [fri'vɔl], *a.* Frivolous, trifling, futile.— *n.m.* That which is frivolous. **frivolement**, *adv.* Frivolously. **frivolité**, *n.f.* Frivolity; trifle; (*Needlework*) tatting.

froc [frɔk], *n.m.* Cowl (monk's garment covering head and shoulders), monk's gown. *Jeter le froc aux orties*, to throw off the cowl, to give up one's profession; *prendre le froc*, to turn monk. **frocaille**, *n.f.* (*colloq.*) People of the cowl, monks. **frocard**, *n.m.* (*colloq.*) Monk.

froid (1) [frwa], *n.m.* Cold, coldness; chilliness, feeling of cold; (*fig.*) unconcern, lukewarmness, dullness; gravity, reserve. *À froid*, coldly, in cold blood; *avoir froid*, to be cold; *être en froid*, not to be on the best terms; *battre froid à quelqu'un*, to give someone the cold shoulder; *cela ne fait ni chaud ni froid*, it makes no difference; *froid de loup*, extreme cold; *n'avoir pas froid aux yeux*, to be game, to be determined; *il est tout raide de froid*, he is quite stiff with cold; *les grands froids*, extreme cold, depth of winter; *mourir de froid*, to be frozen to death; *prendre froid*, to catch cold.

froid (2) [frwa], *a.* (*fem.* **froide**) Cold; (*fig.*) lukewarm, cool, indifferent, dispassionate, frigid, lifeless; reserved, distant. *Froid comme glace*, as cold as ice; *temps froid*, cold weather; *un homme froid*, a cold sort of man. **froidement**, *adv.* Coldly, frigidly; lukewarmly, dispassionately. **froideur**, *n.f.* Coldness; chilliness; indifference, coolness; (*Path.*) frigidity. **froidure**, *n.f.* Coldness (of the weather); cold; (*fig.*) winter.

froissable [frwa'sabl], *a.* Which can be crumpled (of material etc.); (*fig.*) who can be vexed. **froissage**, *n.m.* Crumpling, crushing, rumpling. **froissement**, *n.m.* Rumpling, crumpling; bruising; (*fig.*) clash; hurt, slight affront, annoyance. **froisser**, *v.t.* To rumple, to crumple (paper); to bruise slightly (muscle); (*fig.*) to offend, to hurt, to wound. *Je ne voudrais pas le froisser*, I should not like

to hurt his feelings. **se froisser**, *v.r.* To get bruised (of a muscle); to take offence. **froissure**, *n.f.* Crease, rumple, crumple; bruise.

frôlement [frol'mɑ̃], *n.m.* Grazing, touching lightly; rustle. **frôler**, *v.t.* To graze, to touch slightly in passing; to brush past. **frôleur** (*fem.* **-euse**), *a.* Brushing lightly, caressing.

fromage [frɔ'maːʒ], *n.m.* Cheese. *Au fromage*, with cheese; *fromage blanc* or *fromage à la crème*, cream-cheese; *fromage de chèvre*, goat's milk cheese; *fromage de tête*, brawn; *fromage bien fait*, ripe cheese; (*fig.*) *un* (*bon*) *fromage*, a fine billet, a nice soft job, a well-salaried berth. **fromageon**, *n.m.* Goat's milk or ewe's milk cheese. **fromager**, *n.m.* (*fem.* **-ère**) Cheese-maker or -monger; cheese-mould; kapok-tree. **fromagerie**, *n.f.* Cheese farm or dairy; cheese-trade. **fromageux**, *a.* (*fem.* **-euse**) Cheesy.

froment [frɔ'mɑ̃], *n.m.* Wheat. *De froment*, wheaten. **fromentacé**, *a.* (*fem.* **-ée**) (*Bot.*) Frumentaceous. **fromental**, *a.* (*fem.* **-ale**, *pl.* **-aux**) Frumentaceous.—*n.m.* or *avoine élevée* or *faux froment*. False oat; ryegrass.

fronce [frɔ̃ːs], *n.f.* Gather, pucker (in needlework etc.); crease (in paper). **froncement**, *n.m.* Contraction, knitting, puckering (of the brows etc.); (*fig.*) frowning, frown. **froncer**, *v.t.* To contract, to pucker, to knit (the brows etc.); to wrinkle; to purse (the lips); to gather (needlework). *Froncer le sourcil*, to frown. **se froncer**, *v.r.* To contract, to pucker, to wrinkle. **froncis**, *n.m.* Gathering, fold.

frondaison [frɔ̃dɛ'zɔ̃], *n.f.* Foliation; foliage.

fronde [frɔ̃ːd], *n.f.* Sling; frond (of algae, ferns, etc.); (*Surg.*) bandage; (*Fr. Hist.*) party or war of the Fronde. **frondée**, *n.f.* Sling-shot (distance). **fronder**, *v.t.* To sling, to fling with a sling; to banter; to censure, to find fault with; to jeer at. **frondeur**, *n.m.* Slinger; banterer, censurer, fault-finder; rioter; member of the Fronde.

front [frɔ̃], *n.m.* Forehead, brow; face, countenance; head; front, frontage, fore-part; (*fig.*) boldness, impudence, brass. *À front découvert*, without disguise; *avoir le front de*, to have the face to; *courber le front*, to bow one's head; *de front*, in front, abreast, at a time; *faire front à*, to face; *front de bataille*, battle-front; (*Polit.*) *Front populaire*, Popular Front. **frontal** (1) or **frontail**, *n.m.* Forehead-strap (of harness); head-piece (of horse's armour). **frontal** (2), *a.* (*fem.* **-ale**, *pl.* **-aux**) (*Anat.*) Frontal.—*n.m.* Frontal; frontal bone; head-bandage. **fronteau**, *n.m.* (*pl.* **-eaux**) Frontlet; [FRONTAL (1)].

frontalier [frɔ̃ta'lje], *a.* and *n.* (*fem.* **-ière**) (Person) who lives near the frontier, borderer. (C) **fronteau** [frɔ̃'to], *n.m.* Range line.

frontière [frɔ̃'tjɛːr], *n.f.* Frontier, border; (*fig.*) confine, limit.

frontispice [frɔ̃tis'pis], *n.m.* Frontispiece, title-page.

fronton [frɔ̃'tɔ̃], *n.m.* (*Arch.*) Fronton, pediment; (*Naut.*) stern-rail; high and broad wall used in game of *pelote basque*.

frottage [frɔ'taːʒ], *n.m.* Rubbing; polishing; **frottant**, *a.* (*fem.* **-ante**) Rubbing; suitable for polishing etc. **frottée,** *n.f.* (*colloq.*) Drubbing. **frottement,** *n.m.* Rubbing, friction; (*fig.*) contact, interaction. **frotter,** *v.t.* To rub; to polish; (*fig.*) to rub, to pommel, to warm (the ears of). *Se faire frotter,* to get a drubbing.—*v.i.* To rub. **se frotter,** *v.r.* To rub oneself; to provoke, to come in contact, to meddle (*à*). *Ne vous frottez pas à lui,* do not provoke him; *ne vous y frottez pas,* do not meddle with it; *qui s'y frotte s'y pique,* meddle and smart for it; *se frotter les yeux,* to rub one's eyes. **frotteur,** *n.m.* (*fem.* **-euse**) Rubber; scrubber; rubbing part (of a machine), floor-polisher. **frottis,** *n.m.* (*Paint.*) Thin wash of colour, scumble; (*Med.*) smear. **frottoir,** *n.m.* Rubbing-cloth, rough towel, scrubber, hat-pad, etc.; (*Elec.*) cushion, brush (of dynamo). **frou-frou** [fru'fru], *n.m.* (*pl.* **frou-frous**) Rustling (of silk etc.). *Faire du frou-frou,* to show off. **froufroutant,** *a.* Rustling. **froufrouter,** *v.i.* To rustle; (*fig.*) to show off. **frousse** [frus], *n.f.* (*slang*) Fear, alarm. *Avoir la frousse,* to be in a funk. **froussard,** *a.* (*fem.* **-arde**) Funky.—*n.* A coward. **fructidor** [frykti'dɔːr], *n.m.* Fructidor (twelfth month of calendar of first French republic, 18 August to 16 September). **fructifère** [frykti'fɛːr], *a.* (*Bot.*) Fructiferous (fruit-bearing). **fructification** [fryktifika'sjɔ̃], *n.f.* Fructification. **fructifier,** *v.i.* To fructify, to bear fruit; (*fig.*) to thrive, to bring forth good results. **fructiforme** [frykti'fɔrm], *a.* (*Bot.*) Fructiform. **fructueusement** [fryktɥøz'mɑ̃], *adv.* Fruitfully, profitably. **fructueux,** *a.* (*fem.* **-ueuse**) Fruitful, profitable. **fructuosité,** *n.f.* Fruitfulness. **frugal** [fry'gal], *a.* (*fem.* **-ale**, *pl.* **-aux**) Frugal. **frugalement,** *adv.* Frugally. **frugalité,** *n.f.* Frugality. **frugifère** [FRUCTIFÈRE]. **frugivore** [fryʒi'vɔːr], *a.* Frugivorous. **fruit** [frɥi], *n.m.* Fruit; (*fig.*) offspring; advantage, benefit, profit, utility; (*pl.*) fruits, productions; effect, result; (*Masonry*) batter. *Avec fruit,* profitably; *fruit sec,* dried fruit, (*sch. slang*) a failure, a dud; *producteur de fruits,* fruit-grower; *sans fruit,* without result, fruitlessly. **fruité,** *a.* (*fem.* **-ée**) Fruity (of wine, olives); (*Her.*) fructed. **fruiterie,** *n.f.* Fruit-loft; fruit-trade. **fruitier** (1), *a.* (*fem.* **-ière** (1)) Fruit-bearing. *Arbre fruitier,* fruit-tree; *jardin fruitier,* orchard, fruit-garden. **fruitier** (2), *n.m.* (*fem.* **-ière** (2)) Fruiterer, greengrocer.—*n.m.* Fruit-loft.—*n.f.* Co-operative cheese-dairy. **frusquer** [frys'ke], *v.t.* (*slang*) To dress, to rig out. **frusques,** *n.f. pl.* Clothes, togs. **fruste** [fryst], *a.* Worn, defaced, corroded (of coins, medals, sculpture, etc.); rough, unpolished (persons). **frustration** [frystra'sjɔ̃], *n.f.* Frustration. **frustratoire,** *a.* Frustratory. **frustrer,** *v.t.* To defraud; to frustrate, to disappoint, to baulk, to foil, to baffle. *Il a frustré ses créanciers,* he has defrauded his creditors. **frutescent** [fryte'sɑ̃], *a.* (*fem.* **frutescente**) (*Bot.*) Frutescent. **frutille** [fry'tiːj], *n.f.* Chilean strawberry.

frutillier, frutilier, *n.m.* Chilean strawberry-plant. **fuchsia** [fyk'sja], *n.m.* Fuchsia. **fuchsine,** *n.f.* (*Chem.*) Fuchsine (aniline magenta dye). **fucus** [fy'kyːs], *n.m.* Focus, sea-wrack. **fugace** [fy'gas], *a.* Fugaceous, fugitive, fleeting, transient. **fugacité** *n.f.* Fugacity. **fugitif** [fyʒi'tif], *a.* (*fem.* **fugitive**) Fugitive, transient, fleeting, short-lived. *Des plaisirs fugitifs,* transient pleasures.—*n.* Fugitive, runaway. **fugitivement,** *adv.* Fugitively. **fugue** [fyg], *n.f.* Fugue; (*colloq.*) flight, escapade. *Faire une fugue,* to run away from home (for a few days). **fuie** (1) [fɥi], *n.f.* Small pigeon-house or dove-cot. **fuie** (2), *pres. sub.* [FUIR]. **fuir** [fɥiːr], *v.i. irr.* (*pres.p.* **fuyant,** *p.p.* **fui**) To fly, to flee, to run away, to escape; to elude; to glide or slip away (of water etc.); to leak; (*Paint.*) to recede. *Ce tonneau fuit,* this cask leaks.—*v.t.* To fly, to avoid, to shrink from; to shun, to eschew. **se fuir,** *v.r.* To fly from oneself; to shun or avoid each other. **fuite** [fɥit], *n.f.* Flight, running away, escaping; avoiding, shunning; evasion, shift, subterfuge; running out, leakage, escape (of gas etc.). *Fuite du domicile conjugal,* elopement; *la fuite en Égypte,* the flight into Egypt; *mettre en fuite,* to put to flight; *prendre la fuite,* to run away. **fulgurant** [fylgy'rɑ̃], *a.* (*fem.* **-ante**) Attended with lightning; flashing, vivid, sharp. *Une douleur fulgurante,* a sharp pain. **fulguration** [fylgyra'sjɔ̃], *n.f.* (*Chem.*) Fulguration, lightning. **fulgurite,** *n.m.* Fulgurite. **fuligineux** [fyliʒi'nø], *a.* (*fem.* **fuligineuse**) Fuliginous. **fuliginosité,** *n.f.* Fuliginosity. **fuligule** [fyli'gyl], *n.m.* Name of several duck of the genus *Nyroca. Fuligule milouin,* pochard; *fuligule morillon,* tufted duck; *fuligule milouinan,* scamp. **fulmar** [fyl'mar], *n.m.* Petrel fulmar, *Fulmarus glacialis.* **fulmicoton** [COTON-POUDRE]. **fulminant** [fylmi'nɑ̃], *a.* (*fem.* **-ante**) Fulminant, fulminating. **fulminate,** *n.m.* Fulminate. **fulmination,** *n.f.* Fulmination. **fulminatoire,** *a.* Fulminatory. **fulminer,** *v.i.* To fulminate, to explode; (*fig.*) to storm, to thunder, to inveigh (against).—*v.t.* To fulminate, to send forth (maledictions or religious decrees). **fumage** (1) [fy'maːʒ], *n.m.* Smoking (bacon etc.); lacquering by smoking (silver wire etc.). **fumage** (2) [fy'maːʒ], *n.m.*, or **fumaison,** *n.f.* Spreading of dung on land. **fumant** [fy'mɑ̃], *a.* (*fem.* **fumante**) Smoking, reeking, fuming. **fumé** (1) [fy'me], *a.* (*fem.* **fumée** (1)) Smoked; manured. *Verres fumés,* sun-glasses, dark glasses.—*n.m.* (*Engr.*) Smoke-proof. **fume-cigare** [PORTE-CIGARE]. **fume-cigarette,** *n.m. inv.* Cigarette-holder. **fumée** (2) [fy'me], *n.f.* Smoke; steam; fume, exhalation, reek; (*fig.*) fumes (of drink etc.); phantom, bubble, dream, vain hope; (*pl.*) (*Hunt.*) fumet, dung of deer. *Des tourbillons de fumée,* volumes of smoke; *il n'y a point de fumée sans feu,* there is no smoke without fire; *s'en aller en fumée,* to dissolve into thin air.

fumer [fy'me], *v.i.* To smoke, to emit smoke; to give out vapour etc., to reek, to steam; (*fig.*) to fret and fume.—*v.t.* To smoke (a cigarette etc.), to smoke-dry; to dung; to manure. *Fumer des jambons*, to smoke hams; *fumer un champ*, to manure a field; *défense de fumer*, no smoking.

fumerie [fym'ri], *n.f.* *Smoking (of tobacco etc.). *Fumerie d'opium*, opium den.

fumerolle [fym'rɔl], *n.f.* Fumarole.

fumeron [fym'rɔ̃], *n.m.* Smoking half-burnt charcoal.

fumet [fy'me], *n.m.* Flavour (of meat), bouquet (of wines); (*fig.*) raciness; (*Hunt.*) scent.

fumeterre [fym'tɛːr], *n.f.* (*Bot.*) Fumitory.

fumeur [fy'mœːr], *n.m.* (*fem.* **fumeuse** (1)) Smoker; smoking compartment.—*n.f.* Smoking-chair. **fumeux**, *a.* (*fem.* **-euse** (2)) Smoky, fumose; heady, fumy; not very clear, hazy (of brain, ideas, etc.).

fumier [fy'mje], *n.m.* Manure, dung, dung-hill; (*fig.*) trash, rubbish. **fumière**, *n.f.* Dung heap.

fumifuge [fymi'fyːʒ], *a.* Smoke-expelling.

fumigateur [fymiga'tœːr], *n.m.* Fumigator. **fumigation**, *n.f.* Fumigation. **fumigatoire**, *a.* Fumigating. **fumigène**, *a.* (*Mil.*) *Un obus fumigène*, a smoke shell. **fumiger**, *v.t.* To fumigate.

fumiste [fy'mist], *n.m.* Stove- or chimney-repairer; (*fig.*) practical joker. **fumisterie**, *n.f.* Profession, premises of chimney and stove dealer or repairer; (*fig.*) practical joke, mystification.

fumivore [fymi'vɔːr], *a.* Smoke-consuming. —*n.m.* Smoke-consumer.

fumoir [fy'mwaːr], *n.m.* Smoking-shed, smoking-house (for curing fish etc.); smoking-room.

fumure [FUMAGE (2)].

funambule [fynɑ̃'byl], *a.* Funambulatory— *n.m.* Funambulist, rope-dancer. **funambulesque**, *a.* Funambulatory; (*fig.*) grotesque.

fune [fyn], *n.f.* (*Naut.*) Rope, line (of tent, seine, etc.).

funèbre [fy'nɛbr], *a.* Funeral; funereal, mournful; dismal, ominous. *Marche funèbre*, funeral march. **funérailles**, *n.f. pl.* Funeral ceremonies, obsequies; (*fig.*) death, destruction, ruin. **funéraire**, *a.* Funeral, funereal.

funeste [fy'nɛst], *a.* Fatal, deadly; (*fig.*) baneful, disastrous; distressing. **funestement**, *adv.* Fatally, disastrously.

funiculaire [fyniky'lɛːr], *a.* Funicular.—*n.m.* Funicular railway.

funicule [fyni'kyl], *n.m.* (*Bot.*) Funiculus, funicle. **funiforme**, *a.* Funiform.

fur [fyːr], *n.m.* (*used only in the expressions Au fur et à mesure*, gradually as, as the work etc. goes on; *on le paye au fur et à mesure de l'ouvrage*, he is paid as the work proceeds.

furet [fy're], *n.m.* Ferret. *C'est un furet*, he is a nosey parker; *chasser au furet*, to hunt with a ferret; *jouer au furet*, to hunt the slipper. **furetage**, *n.m.* Hunting with ferrets; (*fig.*) ferreting out, rummaging. **fureter**, *v.i.* To ferret, to hunt with a ferret; (*fig.*) to rummage. **fureteur**, *n.m.* (*fem.* **-euse**) Ferreter; (*fig.*) Nosey Parker. *Fureteur de nouvelles*, news-hunter.—*a.* Ferreting, prying.

fureur [fy'rœːr], *n.f.* Rage, fury, madness, transport, passion, ecstasy; violence, frenzy. *Avec fureur*, furiously; *cette actrice fait fureur*, that actress is all the rage; *être transporté de fureur*, to be beside oneself with rage; *il a la fureur du jeu*, he has a passion for gambling; *lorsque la fureur le prend*, when the fit is on him; *quand il entre en fureur*, when he gets into a fury.

furfuracé [fyrfyra'se], *a.* (*fem.* **-ée**) Furfuraceous, scurfy. **furfures**, *n.m. pl.* (*Med.*) Furfur.

furibond [fyri'bɔ̃], *a.* (*fem.* **-onde**) Furious, raging, wild; furious-looking.—*n.* A furious person.

furie [fy'ri], *n.f.* Fury, rage; heat, ardour, intensity; (*Myth.*) Fury. *C'est une furie*, she is a termagant; *dans la furie du combat*, in the heat of the battle; *entrer* (or *se mettre*) *en furie*, to get into a rage; *la furie française*, battle-ardour of the French. **furieusement**, *adv.* Furiously; (*colloq.*) prodigiously, with a vengeance. **furieux**, *a.* (*fem.* **-ieuse**) Furious, raging; mad, fierce, savage, impetuous; (*colloq.*) excessive, monstrous, tremendous. *Fou furieux*, raging mad.—*n.* Mad person.

furolle [fy'rɔl], *n.f.* Jack-o'-lantern.

furoncle [fy'rɔ̃kl], *n.m.* (*Med.*) Furuncle, boil. **furonculose**, *n.f.* Furunculosis. **furonculeux**, *a.* (*fem.* **-euse**) Furunculous.

furtif [fyr'tif], *a.* (*fem.* **-ive**) Furtive, stealthy, secret. *Entrer d'un pas furtif*, to steal in. **furtivement**, *adv.* Furtively, stealthily, secretly.

fusain [fy'zɛ̃], *n.m.* Spindle-tree; charcoal (for drawing). *Un fusain*, a charcoal sketch.

fusarolle or **fusarole** [fyza'rɔl], *n.f.* (*Arch.*) Fusarole.

fusant [fy'zɑ̃], *a.* Fusing. *Obus fusant*, time shell.

fuseau [fy'zo], *n.m.* (*pl.* **fuseaux**) Spindle; gasteropod with a long, pointed shell. *Fuseau de quenouille*, distaff; *fuseau horaire*, time-belt, hour-zone; *jambes en fuseau*, spindle-legs.

fusée [fy'ze], *n.f.* Spindleful; spindle (of axle); fusee (of a watch etc.); (*Motor.*) stub axle; (*Mil. etc.*) fuse; rocket; (*Vet.*) splint, splinter; (*Surg.*) fistula etc.; (*fig.*) volley (of laughter etc.). (*Av.*) *Avion-fusée*, rocket-propelled aircraft. *Fusée éclairante*, star-shell, flare; *fusée volante*, sky-rocket.

fuselage [fyz'laːʒ], *n.m.* Framework, body, fuselage (of an aeroplane).

fuselé [fyz'le], *a.* (*fem.* **fuselée**) Spindle-shaped, slender, tapering (fingers); stream-lined (of racing-cars, aircraft, etc.). **fuseler**, *v.t.* To give a body the shape of a spindle.

fuser [fy'ze], *v.i.* To spread insensibly; to spirt; to liquefy, to dissolve, to fuse. **fusibilité**, *n.f.* Fusibility. **fusible**, *a.* Fusible. —*n.m.* (*Elec.*) Fuse.

fusiforme [fyzi'fɔrm], *a.* Spindle-shaped, fusiform.

fusil [fy'zi], *n.m.* Steel, strike-a-light; hammer (of obsolete musket); steel for sharpening knives; gun, rifle, rifleman. *À portée de fusil*, within gun-shot; *changer son fusil d'épaule*, (*fig.*) to change one's opinion; *coup de fusil*, gun shot; report of a rifle; (*fam.*) overcharging; fleecing; *fusil à aiguille*, needle-gun; *fusil à deux coups*, double-barrelled gun;

fusil à piston or *à percussion*, percussion-gun; *fusil à vent*, air-gun; *fusil de chasse*, fowling-piece, shot-gun; *fusil de munition*, service rifle; *il est bon fusil*, he is a good shot; *pierre à fusil*, flint, strike-a-light. **fusilier**, *n.m.* Fusilier. *Fusilier marin*, marine. **fusillade**, *n.f.* Discharge of musketry, fusillade; execution by shooting. **fusiller**, *v.t.* To shoot (down); to execute by shooting; (*fam.*) to pelt with (questions, witticisms, ogling glances). **fusil-mitrailleur**, *n.m.* Sub-machine-gun.

fusion [fy'zjɔ̃], *n.f.* Fusion, melting; (*Fin.*) amalgamation (of companies); (*fig.*) coalescence, blending, merger. **fusionnement**, *n.m.* Amalgamation, coalescence. **fusionner**, *v.t.*, *v.i.* To amalgamate, to unite, to merge; to blend.

fustanelle [fysta'nɛl], *n.f.* Fustanella.

fustet [fys'tɛ], *n.m.* (*Bot.*) Venetian sumach, fustic.

fustigation [fystiga'sjɔ̃], *n.f.* Fustigation, whipping, flogging. **fustiger**, *v.t.* To flog, to whip.

fût [fy], *n.m.* Stock (of a gun or pistol); shaft (of a column); part of trunk devoid of branches; cask; barrel (of a drum); case (of an organ).

futaie [fy'tɛ], *n.f.* Forest of high trees; high forest tree. *Arbre de haute futaie*, full-grown forest tree; *bois de haute futaie*, wood of full-grown forest trees, timber trees, timber; *demi-futaie*, forest of half-grown trees.

futaille [fy'taːj], *n.f.* Cask, barrel.

futaine [fy'tɛːn], *n.f.* Fustian.

futé [fy'te], *a.* (*fem.* **-ée** (1)) (*colloq.*) Sharp, cunning, sly.—*n.* Sharp, sly person (mostly of children). *C'est une petite futée*, she is a sly little puss.

futée (2) [fy'te], *n.f.* Joiner's stopping.

futile [fy'til], *a.* Futile, frivolous, trifling. **futilement**, *adv.* Emptily, vainly, futilely. **futilité**, *n.f.* Futility; trifle.

futur [fy'tyːr], *a.* (*fem.* **-ure**) Future.—*n.m.* The future; futurity; (*Gram.*) future.—*n.* Intended husband or wife. *Sa future*, his intended wife. **futurisme**, *n.m.* Futurism. **futuriste**, *a.* Futuristic.—*n.* Futurist. **futurition**, *n.f.* Futurition.

fuyant [fɥi'jɑ̃], *a.* (*fem.* **-ante**) Flying, fleeing, retreating; receding (of the forehead etc.); fleeting, ephemeral, transient.—*n.m.* Perspective, receding line. **fuyard**, *a.* and *n.* (*fem.* **-arde**) Fugitive, runaway.

fy [fi], *n.m.* Leprosy of animals.

G

G, g [ʒe], *n.m.* The seventh letter of the alphabet pronounced (g) before *a*, *o*, *u*, as in *garde*, *gond*, *guise*, and (ʒ) before *e* and *i*, as in *gemme*, *gîte*. The combination *gn* represents *n mouillé* or (ɲ) as in *agneau* (a'ɲo).

gabardine [gabar'din], *n.f.* Gabardine; a coat made of gabardine.

gabare [ga'baːr], *n.f.* Lighter, flat-bottomed barge or smack; lump; store-ship, transport-ship. **gabarier** (1), *n.m.* Lighterman; master of a *gabare*.

gabarier (2) [gaba'rje], *v.t.* To mould or gauge upon a *gabarit*; to verify the dimensions of a body. **gabarit**, *n.m.* Mould or full-sized model of part of a ship etc.; frame-board, mould, gauge; (*Rail.*) carriage-gauge templet, tunnel gauge.

gabegie [gab'ʒi], *n.f.* (*fam.*) Fraud, deceit; waste; muddle.

gabelle [ga'bɛl], *n.f.* Gabelle, salt-tax; similar duty on provisions. *Frauder la gabelle*, to defraud the excise. **gabelou**, *n.m.* [ga'blu]. Workman in salt-magazine; (*slang*) customs-officer; rate collector.

gabier [ga'bje], *n.m.* (*Naut.*) Top-man, A.B.

gabion [ga'bjɔ̃], *n.m.* (*Fort.*) Gabion. **gabionnade**, *n.f.* Gabionade; intrenchment of gabions. **gabionnage**, *n.m.* Gabionage. **gabionner**, *v.t.* To revert with gabions.

gable [gabl] or **gâble** [gɑːbl], *n.m.* Triangular window-canopy; gable.

gabord [ga'bɔːr] or **galbord**, *n.m.* (*Naut.*) Garboard.

gâche (1) [gɑːʃ], *n.f.* Staple, wall-hook.

gâche (2) [gɑːʃ], *n.f.* Trowel; baker's spatula. **gâcher**, *v.t.* To mix (mortar); to slack (lime); (*fig.*) to bungle, to make a mess of, to botch; to waste.

gâchette [gɑ'ʃɛt], *n.f.* Tumbler, sear (of a gun-lock); follower, catch (of a lock).

gâcheur [gɑ'ʃœːr], *n.m.* Mason's labourer; (*fig.*) bungler.

gâcheux [gɑ'ʃø], *a.* (*fem.* **-euse**) Splashy, sloppy. **gâchis**, *n.m.* Wet mortar etc.; sludge, slop, mire; (*fig.*) mess, pickle, hash, confusion, disorder, trouble. *Faire du gâchis de*, to make a mess of; *être dans le gâchis*, to be in a pickle.

gade [gad], *n.m.* Gade, gadoid.

(C) **gadelle** [ga'dɛl], *n.f.* Gooseberry, currant.

gadoïde [gado'id], *n.m.* Gadoid (fish of cod tribe).

gadouard [ga'dwaːr], *n.m.* (*pop.*) Scavenger.

gadoue [ga'du], *n.f.* Night-soil; sewage used as manure; dirt, slush.

gadzarts [gad'zar], *n.m. inv.* Contraction of *gars des arts*, students or former students of *Écoles des Arts et Métiers*.

gaélique [gae'lik], *a.* and *n.m.* Gaelic.

gaffe [gaf], *n.f.* Boat-hook; gaff; (*fam.*) gross blunder, howler. *Avaler sa gaffe*, to die; *gaffe de sauvetage*, life-drag; *se tenir à longueur de gaffe*, to keep oneself at a distance. (*slang*) *Faire gaffe*, to pay attention; *faire une gaffe*, to drop a brick. **gaffeau**, *n.m.* Small boat-hook. **gaffer**, *v.t.* To hook with a gaff.—*v.i.* (*fam.*) To blunder; (*Row.*) to catch a crab. **gaffeur**, *n.m.* (*fem.* **-euse**) (*fam.*) Blunderer, hopeless idiot.

gag [gag], *n.m.* Gag.

gaga [ga'ga], *a.* (*fam.*) [GÂTEUX].

gage [gaːʒ], *n.m.* Pawn, pledge; security, deposit; stake, forfeit, assurance, promise, proof, token, testimony; (*pl.*) wages, hire, pay. *À gages*, hired, paid; *casser aux gages*, to dismiss from service, to cashier; *donner des gages de*, to give proofs of; *donner en gage*, to pawn, *gage d'amitié*, pledge or token of amity or friendship; *jouer aux gages*, to play at forfeits; *mettre en gage*, to pawn; *prendre à gages*, to hire; *prêteur sur gage*, pawnbroker; *retirer un gage*, to redeem a pledge; *tueur à gages*, hired assassin.

gagée [ga'ʒe], *n.f.* or *gagée des champs*, [ORNITHOGALE].

gage-mort [MORT-GAGE].

gager [ga'ʒe], *v.t.* To wager, to bet, to stake; to pay wages to, to pay; to engage (of a domestic, a farm-hand, etc.). *Gage que si, gage que non*, I bet it is, I bet it is not; *gager avec quelqu'un* or *contre quelqu'un*, to lay a wager with or against someone; *gager sa vie*, to stake one's life.

*gagerie [SAISIE-GAGERIE].

gageur [ga'ʒœ:r], *n.m.* (*fem.* **-euse**) Better, one who wagers.

gageure [ga'ʒy:r], *n.f.* Wager, stake; something which seems impossible to do. *Faire* or *accepter une gageure*, to lay a wager; *tenir la gageure*, to stick to a thing, to persevere.

gagiste [ga'ʒist], *n.m.* (*Theat.*) Supernumerary; (*Law*) pledgee, bailee.—*a.* (*Law*) By pledge. *Créancier gagiste*, guaranteed creditor.

gagnable [gɑ'ɲabl], *a.* That can be won.

gagnage [gɑ'ɲaːʒ], *n.m.* Pasturage, pastureland.

gagnant [gɑ'ɲɑ̃], *a.* (*fem.* **-ante**) Winning.—*n.* Winner. ***gagne-deniers**, *n.m.* (*pl.* **gagne-deniers**) Unskilled worker, day-labourer. **gagne-pain**, *n.m. inv.* Means of subsistence, livelihood, daily bread; bread-winner. **gagne-petit**, *n.m. inv.* Knife-grinder (itinerant); cheap-jack.

gagner [gɑ'ɲe], *v.t.* To gain, to get, to earn; to win; to merit, to deserve; to prevail upon, to gain over, to corrupt, to bribe; to allure, to attract, to entice; to take, to make oneself master of, to seize; to overtake, to arrive at; to catch (a cold etc.). *Gagner au change*, to profit by the exchange; *gagner du pays*, to flee, to get away; *gagner du temps*, to gain time; *gagner la partie*, to win the game; *gagner le dessus*, to get the better of; *gagner le devant*, to get the start; *gagner le large*, to escape; *gagner le logis*, to reach home; *gagner quelqu'un à quelque chose*, to win someone over; *gagner quelqu'un de vitesse*, to outstrip someone; *gagner sa vie avec peine*, to work hard for one's living; *gagner son procès*, to win one's case; *gagner une bataille*, to win a battle; *il l'a bien gagné*, he well deserves it, it serves him right; *j'y gagnai une pleurésie*, I caught pleurisy there; *la faim, le sommeil, me gagne*, I am beginning to feel hungry, sleepy; *la nuit nous gagnera*, night will overtake us; *y gagner*, to profit by it.—*v.i.* To spread, to extend, to gain (*à*); to improve, to advance. *Gagner à être connu*, to improve upon acquaintance; *qui épargne gagne*, a penny saved is a penny earned. **se gagner**, *v.r.* To be gained, earned, or won; to be catching, to be contagious.

gai [ge], *a.* (*fem.* **gaie**) Gay, merry, mirthful, cheerful, blithe; lively, exhilarating, pleasant; gaudy, bright, vivid (of colours); (*Naut.*) easy, free. *Avoir le vin gai*, to be merry when in one's cups; *être fort gai*, to be in excellent spirits; *gai comme un pinson*, as gay as a lark; *gai comme un bonnet de nuit*, as dull as ditchwater; *temps gai*, exhilarating weather.

gaïac [ga'jak], *n.m.* Guaiacum. *Bois de gaïac*, lignum vitae; *gomme* or *résine de gaïac*, guaiacum.

gaiement or **gaîment** [gɛ'mɑ̃], *adv.* Gaily,

merrily, cheerfully; briskly, blithely, willingly, heartily. **gaieté** or **gaîté**, *n.f.* Gaiety, mirth, glee, cheerfulness, blitheness, mirthfulness, good humour; a youthful frolic. *Cheval qui a de la gaieté*, mettlesome horse; *de gaieté de cœur*, out of sheer wantonness.

gaillard (1) [ga'jaːr], *n.m.* (*Naut.*) Castle. *Gaillard d'arrière*, quarter-deck; *gaillard d'avant*, forecastle; *sur le gaillard d'avant*, before the mast.

gaillard (2) [ga'jaːr], *a.* (*fem.* **gaillarde** (1)) Strong, vigorous; jolly, merry, lively; wanton; broad; gallant, bold, free; cool, fresh (of the wind). *Vent gaillard*, cool wind.—*n.m.* Lively, merry, jovial fellow; strapping blade, jolly dog. *Gaillard résolu*, determined dog; *gros gaillard*, big fellow. (With admiration) *C'est un gaillard!* some chap! (with anger, irony, etc.) *Je te tiens, mon gaillard!* I have got you, my man!

gaillarde (2) [ga'jard], *n.f.* *Galliard (dance); (*Print.*) brevier; (*fam.*) a strapping wench; (*Bot.*) Gaillardia (a genus of daisies).

gaillardement [gajardə'mɑ̃], *adv.* Joyously, merrily, blithely; boldly, gallantly.

gaillardie [gajar'di], *n.f.* (*Bot.*) Gaillardia.

gaillardise [gajar'diːz], *n.f.* Sprightliness, liveliness, mirth, jollity; broad, free, wanton language, risky story.

gaillet [ga'jɛ], *n.m.* (*Bot.*) Common name of fifteen species of *Galium*, such as *caille-lait*, rennet; *gratteron*, catch-weed, goose-grass.

gailletin [gaj'tɛ̃], *n.m.* Nuts (of coal), also called *tête de moineau*. **gaillette**, *n.f.* Cobbles (of coal).

gaîment [GAIEMENT].

gain [gɛ̃], *n.m.* Gain, profit, advantage; earnings, emolument, lucre; winnings; success, victory. *Amour du gain*, love of lucre; *avoir gain de cause*, to carry the day, to win; *donner gain de cause à*, to yield to (someone); *gain de jeu*, winnings; *gain net*, clear gain, net profit; *gains nuptiaux* or *de survie*, (*Law*) whatever is left to the survivor (husband or wife); *se retirer sur son gain*, to retire while still winning; *vivre de son gain*, to live by one's winnings.

gainage [gɛ'naːʒ], *n.m.* Sheathing, sleeving.

gaine, *n.f.* Sheath; foundation garment; case (of a clock etc.); (*Bot.*) ocrea; (*Arch.*) terminal; (*Mach.*) sheath, sleeve. (*Naut.*) *Gaine de pavillon*, halyard sheath. **gainer**, *v.t.* To sheath, to cover tightly. **gainerie**, *n.f.* Sheath-making, scabbard-making.

gainier, *n.m.* Sheath-maker, scabbard-maker; judas-tree.

gaîté [GAIETÉ].

gala [ga'la], *n.m.* Gala. *Habits de gala*, full or court dress.

galactique [galak'tik], *a.* (*Astron.*) Galactic.

galactomètre [galaktɔ'mɛtr], *n.m.* Lactometer. **galactophage**, *a.* Galactophagous.—*n.* Galactophagist. **galactose**, *n.f.* Galactose.

galamment [gala'mɑ̃], *adv.* Gallantly, with gallantry, courteously; gracefully, handsomely, nobly.

galandage [galɑ̃'daːʒ], *n.m.* Brick partition.

galanga [galɑ̃'ga], *n.m.* (*Bot.*) Galingale.

galant [ga'lɑ̃], *a.* (*fem.* **-ante**) Attentive to ladies; pleasing; elegant; correct, tasteful; courteous, polite, complimentary, flattering. *C'est un galant homme*, he is a man of honour;

en galant homme, like a gentleman, gallantly; *femme galante*, courtesan, gay woman; *humeur galante*, gay humour; *un billet galant*, a love-letter; *un homme galant*, a courteous man, ladies' man.—*n.m.* Gallant; wooer, sweetheart, suitor. lover. *Faire le galant*, to court the ladies; *un vert galant*, an elderly ladies' man. **galanterie**, *n.f.* Politeness, elegance; gallantry (towards the ladies); flattering, courteous compliment or present; intrigue, love-affair; courtesan's profession. *Ce n'est qu'une galanterie*, it is but a compliment; *dire des galanteries*, to pay compliments (to a lady).

galanthe [gaˈlɑ̃:t] or **galanthus**, *n.m.* Snowdrop.

galantin [galɑ̃ˈtɛ̃], *n.m.* Fop, coxcomb.

galantine [galɑ̃ˈtin], *n.f.* Galantine.

galapiat [galaˈpja], *n.m.* (*dial.*) Good-for-nothing, young ruffian.

Galatie [galaˈsi], *f.* Galatia.

galaxie [galakˈsi], *n.f.* Galaxy, Milky Way.

galbanum [galbaˈnɔm], *n.m.* Galbanum.

galbe [galb], *n.m.* (*Arch.*) Entasis; graceful curve, outline, or contour. *Avoir du galbe*, *être galbé*, to be shapely, to have a good figure. **galber**, *v.t.* To shape, to accentuate contours.

gale [gal], *n.f.* Scabies; itch; scab; mange; scurf (of vegetables, fruit, etc.). *Être méchant comme la gale*, to be very spiteful.

galé [gaˈle], *n.m.* Sweet-gale, bog-myrtle.

galéasse or **galéace** [galeˈas], *n.f.* (*Naut.*) Galleass.

galée [gaˈle], *n.f.* *Small galleass; (*Print.*) galley.

galéga [galeˈga], *n.m.* (*Bot.*) Galega, goat's rue.

galène [gaˈlɛ:n], *n.f.* Galena. *Fausse galène*, mock-lead; *galène de fer*, wolfram; *poste à galène*, crystal set.

galénique [galeˈnik], *a.* (*Med.*) Galenic. **galénisme**, *n.m.* Galenism. **galéniste**, *n.m.* Galenist.

galéopsis [galeɔpˈsis], or **galéopside**, *n.m.* (*Bot.*) Hemp-nettle; stinging nettle.

galère [gaˈlɛ:r], *n.f.* Galley; *pl.* galleys, the hulks, imprisonment with hard labour; (*fig.*) drudgery. *C'est une vraie galère*, it's a hell on earth; *être condamné aux galères*, to be condemned to the galleys; *qu'allait-il faire dans cette galère?* whatever was he doing there? *vogue la galère!* come what may! let's chance it! here goes!

galerie [galˈri], *n.f.* Gallery, long room; corridor; picture-gallery; balcony; (*Theat.*) upper circle, gallery; (*fig.*) spectators, lookers on, company; (*Naut.*) stern-gallery; (*Mining*) level, drift, adit, heading; (*Furniture etc.*) beading, rim, cornice (for curtains); fret (of hearth fire). *Faire galerie*, to look on, to be a wallflower; *galerie d'écoute*, (*Mil.*) listening gallery; *galerie de tableaux*, picture-gallery; (*Ten., Theat.*) *jouer pour la galerie*, to play to the gallery.

galérien [galeˈrjɛ̃], *n.m.* Galley-slave, convict.

galerne [gaˈlɛrn], *n.f.* (*W. dial.*) West-north-westerly wind.

galet [gaˈlɛ], *n.m.* Pebble, shingle; friction-roller. *Plage de galets*, shingly beach. *Jeu de galets*, shovel-board.

galetas [galˈta], *n.m. inv.* Garret, attic; (*fig.*) hole, hovel.

galette [gaˈlɛt], *n.f.* Broad thin cake; sea-biscuit; flat cake of saltpetre and charcoal and other substance; (*slang*) brass, dough. *Galette des Rois*, Twelfth-night cake; *galette d'avoine*, bannock; *galette de sarrasin*, buckwheat pancake. *Plat comme une galette*, flat as a pancake. **galetteux, galettard,** *a.* (*slang*) Rich, well off.

galeux [gaˈlø], *a.* (*fem.* **galeuse**) Itchy; scabby; mangy; scurfy (of plants, trees, etc.). *Brebis galeuse*, scabby sheep; (*fig.*) black sheep; *chien galeux*, mangy dog; *il ne faut qu'une brebis galeuse pour infecter un troupeau*, one vicious person will infect a whole company.—*n.* Mangy person.

galhauban [galoˈbɑ̃], *n.m.* (*Naut.*) Backstay. *Galhaubans volants*, preventer backstays; *rides de galhaubans*, lanyards of the backstays.

galibot [galiˈbo], *n.m.* Pit-boy.

Galilée [galiˈle], *m.* Galileo. **La Galilée,** *f.* Galilaea, Galilee.

galimafrée [galimaˈfre], *n.f.* (*Cook.*) Hotchpotch.

galimatias [galimaˈtja], *n.m.* Pompous nonsense; balderdash; farrago, rigmarole.

galion [gaˈljɔ̃], *n.m.* Galleon.

galiote [gaˈljɔt], *n.f.* Galliot, half-galley; Dutch covered barge (in canals); cross-bar to shut the hatchway cover.

galipette [galiˈpɛt], *n.f.* (*pop.*) *Faire la galipette*, to turn a somersault; *faire des galipettes*, to play pranks or antics.

galipot [galiˈpo], *n.m.* White resin. **galipoter,** *v.t.* To pitch with resin.

galle [gal], *n.f.* Gall. *Galle de chêne*, oak-gall; *noix de galle*, gall-nut.

gallérie [galeˈri], *n.f.* Bee-moth.

Galles [gal], **le Pays de,** *m.* Wales.

gallican [galiˈkɑ̃], *a.* (*fem.* **-ane**) Gallican; of the Church of France. **gallicanisme,** *n.m.* Gallicanism.

gallicisme [galiˈsism], *n.m.* Gallicism, French idiom.

gallinacé [galinaˈse], *a.* (*fem.* **-ée**) Gallinaceous.—*n.m. pl.* (*Zool.*) Order of gallinaceous birds. *galline, a.f. L'espèce galline*, cocks and hens.

gallique [gaˈlik], *a.* (*Chem.*) Gallic (acid).

gallois [gaˈlwa], *a.* (*fem.* **galloise**) Welsh; Welsh language.—*n.m.* (**Gallois,** *fem.* **Galloise**) Welshman, Welshwoman. **gallomane,** *n.* Gallomaniac.

gallophobe [galɔˈfɔb], *n.* Gallophobe. **gallophobie,** *n.f.* Gallophobia.

galoche [gaˈlɔʃ], *n.f.* Clog; (*Naut.*) shoe-block. *Un menton en galoche*, slipper chin.

galon [gaˈlɔ̃], *n.m.* Braid, *galloon; lace; grocer's round box; *pl.* (*Mil.*) bands (of officers), stripes (of N.C.O.s); (*Navy*) stripes (of officers), bands (in the Merchant Service); (*Naut.*) canvas band (on sail). *Arroser ses galons*, to give drinks to celebrate one's promotion; *rendre ses galons*, to resign one's rank. **galonner,** *v.t.* To lace, to adorn with gold- or silver-lace. *Habit galonné*, laced coat. **galonnier,** *n.m.* Gold- or silver-lace maker.

galop [gaˈlo], *n.m.* Gallop, galloping; name of dance and music thereto; (*slang*) scolding, reprimand. *Aller au grand galop*, to go full gallop; to run on without a pause; *demi-galop*, canter; *grand galop* or *galop de charge*, full gallop; *petit galop*, hand gallop, canter. **galopade**, *n.f.* Galloping, gallop. *À la galopade*, very quickly. **galoper**, *v.i.* To gallop; (*fig.*) to run on, to go very fast; to dance the galop. *Faire galoper un cheval*, to make a horse gallop.—*v.t.* To gallop (a horse etc.); to run after; to seize upon (of fear, illness, etc.). **galopin** [galɔ'pɛ̃], *n.m.* Errand-boy; (*fig.*) urchin, rogue, imp. **galoubet** [galu'bɛ], *n.m.* (*Prov.*) Three-holed flageolet. **galuchat** [galy'ʃa], *n.m.* Dogfish skin, sharkskin, etc. (for sheaths etc.). **galurin** [galy'rɛ̃], *n.m.* (*slang*) Hat, lid, tile. **galvanique** [galva'nik], *a.* Galvanic. *Pile galvanique*, galvanic battery. **galvanisation**, *n.f.* Galvanization. **galvaniser**, *v.t.* To galvanize; (*fig.*) to stimulate. **galvanisme**, *n.m.* Galvanism. **galvanomètre**, *n.m.* Galvanometer. **galvanoplastie**, *n.f.* Galvanoplasty; electroplating. **galvanoscope**, *n.m.* Galvanoscope.

galvaudage [galvo'da:ʒ], *n.m.* Lowering; muddling. **galvauder**, *v.t.* (*colloq.*) To mess, to ·muddle; to lower, to dishonour. **galvaudeur** or **galvaudeux**, *n.* (*fem.* **-euse**) Vagrant, rogue.

gamache [ga'maʃ], *n.f.* *Gaiter or legging worn in 16th cent.; black-cap (bird).

gamay, gamet [ga'mɛ], *n.m.* A variety of cheap vine grown in Côte d'Or (Burgundy).

gambade [gɑ̃'bad], *n.f.* Skip, bound; antic, gambol. *Faire des gambades*, to gambol about. **gambader**, *v.i.* To skip, to gambol, to romp, to frisk about.

gambe [gɑ̃:b], *n.f.* (*Naut.*) *pl.* Shrouds. *Viole de gambe*, viol da gamba.

gambette [gɑ̃'bɛt], *n.f.* Variety of sandpiper, redshank gambet.

gambeyer [gɑ̃be'je], **gambier** [gɑ̃'bje], *v.t.* (*Naut.*) To gybe.

Gambie [gɑ̃'bi], *f.* Gambia.

gambiller [gɑ̃bi'je], *v.i.* (*colloq.*) To kick about, to fidget; (*slang*) to dance. **gambilleur**, *n.m.* (*fem.* **gambilleuse**) Fidget; (*slang*) dancer.

gambit [gɑ̃'bi], *n.m.* Gambit.

gamelle [ga'mɛl], *n.f.* (*Mil.* and *Naut.*) Messtin, dixie; (*fig.*) company-mess. *Camarade de gamelle*, messmate; *manger à la même gamelle*, to eat out of the same dish, to mess together; *ramasser une gamelle*, (*slang*) to come a cropper.

gamète [ga'mɛt], *n.m.* (*Biol.*) Gamete.

gamin [ga'mɛ̃], *n.m.* Boy, youngster, urchin; street-boy, tomboy; (*fem.* **gamine**) hoyden, chit of a girl. **gaminer**, *v.i.* To play the *gamin* or *gamine*. **gaminerie**, *n.f.* Youth's prank or roguery.

gamme [gam], *n.f.* Gamut, scale. *Faire des gammes*, to practise scales; *changer de gamme*, to alter one's tone, to climb down; *chanter sa gamme à quelqu'un*, to lecture someone soundly; *toute une gamme de couleurs*, a whole gamut of colours.

gammée [ga'me], *a.f.* Used in 'croix gammée', swastika.

ganache (1) [ga'naʃ], *n.f.* Lower jaw (of a horse). —*a.* and *n.f.* (*colloq.*) Booby, blockhead. *Il est un peu ganache*, he is something of a bungler. *Vieille ganache*, old fogey, old dotard.

ganache (2) [ga'naʃ], *n.f.* Well-padded easy chair.

gandin [gɑ̃'dɛ̃], *n.m.* Dandy, dude, swell.

gandoura [gɑ̃du'ra], *n.f.* Long sleeveless shirt of the North Africans.

gang [gɑ̃g], *n.m.* Gang (of thieves).

ganga [gɑ̃'ga], *n.m.* Pin-tailed grouse. *Ganga des sables*, sand-grouse.

Gange [gɑ̃:ʒ], *m.* Ganges.

ganglion [gɑ̃gli'ɔ̃], *n.m.* Ganglion. **ganglionnaire**, *a.* Ganglionary.

gangrène [gɑ̃'grɛ:n], *n.f.* Gangrene, mortification; (*fig.*) corruption, canker. **gangrené**, *a.* (*fem.* **-ée**) Gangrened, mortified; (*fig.*) cankered, corrupt. **gangrener**, *v.t. irr.* (*conjugated like* AMENER) To gangrene, to mortify; (*fig.*) to corrupt. **se gangrener**, *v.r.* To become gangrened, to mortify; (*fig.*) to canker, to corrupt. **gangreneux**, *a.* (*fem.* **-euse**) Gangrenous, cankered.

gangster [gɑ̃gs'tɛ:r], *n.m.* Gangster. **gangstérisme**, *n.m.* Hooliganism.

gangue [gɑ̃:g], *n.f.* Gangue, vein-stone.

gannet [ga'nɛ], *n.m.* Gannet, solan-goose.

ganse [gɑ̃:s], *n.f.* Braid; cord, twist, etc., of silk, gold-thread, etc. (used to trim dresses, furniture, etc.); edging; string; loop (of diamonds); bight, eye (in a rope). *Ganse de soie*, silk cord.

gant [gɑ̃], *n.m.* Glove. *Aller à quelqu'un comme un gant*, to fit someone like a glove; *gant de Notre-Dame*, foxglove; *gant de Neptune*, glove-sponge; *gant-éponge*, washing glove; *il s'en donne les gants*, he takes the credit for it; *jeter le gant*, to throw down the gauntlet; *prendre des gants*, to act with tact; *ramasser* or *relever le gant*, to accept the challenge. **gantelé**, *a.* (*fem.* **-ée**) Wearing a gauntlet; mailed. *Campanule gantelée*, throatwort. **gantelée** or **ganteline**, *n.f.* Fox-glove; bellflower. **gantelet**, *n.m.* Gauntlet; handleather (used by workmen etc. to protect the hands); (*Surg.*) glove-bandage. **ganter**, *v.t.* To glove, to put gloves on; to fit (of gloves); (*fig.*) to fit, to suit. *Cela me gante*, or *me va comme un gant*, that suits me down to the ground. *Je gante du six et demi*, I take six and a half in gloves. **se ganter**, *v.r.* To put on one's gloves; to wear gloves (that fit well or ill); to get one's gloves (at so-and-so's). **ganterie**, *n.f.* Glove-making; glove-trade; glove-shop; glove-wear. **gantier**, *n.m.* (*fem.* **gantière**) Glover.

garage [ga'ra:ʒ], *n.m.* Parking, putting aside; storing away; (*Rail.*) shunting into the siding; siding; (on rivers, canals, etc.) putting into wet dock; (*Motor. etc.*) garage, storage-place; (*Row.*) boat-house. *Voie de garage*, siding. **garagiste**, *n.m.* Garage keeper; garage mechanic or owner.

garançage [garɑ̃'sa:ʒ], *n.m.* Madder dyeing.

garance [ga'rɑ̃:s], *n.f.* Madder; madder-root. —*a.* Madder-coloured. **garancer**, *v.t.* To dye with madder. **garanceur**, *n.m.* Madder-dyer. **garancière**, *n.f.* Madder-ground; madder-dyer's establishment.

garant [ga'rɑ̃], *n.m.* (*fem.* **-ante**) Guarantor, surety, warranter; guaranty, security, warrant voucher, proof; (*Naut.*) tackle-fall; running return. *Comme garant de*, as caution for; *j'en suis garant*, I answer for it; *se rendre garant* or *se porter garant de*, to guarantee or vouch for;

to go bail for. **garanti**, *a.* (*fem.* **garantie** (1)) Guaranteed, warranted.—*n.* Warrantee, person guaranteed. **garantie** (2), *n.f.* Guarantee, guaranty; making good, indemnity; security, safeguard; voucher, pledge. *Avec garantie*, guaranteed, warranted; *être garantie à quelqu'un de quelque chose*, to pledge oneself to someone for something; *sans garantie*, unwarranted. **garantir**, *v.t.* To guarantee, to warrant, to vouch for; to be security for, to ensure; to make good, to indemnify; to protect, to defend, to shield, to guard. *Garantir de tout défaut*, to warrant free from all defects; *garantir du froid*, to screen from cold; *garantir quelqu'un de toutes poursuites*, to secure someone against all demands; *je lui ai garanti le fait*, I vouched for the fact to him; *je ne vous garantis pas que ...*, I will not guarantee that.... **se garantir**, *v.r.* To secure oneself, to preserve oneself; to keep oneself, to steer clear (*de*). **garantissement**, *n.m.* Guaranteeing. **garantisseur**, *n.m.* Warranter.

garbure [gar'byːr], *n.f.* (*S.W. dial.*) Soup of cabbage, ham, bacon and pickled goose.

garce [gars], *n.f.* of *gars* (always in a bad sense). Bitch, drab, trollop.

garcette [gar'set], *n.f.* (*Naut.*) Gasket; rope's end.

garçon [gar'sɔ̃], *n.m.* Boy, lad; young fellow; bachelor; journeyman, workman; shop-boy, shop-man; porter, office-boy; waiter; stable-boy, ostler, groom; servant; steward (on ship). *Bon garçon*, good, amiable fellow, decent chap; *brave garçon*, worthy fellow, trump; *dîner de garçons*, stag-dinner or party; *garçon de cabine*, cabin-steward; *garçon d'honneur*, best man, groom's man; *garçon tailleur*, journeyman tailor; *garçon manqué*, tomboy; *vieux garçon*, bachelor. **garçonne**, *n.f.* Hoyden, fast flapper. **garçonner**, *v.i.* To hoyden, romp (of girls). **garçonnet**, *n.m.* Little boy. **garçonnier** (*fem.* -ière), *a.* Boyish (usually derogatory). **garçonnière**, *n.f.* Bachelor's rooms; (rare) hoyden; romp, tomboy.

garde (1) [gard], *n.f.* Keeping, safe-keeping, care; defence, protection, guard; custody, charge, watch; watching, watch-keeping; heed, attention; nurse; hilt (of sword); ward (of lock); fly-leaf (of books); end-paper; covering card (at cards). *À la garde!* guard, guard! watch, watch! *avoir en garde*, to have in one's keeping; *avoir la garde d'un poste*, to have the custody or defence of a post; *descendre de garde*, to come off guard; *donner en garde à quelqu'un*, to commit to someone's keeping; *droits de garde*, bank-charges; *en garde!* parry! *être de garde*, to be on guard (of a soldier), to be on duty (of a doctor, a nurse); *être* or *se tenir sur ses gardes*, to be upon one's guard; *faire bonne garde*, to keep good watch; *faire la garde*, to be on guard; *fruit de garde*, fruit that will keep; *garde à vous!* attention! *garde d'enfants*, children's nurse; *il a toujours garde à carreau*, he always has a card up his sleeve, he is always ready for every emergency; *j'ai été trop loin sans y prendre garde*, I went too far without realizing it; *jusqu'à la garde*, up to the hilt; *la garde descendante*, the guard coming off duty; *la garde montante*, the relieving guard; *monter*

la garde, to mount guard; *n'avoir garde de faire une chose*, to be far from doing a thing, not to be fool enough to do a thing; *ne prenez pas garde à moi*, don't mind me; *prenez garde à cela*, take care of that; *prenez garde de tomber*, take care not to fall; *mind you don't fall*; *prenez garde qu'on ne vous trompe*, mind they don't cheat you; *relever la garde*, to relieve guard. *La Garde*, the Guards; *la Garde à cheval*, the Horse-guards; *la garde du drapeau*, a colour party.

garde (2) [gard], *n.m.* Guard, guardsman, lifeguardsman; keeper, warder, guardian, watchman. *Garde champêtre*, rural constable; *garde des rôles* or *des archives*, master of the rolls; *garde des sceaux*, keeper of the seals, minister of Justice; **garde du commerce*, sheriff's officer, bailiff; *garde du corps*, lifeguardsman; *garde forestier*, ranger, forester; *garde maritime*, coast-guard; *garde national*, national guard; *les gardes du corps*, the lifeguards. **garde-à-vous**, *n.m. inv.* (*Mil.*) Position at attention. *Être au garde-à-vous*, to stand to attention. *Garde à vous, fixe!* Eyes front! **garde-barrière**, *n.m.* (*pl. unchanged* or **gardes-barrières**) (*Rail.*) Signalman at level-crossing. **garde-bois** [GARDE FORESTIER]. **garde-boue**, *n.m. inv.* Mudguard (of a bicycle etc.), splashboard (of car). **garde-boutique**, *n.m.* (*pl. unchanged* or **garde-boutiques**) Unsaleable article; old shopkeeper. **garde-cendre** or **garde-cendres**, *n.m. inv.* Fender, fire-guard. **garde-chasse**, *n.m.* (*pl. unchanged* or **gardes-chasses**) Game-keeper. **garde-chiourme**, *n.m.* (*pl. unchanged* or **gardes-chiourme**) Overseer of convict-gangs; warder. **garde-corps**, *n.m. inv.* Rail, hand-rail; (*Naut.*) life-line. **garde-côte** or **-côtes**, *n.m.* (*pl.* **garde-** or **gardes-côtes**) Guard-ship, coast-guard. **garde-crotte**, *n.m. inv.* Splash-board, mudguard. **garde-feu**, *n.m.* (*pl. unchanged* or **garde-feux**) Fire-guard; fender. **garde-fou**, *n.m.* (*pl.* **garde-fous**) Parapet (of bridges, quays, etc.); rail, railings. **garde-frein**, *n.m.* (*pl.* **garde-freins** or **gardes-freins**) Brakesman. **garde-ligne**, *n.m.* (*pl.* **garde-lignes** or **gardes-lignes**) Watchman on railway. **garde-magasin**, *n.m.* (*pl. unchanged* or **garde-magasins**) Warehouse-keeper, warehouseman, storekeeper. **garde-malade** *n.* (*pl. unchanged* or **gardes-malades**) Sick-nurse, attendant. **garde-manger**, *n.m. inv.* Larder, pantry, meat (or provision) safe. **garde-meuble**, *n.m.* (*pl. unchanged* oi **garde-meubles**) Furniture repository. **garde-pêche**, *n.m.* (*pl.* **gardes-pêche**) River-keeper, water-bailiff; (*pl.* **garde-pêche**) conservancy boat. **garde-port**, *n.m.* (*pl.* **gardes-port** or **gardes-ports**) Harbour-master.

garder [gar'de], *v.t.* To keep, to preserve; to withhold, to retain, to keep for oneself; to watch over, to tend, to take care of, to look after, to nurse; to guard, to protect, to defend; to keep from escaping; to observe (silence etc.); to remain in or at; to maintain, to keep up; to lay up, to save; to keep down, to keep on one's stomach. *Dieu m'en garde*, God forbid! *garder à vue*, not to lose sight of; *garder la bienséance*, to observe decency;

garder la chambre, to keep to one's room; garder la maison, to take care of the house, to stay indoors; garder les bestiaux, to tend cattle; garder les enjeux, to keep the stakes; garder pour soi, to keep for oneself; garder sa dignité or son rang, to maintain one's dignity or one's rank; garder sous clef, to keep locked up; garder un malade, to nurse a sick person; garder un secret, to keep a secret; gardez votre place, keep your place; je garde cela pour moi, I keep that for myself.—v.i. To avoid, to prevent. Gardez qu'on ne vous soupçonne, don't let anyone suspect you. se garder, v.r. To keep, to last; to keep down, to keep in; to beware, to take care not to; to abstain, to forbear, to refrain (de); to guard. Ce fruit ne peut se garder longtemps, this fruit will not keep long; gardez-vous bien de faire cela, mind you don't do that; il faut savoir se garder à carreau, we must always be prepared for emergencies.

garderie [gardə'ri], n.f. Day-nursery; beat of a keeper.

garde-robe (1) [gardə'rɔb], n.m. (pl. **garde-robes**) Apron; overall. **garde-robe** (2), n.f. (pl. **garde-robes**) Wardrobe (closet or clothes); water-closet, privy; stool, motions. **garde-roues**, n.m. (pl. unchanged or **gardes-roues**) Paddle-box; [GARDE-CROTTE (GARDE (2))]. **garde-temps**, n.m. inv. Chronometer.

gardeur [gar'dœːr], n.m. (fem. **-euse**) Herdboy or girl, keeper, tender. Gardeur de porcs, swineherd; gardeuse d'enfants, baby-farmer, baby-sitter; gardeuse d'oies, goose-girl.

***garde-vaisselle** [gardvɛ'sɛl], n.m. (pl. unchanged) Yeoman of the scullery. **garde-vente**, n.m. (pl. unchanged or **garde-ventes**) Wood-merchant's agent. **garde-voie**, n.m. (pl. **gardes-voie**) Railway-watchman; military railway-watchman. **garde-vue**, n.m. inv. Screen, lamp-shade; eye-shade.

gardian [gar'djã], n.m. (S. Fr.) Cowherd in the Camargue.

gardien [gar'djɛ̃], n.m. (fem. **gardienne**) Guardian, keeper, ward, door-keeper; protector, trustee; superior (of a Franciscan convent). Gardien de but, goal-keeper (football); gardien de musée, attendant (of museum); gardien de nuit, night-watchman; gardien de prison, warder; gardien de la paix, policeman (in Paris); gardien de phare, lighthouse-keeper; gardien judiciaire, bailiff's man, broker's man; gardien des Cinq Ports, Warden of the Cinque Ports.—a. Tutelary, guardian. Ange gardien, guardian angel. **gardiennage**, n.m. Guarding (of harbours, railways, etc.).

gardon [gar'dɔ̃], n.m. Roach. Gardon rouge, rudd.

gare (1) [gaːr], int. Beware; take care; look out. Crier gare! to give warning; sans crier gare, without warning, out of the blue; gare là! look out there! gare l'eau! mind the water!

gare (2) [gaːr], n.f. Railway-station, terminus; (Am.) depot; (wet) dock, basin (canal), wharf; siding. Chef de gare, station-master; gare aérienne, air-terminal; gare d'évitement, siding; gare de triage, marshalling yard; gare de manœuvre, sorting depot; gare de voyageurs, passenger-station; gare maritime, harbour station; le train est en gare, the train is in.

garenne [ga'rɛn], n.f. Warren. Lapin de garenne, wild rabbit.

garer [ga're], v.t. To side-track (a train); to garage or to park (a car); to put (an aeroplane) into a hangar. Garer un bateau, to dock a boat. se garer, v.r. To keep or get out of the way; to take cover; to park.

Gargantua [gargã'tɥa], n.m. Gargantua; glutton. **gargantuesque**, a. Gluttonous.

gargariser (se) [gargari'ze], v.r. To gargle one's throat, to gargle. Se gargariser de grands mots (fig.), to revel in high-flown words. **gargarisme**, n.m. Gargle, throat-wash; gargling.

gargote [gar'gɔt], n.f. Cheap eating-house, cook-shop. **gargoter**, v.i. To eat in cheap cook-shops; to cook wretchedly. **gargotier**, n.m. (fem. **gargotière**) Keeper of a cook-shop; bad cook.

gargouille [gar'guːj], n.f. Gargoyle, water-spout; gutter-spout, drain-pipe.

gargouillement [garguj'mã], n.m. Rumbling (in the stomach); gurgling, bubbling (of water). **gargouiller**, v.i. To rumble, to gurgle; to dabble, to paddle. **gargouillis**, n.m. Gurgling (of water). **gargoulette**, n.f. Goglet, gugglet. Boire à la gargoulette, to drink out of the jug.

gargousse [gar'gus], n.f. Cannon-cartridge. Papier à gargousse, cartridge-paper. **gargoussier**, n.m., or **gargoussière**, n.f. Cartridge-box.

garigue or **garrigue** [ga'rig], n.f. Waste land, moor (in Languedoc).

garnement [garnə'mã], n.m. Scapegrace, scamp, (young) rogue.

garni [gar'ni], a. (fem. **-ie**) Furnished; trimmed, garnished. Chambres garnies, furnished apartments; choucroute garnie, sauerkraut with sausages; bourse (bien) garnie, well-lined purse.—n.m. Furnished lodgings or house. Être en garni or loger en garni, to live in lodgings; loueur or loueuse en garni, lodging-house keeper.

garnir [gar'niːr], v.t. To furnish, to provide with necessary things, to stock; to ornament, to trim, to garnish, to adorn; to line, to fill; to mount; to quilt; (Angling) to bait. Garnir un cheval, to harness a horse; garnir une boutique, to stock a shop; garnir une chaudière, to stoke a boiler; garnir une chemise, to trim a shirt; garnir un fort, to man a fort; garnir une maison, to furnish a house; garnir une robe, to trim a gown. se garnir, v.r. To furnish or provide oneself; to stock oneself; to fill, to be filled; to protect oneself.

garnisaire [garni'zɛːr], n.m. *Bailiff's man; member of a garrison.

garnison [garni'zɔ̃], n.f. Garrison, station; bailiff's men. Troupes en garnison, garrisoned troops; ville de garnison, garrison-town.

garnissage [garni'saːʒ] or **garnissement**, n.m. Trimming (of clothes etc.); facing. **garnisseur**, n.m. (fem. **-euse**) Trimmer.

garniture [garni'tyːr], n.f. Furniture, trimmings; trimming, garniture, ornaments; garnish, garnishing; setting; lining; set; packing; (Naut.) rigging. Garniture de bureau, writing set; garniture de cheminée, set of chimney ornaments; garniture de foyer, set of fire-irons; garniture de frein, (Motor.) brake-lining; garniture de rideau, valance;

garniture de toilette, toilet-set; *garniture d'une pompe*, pump-gear; *la garniture d'une chemise*, the trimming of a shirt; *garniture d'une épée*, sword ornaments; *une garniture de diamants*, a set of diamonds.

garou (1) [ga'ru], *n.m.* (*Bot.*) Mezereon, spurge-flax.

garou (2) [LOUP-GAROU].

garrigue [GARIGUE].

garrot (1) [ga'ro], *n.m.* Withers (of a horse etc.). *Cheval blessé sur le garrot*, witherwrung horse.

garrot (2) [ga'ro], *n.m.* Tightener, garrot; (*Surg.*) tourniquet; [GARROTTE].

garrot (3) [ga'ro], *n.m.* Arctic duck, garrot.

garrottage [garɔ'ta:ʒ], *n.m.* Garrotting.

garrotte [ga'rɔt], *n.f.* Garrotting, strangulation; garrotte. **garrotter**, *v.t.* To tie down, to pinion; to garrotte, to strangle.

garrulité [garyli'te], *n.f.* Garrulity, loquacity.

gars [ga], *n.m.* Lad, stripling, young fellow.

Gascogne [gas'kɔɲ], *f.* Gascony. *Le Golfe de Gascogne*, the Bay of Biscay.

gascon [gas'kɔ̃], *a.* (*fem.* **-onne**) Gascon.— *n.m.* Gascon language; (**Gascon**, *fem.* **-onne**) Gascon; (*fig.*) boaster, braggart. *Une offre de Gascon*, (*fam.*) a hollow promise.

gasconnade [gaskɔ'nad], *n.f.* Gasconade, boast, brag. **gasconner**, *v.i.* To speak with a Gascon accent; to gasconade, to brag.

gaspillage [gaspi'ja:ʒ], *n.m.* Waste, squandering. **gaspiller**, *v.t.* To waste, to lavish, to squander, to fritter away. *Gaspiller son argent*, to squander one's money; *gaspiller son temps*, to waste one's time. **gaspilleur**, *a.* (*fem.* **-euse**) Wasting, squandering.—*n.* Waster, squanderer, spendthrift.

gaster [gas'tɛːr], *n.m.* (*Anat.*) Stomach. **gastéropode**, *n.m.* (*Zool.*) Gasteropod. **gastralgie**, *n.f.* (*Path.*) Gastralgia. **gastrique**, *a.* Gastric. *Embarras gastrique*, stomach disorder. **gastrite**, *n.f.* Gastritis. **gastro-**, *comb. form.* Gastro-. **gastro-entérique**, *a.* Gastro-enteric. **gastro-entérite**, *n.f.* Gastro-enteritis. **gastronome**, *n.m.* Gastronome, gastronomer. **gastronomie**, *n.f.* Gastronomy. **gastronomique**, *a.* Gastronomic. **gastrostomie**, *n.f.* Gastrostomy. **gastro-vasculaire**, *a.* Gastro-vascular.

gastrula [gastry'la], *n.f.* (*Biol.*) Gastrula. **gastrulation**, *n.f.* Gastrulation.

gât [ga], *n.m.* Landing-steps.

gatangier [CHIEN DE MER].

gâté [ga'te], *a.* (*fem.* **-ée**) Marred, deteriorated, damaged, tainted; (*fig.*) spoiled. *Dents gâtées*, decayed teeth; *enfant gâté*, spoiled child; *viande gâtée*, tainted meat.

gâteau [ga'to], *n.m.* (*pl.* **gâteaux**) Cake; object or piece of material like a cake. *Avoir part au gâteau*, to share in the booty; to have a finger in the pie; *gâteau de miel*, honeycomb; *gâteau des rois*, Twelfth-night cake; *partager le gâteau*, to go halves; *trouver la fève au gâteau*, to have good luck in everything.

gâte-maison [gatmɛ'zɔ̃], or **gâte-ménage**, *n.m.* Servant who does his work too well. **gâte-métier**, *n.m.* (*pl. unchanged* or **gâte-métiers**) Spoil-trade, underseller. **gâte-papier**, *n. inv.* Scribbler, poor writer. **gâte-pâte**, *n. inv.* Bad pastry-cook; (*fig.*) bungler, botcher.

gâter [ga'te], *v.t.* To spoil, to damage, to injure, to impair, to mar; to taint, to corrupt to deprave, to make worse. *Gâter du papier*, to waste or blot paper, to scribble; *gâter la main*, to spoil one's hand; *gâter le métier*, to work or sell too cheap, to undercut; *gâter un enfant*, to spoil a child; *la grêle a gâté les vignes*, hail has damaged the vines; *le soleil gâte la viande*, the sun taints meat. **se gâter**, *v.r.* To taint, to spoil, to get spoiled; to break up (of weather). *Ce vin commence à se gâter*, that wine is beginning to spoil; *le temps se gâte*, the weather is breaking up.

gâterie [ga'tri], *n.f.* Spoiling (of children), foolish indulgence. **gâte-sauce**, *n.m.* (*pl.* **gâte-sauce** or **gâte-sauces**) Scullion; (*colloq.*) bad cook. **gâte-tout**, *n. inv.* Marall. **gâteur**, *n.m.* (*fem.* **gâteuse** (1)) Spoiler, waster.—*n.f.* Long and ample overcoat, ulster. **gâteux**, *n.m.* (*fem.* **-euse** (2)) Idiot (one who has lost control over the excretory organs); in senile decay.

gâtine [ga'tin], *n.f.* Marsh-land.

gâtisme [ga'tism], *n.m.* (*fam.*) Senile decay.

gatte [gat], *n.f.* (*Naut.*) Manger.

gattilier [gati'lje], *n.m.* (*Bot.*) Agnus-castus.

gauche [go:ʃ], *a.* Left; (*fig.*) crooked, ugly; clumsy, awkward, uncouth, bashful. *Coup de la main gauche*, left-handed blow; *des manières gauches*, clumsy manners; *être à gauche*, to be on the left; *le côté gauche*, the left side; *mariage de la main gauche*, left-handed marriage; *un air gauche*, an awkward air.—*n.f.* Left hand, left side; (*Mil.*) left wing, left flank, left wheel. *À gauche*, on the left, to the left; *prenez à gauche*, turn to the left. *Jusqu'à la gauche*, (*Mil.*) to the end (of the line), to the last. (*Polit.*) *Parti de gauche*, left-wing party.—*n.m.* Awkwardness, clumsiness; (*Box.*) left. *Direct du gauche*, straight left. **gauchement**, *adv.* Awkwardly, clumsily. **gaucher**, *a.* (*fem.* **-ère**) Left-handed.—*n.* Left-handed person.

gaucherie [go:'ʃri], *n.f.* Awkwardness, clumsiness; clumsy action, blunder.

gauchir [go'ʃiːr], *v.i.* To turn aside, to go away; to flinch; to become warped; (*fig.*) to dodge, to shuffle.—*v.t.* To warp. **gauchissement**, *n.m.* Warping. *Gauchissement des ailes*, warped wings (of an aeroplane); *commande de gauchissement*, warp(ing) control.

gaudage [go'da:ʒ], *n.m.* Dyeing with weld.

gaude [go:d], *n.f.* Weld. *pl.* Yellow weed; hasty porridge.

gaudir (se) [go'diːr], *v.r.* To rejoice, to make merry; (*fig.*) to make fun of, to deride.

gaudriole [godri'ɔl], *n.f.* Broad joke, coarse jest.

gaufrage [go'fra:ʒ], *n.m.* Goffering.

gaufre [go:fr], *n.f.* Wafer, waffle (thin cake). *Gaufre de miel*, honeycomb; *moule à gaufres*, waffle-iron; (*pop.*) duffer.

gaufrer [go'fre], *v.t.* To goffer. *Fer à gaufrer*, goffering-iron. **gaufrette**, *n.f.* Small wafer. **gaufreur**, *n.m.* (*fem.* **-euse**) Gofferer.

gaufrier [gofri'e], *n.m.* Waffle-iron.

gaufrure [go'fryːr], *n.f.* Goffering.

gaulage [go'la:ʒ], *n.m.* Beating (a fruit-tree etc.)

Gaule [go:l], *f.* Gaul.

gaule [go:l], *n.f.* Pole, switch, long stick; fishing-rod; pump-handle. **gauler**, *v.t.* To beat (trees) with a long pole; to knock down (fruit).

gaulis [goˈli], *n.m.* Copse of brushwood; *pl.* young trees.

gaullisme [goˈlism], *n.m.* Policy, or partisanship of General de Gaulle. **gaulliste**, *n.* and *a.* Follower of General de Gaulle.

gaulois [goˈlwa], *a.* (*fem.* -oise) Gaulish, Gallic; (*fig.*) old-fashioned, free. *Esprit gaulois*, Gallic wit; *propos gaulois*, free expressions.—*n.m.* Gallic language. *C'est du gaulois*, it is an old-fashioned expression; (**gaulois**, *fem.* -oise) Gaul (person). **gauloiserie**, *n.f.* Coarse joke.

gaupe [goːp], *n.f.* *Slut; trollop, drab.

gaur [goˈr], *n.m.* Gaur; Indian urus.

gausser (se) [goˈse], *v.r.* (*colloq.*) To banter, to chaff, to make game (*de*). **gausserie**, *n.f.* Mockery, banter. **gausseur**, *a.* (*fem.* -euse) Bantering.—*n.* Banterer.

Gauthier [goˈtje], *m.* Walter.

gavache [gaˈvaʃ], *n.m.* (*S.W. dialect*) Coward, dastard.

gavage [gaˈvaːʒ], *n.m.* Cramming (of poultry); gorging.

gave [gaːv], *n.m.* Torrent, mountain stream (in the Pyrenees).—*n.f.* Crop (of birds).

gaver [gaˈve], *v.t.* (*colloq.*) To cram, to gorge (with food). **se gaver**, *v.r.* To cram oneself, to gorge.

gavial [gaˈvjal], *n.m.* (*pl.* -als) Gavial.

gavion [gaˈvjɔ̃] or **gaviot**, *n.m.* (*slang*) Throat.

gavotte [gaˈvɔt], *n.f.* Gavotte (dance).

gavroche [gaˈvrɔʃ], *n.m.* Parisian urchin.

gaz [gɑːz], *n.m.* Gas. *À la lumière du gaz*, by gas-light; *bec de gaz*; gas-burner; *compteur à gaz*, gas-meter; *éclairage au gaz*, lighting with gas; *fermer le gaz*, to turn off the gas; *gaz asphyxiant*, asphyxiating gas, poison-gas; *gaz hilarant*, laughing-gas; *gaz lacrymogène*, tear-gas; *gaz pauvre* or *à l'eau*, water-gas; *lustre à gaz*, gaselier; *ouvrir le gaz*, to turn on the gas; *réservoir de gaz*, gas-holder; *conduit de gaz*, gas-pipe; *obus à gaz*, gas-shell; *usine à gaz*, gas-works.

gaze [gɑːz], *n.f.* Gauze. **gazé**, *a.* (*fem.* -ée) Covered with gauze, veiled; softened, toned down; (*Mil.*) gassed (soldier).—*n.m.* Hawthorn butterfly.

gazéifier [gazeiˈfje], *v.t.* To gasify. **se gazéifier**, *v.r.* To gasify. **gazéiforme**, *a.* Gasiform.

gazelle [gaˈzɛl], *n.f.* Gazelle.

gazer (1) [gaˈze], *v.t.* To cover with gauze; (*fig.*) to veil, to gloss over, to tone down.

gazer (2) [gaˈze], *v.t.* (*Mil.*) To gas (men).

gazer (3) [gaˈze], *v.i.* To go fast (of a vehicle); to go strong. *Ça gaze*, it is going strong.

gazette [gaˈzɛt], *n.f.* Gazette, newspaper; (*fig.*) newsmonger, blab.

gazeux [gaˈzø], *a.* (*fem.* -euse) Gaseous, aerated. *Eau gazeuse*, effervescent or fizzy water.

gazier (1) [gaˈzje], *n.m.* Gas-fitter.

gazier (2) [gaˈzje], *n.m.* (*fem.* -ière) Gauze-maker.

gazogène [gazoˈʒɛn], *n.m.* Gazogene.—*a.* For making soda-water.

gazolène [gazoˈlɛn], **gazoléine**, or **gazoline**, *n.f.* Gasolene.

gazomètre [gazoˈmɛtr], *n.m.* Gasometer. **gazométrie**, *n.f.* Gasometry.

gazon [gaˈzɔ̃], *n.m.* Grass; sod, turf, sward; lawn. *Abonder en gazon*, to abound in grass; *gazon d'Olympe*, thrift; *gazon mousse*, mossy saxifrage; *gazons plaqués*, facing sods; *touffe de gazon*, divot. **gazonnant**, *a.* (*fem.* -ante) Producing grass; grassy, turfy. **gazonnement** or **gazonnage**, *n.m.* Turfing. **gazonner**, *v.t.* To cover with turf, to turf. **gazonneux**, *a.* (*fem.* **gazonneuse**) Turflike, turfy, swarded.

gazouillement [gazujˈmɑ̃], *n.m.* Chirping, warbling, twittering (of birds); purling, babbling (of a brook etc.); prattle (of children etc.). **gazouiller**, *v.i.* To chirp, to warble; to twitter; to prattle; to purl, to babble, to murmur; (*slang*) to stink, to hum, to pong. *Cet enfant commence à gazouiller*, that child is beginning to prattle.—*v.t.* To warble, twitter, or chirp (a song etc.). **gazouilleur**, *a.* (*fem.* -euse) Who warbles. **gazouillis**, *n.m.* Warbling, twittering, etc.

geai [ʒɛ], *n.m.* Jay; jackdaw. *Le geai paré des plumes du paon*, the jackdaw in borrowed feathers.

géant [ʒeˈɑ̃], *a.* (*fem.* **géante**) Gigantic.—*n.* Giant. *Aller à pas de géant*, to stride like a giant. *La Chaussée des Géants*, the Giant's Causeway; (*Cycl.*) *les géants de la route*, (*fam.*) the racers taking part in the Tour de France. **géantisme** [GIGANTISME].

gecko [ʒɛˈko], *n.m.* Gecko.

géhenne [ʒeˈɛn], *n.f.* Gehenna, hell.

geignant [ʒɛˈɲɑ̃], *a.* (*fem.* -ante) Moaning, whining, fretful, complaining. **geignard**, *a.* (*fem.* -arde) Always whining, querulous. **geignement**, *n.m.* Moan, whine.

geindre (1) [ʒɛ̃ːdr], *v.i. irr.* (*pres.p.* **geignant**, *p.p.* **geint**, *conjugated like* CRAINDRE) To moan, to whine, to fret, to complain.

geindre (2) [GINDRE].

geisha [ʒeˈʃa], *n.f.* Geisha.

gel [ʒɛl], *n.m.* Frost, freezing.

gélatine [ʒelaˈtin], *n.f.* Gelatine. **gélatiné** (*fem.* -ée), *a.* Gelatinized, coated with gelatine. **gélatiner**, *v.t.* To gelatinize. **gélatineux**, *a.* (*fem.* -euse) Gelatinous. **gélatinifier**, *v.t.* To gelatinate. **gélatiniforme**, *a.* Gelatiniform.

gelé [ʒəˈle], *a.* (*fem.* -ée) Frozen, cold; (*fig.*) indifferent, cold; (*Fin.*) frozen (capital). (*fam.*) *Je suis gelé*, I am quite frozen.

gelée [ʒəˈle], *n.f.* Frost; jelly; aspic. *Gelée blanche*, white frost, hoar-frost, rime; *gelée de groseille*, red-currant jelly; *saumon en gelée*, salmon in aspic.

geler [ʒəˈle], *v.t.* To freeze, to convert into ice; to frost-bite. *Ils gèleront nos crédits à l'étranger*, they will freeze our credits abroad. —*v.i.* To freeze. *La rivière a gelé*, the river is frozen; *les doigts lui ont gelé*, his fingers were frozen. *Il gèle à pierre fendre*, it is freezing very hard. **se geler**, *v.r.* To freeze. **gélif**, *a.* (*fem.* -ive) Split or cracked by frost; that freezes easily.

gélignite [ʒeliˈɲit], *n.f.* Gelignite.

géline [ʒəˈlin], *n.f.* Hen, pullet.

gelinotte [ʒəliˈnɔt], *n.f.* Gelinotte des bois, hazel grouse; *gelinotte des Pyrénées*, pin-tailed sand grouse; *gelinotte des prairies*, (*Am.*) prairie chicken.

gélivure [ʒeliˈvyːr], *n.f.* Crack (caused by frost).

Gémeaux [ʒeˈmo], **les,** *n.m. pl.* (*Astron.*) Gemini, the Twins.

gémellaire, *a.* *Grossesse gémellaire,* twin pregnancy.

géminé [ʒemiˈne], *a.* (*fem.* **géminée**) (*Bot.*) Geminate, double. (*sch.*) *Première et seconde géminées,* Sixth and Fifth forms taught together; *écoles géminées,* co-educational schools; *consonnes géminées,* double consonant; (*Arch.*) *colonnes géminées,* twin columns. **géminer,** *v.t.* To geminate, to throw together.

gémir [ʒeˈmiːr], *v.i.* To groan, to moan; to sigh, to lament, to wail, to grieve, to repine; to creak (of wood); (*fig.*) to suffer. *Gémir de douleur,* to groan with pain; *gémir sous le joug,* to groan under the yoke; *gémir sur son sort,* to bemoan one's fate.—*v.t.* To groan (a message etc.). **gémissant,** *a.* (*fem.* **-ante**) Groaning, moaning; lamenting. **gémissement,** *n.m.* Groan, moan; (*fig.*) wail, lament, lamentation; murmuring, cooing (of pigeons etc.).

gemmage [ʒeˈmaːʒ], *n.m.* Tapping (of trees for resin).

gemmation [ʒemaˈsjɔ̃], *n.f.* Gemmation.

gemme [ʒem], *n.f.* Gem, precious stone; resin; (*Biol.*) gemma; (*Bot.*) bud, leaf-bud. *Sel gemme,* rock-salt. **gemmer,** *v.i.* To bud, to gemmate; to tap trees for resin. **gemmeur,** *n.m.* Tapper. **gemmifère,** *a.* Gemmiferous. **gemmiforme,** *a.* (*Bot.*) Bud-shaped. **gemmipare,** *a.* Gemmiparous. **gemmule,** *n.f.* Gemmule.

gémonies [ʒemoˈni], *n.f.* (*used only in pl.*) (*Rom. Ant.*) Gemonian stairs;(*fig.*) pillory, gibbet. *Vouer quelqu'un aux gémonies,* to expose someone to public condemnation or contempt.

génal [ʒeˈnal], *a.* (*fem.* **-ale,** *pl.* **-aux**) (*Anat.*) Pertaining to the cheek.

gênant [ʒeˈnɑ̃], *a.* (*fem.* **-ante**) Troublesome, in the way, inconvenient, embarrassing.

gencive [ʒɑ̃ˈsiv], *n.f.* Gum (of the teeth).

gendarme [ʒɑ̃ˈdarm], *n.m.* Gendarme (armed policeman); constable; virago (woman); spark; flaw (in a diamond). *C'est un vrai gendarme,* she is a regular termagant. **se gendarmer,** *v.r.* To make a violent protest; to get on one's high horse. **gendarmerie,** *n.f.* Gendarmery (armed police); constabulary (French horse and foot police); barracks of gendarmes. **gendarmeux,** *a.* (*fem.* **-euse**) Flawy, spotty (of gems).

gendre [ʒɑ̃ːdr], *n.m.* Son-in-law.

gène [ʒɛn], *n.m.* (*Biol.*) Gene.

gêne [ʒɛːn], *n.f.* *The question (torture), the rack; (*fig.*) constraint, uneasiness, inconvenience, annoyance; difficulty, trouble; narrow circumstances, financial difficulties, straits, penury. *Connaître la gêne,* to know what want is; *éprouver de la gêne (en face de quelqu'un),* to feel ill at ease (in someone's presence); *être dans la gêne,* to be badly off *or* hard up; *être sans gêne,* to be free and easy (to the point of rudeness); *mettre à la gêne,* *to put (someone) to the question, (*fig.*) to cause trouble or embarrassment to; *où il y a de la gêne il n'y a pas de plaisir,* there's nothing like making oneself at home; *il a fait preuve d'un sans-gêne!* he showed such a lack of consideration! **gêné,** *a.* (*fem.* **-ée**) Constrained, uneasy; embarrassed, ill

at ease; short of cash, hard up. *Air gêné,* constrained air; *n'être pas gêné,* to be too free or too familiar.

généalogie [ʒenealɔˈʒi], *n.f.* Genealogy; pedigree. **généalogique,** *a.* Genealogical. *Arbre généalogique,* family tree. **généalogiquement,** *adv.* Genealogically. **généalogiste,** *n.m.* Genealogist.

génépi [ʒeneˈpi] *or* **génipi,** *n.m.* *or* **armoise des glaciers,** (*Bot.*) Alpine mugwort, yarrow.

gêner [ʒɛːˈne], *v.t.* To constrain, to cramp, to constrict, to squeeze; to impede, to obstruct, to clog; to thwart, to restrain, to fetter, to trouble, to inconvenience, to incommode, to embarrass; to straiten, to make short of cash; to irk; to put out, to annoy. *Ce soulier me gêne,* this shoe pinches me; *est-ce que je vous gêne?* am I in your way? *la fumée vous gêne-t-elle?* do you mind my smoking? *il me gêne dans mes projets,* he thwarts me in my plans; *la présence de cet homme me gênait,* the presence of that man annoyed me. **se gêner,** *v.r.* To constrain oneself, to put oneself out, to put oneself to inconvenience. *Ne pas se gêner,* not to be embarrassed, to make oneself at home; *ne vous gênez pas,* don't stand upon ceremony; (*often iron.*) don't mind me; *ce n'est pas la peine de se gêner entre amis,* there is no need of ceremony among friends.

général [ʒeneˈral], *a.* (*fem.* **-ale** (1), *pl.* **-aux**) General, universal; vague. *En règle générale,* as a general rule; *répétition générale,* dress-rehearsal.—*adv. phr.* *En général,* in general, generally.—*n.m.* (*Mil.*) General. *Général de brigade,* brigadier-general; *général de division,* major-general; *général de corps d'armée,* lieutenant-general; (*Av.*) *général de brigade aérienne,* air commodore; *général de division aérienne,* air vice-marshal; *général de corps aérien,* air marshal. **généralat,** *n.m.* Generalship. **générale** (2), *n.f.* General's wife; drum-beat (to give alarm of fire etc.). *Battre la générale,* to sound the alarm. **généralement,** *adv.* Generally, in general. **généralisable,** *a.* Generalizable. **généralisateur,** *a.* (*fem.* **-trice**) Generalizing. **généralisation,** *n.f.* Generalization. **généraliser,** *v.t.* To generalize. **généralissime** [ʒeneraliˈsim], *n.m.* Generalissimo, commander-in-chief of allied armies. **généralité** [ʒeneraliˈte], *n.f.* Generality.

générateur [ʒeneraˈtœːr], *a.* (*fem.* **-trice**) Generating, generative.—*n.m.* Generator.—*n.f.* (*Geom.*) Generant. **génératif,** *a.* (*fem.* **-ive**) Generative.

génération [ʒeneraˈsjɔ̃], *n.f.* Generation; procreation. *De génération en génération,* from generation to generation.

générer [ʒeneˈre], *v.t. irr.* (*conjug. like* ACCÉLÉRER) To generate. **se générer,** *v.r.* To be generated.

généreusement [ʒenerøzˈmɑ̃], *adv.* Generously, bountifully, munificently; nobly, bravely.

généreux [ʒeneˈrø], *a.* (*fem.* **-euse**) Generous, liberal, fertile, bountiful; noble; courageous.

générique [ʒeneˈrik], *a.* Generic.—*n.m.* (*Cine.*) Credits. **génériquement,** *adv.* Generically.

générosité [ʒenerozˈite], *n.f.* Generosity, liberality; nobility of temper etc., magnanimity.

Gênes [ʒɛːn], *f.* Genoa.
genèse [ʒə'nɛːz], *n.f.* Genesis. **génésique,** *a.* Genetic (instinct etc.).
genestrolle [ʒənɛs'trɔl], *n.f.* [PETIT GENÊT].
genet [ʒə'nɛ], *n.m.* Jennet (Spanish horse).
genêt [ʒə'nɛ], *n.m.* (*Bot.*) Genista. *Genêt à balais,* broom; *genêt épineux,* furze, gorse, whin; *genêt des teinturiers* or *petit genêt,* or *genette,* dyer's greenweed, woodwaxen.
généthliaque [ʒenetli'ak], *a.* Genethliac.—*n.m.* Genethliac (birthday poem).
genêtière [ʒənɛ'tjɛːr], *n.f.* Broom-field.
génétique [ʒene'tik], *a.* Genetic (definition etc.).
genette (1) [ʒə'nɛt], *n.f.* Genet, civet cat.
genette (2) [ʒə'nɛt], *n.f.* Ring-curb or bit. *Monter à la genette,* to ride with short stirrups.
genette (3) [GENÊT].
gêneur [ʒɛːˈnœr], *n.* (*fem.* **-euse**) Intruder; spoil-sport.
Genève [ʒə'nɛv], *f.* Geneva.
genevois [ʒən'vwa], *a.* (*fem.* **-oise**) Genevese. —*n.f.* Sauce used with freshwater fish.
genévrette [ʒənɛ'vrɛt] or **genevrette,** *n.f.* Geneva, juniper liqueur.
genévrier [ʒənevri'e], *n.m.* Juniper-tree.
génial [ʒe'njal], *a.* (*fem.* **-iale,** *pl.* **-iaux**) Having genius, inspired.
géniculation [ʒenikyla'sjɔ̃], *n.f.* Geniculation.
géniculé [ʒeniky'le], *a.* (*fem.* **-ée**) (*Bot.*) Geniculate.
génie [ʒe'ni], *n.m.* Genius; spirit, nature, bent, talent; (*pej.*) knack; genie, demon, sylph; (*Mil.*) engineering, corps of engineers. *Le corps du génie,* the engineers; *école du Génie civil,* engineering college; *soldat du génie,* sapper; *le génie d'une langue,* the genius of a language; *mauvais génie,* evil genius; *suivre son génie,* to follow the bent of one's genius.
genièvre [ʒə'njeːvr], *n.m.* Juniper-berry; juniper-tree; gin. *Baies* or *grains de genièvre,* juniper-berries.
génisse [ʒe'nis], *n.f.* Heifer.
génital [ʒeni'tal], *a.* (*fem.* **-ale,** *pl.* **-aux**) Genital. *Organes génitaux,* genitals. **géniteur,** *a.* and *n.m.* Begetter. **génitif,** *n.m.* (*Gram.*) Genitive. *Au génitif,* in the genitive case. **géniture,** *n.f.* *Offspring.
génocide [ʒeno'sid], *n.m.* Genocide.
génois [ʒe'nwa], *a.* (*fem.* **génoise**) Genoese.
genope [ʒə'nɔp], *n.f.* (*Naut.*) Seizing, lashing, belaying; break-stop. **genoper,** *v.t.* To seize, to lash, to belay.
genou [ʒə'nu], *n.m.* (*pl.* **genoux**) Knee; workman's knee-pad; (*Naut.*) lower futtock; (*Mech.*) ball and socket; knee-piece. *Avoir la tête comme un genou,* (*colloq.*) to be as bald as a coot; *être à genoux,* to be on one's knees; *à genoux!* on your knees! *être aux genoux de quelqu'un,* to be deeply devoted to someone; *fléchir le genou,* to bend the knee, to humble oneself; *se mettre à genoux,* to kneel down; *se mettre à genoux devant quelque chose,* (*fam.*) to admire, to be in fits of ecstasy before something; *tenir un enfant sur ses genoux,* to hold a child on one's lap; *tomber, se jeter,* or *se précipiter aux genoux de quelqu'un,* to fall at someone's feet. **genouillère,** *n.f.* Knee-piece (of armour); top (of a high boot); knee-cap; ball-and-socket joint.
genre [ʒɑ̃ːr], *n.m.* Genus; species, kind, sort; fashion, mode, taste, style, manner; airs,

affectation, mannerism; (*Gram.*) gender; (*Paint.*) genre. *De bon genre,* gentlemanly, ladylike, in good taste; *de mauvais genre,* ungentlemanly, unladylike, in bad taste, bad form; *faire* or *se donner du genre,* to put on airs; *il a un genre qui lui est propre,* he has a style peculiar to himself; *je voudrais un article du même genre,* I would like the same kind of article; *le genre comique,* comedy; *le genre tragique,* tragedy; *le genre humain,* mankind; *peintre de genre,* genre-painter.
gens (1) [ʒɑ̃], *n.m. pl.* (All the adjectives in front of *gens* are used in the *feminine* when *gens* is immediately preceded by an adjective, unless this adjective ends with an *e*. In such phrases as *gens de lettres, gens de loi,* etc., *gens* is always *masculine.*) People, persons, folks; men, hands; domestics, servants, attendants. *Ce sont des gens fort dangereux* or *de fort dangereuses gens,* they are very dangerous people; *des gens de bon sens,* sensible people; *des gens fins* or *de fines gens,* cunning folk; *gens d'église,* churchmen; *gens de guerre,* soldiers; *gens de lettres,* men of letters; *gens de sac et de corde,* people who will do anything; *gens du monde,* rich and fashionable people, society; *le droit des gens,* the law of nations; *les petites gens, gens de peu,* or *gens de rien,* humble people; *les vieilles gens sont prudents,* old people are prudent; *tous les gens de bien,* all honest people; *tous les habiles gens,* all clever people; *toutes les vieilles gens,* all old people.
gens (2) [ʒɛ̃s], *n.f.* (*Rom. Ant.*) Gens.
gent (1) [ʒɑ̃], *n.f.* Brood, race, tribe. *La gent marécageuse,* the marshy tribe.
*****gent** (2) [ʒɑ̃], *a.* (*fem.* **gente**) Pretty, graceful.
gentiane [ʒɑ̃'sjan], *n.f.* (*Bot.*) Gentian.
gentil (1) [ʒɑ̃'ti], *n.m.* Gentile. (*usu. pl.*) The Gentiles.
gentil (2) [ʒɑ̃'ti], *a.* (*fem.* **gentille** [ʒɑ̃'tij]) Noble, gentle; pretty, nice, graceful; amiable, pleasing; (*iron.*) ridiculous, fine. *Un gentil enfant,* a pretty, amiable child; *un gentil métier,* a fine occupation, indeed! *c'est gentil de votre part,* it is very kind of you.—*n.* (used only in) *Faire le gentil,* to affect graceful manners.
gentilhomme [ʒɑ̃ti'jɔm], *n.m.* (*pl.* **gentilshommes**) Nobleman, gentleman. *Vivre en gentilhomme,* to live like a gentleman, to do nothing for a livelihood. **gentilhommerie,** *n.f.* Gentility, gentry. **gentilhommière,** *n.f.* Small country-seat.
gentilité [ʒɑ̃tili'te], *n.f.* Gentile nations. **gentilisme,** *n.m.* Heathenism, paganism.
gentilâtre [ʒɑ̃ti'jɑːtr], *n.m.* Lordling, squireen.
gentillesse [ʒɑ̃ti'jɛs], *n.f.* Kindness, niceness, sweetness (of temperament); prettiness, gracefulness; pretty thing, thought, speech; pretty trick, prank. *Voilà de vos gentillesses,* these are some of your fine tricks. **gentillet,** *a.* (*fem.* **-ette**) Rather nice, rather pretty.
gentiment, *adv.* Prettily, gracefully, nicely, like a good boy or girl.
gentleman [dʒɛntl'man] or [ʒɑ̃tl'man], *n.m.* Gentleman. *Il s'est conduit comme un gentleman,* he behaved in a gentlemanly way. *Un gentleman-rider,* an amateur jockey.
génuflexion [ʒenyflɛk'sjɔ̃], *n.f.* Genuflexion.
géocentrique [ʒeosɑ̃'trik], *a.* Geocentric.
géode [ʒe'ɔd], *n.f.* Geode.

géodésie [ʒeɔde'zi], *n.f.* Geodesy. **géodésique**, *a.* Geodesic.

géodique [ʒeɔ'dik], *a.* Geodic. **géodynamique**, *a.* Geodynamic.

Geoffroy [ʒɔ'frwɑ], *m.* Geoffrey, Jeffrey.

géogénie [ʒeɔʒe'ni], *n.f.* Geogeny. **géognosie**, *n.f.* Geognosy.

géographe [ʒeɔ'graf], *n.m.* Geographer. *Ingénieur géographe*, surveyor. **géographie**, *n.f.* Geography. *Cartes de géographie*, (geographical) maps. **géographique**, *a.* Geographical. **géographiquement**, *adv.* Geographically.

geôlage [ʒo'laːʒ], *n.m.* Gaol fee. **geôle** [ʒoːl], *n.f.* Gaol, prison. **geôlier**, *n.m.* Gaoler. **geôlière**, *n.f.* Gaoler's wife.

géologie [ʒeɔlɔ'ʒi], *n.f.* Geology. **géologique**, *a.* Geological. **géologiquement**, *adv.* Geologically. **géologue**, *n.m.* Geologist.

géométral [ʒeɔme'tral], *a.* (*fem.* **géométrale**, *pl.* **géométraux**) Geometrical. *Plan géométral*, ground-plan. **géomètre**, *n.m.* Geometrician; geometer. *Expert-géomètre*, surveyor. **géométrie**, *n.f.* Geometry. *Géométrie plane*, *dans l'espace*, plane, solid geometry. **géométrique**, *a.* Geometrical. **géométriquement**, *adv.* Geometrically. **géométriser**, *v.t.* To geometrize.

géopolitique [ʒeopoli'tik], *n.f.* Geopolitics.

géorama [ʒeora'ma], *n.m.* Georama.

Georges [ʒɔrʒ], *m.* George.

Géorgie [ʒeɔr'ʒi], *f.* Georgia.

géorgien [ʒeɔr'ʒiɛ̃], *a.* and *n.* (*fem.* **géorgienne**) Georgian.

géorgique [ʒeɔr'ʒik], *a.* Georgic.—*n.f. pl.* Georgics.

géotropisme [ʒeɔtrɔ'pism], *n.m.* Geotropism.

gérance [ʒe'rɑ̃ːs], *n.f.* Management, managership; editorship.

géranium [ʒera'njɔm], *n.m.* Geranium. *Géranium des prés*, meadow crane's bill.

gérant [ʒe'rɑ̃], *n.m.* (*fem.* **-ante**) Manager; editor. *Armateur gérant*, ship's husband; *rédacteur gérant*, managing editor.

gerbe [ʒɛrb], *n.f.* Sheaf, bundle; bunch of flowers; (*Pyro.*) gerbe. *Gerbe d'étincelles*, shower of sparks. **gerbée**, *n.f.* Bundle of straw with some ears, for fodder. **gerber**, *v.t.* To make up or bind into sheaves. *Gerber des tonneaux*, to pile casks upon each other.—*v.i.* To produce abundant sheaves (of corn etc.). **gerbeur**, *n.* (*fem.* **-euse**) Stacking machine or workman. **gerbier**, *n.m.* Cornstack. **gerbière**, *n.f.* Harvest-wagon. **gerbillon**, *n.m.* Small sheaf.

gerboise [ʒɛr'bwaːz], *n.f.* Jerboa, jumping-mouse.

gerce [ʒɛrs], *n.f.* Chap, crack; clothes-moth. **gercé**, *a.* (*fem.* **-ée**) Chapped (hands); leaky (boat). **gercement**, *n.m.* Chapping, cracking. **gercer**, *v.t.* To chap, to crack. *Le froid gerce les lèvres*, cold weather chaps the lips.—*v.i.* To chap, to crack. **se gercer**, *v.r.* To chap, to crack. **gerçure**, *n.f.* Chap, crack; chink, cleft.

gérer [ʒe're], *v.t. irr.* (*conjug. like* ACCÉLÉRER) To manage, to administer, to conduct.

gerfaut [ʒɛr'fo], *n.m.* Gerfalcon.

germain (1) [ʒɛr'mɛ̃], *a.* (*fem.* **-aine**) German, first (of cousins etc.); (*Law*) own, full (brother etc.). *Cousin germain* (*fem.* **cousine germaine**), cousin-german, first cousin.—*n.*

First cousin. *Cousins issus de germains*, second cousins.

germain (2) [ʒɛr'mɛ̃], *a.* and *n.* (*fem.* **germaine**) German (native of ancient Germany).

germandrée [ʒɛrmɑ̃'dre], *n.f.* (*Bot.*) Germander. *Germandrée petit chêne*, wall germander; *Germandrée des bois* [SAUGE].

Germanie [ʒɛrma'ni], *f.* Germania.

germanique [ʒɛrma'nik], *a.* Germanic. **germaniser**, *v.t.*, *v.i.* To germanize. **se germaniser**, *v.r.* To become germanized. **germanisme**, *n.m.* German idiom, germanism. **germanophile**, *a.* and *n.* Germanophile. **germanophilie**, *n.f.* Germanomania. **germanophobe**, *a.* and *n.* Germanophobe. **germanophobie**, *n.f.* Germanophobia.

germe [ʒɛrm], *n.m.* Germ, embryo; seed; bud, sprout, shoot; (*fig.*) principle, source, origin. *Pousser des germes*, to sprout. **germer**, *v.i.* To shoot, to sprout, to bud, to germinate; to spring up, to develop. *Le blé commence à germer*, the corn is beginning to spring up.

germinal, *a.* (*fem.* **-ale**, *pl.* **-aux**) Germinal. —*n.m.* Germinal, seventh month of calendar of first French republic, 21 March–19 April. **germinatif**, *a.* (*fem.* **-ive**) Germinal. **germination**, *n.f.* Germination.

germoir [ʒɛr'mwaːr], *n.m.* Malt-house; hot-bed.

gérondif [ʒerɔ̃'dif], *n.m.* (*Gram.*) Gerund, gerundive.

géronte [ʒe'rɔ̃ːt], *n.m.* The 'old man' in comedy; a dotard. **gérontisme**, *n.m.* Senility. **gérontocratie**, *n.f.* A government of old people. **gérontologie**, *n.f.* Study of the problems of old age; gerontology.

gésier [ʒe'zje], *n.m.* Gizzard (of a hawk etc.); (*vulg.*) stomach.

*****gésir** [ʒe'ziːr], *v.i. irr.* To lie. *C'est là que gît le lièvre*, there's the rub; *ci-gît*, here lies.

*****gésine**, *n.f.* Lying-in. *En gésine*, lying in child-bed.

gesse [ʒes], *n.f.* (*Bot.*) Vetch. *Gesse odorante* or *pois à bouquets*, sweet pea.

gestation [ʒesta'sjɔ̃], *n.f.* Gestation. **gestatoire**, *a.* Gestatory. *Chaise gestatoire*, sedan chair, sedia gestatoria (of the Pope).

geste (1) [ʒest], *n.m.* Gesture, action, movement (of the hands etc.); sign. *Faire des gestes*, to gesticulate.

geste (2) [ʒest], *n.f.* Deed, heroic achievement, exploit. *Chanson de geste* [CHANSON]; *faits et gestes*, actions and conduct, behaviour; (*fam.*) doings, movements.

gesticulaire [ʒestiky'lɛːr], *a.* Gesticulatory. **gesticulant** (*fem.* **-ante**), *a.* Gesticulating. **gesticulateur**, *n.m.* (*fem.* **-trice**) Gesticulator. **gesticulation**, *n.f.* Gesticulation. **gesticuler**, *v.i.* To gesticulate.

gestion [ʒes'tjɔ̃], *n.f.* Management, administration, conduct (of a business etc.); period of office in financial administration.

geyser [ge'zeːr], *n.m.* Geyser.

ghetto [ge'to], *n.m.* Jewish quarter, ghetto.

gi [ʒi], *adv.* (*pop.* instead of *oui*) Right!

giaour [ʒja'uːr], *n.m.* Giaour.

gibbeux [ʒi'bø], *a.* (*fem.* **-euse**) Gibbous, hump-backed, crooked.

gibbon [ʒi'bɔ̃], *n.m.* Gibbon (ape).

gibbosité [ʒibozi'te], *n.f.* Gibbosity; hump.

gibecière [ʒib'sjɛːr], *n.f.* Game-bag, satchel;

juggler's pocket; *pouch, bag, poke. *Tours de gibecière*, conjuring, sleight-of-hand tricks.

gibelet [ʒi'blɛ], *n.m.* Gimlet.

gibelin [ʒi'blɛ̃], *a.* and *n.* (*fem.* **gibeline**) (*It. Hist.*) Ghibelline.

gibelotte [ʒi'blɔt], *n.f.* Rabbit-stew.

giberne [ʒi'bɛrn], *n.f.* *Cartridge-box or pouch. *Chaque soldat a son bâton de maréchal dans sa giberne*, any private can become a field-marshal.

gibet [ʒi'bɛ], *n.m.* Gibbet, gallows.

gibier [ʒi'bje], *n.m.* Game. *Gibier à plume*, feathered game; *gibier d'eau*, wild fowl; *gibier à poil*, ground game; *gibier de potence*, gaol-bird, gallows-bird; *gibier braconné*, poached game; *gros gibier*, big game; *menu gibier*, small game; *pièce de gibier*, head of game.

giboulée [ʒibu'le], *n.f.* Sudden shower, hail-shower; (*fig.*) hail (of blows etc.). *Giboulée de mars*, April shower.

*giboyer [ʒibwa'je], *v.i. irr.* (*conjugated like* ABOYER) To go out hunting, to shoot. ***giboyeur**, *n.m.* Fowler, sportsman. **giboyeux**, *a.* (*fem.* **giboyeuse**) Full of game.

gibus [ʒi'by:s], *n.m. inv.* Gibus (crush-hat, opera-hat).

giclage [ʒi'kla:ʒ], *n.m.* Spraying. *Carburateur à giclage*, jet carburettor. **giclée**, *n.f.* Squirt, spirt; (*Motor.*) spray (of petrol). **giclement**, *n.m.* Squirting, spirting (of blood); squelching, splashing up (of mud). **gicleur**, *n.m.* Spray nozzle, jet.

gicler [ʒi'kle], *v.i.* To spout, to squirt out; to spirt (blood); to splash up (mud).

gifle [ʒifl], *n.f.* Slap in the face, box on the ear. **gifler**, *v.t.* To slap in the face, to box the ears of.

gigantesque [ʒigɑ̃'tɛsk], *a.* Gigantic, colossal. **gigantisme**, *n.m.* Abnormal development of the body or a part of it, gigantism.

gigogne [ʒi'gɔɲ], *n.f.* *La mère gigogne*, 'the old woman who lived in a shoe'; *mère gigogne*, woman with many children; *fusée gigogne*, multiple stage rocket; *table gigogne*, nest of tables.

gigolette [ʒigɔ'lɛt], *n.f.* Fast girl, streetwalker.

gigolo [ʒigɔ'lo], *n.m.* Fancy-man, gigolo.

gigot [ʒi'go], *n.m.* Leg of mutton; (*pl.*) hind legs of a horse. **Des manches à gigot*, leg-of-mutton sleeves; *manche à gigot*, carving handle. **gigoté**, *a.* (*fem.* **-ée**) Strong-limbed (of horses and dogs). **gigoter**, *v.i.* To kick; (*colloq.*) to fidget with the legs, to jig it.

gigue (1) [ʒig], *n.f.* Shank, leg, haunch (of venison). *Grande gigue*, lanky woman or girl. *Gigue de crosse*, cheek layer (of rifle-butt).

gigue (2) [ʒig], *n.f.* Jig (dance).

gilet [ʒi'lɛ], *n.m.* Waistcoat; vest. *Gilet d'armes*, fencing-jacket; *gilet de flanelle*, flannel undervest; *gilet de sauvetage*, life-jacket; *gilet tricoté*, cardigan; *gilet droit*, single-breasted waistcoat; *gilet croisé*, double-breasted waistcoat. **giletier**, *a.* (*fem.* **-ière**) Making waistcoats.—*n.* Waistcoat-maker.

Gilles [ʒil], *m.* Giles.

gilles [ʒil], *n.m.* Clown, ninny, simpleton.

gimblette [ʒɛ̃'blɛt], *n.f.* Cracknel, ring-biscuit.

gin [dʒin], *n.m.* Gin.

gindre or **geindre** (2) [ʒɛ̃:dr], *n.m.* Journeyman baker, baker's man.

gingembre [ʒɛ̃'ʒɑ̃:br], *n.m.* Ginger.

gingeole [ʒɛ̃'ʒɔl], *n.f.* Jujube. **gingeolier**, *n.m.* Jujube-tree.

gingin [ʒɛ̃'ʒɛ̃], (*fam.*) *Avoir du gingin*, to have some gumption.

gingival [ʒɛ̃ʒi'val], *a.* (*fem.* **-ale**, *pl.* **-aux**) Gingival. **gingivite**, *n.f.* Gingivitis.

ginglyme [ʒɛ̃'glim], *n.m.* (*Anat.*) Hinge-joint, ginglymus.

ginguer [ʒɛ̃'ge], *v.i.* To jump, to fling out (of animals); to gambol.

ginguet [ʒɛ̃'gɛ], *a.* (*fem.* **ginguette**) (*colloq.*) Poor, weak, sorry, worthless, short, scanty. *Esprit ginguet*, frivolous mind; *habit ginguet*, scanty coat; *style ginguet*, frivolous style. —*n.m.* Thin wine.

giorno [dʒɔr'no, ʒjɔr'no], *n.m.* *Éclairage à giorno*, brilliant illumination.

girafe [ʒi'raf], *n.f.* Giraffe; high diving board.

girande [ʒi'rɑ̃:d], *n.f.* Sheaf or cluster of water-jets or fireworks.

girandole [ʒirɑ̃'dɔl], *n.f.* Girandole, epergne, branched candlestick or fireworks; sprig (of diamonds etc.). *Girandole d'eau*, (*Bot.*) water horsetail.

girasol [ʒira'sɔl], *n.m.* Girasol, fire-opal; sunflower.

giration [ʒira'sjɔ̃], *n.f.* Gyration. **giratoire**, *a.* Gyratory. *Sens giratoire*, one-way circular traffic; roundabout.

giraumon(t) [ʒiro'mɔ̃], *n.m.*, or *giraumon turban*. Small round pumpkin.

giries [ʒi'ri], *n.f. pl.* (*pop.*) Affected complaints or manners.

girl [gœrl], *n.f.* Music-hall dancer, chorus-girl.

girofle [ʒi'rɔfl], *n.m.* Clove. *Griffe de girofle*, clove-stalk; *un clou de girofle*, a clove. **giroflée**, *n.f.* Gillyflower, stock. *Giroflée jaune*, or *ravenelle*, wallflower; *une giroflée (à cinq feuilles)*, slap in the face.—*a.* Of clove. *Cannelle giroflée*, clove-bark. **giroflier**, *n.m.* Clove-tree.

girolle or **girole** [ʒi'rɔl], *n.f.* Chanterelle, skirret.

giron [ʒi'rɔ̃], *n.m.* Lap; (*fig.*) bosom; (*Arch.*) tread (of a step); (*Her.*) gyron; handle-case (of windlass). *Le giron de l'Église*, the bosom of the Church.

girond [ʒi'rɔ̃], *a.* (*fem.* **gironde** (1)) (*vulg.*) Good-looking, pretty.

gironde (2) [ʒi'rɔ̃:d], *n.f.* (*Fr. Hist.*) Girondist party. **girondin**, *a.* and *n.* (*fem.* **-ine**) Girondist.

gironné [ʒirɔ'ne], *a.m.* (*Her.*) Gyronny; winding (steps).

girouette [ʒi'rwɛt], *n.f.* Weathercock, vane. *C'est une girouette*, he is a mere weathercock, a mere time-server; *fer de girouette*, spindle of a vane; *girouette anémomètre*, direction and speed anemometer.

gisant [ʒi'zɑ̃], *a.* (*see* GÉSIR) Lying (ill, dead, etc.); out-stretched, stranded (ship). *Meule gisante*, nether mill-stone.—*n.m.* Recumbent effigy on a tomb.

gisement [ʒiz'mɑ̃], *n.m.* (*Geol. etc.*) Lie (of strata); layer, bed; (*Naut.*) bearing or lie (of coast etc.). *Gisements houillers*, coal-measures.

gisent, *3rd pl. pres. indic.* [GÉSIR].

gît, *3rd sing. pres. indic.* [GÉSIR].

gitan [ʒiˈtɑ̃], *n.m.* (*fem.* gitane) Gitano, Gitana, gipsy.

gîte [ʒit], *n.m.* Home, lodging, resting-place, quarters; refuge; lair (of deer); form (of hare); (*Min.*) seam, bed, layer, stratum; nether millstone. *Dernier gîte*, last long home; *gîte d'étape*, road-post, halt; *gîte à la noix*, silverside; *un lièvre va toujours mourir au gîte*, one likes to come home to die.—*n.f.* (*Naut.*) List, grounding, bed (of stranded ship). *Prendre de la gîte*, to list. gîter, *v.i.* To lie, to lodge; (*fam.*) to perch; (*Naut.*) to list; to run aground.—*v.t.* To lodge, to house, to put up, to shelter. se gîter, *v.r.* To lodge, to sleep; to take up one's abode.

givrage [ʒiˈvraːʒ], *n.m.* (*Av.*) Frosting, icing.

givre (1) [ʒiːvr], *n.f.* (*Her.*) Wyvern.

givre (2), *n.m.* Hoar-frost, rime. givré, *a.* (*fem.* -ée) Rimed, rimy. givrer, *v.t.* To cover, to overlay with frost. givreux, *a.* (*fem.* -euse) Frosted.

glabre [glɑːbr], *a.* (*Bot.*) Glabrous, smooth, without down; hairless.

glaçage [glaˈsaːʒ], *n.m.* Frosting, glazing.

glaçant [glaˈsɑ̃], *a.* (*fem.* -ante) Freezing; icy, chilling.

glace [glas], *n.f.* Ice; freezing-point; frost, intense cold; (*fig.*) chill, insensibility, indifference; glass, plate-glass; looking-glass, mirror; carriage window; flaw (in a diamond etc.); icing (on cakes etc.). *Baisser les glaces*, to lower the windows (of a carriage); *ferré à glace*, rough-shod (of horses' hoofs); *geler à glace*, to freeze hard; *prendre une glace*, to have (eat) an ice-cream; *rompre la glace*, to break the ice, to begin conversation. glacé, *a.* (*fem.* glacée) Frozen, freezing; nipping, biting, chilling, icy-cold; frosted, iced; glazed, glossy (paper); candied. glacer, *v.t.* To freeze; to congeal; to chill, to ice; (*fig.*) to strike a chill into; to paralyse; to glaze, to frost (meat). *Ce récit nous glaça d'horreur*, this story struck us dumb with horror; *glacer la soie*, to give a lustre to silk.—*v.i.* or se glacer, *v.r.* To freeze. glacerie, *n.f.* Ice works; mirror factory. glaceur, *n.m.* Glazer (of paper etc.). glaceux, *a.* (*fem.* -euse) Having flaws, flawy (of gems etc.). glaciaire, *a.* Of glaciers, glacial. *La période glaciaire*, the Ice Age. glacial, *a.* (*fem.* -iale, *pl.* -ials, -iales) Frozen, glacial, icy, frigid. *Air glacial*, nipping air; *mer glaciale* or *océan glacial*, frozen sea, Arctic Ocean; *mine glaciale*, frigid countenance; *vent glacial*, biting wind.—*n.f.* (*Bot.*) Ice-plant. glacialement, *adv.* Glacially. glaciation, *n.f.* Glaciation. glacier, *n.m.* Glacier, field of ice; ice-cream vendor. *Glacier-confiseur*, confectioner and ice-cream maker. glacière, *n.f.* Ice-house; freezing-machine, refrigerator; ice-cave.

glacis [glaˈsi], *n.m. inv.* Slope, sloping bank; (*Fort.*) glacis; (*Paint.*) glazing, scumble.

glaçon [glaˈsɔ̃], *n.m.* Block of ice; floe; ice-cube; (*fig.*) cold person. *Petit glaçon*, icicle.

glaçure [glaˈsyːr], *n.f.* Glazing.

gladiateur [gladjaˈtœːr], *n.m.* Gladiator. gladiatorial (*fem.* -iale, *pl.* -iaux) or gladiatoire, *a.* Gladiatorial. gladié, *a.* (*fem.* -iée) Sword-shaped.

glaïeul [glaˈjœl], *n.m.* Gladiolus, sword-grass. *Glaïeul des marais*, yellow flag, wild iris.

glaire [glɛːr], *n.f.* Glair, white of egg; flaw (of diamond); phlegm, mucus. glairer, *v.t.* To glair. glaireux, *a.* (*fem.* -euse) Glairy. glairine, *n.f.* Glairine. glairure, *n.f.* Glair.

glaise [glɛːz], *n.f.* Clay, loam; potter's earth. —*a.* Clayey. *Terre glaise*, clay. glaiser, *v.t.* To clay. glaiseux, *a.* (*fem.* glaiseuse) Clayey, loamy. glaisière, *n.f.* Clay-pit.

glaive [glɛːv], *n.m.* Sword, glaive, blade, steel. *La balance et le glaive*, the scales and the sword; *la puissance du glaive*, the power of life and death; *tirer le glaive*, to declare or wage war.

glanage [glaˈnaːʒ], *n.m.* Gleaning.

gland [glɑ̃], *n.m.* Acorn; tassel; (*Anat.*) glans. *Gland de soie* or *de rideaux*, silken tassel, curtain tassel; *gland de terre*, earth-nut, pig-nut; *gland de mer*, acorn-shell.

glande [glɑ̃ːd], *n.f.* (*Anat.*) Gland; (*pop.*) tumour; kernel. *Glande lymphatique*, lymphatic gland. glandé, *a.* (*fem.* glandée (1)) Glandered. glandée (2), *n.f.* Crop of acorns, pannage. glandifère, *a.* Glandiferous. glandiforme, *a.* Glandiform.

glandulaire [GLANDULEUX].

glandule [glɑ̃ˈdyl], *n.f.* (*Anat.*) Glandule. glanduleux, *a.* (*fem.* -euse) Glandulous, glandular. glandulifère, *a.* Glanduliferous. glanduliforme, *a.* Glanduliform.

glane [glan], *n.f.* Handful of gleaned ears of corn etc.; wisp of straw. *Glane de poires*, bunch of pears; *glane d'oignons*, rope of onions. glaner, *v.t., v.i.* To glean. glaneur, *n.m.* (*fem.* -euse) Gleaner. glanure, *n.f.* Gleanings.

glapir [glaˈpiːr], *v.i.* To yelp (of puppies etc.); to screech, to scream, to squeak (of persons). glapissant, *a.* (*fem.* -ante) Yelping; screeching, screaming, shrill. glapissement, *n.m.* Yelping; screeching, screaming.

glas [glɑ], *n.m.* Knell, passing-bell, tolling. *Glas funèbre*, funeral-knell, death-bell; *sonner le glas*, to toll the knell.

glaucescence [glosɛˈsɑ̃ːs], *n.f.* Glaucescence. glaucescent, *a.* (*fem.* -ente) Glaucescent.

glaucière [gloˈsjɛːr] or glaucienne, *n.f.* Horned poppy. glaucique, *a.* Pertaining to the poppy, glaucic.

glaucome [gloˈkoːm], *n.m.* (*Path.*) Glaucoma.

glauque [gloːk], *a.* Glaucous, pale sea-green.

glaux [glo], *n.m.* (*Bot.*) Milkwort.

glaviot [glaˈvjo], *n.m.* (*vulg.*) Spittle, gob.

glèbe [glɛb], *n.f.* Glebe; land, soil; sod, clod. *Être attaché à la glèbe*, to be bound to the soil.

glène [glɛn], *n.f.* (*Anat.*) Glene, socket; (*Naut.*) coil. glener, *v.t.* (*Naut.*) To coil. glénoïdal or glénoïde, *a.* (*Anat.*) Glenoid. *Cavité glénoïdale de l'omoplate*, glenoid cavity of the scapula.

glette [glɛt], *n.f.* Litharge.

glissade [gliˈsad], *n.f.* Sliding, slide; slipping, slip; glissade. *Faire une glissade*, to have a slide; *to make a slip. glissage, *n.m.* Trunk or timber sliding operation. glissant [gliˈsɑ̃], *a.* (*fem.* -ante) Slippery; (*fig.*) ticklish, delicate, hazardous. *Terrain glissant*, slippery ground. glissé, *n.m.* Glissade (in dancing). glissement, *n.m.* Slipping, sliding, gliding; the noise made by those motions; (*Polit.*) landslide.

glisser [gli'se], *v.i.* To slip, to slide; to glide; to glance, to pass lightly, quietly, or furtively; to glissade. *Cela m'a glissé des mains*, it slipped out of my hands; *glisser sur la glace*, to slide; *glisser sur l'aile*, (*Av.*) to side-slip; *glissons là-dessus*, let us pass over that; *l'échelle glissa*, the ladder slipped.—*v.t.* To slip, to slide, to insinuate, to insert quietly, furtively, etc. *Il glissa sa main dans ma poche*, he slipped his hand into my pocket. **se glisser,** *v.r.* To slip, to slide, to creep or steal, to insinuate oneself (*dans*). **glisseur,** *n.m.* (*fem.* **-euse**) Slider. **glissière,** *n.f.* Slide, guide-block; window-guide. *Porte à glissière*, sliding door; *banc à glissière* or *glissière* (of a rowing-boat), sliding seat; *glissière pour colis* etc., shoot. **glissoir,** *n.m.* Chute (for timber). **glissoire,** *n.f.* Slide on ice.

global [glɔ'bal], *a.* (*fem.* **-ale,** *pl.* **-aux**) In a mass, entire. *Méthode globale*, whole-word method; *somme globale*, lump sum. **globalement,** *adv.* In a lump, in the aggregate, all in.

globe [glɔb], *n.m.* Globe, sphere, orb; glassshade. *Globe de feu*, fire-ball. **globeux,** *a.* (*fem.* **-euse**) Globose, round.

globulaire [glɔby'lɛːr], *a.* Globular.—*n.f.* (*Bot.*) Globe-daisy.

globule [glɔ'byl], *n.m.* Globule. **globuleux,** *a.* (*fem.* **-euse**) Globulous, globular. **globuline,** *n.f.* Globulin.

gloire [glwa:r], *n.f.* Glory, fame; glorification, homage; halo; vanity, pride. *Être la gloire de*, to be the glory of; *mettre sa gloire à*, to glory in; *rendre gloire à*, to pay tribute to, to glorify; to testify to (the truth); *se faire une gloire de quelque chose*, to pride oneself upon something; (*fam.*) *travailler pour la gloire*, to work for nothing.

glomérule [glɔme'ryl], *n.m.* Glomerule.

gloria [glɔ'rja], *n.m.* Gloria; (*colloq.*) coffee with brandy; an additional brandy.

gloriette [glɔ'rjɛt], *n.f.* Arbour, summerhouse.

glorieusement [glɔrjøz'mã], *adv.* Gloriously. **glorieux,** *a.* (*fem.* **glorieuse**) Glorious, glorified; blessed; vainglorious, conceited, haughty, over-weening.—*n.* Braggart, boaster, vainglorious person. *Faire le glorieux*, to be a braggart. (*Hist.*) *Les trois Glorieuses*, 27, 28, 29 July, 1830.

glorification [glɔrifika'sjɔ̃], *n.f.* Glorification.

glorifier [glɔri'fje], *v.t.* To glorify, to honour. **se glorifier,** *v.r.* To glory in, to boast (*de*). **gloriole,** *n.f.* Vainglory, petty vanity. *C'est la gloriole qui les tient*, they are eaten up with vanity.

glose [glo:z], *n.f.* Glossing; gloss; commentary; criticism; comment; reflection; carping; parody. **gloser,** *v.t.* To gloss, to expound, to comment upon; to criticize, to carp at, to find fault with.—*v.i.* To carp, to find fault, to comment (*sur*). **gloseur,** *n.m.* (*fem.* **-euse**) Carper, fault-finder. **glossaire,** *n.m.* Glossary, vocabulary. **glossateur,** *n.m.* Glossarist.

glossite [glɔ'sit], *n.f.* (*Path.*) Glossitis.

glossographe [glɔsɔ'graf], *n.m.* Glossographer. **glossographie,** *n.f.* Glossography. **glossologie,** *n.f.* Glossology.

glotte [glɔt], *n.f.* (*Anat.*) Glottis. *Coup de glotte*, glottal stop. **glottique,** *a.* Glottal, glottic.

glouglou [glu'glu], *n.m.* Gurgling, gurgle, bubbling; gobbling (of turkeys). **glouglouter,** *v.i.* To gurgle, to bubble; to gobble (of turkeys).

gloussement [glus'mã], *n.m.* Clucking, cluck. **glousser,** *v.i.* To cluck (of hens).

glouteron [glu'trɔ̃], *n.m.* (*Bot.*) Burdock; burr; bedstraw.

glouton [glu'tɔ̃], *a.* (*fem.* **-onne**) Gluttonous, greedy.—*n.* Glutton; (*Zool.*) glutton, carcajou. **gloutonnement,** *adv.* Gluttonously, greedily, ravenously. **gloutonnerie,** *n.f.* Gluttony, greediness.

gloxinie [glɔksi'ni], *n.f.* (*Bot.*) Gloxinia.

glu [gly], *n.f.* Bird-lime, glue. *Avoir de la glu aux doigts*, to be sticky-fingered, *i.e.* to take toll of money etc. passing through one's hands; *elle est collante comme de la glu* or *c'est une vraie glu*, you cannot get rid of her; *glu marine*, marine glue; *prendre à la glu*, to take with bird-lime, to inveigle, to snare. **gluant,** *a.* (*fem.* **-ante**) Glutinous, adhesive, sticky; slimy; gluey. **gluau** [gly'o], *n.m.* Limetwig; (*fig.*) snare. *Tendre des gluaux*, to set lime-twigs or snares.

glucose [gly'ko:z], *n.m.* Glucose.

gluer [glɥe], *v.t.* (*rare*) To lime; to make sticky.

glui [glɥi], *n.m.* Straw for thatching etc.

glume [glym], *n.f.* Glume, husk, chaff.

gluten [gly'tɛn], *n.m.* Gluten. *Pain de gluten*, gluten-bread. **glutinatif,** *a.* (*fem.* **-ive**) Glutinative. **glutination** [AGGLUTINATION]. **glutineux,** *a.* (*fem.* **-euse**) Glutinous, viscous. **glutinosité,** *n.f.* Glutinosity, viscidity, stickiness.

glycémie [glise'mi], *n.f.* Blood-sugar; glycaemia. *Glycémie expérimentale*, sugartolerance test.

glycérie [glise'ri], *n.f.* (*Bot.*) Sweet grass.

glycérine [glise'rin], *n.f.* Glycerine.

glycine [gli'sin], *n.f.* Wistaria.

glycol [gli'kɔl], *n.m.* (*Chem.*) Glycol.

glyconien [glikɔ'njɛ̃] (*fem.* **glyconienne**) or **glyconique,** *a.* (*Pros.*) Glyconic (verse).

glycosurie [glikɔsy'ri], *n.f.* Glucosuria.

glyphe [glif], *n.m.* (*Arch.*) Glyph.

glyptique [glip'tik], *n.f.* Glyptics.

gnaf [naf], *n.m.* (*slang*) Cobbler; bungler.

gnan-gnan or **gnangnan** [nã'nã], *a. inv.* (*fam.*) Slow, inert; spineless, peevish.—*n. inv.* Milksop, slow-coach, peevish person.

gnaphale [gna'fal] or **gnaphalium,** *n.m.* (*Bot.*) Cudweed, everlasting gnaphalium.

gneiss [gnɛs], *n.m.* Gneiss.

gnognotte [nɔ'nɔt], *n.f.* (*pop.*) *C'est de la gnognotte, ça*, it's all trash.

gnole [nɔl], *a.* and *n.* (*slang*) Soft, stupid.—*n.f.* blow [GNON].

gnôle or **gniole** [nɔl], *n.f.* (*Mil. slang*) Brandy.

gnome [gno:m], *n.m.* (*fem.* **gnomide**) Gnome.

gnomique [gno'mik], *a.* Gnomic, sententious.

gnomon [gno'mɔ̃], *n.m.* Gnomon. **gnomonique,** *n.f.* Gnomonics, sundial-making.

gnon [nɔ̃], *n.m.* (*pop.*) Blow, biff (usually on the head).

gnose [gno:z], *n.f.* (*Theol.*) Gnosis; (*Phil.*) Gnosticism. **gnosticisme,** *n.m.* Gnosticism. **gnostique,** *n.* Gnostic.

gnou [gnu], *n.m* Gnu.

go [go] (*Only used in*) *Tout de go*, freely, right off, easily, unceremoniously.

goal [gol], *n.m.* (*Ftb.*) (*fam.*) Goal-keeper.

gobbe or **gobe** [gɔb], *n.f.* Fattening ball (for poultry); poisoned ball (for a dog); wool-ball (in sheep); cave, cave-dwelling in cliffs (near Dieppe).

gobelet [gɔ'blɛ], *n.m.* Goblet, cup, mug, tumbler; thimble, juggler's cup, thimble-rigging; dice-box. *Joueur de gobelets*, thimble-rigger; *tour de gobelet*, juggler's trick. **gobeleterie**, *n.f.* Cup-making or -selling. **gobeletier**, *n.m.* Cup-maker or -seller.

gobelin [gɔ'blɛ̃], *n.m.* Goblin, imp.

gobelotter or **gobeloter** [gɔblɔ'te], *v.i.* (*colloq.*) To tipple, to booze. **gobelotteur**, *n.m.* Tippler, boozer.

gobe-mouches [gɔb'muʃ], *n.m. inv.* Fly-catcher (bird); fly-trap (plant); (*fig.*) simpleton, gull, ninny.

gober [gɔ'be], *v.t.* To gulp down, to swallow; (*colloq.*) to swallow down, to believe easily; to fancy, to have a liking for (a person). *Gober le morceau*, to swallow the bait, to be taken in; *il gobe des mouches*, he moons about; *je ne vais pas gober cela*, I am not going to swallow that; *je ne crois pas qu'il me gobe beaucoup*, I don't think he fancies me very much. **se gober**, *v.r.* (*fam.*) To think a lot of oneself.

goberge [gɔ'bɛrʒ], *n.f.* Screw-stick, handle (of a joiner's press); cross-bar (of a bedstead).

goberger (se) [gɔbɛr'ʒe], *v.r.* To amuse oneself (*de*), to mock at; to enjoy oneself, to take one's ease, to lounge, to do oneself well.

gobet [gɔ'bɛ], *n.m.* (*colloq.*) Gobbet, mouthful; (*fig.*) gull, simpleton. *Prendre au gobet*, to nab.

gobetage [gɔb'ta:ʒ], *n.m.* Pointing, stopping (of masonry). **gobeter**, *v.t.* To stop (cracks).

gobeur [gɔ'bœːr], *n.m.* (*fem.* **gobeuse**) Swallower, gobbler, gulper; gull (person).

gobichonner [gɔbiʃɔ'ne], *v.i.* To feast, to live well, to guzzle.

gobie [gɔ'bi], *n.m.* (*Ichth.*) Common (or freckled) goby.

gobille [gɔ'bi:j], *n.f.* Marble, alley-taw.

godage [gɔ'da:ʒ], *n.m.* Bagging, puckering (of a coat etc.); cockling (of paper).

godaille [gɔ'da:j], *n.f.* (*colloq.*) Tippling, swilling, guzzling. **godailler**, *v.i.* To guzzle, to stuff and swill, to tipple. **godailleur**, *n.m.* (*fem.* **godailleuse**) Guzzler, pub-crawler.

godasse [gɔ'das], *n.f.* (*slang*) Boot.

Godefroi, Godefroy [gɔd'frwa], *m.* Godfrey.

godelureau [gɔdly'ro], *n.m.* (*pl.* **-eaux**) Popinjay, coxcomb, fop.

(*C*) **godendard** [gɔdɑ̃'daːr], *n.m.* Cross-cut saw, whip-saw, two-handle saw.

godenot [gɔd'no], *n.m.* Juggler's puppet; (*fam.*) small misshapen man.

goder [gɔ'de], *v.i.* To crease, to bag (of clothes), to pucker (of needlework etc.); to cockle (of paper).

godet [gɔ'dɛ], *n.m.* Small footless and handleless cup, mug; horn (for drinking); calyx (of flower); cup (of lamp); bowl (of pipe); bucket (of noria or dredger); saucer (of water-colour painters); insulator (of piano etc.).

godiche [gɔ'diʃ], *a.* Clumsy, boobyish, lumpish, simple. **godichon**, *a.* (*fem.* **-onne**)

(*colloq.*) Silly, simple; clumsy, gawky.—*n.* Gawk, bumpkin, ninny, booby.

godille [gɔ'diːj], *n.f.* Stern-oar; scull. **godiller**, *v.i.* To single scull. **godilleur**, *n.m.* Sculler.

godillot [gɔdi'jo], *n.m.* (*slang*) Boot; 'beetle-crusher'.

godiveau [gɔdi'vo], *n.m.* Force-meat ball.

godron [gɔ'drɔ̃], *n.m.* (*Arch.*) Gadroon; round plait. **godronner**, *v.t.* To plait round; to gadroon.

goéland [gɔe'lɑ̃], *n.m.* Gull, sea-gull. *Goéland argenté*, herring gull; *goéland brun*, lesser black-backed gull; *goéland à manteau noir*, great black-backed gull; *goéland pygmée*, little gull.

goélette [gɔe'lɛt], *n.f.* Schooner; trysail; sea-swallow.

goémon [gɔe'mɔ̃], *n.m.* Seaweed. *Goémons épaves*, sea-wrack.

gogaille [gɔ'ga:j], *n.f.* Merry-making, junketing, spree.

gogo (1) [gɔ'go], *n.m.* Gull, simpleton.

gogo (2) [gɔ'go] (*In adv. phr.*) *à gogo*, galore. *Avoir de l'argent à gogo*, to have pots of money; *avoir tout à gogo*, to live in clover.

goguenard [gɔg'na:r], *a.* (*fem.* **goguenarde**) Bantering, jeering, mocking, scoffing.—*n.* Banterer, jeerer, chaffer. **goguenarder**, *v.i.* To jeer, to banter, to chaff. **goguenarderie**, *n.f.* Jeering, bantering. **goguenardises**, *n.f. pl.* Broad jokes.

gogueneau, goguenot [gɔg'no], *n.m.* (*Mil.*) Camp-kettle (in Algeria); pail (of latrines); *pl.* (*vulg.*) (*often abridg.*) *les gogues* [lɛ'gɔg], latrines.

goguette [gɔ'gɛt], *n.f.* (*colloq.*) *Merry story; pleasure-party. *Chanter goguette à quelqu'un*, to abuse someone; *être en goguette*, to be in a merry mood, to be on the spree.

goinfre [gwɛ̃:fr], *n.m.* (*fam.*) Guzzler, gormandizer. **goinfrer**, *v.i.* To gorge, to gormandize. **goinfrerie**, *n.f.* Gluttony.

goitre [gwa:tr], *n.m.* Goitre, wen. **goitreux**, *a.* (*fem.* **-euse**) Goitrous.—*n.* Goitrous person, (*colloq.*) imbecile, idiot.

golf [gɔlf], *n.m.* Golf. *Terrain de golf*, golf-links. *Joueur de golf* or *golfeur* (*fem. golfeuse*), golfer. *Culottes de golf*, plus-fours.

golfe [gɔlf], *n.m.* Gulf, bay.

goménol [gɔme'nɔl], *n.m.* Soothing oil or vaseline.

gommage [gɔ'ma:ʒ], *n.m.* Gumming.

gomme [gɔm], *n.f.* Gum; rubber, eraser; (*Path.*) gumma. *Gomme arabique*, gum arabic; *gomme élastique*, india-rubber; *gomme laque*, shellac; *gomme à encre*, ink-eraser. (*colloq.*) *Faire des affaires à la gomme*, to do bogus transactions. **gomme-gutte**, *n.f.* (*pl.* **gommes-guttes**) Gamboge. **gommer**, *v.t.* To gum; to rub out; to mix with gum or syrup. **gomme-résine**, *n.f.* (*pl.* **gommes-résines**) Gum-resin. **gommeux**, *a.* (*fem.* **-euse**) Gummy; gummous.—*n.* (*slang*) Toff, swell. *Petit gommeux*, fop, coxcomb. **gommier**, *n.m.* Gum-tree. **gommifère**, *a.* Gummiferous. **gommose**, *n.f.* Gum (of fruit-trees).

gomphose [gɔ̃'fo:z], *n.f.* (*Anat.*) Gomphosis.

gonce [GONZE].

gond [gɔ̃], *n.m.* Hinge. *Hors des gonds*, un-hinged, (*fig.*) enraged, beside oneself. *Être* *mis hors de ses gonds*, to lose one's temper, to fly off the handle. **gonder**, *v.t.* To put a hinge or hinges on.

gondolage [gɔ̃dɔ'la:ʒ], *n.m.* Warping; cockling; buckling; blistering.

gondole [gɔ̃'dɔl], *n.f.* Gondola; car or gondola (of a balloon etc.); eye-cup, eye-bath. **gondoler**, *v.i.* (*Naut.*) To turn up at the ends like a gondola (of ships etc.); to bulge; to warp (of wood); to cockle; to buckle; to blister. **se gondoler**, *v.r.* To warp; (*slang*) to shake with laughter. **gondolier**, *n.m.* Gondolier.

gonfalon [gɔ̃fa'lɔ̃] or **gonfanon**, *n.m.* Gonfalon, banner, streamer. **gonfalonier**, *n.m.* Gonfalonier.

gonflage [gɔ̃'fla:ʒ], *n.m.* Air-pumping; inflating (of tyres). **gonflement**, *n.m.* Swelling, inflation, distention. **gonfler**, *v.t.* To swell, to inflate, to distend; to blow up, to pump up (a tyre); to puff up, to bloat. *Des yeux gonflés*, swollen eyes; (*colloq.*) *être gonflé à bloc*, to be full of energy; *il est gonflé*, what a cheek; *il est gonflé d'orgueil*, he has got a swollen head.—*v.i.* To swell, to be swollen. **se gonfler**, *v.r.* To swell, to be swollen, to be puffed up. **gonfleur**, *n.m.* Air-pump, inflator.

gong [gɔ̃:g], *n.m.* Gong.

goniomètre [gɔnjo'mɛtr], *n.m.* Goniometer. **goniométrie**, *n.f.* Goniometry. **goniométrique**, *a.*

gonne [gɔn], *n.f.* Cask, tar-barrel.

gonocoque [gɔnɔ'kɔk], *n.m.* Gonococcus.

gonorrhée [gɔnɔ're], *n.f.* Gonorrhoea.

gonze, gonse, gonce [gɔ̃s], *n.m.* (*slang*) Man, bloke. **gonzesse** [gɔ̃'zɛs], *n.f.* (*slang*) Girl, wench, woman; kept woman.

gord [gɔːr], *n.m.* Kiddle; fishing weir.

gordien [gɔr'djɛ̃], *a.m.* Gordian. *Trancher le nœud gordien*, to cut the Gordian knot.

gorenflot [gɔrɑ̃'flo], *n.m.* A sort of sponge-cake soaked in diluted brandy.

goret [gɔ'rɛ], *n.m.* Young pig, piglet; (*colloq.*) dirty fellow; (*Naut.*) hog, scrub-broom. **goreter**, *v.t.* irr. (*conjug. like* AMENER) (*Naut.*) To clean (decks etc.) with a hog.

gorge [gɔrʒ], *n.f.* Throat, gullet; breast, bosom, neck; defile, strait, narrow pass; (*Bot.*) mouth, orifice; (*Arch.*, *Fort.*) gorge; groove (of pulley); roller (for maps etc.); tumbler (of lock). *À pleine gorge*, at the top of one's voice; *avoir mal à la gorge*, to have a sore throat; *avoir la gorge serrée*, to have a lump in one's throat; *cette fumée vous prend à la gorge*, this smoke nearly chokes one; *couper la gorge à quelqu'un*, to cut someone's throat, (*fig.*) to ruin someone; *prendre quelqu'un à la gorge*, to seize someone by the throat; *rendre gorge*, to disgorge, to refund, to stump up; *rire à gorge déployée*, to split one's sides with laughter. *Gorge chaude*, *titbit given to a hawk; *faire des gorges chaudes*, to gloat over. **gorge-de-pigeon**, *a. inv.* Iridescent, shot (of colours).—*n.m.* (*no plural*) Shot colour. **gorgée**, *n.f.* Draught, gulp, sip. **gorger**, *v.t.* To gorge, to cram, to glut, to stuff. **se gorger**, *v.r.* To gorge oneself, to stuff oneself. **gorgerette**, *n.f.* Collar, lady's ruffle; cap-string (children's bonnets); breast support; (*Orn.*) blackcap. **gorgerin**, *n.m.* Gorget, neck-piece (armour).

gorgone [gɔr'gɔn], *n.f.* Gorgon; (*Zool.*) gorgonia.

gorille [gɔ'ri:j], *n.m.* Gorilla.

gosier [go'zje], *n.m.* Throat, gullet; (*fig.*) voice; (*Anat.*) fauces. *Avoir le gosier pavé* or *ferré*, to have a cast-iron throat; *avoir le gosier sec* or *en pente*, to be always thirsty; *avoir une éponge dans le gosier*, to be insatiably thirsty; *coup de gosier*, single emission (in singing); *s'éclaircir le gosier*, to clear one's throat; (*fam.*) *s'humecter le gosier*, to wet one's whistle.

gosse [gɔs], *n.* (*fam.*) Brat, urchin, kid. *C'est une belle gosse*, she is a nice bit of skirt.

gothique [go'tik], *a.* Pertaining to the Goths; Gothic, ogival; (*Print.*) black-letter. *Écriture gothique*, black-letter, gothic.—*n.f.* (*Print.*) Old English, black-letter, gothic.

goton [gɔ'tɔ̃], *n.f.* (*fam.*) (*abbr. of Margot*, *Margoton*, Peggy). A country lass; strumpet.

gouache [gwaʃ], *n.f.* Gouache, body-colour; painting in this.

gouailler [gwa'je], *v.t.* (*colloq.*) To chaff, to tease.—*v.i.* To banter, to chaff. **gouaillerie**, *n.f.* Bantering, waggishness. **gouailleur**, *n.m.* (*fem.* **gouailleuse**) Chaffer, joker.

goualante [gwa'lɑ̃t], *n.f.* (*slang*) Song. **goualer**, *v.t.* To shout (a song); to cry.

gouape [gwap], *n.f.* Hooligan, cad, blackguard.

gouaper [gwa'pe], *v.i.* To loaf; to go about with '*gouapes*'.

goudron [gu'drɔ̃], *n.m.* Tar; pine-tar. **goudronnage**, *n.m.* Tarring. **goudronner**, *v.t.* To tar. *Eau goudronnée*, tar-water; *toile goudronnée*, tarpaulin; *papier goudronné*, tar-lined paper. **goudronnerie**, *n.f.* Tar-works. **goudronneur**, *n.m.* Tar-spreader (workman). **goudronneuse**, *n.f.* Tar-spraying machine. **goudronneux**, *a.* (*fem.* -**euse**) Tarry, like tar.

gouet [gwɛ], *n.m.* Billhook; (*Bot.*) Cuckoo-pint, lords and ladies, wild arum.

gouffre [gufr], *n.m.* Gulf, abyss, pit; whirlpool.

gouge (1) [gu:ʒ], *n.f.* (*S. Fr.*) Maidservant; daughter, wife; woman; whore.

gouge (2) [gu:ʒ], *n.f.* Gouge. **gouger**, *v.t.* To gouge. **gougette**, *n.f.* Small gouge.

gouin [gwɛ̃], *n.m.* (*fam.*) Bad lot. **gouine**, *n.f.* Street-walker.

goujat [gu'ʒa], *n.m.* *Soldier's servant, camp-follower; mason's hodman; (*S. dial.*) lad; (*fig.*) cad, scurvy, vulgar fellow. **goujaterie**, *n.f.* Caddishness; scurvy trick.

goujon (1) [gu'ʒɔ̃], *n.m.* Gudgeon (iron pin or spindle); coupling-bolt; dowel. *Goujon de chaîne*, link-pin (of bicycle).

goujon (2) [gu'ʒɔ̃], *n.m.* Gudgeon (fish). *Avaler le goujon*, to swallow the bait, to fall for it.

goujonner [guʒɔ'ne], *v.t.* To assemble with the help of gudgeons; to dowel; to bolt.

goule [gul], *n.f.* Ghoul; (*pop.*) throat, mouth; gulp.

goulée [gu'le], *n.f.* (*slang*) Big mouthful.

goulet [gu'lɛ], *n.m.* Narrow entrance (to a harbour etc.); inlet, mouth, neck (of a bottle etc.); gully, gorge (between mountains etc.).

goulot [gu'lo], *n.m.* Neck (of a bottle etc.); (*pop.*) mouth; gullet.

goulotte [gu'lɔt] or **goulette**, *n.f.* Water-channel.

goulu [gu'ly], *a.* Gluttonous, greedy.—*n.* Glutton, greedy person. **goulûment,** *adv.* Greedily.

goum [gum], *n.m.* (*Arab.*) Tribe, family; (*Mil.*) African contingent. **goumier,** *n.m.* Soldier or horseman member of *goum*.

*goupil [gu'pi], *n.m.* Fox.

goupille [gu'pi:j], *n.f.* Pin, peg, bolt. **goupiller,** *v.t.* To pin, to bolt, to key; to fix, to rig up.

goupillon [gupi'jɔ̃], *n.m.* Aspersorium, aspergillum, holy-water sprinkler; brush, bottle-brush, etc. (*fig.*) *Le sabre et le goupillon,* the Army and the Church.

gourbi [gur'bi], *n.m.* Arab hut; shack.

gourd [gu:r], *a.* (*fem.* **gourde** (1)) Benumbed, numb.

gourde (2) [gurd], *n.f.* Gourd, calabash; wicker bottle, flask, wineskin; (*pop.*) idiot, fathead.

gourdin [gur'dɛ̃], *n.m.* Cudgel, club, thick stick.

goure [gu:r], *n.f.* Adulterated drug; (*fig.*) take-in. **gourer,** *v.t.* To adulterate drugs; (*fig.*) to cheat, to take in. **se gourer,** *v.r.* (*vulg.*) To make a mistake. **goureur,** *n.m.* (*fem.* **-euse**) Adulterator of drugs; (*fig.*) cheat, trickster.

gourgandine [gurgɑ̃'din], *n.f.* Harlot, hussy.

gourgane [gur'gan], *n.f.* Small garden bean; Windsor bean.

gourgouran [gurgu'rɑ̃], *n.m.* Indian silk stuff.

gourmade [gur'mad], *n.f.* Smack in the face, cuff, fisticuff.

gourmand [gur'mɑ̃], *a.* (*fem.* **-ande**) Greedy. —*n.* Glutton, epicure, gourmand; sucker (on trees).

gourmander [gurmɑ̃'de], *v.t.* To chide, to reprimand, to reprove harshly; to prune trees.

gourmandise [gurmɑ̃'di:z], *n.f.* Gluttony, greediness; *pl.* sweetmeats.

gourme [gurm], *n.f.* (*Vet.*) Strangles; (*Path.*) ringworm of the scalp. *Jeter sa gourme,* to have a running at the nose (of a horse); (*fig.*) to sow one's wild oats.

gourmé [gur'me], *a.* (*fem.* **-ée**) Stiff, starched, stuck-up, formal, solemn.

gourmer [gur'me], *v.t.* To box, to thump, to pummel; to curb (a horse). **se gourmer,** *v.r.* To thump, to pummel each other; to adopt a starched, stiff air.

gourmet [gur'mɛ], *n.m.* Connoisseur in wines etc.; gourmet, epicure.

gourmette [gur'mɛt], *n.f.* Curb, curb-chain. *Fausse gourmette,* lip strap.

gournable [gur'nabl], *n.f.* Treenail. **gournabler,** *v.t.* To treenail.

gourou [gu'ru], *n.m.* Guru, Indian religious chief; Christian missionary (in India).

goussant [gu'sɑ̃] or **goussaut,** *a.* and *n.m.* Thick-set (horse, dog, etc.).

gousse [gus], *n.f.* Shell, pod, husk. *Gousse d'ail,* clove of garlic; *gousse de vanille,* vanilla pod.

gousset [gu'sɛ], *n.m.* Armpit; fob, pocket; waistcoat-pocket, gusset (of a shirt etc.); bracket. *Avoir le gousset bien garni,* to have one's pockets well lined; *vider un gousset,* to pick a pocket.

goût [gu], *n.m.* Taste, flavour, relish; savour,
tincture, smack; (*pop.*) smell, odour; fancy, inclination, liking; style, manner, fashion. *Avoir bon goût,* to taste nice, to have good taste; *avoir du goût,* to have good taste; to have flavour; *avoir du goût pour,* to like, to have a liking for; *avoir le* (or *un*) *goût de,* to taste of; *avoir le goût dépravé,* to have one's palate out of order; *avoir un goût délicieux,* to taste delicious; *cela est-il de votre goût?* is that to your taste? *ce pain a un goût de noisette,* that bread tastes of nuts; *c'est un critique plein de goût,* he is a critic of great taste; *c'est une affaire de goût,* it is a matter of taste; *ces vers sont dans le goût de Racine,* these verses are in the style of Racine; *chacun à son goût,* every man to his taste; *chacun son goût,* tastes differ; *de bon goût,* in good taste; *de mauvais goût,* in bad taste, vulgar; *des goûts et des couleurs on ne discute pas,* there is no accounting for tastes; *prendre goût à une chose,* to take a liking to a thing; *relever le goût,* to give a relish or zest to; *satisfaire ses goûts,* to satisfy one's tastes; *trouver une chose à son goût,* to find a thing to one's liking, to be partial to; *viande de haut goût,* highly seasoned meat. **goûter** (1), *v.t.* To taste, to try; to approve of, to appreciate, to relish, to like; to enjoy, to delight in; to smell; to feel. *Goûter le repos,* to enjoy repose; *goûter une plaisanterie,* to enjoy, to relish a joke; *voulez-vous goûter notre vin?* will you taste our wine?—*v.i.* To taste, to make trial (*de* or *à*); to have a snack between lunch and dinner. *Goûtez de ce vin,* try this wine. **goûter** (2), *n.m.* A snack taken between lunch and dinner (the equivalent of English tea); collation.

goutte (1) [gut], *n.f.* Drop, small quantity; sip, sup, dram; (*Arch., Pharm.*) drop, gutta. *Boire la goutte,* to have a drop (of liquor); *boire une goutte,* to have a nip, (*fam.*) to be nearly drowned, to lose heavily; *c'est une goutte d'eau dans la mer,* it is a drop in the ocean; *goutte à goutte,* drop by drop; *goutte à goutte on emplit la cuve,* many a mickle makes a muckle; *ils se ressemblent comme deux gouttes d'eau,* they are as like as two peas; *mère goutte,* unpressed wine; *payer la goutte,* to stand a drink.—*adv. phr.* (*ne . . . goutte*). *N'entendre goutte,* not to hear or understand in the least; *n'y voir goutte,* not to make it out at all.

goutte (2) [gut], *n.f.* Gout. *Accès de goutte,* attack of gout; *être travaillé de la goutte,* to suffer from gout; *goutte militaire,* gleet; *goutte sciatique,* sciatica.

gouttelette [gu'tlɛt], *n.f.* Small drop, drip. **goutter,** *v.i.* To drip.

goutteux [gu'tø], *a.* and *n.* (*fem.* **-euse**) Gouty.

gouttière [gu'tjɛ:r], *n.f.* Gutter of a roof; shoot, spout (for rain-water); cornice (of a carriage); fore-edge (of a book); fuller (of blade); (*Anat.*) groove; (*Surg.*) cradle splint. *Un chat de gouttière,* a stray, a common or garden cat.

gouvernable [guvɛr'nabl], *a.* Governable, manageable.

gouvernail [guver'na:j], *n.m.* Rudder, helm; (*Av.*) elevator. (*Av.*) *Gouvernail de profondeur,* elevator, elevating plane. *Tenir le gouvernail,* to be at the helm.

gouvernance [guver'nã:s], *n.f.* Governorship. **gouvernant**, *a.* (*fem.* **-ante**) Governing, ruling.—*n.m.* Governor, ruler. *Les gouvernants*, the powers that be.—*n.f.* Governor's wife; governess; housekeeper (of bachelor). **gouverne** [gu'vern], *n.f.* Guidance, guide, direction; rule of conduct; *pl.* (*Av.*) rudders and ailerons. *Je vous dis cela pour votre gouverne*, I tell you that for your guidance. **gouvernement** [guvernə'mã], *n.m.* Government, direction, rule, sway; management; governorship; government-house. **gouvernemental**, *a.* (*fem.* **-ale**, *pl.* **-aux**) Governmental.

gouverner [guver'ne], *v.t.* To control, to govern, to direct, to steer; to rule, to command, to manage, to regulate, to take care of; to husband; to bring up (children); to rein up (a horse). *Gouverner un ménage*, to direct, to run a household, a home; *gouverner un vaisseau*, to steer a ship; *verbe qui gouverne l'accusatif*, verb governing the accusative.—*v.i.* To steer, to answer the helm. **gouverneur**, *n.m.* Governor; manager; tutor, preceptor; (*Mil.*) commanding officer of a fortified place.

goyave [gɔ'ja:v], *n.f.* Guava. **goyavier**, *n.m.* Guava-tree.

grabat [gra'ba], *n.m.* Pallet, litter (of straw etc.), miserable bed. *Sur le grabat*, laid up; (*fig.*) wretchedly poor. **grabataire**, *n.* (*colloq.*) Bed-ridden person.

grabuge [gra'by:ʒ], *n.m.* (*fam.*) Wrangling, squabble, brawl. *Il va y avoir du grabuge*, there'll be a rumpus.

grâce [grɑ:s], *n.f.* Grace, favour, pardon, mercy, forgiveness, indulgence; thanks; gracefulness, elegance, charm; (*pl.*) thanks; (*Myth.*) Graces. *Accorder une grâce*, to grant a favour; *actions de grâce*, thanksgiving; *à la grâce de Dieu!* in God's hands! (*colloq.*) anyhow; *avec grâce*, gracefully; *coup de grâce*, grace-stroke, quietus, finishing stroke; *de grâce!* for mercy's sake! *demander grâce à*, to ask pardon of, to call for quarter; *demander en grâce*, to ask as a favour, to entreat; *de mauvaise grâce*, reluctantly, grudgingly; *dire ses grâces*, to say grace; *faire grâce à quelqu'un*, to forgive someone, to grant him a free pardon; *faire grâce de*, to spare; *faire une chose de bonne grâce*, to do a thing with a good grace; *faire une grâce à quelqu'un*, to do someone a favour; *faire des grâces*, to preen oneself; *grâce à Dieu!* thank God! *grâce à lui*, thanks to him; *il est dans les bonnes grâces du roi*, he is in the king's good graces; *j'aurais mauvaise grâce à refuser*, it would be ungracious of me to refuse; *je vous en fais grâce*, I let you off; *je vous rends grâce*, I thank you; *l'an de grâce*, the year of grace, the year of our Lord; *perdre les bonnes grâces de quelqu'un*, to lose someone's good graces; *point de grâce*, no mercy, no quarter; *rendre grâces au ciel*, to give thanks to heaven; *rentrer en grâce*, to get into favour again; *sacrifier aux grâces*, to sacrifice to the Graces; *sans grâce*, graceless; *trouver grâce devant quelqu'un*, to find favour with someone.

graciable [gra'sjabl], *a.* Pardonable. **gracier**, *v.t.* (*conjugated like* PRIER) To pardon, to reprieve.

gracieusement [grasjøz'mã], *adv.* Graciously, kindly, gracefully. **gracieuseté**, *n.f.*

Graciousness, kindness, affability; act of courtesy; acknowledgment, gratuity. *Ce serait une gracieuseté de votre part*, it would be an act of kindness on your part.

gracieux [gra'sjø], *a.* (*fem.* **-ieuse**) Graceful, courteous, gracious, affable, amiable, obliging; complimentary, free. *À titre gracieux*, free of charge.

gracilité [grasili'te], *n.f.* Gracility; slimness, slenderness.

Gracques [grak], **les**, *m. pl.* The Gracchi. **gradation** [gradɑ'sjɔ̃], *n.f.* Gradation; climax. *Gradation inverse*, anti-climax.

grade [grad], *n.m.* Grade, rank; degree. *Monter en grade*, to be promoted. **gradé**, *n.m.* (*Mil.*) Non-commissioned officer; (*Naut.*) rated man. *Les gradés*, (*Naut.*) the petty officers; (*Mil.*) *tous les gradés*, all ranks (officers and n.c.o.s). **grader**, *v.t.* To confer a grade or rank on.

gradin [gra'dɛ̃], *n.m.* Step; tier; stope (of mine).

graduation [gradɥa'sjɔ̃], *n.f.* Graduation; division into degrees; scale; graduation house (in salt manufacture).

gradué [gra'dɥe], *a.* (*fem.* **-ée**) Graduated; progressive (exercises).—*n.* Graduate (of a university).

graduel [gra'dɥel], *a.* (*fem.* **-elle**) Gradual.—*n.m.* (*R.-C. Ch.*) Gradual. **graduellement**, *adv.* Gradually, progressively.

graduer [gra'dɥe], *v.t.* To graduate, to proportion; to graduate (a thermometer, rule, etc.); to increase gradually; to confer a degree upon.

gradus [gra'dys], *n.m.* *Le gradus* (*ad Parnassum*), dictionary of prosody.

graffite [gra'fit] or **graffito** [It.], *n.m.* (*pl.* **graffites** or **graffiti**) Graffito. *pl. Graffiti*, defacement of walls in public places.

graillement [graj'mã], *n.m.* Hoarseness, huskiness. **grailler**, *v.i.* To speak huskily; (*Hunt.*) to sound the horn to recall the hounds.

graillon (1) [gra'jɔ̃], *n.m.* *Sentir le graillon*, to smell of burnt meat or fat.—*n.m. pl.* Scraps (of meat etc.) from a meal.

graillon (2) [gra'jɔ̃], *n.m.* (*vulg.*) Thick phlegm or expectoration. **graillonner** (1), *v.i.* To cough in order to expectorate, to hawk.

graillonner (2) [grajɔ'ne], *v.i.* To smell of burnt meat or fat. **graillonneur**, *n.m.* (*fem.* **-euse**) Bad cook.

grain (1) [grɛ̃], *n.m.* Grain, berry; hard food (for fowls); bead; jot, bit, particle; (*Med.*) pustula; (*Pharm.*) minute pill etc.; (*Weight*) grain. *Avoir un grain*, to have a bee in one's bonnet; *avoir un grain de folie*, to have a touch of madness; *avoir son grain*, to be slightly tipsy; *grain de beauté*, mole, beauty-spot; *grain de café*, coffee bean; *grain de chapelet*, bead of a rosary; *grain de plomb*, pellet; *grain de poivre*, peppercorn; *grain de raisin*, grape; *gros grains*, wheat and rye, winter corn; *menus grains*, spring corn; *il n'a pas un grain de bon sens*, he has not a grain of sense; *le grain d'une étoffe*, the grain of a cloth; *mettre son grain de sel*, to chip in, to add fuel (to conversation); *poulets de grain*, corn-fed pullets; *le grain d'orge* (*Mil.*), the bead (of foresight).

grain (2) [grɛ̃], *n.m.* (*Naut.*) Squall, gust of wind with shower. *Essuyer un grain*, to be overtaken by a squall, to go through, to experience a squall; *temps à grains*, squally weather; *veiller au grain*, to forestall danger, to keep one's weather-eye open.

graine [grɛːn], *n.f.* Seed; breed. *C'est une mauvaise graine*, he is a bad lot; *graine de lin*, linseed; *graine de niais*, bait for fools; *graine de vers à soie*, silkworm's eggs; *monter en graine*, to run to seed, (*fig.*) to be growing into an old maid; (*fam.*) *prendre de la graine*, to model oneself on somebody, to learn from example.

graineler etc. [GRENELER].

graineterie [grɛnˈtri], *n.f.* Trade or shop of a seedsman. **grainetier,** *n.m.* (*fem.* **-ière**) Seedsman, seedswoman, corn-chandler.

grainier, *n.m.* (*fem.* **-ière**) Seedsman, seedswoman; collection of seeds.

graissage [grɛˈsaːʒ], *n.m.* Greasing, oiling, lubrication.

graisse [grɛːs], *n.f.* Fat, grease. *Graisse de bœuf*, suet; *graisse de cuisine*, kitchen-stuff; *graisse de rôti*, dripping; *la graisse ne l'étouffe pas* or *ne l'empêche pas de courir*, he is very thin; *prendre de la graisse*, to get fat. **graisser,** *v.t.* To grease; to make greasy; to lubricate, to oil. *Graisser la patte à quelqu'un*, (*fig.*) to give someone a tip, to grease someone's palm.—*v.i.* To get ropy (of wine). **graisseur,** *n.m.* (*fem.* **graisseuse** (1)) Greaser, oiler (man); lubricator, oiler, grease-cup (in engines). **graisseux,** *a.* (*fem.* **graisseuse** (2)) Greasy; oily; fatty. *Vin graisseux*, ropy wine.

*****gralle** [gral], *n.m.* Grallatorial bird, wading-bird. **grallipède,** *a.* Grallatory, long-legged.

gram [gram], *n.m.*, or *Liqueur de Gram*, Gram's solution.

gramen [graˈmɛn], *n.m.* Gramineous plant, lawn-grass. **graminée,** *a.f.* Gramineous. —*n.f. pl.* **les graminées,** Gramineae.

grammaire [graˈmɛːr], *n.f.* Grammar. **grammairien,** *n.m.* (*fem.* **-ienne**) Grammarian. **grammatical,** *a.* (*fem.* **-ale,** *pl.* **-aux**) Grammatical. **grammaticalement,** *adv.* Grammatically.

gramme [gram], *n.m.* Gramme or gram.

grand [grɑ̃], *a.* Great; large, big; high, lofty, tall; wide, spacious, capacious; grown-up, full-grown; full; much; big, capital (of letters); broad (of daylight); grand, noble, majestic. *À mon grand regret*, much to my regret; *grand air*, open air; *grand livre*, ledger; *grand livre de la dette publique*, list of the creditors of the State; *grand seigneur*, great lord; *Grand Seigneur, Grand Turc*, Grand Turk, Sultan of Turkey; *grand homme*, great man; *homme grand*, tall man; *il fait grand jour*, it is broad daylight; *il est grand temps de partir*, it is high time you were off; *il fut grand dans l'adversité*, he bore up well in adversity; *j'ai eu grand'peur*, I was very much frightened; *le grand monde*, the fashionable world; *le grand ressort*, the main spring; *les grandes eaux*, fountains in full play (at Versailles); *les grands crus*, vintage wines; *une grande personne*, a grown-up person; *un grand personnage*, a great personage; *voleur de grand chemin*, highwayman.—*adv. Voir grand*, to have big ideas. *En grand*, on a large

scale; (of portraits) full length.—*n.m.* Great person, magnate; grown-up person; the grand, the sublime; (*pl.*) the great, great people; (*sch.*) the big (or senior) boys or girls. *Grand d'Espagne*, Spanish grandee.

(C) **grand-bois** [grɑ̃ˈbwa], *n.m.* Virgin forest.

grand-chose [grɑ̃ˈʃoz], *adv.* (usually in the negative) *Il ne fait pas grand-chose*, he does not do much; *ça ne vaut pas grand-chose*, it is of no great value, practically worthless.—*n. C'est une pas grand-chose*, (*pop.*) she's not up to much, not much good.

grand-duc (1) [grɑ̃ˈdyk], *n.m.* (*pl.* **grands-ducs**) Grand duke; eagle-owl.

grand-duc (2) etc. [DUC]. **grand-duché,** *n.m.* (*pl.* **grands-duchés**) Grand-duchy. **grande-duchesse,** *n.f.* (*pl.* **grandes-duchesses**) Grand-duchess.

grandelet [grɑ̃ˈdlɛ], *a.* (*fem.* **-ette**) Biggish, pretty tall. **grandement,** *adv.* Greatly, highly, extremely, largely, very much; grandly, nobly, handsomely. **grandesse,** *n.f.* Grandeeship.

grandeur [grɑ̃ˈdœːr], *n.f.* Extent, size, dimensions, height; length; breadth; bulk, bulkiness; greatness, largeness, magnitude, bigness; tallness; grandeur, nobleness, magnificence; grace, highness (titles). *De grandeur naturelle*, life-size; *grandeur d'âme*, magnanimity; *il a un air de grandeur qui impose*, he has an air of distinction that commands respect; *il a la folie des grandeurs*, he has delusions of greatness; *ils sont de même grandeur*, they are of the same size; *regarder quelqu'un du haut de sa grandeur*, to look down upon someone. *Sa Grandeur*, his Grace.

grand-garde [grɑ̃ˈgard], *n.f.* (*pl.* **grand-gardes**) Outpost (picket).

grandiose [grɑ̃ˈdjoːz], *a.* Grandiose.

grandir [grɑ̃ˈdiːr], *v.i.* To grow; to grow larger; to grow tall, to grow big; to grow up. *Grandir trop pour ses habits*, to grow out of one's clothes.—*v.t.* To increase; to exalt; to magnify. **se grandir,** *v.r.* To make oneself appear taller; to grow taller; to raise oneself, to rise. **grandissant,** *a.* (*fem.* **-ante**) Growing, increasing. **grandissement,** *n.m.* Growth, increase; rise; (*Opt.*) magnification.

grandissime [grɑ̃diˈsim], *a.* Very great, very large.

grand-maman [grɑ̃maˈmɑ̃], *n.f.* Granny.

grand-mère [grɑ̃ˈmɛːr], *n.f.* (*pl.* **grand-mères**) Grandmother.

grand-messe [grɑ̃ˈmɛs], *n.f.* High mass.

grand-oncle [grɑ̃ˈtɔ̃kl], *n.m.* (*pl.* **grands-oncles**) Great-uncle. **grands-parents,** *n.m. pl.* Grand-parents. **grand-père,** *n.m.* (*pl.* **grands-pères**) Grandfather.

grand-prêtre [grɑ̃ˈprɛtr], *n.m.* (*pl.* **grands-prêtres**) High priest.

grand-route, *n.f.* High road, main road.

grand-rue, *n.f.* High street, main street.

grand-tante [grɑ̃ˈtɑ̃t], *n.f.* (*pl.* **grand-tantes**) Great-aunt.

grange [grɑ̃ːʒ], *n.f.* Barn. *Batteur en grange*, thresher.

granit [graˈnit or graˈni] or **granite** [graˈnit], *n.m.* Granite. **granitaire,** *a.* Granitoid. **granité,** *n.m.* Pebbly-textured cloth.—*a.* (*fem.* **-ée**) Crackled, pebbled (surface). **granitique,** *a.* Granitic.

granivore [grani'vɔ:r], *a.* Granivorous.
granulaire [grany'lɛ:r], *a.* Granular. **granulation,** *n.f.* Granulation.
granule [gra'nyl], *n.m.* Granule. **granulé,** *a.* (*fem.* -ée) Granulated, granular. **granuler,** *v.t.* To granulate. **granuleux,** *a.* (*fem.* -euse) Granulous, granular. **granulie,** *n.f.* Granulitis.
graphie [gra'fi], *n.f.* **graphisme** [gra'fism], *n.m.* (Way of) writing. **graphique,** *a.* Graphic.—*n.m.* Diagram; graph. **graphiquement,** *adv.* Graphically.
graphite [gra'fit], *n.m.* Graphite; plumbago.
graphologie [grafɔlɔ'ʒi], *n.f.* Graphology. **graphologique,** *a.* Graphological. **graphologue,** *n.* Graphologist.
graphomètre [grafɔ'mɛtr], *n.m.* Graphometer. **graphométrique,** *a.* Graphometric.
grapin [GRAPPIN].
grappe [grap], *n.f.* Bunch (of grapes, currants, etc.); cluster (of fruit etc.); (*Artill.*) grape, grapeshot; (*Vet.*) grape, wart. *A grosses grappes,* in thick clusters; *croître en grappe,* to cluster. *Mordre à la grappe,* to jump at the offer, to swallow the bait.
grappillage [grapi'ja:ʒ], *n.m.* Vine-gleaning or pickings. **grappiller,** *v.t.* To glean (grapes); (*fig.*) to glean.—*v.i.* To glean; to get pickings, to make a little profit. **grappilleur,** *n.m.* (*fem.* **grappilleuse**) Grapegleaner, gleaner; petty thief, profiteer. **grappillon,** *n.* Small bunch of grapes; part of a bunch of grapes.
grappin or **grapin** [gra'pɛ̃], *n.m.* Grapnel, grappling-iron; grab; (*pl.*) climbing-irons. *Grappin de draguage,* sweep. *Mettre* or *jeter le grappin sur quelqu'un,* to get someone into one's clutches, to influence unduly.
grappu [gra'py], *a.* (*fem.* -ue) Loaded with bunches.
gras [grɑ], *a.* (*fem.* **grasse**) Fat; fleshy, fatty, corpulent, obese; greasy, oily, unctuous; rich; slippery; broad, indecent; (*Paint.*) thick; (*Print.*) thick (of letters). *Boue grasse,* slimy mud; *de gras pâturages,* rich pastures; *eaux grasses,* dishwater; *encre grasse,* thick ink; *faire la grasse matinée,* to sleep all the morning, to get up late; *gros et gras,* fat and lusty; *jour gras,* meat-day; *les jours gras,* Shrovetide; *mardi gras,* Shrove Tuesday; *matières grasses,* fats; *pavé gras,* slippery causeway; *plante grasse,* thick-leaved plant; *rire gras,* fat laugh; *soupe grasse,* meat soup; *terre grasse,* clayey soil; *terres grasses,* rich land; *toux grasse,* throaty cough; *tuer le veau gras,* to kill the fatted calf; *vin gras,* ropy wine; *voix grasse,* oily voice.—*n.m.* Fat, fat part (of meat etc.); meat, flesh; meat diet. *Faire gras* or *manger gras,* to eat meat. *Le gras de la jambe,* the calf; *le gras du pouce,* the ball of the thumb.—*adv.* Thick. *Parler gras,* to pronounce strongly the r's and roll them; to speak thickly. **gras-double,** *n.m.* Tripe.
grassement [grɑs'mɑ̃], *adv.* Plentifully, largely; liberally, at ease, in affluence, comfortably. *Payer grassement,* to pay generously; *vivre grassement,* to live on the fat of the land.
grasset (1) [gra'sɛ], *n.m.* (*Vet.*) Stifle; stifle-joint.
grasset (2) [grɑ'sɛ], *a.* (*fem.* **grassette** (1)) Fattish, pretty fat, plump.

grassette (2) [gra'sɛt], *n.f.* (*Bot.*) Butterwort.
grasseyement [grasɛj'mɑ̃], *n.m.* Exaggerated rolling of uvular r. **grasseyer,** *v.i.* To roll one's r's.
grassouillet [grɑsu'jɛ], *a.* (*fem.* -ette) (*fam.*) Plump, chubby.
grateron [gra'trɔ̃], *n.m.* Goose-grass, cleavers.
graticuler [gratiky'le], *v.t.* To divide into squares (a drawing).
gratification [gratifika'sjɔ̃], *n.f.* Gratuity, extra pay or reward. **gratifier,** *v.t.* To confer (a favour) on, to bestow (a present etc.) on; to favour; to attribute, to ascribe.
gratin [gra'tɛ̃], *n.m.* Burnt part; gratin. *Au gratin,* (*Cook.*) dressed with crust of bread-crumbs. (*fam.*) *Le gratin,* the upper crust (of society). **gratiner** [grati'ne]; *v.t.* To prepare (a dish) with bread-crumbs.
gratiole [gra'sjɔl], *n.f.* (*Bot.*) Gratiola. *Gratiole officinale,* hedge-hyssop.
gratis [gra'tis], *adv.* Gratis, for nothing, gratuitously; free of cost.
gratitude [grati'tyd], *n.f.* Gratitude.
grattage [gra'ta:ʒ], *n.m.* Scratching, scraping; scratching out.
gratte [grat], *n.f.* Scraper; (C) leveller; (*colloq.*) pickings (surreptitious profit); perks.
gratteau [gra'to], *n.m.* Gilder's scratcher.
gratte-boësse [grat'bwɛs], *n.f.* (*pl.* **gratte-boësses**) Scratch-brush (used by gilders).
gratte-ciel [grat'sjel], *n.m. inv.* Skyscraper.
gratte-cul, *n.m. inv.* Fruit of dog-rose, hip.
gratte-dos, *n.m. inv.* Back-scratcher.
gratteler [gra'tle], *v.t. irr.* (*conjugated like* APPELER) To scrape (metal etc.) lightly. **gratteleux,** *a.* (*fem.* -euse) Itchy.
grattelle [gra'tɛl], *n.f.* Rash, itching.
grattement [grat'mɑ̃], *n.m.* Scratching.
gratte-papier [gratpa'pje], *n.m. inv.* Scribbler, pen-pusher.
gratte-pieds [grat'pje], *n.m. inv.* Shoe-scraper.
gratter [gra'te], *v.t.* To scratch; to scrape; to scratch out, to erase; to rake; (*fig.*) (*spt.*) *Gratter un concurrent,* to overtake, to pass a competitor.—*v.i.* (*fam.*) To graft; to work. *Gratter à la porte,* to tap lightly on the door. **se gratter,** *v.r.* To scratch oneself; to rub oneself; to flatter each other. *Se gratter la tête,* to scratch one's head. **grattoir,** *n.m.* Scraper; eraser, paint-scraper.
gratteron [GRATERON].
gratuit [gra'tɥi], *a.* (*fem.* **gratuite**) Free (of charge); gratuitous. *Supposition gratuite,* gratuitous supposition. **gratuité,** *n.f.* Gratuitousness; exemption from fee or payment. **gratuitement,** *adv.* Free of charge, for nothing; gratuitously, groundlessly.
gravatier [grava'tje], *n.m.* Rubbish-carter.
gravats [gra'va], *n.m. pl.* Coarse siftings of plaster; rubbish, debris (of a building).
grave [gra:v], *a.* Heavy, grave, serious, solemn, sedate, sober; weighty, momentous, of importance; grievous; dangerous; low, deep, hollow, (*Mus.*) low-pitched. *Accent grave,* grave accent. *Blessure grave,* dangerous, severe wound. *Contenance* or *mine grave,* solemn look. *Note grave,* low note; *ton grave,* deep tone.—*n.m.* (*Mus.*) Low tone.—*n.f. pl.* Gravelly country N. of Bordeaux. (*Vin des*) *Graves,* Graves.
gravé [gra've], *a.* (*fem.* **gravée**) Pitted. *Être gravé de petite vérole,* to be pitted with

smallpox or pock-marked. *Pierre gravée,* engraved stone.

gravelage [gra'vla:ȝ], *n.m.* Gravelling.

gravelée [gra'vle], *n.f.* Wine-lees.

graveler [grav'le], *v.t. irr. (conjugated like* APPELER) To gravel, to cover with gravel.

graveleux [gra'vlø], *a. (fem.* **-euse)** Gravelly, sandy, gritty; troubled with gravel; *(fig.)* smutty.—*n.* Person affected with gravel.

gravelle [gra'vɛl], *n.f. (Path.)* Gravel.

gravelure [gra'vly:r], *n.f.* Dirty story, smut, smuttiness.

gravement [grav'mɑ̃], *adv.* Gravely, seriously, solemnly; grievously; *(Mus.)* deeply.

graver [gra've], *v.t.* To engrave, to grave; to impress, to imprint. *Graver à l'eau-forte,* to etch; *graver en creux,* to sink; *graver en relief,* to emboss. *Graver dans sa mémoire,* to impress on one's memory. **se graver,** *v.r.* To be engraved, to be impressed or imprinted. *Se graver quelque chose dans l'esprit,* to impress something on one's mind.

graveur, *n.m.* Engraver. *Graveur sur bois,* wood engraver; *graveur à l'eau forte,* etcher.

gravide [gra'vid], *a.* Gravid, pregnant.

gravier [gra'vje], *n.m.* Gravel, grit; *(Path.)* gravel. *Couvrir de gravier,* to gravel.

gravière, *n.f.* Gravel-pit; see also *pluvier.*

gravillon [gravi'jɔ̃], *n.m.* Fine gravel.

gravimètre [gravi'metr], *n.m.* Gravimeter.

gravir [gra'vi:r], *v.t.* To clamber up, to climb, to scale, to ascend.

gravitation [gravita'sjɔ̃], *n.f.* Gravitation.

gravité [gravi'te], *n.f.* Gravity; seriousness, solemnity; weight, importance; seriousness, grievousness (of a wound etc.); *(Mus.)* flatness, lowness. *Centre de gravité,* centre of gravity. *Gravité d'un son,* deepness of a sound. **graviter,** *v.i.* To gravitate; to revolve.

gravoir [gra'vwa:r], *n.m.* Graver, burin.

gravois [GRAVATS].

gravure [gra'vy:r], *n.f.* Engraving, cut, print; *(colloq.)* illustration (in book). *Gravure à l'eau forte,* etching; *gravure au trait,* line-engraving; *gravure en taille-douce,* copper-plate-engraving; *gravure sur acier,* steel-engraving; *gravure sur bois,* wood-engraving; *gravure sur pierre,* stone-engraving.

gré [gre], *n.m.* Will, wish; liking, pleasure; mind, taste, inclination; accord, consent. *Au gré des flots,* at the mercy of the waves; *bon gré mal gré* or *de gré ou de force,* whether one will or no, willy nilly; *cela est-il à votre gré?* is that to your liking? *de bon gré,* willingly; *de mauvais gré* or *contre son gré,* unwillingly, against the grain; *elle est assez à mon gré,* I like her well enough; *flotter au gré du vent,* to wave in the wind (of a flag etc.); *il y est allé de son gré,* he went of his own accord; *je lui en sais (bon) gré,* I am deeply grateful to him; *savoir (bon) gré à quelqu'un de quelque chose,* to be thankful to someone for something; *vendre de gré à gré,* to sell by private contract; *vous avez fait cela de votre plein* or *propre gré,* you did it of your own free will.

gréage [gre'a:ȝ], *n.m.* (Action of) rigging.

grèbe [grɛb], *n.m.* Grebe. *Grèbe castagneux,* dabchick or little grebe; *grèbe huppé,* great-crested grebe; *grèbe oreillard,* Slavonian grebe; *grèbe à cou noir,* black-necked grebe; *grèbe à joues grises,* red-necked grebe.

grébige [gre'biȝ] or **grébiche,** *n.f.* Spring binding, loose-leaf file; metallic edging (of portfolios etc.); file number.

grec [grɛk], *a. (fem.* **grecque** (1)) Greek; Grecian.—*n.m.* Greek language; *(fig.)* sharper; **(Grec,** *fem.* **Grecque)** Greek, Grecian. *C'est du grec pour moi,* that is all Greek, or Hebrew, to me. **Grèce,** *f.* Greece.

gréciser, *v.t.* To Hellenize. **grécité,** *n.f.* Greekness. **grecque** (2), *n.f. (Arch.)* Greek key-pattern, border; bookbinder's saw. *Orner de grecques,* to fret. **grecquer,** *v.t. (Bookb.)* To notch with a saw.

gredin [grə'dɛ̃], *n.m. (fem.* **-ine)** Rascal, scoundrel; small spaniel. **gredinerie,** *n.f.* Roguery, rascality.

gréement or **grément** [gre'mɑ̃], *n.m.* Rigging (of ship); gear (of boat). **gréer,** *v.t.* To rig. **gréeur,** *n.m.* Rigger.

greffe (1) [grɛf], *n.m. (Law)* Registry, record-office; registrar's office, clerk's office.

greffe (2) [grɛf], *n.f.* Graft; grafting, engraftment; *(Naut.)* horse-shoe (knot), cut-splice. *Greffe à l'anglaise,* whip-grafting; *greffe en couronne,* crown-graft; *greffe en écusson,* graft by gems, budding; *greffe en fente,* cleft-graft, graft by incision; *greffe par approche,* graft by approach. **greffer,** *v.t.* To graft. **greffeur,** *n.m.* Grafter.

greffier [gre'fje], *n.m.* Registrar, recorder, clerk of the court.

greffoir [gre'fwa:r], *n.m.* Grafting-knife.

greffon [grɛ'fɔ̃], *n.m.* Graft, scion, slip.

grégaire [gre'gɛ:r] or **grégarien** [grega'rjɛ̃] *(fem.* **-ienne),** *a.* Gregarious. **grégarisme,** *n.m.* Gregariousness.

grège [grɛ:ȝ], *a.* Raw (of silk).

grégeois [gre'ȝwa], *a.m.* Only used in *feu grégeois,* Greek fire.

Grégoire [gre'gwa:r], *m.* Gregory.

grégorien [gregɔ'rjɛ̃], *a. (fem.* **-ienne)** Gregorian.

****grègues** [grɛg], *n.f. pl.* Breeches. *Tirer ses grègues,* to run away, to take to one's heels.

grêle (1) [grɛ:l], *a.* Slender, slim, lank; thin, shrill, acute. *Des jambes grêles,* spindly legs. *Intestin grêle,* (Anat.) small intestine. *Voix grêle,* shrill voice.

grêle (2) [grɛ:l], *n.f.* Hail; hailstorm. *Grêle de coups,* shower of blows. *Méchant comme la grêle,* as wicked as the devil. **grêlé,** *a. (fem.* **-ée)** Ravaged by hail; pock-marked, pitted with smallpox; *(Her.)* set with pearls. **grêler,** *v.impers.* To hail. *Il grêle,* it hails. —*v.t.* To ravage, ruin, or spoil by hail.

grelet [grə'lɛ], *n.m.* Gurlet (of mason).

grêlet [grɛ'lɛ], *a. (fem.* **-ette)** Thinnish, puny.

grelin [grə'lɛ̃], *n.m. (Naut.)* Warp, hawser.

grêlon [grɛ'lɔ̃], *n.m.* Hailstone.

grelot [grə'lo], *n.m.* Small (round) bell. *Grelot blanc,* (Bot.) snowdrop. *Attacher le grelot,* to bell the cat, to take the first step. *Faire sonner son grelot,* to attract attention. *Avoir les grelots,* (pop.) to be afraid, to shiver. **grelotter,** *v.i.* To tremble, to shake, to shiver (with cold, fever, fear); to tinkle, to jingle. **grelottement,** *n.m.* Shivering.

****greluchon** [grəly'ʃɔ̃], *n.m.* Favoured lover.

grément [GRÉEMENT].

grémial [gre'mjal], *n.m. (pl.* **-iaux)** Gremial.

grémil [gre'mi], *n.m.,* or *herbe aux perles.* Gromwell.

grémille [gre'miːj] or **gremeuille,** *n.f.* Ruff, pope (fish).

grenade [grə'nad], *n.f.* Pomegranate; (*Mil.*) grenade. *Grenade à main,* hand-grenade; *grenade sous-marine,* depth-charge. **grenadier,** *n.m.* Pomegranate-tree; (*Mil.*) grenadier. *C'est un vrai grenadier,* she's an amazon; *jurer comme un grenadier,* to swear like a trooper. **grenadière,** *n.f.* Grenade-pouch; ring (of a rifle) to which the strap is fastened.

grenadille [grənə'diːj], *n.f.* (*Bot.*) Grana-dilla.

grenadin [grənə'dɛ̃], *n.m.* Small fricandeau; African finch; variety of carnation.

grenadine [grənə'din], *n.f.* Grenadine (silk or syrup).

grenage [grə'naː3], *n.m.* Granulating, reducing to grains (of gunpowder etc.); production of silkworm's eggs.

grenaille [grə'naːj], *n.f.* Granulated metal; small shot; very small potatoes, refuse corn (for poultry). **grenailler,** *v.t.* To granulate (metal).

grenaison [grənɛ'zɔ̃], *n.f.* Seeding, corning (of cereals).

grenat [grə'na], *n.m.* Garnet.—*a.* Garnet-red.

grené [grə'ne], *a.* (*fem.* **grenée**) Granulated; stippled (engraving).

greneler [grən'le], *v.t.* To grain (leather etc.).

grener [grə'ne], *v.i.* To seed, to produce seed. —*v.t.* To granulate; to grain (leather etc.); (*Engr.*) to stipple. *Grener de la poudre à canon,* to reduce gunpowder to grains.

greneter [GRENELER].

grèneterie etc. [GRAINETERIE].

grènetis [grɛn'ti], *n.m.* Milling, milled edge.

grenette [grə'nɛt], *n.f.* Coarse powder, small grain. *pl.* Avignon berries.

grenier [grə'nje], *n.m.* Loft, cock-loft; garret, attic; corn-loft, granary. *Charger en grenier,* (*Naut.*) to load in bulk; *grenier à foin,* hay-loft.

grenouille [grə'nuːj], *n.f.* Frog; (*Mil. slang*) company's mess funds; (*vulg.*) trollop. *Manger la grenouille,* to make away with the money. **grenouillère,** *n.f.* Place full of frogs, marshy place; (*fam.*) paddling-pool; (*fig.*) damp, unhealthy house etc. **grenouillet,** *n.m.* Solomon's seal. **grenouillette,** *n.f.* Frogbit; water crowfoot; (*Path.*) ranula, frog-tongue.

grenu [grə'ny], *a.* (*fem.* **grenue**) Full of corn; rough-grained (of the surface of leather etc.). *Cuir bien grenu,* leather that has a good grain. *Épi bien grenu,* ear full of corn. *Huile grenue,* clotted oil. *Marbre grenu,* grained marble.

grenure [grə'nyːr], *n.f.* Graining, stippling.

grès [grɛ], *n.m.* Sandstone, stoneware. *Grès à meule,* millstone grit; *grès cérame,* stone-ware. **gréseux,** *a.* (*fem.* **gréseuse**) Sandy, gritty. **grésière** or **gréserie,** *n.f.* Sand-stone quarry.

grésil [gre'zi], *n.m.* Sleet. **grésillement,** *n.m.* Pattering (like sleet); shrivelling, shrivelling up, crackling (as of parchment in the fire); chirping (of crickets etc.). **grésiller,** *v.impers.* To sleet, to patter.—*v.i.* To crackle.—*v.t.* To shrivel up.

grésillon [grezi'jɔ̃], *n.m.* Small coal.

gresserie [grɛs'ri], *n.f.* Sandstone; sandstone quarry; stoneware.

grève [grɛːv], *n.f.* Strand, beach of sand or shingle; sand-bank, shoal; strike of work-men. *En grève,* on strike; *faire* or *se mettre en grève,* to strike, to come out on strike; *grève du zèle,* working to rule; *grève sur le tas,* stay-in strike; *grève surprise,* lightning strike; *le droit de grève,* the right to strike.

grever [grə've], *v.t.* To wrong, to injure; to burden; to encumber (with debt etc.). *Grevé,* (*Law*) heir of entail. *Grevé de substitution,* entailed; *terre grevée d'hypothèques,* heavily mortgaged estate; *un pays grevé d'impôts,* a country burdened with taxes.

gréviste [gre'vist], *n.* Striker.

grianneau [gria'no], *n.m.* (*pl.* **grianneaux**) Young heath-cock, young grouse.

griblette [gri'blɛt], *n.f.* Piece of meat basted and grilled.

gribouillage [gribu'jaː3] or **gribouillis,** *n.m.* (*Paint.*) Daub; scrawl, scribble.

Gribouille [gri'buːj], *n.m.* Simpleton, block-head.

gribouiller [gribu'je], *v.t.*, *v.i.* To daub; to scrawl, to scribble.

gribouillette [gribu'jɛt], *n.f.* A scramble (scrambling for a toy etc.). *À la gribouillette,* carelessly, anyhow, at random; *attraper quelque chose à la gribouillette,* to scramble for something.

gribouilleur [gribu'jœːr], *n.m.* (*fem.* **gribouilleuse**) Dauber; scrawler, scribbler.

gribouri [gribu'ri], *n.m.* Vine-grub.

grief [gri'ef], *n.m.* Wrong, injury, grievance; complaint. *Faire grief à quelqu'un d'une chose,* to hold something as a grievance against somebody; *redresser un grief,* to redress a grievance.

grièvement [griɛv'mã], *adv.* Grievously, gravely. **grièveté,** *n.f.* Gravity, seriousness.

griffade [gri'fad], *n.f.* Clawing, scratch.

griffe [grif], *n.f.* Claw, talon; (*pl.*) claws, clutches; signature stamp; tool of claw-like form or function; paper-clip, clamp, dog. *Griffe d'asperge,* root of asparagus. *Apposer sa griffe à,* to put one's signature to. *Coup de griffe,* scratch, blow with claw; (*fig.*) *donner un coup de griffe à quelqu'un,* to do someone a bad turn; *je suis sous* or *entre ses griffes,* I am in his clutches. **griffer,** *v.t.* To seize or take with the claws; to claw, to scratch (of cats etc.); to stamp (with signature etc.).

griffon [gri'fɔ̃], *n.m.* Griffin (fabulous creature); griffon (a variety of terrier); tawny vulture.

griffonnage [grifɔ'naː3], *n.m.* Scrawl, scribble.

griffonner, *v.t.* To scrawl, to scribble; to sketch roughly. **griffonneur,** *n.m.* (*fem.* **griffonneuse**) Scrawler, scribbler.

grigne [griɲ], *n.f.* Pucker (of stuff). *Grigne du pain,* slash of a loaf. **grigner,** *v.i.* To pucker. **grignon,** *n.m.* Part of a loaf near the slash, which can be nibbled.

grignotage [griɲɔ'taː3] or **grignotement,** *n.m.* Nibbling.

grignoter [griɲɔ'te], *v.t.* To nibble, to gnaw; (*fig.*) to get pickings out of.

grignotis [griɲɔ'ti], *n.m.* Engraving in short lines.

grigou [gri'gu], *n.m.* Miserable skinflint, tight-fisted (old) fellow.

gri-gri or **gris-gris** [grigri], *n.m.* Amulet of Negroes, greegree.

gril [gri], *n.m.*　Gridiron, grill, griller; grate (for shot).　*Être sur le gril*, to be on the rack, to be on tenter-hooks.

grillade [gri'jad], *n.f.*　Grilling, broiling; grill, grilled steak.　*Mettre à la grillade*, to broil.

grillage (1) [gri'ja:ʒ], *n.m.*　Grilling, broiling; toasting; (*Metal.*) roasting.

grillage (2) [gri'ja:ʒ], *n.m.*　Wire lattice; wire guard or mesh; light iron railing.　*Grillage de bois*, (*Arch.*) grillage, foundation of timbers etc.

grillager, *v.t.*　To lattice, to grate, to fit or enclose with lattice-work.

grille [gri:j], *n.f.*　Railing, grating; grill; iron gate or bars; iron grate; (*Elec.*) grid.　*Grille en fer forgé*, (ornamental) wrought-iron gate.　*Grille à déchiffrer*, cipher stencil.

grille-pain [grij'pɛ̃], *n.m. inv.*　Toaster.

griller (1) [gri'je], *v.t.*　To broil, to grill (meat); to roast (coffee); to toast (bread); (*Metal.*) to scorch (of the sun); to dry up, to burn.　(*fam.*) *Griller une cigarette*, to smoke a cigarette.—*v.i.*　To broil, to be burned up or scorched; to burn out (elec. bulbs); (*fig.*) to be itching *or* impatient (to do something).　**se griller**, *v.r.*　To be scorched, to be parched; to scorch oneself.

griller (2) [gri'je], *v.t.*　To enclose with iron rails, to rail in; to shut up, to imprison, to cloister.

grillet [gri'jɛ], *n.m.*, *or* **grillette**, *n.f.*　Dog's bell, hawk's bell.　**grilleté**, *a.* (*fem.* **grilletée**) (*Falconry, Her.*) Belled.

grillon [gri'jɔ̃], *n.m.*　Cricket.　*Grillon domestique*, house-cricket; *grillon des champs*, field-cricket.

grimaçant [grima'sɑ̃], *a.* (*fem.* **grimaçante**) Grimacing, grinning; (*fig.*) gaping, creased; ill-fitting (of shoes etc.).

grimace [gri'mas], *n.f.*　Grimace, wry face; (*fig.*) (*pl.*) affectations, airs and graces.　*Cet habit fait la grimace*, that coat puckers.　*Faire des grimaces à quelqu'un*, to make faces at someone, to grin at someone; *faire la grimace*, to make a face, (*fig.*) to be disgusted.

grimacer, *v.i.*　To make faces, to grimace, to grin; to simper, to mince; to sham, to be affected; to pucker.　**grimacerie**, *n.f.*　Grimaces, grinning.　**grimacier**, *a.* (*fem.* **-ière**) Grimacing; simpering; mincing; dissembling, finical.—*n.* Affected, simpering individual; hypocrite, humbug.

grimaud [gri'mo], *a.* and *n.* (*fem.* **-aude**) Scribbler, pedant.

grime [grim], *n.m.*　(*Theat.*) Old fogy, dotard; actor playing this part.　*Jouer les grimes*, to play old men (parts).

grimer [gri'me], *v.t.*　To paint creases or wrinkles on, to make up.　**se grimer**, *v.r.*　To paint oneself, to make up, esp. as an old man, old woman, duenna, etc.

grimoire [gri'mwa:r], *n.m.*　Book of spells, black-book; obscure language, or illegible scrawl.

grimpant [grɛ̃'pɑ̃], *a.* (*fem.* **-ante**) Climbing, creeping, twining (of plants).—*n.m.* (*slang*) Trousers.

grimper [grɛ̃'pe], *v.i.*　To climb, to clamber up; to scale, to mount; to creep up (of plants).　**grimpeur**, *a.* (*fem.* **-euse**) Climbing, twining.—*n.m.* (*Orn.*) Climber (wood-pecker, parrot, etc.); (*spt.*) good at hill-climbing.

grimpereau [grɛ̃'pro], *n.m.* (*pl.* **-eaux**) Tree-creeper (bird).

grimpette [grɛ̃'pɛt], *n.f.*　Short steep incline; steep climb.

grincement [grɛ̃s'mɑ̃], *n.m.*　Gnashing, grinding (of the teeth etc.); grating.　**grincer**, *v.i.*　To grind, to gnash, to grate.　*Faire grincer les dents*, to make the teeth grate, to set the teeth on edge; *grincer des dents*, to grind one's teeth; *la porte grinça sur ses gonds rouillés*, the door grated on its rusty hinges.

grincher [grɛ̃'ʃe], *v.i.* (*fam.*) To growl, to snarl.

grincheux [grɛ̃'ʃø], *a.* (*fem.* **grincheuse**) Ill-tempered, peevish, crabbed, surly.—*n.m.* Grumbler.

gringalet [grɛ̃ga'lɛ], *n.m.*　Weak, puny man.

gringotter [grɛ̃gɔ'te], *v.i.*　To twitter; to hum.　—*v.t.*　To chirrup or hum (a tune).

gringuenaude [grɛ̃g'no:d], *n.f.* (*fam.*) Dirt, filth, picking.

griot [gri'o], *n.m.*　Seconds (of meal or flour).

griotte [gri'ɔt], *n.f.*　Morello cherry; marble with red and brown spots.　**griottier**, *n.m.* Morello cherry-tree.

grippage [gri'pa:ʒ] *or* **grippement**, *n.m.* Friction (of two surfaces); seizing, jamming (of bearing).

grippal [gri'pal], *a.* (*fem.* **-ale**) Influenzal.

grippe [grip], *n.f.*　Influenza, 'flu; (*colloq.*) crotchet, dislike.　*Prendre quelqu'un en grippe*, to take a dislike to someone.　**grippé**, *a.* (*fem.* **-ée**) Shrunk, contracted (of the face); ill with influenza; run hot, seized up (of motors).

grippeminaud [gripmi'no], *n.m.*　Grimalkin; (*fig.*) hypocritical rascal.

gripper [gri'pe], *v.t.*　To pounce upon, to clutch, to seize; to snatch up.—*v.i.*　To rub or adhere together with friction; to run hot, to seize up, to jam.　**se gripper**, *v.r.*　To shrivel, to shrink; to crease.　**grippe-sou**, *n.m.* (*pl.* **grippe-sou** *or* **grippe-sous**) Miser, money-grubber.

gris [gri], *a.* (*fem.* **grise**) Grey; grey-haired, grey-headed, hoary; raw, dull (of the weather); (*fig.*) tipsy, fuddled.　*En faire voir de grises à*, to lead someone a dance; *en voir de grises*, to have an unpleasant time of it; *faire grise mine à*, to give (someone) the cold shoulder; *il fait gris*, it is dull weather.　*Lettres grises*, (*Print.*) flourished letters.　*Papier gris*, brown paper.　*Tabac gris*, shag.—*n.m.* Grey.　*Gris brun*, drab; *gris cendré*, ash-grey; *gris perle*, pearl-grey; *une robe gris bleu*, a blue-grey dress.

grisaille [gri'za:j], *n.f.*　Grisaille; sketch or painting in tones of grey.　**grisailler**, *v.t.* To paint grey; to paint in grisaille.　**grisard**, *n.m.* Grey poplar.　**grisâtre**, *a.* Greyish.

griser [gri'ze], *v.t.*　To give a grey tint to; to intoxicate; (*fam.*) to make tipsy, to fuddle.　**se griser**, *v.r.*　To get tipsy, to be fuddled.

griserie, *n.f.*　Drunkenness, intoxication.　**griset**, *n.m.* (*pop.*) Young goldfinch.

grisette [gri'zɛt], *n.f.*　Grey gown, russet gown; *grisette (gay working-girl). See also fauvette.

gris-gris [GRI-GRI].

grisoller *or* **grisoler** [grizɔ'le], *v.i.*　To warble, to carol (of the lark).

grison [gri'zɔ̃], a. (fem. -onne) Grey, grey-haired, grey-headed, grizzled.—n.m. (colloq.) Grey-beard (old man); donkey. **grisonnant**, a. (fem. -ante) Turning grey, grizzled.
grisonner, v.i. To grow grey (of hair etc.).
grisou [gri'zu], n.m. Fire-damp [see COUP].
grive [gri:v], n.f. Thrush. Grive chanteuse, or musicienne, song-thrush, throstle; grive dorée, golden oriole; grive de brou or grosse grive, or grive draine, mistle-thrush; grive rouge, redwing; grive litorne, fieldfare. Faute de grives on mange des merles, half a loaf is better than no bread; soûl comme une grive, drunk as a lord.
grivelé [gri'vle], a. (fem. -ée) Speckled.
griveler [gri'vle], v.t. To pilfer, to filch.—v.i. To make illicit profits; (esp.) to sneak a meal (in a restaurant). **grivèlerie**, n.f. Pilfering; sponging. **griveleur**, n.m. Pilferer.
grivois [gri'vwa], a. (fem. -oise) Loose, broad, obscene. Conte grivois, improper story.—n. Lusty, merry fellow.—n.f. Jolly wench. **grivoiserie**, n.f. Smutty story.
Groenland [grɔen'lɑ̃d], m. Greenland.
grog [grɔg], n.m. Grog, toddy.
grognard [grɔ'ɲaːr], a. (fem. -arde) Grumbling, growling.—n. Grumbler, grouser; veteran of Napoleon's Old Guard. **grognasse**, n.f. (pop. and pej.) Woman; prostitute.
grognement [grɔɲ'mɑ̃], n.m. Grunt, grunting; growling, snarling, grumbling; snarl.
grogner [grɔ'ɲe], v.i. To grunt; to growl, to grumble, to grouse.—v.t. To moan, snarl, or growl (a sentence etc.). **grogneur**, a. (fem. -euse) Grumbling, grousing.—n. Grumbler, grouser. **grognon**, a. (fem. -onne, but usu. unchanged) Grumbling, peevish, querulous.—n. Grumbler, growler. **grognonner**, v.i. (colloq.) To grunt; to grumble, to grouse.
groin [grwɛ̃], n.m. Snout (of a hog).
groisil [GRÉSIL].
grole or **grolle** [grɔl], n.f. *Rook; (slang) shoe.
grommeler [grɔm'le], v.t., v.i. To mutter, to grumble.
grondant [grɔ̃'dɑ̃], a. (fem. -ante) Scolding; roaring, rumbling. **grondement**, n.m. Rumbling, growling, snarling; roar, peal, boom.
gronder [grɔ̃'de], v.i. To growl, to mutter; to snarl, to rumble, to roar.—v.t. To chide, to scold, to reprimand. **gronderie**, n.f. Scolding, chiding. **grondeur**, a. (fem. -euse) Grumbling, scolding.—n. Scold; grumbler.
grondin [grɔ̃'dɛ̃], n.m. (Ichth.) Gurnard, gurnet. Grondin gris, grey gurnard; grondin rouge or rouget, red gurnard.
groom [grum], n.m. Page, (U.S.) bell-boy; stable lad.
gros [gro], a. (fem. **grosse** (1)) Big, large, bulky; stout, corpulent; thick, coarse; great, considerable; swollen, pregnant, with child; loud (of laughter); gruff, rough (of the voice); heavy (of cavalry); rich, substantial; foul, bad, heavy (of the weather); high, violent (of the sea etc.); dark, deep (in colour). Avoir le cœur gros, to be deeply affected; gros bétail, bovine cattle; gros bonnet, bigwig; gros bon sens, plain common sense; gros drap, coarse cloth; gros lourdaud,

blockhead; gros mots, swear-words; (Cine.) gros plan, close-up; gros rhume, bad cold; grosse somme d'argent, large sum of money; grosse viande, butcher's meat; gros souliers, thick shoes; gros temps, foul, rough, heavy weather; jouer gros jeu, to play high; la mer est grosse, the sea runs high; le gros lot, the biggest prize; une femme grosse, a pregnant woman; une grosse femme, a stout woman; un gros marchand, a substantial tradesman. —n.m. Large, chief, or main part; bulk, mass; main body (of an army); large-hand capitals (writing). En gros, roughly; en gros et en détail, wholesale and retail. Faire le gros de la besogne, to do the heavy work. Gros de l'eau, spring tide; le commerce de gros, wholesale trade.—adv. Much. Gagner gros, to earn or win a great deal. **gros-bec**, n.m. (pl. **gros-becs**) Hawfinch. **gros-bleu**, a. and n.m. Dark blue.
groseille [gro'zɛːj], n.f. Currant. Groseille à maquereau, gooseberry. **groseillier**, n.m. Currant-bush. Groseillier épineux or à maquereau, gooseberry bush; groseillier rouge or castillier, red-currant bush; groseillier noir or cassissier, black-currant bush.
gros-grain [gro'grɛ̃], n.m. Grosgrain, grogram.
gros-jean [gro'ʒɑ̃], n.m. (pl. **gros-jeans**) Bumpkin, countryman. Être Gros-Jean comme devant, to be as you were (i.e. no better off). C'est Gros-Jean qui en remontre à son curé, he wants to teach his grandmother how to suck eggs.
grosse (1) [GROS].
grosse (2) [gros], n.f. Gross (twelve dozen); large-hand, engrossing (writing), engrossed text, draft, or copy; (Comm.) bottomry. Contrat de or à la grosse, bottomry bond; prêt à la grosse, bottomry loan.
grossement [gros'mɑ̃], adv. Grossly, coarsely.
grosserie [gros'ri], n.f. Ironmongery; *wholesale. Il ne fait que la grosserie, he is a wholesale dealer only.
grossesse [gro'sɛs], n.f. Pregnancy.
grosseur [gro'sœːr], n.f. Size, bulk; bigness, largeness, hugeness; swelling, tumour.
grossier [gro'sje], a. (fem. -ière) Gross, coarse, thick; homely, plain, common; clumsy, rough, rude, unpolished, unmannerly, scurrilous, churlish, boorish. Des meubles grossiers, clumsy furniture; erreur grossière, gross mistake; il m'aborda d'un air grossier, he accosted me rudely; mœurs grossières, unpolished manners; vous êtes bien grossier, or un grossier personnage, you are very unmannerly.—n. Unmannerly person.
grossièrement, adv. Coarsely, rudely, roughly, uncouthly, boorishly, churlishly.
grossièreté, n.f. Coarseness, grossness; rudeness, incivility, unmannerliness, churlishness; coarse language. Il lui a dit des grossièretés, he said rude things to him.
grossir [gro'siːr], v.t. To make bigger, larger, or greater; to enlarge, to augment, to increase, to swell, to swell out; to magnify, to exaggerate.—v.i. To grow bigger; to increase, to augment, to swell, to swell out, to be exaggerated. **grossissant**, a. (fem. -ante) Magnifying. Verre grossissant, magnifying-glass. **grossissement**, n.m. Magnifying, magnifying-power; enlargement, increase; exaggeration. **grossiste**, n.m. Wholesaler.

grosso-modo [grɔsomɔ'do], *adv.* Summarily.
grossoyer [groswa'je], *v.t. irr.* (*conjug. like* ABOYER) To engross (a document).
grotesque [grɔ'tɛsk], *a.* Grotesque, ludicrous.— *n.* The grotesque; grotesque (figure, dancer, etc.). **grotesquement**, *adv.* (*Rarely used*) Ludicrously.
grotte [grɔt], *n.f.* Grotto, cave.
grouillant [gru'jɑ̃], *a.* (*fem.* -**ante**) Stirring, teeming, swarming, crawling. *Tout grouillant de vermine*, crawling with vermin. **grouillement, grouillis**, *n.m.* Stirring, swarming; rumbling (of the intestines).
grouiller [gru'je], *v.i.* To stir, to move; to swarm, to be crawling, to be alive (*de*); to rumble (of the intestines). *Cela grouille de vermine*, that is alive with vermin; (*vulg.*) *j'ai le ventre qui grouille*, my tummy is grumbling. **se grouiller**, *v.r.* (*pop.*) To hurry up, to get a move on, to get cracking.
group [grup], *n.m.* Sealed bag of specie.
groupage [gru'pa:ʒ], *n.m.* Collecting (of parcels).
groupe [grup], *n.m.* Group, party (of people), cluster (of stars), clump (of trees etc.); class, division; unit. *Groupe de combat*, (*Mil.*) section; *groupe d'armées*, army group. **groupement,** *n.m.* Grouping. **grouper,** *v.t.* To group. **se grouper,** *v.r.* To form groups, to gather.
gruau (1) [gry'o], *n.m.* Flour of wheat. *Gruau d'avoine*, groats; oatmeal. *Pain de gruau*, finest wheaten bread; *tisane de gruau*, gruel.
gruau (2) [gry'o] or **gruon,** *n.m.* Young crane; small crane for lifting.
grue [gry], *n.f.* Crane (bird); (*Astron.*) the Crane; crane for lifting; (*slang*) prostitute; (*Cine.*) camera crane. *Faire le pied de grue*, to dance attendance, to kick one's heels.
gruger [gry'ʒe], *v.t.* To crunch; to eat, to devour, exploit. *Gruger du sucre*, to crunch sugar. *On nous gruge*, they eat us out of house and home, they fleece us. **grugerie,** *n.f.* Crunching, fleecing, **grugeur,** *n.m.* (*fem.* -**euse**) (*colloq.*) Sponger, parasite.
grume [grym], *n.f.* Bark. *Bois de* or *en grume*, wood with the bark on, rough timber.
grumeau [gry'mo], *n.m.* (*pl.* -**eaux**) Clot, small lump. **se grumeler,** *v.r.* To clot. **grumeleux,** *a.* (*fem.* -**euse**) Clotted, grumous; *Poires grumeleuses*, rough pears; *sang grumeleux*, clotted blood.
grumelure [grym'ly:r], *n.f.* Small cavity (in cast metal).
gruon [GRUAU (2)].
gruppetto [grupɛ'to], *n.m.* (*pl.* -**i**) (*Mus.*) Turn.
gruyère [gry'jɛ:r], *n.m.* Gruyère cheese.
guais [gɛ], *a. Hareng guais,* shotten (or spent) herring.
guano [gwa'no], *n.m.* Guano.
gué (1) [ge], *int.* [GAI].
gué (2) [ge], *n.m.* Ford. *Passer une rivière à gué*, to ford a river; *sonder le gué*, to see how the land lies. **guéable,** *a.* Fordable.
guèbre [gɛ:br], *n.m.* Guebre (fire-worshipper).
guède [gɛd], *n.f.* Woad, dyer's-woad. **guéder,** *v.t. irr.* (*conjug. like* ACCÉLÉRER) To dye with woad.
guédoufle [ge'dufl], *n.f.* Twin cruets (for oil and vinegar).
guéer [ge'e], *v.t.* To ford. *Guéer du linge,* to wash linen (in a stream); *guéer un cheval,* to water a horse.
guelfe [gɥɛlf], *n.m.* (*It. Hist.*) Guelph.
guelte [gɛlt], *n.f.* Commission on sales (for the vendor).
guenille [gə'ni:j], *n.f.* Rag, tatter; (*pl.*) rags, tattered clothes; (*fam.*) instead of *guenipe*. *La guenille*, the (human) body. **guenilleux,** *a.* (*fem.* -**euse**) Tattered, ragged, in rags. **guenillon,** *n.m.* Little rag.
guenipe [gə'nip], *n.f.* Slut; trollop, drab.
guenon [gə'nɔ̃], *n.f.* Monkey, ape; she-monkey; (*fig.*) fright, ugly woman. **guenuche,** *n.f.* Young she-monkey; (*colloq.*) ape in petticoats.
guépard [ge'pa:r], *n.m.* Cheetah.
guêpe [gɛ:p], *n.f.* Wasp. *Taille de guêpe,* wasp-waist. **guêpier,** *n.m.* Wasps' nest; bee-eater (bird); scrape, difficulty. *Tomber dans un guêpier,* to get into a hornets' nest or a scrape.
guère [gɛ:r], *adv.* But little, not much, not very; not long; not many, very few; hardly, scarcely, barely. *Il n'est guère sage,* he is not very wise; *il ne tardera guère à venir,* it will not be long before he comes, he will soon come; *je ne le vois guère,* I hardly ever see him; *n'avoir guère d'argent,* to have but little money; *n'avoir guère moins,* to have little less; *n'avoir guère plus,* to have little more.
guères, (*poet.*) [GUÈRE].
guéret [ge'rɛ], *n.m.* Ploughed but unsown land; fallow-land; furrow; (*pl., poet.*) fields.
guéridon [geri'dɔ̃], *n.m.* (Small) round table; (*Naut.*) scoop.
guérilla [geri'ja], *n.f.* Guerrilla.
guérir [ge'ri:r], *v.t.* To heal, to cure. *Guérir la fièvre,* to cure a fever; *guérir quelqu'un d'une erreur,* to rid someone of an error; *l'art de guérir,* the healing art.—*v.i.* To heal, to heal up; to recover, to be cured. *On ne guérit point de la peur,* fear admits of no cure.
guérison [geri'zɔ̃], *n.f.* Recovery, healing, cure. *Il lui doit sa guérison,* he owes his recovery to him. **guérissable,** *a.* Curable. **guérisseur,** *n.m.* (*fem.* -**euse**) Healer, curer; faith-healer; quack.
guérite [ge'rit], *n.f.* Sentry-box; cabin, shelter (of watchman); look-out turret.
Guernesey [gɛrnə'zɛ], *f.* Guernsey. **guernesiais,** *a. and n.* (*fem.* -**iaise**) (Native) of Guernsey.
guerre [gɛ:r], *n.f.* War; warfare, hostilities; strife, dissension, contest. *À la guerre comme à la guerre,* one must take things as they come; *allumer la guerre,* to kindle war; *c'est de bonne guerre,* it is quite fair; *cri de guerre,* war-cry; *de guerre lasse je cédai,* for the sake of peace and quiet I gave way; *en guerre,* at war, (*fig.*) at variance; *faire la guerre à,* to wage war upon, to be at war with, (*fig.*) to find fault with; *faire la guerre à ses passions,* to struggle against one's passions; *faire la guerre avec,* to serve with, to be a fellow-soldier of; *foudre de guerre,* great warrior; *gens de guerre,* military men; *guerre à outrance* or *à mort,* war to the knife; *guerre des nerfs,* war of nerves; *guerre d'usure,* war of attrition; *guerre éclair,* blitzkrieg; *guerre économique,* economic warfare; *guerre froide,* cold war; (*fam.*) *la drôle de guerre,* the phoney war (1939-40); *la grande guerre,* the great war

(1914–18); *la première guerre mondiale*, the first world war; *nom de guerre*, stage-name, assumed name; *petite guerre*, sham fight, war on a small scale; *place de guerre*, fortified town, fortress; *qui terre a, guerre a*, property may involve lawsuits; *vaisseau de guerre*, man-of-war. **guerrier**, *a.* (*fem.* **-ière**) Warlike, martial.—*n.* Warrior, fighting man or woman. **guerroyant**, *a.* (*fem.* **-ante**) Bellicose, pugnacious. **guerroyer**, *v.i.* To make war, to war. **guerroyeur**, *a.* and *n.m.* (Man) fond of fighting.

guet [gɛ], *n.m.* Watch; watching. *Au guet*, on the watch, on the look-out; *ce chien est de très bon guet*, this is a very good watch-dog; *être au guet, avoir l'œil au guet* or *l'oreille au guet*, to be on the watch, to be on the look-out; *guet de nuit*, patrol, night-watch; *maison du guet*, round-house.

guet-apens [gɛta'pɑ̃], *n.m.* (*pl.* **guets-apens**) Ambush, ambuscade, lying in wait; snare, trap. *Tendre* or *dresser un guet-apens à*, to waylay.

guêtre [gɛːtr], *n.f.* Gaiter. *Grandes guêtres*, leggings; *petites guêtres*, spats. *Laisser ses guêtres quelque part*, to leave one's bones somewhere; *tirer ses guêtres*, to run away, to hook it; *traîner ses guêtres*, to dawdle about. **guêtrer**, *v.t.* To put gaiters on, to gaiter. **se guêtrer**, *v.r.* To put on one's gaiters. **guêtrier**, *n.m.* (*fem.* **-ière**) Gaiter-maker.

guetter [gɛ'te], *v.t.* To lie in wait for; to watch for, to be on the look-out for, to waylay, to await. **guetteur**, *n.m.* Signalman, look-out man, watcher.

gueulard [gœ'laːr], *a.* (*fem.* **-arde**) (*pop.*) Bawling, mouthing; gluttonous; hard-mouthed (of horses).—*n.* Bawler; glutton. —*n.m.* Furnace-mouth; gully-hole; (*Naut.*) speaking-trumpet.

gueule [gœl], *n.f.* Mouth (of animals); (*vulg.*) instead of human mouth or face; jaw, mug, phiz. (*pop.*) *Avoir de la gueule*, to be smashing; *avoir la gueule de bois*, to have a bit of a head, to have a hangover; *fine gueule*, epicure, judge of good living; *gueule de canon*, muzzle of a gun; *gueule renversée*, (*Arch.*) ogive; *homme fort en gueule*, great talker, one with the gift of the gab, foul-mouthed or abusive man; *il est venu la gueule enfarinée*, he came blundering and full of confidence; *il n'a que de la gueule*, he is all talk; *ta gueule!* shut up! *les gueules cassées*, disfigured ex-service men; **gueule-de-lion**, *n.f.* (*pl.* **gueules-de-lion**) or *muflier rouge*, Antirrhinum. **gueule-de-loup**, *n.f.* (*pl.* **gueules-de-loup**) Snapdragon; chimney cowl. **gueule-de-raie**, *n.f.* (*pl.* **gueules-de-raie**) (*Naut.*) Cat's-paw knot. **gueulée**, *n.f.* (*colloq.*) Large mouthful; bawling.

gueulement [gœl'mɑ̃], *n.m.* (*pop.*) Howl, shout.

gueuler [gœ'le], *v.i.* (*pop.*) To bawl, to clamour, to mouth.—*v.t.* To seize; to mouth, to bawl (insults).

gueules [gœl], *n.m.* (*Her.*) Gules.

gueuleton [gœl'tɔ̃], *n.m.* (*vulg.*) A 'slap-up' dinner, banquet. **gueuletonner**, *v.i.* To feast, to carouse.

*****gueusaille** [gø'zɑːj], *n.f.* (*colloq.*) Rabble, riff-raff. **gueusailler**, *v.i.* To go begging; to consort with vagabonds. **gueusard**, *n.m.*

(*fem.* **gueusarde**) Beggar, ragamuffin; scoundrel, blackguard.

gueuse (1) [gøːz], *n.f.* Pig-iron, sow; (*Naut.*) kentledge.

gueuser [gø'ze], *v.i., v.t.* To beg. **gueuserie**, *n.f.* Beggary, beggarliness; poverty, destitution; (*fig.*) trash.

gueux [gø], *a.* (*fem.* **gueuse** (2)) Poor, beggarly, destitute; wretched.—*n.m.* Beggar, tramp, wretch, ragamuffin; knave, rascal. *Tas de gueux*, pack of scoundrels.—*n.f.* Wench, bitch.

gui [gi], *n.m.* Mistletoe; (*Naut.*) boom.

guibolle [gi'bɔl], *n.f.* (*slang*) Leg, pin.

guibre [gibr], *n.f.* (*Naut.*) Cutwater.

guiche [giʃ], *n.f.* Small strap; little curl of hair (near the ears) [*see* AGUICHER *and* ACCROCHE-CŒUR].

guichet [gi'ʃɛ], *n.m.* Wicket-gate (of prison); spyhole (of door); position at counter (banks, post-office), pay-desk; booking-office (railways); wicket (of cricket). *Guichet fermé*, position closed. **guichetier**, *n.m.* Turnkey.

guide (1) [gid], *n.m.* Guide; guide-book.—*n.f.* Girl-guide.

guide (2) [gid], *n.f.* Rein. *Conduire à grandes guides*, to drive four-in-hand.

guide-âne [gi'dɑːn], *n.m.* (*pl.* **unchanged** or **guide-ânes**) Guide-book; faintly ruled lines on stationery. **guide-main**, *n.m.* (*pl.* **unchanged** or **guide-mains**) Hand-guide (on a pianoforte etc.).

guide-rope [gid'rɔp], *n.m.* (*pl.* **guide-ropes**) Trail-rope; drag.

guider [gi'de], *v.t.* To guide, to lead, to conduct; to direct; to steer.

guidon [gi'dɔ̃], *n.m.* (*Mil.*) Guidon, field-colours; (*Navy*) broad pendant, burgee; (fore)sight, bead of fire-arms); reference-mark (in a book); handle-bar (of bicycle).

guifette [gi'fɛt], *n.f.* Sea-swallow, black tern.

guignard [gi'naːr], *n.m.* Dotterel; (*fam.*) unlucky person.

guigne (1) [giɲ], *n.f.* Sweet cherry, heart-cherry.

guigne (2) [GUIGNON].

guigner [gi'ɲe], *v.i.* To peep, to peer.—*v.t.* To peer or peep at; to glance at, to ogle; to have in view, to have a design upon; to covet. *Guigner une charge*, to have an eye to some post.

guignette [gi'ɲɛt], *n.f.* Small hoe; common sandpiper.

guignier [gi'ɲe], *n.m.* Sweet cherry-tree.

guignol [gi'ɲɔl], *n.m.* Punch; puppet-show, Punch and Judy show; (*Av.*) king-post, lever; (*slang*) a constable; (*fig.*) marionette, clown. **guignolant** [GUIGNONNANT].

guignolet [giɲɔ'lɛ], *n.m.* Cherry-brandy.

guignon [gi'ɲɔ̃], *n.m.* Bad luck, ill-luck. *Avoir du guignon*, to be unlucky. **guignonnant**, *a.* (*fem.* **-ante**) Unlucky, provoking.

guillage [gi'jaːʒ], *n.m.* Fermentation (of beer).

Guillaume [gi'joːm], *m.* William. *Guillaume le Conquérant*, William the Conqueror; *Guillaume le Roux*, William Rufus.

guillaume [gi'joːm], *n.m.* Rabbet-plane.

guilledou [gij'du], *n.m.* (*fam.*) *Courir le guilledou*, to frequent places of ill-fame.

guillemet [gij'mɛ], *n.m.* Quotation mark, inverted comma.

guillemeter, *v.t.* To put between quotation marks *or* inverted commas.

guillemot [gij'mo], *n.m.* Guillemot (bird).

guiller [gi'je], *v.i.* To work, to ferment (of beer).

guilleret [gij'rɛ], *a.* (*fem.* **-ette**) Brisk, lively, dapper; broad (joke). *Il a l'air guilleret*, he has a sprightly air.

guilleri [gij'ri], *n.m.* Chirping (of sparrows).

guillochage [gijɔ'ʃaːʒ], *n.m.* Ornamentation with guilloche, engine-turning. **guilloche**, *n.f.* Tool used for this. **guillocher**, *v.t.* (*Arch.*) To decorate with guilloche, to engine-turn. **guillochis**, *n.m.* Guilloche, engine-turning.

guillotine [gijɔ'tin], *n.f.* Guillotine. *Fenêtre à guillotine*, sash-window. **guillotiné**, *a.* (*fem.* **-ée**) Guillotined. **guillotinement**, *n.m.* Guillotining. **guillotiner**, *v.t.* To guillotine.

guimauve [gi'moːv], *n.f.* Marsh-mallow. *Roman à la guimauve*, (*fam.*) insipid novel.

guimbarde [gɛ̃'bard], *n.f.* (*colloq.*) Rickety old coach, boneshaker; jew's-harp; grooving plane.

guimpe [gɛːp], *n.f.* Stomacher, chemisette; wimple (for nuns etc.).

guinche [MOLINIE].

guincher [gɛ̃'ʃe], *v.i.* (*vulg.*) To dance.

guindage [gɛ̃'daːʒ], *n.m.* Hoisting; hoisting-tackle. **guindant**, *n.m.* (*Naut.*) Hoist, height (of flags).

guindas [GUINDEAU].

guinde [gɛ̃:d], *n.f.* Small clothes-press; crane, hoist.

guindé [gɛ̃'de], *a.* (*fem.* **-ée**) Stiff, strained, forced, unnatural; stilted, formal (of style). *Cet homme est toujours guindé*, that man is always as stiff as a poker.

guindeau [gɛ̃'do], *n.m.* (*pl.* **-eaux**) Windlass.

guinder [gɛ̃'de], *v.t.* To hoist, to hoist up; to strain, to force. **se guinder**, *v.r.* To hoist oneself up; to be strained, to be forced; to be high-flown. **guinderesse**, *n.f.* Top-rope.

Guinée [gi'ne], *f.* Guinea. *La Nouvelle Guinée*, New Guinea. **guinéen**, *a.* and *n.* (*fem.* **-éenne**). Guinean.

guinée [gi'ne], *n.f.* Guinea; cotton cloth from W. Africa.

guingan [gɛ̃'gɑ̃], *n.m.* Gingham.

guingois [gɛ̃'gwa], *n.m.* Crookedness, skew. *Avoir l'esprit de guingois*, to be cross-grained; *de guingois*, awry, askew; *marcher tout de guingois*, to walk crookedly.

guinguette [gɛ̃'gɛt], *n.f.* Small suburban tavern (usually with pleasure garden).

guipon [gi'pɔ̃], *n.m.* Mop, tar-brush.

guipure [gi'pyːr], *n.f.* Guipure (lace).

guirlande [gir'lɑ̃:d], *n.f.* Garland, wreath.

guise [giːz], *n.f.* Manner, way, guise; fancy, humour. *Chacun vit à sa guise*, everybody lives as he likes; *en guise de*, by way of; *faire à sa guise*, to have one's own way.

guitare [gi'taːr], *n.f.* Guitar. *Jouer de la guitare*, to play the guitar. **guitariste**, *n.* Guitarist, guitar-player. **guiterne**, *n.f.* Old form of guitar, cithern; (*Naut.*) prop used in masting.

guit-guit [gi'gi], *n.m.* (*pl.* **guits-guits**) American variety of humming-bird.

guitoune [gi'tun], *n.f.* (*Mil. slang*) Dug-out; hut (in Algeria).

---

guivre [GIVRE (1)].

gumène [gy'mɛn], *n.f.* (*Her.*) Cable (of an anchor).

gustatif [gysta'tif], *a.* (*fem.* **-ive**) Gustatory.

gustation [gysta'sjɔ̃], *n.f.* Tasting, gustation.

gutta-percha [gytapɛr'ka], *n.f.* Gutta-percha.

gutte [GOMME-GUTTE].

guttier [gy'tje], *n.m.* Gum-tree.

guttifère [gyti'fɛːr], *a.* Guttiferous. **guttiforme**, *a.* Guttiform.

guttural [gyty'ral], *a.* (*fem.* **-ale**, *pl.* **-aux**) Guttural.—*n.f.* Guttural (sound or letter).

Guyane [gɥi'jan], *f.* Guiana.

gymkhana [ʒimka'na], *n.m.* Gymkhana.

gymnase [ʒim'naːz], *n.m.* Gymnasium. **gymnaste**, *or* ***gymnasiarque**, *n.m.* Gymnast. **gymnastique**, *a.* Gymnastic.—*n.f.* Gymnastics. **gymnique**, *a.* Gymnic.—*n.f.* Gymnastics.

gymnosophie [ʒimnɔsɔ'fi], *n.f.* Gymnosophy. **gymnosophiste**, *n.m.* Gymnosophist.

gymnosperme [ʒimno'spɛrm], *n.m.* (*Bot.*) Gymnosperm.—*a.* Gymnospermous. **gymnospermie**, *n.f.* Order of gymnosperms.

gymnote [ʒim'nɔt], *n.m.* Gymnotus, electric eel.

gynandre [ʒi'nɑ̃:dr], *a.* (*Bot.*) Gynandrous.

gynandrie, *n.f.* Gynandria.

gynécée [ʒine'se], *n.m.* Gynaeceum, women's apartment.

gynécocratie [ʒinekɔkra's], *n.f.* Gynaecocracy, petticoat government.

gynécologie [ʒinekɔlɔ'ʒi], *n.f.* Gynaecology. **gynécologique**, *a.* Gynaecological. **gynécologiste** or **gynécologue**, *n.* Gynaecologist.

gynère [ʒi'nɛːr], **gynérion** [ʒine'rjɔ̃], *n.m.* Gynerium; pampas grass.

gypaète [ʒipa'ɛt], *n.m.*, or *Vautour des agneaux*, Gypaetus, lammergeier.

gypse [ʒips], *n.m.* Gypsum; plaster of Paris. **gypseux**, *a.* (*fem.* **-euse**) Gypseous.

gyratoire [GIRATOIRE].

gyrin [ʒi'rɛ̃], *n.m.* Whirligig.

gyromancie [ʒirɔmɑ̃'si], *n.f.* Gyromancy.

gyroscope [ʒirɔs'kɔp], *n.m.* Gyroscope. **gyroscopique**, *a.* Gyroscopic.

gyrostat [ʒirɔs'ta], *n.m.* Gyrostat.

H

[In words marked thus † the *h* is said 'aspirated'.]

H, h [aʃ], *n.m.* The eighth letter of the alphabet. *H* is mute or aspirated. Mute *h* is a purely ornamental or etymological letter. Aspirated *h* does not exist in pure French, although in some W. and E. provinces a slightly fricative *h* may be heard. The so-called aspirated *h* is a graphic symbol which indicates that there is neither elision nor liaison; *e.g.* *la halle* [la'al], *les halles* [le'al], *un haricot* [ɶ̃ari'ko], *des haricots* [dɛari'ko]. On the contrary, *un homme* [ɶ̃'nɔm], *des hommes* [dɛ'zɔm], etc. **L'heure H.** [lɶr'aʃ], (*Mil.*) zero hour.

habile [a'bil], *a.* Able, clever, adroit; capable; skilful, expert; sharp, quick, knowing, cunning; (*Law*) qualified, competent. *Habile dans les affaires*, skilful in business. **habilement**, *adv.* Cleverly, skilfully, ably, dexterously; artfully, knowingly. **habileté**, *n.f.* Ability, skill, cleverness, skilfulness; artfulness, knowingness.

habilitation [abilita'sjɔ̃], *n.f.* (*Law*) Qualification, aptitude.

habilité [abili'te], *n.f.* (*Law*) Competency, qualification.—*a.* (*fem.* **-ée**) Entitled, qualified. **habiliter**, *v.t.* To qualify, to enable, to entitle.

habillage [abi'jaːʒ], *n.m.* Dressing; trussing (poultry), pruning, trimming (trees, vegetables); fitting (watch).

habillant [abi'jɑ̃], *a.* (*fem.* **-ante**) Dressing or suiting well (of clothes etc.). **habillé**, *a.* (*fem.* **-ée**) Dressed, clothed, clad, decked out. *Habillé de noir*, dressed in black.

habillement [abij'mɑ̃], *n.m.* Clothes, clothing, dress, wearing apparel, attire.

habiller [abi'je], *v.t.* To dress, to clothe; to make clothes for; to become, to fit; to dress out; to wrap up; to accoutre; (*Cook.*) to prepare, to truss (fowls, fish, etc.); (*fig.*) to ornament, to adorn. *Ce tailleur m'habille*, that tailor makes my clothes; *cette étoffe vous habille bien*, that material suits you; *habiller du cuir*, to dress leather; *habiller quelqu'un de toutes pièces*, to speak ill of someone. **s'habiller**, *v.r.* To dress; to have one's clothes made. *Cet homme s'habille bien*, that man dresses well. **habilleur**, *n.m.* (*fem.* **-euse**) (*Theat.*) Dresser.

habit [a'bi], *n.m.* Clothes, apparel, garb; dress-coat; dress (of monk, nun, etc.); (*pl.*) clothes, wearing apparel. *Habit complet*, suit of clothes; *habit de cheval*, riding-habit; *habits de deuil*, mourning; *habit de soirée*, evening dress (tails); *être en habit*, to be in evening dress (for civilians), in mess-dress (for officers); *l'habit ne fait pas le moine*, it is not the cowl that makes the monk; *marchand d'habits*, old clothes dealer; *prendre l'habit*, to become a monk, (of a nun) to take the veil.

habitabilité [abitabili'te], *n.f.* Habitability. **habitable**, *a.* Habitable.

habitacle [abi'takl], *n.m.* *Habitation, abode, dwelling; (*Naut.*) binnacle; (*Av.*) cockpit.

habitant [abi'tɑ̃], *n.m.* (*fem.* **-ante**) Inhabitant, resident; inmate, occupant, occupier; denizen; (*C*) farmer.

habitat [abi'ta], *n.m.* Habitat.

habitation [abita'sjɔ̃], *n.f.* Habitation, residence, abode, tenement, dwelling-place; plantation, settlement (in a colony); (*Zool.*, *Bot.*) habitat, haunt. *Maison d'habitation*, dwelling-house. *Habitation à loyer modéré* or *H.L.M.*, rent-controlled house. **habiter**, *v.t.* To inhabit, to dwell in, to live in; to frequent. *Habiter un lieu*, to live in a place.—*v.i.* To inhabit, to dwell, to reside. *Habiter avec*, (*Law*) to cohabit.

habitude [abi'tyd], *n.f.* Habit, custom, use, practice, wont; (*colloq.*) trick, bad habit; propensity, constitution. *D'habitude*, usual, habitual, usually, habitually; *faire perdre une vilaine habitude à quelqu'un*, to break someone of a bad habit or a nasty trick; *faire quelque chose par habitude*, to do a thing from habit;

il n'en fait pas une habitude, he does not make a habit of it; *l'habitude est une seconde nature*, use is second nature. **habitué**, *n.m.* (*fem.* **-ée**) Frequenter, habitué, customer. *Un prêtre habitué*, a non-beneficed priest, a priest of another diocese, locum tenens of a curate. *Ce monsieur est un de nos habitués*, that gentleman is one of our regular customers. **habituel**, *a.* (*fem.* **-elle**) Habitual, customary, usual. **habituellement**, *adv.* Habitually, customarily, usually.

habituer [abi'tɥe], *v.t.* To accustom, to habituate, to familiarize, to inure (*à*). *Habituer les jeunes gens à la fatigue*, to inure young men to fatigue. **s'habituer**, *v.r.* To accustom oneself; to grow familiar (with); to get used (*à*). *Je m'y habituerai*, I shall get used to it.

†**hâbler** [ɑ'ble], *v.i.* To brag, to boast, to draw the long bow. †**hâblerie**, *n.f.* Bragging, boasting, drawing the long bow. †**hâbleur**, *n.m.* (*fem.* **-euse**) Braggart, boaster.

†**hachage** [a'ʃaːʒ], *n.m.* Chopping, chopping up. †**hachard**, *n.m.* Shears (of tinman).

†**hache** [aʃ], *n.f.* Axe, hatchet. *Fait à coups de hache*, clumsily made, roughly done; *hache d'abordage*, boarding-axe; *hache d'armes*, battle-axe. †**haché**, *a.* (*fem.* **-ée**) Chopped up, mixed; (*fig.*) abrupt, jerky, desultory (of style etc.); hatched, hachured (drawing). †**hache-légumes**, *n.m. inv.* Vegetable mincer. *†**hache-paille**, *n.m. inv.* Chaff-cutter. †**hache-viande**, *n.m. inv.* Mincer.

†**hacher** [a'ʃe], *v.t.* To chop, to hew, to cut up, to cut to pieces; to hash, to mince; to hack, to mangle; to cross-hatch. *Hacher en morceaux*, to cut to pieces; *hacher menu*, to chop small, to mince; *la grêle hache les vignes*, the hail cuts the vines to pieces; *se faire hacher*, to let oneself be cut to pieces (rather than surrender). †**hachereau** or †**hacheron**, *n.m.* Small axe, hatchet. †**hachette**, *n.f.* Small hatchet; bleak (fish). †**hachis**, *n.m.* Minced meat, hash.

†**hachisch**, †**haschisch**, or †**hachich** [a'ʃiʃ], *n.m.* Hashish.

†**hachoir** [a'ʃwaːr], *n.m.* Chopping-board; chopping-knife; mincer; chaff-cutter. †**hachure**, *n.f.* (*Engr.*) Hatching, hachure. †**hachurer**, *v.t.* To hatch, to hachure.

†**hagard** [a'gaːr], *a.* (*fem.* **-arde**) Wild (of a hawk); wild-looking, wild-eyed, haggard.

hagiographe [aʒjɔ'graf], *n.m.* Hagiographer. *a.* Hagiographic. **hagiographie**, *n.f.* Hagiography.

†**haha** [ɑ'ɑ], *n.m.* Ha-ha (sunk fence).

†**hahé!** [a'e], *int.* 'Ware there! (huntsman's cry to check dogs).

†**hai!** [ɛ], *int.* Well! indeed! bless me!

†**haie** [ɛ], *n.f.* Hedge, hedgerow; hurdle; row, line (of bayonets etc.); beam of a plough. *Former la haie*, to line a road (with troops). *Fermer d'une haie*, to hedge in; *haie vive*, quickset hedge. *Course de haies*, hurdling, hurdle-race.

†**haïe!** [a'i], *int.* Oh! (Pain, surprise.)

†**haillon** [ɑ'jɔ̃], *n.m.* Rag, tatter.

†**haine** [ɛːn], *n.f.* Hate, hatred; ill-will, aversion, dislike, abhorrence, grudge, spite. *Avoir de la haine pour* or *avoir en haine*, to hate; *porter de la haine à*, to feel hatred towards.

†**haineusement**, *adv.* Hatefully, spitefully.

†**haineux,** *a.* (*fem.* **-euse**) Hating, full of hatred, malignant, spiteful.

†**haïr** [a'iːr], *v.t.* *irr.* To hate, to detest, to loathe, to dislike, to have an aversion for. *Haïr comme la peste*, to hate like poison; *haïr cordialement*, to detest cordially.

†**haire** [ɛːr], *n.f.* Hair-shirt; hair-cloth.

†**haïssable** [ai'sabl], *a.* Hateful, odious. †**haïsseur,** *n.m.* (*fem.* **haïsseuse**) Hater.

†**halage** [a'laːʒ], *n.m.* Towage, hauling. *Chemin de halage*, towing-path.

†**halbi** [al'bi], *n.m.* (*Norm. dialect*) Drink made of fermented apples and pears.

†**halbran** [al'brɑ̃], *n.m.* Young wild-duck.

†**halbrené,** *a.* (*fem.* **-ée**) Ragged-feathered (of a bird); (*fig.*) worn-out, in a sad plight.

†**halbrener,** *v.i.* *irr.* (*conjugated like* AMENER) To shoot wild-duck.—*v.t.* (*Hawking*) To break the feathers of (a bird of prey).

†**hale** [aːl], *n.m.* Tow-line, tow-rope.

†**hâle** [ɑːl], *n.m.* Heat of the sun; sunburn. *Le hâle fane tout*, the heat of the sun dries up everything. †**hâlé,** *a.* (*fem.* **-ée**) Sunburnt; tanned; swarthy.

†**hale-bas** or †**halebas** [al'bɑ], *n.m.* *inv.* (*Naut.*) Down-haul.

haleine [a'lɛn], *n.f.* Breath, wind. *Courir à perdre haleine*, to run until one is out of breath; *courte haleine*, shortness of breath; *haleine douce*, sweet breath; *haleine forte*, bad breath; *hors d'haleine*, out of breath; *perdre haleine*, to get out of breath; *phrases à perte d'haleine*, long-winded sentences; *reprendre haleine*, to recover one's breath; *tenir en haleine*, to keep going; *tenir les gens en haleine*, to keep people's attention; *tout d'une haleine*, all in one breath; *un ouvrage de longue haleine*, a work requiring time and labour. **halenée,** *n.f.* Smell, breath, whiff. **halener,** *v.i.* *irr.* (*conjug. like* AMENER) To breathe out. —*v.t.* To exhale; (*Hunt.*) to get scent of; (*fig.*) to scent, to get wind of.

†**haler** (1) [a'le], *v.t.* (*Naut.*) To haul, to warp, to heave, to tow. *Haler le vent*, to haul upon the wind.

†**haler** (2) [a'le], *v.t.* (*Hunt.*) To set, to excite. *Haler un chien sur quelqu'un*, to set a dog at someone.

†**hâler** [a'le], *v.t.* To tan, to burn (of the sun). **se hâler,** *v.r.* To become sunburnt or tanned.

†**haletant** [alt'tɑ̃], *a.* (*fem.* **-ante**) Out of breath, panting, puffing.

†**halètement** [alɛt'mɑ̃], *n.m.* Panting, puffing.

†**haleter** [al'te], *v.i.* To pant, to gasp for breath, to puff and blow.

†**haleur** [a'lœːr], *n.m.* (*fem.* **haleuse**) Hauler, tower of a boat etc.

haliotide [aljo'tid], *n.f.* Sea-ear, ear-shell.

halitueux [ali'tɥø], *a.* (*fem.* **-euse**) (*Med.*) Halituous, moist.

†**hall** [ɔl], *n.m.* Large entrance hall (of hotel, station).

hallage [a'laːʒ], *n.m.* Market-dues.

†**hallali** [ala'li], *n.m.* (*Stag-hunting*) Mort; flourish of the horn at the death.

†**halle** [al], *n.f.* Market; market-hall, market-place. *Fort des halles*, market-porter; *halle aux blés*, corn-exchange; *langage des halles*, billingsgate (bad language).

†**hallebarde** [al'bard], *n.f.* Halberd. *Pleuvoir*

or *tomber des hallebardes*, to rain cats and dogs. †**hallebardier,** *n.m.* Halberdier.

†**hallier** (1) [a'lje], *n.m.* Thicket, coppice.

†**hallier** (2) [a'lje], *n.m.* Market-keeper; stall-keeper.

hallucinant [alysi'nɑ̃], *a.* (*fem.* **-ante**) Hallucinating; haunting. **hallucination,** *n.f.* Hallucination, delusion. **hallucinatoire,** *a.* Hallucinatory. **halluciné,** *a.* (*fem.* **-ée**) Hallucinated; (*fig.*) deluded.—*n.* Person suffering from delusions. **halluciner,** *v.t.* To hallucinate; (*fig.*) to delude.

†**halo** [a'lo], *n.m.* Halo; (*Phot.*) halation.

†**halochimie** [aloʃi'mi], *n.f.* (*Chem.*) Preparation of salts.

halogène [alɔ'ʒɛn], *a.* Halogenous.—*n.m.* Halogen.

haloïde [alɔ'id], *a.* and *n.m.* Haloid.

†**haloir** or †**hâloir** [ɑ'lwaːr], *n.m.* Drying-room (for hemp).

†**halot** [a'lo], *n.m.* Rabbit-burrow.

†**halte** [alt], *n.f.* Halt; stand, stop; halting-place; resting-place; wayside station. *Faire halte*, to halt, to stop; *faire une halte*, to make a halt.—*int.* Halt, stop! *Halte-là!* stop! that won't do! halt!

haltère [al'tɛːr], *n.m.* Dumb-bell. **haltérophile,** *n.m.* Dumb-bell wielder. **haltérophilie,** *n.f.* Dumb-bell wielding.

†**hamac** [a'mak], *n.m.* Hammock. *Hamac à l'anglaise*, (*Naut.*) cot.

hamadryade [amadri'jad], *n.f.* (*Myth.*) Hamadryad, wood-nymph; (*Zool.*) hamadryas, king-cobra.

hamamélis [amame'lis], *n.m.* (*Bot.*) Witch hazel.

†**hameau** [a'mo], *n.m.* (*pl.* **hameaux**) Hamlet.

hameçon [am'sɔ̃], *n.m.* Hook, fish-hook; bait. *Mordre à l'hameçon*, to take the bait. **hameçonné,** *a.* (*fem.* **-ée**) Hooked; fitted with hooks; barbed. **hameçonner,** *v.t.* To hook; to fit with hooks.

†**hamman** [a'mam], *n.m.* Turkish baths.

†**hampe** [ɑ̃ːp], *n.f.* Staff (of a lance, flag, etc.); handle (of a brush etc.); stem, flower-stalk; flank (of beef).

†**hamster** [ams'tɛːr], *n.m.* Hamster.

†**han** [ɑ̃], *n.m.* Guttural cry or grunt (of a workman striking a heavy blow).

†**hanap** [a'nap], *n.m.* Hanap, goblet, drinking-bowl.

†**hanche** [ɑ̃ːʃ], *n.f.* Hip; haunch (of horse), hook (of ox); quarter (of ship). *Les poings sur les hanches*, with his or her arms akimbo; *tour de hanches*, (*Wrestl.*) cross-buttock. *Hanche sous le vent*, (*Naut.*) lee quarter.

†**hancher** [ɑ̃'ʃe], *v.i.* To move the hips (while dancing, walking).

†**handicap** [ɑ̃di'kap], *n.m.* Handicap.

†**handicaper** [ɑ̃dika'pe], *v.t.* To handicap. †**handicapeur,** *n.m.* Handicapper.

†**hanebane** [an'ban], *n.f.* (*Bot.*) Henbane.

†**hanet** [a'nɛ], *n.m.* (*Naut.*) Line, nettle, lashing.

†**hangar** [ɑ̃'gaːr], *n.m.* Outhouse, shed, cart-shed; hangar (for aeroplanes).

†**hanneton** [an'tɔ̃], *n.m.* May-bug, cock-chafer; (*fig.*) thoughtless, harum-scarum person.

†**hansart** [ɑ̃'sar], *n.m.* Chopper (of butcher).

†**hanse** [ɑ̃ːs], *n.f.* League of the Hanse towns,

Hanseatic League. †**hanséatique,** *a.* Hanseatic.

†**hanter** [ã′te], *v.t.* To haunt; to frequent, to resort to; to associate with. *Dis-moi qui tu hantes et je te dirai qui tu es,* tell me the company you keep and I will tell you what you are, birds of a feather flock together. †**hantise,** *n.f.* Frequenting, intimacy; obsession.

†**happe** [ap], *n.f.* Axle clout; cramp-iron; staple.

†**happelourde** [a′plurd], *n.f.* Paste jewel, imitation stone.

†**happer** [a′pe], *v.t.* To snap up, to snatch; to seize. †**happeur,** *n.m.* Paper-clip.

†**haquebute** [akə′byt], *n.f.* Harquebus.

†**haquenée** [ak′ne], *n.f.* Hack, quiet horse; *palfrey; (*fig.*) ill-made, ungainly woman. *Aller sur la haquenée des cordeliers,* to ride on Shanks's mare.

†**haquet** [a′kε], *n.m.* Dray; hand-cart. †**haquetier,** *n.m.* Drayman.

hara-kiri [araki′ri], *n.m.* *Faire hara-kiri,* to commit ritual suicide (by ripping open one's stomach).

†**harangue** [a′rã:g], *n.f.* Harangue, speech; (boring) address. *La tribune aux harangues,* the rostrum. †**haranguer,** *v.t.*, *v.i.* To harangue. †**harangueur,** *n.m.* (*fem.* -euse) Haranguer, orator, speechifier.

†**haras** [a′rɑ], *n.m.* Stud, breeding-stud.

†**harasse** [a′ras], *n.f.* Crate.

†**harassement** [aras′mã], *n.m.* Harassing, harassment; exhaustion.

†**harasser** [ara′se], *v.t.* To harass, to tire out, to weary, to jade.

†**harceler** [arsə′le], *v.t.* To worry, to pester, to torment, to harass. *Harceler l'ennemi,* to harass the enemy. †**harcèlement,** *n.m.* Tormenting, worrying, harassing.

†**harde** [ard], *n.f.* Herd (of deer etc.); leash (for hounds). *Harde de chiens,* several couples of hounds leashed together. †**harder,** *v.t.* To leash (hounds).

†**hardes** [ard], *n.f.* (*used only in pl.*) Wearing apparel, attire, worn clothes.

†**hardi** [ar′di], *a.* (*fem.* -ie) Bold, daring, fearless, intrepid; audacious, rash, venturesome; forward, impudent. *Air hardi,* impudent look. *Ce musicien a le jeu hardi,* this musician has a bold touch; *hardi comme un page,* bold as brass. *Manières hardies,* forward manners.—*int.* Courage! go it! †**hardiesse,** *n.f.* Boldness, daring, fearlessness; audacity, rashness; assurance, effrontery, impudence. *Avoir la hardiesse de dire,* to have the effrontery to say. *Hardiesse de style or d'expression,* boldness of style or expression; *il y a beaucoup de hardiesse dans ce dessin,* there is great boldness in this drawing. †**hardiment,** *adv.* Boldly, daringly; impudently. *Marcher hardiment à l'ennemi,* to march boldly against the enemy.

†**harem** [a′rεm], *n.m.* Harem.

†**harelde** [a′rεld], *n.f.,* or *harelde de Miquelon,* long-tailed duck.

†**hareng** [a′rã], *n.m.* Herring. *Hareng frais,* fresh herring; *hareng ouvert et fumé,* kipper; *hareng saur,* red herring; *serrés comme des harengs,* packed like herrings. †**harengaison,** *n.f.* Herring-season; herring-fishing.

†**harengère,** *n.f.* Fish-wife. †**harengerie,**

n.f. Herring-market. †**harenguet,** *n.m.* Sprat.

†**haret** [a′rε], *a.* *Chat haret,* wild cat.

†**harfang** [ar′fã], *n.m.,* or *harfang des neiges,* great white owl.

†**hargne** [arɲ], *n.f.* Bad temper, surliness.

†**hargneux** [ar′ɲø], *a.* (*fem.* -euse) Cross, cross-grained, peevish, surly; snarling, snappish (of dogs); vicious (of horses). *Chien hargneux,* snarling dog; quarrelsome fellow.

†**haricot** [ari′ko], *n.m.* Kidney-bean. *Haricot de mouton,* Irish stew; *haricots blancs,* haricots, (U.S.) bush-beans; *haricots d'Espagne,* scarlet runners; *haricots flageolets,* flageolets; *haricots verts,* French beans. *Table haricot,* kidney-shaped table.

†**haridelle** [ari′dεl], *n.f.* Jade, hack, sorry horse; (*fig.*) jade, gawky woman.

†**harka** [ar′ka], *n.f.* Harka; (in Morocco) raid of native horsemen.

†**harle** [arl], *n.m.* Merganser. *Harle bièvre,* goosander; *harle huppé,* red-breasted merganser; *harle piette* or *petit harle,* smew.

harmonica [armɔni′ka], *n.m.* Harmonica, musical glasses; mouth-organ.

harmonie [armɔ′ni], *n.f.* Harmony; unison, concord, keeping; (*Mus.*) harmonics. *Avec harmonie,* harmoniously; *en harmonie,* in harmony, in time, in keeping; *sans harmonie,* inharmonious, unmusical. **harmonier** [HARMONISER]. **harmonieusement,** *adv.* Harmoniously. **harmonieux,** *a.* (*fem.* -ieuse) Harmonious; musical, sweet, melodious; in keeping, well-proportioned, friendly, blending (of colours). **harmonique,** *a.* Harmonic. *Échelle harmonique,* harmonic progression.—*n.f.* Harmonics. **harmoniquement,** *adv.* Harmonically. **harmonisation,** *n.f.* Harmonization. **harmoniser,** *v.t.* To harmonize. **s'harmoniser,** *v.r.* To harmonize. **harmoniste,** *n.m.* Harmonist. **harmonium,** *n.m.* Harmonium.

†**harnachement** [arna′mã], *n.m.* Harnessing; harness, trappings, housings; accoutrements. †**harnacher,** *v.t.* To harness; to accoutre, to rig out; (C) to harness (a fall). †**harnacheur,** *n.m.* Harness-maker or -dealer; person harnessing, groom.

†**harnais** [ar′nε] or *†**harnois,** *n.m.* Harness; horse-trappings; armour; equipment, tackle. *Blanchir sous le harnois,* to grow grey in the service. *Cheval de harnais,* draught-horse. *Endosser le harnais,* to buckle on one's armour, to don the uniform. *Harnais d'engrenages,* gearing.

†**haro** [a′ro], *n.m.* and *int.* Hue and cry. *Crier haro sur,* to cry shame upon.

†**harpagon** [arpa′gɔ̃], *n.m.* Miser, skinflint.

†**harpail** [ar′pɑːj], *n.m.,* or †**harpaille,** *n.f.* Herd of hinds and young stags; bevy of roe-deer.

†**harpaye** [ar′pεːj], *n.f.* Moor-buzzard, marsh-harrier.

†**harpe** (1) [arp], *n.f.* Harp; (*Conch.*) harp-shell. *Harpe éolienne,* Aeolian harp.

†**harpe** (2) [arp], *n.f.* Dog's claw; toothing-stone, corner iron.

†**harpé** [ar′pe], *a.* (*fem.* -ée) Harp-shaped, well-shaped (of greyhounds, horses).

†**harpeau** [ar′po], *n.m.* (*pl.* -eaux) Grappling-iron.

†**harper** (1) [ar'pe], *v.i.* To play the harp.
†**harper** (2) [ar'pe], *v.t.* *To grip, to grasp, to clutch.
†**harpie** [ar'pi], *n.f.* Harpy, vixen, shrew; crested eagle.
†**harpin** [ar'pɛ̃], *n.m.* Boat-hook.
†**harpiste** [ar'pist], *n.* Harpist.
†**harpon** [ar'pɔ̃], *n.m.* Harpoon; two-handed cross-cut saw [*see also* HARPE (2)]. †**harponner**, *v.t.* To harpoon. †**harponneur**, *n.m.* Harpooner.
†**hart** [a:r], *n.f.* Withe, faggot-band; rope, halter. *C'est un homme qui mérite la hart*, he is a man who deserves hanging; *sous peine de la hart*, under penalty of the gallows.
haruspice [ARUSPICE].
†**hasard** [a'za:r], *n.m.* Chance; accident, hap, hazard; risk, danger, peril. *À tout hasard*, at all events, on the off chance; *au hasard*, at random, at a venture; *corriger le hasard*, to assist fortune, to cheat at cards; *coup de hasard*, lucky chance or stroke; *courir le hasard*, to run the risk; *est-ce que par hasard il ne viendrait pas?* he surely doesn't mean not to come? *jeter quelque chose au hasard*, to leave something to chance; *jeu de hasard*, game of chance; *le connaissez-vous par hasard?* do you happen to know him? *par hasard*, by chance, accidentally; *s'abandonner au hasard*, to rely entirely upon chance; *s'en remettre au hasard*, to leave it to chance. †**hasardé**, *a.* (*fem.* **-ée**) Hazarded, ventured; hazardous, bold; risky, free; tainted, too high (of game etc.). †**hasarder**, *v.t.* To hazard, to risk, to venture, to expose; to stake. **se hasarder**, *v.r.* To hazard, to venture, to take the risk; to go too far; to be hazarded. *Se hasarder à faire une chose*, to venture to do a thing. †**hasardeusement**, *adv.* Hazardously. †**hasardeux**, *a.* (*fem.* **-euse**) Venturesome, daring; hazardous, unsafe, perilous.
†**haschisch** [HACHISCH].
†**hase** [ɑ:z], *n.f.* Doe-rabbit, doe-hare.
***hast** [ast], *n.m.* Shaft. *Arme d'hast*, long-hafted weapon (such as a halberd).
†**haste** [ast], *n.f.* (*Ant.*) Spear. †**hasté**, *a.* (*fem.* **-ée**) (*Bot.*) Hastate. †**hastiforme**, *a.* (*Bot.*) Lance-shaped.
†**hâte** [ɑ:t], *n.f.* Speed, hurry; promptitude, precipitation; eagerness. *À la hâte*, in a hurry; *avec hâte* or *en hâte*, in haste, hastily; *avoir hâte*, to be in a hurry, to be anxious (to); *en toute hâte*, with all possible speed; *faire une chose à la hâte*, to do a thing in a hurry; *faites hâte*, make haste; *s'éloigner à la hâte*, to hasten away, to hurry off.
†**hâtelet** [ɑ'tlɛ], *n.m.* Small skewer. †**hâtelle** or †**hâtelette**, *n.f.* Small morsel roasted on a skewer.
†**hâter** [ɑ'te], *v.t.* To hasten, to forward, to hurry, to urge on; to expedite, to accelerate; to push on, to force (fruit). *Hâter la besogne*, to hurry the job on. **se hâter**, *v.r.* To make haste, to hurry, to look sharp. *Hâtez-vous de partir*, hurry up and get away; *hâtez-vous lentement*, more haste, less speed.
†**hâtier** [ɑ'tje], *n.m.* Spit-rest, kitchen andiron.
†**hâtif** [ɑ'tif], *a.* (*fem.* **-ive**) Forward; precocious, premature; (*Hort.*) early. *Fruit hâtif*, early fruit. †**hâtiveau**, *n.m.* (*pl.* **-eaux**) Hasty pear; early pea. †**hâtivement**, *adv.* Early, prematurely; hastily.

†**hauban** [o'bɑ̃], *n.m.* (*Naut.*) Shroud, guy, stay. *Grands haubans*, main-shrouds; *haubans de misaine*, fore-shrouds; *haubans de cheminée*, funnel stays. †**haubanner**, *v.t.* To stay, to guy.
†**haubert** [o'bɛ:r], *n.m.* Hauberk.
†**hausse** [o:s], *n.f.* Lift, block (for raising anything); (*Comm.*) rise, advance; nut (of violin bow); (*Print.*) overlay; (back) sight (of a rifle). *À la hausse*, (*Comm.*) on the rise (of stocks etc.); *être en hausse*, to be rising; *jouer à la hausse*, to speculate on a rise; to go a bull; *petite hausse*, low range; *grande hausse*, high range; *subir une hausse*, to go up (in price). †**hausse-col** *n.m.* (*pl.* **hausse-cols**) (*Mil.*) Gorget.
†**haussement** [os'mɑ̃], *n.m.* Raising, lifting; (*Comm.*) rising. *Haussement d'épaules*, shrugging of the shoulders. †**hausser**, *v.t.* To raise, to lift up; to increase; to shrug; (*Comm.*) to advance; (*Print.*) to overlay. *Hausser la voix*, to raise one's voice; *hausser le cœur à*, to encourage; *hausser les épaules*, to shrug one's shoulders.—*v.i.* To rise; to get higher; to increase. *La rente hausse*, the funds are going up; *la rivière a bien haussé*, the river has risen very much; *le change hausse*, the rate of exchange is rising; *les actions haussent*, the price of shares is rising; *faire hausser les prix*, to rig. **se hausser**, *v.r.* To be raised, to rise; to raise oneself; to clear up (of the weather); to increase. *Se hausser sur la pointe des pieds*, to stand upon tiptoe. †**haussier**, *n.m.* (*St. Exch.*) Bull. †**haussière** or ***aussière**, *n.f.* Hawser.
†**haut** [o], *a.* (*fem.* **haute**) High, tall, lofty; elevated, erect, uplifted, raised aloft; upper; superior; chief, principal; grand, eminent; important; proud, haughty; high-priced; loud (of sound). *Au plus haut degré*, in the highest degree; *crime de haute trahison*, crime of high treason; *exécuteur des hautes œuvres*, executioner; *gagner la haute mer*, to reach the open sea(s); *haut de dix mètres*, ten metres high; *haut en couleur*, of a ruddy complexion; *haute estime*, great esteem; *haute fréquence*, high frequency; *hauts faits*, great deeds, exploits; *il a juré, la main haute*, he swore with uplifted hand; *il peut aller partout la tête haute*, he can hold up his head anywhere; *la Chambre haute*, the Upper House; *la marée* or *la mer est haute*, it is high tide; *le haut bout de la table*, the upper end of the table; *le Haut-Canada*, Upper Canada; *le haut commerce*, the higher branches of commerce, finance; *le haut mal*, epilepsy; *le Très-Haut*, the Most High; *lire à haute voix*, to read aloud; *marcher la tête haute*, to walk with head erect; *pousser les hauts cris*, to complain loudly; *une personne de haut rang*, a person of high rank.—*n.m.* Height; top, summit; upper part. *Cette maison a quarante pieds de haut*, this house is forty feet high; *de haut en bas* [BAS (1)]; *d'en haut*, from above; *il y a du haut et des bas dans la vie* [BAS (1)]; *le haut d'un clocher*, the top of a steeple; *le haut d'une page*, the top of a page; *le haut d'une rue*, the upper end of a street; *regarder quelqu'un de haut en bas* [BAS (1)]; *tomber de son haut*, to fall flat down, to be thunderstruck; *traiter quelqu'un de haut en bas* [BAS (1)].—*adv. phr.* *En haut*, upstairs; *chambre*

d'en haut, upper room.—*n.f. La haute*, the wealthy, the upper crust, (*fam.*) the nobs.— *adv.* High, high up; loud, aloud, loudly; haughtily, arrogantly. *Ainsi qu'il a été dit plus haut*, as has already been said; **faire haut le pied*, to vanish, to run away; *haut la main*, brilliantly; *haut les mains!* hands up! *haut le pied*, off with you, let us be off at once; *mener un cheval haut la main*, to keep a tight rein on a horse; *montez plus haut*, go up higher; *parler haut*, to speak out; *parlez plus haut*, speak louder, speak up; *reprendre les choses de plus haut*, to begin further back.

†**hautain** [o'tɛ̃], *a.* (*fem.* -**aine**) Haughty, supercilious, proud. †**hautainement**, *adv.* Haughtily, superciliously, proudly.

†**hautbois** [o'bwɑ], *n.m.* Hautboy, oboe; oboe-player. †**hautboïste**, *n.* Oboe-player.

†**haut-de-chausses** or †**haut-de-chausse** [od'ʃoːs], *n.m.* (*pl.* **hauts-de-chausses** or **hauts-de-chausse**) Breeches; trunk-hose.

†**haut-de-forme** [od'fɔrm], *n.m.* (*pl.* **hauts-de-forme**) Top-hat.

†**haute-contre** [ot'kɔ̃:tr], *n.f.* (*pl.* **hautes-contre**) Counter-tenor.

†**hautement** [ot'mɑ̃], *adv.* Boldly, resolutely, stoutly, proudly; aloud; openly.

†**haute-taille** [ot'tɑ:j], *n.f.* (*pl.* **hautes-tailles**) Light tenor.

†**hauteur** [o'tœːr], *n.f.* Height, elevation, altitude; depth; hill, rising ground, eminence; firmness; haughtiness, arrogance; pitch (of the voice etc.); (*Naut.*) bearing, latitude. *De toute sa hauteur*, at its, his, or her full height; *être à la hauteur de quelqu'un*, to be a match for someone; *être à la hauteur du siècle*, to keep pace with the age; *être à la hauteur d'une île*, (*Naut.*) to be off an island; *être à la hauteur d'une tâche*, to be equal to a task; *la hauteur de ses conceptions*, the loftiness of his ideas; *la hauteur d'une montagne*, the height of a hill; *mur à hauteur d'appui*, breast-high wall; *parler avec hauteur*, to speak haughtily; *prendre la hauteur du soleil*, to take the sun's altitude; (*adv. phr.*) *à la hauteur*, up to it, up to standard, (*fam.*) up to snuff.

†**haut-fond** [o'fɔ̃], *n.m.* (*pl.* **hauts-fonds**) Shoal, shallow.

†**haut-le-cœur** [ol'kœːr], *n.m. inv.* Heave of stomach. *Avoir des haut-le-cœur*, to feel sick.

†**haut-le-corps** [ol'kɔːr], *n.m. inv.* Spring, bound; start. *Il fit un haut-le-corps en nous voyant venir*, he started as he saw us coming.

†**haut-le-pied** [ol'pje], *a. inv. Cheval haut-le-pied*, spare horse; *locomotive haut-le-pied*, running light engine.

†**haut-parleur** [opar'lœr], *n.m.* (*pl.* **haut-parleurs**) Loud-speaker; amplifier; monitor (in projection-room).

†**haut-pendu** [opɑ̃'dy], *n.m.* (*pl.* **haut(s)-pendus**) Passing squall.

†**haut-relief** [orə'ljɛf], *n.m.* (*pl.* **hauts-reliefs**) Alto-relievo, high relief.

†**hauturier** [oty'rje], *a.* (*fem.* -**ière**) (*Naut.*) Of the high seas, sea-going. *Pilote hauturier*, deep-sea pilot.

†**Havane** [a'vən], **la**, *f.* Havana.

†**havane** [a'van], *n.m.* Havana cigar.—*a.* Brown, tan.

†**hâve** [ɑːv], *a.* Pale, wan, emaciated; sunken (of cheeks).

†**haveneau** [av'no], *n.m.* (*pl.* -**eaux**) Shrimp-net. †**havenet** [HAVENEAU].

†**haveron** [a'vrɔ̃], *n.m.* Wild oats.

†**havet** [a'vɛ], *n.m.* Square hook; cook's fork.

†**havre** [ɑːvr], *n.m.* Haven, harbour, port.

†**havresac** [ɑvrə'sak], *n.m.* Knapsack, pack.

Hawaï [awa'i], *m.* Hawaii.

†**Haye** [ɛ], **la**, *f.* The Hague.

†**hé!** [e], *int.* Hoy! (for calling, warning, etc.); why! well! I say! (*emphat.*).

†**heaume** [oːm], *n.m.* Helm, helmet.

hebdomadaire [ebdɔma'dɛːr], *a.* Weekly.— *n.m.* Weekly newspaper. **hebdomadairement**, *adv.* Weekly.

hébergement [ebɛrʒə'mɑ̃], *n.m.* Lodging; entertaining.

héberger [ebɛr'ʒe], *v.t.* To lodge; (*rare*) to entertain.

hébété [ebe'te], *a.* (*fem.* -**ée**) Dazed, stupid, bewildered.

hébéter [ebe'te], *v.t. irr.* (*conjugated like* ACCÉLÉRER) To make stupid, to besot. **hébétement**, *n.m.*, **hébétude**, *n.f.* Stupidity, dazed condition.

hébraïque [ebra'ik], *a.* Hebrew, Hebraic. **hébraïquement**, *adv.* Hebraically. **hébraïsant** or **hébraïste**, *a.* and *n.* Hebraist. **hébraïsme**, *n.m.* Hebraism.

hébreu [e'brø], *a.m.* (*in fem.* **hébraïque** *is used*) Hebrew.—*n.m.* Hebrew language. *C'est de l'hébreu pour moi*, that is Greek to me. (**Hébreu**, *pl.* **Hébreux**) a Hebrew (*fem.* **Juive**).

hécatombe [eka'tɔ̃:b], *n.f.* Hecatomb.

hectare [ɛk'taːr], *n.m.* Hectare (2 acres, 1 rood, 35 perches, or 2·4711 acres).

hectique [ɛk'tik], *a.* Hectic. **hectisie** or **hecticité**, *n.f.* Hectic fever.

hectogramme [ɛktɔ'gram] or **hecto**, *n.m.* Hectogramme (3·527 oz. avoirdupois). **hectolitre**, *n.m.* Hectolitre (22·009668 imperial gallons). **hectomètre**, *n.m.* Hectometre (109·936 yds.).

hédonisme [edɔ'nism], *n.m.* Hedonism.

hégélien [eʒe'ljɛ̃], *a.* and *n.m.* (*fem.* -**ienne**) (*Phil.*) Hegelian.

hégémonie [eʒemɔ'ni], *n.f.* Hegemony.

hégire [e'ʒiːr], *n.f.* Hegira (Mohammedan era).

†**hein** [ɛ̃], *int.* (before a sentence) Hey! what! (after a sentence) isn't it?

hélas! [e'lɑːs], *int.* Alas!

Hélène [e'lɛn], *f.* Helen, Helena.

†**héler** [e'le], *v.t. irr.* (*conjug. like* ACCÉLÉRER) To hail, to speak (a ship); to hail, to call (a taxi, a boat, etc.).

hélianthe [e'ljɑ̃ːt], *n.m.* Helianthus, sunflower. *Hélianthe tubéreux*, Jerusalem artichoke. **hélianthème**, *n.m.* Helianthemum, rock-rose.

hélice [e'lis], *n.f.* Screw, helix; propeller. *En hélice*, spiral, winding; *navire à hélice*, screwsteamer. (*Av.*) *Hélice à pas variable*, variable-pitch propeller; *hélice à mise en drapeau*, feathering propeller; *hélice bipale*, two-blade propeller. **hélicoïdal**, *a.* (*fem.* -**ale**, *pl.* -**aux**) Helicoid, spiral.

hélicon [eli'kɔ̃], *n.m.* (*Mus.*) Bombardon.

hélicoptère [elikɔp'tɛːr], *n.m.* Helicopter.

héliocentrique [eljɔsɑ̃'trik], *a.* Heliocentric. **héliographe**, *n.m.* Heliograph. **héliographie**, *n.f.* Heliography. **héliogravure**

n.f. Héliogravure. **hélioscope,** *n.m.* Helioscope. **héliothérapie,** *n.f.* Sunlight treatment. **héliotrope,** *n.m.* (*Bot.*) Heliotrope; turnsole; (*Min.*) heliotrope, blood-stone.

héliport [eli'pɔr], *n.m.* Heliport, helicopter landing-ground.

hélium [e'ljɔm], *n.m.* Helium.

hellébore [ELLÉBORE].

Hellène [ɛl'lɛn], *n.* Hellene. **hellénique,** *a.* Hellenic. **helléniser,** *v.t., v.i.* To hellenize. **hellénisme,** *n.m.* Hellenism. **helléniste,** *a.* and *n.* Hellenist.

helminthe [ɛl'mɛ̃:t], *n.m.* Helminth (intestinal worm). **helminthie,** *n.f.,* or FAUSSE VIPÉRINE. *Helminthia echioides.* **helminthoïde,** *a.* Helminthoid, vermiform.

helvétique [ɛlve'tik], *a.* Helvetic, Helvetian, Swiss. *La Confédération helvétique,* the Helvetic Confederation.

†**hem** [ɛm], *int.* Hem!

hématie [ema'ti], *n.f.* Red blood corpuscle. **hématite** [ema'tit], *n.f.* Haematite. **hématocèle** [ematɔ'sɛl], *n.f.* Haematocele. **hématologie,** *n.f.* Haematology. **hématose,** *n.f.* Haematosis. **hématurie,** *n.f.* Haematuria.

hémérocalle [emerɔ'kal], *n.f.* Day-lily.

hémicycle [emi'sikl], *n.m.* Hemicycle.

hémièdre [e'mjɛdr], *a.* Hemihedral.—*n.m.* Hemihedron. **hémiédrie,** *n.f.* Hemihedrism.

hémione [e'mjɔn], *n.m.* Dziggetai.

hémiplégie [emiple'ʒi], *n.f.* (*Path.*) Hemiplegia.

hémiptère [emip'tɛ:r], *n.m.* (*Ent.*) Hemipter. —*a.* Hemipterous.

hémisphère [emis'fɛ:r], *n.m.* Hemisphere. *L'hémisphère sud* or *austral,* the Southern Hemisphere. **hémisphérique,** *a.* Hemispheric.

hémistiche [emis'tiʃ], *n.m.* Hemistich.

hémoglobine [emɔglɔ'bin], *n.f.* Haemoglobin.

hémophyle [emɔ'fil], *a.* Haemophilic. **hémophylie,** *n.f.* Haemophilia.

hémorragie [emɔra'ʒi], *n.f.* Haemorrhage.

hémorroïdal [emɔrɔi'dal], *a.* (*fem.* **-ale,** *pl.* **-aux**) Haemorrhoidal. **hémorroïdes,** *n.f. pl.* Haemorrhoids, piles.

hémostase [emɔs'ta:z] or **hémostasie,** *n.f.* Haemostasia. **hémostatique,** *a.* Haemostatic. —*n.m.* Haemostat, styptic.

hendécagone [ɛ̃deka'gɔn], *n.m.* Hendecagon. —*a.* Hendecagonal.

hendécasyllabe [ɛ̃dekasi'lab], *n.m.* Hendecasyllable.—*a.* Hendecasyllabic.

hénioque [e'njɔk], *n.m.* Whipfish.

†**henné** [ɛ'ne], *n.m.* (*Bot.*) Henna. *Cheveux teints* (or *passés*) *au henné,* henna'd hair, henna-tinted hair.

†**hennin** [ɛ'nɛ̃], *n.m.* *Hennin.

†**hennir** [ɛ'ni:r], *v.i.* To neigh, to whinny. †**hennissement,** *n.m.* Neighing.

Henri [ã'ri], *m.* Henry.

Henriette [ã'rjɛt], *f.* Henrietta.

hépatique [epa'tik], *a.* Hepatic. —*n.f.* (*Bot.*) Liverwort. **hépatisation,** *n.f.* Hepatization. **s'hépatiser,** *v.r.* To become hepatized. **hépatite,** *n.f.* Hepatitis (inflammation of the liver); (*Min.*) hepatite (liver-stone). **hépatocèle,** *n.f.* Hepatocele.

heptacorde [epta'kɔrd], *n.m.* and *a.* Heptachord.

heptagonal [ɛptagɔ'nal], *a.* (*fem.* **-ale,** *pl.* **-aux**) Heptagonal. **heptagone,** *n.m.* Heptagon.—*a.* Heptagonal.

heptarchie [ɛptar'ʃi], *n.f.* Heptarchy.

héraldique [eral'dik], *a.* Heraldic.—*n.f.* Heraldry. **héraldiste,** *n.* Heraldist.

†**héraut** [e'ro], *n.m.* Herald; (*fig.*) harbinger.

herbacé [ɛrba'se], *a.* (*fem.* **-ée**) (*Bot.*) Herbaceous.

herbage [ɛr'ba:ʒ], *n.m.* Herbage, grass-land; pasture-ground, meadow. **herbager** (1), *n.m.* (*fem.* **-ère**) Grazier. **herbager** (2), *v.t.* To graze (cattle).

herbe [ɛrb], *n.f.* Herb, grass, wort; simple. *Blé en herbe,* corn in the blade; *brin d'herbe,* blade of grass; *couper l'herbe sous le pied à quelqu'un,* to supplant someone, to take the wind out of somebody's sails; *en herbe,* green, in embryo, unfledged; *fines herbes,* herbs for seasoning (parsley, chervil, chive, tarragon, etc.); *herbe à éternuer,* sneezewort; *herbe à la coupure,* stone-crop; *herbe à Nicot,* tobacco, (*fam.*) the weed; *herbe aux chantres,* hedge mustard; *herbe aux charpentiers,* milfoil, yarrow; *herbe aux chats,* cat-mint; *herbe aux cuillers,* scurvy-grass; *herbe aux écus,* moneywort; *herbe aux gueux,* clematis; *herbe aux perles,* gromwell; *herbe de la Saint-Jean,* St. John's wort; *herbe de Saint-Jean,* mugwort; *herbe marine,* seaweed; *herbes potagères,* potherbs, culinary herbs; *manger l'herbe par la racine,* to be buried; *manger son blé en herbe* [BLÉ]; *mauvaise herbe,* weed, (*fig.*) scamp; *mauvaise herbe croît toujours,* ill weeds grow apace; *mettre un cheval à l'herbe,* to put a horse out to grass; *toutes les herbes de la Saint-Jean,* all possible means. (C) *Herbe à feu,* fireweed; *herbe à la puce,* poison oak, poison ivy.

herber [ɛr'be], *v.t.* To lay on the grass (to bleach). **herberie,** *n.f.* Bleaching-ground.

herbette [ɛr'bɛt], *n.f.* (*Poet.*) Short grass, green-sward. **herbeux,** *a.* (*fem.* **-euse**) Grassy, herbous.

herbicide [ɛrbi'sid], *n.m.* Weed-killer.—*a.* Weed-killing.

herbier [ɛr'bje], *n.m.* Herbarium, hortus siccus, collection of plants dried and arranged in a book.

herbière [ɛr'bjɛ:r], *n.f.* Herb-woman; fodder-gatherer.

herbivore [ɛrbi'vɔ:r], *a.* Herbivorous.—*n.m.* Herbivore.

herborisateur [HERBORISEUR].

herborisation [ɛrbɔriza'sjɔ̃], *n.f.* Herborization. **herboriser,** *v.i.* To herborize. **herboriseur,** *n.m.* Botanizer. **herboriste,** *n.* Herbalist, dealer in medicinal herbs. **herboristerie,** *n.f.* Herb trade, herbalist's shop.

herbu [ɛr'by], *a.* (*fem.* **-ue**) Grassy, covered with grass.

†**hercher** [ɛr'ʃe], *v.i.* (*Mining*) To haul or to push a wagon (of ore, coal, etc.). †**hercheur,** *n.m.* (*fem.* **-euse**) Haulage boy, or girl.

Hercule [ɛr'kyl], *m.* Hercules. *Les travaux d'Hercule,* the labours of Hercules; *les Colonnes d'Hercule,* the Pillars of Hercules.

hercule [ɛr'kyl], *n.m.* Hercules, man of herculean strength; strong-arm man. *Travail d'Hercule,* Herculean task. **herculéen,** *a.* (*fem.* **-enne**) Herculean.

†**hère** [ɛ:r], *n.m.* *Un pauvre hère*, a sorry fellow, a poor devil.

héréditaire [eredi'tɛ:r], *a.* Hereditary. **héréditairement,** *adv.* Hereditarily.

hérédité [eredi'te], *n.f.* Hereditary transmission, inheritance, or succession, hereditary right; inheritance; heredity.

hérédosyphilis [eredɔsifi'lis], *n.f.* Hereditosyphilis. **hérédosyphilitique,** *a.* and *n.* Heredito-syphilitic.

hérésiarque [ere'zjark], *n.m.* Heresiarch.

hérésie [ere'zi], *n.f.* Heresy. **héréticité,** *n.f.* Heretical nature or tendency. **hérétique,** *a.* Heretical.—*n.* Heretic.

†**hérissé** [eri'se], *a.* (*fem.* **-ée**) Bristling, on end; bristly, rough, shaggy; (*Bot.*) hairy, prickly; covered with, full of, studded with, armed (*de*). *Avoir un style hérissé de néologismes*, to have a style that bristles with neologisms. *Cheveux hérissés* or *poil hérissé*, shaggy hair *or* mane. †**hérissement,** *n.m.* Bristling, shagginess.

†**hérisser** [eri'se], *v.t.* To bristle, to erect; to arm, to garnish (*de*). *Le lion hérisse sa crinière*, the lion bristles up his mane; *les piquants qui hérissent la tige du rosier*, the prickles bristling on the stalk of a rose-bush. **se hérisser,** *v.r.* To stand on end, to bristle up; to be bristling, to be armed, covered, or studded (*de*). †**hérisson,** *n.m.* Hedgehog; (*rare*) urchin; (*Fort.*) herisson; sprocket-wheel, sprocket, spur-wheel; (*fig.*) cross-grained person. *Hérisson de mer,* sea-urchin.

héritage [eri'ta:ʒ], *n.m.* Heritage, inheritance, estate, patrimony, legacy. *Faire* or *recueillir un héritage*, to inherit property. **hériter,** *v.i.* To inherit, to be heir (*de*); to succeed.—*v.t.* To inherit. *Il a hérité cent mille francs de son oncle*, he inherited a hundred thousand francs from his uncle. **héritier,** *n.m.* (*fem.* **-ière**) Heir or heiress. *Héritier légitime*, heir at law; *héritier naturel*, heir of one's body; *héritier présomptif*, heir apparent; *il est héritier de son oncle*, he is heir to his uncle.

hermaphrodisme [ɛrmafrɔ'dism], *n.m.* Hermaphroditism. **hermaphrodite,** *a.* and *n.m.* Hermaphrodite.

herméneutique [ɛrmenø'tik], *a.* Hermeneutic.—*n.f.* Hermeneutics.

hermétique [ɛrme'tik], *a.* Hermetic, airtight, water-tight. *Clôture hermétique,* hermetic sealing; *colonne hermétique,* column with a bust (of Hermes); *science hermétique,* hermetical science. **hermétiquement,** *adv.* Hermetically.

hermine [ɛr'min], *n.f.* Ermine. *Hermine d'été,* stoat. **herminé,** *a.* (*fem.* **-ée**) (*Her.*) Ermined.

herminette or **erminette** [ɛrmi'nɛt], *n.f.* Adze, howel.

hermitage etc. [ERMITAGE].

†**herniaire** [ɛr'njɛ:r], *a.* Hernial. *Bandage herniaire,* truss.

†**hernie** [ɛr'ni], *n.f.* Hernia, rupture; bulge, swelling (of tyre); (*Bot.*) club-root. †**hernieux,** *a.* (*fem.* **-ieuse**) Ruptured; suffering from hernia.

†**hernute** [ɛr'nyt], *n.m.* Moravian brother, Herrnhuter.

Hérode [e'rɔd], *m.* Herod.

héroï-comique [erɔikɔ'mik], *a.* Heroicomic, mock-heroic.

héroïne (1) [erɔ'in], *n.f.* Heroine.

héroïne (2) [erɔ'in], *n.f.* (*Chem.*) Heroin.

héroïque [erɔ'ik], *a.* Heroic. *Temps héroïques,* heroic ages. **héroïquement,** *adv.* Heroically. **héroïsme,** *n.m.* Heroism.

†**héron** [e'rɔ̃], *n.m.* Heron. *Héron bihoreau,* black-backed heron; *héron cendré,* grey heron; *héron crabier,* crab plover. †**héronneau,** *n.m.* (*pl.* **-eaux**) Young heron. †**héronner,** *v.i.* (*Hawking*) To fly the heron. †**héronnier,** *a.* (*fem.* **-ière** (1)) Heron-like, thin, lank, spare; (*Hawking*) trained to fly the heron. †**héronnière** (2), *n.f.* Heronry.

†**héros** [e'ro], *n.m.* Hero.

†**herpe** [ɛrp], *n.f.* (*Naut.*) *Herpe de guibre,* head-board; (*pl.*) *herpes marines,* valuable sea products washed ashore, viz. coral, amber, seaweed.

herpès [ɛr'pɛs], *n.m.* Herpes; tetter. **herpétique,** *a.* Herpetic.

herpétologie [ERPÉTOLOGIE].

†**hersage** [ɛr'sa:ʒ], *n.m.* Harrowing.

†**herse** [ɛrs], *n.f.* Harrow; portcullis, herse; (*R.-C. Ch.*) triangular candlestick; (*pl.*) (*Theat.*) battens, lights (above stage). †**hersé,** *a.* (*fem.* **-ée**) Harrowed; (*Her.*) represented with a herse. †**hersement** [HERSAGE]. †**herser,** *v.t.* To harrow. †**herseur,** *n.m.* Harrower.

hertzien [ɛr'tsjɛ̃], *a.* (*fem.* **-ienne**) Hertzian. *Ondes hertziennes,* hertzian waves.

hésitant [ezi'tɑ̃], *a.* (*fem.* **-ante**) Hesitating, wavering, undecided, faltering; stammering.

hésitation, *n.f.* Hesitation. **hésiter,** *v.i.* To hesitate, to falter, to pause, to waver; to be in doubt or suspense, to hang back. *Hésiter à parler*, to be reluctant to speak; *sans hésiter*, unhesitatingly.

†**hessois** [ɛ'swa], *a.* and *n.m.* (*fem.* **-oise**) Hessian. *Bottes à la hessoise*, Hessian boots.

hétaïre [eta'i:r] or **hétère**, *n.f.* Hetaera, courtesan. **hétairie** or **hétérie**, *n.f.* Hetaerism; hetaeria.

hétéroclite [eterɔ'klit], *a.* Heteroclite, anomalous; irregular; unusual. *Bâtiment hétéroclite,* irregular building; *objets hétéroclites,* odds and ends, junk.

hétérodoxe [eterɔ'dɔks], *a.* Heterodox. **hétérodoxie,** *n.f.* Heterodoxy.

hétérodyne [eterɔ'din], *a.* and *n.f.* (*Rad.*) Heterodyne.

hétérogène [eterɔ'ʒɛn], *a.* Heterogeneous, incongruous. **hétérogénéité,** *n.f.* Heterogeneity.

hetman [ɛt'mɑ̃], *n.m.* Hetman (of Cossacks).

†**hêtraie** [ɛ:'trɛ], *n.f.* Beech-grove. †**hêtre,** *n.m.* Beech, beech-tree.

†**heu!** (1) [ø], *int.* (*of doubt*) H'm! (*of hesitation*) . . . er . . .

†**heu** (2) [ø], *n.m.* (*Naut.*) Hoy.

†**heuchère** [ø'ʃer], *n.f.* (*Bot.*) Heuchera.

heur [œ:r], *n.m.* *Luck, fortune, chance. *Il n'y a qu'heur et malheur en ce monde,* that's the way of the world. *Je n'ai pas eu l'heur de lui plaire,* it was not my luck to meet with his (her) approval.

heure [œ:r], *n.f.* Hour; o'clock; time of day; moment; (*pl.*) primer (prayer-book). *À cette heure* or *à l'heure qu'il est,* now, at present, nowadays, by this time; *travail à l'heure,* time-work; *à l'heure qu'il faut,* in due time; *à ses heures,* when he (she) feels like it;

occasionally; *chercher midi à quatorze heures,* to create difficulties where there are none, to look for grapes on thorns; *dernière heure,* last moments; *(nouvelles de la) dernière heure,* latest news; *d'heure en heure,* hourly, every hour; *d'une heure à l'autre,* from one moment to another; *faites-le sur l'heure,* do it this very moment; *heures creuses,* slack hours; *heures d'affluence, de pointe,* peak hours; *heure indue,* unseasonable hour; *heure indiquée,* or *dite,* appointed hour; *heures canoniales,* parts of the breviary or the liturgical office; *petites heures,* those not included in this; *heures supplémentaires,* overtime; *heure suprême,* dying hour, supreme moments; *il est une heure et demie,* it is half-past one; *je le ferai à mes heures perdues,* I will do it in my leisure hours *or* in my spare time; *j'y serai dans une heure,* I will be there within an hour; *la belle heure pour arriver!* what a nice time to come; *les Heures,* (*Myth.*) the Hours; *l'heure du berger* [BERGER]; *l'heure H,* zero hour; *l'horloge a sonné deux heures,* the clock has struck two; *Livre d'Heures,* (*R.-C. Ch.*) Book of Hours; *mettre une montre à l'heure,* to set a watch right; *le quart d'heure de Rabelais,* paying or settling time, a trying time; *quelle heure est-il?* what time is it? (*fam.*) *je ne vous demande pas l'heure qu'il est,* mind your own business; *six heures tapant (tapantes)* or *sonnant* or *juste,* six o'clock sharp; *sur les six heures,* about six o'clock; *une bonne heure,* a favourable time; fully an hour; *un mauvais quart d'heure,* a bad time; *venez de meilleure heure,* come earlier; (*adv. phr.*) *à tout à l'heure,* see you later; (*fam.*) *à tout à l'heure,* see you later; *à la bonne heure!* right! very good; *de bonne heure,* early; *à la première heure,* with the milk.

heureusement [œrøz'mã], *adv.* Happily, luckily, fortunately; successfully, prosperously; by good luck.

heureux [œ'rø], *a.* (*fem.* **-euse**) Happy, blissful; blessed, lucky, fortunate; successful, prosperous; favourable, auspicious; pleasing, prepossessing; happy, pleased, delighted. *Heureux au jeu,* lucky at gambling; *heureux hasard,* stroke of luck; *il est né heureux,* he was born lucky; *une heureuse vieillesse,* a happy old age; *un mot heureux,* an apt word, a well-chosen expression; *une physionomie heureuse,* a pleasing countenance.

†**theurt** [œːr], *n.m.* Blow; knock, shock, collision; bruise. *Sans heurt(s),* smoothly. †**theurté,** *a.* (*fem.* **-ée**) Abrupt, harsh, jerky (of style). †**theurtement,** *n.m.* Clash, collision; hiatus. †**theurter,** *v.t.* To knock against, to strike against, to hit against; to run against; to run foul of; to jostle; to shock, to offend, to wound; to run counter to, to jar with, to combat. *Ce vaisseau a heurté l'autre,* this ship ran foul of the other; *heurter les préjugés de,* to shock the prejudices of.—*v.i.* To strike, to knock, to hit; to dash, to knock (at a door) (*contre*). **se heurter,** *v.r.* To strike or hit oneself; to strike against each other, to run foul of each other; to get across each other, to come into collison, to jostle each other, to clash. *Ils se sont heurtés de front,* they clashed head on; *les boucs se heurtent de leurs têtes,* goats butt at each other with their heads. †**theurtoir,** *n.m.*

Knocker; door-stop; (*Fort.*) hurter; (*Rail.*) buffer.

hévéa [eve'a] or **hévé** [e've], *n.m.* Hevea, para-rubber plant.

hexacorde [egza'kɔrd], *n.m.* (*Mus.*) Hexachord.

hexaèdre [egza'ɛdr], *n.m.* Hexahedron.—*a.* Hexahedral.

hexagonal [egzago'nal], *a.* (*fem.* **-ale,** *pl.* **-aux**) Hexagonal. **hexagone,** *n.m.* Hexagon.—*a.* Hexagonal.

hexamètre [egza'mɛtr], *n.m.* Hexameter.—*a.* Hexametric.

hiatus [ja'tyːs], *n.m.* Hiatus; gap.

hibernal [ibɛr'nal], *a.* (*fem.* **-ale,** *pl.* **-aux**) Hibernal.

hibernant [ibɛr'nã], *a.* (*fem.* **-ante**) Hibernating. **hibernation,** *n.f.* Hibernation. **hiberner,** *v.i.* To hibernate.

†**hibou** [i'bu], *n.m.* (*pl.* **-oux**) Owl; (*fig.*) moper. *Hibou brachyote,* short-eared owl; *hibou grand-duc,* eagle owl; *hibou moyen-duc,* long-eared owl; *hibou petit-duc,* scops owl. *Faire le hibou,* to mope like an owl.

†**hic** [ik], *n.m.* Knot, difficulty, rub. *Voilà le hic,* there's the rub, there's the snag.

†**hideur** [i'dœːr], *n.f.* Hideousness.

†**hideusement** [idøz'mã], *adv.* Hideously. †**hideux,** *a.* (*fem.* **-euse**) Hideous, frightful, shocking.

†**hie** [i], *n.f.* Beetle, rammer (for paviours); ram, monkey (for driving piles).

hièble or **yèble** [jɛbl], *n.f.* Dwarf-elder.

hiémal [je'mal], *a.* (*fem.* **-ale,** *pl.* **-aux**) Winter, hiemal. *Plantes hiémales,* winter plants. **hiémation,** *n.f.* Wintering.

hier (1) [iɛːr], *adv.* Yesterday. *Avant-hier,* the day before yesterday; *être né d'hier,* to have no experience; *hier matin,* yesterday morning; *hier (au) soir,* last night, yesterday evening.

†**hier** (2) [ie], *v.t.* To ram down.—*v.i.* To creak, to grate (of machines).

†**hiérarchie** [jerar'ʃi], *n.f.* Hierarchy. †**hiérarchique,** *a.* Hierarchical. †**hiérarchiquement,** *adv.* Hierarchically. †**hiérarchiser,** *v.t.* To make into a hierarchy.

hiératique [jera'tik], *a.* Hieratic.

hiéroglyphe [jero'glif], *n.m.* Hieroglyph. **hiéroglyphique,** *a.* Hieroglyphical.

hiéronymite [jerɔni'mit], *n.m.* Hieronymite.

hiérophante [jero'fɑːt], *n.m.* Hierophant.

†**hi-han** [i'ɑ̃] (*onom.*) Hee-haw (of a donkey).

Hilaire [i'lɛːr], *m.* Hilary.

hilarant [ila'rã], *a.* (*fem.* **-ante**) Screamingly funny, rollicking. *Gaz hilarant,* laughing-gas. **hilare,** *a.* Hilarious.

hilarité [ilari'te], *n.f.* Hilarity, mirth, laughter.

†**hile** [il], *n.m.* (*Bot.*) Hilum.

hiloire [i'lwar], *n.f.* Coaming, strake; weather-board (of outrigger). *Hiloire transversale,* ledge.

†**hindî** [ɛ̃'di], *n.m.* Hindi (language).

hindou [ɛ̃'du], *a.* (*fem.* **-oue**) Hindu; Indian (of India).—*n.m.* (**Hindou,** *fem.* **-oue**) A Hindu; an Indian (of India). **hindouisme,** *n.m.* Hinduism. **hindoustani,** *n.m.* Hindustani or Urdu (language).

hinterland [ɛ̃ter'lɑ̃d], *n.m.* Hinterland.

hippiatrique [ippja'trik], *a.* Pertaining to the veterinary art, hippiatric.—*n.f.* Veterinary art.

hippique [i'ɒik], *a.* Hippic. *Concours hippique,* horse-show. **hippisme,** *n.m.* Horse-racing; show-jumping; equitation.

hippocampe [ippɔ'kã:p], *n.m.* Hippocampus; hippocamp (sea-horse). **hippocentaure,** *n.m.* Hippocentaur.

Hippocrate [ippɔ'krat], *m.* Hippocrates.

hippocratique [ippɔkra'tik], *a.* Hippocratic.

hippocrépis [ippokre'pis], *n.f.* (*Bot.*) Hippocrepis, small horse-shoe.

hippodrome [ippɔ'drɔm], *n.m.* Hippodrome, circus; race-course.

hippogriffe [ippɔ'grif], *n.m.* Hippogriff, winged horse.

hippomobile [ippomɔ'bil], *a.* (as opposed to automobile) Horse-drawn (vehicle).

hippophage [ippɔ'fa:ʒ], *a.* Hippophagous. —*n.m.* Hippophagist. **hippophagie,** *n.f.* Hippophagy. **hippophagique, a.** *Boucherie hippophagique,* horse-butcher's.

hippopotame [ipopɔ'tam], *n.m.* Hippopotamus.

hircin [ir'sɛ̃], *a.* (*fem.* **-ine**) Hircine, goatish.

hirondeau [irɔ̃'do], *n.m.* (*pl.* **-eaux**) Young swallow.

hirondelle [irɔ̃'dɛl], *n.f.* Swallow. *Hirondelle domestique* or *de cheminée,* house-swallow; *hirondelle de fenêtre,* (house) martin; *hirondelle des marais,* swallow-plover; *hirondelle de mer,* sea-swallow, swallow-fish, ray's bream, sapphirine gurnard; *hirondelle* (*de mer*) *Caugek,* Sandwich tern; *hirondelle de rivage,* sand-martin; *hirondelle de rochers,* crag martin; *une hirondelle ne fait pas le printemps,* one swallow does not make a summer.

hirsute [ir'syt], *a.* Hirsute, hairy.

hispanique [ispa'nik], *a.* Hispanic. **hispanisant,** *n.m.* A student of Spanish. **hispano-américain,** *n.m.* and *a.* (*fem.* **-aine**) Spanish-American.

hispide [is'pid], *a.* (*Bot.*) Hispid, setaceous.

†**hisser** [i'se], *v.t.* To hoist, to lift, to run up, to raise. **se hisser,** *v.r.* To raise, hoist, or lift oneself up.

histoire [is'twa:r], *n.f.* History; tale, story, narration; idle story, untruth, falsehood; trifling concern, trifle. *Ça c'est une autre histoire,* that is quite another story; *faire des histoires,* to make a fuss; *histoire de rire,* for the fun of the thing; *la petite histoire, l'histoire anecdotique,* side-lights on history; *le plus beau de l'histoire c'était,* the best of it was; *peintre d'histoire,* historical painter. *En voilà une histoire!* here's a pretty go! *voilà bien des histoires,* what a fuss you make about it. *Surtout pas d'histoires!* above all keep out of trouble!

histologie [istɔlɔ'ʒi], *n.f.* Histology. **histologique, a.** Histological.

historien [istɔ'rjɛ̃], *n.m.* Historian. **historier,** *v.t.* (*conjugated like* PRIER) To illustrate, to embellish, to adorn. **historiette,** *n.f.* Little story, short tale. **historiographe,** *n.m.* Historiographer. **historiographie,** *n.f.* Historiography. **historique, a.** Historic(al). *Cela est historique,* that is a fact.—*n.m.* Historical account. **historiquement,** *adv.* Historically.

histrion [istri'jɔ̃], *n.m.* Histrion, actor; stage-player, mountebank. **histrionique, a.** Histrionic.

†**hitlérien** [itle'rjɛ̃], *a.* (*fem.* **-ienne**) Hitlerite.

La jeunesse hitlérienne, Hitler youth. **hitlérisme,** *n.m.* Hitlerism.

hiver [i'vɛ:r], *n.m.* Winter. *Au cœur, au milieu,* or *au plus fort de l'hiver,* in the depth of winter; *d'hiver,* wintry, winter's, of winter; *hiver doux,* mild winter; *hiver rude,* severe winter; *il compte quarante hivers,* he is forty years old; *l'hiver de la vie,* old age. **hivernage,** *n.m.* Winter season, winter-time; wintering place or port, winter(ing)-quarters; (*Agric.*) winter-ploughing, winter-foddering. **hivernal, a.** (*fem.* **-ale,** *pl.* **-aux**) Wintry, hibernal. **hivernant,** *n.* Winter resident. **hiverner,** *v.i.* To winter.—*v.t.* (*Agric.*) To winter-fallow.

†**ho!** [ho], *int.* Ho! hoy! (*Naut.*) ahoy!

†**hobereau** [ɔ'bro], *n.m.* (*pl.* **hobereaux**) Hobby (bird); country squire, squireen.

†**hoche** [ɔʃ], *n.f.* Notch (of tallies).

†**hochement** [ɔʃ'mã], *n.m.* Shaking, tossing, wagging (of the head).

†**hochepot** [ɔʃ'po], *n.m.* Hotchpotch, ragout of beef or mutton or fowl, turnips and chestnuts.

†**hochequeue** [ɔʃ'kø], *n.m.* Wagtail.

†**hocher** (1) [ɔ'ʃe], *v.t.* To shake, to toss; to wag (the tail etc.). *Hocher la tête,* to shake one's head.

†**hocher** (2) [ɔ'ʃe], *v.t.* To notch.

†**hochet** [ɔ'ʃe], *n.m.* *Coral, rattle (for children); (*fig.*) toy, bauble, plaything. *Il y a des hochets pour tout âge,* every age has its hobby.

†**hockey** [ɔ'kɛ], *n.m.* Hockey; (*C*) hockey, hockey stick. *Hockey sur glace,* ice-hockey; *joueur de hockey,* hockey player.

***hoir** [wa:r], *n.m.* (*Law*) Heir. **hoirie,** *n.f.* Inheritance.

†**holà!** [ɔ'la], *int.* Stop! Hold on! Hallo, there!—*n.m.* Stop, end. *Mettre le holà,* to put a stop to (a quarrel); to re-establish order.

†**hôlement** [ol'mã], *n.m.* Hooting (of owls etc.). **hôler,** *v.i.* To hoot.

†**hollandais** [ɔlã'dɛ], *a.* (*fem.* **-aise**) Dutch. —*n.m.* Dutch language; (**Hollandais,** *fem.* **-aise**) Dutchman, Dutchwoman.

†**Hollande** [ɔ'lãd], *f.* Holland, the Netherlands. †**hollande,** *n.m.* Dutch cheese.—*n.f.* Holland (linen); delft, delft-ware; Dutch potatoes.

holocauste [ɔlɔ'ko:st], *n.m.* Holocaust, burnt-offering; sacrifice.

holographe [OLOGRAPHE].

holothurie [ɔlɔty'ri], *n.f.* Holothurian, sea-slug.

†**hom** [5] [HUM].

†**homard** [ɔ'ma:r], *n.m.* Lobster.

†**hombre** [5:br], *n.m.* Ombre (card-game).

homélie [ɔme'li], *n.f.* Homily, familiar sermon.

homéopathe [ɔmeɔ'pat], *n.* Homoeopath. —*a.* Homoeopathic. **homéopathie,** *n.f.* Homoeopathy. **homéopathique, a.** Homoeopathic.

Homère [ɔ'mɛ:r], *m.* Homer.

homérique [ɔme'rik], *a.* Homeric.

homicide [ɔmi'sid], *n.m.* Homicide, manslaughter; man-slayer, murderer. *Homicide involontaire,* or *homicide par imprudence,* murder by misadventure; manslaughter; *homicide volontaire,* wilful murder.—*a.*

Murderous. *Des yeux homicides,* eyes that could kill; *un fer homicide,* a murderous weapon.

hommage [ɔ'ma:ʒ], *n.m.* Homage; respect, veneration; service; acknowledgment, token, gift, testimony; (*pl.*) respects, homage. *Avec les hommages de l'auteur,* with the author's compliments; *faire hommage à quelqu'un,* to do homage to someone; *hommage de reconnaissance,* token of gratitude; *rendre hommage à la vérité,* to do homage to truth; *rendre ses hommages à quelqu'un,* to pay one's respects to someone.

hommasse [ɔ'mas], *a.* Masculine, mannish (of women).

homme [ɔm], *n.m.* Man; (*colloq.*) husband, old man. *Bon homme* [BONHOMME]; *jeune homme* [JEUNE]; *brave homme,* worthy man, good fellow; *c'est le dernier des hommes* [DERNIER]; *c'est un homme à ménager,* he is a man to be considered; *c'est un homme à pendre,* he is a man who deserves hanging; *ça c'est un homme,* he is every inch a man; *un homme pauvre,* a poor man; *un pauvre homme,* a poor sort of a man; *homme à tout faire,* jack of all trades; *homme bon,* kind-hearted, good, virtuous man; *homme brave,* brave, daring man; *homme d'affaires* [AFFAIRE]; *un homme de bien* [BIEN]; *un homme de cœur* [CŒUR]; *homme de cour, d'église, d'épée, de lettres,* or *d'État,* courtier, churchman, military man, literary man, *or* statesman; *homme de cheval,* horseman; *homme de journée,* day-labourer; *homme de loi,* lawyer; *homme de paille,* man of straw; *homme de peine,* labourer; *homme de robe,* lawyer; *homme des bois,* orang-outang; *homme du monde,* man of the world; *il a trouvé son homme,* he has found his match; *il n'est pas homme à faire pareille chose,* he is not the sort of man to act like this; *tous les hommes,* all men, all mankind; *tout homme,* every man; *un homme comme il faut,* a gentleman; *voilà mon homme,* that is the man for me.

homme-grenouille [ɔmgrə'nu:j], *n.m.* (*pl.* **hommes-grenouilles**) Frogman.

homme-sandwich [ɔmsɑ̃'dwitʃ], *n.m.* (*pl.* **hommes-sandwich(e)s**) Sandwich man.

homocentrique [ɔmɔsɑ̃'trik], *a.* Homocentric.

homogène [ɔmɔ'ʒɛ:n], *a.* Homogeneous.

homogénéité, *n.f.* Homogeneity.

homologatif [ɔmɔlɔga'tif], *a.* (*fem.* **homologative**) Homologative, affirmative. **homologation,** *n.f.* Confirmation, approval, homologation.

homologue [ɔmɔ'lɔg], *a.* Homologous, similar.

homologué [ɔmɔlɔ'ge] *a.* (*fem.* **-ée**), Officially confirmed. (*spt.*) *Record homologué,* officially recognized record.

homologuer [ɔmɔlɔ'ge], *v.t.* (*Law*) To confirm, to homologate, to endorse.

homoncule [ɔmɔ̃'kyl], *n.m.* Little man, manikin, homunculus.

homonyme [ɔmɔ'nim], *a.* Homonymous. *n.* Homonym; namesake. **homonymie,** *n.f.* Homonymy.

homophone [ɔmɔ'fɔn], *a.* Homophonous.

homosexualité [ɔmɔsɛksɥali'te], *n.f.* Homosexuality.

homosexuel [ɔmɔsɛk'sɥɛl], *a.* and *n.m.* (*fem.* **-elle**) Homosexual.

†**hongre** [ɔ̃:gr], *a.* Gelded.—*n.m.* Gelding.

†**hongrer,** *v.t.* To geld (a horse).

†**Hongrie** [ɔ̃'gri], **la,** *f.* Hungary.

†**hongrois** [ɔ̃'grwa], *a.* (*fem.* **hongroise**) Hungarian.—*n.m.* Hungarian language; (**Hongrois,** *fem.* **Hongroise**) A Hungarian.

†**hongroyer** [ɔ̃grwa'je], *v.t.* To tan (leather) after the Hungarian fashion. †**hongroyeur,** *n.m.* Tanner of Hungary leather, saddler's currier.

honnête [ɔ'nɛ:t], *a.* Honest, upright; virtuous, modest (of women); respectable, honourable, genteel; becoming, seemly, decent, decorous; suitable, proper, befitting; civil, courteous, polite; handsome, fair, comely; good, advantageous; moderate, reasonable. *Cet habit est encore honnête,* this coat is still respectable; *famille honnête,* respectable family; *honnête aisance,* decent means; *honnête garçon,* honest fellow; *manières honnêtes,* obliging manners; *peu* or *pas honnête,* dishonest, dishonourable, unseemly, improper, disreputable, uncivil, unfair; *prétexte honnête,* fair pretence; *prix honnête,* reasonable price; *récompense honnête,* fitting reward; *une honnête femme,* a virtuous woman; *un honnête homme,* an honest man; **a gentleman,* a cultivated man.—*n.m.* Honesty, probity. **honnêtement,** *adv.* Honestly, uprightly, honourably; virtuously, modestly; becomingly, decently, decorously; handsomely; suitably, properly; kindly, courteously, politely, handsomely (liberally); moderately, reasonably. **honnêteté,** *n.f.* Honesty, probity, uprightness, integrity; modesty, decency, chastity, virtue; propriety, fitness, suitability; praiseworthiness; respectability, decorum, politeness, courtesy, kindness. *Blesser les règles de l'honnêteté,* to offend against the rules of propriety; *faire mille honnêtetés à quelqu'un,* to be very polite to someone.

honneur [ɔ'nœ:r], *n.m.* Honour; chastity, virtue; rectitude, integrity, probity; repute, credit; distinction; respect; (*Cards*) court-card, honour; (*pl.*) honours, preferments; regalia (crown jewels). *Affaire d'honneur,* duel; *à tout seigneur tout honneur,* give honour where honour is due; *briguer les honneurs,* to seek honours; *champ d'honneur,* field of battle; *dame d'honneur* [DAME (1)]; *demoiselle d'honneur,* bridesmaid; *en quel honneur?* on what special occasion? *en tout bien tout honneur* [BIEN]; *être en honneur,* to be in favour *or* in great demand; *faire à quelqu'un l'honneur de quelque chose,* to ascribe the honour of something to someone; *faire honneur à,* to do credit to, (*Comm.*) to honour (bills); *faire honneur à ses affaires,* to meet one's engagements; *faire les honneurs,* to do the honours; *garçon d'honneur,* best man; *homme d'honneur,* man of honour; *ne jouer que pour l'honneur,* to play for love; *parole d'honneur!* upon my honour! *partie d'honneur,* rubber (at cards), deciding game; *sauf votre honneur,* saving your presence; *se faire honneur de quelque chose,* to esteem something an honour, to glory in or take credit for something; *s'en tirer avec honneur,* to come off with honour; *se piquer d'honneur,* to do something zealously; *sur l'honneur,* upon one's honour; (*sch.*) *table d'honneur,* high table; *tenir à honneur de,* to esteem it a point of honour to; *tout est perdu fors l'honneur*, all is lost but honour; *vous me faites honneur*, you honour me.

†**honnir** [ɔ'niːr], *v.t.* To dishonour, to disgrace, to cover with shame. *Honni soit qui mal y pense*, shame on him who evil thinks.

honorabilité [ɔnɔrabili'te], *n.f.* Honour, respectability. **honorable**, *a.* Honourable; respectable, creditable, reputable; proper, suitable. **honorablement**, *adv.* Honourably, respectably, creditably; properly, suitably; nobly, splendidly.

honoraire [ɔnɔ'rɛːr], *a.* Honorary, titular. *Professeur honoraire*, emeritus professor.—*n.m. pl.* Honorarium, fee (of a professional person). *Les honoraires d'un avocat*, a barrister's fee. **honorariat**, *n.m.* Position of a person having honorary or emeritus title.

honorer [ɔnɔ're], *v.t.* To honour, to pay honour to; to do credit to, to be an honour to. *Honorer une traite*, to honour, to meet a bill; *votre honorée du . . .*, your favour of the . . . . **s'honorer**, *v.r.* To do oneself honour; to acquire honour; to deem it an honour; to pride oneself. **honorifique**, *a.* Honorary, titular, gratuitous.

†**honte** [ɔ̃ːt], *n.f.* Shame; disgrace, discredit, obloquy, infamy; reproach; scandal; confusion, bashfulness. *Avoir honte de*, to be ashamed of; **avoir toute honte bue*, to be lost to all sense of shame; *faire honte à quelqu'un*, to make someone feel ashamed; *il est la honte de sa famille*, he is a disgrace to his family; *mauvaise honte* or *fausse honte*, self-consciousness, bashfulness; *nous lui faisions* (or *avons fait*) *honte*, he was ashamed of us; *perdre toute honte*, to lose all sense of shame; *quelle honte!* for shame! *regarder quelque chose comme une honte*, to look upon something as a disgrace; **revenir avec sa courte honte*, to return without success, to come back as one started, baulked, unsuccessful; *rougir de honte*, to blush for very shame; *sans honte*, shameless, unblushing; shamelessly, unblushingly; *vous me faites honte*, I am ashamed of you. †**honteusement**, *adv.* Shamefully, disgracefully; ignominiously; infamously, scandalously. †**honteux**, *a.* (*fem.* **honteuse**) Ashamed, bashful, shy; sheepish; shameful, disgraceful, scandalous, disreputable, discreditable. *Il a l'air honteux*, he has a bashful look; *il n'y a que les honteux qui perdent*, nothing ask, nothing have; *jamais honteux n'eut belle amie*, faint heart never won fair lady; *les parties honteuses*, the secret parts, pudenda; *morceau honteux*, last bit in the dish; *pauvres honteux*, poor ashamed to beg; *une conduite honteuse*, disgraceful conduct.

†**hop** [ɔp], *int.* Hop! or hop-là! now then, jump! *debout hop!* get up quick! *Allez, hop!* upsadaisy! get going!

hôpital [ɔpi'tal], *n.m.* (*pl.* **hôpitaux**) Hospital. *Hôpital ambulant*, field-hospital; *hôpital d'évacuation*, clearing hospital; *prendre le chemin de l'hôpital*, to be on the road to ruin; *vaisseau-hôpital* (*pl.* *vaisseaux-hôpitaux*), hospital-ship.

hoplite [ɔ'plit], *n.m.* (*Gr. Ant.*) Hoplite.

†**hoquet** [ɔ'kɛ], *n.m.* Hiccup. *Avoir le hoquet*, to have the hiccups; *faire passer le hoquet*, to stop the hiccups; *hoquet de la mort*, death-rattle. **hoqueter**, *v.i.* To hiccup.

horaire [ɔ'rɛːr], *a.* Hourly; horary, horal. *Halte horaire*, (*Mil.*) hourly halt; *vitesse horaire*, speed per hour.—*n.m.* Time-table, schedule.

†**horde** [ɔrd], *n.f.* Horde; pack; (*fig.*) band, host, rabble.

hordéiforme [ɔrdei'fɔrm], *a.* Hordeiform (barley-shaped).

†**horion** [ɔ'rjɔ̃], *n.m.* Blow, thump, punch.

horizon [ɔri'zɔ̃], *n.m.* Horizon, sky-line. *À l'horizon*, on the horizon; *ligne d'horizon*, vanishing line. *Faire un tour d'horizon de la situation*, to make a general survey of the situation; *l'horizon politique*, the political horizon. *Monter sur l'horizon*, (*Astron.*) to ascend. **horizontal**, *a.* (*fem.* **-ale**, *pl.* **-aux**) Horizontal.—*n.f.* *L'horizontale*, the horizontal line; *une horizontale*, (*fam.*) a harlot. **horizontalement**, *adv.* Horizontally.

horloge [ɔr'lɔːʒ], *n.f.* Clock; time-keeper. *Horloge d'eau*, clepsydra; *horloge électrique*, electric clock; *horloge normande*, grandfather's clock; *horloge parlante*, speaking clock (of the Paris Observatory); *horloge qui marche huit jours*, eight-day clock; *l'horloge sonne midi*, the clock is striking twelve; *réglé comme une horloge*, as punctual as the clock. *Horloge de la mort*, death-watch (beetle). **horloger**, *a.* (*fem.* **horlogère**) Pertaining to clock-making.—*n.* Clock-maker, watchmaker. **horlogerie**, *n.f.* Watch- and clock-making or business; horology; clocks and watches.

hormis [ɔr'mi], *prep.* Except, excepting, but.

hormonal [ɔrmɔ'nal], *a.* (*fem.* **-ale**, *pl.* **-aux**) Hormonal, hormonic. **hormone**, *n.f.* Hormone. **hormonothérapie**, *n.f.* Hormonotherapy, hormonal treatment.

horoscope [ɔrɔs'kɔp], *n.m.* Horoscope. *Se faire tirer* (or *dire*) *son horoscope*, to have one's fortune told; *tirer l'horoscope de quelqu'un*, to cast someone's nativity, to predict the fate of someone.

horreur [ɔ'rœːr], *n.f.* Horror, dread; abhorrence, repulsion, detestation, heinousness, atrocity, enormity; atrocious person; fright (very ugly person). *Avoir horreur de* or *avoir en horreur*, to abhor, to hold in detestation; *dire des horreurs*, to say shocking things; *être saisi d'horreur*, to be struck with horror; *faire horreur à*, to horrify, to disgust; *inspirer l'horreur du vice*, to inspire a hatred of vice; *une belle horreur*, an awful spectacle. **horrible**, *a.* Horrible, dreadful, fearful; hideous, frightful, shocking. *Il fait un temps horrible*, it is shocking weather. **horriblement**, *adv.* Horribly, awfully. **horrifier**, *v.i.* To horrify. **horrifique**, *a.* Hair-raising.

horripilant [ɔripi'lã], *a.* (*fem.* **-ante**) Exasperating.

horripilation [ɔripila'sjɔ̃], *n.f.* (*Med.*) Horripilation. **horripiler**, *v.t.* To horripilate; to exasperate.

†**hors** [ɔːr], *prep.* Out of, outside of; without; beyond, past; but, except, save. *Hors d'affaire*, out of danger; *hors de combat*, disabled; *hors de danger*, out of danger; *hors de doute*, beyond doubt; *hors d'haleine*, out of breath; *hors d'ici!* away with you, out of my sight! *hors* (*de*) *la ville*, outside the town; *hors de portée*, out of reach, out of range; *hors de prix*, exorbitant; *hors de saison*, out of place, inopportune; *hors de service*, unserviceable;

out of order (of lift, telephone, etc.); *hors de soi*, beside oneself. *Hors programme*, outside the programme; *hors série*, specially designed (article).

†**hors-bord** [ɔr'bɔr], *n.m. inv.* Outboard; speed-boat.

†**hors-caste** [ɔr'kast], *a.* and *n. inv.* Outcaste, untouchable.

†**hors-concours** [ɔrkɔ̃'kuːr], *a., adv.,* and *n. inv.* Not competing; outstanding; above competition. *Être* (*mis*) *hors(-)concours*, to be disqualified by reason of superiority or as member of jury.

†**hors-d'œuvre** [ɔr'dœvr], *n.m. inv.* (*Arch.*) Outwork, outbuilding; (*Lit.*) digression, excursion, episode; (*Cook.*) dish served at the beginning of a meal.

†**hors-jeu** [ɔr'ʒø], *n.m. inv.* (*Ftb.*) Off-side.

†**hors-la-loi** [ɔrla'lwa], *adv.* and *n.m. inv.* Outlaw.

†**hors-ligne** [ɔr'liɲ], *a. inv.* Outstanding. *Une interprétation hors-ligne*, an outstanding interpretation.

†**hors-montoir** [ɔrmɔ̃'twaːr], *a.* Côté hors-montoir, off-side (of a horse).

†**hors-texte** [ɔr'tɛkst], *a., adv.,* and *n.m. inv.* Inset plate (in book).

hortensia [ɔrtɑ̃'sja], *n.m.* Hydrangea.

horticole [ɔrti'kɔl], *a.* Horticultural. **horticulteur**, *n.m.* Horticulturist. **horticultural,** *a.* (*fem.* -**ale,** *pl.* -**aux**) Horticultural. **horticulture**, *n.f.* Horticulture. *Exposition d'horticulture*, flower-show.

hosanna [ɔzan'na], *int.* and *n.m.* Hosanna.

hospice [ɔs'pis], *n.m.* Refuge; asylum; almshouse; workhouse; convent etc. offering hospitality to pilgrims, travellers, etc; home for the destitute. *Hospice des enfants trouvés*, foundling hospital; *hospice des vieillards* or *hospice*, home for the aged; *finir à l'hospice*, to end up in a workhouse. **hospitalier,** *a.* (*fem.* -**ière**) Pertaining to a hospice or hospital; hospitable. *Sœur hospitalière*, sister of charity.—*n.* Hospitaller. **hospitalièrement,** *adv.* Hospitably. **hospitalisation,** *n.f.* Admission to hospital; hospital care. **hospitaliser,** *v.t.* To place in hospital; to shelter, harbour. **hospitalité,** *n.f.* Hospitality.

hosteau [ɔs'to], *n.m.* (*Mil. slang*) Hospital; prison.

hostellerie [ɔstɛl'ri], *n.f.* Inn.

hostie [ɔs'ti], *n.f.* (*Jewish Ant.*) Offering, victim, sacrifice; (*R.-C. Ch.*) host, consecrated wafer.

hostile [ɔs'til], *a.* Hostile, inimical, adverse. **hostilement,** *adv.* Hostilely, adversely. **hostilité,** *n.f.* Hostility, enmity.

hôte [oːt], *n.m.* (*fem.* **hôtesse**) Host, hostess; landlord, innkeeper; guest, visitor; lodger; traveller; inhabitant, occupier, inmate. *Hôte payant*, paying guest. *Qui compte sans son hôte compte deux fois*, he who reckons without his host must reckon again; *table d'hôte*, table d'hôte, ordinary. *Hôtesse de l'air*, (*Av.*) air-hostess.

hôtel [o'tɛl], *n.m.* Town mansion, large house; hotel, inn. *Hôtel de ville*, town hall; *hôtel des monnaies*, mint; *hôtel des postes*, General Post Office; *hôtel des ventes*, auction mart; *hôtel particulier*, town-house, private residence; mansion; *l'hôtel-Dieu*, the (chief)

hospital of a town. *Descendre à l'hôtel*, to put up at an hotel; *hôtel meublé* or *garni*, furnished lodgings *or* apartments, lodging-house; *maître d'hôtel*, butler. **hôtelier,** *n.m.* (*fem.* **hôtelière**) Innkeeper, host, hostess, landlord (of an inn).—*a. L'industrie hôtelière*, the hotel trade. **hôtellerie,** *n.f.* Inn, hotel, hostelry; hotel trade. **hôtesse** [HÔTE].

†**hotte** [ɔt], *n.f.* Basket (carried on the back); dosser, hod; pannier; hood (of forge, kitchen, etc.). †**hottée,** *n.f.* Basketful.

†**hottentot** [ɔtɑ̃'to], *a.* and *n.* (*fem.* **hottentote**) Hottentot.

†**hotter** [ɔ'te], *v.t.* To carry (grapes) in a basket.

†**hottereau** [ɔ'tro] (*pl.* -**eaux**) or †**hotteret,** *n.m.* Small hod.

†**hotteur** [ɔ'tœːr], *n.m.* (*fem.* -**euse**) Basket-carrier.

†**hou** [u] *int.* Boo! Fie!

†**houache** [wa'ʃ] or †**houaiche,** *n.f.* Wake, track, wash (of a ship); stray-mark (of log).

†**houage** [wa'ʒ], *n.m.* Hoeing.

†**houari** [ua'ri], *n.m.,* or *f.* Wherry. (*Voile à*) *houari*, shoulder of mutton sail.

†**houblon** [u'blɔ̃], *n.m.* Hop. *Four à houblon*, hop-kiln; *perche à houblon*, hop-pole. †**houblonner,** *v.t.* To put hops into (beer). †**houblonnier,** *a.* and *n.* (*fem.* -**ière** (1)) Pertaining to the cultivation and handling of hops; hop(-growing) area; hop-grower. †**houblonnière** (2), *n.f.* Hop-field.

†**houe** [u], *n.f.* Hoe. †**houement,** *n.m.* Hoeing. †**houer,** *v.t.* To hoe. †**houette,** *n.f.* Small hoe.

†**houille** [uːj], *n.f.* Coal, pit-coal. *Chargeur de houille*, coal-whipper; *exploiter une mine de houille*, to work a coal-mine; *mine de houille*, coal-mine, coal-pit, colliery. *Houille blanche*, water-power. †**houiller,** *a.* (*fem.* **houillère** (1)) Coal-bearing. *Terrains houillers*, coal-fields. †**houillère** (2), *n.f.* Coal-mine, coal-pit, colliery. *Propriétaire de houillère*, coal-owner, coal-proprietor. †**houilleur,** *n.m.* Collier, coal-miner. †**houilleux,** *a.* (*fem.* **houilleuse**) Containing coal.

†**houle** [ul], *n.f.* Swell, surge. †**houler,** *v.i.* To swell, surge.

†**houlette** [u'lɛt], *n.f.* (Shepherd's) crook; crosier; trowel; spatula.

†**houleux** [u'lø], *a.* (*fem.* **houleuse**) Swelling, surging, rough; (*fig.*) agitated, turbulent.

†**houlque** [HOUQUE].

†**houp!** [up], *int.* [HOP]. *Houp là!* gee-up! upsadaisy!

†**houppe** [up], *n.f.* Tuft; top-knot; tassel. *Houppe à poudre*, powder-puff. †**houppé,** *a.* (*fem.* **houppée** (1)) Tufted, crested. †**houppée** (2), *n.f.* Crest, foam (of a wave).

†**houppelande** [u'plɑ̃d], *n.f.* (Warm) great-coat, cloak.

†**houpper** [u'pe], *v.t.* To tuft; to comb (wool).

†**houppette** [u'pɛt], *n.f.* Powder-puff.

†**houque** [uk], *n.f.* (*Bot.*) Feather-grass. *Houque laineuse*, velvet grass.

†**hourdage** [ur'daʒ] or †**hourdis,** *n.m.* Rough-walling; pugging. †**hourder,** *v.t.* To rough-work, to rough-wall; to pug, to nog (frame-work).

†**houret** [u'rɛ], *n.m.* Bad hound, lurcher, cur.

†**houri** (1) [u'ri], *n.f.* Houri, (*fam.*) a beautiful girl.

†**houri** (2) [u'ri], *n.m.* Coasting lugger.
†**hourque** [urk], *n.f.* Hooker (Dutch ship); (*fam.*) cranky old tub.
†**hourra** [u'ra], *n.m.* Hurrah. *Pousser des hourras*, to cheer.
†**hourvari** [urva'ri], *n.m.* (*Hunt.*) Cry to call back the dogs; uproar, din, tumult.
†**housard** [HUSSARD].
†**houseau** [u'zo], *n.m.* (*pl.* **houseaux**) (*usu. in pl.*) Spatterdashes, leggings. *Laisser ses houseaux*, to leave one's bones, to die.
†**houspiller** [uspi'je], *v.t.* To manhandle, to rough-house; to rate, to abuse.
†**houssaie** [u'sɛ], *n.f.* Holly-grove.
†**housse** [us], *n.f.* Housing, horse-cloth; saddle-cloth, hammer-cloth; covering, dust-sheet, loose cover (of bed, furniture, etc.).
†**housser** (1) [u'se], *v.t.* To cover up.
†**housser** (2) [u'se], *v.t.* To dust, to sweep (with a feather-broom etc.).
†**houssine** [u'sin], *n.f.* Switch, riding-switch. †**houssiner**, *v.t.* To switch; to beat.
†**houssoir** [u'swaːr], *n.m.* Whisk, holly-broom, feather-broom.
†**housson** [u'sɔ̃], *n.m.* Knee-holly, butcher's-broom.
†**houx** [u], *n.m.* Holly, holly-tree. *Houx-frêlon* or *-fragon* (*pl.* houx-frêlons), butcher's-broom.
†**hoyau** [wa'jo], *n.m.* (*pl.* **-aux**) Mattock, grubbing-hoe.
†**huaille** [ɥaːj], *n.f.* Mob, rabble.
†**huard** [ɥaːr], *n.m.* Osprey; sea-eagle.
†**hublot** [y'blo], *n.m.* (*Naut.*) Side-light, port-hole. *Faux hublot*, dead light.
†**huche** [yʃ], *n.f.* Kneading-trough; hutch, bread-pan; bin-hopper (of a mill). †**hucher** (1) or †**huchier**, *n.m.* Bin-maker.
†**hucher** (2) [y'ʃe], *v.t., v.i.* To call (by whistling etc.). †**huchet**, *n.m.* (*Her.*) Huntsman's horn.
†**hue** [y], *int.* Gee! gee-up! *viz.* turn to the right (to a horse). (*fam.*) *L'un tire à hue et l'autre à dia*, they don't pull together.
†**huée** [ɥe], *n.f.* Whoop, shouting; hoot, hooting; booing.
†**huer** [ɥe], *v.t.* To shout after; to hoot at, to boo.—*v.i.* To hoot, to boo.
†**huette** [HULOTTE].
hugolâtre [ygɔ'laːtr], *n.* Great admirer of Victor Hugo.
†**huguenot** [yg'no], *a.* and *n.* (*fem.* **huguenote**) Huguenot.—*n.f.* Kitchen-stove (in earthen-ware); pipkin. †**huguenotisme**, *n.m.* Huguenotism.
†**huhau** [y'o], *int.* Gee up! to the right!
***hui** [ɥi], *adv.* Today. Only used in *dès hui*, this very day; *d'hui en un an*, a year from today. See *aujourd'hui*.
huilage [ɥi'laːʒ], *n.m.* Oiling.
huile [ɥil], *n.f.* Oil. *Cet ouvrage sent l'huile*, that work smells of the lamp; (*fig.*) *faire tache d'huile*, to spread slowly (of a rumour etc.); *huile à brûler*, lamp-oil; *huile comestible*, salad-oil; *huile à friture*, frying-oil; *huile de bras*, *huile de coude*, or *huile de poignet*, elbow-grease; *huile de pied de bœuf*, neat's-foot oil; *jeter de l'huile sur le feu*, to add fuel to the flame; *les Saintes huiles*, *l'huile sainte*, the holy oil; *tache d'huile*, oil-stain; *pl.* (*fam.*) *être dans les huiles*, to be on top, to be one of (or among) the big shots; (*Mil.*) *les huiles*,

the top brass. **huiler**, *v.t.* To oil; to anoint with oil; to lubricate.—*v.i.* (*Bot.*) To exude oil. **huilerie**, *n.f.* Oil-works, oil-milk; oil-shop. **huileux**, *a.* (*fem.* **huileuse**) Oily, greasy. **huilier**, *n.m.* Cruet-stand; oil-maker, oil-merchant. **huilière**, *n.f.* (*Naut.*) Oil-pitcher.
†***huis** [ɥi], *n.m.* Door. *À huis clos*, with closed doors, in private, in camera. **huis-serie**, *n.f.* Door-frame.
huissier [ɥi'sje], *n.m.* Usher; gentleman-usher; door-keeper; sheriff's officer, bailiff, tipstaff; beadle. *Huissier audiencier*, crier of the court, usher; *huissier saisisseur*, distrainer.
†**huit** [ɥit before a vowel, a silent *h*, and at the end of the phrase; ɥi before a consonant], *a.* Eight; eighth. *Dans huit jours* or *d'aujour-d'hui en huit*, this day week; *il y a huit jours*, a week ago; *le huit juin*, 8 June; *tous les huit jours*, once a week, every week; *je lui ai donné ses huit jours*, I gave her a week's notice.—*n.m.* [ɥit] Eight; eighth; card with eight pips; 8-shaped object. *Le huit du mois*, the eighth of the month. †**huitain**, *n.m.* Stanza or poem of eight lines. †**huitaine**, *n.f.* Eight days, week; about a week. *Dans la huitaine*, in the course of the week; *dans une huitaine de jours*, in about a week's time. †**huitième**, *a.* Eighth.—*n.m.* Eighth, eighth part. †**huitièmement**, *adv.* Eighthly.
†**huit-reflets** [ɥi'rflɛ], *n.m. inv.* (*fam.*) A (de luxe) silk hat.
huître [ɥitr], *n.f.* Oyster; (*fig.*) blockhead, dunce. **huîtrier**, *n.m.* Oyster-catcher (bird). —*a.* (*fem.* **-ière** (1)) Pertaining to oysters. *L'industrie huîtrière*, oyster-farming. **huî-trière** (2), *n.f.* Oyster-bed.
†**hulan** [UHLAN].
†**hulotte** [y'lɔt], *n.f.*, or *chat-huant*, or *chouette des bois*, wood owl, tawny owl.
†**hululer** [ULULER].
†**hum** [hm], *int.* Hem! hm!
humain [y'mɛ̃], *a.* (*fem.* **humaine**) Human; humane, benevolent. *Le genre humain*, man-kind.—*n.m.* Humanity, mankind, the human race; (*pl.*) humans, men. **humainement**, *adv.* Humanly; humanely. **humanisation**, *n.f.* Humanization. **humaniser**, *v.t.* To humanize, to civilize; to soften, to mollify. **s'humaniser**, *v.r.* To become humanized; to become milder or more compliant; to come down to the intellectual level of others. **humanisme**, *n.m.* Humanism. **humaniste**, *a.* and *n.* classical scholar. **humanitaire**, *a.* and *n.* Humani-tarian. **humanitarisme**, *n.m.* Humani-tarianism. **humanité**, *n.f.* Humanity; human nature; mankind; (*pl.*) humanities; classical studies.
humble [œ̃ːbl], *a.* Humble, lowly, meek, mod-est. **humblement**, *adv.* Humbly, meekly.
humectant [ymɛk'tɑ̃], *a.* (*fem.* **humectante**) Humectant, refreshing, moistening.—*n.m.* Humectant. **humectation** [ymɛkta'sjɔ̃], *n.f.* Humectation, moistening. **humecter**, *v.t.* To damp, to wet, to moisten, to bedew, to refresh. **s'humecter**, *v.r.* To be moist-ened, to grow moist; to drink, to refresh oneself. *S'humecter le gosier* [GOSIER]. **humecteur**, *n.m.* Wetting machine.
†**humer** [y'me], *v.t.* To inhale, to suck in, to take in. *Humer l'air*, to inhale the air.

huméral [yme'ral], *a.* (*fèm.* **-ale,** *pl.* **-aux**) (*Anat.*) Humeral. **humérus,** *n.m.* Humerus.
humescent [ymɛs'sã], *a.* (*fem.* **-ente**) Growing damp.
humeur [y'mœːr], *n.f.* Humour; temperament, disposition, turn of mind; mood, caprice, fancy, inclination; ill-humour. *Avec humeur,* peevishly, crossly, ill-humouredly; *avoir de l'humeur,* to be out of temper; *elle a l'humeur gaie,* she is of a cheerful disposition; *être de bonne humeur,* to be in a good mood *or* temper; *être de mauvaise humeur,* to be in a bad temper; *être d'humeur à faire quelque chose,* to be in the mood to do something; *un mouvement d'humeur,* a fit *or* an outburst of temper; *humeurs froides,* king's evil, scrofula; *humeur noire,* spleen.
humide [y'mid], *a.* Damp, wet, moist, humid. ***humidement,** *adv.* In a damp place or manner. **humidification,** *n.f.* Damping. **humidifier,** *v.t.* To damp, to moisten. **humidité,** *n.f.* Humidity, moisture, dampness. *Taches d'humidité,* damp-stains.
humiliant [ymi'ljã], *a.* (*fem.* **humiliante**) Humiliating, degrading.
humiliation [ymilja'sjɔ̃], *n.f.* Humiliation, abasement, mortification. **humilier,** *v.t.* To humble, to humiliate, to abase. **s'humilier,** *v.r.* To humble, humiliate, or abase oneself. **humilité,** *n.f.* Humility, meekness, lowliness.
humoral [ymɔ'ral], *a.* (*fem.* **humorale,** *pl.* **humoraux**) (*Med.*) Humoral. **humorisme,** *n.m.* Humoralism.
humoriste [ymɔ'rist], *a.* Humorous; (*Med.*) humoralistic.—*n.* A humorous writer or painter, humorist. **humoristique,** *a.* Humorous (writer etc.).
humour [y'mur], *n.m.* Humour.
humus [y'mys], *n.m.* Humus, mould.
†**hune** [yn], *n.f.* (*Naut.*) Top. *La grande hune,* the main-top; *mât de hune,* the topmast; *petit mât de hune,* fore-topmast. †**hunier,** *n.m.* Topsail. *Grand hunier,* main-topsail; *petit hunier,* fore-topsail.
†**huppe** [yp], *n.f.* Hoopoe; tuft, crest. †**huppé,** *a.* (*fem.* **huppée**) Tufted, crested (of birds); (*colloq.*) tip-top, well off, smartly dressed. *Des plus huppés,* of the smartest, moving in the highest circles.
†**hure** [yːr], *n.f.* Head (of a wild boar); (*pop.*) big (ugly) head. *Hure de saumon,* jowl of a salmon.
†**hurlement** [yrlə'mã], *n.m.* Howling; howl, roar, yell, yelling, shrieking; shriek, scream. *Pousser des hurlements d'effroi,* to shriek with terror. †**hurler,** *v.i.* To howl, to yell; to roar, to bellow; to shriek, to scream. *Hurler avec les loups,* to do as others do.—*v.t.* Hurler *sa fureur,* to scream out one's fury. †**hurleur,** *a.* (*fem.* **-euse**) Howling.—*n.* Howler.
hurluberlu [yrlyber'ly], *n.* Giddy-pate, harebrained person, harum-scarum (of both sexes).
†**huron** [y'rɔ̃], *a.* and *n.* (*fem.* **-onne**) Huron; ingenuous young man; (*fig.*) boor.
†**hurrah** [HOURRA].
†**hussard** [y'saːr], *n.m.* Hussar. †**hussarde,** *n.f.* Hungarian dance. *À la hussarde,* in a cavalier fashion; *bottes à la hussarde,* riding-boots.
†**hutin** [y'tɛ̃], *a.m.* Headstrong (nickname of Louis X, King of France).

†**hutte** [yt], *n.f.* Hut, cabin, shanty. **se hutter,** *v.r.* To make or lodge in a hut.
hyacinthe [ja'sɛ̃ːt], *n.f.* Jacinth; hyacinth (precious stone or flower).
hyalin [ja'lɛ̃], *a.* (*fem.* **hyaline**) Hyaline.
hybridation [ibrida'sjɔ̃], *n.f.* Hybridization. **hybride,** *a.* and *n.m.* Hybrid, mongrel. **hybrider,** *v.t.* To hybridize. **hybridité,** *n.f.* Hybridity.
hydarthrose [idar'troːz], *n.f.* Hydarthrosis.
hydracide [idra'sid], *n.m.* Hydracid.
hydrangée [idrã'ʒe], *n.f.* (*Bot.*) Hydrangea.
hydratation [idrata'sjɔ̃], *n.f.* Hydration. **hydrate,** *n.m.* Hydrate. *Hydrate de carbone,* carbo-hydrate. **hydraté,** *a.* (*fem.* **-ée**) Hydrated. **hydrater,** *v.t.* To hydrate.
hydraulique [idro'lik], *a.* Hydraulic. *Usine hydraulique,* waterworks.—*n.f.* Hydraulics.
hydravion [idra'vjɔ̃], *n.m.* Flying-boat, sea-plane.
hydre [idr], *n.f.* Hydra.
hydrique [i'drik], *a.* Hydrous.
hydrocarbonate [idrɔkarbɔ'nat], *n.m.* Hydrocarbonate.
hydrocarbure [idrɔkar'byːr], *n.m.* (*Chem.*) Hydrocarbon.
hydrocèle [idrɔ'sɛl], *n.m.* Hydrocele.
hydrocéphale [idrɔse'fal], *a.* and *n.* Hydrocephalous.—*n.f.* Hydrocephalus. **hydrocéphalie,** *n.f.* Hydrocephalus, hydrocephaly.
hydrochlorate [idrɔklɔ'rat], *n.m.* Hydrochlorate. **hydrochlorique,** *a.* Hydrochloric.
hydrocotyle [idrɔkɔ'til], *n.f.* Pennywort.
hydrodynamique [idrɔdina'mik], *a.* Hydrodynamic.—*n.f.* Hydrodynamics.
hydro-électrique [idrɔelɛk'trik], *a.* Hydro-electric.
hydrofuge [idrɔ'fyʒ], *a.* Damp-proof; damp-proofing (material etc.). **hydrofuger,** *v.t.* To waterproof.
hydrogène [idrɔ'ʒɛːn], *n.m.* Hydrogen. *Hydrogène sulfuré,* sulphydric acid (gas). **hydrogéné,** *a.* (*fem.* **-ée**) Hydrogenated, combined with or containing hydrogen. **hydrogéner,** *v.t.* To hydrogenize.
hydrographe [idrɔ'graf], *n.m.* Hydrographer. **hydrographie,** *n.f.* Hydrography. **hydrologie,** *n.f.* Hydrology.
hydrolyse [idrɔ'liːz], *n.f.* Hydrolysis.
hydromel [idrɔ'mɛl], *n.m.* Hydromel. *Hydromel vineux,* metheglin, mead.
hydromètre [idrɔ'mɛtr], *n.m.* Hydrometer. **hydrométrie,** *n.f.* Hydrometry. **hydrométrique,** *a.* Hydrometric.
hydrophile [idrɔ'fil], *a.* Hydrophilous; absorbent (cotton-wool).
hydrophobe [idrɔ'fɔb], *a.* and *n.* Hydrophobic. **hydrophobie,** *n.f.* Hydrophobia, rabies.
hydropique [idrɔ'pik], *a.* Dropsical.—*n.* Dropsical person. **hydropisie,** *n.f.* Dropsy.
hydroplane [idrɔ'plan], *n.m.* Hydroplane.
hydropneumatique [idrɔpnøma'tik], *a.* Hydropneumatic (buffer of gun).
hydroquinone [idrɔki'noːn], *n.f.* Hydroquinone.
hydroscope [idrɔs'kɔp], *n.m.* Water-diviner. **hydroscopie,** *n.f.* Water-divining; dowsing.
hydrostatique [idrɔsta'tik], *a.* Hydrostatic.—*n.f.* Hydrostatics.
hydrosulfate [SULFHYDRATE].

hydrosulfurique [SULFHYDRIQUE].
hydrothérapie [idrɔtera'pi], *n.f.* Hydrotherapy, hydropathy. **hydrothérapique,** *a.* Hydrotherapeutic, hydropathic.
hydrothermique [idrɔter'mik], *a.* Hydrothermal.
hydrure [i'dry:r], *n.m.* Hydride.
hyène [jɛ:n], *n.f.* Hyena.
hygiène [i'ʒjɛ:n], *n.f.* Hygiene. *Hygiène publique,* public health. **hygiénique,** *a.* Hygienic, healthy; sanitary. *Appareils hygiéniques,* sanitation fittings; *ceinture hygiénique,* sanitary belt; *serviettes* or *tampons hygiéniques,* sanitary towels (napkins) or pads.
hygrologie [igrɔlɔ'ʒi], *n.f.* Hygrology.
hygromètre [igrɔ'mɛtr], *n.m.* Hygrometer. **hygrométrie,** *n.f.* Hygrometry. **hygrométrique,** *a.* Hygrometric. **hygroscope,** *n.m.* Hygroscope. **hygroscopique,** *a.* Hygroscopic.
hylozoïque [ilozɔ'ik], *a.* Hylozoic. **hylozoïsme,** *n.m.* Hylozoism.
hymen [i'mɛn] or **hyménée,** *n.m.* Hymen, marriage, wedlock; (*Anat.*) hymen.
hyménoptère [imenɔp'tɛ:r], *a.* Hymenopterous.—*n.m. pl.* (*Ent.*) Hymenoptera.
hymnaire [im'nɛ:r], *n.m.* Hymn-book, hymnal.
hymne [imn], *n.m.* (Patriotic) song, anthem. *L'hymne national,* the national anthem (in France, *la Marseillaise*).—*n.f.* Hymn. *Recueil d'hymnes,* hymn-book (of church).
hyoïde [iɔ'id], *a.* (*Anat.*) Hyoid.—*n.m.* Hyoid bone, tongue-bone.
hyoscyamine [iosja'min] or **hyoscine** [io'sin], *n.f.* Hyoscine.
hypallage [ipa'la:ʒ], *n.f.* Hypallage.
hyperbate [iper'bat], *n.f.* Hyperbaton.
hyperbole [iper'bɔl], *n.f.* Hyperbole, exaggeration; (*Math.*) hyperbola. **hyperbolique,** *a.* Hyperbolic. **hyperboliquement,** *adv.* Hyperbolically.
hyperborée [iperbɔ're] or **hyperboréen,** *a.* (*fem.* **-éenne**) Hyperborean; arctic.
hypercritique [iperkri'tik], *n.f.* Thorough criticism.—*n.m.* Rigorous critic.—*a.* Overcritical, hypercritical.
hyperdulie [iperdy'li], *n.f.* (*R.-C. Ch.*) Hyperdulia (worship of the Virgin Mary).
hyperesthésie [iperɛste'zi], *n.f.* Hyperaesthesia.
hypermétrope [iperme'trɔp], *a.* Long-sighted. **hypermétropie,** *n.f.* Long-sightedness.
hypersensibilité [ipersãsibili'te], *n.f.* Exaggerated sensitivity. **hypersensible,** *a.* Over-sensitive.
hypertension [ipertã'sjɔ̃], *n.f.* Hypertension. *Hypertension artérielle,* high blood-pressure.
hypertrophie [ipɛrtrɔ'fi], *n.f.* Hypertrophy. **hypertrophié,** *a.* (*fem.* **hypertrophiée**) Hypertrophic, enlarged (of the heart etc.).
hypnose [ip'no:z], *n.f.* Hypnosis. **hypnotique,** *a.* and *n.m.* Hypnotic. **hypnotiser,** *v.t.* To hypnotize; to fascinate. **hypnotiseur,** *n.m.* (*fem.* **-euse**) Hypnotist. **hypnotisme,** *n.m.* Hypnotism.
hypocondre [ipɔ'kɔ̃:dr], *n.m.* (*Anat.*) Hypochondrium. **hypocondriaque,** *a.* and *n.* Hypochondriac. **hypocondrie,** *n.f.* Hypochondria, spleen.
hypocras [ipɔ'kra:s], *n.m.* Hippocras.
hypocrisie [ipɔkri'zi], *n.f.* Hypocrisy. *Avec hypocrisie,* hypocritically. **hypocrite,** *a.*

Hypocritical. *D'un air hypocrite,* looking sly, with a sly look on his face.—*n.* Hypocrite.
hypocritement, *adv.* Hypocritically.
hypoderme [ipɔ'derm], *n.m.* (*Bot.*) Hypoderm. **hypodermique,** *a.* Hypodermic, under the skin. *Piqûre, injection hypodermique,* hypodermic injection.
hypogastre [ipɔ'gastr], *n.m.* (*Anat.*) Hypogastrium. **hypogastrique,** *a.* Hypogastric.
hypogé [ipɔ'ʒe], *a.* (*fem.* **-ée** (1)) Hypogeous, hypogean. **hypogée** (2), *n.m.* (*Arch.*) Hypogeum.
hypoglosse [ipɔ'glɔs], *a.* (*Anat.*) Hypoglossal (under the tongue).—*n.m.* Hypoglossal nerve.
hypophyse [ipɔ'fiz], *n.f.* Hypophysis. **hypophysiaire,** *a.* Hypophysial.
hypostase [ipɔs'ta:z], *n.f.* (*Theol.*) Hypostasis. **hypostatique,** *a.* Hypostatic.
hypostyle [ipɔs'til], *a.* (*Arch.*) Hypostyle.
hyposulfate [ipɔsyl'fat], *n.m.* (*Chem.*) Dithionate. **hyposulfite,** *n.m.* Thiosulphate, hyposulphite.
hypotension [ipɔtã'sjɔ̃], *n.f.* Low blood-pressure.
hypoténuse [ipɔte'ny:z], *n.f.* Hypotenuse.
hypothécable [ipɔte'kabl], *a.* Mortgageable.
hypothécaire [ipɔte'kɛ:r], *a.* On mortgage. *Créancier hypothécaire,* mortgagee. **hypothécairement,** *adv.* By or with regard to mortgage.
hypothèque [ipɔ'tɛk], *n.f.* Mortgage. *Créancier sur hypothèque,* mortgagee; *débiteur sur hypothèque,* mortgager; *donner en hypothèque,* to give as a mortgage; *éteindre* or *purger une hypothèque,* to pay off a mortgage. **hypothéquer,** *v.t. irr.* (*conjug. like* ACCÉLÉRER) To mortgage; (*fig.*) to pledge.
hypothèse [ipɔ'tɛ:z], *n.f.* Hypothesis, assumption, supposition. *Par hypothèse,* by supposition. **hypothétique,** *a.* Hypothetical. **hypothétiquement,** *adv.* Hypothetically.
hypsomètre [ipsɔ'mɛtr], *n.m.* Hypsometer. **hypsométrie,** *n.f.* Altimetry, hypsometry.
hysope [i'zɔp], *n.f.* (*Bot.*) Hyssop.
hystérie [iste'ri], *n.f.* Hysteria, hysterics. **hystérique,** *a.* Hysteric, hysterical. **hystérite,** *n.f.* Hysteritis. **hystérocèle,** *n.f.* Hysterocele. **hystérotomie,** *n.f.* Hysterotomy.

I

I, i [i], *n.m.* The ninth letter of the alphabet. *Droit comme un I,* straight as an arrow; *il met les points sur les i,* he is very particular or very precise.
ïambe [jã:b], *n.m.* Iamb, iambus, iambic. **ïambique,** *a.* Iambic.
ibéride [ibe'rid], *n.f.* Iberis, candytuft.
ibérien [ibe'rjɛ̃], *a.* (*fem.* **-ienne**) Iberian.—*n.m.* (**Ibérien,** *fem.* **-ienne**) An Iberian.
ibis [i'bi:s], *n.m.* Ibis.
icaque [ikak], *n.f. Prune d'icaque,* coco-plum.
icaquier [ika'kje], *n.m.* Coco-plum tree.
iceberg [is'bɛrg], *n.m.* Iceberg.
*****icelui** [isə'lɥi], *a.* and *pron.* (*fem.* **icelle**) This, the said.
ichneumon [iknø'mɔ̃], *n.m.* Ichneumon, Egyptian mongoose; ichneumon-fly.
ichnographie [iknɔgra'fi], *n.f.* Ichnography. **ichnographique,** *a.* Ichnographic.

ichor [i'kɔːr], *n.m.* Ichor. **ichoreux**, *a.* (*fem.* **ichoreuse**) Ichorous.
ichtyologie [iktjɔlɔ'ʒi], *n.f.* Ichthyology. **ichtyologique**, *a.* Ichthyological. **ichtyologiste**, *n.* Ichthyologist. **ichtyophage**, *a.* Ichthyophagous.—*n.* Ichthyophagist. **ichtyosaure**, *n.m.* Ichthyosaurus.
ici [i'si], *adv.* Here, in this place; hither, now, this time. *C'est ici*, this is the place, here we are; *d'ici*, hence; *d'ici là*, from here to there, between now and then; *ici-bas*, here below; *près d'ici*, hard by; *il a passé par ici*, he passed this way; *jusqu'ici*, hitherto, up to now; *venez ici*, come here.
icone [i'kɔn], *n.f.* Icon, holy image or picture.
iconoclaste [ikɔnɔ'klast], *a.* Iconoclastic.—*n.m.* Iconoclast. **iconographe**, *n.m.* Iconographer. **iconographie**, *n.f.* Iconography. **iconolâtre**, *n.m.* Image-worshipper. **iconolâtrie**, *n.f.* Image-worship. **iconologie**, *n.f.* Iconology. **iconomètre**, *n.m.* (*Phot.*) Iconometer. **iconométrie**, *n.f.* (*Phot.*) Iconometry. **iconoscope**, *n.m.* (*Tel.*) Iconoscope. **iconostase**, *n.f.* Iconostasis.
icosaèdre [ikɔza'ɛdr], *n.m.* Icosahedron.—*a.* Icosahedral.
ictère [ik'tɛːr], *n.m.* (*Path.*) Icterus, jaundice. **ictérique**, *a.* Icteric, jaundiced.
idéal [ide'al], *a.* (*fem.* **idéale**, *pl.* **idéaux**) Ideal; unreal, imaginary, visionary. *Le beau idéal*, ideal beauty.—*n.m.* (*pl.* -**als** or -**aux**) Ideal. **idéalement**, *adv.* Ideally. **idéalisation**, *n.f.* Idealization. **idéaliser**, *v.t.* To idealize. **idéalisme**, *n.m.* Idealism. **idéaliste**, *n.* Idealist.—*a.* Idealistic. **idéalité**, *n.f.* Ideality.
idée [i'de], *n.f.* Idea; notion, perception; conception, mode of regarding something, view, opinion; intention, purpose, plan; whim, conceit, fancy; sketch, outline, hint, suggestion. *A-t-on idée d'une chose pareille?* did one ever hear of such a thing? *avoir une idée*, to have an idea; *changer d'idée*, to change one's mind; *en idée*, in imagination, in fancy; *idée fixe*, fixed idea, obsession; *idée plaisante*, odd conceit; *il me vient à l'idée*, it occurs to me; *il me vient une idée*, an idea strikes me; *il me vint à l'idée que*, it struck me that; *j'ai idée que*, I rather think that; *n'avoir pas d'idée de*, to have no notion of; *on ne peut lui ôter cela de l'idée*, one cannot get that out of his head; *quelle idée!* well, I never! *se faire des idées*, to imagine things; *se faire une idée*, to form an idea; *se mettre dans l'idée*, to take it into one's head.
idem [i'dem], *adv.* Idem, ditto.
identification [idãtifika'sjɔ̃], *n.f.* Identification. **identifier**, *v.t.* To identify. **s'identifier**, *v.r.* To identify oneself, to become identified.
identique [idã'tik], *a.* Identical, the same. **identiquement**, *adv.* Identically. **identité**, *n.f.* Identity. *Bureau d'identité*, criminal records office; *carte d'identité*, identity card; *photo d'identité*, passport photograph; *plaque d'identité*, (*Mil.*) identity disk.
idéogramme [ideɔ'gram], *n.m.* Ideograph. **idéographie** [ideɔgra'fi], *n.f.* Ideography. **idéographique**, *a.* Ideographic. **idéologie**, *n.f.* Ideology. **idéologique**, *a.* Ideological. **idéologue**, *n.m.* Ideologist.
ides [id], *n.f. pl.* Ides (15 March etc.).

idiomatique [idjɔma'tik], *a.* Idiomatic.
idiome [i'djoːm], *n.m.* Idiom, dialect.
idiopathie [idjɔpa'ti], *n.f.* Idiopathy. **idiopathique**, *a.* Idiopathic.
idiosyncrasie [idjɔsɛ̃kra'zi], *n.f.* Idiosyncrasy.
idiot [i'djo], *a.* (*fem.* **idiote**) Idiotic, absurd, foolish.—*n.* Idiot, imbecile, fool. **idiotement**, *adv.* Idiotically. **idiotie** [idjo'si], *n.f.* Idiocy, imbecility. **idiotisme** [idjɔ'tism], *n.m.* (*Gram.*) Idiom; (*Path.*) idiocy.
*****idoine** [i'dwan], *a.* (*Law*) Fitting, proper, qualified.
idolâtre [idɔ'lɑːtr], *a.* Idolatrous. *Elle est idolâtre de ses enfants*, she dotes on her children.—*n.* Idolater. **idolâtrer**, *v.t.* To idolize, to dote upon. *Il idolâtre cette femme*, he idolizes that woman.—*v.i.* To worship idols. **idolâtrie**, *n.f.* Idolatry. **idolâtrique**, *a.* Idolatrous.
idole [i'dɔl], *n.f.* Idol. *C'est une vraie idole*, she is nothing but a wax doll; *faire son idole de*, to idolize; *il se tient là comme une idole*, he stands there like a statue.
idylle [i'dil], *n.f.* Idyll. **idyllique**, *a.* Idyllic.
ièble [HIÈBLE].
if [if], *n.m.* Yew, yew-tree; triangular lamp-stand (used at illuminations).
igloo, iglou [i'glu], *n.m.* (Eskimo) ice hut, igloo.
igname [i'ɲam], *n.f.*, or *igname de Chine*, (*Bot.*), Chinese yam, *Dioscorea batatas*.
ignare [i'ɲaːr], *a.* Illiterate, ignorant.—*n.* Dunce, ignoramus.
igné [ig'ne], *a.* (*fem.* **ignée**) Igneous. *****ignescent**, *a.* (*fem.* -**ente**) Ignescent. **ignicole**, *a.* Fire-worshipping.—*n.* Fire-worshipper. **ignifuge**, *a.* Fire-resisting, fireproof. *Grenade ignifuge*, fire-extinguisher. **ignifuger**, *v.t.* To fireproof. **ignition**, *n.f.* Ignition. *Entrer or mettre en ignition*, to ignite. **ignitron**, *n.m.* (*Elec.*) Ignitron. **ignivore**, *a.* Fire-eating.
ignoble [i'ɲɔbl], *a.* Ignoble; vile, mean, base; beastly, filthy. **ignoblement**, *adv.* Ignobly, vilely, basely.
ignominie [iɲɔmi'ni], *n.f.* Ignominy, shame, dishonour. **ignominieusement**, *adv.* Ignominiously. **ignominieux**, *a.* (*fem.* **ignominieuse**) Ignominious.
ignorance [iɲɔ'rɑ̃ːs], *n.f.* Ignorance; error, mistake, blunder. *Croupir dans l'ignorance*, to wallow in ignorance; *être dans l'ignorance de*, to be ignorant of; *ignorance crasse*, gross ignorance; *par ignorance*, through ignorance; *prétendre cause d'ignorance*, to plead ignorance. **ignorant**, *a.* (*fem.* -**ante**) Ignorant, illiterate, unlearned; unacquainted, unskilled, uninformed (*de*).—*n.* Ignorant person, ignoramus, dunce. **ignorantin**, *a.* and *n.m.* Ignorantine. **ignorantisme**, *n.m.* Ignorantism.
ignorer [iɲɔ're], *v.t.* To be ignorant of, not to know, not to be aware of, to be unconscious of. *J'ignorais qu'il fût arrivé*, I was not aware he had arrived; *ne pas ignorer*, to know, to be aware of. **s'ignorer**, *v.r.* Not to know oneself; to be ignorant of one's own capabilities.
iguane [i'gwan], *n.m.* Iguana. *Iguane d'Australie*, frilled lizard.
il [il, i], *pron. m.* He; it, there; (*pl.* **ils**) they,

Il est arrivé quatre personnes, four persons have arrived; *il fait froid,* it is cold; *il me parle,* he is speaking to me; *il s'éleva un murmure,* a murmur arose; *il y a des gens,* there are people.

ilang-ilang [ilãi'lã], *n.m.* (*Bot.*) Ylang-ylang.

île [il], *n.f.* Island, isle. *L'Île-de-France,* Paris and the five surrounding *départements;* Mauritius; *Îles du Vent,* Windward Islands; *Îles sous le Vent,* Leeward Islands; *les Îles,* the Antilles; *les Îles Anglo-Normandes,* the Channel Islands.

iléon [ile'ɔ̃] or **iléum** [ile'ɔm], *n.m.* (*Anat.*) Ileum.

iles [il], *n.m. pl.* (*Anat.*) Ilia, flanks. *Os des iles,* os ilium, hip-bone.

îlet [ÎLOT].

iléus [ile'y:s], *n.m.* (*Path.*) Iliac passion.

iliaque [i'ljak], *a.* (*Anat.*) Iliac. *L'os iliaque,* hip-bone.

ilion [i'ljɔ̃] or **ilium** [i'ljɔm], *n.m.* (*Anat.*) Ilium.

illégal [ille'gal], *a.* (*fem.* **illégale,** *pl.* **illégaux**) Illegal, unlawful. **illégalement,** *adv.* Illegally. **illégalité,** *n.f.* Illegality.

illégitime [illeʒi'tim], *a.* Illegitimate; unlawful, unjust; spurious. **illégitimement,** *adv.* Illegitimately, unlawfully. **illégitimité,** *n.f.* Illegitimacy; unlawfulness; spuriousness.

illettré [ille'tre], *a.* and *n.* (*fem.* **illettrée**) Illiterate, unlettered (person).

illicite [illi'sit], *a.* Illicit, unlawful. **illicitement,** *adv.* Illicitly, unlawfully.

illico [illi'ko], *adv.* (*colloq.*) At once, forthwith, then and there.

illimitable [illimi'tabl], *a.* Illimitable. **illimité,** *a.* (*fem.* **illimitée**) Unlimited, unbounded, boundless.

illisibilité [illizibili'te], *n.f.* Illegibility. **illisible,** *a.* Illegible. **illisiblement,** *adv.* Illegibly.

illogique [illɔ'ʒik], *a.* Illogical. **illogiquement,** *adv.* Illogically. **illogisme,** *n.m.* Inconsistency.

illuminant [illymi'nã], *a.* (*fem.* **-ante**) Illuminating.—*n.m.* Illuminant. **illuminateur,** *n.m.* Illuminator, enlightener. **illumination,** *n.f.* Illumination. **illuminé,** *a.* (*fem.* **-ée**) Illuminated, enlightened; visionary.— *n.* Visionary, fanatic (one of the Illuminati).

illuminer [illymi'ne], *v.t.* To illuminate, to illumine, to light up; to enlighten (the mind etc.); to decorate with illuminations. **s'illuminer,** *v.r.* To be illuminated; to brighten up, to beam. **illuminisme,** *n.m.* Illuminism.

illusion [illy'zjɔ̃], *n.f.* Illusion, self-deception, delusion; fallacy, chimera, phantom. *Être dans l'illusion,* to be labouring under a delusion; *se faire illusion à soi-même,* to deceive or delude oneself; *se faire des illusions,* to be too optimistic. **illusionner,** *v.t.* To delude, to deceive. **illusionniste,** *n.m.* Conjurer. **illusoire,** *a.* Illusive, illusory, delusive. **illusoirement,** *adv.* Illusively.

illustrateur [illystra'tœːr], *n.m.* (Book)-illustrator.

illustration [illystra'sjɔ̃], *n.f.* Illustriousness, celebrity, renown; illustrious man; explanation, elucidation; illustration.

illustre [il'lystr], *a.* Illustrious, famous, renowned.

illustré [illys'tre], *a.* (*fem.* **-ée**) Illustrated.— *n.m.* Illustrated magazine.

illustrer [illys'tre], *v.t.* To do honour to, to give lustre to, to render illustrious; to illustrate, to explain, to make clear; to illustrate with prints etc. **s'illustrer,** *v.r.* To win fame, to become illustrious. **illustrissime,** *a.* Most illustrious.

illuter [illy'te], *v.t.* (*Med.*) To coat with, or bathe in, mud.

îlot [i'lo], *n.m.* Islet (in sea); holm (in river); block (of houses).

ilote [i'lɔt], *n.m.* Helot. **ilotisme,** *n.m.* Helotry.

ils, *pl. pron.* [IL].

image [i'ma:ʒ], *n.f.* Image; likeness, resemblance; picture, effigy, statue, description; (*pl.*) imagery; (*Ent.*) imago. *Être sage comme une image,* to be as quiet as a mouse *or* as good as gold; *image très lumineuse,* (*Cine.*) high-key picture; *livre d'images,* picture-book. **imagé,** *a.* (*fem.* **imagée**) Full of imagery or figures (of style). **imager** (1), *v.t.* To adorn (style etc.) with images. **imager** (2) [IMAGIER]. **imagerie,** *n.f.* Image-making or trade. **imagier,** *a.* (*fem.* **imagière**) Pertaining to images.—*n.* Image-maker or seller; *painter and sculptor.

imaginable [imaʒi'nabl], *a.* Imaginable. **imaginaire,** *a.* Imaginary, visionary, fancied, unreal, fantastic; (*Math.*) imaginary, impossible. *Espaces imaginaires,* realms of fancy. **imaginatif,** *a.* (*fem.* **-ive**) Imaginative.—*n.f.* Imagination, imaginative faculty.

imagination [imaʒina'sjɔ̃], *n.f.* Imagination, creative faculty, invention; conception, thought; fancy, conceit. *C'est un effet de l'imagination,* it is all fancy. **imaginative** [IMAGINATIF]. **imaginer,** *v.t.* To imagine, to conceive, to invent; to fancy, to think, to believe, to suppose; to contrive, to devise. **s'imaginer,** *v.r.* To imagine oneself, to imagine, to think to oneself; to fancy, to conjecture, to surmise. *Imaginez-vous,* just fancy.

iman [i'mã], *n.m.* Imam (Mohammedan priest). .

imbattable [ɛ̃ba'tabl], *a.* Unbeatable (horse, racer); unbroken (record).

imbécile [ɛ̃be'sil], *a.* Imbecile; foolish, silly, idiotic.—*n.* Imbecile, idiot; fool, simpleton, ninny. **imbécilement,** *adv.* Foolishly, stupidly. **imbécillité,** *n.f.* Imbecility, idiocy; stupidity, foolishness; *pl.* (*fam.*) nonsense. *Dire des imbécillités,* to talk nonsense.

imberbe [ɛ̃'bɛrb], *a.* Beardless; without barbels (of fish); (*fig.*) raw, green.

imbiber [ɛ̃bi'be], *v.t.* To imbibe; to imbue; to steep. **s'imbiber,** *v.r.* To imbibe, to take in, to drink in; to sink in. **imbibition,** *n.f.* Imbibition, soaking.

imboire [EMBOIRE].

imbricatif [ɛ̃brika'tif], *a.* (*fem.* **imbricative**) Imbricative. **imbrication,** *n.f.* Imbrication, overlapping.

imbrin [ɛ̃'brɛ̃], *n.m.,* or *Grand plongeon* (*Orn.*) Great northern diver.

imbriqué [ɛ̃bri'ke], *a.* (*fem.* **imbriquée**) Imbricated.

imbroglio [ɛ̃brɔ'ljo], *n.m.* Imbroglio, intricacy.

imbu [ɛ̃'by], *a.* (*fem.* **imbue**) Imbued,

saturated. *Imbu de préjugés*, steeped in prejudice.
imbuvable [ɛ̃by'vabl], *a.* Undrinkable.
imitable [imi'tabl], *a.* Imitable. **imitateur,** *a.* (*fem.* **-trice**) Imitative.—*n.* Imitator. **imitatif,** *a.* (*fem.* **-ive**) Imitative. *Les arts imitatifs,* the imitative arts.
imitation [imitɑ'sjɔ̃], *n.f.* Imitation. *À l'imitation de,* in imitation of. **imiter,** *v.t.* To imitate, to copy; to mimic; to take off; to resemble, to counterfeit (the style etc. of).
immaculé [immaky'le], *a.* (*fem.* **-ée**) Immaculate, spotless [*see* CONCEPTION].
immanence [imma'nɑ̃:s], *n.m.* Immanence. **immanent,** *a.* (*fem.* **-ente**) Immanent.
immangeable [ɛ̃mɑ̃'ʒabl], or [imɑ̃'ʒabl], *a.* Uneatable.
immanquable [ɛ̃mɑ̃'kabl], *a.* Infallible, certain, sure. **immanquablement,** *adv.* Infallibly, certainly, without fail.
immarcescible [immarse'sibl], *a.* Incorruptible, unfading.
immariable [ɛ̃ma'rjabl], *a.* Unmarriageable.
immatérialiser [immaterjali'ze], *v.t.* To immaterialize. **immatérialisme,** *n.m.* Immaterialism. **immatérialiste,** *n.* Immaterialist. **immatérialité,** *n.f.* Immateriality.
immatériel, *a.* (*fem.* **-ielle**) Immaterial, incorporeal. **immatériellement,** *adv.* Immaterially, incorporeally.
immatriculation [immatrikylɑ'sjɔ̃], *n.f.* Matriculation; registering; enrolment. (*Motor.*) *Plaque d'immatriculation,* number plate.
immatriculé, *a.* (*fem.* **-ée**) Registered, matriculated. **immatriculer,** *v.t.* To matriculate; to register. (*Mil.*) *Immatriculer un homme,* to enter a man on the rolls.
immaturité [immatyri'te], *n.f.* Unripeness; immaturity.
immédiat [imme'dja], *a.* (*fem.* **-iate**) Immediate. **immédiatement,** *adv.* Immediately.
immémorable [IMMÉMORIAL].
immémorial [immemɔ'rjal], *a.* (*fem.* **-iale,** *pl.* **-iaux**) Immemorial. *De temps immémorial,* in the olden time, since time immemorial. **immémorialement,** *adv.* Immemorially.
immense [im'mɑ̃:s], *a.* Immense, immeasurable; boundless, huge; prodigious. **immensément,** *adv.* Immensely. **immensité,** *n.f.* Immensity.
immensurable [immɑ̃sy'rabl], *a.* Immensurable.
immerger [immɛr'ʒe], *v.t.* To immerse, to plunge. *Il a été immergé,* his body has been dropped overboard.
immérité [immeri'te], *a.* (*fem.* **-ée**) Undeserved, unmerited, unjust.
immersif [immɛr'sif], *a.* (*fem.* **-ive**) Done by immersion. **immersion,** *n.f.* Immersion; submergence (of submarine); committal (of a body) to the deep.
immesurable [immɔzy'rabl], *a.* Unmeasurable, immeasurable.
immeuble [im'mœbl], *a.* Fixed, real (of estate).—*n.m.* Real estate; realty; landed estate, property; house and land; tenement, mansion; premises.
immigrant [immi'grɑ̃], *a.* and *n.* (*fem.* **-ante**) Immigrant. **immigration,** *n.f.* Immigration. **immigré,** *a.* (*fem.* **-ée**) Settler. **immigrer,** *v.i.* To immigrate.

imminence [immi'nɑ̃:s], *n.f.* Imminence. **imminent,** *a.* (*fem.* **-ente**) Imminent, impending.
immiscer [immi'se], *v.t.* To introduce or twist (someone into an affair). **s'immiscer,** *v.r.* To interfere, to intermeddle; (*Law*) to enter upon (possession). *S'immiscer dans les affaires des autres,* to meddle with other people's business. **immiscibilité,** *n.f.* Immiscibility. **immiscible,** *a.* Immiscible.
immixtion [immiks'tjɔ̃], *n.f.* Mixing, mingling, blending; (*Law*) entering on possession; unwarrantable interference, meddling.
immobile [immɔ'bil], *a.* Immovable, motionless, still; unshaken, stable, firm; impassive.
immobilier [immɔbi'lje], *a.* (*fem.* **immobilière**) Real, landed (of estate). *Agent immobilier,* estate agent. *Société immobilière,* building society. *Vente immobilière,* sale of property. **immobilisation,** *n.f.* Immobilization; (*Law*) conversion of movable property into real estate. **immobiliser,** *v.t.* To immobilize (troops etc.); to convert into real estate, to realize. **immobilisme,** *n.m.* Ultra-conservative policy. **immobilité,** *n.f.* Immobility, immovability. *Garder l'immobilité,* (*Mil.*) to stand at attention.
immodération [immɔderɑ'sjɔ̃], *n.f.* Immoderation. **immodéré,** *a.* (*fem.* **immodérée**) Immoderate, intemperate, excessive, violent. **immodérément,** *adv.* Immoderately, intemperately; excessively.
immodeste [immɔ'dɛst], *a.* Immodest, indecent. **immodestement,** *adv.* Immodestly. **immodestie,** *n.f.* Immodesty.
immolateur [immɔla'tœ:r], *n.m.* Immolator, sacrificer.
immolation [immɔla'sjɔ̃], *n.f.* Immolation; (*fig.*) sacrifice. **immoler,** *v.t.* To immolate, to sacrifice; to slay. **s'immoler,** *v.r.* To immolate or sacrifice oneself; to sacrifice one's feelings. *S'immoler pour sa patrie,* to sacrifice oneself for one's country.
immonde [im'mɔ̃:d], *a.* Unclean, impure. **immondice,** *n.f.* (*usu. in pl.*) Filth, dirt; rubbish; (*Bible*) uncleanliness, impurity.
immoral [immɔ'ral], *a.* (*fem.* **-ale,** *pl.* **-aux**) Immoral. **immoralement,** *adv.* Immorally. **immoralité,** *n.f.* Immorality.
immortaliser [immɔrtali'ze], *v.t.* To immortalize. **s'immortaliser,** *v.r.* To immortalize oneself. **immortalité,** *n.f.* Immortality. **immortel** [immɔr'tɛl], *a.* (*fem.* **immortelle**) Immortal, everlasting.—*n.m.* (*fig.*) Member of the French Academy; (*pl.*) the immortals, the gods.—*n.f.* (*Bot.*) Rhodanthe, immortelle. *Immortelle des neiges,* edelweiss. **immortellement,** *adv.* Immortally, for ever.
immuable [im'mɥabl], *a.* Immutable, unalterable, unchangeable. **immuablement,** *adv.* Immutably, unalterably, unchangeably.
immunisation [immynizɑ'sjɔ̃], *n.f.* (*Med.*) Immunization. **immuniser,** *v.t.* To immunize, to immune.
immunité [immyni'te], *n.f.* Immunity; privilege; exemption.
immutabilité [immytabili'te], *n.f.* Immutability, unchangeableness, fixity.
impact [ɛ̃'pakt], *n.m.* Impact; hit. **impaction** [ɛ̃pak'sjɔ̃], *n.f.* (*Surg.*) Impaction. **impair** [ɛ̃'pɛ:r], *a.* (*fem.* **impaire**) Odd, uneven.—*n.m.* Blunder, bloomer.

impalpabilité [ɛ̃palpabili'te], *n.f.* Impalpability. **impalpable,** *a.* Impalpable.
impaludisme [ɛ̃paly'dism] [PALUDISME].
impanation [ɛ̃pɑnɑ'sjɔ̃], *n.f.* Impanation.
impané [ɛ̃pa'ne], *a.* (*fem.* **-ée**) Impanate.
impardonnable [ɛ̃pardɔ'nabl], *a.* Unpardonable, unforgivable.
imparfait [ɛ̃par'fɛ], *a.* (*fem.* **-aite**) Imperfect, incomplete, defective.—*n.m.* (*Gram.*) Imperfect (tense). **imparfaitement,** *adv.* Imperfectly.
imparisyllabique [ɛ̃parisila'bik], *a.* Imparisyllabic.
imparité [ɛ̃pari'te], *n.f.* Imparity, inequality; oddness.
impartageable [ɛ̃parta'ʒabl], *a.* Indivisible.
impartial [ɛ̃par'sjal], *a.* (*fem.* **impartiale,** *pl.* **impartiaux**) Impartial, fair-minded. **impartialement,** *adv.* Impartially, even-handedly. **impartialité,** *n.f.* Impartiality.
impartir [ɛ̃par'tir], *v.t.* (*Law*) To allow.
impasse [ɛ̃'pɑːs], *n.f.* Blind alley, cul-de-sac; deadlock, dilemma, fix; (*Cards*) finesse.
impassibilité [ɛ̃pɑsibili'te], *n.f.* Impassibility, insensibility. **impassible,** *a.* Impassible, impassive, undisturbed, unmoved. **impassiblement,** *adv.* Impassively, impassibly.
impatiemment [ɛ̃pasja'mɑ̃], *adv.* Impatiently, eagerly.
impatience [ɛ̃pa'sjɑ̃ːs], *n.f.* Impatience; restlessness; eagerness, longing. *Avec impatience,* impatiently; *donner* or *causer des impatiences à,* to put out of all patience; *être dans l'impatience de faire une chose,* to be impatient to do a thing; *l'impatience dans les douleurs,* impatience under suffering; *sans impatience,* patiently. **impatient,** *a.* (*fem.* **-iente**) Impatient; anxious, restless, eager. **impatientant,** *a.* (*fem.* **-ante**) Provoking, vexing, tiresome. **impatienter,** *v.t.* To make impatient, to put out of patience; to provoke. **s'impatienter,** *v.r.* To lose one's patience, to grow impatient; to fret (about), to worry (*de*).
impatroniser [ɛ̃patrɔni'ze], *v.t.* To introduce as a master. **s'impatroniser,** *v.r.* To set up as a master; to get a footing.
impavide [ɛ̃pa'vid], *a.* Impavid, fearless.
impayable [ɛ̃pɛ'jabl], *a.* Invaluable, priceless; inimitable, capital, extraordinarily funny. **impayé,** *a.* (*fem.* **-ée**) Unpaid.
impeccabilité [ɛ̃pɛkabili'te], *n.f.* Impeccability. **impeccable,** *a.* Impeccable, faultless.
impécunieux [ɛ̃peky'njø], *a.* (*fem.* **-ieuse**) Impecunious.
impédance [ɛ̃pe'dɑ̃s], *n.f.* (*Elec.*) Impedance.
impedimenta [ɛ̃pedimɛ̃'ta], *n.m. pl.* Impedimenta.
impénétrabilité [ɛ̃penetrabili'te], *n.f.* Impenetrability, imperviousness; inscrutability. **impénétrable,** *a.* Impenetrable, impervious; unfathomable, inscrutable. *Un homme impénétrable,* a very close man. **impénétrablement,** *adv.* Impenetrably.
impénitence [ɛ̃peni'tɑ̃ːs], *n.f.* Impenitence, obduracy. *Mourir dans l'impénitence,* to die impenitent. **impénitent,** *a.* and *n.* (*fem.* **-ente**) Impenitent, obdurate, unrepentant.
impensable [ɛ̃pɑ̃'sabl], *a.* Unthinkable, inconceivable.

impense [ɛ̃'pɑ̃ːs], *n.f.* (*usu. in pl.*) (*Law*) Expenses (for repairs, improvements, etc.).
impératif [ɛ̃pera'tif], *a.* (*fem.* **impérative**) Imperative, imperious, peremptory. *Prendre un ton impératif,* to assume a peremptory tone.—*n.m.* (*Gram.*) Imperative. **impérativement,** *adv.* Imperatively.
impératrice [ɛ̃pera'tris], *n.f.* Empress.
imperceptibilité [ɛ̃pɛrsɛptibili'te], *n.f.* Imperceptibility. **imperceptible,** *a.* Imperceptible, unperceivable. **imperceptiblement,** *adv.* Imperceptibly.
imperdable [ɛ̃per'dabl], *a.* That cannot be lost (of lawsuits, games, etc.).
imperfectibilité [ɛ̃pɛrfɛktibili'te], *n.f.* Imperfectibility. **imperfectible,** *a.* Imperfectible. **imperfection,** *n.f.* Imperfection, defect, flaw.
imperforation [ɛ̃pɛrfɔra'sjɔ̃], *n.f.* (*Med.*) Imperforation. **imperforé,** *a.* (*fem.* **imperforée**) Imperforate.
impérial [ɛ̃pe'rjal], *a.* (*fem.* **impériale** (1), *pl.* **impériaux**) Imperial. **impériale** (2), *n.f.* Top, outside (of a coach); game at cards like piquet; imperial serge; crown imperial (lily); imperial (small beard under the lip). **impérialement,** *adv.* Imperially. **impérialisme,** *n.m.* Imperialism. **impérialiste,** *a.* and *n.* Imperialist.
impérieusement [ɛ̃perjøz'mɑ̃], *adv.* Imperiously. **impérieux,** *a.* (*fem.* **impérieuse**) Imperious, domineering, supercilious, haughty, lordly, pressing.
impérissable [ɛ̃peri'sabl], *a.* Imperishable. **impérissablement,** *adv.* Imperishably.
impéritie [ɛ̃peri'si], *n.f.* Incapacity, unskilfulness.
imperméabilisation [ɛ̃pɛrmeabiliza'sjɔ̃], *n.f.* Waterproofing. **imperméabiliser,** *v.t.* To waterproof. **imperméabilité,** *n.f.* Impermeability. **imperméable,** *a.* Impermeable, impervious. *Imperméable à l'air,* airtight; *imperméable à l'eau,* waterproof, watertight; *imperméable à la lumière,* light-tight.—*n.m.* Raincoat, mackintosh.
impermutabilité [ɛ̃permutabili'te], *n.f.* Unexchangeability. **impermutable,** *a.* That is not permutable, unexchangeable.
impersonnalité [ɛ̃pɛrsɔnali'te], *n.f.* Impersonality. **impersonnel,** *a.* (*fem.* **-elle**) Impersonal.—*n.m.* (*Gram.*) Impersonal verb. **impersonnellement,** *adv.* Impersonally.
impersuasible [ɛ̃pɛrsɥa'zibl], *a.* Unpersuadable.
impertinemment [ɛ̃pɛrtina'mɑ̃], *adv.* Impertinently. **impertinence,** *n.f.* Impertinence, insolence; silliness, offensive thing; (*Law*) irrelevance. **impertinent,** *a.* (*fem.* **-ente**) Impertinent, insolent, pert; (*Law*) irrelevant.—*n.* Impertinent, saucy person.
imperturbabilité [ɛ̃pɛrtyrbabili'te], *n.f.* Imperturbability. **imperturbable,** *a.* Imperturbable. **imperturbablement,** *adv.* Imperturbably.
impétigo [ɛ̃peti'go], *n.m.* (*Med.*) Impetigo.
impétrable [ɛ̃pe'trabl], *a.* Obtainable. **impétrant,** *n.m.* (*fem.* **-ante**) Grantee (of diploma), recipient.
impétueusement [ɛ̃petɥøz'mɑ̃], *adv.* Impetuously. **impétueux,** *a.* (*fem.* **-euse**) Impetuous, vehement, headlong, violent, boisterous. **impétuosité,** *n.f.* Impetuosity, vehemence, impetus.

impie [ɛ'pi], *a.* Impious, godless; irreligious; blasphemous.—*n.* Impious, ungodly, or irreligious person. **impiété,** *n.f.* Impiety, godlessness.

impitoyable [ɛpitwa'jabl], *a.* Pitiless, unpitying, unmerciful, merciless, ruthless; unforgiving, unrelenting, unsparing. **impitoyablement,** *adv.* Pitilessly.

implacabilité [ɛplakabili'te], *n.f.* Implacability. **implacable,** *a.* Implacable. **implacablement,** *adv.* Implacably.

implantation [ɛplãtɑ'sjɔ̃], *n.f.* Implantation. **implanter,** *v.t.* To implant; to plant. **s'implanter,** *v.r.* To be implanted, fixed, rooted, or lodged.

implexe [ɛ'plɛks], *a.* Implex, intricate, implicate.

impliable [ɛpli'jabl], *a.* That cannot be folded; unpliable.

implication [ɛplika'sjɔ̃], *n.f.* Implication, involving, entangling; contradiction, discrepancy.

implicite [ɛpli'sit], *a.* Implicit. **implicitement,** *adv.* Implicitly.

impliquer [ɛpli'ke], *v.t.* To implicate, to involve, to entangle; to imply.

implorateur [ɛplɔra'tœːr], *n.m.* (*fem.* **imploratrice**) Implorer, supplicant.

imploration [ɛplɔra'sjɔ̃], *n.f.* Supplication, imploration. **implorer,** *v.t.* To implore, to supplicate, to entreat, to beseech; to call for, to crave.

imployable [ɛplwa'jabl], *a.* Unbending.

impluviosité [ɛplyvjɔzi'te], *n.f.* Rainlessness.

impolarisable [ɛpɔlari'zabl], *a.* (*Elec.*) Impolarizable.

impoli [ɛpɔ'li], *a.* (*fem.* **impolie**) Impolite, discourteous, uncivil, rude. **impoliment,** *adv.* Impolitely, discourteously. **impolitesse,** *n.f.* Impoliteness, incivility; impolite thing, rudeness. *Faire une impolitesse à,* to behave rudely to.

impolitique [ɛpɔli'tik], *a.* Impolitic, illadvised. **impolitiquement,** *adv.* Impoliticly, unwisely.

impollué [ɛpɔl'lye], *a.* (*fem.* **-ée**) Unsullied, unpolluted.

impondérabilité [ɛpɔ̃derabili'te], *n.f.* Imponderability. **impondérable,** *a.* and *n.m.* Imponderable. *Les impondérables de la politique,* the mysterious factors in politics.

impondéré, *a.* (*fem.* **-ée**) Unbalanced (character); ill-considered (action).

impopulaire [ɛpɔpy'lɛːr], *a.* Unpopular. **impopularité,** *n.f.* Unpopularity.

importable [ɛpɔr'tabl], *a.* Importable.

importance [ɛpɔr'tãːs], *n.f.* Importance, consequence, moment; consideration, authority, credit; self-conceit, consequentiality. *Avoir de l'importance,* to be of moment; *avoir peu d'importance,* to be of slight importance; *cela n'a pas d'importance,* it does not matter; *de la dernière* or *de la plus grande importance,* of the greatest importance; *d'aucune importance,* of no importance whatever; *d'importance,* soundly, sharply, thoroughly; *homme d'importance,* man of consequence; *mettre* or *attacher de l'importance à,* to consider important; *sans importance,* unimportant; *se donner des airs d'importance,* to give oneself consequential airs. **important,** *a.* (*fem.* **-ante**) Important, of consequence, momentous,

weighty, considerable. *Peu important,* immaterial, of little consequence, trifling; *question importante,* weighty question; *un homme important,* a man of note or influence. —*n.m.* The essential, the main point; person of importance; consequential man. *Faire l'important,* to give oneself airs, to be bumptious.

importateur [ɛpɔrta'tœːr], *a.* (*fem.* **-trice**) Importing.—*n.* Importer.

importation [ɛpɔrta'sjɔ̃], *n.f.* Importation; (*pl.*) imports. *Droits d'importation,* import duties.

importer (1) [ɛpɔr'te], *v.t.* To import; (*fig.*) to introduce. *Importer des expressions étrangères,* to introduce foreign expressions.

importer (2) [ɛpɔr'te], *v.i.* (*used only in the inf. and 3rd pers.*) To import, to be of moment, to concern, to matter, to signify. *Cela m'importe beaucoup,* that matters a good deal to me; *cela n'importe guère,* that is of little importance; *il importe que,* it is important that; *n'importe,* no matter, never mind; *n'importe comment,* no matter how; *n'importe où,* anywhere; *n'importe qui,* anyone; *n'importe quoi,* anything; *peu importe,* it does not much matter; *qu'importe?* what does it matter? *que m'importe?* what does it matter to me? *venez n'importe quand,* come when you like.

importun [ɛpɔr'tœ̃], *a.* (*fem.* **importune**) Importunate, troublesome, tiresome, obtrusive, irksome, inconvenient. *Être importun,* to intrude; *visite importune,* unwelcome visit. —*n.* Tiresome, troublesome person; intruder, bore; dun. **importunément,** *adv.* Importunately, obtrusively. **importuner,** *v.t.* To importune, to pester, to trouble, to annoy; to inconvenience, to incommode; to tease, to molest. *Importuner ses débiteurs,* to dun one's debtors. **importunité,** *n.f.* Importunity, obtrusiveness.

imposable [ɛpo'zabl], *a.* Taxable, assessable.

imposant [ɛpo'zã], *a.* (*fem.* **imposante**) Imposing, impressive, striking, grand. *Attitude imposante,* commanding attitude.

imposer [ɛpo'ze], *v.t.* To lay on (hands); to impose, to inflict, to lay, to tax, to charge; to thrust upon, to force (à); (*Print.*) to impose. *C'est au vainqueur d'imposer la loi aux vaincus,* it is for the conqueror to impose laws on the conquered; *imposer des droits,* to levy duties; *imposer des peines,* to inflict punishment: *imposer silence,* to impose silence; *imposer un nom,* to give a name; *imposer un pays,* to tax a country; *je ne prétends pas vous imposer mon opinion,* I don't intend to force my opinion upon you.—*v.i.* To awe, to overawe. *C'est un homme dont la présence impose,* he is a man whose presence overawes one; *sa mine impose,* his looks command respect. *En imposer à quelqu'un,* to impose upon someone; to deceive someone. **s'imposer,** *v.r.* To assert oneself; to thrust oneself (upon somebody); to be imperative, indispensable.

imposition [ɛpozi'sjɔ̃], *n.f.* Imposition, laying on (of hands); inflicting, assigning; tax, rates, assessment; (*Print.*) imposition. *Imposition d'une peine,* infliction of a punishment; *lever les impositions,* to levy taxes.

impossibilité [ɛpɔsibili'te], *n.f.* Impossibility.

Être de toute impossibilité, to be utterly impossible; *se trouver dans l'impossibilité de faire quelque chose,* to find it impossible to do something. **impossible,** *a.* Impossible, impracticable, out of one's power; out of the question, out of all reason.—*n.m.* That which is impossible; one's utmost, a great deal. *À l'impossible nul n'est tenu,* one can't do the impossible; *chercher l'impossible* or *vouloir trouver l'impossible,* to attempt the impossible; *faire l'impossible,* to do one's utmost; *par impossible,* against all probability; *viser l'impossible,* to aim at the impossible.

imposte [ɛ̃'pɔst], *n.f.* (*Arch.*) Impost, fanlight.

imposteur [ɛ̃pɔs'tœːr], *n.m.* Impostor, cheat. **imposture,** *n.f.* Imposture, deception; fallacy, illusion.

impôt [ɛ̃'po], *n.m.* Tax, duty, impost. *Impôt du sang,* blood-tax, compulsory military service; *impôt sur le revenu,* income tax; *lever des impôts,* to raise taxes; *percevoir les impôts,* to collect the taxes.

impotence [ɛ̃pɔ'tɑ̃ːs], *n.f.* Helplessness, infirmity. **impotent,** *a.* (*fem.* **-ente**) Infirm, crippled.—*n.m.* Cripple, helpless invalid.

impraticabilité [ɛ̃pratikabili'te], *n.f.* Impracticability. **impraticable,** *a.* Impracticable; impassable; untractable, unmanageable. *Des chemins impraticables,* impassable roads.

imprécation [ɛ̃preka'sjɔ̃], *n.f.* Imprecation, curse. *Charger d'imprécations,* to load with imprecations. **imprécatoire,** *a.* Imprecatory.

imprécis [ɛpre'si], *a.* (*fem.* **-ise**) Unprecise, indefinite (words); (*Mil.*) inaccurate (fire).

imprécision [ɛ̃presi'zjɔ̃], *n.f.* Lack of precision, vagueness (of statement); looseness (of terms); (*Mil.*) inaccuracy (in firing).

imprégnation [ɛ̃preɲa'sjɔ̃], *n.f.* Impregnation. **imprégner,** *v.t.* To impregnate; (*fig.*) to imbue. **s'imprégner,** *v.r.* To become impregnated, to be imbued (with prejudice etc.).

imprenable [ɛ̃prə'nabl], *a.* Impregnable.

imprésario [ɛ̃preza'rjo], *n.m.* Impresario.

imprescriptibilité [ɛ̃preskriptibili'te], *n.f.* Imprescriptibility, indefeasibility. **imprescriptible,** *a.* Imprescriptible, indefeasible.

impressif [ɛ̃prɛ'sif], *a.* (*fem.* **impressive**) Impressive, striking.

impression [ɛ̃prɛ'sjɔ̃], *n.f.* Impression; stamping, impressing; impress, mark, stamp; printing; print; issue, edition; (*Paint.*) priming. *Avoir l'impression de,* to have the feeling of; *être à l'impression,* to be in the printer's hands, to be in the press; *faire impression,* to make an impression; *faute d'impression,* misprint; *frais d'impression,* printing expenses. **impressionnabilité,** *n.f.* Impressionability; (*Phot.*) sensitivity. **impressionnable,** *a.* Impressionable, sensitive; excitable, nervous. **impressionnant,** *a.* (*fem.* **-ante**) Impressive. **impressionner,** *v.t.* To make an impression on; to move, to affect, to impress. **impressionnisme,** *n.m.* Impressionism. **impressionniste,** *n.* and *a.* Impressionist.

imprévisible [ɛ̃previ'zibl], *a.* Unforeseeable.

imprévision [IMPRÉVOYANCE].

imprévoyance [ɛ̃prevwa'jɑ̃ːs], *n.f.* Want

of foresight, improvidence. **imprévoyant,** *a.* (*fem.* **-ante**) Wanting foresight, improvident, unwary. **imprévu,** *a.* (*fem.* **-ue**) Unforeseen, unexpected, unlooked for. —*n.m.* The unforeseen. *En cas d'imprévu,* for contingencies, in case of an emergency.

imprimable [ɛ̃pri'mabl], *a.* Fit to be printed. **imprimé,** *n.m.* Printed book, paper, document, etc.; (*pl.*) printed matter. *Service des imprimés,* book-post.

imprimer [ɛ̃pri'me], *v.t.* To imprint, to impress, to stamp; to print, to put in print; to implant, to instil; to impart; (*Paint.*) to prime. *Imprimer un mouvement à une machine,* to set a machine in motion; *se faire imprimer,* to appear in print. **s'imprimer,** *v.r.* To be printed; to be impressed, to be stamped, to be imprinted (*sur* or *dans*). **imprimerie,** *n.f.* Printing; printing-office, printing establishment. **imprimeur,** *n.m.* Printer; (*Print.*) press-man. **imprimeuse,** *n.f.* Printing-machine. **imprimure,** *n.f.* (*Paint.*) Priming.

improbabilité [ɛ̃prɔbabili'te], *n.f.* Improbability, unlikelihood. **improbable,** *a.* Improbable, unlikely. **improbablement,** *adv.* Improbably.

improbateur [ɛ̃prɔba'tœːr], *a.* (*fem.* **-trice**) Disapproving. **improbation,** *n.f.* Disapprobation, disapproval. **improbatif,** *a.* (*fem.* **-ive**) Disapproving.

improbité [ɛ̃prɔbi'te], *n.f.* Improbity, dishonesty.

improductible [ɛ̃prɔdyk'tibl], *a.* Unproducible. **improductif,** *a.* (*fem.* **-ive**) Unproductive, idle. **improductivité,** *n.f.* Unproductiveness.

impromptu [ɛ̃prɔ̃p'ty], *a. inv.* Impromptu, extemporary, unprepared.—*n.m.* Impromptu.—*adv.* Offhand, extempore.

imprononçable [ɛ̃prɔnɔ̃'sabl], *a.* Unpronounceable (word).

impropice [ɛ̃prɔ'pis], *a.* Unpropitious.

impropre [ɛ̃'prɔpr], *a.* Improper, wrong, inaccurate; unfit. *Terme impropre,* wrong expression. **improprement,** *adv.* Improperly. **impropriété,** *n.f.* Impropriety; incorrectness; unfitness.

improuvable [ɛ̃pru'vabl], *a.* Unprovable.

*****improuver** [ɛ̃pru've], *v.t.* To disapprove of.

improvisateur [ɛ̃prɔviza'tœːr], *n.m.* (*fem.* **-trice**) Improvisator, improviser, extemporary speaker, extemporizer.

improvisation [ɛ̃prɔviza'sjɔ̃], *n.f.* Improvisation, extemporaneous speech; extemporaneous speaking; (*Mus.*) voluntary. **improviser,** *v.t.* To improvise, to write, speak, etc., extempore, to extemporize.

improviste (à l') [ɛ̃prɔ'vist], *adv. phr.* All of a sudden, unawares, unexpectedly. *Prendre quelqu'un à l'improviste,* to catch someone unawares.

imprudemment [ɛ̃pryda'mɑ̃], *adv.* Imprudently, indiscreetly, incautiously.

imprudence [ɛ̃pry'dɑ̃ːs], *n.f.* Imprudence, rashness, heedlessness; indiscretion, imprudent act. *Commettre une imprudence,* to be guilty of an indiscretion; *faire une imprudence,* to do an imprudent thing. **imprudent,** *a.* (*fem.* **-ente**) Imprudent, foolhardy, unwise, incautious.

impubère [ɛ̃py'bɛːr], *a.* (*Law*) Under the age of puberty. **impuberté**, *n.f.* Impuberty.
impubliable [ɛ̃pybli'abl], *a.* Unpublishable.
impudemment [ɛ̃pyda'mã], *adv.* Impudently, audaciously, shamelessly.
impudence [ɛ̃py'dãːs], *n.f.* Impudence, effrontery, shamelessness; cheek, sauce; impudent conduct, piece of impudence. **impudent**, *a.* (*fem.* -**ente**) Impudent, shameless, saucy, brazen-faced.—*n.* Impudent person. **impudeur**, *n.f.* Immodesty, indecency; extreme impudence, effrontery, shamelessness.
impudicité [ɛ̃pydisi'te], *n.f.* Impudicity, immodesty, unchasteness, lewdness; lewd act. **impudique**, *a.* Unchaste, lewd, immodest. **impudiquement**, *adv.* Immodestly, unchastely, lewdly.
impuissance [ɛ̃pчi'sãːs], *n.f.* Impotence, inability, incapacity, powerlessness; (*Path.*) impotency, impotence. **impuissant**, *a.* (*fem.* -**ante**) Impotent, ineffectual, powerless, unable; feckless.
impulsif [ɛ̃pyl'sif], *a.* (*fem.* -**ive**) Impulsive.
impulsion [ɛ̃pyl'sjɔ̃], *n.f.* Impulsion, impulse; impetus; motive. *Par impulsion*, by impulse.
impunément [ɛ̃pyne'mã], *adv.* With impunity.
impuni [ɛ̃py'ni], *a.* (*fem.* -**ie**) Unpunished. *Laisser un affront impuni*, to put up with an affront. **impunité.** *n.f.* Impunity.
impur [ɛ̃'pyːr], *a.* (*fem.* -**ure**) Impure, foul; unchaste, immodest; unclean. **impurement**, *adv.* Impurely; immodestly. **impureté**, *n.f.* Impurity, foulness, uncleanness, immodesty; obscenity.
imputabilité [ɛ̃pytabili'te], *n.f.* Imputability. **imputable**, *a.* Imputable, chargeable; to be deducted.
imputatif [ɛ̃pyta'tif], *a.* (*fem.* -**ive**) Imputative.
imputation [ɛ̃pyta'sjɔ̃], *n.f.* Imputation, charge; deduction. **imputer**, *v.t.* To impute, to attribute, to ascribe, to charge; to deduct. *Imputer à crime*, to impute as a crime; *imputer ɥne somme payée sur le principal*, to deduct a payment on account from the principal; *on vous imputera cela à négligence*, it will be put down to your negligence.
imputrescible [ɛ̃pytre'sibl], *a.* Not liable to putrefaction; rot-proof.
inabordable [inabor'dabl], *a.* Inaccessible, unapproachable. **inabordé**, *a.* (*fem.* -**inabordée**) Unvisited, unapproached.
inabrité [inabri'te], *a.* (*fem.* -**ée**) Unsheltered, open.
inabrogé [inabrɔ'ʒe], *a.* (*fem.* -**ée**) Unrepealed. **inabrogeable**, *a.* Unrepealable.
inacceptable [inaksɛp'tabl], *a.* Unacceptable. **inacceptation**, *n.f.* Non-acceptance.
inaccessibilité [inaksɛsibili'te], *n.f.* Inaccessibility. **inaccessible**, *a.* Inaccessible, unapproachable, unattainable; impervious (to).
inaccomplissement [inakɔ̃plis'mã], *n.m.* Unaccomplishment, non-fulfilment.
inaccordable [inakɔr'dabl], *a.* Irreconcilable; unallowable, inadmissible.
inaccostable [inakɔs'tabl], *a.* Inaccessible. *C'est un homme inaccostable*, he is unapproachable.

inaccoutumé [inakuty'me], *a.* (*fem.* -**ée**) Unaccustomed, unwonted, unusual.
inachevé [inaʃ've], *a.* (*fem.* -**ée**) Unfinished, incomplete.
inactif [inak'tif], *a.* (*fem.* -**ive**) Inactive; inert, slothful, indolent. **inaction**, *n.f.* Inaction; indolence, inertness. **inactivement**, *adv.* Inactively. **inactivité**, *n.f.* Inactivity.
inadaptation [inadapta'sjɔ̃], *n.f.* Maladjustment. **inadapté**, *a.* (*fem.* -**ée**) Maladjusted. —*n.m.* Social misfit.
inadéquat [inade'kwa], *a.* (*fem.* **inadéquate**) Inadequate, incomplete.
inadhérent [inade'rã], *a.* (*fem.* -**ente**) Not adherent.
inadmissibilité [inadmisibili'te], *n.f.* Inadmissibility. **inadmissible**, *a.* Inadmissible. **inadmission**, *n.f.* Non-admission.
inadvertance [inadvɛr'tãːs], *n.f.* Inadvertence, oversight. *Par inadvertance*, inadvertently, by an oversight.
inaliénabilité [inaljenabili'te], *n.f.* Inalienability. **inaliénable**, *a.* Inalienable. **inaliéné**, *a.* (*fem.* -**ée**) Unalienated.
inalliable [ina'ljabl], *a.* That cannot be alloyed (of metals); (*fig.*) that cannot be combined or associated, incompatible.
inaltérabilité [inalterabili'te], *n.f.* Inalterability, unchangeableness. **inaltérable**, *a.* Unalterable, unchangeable, invariable. **inaltéré**, *a.* (*fem.* -**ée**) Unspoilt.
inamical [inami'kal], *a.* (*fem.* -**ale**, *pl.* -**aux**) Unfriendly.
inamovibilité [inamɔvibili'te], *n.f.* Irremovability, fixity of tenure. **inamovible**, *a.* Irremovable, permanent, appointed (or held) for life; fixed, built in.
inanimé [inani'me], *a.* (*fem.* -**ée**) Inanimate, lifeless; spiritless, senseless.
inanité [inani'te], *n.f.* Inanity, emptiness.
inanition [inani'sjɔ̃], *n.f.* Inanition. *Mourir d'inanition*, to die from starvation; *tomber d'inanition*, to faint for want of food.
inapaisé [inape'ze], *a.* (*fem.* -**ée**) Unappeased (hunger); unquenched (thirst).
inaperçu [inapɛr'sy], *a.* (*fem.* -**ue**) Unperceived, unobserved, unnoticed.
inapparent [inapa'rã], *a.* (*fem.* -**ente**) Unapparent; inconspicuous.
inappétence [inape'tãːs], *n.f.* Inappetence, want of appetite.
inapplicabilité [inaplikabili'te], *n.f.* Inapplicability. **inapplicable**, *a.* Inapplicable. **inapplication**, *n.f.* Inapplication. **inappliqué**, *a.* (*fem.* -**ée**) Inattentive, heedless, unmindful; unapplied; dormant.
inappréciable [inapre'sjabl], *a.* Inappreciable; inestimable, invaluable. **inappréciablement**, *adv.* Inappreciably. **inapprécié**, *a.* (*fem.* -**ée**) Unappreciated.
inapprêté [inaprɛ'te], *a.* (*fem.* -**ée**) Unprepared, undressed, uncooked.
inapprivoisable [inaprivwa'zabl], *a.* Untamable. **inapprivoisé**, *a.* (*fem.* -**ée**) Untamed.
inapprochable [inaprɔ'ʃabl], *a.* Unapproachable.
inapte [i'napt], *a.* Inapt, unfit, unqualified. **inaptitude**, *n.f.* Inaptitude, unfitness, disqualification.
inarticulé [inartiky'le], *a.* (*fem.* -**ée**) Inarticulate.

inasservi [inasɛr'vi], *a.* (*fem.* **-ie**) Unenslaved, unsubdued.

inassiégeable [inasje'ʒabl], *a.* Unbesiegeable.

inassorti [inasɔr'ti], *a.* (*fem.* **-ie**) Ill-assorted, ill-matched.

inassouvi [inasu'vi], *a.* (*fem.* **-ie**) Unsatiated, unappeased, unsatisfied.

inassouvissable, *a.* Unsatiable, insatiable.

inassujetti [inasyʒɛ'ti], *a.* (*fem.* **-ie**) Unsubjected.

inattaquable [inata'kabl], *a.* Unassailable; (*fig.*) unimpeachable, irreproachable, unobjectionable, unquestionable. *Inattaquable aux acides,* acid-proof, incorrodible.

inattendu [inatɑ̃'dy], *a.* (*fem.* **-ue**) Unexpected, unforeseen; unhoped for.

inattentif [inatɑ̃'tif], *a.* (*fem.* **-ive**) Inattentive, unmindful. **inattention**, *n.f.* Inattention, carelessness. *Faute d'inattention,* slip.

inaudible [ino'dibl], *a.* Inaudible.

inaugural [inogy'ral], *a.* (*fem.* **-ale**, *pl.* **-aux**) Inaugural. **inaugurateur**, *n.m.* (*fem.* **-trice**) Inaugurator. **inauguration**, *n.f.* Inauguration. **inaugurer**, *v.t.* To inaugurate, to open; to establish, to institute; to usher in.

inavouable [ina'vwabl], *a.* Unavowable. **inavoué**, *a.* (*fem.* **-ée**) Unconfessed, unavowed.

incalculable [ɛ̃kalky'labl], *a.* Incalculable, countless, numberless.

incandescence [ɛ̃kɑ̃dɛ'sɑ̃:s], *n.f.* Incandescence. **incandescent**, *a.* (*fem.* **-ente**) Incandescent.

incantation [ɛ̃kɑ̃ta'sjɔ̃], *n.f.* Incantation. **incantatoire**, *a.* Incantatory, spell-binding.

incapable [ɛ̃ka'pabl], *a.* Incapable, unable (*de*); unfit, incompetent, inefficient. *C'est un homme incapable,* he is a man of no capacity; *rendre incapable de,* to incapacitate for, to make incapable of. **incapacité**, *n.f.* Incapacity, incapability; inability, unfitness; incompetence, disability, disqualification, (*Mil.*) disablement. *Frapper d'incapacité,* to incapacitate.

incarcération [ɛ̃karserɑ'sjɔ̃], *n.f.* Incarceration. **incarcérer**, *v.t.* To incarcerate, to imprison.

incarnadin [ɛ̃karna'dɛ̃], *a.* (*fem.* **-ine**) Flesh-coloured, pale carnation.—*n.m.* This colour.

incarnat [ɛ̃kar'na], *a.* (*fem.* **-ate**) Flesh-coloured, rosy.—*n.m.* Carnation, flesh-colour, rosiness.

incarnation [ɛ̃karna'sjɔ̃], *n.f.* Incarnation, embodiment. **incarné**, *a.* (*fem.* **-ée**) Incarnate; ingrowing (nail). **incarner**, *v.t.* To incarnate, to embody; (*Theat., Cine.*) to play the part of. **s'incarner**, *v.r.* To become incarnate, to be embodied; to grow in (of nails).

incartade [ɛ̃kar'tad], *n.f.* Thoughtless insult or invective; prank, folly, freak; shy, sudden swerve (of horse).

incassable [ɛ̃ka'sabl], *a.* Unbreakable, foolproof.

incendiaire [ɛ̃sɑ̃'djɛːr], *a.* and *n.* Incendiary. *Des paroles incendiaires,* inflammatory words.

incendie [ɛ̃sɑ̃'di], *n.m.* Fire, conflagration. *Arrêter un incendie,* to get a fire under control; *incendie par malveillance,* incendiary fire, arson; *pompe à incendie,* fire-engine. **incendié**, *a.* (*fem.* **-iée**) Burnt down, burnt out, gutted.—*n.* Sufferer by fire. **incendier**, *v.t.*

To set fire to, to burn down; (*fig.*) to kindle, to inflame.

incertain [ɛ̃sɛr'tɛ̃], *a.* (*fem.* **-aine**) Uncertain, questionable; unsettled, inconstant; vague, wavering; unreliable. **incertainement**, *adv.* Doubtfully. **incertitude**, *n.f.* Uncertainty, doubt, suspense; instability, fickleness. *L'incertitude du temps,* the unsettled state of the weather.

incessamment [ɛ̃sɛsa'mɑ̃], *adv.* Immediately, at once; incessantly, unceasingly. **incessant**, *a.* (*fem.* **-ante**) Incessant, ceaseless, unremitting.

incessible [ɛ̃sɛ'sibl], *a.* Untransferable, inalienable, not negotiable.

inceste [ɛ̃'sɛst], *n.m.* Incest; incestuous person.—*a.* Incestuous. **incestueusement**, *adv.* Incestuously. **incestueux**, *a.* (*fem.* **-ueuse**) Incestuous.—*n.* Incestuous person.

inchangé [ɛ̃ʃɑ̃'ʒe], *a.* (*fem.* **-ée**) Unchanged. **inchangeable**, *a.* Unchangeable.

inchantable [ɛ̃ʃɑ̃'tabl], *a.* Unsingable.

inchavirable [ɛ̃ʃavi'rabl], *a.* Uncapsizable.

inchoatif [ɛ̃kɔa'tif], *a.* (*fem.* **-ive**) (*Gram.*) Inchoative, inceptive.

incicatrisable [ɛ̃sikatri'zabl], *a.* (Wound) that cannot heal, ever open.

incidemment [ɛ̃sida'mɑ̃], *adv.* Incidentally.

incidence [ɛ̃si'dɑ̃:s], *n.f.* Incidence. **incident**, *a.* (*fem.* **-ente**) Incidental; incident.—*n.m.* Incident, occurrence; (*Law*) difficulty, cavil. **incidenter**, *v.i.* (*Law*) To raise difficulties; to start objections.

incinération [ɛ̃sinera'sjɔ̃], *n.f.* Incineration. **incinérer**, *v.t.* To incinerate.

incirconcis [ɛ̃sirkɔ̃'si], *a.* (*fem.* **-ise**) Uncircumcised.—*n.m.* Uncircumcised person. *Les incirconcis,* the Gentiles.

incise [ɛ̃'siːz], *n.f.* (*Gram.*) Incidental clause. **inciser** [ɛ̃si'ze], *v.t.* To make an incision in, to notch, to gash; to tap (a tree). **incisif**, *a.* (*fem.* **-ive**) Sharp, cutting, incisive. *Dents incisives,* incisors; *une critique incisive,* a sharp criticism.—*n.f.* Incisive tooth, incisor. **incision**, *n.f.* Incision. **incisivement**, *adv.* Incisively, sharply.

incitant [ɛ̃si'tɑ̃], *a.* (*fem.* **-ante**) Inciting, stimulating.—*n.m.* (*Med.*) Incitant, stimulant. **incitateur**, *a.* (*fem.* **-trice**) Inciting.—*n.* Inciter. **incitatif**, *a.* (*fem.* **-ive**) Inciting. **incitation** [ɛ̃sita'sjɔ̃], *n.f.* Incitation; incitement, incentive, instigation; (*Med.*) stimulus. **inciter**, *v.t.* To incite; to instigate, to induce.

incivil [ɛ̃si'vil], *a.* (*fem.* **-ile**) Uncivil, unmannerly. **incivilement**, *adv.* Uncivilly. **incivilisé**, *a.* (*fem.* **-ée**) Uncivilized. **incivilité**, *n.f.* Incivility; rude remark.

incivique [ɛ̃si'vik], *a.* Unpatriotic. **incivisme**, *n.m.* Incivism, want of patriotism.

inclémence [ɛ̃kle'mɑ̃:s], *n.f.* Inclemency. **inclément**, *a.* (*fem.* **-ente**) Inclement.

inclinaison [ɛ̃kline'zɔ̃], *n.f.* Inclination (of star); incline, gradient, slope (of hill); dip (of magnetic needle); rake (of mast, of steering column); pitch, slant (of roof). **inclinant**, *a.* (*fem.* **-ante**) Inclined, sloping. **inclination**, *n.f.* Inclination, bow, stooping, bending; bent, tendency, proneness, propensity; attachment, passion. *Mariage d'inclination,* love-match; *par inclination,* from inclination.

incliner
incontestable

incliner [ɛ̃kli'ne], *v.t.* To incline, to slope, to slant; to bow; to bend; (*Mil.*) to dip (the colours); (*fig.*) to dispose, to turn.—*v.i.* To incline, to lean; to be disposed, to be inclined (*à* or *vers*). **s'incliner,** *v.r.* To incline, to lean; to bow, to bend, to yield; to bow down. *S'incliner sur l'aile,* (*Av.*) to bank. **inclinomètre,** *n.m.* Inclinometer.
inclure [ɛ̃'kly:r], *v.t.* To include, to enclose, to insert. **inclus,** *a.* (*fem.* **-use**) Enclosed, included. *Ci-inclus,* herein enclosed; *trouver ci-inclus,* to find enclosed. **inclusif,** *a.* (*fem.* **-ive**) Inclusive. **inclusion,** *n.f.* Enclosing; inclusion. **inclusivement,** *adv.* Inclusively.
incoercible [ɛ̃koɛr'sibl], *a.* Incoercible.
incognito [ɛ̃kɔɲi'to], *adv.* Incognito.—*n.m.* Incognito. *Garder l'incognito,* to preserve one's incognito.
incohérence [ɛ̃koe'rɑ̃:s], *n.f.* Incoherence. **incohérent,** *a.* (*fem.* **-ente**) Incoherent.
incolore [ɛ̃kɔ'lɔ:r], *a.* Colourless.
incomber [ɛ̃kɔ̃'be], *v.i.* (*only in 3rd pers.*) To be incumbent (on any one); to be a duty, to devolve (*d*).
incombustibilité [ɛ̃kɔ̃bystibili'te], *n.f.* Incombustibility. **incombustible,** *a.* Incombustible, fire-proof.
incomestible [ɛ̃kɔmɛs'tibl], *a.* Inedible.
incommensurabilité [ɛ̃kɔmãsyrabili'te], *n.f.* Incommensurability. **incommensurable,** *a.* Incommensurable; irrational (root).
incommode [ɛ̃kɔ'mɔd], *a.* Inconvenient, incommodious, uncomfortable, unhandy; importunate, annoying, disagreeable, troublesome. **incommodé,** *a.* (*fem.* **-ée**) Indisposed, unwell, poorly. **incommodément,** *adv.* Incommodiously, inconveniently. **incommoder,** *v.t.* To incommode, to inconvenience, to trouble; to disturb, to annoy, to embarrass; to disagree with, to make unwell. *J'ai peur de vous incommoder,* I am afraid of troubling you; *si cela ne vous incommode pas,* if it is no trouble to you. **incommodité,** *n.f.* Inconvenience, incommodiousness; trouble, annoyance; indisposition, infirmity.
incommuable [ɛ̃kɔ'mɥabl], *a.* Incommutable.
incommunicable [ɛ̃kɔmyni'kabl], *a.* Incommunicable.
incommutabilité [ɛ̃kɔmytabili'te], *n.f.* Incommutability. **incommutable,** *a.* (*Law*) Incommutable; untransferable.
incomparable [ɛ̃kɔ̃pa'rabl], *a.* Incomparable, unequalled, peerless. **incomparablement,** *adv.* Incomparably.
incompatibilité [ɛ̃kɔ̃patibili'te], *n.f.* Incompatibility. (*Law*) *Incompatibilité d'humeur,* incompatibility of temper. **incompatible,** *a.* Incompatible, inconsistent, incongruous. **incompatiblement,** *adv.* Incompatibly.
incompétence [ɛ̃kɔ̃pe'tã:s], *n.f.* Incompetence. **incompétent,** *a.* (*fem.* **-ente**) Incompetent.
incomplet [ɛ̃kɔ̃'plɛ], *a.* (*fem.* **-ète**) Incomplete. **incomplètement,** *adv.* Incompletely.
incomplexe [ɛ̃kɔ̃'plɛks], *a.* Incomplex, simple; (*Gram.*) having no complement.
incompréhensibilité [ɛ̃kɔ̃preãsibili'te], *n.f.* Incomprehensibility. **incompréhensible,** *a.* Incomprehensible, unintelligible, inscrutable. **incompréhensiblement,** *adv.* In-

comprehensibly. **incompréhension,** *n.f.* Lack of understanding; obtuseness.
incompressibilité [ɛ̃kɔ̃prɛsibili'te], *n.f.* Incompressibility. **incompressible,** *a.* Incompressible.
incompris [ɛ̃kɔ̃'pri], *a.* and *n.* (*fem.* **-ise**) Misunderstood, unappreciated (person).
inconcevable [ɛ̃kɔ̃s'vabl], *a.* Inconceivable, unthinkable; wonderful. **inconcevablement,** *adv.* Inconceivably.
inconciliable [ɛ̃kɔ̃si'ljabl], *a.* Irreconcilable, incompatible. **inconciliablement,** *adv.* Irreconcilably.
inconduite [ɛ̃kɔ̃'dɥit], *n.f.* Misconduct.
inconfort [ɛ̃kɔ̃'fɔ:r], *n.m.* Discomfort, lack of comfort. **inconfortable,** *a.* Uncomfortable.
incongelable [ɛ̃kɔ̃ʒ'labl], *a.* Uncongealable.
incongru [ɛ̃kɔ̃'gry], *a.* (*fem.* **-ue**) Incongruous, improper, unseemly. **incongruité,** *n.f.* Incongruity, impropriety, unseemliness. **incongrûment,** *adv.* Incongruously, improperly, in an unseemly manner.
inconnaissable [ɛ̃kɔnɛ'sabl], *a.* Unknowable.
inconnu [ɛ̃kɔ'ny], *a.* (*fem.* **-ue**) Unknown. *Inconnu de tous,* unknown to all; *le soldat inconnu,* the unknown soldier.—*n.m.* The unknown, that which is unknown. *Porter plainte contre inconnu,* (*Law*) to lodge a complaint against a person unknown.—*n.f.* (*Math.*) Unknown quantity.
inconquis [ɛ̃kɔ̃'ki], *a.* (*fem.* **-ise**) Unconquered.
inconsciemment [ɛ̃kɔ̃sja'mã], *adv.* Unconsciously, unawares. **inconscience,** *n.f.* Unconsciousness; failure to realize. **inconscient,** *a.* (*fem.* **-ente**) Unconscious.—*n.m.* The unconscious.
inconséquemment [ɛ̃kɔ̃seka'mã], *adv.* Inconsistently, inconsequentially.
inconséquence [ɛ̃kɔ̃se'kã:s], *n.f.* Inconsistency, inconsequence. **inconséquent,** *a.* (*fem.* **-ente**) Inconsistent; inconsequential; (*colloq.*) indiscreet, flighty.
inconsidération [ɛ̃kɔ̃sidera'sjɔ̃], *n.f.* Inconsiderateness. **inconsidéré,** *a.* (*fem.* **-ée**) Inconsiderate, thoughtless; done thoughtlessly. **inconsidérément,** *adv.* Inconsiderately, thoughtlessly.
inconsistance [ɛ̃kɔ̃sis'tã:s], *n.f.* Inconsistency. **inconsistant,** *a.* (*fem.* **-ante**) Inconsistent.
inconsolable [ɛ̃kɔ̃sɔ'labl], *a.* Disconsolate; inconsolable. **inconsolablement,** *adv.* Disconsolately, inconsolably. **inconsolé,** *a.* (*fem.* **-ée**) Unconsoled, uncomforted.
inconsommé [ɛ̃kɔ̃sɔ'me], *a.* (*fem.* **-ée**) Unconsummated (marriage); unconsumed (food).
inconstamment [ɛ̃kɔ̃sta'mã], *adv.* Inconstantly, unsteadily.
inconstance [ɛ̃kɔ̃s'tã:s], *n.f.* Inconstancy, fickleness; unsteadiness, changeableness, instability. *L'inconstance du temps,* the changeableness of the weather. **inconstant,** *a.* (*fem.* **-ante**) Inconstant, fickle, wavering; changeable, variable; unsettled, unsteady.—*n.* Fickle man *or* woman.
inconstitutionnel [ɛ̃kɔ̃stitysjɔ'nɛl], *a.* (*fem.* **-elle**) Unconstitutional.
incontestable [ɛ̃kɔ̃tɛs'tabl], *a.* Incontestable, indisputable, unquestionable. **incontestablement,** *adv.* Incontestably.

[417]

incontesté, *a.* (*fem.* **-ée**) Uncontested, unquestioned, undisputed.
incontinence [ɛ̃kɔ̃ti'nɑ̃ːs], *n.f.* Incontinence.
incontinent (1), *a.* (*fem.* **-ente**) Incontinent, unchaste.
incontinent (2) [ɛ̃kɔ̃ti'nɑ̃], *adv.* At once, immediately, forthwith.
incontrit [ɛ̃kɔ̃'tri], *a.* (*fem.* **-ite**) Uncontrite.
incontrôlable [ɛ̃kɔ̃tro'labl], *a.* That cannot be checked or verified.
inconvenance [ɛ̃kɔ̃v'nɑ̃ːs], *n.f.* Impropriety, unseemliness; indecorous act, indecorum, breach of good manners. *Quelle inconvenance!* how very improper! **inconvenant,** *a.* (*fem.* **-ante**) Improper, unbecoming, unseemly.
inconvénient [ɛ̃kɔ̃ve'njɑ̃], *n.m.* Inconvenience, harm, trouble; disadvantage, drawback, objection; ill consequence. *Je ne vois pas d'inconvénient à cela,* I see no objection to that.
inconvertible [ɛ̃kɔ̃vɛr'tibl], *a.* Unconvertible.
incoordination [ɛ̃koɔrdinɑ'sjɔ̃], *n.f.* Incoordination; (*Med.*) ataxia.
incorporalité [ɛ̃kɔrpɔrali'te], *n.f.* Incorporeality. **incorporation,** *n.f.* Incorporation; (*Mil.*) bringing the recruits to their regiments. **incorporéité,** *n.f.* Incorporeity. **incorporel,** *a.* (*fem.* **-elle**) Incorporeal. **incorporer,** *v.t.* To incorporate, to embody; to fuse. *Incorporer un régiment dans un autre,* to combine one regiment with another; *incorporer les jeunes soldats,* to call the recruits to the colours. **s'incorporer,** *v.r.* To be embodied; to unite, to be blended.
incorrect [ɛ̃kɔ'rɛkt], *a.* (*fem.* **-ecte**) Incorrect, inaccurate, erroneous; wrong. *Citation incorrecte,* misquotation. **incorrectement,** *adv.* Incorrectly, inaccurately, wrongly. **incorrection,** *n.f.* Incorrectness, inaccuracy.
incorrigibilité [ɛ̃kɔriʒibili'te], *n.f.* Incorrigibility. **incorrigible,** *a.* Incorrigible, irreclaimable; hopeless. **incorrigiblement,** *adv.* Incorrigibly.
incorruptibilité [ɛ̃kɔryptibili'te], *n.f.* Incorruptibility. **incorruptible,** *a.* Incorruptible, unbribable.
incrédibilité [ɛ̃kredibili'te], *n.f.* Incredibility.
incrédule [ɛ̃kre'dyl], *a.* Incredulous, unbelieving, misdoubting.—*n.* Unbeliever, infidel. **incrédulité,** *n.f.* Incredulity, unbelief.
incréé [ɛ̃kre'e], *a.* (*fem.* **incréée**) Increate, uncreated.
increvable [ɛ̃krə'vabl], *a.* Unpuncturable (tyre).
incriminable [ɛ̃krimi'nabl], *a.* Incriminable, impeachable. **incrimination,** *n.f.* Incrimination; charge, accusation. **incriminer,** *v.t.* To incriminate, to accuse, to charge, to impeach.
incriticable [ɛ̃kriti'kabl], *a.* That cannot be criticized.
incrochetable [ɛ̃krɔ'ʃtabl], *a.* Unpickable (lock).
incroyable [ɛ̃krwɑ'jabl], *a.* Incredible, past belief.—*n.* French dandy, fop (under the Directory) or belle. **incroyablement,** *adv.* Incredibly. **incroyance,** *n.f.* Unbelief. **incroyant,** *n.m.* (*fem.* **-ante**) Unbeliever.—*a.* Unbelieving.

incrustation [ɛ̃krystɑ'sjɔ̃], *n.f.* Incrustation; inlaying, inlaid work; furring (of boilers). *Table couverte d'incrustations de nacre,* table inlaid all over with mother-of-pearl. **incruster,** *v.t.* To encrust, to inlay. **s'incruster,** *v.r.* To become encrusted; to be furred (of boiler). *S'incruster chez quelqu'un,* to outstay one's welcome.
incubateur [ɛ̃kyba'tœːr], *a.* (*fem.* **-trice**) Incubating.—*n.m.* Incubator.
incubation [ɛ̃kyba'sjɔ̃], *n.f.* Incubation, hatching.
incube [ɛ̃'kyb], *n.m.* Incubus.
incuber [ɛ̃ky'be], *v.t.* To incubate.
inculcation [ɛ̃kylka'sjɔ̃], *n.f.* Inculcation.
inculpable [ɛ̃kyl'pabl], *a.* Chargeable.
inculpation [ɛ̃kylpa'sjɔ̃], *n.f.* Inculpation, indictment, charge. **inculpé,** *n.m.* (*fem.* **-ée**) Defendant, accused. **inculper,** *v.t.* To indict, to inculpate, to charge.
inculquer [ɛ̃kyl'ke], *v.t.* To inculcate, to impress.
inculte [ɛ̃'kylt], *a.* Uncultivated; untilled, unploughed, waste; unpolished, rude; neglected, unkempt. *Terres incultes,* waste lands. **incultivable,** *a.* Untillable, uncultivable. **incultivé,** *a.* (*fem.* **-ée**) Uncultivated; (*fig.*) uncultured. **inculture,** *n.f.* Lack of culture; lack of cultivation.
incunable [ɛ̃ky'nabl], *n.m.* Incunabulum (a book printed in the fifteenth century).
incurabilité [ɛ̃kyrabili'te], *n.f.* Incurability. **incurable,** *a.* and *n.* Incurable. *Les incurables,* hospital for incurables. **incurablement,** *adv.* Incurably.
incurie [ɛ̃ky'ri], *n.f.* Carelessness, heedlessness; negligence.
incursif [ɛ̃kyr'sif], *a.* (*fem.* **-ive**) Incursive.
incursion [ɛ̃kyr'sjɔ̃], *n.f.* Incursion, inroad, irruption; foray, raid; expedition; (*fig.*) excursion.
incurver [ɛ̃kyr've], *v.t.* To curve (something) inwards. **s'incurver,** *v.r.* To curve in.
incuse [ɛ̃'kyːz], *a.f.* Badly struck (of medals). —*n.f.* Badly struck medal.
inde [ɛ̃ːd], *n.m.* Indigo, indigo-blue.
Inde [ɛ̃ːd], *f.* India. *Les Indes, the Indies; *les Indes occidentales,* the West Indies; *bois d'Inde,* logwood; *marron d'Inde,* horse-chestnut; *cochon d'Inde* [COCHON]; *œillet d'Inde* [ŒILLET]; *poule d'Inde [DINDE].
indébrouillable [ɛ̃debru'jabl], *a.* Inextricable, inexplicable, that cannot be unravelled.
indécemment [ɛ̃desa'mɑ̃], *adv.* Indecently.
indécence [ɛ̃de'sɑ̃ːs], *n.f.* Indecency, impropriety. **indécent,** *a.* (*fem.* **-ente**) Indecent: indecorous, unbecoming, unseemly.
indéchiffrable [ɛ̃deʃi'frabl], *a.* Undecipherable, illegible; unintelligible; obscure, incomprehensible. **indéchiffré,** *a.* (*fem.* **-ée**) Undeciphered.
indéchirable [ɛ̃deʃi'rabl], *a.* Untearable.
indécis [ɛ̃de'si], *a.* (*fem.* **-ise**) Undecided, doubtful; uncertain, undefined, faint, vague; wavering, irresolute. *Une bataille indécise,* an indecisive battle. **indécision,** *n.f.* Indecision, irresolution; indistinctness.
indéclinable [ɛ̃dekli'nabl], *a.* Indeclinable.
indécomposable [ɛ̃dekɔ̃po'zabl], *a.* Indecomposable.
indécousable [ɛ̃deku'zabl], *a.* That cannot be unsewn.

indécrottable [ɛ̃dekrɔ'tabl], *a.* Uncleanable; (*fig.*) uncouth, incorrigible, unteachable.
indéfectibilité [ɛ̃defɛktibili'te], *n.f.* Indefectibility. **indéfectible,** *a.* Indefectible.
indéfendable [ɛ̃defã'dabl], *a.* Indefensible, untenable.
indéfini [ɛ̃defi'ni], *a.* (*fem.* **-ie**) Indefinite, unlimited; undetermined, undefined. *Pronom indéfini,* indefinite pronoun. **indéfiniment,** *adv.* Indefinitely. **indéfinissable,** *a.* Undefinable; unaccountable, nondescript.
indéformable [ɛ̃defɔr'mabl], *a.* That cannot be put out of shape.
indéfrichable [ɛ̃defri'ʃabl], *a.* Unclearable (of land).
indéfrisable [ɛ̃defri'zabl], *n.f.* Permanent wave.
indéhiscent [ɛ̃deis'sã], *a.* (*fem.* **-ente**) (*Bot.*) Indehiscent.
indélébile [ɛ̃dele'bil], *a.* Indelible, ineffaceable.
indélibéré [ɛ̃delibe're], *a.* (*fem.* **-ée**) Done without deliberation, unconsidered.
indélicat [ɛ̃deli'ka], *a.* (*fem.* **-ate**) Indelicate; unhandsome. **indélicatement,** *adv.* Indelicately; unhandsomely. **indélicatesse,** *n.f.* Tactlessness, unscrupulousness; indelicate, objectionable action.
indémaillable [ɛ̃dema'jabl], *a.* Ladder-proof (stocking).
indemne [ɛ̃'dɛmn], *a.* Uninjured, undamaged, unhurt, unscathed. **indemnisation,** *n.f.* Indemnification, compensation. **indemniser,** *v.t.* To indemnify; to make good, to recoup. **indemnité,** *n.f.* Indemnity. *Indemnité de charges de famille,* child bounty, family allowance; *indemnité de chômage,* dole; *indemnité de résidence,* cost of living allowance; *indemnité de vie chère,* cost of living bonus; (*Mil.*) *indemnité d'équipement* or *d'entrée en campagne,* outfit allowance; *indemnité de logement,* billet money; (*Naut.*) *indemnité de surestarie,* demurrage.
indémontrable [ɛ̃demɔ̃'trabl], *a.* Undemonstrable.
indéniable [ɛ̃de'njabl], *a.* Undeniable; unquestionable; obvious, self-evident.
indépendamment [ɛ̃depãda'mã], *adv.* Independently. **indépendance,** *n.f.* Independence. **indépendant,** *a.* (*fem.* **-ante**) Independent; free (State); self-reliant.
indéracinable [ɛ̃derasi'nabl], *a.* Ineradicable.
indéréglable [ɛ̃dere'glabl], *a.* That cannot get out of order; fool-proof (of mechanism).
indescriptible [ɛ̃dɛskrip'tibl], *a.* Indescribable. **indescriptiblement,** *adv.* Indescribably.
indésirable [ɛ̃dezi'rabl], *a.* and *n.* Undesirable.
indesserrable [ɛ̃dɛsɛr'abl], *a.* Self-locking (nut).
indestituable [ɛ̃dɛsti'tyabl], *a.* Irremovable, not to be dismissed (from office).
indestructibilité [ɛ̃dɛstryktibili'te], *n.f.* Indestructibility. **indestructible,** *a.* Indestructible.
indéterminable [ɛ̃detɛrmi'nabl], *a.* Indeterminable. **indétermination,** *n.f.* Indetermination, irresolution. **indéterminé,** *a.* (*fem.* **-ée**) Undetermined, undecided, irresolute; (*Math.*) indeterminate.

indevinable [ɛ̃dvi'nabl], *a.* Unguessable.
index [ɛ̃'dɛks], *n.m. inv.* Fore-finger, index-finger; index, table of contents; index expurgatorius. *Être à l'index,* to be on the Index (of book), to be forbidden; (*fam.*) to be on the black list; *mettre à l'index,* to prohibit (a book), to black-list (a person).
indicateur [ɛ̃dika'tœ:r], *a.* (*fem.* **-trice**) Indicating, indicatory. *Poteau indicateur,* sign-post.—*n.m.* Indicator, gauge, guide; guide-book; railway guide, time-table; index-finger; (*fig.*) informer, police spy; (*Orn.*) honey-guide. **indicatif,** *a.* (*fem.* **-ive**) Indicative.—*n.m.* (*Gram.*) Indicative mood; (*Rad. Tel.*) station signal, call-sign; signature-tune (of an orchestra). **indication,** *n.f.* Indication, information; sign, mark, token; (*pl.*) directions (for use).
indice [ɛ̃'dis], *n.m.* Indication, sign, mark, token, symptom, clue. *Indice de réfraction,* refractive index; *indice du coût de la vie,* the cost of living index.
indicible [ɛ̃di'sibl], *a.* Inexpressible, unspeakable, unutterable, indescribable. **indiciblement,** *adv.* Inexpressibly.
indien [ɛ̃'djɛ̃], *a.* and *n.* (*fem.* **-ienne** (1)) Indian. **indienne** (2), *n.f.* Printed calico, printed cotton, print. **indienneur,** *n.m.* (*fem.* **-euse**) Calico-printer.
indifféremment [ɛ̃difera'mã], *adv.* Indifferently, indiscriminately; equally, alike.
indifférence [ɛ̃dife'rã:s], *n.f.* Indifference, unconcern. **indifférent,** *a.* (*fem.* **-ente**) Indifferent, immaterial, unimportant; unconcerned, unmindful, heedless, insensible. *Cela m'est parfaitement indifférent,* it is quite immaterial to me; *il lui est indifférent de sortir ou de rester,* it is the same to him whether he goes out or not; *il m'est indifférent,* he doesn't mean anything to me. —*n.* Indifferent person. *Faire l'indifférent,* to feign indifference.
indigénat [ɛ̃diʒe'na], *n.m.* Denizenship and rights of a native (esp. in Algeria); the natives as a whole.
indigence [ɛ̃di'ʒã:s], *n.f.* Indigence, poverty, need.
indigène [ɛ̃di'ʒɛ:n], *a.* Indigenous, native (of a continent etc.).—*n.* Native.
indigent [ɛ̃di'ʒã], *a.* (*fem.* **-ente**) Indigent, poor, needy, necessitous.—*n.* Pauper, destitute.
indigéré [ɛ̃diʒe're], *a.* (*fem.* **-ée**) Undigested, crude. **indigeste,** *a.* Indigestible; undigested, crude; confused, incoherent. **indigestion,** *n.f.* Indigestion, surfeit.
indignation [ɛ̃diɲa'sjɔ̃], *n.f.* Indignation. *Avec indignation,* indignantly; *faire éclater son indignation,* to give vent to one's indignation.
indigne [ɛ̃'diɲ], *a.* Unworthy, undeserving; infamous, worthless, vile; (*Law*) disqualified (*de*). *Indigne de succéder,* debarred from inheriting.—*n.m.* Worthless, infamous wretch; (*Law*) one debarred by law from inheriting. **indigné,** *a.* (*fem.* **-ée**) Indignant, shocked. **indignement,** *adv.* Unworthily, undeservedly; infamously, scandalously. **indigner,** *v.t.* To render indignant, to rouse the indignation of, to shock. **s'indigner,** *v.r.* To be indignant, to be shocked. **indignité,** *n.f.* Unworthiness,

worthlessness; vileness, baseness; indignity; infamy, scandal; (*Law*) disqualification. *Quelle indignité!* what a shame! *indignité nationale*, loss of civil rights.

indigo [ɛ̃di′go], *n.m.* and *a. inv.* Indigo. **indigoterie**, *n.f.* Indigo plantation or manufactory. **indigotier**, *n.m.* Indigo plant or manufacturer.

indiquer [ɛ̃di′ke], *v.t.* To indicate, to show, to point out; to mention; to denote, to betoken; to inform of, to acquaint with; to appoint, to name, to recommend; to sketch out, to outline. *Au lieu indiqué*, at the appointed place; *voulez-vous m'indiquer le chemin de l'église?* will you show me the way to the church?

indirect [ɛ̃di′rɛkt], *a.* (*fem.* **-ecte**) Indirect; circumstantial (of evidence); collateral (of heirs). *Contributions indirectes*, excise revenue. **indirectement**, *a.* Indirectly.

indiscernable [ɛ̃disɛr′nabl], *a.* Indiscriminable, indistinguishable.

indisciplinable [ɛ̃disipli′nabl], *a.* Indisciplinable, ungovernable. **indiscipline**, *n.f.* Indiscipline, insubordination. **indiscipliné**, *a.* (*fem.* **-ée**) Undisciplined, unruly.

indiscret [ɛ̃dis′krɛ], *a.* (*fem.* **indiscrète**) Indiscreet, inconsiderate, unwary; unguarded, prying; injudicious; inquisitive; tell-tale, unable to keep a secret.—*n.* Indiscreet person, esp. a babbler, a pushing person. **indiscrètement**, *adv.* Indiscreetly, inconsiderately. **indiscrétion**, *n.f.* Indiscretion, inconsiderateness; imprudence, unwariness; piece of indiscretion, indiscreet thing. *Serait-ce une indiscrétion de ma part de demander ...?* would it be indiscreet of me to ask ...?

indiscutable [ɛ̃disky′tabl], *a.* Incontestable, indisputable, obvious. **indiscutablement**, *adv.* Indisputably. **indiscuté**, *a.* (*fem.* **-ée**) Unquestioned.

indispensabilité [ɛ̃dispɑ̃sabili′te], *n.f.* Indispensability. **indispensable**, *a.* Indispensable.—*n.m.* The indispensable or strictly necessary. **indispensablement**, *adv.* Indispensably.

indisponibilité [ɛ̃dispɔnibili′te], *n.f.* Unavailability; (*Law*) inalienability. **indisponible**, *a.* (*Law*) Entailed; (*Mil.*) not available (for duty); unavailable.

indisposé [ɛ̃dispo′ze], *a.* (*fem.* **-ée**) Unwell, out of sorts; ill-disposed, unfriendly.

indisposer [ɛ̃dispo′ze], *v.t.* To indispose, to make unwell; to disaffect, to disincline, to set (*contre*). *Je craignais que son intervention ne vous indisposât contre moi*, I was afraid his interference would set you against me. **indisposition**, *n.f.* Indisposition, slight illness; disinclination.

indisputé [ɛ̃dispy′te], *a.* (*fem.* **-ée**) Unquestioned.

indissolubilité [ɛ̃disɔlybili′te], *n.f.* Indissolubility. **indissoluble**, *a.* Indissoluble. **indissolublement**, *adv.* Indissolubly.

indistinct [ɛ̃dis′tɛ̃:kt], *a.* (*fem.* **-te**) Indistinct. **indistinctement**, *adv.* Indistinctly.

individu [ɛ̃divi′dy], *n.m.* Individual; (*colloq.*) person, fellow. **individualisation**, *n.f.* Individualization. **individualiser**, *v.t.* To individualize. **individualisme**, *n.m.* Individualism. **individualiste**, *a.* Individualistic.—*n.* Individualist. **individualité**, *n.f.* Indi-

viduality. **individuel**, *a.* (*fem.* **-elle**) Individual. **individuellement**, *adv.* Individually.

indivis [ɛ̃di′vi], *a.* (*fem.* **-ise**) (*Law*) Undivided; joint, in common. *Par indivis*, in joint-tenancy. **indivisé**, *a.* (*fem.* **-ée**) Undivided. **indivisément**, *adv.* Jointly. **indivisibilité**, *n.f.* Indivisibility. **indivisible**, *a.* Indivisible. **indivisiblement**, *adv.* Indivisibly. **indivision**, *n.f.* Joint-possession, joint-ownership, joint-tenancy, parcenary.

in-dix-huit [ɛ̃di′zɥit], *n.m.* and *a. inv.* Decimo-octavo, 18mo.

Indochine [ɛ̃dɔ′ʃin], *f.* Indo-China. **indochinois**, *a.* and *n.m.* (*fem.* **-oise**) Indo-Chinese.

indocile [ɛ̃dɔ′sil], *a.* Indocile, unmanageable. **indocilement**, *adv.* With indocility. **indocilité**, *n.f.* Indocility, intractability.

indo-européen [ɛ̃dɔœrɔpe′ɛ̃], *a.* (*fem.* **-éenne**) Indo-European.

indolemment [ɛ̃dɔla′mɑ̃], *adv.* Indolently.

indolence [ɛ̃dɔ′lɑ̃:s], *n.f.* Indolence, sloth; indifference, listlessness; (*Med.*) physical insensibility. *Son indolence le perdra*, his indolence will be his undoing. **indolent**, *a.* (*fem.* **-te**) Indolent, sluggish, slothful; indifferent; (*Med.*) insensible.—*n.* Sluggard.

indolore [ɛ̃dɔ′lɔ:r], *a.* Painless.

indomptable [ɛ̃dɔ̃′tabl], *a.* Indomitable, unconquerable, untamable; ungovernable, unmanageable. **indomptablement**, *adv.* Indomitably, untamably; ungovernably. **indompté**, *a.* (*fem.* **-ée**) Untamed, wild; unsubdued; uncontrollable, unconquerable.

Indonésie [ɛ̃dɔne′zi], *f.* Indonesia. **indonésien**, *a.* and *n.m.* (*fem.* **-ienne**) Indonesian.

indou [HINDOU].

in-douze [ɛ̃′duːz], *n.m.* and *a. inv.* Duodecimo, 12mo.

indu [ɛ̃′dy], *a.* (*fem.* **indue**) Undue, unseasonable, late. *Heure indue*, unseasonable or late hour.

indubitable [ɛ̃dybi′tabl], *a.* Indubitable, certain, unquestionable. **indubitablement**, *adv.* Undoubtedly.

inductance [ɛ̃dyk′tɑ̃:s], *n.f.* Inductance. **inducteur**, *n.m.* Inductor, field-magnet.—*a.* (*fem.* **-trice**) inducing, inductive.

inductif [ɛ̃dyk′tif], *a.* (*fem.* **-ive**) Inductive.

induction [ɛ̃dyk′sjɔ̃], *n.f.* Induction, inference, implication. *Bobine d'induction*, induction coil.

induire [ɛ̃′dɥiːr], *v.t. irr.* (*conjug. like* CONDUIRE) To induce, to lead; to infer. *Induire en erreur*, to lead into error. **induit**, *a.* (*Elec.*) Induced (of a current).—*n.m.* Armature.

indulgemment [ɛ̃dylʒa′mɑ̃], *adv.* Indulgently.

indulgence [ɛ̃dyl′ʒɑ̃:s], *n.f.* Indulgence, forbearance, leniency. *Avoir de l'indulgence pour*, to make allowances for; *user d'indulgence envers*, to show indulgence to. **indulgent**, *a.* (*fem.* **-ente**) Indulgent, forbearing.

indult [ɛ̃′dylt], *n.m.* (*R.-C. Ch.*) Indult. **indultaire**, *n.m.* Incumbent or nominee (by virtue of an indult).

indûment [ɛ̃dy′mɑ̃], *adv.* Unduly, improperly.

induration [ɛ̃dyra'sjɔ̃], *n.f.* Induration, hardening. **induré,** *a.* (*fem.* **-ée**) Indurated. **indurer,** *v.t.* To harden, to indurate.
industrialisation [ɛ̃dystrializa'sjɔ̃], *n.f.* Industrialization. **industrialiser,** *v.t.* To industrialize. **s'industrialiser,** *v.r.* To become industrialized. **industrialisme,** *n.m.* Industrialism.
industrie [ɛ̃dys'tri], *n.f.* Dexterity, skill, ingenuity; business, trade; manufacturing; industry, work. *Chevalier d'industrie,* swindler, sharper; *industrie de base* or *industrie clef,* key industry; *vivre d'industrie,* to live by one's wits. **industriel,** *a.* (*fem.* **-ielle**) Industrial, manufacturing. *Les arts industriels,* mechanical arts; *les produits industriels,* industrial products; *richesses industrielles,* industrial wealth.—*n.m.* Manufacturer, mill-owner. **industriellement,** *adv.* Industrially. **industrieusement,** *adv.* Ingeniously, skilfully, industriously. **industrieux,** *a.* (*fem.* **-ieuse**) Ingenious, skilful, industrious.
inébranlable [inebrã'labl], *a.* Immovable, unshakeable; unmoved, unshaken; steady, firm, resolute. **inébranlablement,** *adv.* Immovably, steadily; resolutely.
inéchangeable [ineʃã'ʒabl], *a.* Unexchangeable.
inédit [ine'di], *a.* (*fem.* **-ite**) Unpublished; new.
ineffabilité [inɛfabili'te], *n.f.* Ineffability, unspeakableness. **ineffable,** *a.* Ineffable, inexpressible, unutterable. **ineffablement,** *adv.* Ineffably.
ineffaçable [inɛfa'sabl], *a.* Indelible, ineffaceable. **ineffaçablement,** *adv.* Indelibly, ineffaceably.
inefficace [inɛfi'kas], *a.* Inefficacious, ineffectual, unavailing, ineffective. **inefficacement,** *adv.* Ineffectively, ineffectually. **inefficacité,** *n.f.* Inefficacy, ineffectiveness.
inégal [ine'gal], *a.* (*fem.* **-ale,** *pl.* **-aux**) Unequal; uneven, rough; (*fig.*) disproportioned, ill-matched; irregular (of the pulse etc.). **inégalé,** *a.* (*fem.* **-ée**) Unqualled. **inégalement,** *adv.* Unequally, unevenly. **inégalité,** *n.f.* Inequality; unevenness, ruggedness; irregularity.
inélégamment [inelega'mã], *adv.* Inelegantly.
inélégance [inele'gã:s], *n.f.* Inelegance. **inélégant,** *a.* (*fem.* **-ante**) Inelegant.
inéligibilité [ineliʒibili'te], *n.f.* Ineligibility. **inéligible,** *a.* Ineligible.
inéluctable [inelyk'tabl], *a.* Ineluctable, unavoidable; indisputable, overwhelming, irresistible. **inéluctablement,** *adv.* Ineluctably.
inéludable [inely'dabl], *a.* Which cannot be evaded, inescapable.
inemployé [inãplwa'je], *a.* (*fem.* **-ée**) Unemployed, unused.
inénarrable [inena'rabl], *a.* Untellable; incredible.
inentamé [inãta'me], *a.* (*fem.* **-ée**) Intact; unshaken (faith etc.).
inepte [i'nɛpt], *a.* Foolish, silly, inept, absurd.
ineptie [inɛp'si], *n.f.* Ineptitude, foolishness, absurdity.
inépuisable [inepɥi'zabl], *a.* Inexhaustible. **inépuisablement,** *adv.* Inexhaustibly.

inéquitable [ineki'tabl], *a.* Unfair. **inéquitablement,** *adv.* Unfairly.
inerme [i'nɛrm], *a.* (*Bot.*) Thornless.
inerte [i'nɛrt], *a.* Inert, sluggish, inactive, dull.
inertie [inɛr'si], *n.f.* Inertia, state of inactivity; inertness, indolence. *Force d'inertie,* (*Phys.*) inertia, vis inertiae.
inespéré [inɛspe're], *a.* (*fem.* **-ée**) Unhoped for, unexpected. **inespérément,** *adv.* Unexpectedly.
inesthétique [inɛste'tik], *a.* Unaesthetic.
inestimable [inɛsti'mabl], *a.* Inestimable. **inestimé,** *a.* (*fem.* **-ée**) Unesteemed.
inévitable [inevi'tabl], *a.* Inevitable, unavoidable. **inévitablement,** *adv.* Inevitably, unavoidably.
inexact [ineg'zakt], *a.* (*fem.* **-te**) Inexact, inaccurate, incorrect, wrong. **inexactement,** *adv.* Inaccurately, incorrectly. **inexactitude,** *n.f.* Inexactness, incorrectness; inaccuracy, slip.
inexaucé [inegzo'se], *a.* (*fem.* **-ée**) Unfulfilled (wish); unheard (prayer).
inexcusable [inɛksky'zabl], *a.* Inexcusable, unjustifiable, unwarrantable.
inexécutable [inegzeky'tabl], *a.* Impracticable. **inexécuté,** *a.* (*fem.* **-ée**) Unexecuted, unperformed. **inexécution,** *n.f.* Non-performance, non-fulfilment.
inexercé [inegzɛr'se], *a.* (*fem.* **-ée**) Unexercised, unpractised, untrained.
inexigible [inegzi'ʒibl], *a.* Not demandable, not due.
inexistant [inegzis'tã], *a.* (*fem.* **-ante**) Non-existent.
inexorabilité [inegzɔrabili'te], *n.f.* Inexorability.
inexorable [inegzɔ'rabl], *a.* Inexorable, inflexible; unrelenting, pitiless. **inexorablement,** *adv.* Inexorably.
inexpérience [inɛkspe'rjã:s], *n.f.* Inexperience.
inexpérimenté [inɛksperimã'te], *a.* (*fem.* **-ée**) Inexperienced, unpractised; untried (of things).
inexpiable [inɛks'pjabl], *a.* Inexpiable, unatonable. **inexpié,** *a.* (*fem.* **-iée**) Unatoned.
inexplicable [inɛkspli'kabl], *a.* Inexplicable, unaccountable. **inexpliqué,** *a.* (*fem.* **-ée**) Unexplained.
inexploitable [inɛksplwa'tabl], *a.* Unworkable, uncultivable, useless. **inexploité,** *a.* (*fem.* **-ée**) Untilled, uncultivated (of land); unworked (of mines etc.); untapped (resources).
inexplorable [inɛksplɔ'rabl], *a.* Inexplorable. **inexploré** [inɛksplɔ're], *a.* (*fem.* **-ée**) Unexplored.
inexplosible [inɛksplo'zibl], *a.* Unexplosive.
inexpressible [inɛkspre'sibl], *a.* Inexpressible. **inexpressif,** *a.* (*fem.* **-ive**) Inexpressive, lacking expression. **inexprimable,** *a.* Inexpressible, unutterable, unspeakable.
inexpugnable [inɛkspy'nabl], *a.* Inexpugnable, impregnable.
inextensible [inɛkstã'sibl], *a.* Inextensible.
inextinguible [inɛkstɛ̃'gibl], *a.* Inextinguishable; unquenchable (thirst, fire); irrepressible (laughter).
inextricable [inɛkstri'kabl], *a.* Inextricable. **inextricablement,** *adv.* Inextricably.

infaillibilité [ɛ̃fajibili'te], *n.f.* Infallibility.
infaillible, *a.* Infallible; certain, unfailing.
infailliblement, *adv.* Infallibly, without fail, unerringly.
infaisable [ɛ̃fə'zabl], *a.* Impracticable, infeasible, not to be done.
infamant [ɛ̃fa'mɑ̃], *a.* (*fem.* **-ante**) Infamous, ignominious. *Peine infamante,* degrading punishment.
infâme [ɛ̃'fɑ:m], *a.* Infamous, base; squalid, sordid, filthy. *D'une manière infâme,* infamously.—*n.* Infamous person, wretch, villain. **infamie,** *n.f.* Infamy, ignominy; baseness, infamous action.
infant [ɛ̃'fɑ̃], *n.* (*fem.* **infante**) Infante, infanta (Spanish prince or princess).
infanterie [ɛ̃fɑ̃'tri], *n.f.* Infantry. *Infanterie de ligne,* line infantry; *l'infanterie de marine,* the marines (Engl.); the colonials (France).
infanticide [ɛ̃fɑ̃ti'sid], *n.m.* Infanticide. *n.* Child-murderer. **infantile** [ɛ̃fɑ̃'til], *a.* Infantile. *Mortalité infantile,* infant mortality. **infantilisme,** *n.m.* Infantilism.
infatigable [ɛ̃fati'gabl], *a.* Indefatigable, untiring, unwearied. **infatigablement,** *adv.* Indefatigably.
infatuation [ɛ̃fatɥa'sjɔ̃], *n.f.* Infatuation; self-conceit. **infatuer,** *v.t.* To infatuate. **s'infatuer,** *v.i.* To become infatuated.
infécond [ɛ̃fe'kɔ̃], *a.* (*fem.* **-onde**) Unfruitful, barren, sterile. **infécondité,** *n.f.* Unfruitfulness, barrenness, sterility.
infect [ɛ̃'fɛkt], *a.* (*fem.* **-te**) Infected, foul, noisome, stinking. *Odeur infecte,* stench. **infectant,** *a.* (*fem.* **-ante**) Infecting. **infecter,** *v.t.* To infect, to contaminate; to corrupt, to pollute, to taint.—*v.i.* To stink. **infectieux,** *a.* (*fem.* **-ieuse**) Infectious. **infection,** *n.f.* Infection; infectious disease; stench; (*fig.*) moral contagion. *Foyer d'infection,* hotbed of disease.
infélicité [ɛ̃felisi'te], *n.f.* Infelicity, unhappiness.
inféodation [ɛ̃feɔda'sjɔ̃], *n.f.* Infeudation, enfeoffment. **inféoder,** *v.t.* To enfeoff.
infère [ɛ̃'fɛ:r], *a.* (*Bot.*) Inferior, lower.
inférence [ɛ̃fe'rɑ̃:s], *n.f.* Conclusion, inference.
inférer [ɛ̃fe're], *v.t. irr.* (*conjug. like* ACCÉLÉRER) To infer, to conclude, to deduce.
inférieur [ɛ̃fe'rjœ:r], *a.* (*fem.* **-ieure**) Inferior, lower, nether; under, below.—*n.m.* Inferior; subordinate. **inférieurement,** *adv.* In an inferior manner, degree, etc. **infériorité,** *n.f.* Inferiority.
infermenté [ɛ̃fɛrmɑ̃'te], *a.* (*fem.* **-ée**) Unfermented. **infermentescible,** *a.* Unfermentable.
infernal [ɛ̃fɛr'nal], *a.* (*fem.* **-ale,** *pl.* **-aux**) Infernal, hellish. *Pierre infernale,* lunar caustic. **infernalement,** *adv.* Infernally.
infertile [ɛ̃fɛr'til], *a.* Infertile, unfruitful; sterile, barren. **infertilisable,** *a.* Infertilizable. **infertilité,** *n.f.* Unfruitfulness.
infester [ɛ̃fɛs'te], *v.t.* To infest, to overrun; to haunt.
infibulation [ɛ̃fibyla'sjɔ̃], *n.f.* Infibulation. **infibuler,** *v.t.* To infibulate.
infidèle [ɛ̃fi'dɛl], *a.* Unfaithful, faithless, untrue, false, disloyal; unbelieving, infidel; inaccurate, erroneous. *Infidèle à ses promesses,* false to one's promises; *la Fortune lui*

devint infidèle, Fortune deserted him.—*n.* Unfaithful person; infidel, unbeliever. **infidèlement,** *adv.* Unfaithfully; faithlessly; inaccurately. **infidélité,** *n.f.* Infidelity, faithlessness, disloyalty; unbelief; dishonesty, deceitfulness; inaccuracy. *Faire des infidélités à,* to be unfaithful to.
infiltration [ɛ̃filtra'sjɔ̃], *n.f.* Infiltration. **s'infiltrer,** *v.r.* To infiltrate, to percolate; (*fig.*) to creep, to filter in; (*Mil.*) to progress by infiltration.
infime [ɛ̃'fim], *a.* Lowest, mean (of ranks); tiny, minute.
infini [ɛ̃fi'ni], *a.* (*fem.* **infinie**) Infinite, boundless; endless; numberless; immense.—*n.m.* Infinite, infinity. *À l'infini,* to infinity, infinitely; endlessly. **infiniment,** *adv.* Infinitely, without end; exceedingly, extremely, immensely. *Il a infiniment d'esprit,* he is exceedingly witty; *l'infiniment petit,* the infinitesimal. **infinité,** *n.f.* Infinity, infiniteness, infinitude; (*fig.*) crowd, host, no end.
infinitésimal, *a.* (*fem.* **-ale,** *pl.* **-aux**) Infinitesimal, infinitely small. **infinitif,** *a.* (*fem.* **-ive**) (*Gram.*) Infinitive.—*n.m.* Infinitive mood.
infirmatif [ɛ̃firma'tif], *a.* (*fem.* **-ive**) (*Law*) Annulling, invalidating. **infirmation,** *n.f.* Invalidation, annulment, quashing.
infirme [ɛ̃'firm], *a.* Cripple, crippled, invalid; infirm, disabled; weak, feeble, sickly.—*n.* Invalid, cripple. **infirmer,** *v.t.* To weaken; to invalidate, to nullify, to quash. **infirmerie,** *n.f.* Infirmary, sick-ward; (*sch.*) sanatorium. **infirmier,** *n.m.* (*fem.* **-ière**) Hospital-attendant; nurse. **infirmité,** *n.f.* Infirmity, weakness, failing.
inflammabilité [ɛ̃flamabili'te], *n.f.* Inflammability. **inflammable,** *a.* Inflammable. **inflammation,** *n.f.* Inflammation; ignition (of a blasting charge). **inflammatoire,** *a.* Inflammatory.
inflation [ɛ̃fla'sjɔ̃], *n.f.* Inflation, swelling. **inflationnisme,** *n.m.* Inflationism. **inflationniste,** *a.* Inflationary.—*n.m.* Inflationist.
infléchi [ɛ̃fle'ʃi], *a.* (*fem.* **infléchie**) (*Opt.*) Inflected, bent. **infléchir,** *v.t.* To inflect, to bend. **s'infléchir,** *v.r.* To be inflected. **infléchissable,** *a.* Inflexible, unbendable.
inflexibilité [ɛ̃flɛksibili'te], *n.f.* Inflexibility. **inflexible,** *a.* Inflexible; unyielding, unbending. **inflexiblement,** *adv.* Inflexibly.
inflexion [ɛ̃flɛk'sjɔ̃], *n.f.* Inflexion; modulation, variation (of voice etc.).
inflictif [ɛ̃flik'tif], *a.* (*fem.* **-ive**) Inflictive.
infliction [ɛ̃flik'sjɔ̃], *n.f.* Infliction. **infliger,** *v.t.* To inflict, to impose. *S'infliger des privations,* to impose privations on oneself.
inflorescence [ɛ̃flɔrɛ'sɑ̃:s], *n.f.* Inflorescence.
influençable [ɛ̃flyɑ̃'sabl], *a.* That can be influenced.
influence [ɛ̃fly'ɑ̃:s], *n.f.* Influence; sway, power, authority. *Avoir beaucoup d'influence sur,* to have great influence over; *avoir de l'influence,* to be influential. **influencer,** *v.t.* To influence, to sway, to bias. *Se laisser influencer,* to let oneself be influenced. **influent,** *a.* (*fem.* **-ente**) Influential.
influenza [ɛ̃flyɑ̃'za], *n.f.* Influenza.
influer [ɛ̃fly'e], *v.i.* To have an influence (*sur,* on).

influx [ɛ̃'fly], *n.m.* **influxion** [ɛ̃flyk'sjɔ̃], *n.f.* Influx.

in-folio [ɛ̃fɔ'ljo], *n.m.* and *a. inv.* Folio (book).

informateur [ɛ̃fɔrma'tœːr], *n.m.* (*fem.* **-trice**) Informant.

information [ɛ̃fɔrma'sjɔ̃], *n.f.* Inquiry; information; (*pl.*) news. *Aller aux informations* or *prendre des informations*, to make inquiries; (*Rad.*) *bulletin d'information*, the news; *service des informations*, reporting staff.

informe [ɛ̃'fɔrm], *a.* Formless, shapeless; misshapen; crude, undigested, imperfect; (*Law*) informal.

informé [ɛ̃fɔr'me], *n.m.* (*Law*) *Pour plus ample informé*, for further inquiry.

informer [ɛ̃fɔr'me], *v.t.* (*Phil.*) To give form to; to inform, to acquaint, to give information to, to apprise.—*v.i.* To inquire, to investigate. *La justice informe*, proceedings have been taken. **s'informer**, *v.r.* To inquire, to make inquiries; to ask (*de*). *Il s'est informé de votre santé*, he inquired after your health.

informulé [ɛ̃fɔrmy'le], *a.* (*fem.* **-ée**) Unformulated.

infortune [ɛ̃fɔr'tyn], *n.f.* Misfortune, adversity. **infortuné**, *a.* (*fem.* **-ée**) Unfortunate, unhappy, ill-fated, wretched.—*n.* Unfortunate, unhappy, ill-fated, wretched (person).

infraction [ɛ̃frak'sjɔ̃], *n.f.* Infraction, infringement, breach, violation. *Une infraction à la loi*, a breach of the law.

infranchissable [ɛ̃frɑ̃ʃi'sabl], *a.* Insurmountable, insuperable.

infrangible [ɛ̃frɑ̃'ʒibl], *a.* Infrangible.

infra-rouge [ɛ̃fra'ruʒ], *a.* Infra-red.

infra-structure [ɛ̃frastryk'tyr], *n.f.* Understructure; bed (of road).

infréquenté [ɛ̃frekɑ̃'te], *a.* (*fem.* **-ée**) Unfrequented.

infroissable [ɛ̃frwa'sabl], *a.* Uncreasable.

infructueusement [ɛ̃fryktɥøz'mɑ̃], *adv.* Fruitlessly, to no purpose, in vain. **infructueux**, *a.* (*fem.* **-ueuse**) Unfruitful, vain, unavailing.

infus [ɛ̃'fy], *a.* (*fem.* **-use**) Infused, innate, inborn, native (of knowledge etc.).

infuser [ɛ̃fy'ze], *v.t.* To infuse, to instil. *Infuser à froid*, to steep. **s'infuser**, *v.r.* To infuse; to draw (of tea etc.). **infusibilité**, *n.f.* Infusibility. **infusible**, *a.* Infusible.

infusion, *n.f.* Infusion, decoction.

infusoires [ɛ̃fy'zwaːr], *n.m.* (*used chiefly in pl.*) (*Zool.*) Infusoria.

ingambe [ɛ̃'gɑ̃ːb], *a.* Nimble, brisk, active.

ingénier (s') [ɛ̃ʒe'nje], *v.r.* (*conjugated like* PRIER) To tax one's ingenuity, to employ all one's wits, to contrive. *Je m'ingénie à le faire*, I am leaving no stone unturned in order to accomplish it.

ingénieur [ɛ̃ʒe'njœːr], *n.m.* Engineer. *Ingénieur civil*, civil engineer; (*Cine.*) *ingénieur du son*, sound engineer; *ingénieur maritime*, naval architect; *ingénieur constructeur* (or *des constructions*), shipbuilder; *ingénieur des mines*, mining engineer; *ingénieur des ponts et chaussées*, civil engineer (under government) for bridges and roads in France; *le Corps des ingénieurs-géographes*, the Ordnance Survey.

ingénieusement [ɛ̃ʒenjøz'mɑ̃], *adv.* Ingeniously. **ingénieux**, *a.* (*fem.* **-ieuse**) Ingenious, clever, witty. **ingéniosité**, *n.f.* Ingenuity; cleverness.

ingénu [ɛ̃ʒe'ny], *a.* (*fem.* **-ue**) Ingenuous, frank, open; guileless, unsophisticated, simple, artless.—*n.* Ingenuous person, artless, unsophisticated, simple-minded person. *Faire l'ingénu*, to affect simplicity; *jouer les ingénues*, (*Theat.*) to play the parts of unsophisticated girls. **ingénuité**, *n.f.* Ingenuousness, frankness, openness, simplicity, lack of sophistication. **ingénument**, *adv.* Ingenuously, frankly.

ingérence [ɛ̃ʒe'rɑ̃ːs], *n.f.* Interference, meddling.

ingérer [ɛ̃ʒe're], *v.t. irr.* (*conjug. like* ACCÉLÉRER) To introduce, to ingest into (stomach etc.). **s'ingérer**, *v.r.* To meddle with, to interfere, to obtrude. *S'ingérer dans les affaires d'autrui*, to meddle with other people's business. **ingestion**, *n.f.* Introduction (of food etc.), ingestion.

inglorieusement [ɛ̃glɔrjøz'mɑ̃], *adv.* Ingloriously. **inglorieux**, *a.* (*fem.* **-ieuse**) Inglorious.

ingouvernable [ɛ̃guvɛr'nabl], *a.* Ungovernable, uncontrollable.

ingrat [ɛ̃'gra], *a.* (*fem.* **ingrate**) Unthankful, ungrateful; thankless, unprofitable, unfruitful, sterile; unpleasant. *L'âge ingrat*, the awkward age. **ingratitude**, *n.f.* Ingratitude, thanklessness, piece of ingratitude.

ingrédient [ɛ̃gre'djɑ̃], *n.m.* Ingredient.

inguéable [ɛ̃ge'abl], *a.* Unfordable.

inguérissable [ɛ̃geri'sabl], *a.* Incurable.

inguinal [ɛ̃gɥi'nal], *a.* (*fem.* **-ale**, *pl.* **-aux**) Inguinal.

ingurgitation [ɛ̃gyrʒita'sjɔ̃], *n.f.* Ingurgitation. **ingurgiter**, *v.t.* To ingurgitate, to gulp down.

inhabile [ina'bil], *a.* Unskilful, unskilled, inexpert; (*Law*) disqualified, unfit. **inhabilement**, *adv.* Unskilfully. **inhabileté**, *n.f.* Unskilfulness, incompetency, inability, incapacity; (*Law*) incompetency, disability.

inhabitable [inabi'tabl], *a.* Uninhabitable. **inhabité**, *a.* (*fem.* **-ée**) Uninhabited.

inhabitude [inabi'tyd], *n.f.* Unaccustomedness. **inhabitué**, *a.* (*fem.* **-ée**) Unaccustomed, unused.

inhalateur [inala'tœːr], *n.m.* Inhaler. **inhalation** [inala'sjɔ̃], *n.f.* Inhalation. **inhaler**, *v.t.* To inhale.

inharmonie [inarmɔ'ni], *n.f.* Lack of harmony. **inharmonieux**, *a.* (*fem.* **-ieuse**) Inharmonious, unmusical.

inhérence [ine'rɑ̃ːs], *n.f.* Inherence. **inhérent**, *a.* (*fem.* **-ente**) Inherent.

***inhiber** [ini'be], *v.t.* To prohibit; to inhibit. **inhibition** [inibi'sjɔ̃], *n.f.* (*Law*) Prohibition; (*Med.*) inhibition. **inhibitoire**, *a.* Inhibitory.

inhospitalier [inɔspita'lje], *a.* (*fem.* **-ière**) Inhospitable; (*fig.*) unfriendly, forbidding. **inhospitalièrement**, *adv.* Inhospitably.

inhumain [iny'mɛ̃], *a.* (*fem.* **inhumaine**) Inhuman, cruel.—*n.f. Une belle inhumaine*, a cruel fair one. **inhumainement**, *adv.* Inhumanly. **inhumanité**, *n.f.* Inhumanity, cruelty.

inhumation [inyma'sjɔ̃], *n.f.* Inhumation, interment. **inhumer**, *v.t.* To bury, to inter.

inimaginable [inimaʒi'nabl], *a.* Unimaginable, incomprehensible, inconceivable.

inimitable [inimi'tabl], *a.* Inimitable. **inimitablement**, *adv.* Inimitably.

inimitié [inimi'tje], *n.f.* Enmity, antipathy, aversion. *Avoir de l'inimitié pour*, to have hostile feelings towards, to have an aversion to.
inimprimable [inɛ̃pri'mabl], *a.* Unprintable.
ininflammabilité [inɛ̃flamabili'te], *n.f.* Non-inflammability. **ininflammable**, *a.* Non-inflammable, fire-proof.
inintelligemment [inɛ̃tɛliʒa'mɑ̃], *adv.* Unintelligently.
inintelligence [inɛ̃tɛli'ʒɑ̃:s], *n.f.* Lack of intelligence. **inintelligent**, *a.* (*fem.* -ente) Unintelligent. **inintelligible**, *a.* Unintelligible.
inintéressant [inɛ̃tɛrɛ'sɑ̃], *a.* (*fem.* -ante) Uninteresting.
ininterrompu [inɛ̃tɛrɔ̃'py], *a.* (*fem.* -ue) Uninterrupted.
inique [i'nik], *a.* Iniquitous; unrighteous. **iniquement**, *adv.* Iniquitously. **iniquité**, *n.f.* Iniquity, unrighteousness; evil-doing, injustice.
initial [ini'sjal], *a.* (*fem.* -iale, *pl.* -iaux) Initial.—*n.f.* Initial. **initialement**, *adv.* Initially.
initiateur [inisja'tœ:r], *n.m.* (*fem.* -trice) One who initiates, initiator. **initiation**, *n.f.* Initiation. **initiative**, *n.f.* Initiative. *Prendre l'initiative*, to take the initiative; *syndicat d'initiative*, tourist information bureau. **initié**, *a.* (*fem.* -ée) Initiated.—*n.* Initiate. **initier**, *v.t.* (*conjugated like* PRIER) To initiate, to admit.
injecté [ɛ̃ʒɛk'te], *a.* (*fem.* -ée) Injected. *Yeux injectés de sang*, bloodshot eyes; *bois injecté*, creosoted wood.
injecter [ɛ̃ʒɛk'te], *v.t.* To inject. **s'injecter**, *v.r.* To become injected or bloodshot. **injecteur**, *n.m.* Injector.—*a.* (*fem.* -trice) Injecting. **injection**, *n.f.* Injection.
injonction [ɛ̃ʒɔ̃k'sjɔ̃], *n.f.* Injunction, order, behest. *Faire injonction à*, to enjoin upon.
injouable [ɛ̃'ʒwabl], *a.* Unplayable, unactable.
injudicieusement [ɛ̃ʒydisjøz'mɑ̃], *adv.* Injudiciously. **injudicieux**, *a.* (*fem.* -ieuse) Injudicious.
injure [ɛ̃'ʒy:r], *n.f.* Injury, wrong; insult, offence; (*pl.*) abuse, abusive language; (*Law*) slander. *Avoir toujours l'injure à la bouche*, to be abusive, to be foul-mouthed; *dire des injures à quelqu'un*, to abuse someone; *faire injure à quelqu'un*, to wrong someone; *ils se sont dit mille injures*, they abused each other roundly. **injurier**, *v.t.* To abuse, to call names, to insult. **injurieusement**, *adv.* *Injuriously, wrongfully; abusively, insultingly. **injurieux**, *a.* (*fem.* -ieuse) *Injurious, wrongful; abusive, offensive, insulting.
injuste [ɛ̃'ʒyst], *a.* Unjust, unfair, wrong, wrongful.—*n.m.* What is unjust. *Le juste et l'injuste*, right and wrong. **injustement**, *adv.* Unjustly, wrongly. **injustice**, *n.f.* Injustice; wrong, act of injustice. **injustifiable**, *a.* Unjustifiable. **injustifié**, *a.* (*fem.* -ée) Unjustified, groundless.
inlassable [ɛ̃la'sabl], *a.* Untirable. **inlassablement**, *adv.* Untiringly.
inné [in'ne], *a.* (*fem.* -ée) Innate, inborn. *Les idées innées*, innate ideas.
innégociable [innego'sjabl], *a.* Not negotiable.
innervation [innɛrva'sjɔ̃], *n.f.* Innervation. **innerver**, *v.t.* To innervate.

innocemment [inɔsa'mɑ̃], *adv.* Innocently.
innocence [inɔ'sɑ̃:s], *n.f.* Innocence; guiltlessness; harmlessness; inoffensiveness; artlessness, simplicity, silliness. **innocent**, *a.* (*fem.* -ente) Innocent, guiltless; harmless, inoffensive; guileless, simple. *Il a été reconnu innocent*, he was found not guilty; *se déclarer innocent*, to plead not guilty; *tenir pour innocent*, to hold guiltless.—*n.* Simpleton; idiot, natural. *Faire l'innocent*, to sham innocence; (*Bibl.*) *les Saints Innocents*, the Holy Innocents. **innocenter**, *v.t.* To acquit, to clear of a charge.
innocuité [innɔkɥi'te], *n.f.* Innocuousness, harmlessness.
innombrable [innɔ̃'brabl], *a.* Innumerable, numberless. **innombrablement**, *adv.* Innumerably.
innomé (*Law*) [INNOMMÉ].
innominé [innɔmi'ne], *a.* (*fem.* -ée) Nameless, unnamed. (*Anat.*) *L'os innominé*, the hip-bone.
innommable [innɔ'mabl], *a.* Unnamable.
innommé [innɔm'e], *a.* (*fem.* -ée) Unnamed, nameless.
innovateur [innɔva'tœ:r], *n.m.* (*fem.* -trice) Innovator.—*a.* Innovating.
innovation [innɔva'sjɔ̃], *n.f.* Innovation. **innover**, *v.i.* To innovate, to make innovations.
inobservable [inɔpsɛr'vabl], *a.* Inobservable.
inobservance [inɔpsɛr'vɑ̃:s] or **inobservation**, *n.f.* Non-observance. **inobservé**, *a.* (*fem.* -ée) Unobserved, unnoticed, overlooked.
inoccupation [inɔkypa'sjɔ̃], *n.f.* Inoccupation. **inoccupé**, *a.* (*fem.* -ée) Unoccupied; idle; vacant.
in-octavo [inɔkta'vo], *n.m. and a. inv.* Octavo, 8vo.
inoculable [inɔky'labl], *a.* Inoculable.
inoculateur [inɔkyla'tœ:r], *n.m.* (*fem.* -trice) Inoculator.
inoculation [inɔkyla'sjɔ̃], *n.f.* Inoculation. **inoculer**, *v.t.* To inoculate.
inodore [inɔ'dɔ:r], *a.* Inodorous, scentless, free from smell or effluvia.
inoffensif [inɔfɑ̃'sif], *a.* (*fem.* -ive) Inoffensive, harmless; innocuous. **inoffensivement**, *adv.* Inoffensively.
inofficiel [inɔfi'sjɛl], *a.* (*fem.* -elle) Unofficial. **inofficiellement**, *adv.* Unofficially.
inofficieusement [inɔfisjøz'mɑ̃], *adv.* Inofficiously.
inofficieux [inɔfi'sjø], *a.* (*fem.* -ieuse) (*Law*) Inofficious (will).
inondable [inɔ̃'dabl], *a.* That can be easily flooded.
inondation [inɔ̃dɑ'sjɔ̃], *n.f.* Inundation, flood, deluge. **inonder**, *v.t.* To inundate, to overflow, to deluge; (*fig.*) to overrun, to overspread, to overwhelm.
inopérant [inɔpe'rɑ̃], *a.* (*fem.* -ante) Inoperative, invalid; inefficient.
inopiné [inɔpi'ne], *a.* (*fem.* -ée) Unforeseen, unexpected, sudden. **inopinément**, *adv.* Unawares, unexpectedly, suddenly.
inopportun [inɔpɔr'tœ̃], *a.* (*fem.* -une) Inopportune, unseasonable, untimely. **inopportunément**, *adv.* Inopportunely.

inopportunité, *n.f.* Inopportuneness, unseasonableness.
inorganique [inɔrga'nik], *a.* Inorganic.
inosculation [inɔskyla'sjɔ̃], *n.f.* (*Anat.*) Inosculation, anastomosis.
inostensible [inɔstɑ̃'sibl], *a.* Inostensible.
inostensiblement, *adv.* Inostensibly.
inoubliable [inubli'abl], *a.* Unforgettable.
inoublié, *a.* (*fem.* **-iée**) Unforgotten, well-remembered.
inouï [i'nwi], *a.* (*fem.* **inouïe**) Unheard of, unprecedented, extraordinary, wonderful.
inoxydable [inɔksi'dabl], *a.* Unoxidizable, rustless, rust-proof, stainless.
in-plano [ɛ̃pla'no], *n.m.* and *a. inv.* Full sheet, broadside.
inqualifiable [ɛ̃kali'fjabl], *a.* Unqualifiable, for which no name is too bad, unspeakable.
inquart [ɛ̃'ka:r], *n.m.,* **inquartation** or **quartation,** *n.f.* Quartation.
in-quarto [ɛ̃kwar'to], *n.m.* and *a. inv.* Quarto, 4to.
inquiet [ɛ̃'kjɛ], *a.* (*fem.* **-iète**) Disquieted, anxious, uneasy; unquiet, restless, agitated, fidgety. **inquiétant,** *a.* (*fem.* **-ante**) Disquieting, alarming. **inquiéter,** *v.t.* To disquiet, to make uneasy, to alarm, to worry; to disturb, to trouble; to harass. **s'inquiéter,** *v.r.* To be anxious, to be uneasy. *Ne vous inquiétez pas,* don't worry. **inquiétude,** *n.f.* Disquiet, restlessness; anxiety, uneasiness, concern, solicitude; (*pl.*) slight pains, fidgets. *Avoir des inquiétudes,* to be uneasy; *avoir des inquiétudes dans les jambes,* to have twitchings in the legs; *donner de l'inquiétude à,* to make uneasy; *il est sans inquiétude au sujet de son avenir,* he is without anxiety about the future; *soyez sans inquiétude là-dessus,* make yourself easy on that score.
inquisiteur [ɛ̃kizi'tœ:r], *a.m.* Inquisitorial; inquisitive.—*n.m.* Inquisitor. **inquisitif,** *a.* (*fem.* **-ive**) Inquisitive.
inquisition [ɛ̃kizi'sjɔ̃], *n.f.* Inquisition. **inquisitorial,** *a.* (*fem.* **inquisitoriale,** *pl.* **inquisitoriaux**) Inquisitorial.
inracontable [ɛ̃rakɔ̃'tabl], *a.* Unrelatable.
insaisissable [ɛ̃sezi'sabl], *a.* Unseizable, imperceptible; (*Law*) not distrainable.
insalissable [ɛ̃sali'sabl], *a.* Dirt-proof.
insalubre [ɛ̃sa'lybr], *a.* Insalubrious, unhealthy, unwholesome. **insalubrement,** *adv.* Insalubriously, unhealthily. **insalubrité,** *n.f.* Insalubrity, unhealthiness, unwholesomeness.
insanité [ɛ̃sani'te], *n.f.* Insanity; (*pl.*) complete nonsense.
insatiabilité [ɛ̃sasjabili'te], *n.f.* Insatiability. **insatiable,** *a.* Insatiable.
insatisfaction [ɛ̃satisfak'sjɔ̃], *n.f.* Unsatisfaction. **insatisfait,** *a.* (*fem.* **-aite**) Unsatisfied.
insaturable [ɛ̃saty'rabl], *a.* Non-saturable.
insciemment [ɛ̃sja'mɑ̃], *adv.* Unwittingly, unknowingly.
inscriptible [ɛ̃skrip'tibl], *a.* (*Geom.*) Inscribable.
inscription [ɛ̃skrip'sjɔ̃], *n.f.* Inscription, inscribing; registry, entry, matriculation, term (of schools); stock-receipt, scrip; (*Law*) allegation, plea. *Inscription de faux,* allegation of forgery; *inscription hypothécaire,* registry of mortgage; *prendre ses inscriptions,* (*sch.*)

to enter for the term; (*Naut.*) *l'inscription maritime,* seaboard conscription (for the navy).
inscrire [ɛ̃s'kri:r], *v.t. irr.* (*conjug. like* ÉCRIRE) To inscribe, to enter, to set down, to register. **s'inscrire,** *v.r.* To inscribe oneself; to enter one's name. *S'inscrire en faux contre,* (*Law*) to deny the truth of, to protest against.
inscrit [ɛ̃s'kri], *n.m.* *Inscrit maritime,* man enrolled in the navy.
inscrutabilité [ɛ̃skrytabili'te], *n.f.* Inscrutability. **inscrutable,** *a.* Inscrutable, unfathomable.
insécable [ɛ̃se'kabl], *a.* Insecable, indivisible.
insecte [ɛ̃'sɛkt], *n.m.* Insect. **insecticide,** *a.* Insect-destroying.—*n.m.* Insecticide. **insectivore,** *a.* Insectivorous.—*n.m.* Insectivore.
insécurité [ɛ̃sekyri'te], *n.f.* Insecurity.
in-seize [ɛ̃'sɛ:z], *n.m.* and *a. inv.* Sixteen-mo, sextodecimo, 16mo.
insémination [ɛ̃semina'sjɔ̃], *n.f.* Insemination (cows, ewes, etc.). **inséminer,** *v.t.* To inseminate.
insensé [ɛ̃sɑ̃'se], *a.* (*fem.* **-ée**) Insane, mad; foolish, senseless.—*n.* Insane person, madman, madwoman, maniac; (*fig.*) fool.
insensibilisation [ɛ̃sɑ̃sibiliza'sjɔ̃], *n.f.* Anaesthetization. **insensibiliser,** *v.t.* To anaesthetize.
insensibilité [ɛ̃sɑ̃sibili'te], *n.f.* Insensibility, unconsciousness; unfeelingness, callousness. **insensible,** *a.* Insensible, unconscious; unfeeling, hard-hearted, callous, insensitive; imperceptible. **insensiblement,** *adv.* Insensibly; gradually, by degrees, imperceptibly.
inséparabilité [ɛ̃separabili'te], *n.f.* Inseparability. **inséparable,** *a.* Inseparable.—*n.m. pl.* (*Orn.*) Love-birds. **inséparablement,** *adv.* Inseparably.
insérer [ɛ̃se're], *v.t. irr.* (*conjug. like* ACCÉLÉRER) To insert, to put in; to thrust or wedge in. *Prière d'insérer,* request to publish.
insermenté [ɛ̃sɛrmɑ̃'te], *a.* (*fem.* **-ée**) Unsworn.
insertion [ɛ̃sɛr'sjɔ̃], *n.f.* Insertion.
insidieusement [ɛ̃sidjøz'mɑ̃], *adv.* Insidiously. **insidieux,** *a.* (*fem.* **-ieuse**) Insidious.
insigne [ɛ̃'siɲ], *a.* Distinguished, conspicuous, notorious, arrant. *L'insigne honneur,* the high honour.—*n.m.* Badge, mark; (*pl.*) insignia.
insignifiance [ɛ̃siɲi'fjɑ̃s], *n.f.* Insignificance. **insignifiant,** *a.* (*fem.* **-iante**) Insignificant, trifling, trivial.
insincère [ɛ̃sɛ̃'sɛ:r], *a.* Insincere.
insinuant [ɛ̃si'nɥɑ̃], *a.* (*fem.* **-ante**) Insinuating.
insinuation [ɛ̃sinɥa'sjɔ̃], *n.f.* Insinuation, hint, innuendo. **insinuer,** *v.t.* To insinuate; to hint, to suggest; to instil. **s'insinuer,** *v.r.* To insinuate oneself (*dans*), to creep or worm one's way.
insipide [ɛ̃si'pid], *a.* Insipid, tasteless; dull, flat. **insipidement,** *adv.* Insipidly. **insipidité,** *n.f.* Insipidity.
insistance [ɛ̃sis'tɑ̃:s], *n.f.* Insistence, persistence. **insistant,** *a.* (*fem.* **-ante**) Insistent. **insister,** *v.i.* To insist, to lay stress (*sur*).
insociabilité [ɛ̃sɔsjabili'te], *n.f.* Unsociableness. **insociable,** *a.* Unsociable; difficult to live with. **insociablement,** *adv.* Unsociably.

insolation [ɛsɔlɑ'sjɔ̃], *n.f.* Insolation, sunstroke.

insolemment [ɛsɔla'mɑ̃], *adv.* Insolently, impudently.

insolence [ɛsɔ'lɑ̃:s], *n.f.* Insolence, sauciness; impertinence, rudeness. **insolent,** *a.* (*fem.* -ente) Insolent, impudent, rude.—*n.* Insolent person.

insolite [ɛsɔ'lit], *a.* Unusual, unwonted, unprecedented.

insolubilité [ɛsɔlybili'te], *n.f.* Insolubility. **insoluble,** *a.* Insoluble.

insolvabilité [ɛsɔlvabili'te], *n.f.* Insolvency. **insolvable,** *a.* Insolvent.

insomnie [ɛsɔm'ni], *n.f.* Sleeplessness, insomnia. *Nuits d'insomnie,* sleepless nights.

insondable [ɛsɔ̃'dabl], *a.* Unfathomable.

insonore [ɛsɔ'nɔr], *a.* Sound-proof. **insonorisation,** *n.f.* Sound insulation. **insonorisé,** *a.* (*fem.* -ée) Sound-proofed.

insouciance [ɛsu'sjɑ̃:s], *n.f.* Carelessness, thoughtlessness, heedlessness, recklessness. **insouciant** or **insoucieux,** *a.* (*fem.* -iante or -ieuse) Careless, thoughtless, heedless, unconcerned; listless, indifferent, free from care, easy-going.

insoumis [ɛsu'mi], *a.* (*fem.* -ise) Unsubdued; refractory, contumacious, unruly.—*n.m.* (*Mil.*) Defaulting recruit, absentee. **insoumission,** *n.f.* Insubordination.

insoupçonnable [ɛsupsɔ'nabl], *a.* Above suspicion. **insoupçonné** *a.* (*fem.* -ée) Unsuspected.

insoutenable [ɛsut'nabl], *a.* Indefensible, untenable, unwarrantable; insupportable, unbearable.

inspecter [ɛspɛk'te], *v.t.* To inspect, to survey, to scan. **inspecteur,** *n.m.* (*fem.* **inspectrice**) Inspector, superintendent, surveyor. *Inspecteur (de police),* superintendent; *inspecteur des contributions directes,* inspector of taxes; *inspecteur du travail,* factory inspector. **inspection,** *n.f.* Inspection, survey; superintendence; inspectorship; (*Mil.*) muster. *Faire l'inspection de,* to examine, to inspect; *passer à l'inspection,* to undergo inspection. **inspectorat,** *n.m.* Inspectorate; inspectorship.

inspirant [ɛspi'rɑ̃], *a.* (*fem.* -ante) Inspiring. **inspirateur** [ɛspira'tœ:r], *a.* (*fem.* -trice) Inspiring; (*Anat.*) inspiratory.—*n.* Inspirer; inspiratory muscle.

inspiration [ɛspira'sjɔ̃], *n.f.* Inspiration, suggestion; inhaling. **inspiré,** *a.* and *n.* (*fem.* -ée) Inspired (person). **inspirer,** *v.t.* To inspire, to breathe into; to cause to inhale; (*fig.*) to suggest, to prompt, to instil, to urge. **s'inspirer,** *v.r.* To draw one's inspiration (*de*).

instabilité [ɛstabili'te], *n.f.* Instability, fickleness. **instable,** *a.* Unstable; cranky (ship); unsteady (table); wobbly (chair).

installation [ɛstala'sjɔ̃], *n.f.* Installation; fitting up; equipment, plant. **installer,** *v.t.* To install, to fit or set up; to induct, to inaugurate, to establish; (*Mil. slang*) to set out one's equipment for checking of kit in detail; (*pop.*) to show off, to brag. **s'installer,** *v.r.* To install oneself; to settle oneself (*dans*).

instamment [ɛsta'mɑ̃], *adv.* Earnestly, urgently.

instance [ɛs'tɑ̃:s], *n.f.* Entreaty, solicitation;

urgency, earnestness; (*Law*) instance, suit; (*pl.*) entreaties, request. *Avec instance,* earnestly; *en instance de,* on the point of; *faire de grandes* or *de vives instances,* to entreat earnestly; *tribunal de première instance,* inferior court.

instant (1) [ɛs'tɑ̃], *n.m.* Instant, moment. *À l'instant* or *dans un instant,* in an instant, immediately; *à tout instant* or *à chaque instant,* at every moment.

instant (2) [ɛs'tɑ̃], *a.* (*fem.* -ante) Pressing, urgent; imminent. **instantané,** *a.* (*fem.* -ée) Instantaneous.—*n.m.* Snapshot. **instantanéité,** *n.f.* Instantaneousness. **instantanément,** *adv.* Instantaneously.

instar (à l') [ɛs'ta:r], *prep. phr.* *À l'instar de,* like; in imitation of.

instaurateur [ɛstɔra'tœ:r], *n.m.* (*fem.* -trice) Founder. **instauration,** *n.f.* Founding.

instaurer [ɛstɔ're], *v.t.* To establish, to found, to set up.

instigateur [ɛstiga'tœ:r], *n.m.* (*fem.* -trice) Instigator.

instigation [ɛstiga'sjɔ̃], *n.f.* Instigation. *À l'instigation de,* at the instigation of.

instillation [ɛstila'sjɔ̃], *n.f.* Instillation. **instiller,** *v.t.* To instil.

instinct [ɛs'tɛ̃], *n.m.* Instinct. *D'instinct* or *par instinct,* instinctively. *Instinct de conservation,* self-preservation instinct. **instinctif,** *a.* (*fem.* -ive) Instinctive. **instinctivement,** *adv.* Instinctively.

instituer [ɛsti'tɥe], *v.t.* To institute, to establish; to settle; to appoint. **s'instituer,** *v.r.* To institute oneself; to be established.

institut [ɛsti'ty], *n.m.* Institution; institute; order or rule (of monks). *L'Institut de France,* the Institute (the 5 Academies). **institutes,** *n.f. pl.* (*Law*) Institutes.

instituteur [ɛstity'tœ:r], *n.m.* (*fem.* -trice) Teacher, schoolmaster, schoolmistress (in primary schools). *Institutrice (particulière),* governess.

institution [ɛstity'sjɔ̃], *n.f.* Institution; establishment; (*Law*) appointment.

instructeur [ɛstryk'tœ:r], *n.m.* Instructor, drill-master.—*a.m.* *Juge instructeur,* examining magistrate. *Sergent instructeur,* drill-sergeant. **instructif,** *a.* (*fem.* -ive) Instructive.

instruction [ɛstryk'sjɔ̃], *n.f.* Instruction, tuition, education, knowledge, learning; (*Law*) inquiry, examination; *pl.* directions, orders. *Avoir de l'instruction,* to be well informed, well educated; *homme de grande instruction,* man of high attainments; *sans instruction,* untaught, uneducated, illiterate. *Juge d'instruction,* examining magistrate. *Donner des instructions détaillées,* to give precise instructions.

instruire [ɛs'trɥi:r], *v.t. irr.* (*pres.p.* **instruisant,** *p.p.* **instruit,** *conjug. like* CONDUIRE) To instruct, to teach, to educate, to train up; to give instruction (*dans*); to inform (*de*), to apprise, to acquaint (*de*); (*Law*) to investigate, to examine. **s'instruire,** *v.r.* To instruct, inform, or improve oneself. **instruisable,** *a.* Teachable. **instruit,** *a.* (*fem.* **instruite**) Instructed, informed; aware; well-informed, educated; trained, exercised.

instrument [ɛstry'mɑ̃], *n.m.* Instrument, implement, tool; document (deed, treaty,

etc.). *Instrument tranchant*, edge-tool; *instruments aratoires*, agricultural implements; *servir d'instrument*, to be instrumental. **instrumentaire,** *a.* (*Law*) *Témoin instrumentaire*, witness (required by law) to a deed. **instrumental,** *a.* (*fem.* **-ale,** *pl.* **-aux**) Instrumental. **instrumentation,** *n.f.* (*Mus.*) Instrumentation. **instrumenter,** *v.i.* (*Law*) To draw up deeds, indentures, etc.; to serve writs; to compose instrumental music.—*v.t.* To score (an opera etc.). **instrumentiste,** *n.m.* Instrumentalist.
insu (à l') [ɛ̃'sy], *prep. phr.* Without the knowledge (*de*). *À l'insu de son père*, unknown to his father; *à mon insu* or *à votre insu*, unknown to me *or* to you.
insubmersible [ɛ̃sybmɛr'sibl], *a.* Unsinkable.
insubordination [ɛ̃sybɔrdinɑ'sjɔ̃], *n.f.* Insubordination. **insubordonné, a.** (*fem.* **-ée**) Insubordinate.
insuccès [ɛ̃syk'sɛ], *n.m.* inv. Failure, want of success.
insuffisamment [ɛ̃syfiza'mɑ̃], *adv.* Insufficiently. **insuffisance,** *n.f.* Insufficiency. **insuffisant,** *a.* (*fem.* **-ante**) Insufficient, inadequate, not equal to.
insufflateur [ɛ̃syfla'tœːr], *n.m.* Insufflator, sprayer (for throat or nose).
insufflation [ɛ̃syflɑ'sjɔ̃], *n.f.* Insufflation. **insuffler,** *v.t.* To insufflate, to spray; to blow up, to inflate.
insulaire [ɛ̃sy'lɛːr], *a.* Insular.—*n.* Islander. **insularité** [ɛ̃sylari'te], *n.f.* Insularity.
insuline [ɛ̃sy'lin], *n.f.* Insulin.
insultant [ɛ̃syl'tɑ̃], *a.* (*fem.* **-ante**) Insulting. **insulte** [ɛ̃'sylt], *n.f.* Insult. *Avec insulte,* insultingly; *faire une insulte à quelqu'un*, to insult someone; *supporter une insulte,* to brook an insult. **insulter,** *v.t.* To insult, to affront.—*v.i.* To be insulting (*à*); to offer an insult (*à*). **insulteur,** *n.m.* Insulter, reviler.
insupportable [ɛ̃sypɔr'tabl], *a.* Insupportable, insufferable, intolerable, unbearable. **insupportablement,** *adv.* Insupportably, insufferably, intolerably, unbearably.
insurgé [ɛ̃syr'ʒe], *a.* (*fem.* **-ée**) Insurgent, in a state of insurrection.—*n.* Insurgent, rebel. **insurgence,** *n.f.* Insurrection. **insurgents, *n.m.* *pl.*** Rebels. **s'insurger,** *v.r.* To revolt, to rebel, to rise in insurrection.
insurmontable [ɛ̃syrmɔ̃'tabl], *a.* Insurmountable, insuperable, invincible. **insurmontablement,** *adv.* Insurmountably, insuperably.
insurpassable [ɛ̃syrpɑ'sabl], *a.* Unsurpassable.
insurrection [ɛ̃syrɛk'sjɔ̃], *n.f.* Insurrection, rising. **insurrectionnel,** *a.* (*fem.* **-elle**) Insurrectionary.
intact [ɛ̃'takt], *a.* (*fem.* **intacte**) Intact, unblemished, untainted, irreproachable, entire, whole; untouched, inviolate.
intactile [ɛ̃tak'til], *a.* Intactile.
intaille [ɛ̃'taːj], *n.f.* Intaglio.
intangibilité [ɛ̃tɑ̃ʒibili'te], *n.f.* Intangibility. **intangible, a.** Intangible.
intarissable [ɛ̃tari'sabl], *a.* Inexhaustible, never-failing, perennial. **intarissablement,** *adv.* Endlessly.
intégral [ɛ̃te'gral], *a.* (*fem.* **-ale,** *pl.* **-aux**) Integral, whole, entire.—*n.f.* (*Math.*) Integral. **intégralement,** *adv.* Integrally,

entirely, wholly, in full. **intégralité,** *n.f.* Integrality, completeness. **intégrant,** *a.* (*fem.* **-ante**) Integral, integrant. **intégration,** *n.f.* Integration.
intègre [ɛ̃'tegr], *a.* Honest, upright, just. **intègrement,** *adv.* Honestly, uprightly.
intégrer [ɛ̃te'gre], *v.t.* (*Math.*) To integrate. **intégrité** [ɛ̃tegri'te], *n.f.* Integrity, uprightness, probity; soundness, entireness.
intellect [ɛ̃tɛ'lɛkt], *n.m.* Intellect, understanding. **intellectif,** *a.* (*fem.* **-ive**) Intellective. **intellectuel, a.** (*fem.* **-elle**) Intellectual.— *n.* *Un intellectuel*, an intellectual, a high-brow. **intellectuellement,** *adv.* Intellectually.
intelligemment [ɛ̃tɛliʒa'mɑ̃], *adv.* Intelligently.
intelligence [ɛ̃tɛli'ʒɑ̃ːs], *n.f.* Intelligence, intellect; clear comprehension or understanding; cleverness, skill, ability; mutual understanding, intercourse; correspondence, means of information. *Avec intelligence,* skilfully, cleverly; *avoir des intelligences avec l'ennemi*, to have (secret) dealings with the enemy; *en bonne intelligence avec*, on good terms with; *être d'intelligence avec*, to be in collusion with; *intelligence étroite*, narrow intellect; *intelligence lente*, dull apprehension. **intelligent,** *a.* (*fem.* **-ente**) Intelligent; bright, shrewd, clever, sharp.
intelligibilité [ɛ̃tɛliʒibili'te], *n.f.* Intelligibility. **intelligible,** *a.* Intelligible, comprehensible; audible, distinct, clear. **intelligiblement,** *adv.* Intelligibly, audibly, clearly.
intempéramment [ɛ̃tɑ̃pera'mɑ̃], *adv.* Intemperately, immoderately.
intempérance [ɛ̃tɑ̃pe'rɑ̃ːs], *n.f.* Intemperance, insobriety. **intempérant,** *a.* (*fem.* **-ante**) Intemperate. **intempéré,** *a.* (*fem.* **-ée**) Ill-regulated, ill-conditioned. **intempérie,** *n.f.* (*usu. in pl.*) Inclemency (of the seasons etc.), bad weather.
intempestif [ɛ̃tɑ̃pes'tif], *a.* (*fem.* **-ive**) Unseasonable, untimely. **intempestivement,** *adv.* Unseasonably.
intenable [ɛ̃ta'nabl], *a.* Untenable, insufferable.
intendance [ɛ̃tɑ̃'dɑ̃ːs], *n.f.* Stewardship (of an estate); (*Mil.*) commissariat; the Army Service Corps. *Les bureaux de l'intendance*, the quarter-master general's offices. **intendant, *n.m.*** Intendant, steward; major-domo; (*Mil.*) administrative officer (having rank of a general). *Intendant de la liste civile*, comptroller of the civil list. *Intendant universitaire*, (*sch.*) bursar. **intendante, *n.f.*** Wife of intendant; directress (of some convents); bursar.
intense [ɛ̃'tɑ̃ːs], *a.* Intense, violent; severe (cold); strenuous (life). **intensif,** *a.* (*fem.* **-ive**) Intensive. **intensifier,** *v.t.* to intensify, **intensité,** *n.f.* Intensity, violence, severity. **intensivement,** *adv.* Intensively.
intenter [ɛ̃tɑ̃'te], *v.t.* (*Law*) *Intenter une action* or *un procès à* or *contre quelqu'un*, to enter *or* to bring an action against someone.
intention [ɛ̃tɑ̃'sjɔ̃], *n.f.* Intention; (*Law*) intent; purpose, design; meaning, drift. *À l'intention de,* for the sake of; for, to (the) behoof of; *à mon intention, à votre intention, etc.,* for my sake, for your sake, etc.; *avec intention,* on purpose; *avoir*

l'intention de, to intend to; *dans la meilleure intention,* with the best intentions; *dans l'intention de,* with a view to; *l'intention est réputée pour le fait,* the will is as good as the deed; *sans intention,* unintentionally, without design. **intentionné,** *a.* (*fem.* **-ée**) Intentioned, disposed, meaning. *Une personne bien intentionnée,* a well-intentioned or well-disposed person. **intentionnel,** *a.* (*fem.* **-elle**) Intentional, wilful. **intentionnellement,** *adv.* Wilfully, deliberately.
inter [ɛ̃tɛr], *n.m.* (*Ftb.*) Inside (-forward). *Inter droit,* inside-right. (*Teleph.*) (*fam.*) *L'inter* [ɪNTERURBAIN].
interaction [ɛ̃tɛrak'sjɔ̃], *n.f.* Interaction.
interallié [ɛ̃tɛra'lje], *a.* (*fem.* **-ée**) Interallied.
interarmes [ɛ̃tɛr'arm], *a. inv.* Combined (staff etc.).
interarticulaire [ɛ̃tɛrartiky'lɛ:r], *a.* Interarticular.
interastral [ɛ̃tɛras'tral], *a.* (*fem.* **-ale,** *pl* **-aux**) Interstellar.
interatomique [ɛ̃tɛratɔ'mik], *a.* Interatomic.
intercadence [ɛ̃tɛrka'dɑ̃:s], *n.f.* (*Med.*) Irregular beating of the pulse. **intercadent,** *a.* (*fem.* **-ente**) Irregular (of the pulse).
intercalaire [ɛ̃tɛrka'lɛ:r], *a.* Intercalary (day); interpolated (sheet of paper).
intercalation [ɛ̃tɛrkala'sjɔ̃], *n.f.* Intercalation. **intercaler,** *v.t.* To intercalate; to interpolate; (*Elec.*) to switch in.
intercéder [ɛ̃tɛrse'de], *v.i.* To intercede, to plead.
intercellulaire [ɛ̃tɛrsɛly'lɛ:r], *a.* Intercellular.
intercepter [ɛ̃tɛrsɛp'te], *v.t.* To intercept. **intercepteur,** *n.m.* (*Av.*) Interceptor fighter.
interception, *n.f.* Interception.
intercesseur [ɛ̃tɛrsɛ'sœ:r], *n.m.* Intercessor, interceder. **intercession,** *n.f.* Intercession; mediation.
interchangeable [ɛ̃tɛrʃɑ̃'ʒabl], *a.* Commutable, interchangeable.
intercommunication [ɛ̃tɛrkɔmynika'sjɔ̃], *n.f.* Intercommunication.
interconnecter [ɛ̃tɛrkɔnɛk'te], *v.t.* (*Elec.*) To interconnect.
intercontinental [ɛ̃tɛrkɔ̃tinɑ̃'tal], *a.* (*fem.* **-ale,** *pl.* **-aux**) Intercontinental.
intercostal [ɛ̃tɛrkɔs'tal], *a.* (*fem.* **-ale,** *pl.* **-aux**) (*Anat.*) Intercostal.
intercotidal [ɛ̃tɛrkɔti'dal], *a.* (*fem.* **-ale,** *pl.* **-aux**) Intertidal. *Zone* (or *partie*) *de rivage intercotidale,* intertidal zone; (*U.S.*) tideland.
intercurrent [ɛ̃tɛrky'rɑ̃], *a.* (*fem.* **-ente**) Intercurrent (trouble).
interdépartemental [ɛ̃tɛrdepartəmɑ̃'tal], *a.* (*fem.* **-ale,** *pl.* **-aux**) Interdepartmental.
interdépendance [ɛ̃tɛrdepɑ̃'dɑ̃s], *n.f.* Interdependence. **interdépendant,** *a.* (*fem.* **-ante**) Interdependent.
interdiction [ɛ̃tɛrdik'sjɔ̃], *n.f.* Interdiction, inhibition, prohibition; laying under an interdict; deprivation (of civil rights). *Frapper d'interdiction,* to lay under an interdict. **interdire,** *v.t.* *irr.* (*pres.p.* **interdisant,** *p.p.* **interdit;** *conjugated like* DIRE, *except in 2nd pers. pl. indic. and imperative,* **interdisez**) To interdict, to prohibit, to forbid; to suspend; (*fig.*) to confound, to dumbfound, to stupefy, to nonplus; (*Law*) to deprive of civil rights. *Interdire l'entrée à*

quelqu'un, to refuse someone admission; *s'interdire l'alcool,* to forego liquor. **interdit,** *a.* (*fem.* **-ite**) Forbidden, prohibited; (*fig.*) abashed, confused, dumbfounded. *Entrée interdite,* no admittance; *passage interdit,* no thoroughfare; *représentation interdite par la censure,* performance banned by the Censor. —*n.m.* Interdict; person interdicted from managing his affairs.
intéressant [ɛ̃terɛ'sɑ̃], *a.* (*fem.* **-ante**) Interesting; lucrative, attractive (price). (*fam.*) *Elle est dans une position intéressante,* she is in the family way. (*fam.*) *Il est peu intéressant,* he is a dubious fellow. **intéressé,** *a.* (*fem.* **-ée**) Interested, concerned, having an interest (in); selfish, mercenary.— *n.* Interested party.
intéresser [ɛ̃terɛ'se], *v.t.* To interest, to give an interest or share to; to concern, to affect; to inspire with interest; (*Surg.*) to injure. *Cela ne vous intéresse en rien,* that does not concern you in the least. **s'intéresser,** *v.r.* To take an interest in, to have an interest, to be concerned (*à*).
intérêt [ɛ̃te'rɛ], *n.m.* Interest, concern, share; self-interest, selfishness. *Avoir un intérêt à,* to have an interest or share in; *c'est l'intérêt qui nous guide,* it is interest that guides us; *cet argent porte intérêt,* this money bears interest; *favoriser les intérêts de quelqu'un,* to promote someone's interest; *il est dans mes intérêts,* he is on my side; *il est de mon intérêt de le faire,* it is to my interest to do it; *il y va de mon intérêt,* my interest is at stake; *intérêt composé,* compound interest; *porter intérêt à,* to be a well-wisher to; *prendre intérêt à,* to take an interest in.
interférence [ɛ̃tɛrfe'rɑ̃:s], *n.f.* Interference. *pl.* (*Rad. Tel.*) Interference. **interférer,** *v.i. irr.* (*conjug. like* ACCÉLÉRER) To interfere.
interfoliacé [ɛ̃tɛrfɔlja'se], *a.* (*fem.* **-ée**) Interfoliaceous, interleaved. **interfolier,** *v.t.* (*conjugated like* PRIER) To interleave (a book etc.).
intérieur [ɛ̃te'rjœ:r], *a.* (*fem.* **-ieure**) Inner, inward, internal, interior; inland. *Commerce intérieur,* home trade; *politique intérieure,* home policy. *Conduite intérieure,* saloon car. —*n.m.* Interior, inside, inner part; home, private or family life, domesticity; home department. *À l'intérieur,* inside, on the inside; *à l'intérieur des terres,* inland; *ministre de l'intérieur,* Home Secretary; *une bonne femme d'intérieur,* a good housewife. **intérieurement,** *adv.* Inwardly.
intérim [ɛ̃te'rim], *n.m.* Interim. *Assurer un intérim,* to deputize; *dans l'intérim,* in the interim; *par intérim,* provisionally. **intérimaire,** *a.* Provisional, temporary.
interjection [ɛ̃tɛrʒɛk'sjɔ̃], *n.f.* Interjection; (*Law*) lodging (of an appeal). **interjeter,** *v.t.* To lodge (an appeal).
interligne [ɛ̃tɛr'liɲ], *n.m.* Line space; interlining.—*n.f.* (*Print.*) Lead. **interligner,** *v.t.* (*Print.*) To space out, to lead; to interline. **interlinéaire** [ɛ̃tɛrline'ɛ:r], *a.* Interlinear. **interlinéation,** *n.f.* Interlineation.
interlocuteur [ɛ̃tɛrlɔky'tœ:r], *n.m.* (*fem.* **interlocutrice**) Interlocutor, speaker. **interlocution,** *n.f.* Interlocution. **interlocutoire,** *n.m.* (*Law*) Interlocutory decree.—*a.*

Interlocutory. *Arrêt interlocutoire,* interlocutory judgment.
interlope [ɛ̃tɛr'lɔp], *a.* Interloping, intrusive; suspect, shady; fraudulent, clandestine.—*n.m.* (*Navy*) Interloper, smuggling vessel.
interloquer [ɛ̃tɛrlɔ'ke], *v.t.* (*Law*) To subject to an interlocutory decree; (*fig.*) to nonplus, to disconcert; to abash.
interlude [ɛ̃tɛr'lyd], *n.m.* Interlude.
intermaxillaire [ɛ̃tɛrmaksi'lɛːr], *a.* Intermaxillary.
intermède [ɛ̃tɛr'mɛd], *n.m.* One-act play, interlude; (*Chem.*) intermediate. **intermédiaire** [ɛ̃tɛrme'djɛːr], *a.* Intermediate, intervening; lying between.—*n.m.* Medium, intermediary, middleman. *Par l'intermédiaire de,* through the medium of; through the agency of. **intermédiat,** *a.* (*fem.* **-ate**) Intermediate.
interminable [ɛ̃tɛrmi'nabl], *a.* Interminable, endless; (*fig.*) long-winded; long-drawn. **interminablement,** *adv.* Interminably.
intermission [ɛ̃tɛrmi'sjɔ̃], *n.f.* Intermission, pause.
intermittence [ɛ̃tɛrmi'tɑ̃ːs], *n.f.* Intermission, cessation; intermittent character. **intermittent,** *a.* (*fem.* **-ente**) Intermittent. *Courant intermittent,* make-and-break current.
intermonde [ɛ̃tɛr'mɔ̃ːd], *n.m.* Intermundane space.
intermusculaire [ɛ̃tɛrmysky'lɛːr], *a.* (*Anat.*) Intermuscular.
internat [ɛ̃tɛr'na], *n.m.* Boarding-school; state of being a boarder; resident medical studentship, house-surgeonship (of hospitals).
international [ɛ̃tɛrnasjɔ'nal], *a.* (*fem.* **-ale,** *pl.* **-aux**) International.—*n.f.* *L'internationale,* the International Workmen's Association; the hymn of this association. **internationalement,** *adv.* Internationally. **internationaliser,** *v.t.* To internationalize. **internationalisme,** *n.m.* Internationalism. **internationaliste,** *a.* and *n.* Internationalist. **internationalité,** *n.f.* Internationality.
interne [ɛ̃'tɛrn], *a.* Internal, inward, resident. *Élève interne,* boarder (in school).—*n.* Boarder (in schools); resident medical student in a hospital.
interné [ɛ̃tɛr'ne], *a.* (*fem.* **-ée**) Interned.—*n.* Internee. **internement,** *n.m.* Internment.
interner [ɛ̃tɛr'ne], *v.t.* To confine (in the interior of a country); to intern.
internissable [ɛ̃tɛrni'sabl], *a.* Untarnishable.
internonce [ɛ̃tɛr'nɔ̃ːs], *n.m.* Internuncio.
interocéanique [ɛ̃tɛrɔsea'nik], *a.* Interoceanic.
interoculaire [ɛ̃tɛrɔky'lɛːr], *a.* Interocular.
interosseux [ɛ̃tɛrɔ'sø], *a.* (*fem.* **-euse**) (*Anat.*) Interosseous.
interparlementaire [ɛ̃tɛrparləmɑ̃'tɛr], *a.* *Commission interparlementaire,* joint committee of both Houses.
interpellateur [ɛ̃tɛrpɛla'tœːr], *n.m.* (*fem.* **-trice**) Interpellator, questioner.
interpellation [ɛ̃tɛrpɛla'sjɔ̃], *n.f.* Interpellation; interruption, sharp question; (*Mil.*) challenge. **interpeller,** *v.t.* To interpellate, to summon, to call upon, to challenge; to question, to put a question to (a minister etc.).
interpénétration [ɛ̃tɛrpenetra'sjɔ̃], *n.f.* Interpenetration. **s'interpénétrer,** *v.r.* To interpenetrate.

interplanétaire [ɛ̃tɛrplane'tɛːr], *a.* Interplanetary.
interpolaire [ɛ̃tɛrpɔ'lɛːr], *a.* Interpolar.
interpolateur, *n.m.* (*fem.* **-trice**) Interpolator. **interpolation,** *n.f.* Interpolation. **interpoler,** *v.t.* To interpolate.
interposer [ɛ̃tɛrpo'ze], *v.t.* To interpose. *Personne interposée* (*Law*), person taking the place of one of the parties; intermediary. **s'interposer,** *v.r.* To interpose, to come between. **interposition,** *n.f.* Interposition, intervention.
interprétable [ɛ̃tɛrpre'tabl], *a.* Interpretable. **interprétariat,** *n.m.* Interpretership.
interprétatif [ɛ̃tɛrpreta'tif], *a.* (*fem.* **-prétative**) Interpretative; explanatory.
interprétation [ɛ̃tɛrpreta'sjɔ̃], *n.f.* Interpretation, construction; rendering (of a play). *Donner une mauvaise interprétation à,* to give a bad construction to; *interprétation erronée,* misconstruction.
interprète [ɛ̃tɛr'prɛt], *n.* Interpreter, expounder. **interpréter,** *v.t. irr.* (*conjug. like* ACCÉLÉRER) To interpret, to expound, to explain; to translate, to construe; (*Mil.*) to read (signals). *Mal interpréter,* to misinterpret.
interrègne [ɛ̃tɛr'rɛɲ], *n.m.* Interregnum.
interrogateur [ɛ̃tɛrɔga'tœr], *a.* (*fem.* **-trice**) Interrogative, questioning, examining.—*n.* Interrogator, questioner, examiner. **interrogatif,** *a.* (*fem.* **-ive**) Interrogative.
interrogation [ɛ̃tɛrɔga'sjɔ̃], *n.f.* Interrogation, question, inquiry. *Point d'interrogation,* question mark. **interrogativement,** *adv.* Interrogatively. **interrogatoire,** *n.m.* Examination. *Interrogatoire contradictoire,* cross-examination; *subir un interrogatoire,* to undergo an examination. **interroger,** *v.t.* To interrogate, to question; to consult, to examine.
interrompre [ɛ̃tɛ'rɔ̃ːpr], *v.t. irr.* (*conjug. like* ROMPRE) To interrupt, to break in upon, to break off; to stop, to suspend. **s'interrompre,** *v.r.* To interrupt oneself; to break off. **interrupteur,** *a.* and *n.* (*fem.* **-trice**) Interrupting; interrupter; (*Elec.*) switch, cut-out. **interruption,** *n.f.* Interruption; (*Elec.*) disconnection, breaking.
interscolaire [ɛ̃tɛrskɔ'lɛr], *a.* Inter-school (competition, championship, etc.).
intersecté [ɛ̃tɛrsɛk'te], *a.* (*fem.* **-ée**) Intersected. **intersection,** *n.f.* Intersection.
interstellaire [ɛ̃tɛrstɛ'lɛːr], *a.* (*Astron.*) Interstellar.
interstice [ɛ̃tɛr'stis], *n.m.* Interstice, cleft, chink, crack.
intertropical [ɛ̃tɛrtrɔpi'kal], *a.* (*fem.* **-ale,** *pl.* **-aux**) Intertropical.
interurbain [ɛ̃tɛryr'bɛ̃], *a.* (*fem.* **-aine**) Interurban. (*Teleph.*) *Communication interurbaine,* trunk call.
intervalle [ɛ̃tɛr'val], *n.m.* Interval; distance apart, gap. *Par intervalles,* at intervals, off and on, now and then; *dans l'intervalle,* in the meantime.
intervenant [ɛ̃tɛrvə'nɑ̃], *a.* (*fem.* **-ante**) (*Law*) Intervening.—*n.* Intervening party.
intervenir [ɛ̃tɛrvə'niːr], *v.i. irr.* (*conjug. like* VENIR) To intervene, to interfere; to interpose one's authority; to act as mediator etc.; (*colloq.*) to happen, to occur; (*Law*) to

interplead. *Faire intervenir*, to bring in, to call in; *il intervint un jugement*, a judgment was given. **intervention**, *n.f.* Intervention, interference. *Intervention chirurgicale*, operation.

interventionnisme [ɛ̃tɛrvɑ̃sjɔ'nism], *n.m.* Interventionism. **interventionniste**, *a.* and *n.* Interventionist.

interversion [ɛ̃tɛrvɛr'sjɔ̃], *n.f.* Inversion, change, reversal. **intervertir**, *v.t.* To invert, to change, to reverse.

interview [ɛ̃tɛr'vju:], *n. f.* Interview.

interviewer (1) [ɛ̃tɛrvju've], *v.t.* To interview.

interviewer (2) [ɛ̃tɛrvju'vœr], *n.m.* Interviewer.

intestat [ɛ̃tɛs'ta], *n.m.* and *a. inv.* (*Law*) Intestate. *Héritier ab intestat*, heir of one that dies intestate.

intestin (1) [ɛ̃tɛs'tɛ̃], *n.m.* Intestine, bowel, gut.

intestin (2) [ɛ̃tɛs'tɛ̃], *a.* (*fem.* **-ine**) Intestine, internal, domestic, civil. *Dissensions intestines*, domestic differences.

intestinal [ɛ̃tɛsti'nal], *a.* (*fem.* **-ale**, *pl.* **-aux**) Intestinal.

intimation [ɛ̃tima'sjɔ̃], *n.f.* Notification.

intime [ɛ̃'tim], *a.* Intimate, inmost, inward, deep, secret; close, familiar, confidential; private.—*n.* Intimate.

intimé [ɛ̃ti'me], *n.m.* (*fem.* **-ée**) (*Law*) Defendant, appellee.

intimement [ɛ̃tim'mɑ̃], *adv.* Intimately; deeply; closely, familiarly.

intimer [ɛ̃ti'me], *v.t.* To notify, to give legal notice of; to summon (before a court etc.). *On lui intima l'ordre de partir*, they gave him orders to leave, they gave him notice.

intimidable [ɛ̃timida'bl], *a.* Easily intimidated. **intimidant**, *a.* (*fem.* **-ante**) Intimidating.

intimidateur [ɛ̃timida'tœ:r], *a.* (*fem.* **-trice**) Intimidating.—*n.* Intimidator.

intimidation [ɛ̃timida'sjɔ̃], *n.f.* Intimidation.

intimider, *v.t.* To intimidate, to frighten, to scare, to browbeat.

intimité [ɛ̃timi'te], *n.f.* Intimacy, closeness; close connexion, friendship; privacy; inward life. *Dans l'intimité*, in private.

intitulé [ɛ̃tity'le], *a.* (*fem.* **-ée**) Entitled.— *n.m.* Title (of deeds, books, etc.).

intituler [ɛ̃tity'le], *v.t.* To entitle, to call, to name. **s'intituler**, *v.r.* To entitle or style oneself; to give oneself out for.

intolérable [ɛ̃tɔle'rabl], *a.* Intolerable, insufferable, unbearable. **intolérablement**, *adv.* Unbearably.

intolérance [ɛ̃tɔle'rɑ̃:s], *n.f.* Intolerance. **intolérant**, *a.* (*fem.* **-ante**) Intolerant.

intonation [ɛ̃tɔna'sjɔ̃], *n.f.* Intonation; pitch, ring.

intouchable [ɛ̃tu'ʃabl], *a.* Untouchable; that cannot be cashed.—*n.* Untouchable (in India).

intoxicant [ɛ̃tɔksi'kɑ̃], *a.* (*fem.* **intoxicante**). Poisonous. **intoxication**, *n.f.* Poisoning.

intoxiquer, *v.t.* To poison, to impregnate with toxic substances.

intrados [ɛ̃tra'do], *n.m. inv.* (*Arch.*) Intrados, inner side of soffit; (*Av.*) under-surface of aeroplane wing.

intraduisible [ɛ̃tradɥi'zibl], *a.* Untranslatable. **intraduit**, *a.* (*fem.* **-uite**) Untranslated.

intraitable [ɛ̃trɛ'tabl], *a.* Not affable, difficult of approach, etc.; intractable, unmanageable.

intra-muros [ɛ̃tramy'ro:s], *adv.* and *a. inv.* Inside a town; intramural.

intramusculaire [ɛ̃tramysky'lɛ:r], *a.* In the muscles (injection).

intransférable [ɛ̃trɑ̃sfe'rabl], *a.* Untransferable.

intransigeance [ɛ̃trɑ̃si'ʒɑ̃:s], *n.f.* Intransigence; strictness. **intransigeant**, *a.* (*fem.* **-ante**) Intransigent, uncompromising, irreconcilable.—*n.* Intransigent, diehard.

intransitif [ɛ̃trɑ̃zi'tif], *a.* (*fem.* **-ive**) (*Gram.*) Intransitive. **intransitivement**, *adv.* Intransitively.

intransmissible [ɛ̃trɑ̃smi'sibl], *a.* Intransmissible.

intransportable [ɛ̃trɑ̃spɔr'tabl], *a.* Untransportable; not fit to travel.

intraveineux [ɛ̃travɛ'nø], *a.* (*fem.* **-euse**) In the veins (injection).

intraversable [ɛ̃travɛr'sabl], *a.* Impassable, not to be crossed.

in-trente-deux [ɛ̃trɑ̃t'dø], *n.m.* and *a. inv.* Thirty-two-mo, 32mo.

intrépide [ɛ̃tre'pid], *a.* Intrepid, dauntless, fearless. **intrépidement**, *adv.* Intrepidly, dauntlessly. **intrépidité**, *n.f.* Intrepidity, dauntlessness, fearlessness.

intrigant [ɛ̃tri'gɑ̃], *a.* (*fem.* **-ante**) Intriguing.—*n.* Intriguer; adventurer, schemer.

intrigue [ɛ̃'trig], *n.f.* Intrigue; liaison; scrape, difficulty; plot (of a novel etc.). *Démêler* or *dénouer une intrigue*, to unravel an intrigue or plot; *intrigue secondaire* or *accessoire*, subordinate plot. **intriguer**, *v.t.* To puzzle, to perplex, to set thinking.—*v.i.* and **s'intriguer**, *v.r.* To intrigue; to plot; to take pains, to rack one's brains. **intrigueur**, *n.m.* (*fem.* **-euse**) Intriguer, plotter.

intrinsèque [ɛ̃trɛ̃'sɛk], *a.* Intrinsic. **intrinsèquement**, *adv.* Intrinsically.

introducteur [ɛ̃trɔdyk'tœ:r], *n.m.* (*fem.* **-trice**) Introducer; (gentleman) usher. **introductif**, *a.* (*fem.* **-ive**) (*Law*) Introductory.

introduction [ɛ̃trɔdyk'sjɔ̃], *n.f.* Introduction; preamble; (*Law*) preliminary proceedings. **introductoire**, *a.* Introductory, preliminary.

introduire [ɛ̃trɔ'dɥi:r], *v.t. irr.* (*pres.p.* **introduisant**, *p.p.* **introduit**; *conjugated like* CONDUIRE) To present; to show in, to bring or usher in, to introduce; to conduct; to put in, to insert. *Introduire la sonde dans une plaie*, to insert the probe in a wound; *introduisez monsieur*, show the gentleman in. **s'introduire**, *v.r.* To get in, to find one's way in; to intrude.

introït [ɛ̃trɔ'it], *n.m.* Introit.

intromission [ɛ̃trɔmi'sjɔ̃], *n.f.* Intromission.

intronisation [ɛ̃trɔniza'sjɔ̃], *n.f.* Enthroning (of bishops). **introniser**, *v.t.* To install, to enthrone; (*fig.*) to establish (a fashion). **s'introniser**, *v.r.* To establish oneself.

introrse [ɛ̃'trɔrs], *a.* (*Bot.*) Introrse.

introspectif [ɛ̃trɔspɛk'tif], *a.* (*fem.* **-ive**) Introspective. **introspection**, *n.f.* Introspection.

introuvable [ɛ̃tru'vabl], *a.* Undiscoverable, not to be found; matchless.

introverti [ɛ̃trɔvɛr'ti], *a.* (*fem.* **-ie**) Introverted.—*n.* Introvert.

intrus [ɛ̃'try], *a.* (*fem.* **intruse**) Intruding, intruded.—*n.* Intruder; trespasser. **intrusion,** *n.f.* Intrusion; trespass.

intuitif [ɛ̃tцi'tif], *a.* (*fem.* **intuitive**) Intuitive. **intuition,** *n.f.* Intuition. **intuitivement,** *adv.* Intuitively.

intumescence [ɛ̃tymɛ'sɑ̃:s], *n.f.* Intumescence, swelling up.

intussusception [ɛ̃tysysɛp'sjɔ̃], *n.f.* Intussusception.

inule [i'nyl], *n.f.* (*Bot.*) or *inule conyse.* Inula, elecampane. **inuline,** *n.f.* Inulin.

inusable [iny'zabl], *a.* That will not wear out durable, everlasting. **inusité,** *a.* (*fem.* **-ée**) Unused, unusual; obsolete, antiquated.

inutile [iny'til], *a.* Useless, needless, unnecessary; unavailing, fruitless, vain; unserviceable, profitless. *Il est inutile de faire cela,* it is no use doing that. **inutilement,** *adv.* Uselessly, to no purpose, needlessly. **inutilisable,** *a.* That cannot be utilized, worthless, unusable, unserviceable. **inutilisé,** *a.* (*fem.* **-ée**) Unutilized. **inutilité,** *n.f.* Inutility, uselessness; fruitlessness, unprofitableness; useless thing, thing of no use.

invagination [ɛ̃vaʒina'sjɔ̃], *n.f.* (*Surg.*) Invagination.

invaincu [ɛ̃vɛ̃'ky], *a.* (*fem.* **-ue**) Unvanquished, unconquered.

invalidation [ɛ̃valida'sjɔ̃], *n.f.* Unseating (of an elected deputy); invalidation.

invalide [ɛ̃va'lid], *a.* Invalid, infirm; disabled; (*Law*) not valid, void, without effect.—*n.* Invalid; pensioner. *Hôtel des Invalides,* the Chelsea Hospital of France (*i.e.* for disabled soldiers or sailors). **invalider,** *v.t.* To invalidate, to nullify, to annul. **invalidité,** *n.f.* Invalidity, nullity; disablement.

invariabilité [ɛ̃varjabili'te], *n.f.* Invariability, unchangeableness. **invariable,** *a.* Invariable, unchangeable, unalterable. **invariablement,** *adv.* Invariably.

invasion [ɛ̃va'zjɔ̃], *n.f.* Invasion; inroad.

invective [ɛ̃vɛk'ti:v], *n.f.* Invective, (*pl.*) abuse. **invectiver,** *v.i.* To abuse.—*v.t.* To inveigh against, to revile; to rail at.

invendable [ɛ̃vɑ̃'dabl], *a.* Unsaleable. **invendu,** *a.* (*fem.* **-ue**) Unsold.—*n.m.pl.* Les *invendus,* unsold copies.

inventaire [ɛ̃vɑ̃'tɛ:r], *n.m.* Inventory; evaluation, stock-taking. *Faire* or *dresser l'inventaire de,* to take an inventory of; (*Comm.*) *faire l'inventaire,* to take stock; *sous bénéfice d'inventaire,* without liability for debts exceeding the assets.

inventer [ɛ̃vɑ̃'te], *v.t.* To invent, to contrive, to devise; to discover, to find out; to imagine, to forge, to fabricate. *Il n'a pas inventé la poudre,* he will never set the Thames on fire. **inventeur,** *n.m.* (*fem.* **-trice**) Inventor, contriver, deviser. **inventif,** *a.* (*fem.* **-ive**) Inventive. **invention,** *n.f.* Invention, contrivance; inventiveness, ingenuity; device, trick; fiction, untruth, falsehood. *Brevet d'invention,* patent; *nécessité est mère d'invention,* necessity is the mother of invention; *vivre d'invention,* to live by one's wits. *L'invention de la croix,* the finding of the true Cross.

inventorier [ɛ̃vɑ̃tɔ'rje], *v.t.* To inventory, to draw up an inventory of; to schedule, to catalogue.

invérifiable [ɛ̃veri'fjabl], *a.* Unverifiable. **invérifié,** *a.* (*fem.* **-ée**) Unverified.

inversable [ɛ̃vɛr'sabl], *a.* That cannot be upset.

inverse [ɛ̃'vɛrs], *a.* Inverse, inverted. *En sens inverse,* in the opposite direction; *être en raison inverse de,* to be in inverse ratio to. —*n.m.* The reverse, the contrary, the opposite. *Faire l'inverse,* to do the opposite. **inversement,** *adv.* Inversely. **inverser,** *v.t.* (*Tech.*) To reverse. **inverseur,** *n.m.* Reversing device. **inversible,** *a.* Reversible. **inversion,** *n.f.* (*Gram.*) Inversion; (*Tech.*) reversal.

invertébré [ɛ̃vɛrte'bre], *a.* and *n.* (*fem.* **-ée**) Invertebrate.

inverti [ɛ̃vɛr'ti], *a.* (*fem.* **-ie**) Inverted, reversed.—*n.* A (sexual) invert, a homosexual. **invertir,** *v.t.* To reverse.

investigateur [ɛ̃vɛstiga'tœ:r], *n.m.* (*fem.* **-trice**) Investigator.—*a.* Investigating, searching, scrutinizing, inquiring. **investigation,** *n.f.* Investigation, inquiry. *Faire des investigations dans,* to make inquiries into.

investir [ɛ̃vɛs'ti:r], *v.t.* To invest; to surround, to lay siege to. **investissement,** *n.m.* Investment. **investiture,** *n.f.* Investiture.

invétéré [ɛ̃vete're], *a.* (*fem.* **-ée**) Inveterate. **invétérer (s')** [ɛ̃vete're], *v.r. irr.* (*conjug. like* ACCÉLÉRER) To grow inveterate, to become inveterate. *Cette maladie s'est invétérée,* this disease has become chronic.

invincibilité [ɛ̃vɛ̃sibili'te], *n.f.* Invincibleness. **invincible,** *a.* Invincible, unconquerable, insurmountable. **invinciblement,** *adv.* Invincibly.

in-vingt-quatre [ɛ̃vɛ̃t'katr], *n.m.* and *a. inv.* Twenty-four-mo, 24mo.

inviolabilité [ɛ̃vjɔlabili'te], *n.f.* Inviolability. **inviolable,** *a.* Inviolable. **inviolablement,** *adv.* Inviolably. **inviolé,** *a.* (*fem.* **-ée**) Inviolate.

invisibilité [ɛ̃vizibili'te], *n.f.* Invisibility, invisibleness. **invisible,** *a.* Invisible. **invisiblement,** *adv.* Invisibly.

invitant [ɛ̃vi'tɑ̃], *a.* (*fem.* **-ante**) Inviting, attractive.

invitation [ɛ̃vita'sjɔ̃], *n.f.* Invitation. **invitatoire,** *a.* and *n.f.* (*Eccles.*) Invitatory. **invite,** *n.f.* Call for a suit, lead (at cards); invitation. **invité,** *n.m.* (*fem.* **-ée**) Invited guest. **inviter,** *v.t.* To invite, to call upon, to beg, to engage, to request; to allure, to incite, to attract, to tempt. *Inviter à dîner,* to ask to dinner.—*v.i.* To call for a suit (at cards).

invocation [ɛ̃vɔka'sjɔ̃], *n.f.* Invocation. **invocatoire,** *a.* Invocatory.

involontaire [ɛ̃vɔlɔ̃'tɛ:r], *a.* Involuntary, unwilling. **involontairement,** *adv.* Involuntarily.

involucral [ɛ̃vɔly'kral], *a.* (*fem.* **-ale,** *pl.* **-aux**) (*Bot.*) Involucral. **involucre,** *n.m.* Involucre, envelope, cover, husk.

involutif [ɛ̃vɔly'tif], *a.* (*fem.* **-ive**) Rolled up, folded; (*Bot.*) involute. **involution,** *n.f.* (*Law*) Involvement, complication; (*Bot. etc.*) involution.

invoquer [ɛ̃vɔ'ke], *v.t.* To invoke, to call upon; to appeal to.

invraisemblable [ɛ̃vrɛsɑ̃'blabl], *a.* Unlikely, improbable. **invraisemblablement,** *adv.* Improbably. **invraisemblance,** *n.f.* Unlikelihood, improbability; unlikely thing; lack of realism.
invulnérabilité [ɛ̃vylnerabili'te], *n.f.* Invulnerability. **invulnérable,** *a.* Invulnerable. **invulnérablement,** *adv.* Invulnerably.
iode [jɔd], *n.m.* Iodine. **iodé,** *a.* (*fem.* **-ée**) Iodized. **ioder,** *v.t.* To iodize. **iodeux,** *a.m.* Iodous. **iodifère,** *a.* Iodiferous. **iodique,** *a.* Iodic. **iodisme,** *n.m.* Iodism. **iodoforme,** *n.m.* Iodoform. **iodure,** *n.m.* Iodide. **ioduré,** *a.* (*fem.* **-ée**) Containing an iodide.
ion [jɔ̃], *n.m.* (*Phys.*) Ion.
ionien [jɔ'njɛ̃], *a.* (*fem.* **ionienne**) Ionian. —*n.m.* (**Ionien,** *fem.* **Ionienne**) An Ionian. **ionique,** *a.* Ionic. *L'ordre ionique,* the Ionic order.
ionisation [jɔniza'sjɔ̃], *n.f.* Ionization. **ioniser,** *v.t.* To ionize. **ionosphère,** *n.f.* Ionosphere.
iota [jo'ta], *n.m.* Iota, jot, tittle. **iotacisme,** *n.m.* (*Gram.*) Iotacism, frequent recurrence of the sound i.
iouler [JODLER].
ipécacuana or **ipécacuanha** [ipekakɥa'na] (*abbrev.* **ipéca**), *n.m.* Ipecacuanha; ipecac.
irai, 1st pers. sing. fut. [ALLER].
Irak [i'rak], *m.* Iraq. **irakien,** *a.* (*fem.* **-ienne**) and *n.m.* (**Irakien,** *fem.* **-ienne**) Iraqi.
Iran [i'rɑ̃], *m.* Iran.
iranien [ira'njɛ̃], *a.* (*fem.* **-ienne**) Iranian. *n.m.* (**Iranien,** *fem.* **-ienne**) An Iranian.
irascibilité [irasibili'te], *n.f.* Irascibility, irritability. **irascible,** *a.* Irascible, irritable.
***ire** [i:r], *n.f.* Wrath, anger, ire.
iridescence [iridɛ'sɑ̃:s], *n.f.* Iridescence. **iridescent,** *a.* (*fem.* **-ente**) Iridescent.
iridier [iri'dje], *v.t.* (*Metal.*) To iridize.
iridium [iri'djɔm], *n.m.* Iridium.
iris [i'ri:s], *n.m. inv.* Iris; rainbow. *Iris des marais* or *iris jaune* or *faux acore,* yellow flag; *poudre d'iris,* powdered orris-root. **irisation,** *n.f.* Irisation. **irisé,** *a.* (*fem.* **-ée**) Rainbow-coloured, irisated, iridescent. **iriser,** *v.t.* To give all the colours of the rainbow to. **s'iriser,** *v.r.* To take all the colours of the rainbow, to become iridescent.
irlandais [irlɑ̃'dɛ], *a.* (*fem.* **-aise**) Irish.— *n.m.* Irish language; (**Irlandais,** *fem.* **-aise**) Irishman, Irishwoman.
Irlande [ir'lɑ̃d], *f.* Ireland.
ironie [irɔ'ni], *n.f.* Irony, mockery, raillery. **ironique,** *a.* Ironical. **ironiquement,** *adv.* Ironically. **ironiser,** *v.i.* To speak ironically. **ironiste,** *n.* Ironist.
iroquois [irɔ'kwa], *a.* (*fem.* **-oise**) Iroquois.— *n.m.* Iroquois language; (*fig.*) clown, bizarre person; (**Iroquois,** *fem.* **-oise**) an Iroquois.
irraccommodable [irrakɔmɔ'dabl], *a.* Unmendable.
irrachetable [irraʃ'tabl], *a.* Unredeemable.
irradiation [irradja'sjɔ̃], *n.f.* Irradiation. **irradier,** *v.t.* To radiate through; (*C*) to broadcast.—*v.i.* or **s'irradier,** *v.r.* To irradiate, to radiate.
irraisonnable [irrɛzɔ'nabl], *a.* Irrational. **irraisonnablement,** *adv.* Irrationally.
irrationnel [irrasjɔ'nɛl], *a.* (*fem.* **-elle**)

Irrational. **irrationnellement,** *adv.* Irrationally.
irréalisable [irreali'zabl], *a.* Unrealizable. **irréalité** [irreali'te], *n.f.* Unreality.
irrecevable [irrəsə'vabl], *a.* Inadmissible, unacceptable.
irréconciliable [irrekɔ̃si'ljabl], *a.* Irreconcilable. **irréconciliablement,** *adv.* Irreconcilably. **irréconcilié,** *a.* (*fem.* **-ée**) Unreconciled.
irrécouvrable [irreku'vrabl], *a.* Irrecoverable. **irrécupérable** [irrekype'rabl], *a.* Irrecoverable.
irrécusable [irreky'zabl], *a.* Irrecusable, unexceptionable, unimpeachable.
irrédentisme [irredɑ̃'tism], *n.m.* Irredentism. **irrédentiste,** *a.* and *n.* Irredentist.
irréductibilité [irredyktibili'te], *n.f.* Irreducibility. **irréductible,** *a.* Irreducible.
irréel [irre'ɛl], *a.* (*fem.* **-elle**) Unreal.—*n.m.* Unreality.
irréfléchi [irrefle'ʃi], *a.* (*fem.* **-ie**) Thoughtless, heedless, inconsiderate, rash. **irréflexion,** *n.f.* Thoughtlessness, heedlessness.
irréformable [irrefɔr'mabl], *a.* Incorrigible, unchangeable, irrevocable.
irréfragable [irrefra'gabl], *a.* Irrefragable, irrefutable. **irréfragablement,** *adv.* Irrefragably.
irréfrangible [irrefrɑ̃'ʒibl], *a.* (*Opt.*) Irrefrangible.
irréfutable [irrefy'tabl], *a.* Irrefutable. **irréfuté,** *a.* (*fem.* **-ée**) Unrefuted, not disproved.
irrégularité [irregylari'te], *n.f.* Irregularity. **irrégulier,** *a.* (*fem.* **-ière**) Irregular; (*Mil.*) desultory (firing).—*n.m.* Irregular, guerrilla, partisan. **irrégulièrement,** *adv.* Irregularly.
irréligieux [irreli'ʒjo], *a.* (*fem.* **-ieuse**) Irreligious. **irréligion,** *n.f.* Irreligion.
irrémédiable [irreme'djabl], *a.* Irremediable, irreparable, irretrievable. **irrémédiablement,** *adv.* Irremediably.
irrémissible [irremi'sibl], *a.* Irremissible, unpardonable.
irremplaçable [irrɑ̃pla'sabl], *a.* Irreplaceable.
irréparable [irrepa'rabl], *a.* Irreparable, irretrievable.
irrépréhensible [irrepreɑ̃'sibl], *a.* Irreproachable, blameless.
irrépressible [irrepre'sibl], *a.* Irrepressible.
irréprochable [irreprɔ'ʃabl], *a.* Irreproachable, blameless, unexceptionable. **irréprochablement,** *adv.* Irreproachably; faultlessly.
irrésistibilité [irrezistibili'te], *n.f.* Irresistibility. **irrésistible,** *a.* Irresistible. **irrésistiblement,** *adv.* Irresistibly.
irrésolu [irrezɔ'ly], *a.* (*fem.* **-ue**) Irresolute, wavering; undetermined, unsolved. **irrésolument,** *adv.* Irresolutely. **irrésolution,** *n.f.* Irresolution, indecision.
irrespect [irres'pɛ], *n.m.* Disrespect. **irrespectueusement** [irrespɛktɥøz'mɑ̃], *adv.* Disrespectfully. **irrespectueux,** *a.* (*fem.* **-ueuse**) Disrespectful.
irrespirable [irrespi'rabl], *a.* Unbreathable.
irresponsabilité [irrespɔ̃sabili'te], *n.f.* Irresponsibility. **irresponsable,** *a.* Irresponsible.
irrétrécissable [irretresi'sabl], *a.* Unshrinkable.

irrévéremment [irrevera'mã], *adv.* Irreverently. **irrévérence,** *n.f.* Irreverence, disrespect. **irrévérencieux,** *a.* (*fem.* **-ieuse**) Irreverent; disrespectful. **irrévérent,** *a.* (*fem.* **-ente**) Irreverent.
irréversible [irreversibl], *a.* Irreversible (steering).
irrévocabilité [irrevɔkabili'te], *n.f.* Irrevocability. **irrévocable,** *a.* Irrevocable. **irrévocablement,** *adv.* Irrevocably. **irrévoqué,** *a.* (*fem.* **-ée**) Unrevoked, unrepealed.
irrigable [irri'gabl], *a.* Irrigable. **irrigateur,** *n.m.* Watering-engine; garden-hose; (*Med.*) irrigator, enema. **irrigation,** *n.f.* Irrigation. **irriguer,** *v.t.* To irrigate, to water, to douche.
irritabilité [irritabili'te], *n.f.* Irritability. **irritable,** *a.* Irritable; sensitive. **irritant,** *a.* (*fem.* **-ante**) Irritating, provoking.—*n.m.* (*Med.*) Irritant. **irritation,** *n.f.* Irritation, exasperation, vexation.
irriter [irri'te], *v.t.* To irritate, to incense, to anger; to provoke, to excite. *Il est irrité contre vous,* he is very annoyed with you; *vous irritez sa colère,* you provoke his anger. **s'irriter,** *v.r.* To grow angry; to become irritated.
irroration [irrɔrɑ'sjɔ̃], *n.f.* Dew-bath. **irrorer,** *v.t.* To spray.
irruption [irryp'sjɔ̃], *n.f.* Irruption, raid; overflow, flood. *Faire irruption dans,* to invade, to make an irruption into, to burst into.
Isabelle [iza'bɛl], *f.* Isabel.
isabelle [iza'bɛl], *a. inv.* Isabel, dun- or cream-coloured (of horses), dove-coloured (of birds etc.).
Isaïe [iza'i], *m.* Isaiah.
isard [i'za:r], *n.m.* Izard (Pyrenean chamois).
isba [is'ba], *n.f.* Isba.
ischion [is'kjɔ̃], *n.m.* Ischium.
ischurie [isky'ri], *n.f.* Ischuria.
Islam [is'lam], *n.m.* Islam, the Mohammedan faith; the Mohammedans. **islamique,** *a.* Islamic. **islamisme,** *n.m.* Islamism. **islamite,** *n.* Islamite.
islandais [islɑ̃'dɛ], *a.* (*fem.* **-aise**) Icelandic. —*n.m.* Icelandic (language); (**Islandais,** *fem.* **-aise**) Icelander; French sailor fishing in Iceland waters.
Islande [is'lɑ̃d], *f.* Iceland.
isobare [izɔ'bar] or **isobarique** or **isobarométrique,** *a.* Isobaric. *Courbe isobare,* isobaric curve.—*n.f.* *Une isobare,* an isobar.
isocèle or **isoscèle** [izɔ'sɛl], *a.* (*Geom.*) Isosceles. **isochromatique,** *a.* Isochromatic. **isochrone,** *a.* Isochronal, isochronous. **isochronisme,** *n.m.* Isochronism. **isoclinal,** *a.* (*fem.* **-ale,** *pl.* **-aux**) Isoclinal. **isodynamique,** *a.* Isodynamic.
isolant [izɔ'lɑ̃], *a.* (*fem.* **-ante**) Insulating, isolating. *Corps isolant,* insulating body; *bouteille isolante,* vacuum flask.—*n.m.* Insulator. **isolateur,** *a.* (*fem.* **-trice**) Insulating. —*n.m.* Insulator. **isolation,** *n.f.* Insulation; isolation. **isolationnisme,** *n.m.* Isolationism. **isolationniste,** *a.* and *n.* Isolationist.
isolé [izɔ'le], *a.* (*fem.* **isolée**) Isolated; lonely, solitary; detached, insulated, apart, not contiguous. *Lieu isolé,* lonely spot; (*Mil.*) *poste isolé,* a detached post. **isolement,** *n.m.* Loneliness, isolation, seclusion, solitude;

insulation. *Vivre dans l'isolement,* to live a retired life. **isolément,** *adv.* Separately. *Voyager isolément,* to travel singly.
isoler [izɔ'le], *v.t.* To isolate, to insulate, to detach; to cut off, to separate. **s'isoler,** *v.r.* To be isolated or detached; to live alone or apart, to shun society. **isoloir,** *n.m.* Insulating-stand, electric stool; polling-booth.
isomère [izɔ'mɛːr], *a.* Isomeric. **isotherme,** *a.* Isothermal.—*n.f.* Isotherm. **isothermique,** *a.* Isothermic. **isotope,** *n.m.* Isotope. **isotopique,** *a.* Isotopic. **isotrope,** *a.* Isotropic. **isotropie,** *n.f.* Isotropism.
Israël [isra'ɛl], *m.* Israel. **israélien,** *a.* (*fem.* **-ienne**) and *n.m.* (**Israélien,** *fem.* **-ienne**) Israeli.
israélite [israe'lit], *a.* Israelitic, Israelitish. —*n.* (**Israélite**) Israelite.
issu [i'sy], *a.* (*fem.* **issue** (1)) Born, descended, sprung (*de*).
issue (2) [i'sy], *n.f.* Issue, egress, outlet; escape; (*fig.*) end, event, upshot; refuse grain; offal (of animals). *A l'issue de,* on leaving, at the close of; *chemin sans issue,* blind path, dead end.
isthme [ism], *n.m.* Isthmus. **isthmique,** *a.* Isthmian. *Jeux isthmiques,* Isthmian games.
itague [i'tag], *n.f.* (*Naut.*) Runner-tie.
italianiser [italjani'ze], *v.t.* To Italianize. **italianisme,** *n.m.* Italianism.
Italie [ita'li], *f.* Italy.
italien [ita'ljɛ̃], *a.* (*fem.* **-ienne**) Italian.— *n.m.* Italian language; (**Italien,** *fem.* **-ienne**) an Italian. **italique,** *a.* and *n.m.* Italic. (*Print.*) *En italique,* in italic(s).
item [i'tem], *n.m. inv.* Item, article (of an account).—*adv.* Also, likewise.
itératif [itera'tif], *a.* (*fem.* **-ive**) Iterative, repeated. **itération,** *n.f.* Repetition. **itérativement,** *adv.* Repeatedly, once again.
itinéraire [itine'rɛːr], *n.m.* Itinerary, route; guide, guide-book; *journal of travel.—a.* Pertaining to roads etc. *Colonne itinéraire,* sign-post.
itinérant [itine'rɑ̃], *a.* (*fem.* **-ante**) Itinerant.
itou [i'tu], *adv.* (*dial.*) Also, too, likewise.
iule [jyl], *n.m.* (*Bot.*) Catkin, ament; galley worm.
ive [iːv] or **ivette,** *n.f.* Ground-ivy; (*dial.*)* mare.
ivoire [i'vwaːr], *n.m.* Ivory; (*fig.*) whiteness. *D'ivoire,* ivory; *ivoire des dents,* bone of the teeth. **ivoirerie,** *n.f.* Ivory trade. **ivoirier,** *n.m.* Ivory-carver. **ivorine,** *n.f.* Ivorine.
ivraie [i'vrɛ], *n.f.* Darnel, tare. *Séparer l'ivraie d'avec le bon grain,* to separate the tares from the wheat.
ivre [iːvr], *a.* Drunk; intoxicated; (*fig.*) inebriated, transported. *A moitié ivre,* half-tipsy, half-seas over; *ivre de joie,* beside oneself with joy; *ivre de sang,* drunk with blood; *ivre mort,* dead-drunk. **ivresse,** *n.f.* Drunkenness, intoxication; (*fig.*) inebriation, frenzy, rapture, enthusiasm. **ivrogne,** *n.m.* Drunkard.—*a.* Drunken, tipsy, given to drink. **ivrogner,** *v.i.* To booze, to get drunk. **s'ivrogner,** *v.r.* (*colloq.*) To take to drink. **ivrognerie,** *n.f.* Habitual drunkenness, intoxication. **ivrognesse,** *n.f.* Drunken woman; woman given to drink.
ixia [ik'sja], *n.f.* (*Bot.*) Ixia.
izard [ISARD].

[433]

J

J, j [ʒi], *n.m.* The tenth letter of the alphabet. (*Mil.*) *Le jour J*, Zero day, D-day.
***jà** [ʒα], *adv.* Already.
jable [ʒα:bl], *n.m.* Croze; chimb (of barrel).
jabler, *v.t.* To cut a chimb in a stave.
jabloir, *n.m.*, **jabloire** or **jablière**, *n.f.* Tool for cutting crozes.
jaborandi [ʒabɔrɑ̃'di], *n.m.* (*Bot. Pharm.*) Jaborandi.
jabot [ʒa'bo], *n.m.* Crop (of a bird); frill (of a shirt or blouse); jabot *Faire jabot*, to pout; (*fam.*) to give oneself airs; *se remplir le jabot*, to have a blow-out.
jabotage [ʒabɔ'ta:ʒ], *n.m.* (*colloq.*) Chattering.
jaboter, *v.i.* (*colloq.*) To prattle, to chatter.
jaboteur, *n.m.* (*fem.* **-euse**) Chatterer, jabberer.
jacasse [ʒa'kas], *n.f.* (*pop.*) Magpie; (*fig.*) chatterer, chatterbox, talkative woman.
jacasser, *v.i.* To chatter (of the magpie); (*fig.*) to chatter, to jabber. **jacasserie** *n.f.* Chattering.
jacée [ʒa'se], *n.f.* (*Bot.*) Knapweed [PENSÉE].
jacent [ʒa'sɑ̃], *a.* (*fem.* **-ente**) (*Law*) Vacant, in abeyance.
jachère [ʒa'ʃɛ:r], *n.f.* Fallow. *Être en jachère*, to lie fallow; *terre en jachère*, fallow-land.
jachérer, *v.t.* To work (fallow-land) for the first time.
jacinthe [ʒa'sɛ̃:t] or **hyacinthe** [ja'sɛ̃:t], *n.f.* Hyacinth; jacinth. *Jacinthe des prés*, or *des bois*, bluebell.
jack [dʒak], *n.m.* (*Tech.*) Jack (in weaving and knitting-machines, telephones, etc.).
jacobée [ʒakɔ'be] or **herbe de St Jacques**, *n.f.* Ragwort.
jacobin [ʒakɔ'bɛ̃], *n.m.* (*fem.* **-ine**) Jacobin friar; Jacobin (ultra-radical of the French Revolution). **jacobinisme**, *n.m.* Jacobinism.
jacobite [ʒakɔ'bit], *n.m.* and *a.* Jacobite.
jaconas [ʒakɔ'na], *n.m.* Jaconet.
jacquard [ʒa'ka:r], *n.m.* Jacquard loom; Fair Isle knitting stitch. *Un chandail jacquard*, a Fair Isle jumper.
jacquemart [JAQUEMART].
jacquerie [ʒa'kri], *n.f.* Jacquerie, rising of peasants.
Jacques [ʒa:k], *n.m.* James, Jim. *Jacques bonhomme*, peasant, friend, Hodge (nickname for French peasants as a class); *faire le Jacques*, to play the fool; to try to be funny; *Maître Jacques*, Jack-of-all-trades.
jacquet [ʒa'kɛ], *n.m.* Backgammon; (*vulg.*) squirrel.
jacquot [ʒa'ko], *n.m.* Poll, Polly.
jactance [ʒak'tɑ̃:s], *n.f.* Boasting, boast, bragging. *Plein de jactance*, boastful.
jacter [ʒak'te], *v.i.* (*slang*) To speak, to boast.
jaculatoire [ʒakyla'twa:r], *a.* Ejaculatory. *Oraison jaculatoire*, ejaculatory prayer.
jade [ʒad], *n.m.* Jade.
jadis [ʒa'dis], *adv.* Of old, once upon a time, of yore, formerly. *Au temps jadis*, in days of old, in the olden time; long ago.
jaguar [ʒa'gwar], *n.m.* Jaguar.
jaïet or **jayet** [ʒa'je] [JAIS].
jaillir [ʒa'ji:r], *v.i.* To spout, to gush, to spurt out; to spring, to burst out; to shoot out *or* up. *Faire jaillir*, to cause to shoot

forth. **jaillissant**, *a.* (*fem.* **-ante**) Spouting, gushing; springing, bursting. *Puits jaillissant*, gusher (of mineral oil). **jaillissement**, *n.m.* Gushing, spouting, springing, flashing, burst.
jais [ʒɛ], *n.m.* Jet. *Noir comme du jais, d'un noir de jais*, jet-black.
jalap [ʒa'lap], *n.m.* Jalap.
jale [ʒal], *n.f.* (*dial.*) Large bowl or tub.
jalon [ʒa'lɔ̃], *n.m.* Levelling-staff, surveying-staff; (*Mil.*) picket (for alignment), aiming-post; (*fig.*) landmark, beacon. **jalonnement**, *n.m.* (*Land-surveying*) Staking-out, marking-out. **jalonner**, *v.i.* To place levelling-staves, landmarks, etc.—*v.t.* To mark out or indicate; to stake out. **jalonneur**, *n.m.* (*Mil.*) Marker, pointer; staffman.
jalouse [JALOUX].
jalousement [ʒaluz'mɑ̃], *adv.* Jealously.
jalouser [ʒalu'ze], *v.t.* To be jealous of, to envy.
jalousie [ʒalu'zi], *n.f.* Jealousy, envy; slotted sun-blind; Venetian shutter (of organ); Venetian blind; (*Bot.*) sweet-william. *Donner de la jalousie à quelqu'un*, to make someone jealous; *par jalousie*, out of jealousy; *regarder à travers la jalousie*, to peep through the blind.
jaloux [ʒa'lu], *a.* (*fem.* **jalouse**) Jealous; envious; desirous, anxious, solicitous (to please etc.). *Jaloux d'acquérir de la gloire*, desirous of acquiring glory; *jaloux de plaire*, anxious to please; *être jaloux de sa réputation*, to be jealous of one's good name.—*n.* Jealous person. *Faire des jaloux*, to excite jealousy.
Jamaïque [ʒama'ik], **la**, *f.* Jamaica.
jamais [ʒa'mɛ], *adv.* (*negative*) Never, not ever, at no time whatever; (*affirm.*) ever, at any time; always, for ever. *A jamais*, for ever; *à tout jamais*, for ever and ever; *au grand jamais*, to all eternity; *jamais de la vie*, not on your life! I don't believe it! never in this world; *je ne la vois jamais*, I never see her; *plus riche que jamais*, richer than ever; *presque jamais*, hardly ever; *si jamais je deviens riche*, if ever I become rich; *mieux vaut tard que jamais*, better late than never.
jambage [ʒɑ̃'ba:ʒ], *n.m.* Jamb (of a door etc.); hanger, down-stroke, pot-hook (in writing).
jambe [ʒɑ̃:b], *n.f.* Leg; shank. *A mi-jambe*, to half-way up the leg; *avoir des jambes de quinze ans*, to be as nimble as ever; *cela ne lui rend pas la jambe mieux faite*, he is no better off for it; *courir à toutes jambes*, to run as fast as one's legs can carry one; *écarter les jambes*, to spread one's legs; to stand with one's feet apart; *être haut de jambes*, (of an animal) to be long-legged; *faire la belle jambe*, to play the dandy, to show off; *c'est ça qui me fait une belle jambe!* a lot of good that does me! *faire une chose par-dessous* (or *par-dessus*) *la jambe*, to do something carelessly, without exertion; *jambe arquée*, bow-leg; *jambe de bois*, wooden leg, peg-leg; *jambe de chien*, (*Naut.*) sheepshank; *jambe de force*, principal rafter, strut, stay; *jambe deçà, jambe delà*, astride; *jouer des jambes*, to take to flight; *le gras de la jambe*. the calf of the leg; *prendre ses jambes à son cou*, to take to one's heels, to show a clean pair of heels; *tirer dans les jambes de quelqu'un*, to play a dirty trick on somebody. **jambé**, *a.* (*fem.* **-ée**) Legged.

Bien jambé, with shapely legs, with good strong legs (esp. of child). **jambette,** *n.f.* Small leg; post (in roof etc.); trip; pocket-knife. **jambier,** *a.* (*fem.* **-ière**) (*Anat.*) Tibial, of the leg.—*n.f.* Legging, leg-guard, shin-guard; greave. **jambon,** *n.m.* Ham. **jambonneau,** *n.m.* (*pl.* **-eaux**) Knuckle of ham; fore-leg ham.

jamboree [ʒãbɔ'ri], *n.m.* Jamboree.

jambose [ʒã'boz], *n.f.*, or **jambosier,** *n.m.* (*Bot.*) Jambose, rose-apple (tree).

jan [ʒã], *n.m.* (*Trick-track*) Each of the two tables; (*dial.*) gorse.

janissaire [ʒani'sɛːr], *n.m.* Janissary.

jansénisme [ʒãse'nism], *n.m.* Jansenism. **janséniste,** *n.m.* and *a.* Jansenist. [*See* RELIURE.]

jante [ʒãːt], *n.f.* Felloe, rim (of a wheel). *Jante à talon*, clincher rim. **jantier,** *n.m.*, or **jantière,** *n.f.* Tool for assembling and fitting felloes. **jantille,** *n.f.* Paddle (of a water-wheel).

janvier [ʒã'vje], *n.m.* January.

Japon [ʒa'põ], *m.* Japan.

japon [ʒa'põ], *n.m.* Japan porcelain; Japanese vellum. **japonais,** *a.* (*fem.* **-aise**) Japanese. —*n.m.* Japanese language; (**Japonais,** *fem.* **-aise**), a Japanese. **japonaiserie** or **japonerie,** *n.f.* Article of Japanese craft.

jappement [ʒap'mã], *n.m.* Yelping. **japper,** *v.i.* To yelp, to yap.

jaquemart [ʒak'maːr], *n.m.* Jack or mannikin-striker in a clock.

jaquet [ʒa'kɛ], *n.m.*, or *petite bécasse*, or *bécassine sourde*, jack-snipe [*see also* JACQUET].

jaquette [ʒa'kɛt], *n.f.* Morning coat, tail-coat; woman's jacket; *frock, short petticoat (for boys); dust-cover, wrapper (of book).

jaquier [ʒa'kje], *n.m.* Breadfruit-tree.

jar [ʒar], *n.m.* (*dial.*) Sand-bank in the river Loire [*see also* JARS].

jarde [ʒard], *n.f.*, or **jardon,** *n.m.* Bog-spavin [*see also* ÉPARVIN].

jardin [ʒar'dɛ̃], *n.m.* Garden; (*pl.*) pleasure-grounds; (*Naut.*) quarter-gallery. *Jardin anglais*, landscape garden; *jardin d'agrément*, pleasure-garden; *jardin des plantes*, botanical gardens; *jardin fruitier*, fruit-garden; *jardin japonais*, rock garden; *jardins ouvriers*, allotments; *jardin potager*, kitchen-garden. *Jardin d'enfants*, kindergarten. *Côté jardin*, (*Theat.*) prompt-side. *Cité-jardin*, garden city. **jardinage,** *n.m.* Gardening; garden-produce. **jardiner,** *v.i.* To garden. **jardinet,** *n.m.* Small garden.

jardinier (1) [ʒardi'nje], *n.m.* (*fem.* **jardinière** (1)) Gardener. **jardinier** (2), *a.* (*fem.* **jardinière** (2)) Of the garden. *Plantes jardinières*, garden-plants.—*n.f.* Flower-stand, flower-pot holder; cart or wagon for vegetables; (*Cook.*) jardinière; (*Ent.*) (general name for several pests such as) ground beetle, mole-cricket; (*Orn.*) ortolan; kindergarten teacher. **jardiniste,** *n.m.* Landscape-gardener.

jardon [JARDE].

jargon [ʒar'gõ], *n.m.* Jargon, gibberish; lingo, cant, slang; (*Min.*) jargon, grey or brown zircon. **jargonner,** *v.i.* To talk jargon, to talk twaddle.

Jarnac [COUP DE JARNAC, *see* COUP].

*jarni! [ʒar'ni], **jarnigué,** int. (*dial. corrupt. of je renie Dieu*) By Heaven! zounds!

jarousse [ʒa'rus] or **jarosse,** *n.f.* Vetch.

jarre [ʒaːr], *n.f.* Jar.

jarret [ʒa'rɛ], *n.m.* Ham (of man); hough, hock (of horse); knuckle (of veal); (*Arch.*) unevenness, bulge. *Tendon du jarret*, hamstring. *Avoir du jarret*, to be a good walker or dancer; *couper les jarrets à un cheval*, to hamstring a horse; *être ferme sur ses jarrets*, to keep one's countenance, to stand unmoved; *jarret tendu*, with the leg(s) straight; with the knee(s) braced. **jarreté,** *a.* (*fem.* **-ée**) Close-hammed, close-hocked, knock-kneed; (*Arch.*) protuberant, projecting (of a surface); gartered. **jarretelle,** *n.f.* (Stocking) suspender. **jarreter,** *v.t.* To garter. **se jarreter,** *v.r.* To put one's garters on. **jarretière,** *n.f.* Garter; (*Mil.*) sling (for lifting cannon). *L'Ordre de la Jarretière*, the Order of the Garter.

jars [ʒaːr], *n.m.* Gander (another form of *jargon*), slang. (*pop.*) *Dévider le jars*, to talk slang; *il entend le jars*, he is no fool, (*colloq.*) he knows what's what.

jas [ʒa], *n.m.* (*Anchor*) stock.

jaser [ʒa'ze], *v.i.* To chatter, to chat, to gossip. *Jaser comme une pie borgne*, to chatter like a magpie.

jaseran [ʒaz'rã], *n.m.* Gold neck-chain.

jaserie [ʒaz'ri], *n.f.* Prating, chattering; chatter; gossip. **jaseur,** *n.m.* (*fem.* **-euse**) Chatterer, chatterbox.—*n.m.* *Jaseur de Bohême*, waxwing.—*a.* Talkative.

jasione [ʒa'zjon], *n.f.* (*Bot.*) or *jasione de montagne*, or *herbe bleue*, jasione.

jasmin [ʒas'mɛ̃], *n.m.* Jasmine, jessamine.

jaspe [ʒasp], *n.m.* Jasper. **jasper,** *v.t.* To marble, to vein, to variegate.

jaspiner [ʒaspi'ne], *v.i.* (*pop.*) To talk, to gossip.

jaspure [ʒas'pyːr], *n.f.* Marbling, veining.

jatte [ʒat], *n.f.* Bowl, platter; dog's bowl. **jattée,** *n.f.* Bowlful, platterful.

jauge [ʒoːʒ], *n.f.* Gauge; gauging-rod, dip-rod; measurement; (*Naut.*) tonnage, burthen; (*Hort.*) trench (for temporarily storing young plants). *Jauge d'eau*, water-gauge. **jaugeage,** *n.m.* Gauging. **jauger,** *v.t.* To gauge, to measure the capacity of, to take the gauge of; (*Naut.*) to draw (so many feet of water). **jaugeur,** *n.m.* Gauger.

jaumière [ʒo'mjɛːr], *n.f.* (*Naut.*) Rudder-hole.

jaunâtre [ʒo'nɑːtr], *a.* Yellowish.

jaune [ʒoːn], *a.* Yellow. *Jaune comme un coing*, as yellow as a guinea; *rire jaune*, to give a sickly smile, to laugh on the wrong side of one's face.—*n.m.* Yellow. *Un jaune*, (*pop.*) a blackleg; *jaune d'œuf*, yolk (of an egg).

jauneau [ʒo:'no:], *n.m.* (*pl.* **-eaux**) Lesser celandine.

jaunet [ʒo:'nɛ], *a.* (*fem.* **-ette**) Yellowish.—*n.m.* Gold coin. *Jaunet d'eau*, yellow water-lily. **jauni,** *a.* (*fem.* **-ie**) Yellowed (by age, sun, etc.); faded. **jaunir,** *v.t.* To make yellow, to dye yellow.—*v.i.* To grow yellow, to turn yellow. **jaunissant,** *a.* (*fem.* **-ante**) Turning yellow, yellowing; ripening. **jaunisse,** *n.f.* Jaundice. *Il va en faire une jaunisse*, he'll be green (with envy), he'll have a fit.

javanais [ʒava'nɛ], *a.* and *n.* (*fem.* **-aise**) Javanese.—*n.m.* *A sort of cant in the middle of the 19th century.

javart [ʒa'va:r], *n.m.* (*Vet.*) Ulcer on pastern.

javeau [ʒa'vo], *n.m.* (*pl.* **javeaux**) Sandbank.

javelage [ʒa'vla:ʒ], *n.m.* Laying in swathes; drying (of corn in the fields). **javeler**, *v.t.* To lay in loose swathes.—*v.i.* To turn yellow (of corn). **javeleur**, *n.m.* (*fem.* **-euse**) Harvester; swathe-layer.

javeline [ʒa'vlin], *n.f.* Javelin.

javelle [ʒa'vel], *n.f.* Swathe, loose sheaf (of corn left to dry); bundle of vine-branches.

javelliser [ʒaveli'ze], *v.t.* To sterilize water with *eau de javel* (potassium chloride), to chlorinate.

javelot [ʒa'vlo], *n.m.* Javelin. (*spt.*) *Lancer le javelot*, to throw the javelin.

jazz [(d)ʒɑ:z], *n.m.* Jazz.

je [ʒə], *pron.* I. *Je parle*, I speak; *parlé-je?* do I speak?

Jean [ʒɑ̃], *m.* John. *Jeannot*, Johnny, Jock. (*vulg.*) *Un Jean-foutre*, an idiot, a coward, a God-help-me, a spineless fellow; *la Saint-Jean*, Midsummer Day.

Jeanne [ʒɑ(:)n], *f.* Joan, Jane, Jean.

jeannette [ʒa'nɛt], *n.f.* Peasant's gold cross hung at the neck; sleeve ironing-stand; (*Bot.*) *jeannette jaune* [FAUX NARCISSE]; *jeannette blanche* [ADONIS].

jeep [(d)ʒip], *n.f.* Jeep.

jejunum [ʒeʒy'nɔm], *n.m.* (*Anat.*) Jejunum.

je-m'en-fichiste [ʒmɑ̃fi'ʃist], *n.m.* *fam.* instead of *je m'en foutiste*, (*vulg.*) person who has no care, no interest about anything.

jérémiade [ʒere'mjad], *n.f.* Jeremiad.

Jérémie [ʒere'mi], *m.* Jeremy.

jersey [ʒɛr'ze], *n.m.* Jersey. *Gros jersey*, sweater.

Jérusalem [ʒeryza'lɛm], *f.* Jerusalem.

jésuite [ʒe'zɥit], *a.*, *n.m.* Jesuit. *Jésuite de robe courte*, lay Jesuit. **jésuitique**, *a.* Jesuitic. **jésuitiquement**, *adv.* Jesuitically. **jésuitiser**, *v.i.* To jesuitize. **jésuitisme**, *n.m.* Jesuitism.

Jésus [ʒe'zy], *m.* Jesus.

jésus [ʒə'zy], *a.m.* and *n.m.* Long royal, super-royal (of paper). *Grand jésus*, imperial.

jet [ʒɛ], *n.m.* Casting, throwing, cast, throw; jet, gush, spurt (of water); sudden ray (of light); casting (of metal); shoot, sprout (of plants); spout (of pump etc.). *Arme de jet*, missile weapon; *d'un seul jet*, at one stroke, at a single effort; *du premier jet*, at the first attempt; *jet à la mer*, jettisoning of a cargo or part of it; *jet d'abeilles*, swarm of young bees; *jet d'air comprimé*, compressed air spray; *jet d'eau*, waterspout, water spray, fountain; *jet de flamme*, burst of flame; *jet de lumière*, ray of light; *le jet de dés*, the cast of dice; *le jet d'une draperie*, (*Paint.*) the folds or lay of a drapery; *le jet d'un filet*, the cast of a net; *un jet de pierre*, a stone's throw.

jetage [ʒə'ta:ʒ], *n.m.* Casting, throwing; (*Vet.*) discharge.

jeté [ʒə'te], *n.m.* Dance-step; (*knitting*) wool forward; oblong piece of lace, embroidery, large ornamental mat or doiley thrown across a table, etc.; spray(s) of flowers used in the same way.

jetée [ʒə'te], *n.f.* Jetty, pier; breakwater.

jeter [ʒə'te], *v.t. irr.* (*conjug. like* APPELER)

To throw, to fling, to hurl; to throw up, to toss; to throw down, to fling down, to knock down; to throw out, to fling away, to shed; to pour, to cast, to mould; to emit, to shoot out, to shoot forth; to send forth, to utter; to disembogue, to empty; to discharge, to run, to suppurate. *Jeter à la mer*, to throw overboard, to jettison; *jeter de l'huile sur le feu*, to add fuel to the flame; *jeter de profondes racines*, to become deeply rooted; *jeter l'ancre*, to cast anchor; *jeter les fondements d'une maison* or *d'une fortune*, to lay the foundations of a house or of a fortune; *jeter les yeux sur quelqu'un*, to cast one's eyes on someone, to select someone for a post etc.; *jeter son argent par la fenêtre*, to play ducks and drakes with one's money; *jeter un coup d'œil sur*, to cast a glance at; to look at; to observe; *le sort en est jeté*, the die is cast, the step has been taken. **se jeter**, *v.r.* To throw oneself, to fling oneself; to rush, to pounce, to fall upon (attack); to disembogue, to flow (of rivers etc.). *Se jeter à corps perdu dans*, to rush headlong into; *se jeter à l'eau*, to jump into the water; (*fig.*) to take the plunge; *se jeter au cou de quelqu'un*, to fall on someone's neck; *se jeter dans*, to flow into (of a river); *se jeter sur l'ennemi*, to fall upon the enemy. **jeteur**, *n.m.* (*fem.* **-euse**) (Mostly used in) *Jeteur, jeteuse de sorts*, person who has the evil-eye, who is supposed to cast spells.

jetisse or **jectisse** [ʒɛ(k)'tis], *a.* usually *pl.* (*Terres* or *pierres*) *jetisses*, that can be moved or put in place by hand.

jeton [ʒə'tɔ̃], *n.m.* Mark, counter. *Jeton de présence*, tally, token, voucher for attendance; *faux comme un jeton*, as false as a brass shilling. (*fam.*) *Vieux jeton*, old fellow. (*vulg.*) *Avoir les jetons*, to have the jitters.

jettature [ʒeta'tyr], *n.f.* (*dial.*) Evil-eye.

jeu [ʒø], *n.m.* (*pl.* **jeux**) Play, sport, pastime; game; fun, joke, freak, frolic; game of cards, card-playing; gaming, gambling; (*fig.*) cards, hand; throw, luck, stake; set (of games); pack of cards; (*Naut.*) set (of oars); suit (of sails); set (of keys); manner of playing, way; acting, performance (of players); (*Mach.*) length of stroke, working; interplay; effects; clearance; looseness. *Avoir beau jeu*, to have a good hand; *avoir du jeu*, to have too much play (of machinery); *bonheur au jeu*, good luck at play; *cacher son jeu*, to conceal one's intentions; *cela n'est pas de jeu*, that is not fair; *c'est le jeu*, that's the game; *être à deux de ieux*, to be even, (*Ten.*) deuce; *faire bonne mine à mauvais jeu*, to put a good face on matters; *jeu de cartes*, card game; pack of cards; *jeu d'échecs*, set of chess-men; *jeu de mains, jeu de vilain*, rough play often ends in tears; *jeu de mots*, pun, play on words; *jeu d'esprit*, witticism; *jeu de quilles*, set of nine-pins; (*Theat.*) *jeux de lumière*, lighting effects; *jeux de scène*, stage-effects; *jeux de société*, parlour games; *jeux d'orgue*, organ-stops; *jeux floraux*, floral games; *jouer gros jeu* or *un jeu d'enfer*, to play for high stakes; *le jeu n'en vaut pas la chandelle*, the game is not worth the candle; *maison de jeu*, gambling-house; *mettre au jeu*, to stake; *mettre en jeu*, to set to work; *mettre tout en jeu pour réussir*, to use every possible means to succeed; *mettre une personne en jeu*, to involve someone (in); *se* *piquer au jeu*, to persist in playing; *tenir le jeu de quelqu'un*, to play for someone; *tenir un jeu*, to keep a gaming-table; *vieux jeu*, out-of-date, old-fashioned.

jeudi [ʒø'di], *n.m.* Thursday. *Jeudi gras*, Shrove Thursday; *jeudi saint*, Maundy Thursday; *la semaine des quatre jeudis*, a month of Sundays (never).

jeun (à) [ʒœ̃], *adv.* Fasting, sober. *J'ai pris cela à jeun*, I took it on an empty stomach; *je suis encore à jeun*, I have not yet breakfasted.

jeune [ʒœn], *a.* Young, youthful; younger, junior; recent, new; early, unripe, green. *Corneille le jeune*, Corneille the younger; *faire le jeune homme*, to enjoy oneself; *jeune homme*, young man, stripling, youngster; *jeune personne*, young girl, young lady; *jeune premier* or *jeune première*, (*Theat.*) juvenile lead, leading man, hero, leading lady, heroine; *jeunes gens*, young men, youths, young people; *mon jeune frère*, my younger brother; *qui jeune n'apprend, rien ne saura*, an old dog will learn no tricks; *un jeune Anglais*, an English boy, a young Englishman; *une jeune employée*, a girl assistant; *une tête jeune*, an unripe head.—*adv. S'habiller jeune*, to dress like a young person.—*n.* Young person or animal.

jeûne [ʒøːn], *n.m.* Fasting; fast, abstinence.

jeunement [ʒœn'mɑ̃], *adv.* (*colloq.*) Like a young man; (*Hunt.*) recently. *Cerf de dix cors jeunement*, stag just turned ten years.

jeûner [ʒø'ne], *v.i.* To fast.

jeunesse [ʒœ'nɛs], *n.f.* Youth, young days; youthfulness; freshness, vigour, prime; young people; (*colloq.*) a very young girl or woman, girl, lass. *Avoir un air de jeunesse*, to have a youthful look; *dans la première jeunesse*, in earliest youth; *dès ma jeunesse*, from my youth up; *erreurs de jeunesse*, youthful indiscretions; *il faut que jeunesse se passe*, boys will be boys; *jeunesse d'esprit*, sprightliness of wit; *jeunesse dorée*, gilded youth; *la jeunesse du village*, the youths of the village; *si jeunesse savait, si vieillesse pouvait*, if youth but knew, if age but could.

jeunet [ʒœ'nɛ], *a.* (*fem.* -ette) (*colloq.*) Very young.

jeûneur [ʒø'nœːr], *n.m.* (*fem.* -euse) Faster.

ji [ʒi], *adv.* (*pop.*) Yes.

jiu-jitsu [(d)ʒyʒi'tsy], *n.m.* Ju-jitsu.

joaillerie [ʒwaj'ri], *n.f.* Jeweller's trade or business; jewellery, jewels.

joaillier [ʒwa'je], *n.m.* (*fem.* -ière) Jeweller.

jobard [ʒɔ'baːr], *n.m.* Sucker, mug, fool. **jobarder**, *v.t.* To dupe, to fool. **jobarderie** or **jobardise**, *n.f.* Silliness, credulity.

joc [ʒɔk], *n.m.* Standing (of a mill). *Mettre le moulin à joc*, to stop the mill.

jociste [ʒɔ'sist], *a.* and *n.* Member of J.O.C., *Jeunesse Ouvrière Chrétienne*, Young Workers' Christian Association.

jockey [ʒɔ'kɛ], *n.m.* Jockey.

jocrisse [ʒɔ'kris], *n.m.* Dolt, dupe, simpleton, ninny. *Jouer les jocrisses*, to play silly servants' parts.

jodler [ʒɔd'le], *v.i.* To yodel.

joie [ʒwa], *n.f.* Joy, happiness, joyfulness, gladness; glee, mirth. *Faire la joie* or *être la joie de quelqu'un*, to be someone's joy; *feu de joie*, bonfire; *fille de joie*, prostitute; *ne pas se sentir de joie*, to be beside oneself with joy;

pleurer de joie, to weep for joy; *se faire une joie de*, to be delighted to; *s'en donner à cœur joie*, to do something to one's heart's content.

joignant [ʒwa'ɲɑ̃], *prep.* Next to, adjoining. —*a.* (*fem.* -ante) Adjoining, next to, contiguous.

joindre [ʒwɛ̃:dr], *v.t irr.* (*pres.p.* **joignant**, *p.p.* **joint**, *conjugated like* CRAINDRE) To join, to put together, to unite, to combine, to fix together; to add, to annex; to joint (masonry etc.); to meet or fall in with; to overtake, to come up with; to contact. *Joindre le geste à la parole*, to suit one's action to one's words; *joindre les mains*, to clasp one's hands; *joindre l'utile à l'agréable*, to combine business with pleasure.—*v.i.* To join, to meet, to be in contact. *Ces planches ne joignent pas*, these planks do not join. **se joindre**, *v.r.* To join, to be joined, to be united; to be adjoining, to be adjacent, to be contiguous; to be added. *Se joindre à la conversation*, to join in the conversation; *se joindre à la foule*, to join the crowd.

joint (1) [ʒwɛ̃], *n.m.* Joint; seam, junction. *Joint articulé* or *de coussinet*, knuckle joint; *joint brisé, universel*, or *de Cardan*, double knuckle *or* universal joint; *trouver le joint*, to hit upon the right way.

joint (2) [ʒwɛ̃], *a.* (*fem.* -te) Joined, united; added. *À pieds joints*, feet together; *les mains jointes*, with clasped hands; *prier quelqu'un à mains jointes*, to beg someone on bended knees.

jointé [ʒwɛ̃'te], *a.* (*fem.* -ée) Jointed. *Cheval long jointé*, long-jointed horse. **jointif**, *a.* (*fem.* -ive) Joined, closed (of boards, slabs, etc.).

jointoiement [ʒwɛ̃twa'mɑ̃], *n.m.* Grouting, pointing (of walls).

jointoyer [ʒwɛ̃twa'je], *v.t.* To grout, to point.

jointure [ʒwɛ̃'ty:r], *n.f.* Joint, jointing, articulation.

joli [ʒɔ'li], *a.* (*fem.* **jolie**) Pretty, pleasing, neat; fine, good; nice. *Joli comme un cœur*, pretty as a picture; *un joli coco* or *monsieur*, (*iron.*) a rogue; *il est dans un joli état*, he is in a nice state, in a pretty mess.—*n.m.* What is pretty. *Le joli de la chose c'est que . . .*, the best of the thing is that . . . .

joliet, *a.* (*fem.* **joliette**) Rather pretty.

joliment, *adv.* Prettily; (*iron.*) nicely, finely; (*colloq.*) extremely, awfully, jolly, much, many.

jonc [ʒɔ̃], *n.m.* Rush; cane, rattan, Malacca cane; keeper, guard (ring). *Droit comme un jonc*, straight as a ramrod; *jonc à balais*, reed; *jonc des chaisiers*, bulrush; *jonc d'Inde* or *canne de jonc*, rattan; *jonc fleuri*, flowering rush; *jonc glauque, jonc des jardiniers*, hard rush; *jonc marin*, whin, common furze.

jonchaie, *n.f.* Bed or plantation of rushes.

jonchée [ʒɔ̃'ʃe], *n.f.* Strewing, sprinkling (of flowers). *Jonchée de crème*, cream-cheese.

jonchement, *n.m.* Strewing.

joncher [ʒɔ̃'ʃe], *v.t.* To strew; to heap; to scatter.

jonchets [ʒɔ̃'ʃɛ], *n.m. pl.* Spillikins.

jonciforme [ʒɔ̃si'fɔrm], *a.* Rush-shaped.

jonction [ʒɔ̃k'sjɔ̃], *n.f.* Junction, joining.

jongler [ʒɔ̃'gle], *v.i.* To juggle. **jonglerie**, *n.f.* Juggling, jugglery; (*fig.*) trickery.

jongleur, *n.m.* *Jongleur; juggler; (fig.) trickster.

jonque [ʒɔ̃:k], *n.f.* Junk (Chinese vessel).

jonquille [ʒɔ̃'ki:j], *n.f.* Jonquil.—*a. inv.* and *n.m.* Pale yellow, jonquil (colour).

Jordanie [ʒɔrda'ni], *f.* Jordan.

Joseph [ʒo'zef], *m.* Joseph; [PAPIER].

jouable [ʒwabl], *a.* Playable.

jouail [JAS].

jouailler [ʒwɑ'je], *v.i.* (*colloq.*) To play for small stakes; to strum (on piano).

joubarbe [ʒu'barb], *n.f.* Sempervivum. *Joubarbe des toits* or *grande joubarbe,* houseleek, sengreen; *petite joubarbe* [*see* ORPIN].

joue [ʒu], *n.f.* Cheek; flange (of wheel); side (of arm-chair). *Coucher* or *mettre en joue,* to take aim at; *joue!* (*Mil.*) present! take aim! (*fam.*) *se caler les joues,* to eat copiously.

jouée [ʒwe], *n.f.* (*Arch.*) Reveal (of window); thickness (of wall).

jouer [ʒwe], *v.i.* To play, to amuse oneself, to sport, to gambol, to frolic; to gamble, to game; to run the risk; to speculate (on the funds); to work, to work loose (of machinery etc.); to act, to perform. *À qui de jouer,* whose turn is it to play? *boiserie qui a joué,* woodwork that has given or warped; *faire jouer,* to set going, to let off (a mine etc.), to make act, play, etc., to put in motion or in action, to set going; *ils jouent bien au billard,* they are good at billiards; *jouer à la marchande,* to play at keeping shop; *jouer à coup sûr,* to play without risk; *jouer à quitte ou double,* to play double or quits; *jouer au plus fin,* to vie in cunning with; *jouer au plus sûr,* to play a safe game; *jouer à la Bourse,* to speculate on the Stock Exchange; *jouer aux cartes,* to play cards; *jouer de bonheur,* to be lucky; *jouer du couteau,* to fight with a knife; *jouer de malheur,* to have a run of ill-luck; *jouer des jambes,* to take to one's heels; *jouer du violon,* to play the violin; *ne jouer que pour l'honneur,* to play for love; *qui a joué jouera,* once a gambler, always a gambler.—*v.t.* To play; to venture, to play for, to stake; to gamble away; to move (a piece); to perform, to act; to counterfeit, to pretend to be, to imitate; to ridicule, to make game of; to deceive, to fool, to trick. *Ce papier joue le velours,* this paper looks like velvet; *jouer de l'argent,* to stake money; *jouer la comédie,* to act; to act a sham part; *jouer la surprise,* to pretend to be surprised; *jouer le double jeu,* to double-cross; *jouer une comédie,* to act a comedy; *jouer quelqu'un,* to make a fool of someone; *jouer un air au violon,* to play a tune on the violin; *jouer un cheval,* to back a horse; *jouer une partie,* to play a game; *jouer un rôle,* to play a part; *jouer un tour à quelqu'un,* to play a trick on someone; *on m'a joué,* I have been tricked; *pièce touchée, pièce jouée,* (*Games*) if you touch your piece you must move it; (*fam.*) *jouer la fille de l'air* or *en jouer un air,* to skedaddle.

se jouer, *v.r.* To sport, to play, to frolic, to gambol; to toy, to dally; to make game (of), to laugh, to make light (de). *La fortune se joue des hommes,* fortune makes sport of mankind; *se jouer de quelqu'un,* to make a fool of someone.

jouet [ʒwɛ], *n.m.* Plaything, toy; laughing-stock, jest, sport. *Jouet du vent,* (*Bot.*) *Agrostis spica venti. Etre le jouet de la fortune,* to be the sport of fortune; *être le jouet d'une illusion,* to be the victim of an illusion; *être le jouet de ses passions,* to be led by one's passions.

joueur [ʒwœ:r], *n.m.* (*fem.* **joueuse**) Player; gamester, gambler; speculator, stock-jobber (on the Bourse); player, performer (on an instrument). *Beau joueur,* good-natured player, good loser; poker-faced gambler; *mauvais joueur,* bad loser; *joueur à la baisse* or *à la hausse,* (*St. Exch.*) bear or bull. *Joueur de flûte,* flute-player.—*a.* Fond of playing (of child).

joufflu [ʒu'fly], *a.* (*fem.* **joufflue**) Chubby, chubby-cheeked.

joug [ʒu(g)], *n.m.* Yoke; bondage, slavery. *Atteler au joug,* to yoke; *briser le joug,* to throw off the yoke; *s'affranchir du joug* or *secouer le joug,* to shake off the yoke. **jouguet,** *n.m.* (*W. dial.*) = *palanche.* Single yoke.

jouir [ʒwi:r], *v.i.* To enjoy, to revel; to be in possession (de). *Jouir de l'embarras de quelqu'un,* to revel in someone's embarrassment; *jouir de toutes ses facultés,* to be in possession of all one's faculties; *jouir d'une belle fortune,* to be in possession of a sizeable fortune; *jouir d'une bonne réputation,* to bear a good character; *jouir d'une excellente santé,* to enjoy excellent health.

jouissance, *n.f.* Enjoyment; possession, use; joy, pleasure, delight; interest payable.

jouissant, *a.* (*fem.* **jouissante**) Enjoying, in possession (de).

jouisseur [ʒwi'sœr], *n.m.* **jouisseuse** [ʒwi'søz], *n.f.* Pleasure-seeker, rake.

joujou [ʒu'ʒu], *n.m.* (*pl.* **joujoux**) Plaything, toy. (*Baby talk*) *Faire joujou,* to play.

joule [ʒul], *n.m.* Joule; (1 h.p. = 136 joule-seconds).

jour [ʒu:r], *n.m.* Day, daylight; light; day-break, dawn; day-time; time; aperture, opening, gap, chink, thin patch (in a sock); aspect. *À chaque jour suffit sa peine,* sufficient unto the day is the evil thereof; *à la chute du jour,* at nightfall; *au point, à la pointe du jour,* at break of day; *au grand jour,* in broad daylight; publicly; *au jour le jour,* from hand to mouth; *à un de ces jours!* so long; *broderie à jours,* open-work embroidery; *comptabilité tenue à jour,* books kept up to date; *ce n'est pas tous les jours fête,* Christmas comes but once a year; *c'est le jour et la nuit,* they are as different as chalk and cheese; *de jour en jour,* daily, progressively; *de nos jours,* these days, nowadays, in our time; *donner le jour à,* to give birth to; *du jour au lendemain,* overnight; *du jour où,* since the day when; *d'un jour à l'autre,* from one day to the next; *en plein jour,* in broad daylight; *être à jour,* to be up to date or in apple-pie order; *être dans son bon jour,* to be in a good humour, (*Paint.*) to be in a good light, (*fig.*) to be on one's best behaviour; *être de jour,* to be on duty for the day; *faux jour,* bad light, confusing light; *il commence à faire jour,* it is beginning to be light; *il donne tant par jour,* he gives so much a day; *il fait jour,* it is daylight; *il me remet de jour en jour,* he puts me off from day to day; *je l'attends de jour en jour,* I expect him any day; *jours à fils tirés,* (*Needlework*) drawn-thread work; *jour de l'an,* new year's day; *jour d'atelier*, studio lighting; *jour de réception*, at-home day; *jour maigre*, fish-day; *jour gras*, flesh-day; *les jours gras*, Shrovetide; *jours caniculaires*, dog-days; *l'auteur de vos jours*, the author of your being; *le goût du jour*, the reigning fashion; *le grand jour*, the big day, 'the' day; *plat du jour*, today's special; *le plus beau jour de ma vie*, the happiest day of my life; *le jour baisse*, dusk is coming on; *mettre à jour*, to discover, to lay open; *mettre au jour*, to give birth to, to bring to light; *mourir plein de jours*, to die at a ripe old age; *nuit et jour*, day and night; *petit jour*, first light, dawn; *prendre jour*, to make an appointment; *quel est votre jour?* when are you at home? *se faire jour*, to force one's way through; *sous son vrai jour*, in one's true light; *tôt ou tard la vérité se fait jour*, sooner or later truth will out; *tous les jours*, every day; *de tous les jours*, everyday; second-best (of clothes etc.); *un jour*, some day, one day; *un beau jour*, one fine day; *un jour de fête*, a holiday; *un jour ou l'autre*, some day or other, eventually; *vivre au jour le jour*, to live from hand to mouth; *voir le jour*, to see the light, to come to light; *voir les choses sous un certain jour*, to see things in a certain light.

Jourdain [ʒur'dɛ̃], **le**, *m.* The Jordan.

journal [ʒur'nal], *n.m.* (*pl.* **-aux**) Journal, diary; newspaper; (*Comm.*) day-book. *Journal de bord*, (*Naut.*) log-book; *tenir un journal*, to keep a diary.

journalier, *a.* (*fem.* **-ière**) Daily, diurnal; uncertain, inconstant, fickle, changeable, not the same every day. *Cette femme est très journalière*, this woman varies a great deal (in beauty).—*n.m.* Journeyman, day-labourer; what is done or happens daily.

journalisme, *n.m.* Journalism, the press.

journaliste, *n.* Journalist; pressman.

journée [ʒur'ne], *n.f.* Day (time); day's work or wages; day's journey; battle; historic day. *À grandes journées*, by forced marches; *aller en journée*, to go out to work by the day; *à petites journées*, by short stages; *dans la journée*, in the course of the day, during the day; *femme de journée*, daily help; charwoman; *homme de journée*, day-labourer; *la journée fut rude*, the battle was stubbornly fought; *les journées de Juillet*, the July insurrection (July 27–29, 1830); *pendant la journée*, during the day, in the course of the day; *toute la journée*, all day long. **journellement**, *adv.* Daily, every day.

joute [ʒut], *n.f.* Joust, tilting-match, tilt; fighting, strife, contest, match. *Joutes sur l'eau* or *joutes lyonnaises*, water tournament. (*C*) Game. *Une joute de hockey*, a hockey game.

jouter, *v.i.* To joust, to tilt. **jouteur**, *n.m.* Tilter; (*fig.*) antagonist, adversary.

*****Jouvence** [ʒu'vɑ̃:s], *n.f.* Youth. *Fontaine de Jouvence*, Fountain of Youth.

*****jouvenceau** [ʒuvɑ̃'so], *n.m.* (*pl.* **-eaux**) Lad, stripling, young fellow. **jouvencelle**, *n.f.* Lass, young girl, damsel.

*****jouxte** [ʒukst], *a.* Adjoining, contiguous to.

jovial [ʒɔ'vjal], *a.* (*fem.* **joviale**, *pl.* **joviaux**) Jovial, jolly, merry. **jovialement**, *adv.* Jovially. **jovialité**, *n.f.* Joviality, jollity.

joyau [ʒwa'jo], *n.m.* (*pl.* **joyaux**) Jewel. *Les joyaux de la couronne*, the crown-jewels.

joyeusement [ʒwajøz'mɑ̃], *adv.* Cheerfully, joyfully, merrily. **joyeuseté**, *n.f.* Joyfulness, merriment, gaiety; pleasantry, joke, jest.

joyeux, *a.* (*fem.* **-euse**) Joyful, merry; cheerful, glad.—*n.m.* [BAT' D'AF].

jubé [ʒy'be], *n.m.* Rood-loft or -screen. *Venir à jubé*, to come to terms.

jubilaire [ʒybi'lɛ:r], *a.* Of jubilee; (*fig.*) of fifty years' standing (of persons etc.).

jubilant [ʒybi'lɑ̃], *a.* (*fem.* **-ante**) Jubilant, delighted.

jubilation, *n.f.* Jubilation, rejoicing.

jubilé [ʒybi'le], *n.m.* Jubilee; (*R.-C. Ch.*) plenary indulgence; (*fig.*) golden wedding. *Faire* or *gagner son jubilé*, to reach fifty years' service etc.

jubiler, *v.i.* To jubilate, to exult.

juchée [ʒy'ʃe:], *n.f.* Pheasant's perch or roosting place.

jucher [ʒy'ʃe], *v.i.* To roost, to perch; to lodge (at the top of a house etc).—*v.t.* To perch (something or someone) up. **se jucher**, *v.r.* To go to roost; to perch oneself up.

juchoir, *n.m.* Roosting-place, perch.

judaïque [ʒyda'ik], *a.* Judaical, Jewish. **judaïquement**, *adv.* Judaically. **judaïsant**, *a.* (*fem.* **-ante**) Judaizing. **judaïser**, *v.i.* To Judaize. **judaïsme**, *n.m.* Judaism.

Judas [ʒy'dɑ], *n.m.* Judas, traitor; peep-hole (in a door etc.). *Baiser de Judas*, treacherous kiss.

Judée [ʒy'de], *f.* Judaea.

judicature [ʒydika'ty:r], *n.f.* Judicature, magistracy.

judiciaire [ʒydi'sjɛ:r], *a.* Judiciary, judicial; legal, forensic. *Erreur judiciaire*, miscarriage of justice; *nouvelles judiciaires*, law reports; *poursuites judiciaires*, legal action; *vente judiciaire*, sale by order of the court.—*n.f.* *Judgment, nous. **judiciairement**, *adv.* Judicially, by authority of justice.

judicieusement [ʒydisjøz'mɑ̃], *adv.* Judiciously, discreetly. **judicieux**, *a.* (*fem.* **-ieuse**) Judicious, wise, discreet, well advised.

judo [ʒy'do], *n.m.*, *fam.* for jiu-jitsu.

juge [ʒy:ʒ], *n.m.* Judge; magistrate, justice; (*pl.*) bench. *Être juge et partie*, to be judge of one's own case; *juge d'instruction*, examining magistrate.

jugé, *a.* (*fem.* **jugée**) Judged. *Bien jugé*, well judged.—*n.m.* *Au jugé*, at a guess, at a venture. **jugeable**, *a.* That can be judged.

jugement [ʒyʒ'mɑ̃], *n.m.* Judgment; opinion, view; test; sentence; discrimination, good sense; nous; gumption, perspicacity. *Jugement arbitral*, award; *jugement par défaut*, judgment by default; *jugement provisoire*, decree nisi; *jugement définitif*, decree absolute; *au jugement de*, in the opinion of; *mettre quelqu'un en jugement*, to bring to trial or put someone on trial; *mise en jugement*, arraignment; *passer en jugement*, to be brought up for trial; *prononcer un jugement*, to pass sentence; *rendre un jugement*, to deliver judgment; *rendre un jugement contre*, to sentence; *subir un jugement*, to be under sentence. *Faire preuve de jugement*, to show good sense; *porter un jugement sur*, to pass judgment on. *Le Jugement Dernier*, the Last Judgment, Doomsday.

jugeote [ʒy'ʒɔt], *n.f.* (*fam.*) Gumption.

juger (1) [ʒy'ʒe], *v.t.* To judge; to try, to decide, to determine; to give judgment on, to pass sentence on; to consider, to think, to believe, to deem; to fancy, to imagine. *Mal juger,* to misjudge.—*v.i.* To judge (*de*), to give judgment, to deem, to be of opinion; to appreciate; to distinguish. *À en juger par,* judging by, to judge from; *juger à propos* or *nécessaire de,* to think it proper to; *juger d'autrui par soi-même,* to judge others by oneself; *juger sur l'étiquette du sac,* to judge by the label or by appearances. **se juger,** *v.r.* To judge oneself; to deem oneself (to be); to be judged. *Cette affaire se jugera demain,* this case will be heard *or* will come on tomorrow; *vous en jugez-vous capable?* do you think yourself equal to it?

juger (2), *n.m.* [JUGÉ, *n.m.*]

jugeur, *n.m.* (*fem.* -euse) Judger, hasty judge of things.

jugulaire [ʒygy'lɛːr], *a.* (*Anat.*) Jugular.—*n.f.* Jugular vein; chin-strap.

juguler, *v.t.* To strangle; to jugulate (a disease); (*fig.*) to torment; to fleece.

juif [ʒɥif], *a.* (*fem.* **juive**) Jewish.—*n.* Jew; Jewess; (*pej.*) grasping usurer. *Le Juif errant,* the wandering Jew; *le petit Juif,* the funny bone.

juillet [ʒɥi'jɛ], *n.m.* July. *Le Quatorze juillet,* France's national day, Bastille day.

juin [ʒɥɛ̃], *n.m.* June.

juiverie [ʒɥi'vri], *n.f.* *Jewry (Jews' quarter); (*pej.*) group of Jews; Jew's bargain or trick.

jujube [ʒy'ʒyb], *n.f.* Jujube (fruit).—*n.m.* or *Pâte de jujube,* jujube (lozenge). **jujubier,** *n.m.* Jujube-tree.

julep [ʒy'lep], *n.m.* Julep.

Jules [ʒyl], *m.* Julius.

jules [ʒyl], *n.m.* (*vulg.*) Chamber-pot. (*Mil. slang*) *Pincer l'oreille à Jules,* to carry the latrine-pail.

julien [ʒy'ljɛ̃], *a.* (*fem.* **julienne** (1)) Julian (calendar, year).

julienne (2) [ʒy'ljɛn], *n.f.* Rocket (plant); julienne (vegetable soup).

Juliette [ʒy'ljɛt], *f.* Juliet.

jumeau [ʒy'mo], *a.* (*fem.* -elle, *pl.* -eaux) Twin; double (of fruit etc.). *Des cerises jumelles,* double cherries; *frères jumeaux,* twin brothers; *lits jumeaux,* twin beds; *maisons jumelles,* semi-detached houses.—*n.* Twin.

jumelage, *n.m.* Pairing, matching; joining.

jumelé, *a.* (*fem.* -ée) Twin, in couples; (*Carp. etc.*) joined together by cheeks. *Maison jumelée,* semi-detached house; *villes jumelées,* twin towns; (*Horse-racing*) *pari jumelé,* win and place bet, each-way bet; *pneus jumelés,* dual tyres. **jumeler,** *v.t.* To couple or strengthen with cheeks, to clamp, to join, to pair. *Jumeler un mât,* to fish *or* clamp a mast.

jumelles, *n.f. pl.* (*Carp.*) Cheeks, side-beams; (*Naut.*) fishes (for masts, yards, etc.); binoculars; (*Her.*) gemels. *Jumelles de campagne,* field-glasses; *jumelles de théâtre,* opera-glasses. *Jumelles de manchettes,* cuff-links.

jument [ʒy'mɑ̃], *n.f.* Mare. *Jument poulinière,* brood-mare.

jungle [ʒɔ̃:gl], *n.f.* Jungle.

junte [ʒɔ̃:t], *n.f.* Junta (Spanish council).

jupe [ʒyp], *n.f.* Skirt. *Jupe entravée,* hobble skirt; *jupe plissée,* pleated skirt; *jupe en forme,* gored or flared skirt. (*Mech.*) *Jupe de piston,* piston skirt. **jupe-culotte,** *n.f.* (*pl.* **jupes-culottes**) Divided skirt.

Jupiter [ʒypi'tɛr], *m.* Jupiter, Jove.

jupon [ʒy'pɔ̃], *n.m.* Petticoat. (*fam.*) *Courir le jupon,* to chase the girls; *être élevé dans les jupons de sa mère,* to be brought up at one's mother's apron-strings.

jurande [ʒy'rɑ̃:d], *n.f.* Wardenship (of a guild etc.).

jurassique [ʒyra'sik], *a.* (*Geol.*) Jurassic.

juratoire [ʒyra'twaːr], *a.* Juratory, on oath.

juré [ʒy're], *a.* (*fem.* -ée) Sworn.—*n.m.* Juror, juryman; member of a jury. *Messieurs les jurés,* gentlemen of the jury; *récuser un juré,* to challenge a juror.

jurement, *n.m.* Oath; swearing. *Proférer un jurement,* to utter an oath. **jurer,** *v.t.* To swear by; to swear, to vow, to take an oath that, to promise; to blaspheme.—*v.i.* To swear, to take an oath; to use oaths, to blaspheme; (*fig.*) to contrast, to jar, to clash (of colours etc.). *Il jure comme un charretier,* he swears like a trooper; *il m'a juré ses grands dieux (que),* he swore by all the gods (that); *il ne faut jurer de rien,* one never can tell; *nous nous jurâmes une éternelle amitié,* we swore eternal friendship.

*jureur, *n.m.* Swearer.

juridiction [ʒyridik'sjɔ̃], *n.f.* Jurisdiction; department, province. *Ce n'est pas de sa juridiction,* it is not in his province. **juridictionnel,** *a.* (*fem.* -elle) Jurisdictional.

juridique [ʒyri'dik], *a.* Juridical, judicial, legal. **juridiquement,** *adv.* Juridically, judicially.

jurisconsulte [ʒyriskɔ̃'sylt], *n.m.* Jurisconsult.

jurisprudence [ʒyrispry'dɑ̃:s], *n.f.* Jurisprudence; statute law; case-law.

juriste [ʒy'rist], *n.m.* Jurist.

juron [ʒy'rɔ̃], *n.m.* Oath. *Gros juron,* tremendous oath; *lâcher un juron,* to rap out an oath.

jury [ʒy'ri], *n.m.* (*pl.* **jurys**) Jury; board or commission of examiners; committee. *Chef du jury,* foreman of the jury; *dresser la liste du jury,* to empanel a jury; *jury d'accusation,* grand jury; *jury d'examen,* examination board; *jury de jugement,* petty jury; *récuser un jury,* to challenge a jury.

jus [ʒy], *n.m.* Juice; gravy; glaze (on a painting); (*Mil. slang*) coffee; chic, elegance. *Avoir du jus,* to be smart, stylish; *jeter un jus,* to look smart, chic, stylish; *laisse-le mijoter dans son jus,* let him stew in his own juice.

jusant [ʒy'zɑ̃], *n.m.* Ebb, ebb-tide.

jusée [ʒy'ze], *n.f.* Tan-liquor, tanning infusion.

jusque or ***jusques** [ʒysk], *prep.* Even to, as far as; till, until; down to; up to; the very. *Depuis le premier jusqu'au dernier,* from the first to the last; *depuis Paris jusqu'à Londres,* all the way from Paris to London; *il a vendu jusqu'à sa chemise,* he has sold the very shirt off his back; *il n'est pas jusqu'aux enfants qui ne l'adorent,* the very children adore him; *jusqu'à ce que cela soit fait,* till it be done; *jusqu'à demain,* till tomorrow; *jusqu'à présent,* up to now; *jusqu'au ciel,* to the skies; *jusque-là,* up to that time, up to that point;

jusqu'ici, as far as here, till now, down to here; *jusqu'où?* how far?

jusquiame [ʒys'kjam], *n.f.* (*Bot.*) Henbane.

jussion [ʒy'sjɔ̃], *n.f.* Royal command (to Parliament etc.).

justaucorps [ʒysto'kɔːr], *n.m. inv.* Jerkin; close-fitting body-garment.

juste [ʒyst], *a.* Just, equitable, rightful, righteous; justifiable, permissible, fair, legitimate, lawful; proper, fit, apt, appropriate, apposite; right, true, accurate, exact; sound; well fitting; tight. *Au plus juste prix*, at the lowest price; *avoir l'oreille juste*, to have a good ear (for music); *juste Dieu! juste ciel!* good God! just heaven! *l'heure juste*, the right time; *rien de plus juste*, nothing could be fairer; *un homme juste*, a righteous man; (*Mil.*) *un tir juste*, an accurate fire; *vos souliers sont trop justes*, your shoes are too tight.— *n.m.* Upright man, virtuous man; what is just. *Distinguer le juste de l'injuste*, to distinguish what is just from what is not. *Au juste*, exactly, precisely.—*adv.* Just, exactly, precisely; (*Mus.*) true. *Chanter juste*, to sing true, in tune; *comme de juste*, of course; naturally; *il raisonne juste*, he reasons closely; *juste à temps*, in the nick of time. *Le train part à six heures juste*, the train leaves on the stroke of six.

justement, *adv.* Justly, precisely, exactly; reasonably, justifiably, properly. **justesse**, *n.f.* Justness, exactness, precision, accuracy; appropriateness. *Avec justesse*, correctly, accurately, appropriately; *de justesse*, only just, just in time.

justice [ʒys'tis], *n.f.* Justice; righteousness, goodness, uprightness, probity, integrity; fairness, impartiality, reason; jurisdiction; courts of justice, judges, law. *Appeler, citer, traduire*, or *poursuivre quelqu'un en justice*, to sue at law, to proceed against someone; *avec justice*, with justice, justly; *avoir recours à la justice*, to seek legal redress; *déni de justice*, refusal of justice; *en toute justice*, by rights; *faire justice à*, to do justice to; *faire justice de*, to punish; to treat (someone) as he deserves; to refute; *palais de justice*, law-court; *que justice soit faite*, let execution be done; *rendre justice à*, to do justice to, to right (a person); *rendre la justice*, to administer justice; *se faire justice*, to take the law into one's own hands, to commit suicide (of a criminal). *Les bois de justice*, the guillotine. *Justice de paix*, court of conciliation. **justiciable**, *a.* Justiciable, amenable. *Être justiciable de*, to come under the jurisdiction of.—*n.* Person amenable to a tribunal.

*****justicier** (1), *v.t.* (*conjugated like* PRIER) To punish; to execute; to inflict corporal punishment on. **justicier** (2), *a.* (*fem.* **-ière**) Justiciary, retributive.—*n.* Judge; lover of justice.

justifiable [ʒysti'fjabl], *a.* Justifiable; warrantable. **justifiablement**, *adv.* Warrantably, justifiably. **justifiant**, *a.* (*fem.* **justifiante**) Justifying.

justificateur, *a.* (*fem.* **-trice**) Justifying.—*n.* Justifier. **justificatif**, *a.* (*fem.* **-ive**) Justificative. *Pièce justificative*, proof, voucher, documentary evidence. **justification**, *n.f.* Justification, vindication, proof; (*Print.*) adjustment of line.

justifier [ʒysti'fje], *v.t.* (*conjugated like* PRIER) To justify, to vindicate, to make good; (*Print.*) to adjust, to make even, etc.—*v.i.* To give proof or an account (*de*). **se justifier**, *v.r.* To justify, clear, or vindicate oneself.

jute [ʒyt], *n.m.* Jute.

juter [ʒy'te], *v.i.* To be juicy, to let juice trickle or drop (of fruits etc.).

juteux [ʒy'tø], *a.* (*fem.* **juteuse**) Juicy; (*pop.*) smart, elegant [*see* JUS].—*n.m.* (*Mil. slang*) Battalion sergeant-major.

juvénile [ʒyve'nil], *a.* Juvenile, youthful. **juvénilement**, *adv.* Boyishly, in a juvenile manner. **juvénilité**, *n.f.* Juvenility, youthfulness.

juxtalinéaire [ʒykstaline'ɛr], *a.* (*sch.*) *Traduction juxtalinéaire*, 'construe' or 'crib' with text and translation arranged line by line.

juxtaposer [ʒykstapo'ze], *v.t.* To juxtapose, to place side by side. **se juxtaposer**, *v.r.* To be in juxtaposition.

juxtaposition, *n.f.* Juxtaposition.

K

K, k [ka], *n.m.* The eleventh letter of the alphabet. *Échelle K* (*viz.* Kelvin), absolute scale (of temperature).

kabbale [CABBALE].

kakatoès [CACATOIS].

kaki [ka'ki], *a. inv.* Khaki (colour).—*n.m.* Field-service uniform of American, British, and French forces; (*Bot.*) Chinese persimmon.

kaléidoscope [kaleidɔs'kɔp], *n.m.* Kaleidoscope.

kali [ka'li], *n.m.* Kali, salt-wort.

kalmie [kal'mi:], *n.f.* (*Bot.*) Kalmia, American laurel.

kan [kan], *n.m.* Khan, caravanserai.

kandjar [kɑ̃d'ʒaːr], *n.m.* Oriental dagger.

kangourou [kɑ̃gu'ru], *n.m.* Kangaroo.

kansanien [kɑ̃sa'njɛ̃], *a.* and *n.m.* (*fem.* **-ienne**) (*Geol.*) Kansan.

kantien [kɑ̃'tjɛ̃], *a.* (*fem.* **kantienne**) Kantian. **kantisme**, *n.m.* Kantism. **kantiste**, *n.* Kantist.

kaolin [kaɔ'lɛ̃], *n.m.* Kaolin, porcelain clay, china-clay.

kapok or **kapoc** [ka'pɔk], *n.m.* Kapok.

karatas or **karata** [kara'ta], *n.m.* (*Bot.*) One of the *Bromeliaceae*, silk-grass.

kari [CARI].

karité [kari'te], *n.m.* Karité, butter-tree. *Beurre de karité*, karité-nut butter.

kasbah [CASBA].

kascher, also **kacher, kachir** [ka'ʃɛr, ka'ʃir], *a.* (*Jew. Relig.*) Kosher.

kayac [ka'jak], *n.m.* Eskimo flat canoe, kayak.

kébir [ke'bir], *a.* (*Arab.*) Large, big.—*n.m.* (*Mil. slang*) The general.

képi [ke'pi], *n.m.* Kepi, military cap; peak cap.

kératine [kera'tin], *n.f.* Keratine. **kératinisé**, *a.* (*fem.* **-ée**) Keratinized. **kératique**, *a.* Keratic. **kératite**, *n.f.* Keratitis. **kératoïde**, *a.* Keratoid. **kératose**, *n.f.* Keratose.

kermès [kɛr'mɛːs], *n.m.* Kermes.

kermesse [kɛr'mɛs], *n.f.* Kermis (in the Netherlands); kermesse; village fair.

kérosène [kero′zɛːn], *n.m.* Kerosene, paraffin-oil.

ketch [kɛtʃ], *n.m.* (*Naut.*) Ketch.

ketmie [kɛt′miː], *n.f.* (*Bot.*) Ketmia, gumbo.

khédive [ke′diːv], *n.m.* Khedive.

khmer, khmère [kmɛr], *a.* and *n.* Khmer.

kidnapper [kidna′pe], *v.t.* To kidnap.

kif-kif [kif′kif], *a.* (*pop.*) All the same, exactly alike.

kilo [ki′lo], *n.m.* (*abbr.*) Kilogramme. **kilocalorie,** *n.f.* Great or major calory. **kilocycle,** *n.m.* Kilocycle. **kilogramme,** *n.m.* Kilogramme (2·2 lb. avoirdupois). **kilométrage,** *n.m.* Measuring in kilometres. **kilomètre,** *n.m.* Kilometre (1093·6 yards). **kilométrer,** *v.t.* To measure in kilometres. **kilométrique,** *a.* Kilometrical. **kilowatt,** *n.m.* Kilowatt.

kimono [kimɔ′no], *n.m.* Kimono, Japanese cloak. *Manches kimono,* Magyar sleeves.

kinéscope [kine′skɔp], *n.m.* Kinescope.

kinétographe [kinetɔ′graf], *n.m.* Kinetograph. **kinétoscope,** *n.m.* Kinetoscope.

kinkajou or **kincajou** [kɛ̃ka′ʒu], *n.m.* Kinkajou, honey-bear.

kiosque [kjɔsk], *n.m.* Kiosk; (*Naut.*) house. *Kiosque à journaux,* newspaper kiosk; *kiosque à musique,* bandstand.

kirsch [kirʃ], *n.m.* Kirschwasser (liqueur).

kiwi [ki′vi], *n.m.* Kiwi, apteryx.

klakson or **klaxon** [klak′sɔ̃], *n.m.* Klaxon, hooter, horn. **klaksonner,** *v.i.* To hoot, to sound one's horn (of motor-car etc.).

kleptomane [klɛptɔ′man], *n.m.* and *a.* Kleptomaniac. **kleptomanie,** *n.f.* Kleptomania.

knock-out [nɔ′kaut], *a.* *inv.* and *n.m.* (*Box.*) *Mettre l'adversaire knock-out,* to knock out the opponent; *perdre par knock-out,* to be knocked out (in a fight).

knout [knut], *n.m.* Knout. **knouter,** *v.t.* To knout.

kola or **cola** [kɔ′la], *n.m.* Kola.

kolback [kol′bak], *n.m.* (A sort of) busby.

kominform [kɔmɛ̃′fɔrm], *n.m.* Cominform.

komintern [kɔmɛ̃′tɛrn], *n.m.* Comintern.

kommandantur [kɔmɑ̃dɑ̃′tyr], *n.f.* (*Ger.*) Military command headquarters, Kommandatura.

kommando [kɔmɑ̃′do], *n.m.* (Boer War) Detachment of troops; (1939–45) gang of prisoners-of-war working in Germany; commando(s); commando raid.

kopeck [kɔ′pɛk], *n.m.* Copeck (Russian coin worth about a halfpenny).

koran [CORAN].

korrigan [kɔri′gɑ̃], *n.m.* Goblin, elf.

koumis [ku′mis], *n.m.* Koumiss.

krach [krak], *n.m.* Failure, financial crash.

krypton [krip′tɔ̃], *n.m.* Krypton.

ksar [ksar], *n.m.* Algerian fortified village.

kymrique [kim′rik], *a.* and *n.m.* Cymric.

kyrielle [ki′rjɛl], *n.f.* Litany; (*fig.*) long string (of words etc.), long tedious story.

kyste [kist], *n.m.* (*Path.*) Cyst. **kysteux** (*fem.* **kysteuse**) or **kystique,** *a.* Cystic.

L

L, l [ɛl], *n.m.* The twelfth letter of the alphabet.

l', *art.* and *pron.* (by elision of *le* or *la*). The.

la (1) [la], *art.* and *pr.f.* The; her.

la (2) [la], *n.m.* (*Mus.*) La; the note A. *Donner le la,* to give the tuning A.

là [la], *adv.* and *int.* There, thither; then (of time). *Çà et là,* here and there, up and down; *ce n'est pas là que je vise,* that is not the thing I am aiming at; *de là,* thence, from there, from that time, from that cause; *d'ici là* [ICI]; *il n'est pas là,* he is not there, he is away; *il est un peu là,* (*pop.*) he is strong, good at it; *là là,* now now! there! there now! *là même,* in that very place; *là où,* where; *par là,* that way; *que dites-vous là?* what are you saying? *qui va là?* who goes there?

labadens [laba′dɛ̃s], *n.m.* Old school chum (a name forged by Labiche).

labarum [laba′rɔm], *n.m.* Labarum, standard.

là-bas [la′ba], *adv.* There, over there.

labbe [lab], *n.m.* (*Orn.*) Skua, common name of several species of *Stercorarius,* e.g. *labbe parasite,* Richardson's (or Arctic) skua.

label [la′bɛl], *n.m.* (*Ind.*) Label; brand, mark, sign (of guarantee).

labelle [la′bɛl], *n.m.* (*Bot.*) Labellum.

labeur [la′bœːr], *n.m.* Labour, work, toil; (*Print.*) book-work.

labial [la′bjal], *a.* (*fem.* **-ale,** *pl.* **-aux**) Labial. —*n.f.* Labial (letter). **labialiser,** *v.t.* To labialize.

labié, *a.* (*fem.* **-ée**) (*Bot.*) Labiate.—*n.f.* Labiate plant.

labile [la′bil], *a.* Labile, changing, unstable; (*Bot.*) deciduous. *Mémoire labile,* failing memory.

laborantine [labɔrɑ̃′tin], *n.f.* Female laboratory assistant.

laboratoire [labɔra′twaːr], *n.m.* Laboratory.

laborieusement [labɔrjøz′mɑ̃], *adv.* Laboriously, painfully. **laborieux,** *a.* (*fem.* **-ieuse**) Laborious, hard-working; toilsome, painful. *Les classes laborieuses,* the working class.

labour [la′buːr], *n.m.* Ploughing, tillage; arable land, tilled land. *Bœufs de labour,* plough-oxen; *donner un labour à une terre,* to till a piece of ground.

labourable, *a.* Arable. **labourage,** *n.m.* Tillage, ploughing; dressing.

labourer, *v.t.* To plough, to till; to dig, to turn up; to dress; to scratch, to graze deeply; to rip up, to rip open; to toil through. (*Naut.*) *Labourer le fond,* to graze the bottom with the anchor.

laboureur, *n.m.* Husbandman, ploughman.

laboureuse, *n.f.* Steam plough, tractor plough.

labre [labr], *n.m.* (*Ichth.*) Wrasse. Common name of several Labrus or lip-fish, e.g. *labre bleu* or *trilobé,* cuckoo wrasse; *labre-perdrix,* cockwing wrasse or sea-partridge.

laburne [la′byrn], *n.m.* Laburnum.

labyrinthe [labi′rɛ̃ːt], *n.m.* Labyrinth, maze. **labyrinthique,** *a.* Labyrinthian.

lac [lak], *n.m.* Lake [*see also* LACS]. (*fam.*) *Être dans le lac,* to be lost, to be in difficulties, to be in the soup.

laçage [la′saːʒ], *n.m.* Lacing.

lacer, *v.t.* To lace; (*Naut.*) to attach (a sail to another) by a line; to line (a dog).

lacération [lasera′sjɔ̃], *n.f.* Laceration. **lacérer,** *v.t. irr.* (*conjugated like* ACCÉLÉRER) To lacerate, to tear; to tear or slash to pieces.

laceron [LAITERON].

lacertiforme [laserti'fɔrm], *a.* Lizard-like.
lacet [la'sɛ], *n.m.* Lace, stay-lace, boot-lace; noose, springe, snare; bowstring (for strangling); winding, turning, hairpin bend (of road etc.); (*pl.*) toils. *Ferrer un lacet,* to tag a lace; *mouvement de lacet,* (*Rail.*) oscillation, swaying; *poser des lacets,* to set toils; *route en lacets,* winding road.
lâche [lɑ:ʃ], *a.* Loose, slack, lax; faint-hearted, mean-spirited, dastardly, cowardly; base, mean, shameful. *Ce nœud est trop lâche,* this knot is too loose.—*n.m.* Coward, craven, dastard.—*adv.* Loosely. **lâché,** *a.* (*fem.* -ée) Slovenly, careless, slipshod. **lâchement,** *adv.* In a dastardly or cowardly manner; loosely, slackly; basely, shamefully.
lâcher [la'ʃe], *v.t.* To loosen, to slacken, to make loose; to drop; to let go, to let slip, to let drop, to release, to let go of; to unbind; to let out, to blurt out; to let fly, to discharge; to let down (someone). *Lâcher la bride à un cheval,* to loosen the reins of a horse; *lâchez-le! lâchez tout!* let him go, let go! *lâcher le frein,* (*Motor.*) to release the brake; *lâcher pied,* to waver, to give way; *lâcher prise,* to let go one's hold; *lâcher sa proie,* to let go one's prey; *lâcher une bordée,* to fire a broadside; *lâcher une parole* or *lâcher un mot,* to let out a word; *lâcher un prisonnier,* to release a prisoner.—*v.i.* To slacken, to grow slack, to become loose; to slip; (*spt.*) to give up.—*n.m.* Release (of pigeons, balloons, etc.).
lâcheté [laʃ'te], *n.f.* Cowardice; baseness, meanness; act of cowardice, base action.
lâcheur [la'ʃœr], *n.m.* (*fem.* -euse) (*fam.*) Unreliable fellow (who fails to turn up, who leaves you in the lurch).
lacinie [lasi'ni], *n.f.* (*Bot.*) Lacinia.
lacinié [lasi'nje], *a.* (*fem.* -ée) (*Bot.*) Laciniate, jagged.
lacis [la'si], *n.m.* Network.
(C) lacon [la'kɔ̃], *n.m.* A little lake.
laconique [lakɔ'nik], *a.* Laconic. **laconiquement,** *adv.* Laconically; briefly, concisely. **laconiser,** *v.i.* To speak laconically. **laconisme,** *n.m.* Laconism.
là-contre [la'kɔ̃:tr], *adv.* Against it, contrary to it.
lacrymal [lakri'mal], *a.* (*fem.* -ale, *pl.* -aux) Lachrymal. **lacrymatoire,** *n.m.* and *a.* Lachrymatory. **lacrymogène,** *a.* *Gaz lacrymogène,* tear-gas.
lacs [la], *n.m. inv.* String; noose; springe, trap, toils. *Lacs d'amour,* love-knot; true lovers' knot; *tomber dans les lacs d'une coquette,* to fall into the trap of a coquette.
lactaire [lak'tɛ:r], *a.* Lactary, lacteal, lacteous.
lactate [lak'tat], *n.m.* (*Chem.*) Lactate. **lactation,** *n.f.* Lactation. **lacté,** *a.* (*fem.* -ée) Lacteous, milky. *La voie lactée,* the Milky Way, the Galaxy. *Régime lacté,* milk diet. **lactescent,** *a.* (*fem.* -ente) (*Bot.*) Lactescent. **lactifère,** *a.* Lactiferous. **lactique,** *a.* (*Chem.*) Lactic. **lactomètre** or **lactoscope,** *n.m.* Lactometer. **lactose,** *n.m.* or *f.* Sugar of milk, milk-sugar.
lacune [la'kyn], *n.f.* Gap, break, hiatus, blank; desideratum; (*Bot.*) air-cell, lacuna. **lacuneux,** *a.* (*fem.* -euse) Incomplete (data, report, etc.).
lacustre [la'kystr], *a.* Lacustrine. *Habitation lacustre,* lake-dwelling.

là-dedans [ladə'dã], *adv.* In there.
là-dehors [ladə'ɔ:r], *adv.* Outside.
là-dessous [la'tsu], *adv.* Under there.
là-dessus [la'tsy], *adv.* On that; thereupon; on top of that. *Là-dessus il me dit,* thereupon he said to me.
ladite [la'dit], *a.f.* [LEDIT].
ladre [lɑ:dr], *a.* Leprous; measly (of pigs); (*fig.*) mean, sordid, stingy, niggardly; unfeeling.—*n.m.* (*fem.* **ladresse**) Leper; sordid, scurvy person, shabby person; niggard, churl. *Un vrai ladre,* a regular curmudgeon. **ladrerie,** *n.f.* Leprosy; lazar-house; mustiness (of pigs); sordid avarice, stinginess, sordidness.
lagon [la'gɔ̃], *n.m.* Lagoon.
lagopède [lagɔ'pɛd], *n.m.* (*Orn.*) Lagopus. *Lagopède blanc* or *des Alpes,* white grouse, willow grouse; *lagopède muet,* ptarmigan; *lagopède rouge d'Écosse* or *tétras rouge,* red grouse.
lagune [la'gyn], *n.f.* Lagoon.
là-haut [la'o], *adv.* Up there; upstairs.
lai (1) [lɛ], *n.m.* Lay (poem, song).
***lai** (2) [lɛ], *a.* (*fem.* **laie**) Lay, laic. *Frère lai,* lay-brother.—*n.m.* Layman.
laïc [LAÏQUE].
laîche [lɛʃ], *n.f.* (*usu. pl.*) (*Bot.*) Name given to colonies of carex or sedges.
laïcisation [laisiza'sjɔ̃], *n.f.* Laicization, secularization. **laïciser,** *v.t.* To laicize, to secularize.
laïcité, *n.f.* Undenominational character (of schools etc.).
laid [lɛ], *a.* (*fem.* **laide**) Ugly, ill-favoured, bad-looking, unsightly; unseemly, unhandsome, unbecoming. *Ce que vous dites là est bien laid,* what you say is very improper, mean, unfair, wicked; *laid comme un pou,* or *comme les sept péchés capitaux,* as ugly as sin. —*n.* Ugly person, creature, etc.; naughty boy or girl; ugly part, ugly side; ugliness. **laidement,** *adv.* In an ugly way. **laideron,** *n.m.* (*fem.* -onne) Ugly creature. **laideur,** *n.f.* Ugliness, uncomeliness; unsightliness, hideousness, deformity; unseemliness.
laie (1) [lɛ], *n.f.* Wild sow.
laie (2) [lɛ], *n.f.* Path (in a forest).
laie (3) [lɛ], *n.f.* Stone-cutter's hammer.
lainage [lɛ'na:ʒ], *n.m.* Woollens, woollen goods; wool, fleece, teaseling, raising.
laine [lɛn], *n.f.* Wool; woollen garment. *Laine filée,* yarn; *laine peignée,* worsted; *laine perlée,* crochet wool; *tapis de haute laine,* thick-pile carpet; *tout laine,* pure wool. (*fig.*) *Jambes de laine,* groggy legs; *se laisser manger la laine sur le dos,* to let oneself be eaten out of house and home. **lainer,** *v.t.* To raise, to teasel (wool etc.).—*n.m.* Nap. **lainerie,** *n.f.* Woollen goods, woollens; wool trade, shop, etc. **laineur,** *n.m.* (*fem.* -euse) Teaseler.—*n.f.* Gig (machine for teaseling wool). **laineux,** *a.* (*fem.* -euse) Woolly, fleecy; (*Bot.*) downy, woolly.
lainier, *a.* (*fem.* -ière) Of wool, woollen.—*n.* Wool-merchant; wool-comber, wool-worker.
laïque [la'ik], *a.* Lay, laic, secular. *Une école laïque,* an undenominational school.—*n.* Layman, lay person. *Les laïques,* the laity.
lais [lɛ], *n.m.* Staddle; alluvion; silt, warp.
laise [LAIZE].
laisse (1) [lɛ:s], *n.f.* String, leash, lead. *Laisse de*

lévriers, leash of greyhounds; *tenir un chien en laisse*, to keep a dog on the leash; *tenir quelqu'un en laisse*, to hold someone in leading-strings or by the nose.

laisse (2) [lɛːs], *n.f.* Tirade or set of assonant lines (in *chansons de geste*); fore-shore.

laissées [lɛ'se], *n.f. pl.* Droppings (of bears, wild boars, etc.).

laisser [lɛ'se], *v.t.* To leave, to quit; to leave behind, not to take with one, to part with; to desert, to abandon; to bequeath; to permit, to let, to allow; to confide; to entrust; to let alone; to pass over, to omit; to leave off; to give up, to lose. *C'est à prendre ou à laisser*, take it or leave it; *cela laisse (beaucoup) à désirer*, there is room for improvement; *cela ne laisse pas d'être vrai*, it is true nevertheless; *faites votre devoir et laissez faire aux dieux*, do your duty and leave the rest to the gods; *laisser aller*, to let go; *laisser faire*, to let things alone, to take it easy, to allow to be done; *laisser la vie à quelqu'un*, to spare someone's life; *laisser quelqu'un en paix* or *en repos* or *tranquille*, to leave, to let someone alone; *laisser sortir*, to let out; *laisser tout à l'abandon*, to leave everything in disorder; *laisser tout aller*, to neglect everything; *laisser tout traîner*, to let everything lie about in disorder; *laisser une chose à quelqu'un à un certain prix*, to let someone have something for a certain price; *laissez donc!* don't bother! *laissez-moi faire*, leave it to me; *on n'a qu'à le laisser faire*, he only needs to be let alone. **se laisser**, *v.r.* To allow oneself (to be led etc.). *Se laisser aller à la douleur*, to abandon oneself to grief; *se laisser aller à la tentation*, to give way to temptation; *se laisser conduire*, to let oneself be led; *se laisser dire*, to allow oneself to be told; *se laisser faire*, to offer no resistance; *se laisser lire*, to be readable; *se laisser manger* or *se laisser boire*, to be palatable; *se laisser mener*, to allow oneself to be led, bullied or ordered about; *se laisser mourir*, to die; *se laisser prendre*, to allow oneself (or itself) to be taken; *se laisser surprendre*, to allow oneself to be taken in or caught or taken unawares; *se laisser tomber*, to let oneself fall.

laisser-aller, *n.m.* Unconstraint, negligence; indolence, nonchalance.

laisser-courre or **laissé-courre**, *n.m. inv.* (*Hunt.*) Starting-place (where the dogs are loosed).

laisser-faire, *n.m.* Non-interference.

laissez-passer, *n.m. inv.* Permit, leave, pass.

lait [lɛ], *n.m.* Milk. *Au lait*, with milk; *cochon de lait*, sucking-pig; *dents de lait*, milk-teeth; *fièvre de lait*, milk-fever; *frère de lait*, foster-brother; *lait coupé*, milk and water; *lait de chaux*, whitewash; *lait de ciment*, grout; *lait de poule*, mulled egg, egg-flip; *petit-lait* or *lait clair*, whey; *sœur de lait*, foster-sister; *soupe au lait*, bread-and-milk; milk porridge; *vache à lait*, milch cow.

laitage, *n.m.* Milk puddings; milk products.

laitance [lɛ'tɑ̃ːs] or **laite**, *n.f.* Milt, soft roe. [*see also* LAITERON (2)].

laité, *a.* (*fem.* **laitée** (1)) Soft roed.

laitée (2) [lɛ'te], *n.f.* Litter (of a bitch).

laiterie [lɛ'tri], *n.f.* Dairy, dairy-farm.

laiteron [lɛ'trɔ̃], *n.m.* (1) Yearling (colt). (2) Milk weed. *Laiteron épineux*, corn sow-thistle.

laiteux [lɛ'tø], *a.* (*fem.* **-euse**) Lacteous, milky.

laitier (1) [lɛ'tje], *a.* (*fem.* **-ière**) Pertaining to milk; having milk, milch (of cows).—*n.* Milkman; milkwoman, milkmaid, dairymaid; milch cow. *Cette vache est une bonne laitière*, this cow is a good milker.—*n.f.* Milklorry, milk-cart.

laitier (2) [lɛ'tje], *n.m.* Dross, slag; cinders. *Laitier des volcans*, vitreous lava.

laiton [lɛ'tɔ̃], *n.m.* Brass, latten. *Fil de laiton*, brass wire. **laitonner**, *v.t.* To trim (a hat) with brass wire.

laitue [lɛ'ty], *n.f.* Lettuce [*see* CHICON, ROMAINE].

laïus [la'jys], *n.m.* (*sch. slang*) Speech, lecture. **laïusser**, *v.i.* To deliver a speech, to speechify.

laize or **laise** [lɛːz], *n.f.* Width (of cloth).

lakiste [la'kist], *a.* Lakist.—*n.m.* Lake-poet.

lama [la'ma], *n.m.* Lama (priest); llama.

lamanage [lama'naːʒ], *n.m.* Pilotage (in harbour, roads). **lamaneur**, *n.m.* Harbour-, inshore or river pilot.

lamantin [lamɑ̃'tɛ̃], *n.m.* Lamantin, manatee, sea-cow.

lambeau [lɑ̃'bo], *n.m.* (*pl.* **-eaux**) Shred; rag; bit, fragment, scrap, remains (of flesh etc.). *Mettre en lambeaux*, to tear to shreds; *tomber en lambeaux*, to fall to pieces.

lambel [lɑ̃'bɛl], *n.m.* (*Her.*) Label.

lambin [lɑ̃'bɛ̃], *a.* (*fem.* **-ine**) Slow, dawdling. —*n.* Dawdler, slowcoach. **lambiner**, *v.i.* To dawdle, to trifle, to dilly-dally.

lambourde [lɑ̃'burd], *n.f.* Beam for supporting joists, breastsummer; soft, chalky stone.

lambrequin [lɑ̃brə'kɛ̃], *n.m.* Valance, cut-out, pelmet; (*Her.*) mantling.

lambris [lɑ̃'bri], *n.m.* Wooden, marble, plaster, etc., lining of a wall; plaster ceiling; ceiling. *Lambris d'appui*, dado; *lambris de hauteur*, panelling, wainscoting; *lambris dorés*, (*fig.*) mansion, palace; *lambris sacrés*, (*fig.*) temple, church; *les célestes lambris*, the heavenly canopy.

lambrissage, *n.m.* Wainscoting, panelling. **lambrisser**, *v.t.* To panel, to wainscot. *Chambre lambrissée*, attic.

lambruche [lɑ̃'bryʃ] or **lambrusque**, *n.f.* Wild vine.

lame [lam], *n.f.* Thin plate, leaf of metal; flat gold or silver wire, foil; knife (of mower etc.), blade; (*fig.*) blade, sword; swordsman; wave, billow; (*Bot. etc.*) scale, lamina, lamella. *À deux lames*, two-bladed; *c'est une bonne, une fine lame*, he is a good, a fine swordsman. *Emporté par une lame*, washed away; *entre deux lames*, in the trough of the sea; *lame de fond*, ground-swell. *Lames de persiennes*, slats of Venetian blinds.

lamé [la'me], *a.* (*fem.* **-ée**) Spangled with gold or silver.

lamelle [la'mel], *n.f.* Lamella; slide, object-slide (of microscope). **lamellé** or **lamelleux**, *a.* (*fem.* **-ée** or **-euse**) Lamellar, scaly, foliated. **lamellifère**, *a.* Lamelliferous. **lamelliforme**, *a.* Lamelliform.

lamentable [lamɑ̃'tabl], *a.* Lamentable, mournful, sad, distressing; broken down, pitiful. **lamentablement**, *adv.* Woefully.

lamentation [lamɑ̃ta'sjɔ̃], *n.f.* Lamentation,

wailing; lament; whining. *Mur des Lamenta-tions*, Wailing Wall (in Jerusalem). **se lamenter**, *v.r.* To lament, to bewail; to bemoan oneself, to deplore.

lamie [la'mi], *n.f.* (*Ichth.*) Lamia; white shark or porbeagle.

lamier [la'mje], *n.m.* Heddle-maker; (*Bot.*) name of several labiates, *e.g. le lamier blanc* or *ortie blanche*, dead-nettle, archangel.

laminage [lami'na:ʒ], *n.m.* Laminating; rolling (of gold etc.).

laminaire [lami'nɛ:r], *n.f.* Laminaria.—*a.* Laminar, flaky.

laminer, *v.t.* To laminate, to roll. **laminerie**, *n.f.* Rolling-mill. **lamineur**, *n.m.* Flattener, roller. **lamineux**, *a.* (*fem.* **-euse**) Laminose.

laminoir, *n.m.* Flattening-mill; rolling-mill; embossing calender.

lampadaire [lãpa'dɛ:r], *n.m.* (*Gr. Ch.*) Lampadary, light-bearer; candelabrum; standard-lamp.

lampant [lã'pã], *a.* (*fem.* **-ante**) Refined and illuminating (oil).

lampas [lã'pɑ], *n.m.* Silk damask, figured silk, lampas; a horse disease.

lampe [lã:p], *n.f.* Lamp; (*Rad. Tel.*) valve. *Dessous* or *pied de lampe*, lamp-stand; *lampe à alcool*, spirit lamp; *lampe à arc*, arc-lamp; *lampe à pétrole*, paraffin lamp; *lampe à souder*, blow-lamp; *lampe de bord*, (*Motor.*) dash-board light; *lampe de poche*, electric torch; *lampe de mineur* or *lampe de sûreté* or *lampe de Davy*, safety-lamp; *lampe tempête*, hurri-cane lamp; *sentir la lampe*, to smell of the midnight oil. (*pop.*) *S'en mettre plein la lampe*, to give oneself a good blow-out, to have a slap-up feed.

lampée [lã'pe], *n.f.* Tumblerful, bumper; draught.

lamper [lã'pe], *v.i.* To glow (of phosphores-cent sea); to swallow avidly a liquid.—*v.t.* To toss off (a bumper).

lamperon [lã'prɔ̃], *n.m.* Wick-holder (of a lamp).

lampette [lã'pɛt], *n.f.* Corn-cockle.

lampion [lã'pjɔ̃], *n.m.* Illumination-lamp, fairy-light; Chinese lantern; (*slang*) cocked hat.

lampiste [lã'pist], *n.m.* Lamp-maker; lamp-lighter. *Punir le lampiste*, to blame the cat.

lampisterie, *n.f.* Lamp-making; lamp-room.

lamprillon [lãpri'jɔ̃] or **lamproyon**, *n.m.* Small lamprey.

lampris [lã'pri], *n.m.* (*Ichth.*) *Lampris tacheté*, opah, moon-fish.

lamproie [lã'prwa], *n.f.* Lamprey; lampern.

lampsane [lãp'san], *n.f.* (*Bot.*) Nipplewort.

lampyre [lã'pi:r], *n.m.* Glow-worm; firefly.

lançage [lã'sa:ʒ] or (more frequently) **lance-ment**, *n.m.* Throwing, darting; launching, launch.

lance [lã:s], *n.f.* Lance, spear; staff, flagstaff; nozzle (of a fire-hose). *Baisser la lance*, to strike one's flag, to give in; *coup de lance*, spear-thrust; *rompre une lance pour*, to take up the cudgels for.

lancé [lã'se], *a.* (*fem.* **-ée**) Launched, started; in the swim. (*spt.*) *Un départ lancé*, a flying start, a racing start.—*n.m.* Embroidery stitch.

lancée [lã'se], *n.f.* Impetus; shooting (of pain).

lancement [LANÇAGE].

lance-flammes [lãs'flam], *n.m. inv.* Flame-thrower.

lance-fusées [lãsfy'ze], *n.m. inv.* Rocket-gun.

lance-mines [lãs'min], *n.m. inv.* Mine-thrower.

lancéolé [lãseɔ'le], *a.* (*fem.* **-ée**) (*Bot.*) Lanceolate, lance-shaped.

lance-pierres [lãs'pjɛr], *n.m. inv.* Catapult.

lancer [lã'se], *v.t.* To fling, to hurl, to throw, to cast; to launch; to shoot, to shoot forth, to dart; to emit, to issue (a warrant etc.). *Lancer des regards*, to cast looks; *lancer la ligne*, to cast the line (in fishing); *lancer un arrêt*, to issue a warrant; *lancer un ballon*, to send up a balloon; *lancer un cerf*, to start a stag; *lancer un cheval*, to urge on a horse; *lancer un chien contre quelqu'un*, to set a dog on someone; *lancer une flèche*, to shoot an arrow; *lancer une pierre*, to fling a stone; *lancer un javelot*, to throw a javelin; *lancer un juron*, to rap out an oath; *lancer un moteur*, to start up an engine; *lancer un regard de colère*, to dart an angry look; *lancer un vaisseau*, to launch a ship. (*fig.*) *Lancer une chanson, une mode, une vedette*, to launch a song, a fashion, a star (more often, to start a fashion). **se lancer**, *v.r.* To dart, to spring; to rush, to fly; to launch out; (*fig.*) to make a start. *Se lancer dans les affaires*, to launch out (into business). (*fam.*) *Eh! bien, tu te lances!* I say, you are ambitious!

lancer [lã'se], *n.m.* Release; casting (while fishing). *Un lancer de pigeons*, a release of pigeons; *pêche au lancer*, casting.

lance-torpilles [lãstɔr'pi:j], *n.m. inv.* Tor-pedo-tube.

lancette [lã'sɛt], *n.f.* Lancet.

lanceur [lã'sœ:r], *n.m.* (*fem.* **-euse**) One who launches, starts things going, etc.; pushful person; (*baseball*) pitcher. *Lanceur d'affaires*, company promoter, speculator.

lancier [lã'sje], *n.m.* Lancer. *Danser les lanciers*, to dance the lancers.

lancière [lã'sjɛ:r], *n.f.* Waste-gate (of a mill-dam).

lancinant [lãsi'nã], *a.* (*fem.* **-ante**) Lanci-nating, shooting (of pains).

lanciner, *v.i.* To lancinate, to throb, to shoot.

lançoir [lã'swa:r], *n.m.* Mill-gate (of water-mills).

lançon [lã'sɔ̃], **lanceron**, *n.m.* Sand-eel.

landau [lã'do], *n.m.* (*pl.* **landaus**) Landau; baby's perambulator; (*fam.*) pram.

landaulet, *n.m.* Landaulet.

lande [lã:d], *n.f.* Waste land, moor, heath.

landerira, landerirette [lãdəri'ra, lãdəri'rɛt]. Burden of songs.

landgrave [lãd'gra:v], *n.m.* Landgrave.

landgraviat, *n.m.* Landgraviate.

landier [lã'dje], *n.m.* Kitchen fire-dog, andiron; furze, gorse.

laneret [lan'rɛ], *n.m.* Lanneret (*Falco canarius*).

langage [lã'ga:ʒ], *n.m.* Language; speech, diction. *Changer de langage*, to change one's tune; *ils tiennent tous le même langage*, they all say the same thing.

lange [lã:ʒ], *n.m.* Napkin; swaddling-cloth; (*pl.*) swaddling-clothes, swaddling bands; (*Print.*) blanket.

langoureusement [lăgurøz'mã], *adv.* Languishingly, languidly. **langoureux,** *a.* (*fem.* -euse) Languishing, languid.—*n.* Languishing lover etc.

langouste [lã'gust], *n.f.* Spiny lobster. **langoustier,** *n.m.*, or **langoustière,** *n.f.* Net for catching lobsters. **langoustine,** *n.f.* Norway lobster; large Brittany prawn; Dublin bay prawn.

langue [lã:g], *n.f.* Tongue; language; neck, tongue, or strip (of land); (*Naut.*) gore (of sail). *Avoir la langue bien pendue* or *bien affilée,* to have the gift of the gab; *avoir la langue liée,* to be tongue-tied; *avoir la langue trop longue,* not to be able to hold one's tongue; *avoir un mot sur le bout de la langue,* to have a word on the tip of one's tongue; *beau parler n'écorche point la langue,* civility costs nothing; *c'est une mauvaise langue* or *une langue de vipère,* he or she is a backbiter; *coup de langue,* tonguing; lick; slander, taunt, sarcasm; *donner sa langue au chat* or *jeter sa langue aux chiens,* to give up guessing; *il a avalé sa langue,* he keeps silent, he is tongue-tied; *la langue lui a fourché,* his or her tongue tripped; *langue morte,* dead language; *langue vivante,* modern language; *langue vulgaire,* ordinary language, vulgar tongue; *langue verte,* slang; *quelle langue!* what a tongue he or she has! *tirer la langue,* to put out one's tongue, (*fig.*) to be in distress. **langue-de-chat,** *n.f.* (*pl.* **langues-de-chat**) Finger biscuit. **langue-de-chien,** *n.f.* (*pl.* **langues-de-chien**) (*Bot.*) Hound's tongue. **langue-de-serpent,** *n.f.* (*pl.* **langues-de-serpent**) Adder's tongue (plant).

languette [lã'gɛt], *n.f.* Small tongue; tongue-like strip; partition, languet (in flue chimney); tongue (of organs and reed instruments); index (of a balance); tongue (of shoe); detent (of fire-arm).

langueur [lã'gœ:r], *n.f.* Apathy, languor; languidness, weakness, weariness; debility. *Maladie de langueur,* lingering illness, decline.

langueyer [lãgɛ'je], *v.t.* (*conjugated like* GRASSEYER) To examine the tongue of (a hog). **langueyeur,** *n.m.* Examiner of hogs' tongues.

languier, *n.m.* Smoked hog's-tongue and throat.

languir [lã'gi:r], *v.i.* To languish, to pine away, to droop, to be sickly; to linger; to be dull or stagnant; to flag. *La conversation languit,* the conversation flags; *languir d'amour,* to pine away for love; *languir de misère,* to languish in misery; *ne nous faites pas languir,* don't keep us on tenterhooks. **languissamment,** *adv.* Languishingly. **languissant,** *a.* (*fem.* -ante) Languid, languishing, pining; (*Comm.*) dull, flat, inactive.

laniaire [la'njɛ:r], *a.* and *n.f.* Laniary (teeth). **lanice** [la'nis], *a.f. Bourre lanice,* flock of wool. **lanier** [la'nje], *n.m.* (*Hawking*) Lanner; female lanneret. **lanière** [la'njɛ:r], *n.f.* Thong, lash. **lanifère** [lani'fɛ:r] or **lanigère,** *a.* Laniferous. **lanlaire** [lã'lɛr] Folk-song refrain. (*fam.*) *Envoyer quelqu'un faire lanlaire,* to send someone to Jericho.

lanoline [lanɔ'lin], *n.f.* Lanoline.

lansquenet [lãskə'nɛ], *n.m.* Lansquenet (card game); *German foot-soldier (16th century). **lantanier** [lãta'nje], *n.m.* (*Bot.*) Lantana. **lanterne** [lã'tɛrn], *n.f.* Lantern; street-lamp; (*Arch.*) lantern-light, skylight; lantern-wheel; dawdler, slow person. *À la lanterne!* hang him to the lamp-post! lynch him! *lanterne magique,* magic-lantern; *lanterne sourde,* dark-lantern; *lanterne vénitienne,* Chinese lantern; *prendre des vessies pour des lanternes,* to believe that the moon is made of green cheese. **lanterneau,** *n.m.* (*pl.* -eaux) Lantern (light) at the top of a cupola. **lanterner,** *v.i.* To dawdle, to trifle away one's time. **lanternerie,** *n.f.* (*colloq.*) Trifling, dilly-dallying. **lanternier,** *n.m.* Lantern-maker, lamplighter; trifler, babbler.

lantiponner, *v.i.* To dilly-dally. **lantur(e)lu** [lãtyr'ly], *adv. Il lui a répondu lanturelu,* stuff and nonsense! he said to him. **lanugineux** [lanyʒi'nø], *a.* (*fem.* -euse) Woolly, downy.

Laos [la'ɔs], *m.* Laos. **laotien** [lao'sjɛ̃], *a.* and *n.m.* (*fem.* -ienne) Laotian.

lapalissade [lapali'sad], *n.f.*, or *Vérité de la Palisse,* truism, self-evident remark. **lapement** [lap'mã], *n.m.* Lapping. **laper,** *v.t., v.i.* To lap (up). **lapereau** [la'pro], *n.m.* (*pl.* -eaux) Young rabbit. **lapidaire** [lapi'dɛ:r], *n.m.* Lapidary, gem cutter, gem dealer.—*a.* Lapidary. *Phrase lapidaire,* pithy expression; *inscription lapidaire,* lapidary or monumental inscription. **lapidation** [lapida'sjɔ̃], *n.f.* Lapidation, stoning. **lapider,** *v.t.* To lapidate, to stone to death; to pelt with stones; (*fig.*) to pelt, to abuse. **lapidification** [lapidifika'sjɔ̃], *n.f.* Lapidification. **lapidifier,** *v.t.* (*conjugated like* PRIER) To lapidify. **lapidifique,** *a.* Lapidific. **lapilleux** [lapi'jø], *a.* (*fem.* -euse) Stony, gritty (of fruit). **lapin** [la'pɛ̃], *n.m.* (*fem.* **lapine**) Rabbit. *Lapin de choux* or *lapin domestique,* tame rabbit; *lapin de garenne* or *lapin sauvage,* wild rabbit; *monter* or *voyager en lapin,* to ride beside the driver on the running board; *peau de lapin,* cony; (*pop.*) *poser un lapin à quelqu'un,* to stand someone up, to fail to turn up at a rendezvous. **lapis** [la'pi:s] or **lapis lazuli** [lapislazy'li], *n.m.* (*pl.*) Lapis lazuli. **lapon** [la'pɔ̃], *a.* (*fem.* -one) Lapp.—*n.m.* (**Lapon,** *fem.* -one) Laplander. **Laponie,** *f.* Lapland.

laps (1) [laps], *n.m.* Lapse (of time). **laps** (2) [laps], *a.* (*fem.* **lapse**) *Lapsed, fallen into heresy. *Laps et relaps,* fallen back into heresy. **lapsus** [lap'sy:s], *n.m. inv.* Slip, mistake, *Lapsus calami,* slip of the pen; *lapsus linguae,* slip of the tongue. **laptot** [lap'to], *n.m.* Senegalese soldier; black stevedore or wharfporter. **laquais** [la'kɛ], *n.m. inv.* Lackey, footman, flunkey. **laque** [lak], *n.f.* Lacquer, lac, lake (paint). *Gomme laque,* gum-lac.—*n.m.* Lacquer. *De*

[446]

beaux laques, fine lacquer-ware. *Vernis laque* or *laque de Chine,* japan.

laqué, *a.* (*fem.* **laquée**) Lacquered; japanned; enamelled.

laquelle [LEQUEL].

laquer [la'ke], *v.t.* To lacquer, to japan.

laquet [la'kɛ], *n.m.* Small lake.

laqueux [la'kø], *a.* (*fem.* **laqueuse**) Of the nature of lac.

larbin [lar'bɛ̃], *n.m.* (*slang*) Flunkey.

larcin [lar'sɛ̃], *n.m.* Larceny, pilfering; petty theft. *Larcin littéraire,* plagiarism; (*poet.*) *faire un doux larcin,* to steal a kiss.

lard [la:r], *n.m.* Fat, *esp.* of pigs; bacon. *Flèche de lard,* flitch of bacon; (*pop.*) *il fait du lard,* he grows fat (by sleeping); *pierre à lard,* steatite; *tranche de lard,* rasher of bacon. **lardé** (*fem.* **-ée**), *a.* Streaked; interlarded; (*Geol.*) interbedded.

larder, *v.t.* To lard; to pink, to run through, to pierce; to interlard; (*Naut.*) to thrum. *Larder de coups d'épée,* to stab with a sword several times; *larder de la viande,* to lard meat; *larder un discours de citations,* to interlard a speech with quotations.

lardite, *n.f.* Steatite.

lardoire, *n.f.* Larding-pin.

lardon, *n.m.* Thin slice of bacon, bit of pig's fat (for larding); *(fig.)* cut, jest, jibe; (*fam.*) child, kid, brat; (*Naut.*) thrum. **lardonner,** *v.t.* To cut into slices; *(fig.)* to taunt, to jibe at.

lare [la:r], *n.m.* (*Myth.*) Lar, household god; (*pl.*) fireside, hearth.—*a. Les dieux lares,* the household gods.

large [larʒ], *a.* Broad, wide; large, great, extensive, ample; generous, liberal; easy, lax, loose. *Large de bord* or *à larges bords,* broad-brimmed (hat).—*n.m.* Breadth, width; offing, open sea. *Le grand large,* the open sea. *Au large!* keep off! sheer off! *au large de Dieppe,* off Dieppe; *au long et au large,* far and wide; *avoir l'esprit large,* to be broad-minded; *cette rue a soixante pieds de large,* this street is sixty feet wide; *de long en large,* to and fro, backwards and forwards, up and down; *en long et en large,* in all directions, in every way; *être au large,* to have elbow-room, to be at one's ease, (*Naut.*) to be in the offing; *être logé au large,* to have a great deal of room; *gagner* or *prendre le large,* to put out to sea, to sheer off; *peindre large,* to paint boldly; *pousser au large,* to put off, to push off, to sheer off. **largement,** *adv.* Largely, broadly, abundantly, amply; fully, plentifully; grandly, liberally. **largesse,** *n.f.* Largess, bounty, munificence. *Faire des largesses,* to be very generous.

largeur, *n.f.* Breadth, width; amplitude, boldness. *Grande largeur,* double-width (cloth); (*fam.*) *dans les grandes largeurs,* on a large scale; *largeur d'esprit,* broad-mindedness; *largeur de voie,* gauge (of railway); (*Naut.*) *dans toute sa largeur,* from luff to leach (of sail).

largue [larg], *a.* Slack, flowing.—*n.m. Vent (grand) largue,* wind on the quarter.—*adv. Courir largue,* to sail off the wind, to sail large or free. **larguer,** *v.t.* To let go, to loosen; to let run (ropes); to let out (reefs).

larigot [lari'go], *n.m.* *Ancient flute, pipe, shawm. Boire à tire-larigot,* or *tire la Rigaude* (a heavy bell at Rouen), to drink hard.

larme [larm], *n.f.* Tear; drop. *Avec des larmes,* with tears, tearfully; *avec des larmes dans la voix,* in a tearful voice; *avoir la larme à l'œil,* (*iron.*) to be rather tearful, to feel sentimental; *avoir le don des larmes,* to have tears at command; *fondre en larmes,* to burst into tears; *larmes de crocodile,* crocodile tears; *les larmes lui vinrent aux yeux,* the tears came to her (his) eyes; *pleurer à chaudes larmes,* to shed bitter tears; *sans larmes,* tearless; *verser des larmes,* to shed tears.

larmier [lar'mje], *n.m.* Dripstone, weather-moulding; eye-vein (of horses); corner (of eye).

larmoiement [larmwa'mɑ̃], *n.m.* Watering of the eyes.

larmoyant, *a.* (*fem.* **-ante**) Weeping, in tears; tearful, lachrymose, whining. *Comédie larmoyante,* (18th cent.) sentimental domestic comedy.

larmoyer [larmwa'je], *v.i.* To shed tears; to whine, to whimper, to snivel; to water (of the eyes).

larron [la'rɔ̃], *n.m.* (*fem.* **-onnesse**) Thief, robber; (*Print.*) bite, white spot; (*Bookb.*) leaf folded in and not cut. *L'occasion fait le larron,* opportunity makes the thief; *s'entendre comme larrons en foire,* to be as thick as thieves.

larvaire [lar've:r], *a.* Larval.

larve [larv], *n.f.* Larva, grub; (*Rom. Ant.*) ghost, spectre, phantom.

larvé, *a.* (*fem.* **-ée**) Larval; masked (fever), insidious. **larvicole,** *a.* Larvicolous. **larviforme,** *a.* Larviform.

laryngé [larɛ̃'ʒe] or **laryngien,** *a.* (*fem.* **-ée, -ienne**) Laryngeal. **laryngite,** *n.f.* Laryngitis. **laryngologie,** *n.f.* Laryngology. **laryngoscope,** *n.m.* Laryngoscope. **laryngotomie,** *n.f.* Laryngotomy.

larynx [la'rɛ̃:ks], *n.m. inv.* Larynx.

las! (1) [la], *int.* Alas!

las (2) [la], *a.* (*fem.* **lasse**) Tired, weary; fatigued, bored, disgusted. *Faire quelque chose de guerre lasse,* to do a thing for the sake of peace.

las (3) [la], *n.m.* [MOIE].

lascar [las'ka:r], *n.m.* Lascar (East Indian sailor). (*Mil.* and *pop.*) *Un lascar,* a brave, bold, clever fellow.

lascif [la'sif], *a.* (*fem.* **-ive**) Lascivious, lewd, wanton. **lascivement,** *adv.* Lasciviously, lewdly, wantonly. **lasciveté,** *n.f.* Lasciviousness.

lassant, *a.* (*fem.* **-ante**) Tiresome, wearisome, fatiguing, tedious.

lasser (1) [la'se], *v.t.* To tire, to weary, to fatigue, to wear out. **se lasser,** *v.r.* To tire, to grow tired, to be fatigued, to be wearied.

lasser (2) [la'se], *v.t.* To catch with a lasso, to lasso.

lassitude [lasi'tyd], *n.f.* Lassitude, weariness.

lasso [la'so], *n.m.* Lasso. *Prendre au lasso,* to lasso.

latanier [lata'nje], *n.m.* (Ind. Ocean) Palm-tree, latania.

latent [la'tɑ̃], *a.* (*fem.* **-ente**) Latent, hidden, concealed, secret. *Chaleur latente,* latent heat.

latéral [late'ral], *a.* (*fem.* **-ale,** *pl.* **-aux**) Lateral, side. **latéralement,** *adv.* Laterally.

latérite [late'rit], *n.f.* (*Min.*) Laterite.

latex [la'tɛks], *n.m.* (*Bot.*) Latex.

laticlave [lati'klaːv], *n.m.* Laticlave.

latin [la'tɛ̃], *a.* (*fem.* **latine**) Pertaining to Latium, Latin; (*Naut.*) lateen. *La langue latine*, the Latin language; *thème latin*, Latin composition; *voile latine*, lateen sail.—*n.m.* Latin. *Bas latin*, low Latin; *latin de cuisine*, dog Latin. *Il est au bout de son latin*, he is at his wits' end; *y perdre son latin*, not to be able to make it out; to be all at sea. **latiniser**, *v.t.* To latinize. **latiniste**, *n.* Latinist. **latinité**, *n.f.* Latinity.

latitude [lati'tyd], *n.f.* Latitude; room, space, margin. **latitudinaire** or **latitudinarien** (*fem.* -**ienne**), *a.* Latitudinarian. **latitudinal**, *a.* (*fem.* -**ale**, *pl.* -**aux**) Latitudinal, athwartship.

latrie [la'tri], *n.f.* *Culte de latrie*, latria.

latrines [la'trin], *n.f. pl.* Latrines; (*Mil.*, *fam.*) rears.

lattage [la'taːʒ], *n.m.* Lathing. **latte**, *n.f.* Lath; (*Mil.*) straight sword (of troopers). **latter**, *v.t.* To lath. **lattis**, *n.m.* Lathing, lath-work; laths.

laudanisé [lodani'ze], *a.* (*fem.* -**ée**) Containing laudanum.

laudanum [loda'nɔm], *n.m.* Laudanum.

laudatif [loda'tif], *a.* (*fem.* -**ive**) Laudatory. **laudes** [loːd], *n.f. pl.* Lauds.

lauré [lɔ're], *a.* (*fem.* -**ée**) Crowned with laurels (of medals etc.).

lauréat [lɔre'a], *a.* (*fem.* -**ate**) Laureate. *Poète lauréat*, poet laureate.—*n.* Prize-winner.

lauréole [lɔre'ɔl], *n.f.* (*Bot.*) Mezereon, daphne.

laurier [lɔ'rje], *n.m.* Laurel, bay-tree; (*fig.*) glory, honour. *Couronné de lauriers*, crowned with laurels; *se reposer sur ses lauriers*, to rest on one's laurels; *s'endormir sur ses lauriers*, to cease to work. **laurier-cerise**, *n.m.* (*pl.* **lauriers-cerises**) Cherry-laurel. **laurier-rose** (*pl.* **lauriers-roses**) or **laurose**, *n.m.* Oleander, rose-laurel. **laurier-sauce**, *n.m.* (*pl.* **lauriers-sauce**) Common laurel. **laurier-tin**, *n.m.* (*pl.* **lauriers-tin**) Laurustinus.

lavable [la'vabl], *a.* Washable.

lavabo [lava'bo], *n.m.* Wash-basin, hand-basin; wash-stand; (*pl.*) conveniences, water-closet, toilet.

lavage [la'vaːʒ], *n.m.* Washing; dilution; (*Min.*) panning. (*pop.*) *Lavage de tête*, a good telling-off. *Lavage de cerveau*, brain-washing.

lavallière [lava'ljɛːr], *n.f.* Loose neck-tie.

lavande [la'vãːd], *n.f.* Lavender. *Lavande commune* or *lavande officinale*, common lavender. *Eau de lavande*, lavender water.

lavanderie [lavã'dri], *n.f.* Laundry, wash-house.

lavandière, *n.f.* Laundress, washerwoman; (*Orn.*) grey wagtail.

lavaret [lava'rɛ], *n.m.* Gwyniad, lake-trout.

lavasse [la'vas], *n.f.* Washy soup or wine; watery food.

lave [laːv], *n.f.* Lava.

lavé [la've], *a.* (*fem.* **lavée**) Washed out, faint. *Cheval bai lavé*, light bay horse; *couleur lavée*, light colour.

lave-dos [lav'do], *n.m. inv.* Back-brush.

lave-mains [lav'mɛ̃], *n.m. inv.* Wash-hand basin (in refectory etc.).

lavement [lav'mã], *n.m.* Washing; (*Med.*) injection, clyster, enema; (*pop.*) a bore (of a person).

laver [la've], *v.t.* To wash, to clean with water etc.; to cleanse; to wash off, to wash away; to absolve, to purify; to expiate. *Laver à grande eau*, to swill; *laver la vaisselle*, to wash up; *laver la tête à quelqu'un*, to blow someone up, to give someone a good talking to. *Machine à laver*, washing machine. **se laver**, *v.r.* To wash, to wash oneself, to wash one's hands etc.; to clear or absolve oneself. *Je m'en lave les mains*, I wash my hands of the whole business; *se laver d'un crime*, to clear oneself of a crime.

laverie, *n.f.* Scullery. *Laverie automatique*, modern laundry.

lave-tête, *n.m. inv.* Shampoo-basin.

lavette, *n.f.* Dish-mop.

laveur, *n.m.* (*fem.* **laveuse**) Washer, scourer. *Laveuse de vaisselle*, scullery-maid.

lavis, *n.m.* Wash, tinting. *Dessin (fait au) lavis*, wash drawing.

lavoir, *n.m.* Wash-house; (*Mining*) buddle.

lavure, *n.f.* Dish-water; hogwash; (*Metal.*) washing, scouring; (*pl.*) goldsmith's sweepings.

laxatif [laksa'tif], *a.* (*fem.* -**ive**) Laxative, opening.—*n.m.* Laxative.

laxité, *n.f.* Laxity, looseness.

layer [le'je], *v.t.* (*conjugated like* BALAYER) To cut a path through (a forest); to blaze (trees not to be cut down).

layetier [lɛj'tje], *n.m.* Box-maker, packing-case maker.

layette [lɛ'jet], *n.f.* Box, small drawer; baby garments. **layetterie**, *n.f.* Box-trade.

layon [lɛ'jɔ̃], *n.m.* Tail-board (of cart); small path (cut in a wood) for the shooters.

lazaret [laza'rɛ], *n.m.* Lazaretto (quarantine-station); hospital.

lazulite [lazy'lit], *n.m.* Lazulite, blue spar.

lazzi [la'zi] [It.], *n.m.* (*pl.* **lazzi** or **lazzis**) Buffoonery, jeers.

le [lə], *art. def.* (*fem.* **la**, *pl.* **les**) The. *La nuit*, in the or during the night; *le coquin!* what a scoundrel.—*pron.* Him, her, it; so. *Donnez-le-moi*, give it to me; *il l'aime*, he loves him, her, *or* it; *je le crois*, I think so; *je les vois*, I see them; *je le vois*, I see him *or* it; *je suis enrhumée, mes enfants le sont aussi*, I have got a cold, so have my children; *la voici*, here she is.

lé [le], *n.m.* Breadth (of linen etc.); tow-path.

leader [li'dœr], *n.m.* Political leader; (*Journ.*) editorial, leader.

lebel [lə'bɛl], *n.m.* Magazine rifle of the French Army (model 1885).

lèche [lɛʃ], *n.f.* Thin slice. (*pop.*) *Faire de la lèche auprès de*, to flatter, to suck up to (a person) [*see* LÉCHER].

léché [le'ʃe], *a.* (*fem.* -**ée**) Licked; (*fig.*) over-finished. *Tableau léché*, laboured picture.

lèchefrite [lɛʃ'frit], *n.f.* Dripping-pan.

lécher [le'ʃe], *v.t. irr.* (*conjug. like* ACCÉLÉRER) To lick; to lick up; (*fig.*) to labour, to polish, to elaborate, to overdo. (*pop.*) *Lécher les bottes* (or *les pieds*) *de quelqu'un*, to lick somebody's boots, to suck up to somebody; *lécher les vitrines*, to go window-shopping; *s'en lécher les doigts*, to lick one's chops over it.

lécheur, *n.m.* (*fem.* **lécheuse**) Gourmand, gormandizer; lick-spittle.
leçon [lə'sɔ̃], *n.f.* Lesson; reading (of a text). *Faire la leçon à quelqu'un,* to give someone a lesson, to coach someone; *il a pris des leçons d'un tel,* he took lessons from so and so; *il vit en donnant des leçons particulières,* he earns his living as a private coach; *elle lui a donné une bonne leçon de politesse,* she jolly well taught him manners.
lecteur [lɛk'tœːr], *n.m.* (*fem.* **lectrice**) Reader, lector; proof-reader; assistant (for a foreign language). *Lecteur électromagnétique,* sound pick-up.
lecture [lɛk'tyːr], *n.f.* Reading; perusal. *Cabinet de lecture,* reading-room; *il a beaucoup de lecture,* he is well read; *lecture au son,* sound reading.
ledit [lə'di], *a.* (*fem.* **ladite**, *pl.* **lesdit(e)s**) The (afore)said, the same.
légal [le'gal], *a.* (*fem.* **-ale**, *pl.* **-aux**) Legal, lawful, legitimate. **légalement,** *adv.* Legally, lawfully, legitimately. **légalisation,** *n.f.* Legalization, authentication. **légaliser,** *v.t.* To legalize, to render legal. **légalité,** *n.f.* Legality, lawfulness.
légat [le'ga], *n.m.* Legate.
légataire [lega'tɛːr], *n.* Legatee. *Légataire universel,* residuary legatee.
légation [lega'sjɔ̃], *n.f.* Legateship; legation.
lège [lɛːʒ], *a.* (*Naut.*) Light.
légendaire [leʒɑ̃'dɛːr], *a.* and *n.m.* Legendary, epic.
légende [le'ʒɑ̃ːd], *n.f.* Legend; inscription (on medals etc.); caption (on drawing); explanation of symbols, key. *La légende dorée,* the Golden Legend.
léger [le'ʒe], *a.* (*fem.* **légère**) Light; thin, flimsy, slight; buoyant, airy; fleet, fast; nimble, active; fickle, unsteady, volatile; faint, trifling, inconsiderate, giddy, thoughtless, wanton, light-minded. *À la légère,* lightly, thoughtlessly, inconsiderately, carelessly; *avoir la main légère,* to be light-handed, to be dexterous, to be handy or ready with one's hand; *avoir la tête légère,* to be hare-brained; *cavalerie légère,* light-horse; *conclure à la légère,* to jump to conclusions; *être léger à la course,* to be fleet of foot; *musique légère,* light music; *une faute légère,* a small fault; *une perte légère,* a trivial loss; *vin léger,* light wine. **légèrement,** *adv.* Lightly, slightly; nimbly, swiftly; cursorily, thoughtlessly.
légèreté [leʒɛrte], *n.f.* Lightness; nimbleness, swiftness, fickleness, unsteadiness, instability; levity, frivolity; airiness, inconsiderateness, thoughtlessness; slight fault. *La légèreté d'un cerf,* the fleetness of a stag.
légiférer [leʒife're], *v.i.* To legislate.
légion [le'ʒjɔ̃], *n.f.* Legion; army; a great number, a host. *Les chômeurs sont aujourd'hui légion,* the unemployed are many nowadays. *La Légion d'honneur,* the Legion of Honour. *La Légion étrangère,* the Foreign Legion. **légionnaire,** *n.m.* Legionary; member of the Legion of Honour; soldier of the Foreign Legion.
législateur [leʒisla'tœːr], *a.* (*fem.* **-trice**) Legislative, lawgiving.—*n.* Legislator, lawmaker.

législatif, *a.* (*fem.* **-ive**) Legislative. *Le Pouvoir législatif,* the Legislature.
législation, *n.f.* Legislation.
législature, *n.f.* Period of functions as a Legislative Assembly; legislature.
légiste, *n.m.* Legist, jurist. *Médecin légiste,* medical expert (at trials etc.).
légitimaire [leʒiti'mɛːr], *a.* Secured by law.
légitimation, *n.f.* Legitimation (of child).
légitime [leʒi'tim], *a.* Lawful, legitimate, rightful; justifiable, allowable. *Demande légitime,* legitimate or justifiable demand; *enfant légitime,* child born in wedlock; *légitime défense,* self defence; *une fierté bien légitime,* a fully justified pride.—*n.m.* That which is legitimate.—*n.f.* Lawful portion of a child. (*pop.*) *Ma légitime,* my wife. **légitimement,** *adv.* Legitimately, lawfully; justly, rightfully, justifiably. **légitimer,** *v.t.* To legitimate; to justify; to recognize. *L'ivresse ne légitime aucune mauvaise action,* drunkenness does not justify any bad action.
légitimiste, *n.* and *a.* Legitimist.
légitimité, *n.f.* Legitimacy, lawfulness.
legs [lɛ], *n.m.* Legacy, bequest.
léguer [le'ge], *v.t.* To leave by will, to devise, to bequeath.
légume [le'gym], *n.m.* Vegetable. *Légumes verts,* greens; *légumes secs,* pulse.—*n.f.* (*fam.*) *Les grosses légumes,* the bigwigs. **légumier,** *n.m.* Vegetable-dish.—*a.* Of vegetables.
légumineux, *a.* (*fem.* **-euse**) Leguminous. —*n.f.* (*Bot.*) Leguminous plant.
leitmotiv [laitmɔ'tif], *n.m.* (*pl.* **-e**) Theme-song or tune, leitmotiv.
lemme [lem], *n.m.* (*Math.*) Lemma.
lémur [le'myr], *n.m.* (*Zool.*) Lemur.
lémures [le'myːr], *n.m. pl.* (*Rom. Ant.*) Lemures.
lémurien [lemy'rjɛ̃], *n.m.* (*Zool.*) Lemurid.— *a.* (*fem.* **-ienne**) Lemurian.
lendemain [lɑ̃d'mɛ̃], *n.m.* Morrow, next day, day after, following day. *Du jour au lendemain,* overnight; *il n'y a pas de bonne fête sans lendemain,* there's always a morning after; *le lendemain de ses noces,* the day after one's wedding; *penser au lendemain,* to think of the morrow.
lénifiant [leni'fjɑ̃], *a.* (*fem.* **-iante**) Soothing.
lénifier [leni'fje], *v.t.* (*conjugated like* PRIER) To lenify; to soothe.
lénitif, *a.* (*fem.* **-ive**) and *n.m.* Lenitive.
lent [lɑ̃], *a.* (*fem.* **lente**) Slow, tardy; remiss, backward; sluggish, slack, dull. *Fièvre lente,* slow fever, low fever; *lent à parler,* slow of speech; *lent à payer,* slack in one's payments.
lente [lɑ̃ːt], *n.f.* Nit.
lentement [lɑ̃t'mɑ̃], *adv.* Slowly, tardily; remissly, sluggishly.
lenteur, *n.f.* Slowness; tardiness, dilatoriness, remissness; sluggishness; delay.
lenticulaire [lɑ̃tiky'lɛːr] or **lenticulé** (*fem.* **-ée**), *a.* Lenticular.
lenticule [lɑ̃ti'kyl], *n.f.* (*Bot.*) Duckweed.
lentiforme [lɑ̃ti'fɔrm], *a.* Lentiform.
lentigineux [lɑ̃tiʒi'nø], *a.* (*fem.* **-euse**) Lentiginous, freckled.
lentigo, *n.m.* Lentigo, freckles.
lentille [lɑ̃'tiːj], *n.f.* Lentil; lens; bob of pendulum; (*Naut.*) deck-light, bull's eye; (*pl.*) freckles. *Lentille d'eau,* duckweed; *plat de lentilles (d'Esaü),* mess of pottage;

visage couvert de lentilles, face freckled all over. **lentilleux,** *a.* (*fem.* **-euse**) Freckled.
lentisque [lɑ̃'tisk], *n.m.* Lentisk, mastic-tree.
léonin [leɔ'nɛ̃], *a.* (*fem.* **léonine**) Leonine.
léonure [leɔ'nyːr], *n.m.* Motherwort.
léopard [leɔ'paːr], *n.m.* Leopard.
léopardé, *a.* (*fem.* **-ée**) Spotted (like leopard). (*Her.*) *Deux lions léopardés,* two lions passant gardant.
lépidoptère [lepidɔp'tɛːr], *n.m.* (*Ent.*) Lepidopter.—*a.* Lepidopterous.
lépisme [le'pism], *n.m.* (*Ent.*) Lepisma; silver-fish, silver worm, bristle-tail.
léporide [lepɔ'rid], *n.m.* Leporide.
lèpre [lɛpr], *n.f.* Leprosy. **lépreux,** *a.* (*fem.* **-euse**) Leprous.—*n.* Leper.
léproserie [lepro'zri], *n.f.* Leper-hospital, lazaretto.
lequel [lə'kɛl], *pron.m.* (*fem.* **laquelle,** *pl.m.* **lesquels,** *pl.f.* **lesquelles**) Who, whom, that, which; (*inter.*) which one, which? *Lequel* or *laquelle préférez-vous?* which do you prefer? *lequel* or *laquelle vous plaît davantage?* which do you like best?
lérot [le'ro], *n.m.* Garden dormouse.
les [LE].
***lès** or **lez** [le], *prep.* Near by (only with towns, as *Plessis-lès-Tours, Saint-Pierre-lès-Elbeuf*).
lesbien [lɛs'bjɛ̃], *a.* and *n.* (*fem.* **-ienne**) Lesbian.
lèse-majesté [lɛzmaʒɛs'te], *n.f.* High treason, lese-majesty.
léser [le'ze], *v.t.* irr. (*conjug. like* ACCÉLÉRER) To wrong; to injure, to hurt.
lésine [le'zin], *n.f.* Niggardliness, stinginess.
lésiner, *v.i.* To be stingy or mean; to higgle, to haggle; (*Am.*) to dicker. **lésinerie,** *n.f.* Stinginess, meanness, niggardliness. **lésineur,** *a.* and *n.* (*fem.* **-euse**) Niggardly, stingy, mean, parsimonious (person).
lésion [le'zjɔ̃], *n.f.* (*Law*) Wrong, injury; (*Surg.*) lesion, wound, hurt.
lessivage [lesi'vaʒ], *n.m.* Washing (of floors, walls, etc.). **lessive,** *n.f.* Lye-wash, wash; linen washed or to be washed, washing, lye-washing; lixivium. *C'est mon jour de lessive,* it is my washing day; *donner sa lessive à laver,* to give one's dirty linen to be washed. **lessiver,** *v.t.* To wash in lye; to lixiviate; (*fam.*) to sell (a jewel, a watch). **lessiveur,** *n.m.* (*fem.* **-euse**) Lye-washer.—*n.f.* Washing-copper.
lest [lɛst], *n.m.* Ballast (for balloons). **lestage,** *n.m.* Ballasting.
leste [lɛst], *a.* Brisk, nimble, active; light; smart; sharp; improper, free. **lestement,** *adv.* Briskly; cleverly; flippantly; freely.
lester [lɛs'te], *v.t.* To ballast. **se lester,** *v.r.* (*fam.*) To take in ballast; to line one's stomach. *Je me suis bien lesté avant de me mettre en route,* I had a square meal before setting out. **lesteur,** *n.m.* Ballast-lighter; ballast-heaver.
léthargie [letar'ʒi], *n.f.* Lethargy.
léthargique [letar'ʒik], *a.* Lethargic.
létifère [leti'fɛr], also **léthifère** (*rare*), *a.* Lethiferous, deadly, lethal, death-dealing.
lettre [lɛtr], *n.f.* Letter, note; (*Print.*) letter, character, type; (*pl.*) literature, letters. *Avant la lettre,* prematurely; *avoir des lettres,* to be well-read; *boîte aux lettres,* letter-box; *cela reste lettre close,* that is a secret; *en toutes lettres,* at full length, in full, unmistakably;

expédition des lettres, dispatch of letters; *gravure avant la lettre,* proof engraving; *jeter* or *mettre une lettre à la poste,* to post a letter; *les belles-lettres,* humanities; *lettre de change,* bill of exchange; *lettre d'envoi,* covering letter; *lettre de crédit,* letter of credit; *lettre de mer,* (*Naut.*) pass; *lettre de voiture,* way-bill; *lettre morte,* dead letter; *lettres de marque,* letters of mark; *lettres patentes,* letters patent; *notre lettre du . . .,* ours of . . .; *prendre une chose à la lettre* or *au pied de la lettre,* to take a thing literally; *rendre à la lettre,* to render word for word; *un homme de lettres,* a man of letters. **lettré,** *a.* (*fem.* **-ée**) Cultured, literate, well-read; literary.—*n.m.* Scholar. *Les lettrés,* the literate, the literati, the cultured people. **lettrine,** *n.f.* (*Print.*) Reference letter; capital letter at head of column in dictionary.
leu [lø], *n.m.* (Picard dialect for *loup*—wolf) used in the expression—*à la queue leu leu* or *le leu,* one after the other, in single file.
leucanthème [løkɑ̃'tɛm], *n.m.* (*Bot.*) or *Canesson,* or *grande marguerite.* Ox-eye daisy.
leucémie [løse'mi], *n.f.* Leuchaemia, leukaemia. **leucémique,** *a.* Leuchaemic.
leucocyte [løkɔ'sit], *n.m.* Leucocyte. **leucocytose,** *n.f.* Leucocytosis. **leucome,** *n.m.* Leucoma.
leucorrhée [løkɔ're], *n.f.* Leucorrhoea, whites.
leur [lœːr], *a. poss.* Their. *Leur maison,* their house; *leurs livres,* their books.—*poss.pron.* Theirs. *J'aime mieux ma maison que la leur,* I like my house better than theirs; *je ne veux rien du leur,* I want nothing of theirs; *le leur, la leur,* or *les leurs,* theirs.—*pers. pron.* To them, them. *Donnez-le-leur,* give it to them; *je le leur donne,* I give it to them; *je leur ai dit cela,* I told them that.
leurre [lœːr], *n.m.* Lure, decoy; bait, enticement; snare, trap. *Se laisser prendre à un leurre,* to be caught in a snare, to swallow a bait.
leurrer, *v.t.* To lure, to entice, to decoy; to ensnare. **se leurrer,** *v.r.* To delude oneself. (*Falconry*) *Ces oiseaux ne se leurrent pas facilement,* these birds are not easily decoyed.
levage [lə'vaʒ], *n.m.* Raising, lifting.
levain [lə'vɛ̃], *n.m.* Leaven; (*fig.*) germ. *Pain sans levain,* unleavened bread.
levant [lə'vɑ̃], *n.m.* East; rising sun; Levant. *Du levant au couchant,* from east to west. *a.m.* Rising, orient.
levantin, *a.* (*fem.* **-ine**) Levantine.—*n.f.* Levantine (silk cloth).—*n.m.* (**Levantin,** *fem.* **-ine**) Levantine (person).
levé [lə've], *a.* (*fem.* **levée**) Lifted up, raised; erect, up, risen, out of bed. *Pâte levée,* raised dough; *blé levé,* sprouted wheat; *pierre levée,* menhir; *dessin à main levée,* freehand drawing; *vote à main levée,* vote by a show of hands; *votre maître est-il levé?* is your master up?—*n.m.* (*Mus.*) Rise (of foot, hand), up beat; plan, survey (of land).
levée [lə've], *n.f.* Raising, lifting, taking, removal; levying; gathering (crop, fruit, etc.); (post-office) collection; embankment; earth-bank; breaking up (of a camp, siege, etc.); heaving, swell (of the sea); (*Cards*) trick. *Faire des levées de soldats,* to raise soldiers; *faire la levée,* to take the odd trick; *levée des arrêts* or *des prohibitions,* suspension

of arrest *or* of the prohibition; *levée du corps*, removal of dead body (from residence).

lever [lə've], *v.t.* To lift, to lift up, to raise; to heave, to heave up; to pull up; to weigh (anchor); to remove, to take away; to take out; to cut off, to cut out; to gather, to collect; to levy; to break up (a siege etc.); to relieve (a guard); to strike (camp); to take a copy of, to draw. *Lever la main sur quelqu'un*, to lift up one's hand against someone; *lever la séance*, to dissolve a meeting; *lever la tête*, to raise one's head; *lever le camp*, to break up the camp; *lever le masque*, to throw off the mask; *lever les épaules*, to shrug one's shoulders; *lever les scellés*, to remove the seals; *lever les yeux*, to look up; *lever un lièvre*, to start a hare; *lever une perdrix*, to put up, to flush a partridge; *lever un plan*, to draw a plan, to make a survey; *lever un siège*, to raise a siege.—*v.i.* To come up; to spring up, to rise (of plants, dough, etc.); to heave (of the sea). **se lever**, *v.r.* To rise, to get up; to stand up; (of the sea) to heave; (of the weather) to clear up. *Se lever précipitamment*, to start up.

lever [lə've], *n.m.* Rising, getting up; levee (of king). *Lever du soleil*, sunrise; (*Am.*) sun-up; (*Theat.*) *lever de rideau*, curtain-raiser.

levier [lə'vje], *n.m.* Lever; crowbar, bar, hand-spike; arm, beam. *Levier de commande*, control; *la force du levier*, the power of the lever; leverage; *le point d'appui d'un levier*, the fulcrum of a lever. *Faire levier sur*, to lever, to prise against.

lévite (1) [le'vit], *n.m.* Levite; ecclesiastic, cleric.

lévite (2) [le'vit], *n.f.* Man's long coat (end of 18th cent.).

lévitique [levi'tik], *a.* Levitical.—*n. Le Lévitique*, Leviticus (book).

levraut [lə'vro], *n.m.* Leveret; young hare.

lèvre [lɛ:vr], *n.f.* Lip; rim. *Pincer les lèvres*, to purse one's lips; *du bout des lèvres*, with the tip of one's lips, (*fig.*) contemptuously, half-heartedly, in a forced manner; *je l'ai sur le bord des lèvres*, I have it on the tip of my tongue.

levrette [lə'vrɛt], *n.f.* Female greyhound; Italian greyhound. **levretté**, *a.* (*fem.* -ée) Slim, greyhound-like.

lévrier [levri'e], *n.m.* Greyhound. *Lévrier d'Écosse*, deer-hound; *lévrier russe*, borzoi.

levron, *n.m.* Young greyhound.

levure [lə'vy:r], *n.f.* Yeast; rind, waste (of larding bacon). *Levure de bière*, brewer's yeast.

lexicographe [lɛksikɔ'graf], *n.m.* Lexicographer. **lexicographie**, *n.f.* Lexicography. **lexicographique**, *a.* Lexicographical.

lexicologie, *n.f.* Lexicology.

lexique [lɛk'sik], *n.m.* Lexicon; vocabulary (of an author); abridged dictionary.

lez [LÈS].

lézard [le'za:r], *n.m.* Lizard.

lézarde [le'zard], *n.f.* Crevice, crack, chink. **lézardé**, *a.* (*fem.* -ée) Cracked (of walls etc.). **lézarder**, *v.t.* To crack (walls etc.).— *v.i.* (*fam.*) To lounge. **se lézarder**, *v.r.* To crack, to become cracked.

liais [ljɛ], *n.m.* Lias; (in England) calcareous limestone, blue limestone.

liaison [ljɛ'zɔ̃], *n.f.* Joining, union, conjunction; connexion, acquaintance; intimacy; binding, cement; union (of stones etc. in masonry); (*Mil.*) liaison, communications, concerted action (between bodies of troops); binding-stroke (of writing); liaison (between words); (*Mus.*) slur, binding-note. (*Mil.*) *Effectuer la liaison*, to liaise; *faire la liaison*, to make the liaison, to run on, to run words together; (*Cook.*) *faire une liaison*, to thicken a sauce; *officier de liaison*, liaison officer.

liaisonner, *v.t.* To bind, to cement (stones etc.).

liane [ljan], *n.f.* Liana; tropical creeper.

liant [ljɑ̃], *a.* (*fem.* **liante**) Supple, flexible, pliant; compliant; affable, sociable.—*n.m.* Suppleness, pliability; affability, sociability; gentleness.

liard [lja:r], *n.m.* Liard (half-farthing); (*Bot.*) black poplar; (C) common poplar. *Il n'a pas un rouge liard*, he hasn't a brass farthing.

liarder, *v.i.* To haggle over pennies.

lias [ljɑs], *n.m.* (*Geol.*) Lias. **liasique** or **liassique**, *a.* Liassic.

liasse [ljas], *n.f.* Bundle, file (of papers); wad (of banknotes).

libage [li'ba:ʒ], *n.m.* Rough ashlar (for foundations etc.); rubble.

Liban [li'bɑ̃], *m.* Lebanon. **libanais**, *a.* and *n.m.* (**Libanais**, *fem.* -aise) Lebanese.

libation [liba'sjɔ̃], *n.f.* Libation; (*fig.*) potation. *Faire des libations*, to offer up libations.

libelle [li'bɛl], *n.m.* Libel, lampoon.

libellé [libɛl'le], *a.* (*fem.* -ée) Drawn up, specified.—*n.m.* Wording, contents.

libeller, *v.t.* To draw up, to word (a legal document etc.).

libelliste [libɛl'list], *n.m.* Lampoonist.

libellule [libɛl'lyl], *n.f.* Dragon-fly.

liber [li'bɛ:r], *n.m.* (*Bot.*) Liber, inner bark.

libérable [libe'rabl], *a.* (*Mil.*) Who can be discharged (of a soldier).

libéral [libe'ral], *a.* (*fem.* -ale, *pl.* -aux) Liberal, generous, bountiful, open-handed; (*Polit.*) Liberal. **libéralement**, *adv.* Liberally, bountifully, generously.

libéralisme, *n.m.* Liberalism.

libéralité, *n.f.* Generosity, open-handedness; bounty, act of liberality.

libérateur ·[libera'tœ:r], *n.m.* (*fem.* **libératrice**) Deliverer, liberator, rescuer.

libération [libera'sjɔ̃], *n.f.* Deliverance; rescue, liberation; discharge, riddance. *Libération (d'une hypothèque)*, redemption. **libéré**, *a.* (*fem.* -ée) Liberated, discharged. *Action libérée*, paid-up share; *forçat libéré*, discharged convict.—*n.* *Un libéré provisoire*, prisoner released on parole.

libératoire [libera'twar], *a.* *Monnaie libératoire*, legal tender.

libérer, *v.t. irr.* (*conjugated like* ACCÉLÉRER) To liberate, to free; to discharge. **se libérer**, *v.r.* To free oneself, to clear oneself (*de*); to pay off one's debts.

libertaire [libɛr'tɛ:r], *a.* and *n.* Libertarian, anarchist.

liberté [libɛr'te], *n.f.* Liberty, freedom, ease; (*pl.*) immunities, franchises. *En liberté*, freely; *liberté de parole, de pensée*, freedom of speech, of thought; *liberté du culte*, freedom of worship; *mettre en liberté*, to set at liberty, to release; *mise en liberté sous caution*,

libertin [libɛr'tɛ̃], *a.* (*fem.* **libertine**) Libertine, licentious; wanton, dissolute; *free-thinking.—n.* Libertine, rake, *free-thinker.

libertinage, *n.m.* Libertinism, debauchery; wantonness; *irreligion. Vivre dans le libertinage,* to lead a dissolute life.

libidineux [libidi'nø], *a.* (*fem.* **-euse**) Libidinous, lewd.

libido, *n.f.* (*Psych.*) Libido.

libraire [li'brɛːr], *n.m.* Bookseller. *Libraire-éditeur,* publisher and bookseller. **librairie,** *n.f.* Book-trade, bookselling; bookseller's shop.

libration [librɑ'sjɔ̃], *n.f.* Libration; swinging.

libre [librˌ], *a.* Free; at liberty, at large; independent; unguarded, undisciplined, unconfined; bold, broad; rid, exempt; irregular (of verse). *Avoir le champ libre,* to have free scope for action; *avoir l'esprit libre,* to be free from care; *cette place est libre,* that seat is unoccupied; *ce porteur est libre,* this porter is disengaged *or* free; *école libre,* independent school; *il a tout son temps libre,* all his time is his own; *la libre entreprise,* free enterprise; *le chemin est libre,* the road is open; *libre à vous de sortir ou de rester,* stay or go, as you please; *libre à vous de dire non,* it is all very well for you to say 'no'; *libre sur parole,* (free) on parole; *libre dans ses paroles,* outspoken.

libre-échange, *n.m.* Free trade. *Zone de libre-échange,* free trade area. **libre-échangiste,** *n.m.* (*pl.* **libre-échangistes**) Free-trader.

librement, *adv.* Freely, without restraint; boldly. *En user librement,* to make free with something.

libre-penseur, *n.m.* (*pl.* **libres-penseurs**) Free-thinker.

librettiste [libre'tist], *n.m.* Librettist.

lice (1) [lis], *n.f.* Lists, tilt-yard. *Entrer dans la lice or en lice,* to enter the lists.

lice (2) [lis], *n.f.* Warp. *Basse lice,* low warp; *haute lice,* high warp.

lice (3) [lis], *n.f.* Hound-bitch.

licence [li'sɑ̃ːs], *n.f.* Licence, leave, permission; liberty, licentiousness; licentiate's degree. *Licence ès lettres,* B.A.; *licence ès sciences,* B.Sc. (approximately).

licencié, *a.* and *n.m.* (*fem.* **-iée**) Licentiate. —*a.* (*C*) *Un épicier licencié,* a grocer licensed to sell beer.

licenciement [lisɑ̃si'mɑ̃], *n.m.* Disbanding.

licencier, *v.t.* To disband (troops); to declare redundant (of staff etc.), to lay off.

licencieusement [lisɑ̃sjøz'mɑ̃], *adv.* Licentiously, dissolutely. **licencieux,** *a.* (*fem.* **-ieuse**) Licentious, dissolute.

licet [li'set], *n.m. inv.* Permission, leave, permit.

lichen [li'ken], *n.m.* Lichen. **lichéneux,** *a.* (*fem.* **-euse**) Lichenous.

licher [li'ʃe], *v.t.* (*pop.*) To lick; to drink greedily; to tipple.

lichette [li'ʃet], *n.f.* (*pop.*) Thin slice (of bread etc.).

licitation [lisitɑ'sjɔ̃], *n.f.* Sale by auction.

licite [li'sit], *a.* Licit, lawful, allowable. **licitement,** *adv.* Lawfully, licitly.

liciter [lisi'te], *v.t.* To sell by auction.

licol [LICOU].

licorne [li'kɔrn], *n.f.* Unicorn. *Licorne de mer,* narwhal.

licou [li'ku] or **licol,** *n.m.* Halter.

licteur [lik'tœːr], *n.m.* (*Rom. Ant.*) Lictor.

lie (1) [li], *n.f.* Lees, dregs, grounds; (*fig.*) scum, refuse. *Boire jusqu'à la lie,* to drink to the dregs; *la lie du peuple,* the scum of the people.

*****lie** (2) [li], *a.* Merry, gay (only used in *Faire chère lie,* to lead a merry life, to feast).

lié [lje], *a.* (*fem.* **liée**) Tied, bound, connected. *Une sauce bien liée,* a thick smooth sauce.

liège [ljeːʒ], *n.m.* Cork; cork-tree. *Bouchon de liège,* cork. **liéger,** *v.t.* To cork (a net, line, etc.). **liégeux,** *a.* (*fem.* **-euse**) Like cork (a net, line, etc.).

lien [ljɛ̃], *n.m.* Bond, tie, link; (*pl.*) bonds, chains, shackles. *Briser or rompre ses liens,* to break one's bonds; *les liens du sang,* ties of kinship; *lien conjugal,* matrimonial bond.

lientérie [ljɑ̃te'riː], *n.f.* (*Path.*) Lientery. **lientérique,** *a.* Lienteric.

lier [lje], *v.t.* To fasten, to tie; to bind, to bind down; to tie down, to tie up; to join, to link (*à*), to connect (*avec*); to contract, to form; to enter into, to engage in; (*Mus.*) to slur; to thicken (a sauce etc.). *Avoir la langue liée,* to be tongue-tied; *avoir les mains liées,* to have one's hands tied; *il est fou à lier,* he is as mad as a March hare; he ought to be put into a strait-jacket; *être lié d'intérêt,* to have a common interest; *lier commerce avec quelqu'un,* to establish relations with someone; *lier conversation,* to enter into conversation; *lier des notes,* to slur notes. **se lier,** *v.r.* To become acquainted, intimate (*avec*); to thicken (of sauce etc.). *Se lier d'amitié,* to make friends.

lierne [ljern], *n.f.* Binding timber; (*Arch.*) lierne; (*Naut.*) floor-plank (of small craft).

lierre [ljeːr], *n.m.* Ivy. *Lierre terrestre or rampant,* ground-ivy.

*****liesse** [ljes], *n.f.* Only used in *être en liesse,* to be revelling, merry-making [see LIE (2)].

lieu (1) [ljø], *n.m.* (*pl.* **lieux**) Place, spot; position, rank; lineage, extraction; stead, lieu, room; cause, reason, occasion; (*pl.*) premises, apartments. *Au lieu de,* in the place of, instead of; *au lieu que,* instead of which, whereas; *avoir lieu,* to take place; *avoir lieu de,* to have good reason to; *donner lieu à,* to be the occasion of, to give rise to; *en aucun lieu,* nowhere; *en dernier lieu,* lastly, last of all; *en haut lieu,* in high quarters; *en lieu sûr,* in a safe place; *en premier lieu,* in the first place; *en quelque lieu que ce soit,* anywhere; *en ses lieu et place,* in his place, as his substitute; *en tout lieu,* everywhere; *être sur les lieux,* to be on the spot; *il m'a tenu lieu de père,* he has been a father to me; *il n'y a pas lieu de craindre,* there is no cause to fear; *les hauts lieux,* the high places; *lieu commun,* commonplace; *lieux (d'aisance),* public conveniences; *mauvais lieu,* a place of debauchery; *s'allier en bon lieu,* to marry into a good family; *tenir lieu de,* to do instead of.

lieu (2) [ljø], *n.m.* (*Ichth.*) or *merlan jaune.* Pollack.

lieudit [ljø'di] or **lieu dit** (*pl.* **lieux dits**), *n.m.* Named place.

lieue [ljø], *n.f.* League (4 kilometres, 2½

English miles). *Deux lieues,* five miles; *j'étais à cent lieues de croire . . .,* I was very far from thinking . . . .

lieur [ljœːr], *n.m.* (*fem.* **-euse**) Binder (of hay etc.). *Une moissonneuse-lieuse,* a reaper-and-binder.

lieutenance [ljøt'nɑ̃ːs], *n.f.* Lieutenancy.

lieutenant, *n.m.* Lieutenant; assistant, right-hand man. *Lieutenant de vaisseau,* lieutenant-commander; *lieutenant en second,* second lieutenant; *sous-lieutenant,* sub-lieutenant. **lieutenant-colonel,** *n.m.* (*pl.* **lieutenants-colonels**) (*Mil.*) Lieutenant-colonel; (*Av.*) wing commander.

lièvre [ljɛːvr], *n.m.* Hare. *C'est là que gît le lièvre,* there's the rub; *il ne faut pas courir deux lièvres à la fois,* one must not have too many irons in the fire; *ils courent le même lièvre,* they are both after the same thing; *lever le lièvre,* to bring up a difficult question; *mémoire de lièvre,* bad memory; *lièvre de mer* [LOMPE].

liftier [lif'tje], *n.m.* Lift-boy; lift-attendant.

liftière, *n.f.* Lift-girl, lift-attendant.

ligament [liga'mɑ̃], *n.m.* Ligament. **ligamenteux,** *a.* (*fem.* **-euse**) Ligamentous.

ligature, *n.f.* Ligature; whipping (of rope, fishing rod); (*Mus.*) tie; (*Naut.*) = *épissure.*

ligaturer, *v.t.* To ligature, to ligate, to splice, to bind; to tie (artery).

lige [liːʒ], *a.* Liege. *Fief lige,* vassalage; (*fig.*) *homme lige,* totally *or* unconditionally devoted (to), yes-man.

lignage [li'ɲaːʒ], *n.m.* Lineage. **lignager,** *n.m.* Person of the same descent, kinsman.

lignard [li'ɲaːr], *n.m.* (*pop.*) Soldier of the line.

ligne [liɲ], *n.f.* Line; row, range; path, way; twine, cord; fishing-line, rod-and-line; order, rank, line of descent. *Aller en droite ligne,* to go in a straight line; *aller à la ligne,* to begin a new line or a fresh paragraph; *avoir la ligne,* to have a good figure (of a lady); *en ligne!* (*Mil.*) fall in! *hors ligne,* out of the common, first-rate; *être or venir en première ligne,* to hold the first rank; *ligne d'autobus, aérienne, de chemin de fer,* bus, air, railway line; *ligne de flottaison,* water-line (of a ship); *ligne de fond,* (fishing) ground line; (*Ten.*) base line; *ligne des 22 mètres,* (*Ftb.*) twenty-five line; *ligne de mire,* line of sight; *ligne de portée* [PORTÉE]; *passer la ligne,* to cross the equator; *pêcher à la ligne,* to angle; *pilote de ligne* [see PILOTE]; *troupes de ligne,* troops of the line. **lignée,** *n.f.* Issue, progeny, off-spring. **ligner,** *v.t.* To draw lines on.

lignerolle, *n.f.* Thin twine.

lignette, *n.f.* Twine for making nets.

ligneul, *n.m.* Shoemaker's thread, wax-end.

ligneux [li'ɲø], *a.* (*fem.* **-euse**) Ligneous, woody.

lignifier, *v.t.* To lignify.

lignite, *n.m.* Lignite, brown coal.

ligoter [ligɔ'te], *v.t.* To bind, to tie up firmly.

ligue [lig], *n.f.* League, confederacy. **liguer,** *v.t.* To unite in a league. **se liguer,** *v.r.* To league, to combine.

ligueur, *n.m.* (*fem.* **-euse**) Leaguer; plotter.

ligule [li'gyl], *n.f.* (*Bot.*) Ligula. **ligulé,** *a.* (*fem.* **-ée**) Ligulate, strap-shaped.

lilas [li'lɑ], *n.m.* Lilac. *Lilas d'Espagne,* or *valériane des jardins,* red valerian.—*a. inv.* Lilac-coloured.

liliacé [lilja'se], *a.* (*fem.* **-ée**) Liliaceous.—*n.f.* Liliaceous plant. **lilial,** *a.* (*fem.* **-ale,** *pl.* **-aux**) Lily-like.

lilliputien [lilipy'sjɛ̃], *a.* (*fem.* **-ienne**) Lilliputian.

limace [li'mas], *n.f.* Slug; Archimedean screw.

limaçon, *n.m.* Snail; (*Anat.*) cochlea. *Limaçon de mer,* cockle.

limage [li'maːʒ], *n.m.* Filing. **limaille,** *n.f.* Filings.

limande [li'mɑ̃ːd], *n.f.* (*Ichth.*) Dab; blade (of leaf); (*Carp.*) graving piece (of wood); (*Naut.*) parcelling (of rope).

limbe [lɛ̃ːb], *n.m.* (*Math., Bot., etc.*) Limb; (*Astron.*) border, halo; (*pl.*) limbo. **limbifère,** *a.* Limbiferous. **limbiforme,** *a.* Limbate. **limbique,** *a.* (*Anat.*) Limbic.

lime (1) [lim], *n.f.* File. *Les dents d'une lime,* the teeth of a file; *lime sourde,* dead file. *Lime à ongles,* nail file.

lime (2) [lim] *or* **limette,** *n.f.* Lime, citron; (*Conch.*) lima.

lime-bois [lim'bwɑ], *n.m. inv.* Wood-fretter (larva).

limer [li'me], *v.t.* To file, to smooth; (*fig.*) to polish, to finish. **limeur,** *n.m.* (*fem.* **-euse**) Filer.—*n.f.* Finishing-tool or machine.

limette [LIME (2)].

limier [li'mje], *n.m.* Bloodhound; (*fig.*) police-spy, detective.

liminaire [limi'nɛːr], *a.* Prefatory.

limitatif [limita'tif], *a.* (*fem.* **-ive**) Limiting, restrictive. **limitation,** *n.f.* Limitation. *Limitation des naissances,* birth-control; (*Motor.*) *limitation de vitesse,* speed-limit. **limitativement,** *adv.* Limitedly, with limitation.

limite [li'mit], *n.f.* Limit, boundary, bound; border, extremity; confine, landmark. *Cas limite,* worst possible case; *date limite,* latest date; *limite d'âge,* age limit; *vitesse limite,* speed limit; (*C*) *limite,* or *limite à bois,* forest concession, limit timber berth. **limité,** *a.* (*fem.* **-ée**) Limited, circumscribed, hide-bound. **limiter,** *v.t.* To limit, to bound, to set bounds to; to circumscribe, to confine. **se limiter,** *v.r.* To limit oneself, to be limited.

limitrophe, *a.* Limitrophe, neighbouring, bordering.

limodore [limo'dɔr], *n.m.* (*Bot.*) Limodorum abortivum (a saprophyte wild orchid).

limogeage [limo'ʒaːʒ], *n.m.* Dismissal (of officer).

limoger, *v.t.* To dismiss (a general etc.) from his command.

limon (1) [li'mɔ̃], *n.m.* Silt, ooze, mud, alluvium; (*fig.*) filth, slime.

limon (2) [li'mɔ̃], *n.m.* Sour lime.

limon (3) [li'mɔ̃], *n.m.* Shaft, thill (of a carriage). *Limon d'escalier,* string-board, stringer.

limonade [limo'nad], *n.f.* Lemonade. *Limonade gazeuse,* aerated lemonade. **limonadier,** *n.m.* (*fem.* **-ière**) Seller of lemonade; *café-keeper.

limoneux [limo'nø], *a.* (*fem.* **-euse**) Muddy, turbid, slimy; alluvial.

limonier (1) [limo'nje], *n.m.* Shaft-horse.

limonier (2) [limo'nje], *n.m.* Lemon- or lime-tree.

limonière [limɔ'njɛːr], *n.f.* Pair of shafts (of wagon etc.); wagon with two shafts.
limonite [limɔ'nit], *n.f.* (*Min.*) Limonite.
limousin [limu'zɛ̃], *a.* (*fem.* **limousine**) Pertaining to Limousin.—*n.m.* (**Limousin**, *fem.* **Limousine**) A native or inhabitant of Limousin.—*n.m.* Stone mason.—*n.f.* Limousine car; coarse woollen cloak.
limousinage [limuzi'naːʒ] or **limosinage**, *n.m.* Rough-walling of stone and mortar. **limousiner**, *v.t.* To rough-wall.
limpide [lɛ̃'pid], *a.* Limpid, clear.
limpidité, *n.f.* Limpidity.
limure [li'myːr], *n.f.* Filing; filings; (*fig.*) polish (on metal).
lin [lɛ̃], *n.m.* Flax. *Graine de lin*, linseed; *huile de lin*, linseed oil; *toile de lin*, linen-cloth.
linacée, *n.f.* (*Bot.*) Flax-plant.
linaire, *n.f.*, or **lin sauvage**. Toad-flax.
linceul [lɛ̃'sœl], *n.m.* Winding-sheet, shroud.
linéaire [line'ɛːr], *a.* Linear. *Dessin linéaire*, geometrical drawing.
linéal, *a.* (*fem.* **-ale**, *pl.* **-aux**) Lineal, in a direct line. **linéament**, *n.m.* Lineament, feature; (*fig.*) trace, vestige.
linette [li'nɛt], *n.f.* Flax-seed.
linge [lɛ̃ːʒ], *n.m.* Linen; piece, rag (of linen). *Blanc comme un linge*, as white as a sheet; *changer de linge*, to change one's linen; *il faut laver son linge sale en famille*, (*fig.*) dirty linen should be washed in private; *linge de corps*, underwear; *linge de maison*, household linen.
linger, *n.m.* (*fem.* **-ère**) Linen-draper; maker of linen goods; seamstress (of same).—*n.f.* Wardrobe woman; linen-room keeper; fine laundress.
lingerie, *n.f.* Linen-trade, linen-drapery; linen-room; linen goods (collars, cuffs, underclothing, etc). *Lingerie fine*, lingerie.
lingot [lɛ̃'go], *n.m.* Ingot; slug (bullet); (*Print.*) clump. *Or en lingot*, gold in bullion.
lingotière, *n.f.* Ingot-mould.
lingual [lɛ̃'gwal], *a.* (*fem.* **-ale**, *pl.* **-aux**) Lingual.—*n.f.* *Une linguale*, a lingual consonant.
lingue [lɛ̃ːg], *n.f.* (*Ichth.*) Ling.—*n.m.* *(slang)* Knife.
linguet [lɛ̃'gɛ], *n.m.* Pawl (of a capstan).
linguiforme [lɛ̃gɥi'fɔrm], *a.* Linguiform (tongue shaped).
linguiste [lɛ̃'gɥist], *n.* Linguist. **linguistique**, *a.* Linguistic.—*n.f.* Linguistics.
linier [li'nje], *a.* (*fem.* **linière**) Of flax or linen. *Industrie linière*, linen-trade, linen-manufacture.—*n.f.* Flax-field.
liniment [lini'mɑ̃], *n.m.* Liniment.
linnéen [linne'ɛ̃], *a.* (*fem.* **-éenne**) Linnaean.
linoléum [linɔle'ɔm], *n.m.* Linoleum.
linon [li'nɔ̃], *n.m.* Lawn (fine linen).
linot [li'no], *n.m.*, or **linotte**, *n.f.* Linnet. *Linotte de montagne*, twite; *petite linotte*, lesser redpoll. *Une tête de linotte*, a hare-brained person, a scatterbrain.
linotype [lino'tip], *n.f.* Linotype. **linotypiste**, *n.* Linotype operator.
linteau [lɛ̃'to], *n.m.* (*pl.* **linteaux**) Lintel.
lion [ljɔ̃], *n.m.* (*fem.* **lionne**) Lion, (*fem.*) lioness (*Astron.*) Leo; (*fig.*) a bold, brave fellow. *C'est l'âne couvert de la peau du lion*, he is the ass with the lion's skin; *dent-de-lion*

[DENT]; *lion du Pérou* or *d'Amérique*, cougar; *lion marin* or *lion de mer*, sea-lion.
lionceau, *n.m.* (*pl.* **-eaux**) Young lion, lion's whelp or cub; (*Her.*) lioncel.
lipome [li'poːm], *n.m.* Lipoma.
lippe [lip], *n.f.* Thick lower lip; pouting lip. *Faire sa lippe*, to pout.
lippée, *n.f.* (*colloq.*) Mouthful. *Franche lippée*, good square meal free of cost.
lippu [li'py], *a.* (*fem.* **lippue**) Thick-lipped.
liquation [likwa'sjɔ̃], *n.f.* Liquation.
liquéfaction, *n.f.* Liquefaction. **liquéfiable**, *a.* Liquefiable.
liquéfier [like'fje], *v.t.* To liquefy. **se liquéfier**, *v.r.* To liquefy.
liquette [li'kɛt], *n.f.* (*slang*) Shirt.
liqueur [li'kœːr], *n.f.* Liquid; liqueur, cordial; (*Chem.*) spirit. *Liqueurs fortes*, strong drinks; *vin de liqueur*, very sweet wine.
liquidateur [likida'tœːr], *n.m.* Liquidator.
liquidation, *n.f.* Liquidation, settling; settlement (of debts etc.); winding up (of a business); clearance sale, selling off.
liquide [li'kid], *a.* Liquid; clear, net (of money).—*n.m.* Liquid, fluid; drink; (*Physiol.*) humour.—*n.f.* Liquid consonant. **liquider**, *v.t.* To liquidate, to settle, to discharge; to wind up; to sell off; to get rid of. **se liquider**, *v.r.* To settle one's debts.
liquidité, *n.f.* Liquidity, fluidity.
liquoreux [likɔ'rø], *a.* (*fem.* **liquoreuse**) Luscious, sweet.
liquoriste, *n.m.* Dealer in liqueurs or spirits.
lire (1) [liːr], *v.t.* *irr.* (*pres.p.* **lisant**, *p.p.* **lu**) To read, to peruse, to study. *Continuer de lire*, to read on, to go on reading; *dans l'espoir de vous lire*, in the hope of hearing from you; *lire à haute voix*, to read aloud; *lire dans la pensée de quelqu'un*, to read someone's thoughts; *lire tout bas*, to read to oneself; *se faire lire quelque chose*, to get or to have something read to oneself.
lire (2), *n.f.* Lira.
liron [LÉROT].
lis [lis], *n.m.* Lily. *Fleur de lis*, fleur-de-lis; *teint de lis*, lily-white complexion.
lisant, *pres.p.* [LIRE].
lise [liz], *n.f.* Quicksand.
liséré [lize'reː, also liza'reː], *n.m.* Piping; border, edge. **lisérer**, *v.t.* To trim (a dress etc.) with piping.
liseron [liz'rɔ̃] or **liset**, *n.m.* (*Bot.*) Convolvulus. *Liseron des champs*, bearbine; *liseron des haies*, larger or hooded bindweed.
liseur [li'zœːr], *n.m.* (*fem.* **liseuse**) Reader. *Une liseuse*, bed-jacket; interchangeable book-jacket; bookmarker; study easy-chair; reading stand or lamp.
lisibilité, *n.f.* Legibility, readableness.
lisible, *a.* Legible, readable. **lisiblement**, *adv.* Legibly.
lisière [li'zjɛːr], *n.f.* List, selvedge, edge (of cloth etc.); leading-strings; border, skirt, verge, outskirts. *Lisière de toile*, selvedge of linen-cloth; *lisière d'un bois*, edge of a wood.
lissage [li'saːʒ], *n.m.* Smoothing, glossing; (*Shipbuilding*) railing, rails.
lisse (1) [lis], *a.* Smooth (skin); sleek (hair); glossy. *Mortier à âme lisse*, smooth-bored mortar.—*n.m.* Smoothness, gloss.
lisse (2) [lis], *n.f.* (*Shipbuilding*) Ribband;

rail, railing. *Lisses de bastingage*, quarter-netting rail; *lisses de couronnement*, taffrail.

lisse (3) [LICE (2)].

lisser [li'se], *v.t.* To smooth, to gloss, to polish (stone); to glaze (paper); to sleek (leather); (*dial.*) to iron. *Se lisser les plumes* (of bird), to preen its feathers.

lisseur, *n.* (*fem.* **lisseuse**) Polisher.

lissoir, *n.m.* Polisher (tool).

lissure, *n.f.* Polishing, glazing (of paper etc.).

liste [list], *n.f.* List, roll; catalogue; schedule, panel. *Dresser une liste*, to make out a list; *liste civile*, civil list; *liste électorale*, polling list, election register; *liste des jurés*, panel of jurymen; (*Mil.*) *liste d'ancienneté*, seniority roll; *liste des morts au Champ d'Honneur*, the Roll of Honour.

listeau [lis'to] (*pl.* **listeaux**) or **listel** or **liston**, *n.m.* Listel, fillet; (*Her.*) scroll; rim (of coin).

listéra [liste'ra], *n.f.* (*Bot.*) *Listera ovata*.

liston [LISTEAU].

lit [li], *n.m.* Bed; layer (of clay, mortar); direction, set (of tide, current); (*fig.*) marriage. *Bois de lit*, bedstead; *chambre à un lit*, single(-bedded) room; *chambre à deux lits*, double(-bedded) room; *comme on fait son lit, on se couche*, as you make your bed so you must lie; *enfant du premier lit*, child by the first wife; *garder le lit*, to keep one's bed, (*more often*) to stay in bed; *ils font lit à part*, they do not sleep together; *lit à colonnes*, four-post bedstead, four-poster; *lit de camp*, camp-bed, field-bed; *lit de dessous*, under-stratum (of a quarry); *lit de fer*, iron bed-stead; *lit de justice*, king's throne in old French parliament, session of the parlia-ment; *lit de parade*, bed of state; *lit de Procruste*, Procrustean bed; *lit de repos*, couch, day-bed; *lit de rivière, de fleuve*, river-bed; *prendre le lit*, to take to one's bed. *Lit du vent*, (*Naut.*) the wind's eye; *tenir le lit du vent*, (*Naut.*) to sail close to the wind.

litanie [lita'ni], *n.f.* (*pl.*) Litany; (*fig.*) (*sing.*) rigmarole.

lit-cage [li'ka:ʒ], *n.m.* (*pl.* **lits-cages**) Folding bed.

liteau (1) [li'to], *n.m.* (*pl.* **liteaux**) Stripe (on table-napkins etc.); wooden rail.

liteau (2) [li'to], *n.m.* (*pl.* **liteaux**) Day-haunt (of wolf).

litée [li'te], *n.f.* Litter (of animals).

literie [li'tri], *n.f.* Bedding.

litharge [li'tarʒ], *n.f.* Litharge. **lithargé** or **lithargyré**, *a.* (*fem.* **-ée**) Adulterated with litharge.

lithiase [li'tja:z] or **lithiasie**, *n.f.* Lithiasis.

lithine [li'tin], *n.f.* Lithia. **lithiné**, *a.* (*fem.* **-ée**) Containing lithia. *Eau lithinée*, lithia water.

lithium, *n.m.* Lithium.

lithochromie [litɔkro'mi], *n.f.* Lithochro-matics.

lithocolle [litɔ'kɔl], *n.f.* Cement made of resin and powdered brick (used by lapidaries).

lithographe [litɔ'graf], *n.m.* Lithographer. *Imprimeur lithographe*, lithographic printer. **lithographie**, *n.f.* Lithography; lithograph; lithographic printing-office. **lithographier**, *v.t.* To lithograph. **lithographique**, *a.* Lithographic.

lithologie [litɔlɔ'ʒi], *n.f.* Lithology.

lithophage, *a.* Lithophagous.

lithophyte, *n.m.* Lithophyte.

lithotome, *n.m.* Lithotome. **lithotomie**, *n.f.* Lithotomy.

lithotritie, *n.f.* Lithotrity.

litière [li'tjɛ:r], *n.f.* Stable-litter; litter (for carrying sick persons etc.). *Faire litière de quelque chose*, to throw away; to neglect; to ignore; *il est sur la litière*, he is in the straw (of a horse), he is ill in bed.

litigant [liti'gɑ̃], *a.* (*fem.* **-ante**) Litigant.

litige [li'ti:ʒ], *n.m.* Litigation, legal dispute; (*fig.*) strife. *En litige*, contested, litigated, in dispute; pending.

litigieux, *a.* (*fem.* **-ieuse**) Litigious, given to lawsuits.

litispendance, *n.f.* (*Law*) Pendency (of a suit).

litorne [li'tɔrn], *n.f.* Fieldfare.

litote [li'tɔt], *n.f.* (*Rhet.*) Litotes.

litre (1) [litr], *n.f.* Black mourning band on church walls or front of house.

litre (2) [litr], *n.m.* Litre.

litron, *n.m.* *Measure of 1/16 bushel; (*pop.*) a litre (of wine).

littéraire [lite'rɛ:r], *a.* Literary. *Propriété littéraire*, copyright. **littérairement**, *adv.* In a literary manner or way.

littéral [lite'ral], *a.* (*fem.* **-ale**, *pl.* **-aux**) Literal. **littéralement**, *adv.* Literally, word for word. **littéralité**, *n.f.* Literality, literalness.

littérateur [litera'tœ:r], *n.m.* Literary man, author, man of letters.

littérature [litera'ty:r], *n.f.* Literature; *learning; pamphlets, booklets.

littoral [litɔ'ral], *a.* (*fem.* **-ale**, *pl.* **-aux**) Littoral, coastal.—*n.m.* Littoral, seaboard.

liturgie [lityr'ʒi], *n.f.* Liturgy. **liturgique**, *a.* Liturgic, liturgical. **liturgiste**, *n.* Litur-gist.

liure [ljy:r], *n.f.* Cord, cart-rope; (*Naut.*) lashing, gammoning (of the bowsprit).

livarde [li'vard], *n.f.* (*Naut.*) Sprit. *Voile à livarde*, spritsail.

livarot [liva'ro], *n.m.* Livarot cheese (made at Livarot, south of Lisieux).

livèche [li'vɛʃ], *n.f.* (*Bot.*) Lovage.

livet [li'vɛ], *n.m.* (*Naut.*) *Livet de pont*, beamline.

livide [li'vid], *a.* Livid, ghastly. **lividité**, *n.f.* Lividness.

livrable [li'vrabl], *a.* Deliverable.

livraison [livrɛ'zɔ̃], *n.f.* Delivery (of goods); part, number, issue (of a magazine etc.). *Faire livraison de*, to deliver (goods etc.); *par livraisons*, in parts or numbers, in sections, in instalments (of book, dictionary, etc.); *prendre livraison*, to receive, to take delivery; *payable à la livraison*, payable on delivery, cash on delivery, C.O.D.; *voiture de li-vraison*, delivery van.

livre (1) [li:vr], *n.m.* Book; register, account-book. *Grand livre*, ledger; *grand livre* or *grand livre de la dette publique*, register of the National Debt; (*Naut.*) *livre de bord*, journal, log; *livre de classe*, school-book; *livre de comptes*, book of accounts; *livre d'heures*, (*R.-C. Ch.*) prayer-book, primer; *livre d'images*, picture-book; *livre d'occasion*, secondhand book; *livre jaune*, French equivalent of Blue Book; *tenir les livres*, to

keep the books, to keep the accounts; *traduire à livre ouvert*, to translate at sight.
livre (2) [li:vr], *n.f.* Pound (1·1 lb. av.). *À la livre*, by the pound; *dix francs la livre*, ten francs a pound; *livre sterling*, pound sterling.
livrée [li'vre], *n.f.* Livery; livery-servants; coat (of deer etc.). *En livrée*, in livery; *grande livrée*, full livery; *petite livrée*, undress livery.
livrer [li'vre], *v.t.* To deliver; to give up, to hand over; to betray (a secret); to confide, to entrust. *Livrer bataille*, to engage, to give battle; *livrer de la marchandise à*, to deliver goods to; *livrer passage à*, to let through, to admit; *livrer un assaut*, to make an assault; *livrer une place*, to deliver up, to surrender a fortress; *livrer une ville au pillage*, to give up a town to pillage. **se livrer,** *v.r.* To give oneself up (*à*); to yield, to surrender; to devote or apply oneself; to entrust oneself to; to expose oneself; to indulge in (a vice).
livresque [li'vresk], *a.* Bookish (mind); (knowledge) acquired from books.
livret [li'vrɛ], *n.m.* Little book; memorandum-book; book (of a play), libretto. *Livret de caisse d'épargne*, savings-bank (depositor's) book; *livret de mariage*, marriage lines; *livret militaire* (or *individuel*), soldier's book; *livret scolaire*, (*sch.*) report book.
livreur [li'vrœ:r], *n.m.* (*fem.* **-euse**) Deliverer (of goods); delivery-man, van-man.—*n.f.* Delivery-van.
lixiviation [liksivja'sjɔ̃], *n.f.* Lixiviation. **lixivier,** *v.t.* To lixiviate.
lob [lɔb], *n.m.* (*Ten.*) Lob.
lobe [lɔb], *n.m.* Lobe (of ear, liver, etc.); (*Arch.*) cusp, foil. **lobé,** *a.* (*fem.* **lobée**) (*Bot.*) Lobed, lobate.
lobélie [lɔbe'li], *n.f.* (*Bot.*) Lobelia.
lobiole [lɔ'bjɔl], *n.f.* Small lobe, lobelet (in lichens etc.). **lobulaire,** *a.* Lobular. **lobule,** *n.m.* Lobule.
local [lɔ'kal], *a.* (*fem.* **locale,** *pl.* **locaux**) Local.—*n.m.* Place, premises; quarters. *Local à usage commercial*, shop or office premises; *locaux à usage d'habitation*, residential premises. **localement,** *adv.* Locally.
localisation, *n.f.* Localization. **localiser,** *v.t.* To localize. **se localiser,** *v.r.* To become localized.
localité, *n.f.* Locality.
locataire [lɔka'tɛ:r], *n.* Tenant, lodger, occupier. *Locataire à bail*, lessee, lease-holder. **locatif,** *a.* (*fem.* **-ive**) *Valeur locative*, rental value; *réparations locatives*, repairs for which the tenant is liable.—*n.m.* and *a.* (*Gram.*) Locative.
location [lɔka'sjɔ̃], *n.f.* Letting out; hiring, renting; (*Théat.*) booking of seat. *Bureau de location*, booking-office (in station), box-office (in theatre); *le prix de la location*, the (amount of) rent, hiring fee.
locatis [lɔka'ti], *n.m.* (*colloq.*) *Hack, jade; (*rare*) rented house or apartment.
loch [lɔk], *n.m.* (*Naut.*) Log. *Jeter le loch*, to heave the log; *table de loch*, log-book.
loche [lɔʃ], *n.f.* (*Ichth.*) Loach; (*Conch.*) grey slug. *Loche de rivière* or *épineuse*, groundling, spined loach; *loche de mer* [MOTELLE].
locher [lɔ'ʃe], *v.i.* To be loose (of a horse's shoe).—*v.t.* (*Norm. dial.*) To shake (a fruit-tree).

lochial [lɔ'ʃjal], *a.* (*fem.* **-iale,** *pl.* **-iaux**) Lochial. **lochies,** *n.f. pl.* Lochia.
lock-out [lɔ'kut], *n.m. inv.* Lock-out. **lock-outer** [lɔku'te], *v.t.* To lock-out.
locman [LAMANEUR].
locomobile [lɔkɔmɔ'bil], *a.* Locomobile, movable.—*n.f.* Locomobile, (portable) steam-engine.
locomoteur, *a.* (*fem.* **-trice**) Locomotor.
locomotif, *a.* (*fem.* **locomotive** (1)) Locomotive. **locomotion,** *n.f.* Locomotion. **locomotive** (2), *n.f.* Locomotive, engine.
locuste [lɔ'kyst], *n.f.* Locust; shrimp, prawn.
locustelle [lɔky'stɛl], *n.f.* (*Orn.*) Locustella. *Locustelle tachetée*, grasshopper warbler.
locution [lɔky'sjɔ̃], *n.f.* Locution, expression, form of speech; term, phrase.
lof [lɔf], *n.m.* (*Naut.*) Luff; weather side, windward. *Aller au lof*, to sail near the wind; *virer lof pour lof*, to veer. **lofer,** *v.i.* To luff.
logarithme [lɔga'ritm], *n.m.* Logarithm. **logarithmique,** *a.* Logarithmic.
loge [lɔ:ʒ], *n.f.* Hut; (woodman's) cabin; (porter's, gardener's) lodge; (lunatic's) cell; masonic lodge; (*Theat.*) box; (actor's, actress's) dressing-room; stand, stall; (dog's) kennel; booth (at fair); loggia; chamber (in shell). *Loge d'avant-scène*, stage-box; *loge de côté*, side-box; *loge découverte*, open box; *loge de face*, front box; *entrer en loge*, to compete (in a separate studio) for the *Grand Prix de Rome*; (*fig.*) *être* or *se trouver aux premières loges*, to be at a point of vantage, to have a front seat; *l'influence des loges*, the influence of freemasonry.
logeable, *a.* Tenantable, fit to live in.
logement, *n.m.* Lodgings; dwelling; house-room, accommodation; (*Mil.*) quarters, billet; lodgment; housing, slot (of key, shaft, ball-bearings, etc.). *Billet de logement*, billeting paper. *Logement garni*, furnished apartments; *le logement et la nourriture*, board and lodging.
loger [lɔ'ʒe], *v.i.* To lodge, to live; to put up; to be billeted. *Ici on loge à pied et à cheval*, accommodation for man and beast; *loger à la belle étoile*, to sleep in the open (air); *loger chez l'habitant*, (*Mil.*) to be billeted; *loger dans une auberge*, to put up at an inn; *vin logé*, wine (sold) in the wood or in bottle. —*v.t.* To lodge; to find room for, to put up, to accommodate, to house; to billet, to quarter; to stable. **se loger,** *v.r.* To lodge, to take up one's abode; to lodge itself.
logette, *n.f.* Small lodge.
logeur, *n.m.* (*fem.* **logeuse**) Lodging-house keeper.
loggia [lɔd'ʒja], *n.f.* (*Arch.*) Loggia.
logicien [lɔʒi'sjɛ̃], *n.m.* (*fem.* **-ienne**) Logician.
logique [lɔ'ʒik], *n.f.* Logic.—*a.* Logical. **logiquement,** *adv.* Logically.
logis [lɔ'ʒi], *n.m.* (*rare*) House, dwelling. *Corps de logis*, main building; *la folle du logis*, imagination, fancy.
logographe [lɔgɔ'graf], *n.m.* Logographer.
logogriphe, *n.m.* Word-puzzle.
logomachie, *n.f.* Logomachy, battle of words.
loi [lwa], *n.f.* The law; law, statute, act; rule. *Faire* or *donner la loi*, to give laws or dictate (*à*); *faire loi* or *avoir force de loi*, to have force of law; *homme de loi*, lawyer; *loi du*

bâton, club-law; *mettre hors la loi*, to outlaw; *présenter un projet de loi*, to bring in a Bill; *se faire une loi de*, to make a point of; *voter une loi*, to pass a Bill.

loin [lwɛ̃], *adv.* Far, at a distance; remote, distant. *Au loin*, far away, far and wide; *de loin*, from afar, from a distance; *de loin en loin*, at long intervals, at long distances from each other; *loin de*, far from; *loin des yeux, loin du cœur*, out of sight, out of mind; *loin d'ici*, a great way off, be gone! *loin du monde*, far from the world; *revenir de loin*, to have had a narrow squeak (for one's life).

lointain, *a.* (*fem.* **-aine**) Remote, far off, distant (country, days, etc.).—*n.m.* Distance, distant prospect. *Le lointain d'un tableau*, the background of a picture; *dans le lointain*, in the distance.

loir [lwa:r], *n.m.* Dormouse.

loisible [lwa'zibl], *a.* Optional, lawful, allowable. *Il vous est loisible de le faire*, you have a perfect right to do it.

loisir [lwa'zi:r], *n.m.* Leisure, spare time. *À loisir*, at leisure; *j'ai du loisir*, I have some spare time; *les loisirs*, spare-time activities.

lolo [lo'lo], *n.m.* (*childish*) Milk.

lombaire [lɔ̃'bɛ:r], *a.* Lumbar.

lombard [lɔ̃'ba:r], *a.* (*fem.* **-arde**) Lombard. —*n.m.* A Lombard; *a banker.

lombes [lɔ̃:b], *n.m. pl.* (*Anat.*) Lumbar region, loins.

lombric [lɔ̃'brik], *n.m.* Earth-worm. **lombrical**, *a.* (*fem.* **-ale**, *pl.* **-aux**) Lumbrical.

lomentacé [lɔmɑ̃ta'se], *a.* (*fem.* **-ée**) Lomentaceous.

lompe [lɔ̃p], *n.m.* or *gros mulet*, or *lièvre de mer*. (*Ichth.*) Lump sucker.

londonien [lɔ̃dɔ'njɛ̃], *a.* (*fem.* **-ienne**) Of or pertaining to London.—*n.* Londoner.

Londres ['lɔ̃drə], *f.* London.

londrès [lɔ̃'drɛs], *n.m.* Havana cigar.

long [lɔ̃], *a.* (*fem.* **longue** (1)) Long; slow, tedious; diffuse, drawn out. (*fig.*) *Avoir le bras long* [BRAS]; *les dents longues* [DENT]; *de longue date*, long ago; *long à tout*, slow at everything; *trouver le temps long*, to find the time dragging, to be bored.—*n.m.* Length; extent. (*Tout*) *au long*, in full; *cela a dix aunes de long*, that is ten ells long; *de long* or *en long*, lengthwise; *de long en large*, up and down, to and fro; *être couché de tout son long*, to lie at full length; (*tout*) *le long de*, all along, all through; *prendre par le plus long*, to go the longest way round.—*n.f.* (2) Long syllable; long suit (at cards). *À la longue*, in the long run. *En savoir long*, to know all about it.

longanimité [lɔ̃ganimi'te], *n.f.* Longanimity, forbearance, long-suffering.

long-courrier [lɔ̃ku'rje], *a.m.* (*pl.* **long-courriers**) Ocean-going.—*n.m.* Ocean-going ship; ocean-liner.

longe (1) [lɔ̃:ʒ], *n.f.* Tether, lunge, leading-rein; thong, picket(ing) rope.

longe (2) [lɔ̃:ʒ], *n.f.* *Longe de veau*, loin of veal.

longer [lɔ̃'ʒe], *v.t.* To go, to walk, to run along; to skirt, to hug; to extend along.

longeron [lɔ̃ʒ'rɔ̃], *n.m.* Small beam or girder; *esp.* side-member (of car); longeron, tail-boom or spar (of aeroplane).

longévité [lɔ̃ʒevi'te], *n.f.* Longevity. **longi-**

corne, *a.* and *n.m.* Longicorn. **longimane**, *a.* Longimanous. **longirostre**, *a.* Longirostral.

longitude [lɔ̃ʒi'tyd], *n.f.* Longitude. *Bureau des Longitudes*, Central Astronomical Office; *par 20° de longitude Est*, in the longitude of 20° east; *prendre les longitudes*, to take the longitude. **longitudinal**, *a.* (*fem.* **-ale**, *pl.* **-aux**) Longitudinal. **longitudinalement**, *adv.* Lengthwise.

long-jointé [lɔ̃ʒwɛ̃'te], *a.* (*fem.* **long-jointée**, *pl.* **long-jointé(e)s**) Long in the pastern (of horses).

longrine [lɔ̃'grin], *n.f.* Railway sleeper; side beam; ridge-bar (of roof); slips (to launch a ship).

longtemps [lɔ̃'tɑ̃], *adv.* Long, a long while. *Depuis longtemps*, long since, for a long time past; *il ne viendra pas de longtemps*, he will not come for a long time; *il y a longtemps que je ne l'ai vu*, it is a long time since I saw him, I have not seen him for a long time.

longue [LONG].

longuement [lɔ̃g'mɑ̃], *adv.* Long, a long time, for a great while.

longuerine [LONGRINE].

longuet [lɔ̃'gɛ], *a.* (*fem.* **-ette**) (*colloq.*) Longish, somewhat long, pretty long, too long.

longueur [lɔ̃'gœ:r], *n.f.* Length, extent in time; slowness; prolixity. *En longueur*, lengthwise, to a great length; (*spt.*) *gagner de deux longueurs*, to win by two lengths; *tirer en longueur*, to spin out; *tirer les choses en longueur*, to delay, to cause an affair to drag; *traîner en longueur*, to drag, to be protracted.

longue-vue [lɔ̃g'vy], *n.f.* (*pl.* **longues-vues**) Telescope, spy-glass.

looch [lɔk], *n.m.* (*Pharm.*) Soothing mixture.

looping [lu'piŋ], *n.m.* (*Av.*) *Faire un looping* or *boucler la boucle*, to loop (the loop).

lophophore [lɔfɔ'fɔr], *n.m.* (*Orn.*) Lophophore.

lopin [lɔ'pɛ̃], *n.m.* Small piece or share. *Lopin de terre*, plot of ground.

loquace [lɔ'kwas], *a.* Loquacious, talkative. **loquacement**, *adv.* Talkatively, loquaciously.

loquacité, *n.f.* Loquacity, talkativeness.

loque [lɔk], *n.f.* Rag, tatter.

loquet [lɔ'kɛ], *n.m.* Latch; clasp (of a knife); clip (of gun). *Fermé au loquet*, on the latch.

loqueteau, *n.m.* (*pl.* **-eaux**) Small latch.

loqueter, *v.i.* To rattle the latch.

loqueteux [lɔk'tø], *a.* (*fem.* **-euse**) In rags.—*n.* Tatterdemalion, ragged person.

lord [lɔr], *n.m.* Lord. *Chambre des Lords*, House of Lords; *Lord-Maire*, Lord Mayor.

*****lorette** [lɔ'rɛt], *n.f.* Lorette, woman of easy virtue.

lorgnade [lɔr'nad], *n.f.* Ogle, side-glance.

lorgner [lɔr'ne], *v.t.* To leer at, to ogle, to make eyes at; to have an eye on.

lorgnette [lɔr'nɛt], *n.f.* Opera-glasses [*see also* BOUT].

lorgneur [lɔr'nœ:r], *n.m.* (*fem.* **-euse**) Ogler.

lorgnon [lɔr'nɔ̃], *n.m.* (*sometimes pl.*) Eye-glasses; pince-nez; lorgnette.

lori [lɔ'ri], *n.m.* Lory (a kind of parrot).

loriot [lɔ'rjo], *n.m.* Oriole. *Loriot d'Europe* or *grive dorée*, golden oriole [*see* COMPÈRE-LORIOT].

lorry [lɔ'ri], *n.m.* (*Rail.*) Lorry, trolley (of platelayer).

lors [lɔːr], *adv.* Then. *Depuis* or *dès lors*, from that time, since then; *lors de*, at the time of; *lors donc que*, thus when; *lors même que*, even though; *pour lors*, then, at the time, so, therefore.

lorsque [lɔrsk, 'lɔrskə], *conj.* When; at the time or moment of. *Lorsque j'arrivai*, when I arrived, on my arrival.

losange [lɔ'zɑ̃ːʒ], *n.m.* Diamond-shape, lozenge. *En losange*, lozenge-shaped. **losangé**, *a.* (*fem.* **-ée**) In lozenges; (*Her.*) lozengy.

lot [lo], *n.m.* Lot; portion, share; fate; prize (in a lottery); (*C*) Woodland, farm woodland. *Le gros lot*, the first prize (in a lottery); *le lot qui lui est échu*, the portion which has fallen to his share.

loterie [lɔ'tri], *n.f.* Lottery, raffle. *C'est une loterie*, it is a gamble; *gagner à la loterie*, to win in the lottery; *mettre en loterie*, to raffle.

lotier [lɔ'tje], *n.m.* (*Bot.*) Bird's-foot trefoil.

lotion [lo'sjɔ̃], *n.f.* Lotion; ablution. **lotionner**, *v.t.* To sponge, to bathe.

lotir [lɔ'tiːr], *v.t.* To divide into lots, to portion out; to portion off. *Le voilà bien loti*, he has got a fair share; *mal loti*, badly off.

lotissement, *n.m.* Dividing into lots, allotment; parcelling out (for building houses); building plot.

loto [lɔ'to], *n.m.* Lotto (game of chance); housey-housey. (*fam.*) *Avoir les yeux en boules de loto*, to be goggle-eyed.

lotophages [lɔtɔ'faːʒ], *n.m. pl.* Lotophagi, lotus-eaters.

lotte [lɔt], *n.f.* Lote, eel-pout.

lotus [lɔ'tyːs] or **lotos**, *n.m. inv.* Lotus.

louable [lwabl], *a.* Laudable, praiseworthy, commendable. **louablement**, *adv.* Commendably.

louage [lwaːʒ], *n.m.* Letting out, hiring, renting; hire. *Donner à louage*, to let out on hire, to hire out; *prendre à louage*, to rent, to hire; *prix de louage*, cost of hiring; *un avion à louage*, a charter aircraft; *un cheval de louage*, hired horse, hack; *vélo de louage*, hired bike.

louange [lwɑ̃ːʒ], *n.f.* Praise, commendation, eulogy. *Chanter les louanges de*, to sing the praises of. **louanger**, *v.t.* To praise, to flatter, to extol.

louangeur, *n.m.* (*fem.* **-euse**) Praiser, flatterer. —*a.* Laudatory, eulogistic.

louche (1) [luʃ], *n.f.* (Soup) ladle; (manure) scoop; countersink bit.

louche (2) [luʃ], *a.* Squinting, squint-eyed; dubious, ambiguous, equivocal; suspicious, shady; (*fam.*) fishy.—*n.m.* *Il y a du louche dans sa conduite*, there is something suspicious in his conduct, his behaviour is rather fishy. **louchement**, *n.m.* Squint, squinting. **loucher**, *v.i.* To squint.

louchet [lu'ʃɛ], *n.m.* Long, narrow spade, draining-spade.

loucheur [lu'ʃœr], *n.m.* (*fem.* **-euse**) Squinter. —*a.* Squinting.

louchir, *v.i.* To get muddy, cloudy (of liquids).

louchon, *n.m.* (*fem.* **-onne**) Cross-eyed or squint-eyed person.—*n.f.* Moon.

louer (1) [lwe], *v.t.* To let or hire out; to lease, to rent, to hire; to book, to reserve; to take on (seasonal workers). *Louer une maison*, to let a house; *maison à louer*, house to let; *loué*, (of a house) let; (of a seat) engaged, (of a compartment) reserved. **se louer** (1), *v.r.* To hire oneself out; to be let or rented.

louer (2) [lwe], *v.t.* To praise, to commend, to extol, to eulogize, to speak highly of. **se louer** (2), *v.r.* To praise oneself; to rejoice, to be pleased (*de*). *Se louer de quelqu'un*, to be well pleased with someone.

loueur (1), *n.m.* (*fem.* **-euse** (1)) Hirer, letter out. *Loueur de bateaux*, boat keeper; *loueur de bicyclettes*, hirer out of bicycles.

loueur (2) [LOUANGEUR].

loufoque [lu'fɔk] or **louftingue** [luf'tɛ̃g] *a.* (*fam.*) Touched, loony, eccentric.

lougre [lugr], *n.m.* Lugger.

Louis [lwi], *m.* Lewis.

louis [lwi], *n.m. inv.* Louis (a French coin worth 20 gold francs).

louise-bonne [lwiz'bɔn], *n.f.* (*pl.* **louises-bonnes**) A juicy variety of pear.

loulou [lu'lu], *n.m.* Lap-dog, pom.

loup [lu], *n.m.* Wolf; black velvet mask; fluffed entrance (of actor); pincers for extracting nails; flaw (in wood), defect. *Avoir une faim de loup*, to be ravenously hungry; *avoir vu le loup*, to know what's what; *crier au loup!* to cry wolf; *entre chien et loup*, at dusk; *il fait un froid de loup*, it is bitterly cold; *les loups ne se mangent pas entre eux*, there is honour among thieves; *marcher à pas de loup*, to walk stealthily, like a thief; *quand on parle du loup on en voit la queue*, talk of the devil and he is sure to appear; *qui se fait brebis, le loup le mange* [BREBIS]; *renfermer le loup dans la bergerie*, to set the fox to keep the geese; *se jeter dans la gueule du loup*, to throw oneself into the lion's mouth; *tenir le loup par les oreilles*, to be in a critical situation. *Loup de mer*, (*Ichth.*) cat-fish, sea-perch; (*fig.*) old sea-dog, old salt. *Saut de loup*, ha-ha. *Tête de loup*, ceiling brush.

loup-cerve, *n.f.* (*pl.* **loups-cerves**) She-lynx.

loup-cervier, *n.m.* (*pl.* **loups-cerviers**) Lynx; (*fig.*) profiteer, shark.

loupe [lup], *n.f.* Wen; knob, excrescence, gnarl (on trees); magnifying-glass.

louper [lu'pe], *v.t.* (*pop.*) To botch (a piece of work); to fail at (exam.); to spoil (a picture); to bungle (a landing); to miss (train).

loupeux, *a.* (*fem.* **-euse**) Wenny, knobby.

loupiot [lu'pjo], *n.m.* (*pop.*) Kid, brat.

loup-garou [luga'ru], *n.m.* (*pl.* **loups-garous**) Werwolf; bugbear; surly dog, churlish fellow.

lourd [luːr], *a.* (*fem.* **lourde**) Heavy, lumpish, unwieldy; clumsy, awkward; dull, stupid, thick-headed; sultry, oppressive, muggy (weather). *Poids lourd*, lorry. *Eau lourde*, heavy water.—*n.f.* (*slang*) Door.

lourdaud [lur'do], *n.m.* (*fem.* **-aude**) Lubber, lout; blockhead.—*a.* Loutish, lumpish, clumsy. **lourdement**, *adv.* Heavily, plump; clumsily; grossly. **lourderie** or **lourdise**, *n.f.* Blunder. **lourdeur**, *n.f.* Heaviness, weight; clumsiness; dullness, stupidity; closeness, sultriness (of weather).

*****loure** [luːr], *n.f.* Old Norman bag-pipe; slow stately dance.

lourer [lu're], *v.t.* (*Mus.*) To tie (the notes); to drone out.

lousse [lus], *n.f.*, or **lousseau**, *n.m.* (*pl.* **-eaux**), or **lousset**, *n.m.* (*Naut.*) Bilge-hole (in the bottom of a boat).

loustic [lus'tik], *n.m.* (*fam.*) Wag. *Un drôle de loustic,* a phoney fellow, a queer fish.

loutre [lutr], *n.f.* Otter; otter-fur.

louvart [lu'va:r] or **louvat,** *n.m.* Young wolf.

louve [lu:v], *n.f.* She-wolf; sling, grip, claw (for lifting stones etc.). **louver,** *v.t.* To lift with a sling, claw, etc.

louvet [lu'vɛ], *a.* (*fem.* **louvette**) Wolf-coloured, grey (of horses).—*n.m.* This colour.

louveteau [luv'to], *n.m.* (*pl.* **-eaux**) Young wolf, wolf-cub. **louveter,** *v.i.* To whelp (wolves).—*v.t.* To comb (wool). **louveterie,** *n.f.* Wolf-hunting equipage; wolf-hunting. *Lieutenant de louveterie,* officer in charge of this, (formerly) master of the wolf-hunt. **louvetier,** *n.m.* Wolf-hunter.

louviers [lu'vje], *n.m.* Louviers cloth.

louvoyage [luvwa'ja:ʒ], **louvoiement** [luvwa'mã], *n.m.* Tacking about. **louvoyer,** *v.i.* To tack, to tack about; (*fig.*) to manœuvre; to dodge.

love [lɔ:v], *n.f.* Bar (of soap).

lovelace [lɔv'las], *n.m.* Lothario, libertine.

lover [lɔ've], *v.t.* To coil (rope etc.). **se lover,** *v.r.* To coil up (of snakes).

loxodromie [lɔksɔdrɔ'mi], *n.f.* Loxodromics; rhumb-line. **loxodromique,** *a.* Loxodromic.

loyal [lwa'jal], *a.* (*fem.* **-ale,** *pl.* **-aux**) Fair, honest, fair-dealing, straightforward, upright; loyal, true, faithful; (*Comm.*) of good quality, unadulterated. *Un loyal chevalier,* a true knight. **loyalement,** *adv.* Fairly, honestly, uprightly; loyally.

loyalisme, *n.m.* Loyalty; loyalism. **loyaliste,** *a.* and *n.* Loyalist.

loyauté [lwajote], *n.f.* Honesty, fairness, fair-dealing; loyalty, faithfulness.

loyer [lwa'je], *n.m.* Hire, rent; (*fig.*) reward, guerdon.

lu, *p.p.* (*fem.* **lue**) [LIRE].

lubie [ly'bi], *n.f.* Crotchet, maggot, whim, fad. *À lubies,* crotchety, whimsical; *il lui prend souvent des lubies,* he often gets ideas in his head.

lubricité [lybrisi'te], *n.f.* Lubricity, lewdness, salacity.

lubrifiant [lybri'fjã], *a.* (*fem.* **-iante**) Lubricating.—*n.m.* Lubricant.

lubrificateur [lybrifika'tœr], *a.* (*fem.* **-trice**) Lubricating.—*n.m.* Lubricator.

lubrification [lybrifika'sjɔ̃], *n.f.* Lubrication.

lubrifier [lybri'fje], *v.t.* (*conjugated like* PRIER) To lubricate.

lubrique [ly'brik], *a.* Lubricious, lewd, lascivious, wanton. **lubriquement,** *adv.* Lasciviously, lewdly.

Luc [lyk], *n.m.* Luke.

lucane [ly'kan], *n.m.* Lucanus; stag-beetle.

lucarne [ly'karn], *n.f.* Dormer-window, garret (or attic) window.

lucide [ly'sid], *a.* Lucid, clear. **lucidement,** *adv.* Lucidly.

lucidité, *n.f.* Lucidness, lucidity, clearness.

lucifuge [lysi'fy:ʒ], *a.* Lucifugous, shunning the light.

lucilie [lysi'li], *n.f.* Lucilia; blow-fly.

luciole [ly'sjɔl], *n.f.* (*Ent.*) Fire-fly; winged glow-worm.

lucratif [lykra'tif], *a.* (*fem.* **-ive**) Lucrative. **lucrativement,** *adv.* Profitably.

lucre [lykr], *n.m.* Lucre, gain.

ludion [ly'djɔ̃], *n.m.* Cartesian diver.

luette [lɥɛt], *n.f.* Uvula.

lueur [lɥœ:r], *n.f.* Glimmer, glimmering, glimpse, gleam; flash (of a shot). *Faible lueur,* faint glimmer; *lueur blafarde,* pale glimmer; *une lueur d'espoir,* a glimpse *or* ray of hope.

luffa [ly'fa], *n.m.* or *f.* Loofah.

luge [ly:ʒ], *n.f.* Luge, single toboggan. **luger** [ly'ʒe], *v.i.* To toboggan.

lugubre [ly'gybr], *a.* Lugubrious, doleful, dismal, mournful; ominous. **lugubrement,** *adv.* Ominously; dismally.

lui [lɥi], *pers. pron.* He, it; to him, to her, to it. *C'est à lui,* it's his; *c'est lui,* it is he; *donnez-lui en,* give him some; *lui-même,* himself; *parlez-lui,* speak to him *or* her.

luire [lɥi:r], *v.i. irr.* (*pres.p.* **luisant,** *p.p.* **lui**) To shine; to glitter, to gleam, to glisten; to dawn, to appear (of the day etc.). **luisant,** *a.* (*fem.* **-ante** (1)) Glistening, glittering, shining, bright; dawning; shiny, glossy. *Un ver luisant,* a glow-worm.—*n.m.* Gloss, shine.

luisante (2), *n.f.* The brightest star in a constellation.

lumachelle [lyma'kɛl], *n.f.* Lumachella, iridescent marble.

lumbago [lɔ̃ba'go], *n.m.* Lumbago.

lumière [ly'mjɛ:r], *n.f.* Light; daylight, day; lamp, luminary; touch-hole, vent (of a fire-arm); (*fig.*) information, enlightenment; intelligence, knowledge, insight, wisdom; (*Paint.*) light. *À la lumière de,* by the light of; *craindre la lumière,* to shun the daylight; *éteindre une lumière,* to put out a light; *la lumière du soleil* or *du jour,* the light of the sun or of day; *mettre en lumière,* to bring to light, to elucidate; *sans lumière,* without a light, in the dark, without guidance or a guide.

lumignon, *n.m.* Snuff (of a candle); candle-end.

luminade, *n.f.* Pêche à la luminade, fishing by torchlight.

luminaire, *n.m.* Luminary, light; (*collect.*) lights (of a church etc.); lighting (of a town).

luminariste, *n.m.* Painter given to effects of light.

luminescence, *n.f.* Luminescence. **luminescent,** *a.* (*fem.* **-ente**) Luminescent. **lumineusement,** *adv.* Luminously. **lumineux,** *a.* (*fem.* **-euse**) Luminous; bright (idea).

luminifère, *a.* Luminiferous. **luminosité,** —*n.f.* Luminosity.

lunaire [ly'nɛ:r], *a.* Lunar.—*n.f.* Lunary, honesty, moon-wort. **lunaison,** *n.f.* Lunation.

lunatique, *a.* Fantastical, whimsical; moon-blind (horse).—*n.* Incalculable, whimsical person.

lundi [lœ̃'di], *n.m.* Monday. *Lundi gras,* Shrove Monday.

lune [lyn], *n.f.* Moon; (*fig.*) lunar month, month; caprice, whim; (*pop.*) posterior. *Aboyer à la lune* [ABOYER]; *clair de lune* [CLAIR]; *demander la lune,* to ask the impossible; *être dans la lune,* to be in a brown study, to be wool-gathering; *faire un trou à la lune,* to run from one's creditors, to make a moonlight flit; *lune de miel,* honeymoon; *la lune est*

[459]

dans son plein, the moon is full; *lune d'août*, harvest-moon; *lune rousse*, April moon; *nouvelle lune*, new moon; *pleine lune*, full moon; *vouloir prendre la lune avec les dents*, to attempt impossibilities. (*Bot.*) *Lune d'eau*, white water-lily.

luné, *a.* (*fem.* **lunée**) Lunate. (*fam.*) *Être bien, mal, luné*, to be in a good, bad, mood.

lunetier [lyn'tje], *n.m.* (*fem.* **-ière**) Spectacle-maker; spectacle-seller, optician.

lunette [ly'nɛt], *n.f.* Telescope, field-glass; (*pl.*) spectacles; (*Arch., Fort., etc.*) lunette; rim (of a watch case); seat (of w.c.); wishbone (of fowl). *Lunette d'approche*, (small) telescope. (*Grosses*) *lunettes*, (*Motor., Av., etc.*) goggles; *lunettes de soleil*, sun-glasses. *Serpent à lunettes*, Indian cobra. **lunetté**, *a.* (*fem.* **-ée**) Spectacled. **lunettier** [LUNETIER].

luniforme [lyni'fɔrm], *a.* Luniform, moon-shaped.

luni-solaire, *a.* Lunisolar.

lunule, *n.f.* Half-moon, crescent; lunula. **lunulé**, *a.* (*fem.* **-ée**) (*Bot.*) Lunulate.

lupanar [lypa'naːr], *n.m.* Bawdy-house, brothel.

lupin [ly'pɛ̃], *n.m.* (*Bot.*) Lupine. **lupinelle**, *n.f.* Sainfoin.

lupuline [lypy'lin], *n.f.* Lupulin.

lupus [ly'pyːs], *n.m.* Lupus.

lurette [lyret], *n.f.* Used only in *il y a belle lurette*, long ago. *Il y a belle lurette que je n'ai vu mon frère*, I haven't seen my brother for ages.

luride [ly'rid], *a.* (*Med.*) Lurid, sallow.

luron [ly'rɔ̃], *n.m.* (*fem.* **luronne**) Jolly fellow, gay dog; gay, carefree type of girl.

lustrage [lys'traːʒ], *n.m.* Glossing.

lustral [lys'tral], *a.* (*fem.* **-ale**, *pl.* **-aux**) Lustral. **lustration**, *n.f.* Lustration.

lustre (1) [lystr], *n.m.* Lustre, brilliancy, brightness; (*fig.*) renown, distinction, splendour; chandelier.

lustre (2) [lystr], *n.m.* (*Rom. Ant.*) Lustrum, space of five years.

lustré [lys'tre], *a.* (*fem.* **-ée**) Glossy. *Lustré* (*par l'usure*), shiny with wear.

lustrer [lys'tre], *v.t.* To give a lustre or gloss to, to gloss, to glaze.

lustrine, *n.f.* Lustring, cotton lustre. *Manches en lustrine*, oversleeves.

lustucru [lysty'kry], *n.m.* Simpleton, ass.

lut [lyt], *n.m.* Lute, luting, chemist's clay. **Lutèce** [ly'tɛːs], *f.* Lutetia.

luter [ly'te], *v.t.* To lute, to close hermetically with lute.

luth [lyt], *n.m.* Lute. *Joueur de luth*, lutanist.

luthéranisme [lytera'nism], *n.m.* Lutheranism. **luthérien**, *a.* and *n.* (*fem.* **-ienne**) Lutheran.

lutherie [ly'tri], *n.f.* Stringed-instrument trade or shop. **luthier**, *n.m.* Maker of musical instruments, *esp.* stringed instruments.

lutin (1) [ly'tɛ̃], *n.m.* Goblin, sprite, elf, imp; (*fig.*) (of child) imp.

lutin (2) [ly'tɛ̃], *a.* (*fem.* **lutine**) Roguish, impish, wanton, sprightly. **lutiner**, *v.t.* To plague, to tease, to pester.—*v.i.* To be mischievous, to play the imp.

lutrin [ly'trɛ̃], *n.m.* Music-lectern or desk; body of choristers, the succentors.

lutte [lyt], *n.f.* Wrestling; scuffle, tussle;

struggle, contest, strife. *De bonne lutte*, by fair play; *de haute lutte*, by force, with a high hand; *lutte libre* or *catch*, catch as catch can; *s'exercer à la lutte*, to practise wrestling.

lutter, *v.i.* To wrestle; to struggle, to contend, to strive (*contre*); to vie (*avec*). *Lutter contre la tempête*, to struggle against the storm.

lutteur, *n.m.* (*fem.* **lutteuse**) Wrestler.

luxation [lyksɑ'sjɔ̃], *n.f.* Luxation, dislocation.

luxe [lyks], *n.m.* Luxury; profusion; extravagance, excess. *C'est du luxe*, that is superfluous, uncalled for; *un luxe de végétation*, an exuberance of vegetation.

Luxembourg [lyksɑ̃'buːr], *m.* Luxemburg.

luxer [lyk'se], *v.t.* To luxate, to dislocate. **se luxer**, *v.r.* To dislocate (one's arm etc.).

luxueusement [lyksɥøz'mɑ̃], *a.* Luxuriously, sumptuously, richly. **luxueux**, *a.* (*fem.* **-euse**) Luxurious; magnificent, rich, sumptuous, gorgeous.

luxure [lyk'syːr], *n.f.* Lasciviousness, lust.

luxuriance [lyksy'rjɑ̃s], *n.f.* Luxuriance.

luxuriant, *a.* (*fem.* **-iante**) Luxuriant.

luxurieusement [lyksyrjøz'mɑ̃], *adv.* Lustfully, lewdly. **luxurieux**, *a.* (*fem.* **-ieuse**) Lustful, lecherous.

luzerne [ly'zɛrn], *n.f.* Lucern, lucern-grass. **luzernière**, *n.f.* Lucerne-field.

luzule [ly'zyl], *n.f.* (*Bot.*) Luzula.

lycanthrope [likɑ̃'trɔp], *n.m.* Lycanthrope; person affected with lycanthropy. **lycanthropie**, *n.f.* Lycanthropy.

lycée [li'se], *n.m.* French grammar- or high-school (supported by the State). **lycéen**, *n.m.* (*fem.* **lycéenne**) Pupil attending this.

lychnide [lik'nid], *n.f.*, or **lychnis**, *n.m.* Lychnis, campion [*see also* NIELLE].

lyciet [ly'sjɛ], *n.m.* (*Bot.*) Lycium.

lycope [li'kɔp], *n.m.* (*Bot.*) Lycopus.

lycoperdon [likɔpɛr'dɔ̃], *n.m.* Puff-ball.

lycopode [likɔ'pɔd], *n.m.* Lycopodium. *Lycopode en massue* or *soufre végétal*, club-moss. **lycopodiacée**, *n.f.* Lycopodiaceous plant.

lycopside, *n.f.* (*Bot.*) Lycopsis.

lyddite [li'dit], *n.f.* Lyddite.

Lydie [li'di], *f.* Lydia (name). **La Lydie**, Lydia (country).

lydien [li'djɛ̃], *a.* (*fem.* **lydienne**) Lydian.

lymphangite [lɛ̃fɑ̃'ʒit], *n.f.* (*Med.*) Lymphangitis.

lymphatique [lɛ̃fa'tik], *a.* Lymphatic.

lymphe [lɛ̃ːf], *n.f.* Lymph; (*Bot.*) sap.

lynchage [lɛ̃'ʃaːʒ], *n.m.* Lynching. **lyncher**, *v.t.* To lynch.

lynx [lɛ̃ks], *n.m. inv.* Lynx. *Avoir des yeux de lynx*, to be lynx-eyed.

Lyon [ljɔ̃], Lyons. **lyonnais**, *a.* and *n.m.* (*fem.* **-aise**) (Native) of Lyons.

lyre [liːr], *n.f.* Lyre; (*fig.*) poetic talent, poetry; (*Astron.*) Lyra. *Jouer de la lyre*, to play on the lyre.

lyrique, *a.* Lyric, lyrical. *Poète lyrique*, lyrical poet; *théâtre lyrique*, opera-house; *vers lyriques*, lyrical verses.

lyrisme, *n.m.* Lyric poetry; lyricism; poetic fire.

lysimaque [lizi'mak] or **lysimachie**, *n.f.* (*Bot.*) Loosestrife, yellow pimpernel. *Lysimaque nummulaire* or *herbe aux écus*, money-wort, creeping jenny.

M

M, m [ɛm], *n.m.* The thirteenth letter of the alphabet. M, 1000. *M., MM.,* abbr. of *Monsieur, Messieurs.*

m' [ME].

ma [ma], *a. poss.f.* [MON].

maboul [ma'bull, *a.* (*fem.* **-oule**) (*slang*) Loony, a bit cracked.

macabre [ma'kɑ:br], *a.* Gruesome, macabre, deathly, ghastly. *La danse macabre,* the dance of death.

macadam [maka'dam], *n.m.* Macadam. **macadamisage,** *n.m.,* or **macadamisation,** *n.f.* Macadamization. **macadamiser,** *v.t.* To macadamize.

macaque [ma'kak], *n.m.* Macaco (monkey).

macareux [maka'rø], *n.m.* (*Orn.*) Puffin, coulterneb.

macaron [maka'rɔ̃], *n.m.* Macaroon; coat-hanger.

macaronée [makarɔ'ne], *n.f.* Macaronic verse.

macaroni [makarɔ'ni], *n.m.* Macaroni.

macaronique [makarɔ'nik], *a.* Macaronic.

Macédoine [mase'dwan], *f.* Macedonia.

macédoine [mase'dwan], *n.f. Macédoine de légumes,* vegetable hotchpotch; *macédoine de fruits,* fruit salad; (*fig.*) medley, hotchpotch.

macération [masera'sjɔ̃], *n.f.* Maceration; mortification. **macérer,** *v.t. irr.* (*conjug. like* ACCÉLÉRER) To macerate; (*fig.*) to mortify.— *v.i.* To soak, to stand. **se macérer,** *v.r.* To macerate one's body; (*fig.*) to mortify one-self.

macfarlane [makfar'lan], *n.m.* Inverness (cape).

machabée or **macchabée** [maka'be], *n.m.* (*pop.*) Corpse, dead body, *esp.* of a drowned person; a 'stiff'.

machaon [maka'ɔ̃], *n.m.* Swallow-tail butter-fly.

mâche [mɑ:ʃ], *n.f.* Corn-salad, lamb's-lettuce.

mâché [mɑ'ʃe], *a.* (*fem.* **-ée**) Chewed; jagged (wound); nicked (bullet). (*fam.*) *Avoir un visage de papier mâché,* to be mealy-faced.

mâchefer [maʃ'fɛ:r], *n.m.* Clinker, slag; dross.

mâchelier [maʃə'lje], *a.* (*fem.* **-ière**) Grinding, molar. *Dents mâchelières,* grinders.—*n.f.* Molar, grinder.

mâchement [maʃ'mã], *n.m.* Chewing, masticating, munching. **mâcher,** *v.t.* To chew, to masticate, to grind; (of a horse) to champ (the bit); to mumble (one's words). *Ne pas mâcher ses mots,* not to mince matters, to speak one's mind; *on lui avait mâché la besogne,* the work had been cut and dried for him.

machette [ma'ʃet], *n.f.* Machete, matchet.

machiavélique [makjave'lik], *a.* Machiavellian. **machiavélisme,** *n.m.* Machiavellism. **machiavéliste,** *n.* Machiavellian.

mâchicoulis [maʃiku'li], *n.m.* Machicolation.

machin [ma'ʃɛ̃], *n.m.* (*colloq.*) So-and-so, what's-his-name; thing, gadget.

machinal [maʃi'nal], *a.* (*fem.* **-ale,** *pl.* **-aux**) Mechanical, automatic, instinctive. **machinalement,** *adv.* Mechanically, automatically, instinctively.

machinateur [maʃina'tœ:r], *n.m.* Plotter,

schemer. **machination,** *n.f.* Machination, plot, scheme.

machine [ma'ʃin], *n.f.* Machine, engine, piece of machinery, *esp.* bicycle; apparatus, appliance, system; (*fam.*) thing, gadget, contraption; (*fig.*) machination, scheme, plot. *Fait à la machine,* machine-made; *la machine animale,* the bodily system; *machine à coudre,* sewing-machine; *machine à écrire,* typewriter; *machine à laver,* washing machine; *machine à sous,* penny-in-the-slot machine; *machine à vapeur,* steam-engine; *machine de Gramme,* Gramme-dynamo; *machine hydraulique,* hydraulic engine; *machine pneumatique,* air-pump; *les machines,* machinery, plant; *pièce à machines,* (*Theat.*) play with spectacular changes of scenery. **machine-outil,** *n.f.* (*pl.* **machines-outils**) Machine-tool. **machiner,** *v.t.* To machinate, to contrive, to plot; to supply with machinery. *Il machine votre perte,* he is plotting your ruin. **machinerie,** *n.f.* Plant; engine-room; machine construction. **machinisme,** *n.m.* Mechanism (system, theory). **machiniste,** *n.* Machinist, engineman; (*Theat.*) scene-shifter, stage-hand.

mâchoire [mɑ'ʃwa:r], *n.f.* Jaw; jawbone. *Jouer* or *travailler des mâchoires,* to eat with avidity; *mâchoires d'étau,* jaws of a vice; *mâchoires de frein,* brake-shoes (of car).

mâchonner, *v.t.* To chew with difficulty; to munch; to mumble; to champ (the bit). **mâchonneur,** *n.m.* (*fem.* **-euse**) Mumbler.

mâchure [mɑ'ʃy:r], *n.f.* Defect, flaw in the nap (of cloth); bruise (on fruit etc.) **mâchurer,** *v.t.* To daub, to smudge; (*Print.*) to spoil (a sheet); to bruise.

macis [ma'si], *n.m.* Mace (spice).

maclage [ma'kla:ʒ], *n.m.* Mixing of glass (when in the furnace).

macle [ma:kl], *n.f.* Twin crystals; net with large meshes; (*Min.*) macle; (*Her.*) mascle; (*Bot.*) [MACRE].

macler [ma'kle], *v.t.* To mix hard and soft glass together in the furnace.

maçon [ma'sɔ̃], *n.m.* Mason, bricklayer; (*fig.*) bungler; freemason. **maçonnage,** *n.m.* Mason's work, stonework. **maçonner,** *v.t.* To build; to wall up, to stop up. *Maçonner une porte,* to wall up a door.

maçonnerie, *n.f.* Masonry, mason's work, stone-work; freemasonry. *Maçonnerie en brique,* brickwork. **maçonnique,** *a.* Masonic.

macquage [ma'ka:ʒ], *n.m.* Braking (of hemp).

macque or **maque** [mak], *n.f.* Tool or machine for braking hemp. **macquer,** *v.t.* To brake (hemp).

macre [makr] or **macle,** *n.f.* Water-caltrop.

macreuse [ma'krø:z], *n.f.* Scoter. *Macreuse noire,* common scoter; *macreuse brune,* velvet scoter. *Avoir un sang de macreuse,* to be very cool and calm.

macrocosme [makrɔ'kɔsm], *n.m.* Macrocosm.

macroure [ma'kru:r], *a.* Macrurous, long-tailed; (*Bot.*) spiked.—*n.m.* (*Ichth.*) Macrurus, rat-tail.

maculage [maky'la:ʒ], *n.m.,* or **maculation,** *n.f.* Maculation, spotting, staining.

maculature, *n.f.* (*Print.*) Macule; waste proof-sheet; coarse brown paper.

macule, *n.f.* Macule, stain, spot; macula.

maculer, *v.t.* To blot, to spot, to maculate.

—*v.i.* To become maculated or foxed (engraving).

madame [ma'dam], *n.f.* (*pl.* **mesdames**) Madam, ma'am; Mrs.; my lady, your ladyship; her ladyship; lady. *Jouer à la madame*, to play at lords and ladies; *madame est servie*, dinner is served, madam; *madame la duchesse*, your grace; *madame votre mère*, your mother; *madame y est-elle?* is Mrs. So-and-so at home?

madapolam [madapɔ'lam], *n.m.* Strong calico.

madéfaction [madefak'sjɔ̃], *n.f.* Wetting, damping. **madéfier,** *v.t.* (*conjugated like* PRIER) To wet, to moisten.

Madeleine [ma'dlɛn], *f.* Magdalen(e), Madeline.

madeleine [ma'dlɛn], *n.f.* Shell-shaped sponge-cake; early pear; repentant prostitute, magdalen. *Pleurer comme une madeleine*, to weep abundantly.

Madelon [ma'dlɔ̃], *f.* Maud.

madelonnette [madlɔ'nɛt], *n.f.* Magdalen.

mademoiselle [madmwa'zɛl], *n.f.* (*pl.* **mesdemoiselles**) Miss; young lady. *Mademoiselle désire-t-elle attendre?* would you like to wait, Miss? *mademoiselle votre sœur*, your sister; *merci, mademoiselle*, thank you, Miss (So-and-so); (in a letter) *Chère Mademoiselle*, Dear Miss So-and-so (surname usually omitted in French).

Madère [ma'dɛ:r], *m.* Madeira.

madère [ma'dɛ:r], *n.m.* Madeira wine, Madeira. *Gâteau au madère*, tipsy cake.

madone [ma'dɔn], *n.f.* Madonna.

madrague [ma'drag], *n.f.* Tunny-net.

madras [ma'drɑ:s], *n.m.* Madras (handkerchief).

madré [mɑ'dre], *a.* (*fem.* **madrée**) Veined, mottled; (*fig.*) cunning, sly, sharp. *Léopard madré*, spotted leopard. *C'est un madré compère*, he is a sly fellow, a knowing card.—*n.* Cunning, sharp, or sly person. *Un fin madré*, a cunning, foxy individual.

madrépore [madre'pɔ:r], *n.m.* Madrepore.

madrier [madri'e], *n.m.* Thick plank (of oak, pine, etc.).

madrigal [madri'gal], *n.m.* (*pl.* **madrigaux**) Madrigal; compliment.

madrure [mɑ'dry:r], *n.f.* Mottle (on wood, porcelain, etc.); spotting (on coat of animals).

maestria [mɑɛs'tria], *n.f.* Masterliness. *Avec maestria*, in a masterly manner.

mafflu [ma'fly], *a.* (*fem.* **mafflue**) Chubby-cheeked; heavy jowled.

magasin [maga'zɛ̃], *n.m.* Warehouse, storehouse; shop, store; magazine (of fire-arm, camera, etc.). *Grand magasin*, stores; *courir les magasins*, to scour the shops; *en magasin*, in stock (of goods), in hand; *garçon de magasin*, warehouseman, counter-hand; *demoiselle de magasin*, shop assistant; *magasin de nouveautés*, draper's shop. (*Mil.*) *Magasin d'armes*, armoury; *magasin de poudre*, powder-magazine. **magasinage,** *n.m.* Warehousing; warehouse-rent; (*C*) shopping. (*C*) **magasiner,** *v.i.* To shop. **magasinier,** *n.m.* Warehouse-keeper, storeman.

magazine [maga'zin], *n.m.* Magazine (usu. illustrated).

mage [ma:ʒ], *n.m.* Mage, magus; seer. *Les Rois mages*, the three wise men from the East.

magenta [maʒɛ̃'ta], *a. inv. and n.m.* Magenta (colour).

magicien [maʒi'sjɛ̃], *n.m.* (*fem.* **-ienne**) Magician, wizard, sorcerer, enchanter.

magie [ma'ʒi], *n.f.* Magic. *La magie de son sourire*, her bewitching smile; *magie blanche*, natural magic; *magie noire*, black art, witchcraft. **magique,** *a.* Magical. *Baguette magique*, magic wand; *lanterne magique*, magic lantern. **magisme,** *n.m.* Magianism.

magister [maʒis'tɛ:r], *n.m.* Village schoolmaster; pedant. **magistral,** *a.* (*fem.* **-ale,** *pl.* **-aux**) Magisterial; masterly, authoritative, sovereign. *Ligne magistrale*, principal outline. *Médicament magistral*, medicine prepared according to a prescription. *Parler d'un ton magistral*, to speak in an authoritative tone. **magistralement,** *adv.* Magisterially; in a masterly fashion.

magistrat [maʒis'tra], *n.m.* Magistrate, justice; civic officer. **magistrature,** *n.f.* Magistracy; bench. *Magistrature assise*, judges, bench; *magistrature debout*, body of public prosecutors.

magma [mag'ma], *n.m.* Magma, mixture.

magnan [ma'nɑ̃], *n.m.* (*Prov.*) Silkworm. **magnanarelle,** *n.f.* (*Prov.*) [MAGNANIÈRE]. **magnanerie,** *n.f.* Silkworm nursery. **magnanier,** *n.m.* (*fem.* **-ière**) Silkworm breeder.

magnanime [mana'nim], *a.* Magnanimous, high-minded. **magnanimement,** *adv.* Magnanimously.

magnanimité, *n.f.* Magnanimity.

magnat [mag'na], *n.m.* Magnate.

magnésie [mane'zi], *n.f.* Magnesia. *Sulfate de magnésie*, Epsom salts. **magnésium,** *n.m.* Magnesium. *Photographier au magnésium*, to flash-light.

magnétique [mane'tik], *a.* Magnetic. **magnétiquement,** *adv.* Magnetically. **magnétisation,** *n.f.* Magnetization; mesmerizing. **magnétiser,** *v.t.* To magnetize; *to mesmerize, to hypnotize. **magnétiseur,** *n.m.* Magnetizer; *mesmerist, hypnotist. **magnétisme,** *n.m.* Magnetism, mesmerism, hypnotism; (*fig.*) attraction. **magnétite,** *n.f.* Magnetite.

magnéto, *n.f.* Magneto. **magnéto-électrique,** *a.* Magneto-electric. **magnétophone,** *n.m.* (*Reg. trade mark*) Tape-recorder.

magnificat [magnifi'kat], *n.m.* (*Eccles.*) Magnificat.

magnificence [manifi'sɑ̃:s], *n.f.* Magnificence, splendour. **magnifier,** *v.t.* To magnify, to glorify.

magnifique, *a.* Magnificent, splendid, grand; sumptuous, gorgeous; lavish. **magnifiquement,** *adv.* Magnificently.

magnitude [magni'tyd], *n.f.* (*Astron.*) Magnitude.

magnolia [mano'lja] or **magnolier,** *n.m.* Magnolia.

magnum [mag'nɔm], *n.m.* Magnum.

magot [ma'go], *n.m.* Magot; ape; grotesque figure (of china); (*fig.*) ugly person, fright; (*fam.*) hoard, hidden treasure.

mahaleb [maa'lɛb], *n.m.* Black cherry-tree.

maharajah [maara'ʒa], *n.m.* Maharaja.

maharani [maara'ni], *n.f.* Maharanee.

Mahomet [maɔ'mɛ], *m.* Mohammed.

mahométan [maɔmeˈtɑ̃], *a.* and *n.m.* (*fem.* **mahométane**) Mohammedan. **mahométisme,** *n.m.* Mohammedanism.

mahout [maˈu], *n.m.* Coarse woollen cloth, made in Provence etc.; elephant driver.

mai [mɛ], *n.m.* May; maypole. *Le premier mai,* Mayday. *Planter le mai,* to set up the maypole.

maïanthème [majɑ̃ˈtɛm], *n.m.* (*Bot.*) Maianthemum (*not* sweet woodruff).

maie [mɛ], *n.f.* Kneading-trough, breadpan.

maïeur [maˈjœːr], *n.m.* (*Belgium*) Mayor.

maigre [mɛːgr], *a.* Meagre, lean, thin, spare, gaunt; skinny, scraggy; poor, sorry, scanty; hungry, barren; Lenten, fasting; uninflammable, close-burning (of coal). *Jours maigres,* fast-days, fish-days; *maigre chère,* poor living, poor fare; *maigre comme un hareng,* as thin as a rake; *repas maigre,* meatless meal; *soupe maigre,* vegetable soup (made without meat); *un maigre salaire,* a low wage; *une terre maigre,* a barren piece of land.—*n.m.* Lean; fish and vegetable diet; any food save meat; (*pl.*) shallows (of river); (*Ichth.*) meagre. *Faire maigre,* to abstain from meat. **maigrelet,** *a.* (*fem.* **-ette**), or **maigret,** *a.* (*fem.* **-ette**) or **maigrichon** (*fem.* **-onne**) or **maigriot** (*fem.* **-iotte**) (*fam.*) Thin, thinnish, lean, spare. **maigrement,** *adv.* Meagrely; poorly; sparingly. **maigreur,** *n.f.* Leanness, meagreness; thinness, poorness, barrenness.

maigrir, *v.i.* To grow thin, to waste away. *Il maigrit à vue d'œil,* he is getting perceptibly thinner.

mail [maːj], *n.m.* Mall (game, promenade, avenue of trees); mailcoach, four-in-hand.

maille (1) [maːj], *n.f.* Stitch or knot in netting; mesh; ring of cable; link of mail; stitch. *Cotte de mailles,* coat of mail; *maille tombée,* loose stitch; (*Mil.*) towing rope (of pontoon).

maille (2) [maːj], *n.f.* Speck (on the wings of partridges etc.); web (in the eye), leucoma.

maille (3) [maːj], *n.f.* Obsolete copper coin, worth about a farthing. *N'avoir ni sou ni maille,* not to have a farthing; *avoir maille à partir avec quelqu'un* (*partir* here means to share), to have a bone to pick with someone; *ils ont toujours maille à partir ensemble,* they have always a bone to pick with each other.

maillé [maˈje], *a.* (*fem.* **maillée**) Stitched; mailed. *Fer maillé,* wire netting.

***maillechort** [majˈʃɔːr], *n.m.* German silver, nickel-silver.

mailler (1) [maˈje], *v.t.* To reticulate, to make with meshes, to lattice; to mail.

mailler (2) [maˈje], *v.i.* To grow speckled; to bud.

maillet [maˈjɛ], *n.m.* Mallet; beetle; hammerhead shark.

mailletage [majˈtaːʒ], *n.m.* Studding.

mailloche [maˈjɔʃ], *n.f.* Heavy mallet; stick for the big drum.

maillon [maˈjɔ̃], *n.m.* Link (of chain); (*Naut.*) shackle = 30-metre chain.

maillot (1) [maˈjo], *n.m.* Swaddling-band; swaddling-clothes. *Enfant au maillot,* baby in arms.

maillot (2) [maˈjo], *n.m.* Pair of tights (for theatre); bathing costume; (sports) jersey, vest.

maillure [maˈjyːr], *n.f.* Speckles (on hawks etc.).

main [mɛ̃], *n.f.* Hand; paw, claw (of some animals); handwriting; lead, deal (at cards); hook (at the end of a well-rope); holder, handle; hand-shovel; hook, ring; quire (of paper); (*Bot.*) cirrus, tendril of climbing plant. *À deux mains* or *des deux mains,* with both hands, for two hands, two-handed (of swords etc.); *à la main,* in his or her hand, with his hand, by hand, to hand; *à la portée de la main,* within reach; *à main armée,* by force; *à pleines mains,* by handfuls, largely, liberally, plentifully; *à toute main* (horse), fitted to ride and drive; (*Cards*) *avoir la main,* to have the deal, to lead, to play first; *avoir la main heureuse,* to be lucky; *avoir la main légère,* to be light of hand; *avoir la main leste,* to be ready with a slap; *baiser les mains à* [BAISER]; *battre des mains* [BATTRE]; *bien en main,* well in hand, under control; *changer de main,* to change hands; *coup de main,* (*Mil.*) surprise attack, (*fam.*) help; *de la main à la main,* direct from me to you etc.; *de longue main,* long since, of long standing; *de main en main,* from hand to hand; *donner un coup de main à quelqu'un,* to give someone a (helping) hand; *en main propre,* into one's own hands; *en un tour de main,* in a twinkling; *en venir aux mains,* to come to blows; *faire la main,* to deal (at cards); *faire main basse sur,* to plunder, to lay hands on; *fait (à la) main,* done by hand, hand-made; *hors main* or *hors la main,* off-side; *il a des mains de beurre,* he's a butter-fingers; *haut la main* [HAUT]; *haut les mains!* Hands up! *je m'en lave les mains* [LAVER]; *j'en mettrais ma main au feu* [FEU (1)]; *la main dans la main,* hand in hand; *main chaude,* hot cockles (game); *mettre la dernière main à un ouvrage,* to put the finishing touches to a work; *mettre la main à la pâte,* to put one's shoulder to the wheel; *mettre la main à une chose,* to set one's hand to a thing; *mettre la main sur quelqu'un,* to lay hands upon someone; *perdre la main,* to get rusty; *petite main,* sempstress, machinist; *savoir de bonne main,* to know on good authority; *se faire la main,* to get one's hand in; *sous la main,* at hand, to hand, at one's beck and call; *sous main,* underhand, clandestinely; *tendre la main,* to hold out one's hand, to lend a helping hand; *tenir la main à quelque chose,* to take something in hand, to see that something is done.

main courante, *n.f.* Rough-book, wastebook. **main-courante,** *n.f.* (*pl.* **mains-courantes**) Hand-rail (of stair).

main-d'œuvre, *n.f.* (*pl.* **mains-d'œuvre**). Man-power, labour, workmanship; payment for a job.

main-forte, *n.f.* Assistance, help, aid. *Prêter main-forte à quelqu'un,* to lend a helping hand to someone.

mainlevée, *n.f.* (*Law*) Replevin, withdrawal.

mainmise, *n.f.* (*Law*) Seizure, distraint.

mainmorte, *n.f.* Mortmain. *Biens de mainmorte,* property in mortmain.

maint [mɛ̃], *a.* (*fem.* **mainte**) Many. *Maintes fois* or *mainte et mainte fois,* many a time.

maintenant (1) [mɛ̃tˈnɑ̃], *adv.* Now, at this moment, at present, nowadays.

maintenant (2) [MAINTENIR].

maintenir [mɛt'ni:r], *v.t. irr. (conjug. like* TENIR) To uphold, to sustain, to keep together; to maintain, to keep up; to enforce; to preserve. **se maintenir,** *v.r.* To keep up, to be kept up, to be maintained; to last, to subsist; to hold out, to stand one's ground, to maintain one's position or health; to remain in force. *Se maintenir dans les bonnes grâces de,* to continue in the good graces of.

maintenue [mɛt'ny], *n.f.* (*Law*) Confirmation of possession etc.

maintien [mɛ̃'tjɛ̃], *n.m.* Maintenance, preservation, keeping up; carriage, deportment, bearing, attitude, demeanour. *Perdre son maintien,* to lose one's assurance.

maïolique [MAJOLIQUE].

mairain [MERRAIN].

maire [mɛ:r], *n.m.* Mayor. **mairesse,** *n.f.* Mayoress.

mairie, *n.f.* Mayoralty; town hall.

mais [mɛ], *conj.* But; why. *Mais non,* why, no; no, of course; *mais oui* [mɛ'wi], why, yes; yes, of course; *mais, qu'ai-je fait?* why, what have I done? *n'en pouvoir mais,* not to be able to do any more; to be at the end of one's tether; *non mais!* I'm amazed! *non seulement... mais encore,* not only... but also.

maïs [ma'is], *n.m.* Maize, Indian corn; (*Am.*) corn.

maison [mɛ'zɔ̃], *n.f.* House; premises, home; household; housekeeping; domestic affairs; family, race; (*Comm.*) firm. *À la maison,* at home; *ami de la maison,* friend of the family; *entrer en maison,* to go into service; *garder la maison,* to be confined to the house, to stay indoors; *gens de maison,* servants; *la maison du roi,* the king's household, the household troops; *maison d'arrêt,* gaol; *maison de campagne,* country-house, country-seat; *maison d'éducation,* boarding-school; *maison de jeu,* gaming-house; *maison de repos,* rest-home; *maison de santé,* nursing home, mental home; **maison commune,* town hall; *maison garnie,* furnished house; *maison mère,* main shop, head office; *maison solaire* or *maison du ciel,* (*Astrol.*) one of the houses or divisions of the heavens observed by astrologers; *tenir la maison,* to rule the household; *tenir maison,* to keep house.

maisonnée, *n.f.* (*fam.*) Whole house or family, household. **maisonnette,** *n.f.* Small house, cottage, lodge.

maistrance [mɛs'trɑ̃:s], *n.f.* (*Navy*) Body of petty officers.

maître [mɛ:tr], *n.m.* Master; ruler, lord; owner, proprietor, landlord; instructor, teacher, tutor, governor, director; chief, head; (*Naut.*) boatswain, second mate, petty officer; title given to lawyers, and usually written Mᵉ, *Mᵉ Salaün, notaire,* Mr. Salaün, solicitor. *Ce tableau est d'un grand maître,* that picture is by a great master; *coup de maître,* masterly stroke; *de main de maître,* in a masterly manner; *en maître,* like a master, imperiously; *être maître de soi,* to be self-controlled; *être passé maître en,* to be a past master at; *il a trouvé son maître,* he has met his match; *maître à danser,* dancing-master; *maître canonnier,* master-gunner; *maître d'armes,* fencing-master; *maître de chapelle,* precentor; *maître d'école,* schoolmaster;

maître de conférences, lecturer; *maître de forges,* iron-master; *maître de port,* harbour-master; *maître d'équipage,* boatswain (of a ship-of-war); *maître des hautes œuvres,* executioner; *maître d'étude* or *d'internat,* master to supervise and maintain discipline; *maître de vaisseau,* commander of a merchant-ship; *maître d'hôtel,* steward, butler, head waiter; *maître fripon,* thorough-paced scamp; *Maître Jacques,* factotum, Jack-of-all-work; *maître sot,* a regular fool; *petit-maître,* fop; *tel maître tel valet,* like master like man; *sous l'œil du maître,* under the eye of one's employer; *vous êtes maître d'y aller,* you are at perfect liberty to go there.

maître-autel, *n.m.* (*pl.* **maîtres-autels**) High altar.

maîtresse [mɛ'trɛs], *n.f.* Mistress; ruler, lady; owner, proprietress; teacher, governess; sweetheart. *Maîtresse de maison,* mistress of the house, hostess.—*a.* Chief, head, leading, governing; main, consummate. *Idée maîtresse,* main theme. *Maîtresse ancre,* sheet-anchor. *Maîtresse femme,* dominating, superior woman.

maîtrisable [mɛtri'zabl], *a.* Controllable.

maîtrise [mɛ'tri:z], *n.f.* Mastership; mastery; control; music-school (in a cathedral). *Maîtrise de soi-même,* self-control. *Maîtrise des mers,* command of the sea.

maîtriser, *v.t.* To master, to overcome, to subdue, to control, to manage; to lord it over. *Maîtriser ses passions,* to control one's passions. **se maîtriser,** *v.r.* To control oneself.

maja [ma'ʒa], *n.f.* Spider crab.

majesté [maʒɛs'te], *n.f.* Majesty; stateliness. *Leurs Majestés,* their Majesties; *Sa Majesté,* His or Her Majesty.

majestueusement, *adv.* Majestically. **majestueux,** *a.* (*fem.* -euse) Majestic.

majeur [ma'ʒœ:r], *a.* (*fem.* **majeure** (1)) Major, greater; superior, main, chief, most important; of full age; (*Mus.*) major. *Force majeure,* superior force, absolute necessity.—*n.m.* A male of full age, major; middle finger.

majeure (2), *n.f.* Major premise.

majolique [maʒɔ'lik], *n.f.* Majolica.

major [ma'ʒɔ:r], *n.m.* Major; medical officer, surgeon-major. *Major de place,* town commandant.

majorat, *n.m.* (*Law*) Majorat, right of primogeniture.

majoration [maʒɔrɑ'sjɔ̃], *n.f.* Over-estimate, exaggeration; increased charge (on steamers, books, etc.); increased allowance.

majordome [maʒɔr'dɔm], *n.m.* Major-domo.

majorer [maʒɔ're], *v.t.* To over-estimate, to overvalue; to raise (the price).

majoritaire [maʒɔri'tɛ:r], *a.* Pertaining to a majority. *Vote majoritaire,* majority vote.—*n.* Person holding a majority of shares.

majorité [maʒɔri'te], *n.f.* Majority (full age); majority (greater number). *Arriver à sa majorité,* to come of age.

majuscule [maʒys'kyl], *a.* Capital, large.—*n.f.* Capital letter.

maki [ma'ki], *n.m.* Lemur, macaco.

mal [mal], *n.m.* (*pl.* **maux**) Evil, ill, wrong; harm, hurt, mischief; pain, ache, sore, sickness, ailment; hardship, inconvenience; misfortune; trouble, difficulty, toil; dislike, repugnance. *Aux grands maux les grands remèdes*, desperate diseases need desperate remedies; *avoir du mal* (*à*), to have difficulty (in); *avoir mal* (*à*), to have a pain; *changement en mal*, change for the worse; *de deux maux il faut choisir le moindre*, one must choose the lesser of two evils; *dire du mal de son prochain*, to speak ill of one's neighbour; *en mal*, amiss, wrongly, in a bad sense; *être en mal d'enfant*, to be in labour; *faire du mal à*, to injure, to be injurious to; *faire mal*, to ache, to be painful, to hurt; *il a eu plus de peur que de mal*, he was more frightened than hurt; *il a mal au côté*, he has a pain in his side; *il faut éviter le mal et faire le bien*, do good and shun evil; *il n'y a que demi-mal*, the evil is not so serious after all; *induire quelqu'un à mal*, to lead someone into evil; *la tête me fait mal*, my head aches; *le haut mal*, falling sickness, epilepsy; *les maux de la vie*, the evils of life; *mal blanc*, gathering; *mal d'aventure*, whitlow; *mal de cœur*, queasiness; *mal de dents*, toothache; *mal de gorge*, sore throat; *mal de mer*, sea-sickness; *mal de tête*, headache; *mal du pays*, homesickness, nostalgia; *mal d'yeux*, sore eyes; *mener* or *conduire à mal*, to bring to a bad end; *penser à mal*, to mean harm; *prendre en mal*, to take offence at; *quel mal y a-t-il à cela?* what harm is there in that? *rendre le bien pour le mal*, to return good for evil; *se donner du mal*, to take pains, trouble; *se faire du mal*, to hurt oneself, to do oneself harm; *tourner en mal*, to misinterpret, to put a wrong construction on; *vous me faites mal*, you are hurting me.—*adv.* Wrong, amiss, badly; ill, mis-; uncomfortably; at variance, on bad terms; badly off. *Cela va mal*, things are going badly; *c'est mal à lui de*, it is wrong of him to; *cet habit vous sied mal* or *vous va mal*, that coat does not suit you; *de mal en pis*, from bad to worse; *être au plus mal*, to be past recovery; *être fort mal*, to be very ill; *être mal avec quelqu'un*, to be on bad terms with someone; *il écrit mal*, he writes badly; *le plus mal*, the worst; *mal à l'aise*, ill at ease; *mal à propos*, improperly, unseasonably, out of place; *mal gérer*, to mismanage; *mal tourner*, to go wrong; *n'être pas mal*, to be not bad-looking; *pas mal*, not badly, not a little, not a few; *plus mal*, worse; *se trouver mal*, to feel faint, to faint away, to be the worse (*de*); *trouver mal*, to find something amiss; *vous vous y prenez mal*, you are going the wrong way about it.

malabare [mala′bar], *n.m.* (*fam.*) Big, burly man.

malachite [mala′kit], *n.f.* Malachite.

malacie [mala′si], *n.f.* Morbid appetite; malacia.

malacologie [malakɔlɔ′ʒi], *n.f.* Malacology.

malade [ma′lad], *a.* Sick, ill, poorly; diseased, sickly, infirm, unhealthy; affected, attacked. *Avoir l'air malade*, to look ill; *ces plantes sont malades*, those plants are diseased; *la partie malade*, the diseased part; *rendre malade*, to make ill; *son bras malade*, his injured arm; *tomber malade*, to fall ill.—*n.* Sick person, invalid; patient. *Faire le malade*, to sham sick; *les malades*, the sick.

maladie, *n.f.* Illness, sickness, malady; disease, complaint, disorder; mania. *Faire une forte maladie*, to have a serious illness;

faire une maladie, to fall ill; (*Vet.*) *maladie des chiens*, distemper; *maladie du sommeil*, sleeping sickness; *maladie noire*, hypochondria.

maladif, *a.* (*fem.* **-ive**) Sickly, puny, ailing, unhealthy. **maladivement**, *adv.* Morbidly.

maladministration [maladministra′sjɔ̃], *n.f.* Maladministration.

maladrerie [maladrə′ri], *n.f.* Hospital for lepers.

maladresse [mala′drɛs], *n.f.* Awkwardness, clumsiness, unskilfulness; piece of tactlessness, blunder.

maladroit [mala′drwa], *a.* and *n.* (*fem.* **-te**) Awkward, clumsy, unskilful, blundering, stupid (person). *C'est une maladroite*, she is an awkward, clumsy woman; *vous êtes un maladroit!* what an awkward fellow you are! **maladroitement**, *adv.* Clumsily.

malaga [mala′ga], *n.m.* Malaga (wine).

malaguette [mala′gɛt], *n.f.* Guinea-pepper.

malais [ma′lɛ], *a.* and *n.m.* (*fem.* **-aise**) Malay, Malayan.

malaise [ma′lɛːz], *n.m.* Uneasiness, discomfort; indisposition. *Avoir, éprouver un malaise*, to feel faint; (*fig.*) *le malaise politique*, the political unease.

malaisé, *a.* (*fem.* **-ée**) Hard, difficult, rough, arduous. **malaisément**, *adv.* With difficulty, painfully.

Malaisie [malɛ′zi], *f.* The Malay Archipelago, Malaya.

malandre [ma′lɑ̃ːdr], *n.f.* Malander; rotten knot (in timber). **malandreux**, *a.* (*fem.* **-euse**) Having rotten knots (of wood).

malandrin [malɑ̃′drɛ̃], *n.m.* 14th-cent. robber; highwayman, ruffian, marauder.

malappris [mala′pri], *a.* (*fem.* **-ise**) Unmannerly, ill-bred.—*n.* Ill-bred person, lout.

malard [ma′laːr], *n.m.* Mallard, wild drake.

malaria or **mal'aria** [mala′rja], *n.f.* Malaria.

malart [MALARD].

malavisé [malavi′ze], *a.* (*fem.* **-ée**). Ill-advised, imprudent, ill-judged, indiscreet.

malaxage [malak′saːʒ], *n.m.* Kneading (of dough); mixing (of mortar); working (of butter). **malaxer**, *v.t.* To mix, knead, or work up (drugs); to massage. **malaxeur**, *n.m.* Kneader, mixer (apparatus).

malbâti [malbɑ′ti], *a.* (*fem.* **-ie**) Ill-shaped, gawky.—*n.* Ill-favoured person.

malchance [mal′ʃɑ̃ːs], *n.f.* Ill-luck, bad luck, mishap, mischance. **malchanceux**, *a.* (*fem.* **-euse**) Unlucky.

malcontent [malkɔ̃′tɑ̃], *a.* (*fem.* **malcontente**) Discontented, dissatisfied.—*n.m.* Disaffected person, malcontent. *Les malcontents*, (*Fr. Hist.*) the Malcontents, name of a party at the court of Charles IX.

maldisant [MÉDISANT].

maldonne [mal′dɔn], *n.f.* (*Cards*) Misdeal.

mâle [mɑːl], *a.* Male; manly, virile; masculine, energetic. *Air mâle*, manliness; *style mâle*, vigorous style; *voix mâle*, manly voice.—*n.m.* Male; cock.

malebête [mal′bɛːt], *n.f.* Caulking-iron.

malechance [MALCHANCE].

malédiction [maledik′sjɔ̃], *n.f.* Malediction, curse. *Donner sa malédiction à*, to curse.

maléfice [male′fis], *n.m.* Evil spell, sorcery.

maléfique, *a.* Hurtful, malignant.

*malemort [mal'mɔːr], *n.f.* Tragic death, bad end.

malencontre [malɑ̃'kɔ̃ːtr], *n.f.* Mishap, mischance, untoward accident. **malencontreusement**, *adv.* Unluckily, untowardly. **malencontreux**, *a.* (*fem.* **-euse**) Unlucky, untoward.

malendurant [malɑ̃dy'rɑ̃], *a.* (*fem.* **malendurante**) Not very patient, short-tempered.

mal-en-point [malɑ̃'pwɛ̃], *adv.* Badly off; in a sorry plight.

malentendu [malɑ̃tɑ̃'dy], *n.m.* Misunderstanding, misapprehension, mistake.

malepeste! [mal'pɛst], *int.* Plague on it!

malévole [male'vɔl], *a.* Malevolent, ill-disposed.

malfaçon [malfa'sɔ̃], *n.f.* Bad work; malpractice, illicit profit.

malfaire [mal'feːr], *v.i.* (*used only in the inf.*) To do evil. **malfaisance** [malfə'zɑ̃ːs], *n.f.* Evil-doing, evil-mindedness. **malfaisant**, *a.* (*fem.* **-ante**) Mischievous; spiteful, malevolent; injurious, prejudicial. *Nourriture malfaisante*, unwholesome food. **malfaiteur**, *n.m.* (*fem.* **-trice**) Malefactor, evil-doer; offender.

malfamé [malfa'me], *a.* (*fem.* **malfamée**) Ill-famed, of bad repute.

malformation [malfɔrmɑ'sjɔ̃], *n.f.* Malformation.

malgache [mal'gaʃ], *a.* and *n.* Malagasy, Madagascan.

malgracieusement [malgrasjøz'mɑ̃], *adv.* Ungraciously, rudely, uncivilly. **malgracieux**, *a.* (*fem.* **malgracieuse**) Rude, ungracious, uncivil.

malgré [mal'gre], *prep.* In spite of, notwithstanding. *Il l'a fait malgré moi*, he did it in spite of me; *je l'ai fait malgré moi*, I did it against my will, without wanting to; *malgré cela*, nevertheless, for all that, yet.

malhabile [mala'bil], *a.* Unskilled, awkward, clumsy. **malhabilement**, *adv.* Unskilfully, awkwardly. **malhabileté**, *n.f.* Unskilfulness, awkwardness, clumsiness.

malherbe [ma'lɛrb], *n.f.* (*Bot.*) Mezereon.

malheur [ma'lœːr], *n.m.* Unhappiness, misfortune, bad luck; mischance, mishap; calamity, disaster, accident; woe, misery, adversity; poverty. *À quelque chose malheur est bon*, it is an ill wind that blows no one any good; *avoir du malheur*, to be unfortunate; *c'est un petit malheur*, it is but a slight misfortune; *faire le malheur de*, to bring misfortune on; (*fam.*) *faire un malheur*, to do something desperate; *jouer de malheur*, to have a run of bad luck; *malheur aux vaincus!* woe to the vanquished! *oiseau de malheur*, bird of ill-omen; *par malheur*, unhappily, unluckily; *porter malheur*, to bring ill luck; *pour comble* or *pour surcroît de malheur*, to crown all; *quel malheur!* what a misfortune; *un malheur ne vient jamais seul*, misfortunes never come singly. **malheureusement**, *adv.* Unfortunately. **malheureux**, *a.* (*fem.* **malheureuse**) Unfortunate, unlucky, ill-starred, hapless; ill-omened; unsuccessful, fatal; unpleasant, disagreeable; unhappy, miserable, wretched, sorry; beggarly, poor. *Faire une fin malheureuse*, to come to an unhappy end; *il est né malheureux*, he was born unfortunate; *il mène une vie fort malheureuse*, he leads a most

unhappy life.—*n.* Unhappy person, wretched or unfortunate creature; naughty child. *Ce malheureux fera une mauvaise fin*, the wretch will come to a bad end; *malheureux!* wretch that you are; *tout cela, pour cent malheureux francs!* all that for a paltry hundred francs!

malhonnête [malɔ'nɛːt], *a.* Dishonest; uncivil, rude; indecent.—*n.* Rude fellow. **malhonnêtement**, *adv.* Dishonestly; rudely, uncivilly. **malhonnêteté**, *n.f.* Rudeness, incivility; rude action; dishonesty, knavery. *Il est d'une malhonnêteté révoltante*, he is shockingly rude.

malice [ma'lis], *n.f.* Malice, maliciousness, spite; malicious act, piece of spite; roguishness, mischievousness; prank, trick. **malicieusement**, *adv.* Maliciously; mischievously; slyly. **malicieux**, *a.* (*fem.* **-ieuse**) Malicious, spiteful; mischievous; roguish, sly. *Un enfant malicieux*, a mischievous child.

maligne [MALIN].

malignement [maliɲ'mɑ̃], *adv.* Malignantly, maliciously. **malignité**, *n.f.* Malignity, spite.

malin [ma'lɛ̃], *a.* (*fem.* **maligne**) Malicious, mischievous, malignant; waggish, arch, roguish; shrewd; sly, knowing, cunning, clever. (*fam.*) *Ce n'est pas malin*, it's quite easy; *esprit malin*, the evil one, Satan; *fièvre maligne*, malignant fever; *il est trop malin pour se laisser attraper*, he is too shrewd to be caught; *un regard malin*, an arch look, a knowing look.—*n.* Malignant, malicious person; sly, shrewd, acute person. *C'est un malin*, he is a sly one, a knowing one; *faire le malin*, to try and be clever, to brag; *un vieux malin*, an old fox.—*n.m.* Devil, evil spirit, fiend.

maline [ma'lin], *n.f.* Spring tide.

malines [ma'lin], *n.f.* Mechlin, Mechlin lace.

malingre [ma'lɛ̃ːgr], *a.* Sickly, weakly, puny.

malintentionné [malɛ̃tɑ̃sjɔ'ne], *a.* (*fem.* **-ée**) Evil-minded, ill-disposed. *Il est malintentionné à votre égard*, he is ill-disposed towards you.

malique [ma'lik], *a.* (*Chem.*) Malic.

malitorne [mali'tɔrn], *a.* Awkward, ungainly. —*n.m.* Lout.—*n.f.* Slut.

mal-jugé [malʒy'ʒe], *n.m.* Erroneous judgment; miscarriage of justice.

mallard [ma'laːr], *n.m.* Knife-grinder's stone.

malle [mal], *n.f.* Trunk; pedlar's box; mail; mail-coach, mail-steamer. *Faire* or *défaire sa malle*, to pack up or unpack; *la malle-poste* [MALLE-POSTE].

malléabilité [maleabili'te], *n.f.* Malleability; pliability. **malléable**, *a.* Malleable.

malléole [male'ɔl], *n.f.* (*Anat.*) Malleolus, ankle-bone.

malle-poste [mal'pɔst], *n.f.* (*pl.* **malles-poste(s)**) Mail-coach.

malletier [mal'tje], *n.m.* Trunk-maker.

mallette [ma'lɛt], *n.f.* Small case, suitcase, attaché-case; (*Bot.*) shepherd's-purse.

malmener [malmə'ne], *v.t. irr.* (*conjug. like* AMENER) To ill-treat, to maltreat, to handle roughly; to rate; to abuse.

malodorant [malɔdɔ'rɑ̃], *a.* (*fem.* **-ante**) Malodorous, evil-smelling.

malotru [malɔ'try], *n.m.* (*fem.* **-ue**) Ill-bred person; uncouth person, lout, boor.—*a* Coarse, uncouth, vulgar.

Malouines [ma'lwin], **les Îles,** *f. pl.* The Falkland Islands.

malpeigné [malpɛ'ɲe], *n.m.* (*fem.* **-ée**) Unkempt, slovenly, or dirty person.

malplaisant [malplɛ'zã], *a.* (*fem.* **-ante**) Unpleasant, disagreeable, displeasing.

malpropre [mal'prɔpr], *a.* Slovenly, untidy, dirty; dishonest, immoral; unfit (*à*). **malproprement**, *adv.* In a slovenly way, dirtily; improperly. **malpropreté,** *n.f.* Dirtiness.

malsain [mal'sɛ̃], *a.* (*fem.* **-aine**) Unhealthy, sickly; unwholesome, injurious; (*fig.*) immoral, corrupting, demoralizing.

***malséance** [malse'ã:s], *n.f.* Unseemliness, impropriety. **malséant,** *a.* (*fem.* **-ante**) Unbecoming, unseemly, improper.

malsonnant [malsɔ'nã], *a.* (*fem.* **malsonnante**) Ill-sounding; offensive, scandalous.

malt [malt], *n.m.* Malt. **maltage,** *n.m.* Maltage.

maltais [mal'tɛ], *a.* and *n.m.* (*fem.* **-aise**) Maltese. **Malte,** *f.* Malta.

malter [mal'te], *v.t.* To malt. **malterie,** *n.f.* Malt-house. **malteur,** *n.m.* Maltman, maltster.

malthusianisme [maltyzja'nism], *n.m.* Malthusianism. **malthusien,** *a.* and *n.* (*fem.* **-ienne**) Malthusian.

maltose [mal'to:z], *n.m.* Maltose.

maltôte [mal'to:t], *n.f.* (*Fr. Hist.*) An oppressive tax levied in 1292 and later; oppressive import, exaction; (*pej.*) tax-collecting; (*collect.*) tax-gatherers. **maltôtier,** *n.m.* Tax-gatherer.

maltraiter [maltrɛ'te], *v.t.* To ill-use, to ill-treat, to maltreat, to abuse; to handle roughly.

malvacée [malva'se], *n.f.* (*Bot.*) Malvaceous plant.

malveillamment [malvɛja'mã], *adv.* Malevolently.

malveillance [malvɛ'jã:s], *n.f.* Malevolence, ill-will, malice. **malveillant,** *a.* (*fem.* **-ante**) Malevolent, malignant, ill-disposed, spiteful. —*n.m.* Evil-minded person.

malvenu [malvə'ny], *a.* (*fem.* **-ue**) Ill-advised, without any right (to).

malversation [malvɛrsa'sjɔ̃], *n.f.* Malversation, peculation, embezzlement.

malvoisie [malvwa'zi], *n.f.* Malmsey (wine).

mamamouchi [mamamu'ʃi], *n.m.* A grotesque Turkish title—grand Panjandrum.

maman [ma'mã], *n.f.* Mamma, mummy. *Bonne maman* or *grand-maman*, grandmamma, granny.

mamelle [ma'mɛl], *n.f.* Breast; udder (of animal). *Herbe aux mamelles,* nipplewort; *un enfant à la mamelle,* a child at the breast. **mamelliforme,** *a.* Mamelliform.

mamelon, *n.m.* Nipple, teat; dug (of animals); pap, hillock, knoll. **mamelonné,** *a.* (*fem.* **-ée**) Mamilliform; covered with hillocks or pap-like hills.

mamelu, *a.* (*fem.* **-ue**) (*pop.*) Full-breasted.

mameluk [mam'luk], *n.m.* Mameluke.

***m'amie, ma mie** [ma'mi], *n.f.* My dear.

mamillaire [mami'lɛ:r], *a.* Mamillary. **mammaire,** *a.* Mammary. **mammalogie,** *n.f.* Mammalogy. **mammalogiste,** *n.* Mammalogist. **mammifère,** *a.* Mammiferous.— *n.* Mammal. **mammiforme,** *a.* Mammiform. **mammite,** *n.f.* (*Med.*) Mammitis.

mammouth [ma'mut], *n.m.* Mammoth.

***m'amour** [ma'mu:r] or **mamour,** *n.f.* My love; (*pl.*) caresses. *Faire des mamours à,* to coax, to wheedle.

manade [ma'nad], *n.f.* Herd of bulls (in Camargue).

manager [mana'ʒɛ:r], *n.m.* (*spt.*) Manager.

manant [ma'nã], *n.m.* Peasant, clodhopper, boor.

manceau [mã'so], *n.m.* (*fem.* **mancelle** (1)). Inhabitant of Maine or Le Mans.

mancelle (2) [mã'sɛl], *n.f.* Tug-chain (of horse).

mancenille [mãs'ni:j], *n.f.* Manchineel. **mancenillier,** *n.m.* Manchineel-tree.

manche (1) [mã:ʃ], *n.m.* Handle (of tools), haft (of dagger); neck (of violin etc.); stick (of umbrella); helve (of axe); stock (of whip); loom (of oar); stilt (of plough). *Il est toujours du côté du manche,* he is always on the strongest side; *il branle dans le manche,* his position is shaky; *jeter le manche après la cognée,* to give up; *manche à balai,* broomstick; (*Av.*) direction-stick; *manche à gigot,* holder for a leg of mutton (for carving); *manche de couteau,* knife-handle.

manche (2) [mã:ʃ], *n.f.* Sleeve; flexible pipe, hose; strait, channel; (*spt.*) rubber, game, heat. *À grandes manches,* with large sleeves; *avoir une personne dans sa manche,* to have somebody in one's pocket; *c'est une autre paire de manches,* that is another kettle of fish; *manches à gigot,* shoulder-of-mutton sleeves. *Manche à air,* (*Naut.*) windsail, (*Av.*) wind-sock. *J'ai gagné la première manche,* I have won the first game (of the rubber), or first heat; *manche à manche,* even in a game, neck and neck.

Manche [mã:ʃ], **la,** *f.* The (English) Channel. **Les Îles de la Manche,** the Channel Islands.

mancheron, *n.m.* Stilt (of plough); short sleeve.

manchette, *n.f.* Cuff; ruffle; wrist-band (of shirt-sleeve); gauntlet (of gloves); oversleeve; (*pop.*) (*in pl.*) handcuffs; headline (in a newspaper); (*Print.*) side-note, marginal note.

manchon [mã'ʃɔ̃], *n.m.* Muff; cylindrical coupler for tubes, axles, etc.; gas-mantle. *Chien de manchon,* small lap-dog for carrying about. *Manchon d'accouplement,* coupling-box; *manchon d'embrayage,* clutch; *manchon de renfort,* outer tube (of gun). (*Mil.*) *Manchon blanc,* white képi-cover (to distinguish one side during manœuvres).

manchot [mã'ʃo], *a.* (*fem.* **-ote**) One-handed, one-armed. (*fam.*) *Il n'est pas manchot,* he is clever with his hands.—*n.* One-handed, one-armed person; penguin.

mandant [mã'dã], *n.m.* Employer; constituent.

mandarin [mãda'rɛ̃], *n.m.* and *a.* (*fem.* **-ine** (1)) Mandarin. **mandarinat,** *n.m.* Mandarinate.

mandarine (2), *n.f.* Tangerine. **mandarinier,** *n.m.* Mandarin orange-tree.

mandat [mã'da], *n.m.* Mandate, authority; charge, commission; warrant, writ; draft, cheque, money-order, order. *Mandat d'arrêt* or *mandat d'amener,* warrant; *mandat de comparution,* summons to appear; *mandat de dépôt,* commitment; *mandat du Trésor,* Treasury warrant; *mandat de perquisition,* search-warrant; *mandat-poste,* money order; *mandat télégraphique,* telegraph money order;

notre mandat, our terms of reference; *territoire sous mandat*, mandated territory.
mandataire, *n.* Mandatory; proxy, attorney, representative, agent. *Mandataire aux Halles*, broker (at the *Halles*). **mandater**, *v.t.* To deliver an order for the payment of.
Mandchourie [mɑ̃tʃu'ri], **la**, *f.* Manchuria.
mandement, *n.m.* Mandate, mandamus; bishop's letter.
mander [mɑ̃'de], *v.t.* To write, to send word, to inform, to acquaint, to let know; to send for. *Je lui ai mandé de venir*, I have sent him word to come; *on a mandé le médecin*, the doctor has been sent for.
mandibulaire [mɑ̃diby'lɛːr], *a.* Mandibular.
mandibule, *n.f.* Mandible, jaw.
mandoline [mɑ̃dɔ'lin], *n.f.* Mandolin. **mandoliniste**, *n.* Mandolin-player.
mandragore [mɑ̃dra'gɔːr], *n.f.* Mandragora, mandrake.
mandrill [mɑ̃'dril], *n.m.* Mandrill (baboon).
mandrin [mɑ̃'drɛ̃], *n.m.* Mandrel; chuck, punch. **mandriner**, *v.t.* To fix on a mandrel; to bore with a mandrel.
manducation [mɑ̃dyka'sjɔ̃], *n.f.* Manducation (of the Paschal Lamb); mastication.
manéage [mane'aːʒ], *n.m.* Unpaid work by merchant sailors.
manécanterie [manekɑ̃'tri], *n.f.* Choir school.
manège [ma'nɛːʒ], *n.m.* Horsemanship; riding-school; (*fig.*) stratagem, trick, intrigue; horse-driven mill. *Manège de chevaux de bois*, roundabout, merry-go-round.
mânes [mɑːn], *n.m. pl.* Manes, shades.
maneton [man'tɔ̃], *n.m.* Crank- or winch-handle.
manette [ma'nɛt], *n.f.* Hand-lever, grip; (*Hort.*) trowel. *Manette des gaz*, throttle lever; *manette d'avance à l'allumage*, ignition lever.
manganèse [mɑ̃ga'nɛːz], *n.m.* Manganese.
manganite [mɑ̃ga'nit], *n.f.* Manganite; manganese ore.
mangeable [mɑ̃'ʒabl], *a.* Eatable, edible.
mangeaille, *n.f.* Food (for birds, cats, etc.); (*colloq.*) victuals, grub.
mangeoire, *n.f.* Manger, crib; feeding-trough.
mangeot(t)er, *v.i.* To eat little, to pick at one's food.
manger [mɑ̃'ʒe], *v.t.* To eat; to eat up; (*fig.*) to consume, to squander, to run through. *La barbe lui mangeait la figure*, he had a luxuriant growth of beard; *manger des yeux*, to devour with one's eyes; *manger la consigne*, to forget the order; *manger sa soupe*, to drink one's soup; *manger ses mots*, to clip one's words; *manger son bien*, to squander one's money; *salle à manger*, dining-room; (*pop.*) *manger le morceau*, to make a clean breast of it; to inform (the police); *manger du curé*, to hate and abuse priests.—*v.i.* To eat; to take one's meals; to feed. *Donnez-moi à manger*, give me something to eat; *donner à manger aux oiseaux*, to feed the birds; *il a bien mangé*, he has made a good meal; *manger à sa faim*, to eat one's fill; *manger dans la main (de)*, to eat out of one's hand; *manger du bout des dents*, to nibble at one's food; *on mange bien dans cet hôtel*, the cooking is excellent in that hotel.

—*n.m.* Eating; victuals, food. *Le boire et le manger*, eating and drinking. **se manger**, *v.r.* To eat each other; to eat each other up; to hurt each other; to be eaten; to be edible.
mangerie, *n.f.* (*colloq.*) Eating, guzzling; (*fig.*) exaction, extortion.
mange-tout, *n.m. inv.* Prodigal, spendthrift, squanderer; (*Bot.*) sugar pea; string-bean.
mangeur, *n.m.* (*fem.* **mangeuse**) Eater; great eater; spendthrift, devourer, exploiter.
mangeure [mɑ̃'ʒyr], *n.f.* Place nibbled (by mice, moths, etc.).
mangle [mɑ̃:gl], *n.f.* Mangrove.
manglier, *n.m.* Mangrove-tree.
mangonneau [mɑ̃gɔ'no], *n.m.* (*pl.* **-eaux**) Mangonel.
mangoustan [mɑ̃gus'tɑ̃], *n.m.* Mangosteen.
mangouste [mɑ̃'gust], *n.f.* Mongoose. *Mangouste d'Égypte*, ichneumon; mangosteen (fruit).
mangue [mɑ̃:g], *n.f.* Mango. **manguier**, *n.m.* Mango-tree.
maniabilité [manjabili'te], *n.f.* (*Motor., Av.*) Manœuvrability; handiness.
maniable [ma'njabl], *a.* Easy to handle, handy, workable; tractable, supple, pliable, ductile. (*Naut.*) *Vent maniable*, moderate wind.
maniaque [ma'njak], *a.* Eccentric, crotchety, having a mania, finical.—*n.* Crotchety person; maniac, faddist, crank.
manichéen [manike'ɛ̃], *a.* and *n.* (*fem.* **manichéenne**) Manichaean. **manichéisme**, *n.m.* Manichaeism.
manicle [MANIQUE].
manicure [MANUCURE].
manie [ma'ni], *n.f.* Mania; fancy, fad, hobby; inveterate habit, craze.
maniement [mani'mɑ̃], *n.m.* Handling, fingering; management, use, conduct; handling of money etc.; parts of an animal which are felt by the hand to ascertain the condition. *Le maniement d'armes*, rifle exercise.
manier [ma'nje], *v.t.* To handle; to touch; to use, to wield, to ply; to work; to manage, to govern. *Il sait bien manier le ciseau*, he is a fine sculptor; *il sait manier un aviron*, he knows how to ply an oar. *Manier une affaire*, to manage a business.—*n.m.* The feel (of a stuff). *Au manier*, by the touch, by handling.
manière [ma'njɛːr], *n.f.* Manner, way, fashion, style; sort, kind; mannerism, affectation; (*pl.*) manners. *Chacun a sa manière*, every one has his own little ways; *à la manière de Poussin*, after the manner of Poussin; *de cette manière*, in this way; *de la bonne manière*, handsomely; *de la même manière*, in the same manner; *de manière à*, so as to; *de manière que* or *de manière à ce que*, in such a way that; *de quelle manière*, how; *d'une manière ou d'une autre*, somehow or other; *en*, *par*, *manière de*, by way of; *faire des manières*, to mince, to affect reluctance; *il a des manières agréables*, he has pleasing manners; *la manière dont je lui ai parlé*, the way in which I spoke to him; *manière de parler*, mode of speech; *manière d'être*, bearing, deportment, attitude.
maniéré, *a.* (*fem.* **-ée**) Mannered, affected, unnatural, forced. *Air maniéré*, affected look. **maniérisme**, *n.m.* Mannerism.
***maniériste**, *n.* Mannerist.
manieur [ma'njœːr], *n.m.* Handler, manager

manifestant [manifɛs'tɑ̃], *n.m.* (*fem.* **-ante**) Demonstrator, participator (in political meeting).

manifestation [manifɛstɑ'sjɔ̃], *n.f.* Manifestation; (*Polit.*) demonstration. **manifeste,** *a.* Manifest, evident, obvious.—*n.m.* Manifest; manifesto. *Manifeste de douane,* customs' manifest. **manifestement,** *adv.* Manifestly. **manifester,** *v.t.* To manifest, to make known, to display clearly, to show. *Manifester sa pensée,* to make known one's thought.—*v.i.* To attend a (political) demonstration, to demonstrate. **se manifester,** *v.r.* To manifest oneself, to make oneself known; to be made manifest.

manigance [mani'gɑ̃:s], *n.f.* (*fam.*) Manœuvre, underhand trick, intrigue. **manigancer,** *v.t.* To contrive, to scheme, to plot, to concoct.

maniguette [MALAGUETTE].

Manille [ma'ni:j], *f.* Manila.

manille (1) [ma'ni:j], *n.f.* (*Cards*) Manille.

manille (2) [ma'ni:j], *n.m.* Manilla cigar.

manille (3) [ma'ni:j], *n.f.* Shackle (of convict).

manillon [mani'jɔ̃], *n.m.* The ace (at MANILLE (1)).

manioc [ma'njɔk], *n.m.* Manioc, cassava.

manipulaire [manipy'lɛ:r], *a.* Manipular.

manipulateur, *n.m.* (*fem.* **-trice**) Manipulator. **manipulation,** *n.f* Manipulation.

manipule [mani'pyl], *n.m.* (*Rom. Ant.* and *Eccles.*) Maniple.

manipuler [manipy'le], *v.t.* To manipulate; (*Teleg.*) to operate.

manique [ma'nik] or **manicle,** *n.f.* (*Ant.*) Long sleeve covering the wrist; hand-leather (of shoemaker).

manitou [mani'tu], *n.m.* Manitou; (*fam.*) the boss (of a firm), a big shot.

maniveau [mani'vo], *n.m.* (*pl.* **maniveaux**) Osier-stand; punnet.

manivelle [mani'vɛl], *n.f.* Crank; handle.

manne (1) [ma:n], *n.f.* Manna; (*fig.*) balm, gift. *Manne céleste,* manna from Heaven.

manne (2) [ma:n], *n.f.* Hamper, flat basket.

mannée, *n.f.* Hamperful.

mannequin (1) [man'kɛ̃], *n.m.* Small hamper; narrow wicker crate.

mannequin (2) [man'kɛ̃], *n.m.* Lay figure, dummy, figure for trying on clothes; mannikin, puppet; insignificant person; scarecrow; model girl, mannequin; (*Mil.*) dummy (for drill). **mannequiné,** *a.* (*fem.* **-ée**) Unnatural, lifeless, posed.

manœuvrable [manœ'vrabl], *a.* Manageable; manœuvrable. **manœuvrabilité,** *n.f.* Manœuvrability.

manœuvre [ma'nœ:vr], *n.f.* Action, working; drill, drilling (of soldiers); manœuvre; scheme; contrivance, move; (*Rail.*) marshalling, shunting; (*Naut.*) working (a ship); (*pl.*) rigging. *Bonne* or *mauvaise manœuvre,* good or bad move; *champ de manœuvres,* drill-ground; *grandes manœuvres,* army manœuvres; (*Naut.*) *manœuvres courantes,* running-rigging; *manœuvres dormantes,* standing-rigging. —*n.m.* Unskilled workman, labourer, navvy. *Travail de manœuvre,* manual labour; hack work (of an artist). **manœuvrer,** *v.t.* To manœuvre; to work (a machine); to shunt (trains); to ply (an oar, a spade, etc.); (in a

bad sense) to scheme, to contrive. *Manœuvrer l'ennemi,* to outmanœuvre the enemy.—*v.i.* To manœuvre. *Faire manœuvrer des soldats,* to drill soldiers.

manœuvrier, *n.m.* Expert seaman; tactician. —*a.* (*fem.* **-ière**) *Troupes manœuvrières,* highly trained troops; *habileté manœuvrière,* skill in handling (a ship).

manoir [ma'nwa:r], *n.m.* Manor, manorhouse; country-house.

manomètre [mano'mɛtr], *n.m.* Manometer, pressure-gauge. **manométrique,** *a.* Manometrical.

manouvrier [manuvri'e], *n.m.* (*fem.* **-ière**) Day-labourer.

manquant [mɑ̃'kɑ̃], *a.* (*fem.* **-ante**) Missing, absent, wanting.—*n.* Absentee, defaulter.— *n.m. pl.* Shortages, deficiencies.

manque [mɑ̃:k], *n.m.* Want, lack, need; shortcoming, failure, defect; deficiency; (*Riding*) stumble. *Manque de parole,* breach of one's word; *manque de touche* or *à toucher,* (*Billiards*) miss; (*pop.*) *acteur à la manque,* a wash-out as an actor.

manqué, *a.* (*fem.* **-ée**) Missed, lost; spoilt; defective; unsuccessful, abortive, miscarried. *Une affaire manquée* or *un coup manqué,* a failure; *un coup manqué,* a miss; *un garçon manqué* (of a girl), a tom-boy; *un poète manqué,* a would-be poet.

manquement, *n.m.* Omission, shortcoming, oversight; failure, slip; breach.

manquer, *v.i.* To miss, to fail, to go wrong, to be wanting; to be deficient, to be lacking; to give way, to slip; to misfire, to be short, to stand in need (*de*); to be wanting in respect (*à*); to be regardless or unfaithful (*à*); to be negligent (*à*); to be insolvent, to go bankrupt; to miscarry. *Il a manqué de tomber,* he was very near falling; *il manque de tout,* he is destitute of everything; *il ne manquait plus que cela!* that was the last straw! *il ne manque de rien,* he wants for nothing; *je n'y manquerai pas,* I will not fail; *vous me manquez,* I miss you; *l'affaire a manqué,* the business has miscarried, the affair has fallen through; *l'argent lui manque,* he is short of money; *le cœur lui manque,* her heart fails her; *le pied lui a manqué,* his foot slipped; *les forces lui manquent,* his strength fails him; *manquer à quelqu'un* or *manquer de respect à quelqu'un,* to be disrespectful to someone; *manquer à sa parole,* to break one's word; *manquer à son devoir,* to fail in one's duty; *manquer d'argent,* to be short of money; *manquer de parole,* to fail in one's promise; *ne manquez pas de le faire,* do not fail to do it; *rien ne vous manquera,* you shall want for nothing.—*v.t.* To miss, to lose; to spoil. *Il a manqué son coup,* he has missed his aim; *manquer son train,* to miss one's train; *manquer une occasion,* to lose an opportunity.

mansarde [mɑ̃'sard], *n.f.* Roof-window, dormer; garret. *Fenêtre en mansarde,* mansard window; *toit en mansarde,* mansard roof.

mansardé, *a.* (*fem.* **mansardée**) *Chambre mansardée,* attic; *étage mansardé,* attic story.

mansuétude [mɑ̃sɥe'tyd], *n.f.* Mildness, gentleness, forbearance, mansuetude.

mante (1) [mɑ̃:t], *n.f.* Mantle (woman's).

mante (2) [mɑ̃:t], *n.f.* Mantis. *Mante religieuse,* praying mantis.

manteau [mã'to], *n.m.* (*pl.* **-eaux**) Cloak, mantle; (*Am.*) topcoat; (*fig.*) mask, pretence. *Cela se vend sous le manteau,* that is sold under the counter; *le manteau royal,* the royal mantle; *s'envelopper de son manteau,* to wrap oneself up in one's cloak. *Manteau de cheminée,* mantelpiece.

mantelé [mã'tle], *a.* (*fem.* **-ée**) Hooded (crow).

mantelet, *n.m.* Short cloak; apron, canopy-cover (of a coach etc.); (*Fort.*) mantelet; (*Naut.*) lid.

mantille, *n.f.* Mantilla.

mantisse [mã'tis], *n.f.* Mantissa.

Mantoue [mã'tu], *f.* Mantua.

manucure [many'ky:r], *n.* Manicure, manicurist.

manuel [ma'nцɛl], *a.* (*fem.* **-uelle**) Manual, portable. *Travail manuel,* handicraft.—*n.m.* Manual, handbook, textbook. **manuellement,** *adv.* By hand, manually.

manufacture [manyfak'ty:r], *n.f.* Manufacture, making; (manu)factory, mill, works. **manufacturer,** *v.t.* To manufacture. **manufacturier,** *a.* (*fem.* **-ière**) Manufacturing.—*n.* Manufacturer.

manuscrit [manys'kri], *a.* (*fem.* **-ite**) Handwritten.—*n.m.* Manuscript.

manutention [manytã'sjɔ̃], *n.f.* Management, administration; manipulation, handling (of goods etc.); (*Mil.*) army store, army bakehouse or bakery. **manutentionnaire,** *n.m.* Manager; army storekeeper; army baker. **manutentionner,** *v.t.* To store or bake for the army.

maouss [maus], *a.* (Algerian word) (*Mil. slang*) big; strong; good.

mappemonde [map'mɔ̃:d], *n.f.* Map of the world. *Mappemonde céleste,* planisphere.

maquereau (1) [ma'kro], *n.m.* (*pl.* **-eaux**) Mackerel. *Maquereau bâtard,* horse mackerel, scad.

maquereau (2) [ma'kro], *n.m.* (*pl.* **-eaux,** *fem.* **-elle**) (*slang*) Pimp, pander; procurer, brothel-keeper. **maquerellage,** *n.m.* Pimping.

maquette [ma'kɛt], *n.f.* (*Sculp.*) Small rough model (in clay, wax, etc.); (*Paint.*) rough sketch; lay figure; (*Theat., Cine.*) model, miniature.

maquignon [maki'ɲɔ̃], *n.m.* (*fem.* **-onne**) Horse-dealer, horse-coper; jobber, go-between. **maquignonnage,** *n.m.* Horse-dealing; underhand work, jobbery. **maquignonner,** *v.t.* To jockey, to bishop (a horse for sale); to job, to manage in an underhand way.

maquillage [maki'ja:ʒ], *n.m.* Making up; make-up.

maquiller, *v.t.* To make up; to fake up. **se maquiller,** *v.r.* To make up or paint oneself.

maquilleur (1) [maki'jœ:r], *n.m.* Mackerel-boat.

maquilleur (2) [maki'jœ:r], *n.m.* (*fem.* **-euse**) (*Theat.*) Maker up; faker (of paintings etc.).

maquis [ma'ki], *n.m. inv.* Scrub, piece of wild, bushy land (in Corsica); (1941–44) underground forces. *Prendre* or *gagner le maquis* (1941–44), to take to the wood in order to make guerrilla warfare; to go underground.

maquisard [maki'za:r], *n.* Free fighter in the maquis.

marabout [mara'bu], *n.m.* Marabout (priest or shrine); ugly man; big-bellied coffee-jug; marabou-stork, marabou feathers; fine kind of ribbon.

maraîcher [marɛ'ʃe], *a.* (*fem.* **maraîchère**) Of market-gardening. *Jardin maraîcher,* market-garden.—*n.m.* Market-gardener.

marais [ma'rɛ], *n.m.* Marsh, fen, bog, swamp, morass. *Dessécher un marais,* to drain a marsh; *marais salant,* salt-marsh; *oiseaux de marais,* moor-fowl.

marant, mare [MARRANT, MARRE].

marante [ma'rɑ̃t], *n.f.* Arrow-root.

marasme [ma'rasm], *n.m.* Marasmus, emaciation; (*fig.*) depression, complete apathy; stagnation, standstill, slump.

marasquin [maras'kɛ̃], *n.m.* Maraschino.

marathon [mara'tɔ̃], *n.m.* Marathon; a long-distance race.

marâtre [ma'rɑ:tr], *n.f.* Stepmother; (*fig.*) unkind, harsh mother.

*****maraud** [ma'ro], *n.m.* (*fem.* **maraude**) Scoundrel, rascal, knave, slut, jade. **maraudage,** *n.m.* Marauding. **maraude,** *n.f.* Pilfering; stealing from gardens, orchards, etc. *Être en maraude* or *aller à la maraude,* (*Mil.*) to loot, to plunder. **marauder,** *v.i.* To pilfer, to go scrounging; (*slang*) to crawl, to prowl about looking out for chance fares (of taxi-cabs). **maraudeur,** *n.m.* (*fem.* **maraudeuse**) Marauder; (*slang*) crawler (cab); (*Mil.*) looter, plunderer.

maravédis [marave'di], *n.m.* Maravedi (small Spanish coin).

marbre [marbr], *n.m.* Marble; marble statue etc.; marble-slab; stone for grinding colours etc. on; (*Print.*) imposing-stone, slab; (*Bookb.*) marbling. *Il est de marbre,* he is as cold or impassive as marble. *Marbre du gouvernail,* (*Naut.*) barrel of the steering-wheel. *Sur le marbre,* (*Print.*) in type. **marbré,** *a.* (*fem.* **marbrée**) Marbled. *Du papier marbré,* marbled, mottled paper. **marbrer,** *v.t.* To marble, to vein. **marbrerie,** *n.f.* Marble-cutting, marble-work; marble-yard, marble-works. **marbreur,** *n.m.* (*fem.* **marbreuse**) Marbler. **marbrier,** *a.* (*fem.* **-ière**) Of marble.—*n.m.* Marble-cutter, marble-polisher; marble-grainer; dealer in marble. **marbrière,** *n.f.* Marble-quarry. **marbrure,** *n.f.* Marbling; mottling (on the skin).

*****marc** (1) [ma:r], *n.m.* Mark (former unit of weight). *Au marc le franc,* so many shillings in the pound; *poids de marc,* eight ounces.

marc (2) [ma:r], *n.m.* Residuum (of fruit etc., squeezed, boiled, or strained); dregs, grounds. *Marc de café,* coffee-grounds; *marc de pommes,* pomace; *marc de raisin,* skins of grapes after the last pressing. *Eau-de-vie de marc* or (*fam.*) *marc,* white brandy.

Marc [mark], *m.* Mark. **Marc-Antoine,** Mark Antony. **Marc-Aurèle** [marko'rɛl], Marcus Aurelius.

marcassin [marka'sɛ̃], *n.m.* Young wild boar.

marcassite [marka'sit], *n.f.* Marcasite.

marceau [MARSAUX].

marceline [marsə'lin], *n.f.* Soft-coloured silk fabric; (*Min.*) red silicate of manganese.

marchand [mar'ʃã], *n.m.* (*fem.* **-ande**)

Dealer, tradesman, shopkeeper; purchaser, hawker, pedlar, merchant; buyer, bidder (at auctions). *En être le mauvais marchand*, to get the worst of a bargain; *gros marchand*, substantial tradesman; *marchand d'habits, de puces*, old-clothes dealer; *marchand de soupe*, head of a Dotheboys' Hall; *marchand des quatre saisons*, costermonger, barrow-boy; *marchand en détail*, retail merchant; *marchand en gros*, wholesale dealer, merchant; *n'est pas marchand qui toujours gagne*, we must expect losses sometimes; *petit marchand*, petty tradesman; *trouver marchand*, to find a customer or a purchaser.—*a.* Merchantable, saleable, mercantile, trading; good for trade. *Marine marchande*, merchant-service, mercantile marine; *place marchande*, a good place for trade; *prix marchand*, trade price; *navire marchand*, merchantman, merchant-ship.

marchandage [marʃɑ̃'da:ʒ], *n.m.* Bargaining, haggling; piece-work. *****marchandailler**, *v.i.* To haggle.

marchander, *v.t.* To ask the price of, to bargain for; to haggle over, (*Am.*) to dicker; (*fig.*) to spare; to grudge. *Il ne marchande pas sa vie*, he does not hesitate to expose his life; *ne pas marchander quelqu'un*, not to spare someone, not to mince matters with someone.—*v.i.* To haggle; to be irresolute, to hesitate.

marchandeur, *n.m.* (*fem.* **marchandeuse**) Bargainer, haggler; contractor on small scale.

marchandise, *n.f.* Merchandise, commodity; goods, wares, commodities. *Faire valoir sa marchandise*, to cry up one's goods, to make the most of oneself; *marchandise qui plaît est à demi-vendue*, please the eye and pick the purse.

marche (1) [marʃ], *n.f.* Walk, walking; gait; march, distance, journey; marching; progress, advance; procession; course; movement; move (at chess etc.); conduct, way of proceeding. *À la marche rapide*, swift-moving; *fermer la marche*, to close the procession, to bring up the rear; *la bonne marche (d'une machine*, organisation), the smooth running (of a machine etc.); *l'armée est en marche*, the army is on the march; *marche en avant*, advance; *marche de deux heures*, two hours' walk; *marche arrière*, (of a car) reversing; *marche d'un poème*, progress of a poem; *marche du temps*, march of time; *marche militaire* or *marche triomphale*, military or triumphal march; *marche précipitée*, hurried gait; *mettre en marche*, to set going; *ouvrir la marche*, to lead the way; *navire construit pour la marche*, ship built for speed, clipper.

marche (2) [marʃ], *n.f.* Step, stair; treadle. *Marche d'escalier*, step of a staircase; *marche d'un tour*, treadle of a lathe.

marche (3) [marʃ], *n.f.* March, border; frontier region.

marché [mar'ʃe], *n.m.* Market; market-place; emporium, mart; bargain, agreement to buy; purchase; price, rate; agreement, contract, treaty. *Acheter* or *vendre à bon marché*, to buy *or* to sell cheap; *avoir bon marché de*, easily to get the better of; *bon marché*, cheapness; *cours du marché*, market price; *faire bon marché d'une chose*, to hold something cheap, not to spare it; *faire son marché*, to do one's shopping; *faire un marché de dupe*, to make a

bad bargain, to be taken in; *gagner sur son marché*, to make a profit on what one buys; *jour de marché*, market-day; *le marché se tient tous les jours*, the market is held every day; *marché au blé, aux fleurs, aux herbes*, or *au poisson*, corn, flower, grass, *or* fish-market; *marché à terme*, (*Fin.*) time bargain; *marché au comptant*, (*Fin.*) cash transaction; *marché aux puces*, jumble market; *marché noir*, black market; *meilleur marché* or *à meilleur marché*, cheaper; *mettre le marché à la main à quelqu'un*, to let someone take it or leave it; *par-dessus le marché*, into the bargain; *vous n'en serez pas quitte à si bon marché*, you won't get off so easily.

marche-palier [marʃpa'lje], *n.m.* or *f.* (*pl.* **marches-paliers**) Landing-step.

marchepied [marʃə'pje], *n.m.* Step (of a coach, altar, etc.); step-ladder; footboard (of carriage); running-board (of motor-car); foot-path (on the opposite side to the towpath); (*Row.*) stretcher; (*pl.*) foot-ropes of the yards. *Servir de marchepied*, to serve as a stepping-stone.

marcher [mar'ʃe], *v.i.* To walk, to go on foot; to go up, to advance, to move on, to progress; to step, to tread; to go, to travel, to march; to sail, to run, to ply, to flow; to work; to knead (clay); to full (cloth). *Ce navire marche bien*, this ship sails well *or* is very fast; *cette montre marche bien*, this watch keeps good time; *elle ne marche plus*, it is out of order; *faire marcher*, to set going; *je le ferai marcher droit*, I will take care that he behaves well; *marcher à grands pas*, to stride along; *marcher dans l'eau*, to wade; *marcher à l'ennemi*, to march against the enemy; *marcher à pas de loup*, to walk with stealthy steps; *marcher à quatre pattes*, to go on all-fours; *marcher sur des épines*, to tread a thorny path; *marcher sur la pointe des pieds*, to walk on tiptoe; *marcher sur les pas* or *les traces de quelqu'un*, to follow in someone's footsteps; *marcher sur les talons de quelqu'un*, to tread on someone's heels; *marcher sur quelque chose*, to tread upon something; *une affaire qui marche bien*, a business that is doing well; *faire marcher une montre*, to get a watch to go; (*fam.*) *faire marcher une personne*, to pull someone's leg; *je ne marche pas*, nothing doing; *ça n'a pas marché*, it hasn't worked. —*n.m.* Walk, gait, step, pace, tread; walking; ground (on which one walks).

marcheur, *n.m.* (*fem.* **marcheuse**) Pedestrian, walker. *Bon marcheur*, (man) good walker; (horse) good goer; (ship) good sailer; *vieux marcheur*, gay old dog; old roué.

marcottage [markɔ'ta:ʒ], *n.m.* (*Hort.*) Layering. **marcotte**, *n.f.* Layer. **marcotter**, *v.t.* To layer.

mardi [mar'di], *n.m.* Tuesday. *Mardi gras*, Shrove Tuesday.

mare [ma:r], *n.f.* Pool, pond.

maréage [mare'a:ʒ], *n.m.* (*Naut.*) Sailor's hire or pay (by the voyage).

marécage [mare'ka:ʒ], *n.m.* Marsh, bog, fen, swamp, morass. **marécageux**, *a.* (*fem.* **-euse**) Marshy, fenny, swampy, boggy.

maréchal [mare'ʃal], *n.m.* (*pl.* **maréchaux**) Marshal, field-marshal; farrier. *Grand maréchal*, grand marshal, lord high steward; *****maréchal de camp*, brigadier-general; *maréchal de France, Marshal of France; maréchal des logis, sergeant (in cavalry and artillery); maréchal des logis chef, sergeant-major. **maréchalat,** n.m. Marshalship. **maréchale,** n.f. Field-marshal's wife. **maréchalerie,** n.f. Farriery, smithy.

maréchal-ferrant [mareʃalfɛ'rɑ̃], n.m. (pl. **maréchaux-ferrants**) Farrier, shoeing-smith.

maréchaussée [mareʃo'se], n.f. Marshalsea; (mounted) constabulary.

marée [ma're], n.f. Tide, flood; fresh sea-fish. Aller contre vent et marée, to pursue one's course in spite of all difficulties; avoir vent et marée, to sail with wind and tide; cela arrive comme marée en carême, that comes very seasonally or in the nick of time; grande marée, spring tide; la marée monte, the tide is coming in; marée basse, low water; marée haute, high water; train de marée, boat-train, fish-train.

marégraphe, maréographe, or **maréomètre,** n.m. Tide-gauge.

marelle [ma'rɛl], n.f. Hopscotch.

maremme [ma'rem], n.f. Maremma (marshy land on the seashore in Italy).

marémoteur [maremɔ'tœːr], a. (fem. -trice) Tidal. Usine marémotrice, tide-driven factory.

marengo [marɛ̃'go], n.m. Speckled reddish brown; double-twilled cloth of this colour. Poulet (à la) marengo, fowl fricasseed with mushrooms.

marennes [ma'ren], n.f. Marennes oyster.

mareyage [marɛ'jaːʒ], n.m. Fresh-fish trade. **mareyeur,** n.m. Fish-factor, fish-salesman.

margarine [marga'rin], n.f. Margarine.

margarique, a. Margaric.

margay [mar'gɛ], n.m. Margay, tiger-cat.

marge [marʒ], n.f. Margin (of paper, books, etc.); border, edge; (fig.) freedom, latitude, scope. Laisser assez de marge à quelqu'un, to give someone sufficient scope; nous avons de la marge, we have time to spare, we have sufficient means.

margelle, n.f. Curb, brink, edge (of a well etc.).

marger, v.t. (Print.) To regulate the margin of, to feed. **margeur,** n.m. (Print.) Layer-on.

marginal, a. (fem. -ale, pl. -aux) Marginal. **marginé,** a. (fem. -ée) Margined, marginate. **marginer,** v.t. To write in the margin of.

margot [mar'go], n.f. Magpie; (fig.) talkative woman.

margota(s) [margɔ'ta], n.m. A punt for cleaning out weeds.

margotin [margɔ'tɛ̃], n.m. Small bundle of firewood.

margouillat [margu'ja], n.m. Grey lizard.

margouillet [margu'jɛ], n.m. (Naut.) Bull's eye (in wood).

margouillis [margu'ji], n.m. Puddle; slush, mud; (colloq.) difficulty, fix, embarrassment. Laisser quelqu'un dans le margouillis, to leave someone in the lurch.

margoulette [margu'lɛt], n.f. (fam.) Mouth, jaw.

margoulin [margu'lɛ̃], n.m. (pop.) Cheating shopkeeper; small retailer; difficult customer; bungling workman.

margousier [AZÉDARAC].

margrave [mar'graːv], n.m. Margrave.—n.f. Margravine. **margraviat,** n.m. Margraviate. **margravine,** n.f. Margravine.

Marguerite [margə'rit], f. Margaret.

marguerite [margə'rit], n.f. (Bot.) Petite marguerite, daisy; grande marguerite, ox-eye daisy; marguerite d'automne, Michaelmas daisy; marguerite dorée, or chrysanthème des moissons, corn marigold. Jeter des marguerites aux pourceaux, to cast pearls before swine.

marguillage [margi'jaːʒ], n.m. Body of churchwardens. **marguillerie,** n.f. Church-wardenship; church register. **marguillier,** n.m. Churchwarden.

mari [ma'ri], n.m. Husband.

mariable [ma'rjabl], a. Marriageable.

mariage [ma'rjaːʒ], n.m. Marriage; wedlock, matrimony; match; wedding, nuptial ceremony; union, blending; (Naut.) landing, lashing. Faire une demande en mariage, to propose; mariage de convenance, marriage for money or position; mariage d'inclination, love match; mariage mixte, mixed marriage; prendre en mariage, to take to wife; promettre en mariage, to promise in marriage.

marial [ma'rjal], a. (fem. -iale, pl. -iaux) Marial. **marianisme,** n.m. Marianism.

Marianne [ma'rjan], f. (pop.) Name of the French Republic.

Marie [ma'ri], f. Mary, Maria.

marié [ma'rje], a. (fem. **mariée**) Married. —n.m. Married man; bridegroom; (pl.) married people. Nouveaux mariés, newly married couple.—n.f. Married woman; bride. Se plaindre que la mariée est trop belle, to find fault with a good bargain.

marier [ma'rje], v.t. To marry, to join together in wedlock; to give in marriage, to marry off; to match; to join, to blend, to unite; (Naut.) to lash, to bend. Il a fort bien marié sa fille, he has married his daughter very advantageously. Marier des couleurs, to blend colours. Marier la vigne avec l'ormeau, to marry the vine with the elm. **se marier,** v.r. To marry, to get married; to match, to pair, to blend, to combine (avec). Elle est en âge de se marier, she is of an age to marry; il s'est marié avec sa cousine, he has married his cousin; il s'est marié très richement, he has married money.

marie-salope [marisa'lɔp], n.f. (pl. **maries-salopes**) Mud-lighter; mud-dredger.

marieur [ma'rjœːr], n.m. (fem. **marieuse**) Matchmaker.

marigot [mari'go], n.m. Small W. African river or lake.

marin [ma'rɛ̃], a. (fem. **marine**) Marine; sea-faring, sea-going; pertaining to the sea. Avoir le pied marin, to have good sea-legs, to be a good sailor; carte marine, marine chart; milles marins, nautical miles.—n.m. Sailor. Marin d'eau douce, (fam.) fresh-water sailor, landlubber.

marinade [mari'nad], n.f. Marinade, pickle, souse. **marinage,** n.m. Sousing, pickling.

marine [ma'rin], n.f. Sea-service; naval administration; Admiralty; navy, naval forces; shipping, craft; taste, smell of the sea; (Paint.) sea-piece, seascape. Marine marchande, mercantile marine, merchant navy; marine militaire, navy; officier de

marine, naval officer; *sentir la marine* or *avoir un goût de marine*, to taste of the sea; **infanterie de marine*, marines; *terme de marine*, sea-term.—*a. inv. Bleu marine*, navy-blue.

mariné [mari'ne], *a.* (*fem.* **marinée**) Soused, pickled; (*Her.*) marine, having a fish's tail. *Des marchandises marinées*, merchandise spoiled or damaged by the sea.

mariner [mari'ne], *v.t.* To marinade, to pickle, to souse.

maringote or **maringotte** [marɛ̃'gɔt], *n.f.* Small cart with movable seats.

maringouin [marɛ̃'gwɛ̃], *n.m.* A big innocuous tipula (about 1 inch long) which appears in autumn; crane-fly, daddy-long-legs; (*C*) mosquito.

marinier [mari'nje], *a.* (*fem.* **-ière** (1)) *Officiers mariniers*, petty officers.—*n.m.* Waterman, bargeman, lighter-man. *Maître marinier*, master-bargeman.

marinière (2), *n.f.* (*Swimming*) Side-stroke; (*Cost.*) (women's) sailor blouse; (*Cook.*) onion sauce (for mussels).

marinisme [mari'nism], *n.m.* Marinism. **mariniste**, *n.m.* Marinist.

mariol or **mariole** [ma'rjɔl], *a.* and *n.* (*pop.*) Shrewd, cute; tough. *Faire le mariol*, to talk big.

mariolâtrie [marjɔla'tri], *n.f.* Mariolatry.

marionnette [marjɔ'nɛt], *n.f.* Puppet, marionette; frivolous, weak-minded person, mere puppet; (*pl.*) puppet-show. *Marionnette à fils*, marionette; *marionnette à gaine*, glove puppet.

mariste [ma'rist], *n.m.* (*R.-C.*) Marist (father).

marital [mari'tal], *a.* (*fem.* **-ale**, *pl.* **-aux**) Marital, pertaining to a husband. **maritalement**, *adv.* Maritally, as man and wife.

maritime [mari'tim], *a.* Maritime, naval. *Agent maritime*, shipping agent; *arsenal maritime*, naval dockyard; *assurance maritime*, marine insurance; *gare maritime*, harbour station; *mouvement maritime*, shipping intelligence; *ville maritime*, seaside town.

maritorne [mari'tɔrn], *n.f.* Ugly sluttish woman.

marivaudage [marivo'da:ʒ], *n.m.* Witty, rather affected conversation between lovers; persiflage; an excess of subtlety. **marivauder**, *v.i.* To flirt in that manner.

marjolaine [marʒɔ'lɛn], *n.f.* Sweet marjoram.

marli or **marly** [mar'li], *n.m.* Thread gauze; fillet bordering the inside of a plate, dish, etc.

marlou [mar'lu], *n.m.* (*slang*) Pimp, bully; cad.

marmaille [mar'ma:j], *n.f.* (*colloq.*) Brats, crowd of brats.

marmelade [marmə'lad], *n.f.* Compote; (*fig.*) jelly, soup. *Avoir la mâchoire en marmelade*, to have one's jaw smashed in; *cette viande est en marmelade*, that meat is done to a jelly; *mettre en marmelade*, to beat to a jelly.

marmenteau [marmã'to], *a.* and *n.m.* (*pl.* **marmenteaux**) Preserved, ornamental (trees in a park etc.).

marmitage [marmi'ta:ʒ], *n.m.* Shelling by heavy guns.

marmite [mar'mit], *n.f.* Cooking-pot; potful; (*Mil.*) dixy, mess-tin; (*Mil. slang*) a big shell; (*slang*) mistress of a pimp. *Marmite norvégienne*, hay-box; *marmite à vapeur*, steamer;

nez en pied de marmite, pug-nose; *marmite de campement*, camp kettle; *écumeur de marmites*, sponger, parasite; *elles servent à faire bouillir la marmite*, they help to make the pot boil; *la marmite est renversée*, they give no more parties, see no more company [*see also* SINGE]. **marmiter**, *v.t.* (*Mil. slang*) To bombard with heavy shells.

marmiteux [marmi'tø], *a.* (*fem.* **marmiteuse**) Pitiful, wretched, miserable.—*n.* Poor devil.

marmiton [marmi'tɔ̃], *n.m.* Scullion, cook's boy. **marmitonner**, *v.i.* To play the drudge.

marmonner [marmɔ'ne], *v.t.* To mutter.

marmoréen [marmɔre'ɛ̃], *a.* (*fem.* **marmoréenne**) Marmorean.

marmot [mar'mo], *n.m.* **Little monkey; puppet, grotesque figure; kid, brat, urchin. *Croquer le marmot*, to dance attendance, to kick one's heels.

marmotte [mar'mɔt], *n.f.* Marmot; kerchief tied under chin; (*Naut.*) match-tub. *Dormir comme une marmotte*, to sleep like a top.

marmottement [marmɔt'mã], *n.m.*, or **marmottage** [marmɔ'ta:ʒ]. Muttering, mumbling.

marmotter [marmɔ'te], *v.t.*, *v.i.* To mutter, to mumble. **marmotteur**, *n.m.* (*fem.* **marmotteuse**) Mutterer.

marmouset [marmu'zɛ], *n.m.* Grotesque figure; young monkey (little boy), little chap; fire-dog.

marnage [mar'na:ʒ], *n.m.* (*Agric.*) Marling (earth). **marne**, *n.f.* Marl, chalk, clay. **marner**, *v.t.* To marl. **marneux**, *a.* (*fem.* **-euse**) Marly. **marnière**, *n.f.* Marlpit.

Maroc [ma'rɔk], **(le)**, *m.* Morocco. **marocain**, *a.* (*fem.* **-aine**) and *n.m.* (**Marocain**, *fem.* **-aine**) Moroccan.

maronite [marɔ'nit], *a.* and *n.* Maronite.

maronner [marɔ'ne], *v.t.*, *v.i.* (*colloq.*) To grumble, to growl, to mutter.

maroquin [marɔ'kɛ̃], *n.m.* Morocco leather; (*Naut.*) guy-rope (holding tackle); (*fam.*) minister's portfolio. *Maroquin du Levant*, Turkey leather. **maroquiner**, *v.t.* To morocco (leather). **maroquinerie**, *n.f.* Morocco-leather manufacture, factory, trade, etc. **maroquinier**, *n.m.* Morocco-leather tanner.

marotique [marɔ'tik], *a.* In the style of Marot. **marotiser**, *v.i.* (*colloq.*) To write in this style. **marotisme**, *n.m.* Imitation of Marot's style.

marotte [ma'rɔt], *n.f.* Fool's bauble, cap and bells; hairdresser's dummy head; (*fig.*) fancy, folly, whim, hobby. *Chacun a sa marotte*, everybody has his hobby.

marouflage [maru'fla:ʒ], *n.m.* Canvas backing. ***maroufle** (1) [ma'rufl], *n.m.* Rascal, rogue. **maroufle** (2) [ma'rufl], *n.f.* Lining-paste. **maroufler**, *v.t.* To stick (a (painted) canvas) on a wall; to stick behind an old picture a new canvas backing [*see also* RENTOILER]; (*Av.*) to tape (a seam).

maroute [ma'rut], *n.f.* (*Bot.*) or *marouette* or *camomille puante*. Stinking camomilla, dog-fennel.

marquant [mar'kã], *a.* (*fem.* **marquante**) Conspicuous, striking. *Cartes marquantes*, cards that count; *personne marquante*, person of note.

marque [mark], *n.f.* Mark, imprint, stamp;

cipher, trade-mark, private mark, make; brand, branding-iron; print, trace (of footsteps etc.); badge, sign, token; testimony, proof; counter (at play); mole, pit (of the smallpox etc.); note, distinction; (*Naut.*) marque. *Donner à quelqu'un une marque d'estime*, to give someone a mark of esteem; *homme de marque*, man of note; *lettres de marque*, letters of marque; *liqueurs de marque*, liqueurs of a well-known brand, of superior quality; *marque de fabrique*, trade-mark. (*spt.*) *A vos marques!* on your marks!

marqué, *a.* (*fem.* **-ée**) Marked, evident, conspicuous, obvious; decided, fixed, determined. *Attentions marquées*, marked attentions; *avoir les traits marqués*, to have strongly marked features; *il est né marqué*, he was born with a mole; *marqué de la petite vérole*, pitted with smallpox.

marquer, *v.t.* To mark; to stamp; to brand, to stigmatize; to indicate; to betoken, to denote; to appoint, to state, to tell, to mention; to give marks of, to testify; to score. *Marquer à quelqu'un sa reconnaissance*, to show one's gratitude to someone; (*Mil.*) *marquer le pas*, to mark time; *marquer son jeu*, to mark one's points at play; (*spt.*) *marquer un adversaire*, to mark an opponent; *marquer un but*, to score a goal.—*v.i.* To make its mark or one's mark; to mark, to be remarked, to be remarkable; to show off, to be conspicuous; to show the hour (of sun-dials); to show age by the teeth (of horses). *Cela marquerait trop*, (*colloq.*) that would attract too much attention; *cet homme marque mal*, that man has an unprepossessing appearance.

marqueter [markə'te], *v.t.* To speckle, to spot; to inlay. **marqueterie,** *n.f.* Marquetry, inlaid-work, inlaying; (*fig.*) patchwork, miscellany. **marqueteur,** *n.m.* Inlayer.

marqueur [mar'kœːr], *n.m.* (*fem.* **marqueuse**) Marker; scorer, tally-keeper; stamping-machine; (*Ten.*) court marker.

marquis [mar'ki], *n.m.* Marquess. *Faire le marquis*, to give oneself airs. **marquisat,** *n.m.* Marquisate. **marquise,** *n.f.* Marchioness; marquee, marquise, glass porch or roof, marquise-ring.

marquoir [mar'kwaːr], *n.m.* Marker (used by tailors etc.); sampler.

marraine [ma'rɛn], *n.f.* Godmother; christener (of a bell, a ship etc.); presenter (of debutante), sponsor. *Marraine de guerre*, correspondent (of a soldier).

marrant [ma'rɑ̃], *a.* (*fem.* **-ante**) (*vulg.*) Very funny.

marre [maːr], *n.f.* Mattock, hoe. (*slang*) *En avoir marre*, to have had enough of it. **se marrer,** *v.r.* (*slang*) To laugh, to have a good time.

***marri** [ma'ri], *a.* (*fem.* **-ie**) Sorry, grieved.

marron (1) [ma'rɔ̃], *n.m.* Chestnut; cracker (fireworks); (*Mil.*) mark, tally; (*Mining*) check given to timekeeper; curl tied with a ribbon; (*slang*) blow. *Marron d'Inde*, horse-chestnut; *marrons glacés*, candied chestnuts; *tirer les marrons du feu*, to pull the chestnuts out of the fire.—*a. inv.* Maroon, chestnut-colour.

marron (2) [ma'rɔ̃], *a.* (*fem.* **marronne**) Fugitive, runaway (of slaves); wild (of animals that have been tame); (*Comm.*) unlicensed,

interloping. *Courtier marron*, unlicensed broker; *amateur marron*, sham amateur; *avocat marron*, unqualified lawyer.—*n.m.* Runaway slave; unlicensed broker; unlicensed printer; interloper; (*Print.*) work printed clandestinely. **marronnage,** *n.m.* State of a runaway slave; running away (of slaves); carrying on the business of a broker without a licence. **marronner,** *v.i.* To be a runaway slave, to maroon; to job (at Stock Exch.); (*fam.*) to grouse, to grumble.

marronnier [marɔ'nje], *n.m.* Chestnut-tree. *Marronnier d'Inde*, horse-chestnut-tree.

marrube [ma'ryb], *n.m.* (*Bot.*) Horehound. *Marrube d'eau*, gipsy-wort.

mars [mars], *n.m.* March; (*Astr. Myth.*) Mars; (*pl.*) seed sown in spring. *Arriver comme mars en carême* [CARÊME]; *Champ de Mars*, large parade-ground; *grand mars*, purple emperor (butterfly).

marsaux, marsault, or **marceau** [mar'so], *n.m.* Goat-willow.

Marseillaise [marsɛ'jɛːz], *n.f.* Marseillaise (French national anthem).

marsouin [mar'swɛ̃], *n.m.* Porpoise; (*fig.*) ugly wretch; (*colloq.*) colonial infantry soldier, marine; (*Naut.*) head awning.

marsupial [marsy'pjal], *a.* (*fem.* **-iale**, *pl.* **-iaux**) Marsupial.—*n.m.* Marsupial.

martagon [marta'gɔ̃], *n.m.* (*Bot.*) Martagon, Turk's-cap.

marte [MARTRE].

marteau [mar'to], *n.m.* (*pl.* **marteaux**) Hammer; hammer-head shark; hammer-shell. *Marteau à deux mains*, sledge-hammer; *marteau de porte*, knocker; *marteau pneumatique*, air-hammer, pneumatic drill. *Être entre le marteau et l'enclume* [ENCLUME]; *graisser le marteau*, to tip the hall-porter; *il faut être enclume ou marteau*, you must bite or be bitten; *passer sous le marteau*, to be sold under the hammer. (*fam.*) *Avoir (reçu) un coup de marteau*, (*pop.*) *être un peu* (or *complètement*) *marteau*, to be (a bit) cracked.

marteau-pilon, *n.m.* (*pl.* **marteaux-pilons**) Steam-hammer.

***martel** [mar'tɛl], *n.m.* *Avoir martel en tête*, to be anxious, worried.

martelage, *n.m.* Hammering; marking (of trees). **martelé,** *a.* (*fem.* **martelée**) Hammered; (*Mus.*) brilliant and distinct. *Vaisselle martelée*, hammered plate; *vers martelés*, laboured verses. **marteler,** *v.t.* To hammer; to mark (trees). (*fig.*) *Marteler ses mots en parlant*, to speak emphatically, to articulate every syllable strongly; *marteler des vers*, to hammer out verse. **martelet,** *n.m.* Small hammer. **marteleur,** *n.m.* Hammerman.

Marthe [mart], *f.* Martha.

martial [mar'sjal], *a.* (*fem.* **martiale**, *pl.* **martiaux**) Martial, warlike, soldierly. *Cour martiale*, court martial; *loi martiale*, martial law.

martin [mar'tɛ̃], *n.m.* Martin. *L'ours Martin*, bruin, teddy bear [*see also* SAINT-MARTIN].

martin-bâton, *n.m.* Man armed with a cudgel; cudgel.

martiner [marti'ne], *v.t.* To tilt, hammer.

martinet (1) [marti'nɛ], *n.m.* (*Orn.*) Swift, martlet. *Martinet noir*, black martin; *martinet des Alpes*, alpine martin.

martinet (2) [marti'nɛ], *n.m.* Tilt-hammer;

cat-o'-nine-tails; flat candlestick; (*Naut.*) boom-span.

martingale [martɛ̃ˈgal], *n.f.* Martingale (of harness, of jib-boom); half-belt (of greatcoat). *Jouer la martingale*, to play double or quits.

martin-pêcheur [martɛ̃pɛˈʃœːr], *n.m.* (*pl.* **martins-pêcheurs**) Kingfisher. *Martin-pêcheur d'Australie*, laughing jackass.

martre [martr] or **marte**, *n.f.* Marten. *Martre zibeline*, sable; *prendre martre pour renard*, to take a cow for a bull, to be misled by resemblance.

martyr [marˈtiːr], *n.m.* (*fem.* **martyre** (1)) Martyr. *Le commun des martyrs*, (R.-C. Ch.) office for the general body of martyrs, (*fig.*) the common herd.—*a.* Martyred. **martyre** (2), *n.m.* Martyrdom. *Souffrir le martyre*, to suffer martyrdom. **martyriser**, *v.t.* To martyrize; to torment, to torture. **martyrologie**, *n.m.* Martyrology. **martyrologiste**, *n.m.* Martyrologist.

marxisme [markˈsizm], *n.m.* Marxism. **marxiste**, *a.* and *n.* Marxist.

mas [ma], *n.m.* (*S. dial.*) Farm-house.

(C) **mascabina** [maskabiˈna], *n.m.* (*Bot.*) Service tree.

mascarade [maskaˈrad], *n.f.* Masquerade.

mascaret [maskaˈrɛ], *n.m.* Bore, tidal wave in an estuary.

mascaron [maskaˈrɔ̃], *n.m.* Grotesque mask (on keystone).

mascotte [masˈkɔt], *n.f.* Mascot, charm.

masculin [maskyˈlɛ̃], *a.* (*fem.* **masculine**) Masculine, male. *Rime masculine*, rhyming word not ending in *e* mute.—*n.m.* (*Gram.*) Masculine. **masculiniser**, *v.t.* To make masculine. **masculinité**, *n.f.* Masculinity.

(C) **maskinongé** [maskinɔ̃ˈʒe], *n.m.* Muskelunge, the ugly fish.

masochisme [mazɔˈʃizm], *n.m.* Masochism. **masochiste**, *a,* and *n.* Masochist.

masque [mask], *n.m.* Mask; (*fig.*) blind, cloak, pretence; masker, masquerader, mummer; (*Fenc.*) face-guard; (*Mil.*) hood, shield (of a gun); ugly person, fright; (*fig.*) face, physiognomy, expression. *Arracher les masques*, to tear off the disguise; *il a un bon masque*, (*Theat.*) his features are expressive; *lever le masque*, to throw off the mask; *masque à gaz*, gas-mask; *masque mortuaire*, cast, deathmask; *sans masque*, unmasked.

masqué, *a.* (*fem.* **masquée**) Masked; disguised; concealed. *Bal masqué*, masked ball; *batterie masquée*, concealed battery; *virage masqué*, blind corner.

masquer, *v.t.* To mask; to cloak, to disguise; to conceal, to hide; (*Naut.*) to take (the sails) aback.

massacrant [masaˈkrɑ̃], *a.* (*fem.* **massacrante**) (*Used chiefly in*) *Être d'une humeur massacrante*, to be in an awful temper.

massacre [maˈsakr], *n.m.* Massacre, butchery, slaughter; (*fig.*) havoc, waste, squandering, spoiling; (*Hunt.*) head (of a deer newly killed). *Jeu de massacre*, the French equivalent of Aunt Sally at a fair.

massacrer, *v.t.* To massacre, to butcher, to murder, to slaughter; (*fig.*) to bungle, to mangle; to hack (meat or poultry). *Cet acteur a massacré son texte*, that actor

murdered his part; *massacrer des hardes* or *des meubles*, to spoil clothes or furniture.

massacreur, *n.m.* Slaughterer, slayer; (*fig.*) bungler, spoiler.

massage [maˈsaːʒ], *n.m.* Massage; *shampooing.

masse (1) [mas], *n.f.* Mass, heap, lump; bulk, aggregate; mob; stock, common fund, pool; (*Elec.*) earth. *En masse*, in a body, in the mass, by the bulk; *les masses*, the masses, the mob; *soulever les masses*, to stir up the people; *tomber comme une masse*, to fall like a log.

masse (2) [mas], *n.f.* Sledge-hammer. *Masse en bois*, maul, beetle; *masse d'armes*, mace.

massé [maˈse], *n.m.* (*Billiards*) Perpendicular or massé-stroke.

massepain [masˈpɛ̃], *n.m.* Marzipan.

masser (1) [maˈse], *v.t.* To mass (troops etc.). **se masser**, *v.r.* To come together in a mass; to mass.

masser (2) [maˈse], *v.t.* (*Billiards*) To strike almost vertically; to make a massé (stroke).

masser (3) [maˈse], *v.t.* To massage, *to shampoo.

massette [maˈsɛt], *n.f.* (*Bot.*) Reed-mace, bulrush; roadman's (two-handed) hammer.

masseur [maˈsœːr], *n.m.* (*fem.* **masseuse**) Masseur, masseuse.

massicot [masiˈko], *n.m.* Massicot, yellow oxide of lead; (*Bookb.*) trimmer, guillotine.

massier [maˈsje], *n.m.* (*fem.* **-ière**) Macebearer; art student in charge of the *masse* (common fund) of a studio.

massif [maˈsif], *a.* (*fem.* **massive**) Massive, bulky, massy, solid; lumpish, heavy. *Avoir l'esprit massif*, to be dull-minded; *argent massif*, solid silver.—*n.m.* Clump of (trees, flowers, etc.); solid mass or block (of masonry); mass of mountains. **massivement**, *adv.* Massively, heavily, solidly. **massiveté**, *n.f.* Massiveness.

massue [maˈsy], *n.f.* Club. *Coup de massue*, knock-down blow; (*fig.*) crushing news.

mastic [masˈtik], *n.m.* Mastic; cement; (glazier's) putty; stopping (for teeth, tyres); plastic wood; (*Print.*) transposition; (*pop.*) thick sauce or soup. **masticage**, *n.m.* Cementing, puttying; stopping, filling.

mastication [mastikaˈsjɔ̃], *n.f.* Mastication, chewing. **masticatoire**, *a.* and *n.m.* Masticatory.

mastiquer (1) [mastiˈke], *v.t.* To masticate.

mastiquer (2) [mastiˈke], *v.t.* To putty, to cement.

mastoc [masˈtɔk], *n.m.* and *a.* (*colloq.*) Heavy, clumsy (fellow).

mastodonte [mastɔˈdɔ̃ːt], *n.m.* Mastodon.

mastoïde [mastɔˈid], *a.* Mastoid. *Apophyse mastoïde*, mastoid process. **mastoïdien**, *a.* (*fem.* **-ienne**) Mastoidean. **mastoïdite**, *n.f.* (*Path.*) Inflammation of mastoid process.

mastroquet [mastrɔˈkɛ], *n.m.* (*pop.*) Keeper of a pub.

masturbation [mastyrbaˈsjɔ̃], *n.f.* Masturbation. **se masturber**, *v.r.* To masturbate.

m'as-tu-vu [matyˈvy], *n.m. inv.* A bumptious actor (who often says *m'as-tu-vu dans tel rôle?*)

masure [maˈzyːr], *n.f.* Hovel, tumbledown cottage.

mat (1) [mat], *n.m.* (*Chess*) Mate. *Faire échec*

et mat, to checkmate.—*a. inv.* (Check-)
mated.

mat (2) [mat], *a.* (*fem.* **mate**) Mat, dull, unpolished; dead, dull-sounding; heavy, sod-
den. *Pâte mate*, heavy dough; *coloris mat*,
dull colouring; *or mat*, unpolished gold.—*n.m.*
Dull or mat part, mat.

mât [mɑ], *n.m.* Mast; pole. *Aller à mâts et à
cordes*, to scud under bare poles; *le grand
mât*, the mainmast; *mât de charge*, derrick;
mât de cocagne, greasy pole; *mât de fortune*,
jury-mast; *mât de misaine*, foremast; *mât de
pavillon*, flagstaff; *mât de rechange*, spare
mast; *mât d'artimon*, mizzen-mast.

matador [mata'dɔːr], *n.m.* Matador (killer of
bulls; a game of dominoes); (*slang*) big-wig.

mâtage [mɑ'taːʒ], *n.m.* Fixing the lower masts.

matamore [mata'mɔːr], *n.m.* Blusterer, braggart.

match [matʃ], *n.m.* (*pl.* **matches** [matʃ])
Match. *Un match de football*, a football
match; *match nul*, draw. **matcher**, *v.t.* To
match.—*v.i.* To play a match.

maté [ma'te], *n.m.* Maté, Paraguay tea.

matelas [ma'tlɑ], *n.m.* Mattress; pad, cushion.
Toile à matelas, ticking; *matelas d'air*, air
cushion. **matelasser**, *v.t.* To stuff, to pad,
to cushion; to cover with a mattress. **matelassier**, *n.m.* (*fem.* **-ière**) Mattress-maker.

matelassure, *n.f.* Padding, wadding, padded
lining.

matelot [ma'tlo], *n.m.* Sailor, seaman; consort-
ship; child's sailor-suit. **matelotage**, *n.m.*
Seamanship; seaman's wages, pay; comradeship.

matelote, *n.f.* Sailor's wife; fish-stew; *hornpipe.

mater (1) [ma'te], *v.t.* To checkmate; to bring
down, to subdue. *On a bien maté son orgueil*,
his pride has been sadly brought down.

mater (2) [ma'te], *v.t.* To make mat or dull,
to deaden; to render compact.

mâter [mɑ'te], *v.t.* To mast; to toss (oars);
to up-end (a boat).

mâtereau, *n.m.* (*pl.* **-eaux**) Small mast; spar.

matérialisation [materjaliza'sjɔ̃], *n.f.* Mat-
erialization. **matérialiser**, *v.t.* To materialize.

matérialisme, *n.m.* Materialism. **matérialiste**, *n.* Materialist.—*a.* Materialistic. **matérialité**, *n.f.* Materiality.

matériau, *n.m.* (*Arch.*) Material. **matériaux**,
n.m. pl. Materials.

matériel, *a.* (*fem.* **matérielle**) Material;
gross, rough; heavy, dull; sensual. *C'est un
esprit bien matériel*, he is a dull, matter-of-
fact man; *dégâts matériels*, damage to
property.—*n.m.* That which is material or
corporeal; material, working-stock, implements, plant. (*Rail.*) *Matériel roulant*, rolling
stock; *matériel scolaire*, school furniture.
matériellement, *adv.* Materially; positively; sensually.

maternel [mater'nɛl], *a.* (*fem.* **maternelle**)
Maternal, motherly. *École maternelle* or
(*fam.*) *la maternelle*, infant school. *Langue
maternelle*, mother *or* native tongue; *parents
maternels*, relations on the mother's side.
maternellement, *adv.* Maternally.

maternité, *n.f.* Maternity; lying-in hospital.

mathématicien [matemati'sjɛ̃], *n.m.* (*fem.*
-ienne) Mathematician.

mathématique [matema'tik], *a.* Mathematical.—*n.f.* (*usu. in pl.*) Mathematics. *Étudier
les mathématiques*, to study mathematics;
mathématiques appliquées or *pures*, applied *or*
pure mathematics. *Classe de Mathématiques
Élémentaires*, one of the classes preparing for
the second part of *Baccalauréat*. **mathématiquement**, *adv.* Mathematically.

Mathilde [ma'tild], *f.* Mathilda.

mathurin [maty'rɛ̃], *n.m.* (*fam.*) Jack Tar.

matière [ma'tjɛːr], *n.f.* Matter; material;
subject-matter, theme, topic, subject; cause,
motive, grounds; contents; faeces, stools.
Donner matière à parler, to give occasion for
talking; *en matière de*, in matters of; *entrée en
matière*, introduction (of speech, narrative,
etc.); *entrer en matière*, to broach the matter;
il y a là matière à discussion, that gives good
ground for discussion; *matière première*, raw
material; *matières d'or et d'argent*, bullion;
s'élever au-dessus de la matière, to soar above
material things; *table des matières*, table of
contents.

matin [ma'tɛ̃], *n.m.* Morning, forenoon; prime,
dawn. *Au petit matin*, in the small hours; *de
bon* or *de grand matin*, early in the morning;
demain matin, tomorrow morning; *se lever
de grand matin*, to rise very early; *un beau
matin*, one fine morning; *un de ces quatre
matins*, one of these fine days; *onze heures du
matin*, 11 a.m.—*adv.* Early, early in the
morning. *De grand* or *de bon matin*, very
early.

mâtin [mɑ'tɛ̃], *n.m.* Mastiff; big mongrel
dog; (*fam.*) *le mâtin, la mâtine* (to a boy or a
girl), you little rascal!—*int. Mâtin!* by Jove!

matinal [mati'nal], *a.* (*fem.* **matinale**, *pl.*
matinaux) Morning, early; early-rising.
matinalement, *adv.* Early.

matiné [mati'ne], *a.* (*fem.* **-ée**) Mongrel,
cross-bred.

mâtineau [mɑti'no], *n.m.* (*pl.* **mâtineaux**).
Mastiff-pup.

matinée [mati'ne], *n.f.* Morning, forenoon;
afternoon performance, matinée; woman's
morning dress. *Faire la grasse matinée*, to
lie in bed late in the morning.

mâtiner [mɑti'ne], *v.t.* To serve, to cover (a
bitch of a different breed); (*colloq.*) to abuse,
to disparage, to snub.

matines [ma'tin], *n.f. pl.* Matins. **matineux**,
a. (*fem.* **-euse**) Rising early.

matinière [mati'njɛːr], *a.f.*, used only in *l'étoile matinière*,
the Morning-Star.

matir [ma'tiːr], *v.t.* [MATER (2)].

matois [ma'twa], *a.* (*fem.* **matoise**) Cunning,
artful, sly, deep.—*n.* Cunning person, sly dog.
C'est un fin matois, he's a sly one. **matoise-
ment**, *adv.* Cunningly, slyly. **matoiserie**,
n.f. Cunning; wile, dodge.

matou [ma'tu], *n.m.* Tom-cat; (*fam.*) curmudgeon.

matraque [ma'trak], *n.f.* Arab bludgeon, big,
knotted stick; shillelagh; (rubber) life-
preserver, truncheon.

matraquer, *v.t.* To bludgeon.

matras [ma'trɑ], *n.m. inv.* Matrass.

matriarcal [matriar'kal], *a.* (*fem.* **matriar-
cale**, *pl.* **matriarcaux**) Matriarchal.

matriarcat, *n.m.* Matriarchy.

matricaire [matri'kɛːr], *n.f.* (*Bot.*) *Matricaire
camomille*, wild camomile, feverfew.

matrice [ma'tris], *n.f.* Womb, matrix; standard weight or measure; original register; (*Print.*) type mould; mother record.—*a.f.* *Couleurs matrices*, primary colours; *Église matrice*, Mother Church.

matricide [matri'sid], *a.* Matricidal.—*n.* Matricide (person).—*n.m.* Matricide (crime).

matriculaire [matriky'lɛːr], *a.* and *n.* Matriculate.

matricule [matri'kyl], *n.f.* Register, roll; matriculation, certificate of matriculation.— *a. Registre matricule*, matriculation register. —*n.m.* Regimental number (of a soldier); number (of a rifle etc.). **matriculer**, *v.t.* To enter on the register; to mark a soldier's kit with his regimental number.

matrimonial [matrimɔ'njal], *a.* (*fem.* **matrimoniale**, *pl.* **matrimoniaux**) Matrimonial.

matrone [ma'tron], *n.f.* Matron, dame; midwife.

matte [mat], *n.f.* (*Metal.*) Matte.

Matthieu [ma'tjø], *m.* Matthew.

matthiole [ma'tjɔl], *n.f.* (*Bot.*) Mathiola, stock.

maturatif [matyra'tif], *n.m.* and *a.* (*fem.* -**ive**) Maturative.

maturation, *n.f.* Maturation.

mâture [mɑ'tyːr], *n.f.* Masting, masts and spars; mast-store, wood for masts, mast-yard.

maturité [matyri'te], *n.f.* Maturity, ripeness, mellowness; completion; circumspection, consideration befitting mature age. *Avec maturité*, maturely, with consideration; *manque de maturité*, immaturity.

matutinal [matyti'nal], *a.* (*fem.* **matutinale**, *pl.* **matutinaux**) Matutinal.

maubèche [mo'bɛʃ], *n.f.*, or *bécasseau maubèche*, wood sandpiper. *Grande maubèche*, knot; *petite maubèche*, dunlin.

maudire [mo'diːr], *v.t. irr.* (*pres.p.* **maudissant**, *p.p.* **maudit**; *conjug. like* DIRE, *except in pl. indic. pres. and imper.*) To curse, to execrate; to hate, to rue, to reprove, to censure. **maudissable**, *a.* Execrable, detestable. **maudit**, *a.* (*fem.* **maudite**) Cursed, accursed; miserable, wretched. *C'est un temps maudit*, it is wretched weather; *maudit soit le maladroit!* confound the clumsy fool!—*n.m. Le Maudit*, the Evil One; *les maudits*, the damned.

maugère [mo'ʒɛr], *n.f.* (*Naut.*) (Pump-) leather.

maugréer [mogre'e], *v.i.* To fret and fume, to curse and swear.

maure etc. [MORE].

mauresque [mɔ'rɛsk] or **moresque**, *a.* Moresque.—*n.f.* Loose Oriental trousers; moresque tracery.

Maurice [mɔ'ris], *m.* Maurice. *L'île Maurice*, Mauritius.

Mauritanie [mɔrita'ni], **la**, *f.* Mauritania.

mausolée [mozɔ'le], *n.m.* Mausoleum.

maussade [mo'sad], *a.* Sulky, sullen, cross; disagreeable, unpleasant, dull, tedious. **maussadement**, *adv.* Disagreeably, sullenly, peevishly. **maussaderie**, *n.f.* Sullenness, sulkiness.

mauvais [mɔ've], *a.* (*fem.* **mauvaise**) Bad, ill, evil; wicked, evil-minded; naughty, mischievous, hurtful, injurious; wrong, amiss, foul; unpleasant; sinister, unpropitious, contrary, adverse; wretched, sorry, poor; nasty;

(*Print.*) battered (of letters). *Avoir mauvaise mine*, to look ill; *c'est une mauvaise langue* [see LANGUE]; *les temps sont mauvais*, these are bad times; *mauvaise action*, bad deed; *mauvaise haleine*, foul breath; *mauvaise mer*, rough sea; *mauvaise nouvelle*, bad news; *mauvais sujet*, worthless fellow, rake, libertine; *mauvaise tête*, hot-headed person; *pas mauvais*, not bad, tolerable; *plus mauvais*, worse; *le plus mauvais*, the worst; *prendre quelque chose en mauvaise part*, to take a thing in bad part; *tenir quelque chose par le mauvais bout*, to hold something by the wrong end.—*n.m.* Bad. *Il faut prendre le bon et le mauvais*, one must take the good with the bad.—*adv.* Badly, wrong, amiss, ill. *Il fait mauvais*, it is bad weather; *sentir mauvais*, to have a bad smell; *trouver mauvais que*, to take it amiss that.

mauve (1) [moːv], *n.f.* (*Bot.*) Mallow.—*a.* Mauve.

mauve (2) [moːv], *n.f.* (*pop.*) Sea-gull, seamew.

mauviette [mo'vjet], *n.f.* Lark (when fat in season); (*fam.*) lath, poor stick (thin person). *Manger comme une mauviette*, to eat like a sparrow. (*fam.*) *C'est une mauviette*, he is a softy.

mauvis [mo'vi], *n.m.* Redwing. [*See* GRIVE.]

maxillaire [maksi'lɛːr], *a.* Pertaining to the jaw, maxillary.—*n.m.* Jaw-bone, maxilla, maxillary. *Maxillaire supérieur*, upper jaw.

maxime [mak'sim], *n.f.* Maxim. *Tenir* or *avoir pour maxime de*, to hold it as a maxim to.

maximer, *v.t.* To make a maxim of; to generalize a motive; *to fix the maximum price of.

maximum [maksi'mɔm], *n.m.* (*pl.* **maxima**, *also pl.* **maximums**) Maximum, highest point, price, etc.; the most, the height, the acme.—*a.* (*fem.* **maxima**) Maximum, top, highest.

Mayence [ma'jãːs], *f.* Mainz.

mayonnaise [majɔ'nɛːz], *n.f.* Mayonnaise.

***mazagran** [maza'grã], *n.m.* Cold coffee drunk with water in a glass; glass of coffee.

mazette [mɑ'zet], *n.f.* Worn-out horse; (*fig.*) duffer, rabbit (at games).—*int.* You don't say so!

mazout [ma'ʒut], *n.m.* Residue of refined petrol; oil fuel (for engines, stoves, etc.).

mazurka [mazyr'ka], *n.f.* Mazurka.

me [mə], *pron. pers.* Me; to me. *Me voici*, here I am; *vous me parlez*, you are speaking to me.

mea-culpa [meakyl'pa], *n.m. inv.* (Latin words = my sin). *Dire* or *faire son mea-culpa*, to make confession of one's sins.

méandre [me'ãːdr], *n.m.* Meander, winding.

méat [me'a], *n.m.* (*Anat.*) Meatus, duct, passage.

mec [mɛk], *n.m.* (*slang*) Pimp; bloke.

mécanicien [mekani'sjɛ̃], *n.m.* Mechanic; engine-man, engine-driver, (*Am.*) engineer. *Ingénieur mécanicien*, mechanical engineer; *mécanicien dentiste*, dental mechanic. **mécanicienne**, *n.f.* Machinist; sewing-girl.

mécanique [meka'nik], *a.* Mechanical; machine-made.—*n.f.* Mechanics; mechanism, machinery; machine, piece of machinery.

mécaniquement, *adv.* Mechanically.

[477]

mécanisation, *n.f.* Mechanization.
mécaniser, *v.t.* To make mechanical, to make as a machine; (*Mil.*) to mechanize; (*colloq.*) to tease, to plague.
mécanisme, *n.m.* Mechanism, machinery; technique; clock-work. *Mécanisme de renversement,* reversing gear; *mécanisme de répétition,* repeating apparatus (of a rifle).
mécano [meka′no], *n.m.* (*pop.*) A mechanic.
mécanographe [mekanɔ′graf], *n.* Multicopier.
mécanographie, *n.f.* Multicopying.
mécanothérapie [mekanɔtera′pi], *n.f.* Mechanotherapy.
mécénat [mese′na], *n.m.* Patronage (of arts and letters).
mécène [me′sɛn], *n.m.* Maecenas; patron of letters, arts, sports.
méchamment [meʃa′mɑ̃], *adv.* Wickedly; spitefully, maliciously, ill-naturedly; mischievously.
méchanceté [meʃɑ̃s′te], *n.f.* Wickedness; spitefulness; mischievousness; naughtiness; ill-nature; unkind thing, ill-natured remark, etc.
méchant [me′ʃɑ̃], *a.* (*fem.* **méchante**) Wicked, evil, bad; ill-natured, spiteful, mischievous, malicious; wayward, naughty; wretched, worthless; sorry, paltry; vicious (of a horse); nasty; ugly, ill-looking. *Attention, chien méchant!* beware of the dog; *être de méchante humeur,* to be ill-tempered; *méchant homme,* wicked man; *un méchant poète,* a bad poet; (*C*) *un méchant temps,* bad weather.—*n.* Wicked person, evil-doer, reprobate; naughty child. *Faire le méchant,* to be fractious (of a child).—*n.m. pl. Les méchants,* the wicked.
mèche (1) [mɛ:ʃ], *n.f.* Wick (of a lamp, candle, etc.); linstock, fuse; cracker (of whip); bit, drill, centre-bit; worm (of corkscrews, wimbles, etc.); tent (of surgeon). *Mèche anglaise,* centre-bit; *mèche de cheveux,* lock of hair; *mèche de rabot,* plane-iron. *Découvrir* or *éventer la mèche,* (*Mil.*) to discover the enemy's mine by means of a countermine; (*fig.*) to find out the secret of a plot; (*fam.*) *être de mèche avec,* to be party to; *vendre la mèche,* to blab, to blow the gaff.
mèche (2) [mɛ:ʃ], *n.f.* (*pop.*) *Il n'y a pas mèche,* it's no go, it can't be done.
mécher [me′ʃe], *v.t.* To fumigate with brimstone, to sulphur (a cask etc.).
mécompte [me′kɔ̃t], *n.m.* Miscalculation; mistake, error; disappointment, disillusionment. **mécompter,** *v.i.* To strike wrong (of clocks).
méconnaissable [mekɔnɛ′sabl], *a.* Not to be recognized, unrecognizable.
méconnaissance, *n.f.* Misappreciation, misreading; ungratefulness, ingratitude.
méconnaître [mekɔ′nɛ:tr], *v.t. irr.* (*pres.p.* **méconnaissant,** *p.p.* **méconnu;** *conjug. like* CONNAÎTRE) Not to recognize; to disown; to disregard, to slight, to ignore, to misappreciate, to misjudge. **se méconnaître,** *v.r.* To forget oneself; to forget what one has been.
méconnu, *a.* (*fem.* **méconnue**) Unrecognized, unacknowledged; ignored, disowned, disregarded.
mécontent [mekɔ̃′tɑ̃], *a.* (*fem.* **mécontente**) Displeased, dissatisfied, discontented. *Il est*

mécontent de vous, he is displeased with you; *mécontent de tout,* discontented with everything.—*n.* Dissatisfied person, malcontent.
mécontentement, *n.m.* Dissatisfaction, discontent. *Donner du mécontentement à,* to displease. **mécontenter,** *v.t.* To discontent, to dissatisfy, to displease.
Mecque [mek], **la,** *f.* Mecca.
mécréance [mekre′ɑ̃:s], *n.f.* Disbelief; infidelity, irreligion. **mécréant,** *n.m.* (*fem.* -**ante**) Unbeliever, infidel.
médaille [me′da:j], *n.f.* Medal; (*Arch.*) medallion. *Toute médaille a son revers,* everything has its bright and its dark side; *le revers de la médaille,* the reverse of the medal, (*fig.*) the dark side of the picture; *médaille d'honneur,* prize-medal.
médaillé, *a.* (*fem.* **médaillée**) With a medal as a reward; having a badge (of hawker, porter, etc.).—*n.* Holder of a medal.
médailler [meda:′je], *v.t.* To award a medal to.
médailleur, *n.m.* Die-sinker.
médaillier, *n.m.* Cabinet of medals. **médailliste,** *n.* Collector of medals.
médaillon, *n.m.* Medallion; locket.
médecin [med′sɛ̃], *n.m.* Physician, doctor, medical man. *Faire venir le médecin,* to send for the doctor; *femme médecin,* lady doctor; *il est abandonné des médecins,* the doctors have given him up; *le temps est un grand médecin,* time cures all ills or time is the great healer; *médecin consultant,* consultant; *médecin légiste,* medical expert; *médecin traitant,* doctor in charge.
médecine, *n.f.* Medicine (medical profession); medicine (physic). *Docteur en médecine,* doctor of medicine; *école de médecine,* medical school; *étudiant en médecine,* medical student; *médecine légale,* forensic medicine. (*fig.*) *Avaler la médecine,* to take one's medicine or punishment.
Médée [me′de], *f.* Medea.
médial [me′djal], *a.* (*fem.* **médiale,** *pl.* **médiaux**) (*Gram.*) Medial.
médian, *a.* (*fem.* **médiane**) (*Anat., Geom.*) Median, middle.—*n.f.* Median.
*médianoche [medja′nɔʃ], *n.m.* Meat supper after midnight.
médiante [me′djɑ̃:t], *n.f.* (*Mus.*) Mediant; the note mi.
médiastin [medjas′tɛ̃], *n.m.* (*Anat.*) Mediastinum.
médiat [me′dja], *a.* (*fem.* **médiate**) Mediate. **médiateur,** *n.m.* (*fem.* **médiatrice**) Mediator.—*a.* Mediatory. **médiation,** *n.f.* Mediation.
médiatisation [medjatizɑ′sjɔ̃], *n.f.* Mediatization. **médiatiser,** *v.t.* To mediatize.
médiator [medja′tɔ:r], *n.m.* (*Mus.*) Plectrum.
médical [medi′kal], *a.* (*fem.* -**ale,** *pl.* -**aux**) Medical. *Matière médicale,* materia medica. **médicalement,** *adv.* Medically.
médicament, *n.m.* Medicament, medicine. **médicamentaire,** *a.* Medicamental. **médicamentation** [MÉDICATION]. **médicamenter,** *v.t.* To medicate; to physic, to doctor. **médicamenteux,** *a.* (*fem.* -**euse**) Medicamental, medicinal.
médicastre, *n.m.* Medicaster. **médicateur,** *a.* (*fem.* **médicatrice**) Medicative. **médication,** *n.f.* Medication.

médicinal, *a.* (*fem.* **médicinale**, *pl.* **médicinaux**) Medicinal.
Médicis [medi′si:s], *m.* Medici.
médico-légal, *a.* (*pl.* **-aux**) Medico-legal.
médiéval [medje′val], *a.* (*fem.* **médiévale**, *pl.* **médiévaux**) Medieval.
médiéviste, *n.* Medievalist.
médiocre [me′djɔkr], *a.* Mediocre, middling; moderate, passable, indifferent.—*n.m.* Mediocrity. **médiocrement**, *adv.* Middlingly, indifferently, tolerably, moderately; poorly; hardly, barely.
médiocrité, *n.f.* Mediocrity; moderate fortune; indifferent person, performance, etc.
médique [me′dik], *a.* Pertaining to the Medes.
médire [me′di:r], *v.i. irr.* (*pres.p.* **médisant**, *p.p.* **médit**; *conjug. like* DIRE, *except in 2nd pl. indic. and imper.* **médisez**) To slander, to speak ill of, to traduce (*de*).
médisance, *n.f.* Slander, scandal, backbiting; piece of slander. *L'École de la Médisance*, the School for Scandal. **médisant**, *a.* (*fem.* **-ante**) Slanderous, scandalous.—*n.* Slanderer, scandal-monger. *Il ne faut pas croire les médisants*, slanderers are not to be believed.
méditatif [medita′tif], *a.* (*fem.* **méditative**) Meditative, contemplative, pensive.
méditation, *n.f.* Meditation, musing, reverie.
méditer [medi′te], *v.t.* To meditate, to think over, to consider; to contemplate, to plan, to project. *Méditer la ruine de quelqu'un*, to plot someone's ruin.—*v.i.* To meditate, to muse. *Passer sa vie à méditer*, to spend one's life in meditation.
méditerrané [meditɛra′ne], *a.* (*fem.* **-ée**) *La* (*Mer*) *Méditerranée*, the Mediterranean (Sea).
méditerranéen, *a.* and *n.* (*fem.* **-éenne**) Pertaining to the Mediterranean.
médium [me′djɔm], *n.m.* (*pl.* **médiums**) Medium.
médius [me′djys], *n.m.* Middle finger.
médoc [me′dɔk], *n.m.*, or *Vin de Médoc*. Médoc (claret).
médullaire [medy′lɛ:r], *a.* Medullary, medullar. **médulle**, *n.f.* (*Bot.*) Medulla, pith.
méduse [me′dy:z], *n.f.* Medusa, jelly-fish.
méduser, *v.t.* To stupefy, to paralyse.
meeting [mi′tiŋ], *n.m.* (*Polit., spt.*) Meeting. *Meeting d'aviation*, air display.
méfaire [me′fɛ:r], *v.i. irr.* (*p.p.* **méfait**; *conjug. like* FAIRE) To do evil, to do wrong.
méfait, *n.m.* Misdeed, crime.
méfiance [me′fjɑ̃:s], *n.f.* Mistrust, distrust, suspicion. **méfiant**, *a.* (*fem.* **méfiante**) Mistrustful, distrustful, suspicious; cautious. **se méfier**, *v.r.* (*conjugated like* PRIER) To mistrust, to distrust, to be suspicious (*de*).
mégadyne [mega′din], *n.f.* (*Mech.*) Megadyne.
mégagraphe [mega′graf], *n.m.* Enlarging screen.
mégajoule [mega′ʒul], *n.m.* (*Elec.*) A million joules.
mégalithe [mega′lit], *n.m.* Megalith. **mégalithique**, *a.* Megalithic.
mégalocéphale, *a.* and *n.* Megalocephalous. **mégalocéphalie**, *n.f.* Megalocephaly.
mégalomane, *a.* and *n.* Megalomaniac. **mégalomanie**, *n.f.* Megalomania.
mégalosaure, *n.m.* Megalosaurus.
mégaphone, *n.m.* Megaphone.

mégapode, *n.m.* Megapod, mound-bird.
mégarde [me′gard], *n.f.* Inadvertence. *Par mégarde*,. inadvertently unawares.
mégathérium [megate′rjɔm], *n.m.* (*pl.* **mégathériums**) Megatherium.
mégère [me′ʒɛːr], *n.f.* Shrew, vixen, termagant. *La mégère apprivoisée*, The Taming of the Shrew.
mégie [me′ʒi], *n.f.* Tawing, leather-dressing.
mégir or **mégisser**, *v.t.* To taw.
mégis, *n.m.* Bath for dressing skins.—*a. inv.* Tawed. **mégisserie**, *n.f.* Tawing, leather-dressing. **mégissier**, *n.m.* Tawer, leather-dresser.
mégot [me′go], *n.m.* (*pop.*) Cigar-stump, cigarette-end, fag-end. **mégotier**, *n.m.* Collector of fag-ends (in streets).
méhalla [mea′la], *n.f.* (*Arab.*) Troop in march, column.
méhari [mea′ri], *n.m.* (*pl.* **méhara** or **méharis**) (*Arab.*) Fast dromedary. **méhariste**, *n.m.* Trooper mounted on a *méhari*.
meilleur [mɛ′jœːr], *a.* (*fem.* **meilleure**) Better; preferable. *Le meilleur*, the best. *Meilleur marché*, cheaper; *de meilleure heure*, earlier.—*n.m.* Best, the cream. *Le meilleur de l'affaire*, the cream of the matter; *le meilleur du conte* or *de l'histoire*, the best of the story; *le meilleur n'en vaut rien*, bad's the best.
meistre or **mestre** [mɛstr], *n.m.* Mast, main-mast (of ships with lateen sails).
méjuger [meʒy′ʒe], *v.t.* (*conjugated like* JUGER) To misjudge.
mélampyre [melɑ̃′piːr], *n.m.* (*Bot.*) Cow-wheat.
mélancolie [melɑ̃kɔ′li], *n.f.* Melancholy, sadness, gloom, dejection. *Chasser la mélancolie*, to drive away the spleen; *il n'engendre point la mélancolie*, he is a merry fellow. **mélancolique**, *a.* Melancholy;˙dismal, gloomy, stern. *Séjour mélancolique*, dismal abode. **mélancoliquement**, *adv.* Gloomily.
mélange [me′lɑ̃:ʒ], *n.m.* Mixture, mingling; blending (of tea); medley, jumble; crossing (of breeds); alloy; mash (for brewing); (*pl.*) miscellaneous works, miscellanea. *Mélange confus*, jumble; *sans mélange*, unmixed, unblended, (*fig.*) pure, unalloyed.
mélanger, *v.t.* To mix, to mingle, to blend; to cross, to intermix. **se mélanger**, *v.r.* To mix, to mingle, to blend.
mélangeur, *n.m.* (*fem.* **mélangeuse**) Mixer.
mélanique [mela′nik], *a.* Melanic. **mélanisme**, *n.m.* Melanism.
mélanite, *n.f.* Melanite.
mélanose, *n.f.* Melanosis.
mélasse [me′las], *n.f.* Molasses, treacle. (*slang*) *Être dans la mélasse*, to be in the soup; to be hard up.
melchior [MAILLECHORT].
mêlé [mɛ′le], *a.* (*fem.* **mêlée** (1)) Mixed; miscellaneous; mixed (of rhymes) *De sang mêlé*, mixed (race); *un sang mêlé*, a half-caste.
méléagride [FRITILLAIRE].
mêlé-cass(e) [mɛle′kas], *n.m.* (*Mil. slang*) short for **mêlé-cassis**, a cheap mixture of brandy or vermouth and black-currant liqueur.
mêlée (2) [mɛ′le], *n.f.* Mêlée, conflict, fray; scramble, scuffle, free-fight; (*Rugby*) scrimmage, scrum. *Mêlée ouverte*, loose scrum; *mêlée fermée*, tight scrum.

mêler [mɛ'le], *v.t.* To mingle, to mix, to mix up; to intermingle, to blend; to jumble; to entangle, to implicate, to involve; to shuffle (cards). *Il est mêlé dans une mauvaise affaire*, he is mixed up in a bad business; *mêler de l'eau avec du vin*, to mingle water with wine; *mêler les fils* or *un écheveau*, to entangle the threads *or* a skein. **se mêler**, *v.r.* To mingle, to blend, to intermingle, to trouble oneself (*de*); to interfere (*de*); to have a hand in; to get entangled, to get mixed up (*dans*). *Le diable s'en mêle*, the devil's in the thing; *mêlez-vous de vos affaires*, mind your own business; *se mêler à la foule*, to mingle with the crowd; *se mêler de politique*, to dabble in politics.

mélèze [me'lɛ:z], *n.m.* Larch. *Mélèze d'Amérique*, tamarack.

mélianthe [me'ljɑ̃:t], *n.m.* Melianthus.

mélie [me'li], *n.f.* Bead-tree.

mélilot [meli'lo], *n.m.* Melilot; sweet-clover.

méli-mélo [melime'lo], *n.m.* (*pl.* **mélis-mélos**) (*colloq.*) Medley, jumble, hotch-potch.

mélinet [meli'nɛ], *n.m.* Honeywort.

mélinite [meli'nit], *n.f.* Melinite.

mélique [me'lik], *a.* Melic (poetry).—*n.f.* Melic-grass.

mélisse [me'lis], *n.f.* Melissa. *Eau de mélisse*, melissa cordial.

mellifère [mɛli'fɛ:r], *a.* Melliferous. **mellification**, *n.f.* Mellification. **mellifique**, *a.* Mellific. **mellifiu**, *a.* (*fem.* **melliflue**) Mellifluous, honeyed, sweet. **mellite**, *n.m.* Medicament prepared with honey.

mélo [me'lo], *n.m.* (*fam.*) = MÉLODRAME.

mélodie [melɔ'di], *n.f.* Melody; melodiousness.

mélodieusement, *adv.* Tunefully. **mélodieux**, *a.* (*fem.* **mélodieuse**) Melodious, musical, tuneful. **mélodique**, *a.* Melodic.

mélodiste, *n.* Melodist.

mélodramatique [melɔdrama'tik], *a.* Melodramatic. **mélodramatiser**, *v.t.* To melodramatize.

mélodrame, *n.m.* Melodrama.

mélomane [melɔ'man], *a.* and *n.* Music-lover. **mélomanie**, *n.f.* Rage for music.

melon [mə'lɔ̃], *n.m.* Melon; bowler (hat); freshman (at Saint-Cyr military school). *Melon d'eau*, water-melon.

mélongène [melɔ̃'ʒɛ:n] or **mélongine**, *n.f.* Aubergine, egg-plant.

melonnière [məlɔ'njɛ:r], *n.f.* Melon-bed.

mélopée [melɔ'pe], *n.f.* Recitative chant, recitative, monotonous chant (of poetry etc.).

mélophobe [melɔ'fɔb], *a.* and *n.* (Person) music-hating.

mélusine [mely'zin], *n.f.* Long-haired felt.

***mémarchure** [memar'ʃy:r], *n.f.* Sprain (in a horse's leg).

membrane [mɑ̃'bran], *n.f.* Membrane; web (of duck's foot etc.). **membraneux**, *a.* (*fem.* **membraneuse**) Membranous.

membre [mɑ̃:br], *n.m.* Limb; member; (*Naut.*) rib-timber.

membré, *a.* (*fem.* **membrée**) *Bien membré*, having well-made limbs.

membru, *a.* (*fem.* **membrue**) Stout-limbed. **membrure**, *n.f.* Limbs, frame (of a person etc.); ribs, timbers (of a ship).

même [mɛ:m], *a.* Same; self, self-same, very same; self, himself, herself, itself. *Cela revient au même*, it comes to the same thing; *c'est la bonté même*, she is goodness itself; *c'est la même chose*, it is all one; *en même temps*, at the same time; *eux-mêmes*, themselves; *la chose même*, the thing itself; *la même chose*, the same thing; *moi-même*, myself; *une seule et même origine*, one and the same origin.—*adv.* Even, also. *À même de*, in a position to, able to; *boire à même*, to drink out of (the bottle); *de même*, the same, the same way, likewise; *de même que*, in the same way as, just as, as well as; *faites de même*, do the same; *il lui a tout donné, même ses habits*, he has given him everything even to his clothes; *il vous a mis à même de le faire*, he has enabled you to do it; *même les plus sages le font*, even the wisest do it; *quand même il me l'aurait dit*, even though he had told me so; *tout de même*, all the same, in the same manner. ***même-ment**, *adv.* The same, likewise.

mémento [memɛ̃'to], *n.m.* Memento; agenda; memorandum-book, epitome. **mémento-mori**, *n.m. inv.* Memento mori (skull).

mémère [me'mɛ:r], *n.f.* (*childish, pop.*) Grandmother, granny; (*sometimes*) mammy.

mémoire (1) [me'mwa:r], *n.f.* Memory; recollection, remembrance; commemoration; fame. *À la mémoire de*, in memory of; *avoir la mémoire courte*, to be hare-brained; *avoir des absences de mémoire*, to have slips of memory; *conserver la mémoire de*, to remember; *de mémoire*, from memory; *de mémoire d'homme*, within living memory; *en mémoire de*, in memory of; *mémoire fidèle*, retentive memory; *pour mémoire*, as a reminder; *rafraîchir la mémoire de*, to refresh the memory of; *réhabiliter la mémoire d'un défunt*, to restore the good name of a dead person; *se remettre en mémoire*, to refresh one's memory; *si j'ai bonne mémoire*, if I remember rightly.

mémoire (2) [me'mwa:r], *n.m.* Memorandum, bill, statement of account, report; (*Sci.* or *Lit.*) treatise, memoir; memorial; (*pl.*) memoirs. *Dresser un mémoire*, to draw up a statement; *mémoire acquitté*, bill receipted; *mémoire d'apothicaire*, exorbitant bill.

mémorable [memɔ'rabl], *a.* Memorable, noteworthy. **mémorablement**, *adv.* Memorably.

mémorandum, *n.m.* Memorandum; note-book. (*Mil.*) *Mémorandum de combat*, operation orders.

***mémoratif**, *a.* (*fem.* **-ive**) Recollecting.

mémorial [memɔ'rjal], *n.m.* (*pl.* **mémoriaux**) Memorial; memoirs; (*Comm.*) waste-book. *Le mémorial diplomatique*, the diplomatic gazette. **mémorialiste**, *n.* Memorialist.

mémorisation [memɔriza'sjɔ̃], *n.f.* Memorizing.

menaçant [məna'sɑ̃], *a.* (*fem.* **menaçante**) Menacing, threatening.

menace [mə'nas], *n.f.* Menace, threat. *Menace en l'air*, empty threat; *paroles de menace*, threatening words. **menacer**, *v.t.* To threaten, to menace; to forebode, to portend; to impend. *L'orage menace*, there is thunder about; *menacer du poing*, to shake one's fist at; *menacer ruine* or *menacer de tomber*, to totter, to be on the point of ruin.

ménade [me'nad], *n.f.* Bacchante, maenad.

ménage [me'na:ʒ], *n.m.* Housekeeping, housewifery; household, family, married couple; set of furniture, household equipment; husbandry, economy, thrift. *Dépenses de ménage,* household expenses; *entrer* or *se mettre en ménage,* to set up house; *faire bon ménage,* to live happily together; *faire le ménage,* to do the house or rooms; *faire des ménages,* to go out charring; *femme de ménage,* charwoman; *jeune ménage,* young couple; *ménage à trois,* triangle; *ménage de poupée,* set of doll's furniture; *pain de ménage,* household bread.

ménagement [menaʒ'mã], *n.m.* Regard, circumspection, caution, discretion. *Parler sans ménagements,* to be outspoken, to speak bluntly.

ménager (1) [mena'ʒe], *v.t.* To husband, to be sparing of, to save; to take care of, to be careful of, to treat with caution, to treat kindly, to treat with respect, to humour; to reserve; to procure; to contrive, to manage; to arrange, to prepare, to bring about. *Ménager quelqu'un,* to treat someone tactfully; *ménager ses forces,* to spare one's strength; *ménager ses ressources,* to husband one's resources; *ménager une agréable surprise à,* to prepare a pleasant surprise for; *ménager une étoffe,* to make the most of a piece of material; *ménager un escalier dans un bâtiment,* to contrive a staircase in a house; *pour ménager notre faiblesse,* out of compassion for our weakness; *qui veut voyager loin ménage sa monture,* he who wishes to live long avoids excess. **se ménager,** *v.r.* To take care of oneself; to spare oneself.

ménager (2) [mena'ʒe], *a.* (*fem.* **ménagère**) Thrifty, sparing, frugal; pertaining to the house. *Être ménager de son argent,* to spend one's money sparingly. *Appareil ménager,* domestic appliance; *enseignement ménager,* domestic science; *travaux ménagers,* housework.—*n.f.* Housewife, housekeeper; cruet-stand; canteen.

ménagerie [menaʒ'ri], *n.f.* Menagerie.

mendélien [mãde'ljɛ̃], *a.* (*fem.* **mendélienne**) Mendelian.

mendiant [mã'djã], *n.m.* (*fem.* **mendiante**) Beggar, mendicant. *Les quatre mendiants,* the four orders of mendicant friars. (*fig.*) Raisins, figs, almonds, and nuts (at dessert).

mendicité [mãdisi'te], *n.f.* Begging, mendicity. *La mendicité est interdite,* no begging allowed.

mendier [mã'dje], *v.t.* To beg for; to solicit, to implore. *Il mendie son pain,* he begs his bread; *mendier sa vie,* to live by begging.—*v.i.* To beg.

mendigot [mãdi'go], *n.m.* (*pop.*) Beggar.

meneau [mə'no], *n.m.* (*pl.* **meneaux**) (*Arch.*) *Meneau horizontal,* transom; *meneau vertical,* mullion.

menée [mə'ne], *n.f.* (*Hunt.*) Track of a stag; (*fig. in pl.*) underhand dealings, plots, schemings.

Ménélas [mene'lɑ:s], *m.* Menelaus.

mener [mə'ne], *v.t.* To guide, to conduct, to lead; to drive (a carriage); to steer (a boat etc.); to bring, to convey, to carry, to take; to lead (a dance etc.); to manage, to administer; to carry on. *Mener à bien* or *mener à bonne fin,* to carry out; *mener bien sa barque,* to manage one's affairs well; *mener de front,* to conduct (several things) simultaneously;

mener grand train, to make a great show; *mener les bêtes aux champs,* to drive the cattle to the fields; *mener paître les vaches,* to drive cows to pasture; *mener quelqu'un en prison,* to conduct someone to gaol; *mener une vie déréglée,* to lead an irregular life; *mener quelqu'un par le bout du nez* [see NEZ].—*v.i.* To lead, to conduct, to go. *Ce chemin mène à la ville,* this road leads to the town; *cela ne mène à rien,* that leads to nothing; (*fam.*) *il n'en mène pas large,* he is in a tight corner.

ménestrel [menɛs'trɛl], *n.m.* Minstrel.

ménétrier [menetri'e], *n.m.* Fiddler.

meneur [mə'nœ:r], *n.m.* (*fem.* **meneuse**) Driver, leader; agitator, ringleader.

menhir [mɛ'ni:r], *n.m.* (*Archaeol.*) Menhir.

méniane [me'njan], *n.f.* Veranda, balcony.

ménil, mesnil [me'ni], *n.m.* Farm-house; hamlet.

menin (1) [mə'nɛ̃], *n.m.* (*Fr. Hist.*) Young nobleman attached to the person of the Dauphin.

menin (2) [mə'nɛ̃], *n.m.* (*fem.* **menine**) (*Sp. Hist.*) Young person of noble rank attached to a member of the royal family.

méninge [me'nɛ̃:ʒ], *n.f.* (*Anat.*) Meninx. (*fam.*) *Se creuser les méninges,* to rack one's brains. **méningite,** *n.f.* Meningitis.

ménisque [me'nisk], *n.m.* (*Opt., Anat.*) Meniscus.

ménologe [menɔ'lɔ:ʒ], *n.m.* Menology.

ménopause [menɔ'po:z], *n.f.* Menopause.

menotte [mə'nɔt], *n.f.* (*colloq.*) Little hand (of a child); (*pl.*) handcuffs, manacles. *Mettre les menottes à,* to handcuff.

menotter [mənɔ'te], *v.t.* To handcuff.

mense [mã:s], *n.f.* Income, revenue (of abbeys etc.).

mensole [mã'sɔl], *n.f.* Keystone.

mensonge [mã'sɔ̃:ʒ], *n.m.* Lie, falsehood, untruth, fib, story; (*fig.*) error, illusion, vanity. *Débiter des mensonges,* to tell lies.

mensonger, *a.* (*fem.* **-ère**) Lying, untrue, deceitful; false, counterfeit, illusory. **mensongèrement,** *adv.* Falsely.

menstruation [mãstrɥa'sjɔ̃], *n.f.* Menstruation. **menstruel,** *a.* (*fem.* **-elle**) Menstrual. **menstrues,** *n.f. pl.* Menstrua, periods, menses, catamenia; (*fam.*) monthlies.

mensualité [mãsɥali'te], *n.f.* Monthly remittance. *Payable par mensualités,* to be paid by monthly instalments.

mensuel [mã'sɥɛl], *a.* (*fem.* **-uelle**) Monthly. **mensuellement,** *adv.* Monthly.

mensurabilité [mãsyrabili'te], *n.f.* Mensurability. **mensurable,** *a.* Mensurable.

mensuration, *n.f.* Measurement.

mental [mã'tal], *a.* (*fem.* **-ale,** *pl.* **-aux**) Mental. **mentalement,** *adv.* Mentally.

mentalité, *n.f.* Mentality; mental habit.

menterie [mã'tri], *n.f.* (*fam.*) Story, fib.

menteur, *a.* (*fem.* **-euse**) Lying, false, deceitful.—*n.* Liar, story-teller, fibber. *Un menteur de profession,* a confirmed liar.

menthe [mã:t], *n.f.* Mint. *Crème de menthe,* liqueur flavoured with peppermint; *menthe aquatique,* water-mint; *menthe anglaise* or *menthe poivrée,* peppermint.

menthol [mɛ'tɔl], *n.m.* Peppermint camphor.

mentholé, *a.* (*fem.* **-ée**) Mentholated.

mention [mã'sjɔ̃], *n.f.* Mention. (*sch.*) *Reçu avec mention,* passed with distinction.

mentionner, *v.t.* To mention, to make mention of, to name.

mentir [mãˈtiːr], *v.i. irr.* (*pres.p.* **mentant,** *p.p.* **menti**) To lie, to tell a lie or an untruth; to fib, to tell stories. *Faire mentir le proverbe,* to belie the proverb; *gardez-vous bien de mentir,* beware of lying; *sans mentir,* to tell the truth, candidly, really; *se mentir à soi-même,* to belie oneself.

menton [mãˈtɔ̃], *n.m.* Chin. *Double menton,* double chin; *menton en galoche,* turned-up chin. **mentonnet,** *n.m.* Catch (of latch), stop, cam (of engine). **mentonnier,** *a.* (*fem.* **-ière**) (*Anat.*) Of the chin.—*n.f.* Chin-piece (of helmet or visor); chin-band; chin-strap; bandage for the chin; chin-rest (of violin).

mentor [mãˈtɔ:r], *n.m.* Mentor, guide, tutor.

menu [məˈny], *a.* (*fem.* **menue**) Slender, spare, thin, small; inconsiderable, petty, minor. *Le menu peuple,* the common people, the lower classes; *menu bétail,* small cattle; *menu gibier,* small game; *menu plomb,* small shot; *menus propos,* small talk.—*n.m.* Minute detail, particulars; menu, bill of fare; lower class. *Des gens du menu,* people of the lower class; *par le menu,* minutely, in detail.—*adv.* Small, fine, minutely, in small pieces. *Hacher menu,* to mince; *il pleuvait dru et menu,* the rain fell fine and fast; *trotter menu,* to walk with short, quick steps.

menuchon [MOURON].

menuet [məˈnɥɛ], *n.m.* Minuet.

menuiser [mənɥiˈze], *v.t.* To saw, cut, etc. (wood).—*v.i.* To do joiner's work. **menuiserie,** *n.f.* Woodwork, joinery, joiner's work. **menuisier,** *n.m.* Joiner, carpenter. *Menuisier en bâtiments,* house-carpenter.

ménure [meˈnyːr], *n.m.* Lyre-bird.

menu-vair [mənyˈvɛr], *n.m.* Miniver.

méphitique [mefiˈtik], *a.* Mephitic, noxious, foul. **méphitisme,** *n.m.* Mephitis, mephitism, stench.

Méphistophélès [mefistɔfeˈlɛs], *m.* Mephistopheles.

mephistophélique [mefistɔfeˈlik], *a.* Mephistophelian.

méplat [meˈpla], *a.* (*fem.* **méplate**) Flat. *Lignes méplates,* (*Paint.*) lines forming the transition from one plane to another.—*n.m.* (*Paint.*) Any one of the planes which together form the surface of a body; ledge (of rock).

méprendre (se) [meˈprã:dr], *v.r. irr.* (*conjug. like* PRENDRE) To mistake, to make a mistake, to be mistaken, to misapprehend. *C'est son père à s'y méprendre,* he is the very image of his father; *vous vous méprenez,* you are mistaken.

mépris [meˈpri], *n.m.* Contempt, scorn. *Au mépris des lois,* in defiance of the laws; *avoir du mépris pour quelqu'un,* to feel contempt for someone; *la familiarité engendre le mépris,* familiarity breeds contempt; *témoigner du mépris pour,* to show contempt for; *tomber dans le mépris,* to fall into contempt.

méprisable, *a.* Contemptible, despicable.

méprisant, *a.* (*fem.* **-ante**) Contemptuous, scornful.

méprise, *n.f.* Mistake, oversight, misunderstanding, error. *Faire une grande méprise,* to make a great mistake; *par méprise,* by mistake.

mépriser, *v.t.* To despise, to scorn; to slight, to set at naught, to disregard.

mer [mɛːr], *n.f.* Sea. *Aller au bord de la mer,* to go to the seaside; *à mer basse,* at low tide; *à mer haute,* at high tide; *c'est la mer à boire,* it is an endless task; *embarquer un coup,* or *un paquet, de mer,* to ship a sea; *en pleine mer,* on the open sea, on the high seas; *gens de mer,* seafaring men; *homme de mer,* seafaring man; *jeter* or *tomber à la mer,* to throw or to fall overboard; *loup de mer,* expert seaman, Jack Tar, old salt; *mal de mer,* sea-sickness; *mer d'huile,* very smooth sea; *mer fermée,* inland sea; *mettre à la mer,* to put to sea; *pouvoir tenir la mer,* to be seaworthy (of a ship); *prendre la mer,* to go to sea; *tenir la mer,* to keep out at sea, (*fig.*) to rule the waves; *un homme à la mer!* man overboard!

mercanette [SARCELLE].

mercanti [mɛrkãˈti], *n.m.* (*Mil.*) Camp-follower, sutler; Eastern bazaar-keeper; (*fam.*) profiteer.

mercantile [mɛrkãˈtil], *a.* Mercantile, commercial; (*fig.*) mercenary. *Esprit mercantile,* grabbing spirit.—*n.f.* Petty trading, huckstering.

mercantilisme, *n.m.* Mercantilism; money-grabbing.

mercenaire [mɛrsəˈnɛːr], *a.* Mercenary, venal.—*n.m.* Mercenary, hireling. **mercenairement,** *adv.* For money.

mercerie [mɛrsəˈri], *n.f.* Haberdashery.

mercerisage, *n.m.* Mercerizing. **merceriser,** *v.t.* To mercerize (cotton goods).

merci [mɛrˈsi], *n.f.* (*no pl.*) Mercy, discretion, will, pleasure. *Crier merci,* to cry for mercy; *être à la merci de quelqu'un,* to be at someone's mercy or discretion.—*n.m.* Thanks; (*fam.*) *je vous dis un grand merci,* thank you so much. —*int.* Thank you; no, thanks. *Dieu merci!* thank God! *Voulez-vous encore du pain?—Merci,* Have some more bread? No, thanks.

mercier [mɛrˈsje], *n.m.* (*fem.* **mercière**) Haberdasher; small-ware dealer.

mercredi [mɛrkrəˈdi], *n.m.* Wednesday. *Mercredi des cendres,* Ash-Wednesday.

Mercure [mɛrˈkyːr], *m.* (*Myth., Astron.*) Mercury.

mercure [mɛrˈkyːr], *n.m.* Mercury, quick-silver.

mercuriale, *n.f.* *Judicial assembly held on the first Wednesday after the vacation; *speech at this; (*fig.*) harangue, lecture, reprimand, rebuke; market prices; (*Bot.*) mercury.

mercuriel, *a.* (*fem.* **mercurielle**) Mercurial.

merde [mɛrd], *n.f.* (*indec.*) Excrement (of man and animals); shit, dung.—*Int.* of wonder, of admiration, of anger, of refusal. The euphemism is *zut.*

merdeux, *a.* (*fem.* **merdeuse**) Filthy, nasty.

merdoyer, *v.i.* (*vulg.*) To flounder (in answering), to blunder.

mère (1) [mɛːr], *n.f.* Mother (of animals); (*fig.*) parent, cause, source, reason. *Idée mère,* basic idea (of a literary or other work); *la mère patrie,* the mother-country (of a colony); *mère de famille,* mother of a family; *notre mère commune,* our mother-earth; *mère de vinaigre,* mother (produced by fermentation of vinegar).

mère (2) [mɛːr], *a.f.* Pure. *Mère goutte*, wine from the first pressing; *mère laine*, fine lamb's wool.

méreau [me'ro], *n.m.* (*pl.* **méreaux**) Disk used at hopscotch; counter, ticket, check.

mérelle [MARELLE].

mérétrice [mere'tris] or **mérétrix**, *n.f.* *Courtesan; (*Zool.*) genus of mollusca.

merganser [mɛrgã'sɛr], *n.m.* Goosander.

mergule [mɛr'gyl], *n.m.* (*Orn.*) Rotch.

méridien [meri'djɛ̃], *a.* (*fem.* **-ienne**) and *n.m.* Meridian.—*n.f.* Siesta, afternoon nap; meridian line. *Faire la méridienne*, to take an afternoon nap.

méridional, *a.* (*fem.* **-ale**, *pl.* **-aux**) Meridional, southern.—*n.m.* Person of the Midi.

meringue [mə'rɛ̃ːg], *n.f.* Meringue (confection). **meringuer**, *v.t.* To make a meringue of; to cover with custard.

mérinos [meri'noːs], *n.m.* Merino sheep; merino wool; merino (stuff).

merise [mə'riːz], *n.f.* Wild cherry. **merisier**, *n.m.* Wild cherry-tree.

méritant [meri'tã], *a.* (*fem.* **méritante**) Meritorious, worthy, deserving.

mérite [me'rit], *n.m.* Merit, worth; desert, due; capacity, attainments. *Il sera traité selon ses mérites*, he shall be dealt with according to his deserts; *se donner le mérite de quelque chose*, to assume the credit for something; *se faire un mérite de*, to make a merit of. **mériter**, *v.t.* To deserve, to merit; to earn, to gain; to need, to require. *Cela ne mérite pas qu'on en parle*, that is not worth mentioning; *cette nouvelle mérite confirmation*, that news requires confirmation.—*v.i.* To be deserving (*de*). *Il a bien mérité de la patrie*, he has deserved well of the country; *il mérite d'être récompensé*, he deserves to be rewarded.

mérithalle [meri'tal], *n.m.* (*Bot.*) Internode.

méritoire [meri'twaːr], *a.* Meritorious. **méritoirement**, *adv.* Meritoriously, deservingly.

merl, maërl [mɛrl], *n.m.* Breton ameliorator (made of sand, shell, and seaweeds).

merlan [mɛr'lã], *n.m.* Whiting. *Merlan bleu*, mackerel; *merlan jaune* or *lieu*, pollack; *merlan noir*, coal-fish. (*pop.*) *Faire des yeux de merlan frit*, to goggle.

merle [mɛrl], *n.m.* Blackbird. *Merle d'eau*, water-ousel, dipper; *merle à plastron* or *à collier*, ring-ousel; (*fig.*) *Merle blanc*, person or thing that does not exist or cannot be found; (*colloq.*) *c'est un fin merle*, he is a cunning old thing; *un vilain merle*, a disreputable fellow.

merleau, *n.m.* (*pl.* **-eaux**) Young blackbird.

merlette or **merlesse**, *n.f.* Hen blackbird; (*Her.*) martlet.

merlin (1) [mɛr'lɛ̃], *n.m.* Pole-axe; cleaver.

merlin (2) [mɛr'lɛ̃], *n.m.* (*Naut.*) Marline.

merlon [mɛr'lɔ̃], *n.m.* (*Fort.*) Merlon.

merluche [mɛr'lyʃ], *n.f.* Hake or sea-pike; dried cod; stockfish.

mérovingien [merɔvɛ̃'ʒjɛ̃], *a.* and *n.m.* (*fem.* **-ienne**) (*Hist.*) Merovingian.

merrain or **mairain** [me'rɛ̃], *n.m.* Stavewood, clap-board; beam (of deer horn).

merveille [mɛr'vɛːj], *n.f.* Wonder, marvel, miracle, prodigy. *À merveille*, admirably done, wonderfully well, capitally; *faire des merveilles*, to perform wonders; *mes affaires vont à merveille*, my affairs are going swimmingly; *promettre monts et merveilles*, to promise wonders; *se porter à merveille*, to be in splendid health, to be very fit. **merveilleusement**, *aav.* Wonderfully, admirably; wonderfully well. **merveilleux**, *a.* (*fem.* **merveilleuse**) Wonderful, marvellous; capital.—*n.m.* The wonderful, the marvellous part; the supernatural; *exquisite, swell.

mes, *pl.* [MON].

mésalliance [meza'ljãːs], *n.f.* Misalliance, bad match.

mésallier, *v.t.* To marry off (somebody) badly; (*fig.*) to disparage. **se mésallier**, *v.r.* To disparage oneself; to marry beneath one.

mésange [me'zãːʒ], *n.f.* (*Orn.*) Tit. *Mésange azurée* or *bleue*, blue tit; *mésange à longue queue* or *demoiselle*, long-tailed tit; *mésange à moustaches*, bearded tit; *mésange charbonnière* or *mésangère*, great tit; *mésange noire* or *petite charbonnière*, coal-tit. **mésangette**, *n.f.* Bird-trap.

mésaventure [mezavã'tyːr], *n.f.* Mischance, misadventure, misfortune.

mesdames, *pl.* [MADAME].

mesdemoiselles, *pl.* [MADEMOISELLE].

mésembryanthème [mezãbrijã'tɛːm], *n.m.* Mesembryanthemum, fig-marigold.

mésentente [mezã'tãːt], *n.f.* Misunderstanding.

mésentère [mezã'tɛːr], *n.m.* Mesentery. **mésentérique**, *a.* Mesenteric.

mésestime [mezɛs'tim], *n.f.* Disesteem, low esteem. **mésestimer**, *v.t.* To underestimate, to depreciate, to underrate.

mésintelligence [mezɛ̃teli'ʒãːs], *n.f.* Misunderstanding, variance, disagreement.

mesmérien [mɛzme'rjɛ̃] (*fem.* **mesmérienne**) or **mesmérique**, *a.* Mesmeric. **mesmérisme**, *n.m.* Mesmerism.

mésocarpe [mezɔ'karp], *n.m.* (*Bot.*) Mesocarp.

mésoderme, *n.m.* (*Bot.*, *Anat.*) Mesoderm.

mésogastre [mezɔ'gastr], *n.m.* (*Anat.*) Mesogaster.

Mésopotamie [mezɔpɔta'mi], *f.* Mesopotamia.

mésothorax, *n.m.* Mesothorax.

mésozoïque, *a.* (*Geol.*) Mesozoic.

mesquin [mɛs'kɛ̃], *a.* (*fem.* **mesquine**) Shabby; paltry; mean, niggardly, illiberal. **mesquinement**, *adv.* Shabbily, meanly. **mesquinerie**, *n.f.* Meanness, shabbiness, mean or paltry thing.

mess [mɛs], *n.m. inv.* Mess, officer's table.

message [me'saːʒ], *n.m.* Message.

messager, *n.m.* (*fem.* **messagère**) Messenger; carrier; (*fig.*) forerunner, harbinger. *Les hirondelles sont les messagères du printemps*, swallows are the harbingers of spring.

messagerie, *n.f.* Stage-coach office; carriage of goods, goods traffic, goods department; parcels office. *Messageries maritimes*, liners, steam-packets.

messaline [mɛsa'lin], *n.f.* Dissolute woman.

messe [mɛs], *n.f.* Mass. *Messe basse*, low mass; *grand-messe*, high mass; (*fam.*) *ne dites pas de messes basses*, don't mumble, speak up.

mésséance [mese'ãːs], *n.f.* Unseemliness, impropriety. **mésséant**, *a.* (*fem.* **mésséante**) Unseemly, unbecoming, improper.

messeigneurs, *pl.* [MONSEIGNEUR].

messeoir [me'swaːr], *v.i. irr.* (*pres.p.* **mésséant**, *conjug. like* SEOIR) To be unbecoming.

messianique [mɛsia'nik], *a.* Messianic. *Les temps messianiques*, the millennium.

messidor [mesi'dɔːr], *n.m.* Messidor (10th month of calendar of first French republic, 20 June–19 July).

Messie [me'si], *m.* Messiah.

*__messier__ [me'sje], *n.m.* or *a. Garde messier*, crop watcher.

messieurs, *pl.* [MONSIEUR].

*__messire__ [me'siːr], *n.m.* Sire, master, squire (title given to priests, advocates, etc.). *Messire Jean*, a variety of pear.

*__mestre__ (1) [mɛstr] [MAÎTRE], *n.m.* (*Fr. Hist.*) *Mestre de camp* (*pl. mestres de camp*), colonel (of a horse or infantry regiment).—*n.f.* The first company of a regiment.

mestre (2) (*Naut.*) [MEISTRE].

mesurable [məzy'rabl], *a.* Measurable.

mesurage, *n.m.* Measurement, measuring; metage.

mesure [mə'zyːr], *n.f.* Measure; gauge, standard; measurement, size, bounds, extent, limit, compass; (*fig.*) moderation, decorum, propriety; dimension; (*Mus.*) bar; (*Pros.*) metre. *À la mesure*, by measure, on draught; *à mesure*, in proportion, accordingly; *à mesure que*, in proportion as, as; *à mesure que l'un avançait, l'autre reculait*, as one advanced the other retired; *au fur et à mesure que* [FUR]; *battre la mesure* [BATTRE]; *cela passe toute mesure*, this is really too much; *chanter* or *aller en mesure*, to keep time in singing; *dans une large mesure*, to a large extent; *il a dépassé la mesure*, he has gone too far, he has overstepped the mark; *observer la mesure*, to keep time; *outre mesure*, excessively, beyond measure; *prendre des mesures*, to take measurements; to take steps, to make arrangements; *prendre ses mesures*, to take precautions; *sans mesure*, beyond all measure, immeasurably; *se mettre en mesure de*, to prepare to, to get ready to.

mesuré, *a.* (*fem.* **mesurée**) Measured, regular; proportioned; cautious, circumspect, guarded, prudent; moderate. *Il est très mesuré dans ses discours*, he is very guarded in what he says.

mesurer, *v.t.* To measure; to measure out; to proportion; to calculate; to compare; to consider, to weigh, to examine. *Mesurer ses discours*, to weigh one's words. **se mesurer**, *v.r.* To try one's strength, to measure swords; (*fig.*) to vie, to contend, to cope.

mesureur, *n.m.* Measurer; meter.

mésusage [mezy'zaːʒ], *n.m.* Misuse, abuse.

mésuser, *v.i.* To misuse, to abuse. *Mésuser de sa liberté*, to make bad use of one's freedom.

met, *3rd indic. pres.* [METTRE].

métabole [meta'bɔl] or **métabolique**, *a.* Metabolic. **métabolisme**, *n.m.* Metabolism.

métacarpe [meta'karp], *n.m.* (*Anat.*) Metacarpus. **métacarpien**, *a.* (*fem.* **métacarpienne**) Metacarpal.

métacentre [meta'sɑ̃ːtr], *n.m.* Metacentre.

métagénèse [metaʒe'nɛːz], *n.f.* Metagenesis. **métagénésique**, *a.* Metagenetic.

métairie [metɛ'ri], *n.f.* Land, small farm (held on the principle of *métayage*).

métal [me'tal], *n.m.* (*pl.* **métaux**) Metal. *Métal précieux*, precious metal. **métallifère**,

a. Metalliferous. **métallique**, *a.* Metallic.

métallisation, *n.f.* Metallization. **métalliser**, *v.t.* To metallize. **métallo** [meta'lo], *n.m.* (*pop.*) Metal-worker. **métallographie**, *n.f.* Metallography. **métalloïde**, *n.m.* Metalloid. **métallurgie**, *n.f.* Metallurgy. **métallurgique**, *a.* Metallurgic. **métallurgiste**, *n.m.* Metallurgist.

métamorphique [metamɔr'fik], *a.* Metamorphic. **métamorphisme**, *n.m.* Metamorphism.

métamorphose [metamɔr'foːz], *n.f.* Metamorphosis, transformation. **métamorphoser**, *v.t.* To metamorphose, to transform. **se métamorphoser**, *v.r.* To metamorphose oneself; to change altogether.

métaphonie [metafo'ni:], *n.f.* Mutation of a vowel; umlaut.

métaphore [meta'fɔːr], *n.f.* Metaphor. **métaphorique**, *a.* Metaphorical. **métaphoriquement**, *adv.* Metaphorically.

métaphrase [meta'frɑz], *n.f.* Metaphrase.

métaphysicien [metafizi'sjɛ̃], *n.m.* (*fem.* **-ienne**) Metaphysician.

métaphysique [metafi'zik], *n.f.* Metaphysics. —*a.* Metaphysical. **métaphysiquement**, *adv.* Metaphysically.

métaplasme [meta'plasm], *n.m.* Metaplasm.

métastase [metas'tɑːz], *n.f.* Metastasis.

métatarse [meta'tars], *n.m.* (*Anat.*) Metatarsus.

métathèse [meta'tɛːz], *n.f.* Metathesis.

métayage [metɛ'jaːʒ], *n.m.* Metayage; (*Am.*) sharecropping. **métayer**, *n.m.* (*fem.* **-yère**) Metayer, small farmer.

métazoaires [metazɔ'ɛːr], *n.m. pl.* (*Zool.*) Metazoa.

méteil [me'tɛːj], *n.m.* Maslin (mixture of wheat and rye).

métempsyc(h)ose [metɑ̃psi'koːz], *n.f.* Metempsychosis; transmigration of souls. **métempsychosiste**, *n.* Believer in metempsychosis.

météo [mete'o], *n.f.* (*fam.*) Meteorology; weather-report; meteorological office.

météore [mete'ɔːr], *n.m.* Meteor. **météorique**, *a.* Meteoric.

météorisation [meteɔriza'sjɔ̃], *n.f.* (*Path.*) Wind, flatulence. **météorisé**, *a.* (*fem.* **-ée**) Flatulent, distended. **météoriser**, *v.t.* To distend with flatulence.

météorisme [MÉTÉORISATION].

météorite [meteɔ'rit], *n.m.* or *f.* Meteorite.

météorologie [meteɔrɔlɔ'ʒi], *n.f.* Meteorology. **météorologique**, *a.* Meteorological. *Bulletin météorologique* [*see* BULLETIN]. **météorologiste** or **météorologue**, *n.* Meteorologist.

métèque [me'tɛk], *n.m.* Alien; resident foreigner.

méthane [me'tan], *n.m.* Marsh gas, methane.

méthode [me'tɔd], *n.f.* Method, system; way, manner. *Cet homme a une étrange méthode*, that man has a strange way of doing things. **méthodique**, *a.* Methodical, systematic. **méthodiquement**, *adv.* Methodically.

méthodisme, *n.m.* Methodism. **méthodiste**, *n.* and *a.* Methodist.

méthyle [me'til], *n.m.* Methyl. **méthylène**, *n.m.* Methylene.

méticuleusement [metikyløz'mɑ̃], *adv.* Meticulously. **méticuleux**, *a.* (*fem.* **-euse**)

Meticulous, punctilious, fastidious particular. **méticulosité,** *n.f.* Meticulousness.

métier [me'tje], *n.m.* Trade, business, calling, craft, profession; loom, frame. *Arts et métiers,* arts and crafts; *avoir du métier,* to be a master of one's craft; *chacun son métier,* everyone to his trade; *corps de métier,* corporation, guild; *être du métier,* to be in the (same) trade; *faire métier de,* to make a trade of; *faire son métier,* to mind one's own business; *gens de métier,* professionals; *homme de métier,* craftsman, handicraftsman; *le métier des armes,* the profession of arms, soldiering; *métier manuel,* handicraft. *Métier à bas,* stocking-frame; *métier à broder,* tambour-frame; *métier à tisser,* loom; *sur le métier,* on the anvil, on the stocks, in hand.

métis [me'tiːs], *a.* (*fem.* **métisse**) Half-caste, half-bred, cross-bred; hybrid (plant); mongrel (dog).—*n.* Half-breed; mongrel (dog).

métissage, *n.m.* Cross-breeding, hybridization. **métisser,** *v.t.* To cross-breed.

métonymie [metɔni'mi], *n.f.* Metonymy.

métope [me'tɔp], *n.f.* (*Arch.*) Metope.

métrage [me'traːʒ], *n.m.* Measurement (in metres). (*Cine.*) *Court métrage,* short film; *long métrage,* feature film.

mètre [metr], *n.m.* Metre (1·09 yards); rule, measure (of 1 metre); (*Pros.*) metre, measure. *Mètre à ruban,* tape-measure; *mètre pliant,* folding-rule. **métrer,** *v.t.* To measure (by the metre).

métreur, *n.m.* Quantity-surveyor, appraiser.

métricien, *n.m.* Metrician.

métrique, *a.* Metric (system etc.); (*Pros.*) metrical.—*n.f.* Scansion, metrics.

métro [me'tro], *n.m.* (*colloq.*) Abbr. of *chemin de fer métropolitain.* *Le métro,* the underground (railway), the tube (in Paris); (*Am.*) the subway.

métrologie [metrɔlɔ'ʒi], *n.f.* Metrology.

métromane [metrɔ'man], *n.* Metromaniac.

métronome [metrɔ'nɔm], *n.m.* Metronome.

métropole [metrɔ'pɔl], *n.f.* Mother country; metropolis, capital; metropolitan see.

métropolitain, *a.* (*fem.* **métropolitaine**) Metropolitan; archiepiscopal. *Église métropolitaine,* mother-church.—*n.m.* Metropolitan, archbishop; underground railway, tube.

mets [mɛ] (1), *n.m.* Dish, food, viands. (2) *2nd pers. sing. of* METTRE.

mettable [mɛ'tabl], *a.* Fit to be worn, wearable.

metteur [mɛ'tœːr], *n.m.* (*fem.* **metteuse**) *Metteur en œuvre,* setter, mounter (of jewels); *metteur en pages,* (*Print.*) make-up hand, clicker; *metteur en scène,* (*Theat.*) producer, (*Cine.*) director.

mettre [metr], *v.t. irr.* (*pres.p.* **mettant,** *p.p.* **mis**) To put, to set; to place; to put in, to introduce; to put on, to wear; to bring; to employ; to contribute, to devote, to expend; to translate; to suppose, to imagine. *Il met son nez partout,* he pokes his nose into everything; *mettez que je n'ai rien dit,* forget what I said; *mettre à jour* [JOUR]; *mettre au jour* [JOUR]; *mettre bas* [BAS (1)]; *mettre de côté,* to save; *mettre des paroles en musique,* to set words to music; *mettre en marche* or *en mouvement,* to start up, to set going; *mettre en ordre,* to set in order; *mettre en pages,* (*Print.*) to make up; *mettre la charrue devant les bœufs* [CHARRUE];

mettre le couvert [COUVERT (1)]; *mettre les pieds dans le plat,* to put one's foot in it; *mettre par écrit,* to set down in writing; *mettre à l'amende* [AMENDE]; *mettre quelqu'un à la raison,* to bring someone to his senses; *mettre à la voile,* to set sail; *mettre au désespoir* [DÉSESPOIR]; *mettre quelqu'un au courant,* to inform someone of the state of matters; *mettre quelqu'un dehors* [DEHORS]; *mettre quelqu'un en colère,* to put someone into a passion; *mettre quelqu'un en état de,* to enable someone to; *mettre un arrêt à exécution,* to execute a decree; *mettre un habit,* to put on a coat; *mettre un vaisseau à l'eau,* to launch a ship; (*pop.*) *en mettre un coup,* to work hard; *y mettre du sien,* to make concessions, to meet half-way. **se mettre,** *v.r.* To put or place oneself; to sit down; to lie down; to stand up; to dress; to begin, to set about; to take to, to apply oneself, to turn one's thoughts (*à*); to go, to get; to break out. *Il se met à tout,* he turns his hand to everything; *la peste se mit dans l'armée,* the plague broke out in the army; *le temps se met au beau,* it is turning out fine; *se mettre à la fenêtre,* to place oneself at the window; *se mettre à parler,* to begin to speak; *se mettre à son aise,* to put oneself at one's ease; *se mettre à table,* to sit down to table; (*slang*) to peach, to blab, to give the show away; *se mettre avec quelqu'un,* to cohabit with someone; *se mettre au pas,* to fall into line, to come to heel; *se mettre bien,* to dress well; *se mettre bien avec,* to get on good terms with; *se mettre dans le commerce,* to turn tradesman, to take to trade; *se mettre du fard* or *du rouge* [FARD]; *se mettre en colère* [COLÈRE]; *se mettre en route, en chemin,* or *en marche,* to start, to go forward, to make a move; *se mettre en tête,* to take it into one's head; *se mettre mal avec quelqu'un,* to fall out with someone; *se mettre sur son trente et un,* to dress up to the nines; *s'y mettre,* to set about it, to turn to, to buckle to.

meublant [mœ'blɑ̃], *a.* (*fem.* **-ante**) Serving to furnish, fit for furniture. (*Law*) *Meubles meublants,* movables, household goods.

meuble [mœbl], *a.* Movable. *Biens meubles,* (*Law*) personal property. *Sol* or *terre meuble,* light, mellow soil, loose ground.—*n.m.* Piece of furniture; (*pl.*) furniture; (*Law*) chattels, household goods, belongings; suite of furniture. *Meuble de famille,* heirloom. *Se mettre dans ses meubles,* to furnish a home of one's own. **meublé,** *a.* (*fem.* **-ée**) Furnished. *Avoir la bouche bien meublée,* to have a fine set of teeth. *Chambre meublée,* furnished room; *être bien meublé,* to have one's house or rooms well furnished.—*n.m.* A furnished room or flat.

meubler, *v.t.* To furnish; to stock, to store. *Meubler sa mémoire,* to store one's memory. *Meubler une ferme,* to stock a farm; *meubler une maison,* to furnish a house. **se meubler,** *v.r.* To purchase one's furniture; to furnish one's home.

meuglement etc. [BEUGLEMENT].

meulage [mø'laːʒ], *n.m.* Grinding.

meulard [mø'laːr], *n.m.,* or **meularde,** *n.f.* Large millstone, grindstone.

meule [møl], *n.f.* Millstone, grindstone; (*Agric.*) stack, rick (of corn, hay, etc.); (*Hort.*) hotbed; crown (of deer's horns).

Mettre en meule, to stack; *meule de fromage*, round cheese. **meuler**, *v.t.* To grind (chisel etc.). **meulerie**, *n.f.* Millstone yard. **meulette**, *n.f.* [MEULON].

meulier, *a. (fem. **-ière**)* Pertaining to millstones, burrstone, millstone-quarry.—*n.m.* Millstone or grindstone maker.—*n.f. (Pierre) meulière*, millstone grit. **meulon**, *n.m.* Small stack, shock (of hay etc.), haulm-stack.

meunerie [mønˈri], *n.f.* Miller's trade; *(collect.)* millers. **meunier**, *n.m.* Miller; chub (fish). *Se faire d'évêque meunier*, *(fig.)* to come down in the world. **meunière**, *n.f.* Woman owner of a mill; miller's wife; long-tailed titmouse.

meurs etc. [MOURIR].

meurt-de-faim [mœrdəˈfɛ̃], *n. inv.* Half-starved wretch, starveling.

meurt-de-soif, *n. inv.* Drunkard, toper.

meurtre [mœrtr], *n.m.* Murder; *(fig.)* sin, great shame, great pity. *Crier au meurtre*, to cry murder, to complain bitterly.

meurtri, *a. (fem. **meurtrie**)* Bruised, black and blue, contused. *Il est tout meurtri de coups*, he is covered with bruises.

meurtrier, *n.m. (fem. **meurtrière** (1))* Murderer, murderess.—*a.* Murdering, murderous, deadly; killing. *Un feu meurtrier*, a deadly fire. **meurtrière** (2), *n.f. (Fort.)* Loophole.

meurtrir [mœrˈtriːr], *v.t.* To bruise, to make black and blue.

meurtrissure, *n.f.* Bruise.

meus etc. [MOUVOIR].

meute [møːt], *n.f.* Pack (of hounds etc.). *Chef de meute*, whipper-in; *(fig.)* leader of the band, ringleader.

mévendre [meˈvɑ̃ːdr], *v.t. irr. (conjug. like* VENDRE*)* To sell at a loss. **mévente**, *n.f.* Selling at a loss; lack of sale, slump.

mexicain [mɛksiˈkɛ̃], *a. (fem. **-aine**)* and *n.m.* (**Mexicain**, *fem.* **-aine**) Mexican.

Mexique [mɛkˈsik], **le**, *m.* Mexico.

mézéréon [mezereˈ5], *n.m. (Bot.)* Mezereon.

*mézigue [meˈzig], *pron. (slang)* Me, myself.

mezzanine [mɛdzaˈnin], *n.f.* Mezzanine (floor), small window (of entresol).

mezzo-soprano [mɛdzosɔpraˈno], *n.m. (pl.* **mezzo-sopranos** or **-soprani**) Mezzo-soprano.

mezzo-tinto [mɛdzotɛ̃ˈto], *n.m. inv.* Mezzo-tint.

mi [mi], *n.m. (Mus.)* Mi; the note E.

mi- [mi], *comb. form.* Half, demi-, semi-; mid, middle. *À mi-chemin*, half-way; *à mi-corps*, up to the waist; *à mi-côte*, half-way up the hill; *à mi-jambe*, half-way up the leg; *à mi-mât*, half-mast high; *la mi-août*, the middle of August.

miaou [mjau], *n.m. inv. (fam.)* Mew, miaow, cat.

miasmatique [mjasmaˈtik], *a.* Miasmatic, malarious. **miasme**, *n.m.* Miasma.

miaulement [mjolˈmɑ̃], *n.m.* Mewing.

miauler, *v.i.* To mew; to caterwaul.

miauleur, *a. (fem. **-euse**)* Mewing.

mibora [miboˈra], *n.f.*, or *poil de chat.* (*Bot.*) Mibora.

mica [miˈka], *n.m.* Mica. **micacé**, *a. (fem.* **-ée**) Micaceous.

mi-carême [mikaˈrɛːm], *n.f.* Mid-Lent. *Le dimanche de la mi-carême*, Simnel Sunday.

micaschiste, *n.m.* Mica-schist, mica-slate.

miche [miʃ], *n.f.* Round loaf.

miché [miˈʃe], **michet**, or **micheton**, *n.m. (slang)* Man who pays a woman for 'a short time'; a mug.

Michel [miˈʃɛl], *m.* Michael. *La Saint-Michel*, Michaelmas.

Michel-Ange [mikɛlˈɑ̃ːʒ], *m.* Michael Angelo, Michelangelo.

micheline [miʃˈlin], *n.f.* Rail-car.

micmac [mikˈmak], *n.m.* Underhand dealing, foul-play.

micocoulier [mikokuˈlje], *n.m.* Nettle-tree.

(*C*) **micoine** [miˈkwan], *n.f.* A wooden spoon.

micro [miˈkro], *n.m. (abbr. fam. of microphone)* Mike. *Parler au micro*, to broadcast.

microbalance [mikrobaˈlɑ̃s], *n.f. (Phys.)* Micro-balance.

microbe [miˈkrɔb], *n.m.* Microbe. **microbicide**, *a.* Germ-killing. **microbien** (*fem.* **-ienne**) or **microbique**, *a.* Microbial.

microbiologie, *n.f.* Microbiology.

microbisme, *n.m.* Microbial infection.

microcéphale [mikrɔseˈfal], *a.* Microcephalous.—*n.* Microcephalous person, microcephal. **microcéphalie**, *n.f.* Imbecility due to being microcephalous, microcephaly.

microchimie [mikrɔʃiˈmi], *n.f.* Micro-chemistry.

microcosme [mikrɔˈkɔsm], *n.m.* Microcosm.

microfilm [mikroˈfilm], *n.m.* Microfilm. **microfilmer**, *v.t.* To microfilm.

micrographie [mikrɔgraˈfi], *n.f.* Micrography.

microlithe [mikrɔˈlit], *n.m.* Microlith.

micrologie, *n.f.* Micrology.

micromètre [mikrɔˈmɛtr], *n.m.* Micrometer.

micron [miˈkr5], *n.m.* = micromillimetre = millionth part of a millimetre, micron.

micro-organisme [mikroɔrgaˈnism], *n.m.* Micro-organism.

microphone [mikrɔˈfɔn], *n.m.* Microphone.

microscope [mikrɔsˈkɔp], *n.m.* Microscope. *Microscope électronique*, electron microscope. **microscopie**, *n.f.* Microscopy. **microscopique**, *a.* Microscopic.

microsillon [mikrɔsiˈj5], *n.m.* Microgroove; *(fam.)* long-playing record.

microzoaire, *n.m.* Microscopic animalcule, infusory.

miction [mikˈsj5], *n.f.* Urinating, making water.

micturition, *n.f. (Path.)* Micturition.

midi [miˈdi], *n.m.* Noon, noontide, midday, noonday; twelve o'clock (in the day); meridian; south; southern aspect. *À midi*, at noon, at twelve o'clock; *chercher midi à quatorze heures*, to create difficulties where there are none, to miss the obvious; *en plein midi*, at noon, in broad daylight; *le Midi (de la France)*, the South of France; *le midi de la vie*, the meridian of life; *midi est sonné*, it has struck twelve; *midi et demi*, half past twelve; *sur le coup de midi*, on the stroke of twelve.

midinette [midiˈnɛt], *n.f. (fam.)* Young dress-maker or milliner in Paris.

mie (1) [mi], *n.f.* Crumb, very little bit; soft part of loaf.

mie (2) [mi], *n.f.* (a wrong orthography used after *ma, ta, sa*). *Ma mie* (instead of *m'amie*), my love.

miel [mjɛl], *n.m.* Honey. *Lune de miel,* honeymoon; *mouche à miel,* honey-bee; *rayon de miel,* honeycomb.

miélaison, *n.f.* Honey-time.

miellat [MIELLÉE (2)].

miellé, *a.* (*fem.* **miellée** (1)) Honeyed; like honey; (*fig.*) sweet, bland. **miellée** (2) or **miellure,** *n.f.* Honeydew. **mielleusement,** *adv.* Sweetly, blandly, honey-like.

mielleux, *a.* (*fem.* **mielleuse**) Honeyed; fair-spoken; sweet, bland; mawkish. *Paroles mielleuses,* honeyed words.

mien [mjɛ̃], *a. poss.* and *pron. poss.* (*fem.* **mienne**) Mine. *Je ne demande que le mien,* I only ask for my own; *le mien, la mienne, les miens, les miennes,* mine, my own; *les miens,* my friends, my relations; *un mien frère,* a brother of mine.

miette [mjɛt], *n.f.* Crumb, bit, particle, morsel. *Mettre en miettes,* to crumble; to smash; *ramasser les miettes,* to pick up the crumbs.

mieux [mjø], *adv.* Better; correctly, more agreeably, more comfortably, etc.; rather, more. *À qui mieux mieux,* in emulation of one another, in rivalry; *au mieux,* at best, for the best; *avoir mieux que cela,* to have much better; *c'est ce qu'il y a de mieux* or *c'est on ne peut mieux,* it cannot be improved upon, it is the best of its kind; *de mieux en mieux,* better and better; *disons mieux,* or rather, to speak more correctly; *en mieux,* for the better; *faute de mieux,* for want of something better; *il a fait de son mieux* or *du mieux qu'il a pu,* he has done his best; *j'aimerais mieux,* I had rather, I should prefer; *je me porte le mieux du monde,* I am as well as can be; *je ne demande pas mieux,* nothing would give me greater pleasure; *le mieux que je pourrai,* as well as I can, as best I can; *mieux vaut tard que jamais,* better late than never; *tant mieux,* so much the better; *valoir mieux,* to be better, to be worth more; *vous feriez mieux de venir,* you had better come.—*n.m.* Best thing; improvement. *Faire pour le mieux,* to act for the best; *il y a du mieux dans son état,* he is better; *le mieux est d'aller le voir,* the best course is to go and see him; *le mieux est l'ennemi du bien,* let well alone.

mieux-être, *n.m. inv.* Better or best condition; improvement in one's condition.

mièvre [mjɛːvr], *a.* Finical, affected; delicate (child), fragile. **mièvrement,** *adv.* Affectedly. **mièvrerie** or **mièvreté,** *n.f.* Affectation.

mignard [mi'ɲaːr], *a.* (*fem.* **mignarde**) Delicate, pretty, dainty; mincing, affected. *Manières mignardes,* mincing manners.—*n.m.* Delicacy, prettiness; mincing ways. **mignardement,** *adv.* Delicately, daintily, mincingly.

mignarder, *v.t.* To fondle, to pet, to indulge. *Mignarder son style,* to be over-fastidious in writing; *mignarder un enfant,* to coddle a child. **se mignarder,** *v.r.* To take great care of oneself; to smirk.

mignardise, *n.f.* Delicacy, prettiness, daintiness, affectation, mincing ways; (*Bot.*) garden pink.

mignon [mi'ɲɔ̃], *a.* (*fem.* **-onne**) Delicate, pretty, dainty; sweet; neat, tiny. *Bouche mignonne,* pretty, small mouth; *pied mignon,* neat foot.—*n.* Darling, pet, favourite;

minion.—*n.f.* A scarlet variety of pear; (*Print.*) minion. **mignonnement,** *adv.* Daintily, prettily.

mignonnette [miɲɔ'nɛt], *n.f.* Fine sort of lace; coarse-ground pepper; fine gravel; (*Print.*) minion; (*Bot.*) London Pride, wild succory.

*****mignoter** [miɲɔ'te], *v.t.* (*colloq.*) To fondle.

migraine [mi'grɛːn], *n.f.* Sick headache; migraine. **migraineux,** *a.* (*fem.* **-euse**) Suffering from a headache; headachy.

migrateur [migra'tœːr], *a.* (*fem.* **-trice**) Migratory, migrating (bird).

migration, *n.f.* Migration.

migratoire, *a.* Migratory.

mijaurée [miʒɔ're], *n.f.* (*colloq.*) Affected, conceited woman.

mijoter [miʒɔ'te], *v.t.* To cook slowly, to stew; to let simmer; (*fig.*) to plot, to brew.—*v.i.* To boil gently, to simmer.

mikado [mika'do], *n.m.* Mikado.

mil (1) [MILLE (2)].

mil (2) [mil], *n.m.* Millet.

mil (3) [mil], *n.m.* *Mil persan,* Indian club.

milan [mi'lɑ̃], *n.m.* Kite (bird); red gurnard (fish).

milandre [mi'lɑ̃ːdr], *n.m.* Tope (a dog-fish).

milaneau [mila'no], *n.m.* (*pl.* **-eaux**) Young kite.

mildiou, mildew [mil'dju], *n.m.* Mildew, brown rot. **mildiousé,** *a.* (*fem.* **-ée**) Mildewed.

milésien [mile'zjɛ̃], *a.* and *n.m.* (*fem.* **-ienne**) Milesian.

miliaire [mi'ljɛːr], *a.* Miliary. *Fièvre miliaire,* miliary fever.—*n.f.* Miliary eruption.

milice [mi'lis], *n.f.* Militia; (*fig.*) troops, soldiery. **milicien,** *n.m.* Militiaman.

milieu [mi'ljø], *n.m.* (*pl.* **milieux**) Middle, midst; heart, centre; medium, mean; middle term; environment, habitat; intellectual, moral, etc., sphere, surroundings. *Au beau milieu,* in the very middle; *au milieu de la foule,* in the midst of the crowd; *au milieu des hommes,* among men; *il faut savoir garder le juste milieu,* we must know how to observe the golden mean; *ils n'appartiennent pas au même milieu,* they belong to different social spheres; *l'air est le milieu dans lequel nous vivons,* the air is the medium in which we live. *Le milieu,* (*slang*) the underworld.

militaire [mili'tɛːr], *a.* Military; martial, soldierly, warlike. *L'annuaire militaire,* the army list.—*n.m. Un militaire,* military man, soldier; *les militaires,* the military. **militairement,** *adv.* In a soldierlike manner.

militant [mili'tɑ̃], *a.* (*fem.* **militante**) Militant. *L'église militante,* the Church militant. —*n.* An active member of a political party.

militarisation [militariza'sjɔ̃], *n.f.* Militarization. **militariser,** *v.t.* To militarize.

militarisme, *n.m.* Militarism. **militariste,** *n.* and *a.* Militarist.

militer [mili'te], *v.i.* To militate (*pour* or *contre*). *Cette raison milite en ma faveur,* that reason militates in my favour.

millade [mi'jad], *n.f.* Maize cake.

(*C*) **millage** [mi'laːʒ], *n.m.* Mileage.

mille (1) [mil], *n.m.* Mile (English mile, 1609·3 metres). *Mille marin,* sea-mile (French sea-mile, 1,852 metres).

mille (2) [mil], *a. inv.* and *n.m. inv.* (**mil in**

dates of the Christian era) Thousand, a thousand, one thousand. *Dix mille*, ten thousand; *l'an mil neuf cent quarante*, the year nineteen hundred and forty; *l'an mille*, the year one thousand; *le premier mille*, the first thousand; *les mille et une nuits*, the Arabian nights; *on a dit cela mille et mille fois*, that has been said thousands of times. *Mettre (en plein) dans le mille*, to throw the quoit into the 'thousand' (usually a frog's mouth in the *tonneau* game); to hit the bull's-eye; to win immediately.

millée [mi′je], *n.f.* Millet broth or gruel.

mille-feuille [mil′fœːj], *n.f.* (*pl.* **mille-feuilles**) Genoese pastry; (*Bot.*) milfoil, yarrow.

mille-fleurs [mil′flœːr], *n.f. inv.* Extract distilled from many different flowers.

millénaire [mille′nεːr], *a.* Millenary.—*n.m.* Millennium; millenarian. **millénarisme,** *n.m.* Millenarianism.

mille-pattes [mil′pat], *n.m. inv.* Centipede.

mille-pertuis [milpεr′tɥi], *n.m. inv.* St. John's wort.

mille-pieds [mil′pje] [MILLE-PATTES].

millésime [mile′zim], *n.m.* Date (on a coin, monument, etc.).

millet [mi′jε], *n.m.* Millet, millet grass. *Grand millet*, sorg; *grains de millet*, bird-seed.

milliaire [mi′ljεːr], *a.* Milliary. *Borne milliaire*, or *pierre milliaire* or (*n.m.*) *milliaire*, milestone.

milliard [mi′ljaːr], *n.m.* One thousand millions, one milliard, (*Am.*) one billion.

milliardaire, *n.m.* and *a.* Multi-millionaire.

*****milliasse** [mi′ljas], *n.f.* A (Fr.) trillion, one thousand billions; (*fig.*) thousands, swarms, a vast number.

millibar [milli′bar], *n.m.* (*Meteor.*) Millibar.

millième [mi′ljεm], *a.* and *n.m.* Thousandth.

millier [mi′lje], *n.m.* Thousand, ten hundred-weight. *Des milliers d'arbres*, thousands of trees; *on en trouve par milliers*, they are to be found in thousands.

milligramme [milli′gram], *n.m.* Milligramme (·0154 grain).

millilitre, *n.m.* Millilitre (·061027 cub. in.).

millimètre, *n.m.* Millimetre (·03937 in.).

million [mi′ljɔ̃], *n.m.* Million. **millionième,** *a.* and *n.m.* Millionth.

millionnaire, *a.* and *n.* Millionaire.

milord [mi′lɔːr], *n.m.* Lord; my lord, your lordship. (*colloq.*) *C'est un milord*, he is made of money.

milouin [mi′lwε̃], *n.m.* (*Orn.*) Pochard.

milouinan [milwi′nɑ̃], *n.m.* Scaup.

mime [mim], *n.m.* Mime; mimic. **mimer,** *v.t., v.i.* To mimic, to mime.

mimétisme [mime′tism], *n.m.* (*Zool.*) Mimesis; mimicry.

mimi [mi′mi], *n.m.* (*Childish*) Cat, pussy; darling, ducky.

mimique [mi′mik], *a.* Mimic, mimetic.—*n.f.* Art of mimicry.

mimodrame [mimɔ′dram], *n.m.* Dumb show.

mimosa [mimo′za], *n.m.* Mimosa, sensitive plant.

mimule [mi′myl], *n.m.* (*Bot.*) Mimulus, monkey-flower.

minable [mi′nabl], *a.* (*colloq.*) Seedy, shabby, wretched-looking.

minahouet [mina′wε], *n.m.* (*Naut.*) Serving-board.

minaret [mina′rε], *n.m.* Minaret.

minauder [mino′de], *v.i.* To smirk, to simper.

minauderie, *n.f.* Affected, mincing manners, simpering, smirking.

minaudier, *a.* (*fem.* **minaudière**) Affected, lackadaisical.—*n.* Affected, mincing person.

mince [mε̃:s], *a.* Thin, slender, slim; puny, slight, trivial; scanty, small. *C'est un homme bien mince*, he is a very shallow man; *minces revenus*, small income; *taille mince*, slim waist.—*int.* (*pop.*) Ah! *mince!* or *mince alors!* My word; well I never!

minceur, *n.f.* Slenderness, slimness.

mine (1) [min], *n.f.* Look, bearing; face, look, expression; appearance, aspect, show; (*pl.*) grimaces, airs. *Avoir bonne mine*, to look well; *avoir mauvaise mine*, to look ill; *de mauvaise mine*, suspicious-looking; *faire bonne mine à mauvais jeu*, to put a good face on a bad business; *faire bonne mine à quelqu'un*, to greet someone pleasantly; *faire des mines à*, to ogle, to simper at; *faire la mine*, to look displeased, to sulk; *faire la mine à quelqu'un*, to pout at someone; *faire mauvaise* or *grise mine à*, to receive coldly, to look daggers at; *faire mine d'être fâché*, to pretend to be angry; *homme de bonne mine*, good-looking man; *à la mine trompeuse*, he has a deceitful look; *il ne faut pas juger des gens à la mine*, people should not be judged by their looks; *il ne paye pas de mine*, he is a better man than he looks; *j'ai bien la mine de payer vos folies*, it looks as if I shall have to pay for your follies; *mine fière*, proud look.

mine (2) [min], *n.f.* Mine; *ore*; (*fig.*) source, store. *Mine de charbon de terre*, coal-mine; *mine d'or*, gold-mine; *puits de mine*, mine-shaft. *Mine de plomb*, black-lead; *passer à la mine de plomb*, to black-lead.

mine (3) [min], *n.f.* (*Mil., Pyro.*) Mine; (*fig.*) plot, secret. *Détecteur de mines*, mine detector; *éventer la mine*, to discover the enemy's mine; (*fig.*) to thwart someone's designs; *faire jouer une mine*, to spring a mine; *mouiller* or *poser une mine*, to lay a mine.

*****mine** (4) [min], *n.f.* Old French measure (78 litres); (*Gr. Ant.*) mina.

miner [mi′ne], *v.t.* To mine, to undermine, to sap; to sow with mines; to wear away; to consume, to waste by slow degrees, to impair. *Cette maladie le mine*, that disease is wearing him away; *l'eau mine la pierre*, water wears away stone.

minerai [min′rε], *n.m.* Ore.

minéral [mine′ral], *n.m.* (*pl.* **-aux**) Mineral; ore.—*a.* (*fem.* **-ale**, *pl.* **-aux**) Mineral. *Chimie minérale*, inorganic chemistry.

minéralisable, *a.* Mineralizable. **minéralisateur,** *a.* (*fem.* **-trice**) Mineralizing.—*n.m.* Mineralizer. **minéralisation,** *n.f.* Mineralization. **minéraliser,** *v.t.* To mineralize.

minéralogie, *n.f.* Mineralogy. **minéralogique,** *a.* Mineralogical. *Numéro minéralogique*, (*Motor.*) registration number. **minéralogiste,** *n.m.* Mineralogist.

Minerve [mi′nεrv], *f.* Minerva. *Arbre de Minerve*, (*poet.*) olive-tree; *oiseau de Minerve*, (*poet.*) the owl.

minerve [mi′nεrv], *n.f.* (*colloq.*) *****Brains, sense; (*Print.*) small printing-press.

minet ... **miroir**

minet [mi'nε], *n.m.* (*fem.* **minette** (1)) (*colloq.*) Puss, kitten.

minette (2) [mi'nεt], *n.f.* (*Bot.*) Nonsuch, hop-trefoil.

mineur (1) [mi'nœ:r], *n.m.* Miner, pitman; (*Mil.*) sapper, engineer.

mineur (2) [mi'nœ:r], *a.* (*fem.* **mineure**) Less, minor; under age. *Frère mineur,* Minorite, Franciscan; *l'Asie Mineure,* Asia Minor.—*n.* Minor; (*Law*) infant.—*n.f.* Minor premise.

miniature [minja'ty:r], *n.f.* Miniature; illuminated letter drawn in minium in MS. *Portrait en miniature,* miniature(-portrait).

miniaturiste, *a.* Of miniatures.—*n.* Miniature-painter, miniaturist.

minier [mi'nje], *a.* (*fem.* **minière**) Pertaining to mines, mining.—*n.f.* Open mine or pit.

minime [mi'nim], *a.* Very small, trifling, inconsiderable.—*n.m.* Minim (monk of the order of St. Francesco di Paola).

minimum [mini'mɔm], *n.m.* (*pl.* **minimums** or **minima**) Minimum. *Au minimum,* at the very least; *minimum vital,* minimum living wage; *réduire au minimum,* to reduce to a minimum.—*a.* (*usu. inv.* but also *fem.* **minima** and *pl.* **minima** or **minimums**) Minimum.

ministère [minis'tε:r], *n.m.* Ministry, agency, charge; department; minister's office or function, ministration; offices, medium, services; administration. *Cela n'est pas de mon ministère,* that does not belong to my department; *le ministère des Affaires Étrangères, de l'Intérieur, des Forces armées,* the Foreign Office, the Home Office, Ministry of Defence; *le ministère public,* public prosecutor, prosecuting magistrate; *le ministère du Commerce,* the Board of Trade; *ministère du Ravitaillement,* Ministry of Food.

ministériel, *a.* (*fem.* **-ielle**) Ministerial. *Officiers ministériels,* (*Law*) Law officials.

ministre [mi'nistr], *n.m.* Minister; clergyman. *Le premier ministre,* the prime minister; *les ministres de l'autel,* the priests; *ministre de la Marine,* First Lord of the Admiralty; *ministre de l'Intérieur,* Home Secretary; *ministre des Affaires Étrangères,* Foreign Secretary; *ministre d'État,* Secretary of State; *ministre du Commerce,* President of the Board of Trade.

minium [mi'njɔm], *n.m.* Minium, red lead.

minois [mi'nwa], *n.m. inv.* Pretty face; looks, air, appearance.

minon [mi'nɔ̃], *n.m.* Puss, kitty; (*Bot.*) catkin.

minoritaire [minɔri'tε:r], *a.* Minority.

minorité [minɔri'te], *n.f.* Minority; nonage; (*Law*) infancy.

Minorque [mi'nɔrk], *f.* Minorca.

minot [mi'no], *n.m.* An old measure of 39 litres (8¾ gallons); (*Naut.*) bumpkin.

minotaure [minɔ'tɔ:r], *n.m.* (*Myth.*) Minotaur.

minoterie [minɔ'tri], *n.f.* Flour-mill, flour-store; flour export trade.

minotier, *n.m.* Flour-dealer, corn-factor.

minuit [mi'nɥi], *n.m.* Midnight, twelve o'clock at night. *Minuit et demi,* half past twelve at night.

minuscule [minys'kyl], *a.* Small (of letters), minute, tiny.—*n.f.* Small letter.

minus habens [minysa'bɛ̃s], *n.m. inv.* Mentally defective, simpleton.

minute [mi'nyt], *n.f.* Minute (of time), moment, instant; small-hand (writing); first draft, rough draft; minute, draft. *Faire la minute de,* to make a rough draft of, to take the minutes of. *Homme à la minute,* punctual man; *sablier de minute,* minute-glass. *Minute!* (*fam.*) just a moment! *La minute de vérité,* the moment of truth.

minuter, *v.t.* To minute down, to record; to design, to intend.

minuterie, *n.f.* Minute-wheels; minutes marked on a dial; time switch (which puts on the light only for a minute or so).

minutie [miny'si], *n.f.* Trifle, (*pl.*) minutiae.

minutieusement, *adv.* Minutely. **minutieux,** *a.* (*fem.* **-ieuse**) Minute; meticulous.

miocène [mjɔ'sε:n], *a.* and *n.m.* (*Geol.*) Miocene.

mioche [mjɔʃ], *n.* (*colloq.*) Brat, urchin, mite.

mi-parti [mipar'ti], *a.* (*fem.* **mi-partie**) Bipartite, divided into two equal but different parts; half and half. *Les avis ont été mi-partis,* opinions were equally divided.

miquelet [mi'klε], *n.m.* *Spanish bandit; irregular Spanish soldier.

mirabelle [mira'bεl], *n.f.* Yellow variety of plum.

miracle [mi'ra:kl], *n.m.* Miracle; (*fig.*) wonder, marvel. *À miracle,* wonderfully well; *c'est un miracle de vous voir,* it is a miracle to see you; *crier miracle* or *crier au miracle,* to declare a thing a miracle; *faire des miracles,* to work miracles; *faiseur de miracles,* miracle-worker.

miraculé, *a.* and *n.* (*fem.* **-ée**) Miraculously healed.

miraculeusement, *adv.* Miraculously; wonderfully. **miraculeux,** *a.* (*fem.* **-euse**) Miraculous; wonderful, marvellous.

mirador [mira'dɔr], *n.m.* (*Mil.*) Post of observation (generally in a tree); small platform or stage in a street for a policeman to control traffic; control tower in prison camp; mirador, belvedere.

mirage [mi'ra:ʒ], *n.m.* Mirage; (*Naut.*) looming; (*fig.*) shadow, delusion.

mire [mi:r], *n.f.* Land-surveyor's pole; (*Artill.*) aim; sight, fore-sight (of fire-arms). *Ligne de mire,* line of sight; *point de mire,* aim, point aimed at; object, end in view; *prendre sa mire,* to take aim.

mirer, *v.t.* To aim at; to have in view, to look at; to examine; to covet. *Mirer des œufs,* to test eggs (by holding them up to the light). **se mirer,** *v.r.* To look at oneself; to admire oneself, to be mirrored.

mirette, *n.f.* Mason's, modeller's pointing-tool; (*Bot.*) Venus' looking-glass; *pl.* (*slang*) eyes, peepers.

mirifique [miri'fik], *a.* (*colloq.*) Wonderful; admirable, splendid.

***mirliflore** [mirli'flɔ:r], *n.m.* Fop, dandy.

mirliton [mirli'tɔ̃], *n.m.* Reed-pipe; cream-roll; *conical shako. *Vers de mirliton,* doggerel.

mirmidon [mirmi'dɔ̃], *n.m.* Myrmidon; (*colloq.*) pigmy, little monkey.

mirobolant [mirɔbɔ'lɑ̃], *a.* (*fem.* **-ante**) (*colloq.*) Wonderful, first-rate, prodigious.

miroir [mi'rwa:r], *n.m.* Mirror, looking-glass; speck (on feathers, coat, etc.). *Des œufs au* *miroir*, fried eggs; *miroir ardent*, burning-mirror; *miroir de Vénus* [MIRETTE].

miroitant, *a.* (*fem.* **-ante**) Reflecting (like a mirror), glistening, glittering, shimmering.

miroité, *a.* (*fem.* **miroitée**) Shot, shiny, dappled (of horses). **miroitement**, *n.m.* Reflection of the light by polished surfaces; sheen, brilliancy.

miroiter, *v.i.* To reflect light, to shine, to glisten, to shimmer.

miroiterie, *n.f.* Looking-glass business, mirror-trade or factory.

miroitier, *n.m.* (*fem.* **miroitière**) Looking-glass maker or vendor.

miroton [mirɔ'tɔ̃], *n.m.* Stew containing beef with onions devilled.

mis, *p.p.* (*fem.* **mise** (1)) [METTRE]. *Bien*, or *mal, mis*, well, *or* badly, dressed.

misaine [mi'zɛːn], *n.f.* *Mât de misaine*, foremast; *voile de misaine*, foresail.

misanthrope [mizɑ̃'trɔp], *n.m.* Misanthrope.

misanthropie, *n.f.* Misanthropy. **misanthropique**, *a.* Misanthropic.

miscellanées [misɛla'ne], *n.f. pl.* Miscellanea, miscellany.

miscibilité [misibili'te], *n.f.* Miscibility.

miscible, *a.* Miscible, mixable.

mise (2) [miːz], *n.f.* Laying, placing, putting; stake; deposit, investment, outlay; bidding (at auctions); capital, share of capital; dress, manner of dressing; fashion, mode. *Avoir une mise simple*, to dress plainly; *ce tissu n'est pas de mise*, that material is not worn, is not in fashion; *mise à exécution*, carrying out; *mise à l'eau*, launching (of a ship); *mise à la retraite*, retirement; *mise au point*, restatement (of a question); (*Opt.*) focusing (of a lens); *mise au tombeau*, entombment; *mise en accusation*, indictment; *mise en arrestation*, apprehension; *mise en boîte*, (*fam.*) a leg-pull; *mise en jugement*, trial; *mise en liberté*, release; *mise en marche*, starting; starting-handle; *mise en marche automatique*, self-starter; *mise en musique*, setting to music; *mise en œuvre*, working up, preparation, employing, using; *mise en ondes*, production; *mise en plis*, setting (of the hair); *mise en possession*, putting in possession; *mise en scène*, (*Theat.*) production, staging, setting; (*Cine.*) direction; *mise en train*, setting to work, starting, (*Print.*) making ready; *mise en vente*, putting up for sale; *sa mise était de cent francs*, he had staked a hundred francs.

miser, *v.t.* (*colloq.*) To stage, wager, speculate; to bid (at an auction).

misérable [mize'rabl], *a.* Miserable, unfortunate, pitiable; poor, destitute; sorry, worthless; despicable.—*n.* Wretch, miserable person; miscreant. *C'est une misérable*, she is a wretch; *c'est un misérable*, he is a scoundrel; *les misérables*, the wretched, the outcasts. **misérablement**, *adv.* Miserably.

misère [mi'zɛːr], *n.f.* Misery, wretchedness, distress; poverty, want; trouble, calamity; trifle, trifling thing. *Crier misère*, to plead want, to complain of poverty; *faire des misères à quelqu'un*, to tease someone; to grieve someone; *il est mort de faim et de misère*, he died of starvation and want; *secourir la misère*, to help the destitute; *se fâcher pour des misères*, to make a fuss about trifles.

miserere [mize'rere], *n.m. inv.* Miserere (Ps. li). *Colique de miserere*, iliac passion.

miséreux, *a.* and *n.* (*fem.* **miséreuse**) Poor, destitute; seedy-looking (person).

miséricorde [mizeri'kɔrd], *n.f.* Mercy, pardon, grace; misericord (small rest under the seat of choir-stalls). *Ancre de miséricorde*, sheet-anchor; *à tout péché miséricorde*, no offence is utterly unpardonable; *crier miséricorde*, to cry for mercy; *faire miséricorde*, to show mercy; *il ne mérite point de miséricorde*, he deserves no mercy; *miséricorde! il va se tuer*, mercy on us! he will kill himself.

miséricordieux, *a.* (*fem.* **-ieuse**) Merciful, compassionate.—*n.* Merciful person. **miséricordieusement**, *adv.* Mercifully.

misogame [mizɔ'gam], *a.* Misogamous.

misogyne, *a.* Misogynous.—*n.* Misogynist. **misogynie**, *n.f.* Misogyny.

misonéiste, *n.* Opposed to anything new.

missel [mi'sɛl], *n.m.* Missal, mass-book.

mission [mi'sjɔ̃], *n.f.* Mission; commission, errand; mission station. *Envoyer en mission*, to send on a mission; *remplir une mission*, to perform a mission; *mission scientifique*, scientific expedition.

missionnaire, *n.m.* Missionary.

missive [mi'siːv], *a.* and *n.f.* Missive.

mistelle [mis'tɛl], *n.f.* Must of grapes muted through alcohol to stop fermentation.

mistenflûte [mistɑ̃'flyt], *n.m.* (*fam.*) Thingumajig.

mistigri [misti'gri], *n.m.* (*colloq.*) Cat, puss; pam (card game); jack of clubs.

mistoufle [mis'tufl], *n.f.* (*slang*) Dirty trick; poverty.

mistral [mis'tral], *n.m.* Mistral (cold north wind in southern France).

mitaine [mi'ten], *n.f.* Mitten.

mitan [mi'tɑ̃], *n.m.* (*dial.*) Middle.

mite [mit], *n.f.* Mite, maggot, tick; moth. *Mangé des mites*, moth-eaten. **mité**, *a.* (*fem.* **mitée**) Moth-eaten, maggoty.

mi-temps [mi'tɑ̃], *n.f.* (*Ftb.*) *La mi-temps*, half-time. *La première mi-temps*, the first half; *travailler à mi-temps*, to go on half time (work).

mi-terme (à) [mi'term], *adv. phr.* Half-way through a period.

miteux, *a.* (*fem.* **-euse**) Full of mites, (*fig.*) shabby, poverty-stricken.

Mithridate [mitri'dat], *m.* Mithridates.

mithridatiser [mitridati'ze], *v.t.* To render immune from poison.

mitigation [mitiga'sjɔ̃], *n.f.* Mitigation.

mitigé, *a.* (*fem.* **-ée**) Mitigated. *Peine mitigée*, modified penalty. **mitiger**, *v.t.* To mitigate, to alleviate, to modify.

miton [mi'tɔ̃], *n.m.* Woollen wrist-band or short mitten. (*fig.*) *Onguent miton mitaine*, harmless, useless ointment.

mitonner [mitɔ'ne], *v.i.* To let slices of bread simmer in the broth, to simmer.—*v.t.* To coddle, to fondle; to nurse. *Il aime qu'on le mitonne*, he likes to be coddled; *mitonner quelqu'un*, to humour someone; *mitonner une affaire*, to prepare an affair gradually.

mitose [mi'toːz], *n.f.* Mitosis.

mitoyen [mitwa'jɛ̃], *a.* (*fem.* **mitoyenne**) Mean, middle; intermediate, midway; party, joint. *Mur mitoyen*, party-wall.

mitoyenneté, *n.f.* Joint property, party-right, joint ownership.

mitraillade [mitra'jad], *n.f.* Discharge of grape-shot; machine-gunning.

mitraille [mi'traːj], *n.f.* Scrap-iron; mitraille, grape-shot; (*colloq.*) small change, coppers.

mitrailler, *v.i.* To fire mitraille, to machine-gun.—*v.t.* To riddle with mitraille, to rake with machine-gun fire, to machine-gun.

mitraillette, *n.f.* Tommy-gun.

mitrailleur, *n.m.* Machine-gunner.—*a. Fusil mitrailleur,* Bren gun. **mitrailleuse,** *n.f.* Machine-gun.

mitral [mi'tral], *a.* (*fem.* **mitrale,** *pl.* **mitraux**) Mitral, mitre-shaped.

mitre [mitr], *n.f.* Mitre; chimney-pot or -cowl.

mitré, *a.* (*fem.* **mitrée**) Mitred.

mitron [mi'trɔ̃], *n.m.* Journeyman baker; pastry-cook's boy.

mitte [mit], *n.f.* Cesspool exhalation, stench; eye infection from this.

mixage [mik'saːʒ], *n.m.* (*Cine.*) Mixing.

mixte [mikst], *a.* Mixed. *Commission mixte,* joint committee; *école mixte,* mixed school; *paquebot mixte,* cargo and passenger boat; *train mixte,* composite train.

mixtion [mik'stjɔ̃], *n.f.* Mixing (of drugs etc.).

mixture, *n.f.* Mixture; (*fam.*) stuff.

mnémonique [mnemɔ'nik], *a.* Mnemonic. —*n.f.* Mnemonics. **mnémoniser,** *v.t.* To memorize by mnemonic methods. **mnémotechnique,** *a.* Mnemotechnic.

mobile [mɔ'bil], *a.* Mobile, movable; changeable, unsteady, variable. *Garde mobile,* (*Fr. Hist.*) militia (in 1848, 1868–71); now militarized mounted police.—*n.m.* Body in motion; mover, motive power; a soldier of the militia. *L'intérêt est le plus grand mobile des hommes,* self-interest is the prime mover in human actions; *le premier mobile,* the prime mover; *reliure mobile,* detachable binding.

mobilier, *a.* (*fem.* **mobilière**) Movable; personal (of property). *Saisie mobilière,* distraint on furniture; *succession mobilière,* inheritance of personal property; *valeurs mobilières,* transferable shares.—*n.m.* Movables, furniture; suite of furniture.

mobilisable, *a.* (*Mil.*) That can be mobilized.

mobilisation, *n.f.* Mobilization; (*Law*) conversion into movables; liquidation (of capital).

mobiliser, *v.t.* (*Law*) To mobilize; to liquidate, to convert into movables; (*Mil.*) to mobilize.

mobilité, *n.f.* Mobility; variability; instability, fickleness. *Mobilité de caractère,* excitability of temperament.

mocassin [mɔka'sɛ̃], *n.m.* Moccasin (shoe).

moche [mɔʃ], *a.* (*slang*) Ugly; shoddy (work), dowdy (girl); lousy, rotten.

modal [mɔ'dal], *a.* (*fem.* **-ale,** *pl.* **-aux**) Modal. —*n.f.* Modal.

modalité, *n.f.* Modality. *Modalités de paiement,* methods of payment.

mode (1) [mɔd], *n.f.* Fashion; vogue; manner, way, custom; (*pl.*) millinery. *À la mode de,* after the manner of; *c'est la dernière mode,* it is the latest fashion; (*Cook.*) *du bœuf à la mode,* alamode beef; *être à la mode,* to be in fashion; *gravure de mode,* fashion-plate; *passé de mode,* out of fashion, unfashionable; *se mettre à la mode,* to dress in the fashion;

oncle, tante à la mode de Bretagne, first cousin once removed; a distant relation.

mode (2) [mɔd], *n.m.* (*Mus. etc.*) Mode; (*Gram.*) mood; method, mode. *Mode d'emploi,* directions for use.

modelage [mɔ'dlaːʒ], *n.m.* Modelling.

modèle [mɔ'dɛl], *n.m.* Model; pattern, design; (artist's) model. (*Article*) *petit modèle,* small size; *nouveau modèle,* new type; *conformez-vous au modèle,* keep to the pattern; *modèle parfait,* perfect model, paragon.—*a.* Exemplary. *Un enfant modèle,* a model child.

modelé [mɔ'dle], *n.m.* (*Sculp., Paint.*) Relief, density; imitation, reproduction.

modeler, *v.t.* To model; to shape; to mould (clay). **se modeler,** *v.r.* To model oneself (*sur*). *Il se modèle sur son frère,* he takes his brother as a model.

modeleur, *n.m.* Modeller.

modelliste or **modéliste,** *n.* Dress designer; (*Theat.*) model maker.

modénature [mɔdena'tyːr], *n.f.* (*Arch.*) Profile (of a cornice mouldings).

Modène [mɔ'dɛːn], *f.* Modena.

modérantisme [mɔderɑ̃'tism], *n.m.* Moderatism (in politics etc.).

modérateur [mɔdera'tœːr], *n.m.* (*fem.* **modératrice**) Moderator; (*Mech.*) regulator, governor; volume-control.—*a.* Moderating, restraining.

modération [mɔderɑ'sjɔ̃], *n.f.* Moderation; abatement, diminution, mitigation.

modéré, *a.* (*fem.* **-ée**) Moderate, reasonable, temperate. *Allure modérée,* steady pace.—*n.* (*Polit.*) Conservative, moderate. **modérément,** *adv.* Moderately, in moderation.

modérer, *v.t. irr.* (*conjug. like* ACCÉLÉRER) To moderate, to abate, to mitigate; to restrain, to restrict. *Modérer le zèle de quelqu'un,* to restrain someone's zeal; *modérer ses passions,* to curb one's passions. **se modérer,** *v.r.* To moderate oneself, to keep one's temper; to restrain oneself. *Le temps s'est modéré,* the weather has become calmer.

moderne [mɔ'dɛrn], *a.* Modern, up-to-date. —*n.m.* Modern style.

modernisation, *n.f.* Modernization.

moderniser, *v.t.* To modernize.

modernisme, *n.m.* Modernism. **moderniste,** *n.* Modernist.

modernité, *n.f.* Modernity.

modeste [mɔ'dɛst], *a.* Modest, unassuming, unpretentious; quiet, simple; moderate. **modestement,** *adv.* Modestly, quietly, simply.

modestie, *n.f.* Modesty, simplicity, plainness; moderation.

modicité [mɔdisi'te], *n.f.* Smallness, lowness; small quantity, modicum.

modifiable [mɔdi'fjabl], *a.* Modifiable.

modifiant, *a.* (*fem.* **-ante**) Modifying.

modificateur, *a.* (*fem.* **-trice**) Modifying.—*n.* Modifier.

modificatif, *a.* (*fem.* **-ive**) Modifying.—*n.m.* (*Gram.*) Modifying word.

modification [mɔdifika'sjɔ̃], *n.f.* Modification.

modifier, *v.t.* (*conjugated like* PRIER) To modify, to change, to alter. **se modifier,** *v.r.* To become modified.

modillon [mɔdi'jɔ̃], *n.m.* (*Arch.*) Modillion.

modique [mɔ'dik], *a.* Moderate; small. **modiquement,** *adv.* Moderately; little.

modiste [mɔ'dist], *n.* Modiste, milliner.
modulant [mɔdy'lã], *a.* (*fem.* **-ante**) Modulating.
modulateur, *a.* (*fem.* **-trice**) Modulating.—*n.* Modulator.
modulation, *n.f.* Modulation, inflexion. (*Rad.*) *Modulation de fréquence*, very high frequency, V.H.F.
module [mɔ'dyl], *n.m.* (*Arch.*) Module; (*Math.*) modulus; unit of measurement (*esp.* for running water); diameter of medals, coins, etc.; thickness of metal (in bells). *Cigarettes gros module*, large-sized cigarettes.
moduler [mɔdy'le], *v.t.* To modulate.—*v.i.* To pass from one tone to another; to warble.
modus vivendi [mɔdys vivɛ̃'di], *m. inv.* A working agreement.
moelle [mwal], *n.f.* Marrow (of bone); (*Bot.*) pith; (*Anat.*) medulla. *Jusqu'à la moelle*, to the very marrow, to the backbone; (*fam.*) *être trempé jusqu'à la moelle*, to be soaked through; *moelle épinière*, spinal marrow; *os à moelle*, marrowbone.
moelleusement, *adv.* Softly; (*Paint.*) with mellowness.
moelleux, *a.* (*fem.* **moelleuse**) Full of marrow, marrowy; pithy; soft, velvety; mellow. *Discours moelleux*, pithy discourse; *vin moelleux*, mellow wine (full of body and flavour); *voix moelleuse*, mellow voice.—*n.m.* Softness; mellowness.
moellon [mwa'lɔ̃], *n.m.* Rubble, roughstone. *Moellon (d'appareil)*, ashlar.
moère [mwɛr], *n.f.* (*N. dial.*) Polder.
mœurs [mœrs, *occasionally* mœːr], *n.f. pl.* Morals, morality; manners, habits, ways, manners and customs. *Attentat aux mœurs*, indecent behaviour; *autres temps autres mœurs*, manners change with the times; *avoir des mœurs*, to be a man of morals; *certificat de bonne vie et mœurs*, certificate of good character; *les mœurs des animaux*, the habits of animals.
*mofette (1) [mɔ'fɛt], *n.f.* Choke-damp; noxious fume, poisonous gas.
mofette (2) [mɔ'fɛt], *n.f.* (*Zool.*) Skunk.
Mogol [mɔ'gɔl], *m.* Mogul.
mohair [mɔ'ɛːr], *n.m.* Mohair.
mohatra [mɔa'tra], *a.* (*Law*) *Contrat mohatra*, usurious and illegal loan camouflaged as a bona fide sale; mohatra.
moi [mwa], *pron. pers.* I; me, to me. *À moi!* help! here! *c'est à moi*, it is mine; *ce n'est pas moi qui le ferais*, I'm not the one to do it; *de vous à moi*, between you and me; *donnez-le-moi*, give it (to) me; *moi-même*, myself; *moi! trahir le meilleur de mes amis!* what! I betray my best friend; *parlez-moi*, speak to me; *quant à moi*, as for me; *regardez-moi ça!* just look at that! *venez à moi*, come to me.—*n.m.* Self, ego. *L'identité du moi*, personal identity.
moie [mwa], *n.f.* Mow (of hay).
moignet [mwa'ɲɛ], *n.m.* (*Orn.*) Long-tailed titmouse.
moignon [mwa'ɲɔ̃], *n.m.* Stump (of limbs, trees, etc.).
moindre [mwɛ̃ːdr], *a.* Less, smaller, shorter; slighter, less important, inferior (*que*); the least, the smallest, the slightest. *Je n'en ai pas le moindre souvenir*, I have not the least recollection of it; *la moindre chose*, the least thing; *le moindre*, least, shortest, smallest,

meanest, slightest. *Le dernier, non le moindre*, last, not least; *c'est le moindre de mes soucis*, I don't care a bit; that's the least of my worries. **moindrement**, *adv.* Least. *Pas le moindrement du monde*, not in the least.
moine [mwan], *n.m.* Monk, friar; monk-fish or shark-ray or mongrel skate; monk-seal; bed-warmer; (*Print.*) friar; (*Naut.*) maroon or long-light (used for signalling). *Gras comme un moine*, as fat as a priest; *l'habit ne fait pas le moine*, it is not the cowl that makes the monk.
moineau [mwa'no], *n.m.* (*pl.* **-eaux**) Sparrow. *Moineau des champs*, hedge-sparrow; *moineau franc* or *domestique* or *pierrot*, house-sparrow; *moineau friquet* or *montagnard*, tree-sparrow; *brûler sa poudre aux moineaux*, to waste one's powder and shot; *têtes de moineau*, nuts of coal; (*fam.*) *un vilain moineau*, a disreputable fellow.
moinerie [mwan'ri], *n.f.* (*pej.*) Monks, monastery.
moinesse, *n.f.* (*pej.*) Nun.
moinillon, *n.m.* (*colloq.*) Petty monk, shaveling.
moinotin [mwanɔ'tɛ̃], *n.m.* (*Orn.*) Coaltitmouse.
moins [mwɛ̃], *adv.* Less; fewer (*de* or *que*); not so. *À moins*, for less; *à moins de*, for less than, unless; *à moins qu'il ne le fasse*, unless he does it; *au moins*, at least; *c'est le moins que vous puissiez faire*, it is the least you can do; *c'est moins que rien*, it is next to nothing; *de moins en moins*, less and less, fewer and fewer; *du moins*, at least, at any rate, at all events; *en* or *dans moins de*, in less than; *il a trois ans de moins que moi*, he is three years younger than I; *il ne s'agit de rien moins que de sa vie*, nothing less than his life is at stake; *il n'est rien moins que sage*, he is anything but prudent; *il n'y a rien de moins vrai que cette nouvelle*, no news can be further from the truth than this; *les moins de seize ans*, the under sixteens; *moins il travaille, plus il mange*, the less he works the more he eats; *ni plus ni moins*, neither more nor less; *non moins que*, as well as; *parlez moins*, speak less; *pas le moins du monde*, not in the least; *pour le moins*, at least; *rien moins*, much less; *tout au moins*, at the very least; *vous ne l'aurez pas à moins*, you shall not have it for less.—*prep.* Less, minus. *Une heure moins un quart*, a quarter to one; *il était moins cinq* (or *moins une*), (we had) a narrow squeak; *onze moins cinq égale six*, eleven minus five equals six.—*n.m.* (*Math.*) Minus sign; (*Print.*) dash.
moins-value, *n.f.* (*pl.* **moins-values**) Decrease in value; loss of value.
moirage [mwa'raːʒ], *n.m.* Watering (of silk).
moire [mwar], *n.f.* Watering, moire, watered silk.
moiré [mwa're], *a.* (*fem.* **-ée**) Watered, moiré.—*n.m.* Watered effect.
moirer, *v.t.* To moiré, to give a watered appearance to.
moirure, *n.f.* Watered effect.
mois [mwa], *n.m.* Month; monthly allowance, month's pay. *Au mois*, by the month; *au mois de*, in the month of; *par mois*, monthly, (so much) a month.
moise [mwaːz], *n.f.* (*Carp.*) Brace, binding-piece.

Moïse [mɔ'iːz], *m.* Moses.
moïse [mɔ'iːz], *n.m.* Small wicker-cradle.
moiser [mwa'ze], *v.t.* (*Carp.*) To brace, to tie.
moisi [mwa'zi], *a.* (*fem.* **moisie**) Mouldy, musty.—*n.m.* Mouldiness, mustiness; musty part, thing, etc. *Sentir le moisi*, to smell musty. **moisir**, *v.t.* To make mouldy or musty. *v.i.* or *se moisir*, *v.r.* To grow mouldy or musty. **moisissure**, *n.f.* Mouldiness, mustiness, mildew.
moissine [mwa'sin], *n.f.* Vine-branch with grapes hanging (cut so to be kept).
moisson [mwa'sɔ̃], *n.f.* Harvest, harvest-time, crop. *Faire la moisson*, to gather in the harvest.
moissonnage [mwasɔ'naːʒ], *n.m.* Harvesting.
moissonner, *v.t.* To reap, to gather in, to mow; (*fig.*) to cut down, to destroy. *Moissonner un champ*, to reap a field.
moissonneur, *n.m.* (*fem.* **moissonneuse**) Reaper, harvester.—*n.f.* Reaping-machine.
moissonneuse-batteuse, *n.f.* (*pl.* **moissonneuses-batteuses**) Combine harvester.
moissonneuse-lieuse, *n.f.* (*pl.* **moissonneuses-lieuses**) Reaper and binder.
moite [mwat], *a.* Moist, damp; clammy.
moiteur, *n.f.* Moistness, dampness. *Moiteur froide*, clamminess.
moitié [mwa'tje], *n.f.* Half; (*colloq.*) better half, wife.—*adv.* Half. *À moitié*, half, by halves; *à moitié fait*, half done; *à moitié prix*, for half price; *trop cher de moitié*, too dear by half; *être* or *se mettre de moitié avec quelqu'un*, to go halves with someone; *être plus qu'à moitié convaincu*, to be more than half convinced; *je l'ai laissé à moitié chemin*, I left him half-way.
moitir [mwa'tiːr], *v.t.* To moisten; to make damp.
Moka [mɔ'ka], *m.* Mocha.
moka [mɔ'ka], *n.m.* Mocha (coffee or cake).
mol [MOU].
molaire [mɔ'lɛːr], *a.* Molar.—*n.f.* Molar-tooth.
molard [mɔ'lar], *n.m.* (*vulg.*) Spit.
molasse [mɔ'las], *n.f.* Molasse, sandstone.
Moldavie [mɔlda'vi], **la,** *f.* Moldavia.
môle (1) [moːl], *n.m.* Mole, pier.
môle (2) [moːl], *n.f.* (*Path.*) Mole. (*Ichth.*) Sun-fish.
moléculaire [mɔleky'lɛːr], *a.* Molecular.
molécule, *n.f.* Molecule. **molécule-gramme**, *n.f.* (*pl.* **molécules-grammes**) Gramme-molecule.
molène [mɔ'lɛːn], *n.f.* (*Bot.*) Name of several *Verbascum*, e.g., *bouillon blanc*, mullein (called also *chandelier, cierge de Notre-Dame, verge d'Aaron*). *Molène blattaire*, moth-mullein.
moleskine or **moleskine** [mɔlɛs'kin], *n.f.* Cotton velvet for lining; imitation leather; rexine.
molestation [mɔlɛsta'sjɔ̃], *n.f.* Molestation, annoyance.
molester, *v.t.* To molest, to trouble.
molet(t)age [mɔl'taʒ], *n.m.* Milling.
molette [mɔ'lɛt], *n.f.* Muller (for grinding and mixing colours); rowel (of a spur); (*Vet.*) wind-gall; tool with small wheel and handle (of various kinds); turfing-iron; (rope-making) whirl. *Clef à molette*, adjustable spanner. **molet(t)er**, *v.t.* To mill, to knurl. *Anneau moleté*, milled ring.

molinie [mɔli'ni], *n.f.* (*Bot.*) *Molinia caerulea*.
molinisme [mɔli'nism], *n.m.* Molinism.
moliniste, *n.m.* Molinist.
mollasse [mɔ'las], *a.* Flabby; spineless, apathetic.
molle [MOU].
mollement [mɔl'mɑ̃], *adv.* Softly; gently; feebly; slackly, remissly; indolently; tamely, effeminately. *Vivre mollement*, to lead an indolent life.
mollesse, *n.f.* Softness, mildness; flabbiness; laxity, slackness; tameness; indolence; weakness; effeminacy. *Vivre dans la mollesse*, to lead a life of luxury, to lead a soft life.
mollet [mɔ'lɛ], *a.* (*fem.* **mollette**) Soft; light (of bread). *Des œufs mollets*, soft-boiled eggs; *pain mollet*, light bread.—*n.m.* Calf (of the leg). **molletière**, *n.f.* Legging, puttee.
molleton [mɔl'tɔ̃], *n.m.* Thick flannel, duffel; swanskin. **molletonner**, *v.t.* To line or pad with *molleton*.
mollir [mɔ'liːr], *v.i.* To soften, to grow soft; to mellow (of fruit); to slacken, to flag, to abate, to give way; (*Row.*) to row slowly. *Le vent mollit*, the wind is going down.
mollusque [mɔ'lysk], *n.m.* Mollusc; (*fig.*) weakling; 'slug'.
moloch [mɔ'lɔk], *n.m.* (*Austral.*) Spiny lizard, thorn-devil.
molosse [mɔ'lɔs], *n.m.* Mastiff, watch-dog; American bat.
Moluques [mɔ'lyk], **les,** *f. pl.* The Moluccas.
moly [mɔ'li], *n.m.* Moly; wild garlic.
molybdène [mɔlib'dɛːn], *n.m.* Molybdenum.
môme [moːm], *n.m.* and *f.* (*pop.*) Brat, urchin, girl.
moment [mɔ'mɑ̃], *n.m.* Moment, instant; proper time; favourable occasion; present time; momentum. *À tous moments*, at every turn; *à tout moment*, every instant; *attendez un moment*, wait a moment; *au moment de*, just as; *au moment même*, at the very moment; *au moment où*, the instant that, just as; *du moment que vous le voulez*, since you will have it so; *en ce moment*, at this moment; *il a des moments de bonté*, he has fits of kindness; *je l'attends d'un moment à l'autre*, I expect him any moment; *par moments*, at times, at intervals; *un moment, j'ai à vous parler*, one moment, I want to speak to you; *un petit moment*, just a moment; *voici le moment de se décider*, now is the time for decision.
momentané, *a.* (*fem.* **-ée**) Momentary. **momentanément**, *adv.* Momentarily; for the time being.
momerie [mɔm'ri], *n.f.* Mummery; affected mannerisms.
mômerie [mom'ri], *n.f.* (*slang*) Kids, youngsters.
momie [mɔ'mi], *n.f.* Mummy; (*fig.*) thin, dried-up person; old fogy.
momification, *n.f.* Mummification.
momifier, *v.t.* (*conjugated like* PRIER) To mummify. **se momifier**, *v.r.* To become mummified; (*fig.*) to get very thin; to become an old fogy.
mominette [mɔmi'nɛt], *n.f.* (*pop.*) Small glass of absinthe with water.
mon [mɔ̃], *a.poss.m.* (*fem.* **ma**, *pl.* **mes**) My. *Mon âme*, my soul, my love; *mon bon et digne ami*, my good and worthy friend; *mon père, ma mère, et mes enfants*, my father, mother,

and children; *mon unique ressource*, my only resource. [*Mon* is used instead of *ma* (in the feminine) before a vowel or unaspirated *h*.] N.B.—In the French Army (not in the Navy), when speaking or writing to an officer, any private or N.C.O., and any officer to his superior, *must* use *mon* before the grade of the addressee, e.g. *Oui, mon capitaine; non, mon général*, Yes, Sir; no, Sir. Only officers with the title of *maréchal* and those who occupy special posts are addressed as *Monsieur* (*Monsieur le Maréchal, Monsieur le Gouverneur militaire de Paris*, etc.).

monacal [mɔna′kal], *a.* (*fem.* **monacale,** *pl.* **monacaux**) Monachal, monkish. **monacalement,** *adv.* Like a monk.

monachisme [mɔna′kism], *n.m.* Monachism.

monade [mɔ′nad], *n.f.* Monad.

monadelphe [mɔna′dɛlf], *a.* (*Bot.*) Monadelphous.

monandrie [mɔnɑ̃′dri], *n.f.* (*Bot.*) Monandria.

monarchie [mɔnar′ʃi], *n.f.* Monarchy. **monarchique,** *a.* Monarchical. **monarchiser,** *v.t.* To monarchize.

monarchisme, *n.m.* Monarchism, system of monarchy.

monarchiste, *n.* and *a.* Monarchist.

monarque [mɔ′nark], *n.m.* Monarch.

monastère [mɔnas′tɛːr], *n.m.* Monastery, convent.

monastique, *a.* Monastic.

monaut [mɔ′no], *a.m.* One-eared (of animals).

monbin [mɔ̃′bɛ̃], *n.m.* (*Bot.*) Hog-plum.

monbrétia [mɔ̃bre′sja], *n.f.* Montbretia; common name of varieties of small bulbs, such as, *étoile de feu, gerbe d'or, œil de dragon.*

monceau [mɔ̃′so], *n.m.* (*pl.* **-eaux**) Heap, pile.

mondain [mɔ̃′dɛ̃], *a.* (*fem.* **mondaine**) Worldly, worldly-minded; mundane, earthly. *La vie mondaine*, fashionable society; round of social engagements.—*n.* Worldly person; man about town. *Les mondains*, people in society. **mondainement,** *adv.* In a worldly manner. **mondanité,** *n.f.* Worldliness, worldly vanities; society gossip; (*pl.*) social events.

monde (1) [mɔ̃:d], *n.m.* World; universe; mankind, men; people; society; company, set; men, hands; customers; worldly life; (*Her.*) mond, orb. *Ainsi va le monde*, such is life; *avoir du monde*, to have visitors; *au bout du monde*, miles away; *c'est le bout du monde*, it is the utmost you will get; *c'est le monde renversé*, everything is turned upside down; *connaître son monde*, to know whom one has to deal with; *faire le tour du monde*, to go round the world; *homme du monde*, man of the world; *il n'est plus de ce monde*, he is dead; *il voit beaucoup de monde*, he sees a great deal of company; *l'autre monde*, the next world; *le beau monde*, fashionable society; *le mieux du monde*, the best in the world; *mettre au monde*, to give birth to; *peu de monde* or *pas grand monde*, not many people; *pour rien au monde*, not for anything in the world; *se moquer du monde*, to make fun of people; *tout le monde*, everybody; *venir au monde*, to come into the world; *vieux comme le monde*, as old as the hills.

monde (2), *a.* Only used in *les animaux mondes et immondes*, clean and unclean animals.

monder [mɔ̃′de], *v.t.* To cleanse; to hull (barley), to blanch (almonds) [*see* ORGE].

mondial [mɔ̃′djal], *a.* (*fem.* **-iale,** *pl.* **-iaux**) World-wide. *Guerre mondiale*, world-war.

mondification [mɔ̃difika′sjɔ̃], *n.f.* (*Surg.*) Mundification. **mondifier,** *v.t.* To cleanse.

Monégasque [mɔne′gask], *n.* and *a.* Native of Monaco.

monétaire [mɔne′tɛːr], *a.* Monetary. **monétisation,** *n.f.* Making and stamping of money, minting, monetization. **monétiser,** *v.t.* To monetize.

mongol [mɔ̃′gɔl], *a.* (*fem.* **mongole**) Mongolian. *n.m.* **Mongol** (*fem.* **Mongole**) Mongol. **Mongolie,** *f.* Mongolia.

mongoloïde, *a.* Mongoloid.

*****monial** [mɔ′njal], *a.* (*fem.* **moniale,** *pl.* **moniaux**) Monachal.—*n.f.* Cloistered nun.

Monime [mɔ′nim], *f.* Monima.

Monique [mɔ′nik], *f.* Monica.

monisme [mɔ′nism], *n.m.* Monism. **moniste,** *n.* Monist. **monistique,** *a.* Monistic.

moniteur [mɔni′tœːr], *n.m.* (*fem.* **-trice**) (*sch.*) Prefect, monitor; coach, instructor; gazette. (*Mil.*) *Moniteur de gymnastique*, instructor in gymnastics.

monition [mɔni′sjɔ̃], *n.f.* Monition.

monitoire, *n.m.* and *a.* (*R.-C. Ch.*) Monitory.

monitor [mɔni′tɔːr], *n.m.* (*Naut.*) Monitor.

monitorial [mɔnitɔ′rjal], *a.* (*fem.* **monitoriale,** *pl.* **monitoriaux**) Monitory.

monnaie [mɔ′nɛ], *n.f.* Coin, money; change; mint. *Battre monnaie* [BATTRE]; *donner* or *rendre à quelqu'un la monnaie de sa pièce*, to pay someone back in his own coin; *donnez-moi la monnaie de vingt francs*, give me change for twenty francs; *fausse monnaie*, counterfeit coin; *hôtel de la monnaie* or *des Monnaies* [HÔTEL]; *monnaie blanche* [BLANC]; *monnaie de compte*, nominal money; *monnaie forte*, hard currency; *monnaie de singe*, sham coin, soft sawder, blarney; *payer en monnaie de singe*, to laugh at one's creditors; *monnaie fictive* or *papier monnaie*, paper money; *monnaie légale*, legal tender; *petite monnaie*, small change.

monnaie du pape [*see* LUNAIRE].

monnayage, *n.m.* Coining, minting. *Droit de monnayage*, mintage, seigniorage.

monnayer, *v.t. irr.* (*conjug. like* BALAYER) To coin into money, to mint.

monnayère, *n.f.* (*Bot.*) Money-wort; penny-cress. **monnayeur,** *n.m.* Coiner, minter. *Faux monnayeur*, counterfeiter, forger.

monobase [mɔnɔ′baːz], *a.* Monobasic.

monobloc, *a.* Cast in one piece.

monocamérisme or **monocaméralisme,** *n.m.* Unicameral political régime.

monocarpe, *a.* Monocarpous.

monochrome, *a.* Monochrome.

monochromie, *n.f.* Monochromy.

monocle [mɔ′nɔkl], *n.m.* Monocle, (single) eyeglass.

monoclinique, *a.* (*Cryst.*) Monoclinic.

monocorde, *n.m.* Monochord.—*a.* Monotonous. **monocotylédone,** *a.* (*Bot.*) Monocotyledonous.—*n.f.* Monocotyledon.

monoculaire, *a.* Monocular.

monocycle, *n.m.* Monocycle.

monocylindrique, *a.* One-cylinder, single-cylinder.

monœcie, *n.f.* (*Bot.*) Monoecian.

monogame, *a.* Monogamous. **monogamie,**
n.f. Monogamy. **monogamique,** *a.* Monogamous.

monogenèse or **monogénèse,** *n.f.* Monogenesis. **monogenésique** or **monogénésique,** *a.* Monogenetic.

monogramme, *n.m.* Monogram.

monographie, *n.f.* Monograph.

monogyne, *a.* Monogynous. **monogynie,**
n.f. Monogyny.

monoïque, *a.* (*Bot.*) Monoecious.

monolithe, *n.m.* Monolith.—*a.* Monolithic.

monologue, *n.m.* Monologue, soliloquy.
monolog·ier, *v.i.* To soliloquize.

monomane or **monomaniaque,** *n.* and *a.*
Monomaniac.

monomanie, *n.f.* Monomania.

monôme [mɔ'noːm], *n.m.* (*Alg.*) Monomial;
procession of students in single file.

monométallisme [mɔnɔmetaˈlism], *n.m.*
Monometallism. **monométalliste,** *n.* Monometallist.—*a.* Monometallic.

monomoteur, *a.m.* Single-engined (aircraft).

mononucléaire, *a.* Mononuclear.

monopétale, *a.* (*Bot.*) Monopetalous.

monophasé, *a.* (*fem.* -ée) (*Elec.*) Monophase.

monophone, *n.m.* Monophone.

monophylle, *a.* (*Bot.*) Monophyllous.

monoplace, *n.m.* and *a.* Single-seater.

monoplan, *n.m.* Monoplane.

monoplastide, *n.m.* Monoplast.

monopode, *a.* Monopodous.

monopole, *n.m.* Monopoly. **monopolisateur,** *n.m.* Monopolist. **monopoliser,** *v.t.*
To monopolize. **monopolistique,** *a.* Monopolistic.

monoptère, *a.* (*Arch.*) Monopteral.

monorail, *a.* and *n.m.* Monorail.

monorime, *a.* Monorhyme.

monosépale, *a.* (*Bot.*) Monosepalous.

monosperme, *a.* (*Bot.*) Monospermous.

monostique, *a.* and *n.m.* (*Pros.*) Monostich.

monosyllabe, *a.* Monosyllable.—*a.* Monosyllabic. **monosyllabique,** *a.* Monosyllabic. **monosyllabisme,** *n.m.* Monosyllabism.

monothéisme, *n.m.* Monotheism. **monothéiste,** *a.* Monotheistic.—*n.* Monotheist.

monotone, *a.* Monotonous. **monotonie,** *n.f.*
Monotony, sameness.

monotype, *a.* Monotypic.—*n.m.* Monotype.

monseigneur (1) [mɔ̃sɛ'pœːr], *n.m.* (*pl.* **messeigneurs** or **nosseigneurs**) My lord; your
Grace; your Royal or Imperial Highness.

monseigneur (2) [mɔ̃sɛ'pœːr], *n.m.* (*pl.* **mon-
seigneurs**) Also *pince monseigneur, n.f.*
(Burglar's) jemmy.

monsieur [mə'sjø, msjø], *n.m.* (*pl.* **messieurs**)
Sir; gentleman, this gentleman; the master
of the house; the king of France's eldest
brother. *Ce monsieur,* that gentleman, (*iron.*)
that man, that fellow; *c'est un vilain monsieur,*
he is a nasty fellow; *faire le monsieur,* to play
the fine gentleman; *mon petit monsieur,*
(*iron.*) my lad; *Monsieur A.,* Mr. A.; *monsieur
dit,* the gentleman says, this gentleman says;
monsieur le maire, Mr. Mayor; *Monsieur le
Président,* Mr. President; *monsieur veut-il
déjeuner?* would you like breakfast, sir?
monsieur votre père, your father; *non, monsieur,*
no, sir.

monstrance [mɔ̃s'trãs], *n.f.* (*R.-C. Ch.*)
Monstrance.

monstre [mɔ̃:str], *n.m.* Monster.—*a.* (*fam.*)
Huge. **monstrueusement,** *adv.* Monstrously, prodigiously.

monstrueux, *a.* (*fem.* **monstrueuse**) Monstrous, prodigious, dreadful.

monstruosité, *n.f.* Monstrosity.

mont [mɔ̃], *n.m.* Hill, mount, mountain. *Par
monts et par vaux,* up hill and down dale; *le
mont Etna,* Mount Etna; *promettre monts et
merveilles,* to promise the earth.

montage [mɔ̃'taːʒ], *n.m.* Carrying up; mounting, setting, putting together; fitting on;
assembling; connecting, wiring; (*Cine.*)
editing (of film). (*Ind.*) *Chaîne de montage,*
assembly line.

montagnard [mɔ̃ta'paːr], *a.* (*fem.* **monta-
gnarde**) Mountain, highland.—*n.* Mountaineer, highlander; (*Fr. Hist.*) member of
La Montagne.

montagne [mɔ̃'tap], *n.f.* Mountain; hill; (*Fr.
Hist.*) democratic party in the Convention
and National Assembly, 1793. *La montagne
a enfanté une souris,* the mountain has brought
forth a mouse; *se faire une montagne de . . . ,*
to overestimate the difficulties of . . . ; *pays de
montagnes,* mountainous, hilly country; *montagnes russes,* switchback (railway).

montagneux, *a.* (*fem.* **montagneuse**) Mountainous, hilly.

montaison [mɔ̃tɛ'zɔ̃], *n.f.* Run-up of salmon.

montanisme [mɔ̃ta'nism], *n.m.* Montanism.

montant (1) [mɔ̃'tɑ̃], *n.m.* Upright (of a
ladder etc.); post (of door etc.); (*Naut.*)
stanchion; height (of vault etc.); rising flight
(of falcon); part of horse's bridle; amount,
sum total; coming in or rising tide; high
flavour, pungency; (*Ftb.*) goal-post.

montant (2) [mɔ̃'tɑ̃], *a.* (*fem.* **montante**)
Rising; ascending, uphill, flowing, coming
in; high-necked (of dresses). *Aller en montant,* to rise, to go uphill; *la garde montante,*
the new (or relieving) guard; *la marée montante,* the rising tide; *train montant,* up train;
un chemin montant, a hilly road; *une robe
montante,* a high-necked dress.

mont-de-piété [mɔ̃dpjɛ'te], *n.m.* (*pl.* **monts-
de-piété**) (Municipal) pawnshop (now
officially styled *Crédit Municipal*). *Mettre au
mont-de-piété,* to pawn.

monte [mɔ̃:t], *n.f.* Mounting, mount (of a
jockey); serving (of animals), covering
season.

monté [mɔ̃'te], *a.* (*fem.* **montée** (1)) Mounted
(officer, soldier); raised; set (of gems etc.);
supplied, furnished; equipped; manned (of
ships etc.). *Être bien* or *mal monté,* to be on
a good *or* a poor horse; (of a shopkeeper) to
be well supplied; *un coup monté,* a put-up
job; *être monté,* to be angry; *monté en couleur,*
highly coloured.

monte-charge [mɔ̃t'ʃarʒ], *n.m. inv.* Hoist,
goods lift; (*Am.*) elevator.

montée (2) [mɔ̃'te], *n.f.* Gradient, slope;
ascent; rising; (*Arch. etc.*) height.

monte-en-l'air [mɔ̃tɑ̃'lɛr], *n.m. inv.* (*slang*)
Cat-burglar.

monte-plats [mɔ̃t'pla], *n.m. inv.* Lift for
dishes (from kitchen to dining-room).

monter [mɔ̃'te], *v.i.* (with *avoir* or *être* according as action or condition is meant) To go
up, to ascend, to mount; to climb; to embark;
to rise, to slope up, to be uphill; to grow up,

to shoot; to increase; to amount; to get on, to have advancement. *Faire monter*, to make (a person) go up or get up; (*fam.*) to get a rise out of; *la marée monte*, the tide is coming in; *monter à cheval*, to ride; *monter à bicyclette*, to ride a bicycle; *monter à l'échelle*, to go up the ladder; *monter dans le train*, to get on a train, (*Am.*) to board a train; *monter en avion*, to emplane; *monter en chaire*, to preach; *monter en grade*, to be promoted; *monter en voiture*, to get in a car; *les prix montent*, prices are going up; *monter à la tête* (of wine), to go to the head; *monter et descendre*, to go up and down; *monter sur un arbre*, to climb a tree; (*fig.*) *monter sur ses grands chevaux*, to mount one's high horse.— *v.t.* To mount, to ascend, to go up; to walk, ride, row, etc., up; to get up on, to ride; to carry up, to lift up, to make up, to bring up, to raise; to wind up; to equip, to furnish, to stock; to put together, to make up, to set; to rouse, to work up, to excite, to stir; to establish. *Faire monter*, to make go up, to send up, to make to take up, to bring up, to raise, to have mounted; *monter la garde*, to mount guard; *monter la tête à quelqu'un*, to excite someone; *monter le cou à quelqu'un*, to take someone in; *monter le gouvernail*, to hang the rudder; *monter un cheval*, to mount a horse, to train a horse; *monter un diamant*, to set a diamond; *monter un pneu*, to fit on a tyre; *monter une pièce*, to stage a play. **se monter**, *v.r.* To amount, to rise; to get excited; to supply oneself with (*en*). *Se monter la tête*, to get excited. **monteur**, *n.m.* (*fem.* **-euse**) Setter, mounter (of jewels, machinery, etc.); (*Cine.*) (film-)editor.

montgolfière [mɔ̃gɔlˈfjɛːr], *n.f.* Fire-balloon.

monticule [mɔ̃tiˈkyl], *n.m.* Hillock, knoll.

mont-joie [mɔ̃ˈʒwa], *n.f.* (*pl.* **monts-joie**) Cairn; (*Mil.*) hill serving as observation post; *mound, heap; (*Fr. Hist.*) war-standard. *Mont-joie Saint Denis!* ancient war-cry of the French.

montoir [mɔ̃ˈtwaːr], *n.m.* Horse-block. *Côté du montoir*, near side; *côté hors montoir*, off side; *difficile* or *doux au montoir*, difficult *or* easy to mount.

montrable [mɔ̃ˈtrabl], *a.* Showable, presentable.

montre (1) [mɔ̃ːtr], *n.f.* Show-case, show, exhibition, shop-window; parade, pattern; sample. *En montre*, in the window, prominently; *faire montre de son esprit*, to show off one's wit.

montre (2) [mɔ̃ːtr], *n.f.* Watch. (*Cycl.*) *Course contre la montre*, time-race. *Il est une heure à ma montre*, it is one o'clock by my watch. *Montre à arrêt*, stop-watch; *montre à remontoir*, keyless watch, (*Am.*) stem-winder; *montre à répétition*, repeater; *montre marine*, chronometer. (*Chem.*) *Montre fusible*, temperature indicator. **montre-bracelet**, *n.f.* (*pl.* **montres-bracelets**) Wrist-watch.

montrer [mɔ̃ˈtre], *v.t.* To show, to display; to make manifest, to demonstrate, to point out; to teach; to set forth, to intimate; to evince, to indicate. *Montrer la corde*, to be threadbare; *montrer quelqu'un du doigt*, to point one's finger at someone, to mock someone openly. **se montrer**, *v.r.* To show oneself; to appear; to prove oneself to be, to prove,

to turn out; to be seen, to come out (of the stars etc.).

montreur, *n.m.* (*fem.* **-euse**) Showman, exhibitor. *Montreur d'ours*, bear-leader.

montueux [mɔ̃ˈtɥø], *a.* (*fem.* **-ueuse**) Hilly.

monture [mɔ̃ˈtyːr], *n.f.* Animal for riding, mount; mounting, setting (of gems etc.); frame (of spectacles, umbrella); support, socket; work of assembling parts. *Monture d'un fusil*, stock of a gun; *monture de sabre*, sword hilt; *qui veut voyager loin ménage sa monture*, he who wishes to live long, avoids excess.

monument [mɔnyˈmɑ̃], *n.m.* Monument; memorial. *Monument aux morts*, war memorial; *monument funéraire*, tomb. **monumental**, *a.* (*fem.* **-ale**, *pl.* **-aux**) Monumental.

moquable [mɔˈkabl], *a.* Laughable, ridiculous.

moque [mɔk], *n.f.* Pulley-block; tin-measure; (*Norm.*) large mug (of cider).

***moquer** [mɔˈke], *v.t.* To ridicule, to make fun of. **se moquer**, *v.r.* To mock, to jeer, to laugh at; to make fun (*de*); to trifle, to scoff at, to make a jest (*de*); to be reckless (*de*). *Je m'en moque*, what do I care; *je m'en moque pas mal* or *je m'en moque comme de l'an quarante*, I don't care a straw; *on s'est moqué de lui*, they laughed at him; *vous vous moquez*, you are joking. **moquerie**, *n.f.* Mockery, scoff, jeer, derision; jest, mere mockery.

moquette [mɔˈkɛt] (1), *n.f.* Decoy-bird.

moquette (2), *n.f.* Wilton carpet; velvet pile.

moqueur [mɔˈkœːr], *a.* (*fem.* **-euse**) Mocking, jeering, deriding, derisive.—*n.* Mocker, scoffer, quiz, wag. *Moqueur d'Amérique*, mocking-bird.

***morailles** [mɔˈraːj], *n.f. pl.* Barnacles (for restive horses).

moraillon [mɔraˈjɔ̃], *n.m.* Hasp (of lock).

moraine [mɔˈrɛn], *n.f.* Moraine.

moral [mɔˈral], *a.* (*fem.* **morale** (1), *pl.* **moraux**) Moral, ethical; of good morals; mental, intellectual. *Une certitude morale*, a moral certainty.—*n.m.* Mind, mental or moral faculties, spirit, morale (of troops etc.). *Il faut vous remonter le moral*, you must cheer up.

morale (2), *n.f.* Ethics, moral philosophy; morals, morality; rebuke, lecture; moral (of a story etc.). *Faire la morale à quelqu'un*, to rebuke, to lecture, someone. **moralement**, *adv.* Morally.

moralisateur, *a.* (*fem.* **-trice**) Edifying, improving.

moralisation, *n.f.* Moralization.

moraliser, *v.t., v.i.* To moralize.

moraliseur, *n.m.* (*fem.* **-euse**) Moralizer.

moralisme, *n.m.* Moralism.

moraliste, *n.* and *a.* Moralist.

moralité, *n.f.* Morality; moral reflection; moral (of a story etc.); moral sense, conscience; morals, integrity; morality (play).

morasse [mɔˈras], *n.f.* (*Print.*) Final page-proof.

moratoire [mɔraˈtwaːr], *a.* (*Law*) Entailing a moratorium, delaying.—*n.m.* Moratorium.

morave [mɔˈraːv], *a.* and *n.* Moravian. *Frères moraves*, United Brethren.

Moravie [mɔraˈvi], *f.* Moravia.

morbide [mɔrˈbid], *a.* Morbid; (*Paint. etc.*), soft, delicate. **morbidesse**, *n.f.* (*Paint.*) Morbidezza, life-like delicacy in flesh-tints.

morbidité, *n.f.* Morbidity, morbidness.
morbifique, *a.* Morbific.
morbleu [mɔr'blø], *int.* The devil !
morceau [mɔr'so], *n.m.* (*pl.* **-eaux**) Bit, piece, morsel, fragment; musical composition; snack, mouthful. *Aimer les bons morceaux,* to love good things (to eat); *gober le morceau,* to swallow the bait; *il a ses morceaux taillés,* he has just enough to live on; *manger un morceau,* to eat a mouthful, to have a snack; *manger le morceau,* (*slang*) to blab, to peach; *mettre en morceaux,* to tear to pieces; *morceau délicat* or *bon morceau,* titbit; *morceau de roi,* dish fit for a king; *morceau de sucre,* lump of sugar; *sucre en morceaux,* lump sugar. *Morceaux choisis,* (*Lit.*) selected passages.
morceler, *v.t.* To parcel out, to cut up.
morcellement, *n.m.* Parcelling out.
mordache [mɔr'daʃ], *n.f.* Cap (of lead or copper) for jaws of vice; clamp.
mordacité [mɔrdasi'te], *n.f.* Mordacity, virulence, bitterness.
mordant [mɔr'dɑ̃], *a.* (*fem.* **-ante**) Biting, corrosive, mordant; pungent, keen, cutting, sarcastic.—*n.m.* Mordant; causticity, pungency, keenness; dash (of troops), punch; (*Mus.*) mordent, grace-note.
mordicus [mɔrdi'ky:s], *adv.* (*colloq.*) Tenaciously, stoutly, with tooth and nail.
*****mordieu** [mɔr'djø], *int.* 'sdeath !
mordiller [mɔrdi'je], *v.t.* To nibble, to bite at.
mordoré [mɔrdɔ're], *a.* and *n.m.* (*fem.* **-ée**) Reddish brown, russet, bronze coloured.
mordorure, *n.f.* This colour.
mordre [mɔrdr], *v.t.* To bite; to bite off; to gnaw, to corrode, to eat into; to catch, to take hold of; (*fig.*) to carp at, to find fault with. *Chien qui aboie ne mord pas,* barking dogs do not bite; *mordre la poussière,* to bite the dust.—*v.i.* To bite, to nibble; to catch, to take hold; to take effect, to succeed, to get on; to criticize, to censure. *Je n'ai jamais pu mordre au latin,* I was never able to take to Latin; *mordre à l'hameçon,* to take the bait; *ça mord,* I've got a bite. **se mordre,** *v.r.* To bite oneself. *Se mordre la langue* or *les lèvres,* to bite one's tongue *or* one's lip; *s'en mordre les doigts,* to repent of a thing.
Morée [mɔ're], *f.* Morea.
more [mɔ:r] or **moresque,** *a.* Moorish.
more, *n.m.* Moor. [**maure** etc.]
moreau [mɔ'ro], *a.* (*fem.* **-elle** (1), *pl.* **-eaux**) Dark shiny black.—*n.m.* Jet-black horse; nose-bag.
morelle (2) [mɔ'rɛl], *n.f.* Nightshade, morel. *Morelle noire,* black nightshade; *morelle douce-amère* or *grimpante,* or *bourreau des arbres,* woody nightshade; *morelle tubéreuse* or *pomme de terre,* potato.
moresque [MAURESQUE].
morfil [mɔr'fil], *n.m.* Wire edge (of knives etc.); raw ivory.
morfondre [mɔr'fɔ̃:dr], *v.t.* To chill, to make shiver. **se morfondre,** *v.r.* To be chilled, to shiver; to kick one's heels, to dance attendance. *La pâte se morfond,* the dough is losing its heat.
morfondu, *a.* (*fem.* **morfondue**) Chilled, shivering, benumbed.
morfondure, *n.f.* Cold, chill, catarrh (in horses).

morganatique [mɔrgana'tik], *a.* Morganatic.
morganatiquement, *adv.* Morganatically.
morgeline [mɔrʒə'lin], *n.f.* [MOURON].
morgue [mɔrg], *n.f.* Haughty look, haughtiness, arrogance; self-sufficiency, conceit; *****search-room (of a prison); morgue, mortuary. *****morguer,** *v.t.* To brave, to browbeat, to beard.
moribond [mɔri'bɔ̃], *a.* (*fem.* **moribonde**) Moribund, dying.—*n.* Person in a dying state.
moricaud [mɔri'ko], *a.* (*fem.* **moricaude**) (*pej.*) Dark, darkish.—*n.* (*pej.*) Dark-skinned person, Negro.
morigéner [mɔriʒe'ne], *v.t. irr.* (*conjug. like* ACCÉLÉRER) To scold, to reprimand.
morille [mɔ'ri:j], *n.f.* Morel (mushroom).
morillon [mɔri'jɔ̃], *n.m.* Black grape; small morel; tufted duck; (*pl.*) rough emeralds.
morio [mɔ'rjo], *n.m.* Camberwell beauty (butterfly).
morion [mɔ'rjɔ̃], *n.m.* Morion.
mormon [mɔr'mɔ̃], *n.m.* and *a.* (*fem.* **-one**) Mormon.
mormonisme [mɔrmɔ'nism], *n.m.* Mormonism.
morne (1) [mɔrn], *a.* Gloomy, mournful, dejected, dismal, dull, dreary.
morne (2) [mɔrn], *n.m.* Bluff (in West Indies); knoll.
morne (3) [mɔrn], *n.f.* (*Archaeol.*) Morne, coronal.
morné [mɔr'ne], *a.* (*fem.* **mornée**) Blunted (of arms); (*Her.*) morné.
mornement [mɔrnə'mɑ̃], *adv.* Gloomily, sadly.
mornifle [mɔr'nifl], *n.f.* (*colloq.*) Backhanded slap in the face; (*fig.*) taunt, jibe, dig.
morose [mɔ'ro:z], *a.* Morose, sullen, surly.
morosité, *n.f.* Moroseness, sullenness, surliness.
moro-sphinx [moro'sfɛ̃ks], *n.m. inv.* Hawkmoth.
Morphée [mɔr'fe], *m.* Morpheus. *Être dans les bras de Morphée,* to be asleep.
morphine [mɔr'fin], *n.f.* Morphia.
morphinisme, *n.m.* Morphinism.
morphinomane, *n.* and *a.* Morphinomaniac.
morphinomanie, *n.f.* Morphinomania.
morphologie [mɔrfɔlɔ'ʒi], *n.f.* Morphology.
morphologique, *a.* Morphological.
morphose, *n.f.* Morphosis.
morpion [mɔr'pjɔ̃], *n.m.* Crab-louse; (*slang*) little, dirty fellow; brat.
mors [mɔ:r], *n.m. inv.* Bit (of a bridle); (*fig.*) curb, cheek, restraint. *Mors de bridon,* snaffle; *les chevaux prirent le mors aux dents,* the horses bolted; *prendre le mors aux dents,* to take the bit between one's teeth, to buckle to.
mors du diable [SCABIEUSE].
morse (1) [mɔrs], *n.m.* Morse, walrus.
morse (2) [mɔrs], *n.m.* Morse (code).
morsure [mɔr'sy:r], *n.f.* Bite, biting.
mort (1) [mɔ:r], *n.f.* Death; (*Hunt.*) mort. *À la vie, à la mort,* for ever, in life and death; *à mort,* mortally, to the death; *avoir la mort dans l'âme,* to be sick at heart; *avoir la mort sur les lèvres,* to look like death; *être à l'article de la mort,* to be at the point of death; *guerre à mort,* war to the death; *la peine de mort,* capital punishment; *les affres*

de la mort, the terrors of death; *mettre à mort*, to put to death; *mourir de sa belle mort*, to die a natural death. *Mort aux rats*, ratpoison.

mort (2) [mɔːr], *a.* (*fem.* **morte**) Dead; lifeless, inanimate, still, insensible; dormant, stagnant; spent, out (of a candle etc.); deathlike, pale, leaden, dull. *Balle morte*, spent bullet; *eau morte*, stagnant water; *le feu est mort*, the fire is out; *nature morte*, still-life; *œuvres mortes*, upper works (of a ship); (*Mech.*) *point mort*, dead point, dead centre. —*n.* Dead person, deceased; dead body, corpse; dummy (at cards). *Enterrer les morts*, to bury the dead; *faire le mort*, to pretend to be dead; *jouer le mort*, to play dummy at whist etc.; *le jour* or *la fête des morts*, All Souls' Day.

mortadelle [mɔrta'dɛl], *n.f.* Bologna sausage.

mortaille [mɔr'taːj], *n.f.* (*Feud.*) Right of landlord to property of heirless serf.

mortaisage [mɔrtɛ'zaːʒ], *n.m.* Mortising.

mortaise [mɔr'tɛːz], *n.f.* Mortise. **mortaiser**, *v.t.* To mortise.

mortalité [mɔrtali'te], *n.f.* Mortality.

mort-bois [mɔr'bwɑ], *n.m.* (*no pl.*) Brushwood, undergrowth.

morte-eau [mɔr'to], *n.f.* (*pl.* **mortes-eaux**) Neap tide, neaps.

mortel [mɔr'tɛl], *a.* (*fem.* **mortelle**) Mortal, deadly; grievous, extreme, excessive; long, tedious.—*n.* Mortal. **mortellement**, *adv.* Fatally, deadly.

morte-saison [mɔrtsɛ'zɔ̃], *n.f.* (*pl.* **mortes-saisons**) Slack season, slack time, off season.

mortier [mɔr'tje], *n.m.* Mortar (cement, artillery, vessel); mortier (cap of a president of court of justice). *Mortier liquide*, grout.

mortifère [mɔrti'fɛːr], *a.* Deadly.

mortifiant [mɔrti'fjɑ̃], *a.* (*fem.* **mortifiante**) Mortifying, humiliating.

mortification [mɔrtifika'sjɔ̃], *n.f.* Mortification, humiliation; (*Med.*) gangrene.

mortifier, *v.t.* To mortify; to humiliate. *Mortifier de la viande*, to make meat tender. **se mortifier**, *v.r.* To mortify oneself; to grow tender (of meat).

mort-né [mɔr'ne], *a.* and *n.m.* (*fem.* **mort-née**, *pl.* **mort-nés**, **mort-nées**) Born dead, stillborn (child); (*fig.*) abortive.

mortuaire [mɔr'tɥɛːr], *a.* Funerary, mortuary. *Chambre mortuaire*, death chamber; *le domicile mortuaire*, the house of the deceased; *drap mortuaire*, pall; *droits mortuaires*, burial fee; *extrait mortuaire*, death certificate.

morue [mɔ'ry], *n.f.* Cod, codfish; (*pop.*) prostitute. *Huile de foie de morue*, cod-liver oil. *Queue-de-morue*, (*pop.*) swallow-tails; flat brush (for painting).

morutier [mɔry'tje] or **moruyer** [mɔry'je], *n.m.* Cod-fisher; cod-fishing boat.

morve [mɔrv], *n.f.* Snot, mucus; glanders. **morveau**, *n.m.* (*slang*) Thick mucus.

morveux, *a.* (*fem.* **morveuse**) Snotty; glandered. *Cheval morveux*, horse that has the glanders; *qui se sent morveux se mouche*, if the cap fits, wear it.—*n.* (*pej.*) Child, brat, urchin. *Petit morveux va!* you little brat!

mosaïque (1) [mɔza'ik], *n.f.* Mosaic, mosaicwork; (*Bot.*) a disease of potatoes.

mosaïque (2) [mɔza'ik], *a.* Mosaic, relating to Moses. **mosaïsme**, *n.m.* Mosaism.

mosaïste [mɔza'ist], *n.* and *a.* (Worker) in mosaics.

moscatelle [mɔska'tɛl], *n.f.* Moschatel.

Moscou [mɔs'ku], *m.* Moscow.

moscouade [mɔs'kwad], *n.f.* Muscovado (unrefined sugar).

moscoutaire [mɔsku'tɛːr], *n.* (*pej.*) Great admirer of the Soviet régime.

Moscovie [mɔskɔ'vi], *f.* Muscovy.

mosette or **mozette** [mɔ'zɛt], *n.f.* Camail, mozetta, tippet.

mosquée [mɔs'ke], *n.f.* Mosque.

***moss** [mɔs], *n.m.* (*dial.*) Large glass of lager beer.

Mossoul [mɔ'sul], *f.* Mosul.

mot [mo], *n.m.* Word; remark, saying, sentence; motto; note, line, memorandum; cue, hint, intimation; answer (to a riddle); (*Mil.*) parole, watchword. *Au bas mot*, at the least; *avoir le mot pour rire*, to be ready with a joke; *bon mot*, witticism; *c'est mon dernier mot*, it is my last concession; *donner le mot à quelqu'un*, to give someone the cue; *entendre à demi-mot*, to take a hint; *en un mot*, in a word, in short; *gros mots*, foul words, bad names; *il lui a dit un mot à l'oreille*, he whispered a word in his ear; *ils se sont donné le mot*, they understand one another, they have passed the word round; *jeu de mots*, play upon words, pun; *je vous enverrai un mot*, I shall drop you a line; *mot à double entente*, word bearing a double interpretation; *mot à mot* or *mot pour mot*, word for word; *le mot de Cambronne* [MERDE]; *mot d'ordre*, parole, pass-word; *mot de ralliement*, countersign; *ne dire mot* or *ne pas souffler mot*, not to utter, not to breathe a word; *prendre quelqu'un au mot*, to take someone at his word; *qui ne dit mot consent*, silence gives consent; *savoir le fin mot de l'affaire*, to know the secret or inner meaning of something; *trancher le mot*, to speak out, not to mince matters; *mots croisés*, crossword.

motel [mɔ'tɛl], *n.m.* Motor hotel, motel.

motelle [mɔ'tɛl], *n.f.*, or *loche de mer*. Rockling.

motet [mɔ'tɛ], *n.m.* (*Mus.*) Motet.

moteur [mɔ'tœːr], *a.* (*fem.* **motrice** (1)) Motive, propelling, moving, driving. *Arbre moteur*, driving shaft; *nerf moteur*, motory nerve; *unité motrice*, power unit.—*n.m.* Mover; propeller, motor, engine; motive power, author; (*Anat.*) motor. *Moteur à gaz, à pétrole*, gas, oil engine; *moteur à réaction*, jet-propulsion motor, jet engine; *moteur d'avion*, aeromotor; *moteur rotatif*, rotary motor.

motif [mɔ'tif], *a.* (*fem.* **motive**) Moving, causing, inciting.—*n.m.* Motive, incentive; ground, cause; (*Mus. etc.*) motif, theme, design. *Faire valoir les motifs*, (*Law*) to show cause; *pour quel motif?* on what grounds?

motilité, *n.f.* Motility, motivity.

motion [mo'sjɔ̃], *n.f.* Motion. *Faire, appuyer, or faire adopter une motion*, to propose, to support, or to carry a motion.

motiver [mɔti've], *v.t.* To allege as a motive; to be the motive or cause of, to bring about; to justify.

moto [mɔ'to], *n.f.* (*fam.*) Motor bike.

motoculteur [mɔtokyl'tœːr], *n.m.* Power-driven cultivator.

motoculture [mɔtokyl'tyr], *n.f.* Mechanized farming.
motocyclette [mɔtosi'klɛt], *n.f.* Motor-cycle.
motocycliste, *n.* Motor-cyclist.
motogodille [mɔtogɔ'dij], *n.f.* Boat with an outboard motor near the rudder.
motopompe [mɔto'pɔ̃:p], *n.f.* Motor pump.
motorisation [mɔtoriza'sjɔ̃], *n.f.* Motorization. **motorisé**, *a.* (*fem.* **motorisée**) Motorized (cavalry, unit, etc.).
motoriser, *v.t.* To motorize.
mot-outil [mou'ti], *n.m.* (*pl.* **mots-outils**) Link-word.
motrice (2) [mɔ'tris], *n.f.* (*Rail.*) Motor carriage.
motte [mɔt], *n.f.* Clod; ball of earth; mound (of windmill). *Motte de beurre*, pat of butter; *motte de gazon*, sod (of turf); *motte de tourbe*, block of peat. **motter**, *v.t.* To throw clods at (sheep etc.). **se motter**, *v.r.* To hide behind a clod (of game).
mottereau [mɔ'tro], *n.m.* (*pl.* **-eaux**) Sand-martin.
motteux [mɔ'tø], *n.m.*, or **traquet motteux**. Fallow-finch, wheatear.
motton [GRUMEAU].
motus! [mɔ'ty:s], *int.* (*colloq.*) Mum's the word!
mou [mu], *a.* (**mol** before vowel or *h* mute, *fem.* **molle**) Soft; mellow; weak, feeble; slack, flabby, sluggish, indolent; tame, effeminate, careless, luxurious. *Cire molle*, soft wax; *mer molle*, slack water; *poires molles*, mellow pears; *style mou*, nerveless style.—*n.m.* Soft part of thing; slack (of a rope); lights, lungs (*esp.* of calves).
mouchage [mu'ʃa:ʒ], *n.m.* Snuffing (of candles).
mouchard [mu'ʃa:r], *n.m.* Sneak, *esp.* police-spy, nark, informer, stool-pigeon.
mouchardage [muʃar'da:ʒ], *n.m.* Sneaking.
moucharder, *v.t.*, *v.i.* To inform (on), to spy (on).
mouche [muʃ], *n.f.* Fly; speck, spot; patch (on the face), beauty-spot; tuft (on lower lip); button or cap (of foil); bull's-eye (of a target); catch (of clasp-knife); river passenger-steamer; (*Naut.*) advice-boat; loo (game of cards). *C'est une fine mouche*, he is a sly dog, she is a sly minx; *chiures* or *taches de mouches*, fly-blows; *des pattes de mouches*, scrawl (writing); *faire la mouche du coche*, to play the dun, the busybody; *faire mouche*, to hit the bull's-eye; *mouche à miel*, honey-bee; *mouche à viande*, blow-fly; *mouche bleue*, blue-bottle; *mouche commune*, house-fly; *mouches volantes*, motes in the eyes, floating specks; *on aurait entendu voler une mouche*, you could have heard a pin drop; *on prend plus de mouches avec du miel qu'avec du vinaigre*, more is done by kindness than by harshness; *pêche à la mouche flottante, noyée*, dry-, wet-fly-fishing; (*Box.*) *poids mouche*, fly-weight; *prendre la mouche*, to take umbrage, to be touchy; *quelle mouche vous pique?* what's biting you?
(C) mouche à feu [muʃa'fø], *n.f.* Firefly.
moucher [mu'ʃe], *v.t.* To wipe or blow the nose of; to snuff; (*fam.*) to snub, to sit on. *Moucher une chandelle*, to snuff a candle; *mouchez cet enfant*, wipe that child's nose. *Je l'ai bien mouché*, I told him off; I sat on him good and proper. **se moucher**, *v.r.* To

blow one's nose. *Mouchez-vous*, blow your nose; (*fam.*) *ne pas se moucher du pied*, to do things in grand style.
moucherolle [muʃ'rɔl], *n.f.* (*Orn.*) Fly-catcher.
moucheron, *n.m.* Gnat, very small fly; (*fam.*) brat, urchin; snuff (of a candle).
moucheronner, *v.i.* To rise, to be on the rise (of fish).
mouchet [mu'ʃɛ], *n.m.* Dunnock. *Mouchet chanteur*, or *fauvette d'hiver* or *des haies*, hedge sparrow.
moucheté [muʃ'te], *a.* (*fem.* **mouchetée**) Spotted, speckled, flecked; blunted, capped. *Chat moucheté*, tabby-cat; *cheval moucheté*, flea-bitten horse. *Fleuret moucheté*, capped foil. **moucheter**, *v.t.* To spot, to speckle, to fleck; to cap or button (foils); to mouse (hook).
mouchette [mu'ʃɛt], *n.f.* (*Arch.*) Outer fillet; moulding plane; (*pl.*) snuffers (for candle); barnacles (for horse); nose-ring (for bull, pig.).
moucheture [muʃ'ty:r], *n.f.* Spot, speck, marking (of animal's skin), patterning (of fabric).
mouchoir [mu'ʃwa:r], *n.m.* Handkerchief; (*Shipbuilding*) filling timber. *Jeter le mouchoir à*, to throw the handkerchief at, (*fig.*) to choose out; *mouchoir de poche*, pocket-handkerchief.
mouchure [mu'ʃy:r], *n.f.* Snuff (of a candle); cut end (of a rope); nasal mucus.
moudre [mudr], *v.t. irr.* (*pres.p.* **moulant**, *p.p.* **moulu**) To grind, to mill, to crush; (*fig.*) to thrash soundly; to produce (music) mechanically. *Il viendra moudre à notre moulin*, he will want us some day; *j'ai le corps tout moulu*, I am bruised all over; *moudre de coups*, to beat soundly; *moudre du café*, to grind coffee.
moue [mu], *n.f.* Pout. *Faire la moue*, to pout; *faire la moue à quelqu'un*, to make a wry face at someone; *vilaine moue*, ugly face.
mouette [mwɛt], *n.f.* Gull, sea-mew. *Mouette pillarde* or *stercoraire*, arctic skua; *mouette rieuse*, black-headed gull; *mouette tridactyle*, kittiwake, tarrock.
moufette [mu'fɛt] or **mouffette** [MOFETTE (2)].
moufle (1) [mufl], *n.m.* Muffle (furnace).
moufle (2) [mufl], *n.f.* Fingerless glove, mitten; muffle; tackle, tackle-block; tie-rod (for walls).
mouflé, *a.* (*fem.* **mouflée**) Used only in *poulie mouflée*, single pulley connected with others in a tackle-block.
mouflon [mu'flɔ̃], *n.m.* Moufflon, wild sheep.
mouillage [mu'ja:ʒ], *n.m.* Soaking, wetting, watering; anchorage. *Être au mouillage*, to lie or ride at anchor.
mouillé, *a.* (*fem.* **mouillée**) Wet, damp, watery; liquid (of the letter *l*). (*fig.*) *Poule mouillée*, milksop.
mouille-bouche, *n.f. inv.* Luscious kind of pear. **mouille-étiquettes**, *n.m. inv.* Stamp-damper.
mouiller [mu'je], *v.t.* To wet, to moisten; to steep, to bedew; to water, to dilute; to palatalize (a consonant). *Mouiller l'ancre*, to let go the anchor; *mouiller une mine*, to lay a mine. —*v.i.* To cast anchor.
mouillère, *n.f.* Wet or marshy part of a field etc.

mouillette, *n.f.* Sippet (to eat with boiled eggs).

mouilleur, *n.m.* Pad for damping stamps. (*Naut.*) *Mouilleur de mines,* mine-layer.

mouilloir, *n.m.* Water-can (in which women dip their fingers when they spin).

mouillure, *n.f.* Wetting, watering, sprinkling; wet, dampness.

mouise [mwiz], *n.f.* (*dial.*) Pap; thence *être dans la mouise* (*pop.*), to be in a pretty mess; to be hard up.

moujik [mu'ʒik], *n.m.* Moujik (Russian peasant).

moukère [mu'kɛr], *n.f.* (*Sabir word*) Woman.

(C) moulac [mu'lak], *n.f.* (*Ichth.*) Splake.

moulage (1) [mu'la:ʒ], *n.m.* Moulding, casting; mould; cast.

moulage (2) [mu'la:ʒ], *n.m.* Grinding, milling; machinery of mill.

moulant, *pres.p.* [MOUDRE].

moule (1) [mul], *n.m.* Mould, matrix; pattern, form; pin. *Jeter en moule,* to cast; *faire un moule,* to take a cast; *fait au moule,* moulded, (*fig.*) beautifully shaped; *moule à beurre,* butter-print; *moule à gaufres,* waffle-iron; *moule à gâteaux,* cake-tin.

moule (2) [mul], *n.f.* Mussel; (*pop.*) weak, flabby fellow.

moulé [mu'le], *a.* (*fem.* **moulée**) Moulded; cast; well-shaped, well-formed. *Lettre moulée,* block letter.—*n.m.* (*colloq.*) Print, block letters.

mouler [mu'le], *v.t.* To cast, to mould; to shape, to form; to show the shape of clearly. *Un corsage qui moule le buste,* a corsage that shows up the shape of the bust. **se mouler,** *v.r.* To model oneself. *Se mouler sur un autre,* to take another for one's model.

mouleur, *n.m.* Moulder.

moulin [mu'lɛ̃], *n.m.* Mill; (*Geol.*) pothole. *C'est un moulin à paroles,* she is a chatterbox; *jeter son bonnet par-dessus les moulins,* to throw off all restraint; *moulin à blé,* corn-mill; *moulin à bras,* hand-mill; *moulin à café,* coffee-mill; *moulin à eau,* water-mill; *moulin à prières,* prayer wheel; *moulin à vapeur,* steam-mill; *moulin à vent,* windmill; *faire le moulin* (à vent), (*Row.*) to sky the blade. (*fam.*) *On y entre comme dans un moulin,* it is open to all and sundry.

moulinage [muli'na:ʒ], *n.m.* Throwing silk.

mouliner, *v.t.* To throw (silk); to eat away wood (of worms), to grind or polish (marble).

moulinet, *n.m.* Small mill; small windlass; winch; turnstile; fishing reel; (*fig.*) windmill (rotation of arms). *Faire le moulinet avec une épée,* to twirl a sword about.

moulineur or **moulinier** [muli'nje], *n.m.* (*fem.* **moulineuse** or **moulinière**) Silk-thrower, throwster.

*moult [mult *or* mu], *adv.* (*dial.*) Much, very much.

moulu [mu'ly], *a.* (*fem.* **-ue**) Ground; bruised.

moulure [mu'ly:r], *n.f.* (*Arch.*) Moulding.

moulurer, *v.t.* To cut a moulding on.

mourant [mu'rɑ̃], *a.* (*fem.* **mourante**) Dying, expiring; fading, faltering; disappearing; faint; languishing.—*n.* Dying person.

mourir [mu'ri:r], *v.t. irr.* (*pres.p.* **mourant,** *p.p.* **mort**) To die, to expire; to depart this life; to perish, to drop off, to go off, to die away, to stop, to go out (of fire); to be out (at

play). *Avant de mourir,* before dying; *être mort au monde,* to be dead to the world; *faire mourir,* to put to death; *il est mort hier,* he died yesterday; *laisser mourir le feu,* to let the fire go out; *mourir de chagrin* [CHAGRIN (1)]; *mourir d'envie* [ENVIE]; *mourir de froid* [FROID]; *mourir de rire,* to die of laughter.

se mourir, *v.r.* (*only used in pres. and imp. indic.*) To be dying, to be at the point of death; to die away, to be going out (of fire). *Cet homme se meurt,* this man is dying.

mouron [mu'rɔ̃], *n.m.* (*Bot.*) *Mouron rouge* or *menuchon* or *faux-mouron,* or *mouron des champs,* scarlet pimpernel; *mouron des fontaines,* water blinks; *mouron d'eau,* brookweed; *mouron des oiseaux* or *mouron blanc* or *alsine* or *morgeline,* chickweed.

mourre [mu:r], *n.f.* Mora (the game 'how many fingers do I hold up?').

mousquet [mus'kɛ], *n.m.* Musket. *Mousquet à pierre,* flintlock. **mousquetade,** *n.f.* Musket-shot, volley of musketry. **mousquetaire,** *n.m.* Musketeer. **mousqueter,** *v.t.* To fire at with musketry. **mousqueterie,** *n.f.* Musket-fire. **mousqueton,** *n.m.* Musketoon, (short) snap-hook; safety-clasp; carbine.

mousse (1) [mus], *n.f.* Moss; froth, foam; lather; whipped cream. *Pierre qui roule n'amasse pas mousse,* a rolling stone gathers no moss; *se faire de la mousse,* (*pop.*) to worry, to fret.

mousse (2) [mus], *n.m.* Cabin-boy, ship-boy.

mousse (3) [mus], *a.* Blunt (of tools etc.).

mousseau [mu'so], *n.m. and a.* (*pl.* **-eaux**) Choice wheaten (bread).

mousseline [mus'lin], *n.f.* Muslin; (*Am.*) cheesecloth. *Mousseline de soie,* chiffon.

mousser [mu'se], *v.i.* To froth, to foam; to lather; to sparkle (of wine). *Faire mousser,* to whisk; to puff (a person); to make him foam with rage. *Se faire mousser,* to lay it on thick.

mousseron [mus'rɔ̃], *n.m.* Small edible mushroom.

mousseux [mu'sø], *a.* (*fem.* **mousseuse**) Foaming, frothy; sparkling (of wine etc.). *Vin non mousseux,* still wine.

moussoir [mus'war], *n.m.* (*Cook.*) Instrument for beating or stirring; whisk.

mousson [mu'sɔ̃], *n.f.* Monsoon.

moussu [mu'sy], *a.* (*fem.* **-ue**) Mossy, moss-grown. *Rose moussue,* moss-rose.

moustache [mus'taʃ], *n.f.* Moustache; whiskers (of animals). *Brûler la moustache à quelqu'un,* to fire a pistol in someone's face; *moustache(s) à la gauloise,* walrus moustache; *relever sa moustache,* to twirl one's moustache; *vieille moustache,* veteran, old campaigner. **moustachu,** *a.* (*fem.* **moustachue**) Moustached; with a heavy moustache.

moustérien [muste'rjɛ̃], *a.* (*fem.* **moustérienne**) (*Archaeol.*) Mousterian, pertaining to the Palaeolithic culture of Le Moustier, Dordogne.

moustiquaire [musti'kɛ:r], *n.f.* Mosquito-net.

moustique, *n.m.* Mosquito; gnat; sand-fly; (*fam.*) midget, tiny person. *Une piqûre de moustique,* a mosquito-bite.

moût [mu], *n.m.* Must (wine not fermented); wort (of beer).

moutard [mu'ta:r], *n.m.* (*fam.*) Brat, urchin.

moutarde [mu'tard], *n.f.* Mustard. *Graine de moutarde*, mustard-seed. (*fam.*) *Il m'a fait monter la moutarde au nez*, he made me lose my temper.

moutardier, *n.m.* Mustard-pot; mustard-maker. *Il se croit le premier moutardier du pape*, he's not half proud of himself.

*__moutier__ [mu'tje], *n.m.* Monastery, church.

mouton [mu'tɔ̃], *n.m.* Sheep; wether; (*Cook.*) mutton; sheepskin (leather); ram; beetle, monkey (rammer); timber support for bell; balls (of fluff); (*fig.*) lamb (person), ninny; (*slang*) decoy, prison-spy; (*pl.*) white-crested waves, white horses; skipper's daughters; *mouton du Cap* [ALBATROS]. *Doux comme un mouton*, quite harmless, quite tame; *frisé comme un mouton*, as curly as a poodle; *revenons à nos moutons*, let us return to the subject; *un troupeau de moutons*, a flock of sheep; *saut de mouton*, buck (of horse).—*a.* (*fem.* **moutonne**) Sheep-like.

moutonné, *a.* (*fem.* **moutonnée**) Fleecy, ruffled, curled; white with foam (of the sea). *Roches moutonnées*, glaciated rocks. **moutonnement**, *n.m.* Foaming, breaking into white horses.

moutonner, *v.t.* To make woolly or fleecy; to curl, to frizzle.—*v.i.* To be ruffled, to foam.

moutonneux [mutɔ'nø], *a.* (*fem.* **-euse**) Fleecy; foaming, frothy, whitening (of waves).

moutonnier, *a.* (*fem.* **-ière**) Sheep-like. *Gent moutonnière* or *moutonne*, ovine race.

mouture [mu'tyːr], *n.f.* Grinding; grist; charge for grinding; maslin, a mixture of wheat, rye, and barley. *Tirer d'un sac deux moutures*, to make a double profit out of something.

mouvant [mu'vã], *a.* (*fem.* **mouvante**) Moving, shifting; unfixed, unstable; (*Her.*) issuant; busy; (*Feud. law*) depending on. *Sable mouvant*, quicksand.

mouvement [muv'mã], *n.m.* Movement, motion; move, gesture; progress, advance, march; animation, life, bustle, stir; agitation, emotion, disturbance, commotion; change, mutation; spirit, impulse; (*Mus.*) time; animation, sparkle (of style); (*Mach.*) works, play; stroke (of piston etc.); (*Mil.*) manœuvre, move. *Être dans le mouvement*, (*fam.*) to be in the swim, abreast of the times, up to date; *être en mouvement*, to be in motion; *être toujours en mouvement*, to be always on the go; *faire une chose de son propre mouvement*, to do a thing of one's own accord; *le premier mouvement*, the first impulse; *les mouvements de l'âme*, the emotions; *mouvements de bateaux*, shipping news *or* schedule; *mouvement de colère* (or *d'humeur*), angry impulse, fit of anger (or of impatience); *mouvement d'horlogerie*, clockwork; *mouvements de personnel*, staff changes; *mouvement naturel*, natural impulse; *mouvement perpétuel*, perpetual motion; *obéir à un bon mouvement*, to obey a generous impulse; *sans mouvement*, lifeless, spiritless; *se donner du mouvement*, to bestir oneself; *se mettre en mouvement*, to start, (*Mil.*) to move forward, to advance; *un bon mouvement!* make an effort! buck up!

mouvementé, *a.* (*fem.* **-ée**) Animated, lively, vivacious; eventful; undulating (ground). (*spt.*) *Partie mouvementée*, exciting

game (*or* match); *vie mouvementée*, checkered (chequered) existence, life of ups and downs.

mouver, *v.t.* To loosen, to dig up (soil); to stir (sauce).

mouvette, *n.f.*, or **mouvoir** (1), *n.m.* Wooden spoon, stirring gadget.

mouvoir (2) [mu'vwaːr], *v.t. irr.* (*pres.p.* **mouvant**, *p.p.* **mû**) To move, to stir; to drive, to prompt, to actuate; to start. *Faire mouvoir*, to set in motion. **se mouvoir**, *v.r.* To move, to stir, to be moved.

moxa [mɔk'sa], *n.m.* (*Surg.*) Moxa.

moye, moie [mwa], *n.f.* Soft part (of stone).

moyen (1) [mwa'jɛ̃], *a.* (*fem.* **moyenne** (1)) Mean, middle, medium; middle-sized, average. *Cours moyen*, (*Geol.*) middle course (of river), (*sch.*) intermediary form, remove, (*St. Exch.*) middle price; *d'âge moyen*, middle-aged; *le Français moyen*, the average Frenchman; *le Moyen-Âge*, the Middle Ages; *le Moyen-Orient*, the Middle East; *moyen haut-allemand*, Middle High German; *moyen terme*, middle term, (*Log.*) middle course; *ondes moyennes*, (*Rad.*) medium waves; *temps moyen*, mean time.

moyen (2) [mwa'jɛ̃], *n.m.* Means; way, manner, contrivance; medium; (*Law*) plea, grounds; (*pl.*) resources, pecuniary circumstances; abilities, talents, parts. *Au moyen de*, by means of, with the help of; *contribuer chacun selon ses moyens*, to contribute each according to his means; *employer les grands moyens*, to have recourse to strong measures; *il a beaucoup de moyens*, he is very clever; *il n'y a pas moyen de faire cela*, that is not to be done; *je n'en ai pas les moyens*, I have not the means, I cannot afford it; *le moyen de lui parler?* how can one manage to speak to him? *par tous les moyens*, by every possible means, at all cost; *trouver moyen*, to find means, to contrive.

moyenâgeux [mwajɛnɑ'ʒø], *a.* (*fem.* **moyenâgeuse**) Medieval, *esp.* sham medieval.

moyennant [mwajɛ'nã], *prep.* By means of. *Moyennant finances*, against payment, for a consideration; *moyennant quoi*, in return for which, in consideration of which.—*conj. phr. moyennant que*, on condition that.

moyenne (2) [mwa'jɛn], *n.f.* Average; (*sch.*) pass-mark. *En moyenne*, on an average; *sur une moyenne de*, at an average of; (*sch.*) *obtenir la moyenne*, to get a pass-mark.

moyennement, *adv.* Fairly, moderately; on the average.

moyer [mwa'je], *v.t. irr.* (*conjug. like* ABOYER) To saw (a stone) in two equal parts.

moyette [mwa'jɛt], *n.f.* Shock (of corn etc.).

moyeu [mwa'jø], *n.m.* (*pl.* **moyeux**) Nave (of cartwheel); hub (of bicycle); boss (of fly-wheel, propeller, etc.).

mozarabe *or* **mosarabe** [mɔza'rab], *a.* and *n.* Mozarab. **mozarabique**, *a.* Mozarabic.

mozette [MOSETTE].

m'sieu [*short for* MONSIEUR].

mû [*part. of* MOUVOIR].

muabilité [mɥabili'te], *n.f.* Mutability, changeability, instability, unstableness.

muable, *a.* Mutable, changeable, unstable.

muance, *n.f.* (*Mus.*) Changing a note; breaking of the voice.

mucher [my'ʃe], *v.t.* (*dial.*) To hide, to conceal.

mucilage [mysi′la:ʒ], *n.m.* ˉMucilage. **muci-laﬁneux,** *a.* (*fem.* **-euse**) Mucilaginous.

mucosité [mykozi′te], *n.f.* Mucus, mucosity. **mucus,** *n.m.* Mucus.

mue (1) [my], *n.f.* Moulting; moulting season; skin, slough; mew, coop (cage); breaking of the voice. *Être en mue,* to be moulting; to be breaking (of the voice).

mue (2) [my], *a.f.* Used in *rage mue,* silent rabies, silent hydrophobia.

muer [mɥe], *v.i.* To moult, to cast or slough horns etc.; to break (of the voice). *Ce chien mue,* that dog is shedding its coat.

muet [mɥe], *a.* (*fem.* **muette** (1)) Dumb, mute, speechless; taciturn, secret; silent (of letters). *E muet,* silent *e; la frayeur le rendit muet,* terror struck him dumb; *carte muette,* blank map; *film muet,* silent film; *muet comme une carpe,* as dumb as a fish; (*Theat.*) *personnage muet,* mute; *scène muette,* dumb show.—*n.* Dumb man or woman, mute; mute letter.—*adv. phr.* *À la muette,* by gestures only, without speaking.

muette (2) [mɥet], *n.f.* Mews; hunting-lodge.

muézin or **muezzin** [mɥɛ′zɛ̃], *n.m.* Muezzin.

mufle [myfl], *n.m.* Snout, muzzle (of animals); face, phiz, mug (of persons); (*pop.*) beast, low cad, skunk. *Mufle de veau* [MUFLIER].

muflerie, *n.f.* (*pop.*) Low-down trick or ways.

muflier [myfli′je], *n.m.* (*Bot.*) Antirrhinum. *Grand muflier,* or *mufleau,* or *mufle de veau,* or *gueule-de-loup,* or *tête de singe,* snapdragon; *muflier des champs* or *muflier tête de mort,* antirrhinum orontium.

mufti or **muphti** [myf′ti], *n.m.* Mufti.

muge [my:ʒ], *n.m.* Mullet.

mugir [my′ʒi:r], *v.i.* To bellow (of bull); to low (of cow); (*fig.*) to roar, to moan; to sough (of the wind etc.). **mugissant,** *a.* (*fem.* **-ante**) Bellowing, roaring.

mugissement, *n.m.* Bellowing, lowing, roaring, soughing.

muguet (1) [my′gɛ], *n.m.* Lily of the valley, May-lily; (*Path.*) thrush. *Muguet des bois,* woodruff.

*****muguet** (2), *n.m.* (*fem.* **-ette**) Fop, beau, gallant.

*****mugueter,** *v.t.* To make love to.—*v.i.* To play the gallant, to flirt, to philander.

muid [mɥi], *n.m.* Hogshead (of wine).

mulassier [myla′sje] or **mulatier** [myla′tje], *a.* (*fem.* **mulassière** or **mulatière**) Producing mules; pertaining to the mule industry.

mulâtre [my′la:tr], *a.* and *n.* (*fem. inv.* or **-esse**) Mulatto, half-caste.

mule (1) [myl], *n.f.* Mule, slipper; chilblain in the heel, kibes; (*Vet.*) chaps. *Baiser la mule du pape,* to kiss the Pope's toe; *la mule du pape,* the Pope's slipper.

mule (2) [myl], *n.f.* She-mule. *Ferrer la mule,* to get one's cut *or* payola.

mulet (1) [my′lɛ], *n.m.* He-mule; (*Bot., Zool., etc.*) mule. *Têtu comme un mulet,* as stubborn as a mule, pig-headed; *mulet de bât,* pack mule.

mulet (2) [MUGE] and [LOMPE].

muletier [myl′tje], *a.* (*fem.* **muletière**) Pertaining to mules. *Chemin muletier,* mule-track.—*n.* Muleteer.

mulle [myl], *n.m.* Surmullet.

mulot [my′lo], *n.m.* Field-mouse.

mulsion [myl′sjɔ̃], *n.f.* Milking (of cows).

multiarticulé, *a.* (*fem.* **-ée**) Multiarticulate.

multicolore, *a.* Many-coloured; motley; variegated.

multidigité, *a.* (*fem.* **-ée**) Multidigitate.

multiflore, *a.* Multiflorous.

multiforme, *a.* Multiform.

multilatéral, *a.* (*fem.* **-ale,** *pl.* **-aux**) Multilateral.

multimillionnaire, *a.* and *n.* Multimillionaire.

multipare, *a.* Multiparous.

multiple [myl′tipl], *a.* and *n.m.* Multiple; multifarious. (*Math.*) *Le plus petit commun multiple,* the least common multiple.

multiplex, *a.* Multiplex.

multipliable, *a.* Multipliable.

multipliant, *a.* (*fem.* **-iante**) Multiplying.

multiplicande, *n.m.* Multiplicand.

multiplicateur, *a.* (*fem.* **multiplicatrice**) Multiplying.—*n.m.* Multiplier, multiplicator.

multiplicatif, *a.* (*fem.* **-ive**) Multiplicative.

multiplication, *n.f.* Multiplication; gearing (-ratio). *Table de multiplication,* multiplication table.

multiplicité, *n.f.* Multiplicity.

multiplié, *a.* (*fem.* **multipliée**) Multiplied; multifarious, manifold; repeated, frequent.

multiplier, *v.i., v.t.* To multiply; to gear up to. **se multiplier,** *v.r.* To multiply; to be repeated, to be everywhere.

multipolaire [myltipo′lɛ:r], *a.* Multipolar.

multitube [mylti′tyb] or **multitubulaire,** *a.* Multitubular.

multitude [mylti′tyd], *n.f.* Multitude; crowd, host.

multivalve [mylti′valv], *a.* Multivalvular.—*n.f.* Multivalve.

muni [my′ni], *a.* (*fem.* **munie**) Supplied, furnished, provided (*de*); fortified.

municipal [mynisi′pal], *a.* (*fem.* **municipale,** *pl.* **municipaux**) Municipal. *Arrêté municipal,* by-law; *conseiller municipal,* (city) councillor; *musique municipale,* town band. —*n.m.* Soldier of the municipal guard.

municipalité, *n.f.* Municipality; town council and staff.

munificence [mynifi′sɑ̃:s], *n.f.* Bounty, munificence.

munificent *a.* (*fem.* **-ente**), Bountiful.

munir [my′ni:r], *v.t.* To provide, to supply, to furnish (*de*); to arm, to strengthen, to secure. **se munir,** *v.r.* To provide oneself, to be provided, supplied, or furnished (*de*).

munition [myni′sjɔ̃], *n.f.* Munition, munitioning, ammunition; (*pl.*) munitions, military stores, provisions, etc. *Pain de munition,* ration loaf; *fusil de munition,* regulation rifle; *munitions de bouche,* provisions, food supplies; *munitions (de guerre),* ammunition.

munitionnaire, *n.m.* Commissary.

muphti [MUFTI].

muqueux [my′kø], *a.* (*fem.* **-euse**) Mucous. *Fièvre muqueuse,* (*euph.*) typhoid fever or paratyphoid.—*n.f.* Mucous membrane.

mur [my:r], *n.m.* Wall. *Battre les murs,* to stagger against the walls; *gros murs,* main walls; *le mur du son,* the sound barrier; *mettre quelqu'un au pied du mur,* to drive someone into a corner, to demand a categorical answer; *mur d'appui,* breast-high wall, parapet wall; *mur de clôture,* enclosure-wall;

[502]

mur de refend, partition wall; *mur mitoyen*, jointly owned wall between two properties; [SOUTÈNEMENT]; *vivre entre quatre murs*, to live all cooped-up.

mûr [myːr], *a.* (*fem.* **mûre** (1)) Ripe, mature, matured; (of a person) mellow, drunk; (*fam.*) worn out, shabby (of clothes). *Après mûre réflexion*, after mature consideration; *du vin mûr*, mellow wine; *esprit mûr*, mature, serious mind; *l'âge mûr*, mature age, maturity.

murage [my'raːʒ], *n.m.* Walling.

muraille [my'raːj], *n.f.* Thick, high wall; barrier; (*pl.*) ramparts; (*Naut.*) sides (of ship). *Couleur muraille* or *de muraille*, grey or dim colour (like that of a wall). **muraillement**, *n.m.* Walling; erection of supporting walls. **murailler**, *v.t.* To support with walling.

mural, *a.* (*fem.* **murale**, *pl.* **muraux**) Mural. *Carte murale*, wall-map; *peintures murales*, wall-paintings.—*n.m.* (*Cercle*) *mural*, astrolabe, mural circle.

Murcie [myr'si], *f.* Murcia.

mûre (1) [MÛR].

mûre (2) [myːr], *n.f.* Mulberry. *Mûre bleue*, dewberry; *mûre sauvage*, *mûre de ronce*, or *mûre de haie*, blackberry.

mûrement [myr'mɑ̃], *adv.* Maturely. *J'y ai mûrement réfléchi*, I have given it close consideration.

murène [my'rɛːn], *n.f.* Muraena, marine eel; (*Am.*) moray.

murer [my're], *v.t.* To surround with a wall or walls, to wall in, to wall up, to brick up; to immure; (*fig.*) to screen, to conceal (one's life etc.).

muret [my're], *n.m.*, or **murette** [my'rɛt], *n.f.* Low wall.

murex [my'rɛks], *n.m.* Murex.

muriate [my'rjat], *n.m.* (*Chem.*) Muriate. **muriatique**, *a.* Muriatic.

mûrier [my'rje], *n.m.* Mulberry-tree. *Mûrier sauvage*, blackberry bush, bramble-bush.

mûrir [my'riːr], *v.t.* To ripen, to mature; to bring to perfection or completeness. *Mûrir un projet*, to plan.—*v.i.* To ripen, to grow ripe, to mature.

mûrissant, *a.* (*fem.* **-ante**) Ripening.

murmurant [myrmy'rɑ̃], *a.* (*fem.* **murmurante**) Murmuring, whispering; babbling; purling; muttering, grumbling.

murmurateur, *a.* (*fem.* **-trice**) (*rare*) Murmuring, grumbling.—*n.* Murmurer, grumbler; discontented, grumbling person.

murmure [myr'myːr], *n.m.* Murmur, murmuring; grumbling, muttering; whisper, whispering, babbling, hum, purl (of a brook), soughing (of the wind). **murmurer**, *v.i.* To murmur, to whisper; to grumble, to mutter; to gurgle, to prattle, to purl, to babble; to bicker, to brawl; to sough.—*v.t.* To mutter, to whisper. *Que murmurez-vous là?* what are you muttering there?

mûron [my'rɔ̃], *n.m.* Blackberry; wild raspberry.

murrhe [myr], *n.f.* Murra (also murrha, myrrha). **murrhin**, *a.* (*fem.* **murrhine**) Murrhine. *Vase murrhin*, murrhine vase.

mus, *1st sing. past* [MOUVOIR (2)].

musagète [myza'ʒɛt], *a.* Chief of the Muses (Apollo).

musaraigne [myza'rɛɲ], *n.f.* Shrew-mouse.

musard [my'zaːr], *a.* (*fem.* **musarde**) Loitering, dawdling.—*n.* (*colloq.*) Loiterer, dawdler.

musarder, *v.i.* To loiter, to dawdle.

musarderie or **musardise**, *n.f.* Loitering, dawdling, trifling.

musc [mysk], *n.m.* Musk-deer, musk. *Herbe au musc* [AMBRETTE].

muscade [mys'kad], *n.f.* Nutmeg; juggler's ball. (*fam.*) *Passez, muscade!* Hey, presto!

muscadet [myska'dɛ], *n.m.* A dry, white wine from the Nantes district; small cider apple.

muscadier [myska'dje], *n.m.* Nutmeg-tree.

muscadin [myska'dɛ̃], *n.m.* Musk-lozenge, muscadin; dandy, fop.—*a.* (*fem.* **muscadine**) Foppish.

muscardin [myskar'dɛ̃], *n.m.* Small dormouse.

muscardine [myskar'din], *n.f.* Muscardine or pebrine (silkworm disease).

muscari [myska'ri], *n.m.* Grape hyacinth.

muscat [mys'ka], *n.m.* and *a.* Muscat grape, muscadine; dried muscatel wine; variety of pear.

muscle [myskl], *n.m.* Muscle. **musclé**, *a.* (*fem.* **-ée**) With well-developed or well-marked muscles; muscular; (*fig.*) powerful. **muscler**, *v.t.* To develop muscles in (body, limb).

musculaire, *a.* Muscular.

muscularité, *n.f.* Muscularity.

musculature, *n.f.* Musculature.

musculeux, *a.* (*fem.* **-euse**) Muscular, brawny.

muse [myːz], *n.f.* Muse.

museau [my'zo], *n.m.* (*pl.* **museaux**) Muzzle, snout, nose; (*slang*) face, mug. *Quel vilain museau!* what an ugly mug!

musée [my'ze], *n.m.* Museum, art gallery, picture gallery. *Objet de musée*, museum-piece.

museler [myz'le], *v.t.* To muzzle; (*fig.*) to gag, to silence. **muselière**, *n.f.* Muzzle. **musellement**, *n.m.* Muzzling; (*fig.*) gagging, silencing.

muser [my'ze], *v.i.* To loiter, to moon, to dawdle. *Qui refuse muse*, he that will not when he may, when he fain would shall have nay.

muserolle or **muserole** [myz'rɔl], *n.f.* Noseband (of bridle).

musette [my'zɛt], *n.f.* Bagpipe; tune for this; (*Mil.*) haversack. *Musette de pansage*, stable bag; *musette de pansement*, stretcher-bearer's bag for bandages etc.; *musette* (*mangeoire*), nosebag (for horses). *Bal musette*, popular dancing-hall, (suburban) shilling hop; *orchestre musette*, accordion-band.

muséum [myze'ɔm], *n.m.* Natural history museum.

musical [myzi'kal], *a.* (*fem.* **-ale**, *pl.* **-aux**) Musical. *Soirée musicale*, musical evening. **musicalement**, *adv.* Musically. **musicalité**, *n.f.* Musicality. **music-hall**, *n.m.* (*pl.* **music-halls**) Music-hall, variety show. **musicien**, *n.m.* (*fem.* **-ienne**) Musician; (*Mil.*) bandsman.

musicologue, *n.m.* Music critic.

musique [my'zik], *n.f.* Music; band, musicians. *Être réglé comme du papier à musique*, to be as regular as clockwork; *la musique* *du régiment,* the regimental band; *chef de musique,* bandmaster; *maître de musique,* music-master; *mettre des vers en musique,* to set verses to music; *musique de chambre,* chamber-music; *musique de fond,* background music; *musique de scène,* incidental music; *musique religieuse,* church music; *nous ferons de la musique,* we shall have some music, (*fam.*) we shall kick up a fuss.

musiquer, *v.i.* To make music; to strum (on the piano).—*v.t.* To set to music.

musiquette, *n.f.* Paltry music, cheap music.

(C) muskeg [mɔs'keːg], *n.m.* Swamp.

musoir [my'zwaːr], *n.m.* Pier-head, jetty-head; wing, wall (of a lock).

musqué [mys'ke], *a.* (*fem.* **musquée**) Musked, muscat-flavoured, perfumed; (*fig.*) studied, unnatural, affected (language etc.).

musquer, *v.t.* To perfume with musk. **se musquer,** *v.r.* To scent oneself with musk.

mussif [my'sif], *a.m. Or mussif* (disulphide of tin), ormolu, mosaic gold.

musulman [myzyl'mɑ̃], *a.* and *n.* (*fem.* **-ane**) Mohammedan, Moslem.

mutabilité [mytabili'te], *n.f.* Mutability, changeableness.

mutable, *a.* Mutable.

mutation, *n.f.* Change; (*Biol.*) mutation, saltation; (*Law*) transfer.

muter [my'te], *v.t.* To stop the fermentation of must; (*Mil.* and *Adm.*) to transfer (of persons, property, etc.).

mutilateur [mytila'tœːr], *n.m.* Mutilator, maimer, defacer.

mutilation [mytilɑ'sjɔ̃], *n.f.* Mutilation, maiming; mangling, garbling. **mutilé,** *a.* (*fem.* **-ée**) Disabled.—*n. Les mutilés de guerre,* the disabled ex-servicemen; *un grand mutilé,* a very seriously disabled ex-service-man; *un mutilé (à) 100%,* a one hundred per cent disabled man.

mutiler, *v.t.* To mutilate, to maim; (*fig.*) to disfigure, to garble (of text).

mutin [my'tɛ̃], *a.* (*fem.* **mutine**) Obstinate, unruly; fractious; sprightly, pert, saucy, roguish.—*n.* Mutineer, rebel, rioter. **mutiné** *a.* (*fem.* **mutinée**) Mutinous, riotous. (*poet.*) *Les flots mutinés,* the boisterous waves. **mutinement,** *n.m.* Mutiny, mutineering. **mutiner,** *v.t.* To excite to rebellion. **se mutiner,** *v.r.* To mutiny. *Cet enfant se mutine,* that child is getting unruly.

mutinerie, *n.f.* Unruliness; mutiny, riot; sauciness, pertness.

mutisme [my'tism], *n.m.* Dumbness; speech-lessness, silence.

mutualisation [mytɥaliza'sjɔ̃], *n.f.* Mutualiza-tion. **mutualisme,** *n.m.* Mutualism. **mutualiste,** *a.* and *n.* Belonging to mutual benefit society. **mutualité,** *n.f.* Mutuality.

mutuel, *a.* (*fem.* **mutuelle** (1)) Mutual, reciprocal. *Société de secours mutuels,* benefit or friendly society. **mutuelle** (2), *n.f.* Mutual insurance company. **mutuelle-ment,** *adv.* Mutually.

mutule [my'tyl], *n.f.* (*Arch.*) Mutule.

Mycènes [mi'sɛːn], *f.* Mycenae.

mycète [mi'set], *n.m.* Mushroom.

mycétologie [MYCOLOGIE].

mycoderme, *n.m.* Mycoderma.

mycologie, *n.f.* Mycology.

mycologique, *a.* Mycologic. **mycologue** or **mycétologue,** *n.* Mycologist.

mycophage, *n.m.* Mycophagist.

mycose, *n.f.* Mycosis.

mye [mi], *n.f.* (*Conch.*) Gaper-shell.

myélite [mje'lit], *n.f.* Myelitis, inflammation of the spinal marrow. **myélo-méningite,** *n.f.* Myelomeningitis.

mygale [mi'gal], *n.f.* (*Zool.*) Mygale, trap-door spider.

myocardite [miɔkar'dit], *n.f.* Myocarditis. **myographe,** *n.* Myographist. **myographie,** *n.f.* Myography.

myologie, *n.f.* Myology.

myope [mjɔp], *a.* Myopic, short-sighted.—*n.* Myope; short-sighted person.

myopie, *n.f.* Myopia, short-sightedness. **myopique,** *a.* Myopic.

myosotis [mjɔzɔ'tiːs], *n.m.* Myosotis, forget-me-not; scorpion-grass.

myosure [miɔ'zyːr], *n.f.* (*Bot.*) Mousetail.

myotomie [miɔtɔ'mi], *n.f.* Myotomy.

myriade [mi'rjad], *n.f.* Myriad.

*****myriagramme,** *n.m.* Weight of 10,000 grammes (22·0485 lb. av.).

myriamètre, *n.m.* Measure of 10,000 metres (6·21375 miles).

myriapode, *n.m.* Myriapod.

myrmidon [mirmi'dɔ̃], *n.m.* Myrmidon.

myrobolan [mirɔbɔ'lɑ̃] or **myrobalan,** *n.m.* Myrobalan. **myrobolanier,** *n.m.* Myro-balan-tree.

myrrhe [miːr], *n.f.* Myrrh. **myrrhide,** *n.f.,* or **myrrhis,** *n.m.,* or *cerfeuil musqué.* Sweet cicely.

myrte [mirt], *n.m.* Myrtle. **myrtiforme,** *a.* Like a myrtle in form or habit.

myrtille [mir'tiːj], *n.f. Vaccinium myrtillus,* the berries of which are called *airelles* or *brimbelles,* bilberries, whortle-berries; (*Am.*) huckle-berries.

Mysie [mi'zi], *f.* Mysia.

mystagogue [mista'gɔg], *n.* Mystagogue.

mystère [mis'tɛːr], *n.m.* Mystery; secret, secrecy; (*fig.*) fuss, ado; mystery-play. *Approfondir un mystère,* to probe a mystery; *mettre du mystère à,* to make a mystery of; *sans aucun mystère,* without further ado.

mystérieusement, *adv.* Mysteriously. **mys-térieux,** *a.* (*fem.* **-ieuse**) Mysterious.

mysticisme, *n.m.* Mysticism.

mysticité, *n.f.* Mysticism, ardent piety.

mystificateur, *n.m.* (*fem.* **mystificatrice**) Mystifier, hoaxer.—*a.* Mystifying, hoaxing.

mystification, *n.f.* Hoax.

mystifier, *v.t.* (*conjugated like* PRIER) To mystify; to hoax.

mystique, *a.* Mystical, mystic.—*n.* Mystic.—*n.f.* Study of mysticism; mystical theology; (*neologism*) doctrine, creed, faith. *La mystique totalitaire,* the totalitarian doctrine.

mythe [mit], *n.m.* Myth; fable, fiction; fabu-lous thing.

mythique, *a.* Mythical.

mythographie, *n.f.* Mythography.

mythologie, *n.f.* Mythology. **mythologique,** *a.* Mythological. **mythologiste** or **mytho-logue,** *n.* Mythologist. **mythomane,** *n.* Mythomaniac. **mythomaniaque,** *a.* Mytho-maniac. **mythomanie,** *n.f.* Mythomania.

mytilicole [mitili'kɔl], *a.* Pertaining to mussel-breeding. **mytiliculteur,** *n.m.*

Mussel-breeder. **mytiliculture,** *n.f.* Mussel breeding.

myure [mi'jyr], *a.* *Pouls myure,* progressively sinking pulse.

myxomatose [miksɔma'toz], *n.f.* Myxomatosis. **myxomateux,** *a.* (*fem.* **-euse**) Myxomatous. **myxome,** *n.m.* Myxoma.

myxomycètes, *n.m. pl.* Myxomycetes.

N

N, n [ɛn], *n.m.* or *f.* The fourteenth letter of the alphabet. (*Geom.*) *L'espace à* n *dimensions,* n dimensional space. (*fam.*) *C'est la* n^ième *fois que je vous le dis,* I don't know how many times I have been telling you.

na [na], *int.* (*childish*) always at the end of a sentence. *Je n'en veux pas de ta bouillie, na!* I don't want your porridge, so there!

nabab [na'bab], *n.m.* Nabob.

nable [nɑ:bl], *n.m.* (*Naut.*) Scuttle-hole. *Bouchon de nable,* plug or stopper for this.

nabot [na'bo], *a.* (*fem.* **nabote**) Shrimpish, dwarfish.—*n.* Shrimp, manikin; dwarf.

Nabuchodonosor [nabykɔdɔnɔ'zɔ:r], *m.* Nebuchadnezzar.

nacarat [naka'ra], *a. inv.* and *n.m.* Nacarat.

nacelle [na'sɛl], *n.f.* Wherry, small boat, skiff; (gondola-) car, gondola, nacelle (of airship etc.); (*Arch.*) scotia.

nacre [nakr], *n.f.* Mother-of-pearl.

nacré [na'kre], *a.* (*fem.* **-ée**) Nacreous, pearly.

nacrer, *v.t.* To give a pearly lustre to.

nadir [na'di:r], *n.m.* Nadir.

nævus [ne'vy:s], *n.m.* (*pl.* **nævi**) Naevus, birthmark.

naffe [naf], *n.f.* Only used in *eau de naffe,* orange-flower water.

nage [na:ʒ], *n.f.* Swimming; rowing, sculling, paddling; rowlock. *Passer* or *traverser la rivière à la nage,* to swim across the river; *se jeter à la nage,* to leap into the water. *Nage à la marinière,* side-stroke; *nage libre,* freestyle; *nage sur le dos,* back-stroke. (*Row.*) *Banc de nage,* rowing seat; *chef de nage,* stroke; *être à la nage* or *donner la nage,* to row stroke. (*fam.*) *Être en nage,* to be bathed in perspiration. **nageant,** *a.* (*fem.* **-ante**) Of swimming or floating species, swimmer (bird etc.). **nageoire,** *n.f.* Fin (of a fish); board floating in a pail (to keep the water steady); (*slang*) arm.

nageoter, *v.i.* To swim badly, with difficulty; to flip about. **nager,** *v.i.* To swim; to float, to be buoyed up; to welter; to row, to scull, to pull. *Il nage comme un poisson,* he swims like a fish; *nager dans l'opulence,* to be rolling in money; *nager dans son sang,* to be weltering in one's blood; *nager entre deux eaux,* to swim under water, (*fig.*) to be a trimmer.

nageur, *a.* (*fem.* **nageuse**) *Oiseau nageur,* swimming bird; *poupée nageuse,* swimming-doll.—*n.* Swimmer; rower, oarsman. *Maître nageur,* swimming-coach.

naguère [na'gɛ:r], *adv.* Lately, but lately, not long ago.

naïade [na'jad], *n.f.* Naiad, water-nymph.

naïf [na'if], *a.* (*fem.* **naïve**) Naïve, artless, ingenuous, unaffected; simple, green. *Grâce naïve,* natural grace; *réponse naïve,* ingenuous

answer.—*n.* Artless person. *Ne fais pas le naïf* (*la naïve*), don't pretend (you don't understand).—*n.m.* (*Lit., Paint., etc.*) Naïveté, nature without art.

nain [nɛ̃], *a.* (*fem.* **naine**) Dwarfish. *Arbres nains,* dwarf trees; *œuf nain,* yolkless egg.—*n.* Dwarf. *Nain jaune,* Pope Joan (card game).

naissain [nɛ'sɛ̃], *n.m.* Brood, spat of oysters, mussels (in artificial breeding-ponds).

naissance [nɛ'sɑ̃:s], *n.f.* Birth; descent, extraction, noble birth; (*fig.*) beginning, dawn, rise; root, foundation, base; (*Arch.*) spring, spandrel. *Acte de naissance,* birth-certificate; *donner naissance à,* to give rise to (a rumour), to give birth to (a child); *être aveugle de naissance,* to be blind from birth; *être de haute naissance,* to be high-born; *la naissance de la poésie,* the dawn of poetry; *la naissance des cheveux,* the hair-line, the hair-roots; *lieu de naissance,* birth-place; *prendre naissance,* (*fig.*) to be born, to originate.

naissant, *a.* (*fem.* **naissante**) New-born, infant, in its infancy; beginning, budding, dawning, growing, nascent, rising.

naître [nɛ:tr], *v.i. irr.* (*pres.p.* **naissant**, *p.p.* **né**) To be born, to come into the world; to begin to grow; (*fig.*) to commence, to originate, to arise; to rise, to dawn, to spring up. *Cela peut faire naître des soupçons,* that may give rise to suspicion; *faire naître,* to give birth to, to call into existence, to create, to produce, to excite, to suggest; *il est né poète,* he is a born poet; *Jeanne Manchon, née Barry,* J. M., maiden name Barry or née B.; *je l'ai vu naître,* I have known him from infancy.

naïve [na'if], *see* **naïf.**

naïvement [naiv'mɑ̃], *adv.* Naïvely, ingenuously, artlessly.

naïveté, *n.f.* Artlessness, simplicity, naïvety; greenness.

naja [na'ʒa], *n.m.* Cobra, naja.

nandou [nɑ̃'du], *n.m.* (*Orn.*) Nandu.

naniser [nani'ze], *v.t.* To dwarf (a plant), to stunt in growth. **nanisme,** *n.m.* Dwarfishness, characteristic of a dwarf.

nankin [nɑ̃'kɛ̃], *n.m.* Nankeen.

nansouk [nɑ̃'suk], *n.m.* (*Tex.*) Nainsook.

nantir [nɑ̃'ti:r], *v.t.* To give as a pledge, to secure; (*fig.*) to provide, to furnish. *Être nanti de,* to hold as a pledge; to have (in hand), to be furnished (with). *Elle est partie nantie de quelques livres sterling,* she went off with a few pounds in her pocket. **se nantir,** *v.r.* To hold as a pledge; to provide oneself (*de*); to take possession (*de*); to feather one's nest.

nantissement, *n.m.* Security, pledge, lien, cover.

napalm [na'palm], *n.m.* Napalm.

napée [na'pe], *n.f.* Wood-nymph, mountain-nymph.

napel [na'pɛl], *n.m.,* or **aconit napel**. Monk's-hood, napellus, wolf's-bane.

naphtaline [nafta'lin], *n.f.,* or **naphtalène,** *n.m.* Naphthaline.

naphte, *n.m.* Naphtha.

naphtylamine, *n.f.* Naphthylamine.

napiforme [napi'fɔrm], *a.* Napiform (turnip-shaped).

***napoléon** [napɔle'ɔ̃], *n.m.* French gold coin, worth 20 francs.

napoléonien, *a.* (*fem.* **-ienne**) Napoleonic,

of Napoleon.—*n.* Partisan or descendant of Napoleon (more often *bonapartiste*).

napolitain [napɔli'tɛ̃], *a.* and *n.* (*fem.* **napolitaine**) Neapolitan.

nappe [nap], *n.f.* Table-cloth, cover, cloth; (*Hunt.*) stag's skin; clap-net. *Nappe d'autel*, altar-cloth; *nappe d'eau, d'huile*, or *de pétrole*, sheet or pool of water, oil, or petrol (underground). **napper**, *v.t.* (*Cook.*) To cover with thick gravy *or* sauce. **napperon**, *n.m.* Napkin, small table-cloth, tray-cloth; doily.

naquis, *1st sing. past* [NAÎTRE].

Narcisse [nar'sis], *m.* (*Myth.*) Narcissus. *C'est un vrai Narcisse*, he is enamoured of his person.

narcisse [nar'sis], *n.m.* (*Bot.*) Narcissus. *Narcisse blanc* or *des poètes*, narcissus, pheasant's eye [ADONIS], *narcisse des prés* or *coucou*, or *jeannette jaune*, daffodil.

narcissisme, *n.m.* Narcissism, morbid self-love.

narco-analyse [narkoana'liz], *n.f.* Narco-analysis.

narcomanie [narkoma'ni], *n.f.* Drug addiction.

narcose, *n.f.* Narcosis.

narcotine [narkɔ'tin], *n.f.* Narcotine.

narcotique, *a.* and *n.m.* Narcotic.

narcotiser, *v.t.* To narcotize.

narcotisme, *n.m.* Narcotism.

nard [na:r], *n.m.* Nard, spikenard. *Nard de montagne*, setwall; *nard sauvage* or *asaret d'Europe*, asarabacca.

nargue [narg], *n.f.* (Only used in) *Faire nargue à*, to snap one's fingers at; *nargue pour l'amour*, a fig for love.

narguer, *v.t.* (*colloq.*) To snap one's fingers at, to defy, to flout; to beard, to brave. *Narguer la mort*, to defy death, to snap one's fingers at death.

narguilé [nargi'le], *n.m.* Narghile (Turkish or Persian pipe).

narine [na'rin], *n.f.* Nostril.

narquois [nar'kwa], *a.* (*fem.* **narquoise**) Cunning, sly, chaffing *or* bantering. **narquoisement**, *adv.* Slyly, quizzingly.

narrateur [nara'tœːr], *n.m.* (*fem.* **-trice**) Narrator, relater.

narratif, *a.* (*fem.* **-ive**) Narrative.

narration [nara'sjɔ̃], *n.f.* Narration, narrative. *Présent de narration*, historic present.

***narré**, *n.m.* Narrative, recital, account.

narrer, *v.t.* To narrate, to tell.

narthex [nar'teks], *n.m.* (*Arch.*) Narthex.

narval [nar'val], *n.m.* (*pl.* **narvals**) Narwhal.

nasal [na'zal], *a.* (*fem.* **nasale**, *pl.* **nasaux**) Nasal. *Son nasal*, nasal sound.—*n.f.* Nasal sound or letter.—*n.m.* Nasal (of helmet). **nasalement**, *adv.* Nasally, with a nasal sound.

nasalisation, *n.f.* Nasalization.

nasaliser, *v.t.* To nasalize.

nasalité, *n.f.* Nasality, nasal sound.

nasarde [na'zard], *n.f.* Fillip, rap on the nose; (*fig.*) affront, sneer.

***nasarder**, *v.t.* To fillip, to rap on the nose; to jeer at, to banter, (*Am.*) to rib.

naseau [na'zo], *n.m.* (*pl.* **naseaux**) Nostril (of animals).

nasillant [nazi'jɑ̃], *a.* (*fem.* **nasillante**) Speaking through the nose, snuffling.

nasillard, *a.* (*fem.* **nasillarde**) Snuffling, nasal.

nasillement [nazij'mɑ̃], *n.m.* Speaking through the nose, snuffling; twang. **nasiller**, *v.t.* To utter as if through the nose, to snuffle.—*v.i.* To speak through the nose, to snuffle.

nasique [na'zik], *n.m.* Long-nosed monkey (of Borneo); proboscis monkey.

nasse [nɑːs], *n.f.* Bow-net, weir, eel-pot; (*fig.*) fix, trap. *Il est dans la nasse*, he is in a fix.

natal [na'tal], *a.* (*fem.* **-ale**, *pl.* **-als** (*rare*)) Natal, native. *Jour natal*, birthday; *pays natal*, native country. **natalité**, *n.f.* Birthrate.

natation [nata'sjɔ̃], *n.f.* Swimming.

natatoire, *a.* Swimming, natatory. *Vessie natatoire*, swimming-bladder.

natif [na'tif], *a.* (*fem.* **native**) Native; natural. *Ma fille est native de Londres*, my daughter is London-born; *or natif*, native gold.—*n.* Native.

nation [nɑ'sjɔ̃], *n.f.* Nation. *Société des Nations*, League of Nations; *les Nations Unies*, the United Nations.

national, *a.* (*fem.* **-ale**, *pl.* **-aux**) National. *Assemblée nationale*, national assembly; *garde national*, national guard (man); *garde nationale*, national guard (corps.)—*n.* (used only in *pl.*) Nationals, citizens.

nationalement, *adv.* Nationally.

nationalisation, *n.f.* Nationalization.

nationaliser, *v.t.* To nationalize.

nationalisme, *n.m.* Nationalism.

nationaliste, *n.* Nationalist.

nationalité, *n.f.* Nationality, national status; nation.

national-socialisme [nasjɔnalsɔsja'lism], *n.m.* National Socialism. **national-socialiste**, *a.* and *n.* (*pl.* **nationaux-Socialistes**) National Socialist.

nativité [nativi'te], *n.f.* Nativity, birth.

natron [na'trɔ̃], *n.m.* Natron, soda.

natte [nat], *n.f.* Mat, matting (of straw); plait, twist (of hair, silk, etc.). *Natte (de Chinois)*, pigtail.

natter, *v.t.* To mat; to plait, to twist.

naturalisation [natyraliza'sjɔ̃], *n.f.* Naturalization; taxidermy. *Acte de naturalisation*, certificate of registry (*Naut.*), naturalization papers.

naturalisé [natyrali'ze], *a.* and *n.m.* (*fem.* **-ée**) Naturalized (citizen).

naturaliser, *v.t.* To naturalize; to stuff, to mount (animal).

naturalisme, *n.m.* Naturalness; naturalism.

naturaliste, *n.* Naturalist; taxidermist.—*a.* Naturalistic.

naturalité, *n.f.* (*rare*) Denizenship, citizenship; naturalization.

naturante, *a.f.* (*Phil.*) Naturizing (used by Spinosa of nature as causing phenomena).

nature [na'tyːr], *n.f.* Nature; kind, sort; essence, constitution; disposition, temperament, character; life, life-size. (*fam.*) *C'est une petite nature*, he *or* she is a weakly, delicate person; *contre nature*, unnatural; *de la nature* or *de nature*, by nature, naturally; *de nature à*, likely to; *dessiner d'après nature*, to draw from life; *don de la nature*, gift of nature; *nature morte*, still life; *l'art perfectionne la nature*, nature is improved by art;

l'habitude est une seconde nature, habit is a second nature; *payer en nature,* to pay in kind; *plus grand que nature,* larger than life. —*a. inv. (colloq.)* Natural. *Pommes de terre nature,* plain boiled potatoes.

naturel, *a. (fem.* **naturelle)** Natural; native, innate; artless, plain, home-bred; genuine, unsophisticated. *Enfant naturel,* illegitimate child.—*n.m.* Native (of a country); character, temper, disposition, nature; naturalness, freedom from affectation, genuineness, simplicity; natural ease or unconstraint. *Au naturel,* naturally, to the life, life-size, *(Cook.)* cooked plain; *chassez le naturel, il revient au galop,* the leopard cannot change his spots; *naturel fort et robuste,* strong constitution; *un homme d'un mauvais naturel* or *d'un bon naturel,* an ill-natured *or* a good-natured man. **naturellement,** *adv.* Naturally, by nature; genuinely, sincerely; freely, artlessly. —*int.* Of course. **naturiste,** *a.* Naturistic. —*n.* Naturist.

naufrage [noˈfraːʒ], *n.m.* Shipwreck; *(fig.)* wreck, wrecking. *Faire naufrage,* to be shipwrecked or wrecked.

naufragé, *a. (fem.* **naufragée)** Shipwrecked, wrecked.—*n.* Shipwrecked person, castaway.

naufrager, *v.i.* To suffer shipwreck. **naufrageur,** *n.m.* and *a. (fem.* **-euse)** Wrecker.

naulage [NOLIS, NOLAGE].

naulisateur [NOLISATEUR].

naumachie [nomaˈʃi], *n.f.* Naumachy (spectacle representing a sea-fight); *(Arch.)* small artificial lake with sham ruins of colonnade, as in Parc Monceau, Paris.

Nauplie [noˈpli], *f.* Nauplia.

nauséabond [nozeaˈbɔ̃], *a. (fem.* **nauséabonde)** Nauseous, loathsome, disgusting.

nausée [noˈze], *n.f.* Nausea, qualmishness; sickness; *(fig.)* loathing, disgust. *Cela me donne des nausées,* that makes me feel sick.

nauséeux, *a. (fem.* **nauséeuse).** Nauseating.

nautile [noˈtil], *n.m.* Nautilus.

nautique [noˈtik], *a.* Nautical. **nautonier,** *n.m. (poet.)* Boatman, mariner, pilot.

naval [naˈval], *a. (fem.* **navale,** *pl.* **navals)** Naval, nautical.—*n.f. Navale (fam.)* = *École Navale. Entrer à Navale,* to gain admission to the Naval Training College.

Navarin [navaˈrɛ̃], *m.* Navarino.

navarin [navaˈrɛ̃], *n.m.* Mutton stew with turnips and potatoes.

navet [naˈvɛ], *n.m.* Turnip; *(Art)* daub. *Avoir du sang de navet,* (pop.) to be anaemic, to have no pluck; *(Cine.) c'est un navet! (pop.)* it is a flop! *Navet du diable* [BRYONE].

navette (1) [naˈvɛt], *n.f.* Incense-box; shuttle (for knotting, tatting, etc.), weaver's shuttle. *Faire la navette,* to ply to and fro, to run a shuttle-service.

navette (2) [naˈvɛt], *n.f.* Rape; rape-seed. *Huile de navette,* rape oil.

navicert [naviˈsɛrt], *n.m.* Navicert.

naviculaire [navikyˈlɛːr], *a.* Navicular.

navigabilité [navigabiliˈte], *n.f.* Navigableness; airworthiness, seaworthiness. *Certificat de navigabilité,* certificate of air- (or sea-) worthiness.

navigable, *a.* Navigable; seaworthy, airworthy.

navigant, *a. (fem.* **-ante)** Sailing; *(Av.)* flying.

Le personnel navigant, (Av.) the flying staff, the air-crews.

navigateur [navigaˈtœːr], *n.m.* Navigator.— *a.m.* Seafaring; swimming (birds etc.).

navigation [navigaˈsjɔ̃], *n.f.* Navigation; voyage, sailing. *Navigation au long cours* or *hauturière,* foreign trade; high seas navigation; *navigation de plaisance,* boating, yachting.

naviguer, *v.i.* To navigate; to row, to sail, etc.; to steer well or ill (of a boat etc.). *Naviguer en pleine mer,* to sail in the open sea.

navire [naˈviːr], *n.m.* Vessel, ship. *Navire de charge* (usually *cargo*), cargo vessel; *navire de guerre,* man-of-war; *navire marchand,* merchantman; *navire hôpital,* hospital ship.

navrant [naˈvrɑ̃], *a. (fem.* **navrante)** Heartrending, harrowing, distressing.

navrement [navrəˈmɑ̃], *n.m.* Grief, despair.

navrer, *v.t.* *To wound; to distress, to rend (the heart). *Je suis navré,* I am brokenhearted, I feel this very deeply; *j'en suis navré pour vous,* I feel deeply for you.

nazaréen [nazareˈɛ̃], *a. (fem.* **nazaréenne)** Of Nazareth.—*n.* Nazarene; Nazarite.

nazi [naˈzi], *a.* and *n. (fem.* **-ie)** *(abbr. of National-sozialist)* Nazi. **nazifier,** *v.t.* To nazify. **nazisme,** *n.m.* Nazism.

ne [nə], *adv.* (**n'** before a vowel or unaspirated *h).* No, not. *À moins que cela ne soit,* unless that is so; *cela ne vaut rien,* that is worth nothing; *il ne cesse de gronder,* he is always scolding; *il n'a fait que cela,* he only did that; *il ne fait que dormir,* he does nothing but sleep; *il ne le fera plus,* he will not do it again; *je crains que cela ne soit,* I fear that it is so; *je ne doute pas que cela ne soit,* I do not doubt it; *je ne peux me taire,* I cannot remain silent; *je ne saurais vous dire,* I cannot tell you; *je ne veux pas,* I will not; *je n'ose lui parler,* I dare not speak to him; *ne . . . que,* only, nothing but; *il ne faut pas que vous* (*subj.*) or *vous ne devez pas,* you must not.

né [ne], *a. (fem.* **née)** Born. *Bien né,* of good birth; *premier né,* first-born [*see also* MORT, NAÎTRE, NOUVEAU].

néanmoins [neɑ̃ˈmwɛ̃], *adv.* Nevertheless, however, for all that.

néant [neˈɑ̃], *n.m.* Nothing, naught, nothingness; annihilation, emptiness, nullity; (on report sheet, statement, etc.) nil, none. *Sortir du néant,* to rise from obscurity; *rentrer dans le néant,* to return to nothing; *tirer du néant,* to create out of nothing; *un état néant,* a nil return.

nébulaire [nebyˈlɛːr], *a.* Nebular. **nébuleuse** (1), *n.f.* Nebula. **nébuleusement,** *adv.* Nebulously. **nébuleux,** *a. (fem.* **nébuleuse** (2)) Cloudy, misty, hazy; gloomy; nebulous; *(fig.)* obscure. **nébulosité,** *n.f.* Patch of haze; *(fig.)* lack of clarity.

nécessaire [neseˈsɛːr], *a.* Necessary, requisite, needful; unavoidable, inevitable.—*n.m.* That which is necessary, the needful or indispensable; necessities (of life etc.); dressing-case, work-box, outfit of various forms; cleaning kit (of rifle). *Faire le nécessaire,* to fuss round; to do what is necessary; *se refuser le nécessaire,* to refuse oneself the necessities of life; *un nécessaire de couture,* a sewing set *or* kit. **nécessairement,** *adv.* Necessarily, inevitably, of course.

nécessitant, *a.* (*fem.* **nécessitante**) (*Theol.*) Absolute (of grace).

nécessité, *n.f.* Necessity; need, want. *De nécessité* or *de toute nécessité*, of necessity, necessarily; *de première nécessité*, staple (goods); *faire de nécessité vertu*, to make a virtue of necessity; *la nécessité est mère de l'invention*, necessity is the mother of invention; *les nécessités de la nature*, the wants of nature; *nécessité n'a point de loi*, necessity knows no law [*see also* CHALET].

nécessiter, *v.t.* To necessitate, to require; to compel, to force, to oblige; to imply.

nécessiteux, *a.* (*fem.* **nécessiteuse**) Necessitous, needy.—*n.* Necessitous person, pauper.

nécrobie [nekrɔ'bi], *n.f.* Scavenger-beetle.

nécrologe [nekrɔ'lɔːʒ], *n.m.* Obituary list; death roll. **nécrologie**, *n.f.* Necrology, deaths (in newspaper); obituary. **nécrologique**, *a.* Necrological. *Notice nécrologique*, obituary (notice). **nécrologue**, *n.* Necrologist.

nécromancie [nekrɔmã'si], *n.f.* Necromancy. **nécromancien**, *n.m.* (*fem.* **-ienne**) Necromancer.

nécromant, *n.m.* [NÉCROMANCIEN].

nécrophage, *a.* Necrophagous.

nécrophobie, *n.f.* Necrophobia.

nécrophore, *n.m.* Carrion-beetle.

nécropole, *n.f.* Necropolis.

nécrose, *n.f.* Necrosis (of bones); canker (of wood).

nécroser, *v.t.* To cause necrosis. **se nécroser**, *v.r.* To develop necrosis.

nectaire [nɛk'tɛːr], *n.m.* Nectary, honeycup.

nectar [nɛk'taːr], *n.m.* Nectar.

nectarine, *n.f.* Nectarine.

néerlandais [neɛrlã'dɛ], *a.* and *n.* (*fem.* **-aise**) Dutch; Dutchman; Dutchwoman.

Néerlande [neɛr'lãːd], **la**, *f.* The Netherlands.

nef [nɛf], *n.f.* Nave (of a church); *ship; *piece of plate (in the shape of a ship) for holding the lord's knife and fork etc. *La Blanche Nef*, the White Ship.

néfaste, *a.* Inauspicious, of evil omen; unlucky, disastrous; unfortunate (of decision, measure, etc.). (*Rom. Ant.*) *Jour néfaste*, ill-fated day, dies non (on which business was not allowed).

nèfle [nɛfl], *n.f.* Medlar. *Nèfle du Japon* [BIBASSE]; (*pop.*) *des nèfles!* certainly not! not on your nelly.

néflier, *n.m.* Medlar-tree.

négateur [nega'tœːr], *n.m.* (*fem.* **-trice**) Denier.—*a.* Denying.

négatif [nega'tif], *a.* (*fem.* **-ive**) Negative.— *n.m.* (*Phot.*) Negative.—*n.f.* Negative, refusal.

négation, *n.f.* Negation; (*Gram.*) negative.

négativement, *adv.* In the negative, negatively. **négaton**, *n.m.* Negaton, (negative) electron.

négligé [negli'ʒe], *a.* (*fem.* **négligée**) Neglected, unnoticed, unheeded; unstudied, careless; slovenly. *Extérieur négligé*, slovenly exterior; *style négligé*, careless style.—*n.m.* Undress, negligee.

négligeable, *a.* Negligible; trifling, unimportant. *Quantité négligeable*, (*Math.*) quantity not to be taken into account.

négligemment, *adv.* Nonchalantly, as if by chance, falsely detached; negligently.

négligence [negli'ʒãːs], *n.f.* Negligence, neglect, carelessness, oversight. *Par négligence*, through an oversight.

négligent, *a.* (*fem.* **-ente**) Negligent, neglectful, remiss, careless; unstudied. *D'un air négligent*, in an apparently unstudied fashion, as if by chance.—*n.* Negligent person.

négliger, *v.t.* To neglect, to be careless of; to omit, to slight, to pass over, to disregard. **se négliger**, *v.r.* To neglect oneself; to be negligent or careless. *Il commence à se négliger*, he begins to be careless of his person.

négoce [ne'gɔs], *n.m.* Trade, business; trafficking. *Faire un gros négoce*, to carry on a large trade.

négociabilité, *n.f.* Negotiability.

négociable, *a.* Negotiable, transferable.

négociant, *n.m.* Merchant (wholesale).

négociateur, *n.m.* (*fem.* **négociatrice**) Negotiator, transactor. **négociation**, *n.f.* Negotiation, transaction. *Engager des négociations*, to enter into negotiations.

négocier, *v.i.* (*conjugated like* PRIER) To trade. —*v.t.* To negotiate; to be in treaty for. **se négocier**, *v.r.* To be negotiating; to be negotiated.

nègre [nɛːgr], *a.* and *n.m.* (*fem.* **négresse**) (*pej.*) Negro (*pl.* Negroes); (*fam.*) ghost-writer, stooge; (barrister's) devil. *Travailler comme un nègre*, to work like a beaver, to work like a slave; *avoir un nègre*, (*fam.*) to have a man who does the donkey (*or* routine) work for you; *la race nègre*, the black race; *parler petit nègre*, to talk trading French or 'pidgin'.

négrerie, *n.f.* *Barracoon, slave-compound.

négrier, *a.m.* *(Bâtiment) négrier*, slave-ship; *capitaine négrier*, captain of a slave-ship; *marchand négrier*, slave-dealer.—*n.m.* Slave-ship, slaver; slave-dealer.

négrillon, *n.m.* (*fem.* **-onne**) (*pej.*) Little Negro, Negro boy *or* girl.

négroïde, *a.* Negroid.

négrophile, *a.* and *n.* Negrophile, pro-Negro.

négrophobe, *a.* and *n.* Negrophobe, Negrophobiac, anti-Negro.

Négus [ne'gys], *m.* Negus (Ethiopian royal title).

Néhémie [nee'mi], *m.* Nehemiah.

neige [nɛːʒ], *n.f.* Snow; (*fig.*) whiteness; (*slang*) cocaine. *Amas de neige*, snow-drift; *blanc comme la neige*, snow-white; (*fig.*) spotless; *boule de neige* [BOULE]; *de gros flocons de neige*, large flakes of snow; *d'une blancheur de neige*, as white as snow; *il est tombé de la neige*, there has been a fall of snow; *neiges éternelles*, perpetual snow; *neige fondue*, sleet; slush; *tempête* or *rafale de neige*, blizzard.

neiger, *v.impers.* To snow. *Il neige*, it is snowing.

neigeux, *a.* (*fem.* **neigeuse**) Snowy, snow-covered. *Temps neigeux*, snowy weather.

nélombo or **nélumbo** [nelɔ'bo], *n.m.* Nelumbium, Nile lily.

nématode [nema'tɔd], *n.m.* Nematode.

néméen [neme'ɛ̃], *a.* and *n.* (*fem.* **-éenne**) Nemean.

némoral [nemɔ'ral], *a.* (*fem.* **-ale**, *pl.* **-aux**) Nemoral, growing or living in forests.

Nemrod [nem'rɔd], *m.* Nimrod.

nénies [ne'ni], *n.f. pl.* (*Class. Ant.*) Funeral dirges.

nenni [na'ni], *adv.* *(*fam.*) No, not at all.

nénuphar [neny'fa:r], *n.m.* Nenuphar. *Nénuphar blanc*, or *nymphéa*, or *lis des étangs*, white water-lily; *nénuphar jaune* or *plateau*, yellow water-lily.

néo-catholicisme [neokatɔli'sism], *n.m.* Neo-Catholicism. **néo-catholique**, *a.* and *n.* Neo-Catholic.

néo-chrétien, *a.* (*fem.* **néo-chrétienne**) Neo-Christian. **néo-christianisme**, *n.m.* Neo-Christianity. **néo-gallois**, *a.* and *n.* (*fem.* **-oise**) Of New South Wales.

néographe [neɔ'graf], *a.* Reforming orthography.—*n.* Spelling reformer.

néo-grec [neo'grɛk], *a.* (*fem.* **néo-grecque**) Modern Greek.

néo-impressionnisme [neoɛ̃prɛsjɔ'nism], *n.m.* Post-impressionism.

néo-latin [neola'tɛ̃], *a.* (*fem.* **néo-latine**) Neo-Latin (modern language derived from Latin).

néolithique [neɔli'tik], *a.* Neolithic.

néologie [neɔlɔ'ʒi], *n.f.* Neology. **néologique**, *a.* Neological. **néologisme**, *n.m.* Neologism. **néologue** or **néologiste**, *n.m.* Neologist.

néon [ne'ɔ̃], *n.m.* Neon. *Lampe au néon*, neon glow-lamp; *tube au néon*, neon tube.

néophyte [neo'fit], *n.* Neophyte, novice; tyro.

néoplasme [neo'plasm], *n.m.* (*Path.*) Neoplasm.

néo-platonicien [neoplatɔni'sjɛ̃], *a.* (*fem.* **néo-platonicienne**) Neoplatonic.—*n.* Neoplatonist. **néo-platonisme**, *n.m.* Neoplatonism.

néottie [neo'ti], *n.f.*, or *néottie nid d'oiseau*, (*Bot.*) *Neottia nidus avis* (an orchid).

néo-zélandais [neozelɑ̃'dɛ], *a.* (*fem.* **-aise**), *a.* and *n.* New Zealand (butter, cheese, etc.); New Zealander.

Népal [ne'pɑ:l], *m.* Nepal. **népalais**, *a.* and *n.* (*fem.* **-aise**) Nepalese.

nèpe [nɛp], *n.f.* [SCORPION].

népenthès [nepɛ̃'tɛs], *n.m.* Nepenthes.

néphélion [nefe'ljɔ̃], *n.m.* Nebula (a trouble of the cornea).

néphralgie [nefral'ʒi], *n.f.* Nephralgia. **néphrétique**, *a.* Nephritic.—*n.* Person affected with renal colic.—*n.m.* Remedy for this.

néphrite (1) [ne'frit], *n.f.* Nephritis. *Néphrite chronique*, Bright's disease.

néphrite (2) [ne'frit], *n.f.* Nephrite, greenstone, jade.

népotisme [nepɔ'tism], *n.m.* Nepotism.

neptunien [nɛpty'njɛ̃], *a.* (*fem.* **neptunienne**) Neptunian.

Nérée [ne're], *n.m.* (*Myth.*) Nereus. (*poet.*) *L'empire de Nérée*, the sea. **néréide**, *n.f.* Sea-nymph.

nerf [nɛ:r], *n.m.* Nerve; sinew, tendon; fortitude, vigour, strength, stamina; (*Bookb.*) cord, tape. *Attaque de nerfs*, nervous attack, hysterics; *avoir ses nerfs*, to be on edge, irritable; *donner* or *porter sur les nerfs*, to irritate, to get on (someone's) nerves; *l'argent est le nerf de la guerre*, money is the sinews of war; *manquer de nerf*, to be wanting in energy; *nerfs à vif*, frayed nerves; *nerfs d'acier*, nerves of steel; *nerf de bœuf*, bull's pizzle, lash.

nerf-férure, *n.f.* (*pl.* **nerfs-férures**) (*Vet.*) Overreach cut.

nerf-foulure, *n.f.* (*pl.* **nerfs-foulures**) Sprained ankle.

néroli [nerɔ'li], *n.m.* Neroli.

Néron [ne'rɔ̃], *m.* Nero.

nerprun [nɛr'prœ̃], *n.m.* (*Bot.*) Buckthorn, *Rhamnus cathartica*. *Faux nerprun* or *arbousier*, sea-buckthorn [*see also* BOURDAINE].

nerval [nɛr'val], *a.* (*fem.* **-ale**, *pl.* **-aux**) Nerval, neural.

nervé, *a.* (*fem.* **-ée**) (*Bot.*) Nerved, nervose.

nerver [nɛr've], *v.t.* To cover with sinews. *Nerver un livre*, (*Bookb.*) to cord a book, to rib.

nerveusement [nɛrvøz'mã], *adv.* Impatiently; nervously. **nerveux**, *a.* (*fem.* **nerveuse**) Nervous; sinewy, muscular, wiry, vigorous, excitable; (*fam.*) nervy.

nervin, *a.m.* and *n.m.* (*Med.*) Nervine.

nervosité, *n.f.* Nervousness.

nervure, *n.f.* (*Bot. etc.*) Nervure, nerve; (*Arch.*) moulding on ribs, angles, etc.; (*Carp.*) rib, fillet; (*Bookb.*) tapes, cording, raised band; (*Needlework*) piping.

nescience [nɛs'jãs], *n.f.* Nescience, ignorance.

nestor [nɛs'tɔ:r], *n.m.* Nestor, wise old man.

nestorianisme, *n.m.* Nestorianism. **nestorien**, *a.* and *n.m.* (*fem.* **-ienne**) Nestorian.

net [nɛt], *a.* (*fem.* **nette**) Clean; pure, spotless; clear, plain, distinct, sharp; flat, frank, pointblank; net (of prices). *Avoir la voix nette*, to have a clear voice; *avoir les mains nettes*, to have clean hands, not to be mixed up in any shady enterprise; *cassure nette*, clean break; *il a l'esprit net* or *les idées nettes*, he is clearheaded; *je veux en avoir le cœur net*, I want to get to the bottom of the matter; *prix net*, trade price; *réponse nette*, plain, downright answer; *revenu* or *profit net*, clear profit; *son bien est net*, his estate is clear; *trouver maison nette*, to find the house empty; *un cheval sain et net*, a horse warranted sound and free from any defect; *une chambre nette*, a clean room; *une écriture nette*, a fair hand.—*n.m.* Fair copy. *Mettre au net*, to make a fair copy.—*adv.* Clean off, at once; flatly, point-blank, outright; net. *Coupé net*, cut clean off. *Il me l'a refusé tout net*, he flatly refused me, he refused me point-blank. **nettement**, *adv.* Cleanly; clearly, distinctly; outright, plainly, flatly. *Parlez-lui nettement*, speak to him plainly.

netteté, *n.f.* Cleanness; clearness, distinctness. *Netteté dans la voix*, clearness of voice.

nettoiement [netwa'mã] or **nettoyage**, *n.m.* Cleaning, cleansing; scouring, clearing; sweeping, wiping. *Le grand nettoyage (de printemps)*, spring cleaning.

nettoyer, *v.t. irr.* (*conjug. like* ABOYER) To clean, to cleanse; to scour; to wipe; to free, to clear, to rid (*de*), to purge; (*pop.*) to strip, to plunder, to demolish; to kill. *Nettoyer un habit*, to clean a coat; *nettoyer une pièce à fond*, to turn out a room; (*Mil.*) *nettoyer une tranchée*, to clear a trench of remaining enemy, to mop up.

nettoyeur, *n.m.* (*fem.* **nettoyeuse**) Cleaner; scurfer (of boiler etc.). (*Mil.*) *Nettoyeur de tranchée*, trench mopper-up.

neuf (1) [nœf], *a.* and *n.m.* Nine, ninth. *Neuf heures* [nœv'œr], nine (o'clock); *le neuf août* [nœfu], the ninth of August; *un enfant de neuf ans* [nœ'vã], a nine-year-old child; *un neuf de cœur*, a nine of hearts.

neuf (2) [nœf], *a.* (*fem.* **neuve**) New; inexperienced, young, raw, green. *À neuf*, anew, again, like new; *faire peau neuve*, to brighten up; *habiller de neuf*, to dress in new clothes; *il est tout neuf dans ce métier*, he is quite new to the business; *refaire à neuf*, to do over; *remettre à neuf*, to do up, to make as good as new.—*n.m.* Something new. *Donnez-nous du neuf*, give us something new; *il y a du neuf*, something has happened; *quoi de neuf?* any news?

neume [nø:m], *n.m.* (*Mus.*) Neume.

neurasthénie [nœraste′ni], *n.f.* Neurasthenia.

neurasthénique, *a.* Neurasthenic.—*n.* Person afflicted with neurasthenia.

neurologie [nœrɔlɔ′ʒi], *n.f.* Neurology.

neurologue or **neurologiste**, *n.m.* Neurologist.

neurone, *n.m.* Neurone.

Neustrie [nøs′tri], **la**, *f.* Neustria.

neutralement [nøtral′mɑ̃], *adv.* Neutrally.

neutralisant [nøtrali′zɑ̃], *a.* (*fem.* **neutralisante**) (*Chem.*) Neutralizing.

neutralisation [nøtraliza′sjɔ̃], *n.f.* Neutralization.

neutraliser, *v.t.* To neutralize. **se neutraliser**, *v.r.* To neutralize each other.

neutraliste [nøtra′list], *a.* and *n.* Neutralist.

neutralité, *n.f.* Neutrality. *Neutralité armée*, armed neutrality.

neutre [nø:tr], *a.* and *n.m.* Neuter; neutral. *Au neutre*, in the neuter; *pavillon neutre*, neutral flag; *fleur neutre*, neuter, asexual, flower.

neutron [nø′trɔ̃], *n.m.* Neutron.

neuvaine [nœ′vɛ:n], *n.f.* (*R.-C. Ch.*) Novena.

neuve, *fem.* [NEUF (2)].

neuvième [nœ′vjɛm], *a.* and *n.* Ninth.—*n.f.* (*Mus.*) Ninth.—*n.m.* *Le neuvième*, the ninth part. **neuvièmement**, *adv.* Ninthly.

névé [ne′ve], *n.m.* Névé (consolidated snow).

neveu [nə′vø], *n.m.* (*pl.* **neveux**) Nephew; (*pl. poet.*) descendants, posterity. *Neveu à la mode de Bretagne*, first cousin once removed; *nos neveux, nos arrière-neveux*, our posterity, our children's children; *petit-neveu* (*pl. petits-neveux*), grandnephew, greatnephew.

névralgie [nevral′ʒi], *n.f.* Neuralgia. **névralgique**, *a.* Neuralgic.

névrine or **neurine**, *n.f.* Neurine.

névrite, *n.f.* Neuritis.

névritique, *a.* Neuritic.

névroptère, *a.* Neuropteral, neuropterous. —*n.m.* Neuropteran.

névrose, *n.f.* Neurosis, nervous disorder.

névrosé, *a.* and *n.m.* (*fem.* **-ée**) Neurotic.

névrotomie, *n.f.* Neurotomy.

newtonianisme [nøtɔnja′nism] or **newtonisme**, *n.m.* Newtonian doctrines or system.

newtonien, *a.* and *n.m.* (*fem.* **newtonienne**) Newtonian.

nez [ne], *n.m. inv.* Nose; (*fig.*) snout, brow, head, face; scent (of dogs etc.). *Avoir bon nez* or *avoir du nez*, to have a good nose, to be sagacious, shrewd; *avoir le nez creux*, (*fam.*) to have a nose (for something), to be canny; *avoir quelqu'un dans le nez*, (*pop.*) to hate someone; *cela vous pend au nez*, this will happen to you; *dessiner à vue de nez*, to draw in a rough way; *donner sur le nez à*, to smite; *faire un pied de nez à*, to make a long nose at,

to cock a snook at; *fourrer son nez dans les affaires d'autrui*, to pry into other people's business; *il s'est cassé le nez*, he has broken his nose, he found the door closed; *jeter quelque chose au nez de quelqu'un*, to cast a thing in someone's teeth, to twit someone with a thing; *mener quelqu'un par le bout du nez*, to lead someone by the nose, to twist someone round one's little finger; *ne pas voir plus loin que le bout de son nez*, to see no farther than one's nose; *nez à nez*, face to face; *nez écrasé* or *épaté* [ÉCRASÉ]; *nez retroussé*, turned-up nose; *regarder quelqu'un sous le nez*, to stare someone in the face; *rire au nez de quelqu'un*, to laugh in someone's face; *tirer les vers du nez à quelqu'un*, to pump someone; *piquer du nez* (of a ship), to dive (into it); (of an aeroplane) to nose-dive.

ni [ni], *conj.* Nor, neither . . . nor; (after *sans, sans que*, etc.) either . . . or. *Il n'est ni bon ni mauvais*, it is neither good nor bad; *ni moi non plus*, neither am I, neither do I; *ni Henri ni Jacques ne sont avec moi*, neither Henry nor James is with me; *ni l'un ni l'autre*, neither of them.

niable [njabl], *a.* Deniable; (*Law*) traversable.

niais [njɛ], *a.* (*fem.* **niaise**) Silly, simple, foolish. *Il a l'air niais*, he looks silly.—*n.* Ninny, simpleton. **niaisement**, *adv.* Foolishly. **niaiser**, *v.i.* To stand trifling, to play the fool. **niaiserie**, *n.f.* Silliness, foolishness, foolery; silly thing, nonsense; trifle.

nicaise [ni′kɛ:z], *n.m.* Booby, simpleton.

Nicée [ni′se], *f.* Nicaea.

niche (1) [niʃ], *n.f.* Niche, nook, corner; recess, alcove; kennel.

niche (2) [niʃ], *n.f.* (*fam.*) Trick, prank. *Faire une niche à*, to play a trick upon.

nichée [ni′ʃe], *n.f.* Nestful (of young birds); brood (of animals, children, etc.). **nicher**, *v.i.* To build a nest; to nestle.—*v.t.* To lodge, to put. *Qui vous a niché là?* who put you there? **se nicher**, *v.r.* To nest, to nestle, to fix its (or one's) nest; to hide oneself; to put oneself. *Où la vertu va-t-elle se nicher?* who could expect to find virtue there?

nichet, *n.m.* Nest-egg.

nicheur, *a.* (*fem.* **-euse**) Nesting, nest-building.

nichoir, *n.m.* Breeding-cage.

nichon, *n.m.* (*slang*) Woman's breast.

nickel [ni′kɛl], *n.m.* Nickel. **nickelage**, *n.m.* Nickel-plating. **nickelé**, *a.* (*fem.* **-ée**) Nickel-plated. (*pop.*) *J'ai les pieds nickelés*, I can't walk; nothing doing. **nickeler**, *v.t.* To nickel-plate.

Nicodème [nikɔ′dɛ:m], *m.* Nicodemus.

nicodème [nikɔ′dɛ:m], *n.m.* Noodle, booby, nincompoop.

Nicolas [nikɔ′lɑ], *m.* Nicholas.

Nicosie [nikɔ′zi], *f.* Nicosia.

nicotinamide [nikɔtina′mid], *n.f.* Nicotinamide.

nicotine [nikɔ′tin], *n.f.* Nicotine. **nicotinisme**, *n.m.* Nicotinism.

nictation [nikta′sjɔ̃] or **nictitation**, *n.f.* Nictation.

nicter, *v.i.* To wink, to nictate.

nictitant, *a.* (*fem.* **-ante**) Nictitating, winking.

nid [ni], *n.m.* Nest; berth, post. *Nid de brigands*, robbers' den; *nid d'oiseau*, bird's nest; *petit à petit l'oiseau fait son nid*, little strokes fell great oaks; *trouver la pie au nid*, to find out what one is looking for; *un nid à rats*, a mere hovel; *nid-de-pie*, (*Mil.*) lodgment in an outer work; (*Naut.*) crow's nest.

nidification, *n.f.* Nidification, nest-building.

nidifier, *v.t.* (*conjugated like* PRIER) To nidify.

nièce [njɛs], *n.f.* Niece. *Nièce à la mode de Bretagne*, first cousin once removed; *petite-nièce* (*pl. petites-nièces*), grand-niece, great-niece.

nielle (1) [njɛl], *n.f.* Smut, blight (of wheat), corn cockle (*see* LYCHNIS].

nielle (2) [njɛl], *n.m.* Niello, black enamel.

nieller (1) [njɛˈle], *v.t.* To smut, to blight.

nieller (2) [njɛˈle], *v.t.* To inlay with niello.

nielleur [njɛˈlœːr], *n.m.* Enameller in niello.

niellure, *n.f.* Niello-work; blighting.

nier [nje], *v.t.* (*conjugated like* PRIER) To deny, to deny the existence of; to repudiate, to disown. *Il nie que cela soit*, he denies that it is so; *je nie l'avoir rencontré(e)*, I deny meeting him (her).

nigaud [niˈgo], *a.* (*fem.* **nigaude**) (*colloq.*) Silly, foolish; simple.—*n.* Booby, simpleton, silly person.—*n.m.* (*Orn.*) Booby, gannet; Russian patience (game of cards).

nigauder, *v.i.* To play the fool, to trifle.

nigauderie, *n.f.* Silliness, tomfoolery.

nigelle [niˈʒɛl], *n.f.* (*Bot.*) Nigella, fennel-flower. *Nigelle de Damas* or (*patte d') araignée*, love-in-a-mist.

(C) **nigog** [niˈgɔːg], *n.m.* Spear for eel or salmon fishing.

nihilisme [niiˈlism], *n.m.* Nihilism. **nihiliste,** *a.* Nihilistic.—*n.* Nihilist.

Nil [nil], **le,** *m.* The Nile.

nilgaut [nilˈgo], or **nilgau,** *n.m.* (*pl.* **nil-gau(t)s**) Nylghau (antelope).

nille [niːj], *n.f.* Tendril (of a vine); loose handle (of crank etc.).

nilomètre [niloˈmɛtr], *n.m.* Nilometer.

nimbe [nɛ̃ːb], *n.m.* Nimbus, halo. **nimbé** (*fem.* **-ée**) Haloed. **nimbus,** *n.m.* Nimbus (rain-cloud).

Nimègue [niˈmɛg], *m.* Nimeguen.

nippe [nip], *n.f. usu. pl.* (*colloq.*) Old clothes, togs, toggery. **nipper,** *v.t.* (*colloq.*) To fit out, to rig out. **se nipper,** *v.r.* To rig oneself out. *Il s'est bien nippé*, he has rigged himself out well.

nippon [niˈpɔ̃], *a.* and *n.* (*fem.* **-one**) Japanese.

nique [nik], *n.f.* (*only used in*) *Faire la nique à la fortune*, to despise riches; *faire la nique à quelqu'un*, to make fun of someone, to cock a snook at someone.

nirvana [nirvɑˈna], *n.m.* Nirvana.

nitouche [niˈtuʃ], *n.f.* (*fam.*) *C'est une sainte nitouche*, she is a hypocrite; *faire la sainte nitouche*, to look as if butter would not melt in one's mouth.

nitrate [niˈtrat], *n.m.* Nitrate. **nitration,** *n.f.* Nitration.

nitre [nitr], *n.m.* Nitre, saltpetre. **nitré,** *a.* (*fem.* **-ée**) Nitrated. *Dérivés nitrés*, nitro-compounds. **nitreux,** *a.* (*fem.* **-euse**) Nitrous. **nitrière,** *n.f.* Nitre-bed. **nitrification,** *n.f.* Nitrification. **nitrifier,** *v.t.* To nitrify. **nitrique,** *a.* Nitric. **nitrite,** *n.m.* Nitrite.

nitrobenzine, *n.f.* Nitrobenzene.

nitrogène, *n.m.* Nitrogen.

nitroglycérine, *n.f.* Nitroglycerine.

nivéal [niveˈal], *a.* (*fem.* **nivéale,** *pl.* **nivéaux**) Nival, growing in the snow.

niveau [niˈvo], *n.m.* (*pl.* **niveaux**) Level; standard. *Au même niveau*, on a par with; *au niveau de* or *de niveau avec*, on a level with, even with; *mettre de niveau*, to level, to make even; *niveau à bulle d'air*, spirit-level; *niveau d'eau*, gauge-glass, water-gauge, water-level; *niveau des eaux*, water-mark; *niveau des études*, standard of education; *niveau de pointage*, quadrant; *niveau de vie*, standard of living; *passage à niveau*, level crossing.

niveler [nivˈle], *v.t.* To take the level of; to make even, to level, to flatten (out). **se niveler,** *v.r.* To become levelled.

niveleur, *a.* (*fem.* **-euse**) Levelling.—*n.* Leveller.

nivellement, *n.m.* Surveying; levelling; flattening.

nivéole [niveˈɔl], *n.f.* Snow-flake (plant).

nivernais [niverˈnɛ], *a.* (*fem.* **nivernaise** (1)) Belonging to Nevers.

nivernaise (2), *n.f.* Carrot garnishing.

niverolle [PINSON DE NEIGE].

nivôse [niˈvoːz], *n.m.* Fourth month of calendar of first French republic (from 21 or 22 December to 19 or 20 January).

nixe [niks], *n.f.* Nixie.

nô [no], *n.m.* No (plays), Japanese drama.

nobiliaire [nɔbiˈljɛːr], *a.* Of the nobility, nobiliary. *Particule nobiliaire* [*see* DE].—*n.m.* List of the nobility.

noble [nɔbl], *a.* Noble; great, high, exalted. *Être de sang noble*, to be of noble blood; *il a l'air noble*, he has a noble appearance; (*Theat.*) *père noble*, heavy father.—*n.m.* Noble, noble-man. *Noble à la rose*, rose-noble.

noble-épine, *n.f.* Hawthorn.

noblement, *adv.* Nobly; honourably, hand-somely. *Vivre noblement*, to live like a noble.

noblesse, *n.f.* Nobility; rank of nobleman; the nobility; nobleness, loftiness. *La haute noblesse*, the higher nobility; *la petite noblesse*, the petty nobility, the gentry; *noblesse de cœur*, nobleness of heart; *noblesse de style*, loftiness of style; *noblesse oblige*, rank has its obliga-tions.

noce [nɔs], *n.f.* Wedding, marriage ceremony, nuptials; nuptial feast, bridal feast; wedding-party; (*colloq.*) jollification, drinking-bout; (*pl.*) marriage, nuptials, wedding. *Faire la noce*, to go on the spree; *gâteau de noce*, wedding-cake; *je n'ai jamais été à pareilles noces*, I never had such a time of it; *ne pas être à la noce*, not to be enjoying oneself, to be in a sad plight; *voyage de noces*, honey-moon.

noceur, *n.m.* (*fem.* **noceuse**) Gay dog, gay woman, rake.

nocher [nɔˈʃe], *n.m.* (*poet.*) Pilot, boatman. *Le pâle nocher* or *le nocher des enfers*, the grim boatman, Charon.

nochère [nɔˈʃɛr], *n.f.* Gutter (*usually of wood*) fixed under eaves; roof-light.

nocif [nɔˈsif], *a.* (*fem.* **-ive**) Injurious, noxious.

noctambule [nɔktɑ̃ˈbyl], *a.* Noctambulant, noctambulous.—*n.* Noctambulist, (*fam.*) night prowler; night reveller. **noctambu-lisme,** *n.m.* Noctambulism; night-revelling.

noctiluque [nɔktiˈlyk], *n.f.* Noctiluca.

noctuelle [nɔkˈtɥɛl], *n.f.* Genus of nocturnal lepidoptera, noctua.

nocturne [nɔk'tyrn], *a.* Nocturnal, nightly; of night. *Tapage nocturne*, (*Law*) disorder by night.—*n.m.* (*R.-C. Ch.*) Nocturn; (*Mus.*) nocturne. **nocturnement,** *adv.* By night.

nocuité [nɔkɥi'te], *n.f.* Noxiousness.

nodal [nɔ'dal], *a.* (*fem.* **-ale,** *pl.* **-aux**) Nodal.

nodosité [nɔdozi'te], *n.f.* Nodosity; (*Surg.*) node.

nodulaire, *a.* Nodular.

nodule, *n.m.* Nodule.

nodus, *n.m.* (*Surg.*) Node.

Noé [nɔ'e], *m.* Noah.

Noël [nɔ'ɛl], *n.m.* Christmas, Yule-tide; Christmas carol; Christmas box. *À* (*la*) *Noël*, at Christmas; *arbre de Noël*, Christmas-tree; *bûche de Noël*, Yule-log; *la nuit de Noël*, Christmas Eve; *le père Noël*, Father Christmas; *les fêtes de Noël*, the Christmas holidays.

Noémi [nɔe'mi], *f.* Naomi.

nœud [nø], *n.m.* Knot; (*Naut.*) hitch, bow; difficulty, intricacy, knotty point, rub; tie, bond; knuckle; Adam's apple; knob, node. *Corde à nœuds*, knotted rope; *nœud coulant*, slip-knot; *nœud d'amour*, love-knot; *nœud de bouline*, bowline knot; *nœud d'une pièce de théâtre*, the intrigue in a play; *nœuds d'une planète*, nodes of a planet; *nous filons douze nœuds*, we are making twelve knots; *resserrer les nœuds de l'amitié*, to tighten the bonds of friendship; *trancher le nœud (gordien)*, to cut the (Gordian) knot; *un nœud de diamants*, a cluster of diamonds; *voilà le nœud de l'affaire*, there's the rub.

noir [nwa:r], *a.* (*fem.* **noire** (1)) Black; swarthy, dark; dark, gloomy, dismal; foul, dirty; base, wicked, heinous, vile; (*pop.*) drunk. *Bête noire*, pet aversion; *des idées noires*, gloomy ideas; *gravure à la manière noire*, mezzotint; *il est d'une humeur noire*, he has a fit of the blues; *marché noir*, black market; *misère noire*, extreme poverty; *nourrir de noirs desseins*, (*melodrama*) to harbour criminal intentions; *noir comme dans un four*, pitch dark; *rendre noir*, to blacken; *sur la liste noire*, black-listed; *une chambre noire*, a dark room. —*n.m.* Black; dark colour; Negro; black spot; (*fig.*) misfortune, sorrow. *Broyer du noir*, to have the blues; *en noir*, in black, in a bad light; *la traite des noirs*, the slave trade, black ivory trade; *noir animal*, bone-black, animal charcoal; *noir de fumée*, lampblack; *noir d'ivoire*, ivory-black; *porter le noir*, to be in mourning; *pousser les choses au noir*, to present (*or* paint) a gloomy picture; *teindre en noir*, to dye black; *voir tout en noir*, to take a gloomy view of everything.

noirâtre, *a.* Blackish.

noiraud, *a.* (*fem.* **noiraude**) Dark, swarthy-looking.—*n.* Swarthy person.

noirceur [nwa:r'sœr], *n.f.* Blackness; black spot; heinousness (of a crime); baseness (of soul); atrocity, treacherous action, foul deed; slander, aspersion.

noircir, *v.t.* To blacken, to make black; to smut, to sully; to traduce, to asperse, to defame; to darken, to throw a gloom over. *Noircir la réputation de quelqu'un*, to blacken someone's character.—*v.i.* To blacken, to darken, to grow black. **se noircir,** *v.r.* To blacken, to grow black or dark; to blacken one's hair etc.; to disgrace oneself. *Cela s'est noirci à la fumée*, that has turned black in the

smoke; *le temps se noircit*, the weather is beginning to get cloudy; *se noircir les sourcils*, to blacken one's eyebrows.

noircissement, *n.m.* Blackening.

noircissure, *n.f.* Black spot, smudge.

noire (2), *n.f.* (*Mus.*) Crotchet.

noise [nwa:z], *n.f.* (*only used in*) *Chercher noise à quelqu'un*, to pick a quarrel with someone, (*U.S.*) to pick on someone.

noisetier [nwaz'tje], *n.m.* Hazel (tree or bush).

noisette, *n.f.* Hazel-nut. *Beurre noisette,* brown butter; *couleur noisette,* hazel; nut-brown.

noix [nwa], *n.f. inv.* Walnut; nut; (*Cook.*) pope's eye (of leg of mutton); tumbler (in fire-arms); cone (of wheel); cog-wheel (in coffee-mill etc.); (*Naut.*) head (of capstan), hound (of mast); (*pop.*) head. *Coquille de noix,* walnut-shell; (*fig.*) cockle-shell (small light, apparently unsafe boat); (*Cook.*) *gîte à la noix,* silverside; *noix de coco,* coco-nut; *noix d'acajou,* cashew-nut; *noix d'Amérique* (or *du Brésil*), Brazil nut; *noix muscade,* nutmeg; *noix vomique,* nux vomica; *vieille noix,* (*pop.*) old chap; (*slang*) *à la noix* (*de coco*), bad, badly done, faked, idiotic.

nolis [nɔ'li] or **nolage,** *n.m.* Freight, freighting or chartering (of a ship etc.).

nolisateur or **noliseur,** *n.m.* Freighter, charterer.

nolisement, *n.m.* Freighting, chartering.

noliser, *v.t.* To freight, to charter.

nom [nɔ̃], *n.m.* Name; fame, celebrity; noun. *Au nom de,* in the name of; *avoir nom,* to be called; *cela n'a pas de nom,* it is beyond words; *de nom,* by name, in name; *erreur de nom,* (*Law*) misnomer; *il nomme les choses par leur nom,* he calls a spade a spade; *je ne le connais que de nom,* I only know him by name; *nom de famille,* family-name, surname, patronym; *nom de guerre* or *nom de théâtre,* stage-name; *nom de jeune fille,* maiden name; *nom d'emprunt,* assumed name; *nom de plume,* pseudonym, pen-name; *nom de religion,* name in religion; *nom d'une pipe! nom d'un chien!* by Jingo! my hat! *petit nom* or *nom de baptême,* Christian name; *porter un grand nom,* to bear a great name; *se faire un nom,* to become famous; to gain a reputation, to make a name for oneself.

nomade [nɔ'mad], *a.* Nomad, nomadic, wandering, migratory.—*n.* Nomad.

nombrable [nɔ̃'brabl], *a.* Countable, numerable.

nombrant, *a.* (used only in) *nombre nombrant,* abstract number.

nombre [nɔ̃:br], *n.m.* Number; quantity; plurality; majority; variety; numbers; harmony. *Dans le nombre,* among the number; *être du nombre* or *au nombre des savants,* to be one of the learned; *il y a du nombre dans ces vers,* there is harmony in these verses; *mettre au nombre de,* to number among; *ne pas être en nombre,* (of assemblies) not to form a quorum; *nombre* or *bon nombre de gens,* many people; *nombre d'or,* golden number; *nombre entier,* integer; *nombre impair,* odd number; *nombre pair,* even number; *nombre premier,* prime number; *sans nombre,* countless, very many; *surpasser en nombre,* to outnumber; *tout fait nombre,* every little helps.

nombrer, *v.t.* To number, to reckon.

nombreux, *a.* (*fem.* **nombreuse**) Numerous; various, multifarious; harmonious, well-balanced (prose, style). *Peu nombreux*, few (in number); *une assistance peu nombreuse*, a poor audience, a thin house.

nombril [nɔ̃'bri], *n.m.* Navel; (*Bot.*) hilum, eye. *Nombril de Vénus*, navel-wort.

nomenclateur [nɔmɑ̃kla'tœːr], *n.m.* Nomenclator. **nomenclature**, *n.f.* Nomenclature; list, catalogue.

nominal [nɔmi'nal], *a.* (*fem.* **-ale**, *pl.* **-aux** (1)) Nominal. *Appel nominal*, roll-call, call-over. **nominalement**, *adv.* Nominally.

nominalisme, *n.m.* Nominalism. **nominaliste**, *n.* (*pl.* **nominalistes** or **nominaux** (2)) Nominalist.

nominataire, *n.m.* (*R.-C. Ch.*) Nominee, presentee to a benefice.

nominateur, *n.m.* (*R.-C. Ch.*) Nominator, presenter, patron.

nominatif, *a.* (*fem.* **nominative**) Nominative. *État nominatif*, nominal roll; *titre nominatif*, registered security.—*n.m.* Nominative.

nomination, *n.f.* Nomination; appointment. **nominativement**, *adv.* By name.

nommé [nɔ'me], *a.* (*fem.* **nommée**) Named, called; appointed. *À jour nommé*, on the appointed day; *à point nommé*, in the nick of time; *le nommé Hugues*, one Hugh by name. **nommément**, *adv.* Namely; particularly, especially.

nommer [nɔ'me], *v.t.* To name, to call, to give a name to; to nickname; to mention; to nominate, to appoint; to elect. *Nommer quelqu'un son héritier*, to institute someone one's heir. **se nommer**, *v.r.* To state one's name; to be called. *Comment se nomme-t-il?* what is his name?

non [nɔ̃], *adv.* No, not. *Je crois que non*, I think not, I don't think so; *je dis que non*, I say no; *non (pas) que* (with *subj.*), not that, it is not that; *non pas, s'il vous plaît*, not so, if you please; *non seulement*, not only; *vous n'aimez pas cela*, (*ni*) *moi non plus*, you do not like it, neither do I.—*n.m.* Les *'non' l'emportent, il n'y a que trois 'oui'*, the noes have it, there are only three ayes; *se fâcher pour un oui ou pour un non*, to get angry for a mere nothing.

[In the following compound words *non-* remains *inv.*]

non-acceptation [nɔ̃aksɛpta'sjɔ̃], *n.f.* Non-acceptance.

non-activité [nɔ̃aktivi'te], *n.f.* State of being unattached or unemployed. *En non-activité*, non-effective, on half-pay (of officers etc.).

nonagénaire [nɔnaʒe'nɛːr], *a.* Ninety years of age.—*n.* Nonagenarian. **nonagésime**, *a.* Nonagesimal.

non-agression [nɔ̃agrɛ'sjɔ̃], *n.f.* Non-aggression.

*****nonante** [nɔ'nɑ̃ːt], *a.* (*dial.*) Ninety.

nonanter, *v.i.* (*Piquet*) To make a repique (enabling the player to count from 29 to 90).

*****nonantième**, *a.* (*dial.*) Ninetieth.

non-belligérance [nɔbɛliʒe'rɑ̃ːs], *n.f.* Non-belligerency.

nonce [nɔ̃ːs], *n.m.* Nuncio.

nonchalamment [nɔ̃ʃala'mɑ̃], *adv.* Non-chalantly, carelessly, heedlessly.

nonchalance, *n.f.* Carelessness, heedlessness, nonchalance, off-handedness.

nonchalant, *a.* (*fem.* **-ante**) Nonchalant, careless, listless, detached, off-hand.—*n.* Such a person.

nonciature [nɔ̃sja'tyːr], *n.f.* Nunciature; nuncio's residence.

non-combattant [nɔ̃kɔ̃ba'tɑ̃], *a.m.* and *n.m.* Non-combatant.

non-comparution, *n.f.* Non-appearance (before tribunal).

non-conducteur, *a.* (*fem.* **non-conductrice**) Non-conducting.—*n.m.* Non-conductor, insulating material.

non-conformisme, *n.m.* Non-conformism.

non-conformiste, *n.* and *a.* Nonconformist.

non-disponibilité, *n.f.* Unavailability. **non-disponible**, *a.* Not available; engaged.

none [nɔn], *n.f.* (*Rom. Ant.*) Ninth hour (3 o'clock p.m.); (*pl.*) 9th day before the ides; (*R.-C. Ch.*) nones.

non-être [nɔ̃'ɛːtr], *n.m.* Non-entity, non-existence.

non-exécution, *n.f.* Non-fulfilment; non-performance.

non-existant, *a.* (*fem.* **-ante**) Non-existent.

non-existence, *n.f.* Non-existence.

nonidi [nɔni'di], *n.m.* Ninth day of the decade in calendar of first French republic.

non-intervention [nɔ̃ɛ̃tɛrvɑ̃'sjɔ̃], *n.f.* Non-intervention. **non-interventionnisme**, *n.m.* Policy of non-intervention. **non-interventionniste**, *a.* and *n.* Belonging to that policy, non-interventionist.

non-lieu [nɔ̃'ljø], *n.m.* (*Law*) No sufficient cause or ground to prosecute, no true bill. *Rendre une ordonnance de non-lieu*, to throw out the bill (of indictment), to dismiss the charge.

non-moi, *n.m.* (*Phil.*) Non-ego (the external world).

nonne [nɔn] or (*facet.*) **nonnain**, *n.f.* Nun.

non-négociable [nɔ̃nego'sjabl], *a.* Not negotiable.

nonnerie [nɔn'ri], *n.f.* Nunnery.

nonnette, *n.f.* (*facet.*) Young nun; ginger-bread-nut; (*Orn.*) *nonnette cendrée* or *des marais*, marsh-tit; *nonnette des saules*, black-headed tit [*see also* OIE].

nonobstant [nɔnɔps'tɑ̃], *prep.* Notwithstanding, in spite of.—*adv.* Nevertheless.

non-ouvré [nɔ̃u'vre], *a.* (*fem.* **non-ouvrée**) Raw, unwrought (of materials).

non-paiement [nɔ̃pɛ'mɑ̃], *n.m.* Non-payment. *Être poursuivi pour non-paiement*, to be sued for failure to pay up.

nonpareil [nɔ̃pa'rɛːj], *a.* (*fem.* **nonpareille**) Nonpareil, matchless, unparalleled.—*n.f.* Nonesuch (apple, small sugar-plum, ribbon, etc.); (*Print.*) nonpareil, six-point type.

non-recevoir [FIN].

non-réclamation, *n.f.* Failure to (re)claim. **non-réclamé**, *a.* (*fem.* **-ée**) Left unclaimed, not claimed.

non-réussite, *n.f.* Non-success, failure.

non-sens, *n.m.* Meaningless sentence, translation, or action.

non-syndiqué, *a.* and *n.* (*fem.* **-ée**) Independent not belonging to trade-union, non-union. **non-tarifé**, *a.* (*fem.* **-ée**) Tax-free.

non-toxicité, *n.f.* Non-toxicity. **non-toxique**, *a.* Non-poisonous.

nonupler [nɔny'ple], *v.t.* To increase or repeat nine times.

non-usage [nɔ̃y'zaːʒ], *n.m.* Disuse.
non-valable [nɔ̃va'labl], *a.* Invalid, void; not valid (ticket); (*Law*) invalid.
non-valeur [nɔ̃va'lœːr], *n.f.* Unproductiveness; thing of no value; (*Comm.*) bad debt, worthless bill; (*Mil.*) a non-effective (man).
non-vente, *n.f.* No sale.
non-viabilité, *n.f.* Unlikelihood of living (of new-born infants). **non-viable,** *a.* Non-viable.
non-violence, *n.f.* Non-violence.
nopal [nɔ'pal], *n.m.* (*pl.* **nopals**) Cochineal-cactus.
nord [nɔːr], *n.m.* North; north-wind; Nord (department of France). *Au nord,* in the north, on *or* to the north; *au nord* or *vers le nord,* northwards; *du nord,* of *or* from the north; (*fam.*) *perdre le nord,* to lose one's head.—*a. inv.* North. *Pôle nord,* North Pole.
nord-est [nɔr(d)'ɛst, (*Naut.*) nɔ'rɛ], *n.m.* North-east; north-east wind. *Nord-nord-est,* north north-east. **nord-ester,** *v.i.* To veer to the north-east.
nordique [nɔr'dik], *a.* and *n.* Nordic, Scandinavian.
nordir [nɔr'diːr], *v.i.* To veer northward.
nordiste [nɔr'dist], *a.* and *n.* (*Amer. Civ. War*) Northerner; (*spt.*) player *or* club from North.
nord-ouest [nɔr'wɛst, (*Naut.*) nɔr'wa], *n.m.* North-west; north-west wind. **nord-ouester,** *v.i.* To veer to the north-west.
noria [nɔ'rja], *n.f.* Noria, chain-pump.
normal [nɔr'mal], *a.* (*fem.* **normale,** *m. pl.* **normaux**) Normal; (*Geom.*) perpendicular. *École normale,* (primary) teachers' training-college; (*École*) *Normale Supérieure,* (secondary) teachers' training college (in Paris).—*n.f. La normale,* normal (line, temperature); (*golf*) *la normale du parcours,* bogey for the course. **normalement,** *adv.* Normally; (*Geom.*) perpendicularly.
normalien, *n.m.* (*fem.* **normalienne**) Training-college student *or* ex-student. **normalisation,** *n.f.* Standardization. **normaliser,** *v.t.* To standardize. **normalité,** *n.f.* Normality.
normand [nɔr'mã], *a.* and *n.* (*fem.* **normande**) Norman. *C'est un fin Normand,* he is a shrewd, crafty fellow; *une réponse de Normand,* an evasive answer; *les Îles Anglo-Normandes,* the Channel Islands.—*n.f.* (*Print.*) Full-face, bold type.
Normandie [nɔrmã'di], **la,** *f.* Normandy.
normannique [nɔrma'nik], *a.* Norse.
norme [nɔrm], *n.f.* Norm, average, standard. *Ne pas s'éloigner de la norme,* to conform.
norois *or* **norrois** [nɔ'rwa], *a.* (*fem.* **noroise** *or* **norroise**) North-west; Norman.—*n.m.* North-west wind; old Norse.
Norvège [nɔr'vɛːʒ], **la,** *f.* Norway.
norvégien [nɔrve'ʒjɛ̃], *a.* (*fem.* **-ienne**) Norwegian [*see* MARMITE].—*n.* (**Norvégien, -ienne**) A Norwegian.—*n.f.* A round-stemmed canoe.
nos, *pl.* [NOTRE].
nosographie [nɔsɔgra'fi], *n.f.* Nosography. **nosologie,** *n.f.* Nosology. **nosologiste,** *n.* Nosologist.
nosseigneurs, *pl.* [MONSEIGNEUR].
nostalgie [nɔstal'ʒi], *n.f.* Nostalgia, home-sickness; hankering, pining. **nostalgique,** *a.* Nostalgic; sad.

nostoc [nɔs'tɔk], *n.m.* (an alga) Nostoc, star-jelly, witches' butter.
nota [nɔ'ta], *n.m. inv.* or **nota bene** [nɔtabene], N.B., Please note.
notabilité [nɔtabili'te], *n.f.* Respectability; notability; person of note.
notable, *a.* Notable, considerable, of influence. —*n.* Notable, leading citizen *or* figure, person of note. **notablement,** *adv.* Notably.
notaire [nɔ'tɛːr], *n.m.* Notary; solicitor. *Clerc de notaire,* solicitor's clerk; *étude de notaire,* (notary's *or* solicitor's) chambers; *fait par-devant notaire,* legally drawn up, witnessed and signed.
notamment [nɔta'mã], *adv.* Specially; more particularly.
notarial [nɔta'rjal], *a.* (*fem.* **-iale,** *pl.* **-iaux**) Notarial.
notariat, *n.m.* Profession, business, or function of notary.
notarié, *a.* (*fem.* **-iée**) Notarial, legal. *Acte notarié,* legal document. **notarier,** *v.t.* To prepare such a document.
notation [nɔta'sjɔ̃], *n.f.* Notation.
note [nɔt], *n.f.* Note, minute, memorandum; mark; notice (in newspaper), written observation or remark; statement; bill, account; (*Am.*) check. (*sch.*) *Bonne* or *mauvaise note,* good *or* bad mark; *cahier de notes,* mark-book; *changer de note,* to change one's tune; *chanter sur une autre note,* to change one's tune; *chanter toujours la même note,* to be always saying or doing the same thing; *donner la note,* (*Mus.*) to play or sing the key-note; to give the lead (to choir etc.); (*fig.*) to give the lead, to set the fashion; *faire une fausse note,* to play or sing the wrong note; *forcer la note,* to exaggerate, to overdo it; *notes (de classe),* (class-)marks, school-marks; *notes de cours,* lecture-notes; *note d'élégance, de gaieté, d'originalité,* touch of elegance, gaiety, originality; *note infamante,* note of infamy; *payer la note,* to foot the bill; *prendre bonne note,* to take due note, to duly note; *prendre en note, prendre note,* to note down. **noter,** *v.t.* To note; to mark, to brand; to note down; to observe, to notice, to remark; (*Mus.*) to prick, to set to music. *Cela est à noter,* that is worth remembering; *il est à noter que,* it should be observed that; *mal noté,* ill-famed, of bad reputation; *notez bien!* mark you; *notez bien cela,* take good note of that; *personne notée,* suspicious or questionable person.
notice [nɔ'tis], *n.f.* Notice, account, sketch; review (of a book); notice.
notificatif [nɔtifika'tif], *a.* (*fem.* **-ive**) Notifying, intimating. **notification,** *n.f.* Notification, notice, intimation.
notifier, *v.t.* (*conjugated like* PRIER) To notify; to make known in legal form; to intimate, to signify.
notion [nɔ'sjɔ̃], *n.f.* Notion, idea; (*pl.*) elements, rudiments.
notoire [nɔ'twaːr], *a.* Notorious; reputed, well-known, plain. **notoirement,** *adv.* Notoriously.
notonecte [nɔtɔ'nɛkt], *n.m.* Notonecta, boat-fly.
notoriété, *n.f.* Notoriety (of fact), repute (of person). *Il est de notoriété publique que,* it is common knowledge, well-known, that; *acte de notoriété,* (*Law*) attested affidavit.

notre [nɔtr], *a. poss.* (*pl.* **nos**) Our. *Nos frères et* (*nos*) *sœurs,* our brothers and sisters; *nos père et mère,* our father and mother; *notre maison,* our house.

nôtre [noːtr], *pron. poss.* (*pl.* **nôtres**) Ours; our own; our things, friends, relatives, etc. *Celui-là est-il des nôtres?* is that man one of our people? *c'est votre ami et le nôtre,* he is your friend and ours; *le nôtre,* our own, ours; *les nôtres,* our people, our relations, our friends; *ne serez-vous pas des nôtres?* won't you make one of us *or* join our party? *voilà leur maison, celle-ci est la nôtre,* that is their house, this one is ours.

Notre-Dame, *n.f.* Our Lady; Notre-Dame (church).

notule [nɔˈtyl], *n.f.* (*rare*) Short note, comment; minute.

nouba [nuˈba], *n.f.* Band of Algerian or Moroccan regiments; (noisy) feast; (showy) retinue. *Faire la nouba,* (*pop.*) to paint the town red.

noue (1) [nu], *n.f.* Concave angle in roof, valley channel, gutter-lead or gutter-tile.

noue (2) [nu], *n.f.* Marsh-meadow (used for pasture), water-meadow.

noué, *a.* (*fem.* **nouée**) Knotty, tied; rickety. *Enfant noué,* rickety child; *une pièce* (*de théâtre*) *bien nouée,* a well-knit play.

nouer [nwe], *v.t.* To tie, to knot, to tie with a knot; to tie up; (*fig.*) to get up, to concoct; to begin, to form, to establish. *Nouer conversation avec quelqu'un,* to enter into conversation with someone, to engage someone in conversation; *nouer l'aiguillette à quelqu'un,* to render someone impotent (by witchcraft). —*v.i.* To set (of fruit). **se nouer,** *v.r.* To be twisted or tied; to wreathe; to fasten oneself; to set (of fruits); to grow rickety (of children).

nouet [nwe], *n.m.* Small linen bag to hold herbs for infusing.

noueur, *n.m.* (*fem.* **noueuse** (1)) Tier, binder.

noueux, *a.* (*fem.* **noueuse** (2)) Knotty, gnarled; stiff, anchylosed. *Rhumatisme noueux,* arthritic rheumatism.

nougat [nuˈga], *n.m.* Nougat, almond-cake.

nouilles [nuːj], *n.f.* (*in pl.*) Noodles, spaghetti. (*pop. in sing.*) Noodle, drip.

noumène [nuˈmɛːn], *n.m.* (*Phil.*) Noumenon.

nounou [nuˈnu], *n.m.* (*childish for* NOURRICE) Nanny.

nourrain [nuˈrɛ̃], *n.m.* Fry (fish).

nourri [nuˈri], *a.* (*fem.* **nourrie**) Nourished, fed; full, rich, copious; (*Mil.*) well-sustained, brisk (fire). *Style nourri,* copious style; *une couleur nourrie,* colour thickly laid on; (*Mil.*) *être nourri chez l'habitant,* to have billets with subsistence; *logé, nourri, blanchi,* with board, lodging, and laundry.—*n.m.* Richness; fullness (of colours, sounds).

nourrice [nuˈris], *n.f.* Nurse; wet-nurse; (*Mot., Av.*) feed-tank. *Conte de nourrice,* nursery tale; *enfant changé en nourrice,* changeling; *mettre un enfant en nourrice,* to put a child out to nurse.

nourricerie [nuriˈsri], *n.f.* Baby-farm; stock-farm.

nourricier (*fem.* -**ière**), *a.* and *n.* Life-giving, nourishing, producing food. *Mère nourricière,* foster-mother; *père nourricier,* foster-father; *sol nourricier,* soil that provides food.

nourrir [nuˈriːr], *v.t.* To nourish, to feed, to

nurture; to be nourishing to; to keep, to maintain, to sustain; to suckle, to nurse; to foster; to bring up, to rear, to keep alive; to cherish, to harbour, to entertain; to supply; (*fig.*) to produce. *La Sicile nourrissait Rome,* Sicily supplied Rome with provisions; *l'espérance nourrit l'amour,* hope keeps love alive; *l'étude nourrit l'esprit,* study strengthens the mind. **se nourrir,** *v.r.* To feed, to live upon, to support oneself (*de*); to keep oneself. *Se bien nourrir,* to feed well, to live well.

nourrissage, *n.m.* Rearing or feeding (of cattle).

nourrissant, *a.* (*fem.* -**ante**) Nutritious, nourishing; substantial, sustaining.

nourrisseur, *n.m.* Cow-keeper, cattle-feeder; stock-raiser.

nourrisson, *n.m.* Infant; foster-child; nursling, suckling.

nourriture, *n.f.* Nourishment, food, sustenance; keep, maintenance, living, livelihood. *Son travail lui procure la nourriture,* he earns his keep by his labour; *la nourriture et le logement,* board and lodging.

nous [nu], *pers. pron.* We; us; to us; ourselves; each other. *C'est à nous à,* it is our turn to; *c'est à nous de,* it is our duty to; *entre nous,* between ourselves; *il nous aime,* he loves us; *nous autres,* we, the like of us; *nous disons,* we say; *nous-mêmes,* ourselves; *nous nous aimons,* we love each other; *vous nous parlez,* you speak to us.

nouure [nuˈyːr], *n.f.* Rachitis, rickets; (*Hort.*) setting (of fruit).

nouveau [nuˈvo] (before a vowel or unaspirated *h* **nouvel**), *a.* (*fem.* **nouvelle** (1), *masc. pl.* **nouveaux,** *fem. pl.* **nouvelles** (1)) New; recent, novel; newfangled, new-fashioned; further, additional, fresh, inexperienced, green. *À la nouvelle mode,* in the new fashion; *jusqu'à nouvel ordre,* till further orders; *le nouvel an, la nouvelle année,* the new year; *nouveau débarqué,* (*fig.*) person just up from the country; *un homme nouveau,* an upstart; *un nouveau riche,* an upstart, a 'nouveau riche'; *un nouveau venu* or *une nouvelle venue,* a new-comer; *un tissu nouveau,* a new material.—*n.m.* New, something new; (*sch.*) new boy or girl. *Qu'y a-t-il de nouveau?* what is the news?—*adv.* Freshly, recently. *À nouveau,* afresh; *de nouveau,* again.

nouveau-né, *n.m.* (*fem.* **nouveau-née,** *pl.* **nouveau-nés**) New-born child.

nouveauté, *n.f.* Newness, novelty; change, innovation; (*pl.*) fancy articles, novelties; (*fig.*) new book, new play, etc. *C'est une nouveauté que de vous voir,* it is quite a change to see you; *l'attrait de la nouveauté,* the charm of novelty; *magasin de nouveautés* [MAGASIN]; *marchand de nouveautés,* linen-draper.

nouvelle (2), *n.f.* (*often in pl.*) News, tidings, intelligence, piece of news, account; short story. *Avez-vous de ses nouvelles?* have you heard from him (or her)? *dernières nouvelles,* latest news; *donnez-moi de vos nouvelles,* let me hear from you; *envoyer prendre des nouvelles de quelqu'un,* to send to know how someone is; *nouvelles à la main,* social gossip; *point de nouvelles, bonnes nouvelles,* no news is good news; *quelles sont les nouvelles?* what is the news? *recevoir des nouvelles de,* to hear from; *vous aurez de mes nouvelles*, you shall hear from me; *vous m'en direz des nouvelles*, you'll be astonished at, *or* delighted with, it.

Nouvelle-Calédonie [nuvɛlkaledɔ'ni], **la**, *f.* New Caledonia.

Nouvelle-Écosse [nuvɛle'kɔs], **la**, *f.* Nova Scotia.

Nouvelle-Guinée [nuvɛlgi'ne], **la**, *f.* New Guinea.

nouvellement [nuvɛl'mã], *adv.* Newly, lately, recently.

Nouvelle-Orléans [nuvɛlɔrle'ã], **la**, *f.* New Orleans.

Nouvelle-Zélande [nuvɛlze'lã:d], **la**, *f.* New Zealand.

nouvelliste, *n.* Newsmonger; newswriter; short story writer.

Novare [nɔ'va:r], *f.* Novara.

novateur [nɔva'tœ:r], *n.m.* (*fem.* **novatrice**) Innovator.—*a.* Innovating.

novation, *n.f.* (*Law*) Novation, substitution, change.

novembre [nɔ'vã:br], *n.m.* November.

nover [nɔ've], *v.t.* (*Law*) To novate, to substitute (a debt for another).

novice [nɔ'vis], *n.* Novice, tyro, probationer; (*Naut.*) apprentice.—*a.* Novice, unpractised, inexperienced, green, new. *Il est encore novice dans son métier*, he is yet but a novice in his trade. **noviciat,** *n.m.* Noviciate. *Faire son noviciat*, to be a novice (in convent), to go through one's noviciate *or* apprenticeship.

noyade [nwa'jad], *n.f.* Drowning.

noyau [nwa'jo], *n.m.* (*pl.* **noyaux**) Stone (of fruit), nucleus; core (of statues, casts, etc.); newel (of staircase); noyau (cordial); (*Polit.*) cell. *Fruits à noyau*, stone fruit; *noyau de pêche*, stone of a peach; *ôter les noyaux de*, to stone (fruit). **noyautage,** *n.m.* Coring (of mould); (*Polit.*) infiltration. **noyauter,** *v.t.* To core (mould); (*Polit.*) to infiltrate.

noyé [nwa'je], *a.* (*fem.* **noyée**) Drowned, drowning; embedded (stone); flooded (carburettor); choked (engine). *Vis à tête noyée*, countersunk screw. *Des yeux noyés de larmes*, swimming eyes, eyes brimming with tears. *Secours aux noyés*, first aid to the drowned. —*n.* Drowned person.

noyer (1) [nwa'je], *n.m.* Walnut-tree; walnut (wood). *Noyer blanc d'Amérique*, hickory.

noyer (2) [nwa'je], *v.t. irr.* (*conjug. like* ABOYER) To drown, to put under water, to sink; to swamp; to wet, to deluge (the earth etc.); to flood (carburettor); to countersink, to let in (screws etc.); (*Paint.*) to mix, to blend (colours); to bed (pebbles) in cement; to play (a fish). *Noyer son chagrin dans le vin*, to drown one's sorrows in wine. **se noyer,** *v.r.* To be drowned; to drown oneself; to sink, to be plunged (*dans*), to go to ruin. (*fam.*) *Il se noierait dans un verre d'eau*, he is a ditherer; any little thing swamps him.

noyon [nwa'jɔ̃], *n.m.* Boundary, scratch, mark (at bowls etc.).

noyure [nwa'jy:r], *n.f.* Countersink (for nails, screws, etc.).

nu [ny], *a.* (*fem.* **nue** (1)) Naked, nude, unclothed; bare, stripped, uncovered; (*fig.*) plain, open, without disguise; unadorned; destitute. *À l'œil nu*, with the naked eye; *aller nu-pieds* or (*les*) *pieds nus*, to go barefoot;

c'est la vérité toute nue, it is the naked truth; *épée nue*, naked sword; *il avait la tête nue* or *il était nu-tête*, he was bareheaded; *nu comme un ver*, stark naked.—*n.m.* The nude, nudity; bare part (of a wall etc.); (*pl.*) (*Bibl.*) the naked. *À nu*, naked, bare, open, next the skin; *mettre à nu*, to lay bare or open, to strip; *monter un cheval à nu*, to ride a horse bareback.

nuage [nɥa:ʒ], *n.m.* Cloud; haze, mist; (*fig.*) gloom, shadow, dejection; dissension, jar, unpleasantness. *Couvert de nuages*, overcast (sky); *nuage artificiel*, smoke-screen; *nuage de poudre*, film of (face) powder; *nuages pommelés*, mackerel sky; *sans nuages*, cloudless; (*fam.*) *tu es dans les nuages*, you are dreaming, you are up in the clouds.

nuageux, *a.* (*fem.* **nuageuse**) Cloudy, clouded; overcast; (*fig.*) hazy (ideas).

nuaison [nɥe'zɔ̃], *n.f.* (*Naut.*) Steady breeze.

nuance [nɥã:s], *n.f.* Shade, hue; faint difference, gradation or degree; hint, suggestion, tinge, touch.

nuancer, *v.t.* To shade, to vary slightly; to express the faintest difference in.

Nubie [ny'bi], **la**, *f.* Nubia.

nubile [ny'bil], *a.* Nubile, marriageable.

nubilité, *n.f.* Nubility, marriageable age.

nucléaire [nykle'ɛ:r], *a.* Nuclear. *Énergie nucléaire*, nuclear energy. **nucléé,** *a.* (*fem.* **-ée**) Nucleate. **nucléole,** *n.m.* Nucleolus, nucleole.

nucléus, *n.m.* (*Biol.*) Nucleus.

nudisme [ny'dism], *n.m.* Nudism. **nudiste,** *a.* and *n.* Nudist.

nudité, *n.f.* Nudity, nakedness; bareness (of rock, room); (*pl.*) nude figures.

nue (1) [NU].

nue (2) [ny], *n.f.* (*poet.*) Cloud; (*pl.*) skies. *Élever jusqu'aux nues*, *porter aux nues*, to extol to the skies; *sauter aux nues*, to go wild with joy etc.; *se perdre dans les nues*, to lose oneself in the clouds; *tomber des nues*, (*fig.*) to be, to look thunderstruck. **nuée,** *n.f.* Cloud; (*fig.*) swarm, host, multitude, flock. *Une nuée de barbares*, a swarm of barbarians; *une nuée de traits*, a shower of darts.

nuement [NÛMENT].

nue-propriété, *n.f.* (*pl.* **nues-propriétés**) (*Law*) Property without the usufruct.

nuire [nɥi:r], *v.i. irr.* (*pres.p.* **nuisant,** *p.p.* **nui**) To be hurtful, injurious, or prejudicial (*à*), to jeopardize, to harm; to stand in the way, to be an obstacle or hindrance (*à*). *Cela ne nuira pas*, it won't do any harm; *dans l'intention de nuire*, maliciously; *il cherche à me nuire*, he is trying to injure me (of business, reputation); *ne pas nuire*, to be harmless; to be useful. **nuisibilité,** *n.f.* Harmfulness.

nuisible, *a.* Hurtful, injurious, noxious, detrimental, prejudicial. **nuisiblement,** *adv.* Harmfully.

nuit [nɥi], *n.f.* Night, night-time; darkness. *À la nuit tombante* or *à la tombée de la nuit*, at nightfall; *bonnet de nuit*, night-cap; *de nuit*, by night, in the night-time, nightly; *effet de nuit*, (*Paint.*) night piece; *il fait nuit*, it is night, it is dark; *il se fait nuit*, night is coming on; *la nuit de l'ignorance*, the darkness of ignorance; *la nuit porte conseil*, sleep on it; *nuit blanche*, sleepless night; *passer la nuit* to sit up all night, to live through the night.

nuitamment, *adv.* By night, in the night.
nuitée, *n.f.* (*rare*) Whole night; night's work; cost of a night's lodging.
nul [nyl], *a.* (*fem.* **nulle**) No, not any; void, null, invalid; worthless, of no account. *C'est un homme nul,* he is a mere cipher; *nul et non avenu* (*Law*) [*see* AVENU]; *nulle part,* nowhere; (*spt.*) *partie nulle,* draw; *rendre nul,* to nullify; *sans nul égard,* without any regard.—*pron.* No one, nobody, not one. *Nul n'ose s'en approcher,* nobody dare come near it.—*n.m.* Nullity.—*n.f.* Graphic sign (in cipher) that is meaningless.
nullement, *adv.* Not at all, by no means.
nullification, *n.f.* Nullification.
nullifier, *v.t.* To nullify.
nullité [nyli'te], *n.f.* Nullity; nonentity; (*fig.*) incapacity. *Cet homme est d'une parfaite nullité,* that man is a perfect fool, a ninny.
nûment [ny'mã], *adv.* Frankly; without disguise.
numéraire [nyme're:r], *a.* Legal (of coin). *Valeur numéraire,* legal tender value.—*n.m.* Metallic currency, cash, specie.
numéral [nyme'ral], *a.* (*fem.* **numérale,** *pl.* **numéraux**) Numeral.
numérateur, *n.m.* (*Arith.*) Numerator.
numératif, *a.* (*fem.* **numérative**) Numerical. —*n.m.* Numerical word.
numération, *n.f.* Numeration, notation. *Numération décimale,* decimal notation.
numérique, *a.* Numerical. **numériquement,** *adv.* Numerically.
numéro [nyme'ro], *n.m.* Number; ticket, house, room, vehicle, designated by a number; issue, number (of a periodical); (*colloq.*) sort, kind, quality. *Numéro matricule,* (*Mil.*) regimental number; *numéro minéralogique,* car registration number; *tenue numéro un,* full-dress uniform, (one's) best (clothes); (*fam.*) *un drôle de numéro,* a queer fish.
numérotage, *n.m.* or **numérotation,** *n.f.* Numbering.
numéroter, *v.t.* To number; to tell off. *Numérotez-vous!* (*Mil.*) number!
numéroteur, *n.m.* and *a.* (*fem.* **-euse**) Numbering (machine).
numismate [nymis'mat] or **numismatiste,** *n.* Numismatist. **numismatique,** *a.* Numismatic.—*n.f.* Numismatics.
nummulaire [nymy'le:r], *n.f.* (*Bot.*) Moneywort.
nummulite or **nummuline,** *n.f.* Nummulite (limestone).
nu-propriétaire, *n.m.* (*Law*) Bare owner.
nuptial [nyp'sjal], *a.* (*fem.* **nuptiale,** *pl.* **nuptiaux**) Nuptial, bridal. *Anneau nuptial,* wedding-ring; *chambre nuptiale,* bridal chamber; *cérémonie nuptiale,* wedding, nuptials; *marche nuptiale,* wedding-march.
nuque [nyk], *n.f.* Nape (of the neck).
nutation [nyta'sjɔ̃], *n.f.* Nutation.
nutritif [nytri'tif], *a.* (*fem.* **nutritive**) Nutritious, nutritive, nourishing.
nutrition, *n.f.* Nutrition.
nyctalope [nikta'lɔp], *n.* and *a.* Nyctalope, day-blind (person). **nyctalopie,** *n.f.* Nyctalopia.
nylon [ni'lɔ̃], *n.m.* Nylon. *Bas nylon,* nylon stockings.

nymphe [nɛ̃:f], *n.f.* Nymph; (*Ent.*) nymph, pupa.
nymphéa [nɛ̃fe'a], *n.m.* White water-lily.
nymphée [nɛ̃'fe], *n.f.* Grotto, marble fountain.
nymphomane, *n.f.* Nymphomaniac.
nymphomanie, *n.f.* Nymphomania.
nymphose, *n.f.* (*Ent.*) Pupation.

O

O, o (1) [o], *n.m.* The fifteenth letter of the alphabet.
ô! (2) [o], *int.* (chiefly used for invocation) Oh! [*see* OH].
oasien [oa'zjɛ̃], *a.* and *n.* (*fem.* **-ienne**) Oasis dweller.
oasis [oa'zi:s], *n.f. inv.* Oasis.
obédience [ɔbe'djã:s], *n.f.* (*Eccles.*) Obedience, permission to leave one convent for another; jurisdiction (of the Pope). *Lettre(s) d'obédience,* licence to teach (granted to a member of a teaching order).
obéir [ɔbe'i:r], *v.i.* To obey, to be obedient; to comply, to yield, to submit. *Il faut lui obéir,* he must be obeyed; *il lui obéit au doigt et à l'œil,* he is at his beck and call; (*Av.*) *obéir aux commandes,* to respond to the controls; (*Naut.*) *obéir à la barre,* to answer the helm; *se faire obéir,* to make oneself obeyed; to command obedience.
obéissance, *n.f.* Obedience; dutifulness, submission, compliance, allegiance; dominion (of princes). *Être d'une grande obéissance,* to be very obedient; *être sous l'obéissance de son père,* to be under the legal authority of one's father; *prêter obéissance à un prince,* to yield obedience to a prince.
obéissant, *a.* (*fem.* **obéissante**) Obedient; docile, dutiful, submissive; pliant, obsequious; elastic, supple.
obèle [ɔ'bɛl], *n.m.* (*Print.*) Obelus.
obélisque [ɔbe'lisk], *n.m.* Obelisk; needle.
obérer [ɔbe're], *v.t. irr.* (*conjug. like* ACCÉLÉRER) To encumber or involve in debt. *Ses finances sont fort obérées,* he is greatly in debt.
obèse [ɔ'bɛ:z], *a.* Obese, stout; very fat; corpulent. **obésité,** *n.f.* Obesity, stoutness.
obier [ɔ'bje], *n.m.* Guelder-rose. *Obier boule de neige,* snowball-tree.
obit [ɔ'bit], *n.m.* Obit.
obituaire, *a.* and *n.m.* Obituary, register of deaths; mortuary.
objecter [ɔbʒɛk'te], *v.t.* To object, to raise as an objection (*à*); to allege. *On a objecté que,* it has been objected that; *vous m'objecterez que c'est bien connu,* you will object that it is a well-known thing. **objecteur,** *n.m.* Objector. *Objecteur de conscience,* conscientious objector.
objectif, *a.* (*fem.* **-ive**) Objective.—*n.m.* Objective, aim, end; (*Opt.*) objective; lens; (*Mil.*) target. *Objectif de projection,* projection lens; *objectif composé,* compound objective; *objectif lumineux,* fast lens.
objection, *n.f.* Objection. *Aller au-devant d'une objection,* to meet an objection; *je ne vois pas d'objection à ce que cela se fasse,* I see no objection to its being done.
objectivement, *adv.* Objectively.

objectiver, *v.t.* To objectivize.

objectivité, *n.f.* Objectivity.

objet [ɔb'ʒɛ], *n.m.* Object; thing, article; subject, matter, business; drift, purport, aim, end, view; (*Gram.*) object, complement; (*pl.*) articles, goods. *Être l'objet de la conversation*, to be the subject of the conversation; *il n'a pour objet que son intérêt*, his only aim is self-interest; *il vend toutes sortes d'objets*, he deals in all sorts of articles; *objets de première nécessité*, indispensable articles, necessities; *objets trouvés*, lost property.

objurgation [ɔbʒyrɡɑ'sjɔ̃], *n.f.* Objurgation.

objurgatoire, *a.* Objurgatory.

oblat [ɔ'bla], *n.m.* Oblate, lay brother.

oblation [ɔbla'sjɔ̃], *n.f.* Oblation, offering.

obligataire [ɔbliɡa'tɛːr], *n.m.* Bond-holder, debenture-holder; holder of redeemable stock.

obligation [ɔbliɡɑ'sjɔ̃], *n.f.* Obligation; (*Law*) recognizance, bond; (*Comm.*) debenture, preference share. *Avoir des obligations à quelqu'un*, to be beholden to someone; *contracter une obligation*, to put oneself under an obligation; *être dans l'obligation de*, to be compelled to; *fête d'obligation* (*R.-C. Ch.*), day of obligation; *porteur d'obligations*, bond-holder; *remplir ses obligations*, to fulfil one's obligations; *vous êtes dans l'obligation de lui répondre*, you have to answer him.

obligatoire, *a.* Compulsory, obligatory, incumbent. *Service militaire obligatoire*, compulsory military service. **obligatoirement,** *adv.* Compulsorily.

obligé, *a.* (*fem.* **obligée**) Compelled, bound; necessary; obliged, grateful. *Je suis obligé de sortir*, I am obliged to go out, I have to go out.—*n.* Obligee, debtor.

obligeamment, *adv.* Obligingly.

obligeance, *n.f.* Obligingness.

obligeant, *a.* (*fem.* **obligeante**) Obliging, kind, helpful.

obliger [ɔbli'ʒe], *v.t.* To oblige, to bind, to constrain; to compel; to put under an obligation, to gratify. *Obliger un ami*, to oblige a friend; *votre devoir vous y oblige*, you are bound in duty to do it. **s'obliger,** *v.r.* To put oneself under an obligation.

oblique [ɔ'blik], *a.* Oblique, slanting; (*fig.*) indirect, underhand, devious. *Pont oblique*, skew-bridge.—*n.m.* (*Anat.*) Oblique muscle.—*n.f.* (*Math.*) Oblique line. **obliquement,** *adv.* Obliquely, indirectly; diagonally, slantwise; unfairly, crookedly; by devious means.

obliquer, *v.i.* To go in an oblique direction, to edge, to slant, to swerve; (*Mil.*) to incline to (right or left).

obliquité, *n.f.* Obliquity.

oblitérateur [ɔblitera'tœːr], *n.m.* Rubber-stamp (for cancelling stamps etc.).—*a.* (*fem.* **-trice**) Obliterating. **oblitération,** *n.f.* Obliteration. **oblitéré,** *a.* (*fem.* **-ée**) Used (stamp). **oblitérer,** *v.t.* To obliterate; to cancel (stamps); to obstruct (blood-vessel). **s'oblitérer,** *v.r.* To become defaced, to become obliterated; (*fig.*) to fall into disuse, to disappear.

oblong [ɔ'blɔ̃], *a.* (*fem.* **oblongue**) Oblong.

obnubilation [ɔbnybila'sjɔ̃], *n.f.* Obnubilation. **obnubiler,** *v.t.* To cloud, to darken.

obole [ɔ'bɔl], *n.f.* Obolus; (*fig.*) farthing, stiver, mite.

obreptice [ɔbrɛp'tis], *a.* Obreptitious. **obrepticement,** *adv.* By concealment or craft.

obreption, *n.f.* Obreption; concealment of part of the truth.

obscène [ɔp'sɛːn], *a.* Obscene, (*fam.*) smutty, (book, words, things); lewd (gesture).

obscénité, *n.f.* Obscenity, smuttiness, lewdness; (*pl.*) obscene words or actions. *Dire des obscénités*, to utter obscenities.

obscur [ɔps'kyːr], *a.* (*fem.* **obscure**) Obscure; dark, gloomy, sombre; (*fig.*) abstruse, mysterious; obscure; humble, modest; low, mean. *Ascendance obscure*, humble birth.

obscurantisme, *n.m.* Obscurantism. **obscurantiste,** *a.* and *n.* Obscurantist.

obscuration, *n.f.* Obscuration; occultation.

obscurcir, *v.t.* To obscure, to darken, to dim, to cloud; (*fig.*) to sully, to tarnish; to make (a statement etc.) obscure. *Obscurcir la vue*, to dim the sight. **s'obscurcir,** *v.r.* To become obscure or dark; to grow dim. *Le ciel s'obscurcit*, the sky is clouding over; *le soleil s'obscurcit*, the sun is going in; *son esprit s'obscurcit*, his mind is becoming clouded.

obscurcissement, *n.m.* Darkening; (*Mil.*) black-out.

obscurément, *adv.* Obscurely, dimly.

obscurité, *n.f.* Obscurity, gloom, darkness; (*fig.*) dimness, mysteriousness; unintelligibility.

obsécration [ɔpsekra'sjɔ̃], *n.f.* Obsecration.

obséder [ɔpse'de], *v.t. irr.* (*conjug. like* ACCÉLÉRER) To beset; to haunt, to importune, to obsess; to possess.

obséquent [ɔpse'kɑ̃], *a.* (*fem.* **-ente**) Obsequent (of river etc.).

obsèques [ɔp'sɛk], *n.f. pl.* Obsequies, funeral.

obséquieusement [ɔpsekjoz'mɑ̃], *adv.* Obsequiously. **obséquieux,** *a.* (*fem.* **obséquieuse**) Obsequious, fawning.

obséquiosité, *n.f.* Obsequiousness, fawning.

observable [ɔpsɛr'vabl], *a.* Observable.

observance, *n.f.* Observance.

observantin, *n.m.* Observantine (monk of a Franciscan order).

observateur [ɔpserva'tœːr], *n.m.* (*fem.* **observatrice**) Observer, looker-on.—*a.* Observant. **observation,** *n.f.* Observation; study, observance; remark, objection, hint; reprimand. *Assez d'observations!* that's enough! *corps d'observation*, reconnaissance party; *être en observation*, to be on the look-out; *prendre des observations*, to take observations.

observatoire, *n.m.* Observatory; observation post; look-out.

observer [ɔpsɛr've], *v.t.* To observe, to notice; to watch, to keep a watch over; to remark, to point out; to fulfil, to perform. *Faire observer*, to remark, to point out, to remind, to call (a person's) attention; *faire observer la loi, les règlements*, to enforce the law, the regulations; *lui avez-vous fait observer que?* did you point out to him that? *observer les lois*, to observe the laws; *observer la consigne*, to obey orders; *observer son langage*, to keep a watch upon one's tongue. **s'observer,** *v.r.* To be circumspect, to be on one's guard; to observe each other; to be observed.

obsession [ɔpsɛ'sjɔ̃], *n.f.* Obsession (by an idea, evil spirits, etc.).

obsidiane [ɔpsi'djan] or **obsidienne,** *n.f.* Obsidian; volcanic glass.

obsidional [ɔpsidjɔ'nal], *a.* (*fem.* **-ale,** *pl.* **-aux**) Obsidional. *Couronne obsidionale,* obsidional crown; *fièvre obsidionale,* fever of the besieged.

obstacle [ɔps'takl], *n.m.* Obstacle, bar, hindrance. *Course d'obstacles,* hurdle-race, obstacle race; steeple-chase; *faire obstacle,* to be an obstacle; *mettre obstacle à,* to put an obstacle in the way, to prevent.

obstétrical [ɔpstetri'kal], *a.* (*fem.* **obstétricale,** *pl.* **obstétricaux**) Obstetric(al).

obstétrique, *n.f.* Obstetrics.

obstination [ɔpstinɑ'sjɔ̃], *n.f.* Obstinacy, stubbornness, wilfulness.

obstiné, *a.* (*fem.* **obstinée**) Obstinate, self-willed, stubborn; dogged; persistent; (*fam.*) pig-headed, mulish. **obstinément,** *adv.* Obstinately, doggedly, mulishly, stubbornly.

obstiner [ɔpsti'ne], *v.t.* To make obstinate. **s'obstiner,** *v.r.* To be obstinately resolved (*à*), to insist, to persist. *Il s'obstine dans son opinion,* he clings to his opinion.

obstructif [ɔpstryk'tif], *a.* (*fem.* **obstructive**) Obstructive; (*Med.*) obstruent. **obstruction,** *n.f.* Obstruction; stoppage. *Faire de l'obstruction,* to practise obstruction, (*U.S.*) to filibuster. **obstruer,** *v.t.* To obstruct, to block. *Obstruer le passage,* to block the way.

obtempérer [ɔptɑ̃pe're], *v.i. irr.* (*conjug. like* ACCÉLÉRER) To obey, to comply (*à*); to submit. *Obtempérer à un ordre,* to obey an order.

obtenir [ɔptə'niːr], *v.t. irr.* (*conjug. like* TENIR) To obtain, to procure, to get. *Faire obtenir,* to get or procure (for anybody); *obtenir satisfaction d'un outrage,* to obtain satisfaction for an insult. **s'obtenir,** *v.r.* To be obtained; to be obtainable.

obtention, *n.f.* Obtaining, obtainment.

obturant [ɔpty'rɑ̃], *a.* (*fem.* **-ante**), Obturating, sealing (plate, plug, etc.). **obturateur,** *a.* (*fem.* **-trice**) Obturating, stopping.—*n.m.* Obturator; closing device; stop-cock, stop-valve; throttle; gasket. (*Phot.*) shutter. **obturation,** *n.f.* Obturation, stopping, closing, sealing. **obturer,** *v.t.* To seal, to obturate; to fill (gap), to stop (a tooth etc.).

obtus [ɔp'ty], *a.* (*fem.* **obtuse**) Obtuse; dull, blunt. *Angle obtus,* obtuse angle; *esprit obtus,* dull, heavy mind.

obtusangle, *a.* Obtuse-angular, obtuse-angled.

obus [o'by], *n.m.* Shell. *Obus à balles,* shrapnel; *obus éclairant,* light shell; *obus fusant,* time-shell; *obus incendiaire,* incendiary shell; *obus de valve,* conical valve-plug (of tyre).

obusier, *n.m.* Howitzer.

obvenir [ɔbvə'niːr], *v.i. irr.* (*pres.p.* **obvenant,** *p.p.* **obvenu,** *conjug. like* VENIR) (*Law*) To escheat to.

obvers [ɔb'vɛːr] or **obverse,** *n.m.* Obverse.

obvier [ɔb'vje], *v.i.* (*conjugated like* PRIER) To obviate, to prevent. *Obvier à un inconvénient,* to obviate a disadvantage.

oc [ɔk], *adv.* (*Old Provençal*) Yes. *La langue d'oc* (the dialects spoken south of the Loire).

occase [ɔ'kaːz], *a.* (*Astron.*) Westerly. *Amplitude occase,* occiduous amplitude (of a star). —*n.f.* (*slang*) Occasion, bargain.

occasion [ɔkɑ'zjɔ̃], *n.f.* Opportunity, occasion; cause, reason, subject, sake; bargain, job lot. *À l'occasion,* if the occasion presents itself; *dans les occasions difficiles,* in emergencies; *en*

toute occasion, on all occasions; *il faut attendre l'occasion,* one must bide one's time; *livres d'occasion,* second-hand books; *marchandise d'occasion,* second-hand *or* used goods; *profiter d'une occasion,* to take advantage of an opportunity; *véritable occasion,* genuine bargain; *par occasion,* now and then, by chance; *si l'occasion se présente,* if I get the chance.

occasionnel, *a.* (*fem.* **-elle**) Occasional. **occasionnellement,** *adv.* Occasionally.

occasionner, *v.t.* To occasion, to cause, to produce.

occident [ɔksi'dɑ̃], *n.m.* West. *D'occident,* western. **occidental,** *a.* (*fem.* **-ale,** *pl.* **-aux**) Occidental, western, westerly. *Les Indes occidentales,* the West Indies. *L'Union de l'Europe Occidentale,* Western European Union.

occidentaliser, *v.t.* To occidentalize, to westernize.

Occidentaux, les, *n.m. pl.* Natives or inhabitants of the western countries, members of the western *bloc*.

occipital [ɔksipi'tal], *a.* (*fem.* **-ale,** *pl.* **-aux**) Occipital.

occiput, *n.m.* Occiput.

*****occire** [ɔk'siːr], *v.t.* (*facet.*) To slay, to kill. *****occis,** *p.p.* (*fem.* **-ise**) Killed, slain.

occlure [ɔ'klyr], *v.t.* To close. **occlusif,** *a.* and *n.m.* (*fem.* **-ive**) Occludent, occlusal. **occlusion,** *n.f.* Occlusion; (*Med.*) obstruction (of bowels), closing (of eyelids); closure (of valve etc.).

occultation [ɔkyltɑ'sjɔ̃], *n.f.* Occultation. *Occultation totale des lumières,* black-out.

occulte [ɔ'kylt], *a.* Occult. **occulter,** *v.t.* To occult. **occultement,** *adv.* Occultly, secretly. **occultisme,** *n.m.* Occultism. **occultiste,** *n.m.* Occultist.

occupant [ɔky'pɑ̃], *n.m.* (*fem.* **occupante**) Occupant, occupier; member of occupying forces. *Fraterniser avec l'occupant,* to fraternize with the occupying troops.—*a.* Occupying.

occupation [ɔkypɑ'sjɔ̃], *n.f.* Occupation, pursuit; vocation, business, employment, work; occupancy, taking possession, capture. *Donner de l'occupation à quelqu'un,* to give someone a job. *L'occupation,* (*Hist.*) the German occupation from 1940 to 1944.

occupé, *a.* (*fem.* **-ée**) Occupied, busy, engaged; seized, taken possession of. *En territoire occupé,* in occupied territory.

occuper [ɔky'pe], *v.t.* To occupy; to employ, to busy; to hold, to fill; to take up, to take possession of, to inhabit. *Il faut occuper les jeunes gens,* youth must have occupation; *occuper la place de quelqu'un,* to be in someone's place; *occuper une maison,* to occupy a house.—*v.i.* (*Fr. Law*) *Occuper pour le demandeur,* to act for the plaintiff. **s'occuper,** *v.r.* To occupy oneself; to be busy; to look after; to see to; to trouble oneself (*de*); to handle, to be in a certain business. *Je m'occupe de votre affaire,* I am attending to your business; *est-ce qu'on s'occupe de vous?* are you being attended to? *il s'occupe de cela pour moi,* he is handling the matter for me; *il s'occupe de tableaux,* he is an art-dealer *or* a picture-dealer; *je vais m'en occuper,* I'll look into it; *s'occuper à lire,* to be busy reading.

occurrence [ɔkyˈrãːs], *n.f.* Occurrence; event. *En l'occurrence*, under the circumstances. **occurrent**, *a.* (*fem.* **-ente**) Occurring, occurrent.

Océan [ɔseˈã], *m.* (*Myth.*) Oceanus. **océan** [ɔseˈã], *n.m.* Ocean, high sea. **océanide**, *n.f.* Oceanid, ocean-nymph. **Océanie** [ɔseaˈni], *f.* Oceania. **océanien**, *a.* (*fem.* **-ienne**) Oceanian.—*n.* South Sea islander. **océanique**, *a.* Oceanic.—*n.f.* *L'océanique à couronne*, a jelly-fish. **océaniste**, *n.m.* Oceanist, specialist of Oceanian studies. **océanographe**, *n.m.* Oceanographer. **océanographie**, *n.f.* Oceanography. **océanographique**, *a.* Oceanographic, oceanographical.

ocelle [ɔˈsɛl], *n.m.* Ocellus. **ocellé**, *a.* (*fem.* **-ée**) Ocellate.

ocellure, *n.f.* Spot, marking (of fur etc.). **ocelot** [ɔsˈlo], *n.m.* Ocelot, Mexican wild cat. **ochlocratie** [ɔklɔkraˈsi], *n.f.* (*rare*) Ochlocracy, mob rule. **ochlocratique**, *a.* Ochlocratic.

Ochozias [ɔkɔˈzjɑːs], *m.* Ahaziah.

ocre [ɔkr], *n.f.* Ochre. **ocré**, *a.* (*fem.* **-ée**) Ochreous. **ocrer**, *v.t.* To ochre, to rub with ochre. **ocreux**, *a.* (*fem.* **ocreuse**) Ochrous.

octaèdre [ɔktaˈɛdr], *n.m.* Octahedron. **octaédrique**, *a.* Octahedral.

octandre [ɔkˈtãːdr], *a.* (*Bot.*) Octandrian. **octandrique**, *a.* Octandrous.

octane [ɔkˈtan], *n.m.* Octane.

octant [ɔkˈtã], *n.m.* Octant. ***octante**, *a.* Eighty, fourscore. ***octantième**, *a.* Eightieth.

Octave [ɔkˈtaːv], *m.* Octavius. **octave** [ɔkˈtaːv], *n.f.* Octave. **Octavie** [ɔktaˈvi], *f.* Octavia. **Octavien** [ɔktaˈvjẽ], *m.* Octavian. **octavin** [ɔktaˈvẽ], *n.m.* Octave-flute. **octavo**, *adv.* Eighthly.—*n.m.* [INOCTAVO]. ***octavon**, *n.m.* (*fem.* **octavonne**) Octoroon. **octidi** [ɔktiˈdi], *n.m.* Eighth day of decade in calendar of first French republic. **octobre** [ɔkˈtɔbr], *n.m.* October. **octogénaire** [ɔktɔʒeˈnɛːr], *a.* and *n.* Octogenarian. **octogonal** [ɔktɔgɔˈnal], *a.* (*fem.* **octogonale**, *pl.* **octogonaux**) Octagonal. **octogone**, *n.m.* Octagon.—*a.* Octagonal, eight-sided. **octogyne** [ɔktɔˈʒin], *a.* (*Bot.*) Octogynous. **octopode** [ɔktɔˈpɔd], *a.* and *n.m.* Octopod, octopodan. **octosyllabe** [ɔktɔsiˈlab] or **octosyllabique**, *a.* (*Pros.*) Octosyllabic. **octroi** [ɔkˈtrwɑ], *n.m.* Grant, concession; octroi, town dues, toll or duty; toll-house or office. **octroyer**, *v.t. irr.* (*conjugated like* ABOYER) To grant, to concede. **octuor** [ɔktyˈɔr], *n.m.* Octet. **octuple** [ɔkˈtypl], *a.* Octuple. **octupler**, *v.t.* To octuple (increase eightfold). **oculaire** [ɔkyˈlɛːr], *a.* Ocular. *Témoin oculaire*, eyewitness.—*n.m.* Ocular, eyepiece. **oculairement**, *adv.* Ocularly. **oculariste**, *n.* Ocularist. **oculiforme**, *a.* Oculiform. **oculiste**, *n.m.* Oculist. **odalisque** [ɔdaˈlisk], *n.f.* Odalisque. **ode** [ɔd], *n.f.* Ode. **odelette**, *n.f.* Little ode, odelet.

odéon [ɔdeˈɔ̃], *n.m.* Odeon. **odeur** [oˈdœːr], *n.f.* Odour, smell; scent, fragrancy, perfume. *En odeur de sainteté*, in the odour of sanctity; *ne pas être en odeur de sainteté auprès de quelqu'un*, not to be in someone's good graces. **odieusement** [odjœzˈmã], *adv.* Odiously, hatefully. **odieux**, *a.* (*fem.* **-ieuse**) Odious, hateful, loathsome, obnoxious, very disagreeable.—*n.m.* Odiousness, hatefulness. *L'odieux de la chose*, the hateful part of the business. **odographe** [ɔdɔˈgraf], *n.m.* Odograph. **odomètre** [ɔdɔˈmɛtr], *n.m.* (H)odometer; pedometer. **odométrie**, *n.f.* (H)odometry. **odométrique**, *a.* (H)odometric(al). **odontalgie** [ɔdɔtalˈʒi], *n.f.* Odontalgia, toothache. **odontoglosse**, *n.m.* (*Bot.*) Odontoglossum. **odontoïde**, *a.* (*Anat.*) Odontoid. **odontologie**, *n.f.* Odontology. **odontologique**, *a.* Odontologic(al). **odontologiste**, *n.* Odontologist. **odorant** [ɔdɔˈrã], *a.* (*fem.* **-ante**) Odoriferous, fragrant, sweet-smelling. **odorat**, *n.m.* Smell, sense of smell. **odorer**, *v.t.* To smell; to exhale an odour of.—*v.i.* To have the sense of smell. **odoriférant** (*fem.* **-ante**) or **odorifique**, *a.* Odoriferous, sweet-smelling. **odyssée** [ɔdiˈse], *n.f.* Odyssey.

œcogénie [ekɔʒeˈni], *n.f.* Ecology. **œcogénique**, *a.* Ecological. **œcogéniste**, *n.* Ecologist.

œcuménique [ekymeˈnik], *a.* Oecumenical.

œdémateux [edemaˈtø], *a.* (*fem.* **-euse**) Oedematous, oedematose. **œdème**, *n.m.* Oedema.

Œdipe [eˈdip], *m.* Oedipus. **œdipe** [eˈdip], *n.m.* Riddle-solver.

œil [œːj], *n.m.* (*pl.* **yeux**) [jø]. Eye; look; notice; lustre, gloss; bud, 'eye'; ox-eye, daisy; opening; dint, hole (in bread, cheese); fuse-hole (of shell); (*Print.*) face. (*slang*) *A l'œil*, free, gratis, and for nothing; on tick; *avoir le compas dans l'œil*, to have a good eye for distances; *avoir le coup d'œil juste*, to be sure-sighted; *avoir les yeux cernés*, to have dark circles round the eyes; *avoir l'œil*, to be on guard, to be on the look-out, to keep one's eyes skinned; *avoir l'œil à quelque chose*, to keep an eye on something; *avoir l'œil chez*, (*slang*) to have credit with; *avoir l'œil sur*, to watch, to see to; *avoir mal aux yeux*, to have sore eyes; *avoir quelqu'un à l'œil*, to have one's eye on someone; *avoir un bandeau sur les yeux*, to be blind with prejudice etc.; *à vue d'œil*, visibly, perceptibly; *cela lui blesse les yeux*, that is an eyesore to him; *cela saute aux yeux* or *crève les yeux*, it is as clear as daylight; *coûter les yeux de la tête*, to be frightfully expensive; *couver* or *dévorer des yeux*, to cast greedy eyes on, to look greedily at; *des yeux à fleur de tête*, prominent eyes; *dévorer une chose des yeux*, to look at a thing with greedy eyes; *donner dans l'œil à quelqu'un*, to take someone's fancy; *d'un coup d'œil*, at a glance; (*pop.*) *entre quat'z yeux*, in confidence, between outselves; *en un clin d'œil*, in the twinkling of an eye; *faire de l'œil à quelqu'un*, to tip someone the wink, to give him the glad eye; *faire les yeux doux*, to cast loving glances, to make sheep's eyes; *fermer les yeux de*, to assist at the last moments of; *fermer les yeux sur* *quelque chose*, to wink at something; *il a de bons yeux*, he is sharp-eyed; *il y a des yeux sur le bouillon*, there are rings of fat on the broth; *le premier coup d'œil*, the first glance or sight of; (*pop.*) *mon œil!* my eye! nothing doing! *n'avoir pas froid aux yeux*, not to stick at trifles, to be a cool one; to be tough; *ouvrir de grands yeux*, to stare with amazement; *pour vos beaux yeux*, for love; for your pretty face, without reward; *regarder quelqu'un du coin de l'œil*, to glance at someone out of the corner of one's eye, to cast side-glances at; *regarder quelqu'un dans les yeux, dans le blanc des yeux*, to look someone full in the face; (*fam.*) *se mettre le doigt dans l'œil*, to delude oneself, (*fam.*) to kid oneself, to make a bloomer; (*pop.*) *s'en battre l'œil*, not to care a rap about; *suivre de l'œil*, to follow with the eye; (*pop.*) *taper dans l'œil à quelqu'un*, to please someone, to appeal to someone; *tourner de l'œil*, to die; to faint; *un beau coup d'œil*, a fine view *or* spectacle; *voir d'un bon œil*, to look favourably on; *voir du même œil que*, to see eye to eye with.

œil-de-bœuf, *n.m.* (*pl.* **œils-de-bœuf**) Bull's-eye; round or oval window.

œil-de-chat, *n.m.* (*pl.* **œils-de-chat**) Cat's-eye.

œil-de-paon, *n.m.* (*Bot.*) Tigridia.

œil-de-perdrix, *n.m.* (*pl.* **œils-de-perdrix**) Soft corn (between toes).

œil-de-serpent, *n.m.* (*pl.* **œils-de-serpent**) Serpentine-stone.

œillade [œˈjad], *n.f.* Glance; ogle, leer; wink. *Jeter* or *lancer des œillades à*, to ogle.

œillère [œˈjɛːr], *a.f.* Of the eye. *Dent œillère*, canine tooth, eye-tooth.—*n.f.* Blinker; canine tooth; eye-bath. *Avoir des œillères*, to be narrow-minded.

œillet [œˈje], *n.m.* Little eye; eyelet, eyelet-hole; (*Bot.*) dianthus, pink. *Œillet des fleuristes*, carnation; *œillet tiqueté*, picotee; *œillet de poète*, sweet william; *œillet des prés* or (*fleur de*) *coucou*, ragged robin; *œillet mignardise*, garden pink; *petit œillet d'Inde*, French marigold.

œilleton [œjˈtɔ̃], *n.m.* Offset; young bud; peep-hole (on rifle); eyepiece-shade (of telescope).

œilletonnage, *n.m.* Budding; offset-propagating. **œilletonner**, *v.t.* To remove the buds from; to bud; to propagate (a plant) from offsets.

œillette [œˈjet], *n.f.* Poppy, oil poppy. *Huile d'œillette*, poppy (seed) oil.

œnanthique [enɑ̃ˈtik], *a.* Oenanthic.

œnologie, *n.f.* Oenology (science of wines).

œnomètre, *n.m.* Oenometer.

œnophile, *n.* Oenophilist, wine connoisseur.

œsophage [ezɔˈfaːʒ], *n.m.* Oesophagus, gullet.

œsophagien, *a.* (*fem.* **-ienne**) or **œsophagique**, *a.* Pertaining to the oesophagus.

œsophagotomie, *n.f.* Oesophagotomy.

œstre [ɛstr], *n.m.* Oestrum, gadfly, bot-fly. *Larve d'œstre*, bot.

œuf [œf], *n.m.* (*pl.* **œufs** [øː]) Egg; ovum; spawn, roe (of fish). *Œuf à repriser*, darning egg (or mushroom); *œuf à thé*, tea infuser; *donner un œuf pour avoir un bœuf*, to send a sprat to catch a mackerel; *il tondrait sur un œuf*, he would skin a flint; *la poule aux œufs d'or*, the goose that lays the golden eggs;

mettre tous ses œufs dans le même panier, to put all one's eggs in one basket; *œufs à la coque* [see COQUE]; *œufs de Pâques*, Easter-eggs; *œuf dur*, hard-boiled egg; *œuf mollet*, soft-boiled egg; *œufs sur le plat*, fried eggs; (*slang*) small (woman's) breasts; *plein comme un œuf*, as full as an egg; *tuer dans l'œuf*, to nip in the bud.

œufrier, *n.m.* Egg-holder; egg-boiler, egg-poacher; eggcup(s)-holder.

œuvé, *a.* (*fem.* **-ée**) Hard-roed (of fish); berried (lobster). •

œuvre [œːvr], *n.f.* Work; labour, action, performance; production, deed, act; church-wardens' seat or pew; fabric fund (for the repairs of a church); bezel, setting (of a stone). *À l'œuvre on connaît l'ouvrier*, the workman is known by his work; *banc d'œuvre*, church-wardens' pew, church fund; *bonne œuvre*, good deed; (*bonnes*) *œuvres*, charities; *être à l'œuvre* or *en œuvre*, to be busy or engaged with something; *faire œuvre de*, to do the work of; *la fin couronne l'œuvre* [FIN (1)]; *exécuteur des hautes œuvres*, executioner, hangman; *faire œuvre de ses dix doigts*, to work; *mettre quelqu'un à l'œuvre*, to set someone working or going; *mettre en œuvre*, to work up, to set (jewellery); *mettre tout en œuvre*, to leave no stone unturned; (*Relig.*) *œuvre de chair*, sexual intercourse, adultery, fornication; *œuvre de charité*, charity; *œuvres inédites*, unpublished works; *œuvres mortes* [MORT (2)]; *œuvres posthumes*, posthumous works; *œuvres vives*, bottom (of ship), under the water-line.—*n.m.* Work (of an author, painter, musician, etc.); (*sometimes in pl.*) building. *À pied d'œuvre*, at hand, in the neighbourhood, on site; *grand œuvre*, (*Alch.*) transmutation into gold; *gros œuvre*, foundations of a building; *hors-d'œuvre* [HORS]; *tout l'œuvre de Hugo*, all the works of Hugo; *travail en sous-œuvre*, underpinning; *travailler au grand œuvre*, to seek the philosophers' stone.

œuvrer [OUVRER].

offensant [ɔfɑ̃ˈsɑ̃], *a.* (*fem.* **-ante**) Offensive, insulting.

offense [ɔˈfɑ̃ːs], *n.f.* Offence; injury, wrong, transgression, trespass; (*Law*) contempt. *Demander réparation d'une offense*, to demand satisfaction for an offence.

offensé, *n.m.* (*fem.* **-ée**) Offended party.

offenser [ɔfɑ̃ˈse], *v.t.* To offend, to give offence to; to offend, sin, or trespass against; to hurt, to injure (feelings); to shock, to be offensive to. *Offenser la délicatesse*, to offend against delicacy; *offenser la vue*, to be an eyesore. **s'offenser**, *v.r.* To be offended, to take exception, to take offence. **offenseur**, *n.m.* Offender.

offensif, *a.* (*fem.* **-ive**) Offensive. *Armes offensives*, offensive weapons.—*n.f.* The offensive (attack). **offensivement**, *adv.* Offensively.

offert, *p.p.* (*fem.* **offerte** (1)) [OFFRIR].

offerte (2) [ɔˈfɛrt], *n.f.*, or **offertoire**, *n.m.* Offertory.

office [ɔˈfis], *n.m.* Office; bureau; duty; employment, functions; service, turn; Divine worship, office of the day; domestic staff; household. *Bons offices*, good offices; kind help; *c'est un office d'ami que vous lui avez rendu*, you have done him a friendly turn;

d'office, officially, ex-officio, voluntarily, spontaneously; *exercer un office*, to hold an office; *faire office de*, to act as; *faire quelque chose d'office*, to do a thing of one's own accord, to do a thing ex-officio; *le Saint-Office*, the Holy Office; the Inquisition; *livre d'office*, prayer-book; *l'office divin*, Divine service; *Office de la main-d'œuvre*, Labour Exchange; *office en plein air*, drum-head service; *rendre un mauvais office à quelqu'un*, to do someone a bad turn.—*n.f.* Servants' hall, pantry, larder; servants' room; (*pl.*) dependencies of the kitchen.

official, *n.m.* (*pl.* **-iaux**) (*Eccles.*) Official (Principal); ecclesiastical judge.

officialité, *n.f.* Ecclesiastical court.

officiant, *n.m.* Officiating priest, officiating clergyman.—*a.m.* Officiating.

officiel, *a.* (*fem.* **-ielle**) Official, formal. (*Mil.*) *Le Bulletin Officiel*, the Army orders; *le Journal Officiel* or *l'Officiel*, the Gazette; *la loge, la tribune officielle*, the official box (at theatre), the official stand (at sports meetings) —*n.m.* (often *pl.*) *Les officiels*, the authorities, the official guests accompanying them at functions. **officiellement**, *adv.* Officially.

officier (1) [ɔfiˈsje], *v.i.* (*conjugated like* PRIER) To officiate (at divine service); (*colloq.*) to do one's duty (at table etc.).

officier (2) [ɔfiˈsje], *n.m.* Officer. *Officier de marine*, naval officer; *officiers ministériels* [*see* MINISTÉRIEL]; *officier de paix*, police officer; *officier de police judiciaire*, law-officer; *officier de port*, harbour-master; *officier de santé*, (*Naut.*) health-officer (in a port); formerly, medical practitioner without the degree of M.D.; *officier d'état-major*, staff-officer; *officier général*, high-ranking officer, (*Navy*) flag-officer; *officier d'ordonnance*, orderly staff officer; (*U.S.*) general's aide.

officière, *n.f.* Woman officer (in the Salvation Army).

officieusement [ɔfisjøzˈmɑ̃], *adv.* Officiously; obligingly. **officieux**, *a.* (*fem.* **-ieuse**) Officious; semi-official; obliging.—*n.* Busybody.

officinal [ɔfisiˈnal], *a.* (*fem.* **-ale**, *pl.* **-aux**) Officinal.

officine, *n.f.* Laboratory; dispensary; headquarters of shady transactions; den (of illicit traffic).

offrande [ɔˈfrɑ̃:d], *n.f.* Offertory; offering.

offrant [ɔˈfrɑ̃], *a.m.* Bidding.—*n.m. Au plus offrant*, to the highest bidder.

offre [ɔfr], *n.f.* Offer, tender. *Faire offre (de)*, to give, to offer; *faire des offres de service*, to apply for a job, to offer to help; *l'offre et la demande*, supply and demand.

offrir [ɔˈfriːr], *v.t. irr.* (*pres.p.* **offrant**, *p.p.* **offert**; *conjug. like* OUVRIR) To offer, to proffer, to hold out, to tender; to offer up, to present, to expose to view; to put up (a resistance); to afford, to give; to bid. *Offrir beaucoup de difficultés*, to present many difficulties; *offrir son nom*, to make an offer of one's name (in marriage). **s'offrir**, *v.r.* To offer oneself; to offer; to present itself. *Si l'occasion s'en offrait*, if I got the chance; *s'offrir à faire quelque chose*, to offer, to volunteer to do something.

offuscation [ɔfyskaˈsjɔ̃], *n.f.* Obfuscation (of the sun's rays etc.).

offusquer [ɔfysˈke], *v.t.* To obscure, to

eclipse, to cloud; to dazzle, to blind; to offend, to give umbrage to; to shock. *Cet artiste a un rival qui l'offusque*, that artist has a rival who stands in his light; *le soleil m'offusque les yeux*, the sun dazzles my eyes. **s'offusquer**, *v.r.* (*rare*) To become darkened; (*fig.*) to take offence; to be shocked.

ogival [ɔʒiˈval], *a.* (*fem.* **-ale**, *pl.* **-aux**) (*Arch.*) Pointed; ogival; gothic.

ogive [ɔˈʒiːv], *n.f.* Ogive, pointed arch, rib; cap; nose (of missile, rocket). *En ogive*, ogival, pointed (roof); *voûte d'ogives*, ribbed vault.

ogre [ɔgr], *n.m.* (*fem.* **ogresse**) Ogre; ogress. *Il mange comme un ogre*, he eats like a wolf.

oh! [o], *int.* O! ho! (*Naut.* and tug-of-war) *Oh! hisse!* Yo-heave-ho!

ohé [oe], *int.* (*Naut.*) *Ohé du bateau!* Ship ahoy!

ohm [om], *n.m.* Ohm. **ohmique**, *a.* Ohmic. **ohmmètre**, *n.m.* Ohmmeter.

oïdium [ɔiˈdjɔm], *n.m.* Oïdium, vine-mildew.

oie [wɑ], *n.f.* Goose; (*fig.*) simpleton, ninny. *Confit d'oie*, potted goose; *contes de ma mère l'oie*, tales of Mother Goose, fairy tales; *jeu de l'oie*, game of goose; *marcher au pas de l'oie*, to do the goose step; *patte d'oie* [PATTE]. *Oie à bec court*, pink-footed goose; *oie à collier* or *barnache nonnette*, black-ringed goose; *oie cendrée*, greylag; *oie rieuse*, white-fronted goose. (*fig.*) *Une oie blanche*, a simple and naïve girl.

oignon [ɔˈɲɔ̃], *n.m.* Onion; bulb, bulbous root; bunion; (*fam.*) turnip (watch). *Chapelet d'oignons*, rope of onions; (*pop.*) *occupe-toi de tes oignons*, mind your own business; *oignon bâtard* or *ail des vignes, Allium vineale*; *oignon marin*, sea-onion; *être en rang d'oignons*, to be all in a row; *pelure d'oignon*, onion-skin; kind of French wine; *petits oignons*, spring or pickling onions; *plante* (or *fleur*) *à oignon*, bulb (plant); *aux petits oignons*, (stewed) with spring onions; (*fig.*) nice, first-rate; *soupe à l'oignon*, onion-soup. **oignonade** or **ognonade**, *n.f.* Onion-stew. **oignonière**, *n.f.* Onion-bed.

oignons, *1st pres. pl.* [OINDRE].

oïl [ɔil], *adv.* (*Old French*) Yes. *Langue d'oïl*, language spoken north of the Loire [*see* OC].

oille [ɔːj], *n.f.* Olio.

oindre [wɛ̃:dr], *v.t. irr.* (*pres.p.* **oignant**, *p.p.* **oint**; *conjugated like* CRAINDRE) To anoint. *Oignez vilain* [*see* VILAIN].

oing [wɛ̃], *n.m.* Grease. *Vieux oing*, cart-grease.

oint [wɛ̃], *p.p.* (*fem.* **ointe**) [OINDRE]. *L'Oint du Seigneur*, the Lord's anointed.

oiseau [waˈzo], *n.m.* (*pl.* **-eaux**) Bird; hod; (*colloq.*) fellow, chap. *À vol d'oiseau*, as the crow flies; *il est comme l'oiseau sur la branche*, he is always on the move; *oiseaux de basse-cour*, fowls, poultry; *oiseau de passage*, bird of passage; *oiseau de proie*, bird of prey; *oiseau de volière*, cage-bird; *oiseau rare*, rare bird, rara avis; *petit à petit l'oiseau fait son nid* [NID]; *un bel oiseau!* a fine bird, indeed! *un vilain oiseau*, a disreputable fellow. **oiseau-moqueur**, *n.m.* (*pl.* **oiseaux-moqueurs**) Mocking-bird. **oiseau-mouche**, *n.m.* (*pl.* **oiseaux-mouches**) Humming-bird.

oiseler, *v.t. irr.* (*conjug. like* APPELER) (*Hawking*) To train (a bird).—*v.i.* To catch birds.

oiselet, *n.m.* Small bird.

[522]

oiseleur, *n.m.* Bird-catcher; fowler.
oiselier, *n.m.* Bird-seller; bird-breeder; bird-fancier.
oisellerie, *n.f.* Bird-catching; bird-shop.
oiseusement [wazøz′mã], *adv.* Idly; uselessly. **oiseux**, *a.* (*fem.* **-euse**) Indolent, idle; otiose; useless, trifling. *Mener une vie oiseuse*, to live in idleness; *paroles oiseuses*, idle words.
oisif, *a.* (*fem.* **-ive**) Idle, unoccupied; dormant, lying dead (of money).—*n.* Idler.
oisillon [wazi′jõ], *n.m.* Young bird, fledgeling.
oisivement [waziv′mã], *adv.* Idly. **oisiveté**, *n.f.* Idleness; hours of ease. *Croupir dans l'oisiveté*, to be steeped in indolence.
oison [wa′zõ], *n.m.* Gosling; (*fig.*) simpleton.
okapi [ɔka′pi], *n.m.* (*Zool.*) Okapi.
okoumé [ɔku′me], *n.m.* Gaboon (wood).
oléagineux [ɔleaʒi′nø], *a.* (*fem.* **-euse**) Oleaginous, oily.—*n.m. Le commerce des oléagineux*, the oil-(seed) trade.
oléandre [ɔle′ã:dr], *n.m.*, or *laurier-rose*, Oleander.
oléastre [ɔle′astr], *n.m.*, or *olivier sauvage*, Oleaster.
oléicole [ɔlei′kɔl], *a.* Olive-growing (district); olive-oil (industry).
oléiculteur, *n.m.* Olive-grower; olive-oil manufacturer.
oléiculture, *n.f.* Olive-growing. **oléifère**, *a.* Oil-bearing, oleiferous. **oléifiant**, *a.* (*fem.* **-iante**) Olefiant.
oléine, *n.f.* Olein. **oléique**, *a.* Oleic.
oléoduc [ɔleo′dyk], *n.m.* Pipeline.
oléomètre, *n.m.* Oleometer.
oléorésine, *n.f.* Oleoresin.
olfactif [ɔlfak′tif], *a.* (*fem.* **-ive**) Olfactive. **olfaction**, *n.f.* Olfaction.
oliban [ɔli′bã], *n.m.* Olibanum, frankincense.
olibrius [ɔlibri′y:s], *n.m. inv.* Conceited person; swaggerer.
olifant [ɔli′fã], *n.m.* Horn made of ivory.
oligarchie [ɔligar′ʃi], *n.f.* Oligarchy. **oligarchique**, *a.* Oligarchical. **oligarque**, *n.m.* Oligarch.
oligiste [ɔli′ʒist], *a.* (*Min.*) Oligistic, oligistical.—*n.m.* Oligist (iron).
oligocène [ɔligo′sɛn], *a.* and *n.m.* Oligocene, tertiary.
olivacé [ɔliva′se], *a.* (*fem.* **-ée**) Olivaceous, olive-coloured. **olivaire**, *a.* Olivary. **olivaison**, *n.f.* Olive season; olive-harvest, crop of olives. **olivâtre**, *a.* Olivaceous, olive-hued; sallow.
olive [ɔ′li:v], *n.f.* Olive; olive-shaped object; (*Arch.*) olive-shaped moulding.—*a. inv.* Olive-coloured. **oliverie**, *n.f.* Olive-oil factory.
olivète [ŒILLETTE].
olivette [ɔli′vɛt], *n.f.* Olive-plantation; variety of grapes; (*pl.*) dance marking the end of olive-gathering.
Olivie [ɔli′vi], *f.* Olivia.
Olivier [ɔli′vje], *m.* Oliver.
olivier [ɔli′vje], *n.m.* Olive-tree; olive-wood. *Le Jardin des Oliviers*, the Garden of Olives; *le Mont des Oliviers*, the Mount of Olives; *rameau d'olivier*, olive-branch (symbol of peace).
ollaire [ɔ′lɛ:r], *a.f. Pierre ollaire*, potstone.
olla-podrida [ɔlapɔdri′da], *n.f. inv.* Mixed dish; miscellany.

ollure [ɔ′ly:r], *n.f.* Tanner's leather apron.
olographe [ɔlɔ′graf], *a. Testament olographe*, Holograph(ic) (will), will written in the testator's own hand.
Olympe [ɔ′lɛ̃:p], *f.* Olympia.
Olympe [ɔ′lɛ̃:p], *n.m.* Olympus; (*fig.*) heaven. *Les Dieux de l'Olympe*, the Olympian gods, the Olympians.
olympiade [ɔlɛ̃′pjad], *n.f.* Olympiad.
Olympie [ɔlɛ̃′pi], *f.* Olympia.
olympien [ɔlɛ̃′pjɛ̃], *a.* and *n.m.* (*fem.* **-ienne**) Olympian. **olympique**, *a.* Olympic. *Les Jeux Olympiques*, the Olympic Games.
Olynthe [ɔ′lɛ̃:t], *f.* Olynthus.
ombelle [ɔ̃′bɛl], *n.f.* Umbel; (*Print.*) old form of asterisk. **ombellé**, *a.* (*fem.* **-ée**) (*Bot.*) Umbellate. **ombellifère**, *a.* Umbelliferous.—*n.f.* Umbelliferous plant, umbellifer.
ombilic [ɔ̃bi′lik], *n.m.* (*Anat.*) Umbilicus, navel; (*Bot.*) hilum; umbilic, navel-wort; (*Geom.*) umbilic(us), umbilical-point. **ombilical**, *a.* (*fem.* **-ale**, *pl.* **-aux**) Umbilical. *Cordon ombilical*, umbilical cord, navel-string. **ombiliqué**, *a.* (*fem.* **-ée**) Umbilicated; navel-shaped.
omble [ɔ̃:bl] or **omble-chevalier**, *n.m.* (*Ichth.*) Char, horseman.
ombrage [ɔ̃′bra:ʒ], *n.m.* Shade; umbrage, suspicion, distrust. *Donner de l'ombrage à*, to give umbrage to; *porter ombrage à*, to overshadow, to offend; *tout lui porte ombrage*, he takes umbrage at everything. **ombragé**, *a.* (*fem.* **-ée**) Shaded, shady. **ombrager**, *v.t.* To shade; (*fig.*) to protect. **s'ombrager**, *v.r.* To put oneself under the shade or protection (of), to get shade (from) (*de*).
ombrageux, *a.* (*fem.* **-euse**) Skittish (of horses); suspicious, touchy.
ombre (1) [ɔ̃:br], *n.f.* Shadow; shade; obscurity, darkness; gloom; background; phantom, ghost; a mere shadow, something fugitive, slight, or impalpable; (*Astron.*) umbra; umbrage. *À l'ombre*, in the shade; *avoir peur de son ombre*, to be afraid of one's own shadow; *dans l'ombre*, (*fig.*) in the background; *faire de l'ombre*, to give (some) shade; *faire ombre à quelqu'un*, to eclipse someone, to put someone in the shade, to give umbrage to someone; *n'être plus que l'ombre de soi-même*, to be worn to a shadow; *les ombres de la nuit*, the shades of night; *mettre à l'ombre*, (*colloq.*) to put in prison, to put (someone) out of harm's way; *ombres chinoises*, shadow-theatre, galanty-show; *ombre portée*, cast shadow; *projeter une ombre*, to cast a shadow; *se mettre à l'ombre*, to get into the shade; *sans l'ombre d'un prétexte*, without the slightest pretext.
ombre (2) [ɔ̃:br], *n.m.* (*Ichth.*) Grayling; ombre (game of cards).
ombre (3) [ɔ̃:br], *n.f. Terre d'ombre*, umber.
ombré [ɔ̃′bre], *a.* (*fem.* **-ée**) Tinted, shaded.
ombrelle [ɔ̃′brɛl], *n.f.* Parasol, sunshade.
ombrer [ɔ̃′bre], *v.t.* To shade; to darken, to put eye-shadow (on eyelids etc.). **ombreux**, *a.* (*fem.* **-euse**) Shady (wood, garden, etc.).
ombrette [ɔ̃′brɛt], *n.f.* Umbrette (bird).
ombrine [ɔ̃′brin], *n.f.* Umbrine (fish).
ombromètre etc. [PLUVIOMÈTRE].
oméga [ɔme′ga], *n.m.* Omega.
omelette [ɔm′lɛt], *n.f.* Omelet(te). *On ne fait*

pas d'omelette sans casser d'œufs, (*fig.*) you cannot make an omelet without breaking eggs.

omettre [ɔ'mɛtr], *v.t. irr.* (*p.p.* **omis**) To omit, to leave out, to pass over; to leave undone.

omission, *n.f.* Omission. *Péché par omission*, sin of omission; *sauf erreur ou omission*, errors and omissions excepted; (*Typ.*) *signe d'omission*, caret.

omnibus [ɔmni'byːs], *n.m. inv.* Omnibus, bus. —*a.* Suitable for all (cases *or* people). *Formule omnibus*, blanket formula; *train omnibus*, slow train; (*U.S.*) accommodation train.

omniforme [ɔmni'fɔrm], *a.* Omniform.

omnipotence [ɔmnipɔ'tɑ̃ːs], *n.f.* Omnipotence. **omnipotent**, *a.* (*fem.* **-ente**) Omnipotent.

omniprésence [ɔmnipre'zɑ̃ːs], *n.f.* Omnipresence. **omniprésent**, *a.* (*fem.* **-ente**) Omnipresent.

omniscience [ɔmni'sjɑ̃ːs], *n.f.* Omniscience. **omniscient**, *a.* (*fem.* **-iente**) Omniscient.

omnium [ɔmni'ɔm], *n.m.* (*Comm.*) Omnium, company undertaking any sort of transaction; (*Turf*) open race.

omnivore [ɔmni'vɔːr], *a.* Omnivorous.—*n.m.* Omnivore.

omoplate [ɔmɔ'plat], *n.f.* Shoulder-blade; scapula.

on [ɔ̃], *indef. pron.* One, they, we, I, you, people, men, somebody. *Croire sur un on-dit or sur des on-dit*, to believe upon hearsay; *quand on est femme on est coquette*, all women are coquettes; *on croirait*, one would think; *on croit*, it is thought; *on dit*, it is said; *on est le cinq aujourd'hui*, today is the fifth; *on est tous égaux devant la loi*, we are all equal before the law; *on me l'a dit*, I was told so; *on part demain*, we are leaving tomorrow; *on s'imagine*, people think; *que dira-t-on?* what will people say? *se moquer du qu'en dira-t-on*, not to care what people say; *si l'on m'en croit*, if you will believe me.

onagre [ɔ'nagr], *n.m.* Onager, wild ass; (*Bot.*) evening primrose, oenothera.

***onc, oncques**, or **onques** [ɔ̃ːk], *adv.* Never; ever.

once (1) [ɔ̃ːs], *n.f.* Ounce (weight); (*fig.*) bit, whit, small quantity. *Elle n'a pas une once de vanité*, she's not a bit vain.

once (2) [ɔ̃ːs], *n.f.* Ounce, snow-leopard.

oncial [ɔ̃'sjal], *a.* (*fem.* **-iale**, *pl.* **-iaux**) Uncial (letter).

oncle [ɔ̃ːkl], *n.m.* Uncle. *Oncle à la mode de Bretagne*, first-cousin once removed; Welsh uncle; *oncle d'Amérique*, rich uncle (as a joke).

onction [ɔ̃k'sjɔ̃], *n.f.* Unction, anointing; (*fig.*) impressiveness; unctuousness. *L'extrême-onction* [*see* EXTRÊME]. **onctueusement**, *adv.* Unctuously. **onctueux**, *a.* (*fem.* **-euse**) Unctuous, oily; mellow; (*fig.*) moving; (*pej.*) smooth (of speech etc.). *Une terre onctueuse*, fat earth. **onctuosité**, *n.f.* Unctuosity, unctuousness; smoothness.

ondain [ɔ'dɛ̃], *n.m.* Swath (= ANDAIN).

onde [ɔ̃ːd], *n.f.* Wave, billow; (*fig.*) water, sea, tide, main. *Ondes électromagnétiques*, electromagnetic waves; *onde lumineuse*, light-wave; *onde sonore*, sound wave. (*Rad.*) *Grandes ondes*, long waves; *longueur d'onde*, wavelength; *ondes courtes*, short waves; *ondes*

moyennes, medium waves; *sur les ondes*, on the air. (*poet.*) *L'onde amère*, the briny main.

ondé, *a.* (*fem.* **ondée** (1)) Undulating, wavy; streaked; watered (of silk etc.).

ondée (2), *n.f.* Shower (of rain). **ondemètre**, *n.m.* (*Elec.*) Wave-meter.

ondin, *n.m.* (*fem.* **-ine**) Undine, water-sprite.

on-dit [ɔ̃'di], *n.m. inv.* [*see* ON].

ondoiement, *n.m.* Undulation, waving *or* swaying motion; private baptism.

ondoyant, *a.* (*fem.* **-ante**) Undulating, flowing (of draperies etc.); (*fig.*) inconstant, changeable.

ondoyer, *v.i. irr.* (*conjug. like* ABOYER) To undulate.—*v.t.* To baptize privately.

ondulant, *a.* (*fem.* **-ante**) Undulating; waving, flowing. *Fièvre ondulante*, rock-fever.

ondulation, *n.f.* Undulation; wave (of hair). **ondulatoire**, *a.* Undulatory. *Mouvement ondulatoire*, wave-motion.

ondulé, *a.* (*fem.* **-ée**) Rolling, undulating (ground); waved (hair); corrugated (iron). *Tôle ondulée*, corrugated iron.

onduler, *v.i.* To undulate; to ripple.—*v.t.* To wave (hair). *Se faire onduler*, to have one's hair waved.

onduleux, *a.* (*fem.* **-euse**) Sinuous, wavy.

onéreux [ɔne'rø], *a.* (*fem.* **-euse**) Burdensome, onerous, dear, expensive.

Onésime [ɔne'zim], *m.* Onesimus.

ongle [ɔ̃ːgl], *n.m.* Nail (of fingers, claws, etc.); claw, talon; hoof; (*Zool.*) unguis. *Coup d'ongle*, scratch; *donner sur les ongles*, to rap over the knuckles; *jusqu'au bout des ongles*, to one's finger-tips, every inch; *ongles en deuil*, dirty nails (black-edged); *ongle incarné*, ingrown nail; *payer rubis sur l'ongle*, to pay on the dot; to pay cash; *rogner les ongles à quelqu'un*, to clip someone's wings; *se faire les ongles*, to manicure oneself. **onglé**, *a.* (*fem.* **-ée** (1)) Armed with nails. **onglée** (2), *n.f.* Numbness of the fingers (from cold). **onglet**, *n.m.* Mitre, mitre-joint; (*Bookb.*) guard; binding-strip; (*Print.*) single-leaf cancel; nick, cut (in knife-blade etc.). *Assembler or tailler à onglet*, to mitre; *registre à onglets*, thumb-index register. **onglette**, *n.f.* Flat graver. **onglier**, *n.m.* Manicure-case; (*pl.*) (curved) nail-scissors.

onguent [ɔ̃'gɑ̃], *n.m.* Ointment, salve, unguent. *Onguent gris*, blue ointment; *dans les petits pots les bons onguents*, good things are packed in small parcels.

onguiculé [ɔ̃gɥiky'le], *a.* (*fem.* **-ée**) Unguicular, unguiculate. **onguiforme**, *a.* Unguiform.

ongulé, *a.* (*fem.* **-ée**) Hoofed, ungulate.

onirique [ɔni'rik], *a.* Dream-like; inspired by dreams. (*Med.*) *Délire onirique*, delirious hallucinations; *souvenirs oniriques*, remembered dreams.

onirocritie [ɔnirɔkri'si], *n.f.* Interpretation of dreams, oneirocriticism. **onirocritique**, *a.* Oneirocritical. **oniromancie**, *n.f.* Oneiromancy.

onomastique [ɔnɔmas'tik], *a.* and *n.f.* Onomastic. **onomatologie**, *n.f.* Onomatology. **onomatopée** [ɔnɔmatɔ'pe], *n.f.* Onomatopoeia. **onomatopéique**, *a.* Onomatopoeic(al).

onopordon [onopɔr'dɔ̃], *n.m.* (*Bot.*) or *chardon aux ânes or chardon acanthe*, cotton thistle.

**onques [ɔNC].

ont, *3rd pl. pres. indic.* [AVOIR].

ontogenèse [ɔ̃tɔgə'nɛːz], *n.f.* Ontogenesis. **ontogénétique**, *a.* Ontogenetic. **ontogénie**, *n.f.* Ontogeny.

ontologie, *n.f.* Ontology. **ontologique**, *a.* Ontological. **ontologiste**, *n.m.* Ontologist.

onyx [ɔ'niks], *n.m. and a. inv.* Onyx.

onzaine [ɔ̃'zɛn], *n.f.* About eleven, eleven.

onze [ɔ̃ːz], *a.* and *n.m.* Eleven, eleventh. (*Onze, onzième,* do not admit of elision, therefore, *le onze, du onze, au onzième.*) *Le onze du mois,* the eleventh of the month; (*fam.*) *le train 11,* Shanks' pony; *Louis Onze,* Louis the Eleventh. **onzième**, *a.* and *n.m.* Eleventh.—*n.f.* (*Mus.*) Eleventh. **onzièmement**, *adv.* Eleventhly, in the eleventh place.

oolithe [ɔɔ'lit], *n.m.* Oolite, roe-stone. **oolithique**, *a.* Oolitic.

oospore [ɔɔs'pɔr], *n.f.* Oospore.—*a.* Oosporous.

opacifier [ɔpasi'fje], *v.t.* To render opaque. **s'opacifier**, *v.r.* To become opaque. **opacimètre**, *n.m.* (*Phot.*) Plate-tester. **opacité**, *n.f.* Opacity; (*fig.*) darkness.

opale [ɔ'pal], *n.f.* Opal. **opalescence**, *n.f.* Opalescence. **opalescent**, *a.* (*fem.* -ente) Opalescent.

opalin, *a.* (*fem.* -ine) Opaline.—*n.f.* Opaline, milk-glass. **opalisé**, *a.* (*fem.* -ée) Opalized.

opaque [ɔ'pak], *a.* Opaque.

ope [ɔp], *n.m.* (*Building*) Scaffold-holes, putlog holes.

opéra [ɔpe'ra], *n.m.* Opera; opera-house. **opéra-bouffe**, *n.m.* Comic opera; musical comedy. **opéra-comique**, *n.m.* Opera with spoken dialogue.

opérable [ɔpe'rabl], *a.* Operable.

opérant [ɔpe'rɑ̃], *a.* (*fem.* -ante) Operative; (*Theol.*) operating.

opérateur, *n.m.* (*fem.* -trice) Operator; operative. (*Cine.*) *Opérateur (de cinéma),* cameraman; *opérateur de radio* or *de T.S.F.,* wireless operator; (*St. Exch.*) *opérateur à la hausse,* bull; *opérateur à la baisse,* bear.

opératif, *a.* (*fem.* -ive) Operative.

opération [ɔpera'sjɔ̃], *n.f.* Operation, working, performance; (*Comm.*) transaction, deal. *Opération à chaud,* emergency operation; *salle d'opération,* operating theatre or room; *subir une opération,* to undergo an operation; *terminer une opération,* to close a transaction; *théâtre des opérations (militaires),* war theatre.

opératoire, *a.* Operative, surgical. *Médecine opératoire,* surgery. *Choc opératoire,* surgical shock.

operculaire [ɔpɛrky'lɛːr], *a.* (*Bot.*) Opercular. **opercule**, *n.m.* Operculum, cover. **operculé**, *a.* (*fem.* -ée) Operculated. **operculiforme**, *a.* Operculiform.

opéré [ɔpe'ɾe], *a.* (*fem.* -ée) (*Med.*) Operated. —*n.* Patient (after operation).

opérer [ɔpe'ɾe], *v.t.* To operate, to effect, to bring about, to perform, to operate upon. *Se faire opérer,* to undergo an operation.—*v.i.* To work, to operate. **s'opérer**, *v.r.* To take place, to be brought about.

opérette [ɔpe'ɾɛt], *n.f.* Operetta, light opera.

Ophélie [ɔfe'li], *f.* Ophelia.

ophicléide [ɔfikle'id], *n.m.,* or *serpent à clefs.* Ophicleide.

ophidien [ɔfi'djɛ̃], *a.* (*fem.* -ienne) Ophidian. —*n.m.* Ophidian.

ophioglosse [ɔfiɔ'glɔs], *n.m.* Ophioglossum, adder's tongue.

ophiographie [ɔfiɔgra'fi], *n.f.* Ophiography.

ophiologie, *n.f.* Ophiology.

ophiophage, *a.* Ophiophagous.

ophite [ɔ'fit], *n.m.* Ophite.

ophrys [ɔ'fris], *n.m.* Name of several orchids, such as *ophrys araignée,* spider orchis, *ophrys mouche,* fly-orchis, etc.

ophtalmie [ɔftal'mi], *n.f.* Ophthalmia. **ophtalmique**, *a.* Ophthalmic. **ophtalmologie**, *n.f.* Ophthalmology. **ophtalmologiste**, *n.m.* Ophthalmologist. **ophtalmoscope**, *n.m.* Ophthalmoscope. **ophtalmotomie**, *n.f.* Ophthalmotomy.

opiacé [ɔpja'se], *a.* (*fem.* -ée) Containing opium.

opiat, *n.m.* Opiate, narcotic; tooth-paste.

opilatif [ɔpila'tif], *a.* (*fem.* -ive) (*Med.*) Obstruent. **opilation**, *n.f.* Obstruction. **opiler**, *v.t.* To obstruct.

opimes [ɔ'pim], *a.f. pl. Dépouilles opimes,* spoils of a hostile general killed in action; (*fig.*) rich profits.

opiner [ɔpi'ne], *v.i.* To opine, to speak, to give or be of opinion. *Opiner du bonnet,* to vote blindly, to nod assent. **opineur**, *n.m.* Opiner.

opiniâtre [ɔpi'njaːtr], *a.* Stubborn, obstinate, headstrong, self-willed. *Le combat fut opiniâtre,* the fight was a stubborn one; *un mal opiniâtre,* an obstinate disease.—*n.* Stubborn person. *Je hais les opiniâtres,* I hate stubborn people. **opiniâtrement**, *adv.* Doggedly. **s'opiniâtrer**, *v.r.* To be obstinate, to insist. *Ils s'y sont opiniâtrés,* they obstinately persisted in it. **opiniâtreté**, *n.f.* Obstinacy.

opinion [ɔpi'njɔ̃], *n.f.* Opinion; judgment, view; (*pl.*) votes. *C'est une affaire d'opinion,* it is a mere matter of opinion; *il a bonne opinion de lui-même,* he has a great opinion of himself; *recueillir les opinions,* to collect the votes.

opiomane [ɔpjɔ'man], *a.* and *n.* Opiumeating, opium-smoking (person); opiumaddict; opium-eater or smoker.

opisthodome [ɔpistɔ'dɔm], *n.m.* (*Arch.*) Opisthodomos.

opisthographe, *a.* Opisthographic (written on both sides).

opium [ɔ'pjɔm], *n.m.* Opium.

opobalsamum [ɔpɔbalza'mɔm], *n.m.* (*Pharm.*) Opobalsamum, balm of Gilead.

opodeldoch [ɔpɔdɛl'dɔk], *n.m. Baume opodeldoch,* opodeldoc, soap-liniment.

opopanax, *n.m.* Opopanax.

opossum [ɔpɔ'sɔm], *n.m.* Opossum; (*Austr.*) possum.

opothérapie [ɔpotera'pi], *n.f.* Opotherapy. **opothérapique**, *a.* Opotherapeutic.

opportun [ɔpɔr'tœ̃], *a.* (*fem.* opportune) Opportune, timely; expedient. **opportunément**, *adv.* Seasonably. **opportunisme**, *n.m.* Opportunism. **opportuniste**, *a.* and *n.* Opportunist. **opportunité**, *n.f.* Opportuneness, seasonableness, expediency; advisability; favourable occasion.

opposabilité [ɔpozabili'te], *n.f.* Opposability. **opposable**, *a.* Opposable. **opposant**, *n.*

(*fem.* **-ante**) Opposing, adverse.—*n.* Opponent, adversary.

opposé, *a.* (*fem.* **-ée**) Opposite, contrary; facing, over against (*à*); opposed (*à*). *Deux armées opposées l'une à l'autre*, two armies opposed one to the other.—*n.m.* The opposite, the reverse, the contrary. *Il est tout l'opposé de son père*, he is quite the opposite of his father; *à l'opposé de*, contrary to.

opposer [ɔpo'ze], *v.t.* To oppose; to put in opposition; to place opposite or facing each other; to object, to urge. *Opposer la force à la force*, to oppose force by force. **s'opposer**, *v.r.* To be opposed or contrary (*à*), to set oneself against, to resist, to combat, to stand in the way (*à*). *Je m'oppose absolument à ce que tu y ailles*, I won't hear of your going there; *s'opposer à quelque chose*, to be opposed to something; *vous vous y opposez*, you stand in the way.

opposite [ɔpo'zit], *n.m.* Opposite, contrary, reverse. *À l'opposite*, over against, opposite to; *à l'opposite du camp*, facing the camp; *c'est tout l'opposite de l'autre*, it is quite the reverse of the other.

opposition [ɔpozi'sjɔ̃], *n.f.* Opposition, resistance; antithesis, contrast, contradistinction; obstacle, impediment. *Faire opposition à*, to oppose; *frapper d'opposition*, to stop payment of (a cheque etc.); *le parti de l'opposition*, the opposition; *mettre opposition à*, to oppose; (*Law*) to put in opposition to; *mettre opposition à un mariage*, to enter a caveat against a marriage; *mettre opposition sur les appointements de quelqu'un*, to lodge an objection to the payment of someone's salary; *opposition d'humeur*, incompatibility of temper.

oppressé [ɔprɛ'se], *a.* (*fem.* **-ée**) (*Path.*) Breathless.

oppresser [ɔprɛ'se], *v.t.* *To oppress, to lie heavy upon, to impede; (*fig.*) to vex; to deject. *Le chagrin l'oppresse*, grief weighs heavily on him.

oppresseur, *n.m.* Oppressor.—*a.m.* Oppressive, tyrannical.

oppressif, *a.* (*fem.* **-ive**) Oppressive.

oppression, *n.f.* Oppression; breathlessness.

oppressivement, *adv.* Tyrannically, oppressively.

opprimant [ɔpri'mɑ̃], *a.* (*fem.* **-ante**) Oppressing. **opprimé**, *a.* (*fem.* **-ée**) Oppressed.—*n.* The oppressed.

opprimer [ɔpri'me], *v.t.* To oppress, to crush. *Malheur à ceux qui opprimment!* woe to the oppressors!

opprobre [ɔ'prɔbr], *n.m.* Opprobrium, shame, disgrace. *Être l'opprobre de sa famille*, to be the disgrace of one's family.

optant [ɔp'tɑ̃], *a.* and *n.* (*fem.* **-ante**) *Les optants français*, persons electing to become French nationals. **optatif**, *a.* (*fem.* **-ive**) Optative.—*n.m.* Optative mood. **opter**, *v.i.* To choose, to decide. *Il faut qu'il opte entre ces deux emplois*, he must choose between those two occupations; *opter pour une certaine nationalité*, to opt for a certain nationality.

opticien [ɔpti'sjɛ̃], *n.m.* Optician.

optimisme [ɔpti'mism], *n.m.* Optimism.

optimiste, *a.* and *n.* Optimist, of a sanguine disposition, optimistic.

optimum, *a.* and *n.m.* Optimum. **optima**, *a.f.* Best, most favourable. *La formule*

optima, the best formula.—*pl. m.* and *f. Des conditions optima*, most favourable conditions.

option [ɔp'sjɔ̃], *n.f.* Option, choice. *Option d'achat*, call; *option de vente*, put; *souscrire des valeurs à option*, to buy an option on stock.

optique [ɔp'tik], *a.* Optic, optical. *Illusion d'optique*, optical illusion; *le nerf optique*, the optic nerve.—*n.f.* Optics; perspective; show-box. *L'optique du théâtre*, stage illusion.

opulence [ɔpy'lɑ̃:s], *n.f.* Opulence, wealth, affluence, riches. *Nager dans l'opulence*, to be rolling in money. **opulent**, *a.* (*fem.* **-ente**) Opulent, wealthy (person); abundant (harvest). *Charmes opulents*, buxom figure; *poitrine opulente*, ample bosom.

opuscule [ɔpys'kyl], *n.m.* Opuscule, pamphlet, tract; small opus.

or (1) [ɔ:r], *n.m.* Gold; gold ornament etc.; gold money; (*Her.*) or. *Acheter quelque chose au poids de l'or*, to pay an exorbitant price for something; *chercheur d'or*, gold-digger; *c'est de l'or en barre*, it is as good as ready money; *être tout cousu d'or*, to be rolling in money; *il parle d'or*, he talks admirably; *l'âge d'or*, the golden age; *lettres d'or*, gilt-letters; *l'or des moissons*, harvest gold; *or brut*, gold in nuggets; *or en barres*, ingot gold; *or monnayé*, gold specie; *or vierge*, native gold; *pont d'or*, a golden bridge; *qui vaut son pesant d'or*, worth its weight in gold; *tout ce qui brille n'est pas or*, all that glitters is not gold.

or (2) [ɔ:r], *conj.* But, now; well. *Or çà*, now, well now; **or sus, commençons*, now, let us begin.

oracle [ɔ'ra:kl], *n.m.* Oracle.

orage [ɔ'ra:ʒ], *n.m.* Storm, tempest; thunder; (*fig.*) tumult, disorder. *Chercher un abri contre l'orage*, to seek shelter from the storm; *laisser passer l'orage*, to let the storm blow over; *les orages des passions*, the tempests of the passions; *le temps est à l'orage*, the weather is stormy. **orageusement**, *adv.* Tempestuously; turbulently, boisterously. **orageux**, *a.* (*fem.* **-euse**) Stormy, tempestuous; agitated, restless. *Mener une vie orageuse*, to lead a riotous life; *une mer orageuse*, a stormy sea.

oraison [ɔrɛ'zɔ̃], *n.f.* Speech, oration; prayer, orison. *L'oraison dominicale*, the Lord's Prayer; *une oraison funèbre*, a funeral oration.

oral [ɔ'ral], *a.* (*fem.* **-ale**, *pl.* **-aux**) Oral, by word of mouth.—*n.m.* (*colloq.*) Oral (or *viva voce*) examination. *Être collé à l'oral*, rater l'oral, to fail the oral, to be ploughed in the viva. **oralement**, *adv.* Orally, by word of mouth.

orange [ɔ'ra:ʒ], *n.f.* Orange; orange-colour. *Orange amère*, bitter orange; *orange navel*, navel-orange; *orange sanguine*, blood orange.—*n.m.* and *a. inv.* Orange-colour. *Ruban orange*, orange-coloured ribbon. **orangé**, *a.* (*fem.* **-ée**) Orange-coloured. **orangeade**, *n.f.* Orangeade, orange squash. **orangeat**, *n.m.* Candied orange-peel. **oranger** (1), or *oranger doux*, *n.m.*, Orange-tree. *Oranger amer* [BIGARADIER]. **oranger** (2), *n.* (*fem.* **orangère**) Orange-man, orange-girl. **orangerie**, *n.f.* Orange-house; orange-grove, orangery; orange-plantation.

orang-outan(g) [ɔrɑ̃u'tɑ̃], *n.m.* (*pl.* **orangs-outans**) Orang-utan.

orateur [ɔra'tœːr], *n.m.* (*fem.* **-trice**) Orator, speaker, spokesman.

oratoire (1), *a.* Oratorical; oratorial. *L'art oratoire,* oratory, art of public speaking.

oratoire (2), *n.m.* Oratory; private chapel. *Pères de l'Oratoire,* Oratorians.

oratoirement, *adv.* Oratorically.

oratorien, *a.* and *n.m.* Oratorian.

orbe (1) [ɔrb], *n.m.* Orb, orbit; globe; sphere; fold, coil (snake).

orbe (2) [ɔrb], *a.* Contusing (blows); blind (wall).

orbiculaire [ɔrbiky'lɛːr], *a.* Orbicular.

orbitaire [ɔrbi'tɛːr], *a.* (*Anat.*) Orbital.

orbital, *a.* (*fem.* **-ale,** *pl.* **-aux**) (*Astron.*) Orbital.

orbite [ɔr'bit], *n.f.* Orbit; (*Anat.*) socket; (*fig.*) sphere (of action). *L'orbite de l'œil,* the eye-socket.

Orcades [ɔr'kad], **les,** *f.pl.* The Orkneys, the Orkney Islands.

orcanette [ɔrka'nɛt], *n.f.* (*Bot.*) Alkanet, dyer's bugloss.

orchestral [ɔrkɛs'tral], *a.* (*fem.* **-ale,** *pl.* **-aux**) Orchestral. **orchestration,** *n.f.* Scoring, orchestration.

orchestre [ɔr'kɛstr], *n.m.* Orchestra; band. *Chef d'orchestre,* bandmaster, conductor; *fauteuil d'orchestre,* orchestra stall. **orchestrer,** *v.t.* To score, to orchestrate; (*fig.*) to organize (of publicity or propaganda campaign).

orchidée [ɔrki'de], *n.f.* Orchid; (*pl.*) Orchidaceae. Common name of many varieties, *e.g. l'acéras* or *homme pendu,* green man orchid; *l'orchidée pourpre,* early purple orchid etc.

orchis [ɔr'kis], *n.m.* Orchis, wild orchis.

ordalie [ɔrda'li], *n.f.* Ordeal (old form of trial).

ordinaire [ɔrdi'nɛːr], *a.* Ordinary, common, usual, customary; vulgar, average, mediocre. *Le cours ordinaire de la nature,* the usual course of nature; *le train ordinaire de la vie,* the ordinary course of life; *peu ordinaire,* unusual, out of the common.—*n.m.* Ordinary practice, wont, custom; commons, usual fare; the usual level or standard; (*Eccles.*) ordinary; postal courier; gentleman ordinary of the king; (*Mil.*) company mess. *À l'ordinaire,* usually; *c'est un homme au-dessus de l'ordinaire,* he is above the common run; *comme à l'ordinaire, comme d'ordinaire,* as usual; *d'ordinaire* or *pour l'ordinaire,* usually, ordinarily. **ordinairement,** *adv.* Usually.

ordinal [ɔrdi'nal], *a.* (*fem.* **-ale,** *pl.* **-aux**) Ordinal (of adjectives).—*n.m.* (*Eccles.*) Ordinal.

ordinand [ɔrdi'nɑ̃], *n.m.* Candidate for ordination. **ordinant,** *n.m.* Ordaining bishop, orderer. **ordination,** *n.f.* Ordination.

ordonnance [ɔrdɔ'nɑ̃ːs], *n.f.* Order, ordinance, regulation, statute; disposition, arrangement; (*Med.*) prescription. *Habits d'ordonnance,* regimentals, uniform; *officier d'ordonnance,* aide-de-camp; *ordonnance de police,* police regulation; *ordonnance royale,* order in council.—*n.m.* or *f.* (*Mil.*) Batman, (officer's) servant, orderly.

ordonnancement, *n.m.* Written order for payment. **ordonnancer,** *v.t.* To order the payment of (in writing).

ordonnateur, *n.m.* (*fem.* **-trice**) Organizer, manager; master of ceremonies.—*a.* Ordaining, ordering. *Commissaire ordonnateur,* pay commissioner.

ordonné [ɔrdɔ'ne], *a.* (*fem.* **-ée**) Ordered, regulated; tidy, orderly; prescribed; ordained (priest). *Charité bien ordonnée commence par soi-même,* charity begins at home.—*n.f.* (*Geom.*) Ordinate. **ordonnément,** *adv.* In an orderly fashion.

ordonner [ɔrdɔ'ne], *v.t.* To order, to set in order, to regulate; to direct, to command, to enjoin; to appoint, to decree; to ordain, to confer holy orders on; (*Med.*) to prescribe. *Bien ordonner sa maison,* to order one's house properly.—*v.i.* To dispose (*de*); (*colloq.*) to give orders. *Il est plus aisé d'ordonner que d'exécuter,* ordering and carrying out are two different things; *le roi ordonnait de la vie de ses sujets,* the king disposed of the lives of his subjects.

ordre [ɔrdr], *n.m.* Order, command, mandate, behest; writ, warrant, decree; regulation; line, order of battle, etc.; class, category, division, tribe; (*pl.*) holy orders. *À l'ordre!* order! (*Mil.*) *à mon ordre,* wait for the word; *avec ordre,* methodically; *billet à ordre,* promissory note; *c'est dans l'ordre des choses,* it is in the nature of things; *cet homme n'a pas d'ordre,* that man is untidy; *conférer les ordres,* to ordain; *de l'ordre de dix millions,* running to, in the region of ten million (francs, pounds, etc.); *de premier ordre,* first-rate; *donner ses ordres,* to give one's orders; *d'ordre et pour compte de,* (*Comm.*) by order and on account of; *en bon ordre,* in good order; *entrer dans les ordres,* to take (holy) orders; *il est le premier créancier en ordre,* he stands first on the list of creditors; *jusqu'à nouvel ordre,* until further orders; *j'y mettrai ordre,* I shall see to it; *l'ancien ordre de choses,* the old order of things; *l'ordre nouveau,* the new order; *maintenir l'ordre,* to maintain order or peace; *marcher en ordre de bataille,* to march in battle array; *mettre ordre à, en ordre,* or *de l'ordre à,* to put to rights; *mot d'ordre,* watchword, password; *ordre de chevalerie,* order of knighthood; *ordre du jour,* agenda (of a meeting), (*Mil.*) order of the day; *porter à l'ordre du jour,* (*Mil.*) to mention in dispatches; *procéder par ordre,* to take things in order; *rappeler à l'ordre,* to call to order; *un esprit de premier ordre,* an intellect of the highest order; *un ordre par écrit,* a written order.

ordure [ɔr'dyːr], *n.f.* Ordure, filth, dirt, muck; excrement, ribaldry; (*pl.*) sweepings, refuse, garbage. *Défense de déposer des ordures,* commit no nuisance; *boîte à ordures,* dustbin, refuse-bin, (*Am.*) ashcan; *ordures ménagères,* household refuse. **ordurier,** *a.* (*fem.* **-ière**) Filthy, ribald, lewd.

oréade [ɔre'ad], *n.f.* Oread; mountain nymph.

orée [ɔ're], *n.f.* Border, edge, verge, skirt (of a wood or forest).

oreillard [ɔrɛ'jaːr], *n.m.* Hare, long-eared bat. —*a.* (*fem.* **-arde**) Having long, pendulous ears (of horses etc.).

oreille [ɔ'rɛːj], *n.f.* Ear; hearing; appendage of various forms analogous to an ear, flange; handle (of a vase etc.), mould-board (of plug), fluke (of anchor), (*pl.*) ears (of a bale);

wing, head-rest (on a sofa etc.); dog's-ear (in a book). *Avoir les oreilles chastes*, to be easily shocked; *avoir les oreilles rebattues de quelque chose*, to be tired of hearing a thing; *avoir l'oreille basse*, to be crestfallen; *avoir mal aux oreilles*, to have ear-ache; *boucle d'oreille*, ear-ring; *cela lui entre par une oreille et lui sort par l'autre*, that goes in at one ear and out at the other; *donner sur* or *frotter les oreilles à quelqu'un*, to box someone's ears; *dormir sur les deux oreilles* [DORMIR]; *échauffer les oreilles à quelqu'un*, to annoy, to aggravate someone; *écrou à oreilles*, wing-nut; *faire la sourde oreille*, to turn a deaf ear; *il a de l'oreille*, he has a good ear or an ear for music; *il a l'oreille dure*, he is hard of hearing; *il ne l'entend pas de cette oreille-là*, he will not listen to that; *jusqu'aux oreilles*, up to the eyes (or ears), completely; *les oreilles doivent lui tinter*, her (his) ears must be burning; *montrer le bout de l'oreille*, to show the cloven hoof; *n'écouter que d'une oreille*, to pay little attention to what is said; *parler à l'oreille à quelqu'un* or *dire un mot à l'oreille à quelqu'un*, to whisper a word to someone; *prêter* or *dresser l'oreille*, to lend an ear (to rumours etc.), to prick up one's ears, to be very attentive; *prêter l'oreille à*, to listen to; *se boucher les oreilles* [BOUCHER (1)]; (*fam.*) *se faire tirer l'oreille*, to be reluctant; *ventre affamé n'a point d'oreilles*, a hungry belly has no ears; *oreille d'âne*, (*Naut.*) level; *oreille de Vénus*, (*Conch.*) white ear; *oreille de mer* [HALIOTIDE]; (*Bot.*) *oreille de géant* [BARDANE]; *oreille d'homme* [NARD]; *oreille de lièvre* [SCABIEUSE]; *oreille d'ours* [PRIMEVÈRE]; *oreille de rat* [MYOSOTIS]; *oreille de souris* [PILOSELLE].

oreiller, *n.m.* Pillow. *Prendre conseil de son oreiller*, to sleep on it. **oreillère,** *n.f.* Earwig.

oreillette, *n.f.* (*Anat.*) Auricle; (*Bot., Conch.,* etc.) small-ear.

oreillon, *n.m.* Ear-piece of helmet; earlet of bats; (*pl.*) mumps.

orémus [ɔre'myːs], *n.m. inv.* Orison, prayer.

Orénoque [ɔre'nɔk], l', *m.* The Orinoco.

ores, ors, or **ore** [ɔːr], *adv.,* used only in *d'ores et déjà*, here and now; as I speak.

Oreste [ɔ'rɛst], *m.* Orestes.

orfèvre [ɔr'fɛːvr], *n.m.* Goldsmith or silversmith. *Orfèvre bijoutier*, goldsmith and jeweller; *vous êtes orfèvre*, you are in the trade or that is a bit of special pleading.

orfévré, *a.* (*fem.* -ée) Wrought by the goldsmith.

orfèvrerie, *n.f.* Goldsmith or silversmith's craft or trade; gold or silver ware; jewellery.

orfraie [ɔr'frɛ], *n.f.* Osprey, ossifrage, seaeagle. *Pousser des cris d'orfraie*, to shriek, to screech (by confusion with EFFRAIE).

orfroi [ɔr'frwɑ], *n.m.* Orphrey, orfray.

organdi [ɔrgɑ̃'di], *n.m.* Organdie, bookmuslin.

organe [ɔr'gan], *n.m.* Organ; voice; agent, instrument, medium, agency; mouthpiece, spokesman; component part (of machine). *Avoir un bel organe*, to have a good voice; *l'organe de la vue*, the organ of sight. **organeau,** *n.m.* (*pl.* -eaux) (*Naut.*) Ring, anchorring; mooring-ring.

organique, *a.* Organic.—*n.f.* (*Ant.*) Instrumental music.

organisateur [ɔrganiza'tœr], *n.m.* (*fem.* -**trice**) Organizer.—*a.* Organizing.

organisation [ɔrganiza'sjɔ̃], *n.f.* Organization, arrangement, structure; (*fig.*) organized body; set-up; constitution, nature.

organisé [ɔrgani'ze], *a.* (*fem.* -ée) Organized, constituted; organic. *Une tête bien organisée*, a well-balanced mind.

organiser, *v.t.* To organize; to get up, to arrange. **s'organiser,** *v.r.* To become organized; to get everything ship-shape.

organisme, *n.m.* Organism, structure, constitution (of body); organization (of a society). *L'organisme*, (*Med.*) the system.

organiste, *n.m.* Organist.

organsin [ɔrgɑ̃'sɛ̃], *n.m.* Organzin (silk). **organsinage,** *n.m.* Silk-throwing. **organsiner,** *v.t.* To throw (silk). **organsineur,** *n.m.* Silk-throwster.

orgasme [ɔr'gasm], *n.m.* Orgasm.

orge [ɔrʒ], *n.f.* Barley (masc. in *orge mondé*, hulled barley, and *orge perlé*, pearl barley). *Orge chevalier* or *pamelle*, two-rowed barley; *orge carrée* [ESCOURGEON]; *orge queue-de-souris*, wild barley; *sucre d'orge*, barley-sugar; *toile grains d'orge*, huckaback linen. *Faire ses orges*, to feather one's nest.

orgeat [ɔr'ʒa], *n.m.* Orgeat (syrup).

orgelet [ɔrʒ'lɛ], *n.m.* (*Path.*) Sty (in the eye).

orgiaque [ɔr'ʒjak], *a.* Orgiac; orgiastic.

orgie [ɔr'ʒi], *n.f.* Orgy (frantic revel or drunken bout); (*fig.*) profusion, wealth. *Orgie de fleurs*, profusion of flowers; *orgie de couleurs*, riot of colours.

orgue [ɔrg], *n.m.* (*fem. in pl.*) Organ; (*Geol.*) basalt pillars, organ-pipe. *Buffet d'orgues*, organ-case; *jeu d'orgues*, partial organs, set of organ-stops; *orgue de Barbarie*, barrel-organ, street organ; *orgue de cinéma*, theatre organ; *point d'orgue*, fermata, pause; *tenir l'orgue*, to be at the organ.

orgueil [ɔr'gœij], *n.m.* Pride; arrogance; ostentation. *Être enflé* or *bouffi d'orgueil*, to be puffed up with pride; *mettre son orgueil à*, to take a pride in. **orgueilleusement,** *adv.* Proudly, haughtily. **orgueilleux,** *a.* (*fem.* -**euse**) Proud, haughty, arrogant.—*n.* Proud and haughty person.

orient [ɔ'rjɑ̃], *n.m.* East, Orient; rising, rise; water (of pearls). *Le Grand Orient*, Grand Lodge (*Freemasonry*); *l'Empire d'Orient*, the Byzantine Empire; *le Proche, le Moyen, l'Extrême Orient*, the Near, Middle, Far East; *les peuples d'Orient*, the Eastern nations. **orientable,** *a.* Adjustable, mobile. *Raccord orientable*, swivel joint or connexion or union.

oriental, *a.* (*fem.* -**ale**, *pl.* -**aux**) Oriental, Eastern. *À l'orientale*, in Eastern fashion; *Indes orientales*, the East Indies, India.

orientaliser, *v.t.* To orientalize.

orientalisme, *n.m.* Orientalism. **orientaliste,** *n.* Orientalist.

orientation, *n.f.* Finding the cardinal points, orientation; (*Naut.*) trimming (of sails). (*sch.*) *Orientation professionnelle*, vocational guidance; *sens d'orientation*, sense of direction; *table d'orientation*, panoramic table [*see* ORIENTEUR].

orientement, *n.m.* (*Naut.*) [ORIENTATION].

orienter, *v.t.* To set towards the east, to orient, to orientate; to turn, to point; (*fig.*)

to guide; (*Naut.*) to trim (sails). *Bien orienté*, on the better side (of house or street), looking towards the south, etc.; *mal orienté*, looking the wrong way, looking towards the north, on the wrong side (of house or street); *orienter un cadran*, to set a quadrant. **s'orienter,** *v.r.* To find out the east; to take one's bearings, to ascertain one's position; (*fig.*) to see what one is about. *Laissez-moi m'orienter*, let me see where I am, let me find my bearings.

orienteur, *n.m.* (*Mil.*) Pathfinder; one who reconnoitres; member of advance-party; (*sch.*) vocational adviser, careers master.

orifice [ɔri'fis], *n.m.* Orifice, aperture, hole; (*Naut.*) port. *Orifice d'admission*, intake port; *orifice d'évacuation*, exhaust port; *orifice de soupape*, valve port.

oriflamme [ɔri'flɑ:m], *n.f.* Oriflamme; banner; streamer.

origan [ɔri'gɑ̃], *n.m.* (*Bot.*) Origanum; wild marjoram.

Origène [ɔri'ʒɛ:n], *m.* Origen.

originaire [ɔriʒi'nɛ:r], *a.* Originally (coming) from; native (*de*); aboriginal, primitive. *Il est originaire d'Italie*, he hails or comes from Italy. **originairement,** *adv.* Originally, primitively.

original [ɔriʒi'nal], *a.* (*fem.* **-ale,** *pl.* **-aux**) Original, singular, odd, peculiar, quaint. *Avoir un caractère original*, to have an eccentric character; *le texte original*, the original text; (*Cine.*) *version originale*, original version.—*n.m.* Original manuscript, drawing, etc. (not the copy).—*n.* Original; queer person, character, oddity. *C'est un original*, he is a character *or* an eccentric. **originalement,** *adv.* Originally; in an original manner; singularly, oddly.

originalité, *n.f.* Originality; eccentricity; character, individuality.

origine [ɔri'ʒin], *n.f.* Origin, fountain, source; descent, derivation, extraction, birth. *À l'origine*, originally; *avoir* or *tirer son origine de*, to originate from, in, with; *bureau d'origine*, office of dispatch (of telegram); *dès l'origine*, from the very beginning; *d'origine*, authentic, vintage (wine); *il était de basse origine*, he was of low extraction; *l'origine d'un mot*, the origin of a word; *mots de même origine*, cognate words; *pneus d'origine*, original tyres.

originel, *a.* (*fem.* **-elle**) Original, primitive. *Péché originel*, original sin. **originellement,** *adv.* Originally, from the very start.

orignal [ɔri'nal], *n.m.* Elk (of Canada), moose.

orillard [OREILLARD].

orillon [ɔri'jɔ̃], *n.m.* Ear, lug, mould-board (of a plough); handle (of a porringer etc.); (*Fort.*) mass of masonry in bastion.

orin [ɔ'rɛ̃], *n.m.* Buoy-rope (of an anchor).

Orion [ɔ'rjɔ̃], *n.m.* (*Astron.*) Orion.

oripeau [ɔri'po], *n.m.* (*pl.* **-eaux**) Tinsel; foil; (*pl.*) tawdry finery; (*more usually*) rags.

orle [ɔrl], *n.m.* (*Arch.* and *Her.*) Orle.

orléaniste [ɔrlea'nist], *a.* and *n.* (*Hist.*) Orleanist.

ormaie [ɔr'mɛ] *or* **ormoie,** *n.f.* Elm-grove.

orme [ɔrm], *n.m.* Elm. *Orme à grandes feuilles* or *orme tilleul*, broad-leaved elm; *orme champêtre*, common elm; *orme de montagne*, wych elm; *orme trifolié*, hop-tree.

ormeau, *n.m.* (*pl.* **-eaux**) Young elm.

ormerie, *n.f.* Saddler's craft.

ormille, *n.f.* Very small elm; plantation of young elms.

ormoie [ORMAIE].

orne [ɔrn], *n.m.* Flowering ash.

orné [ɔr'ne], *a.* (*fem.* **-ée**) Ornate (letter); ornate, florid (style).

ornemaniste [ɔrnəma'nist], *n.m.* Sculptor or painter of ornaments.

ornement [ɔrnə'mɑ̃], *n.m.* Ornament, embellishment; (*Mus.*) grace-note; (*pl.*) (*Eccles.*) vestments. *Dessin d'ornement*, decorative drawing; *sans ornement*, plain, bare, unadorned. **ornemental,** *a.* (*fem.* **-ale,** *pl.* **-aux**) Ornamental. **ornementation,** *n.f.* Ornamentation. **orner,** *v.t.* To adorn, to decorate, to deck, to embellish. *Les vertus ornent l'âme*, virtues embellish the soul; *orner son esprit*, to adorn one's mind. **s'orner,** *v.r.* To adorn oneself; to be adorned, to be decked.

ornière [ɔr'njɛ:r], *n.f.* Rut. *Il est retombé dans l'ornière*, (*fig.*) he has fallen back into the same old rut.

ornithogale [ɔrnitɔ'gal], *n.m.* (*Bot.*) Star of Bethlehem.

ornithologie [ɔrnitɔlɔ'ʒi], *n.f.* Ornithology. **ornithologique,** *a.* Ornithological. **ornithologiste** or **ornithologue,** *n.* Ornithologist.

ornithorynque [ɔrnitɔ'rɛ̃:k], *n.m.* Ornithorhynchus; (in Australia) platypus.

orobanche [ɔrɔ'bɑ̃:ʃ], *n.f.* Broom-rape, chokeweed. *Orobanche de Virginie*, beech-drops.

orobe [ɔ'rɔb], *n.f.* Black pea, bitter vetch.

orographie [ɔrɔgra'fi], *n.f.* Orography. **orographique,** *a.* Orographical (map).

orologie, *n.f.* Orology.

oronge [ɔ'rɔ̃:ʒ], *n.f.* Orange agaric. *Fausse oronge* or *tue-mouches*, fly-agaric; *oronge ciguë verte*, death-cup.

***orpailleur** [ɔrpa'jœ:r], *n.m.* Gold-washer, gold-seeker.

Orphée [ɔr'fe], *m.* Orpheus.

orphelin [ɔrfə'lɛ̃], *a.* and *n.m.* (*fem.* **-ine**) Orphan. **orphelinage,** *n.m.* Orphanhood. **orphelinat,** *n.m.* Orphan-home, orphanage.

orphéon [ɔrfe'ɔ̃], *n.m.* Male-voice choir. **orphéoniste,** *n.m.* Member of an *orphéon*.

orphie [ɔr'fi], *n.f.* Garfish, sea-pike, greenbone, snipe-eel.

orphique [ɔr'fik], *a.* Orphic.—*n.m. pl.* Poems of Orpheus.—*n.f. pl.* Orgies; feasts of Orpheus.

orpiment [ɔrpi'mɑ̃], *n.m.* Orpiment, yellow arsenic. **orpimenter,** *v.t.* To mix or colour with orpiment.

orpin [ɔr'pɛ̃], *n.m.* (*Chem.*) Orpiment; (*Bot.*) *orpin* or *joubarbe des vignes*, or *herbe à coupure*, or *reprise*, stone-crop. *Orpin blanc* or *petite joubarbe*, white stone-crop; *orpin jaune* or *poivre de muraille*, biting stone-crop; (*Pharm.*) *orpin confit*, orpin's leaves soaked in olive-oil.

orque [ɔrk], *n.f.* Orc, grampus.

orseille [ɔr'sɛ:j], *n.f.* Orchil, dyer's moss.

ort [ɔ:r], *a. inv.* and *adv.* (*Comm.*) Gross, gross weight.

orteil [ɔr'tɛ:j], *n.m.* Toe, *esp.* the big toe. *Se dresser sur ses orteils*, to stand on tiptoe; *orteil en marteau*, hammer toe.

orthodontie [ɔrtɔdɔ̃'ti] or **orthodontosie**, *n.f.* Orthodontics.
orthodoxe [ɔrtɔ'dɔks], *a.* Orthodox. **orthodoxie**, *n.f.* Orthodoxy, conformity.
orthodromie [ɔrtɔdrɔ'mi], *n.f.* Orthodromy.
orthogonal [ɔrtɔgɔ'nal], *a.* (*fem.* **-ale,** *pl.* **-aux**) Orthogonal.
orthographe, *n.f.* Orthography, spelling. *Faute d'orthographe,* spelling mistake. **orthographie,** *n.f.* (*Arch.*) Orthography. **orthographier,** *v.t.* (*conjugated like* PRIER) To spell correctly. **orthographique,** *a.* Orthographical.
orthopédie, *n.f.* Orthopedics. **orthopédique,** *a.* Orthopedic. **orthopédiste,** *n.m.* Orthopedist.
orthoptère [ɔrtɔp'tɛːr], *a.* Orthopterous.—*n.m.* Orthopteran.
ortie [ɔr'ti], *n.f.* Nettle; (*Vet.*) rowel. *Ortie blanche* [LAMIER]; *ortie jaune,* yellow archangel; *ortie puante,* stinking nettle; *ortie rouge* [GALÉOPSIS]; *ortie de mer,* sea-anemone.
ortié [ɔr'tje], *a.* (*fem.* **-ée**) *Fièvre ortiée,* nettle-rash, urticaria.
ortolan [ɔrtɔ'lɑ̃], *n.m.* Ortolan. *Ortolan jardinière,* garden-bunting.
orvet [ɔr've], *n.m.* Slow-worm.
orviétan [ɔrvje'tɑ̃], *n.m.* Orvietan, nostrum. *Marchand d'orviétan,* quack-doctor.
os [ɔs; *pl.* o], *n.m. inv.* Bone. *Elle n'a que la peau et les os,* she is nothing but skin and bone; *en chair et en os,* in the flesh, in person; *être trempé jusqu'aux os,* to be wet through; *jusqu'à la moelle des os,* to the marrow; *ne pas faire de vieux os,* not to live long; *os à ronger,* bone to pick, (*fig.*) something to live on; *os de seiche,* cuttle bone.
oscillant [ɔsi'lɑ̃], *a.* (*fem.* **-ante**) Oscillating, rocking.
oscillateur [ɔsila'tœːr], *a.* (*fem.* **-trice**) Oscillating (coil).—*n.m.* Oscillator, generator.
oscillation [ɔsila'sjɔ̃], *n.f.* Oscillation, swing, vibration; fluctuation. **oscillatoire** [ɔsila'twaːr], *a.* Oscillatory. **osciller,** *v.i.* To oscillate, to swing, to rock, to vibrate, to flicker; (*fig.*) to fluctuate, to waver between two opinions. **oscillographe,** *n.m.* (*Elec.*) Oscillograph.
osculateur [ɔskyla'tœːr], *a.* (*fem.* **-trice**) (*Geom.*) Osculatory. **osculation,** *n.f.* Osculation (of curves).
osé [o'ze], *a.* (*fem.* **osée**) Attempted, ventured; bold, daring.
Osée [o'ze], *m.* Hosea.
oseille [o'zɛːj], *n.f.* Sorrel. *Oseille sauvage* or *petite oseille,* wood sorrel; *oseille épinard* or *patience,* patience dock. (*pop.*) *Il a voulu me la faire à l'oseille,* he tried to deceive me.
oser [o'ze], *v.t., v.i.* To dare, to be so bold as, to venture. *Je n'oserais* or *je n'ose,* I dare not; *oserai-je le dire?* dare I say so? can I venture to say so? *oseriez-vous le blâmer?* would you dare to blame him? *si j'ose le dire,* if I may venture to say so; *vous n'osez rien,* you won't venture anything.
oseraie [oz'rɛ], *n.f.* Osier-bed.
oseur [o'zœːr], *a.* and *n.* (*fem.* **-euse**) Bold, daring.
osier [o'zje], or *saule des vanniers,* *n.m.* Osier, water willow. *Branche d'osier,* withy; *chaise en osier,* wicker chair; *panier d'osier,* wickerbasket.

osmium [ɔs'mjɔm], *n.m.* Osmium.
osmonde [ɔs'mɔ̃:d] or *osmonde royale,* *n.f.* Osmund, royal fern.
osmose [ɔs'moːz], *n.f.* (*Phys.*) Osmosis.
ossature [ɔsa'tyːr], *n.f.* Osseous framework, skeleton (of man, animals); framework, carcass, structure (of things).
osséine [ɔse'in], *n.f.* (*Chem.*) Ostein (substance extracted from bones).
osselet, *n.m.* Knuckle-bone (of sheep); ossicle (of ear). *Jouer aux osselets,* to play at knucklebones.
ossements [ɔs'mɑ̃], *n.m. pl.* Bones (of the dead); (*fig.*) remains.
osseux, *a.* (*fem.* **-euse**) Bony, osseous.
ossianique [ɔsja'nik], *a.* Ossianic.
ossicule [ɔsi'kyl], *n.m.* Ossicle.
ossification [ɔsifika'sjɔ̃], *n.f.* Ossification. **ossifier,** *v.t.* To ossify. **s'ossifier,** *v.r.* To become ossified.
*ossu [ɔ'sy], *a.* (*fem.* **-ue**) Large-boned, bony.
ossuaire [ɔ'sɥɛːr], *n.m.* Ossuary, charnelhouse; heap of bones.
ostéine [OSSÉINE].
ostéite [ɔste'it], *n.f.* Osteitis.
ostensible [ɔstɑ̃'sibl], *a.* Fit to be seen; open; above-board. **ostensiblement,** *adv.* Openly, publicly.
ostensoir [ɔstɑ̃'swaːr], *n.m.* Monstrance.
ostentateur [ɔstɑ̃ta'tœːr], *a.* (*fem.* **-trice**) Ostentatious.
ostentation [ɔstɑ̃ta'sjɔ̃], *n.f.* Ostentation, show, empty display. *Faire ostentation de ses richesses,* to parade one's wealth; *sans ostentation,* unostentatiously.
ostéoblaste [ɔsteɔ'blast], *n.m.* Osteoblast. **ostéoclasie,** *n.f.* Osteoclasis. **ostéogénie,** *n.f.* Osteogenesis. **ostéographie,** *n.f.* Osteography. **ostéolithe,** *n.m.* Petrified bone. **ostéologie,** *n.f.* Osteology. **ostéopathie,** *n.f.* Osteopathy. **ostéoplastie,** *n.f.* Osteoplasty. **ostéotomie,** *n.f.* Osteotomy.
Ostie [ɔs'ti], *f.* Ostia.
ostraciser [ɔstrasi'ze], *v.t.* To ostracize. **ostracisme,** *n.m.* Ostracism. *Frapper d'ostracisme,* to ostracize.
ostréiculteur [ɔstreikyl'tœːr], *n.m.* Oystergrower. **ostréiculture,** *n.f.* Oyster-culture.
ostrogoth or **ostrogot** [ɔstrɔ'go], *a.* and *n.* Ostrogoth; (*fig.*) barbarian, savage. **ostrogothique** or **ostrogotique,** *a.* Savage, barbarous.
otage [ɔ'taːʒ], *n.m.* Hostage; pledge, guarantee. *En otage,* as a hostage.
otalgie [ɔtal'ʒi], *n.f.* Otalgia, ear-ache.
otarie [ɔta'ri], *n.f.* Otariid; sea-lion, eared seal.
ôté [o'te], *prep.* Except, but, barring. *Ôté cela je ferai tout,* I'll do everything but that.
ôter [o'te], *v.t.* To take away; to remove; to take off, to pull off; to deprive of; to deduct; to deliver, to rid, to relieve. *Cette eau ôte les taches,* that water removes stains; *je ne puis m'ôter cela de la tête,* I can't get that out of my head; *on lui a ôté sa place,* they have deprived him of his situation; *ôter sa cravate, son manteau, son chapeau,* or *ses souliers,* to take off one's tie, coat, hat, or shoes; *ôtez cette table de là,* take that table away; *ôtez la nappe,* take off the cloth. **s'ôter,** *v.r.* To remove oneself, to get away; to rid oneself. *Ôte-toi de là que je m'y mette,* (*fam.*)

make room for me; *ôtez-vous de devant mes yeux*, get out of my sight; *ôtez-vous de mon chemin*, stand aside.

otite [ɔ'tit], *n.f.* Otitis. **otographie,** *n.f.* Otography. **otologie,** *n.f.* Otology.

otoscope [ɔtɔs'kɔp], *n.m.* Ear-speculum.

Otrante [ɔ'trɑ̃ːt], *m.* Otranto.

ottoman [ɔtɔ'mɑ̃], *a.* (*fem.* **-ane** (1)) Ottoman.—*n.m.* **Ottoman** (*fem.* **-ane**). An Ottoman.

ottomane (2), *n.f.* Ottoman (sofa).

ou [u], *conj.* Or, either, else. *Mort ou vif*, either dead or alive; *ou bien*, or else; *ou . . . ou*, either . . . or.

où [u], *adv.* Where; whither; at which, in which, to which, through which; when, that. *D'où*, whence, where . . . from; how; *d'où est-il?* where is he from? *d'où tenez-vous cela?* how do you know that? *d'où vient que?* how is it that? *jusqu'où*, how far, up to what point; *le moment où je vous ai quitté*, just as I left you; *l'état où il est*, the condition in which he is; *où allez-vous?* where are you going? *où en êtes-vous avec lui?* how do you stand with him? *où en êtes-vous de votre travail?* how far have you got with your work? *où en suis-je?* how do matters stand? *où suis-je?* where am I? *où que vous alliez*, wherever you may go; *par où?* which way? *partout où*, wherever.

(C) **ouache** [wa:ʃ], *n.f.* Bear's den.

ouaille [wɑːj], *n.f.* *Sheep.* (*pl.*) Flock (of a pastor, a priest).

ouais! [wɛ], *int.* Well now! my word! well, perhaps.

(C) **ouaouaron** [wawa'rɔ̃], *n.m.* Bullfrog.

ouate [wat], *n.f.* *L'ouate* or *la ouate*. Wadding, padding; cotton-wool. *Doublé d'ouate*, wadded, lined with wadding. **ouaté,** *a.* (*fem.* **-ée**) Velvety. **ouater,** *v.t.* To wad, to pad; to coddle. **ouateux,** *a.* (*fem.* **-euse**) Padded, wadded.

Oubangui [ubɑ̃'gi], *m.* Ubangi.

oubli [u'bli], *n.m.* Forgetfulness; oblivion; oversight, inadvertence, omission, slip; pardon. *Ensevelir dans l'oubli*, to bury in oblivion; *oubli de soi-même*, forgetfulness of self; *tirer quelqu'un de l'oubli*, to rescue someone from oblivion; *tomber dans l'oubli*, to sink into oblivion. **oubliable,** *a.* Liable or deserving to be forgotten. **oublie,** *n.f.* (Cone) wafer. **oublier,** *v.t.* (*conjugated like* PRIER) To forget, to be unmindful of, to omit, to neglect. *Oublier son devoir*, to forget one's duty; *oublier une injure*, to forget an injury; *oublions le passé*, let bygones be bygones. **s'oublier,** *v.r.* To forget oneself; to neglect one's affairs; to be forgotten. **oubliettes,** *n.f. pl.* Oubliette; trap-dungeon. *Mettre aux oubliettes*, to consign to oblivion. **oublieux,** *a.* (*fem.* **-ieuse**) Forgetful, unmindful.

oued [wɛd], *n.m.* (*pl.* **oueds** or **ouadi**) Water course in Algeria, Morocco, etc.; wadi.

Ouen [wɛ̃], *m.* Owen.

Ouessant [wɛ'sɑ̃], *m.* Ushant.

ouest [wɛst], *n.m.* West. *À l'ouest*, westward, in a westerly direction. *Vent d'ouest*, west wind.—*a. inv.* Westerly, western.

ouf! [uf], *int.* Oh! (of relief).

Ouganda [ugɑ̃'da], *m.* Uganda.

oui [wi], *adv.* Yes. *Dire, parier, or assurer que*

oui, to say, to bet, *or* to assure that it is so; *il a dit que oui* or *il a dit oui*, he said yes; *il croit que oui*, he thinks so; *il ne m'a répondu ni oui ni non*, he gave me no positive answer; *oui-da*, yes, indeed.—*n.m.* Yes. *Dire le grand oui*, to marry; *les oui et les non*, the ayes and noes; *pour un oui ou pour un non*, for the least thing.

ouï [wi], *p.p.* (*fem.* **ouïe** (1)) [OUÏR].

ouï-dire [wi'diːr], *n.m. inv.* Hearsay. *Savoir par ouï-dire*, to know from hearsay.

ouïe (2) [wi], *n.f.* *Hearing; hole (of a violin etc.); (pl.)* gills (of fish). *Avoir l'ouïe fine*, to be quick of hearing.

ouillage [u'jaːʒ], *n.m.* Filling up (of a cask).

ouiller [u'je], *v.t.* To fill up, to replace (in a cask) the quantity which has disappeared by leakage etc.

ouïr [wiːr], *v.t. irr.* (used only in the infinitive and compound tenses) To hear. *J'ai ouï dire*, I have heard say.

ouistiti [wisti'ti], *n.m.* Wistiti.

oukase [UKASE].

ouragan [ura'gɑ̃], *n.m.* Hurricane; (*fig.*) storm.

Oural [u'ral], *l', m.* The Ural. *Les Monts Ourals*, The Ural Mountains.

ourdir [ur'diːr], *v.t.* To warp (cloth etc.) before putting on the loom; (*fig.*) to weave, to plot, to concoct. *Ourdir un complot*, to hatch a plot; *ourdir une toile*, to warp a cloth; *ourdir une trahison*, to plot a treacherous deed.

ourdissage, *n.m.,* or **ourdissure,** *n.f.* Warping. **ourdisseur,** *n.m.* and *a.* (*fem.* **-euse**) Warper. **ourdissoir,** *n.m.* Warp-beam.

ourdou [ur'du], *n.m.* Urdu (language), Hindustani.

ourler [ur'le], *v.t.* To hem. *Ourler à jour*, to hemstitch. **ourlet,** *n.m.* Hem.

ours [urs], *n.m.* Bear. *Chasse à l'ours*, bear-hunt; *ours blanc*, Polar bear. *Il ne faut pas vendre la peau de l'ours avant de l'avoir tué*, you must not count your chickens before they are hatched; *un ours mal léché*, an unlicked cub; an unmannerly fellow; *il est (un peu) ours*, he is gruff, unsociable.

ourse, *n.f.* She-bear. *La grande Ourse*, the Great Bear; *la petite Ourse*, the Little Bear.

oursin, *n.m.* Sea-urchin.

ourson, *n.m.* Bear cub.

ourvari [HOURVARI].

oust, ouste [ust], *int.* (*fam.*) *Et oust! Allez ouste!* out you get!

outarde [u'tard], *n.f.* *Petite outarde*, or *canepetière*, bustard, field-duck; *grande outarde*, greater bustard. **outardeau,** *n.m.* (*pl.* **-eaux**) Young bustard.

outil [u'ti], *n.m.* Tool, implement; (*vulg.*) any old gadget, or useless person. **outillage,** *n.m.* Stock of tools, provision of tools; gear, apparatus, plant. **outillé,** *a.* (*fem.* **-ée**) Furnished with tools. *Mal outillé*, badly equipped. **outiller,** *v.t.* To furnish with tools; to equip; to supply the necessary means. **outilleur,** *n.m.* Tool-maker.

outrage [u'traːʒ], *n.m.* Outrage, gross insult; injury, wrong. *Faire un outrage à*, to commit an outrage upon; *outrage à la justice*, contempt of court; *outrage à la pudeur*, indecent act; *souffrir un outrage*, to brook an outrage. **outrageant,** *a.* (*fem.* **-eante**) Outrageous;

insulting, abusive. **outrager**, *v.t.* To outrage; to insult, to offend. **outrageusement**, *adv.* Insultingly. **outrageux**, *a.* (*fem.* **-euse**) Outrageous, scurrilous.

outrance [uˈtrɑ̃ːs], *n.f.* Extreme; excess. *À outrance*, to the death; *guerre à outrance*, war to the knife. **outrancier**, *a.* and *n.* (*fem.* **-ière**) Extremist.

outre (1) [utr], *n.f.* Goatskin, leather bottle. *Outre-de-mer* [ASCIDIE].

outre (2) [utr], *adv.* Further, beyond. *En outre*, besides, further; *passer outre*, to go on, to take no notice of a thing; (*Law*) to proceed; *percer d'outre en outre*, to run through (and through).—*prep.* Beyond; besides, in addition to. *Outre cela*, besides that; *outre que*, besides; *travailler outre mesure*, to overwork.

outré [uˈtre], *a.* (*fem.* **-ée**) Exaggerated, strained, excessive, undue; incensed. *Des louanges outrées*, excessive praise. *Il est outré en tout*, he is far-fetched in everything. *Il est outré de tant d'impertinences*, he is incensed at such impertinences.

outrecuidance [utrəkɥiˈdɑ̃ːs], *n.f.* Presumption, overweening conceit; audacity. **outrecuidant**, *a.* (*fem.* **-ante**) Presumptuous, overweening, bumptious, cheeky, cocksure.

outre-Manche [utrəˈmɑ̃ʃ], *adv.* Across the Channel.

outremer [utrəˈmɛːr], *n.m.* Ultramarine (colour).

outre-mer [utrəˈmɛːr], *adv.* Overseas. *La France d'Outre-mer*, the French Overseas Territories.

outre-monts [utrəˈmɔ̃], *adv.* Beyond the mountains; transmontane.

outrepasser [utrəpɑˈse], *v.t.* To go beyond, to exceed, to transgress. *Outrepasser ses pouvoirs*, to exceed one's powers.

outrer [uˈtre], *v.t.* To overdo; to overstrain; to incense, to put out of patience; to exaggerate; to overwhelm. *Outrer un cheval*, to strain a horse.

outre-tombe [utrəˈtɔ̃ːb], *adv.* Beyond the grave. *Mémoires d'outre-tombe*, posthumous memoirs.

ouvert [uˈvɛːr], *a.* (*fem.* **-te**) Open; unprotected, exposed, bleak, unfortified (of towns); (*fig.*) frank, open-hearted. *À bras ouverts*, with open arms, cordially; *à bureau* or *à guichet ouvert*, on demand; *à l'esprit ouvert*, open-minded; *compte ouvert*, open credit; *café ouvert la nuit*, all-night café; *guerre ouverte*, open warfare; *parler à cœur ouvert*, to speak unreservedly; *traduire* or *chanter à livre ouvert*, to translate *or* to sing at sight. **ouvertement**, *adv.* Openly, frankly.

ouverture, *n.f.* Opening; aperture, mouth, orifice, gap, hole; (*Mus.*) overture; (*fig.*) means, way; (*Arch.*) span, width (of a doorway etc.); (*Av.*) (parachute) drop; (*Opt.*) opening (of a lens). *Faire des ouvertures de paix*, to make overtures of peace; *l'ouverture de la chasse*, the opening of the shooting season; *l'ouverture des hostilités*, the outbreak of war; *ouverture d'esprit*, quick-wittedness; (*Cine.*) *ouverture en fondu*, fade-in.

ouvrable [uˈvrabl], *a.* Working, workable. *Jour ouvrable*, working-day.

ouvrage [uˈvraːʒ], *n.m.* Work, piece of work

(production), work of art, etc.; work (labour); performance, workmanship; result. *Gros ouvrages*, main walls; *l'ouvrage du temps*, the work (or result) of time; *ouvrage à l'aiguille*, needlework; *ouvrages d'art*, construction works; *ouvrages de dames*, ladies' fancy work; *se mettre à l'ouvrage*, to set to work. **ouvragé**, *a.* (*fem.* **-ée**) Wrought, figured. **ouvrager**, *v.t.* To work, to figure.

ouvraison, *n.f.* Act or process of working (material).

ouvrant, *a.* (*fem.* **-ante**) Opening. *À jour ouvrant*, at break of day; (*Motor.*) *toit ouvrant*, sliding roof.

ouvré, *a.* (*fem.* **-ée**) Wrought; diapered, figured.

ouvreau [uˈvro], *n.m.* (*pl.* **-eaux**) Lading-hole (of glass-furnaces).

ouvre-boîte [uvrəˈbwaːt], *n.m.* (*pl.* **ouvre-boîtes**) Tin-opener.

ouvrer [uˈvre], *v.i.* To work.—*v.t.* To work (material); to figure, to diaper (linen).

ouvreur [uˈvrœːr], *n.m.* (*fem.* **-euse**) Opener. *Ouvreuse* (*de loges*), (*Theat.*) box-opener, attendant (who shows to seats), usherette.

ouvrier [uvriˈe], *n.m.* (*fem.* **-ière**) Workman, workwoman, worker, hand, mechanic, operative; labourer. *À l'œuvre on connaît l'ouvrier*, a man is judged by his work; *ouvrier à la journée*, day-labourer; *ouvrière*, workgirl, factory hand, operative.—*a.* Operative, working. *Cheville ouvrière* [CHEVILLE]; *habitations ouvrières*, workmen's dwellings; *la classe ouvrière*, the working classes.

ouvrir [uˈvriːr], *v.t. irr.* (*pres.p.* **ouvrant**, *p.p.* **ouvert**) To open, to unlock, to set, throw, or break open; to broach (opinions etc.). *Cela ouvre l'appétit*, that sharpens the appetite; *faire ouvrir*, to have opened, to open; *on n'ouvre plus*, the doors are closed; *ouvrir un compte en banque*, to open a banking account; *ouvrir la terre*, to dig up the earth; *ouvrir son cœur à quelqu'un*, to unbosom oneself to someone.—*v.i.* To open; to expand. **s'ouvrir**, *v.r.* To open; to open for oneself; to disclose oneself, to open one's mind. *La porte s'ouvrit*, the door opened. *S'ouvrir à quelqu'un*, to unburden oneself to someone; *s'ouvrir un chemin*, to cut a way for oneself.

ouvroir [uˈvrwaːr], *n.m.* Charity workshop; workroom.

ovaire [ɔˈvɛːr], *n.m.* Ovary.

ovalaire [ɔvaˈlɛːr], *a.* (*Anat.*) Oval.

ovale [ɔˈval], *a.* and *n.m.* Oval, egg-shaped.

ovalisation [ɔvalizaˈsjɔ̃], *n.f.* Ovalization.

ovalisé, *a.* (*fem.* **-ée**) Ovalized, out of round.

ovarien [ɔvaˈrjɛ̃], *a.* (*fem.* **-ienne**) Ovarian.

ovariotomie, *n.f.* Ovariotomy.

ovation [ɔvaˈsjɔ̃], *n.f.* Ovation. *Faire une ovation à*, to acclaim someone, to give an ovation to.

ove [ɔːv], *n.m.* (*Arch.*) Ovolo, egg-shape.

ové, *a.* (*fem.* **-ée**) Ovate, egg-shaped.

ovibos [ɔviˈbɔs], *n.m.* Musk-ox.

ovicule, *n.m.* Small ovolo.

oviducte, *n.m.* Oviduct.

ovin [ɔˈvɛ̃], *a.* (*fem.* **-ine**) Ovine. *L'espèce ovine* ou *les ovins*, sheep.

ovipare [ɔviˈpaːr], *a.* Oviparous.—*n.m.* Oviparous animal.

ovoïde [ɔvɔˈid], *a.* Ovoid, egg-shaped.

ovule [ɔˈvyl], *n.m.* Ovule.

oxalate [ɔksa′lat], *n.m.* Oxalate.
oxalide or **oxalis**, *n.f.* (*Bot.*) Oxalis, wood-sorrel.
oxalique, *a.* Oxalic.
oxhydrique [ɔksi′drik], *a.* Composed of oxyhydrogen. *Lumière oxhydrique*, lime-light.
oxyacétylénique [ɔksiasetile′nik], *a.* Oxy-acetylene (welding etc.).
oxydable [ɔksi′dabl], *a.* Oxidable. **oxydant**, *n.m.* Oxidant, oxidizing agent.—*a.* (*fem.* **-ante**) Oxidizing. **oxydation**, *n.f.* Oxidation. **oxyde**, *n.m.* Oxide. **oxyder**, *v.t.* To oxidize. **s'oxyder**, *v.r.* To become oxidized.
oxygénable [ɔksiʒe′nabl], *a.* Oxygenizable. **oxygénation**, *n.f.* Oxygenation.
oxygène [ɔksi′ʒɛːn], *n.m.* Oxygen. **oxygéner**, *v.t.* To oxygenate; to bleach (hair). *Eau oxygénée*, peroxide of hydrogen.
oxymoron [ɔksimɔ′rɔ̃], *n.m.* Oxymoron.
oxyrhinque or **oxyrhynque** [ɔksi′rɛ̃ːk], *n.m.* (*Ichth.*) Oxyrhynchus.
oxyton [ɔksi′tɔ̃], *a.* Oxytone.
oxyure [ɔksi′yr], *n.f.* Small intestinal worm.
oyant [wa′jɑ̃], *pres.p.* *Hearing, listening.—n.m.* (*fem.* **-ante**) (*Law*) Auditor, hearer.
oyat [ɔ′ja], *n.m.* (*Picard. dial.*). Marram (grass).
*oyez** [ɔ′je], 2nd *pers. pl. imperative of Ouïr*, Hearken! Oyez!
ozokérite [ɔzɔke′rit] or **ozocérite**, *n.f.* Ozocerite, fossil wax.
ozone [ɔ′zɔn], *n.m.* Ozone. **ozoniser**, *v.t.* To ozonize. **ozoniseur** or **ozoneur**, *n.m.* Ozonizer. **ozonomètre**, *n.m.* Ozonometer.

P

P, p [pe], *n.m.* The sixteenth letter of the alphabet.
pacage [pa′kaːʒ], *n.m.* Pasture-land; pasturage. *Droit de pacage*, grazing rights. **pacager**, *v.t., v.i.* To pasture, to graze.
pacane [pa′kan], *n.f.* Pecan-nut.
pacha [pa′ʃa], *n.m.* Pasha. **pachalik**, *n.m.* Country governed by a Pasha.
pachyderme [paʃi′dɛrm], *a.* Pachydermatous.—*n.m.* Pachyderm.
pacificateur [pasifika′tœːr], *a.* (*fem.* **-trice**) Pacifying, peace-making.—*n.* Pacificator, pacifier.
pacification [pasifika′sjɔ̃], *n.f.* Pacification, peace-making. **pacifier**, *v.t.* (*conjugated like* PRIER) To pacify, to still, to appease, to calm. **pacifique**, *a.* Pacific, peaceable, gentle, peaceful. **pacifiquement**, *adv.* Peaceably, quietly. **pacifisme**, *n.m.* Pacifism. **pacifiste**, *a.* and *n.* Pacifist.
pacotille [pakɔ′tiːj], *n.f.* Goods carried free of charge by passengers or seamen; trumpery wares; pack, bale, lot, small stock. *Marchandises de pacotille*, private venture; shoddy goods; *maison de pacotille*, jerry-built house; *mobilier de pacotille*, gimcrack furniture.
pacotilleur, *n.m.* (*fem.* **-euse**) Trader in shoddy goods.
pacquer [pa′ke], *v.t.* To pack (herrings etc.).
pacte [pakt], *n.m.* Compact, contract, pact, agreement. *Pacte de préférence*, preference clause.
pactiser, *v.i.* To covenant, to make a compact

(*avec*); (*fig.*) to compound or compromise (*avec*).
pactole [pak′tɔl], *n.m.* (*fig.*) A source of great wealth, a regular gold mine.
padischa [padi′ʃa], *n.m.* Padishah.
padou [pa′du], *n.m.* Ferret, narrow tape (half cotton, half silk).
Padoue [pa′du], *f.* Padua.
paf [paf], *int.* Slap! bang!—*a. inv.* (*pop.*) *Il est paf*, he's a bit tight.
pagaie [pa′gɛ], *n.f.* Paddle (for canoe etc.). *Aller à la pagaie*, to paddle.
pagaïe or **pagaille** [pa′gaj], *n.f.* Hurry; disorder. *En pagaïe*, (*Naut.*) hurriedly; in bulk; (*Mil. slang*) hurriedly, in complete disorder; (*pop.*) all in a clutter, higgledy-piggledy.
paganisme [paga′nism], *n.m.* Paganism; heathendom.
pagayer [page′je], *v.i., v.t. irr.* (*conjug. like* BALAYER) To paddle. **pagayeur**, *n.m.* (*fem.* **-euse**) Paddler.
page (1) [paːʒ], *n.m.* Page (boy). *Être hors de page*, to be one's own master.
page (2) [paːʒ], *n.f.* Page (of a book). *Le haut or le bas d'une page*, the top *or* the bottom of a page; *metteur en pages*, (*Print.*) maker-up. *Être à la page*, (*fam.*) to be up to the minute, in the know.
(*C*) **pagée** [pa′ʒe], *n.f.* Fence section.
pagel, *n.m.*, or **pagelle**, *n.f.* [paʒɛl], or *dorade bilunée*. Sea-bream.
pagination, *n.f.* Pagination. **paginer**, *v.t.* To paginate, to page.
pagne [paɲ], *n.m.* Loin-cloth.
pagnon [pa′ɲɔ̃], *n.m.* Black broadcloth.
pagode [pa′gɔd], *n.f.* Pagoda. *Manche pagode*, wide sleeve.
pagure [pa′gyːr], *n.m.* Hermit-crab.
paiement [PAYEMENT].
païen [pa′jɛ̃], *a.* and *n.* (*fem.* **païenne**) Pagan, heathen.
paillard [pɑ′jaːr], *a.* (*fem.* **-arde**) Lecherous, lewd; broad, racy.—*n.* Wanton, sensual person, bawd. **paillarder**, *v.i.* To practise lewdness. **paillardise**, *n.f.* Lechery.
paillasse (1) [pɑ′jas], *n.f.* Straw mattress, palliasse; (*slang*) belly.
paillasse (2) [pɑ′jas], *n.m.* Clown, buffoon.
paillasson [pɑja′sɔ̃], *n.m.* Straw-mat; doormat; matting for protecting plants etc.
paille [pɑːj], *n.f.* Straw; flaw (in gems, metals, etc.). *Botte de paille*, truss of straw; *brin de paille*, bit of straw; *ce diamant a une paille*, that diamond has a flaw in it; *chapeau de paille*, straw-hat; *couleur paille*, straw-coloured; *être sur la paille*, to be miserably poor; *feu de paille*, (*fig.*) sudden, short blaze, spurt, etc.; *homme de paille*, man of straw; *menue paille* or *paille d'avoine*, chaff; *paille de fer*, iron shavings; *tirer à la courte paille*, to draw lots; *voir la paille dans l'œil du prochain*, to see the mote in one's brother's eye.
paillé, *a.* (*fem.* **-ée**) Straw-coloured; flawy (of metals etc.); rush-bottomed (chair)—*n.m.* Clean litter.
paille-en-queue, *n.m. inv.* Tropic bird, bo'sun bird.
pailler (1) [pɑ′je], *n.m.* Farm-yard; heap of straw, straw-rick. *Être sur son pailler*, to be in one's stronghold.
pailler (2), *v.t.* To mulch (plants).

paillet [pɑ'jɛ], *n.m.* (*Naut.*) Mat, fender.—*a.m.* Pale (of red wine).

pailleter [pɑj'te], *v.t.* To spangle. **paillette,** *n.f.* Grain of gold-dust; spangle; flaw (in a gem). *Savon en paillettes,* soap flakes.

pailleur [pɑ'jœ:r], *n.m.* (*fem.* **-euse**) Dealer in straw [*see* REMPAILLEUR].

pailleux [pɑ'jø], *a.* (*fem.* **-euse**) Flawy (of metals); strawy (manure).

paillis [pɑ'ji], *n.m.* Mulch.

paillon [pɑ'jɔ̃], *n.m.* Large spangle, tinsel; wisp of straw; straw wrapper for bottle.

paillot, *n.m.* Palliasse, door-mat.

paillote, *n.f.* Straw hut.

pain [pɛ̃], *n.m.* Bread; loaf; cake (of soap etc.), pat (of butter); (*pop.*) blow, punch. *Avoir du pain sur la planche,* to have plenty to do; *avoir quelque chose pour une bouchée de pain,* to get something for a mere song; *du pain bis* [BIS (1)]; *du pain frais* [FRAIS (1)]; *du pain rassis,* stale bread; *long comme un jour sans pain,* interminably long; *manger son pain blanc le premier,* to have one's best time first; *ne pas valoir le pain qu'on mange,* not to be worth one's salt; *pain à chanter,* unconsecrated wafer; *pain bénit,* consecrated bread; *c'est pain bénit,* it serves him right; *pain complet,* wholemeal bread; (*Bot.*) *pain de coucou* [OXALIDE], *pain de grenouille* [PLANTAIN]; *pain de pourceau* [CYCLAMEN]; *pain de munition,* regulation bread (for soldiers); *pain d'épice* [ÉPICE]; *pain de savon,* cake of soap; *pain de sucre,* sugar-loaf; *pain grillé,* toast; *pain mollet,* soft bread, milk-roll; *pain quotidien,* daily bread; *un pain,* a loaf; *un pain à cacheter,* a wafer; *un petit pain,* a roll.

pair [pɛ:r], *a.* (*fem.* **paire** (1)) Equal, even. *Pair ou impair,* odd or even; *voie paire,* up line.—*n.m.* Peer; equal; mate (of birds); par, equality; fellow. *Aller* or *marcher de pair avec quelqu'un,* to keep up with, or be on an equal footing with someone; *au pair,* at par, even (with), 'au pair'; *de pair,* on a par, on an equality; *être jugé par ses pairs,* to be tried by one's peers; *hors* (*de*) *pair,* beyond comparison; *le change est au pair,* the exchange is at par; *nous voilà pair à pair,* now we are even; *traiter quelqu'un de pair à compagnon,* to be hail fellow well met with someone.

paire (2), *n.f.* Pair, brace, couple. *Les deux font la paire,* they are well matched; *une paire de bœufs,* a yoke of oxen; *une paire de ciseaux,* a pair of scissors.

pairesse, *n.f.* Peeress.

pairie, *n.f.* Peerage.

paisible [pɛ'zibl], *a.* Peaceable, peaceful, quiet, still, calm. *Mener une vie paisible,* to lead a peaceful life; *sommeil paisible,* peaceful sleep. **paisiblement,** *adv.* Peaceably, peacefully.

paisson [pɛ'sɔ̃], *n.f.* Forest-pasture.

paître [pɛ:tr], *v.t. irr.* (*pres.p.* **paissant,** *p.p.* **pu** (1) *very rare*). To graze, to feed; to tend (flocks etc.).—*v.i.* To graze, to feed. (*fam.*) *Envoyer paître quelqu'un,* to send someone about his business. *Mener paître des moutons,* to drive sheep to pasture.

paix [pɛ], *n.f.* Peace; quiet; calm, stillness, tranquillity; silence; rest, repose; (*R.-C. Ch.*) osculatory, pax. *Il a fait sa paix,* he has made his peace; *ils ont fait la paix,* they have become reconciled, come to terms; *laisser en*

paix, to leave alone; *paix fourrée,* hypocritical peace; *paix plâtrée,* patched-up peace; *troubler la paix de,* to disturb the peace of.—*int.* Be quiet!

pal [pal], *n.m.* (*pl.* **pals**) Pale, stake (punishment); (*Her.*) pale. *Pal injecteur,* injecting tube, sulphurator.

palabre [pa'labr], *n.f.* Palaver. **palabrer,** *v.i.* To palaver.

palace [pa'las], *n.m.* Sumptuous hotel.

palade [pa'lad], *n.f.* (*Row.*) Pull (at the oar) [*see* PASSÉE].

paladin [pala'dɛ̃], *n.m.* Paladin, champion. *C'est un vrai paladin,* he is a perfect knight-errant.

palais (1) [pa'lɛ], *n.m.* Palace; (*fig.*) the Bar; the law. *Jour de palais,* court day; *palais de justice,* law-courts; *révolution de palais,* palace revolution; *style du palais,* law style; *terme de palais,* law term.

palais (2) [pa'lɛ], *n.m.* Palate, roof (of the mouth); (*fig.*) taste. *Le voile du palais,* the soft palate; *palais fendu,* cleft palate.

palan [pa'lɑ̃], *n.m.* Tackle, hoisting gear, pulley-block. *Palan à croc,* luff; *palan de charge,* garnet.

palanche [pa'lɑ̃:ʃ], *n.f.* Yoke (for pails etc.).

palançon [palɑ̃'sɔ̃], *n.m.* Lath (to support mud-walls till they are dry).

palangre [pa'lɑ̃:gr] or **palancre,** *n.f.* Trawl-line.

palanque [pa'lɑ̃:k], *n.f.* (*Fort.*) Timber stockade; (*Naut.*) fishing line.

palanquer [palɑ̃'ke], *v.t.* To stockade.

palanquin [palɑ̃'kɛ̃], *n.m.* Palankeen; (*Naut.*) reef tackle.

palastre [pa'lastr], *n.m.* Lock-plate; box.

palatal [pala'tal], *a.* (*fem.* **-ale,** *pl.* **-aux**) Palatal.—*n.f.* Palatal letter or sound.

palataliser, *v.t.* To palatalize (consonants).

palatin (1) [pala'tɛ̃], *a.* (*fem.* **-ine**) (*Anat.*) Palatine.

palatin (2) [pala'tɛ̃], *a.* (*fem.* **-ine**) (*Hist.*) Palatine.—*n.m.* Palatine.—*n.f.* Palatine princess; fur-tippet.

Palatinat [palati'na], **le,** *m.* The Palatinate.

pale (1) [pal], *n.f.* Blade (of oar, propeller, etc.); float, paddle-board; sluice, flood-gate.

pale (2) [pal] or **palle,** *n.f.* (*R.-C. Ch.*) Linen cover for chalice.

pâle [pɑ:l], *a.* Pale, wan, pallid, ghastly; (*fig.*) vapid, colourless, tame (of style). *Pâle comme la mort,* as pale as death; *pâle de colère,* pale with rage; *visages pâles,* pale-faces (white people).

paléage [pale'a:ʒ], *n.m.* (*Naut.*) Shovelling (of grain etc. by dockers).

palée [pa'le], *n.f.* Row or structure of stakes; pilework.

palefrenier [palfrə'nje], *n.m.* Groom, ostler.

palefroi [pal'frwa], *n.m.* Palfrey.

palémon [pale'mɔ̃], *n.m.* (*Conch.*) Prawn.

paléographe [paleɔ'graf], *a.* Palaeographic. —*n.* Palaeographer. **paléographie,** *n.f.* Palaeography (study of ancient writings). **paléographique,** *a.* Palaeographic.

paléolithique [paleɔli'tik], *a.* Palaeolithic.

paléologue [paleɔ'lɔg], *n.* Palaeologist.

paléontologie [paleɔtɔlɔ'ʒi], *n.f.* Palaeontology. **paléontologique,** *a.* Palaeontological. **paléontologiste,** *n.* Palaeontologist.

Palerme [pa'lɛrm], *f.* Palermo.

paleron [pal'rɔ̃], *n.m.* Shoulder-blade (of horse etc.) *Paleron de bœuf*, chuck.

*****palestine** [palɛs'tin], *n.f.* (*Print.*) Two-line pica.

Palestine [palɛs'tin], *f.* Palestine.

palestre [pa'lɛstr], *n.f.* Palaestra.

palet [pa'lɛ], *n.m.* Quoit; small iron disc to play *au bouchon* or *au tonneau*.

*****paletot** [pal'to], *n.m.* Overcoat, coat; (woman's) woollen jacket.

palette [pa'lɛt], *n.f.* Paddle (of paddle-wheel); vane (of rotary pump); bat (of ping-pong); palette (of painter); slice (of printer); pallet (of gilder); (wooden) butter-pat.

palétuvier [palety'vje], *n.m.* Mangrove.

pâleur [pɑ'lœ:r], *n.f.* Pallor, wanness, ghastliness. *Pâleur mortelle*, deathlike pallor.

pâli [pɑ'li], *a.* (*fem.* **pâlie**) Grown pale.

pâlichon [PÂLOT].

palier [pa'lje], *n.m.* Landing (on a staircase), stair-head; plummer-block, pillow-block; stage, degree; level stretch. *Demeurer sur le même palier*, to live on the same floor. *Par paliers*, by degrees. *Vitesse en palier*, speed on the flat. **palière**, *a.f. Marche palière*, top step.

palification [palifika'sjɔ̃], *n.f.* Palification, pile-driving.

palifier, *v.t.* (*conjugated like* PRIER) To strengthen with piles.

palimpseste [palɛ̃p'sɛst], *n.m.* and *a.* Palimpsest.

palindrome [palɛ̃'drɔm], *n.m.* Palindrome.—*a.* Palindromic.

palingénésie [palɛ̃ʒene'zi], *n.f.* Palingenesy, regeneration, atavism.

palinodie [palinɔ'di], *n.f.* Palinode, recantation. *Chanter la palinodie*, to retract, to recant.

pâlir [pɑ'li:r], *v.i.* To grow, turn, or become pale; to grow dim, to pale; to fade. *Faire pâlir*, to throw into the shade, to eclipse, to frighten; *pâlir sur les livres*, to pore over books; *pâlir d'émotion*, to go pale with excitement, emotion; *son étoile pâlit*, his star is on the wane.—*v.t.* To make pale, to bleach.

palis [pa'li], *n.m.* Stake, pale; paling, enclosure.

palissade [pali'sad], *n.f.* Palisade, paling; wooden fence; hedgerow; stockade. **palissader**, *v.t.* To palisade; to stockade; to fence, to rail in.

palissage, *n.m.* (*Hort.*) Paling or nailing up.

palissandre [pali'sɑ̃:dr], *n.m.* Purple wood; (Brazilian) rose-wood.

pâlissant [pɑli'sɑ̃], *a.* (*fem.* **-ante**) Turning pale, fading.

palisser [pali'se], *v.t.* (*Hort.*) To nail up (a vine etc.).

palladium [palla'djɔm], *n.m.* (*Chem.*) Palladium; safeguard.

palle [PALE (2)].

palliatif [palja'tif], *a.* (*fem.* **-ive**) Palliative.—*n.m.* Palliative. **palliation**, *n.f.* Palliation.

pallier [pa'lje], *v.t.* (*conjugated like* PRIER) To palliate, to excuse, to mitigate.

pallium [pal'ljɔm], *n.m.* Pallium; pall.

palma-christi [palmakris'ti], *n.m.* Castor-oil plant.

palmaire [pal'mɛ:r], *a.* (*Anat.*) Palmar (muscle).

palmarès [palma'rɛ:s], *n.m. inv.* Prize-list, list of honours.

palmarium [palma'rjɔm], *n.m.* Conservatory (for palms).

palme (1) [palm], *n.f.* Palm, palm-branch; palm-tree; (*fig.*) victory, triumph. (*pl.*) *Les palmes* (*académiques*), the insignia of the *Ordre des Palmes Académiques. Huile de palme*, palm-oil; *vin de palme*, palm wine. *La palme du martyre*, the crown of martyrdom; *remporter la palme*, to bear away the palm.

*****palme** (2) [palm], *n.m.* (*anc. Rom. measure*) Palm, hand's breadth.

palmé, *a.* (*fem.* **-ée**) Palmate; web-footed, fin-toed; (*fam.*) holder of the *Palmes*.

palmer (1) [pal'me], *v.t.* To measure by hands; to flatten (the head of needles).

palmer (2) [pal'mɛr], *n.m.* Micrometer, calliper (of planisher, turner).

palmeraie [palmə'rɛ], *n.f.* Grove of palms.

palmette [pal'mɛt], *n.f.* Palmette, palm-leaf (ornament); palm-shaped espalier.

palmier [pal'mje], *n.m.* Palm-tree, palm.

palmifère [palmi'fɛ:r], *a.* (*Bot.*) Palmiferous.

palmipède [palmi'pɛd], *a.* and *n.m.* Palmiped, web-footed (bird).

palmiste [pal'mist], *n.m.* Palmetto, cabbage-tree. *Rat palmiste*, palm-squirrel.

palmite [pal'mit], *n.m.* Palm-marrow.

Palmyre [pal'mi:r], *f.* Palmyra.

palombe [pa'lɔ̃:b], *n.f.* Wood-pigeon, ring-dove.

palonnier [palɔ'nje], *n.m.* Swing-bar, pole (of a coach); (*Motor.*) compensator (of brake); (*Av.*) rudder-bar.

pâlot [pɑ'lo], *a.* (*fem.* **-otte**) Palish, rather pale.

palourde [pa'lu:rd], *n.f.* Clam.

palpabilité [palpabi'lite], *n.f.* Palpability. **palpable**, *a.* Palpable; tangible. **palpablement**, *adv.* Palpably. **palpation**, *n.f.* Palpation.

palpe [palp], *n.f.* Palp, feeler (of insects etc.).

palpébral [palpe'bral], *a.* (*fem.* **-ale**, *pl.* **-aux**) (*Anat.*) Palpebral.

palper [pal'pe], *v.t.* To feel, to touch, to examine by the feel; (*colloq.*) to pocket, to receive. *Palper de l'argent*, to finger money.

palpitant [palpi'tɑ̃], *a.* (*fem.* **-ante**) Palpitating, panting. *Cœur palpitant*, throbbing heart; *des membres palpitants*, quivering limbs. **palpitation**, *n.f.* Palpitation; throbbing, quivering; thrill, flutter.

palpiter, *v.i.* To palpitate, to pant, to throb, to beat; to thrill, to quiver, to flutter. *Le cœur lui palpite*, his heart flutters.

palplanche [pal'plɑ̃:ʃ], *n.f.* Pile-plank.

*****palsambleu** [palsɑ̃'blø], *int.* Zounds! forsooth!

paltoquet [paltɔ'kɛ], *n.m.* Lout, contemptible fellow, mere nobody.

paludéen [palyde'ɛ̃], *a.* (*fem.* **-enne**) Paludal, marshy. *Fièvre paludéenne*, marsh-fever.

paludier, *n.m.* Salt-maker.

paludique [PALUDÉEN].

paludisme, *n.m.* Malaria, marsh-fever.

palus [pa'ly:s], *n.m.* Marsh, fen.

palustre, *a.* Paludal.

pambéotie [pɑ̃beo'si], *n.f.* General stupidity or dullness of mind.

pâmer [pɑ'me], *v.i.* To swoon. *Faire pâmer quelqu'un de rire*, to make someone split his sides with laughter. **se pâmer**, *v.r.* To swoon, to faint away; to lose its temper (of steel). *Se pâmer de joie*, to be overcome with joy; *se pâmer de rire*, to be ready to die with laughter.

pâmoison, *n.f.* Swoon, fainting fit. *Tomber en pâmoison*, to faint away.

pampa [pā'pa], *n.f.* Pampa. *Herbe des pampas*, pampas-grass.

pampe [pāːp], *n.f.* Blade (of corn etc.).

Pampelune [pā'plyn], *f.* Pamplona.

pamphlet [pā'flɛ], *n.m.* Satirical booklet, lampoon. **pamphlétaire,** *n.* Pamphleteer.

pamplemousse [pāplo'mus], *n.f.*, *more usually m.* Grape-fruit; shaddock (tree).

pampre [pāːpr], *n.m.* Vine-branch (full of leaves).

Pan [pā], *m.* Pan.

pan (1) [pā], *n.m.* Flap, coat-tails, panel (of dress); side, section (of a wall etc.). *Pan coupé*, (*Carp.*) cant; *pan de bois*, timber-framing; *pan de ciel*, stretch, patch of sky; *pan de comble*, slope or side of roof; *pan de mur*, bare wall; *tour à six pans*, six-sided tower.

pan! (2) [pā], *int.* Slap! bang! smack!

panacée [pana'se], *n.f.* Panacea, nostrum.

panachage [pana'ʃaːʒ], *n.m.* Mixing (of colours); (*Polit.*) splitting (up) of one's vote.

panache [pa'naʃ], *n.m.* Plume, tuft, bunch of feathers etc.; cap, top (of a church lamp); (*Arch.*) triangular part of pendentive of an arch; (*fig.*) panache, show, swagger. *Panache de fumée*, wreath or trail of smoke; *panache de mer*, sea-palm. *Aimer le panache*, to like military flourish, glamour or displays; *avoir du panache*, to have an air about one; *faire panache*, to be pitched over the horse's head (rider), over the handle-bars (cyclist); to turn right over, to turn turtle (of car, aeroplane).

panaché, *a.* (*fem.* **-ée**) Plumed, tufted; striped, streaked; (*colloq.*) variegated, motley; mixed. *Glace panachée*, mixed ice-cream; *salade panachée*, salad of different herbs. *Liste panachée*, (*Polit.*) electoral list made up of candidates belonging to different parties.

panacher, *v.t.* To plume; to streak, to variegate, to mix.

panachure, *n.f.* Streak, stripe; variety of colours, variegation (on flowers, fruit, etc.).

panade [pa'nad], *n.f.* (*Cook.*) Panada, bread-soup. (*fam.*) *Être dans la panade*, to be in the soup; to be hard up.

panais [pa'nɛ], *n.m.* Parsnip.

panama [pana'ma], *n.m.* Panama-hat, panama. *Bois de panama*, soap-bark.

panaméricanisme [panamerika'nism], *n.m.* Pan-Americanism.

panarabisme, *n.m.* Pan-Arabism.

panard [pa'naːr], *a.* (*fem. inv.* or **-arde**) With out-turned feet (of horses); cow-hocked.— *n.m.* (*slang*) Foot.

panaris [pana'ri], *n.m.* Whitlow.

panca [pā'ka] or **punca,** *n.m.* Punkah.

pancalier [pāka'lje], *n.m.*, or *chou frisé de Milan*, Savoy cabbage.

pancarte [pā'kart], *n.f.* Large placard or bill; paper-holder.

pancrace [pā'kras], *n.m.* Pancratium.

pancréas [pākre'aːs], *n.m. inv.* Pancreas; sweetbread. **pancréatique,** *a.* Pancreatic.

panda [pā'da], *n.m.* Panda.

pandanus [pāda'nys], *n.m.* (*Bot.*) Screw-pine.

pandectes [pā'dɛkt], *n.f. pl.* (*Rom. law*) Pandects.

pandémonium [pādemɔ'njɔm], *n.m.* Pandemonium; the abode of all demons; (*fig.*) a place of disorder.

pandit [pā'di], *n.m.* Pundit.

Pandore [pā'dɔːr], *n.f.* Pandora. *Boîte de Pandore*, Pandora's box, source of many evils.—*n.m.* (*fam.*) Police constable.

*pandour [pā'duːr], *n.m.* Pandour (Hungarian soldier); marauder; coarse, brutal man.

pané [pa'ne], *a.* (*fem.* **-ée**) Covered, or fried, in bread-crumbs. *Soupe panée*, bread soup.

panégyrique [paneʒi'rik], *n.m.* Panegyric.

panégyriste, *n.m.* Panegyrist.

paner [pa'ne], *v.t.* To cover with bread-crumbs.

panerée [pan're], *n.f.* Basketful.

paneterie [pan'tri], *n.f.* Bread-pantry.

panetier, *n.m.* Pantler, store-keeper.

panetière, *n.f.* *Satchel; small hanging cupboard for bread etc.; sideboard, dresser.

pangolin [pāgɔ'lɛ̃], *n.m.* Scaly ant-eater.

panic [pa'nik], *n.m.*, or **panis** [*see* MILLET].

panicaut [pani'ko], *n.m.*, or *Chardon Roland*, Eryngium. *Panicaut maritime* or *chardon bleu*, sea-holly.

panicule [pani'kyl], *n.f.* (*Bot.*) Panicle.

paniculé, *a.* (*fem.* **-ée**) Paniculate.

panier [pa'nje], *n.m.* Basket, hamper, pannier; beehive made of straw; hoop-petticoat, hoop; pony-carriage. *Être dans le même panier*, to be in the same boat; *faire danser l'anse du panier*, to take the market-penny, to make a bit on the side; *le dessus du panier*, the pick of the basket; *panier à ouvrage*, work-basket; *panier à salade*, (wire) salad washer, (*slang*) black Maria; *panier à gibier*, hamper; *panier de pêche*, creel; *panier percé*, spendthrift; *panier roulant*, go-cart.

panification [panifika'sjɔ̃], *n.f.* Panification.

panifier, *v.t.* (*conjugated like* PRIER) To turn (flour) into bread.

panique [pa'nik], *a.* Panic. *Une peur panique*, a panic.—*n.f.* Sudden fright, panic, scare; stampede (of animals).

(C) **panis** [pa'ni], *n.* Pawnis.

panne (1) [pan], *n.f.* Plush; panne; (*Theat.*) a small or bad part; actor or actress fit only for those parts; (*Her.*) pean. *Être* (*tombé*) *dans la panne*, (*fam.*) to be hard up, in a hole.

panne (2) [pan], *n.f.* Fat, lard.

panne (3) [pan], *n.f.* Pane (of a hammer), (*Am.*) peen.

panne (4) [pan], *n.f.* Purlin; pantile.

panne (5) [pan], *n.f.* Breakdown, mishap, failure, standstill. (*Naut.*) *Mettre en panne*, to heave to, to bring to (in order to immobilize the ship). *Panne d'allumage*, (*Motor.*) ignition trouble; *panne d'électricité*, electricity failure; *panne d'essence* or *panne sèche*, shortage of petrol; *panne de métro*, hold-up or stoppage in the tube; *rester en panne*, (*Motor.*) to have a breakdown. *Laisser quelqu'un en panne*, to leave someone in the lurch.

panné [pa'ne], *a.*(*fem.* **-ée**) (*slang*) Hard up.

panneau [pa'no], *n.m.* (*pl.* **-eaux**) Panel; snare, trap; (*Naut.*) hatch; (*Hort.*) glass-frame. *Donner dans le panneau*, to fall into the trap. *Panneau de lambris*, wainscot panel.

panneauter, *v.t.* To catch in snares or trap-nets.

pannequet [pan'kɛ], *n.m.* Pancake.
panneresse [pan'rɛs], *a.* and *n.f.* Stretcher brick.
panneton [pan'tɔ̃], *n.m.* Key-bit; catch (window fastening).
panonceau [panɔ̃'so], *n.m.* (*pl.* **-eaux**) Escutcheon; oval plaque or plate (doctor. lawyer, etc.).
panoplie [panɔ'pli], *n.f.* Panoply; trophy (of arms). *Panoplie de soldat,* (for a small boy) soldier's outfit.
panorama [panɔra'ma], *n.m.* Panorama.
panoramique, *a.* Panoramic.—*n.m.* (*Cine.*) Panning shot, pan shot.
panorpe [pa'nɔrp], *n.f.* Scorpion-fly.
pansage [pã'sa:ʒ], *n.m.* Grooming (of horses etc.); (*Mil.*) stables (*colloq.*) [*see* MUSETTE].
panse [pã:s], *n.f.* Belly, rumen (of ruminating animals). *Grosse panse,* pot-belly, paunch; *panse d'a,* (*Print.*) bowl of an α.
pansement [pãs'mã], *n.m.* Dressing (of wounds). *Pansement sommaire,* first aid; *paquet de pansement,* field dressing.
panser, *v.t.* To dress (wounds); to groom (a horse); to tend (a wounded man).
pansu [pã'sy], *a.* and *n.* (*fem.* **-ue**) Pot-bellied (individual); bulging.
pantagruélique [pãtagrye'lik], *a.* Pantagruelian.
pantalon [pãta'lɔ̃], *n.m.* (Pair of) trousers; name of a dance; pantaloon (pantomime). *Pantalon blanc,* ducks; *pantalon collant,* tight trousers; *pantalon de femme,* women's knickers, panties; *pantalon rouge,* (*fig.*) French soldier (1831–1915).
pantalonnade, *n.f.* Pantaloon's dance; buffoonery; make-believe, piece of humbug.
pantelant [pãt'lã], *a.* (*fem.* **-ante**) Panting, heaving, gasping. *Chair pantelante,* quivering flesh.
panteler, *v.i.* To gasp, to pant.
pantenne [pã'tɛn], *n.f.* Wicker tray (for fruit-drying or silkworms); [PANTIÈRE]. *Mettre en pantenne,* to throw into disorder; *vergues en pantenne,* (*Naut.*) yards apeak (in sign of mourning).
panthéisme [pã'teism], *n.m.* Pantheism.
panthéiste, *n.* and *a.* Pantheist.
panthère [pã'tɛ:r], *n.f.* Panther.
pantière [pã'tjɛ:r], *n.f.* Draw-net (for catching birds).
pantin [pã'tɛ̃], *n.m.* Dancing Jack, puppet; (*fig.*) trimmer, jumping-jack.
pantographe [pãtɔ'graf], *n.m.* Pantagraph, pantograph.
pantois [pã'twa], *a.* (*fem.* **-oise**) *Panting, out of breath; (*fig.*) astonished, aghast, flabbergasted.
pantomime [pãtɔ'mim], *n.f.* Dumb-show, pantomime.—*n.m.* Pantomime (actor).—*a.* Pantomimic.
pantomimer, *v.t.* To pantomime.
pantouflard [pãtu'fla:r], *n.m.* (*fam.*) A stay-at-home fellow.
pantoufle [pã'tufl], *n.f.* Slipper. *En pantoufles,* in one's slippers, slipshod, (*fig.*) in a slipshod way; *fer à pantoufle,* panton (horse-shoe); *raisonner comme une pantoufle,* to reason like a jackass, to talk through one's hat.
pantoufler, *v.i.* (*colloq.*) To act or talk in a silly way.

pantouflerie, *n.f.* *Stupid conversation; piece of absurdity; slipper-making.
pantouflier, *n.m.* (*fem.* **-ière**) Slipper-maker, slipper-vendor.
panure [pa'nyr], *n.f.* Raspings, bread-crumbs.
paon [pã], *n.m.* Peacock; emperor-moth; (*fig.*) vain person. *Paon de mer,* ruff.
paonne [pan], *n.f.* Peahen. **paonneau,** [pa'no], *n.m.* (*pl.* **-eaux**) Pea-chick.
paonner [pa'ne], *v.i.* To strut, to preen oneself.
papa [pa'pa], *n.m.* Papa, daddy. *Bon papa,* grand-dad.
papal [pa'pal], *a.* (*fem.* **-ale**, *pl.* **-aux**) Papal. **papalin,** *a.* (*fem.* **-ine**) Under the papal sovereignty; popish.—*n.m.* Soldier or partisan of the Pope.
papauté, *n.f.* Papacy.
papavéracée [papavera'se], *n.f.* (*Bot.*) Papaveraceous plant.
papaye [pa'pɛ:j], *n.f.* Papaw (fruit). **papayer** [papɛ'je], *n.m.* Papaw-tree, papaw.
pape (1) [pap], *n.m.* Pope. *Le pape Jean XXIII,* Pope John XXIII.
pape (2) [pap], *n.m.* Painted finch.
papegai [pap'gɛ] or **papegeai** [pap'ʒe], *n.m.* Popinjay.
papelard [pa'pla:r], *a.* (*fem.* **-arde**) Canting, hypocritical. *Air papelard,* sanctimonious air. —*n.m.* (*pop.*) Written paper.
papelarder, *v.i.* To cant.
papelardise, *n.f.* Hypocrisy.
paperasse [pa'pras], *n.f.* Old paper; waste paper. (*pl.*) Old documents, red tape. **paperasser,** *v.i.* To rummage among old papers; to scribble. **paperasserie,** *n.f.* Old waste paper; red-tapism. **paperassier,** *n.m.* (*fem.* **-ière**) Everlasting scribbler; rummager of old papers.—*a.* Red-tape, formal.
papesse [pa'pɛs], *n.f.* (only used in) *La papesse Jeanne,* Pope Joan.
papeterie [pap'tri], *n.f.* Paper-mill, paper-factory; paper-manufacture, paper-making; paper-trade; stationery; stationer's shop; stationery case.
papetier, *n.m.* (*fem.* **-ière**) Paper-maker; stationer.—*a.* Paper (industry etc.).
papier [pa'pje], *n.m.* Paper; (*fam.*) article (for newspaper). (*pl.*) Papers, identification documents, passport, etc. (*fam.*) *Être dans les petits papiers de quelqu'un,* to be in someone's good books; *papier à écrire* [ÉCRIRE]; *papier buvard* [BUVARD]; *papier calque,* tracing paper; *papier carbone,* carbon paper; *papier court,* short-dated bills; *papier d'Arménie,* scented paper (when burning); *papier d'emballage,* brown paper; *papier de verre,* glass-paper, sand-paper; *papier Joseph,* filter paper; *papier hygiénique,* toilet paper; *papier libre,* unstamped paper; *papier long,* long-dated bills; *papier timbré,* stamped paper; *payer en papier,* to pay in bills; *rayez cela de vos papiers,* don't count on it; *réglé comme du papier à musique* [MUSIQUE]; *sur le papier,* on paper, in the air.
papier-monnaie, *n.m.* Paper-money.
papilionacé [papiljɔna'se], *a.* (*fem.* **-ée**) (*Bot.*) Papilionaceous.
papillaire [papil'lɛ:r], *a.* Papillary.
papille [pa'pij], *n.f.* Papilla.
papillifère [papilli'fɛ:r], *a.* Papilliferous.
papillon [papi'jɔ̃], *n.m.* Butterfly; fish-tail burner; detachable inset (in a book etc.);

(*Naut.*) sky-sail. (*Cost.*) *Nœud papillon* or (*fam.*) *papillon*, butterfly bow; *papillon de nuit*, moth; *vis à papillon*, thumb screw.
papillonner, *v.i.* To flutter about, to hover; (*fig.*) to trifle, to flirt.
papillotage [papijɔ'taːʒ], *n.m.* Blinking (of the eyes); dazzle, glitter, tinsel (of style); (*Print.*) mackling, slurring.
papillote [papi'jɔt], *n.f.* Curl-paper; bonbon, sweetmeat in paper; oiled paper for cooking. *Côtelette en papillote*, cutlet fried in buttered paper; *fer à papillotes*, curling-irons; *papillotes à pétard*, Christmas crackers. **papillotement**, *n.m.* Flickering. **papilloter**, *v.t.* To put (hair etc.) in paper.—*v.i.* To blink; to dazzle, to be gaudy; (*Print.*) to show a slur.
papisme [pa'pism], *n.m.* Papism, popery. **papiste**, *n.* Papist.—*a.* Popish. **papistique**, *a.* Papistic.
papotage [papɔ'taːʒ], *n.m.* Idle talk.
papoter [papɔ'te], *v.i.* To prattle, to chatter.
papou [pa'pu], *a.* and *n.* (*fem.* **-oue**) Papuan.
Papouasie [papwa'zi], *f.* Papua.
papouille [pa'puj], *n.f.* (*slang*) Caress, cuddle.
pappeux [pa'pø], *a.* (*fem.* **-euse**) (*Bot.*) Pappous, downy.
papule [pa'pyl], *n.f.* Papula, pimple. **papuleux**, *a.* (*fem.* **-euse**) Papulous.
papyracé [papira'se], *a.* (*fem.* **-ée**) Papyraceous, thin and dry like paper.
papyrus [papi'ryːs], *n.m.* Papyrus.
pâque [paːk], *n.f.* Passover (among Jews).
paquebot [pak'bo], *n.m.* Packet-boat, packet, steamer, liner.
pâquerette [paˈkrɛt], *n.f.*, or *petite marguerite*, Daisy.
Pâques [paːk], *n.m.* Easter. *Semaine de Pâques*, Easter-week. In the following expressions *Pâques* is feminine plural: *faire ses pâques*, to receive the Sacrament (at Easter); *Pâques closes*, Low-Sunday; *Pâques fleuries*, Palm-Sunday.
paquet [pa'kɛ], *n.m.* Package, bundle, parcel; mail; mail-boat, packet; slander; (*fig.*) dowdy, clumsy lout; (*Print.*) slip. *Donner à quelqu'un son paquet*, to give someone the sack, to silence someone with the plain truth; *faire ses paquets*, to pack up, to be off; *faire un paquet*, to make up a parcel; *hasarder* or *risquer le paquet*, to chance it; *recevoir son paquet*, to get the sack; *un paquet de mer*, a green (*or* heavy) sea; *un paquet de nerfs*, a bundle of nerves.
paquetage, *n.m.* (*Mil.*) (Soldier's) pack.
paqueter, *v.t.* To tie up in a parcel, to make into a packet, parcel, etc.
paqueteur, *n.m.* (*fem.* **-euse**) Packer.
paquetier, *n.m.* (*Print.*) Slip compositor.
pâquis [pa'ki], *n.m.* Pasturage.
par [paːr], *prep.* By, through, out of, from; about, in, into; for, for the sake of. *De par le roi*, in the king's name; *distribuer par chapitres*, to divide into chapters; *donner tant par tête*, to give so much per head; *elle finit par le persuader*, she at length persuaded him; *il a fait cela par crainte*, he did it from fear; *il entra par la porte*, he entered by the door; *il faut en passer par là*, you must put up with it; *jeter par la fenêtre*, to throw out of the window; *par aventure*, by chance; *par-ci* [CI]; *par deçà*, this side; *par dedans* [DEDANS]; *par dehors*, without; *par delà*, that

side; *par derrière* [DERRIÈRE]; *par devant*, before, forwards; *par ici* [ICI]; *par-là* [LÀ]; *par le bas* or *par en bas*, at the bottom, downwards; *par le haut* or *en haut*, towards the top, upwards; *par passe-temps*, by way of diversion; *par soi-même*, by oneself, unaided; *par trop*, far too much; *par une belle matinée*, on a fine morning; *prenez-le par le bras*, take his arm; *se marier par amour*, to marry for love; *se promener par les rues*, to walk about the streets.
parabase [para'baːz], *n.f.* Parabasis.
parabellum [parabe'lɔm], *n.m.* Automatic pistol.
parabole [para'bɔl], *n.f.* Parabola; parable. *Les paraboles de Salomon*, the Book of Proverbs.
parabolique, *a.* Parabolic.
paracentèse [parasɑ̃'tɛːz or parasɛ̃'tɛːz], *n.f.* (*Surg.*) Paracentesis.
parachèvement [paraʃɛv'mɑ̃], *n.m.* Finishing, completion.
parachever, *v.t.* To finish, to complete.
parachronisme [parakrɔ'nism], *n.m.* Parachronism.
parachutage [paraʃy'taːʒ], *n.m.* Parachuting; parachute landing.
parachute, *n.m.* Parachute. *Sauter en parachute*, to bale out.
parachuter, *v.t.*, *v.i.* To parachute, to drop (by parachute).
parachutiste, *n.* Parachutist, paratrooper. *Les parachutistes*, the paratroops.
paraclet [para'klɛ], *n.m.* Paraclete, comforter.
parade [pa'rad], *n.f.* Parade, show, display; pomp, state, pageantry; (*Fenc.*) parry; burlesque scenes (outside shows at fairs). *Faire parade de son savoir*, to show off one's knowledge; *habit de parade*, state, court, or official dress; *lit de parade*, bed for lying-in-state; *ne pas être prompt à la parade*, to be a bad hand at repartee. **parader**, *v.i.* To show off. *Faire parader un cheval*, to show off the paces of a horse.
paradigme [para'digm], *n.m.* Paradigm.
paradis [para'di], *n.m.* Paradise; heaven; (*Theat.*) upper gallery, the gods; (*Hort.*) apple-stock used for grafting on. *Ce lieu-ci est un vrai paradis*, this place is a heaven on earth; *le paradis terrestre*, earthly paradise; *il ne l'emportera pas en paradis*, I will have my revenge sooner or later; *oiseau de paradis*, bird of paradise.
paradisiaque, *a.* Paradisiac.
paradisier, *n.m.* Bird of paradise.
paradoxal [paradɔk'sal], *a.* (*fem.* **-ale**, *pl.* **-aux**) Paradoxical. **paradoxalement**, *adv.* Paradoxically. **paradoxe**, *n.m.* Paradox.
parafe or **paraphe** [pa'raf], *n.m.* Paraph; flourish (after one's signature); initials and flourish. **parafer** or **parapher**, *v.t.* To paraph, to put one's flourish, dash, or initials to.
paraffine [para'fin], *n.f.* Paraffin. **paraffiner**, *v.t.* To paraffin.
parafoudre [para'fudr], *n.m.* Lightning-protector.
parage (1) [pa'raːʒ], *n.m.* Extraction, descent, lineage. *De haut parage*, of high degree.
parage (2) [pa'raːʒ], *n.m.* (usually in *pl.*) (*Naut.*) Localities, latitudes, waters. *Dans ces parages*, in these parts.

parage (3) [para:ʒ], *n.m.* Paring (of beam); dressing (of ground, cloth).

paragénésie [paraʒene'zi], *n.f.* Paragenesis.

paragraphe [para'graf], *n.m.* Paragraph.

paraître [pa'rɛ:tr], *v.i. irr.* (*pres.p.* **paraissant**, *p.p.* **paru**; *conjugated like* CONNAÎTRE) To appear, to make one's appearance; to come into sight, to become visible; to heave in sight; to prove, to turn out to be; to make a show, to make some figure; to seem, to look like; to come out, to be published. *À ce qu'il paraît*, as it would seem; *ces raisons paraissent bonnes*, these reasons seem plausible; *chercher à paraître*, to try to cut a figure; *faire paraître*, to show, to demonstrate, to publish; *il n'y paraît pas*, one would not have thought it; *il paraît que vous avez tort*, it seems that you are wrong; *quand votre ouvrage paraîtra-t-il?* when will your work be published? *sans qu'il y paraisse*, without its being seen.

paralipse [para'lips], *n.f.* Paralipsis.

parallactique [paralak'tik], *a.* Parallactic.

parallaxe, *n.f.* Parallax.

parallèle [para'lɛl], *a.* Parallel.—*n.f.* Parallel line; (*Fort.*) parallel, trench.—*n.m.* Parallel, comparison, simile; (*Geog.*) parallel of latitude. *Mettre en parallèle*, to draw a parallel between. **parallèlement,** *adv.* In a parallel way or direction.

parallélépipède or **parallélipipède,** *n.m.* Parallelepiped.

parallélisme, *n.m.* Parallelism.

parallélogramme, *n.m.* Parallelogram. *Parallélogramme articulé*, parallel motion.

paralogisme [paralɔ'ʒism], *n.m.* Paralogism.

paralysateur [paraliza'tœ:r] (*fem.* **-trice**) or **paralysant** (*fem.* **-ante**), *a.* Paralysing.

paralyser [parali'ze], *v.t.* To paralyse; (*fig.*) to render powerless. **paralysie,** *n.f.* Paralysis, palsy. *Attaque de paralysie*, paralytic stroke. **paralytique,** *a.* and *n.* Paralytic.

paramètre [para'mɛtr], *n.m.* Parameter.

paramilitaire [paramili'tɛ:r], *a.* Paramilitary, semi-military.

paraneige [para'nɛ:ʒ], *n.m.* Snow-shield.

parangon [parɑ̃'gɔ̃], *n.m.* Model, type, paragon; comparison, parallel; flawless precious stone. *Gros parangon*, (*Print.*) double pica; *petit parangon*, (*Print.*) paragon.

parangonnage, *n.m.* (*Print.*) Ranging. **parangonner,** *v.t.* (*Print.*) To adjust, to range.

paranoïa [parano'ja], *n.f.* (*Med.*) Paranoia. **paranoïaque,** *a.* and *n.* Paranoiac.

parapet [para'pɛ], *n.m.* Parapet, breastwork.

paraphe, parapher [PARAFE].

paraphernal [parafɛr'nal], *a.* (*fem.* **-ale**, *pl.* **-aux**) (*Law*) Paraphernal. *Biens paraphernaux*, paraphernal property, *paraphernalia.

paraphrase [para'frɑːz], *n.f.* Paraphrase, amplification. **paraphraser,** *v.t.* To paraphrase; to amplify. **paraphraseur,** *n.m.* (*fam.*) (*fem.* **-euse**) Paraphraser, verbose writer.

paraplégie [paraple'ʒi], *n.f.* (*Med.*) Paraplegia. **paraplégique,** *a.* Paraplegic.

parapluie [para'plɥi], *n.m.* Umbrella; hood (of chimney). *Manche de parapluie*, umbrella-handle; *monture de parapluie*, umbrella-frame; *ouvrir son parapluie*, to put up one's umbrella.

parasélène [parase'lɛːn], *n.f.* (*Meteor.*) Paraselene.

parasite [para'zit], *n.m.* Parasite; (*fig.*) hanger-on, sponger.—*a.* Parasitic; superfluous; extraneous.—*n.m.* (*pl.*) (*Rad.*) Atmospherics. **parasitisme,** *n.m.* Parasitism.

parasol [para'sɔl], *n.m.* Parasol, sunshade. *Pin parasol*, umbrella pine.

parasoleil, *n.m.* (*Phot.*) Hood, lens-hood.

parasolerie [parasɔl'ri], *n.f.* Umbrella factory or shop.

paratonnerre [paratɔ'nɛːr], *n.m.* Lightning-conductor.

paratyphoïde [paratifɔ'id], *n.f.* and *a.* (*Med.*) Paratyphoid (fever).

paravent [para'vɑ̃], *n.m.* Folding-screen; (*fig.*) screen. *Chinois de paravent*, grotesque figure, guy; *comédie de paravent*, play that requires only a few screens for scenery.

parbleu! [par'blø], *int.* By Jove! Why, of course!

parc [park], *n.m.* Park; pen. *Parc à bestiaux*, cattle-pen; *parc à chevaux*, paddock; *parc à huîtres*, oyster-bed; *parc à moutons*, sheep-fold; *parc à voitures*, car park; *parc d'artillerie*, artillery-park; *parc d'attractions*, fun fair.

parcage, *n.m.* Folding (of sheep); penning (of cattle); laying down (of oysters); parking (of cars).

parcellaire [parsɛ'lɛːr], *a.* By small portions, by lots, in detail. *Cadastre parcellaire*, register of lands divided into small portions.

parcelle [par'sɛl], *n.f.* Part, portion; particle; piece (of land). **parceller,** *v.t.* To portion or parcel out.

parce que [parsə'kə, pars'kə], *conj.* Because, as.—*n.m. inv. Les pourquoi et les parce que*, the whys and the wherefores.

parchemin [parʃə'mɛ̃], *n.m.* Parchment; (*fam.*) diploma; (*pl.*) titles of nobility. *Papier parchemin*, vegetable parchment; *visage de parchemin* or *parcheminé*, shrivelled face. **parcheminé,** *a.* (*fem.* **-ée**) Parchment-like, shrivelled. **parcheminer,** *v.t.* To give a parchment finish (*or* appearance) to. **se parcheminer,** *v.r.* To shrivel up. **parcheminerie,** *n.f.* Parchment making; parchment-trade. **parcheminier,** *n.m.* (*fem.* **-ière**) Parchment-maker.

parcimonie [parsimɔ'ni], *n.f.* Parsimony. **parcimonieusement,** *adv.* Parsimoniously. **parcimonieux,** (*fem.* **-ieuse**) Parsimonious, stingy.

(C) **parcomètre** [parko'mɛtr], *n.m.* Parking-meter.

parcourir [parku'riːr], *v.t. irr.* (*pres.p.* **parcourant**, *p.p.* **parcouru**; *conjugated like* COURIR) To travel through; to run over, to scour; to traverse, to go through; to run through, to pervade; to survey, to look over; to peruse, to glance through (a book). *Il a parcouru toute l'Asie*, he has travelled all over Asia; *parcourir des yeux*, to glance over; *parcourir la ville*, to scour the town.

parcours, *n.m.* Line, course, road, way; route (of bus); distance; green (golf course). *Faire le parcours entre*, to ply between.

pard [paːr], *n.m.* Serval, African tiger-cat.

par-dessous [pardə'su], *prep. adv.* Under, beneath, underneath. (*fam.*) *Faire (un travail) par-dessous la jambe*, to do (work) all anyhow.

par-dessus [pardə'sy], *prep. adv.* Over, above. *Il sauta par-dessus le mur*, he jumped over the wall; *par-dessus le marché*, into the bargain.

pardessus [pardə'sy], *n.m.* Overcoat, greatcoat.

par-devant [pardə'vã], *prep. Par-devant notaire*, (deed signed) before a notary.

pardi [par'di], **pardieu, pardienne,** or **pardine,** *int.* By Jove!

pardon [par'dɔ̃], *n.m.* Pardon, forgiveness; pilgrimage (in Brittany); (*pl.*) indulgences. *Je vous demande pardon*, I beg your pardon; *mille pardons!* I am so sorry; *pardon!* excuse me.

pardonnable, *a.* Pardonable, excusable.

pardonner, *v.t.* To pardon, to forgive; to overlook; to excuse; to spare. *Dieu me pardonne!* God forgive me! *pardonner les offenses*, to forgive offences.—*v.i.* To pardon, to excuse (*d*); to spare (*d*). *Pardonnez à ma franchise de vous dire cela*, excuse my frankness in telling you that; *pardonnez-moi si*, excuse me if.

pardonneur, *n.m.* (*fem.* -**euse**) Pardoner.

paré [pa're], *a.* (*fem.* -**ée**) Adorned, trimmed, got up; dressed; (*Naut.*) ready, clear. *Bal paré*, full-dress ball; *cidre paré*, fermented cider; *côtelette parée*, trimmed chop; *titre paré*, (*Law*) title in due form.

pare-boue [par'bu], *n.m. inv.* Mud-guard.

pare-brise, *n.m. inv.* Wind-screen (of motor-car).

pare-chocs, *n.m. inv.* Fender, bumper (of car).

pare-éclats, *n.m. inv.* Screen for shell splinters.

pare-étincelles, *n.m. inv.* Fire-screen.

pare-feu, *n.m. inv.* Fire-belt (in forest).

parégorique [paregɔ'rik], *a.* Paregoric (elixir).

pareil [pa'rɛːj], *a.* (*fem.* -**eille**) Like, equal, similar; such, like that; same, identical. *À pareil jour*, on the same day; *à pareille heure*, at the identical hour; *comment pouvez-vous me dire chose pareille!* how can you tell me such a thing! *je n'ai rien vu de pareil*, I never saw the like.—*n.* Similar or equal person. *N'avoir pas son pareil* or *sa pareille*, to be without his or her equal.—*n.m.* Equal, fellow, match. *C'est un homme sans pareil*, he has not his equal; *il a trouvé son pareil*, he has found his match; *j'ai le pareil*, I have the fellow to it.—*n.f.* The like, tit for tat. *Je vous souhaite la pareille*, the same to you; *rendre la pareille*, to give tit for tat. **pareillement,** *adv.* In like manner; likewise, also.

parélie [PARHÉLIE].

parelle [pa'rɛl], *n.f.* Parella (lichen); yellow dock.

parement [par'mã], *n.m.* Ornament; facing (of dress); cuff (of sleeves); large sticks (of a faggot); (*Build.*) facing of stone or wall; kerb-stone.

parementer, *v.t.* (*Build.*) To face.

parenchyme [parã'ʃim], *n.m.* Parenchyma.

parent [pa'rã], *n.m.* (*fem.* **parente**) Relative, kinsman, kinswoman; (*pl.*) parents, father and mother; relations, relatives. *Être parent*, to be related; *parents par alliance*, related by marriage; *parent paternel*, relation on the father's side; *parents spirituels*, god-parents; *proche parent*, near relative; *ses parents et amis*, his kith and kin; *son plus proche parent*, his next of kin.

*parentage, *n.m.* Parentage; relations, kindred.

parenté, *n.f.* Relationship, consanguinity, kinship; kindred, relatives, kith and kin, family.

parenthèse [parã'tɛːz], *n.f.* Parenthesis, digression; (*Print.*) bracket. *Entre parenthèses*, in parenthesis; *ouvrir, fermer la parenthèse*, to open, close brackets; *par parenthèse*, incidentally.

parer (1) [pa're], *v.t.* To adorn, to set off, to deck, to embellish; to dress, to attire, to trim; (*Box.*) to parry, to ward off; to screen, to shelter, to guard; (*Naut.*) to clear, to get ready. *Il est assez paré de sa bonne mine*, his good looks set him off sufficiently; *parer du cuir*, to dress leather; *parer sa marchandise*, to set off one's goods; *parer un cap*, (*Naut.*) to clear a cape; *parer un coup*, to ward off a blow; *parer une ancre*, to clear an anchor; *parer un enfant*, to fit out a child; *parer un sabot de cheval*, to pare a horse's hoof.—*v.i.* To fend, to guard (*d*). *On ne peut pas parer à tout*, one can't guard against everything. **se parer,** *v.r.* To adorn oneself; to deck oneself out; to make a show, to boast; to screen, to guard oneself, to ward off. *Elle se pare d'une manière ridicule*, she decks herself out in a ridiculous manner.

*parer (2) [pa're], *v.t.* To stop, to rein in (a horse).—*v.i.* To stop, to pull up (of a horse).

*parère [pa'rɛːr], *n.m.* (*Law*) Expert opinion (of merchants etc. on matters of commercial law, usage, etc.).

parésie [pare'zi], *n.f.* Slight palsy.

pare-soleil [parsɔ'lɛːj], *n.m. inv.* (*Motor.*) Visor.

paresse [pa'rɛs], *n.f.* Idleness, sloth, laziness, indolence; weakness. *Paresse d'esprit*, sluggishness of intellect. **paresser,** *v.i.* To idle, to fritter away one's time. **paresseusement,** *adv.* Lazily, idly, slothfully.

paresseux, *a.* (*fem.* -**euse**) Lazy, idle, slothful; sluggish, slow (of the bowels etc.).—*n.* Sluggard, lazy fellow.—*n.m.* (*Zool.*) Sloth (both two-toed and three-toed).—*n.f.* Ready-made coiffure; laceless corset.

pareur [pa'rœːr], *n.m.* (*fem.* -**euse**) Finisher.

parfaire [par'fɛːr], *v.t. irr.* (*pres.p.* **parfaisant,** *p.p.* **parfait;** *conjugated like* FAIRE) To complete, to perfect; to make up (a sum).

parfait [par'fɛ], *a.* (*fem.* -**te**) Perfect, faultless; finished, complete, full; (*colloq.*) capital, first-rate. *Parfait!* splendid!—*n.m.* Perfection; (*Gram.*) perfect. *Un parfait au café*, a coffee ice-cream. **parfaitement,** *adv.* Perfectly, completely; exactly, just so, decidedly.

parfilage [parfi'laːʒ], *n.m.* Unravelling; unravelled gold or silver threads.

parfiler, *v.t.* To unravel, to undo the threads of.

parfois [par'fwa], *adv.* Sometimes, occasionally, now and then.

parfondre [par'fɔ̃ːdr], *v.t.* To fuse (colours in enamel etc.).

parfum [par'fœ̃], *n.m.* Perfume, odour, scent, fragrance; flavour, bouquet (of wines etc.).

parfumer, *v.t.* To perfume, to sweeten, to scent; to fumigate. **se parfumer,** *v.r.* To use perfumes, to scent oneself.

parfumerie, *n.f.* Perfumery.

parfumeur, *n.m.* (*fem.* -**euse**) Perfumer.

parhélie or **parélie** [pare'li], *n.m.* Parhelion, mock-sun.

pari [pa'ri], *n.m.* Bet, wager, stake. *Faire un pari*, to lay a bet; *pari mutuel*, totalizator system, *(fam.)* tote; *tenir un pari*, to take a bet.

paria [pa'rja], *n.m.* Pariah, outcast.

pariade [pa'rjad], *n.f.* Pairing; pairing-time; couple (of partridges etc.).

parier [pa'rje], *v.t.* *(conjugated like* PRIER*)* To bet, to wager, to stake; to undertake to say, to warrant, to lay. *C'est à parier dix contre un*, it is ten to one; *il y a à parier*, the odds are; *j'en parierais ma tête*, I would stake my head upon it.

pariétaire [parje'tɛːr], *n.f.* *(Bot.)* Pellitory.

pariétal [parje'tal], *a.* *(fem.* -ale, *pl.* -aux) Parietal.—*n.m.* Parietal bone.

parieur [pa'rjœːr], *n.m.* *(fem.* -ieuse) Punter; *(spt.)* backer.

parigot [pari'go], *n.m.* *(fem.* -ote) *(slang)* Parisian.

Paris [pa'ri], *m.* Paris. *Article de Paris*, fancy goods.

Pâris [pɑ'ris], *m.* *(Greek Lit.)* Paris.

parisette [pari'zɛt], *n.f.* Herb Paris, true love.

parisien [pari'zjɛ̃], *a.* and *n.* *(fem.* -ienne) Parisian.

parisyllabe [parisi'lab] or **parisyllabique**, *a.* Parisyllabic.

paritaire [pari'tɛːr], *a.* Equally representative of employers and employees (used in *Commission paritaire*).

parité [pari'te], *n.f.* Parity, likeness, equality; comparison, parallel; *(Fin.)* equivalence (of exchange), par.

parjure [par'ʒyːr], *n.m.* Perjury, false oath.—*n.* Perjurer.—*a.* Perjured, forsworn. **se parjurer**, *v.r.* To perjure or forswear oneself.

parkériser [parkeri'ze], *v.t.* *(Metal.)* To parkerize.

parking [par'kiŋ], *n.m.* Parking place, car park.

*parlage [par'laːʒ], *n.m.* Empty talk, twaddle.

parlant [par'lɑ̃], *a.* *(fem.* -ante) Speaking; *(colloq.)* talkative, chatty; expressive (of portraits etc.); *(Her.)* allusive, canting. *Ce portrait est parlant*, that is a speaking likeness; *cet homme est peu parlant*, that man is very reticent; *film parlant*, *(Cine.)* sound film; *l'horloge parlante*, 'Tim'. **parlé**, *a.* *(fem.* -ée) Spoken, colloquial.

parlement [parlə'mɑ̃], *n.m.* Parliament; *ancient court of justice.

parlementaire, *a.* Parliamentary.—*n.m.* Bearer of a flag of truce; Parliamentarian.

parlementarisme, *n.m.* Parliamentary government.

parlementer, *v.i.* To parley, to come to terms.

parler [par'le], *v.i.* To speak to talk; to discourse, to converse, to treat *(de)*; to have meaning; to sound. *Cela parle de soi*, that is self-evident; *façon de parler*, mode of speaking; *faire parler*, to induce to speak, to make speak, to put words into the mouth of; *faire parler de soi*, to get oneself talked about; *humainement parlant*, humanly speaking; *n'en parlez à personne*, keep it to yourself; *n'en parlons plus*, let us say no more about it; *on n'en parle plus*, it is never mentioned now; *parler de tout*, to talk about everything or anything; *trop parler nuit*, least said soonest

mended; *(pop.)* *tu parles!* right! you're telling me!—*v.t.* To speak, to talk; to speak, talk, or converse about.—*n.m.* Speech, utterance; way or manner of speaking; language, accent, dialect, patois. *Avoir son franc parler*, to speak one's mind; *jamais beau parler n'écorcha la langue*, fair words are always the best, civility costs nothing. **se parler**, *v.r.* To be spoken, to be talked; to talk to oneself; to talk to each other.

parleur, *n.m.* *(fem.* -euse) Talker, speechmaker; *(Teleg.)* sounder. *Un beau parleur*, a good speaker, a glib person.

parloir, *n.m.* Parlour.

parlote or **parlotte** [par'lɔt], *n.f.* Gossip; *(Law)* debating room for lawyers in a court of justice.

Parme [parm], *n.f.* Parma.

parmentier [parmɑ̃'tje], *a.* and *n.m.* *Potage parmentier*, thick potato soup; *(hachis)* parmentier, minced meat with mashed potatoes.

parmesan [parmə'zɑ̃], *n.m.* Parmesan (cheese).

parmi [par'mi], *prep.* Among, amongst, amid, amidst.

Parnasse [par'nas], *m.* *(Geog.)* Parnassus. *Le Parnasse*, Parnassian school of French poetry.

parnassie, *n.f.*, or *gazon du Parnasse*, grass of Parnassus.

parnassien, *a.* *(fem.* -ienne) Parnassian.—*n.m.* Member of the Parnassian school of French poets.

parodie [parɔ'di], *n.f.* Parody, travesty. **parodier**, *v.t.* To parody, burlesque. **parodique**, *a.* Parodic. **parodiste**, *n.m.* Parodist, author of a parody.

paroi [pa'rwa], *n.f.* Wall; partition; inner side or surface; lining; *(Anat.)* coat, wall; *(Theat.)* flat. *Les parois de l'estomac*, the lining of the stomach; *les parois d'un vase*, the inner sides of a vase.

paroir [pa'rwaːr], *n.m.* Paring-knife.

paroisse [pa'rwas], *n.f.* Parish; parish-church; *(collect.)* parishioners. *N'être pas de la paroisse*, *(colloq.)* to be a stranger. **paroissial**, *a.* *(fem.* -iale, *pl.* -iaux) Parochial, parish. *Salle paroissiale*, parish hall. **paroissien**, *n.m.* *(fem.* -ienne) Parishioner; prayer-book. *C'est un pauvre paroissien*, he is a poor sort of a fellow.

parole [pa'rɔl], *n.f.* (Spoken) word; speech, utterance, parole, voice, tone of voice; eloquence, oratory; promise; *(cards)* no bid. *Adresser la parole à* [ADRESSER]; *avoir la parole* [AVOIR]; *céder la parole*, to decline speaking, to give up one's turn to speak; *couper la parole à quelqu'un* [COUPER]; *demander la parole*, to request permission to speak, *(Parl.)* to rise to order; *donner sa parole* [DONNER]; *engager sa parole*, to pledge one's word; *il a la parole lente*, he is slow of utterance; *il est homme de parole*, he is a man of his word; *il est prisonnier sur parole*, he is a prisoner on parole; *ils ont eu des paroles*, they have had words; *la puissance de la parole*, the power of eloquence; *parole d'honneur*, word of honour [HONNEUR]; *paroles mémorables*, notable sayings; *perdre la parole*, to lose the use of speech, to be speechless; *prendre la parole*, to begin to speak, to have one's turn to speak, to speak next; *se dédire de sa parole*, *manquer de parole*, or *manquer à sa parole*, to break one's word; (*sur*) *ma parole!* upon my word! *tenir parole* or *sa parole*, to keep one's word; *un homme d'honneur n'a que sa parole*, an honest man's word is as good as his bond.

paroli [parɔ'li], *n.m.* Double stake (at faro etc.). *Faire paroli*, to double.

parolier [parɔ'lje], *n.m.* (*fem.* **-ière**) Author of the words of a song; librettist.

paronomase [parɔnɔ'mɑːz], *n.f.* Paronomasia.

paronomasie, *n.f.* Resemblance between words of different languages.

paronyme [parɔ'nim], *n.m.* Paronym. **paronymie**, *n.f.* Paronymy. **paronymique**, *a.* Paronymous.

parotide [parɔ'tid], *n.f.* Parotid gland.—*a.* Parotid. **parotidien**, *a.* (*fem.* **-ienne**) Parotid. **parotidite**, *n.f.* Parotitis, mumps.

paroxysme [parɔk'sism], *n.m.* Paroxysm; culminating point. *Au paroxysme de la colère*, in a blazing temper.

paroxyton [parɔksi'tɔ̃], *a.m.* and *n.m.* Paroxytone.

parpaillot [parpa'jo], *n.m.* (*fem.* **-ote**) *Huguenot; infidel, unbeliever.

parpaing [par'pɛ̃], *n.m.* (*Build.*) Parpen, bond-stone; breeze-block.

parquer [par'ke], *v.t.* To fold, to pen; to enclose, to make into a park; (*Artill.*) to park; (*fig.*) to shut up. *Parquer des bœufs*, to pen cattle; *parquer des huîtres*, to lay down a bed of oysters; *parquer des moutons*, to fold sheep; *parquer sa voiture*, to park one's car. —*v.i.* To be penned up (of cattle etc.); (*Artill.*) to be parked. **se parquer**, *v.r.* To be placed in an enclosure; (*Artill.*) to be parked.

Parques [park], *f.pl.* Fates, Parcae.

parquet [par'kɛ], *n.m.* Well (of a court of justice); office of the public prosecutor; prosecuting magistrates; stockbroker's ring or enclosure; floor, inlaid floor; back (of a looking-glass). *Parquet à points de Hongrie*, herring-bone flooring; *parquet ciré*, polished floor; (*Naut.*) *parquet de chargement*, dunnage (for corn in bulk); *parquet de chauffe*, floor-plates. **parquetage**, *n.m.* Making a floor; flooring. **parqueter**, *v.t.* To floor, to lay a floor. **parqueterie**, *n.f.* Floor-making, inlaid floor. **parqueteur**, *n.m.* Floor-layer, parquet-layer.

parr [SAUMONEAU].

parrain [pɑ'rɛ̃], *n.m.* Godfather, sponsor; proposer, introducer.

parrainage, *n.m.* Sponsorship. **parrainer**, *v.t.* To sponsor.

parricide [pari'sid], *n.* Parricide.—*n.m.* Parricide (the crime).—*a.* Parricidal; (*fig.*) murderous.

parsemer [parsə'me], *v.t.* To strew, to sprinkle; to be strewn on, to stud, to spangle. *Le ciel est parsemé d'étoiles*, the sky is studded with stars; *parsemer un chemin de fleurs*, to strew a path with flowers.

parsi [par'si], *n.m.* and *a.* (*fem.* **-ie**) Parsee.

part (1) [paːr], *n.f.* Share, part, portion; collaboration, hand; concern, interest; place (where). *À part*, aside; apart from; *avoir part au gâteau* [GÂTEAU]; *billets de faire part* [BILLET]; *c'est un fait à part* [FAIT (1)]; *de part en part*, through and through; *de part et d'autre* [AUTRE (1)]; *de toutes parts*, on all

sides; *dites-lui de ma part*, tell him from me; *d'une part il considérait que*, on the one hand he considered that; *faire la part des accidents*, to make allowance for accidents; *faire la part du feu*, (*fig.*) to sacrifice something (to save the rest); *faire part de* [FAIRE]; *je le sais de bonne part*, I have it from a good source, I know it on good authority; *la part du lion*, the lion's share; *mettre à part*, to set apart; *naviguer à la part*, to go shares in a voyage; *nulle part*, nowhere; *on ne le trouve nulle part*, he is not to be found anywhere; *pour ma part*, as far as I am concerned; *prendre en bonne part*, to take in good part; *prendre en mauvaise part*, to take amiss; *prendre part à*, to participate in, to be a party to, to take part in; *quelque part*, somewhere (or other); *raillerie à part*, in good earnest, joking aside.

part (2) [paːr], *n.m.* (*Law*) Infant; birth, parturition (of animals).

partage [par'taːʒ], *n.m.* Sharing, distribution, division; share, lot, portion; apportionment; partition. *Entrer en partage à*, to share; *être le partage de*, to be the lot of; *faire le partage du butin*, to divide the spoils; *ligne de partage des eaux*, watershed, (*Am.*) divide; *partage égal*, equal division; *sans partage*, without division, undivided. **partageable**, *a.* Divisible into shares. **partageant**, *n.m.* (*fem.* **-eante**) (*Law*) Sharer. **partager**, *v.t.* To divide, to share out; to share, to participate in, to go shares in; to endow. *Il est bien partagé*, the fates have been kind to him, his bread is well buttered; *il faut partager le différend*, we must split the difference; *je partage votre joie*, I share your joy; *la nature l'a mal partagé*, nature has treated him badly; *la question partage l'opinion publique*, public opinion is divided on the matter; *les avis se trouvent partagés*, the votes are divided; *partager l'avis de*, to agree with; *partager le butin*, to share the spoils; *partagez cela entre vous*, divide that between you.—*v.i.* To share, to go halves, to receive a share. **se partager**, *v.r.* To divide, to be divided, to separate, to part; to divide one's time, affection, etc., between. **partageur**, *a.* (*fem.* **-euse**), or **partageux**, *a.* (*fem.* **-euse**) (*colloq.*) Who shares.—*n.* One who wants to share all goods and wealth.

partance [par'tãːs], *n.f.* (*Naut.*) Sailing, departure. *En partance*, about to sail, outward bound; *pavillon de partance*, Blue Peter.

partant (1) [par'tã], *adv.* Consequently, hence, therefore, thus.

partant (2) [par'tã], *n.m.* *Les partants*, the departing guests, the travellers; (*turf*) the starters.

partant (3), *pres.p.* [PARTIR].

partenaire [partə'nɛːr], *n.* Partner (at games or dancing).

parterre [par'tɛːr], *n.m.* Flower-bed; (*Theat.*) pit. (*facet.*) *Prendre un billet de parterre*, to come a cropper; *réjouir le parterre*, to please the groundlings.

parthe [part], *a.* and *n.* Parthian.

parthénogénèse [partenɔʒe'neːz], *n.f.* Parthenogenesis.

parti (1) [par'ti], *n.m.* (Political) party, side; part, cause; resolution, choice, course; profit, advantage, utility; match (marriage); (*Mil.*) detachment. *Parti pris*, set purpose; rank prejudice; *de parti-pris*, of set purpose; *à parti pris, point de conseil*, when a man's mind is set, advice is useless; *chef de parti*, leader of a party; *en prendre son parti*, to resign oneself to the inevitable; *esprit de parti*, party spirit; *être, se mettre*, or *se ranger du parti de*, to side with; *faire un mauvais parti à*, to handle (somebody) roughly, to kill him; *homme de parti*, party man; *il a épousé un bon parti*, he has made a good match; *il a pris son parti*, he has made up his mind; *il cherche à tirer parti de tout*, he endeavours to turn everything to account; *j'ai pris le parti de me taire*, I chose to be silent; *le parti conservateur*, the Conservative party; *le parti travailliste*, the Labour party; *prendre le parti de quelqu'un*, to take someone's part; *prendre parti pour (contre) quelqu'un*, to side with (against) someone; *tirer le meilleur parti de quelque chose*, to make the best of something; *tirer parti de quelque chose*, to turn something to one's advantage; *voilà le parti qu'il nous faut prendre*, this is what we must do.

parti (2) *p.p.* (*fem.* **-ie**) [PARTIR]. Gone away, gone off. (*fam.*) *Être un peu parti*, to have had a little too much to drink; *nous voilà mal partis!* we started on the wrong foot!

partiaire [par'sjɛːr], *a.* To whom part of the produce is allowed. *Colon partiaire*, farmer who pays part of his rent in kind.

partial [par'sjal], *a.* (*fem.* **-iale**, *pl.* **-iaux**) Partial, biased, unfair. **partialement**, *adv.* Partially, with partiality. **partialité**, *n.f.* Partiality, bias, one-sidedness.

participant [partisi'pã], *a.* (*fem.* **-ante**) Participating.—*n.* Participant, sharer. **participatif**, *a.* (*fem.* **-ive**) Participative. **participation**, *n.f.* Participation; share. *Cela s'est fait sans ma participation*, that was done without my knowledge; *compte en participation*, joint account; *participation aux bénéfices*, profit-sharing.

participe, *n.m.* (*Gram.*) Participle.

participer [partisi'pe], *v.i.* To partake in, to participate in, to share in (*à*); to be a party to, to have a hand in (*à*); to partake of, have the characteristics of (*de*). *Je participe à votre douleur*, I share in your sorrow; *le mulet participe du cheval et de l'âne*, the mule partakes of both the horse and the ass.

participial [partisi'pjal], *a.* (*fem.* **-iale**, *pl.* **-iaux**) (*Gram.*) Participial.

particularisation [partikylariza'sjɔ̃], *n.f.* Particularization.

particulariser, *v.t.* To particularize, to specify.

particularisme, *n.m.* Particularism.

particularité, *n.f.* Peculiarity; particular circumstance; particularity.

particule [parti'kyl], *n.f.* Particle. *La particule nobiliaire*, the word *de* before a name [see DE].

particulier [partiky'lje], *a.* (*fem.* **-ière**) Particular, peculiar; private; special, specific, express; singular, odd, extraordinary; intimate, personal. *Le cas est fort particulier*, it's a very unusual case; *l'intérêt particulier doit céder à l'intérêt général*, private interest must give way to public interest; *on lui a donné une chambre particulière*, they gave him a private room; *particulier au pays*, peculiar to the country; *secrétaire particulier*, private

secretary.—*n.m.* Private person, individual; (*colloq.*) fellow, individual.—*f.* (*pop.*) a woman. *Ce n'est qu'un simple particulier*, he is only a private person; *en particulier*, in particular, privately; *il faut le voir en particulier*, you must see him privately; *quel drôle de particulier!* what a queer cove! *que nous veut ce particulier?* what does that fellow want with us? **particulièrement**, *adv.* Particularly, in particular; peculiarly, especially. ·

partie (1) [PARTI (2)].

partie (2) [par'ti], *n.f.* Part (of a whole); line of business, particular profession; party, diversion, amusement; game, match, contest; client; opponent, adversary; (*Law*) party, contracting party; (*Comm.*) parcel, lot; (*Book-keeping*) methods of accounts, entry; (*Mus.*) part. *Air à quatre parties*, tune in four parts; *avoir affaire à forte partie*, to have to deal with a powerful opponent; *c'est partie remise*, the pleasure is only deferred; *en grande partie*, in a great measure; *en partie*, partly; *faire partie de*, to be a part of; *faire sa partie*, to play or sing one's part; *faire une partie de piquet*, to play a game of piquet; *partie civile* [CIVIL]; *fin de partie*, end game; *la partie n'est pas égale*, it is not an equal match; *les hautes parties contractantes*, the high contracting parties; *lier une partie*, to make up a party (or amusement); *ma partie*, my client (word of counsel); *par partie*, in lots; *partie carrée*, pleasure party consisting of two gentlemen and two ladies; *partie de plaisir*, pleasure trip; *partie double*, (*Book-keeping*) double entry; *partie simple*, single entry; *partie fine*, select party; *partie intéressée*, interested party, party concerned; *partie nulle*, drawn game; *prendre à partie*, to take to task; (*Law*) to sue; *quitter la partie*, to throw in one's hand; *tenir bien sa partie*, to act one's part well; *voulez-vous être de la partie?* will you join us?

partiel [par'sjɛl], *a.* (*fem.* **-ielle**) Partial, in part. *Éclipse partielle*, partial eclipse. **partiellement**, *adv.* Partially, in part; by instalments.

partir [par'tiːr], *v.i. irr.* (*pres.p.* **partant** (3), *p.p.* **parti** (2); *conjugated like* SERVIR) To set out, to start; to depart, to go, to leave, to be off; to start up, to rise (of birds); to crack, to crash, to flash forth; to die; to proceed, to commence, to emanate (from); to go off (of fire-arms). *À partir d'aujourd'hui*, from this day forward; *à partir du règne de*, from the reign of; *cela part d'un bon cœur*, that flows from good-nature; *faire partir*, to send off, to dispatch (troops), to remove (a stain etc.), to fire (gun), to start (a partridge etc.); *il est parti de zéro*, he started from scratch; *il part comme l'éclair*, he is off like lightning; *nous voilà partis*, off we go; *partir d'un éclat de rire*, to burst into a fit of laughter; *partir du pied gauche*, to step off with the left; *partir du port*, to sail.—*v.t.* *To part, to divide. *Avoir maille à partir avec*, to have a bone to pick with [see MAILLE].

partisan [parti'zã], *n.* (*fem.* **-ane**) Partisan, believer (in), supporter (of), guerilla war.

partitif [parti'tif], *n.m.* and *a.* (*fem.* **-ive**) (*Gram.*) Partitive.

partition [parti'sjɔ̃], *n.f.* (*Her.*) Partition, division; (*Mus.*) score.

partout [par′tu], *adv.* Everywhere, on all sides. *Partout où,* wherever, wheresoever. *Quatre, six partout,* all four, all six (dominoes); *trois jeux partout,* (*Ten.*) three all; (*Row.*) *Sur l'avant! dans l'eau! Partout!* Forward! Ready! Paddle! *Dénage partout!* Back all!

parturition [partyri′sjɔ̃], *n.f.* Parturition.

paru, *p.p.* (*fem.* -**ue**) [PARAÎTRE].

parulie [pary′li], *n.f.* Gumboil.

parure [pa′ry:r], *n.f.* Attire, dress, finery, ornament, head-dress; set (of jewellery, underwear); trimmings (of meat), parings. *Parure de diamants,* set of diamonds.

parution [pary′sjɔ̃], *n.f.* Appearance, publication (of book).

parvenir [parvə′ni:r], *v.i. irr.* (*conjugated like* VENIR) To attain, to reach, to succeed, to get, to make one's way; to arrive, to come to; to rise in the world. *Faire parvenir,* to send, to forward; *il parvint à le faire,* he managed to do it; *parvenir à ses fins,* to attain one's ends.

parvenu, *n.m.* (*fem.* -**ue**) Upstart, self-made person, a newly rich.

parvis [par′vi], *n.m.* Parvis, open space (in front of a church); outer sanctuary, court (of the Jewish Temple); (*Poet.*) hall, temple.

pas (1) [pɑ], *n.m. inv.* Step, pace; footprint, trace; stride, walk, gait; dance; precedence; threshold; step of stair; *passage (of arms); strait, pass; pitch, thread (of screw). *Aller à pas mesurés,* to proceed with circumspection; *aller* or *marcher à pas de loup,* to go stealthily; *à petits pas,* toddling, with short steps; *au pas,* at a walking pace; in time; *au pas! keep step! au pas gymnastique,* at the double; *avoir le pas sur quelqu'un,* to have precedence over someone; *ce n'est que le premier pas qui coûte,* beginning is the difficulty; *de ce pas,* directly, at once; *faire un faux pas,* to stumble, (*fig.*) to blunder, to put one's foot in it; *faire un pas en arrière,* to draw back a little; *hâter le pas,* or *presser le pas,* to quicken one's step; *il le suit pas à pas,* he follows him step by step; *il marche à grands pas,* he takes long strides; *il n'y a qu'un pas,* it is but a step from here; *le pas de Calais,* the Straits of Dover; *marcher à pas comptés,* to walk with measured step; *marcher d'un pas léger,* to walk with a light step; *marcher sur les pas de quelqu'un,* to tread in someone's footsteps; *marquer le pas,* to mark time; *mettre au pas,* to discipline, to bring to heel; *mettre un cheval au pas,* to walk a horse; *où allez-vous donc de ce pas?* where are you off to? *pas accéléré,* quick step, (*Mil.*) quick march; *pas à pas,* slowly, little by little; *pas de clerc,* blunder; *pas de deux,* dance for two persons; *pas de parade* or *pas de l'oie,* goose step; *pas de porte,* (*Comm.*) goodwill, premium; *pas de route!* march at ease! *ralentir le pas,* to slow down; *retourner sur ses pas,* to retrace one's steps; *sauter* or *franchir le pas,* to take a decisive step; *se tirer d'un mauvais pas,* to get out of a scrape.

pas (2) [pɑ], *adv.* No; not, not any. *Je n'ai pas de livre,* I have no book; *je ne veux pas,* I will not; *pas du tout,* not at all; *peu ou pas,* little or not at all; *presque pas,* scarcely any; *pourquoi pas?* why not?

pascal [pas′kal], *a.* (*fem.* -**ale**, *pl.* -**aux**) Paschal.

pas-d'âne [pɑ′dɑ:n], *n.m. inv.* Basket-hilt (of a sword); (*Vet.*) gag for horses, dogs, etc., (*Bot.*) colt's-foot.

pasquin [pas′kɛ̃], *n.m.* Pasquin, lampooner.

pasquinade, *n.f.* Lampoon, squib.

passable [pɑ′sabl], *a.* Passable, tolerable; (*fig.*) middling, so-so. *Une note passable,* (*sch.*) a fair mark. **passablement,** *adv.* Fairly, passably.

passade [pɑ′sad], *n.f.* Short stay or sojourn; (*fig.*) passing fancy, brief intimacy; (*Horsemanship*) passade; (*Swimming*) passing over another person in the water.

passage [pɑ′sa:ʒ], *n.m.* Passage, passing across, through, etc., transit, transition, crossing; thoroughfare, corridor, archway, lane, gateway, arcade; crossing (on railway etc.); passage (from a literary or musical work). *Attendre* or *guetter au passage,* to lie in wait for, to waylay; *barrer le passage à,* to bar the way of; *céder le passage à,* to let pass first; *droit de passage,* toll; right of way; *être de passage dans un lieu,* to make only a short stay in a place; *livrer passage à,* to make way for; *oiseaux de passage,* birds of passage; *ôtez-vous de mon passage,* stand out of the way; *passage à niveau,* level crossing; *passage clouté,* pedestrian crossing; *passage interdit,* no thoroughfare; *se faire* or *s'ouvrir un passage,* to make one's way through.

passager, *a.* (*fem.* -**ère**) Passing, transitory, fugitive, short-lived, momentary; migratory. —*n.* Passenger (by sea or air); person passing through; passer-by. (*Naut.*) *Passager de cale,* stowaway. **passagèrement,** *adv.* Transiently.

passant, *a.* (*fem.* -**ante**) Much-frequented; (*Her.*) passant. *Rue passante,* busy street.—*n.m.* Passer-by, wayfarer; runner loop, keeper (on a belt).

passation [pɑsa′sjɔ̃], *n.f.* (*Law*) Drawing up a title-deed, passing (of contracts etc.). (*Polit.*) *Passation des pouvoirs,* transfer of power.

passavant [pɑsa′vɑ̃], *n.m.* Pass, permit; transire; (*Naut.*) gangway.

passe [pɑ:s], *n.f.* Passing, passage; permit, pass; situation, state, case; (*Print.*) extra sheets, overplus; (*Fenc.*) passado, thrust; channel, narrow passage (of harbours, rivers, etc.); stake (at play); (*Ftb.*) pass; (*Cloth.*) part of a hat which surrounds the face. *Être dans une mauvaise passe,* to be in a fix; *être en passe d'avoir quelque emploi,* to be in a fair way to procure employment; *exemplaires de passe,* over copies; *il est en fort belle passe,* he has a very fine prospect before him; *maison de passe,* house of call; *mot de passe,* password; *passe d'armes,* passage of arms; *une longue passe de froid,* a long spell of cold; *la passe de caisse,* allowance to cashier to make good for errors.

passé [pɑ′se], *a.* (*fem.* -**ée**) Past, by, gone; dead, vanished; faded, worn, withered; last. *Étoffe passée,* faded material; *il a trente ans passés,* he is over thirty; *la pluie est passée,* the rain is over.—*n.m.* Past, past life, time past, things past; (*Gram.*) past tense. *Passé composé,* perfect; *passé simple,* past historic; *passé antérieur,* past anterior.—*prep.* After, beyond.

passe-carreau [pɑska′ro], *n.m.* (*pl.* **passe-carreaux**) Sleeve-board.

passe-debout, *n.m. inv.* Permit for transit.
passe-droit, *n.m.* (*pl.* **passe-droits**) Illegitimate favour, unfair promotion.
passée [pɑ'se], *n.f.* (*Hunt.*) Flight, passage (of woodcock etc.), slot (of deer). *Tuer des bécasses à la passée,* to shoot woodcocks as they fly by.
passefilage [pɑs'flœ:r], *n.m.* Darning.
passefiler, *v.t.* To darn.
passefilure, *n.f.* Darn.
passe-fleur [pɑs'flœ:r], *n.f.* (*pl.* **passe-fleurs**) (*Bot.*) Pasque-flower; rose-campion.
passe-lacet [pɑslɑ'sɛ], *n.m.* (*pl.* **passe-lacets**) Bodkin.
passement [pɑs'mɑ̃], *n.m.* Lace (of gold, silk, etc.) **passementer,** *v.t.* To trim with this.
passementerie, *n.f.* Lace, lace-making, lace-trade. **passementier,** *n.m.* (*fem.* **-ière**) Lace-maker, lace-seller.
passe-montagne, *n.m.* (*pl.* **passe-montagnes**) Balaklava helmet.
passe-parole, *n.m. inv.* (*Mil.*) Running order passed from the head to the rear of the column.
passe-partout, *n.m. inv.* Master-key; latch-key; passe-partout (frame); cross-cut saw. *L'argent est un bon passe-partout,* money opens most doors.
passe-passe, *n.m. inv.* Sleight of hand. *Tour de passe-passe,* legerdemain, conjuring trick, hocus-pocus.
passepoil, *n.m.* Piping, braid (for clothes).
passeport [pɑs'pɔ:r], *n.m.* Passport; (*Naut.*) sea-pass.
passer [pɑ'se], *v.i.* (*takes the auxiliary* AVOIR *or* ÊTRE *according as action or condition is implied*) To pass, to go; to pass on; to disappear, to pass away, (time) to elapse; to die, to expire; to fade; to become; to be considered; to be accepted, to be received, to be current; to pass muster; to call on a person; (*Law*) to come up (for trial etc.). *Ce film passe cette semaine,* this film is on this week; *cela est passé en proverbe,* that has become a proverb; *cela m'a passé de l'esprit,* that has slipped my memory; *cette fleur est passée,* that flower is faded; *en passant,* on the way, by the way; *faire passer,* to pass on, to transmit; to hand round; to while away (time); *faire passer un mal,* to cure an illness; *il a passé par de rudes épreuves,* he has gone through painful experiences; *il faut en passer par là,* we must submit, it must be endured; *il faut y passer,* we must put up with it; *il passera un jour par mes mains,* some day or other he will fall into my hands; *il vient de passer,* he has just died; *je passerai chez vous demain,* I will call on you tomorrow; *la fantaisie m'en est passée,* I have no desire for it now; *laisser passer,* to overlook; *mes beaux jours sont passés,* my best days are over; *passer devant une maison,* to pass a house; *passer outre,* to go on, to proceed, to take no notice; *passer par,* to pass through; *passer pour,* to pass for, to be considered; *passez par ici,* come this way; *passez votre chemin,* go about your business; *passons à autre chose,* let us change the subject.—*v.t.* To pass; to traverse, to cross, to go over; to carry, to transport, to carry across, to ferry; to strain (liquids); to sift (flour); to put on (wearing apparel); to omit, to leave out; to overlook,

to pardon, to waive; to allow, to grant; to spend, to while away; to outlive, to go beyond, to surpass, to outstrip; (*Law*) to pass, to enter into (a contract); to take (an examination). *Il ne lui passe rien,* he shows no indulgence for him; (*Teleph.*) *je vous passe sa secrétaire,* I am putting you through to his secretary; *passer sa colère sur,* to have one's temper out on; *passer son envie,* to gratify one's desire (for a thing); *passer son habit,* to put on one's coat; *passer son temps à se divertir,* to spend one's time in amusement; *passer sous silence,* to make no mention of; *passer tout le monde au fil de l'épée,* to put everybody to the sword; *passer un examen,* to sit for *or* take an examination; *passer un soldat par les armes,* to shoot a soldier; *passez-moi cet article,* pass me that article; *passer une rivière à gué,* to ford a river; *passer un mot,* to omit a word; *passez votre chemin,* go your way, go about your business. **se passer,** *v.r.* To pass, to pass away; to fade, to decay, to fall off, to happen, to take place; to be satisfied; to do without, to dispense with. *Il ne saurait se passer de vin,* he cannot do without wine; *il se passe d'étranges choses,* strange things are going on; *je dois l'avertir de tout ce qui se passe,* I must inform him of everything that happens.
passerage [pɑs'ra:ʒ], *n.f.,* or *passerage des décombres,* Pepperwort. *Passerage cultivée* [ALÉNOIS].
passereau [pɑs'ro], *n.m.* (*pl.* **-eaux**) Sparrow. *Les passereaux,* the Passeres.
passerelle [pɑs'rɛl], *n.f.* Foot-bridge; (*Naut.*) bridge, captain's bridge; gangway.
passeresse [pɑs'rɛs], *n.f.* (*Naut.*) Reef-line.
passerine [pɑs'rin], *n.f.* (*Orn.*) Passerine, white-throat; (*Bot.*) sparrow-wort. *Passerine bleue,* indigo bird.
passerinette, *n.f.* [FAUVETTE].
passe-rose [pɑs'ro:z], *n.f.* (*pl.* **passe-roses**) Hollyhock, rose-mallow.
passe-temps [pɑs'tɑ̃], *n.m. inv.* Pastime, hobby.
passe-thé [pɑs'te], *n.m. inv.* Tea strainer.
passette [pɑsɛt], *n.f.* Small strainer.
passeur [pɑ'sœ:r], *n.m.* (*fem.* **-euse**) Ferryman, ferry-woman.
passe-velours [pɑsvə'lu:r], *n.m. inv.* [CÉLOSIE].
passe-vue [pɑs'vu], *n.m.* (*pl.* **passe-vues**) Lantern-slide carrier.
passibilité [pasibili'te], *n.f.* Liability. **passible,** *a.* Passible; liable. *Passible de prison,* liable to imprisonment.
passif, *a.* (*fem.* **-ive**) Passive; (*Comm.*) on debit side. *Dettes passives,* liabilities.—*n.m.* (*Gram.*) Passive; (*Comm.*) liabilities. *Son passif dépasse son actif,* his liabilities exceed his assets.
passiflore [pɑsi'flɔ:r], *n.f.* Passion-flower.
passion [pɑ'sjɔ̃], *n.f.* Suffering, agony; deep or strong emotion, passion, *esp.* love; (*fig.*) liking, fondness; object of this. *Avec passion,* passionately; *déclarer sa passion,* to declare one's love; *il a la passion des médailles,* he has a craze for medals; *sans passion,* dispassionately. *La Passion,* the Passion (of Christ); *la semaine de la Passion,* Passion Week; *une Passion,* a Passion sermon.
passioniste or **passionniste,** *n.* Passionist.
passionnaire, *n.m.* Passionary (book).—*n.f.* (*fam.*) Passion flower.

passionnant, *a.* (*fem.* **-ante**) Exciting, thrilling.

passionné, *a.* (*fem.* **-ée**) Passionate, impassioned; passionately fond, doting. *Amant passionné,* passionate lover; *il est passionné de musique,* he is very fond of music.

passionnel, *a.* (*fem.* **-elle**) Under the influence of the passions, especially love. *Crime passionnel,* crime due to jealous love.

passionnément, *adv.* Passionately, fondly.

passionner, *v.t.* To impassion, to interest deeply, to excite. **se passionner,** *v.r.* To be impassioned; to become enamoured of, to have an intense desire for; to take a deep interest in (*de* or *pour*); to be wild with rage. *Vous vous passionnez trop,* you are too ardent, you get too worked up. **passionnette,** *n.f.* Passing fancy.

passivement [pasiv'mã], *adv.* Passively.

passiveté or **passivité,** *n.f.* Passivity.

passoire [pɑ'swa:r], *n.f.* Strainer. *Passoire à légumes,* colander.

pastel [pas'tɛl], *n.m.* Pastel, crayon. (*Bot.*) *Pastel des teinturiers* or *guède,* woad. **pastelliste,** *n.* Pastellist.

pastèque [pas'tɛk], *n.f.* Water-melon.

pasteur [pas'tœ:r], *n.m.* Shepherd; pastor, (Protestant) minister; clergyman. *Le Bon Pasteur,* The Good Shepherd, Jesus Christ.

pasteurisation [pastœriza'sjɔ̃], *n.f.* Pasteurization, sterilization.

pasteuriser, *v.t.* To pasteurize, to sterilize (milk).

pastiche [pas'tiʃ], *n.m.* Pasticcio, pastiche; imitation (of an author etc.); (*Mus.*) medley.

pasticher, *v.t.* (*Art, Lit., Mus.*) To imitate.

pasticheur, *n.m.* (*fem.* **-euse**) Imitator.

pastille [pas'ti:j], *n.f.* Pastille; lozenge; pellet; rubber patch (for tubes of tyre).

pastis [pas'tis], *n.m.* Aniseed alcoholic drink; (*fam.*) mess, muddle.

pastoral [pastɔ'ral], *a.* (*fem.* **-ale,** *pl.* **-aux**) Pastoral.—*n.f.* Pastoral (play or poem). **pastoralement,** *adv.* Pastorally. **pastorat,** *n.m.* Pastorate. **pastoureau,** *n.m.* (*pl.* **-eaux**) Shepherd boy. **pastourelle,** *n.f.* Shepherd girl; a medieval verse-form; 4th figure of quadrille.

pat [pat], *n.m.* and *a. inv.* (*Chess*) Stalemate.

patache [pa'taʃ], *n.f.* *(Naut.)* *Revenue-cutter; *barge; public conveyance without springs; (*colloq.*) rickety old coach.

patachon, *n.m.* Captain, steersman, or driver of a *patache;* coach-driver. *Vie de patachon,* knockabout life, jolly life.

patagon [pata'gɔ̃], *a.* and *n.m.* (*fem.* **-onne**) Patagonian. **Patagonie,** *f.* Patagonia.

patapouf [pata'puf], *int.* *Faire patapouf,* to fall flop.—*n.m. Gros patapouf,* fat lump of a man, fatty.

pataquès [pata'kɛs], *n.m.* (*colloq.*) Fault which consists in making liaison with *z* instead of with *t,* or vice versa; dreadful slip, bloomer.

patarafe [pata'raf], *n.f.* (*colloq.*) Scrawl.

pataras [pata'rɑ], *n.m.* (*Naut.*) Swifter, or extra shroud. **patarasse,** *n.f.* Reaming iron.

patate [pa'tat], *n.f.* Batata; sweet potato; (*pop.*) potato, spud; bumpkin.

patati (*only used in the following phr.*) *Et patati et patata,* and so on and so forth.

patatras [pata'tra] *int.* Crack! slap! bang!

pataud [pa'to], *n.m.* (*fem.* **-aude**) Pup with large paws; (*fig.*) lout, clumsy fellow.—*a.* Awkward, clumsy.

patauger [pato'ʒe], *v.i.* To splash, to flounder; (*fig.*) to become entangled, to make a mess of anything.

patchouli [patʃu'li], *n.m.* Patchouli.

pâte [pɑ:t], *n.f.* Paste; dough, batter; (*fig.*) constitution, temper, kind, sort; (*Print.*) pie. (*fam.*) *C'est une bonne pâte,* he is a good-natured fellow; *mettre la main à la pâte,* to do a thing oneself; *peindre en pleine pâte,* to lay on the paint (without oil); *vivre comme un coq en pâte,* to live like a fighting cock. *Pâtes alimentaires,* various dried pastes such as macaroni, vermicelli, etc. **pâté,** *n.m.* Pie, pasty, patty, pâté; blot (of ink); block (of buildings); (*Print.*) pie. *Faire un pâté,* to make a pie, (*fig.*) to make a blot; *pâté de foie gras,* goose liver pâté; *pâté de venaison,* venison pasty; *petit pâté,* patty. **pâtée,** *n.f.* Mash (to fatten poultry), hash; mess (for dogs or cats), bran-mash, (*pop.*) coarse food.

patelette [pat'lɛt], *n.f.* (*Mil.*) Flap, or pocket in the flap (of the pack).

patelin [pa'tlɛ̃], *a.* (*fem.* **-ine**) Smooth-tongued, wheedling. *Air patelin,* wheedling look.—*n.m.* Wheedler; (*fam.*) (native) village. **patelinage,** *n.m.,* or **patelinerie,** *n.f.* Wheedling. **pateliner,** *v.i., v.t.* To wheedle. **patelineur,** *n.m.* (*fem.* **-euse**) Wheedler.

patelle [pa'tɛl], *n.f.* (*Rom. Ant.*) Patella (dish or pan); (*Conch.*) limpet.

patène [pa'tɛ:n], *n.f.* Paten.

patenôtre [pat'no:tr], *n.f.* Paternoster; Lord's prayer; (*colloq.*) bead of a rosary. *Dire ses patenôtres,* to tell one's beads, to mutter prayers; *diseur de patenôtres,* hypocrite.

patent [pa'tã], *a.* (*fem.* **-ente** (1)) Patent; obvious, manifest. *Lettres patentes,* letters patent. **patentable,** *a.* Liable to pay a licence. **patente** (2), *n.f.* *Licence (for the exercise of a trade); (*Naut.*) bill of health. *Patente brute,* foul bill; *patente nette,* clean bill. **patenté,** *a.* (*fem.* **-ée**) Licensed.—*n.* Licensed dealer. **patenter,** *v.t.* To license.

pater [pa'tɛ:r], *n.m. inv.* Lord's Prayer, paternoster; great bead (of a chaplet).

patère [pa'tɛ:r], *n.f.* (*Rom. Ant.* and *Arch.*) Patera; clothes-peg, hat-peg, curtain-screw, curtain-hook.

paternalisme [paterna'lism], *n.m.* Paternalism. **paternaliste,** *a.* Paternalistic.

paterne [pa'tɛrn], *a.* Benevolent, kind.

paternel, *a.* (*fem.* **-elle**) Paternal, fatherly; on the father's side. *Amour paternel,* fatherly love; *bénédiction paternelle,* father's blessing; *parents paternels,* relations on the father's side. —*n.m.* (*pop.*) *Le paternel,* the governor, the pater. **paternellement,** *adv.* Paternally.

paternité, *n.f.* Paternity, fatherhood; (*fig.*) authorship (of a book).

pâteux [pa'to], *a.* (*fem.* **-euse**) Pasty, clammy, sticky; doughy (of bread); muddy, greasy (of roads); thick (of the voice); coated (of tongue); milky (of gems); dull, heavy (of style).

pathétique [patⵣ'tik], *a.* Pathetic, moving. —*n.m.* Pathos; the pathetic. **pathétiquement,** *adv.* Pathetically.

pathogène [patɔ'ʒɛ:n], *a.* Pathogenic. **pathogénie,** *n.f.* Pathogenesis.

pathognomonique [patɔgnɔmɔ'nik], *a.* Pathognomonic.

pathologie [patɔlɔ'ʒi], *n.f.* Pathology. **pathologique**, *a.* Pathological. **pathologiste**, *n.m.* Pathologist.

pathos [pa'tɔ:s], *n.m.* Affectation of pathos, bathos; (*fig.*) bombast, fustian, rant.

patibulaire [patiby'lɛ:r], *a.* Patibulary (like a gallows).—*n.m.* *Gallows, gibbet.

patiemment [pasja'mɑ̃], *adv.* Patiently.

patience (1) [pa'sjɑ̃:s], *n.f.* Patience, endurance; perseverance; forbearance; puzzle, game of patience; (*Mil.*) button-stick. *Être à bout de patience*, to be out of patience; *prendre son mal en patience*, to bear one's misfortune patiently; *un jeu de patience*, a puzzle, jig-saw puzzle.

patience (2) [pa'sjɑ̃:s], *n.f.* (*Bot.*) (Patience-) dock [*see also* SANG-DE-DRAGON].

patient [pa'sjɑ̃], *a.* (*fem.* **-iente**) Patient, enduring, forbearing.—*n.* Sufferer; (*Med.*) patient; condemned man (about to be executed). **patienter**, *v.i.* To have patience.

patin [pa'tɛ̃], *n.m.* Patten, skate; flange (of rail); runner, skid (of aeroplane); shoe (of wheel, brake). *Patins à roulettes*, roller skates.

patinage [pati'na:ʒ], *n.m.* Skating; skidding, slipping (of locomotive, car, etc.).

patine [pa'tin], *n.f.* Patina (of bronze).

patiner (1), *v.t.* To give a patina to.

patiner (2) [pati'ne], *v.i.* To skate; to slide, to skid (of wheels).

patinette [pati'nɛt], *n.f.* Scooter.

patineur [pati'nœ:r], *n.m.* (*fem.* **-euse**) Skater.

patinoire, *n.f.* Skating-rink.

patio [pati'o], *n.m.* (Spanish) inner court, patio.

pâtir [pɑ'ti:r], *v.i.* To suffer; to be in distress. *Vous en pâtirez*, you'll suffer for it, you'll regret it.

pâtis [pɑ'ti], *n.m.* Pasture-ground.

pâtisser [pɑti'se], *v.t.* To make pastry.—*v.t.*, *v.i.* To knead (flour). **pâtisserie**, *n.f.* Pastry, fancy cake; pastry-cook's shop or business, cake-shop, tea-rooms. **pâtissier**, *n.m.* (*fem.* **-ière**) Pastry-cook.

pâtisson [pɑti'sɔ̃], *n.m.* Squash-melon.

patoche [pa'tɔʃ], *n.f.* (*pop.*) Stroke of the cane; flabby hand, paw.

patois [pa'twa], *n.m. inv.* Patois, provincial dialect; brogue; jargon. **patoiser**, *v.i.* To speak patois or with a provincial accent.

pâton [pɑ'tɔ̃], *n.m.* Pellet (for fattening poultry).

patouille [pa'tu:j], *n.f.* (*pop.*) Mud.

patouiller, *v.i.* To walk, to splash, to drabble in the mud.—*v.t.* (*pop.*) To paw. **patouillet**, *n.m.* (*Min.*) Machine for washing ore. **patouilleux**, *a.* (*fem.* **-euse**) Muddy, slushy; (*Naut.*) choppy (sea).

patraque [pa'trak], *n.f.* Old crock.—*a.* Seedy, broken-down or worn-out (person or machine).

pâtre [pɑ:tr], *n.m.* Herdsman, shepherd.

patriarcal [patriar'kal], *a.* (*fem.* **-ale**, *pl.* **-aux**) Patriarchal. **patriarcat**, *n.m.* Patriarchate.

patriarche [patri'arʃ], *n.m.* Patriarch.

Patrice [pa'tris], *m.* Patrick.

patrice [pa'tris], *n.m.* Patrician. **patriciat**, *n.m.* Patriciate; patrician dignity; order of patricians. **patricien**, *a.* and *n.* (*fem.* **-ienne**) Patrician.

patrie [pa'tri], *n.f.* Native land, fatherland; home and country; birth-place. *Mère patrie*, motherland; *mourir pour la patrie*, to die for one's fatherland.

patrimoine [patri'mwan], *ɲ.m.* Patrimony, inheritance.

patrimonial, *a.* (*fem.* **-iale**, *pl.* **-iaux**) Patrimonial. **patrimonialement**, *adv.* By right of inheritance.

patriotard [patriɔ'ta:r], *n.m.* (*pej.*) Jingo; flag-wagger.

patriote [patri'ɔt], *a.* Patriotic (person).—*n.* Patriot. **patriotique**, *a.* Patriotic (song, speech, etc.). **patriotiquement**, *adv.* Like a patriot, patriotically. **patriotisme**, *n.m.* Patriotism.

patron (1) [pa'trɔ̃], *n.m.* Pattern, model; template. *Patron ajouré*, stencil.

patron (2) [pa'trɔ̃], *n.m.* (*fem.* **-onne**) Patron; patron saint; master, mistress, employer, principal; proprietor; chief, head; (*colloq.*) governor, boss; (*Naut.*) skipper, coxswain, master of a (small) vessel. *Je veux parler au patron*, I want to speak to the principal; *patron de chaloupe*, coxswain of a long-boat; *patron d'un bénéfice*, patron of a living. **patronage**, *n.m.* Patronage; (*Eccles.*) advowson; church club (for youth). **patronal**, *a.* (*fem.* **-ale**, *pl.* **-aux**) Patronal. *Fête patronale*, patron saint's day.

patronat, *n.m.* (*Rom. Ant.*) Protection, patronage; (*Ind.*) the management.

patronner (1) [patrɔ'ne], *v.t.* To patronize, to protect.

patronner (2) [patrɔ'ne], *v.t.* To cut out on a pattern; to stencil.

patronnesse, *n.f.* Usually *dame patronnesse* (of a charity organization), lady patroness.

patronnet, *n.m.* Pastry-cook's boy.

patronymique [patrɔni'mik], *a.* Patronymic. *Nom patronymique*, surname.

patrouille [pa'tru:j], *n.f.* Patrol. *Faire la patrouille*, to patrol. **patrouiller**, *v.i.* To patrol, to go on patrol. **patrouilleur**, *n.m.* (*Mil.*) Patrol soldier; (*Naut.*) patrol-boat.

patte [pat], *n.f.* Paw (of quadruped); foot (of bird (other than birds of prey), glass, etc.); leg (of insect); fluke (of anchor); hasp, bracket, fastening, cramp, hook, holdfast; flap (of pocket etc.); tab, strap, band (of clothes); root (of plant); cringle (of sail); (*fig.*) claws, clutches; (*slang*) human hand or foot. *Aller à pattes*, (*vulg.*) to hoof it; *avoir de la patte*, to have great ability (of a painter); *faire patte de velours*, to draw in one's claws (of cats etc.), (*fig.*) to cajole, to flatter; *graisser la patte à quelqu'un* [GRAISSER]; *marcher à quatre pattes* [MARCHER]; *mettre la patte sur quelqu'un*, to lay hands upon someone; *pattes de devant*, fore legs; *pattes de derrière*, hind legs; *pattes d'épaule*, shoulder straps; *pattes de lapin*, short side-whiskers; *pattes de mouches*, bad writing, scrawl; *tomber sous la patte de quelqu'un*, to fall into someone's clutches.

patte-d'araignée, *n.f.* (*pl.* **pattes-d'araignée**) (*Bot.*) Love in the mist.

patte-de-griffon, *n.f.* (*pl.* **pattes-de-griffon**) (*Bot.*) Stinking hellebore.

patte-de-lièvre, *n.f.* (*pl.* **pattes-de-lièvre**) (*Bot.*) Hare's-foot trefoil.

patte-d'oie, *n.f.* (*pl.* **pattes-d'oie**) (*Bot.*)

Goose-foot plant; crossroads; crow's-foot (wrinkle); dolphin (of bridge).

patte-fiche, *n.f.* (*pl.* **pattes-fiches**) Holdfast.

pattemouille [pat'mu:j], *n.f.* Pressing cloth.

pattu, *a.* (*fem.* **-ue**) Rough-footed, large-pawed; feather-legged (of pigeons etc).

pâturage [pɑty'ra:ʒ], *n.m.* Pasture, pasture-ground, grazing.

pâture [pɑ'ty:r], *n.f.* Food (for animals); pasturage; pasture; fodder. *Droit de vaine pâture,* common of pasture; *servir de pâture à,* to become the prey of; *vaine pâture,* common. **pâturer,** *v.i.* To pasture, to graze, to feed.—*v.t.* To graze on.

pâturin, *n.m.* Meadow-grass; (*Am.*) spear grass.

pâturon or **paturon** [pɑty'rɔ̃], *n.m.* Pastern.

paul [pol], *m.* Paul.

Paule [pol], *f.* Paula.

paulette [po'lɛt], *n.f.* Tax (formerly paid to the king for certain legal and fiscal offices).

Pauline [po'lin], *f.* Paulina, Pauline.

paulownia [polɔ'nja], *n.m.* (*Bot.*) Paulownia.

paume [po:m], *n.f.* Palm (of the hand); hand (a measure). *Courte paume,* close tennis (a sort of rackets); *jeu de paume,* (court) tennis, 'real' tennis; *longue paume,* a sort of open-air tennis.

paumelle [po'mɛl], *n.f.* Variety of barley; hand-leather, hand-guard; hinge.

paumer [po'me], *v.t.* (*slang*) To catch, to grab, to nab; to slap; to lose. **se paumer,** *v.r.* (*slang*) To get lost.

paumier [po'mje], *n.m.* (*fem.* **-ière**) Tennis-court keeper; maker or vendor of tennis apparatus.

paumoyer [pomwa'je], *v.t. irr.* (*conjug. like* ABOYER) To measure with the palm; (*Naut.*) to haul in, to overhaul.

paumure [po'my:r], *n.f.* Top-antlers.

paupérisme [pope'rism], *n.m.* Pauperism.

paupière [po'pjɛ:r], *n.f.* Eyelid; (*fig.*) eye, eyes. *Fermer la paupière,* to shut one's eyes, to die.

paupiette [po'pjɛt], *n.f.* (*Cook.*) Stuffed slice of meat.

pause [po:z], *n.f.* Pause, stop; (*Mus.*) rest. **pauser,** *v.i.* To pause, to make a pause.

pauvre [po:vr], *a.* Poor, needy, indigent; wretched, sorry, paltry, scanty, mean, beggarly. *C'est un pauvre poète,* he is a wretched poet; *le pauvre homme!* poor devil! *un homme pauvre,* a poor man; *pauvre d'esprit,* weak-headed; *un sujet pauvre,* a barren subject.—*n.m.* Poor person, pauper; beggar; (*pl.*) the poor. **pauvrement,** *adv.* Poorly, wretchedly.

pauvresse, *n.f.* Poor woman, beggar-woman, beggar-girl.

pauvret, *n.m.* (*fem.* **-ette**) Poor creature, poor little thing.

pauvreté, *n.f.* Poverty; wretchedness; sorry thing. *Dire des pauvretés,* to deal in platitudes; *pauvreté n'est pas vice,* poverty is no crime.

pavage [pa'va:ʒ], *n.m.* Paving; pavement.

pavane [pa'van], *n.f.* Pavan (dance). **se pavaner,** *v.r.* To strut, to stalk proudly; to flaunt.

pavé [pa've], *a.* (*fem.* **-ée**) Paved.—*n.m.* Paving-stone; paved part of road, causeway; (*fig.*) public road, street, streets. *Battre*

le pavé, to loaf about the streets; *être sur le pavé,* to be without a home, to be on the streets, to be out of work; *le haut du pavé,* the wall side; *tenir le haut du pavé,* to hold the first rank. **pavement,** *n.m.* Paving; flooring. **paver,** *v.t.* To pave. **paveur,** *n.m.* Pavior.

Pavie [pa'vi], *f.* Pavia.

pavie [pa'vi], *n.f.* Clingstone peach.

pavier [pa'vje], *n.m.* Pavia.

pavillon [pavi'jɔ̃], *n.m.* Pavilion, tent; summerhouse; wing (of a house), outhouse, lodge; (*Eccles.*) veil of the ciborium; (*Anat.*) auricle, pavilion (of the ear); horn (of old gramophone); bell (of a trumpet); (*Naut.*), flag, standard; colours. *Pavillon de banlieue,* suburban house; *pavillon de chasse,* shooting-lodge; (*Naut.*) *amener* or *baisser son pavillon,* to strike her flag (of a ship); (*fig.*) *baisser pavillon,* to yield, to surrender; *hisser le pavillon,* to hoist the flag; *pavillon de partance,* Blue Peter; *pavillon de poupe,* ensign; *pavillon de quarantaine,* yellow flag.

pavois [pa'vwa], *n.m.* Shield; (*Naut.*) bulwark; awning; flags arranged in a certain order. **pavoisement,** *n.m.* Dressing with flags. **pavoiser,** *v.t.* To deck (house) with flags, to dress (ship).

pavot [pa'vo], *n.m.* Poppy. *Pavot cornu,* yellow horned poppy; *pavot somnifère* or *des jardins,* opium poppy.

payable [pɛ'jabl], *a.* Payable.

payant, *a.* (*fem.* **-ante**) Paying; to be paid for. *Hôte payant,* paying guest; *l'entrée est-elle payante?* is there any admission charge?—*n.* Payer.

paye [pɛ:j] or **paie** [pɛ], *n.f.* Pay, wages; payment. *Haute paye,* (*Mil.*) extra pay; *jour de paye,* pay-day.

payement, paiement, *n.m.* Payment.

payer [pɛ'je], *v.t.* To pay; to pay for; to pay off, to discharge; to recompense, to reward, to requite; to expiate, to atone for. *Congés payés,* holiday with pay; *être payé pour le savoir,* to know a thing to one's cost; *il me le payera,* he shall pay for it; *payer argent comptant,* to pay cash down; *payer cher,* to pay dear, (*fig.*) to be sorry for; *payer de belles paroles,* to pay with fine speeches; *payer d'effronterie* or *payer d'audace,* to brazen it out; *payer de retour,* to pay back; *payer de sa personne,* to risk one's skin, (*fig.*) to exert oneself; *payer la note,* to foot the bill; *payer les pots cassés,* to pay for the damage; *payer les violons,* to pay the piper; *payer le tribut à la nature,* to pay the debt of nature; *payer quelqu'un d'ingratitude,* to reward someone with ingratitude; *payer rubis sur l'ongle,* to pay on the nail; *payer un dîner à quelqu'un,* to stand somebody a dinner; *se faire payer,* to get paid, to get one's money. **se payer,** *v.r.* To be paid, recompensed, or satisfied; to be able to be paid; to treat oneself to. *Cela ne peut pas se payer,* that cannot be had for money; *je me paierai un habit neuf,* I shall treat myself to a new coat; *se payer de mots,* to be all talk; *se payer la tête de quelqu'un,* to take a rise out of somebody; (*pop.*) *s'en payer,* to have a good time.

payeur, *n.m.* (*fem.* **-euse**) Payer; pay-clerk; (*Mil.*) pay-master.

pays (1) [pe'i], *n.m. inv.* Country, land; region, district; fatherland, birthplace, native land, home; the country. *Avoir le mal du pays*, to be home-sick; *battre le pays* [BATTRE]; *courir le pays*, to rove about; *être en pays de connaissance*, to be among friends; *faire voir du pays à quelqu'un*, to lead someone a dance; *il est bien de son pays!* what a simpleton! *nul n'est prophète en son pays*, no man is a prophet in his own country; *pays natal*, native country; *pays perdu*, out-of-the-way place, desert; *vin du pays*, local wine; *voir du pays*, to travel about a great deal.

pays (2) [peji, pei], *n.m.* (*fem.* **payse**) (*pop.*) Native of the same village.

paysage, *n.m.* Landscape, scenery; landscape-painting. **paysager**, *a.* Used in *jardin paysager*, landscape garden. **paysagiste**, *n.m* and *a.* Landscape-painter.

paysan [pei'zɑ̃], *a.* (*fem.* **-anne**) Rustic, peasant-like (manners).—*n.* Peasant, countryman, countrywoman, rustic; (*pl.*) the peasantry. **paysannat**, *n.m.* Peasantry. **paysannerie**, *n.f.* Rusticity; peasant people, peasantry; story on rural life.

Pays-Bas [pei'bɑ, **les**, *m.pl.* The Netherlands.

péage [pe'a:ʒ], *n.m.* Toll; toll-house. **péager**, *n.m.* (*fem.* **-ère**) Toll-gatherer.

péan or **pæan** [pe'ɑ̃], *n.m.* Paean, song of triumph or joy.

peau [po], *n.f.* (*pl.* **peaux**) Skin; hide, fell; peel, rind; leather; coating. *À fleur de peau*, skin-deep; *avoir les nerfs à fleur de peau*, to have one's nerves on edge; (*pop.*) *avoir quelqu'un dans la peau*, to have someone on the brain; *entrer dans la peau de son personnage*, (*Theat.*) to live one's part, to get inside one's part; *faire peau neuve*, to cast its slough (of serpent); (*fig.*) to turn over a new leaf; *il ne faut pas vendre la peau de l'ours* [OURS]; *marchand de peaux de lapin*, dealer in rabbit-skins; *n'avoir que la peau et les os*, to be nothing but skin and bones; *peau de soie*, Japanese silk; (*vulg.*) *une* (*vieille*) *peau*, old hag; (*pop.*) *vendre cher sa peau*, (*Mil*,) to die hard, to sell one's life dearly. *La peau!* or *peau de balle!* No! Nothing doing.

Peau-Rouge [po'ru:ʒ], *n.* (*pl.* **Peaux-Rouges**) Redskin, Red Indian.

peausserie [pos'ri], *n.f.* Peltry, skins, leather; leather-dressing; skinner's trade, fellmongery. **peaussier**, *n.m.* Skinner, skin-dresser; (*fam.*) dermatologist.—*a.m.* Pertaining to skins.

pec [pɛk], *a.m.* Newly salted (herring).

pécari [peka'ri], *n.m.* Peccary, Mexican hog.

peccable [pɛ'kabl], *a.* Peccable, faulty.

peccadille [pɛka'di:j], *n.f.* Peccadillo.

*peccant [pɛ'kɑ̃], *a.* (*fem.* **-ante**) (*Med.*) Morbid, not healthy, peccant.

pechblende [pɛʃ'blɑ̃:d *or* -ɛ̃:d], *n.f.* Pitch-blende.

pêche (1) [pɛ:ʃ], *n.f.* Peach.

pêche (2) [pɛ:ʃ], *n.f.* Fishing, angling; catch, fishery. *Aller à la pêche*, to go fishing; *canne à pêche* [CANNE]; *la pêche à la ligne*, angling; *ligne de pêche*, fishing-line; *la grande pêche*, deep-sea fishing; *la pêche miraculeuse*, the miraculous draught of fishes.

péché [pe'ʃe], *n.m.* Sin, trespass, transgression. *À tout péché miséricorde* [MISÉRICORDE]; *péché avoué est à demi pardonné*, a fault confessed is half redressed; *péché mignon*, besetting sin; *racheter ses péchés*, to redeem

one's sins. **pécher**, *v.i.* To sin, to transgress; to offend; to be deficient. *Ce n'est pas par là qu'il pèche*, that is not his failing; *il pèche par excès de zèle*, he is overdoing it; *pécher contre la bienséance*, to offend against decency.

pêcher (1) [pɛ'ʃe], *n.m.* Peach-tree.

pêcher (2) [pɛ'ʃe], *v.t.* To fish for; to fish up, to drag out; (*fig.*) to take, to get hold of, to pick up. *Où avez-vous pêché cela?* where did you get hold of that?—*v.i.* To fish, to angle. *Pêcher à la ligne*, to fish with rod and line; *pêcher en eau trouble*, to fish in troubled waters; *pêcher dans le talon* (at dominoes), to draw from the stock.

pêcheresse, *fem.* [PÉCHEUR].

pêcherie [pɛʃ'ri], *n.f.* Fishing-ground, fishery, fish-pond.

pécheur [pe'ʃœ:r], *n.m.* (*fem.* **-eresse**) Sinner.

pêcheur [pɛ'ʃœ:r], *n.m.* (*fem.* **-euse**) Fisher, angler, fisherman. *Bateau de pêcheur*, fishing-boat; *pêcheur à la ligne*, angler.

pécore [pe'kɔ:r], *n.f.* Stupid creature, blockhead; *esp.* silly girl.

pectiné [pɛkti'ne], *a.* (*fem.* **-ée**) (*Anat.*) Pectinate, comb-shaped.

pectoral [pɛktɔ'ral], *a.* (*fem.* **-ale**, *pl.* **-aux**) Pectoral.—*n.m.* Breast-plate; pectoral.

péculat [peky'la], *n.m.* Peculation, embezzlement.

pécule [pe'kyl], *n.m.* Savings, scrapings; earnings (of a prisoner); (*Mil.*) extra pay given to a soldier when leaving the army.

pécuniaire [peky'njɛ:r], *a.* Pecuniary. **pécuniairement**, *adv.* Pecuniarily.

pécunieux, *a.* (*fem.* **-ieuse**) (*colloq.*) Moneyed.

pédagogie [pedagɔ'ʒi], *n.f.* Pedagogy. **pédagogique**, *a.* Pedagogic. **pédagogue**, *n.* Pedagogue.

pédale [pe'dal], *n.f.* Pedal; treadle. (*Motor.*) *Pédale de frein*, brake pedal; *pédale d'embrayage*, clutch pedal; *pédale de mise en marche*, foot starter. **pédaler**, *v.i.* To pedal; (*colloq.*) to cycle. **pédaleur**, *n.m.* (*fem.* **-euse**) Pedaller. **pédalier**, *n.m.* Pedal-board; crank-gear (of bicycle etc.). **pédalo**, *n.m.* Pedal boat.

pédant [pe'dɑ̃], *a.* (*fem.* **-ante**) Pedantic.—*n.* Pedant. **pédanterie**, *n.f.* Pedantry. **pédantesque**, *a.* Pedantic. **pédantisme**, *n.m.* Pedantry.

pédéraste [pede'rast], *n.m.* Pederast. **pédérastie**, *n.f.* Pederasty.

pédestre [pe'dɛstr], *a.* Pedestrian, on foot. **pédestrement**, *adv.* On foot.

pédiatre [pe'dja:tr], *n.m.* (*Med.*) Pediatrist. **pédiatrie**, *n.f.* Pediatry.

pédicelle [pedi'sɛl], *n.m.* (*Bot.*) Pedicel.

pédiculaire [pediky'lɛ:r], *a.* Pedicular.—*n.f.* Lousewort. *Pédiculaire des bois*, red-rattle; wood-betony.

pédicule [pedi'kyl], *n.m.* (*Bot. and Zool.*) Pedicle. **pédiculé**, *a.* (*fem.* **-ée**) Pediculate.

pédicure, *n.* Pedicure, chiropodist.

pédimane, *a.* Pedimanous.—*n.* Pedimane.

pédologie [pedolɔ'ʒi], *n.f.* Pedology; pediatry.

pédonculaire [pedɔ̃ky'lɛ:r], *a.* (*Bot.*) Peduncular. **pédoncule**, *n.m.* Peduncle, flower-stalk. **pédonculé**, *a.* (*fem.* **-ée**) Pedunculate.

pedzouille [pɛ'dzu:j], *n.m.* (*pop.*) Peasant, bumpkin.

Pégase [pe'gɑ:z], *m.* Pegasus.

pègre [pɛ:gr], *n.f.* Light-fingered gentry.

peignage [pɛˈɲaːʒ], *n.m.* Combing, wool-combing.

peigne [pɛɲ], *n.m.* Comb; graining-tool. *Donner un coup de peigne à,* to comb (someone) hastily; *être sale comme un peigne,* to be very dirty; *peigne fin,* small-tooth comb. **peigné,** *a.* (*fem.* **-ée** (1)) Combed; (*fig.*) arranged, got up, laboured. *Mal peigné,* dirty, slovenly, ill-dressed; *un jardin bien peigné,* a well-kept garden.—*n.m.* Worsted. **peignée** (2), *n.f.* Cardful (of wool); (*pop.*) fight; thrashing.

peigner, *v.t.* To comb; to card; (*fig.*) to elaborate, to polish (style). **se peigner,** *v.r.* To comb one's hair; (*pop.*) to fight (*esp.* of women). **peignerie,** *n.f.* Comb factory, comb-trade; combing works. **peigneur,** *n.m.* (*fem.* **-euse**) Comber, wool-comber.— *n.f.* Carding-machine. **peignier,** *n.m.* Comb-maker or -seller.

peignoir, *n.m.* Dressing-gown; wrapper; (*Am.*) bath-robe.

peignures, *n.f. pl.* Combings.

peinard [pɛˈnaːr], *a.* and *n.* (*fem.* **-arde**) (*pop.*) Quiet, carefree. *Être peinard,* to be well off.

peindre [pɛ̃ːdr], *v.t. irr.* (*pres.p.* **peignant,** *p.p.* **peint**) To paint, to portray, to depict; to represent, to express, to describe, to write. *Il nous a peint sa détresse,* he described his distress to us; *peindre d'après nature,* to paint from nature; *se faire peindre,* to sit for one's portrait. **se peindre,** *v.r.* To paint oneself; to be represented or depicted. *La douleur se peignait sur son visage,* grief was depicted on his face.

peine [pɛn], *n.f.* Punishment, penalty; pain, affliction, grief, sorrow, misery; uneasiness, anxiety; labour, trouble, pains; difficulty; reluctance. *À chaque jour suffit sa peine* [CHAQUE]; *à grand'peine,* with great trouble, with much difficulty; *à peine,* hardly, scarcely; *à peine sait-il lire,* he can hardly read; *cela fait peine à voir,* it hurts one to see it; *cela n'en vaut pas la peine* or *ce n'est pas la peine,* it is not worth while; *être dans la peine,* to be in trouble; *faire de la peine à quelqu'un,* to pain someone; *il a de la peine à parler,* he is scarcely able to speak; *il a eu beaucoup de peine à en venir à bout,* he had much difficulty in bringing it about; *j'ai peine à le croire,* I can hardly believe it; *je suis en peine de savoir ce qu'il deviendra,* I am at a loss to know what will become of him; *je voudrais vous épargner cette peine,* I would willingly spare you that trouble; *la peine de mort,* death penalty; *mourir à la peine,* to die in harness, to work oneself to death; *partager les peines de,* to share the troubles of; *se mettre en peine de,* to trouble oneself to; *sous peine de mort,* under pain of death; *un homme de peine,* a common labourer.

peiné, *a.* (*fem.* **-ée**) Pained, grieved; laboured; elaborate, stiff.

peiner, *v.t.* To pain, to make uneasy, to trouble, to grieve; (*fig.*) to fatigue, to labour, to elaborate.—*v.i.* To labour, to toil; to be reluctant, to be loath.

peintre [pɛ̃ːtr], *n.m.* Painter; (*fig.*) portrayer. *Femme peintre,* woman artist; *peintre en bâtiment,* house-painter. **peinture,** *n.f.* Painting; picture; portraiture, description,

appearance; portrayal (of manners), paint, colour. *En peinture,* painted, in appearance; *peinture à l'huile,* oil-painting; *peinture au pistolet,* spray-painting; *peinture en détrempe,* distemper-painting; *peinture en mosaïque,* mosaic-painting. *Prenez garde à la peinture,* mind the paint; wet paint.

peinturer, *v.t.* To daub. **peintureur,** *n.m.* (*fem.* **-euse**) Bad painter, dauber. **peinturlurer,** *v.t.* To paint in loud colours, to daub (with bright colours).

péjoratif [peʒɔraˈtif], *a.* (*fem.* **-ive**) Pejorative.

Pékin [peˈkɛ̃], *m.* Peking.

pékin [peˈkɛ̃], *n.m.* Pekin (textile fabric); (*Mil. slang*) civilian. *Être en pékin,* to be in mufti. **pékiné,** *a.* (*fem.* **-ée**) (*Text.*) Candy-striped. **pékinois,** *a.* and *n.* (*fem.* **-oise**) Pekinese.—*n.m.* Pekinese (dog).

pelade [pəˈlad], *n.f.* Fox-evil, pelada.

Pélage [peˈlaːʒ], *m.* Pelagius.

pelage [pəˈlaːʒ], *n.m.* Coat, fur (*esp.* of colour); removing the hair (of skins).

pélagianisme [pelaʒjaˈnism], *n.m.* Pelagianism. **pélagien,** *a.* (*fem.* **-ienne**) Pelagian.

pélagique [pelaˈʒik], *a.* Pelagic (of the sea).

pelard [pəˈlaːr], *a.m.* and *n.m.* Barked (wood). *Faire du pelard,* to bark (trees).

pélargonium [pelargɔˈnjɔm], *n.m.* Pelargonium, stork's bill; (*fam.*) geranium.

pélasgien [pelazˈʒjɛ̃], *a.* (*fem.* **-ienne**) Pelasgian.

pelé [pəˈle], *a.* (*fem.* **-ée**) Bald; bare, naked; threadbare, napless; pealed.—*n.* Bald-headed person. *Il n'y avait que quatre pelés et un tondu,* there was nothing but the ragtag and bobtail.

pêle-mêle [pɛlˈmɛl], *adv.* Pell-mell, confusedly, higgledy-piggledy.—*n.m. inv.* Disorder, jumble.

peler [pəˈle], *v.t.* To skin, to peel, to pare, to strip.—*v.i.* To peel off (of the skin etc.). **se peler,** *v.r.* To come off, to peel.

pèlerin [pɛlˈrɛ̃], *n.m.* (*fem.* **-ine** (1)) Pilgrim; peregrine falcon; basking shark.

pèlerinage, *n.m.* Pilgrimage. *Aller en pèlerinage,* to go on a pilgrimage.

pèlerine (2), *n.f.* Tippet, cape (with hood).

pélican [peliˈkɑ̃], *n.m.* Pelican; holdfast bench; dentist's forceps.

pelisse [pəˈlis], *n.f.* Pelisse; fur-lined coat.

pellagre [pɛˈlaːgr], *n.f.* Pellagra.

pelle [pɛl], *n.f.* Shovel, scoop, blade (of an oar); (*fam.*) spill, cropper. *Ôter avec la pelle,* to shovel out; (*fam.*) *ramasser une pelle,* to have a spill (cyclist), to take a toss (rider), to come a cropper; *remuer l'argent à la pelle,* to have heaps of money. **pelletée,** *n.f.* Shovelful. **pelleter,** *v.t.* To shovel. **pelleron,** *n.m.* Baker's peel. **pelletage,** *n.m.* Shovelling up.

pelle-bêche, *n.f.* (*pl.* **pelles-bêches**) (*Mil.*) Portable entrenching tool (used as shovel, spade, hatchet and saw).

pelleterie [pɛlˈtri], *n.f.* Peltry, skins, furs, furriery.

pelletier, *n.m.* (*fem.* **-ière**) Furrier.

pellicule [peliˈkyl], *n.f.* Pellicle; thin skin; scurf (of scalp), dandruff; (*Phot.*) film, (*Cine.*) stock. *Pellicule inversible,* reversible stock; *pellicule vierge,* non-exposed stock.

pelliculeux, *a.* (*fem.* **-euse**) Scurfy.

Péloponnèse   pénétrer

Péloponnèse [pelɔpɔ'nɛːz], **le**, *m.* The
Peloponnesus.
pelotage [pəlɔ'taːʒ], *n.m.* Winding skeins into
balls; (*at Billiards, Tennis*), knocking the
balls about (before playing), knock-up; (*pop.*)
cuddling.
pelote [pəlɔt], *n.f.* Ball; ball of thread; pellet;
pin-cushion; star, blaze (on a horse's forehead). *Avoir les nerfs en pelote*, to be very
nervy; *faire sa pelote*, to make one's pile;
faire la pelote, (*Mil. slang*) to do punishment
drill [*see* PELOTON]; (*spt.*) *pelote basque*,
pelota.
peloter, *v.t.* To make or wind into a ball;
(*fam.*) to cuddle (a woman), to flatter.—*v.i.*
(*spt.*) To knock about, to knock up. **peloteur**,
n.m. (*fem.* **-euse**) Ballmaker; (*fam.*) cuddler.
—*n.f.* Balling-machine.
peloton [pəlɔ'tɔ̃], *n.m.* Ball; clew (of string);
cluster (of bees); lump (of fat etc.); (*Mil.*)
half a company *or* fourth of a squadron.
Le peloton, the bunch (of runners); *ils
entraient par pelotons*, they entered by
groups; *se mettre en peloton*, to roll oneself
up like a ball. (*Mil.*) *Peloton d'exécution*,
firing squad; *peloton de punition*, punishment
squad.
pelotonner, *v.t.* To wind into balls. **se
pelotonner**, *v.r.* To gather into a round
mass, to roll oneself up; to gather into knots
or groups.
pelouse [pəluːz], *n.f.* Lawn, greensward; (*turf*)
ground within the track.
pelu [pəly], *a.* (*fem.* **-ue**) Hairy.
peluche [pəlyʃ], *n.f.* Plush, cotton and woollen
drugget. **peluché**, *a.* (*fem.* **-ée**) Shaggy.
pelucher, *v.i.* To become shaggy, to wear
rough. **pelucheux**, *a.* (*fem.* **-euse**) Shaggy;
fluffy.
pelure [pə'lyːr], *n.f.* Paring; peel, skin; rind.
Papier pelure, copying paper.
pelvien [pɛl'vjɛ̃], *a.* (*fem.* **-ienne**) (*Anat.*)
Pelvic.
pelvimètre, *n.m.* Pelvimeter. **pelvis**, *n.m.*
Pelvis.
*****penaille** [pə'naːj], *n.f.* Rags. *****penaillon**,
n.m. Rag; monk.
pénal [pe'nal], *a.* (*fem.* **-ale**, *pl.* **-aux**) Penal.
pénalisation, *n.f.* (*spt.*) Penalization.
pénaliser, *v.t.* To penalize. **pénalité**, *n.f.*
Penal law; penalty.
pénates [pe'nat], *n.m. pl.* Penates, household
gods; (*fig.*) fireside, home. *Regagner ses
pénates*, to return home.
penaud [pə'no], *a.* (*fem.* **-aude**) Abashed,
sheepish, crestfallen.
penchant [pã'ʃã], *a.* (*fem.* **-ante**) Inclined,
sloping, leaning, inclined (*à*); declining.—
n.m. Declivity, slope; decline; inclination,
propensity, bent, taste. *Le penchant d'une
montagne*, the slope of a mountain; *suivre son
penchant* or *se laisser aller à son penchant*, to
follow one's bent.
penchement, *n.m.* Inclination, leaning;
bending, stoop.
pencher [pã'ʃe], *v.t.* To incline, to bend, to
cause to lean. *Pencher la tête*, to bend one's
head; *pencher un vase*, to incline a vase.—*v.i.*
To lean; to tilt, to slope, to incline, to be
disposed (*à*). *Il penche vers le nord*, it leans
to the north; *pencher du côté de*, to lean in the
direction of; *pencher vers*, to incline towards;

pencher vers la clémence, to lean towards
mercy. **se pencher**, *v.r.* To bend, to
stoop; to slope, to be inclined. *Défense de se
pencher au dehors*, do not lean out (of the
window).
pendable [pã'dabl], *a.* Deserving hanging,
abominable. *Cas pendable*, hanging matter;
un tour pendable, an abominable trick.
pendaison, *n.f.* Hanging (on the gallows),
death by hanging.
pendant [pã'dã], *a.* (*fem.* **-ante**) Pendent,
hanging; pending, depending. *Le procès est
pendant*, the case is pending; *marcher les
bras pendants*, to walk with one's arms
swinging.—*n.m.* Thing hanging, pendant;
counterpart, fellow; frog (of a sword-belt).
C'est son pendant, he is his counterpart; *il
faut un pendant à ce tableau*, this picture
needs a pendant; *pendant d'oreille*, ear-ring.
—*prep.* During. *Pendant que*, while, whilst;
pendant qu'il était là, while he was there.
pendard, *n.m.* (*fem.* **-arde**) (*colloq.*) Rascal,
rogue, jade.
pendeloque, *n.f.* Ear-drop; pendant, drop;
(*colloq.*) tatter, shred.
pendentif [pãdã'tif], *n.m.* (*Arch.*) Pendentive; pendant (of a necklace).
penderie, *n.f.* Drying-house; wardrobe.
pendiller, *v.i.* To hang loose, to dangle.
pendoir, *n.m.* Hook (of a butcher).
pendre [pãːdr], *v.t.* To hang, to hang up, to
suspend; to hang on the gallows. *Il dit pis que
pendre de vous*, he says all kinds of nasty
things about you; *il ne vaut pas la corde pour
le pendre*, he is not worth hanging; *je veux
être pendu si*, I'll be hanged if; *pendre de la
viande au croc*, to hang up meat on a hook.—
v.i. To hang, to be suspended; to hang down,
to dangle, to droop, to sag. *Autant lui en
pend à l'oreille*, he may expect to be served in
the same way; *les joues lui pendent*, his cheeks
are flabby. **se pendre**, *v.r.* To hang oneself.
pendu, *a.* (*fem.* **-ue**) Hanging, hung up,
suspended; hanged, hung. *Avoir la langue
bien pendue*, to have a glib tongue; *il est
toujours pendu à ses côtés*, he is always dangling after her.—*n.* One that has been hanged.
Avoir de la corde de pendu dans sa poche, to
have the devil's own luck; *il est sec comme un
pendu*, he is as thin as a rake [*see also* HOMME].
pendulaire [pãdy'lɛːr], *a.* Pendular.
pendule [pã'dyl], *n.f.* Clock, time-piece.
—*n.m.* Pendulum. **pendulette**, *n.f.* Small
clock, carriage-clock.
pêne [pɛːn], *n.m.* Bolt (of a lock).
Pénélope [pene'lɔp], *f.* Penelope.
pénéplaine [pene'plɛn], *n.f.* (*Geog.*) Pene-
plain.
pénétrabilité [penetrabili'te], *n.f.* Penetrability. **pénétrable**, *a.* Penetrable.
pénétrant, *a.* (*fem.* **-ante**) Penetrating;
piercing, keen; acute; searching; impressive.
Il fait un froid pénétrant, it is piercingly cold.
pénétration [penetra'sjɔ̃], *n.f.* Penetration;
acuteness, shrewdness. *Avoir une grande
pénétration d'esprit*, to have great acuteness
of mind.
pénétré, *a.* (*fem.* **-ée**) Penetrated, moved,
affected, impressed. *Pénétré de douleur*,
grieved to the heart.
pénétrer [pene'tre], *v.t.* To penetrate, to go
through; to pierce; to imbue; to pervade; to

[551]

see through, to fathom; to impress, to affect, to move. *Pénétrer le sens d'un texte*, to see through the real meaning of a text.—*v.i.* To penetrate (*dans*); to reach (*à*). *Il pénétra bien avant dans le pays*, he went a great way into the country. **se pénétrer**, *v.r.* To penetrate each other; to impress one's mind, to be impressed.

pénible [pe'nibl], *a.* Painful, laborious; troublesome, afflicting. **péniblement**, *adv.* Laboriously.

péniche [pe'niʃ], *n.f.* Pinnace; canal boat, barge.

pénicillé [penisi'le], *a.* (*fem.* **-ée**) (*Nat. Hist.*) Penicillate (pencil-shaped).

pénicilline [penisi'lin], *n.f.* Penicillin.

péninsulaire [penɛ̃sy'lɛːr], *a.* Peninsular.

péninsule, *n.f.* Peninsula.

pénitence [peni'tãːs], *n.f.* Penitence, repentance; penance; punishment; penalty (in games). *Faire pénitence*, to do penance for one's sins; *mettre un enfant en pénitence*, to punish a child. **pénitencerie**, *n.f.* (*R.-C. Ch.*) Office of penitentiary. **pénitencier**, *a.* Penitentiary.—*n.m.* Priest presiding over penitentiary; penitentiary, reformatory.

pénitent, *a.* (*fem.* **-ente**) Penitent, repentant. *Pécheur pénitent*, contrite sinner.—*n.* Penitent. **pénitentiaire**, *a.* Penitentiary. *Maison pénitentiaire*, penitentiary.

pénitentiaux, *a.m.pl.* *Psaumes pénitentiaux*, penitential psalms. **pénitentiel**, *a.* (*fem.* **-ielle**) Penitential.—*n.m.* Penitential ritual.

pennage [pɛ'naːʒ], *n.m.* (*Hawking*) Plumage of birds of prey.

penne (1) [pɛn], *n.f.* Tail-feather, wing-feather.

penne (2) [pɛn], *n.f.* (*Naut.*) Peak of a lateen-sail yard.

penné [pɛ'ne], *a.* (*fem.* **-ée**) (*Bot.*) Pinnate.

penniforme [pɛni'fɔrm], *a.* Penniform.

pennon [pɛ'nɔ̃], *n.m.* Pennon.

Pennsylvanie [PENSYLVANIE].

pénombre [pe'nɔ̃ːbr], *n.f.* Penumbra; semi-darkness, half-light.

penon [pə'nɔ̃], *n.m.* (*Naut.*) Dog-vane.

pensant [pã'sã], *a.* (*fem.* **-ante**) Thinking. *Bien pensant*, right-thinking, well-disposed.

pensée (1) [pã'se], *n.f.* Thought; opinion, sentiment; notion, idea, conception; maxim, sentence; meaning; sketch, first draft. *Entrer dans la pensée de quelqu'un*, to follow someone's reasoning or train of thought; *libre pensée*, free-thinking; *s'accoutumer à la pensée de la mort*, to accustom oneself to the idea of death.

pensée (2) [pã'se], *n.f.* (*Bot.*) Pansy, heart's-ease. *Pensée sauvage* or *petite jacée*, wild pansy.

penser [pã'se], *v.i.* To think, to reflect, to consider; to expect, (*Am.*) to guess; to take heed, to take care. *Cela donne bien à penser*, that offers food for thought; *c'est un homme qui pense bien*, he is a man who thinks well; *façon de penser*, way of thinking; *faire penser*, to remind; *il l'a fait sans y penser*, he did it without thinking; *penser à quelque chose*, to think of something; *penser à soi*, to look to oneself, to take care of oneself; *pensez donc!* just imagine!—*v.t.* To think, to think of; to believe, to judge. *Il a pensé mourir*, he nearly lost his life; *il ne dit jamais ce qu'il pense*, he

never says what he thinks; *j'ai pensé tomber*, I was near falling; *penser du bien de*, to think well of; *que pensez-vous de cela?* what do you think of that?—*n.m.* (*poet.*) Inward reasoning, thought.

penseur, *n.m.* (*fem.* **-euse**) Thinker. *Libre penseur*, free-thinker.—*a.* Thinking, reflecting, thoughtful.

pensif, *a.* (*fem.* **-ive**) Pensive, thoughtful.

pension [pã'sjɔ̃], *n.f.* Payment for board or board and lodging; boarding-house; boarding-school; pension, allowance, annuity. *Mettre son fils en pension*, to send one's son to a boarding-school; *obtenir une pension*, to obtain a pension; *pension de famille*, boarding-house, residential hotel; *pension de jeunes filles*, girls' boarding-school; *pension de retraite*, retirement pension; superannuation; *pension viagère*, life-annuity; *prendre quelqu'un en pension*, to take someone in as a boarder.

pensionnaire, *n.* Boarder; school-boy or -girl; pensioner, resident. *Le grand Pensionnaire* (of Holland), the Grand Pensionary; *prendre des pensionnaires*, to take in boarders.

pensionnat, *n.m.* Private boarding-school.

pensionné, *a.* (*fem.* **-ée**) Pensioned.—*n.* Pensioner. **pensionner**, *v.t.* To pension, to grant a pension to.

pensivement, *adv.* Pensively; musingly.

pensum [pɛ̃'sɔm], *n.m.* (*pl.* **pensums**) Imposition, extra task (at school).

Pennsylvanie [pãsilva'ni], *f.* Pennsylvania.

pentacle [pɛ̃'takl], *n.m.* Pentacle.

pentacorde [pɛ̃ta'kɔrd], *n.m.* Pentachord.

pentagonal, *a.* (*fem.* **-ale**, *pl.* **-aux**) Pentagonal. **pentagone**, *a.* Pentagonal.—*n.m.* Pentagon.

pentamère, *a.* Pentamerous.

pentamètre, *n.m.* and *a.* Pentameter.

pentateuque, *n.m.* (*Bible*) Pentateuch.

pentathle or **pentathlon**, *n.m.* Pentathlon.

pente [pãːt], *n.f.* Declivity, inclination, slope; acclivity; (ascent; incline, gradient; pitch (of roofs); (*fig.*) propensity, bent. *Avoir le gosier* (or *la dalle*) *en pente*, (*fam.*) to be fond of tippling; *être* or *aller en pente*, to slope, to shelve; *le terrain va en pente*, the ground slopes down.

Pentecôte [pãt'koːt], *n.f.* Pentecost, Whitsuntide. *Dimanche de la Pentecôte*, Whit-Sunday.

Pentélique [pãte'lik], *m.* Pentelicus.

Penthée [pã'te], *m.* Pentheus.

Penthésilée [pãtezi'le], *f.* Penthesilea.

pentière [pã'tjɛːr], *n.f.* Slope of mountain.

pentstémon [pãtste'mɔ̃], *n.m.* (*Bot.*) *Pentstémon à grandes fleurs*, Pentstemon grandiflorus.

penture [pã'tyːr], *n.f.* Iron brace (on door), hinge. *Penture de sabords*, port-brace.

pénultième [penyl'tjɛm], *a.* Last but one, penultimate.—*n.f.* Penult, penultima.

pénurie [peny'ri], *n.f.* Scarcity, lack, dearth; penury, want.

pépère [pe'pɛr], *n.m.* (*childish*) Grandfather. —*a.* (*pop.*) Big; calm, quiet, comfortable; clever, sly.

pépètes or **pépettes** [pe'pɛt], *n.f. pl.* (*pop.*) Money, brass, dibs.

pépie [pe'pi], *n.f.* Pip (disease of birds). *Elle n'a pas la pépie*, (*fam.*) she is not tongue-tied; *il a la pépie*, he is always thirsty.

pépiement [pepi'mã], *n.m.* Chirping. **pépier,** To chirp, to cheep.

Pépin [pe'pɛ̃], *m.* Pepin. **Pépin le Bref,** Pepin the Short.

pépin [pe'pɛ̃], *n.m.* Pip (of apple etc.); stone (of grape); (*fam.*) umbrella, brolly; (*fam.*) snag. (*pop.*) *Avoir des pépins,* to have a spot of bother.

pépinière, *n.f.* Nursery (of trees); (*fig.*) nursery (of actors etc.). **pépiniériste,** *n.m.* Nurseryman.

pépite [pe'pit], *n.f.* Nugget (of gold).

péplum [pe'plɔm], *n.m.* (*Greek Ant.*) Peplum (cloak).

pepsine [pɛp'sin], *n.f.* Pepsine.

peptique, *a.* Peptic.

peptogène, *n.m.* Peptogen.

peptone, *n.f.* Peptone.

peptoniser, *v.t.* To peptonize.

péquenot [pek'no], *n.m.* (*pop.*) Peasant, bumpkin.

péquin [PÉKIN].

perçage [pɛr'sa:ʒ], *n.m.* Piercing, boring.

percale [pɛr'kal], *n.f.* Cotton cambric, percale. **percaline,** *n.f.* Glazed calico or lining, etc., percaline.

perçant, *a.* (*fem.* **-ante**) Piercing; sharp, keen; shrill, acute. *Des yeux perçants,* piercing eyes; *esprit perçant,* acute mind; *froid perçant,* piercing cold; *voix perçante,* shrill voice.

perce, *n.f.* Piercer, borer; hole (in flute etc.). *En perce,* broached, tapped; *mettre du vin en perce,* to broach a cask of wine. **percé** (1), *a.* (*fem.* **-ée** (1)) Pierced, bored, in holes; out at elbows. *Avoir le cœur percé,* to be struck to the heart; *c'est un panier percé,* money burns a hole in his pocket, he is a spendthrift; *chaise percée,* close-stool; *habit percé,* coat in holes; *percé à jour,* pierced through and through. **perce-bois,** *n.m. inv.* Borer, woodborer (insect). **percée** (2), *n.f.,* or **percé** (2), *n.m.* Opening, cutting (in a wood), vista, glade; (*Mil.*) break-through; (*Ftb.*) run-through. *Faire une percée dans,* to hew a passage through.

perce-feuille, *n.f.* (*pl.* **perce-feuilles**) Hare's ear (plant).

percement, *n.m.* Piercing, boring, perforation.

perce-muraille, *n.f.* (*pl.* **perce-murailles**) [PARIÉTAIRE].

perce-neige, *n.f. inv.* Snowdrop.

perce-oreille, *n.m.* (*pl.* **perce-oreilles**) Earwig.

perce-pierre, *n.f.* (*pl.* **perce-pierres**) [SAXIFRAGE].

percepteur [pɛrsep'tœːr], *n.m.* Collector of taxes, tax-gatherer. ─*a.* (*fem.* **-trice**) (*Anat.*) Of perception.

perceptibilité [pɛrsɛptibili'te], *n.f.* Liability to collection (of taxes etc.); perceptibility. **perceptible,** *a.* Collectible; perceptible. **perceptiblement,** *adv.* Perceptibly. **perceptif,** *a.* (*fem.* **-ive**) Perceptive.

perception [pɛrsep'sjɔ̃], *n.f.* Faculty of perceiving; perception; gathering, collecting, receipt; collectorship, collector's office.

percer [pɛr'se], *v.t.* To pierce, to bore, to drill; to tap, to broach; to open (a door, window, etc.), to make (an opening); to penetrate, to go, pass, or break through; to tunnel; to soak or wet through (of rain etc.);

to thrill. *Machine à percer,* punching-machine; *percer de part en part,* to run through and through; *percer l'avenir,* to dive into the future; *percer le cœur,* (*fig.*) to break the heart; *percer les oreilles,* (*fig.*) to deafen (of a shrill noise); *percer un abcès,* to open an abscess; *percer une dent,* to cut a tooth; *percer une forêt,* to open up or to make a road through a forest; *percer une porte dans un mur,* to open a door in a wall; *percer un tonneau,* to tap a cask.—*v.i.* To pierce through, to break, to come through; to appear, to transpire; to discover or manifest oneself; to make one's way, to attract attention; to enter (*dans*). *Cette tumeur percera d'elle-même,* that tumour will burst of itself; *les dents vont bientôt percer à cet enfant,* that child will soon cut his teeth; *percer par son mérite,* to come into notice by one's merit. **se percer,** *v.r.* To pierce oneself, to be pierced.

perceur, *n.m.* (*fem.* **-euse**) Borer.—*n.f.* Boring-machine, drill.

percevable [pɛrsə'vabl], *a.* Perceivable; leviable (of a tax).

percevoir [pɛrsə'vwaːr], *v.t. irr.* (*conjug. like* RECEVOIR) To gather, to collect (taxes etc.); (*Phil.*) to perceive.

perche (1) [pɛrʃ], *n.f.* Perch, pole; rod or perch (measure); (*Cine.*) boom. *Grande perche,* lanky person; *saut à la perche,* pole-jump, pole-vaulting; *tendre la perche à quelqu'un,* to help someone out of a difficulty.

perche (2) [pɛrʃ], *n.f.* (*Ichth.*) Perch. *Perche goujonnière,* ruff.

perché [pɛr'ʃe], *a.* (*fem.* **-ée**) Perched, perched up, roosting.

percher [pɛr'ʃe], *v.i.,* or **se percher,** *v.r.* To perch, to roost. (*fam.*) *Où perches-tu?* where do you hang out?

percheron [pɛrʃə'rɔ̃], *n.m.* (*fem.* **-onne**) Horse or mare (from the Perche, S.E. of Normandy).

percheur [pɛr'ʃœːr], *a.* (*fem.* **-euse**) Perching, roosting (of birds).

perchlorate [pɛrklɔ'rat], *n.m.* Perchlorate. **perchlorique,** *a.* Perchloric. **perchlorure,** *n.m.* Perchloride.

perchoir [pɛr'ʃwaːr], *n.m.* Roost.

perclus [pɛr'kly], *a.* (*fem.* **-use**) Crippled, anchylosed, impotent. *Avoir le cerveau perclus,* to be wanting in sense; *il est perclus de rhumatismes,* he is crippled with rheumatism.

perçoir [pɛr'swaːr], *n.m.,* or **perçoire,** *n.f.* Piercer (to tap casks etc.).

percolateur [pɛrkɔla'tœːr], *n.m.* Percolator, big percolating coffee-pot.

perçu, *p.p.* (*fem.* **-ue**) [PERCEVOIR].

percussion [pɛrky'sjɔ̃], *n.f.* Percussion. *Arme à percussion,* percussion fire-arm; *instruments de percussion,* (*Mus.*) percussion instruments (drums, cymbals, etc.). **percutant,** *a.* (*fem.* **-ante**) Producing percussion. *Fusée percutante,* percussion-fuse. **percuter,** *v.t.* To strike; to percuss.—*v.i.* To crash. *Sa voiture a percuté contre un arbre,* his car crashed into a tree. **percuteur,** *n.m.* Needle (of rifle); pin (of machine-gun); striker (of gun, torpedo).

perdable [pɛr'dabl], *a.* Losable. **perdant,** *a.* (*fem.* **-ante**) Losing. *Partir perdant,* to have no hope of winning.—*n.* Loser.

perdition [pɛrdi′sjɔ̃], *n.f.* Perdition. *En perdition*, sinking, in distress (of ships).

perdre [perdr], *v.t.* To lose, to be deprived of; to get rid of; to waste, to idle away, to ruin, to destroy, to undo, to corrupt, to lead astray; to deprave, to disgrace, to dishonour; (*Naut.*) to carry away. *Courir à perdre haleine*, to run oneself out of breath; *jouer à qui perd gagne*, to play at the loser wins; *l'inondation a perdu les blés*, the floods have ruined the crops; *perdre la santé*, to lose one's health; *perdre la tête*, to be beheaded, (*fig.*) to lose one's wits; *perdre l'occasion*, to lose the opportunity; *perdre pied*, to be out of one's depth; *perdre quelqu'un de réputation*, to defame someone; *perdre son temps*, to waste one's time; *perdre une chose de vue*, to lose sight of a thing; *perdre une gageure*, to lose a wager; *ses débauches le perdront*, his debauchery will be the ruin of him.—*v.i.* To lose, to be a loser; to be out of pocket; to deteriorate; to leak; to ebb. *La marée perd*, the tide is ebbing. **se perdre**, *v.r.* To be lost; to lose one's way, to go astray; to be cast away; to be bewildered, to be nonplussed; to disappear, to fall into disuse; to go to ruin; to spoil, to be spoilt; (*Naut.*) to be carried away. *Je m'y perds*, I cannot make head nor tail of it; *se perdre dans la foule*, to be lost in the crowd.

perdreau [per′dro], *n.m.* (*pl.* -eaux) Young partridge.

perdrix [per′dri], *n.f. inv.* Partridge. *Couple de perdrix*, brace of partridges; *perdrix de mer*, pratincole, *perdrix des neiges*, ptarmigan; *perdrix grecque* or *bartavelle*, greater red legs; *perdrix grise*, common partridge; *perdrix rouge*, red-legged partridge.

perdu [per′dy], *a.* (*fem.* -ue) Lost; ruined, undone, done for, wasted; wrecked; dishonoured; spoilt; stray, forlorn; obsolete, out of use; out of the way, sequestered; bewildered. *À corps perdu* [CORPS]; *à ses moments perdus*, in his spare time; *courir* or *crier comme un perdu*, to run or cry like a madman; *enfants perdus* [ENFANT]; *femme perdue*, fallen woman; *pays perdu* [PAYS]; *perdu de dettes* [DETTE]; *perdu de réputation*, ruined in reputation; *salle des pas perdus*, outer hall, waiting hall (in courts of law); *sentinelle perdue*, advance sentry; *tirer à coups perdus*, to shoot at random; *un trou perdu*, a dead and alive hole.

père [pɛːr], *n.m.* Father; sire; *gaffer; (*pl.*) forefathers, ancestors. *Beau-père* [BEAU]; *de père en fils*, from father to son; *nos pères*, our forefathers; *père noble*, (*Theat.*) heavy father, old man; *père nourricier*, foster-father; *pères du désert*, the anchorites of the Thebaid; *père spirituel*, father confessor; *le P. Sanson*, Father Sanson; (*Comm.*) *M. Massip père*, Mr. Massip senior; (*fam.*) *le père Gérard*, old Gerard; (*pop.*) *le coup du père François*, an attack from behind with a handkerchief to throttle the victim; (*fig.*) a piece of treachery; *le père Fouettard*, the bogy man.

pérégrination [peregrina′sjɔ̃], *n.f.* Peregrination. **pérégriner**, *v.i.* To peregrinate. **pérégrinité**, *n.f.* Peregrinity.

péremption [perãp′sjɔ̃], *n.f.* (*Law*) Prescription.

péremptoire [perãp′twaːr], *a.* Peremptory. **péremptoirement**, *adv.* Peremptorily.

pérenne [pe′rɛn], *a.* Perennial. **pérennité**, *n.f.* Perenniality, perpetuity.

péréquation [perekwa′sjɔ̃], *n.f.* Equal distribution, equalization.

perfectibilité [perfɛktibili′te], *n.f.* Perfectibility. **perfectible**, *a.* Perfectible.

perfection [perfɛk′sjɔ̃], *n.f.* Perfection; faultlessness; completeness. *À la perfection*, to perfection; *la perfection en personne*, perfection personified, the pink of perfection; *le plus haut degré de perfection*, the acme of perfection.

perfectionnement, *n.m.* Improvement, perfecting, finishing. *Cours de perfectionnement*, finishing lessons, refresher course.

perfectionner, *v.t.* To perfect, to bring to perfection; to improve; to improve upon. *Perfectionner ce que les autres ont inventé*, to improve on the inventions of others. **se perfectionner**, *v.r.* To perfect oneself; to improve oneself, to improve.

perfide [per′fid], *a.* Perfidious, treacherous, false, false-hearted.—*n.* Perfidious, treacherous, false person. **perfidement**, *adv.* Perfidiously, falsely, treacherously, basely.

perfidie, *n.f.* Perfidy, treachery, false-heartedness; treacherous act *or* thing. *Faire une perfidie*, to commit an act of perfidy.

perfolié [perfɔ′lje], *a.* (*fem.* -ée) (*Bot.*) Perfoliate.

perforage [perfɔ′raːʒ], *n.m.* Boring, perforation. **perforant**, *a.* (*fem.* -ante) Perforating, penetrating. *Balle perforante*, penetrating bullet.

perforateur, *a.* (*fem.* -trice) Perforative.—*n.m.* Perforator.—*n.f.* Drilling-machine.

perforatif, *a.* (*fem.* -ive) (*Surg.*) Perforative.

perforation, *n.f.* Perforation; (*Ciné.*) sprockethole, perforation.

perforer, *v.t.* To perforate, to bore, to drill (material); to punch (leather), to puncture (tyre).

perforeuse, *n.f.* Drilling-machine.

performance [perfɔr′mãːs], *n.f.* (*spt.* only) Performance.

perfusion [perfy′zjɔ̃], *n.f.* Perfusion.

pergola [pergɔ′la], *n.f.* Pergola.

péri [pe′ri], *n.* Peri (Persian fairy).

périanthe [pe′rjãːt], *n.m.* Perianth.

péricarde [peri′kard], *n.m.* Pericardium. **péricardite**, *n.f.* Pericarditis.

péricarpe, *n.m.* (*Bot.*) Pericarp, seed-vessel.

périchondre, *n.m.* Perichondrium.

Périclès [peri′klɛːs], *m.* Pericles.

péricliter [perikli′te], *v.i.* To be in jeopardy.

péricrâne [peri′krɑːn], *n.m.* Pericranium.

péridot [peri′do], *n.m.* Peridot, chrysolite, olivine.

périgée [peri′ʒe], *n.m.* Perigee.

périgourdin [perigur′dɛ̃], *a.* (*fem.* -ine) Of Périgord.

périgyne [peri′ʒin], *a.* (*Bot.*) Perigynous.

périhélie, *n.m.* (*Astron.*) Perihelion.—*a.* In its perihelion.

péril [pe′ril], *n.m.* Peril, danger, jeopardy, hazard, risk. *Au péril de ma vie*, at the risk of my life; *mettre en péril*, to put in jeopardy; *prendre une affaire à ses risques et périls*, to take on something at one's own risk. **périlleusement**, *adv.* Perilously. **périlleux**, *a.* (*fem.* -euse) Perilous, dangerous, hazardous. *Saut périlleux* [SAUT].

périmé [peri′me], *a.* (*fem.* **-ée**) Out-of-date, no longer valid.

périmer [peri′me], *v.i.* (*Law*) To be barred by limitation, to pass out of date, to lapse.

périmètre [peri′mɛtr], *n.m.* Perimeter.

périnéal [perine′al], *a.* (*fem.* **-ale**, *pl.* **-aux**) Perineal.

périnée, *n.m.* Perineum.

période [pe′rjɔd], *n.f.* Period (of a planet's revolution); period of time, epoch, age, era; (*Gram.*) period, complete and rounded sentence; (*Mus.*) phrase. *Période bien arrondie*, well-rounded period; *période embarrassée*, involved period; *période lunaire*, lunar period. —*n.m.* Pitch, summit, degree, acme. *À son dernier* or *son plus haut période*, to its utmost pitch. **périodicité**, *n.f.* Periodicity. **périodique**, *a.* Periodic, periodical; characterized by periods (of style); (*Arith.*) recurring, circulating. *Fraction périodique*, (*Arith.*) circulating or recurring decimal; *style périodique*, periodic style.—*n.m.* Periodical. **périodiquement**, *adv.* Periodically.

périoste [pe′rjost], *n.m.* (*Anat.*) Periosteum. **périosté**, or **périostéal**, *a.* (*fem.* **-ée**, **-éale**, *pl.* **-éaux**) Periosteal. **périostite**, *n.f.* Periostitis.

péripatéticien [peripateti′sjɛ̃], *a.* and *n.* (*fem.* **-ienne**) Peripatetic.—*n.f.* Street-walker. **péripatétisme**, *n.m.* Peripateticism.

péripétie [peripe′si], *n.f.* Peripeteia, sudden turn of fortune; (*pl.*) vicissitudes.

périphérie [perife′ri], *n.f.* Periphery. *À la périphérie*, on the outskirts. **périphérique**, *a.* Peripheric.

périphrase [peri′frɑːz], *n.f.* Periphrasis, circumlocution. **périphraser**, *v.i.* To periphrase. **périphrastique**, *a.* Periphrastic.

périple [pe′ripl], *n.m.* Periplus.

périptère [perip′tɛːr], *a.* Peripteral (temple). —*n.m.* Peripter.

périr [pe′riːr], *v.i.* (*takes the auxiliary* AVOIR) To perish, to die a violent death; to be wrecked, destroyed, sunk, etc.; to decay, to fall into ruin; to be lost; to fall off; (*Law*) to be barred by limitation. *Faire périr*, to put to death, to do away with; *faire périr une armée*, to destroy an army; *l'instance est périe*, (*Law*) the suit is barred by limitation; *périr corps et biens*, to be lost with all hands (of ships); *périr de froid*, to perish with cold; *périr d'ennui*, to be bored to death.

périscope [peris′kɔp], *n.m.* Periscope. **périscopique**, *a.* Periscopic.

périssable, *a.* Perishable.

périssoire [peri′swaːr], *n.f.* Flat-bottomed canoe.

péristaltique [peristal′tik], *a.* Peristaltic. **péristaltisme**, *n.m.* Peristalsis. **péristole**, *n.f.* Peristaltic motion (of the intestines).

péristome [peris′tom], *n.m.* Peristome.

péristyle [peris′til], *n.m.* and *a.* Peristyle.

péritoine [peri′twan], *n.m.* Peritoneum. **péritonite**, *n.f.* Peritonitis.

perlasse [pɛr′las], *n.f.* Pearl-ash.

perle [pɛrl], *n.f.* Pearl; bead, bugle (for bracelets, necklaces, etc.); (*fig.*) best, gem, jewel; (*sch.*) howler. *C'est la perle des hommes*, he is the best of men; *nous ne sommes pas ici pour enfiler des perles*, we are not here to trifle our time away; *perles fines*, real pearls; *semence de perles*, seed pearls.—*a. inv. Gris perle*, pearl grey.

perlé, *a.* (*fem.* **-ée**) Pearled, set with pearls; pearly; (*fig.*) finished or executed to perfection; (*Mus.*) brilliant and delicate. *Orge perlé*, pearl-barley; *faire la grève perlée*, to go slow, to ca'canny.

perler, *v.t.* To bead, to form into beads; to pearl (barley); (*fig.*) to give a fine finish to, to polish.—*v.i.* To form beads (of sweat etc.).

perlier, *a.* (*fem.* **-ière**) Of pearl; producing pearls. *Huître perlière*, pearl-oyster.

perlimpinpin [pɛrlɛ̃pɛ̃′pɛ̃], *n.m.* Only used in *c'est de la poudre de perlimpinpin*, that's all bunkum.

permanence [pɛrma′nɑ̃ːs], *n.f.* Permanence; headquarters (of a political party). *Assurer une permanence*, to be on duty; *en permanence*, permanently.

permanent, *a.* (*fem.* **-ente**) Permanent, lasting, constant. *Spectacle permanent*, continuous show.—*n.f.* (*Hairdressing*) Permanent wave.

permanganate [pɛrmɑ̃ga′nat], *n.m.* *Permanganate de potassium*, potassium permanganate. permanganate of potash. **permanganique**, *a.* Permanganic.

perméabilité [pɛrmeabili′te], *n.f.* Permeability. **perméable**, *a.* Permeable, pervious (to).

permettre [pɛr′mɛtr], *v.t. irr.* (*conjugated like* METTRE) To permit, to allow, to let; to suffer, to put up with; to enable, to afford room for. *Permettez!* allow me! excuse me! *permettez-moi de vous dire*, allow me to tell you. **se permettre**, *v.r.* To permit, allow, or suffer oneself; to indulge, to venture, to take the liberty (*de*).

permis, *a.* (*fem.* **-ise**) Allowed, permitted, lawful. *Permis à vous de croire cela*, you may believe that if you like; *s'il m'est permis de le dire*, if I may say so.—*n.m.* Permission, leave, permit; licence, pass. *Permis de chasse*, shooting-licence; *permis de conduire*, driving-licence; *permis de circulation*, (*Rail.*) pass; *permis de séjour*, permission to reside; *permis de travail*, labour permit.

permission, *n.f.* Permission, leave, permit, *Abuser de la permission*, to go beyond bounds; *avec votre permission*, by your leave.

permissionnaire, *n.* Person having a licence or permit; soldier on short leave.

permutabilité [pɛrmytabili′te], *n.f.* Permutability. **permutable**, *a.* Permutable. **permutant**, *a.m.* (*fem.* **-ante**) Permuter, exchanger. **permutation**, *n.f.* Permutation, exchange of posts; (*Mil.*) transfer. *Permutation de consonnes*, transposition of consonants. **permuter**, *v.t.* To exchange, to permute, to transpose.

pernicieusement [pɛrnisjøz′mɑ̃], *adv.* Perniciously, mischievously, injuriously. **pernicieux**, *a.* (*fem.* **-ieuse**) Pernicious, mischievous, hurtful.

péroné [perɔ′ne], *n.m.* Fibula (splint bone).

péronnelle [perɔ′nɛl], *n.f.* Pert hussy, saucy baggage.

péroraison [perɔrɛ′zɔ̃], *n.f.* Peroration.

pérorer [perɔ′re], *v.i.* To hold forth, to speechify. **péroreur**, *n.m.* (*fem.* **-euse**) Speechifier, spouter.

Pérou [pe′ru], *m.* Peru. (*fam.*) *Ce n'est pas*

le Pérou, it is no great thing, no well-paid job.

Pérouse [peˈruːz], *f.* Perugia.

péroxyde [perɔkˈsid], *n.m.* Peroxide.

péroxyder, *v.t.* To peroxidize.

perpendiculaire [pɛrpɑ̃dikyˈlɛːr], *a.* and *n.f.* Perpendicular. *Abaisser une perpendiculaire*, to drop a perpendicular; *élever une perpendiculaire*, to raise a perpendicular. **perpendiculairement**, *adv.* Perpendicularly. **perpendicularité**, *n.f.* Perpendicularity, uprightness.

perpète [pɛrˈpɛt], *abbr.* (*fam.*) of *perpétuité*. (*slang*) *À perpète*, for life, very far away.

perpétration [pɛrpetrɑˈsjɔ̃], *n.f.* Perpetration.

perpétrer, *v.t.* To perpetrate, to commit.

perpétuation [pɛrpetɥɑˈsjɔ̃], *n.f.* Perpetuation. **perpétuel**, *a.* (*fem.* **-elle**) Perpetual, permanent; for life. **perpétuellement**, *adv.* Perpetually, everlastingly. **perpétuer**, *v.t.* To perpetuate. **se perpétuer**, *v.r.* To be perpetuated, to continue. **perpétuité**, *n.f.* Perpetuity. *À perpétuité*, for ever, for life; *condamner aux travaux forcés à perpétuité*, to sentence to hard labour for life.

perpignan [pɛrpiˈɲɑ̃], *n.m.* Flexible handle of whip (made of plaited nettle-tree).

perplexe [pɛrˈplɛks], *a.* Perplexed, embarrassed, irresolute; perplexing.

perplexité, *n.f.* Perplexity.

perquisiteur [pɛrkiziˈtœːr], *n.m.* Searcher.

perquisition, *n.f.* Perquisition, search; investigation. *Mandat de perquisition*, search-warrant. **perquisitionner**, *v.i.* To make a search.

perré [pɛˈre], *n.m.* Stone facing, revetment.

perrier [pɛˈrje], *n.m.* (*W. dial.*) Quarryman. **perrière**, *n.f.* Stone (or slate) quarry.

perron [pɛˈrɔ̃], *n.m.* Flight of steps (before a house); perron.

perroquet [pɛrɔˈkɛ], *n.m.* Parrot; (*Naut.*) topgallant sail. *Grand perroquet*, main-topgallant sail; *mât de perroquet*, topgallant mast; *vergue de grand perroquet*, main-topgallant yard.

perruche [pɛˈryʃ], *n.f.* Small long-tailed parrot, parakeet, budgerigar; (*pop.*) hen-parrot; (*Naut.*) mizzen top-gallant sail; (*fam.*) a talkative flapper.

perruque [pɛˈryk], *n.f.* Wig, periwig; (*Bot.*) white stonecrop. *Perruque à nœuds*, tie-wig; *tête à perruque*, barber's block; *une vieille perruque*, an old fogey. **perruquier**, *n.m.* Wig-maker; hair-dresser, barber. **perruquière**, *n.f.* Barber's wife.

pers [pɛːr], *a.* (*fem.* **perse** (1)) Greenish-blue.

persan [pɛrˈsɑ̃], *a.* (*fem.* **-ane**) Persian.—*n.m.* Persian language.—*n.* (**Persan**, *fem.* **-ane**) A Persian. **perse** (2), *a.* and *n.m.* (**Perse**) (*Anc. Hist.*) Persian.

Perse [pɛrs], *f.* Persia.

perse (3) [pɛrs], *n.f.* Chintz.

persécuter [pɛrsekyˈte], *v.t.* To persecute; (*fig.*) to importune, to bore, to dun. **persécuteur**, *n.m.* (*fem.* **-trice**) Persecutor; troublesome person.—*a.* Persecuting; importunate, troublesome. **persécution**, *n.f.* Persecution; annoyance, importunity.

Persée [pɛrˈse], *m.* Perseus.

persévérance [perseveˈrɑ̃s], *n.f.* Perseverance; firmness, steadiness. **persévérant**, *a.*

(*fem.* **-ante**) Persevering; firm, steady, resolute; dogged.

persévérer [perseveˈre], *v.i. irr.* (*conjug. like* ACCÉLÉRER) To persevere; to be steadfast; to persist. *Persévérer dans un dessein*, to persevere in a design.

persicaire [pɛrsiˈkɛːr], *n.f.* Persicaria [*see* RENOUÉE].

persicot [pɛrsiˈko], *n.m.* Persicot (cordial).

persienne [pɛrˈsjɛn], *n.f.* Venetian shutter.

persiflage [pɛrsiˈflaːʒ], *n.m.* Banter, chaff, persiflage. **persifler**, *v.i.* To rally, to banter, to chaff. **persifleur**, *n.m.* (*fem.* **-euse**) Banterer, quiz.—*a.* Bantering, chaffing.

persil [pɛrˈsi], *n.m.* Parsley.

persillade [pɛrsiˈjad], *n.f.* Beef with oil, vinegar, and parsley.

persillé, *a.* (*fem.* **-ée**) Spotted; blue-moulded (cheese). **persiller**, *v.t.* To spot (with green).

persique [pɛrˈsik], *a.* Ancient Persian. *Le Golfe Persique*, Persian Gulf.

persistance [pɛrsisˈtɑ̃ːs], *n.f.* Persistence. **persistant**, *a.* (*fem.* **-ante**) Persistent.

persister, *v.i.* To persist. *Il persiste dans son opinion*, he maintains his opinion.

personé [PERSONNÉ].

personnage [pɛrsɔˈnaːʒ], *n.m.* Personage, great person, somebody; person, individual; (*Theat.*) character, part. *C'est un sot personnage*, he is a silly fellow; *il joue bien son personnage*, he acts his part well; *je connais le personnage*, I know the fellow; *un grand personnage*, a very important man; *voilà un plaisant personnage!* what an absurd fellow!

personnalisation [pɛrsɔnalizaˈsjɔ̃], *n.f.* Personalization.

personnaliser, *v.t.* To personalize.

personnalité [pɛrsɔnaliˈte], *n.f.* Personality, individuality, personal character; person, personage; self-love, selfishness, egotism; personal remark. *De hautes personnalités*, high officials.

personne [pɛrˈsɔn], *n.f.* Person; own self, one's person; body, exterior, appearance; (*Gram.*) person. *À la première, seconde, or troisième personne*, (*Gram.*) in the first, second or third person; *c'est la bonté en personne*, he is kindness itself; *il aime sa personne*, he loves his dear self; *il est bien fait de sa personne*, he has a fine presence, he is a fine figure of a man; *jeune personne*, young lady, young girl; *j'y étais en personne*, I was there in person; *les grandes personnes*, the grown-ups; *payer de sa personne*, to expose oneself to danger, not to spare oneself, to repay by personal favours. —*pron.m.* Anyone, no one, nobody. *Il n'y a personne à la maison*, there is nobody at home; *je doute que personne y réussisse*, I doubt whether anyone will succeed in it; *personne ne l'aime*, nobody likes him; *qui avez-vous vu?* Personne, whom did you see? No one.

personné, *a.* (*fem.* **-ée**) (*Bot.*) Personate.

personnel, *a.* (*fem.* **-elle**) Personal; egoistic, selfish.—*n.m.* Personnel, staff (of servants, teachers, clerks), hands (of factory), etc. (*Av.*) *Personnel navigant*, flying staff; *personnel rampant*, ground staff. **personnellement**, *adv.* Personally.

personnification, *n.f.* Personification. **personnifier**, *v.t.* (*conjugated like* PRIER) To personify.

perspectif [pɛrspɛk'tif], *a.* (*fem.* **-ive**) Perspective.—*n.f.* Perspective; view, prospect, distance, vista, opening. *En perspective,* in the distance, in prospect, in expectation, (*Art*) in perspective; *il a la perspective d'une grande fortune,* he has a large fortune in prospect; *perspective aérienne,* aerial perspective; *perspective riante,* delightful prospect.

perspicace [pɛrspi'kas], *a.* Perspicacious, shrewd. **perspicacité,** *n.f.* Perspicacity, insight.

persuadant [pɛrsɥa'dã], *a.* (*fem.* **-ante**) Convincing (argument).

persuader [pɛrsɥa'de], *v.t.* To persuade, to induce; to convince, to satisfy. *J'en suis persuadé,* I am convinced of it; *persuader (à) quelqu'un de faire quelque chose,* to prevail upon someone to do something. **se persuader,** *v.r.* To persuade or convince oneself; to be persuaded, to imagine.

persuasible, *a.* Persuadable.

persuasif, *a.* (*fem.* **-ive**) Persuasive; persuasory, convincing.

persuasion, *n.f.* Persuasion; conviction, belief, opinion.

persuasivement, *adv.* Persuasively.

perte [pɛrt], *n.f.* Loss; waste, wastefulness; ruin, fall, doom; (*pl.*) (*Med.*) leucorrhoea. *À perte,* at a loss; *à perte de vue,* as far as the eye can see; *courir à sa perte,* to be on the road to ruin; *en pure perte,* to no purpose, uselessly, in vain; *être en perte,* to be a loser, to be out of pocket; *être en perte de vitesse,* (*Av.*) to be stalled; *faire une perte,* to meet with a loss; *perte à la terre,* (*Elec.*) earth leakage; *perte d'avancement,* (*Mil.*) forfeiture of seniority; *la perte du Rhône,* the place where the Rhône disappears; *perte de temps,* waste of time; *perte sèche,* dead loss, salvage loss; *vendre à perte,* to sell at a loss.

***pertinacité** [pɛrtinasi'te], *n.f.* Pertinacity.

pertinemment [pertina'mã], *adv.* Pertinently.

pertinence, *n.f.* Pertinence.

pertinent, *a.* (*fem.* **-ente**) Pertinent, relevant. (*Law*) *Les faits pertinents et les pièces justificatives,* the relevant facts and papers.

pertuis [pɛr'tɥi], *n.m.* Opening, sluice, narrow opening in a flood-gate etc.; straits; (*Jura*) pass.

pertuisane [pɛrtɥi'zan], *n.f.* Partisan, halberd.

pertuisanier, *n.m.* Halberdier.

perturbateur [pɛrtyrba'tœ:r], *n.m.* (*fem.* **-trice**) Disturber.—*a.* Disturbing.

perturbation, *n.f.* Perturbation, disturbance.

perturber, *v.r.* To perturb, to disturb.

péruvien [pery'vjɛ̃], *a.* (*fem.* **-ienne**) Peruvian.

pervenche [pɛr'vã:ʃ], *n.f.* (*Bot.*) Periwinkle.

pervers [pɛr'vɛ:r], *a.* (*fem.* **-erse**) Perverse, *froward, wicked, depraved.—*n.* Perverse, *froward person; wrong-doer.

perversion, *n.f.* Perversion.

perversité, *n.f.* Perverseness.

pervertir [perver'ti:r], *v.t.* To pervert. **se pervertir,** *v.r.* To become perverted.

pervertissable, *a.* Pervertible.

pervertissement, *n.m.* Perversion.

pervertisseur, *a.* (*fem.* **-euse**) Perverting.—*n.m.* Perverter, corrupter.

pesade [pə'zad], *n.f.* Pesade; standing on its hind legs (of a horse).

pesage [pə'za:ʒ], *n.m.* Weighing; (*Turf.*) weighing-in room; paddock (on race-course), the enclosure.

pesamment [pəza'mã], *adv.* Heavily, ponderously; lumpishly, clumsily.

pesant [pə'zã], *a.* (*fem.* **-ante**) Heavy, ponderous, weighty; unwieldy, cumbersome; sluggish, slow. *Cheval pesant à la main,* hard-mouthed horse; *fardeau pesant,* heavy burden; *il a la main pesante,* he has a heavy hand; *il a l'esprit pesant,* he is dull-minded. —*n.m.* Weight. *Il vaut son pesant d'or,* he is worth his weight in gold.—*adv.* In weight.

pesanteur, *n.f.* Weight; heaviness, weightiness; unwieldiness; sluggishness, dullness, ponderousness; (*Phys.*) gravity. *Pesanteur d'esprit,* dullness of mind; *pesanteur de tête,* heaviness in the head.

pèse or **pèze** [pɛ:z], *n.m.* (*slang*) Money, cash.

pèse-acide [pɛ:za'sid], *n.m.* (*pl.* **pèse-acides**) Acetometer.

pèse-bébé, *n.m.* (*pl.* **pèse-bébés**) Baby-weighing machine.

pesée [pə'ze], *n.f.* Weighing; all that is weighed at once; leverage. *Faire une pesée,* to weigh.

pèse-lait, *n.m. inv.* Lactometer.

pèse-lettre, *n.m.* (*pl.* **pèse-lettres**) Letter-weight, letter-scales.

pèse-liqueur, *n.m.* (*pl.* **pèse-liqueurs**) Alcoholometer, hydrometer.

peser [pə'ze], *v.t. irr.* (*conjug. like* AMENER) To weigh; to weigh out; (*fig.*) to ponder, to consider, to estimate. *Peser ses mots,* to weigh one's words.—*v.i.* To weigh, to be of weight; to be heavy, to be of value or importance; to lie heavy, to be a burden; to lay stress, to dwell (*sur*). *Cela me pèse sur le cœur,* that lies heavy upon my heart; *peser sur un levier,* to bear upon a lever; *viande qui pèse sur l'estomac,* meat that lies heavy on the stomach.

pèse-sel, *n.m.* (*pl.* **pèse-sels**) Araeometer (for salt liquids).

pesette, *n.f.* Assay-scales.

peseur, *n.m.* (*fem.* **-euse**) Weigher.

pèse-vin, *n.m. inv.* Oenometer.

peson, *n.m.* Steelyard; spring balance.

pessaire [pɛ'sɛ:r], *n.m.* Pessary.

pesse [pɛs], *n.f.* (1) Mare's-tail, equisetum; (2) [ÉPICÉA].

pessimisme [pesi'mism], *n.m.* Pessimism.

pessimiste, *n.* Pessimist.—*a.* Pessimistic.

peste [pɛst], *n.f.* Plague, pestilence; (*fig.*) bane, pest, torment, bore, nuisance.—*int.* The deuce! hang it! *Peste soit du fou!* a plague on the fool! **pester,** *v.i.* To inveigh, to storm, to rave. *Il peste contre ses juges,* he rails at his judges.

pesteux, *a.* (*fem.* **-euse**) Pestilential; pestiferous.

pestifère, *a.* and *n.m.* Pestiferous.

pestiféré, *a.* (*fem.* **-ée**) Plague-stricken (person).

pestilence, *n.f.* Pestilence.

pestilent, *a.* (*fem.* **-ente**) Pestilent.

pestilentiel, *a.* (*fem.* **-ielle**) Pestilential.

pet [pɛ], *n.m.* (*vulg.*) Fart. (*pop.*) *Ça ne vaut pas un pet (de lapin),* it is worthless. *Pet d'âne,* (*Bot.*) oropordon.

pétale [pe'tal], *n.m.* Petal. **pétalé,** *a.* (*fem.* **-ée**) Petalous, petalled. **pétaliforme,** *a.*

Pet'aliform. **pétalin**, *a.* (*fem.* **-ine**) Petaline.
pétaloïde, *a.* Petaloid.
pétanque [pe'tãk], *n.f.* (*S. Fr.*) Bowl game.
pétarade [peta'rad], *n.f.* Farting (of animals); cracking noise of crackers, discharge of fire-arms; popping back, back-fire (of car).
pétarader, *v.i.* To make that noise.
pétard [pe'ta:r], *n.m.* Petard; cracker (firework); detonator, fog-signal (of railways); (*fam.*) noise, row; sensational piece of news; (*pop.*) revolver. *Faire du pétard*, (*fam.*) to make a hell of a row. **pétarder**, *v.t.* To blow in with a petard. **pétardier**, *n.m.* One who makes or fires petards.
pétase [pe'ta:z], *n.m.* (*Ant.*) Petasus (broad-brimmed, low-crowned hat).
Pétaud [pe'to], *m.* *C'est la cour du roi Pétaud*, it is Bedlam broken loose.
pétaudière, *n.f.* Bear-garden, noisy or disorderly assembly.
pet-de-nonne [pɛd'nɔn], *n.m.* (*pl.* **pets-de-nonne**) (*Cook.*) Batter-fritter.
pet-en-l'air [pɛɑ̃'lɛ:r], *n.m. inv.* Man's short jacket.
péter [pe'te], *v.i.* (*vulg. and not decent*) To crack, to· crackle, to snap, to make a loud report; to fart; to explode, to burst (of fire-arms).
péteur, *n.m.* (*fem.* **-euse**) (*vulg.*) Farter; coward.
péteux, *n.m.* (*fem.* **-euse**) (*pop.*) Coward.
pètesec, *n.m.* (*fam.*) A stiff, unkind fellow; (*Mil.*) a regular martinet.
pétillant [peti'jã], *a.* (*fem.* **-ante**) Crackling; sparkling. **pétillement**, *n.m.* Crackling; sparkling.
pétiller [peti'je], *v.i.* To crackle; (of burning wood); to sparkle (of eyes); to fizz, to bubble, to sparkle (of wine). *Pétiller d'impatience*, to boil over with impatience; *son ouvrage pétille d'esprit*, his work sparkles with wit.
pétiolaire [pesjɔ'lɛ:r], *a.* (*Bot.*) Petiolar. **pétiole**, *n.m.* Petiole. **pétiolé**, *a.* (*fem.* **-ée**) Petiolate.
petiot [pə'tjo], *a.* (*fem.* **-ote**) (*fam.*) Tiny, wee.—*n.* Little one; darling.
petit [pə'ti], *a.* (*fem.* **-ite**) Little, small; diminutive, short; very young; slender; unimportant, petty, slight, trifling; low, mean, shabby, few, limited; humble; miniature; feeble. *Cela est bien petit*, that's very shabby; *de la petite bière*, small beer; *être aux petits soins pour*, to be all attention to; *en petit*, in miniature, on a small scale; *le petit monde* [MONDE (1)]; *le petit peuple* [PEUPLE (1)]; *petit à petit*, by degrees, little by little; *petit à petit l'oiseau fait son nid* [NID]; *petite vérole*, small-pox; *se faire petit devant quelqu'un*, to abase oneself before someone; *un homme petit*, a mean man; *un petit homme*, a little man; *un petit roi*, a petty king.—*n.* Little child, little one; young one; whelp, pup, kitten, cub. *Faire des petits*, to bring forth young; *les petits*, the poor, the humble, (at school) the junior boys, the juniors; *les petits d'une chienne*, the pups of a bitch; *pauvre petit*, poor little chap; *les tout-petits*, the tiny tots.
(*C*) **petit-calumet** [pətikaly'mɛ], *n.m.* (*Bot.*) Indian pipe.
petite-fille, *n.f.* (*pl.* **petites-filles**) Granddaughter.
petitement, *adv.* In small quantity; not much,

little; slenderly, poorly, meanly. *Il est logé petitement*, he is cramped for room.
petite-nièce [PETIT-NEVEU].
petite-oie, *n.f.* Giblets.
petitesse, *n.f.* Smallness, littleness; diminutiveness; slenderness; insignificance; meanness, shabbiness; mean trick; scantiness, narrowness. *C'est une petitesse de sa part*, it is a piece of meanness on his part; *petitesse d'âme*, meanness of soul; *petitesse d'esprit*, narrowness of mind.
petit-fils, *n.m.* (*pl.* **petits-fils**) Grandson.
petit-gris, *n.m.* (*pl.* **petits-gris**) Miniver, Siberian squirrel.
petit-houx [FRAGON].
pétition [peti'sjɔ̃], *n.f.* Petition, memorial, request. *Faire droit à une pétition*, to grant a petition; *pétition de principe*, petitio principii, begging the question; *présenter une pétition*, to petition, to memorialize.
pétitionnaire, *n.* Petitioner. **pétitionnement**, *n.m.* Petitioning. **pétitionner**, *v.i.* To make a request, to petition.
petit-lait [pəti'lɛ], *n.m.* Whey.
petit-maître, *n.m.* (*pl.* **petits-maîtres**, *fem.* **petite-maîtresse**) Fop, dandy.
petit-nègre, *n.m. inv.* (*fam.*) Used in *parler petit-nègre*, to talk pidgin.
petit-neveu, *n.m.* (*pl.* **petits-neveux**, *fem.* **petite-nièce**) Grand-nephew, great-nephew; grand-niece, great-niece; (*pl.*) descendants.
pétitoire [peti'twa:r], *a.* (*Law*) Petitory (claiming the right of property in real estate).—*n.m.* Claim of ownership.
petit-poivre, *n.m.* [AGNUS-CASTUS].
(*C*) **petit-prêcheur** [pətiprɛ'ʃœ:r], *n.m.* (*Bot.*) Jack-in-the-pulpit.
petits-bois, *n.m. pl.* Window-bars.
petits-enfants, *n.m. pl.* Grand-children.
pétoire [pe'twar], *n.f.* (*pop.*) Pop-gun; (poor) rifle.
peton [pə'tɔ̃], *n.m.* (*colloq.*) Tiny foot.
pétoncle [pe'tɔ̃:kl], *n.m.* Scallop.
Pétrarque [pe'trark], *m.* Petrarch.
pétré [pe'tre], *a.* (*fem.* **-ée**) Stony. *Arabie Pétrée*, Arabia Petraea.
pétrel [pe'trɛl], *n.m.* Petrel. *Pétrel glacial*, fulmar; *pétrel-tempête* or *oiseau des tempêtes*, stormy petrel, Mother Carey's chicken.
pétreux [pe'trø], *a.* (*fem.* **-euse**) (*Anat.*) Stonelike.
pétri [pe'tri], *a.* (*fem.* **-ie**) Kneaded. *C'est un homme tout pétri d'orgueil*, he is eaten up with pride.
pétrifiant [petri'fjã], *a.* (*fem.* **-iante**) Petrifying. **pétrification**, *n.f.* Petrifaction.
pétrifier [petri'fje], *v.t.* To petrify. **se pétrifier**, *v.r.* To turn into stone.
pétrin [pe'trɛ̃], *n.m.* Kneading-trough; (*fig.*) scrape, mess, tight corner. *Être dans un beau pétrin*, to be in a fine pickle, to be in a mess; *se mettre dans le pétrin*, to get into hot water, into trouble.
pétrir [pe'tri:r], *v.t.* To knead; (*fig.*) to mould, to form. *Pétrir l'esprit*, to shape a character. **pétrissable**, *a.* That can be kneaded; (*fig.*) yielding, pliant, easily led. **pétrissage** or **pétrissement**, *n.m.* Kneading; (*fig.*) forming.
pétrisseur, *n.m.* (*fem.* **-euse**) Kneader.—*n.f.* Kneading-machine.

pétrographie [petrɔgra'fi], *n.f.* Petrography.
pétrole [pe'trɔl], *n.m.* Petroleum, (mineral) oil. *Pétrole lampant*, paraffin; (*Am.*) kerosene. **pétroler**, *v.t.* To kindle with paraffin.
pétrolette, *n.f.* (*fam.*) Small motor-bike.
pétroleur, *n.m.* (*fem.* **-euse**) Miscreant who commits arson by means of petroleum.
pétrolier [petrɔ'lje], *a.* (*fem.* **-ière**) Pertaining to oil.—*n.m.* Oil-tanker.
pétrolifère, *a.* Petroliferous, oil-bearing.
pétulance [pety'lɑ̃:s], *n.f.* Petulance, petulancy. **pétulant**, *a.* (*fem.* **-ante**) Petulant.
*__pétun__ [pe'tœ̃], *n.m.* Tobacco; snuff. *__pétuner__, *v.i.* To smoke; to take snuff.
pétunia [pety'nja], *n.m.* Petunia.
pétunsé [petœ̃'se] or **pétunzé**, *n.m.* Petuntse, china-stone.
peu [pø], *adv.* Little, not much; few, not many; not very, not over. *À peu près*, nearly, about; *c'est peu* or *bien peu de chose*, it's a mere trifle; *dans peu de temps*, in a little time; *dans peu de jours*, in a few days; *fort peu*, very little; *peu aimable*, not very likeable; *peu d'argent*, little money; *peu d'hommes*, few men; *peu ou point*, little or none; *pour peu que*, if . . . in the least, . . . if . . . ever so little; *quelque peu*, a little; *si peu que*, however little; (*un*) *tant soit peu*, ever so little; *un peu mieux*, rather better.—*n.m.* Little; bit. *Attendez un peu*, wait a little (while); *encore un peu*, a little longer, a little more; *le peu que je vaux*, the little I am worth; *peu à peu*, little by little, gradually; *peu après*, a little later; *se contenter de peu*, to be content with little; *sous peu*, before long; *vivre de peu*, to live on next to nothing.
peuh [pø], *int.* Pooh!
peulven [pøl'vɛn], *n.m.* Menhir.
peuplade [pœ'plad], *n.f.* Clan, tribe, horde.
peuple (1) [pœpl], *n.m.* People, nation; the people, the multitude, the crowd, the lower classes; small fry (fish). *La lie du peuple* [LIE (1)]; *le menu peuple, le bas peuple*, or *le petit peuple*, the common people; *le peuple singe*, the monkey tribe.—*a.* Plebeian, common, vulgar, gross.
*__peuple__ (2) [pœpl], *n.m.* (*Bot.*) Poplar.
peuplé [pœ'ple], *a.* (*fem.* **-ée**) Heavily populated, populous.
peuplement [pœplə'mɑ̃], *n.m.* Peopling; stocking of a poultry-yard, pond, etc. *Colonie de peuplement*, settlement. **peupler**, *v.t.* To people; to stock with animals, etc.; to populate; to throng. *Peupler un lac de truites*, to stock a lake with trout.—*v.i.* To multiply, to breed. **se peupler**, *v.r.* To become peopled or populous.
peuplier [pœ'plje], *n.m.* Poplar. *Peuplier blanc* or *de Hollande*, or *franc-picard* or *ypréau*, white poplar; *peuplier du Canada*, cottonwood; *peuplier gris* or *grisard*, grey poplar; *peuplier noir d'Italie* or *de Suisse* or *pyramidal*, black Italian poplar.
peur [pœ:r], *n.f.* Fear, dread, terror; apprehension. *Avoir grand'peur*, to be in great fear; *avoir peur*, to be afraid; *avoir peur de son ombre*, to be afraid of one's own shadow; *avoir plus de peur que de mal*, to be more frightened than hurt; *de peur de*, for fear of; *de peur que*, lest, for fear that; *de peur qu'il ne le sache*, lest he should know it; *en être quitte pour la peur*, to get off with a fright, to be

merely frightened; *être mis à faire peur*, to look a fright; *faire peur à quelqu'un*, to frighten someone; *laid à faire peur*, frightfully ugly; *mourir de peur*, to be frightened to death; *sans peur*, fearless, fearlessly; (*fam.*) *une peur bleue*, a blue funk. **peureusement**, *adv.* Timorously. **peureux**, *a.* (*fem.* **-euse**) Fearful, timid, timorous.—*n.m.* A timid person.
peut-être [pø'tɛ:tr], *adv.* Perhaps, maybe; perchance, peradventure. *Peut-être que oui*, perhaps so; *peut-être viendra-t-il* or *peut-être qu'il viendra*, perhaps he will come.—*n.m.* Perhaps, supposition. *Il n'y a pas de peut-être*, there is no perhaps about it.
pff [pf], **pfft**, **pfut**, **pfutt**! *int.* Phew!
phacochère [fakɔ'ʃɛ:r], *n.m.* (*Zool.*) Wart-hog.
phaéton [fae'tɔ̃], *n.m.* Phaeton.
phagocyte [fagɔ'sit], *n.m.* Phagocyte. **phagocytose**, *n.f.* Phagocytosis.
phalange [fa'lɑ̃:ʒ], *n.f.* Phalanx; (*poet.*) army, host; (*Anat.*) phalanx (small bone of finger or toe); (*pop.*) hand. **phalanger**, *n.m.* (*Zool.*) Phalanger. **phalangette**, *n.f.* Ungual phalanx. **phalangien**, *a.* (*fem.* **-ienne**) Phalangeal. **phalangine**, *n.f.* Middle joint of finger.
phalanstère [falɑ̃s'tɛ:r], *n.m.* Phalanstery, viz., house of a phalanx. **phalanstérien**, *a.* and *n.* (*fem.* **-ienne**) Phalansterian.
phalaris [fala'ri:s], *n.m.* Canary grass.
phalarope [fala'rɔp], *n.m.* (*Orn.*) Phalarope.
phalène [fa'lɛn], *n.f.* Phalaena, moth.
phalère [fa'lɛ:r], *n.f.* Phalera moth.
phallique [fa'lik], *a.* Phallic.
phallus, *n.m.* Phallus.
phanérogame [fanerɔ'gam], *a.* (*Bot.*) Phanerogamous.—*n.f. pl.* Phanerogamic plants.
pharamineux [farami'nø], *a.* (*fem.* **-euse**). (*fam.*) Awful, amazing.
pharaon [fara'ɔ̃], *n.m.* Pharaoh; faro (card game).
phare [fa:r], *n.m.* Lighthouse; beacon; (*Motor.*) head-light. *Phare à éclipse*, occulting light; *phare d'atterrissage*, landing-light; *phare flottant*, lightship.
pharisaïque [fariza'ik], *a.* Pharisaic, Pharisaical. **pharisien**, *n.m.* Pharisee; (*fig.*) hypocrite.
pharmaceutique [farmasø'tik], *a.* Pharmaceutical.—*n.f.* Pharmaceutics.
pharmacie, *n.f.* Pharmacy, chemist and druggist's shop, (*U.S.*) drugstore, dispensary; medicine chest. *Pharmacie portative*, medicine chest. **pharmacien**, *n.m.* (*fem.* **-ienne**) Chemist, pharmacist.
pharmacologie, *n.f.* Pharmacology. **pharmacologique**, *a.* Pharmacological.
pharmacopée, *n.f.* Pharmacopoeia.
pharyngite [farɛ̃'ʒit], *n.f.* Pharyngitis.
pharynx [fa'rɛ̃ks], *n.m.* Pharynx.
phase [fa:z], *n.f.* Phasis (of planet); phase; aspect, stage, period, turn. (*Elec.*) *En phase*, in phase; *hors de phase*, out of phase. **phasé**, *a.* (*fem.* **-ée**) Phased.
phaséole [FASÉOLE].
phasme [fasm], *n.m.* (*Ent.*) Phasma.
Phébé [fe'be], *f.* Phoebe.
Phébus [fe'by:s], *m.* (*Myth.*) Phoebus.—*n.m.* (*fig.*) *__bombast, fustian. *Donner dans le phébus*, to write fustian; *parler phébus*, to talk bombast, to rant.

Phèdre [fɛːdr], *m.* Phaedrus.— *f.* Phaedra.
phégoptère [POLYPODE].
phelloderme [fɛlɔ'dɛrm], *n.m.* Phelloderm.
phellogène, *a.* Phellogenetic.
phénacétine [fenase'tin], *n.f.* (*Pharm.*) Phenacetin.
phénakistiscope [fenakistis'kɔp], *n.m.* Phenakistoscope.
phénicien [feni'sjɛ̃], *a.* and *n.m.* (*fem.* -**ienne**) Phoenician.
phénique [fe'nik], *a. Acide phénique,* carbolic acid. **phéniquer,** *v.t.* To carbolize. *Eau phéniquée,* carbolic lotion.
phénix [fe'niks], *n.m.* Phoenix; paragon.
phénol [fe'nɔl], *n.m.* Phenol, carbolic acid.
phénologie [fenɔlɔ'ʒi], *n.f.* Phenology.
phénoménal [fenɔme'nal], *a.* (*fem.* -**ale,** *pl.* -**aux**) Phenomenal; (*colloq.*) extraordinary. **phénoménalement,** *adv.* Phenomenally. **phénoménalisme,** *n.m.* Phenomenalism. **phénomène,** *n.m.* Phenomenon; (*colloq.*) striking thing, event, etc. *Les phénomènes (de la foire),* the freaks (at a fair); *les phénomènes de la nature,* natural phenomena.
phénoménologie, *n.f.* Phenomenology.
phényle [fe'nil], *n.m.* Phenyl.
Philadelphie [filadɛl'fi], *f.* Philadelphia.
philanthrope [filɑ̃'trɔp], *n.m.* Philanthropist. **philanthropie,** *n.f.* Philanthropy. **philanthropique,** *a.* Philanthropic. **philanthropisme,** *n.m.* Philanthropism.
philatélie [filate'li], *n.f.* Philately, stampcollecting. **philatélique,** *a.* Philatelic. **philatéliste,** *n.* Stamp collector.
philharmonique [filarmɔ'nik], *a.* Philharmonic.
philhellène [filɛl'lɛn], *n.* Philhellene. **philhellénisme,** *n.m.* Philhellenism.
Philippe [fi'lip], *m.* Philip.
Philippes [fi'lip], *n.* Philippi.
Philippines [fili'pin], **les,** *f.pl.* The Philippines.
philippique [fili'pik], *n.f.* Philippic; violent speech.
philistin [filis'tɛ̃], *n.m.* (*fem.* -**ine**) Philistine, person of vulgar taste. **philistinisme,** *n.m.* Philistinism.
philologie [filɔlɔ'ʒi], *n.f.* Philology. **philologique,** *a.* Philological. **philologiquement,** *adv.* Philologically. **philologue,** *n.m.* Philologist.
philomèle [filɔ'mɛl], *n.f.* Philomela (nightingale).
philosophailler [filɔzɔfa'je], *v.i.* (*fam.*) To philosophize extravagantly.
philosophale [filɔzɔ'fal], *a.f. La pierre philosophale,* the philosophers' stone.
philosophe [filɔ'zɔf], *n.m.* Philosopher, philosophical person.—*a.* Philosophical.
philosopher, *v.i.* To philosophize.
philosophie, *n.f.* Philosophy; class in French school roughly equivalent to English upper sixth; (*Print.*) small pica. *Faire sa philosophie,* to take a course of philosophy. **philosophique,** *a.* Philosophical. **philosophiquement,** *adv.* Philosophically.
philosophisme, *n.m.* Philosophism.
philtre [filtr], *n.m.* Philtre.
phlébite [fle'bit], *n.f.* Phlebitis.
phlébotome, *n.m.* Lancet (for bleeding).
phlébotomie, *n.f.* Phlebotomy.
phlegmatique [FLEGMATIQUE].

phlegmon [flɛg'mɔ̃], *n.m.* (*Med.*) Phlegmon. **phlegmoneux,** *a.* (*fem.* -**euse**) Phlegmonous.
phléole [FLÉOLE].
phlogistique [flɔʒis'tik], *n.f.* Phlogiston.
phlox [flɔks], *n.m.* Phlox. *Phlox subulé,* moss pink.
phlyctène [flik'tɛːn], *n.f.* Phlyctaena, blister.
phobie [fɔ'bi], *n.f.* Phobia, morbid dread.
pholade [fɔ'lad], *n.f.* (*Conch.*) Pholas.
phonation [fɔna'sjɔ̃], *n.f.* Phonation.
phonème [fɔ'nɛm], *n.m.* Phoneme.
phonéticien [fɔneti'sjɛ̃], *n.m.* Phonetist. **phonétique,** *a.* Phonetic.—*n.f.* Phonetics. **phonétiquement,** *adv.* Phonetically.
phonique [fɔ'nik], *a.* Phonic.
phonogénique [fɔnɔʒe'nik], *a.* (*Cine.*) Suitable for sound recording.
phonographe [fɔnɔ'graf], *n.m.* Phonograph. *Phonographe à disques,* gramophone. **phonographie,** *n.f.* Phonography, phonetic spelling, sound recording. **phonographique,** *a.* Phonographic.
phonologie [fɔnɔlɔ'ʒi], *n.f.* Phonology.
phonomètre [fɔnɔ'mɛtr], *n.m.* Phonometer.
phonoscope, *n.m.* Phonoscope.
phoque [fɔk], *n.m.* Seal. *Phoque à capuchon,* hooded seal; *phoque à trompe,* elephant seal.
phosgène [fɔs'ʒɛn], *n.m.* Phosgene (gas).
phosphate [fɔs'fat], *n.m.* Phosphate. **phosphaté,** *a.* (*fem.* -**ée**) Phosphatic. **phosphater,** *v.t.* To fertilize (land) with phosphates. **phosphite,** *n.m.* Phosphite.
phosphore [fɔs'fɔːr], *n.m.* Phosphorus. **phosphorescence,** *n.f.* Phosphorescence. **phosphorescent,** *a.* (*fem.* -**ente**) Phosphorescent. **phosphoreux,** *a.m.* Phosphorous. **phosphorique,** *a.* Phosphoric. **phosphure,** *n.m.* Phosphide. **phosphuré,** *a.* (*fem.* -**ée**) Phosphoretted.
photo [fɔ'to], *n.f. abbr.* of *photographie.*
photocopie [fɔtɔkɔ'pi], *n.f.* Photographic reproduction, photocopy.
photoélectricité [fɔtɔelɛktrisi'te], *n.f.* Photoelectric current. **photoélectrique,** *a.* Photoelectric. *Cellule photoélectrique,* photoelectric cell.
photogénique [fɔtɔʒe'nik], *a.* Actinic; photogenic.
photographe [fɔtɔ'graf], *n.m.* Photographer. **photographie,** *n.f.* Photography; photograph. **photographier,** *v.t.* To photograph. **photographique,** *a.* Photographic. *Appareil photographique,* camera. **photographiquement,** *adv.* Photographically.
photogravure, *n.f.* Photogravure.
photolithographie, *n.f.* Photolithography.
photomécanique, *a.* Photomechanical.
photomètre, *n.m.* Photometer. **photométrie,** *n.f.* Photometry.
photomicrographie, *n.f.* Microphotography.
photophone, *n.m.* Photophone.
photosphère, *n.f.* Photosphere.
photosynthèse, *n.f.* Photosynthesis.
photothérapie, *n.f.* Phototherapy.
phototype, *n.m.* Phototype. **phototypographie,** *n.f.* Half-tone engraving.
phragmite (1) [frag'mit], *n.m.* or *rousserolle,* or *fauvette des roseaux.* (*Orn.*) Sedge warbler.
phragmite (2) [frag'mit], *n.m.* or (*Bot.*) *phragmite commun* or *roseau à balais.* Reed.
phrase [frɑːz], *n.f.* Sentence; (*Mus.*) phrase.

Faire des phrases, to speak or write in set phrases, in an affected way; *membre de phrase, phrase; phrase toute faite*, commonplace, stock phrase. **phrasé**, *n.m.* (*Mus.*) Phrasing.
phraséologie, *n.f.* Phraseology. **phraser**, *v.i.* To phrase; (*pej.*) to use flowery language.— *v.t.* To express in phrases, to phrase; (*Mus.*) to phrase.
phraseur, *n.m.* (*fem.* **-euse**) (*fam.*) Verbose writer or talker.
phrénique [fre'nik], *a.* (*Anat.*) Phrenic.
phrénologie [frenɔlɔ'ʒi], *n.f.* Phrenology. **phrénologique**, *a.* Phrenological. **phrénologiste**, *n.m.* Phrenologist.
Phrygie [fri'ʒi], *f.* Phrygia.
phrygien [fri'ʒjɛ̃], *a. and n.* (*fem.* **-ienne**) Phrygian. *Bonnet phrygien*, Phrygian cap (cap of liberty).
phtalique [fta'lik], *a.* (*Chem.*) Phthalic.
phtiriase [fti'rjɑːz], *n.f.* (*Med.*) Phthiriasis.
phtisie [fti'zi], *n.f.* Phthisis, consumption. *Être atteint de phtisie*, to be consumptive.
phtisique, *a.* Consumptive.—*n.* Consumptive person.
phylactère [filak'tɛːr], *n.m.* Phylactery.
phyllithe or **phyllite** [fi'lit], *n.f.* Phyllite.
phyllode [fi'lɔd], *n.f.* (*Bot.*) Phyllode. **phylloïde**, *a.* Phylloid. **phyllopode**, *a.* Phyllopodous.—*n.m.* Phyllopod. **phyllotaxie**, *n.f.* Phyllotaxis.
phylloxéra [filɔkse'ra], *n.m.* (*no plural*) Phylloxera. **phylloxéré**, *a.* (*fem.* **-ée**) Phylloxerized (vine).
physalie [fiza'li], *n.f.* (*Zool.*) Physalia.
physalis [fiza'lis], *n.m.* [COQUERELLE].
physicien [fizi'sjɛ̃], *n.m.* (*fem.* **-ienne**) Physicist; natural philosopher.
physicisme, *n.m.* Physicism.
physiocrate [fizjo'krat], *n.m.* Physiocrat.
physiognomonie [fizjɔgnɔmɔ'ni], *n.f.* Physiognomy.
physiographie, *n.f.* Physiography.
physiologie [fizjɔlɔ'ʒi], *n.f.* Physiology. **physiologique**, *a.* Physiological. **physiologiste** or **physiologue**, *n.* Physiologist.
physionomie [fizjɔnɔ'mi], *n.f.* Physiognomy, countenance, aspect, look. **physionomiste**, *n.* Physiognomist.
physiothérapie [fizjɔtera'pi], *n.f.* (*Med.*) Physiotherapy.
physiothérapiste, *n.* Physiotherapist.
physique [fi'zik], *a.* Physical, material, bodily. *Culture physique*, physical culture; *exercices physiques*, (*Mil.*) physical drill, (*fam.*) physical jerks.—*n.f.* Physics.—*n.m.* Physique, natural constitution; outward appearance. *Il a le physique de l'emploi*, he looks the part. **physiquement**, *adv.* Physically, bodily.
phytochimie [fitɔʃi'mi], *n.f.* Phytochemistry.
phytographie, *n.f.* Phytography. **phytologie**, *n.f.* Phytology, botany. **phytophage**, *a.* Plant-eating. **phytozoaire**, *n.m.* (*Zool.*) Phytozoon.
piaculaire [pjaky'lɛːr], *a.* Expiatory.
*****piaffe** [pjaf], *n.f.* Ostentation, show.
piaffement [pjaf'mɑ̃], *n.m.* Pawing the ground.
piaffer [pja'fe], *v.i.* To paw the ground, to prance (of horses); (*fig.*) to fume, to bridle. **piaffeur**, *n.m.* (*fem.* **-euse**) Pawer, prancer. —*a.* Pawing, prancing.
piaillard [pja'jaːr], *a.* (*fem.* **-arde**) Cheeping

(bird); mewling (child). **piailler**, *v.i.* To cheep (of small birds); (*fig.*) to squall, to scream, to bawl; to rant. *Des enfants qui piaillent toujours*, squalling brats. **piaillerie**, *n.f.* Cheeping, squealing. **piailleur**, *n.m.* (*fem.* **-euse**) Cheeper, squaller.
pian [pjɑ̃], *n.m.* Yaws.
pianiste [pja'nist], *n.* Pianist.
piano (1) [pja'no], *n.m.* Piano, pianoforte. *Jouer du piano*, to play (on) the piano; *piano à queue*, grand piano; *piano à demi-queue*, baby grand piano; *piano droit*, upright or cottage piano; *tenir le piano*, to accompany on the piano.
piano (2) [pja'no], *adv.* (*Mus.*) Piano, softly.
pianotage, *n.m.* Strumming on the piano.
pianoter, *v.i.* (*colloq.*) To strum on the piano; to drum with the fingers.
piastre [pjastr], *n.f.* Piastre; (*C*) dollar.
piat [pja], *n.m.* Young magpie.
piaulard [pjo'laːr] or **piauleur**, *a.* (*fem.* **-arde** or **-euse**) Puling, whining; cheeping (of chickens).—*n.* Puler, whiner. **piaule**, *n.f.* (*slang*) House, digs. **piaulement**, *n.m.* Whining, puling; cheeping (of chickens). **piauler**, *v.i.* To cheep (of chickens etc.); (*fig.*) to pule, to whine.
pible [pibl], *n.m.* *Mât à pible*, pole-mast.
pic (1) [pik], *n.m.* Pick, pickaxe; gaff; peak (of a mountain); pique (at piquet). *À pic*, steep, vertical, sheer, perpendicular(ly); (*Naut.*) apeak; (*colloq.*) *tomber* or *arriver à pic*, to happen, to come opportunely, à propos.
pic (2) [pik], *n.m.* Woodpecker. *Pic maçon*, nuthatch [*see also* ÉPEICHE, ÉPEICHETTE, PICVERT].
picador [pika'dɔːr], *n.m.* Picador.
picaillons [pika'jɔ̃], *n.m. pl.* (*slang*) Money, tin. *Avoir des picaillons*, to be rich.
Picardie [pikar'di], *f.* Picardy.
picaresque [pika'rɛsk], *a.* Picaresque.
piccolo or **picolo** [pikɔ'lo], *n.m.* Light wine, new wine (on draught in the locality); (*Mus.*) piccolo.
pichenette [piʃ'nɛt], *n.f.* (*fam.*) Fillip, flick.
pichet [pi'ʃɛ], *n.m.* Small jug; pitcher (for cider or wine).
picholine [piʃɔ'lin], *n.f.* Pickled olive.
pick-up, *n.m. inv.* Gramophone, pick-up, record player. *Bras de pick-up*, pick-up arm.
picoler [pikɔ'le], *v.i.* (*pop.*) To hit the bottle.
picorée [pikɔ're], *n.f.* *Aller à la picorée*, (of birds) to go plundering. **picorer**, *v.i.* To go out marauding, to forage, to pick, to scratch about; (*fig.*) to pilfer.—*v.t.* To pilfer.
picoreur, *n.m.* Marauder.
picot [pi'ko], *n.m.* Splinter (of wood); wooden wedge; pick-hammer; picot (of lace); net for flat fish.
picotage [pikɔ'taːʒ], *n.m.* Wedging; teasing.
picote [pi'kɔt], *n.f.* (*pop.*) Smallpox. **picoté**, *a.* (*fem.* **-ée**) Pricked, marked.
picotement [pikɔt'mɑ̃], *n.m.* Pricking, tingling. **picoter**, *v.t.* To cause to tingle; to prick, to mark with tiny points; to peck (of birds); (*fig.*) to tease. **picoterie**, *n.f.* (*colloq.*) Teasing.
picoteur, *n.m.* (*fem.* **-euse**) Teaser.—*n.f.* Maker of picots in Alençon lace.
picotin, *n.m.* (*Measure*) Peck; peck of oats.
picrate [pi'krat], *n.m.* Picrate. **picrique**, *a.* Picric.

Pictes [pikt], *m. pl.* Picts.
pictique [pik'tik], *a.* Pictish.
pictographie [piktogra'fi], *n.f.* Picture-writing.
pictural, *a.* (*fem.* **-ale**, *pl.* **-aux**) Pictorial.
picvert or **pivert** [pi'vɛːr], *n.m.* Green woodpecker [*see also* ÉPEICHE].
Pie [pi], *m.* Pius.
pie (1) [pi], *n.f.* Magpie. *Pie-grièche grise* or *écorcheuse*, red-backed shrike, butcher bird; *grande pie-grièche grise* or *boiselière*, great grey shrike; *pie de mer* [HUITRIER]. *Elle jase comme une pie,* she chatters like a magpie; *il croit avoir trouvé la pie au nid,* he thinks he has made a great discovery, he has found a mare's nest.—*a. inv.* and *n.* Piebald (horse).
pie (2) [pi], *a.* (used in) *Œuvre pie,* pious *or* charitable deed; (*pl.*) good works.
pièce [pjɛs], *n.f.* Piece, bit, fragment; patch; barrel, cask (of wine etc.); head (of cattle, poultry, etc.); apartment, room; piece of ground, field; sheet (of water); piece of ordnance, cannon; document, paper; piece of poetry, music, etc., play; coin; medal; joint (of meat); (*colloq.*) fellow. *Appartement de deux pièces,* two-roomed flat; *donner la pièce,* to give a tip; *en pièce,* in the cask, in the wood; *être armé de toutes pièces,* to be armed at all points; *être fait de pièces et de morceaux,* to be made of shreds and patches; *faire de toutes pièces,* to do a thing entirely; *mettre* or *tailler en pièces,* to break *or* take to pieces, to tear to pieces, to defame; *mettre quelqu'un en pièces,* to pull someone to pieces; *mettre une pièce à,* to patch; *monter une pièce,* to get up *or* produce a play; *par pièces,* piecemeal; *pièce à conviction,* material *or* circumstantial evidence; *pièce d'échecs,* chess piece; *pièce de monnaie,* coin; *pièce de musée,* museum piece; *pièce de résistance,* principal dish *or* joint; *pièce de théâtre,* play; *pièce justificative,* voucher; *pièce montée,* set piece; *rassemblage de pièces,* patchwork; *tout d'une pièce,* all of a piece; *travailler à la pièce,* to do piece work; *un deux-pièces,* a two-piece garment; *une pièce d'artillerie,* a piece of ordnance.
piécette [pje'sɛt], *n.f.* Small coin; short play.
pied [pje], *n.m.* Foot; footing; footprint, track; leg (of furniture); stand, rest; stalk (of plants); (*pop.*) idiot, fool. *Aller à pied* [ALLER (1)]; *au pied de la lettre* [LETTRE]; *arbre sur pied* [ARBRE]; *avoir bon pied, bon œil,* to be in sound health; *avoir pied,* to have a footing, not to be out of one's depth; (*pop.*) *ça te fera les pieds,* it will serve you right; *cela a tant de pieds de long,* that is so many feet long; *c'est un Virgile au petit pied,* he is a pale imitator of Virgil; *coup de pied,* kick; *coup de pied tombé,* drop kick; *le coup de pied de l'âne,* the unkindest cut of all; *couper l'herbe sous le pied à quelqu'un* [HERBE]; *de pied en cap,* from head to foot; *de pied ferme,* without stirring, firmly; *donner plus de pied à une échelle,* to give more slope to a ladder; *être à pied d'œuvre,* to be ready to start working; *être assis au pied d'un arbre,* to be seated at the foot of a tree; *être en pied,* to be actively employed; *faire des pieds et des mains pour,* to go all out for; *être mis à pied,* to be suspended or dismissed; *être sur pied,* to be up; *faire un pied de nez à* [NEZ]; *haut le pied* [HAUT, *adv.*]; *il a fait cela au pied levé,* he did that offhand;

il l'a pris au pied levé, he has taken him unawares; *il ne sait sur quel pied danser* [DANSER]; *lâcher pied* [LÂCHER]; *le pied du lit,* the foot of the bed; *les doigts de pied,* the toes; *les pieds de devant,* the fore-feet; (*fig.*) *lever le pied,* to bolt; *marcher pieds nus,* to walk barefoot; *marcher sur la pointe des pieds* [MARCHER]; *mettre pied à terre,* to alight, dismount, disembark; *mettre quelqu'un au pied du mur* [MUR]; *ne pouvoir mettre un pied devant l'autre,* to be too weak for walking; *perdre pied* [PERDRE]; *pied à coulisse,* gauge for measuring thickness; *pied à pied,* step by step, by degrees; *pied à terre!* (*Mil.*) dismount; *pied bot* [BOT]; *pied carré,* square foot; *pied de projecteur,* (*Cine.*) stand; *pied plat,* flat foot, (*fig.*) knave, mean rascal; *pied et poings liés,* tied hand and foot; *portrait en pied,* full-length portrait; *prendre pied,* to settle down; *récolte sur pied,* standing corn; *sauter à pieds joints,* to jump over close-legged, (*fig.*) to ride rough-shod over; *sécher sur pied,* to pine away; *sur le pied de,* at the rate of; *sur pied,* on foot, standing, astir, in readiness; *sur le pied de guerre,* on a war footing; *sur un pied d'égalité,* on an equal footing; *tenir pied,* to stand firm; *une coutume qui prend pied,* a custom that is gaining ground; *un pied de céleri* [CÉLERI]; *pied de mouche,* (*Print.*) paragraph mark.
pied-à-terre, *n.m. inv.* Temporary lodging.
pied-d'alouette, *n.m.* (*pl.* **pieds-d'alouette**) (*Bot.*) Larkspur.
pied-de-biche, *n.m.* (*pl.* **pieds-de-biche**) Bell-pull; (*Surg.*) forceps; nail-clench. **pied-de-chat**, *n.m.* (*pl.* **pieds-de-chat**) (*Bot.*) Ground-ivy.
pied-de-cheval, *n.m.* (*pl.* **pieds-de-cheval**) Large oyster.
pied-de-griffon, *n.m.* (*pl.* **pieds-de-griffon**) Setterwort.
pied-de-loup [LYCOPODE].
pied-de-lion, *n.m.* (*pl.* **pieds-de-lion**) (*Bot.*) Lady's mantle.
pied-de-poule, *n.m.* (*Tex.*) Broken check.
(*C*) **pied-de-roi** [pjedə'rwa], *n.m.* Folding-rule (3 feet).
pied-de-veau, *n.m.* (*pl.* **pieds-de-veau**) (*Bot.*) Cuckoo-pint.
pied-d'oiseau, *n.m.* (*pl.* **pieds-d'oiseau**) Bird's-foot (plant).
pied-droit, *n.m.* (*pl.* **pieds-droits**) (*Civ. Eng.*) Upright, pillar, pier; jamb (of door or window).
piédestal [pjedɛs'tal], *n.m.* (*pl.* **-aux**) Pedestal.
piédouche [pje'duʃ], *n.m.* Small pedestal (for a bust, vase, etc.).
piège [pjɛːʒ], *n.m.* Trap, snare. *Il a donné* or *il est tombé dans le piège,* he fell into the trap; *prendre au piège,* to catch in a trap; *tendre* or *dresser un piège,* to set a snare. **piégeage**, *n.m.* Trapping of animals. **piéger**, *v.t.* To trap (animals); (*Mil.*) to attach a booby trap.
pie-grièche [pigri'ɛʃ], *n.f.* (*pl.* **pies-grièches**) (*Orn.*) Shrike; (*fig.*) shrew [*see also* PIE (1)].
pie-mère [pi'mɛːr], *n.f.* (*Anat.*) Pia mater.
Piémont [pje'mɔ̃], **le**, *m.* Piedmont.
pierraille [pjɛ'rɑːj], *n.f.* Mass of broken or small stones, rubble, ballast.
Pierre, *m.* Peter.
pierre [pjɛːr], *n.f.* Stone; (*Path.*) calculus. *Faire d'une pierre deux coups,* to kill two birds

with one stone; *il gèle à pierre fendre* [GELER]; *jeter des pierres dans le jardin de quelqu'un*, to throw out insinuations against someone; *jeter la pierre à quelqu'un*, to accuse someone; *pierre à aiguiser* or *à repasser*, grindstone; *pierre à fusil*, flint; *pierre à plâtre*, gypsum; *pierre d'achoppement*, stumbling-block; *pierre d'attente*, toothing stone; *pierre de taille*, freestone; *pierre de touche*, touchstone; *pierre fine* [FIN (2)]; *pierre infernale* [INFERNAL]; *pierres précieuses*, precious stones, gems; *pierre qui roule n'amasse pas mousse*, a rolling stone gathers no moss; *poser la première pierre*, to lay the foundation-stone; *un cœur de pierre*, a heart of stone. **pierrée**, *n.f.* Stone drain. **pierreries**, *n.f. pl.* Precious stones, gems.

pierrette, *n.f.* Little stone, pebble; hensparrow; woman attired as a pierrot.

pierreux, *a.* (*fem.* **-euse**) Stony, flinty, gritty, gravelly; calculous.

pierrier, *n.m.* *Gun for firing stones; swivelgun; stone drain.

pierrot [pjɛ'ro], *n.m.* Pierrot, merry-andrew; house-sparrow. *Faire le pierrot*, to play the fool; *un drôle de pierrot*, a queer fish.

pierrures [pjɛ'ry:r], *n.f. pl.* Pearls (at base of deer's horns).

piétage [pje'taʒ], *n.m.* (*Naut.*) Draught-marks.

piété [pje'te], *n.f.* Piety, godliness; affection, filial devotion.

piéter [pje'te], *v.i. irr.* (*coniug. like* ACCÉLÉRER) To toe the mark (at bowls); to run (of partridge, pheasant).—*v.t. Piéter le drap*, to give cloth a nap; *piéter l'étrave, l'étambot*, or *le gouvernail*, (*Naut.*) to mark the numbers of feet on the stem, on the stern-post *or* on the rudder; *piéter le gazon*, to mow the lawn closely; *piéter quelqu'un contre quelque chose*, to set someone against something. **se piéter**, *v.r.* To resist strongly, to set oneself (against).

piétin [pje'tɛ̃], *n.m.* Foot-rot (of cattle).

piétinement [pjetin'mɑ̃], *n.m.* Stamping, trampling.

piétiner, *v.i.* To stamp, to move one's feet about; to paw the ground (of horses). *Piétiner de colère*, to stamp with rage.—*v.t.* To tread or trample under foot, to stamp on.

piétisme [pje'tism], *n.m.* (*Relig.*) Pietism.

piéton [pje'tɔ̃], *n.m.* (*fem.* **-onne**) Pedestrian; *rural postman.—**a. Sentier piéton*, footpath.

piètre [pjɛ'tr], *a.* Poor, paltry, pitiful. *Avoir une piètre opinion de quelqu'un*, to have a poor opinion of someone.

piètrement, *adv.* Pitifully, wretchedly.

piètrerie, *n.f.* Shabby thing, wretched stuff.

pieu [pjø], *n.m.* (*pl.* **pieux**) Stake, pile, post; (*slang*) bed.

pieusement [pjøz'mɑ̃], *adv.* Piously, devoutly, religiously; obediently; reverently.

pieuter (se) [pjø'te], *v.r.* (*slang*) To go to bed, to kip down.

pieuvre [pjœ:vr], *n.f.* Octopus, poulpe, devil-fish.

pieux [pjø], *a.* (*fem.* **pieuse**) Pious, godly.

piézo-électricité [pjezɔelektrisi'te], *n.f.* Piezo-electricity. **piézomètre**, *n.m.* Piezometer.

pif (1) [pif], *n.m.* (*slang*) Bottle-nose, big nose.

pif (2) [pif], *int.* Flick. *Pif paf*, flick, flack.

***piffre** [pifr], *n.m.* (*fem.* **-esse**) (*slang*) Stout person; glutton.

pigamon [piga'mɔ̃], *n.m.* (*Bot.*) Meadow-rue.

pige [pi:ʒ], *n.f.* Measure, tape, gauge; (*Print.*) amount to be set up in given time, take; (*pop.*) year. *Faire la pige à quelqu'un*, to outdo someone, to do better than someone.

pigeon [pi'ʒɔ̃], *n.m.* Pigeon, dove; builder's plaster; (*slang*) dupe, gull. *Pigeon bleu* or *colombin*, stock-dove; *pigeon boulant*, pouter; *pigeon bouvreuil*, archangel; *pigeon brésilien*, helmet pigeon; *pigeon à capuchon* or *huppé*, jacobin; *pigeon cavalier*, horseman; *pigeon cravaté*, turbit; *pigeon culbutant*, tumbler; *pigeon grosse gorge*, cropper; *pigeon nonnain*, capuchin; *pigeon paon* or *trembleur*, fantail; *pigeon ramier*, ring-dove; wood-pigeon, (*in* Scots) cushat; *pigeon romain*, runt; *pigeon de rocher*, rock-dove; *pigeon tambour*, tambourine; *pigeon voyageur*, carrier pigeon, homer. *Aile-de-pigeon*, (*Naut.*) skysail; *gorge de pigeon*, dove-coloured (of silks); *pigeon artificiel*, clay-pigeon; *pigeon vole*, a children's game. **pigeonneau**, *n.m.* (*pl.* **-eaux**) Young pigeon, squab; (*fig.*) young dupe. **pigeonnier**, *n.m.* Pigeon-house, dove-cot.

piger, *v.t.* (*pop.*) To catch; to make out; to look at; to measure. *Tu piges?* do you twig?

pigment [pig'mɑ̃], *n.m.* (*Anat.*) Pigment. **pigmentaire**, *a.* Pigmentary. **pigmentation**, *n.f.* Pigmentation. **pigmenté**, *a.* (*fem.* **-ée**) Pigmented. **pigmenteux**, *a.* (*fem.* **-euse**) Pigmental.

pigne [piɲ], *n.f.* Pine-cone; pine-seed.

pignocher [piɲɔ'ʃe], *v.t.* To pick at (one's food).—*v.i.* To nibble at food; to paint with tiny strokes.

pignon (1) [pi'ɲɔ̃], *n.m.* Gable end; gable pinion (cog-wheel), sprocket-wheel [*see also* PIN]. *Avoir pignon sur rue*, to have a house of one's own; *grand pignon*, (of cycle) front chain wheel.

pignon (2) [pi'ɲɔ̃], *n.m.* Kernel of fir-cone.

pignoratif [piɲɔra'tif], *a.* (*fem.* **-ive**) (*Law*) Pignorative, with power of redemption. **pignoration**, *n.f.* Pignoration.

pignouf [pi'ɲuf], *n.m.* (*pop.*) Skunk; stingy fellow.

pilaf [pi'laf], *n.m.* Pilau, pilaff (stewed rice with mussels etc.).

pilage [pi'la:ʒ], *n.m.* Pounding, crushing.

pilaire [pi'lɛ:r], *a.* Pilous, pilose.

pilastre [pi'lastr], *n.m.* (*Arch.*) Pilaster. *Pilastre d'escalier*, newel post.

Pilate [*see* PONCE].

pilau [pi'lo] or **pilaw** [PILAF].

pilchard [pil'ʃar], *n.m.* Pilchard.

pile (1) [pil], *n.f.* Pile, heap; pier (of a bridge etc). mole (masonry); (*Elec.*) battery. *Mettre en pile*, to pile up; *pile atomique*, atomic pile; *pile voltaïque, galvanique*, voltaic or galvanic battery; *pile de rechange*, refill (for a torch); *pile sèche*, dry cell.

pile (2) [pil], *n.f.* Reverse (of coins). *Jouer à pile ou face*, to play at heads or tails, to toss up. (*fam.*) *S'arrêter pile*, to stop abruptly; *tomber pile*, to arrive just right.

pile (3) [pil], *n.f.* Beating-trough (for paper etc.); hence *mettre* (or *flanquer*) *une pile à quelqu'un*, (*fam.*) to give someone a sound thrashing.

piler [pi'le], *v.t.* To pound, to crush, to powder, to bray, to pestle.

pilet [pi'lɛ], *n.m.* Pintail (duck).

pileur [pi'lœ:r], *n.m.* (*fem.* **-euse** (1)) Pounder, beater, grinder.

pileux [pi'lø], *a.* (*fem.* **-euse** (2)) Pilous, hairy. *Avoir le système pileux développé*, to be very hairy; *le système pileux*, the hair.

pilier [pi'lje], *n.m.* Pillar, column, post; strut (of aircraft); (*fig.*) support, supporter, prop, pillar. *Pilier de café*, (*fig.*) a ' regular ' at the pub.

pilifère [pili'fɛ:r], *a.* (*Bot.*) Piliferous.

piliforme [pili'fɔrm], *a.* (*Bot.*) Piliform.

pillage [pi'ja:ʒ], *n.m.* Pillage, plunder, looting; (*fig.*) pilfering. *Livrer au pillage*, to yield to plunder. **pillard,** *n.* (*fem.* **-arde**) Pillager, plunderer.—*a.* Pillaging, plundering; predatory.

piller, *v.t.* To pillage, to plunder; to ransack; to pilfer; to seize (of dogs); to be guilty of plagiarism. *Ce chien pille tous les autres chiens*, that dog flies at all the other dogs; *pille! pille!* seize him! tear him! **pillerie,** *n.f.* Pillage, plunder; extortion.

pilleur, *n.m.* (*fem.* **-euse**) Pillager, plunderer, pilferer. *Pilleurs d'épaves*, wreckers.

pilon [pi'lɔ̃], *n.m.* Pestle; rammer, beetle, stamper;. (*colloq.*) drum-stick (of a cooked fowl); wooden leg, (*pop.*) wooden-legged man; beggar. *Mettre au pilon*, to pulp (books). **pilonnage,** *n.m.* Ramming, pounding, stamping, milling. **pilonner,** *v.t.* To ram, to pound, to mill, to pug (clay); to stamp (ore).

pilori [pilɔ'ri], *n.m.* Pillory. *Clouer quelqu'un au pilori*, to pillory someone. **pilorier,** *v.t.* (*conjugated like* PRIER) To pillory, to put in the pillory.

piloselle [pilɔ'zɛl], *n.f.*, or *épervière piloselle*, hawk weed, mouse-ear.

pilot [pi'lo], *n.m.* (*Civ. Eng.*) Pile, stake; heap of salt.

pilotage (1) [pilɔ'ta:ʒ], *n.m.* (*Civ. Eng.*) Pile-driving, piling.

pilotage (2) [pilɔ'ta:ʒ], *n.m.* (*Naut. and Av.*) Piloting.

pilote [pi'lɔt], *n.m.* Pilot; guide; pilot-fish. *Bateau pilote*, pilot cutter; *pilote aviateur*, pilot of an aeroplane; *pilote côtier*, coasting pilot; *pilote d'essai*, test pilot; *pilote hauturier*, deep-sea pilot; *pilote lamaneur*, coasting, harbour or river pilot.

piloter (1) [pilɔ'te], *v.t.* To pile, to drive piles into.

piloter (2) [pilɔ'te], *v.t.* (*Naut. and Av.*) To pilot; (*fig.*) to guide, to show the way to.

pilotin [pilɔ'tɛ̃], *n.m.* Apprentice in the merchant service.

pilotis [pilɔ'ti], *n.m.* Series of piles forming a foundation etc.; pilework.

pilou [pi'lu], *n.m.* Flannelette.

pilulaire [pily'lɛ:r], *a.* Pilular.

pilule [pi'lyl], *n.f.* Pill. *Avaler la pilule*, (*fig.*) to swallow the pill; *dorer la pilule*, to gild the pill. **pilulier,** *n.m.* Pill-machine.

pimbêche [pɛ̃'bɛʃ], *n.f.* Uppish and impertinent woman.

(C) **pimbina** [pɛ̃bi'na], *n.m.* (*Bot.*) Viburnum.

piment [pi'mɑ̃], *n.m.* Pimento, allspice. **pimentade,** *n.f.* (*Cook.*) Pimento sauce. **pimenté,** *a.* (*fem.* **-ée**) Highly spiced. **pimenter,** *v.t.* To flavour with pimento; (*fig.*) to make pungent or spicy (a story).

pimpant [pɛ̃'pɑ̃], *a.* (*fem.* **-ante**) Natty, spruce, smart.

pimprenelle [pɛ̃prə'nɛl], *n.f.* (*Bot.*) Burnet.

pin [pɛ̃], *n.m.* Pine-tree. *Pin maritime* or *de Bordeaux*, pinaster, sea-pine, cluster pine; *pin noir d'Autriche*, Austrian black pine; *pin parasol* or *à pignon*, parasol pine; *pin sylvestre* or *de Suisse* or *de Genève* or *pin à mâts*, Norway pine. *Pomme de pin*, fir-cone, fir-nut.

pinacle [pi'nakl], *n.m.* Pinnacle. *Il est sur le pinacle*, he is as high as he can go; *mettre quelqu'un sur le pinacle*, to praise someone to the skies.

pinacothèque [pinakɔ'tɛk], *n.f.* Picture-gallery.

pinard [pi'na:r], *n.m.* (*pop.*) Wine.

pinasse [pi'nas], *n.f.* (*Naut.*) Pinnace, shallop.

pinastre [pi'nastr], *n.m.* (*pop.*) Sea pine.

pince [pɛ̃:s], *n.f.* Pinch, pinching, nipping; hold, grip; pincers, nippers, pliers, forceps, gripper, tongs, clip; crowbar (lever); toe (of a horse's foot); claw (of a lobster etc.); pleat (in a garment etc.); incisor (tooth). *Avoir bonne pince*, to have a firm grip; *petites pinces*, tweezers; *pince à gaz*, gas pliers; *pince à linge*, clothes-peg; *pinces à ongles*, nail clippers; *pinces à pantalon*, bicycle clips; *pinces coupantes*, wire cutters; *pince d'un fer à cheval*, front of a horse-shoe; *pinces à sucre*, sugar-tongs; *serrer la pince à quelqu'un*, (*slang*) to shake hands with someone; (*C*) *pince-de-canot*, the sharp end of a birch-bark canoe. **pincé,** *a.* (*fem.* **-ée**) Affected, stiff, prim. *Lèvres pincées*, thin, tight lips.

pinceau [pɛ̃'so], *n.m.* (*pl.* **-eaux**) Paint-brush. *Avoir un beau pinceau*, (*Paint.*) to have a fine touch; *coup de pinceau*, stroke of the brush.

pincée [pɛ̃'se], *n.f.* Pinch (of snuff, salt, etc.).

pincelier [pɛ̃sə'lje], *n.m.* (*Paint.*) Dip-cup.

pincement [pɛ̃s'mɑ̃], *n.m.* Pinching, nipping off of the heads of buds. **pince-monseigneur,** *n.f.* (*pl.* **pinces-monseigneur**) Burglar's jemmy. **pince-nez,** *n.m. inv.* Pince-nez, (folding) eye-glasses. **pince-notes,** *n.m. inv.* Paper-clip. **pincer,** *v.t.* To pinch, to nip, to compress; to hold fast, to grip; to bite (of cold etc.); to catch; to nip off (buds etc.); to pluck (a musical instrument); (*Naut.*) to hug (the wind). *En pincer pour quelqu'un*, (*pop.*) to be gone on someone; *pincer de la harpe*, to play upon the harp; *pincer le vent*, to hug or haul close to the wind; *pincer quelqu'un*, to give someone a nip; *se faire pincer*, (*pop.*) to get caught, to get found out. **se pincer,** *v.r.* To pinch oneself. *Se pincer le doigt*, to pinch, to nip one's finger.

pince-sans-rire, *n.m. inv.* Sly or malicious person, dry joker.

pincette, *n.f.*, or **pincettes,** *n.f. pl.* Tongs; pincers, tweezers, nippers. *On ne le prendrait pas avec des pincettes*, no one would touch him with a pair of tongs, he is awfully touchy.

pinchard [pɛ̃'ʃa:r], *a.* (*fem.* **-arde**) Iron-grey (coat of horse).

pinchina [pɛ̃ʃi'na], *n.m.* Thick, coarse woollen cloth.

pinçon [pɛ̃'sɔ̃], *n.m.* Bruise, mark on the skin (which has been pinched).

pinçure [pɛ̃'sy:r], *n.f.* Pinching; crease in cloth.

Pindare [pɛ̃'da:r], *m.* Pindar.

pindarique [pɛ̃da'rik], *a.* Pindaric. ***pindariser,** *v.i.* To write in the style of Pindar.

pinéal [pine'al], *a.* (*fem.* **-éale**, *pl.* **-éaux**) (*Anat.*) Pineal.

pineau [pi'no], *n.m.* (*pl.* **-eaux**) Burgundy grape; a brand of liqueur.

pinède [pi'nɛd], *n.f.* Pine-land, pine-forest.

pingouin [pɛ̃'gwɛ̃], *n.m.* Auk. *Pingouin manchot*, penguin; *petit pingouin* or *pingouin commun*, razorbill.

ping-pong [piŋ'pɔ̃ŋ], *n.m.* Ping-pong, table-tennis.

pingre [pɛ̃:gr], *n.* Miser, skinflint.—*a.* Avaricious, stingy, close-fisted. **pingrerie**, *n.f.* (*fam.*) Stinginess.

pinière [pi'njɛ:r], *n.f.* Pine wood.

pinné [pi'ne], *a.* (*fem.* **-ée**) (*Bot.*) Pinnate.

pinnule [pi'nyl], *n.f.* Pinnule; sight-vane (of alidad).

pinque [pɛ̃:k], *n.f.* (*Naut.*) Pink.

pinson [pɛ̃'sɔ̃], *n.m.* Finch. *Pinson des Ardennes*, brambling, mountain finch; *pinson des neiges* or *niverolle*, Alpine finch; *pinson commun*, chaffinch. *Gai comme un pinson*, as merry as a lark.

pintade [pɛ̃'tad], *n.f.* Guinea-fowl. **pintadeau**, *n.m.* (*pl.* **-eaux**) Guinea-chick.

pinte [pɛ̃:t], *n.f.* French Canadian quart; *French pint. Se faire une pinte de bon sang*, to have a good laugh.

pinter, *v.t., v.i.* (*fam.*) To tipple, to swill.

piochage [pjɔ'ʃaːʒ], *n.m.* Digging; (*fig.*) working, fagging.

pioche, *n.f.* Pickaxe; kitty (at cards, dominoes, etc.). **pioche-hache**, *n.f.* (*pl.* **pioche-haches**) Mattock.

piocher, *v.t.* To dig.—*v.i.* To dig; (*fig.*) to fag, to work hard, to swot; to draw from the kitty (at cards etc.). **piocheur**, *n.m.* (*fem.* **-euse**) Digger; (*slang*) hard-working student, swotter.—*n.f.* (*Civ. Eng.*) Excavator.

piolet [pjɔ'lɛ], *n.m.* Piolet, ice-axe.

pion [pjɔ̃], *n.m.* Pawn (at chess); piece (at draughts); (*sch. slang*) junior master, usher. *Damer le pion à quelqu'un*, to outdo someone, to take someone down.

pioncer [pjɔ̃'se], *v.i.* (*slang*) To have a nap, to have forty winks.

pionceur, *n.m.* (*fem.* **-euse**) Snoozer, heavy sleeper.

pionne [pjɔn], *n.f.* (*sch. slang*) Junior mistress.

pionner [pjɔ'ne], *v.i.* To take pawns (at chess).

pionnier [pjɔ'nje], *n.m.* Pioneer.

***piot** [pjo], *n.m.* (*pop.*) Wine.

***pioupiou** [pju'pju], *n.m.* (*pl.* **pioupious**) (*pop.*) French foot-soldier, wearing red trousers (1830–1915).

pipe [pip], *n.f.* Pipe; tobacco-pipe; pipe (cask). (*pop.*) *Casser sa pipe*, to die, to kick the bucket; *terre de pipe*, pipe clay.

pipeau, *n.m.* (*pl.* **-eaux**) Pipe, oaten pipe, reed-pipe, shepherd's pipe; bird-call; limed twig, snare (for birds).

pipée, *n.f.* Bird-catching (with a bird-call); (*fig.*) deceit, trickery. *Prendre à la pipée*, to catch with a bird-call, (*fig.*) *to cozen, to take in.

pipelet [pi'plɛ], *n.m.* (*fem.* **-ette**) (*slang*) Concierge, porter.

piper [pi'pe], *v.t.* To catch (birds) with a bird-call etc.; (*fig.*) to trick, to dupe, to decoy; to mark (cards); to load, to cog (dice). (*fam.*) *Ne pas piper mot*, not to say a word.

***piperie**, *n.f.* Cheating (at play); deceit, trickery.

pipette, *n.f.* (*Chem.*) Pipette.

pipeur, *n.m.* (*fem.* **-euse**) One who decoys birds; cheat, trickster (at play), deceiver.—*a.* Cheating, deceitful.

pipi (1) [pi'pi], *n.m.* (*Childish*) Urine, water. *Faire pipi*, to piddle, to 'wee-wee'.

pipi (2) or **pipit** [pi'pi], *n.m.* Pipit. *Pipit des arbres* or *des buissons*, tree-pipit; *pipit des prés* or *farlouse*, meadow-pipit, tit-lark.

pipistrelle [pipis'trɛl], *n.f.* (*Zool.*) Small bat.

pipo [pi'po], *n.m.* (*fam.*) The *École Polytechnique* (Paris); a cadet at this school.

piquage [pi'kaːʒ], *n.m.* Dressing of stones.

piquant [pi'kɑ̃], *a.* (*fem.* **-ante**) Prickling, stinging; sharp, pungent; biting, nipping; cutting, keen; piquant, pointed; smart, lively. *De la moutarde piquante*, hot mustard; *des mots piquants*, pointed, cutting words; *femme piquante*, lively woman; *froid piquant*, biting cold.—*n.m.* Prickle; quill (of porcupine); pungency, pith, point, piquancy. *Le piquant de la chose*, the cream of the thing.

pique [pik], *n.f.* Pike (weapon); ancient measure equal to the length of a pike; pique, spite, quarrel. *Bois de pique*, pike-staff; *demi-pique*, short pike; *être à cent piques de*, to be miles off in guessing; *par pique*, out of pique. —*n.m.* Spade(s) (at cards). *As de pique*, ace of spades.

piqué [pi'ke], *n.m.* Quilting; piqué; vertical dive, nose-dive. *Bombardement en piqué*, (*Av.*) dive-bombing.—*a.* (*fem.* **-ée**) Quilted, pinked; worm-eaten (wood, bark); pitted (metal); spotted (with mould); larded (meat); sour (wine); (*pop.*) dotted, cracked. *Notes piquées*, (*Mus.*) staccato notes.

pique-assiette [pika'sjɛt], *n.m. inv.* Sponger.

pique-bœuf, *n.m.* (*pl.* **pique-bœufs**) Cattle-drover; goad; beef-eater bird.

pique-feu, *n.m. inv.* Poker.

pique-fleurs, *n.m. inv.* Glass flower-block.

pique-nique, *n.m.* (*pl.* **pique-niques**) Picnic. *Faire un pique-nique* or *pique-niquer*, to have a picnic, to picnic.

pique-notes, *n.m. inv.* Spike-file.

piquer [pi'ke], *v.t.* To prick; to sting; to prod, to goad, to spur; to puncture; to bite (of insects); to quilt; to stitch; to pit (of surfaces); to lard; to prick off, to mark off; to dress (stone); to be piquant to; to excite, to stimulate, to pique; to gall, to nettle, to rouse; (*Med.*) to inject. *Cela n'est pas piqué des vers*, (*fam.*) it is a smart bit of work; *il en fut piqué*, he was nettled at it; *piquer de la viande*, to lard meat; *piquer la curiosité de quelqu'un*, to excite someone's curiosity; *piquer l'heure*, (*Naut.*) to strike the hour; *piquer un cheval*, to spur a horse; *piquer une jupe*, to quilt a skirt; *piquer une note de musique*, to play a note staccato; *piquer une tête*, to take a header; *piquer un fard*, to blush; *quelle mouche le pique?* what's biting him?—*v.i.* To turn sour (of wine etc.); to go fast (of a horse). *Piquer des deux*, to spur a horse (with both heels), to gallop off at full speed, (*colloq.*) to get a move on; *piquer du nez*, (*Naut.*) to nose-dive; *piquer sur*, to head for. **se piquer**, *v.r.* To prick oneself, to sting oneself; to be offended, to be nettled, to be piqued; to plume oneself, to pride one-self; to turn sour; to become spotted or pitted, to be worm-eaten. *Ce papier se pique,* this paper is getting covered with spots; *ce vin se pique,* this wine is turning sour; *il se pique de faire cela,* he prides himself on doing that; *se piquer au jeu,* to persist in spite of difficulties; *se piquer d'honneur,* to make it a point of honour; *se piquer d'un rien,* to take offence at the least thing; *se piquer le nez,* to tipple.

piquet, *n.m.* Peg, stake (for tethering horse); (*Mil.*) picket; piquet (card game). *Droit comme un piquet,* as straight as a ramrod; *être au piquet,* to be stood in the corner (as a punishment); *être de piquet,* to be on picket (-duty); *piquet d'incendie,* fire picket.

piquetage [pik'ta:ʒ], *n.m.* Pegging, staking, marking out; picketing. **piqueter,** *v.t.* To set or mark out with stakes or pegs; to mark with little points.

piquette, *n.f.,* or **piqueton,** *n.m.* Thin wine.

piqueur (1), *n.m.* Outrider; overseer (of work-men); stud-groom; whipper-in, huntsman. *Piqueur de vin,* wine-taster.

piqueur (2), *n.m.* (*fem.* -**euse**) Stitcher.

piquier, *n.m.* Pikeman.

piquoir, *n.m.* Pricking tool.

piqûre, *n.f.* Prick, pricking; sting; bite; puncture; worm-hole; pit (in metal), fly-speck, fly-blow; (*Needlework*) quilting, stitching; (*Med.*) hypodermic injection.

pirate [pi'rat], *n.m.* Pirate; (*fig.*) extortioner, plagiarist. **pirater,** *v.i.* To commit piracy. **piraterie,** *n.f.* Piracy; act of piracy or plagiarism.

pire [pi:r], *a.* Worse; the worst. *Il n'est pire eau que celle qui dort* [EAU]; *il n'est pire sourd que celui qui ne veut pas entendre* [ENTENDRE]; *le remède est pire que le mal,* the remedy is worse than the disease.—*n.m. Le pire,* the worst.

piriforme [piri'fɔrm], *a.* Pyriform, pear-shaped.

pirogue [pi'rɔg], *n.f.* Pirogue, dug-out canoe; (*Am.*) pitpan.

pirole or **pyrole** [pi'rɔl], *n.f.* (*Bot.*) Pirola, winter green [*see also* THÉ].

pirouette [pi'rwɛt], *n.f.* Pirouette, whirligig, (*fig.*) sudden change of opinion. **pirouetter,** *v.i.* To pirouette, to whirl about.

pis (1) [pi], *n.m.* Udder, dug (of cow).

pis (2) [pi], *adv.* (*sometimes used with adjectival function*). (*comp.*) Worse. *De mal en pis,* from bad to worse; *de pis en pis,* worse and worse; *dire pis que pendre de,* to say all that is bad about . . .; *qui pis est,* what is worse. —*n.m. Le pis,* (*superl.*) (the) worst; *le pis qui puisse arriver,* the worst that can happen; *mettre les choses au pis,* to suppose the worst. —*n.m. inv. Pis aller,* the worst, last shift, last resource, makeshift; *au pis aller,* at the worst; *c'est votre pis aller,* it is your last resource.

piscicole [pisi'kɔl], *a.* Piscicultural. **piscicul-teur,** *n.m.* Pisciculturist. **pisciculture,** *n.f.* Pisciculture, fish-culture. **pisciforme,** *a.* Pisciform.

piscine [pi'sin], *n.f.* Piscina; bathing pond; public swimming bath; swimming-pool.

piscivore [pisi'vɔ:r], *a.* Piscivorous.

Pise [pi:z], *f.* Pisa.

pisé [pi'ze], *n.m.* Pisé (masonry). *Pisé de terre,* blocks of clay; *mur en pisé,* cob-wall.

pissat [pi'sa], *n.m.* Urine (of animal). **pisse-ment,** *n.m.* Pissing.

pissenlit [pisã'li], *n.m.* Dandelion. (*fam.*) *Manger les pissenlits par la racine,* to push up the daisies.

pisser [pi'se], *v.i.* (*not decent*) To piss, to make water.—*v.t.* To piss (blood etc.). **pisseur,** *n.m.* (*fem.* -**euse**) Pisser. **pisseux,** *a.* (*fem.* -**euse**) (*pop.*) Faded, drab, greenish (fabric colour). **pissoir,** *n.m.* Urinal. **pissoter,** *v.i.* To piss often, to dribble. **pissotière,** *n.f.* Public urinal.

pistache [pis'taʃ], *n.f.* Pistachio, pistachio-nut. (*pop.*) *Avoir sa pistache,* to be drunk. **pistachier,** *n.m.* Pistachio-tree.

piste [pist], *n.f.* Track, footprint, print, trace, trail, scent; course, race-course. *Être à la piste de,* to be on the track of *or* after (some-one); *piste cyclable,* cycle track; *piste d'envol,* (*Av.*) runway; *piste sonore,* (*Cine.*) sound-track; *suivre quelqu'un à la piste,* to follow on the track of someone. **pistage,** *n.m.* Track-ing, touting. **pister,** *v.t.* To track, to shadow. **pisteur,** *n.m.* Tout; tracker, spy.

pistil [pis'til], *n.m.* (*Bot.*) Pistil.

pistole [pis'tɔl], *n.f.* Pistole; ten francs coin (or value); separate room (in prison).

pistolet [pistɔ'lɛ], *n.m.* Pistol; French curve (for drawing); spray gun, air brush (for painting); (*fam.*) men's urinal; (*in Belgium*) bread roll. *Pistolet à amorce,* cap-pistol; *pistolet à bouchon,* pop-gun; *pistolets d'arçon* [ARÇON]; *pistolet (d'embarcation),* davit; *pisto-let éclairant,* flare pistol; *quel drôle de pistolet!* what a queer fellow! *un coup de pistolet,* a pistol-shot.

piston [pis'tɔ̃], *n.m.* Piston; sucker (of a pump); press button; (*fam.*) instead of *cornet à pistons,* cornet, cornet player; (*fig.*) back-stairs influence. *Avoir du piston,* to have friends at court. *Piston à vapeur,* steam-piston. **pistonnage,** *n.m.* (*colloq.*) Recom-mendation, backing. **pistonner,** *v.t.* (*colloq.*) To recommend, to back up.

pitance [pi'tã:s], *n.f.* Pittance; allowance (of food), dole. *Maigre pitance,* short commons.

pitchpin [pitʃ'pɛ̃, piʃ'pɛ̃], *n.m.* Pitch-pine.

pite or **pitte** [pit], *n.f.* Kind of agave; silk-grass; coir.

piteusement [pitøz'mã], *adv.* Piteously, woe-fully, sadly. **piteux,** *a.* (*fem.* -**euse**) Piteous, pitiable, woeful. *Faire piteuse chère,* to fare badly; *faire piteuse mine,* to look the picture of misery.

pitié [pi'tje], *n.f.* Pity, compassion; pitiful thing, object of pity. *À faire pitié,* pitifully, wretchedly; *il vaut mieux faire envie que pitié,* better be envied than pitied; *par pitié,* for pity's sake, out of pity; *prendre quelqu'un en pitié,* to take pity on someone.

piton [pi'tɔ̃], *n.m.* Eye-bolt, screw-ring, ring-bolt; peak (of mountain); (*pop.*) (big) nose.

(C) **pitoune** [pi'tu:n], *n.f.* Pulpwood bolts.

pitoyable [pitwa'jabl], *a.* *Compassionate; piti-ful, pitiable, piteous; contemptible, paltry. **pitoyablement,** *adv.* Pitifully.

pitre [pitr], *n.m.* Clown, buffoon. **pitrerie,** *n.f.* Buffoonery.

pittoresque [pitɔ'rɛsk], *a.* Picturesque; graphic, vivid, pictorial; romantic (site).

—n.m. The picturesque, picturesqueness.
pittoresquement, *adv.* Picturesquely.
pituitaire [pitµi'tɛːr], *a.* Pituitary. **pituite,** *n.f.* Pituita, phlegm, mucus. **pituiteux,** *a.* (*fem.* **-euse**) Pituitous.
pivert [PICVERT].
pivoine [pi'vwan], *n.m.* Bullfinch.—*n.f.* Peony.
pivot [pi'vo], *n.m.* Pivot, pin, spindle, hinge; (*Bot.*) tap-root. *Canon à pivot,* swivel-gun.
pivotal, *a.* (*fem.* **-ale,** *pl.* **-aux**) Pivotal.
pivotant, *a.* (*fem.* **-ante**) Pivoting; tap-rooted. *Racine pivotante,* tap-root. **pivoter,** *v.i.* To turn on a pivot, to revolve, to turn; to wheel; to push straight down (of roots); (*Mil. slang*) to be drilled. *Pivoter sur ses talons,* to turn on one's heel.
placabilité [plakabili'te], *n.f.* Placability.
placage [pla'kaːʒ], *n.m.* Plating (metal-work); veneering (of wood); (*Lit.*) patchwork; (*C*) blazing (of a tree).
plaçage [pla'saːʒ], *n.m.* Placing.
placard [pla'kaːr], *n.m.* Placard, poster, bill; (*Print.*) slip; cupboard (in a wall); woodwork above a door; (*Naut.*) patch (on sail). *Épreuve en placard,* slip-proof. **placarder,** *v.t.* To placard, to post up; (*fig.*) to libel, to expose, to show up. *Placarder un avis au public,* to post up a public notice.
place [plas], *n.f.* Place; position; room; seat; locality, spot; stead; post, employment, situation, office; town, fortress; public square, market-place. *À la place de (quelqu'un),* instead of (someone); *à vos places!* take your seats! *être sans place,* to be out of a job; *faire la place,* to solicit orders, to canvass; *faire place à quelqu'un,* to make room for someone; *il ne saurait demeurer en place,* he can never stand still; *la place de Lille* (*Comm.*), Lille as a trading town; *la place n'est plus tenable,* it is no longer possible to remain; *mettez-vous à ma place,* put yourself in my place; *mettre chaque chose à sa place,* to put each thing in its place; *mise en place,* putting (something) in its place; *ne pas tenir en place,* to be restless; *place!* make way! *place d'armes,* parade-ground, esplanade; *prendre place,* to take one's seat; *place forte,* fortress, stronghold; *prix sur place,* market price; *qui va à la chasse perd sa place,* if you leave your place you lose it; *remettre quelqu'un à sa place,* to put someone in his place; *rester sur place,* to be left dead on the field; *retenir des places,* to book seats; *sur place,* on the spot, on the premises; *une quatre places,* a four-seater; *une voiture de place,* a hackney-cab; *un homme en place,* a man in office.
placé, *a.* (*fem.* **-ée**) Placed, situated. *Haut placé,* in a high position; *il a le cœur bien placé,* his heart is in the right place; *il est bien placé,* he has a good situation.
placement, *n.m.* Placing; sale, disposal; putting out, investment. *Bureau de placement,* agency, registry-office (for servants); *faire des placements,* to make investments.
placenta [plasɛ̃'ta], *n.m.* Placenta. **placentaire,** *a.* Placental.—*n.m.* (*Zool.*) Placentary.
placer [pla'se], *v.t.* To place, to put, to set; to find a place, seat, or situation for; to dispose of; to lay out, or invest; to deposit, to lodge; to dispose of, to sell. *Il place bien ce qu'il dit,* what he says is to the purpose; *mal placé,* misplaced, ill-timed; *placer de*

l'argent à la banque, to deposit money in the bank; *placer quelqu'un,* to get someone a place; *placer son argent à 5%,* to invest one's money at five per cent. **se placer,** *v.r.* To place oneself, to take one's place or one's seat; to obtain a situation.
placet [pla'sɛ], *n.m.* Petition, address.
placeur [pla'sœːr], *n.m.* (*fem.* **-euse**) Placer; registry-office keeper.
placide [pla'sid], *a.* Placid, calm. **placidement,** *adv.* Placidly, calmly. **placidité,** *n.f.* Placidity.
placier [pla'sje], *n.m.* (*fem.* **-ière**) Town traveller; canvasser; sub-letter (of stands).
plafond [pla'fɔ̃], *n.m.* Ceiling; maximum (of budget, speed, height) [*see* ARAIGNÉE]. *Bas de plafond,* stupid, unintelligent. **plafonnage,** *n.m.* Ceiling (action, work); (*Av.*) visibility.
plafonner, *v.t.* To ceil, to put a ceiling to.— *v.i.* To reach the highest point (of prices etc.); (*Av.*) to fly at the ceiling; (*Motor.*) to travel at maximum speed. **plafonneur,** *n.m.* Plasterer. **plafonnier,** *n.m.* Electrical ceiling fitting.
plagal [pla'gal], *a.* (*fem.* **-ale,** *pl.* **-aux**) (*Mus.*) Plagal (cadence).
plage [plaːʒ], *n.f.* Beach, shore; sea-side resort; area, expanse (of land). *Plage à teinter,* (*Phot.*) area (of negative) to be tinted; *plage avant,* (*Naut.*) forecastle; *plage arrière,* quarter-deck; *plage d'écoute,* (*Rad.*) limits for tuning.
plagiaire [pla'ʒjɛːr], *n.m. and a.* Plagiarist.
plagiat, *n.m.* Plagiarism. **plagier,** *v.t.* To plagiarize.
plaid (1) [plɛ], *n.m.* (*Law*) Plea, pleading; sitting.
plaid (2) [plɛd], *n.m.* Plaid, travelling rug.
plaidable [plɛ'dabl], *a.* Pleadable.
plaidant, *a.* (*fem.* **-ante**) Pleading, litigant. *Avocat plaidant,* barrister.
plaider [plɛ'de], *v.i.* To go to law, to litigate; to plead, to argue; to intercede.—*v.t.* To defend; to plead (a cause); to allege; to maintain. *Plaider le faux pour savoir le vrai,* to allege what is false to get at the truth; *plaidez ma cause,* intercede for me; *plaider coupable,* to plead guilty.
plaideur, *n.m.* (*fem.* **-euse**) Litigant, suitor.
plaidoirie, *n.f.* Pleading; counsel's speech.
plaidoyer, *n.m.* Speech for the defence, counsel's address.
plaie [plɛ], *n.f.* Wound; sore; (*fig.*) plague; evil. *Mettre le doigt sur la plaie,* to put one's finger on the evil; *ne demander que plaies et bosses* [BOSSE]; *panser une plaie,* to dress a wound; *plaie envenimée,* rankling sore.
plaignant [plɛ'ɲɑ̃], *n.m.* (*fem.* **-ante**) Complainant, plaintiff, prosecutor.—*a.* Complaining. *La partie plaignante,* the plaintiff.
plaigne etc. [PLAINDRE].
plain [plɛ], *a.* (*fem.* **plaine** (1)) Plain, even, flat, level.
plain-chant [plɛ̃'ʃɑ̃], *n.m.* (*pl.* **plains-chants**) Plain-song, plain-chant.
plaindre [plɛ̃ːdr], *v.t. irr.* (*pres.p.* **plaignant,** *p.p.* **plaint;** *conjugated like* CRAINDRE) To pity, to be sorry for; *to grudge. Il est à plaindre,* he is to be pitied; *je vous plains,* I pity you; *plaindre sa peine,* to grudge one's pains. **se plaindre,** *v.r.* To complain;

to grumble. *J'ai bien lieu de me plaindre de vous,* I have good reason to complain of you: *je n'ai pas à me plaindre de lui,* (*Am.*) I have no kick about him; *se plaindre en justice,* to lodge a complaint in court.

plaine (2) [plɛn], *n.f.* Plain; flat country.

plain-pied [plɛ̃'pje], **de,** *adv. phr.* On a level; (*fig.*) forthwith, without difficulty. *Pièces de plain-pied,* rooms on one floor. *Entrer de plain-pied dans le vif du sujet,* to come straight to the point.

plains, 2nd pres. indic. [PLAINDRE].

plainte [plɛ̃:t], *n.f.* Complaint, plaint; lamentation, wail, moan, groan; plaint at law. *Porter plainte* or *déposer une plainte,* to lodge a complaint.

plaintif, *a.* (*fem.* **-ive**) Plaintive, complaining, doleful; querulous. **plaintivement,** *adv.* Dolefully; querulously.

plaire [plɛːr], *v.i. irr.* (*pres.p.* **plaisant,** *p.p.* **plu** (1)) To please; to be pleasant or agreeable (*à*). *Cela vous plaît à dire,* you are pleased to say so; *plaire à quelqu'un,* to please someone; *si cela ne vous plaît pas,* if you are averse to it; *vous leur plaisez beaucoup,* they like you very much.—*v.impers.* To be pleasing, satisfactory, or desirable (*à*). *À Dieu ne plaise que,* God forbid that; *comme il vous plaira,* as you like; *il ne me plaît pas que vous y alliez,* I do not like your going there; *je ferai ce qu'il vous plaira,* I will do what you want; *plaît-il?* beg pardon! I didn't hear; *plût à Dieu que,* would to God that; *s'il vous plaît,* please. **se plaire,** *v.r.* To delight, to take pleasure; to like, to love; to please oneself; to thrive. *Il se plaît à faire du mal,* he delights in doing mischief.

plaisamment, *adv.* Humorously, amusingly; ludicrously, laughably, ridiculously.

plaisance, *n.f.* Pleasure. *Bateau de plaisance,* pleasure boat; *maison de plaisance,* country seat.

plaisant [plɛ'zɑ̃], *a.* (*fem.* **-ante**) *Pleasant; humorous, amusing, droll, funny, comical; ridiculous; (*iron.*) pretty; odd, strange. *Ce sont de plaisantes gens,* (*iron.*) they are nice people; *c'est assez plaisant,* it is pretty absurd; *c'est le plus plaisant homme du monde,* he is the most amusing fellow alive; *il vous a fait un plaisant régal,* he entertained you right royally; *un plaisant tour,* a humorous trick. —*n.m.* Jester, wag; the humorous, the ludicrous; the funny side, the absurd part. *Il fait le plaisant,* he tries to be funny; *le plaisant de l'histoire,* the funny part of the story; *un mauvais plaisant,* a practical joker. **plaisanter,** *v.i.* To jest, to joke. *C'est un homme qui ne plaisante pas,* he is not a man to be trifled with; *en plaisantant,* in jest, for fun; *il ne plaisante pas là-dessus,* he is in downright earnest about that; *il plaisante sur tout,* he jokes about everything.—*v.t.* To chaff, to banter, to make fun of.

plaisanterie, *n.f.* Facetiousness, humour, pleasantry; jesting, joking, jest, joke, witticism; practical joke; mockery, trifle, a mere bagatelle. *Cela est dit par plaisanterie,* that is said in jest; *entendre la plaisanterie,* to know how to take a joke; *plaisanterie à part,* joking apart; *tourner en plaisanterie,* to see the humorous side of, to laugh off.

plaisantin, *n.m.* (*fam.*) Jester, practical joker.

plaise etc. [PLAIRE].

plaisir [plɛ'ziːr], *n.m.* Pleasure; delight, gratification; diversion, sport, entertainment; favour; cone-shaped wafer. *À plaisir,* wantonly, gratuitously; *à son bon plaisir,* at one's convenience; *avec plaisir,* with pleasure, willingly; *au plaisir (de vous revoir),* I hope we shall meet again; *avoir* or *trouver du plaisir,* or *prendre plaisir à quelque chose,* to delight in something; *cela fait plaisir à voir,* that is a pleasant sight; *cela nous fera beaucoup de plaisir,* that will give us great pleasure; *faites-moi le plaisir,* do me the favour; *jouer pour le plaisir,* to play for love; *la peine passe le plaisir,* the pain exceeds the pleasure; *par plaisir,* for pleasure, for sport, (*colloq.*) to see the result; *partie de plaisir,* pleasure party, picnic; *se faire un plaisir de,* to be pleased to; *train de plaisir,* excursion train; *un conte inventé à plaisir,* a made-up story.

plamée [pla'me], *n.f.* (*Tanning*) Lime-water. **plamer,** *v.t.* To lime (skins).

plan (1) [plɑ̃], *a.* (*fem.* **plane** (1)) Even, level, flat.

plan (2) [plɑ̃], *n.m.* Plane; plan; draught, drawing, groundwork; scheme, project; (*Paint.*) ground, distance. *Arrêter son plan,* to decide upon one's scheme; *arrière-plan* [ARRIÈRE-PLAN]; *dresser un plan,* to draw up a plan; *gros plan,* (*Cine.*) close up; *laisser en plan,* to leave unfinished; *lever un plan,* to make a plan; *plan à vue d'oiseau,* bird's-eye view; *plan en relief,* plan in relief; *plan incliné,* inclined plane; *premier plan,* (*Paint.*) foreground; (*Cine.*) *plan américain,* two-shot; *plan d'ensemble,* long shot; *plan moyen,* medium shot; *plan sommaire,* sketch map; *reléguer au second plan,* to put into the background.

planage [pla'naːʒ], *n.m.* Planing of wood or metal surfaces.

planche [plɑ̃:ʃ], *n.f.* Board, plank; shelf; (*Engr.*) plate, wood, or lino cut; (*Gard.*) rectangular bed, border; (*Agric.*) land (between furrows); (*Naut.*) gang-plank; (*pl.*) (*fam.*) stage, broadwalk (on sand). *Avoir du pain sur la planche,* to have a nest-egg; *faire la planche,* to float on one's back; *jours de planche,* (*Naut.*) lay-days; *monter sur les planches,* (*Theat.*) to tread the boards; *planche à dessin,* drawing-board; *planche à repasser,* ironing-board; *planche de salut,* (*fig.*) sheet-anchor; *planche dorsale,* (*Gym.*) back-plank; *s'appuyer sur une planche pourrie,* to lean upon a broken reed.

planchéiage, *n.m.* Boarding, planking; flooring. **planchéier,** *v.t.* To board over, to floor.

plancher, *n.m.* Floor, floor-board (of car etc.), (*Naut.*) deck planking. (*pop.*) *Débarrasser le plancher,* to clear off; *le plancher des vaches,* dry land, terra firma.

planchette, *n.f.* Small board; (*Math.*) plane-table; range-table (of gun); map-board; (*Spiritualism*) planchette.

plançon [plɑ̃'sɔ̃] or **plantard,** *n.m.* Slip, shoot used as a cutting (of willow etc.); sapling; squared log sawn in two.

plancton [plɑ̃'tɔ̃] or **plankton,** *n.m.* (*Biol.*) Plankton.

plane (1) [PLAN (1)].

plane (2) [plan], *n.f.* Drawing-knife; planisher.

plane (3) [plan], *n.m.* Plane-tree. *Faux-plane*, sycamore.

plané [pla'ne], *a.m.* Soaring, gliding. *Un vol plané*, gliding descent, volplane, glide. *Descendre en vol plané*, to volplane down or glide down.

planer (1) [pla'ne], *v.i.* To hover, to soar; to look down (on) (*sur*); (*Av.*) to glide. *Planer sur les difficultés*, to soar above difficulties; *un milan qui plane*, a kite hovering.

planer (2) [pla'ne], *v.t.* To make smooth, to plane, to shave (wood); to planish (metals).

planétaire [plane'tɛ:r], *a.* Planetary.—*n.m.* (*Motor.*) Sun pinion. **planétarium** or **planétaire**, *n.m.* Planetarium, orrery.

planète [pla nɛ:t], *n.f.* Planet. **planétoïde**, *n.m.* Planetoid.

planeur [pla'nœ:r], *n.m.* Planisher; glider (aeroplane). **planeuse**, *n.f.* Planing-machine.

planification [planifika'sjɔ̃], *n.f.* (*Polit. Econ.*) Planning. **planifier**, *v.t.* To plan.

planimétrie [planime'tri], *n.f.* Planimetry.

planisme [pla'nism], *n.m.* (*Polit. Econ.*) Planning technique.

planisphère [planis'fɛ:r], *n.m.* Planisphere.

planque [plɑ̃:k], *n.f.* (*slang*) Hiding-place; good job. *Il a une bonne planque*, he's got a soft job. **planquer**, *v.t.* To hide. **se planquer**, *v.r.* (*pop.*) To hide oneself; to take cover; to lie down.

plant [plɑ̃], *n.m.* Young plant, seedling; slip; sapling; plantation. *Plant de choux*, cabbage patch; *plant de vigne*, vine-slip. **plantage**, *n.m.* Planting.

plantain [plɑ̃'tɛ̃], *n.m.* Plantain. *Plantain corne-de-cerf* or *coronope*, wart-cress; *plantain d'eau* or *pain de grenouille*, water plantain; *plantain pulicaire*, flea-bane.

plantard [PLANÇON].

plantation [plɑ̃ta'sjɔ̃], *n.f.* Planting; plantation.

plante [plɑ̃:t], *n.f.* Plant. *Jardin des plantes* [JARDIN]; *plante d'appartement*, indoor plant; *plantes marines*, seaweeds; *plantes potagères*, vegetables. *La plante du pied*, (*Anat.*) the sole of the foot.

planter [plɑ̃'te], *v.t.* To plant; to set, to fix, to drive in; to set up, to erect; to plant with flowers, vegetables, etc. *Aller planter des choux*, (*fig.*) to retire to the country; *planter là* (*quelqu'un*), (*fig.*) to give the slip to, to leave in the lurch, to jilt; *planter des oignons* or *des pois*, to sow onions or peas; *planter un poteau*, to drive in a stake. **se planter**, *v.r.* To station oneself, to take up one's stand.

planteur, *n.m.* Planter. **planteuse**, *n.f.* Potato planting-machine.

plantigrade [plɑ̃ti'grad], *a.* and *n.m.* (*Zool.*) Plantigrade.

plantoir [plɑ̃'twa:r], *n.m.* Dibble.

planton [plɑ̃'tɔ̃], *n.m.* (*Mil.*) Orderly. *Être de planton*, to be on orderly duty.

plantule [plɑ̃'tyl], *n.f.* (*Bot.*) Small plant beginning to germinate.

plantureusement [plɑ̃tyrøz'mɑ̃], *adv.* Copiously, abundantly, luxuriantly. **plantureux**, *a.* (*fem.* **-euse**) Plentiful, copious, abundant; fertile, rich. *Repas plantureux*, lavish meal.

planure [pla'ny:r], *n.f.* Shaving (of wood etc.).

plaquage [pla'ka:ʒ], *n.m.* (*pop.*) Jilting (a lover); (*Ftb.*) rugby tackle.

plaque [plak], *n.f.* Plate, slab (of metal etc.); plaque; badge, star; (*Phot.*) sensitive plate; (*C*) blaze (on a tree). *Plaque commémorative*, tablet; *plaque de blindage*, armour-plate; *plaque de fondation*, bed-plate; *plaque de fonte*, plate of cast iron; *plaque de gazon*, sod; *plaque de propreté*, finger-plate; *plaque d'identité*, (*Mil.*) identity disc; *plaque minéralogique*, (*Motor.*) number plate; *plaque photographique*, (*Phot.*) photographic plate; *plaque sensible*, sensitive plate; *plaque tournante*, (*Rail.*) turn-table.

plaqué [pla'ke], *a.* Plated, covered with.—*n.m.* Plated goods.

(*C*) **plaquebière** [plak'bjɛ:r], *n.f.* Blackberry.

plaquemine [plak'min], *n.f.* (*Bot.*) Persimmon. **plaqueminier**, *n.m.* Persimmon-tree.

plaquer [pla'ke], *v.t.* To plate (metal); to veneer (wood); to lay on (plaster), to lay down (turf); to abandon, to jilt (a lover), to leave in the lurch; (*Ftb.*) to tackle and bring down (an opponent); (*C*) to blaze (a tree). *Plaquer un accord*, (on piano) to strike a chord. **se plaquer**, *v.r.* To lie flat; to flatten oneself; to fall flat; to pancake (aeroplane).

plaquette [pla'ket], *n.f.* Small thin book; plaquette; small plate; thin slab.

plaqueur [pla'kœ:r], *n.m.* Silver (etc.)-plater; (*Ftb.*) strong tackler.

plasma [plas'ma], *n.m.* (*Biol.*) Plasma.

plasmode or **plasmodie**, *n.f.* Plasmodium.

plasmologie, *n.f.* Plasmology.

plasmolyse, *n.f.* Plasmolysis.

plastic [plas'tik], *n.m.* Explosive gelatine, jelly.

plasticité [plastisi'te], *n.f.* Plasticity.

plastique, *a.* Plastic. *Matière plastique*, plastics.—*n.f.* Plastic art; figure. *Une plastique sans défaut*, a perfect figure.

plastron [plas'trɔ̃], *n.m.* Breast-plate; (*Fenc. etc.*) plastron, fencing-pad; shirt-front, front, dicky; (*Mech. Eng.*) drill-plate; (*fig.*) laughing-stock, butt. **plastronner**, *v.t.* To furnish with a plastron.—*v.i.* To practise against a fencing-master wearing a plastron, (*fig.*) to throw out one's chest, to strut.

plat (1) [pla], *a.* (*fem.* **plate**) Flat; level, even; regular, uniform, straight; (*fig.*) dull, insipid, shallow, empty, platitudinous. *À plat ventre*, flat on one's face; *avoir la poitrine plate*, to be flat-chested; *calme plat*, dead calm; *c'est un plat personnage*, he is a dull fellow, a worm; *cheveux plats*, straight hair; *sa bourse est bien plate*, his purse is very low; *son armée a été battue à plate couture*, his army was utterly routed; *un pays plat*, a flat country; *un style plat*, dull, platitudinous style; *vaisselle plate*, gold (or silver) plate; *vin plat*, flat wine.—*n.m.* The flat, flat part, side, etc.; flat racing; (*Bookb.*) board. (*Cook.*) *Plat de côtes*, top ribs of beef. *Course de plat*, flat race; *le plat de la main*, the flat of the hand; *le plat d'un sabre*, the flat of a sword. *À plat*, (*Motor.*) flat (of tyre); (*fam.*) exhausted; *pièce qui tombe à plat*, a play which flops. *Faire du plat à*, (*fam.*) to toady to; (*pop.*) to make advances to.

plat (2) [pla], *n.m.* Dish (the vessel and the food), (*Am.*) platter; scale (of a balance); (*Naut.*) mess; course (of a meal). *En faire tout un plat*, (*pop.*) to make a great fuss;

mettre les petits plats dans les grands, to entertain someone regardless of expense; *mettre les pieds dans le plat*, to put one's foot in it; *plat à barbe*, shaving-dish; *plat de campement*, dixie.

Plata [pla'ta] (**Rio de la**), *f.* The river Plate.

platane [pla'tan], *n.m.* Plane-tree, platan.

plat-bord [pla'bɔːr], *n.m.* (*pl.* **plats-bords**) Gunwale.

plate [plat], *n.f.* (*Naut.*) Small flat-bottomed fishing-boat.

plateau [pla'to], *n.m.* (*pl.* **-eaux**) Scale (of a balance); tray; table-land, plateau; flat part, plate, flange (of various machines etc.); turntable (of gramophone); platform, (*Theat.*) floor (of the stage). *Faire pencher le plateau de la balance*, (*fig.*) to tip the scales; *plateau à thé*, tea-tray; *plateau d'argent*, silver salver; *plateau d'embrayage*, clutch-plate.

plate-bande [plat'bãːd], *n.f.* (*pl.* **plates-bandes**) Border, flower-bed; (*Arch.*) platband, flat-moulding. *Plate-bande de baie*, lintel of a door or window. (*fig.*) *Marcher sur les plates-bandes de quelqu'un*, to encroach on someone's rights.

platée [pla'te], *n.f.* Dishful; foundation under the whole area of the building.

plate-forme [plat'fɔrm], *n.f.* (*pl.* **plates-formes**) Platform (of a bus etc.). *Plate-forme d'envol*, flying-off platform; *plate-forme électorale*, (*Polit.*) election manifesto.

plate-longe [plat'lɔ̃ːʒ], *n.f.* (*pl.* **plates-longes**) Kicking-strap; leading-rein.

platement [plat'mã], *adv.* Flatly, dully, plainly, straight.

platinage [plati'naːʒ], *n.m.* Plating with platinum.

platine (1) [pla'tin], *n.f.* Lock (of fire-arms); plate (of lock, watch, machine); stage (of microscope); platen (of typewriter); shell (of knife). *Quelle platine!* (*fam.*) what a tongue!

platine (2) [pla'tin], *n.m.* Platinum. *Platine iridié*, (of standard meter) platino-iridium. **platiné**, *a.* (*fem.* **-ée**) Platinum plated; platinum coloured (of hair). **platiner**, *v.t.* To plate with platinum. **platinifère**, *a.* Platiniferous. **platinoïde**, *a.* Platinoid.

platitude [plati'tyd], *n.f.* Platitude; flatness, dullness; servile action.

Platon [pla'tɔ̃], *m.* Plato.

platonicien [platɔni'sjɛ̃], *a.* (*fem.* **-ienne**) Platonic.—*n.* Platonist. **platonique**, *a.* Platonic. **platonisme**, *n.m.* Platonism.

plâtrage [plɑ'traːʒ], *n.m.* Plaster-work, plastering; lath-and-plaster; (*fig.*) flimsy work.

plâtras, *n.m.* Debris of plaster-work; rubbish.

plâtre [plɑːtr], *n.m.* Plaster; work or figure in plaster; (*colloq.*) paint (on the face); (*pl.*) plaster-work. *Battre quelqu'un comme plâtre*, to beat someone to a jelly; *enduire de plâtre*, to coat with plaster; *essuyer les plâtres*, to live in a newly built house.

plâtré, *a.* (*fem.* **-ée**) Plastered; (*colloq.*) painted; (*fig.*) feigned, insincere. *Paix plâtrée*, patched-up peace; *visage plâtré*, painted face.

plâtrer, *v.t.* To plaster; to clarify (wine) with plaster; (*fig.*) to patch up, to disguise.

plâtrerie, *n.f.* Plaster-work.

plâtreux, *a.* (*fem.* **-euse**) Chalky.

plâtrier, *n.m.* Plasterer.

plâtrière, *n.f.* Chalk or gypsum pit; plaster-kiln. **plâtroir**, *n.m.* Plasterer's trowel.

plat-ventre [pla'vãtr], *n.m. inv.* (*Swimming*) *Faire un plat-ventre*, to do a belly-flop.

platystémon [platiste'mɔ̃], *n.m.* (*Bot.*) or *pavot de Californie*, Californian poppy.

plausibilité [plozibili'te], *n.f.* Plausibility.

plausible, *a.* Plausible. **plausiblement**, *adv.* Plausibly.

plèbe [plɛb], *n.f.* Common people.

plébéien [plebe'jɛ̃], *a.* and *n.* (*fem.* **-ienne**) Plebeian.

plébiscite, *n.m.* Plebiscite. **plébisciter**, *v.t.* To elect by means of a plebiscite.

plectre [plɛktr], *n.m.* (*Mus.*) Plectrum.

pléiade [ple'jad], *n.f.* Pleiad (group of seven stars).

plein [plɛ̃], *a.* (*fem.* **pleine**) Full; fraught (*de*); filled, replete; entire, whole, complete; thorough; copious, stout; solid; big (with young). *À pleines voiles*, all sails set; *arbre en plein vent*, tree in the open air; *avoir le cœur plein*, to have one's heart full; *donner à pleine main* or *à pleines mains*, to give freely; *en plein air*, in the open air; *en pleine classe*, before the whole class; *en plein hiver*, in the heart of winter; *en plein jour* [JOUR]; *en pleine mer* [MER]; *en plein midi* [MIDI]; *être plein*, (*slang*) to be full up (drunk); *livre plein d'érudition*, book stored with learning; *marée pleine*, full tide; *plein comme un œuf* [ŒUF]; *pleine lune* [LUNE]; *une chienne pleine*, a bitch in pup; *visage plein*, full face.—*n.m.* Full part; plenum; middle; (*Naut.*) full tide. *Battre son plein*, to be at the full (of the tide); (*fig.*) to be in full swing (of a party etc.); *dans le plein*, in the middle; (*Motor.*) *faire le plein* (*d'essence*), to fill up; *porter plein*, (*Naut.*) to keep the sails full; *les pleins*, downstrokes (in writing).—*adv.* Full. *En plein*, fully, entirely; in the middle; *plein les deux mains*, both hands full; *tout plein*, very many, fully.

pleine-eau [plɛn'o], *n.f. inv.* *Faire une pleine-eau*, to bathe in deep water.

pleinement, *adv.* Fully, entirely, thoroughly.

plein-fouet, *n.m.* *Un coup de plein-fouet*, a direct hit (with a gun).

plein-vent, *n.m.* and *a. inv.* *Des arbres de plein-vent*, hardy fruit-trees.

plénier, *a.* (*fem.* **-ière**) Plenary; full, complete. *Indulgence plénière*, plenary indulgence.

plénipotentiaire [plenipɔtɑ̃'sjɛːr], *n.m.* and *a.* Plenipotentiary.

plénitude [pleni'tyd], *n.f.* Plenitude, fullness.

pléonasme [pleo'nasm], *n.m.* Pleonasm. **pléonastique**, *a.* Pleonastic.

plésiosaure [plesjo'sɔːr], *n.m.* Plesiosaurus.

plet [plɛ], *n.m.* Each of the turns of a coiled rope.

pléthore [ple'tɔːr], *n.f.* (*Med.*) Plethora; (*fig.*) excessive amount. **pléthorique**, *a.* Plethoric.

pleur [plœːr], *n.m.* (*poet.*) Tear; lament; bleeding (of vine buds). *Essuyer ses pleurs*, to dry one's tears; *verser* or *répandre des pleurs*, to shed tears; *un pleur éternel*, a never-ending lament.

pleurant, *a.* (*fem.* **-ante**) Weeping.

pleurard, *n.m.* (*fem.* **-arde**) Whimperer, blubberer.—*a.* Whimpering, tearful.

pleure-misère [plœrmi'zɛːr], *n. inv.* A person who always has a hard-luck story.

pleurer [plœ´re], *v.i.* To weep, to cry, to shed tears; to bewail, to mourn; to run (of the eyes); to bleed (of vines etc.); to drip (of a tap). *Pleurer à chaudes larmes*, to shed bitter tears; *pleurer de joie*, to weep for joy; *pleurer sur quelqu'un*, to weep over someone.—*v.t.* To weep, to bewail, to lament, to mourn, to deplore the loss of.

pleurésie [plœre´zi], *n.f.* Pleurisy. **pleurétique**, *a.* Pleuritic.

pleureur [plœ´rœːr], *n.m.* (*fem.* -**euse** (1)) Whimperer, weeper; paid mourner, mute, hired weeper.—*n.f. pl.* Weepers (long sleeves formerly worn).—*a.* Whimpering, tearful. *Saule pleureur*, weeping willow.

pleureux, *a.* (*fem.* -**euse** (2)) Weeping, crying.

pleurnichement [plœrniʃ´mã], *n.m.*, or **pleurnicherie**, *n.f.* Whine, whining, whimpering, snivelling. **pleurnicher**, *v.i.* To whimper, to whine, snivel. **pleurnicheur**, *n.m.* and *a.* (*fem.* -**euse**) Whimperer, sniveller.

pleurodynie [plørɔdi´ni], *n.f.* Pleurodynia.

pleuronecte [plørɔ´nɛkt], *n.m.* Pleuronect.

pleutre [plø:tr], *n.m.* Contemptible fellow.

pleutrerie [pløtrə´ri], *n.f.* Cowardly action; caddish trick.

pleuviner [plœ´vine], **pleuvasser** or **pleuvoter**, *v.impers.* To drizzle.

pleuvoir [plœ´vwaːr], *v.impers. irr.* (*pres.p.* **pleuvant**, *p.p.* **plu** (2)) To rain. *Comme s'il en pleuvait*, in quantities, in torrents; *faire pleuvoir*, to shower down, to pour; *il pleut à verse* or *à seaux*, it is pouring in buckets; *pleuvoir des hallebardes*, to rain cats and dogs. —*v.i.* To rain, to pour. *L'argent y pleut*, it rains money there; *les bombes pleuvaient sur Londres*, the bombs were raining down on London.

plèvre [plɛːvr], *n.f.* (*Anat.*) Pleura.

plexus [plɛk´syːs], *n.m. inv.* Plexus.

pleyon [plɛ´jɔ̃], *n.m.* Curved fruiting-branches; osier-tie.

pli [pli], *n.m.* Fold; crease, wrinkle, pucker, rumple; plait; coil; bend; undulation, depression; cover; envelope, letter, message; bent, habit; trick (at cards). *Avoir des plis au front*, to have wrinkles on one's forehead; *cela ne fera pas un pli*, there will not be the slightest difficulty; *cet habit ne fait pas un pli*, that coat fits without a wrinkle; *faire un pli*, to take a trick (at cards); *sonder tous les plis et replis du cœur*, to search into the innermost recesses of the heart; *le pli du bras*, the bend of the arm; *mise en pli*, setting (the hair); *prendre un mauvais pli*, to get into bad habits; *sous le même pli*, under the same cover (of letters etc.); *pli cacheté*, sealed message; *sous pli recommandé*, in a registered envelope; *un faux pli*, a crease; *un pli de terrain*, an undulation of the ground.

pliable, *a.* Pliable, flexible, supple.

pliage or **pliement**, *n.m.* Folding.

pliant, *a.* (*fem.* -**ante**) Pliant, flexible, docile, folding, collapsible.—*n.m.* Folding-chair, campstool, deck-chair.

plie [pli], *n.f. Plie franche* or *carrelet*. Plaice.

plié [pli´e], *n.m.* Bend of the knee in dancing.

pliement [PLIAGE].

plier [pli´e], *v.t.* (*conjugated like* PRIER) To fold, to fold up; to bend; (*fig.*) to bring under.

Plier bagage, to decamp, to pack up; *plier du linge*, to fold up linen; *plier les genoux*, to bend the knees; *plier les tentes*, to strike tents; *plier les voiles*, to furl the sails; *plier son esprit aux volontés d'autrui*, to be ruled by others.—*v.i.* To bend, to bow; to yield; to bend down, to give way. *Faire plier un arc*, to bend a bow; *il vaut mieux plier que rompre*, better bend than break; *le plancher plia*, the floor gave way; *plier sous l'autorité de quelqu'un*, to yield to someone's authority. **se plier**, *v.r.* To bow, to bend, to yield. *Je ne saurais me plier à cela*, I cannot fall in with that.

plieur, *n.m.* (*fem.* -**euse**) Folder.—*n.f.* Folding-machine.

Pline [plin], *m.* Pliny.

plinthe [plɛ̃:t], *n.f.* Plinth; skirting-board.

pliocène [pliɔ´sɛn], *a.* and *n.m.* (*Geol.*) Pliocene.

plioir [pli´waːr], *n.m.* Paper-knife; folder blade (for folding paper); winder (for fishing line).

plion [PLEYON].

plissage [pli´saːʒ], *n.m.* Pleating, kilting.

plissé [pli´se], *n.m.* Kilting, pleats.—*a.* (*fem.* -**ée**) Kilted, pleated. *Un front plissé*, a furrowed brow. **plissement**, *n.m.* Folding, doubling over; crumpling.

plisser [pli´se], *v.t.* To fold, to crease, to crumple, to wrinkle; to kilt, to pleat.—*v.i.* or **se plisser**, *v.r.* To form pleats, to be wrinkled or creased, to pucker.

plissure, *n.f.* Pleating; pleats.

pliure, *n.f.* (*Bookb.*) Folding.

ploc, *n.m.* or **ploque** [plɔk], *n.f.* Cow-hair; (*Naut.*) sheathing hair.

ploiement [plwa´mã], *n.m.*. Folding, bending. *Le ploiement des troupes*, forming column from line.

plomb [plɔ̃], *n.m.* Lead; bullet, shot; plumb-line, plummet; (*Naut.*) line; sink; custom-house seal; fuse. *À plomb*, perpendicularly, vertically; *de la poudre et du plomb*, powder and shot; *de plomb*, heavy, leaden, of a leaden hue (of clouds etc.); *fil à plomb*, plumb-line; *mine de plomb*, plumbago, blacklead; *n'avoir pas de plomb dans la tête*, to be scatter-brained; *plomb* (*fusible*), fuse; *plomb de sûreté*, cut-out; *plomb de sonde*, (*Naut.*) sounding lead; *sommeil de plomb*, very deep sleep; *tomber à plomb*, to fall vertically.

plombage, *n.m.* Leading, lead-work, plumbing; sealing; stopping (of teeth).

plombagine [plɔ̃ba´ʒin], *n.f.* Plumbago, black-lead, graphite.

plombe [plɔ̃b], *n.f.* (*slang*) Hour.

plombé [plɔ̃´be], *a.* (*fem.* -**ée**) Leaded; (*fig.*) of a leaden hue; loaded (of sticks). *Dent plombée*, tooth that has been stopped; *il a le teint plombé*, he has a livid complexion.

plomber [plɔ̃´be], *v.t.* To cover with lead, to apply lead to; to seal; to mark or stamp with lead; to stop (a tooth); to plumb; to glaze with plumbago. *Plomber le faîte d'un toit*, to lead the ridge of a roof; *plomber un mur*, to plumb a wall.—*v.i.* or **se plomber**, *v.r.* To take on a leaden hue.

plomberie, *n.f.* Plumber's shop; plumbing; lead-making; lead-works.

plombeur, *n.m.* (*Custom-house*) Stamper.

plombier, *n.m.* (*fem.* -**ière**) Lead-worker; plumber. **plombières**, *n.f.* Type of ice-cream sundae. **plombifère,** *a.* Plumbiferous.

plonge [plɔ̃:ʒ], *n.f.* *Faire la plonge,* to do the washing-up (in a restaurant).

plongeant [plɔ̃'ʒɑ̃], *a.* (*fem.* **-ante**) Plunging; downward. *Feu plongeant,* plunging fire (coming from above). **plongée,** *n.f.* Slope; dive, plunge; submersion (of a submarine); (*Cine.*) tilt shot.

plongement, *n.m.* Plunging, plunge; dip (of horizon etc.).

plongeoir [plɔ̃'ʒwa:r], *n.m.* Diving-board.

plongeon, *n.m.* Plunge, plunging; dive; (*Orn.*) diver. *Faire le plongeon,* to dive, to duck one's head. *Plongeon catmarin,* red-throated diver; *plongeon glacial* or *imbrim,* great northern diver; *plongeon huard* or *lumme,* black-throated diver.

plonger [plɔ̃'ʒe], *v.t.* To plunge, to dip, to immerse; to throw, to involve. *Plonger quelqu'un dans la douleur,* to plunge someone in grief; *plonger un poignard dans le cœur de quelqu'un,* to plunge a dagger into someone's heart.—*v.i.* To dive, to plunge; to submerge (of submarine); to bob under (of angler's float); to take a header, a ducker; to take a downward direction; to pitch (of ships); to swoop down (on enemy). *Plonger en canard,* to dive when swimming. **se plonger,** *v.r.* To be plunged; to yield completely (to grief etc.).

plongeur, *n.m.* (*fem.* **-euse**) Diver; dishwasher (in hotels etc.).—*a.* Plunging, diving (bird).

ploque [PLOC].

ploquer [plɔ'ke], *v.t.* To felt, to sheath (a ship's bottom etc.) with hair; to mix wools of different colours.

plosive [plo'ziv], *a.f.* and *n.f.* *Consonne plosive,* plosive consonant.

plot [plo], *n.m.* (*Elec.*) (Contact) stud. *Plot mobile,* plug.

ploutocrate [pluto'krat], *n.m.* Plutocrat.

ploutocratie, *n.f.* Plutocracy.

ploutocratique, *a.* Plutocratic.

ployable [plwa'jabl], *a.* Pliable, flexible.

ployer [plwa'je], *v.t. irr.* (*conjug. like* ABOYER) To bend; to fold up.—*v.i.* and **se ployer,** *v.r.* To bend, to bow, to be folded; to yield, to give way, to submit.

plu (1 and 2), *p.p.* [PLAIRE, PLEUVOIR].

pluie [plɥi], *n.f.* Rain; (*fig.*) shower. *Après la pluie le beau temps,* every cloud has a silver lining; *faire la pluie et le beau temps,* to be powerful or influential, to rule the roost; *le temps est à la pluie,* it looks like rain; *parler de la pluie et du beau temps,* to talk of nothing in particular; *petite pluie abat grand vent,* a little rain lays a great dust; *une pluie de fleurs,* a profusion of flowers; *une pluie d'or,* a shower of gold; *un jour de pluie,* a rainy day.

plumage [ply'ma:ʒ], *n.m.* Plumage, feathers.

plumail, *n.m.* (*pl.* **-aux**) Plume; feather-broom.

plumard, *n.m.* (*pop.*) Bed.

plumasseau, *n.m.* (*pl.* **-eaux**) Feather-broom, feather-duster; (*Surg.*) pledget.

plumasserie, *n.f.* Feather-trade.

plumassier, *n.m.* (*fem.* **-ière**) Feather merchant or dresser.

plume [plym], *n.f.* Feather; plume; quill, pen; nib; (*fig.*) writer, author. *Dessin à la plume,* pen-and-ink drawing; *écrire* or *se laisser aller au courant de la plume,* to write offhand; *guerre de plume,* paper war; *il y a laissé des plumes,* he did not get away unscathed; *la belle plume fait le bel oiseau,* fine feathers make fine birds; *mettre la main à la plume,* to take pen in hand; *poids plume,* (Box.) featherweight; *plume d'acier,* steel nib; *une bonne plume,* a good writer.

plumeau, *n.m.* (*pl.* **-eaux**) Feather-broom; feather-duster.

plumée, *n.f.* Penful (of ink); plucking (of poultry).

plumer, *v.t.* To pluck, to plume; (*fig.*) to fleece. *Plumer la poule sans la faire crier,* to fleece the sheep without making it bleat. —*v.i. Plumer (sur l'eau),* (Row.) to feather (along the water).

plumet, *n.m.* Plume; (*Bot.*) feather-grass, *Stipa pennata. Il a son plumet* or *son pompon,* (*fam.*) he's a bit on.

plumetis, *n.m.* Feather-stitch.

plumeux, *a.* (*fem.* **-euse**) (*Bot.*) Plumous, feathery.

plumier, *n.m.* Pen-box, pen-tray.

plumiste, *n.m.* Artist in feathers.

plumitif, *n.m.* (*Law*) Minute-book; (*fig.*) clerk, quill-driver, bureaucrat.

plumule, *n.f.* (*Bot.* and *Zool.*) Plumule.

plupart [ply'pa:r], *n.f. La plupart,* most, most part, the greatest or greater part, the generality or majority (*de*), most people. *La plupart des gens prétendent,* most people say; *la plupart de ses amis l'abandonnèrent,* most of his friends forsook him; *la plupart du temps,* mostly, generally; *les hommes sont pour la plupart intéressés,* the majority of men are selfish; *pour la plupart,* mostly, for the most part.

pluralité [plyrali'te], *n.f.* Plurality; pluralism.

pluriel, *a.* (*fem.* **-ielle**) Plural.—*n.m.* Plural. *Au pluriel,* in the plural.

plus (1) [plys, ply before a consonant, plyz before a vowel], *adv.* More, -er (*que,* than); -est, the most; also, moreover, further, besides; (*Arith.*) plus; (with *ne*) no more, no longer, not again, never again. *D'autant plus que,* the more so as; *c'est elle qui fait le plus de bruit,* she is the one who makes the most noise; *de plus,* besides, moreover; *de plus en plus,* more and more; *deux fois plus loin,* twice as far; *et qui plus est . . . ,* and what is more . . ; *il a plus d'argent que moi,* he has more money than I; *il a plus de vingt ans,* he is over twenty; *il a tout au plus trente ans,* he is thirty at the most; *il m'en coûte plus qu'à vous,* it hurts me more than it does you (to have to say it etc.); *il ne l'a pas fait non plus,* he hasn't done it either; *il s'enrichit de plus en plus,* he grows richer and richer every day; *il y a plus,* what is more; *je n'y retournerai plus,* I will never go there again, I will go there no more; *le plus beau,* the most beautiful; *n'avoir plus rien,* to have nothing left; *n'être plus,* to be no more; *ni moi non plus,* neither do (did etc.) I; *ni plus ni moins,* neither more nor less; *nous sommes plus qu'à moitié persuadés,* we are more than half convinced; *plus de deux fois,* more than twice; *plus de larmes,* no more tears; *plus je la vois, plus je la hais,* the more I see her the more I hate her; *plus loin,* further, farther; *plus on* *est de fous, plus on rit*, the more the merrier; *plus ou moins*, more or less, thereabouts; *plus près, de plus près*, nearer; *plus que huit jours!* only a week left! *plus que je ne croyais*, more than I thought; *plus savant que lui*, more learned than he; *plus tard*, later; *qui plus est*, what is more; *qui plus, qui moins*, some more, some less; *sans plus de façons*, without any more ado; *sans plus tarder*, without further delay; *vous avez beau dire, il n'en sera ni plus ni moins*, you may talk as much as you please, it will be so.—*n.m.* The most, the maximum; the more (opp. to *moins*); (*Arith., Alg.*) plus (sign). *Au plus*, at most; *en plus*, in addition, into the bargain; *tout au plus*, at the (very) most; *le plus que je puisse faire*, the most I can do; *qui peut le plus peut le moins*, he who can do more, can do less.

plus (2), *1st* and *2nd sing. past* [PLAIRE].

plusie [ply'zi], *n.f.* Gamma-moth, silvery moth.

plusieurs [ply'zjœːr], *a. pl.* and *pron. indef.* Several, some. *Un ou plusieurs*, one or more.

plus-pétition [plyspeti'sjɔ̃], *n.f.* Demand for more, pluris petitio.

plus-que-parfait, *n.m.* Pluperfect.

plus-value, *n.f.* (*pl.* **plus-values**) Increase in value, increment.

Plutarque [ply'tark], *m.* Plutarch.

Pluton [ply'tɔ̃], *m.* Pluto.

plutonien [plytɔ'njɛ̃] (*fem.* **-ienne**) or **plutonique**, *a.* (*Geol.*) Plutonian. **plutonisme**, *n.m.* Plutonism. **plutoniste**, *n.* Plutonist.

plutonium [plytɔ'njɔm], *n.m.* Plutonium.

plutôt [ply'to], *adv.* Rather, sooner (*que*). *Elle est plutôt jolie*, she is rather pretty; *plutôt mourir que faire une lâcheté*, rather die than do a dishonourable thing; *voyez plutôt*, see for yourself!

pluvial [ply'vjal], *a.* (*fem.* **-iale,** *pl.* **-iaux**) Pluvial, of rain, rainy. *Eaux pluviales*, rain-water.—*n.m.* (*Eccl.*) Cope.

pluvier [ply'vje], *n.m.* Plover. *Grand pluvier à collier*, ringed plover; *petit pluvier à collier* (or *gravière, f.*), lesser ringed plover; *pluvier à collier interrompu*, Kentish plover; *pluvier argenté*, grey or Swiss plover; *pluvier doré*, golden plover; *pluvier guignard*, dotterel.

pluvieux [ply'vjø], *a.* (*fem.* **-ieuse**) Rainy, wet, pluvious.

pluviomètre, *n.m.* Pluviometer, rain-gauge.

pluviôse, *n.m.* Fifth month of calendar of First French Republic (Jan. 20–Feb. 18 or 19).

pluviosité, *n.f.* Rainfall.

pneu [pnø], *n.m.* (*pl.* **pneus**), *abbrev. fam.* [PNEUMATIQUE] Tyre; (*Am.*) tire. *Pneu à flanc blanc*, white-wall tyre; *pneu à talons*, clincher tyre; *pneu à tringles*, wired-tyre.

pneumatique [pnøma'tik], *a.* Pneumatic. *Machine pneumatique*, air pump.—*n.f.* Pneumatics.—*n.m.* Pneumatic tyre; express letter (in Paris). *Pneumatique démontable*, detachable tyre.

pneumatologie [pnømatɔlɔ'ʒi], *n.f.* Pneumatology.

pneumonie [pnømɔ'ni], *n.f.* Pneumonia. **pneumonique**, *a.* Pneumonic.—*n.* Pneumonic patient.

pneumothorax, *n.m.* Pneumothorax.

pochade [pɔ'ʃad], *n.f.* Rough sketch; (*fig.*) hurried piece of writing etc.

pochard [pɔ'ʃaːr], *a.* (*fem.* **-arde**) (*slang*)

Drunken.—*n.* Drunkard. **pocharder,** *v.t.* To make tipsy. **se pocharder,** *v.r.* To get fuddled.

poche [pɔʃ], *n.f.* Pocket; pouch; sack, bag; purse-net; pucker, wrinkle (in clothes); crop (of a bird); sac (of an abscess etc.); ladle. *Argent de poche*, pocket-money; *connaître comme sa poche*, to know like the palm of one's hand; *en être de sa poche*, to be out of pocket; *faire des poches aux genoux*, to be baggy (of trousers); *faire la poche*, to bag (of skirt); *faire les poches à quelqu'un*, to go through someone's pockets; *fouiller dans ses poches*, to search one's pockets; *mettre quelqu'un dans sa poche* or *en poche*, to be too strong for someone; *mets ça dans ta poche (et ton mouchoir par-dessus)*, put that in your pipe and smoke it; *payer de sa poche*, to pay out of one's own pocket; (*Geol.*) *poche à cristaux*, druse, geode; *poche d'air*, air pocket; *poche rapportée*, patch-pocket; *poche revolver*, hip-pocket; *poches sous les yeux*, pockets, pouches, bags under the eyes; *y aller de sa poche*, to stump up, to foot the bill.

pocher (1) [pɔ'ʃe], *v.t.* To poach (eggs); to give a black eye to. *Avoir l'œil poché*, to have a black eye; *pocher l'œil à quelqu'un*, to give someone a black eye.—*v.i.* To pucker (of clothes etc.); to get baggy, to bag.

pocher (2) [pɔ'ʃe], *v.t.* To stencil; to make a rough sketch of, to dash off (essay etc.).

pochet, *n.m.* Nosebag (of horse).

pochetée, *n.f.* Pocketful. *En avoir une pochetée*, (*pop.*) to be stupid or drunk; *va donc! eh! pochetée!* you silly ass.

pocheter, *v.t.* (*rare*) To keep in one's pocket.

pochette, *n.f.* Small pocket; small net (for rabbits etc.); small fiddle, kit; packet of note-paper; fancy handkerchief; pocket case (of compasses).

pocheuse, *n.f.* Egg-poacher.

pochoir [pɔ'ʃwaːr], *n.m.* Stencil.

pochon, *n.m.* Stencil brush; (*fig.*) black eye.

podagre [pɔ'dagr], *n.f.* Podagra, gout in the feet.—*n.* Gouty person.—*a.* Gouty.

podestat [pɔdɛs'ta], *n.m.* Podesta (magistrate in Italy).

podocarpe, *n.m.* [SANTAL].

podomètre [pɔdɔ'mɛtr], *n.m.* Pedometer.

poêle (1) [pwaːl], *n.f.* Frying-pan. *Tenir la queue de la poêle*, to run the show; *tomber de la poêle dans le feu*, to jump out of the frying-pan into the fire.

poêle (2) [pwaːl] or **poile**, *n.m.* Stove. *Poêle à feu continu*, slow-combustion stove.

poêle (3) [pwaːl], *n.m.* Pall (at a funeral); canopy. *Tenir les cordons du poêle*, to be one of the pall-bearers.

poêlée [pwa'le], *n.f.* Panful. **poêlette**, *n.f.* Small pan.

poêlier [pwa'lje], *n.m.* Stove dealer or maker. **poêlon** [pwa'lɔ̃], *n.m.* Small saucepan, pipkin.

poème [pɔ'ɛm], *n.m.* Poem.

poésie, *n.f.* Poetry, verse; poem.

poète, *n.m.* Poet. *Poète lauréat*, Poet Laureate.

poétesse, *n.f.* Poetess.

poétique, *a.* Poetical.—*n.f.* Poetics. **poétiquement**, *adv.* Poetically.

poétiser, *v.t.* To make poetical, to idealize, to poeticize.

pognon [pɔ'ɲɔ̃], *n.m.* (*slang*) Money, oof, chink, dough.

pogrom [pɔ'grɔm], *n.m.* Pogrom.
poids [pwɑ], *n.m. inv.* Weight; heaviness; gravity; burden, load; (*fig.*) importance, consequence. *Avoir plus de poids que*, to outweigh, (*fig.*) to be more weighty *or* of more importance than; *de poids*, weighty, (*fig.*) of consequence *or* importance; *faire bon poids*, to give good weight, (*fig.*) to be generous; *lancer le poids*, (*spt.*) to put the weight *or* the shot; *le poids des affaires*, the burden of affairs; *les poids lourds*, lorries, heavy vehicles; *poids lourd*, (*Box.*) heavyweight; *poids mort*, dead-weight; *poids utile*, useful load; *un poids de dix livres*, a ten-pound weight; *vendre au poids*, to sell by weight; *vendre une chose au poids de l'or*, to sell a thing extremely dear.
poignant [pwa'nɑ̃], *a.* (*fem.* -**ante**) Poignant; sharp, acute, keen.
poignard [pwa'na:r], *n.m.* Poniard, dagger. *Ce fut un coup de poignard pour elle*, it was a crushing blow for her; *coup de poignard*, stab.
poignarder, *v.t.* To stab with a poniard, to poniard; (*fig.*) to wound, to grieve to the heart. **se poignarder**, *v.r.* To stab oneself.
poigne [pwaɲ], *n.f.* (*colloq.*) Grasp, grip; (*fig.*) strength, vigour. *Un homme à poigne*, a strong man.
poignée [pwa'ɲe], *n.f.* Handful; handle, hilt (of a sword etc.); holder; bunch, small quantity; shake (of the hand). *À poignée(s)*, by handfuls, by the handful; *jeter de l'argent à poignée*, to throw money about like water; *une poignée de soldats*, a handful of soldiers; *poignée de main*, handshake; *poignée de coffre*, guard iron.
poignet [pwa'ɲɛ], *n.m.* Wrist; wristband, cuff.
poil [pwal], *n.m.* Hair (of animals); hair (of persons) other than that of the head; (*fig.*) beard; nap (of cloth, of hats, etc.); wool, bristle, down (of plants etc.); colour (of horses). *À contre-poil*, against the grain; *à longs poils*, long-haired, shaggy; (*vulg.*) *à poil*, naked, with not a stitch on; (*fam.*) *au poil or au quart de poil*, very accurately; *avoir un poil dans la main*, to be work-shy; *brave à trois poils*, intrepid; *chasser à poil et à plume*, to shoot fur and feather; *cheval barbe de tout poil*, perfect barb; *de quel poil est ce cheval?* what is the colour of that horse? *drap à long poil*, cloth with long nap; (*fam.*) *être de bon poil*, to be in a good mood; *être de mauvais poil*, to be in a bad temper; *faire le poil à quelqu'un*, to outdo, to fleece, or insult someone; *monter un cheval à poil*, to ride a horse bareback; *poil de carotte*, (*pop.*) ginger, carrots; *poil de chameau*, camel's hair, camel-hair; *poil de chat*, (a weed) mibora; *poil de chèvre*, mohair; *poil follet*, soft hair, down (coming before the beard).
poile [POÊLE (2)].
poileux, *a.* (*fem.* -**euse**) [POILU].
poilu [pwa'ly], *a.* (*fem.* -**ue**) Hairy, shaggy; (*Bot.*) pilose.—*n.m.* (*pop.*) French infantryman, 1914–18.
poinçon [pwɛ̃'sɔ̃], *n.m.* Punch; point, stiletto; style (of engraver); awl, stamp, die; (*Carp.*) king-post; large cask. *Poinçon à épissures*, (*Naut.*) marlin spike; *poinçon à glace*, icepick; *poinçon de contrôle*, hall-mark.

poinçonnage or **poinçonnement**, *n.m.* Stamping.
poinçonner, *v.t.* To punch, to stamp, to prick; to clip; to hall-mark.
poinçonneuse, *n.f.* Stamping- or punching-machine.
poindre [pwɛ̃:dr], *v.i. irr.* (*conjugated like* CRAINDRE) To dawn, to break; (*fig.*) to appear, to break through, to sprout. *Le jour commençait à poindre*, day was beginning to break; *le poil commence à lui poindre au menton*, his beard is beginning to grow.—*v.t.* *To sting. *Oignez vilain, il vous poindra, poignez vilain, il vous oindra*, save a thief from the gallows and he will cut your throat.
poing [pwɛ̃], *n.m.* Fist, hand; (*fig.*) force, brute strength. *Coup de poing*, blow with the fist, fisticuff; *coup de poing américain*, knuckle-duster; (*fig.*) *dormir à poings fermés*, to sleep like a log; *il sait faire le coup de poing*, he knows how to box; *l'épée au poing*, sword in hand; *pieds et poings liés*, bound hand and foot; *se battre à coups de poing*, to fight with the fists.
point (1) [pwɛ̃], *adv.* (*used with negative*) No, not at all; none (*more emphatic than* **pas**). *Il n'a point d'argent*, he has no money at all; *je ne l'ai point vu*, I have not seen him; *point du tout*, not at all.
point (2) [pwɛ̃], *n.m.* Point; speck; dot, mark; (school) mark; stop, point of punctuation, full stop, period; (*Print.*) line; hole (of a strap etc.); (*Needlework*) stitch; head, part (of a speech etc.); matter, business, question; respect, particular; state, case, terms; instant, moment; height, pitch, degree; place, quarter. *À point*, in the nick of time (*see also* ATTENDRE]; *à point nommé* [NOMMÉ]; *au dernier point*, in the highest degree; *au plus haut point*, to the highest pitch; *cuit à point* [CUIT]; *de point en point*, exactly, in detail; *deux points*, colon; *en tout point*, in every respect; *faire le point*, to take the ship's bearings, (*fig.*) to state the true position; *gagner aux points*, (*Box.*) to win on points; *il était sur le point de sortir*, he was just going out; *j'étais sur le point de lui dire la vérité*, I was on the verge of telling him (her) the truth; *lettre de deux points*, (*Print.*) two-line letter; *marquer le point sur la carte*, to mark the ship's position on the chart; *mettre les points sur les i*, to dot one's i's, to be very punctilious; *mise au point*, adjustment, rectification; (*Phot., Cine.*) focusing; *point d'appui* [APPUI]; *point de chute*, place of fall; *point de côté*, stitch; *point de riz*, (*Knitting*) moss-stitch; *point de vue*, point of view, standpoint; *point d'exclamation* [EXCLAMATION]; *point d'honneur*, point of honour; *point d'interrogation* [INTERROGATION]; *point d'orgue*, (*Mus.*) pause; *point du compas*, point of the compass; *point du vent*, (*Naut.*) tack; *point estimé*, (*Naut.*) dead reckoning; *point et virgule*, semi-colon; *point mort*, (*Motor.*) neutral position; (*fig.*) standstill, deadlock; *rendre des points*, to give odds; *rendre des points à*, to be more than a match for, to give odds to; *sur ce* or *en ce point*, on that score, in that respect; *un point fait à temps en sauve mille*, a stitch in time saves nine; *un point, c'est tout*, nothing else, no more; and that's that.
pointage [pwɛ̃'ta:ʒ], *n.m.* Pointing, levelling

(of guns); laying, sighting; checking, pricking; scrutiny (of votes), tally, tallying, ticking off.

pointal [pwɛ̃'tal], *n.m.* (*pl.* **-aux**) (*Carp.*) Prop, stay.

pointe [pwɛ̃:t], *n.f.* Point, (sharp end); tip, head (of an arrow, lance, etc.); nose (of a bullet); cape, headland, foreland; peak, pinnacle; etching-needle; nail, tack, rivet; (*Print.*) bodkin; (*fig.*) smack, dash, flavour; small quantity, touch; sting, pungency, sharpness; witticism; triangular kerchief *or* scarf, triangular napkin *or* diaper (for infant). (*pl.*) Toe-dancing. *Avoir une pointe de vin*, to be slightly excited with drink; *coup de pointe*, thrust with a sword; *deux de pointe*, (*Row.*) pair oar; *en pointe*, tapering, pointed; *heure de pointe*, peak hour, rush hour; *la pointe du jour*, the break or dawn of day; *marcher sur la pointe des pieds*, to walk on tiptoe; *pointe d'asperge*, asparagus-tip; *pointe de cœur*, apex (of railway crossing); *pointe de feu*, ignipuncture; *pointe sèche*, (*Engr.*) dry-point (tool, etching); *pointe de vitesse*, spurt, sprint; *pousser sa pointe*, to pursue one's point, to persist; *tailler en pointe*, to cut to a point; *tourner la pointe du pied en dehors*, to turn one's toes out.

pointeau, *n.m.* (*pl.* **-eaux**) Centre-punch; needle, float-spindle (of carburettor); valve-needle (of tyre); checker.

pointement [POINTAGE].

pointer [pwɛ̃'te], *v.t.* To point (a gun etc.); to aim (with firearm); to lay, to sight; to pierce, to stab, to prick; to mark, to dot; to point; to tally, to tick off, to scrutinize (votes); to prick up (ears etc.); to sharpen; (*Print.*) to register.—*Pointer la carte*, (*Naut.*) to point the chart.—*v.i.* To point, to spring, rise, or stick up; to soar; to rear; to sprout, to appear, to come up.

pointerolle [pwɛ̃'trɔl], *n.f.* (Miner's) pitching tool.

pointeur [pwɛ̃'tœ:r], *n.m.* (*fem.* **-euse**) Pointer, marker, checker; (*Artill.*) gun-layer; (*Naut.*) fire control man.

pointillage [pwɛ̃ti'ja:ʒ] *or* **pointillement**, *n.m.* Dotting, stippling; dotted line.

pointille, *n.f.* Trifle, trifling point.

pointillé, *n.m.* Stipple drawing or engraving; dotted line.

pointiller, *v.t.* To dot, to stipple; (*fig.*) to tease.—*v.i.* To bicker, to cavil.

pointillerie, *n.f.* Bickering, cavilling, hair-splitting.

pointilleux, *a.* (*fem.* **-euse**) Cavilling, captious; fastidious, finical. *Un critique pointilleux*, a carping critic.

pointillisme, *n.m.* Pointillism.

pointilliste, *n.m.* Stipple engraver, pointillist.

pointomètre [pwɛ̃tɔ'metr], *n.m.* Sculptor's calliper.

pointu [pwɛ̃'ty], *a.* (*fem.* **-ue**) Pointed, sharp; (*fig.*) subtle, acute, captious. *Voix pointue*, shrill voice.

pointure, *n.f.* (*Print.*) Point; size, number (of shoes, gloves, etc.). *Il a sept de pointure*, he takes size seven, he takes sevens.

poire [pwa:r], *n.f.* Pear; powder-flask; bulb (of a camera); (*colloq.*) head, face; (*slang*) mug, simpleton. *Poire d'angoisse* [ANGOISSE]; *poire de vaporisateur*, bulb of a (scent) spray;

poire d'oiseau [AUBÉPINE]. *Couper la poire en deux*, to split the difference; *entre la poire et le fromage*, at dessert; *faire sa poire*, (*fam.*) to put on side; *garder une poire pour la soif*, to put something by for a rainy day. **poiré**, *n.m.* Perry.

poireau [pwa'ro] *or* **porreau** [pɔ'ro], *n.m.* (*pl.* **-eaux**) Leek, wart. (*colloq.*) *Faire le poireau or poireauter*, to be kept waiting; (*fam.*) *le Poireau*, the 'Mérite Agricole' decoration.

poirée [pwa're], *n.f.* White beet.

poirier [pwa'rje], *n.m.* Pear-tree.

pois [pwɑ], *n.m. inv.* Pea, peas. *Étoffe à pois*, spotted material. *Il donne un pois pour avoir une fève*, he throws a sprat to catch a herring; *pois carrés*, marrow-fats; *pois cassés*, split peas, pease; *pois chiche*, chick-pea; *pois de senteur*, sweet-pea; *pois de serpent*, Lathyrus aphaca; *pois verts or petits pois*, green peas; *purée de pois*, thick pea soup; (*fig.*) dense (yellow) fog, pea-soup fog, pea-souper.

poison [pwa'zɔ̃], *n.m.* Poison; poisonous stuff; (*fig.*) poisonous creature.—*n.f.* (*fam.*) A regular pest.

poissard [pwa'sa:r], *a.* (*fem.* **-arde**) Vulgar, low. *Style poissard*, Billingsgate style.—*n.f.* Fishwife; low or vulgar woman.

poisse [pwas], *n.f.* (*pop.*) Bad luck; poverty.

poisser [pwa'se], *v.t.* To pitch; to make sticky; (*slang*) to pinch, to catch, to nab.

poisseux, *a.* (*fem.* **-euse**) Pitchy, gluey, sticky.

poisson [pwa'sɔ̃], *n.m.* Fish; (*Am.*) sea-food; (*Astron.*) Pisces. *Être comme un poisson hors de l'eau*, to be like a fish out of water; *être heureux comme un poisson dans l'eau*, to be happy as Larry; *finir en queue de poisson* [QUEUE]; *poisson d'avril* [AVRIL]; *poisson de mer*, sea-fish; *poisson de rivière*, freshwater fish; *poisson rouge*, goldfish; *poisson Saint-Pierre*, John Dory. **poisson-chat**, *n.m.* (*pl.* **poissons-chats**) Cat-fish. **poisson-lune**, *n.m.* (*pl.* **poissons-lune**) Moon-fish. **poissonnerie**, *n.f.* Fishmarket; fish-counter; fish-shop. **poissonneux**, *a.* (*fem.* **-euse**) Abounding in fish. **poissonnier**, *n.m.* (*fem.* **-ière**) Fishmonger, fishwife.—*n.f.* Fishkettle.

poitrail [pwa'tra:j], *n.m.* Breast (of a horse); poitrel, breast-piece (of harness); (*Build.*) breastsummer.

poitrinaire [pwatri'nɛ:r], *a.* and *n.* Consumptive.

poitrine [pwa'trin], *n.f.* Chest, breast, bosom; lungs; brisket. *Maladie de poitrine*, consumption; *tour de poitrine*, chest measurement; *voix de poitrine*, chest voice.

poivrade [pwa'vrad], *n.f.* Pepper-sauce.

poivre [pwa:vr], *n.m.* Pepper. *Grain de poivre*, peppercorn; *poivre à queue*, cubeb; *poivre de Brabant* [MYRTE]; *poivre de Cayenne*, Cayenne pepper; *poivre de Guinée*, grains of paradise; *poivre et sel*, grey, grizzly, iron-grey. **poivré**, *a.* Peppery, pungent; (*fig.*) spicy. **poivrer**, *v.t.* To pepper, to put pepper or sarcasm into; (*colloq.*) to lay it on, to overcharge for; (*slang*) to infect with venereal disease.

poivrier, *n.m.* Pepper-plant; pepper-box. **poivrière**, *n.f.* Pepper-plantation; (*Fort.*) corner turret; pepper-box. **poivron**, *n.m.* Jamaica pepper, capsicum, allspice.

poivrot, *n.m.* (*fem.* **-otte**) (*slang*) Boozer.

poix [pwɑ], *n.f.* Pitch; shoemakers' wax.

polaire [pɔ'lɛːr], *a.* Polar. *L'étoile polaire*, the pole-star; the lodestar.

polaque [pɔ'lak], *n.m.* Polish cavalryman (in 18th-century French service), Polack.

polarimètre [pɔlari'mɛtr], *n.m.* Polarimeter.

polarisant, *a.* (*fem.* **-ante**) or **polarisateur,** *a.* (*fem.* **-trice**) Polarizing. **polarisation,** *n.f.* Polarization.

polariscope, *n.m.* Polariscope.

polariser, *v.t.* To polarize.

polariseur, *n.m.* Polarizer.

polarité, *n.f.* Polarity.

polatouche [pɔla'tuʃ], *n.m.* Flying-squirrel.

polder [pɔl'dɛːr], *n.m.* (*Dutch*) Polder.

pôle [poːl], *n.m.* Pole. *Pôle arctique*, arctic pole; *pôle nord*, North Pole.

polémique [pɔle'mik], *n.f.* Polemics, controversy, disputation.—*a.* Polemical. **polémiser** or **polémiquer,** *v.i.* To polemize. **polémiste,** *n.* Polemist, controversialist.

polémonie [pɔlemɔ'ni], *n.f.* (*Bot.*) Valerian.

poli [pɔ'li], *a.* (*fem.* **-ie**) Polished, glossy, sleek; polite, civil; refined.—*n.m.* Polish, finish, gloss.

polianthe [TUBÉREUSE].

police [pɔ'lis], *n.f.* Police; police-regulations, regulative administration; (*Print.*) (bill of a) font; insurance policy. *Agent de police*, police-constable; *bonnet de police*, forage cap; *faire la police des rues*, to keep order in the streets; *salle de police*, guard-room; *tribunal de simple police*, police-court.

policer, *v.t.* To establish law and order in; to civilize, to polish, to refine.

polichinelle [pɔliʃi'nɛl], *n.m.* Punch; buffoon, merry-andrew; Punch and Judy show; (*fig.*) a mere puppet. *Un secret de polichinelle*, an open secret; [*see also* PATACHON].

policier [pɔli'sje], *a.* (*fem.* **-ière**) Pertaining to the police. *Roman policier*, detective story *or* novel; thriller.—*n.m.* Policeman; detective.

policlinique [pɔlikli'nik], *n.f.* Out-patients' department.

poliment [pɔli'mã], *adv.* Politely.

poliomyélite [pɔljɔmje'lit], *n.f.* Poliomyelitis.

polir [pɔ'liːr], *v.t.* To polish, to burnish; to give the final touch to; (*fig.*) to make polite, to civilize, to refine. **se polir,** *v.r.* To polish, to become polished; to become refined.

polissable, *a.* Easy to polish.

polissage or **polissement,** *n.m.* Polishing, finishing.

polisseur, *n.m.* (*fem.* **-euse**) Polisher.

polissoir, *n.m.* Polisher, burnisher (tool).

polissoire, *n.f.* Shining brush.

polisson [pɔli'sɔ̃], *n.m.* (*fem.* **-onne**) Mischievous child, scamp, scapegrace; rascally *or* loose person.—*a.* Loose, naughty, licentious, smutty. **polissonner,** *v.i.* To run about the streets (of children); to be a *polisson*.

polissonnerie, *n.f.* Smutty joke, indecent talk, lewd act.

polissure [pɔli'syːr], *n.f.* Polishing.

politesse [pɔli'tɛs], *n.f.* Politeness, civility, good breeding, polite attention, compliment, act of civility. *Avoir de la politesse*, to be polite; *brûler la politesse à quelqu'un*, to leave someone suddenly; to miss an appointment; *échange de politesses*, exchange of compliments; *ce serait une politesse de votre part de*,

it would be kind of you to; *faire une politesse*, to do a kindness.

politicien [pɔliti'sjɛ̃], *n.m.* (*fem.* **-ienne**) (*usu. pej.*) Politician; politicaster.

politique [pɔli'tik], *n.f.* Politics, affairs of state; polity; policy, statecraft, discretion. *Parler politique*, to talk politics; *politique intérieure*, home politics *or* policy; *politique extérieure*, foreign politics, foreign policy.—*a.* Political; (*fig.*) diplomatic, politic, prudent, wise. *Homme politique*, politician, statesman. —*n.m.* Politician, statesman. *C'est un rusé politique*, he is a crafty politician. **politiquement,** *adv.* Politically; (*fig.*) shrewdly.

politisation, *n.f.* Politicizing. **politiser,** *v.t.* To politicize, to make political.

polka [pɔl'ka], *n.f.* Polka. *Pain polka*, bread (-loaf) with a diamond-pattern on the crust.

polker, *v.i.* To polk, to dance the polka.

pollen [pɔl'len], *n.m.* Pollen.

pollicitation [pɔlisita'sjɔ̃], *n.f.* Pollicitation.

pollination [pɔlina'sjɔ̃], *n.f.* Pollination.

pollinisation [pɔliniza'sjɔ̃], *n.f.* Pollinization, fertilization. *Pollinisation croisée*, cross-fertilization.

polluer [pɔl'lɥe], *v.t.* To pollute; to defile; to profane.

pollution, *n.f.* Pollution; defilement; profanation.

polo [pɔ'lo], *n.m.* Polo (on horse, or bicycle); polo jumper; small knitted toque.

polochon [pɔlɔ'ʃɔ̃], *n.m.* (*slang*) Bolster, pillow. *Se battre à coups de polochon*, to have a pillow-fight.

Pologne [pɔ'lɔɲ], *f.* Poland.

polonais [pɔlɔ'nɛ], *a.* (*fem.* **-aise**) Polish.— *n.m.* Polish language; **Polonais** (*fem.* **-aise**) Pole.—*n.f.* Polonaise (dress, dance, tune).

poltron [pɔl'trɔ̃], *a.* (*fem.* **-onne**) Cowardly, chicken-hearted.—*n.* Coward, poltroon, skulker, funk. **poltronnerie,** *n.f.* Cowardice, poltroonery.

polyandre [pɔli'ãːdr], *a.* Polyandrous.

polyandrie, *n.f.* Polyandry; (*Bot.*) polyandria.

polychrome, *a.* Polychrome. **polychromie,** *n.f.* Polychromy.

polycopier, *v.t.* To jellygraph, to cyclostyle.

polyculture, *n.f.* General farming.

polyèdre, *a.* Polyhedral.—*n.m.* Polyhedron.

polygale or **polygala,** *n.m.* (*Bot.*) Milkwort.

polygame, *n.* Polygamist.—*a.* Polygamous.

polygamie, *n.f.* Polygamy.

polyglotte, *a.* and *n.* Polyglot.

polygonal, *a.* (*fem.* **-ale,** *pl.* **aux**) Polygonal. **polygone,** *n.m.* Polygon; ordnance-yard, practice-ground, shooting-range.

polygraphe, *n.m.* Author of many kinds of works.

polymère, *a.* and *n.m.* Polymeric; polymer, polymeride. **polymérie,** *n.f.* Polymerism. **polymérisation,** *n.f.* Polymerization. **polymériser,** *v.t.* To polymerize.

Polynésie [pɔline'zi], *f.* Polynesia.

polynésien (*fem.* **-ienne**), *a.* and *n.* Polynesian.

polynôme [pɔli'noːm], *n.m.* (*Math.*) Polynomial.

polype, *n.m.* Polyp; (*Med.*) polypus.

polypeux, *a.* (*fem.* **-euse**) (*Path.*) Polypous. **polypier,** *n.m.* (*Zool.*) Polyp.

polypode, *n.m.* Polypodium. *Polypode du*

chêne, wall-fern; *polypode du hêtre*, beech-fern.

polysyllabe, *a.* Polysyllabic.—*n.m.* Polysyllable. **polysyllabique,** *a.* Polysyllabic.

polytechnicien, *n.m.* Student of Polytechnique. **polytechnique,** *a.* Polytechnic. *École polytechnique* or *Polytechnique*, the famous high school in Paris.

polythéisme, *n.m.* Polytheism. **polythéiste,** *n.* Polytheist.—*a.* Polytheistic.

Poméranie [pɔmera'ni], *f.* Pomerania.

pomiculteur [pɔmikyl'tœːr], *n.m.* Pip-fruit grower.

pomifère [pɔmi'fɛːr], *a.* Pomiferous.

pommade [pɔ'mad], *n.f.* Pomade, pomatum. *Passer de la pommade à quelqu'un*, (*fam.*) to toady to someone.

pommader, *v.t.* To pomade. **se pommader,** *v.r.* To pomade one's hair; to use (rather a lot of) hair-cream.

pomme [pɔm], *n.f.* Apple; apple-like fruit; ball, knob; head (of a cabbage, lettuce, walking-stick, etc.); truck (of mast); (*pop.*) head, nut. *Bifteck aux pommes*, steak and chips; *canne à pomme d'or*, gold-headed walking-stick; *pomme à cidre*, cider-apple; *pomme à couteau*, eating apple; *pomme d'Adam*, Adam's apple; *pomme d'amour*, tomato; *pomme d'arrosoir*, rose (of watering-can); *pomme de chêne*, oak-apple; *pomme de pin*, fir-cone; *pomme de terre*, potato; *pomme épineuse* [DATURA]; (*fam.*) *tomber dans les pommes*, to faint.

pommé, *a.* (*fem.* **-ée**) Grown to a round head; (*colloq.*) complete, downright, first-class; whopper. *Laitue pommée*, cabbage-lettuce.

pommeau [pɔ'mo], *n.m.* (*pl.* **-eaux**) Pommel (of a saddle, sword, etc.); head, knob.

pommelé, *a.* (*fem.* **-ée**) Dappled, mottled; cloudy, with dappled clouds. *Cheval gris-pommelé*, dapple-grey horse. **se pommeler,** *v.r.* To become dappled. *Le ciel s'est pommelé*, the sky has become dappled.

(C) pomme-de-mai, *n.f.* May apple.

pommelle [pɔ'mɛl], *n.f.* Grating (over a pipe), strainer (over a drain-pipe).

pommer [pɔ'me], *v.i.* To grow to a firm round head (of cabbage, lettuce etc.). **se pommer,** *v.r.* To grow to a firm round head, to cabbage (of lettuce).

pommeraie [pɔm'rɛ], *n.f.* Apple-orchard.

pommette [pɔ'mɛt], *n.f.* Apple-like ball or knob; cheek-bone; (*C*) crab-apple.

(C) pommettier [pɔmɛ'tje], *n.m.* Crab-apple tree.

pommier [pɔ'mje], *n.m.* Apple-tree; (*Cook.*) apple-roaster.

pomologie [pɔmɔlɔ'ʒi], *n.f.* Pomology.

pompadour [pɔ̃pa'duːr], *a. inv.* Pompadour style (chair, hair, etc.).—*n.f.* Variety of domestic fowl.

pompe (1) [pɔ̃p], *n.f.* Pomp, ceremony, state, display. *Entrepreneur de pompes funèbres*, undertaker, (*Am.*) mortician; *marcher en grande pompe*, to march in great state.

pompe (2) [pɔ̃p], *n.f.* Pump, inflator. *Pompe à feu* or *à vapeur*, steam-pump; *pompe à incendie*, fire-engine; *pompe à pneus*, tyre inflator; *pompe aspirante*, suction-pump; *pompe d'arrosage*, watering-engine, garden engine; *serrure à pompe*, Bramah lock;

travail à la pompe, (tailoring) alterations. *Avoir un coup de pompe*, (*slang*) to be pumped out.

pompé [pɔ̃'pe], *a.* (*fem.* **-ée**) (*slang*) Exhausted.

Pompée [pɔ̃'pe], *m.* Pompey.

Pompéi [pɔ̃pe'i], *f.* Pompeii.

pomper [pɔ̃'pe], *v.t.* To pump; (*fig.*) to suck up.—*v.i.* To pump; (*slang*) to booze.

pompette, *a.* (*pop.*) Tipsy, half-seas over.

pompeusement [pɔ̃pøz'mɑ̃], *adv.* Solemnly, with pomp. **pompeux,** *a.* (*fem.* **-euse**) Stately, solemn; high-sounding, high-flown.

pompier [pɔ̃'pje], *n.m.* Pump-maker; fireman; (*fem.* **-ière**) alteration hand.—*a. inv.* Conventional, stereotyped (art, style).

pompiste [pɔ̃'pist], *n.* Pump-attendant (at petrol-pump etc.).

pompon [pɔ̃'pɔ̃], *n.m.* Pompon, top-knot, ornamental tuft; (*fig.*) pretentious ornament. *À lui le pompon*, (*fam.*) he takes the cake; *avoir son pompon*, (*slang*) to be half-seas over.

pomponner, *v.t.* To ornament with pompons, to deck out, to bedizen. *Pomponner son style*, to trick out one's style. **se pomponner,** *v.r.* To bedizen oneself, to titivate.

ponçage [pɔ̃'saːʒ], *n.m.* Pumicing; pouncing (of drawings).

ponce [pɔ̃s], *n.f.* Pumice; (*Drawing*) pounce. *Pierre ponce*, pumice-stone.

ponceau (1) [pɔ̃'so], *n.m.* (*pl.* **-eaux**) Culvert; one-arched small bridge.

ponceau (2) [pɔ̃'so], *n.m.* (*pl.* **-eaux**) Corn-poppy.—*a.* Poppy-red.

Ponce Pilate [pɔ̃spi'lat], *m.* Pontius Pilate.

poncer [pɔ̃'se], *v.t.* To pumice; (*Drawing*) to pounce. **ponceux,** *a.* (*fem.* **-euse**) Pumiceous.

poncif, *n.m.* Pounced drawing; (*fig.*) poor, conventional, commonplace, hackneyed, stereotyped piece of work.

ponction [pɔ̃k'sjɔ̃], *n.f.* Puncture, tapping.

ponctionner, *v.t.* To tap, to puncture; to prick (a blister).

ponctualité [pɔ̃ktɥali'te], *n.f.* Punctuality.

ponctuation [pɔ̃ktɥa'sjɔ̃], *n.f.* Punctuation.

ponctué, *a.* (*fem.* **-ée**) Punctuated; dotted; spotted (leaf). *Ligne ponctuée*, dotted line.

ponctuel, [pɔ̃k'tɥɛl], *a.* (*fem.* **-elle**) Punctual, exact; (*Phys.*) pin-point. **ponctuellement,** *adv.* Punctually.

ponctuer [pɔ̃k'tɥe], *v.t.* To punctuate; to point, to mark.

pondaison [pɔ̃dɛ'zɔ̃], *n.f.* Laying (of eggs); laying-season.

pondérabilité [pɔ̃derabili'te], *n.f.* Ponderability. **pondérable,** *a.* Ponderable.

pondérateur, *a.* (*fem.* **-trice**) Balancing, stabilizing.

pondération, *n.f.* Ponderation, poise; coolness, level-headedness; equilibrium, proper balance (of parts). **pondéré,** *a.* (*fem.* **-ée**) Poised, calm, self-controlled; weighted (average). **pondérer,** *v.t. irr.* (*conjug. like* ACCÉLÉRER) To poise, to balance.

pondeur [pɔ̃'dœːr], *a.* (*fem.* **-euse**) Laying often (of poultry etc.); (*colloq.*) productive, prolific.—*n.* Layer; productive person.

Pondichéry [pɔ̃diʃe'ri], *m.* Pondicherry.

pondre [pɔ̃dr], *v.t.* To lay (eggs); (*colloq.*) to produce (a poem, a speech, etc.).

ponette [pɔ'nɛt], *n.f.* She-pony.

poney [pɔ'ne], *n.m.* Pony.

pongée [pɔ̃'ʒe], *n.m.* Pongee.

pont [pɔ̃], *n.m.* Bridge; deck; fly, flap (of trousers); work-day between a Sunday and a Bank-holiday or vice versa. *Faire le pont*, (*fam.*) to take the intervening day off as well; (*Wrestling*) to land on nape and feet only; (*slang*) (of a sharper) to bend the cards in order to make the gull cut at the right point, hence *couper dans le pont*, (*fam.*) to be taken in; *faire un pont d'or à quelqu'un*, to make great pecuniary concessions to someone; *faux pont*, orlop deck; *Ponts et Chaussées*, (*France*) Department of Bridges and Highways; *pont à bascule* [BASCULE]; (*Av.*) *pont aérien*, air-lift; (*Motor.*) *pont-arrière*, rear-axle; *pont aux ânes* [ÂNE]; *pont d'envol*, flight-deck; *pont dormant*, fixed bridge over ditch; *pont promenade*, promenade-deck; *pont roulant*, gantry; *pont suspendu*, suspension-bridge; *pont tournant*, swing-bridge; *pont volant*, fly-bridge; *premier pont*, lower deck; *troisième pont*, upper deck of a three-decker.

pontage, *n.m.* Bridging; decking; pontooning.

ponte (1) [pɔ̃:t], *n.f.* Laying of eggs. *Lieu de ponte*, breeding-place (of flies etc.).

ponte (2) [pɔ̃:t], *n.m.* Punter (at baccarat etc.); (*Ombre*) ace of hearts or diamonds; (*fam.*) V.I.P.

ponté [pɔ̃'te], *a.* (*fem.* -ée) Decked. *Non ponté*, open (boat).

ponter (1) [pɔ̃'te], *v.i.* To punt, to gamble.

ponter (2) [pɔ̃'te], *v.t.* To deck (a boat etc.).

pontet [pɔ̃'tɛ], *n.m.* Trigger-guard; scabbard-catch (of bayonet); saddle-bow, saddle-tree.

Pont-Euxin [pɔ̃tøk'sɛ̃], **le**, *m.* The Euxine, Black Sea.

pontier [pɔ̃'tje], *n.m.* Keeper of a swing-bridge.

pontife [pɔ̃'tif], *n.m.* Pontiff, (*fig.*) pundit. *Le Souverain Pontife*, the Pope. **pontifical**, *a.* (*fem.* -ale, *pl.* -aux) Pontifical. **pontificalement**, *adv.* Pontifically. **pontificat**, *n.m.* Pontificate.

pontifier, *v.i.* (*fam.*) To act, to speak solemnly, pompously; to pontificate, to lay down the law.

pont l'évêque [pɔ̃le'vɛk], *n.m. inv.* Square cheese, made at Pont-l'Évêque (Calvados).

pont-levis [pɔ̃l'vi], *n.m.* (*pl.* **ponts-levis**) Drawbridge.

pont-neuf, *n.m. Se porter comme le Pont-Neuf*, to be as fit as a fiddle.

ponton [pɔ̃'tɔ̃], *n.m.* Bridge of boats; pontoon; *hulk, convict-ship, landing-stage.

pontonage, *n.m.* Bridge-toll.

pontonnier, *n.m.* Pontoon soldier, pontoneer; toll-collector.

pope [pɔp], *n.m.* Pope (priest of Greek Church).

popeline [pɔ'plin], *n.f.* Poplin.

poplité [pɔpli'te], *a.* (*fem.* -ée) (*Anat.*) Popliteal.

popote [pɔ'pɔt], *n.f.* (*Mil. slang*) Officers' field-mess. (*fam.*) *Faire la popote*, to do the cooking.—*a. Une femme popote*, a stay-at-home woman.

populace [pɔpy'las], *n.f.* Populace, mob, rabble.

populacier, *a.* (*fem.* -ière) Low, vulgar.

populage [pɔpy'la:ʒ], *n.m.* (*Bot.*) Marsh marigold.

populaire [pɔpy'lɛ:r], *a.* Popular; common.

(*Polit.*) *Front populaire*, Popular Front; *République Populaire*, People's Republic.— *n.m.* Populace, mob, rabble. **populairement**, *adv.* Popularly.

populariser, *v.t.* To popularize.

popularité, *n.f.* Popularity.

population [pɔpylɑ'sjɔ̃], *n.f.* Population.

populeux, *a.* (*fem.* -euse) Populous.

populo, *n.m.* (*colloq.*) Lower orders, the rabble.

poracé [pɔrɑ'se], *a.* (*fem.* -ée) Porraceous.

porc [pɔ:r], *n.m.* Pig; swine; pork; (*fig.*) dirty or beastly person, swine. *Côtelette de porc*, pork-chop; *gardeur de porcs*, swineherd; *peau de porc*, pigskin; *porc châtré*, hog; *porc d'engrais*, porker.

porcelaine [pɔrsə'lɛn], *n.f.* Porcelain, china, chinaware; vase of this; porcelain-shell, cowry. *Terre à porcelaine*, china-clay. **porcelainier**, *a.* (*fem.* -ière) Pertaining to porcelain.—*n.m.* Porcelain manufacturer; workman in a porcelain factory.

porcelet [pɔrsə'lɛ], *n.m.* Young pig, piglet; (*pop.*) wood-louse.

porcelle [pɔr'sɛl], *n.f.* (*Bot.*) Hypochaeris, great dandelion.

porc-épic [pɔrke'pik], *n.m.* (*pl.* **porcs-épics**) Porcupine; (*Am.*) hedgehog.

porche [pɔrʃ], *n.m.* Porch.

porcher [pɔr'ʃe], *n.m.* (*fem.* -ère) Swineherd, swine-girl. **porcherie**, *n.f.* Pigsty, piggery; pig-farm. **porcin**, *a.* (*fem.* -ine) Porcine. —*n.m. pl.* Pigs; the pig family.

pore [pɔ:r], *n.m.* Pore. **poreux**, *a.* (*fem.* -euse) Porous.

porillon [pɔri'jɔ̃] or **porion** (1) [pɔ'rjɔ̃], *n.m.* Daffodil.

porion (2) [pɔ'rjɔ̃], *n.m.* (*N. dial.*) Fireman (in coal-mines), overseer.

porisme [pɔ'rism], *n.m.* Porism. **poristique**, *a.* Poristic.

pornographe [pɔrnɔ'graf], *n.* Pornographer. **pornographie**, *n.f.* Pornography. **pornographique**, *a.* Pornographic.

porosité [pɔrozi'te], *n.f.* Porosity.

Porphyre [pɔr'fi:r], *m.* Porphyry.

porphyre [pɔr'fi:r], *n.m.* Porphyry; porphyry slab (for grinding). **porphyrique**, *a.* Porphyritic. **porphyriser**, *v.t.* To porphyrize, to pound, to pulverize.

porque [pɔrk], *n.f.* (*Naut.*) Rider, web-frame. *Allonges de porque*, futtock-riders; *porque de fond*, floor-riders.

porracé [PORACÉ].

porreau [POIREAU].

port (1) [pɔ:r], *n.m.* Haven, harbour, port; seaport town; wharf, quay. *Arriver à bon port*, to arrive safely, (*fig.*) to end happily; *conduire* or *mener à bon port*, to bring to a successful issue; *faire naufrage au port*, to be wrecked in port; *port d'attache*, home port; *port d'escale*, port of call, (*Av.*) putting-in station; *port de guerre*, naval station; *port de marée*, tidal harbour; *port de mer*, seaport; *port franc*, free port; *port naturel*, natural harbour.

port (2) [pɔ:r], *n.m.* Carriage; cost of this; postage; bearing, gait, port; (*Naut.*) burden, tonnage. *Être au port d'armes*, to be at the shoulder-arms position. *Frais de port*, postal charges; *port dû*, carriage forward; *port payé*, postage paid. *Elle a un port de reine*, she walks like a queen. *Port de Voix*, glide, portamento, scoop (in singing).

port (3) [pɔːr], *n.m.* (High) pass or col (in the Pyrenees).

portable [pɔr'tabl], *a.* Portable; wearable.

portage, *n.m.* Carriage, transport, conveyance, porterage; portage (at rapids etc.). *Faire le portage,* to carry a boat overland.

(*C*) **portageage** [pɔrta'ʒaːʒ], *n.m.* Portaging, toting.

(*C*) **portager** [pɔrta'ʒe], *v.t.* To portage, to tote.

(*C*) **portageur** [pɔrta'ʒœːr], *n.m.* Toter, carrier.

portail [pɔr'taːj], *n.m.* (*pl.* -s) Chief doorway, portal, front gate (of a church).

portance [pɔr'tɑ̃ːs], *n.f.* (*Av.*) Lifting power, lift (of aircraft).

portant [pɔr'tɑ̃], *a.* (*fem.* -**ante**) Bearing, carrying. *À bout portant* [BOUT]; *être bien portant,* to be in good health; *vent portant,* fair wind.—*n.m.* Bearer, supporter, upright; (*Theat.*) prop of set-piece. (*Row.*) *Portant-dehors* or *porte-nage,* outrigger; *les bien-portants,* people in good health. **portatif,** *a.* (*fem.* -**ive**) Portable, portative. *Armes à feu portatives,* small arms; *c'est peu portatif,* it is bulky.

porte [pɔrt], *n.f.* Doorway, gateway; door; gate; door-step, threshold; entrance; eye (of hooks etc.); defile, gorge. *À porte close,* in secret; *à portes ouvrantes,* at the opening of the gates; *c'est à la porte,* it is quite near, it is only next door; *de porte en porte,* from house to house; *écouter aux portes,* to eavesdrop; *faire défendre sa porte à,* not to be at home to; *fermer la porte au nez de quelqu'un* [FERMER]; *la Porte ottomane,* the Sublime Porte; *mettre quelqu'un à la porte,* to turn someone out; to eject; to expropriate; *porte à deux battants,* folding-doors; *porte à glissière,* sliding door; *porte battante* [BATTANT (2)]; *porte cochère* [COCHÈRE]; *porte de derrière, porte de service,* tradesmen's entrance; back-door; *porte d'entrée,* street-door, front-door; *porte ouverte,* (*Polit.*) the open door; *porte vitrée,* glass-door; *prendre la porte,* to go out, to slip out; *refuser la porte,* to forbid the house.—*a.* (*Anat.*) Portal. *Veine porte,* portal vein.

porté [pɔr'te], *a.* (*fem.* -**ée**) Carried; inclined, prone, disposed; projected (of shadows). *Article porté au compte de quelqu'un,* article put down to account; *c'est bien porté,* it is done (by the right people), it's U; *c'est mal porté,* it is not done, it's non-U; *il est porté à médire,* he is prone to backbiting; *il est un peu porté sur la boisson,* (*fam.*) he rather likes his drink; *trop porté à,* too prone to.—*n.m.* Appearance, fit, look (of a garment etc.).

porte-à-faux, *n.m. inv.* Overhang. *En porte-à-faux,* overhanging. *Monté en porte-à-faux,* carried on cantilever.

porte-affiches [pɔrtaˈfiʃ], *n.m. inv.* Advertising-board.

porte-aiguilles, *n.m. inv.* Needle-case.

porte-allumettes, *n.m. inv.* Match-box or -holder.

porte-amarre, *n.m. inv.* Life-saving apparatus, line-rocket.

porte-auge, *n.m. inv.* Hodman, mason's labourer.

porte-avions, *n.m. inv.* Aircraft carrier.

porte-bagages, *n.m.* Luggage-rack.

porte-baguette, *n.m. inv.* Ramrod-pipe (in fire-arms).

porte-baïonnette, *n.m. inv.* Bayonet-frog.

porteballe, *n.m.* Pedlar, packman.

porte-billets, *n.m. inv.* Note-case; (*Am.*) billfold.

porte-bonheur, *n.m. inv.* Good-luck charm; mascot, lucky object.

porte-bouquet, *n.m.* (*pl. inv.* or **porte-bouquets**) Bouquet-holder.

porte-bouteilles. *n.m. inv.* Bottle-rack, wine-bin.

porte-bras, *n.m. inv.* Arm-strap (in car).

porte-cartes, *n.m. inv.* Card-case, card-tray; (*Mil.*) map case (or) holder.

porte-chapeau, *n.m. inv.* Hat-peg.

porte-chapeaux, *n.m. inv.* Hat-stand.

porte-cigares, *n.m. inv.* Cigar-case.

porte-clefs, *n.m. inv.* Turnkey; key-ring.

porte-copie, *n.m. inv.* Copy-holder, copy-stand.

porte-couteau, *n.m. inv.* Knife-rest.

porte-crayon, *n.m. inv.* Pencil-case.

porte-croix, *n.m. inv.* (*R.-C. Ch.*) Cross-bearer.

porte-crosse, *n.m. inv.* Crosier-bearer; (*Mil.*) carbine-bucket.

porte-documents, *n.m. inv.* Dispatch-case.

porte-drapeau, *n.m. inv.* Ensign, colour-bearer.

portée [pɔr'te], *n.f.* Brood, litter; reach (of the hand, arm, etc.); hearing; range, shot; scope, compass; capacity, ability; import (extent of significance, consequences); pitch (of a roof etc.); bearing; resting-point; (*Mus.*) stave. *Cela passe ma portée,* that is beyond my comprehension; *esprit d'une haute portée,* intellect of great range; *être à portée de* (*la*) *voix,* to be within hearing, within hailing distance; *à portée de fusil,* within rifle shot; *à portée de la main,* handy, to hand; *hors de la portée du canon,* beyond cannon-range; *hors de portée,* out of reach, out of range; *la portée d'un raisonnement,* the scope of an argument; *se mettre à la portée de quelqu'un,* to come down to someone's level; *canon d'une portée supérieure aux autres,* gun which outranges others.

porte-en-dehors or **portant-dehors,** *n.m. inv.* Outrigger.

*__porte-enseigne__ [PORTE-DRAPEAU].

porte-éperon, *n.m. inv.* Spur-strap.

porte-étendard, *n.m. inv.* Standard-bearer (in cavalry), cornet.

porte-étiquette, *n.m. inv.* (Leather) luggage label, label-holder.

porte-étriers, *n.m. inv.* Stirrup-strap.

*__portefaix,__ *n.m. inv.* Porter, street-porter, stevedore; dockhand.

porte-fanion, *n.m. inv.* N.C.O. carrying a general's flag.

porte-fenêtre, *n.f.* (*pl.* **portes-fenêtres**) French window.

portefeuille [pɔrtəˈfœːj], *n.m.* Portfolio; pocket-book; bill-case; office, department, portfolio of a minister etc. (*Mil. slang*) *Lit en portefeuille,* apple-pie bed. *Cet auteur a plusieurs ouvrages en portefeuille,* that author has several unpublished works in manuscript; *effets en portefeuille,* bills and acceptances; holdings; *ministre sans portefeuille,* minister without portfolio, minister of state.

porte-flambeau [pɔrtflɑ̃'bo], *n.m. inv.* Torch-bearer, linkman.

porte-fleurs, *n.m. inv.* Flower-holder.

porte-fouet, *n.m. inv.* Whip-holder.

porte-fusain, *n.m. inv.* Portcrayon.

porte-fût or **porte-fûts**, *n.m. inv.* Barrel-stand.

porte-greffe, *n.m. inv.* (*Hort.*) Stock.

porte-habit(s), *n.m. inv.* Coat-hanger; coat-stand, clothes-stand.

porte-haubans, *n.m. inv.* (*Naut.*) Channel-chains.

porte-hélice, *n.m.* *Arbre porte-hélice*, propeller shaft, screw-shaft.

porte-jarretelles, *n.m. inv.* Suspender-belt.

porte-jupe, *n.m. inv.* Skirt-hanger.

porte-lanterne, *n.m. inv.* Lamp-bracket (on carriages, bicycles, etc.).

porte-lettres, *n.m. inv.* Letter-case.

porte-livres, *n.m. inv.* Book-rest; (*Naut.*) bumkin.

porte-malheur, *n.m. inv.* Bird of ill-omen, bearer of ill-luck.

portemanteau [pɔrtmɑ̃'to], *n.m.* (*pl.* **portemanteaux**) Coat-stand, coat-rail; peg, (*Naut.*) davit; (cavalry) valise.

porte-masse [pɔrtə'mas], *n.m. inv.* Mace-bearer.

porte-mèche, *n.m. inv.* Wick-holder; (*Surg.*) tent-probe.

portement [pɔrtə'mɑ̃], *n.m.* Carrying, bearing. *Portement de croix*, Christ carrying the Cross or paintings of this.

porte-menu, *n.m. inv.* Menu holder.

porte-mine, *n.m. inv.*, or **porte-mines**. Propelling pencil.

porte-monnaie [pɔrtmɔ'nɛ], *n.m. inv.* Purse.

porte-montre, *n.m. inv.* Watch-stand.

porte-mousqueton [pɔrtəmuska'tɔ̃], *n.m. inv.* Carbine-swivel (on bandolier), snap-hook (of watch chain).

porte-musique, *n.m. inv.* Music-case, music-folio.

porte-objet, *n.m. inv.* Object-slide (in micro-scope), object-plate.

porte-parapluies, *n.m. inv.* Umbrella-stand.

porte-parole, *n.m. inv.* Mouthpiece, spokesman.

porte-pelle or **porte-pincettes**, *n.m. inv.* Fireside set.

porte-plat, *n.m.* (*pl. inv.* or **porte-plats**.) Dish-stand.

porte-plume, *n.m. inv.* Penholder. *Porte-plume réservoir*, fountain-pen [STYLO].

porte-queue, *n.m. inv.* Train-bearer; swallow-tail butterfly.

porte-queues, *n.m. inv.* (*Billiards*) Cue-rack.

porter [pɔr'te], *v.t.* To bear, to support; to sustain, to endure; to carry, to convey; to bring, to take; to wear, to have on; to deal, to give (blows etc.); to turn, to cast (the eyes etc.); to have, to entertain (affection etc.); to excite, to persuade, to incline; to measure; to bring forth, to yield, to produce; to declare, to manifest, to show, to import, to express, to tell. *Cet argent porte intérêt* [INTÉRÊT]; *il a porté la livrée*, he has worn a livery, he has been a servant; *il ne porte jamais d'argent sur lui*, he never carries money on him; *il porte bien son âge*, he doesn't look his age; *la nuit porte conseil*, sleep on it; *l'arrêt porte condamnation*, the sentence carries con-demnation with it; *le porter haut*, (*fig.*) to

carry it with a high hand; *l'un portant l'autre*, taking one thing with another; *porter amitié à quelqu'un*, to bear someone friendship; *porter aux nues*, to laud to the skies; *porter bonheur* [BONHEUR]; *porter coup* [COUP]; *porter envie à*, to envy; *porter intérêt à* [INTÉRÊT]; *porter la culotte* [CULOTTE]; *porter la main à l'épée*, to lay one's hand upon one's sword; *porter la tête haute*, to carry one's head high; *porter le bras en écharpe*, to carry one's arm in a sling; *porter le deuil*, to be in mourning; *porter le nez au vent*, to snuff the air (of a horse); *porter les armes*, to carry arms, to shoulder arms [ARME]; *porter perruque*, to wear a wig; *porter manquant (à l'appel)*, to report (someone) absent from roll-call; *porter préjudice à*, to be prejudicial to; *porter ses vues bien haut*, to have great aspirations; *porter un jugement sur quelque chose*, to pass judgment upon something; *porter les pieds en dedans*, to walk with the feet turned in; *porter témoi-gnage*, to bear witness; *porter un fardeau*, to carry a burden; *porter un toast à*, to propose the health of, to toast; *se faire porter malade*, to report sick.—*v.i.* To bear, to rest, to lie; to tell, to be effective, to take effect; to hit; to reach; to carry (of a gun etc.); (*Naut.*) to stand, to bear off; to be with young (of animals). *Ce vin porte à la tête*, that wine goes to the head; *la musique lui porte sur les nerfs*, the music gets on his nerves; *les voiles portent*, the sails are full; *l'insulte a porté*, the insult went home; *porter au nord-ouest*, to stand to the north-west; *porter de gueules*, (*Her.*) to bear gules; *sa vue porte loin*, he is far-sighted; *tous les coups que l'on tire ne portent pas*, all shots fired do not carry home; *un raisonnement qui porte à faux*, an unsound argument. **se porter**, *v.r.* To go, to repair, to move; to resort, to flock, to fly; to incline, to be prone, to be inclined or disposed, to tend; to be, to do (of health); to be worn; to present oneself, to stand forth; to turn, to be directed. *Comment vous portez-vous?* how do you do? *il se porte bien* [BIEN]; *le vert se porte beaucoup*, green is very fashionable; *ne pas se porter bien*, to be unwell; *portez-vous bien!* good health! take care of yourself; *se porter au secours de quelqu'un*, to go to someone's help; *se porter candidat*, (*Polit.*) to stand for (Parlia-ment etc.); *se porter fort pour quelqu'un* [FORT]; *se porter garant de*, to answer for.

porte-rame [pɔrt'ram], *n.m. inv.* Rowlock.

porte-respect, *n.m. inv.* Life-preserver (weapon); mark of dignity; (*fig.*) person of imposing exterior.

porterie [pɔrtə'ri], *n.f.* Gate-lodge (of convent).

porte-savon, *n.m. inv.* Soap-dish.

porte-serviette or **porte-serviettes**, *n.m. inv.* Towel-horse, towel-rail. *Rouleau* (*porte-serviette*), towel-roller.

porte-toasts [pɔrt'toust], *n.m. inv.* Toast-rack.

porte-torpille, *n.m. inv.* Torpedo-spar.

porteur [pɔr'tœr], *n.m.* (*fem.* **-euse**) Porter, carrier, heaver, bearer; holder; sleeper (on railway track). (*Cheval*) *porteur*, near- (side) horse; *le porteur d'une lettre*, the bearer of a letter; *onde porteuse*, carrier (radio) wave; *payable au porteur*, payable to bearer; *porteur de germes* or *porteur de microbes*, germ-carrier.

porte-vent [pɔrtə'vɑ̃], *n.m. inv.* Air-duct;

(*Metal.*) blast-main; blast-pipe; wind-trunk (of organs); mouth-tube (of bagpipe); trousers (of kite balloon).

porte-verge, *n.m. inv.* Verger, beadle.

porte-vêtements, *n.m. inv.* [PORTE-HABITS].

porte-voix, *n.m. inv.* Speaking-trumpet, megaphone.

portier [pɔr'tje], *n.m.* (*fem.* **-ière**) Porter, door-keeper, janitor.—*n.f.* Door-curtain, portière; door (of vehicle). *Mettre le nez à la portière,* to lean outside one's carriage.—*a.f.* Of an age to bear (of cows).

portillon [pɔrti'jɔ̃], *n.m.* Small gate; side-gate for pedestrians at level-crossings; (in the Pyrenees) small pass.

portion [pɔr'sjɔ̃], *n.f.* Portion, part, share, allowance. *Diminuer la portion de quelqu'un,* to curtail someone's allowance; *portion congrue* [CONGRU]. **portionner,** *v.t.* To share out.

portique [pɔr'tik], *n.m.* Portico; porch; (*Gym.*) cross-bar or beam. *Portique roulant* or *grue à portique,* travelling-gantry crane.

porto [pɔr'to] or **vin de Porto,** *n.m.* Port (wine).

***portraire** [pɔr'trɛːr], *v.t.* (*only in infin.*) To portray, to paint the portrait of.

portrait [pɔr'trɛ], *n.m.* Portrait, likeness, picture; (*fig.*) image; description; (*slang*) face. *Peintre de portraits,* portrait painter; *portrait en pied,* full-length portrait; *portrait parlant,* speaking likeness. *C'est tout le portrait de son père,* he is the spit and image of his father. **portraitiste,** *n.* Portrait painter. ***portraiture,** *n.f.* Portrait.

port-salut [pɔrsa'ly], *n.m. inv.* Cheese made near Laval.

portuaire [pɔrtɥ'ɛːr], *a.* Pertaining to a harbour. *Installations portuaires,* harbour installations.

portugais [pɔrty'gɛ], *a.* (*fem.* **-aise**) Portuguese.—*n.m.* Portuguese (language); (**Portugais,** *fem.* **-aise**) Portuguese.—*n.f.* Portuguese oyster.

Portugal, *m.* Portugal.

portulan [pɔrty'lɑ̃], *n.m.* Book of seaports, map of harbours, etc., portulan.

posage [po'zaːʒ], *n.m.* Placing, laying, laying down.

pose [poːz], *n.f.* Laying, setting, laying down; pose, posture, attitude; posing, affectation, make-believe; sitting (for one's portrait etc.); hanging (of bells); (*Mil.*) stationing, posting (of sentries); (*Phot.*) exposure; time-exposure. *Pose de la première pierre,* laying of the foundation-stone. *Sans pose,* unaffected(ly). (*Phot.*) *Tenez la pose!* hold it!

posé, *a.* (*fem.* **-ée**) Laid, set, poised; bearing, resting, sedate, staid, sober. *Cela posé, il s'ensuit que,* this being granted it follows that; *un homme bien posé dans le monde,* a man of standing; *une voix bien posée,* a well-produced voice; *une voix posée,* a calm, steady voice. **posément,** *adv.* Calmly, steadily; sedately, staidly.

poser [po'ze], *v.t.* To put, to put in (a lock, a window-pane); to place, to set, to lay down; to hang; to suppose, to admit, to grant; to put up; to post, to station (sentries etc.); to lay down, to state; (*Mus.*) to pitch; (*Arith.*) to put down; to pose (at dominoes); to sit (for portrait). *Poser des conditions,* to

lay down conditions, to impose conditions; *poser des jalons,* to mark out a route, to work out a basic plan, (*fig.*) to pave the way; (*Arith.*) *poser deux et retenir un,* to put down two and carry one; *poser l'arme à terre,* to ground arms; *poser le pied,* to set foot; *poser une figure,* to put a figure in the proper position; *poser un lapin,* (*fam.*) [LAPIN]; *posez votre paquet,* lay down your bundle.—*v.i.* To lie, to rest (*sur*); to take a posture, to stand, to pose, to sit (for one's portrait); to show off, to attitudinize. **se poser,** *v.r.* To perch, to pitch (of birds etc.); to set up (*en*), to play the part (*en*).

poseur, *n.m.* (*fem.* **-euse**) One who lays down stones etc., setter, layer; (*Rail.*) plate-layer; (*colloq.*) poseur, snob, prig. *Poseur de sonnettes,* bell-hanger; *poseur de mines,* minelayer.

positif [pɔzi'tif], *a.* (*fem.* **-ive**) Positive, certain, practical, actual, matter-of-fact. *C'est positif!* it's a fact! *c'est un homme positif,* he is a matter-of-fact man; *elle ne m'avait rien promis de positif,* she had made me no definite promise; *un esprit positif,* a practical mind.—*n.m.* Positive reality, actuality; certainty, fact; (*Gram.*) positive; (*Phot., Cine.*) positive.

position [pɔzi'sjɔ̃], *n.f.* Position, situation; station of life, status, standing; case, state, circumstances. *Dans une bonne position,* well off; *dans une position peu élevée,* in an inferior position; *être dans une position intéressante,* (*fam.*) to be pregnant, to be in an interesting condition; *être en position de,* to be able to; (*Motor.*) *feux de position,* parking lights; *position embarrassante,* involved circumstances; *position fatigante,* tiring position; strain; *prendre position,* to take sides; *quelle est sa position?* what's his position?

positivement [pɔzitiv'mɑ̃], *adv.* Positively, exactly, expressly, explicitly. *Répondre positivement,* to answer yes or no.

positivisme, *n.m.* Matter-of-factness; (*Phil.*) Positivism or Comtism. **positiviste,** *n.* Positivist.

Posnanie [pɔsna'ni], *f.* Posen, Posnania.

posologie [pozɔlɔ'ʒi], *n.f.* Posology.

possédant [pose'dɑ̃], *a.* and *n.* (*fem.* **-ante**) *Les possédants,* the men of property.

possédé [pose'de], *n.* (*fem.* **-ée**) Possessed, infatuated.—*n.* Person possessed, madman, maniac. *Il se démène comme un possédé,* he lays about him like a madman; *un homme possédé du démon,* a man possessed of the devil.

posséder [pose'de], *v.t. irr.* (*conjugated like* ACCÉLÉRER) To possess, to be possessed of, to own, to hold, to have; to be master of, to be conversant with; to dominate (a person); (*pop.*) to deceive, to dupe. *Bien posséder son sujet,* to have a thorough command of one's subject; *l'ambition le possède,* he is eaten up with ambition; *les vertus qu'il possède,* the virtues he is possessed of; *posséder quelqu'un,* (*vulg.*) to get the better of someone; to 'have' someone; *posséder un emploi,* to hold a situation; *posséder une femme,* to enjoy a woman. **se posséder,** *v.r.* To command one's temper, to master one's passions, to contain oneself. *Il ne se possède pas de joie,* he is beside himself with joy.

possesseur [pɔsɛ'sœːr], *n.m.* Possessor, owner, occupier.

possessif, *a.* (*fem.* **-ive**) Possessive.—*n.m.* (*Gram.*) Possessive adjective or pronoun.

possession, *n.f.* Possession; property. *Libre possession*, vacant possession; *mettre en possession de*, to give possession of, to invest with; *prise de possession*, occupancy.

possessoire, *a.* (*Law*) Possessory.—*n.m.* Right of possession.

possibilité [pɔsibili'te], *n.f.* Possibility; (*pl.*) facilities.

possible, *a.* Possible. *C'est bien possible*, that may well be; *il est possible de le faire*, it is possible to do it; *il est possible qu'il le fasse*, he may possibly do it; *pas possible!* well, I never! *venez le plus tôt possible*, come as early as you can.—*n.m.* Possibility, what is possible. *Au possible*, extremely; *je ferai tout mon possible*, I'll do the best I can.

postal [pɔs'tal], *a.* (*fem.* **-ale**, *pl.* **-aux**) Postal, of the post. *Chèques postaux*, postal cheques; *sacs postaux*, mail-bags. **postalement**, *adv.* By post.

postcommunion [pɔstkɔmy'njɔ̃], *n.f.* Post-communion.

postdate, *n.f.* Post-date. **postdater**, *v.t.* To post-date.

post-diluvien, *a.* (*fem.* **-ienne**) Post-diluvian.

poste (1) [pɔst], *n.m.* Post, station; guard-house, station-house, or soldiers occupying this; place, employment, post; (*Naut.*) berth, quarters; (*Rail.*) signal-box, station; (*Teleph.*) extension; entry (in books), item, heading. *Être à son poste*, to be at one's post; *mener quelqu'un au poste*, to run someone in; (*Mil.*) *poste avancé*, outpost, *poste de combat*, action station; *poste d'écoute*, listening station; *poste d'essence*, petrol station; *poste de commandement*, (*Naut.*) control room; *poste de police*, police station, (*fam.*) lock-up; (*Mil.*) guard-room; *poste de T.S.F.*, wireless set; *poste des malades*, (*Naut.*) cockpit; *poste d'incendie*, fire-station; hydrant; *poste de secours*, dressing station.

poste (2) [pɔst], *n.f.* Post (relay); post-stage; postal service; post-office, mail; buck-shot. *Aller en poste*, to travel post; *chevaux de poste*, post-horses; *courir la poste*, to go post-haste. *Agent des postes*, post-office employee; *bureau de poste*, post-office; *Grande Poste*, General Post-office; *receveur des postes*, postmaster; *petite poste*, district post-office; *poste aérienne*, air-mail; *poste restante*, 'poste restante', P.O.B.

poster [pɔs'te], *v.t.* To station, to post (sentry or letter). **se poster**, *v.r.* To station oneself.

postérieur [pɔste'rjœːr], *a.* (*fem.* **-eure**) Posterior, subsequent, later; behind.—*n.m.* (*colloq.*) Posterior, bottom. **postérieurement**, *adv.* Subsequently, after.

postériorité, *n.f.* Posteriority.

postérité, *n.f.* Posterity, future descendants. *En appeler à la postérité*, to appeal to posterity; *transmettre son nom à la postérité*, to hand down one's name to posterity.

postface [pɔst'fas], *n.f.* Postscript or notice (at the end of a book).

posthume [pɔs'tym], *a.* Posthumous. *Œuvres posthumes* [ŒUVRE]; *un fils posthume*, a posthumous son.

postiche [pɔs'tiʃ], *a.* Superadded; super-fluous; false, artificial, sham.—*n.m.* Wig.

posticheur, *n.* (*fem.* **-euse**) Wig-maker.

postier [pɔs'tje], *n.m.* (*fem.* **-ière**) Post-office employee.—*n.m.* Post-horse.

postillon [pɔsti'jɔ̃], *n.m.* Postilion; post-boy; messenger (on kite-tail); (*colloq.*) involuntary splutter in speaking. **postillonner**, *v.i.* To splutter.

postnatal [pɔstna'tal], *a.* (*fem.* **-ale**) Postnatal. *Soins postnatals*, postnatal care.

post-opératoire, *a.* Post-operational (care, shock).

***postposer** [pɔstpo'ze], *v.t.* To put after or below. **postposition**, *n.f.* Postposition.

postscolaire, *a.* Continuation (class). *Enseignement postscolaire*, adult education.

post-scriptum (or *abbr.* **p.s.**), *n.m. inv.* Post-script.

post-synchronisation [pɔstsɛ̃krɔnizɑ'sjɔ̃], *n.f.* Post-synchronization, post-scoring.

postulant [pɔsty'lɑ̃], *n.m.* (*fem.* **-ante**) Candidate, applicant; postulant.

postulat [pɔsty'la], *n.m.* Postulate. *Admettre quelque chose en postulat*, to postulate something; to assume something.

postuler, *v.t.* To solicit, to demand, to apply for.—*v.i.* (*Law*) To act on behalf of a client, to be briefed.

posture [pɔs'tyːr], *n.f.* Posture, attitude; situation; plight. *Être en mauvaise posture*, to be in a bad plight; *être en posture de*, to be in a position to.

pot [po], *n.m.* Pot; jug, tankard, flagon, can, jar; (*Stationery*) pott (size of paper); (*C*) half a gallon. (*pop.*) *Avoir du pot*, to be lucky; *c'est le pot de terre contre le pot de fer*, it is the earthen pot against the iron pot; *découvrir le pot aux roses* [DÉCOUVRIR]; *dîner à la fortune du pot*, to take pot-luck; *il faut payer les pots cassés* [CASSER]; *jouer (à la bille) au pot*, to play at pits [*see* BLOQUETTE]; (*pop.*) *manquer de pot*, to have hard luck; *mettre en pot*, to pot (of flowers), to put into jars, to bottle; *pot à eau* [pota'o], water-jug; *pot à tabac*, tobacco jar, (*fam.*) small pot-bellied fellow; ***pot au lait** [poto'lɛ], *pot à lait* [poa'lɛ], milk-jug or -can; *pot au noir* [poto'nwaːr], (*Naut.*) pitch-pot, (*fig.*) dreadful muddle; *pot de chambre* [CHAMBRE]; *pot d'échappement*, exhaust-tank; *pot pourri*, hotchpotch, medley, olio, jar filled with all sorts of flowers, miscellaneous stew; (*fam.*) *prendre un pot*, to have a drink; *tourner autour du pot*, to beat about the bush.

potable [pɔ'tabl], *a.* Potable, drinkable (water). *Eau potable*, drinking water.

potache [pɔ'taʃ], *n.m.* (*sch.*) School-boy of a *Lycée* or *Collège*.

potage [pɔ'taːʒ], *n.m.* Soup. *Potage aux légumes*, vegetable soup; *pour tout potage*, in all, all told.

potager (1), *n.m.* Kitchen-garden; kitchen-stove.

potager (2), *a.* (*fem.* **-ère**) Comestible, culinary; for vegetables. *Herbes* or *plantes potagères*, pot-herbs; *jardin potager*, kitchen-garden.

potard [pɔ'taːr], *n.m.* (*fam.*) Chemist's clerk, chemist.

potasse [pɔ'tas], *n.f.* Potash.

potasser, *v.t., v.i.* (*sch. slang*) To study hard, to grind, to swot (at).

potassique, *a.* Potassic.

potassium, *n.m.* Potassium.

pot-au-feu [pɔtoˈfø], *n.m. inv.* Beef boiled with carrots etc.; broth of this.—*a.* (*fam.*) Stay-at-home (person).

pot-bouille [pɔˈbuːj], *n.f.* *(*colloq.*) *Faire pot-bouille avec*, to live in common with.

pot-de-vin, *n.m.* (*pl.* **pots-de-vin**) Gratuity; bribe; hush-money.

pote [pɔt], *n.m.* (*vulg.*) Chum, pal.—*a.f.* Big, swollen (of hand).

poteau [pɔˈto], *n.m.* (*pl.* **-eaux**) Post, stake. *Poteau de départ*, starting-post; *poteau d'exécution*, place of execution; *au poteau!* down with him! *poteau-frontière*, frontier-post; *poteau indicateur* or *guide*, finger-post, sign-post; *poteau télégraphique*, telegraph pole.

potée [pɔˈte], *n.f.* Potful; kind of hotch-potch; (*colloq.*) swarm (of children etc.); putty; emery-dust; (*Metal.*) moulding or luting loam. *Potée d'émeri*, emery-dust; *potée d'étain*, putty-powder.

potelé [pɔˈtle], *a.* (*fem.* **-ée**) Plump, dimpled (arm); chubby (cheek).

potelet [pɔˈtlɛ], *n.m.* Small post, strut, prop.

potence [pɔˈtãːs], *n.f.* Potence of clock; (*Her.*) tan-cross, cross potent; gallows, gibbet; bracket; crutch; sliding rule for measuring men and horses. *Potence de drôme*, (*Naut.*) gallows-bitt; *potence (de guidon)*, stem (of handlebar); *gibier de potence*, jail-bird.

potentat [pɔtãˈta], *n.m.* Potentate, magnate.

potentiel [pɔtãˈsjɛl], *a.* (*fem.* **-ielle**) Potential. —*n.m.* Potentialities; (*Elec.*) potential. **potentiellement**, *adv.* Potentially.

potentille [pɔtãˈtiːj], *n.f.* (*Bot.*) Potentilla (name of several varieties). See *ansérine*, *quintefeuille*, *tormentille*.

potentiomètre [pɔtãtjɔˈmɛtr], *n.m.* (*Elec.*) Potentiometer.

poterie [pɔˈtri], *n.f.* Pottery, earthenware; pottery (works); earthenware pipe etc. *Poterie de grès*, stoneware; *poterie d'étain*, pewter (ware).

poterne [pɔˈtɛrn], *n.f.* Postern; sally port.

potiche [pɔˈtiʃ], *n.f.* China or Japan porcelain vase.

potier [pɔˈtje], *n.m.* Potter. *Potier d'étain*, pewterer.

potin [pɔˈtɛ̃], *n.m.* Pinchbeck or other alloy of copper, tin, pewter, etc.; (*colloq.*) pother; row, noise, (*pl.*) gossip.

potiner, *v.i.* To gossip. **potinier**, *a.* (*fem.* **-ière**) Gossipy.—*n.f.* Gossip-shop.

potion [pɔˈsjɔ̃], *n.f.* Potion, draught; mixture.

potiron [pɔtiˈrɔ̃], *n.m.* Pumpkin. *Courge potiron*, gourd; (*Am.*) winter squash.

pot-pourri [popuˈri], *n.m.* (*pl.* **pots-pourris**) [POT].

potron-jaquet [pɔtrɔ̃ʒaˈkɛ] or **potron-minet**, *n.m.* Used only in *dès le potron-jaquet*, at early dawn.

pou [pu], *n.m.* (*pl.* **poux**) Louse; (*pl.*) lice. *Œuf de pou* (= *lente*), nit; *pou de bois*, death-watch beetle; *pou du ciel*, (*Av.*) flying flea.

pouacre [pwakr], *a.* Nasty, filthy, disgusting. —*n.* Such a person.

pouah! [pwa], *int.* Faugh! disgusting!

poubelle [puˈbɛl], *n.f.* Dust-bin; (*Am.*) ash-can.

pouce [pus], *n.m.* Thumb; big toe; inch. *Donner le coup de pouce à*, to give the finishing

touches to; *donner un coup de pouce* (*à la balance*), to shove down (the scales); *et le pouce* (*avec*), and a bit more, and a bittock; *il s'en mordra les pouces*, he will regret it; *manger un morceau sur le pouce*, to take a snack; (*pop.*) *mettre les pouces*, to knuckle under; (*C*) *faire du pouce*, *voyager sur le pouce*, to hitch-hike.—*int.* (*sch.*) *Pouce!* Stop! Pax! I give up.

poucet, *n.m.* Small thumb. *Le petit Poucet*, Hop-o'-my-Thumb, Tom Thumb. **poucettes**, *n.f. pl.* *Thumb-screw (for torture), thumb-cuffs.

poucier [puˈsje], *n.m.* Thumb-stall; thumb-piece (of latch).

pou-de-soie [pudˈswa], *n.m.* (*pl.* **poux-de-soie**) **poult-de-soie**, **pout-de-soie** (*pl.* **poults, pouts**) Paduasoy.

pouding [puˈdɛ̃], *n.m.* Plum-pudding.

poudingue, *n.m.* (*Geol.*) Pudding-stone.

poudre [pudr], *n.f.* Powder; gunpowder; dust. *Il n'a pas inventé la poudre* [INVENTER]; *jeter de la poudre aux yeux de quelqu'un*, to throw dust in someone's eyes, to bluff him; *mettre le feu aux poudres*, to start a row; *mettre or réduire en poudre*, to pulverize; *poudre de bois*, bore-dust; *poudre de perlimpinpin*, quack powder, nostrum; *poudre à canon* [CANON]; *poudre de chasse*, sporting-powder; *poudre d'or*, gold dust; *sucre en poudre*, castor sugar.

poudrer [puˈdre], *v.t.* To powder, to sprinkle with powder.—*v.i.* To raise a dust (of hunted beast); (*C*) to drift.

poudrerie, *n.f.* Gunpowder-factory; (*C*) blizzard, drifty snow.

poudrette, *n.f.* Fine powder; dried night-soil. *Faire la poudrette*, (of fowls) to take a dust-bath.

poudreux, *a.* (*fem.* **-euse**) Dusty, powdery; (*C*) drifty (of snow).

poudrier, *n.m.* Gunpowder-maker; pounce-box; (face-powder) compact.

poudrière, *n.f.* Powder-mill, magazine; sand-box.

poudroiement, *n.m.* Dustiness, dusty condition (of road).

poudroyer, *v.i. irr.* (*conjug. like* ABOYER) To rise in dust; to be dusty (of roads etc.).

pouf! (1) [puf], *int.* Plop! flop! plump! wallop! phew!

pouf (2) [puf], *n.m.* Ottoman (seat), pouf, tuffet, humpty, dumpy; puff (advertisement). *Faire un pouf*, to disappear without paying one's debts; *faiseur de poufs*, puffer, charlatan.

pouffant, *a.* (*fem.* **-ante**) (*pop.*) Excruciatingly funny, screamingly funny. **pouffer**, *v.i.* *Pouffer de rire*, to burst out laughing, to guffaw; to bubble over with laughter.

pouffiasse, [puˈfjaːs], *n.f.* (*vulg.*) Slut, wench, prostitute.

Pouille [puːj], la, *f.*, or **Les Pouilles**, *f. pl.* Apulia.

***pouiller** (1) [puˈje], *v.t.* To rail at, to abuse.

***pouiller** (2) [puˈje], *v.t.* To search for lice in, to louse.

pouillerie [pujˈri], *n.f.* Abject poverty; extreme avarice; a filthy hole.

pouilles [puːj], *n.f. pl.* Abuse. *Chanter pouilles à quelqu'un*, to shout abuse at someone.

pouilleux [puˈjø], *a.* (*fem.* **-euse**) Lousy; wretched, mean.—*n.* Such a person.

pouillot [pu'jo], *n.m.* (1) (*Orn.*) *Grand pouillot* or *pouillot véloce*, chiff-chaff; *pouillot siffleur* or *roussette*, wood warbler; *pouillot fitis*, willow warbler. (2) (*Bot.*) [SERPOLET].

poulailler [pula'je], *n.m.* Hen-roost, hen-house; poultry-cart; (of persons) poulterer; (*Theat.*) gallery, gods.

poulaillerie [pulaj'ri], *n.f.* Poultry market.

poulain [pu'lɛ̃], *n.m.* Timber slide-way for barrels, etc.; foal, colt; (*spt.*) trainee.

poulaine [pu'lɛn], *n.f.* Prow (of ship); ship's heads (latrines placed here). *Souliers à la poulaine*, long, pointed medieval shoes.

poularde [pu'lard], *n.f.* Fat pullet.

poulbot [pul'bo], *n.m.* Paris street urchin (named after the painter Poulbot).

poule [pul], *n.f.* Hen; fowl; pool (at games); eliminating round (in a competition); (*fam.*) fast (young) woman, bird; (*Am.*) skirt. *Chair de poule*, (*fig.*) goose-flesh; *faire venir la chair de poule*, to make one's flesh creep, to make one shudder; *plumer la poule sans la faire crier*, to make someone disgorge without any fuss; *poule d'eau* or *des marais*, moor-hen; *poule d'Inde* or *dinde*, turkey-hen; *poule-grasse* (*Bot.*) [ANSÉRINE]; *poule mouillée*, milk-sop; *quand les poules auront des dents*, when pigs fly; *tuer la poule aux œufs d'or*, to kill the goose that lays the golden eggs.

poulet, *n.m.* Chicken; love-letter, billet-doux.

poulette, *n.f.* Young hen, pullet; lass. *Sauce poulette*, a type of white sauce.

pouliche [pu'liʃ], *n.f.* Filly.

poulie [pu'li], *n.f.* Pulley; (*Naut.*) block.

*poulier [pu'lje], *n.m.* (*Naut.*) Shingle-bank.

poulieur, *n.m.* Block-maker or vendor.

pouliner [puli'ne], *v.i.* To foal (of mares).

poulinière, *a.f.* and *n.f.* (*Jument*) *poulinière*, brood mare.

pouliot [pu'ljo], *n.m.* Rear windlass (on dray); (*Bot.*) (*Menthe*) *pouliot* or *herbe aux puces*, pennyroyal.

poulot [pu'lo], *n.m.* (*fem.* **-otte**) (Term of endearment (*fam.*) to children), my ducky.

poulpe [pulp], *n.m.* Octopus, devil-fish.

pouls [pu], *n.m.* Pulse. *Le pouls lui bat*, his pulse is high; *se tâter le pouls*, to feel one's pulse, (*fig.*) to gauge one's strength.

poumon [pu'mɔ̃], *n.m.* Lung. *Poumon d'acier*, iron lung.

poupard [pu'pa:r], *n.m.* Baby; doll.—*a.* (*fem.* **-arde**) Chubby. *Figure pouparde*, baby face.

poupart [pu'pa:r], *n.m.* Large edible crab.

poupe [pup], *n.f.* Stern, poop. *À poupe carrée*, square-sterned; *avoir le vent en poupe*, to sail before the wind, (*fig.*) to be in luck's way.

poupée [pu'pe], *n.f.* Doll; puppet; milliner's block, tailor's dummy; finger-bandage; belay-ing-pin; (*Mech.*) poppet.

poupin [pu'pɛ̃], *a.* (*fem.* **-ine**) Fresh-coloured; rosy. *Face poupine*, baby face.

poupon [pu'pɔ̃], *n.m.* (*fem.* **-onne**) Baby; plump, chubby-cheeked boy or girl. **pou-ponner**, *v.t.* To coddle, to mother.

pouponnière, *n.f.* Room (in crèche) for small babies, (public) day-nursery.

pour [pu:r], *prep.* For; on account of; on behalf of; for the sake of; in the direction of; as regards, in; in order; although. *Comme pour parler*, as if to speak; *en être pour ses frais*, to get nothing for one's trouble; *il* fera cela pour vous*, he will do that for your sake; *je le tiens pour mon ami*, I consider him my friend; *on l'a laissé pour mort*, he was left for dead; *pour ainsi dire*, as it were, to so speak; *pour ce qui est de moi*, *j'y consens*, for my part I consent to it; *pour grand qu'il soit*, big as he is; *pour le moins*, at least; *pour lors*, therefore; *pour moi*, for my part; *pour que* (with subj.), in order that; *pour qui me prenez-vous?* what or whom do you take me for! *pour toujours* or *pour jamais*, for ever; *prendre fait et cause pour quelqu'un* [CAUSE]; *vingt pour cent*, twenty per cent.—*n.m.* For. *Le pour et le contre* [CONTRE].

pourboire [pur'bwa:r], *n.m.* Tip, gratuity.

pourceau [pur'so], *n.m.* (*pl.* **-eaux**) Hog, pig, swine. *C'est un vrai pourceau*, he is a perfect beast; *pourceau de mer*, porpoise.

pour-cent [pur'sɑ̃], **pourcentage** [pursɑ̃'ta:ʒ], *n.m.* Percentage.

pourchasser [purʃa'se], *v.t.* To pursue or seek eagerly; to chase, to run, to badger.

pourchasseur, *n.m.* Eager seeker or pursuer.

pourfendeur [purfɑ̃'dœ:r], *n.m.* Killer; swag-gerer, bully. *Pourfendeur de géants*, giant-killer, braggadocio.

pourfendre, *v.t.* To cleave asunder.

pourlécher [purle'ʃe], *v.t. irr.* (*conjug. like* ACCÉLÉRER) To lick all over. **se pourlécher**, *v.r.* To lick one's lips.

pourparler [purpar'le], *n.m.* (*usu. in pl.*) Par-ley, negotiations, conference. *Entrer en pourparlers*, to enter into negotiations.

pourpier [pur'pje], *n.m.* (*Bot.*) Purslain. *Pourpier de mer*, purslain orach; *pourpier sauvage* or *pourpière*, *f.* water-purslain.

pourpoint [pur'pwɛ̃], *n.m.* Doublet, pour-point. *À brûle-pourpoint* [BRÛLE-POUR-POINT].

pourpre [purpr], *n.f.* Purple (stuff); (*fig.*) sovereign dignity; cardinalate. *Être né dans la pourpre*, to be born in the purple; *porter la pourpre*, to wear the purple.—*n.m.* Purple, crimson (colour); (*Conch.*) purpura; (*Path.*) purples; (*Her.*) purpure.—*a.* Purple, dark red.

pourpré, *a.* (*fem.* **-ée**) Purple. *Fièvre pourprée*, purpura.

pourpris [pur'pri], *n.m.* Enclosure; abode, home. (*poet.*) *Les célestes pourpris*, the heavenly abodes.

pourquoi [pur'kwa], *adv.* and *conj.* Why, wherefore. *Pourquoi cela?* why so? *pourquoi pas?* why not? *C'est pourquoi*, that's why, therefore; *demandez-moi pourquoi*, I should like to know why.—*n.m. inv.* The reason why. *Je voudrais bien savoir le pourquoi*, I should like to know the why and the wherefore.

pourri [pu'ri], *a.* (*fem.* **-ie**) Rotten, rotted, putrid, bad. *Œuf pourri*, addle(d) egg; *temps pourri*, muggy weather.—*n.m.* The rotten part; rottenness.

pourrir [pu'ri:r], *v.i.* To rot, to grow rotten; (*fig.*) to corrupt, to perish; (*fam.*) (of a cold) to come to a head.—*v.t.* To make rotten, to corrupt; (*fam.*) (of a cold) to bring to a head. **se pourrir**, *v.r.* To become rotten, to go bad.

pourrissable, *a.* Perishable, liable to rot.

pourrissage, *n.m.* Maceration (of rags into paper-pulp).

pourrissant, *a.* (*fem.* **-ante**) Rotting, causing rot.

pourrissoir, *n.m.* Macerating-vat.

pourriture, *n.f.* Rot, rottenness, putrefaction; (*fig.*) corruption. **Pourriture d'hôpital,* hospital gangrene.

poursuite [pur'sɥit], *n.f.* Pursuit; prosecution; (*Law*) suit, action, proceedings. *À la poursuite de,* in pursuit of; *entamer* or *faire des poursuites contre,* (*Law*) to institute proceedings against.

poursuivable, *a.* Actionable.

poursuivant, *n.m.* (*fem.* **-ante**) Candidate, applicant; suitor, wooer; prosecutor, plaintiff. *Poursuivant d'armes,* pursuivant (herald).—*a.* Suing, prosecuting.

poursuivre [pur'sɥi:vr], *v.t. irr.* (*conjug. like* SUIVRE) To pursue; to endeavour to obtain, to seek; to prosecute; to beset, to haunt; to go on with, to proceed with; to follow up, to go through with; (*Law*) to sue, to prosecute, to proceed against. *Poursuivre l'ennemi,* to pursue the enemy; *poursuivre quelqu'un en justice,* to prosecute someone at law; *poursuivre son chemin,* to proceed on one's way; *poursuivre son discours,* to proceed with one's speech; *poursuivre un procès,* to carry on a lawsuit.—*v.i.* To pursue, to go on, to continue. *Poursuivez!* go on! **se poursuivre** *v.r.* To be continued, to follow its course.

pourtant [pur'tɑ̃], *adv.* However, yet, still, nevertheless.

pourtour [pur'tu:r], *n.m.* Periphery, circumference, circuit; gangway (in a theatre etc.); precincts (of cathedral).

pourvoi [pur'vwa], *n.m.* (*Law*) Appeal (for reversal of judgment). *Pourvoi en grâce,* petition for mercy.

pourvoir [pur'vwa:r], *v.i. irr.* (*pres.p.* **pourvoyant,** *p.p.* **pourvu**) (followed by *à*) To see to, to attend to, to provide for; to make an appointment to. *Pourvoir à sa subsistance,* to provide for one's living; *pourvoir à un emploi,* to fill a vacancy; *pourvoyez à cette affaire,* see to that business.—*v.t.* To invest with, to appoint; to provide, to supply, to provide for; to endow. *Ce père a bien pourvu tous ses enfants,* that father has made a handsome provision for all his children; *pourvoir une place de vivres,* to victual a garrison. **se pourvoir,** *v.r.* To provide oneself; to appeal, to sue, to petition. *Se pourvoir d'argent,* to provide oneself with money; *se pourvoir en cassation,* to appeal for a reversal of judgment.

pourvoyeur, *n.m.* (*fem.* **-euse**) Purveyor, provider, caterer.

pourvu que [pur'vyka], *conj. phr.* Provided that, provided; *pourvu que vous le fassiez,* provided you do it; *pourvu qu'il arrive à temps!* I only hope he gets here in time.

poussah [pu'sa], *n.m.* Tumbler (toy); (*fig.*) a paunchy fellow.

pousse [pus], *n.f.* Shoot, sprout; (*Vet.*) heaves, broken wind (in horses); over-fermentation (in wines).

pousse-café, *n.m. inv.* (*fam.*) Liqueur (after coffee).

pousse-cailloux, *n.m. inv.* (*fam.*) Footslogger, infantryman, P.B.I.

poussée [pu'se], *n.f.* Pushing; push, shove; growth; lifting force; thrust (of arches etc.); pressure (of business etc.). *La poussée des affaires,* pressure of business.

pousse-pousse [pus'pus], *n.m. inv.* Rickshaw (carriage or man).

pousser [pu'se], *v.t.* To push, to give a push to, to thrust, to shove; to drive on, to impel; to carry on, to extend; to grow, to send forth, to shoot, to put forth (of plants etc.); to urge, to provoke, to incite, to instigate; to bring forward, to assist, to help on; to utter, to heave, to fetch (a sigh etc.); to deal (a blow etc.). *Les arbres commencent à pousser des boutons,* the trees are beginning to put forth buds; *pousser à bout,* to provoke beyond endurance; *pousser dehors,* to thrust out; *pousser des cris,* to utter cries; *pousser des soupirs,* to heave sighs; *pousser la porte,* to push the door to; *pousser les choses au noir,* to look on the black side; *pousser un cheval,* to urge on a horse; *pousser une affaire à bout,* to go through with an affair; *pousser une botte,* (*Fenc.*) to make a thrust; *pousser un élève,* to push on a pupil; *vous me poussez trop,* you urge me too far.—*v.i.* To sprout, to shoot, to come up (of plants); to grow (of the hair, nails, etc.); to push on, to go on; to bulge, to jut out; to be broken-winded (of horses). *Ce mur pousse en dehors,* this wall bulges outwards; *les blés poussent déjà,* the corn is already coming up; *pousser à la roue,* to put one's shoulder to the wheel; *poussons jusqu'à la forêt,* let us push on as far as the forest. **se pousser,** *v.r.* To push forward, to push oneself forward; to push one's fortunes, to make one's way; to push each other, to jostle.

poussette, *n.f.* Pushpin (game); small push-cart (for children, or to go shopping); poussette (a movement in dancing).

*pousseur, *n.m.* (*fem.* **-euse**) Pusher, shover.

poussier [pu'sje], *n.m.* Coal-dust, charcoal-dust; screenings. *Poussier d'anthracite,* culm.

poussière [pu'sjɛ:r], *n.f.* Dust; spray, spindrift (of water). *Mordre la poussière,* to bite the dust; *réduire en poussière,* to reduce to dust; *tirer quelqu'un de la poussière,* to raise someone from the gutter. **poussiéreux,** *a.* (*fem.* **-euse**) Dusty.

poussif [pu'sif], *a.* (*fem.* **-ive**) Shortwinded, broken-winded.—*n.* (*pop.*) Shortwinded person.

poussin [pu'sɛ̃], *n.m.* Chick, chicken just hatched. **poussinière,** *n.f.* Chicken-coop; incubator; *Pleiades.

poussoir [pu'swa:r], *n.m.* Button or push (of electric bell etc.); catch (of bayonet).

poutrage [pu'tra:ʒ], *n.m.* Beams, joisting.

poutre [putr], *n.f.* Beam; girder. *Grosse poutre,* balk; *poutre armée,* trussed girder; *poutre faîtière,* roof-tree; *poutre de plancher,* summertree. **poutrelle,** *n.f.* Small beam.

pouvoir [pu'vwa:r], *v.i. irr.* (*pres.p.* **pouvant,** *p.p.* **pu** (2)) To be able (can etc.); to have power; to be allowed (may etc.); (*impers.*) to be possible. *Cela ne se peut pas,* that cannot be so, that cannot be done; *cela se pourrait bien,* it might be so; *faire tout ce qu'on peut,* to do everything one can; *il peut arriver que,* it may happen that; *il peut* or *pourrait avoir vingt ans,* he may or might be twenty; *il peut se faire* or *il se peut faire que,* it may happen that, it may be possible for me to; *il pourrait se faire que,* it is not at all unlikely that; *il pourrait survenir une circonstance qui changeât* *la face des choses,* some circumstance might arise which would change the whole aspect of things: *il se peut que,* it is possible that; *je ne puis pas le faire,* I cannot do it; *je ne puis vous répondre,* I cannot answer you; *je n'y puis rien,* I cannot help it; *n'en pouvoir plus, n'en pouvoir mais,* to be worn out, to be done up; *on ne peut plus, (followed by adj.)* exceedingly, extremely; *puisse-t-il réussir!* may he succeed; *sauve qui peut,* every man for himself; *vous avez pu ne pas voir,* you may not have seen; *vous avez pu voir,* you may have seen; *vous n'avez pas pu voir,* you cannot have seen.—*v.t.* To be able to do. *Je ne crois pas le pouvoir,* I do not think I can do it; *je ne puis rien à cela,* I can do nothing in the matter; *vous pouvez tout sur lui,* you have great power over him.—*n.m.* Power; might force; sway, authority; command, government; power of attorney, procuration. *Le pouvoir législatif,* the legislature; *le quatrième pouvoir,* the fourth estate. *Abuser de son pouvoir,* to abuse one's power; *excéder ses pouvoirs,* to exceed one's powers; *il est en son pouvoir de,* he has it in his power to.

pouzzolane [puzɔ'lan], *n.f.* Pozzolana.

pragmatique [pragma'tik], *a.* Pragmatic.—*n.f.* Pragmatic Sanction. **pragmatisme,** *n.m.* Pragmatism.

prairial [prɛ'rjal], *n.m.* Ninth month of the revolutionary calendar (May 20-June 18).

prairie [prɛ'ri], *n.f.* Meadow, grass-land, grass-field; (*U.S.*) prairie, savanna.

praline [prɑ'lin], *n.f.* Burnt almond.

praliner, *v.t.* To burn with sugar (like burnt almonds).

praticabilité [pratikabili'te], *n.f.* Practicability, feasibility. **praticable** [prati'kabl], *a.* Practicable, feasible, possible; passable (of roads); accessible, affable, sociable (of persons); (*Theat.*) real. *Porte praticable* or *fenêtre praticable,* real door or window.

praticien, *n.m.* (*fem.* **-ienne**) Practitioner; (*Sculp.*) rougher-out, pointer.—*a.* Practising. *Médecin praticien,* practitioner, practising physician.

pratiquant, *a.* (*fem.* **-ante**) Church-going, practising religion.—*n.* Church-goer.

pratique [pra'tik], *n.f.* Practice, application of science, rules, etc.; execution, action; method; experience; observance, usage; association; custom (of tradesman), practice (of attorneys, physicians, etc.); customer, buyer; (puppet-player's) squeaker; (*pl.*) dealings. *Avoir bien de la pratique,* to have plenty of custom; (*Naut.*) *avoir libre pratique,* to have pratique, to be out of quarantine; *c'est une bonne pratique,* he is a good customer; *cet avoué entend bien la pratique,* that attorney is well versed in the practice of the law; *la pratique des affaires,* business method; *mettre en pratique,* to put into practice; *perdre la pratique,* to be out of practice; *terme de pratique,* law-term.—*a.* Practical; experienced.—*n.m.* (*Naut.*) Pilot or sailor well acquainted with the local waters. **pratiquement,** *adv.* In actual fact; in a practical way.

pratiquer, *v.t.* To practise, to exercise; to frequent, to keep company with; to tamper with, to suborn, to bribe; to obtain, to procure (intelligence); (*Arch.*) to contrive, to let in; to make, to effect. *Pratiquer des témoins,* to suborn witnesses; *pratiquer la médecine,* to practise as a doctor; *pratiquer un chemin,* to open a road; *pratiquer une religion,* to practise a religion; *se garder de pratiquer les méchants,* to avoid associating with the wicked.* **se pratiquer,** *v.r.* To be in use, to be practised, to be customary. *Cela ne se pratique point,* such things are not done.

pré [pre], *n.m.* Meadow, mead; ground (to fight a duel). *Aller sur le pré,* to fight a duel.

préadamite [preada'mit], *n.m.* Preadamite.

préalable [prea'labl], *a.* Preliminary; previous.—*n.m. Au préalable,* previously, first of all.

préalablement, *adv.* Previously, first, to begin with.

préambule [preɑ̃'byl], *n.m.* Preamble, preface.

préau [pre'o], *n.m.* (*pl.* **-aux**) Courtyard (of a convent or prison); (*sch.*) covered part of the play-ground.

préavis [prea'vi], *n.m. inv.* (Previous) notice. *Appel avec préavis,* (*Teleph.*) personal call.

prébende [pre'bɑ̃:d], *n.f.* Prebend. **prébendé,** *a.* (*fem.* **-ée**) In possession of a prebend, prebendal.

prébendier, *a.m.* Prebendal.—*n.m.* Prebendary.

précaire [pre'kɛ:r], *a.* Precarious; uncertain.

précairement, *adv.* Precariously.

précarité [prekari'te], *n.f.* Precariousness.

précaution [preko'sjɔ̃], *n.f.* Precaution; caution, care, prudence. *Agir avec précaution,* to act cautiously; *prendre des précautions auprès de quelqu'un,* to proceed warily with someone.

précautionner, *v.t.* To warn, to caution. **se précautionner,** *v.r.* To be cautious, to take precautions. *Se précautionner contre la chaleur,* to guard against the heat. **précautionneusement,** *adv.* Cautiously. **précautionneux** *a.* (*fem.* **-euse**) Cautious.

précédemment [preseda'mɑ̃], *adv.* Before, previously.

précédence, *n.f.* Precedence, priority.

précédent, *a.* (*fem.* **-ente**) Preceding, former.—*n.m.* Precedent. *Créer un précédent,* to create a precedent; *sans précédent,* unprecedented.

précéder [prese'de], *v.t. irr.* (*conjug.* like ACCÉLÉRER) To precede, to go before; to take precedence (of). *Il était précédé de,* he was preceded by.

préceinte [pre'sɛ̃:t], *n.f.* Wale (of ship).

précelles [pre'sɛl], *n.f. pl.* (Dentist's) forceps.

précepte [pre'sɛpt], *n.m.* Precept, rule.

précepteur, *n.m.* (*fem.* **-trice**) Tutor, teacher.

préceptoral, *a.* (*fem.* **-ale,** *pl.* **-aux**) Tutorial.

préceptorat, *n.m.* Tutorship.

précession [prese'sjɔ̃], *n.f.* (*Astrol.*) Precession.

prêche [prɛ:ʃ], *n.m.* Sermon (Protestant); Protestant church, meeting-house.

prêcher [prɛ'ʃe], *v.t.* To preach; to preach upon; to preach to, to exhort or instruct by sermons; to extol, to praise; to keep telling, to repeat. *Prêcher la parole de Dieu,* to preach the word of God; *prêcher les fidèles,* to exhort the faithful; *prêcher l'Évangile,* to preach the Gospel.—*v.i.* To preach. *Prêcher dans le désert,* to preach to empty benches, (*fig.*) to convince no one; *prêcher d'exemple,* to practise what one preaches; *prêcher pour sa paroisse,* to speak in one's own interests.

prêcheur, *n.m.* (*fem.* **-euse**) Preacher;

sermonizer.—*a.* Preaching. *Frère prêcheur,* predicant friar.

prêchi-prêcha [pre'ʃipre'ʃa], *n.m. inv.* (*fam.*) Wearisome repeating of the same moralizing nonsense; preachifying.

précieusement [presjœz'mɑ̃], *adv.* Preciously; carefully; affectedly. **précieux,** *a.* (*fem.* **-ieuse**) Precious, costly, valuable; affected. *C'est un document des plus précieux,* it is a most valuable document; *les métaux précieux,* precious metals; *tableau d'un fini précieux,* picture of exquisite finish.—*n.m.* Affectation; affected man.—*n.f.* Conceited or pedantic woman, of affected or exaggerated literary tastes.

préciosité, *n.f.* Affectation, preciosity.

précipice [presi'pis], *n.m.* Precipice. *On l'a tiré du précipice,* he has been rescued from destruction.

précipitable [presipi'tabl], *a.* (*Chem.*) Precipitable.

précipitamment [presipita'mɑ̃], *adv.* Precipitately, hurriedly, rashly.

précipitant [presipi'tɑ̃], *n.m.* (*Chem.*) Precipitant.

précipitation [presipita'sjɔ̃], *n.f.* Precipitancy, headlong haste, hurry; (*Chem.*) precipitation.

précipité [presipi'te], *a.* (*fem.* **-ée**) Precipitated, hurled; precipitate, rash, hasty, sudden. *Départ précipité,* sudden departure; *marcher à pas précipités,* to walk with hurried steps; *précipité de haut en bas,* hurled headlong from top to bottom.—*n.m.* (*Chem.*) Precipitate.

précipiter [presipi'te], *v.t.* To precipitate, to hurl, to dash down; to hurry on, to hasten, to accelerate; (*Chem.*) to precipitate. *Précipiter sa retraite,* to hasten one's retreat. **se précipiter,** *v.r.* To precipitate, throw, or hurl oneself; to rush forward, to spring forth, to dart. *Se précipiter sur quelqu'un,* to rush upon someone.

préciput [presi'py], *n.m.* (*Law*) Right to a preference share for one of the coheirs.

précis [pre'si], *a.* (*fem.* **-ise**) Fixed, precise, exact; formal, terse, concise. *Prendre des mesures précises,* to take strict measures; *venir à l'heure précise,* to come exactly at the appointed time.—*n.m.* Summary, abstract, epitome, précis. **précisément,** *adv.* Precisely, exactly; quite, just; just so.

préciser, *v.t.* To state precisely, to specify.

précision, *n.f.* Precision, preciseness; precise detail.

précité [presi'te], *a.* (*fem.* **-ée**) Aforementioned.

précoce [pre'kɔs], *a.* Precocious, early, forward; premature. **précocement,** *adv.* Precociously.

précocité [prekɔsi'te], *n.f.* Precocity.

précombustion [prekɔ̃bys'tjɔ̃], *n.f.* Precombustion.

précompte [pre'kɔ̃:t], *n.m.* Previous deduction. **précompter,** *v.t.* To deduct beforehand.

préconception [prekɔ̃sɛp'sjɔ̃], *n.f.* Prejudice, preconception.

préconcevoir [prekɔ̃sə'vwa:r], *v.t. irr.* (*conjug. like* RECEVOIR) To preconceive.

préconçu, *a.* (*fem.* **-ue**) Preconceived. *Idée préconçue,* preconception, preconceived idea.

préconisation [prekɔniza'sjɔ̃], *n.f.* Preconization, commendation.

préconiser, *v.t.* To preconize, to sanction the appointment of; (*fig.*) to extol, to cry up.

préconnaissance [prekɔnɛ'sɑ̃:s], *n.f.* Foreknowledge. **préconnaître,** *v.t. irr.* To foreknow.

précontraint [prekɔ̃'trɛ̃], *a.* (*fem.* **-ainte**) (*Build.*) Prestressed. *Béton précontraint,* prestressed concrete.

précordial [prekɔr'djal], *a.* (*fem.* **-iale,** *pl.* **-iaux**) (*Anat.*) Praecordial.

précurseur [prekyr'sœ:r], *n.m.* Forerunner, precursor, harbinger.—*a.m.* Premonitory.

prédateur [preda'tœ:r], *a.* (*fem.* **-trice**) (*Ent.*) Predatory.

prédécéder [predese'de], *v.i. irr.* (*conjug. like* ACCÉLÉRER) To predecease someone. **prédécès,** *n.m.* Predecease.

prédécesseur [predesɛ'sœ:r], *n.m.* Predecessor.

prédestination [predɛstina'sjɔ̃], *n.f.* Predestination.

prédestiné, *a.* (*fem.* **-ée**) Predestined; predetermined.—*n.* One of the elect or predestinated.

prédestiner, *v.t.* To predestinate, to foredoom; to predetermine.

prédéterminant [predetermi'nɑ̃], *a.* (*fem.* **-ante**) Predetermining.

prédétermination, *n.f.* Predetermination. **prédéterminer,** *v.t.* To predetermine (of God).

prédial [pre'djal], *a.* (*fem.* **-iale,** *pl.* **-iaux**) Predial. *Des rentes prédiales,* ground-rents [*see also* SERF].

prédicable [predi'kabl], *a.* Predicable.

prédicament, *n.m.* Predicament.

prédicant, *n.m.* Protestant preacher.

prédicat, *n.m.* Predicate.

prédicateur, *n.m.* (*fem.* **-trice**) Preacher, teacher (of a religion).

prédication, *n.f.* Preaching.

prédiction [predik'sjɔ̃], *n.f.* Prediction, forecast.

prédilection [predilɛk'sjɔ̃], *n.f.* Predilection, partiality, preference. *Mon auteur de prédilection,* my favourite author.

prédire [pre'di:r], *v.t. irr.* (*conjug. like* MÉDIRE) To predict, to foretell.

prédisposant [predispo'zɑ̃], *a.* (*fem.* **-ante**) Predisposing. **prédisposer,** *v.t.* To predispose. **prédisposition,** *n.f.* Predisposition.

prédominance [predɔmi'nɑ̃:s], *n.f.* Predominance, ascendancy. **prédominant,** *a.* (*fem.* **-ante**) Predominant.

prédominer, *v.i.* To predominate.—*v.t.* To prevail over.

prééminence [preemi'nɑ̃:s], *n.f.* Preeminence. **prééminent,** *a.* (*fem.* **-ente**) Pre-eminent.

préempter [preɑ̃p'te], *v.t.* To pre-empt, to buy beforehand. **préemption,** *n.f.* Preemption.

préétablir [preeta'bli:r], *v.t.* To pre-establish.

préexistant [preɛgzis'tɑ̃], *a.* (*fem.* **-ante**) Pre-existent. **préexistence,** *n.f.* Pre-existence. **préexister,** *v.i.* To pre-exist.

préfabriqué [prefabri'ke], *a.* (*fem.* **-ée**) Prefabricated. *Maison préfabriquée,* (*fam.*) pre-fab.

préface [pre'fas], *n.f.* Preface; foreword.

préfacer, *v.t.* To write a preface to.

préfectoral [prefɛktɔ'ral], *a.* (*fem.* **-ale**, *pl.* **-aux**) Prefectoral.

préfecture [prefɛk'ty:r], *n.f.* Prefecture, prefectship. *Préfecture de police*, Paris police headquarters; *préfecture maritime*, district administered by a *préfet maritime*.

préférable [prefe'rabl], *a.* Preferable, more advisable. **préférablement**, *adv.* Preferably.

préféré [prefe're], *a.* (*fem.* **-ée**) Favourite. —*n.* *C'est le préféré*, he is their favourite child.

préférence, *n.f.* Preference. *De préférence*, in preference, preferably.

préférentiel, *a.* (*fem.* **-ielle**) Preferential.

préférer [prefe're], *v.t.* To prefer, to like better.

préfet [pre'fɛ], *n.m.* Prefect; chief administrator of a department in France. *Préfet de police*, chief commissioner of Parisian police; *préfet maritime*, naval commander-in-chief (of a district), port-admiral; *préfet des études*, (*sch.*) vice-principal.

préfète, *n.f.* (*colloq.*) Prefect's wife.

préfiguration [prefigyra'sjɔ̃], *n.f.* Prefiguration. **préfigurer**, *v.t.* To foreshadow.

préfix [pre'fiks], *a.* (*fem.* **-ixe** (1)) (*Law*) Prefixed, appointed.

préfixe (2), *n.m.* (*Gram.*) Prefix.—*a.* Prefixed.

préfloraison [preflɔrɛ'zɔ̃], *n.f.* (*Bot.*) Prefloration.

préfoliation, *n.f.* Prefoliation; aestivation; vernation.

prégnante [preɲɑ̃t], *a.f.* Pregnant (of animals). **prégnation, *n.f.* Gestation (of animals).

préhenseur [preɑ̃'sœ:r], *a.m.* Prehensory (organ).

préhensible [preɑ̃'sibl], *a.* Prehensible. **préhensile**, *a.* Prehensile. **préhension**, *n.f.* Prehension, gripping.

préhistoire [preis'twa:r], *n.f.* Prehistory. **préhistorique**, *a.* Prehistoric.

préjudice [preʒy'dis], *n.m.* Detriment, injury, damage, prejudice. *Cela vous portera préjudice*, that will be detrimental to you; *il a obtenu cela à mon préjudice*, he obtained that to my prejudice; *sans préjudice de mes droits*, without prejudice to my rights.

préjudiciable, *a.* Prejudicial, detrimental, injurious. **préjudicial**, *a.* (*fem.* **-iale**, *pl.* **-iaux**) *Frais préjudiciaux*, previous costs.

préjudiciel, *a.* (*fem.* **-ielle**) Interlocutory. *Question préjudicielle*, interlocutory question (to be decided before the principal action).

préjudicier, *v.i.* (*conjugated like* PRIER) To be prejudicial or detrimental.

préjugé [preʒy'ʒe], *n.m.* Presumption, prejudice; (*Law*) precedent. *Exempt de préjugés*, free from prejudices; *homme sans préjugé*, unprejudiced man; *des préjugés de bonnes femmes*, old wives' crotchets.

préjuger [preʒy'ʒe], *v.t.* To prejudge.

prélart [pre'la:r], *n.m.* Wagon-tilt; (*Naut.*) tarpaulin.

prélasser (se) [prela'se], *v.r.* To strut, to stalk along.

prélat [pre'la], *n.m.* Prelate.

prélature [prela'ty:r], *n.f.* Prelacy, episcopacy.

prèle [prɛ:l], *n.f.* (*Bot.*) Horsetail; shavegrass.

prélegs [pre'lɛ], *n.m.* Preference-legacy. **préléguer**, *v.t. irr.* (*conjug. like* ACCÉLÉRER) To give as a preference-legacy.

préler [pre'le], *v.t.* To polish (woodwork) with horsetail.

prélèvement [prelɛv'mɑ̃], *n.m.* Previous deduction; sample; (*Med.*) swab. **prélever**, *v.t.* To deduct previously, to set apart (in advance); to appropriate.

préliminaire [prelimi'nɛ:r], *a.* and *n.m.* Preliminary. **préliminairement**, *adv.* Preliminarily.

prélude [pre'lyd], *n.m.* Prelude.

préluder, *v.i.* To prelude, to flourish, to play a prelude. *Préluder à une chose par une autre*, to make one thing a prelude to another.

prématuré [prematy're], *a.* (*fem.* **-ée**) Premature, untimely.—*n.* Premature child. **prématurément**, *adv.* Prematurely. **prématurité**, *n.f.* Prematurity.

préméditation [premedita'sjɔ̃], *n.f.* Premeditation; (*Law*) malice prepense. *Avec préméditation*, wilfully, with malice aforethought.

préméditer, *v.t.* To premeditate.

prémices [pre'mis], *n.f. pl.* First-fruits; firstlings (of cattle); (*fig.*) beginning, début.

premier [prə'mje], *a.* (*fem.* **-ière**) First; foremost, best, chief, principal; former (of two); ancient, early, pristine, primeval; (*Arith.*) prime. *À la première heure*, with the milk; *au premier abord*, at first sight; *denrées de première nécessité*, primary goods; *en premier lieu*, in the first place; *le premier rang*, the front rank; *les premiers temps du monde*, the early ages of the world; *matières premières*, raw materials; *nos premiers parents*, our first parents; *ouvrage de première main*, a first-hand work; *premier ministre*, Prime Minister; *premier plan*, foreground; *premier venu*, first comer.—*n.* Chief, head, leader. *Jeune premier* or *jeune première*, actor or actress playing lover's part.—*n.m.* First floor; first of the month, etc. *Il demeure au premier*, he lives on the first floor; *le premier janvier*, the first of January.—*n.f.* (*Theat.*) Place in dress-circle or first-tier boxes; first night of a play, première; (*Print.*) first proof; (*sch.*) Sixth form. **premièrement**, *adv.* Firstly, in the first place.

premier-né, *n.m.* (*pl.* **premiers-nés**, *fem.* **premier-née** or **première-née**) Firstborn.

prémilitaire [premili'tɛ:r], *a.* *Formation prémilitaire*, pre-military training.

prémisse [pre'mis], *n.f.* (*Log.*) Premise.

prémolaire [premɔ'lɛ:r], *n.f.* Premolar tooth.

prémonition [premɔni'sjɔ̃], *n.f.* Premonition. **prémonitoire** [premɔni'twa:r], *a.* Premonitory.

prémontré [premɔ̃'tre], *n.m.* Premonstratensian.

prémunir [premy'ni:r], *v.t.* To forewarn, to caution, to secure beforehand. **se prémunir**, *v.r.* To provide (*contre*).

prenable [prə'nabl], *a.* Pregnable, seizable; corruptible.

prenant, *a.* (*fem.* **-ante**) Taking, prehensile; receiving (money etc.). *Partie prenante*, payee; *queue prenante*, prehensile tail.

prendre [prɑ̃:dr], *v.t. irr.* (*pres.p.* **prenant**, *p.p.* **pris**) To take; to take up; to take away, to snatch; to grasp, to lay hold of, to seize; to capture, to apprehend; to contract; to catch (a cold etc.); to choose; to fetch; to accept, to receive; to borrow; to assume, to put on; to call for (someone); to collect (votes etc.); to help oneself to; to manage, to conduct (an affair etc.); to conceive, to entertain (a feeling etc.). *À tout prendre*, on the whole, in the main; *avoir la taille bien prise*, to be well-shaped; *avoir le cœur pris*, to be smitten; *c'est à prendre ou à laisser*, take it or leave it; *en prendre et en laisser* or *en prendre à son aise*, to take it easy; *je vous y prends*, now I have caught you; *la peur le prit*, fear seized him; *l'envie lui prit d'y aller*, he took a sudden fancy to go there; *prendre bien la taille*, (of a garment) to fit close to the waist; *prendre bien* or *mal une affaire*, to go the right *or* the wrong way about something; *prendre bien son temps*, to choose the right moment; *prendre congé de*, to take leave of; *prendre des pensionnaires*, to take in boarders; *prendre exemple sur quelqu'un*, to model oneself on someone; *prendre fait et cause pour quelqu'un*, to take someone's part, to undertake someone's defence, to side with someone; *prendre feu*, to catch fire; to ignite; *prendre garde*, to take heed; *prendre l'air*, to take an airing; *prendre la fuite*, to take to flight; *prendre le chemin de l'hôpital*, to be on the high road to ruin; *prendre le large*, to stand out to sea; *prendre le plus court*, to go the shortest way; *prendre les armes*, to take up arms, to parade under arms, to turn out (of guard); *prendre les avis*, to collect the votes; *prendre les choses de travers*, to take things amiss; *prendre le voile*, to become a nun; *prendre naissance*, to originate, to arise (of things); *prendre parti pour quelqu'un*, to side with someone; *prendre pour dit*, to take for granted; *prendre quelqu'un sur le fait*, to catch someone in the act; *prendre sur ses réserves*, to draw on one's reserves; *prendre une chose en bonne part*, to take a thing in good part; *prendre une ville d'assaut*, to take a town by storm; *que je t'y prenne un peu!* just let me catch you at it! *Qu'est-ce qui te prend?* what's up with you?—*v.i.* To take; to take root; to congeal, to freeze; to curdle (of milk etc.); to succeed, to take; to begin to burn. *Il lui prit une fièvre*, he was attacked by fever; *la Seine a pris cet hiver-là*, the Seine was frozen over that winter; *mal lui en prendra*, it will be the worse for him.—*n.m.* Act of taking. *Au fait et au prendre*, when it comes to the point. **se prendre**, *v.r.* To be taken, to be caught; to catch, to cling, to grasp (à); to freeze, to congeal (of liquids); to begin, to start. *De la manière dont il s'y prend*, by the way he goes to work; *s'y prendre mal*, to go about it the wrong way; *le sirop se prendra bientôt*, the syrup will soon set; *s'en prendre à*, to lay the blame on; *se prendre à pleurer*, to begin to cry; *se prendre d'amitié pour quelqu'un*, to take a liking for someone.

preneur, *n.m.* (*fem.* **-euse**) Taker; lessee; purchaser; catcher (of animals).

prénom [pre'nɔ̃], *n.m.* Christian name; first name; given name.

prénommé, *a.* and *n.* (*fem.* **-ée**) (The) above-named, aforesaid. **prénommer**, *v.t.* To give a forename to.

prénotion [preno'sjɔ̃], *n.f.* Prenotion, surmise.

prénuptial [prenyp'sjal], *a.* (*fem.* **-iale**, *pl.* **-iaux**) Prenuptial.

préoccupant [preɔky'pɑ̃], *a.* (*fem.* **-ante**) Worrying, disquieting.

préoccupation, *n.f.* Preoccupation; anxiety, concern; prejudice.

préoccupé, *a.* (*fem.* **-ée**) Preoccupied, absorbed. **préoccuper**, *v.t.* To engross, to preoccupy; to prepossess, to prejudice, to bias; to disturb, to trouble. **se préoccuper**, *v.r.* To see to, to be engaged in (*de*), to be anxious about.

préopinant [preɔpi'nɑ̃], *n.* (*fem.* **-ante**) Previous speaker; last speaker.

préopiner, *v.i.* To vote or express one's opinion before another.

préordination [preɔrdina'sjɔ̃], *n.f.* Preordination.

préordonner [preɔrdɔ'ne], *v.t.* To preordain, to predetermine.

préparateur [prepara'tœːr], *n.m.* (*fem.* **-trice**) Preparer, assistant (in laboratory or in a dispensing chemist's).

préparatif, *n.m.* Preparation. *Préparatifs de guerre*, war preparations.

préparation [prepara'sjɔ̃], *n.f.* Preparation. *Préparation militaire*, preparatory training; *sans préparation*, extempore. **préparatoire**, *a.* Preparatory.

préparer [prepa're], *v.t.* To prepare, to dispose, to make ready; to fit, to facilitate; to make up, manufacture. *Préparer des élèves*, to prepare, coach, pupils; *préparer les voies à quelqu'un*, to pave the way for someone. **se préparer**, *v.r.* To prepare, to prepare oneself, to get ready. *Préparez-vous à le recevoir*, prepare to meet him; *se préparer au combat*, to prepare for action; *voilà un orage qui se prépare*, there is a storm brewing.

prépondérance [prepɔ̃de'rɑ̃ːs], *n.f.* Preponderance. **prépondérant**, *a.* (*fem.* **-ante**) Preponderant. *Voix prépondérante*, casting-vote.

préposé [prepo'ze], *n.m.* (*fem.* **-ée**) Officer in charge, overseer, superintendent, agent. *Le préposé au guichet*, the booking-clerk; *les préposés*, (*Law*) agents and servants.

préposer [prepo'ze], *v.t.* To set (over), to appoint (to), to put in charge (of).

prépositif [prepozi'tif], *a.* (*fem.* **-ive**) Prepositive.

préposition, *n.f.* Preposition.

prépuce [pre'pys], *n.m.* Prepuce, foreskin.

préputial [prepy'sjal], *a.* (*fem.* **-iale**, *pl.* **-iaux**) Preputial.

prérogative [prerɔga'tiːv], *n.f.* Prerogative.

près [prɛ], *adv.* By, near, hard by; nearly, almost, about; on the point of; in comparison with. *À beaucoup près*, by a great deal; *à cela près*, with that exception; *à peu de chose près*, within a trifle, little short of; *à peu près*, pretty near, nearly so; *à peu près la même chose*, pretty much the same (thing); *un à peu près*, an approximation, a play upon words; *au plus près*, to the nearest place, (*Naut.*) close-hauled, close to the wind; *combattre de près*, to fight hand to hand; *de près*, close, from close to, near, closely, intimately; *de près et de loin*, far and near; *être rasé de près*, to be shaved close; *il demeure ci près*, he lives close by; *je ne suis pas à deux livres près*, two pounds more or less won't make any difference to me; *suivre de près*, to follow on the heels of; *tout près*, very near.—*prep.* Near, close to; in the neighbourhood of. *Près de Londres*, near London; *s'asseoir près de quelqu'un*, to sit down by someone; *près de partir*, on the point of leaving. *Ambassadeur près la cour de St. James*, ambassador accredited to the court of St. James's.

présage [preˈzaːʒ], *n.m.* Presage, omen, foreboding; conjecture. *Un oiseau de sinistre présage*, a bird of ill omen.

présager, *v.t.* To presage, to portend; to conjecture, to prognosticate, to predict.

pré-salé [presaˈle], *n.m.* (*pl.* **prés-salés**) Salt-marsh sheep or mutton.

presbyte [prɛzˈbit], *a.* Presbyopic, long-sighted. *Vue presbyte*, long sight.—*n.* Long-sighted person.

presbytéral [prɛzbiteˈral], *a.* (*fem.* **-ale**, *pl.* **-aux**) Priestly. *Maison presbytérale* = **presbytère**, *n.m.* Parsonage, vicarage, rectory; presbytery (*R.-C. Ch.*).

presbytérianisme, *n.m.* Presbyterianism. **presbytérien**, *a.* and *n.* (*fem.* **-ienne**) Presbyterian.

presbytie [prɛzbiˈsi], *n.f.* Presbyopia; far- or long-sightedness.

prescience [preˈsjɑ̃ːs], *n.f.* Prescience, foreknowledge, foresight. **prescient**, *a.* (*fem.* **-iente**) Prescient.

prescriptible [prɛskripˈtibl], *a.* Prescriptible. **prescription**, *n.f.* Prescription; regulation. *Établi par prescription*, prescriptive.

prescrire [prɛsˈkriːr], *v.t. irr.* (*conjugated like* ÉCRIRE) To prescribe, to stipulate, to set; (*Law*) to bar. *Prescrire des lois*, to prescribe laws; *prescrire un régime*, to prescribe a diet. **se prescrire**, *v.r.* To be prescribed, ordered; (*Law*) to be lost by limitation.

préséance [preseˈɑ̃ːs], *n.f.* Precedence. *Avoir la préséance sur*, to take precedence of.

présélection [preselɛkˈsjɔ̃], *n.f.* Preselecting; (*sch.*) short-listing, short list. (*Motor.*) *Boîte de vitesse à présélection*, preselector gears.

présence [preˈzɑ̃ːs], *n.f.* Presence, attendance, appearance. *Deux armées en présence*, two armies facing each other; *en présence de*, in (the) presence of, in view of; *faire acte de présence*, to put in an appearance; *feuille de présence*, time-sheet; *mettre en présence*, to bring face to face; *présence d'esprit*, presence of mind.

présent [preˈzɑ̃], *a.* (*fem.* **-ente**) Present, attentive to); (at the call-over) *Présent!* Here, sir.—*n.m.* Present, present time; (*Gram.*) present tense; gift, present. *À présent*, at present; *dès à présent*, from now on; *donner en présent*, to give as a present; *faire présent de*, to make a present of; *jusqu'à présent*, till now; *pour le présent*, for the time being. —*n.f.* Present letter; (*pl. Law*) presents.

présentable, *a.* Presentable, fit to be seen.

présentateur, *n.m.* (*fem.* **-trice**) Presenter (to benefices etc.); introducer.—*a.* Presenting.

présentation, *n.f.* Presentation, introduction; appearance. *À présentation*, on demand.

présentement, *adv.* Now, at present.

présenter [prezɑ̃ˈte], *v.t.* To present, to offer, to hold out; to show, to expose; to bring forward, to introduce; to put forward (a candidate); (*Theat.*) to present, to put on.

Présenter à quelqu'un ses respects, to pay one's respects to someone; *présenter les armes*, to present arms; *présenter ses lettres de créance*, to present one's credentials; *présenter une personne à une autre*, to introduce one person to another. **se présenter**, *v.r.* To present oneself, to appear, to offer oneself or itself; to occur. *Il se présenta une difficulté*, a difficulty arose; *il s'est présenté à moi*, he presented himself before me; *la chose se présente bien*, the thing promises well; *se présenter aux élections*, to stand, (*Am.*) to run, for an election; *un homme qui se présente bien*, a man of good appearance.

présenteur, *n.m.* (*fem.* **-euse**) Presenter.

préservateur [prezɛrvaˈtœːr], *a.* (*fem.* **-trice**) Preservative.

préservatif, *a.* (*fem.* **-ive**) Preservative, preventive.—*n.m.* Contraceptive sheath.

préservation, *n.f.* Preservation, safeguarding.

préserver [prezɛrˈve], *v.t.* To preserve; to defend, to keep safe or unharmed. *Le ciel m'en préserve!* heaven forbid! **se préserver**, *v.r.* To preserve oneself, to guard against.

préside [preˈzid], *n.m.* (*Sp.*) Fortified post; presidio.

présidence [preziˈdɑ̃ːs], *n.f.* Presidency, chairmanship; president's house.

président, *n.m.* President (of tribunal), presiding judge; speaker (of the House of Commons), chairman (of a committee, a meeting, etc.); foreman (of a jury). *Président d'âge*, president by seniority.

présidente, *n.f.* Lady president; president's wife, chairwoman.

présidentiel, *a.* (*fem.* **-ielle**) Presidential.

présider, *v.t.* To preside over, to be president or chairman of. *Présider une réunion*, to preside over a meeting.—*v.i.* To preside, to be president, to be in the chair. (*fig.*) *Présider aux destinées d'une nation*, to preside over the destinies of a nation.

presle [PRÈLE].

présomptif [prezɔ̃pˈtif], *a.* (*fem.* **-ive**) Presumptive, apparent, presumed (of heirs). *Héritier présomptif*, heir-apparent.

présomption [prezɔ̃pˈsjɔ̃], *n.f.* Presumption, presumptuousness, self-conceit. *Preuve par présomption*, circumstantial evidence.

présomptueusement, *adv.* Presumptuously.

présomptueux, *a.* (*fem.* **-euse**) Presumptuous, presuming, self-conceited. *Jeune présomptueux!* presumptuous youth!

presque [prɛsk], *adv.* Almost, nearly, all but; hardly, scarcely. *Je ne l'ai presque pas vu*, I scarcely saw him at all; *presque jamais*, hardly ever; *presque plus (de)*, scarcely any left; *presque rien*, hardly anything; *un ouvrage presque achevé*, an almost completed work.

presqu'île [prɛsˈkil], *n.f.* Peninsula.

pressage [preˈsaːʒ], *n.m.* Pressing, condensing.

pressant, *a.* (*fem.* **-ante**) Pressing, urgent, earnest. *D'un ton pressant*, insistently.

presse [prɛːs], *n.f.* Throng, crowd; haste, hurry; pressure, urgency; (*Navy*) impressment (of men), press-gang; press (newspapers); printing-press. *Cet ouvrage est sous presse*, this work is in the press. *Fendre la presse*, to force one's way through the crowd; *il n'y a pas de presse*, there's no hurry. *Presse à copier*, copying-press; *presse d'imprimerie*, printing-press. *Conférence de presse*, press conference; *service de presse*, publicity; press copies.

pressé, a. (*fem.* **-ée**) Pressed; crowded; close, serried, thick; in haste, hurried; pressing, urgent, immediate; eager, anxious; very busy; (*fig.*) condensed, brief, concise. *Cela n'est pas pressé*, there's no hurry for that; *je suis très pressé*, I am very busy; *pressé par l'ennemi*, harried by the enemy; *vous êtes bien pressé*, you are in a great hurry.

presse-citron, *n.m.* (*pl. inv.* or **presse-citrons**) Lemon-squeezer.

pressée, *n.f.* Pressing, pressure; pressful (of print etc.).

presse-étoupe, *n.m. inv.* Stuffing-box (in steam-engine).

presse-fruits, *n.m. inv.* Fruit-squeezer.

pressentiment [presãti'mã], *n.m.* Presentiment; misgiving, foreboding.

pressentir, *v.t.* To have a presentiment of; to ascertain the intentions of, to sound. *Il faut le pressentir*, we must sound him.

presse-papiers [prespa'pje], *n.m. inv.* Paper-weight.

presse-purée, *n.m. inv.* Potato masher.

presser [prɛ'se], *v.t.* To press, to squeeze, to press or weigh upon; to tread down; to crush; to crowd, to throng; to hem in; to harry (an enemy etc.); to push hard; to hasten, to accelerate, to hurry; to entreat, to urge, to impel, to actuate. *Il pressa son départ*, he hastened his departure; *il l'a pressé de partir*, he urged him to depart; *presser la détente*, to pull the trigger; *presser le pas*, to quicken one's pace; *presser vivement un siège*, to carry on a siege vigorously.—*v.i.* To press, to be urgent. *Rien ne presse*, or *il n'y a rien qui presse*, there is no hurry; *le temps presse*, time presses. **se presser,** *v.r.* To press, to squeeze, to crowd; to make haste, to hurry, to look sharp. *Pressons-nous*, let us make haste; *se presser de faire une chose*, to make haste to do a thing.

presse-raquette, *n.m.* (*pl.* **presse-raquettes**) Racket press.

presseur, *n.m.* (*fem.* **-euse**) Presser.

pressier, *n.m.* (*Print.*) Pressman.

pression, *n.f.* Pressure. *Machine à vapeur à haute pression, à moyenne pression,* or *à basse pression*, steam-engine of high, medium, *or* low pressure; *sous pression*, under pressure; *with steam up*. *Faire pression sur quelqu'un*, to bring pressure to bear on someone. *Pression sanguine*, blood pressure.

pressis, *n.m.* Juice (of meat etc.) pressed out by a machine.

pressoir, *n.m.* Press (wine-press, cider-press, etc.); press-house.

pressurage, *n.m.* Pressing (of fruit); (*fig.*) extortion.

pressurer, *v.t.* To press (grapes, apples, etc.); (*fig.*) to squeeze money etc. out of; to grind down, to oppress. *Il ne songe qu'à vous pressurer*, his only thought is to drain you of money.

pressureur, *n.m.* (*fem.* **-euse**) Presser (of fruit etc.); (*fig.*) squeezer, sponger, oppressor.

prestance [prɛs'tã:s], *n.f.* Commanding appearance, fine presence, martial bearing.

prestant [prɛs'tã], *n.m.* Diapason (of an organ).

prestataire [prɛsta'tɛ:r], *n.m.* Person liable to

prestations (in labour or money); (*Mil.*) drawing allowances (in money or in kind).

prestation [prɛsta'sjõ], *n.f.* Payment, loan, lending; taking (of an oath); prestation (payment of toll etc.); (*Mil.*) allowance (in money or in kind).

preste [prɛst], *a.* Agile, nimble; quick, smart, sharp. **preste! int.* Quick! sharp! **prestement,** *adv.* Nimbly, quickly.

prestesse, *n.f.* Agility, quickness, nimbleness.

prestidigitateur [prɛstidiʒita'tœ:r], *n.m.* Conjurer, juggler, (*Am.*) magician. **prestidigitation,** *n.f.* Jugglery, conjuring, sleight of hand.

prestige [prɛs'ti:ʒ], *n.m.* Marvel; glamour; illusion, magic spell; prestige.

prestigieux, a. (*fem.* **-ieuse**) Marvellous, amazing.

(*C*) **presto** [prɛs'to], *n.m.* Pressure cooker.

présumable [prezy'mabl], *a.* Presumable.

présumer [prezy'me], *v.t.* To presume, to suppose. *Il est à présumer*, it is to be supposed; *présumer trop de soi*, to be too presuming; *présumer trop de quelqu'un*, to have too high an opinion of someone; *trop présumer de ses forces*, to overestimate one's strength.

présupposer [presypo'ze], *v.t.* To presuppose.

présupposition, *n.f.* Presupposition.

présure [pre'zy:r], *n.f.* Rennet.

prêt (1) [prɛ], *a.* (*fem.* **prête**) Ready, in readiness, prepared. *Prêt à partir*, ready to depart. *Se tenir prêt*, to keep oneself ready.

prêt (2) [prɛ], *n.m.* Loan; (*Mil.*) pay. (*Naut.*) *Prêt à la grosse aventure*, bottomry loan, loan in respondentia.

prêtable, a. Lendable.

prétantaine [pretã'tɛn], *n.f. Courir la prétantaine*, to gad about, to go on the loose.

prêt-bail [prɛ'ba:j], *n.m.* Lend-lease.

prêté [prɛ'te], *a.* (*fem.* **-ée**) Lent.—*n.m.* Thing lent. *C'est un prêté rendu*, tit for tat.

prétendant [pretã'dã], *n.m.* (*fem.* **-ante**) Claimant, candidate; applicant; suitor; pretender (to the throne).

prétendre [pre'tã:dr], *v.t.* To claim, to lay claim to, to pretend to; to intend, to mean; to affirm, to maintain. *À ce qu'on prétend*, according to report; *on prétend que cela n'est pas vrai*, people maintain that this is untrue; *que prétendent ces misérables?* what do these wretches mean?—*v.i.* To lay claim (to); to aspire (*à*). *Je prétends vous traiter comme mon propre fils*, I mean to treat you as my own son.

prétendu, a. (*fem.* **-ue**) Pretended, supposed, sham, so-called, would-be, alleged. *C'est un prétendu bel esprit*, he is a would-be wit.—*n.* Future husband or wife, fiancé, fiancée.

prête-nom [prɛt'nõ], *n.m.* (*pl.* **prête-noms**) One that lends his name (in a contract etc.); figure-head, man of straw.

prétentieux [pretã'sjø], *a.* (*fem.* **-ieuse**) Pretentious, assuming; affected, stilted (of style).

prétention [pretã'sjõ], *n.f.* Pretension, claim; intention, wish; expectation. *C'est un homme sans prétentions*, he is an unassuming man; *il a des prétentions à l'esprit*, he thinks he is witty; *sa prétention est mal fondée*, his claim is groundless.

prêter [prɛ'te], *v.t.* To lend; to impart, to furnish; to attribute, to ascribe; to bestow, to give. *Prêter attention,* to pay attention; *prêter la main à quelqu'un,* to come to someone's assistance; *prêter le flanc,* to expose oneself; *prêter l'oreille,* to give ear, to listen; *prêter main-forte* [MAIN-FORTE]; *prêter serment,* to take an oath.—*v.i.* To give, to stretch; to invite, to give rise to. *Ce cuir-là prête comme un gant,* that leather stretches like a glove. *Une conduite qui prête à la critique,* conduct which invites criticism. se **prêter,** *v.r.* To give way, to yield; to lend oneself or itself; to countenance, to favour.

prétérit [prete'rit], *n.m.* Preterite (tense).

prétérition [preteri'sjɔ̃], or **prétermission,** *n.f.* (*Rhet.*) Preterition.

préteur [pre'tœ:r], *n.m.* Praetor.

prêteur [prɛ'tœ:r], *n.m.* (*fem.* **-euse**) Lender. *Prêteur sur gages,* pawnbroker.—*a.* Given to lending, willing to lend.

prétexte (1) [pre'tɛkst], *n.m.* Pretext, pretence; plea. *Sous prétexte de le secourir,* on pretence of assisting him.

prétexte (2) [pre'tɛkst], *n.f.* (*Rom. Ant.*) Praetexta (tunic).

prétexter [pretɛks'te], *v.t.* To allege (as pretext), to plead, to pretend, to feign, to affect, to sham.

prétoire [pre'twa:r], *n.m.* (*Rom. Ant.*) Praetorium, judgment hall; law court.

prétorien, *a.* (*fem.* **-ienne**) Praetorian.

prêtraille [prɛ'trɑ:j], *n.f.* (*pej.*) The parsons, the clerical crew.

prêtre [prɛ:tr], *n.m.* Priest. *Grand prêtre,* high priest; *il s'est fait prêtre,* he has taken orders. **prêtresse,** *n.f.* Priestess.

prêtrise [prɛ'tri:z], *n.f.* Priesthood.

préture [pre'ty:r], *n.f.* Praetorship.

preuve [prœ:v], *n.f.* Proof; evidence, testimony; token, mark; proof-sample; essay, proof (of spirits etc.). *Faire preuve de courage,* to prove oneself a man of courage; *il a fait ses preuves,* he has given proof of his capacity; *preuve indirecte,* circumstantial evidence.

preux [prø], *a.m. inv.* Gallant, doughty, valiant.—*n.m.* Valiant warrior, gallant knight.

prévaloir [preva'lwa:r], *v.i. irr.* (*conjug. like* VALOIR, except in subj. pres. *que je prévale, que nous prévalions*) To prevail, to stand good, to be superior. *La faveur prévaut souvent sur le mérite,* favour frequently prevails over merit; *il a fait prévaloir ses idées,* he has won acceptance for his ideas. se **prévaloir,** *v.r.* To take advantage, to avail oneself; to boast, to pride oneself, to glory (*de*). *Se prévaloir de sa naissance,* to pride oneself on one's birth.

prévaricateur [prevarika'tœ:r], *n.m.* (*fem.* **-trice**) Betrayer of trust, dishonest judge.—*a.* Dishonest, unjust.

prévarication, *n.f.* Betrayal of trust, maladministration of justice.

prévariquer, *v.i.* To betray one's trust.

prévenance [prev'nɑ̃:s], *n.f.* Obligingness; (*pl.*) kind attentions.

prévenant, *a.* (*fem.* **-ante**) Obliging, kind; prepossessing, engaging. *Il a un air prévenant,* he has a prepossessing look.

prévenir [prev'ni:r], *v.t. irr.* (*conjugated like* VENIR) To precede; to get the start of, to anticipate, to forestall; to prevent, to hinder; to prepossess, to prejudice, to predispose; to inform, to apprise, to caution, to warn. *On* *vous avait prévenu,* you had been informed of it; *prévenir le mal,* to prevent evil; *prévenir les besoins de quelqu'un,* to anticipate someone's wants; *prévenir les objections,* to forestall objections. se **prévenir,** *v.r.* To be prepossessed or prejudiced. *Se prévenir en faveur de quelqu'un,* to take a liking to someone.

préventif [prevɑ̃'tif], *a.* (*fem.* **-ive**) Preventive; prophylactic. *Détention préventive,* detention awaiting trial.

prévention [prevɑ̃'sjɔ̃], *n.f.* Prepossession, prejudice, bias; suspicion, presumption; accusation. *Être en état de prévention,* (*Law*) to be committed for trial; *vaincre les préventions de quelqu'un,* to overcome someone's prejudices. *Prévention routière,* road safety measures. **préventivement,** *adv.* By way of prevention; while awaiting trial, on suspicion.

prévenu, *a.* (*fem.* **-ue**) Forestalled, preceded, anticipated; prejudiced, biased; accused. *Un esprit non prévenu,* an open, unbiased mind. —*n.* The accused, the prisoner.

préventorium [prevɑ̃tɔ'rjɔm], *n.m.* Preventorium.

prévisible [previ'zibl], *a.* Foreseeable.

prévision [previ'zjɔ̃], *n.f.* Prevision, forecast, conjecture; estimate, expectation.

prévoir [pre'vwa:r], *v.t. irr.* (*conjug. like* VOIR, except in fut. *je prévoirai* and cond. *je prévoirais*) To foresee, to forecast, to anticipate, to look forward to. *Il faut tout prévoir,* we must provide against all eventualities; *la conférence prévue pour demain,* the lecture arranged for tomorrow.

prévôt [pre'vo], *n.m.* Provost. *Grand prévôt,* provost-marshal; *prévôt de salle d'armes,* fencing-master's assistant; **prévôt des marchands,* provost of the guilds (in Paris).

prévôtal, *a.* (*fem.* **-ale,** *pl.* **-aux**) Pertaining to a provost. *Cour prévôtale,* (*Fr. Hist.*) summary court. **prévôtalement,** *adv.* Without appeal.

prévôté, *n.f.* Provostship; military police.

prévoyance [prevwa'jɑ̃:s], *n.f.* Foresight, forethought, prudence, caution. *Rien n'échappe à sa prévoyance,* nothing escapes his foresight.

prévoyant, *a.* (*fem.* **-ante**) Provident, prudent, careful.

prévu [pre'vy], *p.p.* (*fem.* **-ue**) [PRÉVOIR].

Priape [pri'ap], *m.* Priapus.

priapée [pria'pe], *n.f.* Priapean picture or poem. **priapisme,** *n.m.* Priapism.

prié [pri'e], *a.* (*fem.* **-ée**) Invited (to a feast etc.).

prie-Dieu [pri'djø], *n.m. inv.* Praying-stool, prie-Dieu.

prier [pri'e], *v.t.* To pray, to entreat, to beseech, to supplicate; to request; to invite, to bid. *Je vous en prie,* I beg of you; do, please! *on m'a prié de le faire,* I have been requested to do it; *prier à dîner,* to invite to dinner; *se faire prier* or *aimer à se faire prier,* to require much persuading.

prière [pri'ɛr], *n.f.* Prayer; request, entreaty; invitation. *Être en prières,* to be at prayers; *faire une chose à la prière de quelqu'un,* to do a thing at someone's request; *faire une prière à quelqu'un,* to make a request to someone; *instante prière,* earnest prayer; *prière de faire*

renvoyer *la lettre*, kindly return the letter; *prière de faire suivre*, please forward; *prière de fermer la porte*, please close the door.
prieur [pri'œːr], *n.m.* Prior (superior of a convent). **prieure**, *n.f.* Prioress. **prieuré**, *n.m.* Priory.
primage [pri'maːʒ], *n.m.* Primage (allowance paid to the captain of a ship).
primaire [pri'mɛːr], *a.* Primary. *École primaire* or *du premier degré*, elementary school. *Esprit primaire*, elementary type of mind.—*n.m.* (*Elec.*) Primary winding.
primat [pri'ma], *n.m.* Primate, metropolitan; pre-eminence, primacy.
primates, *n.m. pl.* (*Zool.*) Primates.
primatial, *a.* (*fem.* -**iale**, *pl.* -**iaux**) Primatial.
primatie, *n.f.* Primacy, primateship.
primauté [primo'te], *n.f.* Primacy, priority, pre-eminence; the lead (at cards, dice, etc.).
prime [prim], *n.f.* Premium; subsidy; (*Mil.*) bounty; bonus, prize; (*R.-C. Ch.*) prime (first canonical hour succeeding lauds); (*Fenc.*) prime; (*Comm.*) free gift; prime wool; (*Jewellery*) pebble; (*Customs*) drawback. *Certificat de primes*, debenture; *marché à primes*, option market; *prime pour acheter*, call, buyer's option; *prime pour vendre*, put option; seller's option; (*Mil.*) *prime d'engagement*, enlistment bounty; *prime de démobilisation*, gratuity on discharge. *Faire prime*, to be much in demand, at a premium.—*a.* First; (*Alg.*) accented. *b'*, *b prime*, b', b accented; *de prime abord*, at first, at the first blush; *de prime face*, at first sight; *de prime saut*, suddenly; at the first attempt.
primer, *v.t.* To surpass, to excel; to give a prize or medal to (at an agricultural show etc.). *Il prime tous les autres*, he excels all the others; *roman primé*, prize-winning novel.—*v.i.* To play first, to lead (at tennis etc.); to excel. *Il prime en tout*, he excels in everything.
prime-sautier, *a.* (*pl.* **prime-sautiers**, *fem.* **prime-sautière**, *pl.* **prime-sautières**) Impulsive, spontaneous, quick. *Les Français ont, en général, l'esprit prime-sautier*, the French are, as a rule, ready-witted.
primeur, *n.f.* Early vegetables, fruit, flowers, etc.; early sentiment, love, etc.; freshness, bloom. *Je vous en donnerai la primeur*, you will be the first to get the news. *Servir à table un plat de primeurs*, to serve up a dish of early vegetables.
primevère [prim'vɛːr], *n.f.* (*Bot.*) Primula. *Primevère commune* or (*fleur de*) *coucou*, cowslip; *primevère à grandes fleurs*, primrose; *primevère élevée*, oxlip; *primevère farineuse*, bird's eye primrose; *primevère des jardins*, polyanthus [*see also* OREILLE D'OURS].
primidi [primi'di], *n.m.* First day of decade in calendar of first French republic.
primipare [primi'paːr], *a.* Primiparous.—*n.f.* Primipara.
primitif [primi'tif], *a.* (*fem.* -**ive**) First, early, primitive, aboriginal; pristine; (*Gram.*) radical.—*n.m.* (*Gram.*, *Paint.*) Primitive.
primitivement, *adv.* Primitively, originally.
*__primitivité__, *n.f.* Primitiveness.
primo [pri'mo], *adv.* First, in the first place.
primogéniture [primɔʒeni'tyːr], *n.f.* Primogeniture.

primordial [primɔr'djal], *a.* (*fem.* -**iale**, *pl.* -**iaux**) Primordial; of prime importance.
prince [prɛ̃ːs], *n.m.* Prince. *Être bon prince*, (*colloq.*) to be a good fellow; *le fait du prince*, arbitrary act (committed by sovereign); *vivre en prince*, to live like a prince.
princeps [prɛ̃'sɛps], *a. inv.* *Édition princeps*, first edition.
princesse [prɛ̃'sɛs], *n.f.* Princess. *Oui, ma princesse*, (*colloq.*) yes, my charmer.
princier [prɛ̃'sje], *a.* (*fem.* -**ière**) Princely, like a prince.
principal [prɛ̃si'pal], *a.* (*fem.* -**ale**, *pl.* -**aux**) Principal, chief, most important. *Locataire principal*, head-lessee.—*n.m.* Chief thing, principal, chief, or essential point; principal, capital (money); chief, head, chief partner, headmaster (of a *collège*); (*pl.*) chief personages (of a town etc.). *Payer le principal et l'intérêt*, to pay both principal and interest. *Pour vous, le principal est que vous ayez soin de votre santé*, the main thing for you is to take care of your health.
principalat, *n.m.* Principalship, headmastership.
principalement, *adv.* Principally, chiefly.
principat, *n.m.* Principate, sovereignty.
principauté, *n.f.* Principality, princedom.
principe [prɛ̃'sip], *n.m.* Beginning, source, basis, origin; element, principle; (*pl.*) principles, rudiments. *Dès le principe*, from the very first; *en principe*, as a rule; theoretically; *établir* or *poser un principe*, to lay down a principle; *homme sans principes*, unprincipled man; *l'amour-propre est le principe de presque toutes nos actions*, self-love is the motive of almost all our actions; *partir d'un principe*, to start from a principle.
principicule [prɛ̃sipi'kyl], *n.m.* Petty prince, princeling.
printanier [prɛ̃ta'nje], *a.* (*fem.* -**ière**) Spring-like, vernal; (*fig.*) youthful, early. *Étoffes printanières*, spring materials, spring goods. *Potage printanier*, soup made of spring vegetables.
printemps [prɛ̃'tɑ̃], *n.m.* Spring, spring-time; (*fig.*) prime, bloom. *Le printemps de la vie*, the morning of life.
prioritaire [priɔri'tɛːr], *a.* and *n.* Having priority.
priorité [priɔri'te], *n.f.* Priority.
pris [pri], *a.* (*fem.* **prise** (1)) Taken, captured, caught, seized; taken in; congealed, curdled, frozen. *C'est autant de pris sur l'ennemi*, it is so much snatched from the fire; *cela m'a pris deux mois*, it took me two months; *citation prise dans Hugo*, quotation taken from Hugo. *Cet homme est pris de vin*, that man is the worse for liquor. *Homme bien pris dans sa taille*, well-proportioned man. *La rivière est prise*, the river is frozen; *le temps est pris*, the sky is overcast. *Parti pris* [PARTI (1)].
prisable, *a.* Estimable, worthy of esteem.
prise (2) [priːz], *n.f.* Taking, capture; prize; hold, handle, purchase; grasp, grip; quarrel; dose; pinch (of snuff, etc.); (*pl.*) fighting, close quarters. *Décret de prise de corps*, writ of arrest; *donner prise à la critique*, to lay oneself open to criticism; *donner prise sur soi à son ennemi*, to give one's enemy a hold over one; *en prise directe* or (*fam.*) *en prise*, (*Motor.*) in gear, engaged; *en venir aux prises*,

to grapple with one another; *être aux prises avec la mort*, to be at death's door; *être de bonne prise*, to be a lawful prize; *faire une prise de sang*, to take a blood test; *lâcher prise*, to let go one's hold; *mettre en prise*, (*Motor.*) to engage; *la prise d'une ville*, the taking of a town; *mettre aux prises*, to set (together) by the ears; *part de prise*, prize-money; *prise d'air*, air-scoop, air-intake; *prise d'armes*, taking up arms, parade under arms; *prise de corps*, arrest; *prise de possession*, taking possession; *prise de son*, sound recording; *prise de tabac*, pinch of snuff; *prise de tête à terre*, (*Wrest.*) half Nelson; *prise de courant*, (*Elec.*) wall-plug; *prise d'eau*, hydrant; *prise de vues*, (*Cine.*) filming, shooting; *prise rapide*, (of cement) quick setting.

prisée [pri'ze], *n.f.* Appraisement, valuation.

priser (1) [pri'ze], *v.t.*, *v.i.* To take snuff. *Tabac à priser*, snuff.

priser (2) [pri'ze], *v.t.* To appraise, to estimate; to set a high price on; to esteem.

priseur (1) [pri'zœːr], *n.m.* (*fem.* **-euse**) Snuff-taker.

priseur (2) [pri'zœːr], *n.m. Commissaire priseur*, auctioneer, valuer.

prismatique [prisma'tik], *a.* Prismatic.

prisme, *n.m.* Prism.

prison [pri'zɔ̃], *n.f.* Prison, gaol; imprisonment, confinement. *Être condamné à la prison*, to be sentenced to imprisonment; *faire de la prison*, to do time; *mettre* or *faire mettre en prison*, to send to prison; *s'échapper de prison*, to break out of prison.

prisonnier, *n.m.* (*fem.* **-ière**) Prisoner. *Prisonnier de guerre* or *P.G.*, prisoner of war.

privatif [priva'tif], *a.* (*fem.* **-ive**) (*Gram.*) Privative.

privation [priva'sjɔ̃], *n.f.* Privation, deprivation; want, need. *Être dans la privation*, to be in want; *la privation de la vue*, the loss of sight; *privation de sortie*, (*Mil.*) confinement to barracks; (*sch.*) gating; *vivre de privations*, to lead a life of privation.

privauté [privo'te], *n.f.* Extreme familiarity or liberty. *Prendre des privautés*, to take liberties.

privé [pri've], *a.* and *n.m.* (*fem.* **-ée**) Private; familiar, intimate, free; tame (of animals). *De son autorité privée*, of one's own authority; *dans le privé*, in private, privately; *vie privée*, private life. **privément**, *adv.* Familiarly, intimately.

priver [pri've], *v.t.* To deprive, to bereave; to tame (animals etc.). *Priver quelqu'un de ses biens*, to deprive someone of his property.

se priver, *v.r.* To deprive or stint oneself; to abstain (*de*).

privilège [privi'lɛːʒ], *n.m.* Privilege; licence; prerogative, grant. *Accorder un privilège à*, to grant a privilege to, to license (printers etc.); *atteinte portée aux privilèges*, breach of privilege; *privilège diplomatique*, diplomatic privilege; *privilège d'une banque*, bank charter; *privilège général*, general lien; *sans privilèges*, ex all.

privilégié, *a.* (*fem.* **-iée**) Privileged; licensed; entitled to preference (of creditors); preferential (of shares). *C'est un être privilégié*, he is a privileged being.—*n.* Privileged person.

privilégier, *v.t.* To privilege, to license.

prix [pri], *n.m. inv.* Price, cost, value; rate, remuneration, return; reward, prize; stakes (race for prize). *À prix d'argent*, tor money; *à quelque prix que ce soit*, cost what it will; *au prix de*, at the cost of, in comparison with; *à vil prix*, dirt-cheap; *hors de prix*, extravagantly dear; *la vertu trouve son prix en elle-même*, virtue is its own reward; *livre de prix*, prize-book; *mettre la tête d'un homme à prix*, to set a price upon a man's head; *mise à prix*, bid or reserve price (auction); *n'avoir pas de prix*, to be priceless, to be worthless; *prix coûtant*, *prix de revient*, cost price; *prix fait*, settled price; *prix fixe*, fixed price; *prix de gros*, wholesale price; *remporter le prix*, to carry off the prize; *une chose de prix*, a thing of great price; *une chose qui n'a point de prix*, a thing beyond price; *vendre à tout prix*, to sell at any cost.

probabilisme [prɔbabi'lism], *n.m.* Probabilism.

probabilité [prɔbabili'te], *n.f.* Probability, likelihood.

probable, *a.* Probable, likely, credible. *Cela est bien peu probable*, that is anything but probable. **probablement**, *adv.* Probably.

probant [prɔ'bɑ̃], *a.* (*fem.* **-ante**) Convincing, conclusive. *En forme probante*, in an authentic form; *raison probante*, convincing reason.

probation [prɔba'sjɔ̃], *n.f.* (*Eccles.*) Probation.

probatoire [prɔba'twaːr], *a.* Probative.

probe [prɔb], *a.* Honest, upright.

probité [prɔbi'te], *n.f.* Probity, honesty, integrity.

problématique [prɔblema'tik], *a.* Problematical, questionable. **problématiquement**, *adv.* Problematically.

problème [prɔ'blɛm], *n.m.* Problem. *Poser un problème*, to state a problem; *résoudre un problème*, to solve a problem.

proboscide [prɔbɔ'sid], *n.f.* Proboscis. **proboscidien**, *n.m.* and *a.* (*fem.* **-ienne**) (*Zool.*) Proboscidean.

procédé [prɔse'de], *n.m.* Behaviour, proceeding, conduct; process, operation; method; (*Billiards*) cue-tip. *Je n'aime pas ces procédés*, I don't like that kind of behaviour; *manquer aux procédés*, to behave in a discourteous manner.

procéder [prɔse'de], *v.i. irr.* (*conjugated like* ACCÉLÉRER) To proceed, to come, to arise, to originate (*de*); to go on, to operate; to behave, to conduct oneself; (*Law*) to take proceedings. *Procéder criminellement contre quelqu'un*, to take proceedings against someone.

procédure, *n.f.* Procedure; proceedings.

procédurier, *a.* (*fem.* **-ière**) Litigious.—*n.m.* Pettifogger.

procès, *n.m.* Lawsuit, suit, action, trial; (*Anat.*) process. *Être en procès*, to be at law; *faire le procès de quelqu'un*, to try someone, to call someone to account, to find fault with someone; *gagner son procès*, to win one's case; *intenter* or *faire un procès à quelqu'un*, to institute proceedings against someone; *sans autre forme de procès*, without more ado, without further formality; *un procès en divorce*, divorce proceedings.

processif, *a.* (*fem.* **-ive**) Litigious.

procession [prɔse'sjɔ̃], *n.f.* Procession; trail, string. **processionnel**, *a.* (*fem.* **-elle**) Processional. **processionnellement**, *adv.* In procession.

processionner [prɔsesjɔ'ne], *v.i.* To walk in procession.

processus [prɔsɛ'sys], *n.m.* (*Anat.*) Process; progress, course; method. *Processus économique*, economic process.

procès-verbal [prɔsɛvɛr'bal], *n.m.* (*pl.* **procès-verbaux**) Official report; journal, minute of proceedings; police report. *Dresser un procès-verbal contre quelqu'un*, to take someone's name and address.

prochain [prɔ'ʃɛ̃], *a.* (*fem.* **-aine**) Near, nearest, next; approaching, near at hand; immediate, proximate. *Fin prochaine*, approaching end; *le mois prochain*, next month; *le prochain village*, the next village; *son départ est prochain*, his departure is imminent.—*n.m.* Neighbour, fellow-creature.

prochainement, *adv.* Shortly, soon.

proche [prɔʃ], *a.* Near, neighbouring; nigh, approaching. *La ville la plus proche*, the nearest town; *proche parent*, near relation. —*prep.* and *adv.* Near, nigh. *De proche en proche*, gradually nearer and nearer, by degrees.—*n.m.* (*usually in pl.*) Near relation, kin, kindred.

prochronisme [prɔkrɔ'nism], *n.m.* Prochronism, antedating.

procidence [prɔsi'dɑ̃:s], *n.f.* (*Med.*) Prolapse.

*proclamateur [prɔklama'tœ:r], *n.m.* (*fem.* **-trice**) Proclaimer.

proclamation [prɔklama'sjɔ̃], *n.f.* Proclamation.

proclamer, *v.t.* To proclaim, to announce, to publish; to reveal, to disclose. **se proclamer**, *v.r.* To proclaim oneself.

proclitique [prɔkli'tik], *a.* and *n.* (*Gram.*) Proclitic.

proclive [prɔ'kli:v], *a.* Proclivous, inclined.

proclivité, *n.f.* Proclivity, slope, incline.

procombant [prɔkɔ̃'bɑ̃], *a.* (*fem.* **-ante**) (*Bot.*) Procumbent.

proconsul [prɔkɔ̃'syl], *n.m.* Proconsul. **proconsulaire**, *a.* Proconsular. **proconsulat**, *n.m.* Proconsulate.

procréateur [prɔkrea'tœ:r], *a.* (*fem.* **-trice**) Procreative.—*n.* Procreator.

procréation [prɔkrea'sjɔ̃], *n.f.* Procreation.

procréer [prɔkre'e], *v.t.* To procreate, to beget.

procurateur [prɔkyra'tœ:r], *n.m.* Procurator.

procuration [prɔkyra'sjɔ̃], *n.f.* Procuration, power of attorney, proxy (deed).

procuratrice, *fem.* [PROCUREUR].

procurer [prɔky're], *v.t.* To procure, to get. *Procurer une charge à quelqu'un*, to procure a post for someone. **se procurer**, *v.r.* To procure, to get for oneself. *Se procurer de l'argent*, to obtain money.

procureur, *n.m.* (*fem.* **procuratrice**) Attorney, procurator, proxy; bursar (at a convent). *Procureur de la République*, public prosecutor; *procureur général*, attorney-general.

procureuse, *n.f.* Procuress, bawd.

Procuste [prɔ'kyst], *m.* Procrustes. *Lit de Procuste*, Procrustean bed.

prodigalement [prɔdigal'mɑ̃], *adv.* Prodigally, extravagantly, profusely.

prodigalité, *n.f.* Prodigality, lavishness.

prodige [prɔ'di:ʒ], *n.m.* Prodigy, marvel.

prodigieusement, *adv.* Prodigiously.

prodigieux, *a.* (*fem.* **-ieuse**) Prodigious, wonderful; stupendous.

prodigue [prɔ'dig], *a.* Prodigal, lavish; wasteful, thriftless. *L'enfant prodigue*, the

Prodigal Son.—*n.* Prodigal, spendthrift, squanderer.

prodiguer, *v.t.* To be prodigal of; to waste, to squander, to throw away. **se prodiguer**, *v.r.* To make oneself cheap; not to spare oneself.

prodrome [prɔ'drɔ:m], *n.m.* Introduction, preface, preamble; (*Med.*) premonitory symptoms.

producteur [prɔdyk'tœ:r], *n.m.* (*fem.* **-trice**) Producer; (*Cine.*) producer.—*a.* Productive, producing.

*productibilité, *n.f.* Producibility. **productible**, *a.* Producible. **productif**, *a.* (*fem.* **-ive**) Productive.

production [prɔdyk'sjɔ̃], *n.f.* Act of producing, production; produce, product (of nature); yield, output, out-turn (of mine, mills); (*Law etc.*) exhibition (of deeds etc.). *Les moyens de production*, the means of production; *société de production*, (*Cine.*) film company.

productivité, *n.f.* Productivity; productiveness.

produire [prɔ'dɥi:r], *v.t. irr.* (*pres.p.* **produisant**, *p.p.* **produit** (1); *conjug. like* CONDUIRE) To produce, to bring forth; to bear, to yield, to bring in; to turn out; to show, to exhibit, to adduce; to introduce; to allege. *La guerre produit de grands maux*, war begets great evils; *produire dix mille avions par an*, to turn out ten thousand aeroplanes a year; *produire des témoins*, to bring forward witnesses; *produire des titres*, to show title-deeds; *produire un jeune homme dans le monde*, to introduce a young man into society. **se produire**, *v.r.* To put oneself forward; to occur, to happen.

produit (2), *n.m.* Produce, product, production; proceeds, profit, yield; exhibit. *Il vit du produit de sa terre*, he lives on the produce of his land; *produits agricoles*, agricultural produce; *produit chimique*, chemical product; *le produit de A par B*, the product of A into B; *le produit net*, the net profit, earnings.

proème or **proème** [prɔ'ɛ:m], *n.m.* Proem, prelude, introduction.

proéminence [prɔemi'nɑ̃:s], *n.f.* Prominence; protuberance. **proéminent**, *a.* (*fem.* **-ente**) Prominent, protuberant.

profanateur [prɔfana'tœ:r], *n.m.* (*fem.* **-trice**) Profaner.

profanation [prɔfana'sjɔ̃], *n.f.* Profanation.

profane [prɔ'fan], *a.* Profane; secular.—*n.* Profane person; outsider, black sheep; (*pl.*) the vulgar herd, the uninitiated.

profaner, *v.t.* To profane, to desecrate; to defile, to pollute; to misuse.

proférer [prɔfe're], *v.t. irr.* (*conjugated like* ACCÉLÉRER) To utter, to pronounce.

profès [prɔ'fɛ], *a.* (*fem.* **professe**) Professed. —*n.* Professed friar or nun.

professer [prɔfe'se], *v.t.* To profess; to exercise, to practise; to teach, to be a professor of, to lecture on. *Professer le plus grand respect pour quelqu'un*, to profess the greatest respect for someone; *professer une science*, to teach a science.—*v.i.* To be a professor, to lecture, to teach.

professeur, *n.m.* Professor, lecturer (at University); master (or mistress); teacher in secondary schools. *Professeur de droit*, professor of law; *une femme professeur*, a woman teacher.

profession, *n.f.* Profession, declaration; occupation, calling, business. *De quelle profession est-il?* what is his profession? *dévot de profession,* professed bigot; *il fait profession de bel esprit,* he sets up for a wit; *profession libérale,* liberal profession.

professionnel, *a.* (*fem.* **-elle**) Professional; vocational. *Enseignement professionnel,* vocational training.—*n.* (*spt.* etc.) Professional, (*fam.*) pro.

professoral [prɔfɛsɔ'ral], *a.* (*fem.* **-ale,** *pl.* **-aux**) Professorial.

professorat, *n.m.* Professorship, lectureship; mastership (of *lycée* or *collège*).

profil [prɔ'fil], *n.m.* Profile, side face, side-view; outline; (*Drawing*) section. *Un visage de profil,* a face in profile.

profilé, *a.* and *n.m.* Sectional iron. *Profilé en T,* T section, T iron.

profiler, *v.t.* To represent or show in profile. **se profiler,** *v.r.* To appear in profile, to stand out, to be outlined.

profit [prɔ'fi], *n.m.* Profit, gain, emolument; benefit, utility, use; percentage; (*pl.*) perquisites. *Au profit de,* for the benefit of, in aid of, on behalf of; *faire son profit de,* to profit by; *il ne m'en revient aucun profit,* I get nothing by it; *mettre tout à profit,* to turn everything to account; *profits et pertes,* profit and loss; *retirer du profit de,* to benefit by.

profitable, *a.* Profitable, advantageous. **profitablement,** *adv.* Profitably.

profiter, *v.i.* To profit, to gain, to benefit; to avail oneself; to improve, to get on, to thrive; (*impers.*) to be of service (*à*). *Faire profiter son argent,* to lay out one's money advantageously; *bien mal acquis ne profite jamais,* ill-gotten gains never serve; *profiter de l'occasion,* to take advantage of the opportunity; *profiter des bons avis,* to profit by good advice; *profiter en sagesse,* to grow in wisdom.

profiteur [prɔfi'tœ:r], *n.m.* (*fem.* **-euse**) (*pej.*) Profiteer.

profond [prɔ'fɔ̃], *a.* (*fem.* **profonde**) Deep; profound; low; vast; sound (of sleep etc.); downright, consummate; heavy (of sighs); dark (of night etc.). *Profonde révérence,* low bow, low curtsy; *puits profond,* deep well; *raisons profondes,* underlying causes; *science profonde,* profound learning; *un profond scélérat,* a consummate villain.—*n.m.* Depth, abyss. **profondément,** *adv.* Deeply, profoundly, greatly, utterly; soundly, fast. *Dormir profondément,* to sleep soundly; *saluer profondément,* to bow low.

profondeur, *n.f.* Depth; profundity; penetration; extent.

profus [prɔ'fy], *a.* (*fem.* **-use**) Profuse. **profusément,** *adv.* Profusely.

profusion, *n.f.* Profusion; thriftlessness. *À profusion,* in profusion; *donner avec profusion,* to give lavishly.

progéniture [prɔʒeni'ty:r], *n.f.* Progeny, offspring.

prognathe [prɔg'nat], *a.* Prognathous. **prognathisme,** *n.m.* Prognathism.

prognostique [prɔgnɔs'tik], *a.* (*Med.*) Prognostic.

programme [prɔ'gram], *n.m.* (*Theat.* etc.) Programme, bill; (*sch.*) curriculum, syllabus; design, scheme, plan. *Programme électoral,* political platform.

progrès [prɔ'grɛ], *n.m.* Progress; advancement, improvement, development. *Être en progrès,* to be progressing; *il a fait de grands progrès,* he has made great progress; *progrès d'une maladie,* progress of a disease.

progresser, *v.i.* To progress, to get on.

progressif, *a.* (*fem.* **-ive**) Progressive.

progression, *n.f.* Progression.

progressiste, *n.* Progressist.—*a.* Progressive.

progressivement, *adv.* Progressively.

progressivité, *n.f.* Progressiveness.

prohibé [prɔi'be], *a.* (*fem.* **-ée**) Prohibited.

prohiber, *v.t.* To forbid, to prohibit.

prohibitif, *a.* (*fem.* **-ive**) Prohibitive, exorbitant; prohibitory.

prohibition [prɔibi'sjɔ̃], *n.f.* Prohibition.

prohibitionnisme or **prohibitisme,** *n.m.* Prohibitionism. **prohibitionniste,** *n.m.* and *a.* Prohibitionist.

proie [prwa], *n.f.* Prey, prize, booty. *Être en proie à la douleur,* to be a prey to grief; *être en proie à ses valets,* to be robbed by one's own servants; *oiseaux de proie,* birds of prey.

projecteur, *n.m.* Searchlight; projector; floodlight. *Projecteur pour diapositives,* slide-projector.

projectif [prɔʒɛk'tif], *a.* (*fem.* **-ive**) Projective.

projectile, *n.m.* and *a.* Projectile, missile. (*Mil.*) *Projectile à ailettes,* winged shot; *projectile incendiaire,* incendiary shell.

projection, *n.f.* Projection. (*Cine.*) *Appareil de projection,* projector; *conférence avec projections,* lecture with lantern slides.

projectionniste, *n.* (*Cine.*) Projectionist.

projecture, *n.f.* Projecture, projection.

projet [prɔ'ʒɛ], *n.m.* Project, scheme, design, plan, idea; first sketch, rough draft. *Projet de loi,* draft bill. *Homme à projets,* schemer.

projeter [prɔʒ'te], *v.t. irr.* (*conjug. like* APPELER) To project; to delineate, to plan, to design; to contemplate, to intend. *La terre projette son ombre,* the earth projects its shadow. *Projeter d'aller à la campagne,* to contemplate going into the country.—*v.i.* To scheme, to form projects. **se projeter,** *v.r.* To project, to stand out.

projeteur, *n.m.* (*fem.* **-euse**) Projector, person full of projects, schemer.

prolapsus [prɔlap'sy:s], *n.m.* (*Path.*) Prolapsus.

prolégomènes [prɔlegɔ'mɛːn], *n.m. pl.* Prolegomena (prefatory matter).

prolepse [prɔ'lɛps], *n.f.* Prolepsis.

proleptique [prɔlɛp'tik], *a.* Proleptic.

prolétaire [prɔle'tɛːr], *n.m.* and *a.* Proletarian.

prolétariat, *n.m.* Proletariat.

prolétarien, *a.* (*fem.* **-ienne**) Proletarian.

prolétariser, *v.t.* To proletarianize.

prolifération [prɔlifera'sjɔ̃], *n.f.* Proliferation.

prolifère, *a.* Proliferous.

proliférer [prɔlife're], *v.t.,* *v.i. irr.* (*conjug. like* ACCÉLÉRER) To proliferate.

prolifique, *a.* Prolific.

prolixe [prɔ'liks], *a.* Prolix, diffuse, verbose. **prolixement,** *adv.* Verbosely, diffusely.

prolixité, *n.f.* Prolixity.

prologue [prɔ'lɔg], *n.m.* Prologue.

prolongation [prɔlɔ̃ga'sjɔ̃], *n.f.* Prolongation, lengthening, protraction. *Prolongation de congé,* extension of leave.

prolonge, *n.f.* (*Artill.*) *Binding-rope, lashing (of gun and limber); gun-carriage.

prolongement, *n.m.* Prolongation, extension; continuation.

prolonger [prɔlɔ̃'ʒe], *v.t.* To prolong, to lengthen, to protract; to draw out; (*Geom.*) to produce; (*Naut.*) to bring alongside; to sail along, to coast. *Prolonger le temps*, to spin out the time; *prolonger le terme d'un payement*, to extend the time for payment; *prolonger une trêve*, to prolong a truce; *un repas prolongé*, a long-drawn-out meal. **se prolonger**, *v.r.* To be protracted; to extend, to continue. *Les débats se sont prolongés fort avant dans la nuit*, the debate was continued far into the night.

promenade [prɔm'nad], *n.f.* Walk, stroll; walking; walk (place), promenade; drive, excursion, pleasure-trip. *Faire une promenade*, to go for a walk; *faire une promenade en voiture*, to go for a drive; *promenade à cheval*, ride (on horseback); *promenade à pied*, walk; *promenade en bateau*, row, sail; *promenade militaire*, route march.

promener, *v.t.* To take out walking or for exercise; to take out for an airing, for a drive, etc.; to turn (one's eyes, looks, etc.). *Promener sa vue sur une assemblée*, to survey an assembly; *promener ses doigts sur quelque chose*, to run one's fingers over something. **se promener**, *v.r.* To walk, to go for a walk, ramble, drive, row, sail, etc.; to promenade; to wander, to ramble. (*fam.*) *Envoyer quelqu'un (se) promener*, to send someone about his business; *se promener à cheval*, to go out riding; *se promener en voiture*, to drive out; *se promener sur l'eau*, to go for a row, to go for a sail.

promeneur, *n.m.* (*fem.* **-euse**) Walker; rider; person taking a drive; guide.

promenoir, *n.m.* Covered walk; promenade (in a concert-hall etc.).

promesse [prɔ'mes], *n.f.* Promise; promissory note, note of hand. *Tenir sa promesse*, to keep one's promise.

Prométhée [prɔme'te], *m.* Prometheus.

prometteur, *n.m.* (*fem.* **-euse**) Ready promiser.—*a.* Promising.

promettre [prɔ'mɛːtr], *v.t. irr.* (*conjug. like* METTRE) To promise; to forebode. *Il m'a promis de venir*, he promised me that he would come; *promettre monts et merveilles*, to promise miracles; *voilà un temps qui promet un orage*, it looks as if there will be a storm.—*v.i.* To be promising, to bid fair. *Ce jeune homme promet beaucoup*, he is a very promising young man. **se promettre**, *v.r.* To promise oneself; to purpose; to promise each other.

promis [prɔ'mi], *a.* (*fem.* **-ise**) Promised; intended, engaged. *Chose promise, chose due*, promises should be kept; *la Terre promise*, the Promised Land.—*n.* Fiancé or fiancée, betrothed.

promiscuité [prɔmiskɥi'te], *n.f.* Promiscuity.

promission [prɔmi'sjɔ̃], *n.f.* (*only used in*) *La Terre de Promission* [PROMIS].

promontoire [prɔmɔ̃'twaːr], *n.m.* Promontory, headland.

promoteur [prɔmɔ'tœːr], *n.m.* (*fem.* **-trice**) Promoter.

promotion, *n.f.* Promotion, preferment; (*collect.*) persons recently promoted. *Camarade de promotion*, class mate; *ils sont de la même promotion*, they are the same year.

promouvoir [prɔmu'vwaːr], *v.t. irr.* (*conjug.*

like MOUVOIR) To promote, to advance. *Être promu colonel*, to get one's colonelcy.

prompt [prɔ̃], *a.* (*fem.* **prompte**) Prompt, quick, active, ready; sudden, speedy, swift; hasty, irascible. *Avoir l'esprit prompt*, to be quick-witted; *avoir l'humeur prompte*, to be hasty-tempered; *il a la repartie prompte*, he is quick at repartee; *il est prompt à servir ses amis*, he is ever ready to serve his friends.

promptement, *adv.* Promptly.

promptitude, *n.f.* Promptitude, promptness, quickness; suddenness; hastiness.

promu [prɔ'my], *p.p.* (*fem.* **-ue**) [PROMOUVOIR].

promulgateur [prɔmylga'tœːr], *n.m.* (*fem.* **-trice**) Promulgator.

promulgation, *n.f.* Promulgation.

promulguer, *v.t.* To promulgate.

pronateur [prɔna'tœːr], *a.* and *n.m.* (*fem.* **-trice**) (*Anat.*) Pronator. **pronation**, *n.f.* Pronation.

prône [proːn], *n.m.* Sermon (at Mass); (*fig.*) homily, lecture, rebuke. **prôner**, *v.t.* To lecture, to sermonize; to boost, to extol; to preach to.—*v.i.* To sermonize, to remonstrate at length.

prôneur, *n.m.* (*fem.* **-euse**) Long-winded preacher, proser; enthusiast (for theory etc.).

pronom [prɔ'nɔ̃], *n.m.* (*Gram.*) Pronoun. **pronominal**, *a.* (*fem.* **-ale**, *pl.* **-aux**) Pronominal. **pronominalement**, *adv.* Pronominally.

prononçable [prɔnɔ̃'sabl], *a.* Pronounceable.

prononcé [prɔnɔ̃'se], *a.* (*fem.* **-ée**) Pronounced, decided, marked; (*Paint.* etc.) prominent; broad (of speech). *Caractère prononcé*, decided character; *goût prononcé*, pronounced taste; *les muscles en sont bien prononcés*, the muscles are very prominent.—*n.m.* Judgment delivered, sentence, terms of decision.

prononcer [prɔnɔ̃'se], *v.t.* To pronounce, to articulate, to utter, to say, to deliver, to declare; to find, to pass (a verdict etc.).—*v.i.* To declare one's sentiments, to decide with authority. **se prononcer**, *v.r.* To declare oneself, to speak out, to express one's opinion, to give a verdict; to be pronounced, to be marked. *Le 't' ne se prononce pas*, the 't' is not sounded.

prononciation, *n.f.* Pronunciation; utterance, delivery. *Prononciation d'un arrêt*, passing of a sentence. *Prononciation nette or distincte*, clear *or* distinct pronunciation; *vice de prononciation*, speech defect.

pronostic [prɔnɔs'tik], *n.m.* Prognostic, prognostication; (*Med.*) prognosis; weather forecast; (*turf*) tip, selection.

pronostiquer, *v.t.* To prognosticate, to forecast. **pronostiqueur**, *n.m.* (*fem.* **-euse**) (*fam.*) Prognosticator.

propagande [prɔpa'gɑ̃ːd], *n.f.* Propaganda.

propagandiste, *n.m.* Propagandist.

propagateur [prɔpaga'tœːr], *n.m.* (*fem.* **-trice**) Propagator, spreader (of news etc.).—*a.* Propagating, spreading.

propagation, *n.f.* Propagation, spread, spreading, diffusion. *La propagation des connaissances*, the diffusion of knowledge; *la propagation d'une maladie*, the spread of a disease; *la propagation d'une espèce*, the propagation of a species.

propager [prɔpa'ʒe], *v.t.* To propagate, to

spread abroad, to diffuse. 'se propager, *v.r.* To be propagated, to spread.

propédeutique [prɔpedø'tik], *n.f.* Propaedeutics, pre-university instruction or class.—*a.* Propaedeutical.

propension [prɔpā'sjɔ̃], *n.f.* Propensity, tendency, bent, disposition.

prophète [prɔ'fɛːt], *n.m.* Prophet, seer. *Nul n'est prophète en son pays*, no man is a prophet in his own country. **prophétesse,** *n.f.* Prophetess.

prophétie [prɔfe'si], *n.f.* Prophecy, prophesying.

prophétique, *a.* Prophetic, prophetical. **prophétiquement,** *adv.* Prophetically.

prophétiser, *v.t.* To prophesy, to foretell.

prophylactique [prɔfilak'tik], *a.* Prophylactic. **prophylaxie,** *n.f.* Prophylaxis. *Prophylaxie antivénérienne,* control of V.D.

propice [prɔ'pis], *a.* Propitious, favourable, kind. *Rendre propice,* to render propitious, to propitiate.

propitiateur, *n.m.* (*fem.* **-trice**) Propitiator.

propitiation, *n.f.* Propitiation. **propitiatoire,** *a.* Propitiatory.—*n.m.* Propitiatory, mercy-seat.

propitier [prɔpi'sje], *v.t.* (*conjugated like* PRIER) To propitiate.

propolis [prɔpɔ'liːs], *n.f.* Propolis, bee-glue.

Propontide [prɔpɔ̃'tid], *f.* Propontis (Sea of Marmora).

proportion [prɔpɔr'sjɔ̃], *n.f.* Proportion, ratio. *À proportion de* or *en proportion de,* in proportion to, in regard to; *à proportion, en proportion,* or *par proportion,* in proportion, proportionably; *à proportion que,* in proportion as; *en proportion directe,* in direct proportion; *en proportion inverse,* in inverse proportion; *hors de toute proportion,* out of all proportion; *toute proportion gardée,* every allowance being made.

proportionnalité, *n.f.* Proportionality.

proportionné, *a.* (*fem.* **-ée**) Proportioned, suited, harmonious.

proportionnel, *a.* (*fem.* **-elle**) Proportional. **proportionnellement,** *adv.* Proportionally, in proportion (to).

proportionner, *v.t.* To proportion, to adjust, to accommodate, to adapt. *Proportionner sa dépense à son revenu,* to cut one's coat according to one's cloth.

propos [prɔ'po], *n.m.* Talk, words; remark, observation; purpose, resolution, design; (*pl.*) idle remarks, tittle-tattle, gossip. *À propos,* apt, apropos, to the purpose, opportunely, pertinently, at the right moment; incidentally, by the way; *à propos de,* with respect to, in connexion with; *à propos de quoi?* for what reason? *à propos, j'ai oublié de vous dire l'autre jour,* while I think of it, I forgot to tell you the other day; *à quel propos?* what about? *à tout propos,* at every turn; *changeons de propos,* let us talk of something else; *de propos délibéré,* of set purpose; *hors de propos,* irrelevant, not to the purpose, ill-timed; *il est venu me quereller à propos de bottes,* he came to quarrel with me for no earthly reason; *il s'est fâché à propos de rien,* he got angry for nothing at all; *je me moque des propos,* what do I care what people say! *mal à propos,* ill-timed, inappropriate, inappropriately; *propos de table,* table-talk;

propos décousus, desultory talk; *venir fort à propos,* to come in the nick of time.

proposable [prɔpo'zabl], *a.* That may be proposed, appropriate.

proposant, *a.* (*fem.* **-ante**) Proposing.—*n.m.* (Protestant) student in divinity.

proposer [prɔpo'ze], *v.t.* To propose; to offer; to propound, to move; to designate, to set up. *Proposer quelqu'un pour exemple,* to set somebody up as a pattern; *proposer un candidat,* to put up a candidate; *proposer (un officier) pour l'avancement,* to recommend (an officer) for promotion; *proposer une question,* to propound a question; *proposer un sujet à traiter,* to propose a subject for writing upon. —*v.i.* To propose. *L'homme propose et Dieu dispose,* man proposes and God disposes. **se proposer,** *v.r.* To propose oneself, to come forward; to propose to oneself, to intend, to have in view. *Il se propose de vous écrire,* he is intending to write to you.

proposeur, *n.m.* (*fem.* **-euse**) Proposer, propounder.

proposition, *n.f.* Proposal; proposition; motion; (*Gram.*) clause. *Faire des propositions de paix,* to make peace proposals; *faire une proposition,* to put forward a motion; *pain de proposition,* shew bread; *proposition principale,* main clause.

propre [prɔpr], *a.* Own; very, same, selfsame, proper; peculiar; appropriate, fitted, suitable; good, right, correct; clean, neat, tidy. *Ce sont ses propres paroles,* they are his very words; *c'est son propre fils,* it is his own son; *en main propre,* into one's own hands; *il est toujours fort propre,* he is always very neat; *le mot propre,* the right word; *le sens propre,* the right meaning; *nom propre,* proper name, proper noun; *peu propre,* inappropriate; dirty or untidy; *sa propre main,* his own hand; *propre à rien,* good for nothing; *propre à tout, propre à rien,* Jack of all trades and master of none.—*n.m.* Characteristic, property; proper sense; (*Law*) real property; (*R.-C.Ch.*) special prayers or service. *C'est du propre!* what a dirty trick! *c'est le propre des oiseaux de voler,* it is the nature of birds to fly; *le propre et le figuré,* the literal and figurative sense; *mettre au propre,* to make a clean copy of; *n'avoir rien en propre,* to have no property of one's own; *posséder en propre,* to possess in one's own right; *le propre des Saints,* the Proper of Saints. **propre à rien,** *n. inv.* Good for nothing. **proprement,** *adv.* Properly, correctly, rightly; suitably, appropriately; cleanly, neatly, tidily; (*colloq.*) tolerably, passably. *À proprement parler,* properly speaking; *proprement dit,* properly so called; *s'habiller proprement,* to dress neatly.

propret, *a.* (*fem.* **-ette**) Spruce, neat, tidy, natty. **propreté,** *n.f.* Cleanliness; neatness, tidiness.

propréteur [propre'tœːr], *n.m.* (*Rom. Hist.*) Propraetor.

propriétaire [proprie'tɛːr], *n.* Owner, proprietor; landlord, landowner, householder. **propriété,** *n.f.* Property, ownership; estate, landed property; premises; quality, characteristic, particular virtue; (*Gram.*) propriety. *Alarmer la propriété,* to alarm the propertied classes; *doter quelqu'un d'une propriété,* to settle an estate upon someone; *propriété*

industrielle, patent rights; *propriété littéraire*, copyright.
proprio [prɔpri'o], *n.m.* (*pop.*) = PROPRIÉTAIRE.
propulser [prɔpyl'se], *v.t.* (*Naut., Av.*) To propel.
propulseur [prɔpyl'sœːr], *n.m.* Propeller. *Propulseur à hélice*, screw-propeller.—*a.m.* Propulsive, propelling, propellent.
propulsif, *a.* (*fem.* **-ive**) Propelling, propellent.
propulsion, *n.f.* Propulsion.
propylée [prɔpi'le], *n.m.* Propylaeum.
prorata [prora'ta], *n.m. inv.* Proportion, pro rata. *Au prorata de*, in proportion to.
prorogatif [prɔrɔga'tif], *a.* (*fem.* **-ive**) Prorogating, proroguing.
prorogation [prɔrɔga'sjɔ̃], *n.f.* Adjournment, prorogation (of Parliament etc.); (*Law*) prolongation.
proroger [prɔrɔ'ʒe], *v.t.* To prolong or protract the time (of); to adjourn, to prorogue (Parliament etc.).
prosaïque [prɔza'ik], *a.* Prosaic; commonplace, matter-of-fact, banal; prosy. **prosaïquement**, *adv.* Prosaically, unpoetically, in a commonplace way.
prosaïser, *v.t.* To make prosaic.—*v.i.* To write prosily. **prosaïsme**, *n.m.* Prosaism; commonplaceness, dullness. *Le prosaïsme de la vie*, the banality of life.
prosateur, *n.m.* Prose-writer.
proscénium [prɔse'njɔm], *n.m.* Proscenium.
proscripteur [prɔskrip'tœːr], *n.m.* Proscriber, banisher. **proscription**, *n.f.* Proscription.
proscrire [prɔs'kriːr], *v.t. irr.* (*pres.p.* **proscrivant**, *p.p.* **proscrit**; *conjugated like* ÉCRIRE) To proscribe, to outlaw; to banish; to taboo. **se proscrire**, *v.r.* To be proscribed, to proscribe each other.
proscrit, *n.m.* (*fem.* **-ite**) Proscribed person, outlaw; exile; outcast; refugee.—*a.* Proscribed, forbidden, tabooed.
prose [proːz], *n.f.* Prose. *Mettre en prose*, to turn into prose.
prosecteur [prɔsɛk'tœːr], *n.m.* (*Anat.*) Prosector, demonstrator in anatomy.
prosélyte [prɔze'lit], *n.* Proselyte. **prosélytisme**, *n.m.* Proselytism.
Proserpine [prɔzɛr'pin], *f.* Proserpina.
prosodie [prɔzɔ'di], *n.f.* Prosody. **prosodique**, *a.* Prosodical.
prosopopée [prɔzɔpɔ'pe], *n.f.* Prosopopoeia, personification.
prospecter [prɔspɛk'te], *v.t.* To prospect (for oil, minerals); to explore the commercial possibilities of (a region).
prospecteur, *n.m.* Prospector. **prospectif**, *a.* (*fem.* **-ive**) Prospective. **prospection**, *n.f.* Prospecting (of ground), canvassing (of opinion).
prospectus [prɔspɛk'tyːs], *n.m. inv.* Prospectus; handbill.
prospère [prɔs'pɛːr], *a.* Prosperous, thriving; propitious, favourable. **prospérer**, *v.i. irr.* (*conjugated like* ACCÉLÉRER) To prosper, to be prosperous, to thrive. **prospérité**, *n.f.* Prosperity, success, well-being.
prostate [prɔs'tat], *n.f.* (*Anat.*) Prostate (prostate gland). **prostatique**, *a.* Prostatic.
prosternation [prɔstɛrna'sjɔ̃], *n.f.*, or **prosternement**, *n.m.* Prostration, obeisance.
prosterner, *v.t.* To prostrate. **se proster-**

ner, *v.r.* To prostrate oneself, to fall prostrate, to bow low; (*fam.*) to kowtow.
prosthèse [prɔs'tɛːz], *n.f.* Prosthesis.
prostituée [prɔsti'tɥe], *n.f.* Prostitute, harlot, whore. **prostituer**, *v.t.* To prostitute. **se prostituer**, *v.r.* To prostitute oneself.
prostitution, *n.f.* Prostitution.
prostration [prɔstra'sjɔ̃], *n.f.* Prostration. *Prostration nerveuse*, nervous prostration.
prostré [prɔs'tre], *a.* (*fem.* **-ée**) Prostrated, exhausted.
protagoniste [prɔtagɔ'nist], *n.m.* Principal character, protagonist.
protase [prɔ'taːz], *n.f.* Protasis.
prote [prɔt], *n.m.* (*Print.*) Overseer; foreman.
protecteur [prɔtɛk'tœːr], *n.m.* (*fem.* **-trice**) Protector, protectress; patron, patroness, fosterer; (*Eng.*) guard (for machine tool). —*a.* Protective; patronizing, fostering. *Société protectrice des animaux*, society for the prevention of cruelty to animals; *un casque protecteur*, a crash helmet.
protection, *n.f.* Protection, shelter; support, interest, influence, favour, patronage. *Protection contre l'incendie*, fire prevention.
protectionnisme, *n.m.* Protectionism.
protectionniste, *n. and a.* Protectionist.
protectorat, *n.m.* Protectorate.
Protée [prɔ'te], *m.* Proteus.
protée [prɔ'te], *n.m.* (*Zool.*) Proteus.
protégé [prɔte'ʒe], *n.m.* (*fem.* **-ée**) Favourite, dependant, protégé.
protège-oreilles [prɔtɛʒɔ're:j], *n.m. inv.* (*Rugby Ftb.*) Scrum-cap, ear-protector.
protéger [prɔte'ʒe], *v.t. irr.* (*conjugated like* ACCÉLÉRER) To protect, to defend, to shield, to guard, to shelter, to screen; to patronize, to favour. *Protéger contre le mal*, to shield from harm.
protège-vue [prɔtɛʒ'vy], *n.m. inv.* Eye-shade.
protéine [prɔte'in], *n.f.* Protein. **protéique**, *a.* Proteinic.
protestant [prɔtɛs'tɑ̃], *n. and a.* (*fem.* **-ante**) Protestant.
protestantisme, *n.m.* Protestantism.
protestataire [prɔtɛsta'tɛːr], *n.* Protester, objector.
protestation [prɔtɛsta'sjɔ̃], *n.f.* Protestation, protest. *Faire insérer une protestation dans le procès-verbal*, to enter a protest; *protestation d'amitié*, profession of friendship.
protester, *v.t.* To protest, to affirm. *Je vous proteste sur mon honneur*, I swear to you on my honour; *protester une lettre de change*, to protest a bill of exchange.—*v.i.* To protest (*contre*); to make a protest or assurance (*de*). *Protester de sa bonne foi*, to protest one's good faith.
protêt, *n.m.* Protest. *Protêt faute de payement*, protest for nonpayment.
prothèse [prɔ'tɛːz], *n.f.* Artificial substitute (for an organ). *Prothèse dentaire*, set of false teeth; dental prosthesis. **prothétique**, *a.* Prosthetic. *Appareil prothétique*, artificial limb(s).
protocolaire [prɔtɔkɔ'lɛːr], *a.* Pertaining to State etiquette.
protocole [prɔtɔ'kɔl], *n.m.* Protocol; formulary; (*State*) etiquette.
protocoque [prɔtɔ'kɔk], *n.m.* Protococcus.
protogyne [prɔtɔ'ʒin], *n.m.* Protogine.
proton [prɔ'tɔ̃], *n.m.* Proton.

protonotaire [prɔtɔnɔ'tɛːr], n.m. Protonotary.

protoplasma or **protoplasme** [prɔtɔ'plasm], n.m. Protoplasm. **protoplaste**, n.m. Protoplast.

prototype, n.m. Prototype. **prototypique**, a. Prototypal, prototypic.

protoxyde, n.m. Protoxide.

protozoaire, n.m. Protozoan.

protracteur [prɔtrak'tœːr], n.m. and a. (fem. -trice) (Anat.) Protractor.

protubérance [prɔtybe'rãːs], n.f. Protuberance, knob. **protubérant**, a. (fem. -ante) Protuberant.

protuteur [prɔty'tœːr], n.m. (fem. -trice) Acting guardian.

*****prou** [pru], adv. Much; (only used in) Ni peu ni prou, not at all; peu ou prou, little or much.

proue [pru], n.f. Prow, stem, bows (of ship).

prouesse [pru'es], n.f. Prowess, valour; feat; (facet.) doughty deed.

prouvable [pru'vabl], a. Provable.

prouver [pru've], v.t. To prove; to make good, to substantiate; to evince, to show, to give proof of.

provenance [prɔv'nãːs], n.f. Origin, source, provenance; (pl.) produce, commodities.

provençal [prɔvã'sal], a. and n. (fem. -ale, pl. -aux) Provençal, of Provence.—n.m. Provençal language.

provende [prɔ'vãːd], n.f. Provisions, victuals; (Agric.) provender, fodder.

provenir [prɔv'niːr], v.i. irr. (conjugated like VENIR) To issue, to proceed, to spring (de), to originate; to come. Les avantages qui en proviennent, the advantages that arise therefrom.

proverbe [prɔ'verb], n.m. Proverb, saying. Devenir proverbe or passer en proverbe, to become a proverb.

proverbial, a. (fem. -iale, pl. -iaux) Proverbial.

providence [prɔvi'dãːs], n.f. Providence. **providentiel**, a. (fem. -ielle) Providential. **providentiellement**, adv. Providentially.

provignage [prɔvi'naːʒ] or **provignement**, n.m. Layering of vines. **provigner**, v.t. To layer (vines).—v.i. To multiply by means of provins. **provin**, n.m. Layer (of a vine); trench in which the layer is placed.

province [prɔ'vɛ̃ːs], n.f. Province, shire; country. En province, in the country, in the provinces; il a encore un air de province, he is still a bit of a country cousin; les gens de province, country people.

provincial, a. (fem. -iale, pl. -iaux) Provincial; countrified. Manières provinciales, country ways.—n.m. Provincial, country person; superior of a monastic fraternity. **provincialisme**, n.m. Word peculiar to a province, provincialism.

proviseur [prɔvi'zœːr], n.m. Headmaster (of a lycée).

provision [prɔvi'zjɔ̃], n.f. Provision, stock, store, supply; stock in hand; provisional maintenance; deposit; retaining fee (to lawyer); (Comm.) reserve funds; (Eccles. law) appointment (to a benefice), deed conferring title; (pl.) letters conferring an appointment. Chèque sans provision, a returned cheque, a worthless cheque, (fam.) a cheque which bounces; faire la provision d'une lettre de change, to provide for a bill of exchange;

faire provision de, to get in a supply of, to lay in a stock of; faire ses provisions, to provide oneself with necessaries; par provision, provisionally, in the meantime; provisions de bouche, victuals.

provisionnel, a. (fem. -elle) Provisional.

provisoire [prɔvi'zwaːr], a. Provisional, temporary. Gouvernement provisoire, provisional government.—n.m. Provisional nature (of something). **provisoirement**, adv. Provisionally, temporarily, in the meantime.

provisorat [prɔvizɔ'ra], n.m. Headmastership (of a lycée).

provocant [prɔvɔ'kã], a. (fem. -ante) Provoking, provocative; exciting, alluring.

provocateur, n.m. (fem. -trice) Provoker; aggressor.—a. Provoking, instigating, abetting, provocative. Agent provocateur, agent hired to instigate a riot etc.

provocation, n.f. Provocation; challenge (to a duel); inducement.

provoquer [prɔvɔ'ke], v.t. To provoke, to incite, to call forth, to elicit, to bring on; to instigate; to challenge. Provoquer au sommeil, to induce sleep; provoquer des applaudissements, to call forth applause; provoquer en duel, to challenge to a duel.

proxénète [prɔkse'net], n. Go-between, procurer, pander, pimp; procuress; white-slaver.

proximité [prɔksimi'te], n.f. Proximity, nearness; near relationship. À proximité de, in the neighbourhood of; il y a proximité de sang entre vous et moi, you and I are blood relations.

proyer [prwa'je], n.m. (Orn.) Corn-bunting.

(C) pruche [pry:ʃ], n.f. Hemlock.

prude [pryd], n.f. Prude.—a. Prudish.

prudemment [pryda'mã], adv. Prudently, discreetly, cautiously.

prudence, n.f. Carefulness, prudence.

prudent, a. (fem. -ente) Prudent, discreet; advisable.

pruderie [pry'dri], n.f. Prudery, prudishness.

*****prud'homie** [prydɔ'mi], n.f. Integrity, probity; experience of affairs.

prud'homme [pry'dɔm], n.m. *Skilful or able person (in an art or trade); upright, honest man; member of a board of arbitration between employers and workers. Conseil des prud'hommes, board of arbitration in industry.

prudhommesque [prydɔ'mesk], a. Like M. Prudhomme, sententious and empty, pompous and nonsensical.

pruine [prɥin], n.f. Bloom (on fruits).

pruiné, a. (fem. -ée) Covered with bloom, velvety.

prune [pryn], n.f. Plum. Pour des prunes, (colloq.) for nothing, in vain.

pruneau, n.m. (pl. -eaux) Prune, dried plum; French plum; (pop.) black eye; (Mil. slang) (rifle) bullet.

prunelaie, n.f. Plum-orchard.

prunelée, n.f. Plum-jam.

prunelle (1) [pry'nel], n.f. Sloe; sloe-gin.

prunelle (2) [pry'nel], n.f. Prunella (woollen stuff).

prunelle (3) [pry'nel], n.f. Pupil, apple (of the eye), eyeball. Jouer de la prunelle, to cast sheep's eyes, to ogle, to leer.

prunelle (4) [pry'nel], or **brunelle**, n.f. (Bot.) Prunella, self-heal.

prunellier [prynɛ'lje], *n.m.*, or *Prunier épineux*, Sloe-tree, blackthorn.

prunier, *n.m.* Plum-tree. *Prunier des oiseaux* [MERISIER] [*see also* DAMAS].

prurigineux [pryriʒi'nø], *a.* (*fem.* **-euse**) Pruriginous. **prurigo,** *n.m.* Prurigo. **prurit,** *n.m.* Pruritus, itching.

Prusse [prys], *f.* Prussia.

prussianiser [prysjani'ze] or **prussifier,** *v.t.* (*conjugated like* PRIER) To Prussianize.

prussiate [pry'sjat], *n.m.* Prussiate, cyanide.

prussien [pry'sjɛ̃], *a.* and *n.* (*fem.* **-ienne**) Prussian.

prussique [pry'sik], *a.* (*Chem.*) Prussic.

prytanée [prita'ne], *n.m.* (*Gr. Ant.*) Prytaneum; military school of La Flèche (for sons of soldiers).

***psallette** [psa'let], *n.f.* Precentorship; practice-room (for church choir).

psalmiste [psal'mist], *n.m.* Psalmist.

psalmodie, *n.f.* Psalmody, intoning; (*fig.*) sing-song. **psalmodier,** *v.t., v.i.* (*conjug. like* PRIER) To recite, to chant (as the psalms); to read, sing, or recite in a sing-song manner.

psaltérion, *n.m.* Psaltery.

psaume [pso:m], *n.m.* Psalm. **psautier,** *n.m.* Psalter, psalm-book; chaplet of fifty beads; veil (of some nuns); psalterium.

pseudocarpe [psødɔ'karp], *n.m.* (*Bot.*) Pseudocarp.

pseudonyme, *a.* Pseudonymous (writing etc. under an assumed name).—*n.m.* Pseudonym, nom-de-plume.

pseudopode, *n.m.* Pseudopodium.

psitt or **pstt** [pst], *int.* (to call) Here!

psittacisme [psita'sism], *n.m.* Parrot-cry.

psittacose, *n.f.* Psittacosis (disease).

psoque [psɔk], *n.m.* Book-louse; death-watch (beetle), also called *anobie vrillette.*

psore [psɔ:r] or **psora,** *n.f.* (*Path.*) Psora, itch. **psorique,** *a.* Psoric, itchy. **psoriasis,** *n.m.* Baker's itch.

psychanalyse [psikana'liz], *n.f.* Psycho-analysis. **psychanalyser,** *v.t.* To psycho-analyse. **psychanalyste,** *n.* Psycho-analyst. **psychanalytique,** *a.* Psychoanalytical.

psychasthénie [psikaste'ni], *n.f.* Neurasthenia.

Psyché [psi'ʃe], *f.* Psyche.

psyché [psi'ʃe], *n.f.* Psyche, soul; (*Ent.*) psyche; cheval-glass.

psychiatre [psi'kjɑtr], *n.* Psychiatrist. **psychiatrie,** *n.f.* Psychiatry. **psychiatrique,** *a.* Psychiatric.

psychique, *a.* Psychical.

psychographie [psikɔgra'fi], *n.f.* Psychography; 'spirit-writing'.

psychologie [psikɔlɔ'ʒi], *n.f.* Psychology. **psychologique,** *a.* Psychological. **psychologiquement,** *adv.* Psychologically. **psychologue,** *n.* Psychologist.

psychométrie, *n.f.* Psychometry. **psychopathe,** *n.* Psychopath. **psychopathie,** *n.f.* Psychopathy. **psycho-physiologie,** *n.f.* Psycho-physiology. **psychose,** *n.f.* Psychosis. **psycho-somatique,** *a.* Psycho-somatic. **psychotechnie** or **psychotechnique,** *n.f.* Psycho-technics. **psychothérapie,** *n.f.* Psycho-therapy.

psychromètre [psikrɔ'mɛtr], *n.m.* Psychro-meter.

ptarmique [ptar'mik], *n.f.* (*Bot.*), or *achillée sternutatoire,* sneezewort.

ptère [ptɛ:r], *n.f.* Ptere.

ptéris [pte'ris], *n.f.* (*Bot.*) or *ptéris aigle,* or *aigle impériale,* or *fougère-aigle* [FOUGÈRE].

ptérodactyle, *n.m.* Pterodactyl.

ptérosaurien, *n.m.* Pterosaur.

ptolémaïque [ptɔlema'ik], *a.* (*Astron.*) Ptolemaic (system).

Ptolémée [ptɔle'me], *m.* Ptolemy.

ptomaïne [ptɔma'in], *n.f.* Ptomaine.

ptôse [pto:z], *n.f.* Ptosis.

ptyaline [ptja'lin], *n.f.* Ptyalin. **ptyalisme,** *n.m.* Ptyalism.

pu (1) *p.p.* [PAÎTRE]; (2) *p.p.* [POUVOIR].

puant [pyɑ̃], *a.* (*fem.* **-ante**) Stinking; foul; disgusting. *Mensonge puant,* foul lie. **puanteur,** *n.f.* Stench, stink, offensive smell.

pubère [py'bɛ:r], *a.* Pubescent, puberal. **puberté,** *n.f.* Puberty. **pubescence,** *n.f.* (*Bot.*) Pubescence, down. **pubescent,** *a.* (*fem.* **-ente**) (*Bot.*) Pubescent, downy.

pubien, *a.* (*fem.* **-ienne**) (*Anat.*) Pubic.

pubis, *n.m.* Pubis.

publiable [py'bljabl], *a.* Publishable.

public [py'blik], *a.* (*fem.* **-ique**) Public; notorious. *Affaire d'intérêt public,* public matter; *fille publique,* prostitute; *la chose publique,* the common weal, the State; (*Law*) *le ministère public,* the public prosecutor; *maison publique,* brothel; *rendre public,* to make public.—*n.m.* Public. *Au grand public,* to the public at large; *en public,* publicly.

publicain, *n.m.* (*Rom. Ant.*) Publican; (*colloq.*) financier, stockbroker.

publication, *n.f.* Publication; publishing, proclamation.

publiciste, *n.m.* Publicist. **publicitaire,** *a.* Connected with publicity, advertising. **publicité,** *n.f.* Publicity; advertising.

publier [py'blje], *v.t.* (*conjugated like* PRIER) To publish, to make public, to proclaim; to celebrate, to blazon; to bring out, to issue.

publiquement, *adv.* In public.

puce [pys], *n.f.* Flea. *Puce d'eau* or *aquatique,* water beetle; *puce de mer,* sand-hopper; *puce pénétrante,* jigger [*see also* PULICAIRE]. *Avoir la puce à l'oreille,* to be uneasy or anxious; to smell a rat; (*fam.*) *marché aux puces,* flea-market; *mettre la puce à l'oreille de,* to make suspicious; *secouer les puces (de quelqu'un),* to give (somebody) a thrashing.—*a. inv.* Puce, puce-coloured.

***puceau** [py'so], *a.* (*fem.* **pucelle**) Virgin, chaste; (*fig.*) intact, untaken, unused.—*n.* Chaste person, virgin, maid. *La Pucelle d'Orléans,* the Maid of Orleans, Joan of Arc.

pucelage, *n.m.* Maidenhood, virginity.

pucelle [PUCEAU].

puceron [pys'rɔ̃], *n.m.* Plant-louse, aphis. *Puceron vert,* greenfly; *puceron lanigère,* woolly aphis. **puceronnière,** *n.f.* (*Hort.*) Dust-sprayer (for control of greenfly).

puche [pyʃ], *n.f.* Shrimping-net.

***pucher** [py'ʃe], *v.i.* To ladle out (soup, syrup). **puchet** or **pucheux,** *n.m.* Ladle.

puchette, *n.f.* Peatdrag.

pucier [py'sje], *n.m.* (*vulg.*) Bed; flea-bag.

pudding [POUDING].

puddlage [py'dla:ʒ], *n.m.* (*Metal.*) Puddling. **puddler,** *v.t.* To puddle. **puddleur,** *n.m.* Puddler.

pudeur [py'dœːr], *n.f.* Modesty, decency; bashfulness, shame; reserve. *Attentat à la pudeur,* indecent assault; *sans pudeur,* shameless, shamelessly.

pudibond, *a.* (*fem.* **-onde**) Bashful, modest, prudish. **pudibonderie,** *n.f.* Bashfulness; false modesty.

pudicité, *n.f.* Modesty, pudicity, chastity.

pudique, *a.* Chaste, modest, bashful. **pudiquement,** *adv.* Modestly.

puer [pɥe], *v.i.* (*fam.*) To stink, to have an offensive smell.—*v.t.* To smell of, to stink of, to reek of. *Il pue le vin,* he smells strongly of wine.

puériculteur [pɥerikyl'tœːr], *n.m.* (*fem.* **-trice**) Infant welfare specialist; child-nurse.

puériculture, *n.f.* Rearing of children. *Puériculture sociale,* child welfare.

puéril [pɥe'ril], *a.* (*fem.* **-ile**) Juvenile, childish, puerile. **puérilement,** *adv.* Puerilely, childishly. **puérilité,** *n.f.* Puerility, childishness.

puerpéral [pɥerpe'ral], *a.* (*fem.* **-ale,** *pl.* **-aux**) Puerperal (fever).

puffin [py'fɛ̃], *n.m.* (*Orn.*) Shearwater. *Puffin à bec grêle,* mutton bird; short-tailed shearwater; *puffin fuligineux,* sooty shearwater.

pugilat [pyʒi'la], *n.m.* Pugilism, boxing. **pugiliste,** *n.m.* Pugilist, boxer. **pugilistique,** *a.* Pugilistic.

pugnace [py'ɲas], *a.* Pugnacious. **pugnacité,** *n.f.* Pugnacity.

puîné [pɥi'ne], *a.* (*fem.* **-ée**) Younger (brother or sister).

puis [pɥi], *adv.* Then, afterwards, after that, next; besides. *Et puis,* and then, and besides; *et puis après?* (*colloq.*) so what?

puis, puisse [*see* POUVOIR, *v.*].

puisage [pɥi'zaːʒ], *n.m.* Drawing up; drawing water.

puisard [pɥi'zaːr], *n.m.* Cesspool; sump, water-sump.

puisatier, *n.m.* Well-sinker; shaft-sinker (in mining); sump-man.

puisement [PUISAGE].

puiser [pɥi'ze], *v.t.* To draw, to fetch up (a liquid); (*fig.*) to take, to borrow; to imbibe. *Puiser à la source,* to go to the fountain-head; *puiser de l'eau à la rivière,* to draw water out of the river.

puisque [pɥisk], *conj.* Since, as, seeing that.

puissamment [pɥisa'mã], *adv.* Powerfully, forcibly, potently; extremely, very. *Il est puissamment riche,* he is extremely rich.

puissance [pɥi'sãs], *n.f.* Power; force, cogency, efficacy; dominion, sway, empire; influence; influential man; virtue, quality, property. *Élever un nombre à la n-ième puissance,* to raise a number to the nth power; *femme en puissance de mari,* (*Law*) feme covert; *les grandes puissances,* the great Powers; *puissance au frein,* brake power; *puissance de feu,* (*Mil.*) fire power; *les puissances des ténèbres,* the powers of darkness; *moteur de grande puissance,* heavy-duty engine; *poste émetteur de haute puissance,* (*Rad.*) high-powered transmitting station; *puissance en chevaux,* horse-power; *puissance horaire,* output per hour; *puissance paternelle,* authority of father; *puissance réelle,* effective output of power; *soumettre à sa puissance,* to bring under one's dominion; *traiter de*

puissance à puissance, to treat on equal terms.

puissant, *a.* (*fem.* **-ante**) Powerful, potent, mighty; lusty, stout; strong, masterful. *Famille puissante,* influential family; *elle est toute-puissante auprès de lui,* she can get him to do anything; *le Tout-Puissant,* the Almighty.

puits [pɥi], *n.m. inv.* Well; pit, shaft. *C'est un puits de science,* he is a walking dictionary *or* encyclopaedia; *eau de puits,* well-water; *la vérité est au fond du puits,* truth lies at the bottom of a well; *puits artésien,* artesian well; *puits d'aérage,* air-shaft; *puits d'amour,* puff-pastry enclosing jam; *puits de mine,* pit; *puits de pétrole,* oil-well.

pulicaire [pyli'kɛːr], *n.f.,* or *Herbe aux puces,* Flea-bane.

pullulation [pylyla'sjɔ̃], *n.f.,* or **pullulement,** *n.m.* Rapid multiplication, pullulation, swarming. **pulluler,** *v.i.* To multiply, to pullulate, to swarm.

pulmonaire [pylmɔ'nɛːr], *a.* Pulmonary. *Phthisie pulmonaire,* consumption.—*n.f.* (*Bot.*) Lungwort. ***pulmonie,** *n.f.* Pulmonary disease. **pulmonique,** *a.* and *n.* Consumptive; person suffering from disease of the lung.

pulpation [pylpa'sjɔ̃], *n.f.* Reducing to pulp, pulping. **pulpe,** *n.f.* Pulp. **pulper,** *v.t.* To pulp. **pulpeux,** *a.* (*fem.* **-euse**) Pulpous, pulpy.

pulsatif [pylsa'tif], *a.* (*fem.* **-ive**) Pulsatile, pulsatory, throbbing.

pulsatille [pylsa'ti:j], *n.f.* Pasque-flower, pulsatilla.

pulsation [pylsa'sjɔ̃], *n.f.* Beating of the pulse, pulsation, throbbing. **pulsatoire,** *a.* Pulsatory. (*Elec.*) *Courant pulsatoire,* pulsating current.

pulsimètre, *n.m.* (*Med.*) Pulsimeter.

pulsomètre, *n.m.* (*Eng.*) Pulsometer.

pulvérin [pylve'rɛ̃], *n.m.* *Priming powder; *powder-horn; spray (from waterfalls).

pulvérisable, *a.* Pulverizable. **pulvérisateur,** *n.m.* Pulverizer, vaporizer. **pulvérisation,** *n.f.* Pulverization. **pulvériser,** *v.t.* To reduce to powder or to dust, to pulverize; to atomize (of liquid); (*fig.*) to annihilate; to reduce to atoms. (*spt.*) *Pulvériser un record,* to smash a record.

pulvérulent, *a.* (*fem.* **-ente**) Pulverulent, powdery.

puma [py'ma], *n.m.* Puma, cougar.

pumicin [pymi'sɛ̃], *n.m.* Palm-oil.

punais [py'nɛ], *a.* (*fem.* **punaise** (1)) Stinking. *Bois punais,* dogwood. **punaise** (2), *n.f.* Bug; drawing-pin, (*Am.*) thumbtack.

punch (1) [pɔ̃ːʃ], *n.m.* (*Box.*) Punch.

punch (2) [pɔ̃ʃ], *n.m.* Punch (beverage).

punique [py'nik], *a.* Punic.

punir [py'niːr], *v.t.* To punish, to chastise. *Il est puni de sa négligence,* he must pay for his carelessness; *punir de mort,* to punish with death.

punissable, *a.* Punishable. **punisseur,** *n.m.* (*fem.* **-euse**) Punisher; avenger.—*a.* Punishing, avenging.

punitif, *a.* (*fem.* **-ive**) Punitive.

punition, *n.f.* Punishment. *Par punition,* as a punishment; (*Mil.*) *carnet de punitions,* conduct book.

pupe [pyp], *n.f.* Pupa-case; chrysalis.
pupillaire [pypi'lɛ:r], *a.* Pupillary. **pupillarité**, *n.f.* Pupilarity, nonage, minority.
pupille (1) [py'pil], *n.* Ward, minor in charge of guardian. *Pupilles de la Nation*, war-orphans adopted by the State.
pupille (2) [py'pil], *n.f.* Pupil (of the eye).
pupiniser [pypini'ze], *v.t.* To load (a long-distance line) with inductances.
pupitre [py'pitr], *n.m.* Desk; reading-stand; music-stand; (*Mus.*) section (of orchestra). *Le pupitre des flûtes*, the flutes.
pur [py:r], *a.* (*fem.* -e) Pure, unmingled, un-alloyed; unadulterated; unsullied; un-blemished; guiltless, guileless, innocent, chaste; mere, sheer, downright; neat (of liquor). *C'est la pure vérité*, it is the plain unvarnished truth; *cheval pur sang*, thorough-bred; *du vin pur*, wine without water; *en pure perte*, to no purpose; *mathématiques pures*, pure mathematics; *obligation pure et simple*, unconditional obligation; *par pure bonté*, out of sheer kindness; *pure sottise*, downright nonsense; *un dessin pur*, a clean drawing; *une lumière pure*, a clear light.—*n.m.* (*colloq.*) Man of integrity.
pureau [py'ro], *n.m.* (*pl.* -eaux) Part un-covered, bare (of a slate, a tile).
purée [py're], *n.f.* Mash, purée, thick soup. *Purée de pommes de terre*, mashed potatoes; *purée de pois*, pea soup. *Être dans la purée*, (*pop.*) to be very hard up.
purement [pyr'mã], *adv.* Purely; merely. *Purement et simplement*, unconditionally; simply and solely.
pureté, *n.f.* Purity, guilelessness, innocence; chastity.
purgatif [pyrga'tif], *a.* (*fem.* -ive) Purgative, purging.—*n.m.* (*Med.*) Purgative. **purgation**, *n.f.* Purgation, purge.
purgatoire, *n.m.* Purgatory.
purge [pyrʒ], *n.f.* Purge; cleansing; disin-fection; blow-off (cock, pipe); (*pop.*) thrash-ing. *Purge légale*, (*Law*) paying off of a mortgage.
purgeoir, *n.m.* Purifying tank, filtering tank (of water-supply etc.).
purger, *v.t.* To purge; to cleanse, to purify; to clear, to rid, to deliver; to pay off (a mortgage). *Purger son bien de dettes*, to clear one's estate of mortgages; *purger un radiateur*, to let off steam (central heating); *purger une condamnation*, to serve a sentence. **purgeur**, *a.* Purifying, cleansing.—*n.m.* Purifier. *Purgeur de gaz*, gas purifier. **se purger**, *v.r.* To purge oneself; to clear oneself (of).
purifiant [pyri'fjã], *a.* (*fem.* -ante), **purificateur**, *a.* (*fem.* -trice) Purifying.—*n.* Purifier. **purification**, *n.f.* Purification. **purificatoire**, *n.m.* (*R.-C. Ch.*) Purificator.
purifier [pyri'fje], *v.t.* (*conjugated like* PRIER) To purify, to cleanse; to refine (metals etc.). *Purifier le langage*, to refine the language. **se purifier**, *v.r.* To purify oneself, to become refined.
purin [py'rɛ̃], *n.m.* Dung-water, liquid manure.
purisme [py'rism], *n.m.* Purism. **puriste**, *n.* Purist.
puritain, *n.m.* and *a.* (*fem.* -aine) Puritan. **puritainement**, *adv.* Puritanically. **puritanisme**, *n.m.* Puritanism.

purotin [pyrɔ'tɛ̃], *n.m.* (*pop.*) One who is always in the *purée*, always on the rocks.
purpurin [pyrpy'rɛ̃], *a.* (*fem.* **purpurine** (1)) Purplish. **purpurine** (2), *n.f.* Purpurin; madder purple.
pur-sang [pyr'sã], *n.m. inv.* A thoroughbred.
purulence [pyry'lã:s], *n.f.* Purulence. **purulent**, *a.* (*fem.* -ente) Purulent.
pus [py], *n.m.* Pus, matter.
pusillanime [pyzila'nim], *a.* Pusillanimous, faint-hearted. **pusillanimité**, *n.f.* Pusillani-mity.
pustule [pys'tyl], *n.f.* Pustule, pimple, blotch; (*Bot.*) blister, wart. **pustulé**, *a.* (*fem.* -ée), and **pustuleux**, *a.* (*fem.* -euse) Pustulous.
putain [py'tɛ̃], *n.f.* (*indec.*) Whore.
putasser, *v.i.* (*indec.*) To go whoring; to be a prostitute. **putasserie**, *n.f.* (*indec.*) Whoring.
putatif [pyta'tif], *a.* (*fem.* -ive) Putative, reputed, supposed. **putativement**, *adv.* Putatively, reputedly.
***pute** [PUTAIN].
putier [py'tje], *n.m.*, or *Bois puant*, or *cerisier à grappes, Cerasus padus*.
putois [py'twa], *n.m.* Polecat, fitchew. *Putois d'Amérique*, skunk. *Crier comme un putois*, (*fam.*) to yell one's head off.
putréfactif [pytrefak'tif], *a.* (*fem.* -ive) Putre-factive, putrefying. **putréfaction**, *n.f.* Putrefaction; putrescence. **putréfiable**, *a.* Liable to putrefy. **putréfier**, *v.t.* (*con-jugated like* PRIER) To putrefy. **se putréfier**, *v.r.* To putrefy. **putrescence**, *n.f.* Putres-cence. **putrescible**, *a.* Liable to putre-faction. **putride**, *a.* Putrid. **putridité**, *n.f.* Putridity.
puy [pɥi], *n.m.* Conical hill, tor (*esp.* in Auvergne).
pyélite [pje'lit], *n.f.* Pyelitis.
pygargue [pi'garg], *n.m.*, also called *huard, aigle des mers, orfraie*. Osprey, sea-eagle, sea-hawk, erne, white-tailed eagle.
pygmée [pig'me], *n.m.* Pygmy. **pygméen**, *a.* (*fem.* -éenne) Pygmaean.
pyjama [piʒa'ma], *n.m.* Pyjamas; (*Am.*) pajamas.
Pylade [pi'lad], *m.* Pylades.
pylône [pi'lo:n], *n.m.* Pylon; tower (on aero-drome, for conveying electric power etc.); mast, lattice-mast (of telegraph wires); (lofty) signal-post (of railway station).
pylore [pi'lɔ:r], *n.m.* (*Anat.*) Pylorus. **pylorique**, *a.* Pyloric.
pyorrhée [piɔ're], *n.f.* Pyorrhoea.
pyracanthe [pira'kã:t], *n.f.* Pyracanth, Christ's thorn.
pyrale [pi'ral], *n.f.* Meal-moth. *Pyrale des pommes*, codling moth [*see also* GALLÉRIE].
Pyrame [pi'ram], *m.* Pyramus.
pyramidal [pirami'dal], *a.* (*fem.* -ale, *pl.* -aux) Pyramidal. **pyramidalement**, *adv.* Pyra-midally. **pyramide**, *n.f.* Pyramid. **pyra-mider**, *v.i.* *To rise like a pyramid; to tower, to taper.
pyrénéen [pirene'ɛ̃], *a.* (*fem.* -éenne) Of or pertaining to the Pyrenees, Pyrenean.
Pyrénées [pire'ne], **les**, *f. pl.* The Pyrenees. *Les Basses Pyrénées*, the Lower Pyre-nees; *Les Hautes Pyrénées*, the Upper Pyrenees.
pyrèthre [pi'rɛ:tr], *n.m.* (*Bot.*) Pyrethrum, feverfew; pellitory of Spain.

pyrétique [pire'tik], *a.* Pyretic. **pyrétologie,** *n.f.* Pyretology. **pyrexie,** *n.f.* Pyrexia.

pyrite [pi'rit], *n.f.* Pyrites. **pyriteux,** *a.* (*fem.* **-euse**) Pyritic. **pyritifère,** *a.* Pyritiferous.

pyroélectrique [piroelɛk'trik], *a.* Pyro-electric. **pyrogallique,** *a.* Pyrogallic. **pyrogène** or **pyrogéné,** *a.* (*fem.* **-ée**) Pyrogenous.

pyrogravure, *n.f.* Poker-work.

pyrolâtrie, *n.f.* Pyrolatry.

pyroligneux [piroli'nø], *a.m.* Pyroligneous.

pyromanie [piroma'ni], *n.f.* Pyromania.

pyromètre, *n.m.* Pyrometer.

pyrophore, *n.m.* Pyrophorus.

pyroscope, *n.m.* Pyroscope.

pyrosis, *n.f.* Pyrosis, water-brash [*see also* AIGREUR].

pyrotechnicien [pirotɛkni'sjɛ̃], *n.m.* Pyrotechnist.

pyrotechnie, *n.f.* Pyrotechnics, pyrotechny. **pyrotechnique,** *a.* Pyrotechnical.

pyroxène [pirok'sɛːn], *n.m.* Pyroxene.

pyroxyle, *n.m.* Pyroxyle (smokeless powder).

pyrrhique [pi'rik], *a.* Pyrrhic.—*n.f.* Pyrrhic (dance).

Pyrrhon [pi'rɔ̃], *m.* Pyrrho.

pyrrhonien [piro'njɛ̃], *n.m.* (*fem.* **-ienne**) Pyrrhonist, Pyrrhonean.—*a.* Pyrrhonic, sceptical. **pyrrhonisme,** *n.m.* Pyrrho-nism, scepticism.

Pythagore [pita'gɔːr], *m.* Pythagoras.

pythagoricien [pitagɔri'sjɛ̃], *n.m.* and *a.* (*fem.* **-ienne**) Pythagorean. **pythagorique,** *a.* Pythagorean. **pythagorisme,** *n.m.* Pytha-gorism.

Pythie [pi'ti], *n.f.* Pythia (priestess of Apollo). **pythien,** *a.* (*fem.* **-ienne**), and **pythique,** *a.* Pythian. *Jeux pythiques,* Pythian games.

python [pi'tɔ̃], *n.m.* Python (snake).

pythonisse [pito'nis], *n.f.* Pythoness; prophe-tess, fortune-teller.

pyxide [pik'sid], *n.f.* (*Bot.*) Pyxidium, pyxis.

Q

Q, q [ky], *n.m.* The seventeenth letter of the alphabet; phonetically it has the same value as *k*.

qu' [QUE].

quadragénaire [kwadraʒe'nɛːr], *a.* Forty years of age.—*n.* Person forty years old.

quadragésimal, *a.* (*fem.* **-ale,** *pl.* **-aux**) Quadragesimal.

Quadragésime, *n.f.* Quadragesima (Sunday).

quadrangle [kwa'drɑ̃:gl], *n.m.* Quadrangle. **quadrangulaire,** *a.* Quadrangular, four-cornered. **quadrangulé,** *a.* (*fem.* **-ée**) (*Bot.*) Quadrangular.

quadrant [kwa'drɑ̃], *n.m.* Quadrant. **qua-drantal,** *a.* (*fem.* **-ale,** *pl.* **-aux**) Quadrantal.

quadrat (1) [kwa'dra], *a.* (*Astrol.*) *Quadrat aspect,* quartile aspect (of two stars).

quadrat (2) [CADRAT].

quadratique [kwadra'tik], *a.* Quadratic. **quadratrice,** *n.f.* (*Geom.*) Quadratrix.

quadrature, *n.f.* (*Astron., Geom.*) Quadrature. *Chercher la quadrature du cercle,* to try to square the circle, to attempt the impossible.

quadricapsulaire [kwadrikapsy'lɛːr], *a.* (*Bot.*) Quadricapsular.

quadridenté, *a.* (*fem.* **-ée**) (*Bot.*) Quadri-dentate.

quadriennal, *a.* (*fem.* **-ale,** *pl.* **-aux**) Four-yearly.

quadrifide, *a.* (*Bot.*) Quadrifid, four-cleft.

quadrifolié, *a.* (*fem.* **-ée**) Quadrifoliate.

quadrige [kwa'dri:ʒ], *n.m.* (*Ant.*) Quadriga.

quadrijumeaux, *a.m. pl.* (*Anat.*) *Tubercules quadrijumeaux,* four medullary tubercles.

quadrilatéral, *a.* (*fem.* **-ale,** *pl.* **-aux**) Quadri-lateral. **quadrilatère,** *n.m.* Quadrilateral.

quadrillage [kadri'ja:ʒ], *n.m.* Chequer-work, arrangement or pattern in squares; map grid.

quadrille (1) [ka'dri:j], *n.m.* or *f.* Troop of horse in a tournament, or of toreadors in a bullfight.

quadrille (2) [ka'dri:j], *n.m.* Quadrille (card game); quadrille (dance).

quadrille (3) [ka'dri:j], *n.m.* Check (in tapestry). **quadrillé,** *a.* (*fem.* **-ée**) Chequered (of cloth); ruled in squares (of paper). *Papier quadrillé,* squared paper.—*n.m.* Check-cloth.

quadriller, *v.t.* To divide into squares.

quadrillion [kwadri'ljɔ̃], *n.m.* (since 1948 = 1 followed by twenty-four ciphers), quadrillion, one million trillion(s); (*Am.*) septillion.

quadrilobé [kwadrilo'be], *a.* (*fem.* **-ée**) (*Bot.*) Quadrilobate.

quadrimoteur, *a.* and *n.m.* Four-engined (aircraft).

quadriparti, *a.* (*fem.* **quadripartie** or **quadri-partite**) (*Bot.*) Quadripartite.

quadrisyllabe, *n.m.* Quadrisyllable.

quadrisyllabique, *a.* Quadrisyllabic.

quadriréacteur, *n.m.* Four-engined jet plane.

quadrumane, *a.* Quadrumanous.—*n.m.* Quadrumane.

quadrupède, *a.* and *n.m.* Quadruped.

quadruple [kwa'drypl], *a.* Quadruple, four-fold. **quadruplé,** *n.* (*fem.* **-ée**) Quadruplet, (*fam.*) quad. **quadrupler,** *v.t., v.i.* To quadruple, to increase fourfold.

quai [ke], *n.m.* Quay, wharf, pier; embank-ment (along river); platform (railway). *Le train est à quai,* the train is in.

quaiage [QUAYAGE].

quaiche [kɛʃ], *n.f.* Ketch.

qualifiable [kali'fjabl], *a.* Qualifiable, charac-terized (as).

qualificateur, *n.m.* (*R.-C. Ch.*) Qualificator (theologian employed to deal with offences in ecclesiastical courts).

qualificatif, *a.* (*fem.* **-ive**) Qualifying.—*n.m.* (*Gram.*) Qualificative.

qualification, *n.f.* Title; designation, qualifi-cation.

qualifié, *a.* (*fem.* **-ée**) Qualified; (*Law*) indictable. *Ouvrier qualifié,* skilled workman.

qualifier [kali'fje], *v.t.* (*conjugated like* PRIER) To qualify; to style. *Qualifier du nom de,* to give the name of; *qualifier quelqu'un de fourbe,* to call someone a knave. **se qualifier,** *v.r.* To style oneself; to qualify (for).

qualitatif, *a.* (*fem.* **-ive**) Qualitative. **qualita-tivement,** *adv.* Qualitatively.

qualité, *n.f.* Quality; property; excellence, virtue; disposition, nature, talent; qualifica-tion; title, rank. *Avoir de la qualité,* to be of good quality; *en qualité de,* in the capacity of; *il n'a pas les qualités requises pour ce poste,* he is not qualified to fill that position.

quand [kɑ̃], *adv.* When, whenever, what time, what period; while, whilst. *Depuis quand?*

since when? how long is it since? *depuis quand est-il arrivé?* how long has he been here? *jusqu'à quand*, until when; *quand je vous le disais!* (*fam.*) what did I tell you! —*conj.* Though. *Quand même*, even though; all the same, nevertheless.

quant [kɑ̃], *adv.*, followed by *à* or *au*. *Quant à*, as for, with regard to; *quant à moi*, so far as I am concerned.

quant-à-soi, *n.m.* Reserve, dignity. *Se mettre sur son quant-à-soi*, to be stand-offish, to stand on one's dignity.

*quantes, *a.f.*, used only in pl. in the phrase, *Toutes et quantes fois que*, whenever, as often as.

quantième [kɑ̃'tjɛm], *n.m.* Which (day of the month etc.). *Quel est le quantième du mois?* what day of the month is it?

quantitatif [kɑ̃tita'tif], *a.* (*fem.* **-ive**) Quantitative. **quantitativement**, *adv.* Quantitatively.

quantité, *n.f.* Quantity; great deal or number, abundance, plenty; variety. *Quantité de gens l'ont dit*, a lot of people have said so.

quantum [kwɑ̃'tɔm], *n.m.* (*pl.* **quanta**) Quantum, amount, ratio, proportion; quorum.

quarantaine [karɑ̃'tɛn], *n.f.* About forty; age of forty; Lent (forty days); quarantine; (*Bot.*) stock. *Faire quarantaine*, to be in quarantine; *lever la quarantaine*, to admit to pratique; *mettre en quarantaine*, to send to Coventry; *purger sa quarantaine*, to clear one's quarantine.

quarante, *a.* and *n.m.* Forty. *Je m'en moque comme de l'an quarante*, I don't care two straws about it; *la semaine de quarante heures*, the forty-hour week; *les Quarante*, the French Academy.

quarantenier, *n.m.* (*Naut.*) Ratline stuff (or rope).

quarantième, *a.* and *n.* Fortieth.—*n.m.* Fortieth part (of something).

quarderonner [kardərɔ'ne], *v.t.* (*Arch.*) To round off (an angle) (by means of a *quart-de-rond*).

quart (1) [kaːr], *n.m.* Quarter, fourth part; point (of the compass); quart (measure), (*Mil.*) tin cup; (*Naut.*) watch. *Dans un petit quart d'heure*, in a few moments; *faire bon quart*, to keep a good look-out; *bon quart!* all's well! *aux trois quarts mort*, more than half-dead; *trois heures et quart*, a quarter past three; *trois heures moins le quart*, a quarter to three; *le premier quart*, the starboard-watch; *le quart d'heure de Rabelais* [HEURE]; *les trois quarts du temps*, mostly, most frequently; *officier de quart*, officer of the watch; *passer un mauvais quart d'heure*, to have a bad time; *quart de cercle*, quadrant; *quart de vent*, point of the compass; *un quart d'heure*, a quarter of an hour.

quart (2) [kaːr], *a.* (*fem.* **quarte** (1)) Fourth; quartan. *Fièvre quarte*, quartan ague.

quartaine, *a.f.* *Fièvre quartaine*, quartan ague.

quartanier [karta'nje], *n.m.* Wild boar four years old.

quartaut [kar'to], *n.m.* *Quarter-cask (of 72 pints); small cask.

quart-de-rond [kardə'rɔ̃], *n.m.* (*pl.* **quarts-de-rond**) Ovolo; quarter-hollow moulding; plane to make it.

quarte (2) [kart], *n.f.* (*Mus.*) Fourth; (*Fenc.* and *Piquet*) carte.

quarteron [kartə'rɔ̃], *n.m.* The fourth part of a pound, or of a hundred.—*n.* and *a.* (*fem.* **-onne**) Quadroon.

quartidi [kwarti'di], *n.m.* Fourth day of decade in the revolutionary calendar.

quartier [kar'tje], *n.m.* Quarter, fourth part; piece, part; (*Her.*) quartering; quarter (of year, town, moon, etc.), ward, district, neighbourhood; quarter's rent, income, pay, etc.; block (of stone); (*Mil.*) quarters, barracks; *Avoir quartier libre*, to be off duty; *cinéma de quartier*, local cinema; *demander quartier*, to beg for quarter; *il ne donne point de quartier à ses débiteurs*, he shows no mercy to his debtors; *les bas quartiers*, the seedy districts, lower parts; *les beaux quartiers*, the fashionable districts; *le quartier commerçant*, the business quarter; *mettre en quartiers*, to quarter, to tear to pieces; *on n'y fait quartier à personne*, they spare nobody there; *quartier de chevreuil*, haunch of venison; *quartier de lard fumé*, gammon of bacon; *quartier de soulier*, quarter of a shoe; *quartier général*, headquarters; *grand quartier général* or *G.Q.G.*, general headquarters *or* G.H.Q.

quartier-maître, *n.m.* (*pl.* **quartiers-maîtres**) (*Naut.*) Leading seaman. *Quartier-maître de 1ère classe*, petty officer.

quarto [kwar'to], *adv.* Fourthly, in the fourth place.

quartz [kwaːrts], *n.m.* Quartz. **quartzeux**, *a.* (*fem.* **-euse**) Quartzose.

quasi (1) [ka'si], *n.m.* Thick end of loin (of veal etc.), chump end.

quasi (2) [ka'zi], *adv.* Almost, as if, quasi.

quasi-contrat, *n.m.* (*pl.* **quasi-contrats**) Quasi contract, implied contract.

quasi-délit, *n.m.* (*pl.* **quasi-délits**) Injury caused involuntarily.

quasiment, *adv.* (*dial.*) Almost, nearly, as you might say, to all intents and purposes, as good as.

Quasimodo, *n.f.* Low Sunday. *Le lundi de Quasimodo*, Low Monday.

quassia [kwa'sja] or **quassier**, *n.m.* Quassia.

quater [kwa'teːr], *adv.* Fourthly.

quaternaire [kwatɛr'nɛːr], *a.* Quaternary.

quaterne, *n.m.* Quaternion, four winning numbers.

quaterné, *a.* (*fem.* **-ée**) (*Bot.*) Quaternate.

quatorze [ka'tɔrz], *a.* and *n.m.* Fourteen; fourteenth. **quatorzième**, *a.* and *n.* Fourteenth, fourteenth day.—*n.m.* Number fourteen, fourteenth. **quatorzièmement**, *adv.* Fourteenthly.

quatrain [ka'trɛ̃], *n.m.* Quatrain.

quatre ['katrə, katr], *a.* and *n.m. inv.* Four, fourth. *À droite par quatre, droite!* (*Mil.*) form fours, right! *être tiré à quatre épingles*, to be spick and span; *manger comme quatre*, to eat a lot; *marcher à quatre pattes*, to go on all fours; *monter l'escalier quatre à quatre*, to rush upstairs; *morceau de quatre mains*, piano duet; *quatre à quatre*, four steps at a time; *se mettre en quatre pour quelqu'un*, to go through fire for someone; *travailler comme quatre*, to work like a slave; *un de ces quatre matins*, some time soon, one of these fine days.

quatre-épices, *n.f. inv.* (*Bot.*) [*see* NIGELLE].

quatre-feuilles, *n.m. inv.* (*Her.*) Quatrefoil.
quatre-temps, *n.m. pl.* Ember-days.
quatre-vingtième, *a.* and *n.m.* Eightieth.
quatre-vingts, *a.* (takes no *s* when it precedes another number or when used as an ordinal) Eighty. *Ils étaient quatre-vingts*, there were eighty of them; *quatre-vingt-dix*, ninety; *quatre-vingt-dix-neuf*, ninety-nine; *quatre-vingt millions*, eighty millions; *quatre-vingt-un*, eighty-one.
quatrième, *a.* and *n.* Fourth.—*n.m.* Fourth floor; fourth story.—*n.f.* Third form (of upper school); (*Piquet*) quart. **quatrièmement**, *adv.* Fourthly.
quatrillion [QUADRILLION].
quatuor [kwaty'ɔr], *n.m.* (*Mus.*) Quartet.
quayage [kɛ'jaːʒ], *n.m.* Quayage, wharfage.
que (1) [kə, k], *pron. rel.* Whom, that; which; what? during which, on which. *Il ne sait que faire*, he does not know what to do; *l'homme que vous voyez*, the man whom you see; *que dites-vous?* what do you say? *que dit-on de nouveau?* what news have you? *qu'est-ce que c'est?* what is it?
que (2) [kə, k], *conj.* That; than that; as, if, whether; when; without; yet; lest; in order that; oh that, may; let; before; so; only, but. *Afin que*, in order that; *à peine eut-il achevé de parler qu'il expira*, he had hardly done speaking when he expired; *approchez, que je vous embrasse*, come near that I may kiss you; *attendez qu'il vienne*, wait till he comes; *c'est une passion dangereuse que le jeu*, gambling is a dangerous passion; *de sorte que*, so that; *du temps que les reines filaient*, in the good old days; *il croit que non*, he thinks not; *il me verrait périr qu'il n'en serait pas touché*, even if he were to see me perish he would not be in the least concerned; *il n'y a qu'une heure qu'il est parti*, he left but an hour ago; *il y a dix ans que je l'aime*, I have loved her these last ten years; *j'avoue que cela est surprenant*, I confess that this is very surprising; *je dis que oui*, I say yes; *je doute que cela soit ainsi*, I doubt whether it is so; *je gage que si*, I bet you it is so; *je ne suis pas si bête que de la croire*, I am not such a fool as to believe her; *n'approchez pas de ce chien, de peur qu'il ne vous morde*, do not go near that dog, or he may bite you; *plutôt que de le faire*, rather than do it; *qu'il parle*, let him speak; *s'il le souhaite, et que vous le vouliez*, if he desires it and you also wish it; *tout savant qu'il est*, il a bien peu de jugement, learned as he is he has very little judgment.—*adv.* How, how much, how many; why, wherefore? *Imbécile que je suis!* Idiot that I am! *que ne parlez-vous?* why do you not speak? *que n'est-il ici?* why is he not here? *que vous aimez à parler!* how fond you are of talking! *qu'elle est grande!* how tall she is!
quel [kɛl], *a.* (*fem.* **quelle**) What, which, what sort of. *À n'importe quelle heure du jour*, at any time of the day; *quel homme est-ce?* what sort of man is he? *quel qu'il soit*, whatever or whoever he be, whatever it is; *quelle heure est-il?* what time is it? *quelle que soit votre intention*, whatever your intention may be; *quelle taille!* what a figure! *tel quel*, just as it is.
quelconque [kɛl'kɔ̃:k], *a. indef.* Any; any whatsoever; no matter what or which;

mediocre. *D'une manière quelconque*, anyhow; *une raison quelconque*, any sort of reason. *Ce livre est très quelconque*, this book is pretty poor.
*quellement [kɛl'mã], *adv.* Only used in *tellement quellement*, after a fashion; so-so.
quelque ['kɛlkə, kɛlk], *adj.* Some, any; a few; whatever, whatsoever. *En quelque lieu qu'il soit*, wherever he is; *il y a quelques années*, some years ago; *j'ai quelques amis dans cette ville*, I have a few friends in this town; *quelque chose*, something; *quelque chose de bon*, something good; *quelque jour*, some day or other; *quelque part*, somewhere; *quelques centaines de livres*, a few hundred pounds; *quelques efforts que vous fassiez*, whatever efforts you make.—*adv.* However, howsoever; some, about. *Quelque cent francs*, about a hundred francs; *quelque peu*, somewhat; *quelque riches qu'ils soient*, however rich they may be.
quelquefois [kɛlk'fwa], *adv.* Sometimes.
quelqu'un, *pron. indef.* (*fem.* **quelqu'une**, *pl.* **quelques-uns, quelques-unes**) Someone, somebody; anyone, anybody. *C'est quelqu'un*, he is somebody; *quelques-uns de ces messieurs*, some of these gentlemen; *quelqu'un d'autre*, somebody else.
quémander [kemã'de], *v.i.* To beg, to go a-begging.—*v.t.* To beg for, to solicit. **quémanderie**, *n.f.* Begging, solicitation. **quémandeur**, *n.m.* (*fem.* **-euse**) Importunate beggar.
qu'en-dira-t-on [kãdira'tɔ̃], *n.m. inv.* Public talk, tittle-tattle. *Se moquer du qu'en-dira-t-on*, to ignore what people say.
quenelle [kə'nɛl], *n.f.* Quenelle, forcemeat or fish ball.
quenotte [kə'nɔt], *n.f.* (*colloq.*) Tooth (of young children).
quenouille [kə'nuːj], *n.f.* Distaff; bed-post; tree cut in the form of a distaff. *En quenouille*, like a distaff; *tomber en quenouille*, to fall to the female line. **quenouillette**, *n.f.* A small distaff. *Quenouillettes de la poupe*, (*Naut.*) stern-timbers.
quenouillon, *n.m.* Coil of tow.
quérable [ke'rabl], *a.* (*Law*) (said of a rent) which is paid only on application.
quercitron [kɛrsi'trɔ̃], *n.m.* Quercitron (oak).
querelle [kə'rɛl], *n.f.* Quarrel, quarrelling; row, brawl, wrangling, feud; cause of dispute or quarrel. *Chercher querelle à*, to pick a quarrel with; *faire une querelle à*, to quarrel with; *ne pas épouser* or *embrasser une querelle*, not to take up a quarrel for anyone; *querelle d'Allemand*, groundless quarrel.
quereller, *v.t.* To quarrel with; to scold. **se quereller**, *v.r.* To quarrel, to wrangle, to have words.
querelleur, *a.* (*fem.* **-euse**) Quarrelsome.—*n.* Quarreller, wrangler.
quérir [ke'riːr], *v.t.* To fetch. (Employed only in the infinitive with *aller, envoyer, venir.*) *Aller quérir*, to go and fetch; *envoyer quérir*, to send for.
qu'est-ce que [kɛs'kə], **qu'est-ce qui** [kɛs'ki], *inter. pron.* What? (*fam.*) who? *Qu'est-ce qu'il y a?* what's the matter?
questeur [kɥɛs'tœːr], *n.m.* Quaestor.
question [kɛs'tjɔ̃], *n.f.* Question, interrogation; query, point, issue; rack, torture. *Question préjudicielle*, demurrer. *Après cela*

il fut question de moi, then my affair came up; *c'est une question de temps*, it is a matter of time; *de quoi est-il question?* what's the matter? *il est question de faire cela*, that is contemplated, there is talk of doing that; *il n'en est pas question*, this is out of the question; *mettre à la question*, to put to the rack; *mettre en question*, to call in question; *poser une question à*, to put a question to; *résoudre une question*, to solve a question; *sortir de la question*, to wander from the point.

questionnaire, *n.m.* Questionnaire; book of questions.

questionner, *v.t.* To question, to interrogate.

questionneur, *n.m.* (*fem.* **-euse**) Questioner, one given to asking questions.—*a.* Inquisitive.

questure [kɥɛs'tyːr], *n.f.* Quaestorship; quaestors' office.

quête [kɛːt], *n.f.* Quest, search; collection; offertory; (*Hunt.*) beating about. *Se mettre en quête de*, to go in quest of.

quêter, *v.t.* To look for, to seek, to go in quest of, to gather.—*v.i.* To beg; to make a collection.

quêteur, *n.m.* (*fem.* **-euse**) Collector; mendicant (friar).

quetsche [kwɛtʃ], *n.f.* Alsatian plum.

queue (1) [kø] *n.f.* Tail; stalk; stem; end, extremity, fag-end; rear; (of documents) label; billiard-cue; handle; train (of robes etc.); queue, file, string (of persons, carriages, etc.); (*fig.*) balance, remainder (of an account etc.). *Faire fausse queue,* (*Billiards*) to miscue; *faire la queue,* to take one's place in the queue, to queue up; *finir en queue de poisson*, to fizzle out (of a long business); *il est à la queue,* he is at the bottom of the class; *la queue de l'armée,* the rear of the army; *piano à queue,* grand piano; *prendre en queue,* to attack at the rear; *queue écourtée,* bob-tail; *une histoire sans queue ni tête,* a confused, illogical story or explanation; *wagon de queue,* end-carriage.

queue-d'aronde, *n.f.* (*pl.* **queues-d'aronde**) Dovetail. *À queue d'aronde,* dovetailed.

queue-de-chat, *n.f.* (*pl.* **queues-de-chat**) Mare's tail (cloud).

queue-de-cheval, *n.f.* (*pl.* **queues-de-cheval**) Horse-tail, equisetum; pony-tail (of hair).

queue-de-cochon, *n.f.* (*pl.* **queues-de-cochon**) Auger-bit.

queue-de-lion, *n.f.* (*pl.* **queues-de-lion**) Motherwort.

queue-de-loup, *n.f.* [MÉLAMPYRE].

queue-de-morue, *n.f.* (*pl.* **queues-de-morue**) Flat brush (to varnish); (*fam.*) swallow-tail coat, called also **queue-de-pie.**

queue-de-rat, *n.f.* (*pl.* **queues-de-rat**) Rat-tail file; (birch-bark) snuff-box; small wax taper; (*Naut.*) pointed-up rope-end; (*Bot.*) [PRÊLE].

queue-de-renard, *n.f.* Fox-tail (grass).

queuter [kø'te], *v.i.* (*Billiards*) To push.

*****queux** (1) or **queue** (2) [kø], *n.f.* Hone, whetstone.

*****queux** (2) [kø], *n.m.* Only used in *maître queux*, head cook.

qui [ki], *pron. rel.* Who, that, whom, which; whoever, whomsoever, whatever; what, some. *À qui?* to whom? *à qui de droit*, to the person, authority concerned; *à qui est ce*

livre? whose book is this? *c'est à qui l'aura*, it is a question of who gets it first; *c'était à qui*, they vied with each other who; *de qui parle-t-il?* whom is he speaking of? *ils étaient dispersés qui çà, qui là*, they had dispersed some one way, some another; *je ne sais pas qui*, I don't know who; *je sais qui vous voulez dire*, I know whom you mean; *l'homme qui pense*, the man who thinks; *nommez qui vous voulez*, appoint whom you like; *qui d'entre vous oserait?* which of you would dare? *qui est-ce qui?* who? *qui est-ce que?* whom? *qui est là?* who's there? *qui pis est*, what is worse; *qui plus est*, what is more; *qui que ce soit* or *qui que ce puisse être*, whoever it may be; *qui s'excuse, s'accuse*, a guilty conscience needs no accuser.

quia [kɥi'a], *adv.* *Être à quia*, to be at a loss, to be nonplussed.

quiche [kiʃ], *n.f.* *Quiche lorraine*, egg and bacon flan.

Quichotte [ki'ʃɔt], **Don,** *m.* Don Quixote.

quiconque [ki'kɔ̃k], *pron. indef.* Whoever, whosoever; whomsoever, whichever.

quidam [ki'dam], *n.m.* (*Law*) Quidam, a certain person, someone (unknown).

quiétisme [kɥie'tism], *n.m.* Quietism (doctrine). **quiétiste,** *n.* and *a.* Quietist.

quiétude [kɥie'tyd], *n.f.* Quietude.

quignon [ki'ɲɔ̃], *n.m.* Hunch (large piece), hunk (of bread).

quillage [ki'jaːʒ], *n.m.* Keelage (dues).

quille (1) [kiːj], *n.f.* Keel.

quille (2) [kiːj], *n.f.* Skittle, ninepin; (*fam., pl.*) legs, pins. *Jeu de quilles*, game of skittles; *jouer des quilles*, (*pop.*) to run away; *prendre son sac et ses quilles*, to clear out, bag and baggage; *recevoir quelqu'un comme un chien dans un jeu de quilles*, to give someone a cool reception.

quiller, *v.i.* To throw for partners or for first play (at skittles).—*v.t.* To throw skittles or a stick between the legs of.

quillier [ki'je], *n.m.* Skittle-alley.

quillon [ki'jɔ̃], *n.m.* Cross-bar (of sword or bayonet); piling-pin (of Lebel rifle).

*****quinaud** [ki'no], *a.* (*fem.* **-aude**) Bashful, confused.

quincaille [kɛ̃'kaːj], *n.f.* Utensil of ironmongery or hardware. **quincaillerie,** *n.f.* Ironmongery, hardware. **quincaillier,** *n.m.* Ironmonger.

quinconce [kɛ̃'kɔ̃ːs], *n.m.* Quincunx. **quinconcial,** *a.* (*fem.* **-iale**, *pl.* **-iaux**) Quincuncial.

quine [kin], *n.m.* Two fives (at trictrac); five winning numbers (in a lottery). *Un quine à la loterie*, a big prize, advantage, etc.

quiné, *a.* (*fem.* **-ée**) (*Bot.*) Quinate.

quinine [ki'nin], *n.f.* Quinine. **quinique,** *a.* Quinic. **quinisme,** *n.m.* Quinism.

quinquagénaire [kɥɛ̃kwaʒe'neːr], *a.* Fifty years old.—*n.* Person of fifty.

Quinquagésime, *f.* Quinquagesima.

quinquennal, *a.* (*fem.* **-ale**, *pl.* **-aux**) Quinquennial. (*Polit. Econ.*) *Plan quinquennal*, five-year plan.

quinquennium, *n.m.* (*Phil.*) Five years' course of philosophy and theology; quinquennium.

quinquet [kɛ̃'kɛ], *n.m.* Argand lamp; (*fam.*) eye.

quinquina [kɛ̃ki'na], *n.m.* Peruvian bark.

quint [kɛ̃], *a.* and *n.* Fifth. *Charles-Quint,* Charles the Fifth. *Fièvre quinte,* quintan fever.

quintaine [kɛ̃'ten], *n.f.* Quintain.

quintal [kɛ̃'tal], *n.m.* (*pl.* **-aux**) Quintal, hundredweight; 100 kilogr.

quinte [kɛ̃:t], *n.f.* (*Mus.*) Fifth; (*Piquet*) quint; (*fig.*) freak, whim; (*Fenc.*) quinte; tenor violin. *Quinte de toux,* fit of coughing.

quintefeuille [kɛ̃t'fœ:j], *n.f.*, or *Potentille rampante,* Cinquefoil.

quintessence [kɛ̃te'sɑ̃:s], *n.f.* Quintessence; (*fig.*) pith, essential part. **quintessenciel,** *a.* (*fem.* **-ielle**) Quintessential.

quintette [kɛ̃'tet], *n.m.* Quintet.

quinteux [kɛ̃'tø], *a.* (*fem.* **-euse**) Whimsical, crotchety; making dead stops, jibbing (of a horse).

quintidi [kɛ̃ti'di], *n.m.* Fifth day of decade of first French republic.

quintillion [kɛ̃ti'ljɔ̃], *n.m.* Quintillion ((*U.K.*) 1 followed by 30 ciphers; (*Fr.*, *U.S.*) 1 followed by 18 ciphers).

quintuple [kɛ̃'typl], *a.* and *n.m.* Quintuple. **quintuplé,** *n.m.* Quintuplet. *Des quintuplés,* (*fam.*) quins. **quintupler,** *v.t.* To quintuple.

quinzaine [kɛ̃'zen], *n.f.* About fifteen; fortnight.

quinze [kɛ̃:z], *a.* and *n.m.* Fifteen; fifteenth. *D'aujourd'hui en quinze,* this day fortnight; *de lundi en quinze,* next Monday fortnight; *il y a eu hier quinze jours,* yesterday fortnight; *les Quinze-vingts,* hospital in Paris for blind men; *quinze à,* (*Ten.*) fifteen all.

quinzième, *a.* and *n.m.* Fifteenth. **quinzièmement,** *adv.* Fifteenthly.

quiproquo [kipro'ko], *n.m.* Mistake, blunder (taking a thing for something else), quid pro quo.

quittance [ki'tɑ̃:s], *n.f.* Receipt, discharge. *Donner quittance,* to give a receipt; (*fig.*) to hold quit; *quittance pour solde de compte,* receipt in full; *quittance valable,* valid receipt. **quittancer,** *v.t.* To receipt.

quitte [kit], *a.* Discharged (from debt); clear, free; rid at the risk of (*d*). *Il en fut quitte pour la peur,* he got off with a good fright; *je suis quitte d'un grand embarras,* I am rid of a deal of trouble; *je vous tiens quitte de votre parole,* I release you from your word; *jouer à quitte ou double,* to play double or quits; *nous resterons plus longtemps ici, quitte à sacrifier le reste du voyage,* we shall stay here longer, even at the price of sacrificing the remainder of the trip; *nous sommes quittes,* we're quits; *tenir quitte,* to release, to let off; *vous n'en serez pas quitte à si bon marché,* you will not get away with it so easily.

quitter [ki'te], *v.t.* To leave; to hold quit, to discharge; to resign, to abandon, to give up; to leave off, to lay aside, to desist from; to exempt; to depart (life). *Il a quitté le service,* he has left the service; *je vous quitte pour un instant,* I won't be a moment; *ne pas quitter des yeux,* not to take one's eyes off; *ne quittez pas!* (*Teleph.*) Hold the line! hold on! *quitter le monde,* to become a monk, nun; *quitter ses habits,* to take off one's clothes; *quitter une charge,* to give up a post; *qui quitte la partie la perd,* who leaves off the game, loses. **se quitter,** *v.r.* To part company, separate; to leave one another.

quitus [ki'tys], *n.m. inv.* Receipt in full, discharge.

qui va là? [kiva'la], *inter. phr.* Who goes there?

qui-vive [ki'vi:v], *n.m.* (Challenge of a sentry) Who goes there? *Être sur le qui-vive,* to be on the alert.

quoi [kwa], *pron. rel.* Which; what. *À propos de quoi?* on what occasion? with respect to what? *avoir de quoi,* to be comfortably off, to have the wherewithal; *c'est en quoi vous vous trompez,* that's where you are wrong; *dites-moi en quoi je puis vous servir,* what can I do for you?; *il n'y a pas de quoi,* don't mention it! *il n'y a pas de quoi rire,* it is no laughing matter; *le je ne sais quoi,* the indefinable something; *quoi de plus vrai?* what could be truer? *quoi que vous disiez,* whatever you may say; *quoi qu'il en soit,* be that as it may; *sans quoi,* otherwise.—*int.* What! *Quoi, vous avez fait cela?* what! have you done that?

quoique [kwakə, kwak], *conj.* Although, though. *Quoiqu'il soit pauvre,* though he is poor.

quolibet [kɔli'be], *n.m.* Gibe, jeer.

quorum [kɔ'rɔm], *n.m.* Quorum.

quote-part [kɔt'pa:r], *n.f.* (*pl.* **quotes-parts**) Quota, portion, share.

quotidien [kɔti'djɛ̃], *a.* (*fem.* **-ienne**) Daily, quotidian. *Notre pain quotidien,* our daily bread.—*n.m.* Daily (newspaper). **quotidiennement,** *adv.* Daily.

quotient [kɔ'sjɑ̃], *n.m.* Quotient. *Le quotient démographique,* (*Polit.*) quota of deputies by population.

quotité, *n.f.* (*Fin.*) Quota, share; amount, proportion.

R

R, r [e:r], *n.m.* The eighteenth letter of the alphabet.

rabâchage [rabɑ'ʃa:ʒ], *n.m.* Tiresome repetition; drivel.

rabâcher, *v.i., v.t.* To repeat (the same thing) over and over again. **rabâcherie,** *n.f.* Eternal repetition. **rabâcheur,** *n.m.* (*fem.* **-euse**) Eternal repeater, twaddler.

rabais [ra'be], *n.m. inv.* Abatement, reduction; reduction in price, discount, allowance; depreciation (of coinage); fall (of flood etc.). *Être au rabais,* to be at a discount or at a reduced price; *il les a pris au rabais,* he has taken them at the lowest price or by contract; *vendre au rabais,* to sell at a reduction; *vente au rabais,* selling off.

rabaissement, *n.m.* Lowering, depreciation, diminution in value; (*fig.*) humiliation.

rabaisser, *v.t.* To lower; to abate, to diminish, to lessen; to depreciate, to humble, to disparage, to undervalue. *Rabaisser les monnaies,* to depreciate the coinage. *Rabaisser l'orgueil de quelqu'un,* to humble someone's pride. *Rabaisser sa voix,* to lower one's voice.

raban [ra'bɑ̃], *n.m.* Rope-band, small rope; gasket; lashing (of hammock). *Raban de faîte d'une tente,* ridge rope of an awning.

rabane [ra'ban], *n.f.* Matting.

rabaner or **rabanter,** *v.t.* To fit (a sail) with rope-bands and ear-rings.

rabat [ra'ba], *n.m.* Clerical or academic band; beating (for game).

rabat-joie, *n.m. inv.* Damper, wet blanket, spoil-sport, kill-joy.

rabattage, *n.m.* Cutting down, diminution, abatement; beating (for game).

rabatteur, *n.m.* Beater; (hotel) tout.

rabattre [ra'batr], *v.t. irr. (conjugated like* ABATTRE*)* To beat down, to put, bring, pull, or cut down; to press down, to smooth down; to quell, to humble; to beat up (game); to abate, to diminish, to cut back (of trees). *Il n'en veut rien rabattre*, he won't come down a peg; *le vent rabat la fumée*, the wind blows the smoke down; *rabattre l'ennemi*, to head off the enemy; *rabattre l'orgueil de quelqu'un*, to lower someone's pride; *rabattre un coup*, to ward off a blow.—*v.i.* To come down, to reduce one's pretensions. **se rabattre**, *v.r.* To turn off, to change one's road; to come down, to lower one's pretensions; to have to be satisfied with; to change the conversation. *Le bataillon se rabattit sur le village*, the battalion fell back on the village.

rabattu [raba'ty], *a. (fem.* **-ue** (1)*) Col rabattu*, turn-down collar; *chapeau rabattu*, slouch hat.

rabattue (2), *n.f.* (*Naut.*) Drift rail.

rabbin [ra'bɛ̃], *n.m.* Rabbi. **rabbinage**, *n.m.* (*pej.*) Rabbinism. **rabbinique**, *a.* Rabbinical. **rabbinisme**, *n.m.* Rabbinism. **rabbiniste**, *n.* Rabbinist.

rabdomancie [rabdɔmɑ̃'si], *n.f.* Rhabdomancy.

rabelaisien [rablɛ'zjɛ̃], *a. (fem.* **-ienne***) Rabelaisian.

rabibocher [rabibɔ'ʃe], *v.t.* (*fam.*) = *raccommoder*.

rabiot, rabiau [ra'bjo], **rab(e)**, *n.m.* (*Mil. slang*) Supplementary portion (of meat, wine, brandy, etc.), which is shared out among soldiers after the normal distribution of food, wine, forage, etc.; surplus fraudulently set aside by an N.C.O. for personal profit; (*fig.*) overtime, extra work (in case of emergency); supplementary days of military service to make up for the same number of days 'lost' in the military prison.

rabioter, *v.i.* To make illicit profits; to scrounge.

rabioteur, *n.m.* Scrounger.

rabique [ra'bik], *a.* Rabid, rabic.

râble (1) [rɑ:bl], *n.m.* Back (of hare, rabbit, etc.); (*colloq.*) back (of a person); floor timber (of pontoon).

râble (2) [rɑ:bl], *n.m.* Fire-rake.

râblé [rɑ'ble], *a. (fem.* **-ée***) Thick-backed (of a hare, rabbit, etc.); broad-backed, strong-backed; (*fig.*) hardy, vigorous, strapping.

râblure [rɑ'bly:r], *n.f.* (*Naut.*) Rabbet, channel.

rabonnir [rabɔ'ni:r], *v.t., v.i.* To improve (wine).

rabot [ra'bo], *n.m.* Plane; beater (for plaster). *Rabot en caoutchouc*, squeegee. *Passer le rabot sur, passer au rabot*, to plane, to polish; (*fig.*) to give a final polish to. **rabotage** or **rabotement**, *n.m.* Planing. **raboter**, *v.t.* To plane, to smooth with a plane; (*fig.*) to polish; (*slang*) to pilfer, to filch. **raboteur**, *n.m.* Planer. **raboteuse** (1), *n.f.* Planing-machine.

raboteux, *a. (fem.* **-euse** (2)*) Knotty; rough,

rugged, uneven; (*fig.*) harsh, crabbed (of style). *Un chemin raboteux*, an uneven road.

rabougri [rabu'gri], *a. (fem.* **-ie***) Stunted, dwarfed.

rabougrir [rabu'gri:r], *v.t.* To stunt. **se rabougrir**, *v.r.* To grow stunted. **rabougrissement**, *n.m.* Stuntedness, scragginess.

rabouiller [rabu'ie], *v.t.* To stir up, to muddy (the water before fishing).

raboutir [rabu'ti:r] or **rabouter**, *v.t.* To join end to end, to join on.

rabrouer [rabru'e], *v.t.* To snub, to chide, to rebuke sharply. **rabroueur**, *n.m.* (*fem.* **-euse***) Snappish person, scold.

raca [ra'ka], *n.m.* Bibl. word used only in *crier raca (sur* or *à)*, to abuse.

racage [ra'ka:ʒ], *n.m.* (*Naut.*) Hoop or stay round a mast; parrel, truss.

racahout [raka'u], *n.m.* Raccahout.

racaille [ra'kɑ:j], *n.f.* Rabble, riffraff; rubbish, trash.

raccastillage [rakasti'ja:ʒ], *n.m.* (*Naut.*) Repair of the upper works of a ship. **raccastiller**, *v.t.* To repair the upper works of (a ship).

raccommodage [rakɔmɔ'da:ʒ], *n.m.* Mending, repairing; darning.

raccommodement [rakɔmɔd'mɑ̃], *n.m.* Reconciliation.

raccommoder [rakɔmɔ'de], *v.t.* To mend, to repair; to darn; to piece, to patch, to botch; to set right, to correct; to make amends for; to reconcile, to make friends again. *Faire raccommoder quelque chose*, to have something mended. *On les a raccommodés*, they have been reconciled. **se raccommoder**, *v.r.* To mend one's clothes; to be reconciled, to make it up again (of persons), *Le mari et la femme se sont raccommodés*, the husband and wife have made it up again. **raccommodeur**, *n.m.* (*fem.* **-euse***) Mender.

raccompagner [rakɔ̃pa'ɲe], *v.t.* To accompany back.

raccord [ra'kɔ:r], *n.m.* Joining, fitting, junction; linking-up; union (coupling-piece); accord.

raccordement, *n.m.* Joining, union, junction; levelling. *Voie de raccordement*, line of metals connecting two lines, loop line.

raccorder, *v.t.* To join, to unite, to connect. **se raccorder**, *v.r.* To fit together, to blend.

raccourci [rakur'si], *a. (fem.* **-ie***) Shortened, abridged; too short. *À bras raccourcis*, with might and main.—*n.m.* Abridgment, epitome; short cut; (*Paint.*) foreshortening. *En raccourci*, abridged, briefly; in miniature; *prendre un raccourci*, to take a short cut; *tête en raccourci*, foreshortened head.

raccourcir [rakur'si:r], *v.t.* To shorten, to make shorter, to curtail, to abridge; to foreshorten; (*slang*) to guillotine. *Raccourcir le pas*, (*Mil.*) to step short.—*v.i.* To shorten, to become shorter; to take a short cut. **se raccourcir**, *v.r.* To shorten, to grow shorter, to contract, to shrink.

raccourcissement, *n.m.* Shortening, abridgment, shrinking; foreshortening.

raccours, *n.m.* Amount of shrinking.

raccoutrage [raku'tra:ʒ] or **raccoutrement**, *n.m.* Mending (of clothes etc.). **raccoutrer**, *v.t.* To mend, to repair (garment).

raccoutumer (se) [rakuty'me], *v.r.* To reaccustom oneself, to get used to again.

raccroc [ra'kro], *n.m.* Chance, lucky stroke (*esp.* at billiards), fluke. *Faire le raccroc,* (*vulg.*) [RACCROCHER]; *par raccroc,* by chance, by a fluke.

raccrochage [rakrɔ'ʃaːʒ], *n.m.* Accosting, soliciting.

raccrocher [rakrɔ'ʃe], *v.t.* To hook on *or* up again, to hang up again; (*colloq.*) to recover, to get hold of again; (*vulg.*) to solicit (of prostitutes); to secure (by chance). *Raccrocher son argent,* to recover one's money. *Raccrochez ce tableau,* hang up this picture again.—*v.i.* To make flukes (at play); (*Teleph.*) to ring off. **se raccrocher,** *v.r.* To cling, to hook on to again; to retrieve one's losses; to grasp or snatch at. *Se raccrocher à une espérance,* to clutch at a straw.

raccrocheuse, *n.f.* (*vulg.*) Street-walker.

race [ras], *n.f.* Race; stock, breed, blood; family, line, ancestry; tribe, brood, generation. *Ce chien est de bonne race,* this dog is pure-bred; *cette fille chasse de race,* that girl is a flirt like her mother; *croiser les races,* to cross the breeds; *la race future,* future ages; *race de vipères,* generation of vipers; *un cheval de race,* a thoroughbred horse.

racé [ra'se], *a.* (*fem.* **-ée**) Thoroughbred.

racème [ra'sɛm], *n.m.* (*Bot.*) Raceme. **racémeux,** *a.* (*fem.* **-euse**) Racemose.

rachat [ra'ʃa], *n.m.* Repurchase, redemption. *Vendre avec faculté de rachat,* to sell with power of redemption.

rachetable, *a.* Redeemable.

racheter [raʃ'te], *v.t.* To buy back, to repurchase; to buy again, to purchase as a replacement; to redeem, to buy up; to ransom; to compensate, to make up for; to atone, to atone for. *Racheter les prisonniers,* to ransom the prisoners. *Racheter ses vices par ses vertus,* to atone for one's vices by one's virtues. *Racheter une rente,* to redeem an annuity; *racheter des valeurs,* to buy in securities. **se racheter,** *v.r.* To redeem oneself, to buy one's freedom; to be atoned, to be made up for.

rachidien [raʃi'djɛ̃], *a.* (*fem.* **-ienne**) (*Anat.*) Spinal, rachidian. **rachis,** *n.m.* Spinal or vertebral column, spine; (*Bot.*) stalk. **rachitique,** *a.* Rachitic, rickety.—*n.* Rachitic or rickety person. **rachitis** or **rachitisme,** *n.m.* Rachitis, rickets; (*Bot.*) blight, stunted development.

racial [ra'sjal], *a.* (*fem.* **-iale,** *pl.* **-iaux**) Racial.

racinage [rasi'naːʒ], *n.m.* Edible roots, rootcrops; walnut-dye; (*Bookb.*) dendroid pattern; marbling.

racinal [rasi'nal], *n.m.* (*pl.* **-aux**) Beam, sleeper.

racine [ra'sin], *n.f.* Root; (*fig.*) beginning, principle, origin. *Prendre racine,* to take root; *racine carrée,* (*Arith.*) square root; *racine cubique,* cube root.

raciner, *v.i.* To strike root (of cuttings etc.).—*v.t.* To dye with roots; (*Bookb.*) to make a dendriform pattern on; to marble.

racisme [ra'sism], *n.m.* Racialism; (*Am.*) racism. **raciste,** *a.* Racial.—*n.* Racialist, (*Am.*) racist.

raclage [ra'klaːʒ], *n.m.* Scraping, raking.

racle [raːkl], *n.f.* Scraper.

raclée [ra'kle], *n.f.* (*fam.*) Drubbing, thrashing, hiding.

racler [ra'kle], *v.t.* To scrape, to rake; to rasp. *Racler le boyau,* (*fam.*) to scrape the fiddle.

raclette, *n.f.* Scraper; (*Gard.*) small hoe; (*Print.*) doctor.

racleur, *n.m.* Scraper; (*fam.*) catgut-scraper, bad violinist.

racloir, *n.m.* Scraper, road-scraper.

racloire, *n.f.* Strike (for levelling a measure of grain).

raclure, *n.f.* Scrapings.

racolage [rakɔ'laːʒ], *n.m.* Impressing; recruiting, enlisting; soliciting (of prostitutes).

racoler, *v.t.* To entice men to enlist, to tout; to enlist; to pick up (of prostitutes).

racoleur, *n.m.* Tout; *recruiting sergeant.

racoleuse [RACCROCHEUSE].

racontable [rakɔ̃'tabl], *a.* Relatable.

racontar, *n.m.* Gossip, tittle-tattle.

raconter [rakɔ̃'te], *v.t.* To relate, to tell, to narrate, to recount. *Raconter par le menu,* to relate in detail.—*v.i.* To tell stories.

raconteur, *n.m.* (*fem.* **-euse**) Story-teller, narrator, raconteur.

racornir [rakɔr'niːr], *v.t.* To make as hard as horn; to harden; to dry up, to shrivel up. **se racornir,** *v.r.* To grow hard; to shrivel up; to grow callous.

racornissement, *n.m.* Hardening.

racquit [ra'ki], *n.m.* Winning back.

racquitter, *v.t.* To indemnify, to recoup. **se racquitter,** *v.r.* To retrieve one's losses, to recoup oneself.

radar [ra'dar], *n.m.* (*abbr. of* radio-detecting and ranging, *repérage et télémétrie par radio*) Radar. **radariste,** *n.* Radar operator.

rade [rad], *n.f.* (*Naut.*) Roads, roadstead. *Grande rade,* outer roads; *petite rade,* inner roads; *rade foraine,* open roadstead; *vaisseau en rade,* roadster. (*fam.*) *Laisser en rade,* to abandon.

radeau [ra'do], *n.m.* (*pl.* **-eaux**) Raft.

rader (1) [ra'de], *v.t.* (*Naut.*) To anchor in a roadstead.

rader (2) [ra'de], *v.t.* To strike (a measure).

radiaire [ra'djɛːr], *a. and n.m.* Radiate.

radial, *a.* (*fem.* **-iale,** *pl.* **-iaux**) Radial.

radiance [ra'djɑ̃ːs], *n.f.* Radiance, lustre.

radiant, *a.* (*fem.* **-iante**) Radiant.—*n.m.* (*Astron.*) Radiant point; radian.

radiateur, *a.* (*fem.* **-trice**) Radiating.—*n.m.* Radiator.

radiation, *n.f.* Radiation, irradiation; obliteration, erasure, striking out. *Radiation atomique,* atomic radiation.

radical [radi'kal], *a.* (*fem.* **-ale,** *pl.* **-aux**) Radical; complete.—*n.m.* Radical; root. **radicalement,** *adv.* Radically. **radicalisme,** *n.m.* Radicalism.

radicant [radi'kɑ̃], *a.* (*fem.* **-ante**) Radicant, radicating. **radication,** *n.f.* Radication. **radicelle,** *n.f.* Radicle. **radicivore,** *a.* Radicivorous, root-eating. **radiculaire,** *a.* Radicular. **radicule,** *n.f.* Radicle.

radié [ra'dje], *a.* (*fem.* **-ée**) (*Bot. etc.*) Radiant, radiate, stellate; struck off.

radier (1) [ra'dje], *n.m.* Revetment protecting masonry against action of water; floor or apron (of docks, locks, basins, etc.); invert (of tunnel).

radier (2) [ra'dje], *v.t.* To strike out, to erase. (*Mil.*) *Radier des contrôles,* to strike off the rolls.—*v.i.* To radiate, to beam (with satisfaction).

radiesthésie [radjeste′zi], *n.f.* Radio-electric detection; dowsing. **radiesthésiste,** *n.* Dowser, water-diviner.

radieux [ra′djø], *a.* (*fem.* **-ieuse**) Radiant, beaming, shining.

radin [ra′dɛ̃], *a.* (*pop.*) Mean, stingy.

radiner [radi′ne], *v.i.* (*Mil. slang*) = RAPPLIQUER.

radio (1) [ra′djo], *n.f.* *abbr.* of *radiodiffusion,* broadcasting, radio. *À la radio,* on the radio; (*appareil de*) *radio,* wireless set; *écouter la radio,* to listen to the wireless, to listen in.

radio (2) [ra′djo], *n.f.* *abbr.* of *radiographie,* radiography. *Passer à la radio,* to X-ray; *passer une radio,* to be X-rayed.

radio (3) [ra′djo], *n.m. abbr.* of *radiotélégramme* and *radiotélégraphiste.* Wireless message; wireless-operator.

radio-actif, *a.* (*fem.* **-ive**) Radio-active.

radio-activité, *n.f.* Radio-activity.

radio-conducteur, *n.m.* Coherer.

radio-diagnostic, *n.m.* X-ray diagnosis.

radiodiffuser, *v.t.* To broadcast. **radiodiffusion,** *n.f.* Broadcasting.

radiogramme, *n.m.* Radiogram, aerogram; X-ray.

radiographie, *n.f.* Radiography. **radiographier,** *v.t.* To X-ray.

radioguidage, *n.m.* Wireless control. **radioguidé,** *a.* (*fem.* **-ée**) Wireless-controlled.

radiolaire, *a.* and *n.m.* Radiolarian.

radiolé [RADIÉ].

radiolite, *n.m.* Radiolite. **radiologie,** *n.f.* Radiology. **radiologue,** *n.* Radiologist.

radiomètre, *n.m.* Radiometer.

radiophare, *n.m.* Wireless beacon.

radiophone, *n.m.* Radiophone.

radiophonie, *n.f.* Wireless telephony; broadcasting.

radio-reportage, *n.m.* Broadcast account. **radio-reporter,** *n.m.* Commentator.

radioscopie, *n.f.* Radioscopy.

radio-télégramme, *n.m.* Radio-telegram.

radio-téléphonie, *n.f.* Wireless telephony.

radio-thérapie, *n.f.* X-ray treatment, radiotherapy.

radis [ra′di], *n.m.* Radish. (*pop.*) *N'avoir plus un radis,* to be stony-broke.

radium [ra′djɔm], *n.m.* Radium.

radius [ra′djy:s], *n.m. inv.* (*Anat.*) Radius.

radoire [ra′dwa:r], *n.f.* Strike (for levelling measures of corn).

radotage [radɔ′ta:ʒ], *n.m.* Nonsense, drivel; dotage. **radoter,** *v.i.* To talk idly, to talk drivel; to dote. **radoterie,** *n.f.* (*colloq.*) Drivel, rot, twaddle. **radoteur,** *n.m.* (*fem.* **-euse**) Driveller, dotard.

radoub [ra′du], *n.m.* Refitting of a ship, graving. *Bassin* or *forme de radoub,* gravingdock; *en radoub,* undergoing repairs. **radoubage,** *n.m.* Repairing (of hull); regeneration (of gun-powder). **radouber,** *v.t.* To refit, to repair (ships); to re-work (damp) powder. **radoubeur,** *n.m.* Shiprepairer; caulker.

radoucir [radu′si:r], *v.t.* To soften, to make milder; to mitigate, to allay; to appease, to pacify. **se radoucir,** *v.r.* To grow milder; to soften, to become soft; to be appeased, to

relent, to relax, to subside. *Le temps se radoucit,* it is getting milder.

radoucissement, *n.m.* Softening, getting milder (of the weather); mitigation, appeasement.

rafale [ra′fal], *n.f.* Squall; strong gust of wind; (*Mil.*) burst of shots; hail (of bullets).

rafalé, *a.* (*fem.* **-ée**) Caught in a squall; (*fig.*) storm-beaten.

raffermir [rafer′mi:r], *v.t.* To make firm or firmer; to confirm, to secure, to fortify, to strengthen. *Cet événement raffermit son autorité,* that event strengthened his authority; *raffermir le courage de quelqu'un,* to fortify someone's courage. **se raffermir,** *v.r.* To grow stronger, to gather strength; to be established, to become confirmed; to improve in strength or health. *Sa santé se raffermit,* his health is improving. *Ces actions se raffermissent,* these shares are hardening.

raffermissement, *n.m.* Hardening; fastening, securing; strengthening; confirmation.

raffinade [rafi′nad], *n.f.* Best refined sugar. **raffinage,** *n.m.* Refining. **raffiné,** *a.* (*fem.* **-ée**) Refined, delicate; subtle, clever; polished.—*n.* Exquisite, sophisticated person.

raffinement, [rafin′mã], *n.m.* Refinement, affected nicety or subtlety, affectation. *Les raffinements du luxe,* the refinements of luxury.

raffiner, *v.t.* To refine.—*v.i.* To be oversubtle, to split hairs. *Raffiner sur le point d'honneur,* to be over-nice upon the point of honour. **se raffiner,** *v.r.* To become refined.

raffinerie, *n.f.* Refinery; sugar-refinery; refining. **raffineur,** *n.m.* (*fem.* **-euse**) Refiner; sugar-refiner.

raffoler [rafɔ′le], *v.i.* To dote, to be passionately fond (*de*). *Il raffole de cette femme,* he is infatuated with that woman; *raffoler du théâtre,* to be mad on the theatre.

raffut [ra′fy], *n.m.* (*pop.*) Noise, row, shindy. *Faire un raffut du diable,* to kick up the devil of a row.

raffûtage [rafy′ta:ʒ], *n.m.* Sharpening. **raffûter,** *v.t.* To (re)sharpen, reset.

rafiot or **rafiau** [ra′fjo], *n.m.* Skiff.

rafistolage [rafisto′la:ʒ], *n.m.* (*colloq.*) Patching up, mending. **rafistoler,** *v.t.* To mend, to patch up, to do up (clothes etc.).

rafle (1) [rɑ:fl], *n.f.* Grape-stalk; head of maize stripped of all its fruit.

rafle (2) [rɑ:fl], *n.f.* (*Dice*) Pair-royal; clean sweep (by thieves); raid, round-up in the streets by police. *Faire rafle,* (*colloq.*) to sweep off the stakes, to make a clean sweep.

rafler, [rɑ′fle] *v.t.* To sweep off, to carry off; to round up (of police).

rafraîchir [rafre′ʃi:r], *v.t.* To cool; to refresh, to restore, to repair; to renew, to freshen, to renovate, to rub up; to crop, to cut the ends of, to trim. *Rafraîchir du vin,* to cool wine; *rafraîchir sa mémoire,* to refresh one's memory; *rafraîchir les cheveux,* to clip the hair; *rafraîchir un tableau,* to freshen up a picture.—*v.i.* To cool; to be refreshed; to freshen. **se rafraîchir,** *v.r.* To cool, to grow cool; to take refreshment, to refresh oneself; to be refreshed, to recruit one's strength, to rest. *Venez vous rafraîchir,* come and take some refreshment.

rafraîchissant, *a.* (*fem.* **-ante**) Cooling, refreshing; laxative.—*n.m.* Cooling medicine.

rafraîchissement, *n.m.* Cooling; cooling effect; (*pl.*) refreshments, (*Naut.*) provisions, supplies.

rafraîchisseur or **rafraîchissoir,** *n.m.* Refrigerator; wine-cooler.

ragaillardir [ragajar′diːr], *v.t.* To enliven, to cheer up, to buck up.

rage [raːʒ], *n.f.* Rabies; hydrophobia, canine madness; violent pain; rage, fury; passion; mania. *Faire rage,* to cause great disorder or havoc; to be all the rage. *Il a la rage du jeu,* he has a passion for gambling. *Rage de dents,* violent toothache. **rageant,** *a.* (*fem.* **-eante**) (*fam.*) Enraging. **rager,** *v.i.* (*colloq.*) To be in a passion; to be angry, to fume.

rageur, *n.m.* (*fem.* **-euse**) Ill-tempered person, spitfire.—*a.* Ill-tempered. *D′un ton rageur,* in an angry tone. **rageusement,** *adv.* Angrily, passionately.

raglan [ra′glɑ̃], *n.m.* Raglan (overcoat).

ragondin [ragɔ̃′dɛ̃], *n.m.* Nutria (fur).

ragot [ra′go], *a.* (*fem.* **-ote**) Thick and short, thick-set.—*n.m.* Wild boar of two years old; little horse; (*fig.*) malicious gossip, tittle-tattle. **ragoter,** *v.i.* (*fam.*) To gossip.

ragoût [ra′gu], *n.m.* Ragout; stew; (*fig.*) relish, seasoning and spice. *En ragoût,* stewed; *ragoût de mouton,* Irish stew.

ragoûtant, *a.* (*fem.* **-ante**) Relishing, savoury, (*fig.*) inviting, tempting. *Ce mets-là n′est guère ragoûtant,* that dish is not very tempting.

ragoûter, *v.t.* To restore the appetite of; to stimulate, to stir up.

ragrafer [ragra′fe], *v.t.* To reclasp, to hook again.

ragréage [ragre′aːʒ], *n.m.* (*Naut.*) Refitting.

ragréer, *v.t.* To finish, to give the finishing touch to; to renovate, to do up; to repair; (*Naut.*) to rig anew, to refit.

ragrément or **ragréement,** *n.m.* Finishing; restoration, renovation, doing up.

raguer [ra′ge], *v.t., v.i.* To chafe, to gall, to rub (of a rope).

Raguse [ra′gyːz], *f.* Ragusa.

rahat loukoum [raatlu′kum], *n.m.* Turkish delight.

rai [RAIS].

raid [red], *n.m.* A long-distance run or flight; reconnaissance; endurance test; raid. *Un raid aérien,* an air-raid.

raide [red], *a.* Stiff, rigid; tight, taut; steep; inflexible, firm; swift, rapid; (*colloq.*) extraordinary, tall; (*slang*) 'stiff', intolerable. *C′est un peu raide!* that′s a bit stiff! *danser sur la corde raide,* to dance on the tight-rope; *raide comme une barre de fer,* as stiff as a poker; *se tenir raide,* to stand stiffly; *un procédé un peu raide,* that′s rather a harsh proceeding; *vol raide,* strong flight.—*adv.* Quick, swiftly, suddenly. *Tomber raide mort,* to fall dead on the spot, to fall stone dead.

raideur, *n.f.* Stiffness, rigidity; firmness, inflexibility; tightness; steepness; swiftness; tenacity; harshness.

raidillon, *n.m.* Stiff ascent, up-hill path.

raidir, *v.t.* To stiffen, to render rigid; to tighten; to make strong, inflexible, or hard-hearted.—*v.i.* and **se raidir,** *v.r.* To stiffen,

to grow stiff; to be inflexible; (*fig.*) to harden oneself (*contre*), to withstand.

raidissement, *n.m.* Stiffening, tautening.

raidisseur, *n.m.* Wire-strainer; counter-brace.

raie (1) [re], *n.f.* Line, stroke; streak, stripe; furrow; weal; parting (of hair). *Étoffe à raies,* striped material; *faire sa raie,* to part one′s hair.

raie (2) [re], *n.f.* (*Ichth.*) Ray, skate. *Grosse raie* or *raie grosse queue blonde; raie blanche* (or *cendrée*), common skate; *raie bouclée,* thornback; *raie pêcheresse,* angler or fishing frog.

raifort [re′foːr], *n.m.* Horse-radish.

rail [raːj, raːj], *n.m.* (*pl.* **rails**) (*Rail.*) Rail. *Rail conducteur,* live rail; *rail à ornières,* tram-rail; *rail mobile,* switch-rail, point; *rail à patin,* flat-bottomed rail.

railler [rɑ′je], *v.t.* To banter, to chaff; to scoff at.—*v.i.* To banter, to jest. *Je ne raille pas,* I am not joking. **se railler,** *v.r.* To jest, to mock, to make game (*de*).

raillerie, *n.f.* Raillery, bantering; jesting, jest. *Entendre la raillerie,* to be able to take a joke; *raillerie à part* or *sans raillerie,* seriously, without joking; *tourner une chose en raillerie,* to make a joke of something.

railleur, *a.* (*fem.* **-euse**) Bantering, joking; jeering, scoffing. *D′un ton railleur,* in a mocking tone.—*n.* Banterer, joker; scoffer, jeerer.

railleusement, *adv.* Mockingly.

rainer [re′ne], *v.t.* (*Tech.*) To groove; to slot.

rainette [re′net], *n.f.* (*Zool.*) Tree-frog; (*Bot.*) pippin. *Rainette grise,* russet.

rainure [re′nyːr], *n.f.* Groove, rabbet, slot.

raiponce [re′pɔ̃ːs], *n.f.* Rampion.

raire [reːr], *v.i. irr.* (*conjugated like* TRAIRE) or **réer,** *v.i.* To bell, to troat (of bucks etc.).

rais or **rai** [re], *n.m.* Spoke (of a wheel); ray (of light).

raisin [re′zɛ̃], *n.m.* Grapes. *Des raisins secs,* raisins; *grand raisin,* royal (paper); *un grain de raisin,* a grape; *une grappe de raisin,* a bunch of grapes; *raisin d′Amérique,* (*Bot.*) pokeweed; *raisins de Corinthe,* (dried) currants; *raisin de renard,* herb Paris; *raisins de Smyrne,* sultanas; *raisin des tropiques,* bladder wrack; *raisin d′ours,* bearberry; *raisin du diable,* black bryony. *Ton mi-figue, mi-raisin,* half in jest, half in earnest.

raisiné, *n.m.* Grape jam; (*vulg.*) blood.

raison [re′zɔ̃], *n.f.* Reason; sense, judgment, sanity; satisfaction, reparation; justice, right, excuse; answer; proof, ground, matter, argument; cause, motive; (*Arith.*) ratio; (*Law*) claim. *À plus forte raison* [FORT]; *à raison de,* at the rate of; *à telle fin que de raison* [FIN (1)]; *avec raison,* rightly; *avoir raison,* to be right; *avoir raison de,* to overcome, to get the better of; *bonne raison,* good grounds; *comme de raison,* as it is fit, of course; *donner raison à quelqu′un,* to decide in favour of someone, to side with someone; *en raison de,* in proportion to, at the rate of, by reason of, in consideration of; *entendre raison* [ENTENDRE]; *faire raison à,* to give satisfaction to, to pledge (in drinking); *il n′a point de raison,* he is lacking in common sense; *l′âge de raison,* years of discretion; *livre de raison,* ledger; *mariage de raison,* marriage of convenience; *mettre quelqu′un à la raison* [METTRE]; *parler* *raison*, to talk sense; *plus que de raison*, more than is reasonable; *point tant de raisons*, don't argue so much; *raison de plus*, all the more reason; *raison directe, inverse*, direct, inverse ratio; *raison probable*, probable proof; *raisons de famille*, family reasons; *raison d'État* [ÉTAT]; *raison d'être*, justification, grounds; (*Comm.*) *raison sociale*, firm, style or name of a firm; *ramener quelqu'un à la raison*, to bring someone to his senses; *rendre raison de sa conduite*, to give an account of one's conduct; *sans raison*, groundless, groundlessly; *se faire une raison*, to accept the inevitable; *tirer raison d'une injure*, to obtain satisfaction for an injury.

raisonnable, *a.* Rational, reasonable, thinking, sensible; just, equitable, proper, right; adequate, moderate, fair; tolerable. *Il est d'une taille raisonnable*, he is fairly tall; *pension raisonnable*, adequate pension; *prix raisonnable*, moderate price; *peu raisonnable*, unreasonable. **raisonnablement**, *adv.* Reasonably, sensibly, fairly, justly, moderately, pretty well; tolerably.

raisonné, *a.* (*fem.* **-ée**) Rational, intelligent; supported by proof, systematic, methodical; classified, analytical. *Catalogue raisonné*, descriptive, analytical list or catalogue.

raisonnement, *n.m.* Reason; reasoning, argument; answer; (*colloq., pl.*) observations, remarks. *Faire des raisonnements à perte de vue*, to argue endlessly; *point tant de raisonnements*, not so many objections.

raisonner, *v.i.* To reason; to argue; to raise objections; to answer, to murmur.—*v.t.* To apply one's reason to, to study, to consider; to talk or discourse upon; to make (a person) listen to reason; to declare cargo (to customs). **se raisonner**, *v.r.* To reason with oneself.

raisonneur, *n.m.* (*fem.* **-euse**) Reasoner, logician; argufier, pertinacious answerer.—*a.* Reasoning; argumentative.

rajah, raja [ra'ʒa], *n.m.* Rajah.

rajeunir [raʒœ'niːr], *v.t.* To restore to youth, to rejuvenate; to make look young or younger; to revive, to renew; to modernize, to smarten up. *Rajeunir des meubles*, to renew furniture. *Ça ne nous rajeunit pas*, that doesn't make us look any younger.—*v.i.* (*takes the auxiliary* AVOIR *or* ÊTRE *according as action or state is meant*) To grow young again, to be restored to youth; to recover one's freshness or vigour. **se rajeunir**, *v.r.* To make oneself look young again; to understate one's age.

rajeunissant, *a.* (*fem.* **-ante**) That makes one look younger, rejuvenating.

rajeunissement, *n.m.* Making young again; growing young again; rejuvenation; renewal, renovation.

rajouter [raʒu'te], *v.t.* To add again; to add more of.

rajustement [raʒystə'mã], *n.m.* Readjustment, setting in order; (*fig.*) reconciliation.

rajuster, *v.t.* To readjust, to put to rights; (*fig.*) to settle, to reconcile. *On les a rajustés*, they have been reconciled; *rajuster une querelle*, to make up a quarrel. **se rajuster**, *v.r.* To readjust or straighten one's dress; to be reconciled.

râle (1) [rɑːl], *n.m.* Rail (bird). *Râle de genêt*, landrail, corncrake; *râle d'eau*, brook ouzel; water rail; *râle de Baillon*, pink-footed small

crake; *râle marouette*, spotted crake; *râle poussin*, green-footed lesser crake.

râle (2) [rɑːl] or **râlement**, *n.m.* Rattling in the throat. *Râle de la mort*, death-rattle.

ralenti [ralã'ti], *a.* Slackened, slower (pace, speed).—*n.m.* (*Cine.*) Slow motion. *Tourner au ralenti*, (*Motor.*) to tick over.

ralentir [ralã'tiːr], *v.t., v.i.* To slacken; to slow down, to ease up; to lessen, to abate, to moderate. **se ralentir**, *v.r.* To slacken, to slow up; to abate, to relax; to flag.

ralentissement, *n.m.* Slackening; decrease, decline; flagging, cooling (of zeal).

râler [rɑ'le], *v.i.* To be at one's last gasp; (*pop.*) to be angry, in a rage.

râleur [rɑ'lœr], *n.m. and a.* (*fem.* **-euse**) (*pop.*) Stingy (person); nagging, bad-tempered (person).

ralingue [ra'lɛ̃ːg], *n.f.* (*Naut.*) Bolt-rope (of a sail). **ralinguer**, *v.t.* To sew the bolt-ropes to (a sail).—*v.i.* To fly loose to the wind (of sails), to shiver.

raller [RAIRE].

ralliement [rali'mã], *n.m.* Rallying, rally; winning over. *Mot de ralliement*, (*Mil.*) countersign, password; *point de ralliement*, rallying-point; *signe de ralliement*, rallying-sign. *Sonner au ralliement*, to sound the recall.

rallier [ra'lje], *v.t.* (*conjugated like* PRIER) To rally; to rejoin; to win over; (*Naut.*) to stand into (the land etc.). *Rallier la terre*, to stand into the land; *rallier le navire au vent*, to haul the ship into the wind. *Rallier son poste*, to return to one's post. *Ce projet rallia tous les partis*, this plan won the agreement of all parties. **se rallier**, *v.r.* To rally; to join, to adopt (à). *Se rallier à terre*, (*Naut.*) to hug the shore.

rallonge [ra'lɔ̃ːʒ], *n.f.* Lengthening-piece. *Rallonge d'une table*, leaf of a table; *table à rallonges*, draw-table. **rallongement**, *n.m.* Lengthening, extension. **rallonger**, *v.t.* To lengthen; let out (skirt).—*v.i.* To extend, to lengthen.

rallumer [raly'me], *v.t.* To relight, to light again; to rekindle; to revive. **se rallumer**, *v.r.* To light again; (*fig.*) to break out again, to rekindle.

rallye [ra'li], *n.m.* (*Motor.*) Race meeting, rally.

rallye-paper [ralipɛ'pœːr] or **rallie-papier**, *n.m.* (*pl.* **rallye-papers, rallie-papiers**) Paper-chase.

ramadan [rama'dã] or **ramazan**, *n.m.* Ramadan (the holy month of Moslems). *Faire ramadan*, to fast in the daytime (and have a good time at night); (*Mil.*) to make a row, din.

ramage [ra'maːʒ], *n.m.* Floral pattern (on stuffs); singing, chirping, warbling (of birds); (*fig.*) prattle (of children).

ramaigrir [ramɛ'griːr], *v.t.* To make lean or thin again.—*v.i.* To grow thin again. **ramaigrissement**, *n.m.* Emaciation, leanness.

ramas [ra'mɑ], *n.m. inv.* Heap, disorderly collection; set, troop, lot, rabble. *Un ramas de bandits*, a set of robbers; *un ramas d'impostures*, a mass of deception.

ramassage [rama'saːʒ], *n.m.* Gathering, collecting.

ramasse [ra'mɑːs], *n.f.* Sledge (used on mountains).

ramassé [ramɑ'se], *a.* (*femĩ.* **-ée**) Thick-set, squat, stocky; compact.

ramassement [ramɑs'mɑ̃], *n.m.* Gathering, collecting.

ramasse-miettes, *n.m. inv.* Crumb-tray.

ramasser, *v.t.* To collect, to gather; to scrape together, to rake together; to pick up, to take up. *Ramasser toutes ses forces,* to muster all one's strength. (*fam.*) *Ramasser une bûche,* or *une pelle,* to come a cropper; *se faire ramasser,* (*fam.*) to get picked up by the police; to be 'told off'. **se ramasser,** *v.r.* To assemble, to gather together; to roll itself up (of an animal), to be huddled up; to crouch, to gather oneself (before leaping); to gather oneself up, to pick oneself up (after a spill).

ramasseur [ramɑ'sœ:r], *n.m.* (*fem.* **-euse**) Gatherer, collector.

ramassis [ramɑ'si], *n.m.* [RAMAS].

ramazan [RAMADAN].

rambarde [rɑ̃'bard], *n.f.* (*Naut.*) Hand-rail.

ramdam [ram'dam, ram'dɑ̃], *n.m.* (*Mil. slang*) [RAMADAN].

rame (1) [ram], *n.f.* Scull, oar; (*Hort.*) stick, prop; (*Manuf.*) tenter frame. *Être à la rame,* to tug at the sculls, to pull at the oars; (*fig.*) to work hard; (*Cycl.*) to toil along; *faire fausse rame,* to catch a crab.

rame (2) [ram], *n.f.* Ream (of paper); string, row (of barges); lift (of carriages); made-up train or portion of train. *Une rame de Métro,* an Underground train.

ramé [ra'me], *a.* (*fem.* **-ée** (1)) Supported with sticks (of peas), propped, staked (of plants); bar, double-head (of shot); (*Her.*) ramé. **Balles ramées,* double shot; *boulets ramés,* bar-shot.

rameau [ra'mo], *n.m.* (*pl.* **-eaux**) Bough, small branch (of a tree); branch, subdivision; (*Anat.*) ramification; (*pl.*) antlers (of deer). *Le dimanche des Rameaux,* Palm Sunday.

ramée (2), *n.f.* Green boughs, green arbour *Sous la ramée,* under the greenwood tree.

ramendable [ramɑ̃'dabl], *a.* Mendable.

ramendage, *n.m.* Mending (*esp.* of gilt).

ramender [ramɑ̃'de], *v.t.* To manure again; to mend (gilding etc.).

ramener [ram'ne], *v.t. irr.* (*conjugated like* AMENER) To bring back, to bring again; to bring; to put back; to take home; to bring over; to restore, to re-establish; to reclaim; to recall. *Ramener à la maison,* to bring home. *Ramener quelqu'un à son devoir,* to recall someone to his duty. **se ramener,** *v.r.* To amount to; (*pop.*) to come along, to turn up. *Ses remarques se ramènent à ceci,* his remarks amount to this.

rameneur, *n.m.* (*fem.* **-euse**) Bringer back, recaller, restorer.

ramequin [ram'kɛ̃], *n.m.* Ramekin (dish of cheese etc.).

ramer (1) [ra'me], *v.i.* To row, to scull. *Ramer en pointe,* to row; *ramer en couple,* to scull; (*Cycl.*) *ramer* or *être à la rame,* to toil along.

ramer (2) [ra'me], *v.t.* To stick (peas), to stake, to prop (plants).

ramer (3) [ra'me], *v.t.* (*Rail.*) To make lifts (of wagons).

ramette [ra'mɛt], *n.f.* Ream (of note-paper); (*Print.*) fancy-case.

rameur [ra'mœ:r], *n.m.* (*fem.* **-euse** (1)) Rower.

Rameur de pointe, oarsman; *rameur de couple,* sculler.

rameux [ra'mø], *a.* (*fem.* **-euse** (2)) Branching, branchy, ramose.

ramier, *n.m.* Wood-pigeon, ring-dove. *Petit ramier* or *colombin,* stockdove.

ramification [ramifika'sjɔ̃], *n.f.* Ramification.

ramifier, *v.t.* (*conjugated like* PRIER) To ramify. **se ramifier,** *v.r.* To ramify, to separate into branches, to divide.

ramille, *n.f.,* or **ramillon,** *n.m.* Twig.

ramingue [ra'mɛ̃:g], *a.* Restive (horse).

ramollir [ramɔ'li:r], *v.t.* To soften, (*fig.*) to enervate, to unman. **se ramollir,** *v.r.* To soften, to grow soft; (*fig.*) to relent; to grow dull-witted. **ramollissant,** *a.* (*fem.* **-ante**) Softening, emollient.—*n.m.* (*Med.*) Emollient.

ramollissement, *n.m.* Softening. *Ramollissement du cerveau,* softening of the brain.

ramollot, *n.m.* (*pop.*) An old dodderer, crock, fogey.

ramonage [ramɔ'na:ʒ], *n.m.* Chimney sweeping. **ramoner,** *v.t.* To sweep (a chimney).

ramoneur, *n.m.* Chimney-sweeper, sweep.

rampant [rɑ̃'pɑ̃], *a.* (*fem.* **-ante**) Creeping, crawling; (*fig.*) cringing, grovelling, servile; (*Her.*) rampant. *Lierre rampant,* ground-ivy; (*Av.*) *personnel rampant,* ground staff; *style rampant,* pedestrian style.—*n.m.* (*fam.*) *Les rampants,* the ground staff, the maintenance men.

rampe [rɑ̃:p], *n.f.* Flight of stairs; banisters; slope, ramp, incline, gradient; (*Theat.*) footlights; (*Eng.*) inclined plane. *Lâcher la rampe,* (*slang*) to die, to kick the bucket. *Rampe mobile,* moving incline. *Cette pièce ne pourra passer la rampe,* that play won't make a hit, *or* get across.

rampement [rɑ̃p'mɑ̃], *n.m.* Creeping, crawling.

ramper, *v.i.* To creep, to crawl; (*fig.*) to crouch, to cringe, to grovel; (*Arch.*) to slope. *Son style rampe,* his style is uninspired.

Ramsès [ram'zɛs], *m.* Rameses.

ramure [ra'my:r], *n.f.* Branches; boughs; antlers (of a stag).

rancart [rɑ̃'ka:r], *n.m.* *Mettre au rancart,* to throw aside, to cast off; to put on the shelf.

rance (1) [rɑ̃:s], *a.* Rancid, rank; (*fig.*) rusty, worn-out, out-of-date.—*n.m.* Rancidness. *Sentir le rance,* to smell rancid.

rance (2) [rɑ̃:s], *n.f.* Stand for barrel; balk (of timber); (*pl.*) (*Naut.*) kevels.

ranche [rɑ̃:ʃ], *n.f.* Rung of a pole-ladder.

rancher, *n.m.* Pole-ladder; jib.

ranci [rɑ̃'si], *a.* (*fem.* **-ie**) Rancid. **rancidité, rancissure,** *n.f.,* or **rancissement,** *n.m.* Rancidity. **rancir,** *v.i.* To grow rancid.

rancœur [rɑ̃'kœ:r], *n.f.* Rancour, bitterness (of feeling).

rançon [rɑ̃'sɔ̃], *n.f.* Ransom. **rançonnement,** *n.m.* Ransoming; (*fig.*) exaction, extortion. **rançonner,** *v.t.* To set a ransom upon; to ransom; (*fig.*) to fleece. **rançonneur,** *n.m.* (*fem.* **-euse**) One who puts to ransom; (*fig.*) extortioner.

rancune [rɑ̃'kyn], *n.f.* Rancour, spite, grudge, malice. *Il lui garde rancune,* he bears him a grudge; *par rancune,* out of spite; *ne lui gardons pas rancune,* let's bear him no malice; *sans rancune,* no hard feelings! with no ill-feeling.

[614]

rancunier, *a.* and *n.* (*fem.* **-ière**) Rancorous, spiteful (person).
randonnée [rãdɔ'ne], *n.f.* Circuit or doubling (of game); (*fig.*) long walk or round, outing, run, ramble, tour, trip; (*Austral.*) hike.
rang [rã], *n.m.* Row, line, rank; order, class; rank; rate (of ships etc.); (*Print.*) frame; tier (of boxes in theatres); (*C*) country road. *À son rang*, in one's place; *à vos rangs!* fall in! *de premier rang*, first-rate; *compagnie hors rang*, headquarters wing; *en rangs serrés, par rangs serrés*, in close order; *former les rangs, se mettre en rangs*, to fall in; *il aspire au premier rang*, he aspires to the first place; *mettre au rang de ses amis*, to reckon among one's friends; *premier rang des fauteuils d'orchestre*, first row of the stalls; *premier rang de tricot*, first row (or round) of knitting; *prendre rang*, to have one's place; *rang social*, social status; *rompre les rangs*, to dismiss, to fall out; *se mettre sur les rangs*, to enter the lists, to come forward (as a candidate); *ouvrez vos rangs!* open order! *serrez les rangs!* close up! (*officier*) *sorti du rang*, risen from the ranks, ranker.
rangé [rã'ʒe], *a.* (*fem.* **-ée** (1)) Ordered, tidy; steady. *En bataille rangée*, in a pitched battle; *un homme rangé*, a steady man.
rangée (2), *n.f.* Row, range, file, line, tier, set. *Une rangée de livres*, a row of books; *une rangée de points*, a row of stitches (in knitting).
rangement, *n.m.* Arranging, putting in order.
ranger [rã'ʒe], *v.t.* To put in order, to set to rights; to draw up, to marshal; to array, to arrange; to range, to set in order; to rank; to put aside, to turn aside; to keep back; to bring under, to reduce, to subdue; (*Naut.*) to coast, to hug, to range, to sail close to. *Les gardes firent ranger le peuple*, the guards kept the people back; *ranger des gens deux à deux*, to place people in double file; *ranger des livres*, to set books in order; *ranger la côte* [CÔTE]; *ranger une armée en bataille* [BATAILLE]; *rangez cette table*, put that table in its place.
se ranger, *v.r.* To make room, to make way (for), to get out of the way; to range or place oneself; to draw up (of carriages, troops etc.); to pull up (at curb); to pull over to the side; to fall in (of soldiers); to amend, to reform; to veer (of the wind). *Il se rangea dans un coin*, he drew aside into a corner; *il s'est rangé*, he has settled down (after sowing his wild oats); *les troupes se rangèrent en bataille*, the troops drew up in order of battle; *rangez-vous donc!* make room, will you! *se ranger à l'avis de quelqu'un*, to fall in with someone's opinion; *se ranger du parti de quelqu'un*, to go over to someone's side.
rangeur, *n.m.* (*fem.* **-euse**) A person who arranges etc.
Rangoun [rã'gun], *m.* Rangoon.
ranimer [rani'me], *v.t.* To restore to life, to revive, to reanimate; to stir up, to rouse, to enliven; to cheer up, to put new life into. *Le printemps ranime toute la nature*, spring revives all nature; *ranimer les couleurs d'un tableau*, to revive the colour of a picture. **se ranimer**, *v.r.* To revive, to come to life again; to be restored to health; to brighten up, to be enlivened; to cheer up. *La nature se ranime*, nature revives; *le feu se ranime*, the fire is beginning to burn up.

ranule [ra'nyl], *n.f.* (*Path.*) Ranula, frog-tongue.
ranz [rã:s], *n.m. inv.* *Ranz des vaches*, song of the Swiss cowherds.
Raoul [ra'ul], *m.* Ralph.
*****raout** [ra'ut], *n.m.* Rout, party, reception.
rapace [ra'pas], *a.* Rapacious; greedy for gain or for a prey; predacious; grasping (of person).—*n.m.* Rapacious bird, bird of prey. *Les rapaces*, the raptores. **rapacement**, *adv.* Rapaciously. **rapacité**, *n.f.* Rapacity; cupidity.
râpage [rɑ'paːʒ], *n.m.* Rasping; grating.
rapatelle [rapa'tɛl], *n.f.* Hair-cloth.
rapatriement [rapatri'mã], *n.m.* Repatriation, sending back to the home country.
rapatrier, *v.t.* (*conjugated like* PRIER) To repatriate, to send back to their country; (*dial.*) to reconcile, to make friends again. *On les a rapatriés*, they have been repatriated; they have been reconciled.
râpe [rɑːp], *n.f.* Grater; rasp; rough file; stalk, stem (of grapes) [RAFLE (1)].
râpé, *a.* (*fem.* **-ée**) Grated; rasped; shabby, threadbare, worn out (of clothes).—*n.m.* Rape-wine; fresh grapes put into a vessel of spoiled wine to improve it; chips to clarify wine; mixture of left-over wines.
râper, *v.t.* To grate (cheese), to rasp; to grind (snuff); to make threadbare.
rapetassage [rapta'saːʒ], *n.m.* Patching up, mending, cobbling. **rapetasser**, *v.t.* To patch, to patch up, to piece, to botch (up), to mend, to cobble. **rapetasseur**, *n.m.* (*fem.* **-euse**) Piecer, patcher; cobbler; (*fig.*) compiler, adapter.
rapetissement [raptis'mã], *n.m.* Shortening, shrinking, lessening; (*fig.*) belittling. **rapetisser**, *v.t.* To shorten, to make smaller; (*fig.*) to belittle.—*v.i.* To grow less, to shorten, to shrink.
râpeux, *a.* (*fem.* **-euse**) Raspy (tongue); harsh (wine).
Raphaël [rafa'ɛl], *m.* Raphael; Raffael.
raphia [ra'fja], *n.m.* Raffia (grass).
rapiat [ra'pja], *a.* and *n.* (*fem.* **-ate**) (*fam.*) Avaricious, mean (person), stingy; skin-flint.
rapide [ra'pid], *a.* Rapid, quick, speedy, swift, fleet, fast; hasty, sudden; steep. *Une guérison rapide*, a speedy recovery; *une pente rapide*, a steep incline.—*n.m.* Rapid; fast train. *Les rapides*, the rapids (in river). **rapidement**, *adv.* Rapidly, swiftly, fast; suddenly, steeply.
rapidité, *n.f.* Rapidity, swiftness, speed; steepness. *La rapidité du tir*, (*Mil.*) the rate of fire; *sur un rythme rapide*, at a quick rate.
rapiéçage [rapje'saːʒ] or **rapiècement** [rapjɛs'mã], *n.m.* Piecing, patching. **rapiécer** or **rapiéceter**, *v.t. irr.* (*conjug. like* ACCÉLÉRER) To piece, to patch.
rapière [ra'pjɛːr], *n.f.* Rapier.
rapin [ra'pɛ̃], *n.m.* Art student; (*fig.*) dauber.
rapine [ra'pin], *n.f.* Rapine, pillage, robbery; spoil, plunder; graft. **rapiner**, *v.t., v.i.* To pillage, to plunder; to peculate.
rapineur, *n.m.* (*fem.* **-euse**) Plunderer, pillager, pilferer.
raplaplat [rapla'pla], *a. inv.* (*fam.*) Fagged out, washed out, nearly finished (person); trite, uninteresting (work).

rappareillement [rapareːjˈmɑ̃] or **rapparie-ment** [rapariˈmɑ̃], *n.m.* Matching, completing (set *or* pair). **rappareiller**, *v.t.*, or **rapparier**, *v.t.* (*conjugated like* PRIER) To match, to complete.

rappel [raˈpɛl], *n.m.* Recall, recalling, reminder, call (to order); (*Mil.*) bugle-call or drums beating to arms or quarters; tattoo, assembly; revocation, repeal; after-payment, after-account *or* call; (*fig.*) a faint whiff. *Battre le rappel,* (*Mil.*) to beat *or* call to arms or the fall-in; (*Mount.*) *corde de rappel,* double rope; *rappel à l'ordre,* call to order; *rappel de chariot,* (*Typewriting*) return of carriage, back-spacing; *rappel de lumière,* (*Paint.*) highlight, touch of light; *rappel de solde,* further payment, back pay.

rappeler, *v.t. irr.* (*conjug. like* APPELER) To call again; to call back, to call off, to recall, to call home; to keep on calling; to restore (to life etc.); to summon up, to muster (one's courage etc.); to retract, to recant; to recall to mind; to recall to someone's memory, to remind. *Je m'en allais et il m'a rappelé,* I was going and he called me back; *rappeler le chariot (d'une machine à écrire),* to return the carriage; to back-space; *rappeler le temps passé,* to recall the past; *rappeler quelqu'un à la vie,* to restore someone to life; *rappeler quelqu'un à l'ordre,* to call someone to order; *rappeler son chien,* to call off one's dog; *rappeler ses esprits,* to recover oneself; *rappeler un homme à son devoir,* to recall a man to his duty; *rappelez-le moi,* remind me of it; *rappelez-moi à son bon souvenir,* remember me kindly to him. **se rappeler**, *v.r.* To recollect, to remember, to recall to mind. *Je me le rappelle parfaitement,* I recollect it very well; *je me rappelle l'avoir fait,* I remember doing it; *vous rappelez-vous?* do you remember?

rappliquer [rapliˈke], *v.t.* To apply again (an ointment).—*v.i.* (*fam.*) To come back, to turn up.

rapport [raˈpɔːr], *n.m.* Revenue, profit; product, produce; productiveness, bearing; report, account, information, tale, story; return, statement; affinity, analogy, resemblance, conformity, correspondence; harmony, agreement; relation, connexion, reference; communication, intercourse; ratio, proportion; restitution, reimbursement, refunding; rising (in the stomach). *Aimer à faire des rapports,* to love to tell tales; *avoir de bons rapports avec quelqu'un,* to be on good terms with someone; *avoir rapport à,* to relate to; *être de bon rapport,* to bring in a good profit; *être en plein rapport,* to be productive, to be in bearing (of land); *faire un rapport,* to draw up a report, to make a return; *il n'y a aucun rapport entre ces choses,* there is no connexion between these things; *le style n'est pas en rapport avec le sujet,* the style is not in keeping with the subject; *maison de rapport,* tenement house; *mettre une personne en rapport avec une autre,* to bring a person into contact with another; *par rapport à,* in proportion, comparison, or regard to; *pièces de rapport,* odd parts to form a patchwork etc.; inlaid pieces; *salle des rapports,* (*Mil.*) orderly room; *sous le rapport de,* with regard to; *sous tous les rapports,* in every respect.

rapportable, *a.* That must be refunded, restorable; attributable.

rapporté, *a.* (*fem.* **-ée**) Brought back. *Bout rapporté,* toe-cap (of shoe); *ouvrage de pièces rapportées,* inlaid work; *poches rapportées,* patch-pockets; *terres rapportées,* artificial soil.

rapporter [rapɔrˈte], *v.t.* To bring back, to take back; to bring, to bring home; to bring in, to yield; to fetch; to retrieve (of dog); to refund, to return; to repeal, to revoke, to recall; to report, to tell, to give an account of; to quote; to direct, to refer; to attribute; (*Surveying*) to trace, to set down; to post (in ledger); to plot, to join, to fit (a piece). *Cette mauvaise action ne lui rapportera rien,* this bad action will avail him nothing; *il n'en a rapporté que des coups,* he only got blows for it; *il rapporte tout,* he tells everything; *rapporter du journal au grand livre,* to post from the journal to the ledger; *rapporter l'effet à sa cause,* to refer the effect to its cause; *rapporter tout à soi,* to make everything subservient to self; *rapporter un fait comme il s'est passé,* to relate a fact as it happened; *son argent lui rapporte six pour cent,* his money brings him in six per cent; *une terre qui rapporte beaucoup,* an estate that yields a good income.—*v.i.* To retrieve (of the dog); (*sch.*) to tell tales, to sneak; to pay well, to be profitable. *Ce chien rapporte bien,* this dog retrieves well. **se rapporter**, *v.r.* To agree, to correspond, to tally; to relate, to have reference, to be related. *Je m'en rapporte à votre témoignage,* I abide by what you say; *je m'en rapporte à vous,* I leave it to you, I take your word for it; *s'il faut s'en rapporter aux anciennes traditions,* if we are to believe ancient traditions.

rapporteur, *n.m.* (*fem.* **-euse**) Tell-tale, tale-bearer, sneak; reporter, stenographer; (*Geom.*) protractor. *Juge-rapporteur,* judge-advocate; *rapporteur d'un comité,* committee reporter.

rapprendre [raˈprɑ̃ːdr], *v.t. irr.* (*conjugated like* PRENDRE) To learn anew; to teach again.

rapprochement [raprɔʃˈmɑ̃], *n.m.* Drawing closer, placing near, bringing together; (*Polit.*) rapprochement, reconciliation; junction, union; putting together, comparison.

rapprocher, *v.t.* To bring near again, to put near again; to bring nearer, to bring together; to bring into harmony or agreement, to reconcile; to compare. *Rapprocher deux personnes,* to bring two persons together, to reconcile two persons; *rapprochez ces deux planches,* bring these two planks closer. **se rapprocher**, *v.r.* To come near again; to draw nearer; to be brought together; to begin to agree or to be friends again, to become reconciled; to approach, to approximate (*de*).

rapsode [rapˈsɔd], *n.m.* Rhapsode.

rapsodie, *n.f.* Rhapsody.

rapt [rapt], *n.m.* Abduction; kidnapping.

râpure [raˈpyːr], *n.f.* Raspings.

raquette [raˈkɛt], *n.f.* Racket, battledore; snow-shoe; regulating lever (of watch); Indian fig, prickly pear, opuntia. *C'est une bonne raquette* or *il a un bon coup de raquette,* he is good at tennis.

rare [raːr], *a.* Rare, uncommon, unusual; extraordinary; singular; scarce; thin, scanty, sparse; slow (of the pulse). *Devenir rare comme les beaux jours,* to become quite a stranger.—*n.m.* The rare. *Le rare n'est pas* *toujours le beau*, the most extraordinary is not always the most beautiful.

raréfaction, *n.f.* Rarefaction.

raréfiant, *a.* (*fem.* **-iante**) Rarefying.

raréfier, *v.t.* (*conjugated like* PRIER) To rarefy. **se raréfier**, *v.r.* To become rare; to become rarefied.

rarement, *adv.* Rarely, seldom.

rareté, *n.f.* Rarity; scarcity; singularity; rare object.

rarissime, *a.* Very rare, most rare, of the rarest.

ras (1) [rɑ], *a.* (*fem.* **rase**) Close-shaven, close-cropped, shorn; bare, smooth; open, flat, low; low-built, flat-bottomed, undecked. *À ras bord*, to the brim; *du velours ras*, smooth velvet; *faire table rase*, to clear the board of, to sweep away all preconceptions; *il a le menton ras*, he has a bare, smooth chin; *navire ras* or *rasé*, dismasted vessel; *rase campagne*, open country; *un chien à poil ras*, a short-haired dog.—*n.m.* Short-nap cloth; level. *À ras de terre*, flush or level with the ground; *au ras de l'eau*, nearly level with the water.

ras (2) [rɑ], *n.m.* Raft. *Ras de carène*, (*Naut.*) shipwright's floating stage.

ras (3) [RAZ].

rasade [ra'zad], *n.f.* Brimful glass (of wine). *Boire une rasade*, to drink a bumper.

rasant [ra'sɑ̃], *a.* (*fem.* **-ante**) Shaving, grazing; sweeping; (*fam.*) boring, dull, tedious. *Fortification rasante*, low fortification; *tir rasant*, grazing fire; *vol rasant* or *rase-mottes*, flight near the ground; *vue rasante*, view of a flat, open country.

(C) **rasé** [ra'ze], *n.m.* Cleared land (in a forest).

*rasement** [raz'mɑ̃], *n.m.* Razing or levelling to the ground.

rase-mottes [raz'mɔt], *n.m. inv.* Overshoot. *Voler en rase-mottes* or *faire du rase-mottes*, (*Av.*) to hedge-hop, to skim the ground.

raser [ra'ze], *v.t.* To shave; to demolish, to pull down, to raze; to cut down (a ship); to graze, to touch, to skim over; (*fam.*) to bore, to worry. *Raser la côte*, to hug the coast; *raser une maison*, to pull down a house; (*cheval*) *qui rase le tapis*, daisy-cutter; *se faire raser*, to get a shave, to have a shave; *une balle lui rasa le visage*, a bullet grazed his face. **se raser**, *v.r.* To shave, to shave oneself, to be shaved; (*fam.*) to get bored.

raseur [ra'zœːr], *n.m.* (*fem.* **-euse**) Shaver; (*fam.*) bore.

rasibus [razi'bys], *adv.* (*colloq.*) Quite close.

rasoir [ra'zwaːr], *n.m.* Razor; bore. *Cuir à rasoir*, razor-strop; *pierre à rasoir*, hone; *rasoir de sûreté*, safety-razor; *rasoir électrique*, electric shaver or razor; *repasser un rasoir*, to set a razor.

rason, *n.m.* Razor-fish.

rassasiant [rasa'zjɑ̃], *a.* (*fem.* **-iante**) Satiating, cloying; filling (food), satisfying. **rassasiement**, *n.m.* Satiety.

rassasier [rasa'zje], *v.t.* (*conjugated like* PRIER) To satisfy, to fill; to sate, to satiate; to cloy, to surfeit. *Être rassasié d'une chose*, to be tired of a thing; *il n'est jamais rassasié d'argent*, he can never have enough money. **se rassasier**, *v.r.* To sate oneself, to be cloyed; to take one's fill.

rassemblement [rasɑ̃blə'mɑ̃], *n.m.* Assembling, mustering, collecting; assembly, muster, assemblage, crowd, concourse; mob; political group; (*Mil.*) fall-in. *Disperser un rassemblement*, to disperse a mob; *sonner le rassemblement*, to sound the assembly.

rassembler, *v.t.* To reassemble; to gather together, to collect; to bring together again; to put together; to collect, to assemble, to muster (troops). *Rassembler des matériaux pour un ouvrage*, to collect materials for a work; *rassembler un cheval*, to gather a horse. **se rassembler**, *v.r.* To reassemble; to assemble, to congregate, to muster. *Se rassembler en foule*, to flock.

rasseoir [ra'swaːr], *v.t. irr.* (*conjugated like* ASSEOIR) To seat again, to reseat; to replace, to put in its place again; to settle again, to calm, to compose. *Donnez-lui le temps de rasseoir ses esprits*, give him time to compose himself. **se rasseoir**, *v.r.* To sit down again; to settle (of liquids); to become composed again.

rasséréner [rasere'ne], *v.t. irr.* (*conjug. like* ACCÉLÉRER) To clear up; to restore serenity to. *Le soleil parut et rasséréna le temps*, the sun came out and cleared up the weather. **se rasséréner**, *v.r.* To clear up; to recover one's serenity.

rassis [ra'si], *a.* (*fem.* **-ise**) Settled; calm, staid, sedate; stale. *Personne de sens rassis*, person of sober judgment; *pain rassis*, stale bread.

rassortiment [rasɔrti'mɑ̃] or **réassortiment**, *n.m.* Rematching (of colours, materials, etc.), resorting; taking in a stock of goods for a season etc., restocking.

rassortir or **réassortir**, *v.t.* To sort or match again; to stock (a shop etc.).

rassurant [rasy'rɑ̃], *a.* (*fem.* **-ante**) Tranquillizing; encouraging, reassuring.

rassurer, *v.t.* To make firm; to strengthen, to consolidate; to tranquillize, to reassure. **se rassurer**, *v.r.* To recover oneself, to be reassured; to settle, to clear up (of the weather). *Rassurez-vous*, set your mind at rest.

rastaquouère [rasta'kwɛːr], *n.m.* Showy adventurer; foreign nobleman of doubtful antecedents.

rat [ra], *n.m.* Rat. *Rat à bajoues* or *rat du blé*, hamster; *rat à bourse*, gopher; *rat d'Amérique*, guinea-pig; *rat d'eau*, water vole; *rat d'égout* or *surmulot*, brown rat, sewer rat; *rat d'Égypte* or *de Pharaon*, ichneumon; *rat des champs*, field-mouse; *rat musqué*, musquash; (*fig.*) *rat de bibliothèque*, book-worm; (*fig.*) *rat d'église*, churchgoer; *rat d'hôtel*, hotel thief; (*petit*) *rat* (*d'opéra*), young ballet-girl. *La mort aux rats*, rat-poison [*see also* CAVE, CHAT, NID, QUEUE].

rata [ra'ta], *n.m.* (*Mil. slang*) *abbrev. of* **ratatouille**.

ratafia [rata'fja], *n.m.* Ratafia.

rataplan [rata'plɑ̃], *n.m.* Drum-beat, rat-tat.

ratatiné [ratati'ne], *a.* (*fem.* **-ée**) Shrivelled, shrunken. **ratatiner**, *v.t.* To shrink, to wrinkle. **se ratatiner**, *v.r.* To shrink, to shrivel up.

ratatouille [rata'tuːj], *n.f.* (*pop.*) Coarse stew.

rate (1) [rat], *n.f.* Spleen. *Décharger sa rate*, to vent one's spleen; *épanouir, dilater*, or *désopiler la rate*, to drive away the spleen; *ne pas se fouler la rate*, to be rather slack (at work); *s'épanouir la rate*, to be merry.

rate (2) [rat], *n.f.* Female rat. **raté,** *a.* (*fem.* **-ée**) (*rare*) Rat-eaten.—*n.m.* Unsuccessful man, failure; wash-out; misfire (of gun, engine, etc.). *Faire des ratés,* to misfire (of engine).

râteau [rɑ'to], *n.m.* (*pl.* **-eaux**) Rake; rack (of a watch etc.). *Râteau de pont,* (*Naut.*) squeegee.

râtelage, *n.m.* Raking. **râtelée,** *n.f.* Rakeful, raking. **râteler,** *v.t.* To rake. **râteleur,** *n.m.* (*fem.* **-euse**) Raker.

râtelier [rɑtə'lje], *n.m.* Rack (in stables etc.); set of teeth, denture. *Manger à plus d'un râtelier,* (*fig.*) to serve more than one master; *mettre les armes au râtelier,* to quit the service; *râtelier à outils,* tool-rack; *râtelier à pipes,* pipe-rack; *râtelier d'armes,* arms-rack.

rater [ra'te], *v.i.* To misfire, to flash in the pan; to miss (one's shot); (golf) to foozle; (*fig.*) to miscarry.—*v.t.* To miss; (*fig.*) to fail to obtain. *Rater le courrier,* to miss the post; *rater son coup,* (*fig.*) to miss the mark; *rater le coche,* (*fig.*) to miss the bus; *rater un examen,* (*fam.*) to be ploughed.

ratiboiser [ratibwa'ze], *v.t.* (*pop.*) To filch; to fleece (someone).

ratichon [rati'ʃɔ̃], *n.m.* (*slang*) Priest.

ratier [ra'tje], *a.* (*fem.* **-ière** (1)) Pertaining to rats. (*Chien*) *ratier,* ratter.

ratière (2), *n.f.* Rat-trap.

ratification [ratifika'sjɔ̃], *n.f.* Ratification. **ratifier,** *v.t.* To ratify.

ratine [ra'tin], *n.f.* Ratteen, frieze, petersham (cloth).

ratiner [rati'ne], *v.t.* To frieze.

ratiocination [rasjɔsina'sjɔ̃], *n.f.* Ratiocination. **ratiociner,** *v.i.* To ratiocinate.

ration [ra'sjɔ̃], *n.f.* Ration, allowance. *J'ai eu ma ration d'épreuves,* I have had my share of trouble; *mettre à la ration,* to ration, to put on short rations.

rational [rasjɔ'nal], *n.m.* (*pl.* **-aux**) (*Jewish*) Breast-plate, pectoral.

rationalisation, *n.f.* Rationalization. **rationaliser** [rasjɔnali'ze], *v.t.* To rationalize. **rationalisme,** *n.m.* Rationalism. **rationaliste,** *a.* and *n.* Rationalist. **rationalité,** *n.f.* Rationality.

rationnel, *a.* (*fem.* **-elle**) Rational. *Horizon rationnel,* rational horizon; *quantité algébrique rationnelle,* rational quantity.

rationnement [rasjɔn'mɑ̃], *n.m.* Rationing, putting on short allowance *or* rations. **rationner,** *v.t.* To ration, to put on short allowance.

ratissage [rati'saːʒ], *n.m.* Scraping; raking. **ratisser,** *v.t.* To rake; to scrape; to scrape off. **ratissoire,** *n.f.* Scraper, light rake, hoe, scuffle. **ratissure,** *n.f.* Scrapings.

raton [ra'tɔ̃], *n.m.* Little rat; (*fig.*) little pet, darling. *Raton laveur,* raccoon; (*U.S.*) coon.

rattacher [rata'ʃe], *v.t.* To refasten, to tie up again; to attach; (*fig.*) to link. **se rattacher,** *v.r.* To be attached or connected; to be linked up (with).

ratteindre [ra'tɛ̃dr], *v.t.* irr. (*conjugated like* CRAINDRE) To retake, to catch again; to overtake.

rattendrir [ratɑ̃'driːr], *v.t.* To soften again, to make tender again.

rattraper [ratra'pe], *v.t.* To catch again, to

retake, to seize again; to overtake; to recover. *Bien fin qui m'y rattrapera,* once bitten twice shy; *on a rattrapé le prisonnier,* the prisoner has been recaptured. **se rattraper,** *v.r.* To catch hold (*d*); to be caught again; to make up for one's losses etc.; to gloss over inconsiderate words. *Le temps perdu ne se rattrape jamais,* you can't make up for lost time.

rature [ra'tyːr], *n.f.* Erasure; word etc. crossed out. **raturer,** *v.t.* To erase, to scratch or cross out; to scrape (parchment etc.).

raucité [rosi'te], *n.f.* Raucity, hoarseness.

rauque, *a.* Hoarse, raucous, rough.

ravage [ra'vaːʒ], *n.m.* Ravage, havoc. *Faire des ravages,* to ravage, to play havoc; *les puits de mine ont causé des ravages dans le sol,* coal-pits have played havoc with the soil.

ravager, *v.t.* To ravage, to lay waste; to spoil, to ruin.

ravageur, *n.m.* Ravager, spoiler.

ravalement [raval'mɑ̃], *n.m.* Scraping and rejointing (of a wall); rough-casting; trimming (of trees); (*fig.*) depreciation, disparagement.

ravaler [rava'le], *v.t.* To swallow again; to gulp down; (*fig.*) to run down, to disparage; to scrape, to rejoint (stonework); to rough-cast (wall); to trim (tree). *Ravaler la gloire de,* to run down the glory of; *ravaler quelqu'un au niveau de la bête,* to reduce someone to the level of a beast; *ravaler ses paroles,* to check oneself (in speaking); to take back one's words. **se ravaler,** *v.r.* To debase oneself, to lower oneself.

ravaudage [ravo'daːʒ], *n.m.* Mending (of old clothes, etc.); darning stockings; (*fig.*) botching.

ravauder, *v.t.* To mend, to darn, to patch up; to botch; (*dial.*) to scold, to abuse; to twaddle, to talk rot.

ravaudeur, *n.m.* (*fem.* **-euse**) Mender (of stockings, old clothes, etc.).

rave [raːv], *n.f.* (*Bot.*) Grosse rave, French turnip. *Petite rave,* radish. *Rave de serpent or navet du diable,* white bryony.

ravenelle [rav'nɛl], *n.f.* Wallflower [*see also* GIROFLÉE]; wild radish.

ravi [ra'vi], *a.* (*fem.* **-ie**) Carried away, enraptured, entranced, transported, ravished; glad, delighted; overjoyed. *D'un air ravi,* delightedly; *j'en suis ravi,* I am delighted at it; *je suis ravi que vous la connaissiez,* I am delighted you know her; *ravi d'admiration,* enraptured, transported with admiration.

ravier [ra'vje], *n.m.* Radish-dish. **ravière,** *n.f.* Radish-bed.

ravigote [ravi'gɔt], *n.f.* Ravigote-sauce.

ravigoter, *v.t.* To revive, to refresh, to buck up. **se ravigoter,** *v.r.* To recover one's spirits, to perk up.

ravilir [ravi'liːr], *v.t.* To degrade, to lower.

ravin [ra'vɛ̃], *n.m.* Ravine; gully.

ravine [ra'viːn], *n.f.* Mountain torrent; small gully.

ravinement, *n.m.* Hollowing out *or* furrowing (by waters).

raviner, *v.t.* To plough *or* hollow out, to channel, to cut up (ground), to furrow.

ravir [ra'viːr], *v.t.* To carry off, to take away by force; to ravish, to rob of; (*fig.*) to charm, to delight, to enrapture. *À ravir,* wonderfully, to admiration; *elle chante à ravir,* she sings admirably; *on lui a ravi son plus doux espoir*, he has been robbed of his dearest hope; *ravir le bien d'autrui*, to steal the property of another.

raviser (se) [ravi′ze], *v.r.* To alter one's mind, to change one's mind; to think better of it.

ravissant [ravi′sɑ̃], *a.* (*fem.* **-ante**) (*rare*) Rapacious, ravenous; (*fig.*) ravishing, delightful, charming.

ravissement, *n.m.* Carrying off; rape; ecstasy; rapture, ravishment, delight. *Il était dans le ravissement*, he was in raptures.

ravisseur, *n.m.* (*fem.* **-euse**) Ravisher; kidnapper; spoiler, robber.

ravitaillement [ravitaj′mɑ̃], *n.m.* Revictualling, provisioning; food control. *Ministère du Ravitaillement*, Ministry of Food. **ravitailler,** *v.t.* To provision; to revictual; to supply.

ravitailleur [ravita′jœːr], *n.m.* Carrier (of food, ammunition, etc.).—*a.* (*fem.* **-euse**) (*Transport*) *ravitailleur*, supply-ship, parent ship.

ravivage [ravi′vaːʒ], *n.m.* Reviving, freshening up, brightening up, touching up (of colours).

ravivement, *n.m.* Cleaning (of wound); filing up (of metal surface). **raviver,** *v.t.* To revive, to reanimate; to enliven, to cheer, to rouse; to brighten up *or* freshen up (colours), to touch up; to clean (wound); to file up (metal surface). *Raviver le feu*, to blow up, or to poke up a fire; *raviver une plaie*, to trim a wound; (*fig.*) to revive an old sorrow.

ravoir [ra′vwaːr], *v.t.* (*usu. in infin.*) To get back again, to recover.

rayage [rɛ′jaːʒ], *n.m.* Streaking, striping; rifling (of guns).

rayé, *a.* (*fem.* **-ée**) Striped, streaked (garment); rifled, grooved (gun); scratched (glass); struck off (of list).

rayer, *v.t.* (*conjugated like* BALAYER) To scratch (plate, dishes, etc.); to streak, to stripe; to scratch out, to cross out, to erase, to expunge; (*fig.*) to suppress; (*Artill.*) to rifle, to groove. *Rayez cela de vos papiers*, strike that out of your book, don't count upon that any more; *rayer des contrôles*, to strike off the rolls.

rayère [rɛ′jɛːr], *n.f.* Loophole.

ray-grass [rɛ′graːs], *n.m.* Rye-grass. *Ray-grass anglais*, perennial rye-grass.

rayon (1) [rɛ′jɔ̃], *n.m.* Ray; beam, gleam; radius; furrow; spoke (of a wheel); (*fig.*) zone, circuit (guarded by the customs etc.); (*Bot.*) floret of the ray; (*Ichth.*) spine (of fin). *Dans un rayon de dix kilomètres*, within a radius of ten kilometres; *rayon d'action*, range (of bomber etc.); *rayon de lumière*, ray of light; *rayon de soleil*, ray of sunshine; *rayon d'espérance*, ray of hope; *rayons cosmiques*, cosmic rays; *rayons X*, X-rays; *semis en rayons*, sowing in furrows.

rayon (2) [rɛ′jɔ̃], *n.m.* Shelf; department (of a shop). *Chef de rayon*, shop-walker; *ça n'est pas de mon rayon*, (*fam.*) that is not in my line; *miel en rayon*, comb-honey; *rayon de miel*, honeycomb.

rayonnant [rɛjɔ′nɑ̃], *a.* (*fem.* **-ante**) Radiant, radiating; beaming, wreathed in smiles. *Rayonnant de fierté*, beaming with pride.

rayonne, *n.f.* Rayon, long-fibre artificial silk.

rayonné, *a.* (*fem.* **-ée**) Radiate, stellate.—*n.m. pl.* (*Zool.*) Radiata.

rayonnement, *n.m.* Radiance, effulgence; radiation. *Le rayonnement des astres*, the radiance of the stars.

rayonner [rɛjɔ′ne], *v.i.* To radiate; to shine, to beam; to glisten, to sparkle. *Son visage rayonne de joie*, his face is radiant with joy.

rayure, *n.f.* Striping (of textile fabrics), stripe; streak, scratch; groove, rifling (of fire-arms); erasure.

raz or **ras** (3) [rɑ], *n.m. inv.* Race (a violent current). *Le raz d'Aurigny*, the race of Alderney. *Raz de marée*, tidal wave.

razzia [ra′zja], *n.f.* (*Algerian*) Razzia, raid, inroad, foray. *Faire une razzia*, to make a clean sweep.

razzier, *v.t.* To raid and rob.

ré [re], *n.m.* (*Mus.*) Re, D.

réa [re′a], *n.m.* Sheave (of pulley).

réabonnement [reabɔn′mɑ̃], *n.m.* Renewed subscription. **réabonner,** *v.t.* To renew (someone's) subscription. **se réabonner,** *v.r.* To renew one's subscription.

réabsorber [reapsɔr′be], *v.t.* To reabsorb. **réabsorption,** *n.f.* Reabsorption.

réacteur [reak′tœːr], *n.m.* (*fem.* **-trice**) Reactor; (*Av.*) jet-engine.

réactif, *a.* (*fem.* **-ive**) Reactive.—*n.m.* (*Chem.*) Reagent.

réaction, *n.f.* Reaction. *Les avions à réaction*, jet-aircraft.

réactionnaire, *a.* and *n.* Reactionary.

réactionner, *v.t.* To sue again.—*v.i.* (*St. Exch.*) To react against a rise.

réadmettre [read′mɛtr], *v.t. irr.* (*conjug. like* METTRE) To admit again.

réadmission, *n.f.* Readmission, readmittance.

réagir [rea′ʒiːr], *v.i.* To react.

réajournement [reaʒurnə′mɑ̃], *n.m.* Readjournment.

réajourner, *v.t.* To readjourn.

réalgar [real′gaːr], *n.m.* (*Chem.*) Realgar.

réalisable [reali′zabl], *a.* Realizable.

réalisateur, *n.m.* (*Cine.*) Film director.

réalisation, *n.f.* Realization; conversion into money, profit-taking; clearance sale; selling-out.

réaliser, *v.t.* To realize; to convert into money. **se réaliser,** *v.r.* To be realized, to come true.

réalisme, *n.m.* Realism. **réaliste,** *n.* Realist. —*a.* Realistic.

réalité, *n.f.* Reality. *En réalité*, in reality, indeed.

réaménager [reamena′ʒe], *v.t.* To refit.

réanimer [reani′me], *v.t.* To reanimate.

réapparaître, *v.i. irr.* (*conjugated like* CONNAÎTRE) To reappear. **réapparition,** *n.f.* Reappearance.

réapprovisionner [RAVITAILLER].

réargenter, *v.t.* To resilver, to replate. **réargenture,** *n.f.* Resilvering, replating.

réarmement, *n.m.* Rearming, rearmament. **réarmer,** *v.t.* To arm again, to rearm; (*Navy*) to refit, to put into commission again.

réassurance, *n.f.* Reinsurance. **réassurer,** *v.t.* To reinsure.

rebaisser [rəbɛ′se], *v.t.* To lower again.

rébarbatif [rebarba′tif], *a.* (*fem.* **-ive**) Stern, surly, grim, crabbed, forbidding.

rebâtir [rəba′tiːr], *v.t.* To rebuild.

rebattre [rə'batr], *v.t. irr.* (*conjug. like* BATTRE) To beat again; to repeat, to tell over and over again; to shuffle (cards) again.

rebattu, *a.* (*fem.* **-ue**) Hackneyed, trite, oft-told. *J'en ai les oreilles rebattues*, I am sick of hearing it so often; *rester dans les sentiers rebattus*, to stick to the beaten track; *un conte rebattu*, a trite story.

rebec [rə'bɛk], *n.m.* Rebeck.

rebelle [rə'bɛl], *n.* Rebel.—*a.* Rebellious; disobedient, fractious (child); unyielding, obstinate; unwieldy; refractory. *Rebelle à la raison*, impervious to reason; *une chevelure rebelle*, hair that is difficult to manage; *un sujet rebelle à la poésie*, a subject unsuitable for verse. **se rebeller**, *v.r.* To rebel, to revolt.

rébellion [rebɛ'ljɔ̃], *n.f.* Rebellion, revolt; resistance, contumacy.

rebiffer [rəbi'fe], *v.i.* (*pop.*) To do it again; to get one's back up. *Cela m'a fait rebiffer*, it put my back up. **se rebiffer**, *v.r.* (*fam.*) To bridle up, to bristle up, to get one's back up, to kick over the traces; to express open refusal or revolt.

reblanchir, *v.t.* To bleach *or* whitewash again.

reboire [rə'bwa:r], *v.t. irr.* (*conjug. like* BOIRE) To drink again.

reboisement [rəbwaz'mɑ̃], *n.m.* Retimbering, reafforestation. **reboiser**, *v.t.* To retimber, to reafforest.

rebond [rə'bɔ̃], *n.m.* Rebound; bounce (of ball).

rebondi, *a.* (*fem.* **-ie**) Plump, chubby. *Des joues rebondies*, chubby cheeks.

rebondir, *v.i.* To rebound; to bounce. **rebondissement**, *n.m.* Rebounding; bounce, bouncing.

rebord [rə'bɔ:r], *n.m.* Edge, brim, brink; sill (of window); border, hem. **reborder**, *v.t.* To border again, to re-hem.

rebouillir [rəbu'ji:r], *v.i. irr.* (*conjug. like* BOUILLIR) To boil again.

rebours [rə'bu:r], *n.m.* Wrong side (of a stuff etc.); wrong way (of the grain); contrary, reverse. *À rebours* or *au rebours*, the wrong way, against the grain, backwards; *lire à rebours*, to read backwards; *marcher à rebours*, to walk backwards; *prendre à rebours*, to misconstrue.—*a.* (*fem.* **-se**) Cross-grained (wood); intractable (horse).

reboutage [rəbu'ta:ʒ], *n.m.* Bone-setting. **rebouter**, *v.t.* To set (bones). **rebouteur** or **rebouteux**, *n.m.* (*fem.* **-euse**) Bone-setter.

reboutonner [rəbutɔ'ne], *v.t.* To rebutton. **se reboutonner**, *v.r.* To button up one's clothes again.

rebroussement, *n.m.* Turning back, turning up. **rebrousse-poil (à)**, *adv. phr.* Against the grain; the wrong way. **rebrousser**, *v.t.* To turn up (the hair); to strike (skins); to grain (leather). *Faire rebrousser chemin à quelqu'un*, to head someone off; *rebrousser chemin*, to turn back, to retrace one's steps. **rebrousseur**, *n.m.* Striker (of skins).

rebroussoir, *n.m.*, or **rebroussette**, *n.f.* Napping-tool for cloth.

rebuffade [rəby'fad], *n.f.* Rebuff, repulse; snub.

rébus [re'by:s], *n.m.* Rebus; riddle.

rebut [rə'by], *n.m.* Repulse, rebuff, rejection, refusal; refuse, rubbish; outcast, riffraff, scum. *Le rebut de l'humanité*, the scum of the earth; *marchandises de rebut*, waste goods; *mettre au rebut*, to throw aside; *mettre une lettre au rebut*, to send a letter to the dead-letter office; *papier de rebut*, waste paper.

rebutant, *a.* (*fem.* **-ante**) Repulsive, disgusting, forbidding. *Air rebutant*, forbidding look; *travail rebutant*, tedious work.

rebuter, *v.t.* To repulse, to rebuff, to reject, to snub; to disgust, to shock. **Il a rebuté ces marchandises*, he rejected those goods; *rebuter des excuses*, to refuse an apology.—*v.i.* To be repulsive. **se rebuter**, *v.r.* To become discouraged. *Il se rebute aisément*, he is easily disheartened; *se rebuter devant quelque chose*, to baulk at something.

recalcifiant [rəkalsi'fjɑ̃], *a.* and *n.* (*fem.* **-iante**) Having calcifying properties. **recalcification**, *n.f.* Strengthening of teeth and bones. **recalcifier**, *v.t.* To recalcify; to strengthen bones and teeth by giving calcium.

récalcitrant [rekalsi'trɑ̃], *a.* (*fem.* **-ante**) Refractory, recalcitrant; rebellious; averse.

récalcitrer, *v.i.* *To be restive, to kick (of horses); (*fig.*) to be refractory; to resist, to be reluctant.

recaler [rəka'le], *v.t.* To wedge up again, to refix, to readjust; to retouch, to better (a drawing etc.); (*sch.*) to plough, to pluck (at an examination). *Il a été recalé*, he has been ploughed.

récapitulatif [rekapityla'tif], *a.* (*fem.* **-ive**) Recapitulatory.

récapitulation, *n.f.* Recapitulation, summing up; résumé, summary.

récapituler, *v.t.* To recapitulate, to sum up; (*colloq.*) to recap.

recel [rə'sɛl] or **recèlement**, *n.m.* Receiving of stolen goods. **receler** or **recéler**, *v.t. irr.* (*conjug. like* ACCÉLÉRER) To receive (stolen goods); to embezzle; to conceal from justice; to hide; to contain, to possess. *La Bretagne recèle des coins charmants*, in Brittany one comes across some delightful spots. **receleur**, *n.m.* (*fem.* **-euse**) Receiver of stolen goods, fence.

récemment [resa'mɑ̃], *adv.* Recently, newly, lately.

recensement [rəsɑ̃s'mɑ̃], *n.m.* Census; return, statement, inventory; record, review (of events etc.); verification. *Faire le recensement*, to take a census; *recensement des jeunes soldats*, return or census of young men liable to military service.

recenser, *v.t.* To take the census of; to record; to count (votes); to verify, to examine.

recenseur, *n.m.* Census-taker; enumerator.

recension, *n.f.* Recension; collation (of books etc.).

récent [re'sɑ̃], *a.* (*fem.* **-ente**) Recent, new, fresh, late.

recépage [rəse'pa:ʒ], or **recepage**, *n.m.* Cutting down close (vines, young trees, etc.).

recepée or **recépée**, *n.f.* Cut part of a wood, clearing.

receper or **recéper**, *v.t. irr.* (*conjugated like* ACCÉLÉRER) To cut down close; to cut back; to clear (a wood etc.); (*Mil.*) to cut off the tops (of stakes).

récépissé [resepi'se], *n.m.* Receipt, acknowledgment (for documents, papers, etc.).

réceptacle [resɛp'takl], *n.m.* Receptacle; repository; torus (of flower); (*fig.*) resort, haunt. **récepteur,** *a.* (*fem.* **-trice**) Receiving. *Machine réceptrice,* dynamo receiving current from a distance; *poste récepteur,* receiving set.—*n.m.* Receiver, reservoir (in a machine, etc.); receiving instrument (of telegraphs).

réception, *n.f.* Receiving, receipt; admission; (hotel) reception desk; official acceptance; levée, drawing-room, reception (at court); entertainment. *Jour de réception,* at-home day.

réceptionnaire, *n.* Receiver, receiving clerk; consignee.—*a.* Receiving.

réceptionniste, *n.* Receptionist.

réceptivité, *n.f.* Receptivity.

recette [rə'sɛt], *n.f.* Receipts, returns; takings, gate-money; (*Cook.*) recipe; receivership; receiver's office. *Faire recette,* (of a play) to be a draw, to be good box-office; *garçon de recette,* (*Bank* etc.) messenger; *recette buraliste,* tobacconist's (in France); *recettes et dépenses,* revenue and expenditure.

recevabilité [rəsəvabili'te], *n.f.* Receivability, admissibility. **recevable,** *a.* Receivable, admissible, allowed.

receveur, *n.m.* (*fem.* **-euse**) Receiver, collector (of taxes etc.). *Receveur d'autobus,* (bus-) conductor. *Receveuse des Postes,* postmistress.

recevoir [rəsə'vwa:r], *v.t. irr.* (*pres.p.* **recevant** *p.p.* **reçu**) To receive, to accept, to take, to take in, to let in, to admit; to welcome, to harbour; to entertain. *Je reçois vos offres,* I accept your offers; *recevoir bien,* to receive well, to welcome; *recevoir un coup mortel,* to be mortally wounded; *recevoir une excuse,* to accept an excuse; *recevoir un mauvais accueil,* to meet with a bad reception; *se faire recevoir avocat,* to be called to the bar.—*v.i.* To receive, to receive company; to be at home to visitors; to hold a levee or reception. *Elle reçoit beaucoup,* she entertains a great deal; *on recevra ce soir-là,* there will be company that evening; *quand recevez-vous?* when are you at home?

réchampir [reʃã'pi:r] or **échampir,** *v.t.* (*Paint.*) To pick out with colours, to set off; to remove stains before gilding a background.

rechange [rə'ʃã:ʒ], *n.m.* Change of anything, refill; replacement; spare things; (*Naut.*) spare stores; (*Comm.*) re-exchange. *Habits de rechange,* spare clothes; *j'en ai de rechange,* I have some in reserve; *mâts de hune de rechange,* spare topmasts; *pièces de rechange,* spare parts, spares; *pneu de rechange,* spare tyre.

rechanter [rəʃã'te], *v.t.* To sing again; to repeat, to retell.

rechapage [rəʃa'pa:ʒ], *n.m.* Retreading. **rechaper,** *v.t.* To retread (a tyre).

réchapper [reʃa'pe], *v.i.* To escape. *Réchapper d'une maladie,* to recover from an illness. —*v.t.* To save. *Il m'a réchappé de la mort,* he saved me from death.

recharge [rə'ʃarʒ], *n.f.* Fresh or second charge. *En recharge,* in addition.

rechargement [rəʃarʒə'mã], *n.m.* Reloading, relading; reshipment; reballasting.

recharger [rəʃar'ʒe], *v.t.* To load again; to recharge; to charge again. *Recharger les routes,* to remetal roads.

réchaud [re'ʃo], *n.m.* Small portable stove; chafing-dish; dish-warmer; (*Hort.*) hot-bed, mulch. *Réchaud à alcool,* spirit stove; *réchaud à gaz,* gas-ring; *réchaud de table,* hot-plate.

réchauffage [reʃo'fa:ʒ], *n.m.* Warming up again, reheating.

réchauffé, *n.m.* Dish or food warmed up again; rehash, stale stuff or news. *C'est du réchauffé,* it is mere imitation.

réchauffement [reʃof'mã], *n.m.* Warming up again; (*Hort.*) relining a hot-bed; mulching.

réchauffer [reʃo'fe], *v.t.* To warm up again, to make hot again, to warm up, to reheat; to reanimate, to rekindle, to stir up. *Faire réchauffer la soupe,* to warm up the soup. *Réchauffer un serpent dans son sein,* to nurse a viper in one's bosom. **se réchauffer,** *v.r.* To warm oneself, to get warm; to rekindle, to grow warm again. *Le temps se réchauffe,* the weather is getting warmer.

réchauffoir, *n.m.* Plate-warmer, hot-plate.

rechaussement [reʃos'mã], *n.m.* Banking up (of a tree).

rechausser [reʃo'se], *v.t.* To put shoes or stockings on (a person) again; to set new cogs on (a wheel etc.); (*Hort.*) to bank up; (*Build.*) to underpin. *Rechausser un mur,* to underpin a wall.

rêche [rɛ:ʃ], *a.* Rough (to the taste, touch, etc.); (*fig.*) sour, crabbed (of persons).

recherche [rə'ʃɛrʃ], *n.f.* Search, quest, pursuit; inquiry, investigation, examination, scrutiny; research, inquiries; addresses, courtship, suit; (*fig.*) studied elegance or refinement, affectation. *Faire la recherche d'une chose,* to search for a thing; *faire des recherches,* to carry out investigations, to do research, to make researches; *se lancer, se mettre à la recherche de,* to set off in search of; *style naturel et sans recherche,* natural and unaffected style; *travailler à la recherche de la vérité,* to labour in search of truth.

recherché [rəʃɛr'ʃe], *a.* (*fem.* **-ée**) Choice, refined, exquisite; affected, studied, far-fetched; sought after, in great request, in great demand. *Expression recherchée,* far-fetched expression; *ornements recherchés,* choice ornaments.

rechercher [rəʃɛr'ʃe], *v.t.* To seek again, to look for again; to seek, to seek after, to search for; to investigate, to search into, to make an inquiry into, to pry into; to desire, to aspire to, to be eager for; to endeavour to obtain; to court, to woo. *Se faire rechercher,* to be courted.

rechigné [rəʃi'ɲe], *a.* (*fem.* **-ée**) Sour-faced, sour-tempered, sour, surly, cross-grained, crabbed.

rechignement [rəʃiɲə'mã], *n.m.* Sulking, sullenness.

rechigner [rəʃi'ɲe], *v.i.* To look sulky, sullen, grim, etc. *En rechignant,* with a bad grace.

rechoir [rə'ʃwa:r], *v.i. irr.* (*conjug. like* CHOIR) To fall again, to have a relapse.

rechute, *n.f.* Second fall; relapse, set-back; backsliding. **rechuter,** *v.i.* To have a relapse *or* a set-back; to backslide.

récidive [resi'di:v], *n.f.* Recidivism, relapse into crime; second offence, repetition of an offence; recurrence (of disease). *Il y a récidive,* it is not the first offence. **récidiver,**

v.i. To repeat the offence; to relapse; to recur (of disease).
récidiviste, *n.* Recidivist, old offender, old lag.
récif [re'sif], *n.m.* Reef (of rocks).
récipé [resi'pe], *n.m.* Recipe, prescription.
récipiendaire [resipjɑ̃'dɛːr], *n.m.* New member, member-elect (object of ceremonial reception).
récipient [resi'pjɑ̃], *n.m.* Container, receptacle, vessel; reservoir, cistern, well (of a machine etc.), receiver (of air-pump).
réciprocation [resiprɔkɑ'sjɔ̃], *n.f.* Reciprocation, reciprocating. **réciprocité,** *n.f.* Reciprocity, reciprocation. **réciproque,** *a.* Reciprocal, mutual; (*Math.*) converse, reciprocal.—*n.f.* The same, the like; (*Math.*) converse, reciprocal. *Rendre la réciproque,* to return the like, to give tit for tat. **réciproquement,** *adv.* Reciprocally, mutually; vice versa; (*Math.*) conversely.
récit [re'si], *n.m.* Recital, account, story, narrative, report; (*Mus.*) recitative. **récital,** *n.m.* (*pl.* **-als**) Musical recital.
récitant, *a,* (*fem.* **-ante**) (*Mus.*) Solo (instrument, voice).—*n.* Soloist; narrator.
récitateur, *n.m.* (*fem.* **-trice**) Reciter, repeater.
récitatif, *n.m.* (*Mus.*) Recitative.
récitation, *n.f.* Recitation, reciting; repetition.
réciter, *v.t.* To recite, to rehearse; to repeat, to say; to tell, to relate, to recount; (*Mus.*) to sing or execute in recitative; to play in recitative. *Fais-moi réciter (ma leçon),* hear me; *récitez votre leçon,* say your lesson.
réciteur, *n.m.* (*fem.* **-euse**) Reciter, storyteller.
réclamant [rekla'mɑ̃], *a.* (*fem.* **-ante**) Claiming.—*n.* Claimant. **réclamation,** *n.f.* Claim, request, demand; complaint, protest, objection. *Bureau des réclamations,* claims department.
réclame [re'klaːm], *n.f.* Advertisement; publicity; (*Print.*) catch-word; puff, puffing. *Faire de la réclame,* to advertise; *réclame lumineuse,* illuminated sign; *réclame réciproque (entre auteurs),* (*fig.*) log-rolling, back-scratching.
réclamer [rekla'me], *v.t.* To crave, to entreat; to beseech, to demand, to require; to clamour for; to reclaim, to claim back, to demand back; to claim. *Réclamer son droit,* to claim one's right; *réclamer des dommages pour,* to sue for; (*Turf*) *course à réclamer,* selling race.—*v.i.* To object, to make a complaint, to protest (*contre*). *Je réclame contre cela,* I protest against that; *personne ne réclame?* does nobody raise any objection? **se réclamer,** *v.r.* To make use of (someone's name), to refer to. *Voyant qu'on allait le maltraiter, il se réclama d'un tel,* seeing they were about to ill-treat him, he mentioned so-and-so's name.
reclassement [rəklas'mɑ̃], *n.m.* Reclassifying, regrading; regrouping. **reclasser,** *v.t.* To reclassify, to regroup; to regrade (civil servants etc.).
reclure [rə'klyːr], *v.t.* (*only used in the infinitive and compound tenses. p.p.* **reclus**) To shut up, to confine.
reclus [rə'kly], *a.* (*fem.* **-use**) Shut up,

sequestered, secluded.—*n.* Recluse; monk, nun.
reclusion or **réclusion,** *n.f.* Reclusion, confinement; (*Law*) solitary confinement (with hard labour). **reclusionnaire** or **réclusionnaire,** *n.* Person punished thus.
récognitif [rekɔgni'tif], *a.* (*fem.* **-ive**) Recognitory. *Acte récognitif,* ratification of a liability (stating the consideration thereof).
recoin [rə'kwɛ̃], *n.m.* Corner, nook; (*pl.*) innermost recess. *Coins et recoins,* nooks and crannies.
récolement [rekɔl'mɑ̃], *n.m.* (*Law*) Reading of depositions to witnesses; checking, verification.
récoler [rekɔ'le], *v.t.* To read his previous evidence to (a witness); to check, to examine, to verify.
récollet [rekɔ'lɛ], *n.m.* (*fem.* **-ette**) Recollect (Franciscan friar or nun).
récolte [re'kɔlt], *n.f.* Harvest, crop, vintage; (*fig.*) gatherings, result; profits, benefit. *Faire la récolte,* to get in the harvest.
récolter [rekɔl'te], *v.t.* To reap, to gather in; to get in.
recommandable [rəkɔmɑ̃'dabl], *a.* Recommendable; respectable; trustworthy, commendable; advisable.
recommandation, *n.f.* Recommendation; reference, introduction; (*Law*) detainer; (*fig.*) esteem, consideration; (*Post*) registration. *Lettre de recommandation,* letter of introduction; testimonial.
recommander [rəkɔmɑ̃'de], *v.t.* To recommend; to charge, to enjoin, to bid; to request; to advise; to commend; (*Law*) to lodge a detainer against; (*Post*) to register. *Faire recommander une lettre,* to have a letter registered; *je vous recommande le secret,* I enjoin secrecy; *recommander son âme à Dieu,* to commend one's soul to God. **se recommander,** *v.r.* To recommend oneself or itself; to request protection (*à*); to refer to. *Je me recommande à vous,* I appeal to you or to your kindness; *se recommander de quelqu'un,* to give someone as a reference.
recommencement [rəkɔmɑ̃s'mɑ̃], *n.m.* Recommencement, beginning anew, new beginning, new start, fresh start.
recommencer, *v.t., v.i.* To recommence, to begin again, to start again. *C'est toujours à recommencer,* there's no end to it; *recommencer de plus belle,* to begin again more vigorously than ever; *recommencer la guerre,* to start another war; *ne recommencez pas, par exemple,* don't do it again.
récompense [rekɔ̃'pɑ̃ːs], *n.f.* Reward, recompense; prize; requital; compensation, amends, indemnity. *En récompense de,* in return for; *pour récompense de,* as a reward for.
récompenser, *v.t.* To reward, to requite, to recompense; to make amends to, to compensate; to repay, to punish. *Il faut le récompenser de sa peine,* he must be rewarded for his pains.
recomposer [rəkɔ̃po'ze], *v.t.* To recompose; to recombine (chemical elements); to reset (printing).
recomposition, *n.f.* Recomposition.
réconciliable [rekɔ̃si'ljabl], *a.* Reconcilable.
réconciliateur, *n.m.* (*fem.* **-trice**) Reconciler.
réconciliation, *n.f.* Reconciliation. *Amener*

une réconciliation, to bring about a reconciliation.

réconcilier, *v.t.* (*conjugated like* PRIER) To reconcile, to make friends again. *On les a réconciliés*, they have been reconciled. **se réconcilier**, *v.r.* To be reconciled, to become friends again; to make it up. *Il s'est réconcilié avec son père*, he has made it up with his father.

réconduction or **reconduction** [rəkɔ̃dyk'sjɔ̃], *n.f.* (*Law*) Renewal of a lease or tenancy.

reconduire [rəkɔ̃'dɥiːr], *v.t. irr.* (*conjug. like* CONDUIRE) To reconduct, to lead back, to see home, to take back; to show out, to accompany to the door; to drive back (the enemy).

reconduite [rəkɔ̃'dɥit], *n.f.* Showing out or to the door, seeing out, seeing home.

réconfort [rekɔ̃'fɔːr], *n.m.* Comfort, relief.

réconfortation, *n.f.* Comforting, cheering up. **réconforter**, *v.t.* To comfort, to cheer up, to fortify, to revive.

reconnaissable [rəkɔnɛ'sabl], *a.* Recognizable. *Il n'est plus reconnaissable*, you would not know him (again).

reconnaissance, *n.f.* Recognition; discovery; gratitude, thankfulness; review, survey, examination; acknowledgment, avowal, confession; reward, return; recognizance; a pawn-ticket; (*Mil.*) reconnaissance, reconnoitring, reconnoitring party. *Aller en* or *faire une reconnaissance*, to go on a reconnaissance; *avions de reconnaissance*, reconnaissance aircraft; *en reconnaissance de mes services*, as an acknowledgment of my services; *témoigner sa reconnaissance*, to show one's gratitude. *Une reconnaissance de dette*, an IOU.

reconnaissant, *a.* (*fem.* **-ante**) Grateful, thankful.

reconnaître [rəkɔ'nɛːtr], *v.t. irr.* (*conjugated like* CONNAÎTRE) To recognize, to know again, to know, to identify; to find out, to discover; to acknowledge, to confess, to admit; to be grateful for; to reconnoitre, to explore. *Être reconnu coupable*, to be found guilty; *je ne le reconnais plus*, he has grown out of all recognition (of growing child); *je le reconnais à son chapeau*, I know or identify him from his hat; I recognize him by his hat; *je vous reconnais bien là*, that is just like you; *reconnaître son erreur*, to admit one's mistake; *reconnaître un enfant*, to acknowledge a child; *se faire reconnaître*, to make oneself known. **se reconnaître**, *v.r.* To recognize oneself, to see oneself (in one's child etc.); to be recognizable; to make out where one is, to collect oneself; to come to oneself. *Se reconnaître coupable*, to acknowledge one's guilt, to plead guilty, to repent; *il se reconnaît dans son fils*, he sees himself in his son; *je commence à me reconnaître*, I begin to know where I am; *je me reconnais bien là*, that is just like me; *je ne me reconnais plus*, I don't know what I am about; *s'y reconnaître*, to be able to find one's way about, to find one's bearings.

reconquérir [rəkɔ̃ke'riːr], *v.t. irr.* (*conjugated like* ACQUÉRIR) To reconquer; to recover, to regain.

reconquête, *n.f.* Reconquest.

reconsidération [rəkɔ̃sidera'sjɔ̃], *n.f.* Reconsideration.

reconsidérer, *v.t.* To reconsider.

reconstituant [rəkɔ̃sti'tɥɑ̃], *n.m. and a.* Restorative, tonic.

reconstituer, *v.t.* To reconstitute, to restore.

reconstitution, *n.f.* Reconstitution, reorganization; reconstruction (of a murder).

reconstruction [rəkɔ̃stryk'sjɔ̃], *n.f.* Reconstruction, rebuilding; rehabilitation (of devastated regions).

reconstruire, *v.t. irr.* (*coniug. like* CONDUIRE) To rebuild, to reconstruct; to rehabilitate.

reconvention [rəkɔ̃vɑ̃'sjɔ̃], *n.f.* (*Law*) Cross-suit, counter-claim, set-off.

reconventionnel, *a.* (*fem.* **-elle**) Cross, counter. *Demande reconventionnelle*, cross-action, counter-claim.

reconversion [rəkɔ̃ver'sjɔ̃], *n.f.* Reconversion.

reconvoquer [rəkɔ̃vɔ'ke], *v.t.* To convene again, to call together again.

recopier [rəkɔ'pje], *v.t.* To copy again, to make a copy of.

recoquillement [rəkɔkij'mɑ̃], *n.m.* Curling up, dog('s)-earing (of pages of book).

recoquiller, *v.t.* To turn up or back, to dog('s)-ear (pages). **se recoquiller**, *v.r.* To curl up, to be dog('s)-eared, to shrivel.

record [rə'kɔːr], *n.m.* Record (in sports etc.); peak output. *Battre, détenir le record du saut en longueur*, to beat, to hold the record for the long-jump.

recorder (1) [rəkɔr'de], *v.t.* To rehearse (a lesson), to learn by heart.

recorder (2) [rekɔr'de], *v.t.* To rope up again, to tie up again; to measure firewood again. ***se recorder**, *v.r.* To call to mind; (*colloq.*) to concert with someone.

recordman [rəkɔrd'man], *n.m.* (*fem.* **-woman**, *pl.* **-men, -women**) Record-holder.

recors [rə'kɔːr], *n.m.* Bailiff's man.

recoucher [rəku'ʃe], *v.t.* To put to bed again; to lay down again. **se recoucher**, *v.r.* To go to bed again, to lie down again.

recoudre [rə'kudr], *v.t. irr.* (*conjug. like* COUDRE) To sew again, to sew up.

recoupe [rə'kup], *n.f.* Grits (of flour); stone-chips, chippings; shreds (of cloth etc.); filings; second crop.

recoupement, *n.m.* (*Build.*) Off-set; cross-checking.

recouper, *v.t.* To cut again, to cross-check; to blend (wines).

recoupette, *n.f.* Coarse meal; third flour.

recourbé [rəkur'be], *a.* (*fem.* **-ée**) Curved, bent (back). *Poignée recourbée*, crook handle.

recourber, *v.t.* To bend back, to bend round, to crook. **se recourber**, *v.r.* To be curved, to bend.

recourir [rəku'riːr], *v.i. irr.* (*conjug. like* COURIR) To run again; to run back; to have recourse, to resort (*à*); (*Law*) to appeal. *Recourir aux remèdes*, to have recourse to remedies.

recours [rə'kur], *n.m.* Recourse; lieu; (*fig.*) refuge, resort, resource, redress, remedy; (*Law*) appeal. *Recours en cassation*, petition, appeal; *recours en grâce*, petition for pardon or commutation.

recousu [rəku'zy], *a.* (*fem.* **-ue**) Sewn or stitched again.

recouvrable [rəku'vrabl], *a.* Recoverable.

recouvrement (1) [rəkuvrə'mɑ̃], *n.m.* Recovery, regaining; recovering (of debts etc.);

(*pl.*) debts due to one. *Faire un état de recouvrement*, to draw up a statement of debts due; *faire un recouvrement*, to recover an outstanding debt; *recouvrement de la santé*, recovery of one's health.

recouvrement (2) [rəkuvrə'mã], *n.m.* Covering up, overlaying, overlapping; lap (of tiles); lid; cap (of a watch); (*Arch.*) overlapping; (*Geol.*) overstep, overstepping. *À recouvrement*, overlapped, capped.

recouvrer [rəku'vre], *v.t.* To recover, to get (something) back, to retrieve, to recuperate; to get in, to collect. *Créances à recouvrer*, outstanding debts; *recouvrer ses forces*, to recover one's strength, to recuperate; *recouvrer son bien*, to recover one's fortune.

recouvrir [rəku'vriːr], *v.t. irr.* (*conjug. like* OUVRIR) To cover again; to cover up, to cover over, to overlay; to mask, to hide, to conceal; (*Arch.*) to overlap. **se recouvrir,** *v.r.* To cover oneself again; to become overcast again, to cloud over.

recracher [rəkra'ʃe], *v.t.* To spit out again; to disgorge.—*v.i.* To spit again.

récréatif [rékrea'tif], *a.* (*fem.* **-ive**) Recreative, entertaining, diverting, amusing.

récréation [rekrea'sjɔ̃], *n.f.* Recreation, amusement, diversion; play, playtime (of children), break. *Cour de récréation*, playground; *être en récréation*, to be at play.

re-création [rəkrea'sjɔ̃], *n.f.* Re-creation, new creation.

recréer [rəkre'e], *v.t.* To re-create, to create again.

récréer [rekre'e], *v.t.* To entertain; to divert, to amuse. **se récréer,** *v.r.* To amuse oneself, to take recreation.

récrément [rekre'mã], *n.m.* Recrement.

recrépir [rəkre'piːr], *v.t.* To give a fresh coat of plaster to; to repoint (a wall); to paint (one's face); to patch up; to recast. *Recrépir son visage*, to re-do one's face, to put on fresh make-up; *recrépir un vieux conte*, to dress up an old story; *recrépir un vieux mur*, to replaster an old wall. **recrépissement** or **recrépissage,** *n.m.* Replastering; repatching.

récrier (se) [rekri'e], *v.r.* (*conjugated like* PRIER) To exclaim, to cry out; to protest (*contre*); to be amazed, to exclaim in admiration. *Il n'y a pas de quoi se récrier*, there is nothing to make a fuss about.

récriminateur [rekrimina'tœːr], *a.* (*fem.* **-trice**) Recriminative.—*n.* Recriminator.

récrimination [rekrimina'sjɔ̃], *n.f.* Recrimination. **récriminatoire,** *a.* Recriminatory.

récriminer [rekrimi'ne], *v.i.* To recriminate.

récrire [re'kriːr], *v.t. irr.* (*conjug. like* ÉCRIRE) To write again, to rewrite; to write over again; to write back; to put into new shape, to recast.—*v.i.* To write again (to someone).

recroqueviller (se) [rəkrɔkvi'je], *v.r.* To curl up, to shrivel (of withered leaves etc.).

recru (1) [rə'kry], *a.* (*fem.* **recrue** (1)) Tired out, worn out, jaded (*especially in*) *recru de fatigue*, dead tired.

recrû or **recru** (2), *n.m.* New growth (of coppice).

recrudescence [rəkryde'sãːs], *n.f.* Recrudescence; renewed outbreak, new spell. *En*

recrudescence, on the increase. **recrudescent,** *a.* (*fem.* **-ente**) Recrudescent.

recrue (2) [rə'kry], *n.f.* Recruiting; recruit; new adherent or member.

recrutement, *n.m.* Recruiting, recruitment.

recruter, *v.t.* To recruit; to enlist (supporters), to enrol (members). **se recruter,** *v.r.* To be recruited.

recruteur, *n.m.* Recruiter; recruiting officer.

recta [rɛk'ta], *adv.* (*fam.*) Punctually, exactly, on the dot.

rectangle [rɛk'tãːgl], *a.* Rectangular, right-angled.—*n.m.* Rectangle.

rectangulaire, *a.* Rectangular, right-angled.

recteur (1) [rɛk'tœːr], *n.m.* Rector, principal (of each of the 'académies' which comprise the French University); principal of certain religious institutions; parish priest (in Brittany).

recteur (2), *a.* (*fem.* **-trice**) Directing; *aromatic. Pennes rectrices* (or *Rectrices, n.f. pl.*), tail-feathers.

rectifiable [rɛkti'fjabl], *a.* Rectifiable.

rectificateur, *a.* (*fem.* **-trice**) Rectifying.—*n.m.* Rectifier.

rectificatif, *a.* (*fem.* **-ive**) Rectifying.—*n.m.* Corrigendum.

rectification, *n.f.* Rectification; adjustment, amendment.

rectifier [rɛkti'fje], *v.t.* (*conjugated like* PRIER) To rectify; to adjust; to amend, to correct, to make right or straight, to reform. (*Mil.*) *Rectifier le tir*, to correct the range; *rectifiez l'alignement!* Right dress!

rectiligne [rɛkti'liɲ], *a.* Rectilinear.

rectitude, *n.f.* Rectitude, uprightness; straightness (of line).

recto, *n.m.* Recto, first page of a leaf, right-hand page.

rectoral, *a.* (*fem.* **-ale,** *pl.* **-aux**) Rectorial.

rectorat, *n.m.* Rectorship.

rectrice [RECTEUR (2)].

rectum [rɛk'tɔm], *n.m.* (*Anat.*) Rectum.

reçu [rə'sy], *a.* (*fem.* **-ue**) Received; admitted, recognized, customary, usual. *Être reçu (à un examen)*, to pass (an examination); *être reçu médecin*, to qualify as a doctor; *une opinion reçue*, a widely accepted opinion.—*n.m.* Receipt. *Au reçu de*, on receipt of; *donnez-moi un reçu de ce que je vous remets*, give me a receipt for what I give you.

recueil [rə'kœːj], *n.m.* Collection, selection, miscellany. *Recueil choisi* or *de morceaux choisis*, anthology; *recueil des lois*, compendium of laws.

recueillement, *n.m.* Meditation; peaceful contemplation. **recueilli,** *a.* (*fem.* **-ie**) In a meditative or contemplative mood (of persons); quiet and conducive to meditation or prayer (of places, atmosphere etc.), rapt. *C'est un homme très recueilli*, he is a very contemplative man.

recueillir [rəkœ'jiːr], *v.t. irr.* (*conjug. like* CUEILLIR) To gather, to get together, to collect, to gather up; to get in, to reap; to receive, to acquire; to take in, to shelter, to harbour. *Recueillir les paroles de quelqu'un*, to record, to set down, to take down someone's words; *recueillir les voix*, to collect the votes; *recueillir ses forces*, to gather one's strength; *recueillir une succession*, to inherit an estate. **se recueillir,** *v.r.* To collect oneself, to collect one's thoughts; to be plunged in meditation; to commune with oneself.

recuire [rə'kɥiːr], *v.t. irr. (conjugated like* CON-DUIRE*)* To cook again; to boil or bake over again; to anneal (metals).

recuit (1), *a. (fem.* **-uite** (1)) Cooked, boiled, baked, or roasted again. *Cela est cuit et recuit,* that is done to rags.

recuit (2), *n.m.,* or **recuite** (2), *n.f.* Annealing (of metals or glass); reheating, rebaking, tempering, etc.

recul [rə'kyl], *n.m.* Recoil (of cannon), kick (of rifle); retirement, retreat (of glacier); backing (of horse, car); recession (of sea-water); room to move back; run-back (of tennis-court).

reculade, *n.f.* Backing (of carriages etc.); falling back, retreat. *Faire une reculade,* to beat a retreat; *honteuse reculade,* shameful climb-down.

reculé, *a. (fem.* **-ée** (1)) Distant, remote. *La postérité la plus reculée,* the remotest posterity.

reculée (2), *n.f.* Backing-room, backing-space; deep, high valley (in Jura).

reculement, *n.m.* Drawing back, backing (of carriages etc.); breech (of saddles).

reculer, *v.t.* To draw back, to move back, to back; *(fig.)* to put farther off; to put off, to defer; to extend (limits etc.).—*v.i.* To go back, to fall back, to draw back, to retreat, to recede; to back out, to recoil, to shrink, to flinch, to waver; to give way. *En reculant,* (going) backwards; *faire reculer l'ennemi,* to force back the enemy; *il est trop avancé pour reculer,* he is too involved to get out of it; *il ne recule jamais,* he never flinches; *il n'y a plus moyen de reculer,* there's no going back; *reculer pour mieux sauter,* to draw back in order to make a spring; *(fig.)* to put off the evil hour. **se reculer,** *v.r.* To draw back, to become more remote.

reculons (à), *adv. phr.* Backwards.

récupérable [rekype'rabl], *a.* Retrievable, recoverable. **récupérage,** *n.m.,* or **récupération,** *n.f.* Recovery, recuperation.

récupérateur, *n.m.* Recuperator.

récupérer, *v.t. irr. (conjug. like* ACCÉLÉRER*)* To recover, to retrieve, to recuperate; *(fam.)* to scrounge; to make good *or* make up (lost time, etc.). **se récupérer,** *v.r.* To recover one's losses.

récurer [reky're], *v.t.* To scour, to clean.

récurrence [reky'rãːs], *n.f.* Recurrence.

récurrent, *a. (fem.* **-ente**) Recurrent.

récusable [reky'zabl], *a. (Law)* Exceptionable, challengeable, doubtful (of witnesses etc.).

récusant, *a. (fem.* **-ante**) Challenging, taking exception.—*n.* Challenger; recusant.

récusation [rekyza'sjɔ̃], *n.f. (Law)* Challenge; exception.

récuser [reky'ze], *v.t.* To challenge, object to, or take exception to (witnesses, jurors, etc.); to impugn; to deny, to reject. **se récuser,** *v.r.* To excuse oneself, to decline; to decline judging, voting, etc. (of judges, jurors, etc.); to declare oneself incompetent.

rédacteur [redak'tœːr], *n.m. (fem.* **-trice**) Writer, inditer (of deed); clerk (in public

office); editor, editress. *Rédacteur en chef,* (chief) editor; *rédacteur-gérant,* manager.

rédaction [redak'sjɔ̃], *n.f.* Drawing up (deeds etc.); wording; editing (periodicals); editorship; editorial staff *or* office; *(sch.)* composition, essay. *Secrétaire de (la) rédaction,* subeditor.

redan or **redent** [rə'dã], *n.m. (Fort.)* Redan; *(Arch.)* foliated cusp; skewback; step (in gable); *(Naut.)* step (under the hull of a hydroplane).

reddition [redi'sjɔ̃], *n.f.* Surrender; rendering (of accounts).

rédempteur [redãp'tœːr], *a. (fem.* **-trice**) Redeeming, redemptory.—*n.m.* Redeemer, saviour.

rédemption, *n.f.* Redemption, redeeming; ransom.

rédemptoriste, *n.m.* Redemptorist.

redescendre [rədɛ'sãːdr], *v.i.* To come, go, step down again; *(Naut.)* to back (of wind). *La marée est redescendue,* the tide has gone out again.—*v.t.* To carry *or* take down again; to bring down again; to come down (the stairs) again. *Il a redescendu l'escalier en courant,* he came running down the stairs again.

redevable [rəd'vabl], *a.* Indebted, owing; *(fig.)* beholden. *Être redevable à . . . de,* to be indebted to . . . for; *je vous suis redevable,* I am in your debt.

redevance, *n.f.* Rent, due, tax; *(Feud. Law)* tenure, due.

redevenir [rədəv'niːr], *v.t. irr. (conjug. like* VENIR*)* To become (something) again.

redevoir [rəd(ə)'vwaːr], *v.t. irr. (conjug. like* DEVOIR*)* To owe still.

rédhibition [redibi'sjɔ̃], *n.f. (Law)* Annulment of sale. **rédhibitoire,** *a.* Vice *rédhibitoire,* redhibitory defect (in a horse).

rédiger [redi'ʒe], *v.t.* To draw up, to draft, to word, to write (up); to edit (newspaper etc.).

rédimer (se) [redi'me], *v.r.* To buy oneself off; to redeem oneself.

redingote [rədɛ̃'gɔt], *n.f.* Frock-coat; (kind of) mannish woman's overcoat.

redire [rə'diːr], *v.t. irr. (conjugated like* DIRE*)* To repeat, to say again, to tell again; to reveal, to let out, to blab.—*v.i.* To criticize, to find fault. *Je n'y trouve rien à redire,* I see nothing wrong with it; *trouver à redire à,* to find fault with. **se redire,** *v.r.* To be repeated; to tell each other.

rediseur, *n.m. (fem.* **-euse**) Repeater; telltale.

redistribuer [rədistri'bɥe], *v.t.* To redistribute. **redistribution,** *n.f.* Redistribution.

redit [rə'di], *a. (fem.* **-ite**) Repeated.—*n.m.* Report, gossip, tittle-tattle.—*n.f.* Repetition, tautology.

redondance [rədɔ̃'dãːs], *n.f.* Superfluity of words, redundancy. **redondant,** *a. (fem.* **-ante**) Redundant.

redonder, *v.i.* To be redundant. *Expressions qui redondent,* superfluous expressions; *redonder d'adjectifs,* to be crammed with adjectives.

redonner [rədɔ'ne], *v.t.* To give again; to give back again, to restore.—*v.i.* To give oneself up again, to fall again; to begin again; to charge again.

redorer [rədɔ're], *v.t.* To regild. *Redorer son blason* (*fig.*), to marry a rich commoner (of a nobleman).

redoublant [rədu'blã], *n.* (*fem.* -**ante**) Pupil who remains a second year in the same class.

redoublé [rədu'ble], *a.* (*fem.* -**ée**) Redoubled, increased; accelerated; repeated. *Frapper à coups redoublés*, to rain blows on; to belabour (someone); *pas redoublé*, quick step; quick march (played by the band); *rimes redoublées*, double rhymes.

redoublement [rədublə'mã], *n.m.* Redoubling, increase; (*Gram.*) reduplication; (*Med.*) paroxysm.

redoubler [rədu'ble], *v.t.* To redouble, to reiterate; to increase; to reline (dress). *Redoubler une classe*, to stay down; *redoubler ses soins*, to be doubly careful.—*v.i.* To increase, to redouble. *Redoubler de soins*, to be even more attentive.

redoul [rə'dul], **rodoul,** or **roudou,** *n.m.* (*Bot.*) Coriaria, myrtifolia, tanners' sumac.

redoutable [rədu'tabl], *a.* Formidable, redoubtable, terrible.

redoute [rə'dut], *n.f.* Redoubt; ridotto; (*in the sense of) entertainment place, 'Palais de Danse'; gala night in such place.

redouter [rədu'te], *v.t.* To dread, to fear. *Il n'est pas à redouter,* ie is not to be feared.

redresse [rə'drɛs], *n.f.* (*Naut.*) Righting tackle. *Être à la redresse,* (*pop.*) to be clever, knowing.

redressement [rədrɛs'mã], *n.m.* Straightening; amendment, rectification, rectifying, redressing, righting, reparation, redress, recovery.

redresser [rədrɛ'se], *v.t.* To make straight, to true (a wheel); to straighten, to re-erect, to set up again; to put right, to rectify, to reform, to right, to set to rights; (*colloq.*) to rebuke, to reprimand. *Redresser des griefs*, to redress grievances; *redresser la tête*, to hold up one's head. **se redresser,** *v.r.* To become straight again; to sit or stand erect again; to be righted, to right itself (of a ship etc.); to be set right, to be redressed. *Redressez-vous,* sit up.

redresseur, *a.* (*fem.* -**euse**) (*Elec.*) *Dispositif redresseur*, rectifying device; (*Opt.*) erecting device.—*n.m.* Redresser, righter; (*Elec.*) rectifier. *Redresseur de torts*, knight-errant.

redû [rə'dy], *n.m.* Balance due.

réducteur [redyk'tœːr], *a.* (*fem.* -**trice**) Reducing.—*n.m.* (*Chem.*) Reducer.

réductibilité, *n.f.* Reducibleness. **réductible,** *a.* Reducible. **réductif,** *a.* (*fem.* -**ive**) Reductive.

réduction, *n.f.* Reduction; subjugation; allowance, abatement; mitigation (of penalty); disrating (in navy); reducing (in rank). *Réduction des salaires*, cuts in wages; *réduction d'une fracture*, setting of a fracture.

réduire [re'dɥiːr], *v.t. irr.* (*pres.p.* **réduisant,** *p.p.* **réduit**; (*conjugated like* CONDUIRE) To reduce, to bring down, to abate, to diminish, to abridge, to curtail; to resolve, to convert, to transform; to condense, to grind, to boil down, etc.; to subdue, to subjugate; to compel, to oblige. *Faire réduire une sauce*, to boil down a sauce; *réduire au désespoir*, to

drive to despair; *réduire des fractions au même dénominateur*, to reduce fractions to the same denominator; *réduire en atomes*, to grind to atoms; *réduire à une plus petite échelle*, to reduce to a smaller scale; *réduire le capital*, to write down the capital; *réduire les francs en centimes*, to reduce francs to centimes; *réduire une place*, (*Mil.*) to reduce a stronghold. **se réduire,** *v.r.* To be reduced, to diminish, to abate, to vanish, to dwindle away; to confine oneself; to be subdued; to be brought, to come, to amount (à).

réduit [re'dɥi], *n.m.* Retreat, poor habitation or lodging; corner, nook, hovel; (*Fort.*) reduit; keep; (*Navy.*) armoured gun emplacement.—*a.* Reduced; dimmed (of light); substandard (of gauge). *À prix réduit*, at a reduced price; *médaille modèle réduit*, miniature medal. (*Cine.*) *Format réduit*, reduction print.

réduplicatif [redyplika'tif], *a.* (*fem.* -**ive**) Reduplicative. **réduplication,** *n.f.* Reduplication.

réédification [reedifika'sjɔ̃], *n.f.* Rebuilding. **réédifier,** *v.t.* To rebuild.

rééditer [reedi'te], *v.t.* To bring out a new edition of; (*Cine.*) to re-edit. **réédition,** *n.f.* New edition.

rééducatif [reedyka'tif], *a.* (*fem.* -**ive**) *Thérapie rééducative*, occupational therapy. **rééducation,** *n.f.* Re-education; occupational therapy. **rééduquer,** *v.t.* To re-educate (muscles, nerves).

réel [re'ɛl], *a.* (*fem.* **réelle**) Real, actual; genuine, sterling; (*Math.*) material, substantial.—*n.m.* That which is real, reality.

réélection [reelɛk'sjɔ̃], *n.f.* Re-election. **rééligibilité,** *n.f.* Re-eligibility. **rééligible,** *a.* Re-eligible. **réélire,** *v.t. irr.* (*conjug. like* LIRE) To re-elect.

réellement [reɛl'mã], *adv.* Really, in reality; truly, indeed.

réembarquer [REMBARQUER].

réembobinage [reãbɔbi'naːʒ], *n.m.* (*Cine.*) Rewinding. **réembobiner,** *v.t.* To rewind. **réembobineuse,** *n.f.* Rewinder.

réemploi [reã'plwã], *n.m.* Re-employment.

réenregistrement [reãrəʒistrə'mã], *n.m.* Re-recording. **réenregistrer,** *v.t.* To re-record.

réer [RAIRE].

réescompte [rees'kɔ̃ːt], *n.m.* Rediscount. **réescompter,** *v.t.* To rediscount.

réexpédier [reekspe'dje], *v.t.* To send on, to (re)forward; to send back. **réexpédition,** *n.f.* Sending off again; forwarding, return.

réexportation [reeksporta'tjɔ̃], *n.f.* Re-exportation. **réexporter,** *v.t.* To re-export.

refaçon [rəfa'sɔ̃], *n.f.* Remaking. **refaçonner,** *v.t.* To make again, to refashion.

réfaction [refak'sjɔ̃], *n.f.* Rebate, reduction of duty on damaged goods; repairs.

refaire [rə'fɛːr], *v.t. irr.* (*conjugated like* FAIRE) To do again, to remake; to begin anew, to recommence; to do up, to mend, to repair; to deal again (at cards); to refresh, to revive; (*slang*) to diddle, to take in. **se refaire,** *v.r.* To refresh oneself, to recover one's strength; to recoup oneself, to retrieve one's losses, to set oneself up again.

refait [rə'fɛ], *n.m.* Drawn game; new horns (on stag).—*a.* (*fem.* -**te**) Set up, done again;

(*slang*) done, dished, had; robbed. *J'ai été refait(e)*, I have been had.

réfection [refɛk'sjɔ̃], *n.f.* Repairs (to buildings etc.); *refection, repast.

réfectoire [refɛk'twaːr], *n.m.* Refectory, dining-room or -hall (in college, convent, etc.).

refend [rə'fɑ̃], *n.m.* Splitting, sawing, dividing. *Bois de refend*, sawn timber; *lignes de refend*, grooves on walls marking or simulating joints; *mur de refend*, partition wall.

refendre [rə'fɑ̃ːdr], *v.t.* To cleave or split again; to saw or cut lengthwise, to quarter (timber); to saw (stone) into slabs.

référé [refe're], *n.m.* (*Law*) Plea of urgency. *Juger en référé*, to give provisional order.

référence [refe'rɑ̃ːs], *n.f.* Reference; (*pl.*) references, character. *Cadre or système de référence*, (*Math.*) frame of reference.

référendaire [referɑ̃'dɛːr], *n.m.* Referendary. **référendariat**, *n.m.* Position of referendary.

referendum or **référendum**, *n.m.* Referendum.

référer [refe're], *v.t.* To refer; to ascribe.—*v.i.* To refer, to have reference. *En référer à*, to refer to. *Nous en référons à la Cour*, we submit the case to (the judgment of) the Court. **se référer**, *v.r.* To have reference, to relate; to leave it (*à*); to confide, to trust (*à*). *S'en référer à l'avis de quelqu'un*, to refer to the opinion of someone.

refermer [rəfɛr'me], *v.t.* To shut again; to close up. *Refermer une plaie*, to close a wound. **se refermer**, *v.r.* To shut itself; to close up; to heal up (of wound).

refiler [rafi'le], *v.t.* (*pop.*) To fob off, to palm off (something) on (a person).

réfléchi [refle'ʃi], *a.* (*fem.* -**ie**) Reflected; deliberate, well-considered; reflective, thoughtful; guarded, wary; (*Gram.*) reflexive. *Action réfléchie*, deliberate action; *opinion peu réfléchie*, hasty opinion; *personne réfléchie*, reflective, circumspect person; *tout bien réfléchi*, all things considered.

réfléchir [refle'ʃiːr], *v.t.* To reflect, to reflect back, to throw back; to reverberate; to consider, to meditate upon.—*v.i.* To think, to consider, to ponder. *J'y réfléchirai*, I'll think it over. **se réfléchir**, *v.r.* To be reflected.

réfléchissant, *a.* (*fem.* -**ante**) Reflecting. **réfléchissement**, *n.m.* Reflection.

réflecteur, *n.m.* Reflector.—*a.m.* Reflecting.

réflectif, *a.* (*fem.* -**ive**) Reflective.

reflet, *n.m.* Reflection, reflex; reflected light.

refléter, *v.t. irr.* (*conjug. like* ACCÉLÉRER) To reflect (light etc.).—*v.i.* and **se refléter**, *v.r.* To be reflected, to be mirrored back.

refleurir [rəflœ'riːr], *v.i.* To blossom or flower again; (*fig.*) to flourish again. *Faire refleurir*, to revive. **refleurissement**, *n.m.* Second flowering.

réflexe [re'flɛks], *a.* and *n.m.* Reflex. **ré-flexibilité**, *n.f.* Reflexibility. **réflexible**, *a.* Reflexible. **réflexif**, *a.* (*fem.* -**ive**) Reflexive.

réflexion, *n.f.* Reflection; thought, consideration; remark. *Angle de réflexion*, angle of reflection; *avez-vous fini de faire des réflexions?* have you finished criticizing? *Épargnez-moi vos réflexions*, spare me your observations; (*toute*) *réflexion faite*, all things

considered; *un homme de réflexion*, a thinking man.

refluer [rə'flye], *v.i.* To reflow, to ebb.

reflux [rə'fly], *n.m.* Reflux, ebb, ebbing; flowing back. *Le flux et le reflux*, the ebb and flow.

refondre [rə'fɔ̃ːdr], *v.t.* To refound (metal), to melt down again, to cast again, to remould; (*fig.*) to recast, to remodel, to improve, to correct. *Refondre la monnaie*, to recoin money; *refondre un ouvrage*, to recast a work. **se refondre**, *v.r.* To be recast *or* melted down again.

refonte, *n.f.* Refounding, recasting; recoining; remodelling; alteration, correction, repair; reorganization.

reforestation, *n.f.* [REBOISEMENT].

reforger [rəfɔr'ʒe], *v.t.* To reforge.

réformable [refɔr'mabl], *a.* Reformable.

réformateur, *n.m.* (*fem.* -**trice**) Reformer.—*a.* Reforming.

réformation [refɔrma'sjɔ̃], *n.f.* Reformation, reform.

réforme [re'fɔrm], *n.f.* Reform, reformation, amendment; (*Mil.*) reduction, discharge. *Cheval de réforme*, cast horse; *être en réforme*, (*Mil.*) to be on half-pay; *être mis à la réforme*, (*Mil.*) to be put on half-pay; to be dismissed the service; *la Réforme*, the Reformation; *traitement de réforme*, (*Mil.*) half-pay.

réformé [refɔr'me], *a.* (*fem.* -**ée**) Reformed. *La religion réformée*, the Protestant religion; *un officier réformé*, a half-pay officer; *soldat réformé*, man invalided out of the service.—*n.* Reformer, Protestant; man invalided out of the service.

réformer [refɔr'me], *v.t.* To reform, to mend, to improve; (*Mil.*) to invalid (a man), to cast (a horse); to scrap (war materials). *Réformer sa vie*, to amend one's life; *réformer ses mœurs*, to reform one's morals. **se réformer**, *v.r.* To reform, to mend one's ways.

reformer [rəfɔr'me], *v.t.* To form again. **se reformer**, *v.r.* To form anew, to re-form (of troops etc.).

réformiste [refɔr'mist], *n.m. and a.* Reformist.

refouillement [rəfuj'mɑ̃], *n.m.* Deepening.

refouiller, *v.t.* To cut into again or farther, to deepen; to fumble again in (one's pockets etc.).

refoulant [refu'lɑ̃], *a.* (*fem.* -**ante**) *Pompe refoulante*, force-pump.

refoulement [rəful'mɑ̃], *n.m.* Driving back, forcing back; (*Psych.*) inhibition, repression, (of desires, feelings); refulling (of stuffs); tamping (of earth etc.). *Le refoulement d'une armée*, the driving back of an army.

refouler [rəfu'le], *v.t.* To drive back, to back (train etc.); to repel; to compress; to repress, to suppress, to inhibit; to expel (aliens); to refuse entry; to stem (the tide); to tamp; to tread (grapes etc.) again; to full (stuffs) again; to ram home (the charge in a gun). *Refouler sa marée*, to stem, to go against the tide.—*v.i.* To ebb, to flow back. *La marée refoule*, the tide is ebbing.

refouloir, *n.m.* Rammer (for gun); tamping-tool.

réfractaire [refrak'tɛːr], *a.* Refractory, insubordinate, stubborn, obstinate, rebellious; (*Mil.*) defaulting (conscript). *Prêtre réfractaire*, non-juring priest (during French

Revolution); *terre réfractaire*, fire-proof clay. —*n.m.* Refractory person; defaulter.

réfracter [refrak'te], *v.t.* To refract. **se réfracter**, *v.r.* To be refracted.

réfractif, *a.* (*fem.* **-ive**) Refractive.

réfraction, *n.f.* Refraction *Index de réfraction*, refractive index. **réfractomètre**, *n.m.* Refractometer.

refrain [rə'frɛ̃], *n.m.* Refrain, burden of a song; (*fig.*) constant theme. *C'est son refrain continuel*, he is always harping on this; *refrain en chœur*, chorus; *le refrain du régiment*, the regimental song.

réfrangibilité [refrɑ̃ʒibili'te], *n.f.* Refrangibility. **réfrangible**, *a.* Refrangible.

refrapper [rəfra'pe], *v.t.* To strike again. *Refrapper la monnaie*, to restamp coin.

refrènement [rəfrɛn'mɑ̃], *n.m.* Curbing.

refréner, *v.t. irr.* (*conjug. like* ACCÉLÉRER) To curb, to control (passions), to bridle, to restrain, to repress.

réfrigérant [refriʒe'rɑ̃], *a.* (*fem.* **-ante**) Refrigerant, cooling. *Mélange réfrigérant*, freezing mixture.—*n.m.* Refrigerator; cooling apparatus. **réfrigérateur**, *n.m.* Refrigerating chamber *or* plant; refrigerator, (*colloq.*) fridge; (*Am.*) icebox. **réfrigératif**, *a.* (*fem.* **-ive**) Refrigerative.—*n.m.* (*Med.*) Refrigerative. **réfrigération**, *n.f.* Refrigeration, cooling, chilling. **réfrigérer**, *v.t.* To cool, to chill, to freeze (food etc.).

réfringent [refrɛ̃'ʒɑ̃], *a.* (*fem.* **-ente**) Refracting, refringent.

refrogné etc. [RENFROGNÉ].

refroidir [rəfrwa'diːr], *v.t.* To cool, to chill; to damp (feelings), to dash (enthusiasm).—*v.i.* To cool, to become cold. **se refroidir**, *v.r.* To cool, to cool down, to cool off, to grow cold; to catch cold; to slacken, to relax, to abate.

refroidissement, *n.m.* Cooling, refrigeration; coolness; coldness; chill, cold. *J'ai pris un refroidissement*, I have caught a chill.

refuge [rə'fyːʒ], *n.m.* Refuge, shelter; resource, protection; excuse, subterfuge; (street-) refuge, island; lay-by. *Lieu de refuge*, place of safety.

réfugié [refy'ʒje], *n.m.* (*fem.* **-iée**) Refugee. **se réfugier**, *v.r.* To take refuge or shelter; to find shelter; (*fig.*) to have recourse (*dans*), to fall back on, to shelter oneself (*dans*).

refuir [rə'fɥiːr], *v.i. irr.* (*conjug. like* FUIR) (*Hunt.*) To double.

refuite, *n.f.* Shift, doubling; (**fig.*) shuffling, delaying action, evasion, pretext.

refus [rə'fy], *n.m. inv.* Refusal, denial; thing refused. *Ce n'est pas de refus*, I accept gladly, I won't say no to it; *sur leur refus*, as they refused; *ce pieu est (enfoncé) à refus*, this pile is driven home; *essuyer un refus net*, to meet with a flat refusal.

refusable, *a.* Refusable.

refusé [rəfy'ze], *a.* (*fem.* **-ée**) *Lettre refusée*, blind letter.—*n.pl. Les refusés*, the artists whose works have not been accepted by the Jury of the Salon; the candidates ploughed at an examination.

refuser [rəfy'ze], *v.t.* To refuse, to deny, to decline, to reject, not to accept; to withhold, to grudge, to demur; to repulse; to plough (a candidate). *Refuser des présents*, to refuse presents; *refuser la porte à quelqu'un*, to deny

someone admittance.—*v.i.* To refuse; to decline; to refuse to advance, to be restive (of a horse); (*Naut.*) to haul ahead, not to come to the wind. **se refuser**, *v.r.* To deny oneself, to deprive oneself; to grudge oneself; to shun, to object to, to set one's face against, to withstand, to resist; to be refused. *Il se refuse le nécessaire*, he denies himself the necessaries of life.

refuseur, *n.m.* (*fem.* **-euse**) (*rare*) Refuser.

réfutable [refy'tabl], *a.* Refutable. **réfutateur**, *n.m.* (*fem.* **-trice**) Refuter. **réfutatif**, *a.* (*fem.* **-ive**) Refutative. **réfutation**, *n.f.* Refutation, rebutment.

réfuter [refy'te], *v.t.* To refute, to confute, to disprove.

regagner [rəga'ɲe], *v.t.* To regain, to win back, to recover, to retrieve; to win a second time; to return to, to rejoin, to reach. *Regagner sa maison*, to return home; *regagner le dessus*, to get the upper hand again; *regagner quelqu'un*, to win someone back.

regain [rə'gɛ̃], *n.m.* Aftermath; second crop; (*fig.*) recrudescence, renewal, revival, return, new lease (of life). *Regain de jeunesse*, a second youth.

régal [re'gal], *n.m.* (*pl.* **régals**) Feast, entertainment, treat; pleasure, delight. *C'est un vrai régal pour moi*, it is a real treat for me.

régalade [rega'lad], *n.f.* Giving a treat, treating, regaling; blazing fire. *Boire à la régalade*, to pour (wine etc.) from a bottle down one's throat without touching one's lips.

régalant, *a.* (*fem.* **-ante**) Pleasant, entertaining.

régale (1) [re'gal], *a. Eau régale*, aqua regia (nitro-hydrochloric acid).

régale (2) [re'gal], *n.m.* (*usu. in pl.*) Regal (portable organ); vox humana.—*n.f.* Right of French kings to receive revenues of vacant bishoprics.

régalement [regal'mɑ̃], **régalage**, *n.m.* Levelling or smoothing (of ground).

régaler [rega'le], *v.t.* To regale, to treat, to entertain; (*fig.*) to amuse, to divert; to level (ground). (*fam.*) *C'est moi qui régale*, you are my guest(s); it is my treat. **se régaler**, *v.r.* To regale oneself; to enjoy oneself; to entertain or treat each other; (*fam.*) to do oneself well.

régalien [rega'ljɛ̃], *a.* (*fem.* **-ienne**) Pertaining to the royal prerogative.

regard [rə'gaːr], *n.m.* Look; glance; gaze, stare, notice, attention; (*pl.*) eyes; inspection-hole, man-hole (in boiler, sewer, etc.), peep-hole. *Abaisser les regards*, to look down; *adoucir ses regards*, to soften one's looks; *attirer les regards*, to draw the eye, to be conspicuous; *au regard de*, in comparison with; *au regard sombre*, dull-eyed; *chercher quelqu'un du regard*, to look round for someone; *détourner ses regards*, to look away; *d'un seul regard*, at one glance; *en regard*, opposite; *fixer les regards de quelqu'un* [FIXER]; *jeter ses regards de côté et d'autre*, to cast eyes here and there; *lancer des regards* [LANCER]; *promener ses regards sur*, to cast one's eyes over, to eye; *regard appuyé*, stare; *regard en coulisse*, side-glance; *regard tendre*, tender look; *suivre du regard*, to follow with one's eyes; *un regard de côté*, a sidelong glance.

regardant, *a.* (*fem.* **-ante**) Particular, meticulous; stingy, saving, niggardly; (*Her.*) regardant.

regarder [rəgar'de], *v.t.* To look at, to look on, to behold; to glance at, to take a look at; to gaze at, to view; to look into, to consider; to mind, to look up to; to face, to be opposite; to look (on) to; to front, to brave; to regard, to concern. *Cela vous regarde*, that concerns you; *cela ne me regarde pas*, it is none of my business; *ma chambre regarde le midi*, my room looks to the south; *regarder comme*, to look upon as, to consider as; *regarder quelqu'un de haut en bas* [BAS (I)]; *regarder quelqu'un fixement*, to stare at someone.—*v.i.* To look; to mind, to pay heed. *Je n'y regarde pas de si près*, I am not so particular as all that; *ma chambre regarde sur le jardin*, my room overlooks the garden; *regarder par un trou*, to look or to peep through a hole; *regardez-y bien*, take heed; *y regarder à deux fois*, to think twice about it. **se regarder,** *v.r.* To look at oneself or one's face; to look at each other; to look upon oneself (*comme*); to consider one another (*comme*); to face each other. *Je me regarde comme responsable*, I consider myself responsible; *ils se regardaient en chiens de faïence*, they glared at each other; *tu ne t'es pas regardé(e)!* look who's talking!

regarnir [rəgar'ni:r], *v.t.* To furnish again, to regarnish, to retrim (dress); to refill (one's pocket etc.), to re-cover (furniture), etc.

régate [re'gat], *n.f.* Regatta, boat-race; yacht-race; sailor-knot tie.

regayer [rəge'je], *v.t.* To comb (hemp). **regayonner**, *n.m.* Hemp-comb. **regayure,** *n.f.* Refuse of hemp.

regazonnement [rəgazɔn'mã], *n.m.* Returfing. **regazonner**, *v.t.* To returf.

regel [rə'ʒɛl], *n.m.* Renewed frost, freezing again. **regeler**, *v.i., v.t.* To freeze again.

régence [re'ʒã:s], *n.f.* Regency; fob-chain; (*dial.*) a sort of roll.—*a. inv.* Of the Regency.

régénérateur [reʒenera'tœ:r], *n.m.* (*fem.* **-trice**) Regenerator.—*a.* Regenerating.

régénération, *n.f.* Regeneration; reclamation (of land).

régénérer [reʒene're], *v.t.* To regenerate. **régénérescence**, *n.f.* Rejuvenation.

régent [re'ʒã], *a.* (*fem.* **-ente**) Regent.—*n.* Regent; *form-master (of a college); *governor (of the Bank of France).

régenter, *v.t.* *To act as a form-master to; (*fig.*) to domineer, to lord it over.

régicide [reʒi'sid], *n.m.* Regicide (crime and person).—*a.* Regicidal.

régie [re'ʒi], *n.f.* Administration; (public) corporation; management; (*Cine.*) studio management. *Employé de la régie*, exciseman; *régie des contributions indirectes*, excise, excise office; *théâtre en régie*, State managed theatre.

regimbement [rəʒɛ̃bə'mã], *n.m.* Kicking (of horses); resistance, recalcitrance.

regimber [rəʒɛ̃'be], *v.i.* To kick (of horses); (*fig.*) to resist, to be refractory, to jib.

régime [re'ʒim], *n.m.* Regimen; diet; form of government, government; rules, regulations; régime, system, order of things; (*Gram.*)

object, objective case; flow; rate, rhythm, speed (of motor etc.); bunch, cluster (of bananas etc.). *Au régime direct*, in the objective case, in the accusative; *être au régime*, to be on a diet; *être sous le régime du bâton*, to be under the rule of the cudgel; *l'Ancien Régime*, the pre-Revolutionary Régime; *régime des prisons*, prison regulations; *régime d'un fleuve*, the rate of flow of a river; *se mettre au régime*, to put oneself on a diet; *vivre de régime*, to live by rule.

régiment [reʒi'mã], *n.m.* Regiment.

régimentaire, *a.* Regimental.

reginglard [rəʒɛ̃'gla:r], *n.m.* (*fam.*) A small local wine, usually very dry or a bit sharp.

réginglette [reʒɛ̃'glet], *n.f.* Small trap or snare for birds.

région [re'ʒjɔ̃], *n.f.* Region, territory; area, district; sphere. **régional,** *a.* (*fem.* **-ale**, *pl.* **-aux**) Local, of the district.

régionalisme, *n.m.* Regionalism, decentralization. **régionaliste**, *n.* Regionalist.

régir [re'ʒi:r], *v.t.* To govern, to rule; to administer; (*Gram.*) to govern.

régisseur, *n.m.* Manager, steward; (farm) bailiff; (*Theat.*) stage-manager, (*Cine.*) assistant-director. (*Cine.*) *Régisseur général*, production manager.

registre [rə'ʒistr], *n.m.* Register; account-book; damper (in chimneys); register-stove; valve, vane (in steam-engine); (*Mus.*) register, compass. *Il est sur mes registres*, I have him on my books; *inscrire sur les registres de l'état-civil*, to enter (someone *or* something) in the registers of births, marriages, and deaths; *tenir registre*, to keep an account (of).

réglable [re'glabl], *a.* Adjustable.

réglage [re'gla:ʒ], *n.m.* Ruling (of paper); regulating, adjusting, setting, timing (of watches, clocks, etc.); tuning (of motor and radio). *Réglage du tir*, ranging; *réglage par avions*, aircraft spotting; (*Teleg.*) *réglages*, dial readings; *vis de réglage*, set screw, adjusting screw.

règle [regl], *n.f.* Ruler, rule; order, regularity; pattern, model, example, guide; (*fig.*) principle, law; (*pl.*) menses, courses. *Cela est de règle*, that is customary; *dans la règle*, according to strict rule; *en règle générale*, as a general rule; *être en règle* or *se mettre en règle*, to be in order, to have everything in order; *règle à calcul*, slide-rule; *règle de trois*, (*Arith.*) rule of three; *règle divisée*, scale; *selon les règles*, according to rule; *servir de règle*, to serve as an example.

réglé, *a.* (*fem.* **-ée**) Regular, steady; punctual; fixed (set of time); ruled; paid. *À des heures réglées*, at regular hours; *il a le pouls réglé*, his pulse is regular; *réglé comme du papier à musique* [MUSIQUE]; *une vie réglée*, a regular life.

règlement [regla'mã], *n.m.* Regulation, regularity, system; standing order, by-law; payment, settlement (of accounts). *Il faut respecter le(s) règlement(s)*, you must abide by the regulations; *règlement de compte*, settlement of an account (*also fig.*); *règlement de police*, police regulation; *règlement intérieur (d'une assemblée)*, the rule of procedure; *vous manquez au règlement*, you are breaking the rules.

[629]

réglementaire [rɛgləmã'tɛːr], *a.* Pertaining or according to regulations, lawful, usual, customary.

réglementation, *n.f.* Strict regulation by system.

réglementer [rɛgləmã'te], *v.t.* To regulate.— *v.i.* To make regulations.

régler [re'gle], *v.t. irr. (conjug. like* ACCÉLÉRER) To rule (paper etc.); to regulate, to order, to set, to adjust; to time (a watch etc.); to settle; to moderate, to make conform to rule. *Régler sa dépense,* to regulate one's expenses; *régler ses affaires,* to settle one's affairs; *régler un différend,* to settle a dispute; *régler un compte,* to settle an account; *régler ses comptes* or *son compte* [COMPTE]; *(fam.) régler son compte à quelqu'un,* to cook someone's goose; *régler une pendule,* to set a clock right. **se régler,** *v.r.* To regulate oneself, to be regulated; to be guided; to time oneself *(sur). Je me réglerai sur vous,* I shall time myself by you; *je ne me règle pas sur cela,* I don't go by that.

réglet [re'glɛ], *n.m.* (*Print.*) Rule; (*Arch.*) reglet. **réglette,** *n.f.* (*Print.*) Reglet.

régleur, *n.m.* (*fem.* **-euse** (1)) Regulator (of clocks etc.); one who rules paper.

régleuse (2), *n.f.* Ruling-machine.

réglisse [re'glis], *n.f.* Liquorice. *Réglisse sauvage* or *bâtarde,* sweet milk-vetch. *Jus de réglisse,* Spanish liquorice.

réglure [re'glyːr], *n.f.* Ruling (of paper).

régnant [re'ɲã], *a.* (*fem.* **-ante**) Reigning; *(fig.)* prevailing, prevalent, predominant.

règne [rɛɲ], *n.m.* Reign; prevalence, vogue, duration; influence; crown (over the high altar in churches); each of the three crowns forming the papal tiara; (*Nat. Hist.*) kingdom. *Règne animal,* animal kingdom; *sous le règne de,* in the reign of.

régner [re'ɲe], *v.i. irr. (conjug. like* ACCÉLÉRER) To reign, to rule, to bear sway; to prevail, to be in fashion; to reach, to extend. *La maladie qui règne,* the prevailing disease.

régnicole, *n.* and *a.* Native or naturalized (citizen); a national.

regonflement [rəgɔ̃flə'mã], *n.m.* Reinflation, swelling anew. **regonfler,** *v.t.* To swell again, to reinflate; to pump up (tyre).—*v.i.* To swell again.

regorgeant [rəgɔr'ʒã], *a.* (*fem.* **-ante**) Overflowing; abounding; replete, glutted; crammed (with), cram-full. **regorgement,** *n.m.* Overflowing, overflow, superabundance.

regorger [rəgɔr'ʒe], *v.i.* To overflow, to run over; to abound (*de*), to be glutted, to be replete; to be crammed (with); to be packed; to be plentiful, to abound. *Cette province reporge de blé,* that province abounds in corn; *faire regorger,* to compel to disgorge; *l'argent regorge sur le marché,* money abounds on the market; *la salle regorgeait de monde,* the hall was packed with spectators.—*v.t.* To regurgitate, to disgorge.

regrat [rə'gra], *n.m.* Second-hand dealing (in food), huckstering, huckster's wares; retail salt-shop.

regrattage [rəgra'taːʒ], *n.m.* Rescraping (of walls etc.).

regratter [rəgra'te], *v.t.* To scrape again, to clean-scrape.—*v.i.* To make petty profits; to huckster.

regratterie, *n.f.* Huckster's trade.

regrattier [rəgra'tje], *n.m.* (*fem.* **-ière**) Huckster, hucksteress, *esp.* dealer in vegetables, cheese, etc.

régressif [regre'sif], *a.* (*fem.* **-ive**) Regressive, retrogressive.

régression, *n.f.* Regression, recession; retrogression; throw-back; drop (in sales); decline.

regret [rə'grɛ], *n.m.* Regret; repining, yearning. *À mon grand regret,* much to my regret; *à regret,* with reluctance, grudgingly; *avoir du regret,* to feel regret; *j'ai regret de vous quitter,* I am sorry to leave you.

regrettable, *a.* Regrettable, deplorable; unfortunate (mistake). **regrettablement,** *adv.* Regrettably.

regretter [rəgre'te], *v.t.* To regret, to lament; to grieve; to be sorry for, to repent; to miss. *Je regrette de vous avoir manqué,* I am sorry to have missed you; *je regrette qu'il ne soit pas ici,* I am sorry he is not here; *je vous regrette,* I miss you; *tout le monde le regrette,* he is regretted by everybody.—*v.i. Je regrette, mais c'est impossible,* I am sorry, but it is impossible.

régularisation [regylariza'sjɔ̃], *n.f.* Putting in order, regularization.

régulariser, *v.t.* To put in order, to regularize.

régularité, *n.f.* Regularity.

régulateur, *n.m.* (*fem.* **-trice**) Regulator; standard; (*Eng.* etc.) governor. *Le régulateur d'une horloge,* the regulator of a clock.—*a.* Regulating.

régulation, *n.f.* (*Naut.*) Regulation (of compass).

régule [re'gyl], *n.m.* (*Metal., Orn., etc.*) Regulus; kinglet.

régulier [regy'lje], *a.* (*fem.* **-ière**) Regular; steady, punctual, exact; conformable; right, correct. *Traits réguliers,* classical features (of face).—*n.m.* Regular (monk, soldier, etc.). **régulièrement,** *adv.* Regularly.

régurgitation [regyrʒita'sjɔ̃], *n.f.* Regurgitation. **régurgiter,** *v.t.* To regurgitate.

réhabilitation, *n.f.* Rehabilitation.

réhabiliter [reabili'te], *v.t.* To rehabilitate; to reinstate, to restore (*dans*). **se réhabiliter,** *v.r.* To rehabilitate oneself, to recover one's good name.

réhabituer [reabi'tɥe], *v.t.* To reaccustom. **se réhabituer,** *v.r.* To get accustomed again.

rehaussement [rəos'mã], *n.m.* Raising; heightening, enhancing; increase of value (of coin).

rehausser, *v.t.* To raise; to heighten, to enhance; to raise the value of; to enrich; to extol, to cry up; to set off, to throw into relief. *Rehausser d'or et de soie,* to enrich with gold and silk; *rehausser le mérite d'une action,* to extol the merit of an action.

rehaut, *n.m.* (*Paint.*) Retouch bringing out the highlights of a picture.

réimperméabiliser [reɛ̃pɛrmeabili'ze], *v.t.* To reproof (raincoat etc.).

réimportateur [reɛ̃pɔrta'tœːr], *n.m.* Reimporter. **réimportation,** *n.f.* Reimportation. **réimporter,** *v.t.* To reimport.

réimposer, *v.t.* To reassess (tax); (*Print.*) to reimpose. **réimposition,** *n.f.* Further assessment; (*Print.*) reimposition.

réimpression, *n.f.* Reprinting; reimpression, reprint.

réimprimer, *v.t.* To print again, to reprint.

rein [rɛ̃], *n.m.* Kidney; (*pl.*) loins, back; (*Arch.*) extrados (of arch). *Ceindre ses reins,* to gird up one's loins; *chute* or *creux des reins,* small of the back; *douleur de reins* or *mal aux reins,* pain in the back; *il a les reins forts* or *solides,* he is strong-backed, (*fig.*) he is a man of substance; *se casser les reins,* to break one's back; *se donner un tour de reins,* to strain one's back.

réincarnation [reɛ̃karnɑ'sjɔ̃], *n.f.* Reincarnation. **réincarner,** *v.t.* To reincarnate. **se réincarner,** *v.r.* To become reincarnated.

réincorporer [reɛ̃kɔrpɔ're], *v.t.* To reincorporate.

reine [rɛːn], *n.f.* Queen. *Faire la reine,* to act the queen; to queen it; *la reine du bal,* the belle of the ball; *reine des abeilles,* queen-bee; *reine-mère,* queen-mother.

reine-claude, *n.f.* (*pl.* **reines-claude**) Greengage.

reine-des-prés, *n.f.* (*pl.* **reines-des-prés**) or *ulmaire.* Meadowsweet, goat's beard.

reine-marguerite, *n.f.* (*pl.* **reines-marguerites**) China aster.

reinette [rɛ'nɛt], *n.f.* [RAINETTE].

réinscription [reɛ̃skrip'sjɔ̃], *n.f.* Re-registering.

réinstallation [reɛ̃stalɑ'sjɔ̃], *n.f.* Reinstalment, re-establishment. **réinstaller,** *v.t.* To reinstall.

réintégrande [reɛ̃te'grɑ̃:d], *n.f.* (*Law*) Restoration, reinstatement, recovery.

réintégration [reɛ̃tegrɑ'sjɔ̃], *n.f.* Reinstatement.

réintégrer, *v.t. irr.* (*conjug. like* ACCÉLÉRER) To reinstate. *Réintégrer son domicile,* to go home again; to resume occupation of one's domicile.

réinventer, *v.t.* To reinvent.

réitératif [reitera'tif], *a.* (*fem.* **-ive**) Reiterative.

réitération, *n.f.* Reiteration, repetition.

réitérer, *v.t.* To reiterate, to repeat.

reître [rɛːtr], *n.m.* Reiter (German horse-soldier of the 16th and 17th century). *C'est un vieux reître,* he is an old fox.

rejaillir [rəʒa'jiːr], *v.i.* To gush out, to spurt out; to spring, to leap out, to spout; (*fig.*) to flash; to reflect; to fly back, to rebound. *Sa gloire a rejailli sur ses amis,* his friends are basking in his reflected glory; *la honte de cet homme rejaillira sur son parti,* his party will share in his disgrace.

rejaillissement [rəʒajis'mɑ̃], *n.m.* Gushing out, spouting, springing; rebounding, reflection, flashing, spread.

réjection [reʒɛk'sjɔ̃], *n.f.* Rejection.

rejet [rə'ʒɛ], *n.m.* Rejection; throwing out; young shoot, sprout; (*fig.*) sprig, scion; (*Fin.*) carrying, transfer; cast, after-swarm (of bees); (*Geol.*) throw (of fault); (*Pros.*) syllable or syllables carried over to the next verse.

rejetable, *a.* Rejectable.

rejéteau or **rejetteau,** *n.m.* (*pl.* **-eaux**) Weather-board or bead (at bottom of a door or window); drip-moulding; (*Av.*) drip-flap.

rejeter [rəʒ'te], *v.t. irr.* (*conjug. like* APPELER) To throw again; to throw back; to tilt back

(one's hat); to fling back, to drive back, to repel; to throw away; to throw up, to put forth (of plants); to refuse, to reject; to set aside; to deny; to throw, to cast; (*Fin.*) to carry, to transfer. *Faire rejeter un projet de loi,* to have a bill thrown out; *il rejeta son chapeau en arrière,* he tilted back *or* pushed back his hat; *rejeter la faute sur quelqu'un,* to throw the blame on someone else.—*v.i.* To shoot (of plants). **se rejeter,** *v.r.* To have recourse to, to fall back (upon); to throw back to each other; to be rejected. *Se rejeter en arrière,* to leap *or* spring back(wards).

rejeton [rəʒ'tɔ̃], *n.m.* Shoot, sprout, offshoot, sucker; (*fig.*) scion, offspring. **rejettement,** *n.m.* Rejection.

rejoindre [rə'ʒwɛ̃:dr], *v.t. irr.* (*conjugated like* CRAINDRE) To rejoin, to join again, to join; to reunite; to overtake, to catch up.—*v.i.* (*Mil.*) To rejoin one's regiment etc. **se rejoindre,** *v.r.* To be joined together again, to reunite; to join each other, to meet again; to meet; to catch each other up again.

rejointoiement [rəʒwɛ̃twa'mɑ̃], *n.m.* (*Build.*) Rejointing, repointing. **rejointoyer,** *v.t. irr.* (*conjug. like* ABOYER) To rejoint, to repoint.

rejouer [rə'ʒwe], *v.t., v.i.* To play again, to replay.

réjoui [re'ʒwi], *a.* (*fem.* **-ie**) Jovial, joyous, merry. *Figure réjouie,* beaming face.—*n.* Such a person. (*fam.*) *Grosse réjouie,* buxom woman or lass; *gros réjoui,* jovial man, jolly fellow.

réjouir [re'ʒwiːr], *v.t.* To rejoice, to gladden, to delight, to cheer; to divert, to entertain, to make merry. *Cette couleur réjouit la vue,* that colour pleases the eye; *le vin réjouit le cœur de l'homme,* wine maketh glad the heart of man. **se réjouir,** *v.r.* To be or to make merry; to rejoice, to be delighted (*de*).

réjouissance, *n.f.* Rejoicing; (*pl.*) rejoicings, merry-making; make-weight (of bones) thrown in by butcher. *En signe de réjouissance,* as a sign of rejoicing.

réjouissant, *a.* (*fem.* **-ante**) Cheering; diverting, amusing.

relâchant [rəlɑ'ʃɑ̃], *a.* (*fem.* **-ante**) Relaxing, laxative, loosening.—*n.m.* (*Med.*) Opening medicine, laxative.

relâche (1) [rə'lɑːʃ], *n.m.* Intermission, discontinuance, rest, respite; relaxation; (*Theat.*) suspension of performance. *Relâche ce soir,* no performance this evening; *sans relâche,* without intermission, without respite; *théâtres qui font relâche l'été,* theatres that close for the summer.

relâche (2) [rə'lɑːʃ], *n.f.* (*Naut.*) Putting into, or calling at a port; port of call.

relâché [rəlɑ'ʃe], *a.* (*fem.* **-ée**) Lax, relaxed; loose, remiss. *Morale relâchée,* loose morals.

relâchement, *n.m.* Slackening, loosening, relaxing; slackness; intermission, abatement, relaxation; remissness, laxity (of morals); looseness of bowels.

relâcher [rəlɑ'ʃe], *v.t.* To slacken, to loosen, to relax; to release, to set at liberty; to unbend (the mind etc.); to yield, to give up, to abate.—*v.i.* To relax, to flag; (*Naut.*) to put into port, to touch (*d*). **se relâcher,** *v.r.* To grow slack or loose, to slacken, to fall off, to flag; to abate, to give way, to relax, to unbend, to sit back; to get milder (of the weather).

relais (1) [rə'lɛ], *n.m.* Relay (fresh horses); stage (where fresh horses are taken); shift (of workmen); (*Hunt.*) relay (of dogs); (*Elec.*) relay; (*Rad.*) relay station. *Chevaux de relais,* fresh horses; *course de relais,* relay-race; *relais de contrôle,* pilot-relay.

relais (2) [rə'lɛ], *n.m.* (*Geol.*) Sand-flats (left by sea at low tide), sand-banks (left by a bending river on the outside); (*Law*) derelict land.

relance [rə'lɑ̃:s], *n.f.* Raise (in game of poker).

relancer, *v.t.* (*Hunt.*) To start again, to turn out again; (*Ten.*) to return (the ball); (*Cards*) to raise (a bid); (*fig.*) to importune; (*colloq.*) to hunt up (someone); to dig (someone) out; to badger. **relanceur,** *n.m.* (*Ten.*) Striker. *Avantage au relanceur,* advantage striker.

relaps [rə'laps], *a.* (*fem.* **relapse**) Relapsed, relapsed into heresy.—*n.* Relapsed heretic; backslider.

rélargir [relar'ʒi:r], *v.t.* To widen, to let out (clothes etc.). **rélargissement,** *n.m.* Widening.

relater [rəla'te], *v.t.* (*Law*) To relate (the facts).

relateur, *n.m.* Relater, narrator.

relatif, *a.* (*fem.* **-ive**) Relative; relating (*à*).—*n.m.* (*Gram. etc.*) Relative.

relation, *n.f.* Relation, account, recital; report, statement; reference; respect; regard; connexion; intercourse, communication, correspondence; (*pl.*) connexions. *Être en relations avec quelqu'un,* to be in touch or in correspondence with someone; *relation exacte,* exact account. **relativement,** *adv.* Relatively.

relativisme, *n.m.* (*Phil.*) Relativism.

relativité, *n.f.* Relativity.

relaver [rəla've], *v.t.* To re-wash.

relaxation [rəlaksa'sjɔ̃], *n.f.* Relaxation, abatement, remission, laxness; discharge, release. (*Law*) *Relaxation d'un prisonnier,* discharge of a prisoner.

relaxer, *v.t.* To relax; to discharge (a prisoner); to release.

relayer [rəlɛ'je], *v.t. irr.* (*conjug. like* BALAYER) To take the place of, to relieve; (*Elec. Eng., Rad., Teleg., etc.*) to relay.—*v.i.* To change horses. **se relayer,** *v.r.* To relieve each other, to take it in turns; to work in shifts.

relégation [rəlega'sjɔ̃], *n.f.* Relegation; transportation (of convict).

relégué, *a.* (*fem.* **-ée**) Relegated, isolated.—*n.m.* (*Law*) Convict.

reléguer, *v.t. irr.* (*conjug. like* ACCÉLÉRER) To transport (for life), to shut up; to seclude; to relegate, to consign (*à*). **se reléguer,** *v.r.* To shut oneself up, to seclude oneself; to be consigned.

relent [rə'lɑ̃], *n.m.* Mustiness, mouldiness, stale smell. *Relent d'alcool,* stale smell of spirits; *sentir le relent,* to smell mouldy.—*a.* (*fem.* **-ente**) Mouldy, musty.

relevable [rəl'vablə], *a.* Able to be raised; able to be refloated (ship).

relevage [rəl'va:ʒ], *n.m.* Raising, lifting; salving (of sunken ship, submarine); collection (letters).

relevailles, *n.f.* (*only in pl.*) Churching (of woman). *Faire ses relevailles,* to be churched.

relevant [rəl'vɑ̃], *a.* (*fem.* **-ante**) Holding; depending (on the Crown etc.).

relève [rə'lɛ:v], *n.f.* (*Mil.*) Relief. *La relève,* the relieving troops.

relevé [rəl've], *a.* (*fem.* **-ée**) Raised, erect; turned up; elevated, exalted, lofty, refined; pungent, highly seasoned. *De la viande d'un goût relevé,* highly seasoned meat; *d'un ton relevé,* in a refined tone; *pantalon à bords relevés,* turn-up trousers, (*Am.*) cuffed trousers; *pensée relevée,* noble thought; *une condition relevée,* a high rank.—*n.m.* Abstract, extract, summary; statement, return; survey; remove (dish following the soup). *Faire un relevé de compte,* to make a statement of account; *relevé de consommation d'électricité,* electricity meter reading.—*n.f.* Afternoon. *De relevée,* in the afternoon.

relèvement, *n.m.* Raising again; rebuilding; recovery (of business); picking up (of object); relieving (of sentry); re-establishment; rise, increase (of salary); (*Naut.*) bearing. *Relèvement du taux officiel de l'escompte,* rise in the bank-rate.

relever [rəl've], *v.t.* To raise again, to lift up again, to set up again; to pick up, to take up; to weigh (anchor); to turn up; to tuck up; to hold up; to restore, to reinstate, to raise anew; to heighten, to relieve, to set off, to enhance, to adorn; to cry up, to extol; to exalt; to dignify; to notice, to remark; to take up, to accept; to give a relish to; to liberate, to free; to survey; (*Naut.*) to take the bearings of. *La parure relève la bonne mine,* dress sets off a handsome face; *relever des fortifications,* to restore fortifications; *relever de terre,* to raise from the ground; *relever la garde,* to relieve the guard; *relever la tête,* to raise one's head again; *relever le courage de quelqu'un,* to raise someone's courage; *relever le gant,* to accept a challenge; *relever le quart,* (*Naut.*) to set the watch; *relever les bords d'un chapeau,* to turn up the brim of a hat; *relever quelqu'un de ses fonctions,* to relieve someone of his duties; *relever une côte,* to take the bearings of a coast; *relever un mot,* to criticize a word; *relever un vaisseau,* to get a ship afloat again; *relevez votre robe,* tuck up your dress; *se faire relever de ses vœux,* to be released from one's vows. —*v.i.* To recover, to get better; to turn up; to depend, to be dependent (*sur*); to be answerable to (*de*). **relever de maladie,** to recover from illness. **se relever,** *v.r.* To rise again, to get up again; to get up; to recover, to retrieve one's losses; to be raised; to right itself (of a ship); to relieve each other.

releveur, *n.m.* (*Anat.*) Levator.

reliage [rə'lja:ʒ], *n.m.* Hooping (of casks).

relief [rə'ljɛf], *n.m.* Relief, relievo, embossment; set-off, enhancement, lustre; (*pl.*) remains, leavings, broken scraps (from the table). *Bas-relief* [BAS-RELIEF]; *carte en relief,* relief map; *en relief,* in relief, standing out, (*Cine.*) three-dimensional, 3 D; *haut-relief* [HAUT-RELIEF]; *mettre* or *donner du relief à,* to set off, to provide contrast to.

relier [rə'lje], *v.t.* To bind again; to connect, to link, to join; to hoop (casks); to bind (books). (*Elec.*) *Relier à la terre,* to connect to earth.

relieur [rə'ljœ:r], *n.m.* (*fem.* **-ieuse**) Binder, book-binder; spring-back file (for paper).

religieusement [rəliʒøz'mã], adv. Religiously; strictly, scrupulously, faithfully. **religieux**, a. (fem. -**ieuse**) Religious, pious;
serious, spiritual; monastic; exact, strict,
punctilious, scrupulous.—n. Monk or nun.
religion [rəli'ʒjõ], n.f. Religion; religious
doctrine; faith, piety, godliness; (fig.)
scrupulousness, conscientiousness. *Entrer
en religion*, to become a monk or nun;
elle s'appelle en religion sœur Thérèse-Marie,
her name in religion is Sister Theresa-Maria;
la religion réformée, the Protestant religion;
se faire une religion d'une chose, to make a
thing a matter of conscience.
***religionnaire**, n.m. Calvinist, Huguenot.
religiosité, n.f. Religiousness; excessive
scrupulousness in religious matters; religiosity.
reliquaire [rəli'kɛːr], n.m. Reliquary, shrine.
reliquat [rəli'ka], n.m. Balance, remainder of
an account; after-effects (of a disease etc.).
relique [rə'lik], n.f. Relic.
relire [rə'liːr], v.t. irr. (conjug. like LIRE) To
re-read.
reliure [rə'ljyːr], n.f. Binding (of books).
Reliure électrique, spring binding; *reliure
janséniste*, plain leather binding.
reloger [rələ'ʒe], v.t. To provide another
lodging for.
relouer [rəlu'e], v.t. To relet, to sub-let; to
take another lease on.
réluctance [relyk'tãːs], n.f. (Elec.) Reluctance, magnetic resistance.
reluire [rə'lɥiːr], v.i. irr. (conjug. like CONDUIRE)
To shine, to glitter, to glisten; to be striking,
brilliant, excellent, etc. *Tout ce qui reluit
n'est pas or* [OR (1)]
reluisant, a. (fem. -**ante**) Gleaming, shining,
glittering.
reluquer [rəly'ke], v.t. (colloq.) To ogle, to
leer at; (fig.) to have an eye on.
reluqueur, n.m. (fem. -**euse**) Ogler; coveter.
remâcher [rəma'ʃe], v.t. To chew again; (fig.)
to ruminate over again, to revolve in one's
mind.
remaillage [rəma'jaːʒ], n.m. Mending, re-
stitching.
remailler, v.t. To repair (the meshes of
fishing-nets etc.); to graft a piece (into
knitting); to mend a ladder (in stocking).
remailleuse, n.f. Ladder-mender (person
or tool).
remaniement or **remaniment** [rəmani'mã],
n.m. Handling again, touching up, doing
over again; repairing, mending; altering,
changing; (Print.) overrunning. *Remaniement
ministériel*, Cabinet reshuffle.
remanier, v.t. (conjugated like PRIER) To
handle again; to do over again; to remodel,
to recast; to mend, to repair; to adapt, to
alter, to revise; (Print.) to overrun.
remariage [rəma'rjaːʒ], n.m. Re-marriage.
remarier, v.t. To remarry. **se remarier**,
v.i. To marry again.
remarquable [rəmar'kabl], a. Remarkable,
notable. **remarquablement**, adv. Remarkably.
remarque [rə'mark], n.f. Remark, observation; notice; note. *Digne de remarque*, worthy
of notice.
remarquer, v.t. To mark again; to remark
upon, to observe, to note, to notice; to

distinguish. *Faire remarquer*, to point out,
to call attention to; *remarquer quelqu'un dans
la foule*, to pick out someone in the crowd;
se faire remarquer, to attract notice, to distinguish oneself. **se remarquer**, v.r. To be
remarked.
remballer [rãba'le], v.t. To re-pack, to pack
up again.
rembarquement [rãbarkə'mã], n.m. Re-embarkation; re-shipment. **rembarquer**, v.t. To
re-embark, to ship again.—v.i. To re-embark.
se rembarquer, v.r. To re-embark, to go
on board again.
rembarrer [rãba're], v.t. To repulse; to
snub; (fam.) to bite someone's head off, to
tick someone off.
remblai [rã'blɛ], n.m. Filling up, embanking;
embankment, bank. *Déblais et remblais,
cuts and fills; *route en remblai*, embanked
road.
remblayer [rãblɛ'je], v.t. irr. (conjug. like
BALAYER) To embank, to raise (an embankment); to fill up (with rubbish). **rem-
blayeur**, n.m. (Civ. Eng.) Filler-up.
remboîtement [rãbwat'mã], n.m. Resetting
(of a bone); fitting in again, reassembling.
remboîter, v.t. To fit in again; to reassemble; to reset (a bone).
rembourrage or **rembourrement**, n.m.
Stuffing, padding; upholstering. **rembourrer**, v.t. To stuff, to pad; to upholster
(with flock, hair, etc.). *Porte rembourrée,
baize-door.
remboursable [rãbur'sabl], a. Repayable,
reimbursable; redeemable.
remboursement [rãbursə'mã], n.m. Reimbursement, repayment, refunding; retirement (of bill); return (of capital). *Livrable
contre remboursement*, cash on delivery,
(fam.) C.O.D.
rembourser [rãbur'se], v.t. To repay, to
refund; to reimburse; to pay off; to redeem
(an annuity etc.); to return (a loan); to retire
(a bill). *On m'a remboursé*, I got my money
back.
rembrayer [rãbrɛ'je], v.i. (Motor.) To let the
clutch in again.
rembruni [rãbry'ni], a. (fem. -**ie**) Dark,
gloomy. *Un air rembruni*, a gloomy look.
rembrunir [rãbry'niːr], v.t. To make brown,
dusky, dark, or darker; to darken; to cloud
over; (fig.) to sadden, to cast a gloom over.
se rembrunir, v.r. To grow darker; to
become cloudy or gloomy; to grow sombre
or melancholy. *Son front se rembrunit*, his
brow grew darker.
rembuchement [rãbyʃ'mã], n.m. (Hunt.)
Return of an animal to covert.
rembucher [rãby'ʃe], v.t. To pursue into
covert. **se rembucher**, v.r. To return to
covert.
remède [rə'mɛd], n.m. Remedy, medicine,
cure. *À chose faite point de remède*, what is
done cannot be undone; *apporter* or *porter
remède à*, to remedy; *remède de cheval*,
drastic remedy; *sans remède*, without remedy;
un remède à tous maux, a cure-all.
remédiable [rəme'djabl], a. Remediable.
remédier, v.i. (conjugated like PRIER) To bring
or be a remedy or cure. *On ne saurait y
remédier*, that can't be helped; *remédier à un
mal*, to remedy an evil.

remêler [rəmɛ'le], *v.t.* To mix again, to reshuffle.

remembrement [rəmãbrə'mã], *n.m.* Reconstitution, re-grouping (of divided-up estate).

remembrer, *v.t.* To re-group (a divided-up estate).

remémorateur, *a.* (*fem.* **-trice**) Reminding.

remémoratif, *a.* (*fem.* **-ive**) Commemorative.

remémorer [rəmemɔ're], *v.t.* To bring (a thing) to someone's mind. **se remémorer**, *v.r.* To recollect.

remener [rəm'ne], *v.t. irr.* (*conjugated like* AMENER) (*rare*) To lead back, to take back.

remerciement or **remercîment** [rəmɛrsi'mã], *n.m.* Thanking; (*pl.*) thanks. *Faire des remerciements*, to return thanks; *voter des remerciements à quelqu'un*, to pass a vote of thanks to someone.

remercier, *v.t.* (*conjugated like* PRIER) To thank, to give thanks to; to decline politely; to discharge, to dismiss. *Je vous remercie de votre lettre*, thank you for your letter; *non, je vous remercie*, no, thank you.

réméré [reme're], *n.m.* (*Law*) Right of redemption or repurchase. *Vente à réméré*, sale with power of redemption.

remettant [rəmɛ'tã], *n.m.* (*fem.* **-ante**) Sender (of money).

remettre, *v.t. irr.* (*conjugated like* METTRE) To put back, to put back again; to replace; to put on again; to lay down again; to restore, to reinstate; to reconcile; to make well again; to deliver, to give up; to deliver up, to hand over; to put off, to delay, to postpone; to confide, to entrust; to remit, to forgive, to pardon; to remember, to recognize; to send in. (*Ten.*) (*Balle*) *à remettre*, let (ball); *faire remettre*, to send, to forward; *je vous remets*, I remember your face; *le voilà tout à fait remis*, he is quite recovered; *remettre dans l'esprit*, to remind; *remettre de l'argent*, to remit money; *remettre d'un jour à l'autre*, to put off from day to day; *remettre en bonne intelligence*, to reconcile; *remettre en bon ordre*, to put into order again; *remettre un criminel à la justice*, to hand over a criminal to justice; *remettre une cause à quinzaine*, to adjourn a case for a fortnight; *remettre une chose à la décision de quelqu'un*, to refer a matter to someone; *remettre une lettre à son adresse*, to deliver a letter to its address; *remettre un os*, to set a bone.—*v.i.* To set sail. *Remettre à la voile*, to set sail again. **se remettre**, *v.r.* To recover (oneself); to compose oneself; to recommence, to start again; to go back to what one was doing; to call to mind, to recollect; to refer, to rely (*à*); to improve (of weather); to resign oneself. *Le temps se remet*, the weather is clearing up again; *remettez-vous*, compose yourself, pull yourself together; (*dial.*) take a seat; *s'en remettre à quelqu'un*, to refer a thing to someone, to leave (a thing) to someone; to rely on someone; *se remettre à table*, to sit down again to table; *se remettre en route*, to resume one's journey.

remeubler [rəmœ'ble], *v.t.* To refurnish.

rémige [re'mi:ʒ], *n.f.* Wing, quill. *Rémiges primaires*, wing primaries.

réminiscence [remini'sã:s], *n.f.* Reminiscence; vague recollection.

remis [rə'mi], *a.* (*fem.* **remise** (1)) Put back; put off. *Ce n'est que partie remise*, it is only a pleasure deferred.

remisage, *n.m.* Housing, putting into the coach-house or shed.

remise (2), *n.f.* Delivery; remittance; remission; discount, reduction, abatement; commission, allowance; delay, deferring; coach-house, mews; engine-shed; (*Shooting*) cover (for game), alighting-place (for partridges); (*Naut.*) shelter. *Faire remise de*, to remit; *faire une remise*, to make a remittance; *la remise d'une audience*, the deferment of a hearing; *remise en jeu*, (*Ftb.*) throw-in (of ball); *sans remise*, without delay; *sous la remise*, in the coach-house, (*fam.*) on the shelf; *voiture de remise*, livery carriage (hired).—*n.m.* Coach on hire; livery coach.

remiser [rəmi'ze], *v.t.* To put in the coach-house; to house; (*colloq.*) to put by, to lay aside. *Remiser la voiture*, to put the car away; (*fam.*) *remiser quelqu'un*, to superannuate somebody; to snub him; *aller remiser*, to go back to the garage. **se remiser**, *v.r.* To alight, to take cover (of birds).

remisier [rəmi'zje], *n.m.* Half-commission man (*St. Exch.*).

rémissible, *a.* Remissible, pardonable.

rémission, *n.f.* Remission, forgiveness, abatement (of fever).

rémittent, *a.* (*fem.* **-ente**) (*Med.*) Remittent.

remmaillage [rãmɑ'ja:ʒ] [*see* REMAILLAGE].

remmailler [*see* REMAILLER].

remmailloter, *v.t.* To rewrap (an infant in swaddling-clothes).

remmancher, *v.t.* To put a new haft or handle to.

remmener, *v.t.* To take back, to lead back.

remodeler, *v.t.* To remodel.

remontage [rəmɔ̃'ta:ʒ], *n.m.* Going up; going upstream; winding up (of clock etc.); putting together, assembling; refitting (of parts of machinery); fortifying (of wine); restocking (of shop). **remontant**, *a.* (*fem.* **-ante**) Ascending; stimulating, strengthening; (*Hort.*) remontant.—*n.m.* (*Med.*) Stimulant, tonic, (*fam.*) pick-me-up. **remonte**, *n.f.* Remounting, going upstream; ascent (of salmon), run (of fish); (*Mil.*) remount. *Le vent est à la remonte*, wind is blowing upstream; *officier de remonte*, remount officer.

remontée [rəmɔ̃'te], *n.f.* Upward motion.

remonte-pentes, *n.m. inv.* Ski-lift.

remonter [rəmɔ̃'te], *v.i.* To reascend, to go up again; to get up again; to go back; to rise, to rise again; to rise or increase (in value etc.); to go back in time, to date back, to have origin; (*Naut.*) to go towards the north (of wind). *Le baromètre remonte*, the barometer is rising again; *remonter à cheval*, to remount; *remonter à l'origine d'une chose*, to trace a thing back to its origin; *remonter sur sa bête*, to get on one's feet again.—*v.t.* To reascend, to go up again; to take up again; to raise, to raise higher; to remount (cavalry); to fit up, to stock; to wind up (a watch, clock etc.); to re-string (instruments); to re-stage (a play). *Remonter des bottes*, to vamp boots; *remonter le courant*, to stem the current; *remonter le moral à quelqu'un*, to revive the spirits of someone; *remonter un fleuve*, to go upstream; *remonter un fusil*, to new-stock a gun; *remonter un magasin*, to stock a warehouse anew. **se remonter,** *v.r.* To stock oneself again, to take in a fresh supply (*de*); to be wound up (of watches etc.); to recover one's strength, health, or spirits.

remontoir, *n.m.* Keyless action (in watches etc.), winder, keyless watch; key (of clockwork motor).

remontrance [rəmɔ̃'trɑ̃:s], *n.f.* Remonstrance.

remontrant, *n.m.* Remonstrant.

remontrer, *v.t.* To demonstrate again, to represent, to show; to teach. *C'est Gros-Jean qui en remontre à son curé*, it is teaching one's grandmother to suck eggs. **se remontrer,** *v.r.* To show oneself again.

remontreur, *n.m.* (*fem.* **-euse**) Remonstrator.

rémora [remɔ'ra], *n.m.* Remora (suckingfish); (*fig.*) hindrance, impediment, obstacle.

remordre [rə'mɔrdr], *v.t.* To bite again.—*v.i.* To try again. (*fam.*) *Y remordre*, to have another go.

remords [rə'mɔ:r], *n.m.* Remorse, compunction. *Avoir des remords*, to feel remorse; *étouffer ses remords*, to stifle remorse; *sans remords*, remorseless, remorselessly.

remorquage [rəmɔr'ka:ʒ], *n.m.* Towing, hauling.

remorque, *n.f.* Towing; tow; towline; trailer (car). *A la remorque de*, in tow of, (*fig.*) under the lead of, in the wake of; *câble de remorque*, tow-line; *prendre à la remorque*, to take in tow; (*Motor.*) *roulotte remorque*, caravan trailer; *se mettre à la remorque*, to get into tow; *voiture remorque*, slip coach (of railway).

remorquer, *v.t.* To tow, to haul, to drag; to draw along.

remorqueur, *a.* (*fem.* **-euse**) Towing, hauling.—*n.m.* Towing-vessel, tug-boat, tug.—*n.f.* Locomotive hauling train, relief engine.

remoucher [rəmu'ʃe], *v.t.* To wipe the nose of again; (*slang*) to snub.

remoudre [rə'mudrə], *v.t. irr.* (*conjug. like* MOUDRE) To regrind. **rémoudre,** *v.t.* To sharpen or whet again.

remouiller [rəmu'je], *v.t.* To wet again.

rémoulade [remu'lad], *n.f.* Sharp sauce.

remoulage [rəmu'la:ʒ], *n.m.* Remoulding; regrinding; bran.

rémouleur [remu'lœ:r], *n.m.* Knife-grinder.

remous [rə'mu], *n.m.* Eddy, eddy-water, back-water, back-wash (of ship); slip-stream; (*fig.*) stirring (of passions etc.).

rempailler [rɑ̃pa'je], *v.t.* To rebottom or re-seat (a straw-bottomed chair); to re-stuff with straw. **rempailleur,** *n.m.* (*fem.* **-euse**) Chair-mender.

rempaquement [rɑ̃pak'mɑ̃], *n.m.* Barrelling of herrings.

rempaqueter, *v.t.* To pack up again.

remparer (se) [rɑ̃pa're], *v.r.* To recapture, to seize again (*de*).

rempart [rɑ̃'pa:r], *n.m.* Rampart; (*fig.*) bulwark.

rempiéter [rɑ̃pje'te], *v.t.* To re-foot (stockings etc.).

rempilé [rɑ̃pi'le], *n.m.* (*Mil. slang*) A re-engaged N.C.O.

rempiler [rɑ̃pi'le], *v.i.* To re-engage for military service.

remplaçable [rɑ̃pla'sabl], *a.* Replaceable.

remplaçant, *n.m.* (*fem.* **-ante**) Substitute (for another person).

remplacement [rɑ̃plas'mɑ̃], *n.m.* Replacing, replacement; substitution; reinvestment; locum (tenens). *Bureau de remplacement*, office for providing substitutes for the army; *en remplacement de*, in place of; *le remplacement a été aboli en France par la loi de 1872*, the replacing of recruits by substitutes was abolished in France by law in 1872. *De remplacement*, refill; spare (tyre etc.).

remplacer [rɑ̃pla'se], *v.t.* To take the place of, to supersede, to serve as a substitute for, to replace; to put something in the place of, to substitute for; to reinvest. *Se faire remplacer*, to get a substitute; *vous le remplacerez pendant son absence*, you will fill his place during his absence. **se remplacer,** *v.r.* To be replaced; to get a fresh supply.

remplage [rɑ̃'pla:ʒ], *n.m.* Filling up (of wine casks etc.); infilling rubble.

rempli (1) [rɑ̃'pli], *n.m.* Tuck, take-up; turning (for seam or hem of garment).

rempli (2) [rɑ̃'pli], *a.* (*fem.* **-ie**) Filled, full, replete, fulfilled.

remplier [rɑ̃pli'e], *v.t.* (*conjugated like* PRIER) To make a tuck in; to turn in.

remplir [rɑ̃'pli:r], *v.t.* To fill again, to refill, to replenish; to fill, to fill up; to fill in (form); to cram, to stuff; to crowd, to throng; to make complete; to supply, to stock, to furnish; to take up, to occupy (time etc.); to fill, to hold, to keep, to fulfil, to discharge, to perform; to realize, to come up to; to pay back. *Il remplit bien son temps*, he employs his time well; *remplir l'attente de quelqu'un*, to come up to someone's expectations; *remplir ses engagements*, to fulfil one's engagements; *remplir une tâche*, to perform a task; *remplir un poste*, to fill a post. **se remplir,** *v.r.* To fill oneself; to fill, to become full; to cram oneself, to be glutted (*de*).

remplissage, *n.m.* Filling, filling up (of casks etc.); filling in (of embroidery etc.); infilling; (*fig.*) rubbish, trash, padding; (*Rad.*) fill-in.

remplisseur, *n.m.* (*fem.* **-euse**) (*Needlework* etc.) Filler-in, point-lace mender; (*Ind.*) charging hopper.—*n.f.* Bottle-filling machine.

remploi [rɑ̃'plwa], *n.m.* Reinvestment.

remployer, *v.t. irr.* (*conjug. like* ABOYER) To use again; to reinvest.

remplumer [rɑ̃ply'me], *v.t.* To feather again. **se remplumer,** *v.r.* To get new feathers; to retrieve one's losses; to pick up again; (*fig.*) to get plump again.

rempocher [rɑ̃pɔ'ʃe], *v.t.* To put (something) back in one's pocket.

rempoigner, *v.t.* To catch hold of again.

rempoissonner [rɑ̃pwasɔ'ne], *v.t.* To restock with fish.

remporter [rɑ̃pɔr'te], *v.t.* To carry or take back; to carry off, to take away with one; to get, to obtain; to bear away, to win. *Remporter la victoire*, to win the victory; *remporter un prix*, to carry off a prize.

rempotage [rɑ̃pɔ'ta:ʒ], *n.m.* Repotting. **rempoter,** *v.t.* To repot.

remuable [rə'mɥabl], *a.* Movable.

remuage, *n.m.* Moving. *Billet de remuage*, permit to move wine.

remuant, *a.* (*fem.* **-ante**) Moving, restless, unquiet; bustling, busy; turbulent, (*fam.*) on the go.

remue-ménage, *n.m. inv..* Stir, disturbance, bustle, confusion; hullabaloo, to-do.

remuement or **remûment,** *n.m.* Stir, stirring; moving, removal; commotion, disturbance.

remue [rə'my], *n.f.* (*E. dial.*) Moving of cattle to the *alpages.*

remuer [rə'mɥe], *v.t.* To move, to stir; to rouse; to turn up; to shake up; to shake, to wag; to rake up, to stir up, to dig, etc.; to shuffle (dominoes etc.); (*fig.*) to rouse. *Remuer ciel et terre,* to move heaven and earth; *remuer des meubles,* to move furniture; *remuer la queue,* to wag its tail; *remuer la terre,* to dig or turn over the ground; *remuer la tête,* to shake one's head.—*v.i.* To stir, to move; to make a disturbance; to fidget. **se remuer,** *v.r.* To stir, to move; to bestir oneself, to bustle about; to fidget. (*fam.*) *Remuez-vous donc!* get on with it!

remueur, *n.m.* (*fem.* **-euse**) Mover, stirrer. *Remueur d'idées,* introducer of new ideas, (*fam.*) new broom.—*a.* Active, bustling.

rémunérateur [remynera'tœːr], *n.m.* (*fem.* **-trice**) Rewarder, remunerator, requiter.—*a.* Remunerative; paying, profitable.

rémunération, *n.f.* Remuneration, reward; consideration (for services rendered).

rémunératoire, *a.* Remunerative.

rémunérer [remyne're], *v.t. irr.* (*conjug. like* ACCÉLÉRER) To remunerate; to reward; to pay for (services rendered).

renâcler [rənɑ'kle], *v.i.* To snort; (*fam.*) to turn up one's nose; to hang back, to jib (at something).

renaissance [rəne'sɑ̃ːs], *n.f.* Rebirth; regeneration; revival, renewal, renaissance. *Renaissance des lettres,* revival of letters. *Style Renaissance,* Renaissance style.

renaissant [rəne'sɑ̃], *a.* (*fem.* **-ante**) Springing up again, reviving, renascent.

renaître [rə'neːtr], *v.i. irr.* (*conjug. like* NAÎTRE) To be born again; to grow again, to come up again; to appear again, to spring up again, to rise again; to revive; to reappear. *Faire renaître,* to bring to life again, to revive; *le jour renaît,* day reappears; *renaître à la vie,* to return to life; *renaître au bonheur,* to be restored to happiness; *toute la nature renaît,* all nature revives.

rénal [re'nal], *a.* (*fem.* **-ale,** *pl.* **-aux**) (*Anat.*) Renal.

renard [rə'naːr], *n.m.* Fox; (*fig.*) sly fox, cunning fox; (*pop.*) strike-breaker, blackleg, scab; (*Eng.*) leak. *Maître Renard,* Reynard the fox; *renard marin,* fox-shark, thresher; *se confesser au renard,* to tell one's secret to an enemy; *écorcher* or *piquer un renard,* (*pop.*) to vomit, to cat.

renarde [rə'nard], *n.f.* She-fox, vixen.

renardeau [rənar'do], *n.m.* (*pl.* **-eaux**) Fox-cub.

renarder, *v.i.* To play the fox; (*vulg.*) to vomit.

renardier, *a.* (*fem.* **-ière**) Pertaining to the foxes.—*n.m.* Fox-catcher.—*n.f.* Fox's hole; fox's earth; (*Metal.*) refining furnace.

Renaud [rə'no], *m.* Reginald.

renauder [rəno'de], *v.i.* (*pop.*) To grouse.

rencaissage [rɑ̃ke'saːʒ] or **rencaissement,** *n.m.* Putting again into wooden boxes or tubs; paying in again.

rencaisser, *v.t.* To put again into boxes; to pay again into the bank.

renchéri [rɑ̃ʃe'ri], *a.* (*fem.* **-ie**) Particular, over-nice (of a person).—*n.* Particular person, fastidious person. *Faire le renchéri,* to put on airs.

renchérir [rɑ̃ʃe'riːr], *v.t.* To raise the price of.—*v.i.* To get dearer, to rise in price. *Renchérir sur,* to improve upon; *renchérir sur quelqu'un,* to go one better than somebody, to outdo someone; to outbid someone.

renchérissement, *n.m.* Rise in price. **renchérisseur,** *n.m.* (*fem.* **-euse**) Outbidder, outdoer.

rencogner [rɑ̃kɔ'ɲe], *v.t.* (*colloq.*) To drive or push into a corner. **se rencogner,** *v.r.* To retreat, to ensconce oneself in a corner.

rencontre [rɑ̃'kɔ̃ːtr], *n.f.* Meeting, encounter, duel, accidental meeting, discovery, etc.; collision, accidental fight; chance, conjuncture, coincidence. *Aller* or *venir à la rencontre de quelqu'un,* to go to meet or come to meet someone; *marchandise de rencontre,* second-hand goods; *roue de rencontre d'une horloge,* balance-wheel of a clock; *une mauvaise rencontre,* an unpleasant encounter.—*n.m.* or *f.* (*Her.*) Head of an animal represented full-face.

rencontrer, *v.t.* To meet, to meet with, to fall in with; to light upon, to find, to encounter; to experience; to meet, to encounter in a hostile manner; to collide with; to hit upon (a witticism etc.); to refute.—*v.i.* To hit the scent (of hounds etc.). *Le limier rencontre,* the bloodhound is on the scent; *vous avez bien rencontré,* you have hit the nail on the head. **se rencontrer,** *v.r.* To meet, to meet each other, to meet with each other; to be met with, to be found; to tally, to agree, to coincide; to collide; to encounter (in a duel). *Cela ne se rencontre pas tous les jours,* one does not meet with that sort of thing every day; *nos idées se rencontrent,* our ideas coincide.

rendement [rɑ̃d'mɑ̃], *n.m.* Produce, yield, output; efficiency (of a machine etc.); (*spt.*) allowance, handicap; (*Comm.*) return, profit. *Loi du rendement non-proportionnel,* law of diminishing returns; *travailler à plein rendement,* to work to full output.

rendeur [rɑ̃'dœːr], *n.m.* (*fem.* **-euse**) One who renders or gives back.

rendez-vous [rɑ̃de'vu], *n.m. inv.* Rendezvous, appointment; place of meeting, trysting-place; time of meeting; resort, haunt. *Prendre rendez-vous* or *se donner rendez-vous,* to make an appointment.

rendormir [rɑ̃dɔr'miːr], *v.t. irr.* (*conjug. like* DORMIR) To send to sleep again. **se rendormir,** *v.r.* To fall asleep again.

rendosser [rɑ̃dɔ'se], *v.t.* To put on again.

rendre [rɑ̃ːdr], *v.t.* To render, to return, to restore, to give back; to pay back, to repay, to refund; to deliver; to yield up, to give up, to render up, to surrender; to pay; to produce, to yield, to bear, to bring in; to reward, to requite; to carry, to convey, to take; to cast up, to eject, to void, to throw up, to throw off one's stomach; to exhale, to emit, to send forth; to express, to convey, to represent, to reproduce; to translate; (*Law*) to find, to bring in, to give (a verdict etc.). *Ce blé rend beaucoup de farine,* this wheat yields plenty of flour; *Dieu vous le rende!* may God reward you! *je vous rends grâce*, I thank you; *la terre rendra ses morts*, the earth will give up its dead; *l'expérience l'a rendu sage*, experience has made him wise; *montez dans ma voiture, en deux heures je vous rendrai là*, get into my car and in two hours you will be there; *rendez-moi raison de votre conduite*, explain your conduct to me; *rendre à la vie*, to restore to life; *rendre à quelqu'un sa parole*, to release someone from his promise; *rendre avec usure*, to return with interest; *rendre compte de*, to render an account of, to account for; *rendre gorge*, to disgorge, to vomit; *rendre grâce à*, to give thanks to; *rendre hommage*, to render homage; *rendre justice à quelqu'un*, to do someone justice; *rendre la justice*, to dispense justice; *rendre l'âme*, to give up the ghost; *rendre le bien pour le mal*, to return good for evil; *rendre le sens exact de l'auteur*, to convey the author's true meaning; *rendre le salut*, to return a salute; *rendre les armes*, to lay down one's arms; *rendre ses respects* or *ses devoirs à quelqu'un*, to pay one's respects to someone; *rendre témoignage*, to bear witness; *rendre un arrêt*, to issue a decree; *rendre une place*, to surrender a town; *rendre un prisonnier à la liberté*, to set a prisoner free; *rendre visite*, to pay a visit; *se faire rendre*, to get back.—*v.i.* To lead (of roads); to be lucrative; to function, to work. **se rendre**, *v.r.* To betake oneself, to go; to resort; to call (on someone); to run, to flow; to lead (*à*); to make oneself, to render oneself; to become; to yield, to surrender, to give up; to be worn out, to be tired out; to be paid, to be returned. *Je me rends*, I give up; *il se rend à Paris*, he is going to Paris; *le sang se rend au cœur*, the blood flows to the heart; *se rendre à son devoir*, to go where duty calls; *se rendre prisonnier*, to give oneself up.

rendu, *a.* (*fem.* **-ue**) Rendered, delivered; exhausted, tired out, dead beat, spent; arrived.—*n.m.* Return, tit for tat; rendering.

renduire [rɑ̃'dɥiːr], *v.t. irr.* (*conjugated like* CONDUIRE) To plaster or daub over again; to re-coat (with paint etc.).

rendurcir, *v.t.* To make harder. **se rendurcir**, *v.r.* To become hard or harder.

rendurcissement, *n.m.* Hardening.

rêne [rɛːn], *n.f.* Rein. *Lâcher les rênes*, to give the horse his head; *prendre les rênes*, to take the reins; *tenir les rênes du gouvernement*, to hold the reins of government.

renégat [rəne'ga], *n.m. and a.* (*fem.* **-ate**) Renegade, turncoat.

rêner [rɛ'ne], *v.t.* To bridle (a horse).

rénette [re'nɛt], *n.f.* Paring-knife; (*Carp. etc.*) tracing-tool.

rénetter, *v.t.* To pare, to groove (horses' hoofs for shoeing).

renfaîtage [rɑ̃fɛ'taːʒ], *n.m.* Repairing the top of a roof, new-ridging.

renfaîter [rɑ̃fɛ'te], *v.t.* To new-ridge, to mend the top of (a roof).

renfermé [rɑ̃fɛr'me], *n.m.* *Odeur de renfermé*, fustiness; musty or close smell. *Sentir le renfermé*, to smell close, fusty, stuffy.—*a.* *Personne renfermée*, close, uncommunicative person.

renfermer [rɑ̃fɛr'me], *v.t.* To shut up, to lock up; to confine; to enclose, to include, to comprise; to conceal, to hide. **se renfermer**, *v.r.* To shut oneself up; to confine oneself. *Se renfermer en soi-même*, to retire within oneself.

renfiler [rɑ̃fi'le], *v.t.* To thread, to string again.

renflammer [rɑ̃flɑ'me], *v.t.* To rekindle. **se renflammer**, *v.r.* To blaze out again, to flare up again.

renflé [rɑ̃'fle], *a.* (*fem.* **-ée**) Swollen, swelling; (*Bot.*) inflated, puffed out; (*Arch.*) having an entasis.

renflement, *n.m.* Swelling, enlargement, bulge; (*Arch.*) entasis.

renfler [rɑ̃'fle], *v.t., v.i.* To swell, to swell again, to expand; to re-inflate.

renflouage [rɑ̃flu'aːʒ] or **renflouement**, *n.m.* Refloating a ship.

renflouer [rɑ̃flu'e], *v.t.* To refloat, to raise (a ship); to reinflate (a balloon); to set (a person, a firm) up in funds.

renfoncement [rɑ̃fɔ̃s'mɑ̃], *n.m.* Dinting, knocking in; dint, dent, cavity, hollow, recess, corner; (*Geol.*) downcast fault; bruise (on metal); (*Print.*) indentation; (*Paint.*) background, distance, depth.

renfoncer, *v.t.* To drive farther in or deeper; (*Build.*) to recess; to pull (a hat etc.) farther on, to pull over one's eyes; to knock a dent (in a hat); (*Print.*) to indent; to new-bottom (a cask). **se renfoncer**, *v.r.* (*Art*) To recede (of background).

renforçage [rɑ̃fɔr'saːʒ], *n.m.* Strengthening; (*Phot.*) intensification.

renforcé, *a.* (*fem.* **-ée**) Arrant, downright, regular; reinforced. *C'est un bourgeois renforcé*, he is an absolute bourgeois; *renforcé nylon*, nylon reinforced (of socks etc.); *sottise renforcée*, downright stupidity; *une étoffe renforcée*, a thick strong material.

renforcement, *n.m.* Reinforcing, strengthening; reinforcement; intensification (of sound); (*Phot.*) intensification.

renforcer [rɑ̃fɔr'se], *v.t.* To strengthen, to reinforce; to augment, to increase; (*Phot.*) to intensify. *Renforcer le son d'un instrument*, to increase the sound of an instrument. **se renforcer**, *v.r.* To gather strength, to grow stronger; (*Mil.*) to be reinforced.

renforcir [rɑ̃fɔr'siːr], *v.t.* (*pop.*) To strengthen. —*v.i.* To grow stronger.

renformer [rɑ̃fɔr'me], *v.t.* To stretch (gloves).

renformir [rɑ̃fɔr'miːr], *v.t.* (*Build.*) To mend and replaster (a wall etc.). **renformis**, *n.m.* Repairing (of a wall).

renfort [rɑ̃'fɔːr], *n.m.* Reinforcement; (*fig.*) help, aid, relief; strengthening-piece; re-inforce (of gun). *À grand renfort de*, by dint of, with any amount of; *de renfort*, extra, additional; *batterie de renfort* (*Elec.*), booster battery; *cheval de renfort*, trace horse.

renfrogné [rɑ̃frɔ'ɲe], *a.* (*fem.* **-ée**) Frowning, glum, scowling, surly, sullen. *Air renfrogné*, scowling look. **renfrognement**, *n.m.* Frown, scowl, knitting of the brows. **renfrogner**, *v.t.* To knit (the brows). **se renfrogner**, *v.r.* To frown, to knit one's brows; to look glum.

rengagé [rɑ̃ga'ʒe], *n.m. and a.* (*fem.* **-ée**) Re-enlisted (N.C.O.).

rengagement [rɑ̃gaʒ'mɑ̃], *n.m.* Re-engagement; re-enlistment; pledging or pawning again. **rengager**, *v.t.* To re-engage; to pledge or pawn again. *Rengager le combat*, to renew the conflict; *rengager son cœur*, to engage one's heart again.—*v.i.* (*Mil.*) To re-enlist. **se rengager,** *v.r.* To re-engage; to begin afresh; to re-enlist; to re-enter an employment.

rengaine [rɑ̃'gɛːn], *n.f.* Catch-phrase; (*fam.*) hackneyed story, stale excuse. *C'est toujours la même rengaine*, it's always the same old story.

rengainer [rɑ̃gɛ'ne], *v.t.* To sheathe, to put up (one's sword); to withdraw, to put away. *Rengainez votre compliment*, pocket your compliment; (*fam.*) shut up; *rengainer toujours la même histoire*, (*fam.*) to be always harping (on something).

rengorgement [rɑ̃gɔrʒə'mɑ̃], *n.m.* Swaggering, carrying one's head high, puffing out the neck (of peacock). **se rengorger,** *v.r.* To carry one's head high, to puff oneself up; (*fig.*) to give oneself airs, to be high handed.

rengréner [rɑ̃gre'ne] or **rengrener,** *v.t. irr.* (*conjugated like* AMENER) To fill (the threshing-machine) again; to throw into gear again, to engage again.

renhardir '(se) [rɑ̃ar'diːr], *v.r.* To pluck up new courage.

reniable [rə'njabl], *a.* Deniable. **renié,** *a.* (*fem.* -**ée**) Repudiated; one who has repudiated (something). **reniement** or **reniment,** *n.m.* Denying, disowning; denial, repudiation.

renier [rə'nje], *v.t.* (*conjugated like* PRIER) To deny; to disown, to disavow, to abjure, to forswear, to repudiate. *Avant que le coq chante tu me renieras trois fois*, before the cock crow twice thou shalt deny me thrice.

reniflard [rəni'flaːr], *n.m.* Snifting-valve; air-intake, blow-valve.

reniflement [rəniflə'mɑ̃], *n.m.* Sniffing, snuffling, snivelling, sniff. **renifler,** *v.i.* To sniff, to snuffle, to snivel; (*fig.*) to turn up one's nose (*sur*); to demur, to hang back. *Ce cheval renifle sur l'avoine*, this horse is off his feed.—*v.t.* To sniff up (snuff etc.).

reniflerie [rəniflə'ri], *n.f.* Sniffing etc.

renifleur, *n.m.* (*fem.* -**euse**) (*colloq.*) Person that often turns up his nose.

réniforme [reni'fɔrm], *a.* Reniform (kidney-shaped).

rénitence [reni'tɑ̃ːs], *n.f.* (*Med.*) Resistance (to pressure).

rénitent [reni'tɑ̃], *a.* (*fem.* -**ente**) Renitent.

reniveler [rəni'vle], *v.t.* To top up, to restore to former level, to re-level.

renne [rɛn], *n.m.* Reindeer.

renom [rə'nɔ̃], *n.m.* Renown, fame, reputation. *Être en renom*, to be famed.

renommé [rənɔ'me], *a.* (*fem.* -**ée** (1)), *a.* Renowned, noted, famed. **renommée** (2), *n.f.* Renown, fame, reputation, celebrity; report, rumour. *Bonne renommée vaut mieux que ceinture dorée*, a good name is better than riches; *la renommée grossit tout*, rumour exaggerates everything.

renommer [rənɔ'me], *v.t.* To name again, to re-elect; to re-appoint; to make renowned, to make famous, to celebrate, to praise. *Se faire renommer*, to make oneself famous; to get re-appointed or re-elected. **se renommer,** *v.r.* To make use of the name (of someone).

renonce [rə'nɔ̃ːs], *n.f.* Renounce, failure to follow suit (at cards). *Fausse renonce*, revoke.

renoncement, *n.m.* Renouncement; self-denial, renunciation. *Renoncement à soi-même*, self-abnegation.

renoncer, *v.i.* To withdraw, to surrender all claims (*à*); to give up, to renounce; to revoke, to renounce (at cards). *Renoncer à faire quelque chose*, to give up doing something; *renoncer à la couronne*, to renounce the crown; *renoncer à sa foi*, to renounce one's faith; *renoncer à une succession*, to give up an inheritance; *renoncer au tabac*, to give up smoking; *y renoncer*, to give up (the attempt), (*fam.*) to throw in one's hand.—*v.t.* To renounce, to disclaim, to disown, to disavow.

renonciateur, *n.m.* (*fem.* -**trice**) Renouncer.

renonciation, *n.f.* Renunciation, self-denial. (*Law*) *Renonciation à un droit*, waiver of a right.

renoncule [rənɔ̃'kyl], *n.f.* (*Bot.*) Ranunculus, (common name of several species such as) *renoncule âcre*, crowfoot; *renoncule aquatique* [GRENOUILLETTE], water-buttercup; *renoncule bulbeuse* or *bouton d'or* or *pied-de-coq*, buttercup; *renoncule des champs* or *bassinet*, corn crowfoot; *fausse renoncule*, pile-wort.

renouée [rə'nwe], *n.f.* (*Bot.*) Polygonum. *Renouée des oiseaux* or *centinode* or *traînasse*, knot-grass, persicaria; *renouée maritime*, sea-knot-grass.

renouement or **renoument** [rənu'mɑ̃], *n.m.* Tying or engaging again, renewing, renewal.

renouer [rənu'e], *v.t.* To tie again, to knot again; to put together; to resume, to renew. *Renouer amitié*, to become friends again; *renouer connaissance*, to renew acquaintance. —*v.i.* To resume relations (*avec*).

renouveau [rənu'vo], *n.m.* (*pl.* -**eaux**) (*poet.*) Spring, springtime; renewal, renaissance.

renouvelable, *a.* Renewable.

renouveler, *v.t.* To renew; to renovate; to revive, to resuscitate; to regenerate; to recommence, to repeat, to do again. *Renouveler l'air*, to admit fresh air; *renouveler un bail*, to renew a lease; *renouveler un usage*, to revive a custom. **se renouveler,** *v.r.* To be renewed, to be revived, to occur again; to spring up again (of plants).

renouvellement, *n.m.* Renewal, revival, renovation; increase, new growth.

rénovateur, *a.* (*fem.* -**trice**) Renovating.—*n.* Renewer, renovator, restorer.

rénovation, *n.f.* Renovation, renewal.

rénover, *v.t.* To renovate; to revive; to re-model, to re-organize.

renseignement, *n.m.* (Piece of) information, (piece of) intelligence, account; (*pl.*) information; references. *Bureau de renseignements*, information bureau, inquiry-office; *prendre des renseignements* or *aller aux renseignements*, to make inquiries; (*Mil.*) *le service des renseignements*, the Intelligence Service; (*Teleph.*) '*Renseignements*', Inquiries.

renseigner [rɑ̃sɛ'ne], *v.t.* To teach again; to inform, to give information; to direct. **se renseigner,** *v.r.* To seek information, to make inquiries, to inform oneself. *Se renseigner sur quelque chose*, to brief oneself about something.

rentabilité [rɑ̃tabili'te], *n.f.* Rentability.

rentable [rɑ̃'tabl], *a.* Profit-earning.

rente, *n.f.* Yearly income; revenue; stock, funds; annuity; rent; profit. *Acheter des rentes*, to buy stock, to invest in the funds; *avoir des rentes*, to have money invested; *faire une rente à*, to allow a pension to; to pension off; *la rente est en hausse*, the stocks are rising; *racheter une rente*, to redeem an annuity; *rentes sur l'État*, government stock; *rente viagère*, life annuity; *vivre de ses rentes*, to live on one's private means.

renté, *a.* (*fem.* **-ée**) Of independent means; endowed (of hospital etc.). *Bien renté*, wealthy; (*fam.*) well off.

renter [rã'te], *v.t.* To allow a yearly income to, to endow (public services etc.).

rentier, *n.m.* (*fem.* **-ière**) Stockholder, fundholder; person of property, man of independent means; holder of an annuity; rentier. *C'est un petit rentier*, he has a small private income, he is a small investor.

rentoilage [rãtwa'la:ʒ], *n.m.* New lining, relining, recanvassing. *Rentoilage d'un tableau*, stretching a picture upon new cloth.

rentoiler [rãtwa'le], *v.t.* To reline, to put new canvas to. *Rentoiler un tableau*, to stretch an old painting on new canvas.

rentrage [rã'tra:ʒ], *n.m.* Bringing in, taking in, housing (of fire-wood etc.).

rentraire [rã'trɛ:r], *v.t.i rr.* (*conjug. like* TRAIRE) To fine-draw (of seam).

rentraiture, *n.f.* Fine-drawing.

rentrant [rã'trã], *a.* (*fem.* **-ante**) Re-entering, returning; (*Av.*) retractable; (*Geom.*) re-entrant. *Angle rentrant*, re-entrant angle; *courbe rentrante*, re-entrant curve.—*n.m.* New player; recess (in a wall).

rentrayeur [rãtrɛ'jœ:r], *n.m.* (*fem.* **-euse**) Fine-drawer.

rentré [rã'tre], *a.* (*fem.* **rentrée** (1)) Returned; suppressed, driven in; hollow, depressed. *Sueur rentrée*, checked perspiration.

rentrée (2), *n.f.* Re-entrance, re-entering; return, home-coming; reopening (of schools, theatre, law-courts); reassembly (of Parliament); reappearance (of actor); taking in, housing, ingathering (of crops etc.); receipt, payment, collection, getting-in of taxes etc. *À la rentrée des classes*, at the beginning of term; *ce revenu est d'une rentrée difficile*, this revenue is hard to get in; *faire des rentrées*, to make returns; *faire la rentrée de*, to gather in; *frais de rentrée*, collection expenses; (*Ftb.*) *rentrée en touche*, throw-in.

rentrer [rã'tre], *v.i.* To re-enter, to enter again, to come in again, to go in again, to get in again; to return home; to return; to join again; to become again; to begin again; to reopen, to resume (of courts of law, schools, colleges, etc.); to make one's reappearance (of an actor etc.); (*Path.*) to be suppressed, to be driven in; to be got in, to come in (of money); to be contained or comprehended. *Faire rentrer les enfants*, to call the children in; *faire rentrer quelqu'un (à cent pieds) sous terre*, to humble a person in the dust; *les écoles sont rentrées*, the schools have gone back; *rentrer dans sa coquille*, (*fam.*) to go back into one's shell; *rentrer en charge*, to return to one's post; *rentrer en fonctions*, to resume one's duties; *rentrer en grâce*, to come back into favour; *rentrer en possession*, to regain possession; *rentrer en soi-même*,

commune with oneself; *rentrer en son bon sens*, to come to one's senses again; (*Mil.*) *rentrez!* dress back!—*v.t.* To take in, to bring in, to get in, to house; to take back home; to haul in; to turn in, to bend in; to gather in; to suppress, to check, to stifle; (*Print.*) to indent. (*Naut.*) *Rentrer l'ancre*, to take in the anchor; (*Av.*) *rentrer le train d'atterrissage*, to retract the under-carriage. *Voici le moment de rentrer les foins*, now is the season for getting in the hay.

renvelopper [rãvlɔ'pe], *v.t.* To wrap up again.

renversable [rãvɛr'sabl], *a.* Liable to be overthrown or upset; reversible.

renversant [rãvɛr'sã], *a.* (*fem.* **-ante**) (*colloq.*) Stupendous, amazing, stunning. *Un coup renversant*, a knock-down blow.

renverse [rã'vɛrs], *n.f.* (*Naut.*) Change (of wind); turn (of tide). *À la renverse*, backwards, upon one's back.

renversé [rãvɛr'se], *a.* (*fem.* **-ée**) Thrown down, thrown back, overthrown, upset; discomposed, troubled; reversed, inverted; upside-down. (*Cook.*) *Crème renversée*, custard shape, caramel custard; *encolure renversée*, (of horse) ewe-neck; *il a l'esprit renversé*, his brain is turning; *le monde renversé* [MONDE (1)].

renversement [rãvɛrsə'mã], *n.m.* Reversing, overturning, throwing down, overthrow; reversal, inversion; upsetting, turning upside down; turning (of tide), backing (of wind); confusion, disorder; subversion, destruction; (*Mus.*) inversion.

renverser [rãvɛr'se], *v.t.* To turn upside down, to throw down, to upset, to overthrow, to overturn; to reverse; to knock down, to knock over; to spill (a liquid); to subvert, to destroy, to turn topsy-turvy; to disorder, to confuse; to turn (the brain); (*fam.*) to astound, to stupefy; to transpose; to drive back, to rout, to put to rout; (*Arith. and Mus.*) to invert. *Ceci lui renversera l'esprit*, this will drive him out of his mind; *renverser à coups de canon*, to batter down; *renverser la table*, to upset the table; *renverser la vapeur*, (Steam-eng.) to reverse steam; (*Elec.*) *renverser le courant*, to reverse the current; *renverser l'encre*, to spill the ink; *renverser le régime*, to overthrow the government; *renverser une voiture*, to upset a carriage.—*v.i.* To overturn, to upset. **se renverser**, *v.r.* To fall back, to throw oneself back, to be thrown back; to upset, to be thrown down, to fall over, to fall down, to capsize; to lean back; to be spilt; to be thrown into disorder; to throw each other down; to be transposed.

renverseur [rãvɛr'sœ:r], *n.m.* (*fem.* **-euse**) Overthrower, subverter; destroyer; transposer.

renvidage [rãvi'da:ʒ], *n.m.* Winding-up, winding (in spinning). **renvider**, *v.t.* To wind upon the bobbins (in spinning). **renvideur**, *n.m.* Mule jenny.

renvier [rã'vje], *v.i.* To lay heavier stakes (at cards); to outbid.

renvoi [rã'vwa], *n.m.* Sending back, returning, return; sending away, dismissal; discharge; referring (to a committee etc.), (*Law*) sending; (*Parl.*) adjournment; caret, reference (in books etc.); reflection (of light), reverberation (of sound); (*Mus.*) repeat; (*Med.*) rising in the stomach, belch. (*Coup de) renvoi aux 22* (m.), (*Rugby*) kick-out from the 25-line; *renvoi de la cause à huitaine*, adjournment of the case for a week; (*Mech. Eng.*) *renvoi de mouvement*, counter-shaft, counter-motion; *renvoi des mains*, (*Row.*) getting the hands away; *renvoi du son*, reverberation of sound.

renvoyer [rᾶvwa'je], *v.t. irr.* (*conjug. like* ENVOYER) To send again; to send back, to return; to send away, to dismiss; to turn away, to discharge; to reject, to refuse; to refer (a cause etc.) before a judge etc.; to put off, to postpone, to adjourn, to delay; to drive back, to throw back; to reflect (light, heat, etc.); to repeat, to reverberate (sound). *On a renvoyé l'affaire à huitaine*, the case has been adjourned for a week; *renvoyer la balle* [BALLE (1)]; *renvoyer le lecteur à une note*, to refer the reader to a note; *renvoyer un domestique*, to dismiss a servant; *renvoyer un élève*, to expel a boy. **se renvoyer**, *v.r.* To be sent back or returned; to send from one to the other, to exchange, to bandy about. *Se renvoyer la balle*, (*fig.*) to bandy compliments.

réoccupation [reɔkypa'sjɔ̃], *n.f.* Reoccupation. **réoccuper**, *v.t.* To reoccupy.

réorchestrer [reɔrkes'tre], *v.t.* To compose a new score for, to re-score.

réordonner [reɔrdɔ'ne], *v.t.* To ordain again; to reorder.

réorganisation [reɔrganiza'sjɔ̃], *n.f.* Reorganization. **réorganiser**, *v.t.* To reorganize.

réouverture [reuver'ty:r], *n.f.* Reopening (of a theatre).

repaire (1) [rə'pɛ:r], *n.m.* Haunt (of criminals); den, lair (of animals).

repaire (2) [REPÈRE].

repaître [rə'pe:tr], *v.t. irr.* (*conjug. like* PAÎTRE) To feed, to nourish. *Il faut repaître ces animaux*, these animals must be fed; *repaître quelqu'un d'espérances*, to feed someone with hopes.—*v.i.* To feed, to browse. **se repaître**, *v.r.* To feed; to feast (*de*); to delight, to indulge in, to glut oneself (*de*). *Il se repaît d'espérances vaines*, he feeds on vain hopes.

répandre [re'pᾶ:dr], *v.t.* To pour out, to pour, to shed; to spill; to diffuse, to scatter, to sprinkle; to distribute, to lavish; to exhale, to give off, to give out; to spread abroad, to propagate. *Répandre des aumônes*, to distribute alms; *répandre des larmes*, to shed tears; *répandre l'alarme*, to spread alarm; *répandre son cœur*, to open one's heart; *répandre son sang*, to shed one's blood; *répandre un bruit*, to spread a rumour; *répandre un parfum*, to give off a scent. **se répandre**, *v.r.* To be poured out, to be shed, to be spilt; to be spread, to be scattered, to be distributed, to be diffused, to be lavished; to be exhaled; to be spread abroad, to be propagated; to be current, to spread, to flow abroad; to burst out, to break out, to launch out; to go into society. *La lumière se répand beaucoup plus vite que le son*, light is diffused much more quickly than sound; *la nouvelle de la victoire se répandit en un instant*, the news of the victory spread abroad in an instant; *se répandre dans le monde*, to go about in society;

se répandre en compliments, to burst into compliments.

répandu, *a.* (*fem.* **-ue**) Poured out, spilt, shed; widespread, widely prevalent. *Être fort répandu dans le monde*, to go about in society, to be well known in society.

réparable [repa'rabl], *a.* Reparable; atonable; rectifiable.

reparaître [rəpa'rɛ:tr], *v.t. irr.* (*conjugated like* CONNAÎTRE) To reappear; to make one's reappearance; to recur (of disease).

réparateur [repara'tœ:r], *a.* (*fem.* **-trice**) Reparative; restorative, refreshing.—*n.* Repairer, restorer, mender.

réparation [repara'sjɔ̃], *n.f.* Repair, repairing, mending; amends, atonement, satisfaction; compensation, redress, reparation. *En réparation*, under repair; *faire réparation à quelqu'un*, to make amends to someone; *réparation d'honneur*, retraction of an affront; *réparation par les armes*, duel; *réparations d'entretien*, maintenance repairs; *réparations de guerre*, war reparations. *Coup de pied de réparation*, (*Ftb.*) penalty kick.

réparatoire, *a.* Reparative.

réparer, *v.t.* To repair, to mend; to make amends for, to atone for, to redeem, to make up for; to rectify; to re-establish, to restore; to retrieve (a loss etc.); to recruit (health). *Réparer le temps perdu*, to make up for lost time; *réparer les dégâts*, to make good the damage; *réparer ses fautes*, to make amends for one's faults; *réparer ses forces*, to recruit one's strength; *réparer ses pertes*, to retrieve one's losses; *réparer des torts*, to redress grievances.

répareur, *n.m.* (*fem.* **-euse**) Repairer.

reparler [rəpar'le], *v.i.* To speak again. *Nous en reparlerons*, we'll talk about it again some other time.

repartie [rəpar'ti], *n.f.* Repartee, retort, rejoinder, reply. *Avoir la repartie prompte* or *être prompt à la repartie*, to be quick at repartee.

repartir (1) [rapar'ti:r], *v.t., v.i., irr.* (*aux.* AVOIR, *but conjugated like* PARTIR) To answer, to retort.

repartir (2), *v.i. irr.* (*aux.* ÊTRE, *conjugated like* PARTIR) To set out again, to go away again.

répartir [repar'ti:r], *v.t.* (*conjugated like* FINIR) To divide, to distribute; to portion out; to assess.

répartissable, *a.* Divisible, dividable, distributable, allottable; assessable.

répartiteur, *n.m.* Distributor; assessor (of taxes etc.).

répartition, *n.f.* Distribution, division; assessment; allotment (of shares etc.); allocation (under rationing etc.).

repas [rə'pɑ], *n.m. inv.* Meal, repast. *Faire ses quatre repas*, to take one's four meals a day; *faire un repas*, to have a meal; *repas de noces*, wedding breakfast; *repas froid*, cold spread.

repassage [rəpɑ'sa:ʒ], *n.m.* Passing again, repassing; grinding, setting, sharpening (of cutlery); ironing (of linen etc.); dressing, doing up (of a hat etc.).

repasser, *v.i.* To pass again, to repass; to go, come, call, etc., again. *Repasser chez quelqu'un*, to call again on someone.—*v.t.* To pass again; to repass; to cross again, to carry over again; to turn over, to think over, to revolve; to sharpen, to grind (tools), to set (razor); to iron, to iron out; to go over, to say over, to repeat; to look over again, to re-examine. *Repasser du linge*, to iron linen; *repasser les mers*, to recross the seas; *repasser quelque chose dans son esprit*, to revolve something in one's mind; *repasser sur un cuir*, to strop; *repasser une leçon*, to go over a lesson; *repasser une fausse pièce à quelqu'un*, (*pop.*) to palm off a bad coin on someone; *repassez-moi le sel*, pass me the salt again.

repasseur, *n.m.* (*fem.* **-euse**) (*Ind.*) Examiner; grinder. *Repasseur de couteaux*, knife-grinder. —*n.f.* Ironer; ironing-machine.

repavage [rəpa'va:ʒ] or **repavement**, *n.m.* Repaving. **repaver**, *v.t.* To repave.

repayer [rəpɛ'je], *v.t.* To pay again.

repêchage [rəpɛ'ʃa:ʒ], *n.m.* Rescuing. (*spt.*) *Épreuve de repêchage*, supplementary heat (to give a second chance to the second bests of preliminary heats); (*sch.*) second chance (for candidate who has failed an examination).

repêcher, *v.t.* To fish up or out again; (*fig.*) to recover, to retrieve; to rescue. (*sch.*) *Repêcher un candidat*, to give a candidate a second chance.

repeindre [rə'pɛ̃:dr], *v.t. irr.* (*conjugated like* CRAINDRE) To repaint.

repeint, *n.m.* Restored part of a picture.

rependre, *v.t.* To re-hang.

repenser [rəpɑ̃'se], *v.t.*, *v.i.* To think again of; to think over.

repentance [rəpɑ̃'tɑ̃:s], *n.f.* Repentance, contrition. **repentant**, *a.* (*fem.* **-ante**) Repentant. **repenti**, *a.* (*fem.* **-ie**) Penitent.—*n.f.* Repentant woman, Magdalen. *Maison de repenties*, rescue home for unfortunates, Magdalen hospital. **se repentir** (1), *v.r. irr.* (*conjugated like* MENTIR) To repent; to rue, to be sorry. *Il s'en repentira*, he will rue it; *se repentir de ses fautes*, to repent of one's faults.

repentir (2), *n.m.* Repentance, contrition, compunction, regret; (*Paint.*) part that has been corrected or altered; *(pl.)* ringlets.

repérage [rəpe'ra:ʒ], *n.m.* Locating, marking with guide marks; logging (of radio station); (*Cine.*) synchronization (of film and soundtrack); (*Print.*) registering; (*Mil.*) spotting. *Repérage par le son*, sound ranging [*see also* RADAR].

repercer [rəpɛr'se], *v.t.* To pierce again.

répercussif [repɛrky'sif], *a.* (*fem.* **-ive**) (*Med.*) Repellent.—*n.m.* Astringent.

répercussion [repɛrky'sjɔ̃], *n.f.* Repercussion, reverberation.

répercuter, *v.t.* To reverberate, to echo, to reflect; (*Med.*) to drive in. **se répercuter**, *v.r.* To reverberate, to have repercussions.

reperdre [rə'pɛrdr], *v.t.* To lose again.

repère or **repaire** [rə'pɛ:r], *n.m.* Mark; benchmark; joining-mark; (*fig.*) landmark; datum. *Point de repère*, indication, guiding-mark, landmark and synchronizing mark, reference mark.

repérer, *v.t. irr.* (*conjug. like* ACCÉLÉRER) To mark, to make a guiding-mark upon; (*Rad.*) to log (station); (*Print.*) to register; (*Artill.*) to locate; (*fam.*) to spot, to keep an eye on. **se repérer**, *v.r.* To take one's bearings.

répertoire [repɛr'twa:r], *n.m.* Table, index,

list, catalogue; repertory; (*fig.*) collection, fund. *Être un répertoire vivant*, to be a walking encyclopaedia; (*Theat.*) *pièce du répertoire*, stock piece; *répertoire d'adresses*, address-book; directory.

répertorier, *v.t.* To index, to file.

repeser [rəpə'ze], *v.t. irr.* (*conjugated like* AMENER) To re-weigh.

répétailler [repeta'je], *v.t.* To repeat over and over again, to keep on repeating.

répéter [repe'te], *v.t. irr.* (*conjug. like* ACCÉLÉRER) To repeat, to say again, to tell again; to rehearse; to reflect; (*Law*) to claim again, to demand back. *Faire répéter*, to make repeat, to have repeated; *faire répéter à quelqu'un sa leçon*, to hear someone his lesson; *répéter sans cesse*, to keep on repeating; *répéter une comédie*, to rehearse a comedy. **se répéter**, *v.r.* To be repeated; to say the same thing over again; to repeat oneself.

répétiteur, *n.m.* (*fem.* **-trice**) Private teacher, coach; assistant-master (in certain schools); (*Theat.*) chorus-master, repetiteur; (*Teleg.*) repeater; (*Naut.*) repeating-ship.

répétition, *n.f.* Repetition; recurrence, renewal, reproduction; private lesson; (*Law*) claim for recovery (of money etc.); (*Theat.*) rehearsal. *Donner des répétitions*, to give private lessons; *montre à répétition*, repeater (watch); *pièce en répétition*, play in rehearsal.

répétitorat, *n.m.* Assistant mastership; lectureship.

repétrir [repe'tri:r], *v.t.* To remould, to knead again; to re-fashion.

repeuplement [rəpœplə'mɑ̃], *n.m.* Re-peopling, restocking. *Repeuplement d'un étang*, restocking of a pond. **repeupler**, *v.t.* To repeople; to restock. **se repeupler**, *v.r.* To be repeopled; to be restocked; to increase in numbers again.

repic [rə'pik], *n.m.* (*Piquet*) Repique.

repincer [rəpɛ̃'se], *v.t.* To pinch again; (*colloq.*) to nab again.

repiquage [rəpi'ka:ʒ], *n.m.* Transplanting, pricking or planting out again; repairing (of road).

repiquer, *v.t.* To prick again; to prick out, to transplant; to repair (road); to re-stitch (needlework).—*v.i.* (*pop.*) *Repiquer (au truc)*, to begin again.

répit [re'pi], *n.m.* Respite, delay; (*fig.*) rest, breathing space; (*fam.*) breather.

replacement [rəplas'mɑ̃], *n.m.* Replacing, putting or setting again, replacement; reinvestment (of funds).

replacer, *v.t.* To replace, to put in place again; to reinvest (funds); to find a new situation for (servant).

replanir [rəpla'ni:r], *v.r.* To plane down (wood), to finish by planing. **se replacer**, *v.r.* To find oneself a new situation.

replanter [rəplɑ̃'te], *v.t.* To replant.

replâtrage [rəpla'tra:ʒ], *n.m.* Re-plastering, plastering up; patching up; (*fam.*) patched-up reconciliation. **replâtrer**, *v.t.* To re-plaster; to plaster up; patch up (temporarily).

replet [rə'plɛ], *a.* (*fem.* **-ète**) Obese, stout; (*fam.*) podgy.

réplétion [reple'sjɔ̃], *n.f.* Stoutness, obesity, repletion, surfeit.

repli [rə'pli], *n.m.* Fold, crease; (*fig.*) winding, sinuosity, coil, meander (of river); (*Mil.*) withdrawal. *Les plis et les replis du cœur humain*, the secret places of the heart; *les replis du serpent*, the coils of the serpent; *un repli de terrain*, a fold of the ground. **repliable**, *a.* Folding, collapsible.

repliement [rəpli'mã], *n.m.* (*Mil.*) Falling back, retirement; folding up.

replier, *v.t.* (*conjugated like* PRIER) To fold again, to fold up; to make a fold or folds in; to bend back; to coil (a rope etc.). **se replier**, *v.r.* To twist, wind or fold oneself, to writhe, to wind, to coil; (*Mil.*) to fall back, to retreat. *Faire replier des troupes*, to withdraw troops; *se replier sur soi-même*, to retire within oneself.

réplique [re'plik], *n.f.* Reply, answer, retort, rejoinder; (*Mus.*) repeat; (*Theat.*) cue; second striking (of double chime); replica (of statue); (*Cine.*) retake. *Donner la réplique*, to give the cue.

répliquer, *v.t.*, *v.i.* To reply, to answer; to retort; (*Law*) to rejoin (to put in a rejoinder). *Ne répliquez pas!* Don't answer back!

reploiement [REPLIEMENT].

replonger [rəplɔ̃'ʒe], *v.t.* To plunge again, to dip again; to reimmerse.—*v.i.* and **se replonger**, *v.r.* To plunge again, to plunge oneself again; to dive or be immersed again.

reployer [REPLIER].

repolir [rəpɔ'liːr], *v.t.* To repolish, to rub up; (*fig.*) to polish up (literary work etc.).

répondant [repɔ̃'dã], *n.m.* One who responds; candidate (at an examination); bail, surety, security; (*R.-C. Ch.*) lay-clerk; server (at Mass).

répondre [re'pɔ̃:dr], *v.t.*, *v.i.* To lay (eggs) again.

répondre [re'pɔ̃:dr], *v.t.* To answer, to reply, to write back; (*R.-C. Ch.*) to make the responses to (the Mass).—*v.i.* To answer, to reply; to write back; to respond; to make a suitable return, to satisfy, to come up (*à*); to correspond, to be in proportion *or* conformity (*à*); to re-echo; to reach, to be heard (of sound); to be answerable (for), to be accountable, to be responsible, to be security (for); to be bail, to pledge oneself (*pour etc.*). *C'est mal répondre à*, it is a poor return for; *je ne vous réponds que de moi*, I only answer for myself; *je vous en réponds*, take my word for it, I assure you, I'll be bound; (*fam.*) *c'était une belle matinée, je vous en réponds*, it was a fine morning and no mistake; *le candidat a bien répondu*, the candidate satisfied the examiners; *ne pas répondre à l'attente publique*, to fall short of public expectation; *pour répondre à*, in answer to; *qui pourrait répondre de l'événement?* who could answer for the event? *qui répond paye*, go bail and you'll have to pay; *répondre à ceux qui appellent*, to answer those who call; *répondre à l'éperon*, to answer to the spur; *tout répond à nos vœux*, everything falls in with our wishes. **se répondre**, *v.r.* To answer oneself; to answer each other; to correspond, to suit, to agree, to be in sympathy. *Nos cœurs se répondent*, our hearts are in sympathy.

répons [re'pɔ̃], *n.m.* Response (in church).

réponse [re'pɔ̃:s], *n.f.* Answer, reply, response; (*Law*) rejoinder. *À sotte demande point de réponse*, a foolish question deserves no answer; *droit de réponse*, right to reply; *faire réponse*, to answer; *réponse à une réplique*, (*Law*) rejoinder; *réponse de Normand*, evasive answer; *réponse des primes*, declaration of options; *rendre réponse*, to return an answer; *un mot de réponse*, a line in reply.

repopulation [rəpɔpyla'sjɔ̃], *n.f.* Repopulation; restocking.

report [rə'pɔ:r], *n.m.* (*Book-keeping*) Carrying forward, bringing forward; amount brought forward; posting (in ledger); (*St. Exch.*) continuation, contango; (*Phot.*) transfer. *Faire un report*, to bring an amount forward; *taux de report*, contango (rate).

reportage [rəpɔr'ta:ʒ], *n.m.* Reporting.

reporter (1) [rəpɔr'tɛ:r], *n.m.* (Newspaper) reporter.

reporter (2) [rəpɔr'te], *v.t.* To carry back, to take in; to take back; (*Book-keeping*) to carry forward; to post (in ledger); (*St. Exch.*) to carry over; (*Phot.*) to transfer. **se reporter**, *v.r.* To go back, to be carried back (in memory etc.); to refer. '*Se reporter à*', 'please refer to'.

repos [rə'po], *n.m.* Rest, repose; sleep; quiet, peace, tranquillity; resting-place, landing (on stairs); seat in garden; (*Mus.*, *Pros.*, etc.) pause, caesura; (*Fire-arms*) half-cock. *Champ du repos*, cemetery; *en repos*, at rest; *laissez-moi en repos*, let me alone; *lit de repos*, couch; *mettre un fusil au repos*, to half-cock a gun; *servir de repos* or *de lieu de repos*, to be a resting-place; *se tenir en repos*, to keep quiet; *valeur de tout repos*, gilt-edged security, very safe security. (*Mil.*) *Repos!* (when drilling) Stand at ease! *Repos!* (to men in barrack-room) Carry on! **reposant**, *a.* (*fem.* **-ante**) Restful, refreshing; well-founded (argument).

reposé, *a.* (*fem.* **reposée** (1)) Rested, refreshed; quiet, calm, cool. *À tête reposée*, coolly, deliberately.

reposée (2), *n.f.* Lair.

repose-pied, *n.m. inv.* Footrest (on bicycle etc.).

reposer, *v.t.* To place again, to lay, put, or set back again, to replace; to rest, to repose (on anything); to refresh; (*Mil.*) to ground, to order (arms). *Cela repose la vue*, that is restful to the eye; *reposer la tête sur*, to rest one's head upon.—*v.i.* To rest, to repose; to lie down; to sleep; to be at rest; to be inactive or out of use; to lie, to lean, to be based or established (*sur*); to settle (of liquids). *Laisser reposer quelqu'un*, to allow someone to rest or remain undisturbed; *laisser reposer une terre*, to let a piece of ground lie fallow; *la maison repose sur le roc*, the house is built on rock. **se reposer**, *v.r.* To rest, to take a rest, to leave off, to pause; to lie down; to settle, to settle down; to alight (of birds). *Il faut que l'esprit se repose*, the mind has need of rest; *se reposer après le travail*, to rest after labour; *se reposer sur*, to rely on.

reposoir, *n.m.* Resting-place; pause; street-altar for the monstrance (in procession of the *Fête-Dieu*); settling-vat (in dyeing).

repoussant [rəpu'sã], *a.* (*fem.* **-ante**) Repulsive, forbidding; repellent, loathsome.

repoussé [rəpu'se], *n.m.* Repoussé (work), chasing, embossing.—*a.* (*fem.* **-ée**) Repoussé, chased (silver), embossed.

repoussement, *n.m.* Repulsion, dislike; recoil, kick (of fire-arms); rejection (of idea etc.).

repousser [rəpu′se], *v.t.* To push again; to push back, to repel, to drive, to beat or force back; to thrust away, to push aside; to spurn, to reject; to repulse, to resist, to rebuff; to re-utter; to shoot out (branches etc.) again (of trees and plants). *Repousser du cuir,* to emboss leather; *repousser du cuivre,* to chase copper; *repousser la force par la force,* to repel force by force; *repousser la tentation,* to thrust aside temptation; *repousser l'ennemi,* to repulse, to force back, to beat off the enemy; *repousser une demande,* to reject a demand.— *v.i.* To recoil, to kick (of firearms); to spring up or come up again (of plants etc.); to grow again (of hair); to be repulsive.

repoussoir, *n.m.* Driving-bolt, starting-bolt; (*Paint.*) foil, set-off, contrast.

répréhensible [repreã′sibl], *a.* Reprehensible.

répréhensiblement, *adv.* Reprehensibly.

répréhension, *n.f.* Reprehension, reproof.

reprendre [rə′prã:dr], *v.t. irr.* (*conjugated like* PRENDRE) To retake, to get back, to recover, to recapture; to catch again (of diseases); to take up again, to take to again, to resume, to begin again, to return to; to reprove, to find fault with; to repair, to mend. *La fièvre l'a repris,* he has got fever again; *on ne m'y reprendra plus,* I will not be caught napping again; *reprendre aigrement,* to take up sharply; *reprendre connaissance,* to recover consciousness, to come round; *reprendre de plus haut,* to go further back in time; *reprendre haleine,* to recover one's breath, to take breath; *reprendre le dessus,* to get the upper hand again; *reprendre les invendus,* to take back unsold articles etc.; *reprendre ses esprits,* to recover one's senses; *reprendre ses forces,* to recover one's strength; *reprendre ses habits d'hiver,* to take to one's winter clothing again; *reprendre une pièce,* to revive a play; *reprendre l'offensive,* to resume the offensive; *reprendre une ville,* to recapture a town; (*Ten.*) *reprendre une volée basse,* to take a low volley.—*v.i.* To take root again; to freeze again; to close up again (of wounds etc.); to begin again, to set in again, to return; to recover, to improve, to look up again; to reply, to answer; to resume, to go on. *La rivière a repris,* the river has frozen over; *le froid a repris,* the cold has set in again; *reprendre vivement,* (of engine) to pick up smartly. **se reprendre,** *v.r.* To correct oneself, to take oneself up; to recover oneself, to collect one's thoughts; to be caught again; to close up again (of wounds); to begin again. *S'y reprendre à plusieurs fois,* to make several attempts at something; (*fam.*) to have several goes, shots, at something (before succeeding).

représaille [rəpre′za:j], *n.f. usu. plur.* Reprisal. *User de représailles,* to make reprisals, to retaliate.

représentable [rəprezã′tabl], *a.* Representable, performable.

représentant, *n.m.* (*fem.* **-ante**) Representative, deputy, delegate; commission agent, traveller.

représentatif, *a.* (*fem.* **-ive**) Representative.

représentation [rəprezãta′sjɔ̃], *n.f.* Representation; exhibition, production, performance; display, show; remonstrance; state,

display (of a high official); agency. *Avoir la représentation exclusive de,* to be sole agents for; Cyrano *a eu 400 représentations, Cyrano* had a run of 400 nights; *droit de représentation,* performing rights; *droits de représentation,* dramatic fees; *faire des représentations à,* to remonstrate with; *frais de représentation,* entertainment allowance; *représentation à bénéfice,* charity performance.

représenter, *v.t.* To present again; to reintroduce; to show, to exhibit, to produce; to represent; to depict, to portray, to describe; to look like, to resemble; to typify, to symbolize; to perform, to act (a play); to be the representative of; to stand in the place or fill the part of. *Cela est représenté au naturel,* that is depicted to the life; *cet enfant me représente son père,* that child reminds me of his father; *représenter à quelqu'un les inconvénients,* to point out to someone the disadvantages; *représenter quelqu'un* (*Law*), to appear for someone; *se faire représenter,* to send a representative, to get a proxy.—*v.i.* To have an imposing appearance; to keep up one's dignity; to make a good show (in society etc.). **se représenter,** *v.r.* To present oneself again, to make one's appearance again; to picture to oneself; to occur, to present itself again (of a thing); to turn up again. *Se représenter comme acteur,* to make oneself out to be an actor.

répressible [reprɛ′sibl], *a.* Repressible.

répressif, *a.* (*fem.* **-ive**) Repressive.

répression, *n.f.* Repression.

réprimandable [reprimã′dabl], *a.* That may be reprimanded.

réprimande [repri′mã:d], *n.f.* Reprimand, reproof, rebuke. *Faire une réprimande à quelqu'un,* to reprimand someone.

réprimander, *v.t.* To reprimand, to reprove, to rebuke.

réprimant [repri′mã], *a.* (*fem.* **-ante**) Repressive, restraining.

réprimer [repri′me], *v.t.* To repress, to restrain, to curb; to quell, to put down. *Réprimer les abus,* to repress abuses; *réprimer le vice,* to hold vice in check; *réprimer ses désirs,* to suppress one's desires.

repris [rə′pri], *a.* (*fem.* **reprise** (1)) Retaken, recaptured, taken up again; reset (of a bone).—*n.m. Repris de justice,* old offender, (*fam.*) old lag.

reprisage, *n.m.* Darn; darning.

reprise (2), *n.f.* Resumption; taking back; retaking, recapture, recovery; reconquest; revival, renewal; return (of an illness etc.); repair, darn; (*Mus.*) repetition, mark of repetition; burden, refrain (of a song); pick-up, acceleration (of engine); (*Build.*) under-propping, underpinning; (*Riding*) (short) lesson; riding squad; (*Law*) claims (of married parties seeking dissolution); (*Ftb.* etc.) second half; (*Fenc.*) bout; (*Box.*) round; (*Bot.*) *Sedum telephium,* stonecrop. *À deux reprises,* twice; *à plusieurs reprises,* several times, repeatedly; *faire des reprises à,* to darn; *faire des reprises perdues,* to fine-draw; *la reprise d'un procès,* the renewal of a lawsuit; *reprise des invendus,* taking back of unsold goods.

repriser, *v.t.* To mend, to darn. *Œuf à repriser,* darning-ball.

repriseuse, *n.f.* Darner, mender.
réprobateur [reprɔba'tœːr], *a.* (*fem.* **-trice**) Reproachful, reproving.
réprobation [reprɔba'sjɔ̃], *n.f.* Reprobation.
reprochable [rəprɔ'ʃabl], *a.* Reproachable.
reproche [rə'prɔʃ], *n.m.* Reproach; (*pl.*, *Law*) exception, objection. *Faire des reproches amers à,* to reproach bitterly; *faire un reproche à quelqu'un de quelque chose,* to reproach someone with something; *s'attirer des reproches,* to incur reproach; (*Law*) *témoin sans reproche,* unimpeachable witness.
reprocher [rəprɔ'ʃe], *v.t.* To reproach, to upbraid; to taunt, to twit, to cast in the teeth of; (*Law*) to object to. *Il lui a reproché ses défauts,* he reproached him with his faults; *il me l'a reproché,* he cast it in my teeth; *reprocher à une personne d'avoir fait quelque chose,* to reproach a person with having done something; *reprocher des témoins,* to object to or challenge (witnesses); *reprocher les morceaux à quelqu'un,* to grudge someone the food he eats. **se reprocher,** *v.r.* To reproach oneself; to blame oneself.
reproducteur [rəprɔdyk'tœːr], *a.* (*fem.* **-trice**) Reproductive.—*n.m.* Stud animal. *Reproducteur d'élite,* pedigree sire.
reproductible [rəprɔdyk'tibl], *a.* Reproducible. **reproductif,** *a.* (*fem.* **-ive**) Reproductive. **reproduction,** *n.f.* Reproduction; reprinting, republication; copy. (*Cine.*) *Reproduction sonore,* sound reproduction.
reproduire [rəprɔ'dɥiːr], *v.t. irr.* (*conjug. like* CONDUIRE) To reproduce; to reprint, to republish, to copy (newspaper advertisement); to bring forward again. **se reproduire,** *v.r.* To reproduce; to breed; to reappear; to happen again, to recur.
réprouvable [repru'vabl], *a.* Censurable, reprehensible.
réprouvé [repru've], *a.* (*fem.* **-ée**) Reprobate, outcast; (*Theol.*) damned.—*n.* Reprobate, outcast, pariah; (*Theol.*) damned person. *Il a un visage de réprouvé,* he has a sinister-looking face.
reprouver [rəpru've], *v.t.* To prove again.
réprouver [repru've], *v.t.* To disapprove of, to reprobate; (*Theol.*) to condemn, to cast out.
reps [reps], *n.m.* Rep (silk or woollen fabric).
reptation [rɛpta'sjɔ̃], *n.f.* Creeping, reptation.
reptile [rɛp'til], *n.m.* Reptile. *C'est un reptile,* he is a crawling wretch.—*a.* Creeping, crawling.
reptilien, *a.* (*fem.* **-ienne**) Reptilian.
repu [rə'py], *a. and p.p.* of *repaître* (*fem.* **-ue** (1)) Full, satiated.
républicain [repybli'kɛ̃], *a. and n.m.* (*fem.* **-aine**) Republican; (*Orn.*) Republican grosbeak.
républicaniser, *v.t.* To republicanize.
républicanisme, *n.m.* Republicanism.
republier [rəpybli'e], *v.t.* To republish.
république [repy'blik], *n.f.* Republic; commonwealth; state. *La république des lettres,* the republic of letters.
répudiable [repy'djabl], *a.* Repudiable.
répudiation, *n.f.* Repudiation; (*Law*) renunciation. **répudier,** *v.t.* (*conjugated like* PRIER) To repudiate; (*Law*) to renounce.

*repue (2) [rə'py], *n.f.* Eating, feeding; meal, repast. *Repue franche,* free meal.
répugnance [repy'ɲãːs], *n.f.* Repugnance, dislike, aversion; reluctance, unwillingness. *Avec répugnance,* with reluctance. **répugnant,** *a.* (*fem.* **-ante**) Repugnant.
répugner, *v.i.* To be repugnant; to inspire repugnance; to feel repugnance; to clash with, to be contrary; to feel loathing. *Cela me répugne,* I am loath to do it; *cela répugne au sens commun,* that is contrary to common sense; *cet homme me répugne,* that man puts me off; *il me répugne de vous entretenir d'un pareil sujet,* it is repugnant to me to talk to you on such a subject.
répulsif [repyl'sif], *a.* (*fem.* **-ive**) Repulsive, repellent; (*fig.*) disgusting.
répulsion, *n.f.* Repulsion; (*fig.*) aversion, disgust.
réputation [repyta'sjɔ̃], *n.f.* Reputation, character; good repute, fame. *Avoir la réputation de,* to have the reputation of, to pass for; *je ne vous connaissais que de réputation,* I only knew you by repute; *perdre quelqu'un de réputation,* to ruin someone's reputation; *sans réputation,* of no repute; *se faire une réputation,* to get oneself a reputation.
réputé [repy'te], *a.* (*fem.* **-ée**) Well-known, of repute, a good name.
réputer [repy'te], *v.t.* To repute, to consider, to deem.
requérable [rəke'rabl], *a.* (*Law*) Demandable, liable to be requisitioned.
requérant [rəke'rã], *a.* (*fem.* **-ante**) Applying, claiming.—*n.* Plaintiff, applicant, petitioner.
requérir [rəke'riːr], *v.t. irr.* (*conjugated like* ACQUÉRIR) To request; to require, to demand; to claim, to summon; to requisition. *C'est lui qui m'en a requis,* it was he who requested me to do it.
requête [rə'kɛːt], *n.f.* Request, petition, demand, application; (*Hunt.*) new cast, new search. *Faire une requête,* to make a request.
requêter [rəkɛ'te], *v.t.* (*Hunt.*) To search for again.
requiem [rekɥi'ɛm], *n.m.* Requiem.
requin [rə'kɛ̃], *n.m.* Shark. *Requin marsouin* [LAMIE]; *peau de requin,* (for smoothing) shagreen.
requinquer (se) [rəkɛ̃'ke], *v.r.* (*pop.*) To deck oneself out, to spruce oneself up; to pick up (after illness).
requis [rə'ki], *a.* (*fem.* **requise**) Required, requisite, necessary. *Il a l'âge requis,* he is of the required age.—*n. Un requis civil,* a civilian forced to do war work; labour conscript (1939–45 war).
réquisition [rekizi'sjɔ̃], *n.f.* Requisition; commandeering; call, summons, levy. *À la réquisition de,* on the demand of; *mettre en réquisition,* to requisition.
*réquisitionnaire, *n.m.* Soldier called up on a levy.
réquisitionnement, *n.m.* Requisitioning.
réquisitionner, *v.t.* To requisition, to commandeer.
réquisitoire, *n.m.* List of charges, indictment; speech for the prosecution. *Faire son réquisitoire,* to address the court (of the prosecuting officer).
rescapé [rɛska'pe], *a. and n.m.* (*fem.* **-ée**)

Survivor of a disaster (pit explosion, railway mishap, shipwreck).

rescindant [resɛ̃'dã], a. (fem. **-ante**) Rescinding, annulling.

rescinder [resɛ̃'de], v.t. (Law) To rescind, to annul.

rescision [resi'zjɔ̃], n.f. Annulment, rescission.

rescisoire, a. Rescissory.

rescousse [res'kus], n.f. Venir (aller) à la rescousse, to come (to go) to the rescue.

rescription [reskrip'sjɔ̃], n.f. Rescription, rescript; order.

rescrit, n.m. Rescript; (papal) bull.

réseau [re'zo], n.m. (pl. **-eaux**) Net; network, reticulate fabric or tissue; (fig.) web, complication, tangle; (Rail., Elec. etc.) network, system; (Anat.) plexus; (Arch.) tracery; (Mil.) Réseau(x) de (fils de fer) barbelés, wire entanglements.

résection [resek'sjɔ̃], n.f. (Surg.) Resection.

réséda [reze'da], n.m. Reseda; mignonette. Réséda des teinturiers, dyer's weed.

réséquer [rese'ke], v.t. (Surg.) To resect.

réservation [rezerva'sjɔ̃], n.f. Reservation, reserving; booking (of seats).

réserve, n.f. Reserve; reservation, caution, wariness; coyness, modesty, shyness; stock, reserve, store; preserve (for game); (Mil.) the Reserve; reserve troops. À la réserve de, except for; à la réserve que, except that; en réserve, in reserve, in store; faire des réserves, to make reservations; mettre en réserve, to reserve; officier de réserve, a reserve officer; sans réserve, unreservedly; se tenir sur la réserve, to act with reserve; sous réserve de, subject to; sous toute réserve, without any guarantee. **réservé**, a. (fem. **-ée**) Reserved; lying in store; cautious, wary, circumspect; shy, coy. Chasse et pêche réservées, fish and game preserve.

réserver, v.t. To reserve, to keep back; to lay by; to intend, to keep (pour). **se réserver**, v.r. To reserve for oneself; to reserve oneself, to wait. Je me réserve de faire cela, I am waiting for an opportunity to do that; se réserver la réplique, to reserve the right of replying.

réserviste, n.m. (Mil.) Reservist.

réservoir, n.m. Reservoir; container, tank, cistern, well; fish-pond. Réservoir d'essence, petrol tank.

résidant [rezi'dã], a. (fem. **-ante**) Resident.

résidence [rezi'dã:s], n.f. Residence, place of abode, dwelling; office or function of resident.

résident, n.m. Resident (minister at a foreign court).

résidentiel, a. (fem. **-ielle**) Residential. Quartier résidentiel, residential quarter.

résider, v.i. To reside, to dwell; to lie, to consist. Là réside la difficulté, that is where the difficulty lies.

résidu [rezi'dy], n.m. Residue; (Math.) residue (of function), remainder; (Chem.) residuum; fouling (of gunpowder).

résiduaire, a. Waste.

résiduel, a. (fem. **-elle**) Residual.

*****résignant** [rezi'ɲã], n.m. Resigner (of a benefice etc.). **résignataire**, n.m. Resignee.

résignation, n.f. Resignation; submissiveness.

résigné [rezi'ɲe], a. (fem. **-ée**) Resigned, submissive. **résigner**, v.t. To resign, to give up. **se résigner**, v.r. To resign oneself, to submit; to be resigned.

resigner [rəsi'ɲe], v.t. To sign again.

résiliable [rezi'ljabl], a. Which may be cancelled. **résiliation**, n.f. **résiliement** or **résilîment**, n.m. Cancelling, annulment.

résilience [rezi'ljã:s], n.f. Resilience (in metals).

résilier, v.t. To cancel, to annul (agreement, lease).

résille [re'zi:j], n.f. Hair-net; network of lead bars over window.

résine [re'zin], n.f. Resin, rosin.

résiner, v.t. To tap (trees) for resin.

résineux, a. (fem. **-euse**) Resinous.

résinier, n.m. (fem. **-ière**) Resin-tapper.

résinifère, a. Resiniferous, yielding resin.

résinification, n.f. Resinification.

résinifier, v.t. To resinify.

résiniforme, a. Resiniform.

résipiscence [resipi'sã:s], n.f. Resipiscence; repentance. Venir à résipiscence, to become repentant.

résistance [rezis'tã:s], n.f. Resistance, opposition; toughness (of materials); staying-power; (prop.n.) the Resistance Movement (1940–5). Faire de la résistance, to offer resistance; limite de résistance, breaking-point; pièce de résistance, main dish; most striking feature, 'pièce de résistance'; sans résistance, unresistingly. **résistant**, a. (fem. **-ante**) Unyielding; resistant, strong, lasting, firm, tough.—a. and n. A member of the Resistance Movement. Couleur résistante, fast colour; tissu résistant aux intempéries, weatherproof material.

résister [rezis'te], v.i. To resist, to offer opposition, to withstand (à), to hold out against; to endure, to bear, to stand (à); to take (stress). Résister à la tentation, to withstand temptation; résister à l'ennemi, to resist the enemy; résister à la tempête, to weather the storm.

résistible, a. Resistible.

résistivité [rezistivi'te], n.f. (Elec.) Resistivity.

résolu [rezɔ'ly], a. (fem. **-ue**) Resolved, decided, determined; solved. Problème résolu, a problem which has been solved.

résoluble [rezɔ'lybl], a. Soluble; that may be dissolved or annulled.

résolument [rezɔly'mã], adv. Resolutely, boldly, stoutly.

résolutif [rezɔly'tif], a. (fem. **-ive**) (Med.) Resolutive; resolvent.

résolution [rezɔly'sjɔ̃], n.f. Resolution, solution; decision, determination; resolve; (Law) cancelling, annulment. Avec résolution, resolutely, stoutly; changer de résolution, to change one's mind; manquer de résolution, to be weak-willed; prendre une résolution, to make up one's mind; résolution d'un contrat, cancelling of a contract.

résolutoire, a. (Law) Cancelling, abrogating.

résolvant, a. (fem. **-ante**) [RÉSOLUTIF; see RÉSOUDRE].

résonance [rezɔ'nã:s], n.f. Resonance.

résonnant [rezɔ'nã], a. (fem. **-ante**) Resonant, resounding, sonorous. Voix claire et résonnante, clear and sonorous voice.

résonnement [rezɔn'mɑ̃], *n.m.* Resounding, re-echoing.

résonner [rezɔ'ne], *v.i.* To resound, to reverberate, to re-echo.

résorber [rezɔr'be], *v.t.* To reabsorb.

résorption, *n.f.* Reabsorption.

résoudre [re'zuːdr], *v.t. irr. (pres.p.* **résolvant,** *p.p.* **résolu** and *(Phys., Chem.)* **résous)** To resolve; to dissolve; to melt; to solve, to work out; to decide upon, to determine on; to cancel, to make void; to persuade, to induce. *A-t-on résolu la paix ou la guerre?* has peace or war been decided upon? *résoudre une tumeur,* to dissipate a tumour; *résoudre un problème,* to solve a problem. **se résoudre,** *v.r.* To resolve, to determine; to be resolved, to be solved; to dissolve. *Je ne saurais m'y résoudre,* I cannot make up my mind to do it; *l'eau se résout en vapeur,* water is resolved into vapour; *se résoudre à,* to resolve upon.

respect [rɛs'pɛ], *n.m.* Respect, regard, reverence, deference. *Manquer de respect envers,* to be wanting in respect towards; *porter respect à,* to show respect to; *présenter ses respects à,* to pay one's respects to; *sauf le respect que je vous dois,* with all due respect; *sauf votre respect,* saving your presence; *tenir en respect,* to keep in awe. *Respect humain* [rɛspɛky'mɛ̃], fear of what people may say.

respectabilité, *n.f.* Respectability.

respectable, *a.* Respectable, worthy of respect.

respectablement, *adv.* Respectably.

respecter [rɛspɛk'te], *v.t.* To respect, to revere; to spare. *Le temps n'a pas respecté ces monuments,* time has not spared those monuments; *respectez ses sentiments,* spare his feelings; *se faire respecter,* to command respect.

respectif, *a. (fem.* **-ive)** Respective. **respectivement,** *adv.* Respectively.

respectueusement, *adv.* Respectfully, deferentially.

respectueux, *a. (fem.* **-ueuse)** Respectful, deferential. *Respectueux de la loi,* law-abiding.

respirable [rɛspi'rabl], *a.* Respirable, breathable.

respirateur, *a.m.* Respiratory.—*n.m.* Respirator.

respiration, *n.f.* Respiration, breathing. *Couper la respiration à quelqu'un,* to wind someone, *(fig.)* to take someone's breath away; *difficulté de respiration,* shortness of breath.

respiratoire, *a.* Respiratory, breathing. *Casque respiratoire,* smoke-helmet.

respirer [rɛspi're], *v.i.* To breathe, to respire; to take breath, to rest. *Il a de la peine à respirer,* he can scarcely breathe.—*v.t.* To breathe, to inhale; to exhale; *(fig.)* to betoken, to express; to long for. *Il ne respire que la vengeance,* he thirsts for vengeance; *son visage respire la douceur,* his face betokens gentleness.

resplendir [rɛsplɑ̃'diːr], *v.i.* To shine brightly; to be resplendent, to glitter. **resplendissant,** *a. (fem.* **-ante)** Resplendent, bright, glittering. **resplendissement,** *n.m.* Splendour, refulgence.

responsabilité [rɛspɔ̃sabili'te], *n.f.* Responsibility, liability. **responsable,** *a.* Responsible, answerable, accountable. **responsif,** *a. (fem.* **-ive)** *(Law)* Responsory, in reply.

resquillage [rɛski'jaːʒ], *n.m.* or **resquille** [rɛs'kiːj], *n.f. (slang)* Gate-crashing. *Entrer à la resquille,* to gate-crash.

resquiller [rɛski'je], *v.i.* To gate-crash; to wangle.

resquilleur, *n.m. (fem.* **-euse)** One who enters theatre, meeting, etc., without being invited, a gate-crasher.

ressac [rɛ'sak], *n.m.* Surf, breakers; undertow.

ressaigner [rɛsɛ'ɲe], *v.t., v.i.* To bleed again.

ressaisir [rɛsɛ'ziːr], *v.t.* To seize again. **se ressaisir,** *v.r.* To regain possession of oneself; to regain one's self-control.

ressasser [rɛsɑ'se], *v.t.* To sift again; to examine minutely, to scrutinize. *Ressasser les mêmes choses,* to keep on dinning the same thing into one's ears.

ressasseur, *n.m. (fem.* **-euse)** Tiresome repeater.

ressaut [rə'so], *n.m.* Projection; abrupt fall, dip; rise (in saddle).

ressauter, *v.i.* To leap again; *(Arch.)* to project; *(Mil. slang)* to grouse, to be refractory, *(pop.)* to bind.—*v.t.* To leap over again.

ressemblance [rəsɑ̃'blɑ̃ːs], *n.f.* Resemblance, likeness, similarity.

ressemblant, *a. (fem.* **-ante)** Like, similar. *C'est très ressemblant,* it is a striking likeness.

ressembler, *v.i.* To be like, to have a resemblance *(à). Ce portrait ne vous ressemble guère,* this portrait is not much like you; *le fils ressemble à son père,* the son resembles his father. **se ressembler,** *v.r.* To be like each other, to be alike; to be uniform. *Ils se ressemblent comme deux gouttes d'eau,* they are as like as two peas; *qui se ressemble s'assemble,* birds of a feather flock together.

ressemelage [rəsəm'laːʒ], *n.m.* Resoling (of boots). **ressemeler,** *v.t.* To re-sole (boots etc.).

ressenti [rəsɑ̃'ti], *a. (fem.* **-ie)** Felt; *(Paint.)* strongly expressed.

ressentiment, *n.m.* *Slight return, touch of (disease, pain, etc.); resentment. *Plein de ressentiment,* resentful.

ressentir [rəsɑ̃'tiːr], *v.t. irr. (conjug. like* SENTIR) To feel, to experience; to manifest, to show; to resent. *Elle ressent vivement cette injure,* she feels that insult keenly; *ressentir du malaise,* to feel uncomfortable. **se ressentir,** *v.r.* To feel the effects *(de);* to feel deeply; to be felt. *Il se ressent encore de ses pertes,* he still feels the effects of his losses; *les effets se ressentirent très loin,* the effects were felt for a considerable distance.

resserre [rə'sɛːr], *n.f.* Storage (of foodstuffs); store-room; (garden) tool-shed.

resserrement [rəsɛr'mɑ̃], *n.m.* Contraction, tightening; restriction, oppression; stringency, scarcity; constipation, costiveness.

resserrer, *v.t.* To tighten again, to draw closer, to bind tighter; to shut up closer; to coop up, to pen in; to restrain, to confine; to condense, to abridge; to compress, to close up, to contract; to lock up again; *(Mil.)* to invest closely. *Le froid resserre les pores,* cold contracts the pores; *resserrer les liens de* *l'amitié*, to draw closer the bonds of friendship; *resserrer une rivière dans son lit*, to confine a river to its bed. **se resserrer**, *v.r.* To contract, to be contracted; to grow narrower or closer; to confine oneself; to be compressed; to shrink; *to become colder (of the weather); to curtail one's expenses.

ressort (1) [rə'sɔːr], *n.m.* Spring; elasticity; energy, activity, strength; motive, means. *À ressort*, with a spring; *faire jouer tous les ressorts*, to leave no stone unturned; *faire ressort*, to fly back; *il n'agit que par ressort*, he acts only at the instigation of others; *ressort à boudin*, spiral spring.

ressort (2) [rə'sɔːr], *n.m.* Extent of jurisdiction; (*fig.*) department, province, line. *Cela n'est pas de mon ressort*, that is not within my province *or* not in my line; *en dernier ressort*, without appeal, in the last resort.

ressortir (1) [rəsɔr'tiːr], *v.i. irr.* (*conjug. like* SORTIR) To go or come out again; (*fig.*) to stand out, to be thrown into relief; to arise, to proceed, to result (*de*). *Faire ressortir*, to throw into relief, to bring out.

ressortir (2) [rəsɔr'tiːr], *v.i.* (*conjugated like* FINIR) To be under the jurisdiction of, to be dependent on *or* amenable to.

ressortissant, *a.* (*fem.* **-ante**) Under the jurisdiction of; amenable to (a jurisdiction). —*n.* National.

ressouder [rəsu'de], *v.t.* To solder again.

ressoudure, *n.f.* Resoldering; joining together again.

ressource [rə'surs], *n.f.* Resource, resort, expedient, resourcefulness, shift; (*Av.*) flattening-out (after dive); (*pl.*) resources. *C'est ma dernière ressource*, that is my last resort; *c'est un homme de ressource*, he is a man of resource; *il n'y a point de ressource*, there's no help for it; *je suis perdu, ruiné, sans ressource*, I am irretrievably ruined; *ressources personnelles*, private means.

ressouvenir [rəsuv'niːr], *n.m.* Remembrance, recollection, reminiscence. **se ressouvenir**, *v.r. irr.* (*conjug. like* VENIR) To recollect, to remember; to call to mind again. *Faire ressouvenir*, to remind; *vous en ressouvient-il?* do you remember it?

ressuage [rə'sɥaːʒ], *n.m.* Cooling off (of hot bread); sweating (of new-built walls); (*Metal.*) eliquation.

ressuer [rə'sɥe], *v.i.* To sweat, to run with moisture; (*Metal.*) to be eliquated.

ressui [re'sɥi], *n.m.* Lair (where wild animals dry themselves).

ressuscitation [resysita'sjɔ̃], *n.f.* Resuscitation, revival.

ressusciter [resysi'te], *v.t.* To resuscitate, to bring to life again; to revive (a custom etc.). —*v.i.* To come to life again, to be resuscitated. *Ressuscité d'entre les morts*, risen from the dead.

ressuyer [resɥi'je], *v.t. irr.* (*conjugated like* ABOYER) To wipe or dry (again). **se ressuyer**, *v.r.* To dry, to air (of linen, road, vegetables, etc.).

restant [res'tɑ̃], *a.* (*fem.* **-ante**) Remaining, left; surviving. *Poste restante*, department of post office where letters may be left till called for; (*U.S.*) general delivery.—*n.m.* Remainder, rest, residue; remaining person. *Restant d'un compte*, balance of an account.

restaurant [resto'rɑ̃], *a.* (*fem.* **-ante**) Restorative.—*n.m.* Eating-house, restaurant; restorative.

restaurateur, *n.m.* (*fem.* **-trice**) Restorer; restaurant keeper.

restauratif, *a.* (*fem.* **-ive**) Restorative.

restauration, *n.f.* Restoration, repair, re-establishment; (*Hist.*) the Restoration; (*Swiss dialect*) restaurant.

restaurer [resto're], *v.t.* To restore (finances, monarchy, pictures, etc.); to refresh. **se restaurer**, *v.r.* To take refreshment; to build up one's strength (after illness).

reste [rest], *n.m.* Rest, remainder, residue; trace, vestige; (*pl.*) remnants, leavings, relics; change; (*Arith.*) remainder; (*pl.*) remains. *Au reste* or *du reste*, besides, moreover; *de reste*, remaining, over and above; *et le reste* or *et ainsi du reste*, and so on, and so forth; *être en reste*, to be in arrears, (*fig.*) to be behindhand; *jouer son reste*, to play one's last stake; *jouir de son reste*, to make the most of what is left; *le reste des hommes*, the rest of mankind; *les restes*, remnants (of meal), broken meat; *les restes mortels*, the mortal remains; *ne pas demander son reste*, to have had enough; *n'être jamais en reste*, to be always in readiness; *rien de reste*, nothing left.

rester [res'te], *v.i.* (*takes the auxiliary* AVOIR *or* ÊTRE *according as action or condition is meant*) To remain, to be left; to stop, to stay, to dwell; to last, to endure, to continue; to come to a stop, to pause. *Ce livre restera*, that book will live; *en rester là*, to stop at that point; *il ne reste que de*, nothing remains but to; *où reste-t-il?* (*pop.*) where does he live? *que reste-t-il à faire?* what else is to be done? *rester court*, to stop short; *rester debout*, to remain standing; *rester en arrière*, (*Mil.*) to fall behind, to straggle; *rester en route*, to stop on the way, to fail to accomplish something; *rester où l'on est*, to stay where one is; *tout ce qui reste de*, all that is left of; *vous êtes resté trop longtemps à faire cela*, you have been too long about this; *vous reste-t-il de l'argent?* have you any money left?

restituable [resti'tɥabl], *a.* Repayable, returnable, refundable.

restituer [resti'tɥe], *v.t.* To restore; to return, to give back again, to refund; to reinstate (a person). *Restituer un passage d'un livre*, to restore a passage in a book.

restituteur, *n.m.* Restorer (of the text, of authors, etc.).

restitution, *n.f.* Restitution; restoration.

restreindre [res'trɛ̃ːdr], *v.t. irr.* (*conjug. like* CRAINDRE) To restrict, to limit, to curtail; to restrain, to confine, to circumscribe. *Restreindre ses prétentions*, to limit one's claims. **se restreindre**, *v.r.* To restrain oneself, to limit oneself; to curtail one's expenses.

restreint, *a.* (*fem.* **-einte**) Restricted.

restrictif [restrik'tif], *a.* (*fem.* **-ive**) Restrictive.

restriction, *n.f.* Restriction, restraint; reserve. *Faire des restrictions*, to accept with reservations; *restriction mentale*, mental reservation.

restringent [restrɛ̃'ʒɑ̃], *a. and n.m.* (*fem.* **-ente**) (*Med.*) Astringent.

resucée [rəsy'se], *n.f.* (*fam.*) Second-hand thing, repeated speech; re-hash.

résultant [rezyl'tɑ̃], *a.* (*fem.* **-ante**) Resulting. —*n.f.* Resultant.

résultat [rezyl'ta], *n.m.* Result. *Sans résultat,* ineffective (treatment); fruitless (attempt).

résulter [rezyl'te], *v.i. (only used in inf. and third pers.).* To result, to follow, to be the consequence *(de).* *Qu'en peut-il résulter?* what can be the consequences? *que résulte-t-il de là?* what follows from that?

résumé [rezy'me], *n.m.* Recapitulation, summary, résumé, epitome; summing-up. *Au résumé* or *en résumé,* on the whole, after all, in brief, to sum up.

résumer [rezy'me], *v.t.* To recapitulate, to sum up, to give a summary of. **se résumer,** *v.r.* To recapitulate, to sum up; to amount (to).

résurgence [resyr'ʒɑ̃:s], *n.f.* Rising (of underground waters) to the surface. **résurgent,** *a. (fem. -ente)* Resurgent (waters).

resurgir [rəsyr'ʒi:r], *v.i.* To rise again.

résurrection [rezyrɛk'sjɔ̃], *n.f.* Resurrection; revival.

résurrectionniste or **résurrectioniste,** *n.* Resurrectionist.

rétable [re'tabl] or **retable,** *n.m.* (*Arch.*) Retable, reredos.

rétablir [reta'bli:r], *v.t.* To re-establish, to restore; to repair; to recover; to reinstall, to reinstate; to retrieve. *Rétablir quelqu'un,* to set someone up again; *rétablir sa santé,* to recover one's health; *rétablir son honneur,* to retrieve one's honour. **se rétablir,** *v.r.* To recover one's health, to get well again; to be re-established, restored. *Le crédit commence à se rétablir,* credit is gradually being restored.

rétablissement [retablis'mɑ̃], *n.m.* Re-establishment, restoration; repair; recovery, re-instatement; recovery of health; (*Gym.*) leading, lifting oneself on one's hands. *Rétablissement dans les bonnes grâces de quelqu'un,* restoration to someone's favour; *rétablissement du commerce,* revival of commerce; *sans espoir de rétablissement,* past recovery; *rétablissement alternatif,* right- or left-hand leading; *rétablissement simultané,* both hands leading.

retaille [rə'tɑ:j], *n.f.* Piece cut off (a length of cloth etc.); shred, paring.

retailler, *v.t.* To cut again, to prune again. *Retailler un arbre,* to prune a tree again; *retailler une scie,* to re-sharpen a saw.

rétamage [reta'ma:ʒ], *n.m.* Retinning; re-silvering.

rétamé [reta'me], *a. (fem. -ée) (pop.)* Drunk.

rétamer [reta'me], *v.t.* To tin over again; to resilver.

rétameur [reta'mœ:r], *n.m.* Tinker.

retape [rə'tap], *n.f. (pop.) Faire la retape,* to solicit.

retaper [rəta'pe], *v.t. (colloq.)* To do up (a hat etc.), to straighten (bedclothes); to recast (speech, play); (*sch. slang*) to plough (at exams). **se retaper,** *v.r. (fam.)* To pick up again; to buck up.

retard [rə'ta:r], *n.m.* Delay; slowness (of a clock etc.); (*Mus.*) retardation. *Apporter un grand retard à,* to delay considerably; *être en retard,* to be late, to be in arrears; *votre montre est en retard de deux minutes,* your watch is two minutes slow; *retard à l'allumage,* retarded spark.

retardataire, *a.* In arrears, late, behindhand; backward.—*n.* Loiterer, lagger, late-comer; defaulter.

retardateur, *a. (fem. -trice)* Retarding. **retardation,** *n.f.* Retardation. **retardement,** *n.m.* Delay, retardment. *Bombe à retardement,* delayed action bomb.

retarder, *v.t.* To retard, to delay; to defer (payment); to hinder; to put back (clocks and watches).—*v.i.* To lose time; to be slow (of clocks and watches); to be behind the times; to come later. *Ma montre retarde,* my watch loses.

retâter [rətɑ'te], *v.t.* To touch or feel again.—*v.i.* To taste or try again *(de).*

retenir [rət'ni:r], *v.t. irr. (conjugated like* TENIR) To hold back; to retain, to keep back, to withhold; to detain; to remember; to reserve; to confine, to repress, to hold in, to moderate, to check, to restrain, to curb; to bespeak, to secure, to engage, to hinder, to prevent; to get hold of again; (*Arith.*) to carry. *Il ne saurait retenir sa langue,* he cannot restrain his tongue; *je ne sais ce qui me retient,* I don't know what holds me back; *je ne vous retiendrai pas,* I won't keep you a minute; *je pose sept et je retiens deux,* (*Arith.*) I put down seven and carry two; *retenir sa colère,* to restrain one's anger; *retenir un domestique,* to engage a servant; *retenir une leçon,* to keep a lesson in one's head, to remember a lesson; *retenir un cheval,* to rein in a horse; *retenir une place,* to book a seat (in advance). **se retenir,** *v.r.* To control oneself, to hold oneself back; to refrain, to forbear; to catch hold, to clutch or cling (à). *Se retenir de parler,* to curb one's tongue.

retenteur [rətɑ̃'tœ:r], *a. (fem. -trice)* Retaining.

rétentif [retɑ̃'tif], *a. (fem. -ive)* Retentive.

rétention, *n.f.* Reservation; (*Arith.*) carrying over; (*Med.*) retention.

rétentionnaire, *n.* (*Law*) Lienor (of goods).

retentir [rətɑ̃'ti:r], *v.i.* To resound, to re-echo, to reverberate, to ring.

retentissant, *a. (fem. -ante)* Resounding, echoing; ringing, sonorous, loud; (*fig.*) famous.

retentissement, *n.m.* Resounding, echo, reverberation; ringing; (*fig.*) stir, fame, celebrity. *Avoir du retentissement,* to make a great noise.

*****retentum** [rətɑ̃'tɔm], *n.m.* (*Law*) Tacit clause or proviso; (*colloq.*) mental reservation.

retenu [rət'ny], *a. (fem. retenue* (1)) Reserved, cautious, discreet, wary. **retenue** (2), *n.f.* Discretion, circumspection, caution, self-control; reservoir, stretch of water between sluices; keeping in, detention; (*Comm.*) deduction, stoppage; (*Arith.*) number carried forward; guy-rope, stay. *Être en retenue,* to be kept in (at school); *faire une retenue de trois pour cent sur les traitements,* to deduct three per cent from the salaries; *il faut avoir de la retenue,* one must keep within bounds; *palan de retenue,* (*Naut.*) relieving tackle; *sans retenue,* indiscreet, unreservedly; (*Mil.*) *retenue de solde,* stoppage of pay.

rétiaire [re'sjɛ:r], *n.m.* (*Rom. Ant.*) Retiary, gladiatorial net-fighter.

réticence [reti'sɑ̃:s], *n.f.* Reserve, silence, concealment (of some particular); (*Rhet.*) reticence.

réticulaire [retiky'lɛːr], *a.* Reticular. **réti-cule**, *n.m.* *Hair-net; reticule; hand-bag; reticle (in a telescope).

réticulé, *a.* (*fem.* **-ée**) Reticulated.

rétif [re'tif], *a.* (*fem.* **-ive**) Restive, stubborn; mulish, awkward to deal with.

rétiforme [reti'fɔrm], *a.* Retiform.

rétine [re'tin], *n.f.* Retina (of the eye).

retirable [rəti'rabl], *a.* Withdrawable.

retiration [rətirɑ'sjɔ̃], *n.f.* (*Print.*) Working off the outer form; printing of verso.

retiré [rəti're], *a.* (*fem.* **-ée**) Retired, se-questered, secluded; retired, in retirement. *Retiré des affaires,* retired from business.

retirement [rətir'mɑ̃], *n.m.* Contraction, shrinking (of the nerves and muscles); cracking of glaze on pottery.

retirer [rəti're], *v.t.* To draw again; to pull or snatch back, to withdraw; to draw in, to draw out; to take away; to retract; to extract; to reap, to get, to derive; to remove (from school, prison, etc.). *Quel profit en retirera-t-il?* what profit will he get by it? *retirer des choses qui étaient en gage,* to take things out of pawn; *retirer du danger,* to rescue from danger; *retirer sa parole,* to go back on one's word; *retirer son enjeu,* to withdraw one's stakes; *retirer son manteau,* to take off one's cloak; *retirer des billets de la circulation,* to call in bank-notes. **se retirer,** *v.r.* To retire, to withdraw, to retreat; to subside (of waters); to recede (of sea); to ebb (of tide); to shrink, to contract. *Il se retire de bonne heure,* he keeps good hours; *il s'est retiré du service,* he has left the service; *retirez-vous,* leave the room, be gone, stand down (to witnesses); *se retirer en lieu sûr,* to retire to a place of safety.

retirons [rəti'rɔ̃], *n.m. pl.* Combings.

rétiveté [retiv'te] or **rétivité,** *n.f.* Stubborn-ness.

retombe [rə'tɔ̃ːb], *n.f. Feuilles de retombe,* supplementary sheets provided with a docu-ment or plan for remarks or modifications.

retombée [rətɔ̃'be], *n.f.* Springing (of an arch or vault); fall, fall-out. *Retombée de particules radioactives,* radio-active fall-out.

retomber [rətɔ̃'be], *v.i.* To fall again; to have a relapse; to fall, to subside, to sink back; to fall back; to hang down. *Retomber dans la même faute,* to relapse into the same fault; *retomber malade,* to fall ill again; *retomber sur ses pieds,* (*fig.*) to fall on one's feet.

retondre [rə'tɔ̃ːdr], *v.t.* To shear again; (*Arch.*) to clean off, to cut away (useless ornaments etc.).

retordement [rətɔrdə'mɑ̃], or **retordage,** *n.m.* Twisting of silk, thread, etc. **retorderie,** *n.f.* Twisting mill. **retordeur,** *n.* (*fem.* **-euse**) Twister.

retordre, *v.t.* To twist again; to twist (silk, thread, etc.). *Donner du fil à retordre à quelqu'un,* to cause someone trouble.

rétorquer [retɔr'ke], *v.t.* To retort, to turn (an argument etc.) against someone.

retors [rə'tɔːr], *a.* (*fem.* **retorse**) Twisted; artful, cunning, crafty.—*n.m.* Twisted thread; crafty person.

rétorsion [retɔr'sjɔ̃], *n.f.* Act of retorting; (*International law*) retortion.

retouche [rə'tuʃ], *n.f.* Retouching, touching up; finishing (of garments). **retoucher,** *v.t.*

To retouch; to touch up, to improve.—*v.i.* To apply corrections (*à*).

retoucheur, *n.* (*fem.* **-euse**) (*Phot.*) Re-toucher; (*Dress.*) finisher.

retour [rə'tuːr], *n.m.* Return, coming back; repetition, recurrence; sending back; (*fig.*) vicissitude, change; reverse; turning, wind-ing; angle, elbow, return of a wall, façade, etc.; (*Law*) reversion. *À mon retour,* on my return; *billet d'aller et retour,* return ticket; *en retour de,* in return for; *être perdu sans retour,* to be past all hope; *être sur le retour,* to be on the wane, to be past middle age, to be past one's prime; *être sur son retour,* to be on the point of returning; *faire retour à,* to return to, to revert to; *faire un retour offensif,* to launch a counter-attack; *faire un retour sur soi-même,* to examine oneself or one's past seriously; *je serai de retour à midi,* I shall be back at twelve; *la fortune a ses retours,* fortune has its vicissitudes; *le retour sur l'avant,* (*Row.*) the recover; *le retour du printemps,* the return of spring; *les tours et les retours d'un ruisseau,* the meanderings of a stream; *match retour,* return match; *par retour du courrier,* by return of post; *payer de retour,* to requite; *retour d'âge,* the change of life, menopause; *retour de manivelle,* (*Motor.*) kick back on a starting-handle; *sans retour,* for ever, irretrievably.

retourne [rə'turn], *n.f.* Turn-up card, trump-card. *La retourne est carreau,* diamonds are trumps.

retournement [rəturnə'mɑ̃], *n.m.* Reversal.

retourner [rətur'ne], *v.i.* To return, go again, to go back (again); to recoil upon; to turn up (cards). *Il retourne cœur,* hearts are trumps; *n'y retournez pas,* don't do it again, don't go there again; *retourner à son travail,* to return to one's work; *retourner en arrière,* to turn back; *retourner en avion à,* to fly back to; *retourner sur ses pas,* to retrace one's steps; *voyons de quoi il retourne,* (*colloq.*) let us see what is going on, *or* how matters stand.—*v.t.* To turn, to turn up, to turn over, round, about, etc.; to return, to send back; (*fig.*) to ruminate upon. *Retourner du foin,* to turn over hay; *retourner sa veste,* to change one's mind; *retourner une carte,* to turn up a card; *retourner une salade,* to mix a salad; *retourner une situation,* to upset a situation; *retourner un habit,* to turn a coat. **se retourner,** *v.r.* To turn, to turn round, to turn oneself round, to look behind, to look round; (*fig.*) to take different steps or a new line of action. *Il sait toujours se retourner,* he can always wriggle out of it; *s'en retourner,* to go back.

retracer [rətra'se], *v.t.* To trace again, to retrace; to recount, to relate. **se retracer,** *v.r.* To recall to mind, to remember; to recur, to be retraced (in mind).

rétractation [retraktɑ'sjɔ̃], *n.f.* Retractation, recantation.

rétracter [retrak'te], *v.t.* To retract; to unsay, to recant. **se rétracter,** *v.r.* To retract, to shrink; to recant.

rétractile, *a.* Retractile. **rétractilité,** *n.f.* Retractility.

rétraction, *n.f.* (*Path.*) Retraction, contrac-tion (of organs).

retraduire [rətra'dɥir], *v.t. irr.* (*conjugated like* CONDUIRE) To re-translate.

retraire (1) [rə'trɛːr], v.t. irr. (conjug. like TRAIRE) (Law) To repurchase, redeem (an estate).

retraire (2) [rə'trɛːr], v.t. irr. (conjug. like TRAIRE) To milk again.

retrait (1) [rə'trɛ], a. (fem. **retraite** (1)) Shrunk (of grain, wood, etc.). **retrait** (2), n.m. Shrinkage, contraction; recess (in wall), closet; withdrawal; (Law) right of pre-emption; (Arch.) off-set. En retrait, withdrawn, recessed, back from the front or alinement, le retrait d'un projet de loi, the withdrawal of a Bill; retrait d'emploi, dismissal, discharge.

retraite (2), n.f. Retreat, retiring; seclusion, privacy, retirement; refuge, hiding-place, shelter; lair, haunt, resort; retirement from office; superannuation; retiring pension; (Arch.) set-back; (Comm.) redraft; (Mil.) signal (drum-beat, sound of bugle, etc.) of retreat; sunset-gun; retraite du soir, tattoo. Battre en retraite, to beat a retreat; battre la retraite, to beat the retreat or tattoo; caisse de retraite, superannuation fund; maison de retraite, (old people's) home; mettre à la retraite, to pension off, to superannuate; prendre sa retraite, to retire on a pension; retraite aux flambeaux, torchlight tattoo; retraite de voleurs, den of thieves; sonner la retraite, (Hunt.) to call off the hounds, (Mil.) to sound the retreat.

retraité [rətre'te], a. (fem. -ée) Superannuated, pensioned off; on the retired list.—n. One who is pensioned off.

retraiter [rətre'te], v.t. To retire, to pension off; to treat again.

retranché [rətrã'ʃe], a. (fem. -ée) Deducted; (Mil.) fortified.

retranchement [rətrãʃ'mã], n.m. Retrenchment, abridging, curtailment; (Mil.) retrenchment, entrenchment. Forcer quelqu'un dans ses retranchements, to storm someone in his stronghold, (fig.) to get someone with his back to the wall.

retrancher, v.t. To retrench, to curtail, to cut short; to cut off, to cut out, to strike off, to suppress; to diminish, to abridge; (Arith.) to subtract, to deduct; (Mil.) to entrench. **se retrancher**, v.r. To restrain oneself; to retrench, to curtail one's expenses; (Mil.) to entrench oneself, to throw up retrenchments; (fig.) to fall back upon, to take refuge behind. Se retrancher derrière un prétexte, to take refuge behind a pretext.

retransmettre [rətrãs'mɛtr], v.t. irr. (conjug. like METTRE) To retransmit.

retransmission, n.f. Retransmission.

retravailler [rətrava'je], v.t. To touch up, to go over (a speech).—v.i. To rework.

retraverser [rətraver'se], v.t. To cross again, to recross.

rétrécir [retre'siːr], v.t. To take in, to contract, to make narrower; to narrow, to limit. —v.i. and **se rétrécir**, v.r. To narrow, to grow narrower; to shrink, to contract; to become narrow-minded. Toile qui (se) rétrécit au lavage, material which shrinks when washed. **rétrécissement**, n.m. Narrowing, cramping; shrinking, contracting; narrowness; (Med.) stricture.

retremper [rətrã'pe], v.t. To soak again; to temper again; (fig.) to give renewed force to, to strengthen. **se retremper**, v.r. To be strengthened or invigorated; to recruit.

rétribuer [retri'bɥe], v.t. To remunerate.

rétribution, n.f. Recompense, salary, reward.

rétro [re'tro], n.m. (fam.) (at Billiards) [see RÉTROGRADE].

rétroactif [retrɔak'tif], a. (fem. -ive) Retroactive. **rétroaction**, n.f. Retroaction; (Rad. Teleg.) feed-back. **rétroactivement**, adv. Retroactively. **rétroactivité**, n.f. Retroactivity.

rétroagir, v.i. To retroact.

rétrocéder, v.t. irr. (conjugated like ACCÉLÉRER) To retrocede.

rétrocessif, a. (fem. -ive) Retrocessive. **rétrocession**, n.f. Retrocession. **rétrocessionnaire**, n. Assignee.

rétrogradation, n.f. Retrogradation, retrogression; (Mil.) reduction (of a N.C.O.) to lower rank (as a punishment). **rétrograde**, a. Retrograde; backward. Effet rétrograde, (Billiards) pull-back stroke; faire de l'effet rétrograde or faire un rétro, to put bottom on the ball. **rétrograder**, v.i. To retrograde, to go back, (Mil.) to fall back.—v.t. To reduce (a N.C.O.) to a lower rank.

rétrogressif, a. (fem. -ive) Retrogressive. **rétrogression**, n.f. Retrogression.

rétropédalage, n.f. Back-pedalling.

rétrospectif, a. (fem. **rétrospective** (1)) Retrospective. **rétrospection**, n.f. Retrospection. **rétrospective** (2), n.f. Retrospect. **rétrospectivement**, adv. Retrospectively.

retroussé [rətru'se], a. (fem. -ée) Turned up; tucked up. Nez retroussé, turned-up nose, snub nose.

retroussement, n.m. Turning up, tucking up.

retrousser [rətru'se], v.t. To turn up, to roll up (trousers); to tuck up, to pull up (shirt); to curl up (one's lip); to cock (one's hat). Retrousser sa moustache, to twist up one's moustache. **se retrousser**, v.r. To tuck up one's gown or other garment.

retroussis [rətru'si], n.m. Cock (of a hat); (of a boot); facing (of a uniform, livery, etc.). Bottes à retroussis, top boots.

retrouver [rətru've], v.t. To find again, to regain, to recover; to recognize; to meet again. Aller retrouver quelqu'un, to go and join someone; je le retrouverai bien, he will not escape me. **se retrouver**, v.r. To find each other again; to find oneself again; to be oneself again; to find one's way again; to be met with again.

rétroviseur [retrɔvi'zœːr], n.m. (Motor.) Driving mirror.

rets [rɛ], n.m. inv. Net; (fig.) snare, toils.

réunion [rey'njɔ̃], n.f. Reunion, joining again; reconciliation; union, junction; meeting, assembly, gathering; party, function, reception. Salle de réunion, assembly-room.

réunir [rey'niːr], v.t. To reunite, to join again, to bring together again, to reconcile; to unite, to join, to bring together; to connect; to collect, to assemble, to muster, to call together; to combine. Réunir des faits, to put facts together. **se réunir**, v.r. To assemble again, to reunite; to join together again, to unite again; to collect; to meet, to gather together, to muster; to club together, to combine, to blend, to amalgamate.

réussi [rey'si], *a.* (*fem.* **-ie**) Successful, brilliant, well executed. *Bien réussi*, well done, well performed.

réussir [rey'si:r], *v.i.* To succeed, to be successful, to do well; to prosper, to thrive, to have successful results. *Cela m'a bien réussi*, that turned out well for me; *ce projet n'a pas réussi*, the plan did not succeed; *il a mal réussi*, he was unsuccessful; *les pommiers réussissent dans ce terrain*, apple-trees thrive in this soil; *réussir à faire quelque chose*, to succeed in doing something.—*v.t.* To carry out well, to make a success of, to bring off, to accomplish, to perform successfully.

réussite, *n.f.* Success; (happy) issue or result; (*Cards*) patience; (*Am.*) solitaire.

revaccination [rəvaksinɑ'sjɔ̃], *n.f.* Revaccination. **revacciner**, *v.t.* To revaccinate.

revaloir, *v.t. irr.* (*conjugated like* VALOIR) To return like for like, to be even with. *Il me le revaudra*, he shall pay for it; *je vous revaudrai cela*, (*fam.*) I'll get even with you.

revaloriser [rəvalɔri'ze], *v.t.* To revalorize or revalue (money).

revanche [rə'vɑ̃:ʃ], *n.f.* Return; return match; requital, revenge. *À charge de revanche*, on condition that you let me do as much for you; *en revanche*, in return; *jouer la revanche*, to play the return match; *prendre sa revanche sur*, to get even with. **se revancher**, *v.r.* To return tit for tat; to have one's revenge. *Se revancher d'un bienfait*, to return a kindness.

rêvasser [rɛva'se], *v.i.* To dream idly, to day-dream, to muse. *Rêvasser à une affaire*, to muse over a matter.

rêvasserie, *n.f.* Day-dreams; idle musing, dreaming of castles in Spain.

rêvasseur, *n.m.* (*fem.* **-euse**) (*colloq.*) Dreamer, muser.

rêve [rɛ:v], *n.m.* Dream; day-dream, illusion. *C'est le rêve*, it's perfect.

revêche [rə'vɛ:ʃ], *a.* Harsh, rough; cross, ill-natured, cross-grained, crabbed, cantankerous.

réveil [re'vɛ:j], *n.m.* Waking, awaking; (*fig.*) disillusionment; alarm-clock; (*Mil.*) reveille. *À mon réveil*, when I awoke; *avoir un fâcheux réveil*, to be badly disillusioned, to have a rude awakening.

réveille-matin, *n.m. inv.* Alarm-clock, alar(u)m. (*Bot.*) (*Euphorbe*) *réveille-matin*, or *herbe aux verrues*, sun-sponge, wart-weed.

réveiller [revɛ'je], *v.t.* To awake, to wake, to wake up, to arouse; to rouse up, to stir up, to quicken; to revive, to recall, to evoke. *Réveiller des souvenirs fâcheux*, to bring back unpleasant memories. **se réveiller**, *v.r.* To awake, to wake up; to be roused; to be renewed, to revive. *Sa haine se réveilla*, his hatred was aroused; *se réveiller de son assoupissement*, to awake from one's lethargy; *se réveiller en sursaut*, to wake with a start.

réveilleur [revɛ'jœ:r], *n.m.* (*fem.* **-euse**) Monk or nun charged with the duty of awakening others.

réveillon [revɛ'jɔ̃], *n.m.* Midnight repast, *esp.* Christmas Eve revel; (*Paint.*) strong touch of light. *Réveillon de la Saint-Sylvestre*, New Year's Eve celebration.

réveillonner [revɛjɔ'ne], *v.i.* To take part in a *réveillon*.

révélateur [revela'tœ:r], *n.m.* (*fem.* **-trice**) Revealer, discoverer, informer; (*Phot.*) developer. *Révélateur d'un complot*, revealer of a plot.—*a.* Revealing, tell-tale.

révélation [revela'sjɔ̃], *n.f.* Revelation, disclosure; thing revealed or thing that explains, or throws a light on; (*Law*) information. *Les Révélations de Saint Jean*, the Book of Revelation.

révéler [reve'le], *v.t. irr.* (*conjugated like* ACCÉLÉRER) To reveal, to disclose; to betray; to inform against; (*Phot.*) to develop. **se révéler**, *v.r.* To show itself, himself, etc., to be revealed or disclosed; to prove (to be).

revenant [rəv'nɑ̃], *a.* (*fem.* **-ante**) Pleasing, prepossessing. *Physionomie revenante*, pleasing countenance.—*n.m.* Ghost. *Histoire de revenants*, ghost-story; *il y a des revenants dans cette maison*, that house is haunted.

*****revenant-bon**, *n.m.* (*pl.* **revenants-bons**) Casual profit; perquisite; bonus, windfall.

revendeur [rəvɑ̃'dœ:r], *n.m.* (*fem.* **-euse**) Retail dealer, dealer in old clothes, etc. *Revendeuse à la toilette*, wardrobe dealer.

revendicable [rəvɑ̃di'kabl], *a.* Claimable.

revendicateur [rəvɑ̃dika'tœ:r], *n.m.* Claimant.

revendication, *n.f.* Claiming, reclaiming; claim, demand. *Action en revendication*, action in pursuit of a claim.

revendiquer, *v.t.* To claim back, to claim, to enter a claim to; (*fig.*) to lay claim to. *Revendiquer une responsabilité*, to accept full responsibility.

revendre [rə'vɑ̃:dr], *v.t.* To sell again, to resell. *En revendre à quelqu'un*, to be more than a match for someone; *il en a à revendre*, he has enough and to spare.

revenez-y [rəvne'zi], *n.m. inv.* (*fam.*) Return to bygone things, tastes, habits, etc.; renewal, repetition. *Un plat qui a un goût de revenez-y*, a cut-and-come-again (dish).

revenir [rəv'ni:r], *v.i. irr.* (*conjugated like* VENIR) To come again, to come back, to return; to reappear, to haunt, to walk (of ghosts, spirits, etc.); to rise (of food in the stomach); to happen again, to arise again, to recur; to grow again, to begin again; to recover, to come to oneself or revive, to be restored; to occur, to present oneself, itself, etc.; to accrue; to amount, to come to, to be tantamount; to cost; to recant, to withdraw, to retract; to correct oneself; to please, to inspire confidence. *Cet habit revient à tant*, that coat costs so much; *en revenir d'une belle*, to have had a narrow escape; *faire revenir de la viande*, to brown meat; *faire revenir quelqu'un*, to call someone back; *il me revient que*, I am told or I understand that; *il ne m'en revient rien*, I get nothing by it; *il revient à vue d'œil*, he is recovering visibly; *j'en reviens toujours là que . . .*, I still persist in thinking that . . .; *je n'en reviens pas*, I can't get over it; I am lost in astonishment; *les deux choses reviennent au même*, the two things come to the same; *quand on m'a fait de ces tours, je ne reviens pas*, when people play me such tricks I never forgive them; *revenez!* (*Mil.*) as you were; *revenir à la charge*, to begin again, to return to the fray; *revenir à l'avis de*, to come over to the opinion of; *revenir à ses moutons*, to return to the matter in hand; *revenir à soi*, to come to, to revive, to reform, to return to the right path; *revenir de loin*, to have a narrow escape, to recover from a dangerous illness etc.; *revenir doucement sur l'avant, (Row.)* to swing forward slowly; *revenir sur l'eau*, to find one's feet again, to recover one's losses; *revenir sur le compte de*, to alter one's views with regard to; *revenir sur ses pas*, to retrace one's steps; *revenons à notre propos*, let us return to our business; *sa tête ne me revient pas*, I don't like his face, I don't like the look of him; *son nom ne me revient pas*, I do not recollect his name. **s'en revenir,** *v.r.* To come back (from a place mentioned).

revente [rə'vã:t], *n.f.* Resale. *De revente*, second-hand; *marchandise de revente*, second-hand goods.

revenu [rəv'ny], *n.m.* Revenue, income; *(fig.)* profit. *(Metal.)* Tempering of steel. *Impôt sur le revenu*, income tax; *revenus casuels*, perquisites. **revenue,** *n.f.* Young wood, aftergrowth.

rêver [rɛ've], *v.i.* To dream, to be in a dream; to have day-dreams; to muse, to ponder, to reflect. *Il rêve tout éveillé*, he indulges in day-dreams; *j'ai rêvé longtemps sur cette affaire*, I have pondered long over that matter; *je regagnai mon hôtellerie en rêvant*, I trudged back to my inn in a thoughtful mood.—*v.t.* To dream, to dream of. *Il ne rêve que fortune*, he thinks of nothing but riches.

réverbérant [reverbe'rã], *a.* (*fem.* **-ante**) Reverberating.

réverbération [reverbera'sjɔ̃], *n.f.* Reverberation.

réverbère, *n.m.* Reverberator, reflector; street lamp. *Four à réverbère*, reverberating furnace.

réverbérer, *v.t., v.i. irr.* (*conjugated like* ACCÉLÉRER) To reverberate, to reflect.

reverdir [rəver'di:r], *v.i.* To grow or become green again; *(fig.)* to grow young again, to bloom again.—*v.t.* To make green again, to revive.

reverdissement, *n.m.* Growing green again.

révéremment [revera'mã], *adv.* Reverently.

révérence [reve'rã:s], *n.f.* Reverence; bow, curtsy. *Avec révérence*, reverently; *faire une profonde révérence*, to make a low bow; *tirer sa révérence*, to bow oneself out, to take one's leave.

révérenciel, *a.* (*fem.* **-ielle**) Reverential.

révérencieusement, *adv.* Reverentially.

révérencieux, *a.* (*fem.* **-ieuse**) Ceremonious and over-polite, obsequious.

révérend [reve'rã], *a.* (*fem.* **-ende**) Reverend. *Très révérend*, right reverend, very reverend.

révérendissime [reverãdi'sim], *a.* Most reverend, right reverend (bishop, cardinal).

révérer [reve're], *v.t. irr.* (*conjugated like* ACCÉLÉRER) To revere.

rêverie [rɛ'vri], *n.f.* Reverie, musing, dreaming. *Plongé dans ses rêveries*, in a brown study.

revers [rə've:r], *n.m.* Back, reverse, other or wrong side; counterpart; facing (of clothes); lapel (of a coat); turn-up (of trousers); top (of boots); *(Ten.)* back-hander; misfortune, change for the worse, set-back. *À revers*, *(Mil.)* in the rear, on the flank; *coup de revers*, back-handed stroke; *le revers de la main*, the back of the hand; *le revers de la médaille*, the reverse side of the medal, *(fig.)* the dark side

of the picture; *le revers de la tranchée, (Fort.)* the reverse of the trench.

réversal, *a.* (*fem.* **-ale**, *pl.* **-aux**) *(*Law*) Confirmatory. (*Lettres*) *réversales*, letters to ratify a compromise.

réverseau, *n.m.* (*pl.* **-eaux**) Weather-board (for doors, windows, etc.).

reverser [rəver'se], *v.t.* To pour out again; to pour back; to transfer, to carry forward or over [TRANSBORDER]. *Reverser la faute sur quelqu'un*, to shift the blame on to someone.

reversi or **reversis,** *n.m.* Reversi (card game).

réversibilité, *n.f.* Reversibility. **réversible,** *a.* Reversible; revertible. **réversion,** *n.f.* Reversion.

reversoir, *n.m.* Weir.

revêtement [rəvɛt'mã], *n.m.* Revetment (wall); lining, casing, facing (of masonry etc.); surface, carpet (of road).

revêtir [rəvɛ'ti:r], *v.t. irr.* (*conjug. like* VÊTIR) To clothe or dress again; to give clothes to, to dress; to put on, to don; to assume; to array, to adorn (*de*); to cover, to coat, to line; to revet; *(fig.)* to invest or endow with, to cloak. *Je me suis dépouillé de cet emploi pour l'en revêtir*, I threw up this employment in his favour, or to bestow it on him; *revêtir les pauvres*, to clothe the poor; *mur revêtu de boiseries*, panelled wall; *revêtir ses pensées d'un style brillant*, to clothe one's thoughts in brilliant language; *revêtir une terrasse de gazon*, to cover a terrace with turf; *revêtir de claies un talus*, to revet a bank with hurdles; *revêtir un habit*, to put on a coat; *revêtir un personnage*, to assume a character. **se revêtir,** *v.r.* To clothe oneself, to array oneself; to put on, to assume.

rêveur [rɛ'vœ:r], *a.* (*fem.* **-euse**) Dreaming; *(fig.)* pensive, dreamy, musing.—*n.* Dreamer; muser. **rêveusement,** *adv.* Dreamily.

revidage [rəvi'da:ʒ], *n.m.* Emptying again; re-boring; settlement of knock-out (at auction).

revider [rəvi'de], *v.t.* To empty again; to re-bore; to make a knock-out or barter of (things bought at an auction).

revient [rə'vjɛ̃], *n.m.* Prix de revient, net cost, cost price, prime cost. *L'établissement du prix de revient*, costing.

revigorer [rəvigɔ're], *v.t.* To reinvigorate.

revirement [rəvir'mã], *n.m.* Tacking about; *(fig.)* sudden change; *(Comm.)* transfer.

revirer, *v.i.* To tack, to put about; *(fig.)* to turn round, to change sides, to rat.

revisable [rəvi'zabl] or **révisable,** *a.* Revisable.

reviser [rəvi'ze] or **réviser,** *v.t.* To revise, to review, to examine. *Réviser un compte*, to audit an account; *réviser une machine*, to recondition an engine.

reviseur or **réviseur,** *n.m.* Reviser, examiner; auditor; proof-reader.

revision or **révision,** *n.f.* Revisal, revision re-examination, review; proof-reading; audit (of accounts); overhaul (of engine). *Conseil de révision, (Mil.)* medical examining board (for recruits); *faire la revision d'une feuille, (Print.)* to revise a sheet; *revision de procès*, rehearing.

revisionniste, *n. and a.* Revisionist, one who advocates the reform (of the constitution).

revivification

revivification [rəvivifikɑ'sjɔ̃], *n.f.* Revivification. **revivifier,** *v.t.* To revivify, to regenerate, to revive.

revivre [rə'viːvr], *v.i. irr. (conjugated like* VIVRE) To come to life again, to live again. *Faire revivre,* to bring to life again; to revive, to restore; *les pères revivent dans leurs enfants,* fathers live again in their children. —*v.t.* To relive, to live over again, to recall. *Revivre son enfance,* to relive one's childhood.

révocabilité [revɔkabili'te], *n.f.* Revocability. **révocable,** *a.* Revocable; removable (of an official).

révocation [revɔkɑ'sjɔ̃], *n.f.* Revocation (of will), repeal, cancellation; removal, dismissal (of an official).

révocatoire, *a.* Revocatory.

revoici [rəvwa'si] or **revoilà,** *adv. (colloq.)* Once more, here (or there) . . . again. *Me revoici,* here I am again; *le revoilà,* there he is again.

revoir [rə'vwaːr], *v.t. irr.* To see again; to meet again; to revise, to review, to re-examine. *À revoir,* to be revised.—*n.m. inv. Au revoir,* good-bye (for the present). **se revoir,** *v.r.* To see or meet each other again; to be seen again. *Nous nous reverrons,* we shall meet again.

revoler [rəvɔ'le], *v.t.* (1) To steal again.—(2) *v.i.* To fly again; to fly back.

revolin [rəvɔ'lɛ̃], *n.m.* (*Naut.*) Eddy-wind.

révoltant [revɔl'tɑ̃], *a. (fem. -ante)* Revolting, shocking.

révolte [re'vɔlt], *n.f.* Revolt, rebellion; mutiny.

révolté, *n.m. (fem. -ée)* Rebel; mutineer.

révolter, *v.t.* To cause to revolt or rebel; to stir up, to rouse, to excite; to shock, to disgust, to horrify. **se révolter,** *v.r.* To revolt, to rebel; to mutiny; to be indignant, to be shocked.

révolu [revɔ'ly], *a. (fem. -ue)* Revolved; accomplished, completed, finished; elapsed, ended.

révolutif, *a. (fem. -ive)* or **révoluté** *(fem. -ée)* (*Bot.*) Revolute.

révolution [revɔly'sjɔ̃], *n.f.* Revolution. **révolutionnaire,** *a.* Revolutionary.—*n.* Revolutionary; revolutionist. **révolutionnairement,** *adv.* In a revolutionary manner. **révolutionner,** *v.t.* To revolutionize; (*fig.*) to upset, to alarm.

revolver [revɔl've:r], *n.m.* Revolver. *Revolver de microscope,* revolving eye-piece of a microscope; *tour revolver,* turret-lathe.

revomir [rəvɔ'miːr], *v.t.* To vomit, to throw up.

révoquer [revɔ'ke], *v.t.* To dismiss (an official etc.); to recall (an ambassador etc.); to revoke, to repeal, to cancel. *Révoquer en doute,* to call in question.

revoyeur [rəvwa'jœːr], *n.m.* Dredge-boat (for canals, rivers).

revoyure [rəvwa'jyːr], *n.f. (fam.) À la revoyure,* bye-bye, so long.

revu, *p.p. (fem.* **revue** (1)) [REVOIR].

revue (2) [rə'vy], *n.f.* Review; survey, examination, revision; review (periodical), magazine; review (critical article); (*Mil.*) review; (*Theat.*) topical ballet or farcical piece, revue; (*Mil.*) *revue de détail,* kit inspection. *Être gens de revue,* to meet often; *faire la revue de,* to examine; (*fam.*) *je suis (encore) de la revue,* I'm for it (again), I'm done (again); *passer en revue,* (*Mil.*) to be inspected, to inspect.

révulsif [revyl'sif], *a.* and *n.m. (fem. -ive)* (*Med.*) Revulsive.

révulsion, *n.f.* Revulsion.

rez [re], *prep.* On a level with, even with. *À rez de terre,* level with the ground.

rez-de-chaussée, *n.m. inv.* Ground-level; ground floor; (*fig.*) the foot of the page in a newspaper. *À rez-de-chaussée,* level with the ground; *au rez-de-chaussée,* on the ground floor.

rhabillage [rabi'jaːʒ], *n.m.* Mending, repairing, overhaul; patching up. **rhabiller,** *v.t.* To dress again, to provide with new clothes; to mend, to patch up; (*fig.*) to set to rights; to put in better form. *Rhabiller une montre,* to repair a watch. **se rhabiller,** *v.r.* To put one's clothes on again. **rhabilleur,** *n.m.* (*fem. -euse*) Mender [REBOUTEUR].

rhapsode [RAPSODE].

rhénan [re'nɑ̃], *a. (fem. -ane)* Rhenish.—*n.* Rhinelander.

Rhénanie [rena'ni] (la), *f.* The Rhineland.

rhéomètre [reɔ'metr], *n.m.* Rheometer.

rhéostat, *n.m.* Rheostat.

rhéteur [re'tœːr], *n.m.* (*Ant.*) Rhetor; rhetorical orator, a flowery talker.

rhétien [re'tjɛ̃], *a. (fem. -ienne)* (*Geol.*) Rhaetian; Rhaetic.

rhétoricien [retɔri'sjɛ̃], *n.m.* Rhetorician.

rhétorique [retɔ'rik], *n.f.* Rhetoric. *Ce n'est que de la rhétorique,* that is only bombast; *faire sa rhétorique,* to be in the class of rhetoric (in the highest form but one) (during 19th century; now called *classe de première,* sixth form); *figure de rhétorique,* rhetorical figure.

Rhin [rɛ̃] (le), *m.* The Rhine.

rhinanthe [ri'nɑ̃ːt], *n.f.* (*Bot.*) or *cocriste* or *croquette.* Rhinanthus, corn-rattle.

rhingrave [rɛ̃'graːv], *n.m.* *Rhinegrave (Count of the Rhine).—*n.f.* 17th-century variety of knee-breeches.

rhinocéros [rinɔse'rɔs], *n.m. inv.* Rhinoceros.

rhinologie [rinɔlɔ'ʒi], *n.f.* (*Med.*) Rhinology. **rhinoplastie,** *n.f.* Rhinoplasty. **rhinoscopie,** *n.f.* Rhinoscopy.

rhodamine [rɔda'min], *n.f.* (*Chem.*) Rhodamin.

rhodium [rɔ'djɔm], *n.m.* Rhodium.

rhododendron [rɔdɔdɛ̃'drɔ̃], *n.m.* Rhododendron.

rhombe [rɔ̃:b], *n.m.* Rhomb; rhombus.—*a.* Rhombic.

rhomboïdal, *a. (fem. -ale, pl. -aux)* Rhomboidal. **rhomboïde,** *n.m.* Rhomboid.

Rhône [ron] (le) *m.* The Rhône.

rhubarbe [ry'barb], *n.f.* Rhubarb. *Tarte à la rhubarbe,* rhubarb-tart [see SÉNÉ]. *Rhubarbe des pauvres* or *rue des prés* or *pigamon jaunâtre,* meadow rue.

rhum [rɔm], *n.m.* Rum.

rhumatisant [rymati'zɑ̃], *a. (fem. -ante)* Suffering from rheumatism, rheumatic.—*n.* Such a person. **rhumatismal,** *a. (fem. -ale, pl. -aux)* Rheumatic (pain, fever). **rhumatisme,** *n.m.* Rheumatism. *Rhumatisme articulaire aigu,* rheumatic fever.

rhume [rym], *n.m.* Cold. *Attraper un rhume,* to catch a cold; *rhume de cerveau,* cold in the head; *un gros rhume*, a violent cold; (*pop.*) *qu'est-ce qu'il a pris pour son rhume!* He was hauled over the coals and no mistake.

rhythme etc. [RYTHME].

riant [ri'ɑ̃], *a.* (*fem.* **riante**) Smiling, cheerful, pleasant, pleasing.

ribambelle [ribɑ̃'bɛl], *n.f.* (*colloq.*) Swarm, string, lot (of children, animals, etc.).

ribaud [ri'bo], *a.* and *n.m.* (*fem.* **-aude**) Ribald. **ribauderie,** *n.f.* Ribaldry.

riblette [ri'blɛt], *n.f.* Collop, rasher.

riblon [ri'blɔ̃], *n.m.* (*usu. in pl.*) Scrap-iron, swarf.

ribord [ri'bɔːr], *n.m.* (*Naut.*) Garboard strake.

ribordage [ribɔr'daːʒ], *n.m.* Damage by fouling.

ribote [ri'bɔt], *n.f.* (*pop.*) *Être en ribote,* to be drunk, to be on the spree; *faire (une) ribote,* to have a drinking bout, to booze.

riboter, *v.i.* To get drunk.

riboteur, *n.m.* (*fem.* **-euse**) Tippler, boozer.

ribouis [ri'bwi], *n.m.* (*vulg.*) Second-hand boots; cheap boots or shoes.

ribouldingue [ribul'dɛ̃ːg], *n.f.* (*pop.*) *Faire la ribouldingue,* to go on the spree.

ribouler, *v.t.* (*pop.*)=**rouler** [CALOT].

ricanement [rikan'mɑ̃], *n.m.* Sneering, sneer; sniggering, mocking laughter.

ricaner, *v.i.* To sneer, to snigger.

ricaneur, *n.m.* (*fem.* **-euse**) Sneerer.—*a.* Sneering, derisive. **ric-à-ric** [rika'rik] or **ric-(à)-rac,** *adv.* (*fam.*) Rigorously, strictly, punctually, to the last farthing.

richard [ri'ʃaːr], *n.m.* (*fam.* and *pej.*) (*fem.* **-arde**) Moneyed person, capitalist.

Richard [ri'ʃaːr], *m.* Richard.

richardie [riʃar'di], *n.f.* (*Bot.*) Arum-lily.

riche [riʃ], *a.* Rich, wealthy, opulent; copious, abundant; costly, valuable, precious. *Langue riche,* rich language; *riche moisson,* abundant harvest; *un riche parti,* a wealthy match (marriage); (*fam.*) *une riche idée,* a jolly good idea.—*n.* Rich person; (*pl.*) the rich. *Le mauvais riche,* Dives (the rich man of the Gospel). **richement,** *adv.* Richly; copiously; splendidly.

richesse, *n.f.* Riches, wealth, opulence; copiousness; richness, costliness. *Contentement passe richesse,* contentment surpasses riches; *la richesse d'une langue,* the copiousness of a language.

richissime, *a.* (*colloq.*) Inordinately rich, rolling in money.

ricin [ri'sɛ̃], *n.m.* Castor-oil plant. *Huile de ricin,* castor-oil.

ricocher [rikɔ'ʃe], *v.i.* To rebound; to ricochet.

ricochet, *n.m.* Rebound (on the water); (*Artill.*) ricochet; (*fig.*) series, chain, succession (of events). *Coup de ricochet,* chance stroke; *faire des ricochets sur l'eau,* to play ducks and drakes; *par ricochet,* indirectly, by accident; *tir à ricochet,* (*Artill.*) firing indirectly by richochet.

rictus [rik'tyːs], *n.m. inv.* Grin; rictus.

ride [rid], *n.f.* Wrinkle; ripple; (*Naut.*) lanyard.

ridé, *a.* (*fem.* **-ée**) Wrinkled; rippling; corrugated; (*Bot.*) rugose. *Un front ridé,* a wrinkled brow; *une pomme ridée,* a shrivelled apple.

rideau [ri'do], *n.m.* (*pl.* **-eaux**) Curtain; screen (of trees etc.); (*Fort.*) rideau. *Baisser le rideau,* (*Theat.*) to drop the curtain; *lever de rideau,* curtain-raiser; *le Rideau de Fer,* the Iron Curtain; *tirer le rideau,* to draw the curtain; *tirer le rideau sur,* to draw a veil over; *un rideau de fumée,* a smoke screen.

ridelle [ri'dɛl], *n.f.* Light rail (at side of a cart).

rider [ri'de], *v.t.* To wrinkle; to corrugate, to shrivel, to ripple, to ruffle (water); (*Naut.*) to tighten (the shrouds). **se rider,** *v.r.* To wrinkle; to be wrinkled; to shrivel up; to ripple (of water).

ridicule [ridi'kyl], *a.* Ridiculous. *Se rendre ridicule,* to make oneself ridiculous.—*n.m.* Ridicule; ridiculousness, the ridiculous; ridiculous thing. *Tomber dans le ridicule,* to become ridiculous; *tourner quelqu'un en ridicule,* to ridicule someone. **ridiculement,** *adv.* Ridiculously.

ridiculiser [ridikyli'ze], *v.t.* To ridicule, to make fun of.

rien [rjɛ̃], *n.m.* Trifle, mere nothing, insignificant thing or quantity. *Il se fâche pour des riens,* he gets annoyed over nothing at all.—*indef. pron.* Nothing, nought, not anything; anything; (*Ten.*) love. *Cela ne fait rien,* that does not matter; *ce n'est rien moins que cela,* it is anything but that; *cet homme ne m'est rien,* that man is nothing to me; *cette montre ne vous sert à rien,* that watch is of no use to you; *de rien,* don't mention it, it's no trouble; *en moins de rien,* in a trice, in less than no time; *homme de rien,* a nobody; *il ne sert à rien de,* it is of no use to; *je n'en ferai rien,* I shall do nothing of the sort; *je ne pense à rien moins qu'à cela,* nothing is further from my thoughts; *n'aboutir à rien,* to come to nothing; *n'être pour rien dans une affaire,* to have no part in the matter; *ne faites semblant de rien,* pretend not to mind it *or* not to see it; *on ne peut faire rien de rien,* nothing can be made out of nothing; *pour rien,* for nothing, for next to nothing; *rien à quinze,* (*Ten.*) love fifteen; *rien au monde ne me fera oublier cela,* nothing in the world will make me forget that; *rien de plus beau,* nothing finer; *rien de rien,* nothing whatever; *rien du tout,* nothing at all; *rien que,* merely; *s'il y a rien qui me plaise,* if anything pleases me; *tout comme si de rien n'était,* as if nothing at all was the matter; *y a-t-il rien de nouveau?* is there any news?

rieur [ri'œːr], *a.* (*fem.* **rieuse**) Laughing, joking.—*n.* Laughter. *Il a les rieurs de son côté,* he has the laugh(ers) on his side.

riflard [ri'flaːr], *n.m.* Large two-handed plane, jack-plane; mason's chisel or trowel; rough file (for metal); (*pop.*) big umbrella, gamp.

rifler, *v.t.* To plane, to file. **rifloir,** *n.m.* Rasp, file.

rigaudon or **rigodon** [rigɔ'dɔ̃], *n.m.* *Rigadoon (an old dance); (*Mil.*) short bugle-call to announce a bull's-eye.

rigide [ri'ʒid], *a.* Rigid, stiff; strict, severe. **rigidement,** *adv.* Rigidly, strictly.

rigidité, *n.f.* Rigidity, stiffness; strictness, severity.

rigodon [RIGAUDON].

rigolade [rigɔ'lad], *n.f.* (*pop.*) Fun; lark.

rigole [ri'gɔl], *n.f.* Trench, small ditch or channel; gutter.

rigoler (1) [rigɔ'le], *v.t.* To furrow, to trench.
rigoler (2), *v.i.* (*pop.*) To have fun; to have a lark, to go on the spree.
rigolo, *a.* (*fem.* **rigolote**) (*pop.*) Funny, amusing, jolly.—*n.m.* (*slang*) Revolver.
rigorisme [rigɔ'rism], *n.m.* Rigorism, austerity; hypercriticism. **rigoriste**, *n.* Rigorist, stickler, precisian; harsh critic.—*a.* Over-rigid, over-severe; hypercritical. **rigoureusement**, *adv.* Rigorously, severely, strictly. *Rigoureusement interdit*, strictly prohibited. **rigoureux**, *a.* (*fem.* **-euse**) Rigorous, strict; severe, stern, harsh; inclement. *Climat rigoureux*, harsh climate.
rigueur [ri'gœːr], *n.f.* Rigour, strictness; precision; severity, harshness; sternness, sharpness; inclemency. *À la rigueur*, strictly, in a strict sense, if absolutely necessary; *de rigueur*, indispensable, compulsory; *être de rigueur*, (of behaviour or of a thing) to be strictly required; *la rigueur de l'hiver*, the inclemency of the winter; *la rigueur du sort*, the sternness of fate; *traiter quelqu'un avec rigueur*, to be severe with someone.
rillettes [ri'jɛt], *n.f.* (*used only in pl.*) Rillettes (minced pork).
rimailler [rima'je], *v.i.* To write doggerel.
rimailleur, *n.m.* Sorry rhymer, rhymester.
rimaye [ri'maːj], *n.f.* Bergschrund, crevasse.
rime [rim], *n.f.* Rhyme; (*fig.*) verse. *Il n'y a ni rime ni raison dans ce qu'il dit*, there is neither rhyme nor reason in what he says; *rimes croisées*, alternate masculine and feminine rhymes; *rimes plates* or *suivies*, following rhymes in which masculine couplets alternate with feminine couplets.
rimer [ri'me], *v.i.* To rhyme; to write verses. *Cela ne rime à rien*, there's no sense in that; *de la prose rimée*, rhymed prose (doggerel).— *v.t.* To versify, to put into rhyme.
rimeur [ri'mœːr], *n.m.* Rhymer, versifier.
rinçage [rɛ̃'saːʒ], *n.m.* Rinsing, washing, cleansing.
rinceau [rɛ̃'so], *n.m.* (*pl.* **-eaux**) Scroll-pattern or ornament; (*Her.*) bough.
rince-bouche [rɛ̃s'buʃ], *n.m. inv.* Vessel formerly used to hold water for rinsing the mouth after a meal.
rince-bouteilles, *n.m. inv.* Bottle-washing machine.
rince-doigts, *n.m. inv.* Finger-bowl.
rincée [rɛ̃'se], *n.f.* (*pop.*) Drubbing; downpour.
rincer [rɛ̃'se], *v.t.* To rinse, to wash, to cleanse; (*fam.*) to stand drinks to (somebody). **se rincer**, *v.r.* To rinse. *Se rincer la bouche*, to rinse one's mouth; (*vulg.*) *se rincer la dalle*, to wet one's whistle; *se rincer l'œil*, to feast one's eyes.
rincette, *n.f.* A nip of brandy etc.
rinçure, *n.f.* (*colloq.*) Rinsings; slops (poor wine etc.).
ringard [rɛ̃'gaːr], *n.m.* Fire-rake, poker for ovens, furnaces, etc.; clinker-bar.
ripage [ri'paːʒ] or **ripement**, *n.m.* Scraping, polishing with a scraper; skidding (of wheels), slipping.
ripaille [ri'paːj], *n.f.* Feasting, junketing. *Faire ripaille*, to feast, to make good cheer.
ripailler, *v.i.* To feast, to make good cheer.
ripailleur, *n.m.* (*fem.* **-euse**) Feaster, carouser.
ripe [rip], *n.f.* (*Sculp.*) Scraper; (*C*) wood

shavings. **riper**, *v.t.* To scrape; to let slip, to let slide.—*v.i.* To skid (of wheels), to rub; to slip.
ripolin [ripɔ'lɛ̃], *n.m.* (Ripolin) enamel paint.
ripoliner, *v.t.* To paint with ripolin.
ripopée [ripɔ'pe], *n.f.* Slops (of wine); medley, hotch-potch.
riposte [ri'pɔst], *n.f.* (*Fenc.*) Ripost, return; (*fig.*) smart reply, retort, repartee.
riposter, *v.i.* (*Fenc.*) To ripost, to parry and thrust; (*fig.*) to make a smart reply, to retort. *Il riposta d'un soufflet*, he replied with a slap in the face.
ripuaire [ri'pɥɛːr], *a. and n.* (*Hist.*) Ripuarian.
riquiqui [riki'ki], *n.m.* (*pop.*) Cheap brandy; rot-gut; anything mean or small; an undersized person; the little finger.
rire (1) [riːr], *v.i. irr.* (*pres.p.* **riant**, *p.p.* **ri**) To laugh; to smile; to look pleasant; to be favourable, to be propitious; to jest, to joke; to mock, to scoff, to make game; to gape (of a hole in one's clothes etc.). *Avoir le mot pour rire* [MOT]; *cela fait rire*, that makes one laugh; *c'est à mourir de rire*, it is killingly funny; *éclater de rire* [ÉCLATER]; *en riant* or *pour rire*, jokingly, in jest; *est-ce que vous riez?* are you joking? *et la foule de rire!* up went a shout of laughter from the crowd! *étouffer de rire* [ÉTOUFFER]; *histoire de rire*, for fun; *il n'y a pas de quoi rire* [QUOI]; *je le disais pour rire*, I said it in jest; *la fortune lui rit*, fortune smiles upon him; *prêter à rire*, to make oneself a laughing-stock; *nous rirons bien*, we shall have great fun; *rira bien qui rira le dernier*, he who laughs last laughs longest; *rire à gorge déployée*, to roar with laughter; *rire bruyamment* or *d'un gros rire*, to guffaw; *rire au nez de quelqu'un* [NEZ]; *rire aux dépens d'autrui*, to laugh at other people's expense; *rire dans sa barbe* or *rire sous cape* [BARBE (1)]; *rire de*, to laugh at, not to mind; *rire de quelqu'un*, to laugh at someone; *rire du bout des dents* or *des lèvres* [BOUT]; *rire jaune*, to force a laugh, to give a sickly smile; *se pâmer de rire* [PÂMER]; *se tenir les côtes de rire* [CÔTE]; *tel qui rit vendredi, dimanche pleurera* [DIMANCHE]; *un conte pour rire*, a laughable story; *un roi pour rire*, a sham king; *vous voulez rire*, you are joking, you are not serious. **se rire**, *v.r.* To make sport, to poke fun, to scoff; to make light. *On se rit de lui*, he is laughed at.
rire (2) [riːr], *n.m.* Laughter, laughing. *Accès de (fou) rire*, fit of (uncontrollable) laughter; *partir d'un éclat de rire* [PARTIR]; *rire étouffé*, suppressed laugh; *un rire*, a laugh; *un gros rire*, loud laughter, a horse-laugh; a guffaw; *un rire moqueur*, a sneer; *un rire niais*, a silly laugh.
ris (1) [ri], *n.m. inv.* Laugh, smile, laughter. *Un ris moqueur*, a sneer.
ris (2) [ri], *n.m. inv.* (*Naut.*) Reef (of sails). *Prendre un ris*, to take in a reef.
ris (3) [ri], *n.m. inv.* Sweetbread. *Ris de veau*, calf's sweetbread.
risée [ri'ze], *n.f.* Laugh; laughter, mockery, derision; butt, laughing-stock; (*Naut.*) gust, squall. *Être la risée de tout le monde*, to be the laughing-stock of everyone; *objet de risée*, laughing-stock.
risette, *n.f.* Pleasant little laugh, smile; (*Naut.*) cat's paw.

risibilité [rizibili'te], *n.f.* Risibility. **risible**, *a.* Risible; comical, laughable; ridiculous. **risiblement**, *adv.* Laughably, ludicrously.
risquable [ris'kabl], *a.* That may be risked.
risque [risk], *n.m.* Risk, hazard. *À ses risques et périls*, at one's own risk; *à tout risque*, at all hazards; *au risque de*, at the risk of; *j'en courrai le risque*, I will chance it.
risqué, *a.* (*fem.* -ée) Risky. *Une aventure risquée*, a hazardous adventure; *une plaisanterie risquée*, a doubtful joke.
risquer, *v.t.* To risk, to hazard, to venture; to run the risk of; (*fam.*) to chance. *Qui ne risque rien n'a rien*, nothing venture, nothing have. **se risquer**, *v.r.* To risk, to venture, to take the risk., to take risks.
risque-tout, *n.m. inv.* (*colloq.*) Dare-devil.
risse [SAISINE].
risser [ri'se], *v.t.* (*Naut.*) To lash, to frap.
rissole [ri'sɔl], *n.f.* Rissole (minced-meat fritter); an anchovy net in the Mediterranean.
rissoler, *v.t.* (*Cook.*) To brown. *Il a le visage rissolé*, his face is sunburnt. **se rissoler**, *v.r.* To brown.
ristourne [ris'turn], *n.f.* Partial or total cancelling of an insurance for the benefit of insurer; refund (of a sum overcharged); transferring to another account [CONTRE-PASSEMENT].
ristorner or **ristourner**, *v.t.* To cancel or surrender (an insurance); (*Comm.*) to carry to another account; to refund.
rit or **rite** [rit], *n.m.* Rite.
ritournelle [ritur'nɛl], *n.f.* (*Mus.*) Ritornello, flourish; (*fig.*) harping on the same tune.
ritualisme [rityɑ'lism], *n.m.* Ritualism. **ritualiste**, *n.* Ritualist.—*a.* Ritualistic. **rituel**, *a.* (*fem.* -elle) Ritual.—*n.m.* Ritual (prayer-book).
rivage [ri'vaːʒ], *n.m.* Shore, strand, beach; bank, waterside. *Être jeté sur le rivage*, to be cast ashore; *quitter le rivage*, to put off.
rival [ri'val], *a.* (*fem.* -ale, *pl.* -aux) Rival, competitive.—*n.* Rival. *Ils sont rivaux de gloire*, they are rivals in glory; *sans rival*, unrivalled.
rivaliser [rivali'ze], *v.i.* To rival, to vie, to compete. *Ils ont rivalisé d'efforts*, they vied with each other.
rivalité [rivali'te], *n.f.* Rivalry, emulation.
rive [riːv], *n.f.* Bank, shore (of rivers, lakes, etc.); (*fig.*) seashore; margin, border, skirt (of woods etc.).
rivelaine [riv'lɛːn], *n.f.* Miner's pick.
rivement [riv'mã], *n.m.* Riveting.
river, *v.t.* To clinch, to rivet. *River son clou à quelqu'un*, to give someone a clincher; to shut someone up.
riverain [ri'vrɛ̃], *a.* (*fem.* -aine) Riparian; bordering (on rivers or woods); possessing property situated along a forest, road, or street; riverside, wayside (property etc.).—*n.* Riverside resident; borderer.
rivet [ri'vɛ], *n.m.* Rivet; clinch. **rivetage**, *n.m.* Riveting. **riveter**, *v.t.* To rivet. **riveteur** or **riveur**, *n.m.* Riveter. **riveteuse** or **riveuse**, *n.f.* Riveting-machine.
rivière [ri'vjɛːr], *n.f.* River, stream. *Bras d'une rivière*, reach of a river; *les petits ruisseaux font les grandes rivières*, many a little makes a mickle, little strokes fell great oaks;

rivière de diamants, diamond necklace; *rivière marchande*, navigable river.
rivoir [ri'vwaːr], *n.m.*, or **rivoire**, *n.f.* Riveting-hammer or machine.
rivure, *n.f.* Clinching, riveting; rivet(ed) joint; hinge-pin.
rixdale [riks'dal], *n.f.* Rix-dollar.
rixe [riks], *n.f.* Fight, scuffle; brawl, affray.
riz [ri], *n.m.* Rice. *Eau de riz*, rice-water; *poudre de riz*, face-powder; *riz au lait*, rice-pudding. **rizerie**, *n.f.* Rice-mill. **riziculture**, *n.f.* Rice-growing. **rizier**, *a.* (*fem.* -ière) Pertaining to rice.—*n.f.* Rice-field, rice-plantation; rice-swamp.
riz-pain-sel [ripɛ̃'sel], *n.m. inv.* (*Mil. slang*) Soldier of the Commissariat.
rob [rɔb], *n.m.* (*Pharm.*) Rob (a conserve).
robe [rɔb], *n.f.* Gown, dress, frock; robe; (*fig.*) the law, the magistracy; long robe (lawyers), the clergy, the cloth; coat (of certain animals); skin, husk, peel (of certain fruits etc.). *Gens de robe*, legal profession; *robe de chambre*, dressing-gown; (*Am.*) bath-robe; *pommes (de terre) en robe de chambre*, potatoes in their jackets.
rober, *v.t.* To bark (madder); to wrap (cigars).
robin, *n.m.* (*colloq.*) Lawyer, man of the long robe.
Robin, *m.* Robin.
robinet [rɔbi'nɛ], *n.m.* Cock; tap; plug, water-cock; (*Am.*) faucet. *Fermer le robinet*, to turn off the tap; *ouvrir le robinet*, to turn on the tap.
robinetier, *n.m.* Brass-smith.
robinetterie, *n.f.* Brass-founding.
robinier [rɔbi'nje], *n.m.* Robinia, false acacia.
robot [rɔ'bo], *n.m.* Automaton, robot.—*a. inv.* *Avion robot*, pilotless plane; *fusée, satellite robot*, unmanned rocket, satellite.
robre [rɔbr], *n.m.* (*Whist etc.*) Rubber.
robuste [rɔ'byst], *a.* Robust, vigorous, sturdy; hardy, strong. **robustement**, *adv.* Robustly, athletically. **robustesse**, *n.f.* Robustness, strength, vigour.
roc [rɔk], *n.m.* Rock; *(Chess)* rook, castle.
rocade [rɔ'kad], *n.f.* Voie or ligne de rocade, (*Mil.*) road or railway parallel to the front.
rocaille [rɔ'kaːj], *n.f.* Rock-work, grotto-work. *(Jardin en) rocaille*, rock-garden, rockery. **rocailleur**, *n.m.* Rockwork-maker.
rocailleux, *a.* (*fem.* -euse) Pebbly, stony, flinty; rugged, rough. *Style rocailleux*, harsh style.
rocambeau [rɔkã'bo], *n.m.* (*pl.* -eaux) (*Naut.*) Traveller; iron ring (holding the sails etc.).
rocambole [rɔkã'bɔl], *n.f.* Rocambole, Spanish garlic; (*fig.*) stale joke; piquancy, point, zest. **rocambolesque**, *a.* Grotesque, incredible (of story, adventures).
rochassier [rɔʃa'sje], *n.m.* Rock-climber.
roche [rɔʃ], *n.f.* Rock; a rock, boulder; any hard stone or stony mass. *Cœur de roche*, heart of stone; *eau de roche*, spring water; *homme de la vieille roche*, man of the good old stock; *il y a anguille sous roche* [ANGUILLE].
rocher (1), *n.m.* High, steep, or prominent rock, crag; (*Conch.*) murex; (*Anat.*) hard part of temporal bone. *Cœur de rocher*, heart of flint; *plein de rochers*, rocky; *le rocher de Gibraltar*, the rock of Gibraltar.
rocher (2), *v.t.* To flux (a welding).—*v.i.* To froth; to sprout (of silver).

rochet (1) [rɔ'ʃɛ], *n.m.* Rochet (surplice).
rochet (2) [rɔ'ʃɛ], *n.m.* Ratchet; blunt lance-head (used in jousting); bobbin. *Roue à rochet*, ratchet-wheel.
rocheux [rɔ'ʃø], *a.* (*fem.* **-euse**) Rocky, stony.
rochier, *n.m.* (*pop.*) Smaller dog-fish.
rock [rɔk], *n.m.* Roc (fabulous bird).
rococo [rɔkɔ'ko], *n.m.* Rococo, antiquated style.—*a. inv.* Rococo; antiquated, quaint, debased (of style in arts).
rocou [rɔ'ku] or **roucou**, *n.m.* Anatta.
rocouyer, *n.m.* Anatta-tree.
rodage [rɔ'daːʒ], *n.m.* Grinding in, lapping; polishing. *En rodage*, (engine) not yet run in; 'running in'.
roder [rɔ'de], *v.t.* To grind, to polish (two pieces, one against the other).
rôder [ro'de], *v.i.* To prowl.
rôdeur, *n.m.* (*fem.* **-euse**) Prowler; vagrant. —*a.* Prowling.
rodoir [rɔ'dwaːr], *n.m.* Grinding-tool.
Rodolphe [rɔ'dɔlf], *m.* Rudolph, Ralph.
rodomont [rɔdɔ'mɔ̃], *n.m.* Braggart, blusterer.
rodomontade, *n.f.* Rodomontade, bluster, swagger.
Rodrigue [rɔ'drig], *m.* Roderick, Roderigo.
rogation [rɔga'sjɔ̃], *n.f.* Rogation; (*pl.*) Rogation Days. *Semaine des Rogations*, Rogation Week.
rogatoire, *a.* Of inquiry, rogatory. *Commission rogatoire*, judicial commission (to another court etc.).
rogaton [rɔga'tɔ̃], *n.m.* Broken meat; (*pl.*) scraps, odds and ends.
Roger [rɔ'ʒe], *m.* Roger. *C'est un vrai Roger Bontemps*, he is a happy-go-lucky sort of chap.
rognage [rɔ'naːʒ] or **rognement**, *n.m.* Cutting, paring, clipping.
rogne [rɔɲ], *n.f.* (*pop.*) Itch, scab, mange; (*slang*) bad humour.
rogne-pied, *n.m. inv.* Farrier's knife.
rogner [rɔ'ne], *v.t.* To cut, to pare, to crop; to clip, to prune, to lop; to curtail, to cut short; (*pop.*) to be cross, to grouse. *Rogner les ailes* or *les ongles à quelqu'un*, to clip someone's wings, to render someone harmless; *trop rogner* (*un livre*), to bleed (a book).
rogneur, *n.m.* (*fem.* **-euse** (1)) Cutter, clipper (of coin etc.).—*n.f.* Clipping or cutting machine.
rogneux [rɔ'nø], *a.* (*fem.* **-euse** (2)) Mangy, scabby.
rognoir [rɔ'nwaːr], *n.m.* (*Bookb.*) Plough, cutting-press, parer.
rognon [rɔ'nɔ̃], *n.m.* Kidney (as food); testicle (of some animals). *Rognons en brochette*, kidneys grilled on a skewer.
rognonner, *v.i.* (*slang*) To grumble.
rognure [rɔ'nyːr], *n.f.* A paring, a clipping; (*pl.*) scraps, shreds, refuse, leavings, clippings.
rogomme [rɔ'gɔm], *n.m.* Spirits. *Voix de rogomme*, drunkard's voice, gin-croak.
rogue (1) [rɔg], *a.* Arrogant, haughty.
rogue (2) [rɔg], *n.f.* Salted cod's-roe.
rogué, *a.* (*fem.* **-ée**) Roed (fish).
rohart [rɔ'ar], *n.m.* Ivory of hippopotamus or walrus.
roi [rwa], *n.m.* King. *De par le roi*, in the king's name; *les Rois, la fête des Rois*, Twelfth Night; *la galette des Rois*, the Twelfth-night cake; *le jour des Rois*, Twelfth Day; *la*

maison du roi, the royal household; *le roi de cœur*, the king of hearts; *morceau de roi*, dish fit for a king; *nous fêtons les Rois*, we celebrate Twelfth Night; *roi d'armes*, King at Arms; *travailler pour le roi de Prusse*, to work for nothing, to work for love; *vive le roi*, long live the king; *vivre en roi*, to live like a king.
roide etc. [RAIDE].
roitelet [rwa'tlɛ], *n.m.* Petty king, kinglet; wren. *Roitelet huppé*, goldcrest.
rôle [roːl], *n.m.* Roll; list, roster, catalogue; (*Theat.*) part, character, rôle. *À tour de rôle*, in turn, in rotation; *distribution des rôles*, cast; *bien jouer son rôle*, to play one's part well; *rôle de combat*, (*Naut.*) quarter-bill; *rôle d'équipage*, muster-roll.
romain [rɔ'mɛ̃], *a.* (*fem.* **-aine**) Roman. *L'Église Catholique romaine*, the Church of Rome.—*n.m.* (*Print.*) Roman, primer. *Gros romain*, great primer; *petit romain*, long primer.—*n.m.* (**Romain**, *fem.* **-aine**) A Roman.—*n.f.* Steelyard; cos lettuce.
romaïque [rɔma'ik], *a.* and *n.m.* Romaic, modern Greek.
roman (1) [rɔ'mɑ̃], *a.* (*fem.* **-ane**) Romance, Romanic; (*Arch.*) Romanesque, (in England) Norman (style). *Une église de style roman, une église romane*, a Romanesque church; *les langues romanes*, Romance languages.
roman (2) [rɔ'mɑ̃], *n.m.* Novel; romance, fiction; (in Middle Ages) work written in Old French (not in Latin), romance. *Cela tient du roman*, it is like a romance; *c'est une aventure de roman*, it is a romantic adventure. *Roman-fleuve*, saga novel; *roman policier*, detective novel.
romance [rɔ'mɑ̃ːs], *n.f.* (*Mus.*) Ballad, sentimental song.—*n.m.* Spanish metrical romance.
romancé, *a.* (*fem.* **-ée**) In the form of a novel. *Une biographie romancée*, a biographical novel. **romancero**, *n.m.* Collection of Spanish romances.
romanche [rɔ'mɑ̃ːʃ], *n.m.* Romansh.
romancier [rɔmɑ̃'sje], *n.m.* (*fem.* **-ière**) Novelist.
romanciser, *v.t.* To romanticize.
romand [rɔ'mɑ̃], *a.* (*fem.* **-ande**) Pertaining to the French-speaking cantons of Switzerland.
romanesque [rɔma'nɛsk], *a.* Romantic.—*n.m.* The romantic.
roman-feuilleton [rɔ'mɑ̃fœj'tɔ̃], *n.m* (*pl.* **romans-feuilletons**) Newspaper serial (story).
romanichel [rɔmani'ʃɛl], *n.m.* (*fem.* **-elle**) Gipsy.
romaniser [rɔmani'ze], *v.t., v.i.* To romanize. **romanisme**, *n.m.* Romanism. **romaniste**, *n.* Romanist.
romantique [rɔmɑ̃'tik], *a.* Romantic.—*n.* Romanticist; romantic genre, art, etc. **romantiquement**, *adv.* Romantically. **romantisme**, *n.m.* (*Lit. Hist.*) Romanticism.
romarin [rɔma'rɛ̃], *n.m.* Rosemary.
rombière, rhombière [rɔ̃'bjɛːr], *n.f.* (*pop.*) Woman, old woman.
Rome [rɔm], *f.* Rome. *Tous les chemins mènent à Rome*, all roads lead to Rome.
rompre [rɔ̃ːpr], *v.t. irr.* To break, to break asunder, to snap; to break off; to break up, to disperse, to rout; to break up, to dissolve; to break in, to train, to inure; to divert, to

turn off; to break the force of, to deaden; to interrupt; to refract; (*Med.*) to rupture; (*Paint.*) to blend. *À tout rompre*, furiously, like mad; *cet acteur a été applaudi à tout rompre*, that actor received frantic applause; *rompre la glace*, (*fig.*) to break the ice; *rompre la tête à quelqu'un*, to split someone's head, to worry someone; *rompre l'eau à un cheval*, to interrupt a horse in drinking; *rompre les chiens*, (*Hunt.*) to call off the dogs; (*fig.*) to change the subject; *rompre son ban*, to break one's bounds, to break one's banns; *rompre un cheval*, to break in a horse; *rompre un choc*, to deaden a shock; **rompre un criminel*, to break a criminal upon the wheel; *rompre un homme aux affaires*, to train a man up to business.—*v.i.* To break, to break asunder, to break off, to snap, to break up; to fall out; (*Box.*) to retreat. *Rompre court*, to break off short; *rompre d'une semelle*, (*Fenc.*) to draw back a step; *rompez!* (*Mil.*) Dismiss! **se rompre**, *v.r.* To break, to break off, to snap; to break one's head, arm, etc.; to be inured, to get used (*à*). *Tu vas te rompre le cou*, you'll break your neck.

rompu, *a.* (*fem.* **-ue**) Broken, snapped; broken in, trained, inured; tired out, overwhelmed (with fatigue etc.); (*Her.*) [BRISÉ]; (*Navy*) hogged (of a ship). *Être rompu aux affaires*, to be used to business; *nombre rompu*, fraction; *tout rompu de fatigue*, completely worn out [BÂTON].

romsteck [rɔm'stɛk], *n.m.* Rump-steak.

ronce [rɔ̃ːs], *n.f.* Bramble, blackberry-bush; thorns; curl (in grain of wood). *Ronce artificielle*, barbed wire. *Ronce de noyer*, burr-walnut.

ronce-framboise, *n.f.* (*pl.* **ronces-framboises**) Loganberry.

ronceraie, *n.f.* Brake, brambly ground.

ronceux, *a.* (*fem.* **-euse**) Brambly.

ronchon [rɔ̃'ʃɔ̃], *a.* and *n. inv.* Grumbler; scold. **ronchonner**, *v.i.* To grouse, to grumble; (*Rad. Teleph.*) to hum.

ronchonneur, *n.m.* (*fem.* **-euse**) Grumbler.

ronchonnot, *n.m.* Old retired officer, old crock.

rond [rɔ̃], *a.* (*fem.* **ronde** (1)) Round; plump, rotund; frank, open, plain-dealing; even (of money or accounts); (*pop.*) tipsy. *C'est un homme tout rond*, he is a plain-dealing man; *compte rond*, round sum; *du fil rond*, coarse thread; *en nombres, en chiffres ronds*, in round numbers *or* figures; *pain rond*, coarse bread; *période ronde*, rounded period; *un peu rond*, roundish; *voix ronde*, full-toned voice.—*adv.* Normally, true. *Tourner rond*, to run smoothly, to run true (of motor, wheel).—*n.m.* Round, ring, orb, circle, disk; (*pop.*) sou. *Danser en rond*, to dance in a ring; *faire des ronds (de fumée)*, to blow smoke-rings; *il n'a pas un rond*, he has not got a brass farthing; *rond de cuir*, air-cushion, (*fig.*) clerk, *esp.* in Government service, quill-driver, penpusher; *Messieurs les rond-de-cuir*, the gentlemen of the red tape, the bureaucrats; *rond de saucisson*, round of sausage; *rond de serviette*, napkin-ring.

rondache, *n.f.* Round buckler or shield.

ronde (2), *n.f.* Round; patrol; beat; (*Mus.*) semibreve; roundelay; round-hand (writing). *À la ronde*, in turn, roundabout; *à quinze*

kilomètres à la ronde, within a radius of ten miles, for ten miles round; *boire à la ronde* [BOIRE]; *faire la ronde*, to go the rounds; *passer à la ronde*, to hand round; *ronde de table*, table roundelay.

rondeau [rɔ̃'do], *n.m.* (*pl.* **-eaux**) Rondeau (French poem); (*Mus.*) rondo; roller.

rondel, *n.m.* Rondel.

rondelet, *a.* (*fem.* **rondelette** (1)) Roundish, plump, plumpish, podgy.

rondelette (2), *n.f.* Sail-cloth (made in Brittany in 15th–18th century); (*pop.*) ground-ivy.

rondelle, *n.f.* Rondelle, washer; rundle, ring; sculptor's rounded chisel; round shield.

rondement, *adv.* Roundly; quickly; briskly, vigorously; plainly, frankly, bluntly. *Il va rondement en besogne*, he goes briskly to work; *mener une affaire rondement*, not to dilly-dally.

rondeur, *n.f.* Roundness, rotundity; fullness; openness, plain dealing.

rondier, *n.m.* (*Bot.*) Palmyra; roundsman.

rondin, *n.m.* Billet, round log; cudgel.

rondouillard, *a.* (*fem.* **-arde**) (*fam.*) Plump, podgy.

rond-point, *n.m.* (*pl.* **ronds-points**) (*Arch.*) Apsis; circus (place where several roads etc. meet); roundabout; (*Am.*) traffic circle.

ronflant ([rɔ̃'flɑ̃], *a.* (*fem.* **-ante**) Snoring; booming, humming, rumbling, throbbing, whirring; sonorous, high-sounding.

ronflement, *n.m.* Snoring, snore; roaring, rumbling; peal, roar, boom; snorting (of horses). *Ronflement du vent*, roaring of the wind; *ronflement d'une toupie*, humming of a top.

ronfler [rɔ̃'fle], *v.i.* To snore; to snort (of horses); to roar (of cannon, thunder, etc.); to boom; to peal (of organs); to hum (of spinning-tops).

ronfleur [rɔ̃'flœːr], *n.m.* (*fem.* **-euse**) Snorer.

ronge [rɔ̃ːʒ], *n.m.* *Le cerf fait le ronge*, the stag is ruminating.

rongeant, *a.* (*fem.* **-ante**) Gnawing, corroding; (*Path.*) rodent (ulcer); (*fig.*) tormenting.

ronge-maille, *n.m. inv.* Nibbler (rat). *Maître ronge-maille*, Squire Nibbler (La Fontaine).

ronger [rɔ̃'ʒe], *v.t.* To gnaw, to nibble, to pick; to eat up, to waste, to consume, to corrode; to fret, to torment, to prey upon (the mind etc.). *La rouille ronge le fer*, rust corrodes iron; *ronger ses ongles*, to bite one's nails; *ronger son frein*, to champ the bit, to fret, to chafe. **se ronger**, *v.r.* To fret, to be tormented with worry. *Se ronger les poings*, to fume, to be in a (quiet) rage.

rongeur, *a.* (*fem.* **-euse**) Gnawing, biting; corroding; consuming; casking (case). *Ver rongeur*, ever-gnawing worm.—*n.m.* (*Zool.*) Rodent.

ronron [rɔ̃'rɔ̃], *n.m.* Purr, purring. *Faire ronron*, to purr. **ronronner**, *v.i.* To purr, to hum. **ronronnement**, *n.m.* Purring; humming; drone (of engine).

roque [rɔk], *n.m.* (*Chess*) Castling.

roquefort [rɔk'fɔːr], *n.m.* Roquefort cheese.

roquer [rɔ'ke], *v.i.* (*Chess*) To castle, to rook; to croquet.

roquet [rɔ'kɛ], *n.m.* Pug-dog; cur, mongrel.

roquette [rɔ'kɛt], *n.f.* Rocket (plant); *(war) rocket.

rorqual [rɔr'kwal], *n.m.* (*Zool.*) Rorqual, fin-back.

rosace [ro'zas], *n.f.* (*Arch.*) Rose; rose-window. **rosacé**, *a.* (*fem.* **-ée**) (*Bot.*) Rosaceous.—*n.f.* Rosaceous plant.

rosage, *n.m.* Rhododendron; azalea; (*Tex.*) retting (of flax).

rosaire [ro'zɛːr], *n.m.* (*R.-C. Ch.*) Rosary.

rosat, *a.* (*fem. inv.*) (*Pharm.*) Of roses, roseate. *Miel rosat*, honey of roses. **rosâtre**, *a.* Pinkish.

rosbif [rɔs'bif], *n.m.* Roast beef.

rose [roːz], *n.f.* Rose; rose-window; rose-diamond. *Bois de rose*, tulip-wood; *couleur de rose*, rose-colour, rose-coloured, pink; *découvrir le pot aux roses* [DÉCOUVRIR]; *de rose*, rosy; *eau de rose*, rose-water; *essence de rose*, attar of roses; *il n'est point de rose sans épines*, there is no rose without a thorn; *laurier-rose* [LAURIER]; *rose de Gueldre*, Guelder-rose; *rose d'Inde*, African marigold; *rose des quatre saisons*, monthly rose; *rose des vents*, compass-card; *rose mousseuse*, moss-rose; *rose pompon*, fairy rose; *rose sauvage*, dog-rose; *rose thé*, tea-rose; *rose trémière*, hollyhock.—*n.m.* Rose-colour, pink.—*a.* Rosy; pink, rose-coloured.

rosé, *a.* (*fem.* **-ée**) Pale pink, rosy, roseate. *Vin rosé*, light-red wine, 'vin rosé'. **roseau**, *n.m.* (*pl.* **roseaux**) Reed. *C'est un roseau peint en fer*, he is a lath painted to look like iron; *roseau des sables*, beach-grass; *s'appuyer sur un roseau*, to lean on a broken reed.

rose-croix [roz'krwa], *n.m. inv.* Rosicrucian.

rosée [ro'ze], *n.f.* Dew. *Goutte de rosée*, dew-drop; *couvert, humecté de rosée*, dewy; *rosée de larmes*, shower of tears; *rosée du matin*, morning dew; *tendre comme une rosée*, beautifully tender.

roselet [roz'lɛ], *n.m.* (*Comm.*) Ermine.

roselière [rozə'ljɛːr], *n.f.* Reed-bed.

roséole [roze'ɔl], *n.f.* Roseola, scarlet rash; German measles.

roser [ro'ze], *v.t.* To rose; to give a roseate tint to; to make pink.

roseraie, *n.f.* Rosery, rose garden.

rosette, *n.f.* Small rose; bow; rosette; rose-shaped object, tool, etc.; pink ink; red chalk; rose-copper; (*Paint.*) roset.

rosier, *n.m.* Rose-tree, rose-bush.

rosière, *n.f.* Rose-queen (maiden awarded a chaplet of roses); virtuous maiden; queen of the May. **rosiériste**, *n.m.* Rose-grower.

rosir, *v.i.* To blush, to go pink.—*v.t.* To turn rosy.

rossard [rɔ'saːr], *n.m.* (*pop.*) Jade; (*fig.*) scamp, ne'er-do-well.

rosse [rɔs], *n.f.* Jade, screw; broken-down hack; (*fig.*) worthless person.—*a.* Bad, malicious. *Chanson rosse*, nasty song; *pièce rosse*, cynical play; *un professeur, un patron rosse*, a perfect beast of a master (boss).

rosserie [rɔ'sri], *n.f.* Nasty, malicious, catty word or trick.

rossée [rɔ'se], *n.f.* Shower of blows, thrashing.

rosser [rɔ'se], *v.t.* (*colloq.*) To belabour, to thrash, to give a drubbing to.

rossignol [rɔsi'nɔl], *n.m.* Nightingale; pick-lock, skeleton key; whistle; flute (made of bark); old organ-stop imitating nightingale; (*Carp.*) wedge; (*fig.*) unsaleable article (in a shop). *Rossignol d'Arcadie*, braying jackass.

rossinante [rɔsi'nãːt], *n.f.* Sorry horse etc.; Don Quixote's horse, Rosinante.

rossolis [rɔsɔ'li], *n.m.* Rosolio (variety of liqueur); sundew (plant).

rostral [rɔs'tral], *a.* (*fem.* **-ale**, *pl.* **-aux**) Rostral (column).

rostre [rɔstr], *n.m.* Rostrum. **rostré**, *a.* (*fem.* **-ée**) Rostrate. **rostrifère**, *a.* Rostriferous. **rostriforme**, *a.* Rostriform.

rot [ro], *n.m.* (*pop.*) Belch, eructation. *Faire un rot*, to belch.

rôt [ro], *n.m.* Roast, roast meat; first course.

rotacé [rɔta'se], *a.* (*fem.* **-ée**) (*Bot.*) Rotate.

rotang [ROTIN].

rotarien [rɔta'rjɛ̃], *n.m.* Member of a Rotary Club.

rotateur [rɔta'tœːr], *a.* (*fem.* **-trice**) (*Anat.*) Rotatory.—*n.m.* (*Anat.*) Rotator; (*Zool.*) rotifer. **rotative**, *n.f.* Rotary printing-press.

rotation, *n.f.* Rotation; rolling (of body) in swimming. **rotatoire**, *a.* Rotatory.

rote [rɔt], *n.f.* (*R.-C. Ch.*) Rota.

roter [rɔ'te], *v.i.* To belch. (*pop.*) *En roter*, to be angry, flabbergasted.

rôti [ro'ti], *n.m.* Roast, roast meat. *Il ne faut pas s'endormir sur le rôti*, (*prov.*) we must have our wits about us. **rôtie**, *n.f.* Slice of toast. *Rôtie à l'anglaise*, Welsh rarebit; *rôtie beurrée*, buttered toast; *rôtie sans beurre*, dry toast.

rotifère [roti'fɛːr], *n.m.* (*Zool.*) Rotifer, wheel-animalcule. **rotiforme**, *a.* (*Zool.*) Wheel-shaped.

rotin [rɔ'tɛ̃] or **rotang**, *n.m.* Rattan, rattan-cane. *Chaise en rotin*, cane chair; (*fam.*) *il n'a pas un rotin*, he's penniless.

rôtir [ro'tiːr], *v.t., v.i.* To roast; to broil; to toast (bread etc.); (*fig.*) to burn, to parch. *N'être bon ni à rôtir ni à bouillir*, to be fit for nothing.

rôtissage, *n.m.* Roasting.

rôtisserie, *n.f.* Cook-shop, roasting-shop.

rôtisseur, *n.m.* (*fem.* **-euse**) Cook-shop keeper, roasting specialist.

rôtissoire, *n.f.* Roaster, Dutch oven. *Rôtissoire électronique*, electronic spit-roaster.

rotonde [rɔ'tɔ̃ːd], *n.f.* Rotunda; boot (of a diligence); long sleeveless cloak.

rotondité, *n.f.* Rotundity, roundness; plumpness.

rotor [rɔ'tɔr], *n.m.* Rotor.

rotule [rɔ'tyl], *n.f.* (*Anat.*) Patella, knee-cap. **rotulien**, *a.* (*fem.* **-ienne**) Patellar.

roture [rɔ'tyr], *n.f.* Plebeian condition, roture. **roturier**, *a.* (*fem.* **-ière**) Plebeian, of mean birth; vulgar, mean.—*n.* Commoner, roturier.

rouable [rwabl], *n.m.* Baker's fire-rake.

rouage [rwaːʒ], *n.m.* Wheelwork, wheels; cog-wheel; machinery; (*Horol.*) movement.

rouan [rwɑ̃], *a.* (*fem.* **rouanne** (1)) Roan (of horses, cattle, etc.).—*n.m.* Roan horse.

rouanne (2) [rwan], *n.f.* Brand, marking-iron; gouge; auger, wimble. **rouanner**, *v.t.* To mark (with a *rouanne*); to pierce with an auger. **rouannette**, *n.f.* Small *rouanne*.

roublard [ru'blaːr], *a.* (*fem.* **-e**) (*fam.*) Knowing, sharp.

roublarder, *v.i.* To be cunning or sharp.

roublardise, *n.f.* Foxiness; cunning trick.

rouble [rubl], *n.m.* Rouble (Russian coin).

roucou [ROCOU]. **roucouyer** [ROCOUYER].

roucoulement [rukul′mã], *n.m.* Cooing; gurgling (of babies).

roucouler, *v.i.*, *v.t.* To coo.

roue [ru], *n.f.* Wheel; paddle-wheel; wheel for torture. *Faire la roue,* to spread (out) his tail (of peacocks etc.); to turn cartwheels; to strut, to show off; *mettre à la roue,* to put to the rack; *mettre* or *jeter des bâtons dans les roues,* to put spokes into the wheel (of); *pousser à la roue,* to put one's shoulder to the wheel; *roue hydraulique,* water-wheel; *roue libre,* free wheel (bicycle); *roue voilée,* buckled wheel.

roué [rwe], *a.* (*fem.* **-ée**) Cunning, sharp, artful; exhausted, broken down. *Être roué de fatigue,* to be worn out.—*n.m.* Roué, rake, profligate; trickster.

rouelle [rwɛl], *n.f.* Round slice (meat). *Rouelle de citron,* slice of lemon; *rouelle de veau,* fillet of veal.

rouennais [rwa′nɛ], *a.* and *n.* (*fem.* **-aise**) Inhabitant, native of Rouen; originating from Rouen.

rouennerie [rwan′ri], *n.f.* Coarse printed cotton, cotton print, Rouen goods. **rouennier,** *n.m.* (*fem.* **-ière**) Cotton-printer; seller of cotton print.

rouer [rwe], *v.t.* To break upon the wheel; to crush with fatigue etc.; to jade. *Rouer de coups,* to beat unmercifully; *rouer un câble,* to coil a cable.

rouerie [ru′ri], *n.f.* Piece of knavery, trick, dodge, sharp practice, trickery.

rouet [rwɛ], *n.m.* Spinning-wheel; wheel in an old flint-lock; (*Naut.*) sheave.

rouette [rwɛt], *n.f.* Osier-band (of a faggot).

rouf [ruf] or **roufle,** *n.m.* (*Naut.*) Deckhouse.

rouflaquette [rufla′kɛt], *n.f.* (*pop.*) Lock of hair on temple, 'Newgate knocker'.

rouge [ru:ʒ], *a.* Red, red-hot; bloodshot; (*fam.*) liberal, left-wing, communist.—*n.m.* Red colour; rouge; redness, blush; (*pop.*) red wine; distemper (disease of animals); (*fam.*) liberal, left-winger, communist.—*adv.* Se fâcher tout rouge, to get downright angry; *voir rouge,* to see red.

rougeâtre, *a.* Reddish.

rougeaud, *a.* (*fem.* **-aude**) (*colloq.*) Red-faced, ruddy.—*n.* Red-faced person.

rouge-gorge, *n.m.* (*pl.* **rouges-gorges**) Redbreast, robin redbreast.

rougeole, *n.f.* Measles; field cow-wheat.

rougeoyer, *v.i. irr.* (*conjug. like* ABOYER) To turn red; to glow.

rouge-queue, *n.m.* (*pl.* **rouges-queues**) Redstart.

rouget, *a.* (*fem.* **-ette**) Reddish.—*n.m.* (*Ichth.*) Red mullet, surmullet; (*Vet.*) swine-fever; (*Ent.*) harvest-bug [TROMBIDION].

rougeur, *n.f.* Redness; flush, glow, colour, blush; (*pl.*) inflamed, red spots on skin; blotches. *La rougeur lui est montée au visage,* the colour came into her cheeks.

rougir, *v.t.* To redden, to tinge with red.—*v.i.* To redden, to grow red, to colour, to blush, (*fig.*) to be ashamed. *Eau rougie,* wine with water; *faire rougir,* to make blush, to put to shame; *rougir de honte,* to blush with shame; *rougir jusqu'au blanc des yeux,* to colour up to the eyes.

roui [rwi], *n.m.* Steeping, soaking, retting of flax; fustiness. *Sentir le roui,* to have a rancid taste.

rouille [ru:j], *n.f.* Rust, rustiness; flaw (in a mirror); (*Agric.*) mildew, blight, blast. *Ces fromens sont chargés de rouille,* this wheat is mildewed; *la rouille mange le fer,* rust corrodes iron.

rouillé, *a.* (*fem.* **-ée**) Rusty; blighted (of corn).

rouiller, *v.t.*, *v.i.* To rust, to make rusty; to blight; to impair. **se rouiller,** *v.r.* To rust, to grow rusty; to be impaired; (*fig.*) to get rusty, to get out of practice.

rouilleux, *a.* (*fem.* **-euse**) Rust-coloured.

rouillure, *n.f.* Rustiness; (*Agric.*) rust.

rouir [rwi:r], *v.t.* To steep, to soak, to ret.

rouissage, *n.m.* Steeping, retting.

rouissoir [ROUTOIR].

roulade [ru′lad], *n.f.* Roll, rolling down; (*Mus.*) roulade, trill, shake.

roulage, *n.m.* Rolling; haulage, carriage (in wagons etc.); wagon-office; road traffic. *Voiture de roulage,* goods-wagon, dray.

roulant [ru′lã], *a.* (*fem.* **-ante**) Rolling; travelling (crane); easy (of roads); (*Surg.*) moving (of veins); (*Print.*) at work; (*slang*) funny, screamingly funny. *Feu roulant,* (*Mil.*) running fire; *escalier roulant,* escalator; *fonds roulant,* working capital; *matériel roulant,* rolling-stock; *trottoir roulant,* moving stairway, escalator.

rouleau, *n.m.* (*pl.* **-eaux**) Roll; roller; rolling-pin; twist (tobacco); coil (rope); scroll. *Être au bout de son rouleau,* to be at the end of one's tether; *mettre* or *plier en rouleau,* to roll up; *passer le gazon au rouleau,* to roll the grass; *rouleau à pâtisserie,* rolling-pin; *rouleau compresseur,* steam-roller; *rouleau d'imprimeur,* printer's roller.

roulée, *n.f.* (*pop.*) Thrashing, drubbing.

roulement [rul′mã], *n.m.* Rolling, roll; rumbling, rattle, etc.; rotation. *Bande de roulement,* tread (of tyre); *faire un roulement de tambour,* to beat a roll of the drum; *fonds de roulement,* cash in hand, floating capital; (*Av.*) *longueur de roulement au départ,* length of take-off; *par roulement,* in rotation; *roulement à billes,* ball-bearing; *roulement de fonds,* circulation of capital; *roulement d'yeux,* rolling of the eyes.

rouler [ru′le], *v.t.* To roll; to roll up; to wind up; to lead, to pass (one's life etc.); to revolve, to turn over in one's mind; (*colloq.*) to take in, to cheat. (*Golf*) *Coup roulé,* putt; *je l'ai roulé,* I diddled him; *rouler carrosse,* to keep a carriage.—*v.i.* To roll, to roll along, to revolve, to drive, to ride (*en*), to ramble, to wander; to keep going; to be plentiful. *La conversation roula sur ce sujet,* the conversation turned upon this subject; *pierre qui roule n'amasse pas mousse,* a rolling stone gathers no moss; *rouler sur l'or,* to be rolling in money; *tout roule là-dessus,* everything turns upon that. **se rouler,** *v.r.* To roll, to turn over and over; to tumble, to wallow; (*fam.*) to split with laughter.

roulette [ru′lɛt], *n.f.* Small wheel; roller, castor, truckle, trundle; bath-chair; roulette (game). *Tout marche comme sur des roulettes,* everything is going swimmingly; *lit à roulettes,* bedstead on castors; *patins à roulettes,* roller-skates; *roulette à patrons* tracing-wheel; *roulette de relieur*, book-binder's fillet.

rouleur, *a.* (*fem.* **-euse**) Rolling.—*n.m.* Travelling journeyman; vine-fretter, vine-grub; (*Naut.*) rolling vessel. *Rouleur de cabarets*, pub-crawler.—*n.f.* Leaf-roller (caterpillar).

roulier, *n.m.* Wagoner, carter, carrier.—*a.* Carrying (trade).

roulière [ru'ljɛ:r], *n.f.* Wagoner's smock.

roulis, *n.m.* Rolling, roll (waves or ships), lurch.

rouloir, *n.m.* Rolling-board (for candles); roller, cylinder.

roulotte, *n.f.* Gipsy-van; (*Motor.*) caravan; (*Am.*) trailer.

roulure, *n.f.* Rolling; disease of trees causing splitting; (*slang*) trollop.

roumain [ru'mɛ̃], *a.* and *n.* (*fem.* **-aine**) Rumanian.

Roumanie [ruma'ni], *f.* Rumania.

roumi [ru'mi], *n.m.* Christian (for the Arabs).

roupie (1) [ru'pi], *n.f.* Rupee.

roupie (2) [ru'pi], *n.f.* Snivel, drop (at end of nose). (*fam.*) *C'est de la roupie de sansonnet* (or *de singe*), it is not worth a dime. **roupieux**, *a.* (*fem.* **-ieuse**) Snivelly, snivelling.

roupiller [rupi'je], *v.i.* (*colloq.*) To doze, to snooze.

roupilleur, *n.m.* (*fem.* **-euse**) Dozer, snoozer.

rouquin [ru'kɛ̃], *a.* (*fem.* **-ine**) (*pop.*) Ginger-haired, carroty-haired.—*n.* Ginger, Carrots.

rouscailler [ruska'je], *v.i.* (*pop.*) [ROUSPÉTER].

rouscailleur, *n.m.* [ROUSPÉTEUR].

rouspétance [ruspe'tã:s], *n.f.* (*fam.*) Protestations, protesting; refractoriness. *Pas de rouspétance!* Don't argue!

rouspéter, *v.i. irr.* (*conjugated like* ACCÉLÉRER) To protest, to resist; to be refractory.

rouspéteur, *n.m.* (*fem.* **-euse**) Refractory person; quarrelsome person.

roussâtre [ru'sɑ:tr], *a.* Reddish, russet.

rousse (1) [rus] [ROUX].

rousse (2), *n.f.* (*slang*) Police [*see also* ROUSSER].

rousseau, *n.m.* (*pl.* **-eaux**) (*pop.*) Red-haired fellow.

rousselet [rus'lɛ], *n.m.* Russet pear.

rousser [ru'se], *v.i.* (*pop.*) or *faire de la rousse*, to grumble, to grouse; to resist.

rousserolle [rus'rɔl], *n.f.* Great sedge-warbler.

roussette, *n.f.* Lesser spotted dog-fish; flying fox (bat); wood-warbler; fritter.

rousseur, *n.f.* Redness. *Tache de rousseur*, freckle.

roussi (1) [ru'si], *n.m.* Burnt smell; burning, smell of burning.—*a.* Browned, scorched.

roussi (2) [ru'si], *n.m.* Russia leather.

roussin [ru'sɛ̃], *n.m.* Cob (thick-set horse); (*slang*) police-spy. *Roussin d'Arcadie*, jackass, Jerusalem pony.

roussir [ru'si:r], *v.t., v.i.* To redden; to singe, to scorch. *Faire roussir*, to brown (meat etc.).

roussissage or **roussissement**, *n.m.* Reddening; browning; scorching.

rouster [rus'te] or **roster**, *v.t.* (*Naut.*) To woold. **rousture** or **rosture**, *n.f.* Woolding.

roustir [rus'ti:r], *v.t.* (*pop.*) To do (someone) brown; to spoil (a thing).

roustissure, *n.f.* Thing or person of no value, trash.

routage [ru'ta:ʒ], *n.m.* Sorting (of letters).

route [rut], *n.f.* Road, way; route, direction, path, course; track, course, way (of a ship etc.). *Faire fausse route*, to take the wrong road, or (*fig.*) a wrong step, (*Naut.*) to be off course; *faire route pour*, to make for, to sail to; *feuille de route*, (*Mil.*) route, marching-orders; *grande route*, highway; *il est en route*, he is on his way; *il est resté en route*, he remained behind; *mettre le moteur en route*, to start up the engine; *on lui a tracé sa route*, his course is marked out for him; *prendre la route de*, to go in the direction of; *route aérienne*, air-lane; *route principale*, main road, high road; (*Am.*) pike; *se mettre en route*, to set out.

router [ru'te], *v.t.* To sort (letters).

routier (1), *n.m.* Track chart, road-book; one used to the roads; lorry-driver; (*fig.*) old hand; mercenary soldier in the Middle Ages; road racer (cyclist). *Restaurant de routiers*, transport café; *vieux routier*, old stager.

routier (2), *a.* (*fem.* **-ière**) Of roads. *Carte routière*, road-map; (*bicyclette*) *routière*, road-ster.

routine [ru'tin], *n.f.* Routine, habit, practice. *Par routine*, out of habit, by rote.

routiner, *v.t.* To teach by routine; to accustom.

routinier, *a.* (*fem.* **-ière**) Routine, following a routine.—*n.* Routineer, person following a routine, stick-in-the-mud.

routoir [ru'twa:r], *n.m.* Retting-pond, retting-pit.

rouverin or **rouverain** [ru'vrɛ̃], *a.m.* (*Metal.*) Brittle, red-short.

rouvieux or **roux-vieux** [ru'vjø], *n.m.* Mange. —*a.m. inv.* Mangy (horse, dog).

rouvre [ru:vr] or **roure**, *n.m.* Austrian oak.

rouvrir [ru'vri:r], *v.i., v.t.* To reopen.

roux [ru], *a.* (*fem.* **rousse**) Reddish, reddish-brown; red-haired, sandy. *Lune rousse*, April moon; *vent roux*, cold, dry wind.—*n.* Red-haired or sandy person.—*n.m.* Reddish colour; brown sauce.

roux-vieux [ROUVIEUX].

royal [rwa'jal], *a.* (*fem.* **-ale**, *pl.* **-aux**) Royal; regal, kingly, kinglike; (*Mil. slang*) **le Royal Cambouis* or *les Royaux*, Army Service Corps.

royalement, *adv.* Royally; regally, in a kingly manner. **royalisme**, *n.m.* Royalism. **royaliste**, *a.* and *n.* Royalist.

royaume [rwa'jo:m], *n.m.* Kingdom, realm. *Le Royaume-Uni*, the United Kingdom.

royauté, *n.f.* Royalty. *Abdiquer la royauté*, to abdicate the throne; *les insignes de la royauté*, the regalia.

ru [ry], *n.m.* Channel (of small stream).

ruade [rɥad], *n.f.* Kick (by horse etc.); lashing out.

rubace [ry'bas], **rubacelle**, or **rubicelle**, *n.f.* Rubicel (ruby).

ruban [ry'bã], *n.m.* Ribbon; (*fig.*) strip, border; band; tape(s). *Porter le ruban rouge*, to wear the ribbon of the Legion of Honour; *ruban-d'eau* (*pl. rubans-d'eau*), reed-grass; *ruban de fil*, tape; *ruban roulant*, conveyor-belt. **rubanaire** or **rubaneux**, *a.* (*fem.* **-euse**) Ribbon-like. **rubané**, *a.* (*fem.* **-ée**) Covered with ribbons. *Canon rubané*, gun-barrel made of narrow bands of steel.

rubaner, *v.t.* To trim with ribbons; to cut into ribbons or ribbon-like strips; to roll (iron) into strips for making guns. **rubane-rie,** *n.f.* Ribbon-weaving; ribbon-trade.

rubanier, *a.* (*fem.* **-ière**) Pertaining to ribbons. *Industrie rubanière,* ribbon-manufacture; ribbon-trade.—*n.* Ribbon-maker or -vendor.

rubéfaction [rybefak'sjɔ̃], *n.f.* Rubefaction.

rubéfiant, *a.* and *n.m.* (*fem.* **-ante**) Rubefacient.

rubéfier, *v.t.* To rubefy; to cause redness (of skin).

rubéole [rybe'ɔl], *n.f.* Rubeola, German measles.

rubescent [rybɛ'sɑ̃], *a.* (*fem.* **-ente**) Reddish; growing red.

rubiacé [rybja'se], *a.* (*fem.* **-ée**) (*Bot.*) Rubiaceous.—*n.f. pl.* Rubia (plants of the madder family).

rubican [rybi'kɑ̃], *a.m.* Black or bay horse flecked with white.

Rubicon [rybi'kɔ̃], *m.* The Rubicon. *Franchir* or *passer le Rubicon,* to cross the Rubicon.

rubicond [rybi'kɔ̃], *a.* (*fem.* **-onde**) Rubicund.

rubigineux, *a.* (*fem.* **-euse**) Rubiginous.

rubis [ry'bi], *n.m. inv.* Ruby; (*fig.*) red pimple, grog-blossom. *Faire rubis sur l'ongle,* to drink to the last drop; *monté sur rubis,* jewelled; *payer rubis sur l'ongle,* to pay to the last farthing [*see* BALAIS].

rubrique [ry'brik], *n.f.* Red chalk, ruddle; (*pl.*) rubric; (*fig.*) head, heading (of article), title; practice; *(fam.)* tricks, tips, wrinkles. *Sous la rubrique,* under the heading.

ruche [ryʃ], *n.f.* Hive; (*Needlework*) frilling, ruche. *Ruche d'abeilles,* bee-hive; *ruche à cadres,* frame hive. **ruchée,** *n.f.* Hiveful.

rucher (1), *n.m.* Stand or shed for bees; apiary.

rucher (2), *v.t.* (*Needlework*) To ruche, to frill.

rude [ryd], *a.* Harsh, rough, uneven, rugged; disagreeable, grating; violent, impetuous, boisterous; severe, rigid, strict; rude, uncouth, unpolished; churlish, unkind; hard, troublesome, arduous, difficult. *Avoir la peau rude,* to have a rough skin; *avoir la voix rude,* to have a harsh voice; *chemin rude,* rugged road; *des manières rudes,* coarse, uncouth manners; *les temps sont rudes,* times are hard; *une rude épreuve,* a severe trial; *un rude assaut,* a fierce assault. **rudement,** *adv.* Roughly ruggedly, harshly, severely, violently, rudely; (*pop.*) awfully, jolly, very. *Aller rudement en besogne,* to work with a vengeance; *c'est rudement chic de sa part,* it is jolly decent of him; *traiter rudement,* to treat roughly.

rudenté [rydɑ̃'te], *a.* (*fem.* **-ée**) (*Arch.*) Cabled (of columns). **rudenture,** *n.f.* Cabling.

rudesse [ry'dɛs], *n.f.* Roughness, coarseness, ruggedness, uncouthness, primitiveness (of manners, life); harshness; severity, austerity; unkindness; rudeness, ungentle action. *Traiter quelqu'un avec rudesse,* to browbeat someone; to give someone the rough edge of one's tongue.

rudiment [rydi'mɑ̃], *n.m.* Rudiment; primer; (*pl.*) rudiments (of knowledge). **rudimentaire,** *a.* Rudimentary.

rudoiement [rydwa'mɑ̃], *n.m.* Bullying, browbeating, rough treatment.

rudoyer [rydwa'je], *v.t. irr.* (*conjugated like* ABOYER) To treat roughly or harshly; to bully, to ill-treat.

rue (1) [ry], *n.f.* Street. *Courir les rues,* to run about the streets, (*fig.*) to be in everybody's mouth (of news), to be very common; *descendre dans la rue,* to start street-fighting; *grande rue, grand-rue,* high street, main street; *rue écartée,* back street.

rue (2) [ry], *n.f.* Rue (plant). *Rue de chèvre,* goat's-rue; *rue de muraille,* wall-rue.

ruée [rɥe], *n.f.* Rush; onslaught. *La ruée vers l'or,* the gold-rush.

ruelle [rɥɛl], *n.f.* Lane, alley; right-of-way; *space between bedside and wall.

ruer [rɥe], *v.t.* *To fling, to hurl.—*v.i.* To kick (of horses etc.). *Ruer dans les brancards,* to kick over the traces; to jib. **se ruer,** *v.r.* To throw oneself, to rush (*sur*). *Les spectateurs se ruèrent vers la sortie,* there was a stampede of spectators towards the exit.

rueur, *a.* (*fem.* **-euse**) Given to kicking.—*n.* Kicker.

rugby [ryg'bi], *n.m.* Rugby football, rugger. **rugbyman,** *n.m.* (*pl.* **rugbymen**) Rugby player.

rugine [ry'ʒin], *n.f.* (*Surg.*) Raspatory, xyster; scaler (of dentist).

ruginer, *v.t.* To scrape (bone); to scale (teeth).

rugir [ry'ʒiːr], *v.i.* To roar, to bellow. **rugissant,** *a.* (*fem.* **-ante**) Roaring. **rugissement,** *n.m.* Roaring, roar.

rugosité [rygozi'te], *n.f.* Rugosity, roughness, unevenness; corrugation, wrinkle. **rugueux,** *a.* (*fem.* **-euse**) Rugose, rough, uneven; wrinkled.—*n.m.* (*Artill.*) Striker.

ruilée [rɥi'le], *n.f.* (*Arch.*) Plaster or mortar laid between roof and wall.

ruine [rɥin], *n.f.* Ruin; decay, decline; overthrow, destruction, downfall. *Courir à sa ruine,* to go to one's ruin; *sortir de ses ruines,* to rise from its ruins; *tomber en ruines,* to fall into ruins, to go to (w)rack and ruin.

ruiner, *v.t.* To ruin, to lay waste; to overthrow, to destroy; to spoil. **se ruiner,** *v.r.* To ruin oneself; to go to ruin, to fall into decay. *Se ruiner la santé,* to ruin one's health.

ruineux, *a.* (*fem.* **-euse**) Ruinous.

ruinure [rɥi'nyːr], *n.f.* (*Carp.*) Notch, nick, etc. (in joists for securing hold on stonework etc.).

ruisseau [rɥi'so], *n.m.* (*pl.* **-eaux**) Brook, stream, rivulet; gutter, runnel, *street-kennel. *Les petits ruisseaux font les grandes rivières,* many a mickle makes a muckle.

ruisselant, *a.* (*fem.* **-ante**) Streaming, dripping, running, very wet.

ruisseler, *v.i.* To stream, to run down, to be streaming or very wet (*de*).

ruisselet, *n.m.* Rivulet, brooklet, rill, streamlet.

rumb or **rhumb** [rɔ̃:b], *n.m.* Rhumb. *Rumb du vent,* air-line.

rumen [ry'mɛn], *n.m.* Rumen, paunch.

rumeur [ry'mœːr], *n.f.* Confused noise; clamour, uproar; (*fig.*) report, rumour. *Si l'on en croit la rumeur publique,* if the rumours are to be believed.

ruminant [rymi'nɑ̃], *a.* (*fem.* **-ante**) Ruminant, ruminating.—*n.m.* Ruminant.

rumination, *n.f.* Rumination (chewing the cud).

ruminer [rymi'ne], *v.i.* To ruminate, to chew the cud; (*fig.*) to ponder, to muse.—*v.t.* To ruminate; (*fig.*) to think over, to muse over. *Que ruminez-vous là?* what are you turning over in your mind?

runes [ryn], *n.f. pl.* Runes (runic characters). **runique**, *a.* Runic.

ruolz [ry'ɔlʒ], *n.m.* Electro-plated ware.

rupestre [ry'pɛstr], *a.* (*Bot.*) Rupestral.

rupin [ry'pɛ̃], *a.* and *n.* (*pop.*) Rich, smart, well dressed. *Les rupins*, the nobs, the toffs.

rupiner [rypi'ne], *v.i.* (*sch. slang*) To do well.

rupture [ryp'ty:r], *n.f.* Break, breaking, rupture; separation; abrogation; annulment; hernia; (*Paint.*) mixing of colours. *En rupture de ban*, breaking bounds; *ils en sont venus à une rupture*, all is at an end between them; *rupture de contrat*, breach of contract; *rupture des négociations*, breaking off of negotiations; *rupture d'équilibre*, upsetting the balance; *rupture d'un mariage*, the breaking off of a match.

rural [ry'ral], *a.* (*fem.* **-ale**, *pl.* **-aux**) Rural, rustic, country.—*n. Les ruraux*, country-people; rustics.

ruse [ry:z], *n.f.* Guile, craft, cunning; trick, wile, ruse, dodge; (*Hunt.*) double. *Ruse de guerre*, stratagem of war; *user de ruses*, to practise deceit.

rusé, *a.* (*fem.* **-ée**) Artful, crafty, sly.—*n.* Such a person. *Un rusé matois*, a knowing card.

ruser, *v.i.* To use deceit, craft, or guile; (*Hunt.*) to double.

russe [rys], *a.* Russian.—*n.* (**Russe**) A Russian. *Chaussettes russes*, (*Mil. slang*) bands (or rags) of cloth to wrap the feet.

Russie [ry'si], *f.* Russia.

russifier [rysi'fje], *v.t.* To Russify.

rustaud [rys'to], *a.* Rustic, boorish, uncouth. —*n.* Rustic, clodhopper.

rusticité [rystisi'te], *n.f.* Rusticity, simplicity; hardiness (of plant).

rustique, *a.* Rustic, rural; artless, homely, simple; hardy (of plant).—*n.m.* Rustic genre etc. **rustiquement**, *adv.* Rustically; boorishly, uncouthly.

rustiquer, *v.t.* (*Arch.*) To make (masonry etc.) rustic.

rustre, *a.* Boorish, loutish, clownish, rude.— *n.m.* Boor, clown, churl, lout.

rusturer [ROUSTER].

rut [ry], *n.m.* Rut, rutting (of deer etc.). *Être en rut*, to rut.

rutabaga [rytaba'ga], *n.m.* Swede, Swedish turnip.

rutilant [ryti'lɑ̃], *a.* (*fem.* **-ante**) Glowing, gleaming, rutilant. **rutiler**, *v.i.* To glow, to gleam (red).

rythme [ritm], *n.m.* Rhythm. **rythmé**, *a.* (*fem.* **-ée**) Rhythmical; having well-marked beats. **rythmer**, *v.t.* To punctuate; to put rhythm into. **rythmique**, *a.* Rhythmical.

S

S, s [ɛs], *n.m.* or *f.* The nineteenth letter of the alphabet. *Faire des S*, to go in zigzag fashion; *en S*, S-shaped; *un crochet en S*, an S-shaped hook.

s', contraction of SE.

sa [sa], *a.f.* [SON (1)].

Saba [sa'ba], *f.* Sheba.

sabbat [sa'ba], *n.m.* Sabbath (seventh day of week among Jews); nocturnal meeting or nightly revels (of witches); (*fig.*) racket, uproar, tumult, scolding. *Faire un sabbat (de tous les diables)*, to kick up a shindy; *sabbat de chats*, caterwauling. **sabbataire**, *n.m.* Sabbatarian; Seventh-day Baptist. **sabbatique**, *a.* Sabbatical (of years). **sabbatisme**, *n.m.* Sabbatism, sabbatarianism.

sabéen [sabe'ɛ̃], *a.* (*fem.* **-éenne**) Sabaean. **sabéisme**, *n.m.* Sabaism.

sabellianisme [sabɛlja'nism], *n.m.* Sabellianism. **sabellien**, *a.* (*fem.* **-ienne**) Sabellian.

sabin [sa'bɛ̃], *a.* (*fem.* **sabine** (1)) Sabine.— *n.m.* (**Sabin**, *fem.* **Sabine**) A Sabine.

sabine (2) [sa'bin], *n.f.* Savin.

Sabine [sa'bin], *f.* Sabina.

sable (1) [sa:bl], *n.m.* Sand; gravel.

sable (2) [sa:bl], *n.m.* (*Zool.* and *Her.*) Sable.

sablé [sa'ble], *a.* (*fem.* **-ée**) Laid or covered with sand, sanded. *Allée sablée*, gravel-walk; *galette sablée*, shortbread.—*n.m.* Shortbread biscuit.

sabler, *v.t.* To sand, to gravel; (*fig.*) to drink off. *Sabler le champagne*, to celebrate in champagne.

sableux, *a.* (*fem.* **-euse**) Sandy.

sablier, *n.m.* Sandman, dealer in sand; sandglass, hour-glass; sand-box (for drying ink etc.); egg-timer.

sablière, *n.f.* Sand-pit; gravel-pit; sand-box (of locomotive); (*Carp.*) raising-piece; (*Arch.*) wall-plate.

sablon, *n.m.* Fine sand, scouring sand.

sablonner, *v.t.* To scour with sand.

sablonneux, *a.* (*fem.* **-euse**) Sandy, gritty.

sablonnier, *n.m.* Dealer in sand.

sablonnière, *n.f.* Sand-pit.

sabord [sa'bɔ:r], *n.m.* (*Naut.*) Port-hole; (square) port. *Sabord de charge*, cargo-door.

sabordage or **sabordement**, *n.m.* Scuttling.

saborder, *v.t.* To scuttle.

sabot [sa'bo], *n.m.* Sabot, clog, wooden shoe; hoof (of horse etc.); shoe, skid, drag (of carriages); slipper-bath, or other sabot-shaped utensil; socket (in furniture etc.); whip-top (play-thing); (*Conch.*) turban shell; (*fam.*) any bad, worn-out article (old crock, old tub, sorry fiddle, etc.); a bad worker, a bungler. *Dormir comme un sabot*, to sleep like a top; *sabot de Vénus*, (*pop.*) lady's-slipper, cypripedium.

sabotage, *n.m.* Wooden-shoe making; (*fig.*) sabotage (wilful destruction of property etc.).

saboter, *v.t.* To arm (a stake) with iron; (*colloq.*) to bungle, to botch; to garble, tc damage wilfully, to sabotage.

saboteur, *n.m.* (*fem.* **-euse**) Bungler; (wartime) person engaged in sabotage, saboteur.

sabotier, *n.m.* (*fem.* **sabotière** (1)) Sabot maker.

sabotière (2), *n.f.* Dance in wooden shoes; wooden-shoe shop; slipper-bath.

sabouler [sabu'le], *v.t.* (*fam.*) To push about, to jostle, to hustle; (*fig.*) to scold, to rate, to haul over the coals.

sabre [sa:br], *n.m.* Sabre; broadsword. *Sabre au clair*, drawn sword; with drawn swords.

sabre-baïonnette, *n.m.* (*pl.* **sabres-baïonnettes**) Sword-bayonet.

sabrer, *v.t.* To strike or cut with a sabre, to sabre; (*colloq.*) to hurry over, to botch; to make drastic (*or sometimes* undiscerning cuts) in a MS. *Sabrer un travail,* to scamp a job; *sabrer une pièce de théâtre,* to make drastic cuts in a play.

sabretache, *n.f.* Sabretache.

sabreur, *n.m.* Swashbuckler; (*colloq.*), botcher. *Beau sabreur,* dashing cavalry soldier.

saburral [saby'ral], *a.* (*fem.* **-ale,** *pl.* **-aux**) Saburral. **saburre,** *n.f.* (*Old Med.*) Saburra, foulness of the stomach.

sac (1) [sak], *n.m.* Sack, bag; sackcloth; poke-net; pouch (of certain animals); (*Surg.*) sac; (*pop.*) stomach, belly. *Sac (de soldat),* pack, knapsack, kitbag; *sac à dos* or *sac tyrolien,* rucksack; *sac (en) bandoulière,* shoulder-bag; *sac de couchage,* sleeping-bag; *sac à main,* hand-bag; *sac de nuit* or *de voyage,* travelling bag. *Avoir le sac,* (*slang*) to be rich; *emplir son sac,* (*pop.*) to fill one's belly; *homme de sac et de corde* [CORDE]; *l'affaire est dans le sac,* it's as good as done, it's in the bag; *mets ça dans ton sac!* Put that in your pipe and smoke it! *prendre quelqu'un la main dans le sac,* to catch someone red-handed; *sac à papier!* hang it! *sac à vin,* drunkard; *sac percé,* prodigal, spendthrift; *vider son sac,* to have one's say, to unbosom oneself; *voir le fond du sac* [FOND].

sac (2) [sak], *n.m.* Sack (plunder); sacking, pillage. *Mettre une ville à sac,* to sack a town.

saccade [sa'kad], *n.f.* Jerk, jolt. *Par saccades,* by fits and starts, jerkily.

saccadé, *a.* (*fem.* **-ée**) Jerky, broken, abrupt, irregular. *Style saccadé,* jerky style; *voix saccadée,* staccato voice.

saccader, *v.t.* To jerk.

saccage [sa'ka:ʒ], *n.m.* Upset, confusion; pillage.

saccagement [sakaʒ'mã], *n.m.* Sacking, pillaging.

saccager [saka'ʒe], *v.t.* To sack, to plunder; (*fig.*) to play havoc with, to throw into confusion.

saccageur [saka'ʒœ:r], *n.m.* (*fem.* **-euse**) Sacker, ravager, ransacker.

saccharate [saka'rat], *n.m.* Saccharate.

sacchareux, *a.* (*fem.* **-euse**) Saccharine.

saccharifère, *a.* Sacchariferous.

saccharifier, *v.t.* To saccharify.

saccharimètre, *n.m.* Saccharimeter.

saccharin, *a.* (*fem.* **saccharine**) Saccharine. —*n.f.* Saccharine.

saccharique, *a.* Saccharic.

saccharisme, *n.m.* Saccharism.

saccharoïde, *a.* Saccharoid.

saccharose, *n.m.* Saccharose.

sacciforme [saksi'fɔrm], *a.* (*Bot.*) Sacciform (bagged).

sacerdoce [saser'dɔs], *n.m.* Priesthood.

sacerdotal, *a.* (*fem.* **-ale,** *pl.* **-aux**) Sacerdotal. ***sacerdotalisme,** *n.m.* Sacerdotalism.

sachée [sa'ʃe], *n.f.* Sackful, bagful.

sachem [sa'ʃɛm], *n.m.* Sachem (Indian chief).

sachet [sa'ʃɛ], *n.m.* Small bag (of various kinds); sachet.

sacoche [sa'kɔʃ], *n.f.* (*Mil.*) Saddle-bag; satchel; (leather) money-bag; tool-bag (for cycle, car, etc.).

sacquer [SAQUER].

sacramentaire [sakramã'tɛ:r], *n.m.* Sacramentary (book of ritual); sacramentarian.

sacramental (*fem.* **-ale,** *pl.* **-aux**) or **sacramentel** (*fem.* **-elle**), *a.* Sacramental.

sacre (1) [sakr], *n.m.* Anointing and coronation of a king. *Sacre d'un évêque,* consecration of a bishop.

sacre (2) [sakr], *n.m.* Saker (falcon and piece of artillery); *(fig.*) blackguard.

sacré [sa'kre], *a.* (*fem.* **-ée**) Holy, consecrated; sacred, inviolable; (*vulg.*) damned, cursed, confounded; (*Anat.*) sacral. *C'est un sacré menteur,* he is a damned liar.—*n.m.* Sacred thing, part, etc.

sacrebleu! *int.* Confound it! curse it!

Sacré-Cœur, *n.m.* (*R.-C. Ch.*) Sacred Heart of Jesus.

sacrement, *n.m.* Sacrament, *esp.* matrimony. *Avoir tous les sacrements,* (*fam.*) to be perfect or complete; *Saint Sacrement,* Holy Sacrament, monstrance.

sacrer [sa'kre], *v.t.* To anoint, to crown; to consecrate (a bishop etc.). *On l'a sacrée reine,* she was (has been) crowned queen.—*v.i.* To curse and swear.

sacret [sa'krɛ], *n.m.* (*Hawking*) Sakeret.

sacrificateur [sakrifika'tœ:r], *n.m.* (*fem.* **-trice**) Sacrificer. *Grand sacrificateur,* high-priest.

sacrificatoire, *a.* Sacrificial.

sacrificature, *n.f.* Office of sacrificer.

sacrifice [sakri'fis], *n.m.* Sacrifice; renunciation, self-immolation. *Le Saint-Sacrifice (de la messe),* The Holy Mass; *offrir quelque chose en sacrifice,* to offer up something as a sacrifice.

sacrifier, *v.t.* (*conjugated like* PRIER) To sacrifice; to immolate; to devote; to give up, to renounce; to sell very cheaply, at a sacrifice. *Sacrifier tout à ses intérêts,* to sacrifice everything to one's interest.—*v.i.* To sacrifice. *Sacrifier aux Muses,* to compose poetry or music, to paint, etc. **se sacrifier,** *v.r.* To sacrifice oneself.

sacrilège [sakri'lɛ:ʒ], *n.m.* Sacrilege.—*a.* Sacrilegious.—*n.* Sacrilegious person. (*rare*) **sacrilègement,** *adv.* Sacrilegiously.

sacripant [sakri'pã], *n.m.* Rascal, scoundrel.

sacristain [sakris'tɛ̃], *n.m.* Sacristan, sexton.

sacristi! [sakris'ti], *int.* Good God! damnation!

sacristie [sakris'ti], *n.f.* Sacristy, vestry; church plate, sacred vessels, etc.

sacristine, *n.f.* Vestry-nun, sacristine.

sacro-iliaque [sakrɔi'ljak], *a.* (*Anat.*) Sacro-iliac.

sacro-saint, *a.* Sacrosanct, doubly holy.

sacrum [sa'krɔm], *n.m.* (*Anat.*) Sacrum.

sadique [sa'dik], *a.* Sadistic.—*n.* Sadist.

sadisme [sɑ'dism], *n.m.* Sadism.

saducéen [sadyse'ɛ̃], *a.* (*fem.* **-éenne**) Sadducean.—*n.* Sadducee.

safran [sa'frã], *n.m.* Saffron; crocus. *Safran bâtard,* safflower; *safran de gouvernail,* afterpiece of a rudder.—*a. inv.* Saffron-coloured.

safrané [safra'ne], *a.* (*fem.* **-ée**) Saffron-coloured, saffroned.

safraner, *v.t.* To saffron.

safranière, *n.f.* Saffron-plantation.

safranine, *n.f.* (*Chem.*) Safranin.

safranum [safra'nɔm], *n.m.* (*Chem.*) Safflower.

safre [safr], *n.m.* (*Chem.*) Zaffre.

saga [sa'ga], *n.f.* Saga.

sagace [sa'gas], *a.* Sagacious, shrewd.
sagacité, *n.f.* Sagacity.
sagaie [sa'gɛ], *n.f.* Assegai.
sage [sa:ʒ], *a.* Wise; sage, sensible, discreet, prudent; sober, well-behaved, good, steady; virtuous, modest, cheap; quiet, gentle (of animals). *Conduite sage,* steady, prudent conduct; *des lois sages,* wise laws; *être sage,* to be good, to be well behaved (of children); *femme sage,* virtuous woman; *sage comme une image,* as good as gold; *sage politique,* wise policy; *une politique peu sage,* an unwise policy.—*n.m.* Wise man, sage.
sage-femme, *n.f.* (*pl.* **sages-femmes**) Midwife.
sagement, *adv.* Sagely, wisely; prudently, discreetly; soberly, steadily.
sagesse, *n.f.* Wisdom; discretion, prudence; steadiness, sobriety; chastity; good behaviour (of children); gentleness (of animals). *Dent de sagesse,* wisdom tooth.
*sagette [sa'ʒet], *n.f.* Arrow; (*Bot.*) arrowhead.
sagine [sa'ʒin], *n.f.* (*Bot.*) Pearlwort, pearlweed.
sagittaire [saʒi'te:r], *n.m.* (*Rom. Ant.*) Archer; (*Astron.*) Sagittarius.—*n.f.* (*Bot.*) Arrowhead.
sagittal, *a.* (*fem.* **-ale,** *pl.* **-aux**) (*Anat.*) Sagittal.
sagitté, *a.* (*fem.* **-ée**) Sagittate, arrow-shaped.
sagou [sa'gu], *n.m.* Sago. **sagouier** or (*preferably*) **sagoutier,** *n.m.* Sago-tree.
sagouin [sa'gwɛ̃], *n.m.* (*fem.* **-ine**) Squirrel-monkey; (*fig.*) slovenly fellow or woman.
sagum [sa'gɔm], *n.m.,* or **saie,** *n.f.* (*Rom. Ant.*) Sagum (military cloak).
Sahara [saa'ra], **le,** *m.* The Sahara.
saharien [saa'rjɛ̃], *a.* (*fem.* **-ienne**) Saharian.—*n.f.* Bush-shirt.
saignant [sɛ'ɲɑ̃], *a.* (*fem.* **-ante**) Bleeding, bloody; nearly raw, underdone (of meat), (*Am.*) rare.
saignée, *n.f.* Bleeding, blood-letting, phlebotomy; small of the arm; trench (for draining), cut, groove (for oil); (*fig.*) heavy payment, drain on the purse.
saignement, *n.m.* Bleeding. *Saignement de nez,* bleeding at the nose.
saigner [sɛ'ɲe], *v.t.* To bleed; to stick (an animal); (*fig.*) to drain, to get money out of.—*v.i.* To bleed. *Le cœur m'en saigne,* it makes my heart bleed; *saigner du nez,* to bleed at the nose, (*fig.*) to show the white feather. **se saigner,** *v.r.* To bleed oneself; to drain oneself or one's purse. *Se saigner aux quatre membres,* to make every sacrifice.
saigneur, *n.m.* Bleeder (of pigs etc.); *blood-letter.
saigneux, *a.* (*fem.* **-euse**) Bloody. *Bout saigneux,* scrag end (of lamb, mutton, or veal, etc.).
saillant [sa'jɑ̃], *a.* (*fem.* **-ante**) Jutting out, projecting; (*fig.*) striking, remarkable; (*Her.*) salient. *Des pommettes saillantes,* prominent cheek-bones.—*n.m.* (*Fort.*) Salient.
saillie [sa'ji], *n.f.* Start, sudden gush or spurt; sudden fit, sally; (*fig.*) flash of wit, witticism; (*Arch. etc.*) jut, projection; rabbet, ledge; spindle (of a steam-engine); covering (by male). *Fenêtre en saillie,* bay-window; *faire saillie,* to project, to jut out; *par bonds et saillies,* in leaps and bounds.

saillir [sa'ji:r], *v.i. irr.* To gush, to spout out (of liquids); *to project, to jut; to ripple (of muscles); (*Paint.*) to stand out. *Faire saillir,* to bring out, to show up.—*v.t.* To cover, to serve (of animals).
sain [sɛ̃], *a.* (*fem.* **saine**) Hale, healthy; sound; healthful, wholesome; sane; (*Naut.*) clear, safe (anchorage). *Jugement sain,* sound judgment; *nourriture saine,* wholesome food; *sain et sauf,* safe and sound; *sain de corps et d'esprit,* sound in body and mind.
saindoux [sɛ̃'du], *n.m. inv.* Lard.
sainement [sɛn'mɑ̃], *adv.* Wholesomely; healthily, soundly; judiciously.
sainfoin [sɛ̃'fwɛ̃], *n.m.* Sainfoin.
saint [sɛ̃], *a.* (*fem.* **sainte**) Holy, sacred; godly, pious, saintly; sainted, sanctified, consecrated. *La Semaine sainte,* Holy Week; *l'Écriture sainte, les Saintes Écritures,* Holy Scripture, the Scriptures, Holy Writ; *le vendredi saint,* Good Friday; *le Saint des Saints,* the Holy of Holies; *terre sainte,* consecrated ground (for burying in). *Feu saint-Antoine,* erysipelas; *toute la sainte journée,* (*colloq.*) the whole blessed day; *les lieux saints* or *la Terre Sainte,* the Holy Land; *lieu saint,* sanctuary; *rendre saint,* to sanctify; *saint-office,* holy office, Inquisition. *(*Saint*) *Crépin,* kit (of a journeyman shoemaker).—*n.m.* Saint. *À chaque saint sa chandelle,* honour to whom honour is due; *il ne sait à quel saint se vouer,* he does not know which way to turn, he is at his wits' end; *mettre au nombre des saints,* to canonize; *saint (patron) d'une ville,* patron saint of a town.
Saint-Ange [sɛ̃'tɑ̃:ʒ], *m.* Sant' Angelo.
Saint-Domingue [sɛ̃dɔ'mɛ̃:g], **L'Île de,** *f.* San Domingo.
Sainte-Hélène [sɛ̃te'len], *f.* Saint Helena.
saintement [sɛ̃t'mɑ̃], *adv.* Holily, sacredly; righteously, piously, religiously.
sainteté, *n.f.* Holiness, sanctity, sacredness, saintliness. *Sa Sainteté le Pape,* His Holiness the Pope.
Saint-Elme [sɛ̃'telm], *n.m. Le feu St-Elme,* corposant, St. Elmo's fire.
Saint-Esprit [sɛ̃tes'pri], **le,** *n.m.* The Holy Ghost.
saint-frusquin [sɛ̃frys'kɛ̃], *n.m.* (*fam.*) *Tout le saint-frusquin,* all the kit (of a person); the whole caboodle.
saint-glinglin [sɛ̃glɛ̃'glɛ̃], *n.f.* (*fam.*) *À la saint-glinglin,* never, when the moon is made of green cheese.
saint-honoré [sɛ̃tɔnɔ're], *n.m.* A kind of cake with cream.
Saint-Jean [sɛ̃'ʒɑ̃], **la,** *n.f.* Midsummer Day.
Saint-Marin [sɛ̃ma'rɛ̃], *m.* San Marino.
(C) **Saint-Michel** [sɛ̃mi'ʃel], *n.m.* Young fir.
Saint-Père [sɛ̃'pe:r], **le,** *m.* The Holy Father, the Pope.
Saint-Siège [sɛ̃'sje:ʒ], **le,** *m.* The Holy See.
saint-simonien [sɛ̃simɔ'njɛ̃], *a.* and *n.* (*fem.* **saint-simonienne**) Saint-Simonian.—*n.* Saint-Simonist. **saint-simonisme,** *n.m.* Saint-Simonianism.
Saint-Sylvestre [sɛ̃sil'vestr], **la,** *f.* New Year's Eve.
saisi [sɛ'zi], *a.* (*fem.* **saisie** (1)) Seized, possessed, struck (*de*); suddenly exposed to great heat (*esp.* of meat); distrained.—*n.m.*

Person distrained. **saisie** (2), *n.f.* (*Law*) Seizure; distraint, execution.
saisie-arrêt, *n.f.* (*pl.* **saisies-arrêts**) (*Law*) Attachment, garnishment. *Ordonnance de saisie-arrêt*, garnishee order.
saisie-brandon, *n.f.* (*pl.* **saisies-brandons**) Execution on growing crops.
saisie-exécution, *n.f.* (*pl.* **saisies-exécutions**) Execution; distress.
saisie-gagerie, *n.f.* (*pl.* **saisies-gageries**) Writ of execution (by way of security).
saisie-revendication, *n.f.* (*pl.* **saisies-revendications**) Attachment of goods claimed (pending litigation).
saisine, *n.f.* (*Feud. law*) Seisin; (*Naut.*) lashing.
saisir [sɛ'ziːr], *v.t.* To seize, to seize upon, to lay hold of; to take hold of; to apprehend, understand, to grasp, to perceive, to comprehend; (*fig.*) to strike, to impress, to shock, to startle; (*Cook.*) to fry (*or* broil) very quickly, to expose meat to sudden heat; to avail oneself of; to make cognizant of, to lay before; to distrain; (*Law*) to vest, to put (someone) in possession (*de*); to attach; (*Naut.*) to lash. *La peur les a saisis*, they were struck with fear; *le désespoir le saisit*, despair seized him; *saisir le sens*, to grasp the meaning; *saisir l'occasion*, to seize the opportunity; *saisir un prétexte*, to avail oneself of an excuse; *saisir un tribunal d'une affaire*, to lay (an affair) before a court. **se saisir**, *v.r.* To seize, to catch hold (*de*); to take possession (*de*); to arrest, to apprehend.
saisir-arrêter, *v.t.* (*p.p.* **saisi-arrêté**) To attach.
saisissable, *a.* Distrainable, attachable; seizable; distinguishable.
saisissant, *a.* (*fem.* **-ante**) Keen, sharp, piercing (of cold); striking, thrilling, startling, impressive. *La ressemblance est saisissante*, there is a striking resemblance.—*n.* Distrainer.
saisissement, *n.m.* Chill, shock, violent impression, seizure.
saison [sɛ'zɔ̃], *n.f.* Season. *Arrière-saison* [ARRIÈRE-SAISON]; *ces mets ne sont plus de saison*, those dishes are out of season; *dans la saison*, in due season; *de saison*, in season; *en toute saison*, in any weather, in all weathers; *être en pleine saison*, to be in their prime (of flowers etc.); *faire une saison dans une station thermale*, to follow a treatment (at spa); *hors de saison*, out of season, (*fig.*) out of place, tactless; *la saison est avancée*, the season is forward; *marchand des quatre saisons*, costermonger, hawker of fresh vegetables, barrowboy; *morte-saison* [MORTE-SAISON]. **saisonnier**, *a.* (*fem.* **-ière**) Seasonal.
salacité [salasi'te], *n.f.* Salaciousness, salacity.
salade (1) [sa'lad], *n.f.* Salad; (*fig.*) hotchpotch, jumble, medley, miscellany, confusion. *Fatiguer la salade*, to mix the salad thoroughly; *le panier à salade*, (*slang*) prisonvan, Black Maria; *salade de fruits*, fruit salad.
salade (2) [sa'lad], *n.f.* Sallet (helmet).
saladier [sala'dje], *n.m.* Salad-bowl.
salage [sa'laːʒ], *n.m.* Salting.
salaire [sa'lɛːr], *n.m.* Wages, pay, hire; recompense, reward, retribution. *Le salaire du péché*, the wages of sin; *toute peine mérite salaire*, the labourer is worthy of his hire.

salaison [salɛ'zɔ̃], *n.f.* Salting; salt provisions; curing (of bacon etc.).
salamalec [salama'lɛk], *n.m.* (*used chiefly in pl.*) Salaam; (*fig.*) low bow, exaggerated politeness. *Faire des salamalecs*, to bow and scrape.
salamandre [sala'mɑ̃ːdr], *n.f.* Salamander; slow-combustion stove. *Salamandre aquatique*, newt.
salangane [salɑ̃'gan], *n.f.* Salangane (swallow that builds edible nests).
salanque [sa'lɑ̃ːk], *n.f.* Salt-marsh. **salant**, *a.m.* *Marais salant*, salt-marsh, salt-pans, saline, saltern.
salariat [sala'rja], *n.m.* Wage-earning; (*collect.*) wage-earners, wage-earning class.
salarié, *a.* (*fem.* **-ée**) Paid, wage-earning.—*n.* Wage-earner; hireling.
salarier, *v.t.* (*conjugated like* PRIER) To pay, to give wages to.
salaud [sa'lo], *n.m.* (*pop.* and *rude*) Sloven, dirty person, slut. *Quel salaud!* dirty beast, skunk, bastard!
sale [sal], *a.* Dirty, nasty, filthy, foul; coarse, indecent, obscene; squalid; dingy, dull (of colours); (*pop.* term of scorn or insult) *sale type*, rotter, beast; *sale bête*, dirty dog; *sale coup*, dirty trick etc.; *sale temps*, beastly weather. *Vaisseau sale*, (*Naut.*) foul ship.
salé [sa'le], *a.* (*fem.* **-ée**) Salted, salt; briny; (*fig.*) keen, pungent, biting; loose, coarse, broad, spicy, salty; (*colloq.*) exaggerated, too dear. *Raillerie salée*, biting raillery; *sources salées*, salt-springs; *un peu salé*, saltish; *un propos salé*, a coarse remark.—*n.m.* Salt pork. *Du petit salé*, pickled pork.
salement [sal'mɑ̃], *adv.* Dirtily, nastily, filthily; (*fig.*) in a slovenly manner; (*colloq.*) smuttily, indecently.
salep [sa'lɛp], *n.m.* Salep.
saler [sa'le], *v.t.* To salt; to preserve with salt; (*fig.*) to overcharge for, to put an exorbitant price on (goods); to sting, to fleece (customers). **saleron**, *n.m.* Bowl of a salt-cellar.
saleté [sal'te], *n.f.* Dirtiness, nastiness, filthiness; filth, dirty thing; dirty trick; coarseness, ribaldry, obscenity.
saleur [sa'lœːr], *n.m.* (*fem.* **-euse**) Salter, curer.—*n.f.* (*Rail.*) Wagon carrying salt for clearing the line of snow.
salicaire [sali'kɛːr], *n.f.* Purple loosestrife.
salicole [sali'kɔl], *a.* Salt-producing.
salicoque [sali'kɔk], *n.f.* Prawn.
salicorne [sali'kɔrn], *n.f.*, *or* **salicor**, *n.m.* (*Bot.*) Saltwort.
saliculture [salikyl'tyːr], *n.f.* Salt-manufacture.
salière [sa'ljɛːr], *n.f.* Salt-cellar; salt-box; eyepit (in horses); hollow behind the collarbone (in thin persons).
salifère [sali'fɛːr], *a.* Saliferous.
salifiable, *a.* Salifiable.
salification, *n.f.* Salification.
salifier, *v.t.* (*conjugated like* PRIER) To salify.
saligaud [sali'go], *n.m.* Dirty person, sloven, slut; dishonest person.
salignon [sali'ɲɔ̃], *n.m.* Salt-deposit, block of salt.
salin [sa'lɛ̃], *a.* (*fem.* **saline** (1)) Salt, saline, briny.—*n.m.* Salt-works; salt-marsh; red potash (used as flux in glass-works).

[666]

salinage, *n.m.* Place where salt is obtained; salt-making by precipitation.
saline (2) [sa'lin], *n.f.* Salt-marsh, salt-mine, salt-pit; salt provisions; salt fish.
salinier, *n.m.* Owner of salt-works; salt-worker or -vendor.
salinité, *n.f.* Salinity.
salinomètre, *n.m.* Salinometer.
salique [sa'lik], *a.* Salic. *Loi salique*, Salic law.
salir [sa'liːr], *v.t.* To dirty, to soil; to stain, to taint, to defile, to sully, to tarnish. **se salir**, *v.r.* To dirty oneself; to get dirty; to sully one's reputation.
salissant, *a.* (*fem.* **-ante**) That soils or gets dirty easily; dirty, messy (of job, work, etc.).
salisson, *n.f.* (*colloq.*) Dirty, untidy little girl.
salissure, *n.f.* Spot of dirt, stain.
salivaire [sali'vɛːr], *a.* (*Anat.*) Salivary.
salival, *a.* (*fem.* **-ale**, *pl.* **-aux**) Salival.
salivation, *n.f.* Salivation. **salive**, *n.f.* Saliva, spittle. *Je perds ma salive*, I am wasting my breath. **saliver**, *v.i.* To salivate.
salle [sal], *n.f.* Hall; large room; gallery (of museum); ward (in hospitals); (*Theat.*) house; *bower, arbour. *Salle à manger*, dining-room; *salle d'armes*, fencing-school, school of arms; *salle d'attente*, waiting-room; *salle d'audience*, court-room; *salle de bains*, bathroom; *salle de conférences* (or *de cours*), lecture-room (*or* hall); *salle de danse*, dance-hall; dancing-room, dancing-school; *salle de police*, (*Mil.*) guard-room; *salle des pas perdus*, ante-chamber of a court of justice; main hall (of railway station); *salle de séjour*, living-room; *salle de spectacle*, playhouse; *salle de(s) ventes*, auction-room, sale-room; *salle de verdure*, green arbour; *salle d'opération*, operating theatre; *salle pleine*, full house.
salmigondis [salmigɔ̃'di], *n.m.* Salmagundi; hotchpotch; (*fig.*) medley, farrago.
salmis [sal'mi], *n.m.* Salmi, ragout of game (previously roasted).
Salomon [salɔ'mɔ̃], *m.* Solomon.
saloir [sa'lwaːr], *n.m.* Salt-box; salting-tub.
salon [sa'lɔ̃], *n.m.* Drawing-room, parlour; saloon; exhibition (art); (*pl.*) fashionable world, fashionable circles. *Fréquenter les salons*, to be a man of fashion; *salon de coiffure*, hairdressing salon; *salon de thé*, tea-room. *Le salon de l'automobile*, the Paris motor show.
salope [sa'lɔp], *n.f.* (*vulg.*) Slut; drab; trollop.
saloper, *v.t.* To botch.
saloperie, *n.f.* Slovenliness, sluttishness; beastliness, filth; trash, rubbish, trashy goods; dirty trick; coarse language, ribaldry [MARIE-SALOPE].
salopette [salɔ'pɛt], *n.f.* Overall, dungarees.
salopiaud or **salopard**, *n.m.* (*pop.*) [SALAUD].
salpêtrage [salpe'traːʒ], *n.m.* Saltpetre-making; nitrification. **salpêtre**, *n.m.* Salt-petre. **salpêtrer**, *v.t.* To cover with saltpetre. **se salpêtrer**, *v.r.* To turn to or get covered with saltpetre. **salpêtrerie**, *n.f.* Saltpetre-works. **salpêtreux**, *a.* (*fem.* **-euse**) Saltpetrous. **salpêtrier**, *n.m.* Saltpetre-maker. **salpêtrière**, *n.f.* Saltpetre-works. *La Salpêtrière*, asylum in Paris for aged and mentally afflicted women.
salse [sals], *n.f.* Salse, mud, volcano.
salsepareille [salspa'rɛːj], *n.f.* Sarsaparilla.
salsifis [salsi'fi], *n.m.* Salsify. *Salsifis sauvage*

or *salsifis des prés*, goat's beard; *salsifis d'Espagne* or *salsifis noir*, scorzonera.
saltarelle [salta'rɛl], *n.f.* Saltarello (Italian dance).
saltimbanque [saltɛ̃'bãːk], *n.m.* Mountebank, showman, buffoon; (*fig.*) humbug, quack.
salubre [sa'lybr], *a.* Salubrious, bracing, healthy (climate), wholesome, healthful.
salubrement, *adv.* Salubriously. **salubrité**, *n.f.* Salubrity, healthfulness, wholesomeness. *Salubrité publique*, public health, sanitation.
saluer [sa'lɥe], *v.t.* To salute, to bow to; to hail, to greet; to cheer; to proclaim. *Je vous salue* or *j'ai l'honneur de vous saluer*, (in letters) your obedient servant; *passer sans saluer quelqu'un*, to cut someone; *saluer de la main*, to wave to; *saluer de onze coups de canon*, to fire a salute of eleven guns in honour of; *saluer (du pavillon)*, to dip the flag; *saluer empereur*, to acclaim emperor; *saluez-le de ma part*, remember me to him. **se saluer**, *v.r.* To bow to or salute each other.
salure [sa'lyːr], *n.f.* Saltness, salinity.
salut [sa'ly], *n.m.* Safety; salvation; welfare, preservation, escape; hope or chance of success; salutation, salute, greeting, bow; hail, cheers; evensong, evening service. *Armée du Salut*, Salvation Army. *À bon entendeur salut!* a word to the wise is sufficient, if the cap fits, wear it; *faire un salut*, to bow; *faire un salut de la main*, to wave; *il a cherché son salut dans la fuite*, he sought safety in flight; *léger salut*, nod; *un profond salut*, a low bow.
salutaire, *a.* Salutary, wholesome, advantageous, beneficial. **salutairement**, *adv.* Beneficially.
salutation, *n.f.* Salutation, greeting, salute, bow; (*pl.*) compliments. *Recevez mes salutations empressées*, (in letters) yours very truly.
salutiste, *n.* Member of the Salvation Army.
salve [salv], *n.f.* Salvo, volley; salute (of artillery). *Salve d'applaudissements*, burst, round of applause.
samaritain [samari'tɛ̃], *a.* and *n.* (*fem.* **-aine**) Samaritan.
samedi [sam'di], *n.m.* Saturday. *Samedi saint*, Easter-eve.
sanatorium [sanatɔ'rjɔm], *n.m.* (*pl.* **sanatoriums** or (*rare*) **sanatoria**) Sanatorium.
sancir [sã'siːr], *v.i.* (*Naut.*) To founder, to sink by the bows.
sanctifiant [sãkti'fjã], *a.* (*fem.* **-iante**) Sanctifying.
sanctificateur, *n.* (*fem.* **-trice**) Sanctifier.—*a.* Sanctifying.
sanctification, *n.f.* Sanctification.
sanctifier, *v.t.* (*conjugated like* PRIER) To sanctify, to make holy, to hallow. *Que votre nom soit sanctifié*, hallowed be Thy Name.
sanction [sãk'sjɔ̃], *n.f.* Sanction; approbation, assent; penalty. **sanctionner**, *v.t.* To sanction, to approve; to penalize.
sanctuaire [sãk'tɥɛːr], *n.m.* Sanctuary (of the temple etc.); chancel (of church); (*fam.*) den, sanctum.
sandal [SANTAL].
sandale [sã'dal], *n.f.* Sandal; fencing-shoe, gymnasium-shoe, sand-shoe. **sandalier**, *n.m.* Sandal-maker.
sandaraque [sãda'rak], *n.f.* Sandarach (resin).

sandjak [sã'ʒjak], *n.m.* Sanjak.
sandow [sã'dɔf], *n.m.* Chest-expander; rubber shock-absorber.
sandwich [sã'dwitʃ], *n.m.* (*pl.* **sandwichs** or **sandwiches**) Sandwich. *Homme-sandwich,* sandwich-man.
sang [sã], *n.m.* Blood; (*poet.*) gore; race, parentage, ancestry; relationship, kindred. *Bon sang ne peut mentir,* blood will tell; *cela glace le sang,* that makes one's blood run cold; *cela est dans le sang,* that runs in the blood; *coup de sang* [COUP]; *histoire à vous tourner les sangs,* blood-curdling tale; *injecté de sang,* blood-shot (eyes); *impôt du sang* [IMPÔT]; *mettre tout à feu et à sang* [FEU (I)]; *prince du sang,* prince of the blood (royal); *pur sang,* thoroughbred; *sans effusion de sang,* without shedding blood; without bloodshed; *se battre au premier sang,* to fight till the first blood is drawn; *se faire du bon sang,* to have a jolly time; *se faire du mauvais sang, se manger les sangs,* to fret, to worry; *son propre sang,* one's own flesh and blood; *suer sang et eau,* to toil away, to 'sweat blood'; *un buveur de sang,* a bloodthirsty man.
sang-dragon or **sang-de-dragon**, *n.m. inv.* Dragon's-blood, resin.
sang-froid, *n.m.* Coolness, composure, sang-froid. *De sang-froid,* in cold blood, with composure; *perdre son sang-froid,* to lose one's presence of mind, or one's temper.
sanglade [sã'glad], *n.f.* Lash, cut (with a whip).
sanglant [sã'glã], *a.* (*fem.* **-ante**) Bloody, covered with blood, gory; bleeding, blood-shot; (*fig.*) keen, biting, cutting, outrageous, gross. *Affront sanglant,* deadly insult.
sangle [sã:gl], *n.f.* Strap, band, belt; saddle-girth, webbing, sacking. *Lit de sangle,* folding bed, camp-bed.
sangler [sã'gje], *v.t.* To bind with a girth, to girth, to strap; to compress, to lace too tightly; to deal (a slashing blow). **se sangler,** *v.r.* To lace oneself tightly.
sanglier [sã'glje], *n.m.* Wild boar. *Sanglier de mer,* boar-fish.
sanglot [sã'glo], *n.m.* Sob. **sangloter,** *v.i.* To sob.
sang-mêlé [sãmɛ'le], *n.m. inv.* Half-caste.
sangsue [sã'sy], *n.f.* Leech; (*fig.*) blood-sucker, extortioner.
sanguin [sã'gɛ̃], *a.* (*fem.* **sanguine** (I)). Of blood; full-blooded, sanguine; blood-coloured, blood-red. *Vaisseau sanguin,* blood-vessel. **sanguinaire,** *a.* Sanguinary, bloody, murderous, bloodthirsty.—*n.f.* (*Bot.*) Blood-root.
sanguine (2), *n.f.* Red chalk; bloodstone; blood-orange.
sanguinelle, *n.f.* Cornel, dogwood.
sanguinolent, *a.* (*fem.* **-ente**) Tinged with blood.
sanhédrin [sane'drɛ̃], *n.m.* Sanhedrin.
sanicle [sa'nikl], *n.f.,* or **sanicule,** *n.f.* Sanicle.
sanie [sa'ni], *n.f.* (*Path.*) Sanies, pus. **sanieux,** *a.* (*fem.* **-ieuse**) Sanious.
sanitaire [sani'tɛ:r], *a.* Sanitary. *Cordon sanitaire,* sanitary cordon; *train sanitaire,* hospital train.
sans [sã], *prep.* Without; free from; but for; *Cela va had it not been for, were it not for. Cela va*

sans dire, of course, that goes without saying; *sans abri, sans gîte, sans logis,* homeless; *sans amis,* friendless; *sans cela,* were it not for that, otherwise; *sans doute,* no doubt, doubtless; *sans le sou,* penniless; *sans pareil,* unique, peerless; *sans peur,* fearless(ly); *sans pitié,* pitiless(ly); *sans quoi,* otherwise, else, but for that; *sans souci,* light-hearted, care-free; *sans y penser,* unawares, unthinkingly; *sans que,* without, unless; *il a passé sans que je l'aie aperçu,* he passed without my seeing him; *ne répondez pas sans qu'on vous interroge,* don't answer unless you are questioned.
sans-abri, sans-gîte, sans-logis, *n. inv.* Homeless person.
sans-atout [sãza'tu], *n.m. Appeler, demander sans-atout,* to call no trumps.
sans-cœur, *n. inv.* Heartless, unfeeling person.
sanscrit [sãs'kri], *a.* (*fem.* **-ite**) Sanskrit.—*n.m.* Sanskrit (language). **sanscritiste,** *n.* Sanskrit scholar.
sans-culotte [sãky'lɔt], *n.m.* (*pl.* **sans-culottes**) Fellow without breeches, sans-culotte; ultra-violent republican.
sans-culottide, *n.f.* One of the five complementary days of the French republican calendar; festivals held during those days.
sans-dent [sã'dã], *n.f.* (*pl.* **sans-dents**) Toothless old woman.
sans-façon, *n.m.* Bluntness, homeliness, honesty (of speech); off-handedness.
sans-filiste, *n.* Wireless operator; listener-in.
sans-gêne, *n.m.* Unceremoniousness, coolness, off-handedness; (*fam.*) cheek; blunt person; (*fam.*) cool customer.
sans-gîte [SANS-ABRI].
sansonnet [sãsɔ'nɛ], *n.m.* (*Orn.*) Starling; (small) mackerel.
sans-patrie [sãpa'tri], *n. inv.* Person who has no nationality; stateless person.
sans-souci [sãsu'si], *n. inv.* (*colloq.*) Carefree, easy-going fellow; free-and-easy manners.—*a.* Carefree, free-and-easy, happy-go-lucky.
sans-travail [sãtra'vaj], *n.m. inv. Les sans-travail,* the unemployed.
santal [sã'tal], *n.m.* (*pl.* **-als**) Sandalwood, santal. **santaline,** *n.f.* Santalin.
santé [sã'te], *n.f.* Health, healthiness; state of health. *À votre santé!* here's to you! your health! *boire à la santé de quelqu'un,* to drink someone's health; *être en bonne santé,* to be in good health; *maison de santé,* (private) nursing home; mental hospital. *Ministère de la santé publique,* Ministry of Health; Public Health Office; *officier de santé,* licensed medical practitioner; (*Naut.*) (port) health officer. *Santé passe richesse,* health before wealth.
santoline [sãtɔ'lin], *n.f.* Santolina.
Santon [sã'tɔ̃], *n.m.* Santon (Mohammedan hermit); Santon's tomb (in Algeria).
santon [sã'tɔ̃], *n.m.* Little coloured clay figure used to group round the Christmas crib (in Provence).
santonine [sãtɔ'nin], *n.f.* Santonica; (*Chem.*) santonin.
sanve [sã:v], *n.f.* (*Bot.*) Charlock.
saoul etc. (SOÛL).
sapa [sa'pa], *n.m.* (*Pharm.*) Grape-jelly.
sapajou [sapa'ʒu], *n.m.* Sapajou; (*fig.*) monkey.
sapan [sa'pã], *n.m.* Sapan-wood.

sape [sap], *n.f.* Sap, sapping, undermining, mine, trench. *Sape d'un piolet*, adze of an ice-axe. **sapement**, *n.m.* Sapping.
sapèque [sa'pɛk], *n.f.* Cash (Chinese coin).
saper, *v.t.* To sap, to undermine.
saperlipopette [SAPRISTI].
sapeur, *n.m.* Sapper.
sapeur-pompier, *n.m.* (*pl.* **sapeurs-pompiers**) Military fireman (in France).
sapeur-télégraphiste, *n.m.* (*pl.* **sapeurs-télégraphistes**) Soldier of the signal corps; (*pl.*) (*fam.*) signals.
saphène [sa'fɛ:n], *n.f.* (*Anat.*) Saphena.
saphique [sa'fik], *a.* Sapphic. *Vers saphiques*, sapphics.
saphir [sa'fi:r], *n.m.* Sapphire. **saphirin**, *a.* (*fem.* **-ine**) Sapphirine.—*n.f.* Sapphirine.
saphisme [sa'fism], *n.m.* Sapphism, Lesbianism.
Sapho [sa'fo], *f.* Sappho.
sapide [sa'pid], *a.* Sapid, savoury, palatable. **sapidité**, *n.f.* Sapidity, flavour, savouriness.
*sapience [sa'pjɑ̃:s], *n.f.* Sapience, wisdom.
sapin [sa'pɛ̃], *n.m.* Fir, fir-tree; coffin. (*Bois de*) *sapin*, deal. *Sentir le sapin*, to have one foot in the grave. (*C*) *Sapin traînard*, Canadian yew-tree.
(*C*) **sapinages** [sapi'na:ʒ], *n.m. pl.* Fir bush, fir branches.
sapine, *n.f.* Fir-plank, deal-board; (*Build.*) scaffolding; crane-tower.
sapineau, *n.m.* (*pl.* **-eaux**) Young fir.
sapinette, *n.f.* Spruce; spruce beer.
sapinière, *n.f.* Fir wood, fir plantation.
saponacé [sapɔna'se], *a.* (*fem.* **-ée**) Saponaceous, soapy. **saponaire**, *n.f.* Saponaria, soapwort. **saponifiable**, *a.* Saponifiable. **saponification**, *n.f.* Saponification. **saponifier**, *v.t.* (*conjugated like* PRIER) To saponify. **saponine**, *n.f.* (*Chem.*) Saponin. **saponite**, *n.f.* Saponite.
sapotille [sapɔ'ti:j] or **sapote**, *n.f.* Sapodilla, naseberry. **sapotillier** or **sapotier**, *n.m.* Sapodilla, naseberry (tree).
sapristi, *saperlotte, saprelotte, saperlipopette*, (*fam.*) euphemisms instead of *sacristi*.
saprogène [saprɔ'ʒɛn], *a.* Saprogenic.
saprophage [saprɔ'fa:ʒ], *a.* Saprophagous.—*n.m.* Saprophagan (beetle).
saprophyte, *a.* Saprophytic.—*n.m.* Saprophyte.
saquebute [sak'byt], *n.f.* Sackbut.
saquer [sa'ke], *v.t.* (*pop.*) To sack, to fire (someone); to punish severely.
sarabande [sara'bɑ̃:d], *n.f.* Saraband (dance); (*fam.*) row, song-and-dance.
sarbacane [sarba'kan], *n.f.* Blow-tube, blowpipe (a weapon), pea-shooter (a toy).
sarcasme [sar'kasm], *n.m.* Sarcasm, sarcastic remark. **sarcastique**, *a.* Sarcastic.
sarcelle [sar'sɛl], *n.f.* (*Orn.*) Teal.
sarcine [sar'sin], *n.f.* (*Chem.*) Sarcine.
sarclage [sar'kla:ʒ], *n.m.* Weeding. **sarcler**, *v.t.* To weed; to hoe, to clean; (*fig.*) to extirpate, to suppress. **sarcleur**, *n.m.* (*fem.* **-euse** (1)) Weeder. **sarcleuse** (2), *n.f.* Mechanical weeder.
sarcloir, *n.m.* Hoe.
sarclure, *n.f.* Weed (pulled up); weeds.
sarcocèle [sarkɔ'sɛl], *n.f.* (*Path.*) Sarcocele.
sarcocollier, *n.m.* Sarcocolla, sarcocol-tree.

sarcode, *n.m.* Sarcode. **sarcoderme**, *n.m.* Sarcoderm.
sarcologie, *n.f.* Sarcology.
sarcomateux, *a.* (*fem.* **-euse**) Sarcomatous.
sarcomatose, *n.f.* Sarcomatosis.
sarcome [sar'ko:m], *n.m.* Sarcoma.
sarcophage, *a.* (*Ent.*) Sarcophagous.—*n.m.* Sarcophagus.—*n.f.* (*Ent.*) Blow-fly.
sarcoplasma, *n.m.* Sarcoplasm.
sarcopte, *n.m.* (*Zool.*) Itch-mite (of *Sarcoptes* genus).
sarcose, *n.f.* Sarcosis.
Sardanapale [sardana'pal], *m.* Sardanapalus.
Sardaigne [sar'dɛɲ], *f.* Sardinia.
sarde [sard], *a.* Sardinian.—*n.* (**Sarde**) A Sardinian.
sardine [sar'din], *n.f.* Sardine; (*Mil. slang*) (metal) stripe(s) of N.C.O.
sardinerie, *n.f.* Sardine packing and curing factory.
sardinier, *n.m.* (*fem.* **-ière**) Sardine fisher; sardine packer or curer; sardine-net; sardine-boat.
sardoine [sar'dwan], *n.f.* Sardonyx.
sardonique [sardɔ'nik], *a.* Sardonic.
sargasse [sar'gas], *n.f.* Sargasso (gulf-weed). *La Mer des Sargasses*, the Sargasso Sea.
sargue [sarg], *n.m.* Sargus (fish); sea-bream.
sari [sa'ri], *n.m.* Sari (Indian women's dress).
sarigue [sa'rig], *n.m. and f.* Sarigue (opossum).
sarisse [sa'ris], *n.f.* Macedonian phalanx's long pike, sarissa.
sarmatique [sarma'tik], *a.* Sarmatian.
sarment [sar'mɑ̃], *n.m.* Vine-shoot, vine-branch.
sarmenteux, *a.* (*fem.* **-euse**) (*Bot.*) Sarmentous, branchy, climbing; rambling (of roses).
sarracénie [sarase'ni], *n.f.* (*Bot.*) Pitcher-plant, sarracenia.
Sarrasin [sara'zɛ̃], *n.m.* (*fem.* **Sarrasine**) A Saracen.—*a.* (**sarrasin** (1), **sarrasine** (1)) Saracen; Saracenic (style of architecture).
sarrasin (2) [sara'zɛ̃], *n.m.* Buckwheat.
sarrasine (2) [sara'zin], *n.f.* Portcullis.
sarrau [sa'ro], *n.m.* (*pl.* **-aux**) Smock-frock; child's blouse.
Sarre [sa:r], *la,* *f.* The Saar.
sarrette [sa'rɛt], *n.f.* (*Bot.*) Saw-wort.
sarriette [sa'rjɛt], *n.f.* Savory.
sas [sɑ], *n.m. inv.* Sieve, screen; chamber (of a lock); (*Naut.*) floating chamber (of submarine); air-lock. *Passer au gros sas*, to examine superficially.
sassafras [sasa'frɑ], *n.m.* Sassafras.
sassage [sa'sa:ʒ] or **sassement**, *n.m.* Sifting, bolting; passing boats through a lock.
sasse [sas], *n.f.* (*Naut.*) Scoop for bailing, bailer; bolting-machine (for flour).
sasser [sa'se], *v.t.* To sift, to bolt; to winnow; (*fig.*) to scan, to scrutinize; to pass boats through a lock.
sasseur [sa'sœ:r], *n.m.* (*fem.* **-euse**) Sifter, bolter; winnower.
Satan [sa'tɑ̃], *m.* Satan.
satané [sata'ne], *a.* (*fem.* **-ée**) (*colloq.*) Devilish, confounded.
satanique, *a.* Satanic, diabolical, fiendish. **sataniquement**, *adv.* Fiendishly, diabolically.
satanisme, *n.m.* Satanism.
satellite [satɛ'lit], *a.* Satellite.—*n.m.* Satellite;

henchman; (*Eng.*) planet wheel. *Veines satel-
lites,* companion veins.

sâti [sɑ′ti], *n.m.* or *f.* Suttee.

satiété [sasje′te], *n.f.* Satiety, repletion.

satin [sa′tɛ̃], *n.m.* Satin. **satinage,** *n.m.*
Satining; glazing (of paper etc.); (*Phot.*)
burnishing (of print). **satiné,** *a.* (*fem.* **-ée**)
Satin-like, satiny; glazed (of paper etc.).
Peau satinée, skin as soft as velvet.—*n.m.*
Satin-like gloss.

satiner [sati′ne], *v.t.* To satin; to glaze (paper
etc.). *Satiner à chaud,* to hot-press; *satiner
à froid,* to cold-press.—*v.i.* To look like satin.
satinette, *n.f.* Satinette. **satineur,** *n.m.*
(*fem.* **satineuse** (1)) Satiner, glazer.
satineuse (2), *n.f.* Satining-machine.

satire [sa′ti:r], *n.f.* Satire. *Satire personnelle,*
lampoon. **satirique,** *a.* Satirical.—*n.m.*
Satirist. **satiriquement,** *adv.* Satirically.
satiriser, *v.t.* To satirize.

satisfaction [satisfak′sjɔ̃], *n.f.* Satisfaction;
gratification; reparation, atonement. **satis-
factoire,** *a.* (*Theol.*) Satisfactory, atoning.

satisfaire [sɑtis′fɛ:r], *v.t. irr.* (*conjug. like* FAIRE)
To satisfy; to please, to gratify; to answer,
to meet; to give satisfaction to, to make
amends to. *Satisfaire l'attente de quelqu'un,*
to come up to someone's expectation; *satisfaire sa passion,* to gratify one's passion.—*v.i.*
To be satisfactory (*à*); to gratify; to answer,
to meet, to fulfil (*à*); to make reparation or
atonement (*à*). *Satisfaire à ses engagements,*
to fulfil one's engagements. **se satisfaire,**
v.r. To satisfy oneself, to indulge oneself; to
obtain satisfaction (for an insult etc.). **satisfaisant,** *a.* (*fem.* **-ante**) Satisfactory. **satisfait,** *a.* (*fem.* **-aite**) Satisfied, contented,
pleased. *Il est satisfait de vos progrès,* he is
satisfied with your progress.

satisfecit [satisfesit], *n.m. inv.* Certificate or
testimonial of complete satisfaction.

satrape [sa′trap], *n.m.* Satrap. **satrapie,** *n.f.*
Satrapy.

saturable [saty′rabl], *a.* Saturable. **saturant,**
a. (*fem.* **-ante**) Saturating. **saturateur,** *n.m.*
Saturator (apparatus for aerating liquids).
saturation, *n.f.* Saturation. **saturé,** *a.*
(*fem.* **-ée**) Saturated. **saturer,** *v.t.* To
saturate, (*fig.*) to surfeit.

saturnales [satyr′nal], *n.f. pl.* Saturnalia.

Saturne [sa′tyrn], *n.m.* Saturn; lead (in
alchemy). **saturnien,** *a.* (*fem.* **-ienne**)
Saturnian.

saturnin, *a.* (*fem.* **-ine**) (*Med.*) Relating to
lead. *Colique saturnine,* lead colic. **saturnisme,** *n.m.* Saturnism (lead-poisoning).

saturomètre [satyrɔ′mɛtr], *n.m.* Brine-gauge.

satyre [sa′ti:r], *n.m.* Satyr. **satyresse,** *n.f.*
She-satyr. **satyrion,** *n.m.* (*Bot.*) Satyrium.
satyrique, *a.* Satyric, pertaining to satyrs.

sauce [so:s], *n.f.* Sauce; soft crayon (made of
lamp-black) used with *tortillons*; (*Tobacco
Ind.*) sauce. *À toute sauce,* for any sort of
work; *être dans la sauce,* (*fam.*) to be in the
soup; *il n'est sauce que d'appétit,* a good
appetite is the best sauce; *on ne sait à quelle
sauce le mettre,* there is no knowing what to
do with him; *sauce blanche* or *sauce hollandaise,* melted butter; (*Motor.*) *mettre toute la
sauce,* to open the throttle; (*fam.*) to step on
the gas. **saucé,** *a.* (*fem.* **saucée** (1)) Soused, wet

through; (*Num.*) thinly plated. *Médailles
saucées,* plated medals.

saucée (2), *n.f.* (*fam.*) Downpour; soaking;
scolding, blowing-up.

saucer, *v.t.* To dip in sauce; to sop, to souse;
(*colloq.*) to wet through; to scold, to blow up.

saucier, *n.m.* Sauce-maker; sauce-setter;
(*Naut.*) saucer (of a capstan).

saucière, *n.f.* Sauce-boat.

saucisse [so′sis], *n.f.* (Fresh) sausage; (*vulg.*)
silly, fathead; (*Mil. slang*) sausage balloon;
observation balloon.

saucisson, *n.m.* Large dry sausage; salami;
(*Artill.*) saucisson; (*Fort.*) bundle of fascines;
(*Av. slang*) aerial torpedo.

sauf (1) [so:f], *a.* (*fem.* **sauve**) Safe; unhurt,
unscathed. *Il en est revenu sain et sauf,* he
returned safe and sound; *s'en tirer la vie
sauve,* to escape with one's life.

sauf (2) [sɔf, sof], *prep.* Save, except, except
for; barring, failing, unless. *Sauf correction,*
subject to correction; *sauf contre-ordre,* unless
I hear to the contrary; *sauf erreur ou omission,*
errors and omissions excepted; *sauf que,*
except that; *sauf votre respect,* saving your
presence.

sauf-conduit, *n.m.* (*pl.* **sauf-conduits**) Safe-
conduct.

sauge [so:ʒ], *n.f.* Sage (herb). *Sauge des bois,*
wood-sage.

saugrenu [sogrə′ny], *a.* (*fem.* **-ue**) Absurd,
ridiculous, preposterous.

Saül [sa′yl], *m.* Saul.

saulaie [so′lɛ], *n.f.* Willow-grove. **saule,** *n.m.*
Willow. *Saule blanc,* white willow, bat
willow; *saule pleureur,* weeping willow; *saule
pourpre,* red osier. **saulée,** *n.f.* Row or
avenue of willows.

saumâtre [so′mɑ:tr], *a.* Brackish, briny.

saumier [so′mje], *n.m.* Salmon-gaff.

saumon [so′mɔ̃], *n.m.* Salmon; (*Metal.*) pig,
block. *Saumon de fonte,* pig-iron.—*a. inv.*
Salmon-coloured. **saumoné,** *a.* (*fem.* **-ée**)
Truite saumonée, salmon-trout. **saumoneau,**
n.m. (*pl.* **-eaux**) Young salmon, grilse,
samlet, parr.

saumurage [somy′ra:ʒ], *n.m.* Pickling (in
brine), brining.

saumure, *n.f.* Brine, pickle.

saumuré, *a.* (*fem.* **-ée**) Pickled, brined.

saunage [so′na:ʒ], *n.m.,* or **saunaison,** *n.f.*
Salt-making; salt-trade. **sauner,** *v.i.* To
make salt.—*v.t.* To extract the salt from
(salt-marsh). **saunerie,** *n.f.* Saltworks.
saunier, *n.m.* Salt-maker; salt-merchant.
Faux-saunier, (*Fr. hist.*) dealer in contraband
salt. **saunière,** *n.f.* Salt-bin; salt-lick (to
attract deer etc.).

saupoudrage [sopu′dra:ʒ], *n.m.* Salting;
sprinkling, powdering. **saupoudrer,** *v.t.*
To sprinkle with salt, pepper, etc.; to powder,
to sprinkle; to dredge (with flour etc.); (*fig.*)
to intersperse, to interlard. **saupoudroir,**
n.m. Dredger, sifter, castor.

saur or **sor** [sɔ:r], *a.m.* Smoked and salted; red
(of herrings).

saure [sɔr], *a.* Yellowish-brown; sorrel (of
horses); red, smoked (of herrings). *Hareng
saur* or *saure,* red herring.

saurel [so′rɛl], *n.m.* Horse-mackerel, scad.

saurer [so′re], *v.t.* To smoke (herrings).

sauret [so′rɛ], *a.m.* Lightly cured (herring).

saurien [so'rjɛ̃], *n.m.* Saurian.

saurin [so'rɛ̃], *n.m.* Freshly smoked herring, bloater.

saurissage [sori'sa:ʒ], *n.m.* Curing, kippering (of herrings).

saurisserie [soris'ri], *n.f.* Kippering factory.

saurographie [sorogra'fi] or **saurologie**, *n.f.* Science of saurians.

saussaie (SAULAIE).

saut [so], *n.m.* Leap, jump, hop, skip, bound; fall, waterfall; vault; (*Theat.*) tumble, somersault. *Au saut du lit*, on getting out of bed; *de plein saut*, at once, suddenly; *faire le saut*, to admit defeat, to throw in the sponge; *faire un saut*, to take a leap; *il s'élança tout d'un saut*, he rushed forward at a bound; *saut de loup*, ha-ha, sunk fence; *saut en hauteur*, high jump; *saut en longueur*, long jump; *saut de pied ferme*, standing jump; *saut d'obstacles*, hurdling; *saut à la perche*, pole vaulting; *saut périlleux*, somersault. **sautage**, *n.m.* Exploding (mines); (*typing*) skipping of space.

saut-de-lit, *n.m.* (*pl.* **sauts-de-lit**) Woman's dressing-gown.

saut-de-mouton, *n.m.* (*pl.* **sauts-de-mouton**) Fly-over crossing, overpass.

saute, *n.f.* (*Naut.*) Sudden veering or chopping of the wind.

sauté, *a.* (*fem.* **-ée**) Fried, tossed in the pan.

saute-en-barque, *n.m. inv.* Boating-jacket.

sautelle, *n.f.* Vine-shoot.

saute-mouton, *n.m.* Leap-frog (game).

sauter [so'te], *v.i.* To leap, to jump, to hop, to skip; to blow up, to explode; to jump off, to fly off; to pass over, to overlook; to spring; (*Theat.*) to tumble; (*Naut.*) to veer, to shift, to chop round (of the wind); (*Elec.*) to blow, to blow out (of fuse); (*fig.*) to skip. *Cela saute aux yeux*, that is self-evident; *faire sauter*, to make jump, to blow up, to toss up, to fry; *faire sauter la banque* [BANQUE]; *faire sauter une mine*, to explode a mine; *il sauta par-dessus la barrière* [DESSUS]; *reculer pour mieux sauter* [RECULER]; *sauter du lit*, to jump out of bed; *sauter à la corde*, to skip; *sauter au collet de*, to collar or fly at the throat of; *sauter aux nues*, to go wild with joy, indignation, etc.; *sauter de joie*, to jump for joy; *sauter en avant*, to leap forward.—*v.t.* To leap, to leap over; to overlook, to leave out, to skip; to toss in the pan. *Il a sauté une phrase*, he has skipped a sentence; *sauter une classe* (*sch.*), to skip a grade; *sauter une maille*, to drop a stitch; *sauter un fossé*, to clear a ditch.

sautereau [so'tro], *n.m.* (*pl.* **-eaux**) Jack or hopper (of harpsichords).

sauterelle, *n.f.* Grasshopper, locust; birdsnare; instrument for marking angles, used by masons, carpenters, etc., bevel square.

sauterie, *n.f.* (*fam.*) Informal dance, hop.

saute-ruisseau, *n.m. inv.* Messenger-boy (in offices).

sauteur, *n.m.* (*fem.* **-euse**) Leaper, jumper; tumbler; vaulter; bucking-horse. *Grand sauteur* (horse) show-jumper.—*n.f.* Flat stew-pan or frying-pan.—*a.* Jumping, leaping.

sautillage [soti'ja:ʒ] or **sautillement**, *n.m.* Hopping, skipping. **sautillant**, *a.* (*fem.* **-ante**) Hopping, skipping; (*fig.*) jerky (of style). **sautiller**, *v.i.* To hop, to skip, to jump about; (*fig.*) to be jerky (of style etc.).

sautoir [so'twa:r], *n.m.* Saltire, Saint Andrew's cross; watch-guard; (*Cook.*) [SAUTEUSE]; (*Horol.*) jumper. *En sautoir*, crosswise, (*Her.*) saltirewise; *porter son bagage en sautoir*, to carry one's baggage slung over the shoulder.

sauvage [so'va:ʒ], *a.* Savage, wild; (of animals) feral; untamed, uncivilized; rude, brutal, barbarous; shy, timid; unsociable.— *n.* Savage; unsociable person. **sauvagement**, *adv.* Wildly, savagely; barbarously, fiercely.

sauvageon, *n.m.* (*Agric.*) Wild stock (for grafting); briar (of roses); wild shoot.

sauvagerie, *n.f.* Unsociableness; shyness, wildness.

sauvagesse, *n.f.* Uncivilized woman; hoyden.

sauvagin, *a.* (*fem.* **-ine**) Fishy (in taste, smell, etc.).—*n.m.* Fishy taste or smell. *Sentir le sauvagin*, to taste fishy, to smell fishy.—*n.f.* Wild waterfowl; common unprepared skins or furs.

sauvegarde [sov'gard], *n.f.* Safe-keeping, safeguard; safe-conduct; (*fig.*) shield, buckler, protection; (*Naut.*) life-line, rudder pendant. *Sauvegardes de beaupré*, (*Naut.*) man-ropes of the bowsprit. **sauvegarder**, *v.t.* To watch over, to protect, to safeguard.

sauve-qui-peut [sovki'pø], *n.m. inv.* Headlong flight, rout, stampede.

sauver [so've], *v.t.* To save; to deliver, to rescue; to preserve; to spare, to exempt; to palliate, to excuse, to conceal. *Sauve qui peut*, every man for himself; *sauver la vie à quelqu'un*, to save someone's life; *sauver les apparences*, to keep up appearances; *sauver les défauts d'un ouvrage*, to conceal the imperfections of a work. **se sauver**, *v.r.* To escape, to make good one's escape; to run away; to make off; (*fam.*) to clear out; to abscond; to take refuge; to indemnify oneself; to work out one's salvation; to boil over (of liquid).

sauvetage, *n.m.* Salvage; saving, life-saving, rescue. *Appareil de sauvetage*, rescue apparatus, fire-escape; *bouée de sauvetage*, life-buoy; *canot de sauvetage*, life-boat; *ceinture de sauvetage*, life-belt; *société de sauvetage*, life-boat institution.

sauveteur, *a.m.* Saving, preserving.—*n.m.* Rescuer, lifeboatman.

sauvette, *n.f.* (*pop.*) *À la sauvette*, ready for a quick get-away. *Vendeur à la sauvette*, street-trader with one eye on the police, spiv.

sauveur, *n.m.* Saver, deliverer; Saviour, Redeemer.—*a.m.* Saving, redeeming; preserving health etc. **sauve-vie**, *n.f. inv.* Wall-rue.

savamment [sava'mã], *adv.* Learnedly, knowingly.

savane [sa'van], *n.f.* Savanna; (*C*) swamp, swampy ground.

savant [sa'vã], *a.* (*fem.* **-ante**) Learned, well-informed, expert (*en*); scholarly; clever, able, skilful. *Chien savant*, performing dog; *femme savante*, bluestocking.—*n.* Scholar, scientist. *Les savants*, the learned.

savantasse [savã'tas], *n.* (*colloq.*) Pedant, sciolist, pseudo-intellectual.

savarin [sava'rɛ̃], *n.m.* Round, hollow cake (named after Brillat-Savarin).

savary [sava'ri], *n.m.* Dragonet (fish).

savate [sa'vat], *n.f.* Old shoe; shoe down at the heel; hunt-the-slipper (game); awkward,

clumsy person; boxing with the feet. *Tirer la savate*, to box with feet and fists; *traîner la savate*, (*fig.*) to be down at heel.
savaterie, *n.f.* Old-shoe trade; old-shoe shop.
saveter [sav'te], *v.t.* (*fam.*) To bungle, to botch.
savetier, *n.m.* Cobbler; (*fig.*) bungler, duffer.
saveur [sa'vœːr], *n.f.* Savour, flavour, taste, relish, zest.
Savoie [sa'vwɑ], *f.* Savoy.
savoir [sa'vwaːr], *v.t. irr.* (*pres.p.* **sachant**, *p.p.* **su**) To know, to be aware of; to understand; to be acquainted with; to be informed of; to be instructed, trained, or practised in; to know how (can), to be able. *Autant que je sache*, to the best of my belief, as far as I know; *en savoir gré à quelqu'un*, to be grateful to someone; *en savoir trop long*, to know too much; *faire savoir*, to acquaint, to inform; *il n'en sait rien*, he knows nothing about it; *il ne sait ni A ni B* [A]; *je ne sais où j'en suis*, I do not know which way to turn; *je ne sais que faire*, I don't know what to do; *je n'en sais trop rien*, I am not very sure; *je ne sais qu'en croire*, I don't know what to think of it; *je ne saurais qu'y faire*, I cannot help it; *on ne sait jamais*, one never knows; *pas que je sache*, not to my knowledge; *puisque vous en savez tant*, since you know so much (about it); *sans le savoir*, unwittingly; *savoir écrire*, to be able to write; *savoir vivre*, to know how to behave, to be well bred; *si l'on vient à savoir cela*, if that comes to be known; *un je ne sais quoi*, indefinable something, something or other.—*v.i.* To know, to be learned. *À savoir* or *savoir*, namely, that is to say; *reste à savoir si*, it remains to be seen if.—*n.m.* Knowledge, learning, scholarship. *Demi-savoir*, half-knowledge. **se savoir**, *v.r.* To get known. *Tout se sait avec le temps*, everything becomes known in time.
savoir-faire, *n.m.* Tact; savoir-faire; cleverness; (*fam.*) gumption, nous. *Il vit de son savoir-faire*, he lives by his wits.
savoir-vivre, *n.m.* Good manners, good breeding.
savoisien [savwa'zjɛ̃], *a.* (*fem.* **-ienne**) Of or from Savoy.—*n.m.* (**Savoisien**, *fem.* **-ienne**) Savoyard.
savon [sa'vɔ̃], *n.m.* Soap; piece or cake of soap; (*colloq.*) scolding. *Eau de savon*, soap-suds; *savon à barbe*, shaving soap; *savon de Marseille*, household soap; *savon noir*, soft soap. *Savon métallique*, suds grease. (*fig.*) *Passer un savon à quelqu'un*, to give someone a good dressing-down.
savonnage, *n.m.* Soaping, washing with soap.
savonner, *v.t.* To soap; to wash with soap, to lather; (*colloq.*) to rebuke, to scold, to blow up. **se savonner**, *v.r.* To bear washing, to wash (of fabrics); to lather. *Cette étoffe se savonne*, this material will wash.
savonnerie, *n.f.* Soap-manufacture; soap-trade; soap-works.
savonnette, *n.f.* Cake of toilet soap. *Montre à savonnette*, hunting-watch.
savonneux, *a.* (*fem.* **-euse**) Soapy.
savonnier, *a.* (*fem.* **-ière**) Pertaining to soap. —*n.m.* Soap-boiler, soap-manufacturer; (*Bot.*) soapberry-tree.
savourer [savu're], *v.t.* To savour, to relish; (*fig.*) to enjoy.

savouret, *n.m.* Marrow-bone (tor flavouring soup etc.).
savoureusement, *adv.* With relish. **savoureux**, *a.* (*fem.* **-euse**) Savoury, tasty (dish); racy (story).
(*C*) **savoyane** [savwa'jan], *n.f.* (*Bot.*) Golden seal.
savoyard [savwa'jaːr], *a.* (*fem.* **-arde**) Of Savoy.—*n.* Savoyard. *Petit Savoyard*, little chimney-sweep, climbing boy.
saxatile [saksa'til], *a.* Saxatile.
Saxe [saks], *f.* Saxony.
saxifrage [saksi'fraːʒ], *a.* Saxifragous.—*n.f.* Saxifrage. *Saxifrage ombreuse*, London pride.
saxon [sak'sɔ̃], *a. and n.* (*fem.* **-onne**) Saxon.
saxophone [saksɔ'fɔn], *n.m.* Saxophone.
saynète [sɛ'nɛt], *n.f.* Playlet, sketch, drawing-room comedy.
sayon [sɛ'jɔ̃], *n.m.* Sleeveless tunic.
sbire [zbiːr], *n.m.* Sbirro; (*fig.*) limb of the law.
scabieuse (1) [ska'bjøːz], *n.f.* Scabious (plant). *Scabieuse tronquée*, devil's-bit scabious.
scabieux [ska'bjø], *a.* (*fem.* **scabieuse** (2)) Scabious, scabby.
scabre [ska:br], *a.* (*Bot.*) Scabrous, rough.
scabreux [ska'brø], *a.* (*fem.* **-euse**) Scabrous, rugged, rough; (*fig.*) dangerous, difficult, slippery, ticklish; improper, indelicate.
scaferlati [skafɛrla'ti], *n.m.* Standard tobacco sold by the French Government.
scalaire [ska'lɛːr], *n.f.* (*Conch.*) *Scalaire précieuse*, wentletrap.
scalde [skald], *n.m.* Scald (Scandinavian bard).
scalène [ska'lɛːn], *a.* Scalene; scalenus.—*n.m.* (*Anat.*) Scalenus (muscle).
scalp(e) [skalp], *n.m.* Scalp (of an enemy).
scalpel, *n.m.* Scalpel. **scalper**, *v.t.* To scalp.
scammonée [skamɔ'ne], *n.f.* Scammony.
scandale [skã'dal], *n.m.* Scandal; shame, dismay, disgust. *Au grand scandale de tout le monde*, to everyone's horror; *faire du scandale*, to make a scene; *pierre de scandale*, stumbling-block.
scandaleusement, *adv.* Scandalously. **scandaleux**, *a.* (*fem.* **-euse**) Scandalous. **scandaliser**, *v.t.* To scandalize, to shock. **se scandaliser**, *v.r.* To be scandalized, to be shocked. *Il se scandalise de tout*, he takes offence at everything.
scander [skã'de], *v.t.* To scan; to stress (a phrase); to punctuate (one's words etc.).
scandinave [skãdi'naːv], *a.* Scandinavian.—*n.* (**Scandinave**) A Scandinavian.
Scandinavie [skãdina'vi], *f.* Scandinavia.
scandium [skã'djɔm], *n.m.* (*Chem.*) Scandium.
scandix [skã'diks], *n.m.* Scandix, shepherd's needle.
scansion [skã'sjɔ̃], *n.f.* Scansion.
scape [skap], *n.m.* (*Bot.*) Flower-supporting stem; (*Ent.*) scape.
scaphandre [ska'fãːdr], *n.m.* Diving-suit. **scaphandrier**, *n.m.* Diver.
scaphocéphale [skafɔse'fal], *a.* Scaphocephalic. **scaphocéphalie**, *n.f.* Scaphocephaly.
scaphoïde, *a. and n.m.* Scaphoid.
scapin [ska'pɛ̃], *n.m.* (*Theat.*) Knave, rogue.
scapulaire [skapy'lɛːr], *a.* Scapular.—*n.m.* Scapular.
scarabée [skara'be], *n.m.* Scarabaeus (beetle); scarab.

scaramouche [skara'muʃ], *n.m.* Scaramouch.
scare [ska:r], *n.m.* Scarus (parrot-fish).
scarieux [ska'rjø], *a.* (*fem.* **-ieuse**) (*Bot.*) Scarious.
scarificateur [skarifika'tœ:r], *n.m.* (*Surg.*) Scarificator; (*Agric.*) hoeing-machine.
scarification, *n.f.* Scarification.
scarifier [skari'fje], *v.t.* To scarify.
scarlatine [skarla'tin], *n.f.* and *a.* La (*fièvre*) *scarlatine*, scarlet fever.
scarole [ska'rɔl], *n.f.* [ESCAROLE].
scatologie [skatɔlɔ'ʒi], *n.f.* Scatology.
scatophage, *a.* Scatophagous.
sceau [so], *n.m.* (*pl.* **-eaux**) Seal; (*fig.*) act of confirmation, sanction. *Apposer son sceau*, to affix one's seal; *mettre le sceau à*, to seal, (*fig.*) to complete, to put the finishing touch to; *petit sceau*, privy seal; *porter le sceau du génie*, to have the mark of genius; (*Bot.*) *sceau de la Vierge* or *de Notre-Dame*, black briony; (*Bot.*) *sceau de Salomon*, Solomon's seal; *sceaux de l'État*, seals of State; *sous le sceau du secret*, under the seal of secrecy.
scélérat [sele'ra], *a.* (*fem.* **scélérate** (1)) Wicked, villainous, criminal, vile.—*n.* Scoundrel, villain, miscreant. **scélérate** (2), *n.f.* (*Bot.*) Celery-leaved crowfoot. **scélératesse**, *n.f.* Villainy.
scellé [sɛ'le], *n.m.* Slip carrying seal placed officially on locks, closets, etc.; seal. *Apposer les scellés*, to affix the seals; *lever les scellés*, to take off the seals. **scellement**, *n.m.* Sealing; fastening; setting, bedding (in concrete etc.); plug (in wall). **sceller**, *v.t.* To put an official seal on, to seal, to seal up; (*Build.*) to fasten, to fix, to plug (in wall), to bed; (*fig.*) to ratify, to confirm. **scelleur**, *n.m.* Sealer.
scénario [sena'rjo], *n.m.* (*pl.* **scénarios** or **scénarii**) Scenario (of ballet etc.); (*Cine.*) film scenario, film script. **scénariste**, *n.* Script-writer, scenario-writer.
scène [sɛ:n], *n.f.* Stage; scenery, scene; (*fig.*) theatre, the boards; (*colloq.*) scene, quarrel, row. *Être toujours en scène*, to be on the stage all the time, (*fig.*) to be always acting; *faire une scène à quelqu'un*, to have a row with someone; *la mise en scène d'une pièce*, the production or staging of a play; *la scène se passe à Londres*; the action takes place in London; *paraître sur la scène*, to become an actor. **scénique**, *a.* Scenic, theatrical. *Indications scéniques*, stage directions.
scénographie [senɔgra'fi], *n.f.* Scenography.
scénographique, *a.* Scenographical.
scepticisme [sɛpti'sism], *n.m.* Scepticism.
sceptique, *a.* Sceptical.—*n.* Sceptic. **sceptiquement**, *adv.* Sceptically.
sceptre [sɛptr], *n.m.* Sceptre; (*fig.*) sway, empire, dominion.
schabraque [ʃa'brak] or **chabraque**, *n.f.* Shabrack, (*fam.*) used as a mild swear-word.
schah [ʃa], *n.m.* Shah (of Persia).
schako [SHAKO].
scheik or **cheik** [ʃɛk], *n.m.* Sheik.
schéma [ʃe'ma] or **schème**, *n.m.* Diagram.
schématique, *a.* Diagrammatic. *Dessin schématique*, draft, diagram.
schématiser, *v.t.* To diagrammatize.
schibboleth [ʃibɔ'let], *n.m.* Catchword, shibboleth.
schiite or **chiite** [ʃi'it], *n.m.* Shiite.
schipperke [ʃipɛr'ke], *n.m.* Schipperke (dog).

schismatique [ʃisma'tik], *a.* Schismatical.—*n.* Schismatic. **schisme**, *n.m.* Schism.
schiste [ʃist], *n.m.* Schist, slaty rock, shale.
schisteux, *a.* (*fem.* **-euse**) Schistose.
schizanthe [ski'zɑ̃:t], *n.m.* (*Bot.*) Schizanthus.
schizoïde [skizɔ'id], *a.* and *n.* Schizoid.
schizoïdie, *n.f.* Schizoid tendency.
schizomycètes, *n.m. pl.* Schizomycetes.
schizophrène, *a.* and *n.* Schizophrenic.
schizophrénie, *n.f.* Schizophrenia.
schlague [ʃlag], *n.f.* *Donner la schlague*, to flog, to beat.
schlass [ʃlas], *a.* (*slang*) Drunk.
schlich [ʃlik], *n.m.* Crushed ore, slick.
schlinguer [ʃlɛ̃'ge], *v.i.* (*vulg.*) To stink, to pong.
schlittage [ʃli'ta:ʒ], *n.m.* (*E. dial.*) Transport in a *schlitte*. **schlitte**, *n.f.* Sled on timber trackway (for felled trees). **schlitteur**, *n.m.* Man in charge of this.
schloff [ʃlɔf], (*pop.*) *Aller à schloff*, to go to bed.
schnaps [ʃnaps] or **schnick** [ʃnik], *n.m.* (*pop.*) (poor) Brandy.
schooner [sku'nœ:r], *n.m.* Schooner.
schnorkel [ʃnɔr'kel], *n.m.* Schnorkel, submarine's air-tube.
sciage [sja:ʒ], *n.m.* Sawing.
scialytique [siali'tik], *n.m.* and *a.* Shadowless lamp (used in operating theatre).
sciant [sjɑ̃], *a.* (*fem.* **-iante**) (*pop.*) Boring, annoying, tiresome.
sciatique [sja'tik], *a.* Sciatic.—*n.m.* Sciatic nerve.—*n.f.* Sciatica.
scie [si], *n.f.* Saw; saw-fish; (*pop.*) nuisance; practical joke repeated *ad nauseam*. *Quelle scie!* what a bore! *scie à découper*, fret-saw; *scie à chantourner*, scroll-saw; *scie circulaire*, circular saw, (*Am.*) buzz-saw; *scie passepartout*, compass saw; *scie à refendre*, rip-saw; *scie de scieur de long*, pit-saw.
sciemment [sja'mɑ̃], *adv.* Wittingly, knowingly.
science [sjɑ̃:s], *n.f.* Science, knowledge, learning; skill, expertness. *Homme de science*, scientist; *la science infuse*, intuitive knowledge; *posséder une science à fond*, to be thoroughly master of a science; *s'adonner aux sciences*, to devote oneself to the sciences; *sciences naturelles*, natural science.
sciène [sjɛn], *n.f.* Sciaena (fish).
scientifique [sjɑ̃ti'fik], *a.* Scientific.—*n.* (*fam.*) Scientist. **scientifiquement**, *adv.* Scientifically.
scier [sje], *v.t.* (*conjugated like* PRIER) To saw; to saw off; to reap, to cut down. (*fam.*) *Scier le dos à quelqu'un*, to bore someone stiff.—*v.i.* (*Row.*) To back water, to hold (boat). *Scie, bâbord*, hold her, stroke side!
scierie, *n.f.* Sawmill.
scieur [sjœ:r], *n.m.* Sawyer; reaper. *Fosse de scieur de long*, saw-pit.
scille [sil], *n.f.* Scilla, squill.
scinder [sɛ̃'de], *v.t.* To divide, to split up.
scinque [sɛ̃:k], *n.m.* Skink.
scintillant [sɛ̃ti'jɑ̃], *a.* (*fem.* **-ante**) Scintillant, scintillating; twinkling. **scintillation**, *n.f.* or **scintillement**, *n.m.* Scintillation, sparkling; twinkling. **scintiller**, *v.i.* To scintillate, to sparkle; to twinkle (of star); (*Cine.*) to flicker.
sciographie [sjɔgra'fi], *n.f.* Skiagraphy.
sciographique, *a.* Skiagraphical, (drawing) in vertical section.

scion [sjɔ̃], *n.m.* Scion, shoot; tip (of fishing rod).

Scipion [si'pjɔ̃], *m.* *Scipion l'Africain*, Scipio Africanus.

scirpe [sirp], *n.m.* Club-rush, bulrush.

scissile [si'sil], *a.* Scissile. **scission,** *n.f.* Scission; split, secession, division. *Faire scission*, to secede; *faire une scission*, to bring about a secession. **scissionnaire,** *a.* Seceding.—*n.m.* Seceder.

scissure, *n.f.* Fissure, crack, cleft.

sciure [sjy:r], *n.f.* *Sciure de bois*, sawdust.

sclérite [skle'rit], *n.f.* Sclerite; (*Med.*) scleritis.

scléroderme, *n.m.* Scleroderm.

sclérogène, *a.* Sclerogenous.

sclérose, *n.f.* Sclerosis.

scléroser, *v.t.* To harden.

sclérotique, *a.* and *n.f.* Sclerotic.

scolaire [skɔ'lɛ:r], *a.* (Of schools) *Année scolaire*, school year (October to July).

scolarité, *n.f.* Course of study; (*pl.*) school fees. *Scolarité obligatoire*, compulsory school attendance.

scolasticat, *n.m.* Religious training-college; course of study followed there.

scolastique, *a.* and *n.m.* Scholastic, schoolman.—*n.f.* Scholasticism. **scolastiquement,** *adv.* Scholastically.

scoliaste [skɔ'ljast], *n.m.* Scholiast.

scolie, *n.f.* Scolion, drinking-song; (*Ent.*) scolia.

scoliose [skɔ'ljo:z], *n.f.* Curvature of the spine, scoliosis.

scolopendre [skɔlɔ'pɑ̃:dr], *n.f.* Hart's-tongue; (*Zool.*) scolopendra (centipede).

scombre [skɔ̃:br], *n.m.* Scomber; mackerel.

sconse [skɔ̃:s], *n.m.* Skunk fur.

scooter [sku'tɛ:r], *n.m.* Motor-scooter. *Autos scooters,* light three-wheeled delivery vans.

scops [skɔps], *n.m.* (*Orn.*) Scops' owl.

scorbut [skɔr'by], *n.m.* Scurvy. **scorbutique,** *a.* and *n.* Scorbutic.

scorie [skɔ'ri], *n.f.* Scoria, slag, dross; scale (of boilers etc.). **scorification,** *n.f.* Slagging. **scorificatoire,** *n.m.* Scorifier. **scorifier,** *v.t.* (*conjugated like* PRIER) To scorify.

scorpène [skɔr'pɛn], *n.f.* Scorpion-fish.

scorpioïde [skɔrpjɔ'id], *a.* (*Bot.*) Scorpioid (curled up like a scorpion's tail).

scorpion [skɔr'pjɔ̃], *n.m.* Scorpion.

scorsonère [skɔrsɔ'nɛ:r] or **scorzonère,** *n.f.* Scorzonera, viper's grass, wild salsify.

scotie [skɔ'si], *n.f.* (*Arch.*) Scotia.

scout [skut], *a.* (*fem.* **scoute**) Of scouting.—*n.m.* (Boy) scout. **scoutisme,** *n.m.* Scouting, boy-scout movement.

scratch [skratʃ], *n.m.* (*spt.*) *Être* or *partir scratch,* to start at scratch. **scratcher,** *v.t.* (*spt.*) To scratch (horse, competitor, etc.).

scribe [skrib], *n.m.* Scribe; copyist. **scribouillard,** *n.m.* Clerk, pen-pusher.

script [skript], *n.m.* Script (film or play). **scripteur,** *n.m.* Writer of the Pope's bulls; manuscript writer. **script-girl,** *n.f.* (*pl.* **script-girls**) (*Cine.*) Continuity-girl.

scriptural [skripty'ral], *a.* (*fem.* **-ale,** *pl.* **-aux**) Scriptural.

scrofulaire [skrɔfy'lɛ:r], *n.f.* Figwort.

scrofule, *n.f.* Scrofula, king's evil. **scrofuleux,** *a.* (*fem.* **-euse**) Scrofulous.—*n.* Scrofulous person.

scrotal [skrɔ'tal], *a.* (*fem.* **-ale,** *pl.* **-aux**) (*Anat.*) Scrotal. **scrotiforme,** *a.* Scrotiform. **scrotocèle,** *n.f.* Scrotocele. **scrotum,** *n.m.* Scrotum.

scrupule [skry'pyl], *n.m.* Scruple, qualm, doubt; scrupulousness; scruple (weight). *Avoir trop de scrupules,* to be over-scrupulous; *je m'en ferais scrupule,* I would hesitate to do it; *lever des scrupules,* to remove scruples.

scrupuleusement, *adv.* Scrupulously. **scrupuleux,** *a.* (*fem.* **-euse**) Scrupulous, strict, punctilious.

scrutateur [skryta'tœ:r], *n.* (*fem.* **-trice**) Investigator, scrutinizer; scrutineer, teller (of a ballot etc.).—*a.* Searching, scrutinizing.

scruter [skry'te], *v.t.* To scrutinize, to search closely into, to investigate.

scrutin, *n.m.* Ballot, balloting, poll. *Au scrutin secret,* by secret vote; *scrutin de liste,* vote by list; *scrutin majoritaire,* election by absolute majority; *second tour de scrutin,* second ballot.

sculptable [skyl'tabl], *a.* Suitable to be sculptured or carved.

sculpter [skyl'te], *v.t.* To sculpture, to carve.

sculpteur, *n.m.* Sculptor, carver.

sculptural, *a.* (*fem.* **-ale,** *pl.* **-aux**) Sculptural.

sculpture, *n.f.* Sculpture, carving; carved work.

scutellaire [skyte'lɛ:r], *n.f.* Skull-cap.

scutiforme [skyti'fɔrm], *a.* Shield-shaped.

scytale [si'tal], *n.f.* Scytale (staff used in Sparta to send secret dispatches).

scythe [sit], *a.* and *n.* Scythian.

Scythie [si'ti], **la,** *f.* Scythia.

se [sə, s], *pron. inv.* Oneself, himself, herself, itself, themselves; to oneself etc.; each other. *Cela se peut,* that may be; *ils s'aiment,* they love each other; *ils se connaissent,* they know each other; *ils se parlent,* they speak to each other; *il se ruine,* he is ruining himself.

séamment [sea'mɑ̃], *adv.* Decently, becomingly.

séance [se'ɑ̃:s], *n.f.* Seat (right of sitting); sitting; session, duration, meeting; sitting (for one's portrait, etc.); performance (conjuring etc.); seance. *Avoir séance,* to have a seat (on committee etc.); *être en séance,* to be in session; *faire une longue séance,* to sit a long time, to pay a long call; *lever la séance,* to close the meeting; *prendre séance,* to take one's seat; *séance de cinéma,* film-show; *séance tenante,* there and then, forthwith.

séant [se'ɑ̃] (1), *a.* (*fem.* **-ante**) Sitting; fitting, seemly, becoming.—*n.m.* Sitting posture; seat; (*fam.*) behind, bottom. *Être sur son séant,* to be sitting up; *se mettre sur son séant,* to sit up.

séant (2), *pres.p.* [SEOIR (1)].

seau [so], *n.m.* (*pl.* **seaux**) Pail, bucket. *Il pleut à seaux,* it is raining in torrents.

sébacé [seba'se], *a.* (*fem.* **-ée**) Sebaceous.

Sébastien [sebas'tjɛ̃], *m.* Sebastian.

sébeste [se'bɛst], *n.m.* Sebesten (plum). **sébestier,** *n.m.* Sebesten-tree.

sébifère [sebi'fɛ:r], *a.* (*Bot.*) Sebiferous.

sébile [se'bil], *n.f.* Small wooden bowl (used by beggars); pan (in gold-mining).

séborrhée [sebɔ're], *n.f.* (*Med.*) Seborrhoea.

sec [sek], *a.* (*fem.* **sèche** (1)) Dry, arid; dried up, withered; lean, spare, gaunt; barren, jejune, plain, unattractive; cold, unfeeling, sharp, severe (of reprimands etc.). *À pied* *sec*, dry-shod; *avoir le gosier sec*, to be thirsty, to feel dry; *cœur sec*, unfeeling heart; *coup sec*, sharp stroke; *il a le pouls sec*, his pulse is sharp; *perte sèche*, dead loss; *sec comme un pendu*, as thin as a rake; *en cinq sec*, in a jiffy. —*n.m.* Dryness; dry fodder; dry weather; (*colloq.*) without money. *À sec*, dried up, run dry; (*fig.*) hard-up; *à sec sur le rivage*, high and dry (of ships); *mettre un étang à sec*, to drain a pond.—*adv.* Dryly, sharply. *Boire sec*, to drink hard, to drink (whisky etc.) neat; *répondre sec*, to answer sharply.

sécable [se'kabl], *a.* That can be cut, divisible.

sécant [se'kɑ̃], *a.* (*fem.* **-ante**) Cutting; (*Geom.*) secant.—*n.f.* Secant.

sécateur, *n.m.* (*Gard.*) Pruning-shears; secateurs.

seccotine [sɛkɔ'tin], *n.f.* Seccotine.

sécession [sesɛ'sjɔ̃], *n.f.* Secession. **sécessionniste**, *a.* and *n.* Secessionist.

séchage [se'ʃaːʒ], *n.m.* Drying.

sèche (1) [sɛʃ], *fem.* [SEC].—*n.f.* (*fam.*) Cigarette, fag.

sèche (2) [SEICHE].

séchée [se'ʃe], *n.f.* Drying. **sèchement**, *adv.* Dryly; curtly, sharply.

sécher [se'ʃe], *v.t. irr.* (*conjug. like* ACCÉLÉRER) To dry; to dry up; to cure, to season; (*sch. slang*) to shun, to cut, to avoid.—*v.i.* To dry; to dry up, to wither; to pine away; (*sch. slang*) to fail to answer, to be stumped. **se sécher**, *v.r.* To dry oneself; to dry (of a thing).

sécheresse, *n.f.* Dryness; drought; (*fig.*) harshness, curtness, sharpness; barrenness, aridity. **sécherie**, *n.f.* Drying-house.

sécheur, *n.m.* Drying or desiccating plant.

séchoir, *n.m.* Drying-room; dryer, clothes-horse; clothes-airer; (hairdresser's) drying machine.

second [sə'gɔ̃, zgɔ̃], *a.* (*fem.* **-onde**) Second. *De seconde main*, second-hand, not original; *de second ordre*, inferior; (*Phil.*) *les causes secondes*, the secondary causes; (*Naut.*) *second maître*, petty officer; *seconds violons*, second violins.—*n.* Second, assistant; second in duel; first officer, mate. *Audace sans seconde*, unparalleled audacity; *en second*, second, second in command, in the second place, in a subordinate capacity.—*n.m.* Second story, second floor.—*n.f.* Second class; (*sch.*) fifth form; second of time, circle, etc.; (*Mus.*) second; (*Fenc.*) seconde; (*Print.*) revise.

secondaire [səgɔ̃'dɛːr], *a.* Secondary; subordinate, subservient, accessory. *Enseignement secondaire* or *du second degré*, secondary education.—*n.m.* (*Elec.*) Secondary winding; secondary (transformer). **secondairement**, *adv.* Secondarily.

secondement, *adv.* Secondly, in the second place.

seconder, *v.t.* To second, to assist; to back (up), to support; to promote, to further, to forward.

secondine, *n.f.* (*Bot.*) Secundine; (*Obstetrics, pl.*) secundines (after-birth).

sécot [se'ko], *a.* (*pop.*) Thin, lanky.

secouement [səku'mɑ̃] or **secouage**, *n.m.* Shaking, jogging, jolting.

secouer [sə'kwe], *v.t.* To shake, to jog, to jolt; to shake off, to discard, to throw off; to shock, to handle roughly; to rouse. **se**

secouer, *v.r.* To shake oneself, to bestir or exert oneself; (*fam.*) to get a move on; to snap out of it.

secourable [səku'rabl], *a.* Helpful, helping, willing to help; relievable.

secourir [səku'riːr], *v.t. irr.* (*conjugated like* COURIR) To succour, to assist, to help, to relieve.

secourisme, *n.m.* First-aid; course in first-aid. **secouriste**, *n.* Qualified first-aider.

secours, *n.m.* Help, assistance, aid, succour, relief; rescue. *Appeler police secours*, to dial 999; *au secours!* help! *caisse de secours*, relief fund; *crier au secours*, to cry out for help; *donner du secours*, to render assistance; *premiers secours*, first-aid; *secours à domicile*, outdoor relief; *société de secours mutuels*, friendly society, benefit society; *roue de secours*, (*Motor.*) spare wheel; *terrain de secours*, emergency landing-ground; *troupes de secours*, relieving force.

secousse [sə'kus], *n.f.* Shake, shock; blow, concussion; jog, jerk, jolt. *Secousse sismique*, earth tremor.

secret [sə'krɛ], *a.* (*fem.* **-ète**) Secret, private, hidden; reserved, reticent, discreet. *Escalier secret*, private staircase; *tenir secret*, to keep secret.—*n.m.* Secret; secrecy, privacy, mystery; explanation, reason; secret drawer, secret spring; solitary confinement. *En secret*, secretly; *être du secret*, to be in the secret; *le secret de Polichinelle*, an open secret; *mettre un prisonnier au secret*, to put a prisoner in solitary confinement; *secret de deux secret de Dieu, secret de trois secret de tous*, no secret but between two.—*n.f.* Secret prayer; (*pop.*) secret police.

secrétaire [səkre'tɛːr], *n.* Secretary. *Secrétaire d'ambassade*, secretary to an embassy; *secrétaire d'État*, Secretary of State; *secrétaire général*, chief secretary.—*n.m.* Writing-desk, secrétaire; (*Orn.*) secretary-bird.

secrétairerie, *n.f.* Secretary's office.

secrétariat, *n.m.* Secretaryship; secretary's office; secretariat.

secrète [SECRET].

secrètement [səkrɛt'mɑ̃], *adv.* Secretly, in secret, inwardly.

sécréter [sekre'te], *v.t. irr.* (*conjugated like* ACCÉLÉRER) To secrete (of glands etc.).

sécréteur, *a.* (*fem.* **-euse** or **-trice**) Secretory, secreting. **sécrétion**, *n.f.* Secretion. **sécrétoire**, *a.* Secretory.

sectaire [sɛk'tɛːr], *n.* Sectary.—*a.* Sectarian.

sectarisme [sɛkta'rism], *n.m.* Sectarianism.

sectateur, *n.m.* (*fem.* **-trice**) Follower, votary.

secte [sɛkt], *n.f.* Sect. *Faire secte*, to form a sect, to differ from most people.

secteur [sɛk'tœːr], *n.m.* Sector, section; district, area (served by electricity supply etc.).

sectile [sɛk'til], *a.* Sectile.

section [sɛk'sjɔ̃], *n.f.* Section; division, (*Mil.*) platoon (*Infantry*); section (*Artill.*); stage on bus route; municipal or electoral ward. *Sections coniques*, conic sections.

sectionnement, *n.m.* Division into parts.

sectionner, *v.t.* To divide into sections.

séculaire [seky'lɛːr], *a.* Secular, coming once in a century; century-old; ancient; time-honoured.

sécularisation, *n.f.* Secularization. **séculariser,** *v.t.* To secularize. **sécularisme,** *n.m.* Secularism. **sécularité,** *n.f.* Secularity; secular jurisdiction.

séculier, *a.* (*fem.* **-ière**) Secular, lay; temporal, worldly. *Le bras séculier,* the secular power.—*n.m.* Layman. **séculièrement,** *adv.* Secularly.

secundo [səgɔ̃'do], *adv.* Secondly.

sécurité [sekyri'te], *n.f.* Security, confidence, safety. *Dispositif de sécurité,* safety device; *sécurité de la route,* road safety; *Sécurité Sociale,* social security, National Health Service.

sedan [sə'dɑ̃], *n.m.* Sedan-cloth.

sédatif [seda'tif], *a.* (*fem.* **-ive**) Sedative.— *n.m.* Sedative. **sédation,** *n.f.* Sedation.

sédentaire [sedɑ̃'tɛ:r], *a.* Sedentary; fixed, settled, stationary; (*Orn.*) non-migratory. **sédentarité,** *n.f.* Sedentary life.

sédiment [sedi'mɑ̃], *n.m.* Sediment. **sédimentaire,** *a.* Sedimentary.

séditieusement [sedisjøz'mɑ̃], *adv.* Seditiously. **séditieux,** *a.* (*fem.* **-ieuse**) Seditious; mutinous, rebellious, treasonable.— *n.m.* Rebel, mutineer.

sédition, *n.f.* Sedition, mutiny, riot.

séducteur [sedyk'tœ:r], *n.m.* (*fem.* **-trice**) Seducer, enticer.—*a.* Seductive; enticing, alluring.

séduction, *n.f.* Seduction; enticement; allurement; bribing, subornation. *La séduction des richesses,* the allurements of wealth; *séduction de témoins,* bribing of witnesses.

séduire [se'dɥi:r], *v.t. irr.* (*conjug. like* CONDUIRE) To seduce; to attract, to beguile; to charm, to win over; to fascinate, to captivate; to suborn, to bribe. **séduisant,** *a.* (*fem.* **-ante**) Seductive, alluring, fascinating; tempting, enticing.

sédum [se'dɔm], *n.m.* (*Bot.*) Sedum.

ségétal [seʒe'tal], *a.* (*fem.* **-ale**, *pl.* **-aux**) Growing in cornfields.

segment [seg'mɑ̃], *n.m.* Segment. *Segment de piston,* piston ring. **segmentaire,** *a.* Segmental; (*Geom.*) segmentary. **segmentation,** *n.f.* Segmentation. **segmenter,** *v.t.* To divide into segments.

ségrairie [segrɛ'ri], *n.f.* Wood held in common. **ségrais,** *n.m.* Detached wood.

ségrégatif [segrega'tif], *a.* (*fem.* **-ive**) Segregative. **ségrégation,** *n.f.* Segregation.

seiche [sɛʃ], *n.f.* Cuttle-fish; tidal-wave (on Swiss lakes).

séide [se'id], *n.m.* Fanatical partisan; blind supporter.

seigle [sɛgl], *n.m.* Rye. *Seigle ergoté,* spurred rye; *faux seigle,* rye-grass.

seigneur [sɛ'ɲœːr], *n.m.* Lord; lord of the manor, squire; nobleman; the Lord. *À tout seigneur tout honneur,* honour to whom honour is due; *en grand seigneur,* in lordly style; *un grand seigneur,* a great lord; *Le Seigneur,* the Lord God; *Notre-Seigneur,* our Lord; *petit seigneur,* lordling; *seigneur suzerain,* lord paramount. **seigneurial,** *a.* (*fem.* **-iale**, *pl.* **-iaux**) Seigneurial, manorial; lordly. **seigneurie,** *n.f.* Seigniory; lordship; manor. *Votre Seigneurie,* your Lordship.

seille [sɛːj], *n.f.* (Wooden) pail, bucket.

seime [sɛm], *n.f.* (*Vet*) Wire-heel.

sein [sɛ̃], *n.m.* Breast, bosom; (*fig.*) heart,

midst; womb; gulf. *Au sein de l'Église,* in the bosom of the Church; *donner le sein à un enfant,* to give a child the breast; *le sein de la terre,* the bowels of the earth.

seine [sɛːn], *n.f.* Seine (fishing-net). *Pêche à la seine,* seine-fishing.

seing [sɛ̃], *n.m.* Sign manual, signature. *Acte sous seing privé,* private agreement.

séisme [se'ism], *n.m.* Earthquake, seism, shock.

seize [sɛːz], *a. and n.m. inv.* Sixteen, sixteenth. **seizième,** *a. and n.m.* Sixteenth. **seizièmement,** *adv.* Sixteenthly.

séjour [se'ʒuːr], *n.m.* Stay, abode, sojourn; place where one sojourns; dwelling, habitation; continuance. *Interdiction de séjour,* local banishment; *permis de séjour,* permission to reside.

séjournement, *n.m.* Sojourning.

séjourner [seʒur'ne], *v.i.* To stay, to sojourn, to make a stay; to remain, to continue; (of water) to lie stagnant.

sel [sɛl], *n.m.* Salt; (*fig.*) wit, pungency; smelling-salts. *Au gros sel,* coarse; *de bon sel,* properly salted; *sel anglais,* Epsom salts; *sel attique,* Attic wit; *sel blanc,* table-salt; *sel gris,* kitchen salt; *beurre demi-sel,* slightly salted butter.

sélacien [sela'sjɛ̃], *a.* (*fem.* **-ienne**) (*Ichth.*) Selachian.—*n.m. pl.* Cartilaginous fishes.

sélam [se'lam], *n.m.* Emblematic nosegay (in the East).

sélecteur [selɛk'tœːr], *a.* (*fem.* **-trice**) Selecting; selective.—*n.m.* (*Elec.*) Selector switch.

sélectif, *a.* (*fem.* **-ive**) Selective (of radio receiver).

sélection, *n.f.* Selection. **sélectionner,** *v.t.* To choose (team).

sélectivité, *n.f.* Selectivity.

séléniate [sele'niat], *n.m.* Seleniate. **sélénien,** *a.* (*fem.* **-ienne**) Selenian. **sélénieux** [SÉLÉNIQUE]. **sélénifère,** *a.* Seleniferous. **sélénique,** *a.* (*Chem.*) Selenic. **sélénite,** *n.f.* (*Chem.*) Selenite.—*n.m.* Inhabitant of the moon. **sélénium,** *n.m.* Selenium. **sélénographie,** *n.f.* Selenography, 'lunar geography'.

self [sɛlf], *n.f. abbr. of* **self-induction,** *n.f.* (*Elec.*) Self-induction. (*Bobine de*) *self,* self-induction coil.

sellage [sɛ'laːʒ], *n.m.* Saddling.

selle [sɛl], *n.f.* Saddle; stool, water-closet; motion of the bowels; washing-board; turntable (of modeller); (*pl.*) (*Med.*) faeces. *Aller à la selle,* to go to stool; *cheval de selle,* saddle-horse; *être toujours en selle,* never to be out of the saddle; *selle de calfat,* (*Naut.*) caulking-box; *selle de femme,* side-saddle, lady's saddle; *se remettre en selle,* to remount, (*fig.*) to re-establish oneself in business etc.

seller [sɛ'le], *v.t.* To saddle.—*v.i. and* **se seller,** *v.r.* To settle down, to harden (of land).

sellerie, *n.f.* Saddlery, saddle-room; harness-room.

sellette [sɛ'lɛt], *n.f.* Culprits' seat, stool of repentance; small saddle; shoeblack's box; (*Naut.*) caulking-box, slung cradle. *Être sur la sellette,* to be at the bar (of criminals); *tenir sur la sellette,* to cross-question, to heckle.

sellier [sɛ'lje], *n.m.* Saddler.

selon [sə'lɔ̃], *prep.* According to, conformably to, pursuant to. *C'est selon,* that depends; *on l'a traité selon son mérite,* he was treated according to his deserts; *selon moi,* in my opinion; *selon que,* according as.

seltz [sɛls], *n.m. Eau de Seltz,* soda water.

seltzogène [sɛlsɔ'ʒɛːn], *n.m.* Seltzogene.

semailles [sə'maːj], *n.f. pl.* Sowings; seeds; sowing; sowing-time.

semaine [sə'mɛn], *n.f.* Week; week's work; week's wages, week's money; week's pocket-money, week's allowances. *À la semaine,* by the week; *être de semaine,* to be on duty for the week; *la semaine des quatre jeudis,* when two Sundays come together (*i.e.* never); *la semaine prochaine,* next week; *par semaine,* per week; *prêter à la petite semaine,* to lend money (for a short time) at high interest; *semaine anglaise,* five-day (working) week; *semaine sainte,* Holy Week. (C) *Fin de semaine,* week-end.

semainier, *n.m.* (*fem.* **-ière**) Officer, monk, actor, etc., on duty for the week; case of seven razors; (*Ind.*) time-sheet; weekly output.—*a.* Once a week; weekly.

semaison [s(ə)mɛ'zɔ̃], *n.f.* (*Agric.*) Sowing-time; self-seeding.

sémantique [semɑ̃'tik], *a.* Semasiological, semantic.—*n.f.* Semasiology, semantics.

sémaphore [sema'fɔːr], *n.m.* Semaphore, signal-post.

semblable [sɑ̃'blabl], *a.* Like, similar, alike, such. *Semblable à un torrent,* like a torrent. —*n.* Like; fellow, match, equal.—*n.m.* Fellow-creature, fellow-man. **semblablement,** *adv.* Likewise, also, in like manner.

*semblance, *n.f.* Semblance.

semblant [sɑ̃'blɑ̃], *n.m.* Appearance, semblance, seeming, look; pretence, show. *Faire semblant,* to feign, to pretend, to make believe, to appear as if; *faux semblant,* false show, pretence; *il fait semblant de ne pas le voir,* he pretends not to see it; *ne faire semblant de rien,* to appear to take no notice, to act surreptitiously.

sembler [sɑ̃'ble], *v.i.* To seem, to appear. *Cela me semble ainsi,* it appears so to me; *c'est ce qui me semble,* precisely as I thought; *faites comme bon vous semblera,* do as you think fit; *il lui semble que cela n'est rien,* he thinks it is nothing; *il me semble que je le vois,* I fancy I see him; *que vous en semble?* what do you think of it? *si bon lui semble,* if he thinks fit.

semé [sə'me], *a.* (*fem.* **-ée**) Sowed, sown; strewn (*de*); (Her.) semé. *Semé de fleurs,* strewn with flowers; *semé d'étoiles,* spangled with stars.

semelle [sə'mɛl], *n.f.* Sole (of boots, shoes, etc.); foot (of stockings); length of a foot; sleeper, groundsill; shoe (of sledge etc.); bedplate (of machine). *Battre la semelle,* to stamp one's feet to get warm; to tramp; *ne pas reculer d'une semelle,* not to give way an inch.

semen [sə'mɛn], *n.f.,* or **semen-contra,** *n.m.* Worm-seed, santonica.

semence, *n.f.* Seed; semen; (*fig.*) seeds, cause; seed-pearls; fine sprigs (small nails, tin-tacks).

semer [sə'me], *v.t. irr.* (*conjugated like* AMENER) To sow; to scatter, to strew, to sprinkle; to disseminate; to shed; (*pop.*) to get rid of. *Semer la discorde,* to sow discord.

semestre [sə'mɛstr], *n.m.* Half-year, six months; half-year's income; six months' furlough; (*Am. sch.*) semester. *Par semestre,* half-yearly.

semestriel, *a.* (*fem.* **-ielle**) Half-yearly; of six months' duration.

semeur [sə'mœːr], *n.m.* (*fem.* **-euse**) Sower; (*fig.*) disseminator.—*n.f.* Seed-drill; (Orn.) wagtail.

semi-circulaire [səmisirky'lɛːr], *a.* Semi-circular.

semi-hebdomadaire, *a.* Semi-weekly, bi-weekly.

semi-illettré, *a.* (*fem.* **-ée**) Semi-literate.

sémillance [semi'jɑ̃ːs], *n.f.* Sprightliness, liveliness. **sémillant,** *a.* (*fem.* **-ante**) Brisk, lively, sprightly.

*sémiller [semi'je], *v.i.* To be sprightly or lively.

semi-lunaire [səmily'nɛːr], *a.* Semilunar.

semi-mensuel, *a.* (*fem.* **-uelle**) Fortnightly.

séminaire [semi'nɛːr], *n.m.* Seminary, theological college; course followed at college; (*Agric.*) fattening coop.

séminal [semi'nal], *a.* (*fem.* **-ale,** *pl.* **-aux**) Seminal.

séminariste [semina'rist], *n.m.* Seminarist, student of theological college.

sémination [semina'sjɔ̃], *n.f.* Semination.

séminifère, *a.* Seminiferous.

semi-officiel [səmiɔfi'sjɛl], *a.* (*fem.* **-ielle**) Semi-official.

semi-périodique [səmiperjɔ'dik], *a.* Semi-periodic.

semi-preuve, *n.f.* (*Law*) Imperfect proof.

semis [sə'mi], *n.m.* Sowing; seed-bed; seedlings.

semi-solide [səmisɔ'lid], *a.* Semi-solid.

Sémite [se'mit], *n.* Semite. **sémitique,** *a.* Semitic. **sémitisme,** *n.m.* Semitism.

semi-ton [səmi'tɔ̃], *n.m.* (*pl.* **semi-tons**) Semi-tone.

semi-voyelle, *n.f.* (*pl.* **semi-voyelles**) Semi-vowel.

semoir [sə'mwaːr], *n.m.* Seed-bag; seed-drill.

semonce [sə'mɔ̃ːs], *n.f.* Rebuke, reprimand, lecture; **invitation to appear, call; (Naut.)* summons to show colours. *Coup de semonce,* warning shot. **semoncer,** *v.t.* To reprimand, to lecture; to summon (a ship) to show its colours.

semoule [sə'mul], *n.f.* Semolina.

sempiternel [sɛ̃piter'nɛl], *a.* (*fem.* **-elle**) Sempiternal, everlasting. **sempiternellement,** *adv.* Sempiternally.

sénat [se'na], *n.m.* Senate; senate-house.

sénateur [sena'tœːr], *n.m.* Senator. **sénatorial,** *a.* (*fem.* **-iale,** *pl.* **-iaux**) Senatorial. **sénatrice,** *n.f.* Senator's wife.

sénatus-consulte, *n.m.* (*pl.* **sénatus-consultes**) Senatus Consultum (decree of the senate).

senau [sə'no], *n.m.* (*Naut.*) Snow (vessel). *Voile de senau,* trysail.

séné [se'ne], *n.m.* Senna. *Passe-moi la rhubarbe (or la casse), je te passerai le séné,* you scratch my back and I'll scratch yours.

sénéchal [sene'ʃal], *n.m.* (*pl .* **-aux**) Seneschal.

Grand sénéchal, high seneschal. **sénéchale,**
n.f. Seneschal's wife.
sénéchaussée [seneʃɔ'se], *n.f.* Seneschalship;
seneschal's jurisdiction; seneschal's court.
seneçon [sən'sɔ̃], *n.m.* Groundsel.
sénegré [sen'gre], *n.m.* (*Bot.*) Fenugreek.
Sénèque [se'nɛk], *m.* Seneca.
sénescence [senɛ'sã:s], *n.f.* Senescence.
sénescent, *a.* (*fem.* -**ente**). Senescent,
elderly.
sénestre [se'nɛstr] or **senestre,** *a.* Left,
(*Her.*) sinister.
sénevé [sen've], *n.m.* Black mustard (plant).
sénile [se'nil], *a.* Senile.
sénilité, *n.f.* Senility, old age.
senne [SEINE].
sens [sã:s], *n.m. inv.* Sense; senses, feelings;
judgment, wits, intelligence; consciousness;
meaning, import; acceptation, interpretation,
construction; opinion, sentiment; way,
direction. *A contre-sens,* in a wrong sense; *à
double sens,* with double meaning; *bon sens,*
good sense; *ce mot a deux sens,* that word has
two meanings; *dans tous les sens,* in all
directions; *dans le sens inverse,* in the opposite direction; *dans le sens des aiguilles d'une
montre,* clockwise; *être dans son bon sens,* to
be in one's right senses; *j'abonde dans votre
sens,* I am entirely of your opinion; *le sens
commun,* common sense; *le sens intime* or
interne, consciousness; *le sens de la circulation,* the direction of traffic; *sens dessus
dessous,* upside down; *sens devant derrière,*
back to front; *sens figuré,* figurative sense;
sens giratoire, roundabout, (*Am.*) traffic circle;
sens interdit, no entry; *sens propre,* proper
meaning; *sens unique,* one way street.
sensation, *n.f.* Sensation, feeling. *Faire
sensation,* to cause a sensation; *sensation de
chaleur,* glow of warmth; *un roman à sensation,* a sensational, thrilling novel.
sensationnel, *a.* (*fem.* -**elle**) Sensational.
sensé, *a.* (*fem.* -**ée**) Sensible, intelligent.
sensément, *adv.* Sensibly, judiciously.
sensibilisateur [sãsibiliza'tœ:r], *a.* (*fem.*
-**trice**) Sensitizing (to light).—*n.f.* (*Biol.*)
Sensitizer. **sensibilisation,** *n.f.* Sensitiza-
tion, sensitizing. **sensibiliser,** *v.t.* To
sensitize.
sensibilité [sãsibili'te], *n.f.* Sensibility, sensitiveness, feeling, compassion.
sensible, *a.* Sensible, palpable, perceptible;
lively, acute (of feelings); sensitive, impressionable, susceptible, responsive; sympathetic; tender, sore (of flesh etc.); evident,
obvious; visible (of the horizon). *C'est son
endroit sensible,* that's his tender spot; *il se
montra sensible à ma douleur,* he seemed
moved by my sorrow; *note sensible,* (*Mus.*)
leading note.—*n.m.* The sensible or perceptible to sense. **sensiblement,** *adv.* Appreciably, noticeably; feelingly, keenly, deeply;
obviously, visibly, considerably.
sensiblerie, *n.f.* Sentimentality; (*fam.*) sob-
stuff.
sensitif, *a.* (*fem.* -**ive**) Sensitive; sensory.—
n.f. Sensitive plant.
sensitivité [sãsitivi'te], *n.f.* Sensitivity.
sensitomètre, *n.m.* Sensitometer.
sensoriel, *a.* (*fem.* -**ielle**) Sensorial, sensory.
sensorium, *n.m.* Sensorium, brain.

sensualisme [sãsɥa'lism], *n.m.* Sensualism.
sensualiste, *n.* Sensualist.—*a.* Sensual.
sensualité [sãsɥali'te], *n.f.* Sensuality.
sensuel [sã'sɥel], *a.* (*fem.* -**uelle**) Sensual,
voluptuous.—*n.* Sensualist. **sensuellement,**
adv. Sensually.
sentant [sã'tã], *a.* (*fem.* -**ante**) Sentient.
sent-bon [sã'bɔ̃], *n.m. inv.* (*Bot.*) Tansy.
sente [sã:t], *n.f.* Footpath.
sentence [sã'tã:s], *n.f.* Aphorism, maxim;
sentence, judgment, decision, verdict.
sentencieusement, *adv.* Sententiously.
sentencieux, *a.* (*fem.* -**ieuse**) Sententious.
senteur [sã'tœ:r], *n.f.* Smell; scent, perfume.
Pois de senteur, sweet pea.
senti [sã'ti], *a.* (*fem.* -**ie**) Felt, experienced.
Bien or *vivement senti,* heartfelt, deeply felt;
(*fig.*) impressive, well expressed.
sentier [sã'tje], *n.m.* Path, footpath. *Sentier
battu,* beaten track.
sentiment [sãti'mã], *n.m.* Feeling; sensation;
sentiment; affection, *esp.* love; perception,
sense, consciousness; sensibility; opinion.
Avoir le sentiment de, to be conscious of, to
have a feeling that; *juger par sentiment,* to
judge from feeling; *selon mon sentiment,* in
my opinion; *sentiment d'amour,* feeling of
love.
sentimental, *a.* (*fem.* -**ale,** *pl.* -**aux**) Sentimental. **sentimentalement,** *adv.* Sentimentally.
sentimentaliste, *n.* Sentimentalist.
sentimentalité, *n.f.* Sentimentality.
sentine [sã'tin], *n.f.* Well, bilge (of a ship);
ventilating-pipe to sewer; (*fig.*) sink (of
vice etc.).
sentinelle [sãti'nɛl], *n.f.* Sentinel, sentry;
(*vulg.*) turd. *En sentinelle,* on sentry-duty;
faire sentinelle, to mount guard, to be on the
watch; *sentinelle perdue,* advanced sentry.
sentir [sã'ti:r], *v.t. irr.* To feel, to be sensible
or conscious of; to foresee, to guess, to know,
to perceive, to experience; to smell, to scent;
to taste of, to savour of, to smell of; to look
like, to seem. *Cette carpe sent la vase,* this
carp tastes of mud; *faire sentir quelque chose
à quelqu'un,* to impress someone with a sense
of something; *il sent les choses de loin,* he can
foretell events; *je ne peux pas la sentir,* I can't
bear her; *je sens qu'il a raison,* I have a feeling
he is right; *se faire sentir,* to make oneself or
itself felt.—*v.i.* To smell, to have an odour;
to have a bad smell. *Cela ne sent pas bon,* I
don't like the smell *or* look of it; *cette viande
commence à sentir,* this meat is beginning to go
bad; *sentir mauvais,* to smell bad. **se sentir,**
v.r. To feel oneself, to feel; to be conscious;
to feel the effects (*de*); to be perceived, felt,
etc. *Il ne se sent pas de joie,* he is quite overjoyed; *il se sentait mourir,* he felt that he was
dying; *il se sent honoré,* he feels honoured.
seoir (1) [swa:r], *v.i. irr.* (used in *pres.p.* **séant**
(2) *and p.p.* **sis**) To sit, to be sitting.
seoir (2) [swa:r], *v.i. irr.* (*pres.p.* **seyant,** *no
p.p.*) To suit, to become. *Cette couleur vous
sied à merveille,* that colour suits you beautifully; *il vous sied mal* or *il ne vous sied pas,* it ill
becomes you.
sep [sɛp], *n.m.* Frame of plough [CEP].
sépale [se'pal], *n.m.* (*Bot.*) Sepal. **sépaloïde,**
a. Sepaloid.
séparable [sepa'rabl], *a.* Separable.

séparateur [separaˈtœːr], *a.* (*fem.* **-trice**) Separative.—*n.m.* (*Tech.*) Separator.

séparatif, *a.* (*fem.* **-ive**) Separating, dividing.

séparation, *n.f.* Separation, severing, parting; partition. *Mur de séparation,* partition wall; *séparation de biens,* separation by contract; *séparation de corps,* judicial separation.

séparatisme, *n.m.* Separatism. **séparatiste,** *n.* and *a.* Separatist.

séparé, *a.* (*fem.* **-ée**) Separate; distinct. **séparément,** *adv.* Separately; apart, asunder.

séparer, *v.t.* To separate, to divide, to part; to sever, to disjoin; to distinguish; to divorce. *Séparer deux hommes qui se battent,* to part two men fighting; *séparer le bon grain de l'ivraie,* to separate the good seed from the bad; *séparer les cheveux sur le front,* to part the hair on the forehead; (*Box.*) *séparez!* Break! **se séparer,** *v.r.* To separate, to part; to part company (*de*); to divide; to break up (of assemblies etc.); to fall or come off. *Il n'y a si bonne compagnie qui ne se sépare,* the best of friends must part.

sépia [seˈpja], *n.f.* Sepia (fish, pigment, drawing).

seps [seps], *n.m. inv.* Seps.

sept [set], *n.m.* and *a. inv.* Seven; seventh.

septain, *n.m.* Seven-lined stanza.

*****septante** [sepˈtãːt], *a.* (used in Belgium, Switzerland, and some provinces) Seventy. *La version des Septante,* the Septuagint.

septembre [sepˈtãːbr], *n.m.* September. **septembrisades,** *n.f. pl.* (*Fr. Hist.*) September massacres, of 1792.

septembriseur, *n.m.* (*Fr. Hist.*) Septembrist.

septemvir [septemˈviːr], *n.m.* Septemvir. **septemvirat,** *n.m.* Septemvirate.

septénaire [septeˈnɛːr], *a.* and *n.m.* Septenary.

septennal, *a.* (*fem.* **-ale,** *pl.* **-aux**) Septennial. **septennalité,** *n.f.* Seven years' duration. **septennat,** *n.m.* Septennate.

septentrion [septãtriˈɔ̃], *n.m.* North; (*Astron.*) Lesser Bear.

septentrional, *a.* (*fem.* **-ale,** *pl.* **-aux**) North, northern.—*n.m. pl.* The peoples of the North, Northerners.

septicémie [septiseˈmi], *n.f.* (*Med.*) Septicaemia, blood poisoning.

septicémique, *a.* Septicaemic.

septidi [septiˈdi], *n.m.* Seventh day of the ten-day week of the first French republic.

septième [seˈtjɛm], *a.* and *n.* Seventh; seventh day; seventh form (in France); top form of lower school (in England). *Être au septième ciel,* to be in the seventh heaven.—*n.m.* Seventh part (of anything); seventh story (of building).—*n.f.* Seventh class; sequence of seven cards; (*Mus.*) seventh. **septièmement,** *adv.* Seventhly.

septime [sepˈtim], *n.f.* (*Fenc.*) Septime.

septimo [septiˈmo], *adv.* In the seventh place.

septique [sepˈtik], *a.* Septic. *Fosse septique,* septic tank.

septivalent [septivaˈlã], *a.* (*Chem.*) Septivalent.

septuagénaire [septɥaʒeˈnɛːr], *a.* and *n.* Septuagenarian.

Septuagésime, *f.* Septuagesima.

septuor, *n.m.* (*Mus.*) Piece for seven voices or seven instruments, septet.

septuple [sepˈtypl], *a.* and *n.m.* Septuple.

septupler, *v.t., v.i.* To increase sevenfold.

sépulcral [sepylˈkral], *a.* (*fem.* **-ale,** *pl.* **-aux**) Sepulchral.

sépulcre, *n.m.* Sepulchre. *Sépulcre blanchi,* whited sepulchre.

sépulture, *n.f.* Burial, sepulture, interment; vault (tomb). *Privé de sépulture,* left unburied.

séquelle [seˈkɛl], *n.f.* Gang, crew (of persons); set, string (of things); (*pl.*) after-effects (of illness).

séquence [seˈkãːs], *n.f.* Sequence (music, cards, cinema).

séquestration [sekɛstrɑˈsjɔ̃], *n.f.* Sequestration.

séquestre, *n.m.* Sequestration; sequestrator; depository; depositor. *Mettre en* or *sous séquestre,* to sequester.

séquestrer [sekɛsˈtre], *v.t.* To sequester, to sequestrate; to shut up illegally. **se séquestrer,** *v.r.* To sequester oneself.

sequin [səˈkɛ̃], *n.m.* Sequin (coin, ornament).

sequoia [sekɔˈja], *n.m.* Sequoia (tree).

sérac [seˈrak], *n.m.* Sérac, block of ice at the end of a glacier; (Swiss) white cheese.

sérail [seˈraːj], *n.m.* (*pl.* **sérails**) Seraglio.

séran [seˈrã] or **sérançoir,** *n.m.* Hackle, flax-comb. **sérançage,** *n.m.* Hackling. **sérancer,** *v.t.* To hackle, to dress (flax). **séranceur,** *n.m.* Hackler.

séraphin [seraˈfɛ̃], *n.m.* Seraph.

séraphique [seraˈfik], *a.* Seraphic; (*fig.*) blissful.

séraskier or **sérasquier** [serasˈkje], *n.m.* Seraskier (Turkish general).

serbe [sɛrb], *a.* and *n.* Serbian, Serb. **Serbie** [sɛrˈbi], *f.* Serbia.

serein (1) [səˈrɛ̃], *n.m.* Night-dew, evening-damp.

serein (2) [səˈrɛ̃], *a.* (*fem.* **-e**) Serene, placid, calm; (of weather) fine and calm.

sérénade [sereˈnad], *n.f.* Serenade.

sérénissime [sereniˈsim], *a.* Most Serene (title).

sérénité, *n.f.* Serenity, calmness, placidity; equanimity. *Avec sérénité,* serenely, calmly.

séreux [seˈrø], *a.* (*fem.* **-euse**) Serous, watery.

serf [sɛrf], *a.* (*fem.* **serve**) In bondage, servile. —*n.* Serf, thrall, bondman.

serfouette [sɛrˈfwɛt], *n.f.* Small hoe with a fork.

serfouir, *v.t.* To grub up; to hoe.

serfouissage, *n.m.* Hoeing.

serge [sɛrʒ], *n.f.* Serge.

sergent [sɛrˈʒã], *n.m.* Sergeant; cramp (joiner's tool); (*Naut.*) iron hook for hoisting, hold-fast. **sergent-chef,** *n.m.* (*pl.* **sergents-chefs**) (*Mil.*) Quartermaster-sergeant; (*Av.*) flight-sergeant. *Sergent d'armes,* sergeant-at-arms; *sergent de ville,* police constable.

sergent-major [SERGENT-CHEF].

serger [sɛrˈʒe] or **sergier,** *n.m.* Serge-weaver. **sergerie,** *n.f.* Serge-manufactory; serge-trade.

sérial [seˈrjal], *a.* (*fem.* **-iale,** *pl.* **-iaux**) Serial.

séricicole [serisiˈkɔl], *a.* Silk-producing.

sériciculteur, *n.m.* Sericulturist, silk-grower, silk-worm breeder. **sériciculture,** *n.f.* Sericulture, silk-culture. **séricigène,** *a.* Silk-producing (gland).

série [seˈri], *n.f.* Series; (*Billiards*) break, run; (*spt.*) heat. *Fabrication en série,* mass-production; *hors série,* specially manufactured; *prix de série,* contract price; *série de* *piqûres*, course of injections; *série parallèle*, (*Elec.*) series in parallel.

sérier, *v.t.* To arrange in series; to standardize.

sérieusement [serjøz′mã], *adv.* Seriously, gravely; in earnest; coolly, coldly. **sérieux**, *a.* (*fem.* **-ieuse**) Serious, grave; sincere, earnest; real, true, solid, substantial; momentous. *Peu sérieux*, irresponsible (person), unsound (business).—*n.m.* Seriousness, importance, gravity; (*Theat.*) serious business, serious part. *Garder son sérieux*, to preserve one's gravity, (*fam.*) to keep a straight face; *prendre au sérieux*, to take (a thing) seriously.

serin [sə′rɛ̃], *n.m.* Canary; (*fig.*) duffer, silly, fool.

serinage, *n.m.* Cramming.

serine, *n.f.* Hen canary; silly girl.

seriner, *v.t.* To teach (a bird) with the bird-organ; to grind, thump out (a tune); (*fig.*) to coach, to cram.

serinette, *n.f.* Bird-organ; insipid or indifferent singer.

seringa or **seringat** [sərɛ̃′ga], *n.m.* Syringa.

seringue [sə′rɛ̃:g], *n.f.* Syringe, squirt. *Seringue à graisse*, (*Motor.*) grease-gun; *seringue injectrice*, hypodermic syringe.

seringuer, *v.t.* To syringe; to squirt; to inject; (*fig.*) to enfilade, to rake with shot.

sérique [se′rik], *a.* (*Med.*) Of the serum.

serment [ser′mã], *n.m.* Oath, promise, solemn declaration; (*pl.*) swearing. *Faux serment*, false oath; *prêter serment*, to take an oath, to be sworn in; *rompre son serment* or *manquer à son serment*, to break one's oath.

sermon [ser′mɔ̃], *n.m.* Sermon; lecture, admonition. **sermonnaire**, *n.m.* Collection of sermons; author of sermons. **sermonner**, *v.t.*, *v.i.* To sermonize, to lecture, to reprimand. **sermonneur**, *n.m.* (*fem.* **-euse**) Sermonizer, preacher, fault-finder.

sérologie [serɔlɔ′ʒi], *n.f.* Serology.

séro-réaction, *n.f.* (*pl.* **séro-réactions**) Sero-reaction.

sérosité, *n.f.* Serosity, wateriness.

sérothérapie, *n.f.* Sero-therapy.

sérotine [serɔ′tin], *n.f.* Serotine (bat).

serpe [serp], *n.f.* Bill-hook, hedge-bill. *C'est fait à la serpe*, it is just hacked out.

serpent [ser′pã], *n.m.* Serpent, snake; serpent (mus. instrument); (*fig.*) snake in the grass, treacherous person. *Serpent à sonnettes*, rattlesnake.

serpentaire, *n.m.* Serpent-eater, secretary-bird.—*n.f.* Serpentaria, snake-root.

serpentant, *a.* (*fem.* **-ante**) Winding, meandering.

serpente, *n.f.* Tissue-paper.

serpenteau, *n.m.* (*pl.* **-eaux**) Young serpent; serpent (firework), squib, jumping cracker.

serpenter [serpã′te], *v.i.* To meander, to wind; to twine.

serpentin [serpã′tɛ̃], *a.* (*fem.* **-ine**) Serpentine, snaky.—*n.m.* Worm (of a still); paper streamer.—*n.f.* Serpentine (stone); snake-wood.

serpette [ser′pet], *n.f.* Pruning-knife, serpette.

serpigineux [serpiʒi′nø], *a.* (*fem.* **-euse**) Serpiginous. **serpigo**, *n.f.* Serpigo.

serpillière [serpi′ljɛ:r], *n.f.* Packing-cloth; sacking; coarse apron.

serpolet [serpɔ′le], *n.m.* Serpolet, wild thyme.

serpule [ser′pyl], *n.f.* Serpulla (tube-worm).

serrage [se′ra:ʒ], *n.m.* Tigntening, pressing, securing. *Clef de serrage*, wedge-key; *écrou de serrage*, adjusting nut; *vis de serrage*, set-screw.

serratule [sera′tyl], *n.f.* Saw-wort.

serre [se:r], *n.f.* Squeeze, pressure, squeezing; talon, claw (of birds); clip; hot-house, greenhouse, conservatory. *Avoir la serre bonne*, to have a strong grip, (*fig.*) to be close-fisted.

serré [se′re], *a.* (*fem.* **-ée**) Close, serried; compact; tight, fast; narrow; clasped, clenched; close-fisted, avaricious; pressing (of arguments etc.); condensed, concise, terse. *Avoir le cœur serré*, to have a heavy heart; *drap bien serré*, close-woven cloth; *un nœud serré*, a tight knot.—*adv.* Very much; strongly, hard (of freezing etc.). *Jouer serré*, to play a careful game.

serre-bosse, *n.m. inv.* (*Naut*) Shank-painter.

serre-file, *n.m. inv.* (*Mil.*) Bringer-up of the rear, last man; (*Naut.*) sternmost ship.

serre-fine, *n.f.* (*pl.* **serre(s)-fines**) Suture forceps.

serre-fils, *n.m. inv.* (*Elec.*) Binding screw (of terminal); clamp; connector.

serre-frein or **serre-freins**, *n.m. inv.* (*Rail.*) Brakesman.

serre-livres, *n.m. inv.* Book-end.

serrement, *n.m.* Pressing, squeeze, squeezing. *Serrement de cœur*, pang (of grief); *serrement de main*, hand-squeeze; handshake.

serre-nez, *n.m. inv.* Twitch (for horses).

serre-papiers, *n.m. inv.* Paper-holder; paper-clip; file (for papers); set of pigeon-holes for papers.

serrer [se′re], *v.t.* To press to tighten, to squeeze, to strain; to tie, to fasten, to clasp, to lock, to lock up; to pinch, to grip, to wring; to crowd, to condense, to put close together; to press, to push hard; to oppress (the heart); to close (the ranks); to clench (one's fist, teeth, etc.); to put away; to hug (the coast etc.); to take in (sail). *Cela serre le cœur*, it is a heart-rending sight; *serrer de près*, to press hard; *serrer la forme*, (*Print.*) to lock up the form; *serrer la main à quelqu'un*, to shake hands with someone; *serrer la muraille*, to skirt the wall; *serrer du blé* [BLÉ]; *serrer les dents* [DENT]; *serrer les pouces à quelqu'un* [POUCE]; *serrer le vent*, to haul close to the wind; *serrer son écriture*, to write close; *serrez les rangs!* close up! **se serrer**, *v.r.* To press each other close; to sit, lie, or stand close together, to crowd; to grow tighter; to pinch or stint oneself.

serre-rayons, *n.m. inv.* Spoke-setter.

serre-tête, *n.m. inv.* Headband, headkerchief; crash-helmet.

serricorne [seri′kɔrn], *a.* Serricorn.—*n.m. pl.* Serricorn beetles.

serriforme, *a.* Serriform.

serron [se′rɔ̃], *n.m.* Seron, fruit-crate.

serrure [se′ry:r], *n.f.* Lock. *Serrure de sûreté*, safety lock; *trou de la serrure*, key-hole. **serrurerie**, *n.f.* Locksmith's trade; locksmith's work; metal work. **serrurier**, *n.m.* Locksmith; metal-worker.

serte [sert], *n.f.* Mounting, setting (of jewels). **sertir**, *v.t.* To set, to mount. **sertissage**, *n.m.* Setting. **sertisseur**, *n.m.* Setter, mounter. **sertissure**, *n.f.* Setting.

sérum [se′rɔm], *n.m.* Serum.

servage [sɛr'vaːʒ], *n.m.* Serfdom, thraldom; servitude, bondage.

serval [sɛr'val], *n.m.* (*pl.* **-als**) Tiger-cat.

servant [sɛr'vɑ̃], *a.m.* Serving; in waiting; lay (brother).—*n.m.* (*Artill.*) Gunner; *les servants*, the gun-crew. **servante**, *n.f.* Maidservant; servant, handmaid; dumbwaiter, dinner-wagon; (*Print.*) frisketstand.

serve, *fem.* [SERF].

serveur, *n.m.* (*fem.* **-euse**) (*Ten.*) Server; carver (at an hotel), barman; (*Cards*) dealer.

serviabilité [sɛrvjabili'te], *n.f.* Obligingness. **serviable**, *a.* Willing, obliging.

service [sɛr'vis], *n.m.* Service; attendance; duty; office, function; department; divine service; set (of utensils, linen, etc.); course (of dishes at meals). *Au service*, in the army or navy; *de bon service*, serviceable; *en service commandé*, on active service; when on duty; *être au service de*, to be in the service of; *être de service*, to be on duty; *faire le service*, to officiate, to ply (coaches); *hors de service*, out of use, unfit; *chef de service*, departmental head; *escalier de service*, backstairs; *il a trente ans de service*, he has served thirty years; *libre service*, self-service; *premier service*, first sitting (in restaurant car); *qu'y a-t-il pour votre service?* what can I do for you? *rendre service* or *un service*, to do service or a service; *se mettre en service*, to go into service; (*Ten.*) *service canon*, cannonball service; *service de table*, dinner set; (*Mil.*) *bon pour le service*, fit for duty; *faire son (temps de) service*, to do one's military service.

serviette [sɛr'vjɛt], *n.f.* Napkin, serviette; towel; portfolio, briefcase. *Serviette nid d'abeilles*, honeycomb towel; *serviette sans fin*, roller towel.

servile [sɛr'vil], *a.* Servile, menial; slavish, cringing; time-serving. **servilement**, *adv.* Servilely, slavishly.

servilité [sɛrvili'te], *n.f.* Servility, slavishness.

servir [sɛr'viːr], *v.t. irr.* (*pres.p.* **servant,** *p.p.* **servi**) To serve, to wait on, to attend; to be a servant to; to serve up, to spread (a table); to help to; to be serviceable or of service to, to minister to; to assist, to help; to furnish, to supply (with goods); to present, to offer; to work, to operate; (*Hunt.*) to dispatch. *Madame est servie*, dinner is served, madam; *se faire servir*, to be waited upon.—*v.i.* To serve, to be of use; to be useful or good (*à*); to perform the office or function (*de*); to be employed, to be conducive; to be a servant; to serve up a meal; to be in the service. *Cela ne sert à rien*, that is no good; *cela sert à plusieurs choses*, that is used for several purposes; *il m'a servi de père*, he has been as a father to me; *il ne sert à rien de s'emporter*, it is no use flying into a passion; *servir de*, to serve as, to be used as; *servir sur mer* or *sur terre*, to serve in the navy or the army. **se servir,** *v.r.* To serve oneself, to help oneself; to avail oneself; to be served up (of dishes). *Se servir de*, to avail oneself of, to use, to make use of; *servez-vous*, help yourself.

serviteur [sɛrvi'tœːr], *n.m.* Servant, manservant. *Serviteur de l'État*, servant of the State.

servitude [sɛrvi'tyd], *n.f.* Servitude, slavery; (*Law*) disability, charge, easement.

servo-frein, *n.m.* (*pl.* **servo-freins**) (*Motor.*) Servo-brake.

ses [sɛ], *a. poss. pl.* His, her, its, one's.

sésame [se'zam], *n.m.* Sesame (plant). *Sésame, ouvre-toi!* open, sesame!

sésamoïde, *a.* (*Anat.*) Sesamoid (bone).

séséli [seze'li], *n.m.* Seseli (plant).

sesquialtère [sɛskɥial'tɛːr], *a.* (*Math.*) Sesquialter. **sesquitierce,** *a.* Sesquitertial.

sessile [se'sil], *a.* Sessile.

session [sɛ'sjɔ̃], *n.f.* Session, sitting; term (of law courts etc.).

sesterce [sɛs'tɛrs], *n.m.* (*Rom. Ant.*) Sesterce.

sétacé [seta'se], *a.* (*fem.* **-ée**) Setaceous, bristly.

setier [sə'tje], *n.m.* Obsolete measure for liquids (8 French pints) and grain (about 37 hectolitres) [*see* DEMI-SETIER].

sétifère [seti'fɛːr] or **sétigère,** *a.* Setiferous, bristle-bearing. **sétiforme,** *a.* Setiform.

séton [se'tɔ̃], *n.m.* (*Surg.*) Seton. *Plaie en séton*, flesh wound.

seuil [sœːj], *n.m.* Threshold; sill; shelf (of ocean bed).

seul [sœl], *a.* (*fem.* **seule**) Alone, by oneself; unaided; single, only, sole; mere, bare. *Cela n'ira pas tout seul*, it won't be easy; *la pensée seule*, the mere thought; *mon bras seul suffit*, my unaided arm is sufficient; *tout seul*, all alone, all by oneself; *un homme seul*, a lonely man, a man by himself; *un seul homme*, one man, one man only.—*n.m.* One only. *Pas un seul*, absolutely none, not one; *seul à seul*, tête-à-tête. **seulement,** *adv.* Only; but; solely, merely. *Un mot seulement*, but one word.

seulet [sœ'lɛ], *a.* (*fem.* **-ette**) (*poet.*) Alone, all alone.

sève [sɛːv], *n.f.* Sap; (*fig.*) pith, vigour, strength.

Sévère [se'vɛːr], *m.* Severus.

sévère [se'vɛːr], *a.* Severe, stern, harsh, austere; rigid, strict; correct, pure. **sévèrement,** *adv.* Severely, sternly; strictly; correctly.

sévérité [severi'te], *n.f.* Severity; strictness; purity, correctness.

séveux [se'vo], *a.* (*fem.* **-euse**) (*Bot.*) Sappy; (*fig.*) pithy, vigorous.

sévices [se'vis], *n.m. pl.* (*Law*) Cruelty, ill-treatment.

sévir [se'viːr], *v.i.* To deal severely (*contre*); to rage (of war etc.).

sevrage [sə'vraːʒ], *n.m.* Weaning **sevrer,** *v.t.* To wean; (*fig.*) to deprive (*de*).

sèvres [sɛːvr], *n.m.* Sèvres porcelain.

sevreuse [sə'vro:z], *n.f.* Dry nurse.

sexagénaire [sɛksaʒe'nɛːr], *a. and n.* Sexagenarian.

sexagésimal, *a.* (*fem.* **-ale,** *pl.* **-aux**) (*Math.*) Sexagesimal.

Sexagésime, *n.f.* Sexagesima (Sunday).

sexangulaire or **sexangulé,** *a.* (*fem.* **-ée**) Sexangular.

sexdigitaire or **sexdigital,** *a.* (*fem.* **-ale,** *pl.* **-aux**) Six-fingered or six-toed.

sexe [sɛks], *n.m.* Sex. *Le beau sexe* or *le sexe faible*, the fair sex.

sexennal [sɛksɛn'nal], *a.* (*fem.* **-ale,** *pl.* **-aux**) Sexennial.

sextant [sɛks'tɑ̃], *n.m.* Sextant.

sexte [sɛkst], *n.f.* (*R.-C. Ch.*) Sext, sixth canonical hour.

sextidi [sɛksti'di], *n.m.* Sixth day of ten-day week of French republican calendar.

sextil [sɛks'til], *a.* (*fem.* **-ile**) (*Astrol.*) Sextile.

sexto, *adv.* Sixthly.

sextuor, *n.m.* Sextet.

sextuple, *a.* and *n.m.* Sextuple, sixfold.

sextupler, *v.t., v.i.* To increase sixfold; to sextuple.

sexualisme [sɛksɥa'lism], *n.m.* Sexualism.

sexualité, *n.f.* Sexuality.

sexuel, *a.* (*fem.* **-elle**) Sexual. *Rapports sexuels*, sexual intercourse.

shako or **schako** [ʃa'ko], *n.m.* Shako.

shampooing [ʃɑ̃'pwɛ̃], *n.m.* Shampoo, hair-wash. *Faire un shampooing*, to shampoo.

shérif [ʃe'rif], *n.m.* Sheriff.

shibboleth [SCHIBBOLETH].

shintoïsme [ʃɛ̃tɔ'ism], *n.m.* Shintoism.

shogoun [ʃɔ'gun], *n.m.* Shogun.

shoot [ʃut], *n.m.* Shot. *Quel shoot il a!* or *c'est un fameux shooteur*, what a shot! **shooter**, *v.t.* (*pop.*) To shoot (the ball).

short [ʃɔrt], *n.m.* (*Cost.*) Shorts.

shrapnel [ʃrap'nɛl], *n.m.* Shrapnel shell.

shunt [ʃœ̃t], *n.m.* (*Elec.*) Shunt. **shunter**, *v.t.* To shunt.

si (1) [si], *conj.* If; whether; supposing, what if. *C'est comme si l'on disait*, that is as if one said; *je ne sais si elle le fera*, I do not know whether she will do it; *si j'avais pu prévoir*, if I could have foreseen; *s'ils veulent*, if they like; *si . . . et que . . ., if . . . and if . . .; si vous le faites*, if you do it; *et s'il vient?* and what if he turns up? *si l'on faisait un tour!* what about a stroll?—*n.m. inv.* If.

si (2) [si], *adv.* So, so much, however much; yes. *N'allez pas si vite*, do not go so fast; *si bien que*, so that; *si petit qu'il soit*, small as he is. *Je dis que si*, I say yes; *je gage que si*, I bet that it is so; *si fait*, yes indeed; *vous ne l'avez pas vu!—Si, je l'ai vu*, you have not seen it.—Yes, I have.—*n.m. inv.* Yes.

si (3) [si], *n.m. inv.* (*Mus.*) Si; the note B.

sialagogue [sjala'gɔg], *n.m.* and *a.* Sialagogue, sialagogic.

sialisme [sja'lism], *n.m.* Ptyalism, sialorrhoea.

Siam [sjam], *m.* Thailand, Siam.

siam [sjam], *n.m.* Game of ninepins played with a wooden disc (instead of bowl).

siamois [sja'mwa], *a.* and *n.* (*fem.* **-oise**) Siamese.

Sibérie [sibe'ri], *f.* Siberia.

sibérien [sibe'rjɛ̃], *a.* and *n.* (*fem.* **-ienne**) Siberian.

sibilant [sibi'lɑ̃], *a.* (*fem.* **-ante**) Sibilant, hissing.

sibylle [si'bil], *n.f.* Sibyl. **sibyllin**, *a.* (*fem.* **-ine**) Sibylline.

sicaire [si'kɛːr], *n.m.* Hired assassin.

siccatif [sika'tif], *a.* (*fem.* **-ive**) Siccative, desiccative, drying.—*n.m.* Siccative, drying agent. **siccité** [siksi'te], *n.f.* Siccity, dryness.

Sicile [si'sil], **la**, *f.* Sicily.

sicilien [sisi'ljɛ̃], *a.* (*fem.* **-ienne**) Sicilian.—*n.m.* (**Sicilien**, *fem.* **-ienne**) A Sicilian.

sicle [sikl], *n.m.* Shekel.

sidecar [sid'kar], *n.m.* Side-car.

sidéral [side'ral], *a.* (*fem.* **-ale**, *pl.* **-aux**) Sidereal. **sidération**, *n.f.* Sideration,

stroke; blasting (of tree etc.). **sidéré**, *a.* (*fem.* **-ée**) Struck down, struck dead; (*fig.*) thunderstruck; (*fam.*) flabbergasted.

sidérite [side'rit], *n.f.* Siderite; (*Bot.*) ironwort. **sidérographie**, *n.f.* Siderography.

sidérolithe, *n.f.* Siderolite. **sidéroscope**, *n.m.* Sideroscope. **sidérostat**, *n.m.* Siderostat. **sidérotechnie**, *n.f.* Metallurgy of iron. **sidéroxyle**, *n.m.* Ironwood.

sidérurgie, *n.f.* Metallurgy of iron. **sidérurgique**, *a.* Of the metallurgy of iron.

sidi [si'di], *n.m.* (*Arab word*) Algerian or Moroccan native.

siècle [sjɛkl], *n.m.* Century; age, period. *Dans les siècles des siècles*, for ever and ever; *il y a un siècle qu'on ne vous a vu*, we have not seen you for ages; *les mœurs de notre siècle*, the customs of our time.

sied, *3rd pres. indic.* [SEOIR (2)].

siège [sjɛː3], *n.m.* Seat; bench (of a court of justice); headquarters (of society etc.); (*Eccles.*) see; siege; (*Eng.*) seating (of machine etc.). *En état de siège*, in a state of siege; *bain de siège*, hip-bath; *le siège d'une société*, the office of a society; *lever le siège*, to raise the siege; (*fig.*) to retire; (*fam.*) to take oneself off; *mettre le siège devant une ville*, to lay siege to a town.

siéger [sje'3e], *v.i. irr.* (*conjug. like* ACCÉLÉRER) To sit (of assemblies, courts, etc); to hold one's see (of bishops); to be seated; (*fig.*) to lie, to reside (of a thing); to have one's headquarters (of business, society).

sien [sjɛ̃], *a. poss. 3rd pers. sing.* (*fem.* **sienne**) His, hers, its, one's.—*pron.* His own, her own, etc. *Ma sœur et la sienne*, my sister and his or hers; *mon père et le sien*, my father and his or hers.—*n.* One's own property, work, etc. *Chacun le sien*, let each have his own; *faire des siennes*, (*fam.*) to lark about; *faire sienne une opinion*, to accept an opinion as one's own; *les siens*, one's people (relations and friends); *y mettre du sien*, to accept a compromise, to show goodwill, to contribute to something.

Sienne [sjɛn], *f.* Sienna. *Terre de Sienne brûlée*, burnt Sienna.

sieste [sjɛst], *n.f.* Siesta. *Faire la sieste*, to take one's afternoon nap.

sieur [sjœːr], *n.m.* (*Law*) *Le sieur Vigne*, Mr. Vigne.

sifflable [si'flabl], *a.* That deserves to be hissed.

sifflage [CORNAGE].

sifflant, *a.* (*fem.* **-ante**) Hissing, whistling, wheezing; sibilant.

sifflement [siflə'mɑ̃], *n.m.* Hissing, hiss; whistling, whistle; whizzing (of an arrow, a bullet); wheezing.

siffler [si'fle], *v.i.* To hiss; to whistle; to whizz; to wheeze; to sizzle.—*v.t.* To whistle; to call with whistling; to hiss; to swig off (glass of wine). *Siffler un acteur*, to hiss, to boo an actor, to give him the bird.

sifflerie, *n.f.* Whistling, hissing, booing.

sifflet, *n.m.* Whistle (instrument and sound); catcall; hiss; (*colloq.*) windpipe; (*Naut.*) boatswain's pipe. *Couper le sifflet à quelqu'un* [COUPER]; *un coup de sifflet* [COUP].

siffleur [si'flœːr], *n.m.* (*fem.* **-euse**) Whistler; hisser; wood-wren.—*a.* Whistling, piping (of birds); wheezing (of horses).

(C) **siffleux** [si'flø], *n.m.* Ground hog.
siffloter, *v.i.* To whistle softly or under one's breath.
sigillaire [siʒi'lɛːr], *n.f.* Sigillaria.—*a.* Sigillary. **sigillé,** *a.* (*fem.* -ée) Sigillate. **sigillographie,** *n.f.* Sigillography.
sigisbée [siʒis'be], *n.m.* Cicisbeo, lover.
sigle [sigl], *n.m.* Initial letter (used in inscriptions etc.); group of initial letters used as abbreviation of phrase (U.N., etc.); outline (shorthand).
sigma [sig'ma], *n.m.* Sigma. **sigmatique,** *a.* Sigmatic. **sigmatisme,** *n.m.* Sigmatism.
sigmoïde, *a.* (*Anat.*) Sigmoid.
signal [si'ɲal], *n.m.* (*pl.* -aux) Signal. **signalé,** *a.* (*fem.* -ée) Signal, remarkable, conspicuous. **signalement,** *n.m.* Description (of a man etc.), particulars.
signaler [siɲa'le], *v.t.* To signal; to give the description of; to point out, to mark out; to signalize. *Rien à signaler,* nothing to report. **se signaler,** *v.r.* To signalize or distinguish oneself. **signalétique,** *a.* Descriptive. *Fiche signalétique,* dossier.
signaleur, *n.m.* Signalman; (*Mil.*) signaller.
signalisateur [siɲaliza'tœːr], *n.m.* Traffic indicator, trafficator. **signalisation,** *n.f.* Signalling system. *Signalisation routière internationale,* international system of road signs.
signataire [siɲa'tɛːr], *n.* Signer, subscriber, signatory.
signature [siɲa'tyːr], *n.f.* Signature; signing.
signe [siɲ], *n.m.* Sign; nod; mark, indication, symptom; token, badge; omen. *Faire le signe de la croix,* to cross oneself. *faire signe,* to make signs; *faire signe de la main,* to beckon; *signe de la tête,* nod.
signer, *v.t., v.i.* To sign, to subscribe. **se signer,** *v.r.* To cross oneself.
signet [si'ɲɛ], *n.m.* Signet; book-mark (*esp.* for a missal); signet-ring.
significatif [siɲifika'tif], *a.* (*fem.* -ive) Significant, meaningful. **signification,** *n.f.* Signification, meaning, import; sense, acceptation; (*Law*) legal notice. **significativement,** *adv.* Significantly.
signifier [siɲi'fje], *v.t.* To signify, to mean; to notify, to intimate; (*Law*) to serve. *Faire signifier,* to give notice of; *je lui ai signifié d'avoir à s'y trouver,* I gave him notice to be sure and be there; *que signifie ce mot?* what is the meaning of this word?
silence [si'lɑ̃ːs], *n.m.* Silence; stillness; secrecy; pause; (*Mus.*) rest. *Dans le silence,* in secret; *en silence,* silently; *faire silence,* to stop talking, to be silent; *garder* or *observer le silence,* to keep silent; *passer sous silence,* to pass over in silence; *réduire au silence,* to silence; *rompre le silence,* to break the silence.
silencieusement, *adv.* Silently. **silencieux,** *a.* (*fem.* -ieuse) Silent; still.—*n.m.* (*Motor.*) Muffler.
Silène [si'lɛːn], *m.* (*Myth.*) Silenus.
silène [si'lɛːn], *n.m.* Silene (plant); catchfly. *Silène enflé,* bladder campion.
Silésie [sile'zi], **la,** *f.* Silesia.
silésienne [sile'zjɛn], *n.f.* Silesia (for linings).
silex [si'lɛks], *n.m.* Silex, flint. *Fusil à silex,* flint-lock gun.
silhouette [si'lwɛt], *n.f.* Silhouette; outline; profile. **silhouetter,** *v.t.* To silhouette, to

outline; (*Phot.*) to block out. **se silhouetter,** *v.r.* To be silhouetted, to stand out.
silicate [sili'kat], *n.m.* Silicate. **silice,** *n.f.* (*Chem.*) Silica, flint. **siliceux,** *a.* (*fem.* -euse) Siliceous. **silicification,** *n.f.* Silicification. **silicique,** *a.* Silicic. **silicium,** *n.m.* Silicon. **siliciure,** *n.m.* Silicide. **silicone,** *n.f.* Silicone. **silicose,** *n.f.* (*Med.*) Silicosis.
silicule [sili'kyl], *n.f.* (*Bot.*) Silicle, silicula (seedpod). **siliculeux,** *a.* (*fem.* -euse) Siliculose. **silique,** *n.f.* Siliqua, silique. **siliqueux,** *a.* (*fem.* -euse) Siliquose.
sillage [si'jaːʒ], *n.m.* Wake, wash, track; slipstream; steerage-way, sea-way; (*Fishing*) drag.
sillée, *n.f.* (*Agric.*) Trench (for planting vines in).
siller [si'je], *v.i.* (*Naut.*) To make headway.
sillet [si'jɛ], *n.m.* Nut (of stringed instruments).
sillon [si'jɔ̃], *n.m.* Furrow made by plough; seed-drill; (*fig.*) track, trail, wake (of a ship etc.), wrinkle; (*poet., pl.*) fields, plains; (*Anat.*) groove. **sillonner,** *v.t.* *To plough, to furrow; to streak; to flash through (of lightning etc.); to groove, to wrinkle. **sillonneur,** *n.m.* Drill-plough.
silo [si'lo], *n.m.* Silo (for preserving fodder). **silotage,** *n.m.* Silage.
silphion [sil'fjɔ̃], *n.m.* Silphium (herb).
silure [si'lyːr], *n.m.* Silurus (sheat-fish); catfish.
silurien [sily'rjɛ̃], *a.* (*fem.* -ienne) (*Geol.*) Silurian.
simagrée [sima'gre], *n.f.* Pretence, affectation; (*pl.*) affected ways, fuss.
simarre [si'maːr], *n.f.* Justice's robe.
simaruba [simary'ba] or **simarouba,** *n.m.* *Simaruba* (genus of trees).
simbleau [sɛ̃'blo], *n.m.* (*pl.* -eaux) Carpenter's line for tracing circles etc.
simien [si'mjɛ̃], *a.* (*fem.* -ienne) Simian. **simiesque,** *a.* Ape-like, apish (face).
similaire [simi'lɛːr], *a.* Similar. **similarité,** *n.f.* Similarity, likeness.
simili or **similigravure,** *n.f.* Half-tone engraving.
similitude, *n.f.* Similitude, resemblance; analogy, comparison; simile.
similor [CHRYSOCALE].
Simon [si'mɔ̃], *m.* Simon.
simoniaque [simɔ'njak], *a.* Simoniacal.—*n.m.* Simoniac. **simonie,** *n.f.* Simony.
simoun [si'muːn], *n.m.* Simoom or simoon.
simple [sɛ̃ːpl], *a.* Simple, single; easy; only, bare, mere; common, plain, unadorned, unpretentious; simple-minded, silly, naïve, credulous; natural, of course. *C'est tout simple,* it is quite natural, it's a matter of course, it's perfectly easy; *temps simples,* simple (not compound) tenses; *un simple soldat,* a private.—*n.m.* That which is simple; simple-minded person; simpleton; (*Ten.*) single; (*pl.*) simples, medicinal plants. *Simple dames,* women's singles. **simplement,** *adv.* Simply.
simplet, *a.* (*fem.* -ette) Naïve, simple; (*fam.*) a bit daft; (*Am.*) green.—*n.* Simpleton, silly.
simplicité, *n.f.* Simplicity; artlessness, plainness; silliness.
simplifiable, *a.* Able to be simplified.

simplificateur [sɛ̃plifika'tœːr] *a.* (*fem.* -**trice**) Simplifying.—*n.* Simplifier.
simplification, *n.f.* Simplification.
simplifier, *v.t.* (*conjugated like* PRIER) To simplify.
simpliste, *n.* and *a.* Over-simple, simplistic.
simulacre [simy'lakr], *n.m.* Image; phantom, apparition; semblance, mere shadow, appearance, feint, sham. *Un simulacre de combat*, a sham fight.
simulateur, *n.m.* (*fem.* -**trice**) Simulator, shammer.
simulation, *n.f.* Simulation, feigning.
simulé, *a.* (*fem.* -**ée**) Feigned, counterfeit, sham.
simuler, *v.t.* To simulate, to feign, to counterfeit, to sham. *Simuler une attaque*, to feign an attack.
simultané [simylta'ne], *a.* (*fem.* -**ée**) Simultaneous. **simultanéité**, *n.f.* Simultaneousness. **simultanément**, *adv.* Simultaneously.
sinanthrope [sinɑ̃'trɔp], *n.m.* Pekin man (fossil skeleton).
sinapine [sina'pin], *n.f.* (*Chem.*) Sinapine. **sinapisation**, *n.f.* (*Med.*) Application of sinapism. **sinapisé**, *a.* (*fem.* -**ée**) Infused with mustard. **sinapiser**, *v.t.* To infuse with mustard. **sinapisme**, *n.m.* Sinapism (mustard plaster).
sincère [sɛ̃sɛːr], *a.* Sincere, frank; unfeigned, honest. **sincèrement**, *adv.* Sincerely, honestly. **sincérité**, *n.f.* Sincerity.
sincipital [sɛ̃sipi'tal], *a.* (*fem.* -**ale**, *pl.* -**aux**) Sincipital. **sinciput**, *n.m.* Sinciput.
sindon [sɛ̃'dɔ̃], *n.m.* Christ's shroud; (*Surg.*) pledget.
sinécure [sine'kyːr], *n.f.* Sinecure. **sinécuriste**, *n.* Sinecurist.
Singapour [sɛ̃ga'puːr], *m.* Singapore.
singe [sɛ̃ːʒ], *n.m.* Ape, monkey; hoist, windlass; monkey (of pile-drivers); pantograph (copying-machine); mimic; ugly, grimacing, or malicious person, (*Mil. slang*) bully beef; (*pop.*) the boss. *Payer en monnaie de singe* [MONNAIE].—*a.* Mimicking, aping.
singer, *v.t.* To ape, to mimic.
singerie, *n.f.* Monkey-house (in zoo); monkey trick, grimace; antic; mimicry.
singesse, *n.f.* Female monkey, ape.
singeur, *a.* (*fem.* -**euse**) Aping, mimicking.—*n.* Ape, mimic.
singleton [sɛ̃glə'tɔ̃], *n.m.* Singleton (cards).
singulariser [sɛ̃gylari'ze], *v.t.* To singularize, to render singular or odd or conspicuous. **se singulariser**, *v.r.* To render oneself singular, to make oneself conspicuous.
singularité, *n.f.* Singularity; peculiarity; oddness.
singulier [sɛ̃gy'lje], *a.* (*fem.* -**ière**) Singular, peculiar; odd, curious, strange, queer; single (of a combat etc.).—*n.m.* (*Gram.*) Singular. *Au singulier*, in the singular. **singulièrement**, *adv.* Singularly, in a singular manner, oddly.
sinistre [si'nistr], *a.* Sinister, ominous; grim, dismal; evil; criminal.—*n.m.* Grim event, disaster, calamity.
sinistré, *a.* (*fem.* -**ée**) Affected by disaster, (shipwreck, fire, etc.).—*n.* Victim of disaster; casualty. **sinistrement**, *adv.* Sinisterly, evilly.

sinistrorse, *a.* Sinistrorse. **sinistrorsum**, *adv.* Anti-clockwise.
sinologie [sinɔlɔ'ʒi], *n.f.* Sinology. **sinologique**, *a.* Sinological. **sinologue**, *n.m.* Sinologist (student of Chinese).
sinon [si'nɔ̃], *conj.* Otherwise, if not, else, or else; except, unless. *Sinon que*, except that.
sinople [si'nɔpl], *n.m.* (*Her.* and *Min.*) Sinople.
sinué [si'nɥe], *a.* (*fem.* -**ée**) (*Bot.*) Sinuate.
sinueux, *a.* (*fem.* -**euse**) Sinuous, winding, meandering.
sinuosité, *n.f.* Sinuosity, winding, meander; bend (of a river).
sinus [si'nyːs], *n.m. inv.* Sine; (*Anat.*) sinus.
sinusite [siny'zit], *n.f.* Sinusitis.
sinusoïdal, *a.* (*Math.*) (*fem.* -**ale**, *pl.* -**aux**) Sinusoidal. **sinusoïde**, *n.f.* (*Math.*) Sinusoid.
Sion [sjɔ̃], *m.* Zion.
sionisme [siɔ'nism], *n.m.* Zionism. **sioniste**, *n.* and *a.* Zionist.
siphon [si'fɔ̃], *n.m.* Siphon; (*Naut.*) waterspout. *Siphon d'eau de Seltz*, soda water siphon. **siphonner**, *v.t.* To siphon.
siphonophore [sifɔnɔ'fɔːr], *n.m.* (*Zool.*) Siphonophore.
sire [siːr], *n.m.* Sir, lord; sire (title of kings and emperors). *Un pauvre sire* or *triste sire*, a contemptible fellow.
sirène [si'ren], *n.f.* Siren, mermaid; hooter, fog-horn.
sirocco [sirɔ'ko], *n.m.* Sirocco.
sirop [si'ro], *n.m.* Syrup.
siroter [sirɔ'te], *v.t.*, *v.i.* To sip; (*pop.*) to tipple.
siroteur, *n.m.* (*fem.* -**euse**) Tippler.
sirupeux [siry'pø], *a.* (*fem.* -**euse**) Syrupy.
sirvente [sir'vɑ̃ːt], *n.m.* Sirvente (Provençal lay).
sis [si], *a.* (*fem.* **sise**) Seated, situated [SEOIR (1)].
sisal [si'zal], *n.m.* Sisal (hemp, grass).
sismal [sis'mal] or **séismal**, *a.* (*fem.* -**ale**, *pl.* -**aux**) Sismal. **sismique** or **séismique**, *a.* Seismic. **sismographe** or **séismographe**, *n.m.* Seismograph. **sismographie** or **séismographie**, *n.f.* Seismography. **sismologie** or **séismologie**, *n.f.* Seismology.
sistre [sistr], *n.m.* (*Ant.*) Sistrum (Egyptian timbrel).
Sisyphe [si'zif], *m.* Sisyphus.
site [sit], *n.m.* Site (situation with regard to scenery etc.). *Un beau site*, a beauty spot. *Angle de site*, (*Mil.*) angle of sight.
sitiologie [sitjɔlɔ'ʒi], *n.f.* Sitiology, dietetics.
sitôt [si'to], *adv.* So soon, as soon. *Sitôt dit, sitôt fait* or *sitôt pris, sitôt pendu*, no sooner said than done; *je ne reviendrai pas de sitôt*, it will be a good while before I return; *sitôt que*, as soon as.
situation [sitɥa'sjɔ̃], *n.f.* Situation, site, position; state of affairs, predicament; (*Naut.*) bearing; post, job. *En situation*, in one's proper place or character; *situation en banque*, bank statement.
situé, *a.* (*fem.* -**ée**) Situated, lying.
situer, *v.t.* To place; to assign his or her place to.
six [si *before a consonant*, siz *before a vowel*, sis *at the end of a sentence*], *a.* Six; sixth.—*n.m. inv.* [sis] Six; sixth; sixth day.
sixième [si'zjɛm], *a.* and *n.* Sixth.—*n.m.* Sixth

part; sixth floor.—*n.f.* (in France) Sixth class, (in England) the first form (of upper school); (*Piquet*) six cards of the same suit. **sixième-ment**, *adv.* Sixthly.

sixte, *n.f.* (*Mus.*) Sixth.

sizain [si'zɛ̃] or ***sixain**, *n.m.* Stanza of six lines; six packs of cards. **sizaine**, *n.f.* Group of six (scouts etc.).

sketch [skɛtʃ], *n.m.* (Revue) sketch.

ski [ski], *n.m.* Ski. *Faire du ski*, to go in for ski-ing; *bâtons de ski*, ski-sticks; *saut à ski*, ski jump; *ski nautique*, water-ski-ing.. **skier**, *v.i.* To ski. **skieur**, *n.m.* (*fem.* -**ieuse**) Skier.

skiff [skif], *n.m.* Sculling boat, skiff.

slave [slav], *a.* Slav, Slavonic.—*n.m.* (*pl.* **Slaves**) Slav. **slaviser**, *v.t.* To slavonicize. **slavisme**, *n.m.* Slavism. **slavophile**, *n.* and *a.* Slavophil.

Slesvig [slɛs'vig], *m.* Schleswig.

slip [slip], *n.m.* (Cost.) Trunks, slip; (*Naut.*) slipway.

slogan [slɔ'gɑ̃], *n.m.* Slogan.

sloop, sloup or **sloupe** [slup], *n.m.* (*Naut.*) Sloop.

sloughi [slu'gi], *n.m.* Algerian hound; saluki.

Slovaque [slɔ'vak], *a.* Slovakian.—*n.* (**Slovaque**) Slovak.

Slovène [slɔ'vɛn], *n.* Slovene.—*a.* Slovenian.

smalah [sma'la], *n.f.*, or **smala**. Family, household, retinue of an Arab chief; (*fam.*) large family, tribe.

smalt [smalt], *n.m.* Smalt (blue glass).

smash [smaʃ], *n.m.* (*Ten.*) Smash.

smérinthe [sme'rɛ̃:t], *n.m.* Hawk-moth.

smilax [smi'laks], *n.m.* (*Bot.*) Smilax.

smille [smi:j], *n.f.* (Double pointed) hammer for scappling stone etc. **smiller**, *v.t.* To scapple, to spall.

smoking [smɔ'kiŋ], *n.m.* Dinner-jacket.

Smyrne [smirn], *f.* Smyrna, Izmir.

snob [snɔb], *n.m.* and *a.* Person who tries to be always in the swim; pretentious admirer of everything new and fashionable; (*fam.*) swanky, smart. **snobisme**, *n.m.* Affected up-to-dateness.

sobre [sɔbr], *a.* Sober, moderate, well-balanced. **sobrement**, *adv.* Soberly.

sobriété, *n.f.* Sobriety.

sobriquet [sɔbri'kɛ], *n.m.* Nickname.

soc [sɔk], *n.m.* Ploughshare.

sociabilité [sɔsjabili'te], *n.f.* Sociability, good fellowship.

sociable, *a.* Sociable, companionable. **sociablement**, *adv.* Sociably.

social [sɔ'sjal], *a.* (*fem.* -**iale**, *pl.* -**iaux**) Social. *Siège social*, registered office; head office; *sous la raison sociale*, under the style of (of commercial firms). **socialement**, *adv.* Socially, in a social manner.

socialiser, *v.t.* To socialize, to pool.

socialisme, *n.m.* Socialism. **socialiste**, *n.* and *a.* Socialist.

sociétaire [sɔsje'tɛ:r], *n.* Associate, member; partner; shareholder. **sociétariat**, *n.m.* Full membership of an association (*esp.* of the Comédie Française).

société [sɔsje'te], *n.f.* Society, association; community; company, firm; partnership, fellowship. *La Société des Nations*, the League of Nations; *société anonyme*, private company; *société à responsabilité limitée*, limited company; *société savante*, learned society.

socinianisme [sɔsinja'nism], *n.m.* Socinianism. **socinien**, *a.* and *n.* (*fem.* -**ienne**) Socinian.

sociologie [sɔsjɔlɔ'ʒi], *n.f.* Sociology. **sociologique**, *a.* Sociological. **sociologiste** or **sociologue**, *n.* Sociologist.

socle [sɔkl], *n.m.* Socle, pedestal, plinth, stand, base.

socque [sɔk], *n.m.* Clog, patten; (*fig.*) sock (comedy). **socquette**, *n.f.* Short or ankle sock.

Socrate [sɔ'krat], *m.* Socrates.

socratique [sɔkra'tik], *a.* Socratic. **socratiquement**, *adv.* Socratically.

soda [sɔ'da], *n.m.* Soda water.

sodalité [sɔdali'te], *n.f.* Sodality, fraternity; conviviality.

sodium [sɔ'djɔm], *n.m.* Sodium.

Sodome [sɔ'dɔm], *f.* Sodom.

sodomie [sɔdɔ'mi], *n.f.* Sodomy. **sodomique** or **sodomitique**, *a.* Sodomitic, sodomitical. **sodomite**, *n.m.* Sodomite.

sœur [sœ:r], *n.f.* Sister; nun; (*pl.*) sisterhood. *Les neuf sœurs*, the Muses; *sœur de lait*, foster-sister.

sœurette, *n.f.* (*colloq.*) Little sister, sissie, sis(s).

sofa [sɔ'fa], *n.m.* Sofa, settee.

soffite [sɔ'fit], *n.m.* Soffit.

sofi or **sophi** [sɔ'fi], *n.m.* Sufi (dervish); ancient title of the Shah of Persia.

soi [swa] or **soi-même**, *pron.* *3rd pers. sing.* Oneself, himself, herself, itself; self. *Chacun pour soi*, every man for himself; *chez soi*, at home; *de* or *en soi*, in itself, of its own nature; *de soi-même*, of oneself; *être à soi*, to be one's own master; *être soi*, to be oneself, to be perfectly natural; *penser à soi*, to think of oneself; *prendre sur soi* (*de*), to take it upon oneself (to); *rentrer en soi-même*, to withdraw into oneself.

soi-disant, *a. inv.* Self-styled, would-be, so-called.—*adv.* Supposedly, ostensibly.

soie [swa], *n.f.* Silk; silken hair; bristle (of hogs); tongue (of knives, swords, etc.). *Des jours filés d'or et de soie*, halcyon days; *papier de soie*, tissue paper. **soierie**, *n.f.* Silks, silk goods; silk-trade; silk-factory. *Marchand de soierie*, silk-mercer.

soif [swaf], *n.f.* Thirst. *Avoir grand'soif*, to be very thirsty; *avoir soif*, to be thirsty; *boire à sa soif*, to drink one's fill; *étancher sa soif*, to quench one's thirst.

soiffard or **soiffeur**, *n.m.* (*fem.* -**arde** or -**euse**) (*vulg.*) Toper.

soigné [swa'ɲe], *a.* (*fem.* -**ée**) Carefully done, highly finished; well got up, neat, smart; (*colloq.*) remarkable, first-rate.

soigner [swa'ɲe], *v.t.* To take care of, to look after, to attend to, to mind; to nurse; to take great pains with. **se soigner**, *v.r.* To take care of oneself; to nurse oneself.

soigneur, *n.m.* (*Box.*) Second.

soigneusement, *adv.* Carefully. **soigneux**, *a.* (*fem.* -**euse**) Careful; mindful; solicitous.

soi-même [sɔɪ].

soin [swɛ̃], *n.m.* Care; attention; attendance (on a sick person etc.); (*pl.*) attentions, solicitude, pains, trouble. *Aux soins de*, care of; *avec soin*, carefully; *avoir soin de quelque chose*, to take care of something; *être aux petits soins pour quelqu'un*, to be full of attentions for someone; *je vous en laisse le soin,*

I leave it to your care; *manque de soin*, carelessness; *petits soins*, delicate attentions; *premiers soins*, first-aid; *rendre des soins à quelqu'un*, to be attentive to someone.

soir [swaːr], *n.m.* Evening; night; afternoon. *Bon soir*, good evening, good night; *ce soir*, this evening, tonight; *du matin au soir*, from morning till night; *hier au soir*, last evening, last night; *journal du soir*, evening paper; *le lendemain soir*, the evening of the next day; *le soir de la vie*, old age; *sur le soir*, towards evening, at night-fall.

soirée, *n.f.* Evening (duration); evening party; (*Theat.*) evening performance. *Donner une soirée dansante*, to give an evening dance; *passer la soirée*, to spend the evening.

soiriste, *n.* Dramatic critic.

soit [swat, swa], *adv.* Be it so, well and good, agreed, granted; suppose, let us say; that is to say. *Ainsi soit-il*, so be it; *hé bien! soit*, well, be it so; *soit dit en passant*, incidentally. —*conj.* Either, or; whether. *Soit l'un, soit l'autre*, either one or the other; *soit que*, whether (with verb); *soit qu'il vienne ou qu'il ne vienne pas*, whether he comes or not.

soixantaine [swasɑ̃'tɛn], *n.f.* About sixty; some sixty years (of age).

soixante, *a.* and *n.m.* Sixty. *Soixante-dix*, seventy; *soixante-douze*, seventy-two.

soixantième, *a.* and *n.m.* Sixtieth.

sol (1) [sɔl], *n.m.* Ground; soil; earth; (*Her.*) field.

sol (2) [sɔl], *n.m.* (*Mus.*) Sol, the note G.

*sol (3), *n.m.* [SOU].

solaire [sɔ'lɛːr], *a.* Solar. *Cadran solaire*, sundial.

solanacée [sɔlana'se] or **solanée**, *n.f.* (*Bot.*) Solanaceous plant. **solandre**, *n.f.* Sallenders. **solanum**, *n.m.* Solanum.

solarium [sɔla'rjɔm], *n.m.* Solarium.

solbatu [sɔlba'ty], *a.* (*fem.* **-ue**) Footsore (of horses). **solbature**, *n.f.* Bruised hoof.

soldanelle [sɔlda'nɛl], *n.f.* Soldanella.

soldat [sɔl'da], *n.m.* Soldier. *Se faire soldat*, to enlist; *simple soldat*, private; *les simples soldats*, the rank and file; *le soldat inconnu*, the Unknown Warrior; *soldat de plomb*, tin soldier.

soldatesque [sɔlda'tɛsk], *n.f.* (*usu. pej.*) Soldiery.—*a.* Soldier-like, barrack-room (language etc.).

solde (1) [sɔld], *n.f.* (*Mil.*) Pay. *Demi-solde*, half-pay; *à la solde de*, in the pay of.

solde (2) [sɔld], *n.m.* Balance (between debit and credit); balance owing; clearance sale; (*pl.*) sale bargains, reductions. *En solde*, to clear; *pour solde de tout compte*, in full settlement; *solde après inventaire*, stock-taking sale.

solder (1) [sɔl'de], *v.t.* To pay (soldiers); to have in one's pay.

solder (2) [sɔl'de], *v.t.* To settle, to discharge (an account); to sell off, to clear.

sole (1) [sɔl], *n.f.* Sole (of animal's foot); sole-plate, foundation-plate; bottom-frame (of vehicle); (*Shipbuilding*) bottom plank of cradle.

sole (2) [sɔl], *n.f.* Sole (fish).

soléaire [sɔle'ɛːr], *a.* (*Anat.*) Solear, soleus.

solécisme [sɔle'sism], *n.m.* Solecism.

soleil [sɔ'lɛːj], *n.m.* Sun; sunshine; (*fig.*) star; monstrance; catherine-wheel (firework); sunflower. *Au grand soleil*, in bright sunshine;

au soleil, in the sun; *avoir du bien au soleil*, to have landed property; *bains de soleil*, sunbathing; *coup de soleil*, sunstroke; sunburn; *en plein soleil*, right in the sun; *entre deux soleils*, from sunset to sunrise; *il fait du soleil*, the sun is shining; *il fait le grand soleil*, he can do the grand circle (on the bar); *le roi-soleil*, Louis XIV; *le soleil luit pour tout le monde*, the sun shines upon all alike; *ôte-toi de mon soleil*, get out of my light; (*fam.*) get out of my way; *piquer un soleil*, to blush suddenly; *se chauffer au soleil*, to bask in the sun; *sous le soleil*, on earth.

solen [sɔ'lɛn], *n.m.* Solen (razor-fish).

solennel [sɔla'nɛl], *a.* (*fem.* **-elle**) Solemn. **solennellement**, *adv.* Solemnly.

solenniser, *v.t.* To solemnize. **solennité**, *n.f.* Solemnity; solemn ceremony or occasion.

solénoïde [sɔlenɔ'id], *n.m.* Solenoid, coil-winding.

solfatare [sɔlfa'taːr], *n.f.* Solfatara.

solfège [sɔl'fɛːʒ], *n.m.* (*Mus.*) Solfeggio, sol-fa. **solfier**, *v.i.* (*conjugated like* PRIER) To sol-fa.

solidaire [sɔli'dɛːr], *a.* Binding on several; jointly and separately liable; interdependent, bound up (with). **solidairement**, *adv.* Jointly and severally.

solidariser, *v.t.* To render jointly liable. **se solidariser**, *v.r.* To join together in liability; to be mutually dependent, to make common cause.

solidarité, *n.f.* Joint and separate liability; solidarity, fellowship; interdependence.

solide [sɔ'lid], *a.* Solid; strong; firm, stable; fast, permanent (of colours etc.); substantial, sound; trustworthy, reliable, solvent. *Un jugement solide*, a sound judgment; *un ami solide*, a reliable friend.—*n.m.* Solid, solid body, solid figure; (*fig.*) that which is substantial, permanent, etc. *Viser au solide*, to have an eye to the main chance. **solidement**, *adv.* Solidly, substantially; firmly; soundly.

solidification [sɔlidifika'sjɔ̃], *n.f.* Solidification.

solidifier [sɔlidi'fje], *v.t.* To solidify. **se solidifier**, *v.r.* To solidify, to become solid.

solidité [sɔlidi'te], *n.f.* Solidity; strength; stability, firmness; soundness.

soliloque [sɔli'lɔk], *n.m.* Soliloquy.

solin [sɔ'lɛ̃], *n.m.* Space between two joists or rafters; plaster filling up such a gap.

solipède [sɔli'pɛd], *a.* Solipedal.—*n.m.* Soliped.

solipsisme [sɔlip'sism], *n.m.* Solipsism.

soliste [sɔ'list], *n.* Soloist, solo singer, solo player.—*a.* Solo.

solitaire [sɔli'tɛːr], *a.* Solitary, single, alone; lonely, desert.—*n.m.* Lonely person, recluse; solitaire (diamond or game). **solitairement**, *adv.* Solitarily, alone.

solitude, *n.f.* Solitude, loneliness; seclusion; wilderness, desert.

solive [sɔ'liːv], *n.f.* Joist.

soliveau [sɔli'vo], *n.m.* (*pl.* **-eaux**) Small joist; (*fig.*) blockhead, nonentity.

sollicitation [sɔlisita'sjɔ̃], *n.f.* Solicitation, entreaty; application (to a judge etc.); pull (of magnet); care.

solliciter [sɔlisi'te], *v.t.* To incite, to urge; to solicit, to entreat; to beg, to canvass; to impel, to call into action; to attract (of magnet).

solliciteur, *n.m.* (*fem.* **-euse**) One who solicits; petitioner.

sollicitude, *n.f.* Solicitude, care; anxiety, concern.

solo [sɔ'lo], *n.m.* (*pl.* **solos** or **soli**) Solo.—*a. inv.* Solo.

solstice [sɔls'tis], *n.m.* Solstice. *Solstice d'été*, summer solstice. **solsticial**, *a.* (*fem.* **-iale**, *pl.* **-iaux**) Solstitial.

solubilité [sɔlybili'te], *n.f.* Solubility.

soluble, *a.* Soluble, dissolvable, solvable.

solution, *n.f.* Solution; resolution; (*Law*) discharge. *Solution de continuité*, interruption, break, fault.

solvabilité [sɔlvabili'te], *n.f.* Solvency. **solvable**, *a.* Solvent. **solvant**, *n.m.* Solvent.

Somalie [sɔma'li], **la**, *f.* Somaliland, Somalia.

somatique [sɔma'tik], *a.* Somatical, somatic.

somatologie [sɔmatɔlɔ'ʒi], *n.f.* Somatology.

sombrage [sɔ̃'braːʒ], *n.m.* First dressing (of vines).

sombre [sɔ̃:br], *a.* Dark, sombre, gloomy; dull, dim, dingy; overcast, cloudy; melancholy, dismal, sullen. **sombrement**, *adv.* Gloomily.

sombrer (1) [sɔ̃'bre], *v.i.* (*Naut.*) To founder, to go down; (*fig.*) to come to grief, to fail.

sombrer (2) [sɔ̃'bre], *v.t.* (*Agric.*) To give a first dressing to.

sombrero [sɔ̃bre'ro], *n.m.* Sombrero (broad-brimmed hat).

sommaire [sɔ'mɛːr], *a.* Summary, concise, succinct; hasty; scanty.—*n.m.* Summary, abridgment, abstract, synopsis.

sommairement, *adv.* Summarily; hastily.

sommation (1) [sɔma'sjɔ̃], *n.f.* (*Math.*) Summation.

sommation (2) [sɔma'sjɔ̃], *n.f.* Summons, appeal, demand. *Faire les trois sommations*, to read the Riot Act.

somme (1) [sɔm], *n.f.* Sum, total; amount; summary, compendium. *Somme totale*, sum-total; *somme toute* or *en somme*, finally, in short; on the whole.

somme (2) [sɔm], *n.f.* Burden, pack-saddle. *Bête de somme*, beast of burden, (*fig.*) drudge.

somme (3) [sɔm], *n.m.* Nap, sleep. *Faire un somme*, to have forty winks; *ne faire qu'un somme*, to sleep the night through.

sommeil [sɔ'mɛːj], *n.m.* Sleep; sleepiness, drowsiness. *Accablé de sommeil*, dreadfully sleepy; *avoir le sommeil léger*, to be a light sleeper; *avoir sommeil*, to be sleepy; *cela porte au sommeil*, that induces sleep; *dormir d'un profond sommeil*, to sleep soundly; *la maladie du sommeil*, sleeping sickness; *tomber de sommeil* or *n'en pouvoir plus de sommeil*, to be overcome or dropping with sleep.

sommeiller [sɔme'je], *v.i.* To slumber; to doze, to snooze; (*fig.*) to lie dormant.

sommelier [sɔmə'lje], *n.m.* (*fem.* **-ière**) Butler, cellarman, wine-waiter. **sommellerie**, *n.f.* Butler's pantry.

sommer (1) [sɔ'me], *v.t.* To summon, to call upon. *Sommer quelqu'un de tenir sa parole*, to call upon someone to keep his promise; *sommer une place de se rendre*, to summon a fortress to surrender.

sommer (2) [sɔ'me], *v.t.* To sum up, to find the sum of; (*Her.*) to surmount.

sommet [sɔ'mɛ], *n.m.* Top, summit; apex; acme, zenith; crown (of the head etc.); (*Zool.*) extremity; (*Bot.*) vertex.

sommier (1) [sɔ'mje], *n.m.* *Beast of burden, pack-horse; box-mattress; wind-chest (of organ); timber or metal plate supporting parts of various machines etc.; (*Arch.*) crossbeam, summer, breast-summer.

sommier (2) [sɔ'mje], *n.m.* Cash-book, register.

sommité [sɔmi'te], *n.f.* Summit, top; head, principal; chief point; prominent person. *Une des sommités*, an eminent person.

somnambule [sɔmnɑ̃'byl], *n.* Somnambulist, sleep-walker.—*a.* Somnambulistic. **somnambulisme**, *n.m.* Somnambulism, sleep-walking.

somnifère [sɔmni'fɛːr], *a.* Somniferous.—*n.m.* (*Med.*) Sleeping-draught; narcotic.

somniloque, *a.* Somniloquous.

somnolence, *n.f.* Somnolence.

somnolent, *a.* (*fem.* **-ente**) Somnolent, sleepy.

somnoler, *v.i.* To drowse, to doze.

somptuaire [sɔ̃p'tɥɛːr], *a.* Sumptuary. **somptueusement**, *adv.* Sumptuously. **somptueux**, *a.* (*fem.* **-euse**) Sumptuous; magnificent, splendid.

somptuosité, *n.f.* Sumptuousness.

son (1) [sɔ̃], *a.* (*fem.* **sa**, *pl.* **ses**) His, her, its; one's. *Son âme*, his (or her) soul; *son frère*, *sa sœur et ses enfants*, his (or her) brother, sister and children. [*Son* is used for the *fem.* instead of *sa* before a vowel or silent *h*.]

son (2) [sɔ̃], *n.m.* Sound. *Ingénieur du son* (*Cine.*, *Rad. Tel.*), sound engineer; *mur du son*, sound barrier; *son aigu*, shrill sound; *son de cloches*, ringing of bells; *son du tambour*, drumbeat or roll; *un autre son de cloche*, (*fig.*) a change of tune.

son (3) [sɔ̃], *n.m.* Bran. *Tache de son*, freckle.

sonate [sɔ'nat], *n.f.* Sonata. **sonatine**, *n.f.* Sonatina.

sondage [sɔ̃'daːʒ], *n.m.* Sounding; (*Mining*) boring; (*Med.*) probing (of a wound). *Sondage de l'opinion*, Gallup poll.

sonde [sɔ̃d], *n.f.* Sounding-line, lead; cheese-taster; (*Surg.* etc.) probe; (*Manuf.*) proof-stick; (*Mining*) bore. *Jeter la sonde*, to heave the lead; *sonde aérienne*, sounding balloon.

Sonde [sɔ̃d], **l'Archipel de la**, *m.* The Sunda Isles. *Le Détroit de la Sonde*, Sunda Strait.

sonder [sɔ̃'de], *v.t.* To sound; to try, to taste; to probe, to search, to fathom, to scrutinize, to investigate, to explore. *Sonder le terrain*, to feel one's way, to see how the land lies; *sonder quelqu'un*, to sound someone; *sonder une plaie*, to probe a wound; *sonder un fromage*, to pierce a cheese.

sondeur [sɔ̃'dœːr], *n.m.* (*Naut.*) Leadsman; sounding apparatus. **sondeuse**, *n.f.* Boring machine.

songe [sɔ̃:ʒ], *n.m.* Dream; dreaming. *Faire un songe*, to have a dream; *voir en songe*, to see in a dream, to dream. **songe-creux**, *n.m. inv.* Dreamer, visionary. **songer**, *v.i.* To dream; (*fig.*) to muse; to day-dream; to think; to mean, to intend, to purpose, to propose; to bear in mind. *Il songe à se marier*, he is thinking of getting married; *maintenant que j'y songe*, now that I think of

it; *sans y songer*, unawares, unthinkingly; *songez à ce que vous faites*, mind what you are about; *songez-y* or *songez-y bien*, think it over carefully, mind what you are about.— *v.t.* To dream; (*fig.*) to imagine; to think of. *Ne songer que bals, que fêtes*, to think of nothing but balls and parties. **songerie,** *n.f.* Dreaming; musing; day-dreaming.
songeur [sɔ̃ʒœːr], *n.m.* (*fem.* **-euse**) Dreamer.— *a.* Thoughtful, dreamy.
sonique [sɔ'nik], *a.* Sonic.
sonnaille [sɔ'naːj], *n.f.* Cattle-bell.
sonnailler [sɔna'je], *v.i.* To keep on ringing.—*n.m.* Bell-wether.
sonnant [sɔ'nɑ̃], *a.* (*fem.* **-ante**) Sounding; sonorous. *À sept heures sonnantes*, just as the clock was striking seven; *espèces sonnantes*, hard cash.
sonner [sɔ'ne], *v.i.* To sound; to ring, to toll, to strike (of clocks etc.); to pull the bell. *On sonne*, there is a ring at the door; *sonner creux*, to sound hollow; *sonner faux*, to ring false; *voilà midi qui sonne*, it is striking twelve.—*v.t.* To sound, to ring, to toll; to ring for (a servant etc.); to toll for; to announce by ringing etc.; to strike (of clocks etc.), to sound (the horn), to drive down (a pile). *Il a vingt ans bien sonnés*, he is well over twenty; *il est trois heures sonnées*, it is past three o'clock; *ne sonner mot*, not to say a word, not to let the least hint drop; *sonner la messe*, to ring for mass; *sonner le dîner*, to ring for dinner; *sonner les cloches*, to ring the bells; (*pop.*) *sonner les cloches à quelqu'un*, to give someone a good talking to. **sonnerie,** *n.f.* Ring, ringing (of bells); bells, chimes; striking part (of a clock etc.); (*Mil.*) bugle- (or trumpet-) call.
sonnet [sɔ'nɛ], *n.m.* Sonnet.
sonnette [sɔ'nɛt], *n.f.* Small bell; house-bell, hand-bell; pile-driver. *Agiter* or *tirer la sonnette*, to ring the bell; *serpent à sonnettes* [SERPENT].
sonneur [sɔ'nœːr], *n.m.* Bell-ringer. **sonomètre,** *n.m.* Sonometer.
sonore [sɔ'nɔːr], *a.* Resonant, deep-toned; clear, emphatic; voiced (consonant). (*Cine.*) *Bande sonore*, sound track; *ondes sonores*, sound waves. **sonorisation,** *n.f.* (*Cine.*) Scoring; provision of sound; sound recording. **sonoriser,** *v.t.* To add sound to (a film). **sonorité,** *n.f.* Resonance.
sopha [SOFA]. **sophi** [SOFI].
Sophie [sɔ'fi], *f.* Sophia. *Faire sa Sophie*, (*fam.*) to put on airs, to be goody-goody.
sophisme [sɔ'fism], *n.m.* Sophism, fallacy.
sophiste, *n.m.* Sophist.—*a.* Sophistical.
sophistication, *n.f.* Sophistication; adulteration. **sophistique,** *a.* Sophistical.—*n.f.* Sophistry. **sophistiqué,** *a.* (*fem.* **-ée**) Sophisticated, affected. **sophistiquer,** *v.t.* To adulterate.—*v.i.* To subtilize, to indulge in sophistry. **sophistiquerie,** *n.f.* Sophistry, quibbling.
Sophocle [sɔ'fɔkl], *m.* Sophocles.
sophore [sɔ'fɔːr] or **sophora,** *n.m.* Sophora (plant).
soporatif [sɔpɔra'tif], *a.* (*fem.* **-ive**) Soporiferous, soporific.
soporeux, *a.* (*fem.* **-euse**) Soporous.
soporifique or **soporifère,** *a.* Soporiferous; (*fig.*) boring, tedious.—*n.m.* Soporific.

soprano [sɔpra'no], *n.* (*pl.* **soprani** or **sopranos**) Soprano, treble.
sorbe [sɔrb], *n.f.* Sorb-apple.
sorbet [sɔr'bɛ], *n.m.* Sorbet, sherbet, water-ice.
sorbétière [sɔrbe'tjɛːr], *n.f.* Ice-pail.
sorbier [sɔr'bje], *n.m.* Sorb; service-tree; mountain-ash.
sorcellerie [sɔrsɛl'ri], *n.f.* Sorcery, witchcraft, enchantment.
sorcier [sɔr'sje], *n.m.* (*fem.* **-ière**) Sorcerer, sorceress, wizard, witch; magician, enchanter, enchantress; conjurer. *Il n'est pas grand sorcier*, he is no conjurer; *sabbat de sorcières*, witches' Sabbath; *vieille sorcière*, old hag.
sordide [sɔr'did], *a.* Sordid, filthy; mean, vile. **sordidement,** *adv.* Sordidly. **sordidité,** *n.f.* Sordidness.
sore [sɔːr], *n.m.* (*Bot.*) Sorus (of ferns).
sorgho or **sorgo** [sɔr'go], *n.m.* Sorghum.
sorite [sɔ'rit], *n.m.* Sorites.
Sorlingues [sɔr'lɛ̃ːg], **les,** *f. pl.* The Scillies, the Scilly Isles.
sorne [sɔrn], *n.f.* Sinter-slag.
sornette [sɔr'nɛt], *n.f.* (*usu. in pl.*) Idle talk, small talk. *Conter des sornettes*, to talk nonsense; to humbug.
sort [sɔːr], *n.m.* Fate, destiny; lot, state; condition; fortune, hazard, chance; spell, charm. *Au sort*, by lot; *être son sort*, to be one's lot, to fall to one's lot; *faire un sort à quelqu'un*, to provide for someone; to dispose of someone; *jeter un sort à quelqu'un*, to cast a spell over someone; *le sort des armes*, the fortunes of war; *le sort en est jeté*, the die is cast; *tirer au sort*, to draw lots; to toss.
sortable [sɔr'tabl], *a.* Suitable. **sortablement,** *adv.* Suitably.
sortant [sɔr'tɑ̃], *a.* (*fem.* **-ante**) Going out, outgoing, retiring, leaving (office etc.); drawn, coming out (of numbers in lotteries).—*n.m.* Person going out; person leaving office etc. *Les entrants et les sortants*, the incomers and outgoers.
sorte [sɔrt], *n.f.* Sort, kind, species; manner, way; (*Print.*) cast. *D'aucune sorte* or *en aucune sorte*, in no wise; *de la sorte*, thus, in that way; *de quelque sorte que ce soit*, in any way whatever; *de sorte que* or *en sorte que*, so that; *de telle sorte*, to such a degree, in such a way; *de toute sorte*, of every kind; *de toutes sortes*, of all kinds; *faire en sorte que*, to manage so that, to see (to it) that.
sorteur [sɔr'tœːr], *n.m.* (*fem.* **-euse**) Person given to going out; gadabout.
sortie [sɔr'ti], *n.f.* Going out, coming out; exit, outlet, way out, escape; holiday, outing, trip; exportation; sally, sortie; (*colloq.*) outburst, attack, outbreak, tirade; low card (at cards). *À la sortie du dîner*, at the end of the dinner; *droit de sortie*, export duty; *faire une sortie*, to make a sally; *faire une sortie à quelqu'un*, to blow someone up, to pitch into someone; *fausse sortie*, pretended exit of a person who at once returns (on the stage); *jour de sortie*, holiday, day out; *se ménager une sortie*, to arrange a way out (of some difficulty); *sortie de bal*, opera cloak; *sortie de bain*, bath-wrap, bath-robe; *sortie de secours*, emergency exit; *par ici la sortie*, this way out.
sortilège [sɔrti'lɛːʒ], *n.m.* Sorcery, magic, sortilege.

sortir (1) [sɔr'tiːr], *v.i. irr.* (*pres.p.* **sortant**, *p.p.*
sorti, *takes the auxiliary* AVOIR *or* ÊTRE
according as action or condition is meant) To
go out, to come out, to come forth, to emerge,
to issue; to make one's exit; to leave; to
depart; to swerve, to deviate; to wander
(from a subject); to proceed, to result; to
spring, to come up; to sally forth; to burst
or gush forth; to get off, to escape; (*Paint.*
etc.) to stand out; to be in relief; to come up
(at an examination). *Faire sortir*, to bring,
send, drive, or thrust out, to call out, to
elicit, to bring out; *faire sortir un homme de
prison*, to get a man out of prison; *il ne fait
qu'entrer et sortir*, he does nothing but go in
and out; *il ne sort pas de là*, he sticks to his
opinion; *il sort d'une bonne école*, he was at a
good school; *il vient de sortir* or *il ne fait
que de sortir*, he has just gone out; *la rivière
est sortie de son lit*, the river has overflowed
its banks; *les yeux lui sortent de la tête*, his
eyes are starting out of his head; *sortir beaucoup*, to go to lots of parties; *sortir de la
chambre*, to go out of the room; *sortir de
l'enfance*, to be no longer a child; *sortir de
maladie*, to recover from an illness; *sortir
des bornes de la bienséance*, to overstep the
bounds of decency; *sortir de son devoir*, to
deviate from one's duty; *sortir de table*, to
rise from table; *sortir du port*, to leave the
harbour; *sortir des rangs*, to step out of the
ranks; to have risen from the ranks; *sortir en
courant*, to run out.—*v.t.* To bring out, to
take out; to pull out, to extricate. *Sortir la
voiture*, to get out the car; *sortir des livres*, to
take out books (from a library); to publish
books; *sortir quelqu'un*, (*fam.*) to dismiss
someone; to chuck someone out.—*n.m.*
Going out, leaving, rising. *Au sortir de sa
lecture*, when we close his book; *au sortir du
lit*, on getting out of bed.

sortir (2) [sɔr'tiːr], *v.t.* (*conjugated like* FINIR)
(*Law*) To obtain, to have.

sosie [sɔ'zi], *n.m.* Double, second self, counterpart.

sot [so], *a.* (*fem.* **sotte**) Stupid, silly, foolish; (*fig*).
embarrassed, sheepish; ridiculous, absurd. *A
sotte demande point de réponse* [RÉPONSE];
il est resté sot, he looked somewhat foolish; *le
voilà bien sot*, he looks rather sheepish now.—
n. Fool, blockhead, ass, idiot. *C'est un sot en
trois lettres*, he is a downright fool.

sotie [sɔ'ti], *n.f.* 14th-century farce.

sot-l'y-laisse, *n.m. inv.* Parson's nose (in
poultry).

sottement, *adv.* Sillily, foolishly. **sottise**, *n.f.*
Silliness, foolishness, folly; silly thing, foolish
trick, nonsense; insult; (*pl.*) abusive language. *Dire des sottises à quelqu'un*, to call
someone names, to slang him. **sottisier**, *n.m.*
Collection of jokes, tales, etc.

sou [su], *n.m.* Sou (copper coin worth 5 centimes); a copper, a halfpenny. *Amasser sou
à sou*, to scrape together penny by penny;
cent sous, five-franc piece; *n'avoir pas le
premier sou*, not to have a coin to start
with; *n'avoir pas le sou* or *n'avoir pas un sou*
or *pas un sou vaillant*, to be penniless, not
to be worth a farthing; *n'avoir pas pour
deux sous de courage*, not to have a ha'p'orth
of pluck; *sans le sou*, penniless; *une affaire de
deux sous*, a twopenny-halfpenny business.

Souabe [swab], **la**, *f.* Swabia.—*a.* and *n.*
Swabian.

soubarbe [SOUS-BARBE].

soubassement [subas'mã], *n.m.* Base; stylobate; bed-valance; bed-rock.

soubresaut [subrə'so], *n.m.* Sudden leap or
bound; plunge (of a horse); start; jolt.
soubresauter, *v.i.* To start, to jump, to
plunge.

soubrette [su'brɛt], *n.f.* Soubrette, lady's
maid, waiting-woman.

souche [suʃ], *n.f.* Stump, stock, stub, stem;
(*fig.*) block, blockhead; head, founder (of a
family etc.); source, origin, root; chimney-
stack; counterfoil (of passports, cheques,
etc.); tally. *C'est une vraie souche*, he is a
regular blockhead; *de bonne souche*, of sound
stock, of good pedigree; *faire souche*, to found
a family.

souchet [su'ʃɛ], *n.m.* Ragstone; galingale;
shoveller (duck).

soucheter [suʃ'te], *v.t.* To count or verify
(the stumps left after a felling). **souchéteur**,
n.m. Surveyor of stocks or stubs in a
forest.

souci [su'si], *n.m.* Care, solicitude, anxiety;
(*Bot.*) marigold. *C'est le moindre de mes soucis*,
that is the least of my worries; *être dévoré
de soucis*, to be careworn; *être en souci de*, to be
anxious about; *sans souci*, free from care; *un
sans-souci*, a care-free fellow. (*Bot.*) *Souci des
marais*, marsh-marigold.

*****soucier**, *v.t.* (*conjugated like* PRIER) To trouble,
to upset. **se soucier**, *v.r.* To care, to mind,
to be concerned, to trouble oneself, to be
anxious (*de*). *Il ne s'en soucie guère*, he cares
little about it; *s'en soucier comme de l'an
quarante*, not to care a rap about it.

soucieusement, *adv.* Anxiously, thoughtfully.

soucieux, *a.* (*fem.* **-ieuse**) Anxious, full of
care; pensive, thoughtful.

soucoupe [su'kup], *n.f.* Saucer. *Soucoupe
volante*, flying saucer.

soudable [su'dabl], *a.* That can be soldered.
soudage, *n.m.* Soldering; (*fig.*) welding,
union; reconciliation.

soudain (1) [su'dɛ̃], *a.* (*fem.* **-aine**) Sudden,
unexpected. **soudain** (2) or **soudainement**,
adv. Suddenly, all of a sudden. **soudaineté**,
n.f. Suddenness.

Soudan [su'dã], **le**, *n.m.* The Sudan. **soudanais**, *a.* and *n.* (*fem.* **-aise**) Sudanese.

soudanien, *a.* (*fem.* **-ienne**) Of the Sudan.

soudard [su'daːr], *n.m.* *Old soldier; mercenary, ruffian.

soude [sud], *n.f.* Kali, salt-wort, glass-wort;
soda.

souder [su'de], *v.t.* To solder, to braze, to
weld; (*fig.*) to unite, to join. *Lampe à souder*,
blow-lamp. **se souder**, *v.r.* To be soldered
or welded; to knit (of bones). **soudeur**, *n.m.*
Welder. **soudeuse**, *n.f.* Welding machine

soudier [su'dje], *a.* (*fem.* **-ière**) Soda (works,
industry, etc.).

soudoir [su'dwaːr], *n.m.* Soldering-iron.

soudoyer [sudwa'je], *v.t. irr.* (*conjugated like*
ABOYER). To keep in one's pay; to hire; to
bribe.

soudure [su'dyːr], *n.f.* Solder; soldering;
union, joint; welding. *Sans soudure*, seamless; *soudure à l'arc électrique*, arc-welding;
soudure autogène, oxy-acetylene welding.

soue [su], *n.f.* Pigsty.

soufflage [su'fla:ʒ], *n.m.* Glass-blowing; blowing, blast; (*Naut.*) sheathing. **soufflant**, *a.* (*fem.* **-ante**) Blowing.

souffle [sufl], *n.m.* Breath, breathing; expiration; puff (of wind etc.); exhalation; (*fig.*) inspiration, influence. *Cela me coupa le souffle*, it made me gasp; *manquer de souffle*, to be short-winded; (*fig.*) to lack inspiration. **soufflé**, *a.* (*fem.* **-ée**) Soufflé (of pastry etc.); exaggerated (reputation).—*n.m.* Soufflé (light dish). **soufflement**, *n.m.* Blowing.

souffler [su'fle], *v.i.* To blow, to breathe; to pant, to puff; to recover one's breath; (*fig.*) to open one's mouth, to breathe a word etc.; to whisper. *Il n'oserait souffler*, he dare not speak; *souffler aux oreilles de quelqu'un*, to whisper in someone's ear; *souffler dans ses doigts*, to blow on one's fingers.—*v.t.* To blow, to blow out; to inflate; to whisper; (*Theat.*) to prompt; to huff (at draughts); (*Naut.*) to sheathe. *Ne pas souffler mot*, not to say a word; *souffler la haine*, to fan hatred; *souffler le feu*, to blow the fire; *souffler le froid et le chaud*, to blow hot and cold; *souffler l'orgue*, to blow the organ; *souffler un emploi à quelqu'un*, to rob someone of a situation by forestalling him.

soufflerie, *n.f.* Bellows (of an organ); blast-apparatus, blowing-apparatus; wind-tunnel.

soufflet, *n.m.* Bellows, pair of bellows; hood (of a carriage); box on the ear, slap in the face; affront, mortification, humiliation. *Donner un soufflet au bon sens*, to outrage common sense.

souffleter, *v.t.* To slap in the face, to box the ears of; (*fig.*) to insult, to outrage.

souffleteur, *n.m.* (*fem.* **-euse**) Striker, slapper; insulter.

souffleur (1) [su'flœ:r], *n.m.* Blower (species of dolphin). **souffleur** (2), *n.m.* (*fem.* **-euse** (1)) Blower; one that puffs and pants; (*Theat.*) prompter. *Le trou du souffleur*, the prompter's box; *souffleur de verre*, glass-blower.—*a.* Blowing, puffing. *Cheval souffleur*, panting horse; roarer.

(**C**) **souffleuse** (2), *n.f.* Snow blower.

soufflure, *n.f.* Flaw (in glass); blister (paint etc.).

souffrance [su'frã:s], *n.f.* Suffering, pain; suspense; (*Law*) sufferance. *En souffrance*, awaiting delivery; suspended, standing over, in abeyance; *Jour de souffrance*, borrowed light; window on sufferance. **souffrant**, *a.* (*fem.* **-ante**) Suffering, in pain; injured, affected; unwell, poorly, ailing; patient, long-suffering.

souffre-douleur, *n.m. inv.* Drudge, butt, laughing-stock.

souffreteux, *a.* (*fem.* **-euse**) Needy; poorly, sickly, weakly.

souffrir [su'fri:r], *v.t. irr.* To suffer; to bear, to endure, to undergo, to sustain; to stand, to tolerate; to allow, to put up with; to admit of, to brook. *Cela ne souffre point de retard*, that admits of no delay; *faire souffrir*, to pain, to grieve, to torture; *je ne saurais souffrir cet homme-là*, I cannot endure that man; *pourquoi souffrez-vous cela?* why do you put up with that? *souffrir la faim*, to endure hunger; *souffrir un assaut*, to withstand an assault.—*v.i.* To suffer, to be in pain; to be pained; to be in trouble, to be injured. *Souffrir de la tête*, to have a pain in the head; *souffrir de rhumatismes*, to suffer from rheumatism. **se souffrir**, *v.t.* To endure each other; to be tolerated, to be suffered (of things).

soufi [SOFI].

soufrage [su'fra:ʒ], *n.m.* Sulphuring, smoking with brimstone.

soufre [sufr], *n.m.* Sulphur, brimstone. *Fleur de soufre*, flowers of sulphur. **soufrer**, *v.t.* To dip in brimstone, to sulphur. **soufrière**, *n.f.* Sulphur-mine. **soufroir**, *n.m.* Sulphuring-stove.

souhait [swɛ], *n.m.* Wish, desire. *À souhait*, to one's heart's content, as one would have it; *avoir tout à souhait*, to have everything to one's liking; *à vos souhaits*, God bless you! (after sneezing). **souhaitable**, *a.* Desirable.

souhaiter, *v.t.* To desire, to wish for. *Il serait à souhaiter que*, it is desirable that; *je vous en souhaite*, (*iron.*) wouldn't you like to get it! *je vous souhaite le bonjour*, I wish you good morning.

souillard [su'ja:r], *n.m.* Hole (for water) in stone; stone so perforated. **souillarde**, *n.f.* Rinsing-tub; rinsing-room; scullery.

souille [su:j], *n.f.* Wallowing-place (of wild boars); bed, impression (made by a ship in mud).

souiller [su'je], *v.t.* To soil, to dirty; to stain, to blemish, to sully; to defile, to pollute, to contaminate. **se souiller**, *v.r.* To soil oneself, to get dirty; to disgrace oneself, to tarnish one's good name.

souillon [su'jɔ̃], *n.* Sloven, slut; scullion.

souillure [su'jy:r], *n.f.* Dirt, spot, stain; blot, blemish; impurity, contamination, defilement.

soûl [su], *a.* (*fem.* **soûle**) Glutted, surfeited (*de*); drunk; satiated, cloyed, heartily sick (*de*). *Il est soûl de musique*, he is surfeited with music; *soûl comme une grive*, as drunk as a lord.—*n.m.* Fill, bellyful. *Tout son soûl*, to one's heart's content.

soulagement [sulaʒ'mã], *n.m.* Relief, alleviation, assuagement; solace, help. *C'est un soulagement à ses peines*, it is an alleviation of his troubles.

soulager [sula'ʒe], *v.t.* To relieve, to ease, to lighten; to alleviate, to allay; to soothe, to comfort; to assist, to succour. **se soulager**, *v.r.* To relieve oneself; to relieve one's feelings; to ease up; to help each other; to relieve nature.

soûlard [su'la:r], *a.* (*fem.* **-arde**) Drunken.—*n.* Drunkard, sot.

soûler [su'le], *v.t.* To fill, to glut, to surfeit; to intoxicate, to make drunk. **se soûler**, *v.r.* To gorge; to get drunk.

soûlerie [sul'ri], *n.f.* Drinking bout, 'binge'.

soulèvement [sulɛv'mã], *n.m.* Heaving; swelling, upheaval, upheaving (of the waves etc.); rising (of the stomach); (*fig.*) insurrection, revolt; burst of indignation. *Soulèvement de cœur*, nausea. **soulever**, *v.t. irr.* (*conjugated like* AMENER) To raise, to lift up, to heave; to take up, to lift; (*fig.*) to excite, to stir up, to urge to insurrection; to excite to action; to sicken, to cause (the stomach etc.) to revolt; to rouse the indignation of; to start, to moot (a question etc.). *Cela me soulève le cœur*, that makes me sick. **se**

soulever, *v.r.* To raise oneself, to rise; to heave, to swell; to be urged (to indignation etc.); to revolt, to rise in insurrection.

soulier [suˈlje], *n.m.* Shoe. *Être dans ses petits souliers,* to be ill at ease, to be in an embarrassing situation; *souliers ferrés,* hobnailed shoes.

soulignement [suliɲˈmã], *n.m.* Underlining.

souligner, *v.t.* To underline, (*fig.*) to emphasize.

soûlographie [sulɔgraˈfi], *n.f.* (*pop.*) Drunkenness; orgy.

soulte [sult], *n.f.* (*Comm.*) Balance, compensation (in cash), to make shares equal.

soumettre [suˈmɛtr], *v.t. irr.* (*conjugated like* METTRE) To subdue, to bring under subjection, to subject; to submit, to defer, to refer; to subordinate. **se soumettre,** *v.r.* To submit, to yield; to comply, to assent (*à*). *Il faut se soumettre ou se démettre,* you must submit or resign.

soumis [suˈmi], *a.* (*fem.* **-ise**) Submissive; subject; amenable (*à*). *Fille soumise,* prostitute under police control. *Non soumis,* unconquered.

soumission, *n.f.* Submission, compliance, obedience; subjection; mark of respect; submissiveness; tender for a contract etc.; contract, deed of contract; bond. *Soumissions sous pli cacheté,* sealed tenders. **soumissionnaire,** *n.* Tendering party. **soumissionner,** *v.t.* To tender for.

soupape [suˈpap], *n.f.* Valve; plug. *À soupape,* with a valve; *soupape à gorge,* throttle valve; *soupape de sûreté,* safety-valve; *soupape d'échappement,* exhaust valve; *sans soupapes,* valveless.

soupçon [supˈsɔ̃], *n.m.* Suspicion; surmise, conjecture; (*fig.*) slight taste, dash, touch. *Exempt de soupçon,* free from suspicion; *un soupçon d'ail,* just a taste of garlic. **soupçonnable,** *a.* Liable to suspicion. **soupçonner,** *v.t.* To suspect; to surmise. **soupçonneur,** *n.m.* (*fem.* **soupçonneuse** (1)) Suspecter. **soupçonneux,** *a.* (*fem.* **soupçonneuse** (2)) Suspicious, distrustful.

soupe [sup], *n.f.* Soup; sop (soaked slice of bread); (*Mil.*) food, meal, signal for dinner. *C'est une soupe au lait,* he has a quick temper; *marchand de soupe,* head of an inferior boarding school; *trempé comme une soupe,* drenched to the skin.

soupente [suˈpãːt], *n.f.* Braces (of a coach); straps (of a horse); loft, garret. *Soupente d'escalier,* cupboard under a staircase.

souper (1) [suˈpe], *v.i.* To sup, to have supper. *J'en ai soupé,* (*fam.*) I have had enough of it. **souper** (2), *n.m.* Supper.

soupeser [supəˈze], *v.t. irr.* (*conjugated like* AMENER) To weigh in one's hand, to try the weight of.

soupière [suˈpjɛːr], *n.f.* Soup-tureen.

soupir [suˈpiːr], *n.m.* Sigh; breath, gasp; (*Mus.*) crotchet-rest, crotchet; (*pl.*) sighing. *Pousser un soupir,* to heave a sigh; *rendre le dernier soupir,* to breathe one's last.

soupirail, *n.m.* (*pl.* **-aux**) Air-hole, ventilator.

soupirant, *a.* (*fem.* **-ante**) Sighing.—*n.m.* Wooer, lover.

soupirer, *v.i.* To sigh; to gasp; to long. *Soupirer après une chose,* to long for a thing; *soupirer de douleur,* to sigh for grief.—*v.t.* To

breathe forth, to sigh out. **soupireur,** *n.m.* Sigher, wooer.

souple [supl], *a.* Supple, pliant, flexible, yielding; lithe, lissom (body); tractable, docile, compliant; tough. **souplement,** *adv.* Flexibly, compliantly, supply.

souplesse [suˈples], *n.f.* Suppleness, flexibility; compliance, pliancy; versatility; toughness. *Tours de souplesse,* feats of agility, cunning tricks.

souquenille [sukˈniːj], *n.f.* Smock-frock; (shabby) old garment.

souquer [suˈke], *v.t.* (*Naut.*) To stiffen (a rope), to haul it taut; (*pop.*) to thrash, to dress down.—*v.i.* (*Row.*) *Souquer (sur les avirons),* to tear the finish.

source [surs], *n.f.* Spring, origin; source, fountain, fountain-head; well-spring, fount, rise. *Avoir sa source dans,* to have its origin in; *couler de source* [COULER]; *de bonne source,* on good authority; *eau de source,* spring-water; *prendre sa source,* to rise (of a river); *remonter aux sources,* to consult the original texts, to go back to the sources. **sourcier,** *n.m.* (*fem.* **-ière**) Spring-finder, water-diviner.

sourcil [surˈsi], *n.m.* Eyebrow, brow. *Froncer le sourcil,* to knit one's brow, to frown.

sourcilier, *a.* (*fem.* **-ière**) (*Anat.*) Superciliary. *Arcade sourcilière,* brow ridge.

***sourciller,** *v.i.* To knit one's brows, to frown; to wince, to flinch; (*fam.*) to bat an eyelid. *Sans sourciller,* without wincing; without turning a hair.

sourcilleux, *a.* (*fem.* **-euse**) Haughty, proud, supercilious; frowning, uneasy.

sourd [suːr], *a.* (*fem.* **sourde**) Deaf; (*fig.*) dull; insensible, dead; hollow, rumbling, muffled (of sound); secret, underhand. *Douleur sourde,* dull pain; *faire la sourde oreille* [OREILLE]; *faire un bruit sourd* [BRUIT]; *il est sourd d'une oreille,* he is deaf in one ear; *lanterne sourde* [LANTERNE]; *rumeur sourde,* faint rumour; *sourd comme un pot,* as deaf as a post; *voix sourde,* hollow voice.—*n.* Deaf person. *Faire le sourd,* to sham deafness; *frapper comme un sourd,* to beat mercilessly; *il n'est pire sourd que celui qui ne veut pas entendre* [ENTENDRE]. **sourdement,** *adv.* Indistinctly; with a hollow voice, rumblingly; secretly, in an underhand manner.

sourdine, *n.f.* Sordine (of a musical instrument); damper (of a piano etc.). *En sourdine,* with muted strings; secretly, on the sly.

sourd-muet, *a.* and *n.* (*fem.* **sourde-muette,** *pl.* **sourds-muets**) Deaf-and-dumb (person), deaf-mute.

sourdre [surdr], *v.i.* To spring, to gush, to well; (*fig.*) to result, to proceed, to arise.

souriant [suˈrjã], *a.* (*fem.* **-iante**) Smiling.

souriceau [suriˈso], *n.m.* (*pl.* **-eaux**) Small mouse. **souricier,** *n.m.* Mouser. **souricière,** *n.f.* Mouse-trap; (*fig.*) trap, snare, ambush.

sourire (1) [suˈriːr], *v.i. irr.* (*conjug. like* RIRE) To smile; to be agreeable, to delight, to please; to be favourable or propitious. *Sourire à quelqu'un,* to smile upon someone; *sourire des efforts de quelqu'un,* to smile at someone's efforts.

sourire (2) or ***souris** (1), *n.m.* Smile. *Large sourire,* grin; *sourire affecté,* smirk; *sourire* *niais*, simper; *sourire moqueur* (*et dédaigneux*), sneer; *sourire méprisant*, scornful smile.

souris (2) [su'ri], *n.f.* Mouse; mouse-colour; knuckle (of a leg of mutton). *On entendrait trotter une souris*, you could hear a pin drop; *souris d'hôtel*, hotel-thief; *souris qui n'a qu'un trou est bientôt prise*, it is as well to have more than one string to one's bow.—*a. inv.* Mouse-coloured. *Cheval souris*, mouse-coloured horse; *gris souris*, mouse-grey.

sournois [sur'nwa], *a.* (*fem.* **-oise**) Artful, cunning, sly; shifty.—*n.* Sneak. **sournoisement**, *adv.* Cunningly, on the sly, sneakingly.

sournoiserie, *n.f.* Slyness, artfulness, cunning; underhand trick.

sous [su], *prep.* Under, beneath, below; on, upon; with; in; by. *Affirmer sous serment*, to swear on oath; *regarder quelqu'un sous le nez*, to stare someone in the face; *sous dix jours*, within ten days; *sous la main*, close at hand, ready to hand; *sous l'équateur*, at the equator; *sous les drapeaux*, with the colours; *sous peu*, in a short time; *sous presse*, printing, being printed; *sous terre*, underground; *sous vos yeux*, before your eyes.

sous-affermer [suzafɛr'me], *v.t.* To sublet; to take an under-lease of.

sous-aide, *n.* (*pl.* **sous-aides**) Under-assistant.

sous-alimentation, *n.f.* Malnutrition. **sous-alimenté**, *a.* (*fem.* **-ée**) Underfed.

sous-amendement, *n.m.* Additional amendment, amendment to an amendment. **sous-amender**, *v.t.* To amend (an amendment).

sous-arbrisseau, *n.m.* (*pl.* **-eaux**) Herbaceous plant (between a herb and a shrub).

sous-axillaire [suzaksi'lɛːr], *a.* (*Bot.*) Subaxillary. **sous-bail**, *n.m.* (*pl.* **sous-baux**) Sub-lease, sub-let.

sous-barbe, *n.f. inv.*, or **soubarbe**, *n.m.* Under-jaw (of a horse); (*Naut.*) bob-stay.

sous-bibliothécaire, *n.m.* Sub-librarian.

sous-bois, *n.m. inv.* Underwood, undergrowth.

sous-brigadier, *n.m.* Lance-corporal (of police etc.).

sous-carbonate, *n.m.* Sub-carbonate.

sous-chef, *n.m.* Deputy head-clerk, second head-clerk; assistant manager.

sous-chevron, *n.m.* Under-rafter.

sous-clavier, *a.* (*fem.* **-ière**) (*Anat.*) Subclavian.

sous-commissaire, *n.m.* (*Navy*) Under-commissary, assistant paymaster.

sous-commission, *n.f.* Sub-committee.

sous-costal, *a.* (*fem.* **-ale**, *pl.* **-aux**) (*Anat.*) Subcostal.

souscripteur, *n.m.* Subscriber; (*Comm.*) underwriter.

souscription, *n.f.* Subscription; signature; entering (of horse).

souscrire [sus'kriːr], *v.t. irr.* (*conjugated like* ÉCRIRE) To subscribe, to sign, to take up (shares).—*v.i.* To subscribe, to consent, to agree (à); to engage oneself.

*souscrivant, *n.m.* Underwriter.

sous-cutané [sukyta'ne], *a.* (*fem.* **-ée**) Subcutaneous.

sous-délégué [SUBDÉLÉGUÉ].

sous-développé, *a.* (*fam.* **-ée**) Under-developed (country).

sous-diaconat, *n.m.* Subdeaconry.

sous-diacre, *n.m.* Subdeacon.

sous-directeur, *n.m.* (*fem.* **-trice**) Sub-manager; deputy headmaster.

sous-dit, *a.* (*fem.* **-dite**) Undermentioned.

sous-dominante, *n.f.* (*Mus.*) Sub-dominant.

sous-économe, *n.m.* Sub-treasurer.

sous-entendre, *v.t.* Not to express fully, to hint, to imply. **sous-entendu**, *n.m.* Thing understood, implication, innuendo. **sous-entente**, *n.f.* Mental reservation.

sous-estimer, *v.t.* To undervalue, to under-estimate.

sous-exposer, *v.t.* (*Phot.*) To under-expose.

sous-faîte, *n.m.* Under-ridgeboard.

sous-fermier, *n.m.* (*fem.* **-ière**) Under-lessee.

sous-fréter, *v.t. irr.* (*conjugated like* ACCÉLÉRER) To underlet or under-freight (a ship).

sous-garde, *n.f.* Trigger-guard.

sous-genre, *n.m.* Sub-genus.

sous-gorge, *n.f. inv.* Throat-band (of a bridle).

sous-gouverneur, *n.m.* Deputy-governor.

sous-intendance, *n.f.* Deputy-commissary-ship; deputy-commissary's office. **sous-intendant**, *n.m.* Deputy-commissary.

sous-jacent, *a.* (*fem.* **-ente**) Subjacent.

sous-jupe, *n.f.* Underslip.

sous-lieutenant, *n.m.* Second-lieutenant. *Sous-lieutenant aviateur*, pilot officer.

sous-locataire, *n.* Under-tenant, subtenant. **sous-location**, *n.f.* Sub-letting; under-tenancy.

sous-louer, *v.t.* To sub-let; to rent from a tenant.

sous-main, *n.m. inv.* Writing-pad. *Faire quelque chose en sous-main*, to do something behind the scenes.

sous-marin, *a.* (*fem.* **-ine**) Submarine.—*n.m.* Submarine. **sous-marinier**, *n.m.* Submariner.

sous-maxillaire, *a.* Submaxillary.

sous-multiple, *a.* and *n.m.* Submultiple.

sous-normale, *n.f.* (*Geom.*) Subnormal.

sous-occipital, *a.* (*fem.* **-ale**, *pl.* **-aux**) Sub-occipital.

sous-œuvre, *n.m. inv.* Underpinning. *Reprendre un mur en sous-œuvre*, to underpin a wall.

sous-off, *abbr. fam.* of **sous-officier**, *n.m.* Non-commissioned officer, N.C.O.

sous-ordre, *n.m. inv.* Subordinate. *En sous-ordre*, subordinately; (*Nat. Hist.*) (*pl.* **sous-ordres**) suborder.

sous-peuplé, *a.* (*fem.* **-ée**) Under-populated.

sous-pied, *n.m.* Trouser-strap.

sous-préfecture, *n.f.* Sub-prefecture. **sous-préfet**, *n.m.* Subprefect, under-sheriff.

sous-prieur, *n.m.* Subprior. **sous-prieure**, *n.f.* Subprioress.

sous-principal, *n.m.* (*pl.* **-aux**) Vice-principal.

sous-production, *n.f.* Under-production.

sous-produit, *n.m.* By-product.

sous-secrétaire, *n.* Under-secretary. **sous-secrétariat**, *n.m.* Under-secretaryship.

sous-seing [su'sɛ̃], *n.m.* Private deed or contract.

soussigné, *a.* (*fem.* **-ée**) Undersigned. *Nous soussignés certifions*, we, the undersigned, certify. **soussigner**, *v.t.* To undersign.

sous-sol, *n.m.* Subsoil, substratum; basement.

sous-station, *n.f.* (*Elec.*) Sub-station.

sous-tangente, *n.f.* Subtangent.

sous-tendante, *n.f.* Subtense.

sous-tendre, *v.t.* To subtend.

sous-titre, *n.m.* Sub-title.

soustraction [sustrak'sjɔ̃], *n.f.* Taking away, abstraction; subtraction.

soustraire [sus'trɛːr], *v.t. irr.* (*conjugated like* TRAIRE) To take away, to abstract; to withdraw, to remove, to screen; (*Arith.*) to subtract. **se soustraire**, *v.r.* To escape, to flee, to avoid; to withdraw, free, or exempt oneself; to be subtracted. *Se soustraire à la justice,* to abscond from justice; *se soustraire à la tyrannie,* to flee from tyranny; *se soustraire au châtiment,* to avoid punishment.

sous-traitant [sutrɛ'tã], *n.m.* Subcontractor; under-farmer (of taxes etc.). **sous-traité**, *n.m.* Subcontract. **sous-traiter**, *v.t.* To subcontract; to under-farm (taxes etc.).

sous-variété, *n.f.* Subvariety.

sous-ventrière, *n.f.* Belly-band.

sous-verge, *n.m. inv.* Unmounted horse on off-side of one carrying a rider. *Sous-verge de derrière,* off-wheeler; *sous-verge de devant,* off-leader.

sous-verre, *n.m. inv.* Passe-partout (picture).

sous-vêtement, *n.m.* Undergarment.

sous-voltage, *n.m.* (*Elec.*) Under-voltage.

soutache [su'taʃ], *n.f.* Braid (used on soldier's uniform etc.).

soutacher [suta'ʃe], *v.t.* To braid.

soutane [su'tan], *n.f.* Cassock; (*fig.*) the cloth, priests. **soutanelle**, *n.f.* Short cassock.

soute [sut], *n.f.* (*Naut.*) Store-room; (*Av.*) luggage-, bomb-bay. *Soute à charbon,* coalbunker; *soute aux poudres,* powder-magazine.

soutenable [sut'nabl], *a.* Sustainable, maintainable; supportable; tenable.

soutenance [sut'nãs], *n.f.* Sustaining or defence (of a thesis). **soutenant**, *n.m.* Sustainer, defender (of a thesis); (*Her.*) supporter.

soutènement [suten'mã], *n.m.* (*Arch.*) Support; (*Law*) written explanation. *Mur de soutènement,* supporting-wall.

souteneur [sut'nœːr], *n.m.* Bully, pimp, ponce; upholder (of system etc.).

soutenir [sut'niːr], *v.t. irr.* (*conjugated like* TENIR) To hold up, to support, to sustain, to bear up; to keep up, to buoy up; to prop, to prop up; (*fig.*) to maintain, to uphold, to affirm; to back, to stand by; to countenance, to favour; to afford (an expense); to endure, to hold out against; to wage. *Il ne peut soutenir la raillerie,* he cannot stand being teased; *le vin vous soutient,* wine strengthens one; *soutenir la conversation,* to keep up the conversation; *soutenir le combat,* to maintain the fight; *soutenir son rang,* to keep up one's position; *soutenir une famille,* to support a family; *soutenir une thèse,* to sustain a thesis; *soutenir un siège,* to withstand a siege. **se soutenir**, *v.r.* To support oneself, to maintain oneself; to stand up, to hold oneself up; to bear up, to hold out; to stand firm; to be buoyed up, to keep afloat; to succeed; to get on; to continue; to sustain one another. *Elle se soutient bien,* she wears well; *se soutenir contre,* to resist, to withstand; *son style ne se soutient pas,* his style is not sustained; *une thèse qui ne peut se soutenir,* a thesis that cannot be defended.

soutenu [sut'ny], *a.* (*fem.* **-ue**) Sustained; unremitting, unceasing, constant; lofty, elevated.

souterrain [sutɛ'rɛ̃], *a.* (*fem.* **-aine**) Underground, subterranean; (*fig.*) underhand. *Voies souterraines,* underhand methods.— *n.m.* Underground vault, cavern; (*Rail.*) tunnel; subway. **souterrainement**, *adv.* Underground; (*fig.*) underhandedly.

soutien [su'tjɛ̃], *n.m.* Support, prop, stay, staff; supporter, upholder, vindicator.

soutien-gorge, *n.m. inv.* Brassière.

soutier [su'tje], *n.m.* (*Naut.*) Trimmer, bunker-hand.

soutirage [suti'raːʒ], *n.m.* Drawing off (of wine etc.).

soutirer [suti're], *v.t.* To draw off, to rack (liquors); (*fig.*) to worm out (*à*), to extract (money, information).

***souvenance** [suv'nãːs], *n.f.* (Distant) recollection.

souvenir (1) [suv'niːr], *n.m.* Remembrance, recollection, memory; reminder, souvenir, memento, keepsake. *Avoir bon souvenir de,* to remember (something) well; *rappeler une chose au souvenir de quelqu'un,* to remind someone of a thing; *rappelez-moi à son bon souvenir,* remember me kindly to him.

souvenir (2) [suv'niːr], *v.impers. irr.* (*conjugated like* VENIR) To occur to the mind. *Il m'en souvient,* I remember it; *il me souvient de,* I remember; *s'il m'en souvient bien,* if I remember rightly. **se souvenir**, *v.r. irr.* (*conjug. like* VENIR) To remember, to call to mind, to recollect; to bear in mind. *Autant que je puis m'en souvenir,* to the best of my recollection; *faire souvenir quelqu'un de quelque chose,* to remind someone of something; *se souvenir du temps passé,* to remember past times.

souvent [su'vã], *adv.* Often, frequently. *Peu souvent,* rarely; ***souventefois** or **souventes fois**, *adv.* Oftentimes.

souverain [su'vrɛ̃], *a.* (*fem.* **-aine**) Sovereign, supreme; superlative, highest, extreme, most excellent; infallible; (*Law etc.*) final, without appeal. *Au souverain degré,* to a sovereign degree.—*n.* Sovereign (monarch).—*n.m.* Sovereign (coin). **souverainement**, *adv.* In the extreme; supremely; superlatively; (*Law*) without appeal.

souveraineté [suvren'te], *n.f.* Sovereignty, supremacy, dominion; dominions.

soviet [sɔ'vjet], *n.m.* Soviet. **soviétique**, *a.* *L'Union des Républiques socialistes soviétiques* (*U.R.S.S.*), the Union of Socialist Soviet Republics (U.S.S.R.).—*n.* Soviet citizen. **soviétiser**, *v.t.* To sovietize.

soyer [swa'je], *a.* (*fem.* **soyère**) Pertaining to silk.—*n.m.* Silk-mercer, seller; (glass of) iced champagne (sipped through a straw).

soyeux [swa'jø], *a.* (*fem.* **-euse**) Silky, silken. —*n.m. Les soyeux de Lyon,* the silk manufacturers of Lyons.

soyez etc. [ÊTRE].

spacieusement [spasjøz'mã], *adv.* Spaciously. **spacieux**, *a.* (*fem.* **-ieuse**) Spacious, wide, roomy.

spadassin [spada'sɛ̃], *n.m.* Bravo, bully. *Spadassin à gages,* hired assassin.

spahi [spa'i], *n.m.* Spahi (Algerian native trooper).

spalme [spalm], *n.m.* (*Naut.*) Tar, paying-stuff.

spalt [spalt], *n.m.* Spalt, Jew's pitch.
sparadrap [spara'dra], *n.m.* Sticking-plaster.
spartan [spar'tã], *n.m.* (*Naut.*) Rope made of esparto.
Sparte [spart], *f.* Sparta.
sparte, *n.f.* Esparto. **sparterie**, *n.f.* Manufacture of esparto, sparterie (esparto articles).
spartiate [spar'sjat], *a.* and *n.* Spartan.
spasme [spasm], *n.m.* Spasm. **spasmodique**, *a.* Spasmodic. **spasmodiquement**, *adv.* Spasmodically. **spasmologie**, *n.f.* Spasmology.
spath [spat], *n.m.* (*Min.*) Spar. *Spath fluor*, fluor-spar.
spathe [spat], *n.f.* (*Bot.*) Spathe. **spathé** or **spathacé**, *a.* (*fem.* -ée) Spathaceous. **spathiforme**, *a.* (*Min.*) Spathiform; (*Bot.*) spathose. **spathique**, *a.* Spathic, sparry.
spatial [spa'sjal], *a.* (*fem.* -iale, *pl.* -iaux) Spatial, spacial.
spatule [spa'tyl], *n.f.* Spatula, palette-knife; spoon-bill (bird). **spatulé**, *a.* (*fem.* -ée) Spatulate.
speaker [spi'kœːr], *n.m.* (*fem.* **speakerine**) (*Rad.*) Announcer.
spécial [spe'sjal], *a.* (*fem.* -iale, *pl.* -iaux) Special, especial, particular; professional. *Armes spéciales*, technical arms (artillery, engineers). **spécialement**, *adv.* Especially, particularly.
spécialisation, *n.f.* Specialization.
spécialiser [spesjali'ze], *v.t.* To specialize. **se spécialiser**, *v.r.* To be a specialist.
spécialisme, *n.m.* Specialism.
spécialiste, *n.* Specialist, expert.
spécialité, *n.f.* Peculiarity, special feature; speciality; line or department of business etc.; patent medicine.
spécieusement [spesjøz'mã], *adv.* Speciously, plausibly. **spécieux**, *a.* (*fem.* -ieuse) Specious, plausible.
spécificatif [spesifika'tif], *a.* (*fem.* -ive) Specifying.
spécification, *n.f.* Specification.
spécificité, *n.f.* Specific feature.
spécifier, *v.t.* To specify, state definitely; to determine specifically.
spécifique, *a.* and *n.m.* Specific. **spécifiquement**, *adv.* Specifically.
spécimen [spesi'mɛn], *n.m.* Specimen.
spéciosité [spesjozi'te], *n.f.* Speciousness.
spectacle [spɛk'takl], *n.m.* Spectacle, scene, sight; play-house, theatre; play, performance; pomp, parade, show. *Être en spectacle*, to be exposed to public ridicule; *se donner en spectacle*, to make an exhibition of oneself; *taxe sur les spectacles*, entertainment tax.
spectaculaire, *a.* Spectacular.
spectateur, *n.m.* (*fem.* -trice) Spectator, looker-on, bystander.
spectral [spɛk'tral], *a.* (*fem.* -ale, *pl.* -aux) Spectral; pertaining to the spectrum.
spectre, *n.m.* Spectre, phantom, ghost; spectrum.
spectrographe, *n.m.* (*Phot.*) Spectrograph.
spectromètre, *n.m.* Spectrometer.
spectroscope, *n.m.* Spectroscope. **spectroscopie**, *n.f.* Spectroscopy.
spéculaire [speky'lɛːr], *a.* Specular (mineral); transparent. *Écriture spéculaire*, mirror writing.

spéculateur [spekyla'tœːr], *n.m.* (*fem.* -trice) Speculator.
spéculatif, *a.* (*fem.* -ive) Speculative.—*n.m.* Man of speculative mind.
spéculation, *n.f.* Speculation. **spéculativement**, *adv.* In a speculative manner.
spéculer, *v.i.* To speculate.
speculum or **spéculum**, *n.m.* Speculum.
spéléologie [speleɔlɔ'ʒi], *n.f.* Speleology. **spéléologique**, *a.* Speleological. **spéléologue**, *n.m.* Speleologist, cave explorer.
spergule [spɛr'gyl], *n.f.* Spurry (plant).
spermaceti [spɛrmase'ti], *n.m.* Spermaceti, sperm. **spermathèque** or **spermatothèque**, *n.f.* Spermatheca. **spermatique**, *a.* Spermatic.
spermatocèle [spɛrmatɔ'sɛl], *n.f.* Spermatocele. **spermatogénèse**, *n.f.* Spermatogenesis. **spermatologie**, *n.f.* Spermatology. **spermatophore**, *n.m.* Spermatophore. **spermatozoïde** or **spermatozoaire**, *n.m.* Spermatozoon.
sperme [spɛrm], *n.m.* Sperm, seed. *Sperme de baleine*, spermaceti.
spermophile [spɛrmɔ'fil], *n.m.* Spermophile.
sphacèle [sfa'sɛl], *n.m.* Sphacelus (gangrene). **sphacélé** [sfase'le], *a.* (*fem.* -ée) Sphacelate.
sphaigne [sfɛːɲ], *n.f.* Sphagnum moss.
sphénoïdal [sfenɔi'dal], *a.* (*fem.* -ale, *pl.* -aux) Sphenoidal.
sphénoïde, *a.* and *n.m.* Sphenoid.
sphère [sfɛːr], *n.f.* Sphere, orb, globe; (*fig.*) circle, orbit, quarters. *Sortir de sa sphère*, to go out of one's sphere. **sphéricité**, *n.f.* Sphericity, curvature. **sphérique**, *a.* Spherical. **sphériquement**, *adv.* Spherically. **sphéroïdal**, *a.* (*fem.* -ale, *pl.* -aux) Spheroidal. **sphéroïde**, *n.m.* Spheroid.
sphéromètre, *n.m.* Spherometer.
sphincter [sfɛk'tɛːr], *n.m.* (*Anat.*) Sphincter.
sphinge [sfɛ̃ːʒ], *n.f.* Female sphinx.
sphinx [sfɛ̃ːks], *n.m.* Sphinx; (*Ent.*) hawkmoth.
spic [spik], *n.m.* Spike lavender.
spica [spi'ka], *n.m.* (*Surg.*) Spica, spicabandage.
spicanard [spika'naːr], *n.m.* Spikenard.
spiciforme [spisi'fɔrm], *a.* Spike-shaped.
spicule [spi'kyl], *n.m.* Spicule (in sponges), spikelet.
spicilège [spisi'lɛːʒ], *n.m.* Collection of thoughts and observations.
spider [spi'dɛːr], *n.m.* Dickey (seat).
spinal [spi'nal], *a.* (*fem.* -ale, *pl.* -aux) Spinal.
Spinalien [spina'ljɛ̃], *n.m.* (*fem.* -ienne) Inhabitant of Épinal.
spinelle [spi'nɛl], *n.m.* and *a.* (*Min.*) Spinel.— *n.f.* Spinule.
spinescence [spinɛ'sãːs], *n.f.* Spinescence. **spinifère**, *a.* Spiniferous. **spiniforme**, *a.* Spine-shaped. **spinigère**, *a.* Spinigerous.
spinozisme [spino'zism] or **spinosisme**, *n.m.* Spinozism. **spinoziste** or **spinosiste**, *n.m.* and *a.* Spinozist.
sphinthariscope [spɛ̃taris'kɔp], *n.m.* Spinthariscope.
spiral [spi'ral], *a.* (*fem.* -ale, *pl.* -aux) Spiral. —*n.m.* Hair-spring (of watch). **spirale**, *n.f.* Spiral. *Aller en spirale*, to wind; *en spirale*, spirally.
spiralé [spira'le], *a.* (*fem.* -ée) Helical, spirated. **spiralement**, *adv.* In a spiral form.

[694]

spirant [spi'rɑ̃], *a.* (*fem.* **-ante**) Spirant.
spire [spi:r], *n.f.* Whorl, single turn of a spiral; helix.
Spire [spi:r], *f.* Speyer.
spirée [spi're], *n.f.* Spiraea; meadow-sweet.
spirite [spi'rit], *n.* Spiritist, spiritualist.—*a.* Spiritualistic. **spiritisme**, *n.m.* Spiritualism. **spiritiste**, *a.* Spiritualistic.
spiritualisation [spirityaliza'sjɔ̃], *n.f.* Spiritualization. **spiritualiser**, *v.t.* To spiritualize; *to distil. **spiritualisme**, *n.m.* Spiritualism. **spiritualiste**, *n.* and *a.* Spiritualist. **spiritualité**, *n.f.* Spirituality.
spirituel [spiri'tyɛl], *a.* (*fem.* **-elle**) Spiritual (incorporeal); spiritual (religious); mental, intellectual; witty, shrewd, ingenious, sprightly, lively, intelligent. *Concert spirituel*, sacred concert; *un homme fort spirituel*, a very witty man; *une réponse spirituelle*, a witty answer.—*n.m.* Spiritual or religious matters.
spirituellement, *adv.* Spiritually; ingeniously, wittily, cleverly, shrewdly.
spiritueux [spiri'tyø], *a.* (*fem.* **-euse**) Spirituous.—*n.m.* Spirit, spirituous liquor.
spiromètre [spirɔ'mɛtr], *n.m.* Spirometer.
spirométrie, *n.f.* Spirometry.
spirophore, *n.m.* Spirophore.
Spitzberg [spitz'bɛr], *m.* Spitzbergen.
splanchnique [splɑ̃k'nik], *a.* Splanchnic.
splanchnologie, *n.f.* Splanchnology.
spleen [splin], *n.m.* Spleen. (*fam.*) *Avoir le spleen*, to be in the dumps.
splendeur [splɑ̃'dœ:r], *n.f.* Splendour, lustre, brilliance; magnificence, pomp.
splendide [splɑ̃'did], *a.* Sumptuous, magnificent, gorgeous. **splendidement**, *adv.* Splendidly.
splénétique [splene'tik], *a.* Splenetic; morose. **splénification** or **splénisation**, *n.f.* Splenization. **splénique**, *a.* Splenic. **splénite**, *n.f.* Splenitis. **splénologie**, *n.f.* Splenology. **splénotomie**, *n.f.* Splenotomy.
spoliateur [spɔlja'tœ:r], *n.m.* (*fem.* **-trice**) Spoiler, despoiler.—*a.* Despoiling, of spoliation. **spoliation**, *n.f.* Spoliation, plundering.
spolier [spɔ'lje], *v.t.* To despoil, to plunder.
spondaïque [spɔ̃da'ik], *a.* Spondaic.
spondée [spɔ̃'de], *n.m.* Spondee.
spondyle [spɔ̃'dil], *n.m.* Spondyl (vertebra); (*Conch.*) spondylus (mollusc.) **spondylite**, *n.f.* Spondylitis, inflammation of the vertebrae, Pott's disease.
spongieux [spɔ̃'ʒjø], *a.* (*fem.* **-ieuse**) Spongy. **spongiforme**, *a.* Spongiform. **spongiole**, *n.f.* (*Bot.*) Spongiole. **spongiosité**, *n.f.* Sponginess. **spongite**, *n.f.* (*Min.*) Spongite. **spongoïde**, *a.* Spongoid.
spontané [spɔ̃ta'ne], *a.* (*fem.* **-ée**) Spontaneous. *Aveu spontané*, voluntary confession. **spontanéité**, *n.f.* Spontaneity. **spontanément**, *adv.* Spontaneously.
sporadique [spɔra'dik], *a.* Sporadic. **sporadiquement**, *adv.* Sporadically.
sporange [spɔ'rɑ̃:ʒ], *n.m.* Sporangium.
spore [spɔ:r] or **sporule**, *n.f.* Spore.
sporocyste [spɔrɔ'sist], *n.m.* Sporocyst.
sporozoaire, *n.m.* Sporozoon.
sport [spɔ:r], *n.m. Le sport*, more usually *les sports*, games, outdoor games. (For a Frenchman shooting, fishing, are not *des sports*.) *Faire du sport*, to play games; *terrain de sport*,

pitch, field. *Être sport*, (*fig.*) to have the sporting spirit, to play the game, to be a good sportsman.
sportif [spɔr'tif], *a.* (*fem.* **-ive**) *Réunion sportive*, athletic meeting; *un grand quotidien sportif*, a great sporting newspaper; *l'esprit sportif*, the sporting spirit.—*n. Un sportif*, a devotee of outdoor games. **sportman** or **sportsman**, *n.m.*=UN SPORTIF.
sportule [spɔr'tyl], *n.f.* (*Rom. Ant.*) Dole, alms.
spume [spym], *n.f.* Spume, froth. **spumescent**, *a.* (*fem.* **-ente**) Spumescent. **spumeux**, *a.* (*fem.* **-euse**) Spumous, spumy. **spumosité**, *n.f.* Spuminess.
squame [skwam], *n.f.* Squama, scale.
squameux [skwa'mø], *a.* (*fem.* **-euse**) Squamous, scaly. **squamifère**, *a.* Squamiferous.
square [skwa:r], *n.m.* Residential square with enclosed garden.
squarreux [skwa'rø], *a.* (*fem.* **-euse**) Squarrose.
squelette [skə'lɛt], *n.m.* Skeleton; carcass, frame (of a ship). *C'est un vrai squelette*, he *or* she is a living skeleton.
squille [ski:j], *n.f.* (*Zool.*) Crustaceous animal, squilla.
squine [skin] or **esquine**, *n.f.* China-root.
squirre or **squirrhe** [ski:r], *n.m.* Scirrhus, schirrosity. **squirreux** or **squirrheux**, *a.* (*fem.* **-euse**) Schirrhous.
st! [st], *int.* Here! hi! I say!
stabilisateur [stabiliza'tœ:r], *a.* (*fem.* **-trice**) Stabilizing.—*n.m.* (*Av.*, *Naut.*) Stabilizer. **stabilisation**, *n.f.* Stabilization. **stabiliser**, *v.t.* To stabilize. **stabilité**, *n.f.* Stability, durability; steadfastness. **stable**, *a.* Stable, firm; durable, lasting, permanent.
stabulation [stabyla'sjɔ̃], *n.f.* Stabling (of horses); stalling (of cattle); keeping of fish, oysters in storage-tanks, of patients in sanatorium, or of patient indoors. **stabuler**, *v.t.* To stall (cattle).
stade [stad], *n.m.* (*Gr. Ant.*) Stadium (about 202 yards); course for foot-racing; sports ground, stadium; (*fig.*) stage, period.
stage [sta:ʒ], *n.m.* Term of probation, study, residence, etc. (for law students etc.); training course; (*fig.*) probation. *Faire son stage*, to go through one's probation.
stagiaire [sta'ʒjɛ:r], *a.* Attending terms, going through one's course.—*n.* Probationer.
Stagire [sta'ʒi:r], *f.* Stagira. **Stagirite, le**, *m.* Aristotle.
stagnant [stag'nɑ̃], *a.* (*fem.* **-ante**) Stagnant, at a standstill. **stagnation**, *n.f.* Stagnation. **stagner**, *v.i.* To stagnate.
stalactite [stalak'tit], *n.m.* Stalactite.
stalagmite [stalag'mit], *n.m.* Stalagmite.
stalle [stal], *n.f.* Stall; box (for horses); (*Theat.*) stall, seat. *Stalle de chœur*, (choir) stall.
staminaire [STAMINAL].
staminal [stami'nal], *a* (*fem.* **-ale**, *pl.* **-aux**) (*Bot.*) Staminal. **staminé**, *a.* (*fem.* **-ée**) Staminate, stamened. **stamineux**, *a.* (*fem.* **-euse**) Stamineous. **staminifère**, *a.* Staminiferous. **staminiforme**, *a.* Staminiform.
stance [stɑ̃:s], *n.f.* Stanza.
stand [stɑ̃:d], *n.m.* Rifle-range; shooting-gallery; stall, stand (at exhibitions etc.).

standard [stă'daːr], *n.m.* (House or office) switchboard; standard (of living).
standardisation, *n.f.* Standardization.
standardiser, *v.t.* To standardize.
standardiste, *n.* Switchboard operator.
stangue [stă:g], *n.f.* (*Her.*) Shank of an anchor.
Stanislas [stanis'la:s], *m.* Stanislaus.
stannate [sta'nat], *n.m.* Stannate. **stanneux**, *a.* (*fem.* **-euse**) Stannous. **stannifère**, *a.* Stanniferous. **stannique**, *a.* Stannic.
staphylin [stafi'lɛ̃], *a.* (*fem.* **-ine**) Staphyline (shaped like a bunch of grapes).—*n.m.* Cocktail beetle, rove-beetle. **staphylomateux**, *a.* (*fem.* **-euse**) Staphylomatous. **staphylome**, *n.m.* Staphyloma.
star [sta:r], *n.f.* (*Cine.*) Star. **starlette**, *n.f.* Starlet.
starter [star'tɛːr], *n.m.* (*Motor.*) Choke; (*Racing*) starter.
stathouder [statu'dɛːr], *n.m.* (*Hist.*) Stadholder.
statice [sta'tis], *n.m.* Statice (sea-lavender).
station [sta'sjɔ̃], *n.f.* Station, standing; stage (of bus, .trams), taxi-rank; resort. *Station balnéaire*, seaside resort; *station thermale*, spa. *Station-service*, service station.
stationnaire, *a.* Stationary.—*n.m.* Guardship.
stationnement, *n.m.* Stationing, standing; parking. *Stationnement interdit*, no parking, no waiting.
stationner, *v.i.* To take station, to stop, to stand, to park (of cars).
statique [sta'tik], *a.* Static.—*n.f.* Statics.
statisticien, *n.m.* Statistician.
statistique, *n.f.* Statistics.—*a.* Statistical.
stator [sta'tɔr], *n.m.* Stator (of turbine, electric motor).
statuaire [sta'tɥɛ:r], *n.* Sculptor of statues.—*n.f.* Statuary (art).—*a.* Statuary.
statue [sta'ty], *n.f.* Statue.
statuer [sta'tɥe], *v.t.* To decree, to resolve, to ordain, to enact.—*v.i.* To make laws, to pronounce.
statuette [sta'tɥɛt], *n.f.* Statuette.
statufier [staty'fje], *v.t.* (*fam.*) To erect a statue to (someone).
stature [sta'ty:r], *n.f.* Stature, height.
statut [sta'ty], *n.m.* Statue, ordinance, article, regulation, by-law; status.
statutaire [staty'tɛr], *a.* Statutory. *Actions statutaires*, qualifying shares.
stéarine [stea'rin], *n.f.* (*Chem.*) Stearine.
stéarique, *a.* Stearic.
stéatite, *n.f.* Steatite, soapstone.
stéatocèle, *n.f.* (*Med.*) Steatocele.
stéatome, *n.m.* Steatoma.
stéatopyge, *a.* Steatopygous.
stéatose, *n.f.* Fatty degeneration, steatosis.
steeple-chase [stiplə'tʃɛs] or **steeple**, *n.m.*, Steeplechase.
stégomyie [stegɔ'mji], *n.f.* Yellow-fever mosquito.
stèle [stɛːl], *n.f.* (*Ant.*) Stele.
stellaire (1) [stɛl'lɛːr], *n.f.* Stellaria, stitchwort.
stellaire (2) [stɛl'lɛːr], *a.* Stellar, stellary, starry. **stelliforme**, *a.* Stelliform, star-shaped.
stellion [stɛ'ljɔ̃], *n.m.* Stellion, star-lizard.
stellionat [stɛljɔ'na], *n.m.* (*Law*) Fraudulent

selling, pledging, assigning, etc. **stellionataire**, *n.m.* and *a.* Person guilty of this.
stencil [sten'sil], *n.m.* Stencil.
sténo [ste'no], *abbr.* of **sténographe** or **sténographie**.
sténo-dactylo(graphe) [stenodaktilɔ'graf], *n.* Shorthand typist.
sténographe [stenɔ'graf], *n.* Stenographer, shorthand writer, shorthand reporter. **sténographie**, *n.f.* Stenography, shorthand.
sténographier, *v.t.* (*conjugated like* PRIER) To take down in shorthand, to report. **sténographique**, *a.* Stenographic, shorthand. **sténographiquement**, *adv.* Stenographically.
sténotype, *n.f.* Stenotypic machine; shorthand typewriter.—*n.m.* Stenotype. **sténotypé**, *a.* (*fem.* **-ée**) Stenotyped. **sténotyper**, *v.t.* To stenotype. **sténotypie**, *n.f.* Stenotypy. **sténotypiste**, *n.* Stenotypist.
stentor [stă'tɔːr], *n.m.* Stentor. *D'une voix de stentor*, in a stentorian voice.
steppe [stɛp], *n.m.* or *f.* Steppe.
stepper [ste'pe], *v.i.* To step well (of horses).
steppeur, *n.m.* (*fem.* **-euse**) High-stepper.
stercoraire [stɛrkɔ'rɛːr], *a.* Stercoraceous.—*n.m.* Dung-beetle.
stère [stɛːr], *n.m.* Stere, cubic metre (of firewood).
stéréobate [stereɔ'bat], *n.m.* Stereobate.
stéréochimie, *n.f.* Stereo-chemistry.
stéréochromie, *n.f.* Stereochromy.
stéréographie, *n.f.* Stereography.
stéréographique, *a.* Stereographic.
stéréométrie, *n.f.* Stereometry.
stéréoscope, *n.m.* Stereoscope.
stéréotomie, *n.f.* Stereotomy.
stéréotypage, *n.m.* Stereotyping. **stéréotype**, *a.* Printed by stereotype.—*n.m.* [CLICHÉ]. **stéréotypé**, *a.* (*fem.* **-ée**) Stereotyped, hackneyed. *Expression stéréotypée*, hackneyed phrase. **stéréotyper**, *v.t.* To stereotype. **stéréotypeur**, *n.m.* Stereotyper.
stérile [ste'ril], *a.* Sterile, barren, unfruitful; childless; (*fig.*) fruitless, unprofitable, vain. *Année stérile*, year of dearth. **stérilement**, *adv.* Barrenly, unfruitfully. **stérilisant**, *a.* (*fem.* **-ante**) Sterilizing.—*n.m.* Sterilizing agent. **stérilisation**, *n.f.* Sterilization. **stériliser**, *v.t.* To sterilize. **stérilité**, *n.f.* Sterility, barrenness, unfruitfulness.
sterling [stɛr'lɛ̃], *a.m. inv.* and *n.m.* Sterling.
sternal [stɛr'nal], *a.* (*fem.* **-ale**, *pl.* **-aux**) Sternal. **sterne**, *n.m.* Tern, sea-swallow.
sternum [stɛr'nɔm], *n.m.* Sternum, breast-bone.
sternutatif [stɛrnyta'tif], *a.* (*fem.* **-ive**) Sternutatory.—*n.m.* Sneezing-powder.
sternutation [stɛrnyta'sjɔ̃], *n.f.* Sternutation.
sternutatoire, *a.* and *n.m.* Sternutatory.
stertoreux [stɛrtɔ'rø], *a.* (*fem.* **-euse**) Stertorous.
stéthoscope [stetɔs'kɔp], *n.m.* Stethoscope.
stibial [sti'bjal] (*fem.* **-iale**, *pl.* **-iaux**) or **stibié** (*fem.* **-ée**), *a.* Containing antimony, stibiated. *Tartre stibié*, tartar emetic.
stick [stik], *n.m.* Swagger-stick; (riding-) switch; riding-whip.
stigmate [stig'mat], *n.m.* Scar, mark, spot, trace, stain; brand, mark of infamy; (*Bot. etc.*) stigma; (*pl.*) (*Theol.*) stigmata. *Porter les stigmates de la petite vérole*, to be pockmarked; *stigmate flétrissant*, mark of infamy.

stigmatisé, *n.m.* (*fem.* **-ée**) Stigmatist.—*a.* Stigmatized.

stigmatiser, *v.t.* To stigmatize, to brand.

stil-de-grain [stildə'grɛ̃], *n.m.* (*Paint.*) Yellow lake.

stillation, *n.f.* Dripping, falling drop by drop.

stimulant [stimy'lɑ̃], *a.* (*fem.* **-ante**) Stimulating.—*n.m.* Stimulant; stimulus; incentive, inducement, spur. *****stimulateur**, *a.* (*fem.* **-trice**) Stimulating. **stimulation**, *n.f.* Stimulation. **stimuler**, *v.t.* To stimulate; to excite, to rouse, to spur on. **stimulus**, *n.m.* Stimulus.

stipe (1) [stip], *n.f.* (*Bot.*) Feather grass.

stipe (2) [stip], *n.m.* Stipe, stem. **stipelle**, *n.f.* (*Bot.*) Stipel.

stipendiaire [stipɑ̃'djɛːr], *a.* and *n.m.* Stipendiary, hireling, mercenary. **stipendié**, *a.* (*fem.* **-ée**) Hired.—*n.* Stipendiary, hireling. **stipendier**, *v.t.* To hire, to keep in pay.

stipulacé [stipyla'se], *a.* (*fem.* **-ée**) (*Bot.*) Stipulaceous. **stipulaire**, *a.* Stipular.

stipulant [stipy'lɑ̃], *a.* (*Law*) Stipulating.

stipulation, *n.f.* Stipulation, provision. *Les stipulations d'un contrat*, the articles of a contract.

stipule [sti'pyl], *n.f.* (*Bot.*) Stipule.

stipuler [stipy'le], *v.t.* To stipulate; to covenant, to contract.

stock [stɔk], *n.m.* (*Comm.*) Stock.

stockage, *n.m.* Stocking.

stocker [stɔ'ke], *v.t.* To stock; to stockpile. **stockiste**, *n.m.* Warehouseman; stockist; agent (for a certain make of car); servicestation (with spare parts).

stoff [stɔf], *n.m.* Stuff (cotton or woollen).

stoïcien [stɔi'sjɛ̃], *a.* and *n.* (*fem.* **-ienne**) Stoic. **stoïcisme**, *n.m.*, or (*rare*) **stoïcité**, *n.f.* Stoicism. **stoïque**, *a.* Stoic.—*n.* Stoical person. **stoïquement**, *adv.* Stoically.

stola [stɔ'la] or **stole**, *n.f.* Stole.

stolon [stɔ'lɔ̃], *n.m.* Stolon. **stolonial**, *a.* (*fem.* **-iale**, *pl.* **-iaux**) Stolonate. **stolonifère**, *a.* Stoloniferous.

stomacal [stɔma'kal], *a.* (*fem.* **-ale**, *pl.* **-aux**) Stomachal. **stomachique** [stɔma'ʃik], *a.* Stomachic, of the stomach.—*n.m.* Stomachic.

stomate [stɔ'mat], *n.m.* (*Bot.*) Stoma. **stomatique**, *a.* Stomatic. **stomatite**, *n.f.* Stomatitis.

stomatologie, *n.f.* Stomatology. **stomatologiste**, *n.m.* Stomatologist.

stop [stɔp], *int.* Stop! *n.m.* (*Motor.*) Stoplight.

stoppage [stɔ'paːʒ], *n.m.* Invisible mending, fine-darning; stoppage (of motion, current). **stopper**, *v.i.* To stop (of a train, steamboat, etc.).—*v.t.* To fine-darn, to darn, mend invisibly; to stop. **stoppeur**, *n.m.* (*fem.* **-euse**) Fine-darner.

storax [stɔ'raks], *n.m.* Storax (resin).

store [stɔːr], *n.m.* (Spring-roller) blind, (*Am.*) shade. *Store à l'italienne*, awning-blind.

strabique [stra'bik], *a.* Squinting, squint-eyed.—*n.* Squinter. **strabisme**, *n.m.* Strabism, squinting.

stramoine [stra'mwan], *n.f.*, or **stramonium** [stramɔ'njɔm], *n.m.* Stramonium, thorn-apple.

strangulation [strɑ̃gyla'sjɔ̃], *n.f.* Strangulation; strangling, throttling.

strangurie [strɑ̃gy'ri], *n.f.* (*Path.*) Strangury.

strapontin [strapɔ̃'tɛ̃], *n.m.* Bracket seat (in a carriage); folding-seat, flap-seat, tip-up seat.

strass or **stras** [stras], *n.m.* Strass, paste jewels.

strasse [straːs], *n.f.* Floss-silk; thick wrapping paper.

stratagème [strata'ʒɛm], *n.m.* Stratagem.

strate [strat], *n.f.* Stratum.

stratège [stra'tɛːʒ], *n.m.* (*Gr. Ant.*) Strategus; (*fam.*) strategist.

stratégie [strate'ʒi], *n.f.* Strategy. **stratégique**, *a.* Strategic. **stratégiquement**, *adv.* Strategically. **stratégiste**, *n.m.* Strategist.

stratification [stratifika'sjɔ̃], *n.f.* Stratification. **stratifier**, *v.t.* To stratify. **stratiforme**, *a.* Stratiform.

stratigraphie, *n.f.* Stratigraphy.

stratosphère [stratɔs'fɛːr], *n.f.* Stratosphere. **stratosphérique**, *a.* Stratospheric. *Avion stratosphérique*, stratocruiser.

stratus [stra'tyːs], *n.m.* *inv.* Stratus (cloud).

streptocoque [strɛptɔ'kɔk], *n.m.* Streptococcus. **streptomycine**, *n.f.* Streptomycin.

strette [strɛt], *n.f.* (*Mus.*) Finale (of a fugue).

strict [strikt], *a.* (*fem.* **-e**) Strict, precise; severe. *Le strict nécessaire*, no more than is strictly necessary. **strictement**, *adv.* Strictly; severely. *Strictement parlant*, strictly speaking.

stridemment [strida'mɑ̃], *adv.* Stridently.

stridence [stri'dɑ̃ːs], *n.f.* Stridency, shrillness; harshness (of sound).

strident, *a.* (*fem.* **-ente**) Strident, jarring, grating, shrill. **stridulant**, *a.* (*fem.* **-ante**) Piercing, acute. **stridulation**, *n.f.* Chirring. **striduler**, *v.i.* To chirr.

strie [stri], *n.f.* Stria; streak (of colour). **strié**, *a.* (*fem.* **-ée**) Striate, channelled, streaked, striped; fluted; corrugated; scored. **strier**, *v.t.* To striate, to groove, to flute.

strige [stri:ʒ], *n.f.* (sometimes **stryge**, *n.m.*) Vampire, ghoul.

strigile [stri'ʒil], *n.m.* (*Ant.*) Strigil.

striure [stri'y:r], *n.f.* Striation, scoring, grooving; stria, score, groove.

strobile [strɔ'bil], *n.m.* Strobile, pine-cone. **strobilifère**, *a.* Strobiliferous. **strobiliforme**, *a.* Strobiliform.

strontiane [strɔ̃'sjan], *n.f.* Strontia, strontianite, *n.f.* Strontianite. **strontium**, *n.m.* Strontium.

strophe [strɔf], *n.f.* Strophe; stanza, verse.

structural [strykty'ral], *a.* (*fem.* **-ale**, *pl.* **-aux**) Structural.

structure [stryk'ty:r], *n.f.* Structure; form, make; (*fig.*) arrangement, disposition.

strumeux [stry'mø], *a.* (*fem.* **-euse**) Strumous, scrofulous.

strychnine [strik'nin], *n.f.* Strychnin(e). **strychnisme**, *n.m.* Strychnism. **strychnos**, *n.m.* Genus of plants yielding strychnine.

stuc [styk], *n.m.* Stucco. **stucage**, *n.m.* Stucco-work. **stucateur**, *n.m.* Stuccoer.

studieusement [stydjøz'mɑ̃], *adv.* Studiously. **studieux**, *a.* (*fem.* **-ieuse**) Studious.

studio [sty'djo], *n.m.* (*Cine.*) Film-studio; (*Rad. Tel.*) broadcasting studio; one-roomed flat.

studiosité [stydjozi'te], *n.f.* Studiousness.

stupéfactif [stypefak'tif], *a.* (*fem.* **-ive**) Stupefactive. **stupéfaction**, *n.f.* Stupefaction, great astonishment. **stupéfait**, *a.*

(*fem.* **-aite**) Stupefied, dumbfounded, thunderstruck. **stupéfiant,** *a.* (*fem.* **-iante**) Stupefactive; amazing, astounding.—*n.m.* Narcotic. *Trafic de stupéfiants,* drug-traffic. **stupéfier,** *v.t.* To stupefy, to astound, to dumbfound. **stupeur,** *n.f.* Stupor; amazement. *Muet de stupeur,* dumbfounded, stunned.

stupide [sty′pid], *a.* Stunned, bemused; stupid, foolish, silly, dull.—*n.* Stupid person, blockhead. **stupidement,** *adv.* Stupidly. **stupidité,** *n.f.* Stupidity; piece of stupidity.

stupre [stypr], *n.m.* Debauchery.

stuquer [sty′ke], *v.t.* To stucco.

stygien [sti′ʒjɛ̃], *a.* (*fem.* **-ienne**) Stygian.

stylaire [sti′lɛ:r], *a.* (*Bot.*) Stylar.

style (1) [stil], *n.m.* Stylus, graver, cutter (of records); pin, gnomon; (*Bot.*) style.

style (2) [stil], *n.m.* Style. *Le style c'est l'homme,* the style is the man himself; *meubles de style,* period furniture; *robe de style,* period dress, picture frock; *vieux style,* old style, old-fashioned. **stylé,** *a.* (*fem.* **-ée**) Having or furnished with a style, stylate; (*colloq.*) trained, taught, clever. *Bien stylé,* well-schooled. **styler,** *v.t.* To train, to form, to school. **stylet,** *n.m.* Stiletto; (*Surg.*) stylet, probe. **styliforme,** *a.* (*Bot.*) Styliform. **stylisé,** *a.* (*fem.* **-ée**) Stylized. **styliste,** *n.* Stylist.

stylite [sti′lit], *a.* and *n.m.* Stylite.

stylo [sti′lo], *n.m.* [STYLOGRAPHE].

stylobate [stilɔ′bat], *n.m.* Stylobate.

stylographe [stilɔ′graf], *n.m.* Fountain-pen. *Stylo(graphe) à pointe,* stylograph; *stylo à bille,* ball-point pen. *Encre à stylo* (or *stylographique*), fountain-pen ink.

styloïde [stilɔ′id], *a.* Styloid.

stylomine [stilo′min], *n.m.* Propelling pencil.

styptique [stip′tik], *a.* and *n.m.* Styptic, astringent.

styrax [sti′raks], *n.m.* Styrax.

Styx [stiks], *m.* (*Myth.*) The (river) Styx. *Les bords du Styx,* the Stygian shores.

su (1) [sy], *n.m.* Knowledge. *Au su de,* to the knowledge of; *au vu et au su de tout le monde,* as everybody knows.

su (2), *p.p.* (*fem.* **sue**) [SAVOIR].

suage [sɥa:ʒ], *n.m.* Dampness, humidity; oozing or sweating (of a wall etc.); (*Naut.*) tallowing a vessel, tallow for this. **suager,** *v.t.* (*Metal.*) To swage, to crease; (*Naut.*) to pay, to tallow.

suaire [sɥɛ:r], *n.m.* Winding-sheet, shroud. *Le Saint Suaire,* the Sindon (of Christ).

suant [sɥɑ̃], *a.* (*fem.* **-ante**) Sweating, in a sweat; dripping with moisture; at welding-point (of metal).

suave [sɥa:v], *a.* Sweet, agreeable; suave, bland; soft. **suavement,** *adv.* Suavely, sweetly. **suavité,** *n.f.* Suavity, sweetness.

subalpin [sybal′pɛ̃], *a.* (*fem.* **-ine**) Subalpine.

subalterne, *a.* and *n.* Subaltern, subordinate; inferior.

subconscience, *n.f.* Subconsciousness. **subconscient,** *a.* (*fem.* **-iente**) Subconscious. —*n.m. Le subconscient,* the subconscious.

subdélégation, *n.f.* Subdelegation. **subdélégué,** *n.m.* Subdelegate. **subdéléguer,** *v.t.* To subdelegate.

subdiviser, *v.t.* To subdivide. **se subdiviser,**

v.r. To be subdivided. **subdivision,** *n.f.* Subdivision.

suber [sy′bɛ:r], *n.m.* Cork-oak; suber.

subéreux [sybe′rø], *a.* (*fem.* **-euse**) Suberous. *Couche subéreuse,* cork layer. **subérification,** *n.f.* Suberification. **subérine,** *n.f.* Suberin. **subérique,** *a.* (*Chem.*) Suberic.

subir [sy′bi:r], *v.t.* To sustain, to support, to go through; to undergo, to suffer, to submit to. **Subir la question,* to undergo torture; *subir son sort,* to submit to one's fate; *subir un examen,* to undergo an examination.

subit [sy′bi], *a.* (*fem.* **-ite**) Sudden, unexpected. **subitement,** *adv.* Suddenly, all of a sudden. **subito,** *adv.* (*fam.*) Suddenly.

subjacent [sybʒa′sɑ̃], *a.* (*fem.* **-ente**) Subjacent.

subjectif [sybʒɛk′tif], *a.* (*fem.* **-ive**) Subjective. **subjection,** *n.f.* Subjection. **subjectivement,** *adv.* Subjectively. **subjectivisme,** *n.m.* Subjectivism. **subjectivité,** *n.f.* Subjectivity.

subjonctif [sybʒɔ̃k′tif], *a.* (*fem.* **-ive**) Subjunctive.—*n.m.* Subjunctive. *Verbe au subjonctif,* verb in the subjunctive (mood).

subjugation [sybʒyga′sjɔ̃], *n.f.* Subjugation. **subjuguer** [sybʒy′ge], *v.t.* To subjugate, to subdue; to master, to overcome; to captivate.

sublimation [syblima′sjɔ̃], *n.f.* Sublimation. **sublimatoire,** *n.m.* Sublimatory. **sublime** [sy′blim], *a.* Lofty, grand, sublime, splendid.—*n.m.* The sublime. **sublimé,** *n.m.* (*Chem.*) Sublimate. **sublimement,** *adv.* Sublimely. **sublimer,** *v.t.* To sublimate. **subliminal,** *a.* (*fem.* **-ale,** *pl.* **-aux**) (*Psych.*) Subliminal **se sublimiser,** *v.r.* (*Psych.*) To become sublimated. **sublimité,** *n.f.* Sublimity.

sublingual [syblɛ̃′gwal], *a.* (*fem.* **-ale,** *pl.* **-aux**) Sublingual.

sublunaire [sybly′nɛ:r], *a.* Sublunary.

submerger [sybmɛr′ʒe], *v.t.* To submerge, to swamp; to flood; (*fig.*) to overwhelm. *Être submergé de travail,* to be snowed under with work. **submersible,** *n.m.* Submarine (boat). —*a.* Submersible. **submersion,** *n.f.* Submersion.

subodorer [sybɔdɔ′re], *v.t.* To scent at a distance. (*fam.*) *Je subodore quelque chose de louche,* I smell a rat.

subordination [sybɔrdina′sjɔ̃], *n.f.* Subordination. **subordonné,** *a.* and *n.m.* (*fem.* **-ée**) Subordinate, dependent. *Proposition subordonnée,* subordinate clause. **subordonnément,** *adv.* Subordinately. **subordonner,** *v.t.* To subordinate.

subornation [sybɔrna′sjɔ̃], *n.f.* or **subornement,** *n.m.* Subornation, bribery, embracery. **suborner,** *v.t.* To suborn, to bribe, to tamper with; to embrace, (*fam.*) to get at (jury etc.). **suborneur,** *n.m.* (*fem.* **-euse**) Suborner, briber; embracer.—*a.* Suborning, bribing, seductive.

subrécargue [sybre′karg], *n.m.* Supercargo.

subreptice [sybrɛp′tis], *a.* Surreptitious. **subrepticement,** *adv.* Surreptitiously. **subreption,** *n.f.* Subreption.

subrogateur [sybrɔga′tœ:r], *a.m.* *Acte subrogateur,* act of subrogation.—*n.m.* Judge advocate.

subrogation [sybrɔga′sjɔ̃], *n.f.* Subrogation. **subrogatoire,** *a.* Of subrogation. **subrogé,** *a.* (*fem.* **-ée**) Surrogated, deputy. *Subrogé* *tuteur,* deputy-guardian (to watch over trustees). **subroger,** *v.t.* To substitute, to appoint as deputy. *Se faire subroger,* to get oneself appointed deputy.

subséquemment [sybseka'mã], *adv.* Subsequently, after. **subséquent,** *a.* (*fem.* -ente) Subsequent, ensuing.

subside [syb'sid], *n.m.* Subsidy; (*colloq.*) aid. **subsidence,** *n.f.* Subsidence. **subsidiaire,** *a.* Subsidiary, auxiliary, additional. **subsidiairement,** *adv.* Further, also, additionally.

subsistance [sybzis'tã:s], *n.f.* Subsistence, sustenance, maintenance; (*pl.*) provisions, supplies. *Tirer sa subsistance de,* to get one's living by; *soldat en subsistance à,* soldier (of another unit) detailed for pay and rations to. **subsistant,** *a.* (*fem.* -ante) Subsisting, existing. **subsister** [sybzis'te], *v.i.* To subsist, to stand; to be extant; to be in force, to hold good; to exist, to live. *J'ai de la peine à subsister,* I can hardly get a livelihood.

substance [sybs'tã:s], *n.f.* Substance. *En substance,* in short, in substance. **substantialiser,** *v.t.* To substantialize. **substantialisme,** *n.m.* Substantialism. **substantialiste,** *n.* Substantialist. **substantialité,** *n.f.* Substantiality. **substantiel,** *a.* (*fem.* -ielle) Substantial. **substantiellement,** *adv.* Substantially. **substantif,** *a.* (*fem.* -ive) Substantive.—*n.m.* (*Gram.*) Substantive, noun. **substantifier, substantiver,** *v.t.* To substantivize.

substituer [sybsti'tɥe], *v.t.* To substitute; to appoint; (*Law*) to entail. *Propriété substituée,* entailed estate. **se substituer,** *v.r.* To substitute oneself (*à*). **substitut,** *n.m.* Substitute, deputy (in France). *Substitut du Procureur (de la République),* deputy public prosecutor. **substitutif,** *a.* (*fem.* -ive) Substitutive. **substitution,** *n.f.* Substitution; (*Law*) entail.

substratum [sybstra'tɔm] or **substrat,** *n.m.* (*Phil.*) Substratum.

substruction [sybstryk'sjɔ̃], *n.f.* Substruction, substructure. **substructure,** *n.f.* Substructure.

subterfuge [sybter'fy:ʒ], *n.m.* Subterfuge, evasion, shift.

subtil [syb'til], *a.* (*fem.* -ile) Subtile, thin, tenuous; penetrating; acute, keen, sharp, quick (of hearing etc.); cunning, artful, crafty; fine-spun, subtle. **subtilement,** *adv.* Subtly, craftily. **subtilisation,** *n.f.* Subtilization. **subtiliser,** *v.i.* To refine (of thought). —*v.t.* To subtilize, to refine; (*colloq.*) to sneak, to steal. **subtiliseur,** *n.m.* (*fem.* -euse) Subtilizer. **subtilité,** *n.f.* Subtlety, fineness; penetration, acuteness; shrewdness, nicety of discrimination, subtility; cunning artfulness.

subtropical [sybtrɔpi'kal], *a.* (*fem.* -ale, *pl.* -aux) Subtropical.

subulé [syby'le], *a.* (*fem.* -ée) (*Bot.*) Subulate, awl-shaped.

suburbain [sybyr'bɛ̃], *a.* (*fem.* -aine) Suburban. **suburbicaire,** *a.* (*Rom. Ant.*) Suburban, living near Rome; (*R.-C. Ch.*) within the diocese of Rome.

subvenir [sybvə'ni:r], *v.i. irr.* (*conjugated like* VENIR) To be helpful; to supply, to provide. *Subvenir aux besoins de quelqu'un,* to provide

for someone('s needs); *subvenir aux frais,* to meet, to defray the expense(s).

subvention [sybvã'sjɔ̃], *n.f.* Subsidy, aid, subvention. **subventionnel,** *a.* (*fem.* -elle) Subventional. **subventionner,** *v.t.* To subsidize, to make a grant to.

subversif [sybver'sif], *a.* (*fem.* -ive) Subversive. **subversion,** *n.f.* Subversion, overthrow, destruction. ***subvertir,** *v.t.* To subvert, to overthrow.

suc [syk], *n.m.* Juice; (*fig.*) essence, quintessence. *Suc gastrique,* gastric juice.

succédané [sykseda'ne], *a.* (*fem.* -ée) Substitute, succedaneous.—*n.m.* Succedaneum, substitute.

succéder [sykse'de], *v.i. irr.* (*conjugated like* ACCÉLÉRER) To succeed, to follow after; to take the place (*à*); to inherit (*à*). *La nuit succède au jour,* night follows day; *succéder à quelqu'un,* to succeed someone. **se succéder,** *v.r.* To succeed each other.

succès [syk'sɛ], *n.m.* Success. *Livre à succès,* best-seller; *chanson, pièce à succès,* hit; *ses efforts sont restés sans succès,* his efforts remained unsuccessful; *succès de circonstance,* accidental success; *succès d'estime,* indifferent success. **successeur,** *n.m.* Successor. **successibilité,** *n.f.* Right of succession. **successible,** *a.* Heritable, capable of inheriting. **successif,** *a.* (*fem.* -ive) Successive, in succession.

succession [syksɛ'sjɔ̃], *n.f.* Succession; inheritance; heritage, estate. *Droit de succession,* right of succession; *droits de succession,* death-duties, probate duty; *par succession de temps,* in process of time; *prendre la succession de quelqu'un,* to succeed someone; *prendre la succession d'une affaire,* to take over a business; *recueillir une succession,* to acquire an inheritance.

successivement, *adv.* Successively, in succession.

successoral [syksɛsɔ'ral], *a.* (*fem.* -ale, *pl.* -aux) Concerned with succession. *Loi successorale,* law on inheritance.

succin [syk'sɛ̃], *n.m.* Succin, amber.

succinct [syk'sɛ̃], *a.* (*fem.* -e) Succinct, concise; scanty (meal). **succinctement,** *adv.* Succinctly.

succion [syk'sjɔ̃], *n.f.* Suction.

succomber [sykɔ̃'be], *v.i.* To sink, to faint; to yield, to succumb; to fail, to be worsted; to die, to perish. *Succomber à la douleur,* to be overcome with grief; *succomber à la tentation,* to yield to temptation.

succube [sy'kyb], *n.m.* Succubus.

succulemment [sykyla'mã], *adv.* Succulently. **succulence,** *n.f.* Succulence. **succulent,** *a.* (*fem.* -ente) Succulent, juicy, rich.

succursale [sykyr'sal], *n.f.* Branch (of a bank etc.). *Église succursale,* chapel of ease. ***succursaliste,** *n.m.* Priest in charge of a chapel of ease.

sucement [sys'mã], *n.m.* Sucking, suck. **sucer,** *v.t.* To suck, to suck in; to absorb, to imbibe; to suck out, to suck up, to draw, to drain. (*vulg.*) *Sucer la pomme à quelqu'un,* to kiss someone. **sucette,** *n.f.* Lollipop; comforter (for baby). **suceur,** *a.* (*fem.* -euse) Sucking; (*Zool.*) suctorial.—*n.m.* Sucker; nozzle (of a vacuum cleaner).

suçoir [sy'swa:r], *n.m.* Sucker.

suçon [sy's5], *n.m.* Mark (on skin) made by sucking; (*colloq.*) stick of barley-sugar. **suçoter,** *v.t.* To keep sucking, to suck away at (something).

sucre [sykr], *n.m.* Sugar. *Pain de sucre,* sugarloaf; *sucre brut,* raw sugar, moist sugar, brown sugar; *sucre cassé, sucre en morceaux,* lump sugar; *sucre cristallisé,* granulated sugar; *sucre de canne,* cane sugar; *sucre d'orge,* barley sugar;*sucre en poudre,*powdered sugar. *Casser du sucre sur le dos de quelqu'un,* to be catty about someone, to make an attack on a person (who is not there). **sucré,** *a.* (*fem.* **-ée**) Sugared, sweet, sweetened, sugary; (*fig.*) demure, prim. *Eau sucrée,* sugar and water; *j'aime le thé très sucré,* I like my tea very sweet. **sucrer,** *v.t.* To sugar, to sweeten, to put sugar in. **sucrerie** (1), *n.f.* Sugar-works, sugar-refinery; (*pl.*) sweetmeats, confectionery, sweets. *Il adore les sucreries,* he has a very sweet tooth. (*C*) **sucrerie** (2), *n.f.* Maple-tree grove, sugar bush. **sucrier,** *a.* (*fem.* **-ière**) Sugar, of sugar. *Industrie sucrière,* sugar-trade.—*n.m.* sugar-basin; sugar-maker, (*fam.*) person fond of sugar. *Êtes-vous sucrier?* Have you a sweet tooth?

sucrin [sy'krɛ̃], *n.m.* Sugary melon.

sud [syd], *n.m.* South; south wind. *Courir au sud,* to steer a southerly course; *au sud,* in the south, to the south, southwards; *du sud,* southern; *vers le sud,* southward. *La Croix du Sud,* the Southern Cross; *le vent du sud,* the south wind; *un vent du sud,* a southerly wind.—*a. inv.* South, southerly (of the wind). **sud-africain** [sydafri'kɛ̃], *a.* and *n.* (*fem.* **-aine**) South African. *L'Union Sud-africaine,* the Union of South Africa.

sud-américain [sydameri'kɛ̃], *a.* and *n.* (*fem.* **-aine**) South American.

sudation [syda'sjɔ̃], *n.f.* Sudation, sweating; steam-bath. **sudatoire,** *a.* Sudatory.—*n.m.* (*Rom. Ant.*) Sudatorium.

sud-est [sy'dɛst; (*Naut.*) sy're, sy'e], *n.m.* and *a. inv.* South-east.

Sudètes [sy'dɛt], **les,** *m. pl.* Sudetenland.

sudiste [sy'dist], *n.* Southerner (in American Civil War).—*a.* Southern.

sudorifère [sydɔri'fɛːr] or **sudoripare,** *a.* Sudoriferous, sudoriparous. *Glande sudoripare,* sweat-gland. **sudorifique,** *n.m.* and *a.* Sudorific.

sud-ouest [sy'dwɛst; (*Naut.* and *W. dialect*) sy'rwa, sy'rwe], *n.m.* and *a. inv.* South-west.

Suède [sɥɛd], *f.* Sweden.—*n.m.* Suède (glove leather). **suéder** [sɥe'de], *v.t.* To give a suède finish to. **suédine,** *n.f.* Imitation suède. **suédois,** *a.* (*fem.* **-oise**) Swedish. *Gymnastique suédoise,* Swedish exercises.—*n.m.* (**Suédois,** *fem.* **-oise**) Swede.

suée [sɥe], *n.f.* Sweating; (*colloq.*) sudden fright; accumulation of work and fatigue, of alarms.

suer [sɥe], *v.i.* To sweat, to perspire, to be in a sweat; (*fig.*) to toil, to drudge; to be damp, to ooze (of walls). *Faire suer,* to throw into a perspiration, (*vulg.*) to annoy; *suer à grosses gouttes,* to perspire profusely.—*v.t.* To sweat. *Suer du sang,* to sweat blood; *suer la pauvreté,* to reek of poverty; *suer sang et eau,* (*fig.*) to strain every nerve.

suerie, *n.f.* Drying-place (for tobacco); [SUÉE].

Suétone [sɥe'tɔn], *m.* Suetonius.

suette [sɥɛt], *n.f.* Sweating sickness. *Suette miliaire,* miliary fever, prickly heat.

sueur [sɥœːr], *n.f.* Sweat, perspiration; sweating; (*pl.*) labour, toil, pains. *A la sueur de son front,* by the sweat of one's brow.

suffire [sy'fiːr], *v.i. irr.* (*pres.p.* **suffisant,** *p.p.* **suffi**) To suffice, to be sufficient, to be enough; to be adequate, to be equal (*à*). *À chaque jour suffit sa peine,* sufficient unto the day is the evil thereof; *cela suffit,* that's enough; *il suffit que vous le disiez pour que je le croie,* enough that you should say so; *le peu que j'ai me suffit,* the little I have suffices me; *on ne peut pas suffire à tout,* it is impossible to cope with everything. **se suffire,** *v.r.* To suffice for oneself, or itself; to provide for oneself. **suffisamment,** *adv.* Sufficiently, enough. **suffisance,** *n.f.* Sufficiency, adequacy; conceit, self-sufficiency. *À suffisance* or *en suffisance,* sufficiently; *un air de suffisance,* a conceited air. **suffisant,** *a.* (*fem.* **-ante**) Sufficient, adequate, enough; consequential, conceited, self-sufficient, stuck-up.—*n.* Conceited person.

suffixe [sy'fiks], *n.m.* Suffix.

suffocant [syfɔ'kɑ̃], *a.* (*fem.* **-ante**) Suffocating, stifling, choking. **suffocation,** *n.f.* Suffocation, stifling. **suffoquer,** *v.t.* To suffocate, to stifle, to choke.—*v.i.* To choke. *Suffoquer de rage* or *de colère,* to be choking with rage or anger.

suffragant [syfra'gɑ̃], *n.m.* and *a.m.* Suffragan. **suffrage** [sy'fraːʒ], *n.m.* Suffrage, vote; franchise; approbation, commendation. **suffragette,** *n.f.* Suffragette.

suffusion [syfy'zjɔ̃], *n.f.* Suffusion; flush.

suggérer [sygʒe're], *v.t. irr.* (*conjugated like* ACCÉLÉRER) To suggest. **suggestibilité,** *n.f.* Suggestibility; susceptivity. **suggestif,** *a.* (*fem.* **-ive**). Suggestive; erotic. **suggestion,** *n.f.* Suggestion, hint, instigation. *Il a fait cela à ma suggestion,* he did it on my advice.

suicide [sɥi'sid], *n.m.* Suicide, self-murder. **suicidé,** *n.m.* (*fem.* **-ée**) Self-murderer, suicide, (*Law*) felo-de-se. **se suicider,** *v.r.* To commit suicide.

suie [sɥi], *n.f.* Soot.

suif [sɥif], *n.m.* Tallow. *Cuir en plein suif,* leather dressed with tallow; *donner un suif à quelqu'un,* (*pop.*) to give someone a good talking-to. **suiffer,** *v.t.* To tallow; to pay (a ship). **suiffeux,** *a.* (*fem.* **-euse**) Tallowy, greasy.

suint [sɥɛ̃], *n.m.* Grease of wool, yolk; sandiver (of glass).

suintement [sɥɛ̃t'mɑ̃], *n.m.* Oozing, sweating, leaking. **suinter,** *v.i.* To ooze, to sweat (of walls etc.); to leak, to run (of vessels).

Suisse [sɥis], **la,** *f.* Switzerland.

suisse (1) [sɥis], *a.* (*fem.* **suissesse**) Swiss.—*n.m.* Porter (of a mansion); church officer.—*n.m.* (**Suisse,** *fem.* **Suissesse**) A Swiss. (*pop.*) *Faire suisse,* to drink or eat alone (instead of inviting friends). *Un petit suisse,* a small cream cheese. (*C*) **suisse** (2), *n.m.* Jumper, tote sled.

suite [sɥit], *n.f.* Rest; those that follow, the rest; retinue, train, attendants; sequel, continuation; series, succession; set; connexion, order, nexus; consequence, effect, issue, result; continuance, progress, course; consistency, coherence. *À la suite,* after, behind; *cela peut avoir de fâcheuses suites,* that may have disagreeable consequences; *(comme) suite à notre lettre du 10 courant,* with reference to ours of the 10th instant; *dans la suite,* eventually, afterwards; *de suite,* one after another, consecutively, on end, running; *donner suite à,* to follow up, to carry out, to proceed with, to give effect to; *et ainsi de suite,* and so on; *être de la suite de quelqu'un,* to be a member of someone's train; *faire suite à,* to be a continuation of, to follow; *la suite au prochain numéro,* to be continued in our next; *n'avoir pas d'esprit de suite,* not to be consistent, to keep at nothing long; *n'avoir pas de suites,* to have no bad consequences, to have no relatives, not to be followed up; *officier à la suite,* officer attached to a corps etc.; *par suite de,* in consequence of, because of; *plusieurs pages de suite,* several pages on end; *propos sans suite,* desultory talk; *sans suite* (of article), *(Comm.)* cannot be repeated; *(Mus.) suite d'orchestre,* orchestral suite; *tout de suite,* immediately, at once, right away.

suitée [sɥi'te], *a.f. Jument suitée,* mare and foal.

suivant [sɥi'vɑ̃], *prep.* According to, in accordance with, agreeably to; in pursuance of; in proportion to, conformably to; in the direction of. *Suivant que,* as, according as.—*a. (fem. -ante)* Next, following, subsequent.—*n.* Follower, attendant.—*n.f.* Waiting-maid, lady's maid; *(Theat.)* soubrette.

suivi [sɥi'vi], *a. (fem. -ie)* Followed; connected; consistent, coherent, regular; sought after, popular. *Discours bien suivi,* coherent speech.

suivre [sɥivr], *v.t. irr. (pres.p.* **suivant,** *p.p.* **suivi)** To follow, to go after, to come after; to be next to, to come next to; to attend, to go with, to accompany; to watch, to observe, to watch over; to pursue; to exercise, to practise (a profession etc.); to give way to, to indulge. *Faire suivre,* to have (a person) followed, to send on, to forward (letters etc.), *(Comm.)* to charge forward; *suivre de loin,* to follow at a distance; *suivre de près,* to follow close on the heels of; *suivre la mode,* to follow the fashion; *suivre la balle, (Ten.)* to follow through; *suivre son chemin,* to go one's way. —*v.i.* To follow; to come after; to result, to ensue. *À faire suivre,* to be forwarded, please forward (letters etc.); *ce qui suit,* what follows; *faites suivre, (Print.)* run on; *(sch.) suivre avec quelqu'un,* to share a book with someone. **se suivre,** *v.r.* To follow each other, to succeed each other; to be continuous, to be coherent.

sujet [sy'ʒɛ], *a. (fem. -ette)* Subject, subjected, amenable, liable, exposed; apt, addicted, inclined (*à*).—*n.m.* Subject (person); *(Gram.)* subject; subject (theme), matter, topic; cause, reason; occasion, ground, account; *(Hort.)* stock. *Au sujet de,* concerning, about; *j'ai sujet de me plaindre,* I have reason to complain; *mauvais sujet,* scamp, bad lot; *s'éloigner de son sujet,* to wander from one's subject.

sujétion [syʒe'sjɔ̃], *n.f.* Subjection, servitude; constraint, continual slavery.

sulfamide [sylfa'mid], *n.f.* Sulphamide, sulpha drug.

sulfatage [sylfa'ta:ʒ], *n.m.* Sulphating; *(Agric.)* spraying of copper sulphate (on vines and fruit-trees).

sulfate [syl'fat], *n.m.* Sulphate. *Sulfate de cuivre,* copper sulphate. **sulfaté,** *a. (fem. -ée)* Sulphatic. **sulfater,** *v.t.* To sulphate; *(Agric.)* to treat with copper sulphate. **sulfhydrate,** *n.m. (Chem.)* Hydrosulphate. **sulfhydrique,** *a.* Hydrosulphuric. **sulfuration,** *n.f.* Sulphuration. **sulfure,** *n.m.* Sulphide, sulphuret. **sulfuré,** *a. (fem. -ée)* Sulphuretted. *Hydrogène sulfuré,* hydrogen sulphide. **sulfureux,** *a. (fem. -euse)* Sulphurous, sulphureous, sulphury. **sulfurique,** *a.* Sulphuric (acid).

sultan [syl'tɑ̃], *n.m.* Sultan; scent-sachet. **sultanat,** *n.m.* Sultanate. **sultane,** *n.f.* Sultana, sultaness.

sumac [sy'mak], *n.m.* Sumac.

summum [sɔm'mɔm], *n.m.* Summit, acme.

sunnite [sy'nit], *n.* Sunnite (orthodox Mohammedan).

super (1) [sy'pe], *v.t. (Naut.)* To suck (of a pump); *(dial.)* to suck (an egg).—*v.i.* To be stopped up (of a pipe).

super (2) [sy'pɛːr], *n.m. (fam.* abbr.) [SUPERCARBURANT].

superbe [sy'pɛrb], *a.* Proud, haughty, arrogant; superb, splendid; stately; lofty; boastful, vainglorious. *Un dîner superbe,* a splendid dinner; *un superbe tableau,* a magnificent painting; *un temps superbe,* glorious weather. —*n.m.* Proud man.—*n.f.* Arrogance; vainglory. **superbement,** *adv.* Haughtily, superbly.

supercarburant [sypɛrkarby'rɑ̃], *n.m.* Highgrade petrol.

supercherie [sypɛrʃə'ri], *n.f.* Deceit, fraud, swindle, trickery; hoax.

superfétation [sypɛrfetɑ'sjɔ̃], *n.f.* Superfoetation; superfluity, redundancy. **superfétatoire,** *a.* Superfluous.

superficie [sypɛrfi'si], *n.f.* Superficies, surface, area; *(fig.)* superficiality. **superficiel,** *a. (fem. -ielle)* Superficial; on the surface only, shallow, skin-deep. **superficiellement,** *adv.* Superficially.

superfin [sypɛr'fɛ̃], *a. (fem. -ine)* Superfine, of superior quality.

superflu [sypɛr'fly], *a. (fem. -ue)* Superfluous; needless, unnecessary; vain.—*n.m.* Superfluity, excess. **superfluité,** *n.f.* Superfluity; superabundance.

supérieur [sype'rjœːr], *a. (fem. -ieure)* Superior; upper, higher. *Être supérieur aux événements,* to rise above events; *cours supérieur d'un fleuve,* upper reaches, headwaters of a river; *les classes supérieures,* the upper classes.—*n.* Superior.—*n.f. La (Mère) Supérieure,* the Mother Superior. **supérieurement,** *adv.* In a superior manner; superlatively, capitally.

supériorité, *n.f.* Superiority; superiorship (of a convent). *Supériorité d'âge,* seniority.

superlatif [sypɛrla'tif], *a. (fem. -ive)* Superlative.—*n.m. (Gram.)* Superlative. *Au superlatif,* superlatively, *(Gram.)* in the superlative; *cet homme est bête au superlatif,* that man is stupid to a degree. **superlativement,** *adv.* Superlatively.

supermarché [sypɛrmar'ʃe], *n.m.* Supermarket.
superposer [sypɛrpo'ze], *v.t.* To superpose; to superimpose. **superposition,** *n.f.* Superposition; superimposition (of colours, etc.).
supersonique [sypɛrsɔ'nik], *a.* Supersonic.
superstitieusement [sypɛrstisjøz'mɑ̃], *adv.* Superstitiously. **superstitieux,** *a.* (*fem.* **-ieuse**) Superstitious. **superstition,** *n.f.* Superstition.
superstructure [sypɛrstryk'ty:r], *n.f.* Superstructure; upper works (of ship); permanent way (of railway).
superviser [sypɛrvi'ze], *v.t.* (*Cine. Theat.*) To supervise.
supin [sy'pɛ̃], *n.m.* (*Gram.*) Supine. *Au supin,* in the supine.
supinateur [sypina'tœ:r], *n.m. and a.m.* (*Anat.*) Supinator. **supination,** *n.f.* Supination.
supplantateur [syplɑ̃ta'tœ:r], *n.m.* (*fem.* **-trice**) or **supplanteur,** *n.m.* (*fem.* **-teuse**) Supplanter. **supplantation,** *n.f.* Supplantation; supplanting, supersession. **supplanter,** *v.t.* To supplant, to oust, to supersede.
suppléance [syple'ɑ̃:s], *n.f.* Substitution, deputyship. *Faire des suppléances,* to be on supply. **suppléant,** *a. and n.m.* (*fem.* **-ante**) Substitute, assistant, deputy, locum tenens, acting; understudy. *Juge suppléant,* assistant-judge; (*instituteur*) *suppléant,* supply-teacher.
suppléer, *v.t.* To supply, to fill up, to make up; to act as, to take the place of, to do duty for.—*v.i.* To make up the deficiency (*à*). *La valeur supplée au nombre,* valour makes up for deficiency of numbers; *se faire suppléer,* to find a substitute; *suppléer à une vacance,* to fill a vacant post.
supplément [syple'mɑ̃], *n.m.* Supplement; additional price, extra charge, excess fare. **supplémentaire,** *a.* Supplementary, supplemental, additional, extra. *Heures supplémentaires,* overtime; (*Mus.*) *lignes supplémentaires,* ledger-lines.
supplétif, *a.* (*fem.* **-ive**) Suppletory; (*Mil.*) auxiliary (of troops).
suppliant [sypli'ɑ̃], *a.* (*fem.* **-iante**) Suppliant, supplicating, beseeching, entreating.—*n.* Suppliant, supplicant, petitioner.
supplication [syplika'sjɔ̃], *n.f.* Supplication, entreaty.
supplice [sy'plis], *n.m.* Corporal punishment; (*fig.*) torment, pain, anguish. *Dernier supplice,* capital punishment; *être au supplice,* to be upon the rack, to be on thorns.
supplicié [sypli'sje], *n.m.* (*fem.* **-iée**) Executed criminal. **supplicier,** *v.t.* To put to death, to execute.
supplier [sypli'e], *v.t.* To beseech, to entreat, to beg, to supplicate.
supplique [sy'plik], *n.f.* Petition, supplication, entreaty.
support [sy'pɔ:r], *n.m.* Support, prop, pillar; rest, stand, bracket; fulcrum; (*Carp.*) strut; (*Her.*) supporter. **supportable,** *a.* Supportable, bearable, tolerable. **supportablement,** *adv.* Tolerably.
supporter (1) [sypɔr'tœ:r], *n.m.* (*spt.*) Supporter, partisan.
supporter (2) [sypɔr'te], *v.t.* To support, to sustain, to uphold; to endure, to suffer, to bear; to tolerate, to put up with; to stand. **se supporter,** *v.r.* To be supported, to be borne; to bear with each other.

supposable [sypo'zabl], *a.* Supposable.
supposé [sypo'se], *a.* (*fem.* **-ée**) Pretended, counterfeit, forged, fictitious, assumed; putative, reputed; supposititious; supposed, admitted. *Supposé qu'il y consente,* suppose he consents to it.
supposer [sypo'ze], *v.t.* To suppose; to grant, to admit, to imply; to forge, to allege; to substitute for what is genuine; to conjecture. *Supposer un enfant,* to palm off a child; *supposer un testament,* to forge a will. **supposition,** *a.* (*fem.* **-ive**) Suppositive. **supposition,** *n.f.* Supposition, assumption; substitution; forgery. **suppositoire,** *n.m.* Suppository.
suppôt [sy'po], *n.m.* Member, agent, henchman, tool, abettor; imp (of the devil). *Suppôt de Satan,* fiend, hell-hound.
suppressif [sypre'sif], *a.* (*fem.* **-ive**) Suppressive. **suppression,** *n.f.* Suppression; cancelling (of passage); quelling (of revolt); concealment.
supprimer [sypri'me], *v.t.* To suppress, to pass over in silence; to omit, to abolish, to cut off or down, to cancel; (*fam.*) to kill, to liquidate; to do away with (someone). *Supprimer des impôts,* to take off taxes; *supprimer une loi,* to abolish a law.
suppuratif [sypyra'tif], *a.* (*fem.* **-ive**) Suppurative.—*n.m.* (*Med.*) Suppurative. **suppuration,** *n.f.* Suppuration, running. **suppurer,** *v.i.* To suppurate, to run.
supputation [sypyta'sjɔ̃], *n.f.* Computation, calculation, reckoning. **supputer,** *v.t.* To calculate, to compute, to reckon.
supraliminal [sypralimi'nal], *n.m. and a.* (*fem.* **-ale,** *pl.* **-aux**) (*Psych.*) Supraliminal.
supramondain [sypramɔ̃'dɛ̃], *a.* (*fem.* **-aine**) Supramundane.
suprasensible, *a.* Suprasensible.
suprématie [syprema'si], *n.f.* Supremacy.
suprême [sy'prɛ:m], *a.* Supreme, highest; last. *À l'heure suprême,* at the last hour (death); *au suprême degré,* in the highest degree.—*n.m.* (*Cook.*) Entrée consisting of the best parts of poultry with a rich sauce. **suprêmement,** *adv.* Supremely.
sur (1) [syr], *prep.* On, upon; over, above; in, into; on to; on board; towards; about; respecting, concerning, on account of; out of, from. *Compter sur,* to rely on, to make sure of; *dix sur quinze,* ten out of fifteen; *donner sur,* to look out upon or over; *faire faute sur faute,* to make one mistake after another; *il prend trop sur lui,* he takes too much upon himself; *il s'excusa sur son âge,* he excused himself on account of his age; *j'ai pris cent francs sur la monnaie,* I took a hundred francs out of the change; *n'avoir pas d'argent sur soi,* to have no money on one; *six pieds sur deux,* six feet by two; *sur ces entrefaites,* in the meantime; at that moment; *sur la fin de la semaine,* towards the end of the week; *sur le soir,* towards evening; *sur le tout,* (*Her.*) over all; *sur ma parole,* upon my word; *sur toute chose* or *sur toutes choses,* above all, above all things; *sur ce,* thereupon, now then; *une fois sur cent,* once in a hundred times.
sur (2) [sy:r], *a.* (*fem.* **sure**) Sour.
sûr [sy:r], *a.* (*fem.* **sûre**) Sure, certain, unfailing, infallible; safe, secure; firm, steady; unerring, trustworthy. *À coup sûr* or *pour*

sûr, for certain, for sure; *bien sûr!* of course! *c'est un ami sûr*, he is a trusty friend; *être sûr de soi*, to be self-assured; *il est en lieu sûr*, he is in a place of safety; *il est sûr de son fait* or *de son coup*, he is sure of success; *je suis sûr de vous*, I can depend on you; *les chemins sont sûrs*, the roads are safe; *le temps n'est pas sûr*, the weather is uncertain; *peu sûr*, unsafe; *pour le plus sûr*, to be on the safe side; *sûr et certain*, positive.

surabondamment [syrabɔ̃daˈmɑ̃], *adv.* Superabundantly. **surabondance**, *n.f.* Superabundance; glut. **surabondant**, *a.* (*fem.* **-ante**) Superabundant **surabonder**, *v.i.* To superabound; to be glutted (*de*).

surah [syˈra], *n.m.* Surah; a soft, twilled silk.

suraigu [syreˈgy], *a.* (*fem.* **-uë**) Overshrill; very high-pitched (note, voice); peracute, very acute (inflammation).

surajouter, *v.t.* To superadd.

suralimentation, *n.f.* (*Med.*) Intensive feeding; over-feeding; (*Motor.*) supercharging. **suralimenté**, *a.* (*fem.* **-ée**) Overfed. **suralimenter**, *v.t.* To feed up; to supercharge.

suranné, *a.* (*fem.* **-ée**) Expired; superannuated, out-of-date, antiquated; old-world; ancient.

sur-arbitre [syrarˈbitr], *n.m.* (*pl.* **sur-arbitres**) Referee (between umpires).

surard [syˈraːr], *a.m.* Elder-flower (vinegar).

surate [syˈrat], *n.f.* Sura (chapter of the Koran).

surbaissé [syrbɛˈse], *a.* (*fem.* **-ée**) Depressed, flattened, less than semicircular (of arches and vaults); very low, underslung (chassis). **surbaisser**, *v.t.* To make (an arch etc.) *surbaissé*; to surbase; to drop, to undersling (frame, chassis).

surcharge, *n.f.* Additional burden, overloading; overcharge; (stamp) surcharge; excess, overplus; weight handicap (of race-horse); word written over another. **surcharger**, *v.t.* To overload, to overburden, to surcharge, to overtax, to overstock; (*fig.*) to overwhelm; to oppress; to weigh down; to overprint (a stamp), to write over other words. *Surcharger d'impôts*, to overtax. **surchauffage**, *n.m.* or **surchauffe**, *n.f.* Superheating; overheating. **surchauffer**, *v.t.* To overheat; to superheat.

surchoix, *n.m.* First choice, prime quality.

surclasser, *v.t.* To outclass.

surcomposé, *a.* (*fem.* **-ée**) (*Gram.*) Double compound.

surcompresseur, *n.m.* Supercharger. **surcompression**, *n.f.* Supercharging. **surcomprimé**, *a.* (*fem.* **-ée**) Supercharged.

surcontre, *n.m.* (*Cards*) Redouble. **surcontrer**, *v.i., v.t.* To redouble.

surcot, *n.m.* Surcoat.

surcoupe, *n.f.* Over-trumping. **surcouper**, *v.t.* To over-trump.

surcroissance [syrkrwaˈsɑ̃ːs], *n.f.* Overgrowth, excrescence. **surcroît**, *n.m.* Addition, increase; surplus, excess. *De* or *par surcroît*, to boot, in addition; *pour surcroît de malheur*, to make matters worse; *un surcroît de besogne*, more work.

surcuit [syrˈkɥi], *a.* (*fem.* **-uite**) Overdone.

surdent [syrˈdɑ̃], *n.f.* Irregular tooth; wolf's tooth (in horses).

surdi-mutité [syrdimytiˈte], *n.f.*, **surdimutisme**, *n.m.* Deaf-(and)-dumbness, surdo-mutism.

surdité [syrdiˈte], *n.f.* Deafness.

surdon [syrˈdɔ̃], *n.m.* Right of non-acceptance (of damaged goods); compensation paid to buyer (of damaged goods).

surdorer [syrdɔˈre], *v.t.* To double-gild.

surdos [syrˈdo], *n.m. inv.* Back-strap (on horse); carrying-pad.

sureau [syˈro], *n.m.* (*pl.* **-eaux**) Elder-(tree).

surélever [syrelˈve], *v.t.* To raise higher, to add storey(s) to; (*Golf*) to tee.

surelle [syˈrɛl], *n.f.* Wood-sorrel.

sûrement [syrˈmɑ̃], *adv.* Surely, certainly, to be sure; safely, securely; confidently.

suréminent [syremiˈnɑ̃], *a.* (*fem.* **-ente**) Supereminent.

surémission, *n.f.* Over-issue.

surenchère, *n.f.* Higher bid, outbidding. **surenchérir**, *v.i.* To overbid, to bid higher. **surenchérissement**, *n.m.* Overbidding. **surenchérisseur**, *n.m.* (*fem.* **-euse**) Overbidder.

surérogation, *n.f.* Supererogation. **surérogatoire**, *a.* Supererogatory.

surestarie [syrestaˈri], *n.f.* (*Naut.*) Demurrage. *Jours de surestarie*, extra lay days.

surestimation [syrestimaˈsjɔ̃], *n.f.* Overestimate, overvaluation. **surestimer**, *v.t.* To overestimate; to overrate.

suret [syˈrɛ], *a.* (*fem.* **surette** (1)) Sourish.

surette (2) [SURELLE].

sûreté [syrˈte], *n.f.* Safety, security; sureness; guarantee, precaution, surety, warranty. *Agent de la sûreté*, detective; *cran de sûreté*, safety-catch, half-cock (on gun); *être en sûreté*, to be out of harm's way, to be in safe keeping; *la Sûreté* (in France), Criminal Investigation Department; *mécanisme de sûreté*, fool-proof mechanism; *prendre toutes ses sûretés*, to take every precaution; *serrure de sûreté*, safety-lock; (*Mil.*) *service de sûreté*, protection.

surévaluation [syrevalɥaˈsjɔ̃], *n.f.* Overvaluation, overestimate. **surévaluer**, *v.t.* To overestimate.

surexcitation, *n.f.* Excitement. **surexciter**, *v.t.* To excite.

surexposer [syrɛkspoˈze], *v.t.* (*Phot.*) To overexpose. **surexposition**, *n.f.* Overexposure.

surface [syrˈfas], *n.f.* Surface; outside. *Faire surface* or *revenir en surface*, (of submarine) to break surface, to surface; *surface d'appui*, bearing surface; (*Geom.*) *surface de révolution*, surface of revolution; *surface portante*, (of aeroplane) aerofoil; *tout en surface*, superficial; *vitesse en surface*, surface speed.

surfaire [syrˈfɛːr], *v.t. irr.* (*conjug. like* FAIRE) To ask too much for; to overrate, to overpraise. **surfait**, *a.* (*fem.* **-aite**) Overpraised, overrated.

surfaix [syrˈfɛ], *n.m. inv.* Surcingle.

surfiler [syrfiˈle], *v.t.* To overcast (seam); to baste.

surfin [syrˈfɛ̃], *a.* (*fem.* **surfine**) (*Comm.*) Superfine.

surfleurir, *v.i.* To flower again.

surge [syːrʒ], *n.f.* and *a.* Raw, unwashed wool.

surgeon, *n.m.* (*Hort.*) Sucker. *Pousser des*

surgeons, to sucker. **surgeonner,** *v.i.* To sucker, to put forth suckers.

surgir [syr'ʒiːr], *v.i.* To rise, to surge; to rise into view, to appear, to loom up; to crop up. *Faire surgir,* to give rise to, to bring about; to call forth. **surgissement,** *n.m.* Upheaval.

surglacer [syrgla'se], *v.t.* To coat (pastry etc.) with sugar, to ice (cake); to glaze (paper).

surhaussement, *n.m.* Raising, forcing up (of prices etc.). **surhausser,** *v.t.* To raise the height of; to bank (road); to force up the price of.

surhomme, *n.m.* Superman.

surhumain, *a.* (*fem.* **-aine**) Superhuman.

surimposer, *v.t.* To overtax.

surimpression, *n.f.* (*Phot. Cine.*) Over-printing. **surimprimer,** *v.t.* To overprint.

surin [sy'rɛ̃], *n.m.* Young apple-tree not yet grafted; (*slang*) *knife. **suriner,** *v.t.* To knife; to do (someone) in.

surintendance [syrɛ̃tɑ̃'dɑ̃:s], *n.f.* Super-intendance; stewardship; superintendent's offices. **surintendant,** *n.m.* Superintendent, overseer; steward (of large estate). **surintendante,** *n.f.* Woman superintendent; superintendent's wife.

surir [sy'riːr], *v.i.* To turn sour.

surjacent [syrʒa'sɑ̃], *a.* (*fem.* **-ente**) Super-jacent (of strata etc.).

surjaler [syrʒa'le], *v.t.* (*Naut.*) To foul (an anchor).—*v.i.* To clear (of anchors).

surjet [syr'ʒe], *n.m.* Overcasting (of seams).

surjeter [syrʒə'te], *v.t. irr.* (*conjug. like* APPELER) To overcast, to whip-stitch.

sur-le-champ [syrlə'ʃɑ̃], *adv.* At once, forth-with.

surlendemain [syrlɑ̃d'mɛ̃], *n.m.* Day after tomorrow. *Le surlendemain de son départ,* the second day after his departure.

surlier [syr'lje], *v.t.* (*Naut.*) To whip (a rope).

surliure, *n.f.* Serving, whipping.

surlonge [syr'lɔ̃:ʒ], *n.f.* Part (of beef) between the chuck and the clod.

surlouer [syr'lwe], *v.t.* To let or rent (at an exorbitant charge).

surmenage, *n.m.* Excess fatigue; overwork-ing. *Le surmenage intellectuel,* brain-fag, mental strain; *le surmenage scolaire,* the mental strain of schoolboys.

surmené, *a.* (*fem.* **-ée**) Jaded, over-tired, fagged (out).

surmener, *v.t.* To overdrive, to override; to overwork. **se surmener,** *v.r.* To overwork oneself; to over-exert oneself, to overdo it.

surmontable [syrmɔ̃'tabl], *a.* Surmountable, superable.

surmonter [syrmɔ̃'te], *v.t.* To surmount; to overcome, to subdue; to outdo, to surpass; to rise above (of fluids etc.). **se surmonter,** *v.r.* To control oneself, one's feelings.

surmoulage [syrmu'la:ʒ], *n.m.* Retreading (of tyres); duplicating (of block); cast, mould.

surmouler [syrmu'le], *v.t.* To cast in a mould taken from a moulded object; to retread (a tyre).

surmoût [syr'mu], *n.m.* Must taken from the vat before fermentation.

surmulet [syrmy'le], *n.m.* Surmullet.

surmulot [syrmy'lo], *n.m.* Brown rat.

surmultiplication [syrmyltiplika'sjɔ̃], *n.f.* (*Motor.*) Overdrive.

surmultiplié, *a.* (*fem.* **-iée**) Overgeared.

surmultiplier, *v.t.* To fit with an over-drive.

surnager [syrna'ʒe], *v.i.* To float on the surface; (*fig.*) to survive, to remain.

surnaturalité [syrnatyrali'te], *n.f.* (*Theol.*) Supernaturalness. **surnaturel,** *a.* (*fem.* **-elle**) Supernatural, preternatural, un-canny.—*n.m.* Supernatural. **surnaturelle-ment,** *adv.* Supernaturally.

surnom [syr'nɔ̃], *n.m.* Surname, cognomen, nickname. **surnommer,** *v.t.* To nickname, to call.

surnombre [syr'nɔ̃:br], *n.m.* Surplus, excess. *En surnombre,* supernumerary.

surnuméraire [syrnyme'rɛːr], *a. and n.m.* Supernumerary. **surnumérariat,** *n.m.* Position of supernumerary; time during which one is supernumerary.

suroît [sy'rwa], *n.m.* (*Naut.*) Sou'wester (hat or wind).

suros [sy'ro], *n.m. inv.* Splint, tumour (on horses).

suroxydation [syrɔksida'sjɔ̃], *n.f.* Super-oxidation. **suroxyde** [PÉROXIDE]. **suroxy-der** or **suroxygéner,** *v.t.* To overcharge with oxygen.

surpasser [syrpa'se], *v.t.* To be higher than; to surpass, to excel, to outdo, to exceed; (*colloq.*) to astonish. *Il me surpasse de trois pouces,* he is three inches taller than I am. **se surpasser,** *v.r.* To surpass oneself.

surpaye [syr'pɛːj], *n.f.* Extra pay, additional pay, bonus. **surpayer,** *v.t.* To overpay, to give extra pay to; to pay too much for.

surpeuplé [syrpœ'ple], *a.* (*fem.* **-ée**) Over-populated.

surpeuplement, *n.m.* Over-population, over-crowding. **surpeupler,** *v.t.* To over-populate. **se surpeupler,** *v.r.* To become over-populated.

surplis [syr'pli], *n.m. inv.* Surplice.

surplomb [syr'plɔ̃], *n.m.* Overhang (of build-ings); belting (of building). *En surplomb,* overhanging. **surplomber,** *v.i., v.t.* To overhang.

surplus [syr'ply], *n.m. inv.* Surplus, remainder, excess. *Au surplus,* besides, moreover.

surpoids [syr'pwɑ], *n.m.* Overweight, excess weight.

surprenant [syrprə'nɑ̃], *a.* (*fem.* **-ante**) Sur-prising, astonishing, extraordinary. *Chose surprenante . . .,* strange to say. . . .

surprendre [syr'prɑ̃:dr], *v.t. irr.* (*conjugated like* PRENDRE) To surprise, to take by sur-prise, to catch; to overhear; to entrap, to overreach; to intercept; to astonish, to amaze. *La nuit nous surprit,* night overtook us; *la pluie me surprit,* I was caught in the rain; *on a surpris ma bonne foi,* my good faith has been abused; *surprendre une ville,* to take a town by surprise. **se surprendre,** *v.r.* To surprise oneself; to catch oneself (napping etc.).

surpression [syrprɛ'sjɔ̃], *n.f.* High pressure; over-pressure.

surpris [syr'pri], *a.* (*fem.* **surprise** (1)) Sur-prised, taken aback, caught (in the act).

surprise (2) [syr'pri:z], *n.f.* Surprise; amaze-ment; deceit; surprise-packet. *Boîte-à-surprise,* Jack-in-the-box. *Ménager une sur-prise à quelqu'un,* to prepare a surprise for someone; *pêche-surprise,* lucky dip; *revenir*

de sa surprise, to recover from one's surprise; *surprise-partie,* party at friends' where everyone brings his share for the buffet.
surproduction [syrprɔdyk'sjɔ̃], *n.f.* Overproduction.
surréalisme [syrrea'lism], *n.m.* Surrealism. **surréaliste,** *a.* and *n.* Surrealist.
surrénal, *a.* (*fem.* **-ale,** *pl.* **-aux**) Suprarenal.
sursaturation, *n.f.* Supersaturation. **sursaturer,** *v.t.* To supersaturate.
sursaut [syr'so], *n.m.* Start, jump; (*Box.*) side-jump. *S'éveiller en sursant,* to wake with a start. **sursauter,** *v.i.* To start up; to side-jump. *Faire sursauter (quelqu'un),* to startle (someone).
surséance [syrse'ã:s], *n.f.* Suspension (of hearing); stay (of proceedings).
sursel [syr'sɛl], *n.m.* (*Chem.*) Supersalt.
sursemer, *v.t.* irr. (*conjug.* like AMENER) To sow over again.
surseoir [syr'swa:r], *v.t., v.i.* irr. (*pres.p.* **sursoyant,***p.p.* **sursis** (1)) To suspend, to delay, to postpone. **sursis** (2), *n.m.* Delay, respite, reprieve. (*Mil.*) *Sursis d'appel,* deferment; (*Law*) *condamné avec sursis,* sentenced with benefit of the First Offenders Act. **sursitaire,** *n.m.* Deferred conscript.
surtare [syr'ta:r], *n.f.* (*Comm.*) Extra tare.
surtaux [syr'to], *n.m.* Excessive rate (of assessment).
surtaxe, *n.f.* Surtax, additional tax; surcharge, extra postage. **surtaxer,** *v.t.* To overtax, to put an extra tax on.
surtension [syrtã'sjɔ̃], *n.f.* Excess pressure, over-pressure; (*Elec.*) over-voltage, volt-rise.
surtout (1) [syr'tu], *adv.* Above all, chiefly. **surtout** (2), *n.m.* Overcoat, surtout; epergne, centrepiece (for table); light luggage-cart; beehive cover.
surveillance [syrvε'jã:s], *n.f.* Superintendence, inspection, supervision; surveillance, watch. **surveillant,** *n.m.* (*fem.* **-ante**) Inspector, overseer, superintendent; guardian, watcher. *Surveillant d'examen,* invigilator, supervisor; *surveillant(e) général(e),* vice-principal. **surveille** [AVANT-VEILLE].
surveiller, *v.t.* To superintend, to inspect; to watch, to keep an eye on; to supervise; to tend (a machine).—*v.i.* To watch (*sur*). **se surveiller,** *v.r.* To watch oneself; to mind one's p's and q's.
survenance [syrvə'nã:s], *n.f.* (*Law*) Unexpected birth; unforeseen arrival. **survenant,** *a.* (*fem.* **-ante**) Chance-comer; unexpected heir.
survendre [syr'vã:dr], *v.t.* To overcharge for (a thing sold).
survenir [syrvə'ni:r], *v.i.* irr. (*conjugated like* VENIR) To arrive or happen unexpectedly; to befall; to drop in.
surventer [syrvã'te], *v.i.* (*Naut.*) To blow hard etc., to blow a gale.
survenue, *n.f.* Chance arrival; unexpected arrival.
survêtement [syrvɛt'mã], *n.m.* (*spt.*) Tracksuit.
survider [syrvi'de], *v.t.* To empty partly, to lighten.
survie [syr'vi], *n.f.* Survivorship; survival.
survivance [syrvi'vã:s], *n.f.* Reversion (of offices etc.); survival. **survivancier,** *n.m.* (*fem.* **-ière**) Reversioner (to an office).

survivant, *a.* (*fem.* **-ante**) Surviving.—*n.* Survivor.
survivre [syr'vi:vr], *v.i.* irr. (*conjugated like* VIVRE) To survive, to outlive someone; to outlast (*d*). *Survivre à son père,* to outlive one's father. **se survivre,** *v.r.* To outlive one's faculties etc.; to live or exist again. *Se survivre dans ses enfants* or *dans ses ouvrages,* to live again in one's children *or* in one's works.
survol [syr'vɔl], *n.m.* Flight over (an area). **survoler,** *v.t.* To fly over (of aircraft).
survoltage [syrvɔl'ta:ʒ], *n.m.* Boosting (of current). **survolter,** *v.t.* To boost, to step up current. **survolteur,** *n.m.* Booster, (step-up) transformer.
sus [sys], *prep.* Upon. *Courir sus à quelqu'un,* to fall upon someone; *en sus,* over and above, to boot.—*int.* Courage! come on!
susceptibilité [sysεptibili'te], *n.f.* Susceptibility, sensitiveness; irritability, touchiness, irascibility. **susceptible,** *a.* Susceptible, capable, admitting (*de*); open to (improvement etc.); apt to; likely to; sensitive, thin-skinned, touchy; irascible.
susception, *n.f.* Taking (of holy orders); (*R.-C. Ch.*) reception (of the crown, cross, etc.).
*****suscitation** [sysita'sjɔ̃], *n.f.* Suscitation, instigation.
susciter [sysi'te], *v.t.* To suscitate, to raise up, to set up; to create, to give birth to; to arouse, to stir up, to rouse, to instigate.
suscription [syskrip'sjɔ̃], *n.f.* Superscription, address.
susdénommé, *a.* and *n.m.* (*fem.* **-ée**) Above-mentioned.
susdit, *a.* and *n.m.* (*fem.* **-ite**) Aforesaid.
susmentionné, *a.* and *n.m.* (*fem.* **-ée**) Above-mentioned.
susnommé, *a.* and *n.m.* (*fem.* **-ée**) Above-named.
suspect [sys'pεkt *or* sys'pε], *a.* (*fem.* **-ecte**) Suspected, suspicious, suspect, doubtful. *Cela m'est suspect,* I don't like the look of it; *je le tiens pour suspect,* I hold him in suspicion; *vous me seriez suspect pour cent raisons,* there are a hundred reasons for my suspecting you.—*n.m.* Suspect, a suspected person. *La liste des suspects,* the black list.
suspecter [syspεk'te], *v.t.* To suspect, to doubt, to question.
suspendre [sys'pã:dr], *v.t.* To suspend, to hang up; to interrupt, to intermit, to delay, to postpone, to defer. *Suspendre son travail,* to lay aside one's work. **se suspendre,** *v.r.* To suspend oneself; to hang.
suspendu [syspã'dy], *a.* (*fem.* **-ue**) Suspended, hung up, hanging; in suspense; on springs (of carriages). *Pont suspendu,* suspension-bridge.
suspens [sys'pã], *a.m.* Suspended; inhibited (priest).—*adv. phr.* *En suspens,* in suspense; (person) in doubt; (thing) in abeyance, outstanding. **suspense,** *n.f.* (*Eccl.*) Suspension, inhibition. **suspenseur,** *a.m.* (*Anat.*) Suspensory. **suspensif,** *a.* (*fem.* **-ive**) Suspensive, suspension; (*Law*) being a bar to subsequent proceedings. *Points suspensifs* or *de suspension,* points of suspension. **suspension,** *n.f.* Suspension, interruption; hanging-lamp, electrolier.

Suspension d'armes, truce; *suspension d'un fonctionnaire*, suspension of an official. **suspensoir**, *n.m.* (*Surg.*) Suspensory bandage. **suspente**, *n.f.* (*Naut.*) Sling (of a yard etc.); ropes (of balloon car). **suspicion** [syspi'sjɔ̃], *n.f.* Suspicion. **sustentateur** [systɑ̃ta'tœːr], *a.* (*fem.* **-trice**) Supporting. (*Av.*) *Aile sustentatrice*, main wing.—*n.m. Sustentateur rotatif*, rotor (of helicopter). **sustentation**, *n.f.* Sustentation, sustenance. *Base de sustentation*, basis of support; *force de sustentation*, (*Av.*) lifting force. **sustenter**, *v.t.* To sustain, to support, to maintain, to nourish.. **se sustenter**, *v.r.* To feed oneself, to sustain oneself. **susucre** [sy'sykr], *n.m.* (childish) Sugar. **susurration** [sysyrɑ'sjɔ̃], *n.f.*, or **susurrement**, *n.m.* Susurration, whispering, murmur; rustling, soughing (of the wind etc.). ***susurrer**, *v.i.*, *v.t.* To murmur, to whisper. **suttée** [sy'te], **suttie**, or **sâti**, *n.f.* Suttee. **suture** [sy'tyːr], *n.f.* Suture; seam, joint; stitching. *Point de suture*, stitch. **suturer**, *v.t.* To suture, to join, to stitch. **Suzanne** [sy'zan], *f.* Susan. **suzerain** [syz'rɛ̃], *n.m.* (*fem.* **-aine**) Suzerain, lord or lady paramount.—*a.* Paramount, suzerain. **suzeraineté**, *n.f.* Suzerainty. **svastika** [zvasti'ka], *n.m.* Swastika. **svelte** [zvelt], *a.* Slender, slim. **sveltesse**, *n.f.* Slenderness, slimness. **sybarite** [siba'rit], *a.* Sybaritic.—*n.* Sybarite, voluptuary; inhabitant of Sybaris. **sycomore** [sikɔ'mɔːr], *n.m.* Sycamore. **sycophante** [sikɔ'fɑ̃ːt], *n.m.* Sycophant; hypocrite, impostor. **syllabaire** [silla'bɛːr], *n.m.* Spelling-book. **syllabe** [sil'lab], *n.f.* Syllable. **syllabique**, *a.* Syllabic. **syllabisation**, *n.f.* Syllabification. **syllabiser**, *v.t.* To syllabize. **syllabus**, *n.m.* (*Relig.*) Syllabus, abstract, summary. **syllepse** [sil'lɛps], *n.f.* Syllepsis. **syllogisme** [sillɔ'ʒism], *n.m.* Syllogism. **syllogistique**, *a.* Syllogistic. **sylphe** [silf], *n.m.* or **sylphide**, *n.f.* Sylph. **Sylvain** [sil'vɛ̃], *m.* Sylvanus. **sylvain** [sil'vɛ̃], *n.m.* Sylvan. **sylvatique**, *a.* (*Bot.*) Sylvan. **sylvestre**, *a.* Sylvan, growing in woods. **Sylvestre**, *m.* Sylvester. **sylvicole**, *a.* Living in woods; relating to forestry. **sylviculture**, *n.f.* Sylviculture, forestry. **Sylvie** [sil'vi], *f.* Sylvia. **sylvie** [sil'vi] or **sylvia**, *n.f.* (*Orn.*) Warbler; (*Bot.*) wood-anemone. **symbole** [sɛ̃'bɔl], *n.m.* Symbol, sign, emblem; creed. *Symbole des Apôtres*, Apostles' creed. **symbolique**, *a.* Symbolic, symbolical.—*n.f.* Symbolism, system of symbols. **symboliquement**, *adv.* Symbolically. **symbolisation**, *n.f.* Symbolization. **symboliser**, *v.t.* To symbolize. **symbolisme**, *n.m.* Symbolism. **symboliste**, *a.* Symbolistic.—*n.* Symbolist. **symétrie** [sime'tri], *n.f.* Symmetry. **symétrique**, *a.* Symmetrical. **symétriquement**, *adv.* Symmetrically. **sympathie** [sɛ̃pa'ti], *n.f.* Sympathy, fellow-feeling. *J'ai de la sympathie pour lui*, I like him, I feel drawn to him; *nous nous sommes pris de sympathie pour eux*, we have taken a

liking to them. **sympathique**, *a.* Sympathetic; congenial, likeable. *Encre sympathique*, invisible ink; *il m'est sympathique*, I like him; (*Biol.*) *le grand sympathique*, the sympathetic nerve. **sympathisant**, *n.m.* (*fem.* **-ante**) (*Pol.*) Fellow-traveller; sympathizer. —*a.* Sympathizing. **sympathiser**, *v.i.* To sympathize, to get on well together, to feel alike; to correspond, to harmonize. **symphonie** [sɛ̃fɔ'ni], *n.f.* Symphony. **symphonique**, *a.* Symphonic. **symphoniste**, *n.m.* Composer of symphonies; orchestral player. **symphyse** [sɛ̃'fiːz], *n.f.* Symphysis. **symptomatique** [sɛ̃ptɔma'tik], *a.* Symptomatic. **symptomatologie**, *n.f.* Symptomatology. **symptôme**, *n.m.* Symptom, indication, sign, token. **synagogue** [sina'gɔg], *n.f.* Synagogue. **synalèphe** [sina'lɛf], *n.f.* Synalepha. **synallagmatique** [sinallagma'tik], *a.* (*Law*) Reciprocal. *Contrat synallagmatique*, indented deed. **synanthéré**, *a.* (*fem.* **-ée**) (*Bot.*) Synantherous. **synanthérées**, *n.f. pl.* (*Bot.*) Compositae. **synarthrose**, *n.f.* Synarthrosis. **synchrone** [sɛ̃'krɔn] or **synchronique**, *a.* Synchronous. **synchronisateur**, *n.m.* Synchronizer; (*Motor.*) synchromesh (device). **synchronisation**, *n.f.* Synchronization. **synchroniser**, *v.t.* To synchronize. **synchronisme**, *n.m.* Synchronism. **synclinal** [sɛ̃kli'nal], *a.* (*fem.* **-ale**, *pl.* **-aux**) (*Geol.*) Synclinal. **syncope** [sɛ̃'kɔp], *n.f.* Syncope, swoon, fainting fit; (*Mus.*) syncopation; (*Gram.*) elision. **syncopé, *a.* (*fem.* **-ée**) Syncopated. *Musique* (*nègre*) *syncopée*, rag-time. **syncoper**, *v.t.* To syncopize; (*Mus.*) to syncopate. **syncrétique** [sɛ̃kre'tik], *a.* Syncretic. **syncrétisme**, *n.m.* Syncretism. **syndic** [sɛ̃'dik], *n.m.* Syndic, trustee; assignee (in bankruptcy). *Syndic d'office*, official trustee. **syndical**, *a.* (*fem.* **-ale**, *pl.* **-aux**) Pertaining to a syndic. *Chambre syndicale*, trade-union committee. **syndicalisme**, *n.m.* Syndicalism. *Syndicalisme ouvrier*, trade-unionism. **syndicaliste**, *n.* and *a.* Trade-unionist. **syndicat**, *n.m.* Syndicate, trusteeship. *Syndicat d'initiative*, association for encouraging tourism, tourists' information bureau; *syndicat ouvrier*, trade-union; *syndicat patronal*, employers' federation; *syndicat professionnel* or *corporatif*, trade association. **syndiqué**, *a.* and *n.* (*fem.* **-ée**) Member of a trade-union, union man, trade-unionist. **syndiquer**, *v.t.* To form into a syndicate. **se syndiquer**, *v.r.* To form themselves into a syndicate or a trade-union. **synecdoche** or **synecdoque** [sinɛg'dɔk], *n.f.* Synecdoche. **synérèse**, *n.f.* Synaeresis. **synergie** [sinɛr'ʒi], *n.f.* Synergy. **synergique**, *a.* Synergic. **syngénésie** [sɛ̃ʒene'zi], *n.f.* (*Bot.*) Syngenesia. **syngnathe** [sɛ̃g'nat], *n.m.* (*Ichth.*) Horn-fish, garfish. **synizèse** [sini'zɛz], *n.f.* (*Path.*) Synizesis. **synodal** [sinɔ'dal], *a.* (*fem.* **-ale**, *pl.* **-aux**) Synodic, synodal. **synode**, *n.m.* Synod. **synodique**, *a.* Synodic. **synonyme** [sinɔ'nim], *a.* Synonymous.—*n.m.*

Synonym. **synonymie**, *n.f.* Synonymy. ~**synonymique**, *a.* Synonymic.
synopse [si'nɔps], *n.f.* Synopsis of the Gospels. **synopsis**, *n.f.* Synopsis. **synoptique**, *a.* Synoptic.
synostose, *n.f.* Synostosis.
synovial, *a.* (*fem.* -**iale**, *pl.* -**iaux**) Synovial. **synovie**, *n.f.* Synovia. *Épanchement de synovie*, housemaid's knee. **synovite**, *n.f.* Synovitis.
syntaxe [sɛ̃'taks], *n.f.* Syntax. **syntaxique** or **syntactique**, *a.* Syntactic, syntactical.
synthèse [sɛ̃'teːz], *n.f.* Synthesis, composition. **synthétique**, *a.* Synthetic. **synthétiquement**, *adv.* Synthetically. **synthétiser**, *v.t.* To synthesize.
syntonie [sɛ̃tɔ'ni], *n.f.* Syntony.
syphilis [sifi'lis], *n.f.* Syphilis. **syphilitique**, *a.* and *n.* Syphilitic.
syriaque [si'rjak], *a.* Syriac.—*n.m.* Syriac (language).
Syrie [si'ri], *f.* Syria. **syrien**, *a.* (*fem.* -**ienne**) Syrian.—*n.m.* (**Syrien**, *fem.* -**ienne**) A Syrian.
syringe [si'rɛ̃ːʒ] or **syrinx**, *n.f.* Syrinx, Pan's pipes.
syringotomie, *n.f.* Syringotomy.
systaltique [sistal'tik], *a.* Systaltic.
systématique [sistema'tik], *a.* Systematic(al). **systématiquement**, *adv.* Systematically. **systématisation**, *n.f.* Systematization. **systématiser**, *v.t.* To systematize. **systématiseur**, *n.m.* Systematizer.
système [sis'tɛm], *n.m.* System, scheme, plan; device; ensemble; mode (of government); (*Row.*) swivel rowlock. *Employer le système D*, (*slang*) to shift for oneself (out of mess, by any means); *il me tape* (or *porte*) *sur le système*, (*fam.*) he bores me, he gets on my nerves; *le système féodal*, feudalism; *le système solaire*, the solar system.
systole [sis'tɔl], *n.f.* Systole. **systolique**, *a.* Systolic.
systyle, *a.* and *n.m.* (*Arch.*) Systyle.
syzygie, *n.f.* Syzygy. *Marée de syzygie*, syzygial tide, spring tide.

T

T, t [te], *n.m.* The twentieth letter of the alphabet. [When the 3rd pers. sing. of a verb ends in **-e** or **-a** (*il aime, elle viendra, on y va*), if the sentence becomes interrogative and admits inversion, these endings in **-e** and **-a**, out of analogy with all other parts of verbs (*vient-il* etc.), are followed by a **-t** and thus written: *aime-t-il? viendra-t-elle? y va-t-on?*] [*see also* TÉ].
**t', ** *elision* [TE].
ta [ta], *poss.a.f.* [TON (1)].
tabac [ta'ba], *n.m.* Tobacco; snuff. *Débitant de tabac*, tobacconist; *tabac à chiquer*, chewing tobacco; *tabac à fumer*, smoking tobacco; *tabac à priser*, snuff. *Il va y avoir du tabac*, (*Naut.*) there is rough water ahead; (*Mil.*) we're in for a scrap. *Passer quelqu'un à tabac*, (*slang*) to beat somebody up.—*a. inv.* Tobacco-coloured. **tabagie**, *n.f.* Room full of tobacco-smoke, reeking of stale smoke. **tabagisme** [NICOTINISME].

tabarinade [tabari'nad], *n.f.* Broad farce, slapstick.
tabatière [taba'tjɛːr], *n.f.* Snuff-box. *Fenêtre* or *châssis à tabatière*, hinged skylight; *fusil à tabatière*, breech-loading rifle introduced in 1867.
tabellion [tabɛl'ljɔ̃], *n.m.* Scrivener; notary.
tabernacle [tabɛr'nakl], *n.m.* Tent; tabernacle.
tabes [ta'bɛs], *n.m.* (*Path.*) Tabes. **tabescence**, *n.f.* Emaciation. **tabescent**, *a.* (*fem.* -**ente**) Tabescent. **tabétique**, *a.* and *n.* Tabetic.
tabi or **tabis** [ta'bi], *n.m.* Tabby (watered silk). **tabiser**, *v.t.* To tabby, to give a watered appearance to.
tablature [tabla'tyːr], *n.f.* (*Mus.*) Tablature; fingering chart (of wind instrument). *Donner de la tablature à quelqu'un*, to cause trouble to someone, to be a nuisance to someone.
table [tabl], *n.f.* Table; board (food, fare); meal; mess (of officers etc.); slab, plaque; face (of anvil etc.); table of contents etc. *Aimer la table*, to like good living; *faire table rase*, to make a clean sweep; *jouer cartes sur table*, to act above-board, to put all one's cards on the table; *la Sainte Table*, the communion table; *la table d'honneur*, the high table; *la table du festin*, the festive board; *mettre* or *dresser la table*, to set, to lay the table; *se lever de table, sortir de table*, or *quitter la table*, to get up from table; *se mettre à table*, to sit down at table, (*slang*) to confess, to split, to blow the gaff; *table à écrire*, writing-table; *table à ouvrage*, work-table; *table d'écoute*, listening-table; *table de cuisine*, kitchen-table; *table de jeu*, card-table; *table de malade*, bed-table; *table de multiplication*, multiplication table; *table de nuit*, bedside table; *table d'opération*, operating table; *table des matières*, table of contents; *table de tir*, range table; *table de toilette*, washstand; *table d'harmonie*, sound-board (of a musical instrument); *table roulante*, trolley; *tenir table ouverte*, to keep open house; *vivre à la même table*, to mess together.
tableau [ta'blo], *n.m.* (*pl.* -**eaux**) Picture, painting, tableau; scene, sight; description; list, catalogue, table; panel (of juries); blackboard, board (for writing on etc.); bill-frame. *Encadrer un tableau*, to frame a picture; *être rayé du tableau*, to be struck off the rolls; *faire tableau*, to make a picture, to look striking; *former un tableau*, to empanel a jury; *tableau d'annonces*, advertising board; *tableau d'avancement*, promotion list; *tableau de chasse*, bag; *tableau de chevalet*, easel-piece; *tableau de distribution*, switchboard; *tableau de graissage*, lubrication chart; *un vieux tableau*, (*fam.*) a painted old hag; *un tableau de maître*, a masterpiece.
tableautin [tablo'tɛ̃], *n.m.* Small picture.
tablée [ta'ble], *n.f.* Company at table. **tabler**, *v.i.* To dress the board (at backgammon). *Vous pouvez tabler là-dessus*, you may depend upon it.
tabletier [tablə'tje], *n.m.* (*fem.* -**ière**) Dealer in fancy turnery, chess-boards, etc.
tablette [ta'blɛt], *n.f.* Shelf; tablet; cake (of chocolate); (*Pharm.*) lozenge; (*Naut.*) rising-staff; (*pl.*) tablets, note-book. *Rayez cela de*

vos tablettes, don't depend upon that; *tablette de cheminée*, mantelpiece.

tabletterie [tablɛ'tri], *n.f.* Fancy-turnery trade, toy-trade; inlaid work.

tablier [tabli'e], *n.m.* Apron (in all senses); flooring, platform (of a bridge etc.); chess- or draughtboard. *Rendre son tablier*, (*fam.*) to give notice; *tablier de cheminée*, fire-place hood; *tablier d'enfant*, pinafore.

tabloïde [tablɔ'id], *n.m.* (*Pharm.*) Tablet.

tabou [ta'bu], *n.m.* and *a.* Taboo.

tabouer [ta'bwe], *v.t.* To taboo.

tabouret [tabu'rɛ], *n.m.* Stool, foot-stool; settle; shepherd's purse (plant).

tabourin [tabu'rɛ̃], *n.m.* Chimney-cowl.

tabulaire [taby'lɛːr], *a.* Tabular. **tabulateur,** *n.m.* Tabulator; (*Teleph.*) dial.

tac [tak], *n.m.* Rot (in sheep); click, clack. (*colloq.*) *Répondre du tac au tac*, to parry with the riposte, to retort quickly.

tacaud [ta'ko], *n.m.* Whiting-pout; pouting, bib.

***tacet** [ta'sɛt], *n.m.* (*Mus.*) Pause; (*fig.*) silence.

tachant [ta'ʃɑ̃], *a.* (*fem.* **-ante**) Easily soiled.

tache [taʃ], *n.f.* Spot, stain; speckle; (*fig.*) blot, blemish. *Faire tache*, to stain, to spot; to stand out as a blemish; *faire tache d'huile*, (*fig.*) to spread all 'around; *sans tache*, stainless, undefiled, unblemished, spotless; *tache de rousseur*, freckle; *tache de vin*, strawberry mark; *tache d'humidité*, mildew; *tache solaire*, sun-spot.

tâche [tɑːʃ], *n.f.* Task, job. *Ouvrage à la tâche*, piece-work; jobbing; *prendre à tâche de faire une chose*, to make it one's business to do a thing; *travailler à la tâche*, to work by the job, to do piece-work.

tachéographe [takeɔ'graf], *n.m.* Recording tacheometer. **tachéomètre,** *n.m.* Tacheometer. **tachéométrie,** *n.f.* Tacheometry.

tacher [ta'ʃe], *v.t.* To stain, to spot; (*fig.*) to taint, to tarnish, to blemish. **se tacher,** *v.r.* To soil oneself or one's clothes.

tâcher [tɑ'ʃe], *v.i.* To try, to endeavour, to strive, to seek. *Il a tâché d'oublier*, he tried to forget. **tâcheron,** *n.m.* One working by the job, jobbing labourer.

tacheter [taʃ'te], *v.t.* To mark with spots, to fleck, to speckle, to mottle.

tachygraphe [taki'graf], *n.* Tachygrapher, shorthand-writer. **tachygraphie,** *n.f.* Tachygraphy. **tachymètre,** *n.m.* Tachymeter.

Tacite [ta'sit], *m.* Tacitus.

tacite [ta'sit], *a.* Tacit, implied. **tacitement,** *adv.* Tacitly. **taciturne,** *a.* Taciturn. **taciturnité,** *n.f.* Taciturnity.

tacot [ta'ko], *n.m.* (*fam.*) Old crock (car, train, boat, engine, etc.).

tact [takt], *n.m.* Feeling, touch; tact.

tacticien [takti'sjɛ̃], *n.m.* Tactician.

tactile [tak'til], *a.* Tactile. **tactilité,** *n.f.* Tactility. **taction,** *n.f.* Taction, touch.

tactique [tak'tik], *n.f.* Tactics; (*fig.*) manœuvres, stratagem, way, move.—*a.* Tactical.

tadorne [ta'dɔrn], *n.m.* Sheldrake.

tael [ta'ɛl], *n.m.* Tael (Chinese silver coin).

tænia [TÉNIA].

taffetas [taf'ta], *n.m.* Taffeta. *Taffetas d'Angleterre*, *taffetas gommé*, sticking-plaster.

tafia [ta'fja], *n.m.* Tafia (rum).

Tage [taːʒ], **le,** *m.* The Tagus river.

taïaut or **tayaut** [ta'jo], *n.m.* and *int.* (*Hunt.*) Tally-ho.

taïcoun or **taïkoun** [tai'kun], *n.m.* Tycoon.

taie (1) [tɛ], *n.f.* *Taie d'oreiller*, pillow-slip, pillow-case.

taie (2) [tɛ], *n.f.* (*Med.*) Albugo, film, speck (in the eye).

taillable [tɑ'jabl], *a.* Taxable.

taillade [tɑ'jad], *n.f.* Slash, gash, cut.

taillader [tɑja'de], *v.t.* To slash, to cut, to gash. *Des manches tailladées*, slashed sleeves.

taillanderie, *n.f.* Edge-tool trade; edge-tools. **taillandier,** *n.m.* Edge-tool maker.

taillant, *n.m.* Edge (of a knife etc.).

taille [tɑːj], *n.f.* Cutting, cut, fashion; (*Min.*) coal-face; edge (of a sword); height, stature, size; shape, waist, waistline, figure; tally-stick; copsewood, copse; (*Hort.*) pruning; (*Surg.*) cystotomy; (*Mus.*) tenor part; (*Feud.*) poll-tax; subsidy; deal (at cards). *Avoir la taille bien prise*, to have a good figure; *basse-taille*, bass; *de bonne taille*, good-sized; *de taille à*, big enough to, quite capable of; *être bien pris de taille* or *dans sa taille*, to be well-proportioned; *faire des coches sur une taille*, to tally; *frapper d'estoc et de taille* [ESTOC]; *haute-taille*, light tenor; *il est de ma taille*, he is my height; *la taille des arbres*, the pruning of trees; *pierre de taille*, freestone; *tour de taille*, waist measurement.

taillé [tɑ'je], *a.* (*fem.* **-ée**) *Cristal taillé*, cut-glass; [COTE]; (*Her.*) *écu taillé*, shield parted per bend sinister; *un homme bien taillé*, a well set-up man; *taillé-en athlète*, of athletic build, built like an athlete.

taille-buissons [tɑjbɥi'sɔ̃], *n.m. inv.* Hedge-cutter; clippers.

taille-crayon [tɑjkrɛ'jɔ̃] or **taille-crayons,** *n.m.* (*pl.* **taille-crayons**) Pencil-sharpener.

taille-douce, *n.f.* (*pl.* **tailles-douces**) Copper-plate engraving.

taille-légumes, *n.m. inv.* Vegetable cutter.

taille-mer, *n.m. inv.* Cutwater.

taille-ongles [tɑj'ɔ̃gl], *n.m. inv.* Nail-cutter.

tailler [tɑ'je], *v.t.* To cut, to cut out; to carve; to cut up; to hew; to prune, to trim; to sharpen; to frame, to shape; to cut for the stone; to deal (cards); [BAVETTE]. *Tailler de la besogne* or *des croupières à*, to cut out work for; *tailler la haie*, to cut the hedge; *tailler un crayon*, to sharpen a pencil; *tailler un habit*, to cut out a coat. **taille-racines,** *n.m. inv.* Vegetable-cutter. **taillerie,** *n.f.* Cutting of diamonds etc.

tailleur [tɑ'jœːr], *n.m.* Tailor; cutter; hewer; (at cards) banker; (tailor-made) costume. *Tailleur de pierre*, stone-cutter. **tailleuse,** *n.f.* Tailoress.

taille-vent [tɑj'vɑ̃], *n.m. inv.* Lug mainsail.

taillis [tɑ'ji], *n.m. inv.* Copse; underwood, brushwood. *Bois taillis*, copsewood.

tailloir [tɑ'jwaːr], *n.m.* Trencher, wooden platter; (*Arch.*) abacus. **taillole,** *n.f.* (*Prov.*) Woollen sash for trousers. ***taillon,** *n.m.* Nib (of a quill pen).

tain [tɛ̃], *n.m.* Foil, tinfoil; silvering (for mirrors). *Glace sans tain*, plate-glass.

taire [tɛːr], *v.t. irr.* (*conjug. like* PLAIRE) To say nothing of, to pass over in silence, to suppress, to keep dark. *Faire taire*, to silence, to reduce to silence, to stop the mouth of, to

gag (the press etc.); to hush. **se taire,** *v.r.*
To hold one's tongue, to be silent; to be kept
secret, to remain unsaid. *Taisez-vous,* hold
your tongue, be quiet.
talapoin [tala'pwɛ̃], *n.m.* Talapoin (Buddhist
priest; monkey).
talc [talk], *n.m.* Talc. **talcique,** *a.* Talcose.
talcite, *n.f.* Talcite.
talent [ta'lɑ̃], *n.m.* Talent; (*fig.*) ability.
Homme de talent, talented man; *il a le talent
de m'exaspérer,* he has the knack of exasperating me.
talion [ta'ljɔ̃], *n.m.* Talion, retaliation. *Loi
du talion,* law of retaliation.
talisman [talis'mɑ̃], *n.m.* Talisman. **talismanique,** *a.* Talismanic.
talle [tal], *n.f.* Sucker (shoot from root).
taller, *v.i.* To throw out suckers.
tallipot [tali'po], *n.m.* Talipot (fan-palm).
talmouse [tal'mu:z], *n.f.* Puff-cake; (*dial.*)
clap, whack.
talmud [tal'myd], *n.m.* Talmud. **talmudique,**
a. Talmudic. **talmudiste,** *n.* Talmudist.—
a. Talmudistic.
taloche [ta'lɔʃ], *n.f.* Cuff, thump, buffet;
plasterer's hawk. **talocher,** *v.t.* To cuff, to
box (someone's) ears.
talon [ta'lɔ̃], *n.m.* Heel; stock (at cards etc.);
butt (of cue); sole (of a rudder etc.); shoulder
(of a sword etc.); counterfoil; ogee-moulding.
Pneu à talons, beaded tyre; *donner un coup
de talon,* (*Naut.*) to ground, to strike;
marcher sur les talons de quelqu'un [MARCHER];
mettre des talons à, to heel; *montrer* or *tourner
les talons,* to take to one's heels; **talon rouge,*
aristocrat, nobleman (who wore red heels).
talonner, *v.t.* To be close at the heels of; to
press hard, to urge, to spur, to dun.—*v.i.*
(*Naut.*) To ground; (*Ftb.*) to heel out (of the
scrum). **talonnette,** *n.f.* Heel-piece. **talonneur,** *n.m.* (*Ftb.*) Hooker. **talonnier,** *n.m.*
Heel-maker. **talonnière,** *n.f.* Heel-piece;
(*Naut.*) heel (of a rudder); (*pl.*) talaria,
Mercury's heel-wings.
talpack [tal'pak], *n.m.* Busby.
talquer [tal'ke], *v.t.* To sprinkle with talcum,
soap-stone, to chalk. **talqueux,** *a.* (*fem.*
-euse) Talcose.
talus [ta'ly], *n.m.* Slope, batter, ramp; bank,
embankment; talus. *Aller en talus,* to slope
down, to shelve; *en talus,* sloping, battered.
talutage, *n.m.* Sloping; embanking.
***taluter,** *v.t.* To slope; to embank; to batter.
tamanoir [tama'nwa:r], *n.m.* Great ant-eater.
tamarin [tama'rɛ̃], *n.m.* Tamarind; tamarind-
tree; tamarin (marmoset). **tamarinier,** *n.m.*
Tamarind-tree.
tamaris [tama'ri], **tamarisc,** *n.m.* Tamarisk.
tambouille [tɑ̃'bu:j], *n.f.* (*Mil. slang*) Kitchen;
cooking.
tambour [tɑ̃'bu:r], *n.m.* Drum; drummer;
(*Horol.*) barrel; drum of a column; barrel,
tympan; tambour, embroidery frame; (*Anat.*)
tympanum; paddle-box (on steamboats).
Battre le tambour, to beat the drum (of town-
crier); *battre du tambour, jouer du tambour,* to
play the drum; *coup de tambour, roulement de
tambour,* beat or roll on the drum; *mener
tambour battant,* to treat high-handedly; to
hustle along; *partir sans tambour ni trompette,*
to leave unnoticed, without fuss; *sortir tambour battant,* to leave with the honours of

war; *tambour de Basque,* tambourine with
jingles; *tambour de frein,* brake-drum; *tambour de ville,* town-crier; *tambour voilé,*
muffled drum. **tambourin,** *n.m.* Provençal
tabor; round parchment-racquet (to play
ball). **tambourinage,** *n.m.* Drumming.
tambourinaire, *n.m.* (*Prov.*) Tambourin-
player. **tambouriner,** *v.i.* To beat the
drum; to drum, to tattoo.—*v.t.* To cry by
the town drummer; to advertise, to boast.
tambourineur, *n.m.* Player on the tambourine. **tambour-major,** *n.m.* (*pl.* **tam-
bours-majors**) Drum-major.
Tamerlan [tamer'lɑ̃], *m.* Tamerlane.
taminier [tami'nje], *n.m.* Black briony.
tamis [ta'mi], *n.m.* **inv.** Sieve, sifter, strainer.
Passer au tamis, to sift, to screen, to strain,
(*fig.*) to examine thoroughly. **tamisage,**
n.m. Sifting, straining.
Tamise [ta'mi:z], **la,** *f.* The Thames.
tamiser [tami'ze], *v.t.* To sift, to bolt, to
strain; to filter; to soften (light etc.).—*v.i.*
(*Naut.*) To let the wind through; to filter
through. **tamiserie,** *n.f.* Sieve-making or
-factory. **tamiseur,** *n.m.* (*fem.* -euse) Sifter.
tamisier, *n.m.* Sieve-maker or -vendor.
tampe [tɑ̃:p], *n.f.* Wedge (in cloth-manufac-
ture). **tamper,** *v.t.* To fix the wedge on
(the friezing-table).
tampon [tɑ̃'pɔ̃], *n.m.* Stopper; plug; bung;
tampion; buffer; pad (used in engraving etc.);
rubber stamp; (*Surg.*) tampon; (*slang*) batman. *Tampon de coton* (*hydrophile*), pad of
cotton wool. **tamponnement,** *n.m.* Plugging, stopping; dabbing; (*Rail.*) end-on
collision. **tamponner,** *v.t.* To plug, to
stop up; to dab with a pad; to run into
(another train etc.); (*pop.*) to hit, to knock
about. **se tamponner,** *v.r.* To collide.
tamponnoir [tɑ̃pɔ'nwa:r], *n.m.* Plugging tool,
wall-bit.
tam-tam [tam'tam], *n.m.* (*pl.* **tam-tams**)
Gong, tom-tom. *Faire du tam-tam,* to kick
up a row.
tan [tɑ̃], *n.m.* Tan; tanner's bark.—*a.* **inv.**
Tan(-coloured).
tanaisie [tanɛ'zi], *n.f.* Tansy.
tancer [tɑ̃'se], *v.t.* To rate, to lecture, to
scold. *Tancer quelqu'un vertement,* to give
someone a good talking-to.
tanche [tɑ̃:ʃ], *n.f.* Tench.
Tancrède [tɑ̃'krɛd], *m.* Tancred.
tandem [tɑ̃'dɛm], *n.m.* Tandem. *Conduire en
tandem,* to drive tandem; *monter en tandem,*
to ride a tandem (bicycle).
tandis [tɑ̃'di] **que,** *conj. phr.* While; whereas.
tangage [tɑ̃'ga:ʒ], *n.m.* Pitching (of ship,
aeroplane).
tangara [tɑ̃ga'ra], *n.m.* Tanager (bird).
tangence [tɑ̃'ʒɑ̃:s], *n.f.* Tangency, contact.
tangent, *a.* (*fem.* -ente) Tangential,
tangent.—*n.f.* Tangent. *Prendre la tangente,*
to go off at a tangent. **tangentiel,** *a.* (*fem.*
-ielle) Tangential.
Tanger [tɑ̃'ʒe], *m.* Tangier(s).
tangibilité [tɑ̃ʒibili'te], *n.f.* Tangibility. **tangible,** *a.* Tangible. **tangiblement,** *adv.*
Tangibly.
tango [tɑ̃'go], *n.m.* Tango (dance); tango
(colour).
tangon [tɑ̃'gɔ̃], *n.m.* Foresail boom. *Tangon
de spinnaker,* spinnaker boom.

tangue [tɑ̃:g], *n.f.* Slimy sand (used as manure).

tanguer [tɑ̃'ge], *v.i.* (*Naut.*) To pitch; to tango.

tanière [ta'njɛ:r], *n.f.* Den, hole, lair (of beasts).

tanin [ta'nɛ̃], *n.m.* Tannin.

tank [tɑ̃k], *n.m.* (*Mil.*) Tank.

tannage [ta'na:ʒ], *n.m.* Tanning, tannage.

tannant, *a.* (*fem.* **-ante**) Tanning; (*pop.*) tiresome, annoying. *Un homme tannant*, a bore. **tanné**, *a.* (*fem.* **-ée**) Tanned, sunburnt (skin); tan-coloured, tawny.—*n.m.* Tan-colour.—*n.f.* Waste tan, (*fig.*) hiding, thrashing. **tanner**, *v.t.* To tan; (*pop.*) to tease, to annoy, to beat, to give (someone) a hiding. **tannerie**, *n.f.* Tan-yard, tannery. **tanneur**, *n.m.* Tanner. **tannin** [TANIN]. **tannique**, *a.* Tannic.

tant [tɑ̃], *adv.* So much, such; so many; as much, as many, as well as; to such a degree, so; so far; so long, as long, while. *En tant qu'homme*, as a man; *si tant est que je le puisse*, if indeed I can at all; *tant bien que mal*, somehow or other, after a fashion; *tant de fois*, so many times; *tant de monde*, so many people; *tant et plus*, so much and more; *tant il est vrai*, so true is it; *tant le monde est crédule*, such is the credulity of the world; *tant mieux*, so much the better; *tant pis*, so much the worse, too bad; *tant pour vous que pour lui*, as much for your sake as for his; *tant que je vivrai*, as long as I live; *tant qu'il vivra*, as long as he lives; *tant s'en faut*, far from it; *tant s'en faut que*, so far from; *tant soit peu*, ever so little; *tant y a que*, at all events, the fact remains that; *tous tant que nous sommes*, every one of us.

Tantale [tɑ̃'tal], *m.* Tantalus. *Supplice de Tantale*, tortures of Tantalus.

tantale [tɑ̃'tal], *n.m.* (*Metal.*) Tantalum.

tantaliser [tɑ̃tali'ze], *v.t.* To tantalize. **tantalisme**, *n.m.* Tantalism.

tante [tɑ̃:t], *n.f.* Aunt; (*slang*) invert, pansy, pederast. *Ma tante*, (*pop.*) pawn-broker, 'uncle'.

tantet [tɑ̃'tɛ] or (*more usually*) **tantinet**, *n.m.* The least bit, the least little drop, a dash, a wee bit. **tantième**, *a.* and *n.m.* Such a quantity, part, percentage.

tantôt [tɑ̃'to], *adv.* Presently, by and by, anon; soon, early; a little while ago, just now; sometimes. *À tantôt!* good-bye for the present; *il se porte tantôt bien, tantôt mal*, sometimes he is well, sometimes ill; *je finirai cela tantôt*, I shall finish that by and by (or) in the afternoon; *sur le tantôt*, towards the evening.

taon [tɑ̃], *n.m.* Ox-fly, breeze, gadfly, cleg.

tapage [ta'pa:ʒ], *n.m.* Noise, uproar, row, racket, disturbance; (*colloq.*) show, display.

tapageur [tapa'ʒœ:r], *n.m.* (*fem.* **-euse**) Noisy person, blusterer.—*a.* Rackety, boisterous, noisy, loud, blustering; flashy, showy.

tape (1) [tap], *n.f.* Rap, slap, tap, thump. (*fam.*) *Ramasser une tape*, to fail utterly (of a play).

tape (2) [tap], *n.f.* Plug, bung.

tape-à-l'œil [tapa'lœj], *a. inv.* (*fam.*) Flashy, gaudy.—*n.m. C'est du tape-à-l'œil*, it's flashy stuff.

tapé [ta'pe], *a.* (*fem.* **-ée**) Dried (of fruit); painted in a bold style; smart (answer).

tapecu or **tapecul** [tap'ky], *n.m.* (*Naut.*) Jigger; jolting carriage; gig.

tapée [ta'pe], *n.f.* (*pop.*) Lot, heap, swarm, host, oodles.

tapement [tap'mɑ̃], *n.m.* Striking, tapping.

taper [ta'pe], *v.t.* To hit, to slap; to smack, to tap; to plug; (*Paint.,* to paint in a free, bold style; (*slang*) to borrow from, to touch. *Taper une lettre* (*à la machine*), to type a letter.—*v.i.* To hit, to tap, to stamp; to strum; to beat down (of sun). *Ce vin tape à la tête*, this wine is heady; (*fam.*) *elle lui a tapé dans l'œil*, he has fallen for her; *le soleil tape*, the sun is very strong; *ça tape*, it is jolly hot; *taper du pied*, to stamp with one's foot; *taper sur le ventre à quelqu'un*, to treat someone with great familiarity. **se taper**, *v.r.* (*pop.*) *Se taper la cloche*, to have a regular tuck in; *tu peux te taper!* it's no good, don't count on it!

tapette, *n.f.* Tap; wood-hammer with flexible hand to push corks in; engraver's pad; game of wall marbles; (*slang*) pansy. (*pop.*) *Quelle tapette* or *il a une fière tapette*, he is a great chatterbox.

tapeur [ta'pœ:r], *n.m.* (*fem.* **-euse**) Bad pianist; (*slang*) great borrower, cadger.

tapin [ta'pɛ̃], *n.m.* Drum; drummer.

tapinois [tapi'nwa], *En tapinois*, (*adv. phr.*) stealthily, clandestinely, slyly.

tapioca [tapjɔ'ka], *n.m.* Tapioca.

tapir (1) [ta'pi:r], *n.m.* Tapir (animal); (*sch. slang*) pupil taking private lessons.

tapir (2) **(se)** [ta'pi:r], *v.r.* To squat, to crouch, to cower, to lurk.

tapis [ta'pi], *n.m.* Carpet, rug; tapis, cover-cloth (for tables etc.). *Amuser le tapis*, to talk the time away; *être sur le tapis*, to be under discussion; *mettre sur le tapis*, to bring forward; *tapis de laine rase*, short-pile carpet; *tapis de haute laine*, thick-pile, long-pile carpet; *tapis de sol*, ground sheet; *tapis de verdure*, a carpet of greensward; *tapis roulant*, moving band, (*Ind.*) endless belt; *tapis vert*, green baize; gaming-table. **tapis-brosse**, *n.m.* (*pl.* **tapis-brosses**) Door-mat. **tapisser**, *v.t.* To hang with tapestry, to hang; to cover; to line (inside an organ), to plaster (with posters etc.); to deck, to adorn; to paper, to carpet.—*v.i.* To make tapestry. **tapisserie**, *n.f.* Tapestry, hangings; wallpaper; tapestry or fancy needlework; upholstery. *Faire de la tapisserie*, to make tapestry, to do fancy-work; *faire tapisserie*, to be a wallflower (at a ball etc.). **tapissier**, *n.m.* (*fem.* **-ière**) Upholsterer; tapestry-worker. —*n.f.* Spring van; delivery van.

tapon [ta'pɔ̃], *n.m.* (old form of *tampon*). Bundle (of clothes etc.); (*Naut.*) plug.

taponner [tapɔ'ne], *v.t.* To screw up.

tapoter [tapɔ'te], *v.t.* To pat, to tap; to strum.

tapotis [tapɔ'ti], *n.m.* Rattle (of typewriter).

taque [tak], *n.f.* Cast-iron plate.

taquer [ta'ke], *v.t.* (*Print.*) To plane down.

taquet [ta'kɛ], *n.m.* Angle-block; stop (for a door etc.); picket; (*Naut.*) (belaying) cleat; button (of oar).

taquin [ta'kɛ̃], *a.* (*fem.* **-ine**) Teasing, of a teasing disposition.—*n.* Tease, teasing person. **taquiner**, *v.t.* To tease, to plague, to torment. *Taquiner le goujon*, to go (line) fishing. **se taquiner**, *v.r.* To tease one another. **taquinerie,** *n.f.* Teasing; teasing disposition.

taquoir [ta'kwaːr], *n.m.* (*Print.*) Planer.

tarabiscot [tarabis'ko], *n.m.* Groove (in mouldings); moulding plane. **tarabiscoté,** *a.* (*fem.* **-ée**) Finicky, over-elaborate (of style).

tarabuster [tarabys'te], *v.t.* (*colloq.*) To pester, to plague, to bother; to handle roughly.

***tarare!** (1) [ta'raːr], *int.* Pshaw! fiddlesticks!

tarare (2) [ta'raːr], *n.m.* Winnowing-machine.

taratata [tarata'ta], *int.* (*fam.*) Nonsense!

taraud [ta'ro], *n.m.* Screw-cutter. **taraudage,** *n.m.* Tapping (of screws, nuts, etc.). **tarauder,** *v.t.* To tap (screws, nuts, etc.); (*fam.*) to torment, to pester. **taraudeuse,** *n.f.* Tapper.

tarbouch(e) [tar'buʃ], *n.m.* Tarboosh.

tard [taːr], *adv.* Late. *Au plus tard*, at the latest; *il est tard*, it is late; *il se fait tard*, it is getting late; *mieux vaut tard que jamais*, better late than never; *plus tard*, later, afterwards, in after years; *tôt ou tard*, sooner or later; *trop tard*, too late.—*n.m.* Late hour. *Sur le tard*, towards the end of the day, or (*fig.*) of life.

tarder [tar'de], *v.i.* To delay, to put off; to tarry, to loiter, to dally; to be long; (*impers.*) to long. *Il me tarde de le faire*, I long to do it; *il me tarde de parler*, I am most anxious to speak; *il ne tardera pas à venir*, he will soon be here; *tarder à repondre*, to put off replying.

tardif [tar'dif], *a.* (*fem.* **-ive**) Tardy, late; slow, sluggish; backward. *Fruits tardifs*, late fruit. ***tardiflore,** *a.* Late blooming. **tardigrade,** *a.* and *n.m.* Tardigrade. **tardillon** or **tardon,** *n.m.* Last-born lamb, chick, etc.; last child. **tardivement,** *adv.* Tardily, slowly. **tardiveté,** *n.f.* (*Hort.*) Lateness, backwardness.

tare (1) [taːr], *n.f.* Tare.

tare (2) [taːr], *n.f.* Waste, damage; (*fig.*) blemish, defect, imperfection.

taré [ta're], *a.* (*fem.* **-ée**) Damaged, spoiled; depraved, disreputable.

Tarente [ta'rãːt], *f.* Taranto.

tarentelle [tarã'tɛl], *n.f.* Tarantella (Italian dance).

tarentule, *n.f.* Tarantula.

tarer [ta're], *v.t.* To injure, to damage, to spoil; (*Comm.*) to tare. *Tarer une réputation*, to damage a reputation. **se tarer,** *v.r.* To spoil, to deteriorate.

taret [ta'rɛ], *n.m.* Teredo, ship-worm.

targe [tarʒ], *n.f.* Targe, target (shield). **targette,** *n.f.* Flat bolt, slide-bolt.

targuer (se) [tar'ge], *v.r.* To boast, to brag, to plume oneself (*de*).

tarier [ta'rje], *n.m.* (*Orn.*) Whinchat.

tarière [ta'rjɛːr], *n.f.* Auger, borer; terebra.

tarif [ta'rif], *n.m.* Tariff, rate, scale of prices; price-list, list of charges. *Billet à plein, à demi-tarif*, full (or half) fare ticket. **tarifaire,** *a.* Relating to tariffs. **tarifer,** *v.t.* To tariff, to price, to rate. **tarification,** *n.f.* Pricing.

tarin [ta'rɛ̃], *n.m.* Siskin (bird); (*slang*) nose.

tarir [ta'riːr], *v.t.* To dry up; to exhaust.—*v.i.* To dry up; to be exhausted; to cease, to stop, to end. *Ne pas tarir*, (*fig.*) to talk incessantly, never to have done. **se tarir,** *v.r.* To dry up. **tarissable,** *a.* Exhaustible.

tarissement, *n.m.* Running dry, exhausting, drying up.

tarlatane [tarla'tan], *n.f.* Tarlatan (muslin).

taroté [taro'te], *a.* (*fem.* **-ée**) (*of playing cards*): With a grilled or chequered back. **tarots,** *n.m. pl.* Tarots (cards with grey chequered backs).

taroupe [ta'rup], *n.f.* Hair growing between the eyebrows.

tarpéienne [tarpe'jɛn], *a.f.* Tarpeian. *Roche Tarpéienne*, Tarpeian rock.

tarpon [tar'pɔ̃], *n.m.* Tarpon.

Tarquin [tar'kɛ̃], *m.* Tarquinius, Tarquin.

Tarragone [tara'gɔn], *f.* Tarragona.

Tarse (1) [tars], *f.* Tarsus.

tarse (2) [tars], *n.m.* (*Anat.*) Tarsus, (*fam.*) instep. **tarsien,** *a.* (*fem.* **-ienne**) Tarsal. **tarsier,** *n.m.* (*Zool.*) Tarsier.

tartan [tar'tã], *n.m.* Tartan, plaid.

tartane [tar'tan], *n.f.* Tartan (vessel).

tartare [tar'taːr], *a.* Tartar.—*n.m.* Tartar (language); (*Myth.*) Tartarus, hell. *À la tartare*, with cold mustard sauce. *Sauce tartare*, a mayonnaise sauce.—*n.* (**Tartare**) A Tartar or Tatar.

tartareux [tarta'rø], *a.* (*fem.* **-euse**) Tartareous.

Tartarie [tarta'ri] or **Tatarie,** *f.* Tartary.

tartarique [TARTRIQUE].

tartariser [tartari'ze], *v.t.* To tartarize.

tarte [tart], *n.f.* Tart, flan. *C'est sa tarte à la crème*, (*fig.*) it is his one and constant objection. **tartelette,** *n.f.* Tartlet. **tartine,** *n.f.* Slice of bread (with butter, jam, etc.); (*colloq.*) tirade, rigmarole. **tartiner,** *v.t.* To spread with butter, jam, etc.—*v.i.* To ramble (in speech or writing).

tartrate [tar'trat], *n.m.* Tartrate. **tartre,** *n.m.* Tartar (argol); scale (on a boiler etc.). **tartrique,** *a.* Tartaric.

tartufe [tar'tyf], *n.m.* Hypocrite. **tartuferie,** *n.f.* Hypocrisy. **tartufier,** *v.i.* To play the hypocrite.—*v.t.* To hoodwink.

tas [tɑ], *n.m. inv.* Heap, pile; (*fig.*) lot, set (of persons etc.); hand-anvil; building under construction. *Mettre en tas*, to put into a heap or mass; *prendre au tas*, to help oneself to; *tas de fumier*, dunghill, heap of manure; *un tas de filous*, a set of sharpers.

Tasmanie [tasma'ni], *f.* Tasmania.

Tasse [taːs] or **Le Tasse,** *m.* Tasso.

tasse [taːs], *n.f.* Cup. *Tasse à café*, coffee cup; *tasse à thé*, tea-cup; *tasse de thé*, cup of tea. (*fam.*) *La grande tasse*, to be drowned at sea; *boire à la grande tasse*, to be drowned at sea; *boire une tasse*, to swallow some water (while bathing).

tasseau [ta'so], *n.m.* (*pl.* **-eaux**) Batten, cleat.

tassement [tas'mã], *n.m.* Settling, sinking, subsidence, cramming, compressing.

tasser [ta'se], *v.t.* To heap or pile up; to compress, to squeeze, to cram, to pack into a small space.—*v.i.* To grow thick. **se tasser,** *v.r.* To sink, to settle, to subside; (*fam.*) to settle down (of opinions), to huddle together (of persons).

tassette [ta'sɛt], *n.f.* Tasse (thigh-armour).

taste-vin [tastə'vɛ̃], *n.m. inv.* Wine-taster.

tata [ta'ta], *n.f.* Childish for *tante*, auntie. *Faire sa tata* (of a girl), to make a fuss, to play the busybody. *Ta, ta, ta*, (*int. fam.*) (of denegation) Nonsense.

tête-au-pot [tɑto'po], *n.m. inv.* Man who interferes in household affairs.

tâter [tɑ'te], *v.t.* To feel; to try, to taste; to sound, to test. *Tâter le courage de quelqu'un,* to put someone's courage to the test or proof; *tâter le pouls,* to feel the pulse; *tâter le terrain,* to see how the land lies; *tâter le vent,* to hug the wind.—*v.i.* To taste, to try (*de* or *à*). *Tâter de quelque chose,* to taste something; *tâter d'un métier,* to try one's hand at a trade. **se tâter,** *v.r.* To examine oneself; to think something over (before making up one's mind). **tâteur,** *n.m.* (*fem.* **-euse**) Feeler, taster; waverer. **tâte-vin,** *n.m. inv.* Wine-tester (instrument).

tatillon [tati'jɔ̃], *n.m.* (*fem.* **-onne**) Meddler.—*a.* Meddling, niggling, finical. **tatillonnage,** *n.m.* Meddling, niggling. **tatillonner,** *v.i.* To meddle; to fuss over trifles.

tâtonnement [tɑtɔn'mɑ̃], *n.m.* Groping; tentative procedure. **tâtonner,** *v.i.* To feel one's way, to grope; to proceed tentatively. **tâtonneur,** *n.m.* (*fem.* **-euse**) Groper, fumbler; waverer, irresolute person. **à tâtons,** *adv. phr.* Gropingly. *Chercher à tâtons,* to grope for; *marcher* or *aller à tâtons,* to feel one's way.

tatou [ta'tu], *n.m.* Armadillo.

tatouage [ta'twaːʒ], *n.m.* Tattooing; tattoo. **tatouer,** *v.t.* To tattoo. **tatoueur,** *n.m.* Tattooer.

tatouille [ta'tuːj], *n.f.* (*pop.*) Licking, thrashing.

tattersall [tater'sal], *n.m.* Horse fair.

taud [to], *n.m.,* or **taude,** *n.f.* (*Naut.*) Awning. **tauder,** *v.t.* To cover with an awning.

taudion [to'djɔ̃], *n.m.* (*pop.*) Miserable hovel.

taudis [to'di], *n.m.* Hole, hovel, slum.

taule [toːl], *n.f.* (*slang*) Room, house; (*Mil.*) prison.

taupe [toːp], *n.f.* Mole; moleskin; (*fig.*) person lacking in sagacity; (*sch.*) class preparatory to *École Polytechnique;* (*slang*) prostitute; hag. ***taupe-grillon,** *n.m.* (*pl.* **taupes-grillons**) Mole-cricket. **taupier,** *n.m* Mole-catcher. **taupière,** *n.f.* Mole-trap.

taupin [to'pɛ̃], *n.m.* (*Nickname*) Sapper; (*sch.*) student preparing for the Polytechnic School; spring-beetle.

taupinière or **taupinée,** *n.f.* Mole-hill; hillock, knoll.

taure [toːr], *n.f.* Heifer.

taureau, *n.m.* (*pl.* **-eaux**) Bull; (*Astron.*) Taurus. *Cou de taureau,* bull neck; *prendre le taureau par les cornes,* to take the bull by the horns. **taurillon,** *n.m.* Young bull. **tauromachie,** *n.f.* Tauromachy, bull-fighting.

tautochrone [totɔ'krɔn], *a.* Tautochronous, isochronous. **tautogramme,** *n.m.* Poem, every word of which begins with the same letter. **tautologie,** *n.f.* Tautology. **tautologique,** *a.* Tautological, redundant.

taux [to], *n.m.* Price, rate; rate of interest; assessment. *Au taux de . . . ,* at the rate of. . . .

tavaillon [tava'jɔ̃], *n.m.* Sheeting-plank (of roof).

tavaïole [tava'jɔl], *n.f.* Chrisom-cloth.

tavelage [ta'vlaːʒ], *n.m.* Spotting or speckling (on fruit). **taveler,** *v.t. irr.* (*conjugated like* APPELER) To spot, to speckle. **tavelure,** *n.f.* Spots, speckles (on fruit and on animal's coat).

taverne [ta'vɛrn], *n.f.* Tavern, café, restaurant. **tavernier,** *n.m.* (*fem.* **-ière**) Tavern-keeper.

taxateur [taksa'tœːr], *n.m.* Taxer, assessor; (*Law.*) taxing-master.—*a.m.* Taxing. **taxation,** *n.f.* Taxation; fixing of prices; (*Law.*) taxing.

taxe [taks], *n.f.* Tax; charge, duty, rate, taxation; fixing of prices etc.; fixed price, controlled price. **taxer,** *v.t.* To tax; to rate, to fix the price of; to assess; to charge, to accuse (*de*). *On le taxa d'avarice,* they accused him of avarice.

taxi [tak'si], *n.m.* Taxi (cab). *Appeler un taxi,* to call a taxi; *chauffeur de taxi,* taxi-driver.

taxidermie [taksidɛr'mi], *n.f.* Taxidermy. **taxidermique,** *a.* Taxidermal. **taxidermiste,** *n.m.* Taxidermist.

taximètre [taksi'mɛtr], *n.m.* Taximeter (in a cab etc.).

taxiphone [taksi'fɔn], *n.m.* Public telephone (box).

taxis [tak'siːs], *n.m.* (*Surg.*) Taxis.

taxologie [taksɔlɔ'ʒi], **taxonomie,** or **taxinomie,** *n.f.* Taxonomy. **taxonomique,** *a.* Taxonomical. **taxonomiste,** *n.m.* Taxonomist.

tayaut [TAÏAUT].

Tchécoslovaquie [tʃekɔslɔva'ki], *f.* Czechoslovakia. **tchèque,** *n.m.* Czech (language). —*a.* Czech.—*n.* (**Tchèque**) Czech.

te [tə, t], *pron. obj.* [TU].

té [te], *n.m.* Anything in the shape of a T, T-square; cross-bar; (*Fort.*) mines having the shape of a T.

technicien [tɛkni'sjɛ̃], *n.m.* (*fem.* **-ienne**) Technician. **technicité,** *n.f.* Technicality. **technique,** *a.* Technical.—*n.f.* Technique; technics. **techniquement,** *adv.* Technically. **technocratie,** *n.f.* Technocracy. **technographie,** *n.f.* Technography. **technographique,** *a.* Technographic. **technologie,** *n.f.* Technology. **technologique,** *a.* Technological. **technologue,** *n.m.* Technologist.

teck or **tek** [tɛk], *n.m.* Teak, teak-wood.

tectologie [tɛktɔlɔ'ʒi], *n.f.* Tectology. **tectonique,** *a.* Tectonic.—*n.f.* Tectonics. **tectrices,** *a.f.* and *n.f.* (*usu. in pl.*) Tectrices (wing and tail feathers).

tégument [tegy'mɑ̃], *n.m.* Tegument. **tégumentaire,** *a.* Tegumentary.

Téhéran [tee'rɑ̃], *m.* Tehran.

teigne [tɛɲ], *n.f.* Tinea (moth); tinea (skin-disease, such as ringworm, scald-head, etc.); corn-moth (in wheat); (*Vet.*) thrush, (*fam.*) a pest of a child, a shrew. **teigneux,** *a.* (*fem.* **-euse**) Scurvy.—*n.* Scurfy person.

teillage [tɛ'jaːʒ] or **tillage,** *n.m.* Stripping (of hemp etc.), scutching. **teille** or **tille,** *n.f.* Hemp-herb. **teiller,** or **tiller,** *v.t.* To strip, to scutch (hemp etc.). ***teilleur** or **tilleur,** *n.m.* (*fem.* **-euse**) Scutcher.—*n.f.* Scutching machine.

teindre [tɛ̃ːdr], *v.t. irr.* (*conjug. like* CRAINDRE) To dye, to tinge, to stain, to colour; to tincture; to give a smattering (*de*). **teint,** *n.m.* Dye, colour; complexion; hue. *Étoffe bon teint* or *grand teint,* fast colour material; *un Conservateur bon teint,* a staunch Conservative, a true blue Tory; *un teint pâle,* a pale complexion. **teinte,** *n.f.* Tint, colour, shade, hue; (*fig.*) tincture, smack, touch. *Demi-teinte* (*pl. demi-teintes*), mezzotint. **teinter,** *v.t.* To tint; to give a colour to. *Teinter légèrement*, to tinge. **teinture,** *n.f.* Dye; dyeing; colour, hue; (*Pharm.*) tincture; (*fig.*) smattering. *Une vague teinture d'allemand*, a smattering of German. *Teinture d'iode*, tincture of iodine. **teinturerie,** *n.f.* Dyeing; dye-works. **teinturier,** *n.m.* (*fem.* **-ière**) Dyer.—*a.* Dyeing (industry etc.).

tek [TECK].

tel [tɛl], *a.* (*fem.* **telle**) Such; like, similar. *J'irai dans telle ville à telle époque*, I shall go to such and such a town at such and such a time; *les hommes tels qu'ils sont*, men as they are; *telle ou telle chose*, such and such a thing; *tel maître, tel valet*, like master, like man; *tel père, tel fils*, like father, like son; *tel que*, such as, just as; *tel quel*, such as it is; *un tel homme*, such a man.—*pron. indef.* Such a one. *M. un tel*, Mr So-and-so; *tel est pris qui croyait prendre*, it is a case of the biter bit.

télécommande [telekɔ'mã:d], *n.f.* Remote control. **télécommander,** *v.t.* To operate by remote control.

télécommunications [telekɔmynika'sjɔ̃], *n.f. pl.* Telecommunications.

télégramme [tele'gram], *n.m.* Telegram. **télégraphe,** *n.m.* Telegraph. **télégraphie,** *n.f.* Telegraphy. *Télégraphie sans fil*, wireless telegraphy. **télégraphier,** *v.t., v.i.* To telegraph; to wire, to cable. **télégraphique,** *a.* Telegraphic. **télégraphiste,** *a.* and *n.* Telegraphist.

téléguidage [telegi'da:ʒ], *n.m.* Radio-control. **téléguidé,** *a.* (*fem.* **-ée**) Guided. *Engin téléguidé*, guided missile. **téléguider,** *v.t.* To radio-control.

téléimprimeur [teleɛ̃pri'mœ:r], *n.m.* Teleprinter.

Télémaque [tele'mak], *m.* Telemachus.

télémètre [tele'metr], *n.m.* Telemeter; rangefinder. **téléologie,** *n.f.* Teleology.

télépathie, *n.f.* Telepathy. **télépathique,** *a.* Telepathic.

téléphérique [telefe'rik], *a.* and *n.m.* Teleferic.

téléphone, *n.m.* Telephone. *Un coup de téléphone*, a telephone call. **téléphoner,** *v.i., v.t.* To telephone, to ring up. *Téléphoner à quelqu'un*, to ring someone up; *téléphoner une nouvelle*, to telephone a piece of news. **téléphonie,** *n.f.* Telephony. **téléphonique,** *a.* *Cabine téléphonique*, call-box. **téléphoniste,** *n.* Telephone operator.

téléphotographie [telefɔtɔgra'fi], *n.f.* Telephotography, phototelegraphy.

télescope [telɛs'kɔp], *n.m.* Telescope. **télescoper,** *v.t.* To telescope (of trains etc.). **se télescoper,** *v.r.* To telescope (into each other). **télescopique,** *a.* Telescopic.

téléscripteur, *n.m.* [TÉLÉIMPRIMEUR].

téléspectateur, *n.m.* (*fem.* **-trice**) Televiewer.

télévisé [televi'ze], *a.* (*fem.* **-ée**) Televised. **téléviser,** *v.t.* To televise. **téléviseur,** *n.m.* Television (receiving-)set. **télévision,** *n.f.* Television. *Appareil de télévision*, television set; *émission de télévision*, television broadcast.

tellement [tɛl'mã], *adv.* So, in such a manner; so much, so far. *Tellement que*, so that; *tellement quellement*, indifferently, so-so.

tellière [tɛl'ljɛ:r], *n.m.* and *a. inv.* A size of paper about 44 cm. by 34 cm. (17½ in. by 13½ in.), foolscap.

tellure [tɛl'ly:r], *n.m.* (*Chem.*) Tellurium. **tellurique,** *a.* Telluric.

téméraire [teme'rɛ:r], *a.* Rash, reckless, daring, foolhardy.—*n.* Reckless person, daredevil. **témérairement,** *adv.* Rashly, foolhardily, recklessly. **témérité,** *n.f.* Temerity.

témoignage [temwa'ɲa:ʒ], *n.m.* Testimony, evidence, witness; testimonial, certificate, character; (*fig.*) token, mark, proof; stick (or any object) passed from hand to hand in relay races. *Appeler en témoignage*, to call to witness; *en témoignage de quoi*, in witness whereof; *rendre témoignage à la vérité de*, to testify to the truth of. **témoigner,** *v.t.* To testify, to bear witness to; to show, to prove, to evince, to be the sign of.—*v.i.* To testify, to bear witness, to give evidence (*de*).

témoin, *n.m.* Witness, evidence, proof, mark; second (in duels); (*pl.*) boundary marks. *Être témoin de*, to witness; *prendre à témoin*, to call to witness; *témoin à charge*, witness for the prosecution; *témoin à décharge*, witness for the defence; *témoin auriculaire*, ear-witness; *témoin oculaire*, eye witness.

tempe [tã:p], *n.f.* (*Anat.* and *Tex.*) Temple.

tempérament [tãpera'mã], *n.m.* Constitution, temperament; temper, character; (*fig.*) moderation, middle-course, compromise. *Par tempérament*, constitutionally, naturally; *tempérament nerveux*, nervous disposition. *À tempérament*, by instalments.

tempérance [tãpe'rã:s], *n.f.* Temperance. **tempérant,** *a.* (*fem.* **-ante**) Temperate, sober; (*Med.*) sedative.—*n.* Temperate person. **température,** *n.f.* Temperature; (*Med.*) *Avoir de la température*, to have a (high) temperature. **tempéré,** *a.* (*fem.* **-ée**) Temperate (of climate); limited, constitutional (of governments); tempered, restrained, sober (of style).—*n.m.* Temperate climate; temperate style.

tempérer [tãpe're], *v.t. irr.* (*conjugated like* ACCÉLÉRER) To temper, to moderate, to regulate, to allay, to assuage, to check. **se tempérer,** *v.r.* To become temperate or mild (of the weather).

tempête [tã'pe:t], *n.f.* Storm, tempest. *Essuyer une tempête*, to weather a storm; *tempête de neige*, blizzard. **tempêter,** *v.i.* To storm, to bluster, to fume. **tempétueusement,** *adv.* Tempestuously, violently; **tempétueux,** *a.* (*fem.* **-euse**) Tempestuous, boisterous, stormy. *Mer tempétueuse*, stormy sea.

temple [tã:pl], *n.m.* Temple; French Protestant church; (*poet.*) fane. **templier,** *n.m.* Knight-Templar.

tempo [tem'po], *n.m.* (*Mus.*) Tempo.

temporaire [tãpɔ'rɛ:r], *a.* Temporary. **temporairement,** *adv.* Temporarily, provisionally.

temporal [tãpɔ'ral], *a.* (*fem.* **-ale**, *pl.* **-aux**) (*Anat.*) Temporal.—*n.m.* Temporal bone.

temporel [tãpɔ'rɛl], *a.* (*fem.* **-elle**) Temporal. —*n.m.* Temporal power; temporalities, revenue (of a benefice).

temporisateur [tãpɔriza'tœ:r], *a.* (*fem.* **-trice**)

Procrastinating, temporizing.—*n.* Temporizer; procrastinator. **temporisation**, *n.f.* Temporizing, procrastination. **temporiser**, *v.i.* To temporize, to delay.

temporiseur [TEMPORISATEUR].

temps [tɑ̃], *n.m. inv.* Time, while, period, term, age, epoch; hour; moment, occasion; season; weather; (*Gram.*) tense; (*Mus.*) measure. *À temps*, in time; *au temps! (Mil.)* as you were; *au temps jadis, autres temps autres mœurs*, manners change with the times; *avec le temps*, in course of time; *avoir bien le temps*, to have plenty of time, *combien de temps?* how long? *dans le temps*, formerly, of yore; *de temps en temps*, from time to time; *de tout temps*, always, ever; *du temps d'Auguste*, in the time of Augustus; *du temps que la reine Berthe filait*, when the world was young; *en même temps*, at the same time; *en moins de temps que*, in less time than; *en temps et lieu*, in proper time and place; *en temps utile*, in due course; *en tout temps* at any time; *entre temps*, meanwhile; *gros temps*, (*Naut.*) stormy weather; *il a fait son temps*, he has had his day, he has served his time; *il fait beau temps*, it is fine weather; *il est grand temps de partir*, it's high time to start off; *le bon vieux temps*, the good old days; *le temps perdu ne se retrouve point*, lost time is never found again; *mesure à trois temps*, (*Mus.*) three part time; *moteur à quatre temps*, four-stroke engine; *parler de la pluie et du beau temps*, to indulge in idle conversation; *par le temps qui court*, nowadays, as times go; *par le temps qu'il fait*, in weather like this; *passer son temps à étudier*, to spend one's time in study; *peu de temps après*, a little later; *prendre bien son temps*, to choose one's time well; *prendre le temps comme il vient*, to take things easily; *quel temps fait-il?* what sort of weather is it? *s'accommoder au temps*, to conform to the times; *se donner du bon temps*, to take it easy, to enjoy oneself; *temps moyen*, mean time; *tout n'a qu'un temps*, everything comes to an end.

tenable [tə'nabl], *a.* Tenable; habitable. *Ce n'est pas tenable*, it is unbearable.

tenace [tə'nas], *a.* Tenacious, adhesive, sticky.

ténacité [tenasi'te], *n.f.* Tenacity, toughness, retentiveness (of memory).

tenaille [tə'nɑːj], *n.f.* (*usu. in pl.*) Pincers, nippers, pliers; (*Fort.*) tenail. *Tenailles de forge*, tongs. **tenaillement**, *n.m.* Torture by pincers. **tenailler**, *v.t.* To torture with red-hot pincers; (*fig.*) to torture.

tenancier [tənɑ̃'sje], *n.m.* (*fem.* -ière) Holder, occupier; tenant-farmer, tenant; keeper (of ill-famed place). *Franc tenancier*, freeholder.

tenant [tə'nɑ̃], *a.* (*fem.* -ante) *Séance tenante*, during the sitting; forthwith, then and there. —*n.m.* Holder (at a tournament); (*fig.*) champion, defender. *Les tenants et les aboutissants*, the adjacent lands, houses, etc.; (*fig.*) the particulars, the ins and outs (of). *D'un seul tenant*, all of a piece, lying together.

tendance [tɑ̃'dɑ̃ːs], *n.f.* Tendency; leaning, bent, inclination. **tendancieux**, *a.* (*fem.* -ieuse) Tendentious; insinuating, suggestive. **tendant**, *a.* (*fem.* -ante) Tending.

tendelet [tɑ̃'dlɛ], *n.m.* Awning, canopy (on a vessel).

tender [tɑ̃'dɛːr], *n.m.* (*Rail.*) Tender.

tendeur [tɑ̃'dœːr], *n.m.* (*fem.* -euse) Spreader, layer, setter (of snares); stretcher, hanger.— *n.m.* Wire-strainer; tightener.

tendineux [tɑ̃di'nø], *a.* (*fem.* -euse) Tendinous. *Viande tendineuse*, stringy meat.

tendoir [tɑ̃'dwaːr], *n.m.* Clothes-line.

tendon [tɑ̃'dɔ̃], *n.m.* Tendon, sinew. *Tendon d'Achille*, Achilles tendon; *tendon du jarret*, hamstring.

tendre (1) [tɑ̃ːdr], *a.* Tender, soft; delicate, sensitive; fond, affectionate, loving; affecting, moving; early, young, new. *Avoir le cœur tendre*, to be tender-hearted; *couleur tendre*, delicate colour; *du pain tendre*, new bread.— *n.m.* *Tenderness, affection, liking; love.

tendre (2) [tɑ̃ːdr], *v.t.* To stretch, to strain; to bend (a bow etc.); to spread, to lay, to set; to hold out; to pitch (tents); to hang (tapestry etc.). *Il me tendit la main*, he held out his hand to me; *tendre la joue*, to offer one's cheek; *tendre l'oreille*, to lend an ear.—*v.i.* To lead; to tend, to conduce. **se tendre**, *v.r.* To become taut, (of relations) strained.

tendrement [tɑ̃drə'mɑ̃], *adv.* Tenderly, affectionately. **tendresse**, *n.f.* Tenderness, fondness; (*pl.*) endearments. **tendret**, *a.* (*fem.* -ette) Rather tender. **tendreté**, *n.f.* Tenderness (of food).

tendron [tɑ̃'drɔ̃], *n.m.* Shoot (of plants); (*pl.*) gristle of veal; (*colloq.*) young lass.

tendu [tɑ̃'dy], *a.* (*fem.* -ue) Stretched, held out; tight, taut, tense; strained, stiff. *Situation tendue*, a strained or delicate situation; *style tendu*, affected, stilted style.

ténèbres [te'nɛbr], *n.f.* (used only in pl.) Darkness, night, gloom; (*R.-C. Ch.*) tenebrae. **ténébreusement**, *adv.* Darkly, gloomily; secretly. **ténébreux**, *a.* (*fem.* -euse) Dark, gloomy, overcast; obscure, mysterious, deep. **ténébrion** [tenebri'ɔ̃], *n.m.* Meal-worm.

ténesme [te'nɛsm], *n.m.* (*Med.*) Tenesmus.

teneur (1) [tə'nœːr], *n.f.* Tenor, terms, text; purport; amount, percentage (*de*); grade (of ore).

teneur (2) [tə'nœːr], *n.m.* (*fem.* -euse) Holder. *Teneur de livres*, book-keeper.

tenez! *int.* [TIENS].

ténia or **tænia** [te'nja], *n.m.* Tape-worm.

tenir [tə'niːr], *v.t. irr.* (*pres.p.* **tenant**, *p.p.* **tenu**) To hold, to have hold of; to have, to possess, to keep; to direct; to take hold of, to seize; to occupy, to take up; to keep, to keep to, to pursue; to follow; to hold back, to keep in, to rein in, to manage; to retain; to hold (*de*), to owe; to keep up; to perform, to do; to look upon, to consider, to deem; to maintain; to side with. *Cessez de tenir ce langage*, stop speaking in that way; *faire tenir des lettres à quelqu'un*, to send letters to someone; *il m'a tenu lieu de père*, he has been like a father to me; *je le tiens pour honnête homme*, I look upon him as an honest man; *je tiendrai compte de cela*, I shall take that into consideration; *je tiens cela de bonne source*, I have it on the best authority; *qu'est-ce qui le tient?* what has come over him? *tenir la caisse*, to have charge of the cash; *tenir la campagne*, (*Mil.*) to keep the field; *tenir un cheval*, to control a horse; *tenir la tête droite*, to hold one's head up; *tenir maison*, to keep house; *tenir quelqu'un à distance*, to keep someone at a distance; *tenir sa chambre*, to be confined to one's room; *tenir sa droite*, to keep to the right; *tenir sa parole*, to keep one's word; *tenir son homme*, to have one's man (at the point required); *tenir table ouverte*, to keep open house; *tenir tête à*, to resist; *tenir un café*, to run a café; *vous tenez trop de place*, you take up too much room.—*v.i.* To hold, to hold fast, to adhere, to stick; to hold together; to cling, to be wedded (*à*); to value, to prize (*à*); to be attached, connected, or related (*à*); to be contiguous; to depend, to proceed, to result, to take its rise (*de*); to be held (of fairs, markets, assemblies, etc.); to take after, to be akin, to be of the nature; to savour, to smack; to persist, to remain; to hold good, to subsist; to withstand, to resist; to be desirous, to be anxious (*à*); (*Naut.*) to sail close to the wind. *À quoi cela tient-il?* what is it owing to? *cela lui tient au cœur*, he thinks of nothing else; *ce clou ne tient pas*, this nail does not hold; *en tenir*, to be caught, to be hit, to be in for it, to be fuddled; *en tenir pour*, to be fond of, to be in love with; *il ne tient pas à moi qu'elle ne vienne pas*, it is not my fault that she does not come; *il ne tient qu'à vous de*, it only depends on you to; *il n'y a pas d'amitié qui tienne*, friendship has nothing to do with the question; *il tient à le faire*, he is anxious to do it; *il tient de son père*, he takes after his father; *il tient pour le communisme*, he is all for communism; *je n'y tiens pas*, I am not particular about it; *je n'y tiens plus*, I cannot stand it any longer; *la vie ne tient qu'à un fil*, life hangs by a thread; *qu'à cela ne tienne*, never mind about that, don't let that be an objection; *s'il ne tient qu'à cela*, if that is all; *tenir bon*, to hold out, to stick to it; *tiens! c'est vous?* hullo! is that you? *se tenir*, *v.r.* To hold fast, to remain, to stand; to be held; to hold each other, to cling, to adhere, to stick; to think oneself, to consider oneself; to contain oneself, to refrain, to be content, to be satisfied. *Tenez-vous!* or *tenez ferme!* Hold tight! (*Naut.*) avast! *Je m'en tiens à votre avis*, I stick to your advice; *je m'y tiens*, stop there, I stand (at cards); *ne pas savoir à quoi s'en tenir*, not to know what to believe; *se le tenir pour dit*, (*fam.*) to take it as read; *s'en tenir à*, to abide by, to rest content with, to think; *se tenir à genoux*, to remain on one's knees; *se tenir debout*, to stand; *se tenir les bras croisés* [CROISÉ]; *se tenir mal à cheval*, to have a poor seat (on horseback); *se tenir sur ses gardes*, to be on one's guard.

tennis [tɛ'nis], *n.m.* Lawn-tennis; (*Court de*) *tennis*, tennis-court; *tennis de table*, table-tennis. **tennisman,** *n.m.* (*pl.* -men) Tennis player.

tenon [tə'nɔ̃], *n.m.* Tenon; bolt (of fire-arms); nut (of an anchor).

ténor [te'nɔːr], *n.m.* (*Mus.*) Tenor.

ténotomie [tenɔtɔ'mi], *n.f.* (*Surg.*) Tenotomy.

tenseur [tɑ̃'sœːr], *a.* and *n.m.* Tensor.

tensif [tɑ̃'sif], *a.* (*fem.* -ive) (*Path.*) Tensive.

tension [tɑ̃'sjɔ̃], *n.f.* Tension, strain, straining; intensity, tenseness; (*Elec.*) voltage. (*Elec.*) *Chute de tension*, potential drop; *fil sous tension*, live wire; *haute tension*, high voltage. *Tension artérielle*, blood pressure; *tension d'esprit*, intense strain on the mind; (*Phys.*) *tension superficielle*, surface tension.

tentaculaire [tɑ̃taky'lɛːr], *a.* Tentacular. **tentacule,** *n.m.* Tentacle, feeler.

tentant [tɑ̃'tɑ̃], *a.* (*fem.* -ante) Tempting, enticing, alluring. **tentateur,** *n.m.* (*fem.* -trice) Tempter, temptress. *Le Tentateur*, the Devil.—*a.* Tempting.

tentatif [tɑ̃ta'tif], *a.* (*fem.* **tentative** (1)) Tentative.

tentation [tɑ̃ta'sjɔ̃], *n.f.* Temptation. *Succomber à la tentation*, to yield to temptation.

tentative (2), *n.f.* Attempt, trial, endeavour.

tente (1) [tɑ̃ːt], *n.f.* Tent, pavilion; (*Naut.*) awning. *Coucher sous la tente*, to sleep under canvas; *dresser une tente*, to pitch a tent; *se retirer sous sa tente*, to sulk in one's tent (ref. to Achilles).

tente (2) [tɑ̃ːt], *n.f.* (*Surg.*) Tent.

tenter [tɑ̃'te], *v.t.* To attempt, to try, to endeavour; to tempt; to put a tent or awning over.

tenture [tɑ̃'tyːr], *n.f.* Hangings, tapestry; coloured wall-paper etc.; paper-hanging.

tenu [tə'ny], *a.* (*fem.* **tenue** (1)) Kept; obliged. *Un jardin bien tenu*, a well-kept garden; *être tenu à la discrétion*, to be bound to secrecy; *tenu de payer*, obliged to pay.

ténu [te'ny], *a.* (*fem.* **ténue**) Tenuous, thin, slender.

tenue (2) [tə'ny], *n.f.* Holding (of assemblies etc.); session; attitude (of a person); behaviour, deportment, carriage, bearing; good behaviour, good manners; dress, appearance; seat (on horseback); steadiness; keeping (of books); holding (of the pen); (*Mus.*) holding-note; (*Naut.*) anchor-hold. *Grande tenue*, (*Mil.*) full dress; *petite tenue*, undress; *tenue de campagne*, battle-dress; *tenue d'exercice*, drill uniform; (*Motor.*) *tenue de route*, road-holding quality (of a car); *tenue des livres*, book-keeping; *tout d'une tenue*, all of a piece, uninterrupted, contiguous.

ténuifolié [tenɥifɔ'lje], *a.* (*fem.* -iée) (*Bot.*) Tenuifolious.

ténuité [tenɥi'te], *n.f.* Tenuity, tenuousness, thinness; (*fig.*) insignificance.

tenure [tə'nyːr], *n.f.* Tenure.

téorbe or **théorbe** [te'ɔrb], *n.m.* Theorbo.

ter [tɛːr], *adv.* Thrice, three times; for the third time.

tératologie [teratɔlɔ'ʒi], *n.f.* Teratology (natural history of monsters). **tératologique,** *a.* Teratological.

tercet [tɛr'sɛ], *n.m.* (*Pros.*) Tercet, triplet.

térébenthine [terebɑ̃'tin], *n.f.* Turpentine.

térébinthe [tere'bɛ̃ːt], *n.m.* Turpentine-tree, terebinth.

térébrant [tere'brɑ̃], *a.* (*fem.* -ante) Terebrant, boring (of insects); acute (of pain).—*n.m.* Terebrant. **térébration,** *n.f.* Terebration, boring.

Térence [te'rɑ̃ːs], *m.* Terence.

tergiversateur [tɛrʒiversa'tœːr], *n.m.* (*fem.* -trice) Tergiversator, shuffler. **tergiversation,** *n.f.* Tergiversation, evasion, shuffling.

tergiverser, *v.i.* To tergiversate, to practise evasion, to beat about the bush.

terme [tɛrm], *n.m.* Term; termination, end; bound, limit, boundary; time, appointed time; three months, a quarter; quarter's rent; word, expression; (*pl.*) state, conditions, wording, terms. *À court* or *long terme*, short- or long-dated (bills), short- or long-term (agreement etc.); *approcher de son terme*, to draw to a close; *aux termes de l'art. 16 du Pacte*, by the terms of article XVI of the Covenant; *avant terme*, before one's time, prematurely, untimely; *dans les meilleurs termes avec*, on the best of terms with; *ménager* or *mesurer ses termes*, to moderate one's expressions; *mener à bon terme*, to bring to a satisfactory conclusion; *mettre un terme à*, to put an end to; *opérations à terme*, business for the account, forward deals (*St. Exch.*); *payer son terme*, to pay one's rent; *qui a terme ne doit rien*, no one need pay before a debt is due; *termes techniques*, technical terms; *toucher à son terme*, to be near one's end (death).

terminaison [tɛrminɛ′zɔ̃], *n.f.* Termination, ending. **terminal,** *a.* (*fem.* **-ale,** *pl.* **-aux**) (*Bot.*) Terminal. **terminatif,** *a.* (*fem.* **-ive**) (*Gram.*) Terminative.

terminer [tɛrmi′ne], *v.t.* To bound, to limit; to put an end to, to terminate, to conclude, to bring to a close, to finish. **se terminer,** *v.r.* To come to an end, to terminate; to be bounded; to conclude, to draw to a close.

terminologie, *n.f.* Terminology. **terminologique,** *a.* Terminological.

terminus [tɛrmi′nys], *n.m.* Terminus (of railway).—*a. inv. La gare terminus*, the terminus.

termite [tɛr′mit], *n.m.* Termite (white ant).

ternaire [tɛr′nɛːr], *a.* Ternary.

terne (1) [tɛrn], *a.* Dull, dim; wan; lustreless; tame, spiritless.

terne (2) [tɛrn], *n.m.* Tern (in a lottery); two threes (at dice).

terné [tɛr′ne], *a.* (*fem.* **-ée**) (*Bot.*) Ternate.

ternir [tɛr′niːr], *v.t.* To dull, to deaden; to sully, to tarnish, to stain. *Ternir sa gloire*, to tarnish one's glory. **se ternir,** *v.r.* To tarnish, to grow dull; to be sullied; to fade (of colours). **ternissure,** *n.f.* Tarnishing, fading; blemish, stain.

terrage [tɛ′raːʒ], *n.m.* Claying (of sugar); tithe.

terrain [tɛ′rɛ̃], *n.m.* Piece of ground; ground, soil, earth; (*Geol.*) formation; ground-plot, position, site; field, course. *Aller sur le terrain*, to fight a duel; *céder le terrain*, to yield ground, to give way; *disputer le terrain*, to dispute every inch of the ground; *être sur son terrain*, to be in one's element, to be on familiar ground; *gagner du terrain*, to gain ground; *ménager le terrain*, to make the most of the space available; (*fig.*) to act cautiously; *sur le terrain*, on the field; *tâter le terrain*, to feel one's way, to see how the land lies; *terrain à bâtir*, building-site or plot, (*Am.*) lot; *terrain de jeux* or *de sports*, playing-field; *terrain vague*, waste ground.

terral [tɛ′ral], *n.m.* (*Naut.*) Land wind. **terraqué,** *a.* (*fem.* **-ée**) Terraqueous.

terrassant [tɛra′sɑ̃], *a.* (*fem.* **-ante**) Crushing (news etc.). **terrasse,** *n.f.* Terrace; flat roof, balcony; earthwork; (*Paint.*) foreground. **terrassement,** *n.m.* Earthwork, embankment; ballasting, banking. **terrasser,** *v.t.* To fill in with earth-work, to embank; to throw to the ground, to fell, to knock down; to beat, to vanquish; to confound, to nonplus, to dismay, to crush. **terrassier,** *n.m.* Digger, excavator, navvy; earthwork contractor.

terre [tɛːr], *n.f.* Earth, the world; land, shore;

ground, soil; loam, clay, etc.; dominion, territory; grounds, estate, property; (*C*) farm. *Armée de terre* [ARMÉE]; *à terre*, ashore, on land, to the ground, on the floor; *cultiver la terre*, to till the ground; *entre deux terres*, a little above the level of the ground; *être sur terre*, to be alive, to exist; *les biens de la terre*, the fruits of the earth; *mettre à terre*, to put down; *mettre en terre*, to bury; *mettre pied à terre*, to alight; *mettre quelqu'un à terre*, to knock someone down; *par terre*, on the ground, on the floor, by land; *pipe de* or *en terre*, clay pipe; *porter en terre*, to inter; *prendre terre*, to go ashore, to land; *qui terre a, guerre a*, much coin much care; *remuer ciel et terre*, to move heaven and earth, to make great efforts; *se coucher à terre*, to lie flat on the ground; *terre à potier*, potter's earth; *terre à terre*, commonplace, vulgar, of the earth, earthy, down to earth; *terre cuite*, terra-cotta; *terre ferme*, dry land, mainland; *terre sainte*, consecrated ground; *tomber à terre*, to fall to the ground (from a height); *tomber par terre*, to fall down (from a standing position); *tremblement de terre*, earthquake; *vaisselle de terre*, earthenware; *ventre à terre*, at full gallop, (*fam.*) flat out; *vivre de ses terres*, to live on the income of one's property; *vivre sur ses terres*, to live on one's property. **terreau,** *n.m.* (Vegetable) mould; compost.

Terre-de-Feu [tɛrdə′fø], **la,** *f.* Tierra del Fuego.

Terre-Neuve [tɛr′nœːv], *f.* Newfoundland.—*n.m. inv.* Newfoundland dog. **terre-neuvier,** *n.m.* (*pl.* **terre-neuviers**) or **terre-neuvien** (*fem.* **-ienne,** *pl.* **terre-neuviens**) or (*dial.*) **terre-neuvas,** *n.m. inv.* Newfoundland fisherman; Newfoundland trader (vessel); Newfoundland dog; Newfoundlander.

terre-noix [tɛr′nwa], *n.f. inv.* Pig-nut; earthnut. **terre-plein,** *n.m.* (*pl.* **terre-pleins**) (*Fort.*) Terreplein; platform; raised strip (planted with trees) in a street.

terrer [tɛ′re], *v.t.* To earth up (a tree etc.), to spread mould over; to clay (sugar), to full (cloth etc.).—*v.i.* To burrow. **se terrer,** *v.r.* To go to ground; to burrow; to dig oneself in.

Terre-Sainte [tɛr′sɛ̃t], **la,** *f.* The Holy Land.

terrestre [tɛ′rɛstr], *a.* Terrestrial, earthly.

terrette [tɛ′rɛt], *n.f.* Ground-ivy.

terreur [tɛ′rœːr], *n.f.* Terror, fright; awe, dread.

terreux ,[tɛ′rø], *a.* (*fem.* **-euse**) Terreous, earthy; dirty; dull (of colours); unhealthy, ashen (of the face).

terrible [tɛ′ribl], *a.* Terrible, dreadful, awful; unmanageable (of children). **terriblement,** *adv.* Terribly; (*colloq.*) with a vengeance.

terrien [tɛ′rjɛ̃], *n.* and *a.* (*fem.* **-ienne**) Landowner, landed proprietor; (*Naut.*) land-lubber.

terrier (1) [tɛ′rje], *n.m.* Burrow, hole; earth (of fox); terrier (dog).

*terrier (2) [tɛ′rje], a.m. Pertaining to lands. *Papier terrier*, court-roll, terrier.

terrifiant [tɛri′fjɑ̃], *a.* (*fem.* **-iante**) Terrifying. **terrifier,** *v.t.* To terrify, to dismay.

terrine [tɛ′rin], *n.f.* Earthen pan, dish; terrine, potted-meat container; potted meat.

terrinée [tɛri′ne], *n.f.* Panful, terrineful, potful.

terrir [tɛ′riːr], *v.i.* To come ashore, to lay

eggs in sand (of the turtle etc.); (*Naut.*) to approach land.

territoire [tɛri'twaːr], *n.m.* Territory, area of jurisdiction etc. **territorial,** *a.* (*fem.* -iale, *pl.* -iaux) Territorial.—*n.m.* Territorial soldier.—*n.f.* Territorial army. **territorialement,** *adv.* Territorially. **territorialité,** *n.f.* Territoriality. **terroir,** *n.m.* Soil, ground. *Goût de terroir,* raciness (of style), native tang (of wine); *sentir le terroir,* to smack of the soil.

terroriser [terɔri'ze], *v.t.* To terrorize. **terrorisme,** *n.m.* Terrorism. **terroriste,** *n.m.* Terrorist.

tertiaire [tɛr'sjɛːr], *a.* Tertiary.

tertio [tɛr'sjo], *adv.* Thirdly.

tertre [tɛrtr], *n.m.* Knoll, hillock. *Tertre artificiel,* mound; *tertre de départ,* (*Golf*) teeing ground.

tes [te], *a.poss.pl.* Thy [TON (1)].

tesselle [tɛ'sɛl], *n.f.* Tessera. **tessellé,** *a.* (*fem.* -ée) Tessellated.

tesson [te'sɔ̃], *n.m.* Potsherd, fragment of broken glass etc.

test [tɛst], *n.m.* Shell; trial, test.

testacé [testa'se], *a.* (*fem.* -ée) Testaceous.—*n.m.* Testacean.

testament [testa'mɑ̃], *n.m.* Will, last will and testament; testament. *Faire son testament,* to draw up one's will; *l'Ancien Testament,* the Old Testament; *le Nouveau Testament,* the New Testament. **testamentaire,** *a.* Testamentary. **testateur,** *n.m.* (*fem.* -trice) Testator, testatrix. **tester,** *v.i.* To make one's will.—*v.t.* To test.

testiculaire [testiky'lɛːr], *a.* Testicular. **testicule,** *n.m.* Testicle.

testif [tɛs'tif], *n.m.* Camel's hair.

testimonial [testimɔ'njal], *a.* (*fem.* -iale, *pl.* -iaux) Testifying, testimonial. *Preuve testimoniale,* oral evidence.

têt [TEST].

tétanie [teta'ni], *n.f.* Tetany. **tétanique,** *a.* Tetanic. **tétaniser,** *v.t.* To tetanize. **tétanos,** *n.m.* Tetanus (lock-jaw).

têtard [te'taːr], *n.m.* Tadpole; pollard (tree); pole-socket (in carriages); bull-head, miller's thumb.

tétasses [te'tas], *n.f. pl.* (*vulg.*) Flabby, pendulous breasts.

tête [tɛːt], *n.f.* Head; head-piece, cranium; head of hair; face; front, beginning; top; van, vanguard; (*fig.*) brains, sense, judgment; presence of mind, self-possession. *Avoir la tête fêlée,* to be crack-brained; *avoir la tête sur les épaules,* to have a good head on one's shoulders; (*fam.*) *avoir une bonne tête,* to look a decent type; *avoir une chose en tête,* to be bent upon a thing; *coup de tête* [COUP]; *crier à tue-tête* [CRIER]; *de la tête aux pieds,* from head to foot; *donner de la tête contre un mur,* to hit one's head against a stone wall; *donner tête baissée contre,* to go bald-headed at; *en tête,* in one's head, in front, ahead; *en tête à tête,* (two) alone together; *en tête du train,* at the front of the train; *en faire à sa tête,* to go one's own way; *faire or tenir tête à quelqu'un,* to cope with someone; *faire la tête,* to pout, to sulk; *faire sa tête,* to give oneself airs; *faire tête,* to stand at bay, to make headway (against); *faire un signe de tête,* to nod; *il a la tête dure,* he is dull-witted;

il est homme de tête, he is a man of resource *or* of resolution; *il ne sait où donner de la tête,* he does not know which way to turn; *il y va de votre tête,* your life is at stake; *la tête baissée,* with head down; *la tête la première,* head first; *la tête me tourne,* I feel giddy; *mal de tête,* headache; *mauvaise tête* [MAUVAIS]; *payer tant par tête,* to pay so much a head; *perdre la tête* [PERDRE]; *piquer une tête,* to take a header; *se monter la tête* [MONTER]; *tête à perruque* [PERRUQUE]; *tête de ligne,* starting-point, terminus, port of departure; *tête de mort,* death's head, skull; *tête de pont* (*Mil.*), bridgehead; beachhead; *tête nue,* bare-headed; *vous en répondrez sur votre tête,* your head will answer for it.

tête-à-queue, *n.m. inv.* Slew round.

tête-à-tête, *n.m. inv.* Tête-à-tête, private interview or conversation; settee (for two).

tête-bêche, *adv.* Top against bottom; head to tail.

tête-de-loup, *n.f.* (*pl.* **têtes-de-loup**) Turk's head brush (with a long handle).

tête-de-nègre, *a. inv.* Dark brown.

tétée [te'te], *n.f.* Suck. *L'heure de la tétée,* feeding-time (of baby). **téter,** *v.t.* To suck. *Donner à téter à,* to give suck to, to suckle.

têtière [tɛ'tjɛːr], *n.f.* Infant's cap; head-stall (of a bridle); antimacassar.

tétin [te'tɛ̃], *n.m.* Nipple, teat; breast. **tétine,** *n.f.* Udder; rubber nipple, teat (of feeding bottle); baby's comforter. **téton,** *n.m.* Teat; (*fam.*) breast. **tétonnière,** *n.f.* Full-breasted woman; breast-band.

tétrachlorure [tetraklɔ'ryːr], *n.m.* Tetrachloride.

tétracorde [tetra'kɔrd], *n.m.* Tetrachord.

tétradactyle, *a.* Tetradactylous. **tétraèdre,** *n.m.* Tetrahedron. **tétraédrique,** *a.* Tetrahedral. **tétragone,** *n.m.* Tetragon.—*a.* Tetragonal. **tétralogie,** *n.f.* Tetralogy. **tétramètre,** *n.m.* Tetrameter. **tétrandre,** *a.* (*Bot.*) Tetrandrous. **tétrapétale,** *a.* Tetrapetalous.

tétrarchat [tetrar'ka], *n.m.* Tetrarchate. **tétrarchie,** *n.f.* Tetrarchy.

tétrarque, *n.m.* Tetrarch.

tétras [te'tra], *n.m. inv.* (*Orn.*) Grouse.

tétrastyle [tetras'til], *a.* and *n.m.* (*Arch.*) Tetra-style. **tétrasyllabe** or **tétrasyllabique,** *a.* Tetrasyllabic.

tette [tɛt], *n.f.* Teat, dug (of animals); nipple.

têtu [tɛ'ty], *a.* (*fem.* -ue) Headstrong, stubborn, obstinate.—*n.m.* Granite hammer.

teuton [tø'tɔ̃], *a.* (*fem.* -onne) Teutonic.— *n.m.* (**Teuton,** *fem.* -onne) A Teuton, a German. **teutonique,** *a.* Teutonic.

texte [tɛkst], *n.m.* Text; theme, matter, subject; passage (of Scripture). *Gravure hors-texte,* plate; *gros texte,* (*Print.*) two-line brevier; *petit texte,* brevier; *restituer un texte,* to restore a text; *revenir à son texte,* to return to the point.

textile [tɛks'til], *a.* Textile.—*n.m.* Textile material or industries.

textuaire [tɛks'tɥɛːr], *a.* and *n.m.* Textuary.

textuel, *a.* (*fem.* -elle) Textual, word for word. **textuellement,** *adv.* Textually.

texture [tɛks'tyːr], *n.f.* Texture; disposition, arrangement.

Thaïlande [tai'lɑ̃ːd], *f.* Thailand, Siam.

thalame [ta'lam], *n.m.* (*Bot.*) Thalamus.
thalamiflore, *a.* Thalamiflorous.
thalassique [tala'sik], *a.* Thalassic. **thalasso-cratie**, *n.f.* Thalassocracy.
thaler [ta'lɛːr], *n.m.* Thaler (old German coin).
Thalie [ta'li], *f.* Thalia.
thalle [tal], *n.m.* (*Bot.*) Thallus. **thalleux**, *a.* (*fem.* **-euse**) Thallous. **thallique**, *a.* Thallic. **thallium**, *n.m.* Thallium.
thalweg or **talweg** [tal'vɛg], *n.m.* Thalweg (middle line of a river).
thapsia [tap'sja], *n.m.* Deadly carrot. *Thapsia garganica*, resicant plaster (made of it).
thaumaturge [toma'tyːrʒ], *a.* and *n.m.* Thaumaturge. **thaumaturgie**, *n.f.* Thaumaturgy.
thé [te], *n.m.* Tea; tea-party. *Boîte à thé*, tea caddy.
théatin [tea'tɛ̃], *n.m.* Theatine (monk).
théâtral [tea'tral], *a.* (*fem.* **-ale**, *pl.* **-aux**) Theatrical. **théâtralement**, *adv.* Theatrically. **théâtre**, *n.m.* Theatre, playhouse; stage; plays (collection), dramatic works; scene, place of action. *Coup de théâtre*, unexpected stage-effect, striking event; *faire du théâtre*, to be an actor; *le théâtre de Corneille*, Corneille's plays; *pièce de théâtre*, play; *roi de théâtre*, mere shadow of a king; *théâtre de la guerre*, seat of war; *théâtre d'eau*, ornamental fountains; *théâtre de verdure*, open-air theatre.
Thébaïde [teba'id], **la**, *f.* The Thebaid.
thébaïde [teba'id], *n.f.* (*fig.*) Solitude.
thébain, *a.* (*fem.* **-aine**) Theban.—*n.m.* (**Thébain**, *fem.* **-aine**) A Theban.
Thèbes [tɛːb], *f.* Thebes.
théerie [te'ri], *n.f.* Tea-factory; tea-plantation.
théière, *n.f.* Teapot. **théine**, *n.f.* Theine.
théisme (1) [te'ism], *n.m.* (*Path.*) Theism.
théisme (2) [te'ism], *n.m.* Theism (belief in God). **théiste**, *n.* and *a.* Theist.
thème [tɛm], *n.m.* Topic, subject, theme; (*sch.*) prose, composition. *Fort en thème*, good at school work (but lacking personality); *thème dirigé*, guided composition.
Thémistocle [temis'tɔkl], *m.* Themistocles.
théocratie [teɔkra'si], *n.f.* Theocracy. **théocratique**, *a.* Theocratic.
Théocrite [teɔ'krit], *m.* Theocritus.
théodicée, *n.f.* Theodicy.
théodolite [teɔdɔ'lit], *n.m.* Theodolite.
Théodore [teɔ'dɔr], *m.* Theodore.
théodose [teɔ'doːz], *m.* Theodosius.
théodosien [teɔdo'zjɛ̃], *a.* (*fem.* **-ienne**) Theodosian.
théogonie [teɔgo'ni], *n.f.* Theogony. **théogonique**, *a.* Theogonic.
théologal [teɔlɔ'gal], *a.* (*fem.* **-ale**, *pl.* **-aux**) Theological; divine.—*n.m.* Lecturer on divinity (in a church).—*n.f.* Such lectureship. **théologie**, *n.f.* Theology; divinity. *Docteur en théologie*, doctor of divinity. **théologien**, *n.m.* Theologian. **théologique**, *a.* Theological. **théophanie**, *n.f.* Theophany. **théophilanthropie**, *n.f.* Theophilanthropy.
Théophile [teɔ'fil], *m.* Theophilus.
Théophraste [teɔ'frast], *m.* Theophrastus.
théorbe [TÉORBE].
théorème [teɔ'rɛm], *n.m.* Theorem.
théoricien, *n.m.* (*fem.* **-ienne**) Theorist. **théorie**, *n.f.* Theory, speculation; (*Gr.*

Ant.) deputation; procession, long line (of persons). *Faire une théorie* or *des théories*, to theorize. **théorique**, *a.* Theoretical. **théoriquement**, *adv.* Theoretically. **théoriser**, *v.t.*, *v.i.* To theorize. **théoriste**, *n.* Theorist.
théosophe [teɔ'zɔf], *n.m.* Theosophist. **théosophie**, *n.f.* Theosophy. **théosophique**, *a.* Theosophical.
thérapeute [tera'pøːt], *n.m.* Member of religious order of therapeutic monks; (*Med.*) therapeutist, therapist. **thérapeutique**, *a.* Therapeutic.—*n.f.* Therapeutics. **thérapeutiste**, *n.m.* Therapeutist. **thérapie**, *n.f.* Therapy. *Thérapie rééducative*, occupational therapy.
Thérèse [te'rɛːz], *f.* Theresa.
thériacal [terja'kal], *a.* (*fem.* **-ale**, *pl.* **-aux**) Theriacal. **thériaque**, *n.f.* Theriac.
thermal [tɛr'mal], *a.* (*fem.* **-ale**, *pl.* **-aux**) Thermal. *Eaux thermales*, hot springs; *station thermale*, watering-place, spa.
thermes [tɛrm], *n.m. pl.* Thermal baths.
thermidor [tɛrmi'dɔːr], *n.m.* Thermidor (eleventh month of calendar of first French republic, 19 July–17 August). **thermidorien**, *a.* and *n.m.* (*fem.* **-ienne**) Thermidorian.
thermie [tɛr'mi], *n.f.* (*Phys.*) Thermal unit.
thermique [tɛr'mik], *a.* Thermic.
thermobaromètre, *n.m.* Thermobarometer. **thermo-cautère**, *n.m.* (*Surg.*) Thermocautery. **thermochimie**, *n.f.* Thermochemistry. **thermodynamique**, *a.* and *n.f.* Thermodynamics. **thermo-électricité**, *n.f.* Thermo-electricity. **thermogène**, *a.* Thermogenic. *Ouate thermogène*, thermogene wool. **thermogénèse**, *n.f.* Thermogenesis. **thermologie**, *n.f.* Thermology. **thermomètre**, *n.m.* Thermometer. **thermométrique**, *a.* Thermometrical. **thermonucléaire**, *a.* Thermonuclear. **thermostat**, *n.m.* Thermostat. **thermothérapie**, *n.f.* Thermotherapy.
Thermopyles [tɛrmɔ'pil], **les**, *f. pl.* Thermopylae.
thermos [tɛr'mɔs], *n.m.* Thermos (flask).
thésaurisation [tezɔriza'sjɔ̃], *n.f.* Hoarding of treasure. **thésauriser**, *v.t.* To treasure up.—*v.i.* To hoard treasure. **thésauriseur**, *n.m.* (*fem.* **-euse**) Hoarder.—*a.* Hoarding, acquisitive. **thésaurus**, *n.m.* Thesaurus.
thèse [tɛːz], *n.f.* Thesis, proposition; (*sch.*) thesis (submitted for a degree). *Pièce à thèse*, problem play.
Thésée [te'ze], *m.* Theseus.
Thessalie [tesa'li], *f.* Thessaly. **thessalien**, *a.* and *n.m.* (*fem.* **-ienne**) Thessalian.
thessalonicien [tesalɔni'sjɛ̃], *a.* and *n.m.* (*fem.* **-ienne**) Thessalonian.
théurgie [teyr'ʒi], *n.f.* Theurgy.
thibaude [ti'boːd], *n.f.* Hair-cloth, coarse drugget.
Thibau(l)t [ti'bo], *m.* Theobald.
Thibet [TIBET].
thlaspi [tlas'pi], *n.m.* Pennycress.
Thomas [tɔ'ma], *m.* Thomas.
thomas [tɔ'ma], *n.m.* (*vulg.*) Chamber (-pot) (a pun upon the Latin hymn *vide*, *Thoma*, *vide* etc.).
thomisme [tɔ'mism], *n.m.* (*Theol.*) Thomism. **thomiste**, *a.* and *n.m.* Thomist.

thon [tɔ̃], *n.m.* Tunny-fish.
thoracique [tɔra'sik], *a.* Thoracic. **thorax**, *n.m.* Thorax, chest.
thridace [tri'das], *n.f.* Thridacium, lettuce-juice.
thrombose [trɔ̃'boːz], *n.f.* Thrombosis.
thrombus, *n.m.* Thrombus.
thuriféraire [tyrife'rɛːr], *n.m.* Thurifer, censer-bearer; (*fig.*) flatterer. **thurifère**, *a.* (*Bot.*) Thuriferous.
Thuringe [ty'rɛ̃ːʒ], *f.* Thuringia.
thuya [ty'ja], *n.m.* Thuya, arbor vitae.
thym [tɛ̃], *n.m.* Thyme (*Thymus*).
thymol [ti'mɔl], *n.m.* Thymol.
thymus [ti'myːs], *n.m.* Thymus.
thyroïde [tirɔ'id], *a.* Thyroid; shield-shaped; connected with the thyroid gland; (*Bot.*) peltate.
thyrse [tirs], *n.m.* Thyrsus.
tiare [tja:r], *n.f.* Tiara.
Tibère [ti'bɛːr], *m.* Tiberius.
Tibet [ti'bɛ], **le**, *m.* Tibet. **tibétain**, *a.* and *n.m.* (*fem.* **-aine**) Tibetan.
tibia [ti'bja], *n.m.* (*Anat.*) Tibia, shin-bone. **tibial**, *a.* (*fem.* **-iale**, *pl.* **-iaux**) Tibial. **tibio-tarsien**, *a.* (*fem.* **-ienne**) Tibio-tarsal.
Tibre [tibr], **le**, *m.* The Tiber.
tic [tik], *n.m.* Tic, twitching; bad habit. *Tic douloureux*, facial neuralgia.
ticket [ti'kɛ], *n.m.* Ticket (for bus, underground, etc., but not railways).
tic-tac [tik'tak], *n.m. inv.* Tick-tack (regular sound). *Faire tic-tac*, to go pit-a-pat (of heart), to go tock-tock etc.
tiède [tjɛd], *a.* Lukewarm, tepid, mild, soft; (*fig.*) indifferent. **tièdement**, *adv.* Lukewarmly, with indifference. **tiédeur**, *n.f.* Lukewarmness, tepidity; (*fig.*) indifference.
tiédir [tje'diːr], *v.i.* To cool, to grow lukewarm.—*v.t.* To make tepid *or* lukewarm; to take the chill off, to tepefy.
tien [tjɛ̃], *a.poss.* (*fem.* **tienne**) *Thine, thy own, yours.—pron.poss. *Thine, yours.—n.* (*pl.*) *Thy, your people. *Les tiens*, *thy, your relations and friends.
tiens, *2nd sing. imper.* [TENIR] (*int.*) Well, hello! look here! Here! Really? you don't say so! *Un 'tiens' vaut mieux que deux 'tu l'auras'*, a bird in the hand is worth two in the bush.
tierce (1) [tjɛrs], *n.f.* A third (of time); tierce (at cards etc.). **tiercelet**, *n.m.* Tiercel (falcon). **tiercement**, *n.m.* Increase by a third. **tiercer**, *v.t.* To raise or increase by one third; to plough a third time.
tierceron, *n.m.* (*Arch.*) Intermediate rib in Gothic vaulting.
tierçon, *n.m.* Tierce (cask).
tiers [tjɛːr], *a.* (*fem.* **tierce** (2)) Third. *En main tierce*, in the hands of a third party; *fièvre tierce*, tertian ague; *le tiers état*, the people, the commons; *tiers porteur*, second endorser.—*n.m.* Third person; (*fig.*) stranger; third part. *Être en tiers*, to be a third party; *le tiers et le quart*, everybody, all the world.
tiers-point, *n.m.* (*pl.* **tiers-points**) Apex of equilateral triangle; (*Arch.*) point of intersection of arcs in a Gothic arch etc.; saw-file; triangular file.
tifs [tif], *n.m. pl.* (*pop.*) Hair.
tige [tiːʒ], *n.f.* Stem, stalk; trunk (of tree); straw (of corn); shank (of a key, anchor, etc.);

shaft (of column); (*fig.*) leg (of a boot); stock (of a family). (*Arbres à*) *hautes tiges*, tall standards; *tige* (*de porte-plume*), body (of penholder); *tige de frein*, brake-rod; *tige de selle*, saddle-pin (of bicycle).
tignasse [ti'ɲas], *n.f.* Old wig; (*pop.*) mop, shock (of hair).
***tignon** [CHIGNON].
tignonner [tiɲɔ'ne], *v.t.* To curl or frizz (the hair).
Tigre [tigr], **le**, *m.* The Tigris.
tigre [tigr], *n.m.* (*fem.* **tigresse**) Tiger, tigress; small groom.
tigré [ti'gre], *a.* (*fem.* **-ée**) Striped, spotted, speckled. **tigrer**, *v.t.* To stripe, to spot, to speckle.
tilbury [tilby'ri], *n.m.* Tilbury (gig).
tilde [tild], *n.m.* Tilde.
tillac [ti'jak], *n.m.* Deck. *Franc tillac*, main-deck.
tillage etc. [TEILLAGE].
tille [tiːj], *n.f.* Slater's hammer.
tilleul [ti'jœl], *n.m.* Lime-tree, linden-tree, lime-blossom (tea).
***tilleur** [TEILLEUR].
timbale [tɛ̃'bal], *n.f.* Kettledrum, timbal; footless metal cup or mug; kitchen-mould; timbale (dish of fowl etc.). *Décrocher la timbale*, to win the prize. **timbalier**, *n.m.* Kettledrummer.
timbrage [tɛ̃'braːʒ], *n.m.* Stamping (of a document).
timbre [tɛ̃ːbr], *n.m.* Bell, clock-chime; cord (of a drum); sound, tone, timbre, quality; stamp; stamp-office; stamp-duty; postmark; (*Her.*) crest. *Il a le timbre fêlé*, (*fam.*) he is a bit cracked; *porter le timbre de Londres*, to have the London postmark; *sa voix a un timbre argentin*, he has a silver-toned voice; *timbre de quittance*, receipt stamp; *timbre humide*, rubber stamp. **timbré**, *a.* (*fem.* **-ée**) Stamped. *Il est un peu timbré*, (*fam.*) he is a bit cracked; *papier timbré*, stamped paper.
timbre-poste, *n.m.* (*pl.* **timbres-poste**) Postage-stamp. **timbrer**, *v.t.* To stamp; to stick a stamp on (a letter). **timbre-taxe**, *n.m.* (*pl.* **timbres-taxe**) Postage-due stamp.
timbreur, *n.m.* (*fem.* **-euse**) Stamper.
timide [ti'mid], *a.* Timid, timorous; shy, bashful.—*n.* A timid, shy person. **timidement**, *adv.* Timidly; shyly. **timidité**, *n.f.* Timidity; shyness, bashfulness.
timon [ti'mɔ̃], *n.m.* Pole (of a carriage, cart, etc.); shaft; beam (of a plough); (*Naut.*) helm, tiller; (*fig.*) direction, government.
timonerie, *n.f.* Steerage, steering, steering-gear; signalling.
timonier, *n.m.* Steersman, helmsman; signal-man; wheeler, wheel-horse.
timoré [timɔ're], *a.* (*fem.* **-ée**) Timorous, fearful.
Timothée [timɔ'te], *m.* Timothy, Timotheus.
tin [tɛ̃], *n.m.* Block of wood; stock; cask-stand.
tincal or **tinkal** [tɛ̃'kal], *n.m.* Tincal (crude borax).
tinctorial [tɛ̃ktɔ'rjal], *a.* (*fem.* **-iale**, *pl.* **-iaux**) Tinctorial, for dyeing.
tine [tin], *n.f.* Tub, water-cask.
tinet [ti'nɛ], *n.m.* Gambrel, bent stick (for suspending carcasses etc.). **tinette**, *n.f.* (Half-)tub or firkin (of butter); soil-tub.

tintamarre [tɛ̃ta'maːr], *n.m.* Hubbub, uproar, hurly-burly, din.

tintement, *n.m.* Ringing sound, tinkling; toll, tolling; singing or buzzing (in the ears etc.).

tinter (1) [tɛ̃'te], *v.t.* To ring, to toll; to sound (a knell etc.).—*v.i.* To ring; to toll; to tinkle, to jingle; to tingle. *Les oreilles me tintent*, my ears are burning (as if someone were talking about me).

tinter (2) [tɛ̃'te], *v.t.* (*Naut.*) To put (a ship etc.) upon the stocks; to prop, to support.

tintin [tɛ̃'tɛ̃], *n.m.* Ting-a-ling, clink (imit. of tinkling of bells, glasses, etc.).

Tintoret [tɛ̃tɔ'rɛ], *m.* Tintoretto.

tintouin [tɛ̃'twɛ̃], *n.m.* Tingling, ringing, buzzing (in one's ears); (*fam.*) anxiety, uneasiness. *Avoir du tintouin*, to be upon thorns; *donner du tintouin*, to give trouble.

tipule [ti'pyl], *n.f.* (*Ent.*) Daddy-long-legs, crane-fly.

tique [tik], *n.f.* Tick (acarid). **tiquer**, *v.i.* To have a tick, to twitch, to wink (of a person); to bite its crib, to be vicious (of a horse).

tiqueté [tik'te], *a.* (*fem.* **-ée**) Speckled, spotted. **tiqueture**, *n.f.* Mottling, speckles.

tiqueur [ti'kœːr], *a.* and *n.m.* (*fem.* **-euse**) Having a tick, a stable-vice, crib-biting (of horses).

tir [tiːr], *n.m.* Shooting; firing, fire; shooting-gallery, rifle-range. *Allonger le tir*, to lengthen the range; *concours de tir*, shooting match; *instructeur de tir*, musketry instructor; *tir à la cible*, target firing; *tir à l'arc*, archery; archery ground; *tir rasant*, grazing fire.

tirade [ti'rad], *n.f.* Passage (of prose or verse); tirade. *Tout d'une tirade*, all in one speech or at one stretch.

tirage [ti'raːʒ], *n.m.* Drawing, pulling, hauling; towing; tow-path; (*fig.*) difficulty, obstacle; working, working off, pulling, printing; winding-off (of silk); drawing (of a lottery); extension, focal length (of camera); drawing (of wire). *Journal à fort tirage*, newspaper with a big circulation; *le tirage d'une cheminée*, the draught of a chimney; *tirage au sort*, drawing lots.

tiraillement [tiraj'mã], *n.m.* Pulling, hauling about; twitching; twinge, pain; (*fig.*) jarring, jar, wrangling, discord, vexation. *Tiraillements d'estomac*, pangs of hunger. **tirailler**, *v.t.* To pull about; to tease, to plague, to pester.—*v.i.* To shoot wildly, to blaze away; to snipe, to skirmish. **se tirailler**, *v.r.* To pull each other about. **tiraillerie**, *n.f.* Desultory, aimless firing. **tirailleur**, *n.m.* Sharpshooter; skirmisher. *En tirailleurs*, in extended order.

tirant [ti'rã], *n.m.* String (for pulling); purse-string; boot-strap; (*Carp.* etc.) tie-beam, iron bar, bolt, tie; brace (of a drum). *A égal tirant d'eau*, (*Naut.*) on an even keel; *tirant d'eau*, ship's gauge, ship's draught.

tirasse [ti'ras], *n.f.* Draw-net. **tirasser**, *v.t.* To catch (quails etc.) with a draw-net.

tire [tiːr], *n.f.* Pull. *Tout d'une tire*, at one stretch; *vol à la tire*, pocket-picking. (*C*) *Tire d'érable*, maple wax.

tiré [ti're], *a.* (*fem.* **-ée**) Drawn; fatigued, worn-out. *Tiré par les cheveux*, far-fetched. —*n.m.* (*Comm.*) Drawee (of a bill); shooting preserve, shoot.

tiré-à-part [tirea'paːr], *n.m.* (*pl.* **tirés-à-part**) (*Print.*) Offprint. **tire-au-flanc**, *n.m. inv.* (*Mil. slang*) Shirker, malingerer. **tire-bonde**, *n.m.* (*pl.* **tire-bondes**) Bung drawer. **tire-botte**, *n.m.* (*pl.* **tire-bottes**) Boot-jack; boot-hook.

tire-bouchon, *n.m.* (*pl.* **tire-bouchons**) Corkscrew; ringlet (of hair). **tire-bouchonné**, *a.* (*fem.* **-ée**) In ringlets (of hair), screwed up (of scarf etc.) **tire-bouchonner**, *v.t.*, *v.i.* To curl up (of smoke); to twist (hair) in curls; to screw up (a scarf etc.).

tire-bouton, *n.m.* (*pl.* **tire-boutons**) Button-hook. **tire-clou**, *n.m.* (*pl.* **tire-clous**) Nail extractor.

tire-d'aile (à), *adv. phr.* At full speed (of a bird flying).

tire-feu, *n.m. inv.* Lanyard (for firing cannon).

tire-fond, *n.m. inv.* Hook or ring in ceiling; eye-bolt. **tire-lait**, *n.m. inv.* Breast-reliever.

tire-larigot (à), *adv. phr.* To one's heart's content.

tire-ligne, *n.m.* (*pl.* **tire-lignes**) Pen for drawing lines.

tirelire, *n.f.* Money-box; (*pop.*) face, mug. *****tire-lire**, *n.m.* (Lark's) carol. *****tire-lirer**, *v.i.* To sing like a lark.

tire-pied, *n.m.* (*pl.* **tire-pieds**) Shoemaker's stirrup.

tire-point, *n.m.* (*pl.* **tire-points**) Pricker (used in stitching leather).

tirer [ti're], *v.t.* To draw, to pull, to drag, to haul, to tug; to pull in, up, out, etc.; to take out, to extract; to let (blood); to tap (liquors); to stretch, to tighten, to draw (wire); to draw apart or close (curtains etc.); to receive, to gather, to elicit, to reap; to conclude, to infer, to deduce; to draw on, to put on; to get, to extort; to trace, to delineate; to shoot, to fire, to discharge; to fire at, to shoot at; (*Print.*) to work off, to print, to pull; (*Comm.*) to draw (a bill). *Se faire tirer l'oreille* [OREILLE], *tirer avantage* [AVANTAGE]; *tirer de l'argent de sa poche*, to pull money out of one's pocket; *tirer d'erreur*, to undeceive; *tirer les cartes* [CARTE], *tirer les oreilles à quelqu'un*, to pull someone's ears; *tirer les rideaux* [RIDEAU]; *tirer les vers du nez à quelqu'un* [NEZ]; *tirer l'œil*, to attract attention; *tirer parti de*, to make the best of, to turn to account; *tirer son chapeau*, to raise one's hat; *tirer une loterie*, to draw a lottery; *tirer un lapin*, to shoot at a rabbit; *tirer vanité d'une chose*, to be vain about a thing; *tirez le rideau, la farce est jouée*, ring down the curtain, the play is over.—*v.i.* To draw; to pull; to fire; (*pop.*) to be off, to beat it; to tend, to border, to verge (*sur*); to fence. *Bon à tirer*, ready for the press, passed for press; *cette pierre tire sur le vert*, that stone is greenish; *cheminée qui tire bien*, chimney which draws well; *tirer à sa fin* [FIN (1)]; *tirer au large*, (*pop.*) to skedaddle; *tirer en longueur*, to be lengthy (of speech etc.), to drag on. **se tirer**, *v.r.* To extricate oneself; to get out; to recover (from illness); (*slang*) to be off. *S'en tirer*, to pull through, to manage; *se tirer d'affaire*, to get out of a difficulty.

tire-sou, *n.m.* (*pl.* **tire-sous**) Money-grubber.

tiret [ti'rɛ], *n.m.* Slip of parchment; hyphen, dash.

tiretaine [tir'tɛːn], *n.f.* Linsey-woolsey.

tirette [ti'rɛt], *n.f.* Cords for drawing curtains; sliding writing leaf of a desk.

tireur [ti'rœːr], *n.m.* (*fem.* **-euse**) One who draws, drawer; marksman, shot; rifleman, sharpshooter; fencer; drawer (of a bill of exchange); fine-drawer. *C'est un bon* or *fin tireur*, he is a good shot; *tireur d'or*, gold wire-drawer; *tireuse de cartes*, fortune-teller; *un franc-tireur*, a sniper.

tire-veille [tir'vɛːj] or **tire-vieille**, *n.f.* inv. (*Naut.*) Ladder-rope, man-rope, (*pl.*) yoke-lines.

tiroir [ti'rwaːr], *n.m.* Drawer (in a table etc.); (*Steam engine*) slide, slide-valve. *Pièce à tiroirs*, (*Theat.*) comedy of episodes.

tisane [ti'zan], *n.f.* Infusion of herbs etc. *Tisane d'orge*, barley-water.

tison [ti'zɔ̃], *n.m.* Brand, fire-brand; (*fig.*) embers. (*Allumette-*)*tison*, fusee; *tison de discorde*, mischief-maker, fire-brand. **tisonné**, *a.* (*fem.* **-ée**) Marked with black spots (of horses). **tisonner**, *v.i.*, *v.t.* To poke (the fire). **tisonnier**, *n.m.* Poker, fire-iron.

tissage [ti'saːʒ], *n.m.* Weaving; cloth mill.

tisser [ti'se], *v.t.* To weave. *Métier à tisser*, weaving-loom. **tisserand**, *n.m.* Weaver. **tisseranderie**, *n.f.* Weaver's business. **tisserin**, *n.m.* Weaver-bird. **tisseur**, *a.* and *n.m.* (*fem.* **-euse**) Weaver.

tissu [ti'sy], *n.m.* Texture, textile, fabric; tissue, web, contexture. *Tissu de mensonges*, tissue of lies; *tissu métallique*, wire gauze.—*a.* (*fem.* **tissue**) Woven. **tissure**, *n.f.* Tissue, texture.

***tistre** [tistr], *v.t.* (used only in *p.p.* (*tissu*) and compound tenses) To weave.

titan [ti'tɑ̃], *n.m.* Titan.

titane [ti'tan] or **titanium**, *n.m.* (*Chem.*) Titanium.

titanifère, *a.* Titaniferous.

Tite [tit], *m.* Titus.

titanesque [tita'nɛsk] or **titanique**, *a.* Titanic.

Tite-Live [tit'liːv], *m.* Livy.

titi [ti'ti], *n.m.* (*pop.*) Gay apprentice; cheeky urchin (in Paris).

Titien [ti'sjɛ̃], *m.* Titian.

titillant [titil'lɑ̃], *a.* (*fem.* **-ante**) Titillating, tickling. **titillation**, *n.f.* Titillation, tickling. **titiller**, *v.t.*, *v.i.* To titillate, to tickle.

titrage [ti'traːʒ], *n.m.* (*Chem.*) Titration; assaying (of ore etc.); (*Cine.*) insertion of titles.

titre [titr], *n.m.* Title, style, denomination; title-page; head, heading; right, claim, reason, qualification (of coins etc.); voucher; title-deed, deed; (*pl.*) securities. *Titre au porteur*, bearer bond, negotiable instrument; *titre de rente*, Government bond; *titre nominatif*, registered scrip. *Titre de circulation*, (railway) ticket or pass; *titre de noblesse*, a title; *titre de permission*, (*Mil.*) pass (for leave); *titre d'une solution*, (*Chem.*) strength of a solution. *À bon titre* or *à juste titre*, deservedly, justly; *à titre de*, by right of, in virtue of; *à plus d'un titre*, on more grounds than one; *donner un titre à*, to entitle to; *en titre*, titular, acknowledged; *faux titre*, false title, falsehood, sham, (*Print.*) half-title.

titré [ti'tre], *a.* (*fem.* **-ée**) Titled. **titrer**, *v.t.* To give a title to; (*Chem.*) to titrate; to make a standard solution of; to assay (ore etc.); to

put titles to (newspaper, film). **titreuse**, *n.f.* (*Cine.*) Titler.

titubant [tity'bɑ̃], *a.* (*fem.* **-ante**) Staggering, reeling. **titubation**, *n.f.* Titubation, reeling, staggering. **tituber**, *v.i.* To stagger, to reel, to lurch.

titulaire [tity'lɛːr], *a.* Titular.—*n.* Titular incumbent, bearer, holder, chief. **titulariser**, *v.t.* To put (someone) on the establishment. **titulateur**, *n.m.* (*Cine.*) Caption writer.

toast [tost], *n.m.* Toast, health; toast(ed bread). *Porter un toast*, to propose a toast. **toaster** or **toster**, *v.t.* To toast (someone).

Tobie [tɔ'bi], *m.* Tobias, Toby.

toboggan [tɔbɔ'gɑ̃], *n.m.* Toboggan.

toc [tɔk], *int.* Tap, rap.—*n.m.* Rap, knock (at a door etc.); (*slang*) sham or imitation jewellery etc., paste, brummagem goods.

tocade [TOQUADE].

tocane [tɔ'kan], *n.f.* New champagne.

tocante [tɔ'kɑ̃ːt], *n.f.* (*slang*) Ticker, watch.

tocard [tɔ'kaːr], *a.* (*slang*) Valueless (thing).—*n.m.* (Bad) horse or racer.

tocasson [tɔka'sɔ̃], *n.m.* Silly, or ugly person.

tocsin [tɔk'sɛ̃], *n.m.* Tocsin, alarm-bell.

toc-toc [tɔk'tɔk], *a.* inv. (*fam.*) *Être un peu toc-toc* (=*toque*), to be a bit cracked or gone in the head.

toge [tɔːʒ], *n.f.* Toga; (*fig.*) robe, gown (of a judge etc.).

Togo [tɔ'go], **le**, *m.* Togoland.

tohu-bohu [tɔybɔ'y], *n.m.* Chaos; (*fig.*) confusion, disorder; jumble, medley, hubbub.

toi [twa], *pron. pers.* [TU].

toile [twal], *n.f.* Linen, linen cloth; cloth; canvas; sail-cloth, sail; (*Paint.*) canvas for painting, painting, picture, piece; (*pl.*) (*Hunt.*) toils; (*vulg.*) bedsheet. *Augmenter de toile*, to put on more sail; *faire de la toile*, to make sail; *marchand de toiles*, linen-draper; *toile à calquer*, tracing cloth; *toile à sac*, sackcloth; *toile cirée*, oil-cloth, American cloth; *toile métallique*, wire gauze; *toile d'araignée*, cobweb, spider's web; *toile d'emballage*, packing-cloth; *toile de fond*, (*Theat.*) backcloth; *toile de Pénélope*, Penelope's web; *toiles d'un moulin à vent*, sails of a windmill; *toile pour chemises*, shirting; *toile pour draps de lit*, sheeting. **toilerie**, *n.f.* Linen drapery; linen-trade.

toilette [twa'lɛt], *n.f.* Small linen cloth, doily; toilet-set; dressing-table, wash-stand; toilette-glass; lavatory; dress, attire; (*fig.*) dressing, trimming (of horses etc.). *Cabinet de toilette*, dressing-room; *faire un brin de toilette*, to tidy oneself up; *grande toilette*, full dress; *il fait sa toilette* or *il est à sa toilette*, he is dressing.

toilier [twa'lje], *a.* (*fem.* **-ière**) Pertaining to linen.—*n.* Dealer in linen; linen manufacturer.

toise [twaːz], *n.f.* *Fathom; fathom-measure; (*fig.*) measure, standard, stature. *On ne mesure pas les hommes à sa toise*, men ought not to be judged by one's own standards. **toisé**, *n.m.* Measuring; mensuration; (*Civ. Eng.*) quantity surveying.—*a.* (*fem.* **-ée**) Measured. **toiser**, *v.t.* To measure; to survey; (*fig.*) to eye from head to foot. **toiseur**, *n.m.* Measurer; quantity surveyor.

toison [twa'zɔ̃], *n.f.* Fleece; (*fig.*) mop, thick

head of hair. *La Toison d'or*, the Golden Fleece.

toit [twɑ], *n.m.* Roof, house-top; top, roof (of a mine); (*fig.*) roof-tree, house, cottage, home. *Habiter sous les toits*, to live in a garret; *publier* or *crier quelque chose sur les toits*, to proclaim something from the house-tops; *toit à cochons*, pigsty; (*Motor.*) *toit ouvrant*, sunshine roof. **toiture**, *n.f.* Roofing, roof.

tokai or **tokay** [tɔ'kɛ], *n.m.* Tokay (wine).

tôle [toːl], *n.f.* Sheet-iron; plate of steel. *Tôle ondulée*, corrugated iron [*see also* TAULE].

Tolède [tɔ'lɛd], *f.* Toledo.

tolérable [tɔle'rabl], *a.* Tolerable, bearable; middling. **tolérablement**, *adv.* Tolerably.

tolérance [tɔle'rɑ̃ːs], *n.f.* Tolerance, toleration; endurance, forbearance; indulgence; (in coins) deduction, allowance; (*Eng.*) limits. *Maison de tolérance*, brothel under police supervision. **tolérant**, *a.* (*fem.* **-ante**) Tolerant. **tolérantisme**, *n.m.* System of religious toleration, latitudinarianism.

tolérer [tɔle're], *v.t. irr.* (*conjug. like* ACCÉLÉRER) To tolerate, to allow; to endure, to bear; to wink at.

tôlerie [tol'ri], *n.f.* Sheet-iron goods; sheet-iron mills or trade.

tolet [tɔ'lɛ], *n.m.* (*Naut.*) Thole-pin.

toletière, *n.f.* Rowlock.

tôlier [to'lje], *n.m.* Manufacturer of sheet-iron.

tollé [tɔl'le], *n.m.* Outcry (of indignation). *Cette remarque souleva un tollé général*, that remark raised a general outcry.

toluène [tɔ'lɥɛn], *n.m.* Methyl benzine.

tomahawk [tɔma'ɔk], *n.m.* Tomahawk.

tomaison [tɔmɛ'zɔ̃], *n.f.* (*Print.*) Number (of the volume on a sheet).

tomate [tɔ'mat], *n.f.* Tomato. *Jus de tomate*, tomato juice; *sauce tomate*, tomato sauce.

tombal [tɔ̃'bal], *a.* (*fem.* **-ale**, *pl.* **-aux**) Pertaining to a tomb. *Pierre tombale*, tombstone.

tombant [tɔ̃'bɑ̃], *a.* (*fem.* **-ante**) Falling down; drooping, flowing (of hair etc.). *À la nuit tombante*, at nightfall.

tombe [tɔ̃ːb], *n.f.* Tomb, grave; tombstone, gravestone. *Descendre dans la tombe*, to sink into the grave; *être au bord de la tombe*, to have one foot in the grave.

tombeau [tɔ̃'bo], *n.m.* (*pl.* **-eaux**) Tomb, grave; (*fig.*) sepulchre, death. *Mettre* or *conduire au tombeau*, to bring down to the grave; *descendre au tombeau*, (*fig. and poet.*) to die; *descendre une côte à tombeau ouvert*, to rush down a hill at break-neck speed.

tombé [tɔ̃'be], *a.* *Coup* (*de pied*) *tombé*, (*Ftb.*) drop-kick.

tombée [tɔ̃'be], *n.f.* Fall (of night etc.). *À la tombée de la nuit*, at nightfall.

tomber [tɔ̃'be], *v.i.* To fall, to fall down; to drop down, to tumble down; to sink; to decay, to fall away, to droop, to dwindle, to fail; to flag; to abate; to sag; to hang; to fall into; to become; to meet, to light (upon) (*sur*). *Cela m'est tombé entre les mains*, that fell into my hands; *faire tomber*, to throw, push, or knock down; *laisser tomber*, to let fall, to drop; *laisser tomber la conversation*, to let the conversation flag; *le jour tombe*, day is closing in; *les bras m'en tombèrent*, I was struck dumb with surprise; *le sort est tombé sur lui*, the lot has fallen upon him; *se laisser*

tomber, to get a fall; *son anniversaire tombe un dimanche*, his birthday falls on a Sunday; *tomber à terre* or *par terre*, to fall down, to fall to the ground; *tomber amoureux*, to fall in love; *tomber bien* or *mal*, to come seasonably or unseasonably, to come at the right *or* wrong moment; *tomber d'accord*, to agree; *tomber dans les bras de quelqu'un*, to fall into someone's arms; *tomber de faiblesse*, to faint away; *tomber de son haut* or *tomber des nues*, to be astounded; *tomber du haut mal*, to have an epileptic fit; *tomber malade*, to fall ill; *tomber raide mort*, to fall down dead; *tomber sur l'ennemi*, to fall upon the enemy; *tomber sur une maison*, to come across a house; *une mode qui commence à tomber*, a fashion which is going out.—*v.t.* To throw (an opponent).

tombereau [tɔ̃'bro], *n.m.* (*pl.* **-eaux**) Tip-cart, cart-load.

tomberelle, *n.f.* Partridge-net.

tombeur [tɔ̃'bœːr], *n.m.* Housebreaker, demolition worker; (*pop.*) invincible wrestler. (*pop.*) *Tombeur de femmes*, great seducer.

tombola [tɔ̃bɔ'la], *n.f.* Tombola; raffle.

Tombouctou [tɔ̃buk'tu], *m.* Timbuctoo.

tome [toːm], *n.m.* Volume, tome.

tomenteux [tɔmɑ̃'tø], *a.* (*fem.* **-euse**) Tomentous, downy.

tom-pouce [tɔm'pus], *n.m.* (*pl. inv.* or **tom-pouces**) Tom Thumb, dwarf; woman's stumpy umbrella.

ton (1) [tɔ̃], *a. poss.* (*fem.* **ta**, *pl.* **tes**) *Thy (your). Ton frère, ta sœur, et tes cousins, *thy (your) brother, sister, and cousins. [*Ton* is used in the fem. before a vowel or silent *h*.]

ton (2) [tɔ̃], *n.m.* Tone; intonation, accent; tint; (*fig.*) manner, strain, style; manners, breeding; vigour, energy; (*Mus.*) pitch, key. *C'est le ton qui fait la musique*, it is the manner that shows the intent; *changer de ton*, to change one's tone or tune; *donner le ton*, to give the tone, to lead the fashion, (*Mus.*) to pitch; *le bon ton*, good form; *le prendre sur un ton*, to put on airs; *mauvais ton*, ill-breeding, vulgarity; *parler d'un ton de maître*, to speak in a magisterial manner.

tonal [tɔ'nal], *a.* (*fem.* **-ale**, *pl.* **-aux**) Tonal. **tonalité**, *n.f.* (*Mus., Art*) Tonality.

tonca [TONKA].

tondaison [TONTE].

tondeur [tɔ̃'dœːr], *n.m.* (*fem.* **-euse**) Shearer, clipper. *Tondeur de drap*, cloth-shearer.— *n.f.* Shearing-machine, clipper. *Tondeuse (de gazon)*, lawn-mower.

tondre [tɔ̃:dr], *v.t.* To shear, to clip, to crop; to cut, to mow, to trim; (*fig.*) to graze; to fleece. *Tondre sur un œuf*, to skin a flint.

(C) **tondrière** [tɔ̃'drjɛːr], *n.f.* Punker.

tondu [tɔ̃'dy], *a.* (*fem.* **-ue**) Shorn.—*n.m. Il n'y avait que quatre pelés et un tondu*, there was nothing but the ragtag and bobtail.

tonicité [tɔnisi'te], *n.f.* Tonicity. **tonifiant**, *a.* (*fem.* **-iante**) Bracing. **tonifier**, *v.t.* To brace, to invigorate. **tonique**, *a.* Tonic. *Accent tonique*, tonic accent. *Vin tonique*, tonic wine.—*n.m.* (*Med.*) Tonic.— *n.f.* (*Mus.*) Keynote.

tonitruant [tɔnitry'ɑ̃], *a.* (*fem.* **-ante**) Thundering. **tonitruer**, *v.i.* To thunder (of speech).

tonka or **tonca** [tɔ̃'ka], *n.f.* Tonka-bean.

tonnage [tɔ'naːʒ], *n.m.* Tonnage, burthen;

displacement. *Droit de tonnage,* tonnage dues; *tonnage brut,* gross tonnage.
tonnant [tɔ'nɑ̃], *a.* (*fem.* **-ante**) Thundering. *Jupiter tonnant,* Jupiter the Thunderer.
tonne [tɔn], *n.f.* Tun (wooden vessel); ton (20 cwt., 1000 kil.). **tonneau,** *n.m.* (*pl.* **-eaux**) Tun (cask); tun (measure); ton [TONNE]; (*colloq.*) drunkard, beer-barrel; (*Motor.*) tonneau; garden game played with small shying quoits; (*Av.*) roll, spin. *Être d'un bon tonneau,* to be of first-rate quality; *mettre un tonneau en perce,* to broach a cask; *tonneau d'arrosage,* water-cart; *tonneau percé,* leaky cask, (*fig.*) spendthrift. **tonnelage,** *n.m.* Cooperage.
tonneler [tɔn'le], *v.t.* (*Hunt.*) To tunnel, to catch (partridges) in a tunnel-net.
tonnelet [tɔn'lɛ], *n.m.* Small cask, (*Naut.*) keg.
tonnelier [tɔnə'lje], *n.m.* Cooper.
tonnelle [tɔ'nɛl], *n.f.* Arbour, bower; semicircular vault; (*Hunt.*) tunnel-net.
tonnellerie [tɔnɛl'ri], *n.f.* Cooperage; cooper's trade; cooper's shed.
tonner [tɔ'ne], *v.i.* To thunder; (*fig.*) to inveigh. *Il tonne,* it is thundering. **tonnerre,** *n.m.* Thunder, thunderclap; thunderbolt; thundering noise; breech (of a gun). *Coup* or *éclat de tonnerre,* clap of thunder; *pierre de tonnerre,* thunder-bolt; *tonnerre de Dieu! mille tonnerres!* by thunder!
tonsille [tɔ̃'si:j], *n.f.* Tonsil.
tonsure [tɔ̃'sy:r], *n.f.* Tonsure. *Recevoir la tonsure,* to enter the priesthood. **tonsuré,** *a.m.* Tonsured, shaven.—*n.m.* Cleric, priest.
tonsurer, *v.t.* To tonsure.
tonte [tɔ̃:t] or **tondaison,** *n.f.* Sheep-shearing; clipping; clippings, clip; shearing-time.
tontine [tɔ̃'tin], *n.f.* Tontine.
tontisse [tɔ̃'tis], *a.* Said of flock sheared from woollen cloth.—*n.f.* Hangings coated with the shearings of cloth. *Papier-tontisse,* flock-paper.
tonton [tɔ̃'tɔ̃], *n.m.* (*Childish*) Uncle.
tonture [tɔ̃'ty:r], *n.f.* Shearing; shearings, clippings, flock (of cloth); (*Naut.*) sheer. *Tonture des ponts,* sheer (of a ship's decks).
top [tɔp], *n.m.* Time signal. *Les tops,* the pips.
topaze [tɔ'pɑ:z], *n.f.* Topaz.
toper [tɔ'pe], *v.i.* To agree. *Je tope à cela,* I agree to that; *tope là!* done! agreed!
topette [tɔ'pɛt], *n.f.* Phial.
tophacé [tɔfa'se], *a.* (*fem.* **-ée**) (*Med.*) Tophaceous, gouty. **tophus,** *n.m.* Toph, tophus.
topinambour [tɔpinɑ̃'bu:r], *n.m.* Jerusalem artichoke.
topique [tɔ'pik], *a.* (*Med. etc.*) Topical; local. —*n.m.* (*Med.*) Topic; topical or relevant.— *n.f.* The art of finding topics or arguments.
topo [tɔ'po], *n.m.* (*sch. slang*) Brief exposition or demonstration (written or oral) of a point, a commonplace etc.; (*fam.*) plan (of a house etc.).
topographe [tɔpɔ'graf], *n.m.* Topographer. **topographie,** *n.f.* Topography. **topographique,** *a.* Topographical.
toponymie [tɔpɔni'mi], *n.f.* Toponymy.
toquade or **tocade** [tɔ'kad], *n.f.* (*colloq.*) Infatuation, whim, fad, craze.
toque [tɔk], *n.f.* Toque; jockey's cap; magistrate's cap.
toqué [tɔ'ke], *a.* (*fem.* **-ée**) (*fam.*) Cracked,

touched; infatuated, in love (*de*). **toquer,** *v.t.* To touch, to hit, to strike; to infatuate. **se toquer,** *v.r.* To become infatuated (*de*).
*toquet [tɔ'ke], *n.m.* Child's cap.
torche [tɔrʃ], *n.f.* Torch, link; twist (of straw etc.); pad (on head); paint-rag. **torche-nez** [TORD-NEZ]. **torche-pot,** *n.m.* (*pl.* **torche-pots**) (*pop.*) Nuthatch. **torcher,** *v.t.* To wipe, to clean; (*fig.*) to polish off, to botch (a job). **se torcher,** *v.r.* To wipe oneself.
torchère, *n.f.* Torch-holder, tall candelabrum, hall-lamp. **torchis,** *n.m.* Cob, loam. *Mur de torchis,* mud-wall.
torchon [tɔr'ʃɔ̃], *n.m.* Duster, house-cloth, dish-cloth. (*fam.*) *Le torchon brûle,* there are squalls in the home; *un coup de torchon,* a dust-up, a set-to. **torchonner,** *v.t.* (*fam.*) To wipe; to botch (a job).
torcol [tɔr'kɔl] or **torcou,** *n.m.* (*Orn.*) Wryneck.
tordage [tɔr'da:ʒ], *n.m.* Twisting, twist. **tordant,** *a.* (*fem.* **-ante**) (*colloq.*) Side-splitting (of laughter). *C'est tordant,* it is a scream. **tord-boyaux,** *n.m. inv.* (*colloq.*) Fiery brandy; rot-gut. **tordeur,** *n.m.* (*fem.* **-euse**) Twister; (silk) throwster.—*n.f.* Cable-twisting or -wringing machine. **tord-nez,** *n.m. inv.* Twitch (for horses). **tordoir,** *n.m.* Apparatus for twisting, mangle, wringer.
tordre [tɔrdr], *v.t.* To twist, to wring, to wring out; to contort, to disfigure; to wrest; (*colloq.*) to beat, to vanquish. *Tordre du linge,* to wring out washing; *tordre la bouche,* to make a wry mouth; *tordre le cou à quelqu'un,* to wring someone's neck. **se tordre,** *v.r.* To twist; to writhe. *Se tordre de rire,* to be convulsed with laughter; *se tordre les mains,* to wring one's hands. **tordu,** *a.* (*fem.* **-ue**) Twisted, distorted.
tore [tɔ:r], *n.m.* (*Arch. etc.*) Torus.
toréador [tɔrea'dɔ:r], *n.m.* Toreador, bullfighter. **toréer,** *v.i.* To fight (of toreador).
torgnole [tɔr'ɲɔl], *n.f.* (*pop.*) Blow, slap.
toril [tɔ'ril], *n.m.* Pen in a bull ring.
tormentille [tɔrmɑ̃'ti:j], *n.f.* Tormentil.
tornade [tɔr'nad], *n.f.* Tornado.
toron [tɔ'rɔ̃], *n.m.* (*Naut.*) Strand (of a rope); (*Arch.*) lower torus.
torpédo [tɔrpe'do], *n.f.* or *m.* (*Motor.*) Open tourer.
torpeur [tɔr'pœ:r], *n.f.* Torpor. **torpide,** *a.* Torpid.
torpillage [tɔrpi'ja:ʒ], *n.m.* Torpedoing. **torpille,** *n.f.* Torpedo (numb-fish); (*Navy, Av.*) torpedo; mine. **torpiller,** *v.t.* To torpedo; to mine. **torpilleur,** *n.m.* Torpedo-boat; sailor in charge of torpedoes.
torque [tɔrk], *n.f.* Torque, coil (of wire); (*Her.*) crest, wreath. **torquer,** *v.t.* To twist or roll (tobacco etc.). **torquet,** *n.m.* Snare. *Donner dans le torquet,* to fall into the trap; *donner un torquet* or *donner le torquet à quelqu'un,* to take someone in, to gull him.
torquette [tɔr'kɛt], *n.f.* *Wicker-basket (for fish); lot of fish; roll of tobacco.
torréfaction [tɔrefak'sjɔ̃], *n.f.* Torrefaction, roasting. **torréfier,** *v.t.* To torrefy, to roast, to grill.
torrent [tɔ'rɑ̃], *n.m.* Torrent, stream; flood (of tears etc.); flow (of words etc.). **torrentiel** or **torrentueux,** *a.* (*fem.* **-ielle, -ueuse**)

Torrential; impetuous. **torrentiellement,**
adv. Torrentially.
torride [tɔ'rid], *a.* Torrid.
tors [tɔr], *a.* (*fem.* **torse** (1) or **torte**) Twisted,
wreathed, contorted; wry, crooked. *Bouche
torse,* wry mouth; *jambes torses,* bandy or
bow legs.—*n.m.* Twisting (of ropes etc.);
torsion.
torsade [tɔr'sad], *n.f.* Twisted fringe or cord;
bullion (on epaulets etc.). **torsader,** *v.t.* To
twist (together).
torse (2) [tɔrs], *n.m.* Torso, trunk, bust.
torsion [tɔr'sjɔ̃], *n.f.* Torsion, twisting. *Barre
de torsion,* torsion bar.
tort [tɔ:r], *n.m.* Wrong, injustice; harm, injury,
mischief, offence; prejudice, detriment;
fault, error. *À tort ou à raison,* rightly or
wrongly; *avoir tort,* to be in the wrong, to be
wrong; *donner tort à quelqu'un,* to decide
against someone; *faire tort à,* to wrong; *il
parle à tort et à travers,* he speaks at random;
se faire tort, to harm oneself.
tortelle [tɔr'tɛl], *n.f.* Hedge-mustard.
torticolis [tɔrtikɔ'li], *n.m.* Wry neck, stiff
neck; crick (in the neck).
tortil [tɔr'ti], *n.m.* (*Her.*) Baron's coronet.
tortillage [tɔrti'ja:ʒ], *n.m.* Confused or embarrassed language; (*colloq.*) shuffling, shifty
manœuvre, trickery. **tortillard,** *a.* Cross-
grained (wood).—*n.m.* (*fam.*) Small local
railway. **tortille** or **tortillère,** *n.f.* Winding
walk (in a park etc.). **tortillé,** *a.* (*fem.* **-ée**)
(*Her.*) Twisted, wreathed. **tortillement,**
n.m. Twisting, twist; (*fig.*) subterfuge,
quibbling, wriggling. **tortiller,** *v.t.* To
twist.—*v.i.* To wriggle, to shuffle; to prevaricate. (*pop.*) *Il n'y a pas à tortiller,* there is no
getting out of it. **se tortiller,** *v.r.* To
wriggle, to writhe.
tortillère [TORTILLE].
tortillon [tɔrti'jɔ̃], *n.m.* Pad (on the head);
wisp (of straw etc.); small paper stump.
tortionnaire [tɔrsjɔ'nɛːr], *a.* Pertaining to
torture; wrongful and cruel.—*n.m.* Executioner, torturer.
tortis [tɔr'ti], *n.m.* Twist (of threads etc.);
wreath, garland.
tortu [tɔr'ty], *a.* (*fem.* **-ue** (1)) Crooked,
tortuous. *Jambes tortues,* bandy legs.
tortue (2) [tɔr'ty], *n.f.* Tortoise; (*Rom. Ant.*)
testudo; (*Mil. slang*) hand-grenade. *À pas de
tortue,* at a snail's pace; *soupe à la tortue,*
turtle-soup; *tortue de mer,* turtle.
*****tortuer** [tɔr'tɥe], *v.t.* To make crooked, to
crook, to bend.
tortueusement [tɔrtɥøz'mɑ̃], *adv.* Crookedly,
tortuously. **tortueux,** *a.* (*fem.* **-ueuse**)
Tortuous, winding, crooked; (*fig.*) artful,
crafty, disingenuous. **tortuosité,** *n.f.* Tortuosity, crookedness; winding.
torturant [tɔrty'rɑ̃], *a.* (*fem.* **-ante**) Torturing,
tormenting. **torture,** *n.f.* Torture; the rack.
Mettre à la torture, to put to the rack. **torturer,** *v.t.* To torture, to put to the rack;
(*fig.*) to strain, to twist. *Se torturer l'esprit,*
to rack one's brains; *torturer un texte,* to
strain (the meaning of) a text.
torve [tɔrv], *a.* Scowling, menacing (look).
tory [tɔ'ri], *n.m. and a.* (*pl.* **tories**) Tory.
torysme, *n.m.* Toryism.
ɔscan [tɔs'kã], *a. and n.m.* (*fem.* **-ane**)
Tuscan.

Toscane [tɔs'kan], *f.* Tuscany.
tôt [to], *adv.* Soon, quickly, speedily; early.
Au plus tôt or *le plus tôt possible,* as soon as
possible; *le plus tôt,* the earliest; *le plus tôt
que,* as early as; *le plus tôt sera le mieux,* the
sooner the better; *se lever tôt,* to get up early;
plus tôt que, sooner than; *tôt ou tard,*
sooner or later; *trop tôt,* too soon.
total [tɔ'tal], *a.* (*fem.* **-ale,** *pl.* **-aux**) Total,
whole, entire; utter, universal, complete.—
n.m. Whole, total, sum-total. *Au total,* on
the whole, after all. **totalement,** *adv.*
Totally, wholly; utterly, completely. **totalisateur,** *a.* (*fem.* **-trice**) Calculating, adding.
—*n.m.* Calculating-machine; totalisator,
(*fam.*) tote. **totaliser,** *v.t.* To tot up or
total up. **totalitaire,** *a.* Totalitarian.
totalitarisme, *n.m.* Totalitarianism. **totalité,** *n.f.* Totality, whole.
totem [tɔ'tɛm], *n.m.* Totem. **totémique,** *a.*
Totemic. **totémisme,** *n.m.* Totemism.
tôt-fait [to'fɛ], *n.m.* (*pl.* **tôt-faits**) A quickly
made soufflé.
toto [tɔ'to], *n.m.* (*pop.*) Louse.
toton [tɔ'tɔ̃], *n.m.* Teetotum. *Faire tourner
quelqu'un comme un toton,* to twist someone
round one's little finger.
touage [twa:ʒ], *n.m.* Towage, towing, warping.
*****touaille** [twɑ:j], *n.f.* Roller-towel, jack-
towel.
toubib [tu'bib], *n.m.* (*slang*) Medical officer,
'M.O.'; doctor.
toucan [tu'kã], *n.m.* Toucan.
touchable [tu'ʃabl], *a.* Touchable; which can
be cashed. **touchant,** *a.* (*fem.* **-ante**) Touching, moving, affecting.—*n.m.* The moving,
affecting, or impressive part.—*prep.* Concerning, with regard to, touching. **touchau,
touchaud,** or **toucheau,** *n.m.* (*pl.* **-aux,
-auds, -eaux**) Touch-needle.
touche [tuʃ], *n.f.* Touch; assay, trial; (*Paint.
etc.*) stroke, manner, style; fret (of violin etc.);
key (of piano, typewriter, etc.); stop (of
organ); (*Fishing*) nibble, bite; (*Print.*) inking;
(*Fenc. etc.*) hit; goad for driving cattle, drove
of cattle; (*colloq.*) look, appearance. *Pierre
de touche,* touchstone. (*Ftb.*) (*Ligne de*)
touche, touch-line; *coup de pied en touche,*
kick into touch. *Il a une drôle de touche,* he's
a queer-looking customer; *quelle touche il a!*
what a guy! **touche-à-tout,** *n. inv.* Meddler,
Jack of all trades; child who touches everything.—*a. inv.* Meddling.
toucher [tu'ʃe], *v.t.* To touch; to handle, to
feel, to finger; to assay, to try (precious
metals etc.); to receive (money); to hit; to
gall, to offend; to move, to affect; to whip,
to drive (animals); to play on (a musical
instrument); to express, to convey, to depict,
to describe; (*Print.*) to ink; to touch on,
to allude to; to concern, to regard. *Bien
touché,* well said, well done, well hit; *cela
ne me touche point,* that does not concern me;
(*fam.*) *je lui en toucherai un mot,* I'll have a
word with him about it; *pièce touchée, pièce
jouée,* (*Chess*) if you touch your piece you
must play it; *se laisser toucher par les larmes
de quelqu'un,* to be affected by someone's
tears; *toucher juste,* to hit the nail on the head;
toucher quelqu'un de près, to be closely related
to someone; *toucher ses appointements,* to
receive one's salary; *toucher un chèque,* to cash

a cheque; *toucher un ulcère*, to touch an ulcer with caustic; *touchez là!* put it there! shake on it! *touchons du bois!* touch wood!—*v.i.* To touch, to meddle (*à*); to reach; to play (on a musical instrument); to draw near, to approach, to be very close (*à*), to be related, to be akin, to be like; to concern, to regard, to interest; to allude, to hint; to drive on; to touch; (*Naut.*) to go aground, to strike, to put in (*à*), to land (*sur*). *Il n'osa toucher à la religion*, he dared not meddle with religion; *il touche à la soixantaine*, he is approaching sixty; *il y a touché*, he had.a hand in it; *l'année touche à sa fin*, the year is drawing to a close; *n'avoir pas l'air d'y toucher*, to look as if butter would not melt in one's mouth; *ne touchez pas à la reine!* hands off the queen! *nous touchons à·l'hiver*, winter will soon be here; (*fam.*) *toucher du piano*, to play the piano.—*n.m.* Touch, feeling; (*fig.*) manner of playing an instrument etc. **se toucher,** *v.r.* To touch, to touch each other; to be adjoining; to meet.

toucheur, *n.m.* (*fem.* **-euse**) Cattle-drover.—*n.m.* (*Print.*) Inking-roller.

toue [tu], *n.f.* Barge; ferry boat. **touée,** *n.f.* (*Naut.*) Scope (length of cable, 120 fathoms); towing, warping; towline. *Ancre de touée,* kedge (anchor for towing).

touer [tu'e], *v.t.* To tow, to warp.

toueur [tu'œːr], *a.* (*fem.* **-euse**) Towing; warping.—*n.m.* Tower; tow-boat, tug.

touffe [tuf], *n.f.* Tuft, clump, bunch, wisp (of straw, hay, hair, etc.).

touffer [tu'fe], *v.i.* To grow in a tuft or tufts.—*v.t.* To arrange in tufts.

touffeur [tu'fœːr], *n.f.* Stifling heat (of room), (*fam.*) fug.

touffu [tu'fy], *a.* (*fem.* **-ue**) Tufted, bushy; branchy, leafy; full, thick, luxuriant; laboured (of style).

touiller [tu'je], *v.t.* (*pop.*) To stir up (soup, mud, etc.).

toujours [tu'ʒuːr], *adv.* Always, ever, for ever; still; all the same, nevertheless, at least. *Allez toujours!* lead on! *est-il toujours à Paris?* is he still in Paris? *se dire adieu pour toujours*, to say good-bye for ever; *toujours est-il que*, still, the fact remains that.

(C) touladi [tula'di], *n.f.* Grey trout.

toundra [tun'dra], *n.f.* (*Geog.*) Tundra.

toupet [tu'pɛ], *n.m.* Tuft of hair; forelock; front, foretop (on a horse); (*colloq.*) effrontery, cheek, impudence. *Avoir du toupet,* to have any amount of cheek; *payer de toupet*, to brazen it out. *Se prendre au toupet*, to take each other by the hair.

toupie [tu'pi], *n.f.* Top, spinning-top, pegtop; spindle moulding machine; (*pop.*) flighty wench. *Dormir comme une toupie*, to sleep like a top; *faire aller une toupie*, to spin a top; *toupie d'Allemagne*, humming-top.

toupiller [tupi'je], *v.i.* To spin, to whirl round and round; (*fig.*) to run up and down or about.—*v.t.* To shape (wood).

toupillon [tupi'jɔ̃], *n.m.* Small tuft of hair; small top; waste branches (of an orange-tree).

tour (1) [tuːr], *n.f.* Tower; (*Chess*) rook, castle. *La Tour Eiffel*, the Eiffel Tower; *tour de contrôle*, (*Av.*) control tower; *tour d'ivoire,* ivory tower.

tour (2) [tuːr], *n.m.* Turn, round, twining;

winding; revolution; circumference, circuit, compass; twist, strain; tour, trip; trick, dodge, wile; feat; office, service; vein, manner, style; place, order. *À chacun son tour*, every dog has his day; *à tour de bras*, with all one's strength; *à tour de rôle*, in turn, by the list; *chacun son tour*, turn and turn about; *faire le tour de*, to go round; *faire or jouer un mauvais tour à quelqu'un*, to play a dirty trick on someone; *faire un tour*, to take a stroll; *faire le tour du monde*, to journey round the world; *faire le tour du cadran*, to sleep the clock round; *fermer à double tour*, to double-lock; *le Tour de France*, annual cycle race round France; *le tour du bâton*, (*fam.*) perks, pickings; *second tour de scrutin*, second round of voting; *mon sang n'a fait qu'un tour*, I turned deadly pale, I was thoroughly upset; *prendre un tour à son concurrent*, to lap one's opponent; *tour à tour*, by turns, in turn; *tour de promenade*, turn, walk, stroll; *tour de force*, feat of strength; *tour de reins*, twist or sprain in the back; *tours et détours*, twists and turns; *tours de gobelets*, juggler's tricks, legerdemain; *vous aurez votre tour*, your turn will come.

tour (3) [tuːr], *n.m.* Lathe; potter's wheel; turning-box (in a convent). (*fig.*) *Elle est faite au tour*, she has a fine figure.

touraillage [tura'jaːʒ], *n.m.* Kilning of malt. **touraille,** *n.f.* Malt-kiln. **touraillon,** *n.m.* Malt combs.

tourangeau [turɑ̃'ʒo], *a.* (*fem.* **-elle,** *pl.* **-eaux**) Of Touraine.—*n.* Native of Touraine.

tourbe (1) [turb], *n.f.* Mob, vulgar herd; rabble.

tourbe (2) [turb], *n.f.* Peat, turf.

tourber, *v.i.* To cut peat.—*v.t.* To cut peat from (bog etc.). **tourbeux,** *a.* (*fem.* **-euse**) Peaty. **tourbier,** *n.m.* Peat-worker; owner of peat-bog. **tourbière,** *n.f.* Peat-bog, peat-moss.

tourbillon [turbi'jɔ̃], *n.m.* Whirlwind; whirlpool, eddy; (*Phil.*) vortex; (*fig.*) hurly-burly, bustle; tourbillion (firework). *Tourbillon de poussière*, a swirling cloud of dust. **tourbillonnant,** *a.* (*fem.* **-ante**) Whirling. **tourbillonnement,** *n.m.* Whirling, eddying. **tourbillonner,** *v.i.* To whirl, to eddy, to swirl.

tourdille [tur'diːj], *a.* Spotty or dirty grey.

tourelle [tu'rɛl], *n.f.* Turret; gun-turret. *Tourelle de veille*, conning-tower.

touret [tu're], *n.m.* Spinning-wheel, wheel (of a lathe etc.); angler's reel; bow-drill; (*Naut.*) thole-pin.

tourie [tu'ri], *n.f.* Carboy.

tourier [tu'rje], *n.m. and a.* (*fem.* **-ière**) Monk or nun in attendance (at the turning-box in a convent).

tourillon [turi'jɔ̃], *n.m.* Axle; axle-tree, arbor; spindle, pivot; trunnion (of gun); gudgeon-pin, crank-pin.

tourisme [tu'rism], *n.m.* Touring, tourism. *Bureau de tourisme*, tourist agency. **touriste,** *n.* Tourist, tripper. **touristique,** *a.* Touristic, tourist.

tourlourou [turlu'ru], *n.m.* (*pop.*) Infantry soldier, tommy.

tourmaline [turma'lin], *n.f.* Tourmaline.

tourment [tur'mɑ̃], *n.m.* Torment, torture;

anguish, pain; agony of mind. **tourmen-tant**, *a.* (*fem.* **-ante**) Tormenting, trouble-some. **tourmente**, *n.f.* Tempest, storm; (*fig.*) disturbance, turmoil.

tourmenté [turmɑ̃ˈte], *a.* (*fem.* **-ée**) Tormented, tortured; uneasy (mind); broken (coast-line etc.); over-elaborate (style). **tourmenter**, *v.t.* To torment, to torture, to rack; to distress, to trouble, to harass; to worry, to pester; to jolt; to agitate, to toss, to rock; to elaborate (style etc.). *Que cela ne vous tourmente point*, don't let that worry or trouble you; *son procès le tourmente*, his lawsuit is worrying him. **se tourmenter**, *v.r.* To torment oneself; to be uneasy, to fret; to warp (of wood); to labour hard (of a ship).

tourmenteur, *a.* (*fem.* **tourmenteuse** (1)) Torturing, tormenting.—*n.* Torturer, tormentor. ***tourmenteux**, *a.* (*fem.* **tourmenteuse** (2)) Stormy (of regions).

tourmentin, *n.m.* (*Naut.*) Storm-jib.

tournage [turˈnaːʒ], *n.m.* (*Naut.*) Turning, belaying; (*Cine.*) shooting. **tournailler**, *v.i.* (*colloq.*) To go round and round *or* to and fro; to prowl round. **tournant**, *a.* (*fem.* **-ante**) Turning, winding. *Escalier tournant*, spiral staircase; *mouvement tournant*, (*Mil.*) outflanking movement; *plaque tournante*, turn-table; *pont tournant*, revolving- *or* swing-bridge.—*n.m.* Turn, turning, bend; street corner; turning-space (for a vehicle); (*fig.*) shift, contrivance, indirect means; turning-point; (*Naut.*) whirlpool, eddy; waterwheel; (*Path.*) [TOURNIOLE]. *Au tournant de la rue*, at the corner of the street; (*fam.*) *attendre quelqu'un au tournant*, to wait for a chance of revenge. **tournasser**, *v.t.* To throw (pottery), to shape on the potter's wheel. **tournasseur**, *n.m.* Thrower (of pottery). **tourné**, *a.* (*fem.* **-ée**) Turned, shaped, made; expressed, etc. (in a certain way); sour, spoilt. *Avoir l'esprit mal tourné*, to be cross-grained; *avoir la tête tournée*, to have one's head turned (by success), to be distracted (with fear etc.); *lait tourné*, sour milk; *lettre mal tournée*, badly phrased letter; *personne bien tournée*, handsome person.

tourne-à-gauche [turnaˈgoːʃ], *n.m. inv.* Wrench.

tournebroche, *n.m.* Roasting-jack; turnspit.

tourne-disques [turnəˈdisk], *n.m. inv.* Pick-up and turn-table.

tournedos, *n.m. inv.* Fillet steak.

tournée [turˈne], *n.f.* Round, turn, visit, journey; circuit. *Il est en tournée*, he is on his round (of postman, inspector, etc.), he is on circuit (of judges, barristers, etc.). *Payer une tournée*, (*pop.*) to stand drinks all round.

tourne-feuille [turnəˈfœːj], *n.f.* (*pl.* **tourne-feuilles**) Leaf-turner of music.

tourne-gants, *n.m. inv.* Glove-stick, glove-stretcher.

tournemain [turnəˈmɛ̃], *n.m.* (*Only in*) *En un tournemain*, in a trice.

tournement [turnəˈmɑ̃], *n.m.* *Tournement de tête*, swimming in the head, giddiness.

tourne-oreille [turnɔˈrɛːj], *n.m. inv.* Plough with turning mould-board. *Charrue tourne-oreille*, such a plough.

tourne-pierre [turnəˈpjɛːr], *n.m.* (*pl.* **tourne-pierres**) Turnstone (bird).

tourner [turˈne], *v.t.* To turn; to turn round,

to revolve, to twirl, to slew; to turn over, to turn up; to wind; to go or get round, to circumvent; (*Cine.*) to shoot (a film); (*Mil.*) to outflank; to manage; to translate; to construe, to convert, to interpret; to fashion, to shape. *Il tourne bien un vers*, he is a good hand at turning a verse; *tourner du latin en français*, to turn Latin into French; *tourner et retourner une idée dans son esprit*, to go over and over an idea in one's mind; *tourner la conversation*, to change the subject of conversation; *tourner la difficulté*, to side-step the issue, to evade the difficulty; *tourner la tête à quelqu'un*, to turn someone's head, to infatuate someone; *tourner le dos à quelqu'un*, to turn one's back on someone, to give someone the cold shoulder; *tourner le sang à quelqu'un*, to upset someone, to give someone quite a turn; *tourner ses souliers*, to wear one's shoes down on one side; *tourner la mêlée*, (*Ftb.*) to wheel the scrum; *tourner les talons*, to turn on one's heel; *tourner tout en mal*, to put a wrong construction on everything; *tourner une carte*, to turn up a card; *tourner une chose en raillerie*, to make a joke of something; *tourner une page*, to turn over a page; *tourner une personne à son gré*, to twist a person round one's little finger.—*v.i.* To turn, to turn round, to revolve, to wheel round, to wind; to turn out; to change; to colour, to ripen; to turn up (of cards); to spoil, to curdle (of liquids); (*Cine.*) to shoot a film; to play in a film. *Cela tournera mal*, no good will come of that; *faire tourner*, to turn, to spin, to curdle; *faire tourner une machine*, to start a machine; *il tourne comme une girouette*, he is for ever changing his mind; *la chance a tourné*, the luck has changed, (*fig.*) the tables are turned; *la tête lui a tourné*, he lost his head; *la tête me tourne*, I feel quite giddy; *le temps tourne au beau*, the weather is changing to fair; *tourner autour du pot*, to beat about the bush; *tourner court*, to turn sharply, to stop abruptly, to make off; *tourner du côté de quelqu'un*, to go over to someone's side; *tourner vers*, to turn towards. **se tourner**, *v.r.* To turn round, to turn about; to turn (towards or against); to turn, to change. (*fig.*) *Il ne sait plus de quel côté se tourner*, he does not know which way to turn.

tournerie [turnəˈri], *n.f.* Turner's shop.

tournesol [turnəˈsɔl], *n.m.* Turnsole, sun-flower; (*Chem.*) litmus.

tournette [turˈnet], *n.f.* Cotton winder; skein-holder; squirrel's cage; circular glass-cutter.

tourneur [turˈnœːr], *n.m.* Turner.—*a. Derviche tourneur*, dancing dervish. **tourneuse**, *n.f.* Reeler, winder (of silk).

tournevent [turnəˈvɑ̃], *n.m.* Cowl (for chimney).

tournevire [turnəˈviːr], *n.f.* or *m.* (*Naut.*) Messenger (for weighing an anchor).

tournevis [turnəˈvis], *n.m.* Turnscrew, screwdriver.

tourniole [turˈnjɔl], *n.f.* Whitlow.

tourniquer [TOURNAILLER].

tourniquet [turniˈke], *n.m.* Turnstile; whirligig; screw-jack; swivel; sash-pulley; (*Surg.*) tourniquet. (*Mil. slang*) *Passer au tourniquet*, to be court-martialled.

tournis [turˈni], *n.m.* (*Vet.*) Sturdy, staggers.

tournoi [turˈnwa], *n.m.* Tournament.

tournoiement [turnwa′mɑ̃], *n.m.* Turning round, wheeling, whirling, swirling; dizziness, staggers.

tournoyant [turnwa′jɑ̃], *a.* (*fem.* **-ante**) Turning, wheeling, whirling, swirling, eddying. **tournoyer**, *v.i. irr.* (*conjug. like* ABOYER) To turn round and round, to wheel or whirl round, to wind; to eddy; (*fig.*) to beat about the bush, to shilly-shally.

tournure [tur′ny:r], *n.f.* Turn, direction, course; figure, shape, tournure; bustle (part of dress); (*fig.*) cast (of mind, style, etc.). *Avoir mauvaise tournure*, to have a bad figure, (*fig.*) to look bad; *les choses commencent à prendre une mauvaise tournure*, things are beginning to look bad.

tourte [turt], *n.f.* Raised pie (with fish, meat, or fruit inside); big round loaf; (*fam.*) idiot, dolt, bumpkin. *Tourte aux pommes*, apple pie, apple tart.

tourteau [tur′to], *n.m.* (*pl.* **-eaux**) Oilcake; cattle cake; hermit-crab; (*Her.*) roundel.

tourtereau [turtə′ro], *n.m.* (*pl.* **-eaux**) Young turtle-dove; (*pl.*) (*fam.*) lovers. **tourterelle**, *n.f.* Turtle-dove.

tourtière [tur′tjɛ:r], *n.f.* Pie-dish, tart-tin.

tous [tu:s], *a.m.pl.* [TOUT].

touselle [tu′zɛl], *n.f.* Beardless wheat.

toussailler [tusa′je], *v.i.* To cough often (but not loudly). **toussailleur**, *n.m.* One who does that.

Toussaint, la [tu′sɛ̃], *f.* All Saints' Day.

tousser [tu′se], *v.i.* To cough. *Tousser un coup*, to clear one's throat. **tousserie**, *n.f.* Habitual or repeated coughing. **tousseur**, *n.m.* (*fem.* **-euse**) Cougher. **toussoter**, *v.i.* [*see* TOUSSAILLER].

tout [tu; *liaison-form*, tut], *a.* (*fem.* **toute**, *pl. m.* **tous**, *fem.* **toutes**) All; whole, the whole of; every; each; any. *C'est tout un*, it's all the same; *courir à toutes jambes*, to run as fast as one can; *tous* (*les*) *deux*, both; *tous les deux jours*, every other day; *tous les huit jours*, every week; *tous les jours*, every day; *tous les quinze jours*, every fortnight; *tous mes livres*, all my books; *tout autre que lui*, anybody but he (him); *toute la famille*, all the *or* the whole family; *toutes les fois que*, as often as, every time that; *toute une histoire*, a long story; *tout homme qui*, any man who; *toute la journée*, the whole day; *tout le monde*, all the world, everybody.—*pron. indef.* (*m.pl.* pronounced tu:s) All, everything; all men. *À tout prendre*, on the whole, all things considered; *avez-vous tout dit?* have you had your say? *une bonne à tout faire*, a general (maid); *c'est tout*, that is all; *comme tout*, exceedingly, extremely, like anything; *du tout*, not at all; *en tout*, in all, on the whole; *est-ce tout?* is that all? *il est propre à tout*, he is fit for anything; *il n'aura rien du tout*, he shall have nothing at all; *il veut tout avoir*, he wants to have everything; *par-dessus tout*, above all; *point du tout*, not at all; *tout bien considéré*, all things considered; *tout ce qui vous plaira*, whatever you like, anything you like; *tout est bien qui finit bien*, all's well that ends well; *voilà tout*, that is all.—*n.m.* Whole, the whole; the chief point, only thing. *Il est son tout*, he is her all or the particular object of her affection etc.; *le grand tout*, the whole

of things; *plusieurs tous distincts*, several distinct wholes; *risquer le tout pour le tout*, to risk all to win all.—*adv.* (**toute** or **toutes** before fem. adj. beginning with a consonant or aspirated *h*) Wholly, entirely, quite, thoroughly; all, altogether; although, however, for all. *Ces fleurs sont toutes fraîches*, these flowers are quite fresh; *c'est une tout autre chose*, that's quite a different matter; *des femmes tout éplorées*, women all in tears; *être tout yeux, tout oreilles*, to be all eyes, all ears; *je suis tout à vous*, I am entirely at your service; *parler tout haut*, to speak aloud; *tout à coup*, suddenly; *tout à fait*, quite, entirely; *tout à l'heure*, just now; presently; *tout au moins*, at the very least; *tout au plus*, at the most; *tout à vous*, sincerely yours; *tout beau* or *tout doux*, softly, gently, not so fast; *tout comme vous voudrez*, just as you please; *tout de bon*, in earnest; *tout de suite*, immediately; *tout d'un coup*, all at once; *tout en le disant*, while saying so; *toute femme qu'elle est*, woman though she is; *toutes bonnes qu'elles sont*, however good they may be; *toutes malades qu'elles sont*, ill as they are; *tout nu*, stark naked.

tout-à-l'égout [tutale′gu], *n.m.* Direct to sewer drainage.

toute-épice [tute′pi:s], *n.f.* (*pl.* **toutes-épices**) All-spice.

toutefois [tut′fwa], *adv.* Yet, nevertheless, however, still.

toute-présence [tutpre′zɑ̃:s], *n.f.* Omnipresence, ubiquity.

toute-puissance [tutpɥi′sɑ̃:s], *n.f.* Omnipotence, almighty power.

toute-saine [tut′sen], *n.f.* (*Bot.*) Tutsan.

toute-science [tut′sjɑ̃:s], *n.f.* (*Theol.*) Omniscience.

toutou [tu′tu], *n.m.* Bow-wow, doggy.

tout-ou-rien [tutu′rjɛ̃], *n.m. inv.* Repeating-spring in watch or clock.

tout-puissant [tupɥi′sɑ̃], *a.* (*fem.* **toute-puissante**) Almighty.—*n.m.* The Almighty.

toux [tu], *n.f. inv.* Cough. *Toux grasse*, loose cough; *toux d'irritation*, tickling cough.

toxémie [tɔkse′mi], *n.f.* (*Med.*) Toxaemia, blood poisoning. **toxicité**, *n.f.* Toxicity, poisonousness. **toxicologie**, *n.f.* Toxicology. **toxicologique**, *a.* Toxicological. **toxicologue**, *n.* Toxicologist. **toxicomane**, *n.* Drug-addict, dope-fiend. **toxicomanie**, *n.f.* Toxicomania, addiction to drugs. **toxicose**, *n.f.* Toxicosis. **toxine**, *n.f.* Toxin. **toxique**, *n.m.* Poison.—*a.* Toxic, poisonous.

trabéation [trabea′sjɔ̃], *n.f.* Trabeation, entablature.

trabéculaire [trabeky′lɛ:r], *a.* (*Anat.*) Trabecular.

trac (1) [trak], *n.m.* (*fam.*) Funk. *Avoir le trac*, to get the wind up; (*esp.*) to have stage-fright.

trac (2) [trak], *n.m. Tout à trac*, thoughtlessly, without thinking.

traçage [tra′sa:ʒ], *n.m.* Tracing, marking, setting-out.

traçant [tra′sɑ̃], *a.* (*fem.* **-ante**) (*Bot.*) Running (of roots). *Balle traçante*, tracer-bullet.

tracas [tra′ka], *n.m.* Bustle, turmoil, stir, disturbance; worry, annoyance. *Tracas des affaires*, turmoil of business. **tracassant**, *a.*

(fem. **-ante)** Worrying, bothersome. **tra-cassement,** *n.m.* Worrying. **tracasser,** *v.i.* To bustle about; to fidget, to make a fuss.— *v.t.* To worry, to pester. **se tracasser,** *v.r.* To worry. **tracasserie,** *n.f.* Worry, pestering, annoyance, vexation; *(pl.)* bickering, pin-pricks. **tracassier,** *a. (fem.* **-ière)** Pestering, worrying, annoying; fussy; mischief-making.—*n.* Pesterer, busybody; troublesome person, mischief-maker.

trace [tras], *n.f.* Trace, track, footprint; spoor, trail, slot; mark, impression, vestige; outline, sketch. **tracé,** *n.m.* Outline, sketch (of figure); setting out (of curve); marking out; laying out (of grounds etc.); direction, line. *Faire le tracé de,* to sketch, to lay out. **tracelet** or **traceret,** *n.m.* Tracer, tracing-point. **tracement,** *n.m.* Tracing, laying out (of grounds, roads, etc.). **tracer,** *v.t.* To trace, to draw, to trace out; to sketch; to draw, to delineate, to portray; to lay out (grounds, roads, etc.); *(fig.)* to set forth, to mark out. *v.i.* To spread their roots, to run out (of trees); to burrow (of moles).

traceret [TRACELET].

traceur, *n.m. (fem.* **-euse)** Tracer.

trachéal [trake'al], *a. (fem.* **-ale,** *pl.* **-aux)** *(Anat.)* Tracheal.

trachée [tra'ʃe], *n.f.* Trachea, air-vessel. **trachée-artère,** *n.f. (pl.* **trachées-artères)** Trachea, windpipe.

trachéite [trake'it], *n.f.* Tracheitis. **trachéotomie,** *n.f.* Tracheotomy.

trachyte [tra'kit], *n.m. (Min.)* Trachyte.

traçoir [tra'swa:r], *n.m.* Tracer [TRACELET].

tract [trakt], *n.m.* Tract, leaflet (for propaganda).

tractation [traktɑ'sjɔ̃], *n.f.* *(Often pej.)* Transaction, dealing, bargaining.

tracté [trak'te], *a. (fem.* **-ée)** *(Mil.)* Tractor-drawn (gun etc.).

tracteur [trak'tœ:r], *n.m.* Tractor, traction-engine. **tractif,** *a. (fem.* **-ive)** Tractive.

traction [trak'sjɔ̃], *n.f.* Traction; pulling; draught; *(Gym.)* pull-up (to the bar). *Traction à bras,* man-haulage; *résistance à la traction,* tensile strength. *(Motor.)* *Une traction avant,* a front-wheel-drive car.

tractoire, *a.* Tractive.

traditeur [tradi'tœ:r], *n.m.* *(Eccles. Hist.)* Traditor.

tradition [tradi'sjɔ̃], *n.f.* Tradition; *(Law)* delivery. *De tradition,* traditional; *tradition de la chose vendue,* delivery of the thing sold. **traditionalisme,** *n.m.* Traditionalism. **traditionaliste,** *n.* and *a.* Traditionalist. **traditionnaire,** *n.m.* and *a.* *(Jewish Relig.)* Traditionary.

traditionnel, *a. (fem.* **-elle)** Traditional. **traditionnellement,** *adv.* Traditionally.

traducteur [tradyk'tœ:r], *n.m. (fem.* **-trice)** Translator.

traduction, *n.f.* Translation, *(sch.)* crib.

traduire [tra'dɥi:r], *v.t. irr. (conjugated like* CONDUIRE) To translate; to interpret, to construe, to render; to convey, to express; to indicate, to denote; *(Law)* to arraign, to indict, to sue. *Traduire à livre ouvert,* to translate at sight. **traduisible,** *a.* Translatable. *Traduisible en justice,* liable to prosecution.

trafic [tra'fik], *n.m.* Traffic; trading, trade; dealings. *Il fait trafic de toute sorte de marchandises,* he deals in all sorts of goods; *trafic d'influence,* corruption. **trafiquant,** *n.m.* Trafficker. **trafiquer,** *v.i.* To traffic, to trade, to deal *(de)*; to make a traffic *(de)*.

tragacanthe [traga'kɑ̃:t], *n.f.* Tragacanth.

tragédie [traʒe'di], *n.f.* Tragedy. **tragédien,** *n.m. (fem.* **-ienne)** Tragedian. **tragi-comédie,** *n.f. (pl.* **tragi-comédies)** Tragicomedy. **tragi-comique,** *a. (pl.* **tragi-comiques)** Tragi-comic. **tragique,** *a.* Tragic, tragical.—*n.m.* Tragedy, tragic art; tragic writer; tragicalness, tragic part. *Prendre une chose au tragique,* to take a thing too seriously. **tragiquement,** *adv.* Tragically.

trahir [tra'i:r], *v.t.* To betray; to be false to, to deceive; to divulge, to reveal, to give away. *Trahir le secret de quelqu'un,* to betray someone's secret. **se trahir,** *v.r.* To be false to oneself, to betray oneself; to betray each other.

trahison, *n.f.* Treachery, treacherousness, treason, perfidy, foul play; breach of faith. *Trahison des clercs,* breach of trust.

traille [trɑ:j], *n.f.* Trail-ferry; trawl-net.

train [trɛ̃], *n.m.* Pace, rate; train, suite, attendants; way, course, manner; mood, spirits; noise, clatter, dust; carriage, skeleton (of carriages); quarters (of a horse etc.); train of boats etc.; raft, float of wood; railway-train; *(Print.)* carriage. *À fond de train,* at full speed; *aller grand* or *bon train,* to go at a great rate; *aller son train,* (of a thing) to have its course; *au train où il va,* at the rate he goes on; *être en train,* to be in good spirits, to be in the mood; *être en train de faire quelque chose,* to be (in the act of) doing something; *faire du train,* to make a fuss, to kick up a shindy; *il va toujours son train,* he goes on in the same old way; *l'affaire est en bon train,* the business is in a fair way; *le train des équipages,* *(Mil.)* Army Service Corps; *mener bon train,* to drive hard, *(fig.)* to lead a pretty dance; *(spt.)* *mener le train,* to set the pace; *mener un grand train,* to live in great style; *mettre en train,* to set going, to put in hand; *mise en train,* *(Print.)* making ready; *train d'aller,* down train; *train d'atterrissage,* undercarriage; *train de devant,* forepart, forequarters; *train de maison,* establishment; *train de marchandises,* goods train; *train de plaisir,* (short) excursion train; *train de retour,* up train; *train de vie,* way of living; *train omnibus,* slow or stopping train; *train supplémentaire,* relief train.

traînage [trɛ'naːʒ], *n.m.* Dragging, drawing; sledging, sleighing. **traînailler,** *v.i.* [TRAÎNASSER]. **traînant,** *a. (fem.* **-ante)** Dragging, trailing (dress); drawling (voice); prolix, tiresome (style); shuffling (gait). **traînard,** *n.m.* Straggler, laggard; slow-coach. **traînasse,** *n.f.* Knot-grass; drag-net for partridges etc. **traînasser,** *v.t. (colloq.)* To spin out, to drag out, to protract.—*v.i.* To linger, to loiter about.

traîne [trɛ:n], *n.f.* Dragging, being dragged or drawn; train (of a dress etc.); *(Naut.)* rope's end; drag-net. *Bateau à la traîne,* boat in tow (at the stern of a ship); *perdreaux en traîne,* unfledged partridges.

traîneau [trɛ'no], *n.m. (pl.* **-eaux)** Sledge, sleigh; drag-net; truck.

traîne-buisson [trɛnbҷi'sɔ̃], *n.m.* (*pl.* **traîne-buissons**) Hedge-sparrow.

traînée [trɛ'ne], *n.f.* Train (of gunpowder etc.); trail, track; (*slang*) street-walker. (*Av.*) *Effort de traînée*, drag.

traîne-malheur [trɛnma'lœːr] or **traîne-misère**, *n. inv.* Wretch.

traîner [trɛ'ne], *v.t.* To drag, to draw, to drag along; to track; to spin out, to drag out, to protract; to drawl; to put off. *Traîner dans la boue*, to trail, (*fig.*) to drag (someone's) name through the mud, to defame; *traîner un homme en prison*, to drag a man off to prison. —*v.i.* To trail, to draggle, to lag; to droop; to languish, to flag; to lie about; to loiter, to linger, to be in abeyance or in suspense; to be spun out, to be protracted; to be found everywhere. *Cela traîne dans tous les livres*, that is found in every book; *faire traîner les choses en longueur*, to drag things out; *l'affaire traîne*, the matter hangs fire; *votre robe traîne*, your gown is trailing. **se traîner**, *v.r.* To crawl along, to creep; to lag, to drag oneself along.

traînerie, *n.f.* Dragging, drawling; delay.

traîneur, *n.m.* (*fem.* **-euse**) Straggler, lagger; poacher (with a trammel). *Traîneur d'épée* or *traîneur de sabre*, swashbuckler.

trainglot [*see* TRINGLOT].

train-poste [trɛ̃'pɔst], *n.m.* (*pl.* **trains-poste(s)**) Mail-train.

train-train [trɛ̃'trɛ̃], *n.m.* (*colloq.*) Routine, regular course.

traire [trɛːr], *v.t. irr.* (*pres.p.* **trayant**, *p.p.* **trait** (1)) To milk; to draw (milk). **trait** (2), *a.* (*fem.* **traite** (1)) Wire-drawn (of metals).

trait (3) [trɛ], *n.m.* Arrow, dart, bolt, shaft; thunderbolt; stroke, hit; trace (of harness); leash (for dogs); turn (of the scale); draught, gulp (of liquor); dash (of the pen etc.); flash (of light); idea, burst (of eloquence etc.); stroke, touch; kerf (of a saw); trait, feature, lineament; act, deed; fact; relation, connexion; prime move (at chess, draughts, etc.); (*Theol.*) tract. *Avoir trait à*, to have reference to; *boire à longs traits*, to drink long draughts of; *cheval de trait*, draught-horse; *copier trait pour trait*, to copy stroke for stroke; *décocher* or *lancer un trait*, to let fly an arrow; *dessiner au trait*, to delineate; *d'un seul trait*, at one gulp; *il partit comme un trait*, he was off like a flash; *tout d'un trait*, at a stroke, at one stretch; *trait de génie*, stroke of genius, (*fam.*) brain-wave; *trait de satire*, satirical stroke; *trait d'esprit*, witticism; *trait d'union*, hyphen, connecting link.

traitable [trɛ'tabl], *a.* Tractable, manageable; ductile, malleable.

traitant [trɛ'tɑ̃], *a. Médecin traitant*, practising doctor.—**n.m.* Tax-farmer.

traite (2) [trɛt], *n.f.* Stage, journey, stretch; traffic, trading (on the African coast); milking; (*Comm.*) draft, bill. *Je m'y rendis d'une seule traite*, I did the journey there non-stop. *Faire la traite*, to carry on the slave-trade; *traite des blanches*, white-slave traffic; *traite des noirs*, slave-trade. *Faire traite sur*, to draw (a bill) on.

traité [trɛ'te], *n.m.* Treatise, tract, dissertation; treaty; agreement. *Traité de paix*, peace-treaty.

traitement [trɛt'mɑ̃], *n.m.* Treatment; (*Ind.*) processing; reception; salary, pay. *Mauvais traitements*, ill-usage.

traiter [trɛ'te], *v.t.* To treat; (*Ind.*) to process; to entertain, to board; to use, to behave to; to deal by; to discuss, to handle, to discourse upon; to call, to style; to negotiate, to be in treaty for; to execute, to do. *Il l'a traité de lâche*, he called him a coward; *il m'a traité en frère*, he treated me like a brother; *traiter de haut en bas*, to treat with contempt; *traiter quelqu'un de Turc à More*, to treat someone harshly, to use someone shamefully.—*v.i.* To treat, to negotiate, to come to terms; to treat of, to deal with (*de*). *Traiter d'une matière*, to treat of a matter. **traiteur**, *n.m.* Restaurant-keeper; caterer; trader (with savages).

traître [trɛːtr], *a.* (*fem.* **-esse**) Treacherous, false, perfidious.—*n.* Treacherous person, traitor, traitress; (*Theat.*) villain. *Prendre en traître*, to fall upon in a treacherous manner. *Traître à sa foi*, betrayer of his faith. **traîtreusement**, *adv.* Treacherously. **traîtrise**, *n.f.* Treachery.

trajectoire [traʒɛk'twaːr], *n.f.* and *a.* Trajectory.

trajet [tra'ʒɛ], *n.m.* Distance, way; passage, journey, crossing, voyage; (*Med.*) course. *Faire le trajet*, to make the passage; *trajet d'une heure*, an hour's walk.

tralala [trala'la], *n.m.* (*fam.*) *Être sur son tralala* or *en grand tralala*, to be decked out in all one's finery, to be dressed up to the nines; *faire du tralala*, to make a fuss or a display of one's finery.

tram [tram], *n.m. abbr.* of *tramway*.

tramail [tra'maːj] or **trémail**, *n.m.* (*pl.* **-ails**) Trammel, drag-net.

trame [tram], *n.f.* Weft, woof; plot, conspiracy; course, progress, thread. *La trame de sa vie*, the course of his life; *ourdir une trame*, to hatch a plot. **tramer**, *v.t.* To weave; (*fig.*) to plot, to contrive, to hatch.

tramontane [tramɔ̃'tan], *n.f.* Tramontane, north wind; north; North Star. *Perdre la tramontane*, to be at one's wits' end, to lose one's bearings.

tramway [tra'mwɛ], *n.m.* Tramcar, (*fam.*) tram, (*Am.*) street car. *Ligne de tramway*, tramway.

tranchant [trɑ̃'ʃɑ̃], *a.* (*fem.* **-ante**) Sharp, cutting; (*fig.*) trenchant, peremptory, decisive; salient, prominent. *Couleurs tranchantes*, glaring colours; *écuyer tranchant*, gentleman-carver.—*n.m.* Edge. *Épée à deux tranchants*, two-edged sword.

tranche [trɑ̃ʃ], *n.f.* Slice, chop; slab; edge (of a book); (*Fin.*) instalment, block (of shares); (*Arith.*) period, series. *Doré sur tranche*, gilt-edged (of a book); *tranche de lard*, rasher of bacon. **tranchée**, *n.f.* Trench, cut, cutting, ditch; entrenchment; (*pl.*) gripes, griping pains, colic. *Tranchée-abri*, rifle-pit. *Tranchées rouges*, gripes (in horses).

tranchefile, *n.f.* (*Bookb.*) Headband; bar (in a shoe).

tranche-gazon, *n.m. inv.* Turfing-iron.

tranche-lard, *n.m. inv.* Cook's knife.

trancher [trɑ̃'ʃe], *v.t.* To cut; to cut off; to slice; to decide, to determine, to solve, to settle. *Ceci tranche la difficulté*, this removes the obstacle; *trancher le mot*, to say the word, to speak out; *trancher la question*, to clinch the matter, to cut the Gordian knot.—*v.i.* To cut; to decide, to determine, to resolve; to set up for, to affect; to be glaring, to stand out clearly (of colours). *Ces couleurs ne tranchent pas assez*, those colours do not contrast sufficiently; *trancher court*, to cut short; *trancher dans le vif*, to cut to the quick, *(fig.)* to set to work in earnest; *trancher du grand seigneur*, to lord it; *trancher du petit-maître*, to affect the dandy.

tranchet [trɑ̃'ʃɛ], *n.m.* Shoemaker's knife, paring-knife, etc.

tranchoir [trɑ̃'ʃwaːr], *n.m.* Trencher, cutting-board.

tranquille [trɑ̃'kil], *a.* Quiet, calm, still, tranquil, placid, peaceful; easy, undisturbed (in mind etc.). *Laissez-moi tranquille*, leave me alone, nonsense! *soyez tranquille*, set your mind at ease. **tranquillement**, *adv.* Peacefully, quietly. **tranquillisant**, *a.* (*fem.* **-ante**) Tranquillizing. **tranquilliser**, *v.t.* To tranquillize, to make easy, to soothe. **se tranquilliser**, *v.r.* To become tranquil, to make oneself easy, to calm down. **tranquillité**, *n.f.* Tranquillity, quiet, peace.

transaction [trɑ̃zak'sjɔ̃], *n.f.* Transaction, compromise, arrangement. **transactionnel**, *a.* (*fem.* **-elle**) Transactional.

transalpin [trɑ̃zal'pɛ̃], *a.* (*fem.* **-ine**) Transalpine.

transat [trɑ̃'zat], *n.m.* (*fam.*) *abbr. for transatlantique*, deck-chair.

transatlantique [trɑ̃zatlɑ̃'tik], *a.* Transatlantic.—*n.m.* Liner; deck-chair.

transbordement [trɑ̃sbɔrdə'mɑ̃], *n.m.* Transhipment. **transborder**, *v.t.* To tranship. **transbordeur**, *n.m.* Transporter (travelling-platform etc.). *Pont transbordeur*, transporting-bridge.

transcendance [trɑ̃sɑ̃'dɑ̃ːs], *n.f.* Transcendency. **transcendant**, *a.* (*fem.* **-ante**) Transcendent. **transcendantal**, *a.* (*fem.* **-ale**, *pl.* **-aux**) Transcendental. **transcendantalisme**, *n.m.* Transcendentalism. **transcendantaliste**, *n.* Transcendentalist.

transcontinental [trɑ̃skɔ̃tinɑ̃'tal], *a.* (*fem.* **-ale**, *pl.* **-aux**) Transcontinental.

transcripteur [trɑ̃skrip'tœːr], *n.m.* Transcriber. **transcription**, *n.f.* Transcription, transcript, copy. **transcrire**, *v.t. irr.* (*conjug. like* ÉCRIRE) To transcribe, to copy out.

transe [trɑ̃ːs], *n.f.* Fright, apprehension; trance. *Être dans les transes*, to be in mortal terror.

transept [trɑ̃'sɛpt], *n.m.* Transept.

transférable [trɑ̃sfe'rabl], *a.* Transferable. **transfèrement**, *n.m.* Transference, conveying (of convicts).

transférer [trɑ̃sfe're], *v.t. irr.* (*conjugated like* ACCÉLÉRER). To transfer, to transport, to convey; to translate (bishops etc.); to put off, to postpone. *Transférer son droit*, to make over one's right; *transférer une fête*, to postpone a fête.

transfert [trɑ̃s'fɛːr], *n.m.* Transfer; (*Law*) conveyance.

transfiguration [trɑ̃sfigyrɑ'sjɔ̃], *n.f.* Transfiguration. **transfigurer**, *v.t.* To transfigure. **se transfigurer**, *v.r.* To be transfigured.

transfilage [trɑ̃sfi'laːʒ], *n.m.* (*Naut.*) Lashing.

transfiler, *v.t.* To lash (two ropes etc.) together.

transformable [trɑ̃sfɔr'mabl], *a.* Transformable, convertible. **transformateur**, *n.m.* (*Elec.*) Transformer.—*a.* (*fem.* **-trice**) Transforming.

transformation [trɑ̃sfɔrmɑ'sjɔ̃], *n.f.* Transformation. **transformer**, *v.t.* To transform; to change, to convert. **se transformer**, *v.r.* To be transformed; to transform oneself or itself.

transformisme [trɑ̃sfɔr'mism], *n.m.* (*Phil.*) Transformism. **transformiste**, *a. and n.* Transformist.

transfuge [trɑ̃s'fyːʒ], *n.m.* Deserter; fugitive; turncoat.

transfuser [trɑ̃sfy'ze], *v.t.* To transfuse. **transfuseur**, *n.m.* Transfuser. **transfusion**, *n.f.* Transfusion.

transgresser [trɑ̃sgrɛ'se], *v.t.* To transgress, to infringe, to contravene. **transgresseur*, *n.m.* Transgressor. **transgression**, *n.f.* Transgression.

transhumance [trɑ̃zy'mɑ̃ːs], *n.f.* Transhumance. **transhumants**, *n.m. pl.* Flocks on transhumance. **transhumer**, *v.t., v.i.* To transhume.

transi [trɑ̃'si], *a.* (*fem.* **-ie**) Chilled, benumbed. *Amoureux transi*, bashful lover; *transi de froid*, perished with cold.

transiger [trɑ̃zi'ʒe], *v.i.* To compound, to compromise, to come to terms (*avec*).

transir [trɑ̃'siːr], *v.t.* To chill, to benumb; to overcome with fear etc., to paralyse.—*v.i.* To be chilled; to be paralysed with fear etc. **transissement**, *n.m.* Chill, numbness; shivering (with terror etc.).

transistor [trɑ̃zis'tɔr], *n.m.* Transistor.

transit [trɑ̃'zit], *n.m.* Transit. **transitaire**, *a.* Pertaining to the transit of goods. *Pays transitaire*, country through which goods are in transit.—*n.m.* Transport agent. **transiter**, *v.t.* To forward.—*v.i.* To be in transit. **transitif**, *a.* (*fem.* **-ive**) Transitive. **transition**, *n.f.* Transition. **transitivement**, *adv.* (*Gram.*) Transitively. **transitoire**, *a.* Transitory. **transitoirement**, *adv.* Transitorily.

translateur [trɑ̃sla'tœːr], *n.m.* Translator, *a.* (*Elec.*) transmitter, repeater.

translatif [trɑ̃sla'tif], *a.* (*fem.* **-ive**) (*Law*) Transferring, pertaining to conveyancing.

translation [trɑ̃slɑ'sjɔ̃], *n.f.* Transfer(ring), relaying, translation.

translucide [trɑ̃sly'sid], *a.* Translucent. **translucidité**, *n.f.* Translucence.

transmarin, *a.* (*fem.* **-ine**) Transmarine, oversea.

transmetteur [trɑ̃smɛ'tœːr], *n.m.* (*Rad.*) Transmitter.—*a.* (*fem.* **-trice**) Transmitting.

transmettre [trɑ̃s'metr], *v.t. irr.* (*conjug. like* METTRE) To transmit, to convey, to send on; to transfer, to make over. *Transmettre son nom à la postérité*, to hand down one's name to posterity. **se transmettre**, *v.r.* To be transmitted.

transmigration [trɑ̃smigrɑ'sjɔ̃], *n.f.* Transmigration. **transmigrer**, *v.i.* To transmigrate.

transmis, *p.p.* (*fem.* **-ise**) [TRANSMETTRE].

transmissibilité [trăsmisibili'te], *n.f.* Transmissibility. **transmissible,** *a.* Transmissible. **transmission,** *n.f.* Transmission, transmittal, passing on. *Arbre de transmission,* driving-shaft; *courroie de transmission,* belt drive; (*Mil.*) *les Transmissions,* the Signals.

transmuable [trăs'mŭabl], *a.* Transmutable. **transmuer,** *v.t.* To transmute. **transmutabilité,** *n.f.* Transmutability. **transmutation,** *n.f.* Transmutation. **transmuter,** *v.t.* To transmute.

transparaître [trăspa're:tr], *v.i. irr.* (*conjug. like* CONNAÎTRE) To appear through.

transparence [trăspa'rā:s], *n.f.* Transparency. **transparent,** *a.* (*fem.* -ente) Transparent.—*n.m.* Paper ruled with black lines, underlines; transparency.

transpercer [trăspɛr'se], *v.t.* To transpierce, to pierce through; to run through (with a sword etc.).

transpiration [trăspirɑ'sjɔ̃], *n.f.* Perspiring, transpiring. **transpirer,** *v.i.* To perspire; to exhale, to ooze out; to transpire; to get abroad (news etc.).

transplantable [trăsplă'tabl], *a.* Transplantable. **transplantation,** *n.f.* Transplantation. **transplanter,** *v.t.* To transplant. **transplanteur,** *n.m.* Transplanter (person). **transplantoir,** *n.m.* Transplanter (instrument).

transport [trăs'pɔ:r], *n.m.* Carriage, conveyance; transport, removal; transfer, assignment; (*fig.*) rapture, ecstasy, delirium; transport-ship. *Compagnie de transport,* forwarding company; *frais de transport,* carriage. *Transport au cerveau,* stroke, fit of delirium. *Transport de joie,* transport of joy. **transportable,** *a.* Transportable. **transportation,** *n.f.* Transportation. **transporté,** *n.* (*fem.* -ée) Transported person, convict. **transporter,** *v.t.* To convey, to transport; to transfer, to make over; to carry over (a balance etc.); to banish; to enrapture. *La joie l'a tout transporté,* he is quite overcome with joy. **se transporter,** *v.r.* To transport oneself, to go, to repair. *Se transporter sur les lieux,* to repair to the spot, to visit the scene of the occurrence. **transporteur,** *n.m.* Carrier, conveyor.

transposable [trăspo'zabl], *a.* Transposable. **transposer,** *v.t.* To transpose. **transpositeur,** *a.* (*fem.* -trice) *Piano transpositeur,* transposing piano. **transpositif,** *a.* (*fem.* -ive) Transpositive. **transposition,** *n.f.* Transposition.

transrhénan [trăsre'nă], *a.* (*fem.* -ane) From beyond the Rhine.

transsaharien [trăssaa'rjɛ̃], *a.* (*fem.* -ienne) Trans-Saharan.

transsibérien [trăssibe'rjɛ̃], *a.* (*fem.* -ienne) Trans-Siberian.

transsubstantiation [trăssybstăsja'sjɔ̃], *n.f.* Transubstantiation. **transsubstantier,** *v.t.* To transubstantiate.

transsudation [:răssydɑ'sjɔ̃], *n.f.* Transudation. **transsuder,** *v.i.* To transude.

transvasement, *n.m.* Decanting, transfusion. **transvaser,** *v.t.* To decant. **transvaseur,** *n.m.* Decanter (person or container).

transversal [trăzver'sal], *a.* (*fem.* -ale, *pl.* -aux) Transversal, transverse. **transver-salement,** *adv.* Crosswise, athwart, transverse, *a.* Transverse.

transvider [trăsvi'de], *v.t.* To pour into another container.

Transylvanie [trăsilva'ni], *f.* Transylvania.

trapèze [tra'pɛ:z], *n.m.* Trapezium; trapeze. *Os trapèze,* trapezium (bone). **trapéziforme,** *a.* Trapeziform. **trapéziste,** *n.* Trapezist. **trapézoïdal** (*fem.* -ale, *pl.* -aux) or **trapézoïde,** *a.* (*Anat.*) Trapezoidal.

trappe [trap], *n.f.* Trap-door; trap, pitfall; curtain, register (of chimney). **trappeur,** *n.m.* Trapper.

trappiste [tra'pist], *n.m. and a.* Trappist.

trapu [tra'py], *a.* (*fem.* -ue) Squat, dumpy, thick-set, stocky.

traque [trak], *n.f.* (*Hunt.*) Enclosing; beating (for game). **traquenard,** *n.m.* Trap (for noxious animals); (*fig.*) snare; (horse's) racking gait. **traquer,** *v.t.* (*Hunt.*) To beat for game; to enclose, to encircle; to ferret out; to round up, to hem in. *Traquer des voleurs,* to round up thieves. **traquet,** *n.m.* Trap (for animals); mill-clapper; (*Orn.*) stonechat. *Donner dans un traquet,* to fall into a trap. **traqueur,** *n.m.* Beater.

trass [tras], *n.m.* (*Min.*) Tarras.

traumaticine [tromati'sin], *n.f.* (*Med.*) Pigment (of gutta-percha).

traumatique [troma'tik], *a.* Traumatic. **traumatisme,** *n.m.* Traumatism. **traumatologie,** *n.f.* Traumatology.

travail (1) [tra'va:j], *n.m.* (*pl.* **travaux**) Labour, work; industry; toil, trouble, pains; travail, childbirth; piece of work, task, job; workmanship; employment, occupation; study; (*pl.*) works, constructions, transactions, proceedings. *A force de travail,* by dint of hard work; *cabinet de travail,* study; *d'un travail exquis,* of exquisite workmanship; *en travail d'enfant,* in labour, in travail; *faire son travail,* to perform one's task; *il a le travail facile,* it is no labour to him; *se mettre au travail,* to set to work; *travaux forcés,* hard labour; *vivre de son travail,* to live by one's labour. *Le Bureau International du Travail,* the International Labour Office. *Les sans-travail,* the unemployed.

travail (2) [tra'va:j], *n.m.* (*pl.* **travails**) Trave (for confining refractory horses whilst they are shod).

travaillé [trava'je], *a.* (*fem.* -ée) Worked, wrought; laboured, elaborate, labouring (under). *Travaillé par une idée,* obsessed by an idea.

travailler [trava'je], *v.i.* To labour, to work; to toil, to be industrious, to be at work; to take pains, to apply oneself (*à*), to study, to make it one's study; to strive, to endeavour; to digest with difficulty; to ferment (of wines); to be strained (of a ship); to warp (of wood); to crack (of a wall). *Faire travailler son argent,* to put one's money out to interest; *se tuer à travailler,* to work oneself to death; *travailler à l'aiguille,* to do needlework; *travailler à la terre,* to till the ground.—*v.t.* To work, to work at, to labour at; to do with care, to take great pains with; to fashion, to work up; to cultivate, to till (the ground); to exercise, to overwork, to fatigue; to torment. *Travailler les esprits,* to excite the minds (of the populace); *travailler son style,* to elaborate one's style. **se travailler,** *v.r.* To torment oneself, to make oneself uneasy; to strain; to be overwrought; to endeavour, to study.

travailleur [travaˈjœːr], *a.* (*fem.* **-euse**) Industrious, hard-working; painstaking.—*n.* Workman, labourer; industrious, hard-working person. **travailleuse,** *n.f.* Work-box table.

travailliste, *n.* Member of the Labour Party.—*a.* Labour, Socialist.

travée [traˈve], *n.f.* (*Arch.*) Bay; truss (of bridges); (*Av.*) rib (of wing).

travelling [travəˈliŋ], *n.m.* (*Cine.*) Dolly shot, travelling shot; travelling platform.

travers [traˈvɛːr], *n.m.* Breadth; irregularity; oddity, eccentricity; (*Naut.*) side, broadside. *À travers champs,* across country; *au travers du corps,* through the body; *avoir l'esprit de travers,* to be wrong-headed; *de travers,* obliquely, awry, askew; *en travers,* across, crosswise; *il prend* or *entend tout de travers,* he puts a wrong construction upon everything; *parler à tort et à travers,* to talk at random; *regarder quelqu'un de travers,* to scowl at someone; *par le travers* (*Naut.*) abeam, athwartships. **traverse,** *n.f.* Crossbar, cross-piece, transom; cross-road, short cut; splinter-bar (of a carriage); (*Rail.*) sleeper; (*Fort.*) traverse; (*fig.*) hitch, setback, misfortune. *Chemin de traverse,* cross-lane; short cut; *prendre la traverse,* to take the short cut; *se jeter* or *se mettre à la traverse,* to place oneself in the way, to oppose, to intervene. **traversée,** *n.f.* Passage, crossing. *La traversée de la Manche à la nage,* the cross-Channel swimming contest. **traversement,** *n.m.* Crossing.

traverser, *v.t.* To cross, to go over or through, to travel through, to traverse, to get through or across; to run through (with a sword etc.); to lie across, to span; to intersect; to penetrate, to drench; to thwart, to cross. *Traverser l'esprit,* to cross the mind (of an idea etc.); *traverser une rivière à la nage,* to swim across a river; *traverser un projet,* to thwart a project. **se traverser,** *v.r.* To traverse (of a horse).

traversier [travɛrˈsje], *a.* (*fem.* **-ière**) Cross; that plies across. *Barque traversière,* ferry-boat; *flûte traversière,* German flute.—*n.m.* Cross-piece (of a hammer).—*n.f.* Cross-bar (in weaving-machine).

traversin [travɛrˈsɛ̃], *n.m.* Bolster; (*Carp. etc.*) cross-beam, cross-piece; (*Naut.*) cross-tree, stretcher (in boats). **traversine,** *n.f.* Cross-piece; transom.

travertin [travɛrˈtɛ̃], *n.m.* Travertine (stone).

travesti [travɛsˈti], *a.* (*fem.* **-ie**) Disguised, masked; travestied, parodied, burlesqued. *Bal travesti,* masked ball; *travesti en paysan,* disguised as a peasant.—*n.m.* Fancy dress. **travestir,** *v.t.* To disguise, to travesty; (*fig.*) to parody, to burlesque; to misinterpret, to misrepresent. **se travestir,** *v.r.* To disguise oneself. **travestissement,** *n.m.* Disguise; travesty. **travestisseur,** *n.m.* (*fem.* **-euse**) Parodist; misinterpreter.

trayeur [trɛˈjœːr], *n.m.* (*fem.* **-euse**) Milker.—*n.f.* Milking-machine.

trayon [trɛˈjɔ̃], *n.m.* Dug, teat (of cows etc.).

trébuchage [trebyˈʃaːʒ], *n.m.* Weighing and sorting of money. **trébuchant,** *a.* (*fem.*

-ante) Of full weight (of coins); stumbling. —*n.m.* Extra weight given to ensure full weight. **trébuchement,** *n.m.* Stumbling, fall, blunder. **trébucher,** *v.i.* To stumble, to slip; to trip, to err; (*fig.*) to turn the scale, to weigh down (of coins etc.). **trébuchet,** *n.m.* Bird-trap, snare; assay-balance. *Prendre quelqu'un au trébuchet,* to entrap someone.

(*C*) **trécarré** [trekaˈre], *n.m.* Range line.

tréfilage [trefiˈlaːʒ], *n.m.* Wire-drawing. **tréfiler,** *v.t.* To wire-draw. **tréfilerie,** *n.f.* Wire-mill; wire-drawing machine. **tréfileur,** *n.m.* Wire-drawer.

trèfle [trɛfl], *n.m.* Trefoil, clover; (*Cards*) clubs; (*Arch.*) trefoil. *Trèfle blanc (d'Irlande),* shamrock.

tréflière [treˈfljɛːr], *n.f.* Clover-field.

tréfoncier [trefɔ̃ˈsje], *a.* (*fem.* **-ière**) Pertaining to the subsoil.—*n.m.* Owner of the subsoil (mine-owner etc.). **tréfonds,** *n.m.* Subsoil; (*fig.*) bottom. *Savoir le fonds et le tréfonds d'une affaire,* to know the ins and outs of an affair. *Le tréfonds d'une âme,* the innermost soul.

treillage [trɛˈjaːʒ], *n.m.* Trellis-(work), lattice-work. **treillager,** *v.t.* To cover or furnish with trellis. **treillageur** or **treillagiste,** *n.m.* Trellis-maker, lattice-maker. **treille,** *n.f.* Vine-trellis; vine-arbour; shrimp-net. *Le jus de la treille,* the juice of the grape. **treillis,** *n.m.* Trellis, trellis-work, lattice; coarse canvas etc., sack-cloth. (*Mil.*) (*Effets de*) *treillis,* dungarees. **treillissé,** *a.* (*fem.* **-ée**) Trellised. **treillisser,** *v.t.* To trellis; to lattice.

treizaine [trɛˈzɛn], *n.f.* Baker's dozen.

treize [trɛːz], *a.* and *n.m. inv.* Thirteen; thirteenth. **treizième,** *a.* and *n.* Thirteenth (part). **treizièmement,** *adv.* Thirteenthly.

tréma [treˈma], *n.m.* Diaeresis.

trémail [TRAMAIL].

trémat [treˈma], *n.m.* or **trémate** [treˈmat], *f.* Sand-bank in the bends of the Seine.

tremblade [trɑ̃ˈblad], *n.f.* (*fam.*) *Avoir la tremblade,* to quiver, to shake.

tremblaie [trɑ̃ˈblɛ], *n.f.* Aspen-grove.

tremblant [trɑ̃ˈblɑ̃], *a.* (*fem.* **-ante**) Trembling, tremulous, quivering; flickering (of light etc.). **tremble,** *n.m.* Aspen. **tremblé,** *a.* (*fem.* **-ée**) Wavy (of lines); shaky (of writing).—*n.m.* (*Print.*) Waved rule. **tremblement,** *n.m.* Trembling, shaking, quaking, trepidation, tremor; tremulousness, agitation; flickering (of light); (*Mus.*) shake, quaver, tremolo. *Et tout le tremblement!* (*colloq.*) and all the rest of it, and the whole cabooq; *tremblement de terre,* earthquake.

trembler [trɑ̃ˈble], *v.i.* To tremble, to shake, to shiver; to quake, to fear; to flutter (of wings), to quiver (of light). *À faire trembler,* enough to make one shiver (of noise etc.); *la main lui tremble,* his hand shakes; *trembler de froid,* to shiver with cold.

trembleur, *n.m.* (*fem.* **-euse**) Trembler; quaker; shaker; (*Elec.*) vibrator; make-and-break.

tremblotant, *a.* (*fem.* **-ante**) Trembling, tremulous (of sound etc.); shivering, quivering, fluttering. **tremblote,** *n.f.* (*pop.*) *Avoir la tremblote,* to have the shivers. **tremblotement,** *n.m.* Trembling, shivering. **trembloter,** *v.i.* To tremble (of sound); to quiver, to shiver; to flutter (of wings); to flicker (of light).

trémie [tre′mi], *n.f.* Hopper, mill-hopper; funnel.

trémière [tre′mjɛːr], *a.f. Rose trémière*, hollyhock.

trémolo [tremɔ′lo], *n.m.* (*Mus.*) Tremolo.

trémoussement [tremus′mã], *n.m.* Moving about, fluttering, frisking, flutter. *Se donner du trémoussement*, to bestir oneself. **trémousser**, *v.t.* To bestir, to move about, to flutter.—*v.i.* To shake, to stir. **se trémousser**, *v.r.* To flutter or frisk about; to bestir oneself, to bustle about; to fidget. **trémoussoir**, *n.m.* Swinging-chair, revolving-chair.

trempage [trã′pa:ʒ], *n.m.* Steeping, soaking; (*Print.*) wetting.

trempe [trã:p], *n.f.* Temper (of steel etc.); tempering, steeping; (*fig.*) character, stamp, quality, constitution; (*Print.*) wetting. *Ce sont des gens de la même trempe*, they are people of the same stamp; *donner la trempe à*, to temper. **trempée**, *n.f.* Steeping, wetting; (*fig.*) whacking, drubbing. **tremper**, *v.t.* To soak, to steep, to wet, to drench; to temper (iron, steel, etc.); to dilute (wine etc.); (*Print.*) to wet (paper); to imbrue. *Il est tout trempé*, he is soaked to the skin; *tremper de larmes*, to wet with tears; *tremper la soupe*, to pour the soup on the bread; *tremper ses mains dans le sang*, to soak one's hands in blood.—*v.i.* To soak, to be steeped; to be imbrued (*dans*); to be implicated (*dans un crime*). **tremperie**, *n.f.* (*Print.*) Wetting-room, sink. **trempette**, *n.f.* (*colloq.*) Slice of bread (for soaking in wine etc.). (*fam.*) *Faire trempette*, to have a dip. **trempeur**, *n.m.* Temperer; (*Print.*) wetter.

tremplin [trã′plɛ̃], *n.m.* Spring-board, diving-board; trampoline; (*fig.*) stepping-stone (to a better job).

trentaine [trã′tɛn], *n.f.* About thirty, some thirty; age of thirty. *Il a passé la trentaine*, he is over thirty.

Trente [trã:t], *f.* Trent. *Le Concile de Trente*, the Council of Trent.

trente [trã:t], *a.* and *n.m. inv.* Thirty; thirtieth. *Trente-six*, thirty-six; (as an indefinite number) *ne pas y aller par 36 chemins*, not to beat about the bush; (with a negative meaning) *il n'y a pas 36 façons de s'y prendre*, there are no two ways of doing it; *tous les 36 du mois*, once in a blue moon, never; *trente-six fois*, umpteen times; *voir 36 chandelles*, (after a blow on the head) to see stars.

trentenaire, *a.* Of thirty years' duration.

trentième, *a.* and *n.* Thirtieth.—*n.m.* Thirtieth (part).

trentin [trã′tɛ̃], *a.* (*fem.* **-ine**) Trentine, Tridentine. *Le Trentin*, *m.* Trentino.

tréou [tre′u], *n.m.* (*Naut.*) Lug-sail.

trépan [tre′pã], *n.m.* Trepan (instrument); trepanning. **trépanation**, *n.f.* Trepanning. **trépaner**, *v.t.* To trepan.

trépang [TRIPANG].

trépas [tre′pɑ], *n.m. inv.* *Passage; (*poet.*) decease, death. **trépassé**, *n.m.* (*fem.* **-ée**) Dead person. *Les trépassés*, the dead. **trépasser**, *v.i.* To depart this life, to pass away.

trépidant [trepi′dã], *a.* (*fem.* **-ante**) Agitated; vibrating. *Ils mènent une vie trépidante*, they lead a hectic life.

trépidation, *n.f.* Trepidation, trembling, tremor; agitation. **trépider**, *v.i.* To vibrate, to shake.

trépied [tre′pje], *n.m.* Trivet; tripod.

trépignement [trepiɲ′mã], *n.m.* Stamping (of feet). **trépigner**, *v.i.* To stamp, to stamp one's foot. *Trépigner de colère*, to stamp with rage.

trépointe [tre′pwɛ̃:t], *n.f.* Welt (of a shoe).

très [trɛ], *adv.* Very; most; very much.

trésaillé [treza′je], *a.* (*fem.* **-ée**) Cracked, crackled, flawed (of pictures, porcelain, etc.).

trésor [tre′zɔːr], *n.m.* Treasure; hoard; treasury; exchequer; (*R.-C. Ch.*) relics and ornaments; thesaurus. *Amasser des trésors*, to heap up riches; (*fam.*) *c'est un trésor*, she is a gem; *mon trésor*, my pet. **trésorerie**, *n.f.* Treasury; treasurership; treasurer's office. **trésorier**, *n.m.* Treasurer; treasure-keeper (in cathedral, etc.); (*Mil.*) paymaster. *Trésorier-payeur général*, chief-paymaster (in French '*département*'). **trésorière**, *n.f.* Treasurer.

tressage [trɛ′sa:ʒ], *n.m.* Plaiting, braiding.

tressaillement [trɛsaj′mã], *n.m.* Start, bound, thrill; shudder; flutter, disturbance.

tressaillir [trɛsa′jiːr], *v.i. irr.* (*conjug. like* ASSAILLIR) To start, to give a start, to thrill; to quake, to tremble, to shudder, to wince. *Faire tressaillir*, to thrill, to startle; *tressaillir de joie*, to leap for joy.

tressauter [trɛso′te], *v.i.* To jump, to start; to jolt.

tresse [trɛs], *n.f.* Tress, plait (of hair); braid; (*Arch.*) strap-work; thick brown paper. **tresser**, *v.t.* To weave, to plait, to braid; to wreathe. **tresseur**, *n.m.* (*fem.* **-euse**) Plaiter, braider.

tréteau [tre′to], *n.m.* (*pl.* **-eaux**) Trestle; (*pl.*) stage, boards, mountebank's booth; (*slang*) horse. *Monter sur les tréteaux*, to become an actor; *tréteau de meule*, (*Agric.*) stack-stand.

treuil [trœːj], *n.m.* Windlass; hand-winch. *Treuil à vis sans fin*, worm-winch.

trêve [trɛːv], *n.f.* Truce; intermission, respite; let-up. *Sans trêve*, ceaselessly, unceasingly, without intermission; *trêve à ces niaiseries!* no more of these fooleries! *trêve de compliments*, let's forget the compliments.

Trèves [trɛv], *m.* Treves, Trier.

trévire [tre′viːr], *n.f.* (*Naut.*) Parbuckle. **trévirer**, *v.t.* To parbuckle.

tri (1) [tri] or **trick**, *n.m.* Three-handed ombre. (*Whist*) *Faire le tri*, to make the odd trick.

tri (2) [tri], *n.m.* Sorting out (of letters etc.). *Faire le tri. faire un tri*, to sort out.

triable [tri′abl], *a.* Choosable, sortable.

triade [tri′ad], *n.f.* Triad.

triage [tri′a:ʒ], *n.m.* Picking, sorting; choice, selection. *Voie de triage*, siding; *gare de triage*, marshalling yard.

triandre [tri′ã:dr], *a.* (*Bot.*) Triandrous.

triandrie [triã′dri], *n.f.* Triandria.

triangle [tri′ã:gl], *n.m.* Triangle; (*Naut.*) hanging stage of three planks (for caulking etc.); triangular flag.

triangulaire [triãgy′lɛːr], *a.* Triangular. *Élection triangulaire*, three-cornered contest. **triangulairement**, *adv.* Triangularly. **triangulation**, *n.f.* Triangulation. **trianguler**, *v.t.* To triangulate.

[733]

trias [tri'ɑːs], *n.m.* (*Geol.*) Trias. **triasique**, *a.* Triassic.

triballe [tri'bal], *n.f.* Small iron rod to beat furs.

tribart [tri'baːr], *n.m.* (Triangular) clog, yoke (for pigs, calves, dogs, etc.).

tribasique [triba'zik], *a.* (*Chem.*) Tribasic.

tribomètre [tribɔ'mɛtr], *n.m.* Tribometer.

tribord [tri'bɔːr], *n.m.* (*Naut.*) Starboard. *Tribord tout!* hard a-starboard! **tribordais**, *n.m.* Sailor of the starboard-watch.

triboulet [tribu'lɛ], *n.m.* Triblet, ring-stick.

tribu [tri'by], *n.f.* Tribe.

tribulation [tribylɑ'sjɔ̃], *n.f.* Tribulation, trouble.

tribun [tri'bœ̃], *n.m.* Tribune; (*fig.*) democratic leader or orator. **tribunal**, *n.m.* Tribunal, bench, judgment-seat; court of justice, law-court, magistrates. *Gazette des Tribunaux*, law reports; *tribunal de simple police*, police-court; *tribunal des prises*, (*Naut.*) prize court; *tribunal pour enfants et adolescents*, *tribunal d'enfants*, juvenile court. **tribunat**, *n.m.* Tribunate. **tribune**, *n.f.* Tribune (rostrum); hustings; gallery. *Monter à la tribune*, to mount the rostrum; *tribune d'honneur*, grand-stand; *tribune d'orgues*, organ-loft. **tribunitien**, *a.* (*fem.* **-ienne**) Tribunicial.

tribut [tri'by], *n.m.* Tribute; grant, contribution; *duty; (*fig.*) debt. *Payer le tribut à la nature*, to pay the debt of nature; to die.

tributaire [triby'tɛːr], *a.* and *n.m.* Tributary.

tricentenaire [trisɑ̃t'nɛːr], *a.* and *n.m.* Tercentenary.

tricéphale [trise'fal], *a.* Tricephalous.

triceps [tri'sɛps], *n.m. inv.* Triceps.

tricher [tri'ʃe], *v.t.*, *v.i.* To cheat, to trick. **tricherie**, *n.f.* Cheating, trick, trickery. **tricheur**, *n.m.* (*fem.* **-euse**) Cheat, trickster.

trichine [tri'ʃin or tri'kin], *n.f.* Thread-worm, trichina. **trichiné**, *a.* (*fem.* **-ée**) Trichinous. **trichinose**, *n.f.* Trichinosis.

trichocéphale [trikɔse'fal], *n.m.* Trichocephalus. **trichologie**, *n.f.* Trichology. **trichoma** or **trichome**, *n.m.* Trichoma. **trichotomie**, *n.f.* Trichotomy.

tricoises [tri'kwaːz], *n.f. pl.* Farrier's pincers.

tricolore [trikɔ'lɔːr], *a.* Tricoloured. *Le drapeau tricolore*, the Tricolour.

tricorne [tri'kɔrn], *a.* Three-cornered.—*n.m.* Three-cornered hat; hunt hat (for ladies).

***tricot** (1) [tri'ko], *n.m.* Cudgel.

tricot (2) [tri'ko], *n.m.* Knitting; jersey, jumper, (*fam.*) woolly. *Tricot de corps*, vest, (*Am.*) undershirt. **tricotage**, *n.m.* Knitting. **tricoter**, *v.t.*, *v.i.* To knit; (*spt.*) to run fast, to pedal quickly. **tricoteur**, *n.m.* (*fem.* **-euse**) Knitter.—*n.f.* Knitting-machine.

trictrac [trik'trak], *n.m.* Tric-trac (form of backgammon); trictrac-board, backgammon-board.

tricycle [tri'sikl], *n.m.* Three-wheeled vehicle; tricycle.

tride [trid], *a.* Swift, quick (of horses etc.). *Mouvement tride*, quick and strong movement.

trident [tri'dɑ̃], *n.m.* Trident; fish-gig; fish-spear; three-pronged fork. **tridenté**, *a.* (*fem.* **-ée**) Tridentate, three-pronged.

tridi [tri'di], *n.m.* Third day of decade in calendar of first French republic.

triduo [tridy'o] or **triduum** [tridy'ɔm], *n.m.* (*R.-C. Ch.*) Triduo (religious exercises which last three days).

trièdre [tri'ɛdr], *a.* and *n.m.* Trihedral.

triennal, *a.* (*fem.* **-ale**, *pl* **-aux**) Triennial. (*Agric.*) *Assolement triennal*, three-course rotation; *magistrat triennal*, judge appointed for three years. **triennat**, *n.m.* Term of three years.

trier [tri'e], *v.t.* (*conjugated like* PRIER) To pick, to choose, to sort, to select, to marshal (trucks). *Des hommes triés sur le volet*, hand-picked men. **trieur**, *n.m.* (*fem.* **-euse**) Sorter, picker.—*n.f.* Sorting-machine; wool-gin; screening-machine.

trifide [tri'fid], *a.* (*Bot.*) Trifid.

triflore [tri'flɔr], *a.* (*Bot.*) Triflorous, three-flowered.

triforium [trifɔ'rjɔm], *n.m.* (*Arch.*) Triforium, blind-story.

trifouiller [trifu'je], *v.t.*, *v.i.* (*vulg.*) To rummage, to fiddle about, to meddle.

trigame [tri'gam], *a.* Trigamous.—*n.* Trigamist. **trigamie**, *n.f.* Trigamy.

trigle [trigl], *n.m.* Trigla, gurnard.

triglyphe [tri'glif], *n.m.* (*Arch.*) Triglyph.

trigone [tri'gon], *n.m.* Trigon.—*a.* Trigonal. **trigonométrie** [trigonome'tri], *n.f.* Trigonometry. **trigonométrique**, *a.* Trigonometrical.

trigrille [tri'griːj], *n.f.* (*Rad. Tel.*) Pentode.

trijumeau [triʒy'mo], *a.* (*fem.* **-elle**, *pl.* **-eaux**) (*Anat.*) Trigeminal (nerve).

trilatéral [trilate'ral], *a.* (*fem.* **-ale**, *pl.* **-aux**) Trilateral.

trilingue [tri'lɛ̃ːg], *a.* Trilingual.

trilittéral [trilite'ral] (*fem.* **-ale**, *pl.* **-aux**) or **trilittère**, *a.* Triliteral.

trille [triːj], *n.m.* Quaver, trill, shake. **triller** *v.t.* To trill, to quaver.

trillion [tri'ljɔ̃], *n.m.* (since 1948=1 followed by eighteen ciphers), trillion, one million billion(s); (*Am.*) quintillion.

trilobé [trilɔ'be], *a.* (*fem.* **-ée**) (*Bot.*) Trilobate; (*Arch.*) three-cusped. **trilobite**, *n.m.* Trilobite.

triloculaire [trilɔky'lɛːr], *a.* (*Bot.*) Trilocular.

trilogie [trilɔ'ʒi], *n.f.* Trilogy.

trimard [tri'maːr], *n.m.* (*slang*) Road. **trimarder**, *v.t.*, or *être sur le trimard*, to go on tramp, to pad the hoof. **trimardeur**, *n.m.* Tramp, vagabond workman.

trimbaler [trɛ̃ba'le], *v.t.* (*fam.*) To drag or lug about (parcels); to trail (children) about. **se trimbaler**, *v.r.* (*pop.*) To traipse round.

trimer [tri'me], *v.i.* (*pop.*) To drudge, to wear oneself out.

trimestre [tri'mɛstr], *n.m.* Quarter (three months), quarter's pay, salary, or income; (*sch.*) term. *Par trimestre*, quarterly; *toucher son trimestre*, to receive one's (quarter's) salary. **trimestriel**, *a.* (*fem.* **-ielle**) Quarterly. (*sch.*) *Bulletin trimestriel*, end of term report.

trimètre [tri'mɛtr], *n.m.* and *a.* Trimeter.

trimorphe, *a.* (*Bot.*, *Cryst.*) Trimorphous. **trimorphisme**, *n.m.* Trimorphism.

trin [trɛ̃] or **trine**, *a.* (*Astrol.*) Trine. *Trin(e) aspect*, trine aspect.

tringa [trɛ̃'ga], *n.m.* (*Orn.*) Tringa (sand-piper).

tringle [trɛ̃ːgl], *n.f.* Rod; (*Arch.*) tringle; (measuring-)rod; (*Carp.*) mark. *Tringle de* *rideau*, curtain-rod; *tringle d'escalier*, stair-rod; (*Naut.*) *tringles de panneaux*, hatch-battens; *tringle de pneu*, wire of a tyre. **tringler**, *v.t.* (*Carp.*) To mark out, to chalk. **tringlette**, *n.f.* Small curtain-rod; glazier's knife.

tringlot [trɛ̃'glo], *n.m.* (*Mil. slang*) Trooper in the *train des équipages* (Service Corps).

trinitaire [trini'tɛːr], *n.* Trinitarian.

Trinité [trini'te], *n.f.* Trinity. *La Trinité*, Trinity Sunday. (**Île de**) **La Trinité**, *f.* Trinidad.

trinôme [tri'noːm], *n.m.* and *a.* Trinomial.

trinquart [trɛ̃'kaːr], *n.m.* Small fishing-boat, herring-boat.

trinquer [trɛ̃'ke], *v.i.* To clink glasses in drinking; (*fam.*) to drink; (*fig.*) to hobnob (*avec*); (*vulg.*) to be hit, to be hurt.

trinquet [trɛ̃'kɛ], *n.m.* (*Naut.*) Foremast (in a lateen vessel). **trinquette**, *n.f.* Fore-staysail.

trio [tri'o], *n.m.* Trio. **triolet**, *n.m.* (*Pros.*) Triolet; (*Mus.*) triplet; (*Bot.*) Dutch clover.

triomphal [triɔ̃'fal], *a.* (*fem.* **-ale**, *pl.* **-aux**) Triumphal. **triomphalement**, *adv.* Triumphantly. **triomphant**, *a.* (*fem.* **-ante**) Triumphant. **triomphateur**, *a.* (*fem.* **-trice**) Triumphing.—*n.* Triumpher. **triomphe**, *n.m.* Triumph.—*n.f.* Card game (variant of écarté); trump. **triompher**, *v.i.* To triumph, to be triumphant; to exult, to glory; to excel. *Triompher de ses passions*, to overcome one's passions.

tripaille [tri'paːj], *n.f.* (*fam.*) Garbage, offal.

tripale [tri'pal], *a.* (*Av.*) Three-bladed (of propellers).

tripang [tri'pɑ̃] or **trépang**, *n.m.* Trepang (holothurian).

triparti [tripar'ti], *a.* (*fem.* **-ie**), or **tripartite**, *a.* Tripartite. *Accord tripartite*, tripartite agreement; *gouvernement tripartite*, three-party government. **tripartisme**, *n.m.* Three-party government.

tripatouiller [tripatu'je], *v.t.* (*pop.*) To handle wrongly, to tinker, to fake, to cook (accounts); to paw (a girl).

tripe [trip], *n.f.* Tripe; guts, intestine; imitation velvet, velveteen (also called *tripe de velours*). *Rendre tripes et boyaux*, to be violently sick. *Tripes à la mode de Caen*, braised tripe and onions. **tripée** (*fem.*) [TRIPAILLE]. **tripe-madame** [TRIQUE-MADAME]. **triperie**, *n.f.* Tripe-shop. **tripette**, *n.f.* Small tripe. *Il ne vaut pas tripette*, he is not worth a straw.

triphasé [trifa'ze], *a.* (*fem.* **-ée**) (*Elec.*) *Courant triphasé*, three-phase current.

triphtongue [trif'tɔ̃:g], *n.f.* Triphthong.

triphylle [tri'fil], *a.* (*Bot.*) Triphyllous.

tripier [tri'pje], *n.m.* (*fem.* **-ière**) Tripe-seller; tripe-casserole.

triplan [tri'plɑ̃], *a.* (*fem.* **-ane**) Triplane (of aeroplanes).—*n.m.* Triplane.

triple [tripl], *a.* and *n.m.* Treble, triple, three-fold. *Au triple galop*, hell for leather; *raison triple*, triple ratio. **triplement** (1), *n.m.* Trebling, tripling. **triplement** (2), *adv.* Trebly, triply. **tripler**, *v.t., v.i.* To treble, to triple. **triplicata**, *n.m. inv.* Triplicate. *Faire un acte en triplicata*, to draw up a deed in triplicate. **triplice**, *n.f.* Triple alliance. **triplicité**, *n.f.* Triplicity. **triplique**, *n.f.* (*Law*) Rebutter (of a rejoinder), surrejoinder.

tripode [tri'pɔd], *a.* and *n.m.* Tripod.

Tripoli [tripɔ'li], *m.* Tripoli. **Tripolitaine**, *f.* Tripolitania.

tripoli [tripɔ'li], *n.m.* Tripoli, rottenstone. **tripolir** or **tripolisser**, *v.t.* To sharpen or polish with rottenstone.

triporteur or **tri-porteur** [tripɔr'tœːr], *n.m.* Tricycle-carrier (for goods).

tripot [tri'po], *n.m.* Gambling-den; house of ill-fame. **tripotage**, *n.m.* Mess, medley, jumble; intrigue, jobbery, underhand dealing; odd job, chore. **tripotée**, *n.f.* (*slang*) Beating, dressing down, a drubbing; crowd (of children etc.). **tripoter**, *v.t.* To meddle with, to pull about, to handle roughly; to speculate in.—*v.i.* To make mischief, to mess about, to act in an underhand way. **tripoteur**, *n.m.* (*fem.* **-euse**) Mischief-maker, shady speculator. **tripotier**, *n.m.* (*fem.* **-ière**) Low intriguer; gaming-house keeper.

triptyque [trip'tik], *n.m.* (*Paint.*) Triptych; triptyque (document).

trique [trik], *n.f.* (*fam.*) Cudgel, stick, bludgeon. *Sec comme un coup de trique*, (*fig.*) as thin as a rake.

triqueballe [trik'bal], *n.m.* or *f.* (*Artill.*) Sling-cart; timber-cart.

trique-madame [trikma'dam], *n.f. inv.* (*pop.*) White stone-crop.

triquer [tri'ke], *v.t.* To cudgel, to beat; to sort, to range (timber etc.).

triquet [tri'kɛ], *n.m.* Bat (for playing *la paume*); workman's trestle; a kind of step-ladder.

trirème [tri'rɛm], *n.f.* Trireme.

trisaïeul [triza'jœl], *n.m.* (*pl.* **-s**) Great-great-grandfather. **trisaïeule**, *n.f.* Great-great-grandmother.

trisannuel [triza'nɥɛl], *a.* (*fem.* **-elle**) Triennial.

trisme [trism], *n.m.* Trismus, lock-jaw.

trismégiste [trisme'ʒist], *n.m.* Trismegistus. —*a.m.* (*Print.*) Two-line double pica.

trisser [tri'se], *v.t.* To encore a second time. —*v.i.* To twitter (of swallows).

trissyllabe or **trisyllabe** [trisil'lab], *a.* Trisyllabic.—*n.m.* Trisyllable.

Tristan [tris'tɑ̃], *m.* Tristram.

triste [trist], *a.* Sorrowful, mournful, sad, melancholy, dejected; calamitous, unfortunate, painful; dull, dreary, gloomy, dismal, poor, sorry (of persons); mean, wretched, paltry. *Faire triste figure*, to look sadly out of place; *tu pull a long face*; *faire triste mine à*, to give a cold welcome to; *faire un triste repas*, to make a sorry meal; *le temps est triste*, the weather is dull; *triste comme un bonnet de nuit*, as dull as ditch-water; *un triste individu, un triste sire*, a bad lot, an unsavoury character; *une triste nouvelle*, a sad piece of news. **tristement**, *adv.* Sadly.

tristesse, *n.f.* Sadness; melancholy; dreariness, dullness; gloom; cheerlessness, bleakness.

tritome [tri'tɔm], *n.m.* Red-hot poker.

triton (1) [tri'tɔ̃], *n.m.* Triton, newt.

triton (2) [tri'tɔ̃], *n.m.* (*Mus.*) Tritone; augmented fourth.

triturable [trity'rabl], *a.* Triturable. **trituration**, *n.f.* Trituration. **triturer**, *v.t.* To triturate, to grind, to masticate.

triumvir [triɔm'viːr], *n.m.* Triumvir. **triumviral**, *a.* (*fem.* **-ale**, *pl.* **-aux**) Triumviral. **triumvirat**, *n.m.* Triumvirate.

trivalve [tri′valv], *a.* (*Bot.* etc.) Trivalvular.
trivelin [tri′vlɛ̃], *n.m.* *Buffoon; dentist's forceps, elevator.
trivelinade [trivli′nad], *n.f.* Buffoonery.
triviaire [tri′vjɛːr], *a.* *Carrefour triviaire*, junction of three roads.
trivial [tri′vjal], *a.* (*fem.* **-iale**, *pl.* **-iaux**) Vulgar, trifling; trite, hackneyed.—*n.m.* Vulgarity. **trivialement**, *adv.* Vulgarly. **trivialiser**, *v.t.* To vulgarize. **trivialité**, *n.f.* Vulgarity; triteness.
troc [trɔk], *n.m.* Truck; barter; swop.
trocart [trɔ′kaːr], *n.m.* (*Surg.*) Trocar.
trochaïque [trɔka′ik], *a.* and *n.m.* Trochaic.
trochanter [trɔkɑ̃′tɛːr], *n.m.* (*Anat.*) Trochanter.
troche [trɔʃ], *n.f.* Bunch, cluster (of flowers); tuft (of onions), mass; (*pl.*) fumet, dung (of deer etc.).
trochée (1) [trɔ′ʃe], *n.m.* (*Pros.*) Trochee.
trochée (2) [trɔ′ʃe], *n.f.* Bunch of sprouting twigs (from a tree-stump).
trochet [trɔ′ʃɛ], *n.m.* Cluster (of fruit or flowers); cooper's block.
trochile [trɔ′kil] or **trochilus**, *n.m.* Trochil (humming-bird).
trochin [trɔ′kɛ̃], *n.m.* Small tuberosity at the top of the humerus.
trochisque [trɔ′ʃisk], *n.m.* (*Pharm.*) Troche (small cone-shaped cake).
troène [trɔ′ɛn], *n.m.* Privet.
troglodyte [trɔglɔ′dit], *n.m.* Troglodyte; cave-dweller; cave-man (*or* woman); (American) wren.
trogne [trɔɲ], *n.f.* Reddish, bloated face. *Trogne d'ivrogne*, drunkard's face.
trognon [trɔ′ɲɔ̃], *n.m.* Core (of a pear or apple); stump (of a cabbage); runt.
Troie [trwa], *f.* Troy. *La guerre de Troie*, the Trojan War.
trois [trwɑ], *a.* and *n.m.* Three; third. *Règle de trois*, rule of three; *la grande scène du trois*, the great scene in the third act (in Act three); (*fam.*) *on vous met au 3*, you are being put in Room 3. (*Polit.*) *Les Trois Grands*, the Big Three. **troisième**, *a.* and *n.* Third.—*n.m.* Third; third story, third floor.—*n.f.* A secondary class (in England the fourth form). **troisièmement**, *adv.* Thirdly. **trois-mâts**, *n.m. inv.* Three-master. **trois-ponts**, *n.m. inv.* Three-decker. **trois-quarts**, *n.m. inv.* (*Mus.*) Three-quarter violin; triangular rasp; (*Ftb.*) three-quarters; (*Cost.*) three-quarter length coat. **trois-six**, *n.m.* Proof spirit (at 36 deg.).
trôle [troːl], *n.f.* Furniture-hawking; trawling. *Filet à la trôle*, drag-net; *ouvrier à la trôle*, furniture-hawker. **trôler**, *v.t.* To lead (somebody) about; to drag (something) about for sale.—*v.i.* To stroll, to tramp about. **trôleur**, *n.m.* Hawker, tramp.
trolle [trɔl], *n.m.* Globe-flower, trollius.
trolley [trɔ′le], *n.m.* Trolley. **trolleybus**, *n.m.* Trolley-bus.
trombe [trɔ̃b], *n.f.* Waterspout. *Arriver en trombe*, to dash in.
trombidion [trɔ̃bi′djɔ̃], *n.m.* A kind of acarus (called also *aoûtat* or *rouget*), harvest-tick.
trombine [trɔ̃′bin], *n.f.* (*pop.*) Mug, face.
tromblon [trɔ̃′blɔ̃], *n.m.* Blunderbuss; grenade-sleeve. *Chapeau tromblon*, wide-crowned hat.

trombone [trɔ̃′bɔn], *n.m.* Trombone; (wire) paper-clip. *Trombone à coulisse*, slide-trombone. **tromboniste**, *n.m.* Trombone-player.
trompe [trɔ̃ːp], *n.f.* Trump, horn; proboscis, trunk (of elephants); blast-engine; (*Arch.*) pendentive. *Publier à son de trompe*, to trumpet abroad; *trompe à vide*, air-pump; *trompe d'Eustache*, Eustachian tube; *trompes de Fallope*, Fallopian tubes; *trompe de Béarn*, Jew's harp.
trompe-la-mort [trɔ̃pla′mɔːr], *n. inv.* Death's cheat (person desperately ill who recovers).
trompe-l'œil [trɔ̃′plœːj], *n.m. inv.* (*Paint.*) Still-life deception; (*fig.*) illusion, sham, camouflage.
tromper [trɔ̃′pe], *v.t.* To deceive, to impose upon; to delude, to beguile; to cheat, to out-wit, to take in; to betray, to be unfaithful to (wife, husband); to elude. *C'est ce qui vous trompe*, that is where you are wrong; *tromper la confiance de quelqu'un*, to abuse someone's trust; *tromper son ennui*, to while away the time. **se tromper**, *v.r.* To be mistaken, to be taken in, to make a mistake, to be wrong, to deceive oneself, to deceive each other. *À s'y tromper*, so as to take one for the other; *se tromper de chemin*, to take the wrong road; *vous vous trompez*, you are mistaken. **tromperie**, *n.f.* Cheat, fraud, imposture; illusion, delusion.
trompeter [trɔ̃pə′te], *v.t.* To publish, pro-claim, or summon by sound of trumpet; to trumpet abroad; to scream (of the eagle).
trompette [trɔ̃′pɛt], *n.f.* Trumpet; (*fig.*) (*Conch.*) trumpet-shell; (*slang*) face. *Déloger sans tambour ni trompette*, to decamp on the quiet; *nez en trompette*, turned-up nose; *sonner de la trompette*, to blow the trumpet; *trompette marine* or *trompette parlante*, speaking-trumpet.—*n.m.* Trumpeter. **trompettiste**, *n.* Trumpet-player (chiefly jazz).
trompeur [trɔ̃′pœːr], *a.* (*fem.* **-euse**) Deceitful, delusive; designing, false, misleading.—*n.* Deceiver, cheat, impostor; betrayer. *À trompeur trompeur et demi*, diamond cut diamond. **trompeusement**, *adv.* Deceitfully, deceptively.
trompillon [trɔ̃pi′jɔ̃], *n.m.* (*Arch.*) Small pendentive.
tronc [trɔ̃], *n.m.* Trunk; bole (of tree); stock, parent-stock; poor-box; (*Arch.*) drum (of column); (*Geom.*) frustum. (*Geom.*) *Tronc de cône*, truncated cone. **troncature**, *n.f.* Truncation.
tronche [trɔ̃ːʃ], *n.f.* Log; end (of rope); *(vulg.)* head.
tronchet [trɔ̃′ʃɛ], *n.m.* (Cooper's, butcher's) block.
tronçon [trɔ̃′sɔ̃], *n.m.* Broken piece, fragment, stump; portion, section (of a line of railway).
tronconique [trɔ̃kɔ′nik], *a.* In the shape of a truncated cone.
tronçonnement [trɔ̃sɔn′mɑ̃], *n.m.* Cutting up. **tronçonner**, *v.t.* To cut into pieces.
trône [troːn], *n.m.* Throne. *Discours du trône*, speech from the throne. **trôner**, *v.i.* To sit on a throne; (*fig.*) to lord it.
tronquer [trɔ̃′ke], *v.t.* To mutilate, to trun-cate; to cut; (*fig.*) to garble, to mangle.
trop [tro], *adv.* Too much, too, over, too many, too far, too long, too well, etc. *De trop*, too

much, too many, superfluous; *être de trop*, to be in the way, not to be wanted; *je ne sais trop*, I hardly know; *nous sommes trop*, there are too many of us; *par trop*, excessively; *pas trop bien*, not very, not over well; *pas trop bon*, not too good; *trop de peine*, too much trouble; *trop peu*, too little.—*n.m.* Excess, superfluity.

trope [trɔp], *n.m.* Trope.

trophée [trɔ'fe], *n.m.* Trophy.

trophique [trɔ'fik], *a.* Trophic.

tropical [trɔpi'kal], *a.* (*fem.* **-ale**, *pl.* **-aux**) Tropical. **tropique**, *n.m.* Tropic. *Les Tropiques*, the tropics.—*a.* (*Bot.*) Diurnal.

tropisme [trɔ'pism], *n.m.* Tropism.

tropologie [trɔpɔlɔ'ʒi], *n.f.* Tropology. **tropologique**, *a.* Tropological.

trop-plein [trɔ'plɛ̃], *n.m.* (*pl.* **trop-pleins**) Overflow, waste; surplus, excess.

troquer [trɔ'ke], *v.t.* To truck, to barter, to exchange, to swap. *Troquer son cheval borgne contre un aveugle*, to exchange bad for worse. **troqueur**, *n.m.* (*fem.* **-euse**) Barterer.

trot [tro], *n.m.* Trot. *Au petit trot*, at a jog-trot; *au grand trot*, speedily, briskly; *cheval de trot*, trotter; *trot assis*, close trot. **trotte**, *n.f.* Trot, run, walk, distance. *Tout d'une trotte*, without stopping. **trotte-menu**, *a. inv.* Running with little steps, pitter-patter. *La gent trotte-menu*, mice. **trotter**, *v.i.* To trot; to run about, to toddle (children). *Cette idée me trotte dans la tête*, this idea keeps haunting me; *être toujours à trotter*, to be always on the go. **se trotter**, *v.r.* (*fam.*) To go away, to take oneself off. **trotterie**, *n.f.* Jaunt, trip. **trotteur**, *n.m.* (*fem.* **-euse**) Trotter, *n.f.* (Split-)second hand (of watch).—*a. inv. Jupe trotteur*, walking-skirt.

trottin [trɔ'tɛ̃], *n.m.* Errand girl. **trottine-ment**, *n.m.* Toddling. **trottiner**, *v.i.* To go at a jog-trot; to toddle along. **trottinette**, *n.f.* Scooter.

trottoir [trɔ'twaːr], *n.m.* Foot-path, pavement, (*Am.*) sidewalk. (*vulg.*) *Faire le trottoir*, to walk the streets; *trottoir roulant*, escalator.

trou [tru], *n.m.* Hole; gap; cave, pot-hole, natural cavity; orifice, mouth; (*Anat.*) foramen. (*pop.*) *Boire comme un trou*, to drink like a fish; *boucher un trou*, to stop a gap, to pay a debt; *faire un trou à la lune*, to shoot the moon, to fly from one's creditors; *loger dans un trou*, to live in a hole; *petit trou pas cher*, a cheap little place; *trou d'air*, air pocket; *trou de la serrure*, keyhole; *trou d'homme*, man-hole; *trou de chat*, (*Naut.*) lubber's hole; *trou du souffleur*, (*Theat.*) prompter's box.

troubadour [truba'duːr], *n.m.* Troubadour.

troublant [tru'blɑ̃], *a.* (*fem.* **-ante**) Disturbing, troubling, disquieting. *Déshabillé troublant*, suggestive deshabille; *parfum troublant*, heady perfume.

trouble (1) [trubl], *a.* Thick, muddy, turbid, cloudy, overcast; dim, dull. *Avoir la vue trouble*, to be dim-sighted; *pêcher en eau trouble*, to fish in troubled waters, to take advantage of confusion.—*adv.* Dimly, confusedly.—*n.m.* Confusion, disorder, disturbance, turmoil; perplexity, uneasiness; misunderstanding, dispute, quarrel; (*pl.*) broils, disturbances, dissensions. *Exciter des troubles dans un État*, to stir up trouble in a State; *troubles civils*, civil disturbances.

trouble (2), **troubleau** [TRUBLE].

trouble-fête [trublə'feːt], *n.m. inv.* Kill-joy, spoil-sport; wet blanket; (*Australia*) wowser.

troubler [tru'ble], *v.t.* To disturb, to make thick, to make muddy; to muddle, to turn; to disturb, to disorder, to confuse, to agitate; to perplex, to disconcert, to unsettle; to trouble; to interrupt, to break in upon; to destroy the harmony of; to ruffle, to annoy, to discompose; to dim, to dull. *La peur lui trouble la raison*, fear unhinges his mind; *troubler la fête*, to mar the festivities, to spoil the fun. **se troubler**, *v.r.* To grow thick, to become muddy; to be confused, to be disconcerted; to become overcast or cloudy; to become confused or dim.

trouée [tru'e], *n.f.* Opening, gap, breach; pass. **trouer**, *v.t.* To bore, to make a hole in. **se trouer**, *v.r.* To get holes in it.

trou-madame, *n.m.* (*pl.* **trous-madame**) Game played with ivory balls rolled into numbered compartments.

troufion [tru'fjɔ̃], *n.m.* (*pop.*) Soldier, private.

trouillard [tru'jaːr], *a.* (*vulg.*) Coward.

trouille, *n.f.* (*vulg.*) Fear, funk. *Flanquer la trouille*, to give the jitters.

troupe [truːp], *n.f.* Troop, band; crew, gang, set; company (of actors); herd, flock, drove, crowd; (*pl.*) troops, forces. *Aller en troupe*, to herd together. **troupeau**, *n.m.* (*pl.* **-eaux**) Flock, herd, drove. *Troupeau de gros bétail*, drove of cattle; *troupeau de moutons*, flock of sheep. **troupier**, *n.m.* Soldier. *Vieux troupier*, old campaigner.

trousse [truːs], *n.f.* Bundle, truss; (*Surg.*) case of instruments; case for razors, toilet articles, etc. *Trousse (de couture)*, housewife; *trousse de toilette*, dressing-case. *Être aux trousses de l'ennemi*, to be upon the enemy's heels; *je suis à ses trousses*, I am after him. **troussé**, *a.* (*fem.* **-ée**) Tucked up. *Bien troussé*, well set up, neat, dapper; *compliment bien troussé*, neatly turned compliment.

trousseau [tru'so], *n.m.* (*pl.* **-eaux**) .Bunch (of keys); school outfit; trousseau, wedding-outfit; outfit, kit; (*Anat.*) fasciculus. **trousse-queue**, *n.m. inv.* Crupper, dock-piece (of harness). **troussequin**, *n.m.* Cantle (of a saddle).

trousser [tru'se], *v.t.* To tuck up, to turn up, to pin up; to truss; to dispatch (business etc.). *Trousser bagage*, to decamp, to be off. **se trousser**, *v.r.* To tuck up one's clothes.

trouvable [tru'vabl], *a.* That can be found.

trouvaille [tru'vaːj], *n.f.* Godsend, windfall; discovery, find, lucky hit; bright, original idea.

trouvé [tru've], *a.* (*fem.* **-ée**) Found. *Bien trouvé*, felicitous, happy, original; *enfant trouvé*, foundling; *objets trouvés*, lost property. **trouver**, *v.t.* To find, to discover, to meet with, to hit upon; to detect; to get; to seek, to look for, to find out; to think, to deem, to judge; to like; to contrive, to manage. *Aller trouver* or *venir trouver*, to go to, to go and see, to visit; *comment le trouvez-vous?* how do you like it? what do you think of him (his health, looks)? *je lui trouve bon visage*, I think he looks well; *où avez-vous trouvé cela?* what made you think of that? what put that into your head? *trouver à dire* or *à redire à*, to find fault with; *trouver à vendre*, to contrive to sell; *trouver beau* or *belle*, to admire, to think handsome; *trouver bon*, to think fit; *trouver mauvais*, to blame, to dislike, to be displeased with; *vous trouvez?* you think so, do you? **se trouver,** *v.r.* To find oneself; to be met with, to be, to exist; to feel, to feel oneself; to prove, to turn out; to find for oneself. *Cela se trouve bien*, that is lucky; *il se trouvait là*, he happened to be there; *il se trouve*, there is, there are, it happens, it turns out; *se trouver mal*, to faint.

trouvère [tru'vɛːr], *n.m.* Trouvère (minstrel of N. France).

trouveur, *n.m.* (*fem.* **-euse**) Discoverer, inventor.—*a.* Inventive.

troyen [trwa'jɛ̃], *a.* (*fem.* **troyenne**) Trojan.

truand [try'ɑ̃], *n.m.* (*fem.* **truande**) Vagrant, beggar, tramp; crook, gangster.—*a.* Vagrant etc. *****truander,** *v.i.* To mump, to tramp. **truanderie,** *n.m.* Mumping, vagrancy.

truble [trybl] or **trouble** (2), *n.f.* Hoop-net.

trubleau or **troubleau,** *n.m.* (*pl.* **-eaux**) Small hoop-net.

truc (1) [tryk], *n.m.* Knack, dodge, trick; (*Theat.*) machinery; (*pop.*) thing, thingumbob, gadget. *Il a le truc*, he has the knack (of doing it).

truc (2) or **truck** [tryk], *n.m.* Truck, bogie, (*Rail.*) open wagon.

trucage or **truquage** [try'kaːʒ], *n.m.* (*pop.*) Faking (of things); cooking (of accounts); (*Cine.*) trick shot.

trucheman [tryʃ'mɑ̃] or **truchement,** *n.m.* Interpreter, dragoman; go-between. *Par le truchement de*, by means of, through.

trucider [trysi'de], *v.t.* (*fam.*) To kill.

truculence [tryky'lɑ̃ːs], *n.f.* Truculence. **truculent,** *a.* (*fem.* **-ente**) Truculent.

trudgen [tryd'ʒɛn] or **trudgeon** [tryd'ʒɔ̃] or even **strudgeon,** *n.m.* Trudgen stroke (in swimming).

truelle [try'el], *n.f.* Trowel. *Truelle à poisson*, fish-slice, fish-carver. **truellée,** *n.f.* Trowelful.

truffe [tryf], *n.f.* Truffle; (*pop.*) big nose; nose; fool. **truffer,** *v.t.* To stuff with truffles; (*fig.*) to stuff, to cram (*de*). *Sa dissertation était truffée de fautes d'orthographe*, his (her) essay was crammed with spelling mistakes. **truffière,** *n.f.* Truffleground.

truie [trɥi], *n.f.* Sow.

truisme [trɥ'ism], *n.m.* Truism.

truite [trɥit], *n.f.* Trout. *Truite saumonée*, salmon-trout, sea-trout. **truité,** *a.* (*fem.* **-ée**) Spotted, mottled, speckled; crackled (of porcelain). *Fonte truitée*, white and grey pig-iron.

trumeau [try'mo], *n.m.* (*pl.* **-eaux**) Wall between windows etc., pier; pier-glass; leg of beef.

truquer [try'ke], *v.t.* To fake, to cook.—*v.i.* To dodge, to cheat, to sham. **truqueur,** *n.m.* (*fem.* **-euse**) Faker, fraud.

trusquin [trys'kɛ̃], *n.m.* (*Carp.*) Markinggauge.

tsar [tsaːr], *n.m.* Tsar. **tsarévitch,** *n.m.* Tsarevitch.

tu [ty], *pron.* Thou, you. *Être à tu et à toi avec*, to be on very familiar terms with.

tuable [ty'abl], *a.* Fit for killing. **tuage,** *n.m.* Killing, slaughter (of an animal).

tuant [ty'ɑ̃], *a.* (*fem.* **-te**) Killing, exhausting, tiresome, laborious. *C'est un homme tuant*, he is a regular bore.

tub [tœb], *n.m.* Tub.

tuba [ty'ba], *n.m.* (*Mus.*) Tuba.

tube [tyb], *n.m.* Tube, pipe; (*Anat.*) duct, (*fam.*) top-hat, topper. *Tube à essai*, testtube; *tube de Branly*, Branly coherer; *tube de direction*, (*Motor.*) steering-column. **tuber,** *v.t.* To tube (well etc.).

tubéracé [tybera'se], *a.* (*fem.* **-ée**) (*Bot.*) Tuberaceous.

tubercule [tyber'kyl], *n.m.* Tubercle. **tuberculé,** *a.* (*fem.* **-ée**) Tuberculate, tubercled. **tuberculeux,** *a.* (*fem.* **-euse**) Tuberculous; (*Bot.*) tubercular; (*Path.*) tuberculous.—*n.* Consumptive person. **tuberculisation,** *n.f.* Tuberculisation. **tuberculiser,** *v.t.* To tuberculize. **tuberculose,** *n.f.* Tuberculosis. *Tuberculose pulmonaire*, phthisis, consumption, tuberculosis of the lungs.

tubéreuse (1) [tybe'røːz], *n.f.* Tuberose. **tubéreux,** *a.* (*fem.* **tubéreuse**) (2) Tuberous. **tubérifère,** *a.* Tuberiferous. **tubérosité,** *n.f.* (*Path.*) Tuberosity.

tubiforme [tybi'fɔrm], *a.* Tubiform.

tubulaire [tyby'lɛːr], *a.* Tubular. **tubule,** *n.m.* Small tube, tubule. **tubulé,** *a.* (*fem.* **-ée**) Tubular, tubulous. **tubuleux,** *a.* (*fem.* **-euse**) Tubulous, tubulate. **tubulure,** *n.f.* Opening of a vessel for receiving a tube; pipe, neck; (*Physiol.*) natural tube or conduit.

tudesque [ty'desk], *a.* Teutonic; rough, coarse.—*n.m.* Teutonic language.

*****tudieu** [ty'djø], *int.* Zounds!

tue-chien [ty'ʃjɛ̃], *n.m. inv.* Meadow-saffron, colchicum.

tue-mouche, *n.m. inv.*, or **tue-mouches.** Fly-swatter; fly-bane (fungus). *Papier tuemouches*, fly-paper.

tuer [tɥe], *v.t.* To kill, to slay; to slaughter, to butcher; to damn (a play etc.); to tire to death, to be the death of; to while away. *Se faire tuer*, to get killed, to expose one's life. **se tuer,** *v.r.* To kill oneself, to commit suicide; (*fig.*) to wear oneself out. **tuerie,** *n.f.* Slaughter, butchery, carnage; slaughterhouse.

tue-tête [tu'tɛt], **à,** *adv. phr.* At the top of one's voice.

tueur [ty'œːr], *n.m.* (*fem.* **-euse**) Killer, slayer, thug.

tuf [tyf], *n.m.* Tuff, tufa; (*fig.*) bottom, bedrock. **tufacé,** *a.* (*fem.* **-ée**) Tufaceous. **tuffeau** or **tufeau,** *n.m.* Micaceous chalk.

tuile [tɥil], *n.f.* Tile. *Loger sous les tuiles*, to live in a garret; (*fam.*) *quelle tuile!* what rotten luck! **tuileau,** *n.m.* (*pl.* **-eaux**) Broken tile. **tuilerie,** *n.f.* Tile-works. *Les Tuileries*, the Tuileries (before 1871 a Royal palace, now a garden in Paris). **tuilier,** *n.m.* Tile-maker.

tulipe [ty'lip], *n.f.* Tulip. **tulipier,** *n.m.* Tulip-tree.

tulle [tyl], *n.m.* Tulle, net. **tulliste,** *n.* Tullemaker or -seller.

tuméfaction [tymefak'sjɔ̃], *n.f.* Tumefaction. **tuméfier,** *v.i.*, or **se tuméfier,** *v.r.* To tumefy. **tumeur,** *n.f.* Tumor, swelling.

tumulaire [tymy'lɛːr], *a.* Of the grave, sepulchral. *Pierre tumulaire*, tombstone.

tumulte   typhus

tumulte [ty'mylt], *n.m.* Tumult, uproar; hubbub, confusion. **tumultuaire**, *a.* Tumultuary. **tumultueusement**, *adv.* Tumultuously. **tumultueux**, *a.* (*fem.* -euse*) Tumultuous, riotous, noisy.

tumulus [tymy'ly:s], *n.m.* Tumulus, barrow.

tungstène [tœks'tɛn], *n.m.* Tungsten.

tunique [ty'nik], *n.f.* Tunic; envelope, film, coat (of the eye etc.).

Tunis [tɥ'nis], *n.* Tunis. **Tunisie,** *f.* Tunisia. **tunisien,** *a.* (*fem.* -ienne*) and *n.m.* (**Tunisien,** *fem.* -ienne*) Tunisian.

tunnel [ty'nɛl], *n.m.* Tunnel.

(*C*) **tuque** [tyk], *n.f.* Woollen cap.

turban [tyr'bɑ̃], *n.m.* Turban. *Prendre le turban*, to turn Mohammedan.

turbidité [tyr'bidite], *n.f.* Turbidity, muddiness.

turbin [tyr'bɛ̃], *n.m.* (*pop.*) Work, grind.

turbine [tyr'bin], *n.f.* Turbine; (rotary) fan (of vacuum-cleaner etc.). *Turbine à choc*, impulse turbine; *turbine à réaction*, reaction turbine; *turbine à vapeur*, steam-turbine; *turbine hydraulique*, water-wheel, water-turbine. **turbiné,** *a.* (*fem.* -ée*) (*Bot. Zool.*) Turbinate.

turbiner [tyrbi'ne], *v.i.* (*pop.*) To slave away, to grind.

turbo-compresseur [tyrbokɔ̃prɛ'sœːr], *n.m.* Turbo-compressor. **turbopropulseur,** *n.m.* Turbo-prop(ulsor). **turboréacteur,** *n.m.* Jet-engine; turbo-jet.

turbot [tyr'bo], *n.m.* Turbot. **turbotière,** *n.f.* Turbot-kettle. **turbotin,** *n.m.* Young turbot.

turbulence [tyrby'lɑ̃:s], *n.f.* Turbulence. **turbulent,** *a.* (*fem.* -ente*) Turbulent, boisterous; noisy, rowdy, wild (of children etc.).

turc [tyrk], *a.* (*fem.* **turque**) Turkish.—*n.m.* Turkish language; (**Turc,** *fem.* **Turque**) Turk. *Être assis à la turque*, to sit cross-legged; *fort comme un Turc*, as strong as an ox; *le Grand Turc*, the Sultan of Turkey; *se faire Turc*, to turn Turk; *tête de Turc*, butt, scape-goat.

turco [tyr'ko], *n.m.* Turco (Algerian tirailleur).

turcoin [tyr'kwɛ̃], *n.m.* Mohair.

turelure [tyr'ly:r], *n.f.* Tol-de-rol, fol-de-rol (burden of a song). *C'est toujours la même turelure*, it is always the same thing over and over again.

turf [tyrf], *n.m.* The turf (horse-racing). **turfiste,** *n.m.* Race-goer, follower of horse-races.

turgescence [tyrʒɛ'sɑ̃:s], *n.f.* Turgescence, turgidity. **turgescent,** *a.* (*fem.* -ente*) Turgescent, turgid.

turlupin [tyrly'pɛ̃], *n.m.* Punster; sorry jester. **turlupinade,** *n.f.* Sorry jesting, poor joke. **turlupiner,** *v.i.* To pun or joke badly.—*v.t.* To crack poor jokes about, to annoy; to worry.

turlutaine [tyrly'tɛn], *n.f.* A word, a sentence that one likes to repeat. *C'est sa turlutaine*, he is always harping on that.

turlututu [tyrlyty'ty], *n.m.* (*fam.*) = *mirliton* (the American hewgag); (*int.*) of mockery or refusal; used also as a French shibboleth to detect a foreign accent.

turne [tyrn], *n.f.* (*pop.*) Dirty, ramshackle house; (*sch.*) study (room).

turnep or **turneps** [tyr'nɛp], *n.m.* Field-turnip.

turpitude [tyrpi'tyd], *n.f.* Turpitude, baseness, ignominy.

turque [TURC].

turquet [tyr'kɛ], *n.m.* (*dial.*) Maize.

turquette [tyr'ket], *n.f.* Rupture-wort.

Turquie [tyr'ki], *f.* Turkey.

turquin [tyr'kɛ̃], *a.* Dark, deep (of blue). **turquine,** *n.f.* Inferior variety of turquoise. **turquoise,** *n.f.* Turquoise.—*a.* Turquoise blue.

tussilage [tysi'la:ʒ], *n.m.* Colt's-foot (plant).

tussor [ty'sɔːr], *n.m.* Tussore (silk).

tutélaire [tyte'lɛːr], *a.* Tutelary, guardian. **tutelle,** *n.f.* Tutelage, guardianship; (*fig.*) protectorship, (*Polit.*) trusteeship. *Enfants en tutelle*, children under the care of a guardian; *prendre quelqu'un sous sa tutelle*, to take someone under one's wing; *tenir quelqu'un en tutelle*, to keep someone under one's thumb.

tuteur, *n.m.* (*fem.* **tutrice**) Guardian, trustee, protector; (*Hort.*) prop, stake, support. *Mettre des tuteurs aux rosiers*, to stake the roses.

tutie [ty'ti], *n.f.* (*Chem.*) Tutty.

tutoiement or **tutoîment** [tytwa'mɑ̃], *n.m.* 'Theeing and thouing.' **tutoyer,** *v.t. irr.* (*conjug. like* ABOYER) To 'thee and thou'; (*pop.*) to insult (somebody). **se tutoyer,** *v.r.* To 'thee and thou' each other; to be on familiar terms.

tutrice, *fem.* [TUTEUR].

tutu [ty'ty], *n.m.* (Ballet-dancer's) short bouffant skirt.

tuyau [tɥi'jo], *n.m.* (*pl.* **-aux**) Pipe; tube, hose; (chimney-)flue; shaft, funnel; barrel (of a quill); stalk (of corn); stem (of a feather); nozzle (of bellows etc.); stem (of a tobacco-pipe); flute (of frills etc.); (*slang*) tip, wrinkle, hint. *Tuyau acoustique*, speaking-tube; *tuyau d'arrosage*, garden-hose; *tuyau d'incendie*, fire-hose; *tuyau de poêle*, stove-pipe; (*fam.*) top-hat. *Dire quelque chose dans le tuyau de l'oreille*, to whisper something in someone's ear. **tuyautage,** *n.m.* Frilling, quilling, fluting; tubing. **tuyauter,** *v.t.* To goffer, to quill, to frill, to plait; (*slang*) to give a tip to. *Fer à tuyauter*, goffering-tongs. **tuyauterie,** *n.f.* System of pipes; plumbing; pipe-store; pipe-trade. **tuyauteur,** *n.m.* Tipster.

tuyère, *n.f.* Tuyere, twyer, nozzle, blast-pipe; (*Av.*) jet-pipe.

tympan [tɛ̃'pɑ̃], *n.m.* Tympanum, ear-drum; tympan, drum; spandrel (of bridges). **tympanique,** *a.* Tympanic. *****tympaniser,** *v.t.* To run down, to decry, to traduce; to advertise. **tympanite,** *n.f.* Tympanitis, tympany.

tympanon, *n.m.* Dulcimer.

type [tip], *n.m.* Type; model, pattern; sample; symbol, emblem; standard; (*Astron.*) plan, drawing; (*colloq.*) bloke, chap, fellow. *C'est un chic type*, he is a good chap, a brick; *quel type!* what a person! **typer,** *v.t.* To stamp, to mark as of a certain type.

typha [ti'fa], *n.m.* (*Bot.*) Typha, cat's-tail.

typhoïde [tifɔ'id], *a.* Typhoid. **typhoïque** or **typhoïdique,** *a.* Typhoidal.

typhon [ti'fɔ̃], *n.m.* Typhoon.

typhus [ti'fy:s], *n.m.* Typhus, gaol-fever.

typifié [tipi'fje], a. (fem. **-iée**) Typified; standardized.

typique [ti'pik], a. Typical, symbolical; characteristic; true to type. **typiquement,** adv. Typically.

typographe [tipɔ'graf], n.m. Typographer, printer. **typographie,** n.f. Typography; letterpress, print; printing-office. Atelier de typographie, printing-works. **typographique,** a. Typographic. Erreur typographique, misprint. **typolithographie,** n.f. Typolithography.

Tyr [tir], f. Tyre.

tyran [ti'rɑ̃], n.m. Tyrant. **tyranneau,** n.m. (pl. **-eaux**) Petty tyrant. **tyrannicide,** n.m. Tyrannicide. **tyrannie,** n.f. Tyranny. S'affranchir de la tyrannie, to free oneself from tyranny. **tyrannique,** a. Tyrannical. **tyranniquement,** adv. Tyrannously. **tyranniser,** v.t. To tyrannize over, to oppress.

Tyrol [ti'rɔl], m. Tirol.

tyrolien, a. (fem. **-ienne**) Tirolean, Tirolese. —n.f. Mountain song or waltz popular in the Tirol.—n.m. (**Tyrolien,** fem. **-ienne**) A Tirolese.

tzar [TSAR].

tzigane or **tsigane** [tsi'gan], n. and a. Gipsy.

U

U, u [y], n.m. The twenty-first letter of the alphabet. Fer en U, channel iron; en U, stirrup-shaped.

ubiquiste [ybi'kɥist], n. and a. (colloq.) Ubiquitous person; [UBIQUITAIRE]. **ubiquitaire,** n.m. and a. (Rel. Hist.) Ubiquitarian. **ubiquité,** n.f. Ubiquity. (iron.) Avoir le don d'ubiquité, to be able to be in several places at the same time.

udomètre [ydɔ'mɛtr], n.m. Udometer (rain-gauge). **udométrique,** a. Udometrical.

uhlan or ***hulan** [y'lɑ̃], n.m. Uhlan (German lancer). Les uhlans [leɥlɑ̃], the uhlans.

ukase [y'kɑ:z], n.m. Ukase, edict.

ulcération [ylsera'sjɔ̃], n.f. Ulceration. **ulcère,** n.m. Ulcer. **ulcéré,** a. (fem. **-ée**) Ulcerated; (fig.) embittered, cankered. Il a la conscience ulcérée, he suffers pangs of conscience. **ulcérer,** v.t. irr. (conjugated like ACCÉLÉRER) To ulcerate; (fig.) to embitter, to gall, to incense. **s'ulcérer,** v.r. To ulcerate; (fig.) to grow embittered or exacerbated. **ulcéreux,** a. (fem. **-euse**) Ulcerous; ulcerated.

uléma [yle'ma], n.m. Ulema (Moslem doctor of law).

ulex [y'lɛks], n.m. (Bot.) Ulex, whin, gorse.

uligineux, a. (fem. **-euse**) (Bot.) Uliginous.

ulmaire [yl'mɛːr], n.f. Common meadow-sweet.

ulmine [yl'min], n.f. (Chem.) Ulmin. **ulmique,** a. Ulmic. Acide ulmique, ulmic acid.

ultérieur [ylte'rjœːr], a. (fem. **-ieure**) Ulterior, further, thither, subsequent. **ultérieurement,** adv. Later on. **ultimatum,** n.m. Ultimatum. **ultime,** a. Final (of syllables etc.). **ultimo,** adv. Lastly.

ultra [yl'tra], n.m. Ultra (person of extremist opinions). **ultra-court,** a. (Phys.) Ultra-short (waves). **ultramontain,** a. and n.m. (fem. **-aine**) Ultramontane. **ultramontanisme,** n.m. Vaticanism. **ultra-son,** n.m. Ultra-sound. (Naut.) Sondage par ultra-sons, supersonic sounding. **ultra-sonore,** a. Supersonic, above the audible range. **ultra-violet,** a. (fem. **-ette**). Ultra-violet. **ultra-zodiacal,** a. (fem. **-ale,** pl. **-aux**) (Astron.) Ultra-zodiacal.

ululation [ylyla'sjɔ̃], n.f., or **ululement,** n.m. Ululation (howling, hooting, etc.). **ululer,** v.i. To ululate, to hoot.

Ulysse [y'lis], m. Ulysses.

umbre [ɔ:br], also **omble** or **ombre,** n.m. Grayling.

un [œ̃], a. and art. indef. (fem. **une** [yn]). One, the first; single; a, an; any, a certain. Sur les une [leyn] heure, about one o'clock; il a fait une de ces têtes! you should have seen his face!—pron. indef. One thing; one. C'est tout un, it is all one; il est menteur comme pas un, he is a terrible liar; les uns disent oui, les autres disent non, some say yes, others say no; les uns et les autres, all, all together; l'un et l'autre, both; l'un ou l'autre, the one or the other; l'un portant l'autre, one with another, on an average; l'un vaut l'autre, one is as good as the other; ne faire ni une ni deux, to make no bones about it, not to hesitate, to decide there and then; un à un, one by one; ni l'un ni l'autre, neither; un pour cent, one per cent. —n.m. One; (Theat. slang) the first act. En scène pour le un! overture beginners (on stage)!—n.f. (Press slang) Ça, c'est pour la une, this is for page one.

unanime [yna'nim], a. Unanimous. **unanimement,** adv. With one accord, unanimously. **unanimité,** n.f. Unanimity. À l'unanimité, by common consent, unanimously.

unau [y'no], n.m. (pl. **-aux**) Sloth (animal).

uncial [ONCIAL].

undécennal [ɔ̃dese'nal], a. (fem. **-ale,** pl. **-aux**) Undecennial.

unguéal [ɔ̃gɥe'al] or **unguinal,** a. (fem. **-ale,** pl. **-aux**) (Anat.) Ungual. **unguifère,** a. Unguiferous.

uni [y'ni], a. (fem. **-ie**) United; smooth, even, level; uniform, regular; plain, simple, unaffected. Du linge uni, plain linen; robe unie, plain, unrelieved frock; tissu uni, plain, unpatterned material; vie unie, regular, uniform life.—n.m. Uniform, even, or plain thing, stuff, etc.—adv. Evenly. Bien uni, quite smooth.

uniarticulé [yniartiky'le], a. (fem. **-ée**) Uniarticulate. **unicapsulaire,** a. Unicapsular. **unicellulaire,** a. Unicellular.

unicité [ynisi'te], n.f. Uniquity, oneness; uniqueness, singleness.

unicolore [yniko'lɔr], a. Unicolour, of one colour all over.

unicorne [yni'kɔrn], n.m. Unicorn.

unième [y'njɛm], a. (in compounds only) First. Vingt et unième, 21st. **unièmement,** adv. (in compounds only) Firstly.

unification [ynifika'sjɔ̃], n.f. Unification, standardization. **unifier,** v.t. (conjugated like PRIER) To unify, to unite, to standardize; to amalgamate.

uniforme [yni'fɔrm], *a.* Uniform, even, unvarying; flat (rate etc.).—*n.m.* Uniform, regimentals. *Grand uniforme*, full-dress uniform; *quitter l'uniforme*, to leave, to quit the service. **uniformément,** *adv.* Uniformly. **uniformiser,** *v.t.* To render uniform; to standardize. **uniformité,** *n.f.* Uniformity.

unijambiste [yniʒɑ̃'bist], *a.* and *n.* One-legged (person).

unilatéral [ynilate'ral], *a.* (*fem.* **-ale,** *pl.* **-aux**) (*Bot.*) Unilateral; binding on one party only, one-sided (of contracts). **unilatéralement,** *adv.* Unilaterally.

uniment [yni'mɑ̃], *adv.* Evenly, even, smoothly; plainly, simply. *Parler tout uniment,* to speak plainly.

uninominal [yninɔmi'nal], *a.* (*fem.* **-ale,** *pl.* **-aux**) Of one name. *Scrutin uninominal,* ballot for one candidate only.

union [y'njɔ̃], *n.f.* Union; concord, agreement, harmony; blending, mixture; marriage, match; unity, concord. **unionisme,** *n.m.* Unionism. **unioniste,** *n.m.* Unionist; trade-unionist.

unipare [yni'paːr], *a.* Uniparous.

unipersonnel, *a.* (*fem.* **-elle**) Unipersonal; impersonal (verb).

uniphasé [ynifa'ze], *a.* (*fem.* **-ée**) Single-phase (current, generator, etc.).

unipolaire [ynipɔ'lɛːr], *a.* Single-pole (dynamo etc.), unipolar.

unique [y'nik], *a.* Only, sole; single, unique, unrivalled, unparalleled, unprecedented; odd, singular. *Fils unique,* only son. *Sens unique,* one-way (street). (*fam.*) *Ça, c'est unique!* that's the limit; did you ever? **uniquement,** *adv.* Solely.

unir [y'niːr], *v.t.* To unite, to join, to combine; to connect, to link; to smooth, to level, to plane; to pair. **s'unir,** *v.r.* To unite, to join together, to coalesce.

uniréfringent [ynirefrɛ̃'ʒɑ̃], *a.* (*fem.* **-ente**) Monorefringent (crystal).

unisexuel [ynisek'sɥel] or **unisexué,** *a.* (*fem.* **-elle** or **-ée**) (*Bot.* etc.) Unisexual.

unisson [yni'sɔ̃], *n.m.* Unison; (*fig.*) harmony, concert. *À l'unisson,* in unison, in concert; in keeping (with).

unitaire [yni'tɛːr], *a.* and *n.* Unitarian, unitary. **unitarisme,** *n.m.* Unitarianism.

unité [yni'te], *n.f.* Unity; unit; (*fig.*) concord, agreement. *L'unité de lieu,* the unity of place; *les (trois) unités,* the (dramatic) unities. **unitif,** *a.* (*fem.* **-ive**) (*Theol.*) Unitive (with God).

univalve [yni'valv], *a.* (*Bot.* etc.) Univalve, univalvular.

univers [yni'vɛːr], *n.m. inv.* Universe. **universaliser,** *v.t.* To make universal. **universalité,** *n.f.* Universality, universalness; the sum total; the whole. **universaux,** *n.m. pl.* (*Phil.*) The universals. **universel,** *a.* (*fem.* **-elle**) Universal; *world-wide; residuary, sole (of legacies). *C'est un homme universel,* he knows everything about everything, he is an all-rounder. **universellement,** *adv.* Universally.

universitaire [yniversi'tɛːr], *a.* Of or belonging to the university, academic. *Grade universitaire,* (university, college) degree; *ville universitaire,* university town; *Cité Universitaire,* Students' Hostels Centre.—*n.* Member of the university; in the teaching profession.

université [yniversi'te], *n.f.* University. *Universités populaires,* Associations for the education of the masses.

upas [y'paːs], *n.m. inv.* Upas, poison-tree.

Upsal [yp'sal], *n.* Upsala.

urane [y'ran], *n.m.* (*Chem.*) Oxide of uranium. **uraneux,** *a.* (*fem.* **-euse**) Uranous. **uranique,** *a.* Uranic. **uranite** *n.f.* Uranite. **uranium,** *n.m.* Uranium.

uranographie [yranɔgra'fi], *n.f.* Uranography. **uranographique,** *a.* Uranographic, uranographical. **uranoscopie,** *n.f.* Uranoscopy.

urate [y'rat], *n.m.* (*Chem.*) Urate.

Urbain [yr'bɛ̃], *m.* Urban.

urbain [yr'bɛ̃], *a.* (*fem.* **-aine**) Urban. *Population urbaine,* city dwellers. **urbanisme,** *n.m.* Town-planning. **urbaniste,** *a.* *Architecte, ingénieur urbaniste,* city-designer, urbanist, town-planning architect, *or* engineer.—*n.m.* Town-planner.

urbanité [yrbani'te], *n.f.* Urbanity.

urcéole [yrse'ɔl], *n.m.* (*Bot.* etc.) Urceolus (urn-shaped organ). **urcéolé,** *a.* (*fem.* **-ée**) Urceolate.

ure [yːr] or **urus,** *n.m.* Urus, aurochs.

urédo [yre'do], *n.m.* (*Bot.*) Uredo.

urée [y're], *n.f.* (*Chem.*) Urea. **uréique,** *a.* Ureal. **urémie,** *n.f.* Uraemia. **urémique,** *a.* Uraemic. **uréomètre,** *n.m.* Ureameter. **uretère,** *n.m.* (*Anat.*) Ureter. **urètre,** *n.m.* Urethra.

urgence [yr'ʒɑ̃ːs], *n.f.* Urgency. *D'urgence,* urgently, on the spot, immediately. **urgent,** *a.* (*fem.* **-ente**) Urgent, pressing. *Cas urgent,* emergency.

urinaire [yri'nɛːr], *a.* Urinary. **urinal,** *n.m.* (*pl.* **-aux**) Urinal (vessel). **urine,** *n.f.* Urine. **uriner,** *v.i.* To urinate, to make water. **urineux,** *a.* (*fem.* **-euse**) Urinous. **urinoir,** *n.m.* (Public) urinal. **urique,** *a.* (*Chem.*) Uric (acid).

urne [yrn], *n.f.* Urn. *Urne électorale,* ballot-box. *Aller aux urnes,* to vote, to go to the polls.

urogénital [yrɔʒeni'tal], *a.* (*fem.* **-ale,** *pl.* **-aux**) Urogenital. **uroscopie,** *n.f.* Uroscopy.

Ursule [yr'syl], *f.* Ursula.

Ursuline [yrsy'lin], *n.f.* Ursuline nun.

urticaire [yrti'kɛːr], *n.f.* Nettle-rash; urticaria. **urticant,** *a.* (*fem.* **-ante**) Stinging. **urtication,** *n.f.* Urtication, stinging.

urus [URE].

us [ys, yz], *n.m. pl. Les us et coutumes,* the ways and customs.

usable [y'zabl], *a.* Liable to wear out.

usage [y'zaːʒ], *n.m.* Custom, practice, usage; use, employment, enjoyment; wear (of clothes etc.). *À l'usage de,* for the use of; *avoir de l'usage,* to have manners or breeding; *cela est hors d'usage,* that's out of use, unfit for use; *faire de l'usage or faire un bon usage,* to last *or* wear a long time; *il n'a plus l'usage de ses mains,* he has lost the use of his hands; (*Pharm.*) *pour l'usage externe,* for external application, not to be taken; *selon l'usage, suivant l'usage,* according to custom. **usagé,** *a.* (*fem.* **-ée**) (Article) which has been used or worn, which is not new, second-hand. **usager,** *a.* (*fem.* **-ère**) (Article) that one uses personally.—*n.pl. Les usagers* (*de la route*), the road-users; *les usagers* (*des biens communaux*), those entitled to the right of common. **usance,** *n.f.* Usance. **usant,** *a.* (*fem.* **-ante**) (*Law*) Making use of, using (of spinsters etc.).

usé [y'ze], *a.* (*fem.* **-ée**) Worn-out, threadbare; stale, trite, hackneyed.

user [y'ze], *v.i.* To make use; to have recourse, to avail oneself; to enjoy. *En user bien avec quelqu'un,* to treat someone well; *en user bien* or *mal,* to make a good or bad use of; *user de douceur,* to use gentle means; *user de violence,* to use violence.—*v.t.* To use up, to consume; to wear out, to wear away, to wear down; to spend, to waste. *User des souliers,* to wear out shoes. **s'user,** *v.r.* To wear oneself out; to wear away.

usinage [yzi'na:ʒ], *n.m.* Machine finishing.

usine [y'zin], *n.f.* Works, mills, factory. *Usine hydraulique,* waterworks; *usine à gaz,* gas-works. **usiner,** *v.t.* To machine, to machine-finish. **usinier,** *n.m.* Manufacturer, mill-owner.

usité [yzi'te], *a.* (*fem.* **-ée**) Used, in use, usual, in common use. *Mot qui n'est plus usité,* obsolete word.

ustensile [ystɑ̃'sil], *n.m.* Utensil; tool, implement. *Ustensiles de cuisine,* kitchen utensils.

usuel [y'zɥel], *a.* (*fem.* **-elle**) Usual, customary, ordinary. *Connaissances usuelles,* knowledge of everyday things, common knowledge. **usuellement,** *adv.* Habitually, ordinarily.

usufructuaire [yzyfryk'tɥe:r], *a.* Usufructuary. **usufruit,** *n.m.* Usufruct, use; life-interest. **usufruitier,** *n.m.* and *a.* (*fem.* **-ière**) Usufructuary; life-tenant.

usuraire [yzy'rɛ:r], *a.* Usurious. **usure,** *n.f.* Usury, excessive interest; wear, wear and tear; (*Geol.*) erosion, wearing away. *Rendre avec usure,* to return with interest; *guerre d'usure,* war of attrition. **usurier,** *n.m.* (*fem.* **-ière**) Usurer.—*a.* Usurious.

usurpateur [yzyrpa'tœ:r], *n.m.* (*fem.* **-trice**) Usurper.—*a.* Usurping. **usurpation,** *n.f.* Usurpation; encroaching, encroachment. **usurpatoire,** *a.* Usurpatory. **usurper,** *v.t.* To usurp; to encroach upon.

ut [yt], *n.m.* (*Mus.*) Ut, do, the note C. *Clé d'ut quatrième ligne,* tenor clef.

utérin [yte'rɛ̃], *a.* (*fem.* **-ine**) Uterine; (half-brother or -sister) on the mother's side.

utérus [yte'rys], *n.m.* Uterus, womb.

utile [y'til], *a.* Useful, of use, serviceable; advantageous, expedient, beneficial. *En temps utile,* in due or good time.—*n.m.* Utility, usefulness; what is useful. *Joindre l'utile à l'agréable,* to combine business with pleasure. **utilement,** *adv.* Usefully. **utilisable,** *a.* Utilizable, available. **utilisation,** *n.f.* Utilization, the turning of something to account. **utiliser,** *v.t.* To find use for, to employ. **utilitaire,** *n.m.* and *a.* Utilitarian. **utilitarien,** *a.* (*fem.* **-ienne**) Utilitarian. **utilitarisme,** *n.m.* Utilitarianism. **utilité,** *n.f.* Utility, usefulness; benefit, profit, service, avail; (*Theat.*) utility-man. *D'aucune utilité,* of no use.

utopie [ytɔ'pi], *n.f.* Utopia. **utopique,** *a.* Utopian. **utopiste,** *n.m.* and *a.* Utopian.

utricule [ytri'kyl], *n.m.* Utricle.

uval [y'val], *a.* (*fem.* **-ale,** *pl.* **-aux**) Pertaining to grapes. *Station uvale,* grape-juice bar.

uvée [y've], *n.f.* (*Anat.*) Uvea.

uviforme [yvi'fɔrm], *a.* Uviform, grape-shaped.

uvulaire [yvy'lɛ:r], *a.* (*Anat.*) Uvular; (*Bot.*) uvularia. **uvule,** *n.f.* Uvula.

uxorieux [yksɔ'rjø], *a.* (*fem.* **-ieuse**) Uxorious; doting (husband).

V

V, v [ve], *n.m.* The twenty-second letter of the alphabet.

va [va], *2nd pers. sing. imper.* [ALLER], *int.* Go. *3rd pers. sing. ind. pres. Va pour cela,* I consent, done, agreed.

vacance [va'kɑ̃:s], *n.f.* Vacancy; (*pl.*) vacation, holidays; recess (of parliament etc.). *Entrer en vacances,* to break up (of schools); *les grandes vacances,* the summer holidays; the long vacation (University). **vacant,** *a.* (*fem.* **-ante**) Vacant; unfilled, unoccupied, empty; (*Law*) in abeyance, unclaimed. *Place vacante,* vacant seat, vacant post.

vacarme [va'karm], *n.m.* Hubbub, uproar, fuss. *Faire du vacarme,* to kick up a shindy.

vacation [vaka'sjɔ̃], *n.f.* Attendance, sitting (of public officers etc.); fee for this; day's sale (at auctions); vacation, recess (of courts).

vaccin [vak'sɛ̃], *n.m.* Vaccine matter, lymph. **vaccinal,** *a.* (*fem.* **-ale,** *pl.* **-aux**) Vaccinal. **vaccinateur,** *n.m.* Vaccinator. **vaccination,** *n.f.* Inoculation, vaccination. **vaccine,** *n.f.* Vaccinia, cowpox. **vacciner,** *v.t.* To inoculate, to vaccinate; to immunize.

vache [vaʃ], *n.f.* Cow; cow-hide; leather covering for luggage boot; (in a diligence etc.); (*slang*) obese woman, trollop, bitch; beast, swine; (*pl.*) police. *Manger de la vache enragée,* to rough it; *parler français comme une vache espagnole,* to murder the French language; *vache à lait* or *laitière,* milch cow; *le plancher* or *le parquet des vaches,* terra firma. **vacher,** *n.m.* (*fem.* **-ère**) Cow-herd, neat-herd. **vacherie,** *n.f.* Cow-house, byre; (*vulg.*) dirty trick.

vaciet [va'sjɛ], *n.m.* Whort, whortleberry.

vacillant [vasi'jɑ̃], *a.* (*fem.* **-ante**) Vacillating, wavering, flickering; shaky, uncertain, staggering, unsteady; (*Bot.*) versatile. **vaciller,** *v.i.* To vacillate; to waver, to reel, to stagger; to flicker (of light etc.). **vacillation,** *n.f.* wobbling, flickering.

va-comme-j'te-pousse [vakɔmʒtə'pus], *adv. phr.* Happy-go-lucky way. *C'est fait à la va-comme-j'te-pousse,* it is a slap-dash job.

vacuité [vakɥi'te], *n.f.* Vacuity, emptiness.

vacuum [vakɥ'ɔm], *n.m.* Vacuum.

vade-mecum [vademe'kɔm], *n.m. inv.* Vade-mecum, handbook.

vadrouille [vad'ru:j], *n.f.* (*Naut.*) Pitch-mop; deck-swab; (C) mop. (*pop.*) *Aller en vadrouille* or **vadrouiller,** *v.i.*, to go on the spree, to go on the loose, to gallivant. **vadrouilleur,** *n.m.* (*fem.* **-euse**) Gadabout.

va-et-vient [vae'vjɛ̃], *n.m. inv.* Reciprocating motion, swing, see-saw motion, oscillation; ferry-boat drawn by rope; wherry used between two ships etc.; pass-rope, traversing gear; (*fig.*) coming and going. *Commutateur va-et-vient*, two-way switch; *porte va-et-vient*, swing-door.

vagabond [vaga'bɔ̃], *a.* and *n.* (*fem.* **-onde**) Vagabond, vagrant. **vagabondage,** *n.m.* Vagrancy. **vagabonder,** *v.i.* To be a vagabond, to roam; (*fig.*) to flit from one thing to another.

vagin [va'ʒɛ̃], *n.m.* (*Anat.*) Vagina. **vaginal,** *a.* (*fem.* **-ale,** *pl.* **-aux**) Vaginal. **vaginite,** *n.f.* Vaginitis.

vagir [va'ʒiːr], *v.i.* To wail, to pule (of infants). **vagissant,** *a.* (*fem.* **-ante**) Wailing, puling. **vagissement,** *n.m.* Cry, wailing.

vague (1) [vag], *n.f.* Wave, billow. *Vague de fond,* undertow, undercurrent; *vague de chaleur,* heat-wave.

vague (2) [vag], *a.* Vague, indeterminate, uncertain; faint, indistinct, hazy; sketchy; waste, empty, vacant. *Terres vagues,* wasteland; *un terrain vague,* a vacant site, a piece of waste ground.—*n.m.* Vagueness, looseness, uncertainty; empty space, emptiness, vacancy. *Avoir du vague à l'âme,* to have vague yearnings. **vaguelette,** *n.f.* Wavelet. **vaguement,** *adv.* Vaguely, dimly.

vaguemestre [vag'mestr], *n.m.* (*Mil.*) Baggage-master; regimental postman, (ship's) postman.

vaguer [va'ge], *v.i.* To ramble, to wander, to stray.—*v.t.* To mash (in brewing).

vaigrage [vɛ'graːʒ], *n.m.* (*Naut.*) Inner-planking. **vaigre,** *n.f.* Plank for lining boat.

vaillamment [vaja'mɑ̃], *adv.* Valiantly, courageously, stoutly. **vaillance,** *n.f.* Valour, bravery. **vaillant,** *a.* (*fem.* **-ante**) Valiant, brave, courageous, gallant, spirited; stout (heart). *N'avoir pas un sou vaillant,* to be penniless.

vaillantise [vajɑ̃'tiːz], *n.f.* Deed of prowess, derring-do.

vaille, *1st sing. subj.* [VALOIR].

vain [vɛ̃], *a.* (*fem.* **vaine**) Vain, fruitless, ineffectual; empty, hollow, shadowy; trifling, frivolous; vainglorious, presumptuous, conceited. *En vain,* vainly, in vain.

vaincre [vɛ̃ːkr], *v.t. irr.* (*pres.p.* **vainquant,** *p.p.* **vaincu**) To vanquish, to conquer, to overcome, to defeat, to get the better of; to master, to subdue; to outdo, to surpass, to excel. *Faire vaincre,* to cause to conquer, to cause to be conquered; *s'avouer vaincu,* to admit defeat; *se laisser vaincre,* to give way to, to yield, to be outdone or overruled, to relent; *se laisser vaincre à la pitié,* to be moved to pity. **se vaincre,** *v.r.* To conquer oneself; to conquer one's passions.

vaincu [vɛ̃'kɥ], *a.* (*fem.* **-ue**) Conquered, vanquished.—*n.* Conquered person, loser.

vainement [vɛn'mɑ̃], *adv.* Vainly, in vain, to no purpose.

vainqueur [vɛ̃'kœːr], *n.m.* Vanquisher, conqueror, victor; prize-winner.—*a.m.* Conquering, victorious, triumphant.

vair [vɛːr], *n.m.* (*Her.*) Vair; (whole) squirrel fur. **vairé,** *a.* (*fem.* **-ée**) (*Her.*) Charged with vair.

vairon (1) [vɛ'rɔ̃], *n.m.* Minnow.

vairon (2) or **véron** [vɛ'rɔ̃], *a.m.* Wall-eyed (of horses); (eyes) of different colours.

vaisseau [vɛ'so], *n.m.* (*pl.* **-eaux**) Vessel, receptacle, vase; ship; large covered space (of a building); (*Anat.*) tube, duct; (*pl.*) shipping. *Brûler ses vaisseaux,* to burn one's boats; *vaisseau-école,* training-ship. *Le vaisseau fantôme,* The Flying Dutchman.

vaisselier [vɛsə'lje], *n.m.* Dresser.

vaisselle, *n.f.* Plates and dishes; plate (of gold or silver). *Eau de vaisselle,* dish-water; *faire la vaisselle,* to wash up, to do the washing-up; *vaisselle d'or,* gold plate; *vaisselle plate,* plate. **vaissellerie,** *n.f.* Manufacture of pots and pans; ware of this kind.

val [val], *n.m.* (*pl.* **vals** or **vaux**) Narrow valley, vale, dale. *Par monts et par vaux,* up hill and down dale.

valable [va'labl], *a.* Valid, good, live (claim); available. **valablement,** *adv.* Validly.

Valence [va'lɑ̃ːs], *f.* Valencia.

valence [va'lɑ̃ːs], *n.f.* (*Chem.*) Valence.

valenciennes [valɑ̃'sjɛn], *n.f.* Valenciennes (lace).

Valentin [valɑ̃'tɛ̃], *m.* Valentine.

Valentine [valɑ̃'tin], *f.* Valentine.

Valère [va'lɛːr], *m.* Valerius.

Valérie [vale'ri], *f.* Valeria.

valériane [vale'rjan], *n.f.* Valerian.

valet [va'lɛ], *n.m.* Footman, valet, man-servant; servitor; menial, hireling, servant; knave, (at cards) jack; door-weight; hold-fast, claw, dog; support, rest, stand (for a looking-glass etc.); wad. *Âme de valet,* obsequious, servile nature; *faire le bon valet,* to be officious; *faire le plat valet,* to cringe, to fawn; to toady; *il n'y a pas de grand homme pour son valet de chambre,* no man is a hero to his valet; *je suis votre valet,* I am your humble servant; *maître valet,* head man; *tel maître, tel valet,* like master, like man; *valet de bourreau,* assistant-executioner; *valet de chambre,* valet, manservant; *valet de chiens,* whipper-in; *valet de ferme,* farm-servant; *valet de limiers,* harbourer; *valet de pied,* footman; (*fam.*) flunkey. **valetage,** *n.m.* Duty of a valet; (*fig.*) servility. **valetaille,** *n.f.* Pack of men servants, footmen, flunkeys, lackeys, menials.

valet-à-patin, *n.m.* (*Surg.*) Forceps (for ligatures).

valeter [val'te], *v.i. irr.* (*conjugated like* AMENER) To cringe, to dance attendance.

valétudinaire [valetydi'nɛːr], *a.* Valetu-dinary.—*n.* Valetudinarian, invalid.

valeur [va'lœːr], *n.f.* Value, worth, price; weight, consideration; import, meaning; valour, bravery, courage, gallantry; (*pl.*) bills, paper, stocks, shares, securities. *Avoir de la valeur,* to be of value, importance, or weight; *mettre en valeur,* to improve (land); to empha-size, to enhance; *sans valeur,* valueless, worthless, of no account; *valeur en espèces,* value in cash; *valeurs mobilières,* transferable securities. **valeureusement,** *adv.* Bravely, courageously. **valeureux,** *a.* (*fem.* **-euse**) Brave, courageous, gallant.

validation [valida'sjɔ̃], *n.f.* Validation, render-ing valid. **valide,** *a.* Valid, good; in health, healthy, able-bodied.—*n.* Person in health. **validement,** *adv.* Validly. **valider,** *v.t.* To make valid; to ratify, to validate; to authenticate. **validité,** *n.f.* Validity; avail-ability (of a ticket). *Peut-on établir la* *validité de ce testament?* Can this will be proved?

valise [va'liːz], *n.f.* Suit-case; valise, portmanteau. *La valise diplomatique,* the diplomatic bag, the bag.

vallée [va'le], *n.f.* Valley. (*fig.*) *Cette vallée de larmes,* this vale of tears.

vallon [va'lɔ̃], *n.m.* Small valley, vale, dale. **vallonnement,** *n.m.* Disposing in vales (in landscape gardening).

valoir [va'lwaːr], *v.i. irr.* (*pres.p.* **valant,** *p.p.* **valu**) To be worth, to be as good as, to be equal to; to deserve, to merit. *Autant vaut,* to all intents and purposes; *autant vaut faire cela,* we may as well do that; *à valoir,* on account; *cela ne vaut pas la peine d'y penser,* that is not worth a moment's thought; (*pop.*) *cela ne vaut pas le coup,* it is not worth it; *cela ne vaut rien,* that is good for nothing; *cela vaut son pesant d'or,* that is worth its weight in gold; *chaque chose vaut son prix,* everything has its price; *combien vaut ce poulet?* how much do you charge for that chicken? *faire valoir sa marchandise,* to set off one's goods; *faire valoir son argent,* to turn one's money to account; *faire valoir son droit,* to assert one's right; *faire valoir son teint, sa taille,* to set off, to show off one's complexion, one's figure; *faire valoir une terre,* to improve an estate; *il ne vaut pas la peine qu'on lui réponde,* he is not worth answering; *il vaut mieux ne pas y aller,* it is better not to go there; *se faire valoir,* to push oneself forward, to boast; *vaille que vaille,* at all events, for better or worse; *vous ne faites rien qui vaille,* nothing you do is any good.— *v.t.* To yield, to bring in; to procure, to furnish. **valorisation,** *n.f.* Valorization. **valoriser,** *v.t.* To valorize.

valse [vals], *n.f.* Waltz. **valser,** *v.i.* To waltz. (*fam.*) *Envoyer quelqu'un, quelque chose valser,* to send someone packing, to throw about, to fling off something; *faire valser une jeune fille,* to waltz with a girl; *faire valser les millions,* to spend money like water; *il nous a bien fait valser,* he led us a merry dance. **valseur,** *n.m.* (*fem.* **-euse**) Waltzer.

*value [va'ly], *n.f.* Value. (*Now only used in*) *moins-value,* inferior value; *plus-value,* superior value, excess yield.

valvaire [val'vɛːr], *a.* (*Bot.*) Valvar, valvate. **valve,** *n.f.* Valve, clack, trap-door. **valvé,** *a.* (*fem.* **-ée**) Valved, valvate. **valvule,** *n.f.* Valvule. **valvulé,** *a.* (*fem.* **-ée**) Valvulate.

vampire [vã'piːr], *n.m.* Vampire; (*Zool.*) vampire-bat; (*fig.*) blood-sucker. **vampirisme,** *n.m.* Vampirism; belief in vampires; extortion, blood-sucking.

van [vã], *n.m.* Fan, van, winnowing-basket or machine; aspirator.

vandale [vã'dal], *n.m.* Vandal. **vandalisme,** *n.m.* Vandalism.

vanesse [va'nɛs], *n.f.* Vanessa, red admiral (butterfly).

vandoise [vã'dwaːz], *n.f.* Dace (fish).

vanille [va'niːj], *n.f.* Vanilla. *Gousse de vanille,* vanilla bean. **vanillier,** *n.m.* Vanilla-plant.

vanité [vani'te], *n.f.* Vanity, futility; conceit. *La foire aux vanités,* vanity fair; *que vous avez de vanité!* how vain you are! *sans vanité,* without wishing to boast; *tirer vanité de,* to

take an empty pride in. **vaniteusement,** *adv.* Conceitedly. **vaniteux,** *a.* (*fem.* **-euse**) Vainglorious, vain.—*a.* Vain person, full of self-conceit.

vannage (1) [va'naːʒ], *n.m.* Winnowing.

vannage (2) [va'naːʒ], *n.m.* System of watergates in a dam etc.; sluicing. **vanne,** *n.f.* Water-gate, sluice, sluice-gate. *Vanne de décharge,* overflow sluice.—*a.* Eaux vannes, waste-water, cess-water (from houses).

vanneau [va'no], *n.m.* (*pl.* **-eaux**) Lapwing, peewit. *Œufs de vanneaux,* plovers' eggs.

vanner (1) [va'ne], *v.t.* To winnow, to fan, to sift; (*pop.*) to tire out, to exhaust. *Je suis vanné,* I am dead beat, all in.

vanner (2) [va'ne], *v.t.* To fit with sluices.

vannerie [van'ri], *n.f.* Basket-making or -trade; basket-work; wicker-work. **vannette,** *n.f.* Winnowing-basket (for sifting corn for horses). **vanneur,** *a.* (*fem.* **-euse**) Winnowing.—*n.* Winnower.—*n.f.* Winnowing-machine.

vannier [va'nje], *n.m.* Basket-maker.

vannure [va'nyːr], *n.f.* Chaff, husks.

vantail [vã'taːj], *n.m.* (*pl.* **-aux**) Leaf (of door, sluice-gate, etc.). *Porte à deux vantaux,* folding-door.

vantard [vã'taːr], *a.* (*fem.* **-arde**) Boasting, boastful, bragging.—*n.* Boaster, braggart. **vantardise,** *n.f.* Boasting, bragging; braggadocio; boast, piece of bluff.

vanter [vã'te], *v.t.* To vaunt, to cry up, to praise. **se vanter,** *v.r.* To boast, to vaunt, to praise oneself; to plume oneself; to pride oneself on (*de*). *Il n'y a pas de quoi se vanter,* there is nothing to boast about. **vanterie,** *n.f.* Boasting, bragging; boast, brag.

va-nu-pieds [vany'pje], *n. inv.* Tatterdemalion, ragamuffin; (barefoot) tramp.

vapeur [va'pœːr], *n.f.* Vapour; steam; fume, haze, mist, exhalation; (*pl.*) vapours; (*Paint.*) air. *À la vapeur* or *à toute vapeur,* at full speed; *bateau à vapeur,* steamboat, steamer; *machine à vapeur,* steam-engine.—*n.m.* Steamer, steamship. **vaporeux,** *a.* (*fem.* **-euse**) Vaporous; vapoury; steamy, hazy; (*Path.*) vapourish; (*Paint.*) aerial.

vaporisateur, *n.m.* Vaporizer, sprayer; atomizer; scent-spray. **vaporisation,** *n.f.* Vaporization; evaporation; atomization. **vaporiser,** *v.t.* To vaporize; to atomize. **se vaporiser,** *v.r.* To be vaporized; to spray oneself (with scent etc.).

vaquer [va'ke], *v.i.* To be vacant; to be in vacation; to attend, to devote oneself (*à*). *Il vaque à ses affaires,* he is attending to his business.

varaigne [va'rɛɲ], *n.f.* Tide-sluice (in a salt-marsh).

varaire [va'rɛːr], *n.f.* White hellebore.

varangue [va'rãːg], *n.f.* Floor-timber or floorplate (in a ship).

varappe [va'rap], *n.f.* Well-known corridor in the Alps, where rock-climbers train; rock-surface (where same methods must be used). **varapper,** *v.i.* To climb up a rocky corridor or chimney with the help of hands, elbows, feet, and knees. **varappeur,** *n.m.* Specialist of this kind of climbing; cliffs-man.

varech or **varec** [va'rek], *n.m.* Varec, sea-wrack, sea-weed.

*varenne [GARENNE].

vareuse [va'rø:z], *n.f.* Pea-jacket, pilot-jacket; jersey; dark-blue close-fitting jacket, blazer.
variabilité [varjabili'te], *n.f.* Variability, changeableness. **variable,** *a.* Variable, changeable, fickle, unsettled, unsteady.—*n.f.* (*Math.*) Variable. **variant,** *a.* (*fem.* **-iante**) Variable, fickle.—*n.f.* Variant (reading or interpretation). **variation,** *n.f.* Variation. *Air et variations*, theme and variations.
varice [va'ris], *n.f.* Varix, varicose vein.
varicelle [vari'sɛl], *n.f.* Varicella, chicken-pox. **varicocèle**, *n.f.* Varicocele.
varié [va'rje], *a.* (*fem.* **-iée**) Varied, diversified, variegated; miscellaneous; chequered (existence). (*Mus.*) *Air varié,* air with variations; *mouvement varié,* variable motion.
varier [va'rje], *v.t.* (*conjugated like* PRIER) To vary, to change; to diversify; to variegate.—*v.i.* To vary, to change, to veer; to be changeable, to be fickle; to disagree, to be at variance.
variété [varje'te], *n.f.* Variety, diversity, change; (*pl.*) miscellanea, varieties.
variole [va'rjɔl], *n.f.* Variola, smallpox. *Variole des vaches,* cow-pox. **varioleux,** *a.* (*fem.* **-euse**) Suffering from smallpox.—*n.* Smallpox patient. **variolique,** *a.* Variolous. **variolisation,** *n.f.* Variolation.
variolite, *n.f.* (*Min.*) Variolite.
variqueux [vari'kø], *a.* (*fem.* **-euse**) Varicose.
***varlet** [var'le], *n.m.* Varlet, page.
varlope [var'lɔp], *n.f.* Jointing-plane; trying-plane. *Demi-varlope,* jack-plane. **varloper,** *v.t.* To plane, to try up. **varlopeuse,** *n.f.* Planing-machine.
Varsovie [varsɔ'vi], *f.* Warsaw.
vas, *2nd indic. pres.* [ALLER].
vasard [va'za:r], *a.* (*fem.* **-arde**) Muddy.—*n.m.* Muddy bottom (sea etc.).
vasculaire [vasky'lɛ:r] or **vasculeux,** *a.* (*fem.* **-euse**) (*Anat.*) Vascular. *Pression vasculaire,* blood-pressure.
vase (1) [vɑ:z], *n.m.* Vase, vessel. *Vase de chapiteau,* vase of Corinthian capital; *vase de nuit,* chamber-pot. *Vase clos,* retort; *vases communicants,* communicating vessels.
vase (2) [vɑ:z], *n.f.* Slime, mud, mire, ooze.
vaseline [vaz'lin], *n.f.* Petroleum jelly, Vaseline (proprietary mark).
vaseux [va'zø], *a.* (*fem.* **-euse**) Slimy, muddy, miry; (*fam.*) tired, seedy. **vasier,** *a.* (*fem.* **-ière**) Of ɔr for mud.—*n.f.* Slimy place, mud-hole.
vasistas [vasiz'tɑ:s], *n.m.* (*pl. inv.*) Opening, fan-light (over a door or a window).
vaso-moteur [vazɔmo'tœ:r], *a.* (*fem.* **-trice**) Vasomotor.—*n.m.* (*pl.* **vaso-moteurs**) Vaso-motor.
vason [va'zɔ̃], *n.m.* Clay ready for the potter; (*Tech.*) body.
vasque [vask], *n.f.* Basin (of a fountain).
vassal [va'sal], *a.* (*fem.* **-ale,** *pl.* **-aux**) Vassal.—*n.* Vassal, retainer. **vasselage,** *n.m.* **vassalité,** *n.f.* Vassalage; subjection.
vaste [vast], *a.* Vast, wide, spacious; capacious, comprehensive. **vastement,** *adv.* Vastly, widely.
Vatican [vati'kɑ̃], **le,** *m.* The Vatican. **vaticane,** *a.f.* Of the Vatican.
vaticination [vatisina'sjɔ̃], *n.f.* Vaticination, prophecy. **vaticiner,** *v.i.* To prophesy, to vaticinate.

va-tout [va'tu], *n.m. inv.* One's all (at cards). *Jouer son va-tout,* to stake one's all.
vau-de-route [vo'drut], **à,** *adv. phr.* At sixes and sevens, in disorder.
vaudeville [vod'vil], *n.m.* Vaudeville; ballad; light form of comedy. **vaudevilliste,** *n.* Vaudeville-writer.
vaudou [vo'du], *n.m.* Voodoo; witch-doctor.
vau-l'eau [vo'lo], **à,** *adv. phr.* With the current, down-stream; to rack and ruin.
vaurien [vo'rjɛ̃], *n.m.* (*fem.* **-ienne**) Good-for-nothing, scamp, scapegrace; rogue; (*fam.*) rotter.
vaut, *3rd indic. pres.* [VALOIR].
vautour [vo'tu:r], *n.m.* Vulture.
vautrait [vo'trɛ], *n.m.* Boar-hunting pack. **vautre,** *n.m.* Boar-hound. **vautrer** (1), *v.t.* To hunt boar with hounds.
vautrer (2) [vo'tre], **se,** *v.r.* To wallow, to welter; to sprawl; (*fig.*) to revel (*dans*).
vau-vent [vo'vɑ̃], **à,** *adv. phr.* Down-wind.
vavasseur [vava'sœ:r] or **vavassal,** *n.m.* (*pl.* **-aux**) Vavasour (vassal holding of a vassal).
veau [vo], *n.m.* (*pl.* **veaux**) Calf; (*Cook.*) veal; calf-skin, calf-leather; (*fig.*) lump, lout, slow-witted fellow. *Faire le veau,* to sprawl about; *pleurer comme un veau,* to blubber; *longe de veau,* loin; *tuer le veau gras,* to kill the fatted calf; *veau marin,* seal, sea-calf, seal-skin.
vecteur [vɛk'tœ:r], *a.m.* and *n.m.* Vector. *Rayon vecteur,* radius vector. **vectoriel,** *a.* (*fem.* **-ielle**) Vectorial.
vécu, *p.p.* (*fem.* **vécue**) [VIVRE].
vedette [və'dɛt], *n.f.* Vedette, mounted sentinel; scout; observation post, watch-tower; (*Naut.*) vedette-boat; (*Theat.*) star. *Être en vedette,* to be in the limelight; *mettre un nom en vedette,* to make a name stand out; *vedette policière,* police launch; *vedette de l'écran,* film star.
védique [ve'dik], *a.* Vedic.
végétal [veʒe'tal], *a.* (*fem.* **-ale,** *pl.* **-aux**) Vegetable.—*n.m.* Vegetable, plant. **végé-tant,** *a.* (*fem.* **-ante**) Vegetating. **végé-tarianisme** or **végétarisme,** *n.m.* Vegetarianism. **végétarien,** *a.* and *n.m.* (*fem.* **-ienne**) Vegetarian. **végétatif,** *a.* (*fem.* **-ive**) Vegetative. **végétation,** *n.f.* Vegetation; (*pl.*) adenoids. **végéter,** *v.i. irr.* (*conjug. like* ACCÉLÉRER) To vegetate. *Il ne fait plus que végéter,* he merely vegetates.
véhémence [vee'mɑ̃:s], *n.f.* Vehemence. **véhément,** *a.* (*fem.* **-ente**) Vehement, impetuous, hot, passionate. **véhémente-ment,** *adv.* Violently, vehemently.
véhiculaire [veiky'lɛ:r], *a.* Vehicular.
véhicule [vei'kyl], *n.m.* Vehicle; medium; excipient; carrier (of disease). **véhiculer,** *v.t.* To carry, to convey.
vehme [vɛ:m], *n.f.* Vehmgericht (medieval German court). **vehmique,** *a.* Vehmic.
veille [vɛ:j], *n.f.* Sleeplessness, wakefulness, insomnia, watching; waking, being awake; sitting up; vigil; eve, day before; point, verge; (*pl.*) midnight work, late nights, nightly labours. (*Naut.*) *Chambre de veille,* chart-house; *entre le sommeil et la veille,* between sleeping and waking; *être à la veille de,* to be on the point of, on the verge of; *homme de veille,* look-out man; *la veille de Noël,* Christmas Eve.

veillée [vɛ'je], *n.f.* Time from supper to bedtime, evening (in company); sitting up to work etc. in company; night attendance (upon a sick person). *Les veillées d'hiver*, the winter evenings; *veillée funèbre*, (night) watch beside a dead person; (Irish) wake. **veiller,** *v.i.* To sit up, to watch, to be awake, to lie awake; to be on the watch; to attend, to take care, to see, to have an eye (*à*). *Faire veiller quelqu'un*, to keep someone up; *veiller au grain*, to keep one's weather eye open; *veiller au salut de l'État*, to watch over the safety of the State; *veiller sur soi-même*, to be on one's guard; *veillez à ce que cela se fasse*, see to it that that is done.—*v.t.* To watch by, to nurse, to look after, to sit up with. *Veiller un malade*, to watch by the bedside of a sick person.

veilleur [vɛ'jœːr], *n.m.* (*fem.* **-euse**) Watcher. *Veilleur de nuit*, night-watchman.—*n.f.* Night-light; float-light, watch-light; pilot-light; by-pass (gas). *Lampe mise en veilleuse*, lamp turned low. *Mettre le gaz en veilleuse*, to turn down the gas to a peep; *mettre les phares en veilleuse*, to dim the head-lights; *mettre un projet en veilleuse*, to slow down work on a plan; (*fam.*) to put it on ice.

veillotte [vɛ'jɔt], *n.f.* Meadow-saffron; hay-cock.

veinard [vɛ'naːr], *n.m.* and *a.* (*fem.* **-arde**) (*pop.*) Lucky person, lucky dog.

veine [vɛːn], *n.f.* Vein; (*Geol.* etc.) seam; (*pop.*) good luck. *Avoir de la veine*, to be in luck; *en veine de*, in the mood for; *je suis en veine*, I am in luck; *un coup de veine*, a fluke. **veiné,** *a.* (*fem.* **-ée**) Veined, veiny; (*Paint.*) grained. **veiner,** *v.t.* (*Paint.*) To vein, to grain. **veineux,** *a.* (*fem.* **-euse**) Veined, veiny; venous. **veinule,** *n.f.* Small vein. **veinure,** *n.f.* Veining (of marble).

vêlage [vɛ'laːʒ] or **vêlement,** *n.m.* Calving (of cows).

vélaire [ve'lɛːr], *a.* and *n.f.* Velar.

vélar [ve'laːr], *n.m.* (*Bot.*) Hedge-mustard.

vélarium [vela'rjɔm], *n.m.* (*pl.* **vélariums**) (*Rom. Ant.*) Velarium (awning above amphi-theatre).

velche [vɛlʃ] or **welche,** *n.m.* Goth, ignora-mus.

veld [vɛlt] or **veldt,** *n.m.* Veldt, veld.

vêler [vɛ'le], *v.i.* To calve (of cows).

vélin [ve'lɛ̃], *n.m.* Vellum; fine Alençon lace; a kind of paper.

vélique [ve'lik], *a.* (*Naut.*) Concerned with sails.

vélite [ve'lit], *n.m.* (*Rom. Ant.*) Light-armed soldier, skirmisher.

vélivoler [velivɔ'le], *v.i.* (*Av.*) To glide.

velléitaire [vɛlei'tɛːr], *a.* Impulsive, erratic.—*n.* A person who has only stray impulses, but no efficient will; person of fits and starts.

velléité, *n.f.* Velleity, slight degree of volition; passing fancy, mind, whim.

vélo [ve'lo], *n.m.* (*fam.*) Bike; push-bike. *Aller, monter à vélo*, to bike, to cycle.

véloce [ve'lɔs], *a.* Swift, rapid. **vélocimane,** *n.m.* (Hand-propelled) invalid tricycle. **vélocipède,** *n.m.* Velocipede; cycle. **vélo-cité,** *n.f.* Velocity. **vélodrome,** *n.m.* Cycle racing-track. **vélomoteur,** *n.m.* Motor-bicycle (maximum weight 75 kilogr.); auto-cycle.

velours [və'luːr], *n.m.* Velvet; (*fam.*) false liaison. *Être sur le velours*, to be on velvet, to be safe from losing; *faire patte de velours*, to draw in one's claws; *habits de velours*, *ventre de son*, silks and satins put out the kitchen fire; *le chemin de velours*, the primrose path; *velours à côtes*, corduroy; *velours de coton*, velveteen; *velours de soie*, silk velvet; *velours ras*, short-nap velvet.

velouté [vəlu'te], *a.* (*fem.* **-ée**) Velvet, velvety, velvet-like; soft as velvet; soft and smooth to the palate (of wines).—*n.m.* Velveting, flock-surface, velvet-pile; softness; bloom (of fruit); smooth rich soup or sauce. *Velouté de laine*, velours cloth. **velouter,** *v.t.* To give (a material) the appearance of velvet, to make like velvet. **velouteux,** *a.* (*fem.* **-euse**) Velvety, downy. **veloutier,** *n.m.* Velvet-weaver.

velpeau [vɛl'po], *n.m.* Crape bandage.

veltage [vɛl'taːʒ], *n.m.* Measuring liquids by the velte. **velte,** *n.f.* Obsolete measure of capacity (about 7 quarts English); gauge. **velter,** *v.t.* To measure (liquids).

velu [və'ly], *a.* (*fem.* **-ue**) Hairy, shaggy, rough.—*n.m.* Shagginess; hairy part.

vélum [ve'lɔm], *n.m.* Awning.

velventine [vɛlvã'tin], *n.f.* Velveteen.

velvote [vɛl'vɔt], *n.f.* Toad-flax.

venaison [vənɛ'zɔ̃], *n.f.* Venison.

vénal [ve'nal], *a.* (*fem.* **-ale**, *pl.* **-aux**) Venal, mercenary. **vénalement,** *adv.* Venally. **vénalité,** *n.f.* Venality.

venant [və'nɑ̃], *a.* (*fem.* **-ante**) Coming, thriving. *Bien venant*, thriving.—*n.m.* Comer. *À tout venant*, to all comers; *les allants et les venants*, comers and goers; *tout-venant*, un-sorted (of a produce).

vendable [vɑ̃'dabl], *a.* Saleable, vendible; marketable.

vendange [vɑ̃'dɑ̃ːʒ], *n.f.* Vintage, grape-gathering, season of this. *Faire la vendange* or *les vendanges*, to gather in the grapes. **vendangeoir,** *n.m.* Grape-basket. **ven-danger,** *v.t.* To gather in the grapes from; (*fig.*) to ravage, to spoil.—*v.i.* To make the vintage; (*fig.*) to make illicit profits. **ven-dangerot,** *n.m.* Grape-picker's willow basket. **vendangeur,** *n.m.* (*fem.* **-euse**) Vintager, grape-gatherer.

vendéen [vɑ̃de'ɛ̃], *a.* (*fem.* **-éenne**) Vendean. —*n.m.* (**Vendéen,** *fem.* **-éenne**) A Vendean.

vendémiaire [vɑ̃de'mjɛːr], *n.m.* First month of calendar of first French republic (Sept. 22nd or 23rd to Oct. 21st or 22nd).

venderesse, *fem.* [VENDEUR (1)].

vendetta [vɛ̃dɛt'ta], *n.f.* (*It.*) Vendetta, family blood-feud.

vendeur (1) [vɑ̃'dœːr], *n.m.* (*Law*) (*fem.* **ven-deresse**) Vendor.

vendeur (2) [vɑ̃'dœːr], *n.m.* (*fem.* **-euse**) Seller, dealer; salesman, shop assistant; shopgirl, (*Am.*) salesgirl.

vendre [vɑ̃:dr], *v.t.* To sell; (*fig.*) to betray; (*pop.*) to squeal on, to turn Queen's evidence against; (*Law*) to sell up (a person). *À vendre*, to be sold, for sale; *vendre à bon marché*, to sell cheap; *vendre cher*, to sell dear. **se vendre,** *v.r.* To sell oneself; to sell, to be sold, to go off (well etc.). *Ça se vend comme des petits pains*, it is selling like hot cakes.

vendredi [vãdrə'di], *n.m.* Friday. *Le Vendredi saint*, Good Friday.

vendu [vã'dy], *n.m.* (*pop.*) A traitor; a re-enlisted soldier.

vené [və'ne], *a.* (*fem.* **-ée**) High (of meat).

venelle [və'nɛl], *n.f.* Small street, alley. *Enfiler la venelle*, to take to one's heels.

vénéneux [vene'nø], *a.* (*fem.* **-euse**) Poisonous (chiefly of plants, mushrooms, shellfish, etc.) (when eaten).

vener [və'ne], *v.t. irr.* (*conjug. like* AMENER) To hang meat to make it tender. *Faire vener de la viande*, to keep meat until it gets high.

vénérable [vene'rabl], *a.* Venerable.—*n.m.* Master (of Masonic lodge). **vénérateur,** *n.m.* (*fem.* **-trice**) Venerator. **vénération,** *n.f.* Veneration. **vénérer,** *v.t. irr.* (*conjug. like* ACCÉLÉRER) To venerate, to hold in reverence.

vénerie [ven'ri], *n.f.* Venery, hunting; hunt, hunting-train; kennel.

vénérien [vene'rjɛ̃], *a.* (*fem.* **-ienne**) Vene-real.

venette [və'nɛt], *n.f.* (*fam.*) Fright, funk. *Avoir la venette*, to be in a funk.

veneur [və'nœːr], *n.m.* Huntsman. *Grand veneur*, master of the hounds, M.F.H.

vengeance [vã'ʒãːs], *n.f.* Vengeance, revenge. *Demander* or *crier vengeance*, to cry for vengeance; *par vengeance*, out of revenge; *tirer vengeance d'un affront*, to be revenged for an affront. **venger,** *v.t.* To revenge, to avenge. **se venger,** *v.r.* *Se venger sur quelqu'un*, to revenge oneself on someone. **vengeur,** *n.m.* (*fem.* **-eresse**) Avenger, revenger.—*a.* Revengeful, avenging.

véniel [ve'njɛl], *a.* (*fem.* **-ielle**) Venial. **véniellement,** *adv.* Venially.

venimeux [vəni'mø], *a.* (*fem.* **-euse**) Communicating poison (from outside), venomous (snake etc.); (*fig.*) malignant, spiteful, harmful.

venimosité [vənimozi'te], *n.f.* Venomousness.

venin [və'nɛ̃], *n.m.* Venom, poison; (*fig.*) virulence, spite, rancour, malice. *Il a jeté tout son venin*, he has vented all his spite; *sans venin*, harmless.

venir [və'niːr], *v.i. irr.* (*pres.p.* **venant,** *p.p.* **venu**) To come, to be coming; to come to, to arrive; to reach; to occur, to happen, to chance; to grow, to grow up; to thrive; to issue, to emanate, to proceed, to arise; to be descended. *Cette nouvelle est venue jusqu'à moi*, that news reached even me; *dans les temps à venir*, in the days to come; *d'où venez-vous?* where do you come from? where were you brought up? *d'où vient cela?* what is the cause of that? *d'où vient que vous faites cela?* how is it that you do that? *en venir aux extrémités*, to come to extremities; *en venir aux mains*, to come to blows; *faire venir le médecin*, to send for the doctor; *il faut en venir là*, we must come to that at last; *il en vint jusqu'à le menacer*, he went so far as to threaten him; *il me vint une pensée*, a thought came into my head; *il va et vient*, he goes in and out; *il vient de partir*, he has only just gone; *je ne ferai qu'aller et venir*, I will not stay, I shall come straight back; *je venais de le quitter*, I had just left him; *je viens de le voir*, I have just seen him; *je viens le voir*, I am coming to see him; *le voilà qui vient,*

here he comes; *où voulez-vous en venir?* what are you getting at? (*fam.*) what's the idea? (*Am.*) where do we go from here? *quand il vint à parler de*, when he came to speak of; *s'en venir*, to come away, to come along; *si ma lettre venait à se perdre*, if my letter should happen to go astray; *tout lui vient à souhait*, everything goes according to his wishes; *tout vient à point à qui sait attendre*, everything comes to him who waits; *venez donc, do come along; *venez ici*, come here; *venir à bout de*, to master, to get through with, to defeat; *venir au monde*, to come into the world, to be born; *venir de*, to come from, (*followed by an infinitive*) to have just; *voulez-vous venir avec nous à Londres?* will you go with us to London?—*n.m.* Coming.

Venise [və'niːz], *f.* Venice.

vénitien [veni'sjɛ̃], *a.* (*fem.* **-ienne**) Venetian. *Lanterne vénitienne* [LANTERNE].—*n.m.* (**Vénitien,** *fem.* **-ienne**) A Venetian.

vent [vã], *n.m.* Wind; breeze; breath, breathing; (*Med.*) (*pl.*) flatulence, wind; (*Hunt.*) scent; (*fig.*) vanity, emptiness; (*Artill.*) windage; vent (of a barrel etc.). *Aller comme le vent*, to go like the wind; *aller contre vent et marée*, to go against wind and tide; *aller selon le vent*, to sail with the wind, (*fig.*) to move with the times; *autant en emporte le vent*, all that is idle talk; *au vent*, to windward; *avoir vent de*, to get wind of; *coup de vent*, gust of wind; *en plein vent*, in the open air; *être logé aux quatre vents*, to be exposed to every wind that blows; *filer vent arrière*, to sail before the wind; *flotter au gré du vent*, to float in the breeze; *grand coup de vent*, strong gale; *Îles du Vent*, Windward Islands; *Îles sous le Vent*, Leeward Islands; *il fait du vent*, it is windy; *instruments à vent*, wind instruments; *prendre le vent*, to catch the wind (of sails); (*fig.*) to see how the land lies; *prendre vent*, to recover one's breath; *sous le vent*, to leeward; *tout cela n'est que du vent*, all that means nothing; *vent coulis*, draught; *vent de mer*, sea-breeze; *vent de terre*, land-breeze.

ventage [vã'taːʒ], *n.m.* Winnowing.

ventail [vã'taːj], *n.m.* (*pl.* **-aux**) or **ventaille,** *n.f.* Ventail.

vente [vã:t], *n.f.* Sale; selling, auction; a felling or cutting (of timber). *En vente*, for sale, on sale, now ready (of a book); *marchandise de bonne vente*, goods that sell well; *mettre en vente*, to put up for sale; *vente aux enchères*, sale by auction; *vente publique*, auction(-sale).

venté [vã'te], *a.* (*fem.* **-ée**) Wind-shaken; exposed (to wind).

venteaux [vã'to], *n.m. pl.* Air-holes; valves (of bellows).

venter [vã'te], *v.i.* (*usu. impers.*) To blow, to be windy. *Il vente*, the wind is blowing.

venteux, *a.* (*fem.* **-euse**) Windy, gusty; causing flatulence; blistered (of casting).

ventilateur [vãtila'tœːr], *n.m.* Ventilator, fan, air-exhaust, blower. *Ventilateur électrique*, electric fan. **ventilation,** *n.f.* Ventilation, airing; (*Law*) separate valuation of objects sold together. **ventiler,** *v.t.* To ventilate, to air; (*Law*) to value (things sold together); (*fig.*) to discuss. **ventileuse,** *n.f.* Fanner (bee).

ventis [vã'ti], *n.m.* Wind-fallen timber.

ventôse [vã'toːz], *n.m.* Sixth month of calendar

of first French republic (February 19th or 20th to March 20th).

ventosité [vãtozi'te], *n.f.* Flatulence.

ventouse [vã'tu:z], *n.f.* Cupping-glass; vent, vent-hole, air-hole; sucker (of leech); nozzle (of vacuum-cleaner). *Appliquer des ventouses,* to cup. **ventouser,** *v.t.* To cup.

ventral [vã'tral], *a.* (*fem.* **-ale,** *pl.* **-aux**) Ventral.

ventre [vã:tr], *n.m.* Belly, abdomen; stomach; womb; bowels, one's inside; bulge. *À plat ventre,* flat on one's face; *ça vous donne du cœur au ventre,* that bucks you up; *courir ventre à terre,* to run, go, or gallop at full speed; *j'ai mal au ventre,* I have a stomach-ache, I have got a pain in my middle; *n'avoir rien dans le ventre,* to have no guts; *prendre du ventre,* to get fat; *quand on a faim tout fait ventre,* when one is hungry, anything helps to make a meal; *ventre affamé n'a point d'oreilles,* a hungry man will not listen to reason. (*C*) *Ventre de bœuf,* bog hole.

ventrebleu! *int.* Zounds! **ventrée,** *n.f.* Litter (of animals); (*vulg.*) bellyful. **ventriculaire,** *a.* Ventricular. **ventricule,** *n.m.* Ventricle. **ventriculographie,** *n.f.* Ventriculography. **ventrière,** *n.f.* Belly-band, abdominal belt; sling, purlin, brace.

ventriloque [vãtri'lɔk], *n.* Ventriloquist.—*a.* Ventriloquial. **ventriloquie,** *n.f.* Ventriloquy.

ventripotent [vãtripɔ'tã], *a.* (*fem.* **-ente**) Pot-bellied.

ventru [vã'try], *a.* (*fem.* **-ue**) Big-bellied, corpulent; bulging.—*n.* Pot-bellied person, (*fam.*) someone with a corporation.

venu [və'ny], *a.* (*fem.* **-ue**) Come; done; come up, grown. *Bien venu* [BIENVENU]; *enfant bien venu,* well-grown child; *mal venu,* unwelcome, ill-received; open to censure.—*n. Le dernier venu,* the last comer; *le premier venu* or *la première venue,* the first comer, the first that comes, anyone; *nouveau venu* [NOUVEAU].— *n.f.* Coming, arrival, advent; growth. *Allées et venues,* comings and goings; *tout d'une venue,* all of a size or growth.

vénule [VEINULE].

Vénus [ve'nys], *f.* Venus.

***vénusté** [venys'te], *n.f.* Handsomeness, gracefulness, elegance.

vêpres [vɛ:pr], *n.f. pl.* Vespers.

ver [vɛ:r], *n.m.* Worm; maggot, mite; moth. *Avoir le ver solitaire,* (*colloq.*) to eat ravenously; *mangé* or *rongé des vers,* worm-eaten; *nu comme un ver,* stark naked; *tuer le ver,* (*colloq.*) to have a morning nip; *ver blanc,* grub; *ver à soie,* silkworm; *ver de fromage,* cheese-mite; *ver de fumier,* muckworm; *ver de mer,* ship-worm, teredo; *ver de terre,* earth-worm; *ver luisant,* glow-worm; *ver rongeur,* canker; *ver solitaire,* tapeworm; (*fam.*) *tirer les vers du nez à quelqu'un,* to pump someone.

véracité [verasi'te], *n.f.* Veracity.

véraison [verɛ'zɔ̃], *n.f.* Turning, ripening (*esp.* of grapes).

véranda [verã'da], *n.f.* Veranda.

vératre [ve'ratr], *n.m.* Veratrum (hellebore). **vératrine,** *n.f.* (*Chem.*) Veratria, veratrine.

verbal [vɛr'bal], *a.* (*fem.* **-ale,** *pl.* **-aux**) Verbal; (*colloq.*) oral; by word of mouth. *Promesse verbale,* promise by word of mouth. **verbalement,** *adv.* Verbally; (*colloq.*) by word of mouth. **verbalisation,** *n.f.* Taking down of notes (by police etc.). **verbaliser,** *v.i.* To draw up a written statement. **verbalisme,** *n.m.* Verbosity, prolixity.

verbe [vɛrb], *n.m.* Verb; (*Theol.*) the Word. *Avoir le verbe haut,* to be loud of speech.

verbénacée [vɛrbena'se], *n.f.* Verbenaceous plant.

verbeusement [vɛrbøz'mã], *adv.* Verbosely, with many words. **verbeux,** *a.* (*fem.* **-euse**) Verbose, long-winded, wordy. **verbiage,** *n.m.* Mere talk, verbiage. **verbosité,** *n.f.* Verbosity, wordiness.

ver-coquin [vɛrkɔ'kɛ̃], *n.m.* (*pl.* **vers-coquins**) Stagger-worm or maggot; vine-grub; (*fig.*) caprice, whim.

verdage [vɛr'da:ʒ], *n.m.* Green manure.

verdâtre [vɛr'dɑ:tr], *a.* Greenish. **verdelet,** *a.* (*fem.* **-ette**) Greenish; tart (of wine); vigorous, hale (of old people).

verderie [vɛrdə'ri], *n.f.* Verderer's range; verderer's jurisdiction.

verdet [vɛr'dɛ], *n.m.* (*Chem.*) Verdigris; verditer.

verdeur [vɛr'dœ:r], *n.f.* Greenness, sap (of wood); tartness, harshness (of wine); vigour; spryness (of old people); (*fig.*) acrimony.

verdict [vɛr'dikt], *n.m.* Verdict, finding.

verdier [vɛr'dje], *n.m.* Greenfinch; verderer, ranger.

verdir [vɛr'di:r], *v.t.* To make or paint green. —*v.i.* To grow green, to become green; to get covered with verdigris (of copper). **verdoyant,** *a.* (*fem.* **-ante**) Verdant, green. **verdoyer,** *v.i. irr.* (*conjug. like* ABOYER) To become green.

verdunisation [vɛrdyniza'sjɔ̃], *n.f.* Chlorination (of water).

verdure [vɛr'dy:r], *n.f.* Verdure, greenness; greenery; green stuff, pot-herbs; foliage or forest-scenery (on tapestry). **verdurier,** *n.m.* (*fem.* **-ière**) Greengrocer.

véreux [ve'rø], *a.* (*fem.* **-euse**) Worm-eaten, maggoty; rotten; (*fig.*) suspicious, suspect, shady; insecure, doubtful (of bills etc.).

verge [vɛr:ʒ], *n.f.* Rod, wand, staff, switch, verge; shaft, pin; shank (of an anchor etc.); (*Anat.*) penis; obsolete measure for land (one quarter of an *arpent*); (*C*) yard (measure of length). *Donner des verges pour se faire fouetter,* to lay up a rod for one's own back; *faire passer un soldat par les verges,* to make a soldier run the gauntlet; *verge de bedeau,* verger's rod; *verge d'or,* golden-rod (plant). **vergé,** *a.* (*fem.* **-ée** (1)) Laid (of paper); streaky (of textile fabrics).

vergée (2) [vɛr'ʒe], *n.f.* Obsolete measure (about a rood). **verger** (1), *v.t.* To measure with this.

verger (2) [vɛr'ʒe], *n.m.* Orchard.

vergeté [vɛrʒə'te], *a.* (*fem.* **-ée**) Streaky; (*Her.*) paly.

vergeter, *v.t. irr.* (*conjugated like* APPELER) To beat, to whisk, to brush, to dust (clothes). **vergetier,** *n.m.* (*fem.* **-ière**) Brushmaker. **vergette,** *n.f.* Clothes-brush; bundle of rods, switch; hoop (of a drum); (*Her.*) pallet. **vergeture,** *n.f.* Weal.

vergeure [vɛr'ʒy:r], *n.f.* Wire (used in paper-making); wire-mark.

verglacé [vɛrgla'se], *a.* (*fem.* **-ée**) Covered with glazed frost; icy. **verglas,** *n.m.* Thin

coating of ice, frost after a thaw or rain;
glazed frost.

vergne [vɛrɲ] or **verne**, *n.m.* Alder(-tree).

vergogne [vɛrˈgɔɲ], *n.f.* Shame. *Sans
vergogne*, shameless(ly).

vergue [vɛrg], *n.f.* Yard (for sail). *Grande
vergue*, main-yard; *vergues de T.S.F.*, wireless
yards.

véridicité [veridisiˈte], *n.f.* Veracity, truthfulness. **véridique**, *a.* Veracious, truthful.

vérifiable [veriˈfjabl], *a.* Verifiable.

vérificateur [verifikaˈtœːr], *n.m.* Verifier,
examiner, inspector, checker, tester; *(Eng.)*
calipers, gauge. *Vérificateur des comptes*,
auditor. **vérification**, *n.f.* Verification,
examination, auditing, probate.

vérifier [veriˈfje], *v.t.* (*conjugated like* PRIER)
To verify, to inspect, to examine, to audit;
to check; to prove, to confirm; to test, to
overhaul.

vérin [veˈrɛ̃], *n.m.* Jack. *Vérin à vis*, screwjack.

vérine [veˈrin] or **verrine**, *n.f.* (*Naut.*)
Binnacle-lamp; lantern; barometer-glass;
hook-rope.

véritable [veriˈtabl], *a.* True, genuine, real;
staunch, downright, thorough. *Une véritable
friponnerie*, a downright fraud; *un véritable
ami*, a true friend. **véritablement**, *adv.*
Truly, in reality, indeed, in truth. **véritas**,
n.m. Bureau Véritas, the French Lloyd's.

vérité, *n.f.* Truth, verity, truthfulness. *À la
vérité*, indeed, it is true, I admit; *dire à quelqu'un ses* (*quatre*) *vérités*, to tell someone his
faults, to tell someone a few home truths; *dire
la vérité*, to speak the truth; *en vérité*, indeed,
truly; *toute vérité n'est pas bonne à dire*, all
truths are not to be spoken at all times.

verjus [vɛrˈʒy], *n.m.* Verjuice; sour grapes.
C'est jus vert ou verjus, it is six of one and
half a dozen of the other. **verjuté**, *a.* (*fem.
-ée*) Sharp, tart, acid.

vermée [vɛrˈme], *n.f.* Bait of worms (in
fishing).

vermeil [vɛrˈmɛːj], *a.* (*fem. -eille*) Vermilion,
ruddy, rosy. *Teint vermeil*, rosy complexion.
—*n.m.* Vermeil, silver-gilt.

vermicelle [vɛrmiˈsɛl], *n.m.* Vermicelli.

vermicide [vɛrmiˈsid], *a.* and *n.m.* Vermicide.

vermiculaire [vɛrmikyˈlɛːr], *a.* Vermicular
(worm-shaped).—*n.f.* Stone-crop. **vermiculé**, *a.* (*fem. -ée*) (*Arch.*) Vermiculated.
vermiculure, *n.f.* (*Arch.*) Vermiculation
(on masonry). **vermiforme**, *a.* Vermiform
(worm-shaped). **vermifuge**, *a.* and *n.m.*
(*Med.*) Vermifuge. **vermiller**, *v.i.* To root,
to scratch for worms etc. (of boars, fowls,
etc.).

vermillon [vɛrmiˈjɔ̃], *a. inv.* and *n.m.* Vermilion. **vermillonner**, *v.t.* To paint red.

vermine [vɛrˈmin], *n.f.* Vermin; (*fig.*) rabble.
vermineux, *a.* (*fem. -euse*) Caused by
intestinal worms (of diseases). **vermisseau**,
n.m. (*pl. -eaux*) Small worm, grub. **vermivore**, *a.* Vermivorous.

vermouler [vɛrmuˈle], **se**, *v.r.* To get worm-
eaten. **vermoulu**, *a.* (*fem. -ue*) Worm-
eaten. **vermoulure**, *n.f.* Worm-hole,
rottenness caused by worms (in wood); dust
from worm-holes.

vermout(h) [vɛrˈmut], *n.m.* Vermouth.

vernaculaire [vɛrnakyˈlɛːr], *a.* and *n.m.*
Vernacular.

vernal [vɛrˈnal], *a.* (*fem. -ale, pl. -aux*) Vernal,
spring-like. **vernation**, *n.f.* (*Bot.*) Vernation.

verne [VERGNE].

verni [vɛrˈni], *a.* (*fem. -ie*) Varnished; (*slang*)
lucky, never losing, never hurt; drunk,
plastered.

vernier [vɛrˈnje], *n.m.* Vernier, sliding-scale.

vernir [vɛrˈniːr], *v.t.* To varnish; to glaze, to
polish. **vernis**, *n.m.* Varnish, polish, glaze.
Vernis au tampon, French polish; *vernis
japonais*, japan. *Donner un vernis à*, to give
a gloss to, to set off. **vernissage**, *n.m.*
Varnishing; varnishing day. **vernisser**, *v.t.*
To glaze (pottery etc.). **vernisseur**, *n.m.*
(*fem. -euse*) Varnisher; japanner. **vernissure**, *n.f.* Varnish(ing); glazing, glaze.

vérole [veˈrɔl], *n.f.* (*indec.*)=Pox, syphilis.
Petite vérole, smallpox; *petite vérole volante*,
chicken-pox. **vérolé**, *a.* (*fem. -ée*) (*indec.*)
Poxed, syphilitic.

véron [VAIRON (2)].

véronal [veroˈnal], *n.m.* (*Chem.*) Veronal,
barbitone.

Véronique [veroˈnik], *f.* Veronica.

véronique [veroˈnik], *n.f.* Veronica, speedwell.

verraille [vɛˈraːj], *n.f.* Small glass-ware, old
glass.

verranne [vɛˈran], *n.f.* Glass fibre.

verrat [vɛˈra], *n.m.* Boar.

verre [vɛːr], *n.m.* Glass. *Porter verres*, to wear
glasses; *verre (à boire)*, (drinking-)glass; *verre
à eau* or *verre gobelet*, tumbler; *verre à vin*,
wine-glass *or* stemmed glass; *verre de vin*,
glass of wine; *verre armé*, reinforced glass;
verre de lunettes, lens; *verres dalles*, pavement
lights. **verré**, *a.* (*fem. -ée*) Glazed, glass-
lined. **verrerie**, *n.f.* Glass-works; glass-
making, glass-ware. **verrier**, *a.* *Peintre
verrier*, painter on glass, maker of stained-
glass windows.—*n.m.* Glass-maker, glass-
blower; glass basket or rack. **verrière**, *n.f.*
Glass-stand, glass case, glass frame, stained-
glass window. **verrine**, *n.f.* (*Gard.*) Bell-
glass, cloche. **verroterie**, *n.f.* Small glass-
ware, glass trinkets, glass beads.

verrou [vɛˈru], *n.m.* Bolt. *Fermer une porte au
verrou* or *s'enfermer au verrou*, to bolt a door.
verrouiller, *v.t.* To bolt. **se verrouiller**,
v.r. To bolt oneself in.

verrucaire [veryˈkɛːr], *n.f.* Wartwort (plant).
verrucosité, *n.f.* Warty swelling. **verrue**,
n.f. Wart. *Verrue plantaire*, verruca.
verruqueux, *a.* (*fem. -euse*) Warty,
verrucose.

vers (1) [vɛːr], *n.m. inv.* Verse, line (of poetry).
Faire des vers, to write verses; *vers blancs*,
blank verse; *vers libres*, free verse.

vers (2) [vɛːr], *prep.* Towards, to; about.
Tournez-vous vers moi, turn towards me; *vers
(les) quatre heures*, about four o'clock.

versable [vɛrˈsabl], *a.* Apt to overturn, liable
to upset. **versage**, *n.m.* Emptying, tipping;
(*Agric.*) first ploughing (of fallow land). **versant** (1), *a.* (*fem. -ante*) Liable to be overturned. **versant** (2), *n.m.* Declivity, side,
slope; watershed. **versatile**, *a.* Inconstant,
changeable. **versatilité**, *n.f.* Inconstancy.

verse, *a.* (*Geom.*) Versed. *Sinus verse*, versed

sine.—*n.f.* (*Agric.*) Laying (of crops by storm).—*adv.* *À verse*, abundantly; *il pleut à verse*, it is pouring (with rain). **versé,** *a.* (*fem.* **-ée**) Spilt; well versed, conversant; laid (of crops).

Verseau, *m.* (*Astron.*) Aquarius.

versement, *n.m.* Payment; deposit.

verser [vɛr'se], *v.t.* To pour, to pour out; to pour forth, to discharge, to empty; to shed, to spill; to pay in, to deposit; to overturn, to upset, to beat down, to lay (corn).—*v.i.* To overturn, to upset (of vehicles); to be laid, to be beaten down (of standing corn); (*fig.*) to have a bad fall.

verset [vɛr'sɛ], *n.m.* (*Bibl.* etc.) Verse.

verseuse, *n.f.* Coffee pot (with a long handle); waitress who pours out the coffee (in restaurant).

versicolore [vɛrsikɔ'lɔːr], *a.* Variegated, chameleon-like.

versicule [vɛrsi'kyl] or **versiculet,** *n.m.* Little verse, versicle.

versificateur [vɛrsifika'tœːr], *n.m.* (*fem.* **-trice**) Versifier. **versification,** *n.f.* Versification.

versifier, *v.i.*, *v.t.* (*conjugated like* PRIER) To versify.

version [vɛr'sjɔ̃], *n.f.* Version, translation. (*Cine.*) *Version doublée*, dubbed version.

verso [vɛr'so], *n.m.* Verso, back, left-hand page.

versoir [vɛr'swaːr], *n.m.* Mould-board (of a plough).

verste [vɛrst], *n.f.* Verst (Russian measure of length, 1067 metres or two-thirds of a mile).

Vert [vɛːr], **le Cap,** *m.* Cape Verde.

vert [vɛːr], *a.* (*fem.* **-e**) Green; verdant, grassy, sharp, harsh (of things); sharp (of wine); fresh, raw; unripe, sour; (*fig.*) vigorous, robust, hale, hearty; trenchant, sharp (of answers etc.); spicy (of stories). *Il en a raconté de vertes*, he told some very risky stories; *ils sont trop verts*, the grapes are sour; *langue verte*, slang; *l'heure verte*, (*pop.*) the time for absinthe; *pierres vertes*, stones just cut out of the quarry; *une verte réponse*, a sharp answer; *une verte vieillesse*, a vigorous old age.—*n.m.* Green, green colour; green cloth or clothes; green food; sharpness (of wine etc.); (*Golf*) (putting-)green. *Employer le vert et le sec*, to leave no stone unturned; *mettre des chevaux au vert*, to turn horses out to grass; *vous ne le prendrez pas sans vert*, you will not catch him napping.

vert-de-gris, *n.m.* and *a.* *inv.* Verdigris. **vert-de-grisé,** *a.* (*fem.* **-ée**) Covered with verdigris.

vertébral [vɛrte'bral], *a.* (*fem.* **-ale,** *pl.* **-aux**) Vertebral. **vertèbre,** *n.f.* Vertebra. **vertébré,** *a.* (*fem.* **-ée**).—*n.m.* (*Zool.*) Vertebrate. *Les vertébrés*, the vertebrates.

vertébro-iliaque, *a.* Vertebro-iliac.

vertement [vɛrtə'mã], *adv.* Vigorously, briskly, sharply; harshly, severely. *Je l'ai tancé vertement*, I gave him a good talking to.

vertical [vɛrti'kal], *a.* (*fem.* **-ale,** *pl.* **-aux**) Vertical. **verticalement,** *adv.* Vertically. **verticalité,** *n.f.* Verticality, uprightness.

verticille [vɛrti'sil], *n.m.* (*Bot.*) Verticil (whorl). **verticillé,** *a.* (*fem.* **-ée**) Verticillate.

vertige [vɛr'tiːʒ], *n.m.* Dizziness, giddiness, vertigo, swimming in the head; (*fig.*) madness, intoxication. *Avoir des vertiges*, to have

fits of giddiness. **vertigineux,** *a.* (*fem.* **-euse**) Dizzy, giddy. **vertigo,** *n.m.* Staggers; (*fig.*) whim, crotchet.

vertu [vɛr'ty], *n.f.* Virtue, chastity; property, faculty, quality; efficacy, force. *En vertu de*, by virtue of, in pursuance of; *faire de nécessité vertu*, to make a virtue of necessity; *vertu de ma vie!* why, bless my heart! ***vertubleu!*** or **vertuchou!** *int.* Bless my heart! For goodness' sake! **vertueusement,** *adv.* Virtuously. **vertueux,** *a.* (*fem.* **-euse**) Virtuous.

verve [vɛrv], *n.f.* Warmth, animation, verve, spirit, zest.

verveine [vɛr'vɛn], *n.f.* Vervain, verbena.

vervelle [vɛr'vɛl], *n.f.* (*Hawking*) Varvel.

verveux (1) or **vervier,** *n.m.* Pannier; hoop-net (for fishing).

verveux (2) [vɛr'vø], *a.* (*fem.* **-euse**) Animated, full of verve, spirited, full of go.

vésanie [veza'ni], *n.f.* (*Path.*) Vesania, insanity.

vesce [vɛs], *n.f.* Vetch.

vésical [vezi'kal], *a.* (*fem.* **-ale,** *pl.* **-aux**) Vesical. **vésicant,** *a.* (*fem.* **-ante**) Vesicant, causing blisters. **vésication,** *n.f.* Vesication. **vésicatoire,** *a.* and *n.m.* Vesicatory. **vésiculaire,** *a.* Vesicular. **vésicule,** *n.f.* Vesicle, bladder. *Vésicule biliaire*, gallbladder. **vésiculeux,** *a.* (*fem.* **-euse**) Blistered, vesiculose.

vesou [və'zu], *n.m.* Sugar-cane juice.

Vespasien [vɛspa'zjɛ̃], *m.* Vespasian.

vespasienne [vɛspa'zjɛn], *n.f.* Public urinal; public convenience.

Vesper [vɛs'pɛːr], *n.m.* Vesper, Venus. **vespéral,** *a.* (*fem.* **-ale,** *pl.* **-aux**) Vespertine; vesperal.—*n.m.* Vesperal.

vespertilion or **vespertilio,** *n.m.* (*Zool.*) Vespertilio (bat).

vespétro [vɛspe'tro], *n.m.* Liqueur flavoured with angelica, fennel, aniseed, coriander, etc.

vespiforme [vɛspi'fɔrm], *a.* Vespiform (wasplike).

vesse [vɛs], *n.f.* (*indec.*) Silent evacuation of wind.—*int.* (*slang*) Cave! (there is danger).

vesse-de-loup, *n.f.* (*pl.* **vesses-de-loup**) (*pop.*) Puff-ball.

vessie [vɛ'si], *n.f.* Bladder. *Prendre des vessies pour des lanternes*, to believe that the moon is made of green cheese; *vessie natatoire*, swimming-bladder. **vessigon,** *n.m.* (*Vet.*) Vessignon, wind-gall.

vestale [vɛs'tal], *n.f.* Vestal (virgin).

veste [vɛst], *n.f.* (Short) jacket as worn by waiters, fencers, etc. *Remporter* (or *ramasser*) *une veste*, to fail utterly; to be beaten, ploughed or rebuffed; *tomber la veste*, to take off one's jacket or coat in order to work or to fight. **vestiaire,** *a.* Vestiary, relating to clothes.—*n.m.* Cloakroom; changing-room; robing-room (for judges); hat-and-coat rack.

vestibulaire [vɛstiby'lɛːr], *a.* (*Anat.*) Vestibular.

vestibule, *n.m.* Vestibule, lobby, hall; (*Anat.*) vestibule (of ear).

vestige [vɛs'tiːʒ], *n.m.* Footprint, vestige, sign, mark; trace, remains.

veston [vɛs'tɔ̃], *n.m.* Jacket, lounge-coat. *Complet veston*, lounge-suit; *veston* or *veste d'intérieur*, indoor jacket.

Vésuve [ve'zyːv], **le,** *m.* Vesuvius.

vêtement [vɛt'mã], *n.m.* Garment; (*pl.*) dress, clothes; (*poet.*) vestment, raiment, vesture; (*fig.*) cloak, disguise. *Vêtements de dessous,* underwear; *vêtements sacerdotaux,* canonicals.

vétéran [vete'rã], *n.m.* Veteran; (*sch.*) boy who stays in a form a second year. **vétérance,** *n.f.* Quality of veteran.

vétérinaire [veteri'nɛːr], *a.* Veterinary.—*n.m.* Veterinary surgeon, vet.

vétillard [VÉTILLEUR].

vétille [ve'tiːj], *n.f.* Trifle, bagatelle. **vétiller,** *v.i.* To trifle; to stand upon trifles.—*v.t.* To quibble or carp at. **vétillerie,** *n.f.* Hairsplitting, quibbling. **vétilleur,** *n.m.* (*fem.* **vétilleuse** (1)) Trifler; hair-splitter, quibbler. **vétilleux,** *a.* (*fem.* **vétilleuse** (2)) Particular, finicky, captious, hair-splitting (of a person); tricky, requiring minute care.

vêtir [ve'tiːr], *v.t. irr.* (*pres.p.* **vêtant,** *p.p.* **vêtu**) To clothe; to array, to dress; to invest oneself with, to put on. **se vêtir,** *v.r.* To dress oneself.

vétiver or **vétyver** [veti'vɛːr], *n.m.* Cuscus.

veto [ve'to], *n.m.* Veto.

vêtu [ve'ty], *a.* (*fem.* **-ue**) Dressed, clothed, arrayed. *Mal vêtu,* ill-dressed; *vêtu de blanc,* dressed in white. **vêture,** *n.f.* Taking the habit or the veil; provision of clothing for the needy.

vétuste [ve'tyst], *a.* Old, antiquated; dilapidated, worn out. **vétusté,** *n.f.* Antiquity, old age, decay.

vétyver [VÉTIVER].

veuf [vœf], *a.* (*fem.* **veuve**) Widowed; (*fig.*) bereft, deprived. *Cette église est veuve de son évêque,* this church is deprived of its bishop. —*n.m.* Widower.—*n.f.* Widow; (*Bot.*) sweet scabious; (*pop.*) the guillotine. *Épouser la veuve,* (*pop.*) to be guillotined.

veuillez, *2nd subj. and imper.* [VOULOIR].

veule [vœːl], *a.* Soft, weak, feeble. **veulerie,** *n.f.* Flabbiness, slackness, listlessness.

veuvage [vœ'vaːʒ], *n.m.* Widowhood, widowerhood.

vexant [vɛk'sã], *a.* (*fem.* **-ante**) Vexing, provoking. **vexateur,** *a.* (*fem.* **-trice**) Vexatious. **vexation,** *n.f.* Vexation, molestation, annoyance. **vexatoire,** *a.* Vexatious, annoying. **vexer,** *v.t.* To vex, to plague, to annoy.

vexillaire [vɛksi'lɛːr], *a.* Vexillar; (*Bot.*) having the shape of a flag.—*n.m.* (*Rom. Ant.*) Standard-bearer.

via [via], *prep.* Via, by way of.

viabilité [vjabili'te], *n.f.* Viability, likelihood of living (of infants); condition (of the roads). **viable,** *a.* Likely to live, viable; fit for traffic.

viaduc [vja'dyk], *n.m.* Viaduct.

viager [vja'ʒe], *a.* (*fem.* **-ère**) For life, during life. *Rente viagère,* life-annuity.—*n.m.* *Placer en viager,* to invest in a life-annuity. **viagèrement,** *adv.* For life.

viande [vjãːd], *n.f.* Meat. *Basse viande,* coarse meat; *menue viande,* fowl and game; *viande blanche,* white meat (poultry, veal, etc.); *viande creuse,* meagre diet, (*fig.*) poor mental nourishment; *viande de boucherie* or *grosse viande,* butcher's meat; *viande de cheval,* horse-flesh; *viande noire,* brown meat (game); *viandes froides,* cold buffet; *viandes*

rouges, red meat (beef, mutton). **viander,** *v.i.* To graze (of deer). **viandis,** *n.m.* Pasture, grazing (of deer etc.).

viatique [vja'tik], *n.m.* Viaticum, provisions for a journey, travelling money; last sacrament.

vibord [vi'bɔːr], *n.m.* (*Naut.*) Waist (of a ship).

vibrant [vi'brã], *a.* (*fem.* **-ante**) Vibrating; vibrant, ringing, resonant. **vibrateur,** *n.m.* (*Teleg.*) Vibrator, buzzer. **vibration,** *n.f.* Vibration. **vibratoire,** *a.* Vibratory, (*Elec.*) oscillatory. **vibrer,** *v.i.* To vibrate. **vibreur,** *n.m.* (*Teleg.*) Vibrator, (*Elec.*) buzzer; trembler. **vibrion,** *n.m.* Vibrio (bacterium). **vibrisses,** *n.f. pl.* Vibrissae (hairs, bristles). **vibrographe,** *n.m.* Vibrograph.

vicaire [vi'kɛːr], *n.m.* Curate (of a parish). *Grand vicaire* or *vicaire général,* vicargeneral; *le vicaire de Jésus-Christ,* the Pope.

vicarial, *a.* (*fem.* **-iale,** *pl.* **-iaux**) Vicarial. **vicariat,** *n.m.,* or **vicairie,** *n.f.* Curacy, curateship, chapel of ease.

vice [vis], *n.m.* Fault, defect, flaw, blemish; vice, viciousness. *Vice de forme,* flaw, faulty drafting (of deed).

vice-amiral [visami'ral], *n.m.* (*pl.* **vice-amiraux**) Vice-admiral; second ship of a fleet. **vice-amirauté,** *n.f.* (*pl.* **vice-amirautés**) Vice-admiralty.

vice-chancelier, *n.m.* (*pl.* **vice-chanceliers**) Vice-chancellor.

vice-consul, *n.m.* (*pl.* **vice-consuls**) Vice-consul. **vice-consulat,** *n.m.* (*pl.* **vice-consulats**) Vice-consulate.

vice-gérant, *n.m.* (*pl.* **vice-gérants**) Deputy-manager.

vice-gérent, *n.m.* (*pl.* **vice-gérents**) Vice-gerent.

vice-légat, *n.m.* (*pl.* **vice-légats**) Vice-legate. **vice-légation,** *n.f.* (*pl.* **vice-légations**). Vice-legation.

vicennal [visɛ'nal], *a.* (*fem.* **-ale,** *pl.* **-aux**) Vicennial (of twenty years).

vice-présidence, *n.f.* (*pl.* **vice-présidences**) Vice-presidency. **vice-président,** *n.m.* (*pl.* **vice-présidents**) Vice-president.

vice-reine, *n.f.* (*pl.* **vice-reines**) Wife of viceroy.

vice-roi, *n.m.* (*pl.* **vice-rois**) Viceroy. **vice-royauté,** *n.f.* (*pl.* **vice-royautés**) Vice-royalty.

vicésimal [visezi'mal], *a.* (*fem.* **-ale,** *pl.* **-aux**) Vicenary.

viciation [visja'sjɔ̃], *n.f.* Vitiation; invalidation; corruption.

vicié [vi'sje], *a.* (*fem.* **-iée**) Vitiated, depraved, corrupted; tainted, stale, foul (of air etc.).

vicier [vi'sje], *v.t.* To vitiate, to taint, to corrupt, to render foul. **se vicier,** *v.r.* To become vitiated or corrupt; to become tainted or foul. **vicieusement,** *adv.* Viciously; (*Gram.*) incorrectly; faultily. **vicieux,** *a.* (*fem.* **-ieuse**) Vicious; faulty, defective; tricky, restive (horse). *Les cercles vicieux de la pauvreté,* the vicious circles of poverty; *un cercle vicieux,* a syllogistic or vicious circle.—*n.m.* Profligate, person addicted to vice.

vicinal [visi'nal], *a.* (*fem.* **-ale,** *pl.* **-aux**) Local, connecting (of roads). *Chemin vicinal,* by-road, minor road. **vicinalité,** *n.f.* Local status (of roads). *Chemin de grande* *vicinalité*, road connecting parts of a commune, etc., or connecting these with the main roads.

vicissitude [visisi′tyd], *n.f.* Vicissitude, change, succession (of seasons etc.); (*pl.*) ups and downs.

vicomte [vi′kɔ̃:t], *n.m.* Viscount. **vicomté,** *n.f.* Viscountship, viscounty. **vicomtesse,** *n.f.* Viscountess.

victime [vik′tim], *n.f.* Victim; sufferer. *Être victime de*, to be a victim of; *il était victime d'une bronchite*, he was down with bronchitis.

Victoire [vik′twa:r] or **Victoria,** *f.* Victoria. **victoire** [vik′twa:r], *n.f.* Victory. *Remporter la victoire*, to gain the victory.

victoria [viktɔ′rja], *n.f.* Victoria (four-wheeled carriage).

victorien [viktɔ′rjɛ̃], *a.* (*fem.* **-ienne**) Victorian (period).

victorieusement [viktɔrjøz′mɑ̃], *adv.* Victoriously. **victorieux,** *a.* (*fem.* **-ieuse**) Victorious.

victuaille [vik′tɥɑːj], *n.f.* (*colloq.*) Provisions, victuals, eatables.

vidage [vi′da:ʒ], *n.m.* Emptying.

vidame [vi′dam], *n.m.* Vidame (minor noble). **vidamé,** *n.m.*, or **vidamie,** *n.f.* Dignity of a vidame. **vidamesse,** *n.f.* Wife of a vidame.

vidange [vi′dɑ̃:ʒ], *n.f.* Emptying; draining of; blowing off (boiler); night-soil; (*Med.*) *lochia. Tonneau en vidange*, broached cask. **vidanger,** *v.t.* To empty, to clean out, to drain, to blow off. **vidangeur,** *n.m.* Nightman, scavenger.

vide [vid], *a.* Empty; void, vacant, blank; devoid, destitute. *Vide de sens*, meaningless. —*n.m.* Empty space, blank, void; vacuum; gap, chasm, hole; emptiness, vanity.—*adv. phr. À vide*, empty; *mâcher à vide*, (*fig.*) to feed on false hopes.

vidé [vi′de], *a.* (*fem.* **-ée**) Emptied, exhausted. *Jarrets (bien) vidés*, clean hocks (of a horse).

vide-bouteille or **vide-bouteilles,** *n.m.* (*pl.* **vide-bouteilles**) Siphon. **vide-citron,** *n.m.* (*pl.* **vide-citrons**) Lemon-squeezer. *vide-gousset,** *n.m.* (*pl.* **vide-goussets**) (*colloq.*) Pick-pocket, thief. **vide-ordures,** *n.m. inv.* Rubbish-shoot. **vide-poche** or **vide-poches,** *n.m. inv.* Pin-tray, tidy. **vide-pomme,** *n.m.* (*pl.* **vide-pommes**) Apple-corer.

vider [vi′de], *v.t.* To empty; to draw off, to drain; to bore, to hollow out; to draw (poultry); to gut (fish); to vacate; to decide, to end; to settle. *Vider les lieux, une province, etc.*, to leave or vacate a place; *vider ses comptes*, to make up one's accounts; *vider une clef*, to bore a key; *vider un étang*, to drain a pond; *vider un procès*, to settle a lawsuit.

vide-tasses [vid′ta:s], *n.m. inv.* Slop-basin.

viduité [vidɥi′te], *n.f.* Widowhood.

vidure [vi′dy:r], *n.f.* Things drawn out; (*Dress.*) open-work, pinking.

vie [vi], *n.f.* Life; lifetime; existence, days; vitality; livelihood, living; food, subsistence; way of living, course of life, profession; spirit, animation; row, noise; biography, memoir. *À la vie, à la mort*, in life and in death; *avoir la vie dure*, to have a hard time, to be tenacious of life; to die hard; *être en vie*, to be alive; *faire la vie*, to live fast, to kick

up a row; *gagner sa vie*, to earn one's living; *il a écrit lui-même sa vie*, he has written his own life; *il y va de la vie*, it is a matter of life and death; *je n'ai rien vu de pareil de ma vie*, I never saw anything like it in all my life; *le prix de la vie*, the cost of living; *mener la bonne vie*, to lead a merry life; *mener une vie réglée*, to lead a regular life; *niveau de vie*, standard of living; *rendre la vie à quelqu'un*, to restore life to someone; *rendre la vie dure à quelqu'un*, to make life a burden to someone; *sa vie durant*, during his life; *telle vie, telle fin*, people die as they live; *train de vie*, way of living; *une pension à vie*, a life pension.

vieil [VIEUX].

vieillard [vjɛ′ja:r], *n.m.* Old man.

vieille [VIEUX].

vieille-de-mer [vjɛjdə′mɛr], *n.f.* [LABRE].

vieillement, *adv.* In an old way.

vieillerie, *n.f.* (*usu. pl.*) Old things, old clothes, old lumber, rubbish; obsolete ideas.

vieillesse, *n.f.* Old age; oldness. *Elle est morte de vieillesse*, she died of old age.

vieillir [vjɛ′ji:r], *v.i.* To grow old, to age; to look old; to become obsolete or old-fashioned. *Elle portait des modes vieillies*, her style of dress was old-fashioned; *il avait beaucoup vieilli depuis la guerre*, he had aged greatly since the war; *vieillir dans le service de son pays*, to grow old in the service of one's country.—*v.t.* To make old; to make look old. **se vieillir,** *v.r.* To make oneself look old; to give oneself out as older than one actually is. **vieillissant,** *a.* (*fem.* **-ante**) Growing old. **vieillissement,** *n.m.* Ageing; obsolescence. **vieillot,** *a.* (*fem.* **-otte**) Oldish; old-fashioned.

vielle [vjɛl], *n.f.* *Hurdy-gurdy. Il est du bois dont on fait les vielles*, he is of a pliant temperament. **vieller,** *v.i.* To play upon the hurdy-gurdy. **vieilleur** [vjɛ′lœ:r], *n.m.* (*fem.* **-euse**) Hurdy-gurdy player.

Vienne [vjɛn], *f.* Vienna. **viennois,** *a.* and *n.m.* (**Viennois,** *fem.* **-oise**) Viennese.

vierge [vjɛrʒ], *n.f.* Virgin, maid. *La (Sainte) Vierge*, the Blessed Virgin. (*Astron.*) *La Vierge*, Virgo.—*a.* Virgin, virginal, maiden; pure, untrodden, unwrought; free (from). *Épée vierge*, unfleshed sword; *forêt vierge*, virgin forest; *page vierge*, blank page.

Viet-Nam [vjɛt′nam], *m.* (*Geog.*) Viet-Nam.

vietnamien [vjɛtna′mjɛ̃], *a.* (*fem.* **-ienne**) and *n.m.* (**Vietnamien,** *fem.* **-ienne**) Vietnamese.

vieux [vjø], *a.* (before a vowel or *h* mute, **vieil,** *fem.* **vieille** [vjɛj]). Old, aged, advanced in years; ancient, venerable; olden, old-fashioned; out of date, obsolete; veteran. *Vieux comme Hérode*, as old as Adam; *il est vieux jeu*, he is old-fashioned; *le bon vieux temps*, the good old days; (C) *les vieux pays*, Europe and Asia; *ne pas faire de vieux os*, not to make old bones, not to be long-lived.—*n. inv.* Old person. *La retraite des vieux*, old-age pension; (*fam.*) (*pl.*) *les vieux*, my parents, my old people; *mon vieux*, (a term of endearment) old friend, old chap; *un vieux de la vieille*, a veteran of the Old Guard, one of the old stalwarts.—*n.m.* Anything that is old (especially clothes, shoes, etc.). *Le vieux vaut mieux que le nouveau*, old things are better than newfangled ones.

vif [vif], *a.* (*fem.* **vive** (1)) Alive, live, living; quick; lively, brisk, sprightly, animated, fiery, mettlesome, ardent, eager, hasty, passionate; keen; sharp, violent (of pain etc.); sharp, bracing (of air etc.); vivid, bright (of colours). *Chaux vive*, quicklime; *couleur vive*, bright colour; *de vive force*, by sheer force; *de vive voix*, by word of mouth; *des yeux vifs*, sparkling eyes; *eau vive*, spring-water; *être brûlé vif*, to be burned alive; *haie vive*, quickset hedge; *il est vif comme la poudre*, he is as hot as ginger, fiery-tempered; *mort ou vif*, dead or alive; *cheval vif*, high-spirited horse; *œuvres vives* [ŒUVRES]; *un froid vif*, a piercing cold; *vive arête*, a sharp edge; *vives eaux*, spring tide.—*n.m.* The quick (live flesh); living person. (*Law*) *Donation entre vifs*, donation inter vivos; *entrer dans le vif du sujet*, to come to the heart of the matter; *être pris sur le vif*, to be very lifelike (of pictures, descriptions, etc.); *être touché au vif*, to be touched to the quick; *piquer au vif*, to sting to the quick; *trancher* or *couper dans le vif*, to cut to the quick, (*fig.*) to set to work in earnest.

vif-argent [vifar'ʒɑ̃], *n.m.* Quicksilver.
vigie [vi'ʒi], *n.f.* Look-out man; look-out (station or ship); (*Rail.*) seat on the top of guard's van. *Être en vigie*, to be on the look-out.
vigilamment [viʒila'mɑ̃], *adv.* Vigilantly. **vigilance**, *n.f.* Vigilance. **vigilant**, *a.* (*fem.* **-ante**) Vigilant, watchful.
vigile [vi'ʒil], *n.f.* Vigil, eve.
vigne [viɲ], *n.f.* Vine; vineyard. *Être dans les vignes du Seigneur*, to be in one's cups; *vigne blanche*, white briony, traveller's joy; *vigne de Judée* or *de Judas*, woody nightshade, bitter-sweet; *vigne de Salomon*, clematis; *vigne noire*, black briony; *vigne sauvage*, wild vine; *vigne vierge*, wild-grape, wild-briony, virginia-creeper. **vigneron**, *n.m.* (*fem.* **-onne**) Vine-dresser, wine-grower.
vignette [vi'ɲɛt], *n.f.* Vignette; (*pop.*) meadow-sweet. **vignettiste**, *n.m.* Vignette-engraver.
vignoble [vi'ɲɔbl], *n.m.* Vineyard.—*a.* Wine-growing (district).
vigogne [vi'ɡɔɲ], *n.f.* Vicuna; vicuna-wool, swan's down.—*n.m.* Vicuna-felt hat.
vigoureusement [viɡurøz'mɑ̃], *adv.* Vigorously, energetically. **vigoureux**, *a.* (*fem.* **-euse**) Vigorous, forcible, energetic; stout, stalwart.
vigueur [vi'ɡœːr], *n.f.* Vigour, strength; force, power, energy. *Entrer en vigueur*, to come into force (of laws etc.); *mise en vigueur d'une loi*, enforcement of a law; *vigueur d'esprit*, strength of mind.
vil [vil], *a.* (*fem.* **vile**) Vile, base, mean; abject, low; paltry, worthless. *À vil prix*, dirt cheap.
vilain [vi'lɛ̃], *n.m.* (*fem.* **-aine**) *Villein (bondman); nasty fellow; (*childish*) naughty boy. *Oignez vilain il vous poindra, poignez vilain il vous oindra*, a bad man will return evil for good. (*fam.*) *Il va y avoir du vilain*, there'll be trouble.—*a.* Ugly; unsightly; pitiful; nasty; sordid, wretched; naughty (of a child). *Il m'a joué un vilain tour*, he has played me a mean, dirty trick; *vilain temps*, vile weather; (*fam.*) *un vilain monsieur*, or *un vilain coco*, a bad lot. **vilainement**, *adv.*

Uglily; basely, shamefully, scandalously, unworthily, villainously, improperly, deplorably.
vilebrequin [vilbrə'kɛ̃], *n.m.* Brace, wimble. *Vilebrequin à cliquets*, ratchet-brace; *vilebrequin à conscience*, breast-drill. *Arbre à vilebrequin*, crankshaft.
vilement [vil'mɑ̃], *adv.* Vilely, basely, meanly.
vilenie, *n.f.* Nastiness, foulness; vile action; stinginess, meanness; (*pl.*) offensive words. **vileté**, *n.f.* Cheapness, low price; vileness; mean action.
vilipender [vilipɑ̃'de], *v.t.* To vilipend, to vilify; to disparage.
villa [vi'la], *n.f.* Villa, country-house, suburban dwelling.
village [vi'laːʒ], *n.m.* Village. *Des gens de village*, country-folk; *il est bien de son village*, he knows nothing of the world. **villageois**, *n.m.* (*fem.* **-oise**) Villager, bumpkin.—*a.* Rustic.
villanelle [vila'nɛl], *n.f.* Villanelle (pastoral poem).
ville [vil], *n.f.* Town, city; the inhabitants of a town or city; town life. *Être en ville*, to be out (not at home); *hôtel* or *maison de ville*, town hall; *il est allé dîner en ville*, he is dining out. *Ville d'eaux*, spa.
villégiature [vileʒa'tyːr], *n.f.* Sojourn in the country. *En villégiature*, staying in the country; on holiday. **villégiaturer**, *v.i.* (*colloq.*) To stay in the country.
villeux [vi'lø], *a.* (*fem.* **-euse**) Hairy, villous. **villifère**, *a.* Hairy. **villosité**, *n.f.* Villosity.
***vimaire** or **vimère** [vi'mɛːr], *n.f.* Damage, ravage (by storm etc.); outrage, insult.
vin [vɛ̃], *n.m.* Wine. *À bon vin point d'enseigne*, good wine needs no bush; *être entre deux vins*, to be half-seas over; *être pris de vin*, to be the worse for drink; *il a le vin mauvais*, he is quarrelsome in his cups; *le vin est tiré, il faut le boire*, there is no going back now, we must face the music; *mettre de l'eau dans son vin*, to moderate one's pretensions, to go slow; *un doigt de vin*, a drop of wine; *vin chaud*, mulled wine; *vin de Bordeaux rouge*, claret; *vin de marque*, vintage wine; *vin d'honneur*, reception held in honour of somebody who leaves, farewell-party; *vin doux*, sweet wine (not yet finished fermenting); *vin mousseux*, sparkling wine; *vin non mousseux*, still wine; *vin ordinaire*, dinner wine.
vinage [vi'naːʒ], *n.m.* Putting alcohol into wine.
vinaigre [vi'nɛːɡr], *n.m.* Vinegar; quick turning of the rope (in skipping). **vinaigré**, *a.* (*fem.* **-ée**) Seasoned with vinegar. **vinaigrer**, *v.t.* To season with vinegar; (*fig.*) to make piquant. **vinaigrerie**, *n.f.* Vinegar factory. **vinaigrette**, *n.f.* Vinegar sauce; French dressing; meat seasoned with vinegar; *two-wheeled sedan. **vinaigrier**, *n.m.* Vinegar-maker or merchant; vinegar cruet; (*Bot.*) sumac.
vinaire [vi'nɛːr], *a.* For wine. *Vaisseaux vinaires*, wine-vessels, wine-casks. **vinasse**, *n.f.* Very weak bad wine.
vindas [vɛ̃'daːs] or **vindau**, *n.m.* (*pl.* **-aux**) Windlass.
vindicatif [vɛ̃dika'tif], *a.* (*fem.* **-ive**) Vindictive, revengeful. **vindicte**, *n.f.* Prosecution

(of crime); vengeance. *La vindicte publique*, public obloquy or outcry.

vinée [vi′ne], *n.f.* Crop of wine, vintage.

viner [vi′ne], *v.t.* To put alcohol into (wine).

vinette [vi′nɛt], *n.m.* or *f.* Barberry.

vineux [vi′nø], *a.* (*fem.* **-euse**) Vinous; winy, wine-coloured.

vingt [vɛ̃], *a.* and *n.m.* Twenty, score; twentieth. *Le vingt mai*, the twentieth of May; *quatre-vingts hommes*, eighty men; *quatre-vingt-six bœufs*, eighty-six oxen [vingt takes an *s* when preceded by another number, but remains invariable when followed by another number]; *son père lui a reproché vingt fois son erreur*, his father reproached him for his mistake time and time again. **vingtaine**, *n.f.* A score, about twenty. **vingt-et-un**, *n.m.* Vingt-et-un (card game). **vingt-deux** [vɛ̃d′dø], *int.* (*Rugby Ftb.*) abbr. of *aux vingt-deux mètres!* come back to the 25 yards line for a kick-out [*see* RENVOI]; (*slang*) two cops [*see* FLIC] are coming! (*fig.*) there is danger ahead; look out! Shut up! **vingtième**, *a.* and *n.m.* Twentieth. **vingtuple**, *a.* and *n.m.* Twentyfold. **vingtupler**, *v.t.*, *v.i.* To increase twentyfold.

vinicole [vini′kɔl], *a.* Wine-growing, wine-producing. **viniculture** [VITICULTURE]. **vinifère**, *a.* Viniferous. **vinification**, *n.f.* Vinification. **vinique**, *a.* Vinic.

vinomètre, *n.m.* Vinometer. **vinosité**, *n.f.* Vinosity.

viol [vjɔl], *n.m.* Rape, violation (of a woman).

violacé [vjɔla′se], *a.* (*fem.* **-ée** (1)) Violaceous, purplish-blue. **violacée** (2) or **violariée**, *n.f.* (*Bot.*) Violaceous plant.

violat, *a.m.* *Miel violat*, syrup of violets.

violateur [vjɔla′tœ:r], *n.m.* (*fem.* **-trice**) Violator, infringer, breaker.—*a.* Violating, transgressing, infringing. **violation**, *n.f.* Violation, breach, infringement.

violâtre [vjɔ′lɑ:tr], *a.* Purplish.

viole [vjɔl], *n.f.* Viol.

violement [VIOLATION].

violemment [vjɔla′mɑ̃], *adv.* With violence, violently. **violence**, *n.f.* Violence; (*Law*) force, duress; (*fig.*) stress, height, fury. *Faire violence à*, to do violence to. **violent, a.** (*fem.* **-ente**) Violent; strong (of suspicion etc.); (*colloq.*) considerable, excessive, extraordinary. *C'est par trop violent*, it really is too bad. **violenter**, *v.t.* To offer *or* do violence to, to force; to constrain; to violate, to outrage.

violer [vjɔ′le], *v.t.* To violate; to ravish, to rape; to outrage, to transgress. *Violer le droit des gens*, to break the law of nations; *violer sa promesse*, to break one's promise.

violet [vjɔ′lɛ], *n.m.* Violet-colour.—*a.* (*fem.* **-ette** (1)) Violet-coloured. **violette** (2), *n.f.* (*Bot.*) Violet.

violeur [vjɔ′lœ:r], *n.m.* (*fem.* **-euse**) Violator, ravisher.

violier [vjɔ′lje], *n.m.* Wallflower, gillyflower.

*violiste [vjɔ′list], *n.m.* Violist.

violon [vjɔ′lɔ̃], *n.m.* Violin, fiddle; violinist, violin-player, fiddler; (*pop.*) lock-up, cells (prison). *Il a payé les violons*, he paid the piper; *jouer du violon*, to play (on) the violin; *mettre quelqu'un au violon*, to put someone in the cells. **violoncelle**, *n.m.* Violoncello,

'cello. **violoncelliste**, *n.m.* Violoncellist, 'cellist. **violoniste**, *n.* Violinist.

viorne [vjɔrn], *n.f.* Viburnum, wayfaring-tree.

vipère [vi′pɛ:r], *n.f.* Viper, adder. **vipereau**, *n.m.* (*pl.* **-eaux**) Young viper. **vipérin, a.** (*fem.* **-ine**) Viperine.—*n.f.* (*Bot.*) Viper's-bugloss.

virage [vi′ra:ʒ], *n.m.* Turning, cornering; turn, bend, corner; (*Naut.*) tacking; (*Phot.*) toning. *Virage incliné*, bank; *virage en épingle à cheveux*, hair-pin bend.

virago [vira′go], *n.f.* Virago, termagant.

vire [vi:r], *n.f.* Traverse; winding mountain-path.

virée [vi′re], *n.f.* Turning; winding.

*virelai [vir′lɛ], *n.m.* Virelay (French poem).

virement [vir′mɑ̃], *n.m.* Turning; (*Naut.*) veering about, tacking; (*Book-keeping*) clearing, transfer. *Virement d'eau*, turn of the tide; *banque de virement*, clearing-bank.

virer [vi′re], *v.i.* To turn, to twist, to turn about; to change colour; (*Naut.*) to tack, to veer about; (*Phot.*) to be toned. *Vire!* 'bout ship! *Virer au cabestan*, to heave, to hoist with the capstan; *virer de bord*, (*Naut.*) to tack about, to put about; (*fig.*) to change sides, to rat.—*v.t.* To transfer, to clear (a sum of money), (*Phot.*) to tone.

vireur [vi′rœ:r], *n.m.* Turning-gear.

vireux [vi′rø], *a.* (*fem.* **-euse**) Poisonous, noxious, nauseous.

virevaude [VIRE-VIRE].

vireveau [vir′vo], *n.m.* (*pl.* **-eaux**) or **virevaut**, *n.m.* Small windlass.

vire-vire [vir′vi:r], *n.m.*, or **virevaude**, *n.f.* Whirlpool (in a river).

virevolte [vir′vɔlt], *n.f.* Quick turning or wheeling (of a horse); (*fig.*) sudden change. *Les virevoltes d'un politicien*, a politician's changes of front. **virevolter**, *v.i.* To circle (of a horse); to spin round (of a person).

virevouster or **virevousser**, *v.i.* (*fam.*) To spin round.

Virgile [vir′ʒil], *m.* Vergil, Virgil.

virginal [virʒi′nal], *a.* (*fem.* **-ale**, *pl.* **-aux**) Virginal, maidenly. **virginalement**, *adv.* Virginally.

Virginie [virʒi′ni], *f.* Virginia. *La Virginie*, Virginia.

virginité [virʒini′te], *n.f.* Virginity, maidenhood.

virgule [vir′gyl], *n.f.* Comma. *Observer les points et les virgules*, to dot one's i's and cross one's t's; (in decimal numbers) point. *Deux virgule un* (2,1), two point one (2·1); *point et virgule*, semi-colon.

viril [vi′ril], *a.* (*fem.* **-e**) Virile, male; manly. *Âge viril*, manhood, man's estate. **virilement**, *adv.* Like a man; in a manly way. **virilité**, *n.f.* Virility; manhood, man's estate; vigour, energy.

virole [vi′rɔl], *n.f.* Ferrule, collar; (*Her.*) virole (hook or ring); die (for stamping), locking-ring (of bayonet). **virolé, a.** (*fem.* **-ée**) (*Her.*) Having viroles. **viroler**, *v.t.* To ferrule, to hoop; (*Die-stamping*) to put (the disk) into the stamp.

virtualité [virtɥali′te], *n.f.* Virtuality. **virtuel, a.** (*fem.* **-elle**) Virtual. **virtuellement**, *adv.* Virtually; potentially.

virtuose [vir′tɥo:z], *n.* Virtuoso. **virtuosité**, *n.f.* Virtuosity.

virulence [viry'lā:s],`n.f.` Virulence. **virulent,** a. (fem. **-ente**) Virulent.

virure [vi'ry:r], n.f. (Naut.) Strake.

virus [vi'ry:s], n.m. Virus.

vis [vis], n.f. inv. Screw. Escalier à vis, spiral staircase; vis sans fin, worm, endless screw; (fam.) serrer la vis à quelqu'un, to put the screw on someone.

visa [vi'za], n.m. Visa, signature, endorsement (on passports etc.). Visa de censure, (Cine.) censor's certificate.

visage [vi'za:3], n.m. Face, visage, countenance; aspect, look, air. À deux visages, double-faced; à visage découvert, openly, barefacedly; avoir bon visage, to look well; changer de visage, to change countenance, to turn pale; faire bon or mauvais visage à quelqu'un, to look pleasantly or unpleasantly at someone, to give someone a good or bad reception; se composer le visage, to compose one's countenance.

vis-à-vis [viza'vi], prep. phr. Opposite, over against; towards, relatively to. Vis-à-vis de l'église, opposite the church.—adv. phr. Opposite.—n.m. inv. Vis-à-vis (in dancing etc.), opposite neighbour (at table etc.); vis-à-vis (carriage).

viscéral [vise'ral], a. (fem. **-ale**, pl. **-aux**) Visceral. **viscère,** n.m. Any of the viscera or vital organs.

*****viscope** [vis'kɔp], n.f. (Mil. slang) Peak (of képi).

viscosité [viskozi'te], n.f. Viscosity, viscidity, stickiness.

visée [vi'ze], n.f. Aim; end, design, plan.

viser [vi'ze], v.i. To aim, to take aim; to aspire (à). Il visait à ce but, that was his goal.—v.t. To aim at, to take aim at; to allude to; to seek, to pursue; to visa, to countersign, to endorse. Faire viser un passeport, to get a passport visaed.

viseur [vi'zœːr], n.m. (fem. **-euse**) Aimer.— n.m. (Phot.) View-finder.

visibilité [vizibili'te], n.f. Visibility. **visible,** a. Visible; evident, manifest, obvious; ready to receive a visit. M. Lebrun n'est pas visible, M. Lebrun is not at home. **visiblement,** adv. Visibly, obviously.

visière [vi'zjɛːr], n.f. Visor (of a helmet); peak (of caps etc.), eye-shade; sight (on firearms); eye, insight, penetration; (colloq.) eyesight. Rompre en visière à quelqu'un, (fig.) to fall out with, to break openly with someone.

vision [vi'zjɔ̃], n.f. Vision, sight; dream, phantom, chimera, fancy. **visionnaire,** a. Visionary, fanciful.—n. Seer; dreamer, visionary.

visionner [vizjɔ'ne], v.t. (Cine.) To view. **visionneuse,** n.f. Film viewer.

visir, visirat, etc. [VIZIR etc.].

visitandine [vizitã'din], n.f. Nun of the Order of the Visitation.

visitation [vizita'sjɔ̃], n.f. Visitation of the Virgin to St. Elizabeth.

visite [vi'zit], n.f. Visit; call; visitation (of a bishop etc.); examination, inspection; search. Aller en visite, to go visiting; droit de visite, right of search; être en visite, to be on a visit; faire la visite des bagages, to examine luggage; faire la visite des caves, to search the cellars; faire une visite, to pay a visit; rendre sa visite

à quelqu'un, to return someone's call; rendre visite à quelqu'un, to pay a call on someone, to pay someone a visit.

visiter [vizi'te], v.t. To visit (patients, clients, etc.); to go over (cathedral etc.); to search, to examine, to inspect. **visiteur,** n.m. (fem. **-euse**) Visitor, caller; inspector, searcher. (spt.) Les visiteurs, the visiting team.

vison [vi'zɔ̃], n.m. Mink (animal).

*****vison-visu** [vi'zɔ̃vi'zy], adv. (colloq.) Opposite one another.

visorium [vizɔ'rjɔm], n.m. (Print.) Copyholder.

visqueux [vis'kø], a. (fem. **-euse**) Viscous, sticky, slimy, clammy.

vissage [vi'sa:3], n.m. Screwing. **visser,** v.t. To screw, to screw on, up, or down, to fix with a screw; (Mil. slang) to put (a soldier) in clink. **se visser,** v.r. To fix or attach oneself firmly. **visserie,** n.f. Screws, bolts, etc.

Vistule [vis'tyl], **la,** f. The Vistula.

visuel [vi'zɥɛl], a. (fem. **-elle**) Visual. **visuellement,** adv. Visually.

vital [vi'tal], a. (fem. **-ale,** pl. **-aux**) Vital; (fig.) essential, fundamental. **vitalement,** adv. Vitally. **vitaliser,** v.t. To vitalize. **vitalisme,** n.m. Vitalism. **vitaliste,** a. and n.m. Vitalist. **vitalité,** n.f. Vitality. **vitamine,** n.f. Vitamin.

vite [vit], a. Swift, quick, speedy, rapid. Vite comme le vent, as fleet as the wind.—adv. Quick, quickly, fast, rapidly, expeditiously. Aller vite en besogne, to be quick at work, to get to work promptly; au plus vite, as fast as possible; faire vite, to be quick, to make haste; vite! quick! look sharp!

vitellin [vitɛ'lɛ̃], a. (fem. **-ine**) (Biol.) Vitelline. **vitellus,** n.m. Vitellus; yolk of egg.

vitelotte [vit'lɔt], n.f. Kidney potato.

*****vitement** [vit'mã], adv. Quickly, speedily.

vitesse [vi'tes], n.f. Quickness, rapidity, celerity, swiftness, speed; (Motor.) gear. À grande or à toute vitesse, at full speed; à la vitesse de, at the rate of; gagner quelqu'un de vitesse, to outstrip or outrun someone; train de grande vitesse, express train; train de petite vitesse, slow train; boîte de vitesses, gear-box; changement de vitesse, change of gear; première vitesse, first (or low) gear; en (quatrième) vitesse, at full speed. Perdre de la vitesse, (of an aeroplane) to stall.

Viti [vi'ti], n. **Les îles,** The Fiji Islands.

viticole [viti'kɔl], a. Pertaining to vine culture, viticultural. **viticulteur,** n.m. Viticulturist. **viticulture,** n.f. Vine-growing.

vitonnière [vitɔ'njɛːr], n.f. (Naut.) Ironwork of rudder [AIGUILLOT].

vitrage [vi'tra:3], n.m. Glazing; glass windows, glass of partition, etc. **vitrail,** n.m. (pl. **-aux**) Stained-glass window. **vitre,** n.f. Pane of glass; window. (fam.) Casser les vitres, to break the windows, (fig.) to speak one's mind, to kick up a row. **vitré,** a. (fem. **-ée**) Glazed, of glass; (Anat. etc.) vitreous. Porte vitrée, glass door. **vitrer,** v.t. To furnish with glass windows, to glaze. **vitrerie,** n.f. Glaziery, glazier's work. **vitrescible,** a. Vitrescible. **vitreux,** a. (fem. **-euse**) Vitreous, glassy. **vitrier,** n.m. Glass-maker; glazier. **vitrière,** n.f. Iron framing for glass in windows. **vitrifiable,** a.

Vitrifiable. **vitrification**, *n.f.* Vitrification.
vitrifier, *v.t.* (*conjugated like* PRIER) To vitrify. *Brique vitrifiée*, glazed brick. **se vitrifier**, *v.r.* To vitrify. **vitrine**, *n.f.* Shop-window; show-case, glass case (in museums etc.).
vitriol [vitri'ɔl], *n.m.* Vitriol. (*Comm.*) *Vitriol bleu*, copper sulphate. **vitriolé**, *a.* (*fem.* -**ée**) Vitriolized. **vitrioleur**, *n.m.* (*fem.* -**euse**) Vitriol-thrower. **vitriolique**, *a.* Sulphuric.
vitupération [vitypera'sjɔ̃], *n.f.* Vituperation. **vitupérer**, *v.t. irr.* (*conjug. like* ACCÉLÉRER) To vituperate, to reprimand.
vivable [vi'vabl], *a.* Livable (in).
vivace [vi'vas], *a.* Long-lived, tenacious of life; perennial (of plants); inveterate, deep-rooted. *Préjugés vivaces*, deep-rooted prejudices.
vivacité [vivasi'te], *n.f.* Vivacity, liveliness, sprightliness, animation; spirit, life, ardour; vividness, brightness; penetration, acuteness; hastiness (of temper). *Avoir de la vivacité*, to be vivacious.
vivandier [vivã'dje], *n.m.* (*fem.* -**ière**) Sutler, canteen-manager.
vivant [vi'vã], *a.* (*fem.* -**ante**) Living, alive; lively, animated. *Pas une âme vivante*, not a living soul; *langue vivante*, modern language; *portrait vivant*, lifelike portrait; *rue vivante*, lively street.—*n.m.* Living person, person alive; (*pl.*) the living, the quick; life, lifetime. *De son vivant*, in his lifetime; *du vivant de son frère*, when his brother was alive; *un bon vivant*, one fond of good living.
vivat [vi'vat], *int.* Hurrah! huzza!—*n.m.* Huzza. *Crier vivat* or *pousser des vivats*, to cheer.
vive (1) [VIF].
vive (2) [viːv], *n.f.* Weever (fish).
vive (3) *subj.* [VIVRE].
vive-la-joie [vivla'ʒwa], *n.m. inv.* Jolly fellow, boon companion.
vivement [viv'mã], *adv.* Quickly, briskly, sharply, vigorously; eagerly; keenly, poignantly, acutely; smartly, angrily; spiritedly, vividly. *Partir vivement*, to hurry off; *mon père me reproche vivement mes fautes*, my father reproaches me sharply for my failings.
viveur [vi'vœːr], *n.m.* Rake, gay dog.
Vivien [vi'vjɛ̃], *m.* Vivian.
vivier [vi'vje], *n.m.* Fish-pond, stew; fish-well (in boat).
vivifiant [vivi'fjã], *a.* (*fem.* -**iante**) Vivifying, quickening; refreshing, invigorating. **vivification**, *n.f.*, or **vivifiement**, *n.m.* Vivification, vivifying; revival. **vivifier**, *v.t.* (*conjugated like* PRIER) To vivify, to quicken, to give life to; to enliven, to refresh, to revive. ***vivifique**, *a.* Reviving.
vivipare [vivi'paːr], *a.* Viviparous. **viviparité**, *n.f.*, or **viviparisme**, *n.m.* Viviparity.
vivisecteur [vivisɛk'tœːr], *n.m.* Vivisector.
vivisection [vivisɛk'sjɔ̃], *n.f.* Vivisection.
(C) **vivoir** [vi'vwaːr], *n.m.* Living-room.
vivoter [vivɔ'te], *v.i.* To live poorly, to rub along.
vivre [viːvr], *v.i. irr.* (*pres.p.* **vivant**, *p.p.* **vécu**) To live, to be alive; to subsist, to be maintained; to board, to take one's meals; to behave; to last, to endure. *Apprendre à vivre à*, to teach (someone) manners; *avoir de quoi vivre*, to have enough to live on; *avoir juste*

de quoi vivre, to have a bare competence; *faire vivre*, to keep alive, to feed, to maintain, to support; *il a vécu*, he has lived (*i.e.* he is dead); *vive la France!* long live France! *Qui vive?* Who goes there? *il fait bon vivre ici*, this is a good place to live in; *il faut que tout le monde vive*, everybody must live; *il ne sait pas vivre*, he has no manners; *il vit aux dépens d'autrui*, he lives at other people's expense; *il vit mal*, he lives badly; *il vit mal avec son frère*, he is on bad terms with his brother; *le bien-vivre*, an easy life; *ne pas trouver âme qui vive*, not to find a soul at home; *qui vivra verra*, live and learn, he who lives longest will see most; *savoir vivre* [SAVOIR-VIVRE]; *vivre bien*, to live an upright or honourable life; *vivre de son travail*, to live by one's labour; *vivre d'espérance*, to live in hopes; *vivre de ses rentes*, to be of independent means; *vivre d'industrie*, to live by one's wits; *vivre en prince*, to live like a prince.— *n.m.* Living, board, food; (*pl.*) provisions, victuals, rations. *Couper les vivres à quelqu'un*, to cut off someone's supplies.
vivrier [vi'vrje], *a.* (*fem.* -**ière**) Alimentary. —*n.m.* Victualler.
vizir [vi'ziːr], *n.m.* Vizier. **vizirat, visirat**, **viziriat**, or **visiriat**, *n.m.* Vizierate, viziership.
vlan [vlã], *interj.* (*pop.*) Bang!
vocable [vɔ'kabl], *n.m.* Vocable, word, name.
vocabulaire, *n.m.* Vocabulary.
vocal [vɔ'kal], *a.* (*fem.* -**ale**, *pl.* -**aux**) Vocal.— *n.* *Monk or nun having the right of voting in an election. **vocalement**, *adv.* Vocally.
vocalique, *a.* (Phon.) Vocalic (sound).
vocalisation [vɔkaliza'sjɔ̃], *n.f.* Vocalization.
vocalise, *n.f.* Piece of music for exercising the voice; vocalization; method of vocalizing.
vocaliser, *v.i., v.t.* (*Mus.*) To vocalize.
vocatif [vɔka'tif], *n.m.* (*Gram.*) Vocative case. *Au vocatif*, in the vocative.
vocation [vɔka'sjɔ̃], *n.f.* Vocation, calling, call; inclination; bent, turn, talent. *Suivre sa vocation*, to follow one's bent.
vociférant [vɔsife'rã], *a.* (*fem.* -**ante**) Vociferous. ***vociférateur**, *n.m.* (*fem.* -**trice**) Clamourer. **vociférations**, *n.f. pl.* Vociferations. **vociférer**, *v.t. irr.* (*conjugated like* ACCÉLÉRER) To vociferate, to bawl.
vœu [vø], *n.m.* (*pl.* **vœux**) Vow; votive offering; prayer, wish, desire; vote, suffrage. *Être au comble de ses vœux*, to have reached the summit of one's hopes; *faire des vœux pour quelqu'un*, to offer up prayers for someone, to wish someone success; *faire vœu de jeûner*, to make a vow of abstinence.
vogue [vɔg], *n.f.* Vogue, fashion; credit, craze; (*dial. S.E.*) patronal festival. *Avoir de la vogue*, to be in fashion.
voguer [vɔ'ge], *v.i.* To move forward by rowing (of a galley etc.); to sail, to go, to move along, to scud along. *Vogue la galère!* [GALÈRE].
voici [vwa'si], *prep.* See here, behold; here is, here are, this is, these are; ago, past. *Le voici qui vient*, here he comes; *le voilà, me voici*, there he is, here I am; *monsieur que voici*, this gentleman; *nous y voici*, here we are; *voici mon livre, voilà le vôtre*, here is my book, there is yours; *voici venir le printemps*, spring is coming, is at hand, or is near; *voici venir*

votre frère, here comes your brother. *J'ai quitté Londres voici deux ans,* I left London two years ago; *voici trois mois que je suis à l'hôpital,* I have been in hospital for the past three months.

voie [vwɑ], *n.f.* Way, road, highway; line, route, path, track, trail; (*fig.*) means, organ, medium, channel, course; conveyance, means of conveyance; gauge, breadth (between the wheels of carriages); load, two pailfuls; (*Chem.*) process; (*Rail.*) permanent way, four-foot way. *Changement de voies,* (*Rail.*) points; switch; *voie libre,* line clear; *être en voie de,* to be in a fair way to; *donner de la voie à une scie,* to set a saw; *la voie lactée,* the Milky Way; *mettre sur la voie,* to put on the track or on the scent; *voies biliaires,* bile ducts; *voie d'eau,* two pailfuls of water; (*Naut.*) leak; *voie ferrée,* railway, railroad; *voies de fait,* (*Law*) assault, blows; *voies et moyens,* ways and means; *voies respiratoires,* respiratory tracts; *voies urinaires,* urinary passages.

voilà [vwa'la], *prep.* There, behold, there now, there is, there are, that is. *Ah! vous voilà,* oh! there you are! *comme vous voilà fait!* what a strange figure you cut! what a plight you are in! *en voilà assez,* that is enough; *je l'ai vu voilà cinq ans,* I saw him five years ago; *le voilà,* there he is; *le voilà qui arrive,* there he comes; *ne voilà-t-il pas qu'il pleut,* well! I declare, it is raining; *voilà ce que c'est,* that is what it is; *voilà comme je suis,* you must take me as I am, I'm that sort of man; *voilà qui va bien,* that's all right now, that's capital; *voilà tout,* that is all; *voilà une heure qu'il parle,* he has been speaking for an hour.

voile (1) [vwal], *n.m.* Veil; (*fig.*) cover, mask, disguise, show, pretence. *Avoir un voile devant les yeux,* to have a mist before one's eyes; *prendre le voile,* to take the veil (of a nun).

voile (2) [vwal], *n.f.* Sail; canvas; (*fig.*) ship. *Aller à voiles et à rames,* to go with sails and oars; *à pleines voiles,* all sails set; *déployer les voiles,* to unfurl the sails; *faire force de voiles,* to crowd all sail; *faire voile,* to sail, to set sail; *grand-voile,* mainsail; *la voile de misaine,* the foresail; *mettre à la voile,* to set sail.

voilé [vwa'le], *a.* (*fem.* **-ée**) Rigged; veiled; clouded, dull, dim, soft; (*Phot.*) fogged; (wheel) buckled, bent. *Peu voilé,* broad (of hints, etc.). **voiler,** *v.t.* To veil; to cover, to cloak, to blind, to disguise, to conceal; (*Naut.*) to rig, to set sails on; (*Phot.*) to fog; to bend, to buckle, to warp (wheel, wood).— *v.i.* or **se voiler,** *v.r.* To wear a veil; to cloud over (of the sky); to buckle (of a wheel).

voilerie [vwal'ri], *n.f.* Sail-loft; sail-making.

voilette, *n.f.* Small veil, puggaree, fall; antimacassar.

voilier, *n.m.* Sail-maker; sailer (ship). *Un bon voilier,* a fast sailer.

voilure, *n.f.* (Set of) sails; trim of the sails; (*Av.*) wings, flying surface; buckle (of wheel), warp (of wood).

voir [vwaːr], *v.t. irr.* (*pres.p.* **voyant,** *p.p.* **vu**) To see; to behold, to perceive; to witness; to look at, to observe, to view; to inspect, to superintend; to overlook; to visit; to attend (a sick person); to have to do with, to deal with; to know, to understand, to comprehend; to be on visiting terms with, to frequent the society of. *Ceci est à voir,* it remains to be seen; *faire voir,* to show, to let see; *faire voir du pays à quelqu'un,* to lead someone a dance; *il ne voit personne,* he sees no company; *il veut tout voir par lui-même,* he insists on seeing everything for himself; *je l'ai vu de mes propres yeux,* I have seen it with my own eyes; *je ne vois point à quoi cela peut servir,* I don't see what purpose that can serve; *je vois bien quelle est son intention,* I see plainly what he is driving at; *je vous vois venir,* I see what you are driving at; *n'y voir goutte,* not to see a bit; *on n'a jamais rien vu de pareil,* the like was never seen before; *que vois-je?* what do I see? *se faire voir,* to show oneself, to appear; *vit-on jamais rien d'égal?* was anything like it ever seen? *voir de loin,* to be far-sighted; *voir le jour,* to be born, to see the light of day; *voir tout en beau,* to see the bright side of everything; *voyons!* let us see! now then! surely! come, come!—*v.i.* To see, to look, to watch; to have one's sight. *Voir à* or *voir à ce que,* to see to it that. **se voir,** *v.r.* To see oneself; to see each other; to visit each other; to be or to find oneself. *Cela se voit tout seul,* that is obvious; *ils ne se voient point,* they are not on visiting terms.

voire [vwaːr], *adv.* *Indeed, truly. *Voire même,* nay even, and indeed.

voirie [vwa'ri], *n.f.* Roads, the system of roads; refuse-dump; commission of public streets and highways.

voisin [vwa'zɛ̃], *a.* (*fem.* **-ine**) Bordering, adjacent, next; next door, neighbouring. *Être voisin de sa ruine,* to be on the verge of ruin; *la maison voisine,* the next house.—*n.* Neighbour. *Médire du voisin,* to speak ill of one's neighbour. **voisinage,** *n.m.* Neighbourhood; vicinity; proximity, nearness; neighbours. (*Rapports de*) *bon voisinage,* neighbourliness. **voisiner,** *v.i.* To visit one's neighbours.

voiturage [vwaty'raːʒ], *n.m.* Carriage, cartage (of goods etc.). **voiture,** *n.f.* Vehicle, conveyance; carriage; coach; cart, car; cost of carriage, fare; coachful, carriage-load, cart-load. *Descendre de voiture,* to alight from a carriage; *en voiture!* take your seats! *se promener en voiture* or *aller en voiture,* to drive; *voiture à deux chevaux,* carriage and pair; *voiture d'enfant,* perambulator, baby-carriage, (*fam.*) pram; *voiture de roulier,* wagon; *voiture de livraison,* delivery van; *voiture de laitier,* milk cart; *voiture à bras,* barrow; *voiture à deux places,* two-seater; *voiture-radio,* radio-car. **voiturée,** *n.f.* Carriageful; cart-load. **voiturer,** *v.t.* To carry, to convey, to cart. **voiturette,** *n.f.* Light (motor-) car. **voiturier,** *n.m.* Carrier, carter.—*a.* (*fem.* **-ière**) Carrying; carriage-able.

voïvodat [vɔivɔ'da], *n.m.* Voivodeship. **voïvode,** *n.m.* Voivode (Polish or Turkish governor).

voix [vwa], *n.f. inv.* Voice; tone, sound; vote, suffrage; opinion, judgment; singer. *A demi-voix,* in a low voice; *à haute voix,* aloud; loudly; *aller aux voix,* to come to the vote, to divide; *chanter à trois voix,* to sing in three parts; *de vive voix,* by word of mouth; *donner* *de la voix*, to give tongue; (*Gram.*) *la voix active*, the active voice; *mettre aux voix*, to put to the vote.

vol (1) [vɔl], *n.m.* Flying, soaring; flight; flock (of birds); spread (of wings); hawking; cast of hawks. *Au vol*, on the wing; *à vol d'oiseau*, as the crow flies; *prendre son vol*, to take wing (of birds), to fly off (of aeroplane); *prendre un vol trop haut*, to soar too high; *saisir l'occasion au vol*, to grasp the opportunity; *vol à voiles*, gliding; *vol de nuit*, night flying.

vol (2) [vɔl], *n.m.* Theft, robbery, stealing, larceny; stolen goods. *Vol à l'étalage*, shoplifting; *vol à la tire*, pocket-picking; *vol avec effraction*, burglary; *vol de grand chemin*, highway robbery.

volable [vɔ'labl], *a.* Worth stealing.

volage [vɔ'laːʒ], *a.* Fickle, inconstant, flighty.

volaille [vɔ'lɑːj], *n.f.* Poultry, fowls; bird. *Marchand de volaille*, poulterer. **volailler**, *n.m.* Poulterer; poultry-yard.

volant [vɔ'lɑ̃], *a.* (*fem.* **-ante**) Flying; loose, floating; movable, portable; travelling; (*Her.*) volant. *Feuille volante*, loose sheet; *fusée volante*, sky-rocket; *pont volant*, flying-bridge; —*n.m.* Shuttlecock; flounce (of a dress); flywheel (of machinery); hand-wheel (of lathe etc.), steering-wheel (of a car); sail (of a windmill). *Jouer au volant*, to play at battledore and shuttlecock. (*Motor.*) *Prendre le volant*, to take the wheel.

volatil [vɔla'til], *a.* (*fem.* **-ile** (1)) (*Chem.*) Volatile; (*fig.*) volatile (of temperament).

volatile (2) [vɔla'til], *a.* Winged.—*n.m.* or *n.f.* Winged creature, bird.

volatilisation [vɔlatiliza'sjɔ̃], *n.f.* Volatilization. **volatiliser**, *v.t.* To volatilize. **se volatiliser**, *v.r.* To become volatilized.

vol-au-vent [vɔlo'vɑ̃], *n.m. inv.* Vol-au-vent, puff-pie.

volcan [vɔl'kɑ̃], *n.m.* Volcano. **volcanique**, *a.* Volcanic, fiery.

vole [vɔl], *n.f.* Vole, all the tricks (at cards), slam.

volée [vɔ'le], *n.f.* Flight (of birds etc.); flock, covey; brood; bevy; troop; rank; volley (of guns); shower (of blows); thrashing; peal (of bells); splinter-bar (on coach); chase (of a cannon). *À la volée*, flying, as it flies, in the air, (*fig.*) quickly, precipitately, rashly, unthinkingly, at random; *coup (de pied) de volée*, (*Ftb.*) punt; *entre bond et volée*, at a lucky moment, (*Ten.*) on the half-volley; *être de la première volée*, to be of the first water, of high rank; *il a pris sa volée*, he has taken wing; *semer à la volée*, to (sow) broadcast; *sonner à toute volée*, to ring a full peal; *tirer à toute volée*, to fire at random or as far as a gun will carry; *une volée de coups de bâton*, a shower of blows; *volée basse*, (*Ten.*) low volley; *volée d'escalier*, flight of stairs.

voler (1) [vɔ'le], *v.i.* To fly; to take wing, to soar. *Entendre voler une mouche*, to hear a pin drop; *le temps vole*, time flies; *voler en éclats*, to fly into pieces.—*v.t.* (*Hawking*) To chase, to fly at.

voler (2) [vɔ'le], *v.t.* To steal, to rob; to fleece, to plunder; (*fig.*) to embezzle, to usurp. *Ne l'avoir pas volé*, to have got one's deserts, to have got what was coming to one.—*v.i.* To

steal. *Voler sur les grands chemins*, to rob on the highway.

volerie [vɔl'ri], *n.f.* Robbery; pilfering; (*Hawking*) flying.

volet [vɔ'lɛ], *n.m.* (Window)-shutter; pigeon-house, dove-cot; *boat-compass, sorting-board; (*Av.*) flap. *Trié(s) sur le volet*, very select (people).

voleter [vɔl'te], *v.i. irr.* (*conjugated like* AMENER) To flutter.

volette [vɔ'lɛt], *n.f.* Small wattle (for draining cheese); fly-net (for horses).

volettement, *n.m.* Fluttering.

voleur [vɔ'lœːr], *n.m.* (*fem.* **-euse**) Thief, robber; plunderer, extortioner; stealer. *Crier au voleur*, to cry out 'stop thief!'; *être fait comme un voleur*, to be in tatters; *voleur de grand chemin*, highwayman, footpad.—*a.* Thieving; pilfering.

volière [vɔ'ljɛːr], *n.f.* Aviary, large bird-cage.

volige [vɔ'liːʒ], *n.f.* Scantling. batten.

volition [vɔli'sjɔ̃], *n.f.* Volition. **volitionnel**, *a.* (*fem.* **-elle**) Volitional.

volontaire [vɔlɔ̃'tɛːr], *a.* Voluntary, willing; intended, intentional; spontaneous; obstinate, wilful, headstrong.—*n.* Volunteer; obstinate, headstrong person. **volontairement**, *adv.* Willingly, voluntarily; wilfully.

volontariat [vɔlɔ̃ta'rja], *n.m.* Voluntariate.

volonté [vɔlɔ̃'te], *n.f.* Will; (*pl.*) whims, caprices. *Avoir de la bonne volonté*, to be willing; *à volonté*, at pleasure, at will; *dernières volontés*, last will and testament; *faire ses quatre volontés*, (*colloq.*) to do as one pleases; *il aime à faire ses volontés*, he uses to have his own way; *mauvaise volonté*, ill-will, unwillingness; *tout plie sous sa volonté*, everything yields to his will. **volontiers**, *adv.* Willingly, gladly, with pleasure.

volt [vɔlt], *n.m.* (*Elec.*) Volt. **voltage**, *n.m.* Voltage. **voltaïque**, *a.* Voltaic. **voltamètre**, *n.m.* Voltameter.

volte [vɔlt], *n.f.* Volt (of horse, in fencing etc.). **volte-face**, *n.f. inv.* Turning round, volte-face. *Faire volte-face*, to face about; (*fig.*) to reverse one's opinions completely, to change loyalties, to change sides. (*Bayonet fencing*) *Double pas en arrière*, volte-face, two paces back and turn about.

volter [vɔl'te], *v.i.* (*Fenc.*) To make a volt.

voltige [vɔl'tiːʒ], *n.f.* Slack-rope gymnastics, flying-trapeze exercises; mounted gymnastics. **voltigeant**, *a.* (*fem.* **-ante**) Fluttering, hovering. **voltigement**, *n.m.* Tumbling; fluttering. **voltiger**, *v.i.* To flutter, to fly about, to hover; to practise *voltige*. **voltigeur**, *n.m.* Vaulter; light-infantry soldier, rifleman; kind of cigar.

voltmètre [vɔlt'mɛtr], *n.m.* Voltmeter.

volubile [vɔly'bil], *a.* (*Bot.*) Volubile, twining. **volubilis**, *n.m.* Convolvulus. **volubilité**, *n.f.* Volubility, fluency, glibness.

volume [vɔ'lym], *n.m.* Volume; bulk, size, mass; compass (of the voice etc.). **voluménomètre**, *n.m.* Volumenometer. **volumètre**, *n.m.* Volumeter. **volumineux**, *a.* (*fem.* **-euse**) Voluminous, bulky.

volupté [vɔlyp'te], *n.f.* Voluptuousness, sensual pleasure. **voluptuaire**, *a.* Voluptuary, luxurious. **voluptueux**, *a.* (*fem.* **-ueuse**) Voluptuous, sensual.—*n.* Voluptuary.

volute [vɔ'lyt], *n.f.* Volute; scroll.

volva [vɔl'va] or **volve**, *n.f.* (*Bot.*) Envelope, skin (of mushrooms).

volvulus [vɔlvy'ly:s], *n.m.* (*Path.*) Volvulus (twisting of intestinal canal).

vomer [vɔ'me:r], *n.m.* (*Anat.*) Vomer; (*Ichth.*) moon-fish.

vomique [vɔ'mik], *a.* Vomic. *Noix vomique,* nux vomica.—*n.f.* Vomica. **vomiquier,** *n.m.* (*pop.*) Nux vomica tree.

vomir [vɔ'mi:r], *v.t.* To vomit, to throw up, (*fig.*) to belch forth, to pour out. *Vomir de la flamme,* to belch out flame.—*v.i.* To vomit, to be sick. *Faire des efforts pour vomir,* to heave, to retch. **vomissement,** *n.m.* Vomit(ing). **vomitif,** *a.* (*fem.* -**ive**) Vomitory.—*n.m.* Emetic. **vomitoire,** *n.m.* (*Rom. Ant.*) Vomitory (large door of circus etc.).—*a.* [VOMITIF].

vorace [vɔ'ras], *a.* Voracious, ravenous. **voracement,** *adv.* Voraciously. **voracité,** *n.f.* Voracity.

vortex [vɔr'teks], *n.m.* Vortex-ring. **vorticelle,** *n.f.* Vorticel.

vos, *a.poss. pl.* [VOTRE].

votant [vɔ'tɑ̃], *a.* (*fem.* -**ante**) Voting, having a vote.—*n.m.* Voter. *Liste des votants,* register. **votation,** *n.f.* Voting. **vote,** *n.m.* Vote; division, voting, poll. *Vote à main levée,* vote by show of hands; *vote d'une loi,* passing of a bill. **voter,** *v.i., v.t.* To vote; to pass (a bill). *Voter des remercîments à quelqu'un,* to pass a vote of thanks to someone.

votif [vɔ'tif], *a.* (*fem.* -**ive**) Votive.

votre [vɔtr], *a.poss.* (*pl.* **vos**) Your. *Vos parents,* your relations; *votre serviteur,* your servant. **le vôtre,** *pron.poss.* (*fem.* **la vôtre,** *pl.* **les vôtres**) Yours. *Il a pris ses livres et les vôtres,* he has taken his books and yours. —*n.m.* Your own, your own property; (*pl.*) your relations, friends, etc.; your pranks, tricks. *Je suis des vôtres,* I am one of your party; *vous avez fait des vôtres,* you have been up to one of your tricks.

vouer [vwe], *v.t.* To devote, to dedicate, to consecrate; to give up; to vow, to swear. *Des soldats voués à la défaite,* soldiers doomed to defeat. **se vouer,** *v.r.* To devote oneself. *Ne pas savoir à quel saint se vouer,* not to know which way to turn.

vouge [vu:ʒ], *n.m.* Bill-hook; *halberd or voulge.

voui [vwi], *adv.* A familiar form of *oui,* not uncommon in the Parisian region; other similar deformations are *vouate, vuissier* (*pop.*) instead of *ouate, huissier.*

vouloir [vu'lwa:r], *v.t. irr.* (*pres.p.* **voulant**, *p.p.* **voulu**) To will; to desire, to wish, to require, to want, to need; to consent; to please; to choose; to resolve, to determine; to try, to seek, to attempt, to endeavour; to admit, to grant; to mean, to signify. *Ce bois ne veut pas brûler,* this wood will not burn; *Dieu le veuille!* God grant it! *en vouloir à quelqu'un,* to bear or owe someone a grudge; *il ne sait ce qu'il veut,* he does not know his own mind; *il nous demanda ce que nous lui voulions,* he asked us what we wanted of him; *il veut que cela soit,* he will have it so; *il veut que vous obéissiez,* he will have you obey, he requires you to obey; *je le veux ainsi,* I will

have it so; *je ne veux pas,* I won't, I don't mean to; *je veux que vous sachiez,* I wish you to know; *oui, je (le) veux bien,* yes, I am willing; *que veut dire cela?* what does that mean? *que voulez-vous?* what do you want? what can I do for you? what can you expect? *savoir ce que parler veut dire,* to take the hint; *s'en vouloir de,* to be angry with oneself for; *veuillez agréer,* be pleased to accept; *veuillez me dire,* please tell me; *vouloir c'est pouvoir,* where there's a will, there's a way; *vouloir du bien à quelqu'un,* to wish someone well; *vous l'avez voulu!* you would have it, you have only yourself to blame.—*n.m.* Will. *Bon vouloir,* goodwill; *mauvais vouloir,* ill-will; *votre vouloir sera le mien,* your desire shall be mine.

voulu [vu'ly], *a.* (*fem.* -**ue**) Wished, desired; required, requisite; due, received; deliberate, studied. *Indifférence voulue,* studied indifference.

vous [vu], *pron.pers. pl.* You, *ye; to you. *De vous à moi,* between you and me; *vous-même,* yourself; *vous-mêmes,* yourselves.

voussoir [vu'swa:r] or **vousseau,** *n.m.* (*pl.* -**eaux**) Voussoir, wedge-shaped arch-stone.

voussure, *n.f.* Curve (of arch or vault), coving.

voûte [vut], *n.f.* Arch, vault; hollow (of a horseshoe); (*fig.*) roof, canopy. *Clef de voûte,* keystone; *la voûte du ciel* or *voûte céleste,* the canopy of heaven; *voûte d'arête,* groined vault. **voûté,** *a.* (*fem.* -**ée**) Vaulted, curved, bent. **voûter,** *v.t.* To vault, to arch over; to arch, to bend. **se voûter,** *v.r.* To arch, to vault; to be bent, to stoop.

vouvoiement [vuvwa'mɑ̃], *n.m.* Use of the conventional *vous.* **vouvoyer,** *v.t.* To say *vous* instead of *tu* when addressing somebody.

voyage [vwa'ja:ʒ], *n.m.* Travelling, travel; journey, voyage, tour, run, trip; visit, sojourn, stay; progress (of a magnate); (*pl.*) travels. *Bon voyage!* pleasant journey to you! *être en voyage,* to be travelling, to be abroad; *faire le grand voyage,* to go on one's last journey, to die; *faire un voyage,* to travel, to make a journey; *un petit voyage d'agrément,* a pleasure trip; *voyage d'aller,* outward voyage; *voyage au long cours,* voyage in foreign parts; *voyage de retour,* homeward voyage. **voyager,** *v.i.* To travel, to voyage, to journey. *Voyager à pied,* to travel on foot.

voyageur, *n.m.* (*fem.* -**euse**) Traveller; passenger.—*a.* Travelling; pertaining to travel; migrating. *Commis voyageur,* commercial traveller, traveller; *oiseau voyageur,* migratory bird; *pigeon voyageur,* carrier pigeon.

voyant [vwa'jɑ̃], *a.* (*fem.* -**ante**) Gaudy, showy (of colours).—*n.* Seer, clairvoyant, prophet. —*n.m.* Signal, mark; sighting-board, sight; sphere (of light-ship). *Voyant de mire,* particoloured plate used in surveying.

voyelle [vwa'jɛl], *n.f.* Vowel.

voyer (1) [vwa'je], *n.m.* and *a.m. Agent voyer,* surveyor of roads, inspector of highways.

voyer (2) [vwa'je], *v.t. irr.* (*conjug. like* ABOYER) To cause (liquid etc.) to run. **voyette,** *n.f.* Hand-bowl.

voyeur [vwa'jœ:r], *n.m.* (*fem.* -**euse**) Voyeur (sexual pervert).

[759]

voyou [vwa'ju], *n.m.* (*fam.*) Street arab; loafer, corner-boy. **voyoucratie,** *n.f.* Mob rule, riff-raff.

vrac [vrak], *adv. phr. En vrac,* in bulk, loose, pell-mell. *Charger en vrac,* to load with a loose cargo.

vrai [vrɛ], *a.* True, real, genuine; veracious, speaking the truth; right, proper, fit; regular, downright, arrant, very. *Il est vrai que je l'ai dit,* it is true I said so; *un vrai coquin,* a real scoundrel, **an arrant knave; un vrai savant,* a real scholar.—*int.* Truly, really, in truth!—*n.m.* Truth. *Au vrai, pour vrai, dans le vrai,* in truth, truly; *à vrai dire,* to tell the truth, as a matter of fact; *vous êtes dans le vrai,* you are perfectly right. **vraiment,** *adv.* Truly, in truth; indeed, really! *Il est vraiment trop bête,* he is really too stupid.

vraisemblable [vrɛsɑ̃'blabl], *a.* Likely, probable.—*n.m.* Probability, likelihood. **vraisemblablement,** *adv.* Very likely, probably. **vraisemblance,** *n.f.* Probability, likelihood, verisimilitude.

vrillage [vri'ja:ʒ], *n.m.* Kinking. **vrille,** *n.f.* Gimlet, borer, piercer; (*Bot.*) tendril; (*Av.*) tail-spin. **vrillé,** *a.* (*fem.* -ée (1)) Bored; spiral, curled; (*Bot.*) having tendrils. **vrillée** (2), *n.f.* (*fam.*) Bindweed. **vriller,** *v.t.* To bore.—*v.i.* To ascend spirally; to twist, to kink. **vrillette,** *n.f.* Death-watch beetle. **vrillier** [vri'je], *n.m.* Gimlet-maker. **vrillon,** *n.m.* Small auger.

vrombir [vrɔ̃'bi:r], *v.i.* To buzz, to hum, to whirr, to purr, to throb. **vrombissement,** *n.m.* Humming, buzzing, throbbing, purring.

vu [vy], *a.* (*fem.* **vue** (1)) Considered, regarded; seen, observed. *Mal vu,* held in poor esteem; *ni vu, ni connu,* (*colloq.*) you won't discover anything.—*prep.* Considering, in view of. *Vu ses services à la patrie,* in view of his services to the country.—*n.m.* Sight, examination, inspection; (*Law*) preamble. *Au vu et au su de tout le monde,* with everyone's knowledge, openly.—*conj. phr.* Seeing that, whereas. *Vu que les contrevenants s'exposent à des poursuites correctionnelles . . .,* whereas the offenders are liable to penalties. . . .

vue (2) [vy], *n.f.* Sight, eyesight; eyes; view, survey, inspection; prospect; appearance, presence; light, window; design; insight, penetration. *À dix jours de vue,* (*Comm.*) ten days after sight; *à perte de vue,* as far as the eye can reach, out of sight; *avoir des vues sur,* to have designs upon; *avoir la vue basse,* to be near-sighted; *avoir la vue courte,* to be short-sighted; *avoir la vue sur quelqu'un,* to keep a watch over someone; *dessin à vue,* freehand drawing; *à vue de pays,* at a cursory glance, by guess-work; *à vue d'œil,* visibly; *cette maison a une belle vue,* that house has a fine view; *connaître de vue,* to know by sight; *des compliments à perte de vue,* long-winded compliments; *donner dans la vue,* to catch the eye; *en vue de,* with a view to; *en vue de terre,* within sight of land; *garder un prisonnier à vue,* not to let a prisoner out of sight; *il a de grandes vues,* he aims high; *il a perdu la vue,* he has lost his sight; *jouer à vue,* (*Mus.*) to play at sight; *navire en vue!* sailho! *perdre de vue,* to lose sight of, to forget; (*Cine.*) *prise de vues,* shooting of a film; *une*

vue de côté, a side view; *vues fixes,* (lantern-) slides.

Vulcain [vyl'kɛ̃], *m.* Vulcan.

vulcanien [vylka'njɛ̃], *a.* (*fem.* -ienne) (*Geol.*) Plutonian, vulcanian. **vulcanisation,** *n.f.* Vulcanization. **vulcanisé,** *a.* (*fem.* -ée) Vulcanized. **vulcaniser,** *v.t.* To vulcanize. **vulcanite,** *n.f.* Vulcanite, ebonite.

vulgaire [vyl'gɛːr], *a.* Vulgar, common. *Langue vulgaire,* vernacular.—*n.m.* The common herd. **vulgairement,** *adv.* Vulgarly, commonly. **vulgarisateur,** *n.m.* (*fem.* -trice) Vulgarizer, popularizer (of knowledge etc.).—*a.* Vulgarizing, popularizing. **vulgarisation,** *n.f.* Popularization. **vulgariser,** *v.t.* To popularize. **se vulgariser,** *v.r.* To become vulgar. **vulgarisme,** *n.m.* Vulgarism. **vulgarité,** *n.f.* Vulgarity, vulgar thing, triviality. **vulgate,** *n.f.* Vulgate (the Latin Bible).

vulnérabilité [vylnerabili'te], *n.f.* Vulnerability. **vulnérable,** *a.* Vulnerable. **vulnéraire,** *a.* and *n.m.* (*Pharm.*) Vulnerary.—*n.f.* (*Bot.*) Wound-wort. **vulnérant,** *a.* (*fem.* -ante) Wounding. **vulnération,** *n.f.* Wounding, wounds.

vulpin [vyl'pɛ̃], *n.m.* Foxtail (grass).

vultueux [vyl'tɥø], *a.* (*fem.* -euse) Flushed, bloated (of the face). **vultuosité,** *n.f.* Puffiness (of the face).

vulve [vylv], *n.f.* (*Anat.*) Vulva. **vulvite,** *n.f.* Vulvitis.

W

W, w [dublə've], *n.m.* (This twenty-third letter of the alphabet is used only in borrowed words.)

wacke [vak], *n.f.* (*Geol.*) Wacke.

wagage [va'ga:ʒ], *n.m.* River mud.

wagnérien [vagne'rjɛ̃], *a.* and *n.m.* (*fem.* -ienne) Wagnerian.

wagon [va'gɔ̃], *n.m.* (*Rail.*) Carriage, truck, van.

wagon-bar, *n.m.* (*pl.* **wagons-bars**) Refreshment-car. **wagon-couloir,** *n.m.* (*pl.* **wagons-couloirs**) Corridor carriage. **wagon-foudre,** *n.m.* (*pl.* **wagons-foudres**) Tank-car. **wagon-lit,** *n.m.* (*pl.* **wagons-lits**) Sleeping-car. **wagonnet,** *n.m.* Tip-truck. **wagon-poste,** *n.m.* (*pl.* **wagons-poste**) Mail-van. **wagon-restaurant,** *n.m.* (*pl.* **wagons-restaurants**) Restaurant-car, dining-car. **wagon-salon,** *n.m.* (*pl.* **wagons-salons**) Saloon, Pullman car.

Wallace [va'las], *n.f.,* or *fontaine Wallace,* drinking-fountain, as presented to the Parisians by Richard Wallace.

Wallon [wa'lɔ̃], *a.* and *n.m.* (*fem.* -onne) Walloon.—*n.m.* Walloon (language).

warrant [va'rɑ̃], *n.m.* Warrant. **warranter,** *v.t.* To warrant, to guarantee, to certify.

water [wa'tɛr or va'tɛr], *n.m. pl. Les water,* or *les water-closets,* or *les W.C.* [lɛvɛ've:se], water-closet, lavatory, W.C.

wateringue [vatə'rɛ̃:g], *n.f.* (*N. France*) Draining system; draining syndicate.

waterproof [watɛr'pruf], *n.m.* Waterproof.

watt [wat], *n.m.* (*Elec.*) Watt. **wattman,** *n.m.* (*pl.* **-men**) Tram-driver.

week-end [wik'ɛnd], *n.m.* (*pl.* **week-ends**) Week-end.

welche [VELCHE].

wesleyen [wesle'jɛ̃], *a.* and *n.m.* (*fem.* **-enne**) Wesleyan.

Westphalie [vɛsfa'li], *f.* Westphalia.

whig [wig], *n.m.* Whig. **whiggisme**, *n.m.* Whiggery.

whisk(e)y [wis'ki], *n.m.* Whisky.

whist [wist], *n.m.* Whist. **whisteur**, *n.m.* (*fem.* **-euse**) Whist-player.

wicléfisme [wikle'fism], *n.m.* Wycliffism. **wicléfiste**, *n.* Wycliffite.

wigwam [wig'wam], *n.m.* Wigwam.

wisigoth [viʒi'go], *a.* (*fem.* **-gothe**) Visigothic; (*fig.*) rude, barbarous.—*n.* Goth, barbarian.

wistarie [vista'ri], *n.f.* (*Bot.*) Wistaria.

witloof [wit'lɔf], *n.f.*, or *chicorée de Bruxelles.* Its bleached roots become either chicory or *barbe de capucin.*

wolfram [vɔl'fram], *n.m.* Wolfram (tungsten-ore).

X

X, x [iks], *n.m.* The twenty-fourth letter of the alphabet. *Jambes en* X, knock-kneed; *rayons* X, X-rays; *l'*X, (*school slang*) the Polytechnic School (in Paris); *un* X, a cadet of that school.

xanthéine [gzɑ̃te'in], *n.f.* (*Chem.*) Xanthein (colouring-matter in flowers). **xanthine**, *n.f.* Xanthin. **xanthoma** or **xanthome**, *n.m.* (*Path.*) Xanthoma. **xanthophylle**, *n.f.* Xanthophyll.

xénogénèse [ksenɔʒe'nɛːz], *n.f.* (*Biol.*) Xenogenesis, heterogenesis.

xénophobe [ksenɔ'fɔb], *a.* and *n.* Xenophobe. **xénophobie**, *n.f.* Xenophobia; hatred of foreigners.

xérasie [ksera'zi], *n.f.* (*Path.*) Xerasia, alopecia.

xérès [kse'rɛs], *n.m.* Sherry (wine).

xérodermie [kserɔdɛr'mi], *n.f.* Xerodermia. **xérophagie** [kserɔfa'ʒi], *n.f.* Xerophagy.

Xerxès [ksɛr'sɛːs], *m.* Xerxes.

xiphias [ksi'fjas], *n.m.* Sword-fish. **xiphoïde**, *a.* (*Anat.*) Xiphoid, sword-shaped.

xylème [ksi'lɛm], *n.m.* (*Bot.*) Xylem (woody tissue). **xylène**, *n.m.* (*Chem.*) Xylene.

xylocope [ksilɔ'kɔp], *n.m.* (*Ent.*) Carpenter-bee.

xylographe [ksilɔ'graf], *n.m.* Xylographer, wood-engraver. **xylographie**, *n.f.* Wood-engraving.

xylonite [ksilɔ'nit], *n.f.* Xylonite, celluloid.

xylophage [ksilɔ'faːʒ], *a.* Xylophagous (living or growing on wood).—*n.m.* Xylophagan (wood-boring insect).

xylophone [ksilɔ'fɔn], *n.m.* (*Mus.*) Xylophone.

xyste [ksist], *n.m.* (*Anat.*) Xystus (gymnasium).

Y

Y, y [i grɛk], *n.m.* The twenty-fifth letter of the alphabet.

y [i], *adv.* There; here; thither; within, at home. *Allez-y*, go there; *il y a*, there is, there are, there exists; *je l'y ai vu*, I saw him there; *j'y suis*, I follow you, I get you.—

pron. By, for, in, at, or to him, her, it, them. *Il n'y gagnera rien*, he will gain nothing by it; *ne vous y fiez pas*, be careful, don't be too sure; *sans y penser*, without thinking of it; *je n'y suis pour rien*, I have nothing at all to do with it.

yachmak [jaʃ'mak], *n.m.* Veil (worn by Moslem women), yashmak.

yacht [jɔt] or [jak], *n.m.* Yacht. **yachting**, *n.m.* Yachting. **yachtman**, *n.m.* (*pl.* **-men**) Yachtsman. **yachtwoman**, *n.f.* (*pl.* **-women**) Yachtswoman.

yaourt, yahourt [ja'urt], *n.m.* Yaourt, yogurt.

yatagan [jata'gɑ̃], *n.m.* Yataghan.

yèble [HIÈBLE].

yeuse [jøːz], *n.f.* Ilex, holm-oak.

yeux [ŒIL].

ylang-ylang [ilɑ̃'ilɑ̃], *n.m.* Ylang-ylang.

yod [jɔd], *n.m. Le yod*, the semi-vowel [j].

yodler [jɔ'dle], *v.i.* (*Mus.*) To yodel.

yogi or **yogui** [jɔ'gi], *n.m.* Yogi.

yole [jɔl], *n.f.* Yawl, gig.

Yougoslave [jugɔs'lav], *a.* and *n.* Yugoslav. **Yougoslavie** [jugɔsla'vi], *f.* Yugoslavia.

youpin [ju'pɛ̃], *a.* and *n.m.* (*fem.* **-ine**), or **youtre**. (*pej.*) Jew, Jewish, Yid, sheeny.

youyou [ju'ju], *n.m.* Dinghy.

ypérite [ipe'rit], *n.f.* (*Chem.*) Yperite, mustard-gas. **ypérité**, *a.* (*fem.* **-ée**) Gassed.

ypréau [ipre'o], *n.m.* (*pl.* **-aux**) Broad-leaved elm.

*****ysopet** [izɔ'pɛ], *n.m.* Collection of medieval fables.

yucca [ju'ka], *n.m.* Yucca.

Z

Z, z [zed], *n.m.* The twenty-sixth letter of the alphabet.

zabre [zɑːbr], *n.m.* Species of carrion-eating beetles, zabrus.

Zacharie [zaka'ri], *m.* Zachariah, Zachary.

Zachée [za'ʃe], *m.* Zaccheus.

zagaie [za'gɛ], **sagaie**, or **sagaye**, *n.f.* Assegai.

zain [zɛ̃], *a.m.* Whole-coloured (of horses etc.).

Zambèze [zɑ̃'bɛːz], (**le**), *m.* The Zambezi (river).

zanzibar [zɑ̃zi'baːr], or **zanzi**, *n.m.* A popular game of dice played in the pubs.

Zébédée [zebe'de], *m.* Zebediah.

zèbre [zɛbr], *n.m.* Zebra. **zébré**, *a.* (*fem.* **-ée**) Striped like the zebra. **zébrure**, *n.f.* Stripes.

zébu [ze'by], *n.m.* Zebu (Indian ox).

zée [zeː], *n.m.* (*Ichth.*) *Zée forgeron*, John Dory.

zef [zɛf], *n.m.* (*abbr. of* **zéphyr**) (*Av.*) Breeze, wind.

zélateur [zela'tœːr], *n.m.* (*fem.* **-trice**) Zealot, zealous person.—*a.* Zealous.

zèle [zɛːl], *n.m.* Zeal, warmth, ardour, enthusiasm. *Avec zèle*, zealously; *avoir du zèle pour*, to be zealous in; *surtout, pas de zèle*, above all beware of zeal, don't overdo it.

zélé [ze'le], *a.* (*fem.* **-ée**) Zealous.

zélote, *n.m.* Zealot. **zélotisme**, *n.m.* Zealotry.

zend [zɛ̃ːd], *n.m.* and *a.* Zend (language).

zénith [ze'nit], *n.m.* Zenith. **zénithal,** *a.* (*fem.* **-ale,** *pl.* **-aux**) Zenithal.

Zéphir [ze'fiːr], *m.* Zephyr, Zephyrus.

zéphire, zéphyr, or **zéphyre** [ze'fiːr], *n.m.* Zephyr, gentle breeze; *(Mil. slang)* soldier in the *Compagnies de discipline.* **zéphirien,** *a.* (*fem.* **-ienne**) Like a zephyr.

zeppelin [ze'plɛ̃], *n.m.* Zeppelin.

zéro [ze'ro], *n.m.* Naught; zero (of the thermometer); (*fig.*) a mere cipher, a nonentity. *À zéro,* at zero; (*Ten.*) *deux à zéro,* two love; *un zéro* or *zéro point,* (*cricket*) duck's egg, duck; (*Naut.*) *zéro la barre!* Helm amidships! (*Mil. slang*) Nothing; nothing doing. *Dans l'équipe c'est un pur zéro,* he is a complete passenger in the team.

zest [zɛst], *int.* Pshaw! nonsense!— *n.m.* Used only in the expression *entre le zist et le zest,* so-so, middling, neither one thing nor the other.

zeste [zɛst], *n.m.* Woody skin dividing sections of a walnut; peel (of orange, lemon, etc.); (*fig.*) straw, fig, nothing. *Cela ne vaut pas un zeste,* it is not worth a straw. **zester,** *v.t.* To take the peel off (orange, lemon). **zesteuse,** *n.f.* Orange or lemon peeler.

zététique [zete'tik], *a.* Zetetic, proceeding by inquiry.—*n.f.* Zetetics.

zeugme [zø:gm] or **zeugma,** *n.m.* Zeugma.

zézaiement or **zézayement** [zeze(j)'mɑ̃], *n.m.* Lisping, lisp (vicious pronunciation of [z] instead of [ʒ]). **zézayer,** *v.i.* (*conjugated like* BALAYER) To lisp.

zibeline [zi'blin], *n.f.* Sable.

zigoteau, zigotot [zigɔ'to], *n.m.* (*pop.*) Chap, fellow. *Faire le zigoteau,* to play the giddy goat.

zigouiller [zigu'je], *v.t.* (*slang*) To kill.

zigue, zig [zig], *n.m.* (*slang*) Man, fellow (always in a good sense). *Un bon zigue,* a nice fellow, a decent sort.

zigzag [zig'zag], *n.m.* Zigzag. *Éclair en zigzag,* forked lightning; *faire des zigzags,* to move in zigzags, to stagger. **zigzaguer,** *v.i.* To zigzag.

zinc [zɛ̃:g], *n.m.* Zinc; (*slang*) bar or counter of public-house, aeroplane. **zincage** or **zingage,** *n.m.* Covering with zinc; zinking, zinc-plating. **zincographe,** *n.m.* Zincographer. **zincographie,** *n.f.* Zincography.

zingaro [zɛ̃ga'ro], *n.m.* (*pl.* **zingari**) Gipsy.

zinguer [zɛ̃'ge], *v.t.* To cover with zinc; to zinc. **zinguerie,** *n.f.* Zinc-works; zinc-trade. **zingueur,** *n.m.* Zinc-worker.

zinnia [zi'nja], *n.m.* Zinnia.

zinzolin [zɛ̃zɔ'lɛ̃], *n.m.* Reddish violet.

zircon [zir'kɔ̃], *n.m.* Zircon.

zist [ZEST].

zizanie [ziza'ni], *n.f.* *Tare, darnel; (*fig.*)

discord, bickering. *Semer la zizanie,* to sow dissension.

zodiacal [zɔdja'kal], *a.* (*fem.* **-ale,** *pl.* **-aux**) Zodiacal. **zodiaque,** *n.m.* Zodiac.

zoïle [zɔ'il], *n.m.* Snarling critic.

zona [zo'na], *n.m.* Shingles.

zonal, *a.* (*fem.* **-ale,** *pl.* **-aux**) Zonal.

zone [zo:n], *n.f.* Zone, belt, area. *Zone glaciale,* frigid zone; *zone torride,* torrid zone; *zone verte,* green belt. *La zone (militaire),* the unbuilt ground outside the fortifications of Paris. **zonier,** *n.m.* (Poor) dweller in the hutments of the military zone outside Paris. **zoné,** *a.* (*fem.* **-ée**) Zoned.

zoo [zo'o], *n.m.* (*fam.*) Zoo.

zoochimie [zɔɔʃi'mi], *n.f.* Zoochemistry. **zoochimique,** *a.* Zoochemical. **zoographe,** *n.m.* Zoographer. **zoographie,** *n.f.* Zoography. **zoolâtre,** *n.m.* Zoolater. **zoolâtrie,** *n.f.* Zoolatry. **zoolithe** or **zoolite,** *n.m.* Zoolite. **zoologie,** *n.f.* Zoology. **zoologique,** *a.* Zoological. *Jardin zoologique,* zoological garden(s), zoo. **zoologiste,** *n.* Zoologist. **zoomorphie,** *n.f.* Zoomorphism. **zoonomie,** *n.f.* Zoonomy. **zoophage,** *a.* Zoophagous. **zoophagie,** *n.f.* Zoophagous instinct. **zoophore,** *n.m.* Zoophorus. **zoophyte,** *n.m.* Zoophyte. **zoophytologie,** *n.f.* Zoophytology. **zoospore,** *n.f.* Zoospore. **zootomie,** *n.f.* Zootomy. **zootomiste,** *n.* Zootomist.

Zoroastre [zɔrɔ'astr], *m.* Zoroaster. **zoroastrien** [zɔrɔas'trjɛ̃], *a.* and *n.m.* (*fem.* **-ienne**) Zoroastrian. **zoroastrisme,** *n.m.* Zoroastrianism.

zostère [zɔs'tɛːr], *n.f.* (*Bot.*) Genus of seaweed, wrack-grass.

zouave [zwa:v], *n.m.* Zouave (soldier) (Algerian infantry). *Faire le zouave,* (*Mil. slang*) to play the fool; to try to be funny (in dress and manners).

zozoter [zɔzɔ'te], *v.i.* (*pop.*)=ZÉZAYER.

zut [zyt], *int.* (*fam.*) (to convey anger, scorn, disappointment, flat refusal). *Zut! Zut alors! non, zut!* Be blowed! No go! Never! Bother! Dash it! *Avoir un œil qui dit zut à l'autre,* to squint.

Zuyderzée [zɥidɛr'ze], **le,** *m.* Zuyder Zee.

zyeuter [zjø'te] or **ziotter** [zjɔ'te], *v.t.* (*vulg.*) To look at, to have a squint at.

zygoma [zigɔ'ma], *n.m.* (*Anat.*) Zygoma. **zygomatique,** *a.* Zygomatic. **zygomorphe,** *a.* Zygomorphous.

zymogène [zimɔ'ʒɛn], *n.m.* (*Biol.*) Zymogen. **zymologie,** *n.f.* Zymology (science of fermentation). **zymosimètre,** *n.m.* Zymometer (instrument for measuring degree of fermentation). **zymotique,** *a.* Zymotic.

CASSELL'S FRENCH-ENGLISH
ENGLISH-FRENCH DICTIONARY
PART II
ENGLISH-FRENCH

CASSELL'S
ENGLISH-FRENCH DICTIONARY

A

A, a [ei]. La première lettre de l'alphabet; (*Mus.*) la, *m.* *A* 1, (*Naut.*) de première cote, (*fig.*) de première qualité; *A.D.*, anno Domini, l'an du Seigneur; *A.M.*, antemeridiem, du matin; *not to know A from B*, ne savoir ni A ni B.

a [ε, ei, ə], **an** (before a vowel), *indef. art.* Un, *m.*, une, *f.* *A man*, un homme; *a shilling a pound*, un shilling la livre; *three a day*, trois par jour.

Aargau [ˈɑːgau]. Argovie, *f.*

aback [əˈbæk], *adv.* En arrière; (*fig.*) à l'improviste, au dépourvu; (*Naut.*) (voile) sur le mât, coiffé. *To be taken aback*, être surpris, déconcerté, interloqué. (*Naut.*) *To be aback*, avoir le vent dessus; *to lay a sail aback*, coiffer une voile.

abacus [ˈæbəkəs] (*pl.* **abaci**), *n.* (*Arch.*, *Math.*) Abaque; tailloir, *m.*

abaft [əˈbɑːft], *adv.* Sur l'arrière, en arrière. —*prep.* En arrière de, à l'arrière de.

abandon [əˈbændən], *v.t.* Abandonner; délaisser, quitter; renoncer à, se désister de. *To abandon oneself to*, se livrer à.—*n.* Abandon, *m.*; laisser aller, *m.*, désinvolture, *f.*

abandoned, *a.* Abandonné; dépravé, perdu (de débauches). *Abandoned wretch*, misérable, *m.* **abandoning**, *n.* Abandonnement; délaissement, *m.* **abandonment**, *n.* Abandonnement; délaissement; abandon, *m.*; cession, *f.* (de biens).

abase [əˈbeis], *v.t.* Abaisser; ravaler. **abasement**, *n.* Abaissement; ravalement, *m.*; humiliation, *f.*

abash [əˈbæʃ], *v.t.* Déconcerter, décontenancer; interdire, confondre. **abashed**, *a.* Confus (de).

abate [əˈbeit], *v.t.* Diminuer; rabattre; affaiblir, atténuer, amortir; calmer, apaiser. —*v.i.* Diminuer; s'affaiblir; se calmer, s'apaiser (of the weather etc.); tomber, baisser, s'abattre, perdre de sa force (of the wind etc.). **abatement**, *n.* Diminution, réduction, remise, *f.*, rabais, *m.*; affaiblissement, adoucissement, *m.*; apaisement, *m.*; (*Law*) annulation, *f.*

abatis [əˈbæti], *n.* Abattis, *m.* (of trees).

abbacy [ˈæbəsi], *n.* Dignité d'abbé, *f.*; abbatiat, *m.*; droits abbatiaux, *m.pl.*; abbaye, *f.* **abbatial** [əˈbeiʃəl], *a.* Abbatial. **abbé**, *f.* Abbé, *m.* **abbess**, *n.* Abbesse, *f.* **abbey**, *n.* Abbaye, église abbatiale, *f.* **abbot**, *n.* Abbé, supérieur (d'abbaye), *m.* **abbotship**, *n.* Dignité *or* fonctions d'abbé *or* d'abbesse.

abbreviate [əˈbriːvieit], *v.t.* Abréger; raccourcir.

abbreviation [əbriːviˈeiʃən], *n.* Abréviation, *f.* **abbreviator**, *n.* Abréviateur, *m.* **abbreviatory**, *a.* Qui abrège, abréviatif.

ABC [ˈeiˈbiːˈsiː], *n.* A b c (alphabet); abécédaire, *m.* *The A B C Guide*, l'Indicateur (alphabétique) des chemins de fer; *An A B C* (*shop*), un restaurant bon marché de l'Aerated Bread Co.; *the A B C of a subject*, les principes élémentaires d'une question.

abdicant [ˈæbdikənt], *a.* and *n.* Abdicataire.

abdicate [ˈæbdikeit], *v.t.* Abdiquer, se démettre de; renoncer à.—*v.i.* Abdiquer. **abdication**, *n.* Abdication, *f.*

abdomen [æbˈdoumən, ˈæbdəmən], *n.* Abdomen, bas-ventre, *m.*

abdominal [æbˈdɔminəl], *a.* Abdominal.

abducent [æbˈdjusənt], *a.* and *n.* (*Anat.*) Abducteur, *m.*

abduct [æbˈdʌkt], *v.t.* Détourner, enlever (clandestinement *or* par force). **abduction**, *n.* Abduction, *f.*, enlèvement (de mineur etc.), détournement, *m.* **abductor**, *n.* (*Anat.*) Abducteur; (*Law*) ravisseur, *m.*

abeam [əˈbiːm], *adv.* (*Naut.*) Par le travers.

abecedarian [eibiːsiːˈdɛəriən], *a.* and *n.* Abécédaire, *m.*

abed [əˈbed], *adv.* Au lit, couché; alité (ill).

aberdevine [æbədiˈvain], *n.* (*Orn.*) Tarin, *m.*

aberrance [æˈberəns], *n.* Déviation, aberration, erreur, *f.*; égarement, *m.* **aberrant**, *a.* Aberrant, qui s'écarte, égaré. **aberration** [æbəˈreiʃən], *n.* Aberration, *f.*; éloignement, écart, égarement, *m.*; erreur, *f.* (de jugement).

abet [əˈbet], *v.t.* Soutenir, encourager (à un crime). *To aid and abet*, être le complice. **abetment** *or* **abetting**, *n.* Encouragement (à un crime), *m.*; complice, *m.* **abettor**, *n.* Instigateur (d'un crime); complice, *m.*

abeyance [əˈbeiəns], *n.* Vacance; suspension, *f.* *In abeyance*, en suspens; *to fall into abeyance*, tomber en désuétude.

abhor [əbˈhɔː], *v.t.* Abhorrer, avoir en horreur, détester.

abhorrence [æbˈhɔrəns], *n.* Aversion extrême, horreur, *f.* **abhorrent**, *a.* Odieux, répugnant (à); incompatible, contraire; saisi d'horreur. **abhorrently**, *adv.* Avec horreur.

abhorrer [æbˈhɔːrə], *n.* Personne qui abhorre, *f.*; ennemi juré *or* déclaré, *m.*

abide [əˈbaid], *v.i.* (*past* **abode** (2)) Demeurer, rester; séjourner, habiter; durer, être durable; rester fidèle (à). *To abide by* (*a decision etc.*), rester fidèle à; *to abide by* (*the laws etc.*), s'en tenir à, se conformer à.—*v.t.* Attendre; supporter, endurer; subir, souffrir. **abider**, *n.* Personne qui demeure, *f.*, habitant, *m.*

abiding, *a.* Constant, ferme, durable, immuable. **abidingly**, *adv.* Constamment.

abigail [ˈæbigeil], *n.* Suivante, soubrette, *f.*

ability [əˈbiliti], *n.* Capacité, *f.*; pouvoir, *m.*; talent, *m.*; habileté, *f.*; (*pl.*) dons intellectuels, *m.pl.* *To the best of my ability*, de mon mieux.

abject [ˈæbdʒekt], *a.* Abject, bas, vil, misérable. **abjectness**, *n.* Abjection, *f.* **abjection** [æbˈdʒekʃən], **abjectness** [ˈæbdʒektnis], *n.* Abjection, *f.*, misère, *f.* **abjectly**, *adv.* D'une manière abjecte.

abjuration [æbdʒuˈreiʃən], *n.* Abjuration, *f.*

abjure [æbˈdʒuə], *v.t.* Abjurer; renoncer à, renier. **abjurer**, *n.* Personne, *f.*, qui abjure *or* qui renie.

ablation [əb'leiʃən], *n.* (*Med.*) Ablation, *f.*; enlèvement, *m.*

ablative ['æblətiv], *a.* and *n.* (*Gram.*) Ablatif, *m. In the ablative,* à l'ablatif.

ablaut ['æblaut], *n.* Apophonie, *f.*

ablaze [ə'bleiz], *a.* En feu, en flammes; (*fig.*) enflammé. *Ablaze with anger,* enflammé de colère.

able ['eibl], *a.* Capable (de), à même (de); habile. *As one is able,* selon ses moyens; *better able,* plus capable, mieux à même de; *to be able to,* pouvoir, être à même de. **able-bodied,** *a.* Fort, robuste, vigoureux; (*Mil.*) bon pour le service. *Able-bodied seaman,* matelot de deuxième classe, *m.*

ablet ['æblet] or **ablen,** *n.* (*Ichth.*) Ablette, *f.*

abloom [ə'blu:m], *adv.* and *pred. a.* En fleur; refleuri.

ablution [a'blu:ʃən], *n.* Ablution, *f.* (*colloq.*) *The ablutions,* le lavabo, *m.*

ably ['eibli], *adv.* Habilement, avec talent.

abnegation [æbni'geiʃən], *n.* Abnégation, renonciation, *f.*; désaveu, *m.* **abnegate,** *v.t.* Renoncer à, nier. **abnegator,** *n.* Renonciateur, *m.*; personne qui désavoue, *f.*

abnormal [æb'nɔːməl], *a.* Anormal. **abnormality** [æbnɔː'mæliti], *n.* Anomalie; difformité, *f.* **abnormally,** *adv.* Anormalement.

aboard [ə'bɔːd], *adv.* À bord (de). *All aboard!* embarquez! (a ship); en voiture! (a train). *To fall aboard a ship,* aborder un navire; *to go aboard,* aller à bord, s'embarquer.

abode (1) [ə'boud], *n.* Demeure, habitation, *f.*; séjour, *m. Of no fixed abode,* sans domicile fixe.

abode (2) [ə'boud], *past* [ABIDE].

abolish [ə'bɔliʃ], *v.t.* Abolir; supprimer. **abolishable,** *a.* Abolissable. **abolishment,** *n.* **abolition** [æbo'liʃən], *n.* Abolition, suppression, *f.*; abolissement, *m.* **abolitionism,** *n.* Abolitionnisme, *m.* **abolitionist,** *n.* Abolitionniste.

abominable [ə'bɔminəbl], *a.* Abominable, infâme, détestable. **abominableness,** *n.* Nature abominable, *f.*; l'odieux (d'une chose), *m.* **abominably,** *adv.* Abominablement.

abominate, *v.t.* Abominer, détester.

abomination, *n.* Abomination, horreur, *f.*

aboriginal [æbə'ridʒinəl], *a.* Aborigène, primitif.—*n.* Aborigène, indigène, *m.* **aborigines,** *n.* (*used only in pl.*) Aborigènes, *m.pl.*, spécialement indigènes d'Australie.

abort [ə'bɔːt], *v.i.* Avorter.

abortion [ə'bɔːʃən], *n.* Avortement (action); avorton (product), *m.* **abortive,** *a.* Abortif, manqué; avorté. **abortively,** *adv.* Avant terme; (*fig.*) sans résultat, sans succès. **abortiveness,** *n.* (*fig.*) Insuccès, *m.*

abound [ə'baund], *v.i.* Abonder (de). *To abound with,* avoir en abondance, avoir abondance de; *to abound in,* abonder en. **abounding,** *a.* Abondant. *Abounding in,* abondant en.

about [ə'baut], *prep.* Autour de; auprès de; sur; vers; environ; touchant, au sujet de, à l'égard de; à peu près; sur le point de; dans, par; en train de. *About that,* là-dessus, à ce sujet, à cet égard; *about the streets,* dans les rues; *about thirty men,* trente hommes environ, une trentaine d'hommes; *about two*

o'clock, vers (les) deux heures; *much ado about nothing,* beaucoup de bruit pour rien; *I have no money about me,* je n'ai pas d'argent sur moi; *to be about something,* être à faire une chose, s'occuper d'une chose; *to set about something,* se mettre à quelque chose; *to talk about,* parler de; *what is it all about?* de quoi s'agit-il? qu'est-ce que c'est? *what's he about?* que fait-il?—*adv.* Tout autour, à l'entour, à la ronde; çà et là; en faisant un détour. *All about,* partout; *ready about,* (*Naut.*) pare à virer! *round about,* tout autour; *somewhere about here,* (*colloq.*) *round and about,* quelque part près d'ici, de ce côté, dans les environs; *to be about to,* être sur le point de; *to bring about,* accomplir, faire réussir, venir à bout de; *to go about,* (*Naut.*) virer de bord.

above [ə'bʌv], *prep.* Au-dessus de, par-dessus; en amont de; plus de; au delà de. *Above all,* surtout, par-dessus tout; *above board,* ouvertement, franchement, à jeu découvert; *above ground,* sur la terre, de ce monde, en vie; *to be above* (*doing a thing*), être trop fier pour; *to get above oneself,* s'en faire accroire; *to play fair and above board,* jouer cartes sur table.—*adv.* En haut; là-haut; au-dessus; ci-dessus, précédemment. *Above named,* susdit, précité, dont on a parlé plus haut; *over and above,* en outre, en sus.

abrade [ə'breid], *v.t.* User par le frottement, roder; produire une abrasion, écorcher.

Abraham ['eibrəhæm]. Abraham, *m. To sham Abraham,* faire le malade (pour éviter de travailler).

abrasion [ə'breiʒən], *n.* (Action d'enlever par) frottement, *m.*; abrasion, écorchure, *f.*; frai (in coins etc.), *m.* **abrasive,** *a.* and *n.* Abrasif, *m.*

abreast [ə'brest], *adv.* De front, à côté l'un de l'autre; (*Naut.*) par le travers; (*fig.*) de pair avec. *To keep abreast of the times,* marcher de pair avec son époque, suivre son temps.

abridge [ə'bridʒ], *v.t.* Abréger, raccourcir; restreindre, retrancher (les droits de); priver. *Abridged edition* (*of book*), édition réduite, *f.* **abridger,** *n.* Abréviateur, *m.* **abridgment,** *n.* Abrégé, précis, *m.*; réduction, diminution, *f.*

abroach [ə'broutʃ], *adv.* En perce (tonneau).

abroad [ə'brɔːd], *adv.* À l'étranger; au loin, de tous côtés. *To be all abroad,* être tout désorienté, divaguer; (*Row.*) ne pas ramer ensemble, (*fam.*) cafouiller; *to get abroad,* courir, se répandre, transpirer (of news).

abrogate ['æbrogeit], *v.t.* Abroger. **abrogation,** *n.* Abrogation, *f.*

abrupt [ə'brʌpt], *a.* Brusque; brisé, saccadé; précipité, soudain; (ton) cassant, abrupt, escarpé, à pic. **abruptly,** *adv.* Brusquement, tout à coup; avec brusquerie (way of speaking etc.). **abruptness,** *n.* Précipitation; (*fig.*) brusquerie, rudesse, *f.*; escarpement, *m.*

Abruzzi [ə'brutsi]. Les Abruzzes, *f.pl.*

abscess ['æbses], *n.* Abcès, dépôt, *m.*

abscissa [æb'sisə], *n.* (*pl.* **abscissae**) (*Geom.*) Abscisse, *f.* **abscission,** *n.* Abscission, excision, *f.*

abscond [əb'skɔnd], *v.i.* Se soustraire (furtivement) aux poursuites de la justice; disparaître; (*fam.*) déguerpir, décamper. **absconder,** *n.* Fugitif, *m.*; (*Law*) contumace, défaillant, *m.*

absence ['æbsəns], *n.* Absence, *f.*; éloignement, *m.*; absence d'esprit, distraction, *f.*; manque, *m.*
absent (1) ['æbsənt], *a.* Absent. **absent-minded,** *a.* Distrait.
absent (2) [æb'sent], *v.r.* *To absent oneself,* s'absenter.
absentee [-sən'tiː], *n.* Absent, *m.*, manquant, *m.* *Absentee landlord,* absentéiste; (*Law*) propriétaire forain. **absenteeism,** *n.* Chômage volontaire; absentéisme, *m.*
absently, *adv.* D'un air distrait.
absinthe ['æbsinθ], *n.* Absinthe, *f.* **absinthiated,** *a.* Absinthé. **absinthism,** *n.* Absinthisme, *m.*
absolute ['æbsəluːt], *a.* Absolu, illimité; (décret) irrévocable; parfait, véritable, fieffé. *He is an absolute scoundrel,* c'est un franc coquin.—*n.* *The absolute,* l'absolu, *m.* **absolutely,** *adv.* Absolument; (*colloq.*) complètement. **absoluteness,** *n.* Pouvoir absolu; caractère absolu, *m.* **absolution,** *n.* Absolution; (*R.-C.Ch.*) absoute, *f.*; acquittement, *m.* **absolutism,** *n.* Absolutisme, *m.* **absolutist,** *n.* Absolutiste. **absolutory,** *a.* Absolutoire.
absolve [əb'zɔlv], *v.t.* Absoudre (de); délier, décharger, dégager, affranchir.
absorb [əb'sɔːb], *v.t.* Absorber; amortir (un choc); (*fig.*) absorber. **absorbable,** *a.* Absorbable. **absorbent,** *a.* and *n.* Absorbant, *a.* and *n.m.*, hydrophile (coton). **absorbing,** *a.* Absorbant. **absorption,** *n.* Absorption, *f.*; absorbement, *m.*; amortissement, *m.* **absorptive,** *a.* (*Chem.*) Absorbant.
abstain [əb'stein], *v.i.* S'abstenir (de). **abstainer,** *n.* Buveur d'eau, abstème, *m.* *Total abstainer,* personne qui ne boit jamais d'alcool, *f.* **abstaining,** *n.* Abstinence, *f.*
abstemious [əb'stiːmiəs], *a.* Tempérant, sobre. **abstemiously,** *adv.* Sobrement, avec modération. **abstemiousness,** *n.* Abstinence; modération, sobriété, *f.* **abstention,** *n.* Abstention, *f.*
absterge [əb'stəːdʒ], *v.t.* (*Surg.*) Nettoyer. **abstergent,** *a.* and *n.* Abstergent; détersif, *a.* and *n.m.* **abstersive,** *a.* Détersif.
abstinence ['æbstinəns], *n.* Abstinence, *f.* **abstinent,** *a.* Abstinent, sobre.
abstract (1) [æb'strækt], *v.t.* Soustraire, dérober, détourner; faire abstraction de; résumer, abréger.
abstract (2) ['æbstrækt], *n.* Abrégé, résumé, précis, *m.*; analyse, *f.*; (*Comm.*) relevé, *m.* *In the abstract,* par abstraction, en théorie. —*a.* Abstrait. **abstracted,** *a.* Séparé, détaché; distrait, rêveur, pensif; soustrait, dérobé. **abstractedness,** *n.* Caractère abstrait, *m.*; préoccupation, *f.* **abstracter,** *n.* Détourneur, subtiliseur, *m.*; abréviateur, *m.* **abstraction,** *n.* Soustraction, distraction, *f.*, détournement, *m.*; abstraction, *f.*; préoccupation, *f.* **abstractive,** *a.* Abstractif. **abstractly,** *adv.* Abstractivement, d'une manière abstraite.
abstruse [æb'struːs], *a.* Caché; abstrus, obscur. **abstrusely,** *adv.* D'une manière abstruse, obscurément. **abstruseness,** *n.* Caractère abstrus, *m.*, obscurité, *f.*
absurd [əb'səːd], *a.* Absurde. **absurdity** or **absurdness,** *n.* Absurdité, *f.* **absurdly,** *adv.* Absurdement.
abundance [ə'bʌndəns], *n.* Abondance,

grande quantité, *f.*; grand nombre, *m.*; (*fig.*) prospérité, *f.* **abundant,** *a.* Abondant. **abundantly,** *adv.* Abondamment, en abondance, à foison.
abuse (1) [ə'bjuːz], *v.t.* Abuser de; maltraiter; médire de, dire du mal de; iniurier, dire des injures à; tromper; séduire.
abuse (2) [ə'bjuːs], *n.* Abus, *m.*; insultes, injures, *f.pl.* **abuser,** *n.* Détracteur; séducteur; trompeur, *m.* **abusive,** *a.* Abusif; injurieux, grossier. **abusively,** *adv.* Abusivement; injurieusement. **abusiveness,** *n.* Langage injurieux *or* grossier, *m.*
abut [ə'bʌt], *v.i.* Aboutir (à), confiner (à); (*Build.*) s'appuyer (contre). **abutment,** *n.* Aboutement, *m.*; contre-fort, pied-droit, *m.*; culée (of a bridge), *f.* **abutter,** *n.* Riverain, *m.*
abuzz [ə'bʌz], *adv.* and *pred. a.* Bourdonnant.
abysmal [ə'bizməl], *a.* Sans fond, (ignorance) profonde.
abysmally, *adv.* *Abysmally ignorant,* d'une ignorance profonde.
abyss [ə'bis], *n.* Abîme, gouffre, *m.*
Abyssinia [æbi'sinjə]. L'Abyssinie, l'Éthiopie, *f.*
acacia [ə'keifə], *n.* Acacia, *m.* *False acacia,* acacia vulgaire, robinier, *m.*
academic [ækə'demik] or **academical,** *a.* Académique, universitaire, classique, scolaire; sans portée pratique, abstrait, stérile. **academically,** *adv.* Académiquement. **academicals,** *n.pl.* Costume, *m.*, *or* robe universitaire, *f.*
academician [əkædə'mifən], *n.* Académicien, *m.* *Royal Academician,* membre de la Royal Academy. **academism,** *n.* Platonisme, *m.*; académisme, *m.* **academist,** *n.* Académiste.
academy [ə'kædəmi], *n.* Académie (société savante), *f.*; école libre, *f.*, pensionnat, *m.*, institution, *f.*, (in Scotland) lycée, *m.* *Academy of music,* conservatoire, *m.*; *academy* (*figure*) (Paint. etc.), académie, étude, *f.*
Acadia [ə'keidiə]. L'Acadie, *f.*
acanthus [ə'kænθəs], *n.* Acanthe, *f.*
Acaridae [æ'kæridiː], *n.pl.* Acarides, acariens, *m.pl.*
accede [æk'siːd], *v.i.* Accéder, consentir (à), se joindre à, écouter; monter (sur le trône).
accelerate [æk'seləreit], *v.t.* Accélérer; hâter, activer, précipiter.—*v.i.* S'accélérer. **acceleration,** *n.* Accélération, *f.* **accelerative** or **acceleratory,** *a.* Accélérateur. **accelerator,** *n.* Accélérateur, *m.*
accension [æk'senfən], *n.* (*Chem.*) Inflammation, *f.*
accent (1) [æk'sent], *v.t.* Accentuer.
accent (2) ['æksənt], *n.* Accent, *m.*
accentuate [æk'sentjueit], *v.t.* Accentuer, appuyer sur. **accentuation,** *n.* Accentuation, *f.*
accept [æk'sept], *v.t.* Accepter, agréer, admettre; *comprendre, entendre. *To accept the consequences,* subir les conséquences. **acceptability** or **acceptableness,** *n.* Acceptabilité, *f.*; droit au bon accueil, *m.* **acceptable,** *a.* Acceptable; agréable. **acceptably,** *adv.* Agréablement. **acceptance,** *n.* Acceptation, *f.*; réception, *f.*; accueil favorable, *m.*; approbation, *f.* *To beg someone's acceptance of something,* prier quelqu'un d'accepter quelque chose; *to cancel* ⁓

acceptance, (*Comm.*) annuler une acceptation; *worth acceptance,* qui vaut la peine d'être offert.

acceptation [æksep'teiʃən], *n.* *Acceptation; acception, *f.*, sens (d'un mot), *m.* **accepter,** *n.* Personne qui accepte, *f.* **acceptor,** *n.* (*Comm.*) Accepteur, avaliste, tiré, *m.*

access ['ækses], *n.* Accès, abord, *m.*; entrée, admission, *f.* *Difficult of access,* d'un accès *or* abord difficile; *to have access to,* avoir accès à. **accessary** [ACCESSORY]. **accessible,** *a.* Accessible, abordable. **accession** [æk'seʃən], *n.* Acquisition; augmentation, addition, *f.*, accroissement; avènement (to a throne etc.), *m.* **accessory,** *a.* Accessoire; complice (de), participant (à).—*n.* Accessoire (thing), complice (person), *m.* *Accessory after the fact,* complice par assistance.

accidence ['æksidəns], *n.* Morphologie, *f.*; rudiments (de grammaire), *m.pl.*

accident ['æksidənt], *n.* Accident, *m.*, avarie, *f.*, cas fortuit; hasard; incident; malheur, *m.* *By accident,* accidentellement; par hasard; *to meet with a fatal accident,* être victime d'un accident mortel. *Accident of the ground,* irrégularité de terrain, *f.*

accidental ['æksi'dentəl], *a.* Accidentel, fortuit; accessoire.—*n.* (*Mus.*) Signe accidentel; accident; (*Paint.*) (light) contre-jour, reflet, *m.* **accidentally,** *adv.* Accidentellement; par hasard. **accidentality** *or* **accidentalness,** *n.* Nature accidentelle *or* fortuite, *f.*

acclaim [ə'kleim], *v.t.* Acclamer, applaudir à; proclamer.—*n.* Acclamation, *f.*

acclamation [æklə'meiʃən], *n.* Acclamation, *f.* **acclamatory,** *a.* D'acclamation; acclamatif.

acclimation [æklai'meiʃən] *or* **acclimatation** [æklaimə'teiʃən], *n.* Acclimatement, *m.*; acclimatation, *f.* **acclimatization,** *n.* Acclimatation, *f.*

acclimatize [ə'klaimətaiz], *v.t.* Acclimater. *To become acclimatized,* s'acclimater; s'accoutumer.

acclivity [ə'kliviti], *n.* Montée, côte, rampe, *f.* **acclivous** [ə'klaivəs], *a.* En rampe, montant, escarpé.

accolade [æko'leid], *n.* Accolade, *f.*

accommodate [ə'kɔmədeit], *v.t.* Accommoder, ajuster, mettre d'accord; loger, recevoir, contenir; fournir, donner; obliger (par), servir (de). *To accommodate oneself to,* s'accommoder à, se prêter à; *to accommodate with a seat,* donner un siège *or* une place à. **accommodating** *or* **accommodative,** *a.* Accommodant, obligeant; complaisant. **accommodation** [əkɔmə'deiʃən], *n.* Ajustement, accommodement, *m.*; complaisance; convenance, commodité, *f.*; logement, *m.*; facilités, *f.pl.*, aménagements, *m.pl.* *Accommodation bill,* billet de complaisance, *m.*; *accommodation for man and beast,* on loge à pied et à cheval; *accommodation ladder,* (*Naut.*) échelle de commandement, *f.*; *the accommodation is very good in this hotel,* on est très bien dans cet hôtel. **accommodator,** *n.* Personne qui accommode, *f.*

accompaniment [ə'kʌmpənimənt], *n.* Accompagnement, *m.* **accompanist,** *n.* (*Mus.*) Accompagnateur, *m.*, accompagnatrice, *f.* **accompany,** *v.t.* Accompagner; reconduire (à sa voiture etc.). *To be accompanied by,* *with,* être accompagné de.

accomplice [ə'kʌmplis *or* ə'kɔmplis], *n.* Complice, compère, *m.*

accomplish [ə'kʌmpliʃ *or* ə'kɔmpliʃ], *v.t.* Accomplir, achever; effectuer; réaliser (une prédiction etc.); parfaire (son éducation). **accomplished,** *a.* Accompli, achevé; parfait. **accomplisher,** *n.* Exécuteur, *m.* **accomplishment,** *n.* Accomplissement, *m.* exécution, *f.*; (*usu. pl.*) arts d'agrément, talents, *m.pl.*

accord [ə'kɔːd], *v.t.* Accorder, concéder; mettre d'accord.—*v.i.* S'accorder, être d'accord.—*n.* Accord, consentement, *m.* *In accord, d'accord* (avec), conformément (à); *of one's own accord,* de lui-même, de son propre mouvement; *with one accord,* d'un commun accord. **accordance,** *n.* Accord, rapport, *m.*; conformité, *f.*; octroi, *m.*, concession (d'un privilège), *f.* **accordant,** *a.* D'accord (avec); conforme (à). **according,** *a.* Conforme (à). *According as,* selon que, suivant que; *according to,* selon, suivant, conformément à, d'après; *according to you,* à vous entendre. **accordingly,** *adv.* En conséquence; donc, aussi.

accordion [ə'kɔːdiən], *n.* Accordéon, *m.*

accost [ə'kɔst], *v.t.* Accoster, aborder. **accostable,** *a.* Abordable.

accouchement [ə'kuːʃmɑ̃], *n.* Accouchement, *m.* **accoucheur,** *n.* Accoucheur, *m.*; accoucheuse, *f.*

account [ə'kaunt], *n.* Compte, *m.*; mémoire, rapport, exposé, compte rendu, *m.*; relation, histoire, *f.*, récit, *m.*; raison, *f.*; motif, *m.*; cause, *f.*; (*fig.*) considération, valeur, *f.*; parti, profit, *m.*; cas *or* poids, *m.* *As per account rendered,* suivant compte remis; *by all accounts,* au dire de tout le monde; *current account,* compte courant; *for account,* à terme; *in account with,* en compte avec; *on account of,* à cause de; *on joint or mutual account,* de compte à demi; *on no account,* pour rien au monde; *on that account,* pour cela; *on your account,* par égard pour vous; *to call to account,* demander compte à; *to carry to account,* porter en compte; *to give an account of,* rendre raison *or* compte de; *to have a current account with,* être en compte courant avec; *to keep accounts,* tenir les livres; *to make no account of,* ne faire aucun cas de; *to take into account,* tenir compte de, (*Comm.*) faire entrer en ligne de compte; *to turn to account,* tirer parti de, mettre à profit.—*v.t.* Compter; estimer (de), regarder (comme), tenir (pour).—*v.i.* *To account for,* rendre compte de, expliquer; répondre de, rendre raison de; (*fam.*) tuer, faire son affaire à. **accountability** *or* **accountableness,** *n.* Responsabilité, *f.* **accountable,** *a.* Responsable; comptable. **accountancy,** *n.* Comptabilité; tenue des livres, *f.* **accountant,** *n.* Comptable, agent comptable, *m.* *Accountant general,* chef de la comptabilité, *m.* *Chartered accountant,* expert comptable, *m.* **account-book,** *n.* Livre de comptes, *m.* **accountantship,** *n.* Charge *or* place de comptable, *f.*

accoutre [ə'kuːtə], *v.t.* Habiller, équiper; accoutrer (un chevalier etc.). **accoutrement,** *n.* Harnachement; équipement (du soldat), *m.*

accredit [ə'kredit], *v.t.* Accréditer.

accretion [ə'kriːʃən], *n.* Accroissement, *m.*

[4]

accrue [ə'kru:], *v.i.* Provenir, résulter (de), revenir (à); courir (interest); s'accumuler.
accumbent [ə'kʌmbənt], *a.* À demi couché.
accumulate [ə'kju:mjuleit], *v.t.* Accumuler, entasser; amonceler.—*v.i.* S'accumuler, s'amonceler. **accumulation** [-'leiʃən], *n.* Accumulation, *f.*; amoncellement, amas, entassement, *m.* **accumulative**, *a.* (Chose) qui s'accumule; (personne) qui accumule, thésauriseur. **accumulatively**, *adv.* Par accumulation, **accumulator**, *n.* Accumulateur, *m.*, accumulatrice, *f.*; (*Mech.*) accumulateur (d'énergie), *m. Accumulator capacity indicator*, accumètre, *m.*
accuracy ['ækjurəsi] or **accurateness**, *n.* Exactitude, justesse, *f.*; précision, *f.*; soin, *m.* **accurate**, *a.* Exact, juste, correct, précis. **accurately**, *adv.* Exactement, avec justesse.
accursed [ə'kə:sid], *a.* Maudit; détestable, exécrable.
accusable [ə'kju:zəbl], *a.* Accusable. **accusation** [ækju'zeiʃən], *n.* Accusation, *f.*; (*Law*) acte d'accusation, *m.*
accusative [ə'kju:zətiv], *n.* (*Gram.*) Accusatif, régime direct, *m.*—*a.* De l'accusatif.
accuse [ə'kju:z], *v.t.* Accuser. **accused**, *n.* (*Law*) *The accused*, le prévenu, la prévenue, l'accusé(e). **accuser**, *n.* Accusateur, *m.*, accusatrice, *f.*
accustom [ə'kʌstəm], *v.t.* Accoutumer, habituer. *To accustom oneself to*, s'accoutumer à, s'habituer à. **accustomed**, *a.* Accoutumé, habitué; habituel, coutumier.
ace [eis], *n.* As; (*Ten.*) service qui bat l'adversaire; (*fig.*) point, iota, *m. Within an ace of*, à deux doigts de.—*a.* (*colloq.*) Épatant.
acephalous [ə'sefələs], *a.* Acéphale, sans chef.
acerb [ə'sə:b], *a.* Acerbe, aigre. **acerbity**, *n.* Acerbité, aigreur; (*fig.*) âpreté, sévérité, *f.*
acescence, *n.* Acescence, *f.* **acescent**, *a.* Acescent (qui tourne à l'aigre).
acetate ['æsiteit], *n.* (*Chem.*) Acétate, *m.*
acetic [ə'si:tik, ə'setik], *a.* Acétique. **acetification** [əsetifi'keiʃən], *n.* Acétification, *f.* **acetify** [æ'setifai], *v.t.* Acétifier.—*v.i.* S'acétifier.
acetone ['æsitoun], *n.* Acétone, *f.*
acetous ['æsitəs], *a.* Acéteux.
acetylene [ə'setili:n], *n.* Acétylène, *f.*
ache [eik], *n.* Mal, *m.*; douleur, *f. Headache*, mal de tête; *toothache*, mal de dents.—*v.i.* Faire mal; (*fig.*) souffrir (de). *My feet ache*, les pieds me font mal; *my head aches*, j'ai mal à la tête.
Acheron ['ækərən]. Achéron, *m.*
achievable [ə'tʃi:vəbl], *a.* Exécutable, faisable.
achieve [ə'tʃi:v], *v.t.* Exécuter, accomplir; remporter (une victoire); atteindre (à). *To achieve a reputation*, se faire une réputation.
achievement, *n.* Exploit, fait d'armes; accomplissement, succès, achèvement, *m.*; réalisation, *f.*; (*Her.*) armoiries, *f.pl.*
achieving [ə'tʃi:vin], *n.* Accomplissement, *m.*; obtention, *f.* (d'un résultat).
Achilles [ə'kili:z]. Achille, *m. Achilles tendon*, tendon d'Achille, *m.*; *that is his Achilles heel*, c'est là son faible *or* son talon d'Achille.
aching ['eikin], *a.* Endolori, douloureux. *An aching heart*, un cœur dolent.
achromatic [ækro'mætik], *a.* (*Opt.*) Achromatique.
achromatism [ə'kroumətizm], *n.* Achromatisme, *m.* **achromatize**, *v.t.* Achromatiser.

achy ['eiki], *a.* Douloureux. *Rather achy*, un peu douloureux.
acicular [ə'sikjulə], *a.* Aciculaire.
acid ['æsid], *a.* Acide.—*n.* Acide, *m. Acid drops*, bonbons anglais *or* acidulés.
acidification [əsidifi'keiʃən], *n.* Acidification, *f.*
acidify [ə'sidifai], *v.t.* Acidifier.—*v.i.* S'acidifier. **acidimeter**, *n.* Acidimètre, *m.*
acidity [ə'siditi], *n.* Acidité, *f.* **acidly**, *adv.* Aigrement, avec acerbité. **acidulate**, *v.t.* Aciduler. **acidulous**, *a.* Acidulé.
acierage ['æsiəridʒ], *n.* Aciérage, *m.* **acierate**, *v.t.* Aciérer.
aciniform [ə'sinifɔ:m], *a.* Acineux. **acinus**, *n.* Acine, acinus, *m.*
ack-ack ['æk'æk], *n.* (*colloq.*) Défense anti-aérienne, *f.*
acknowledge [æk'nɔlidʒ], *v.t.* Reconnaître; avouer, confesser; accuser réception de (letters); répondre à. *I acknowledged receipt of his letter*, je lui ai accusé réception de sa lettre. **acknowledgment**, *n.* Reconnaissance, *f.*; aveu, *m.*; accusé de réception, *m.*; remerciements, *m.pl.*
acme ['ækmi], *n.* Le plus haut point; comble, summum, faîte, *m.*; apogée, *m.*
acne ['ækni], *n.* (*Med.*) Acné, *f.*
acock [ə'kɔk], *adv.* (Chapeau) sur l'oreille, en bataille.
acolyte ['ækolait], *n.* Acolyte, *m.*
aconite ['ækonait], *n.* (*Bot.*) Aconit, *m.*
acorn ['eikɔ:n], *n.* Gland, *m.* **acorn-shell**, *n.* (*Conch.*) Gland de mer, balane, *m.* **acorned**, *a.* (*Her.*) Glandé.
acotyledon [əkɔti'li:dən], *n.* (*Bot.*) Acotylédone, *f.* **acotyledonous**, *a.* Acotylédoné.
acoustic [ə'ku:stik], *a.* Acoustique. **acoustics**, *n.* Acoustique, *f.*
acquaint [ə'kweint], *v.t.* Informer (de); faire savoir à, faire part à. *To be acquainted with*, connaître, savoir; *to be intimately acquainted with someone*, être très lié avec quelqu'un; *to get acquainted with someone*, faire la connaissance de quelqu'un. **acquaintance**, *n.* Connaissance (de); personne de ma (sa etc.) connaissance, *f. To have a wide circle of acquaintances*, avoir beaucoup de relations; *to improve upon acquaintance*, gagner à être connu; *to make the acquaintance of*, faire connaissance avec; *to make his or her acquaintance*, faire sa connaissance. **acquainted**, *a.* Connu; instruit (de), familier (avec).
acquest [ə'kwest], *n.* (*Law*) Acquêt, *m.*
acquiesce [ækwi'es], *v.i.* Acquiescer (à); accéder (à). **acquiescence**, *n.* Acquiescement, *m.*; consentement, *m.* **acquiescent**, *a.* Résigné, soumis; consentant.
acquirable [ə'kwaiərəbl], *a.* Acquérable.
acquire [ə'kwaiə], *v.t.* Acquérir, obtenir, gagner. *An acquired taste*, un goût acquis, *m.* **acquirement**, *n.* Acquisition; connaissance, *f.*; (*pl.*) acquis, *m.pl.* or *sing.* **acquirer**, *n.* Acquéreur, *m.*, acquéreuse, *f.*
acquisition [ækwi'ziʃən], *n.* Acquisition, *f.*
acquisitive [ə'kwizitiv], *a.* Porté à acquérir, âpre au gain.
acquit [ə'kwit], *v.t.* Régler (une dette); absoudre, acquitter (un accusé); s'acquitter (d'un devoir). *To acquit oneself well*, se comporter bien, faire son devoir. **acquittal**, *n.* Acquittement, *m.* **acquittance**, *n.*

Acquittement, *m.*; décharge, quittance, *f.*;
(*Comm.*) acquit, *m.*
acre [ˈeikə], *n.* Arpent, *m.*, acre, *f.* (environ 40
ares). *God's acre*, le cimetière. **acreage**
[ˈeikəridʒ], *n.* Superficie, *f.*
acrid [ˈækrid], *a.* Âcre; (*fig.*) acerbe. **acridity**,
n. Âcreté, *f.*
acrimonious [ækriˈmouniəs], *a.* Acrimonieux.
acrimoniously, *adv.* Avec aigreur, avec
acrimonie.
acrimony [ˈækriməni], *n.* Acrimonie, aigreur, *f.*
acrobat [ˈækrəbæt], *n.* Acrobate.
acrobatic [ækroˈbætik], *a.* Acrobatique.
acrobatics, *n.* Acrobatie, *f.* **acrobatism**,
n. Acrobatisme, *m.*
acronychal or **acronycal** [əˈkrɔnikəl], *a.*
(*Astron.*) Acronyque.
acropolis [əˈkrɔpəlis], *n.* Acropole, *f.*
across [əˈkrɔs, əˈkrɔːs], *prep.* À travers, sur.
To come across (*something or someone*), rencontrer, tomber sur; (*pop.*) *to put it across
someone* (*at a game*), battre quelqu'un à plate
couture; *to swim across a river*, traverser une
rivière à la nage.—*adv.* À travers, en travers;
de l'autre côté. *When did you come across?*
quand avez-vous fait la traversée? *the distance across*, la distance en largeur.
acrostic [əˈkrɔstik], *n.* Acrostiche, *m.*
acroterium [ækroˈtiəriəm], *n.* Acrotère, *m.*
act [ækt], *n.* Acte, *m.*, loi, *f.*; action, *f.*; acte
(d'une pièce), *m.* *In the act*, sur le fait; *in
the act of doing it*, en train de le faire; *in the
very act*, en flagrant délit; *it is not the act of
an honest man*, ce n'est pas le fait d'un
honnête homme.—*v.t.* Jouer, représenter,
feindre, contrefaire; remplir (les fonctions
etc.).—*v.i.* Agir (en, sur, etc.); se conduire;
se comporter; opérer. *Please act as you think
best*, veuillez faire pour le mieux. **acting**, *n.*
(*Theat.*) Jeu, *m.*; (*fig.*) feinte, *f.* *His affection
is not sincere, it is mere acting*, son affection
est jouée, ce n'est qu'une feinte.—*a.* Qui
agit; (*Comm.*) gérant; (*taking the place of*)
suppléant. *Acting manager*, directeur gérant;
gérant provisoire, *m.* *Acting allowance*, indemnité de fonction, *f.*
actinic [ækˈtinik], *a.* Actinique.
action [ˈækʃən], *n.* Action, *f.*, fait; (*Law*)
procès; (*Mil.*) combat, *m.*, bataille, *f.* *Civil
action*, action au civil; *killed in action*, tué à
l'ennemi; *naval action*, combat naval; *the
action* (*of the play*) *takes place at London*, la
scène se passe à Londres; *to bring an action
against*, intenter une action à, poursuivre *or*
citer en justice; *to call into action*, mettre en
action, mettre en jeu, faire jouer, employer;
to come into action, entrer en jeu; *to go into
action*, aller au feu; *to take action*, agir,
prendre des mesures, intervenir. **actionable**,
a. Actionnable, sujet à procès.
Actaeon [ækˈtiːən]. Actéon, *m.*
activate [ˈæktiveit], *v.t.* Activer; rendre radio-
actif.
active [ˈæktiv], *a.* Actif, agile, alerte. *On
active service*, en campagne. (*Elec.*) *Active
cell*, élément chargé, *m.* **actively**, *adv.*
Activement.
activity [ækˈtiviti], *n.* Activité, *f.* *Sphere of
activity*, sphère d'action, *f.* (*pl.*) **activities**,
fonctions, occupations (of a person), *f.pl.*
actor [ˈæktə], *n.* Acteur, comédien, *m.*
actress, *n.* Actrice, comédienne, *f.*

actual [ˈæktjuəl], *a.* Réel, véritable, effectif;
positif. **actuality** [æktjuˈæliti], *n.* Réalité,
actualité, *f.* (*pl.*) **actualities**, conditions
réelles, actuelles, *f.pl.* **actualization**, *n.*
Réalisation, *f.* **actualize**, *v.t.* Réaliser.
actually, *adv.* Réellement, en effet, positivement, véritablement; à vrai dire. **actualness**
[REALITY].
actuarial [æktjuˈɛəriəl], *a.* Actuariel.
actuary [ˈæktjuəri], *n.* Actuaire, *m.* *Actuaries'
tables*, tables de mortalité, *f.pl.*
actuate [ˈæktjueit], *v.t.* Mettre en action;
pousser, animer. **actuation**, *n.* Mise en
action, *f.*
acuity [əˈkjuiti], *n.* Acuité, *f.*
aculeate [əˈkjuːliеit] or **aculeated**, *a.* (*Bot.*)
Aiguillonné, pointu, aculéiforme; (*fig.*)
piquant.
acumen [əˈkjuːmən], *n.* Finesse, pénétration,
f. **acuminate**, *a.* (*Bot.*) Acuminé.
acute [əˈkjuːt], *a.* Aigu, pointu, fin; (*fig.*)
violent, poignant; perçant, pénétrant.
acutely, *adv.* Vivement; avec finesse.
acuteness, *n.* Acuité; intensité; finesse,
pénétration, *f.*
adage [ˈædidʒ], *n.* Adage, proverbe, *m.*
Adam [ˈædəm]. Adam, *m.* (*Anat.*) *Adam's
apple*, pomme d'Adam, *f.*; *the old Adam*, le
vieil homme, le vieil Adam.
adamant [ˈædəmənt], *n.* Diamant, *m.*—*a.* Fort,
dur, inflexible, intransigeant. **adamantine**,
a. Adamantin, inflexible, indomptable.
adapt [əˈdæpt], *v.t.* Adapter, approprier,
ajuster (à). **adaptability** [ədæptəˈbiliti], *n.*
Faculté d'adaptation, souplesse, *f.* **adaptable**, *a.* Adaptable, qui peut s'adapter.
adaptation [ædæpˈteiʃən], *n.* Adaptation, *f.*
adapted, *a.* Approprié; adapté. **adapter**, *n.*
Qui adapte; (*Elec.*) raccord, *m.* (de lampe).
add [æd], *v.t.* Ajouter, joindre; additionner.
Added to which, en outre de quoi; *to add to*
(*joy, troubles, etc.*), ajouter à, accentuer,
rehausser, accroître; *to add up*, additionner;
s'accorder.
addendum [əˈdendəm], *n.* (*pl.* **addenda**)
Supplément, *m.*, addition, *f.*, appendice, *m.*
adder [ˈædə], *n.* Vipère, *f.* **adder's-tongue**,
n. Langue de serpent (plant), *f.* **adderwort**,
n. Bistorte, *f.*
addible [ˈædibl], *a.* Qui peut être ajouté,
additionnable.
addict (1) [ˈædikt], *n.* Personne adonnée à
(stupéfiants etc.).
addict (2) [əˈdikt], *v.t.* S'adonner, se livrer
(à). *To be addicted to*, s'adonner à, être
adonné à. **addictedness** or **addiction**, *n.*
Attachement, goût (pour), penchant (à), *m.*
adding-machine, *n.* Additionneuse, *f.*
addition [əˈdiʃən], *n.* Addition, *f.*; surcroît,
supplément, accroissement, *m.* *In addition
to*, outre, en plus de. **additional**, *a.* Additionnel, supplémentaire, de plus. **additionally**, *adv.* Par addition, en sus, de plus, en
outre.
addle [ædl], *a.* Couvi (of eggs); pourri; (*fig.*)
stérile.—*v.t.* Rendre couvi, corrompre.
addle-headed, *a.* À cerveau vide, écervelé,
à l'esprit brouillon.
address [əˈdres], *n.* Adresse; habileté, dextérité; allocution, *f.*, discours, *m.*; (*fig.*) abord,
m. *My present address*, mon adresse actuelle;
of good address, à l'air distingué; *to pay one's*

addresses to, faire la cour à, rechercher en mariage; *style of address,* titre, *m.*—*v.t.* Adresser (une lettre); adresser la parole à, aborder (quelqu'un). *To address oneself to a task,* entreprendre une tâche; *to address the ball* (*at golf*), viser la balle. **addressee** [ædre'si:], *n.* Destinataire. **addresser,** *n.* Expéditeur, pétitionnaire, *m. My addresser,* la personne qui me parle (*or* me parlait), mon interlocuteur, *m.* **addressograph,** *n.* Machine à adresser les circulaires, *f.*

adduce [ə'dju:s], *v.t.* Alléguer; apporter, avancer, produire. **adducible,** *a.* Qu'on peut avancer.

adduction [ə'dʌkʃən], *n.* Adduction; citation, *f.* **adductor,** *n.* (*Anat.*) Adducteur, *m.*

Adela ['ædilə]. Adèle, *f.*

Adelaide ['ædəleid]. Adélaïde, *f.*

ademption [ə'dempʃən], *n.* (*Law*) Ademption, révocation (d'un legs), *f.*

adenitis [ædə'naitis], *n.* Adénite, *f.* **adenoid,** *a.* Adénoïde.—*n.pl.* Adénite, *f.*; végétations, *f.pl.*

adept (1) [ə'dept], *a.* Adepte, habile, versé (dans).

adept (2) ['ædept], *n.* Adepte.

adequacy ['ædikwəsi] *or* **adequateness,** *n.* Juste proportion, suffisance, *f.* **adequate,** *a.* Proportionné, suffisant (à), compétent. **adequately,** *adv.* En juste proportion, suffisamment, convenablement.

adhere [əd'hiə], *v.i.* Adhérer, s'attacher, s'en tenir (à). **adherence,** *n.* Adhérence, *f.*, attachement, *m.* **adherent,** *n.* Adhérent, *m.* ***adherer,** *n.* Adhérent, partisan, *m.*

adhesion [əd'hi:ʒən], *n.* Adhésion, *f.* **adhesive,** *a.* Adhésif, tenace; visqueux, gommé, agglutinant. **adhesiveness,** *n.* Propriété d'adhérer; (*fig.*) ténacité, *f.*

adiabatic [ædiə'bætik], *a.* Adiabatique. **adiabatically,** *adv.* Adiabatiquement.

adiantum [ædi'æntəm], *n.* (*Bot.*) Adiante, *m.*

adiaphorous [ædi'æfərəs], *a.* Indifférent, neutre.

adieu [ə'dju:], *adv.* and *n.m.* Adieu. *To bid someone adieu,* faire ses adieux à quelqu'un.

adipose ['ædipous], *a.* Adipeux. **adiposity,** *n.* Adiposité, *f.*

adit ['ædit], *n.* (*Mining*) Galerie d'écoulement, *f.*; accès d'un lieu, *m.*

adjacency [ə'dʒeisənsi], *n.* Contiguïté, *f.*, voisinage, *m.* **adjacent,** *a.* Adjacent, contigu (à), avoisinant; (*Law*) jouxtant.

adjectival [ædʒək'taivəl], *a.* Comme adjectif. **adjectivally** *or* **adjectively,** *adv.* Adjectivement. **adjective** ['ædʒektiv], *a.* and *n.* Adjectif, *m.*

adjoin [ə'dʒɔin], *v.i.* Se toucher, être contigu. —*v.t.* Adjoindre, joindre; toucher, se joindre à. **adjoining,** *a.* Adjacent, avoisinant, contigu (à).

adjourn [ə'dʒə:n], *v.t.* Ajourner, différer, remettre.—*v.i.* S'ajourner, lever la séance. **adjournment,** *n.* Ajournement, *m.*; suspension, remise, *f.*

adjudge [ə'dʒʌdʒ], *v.t.* Adjuger; juger, condamner; (*fig.*) estimer. **adjudgment,** *n.* Jugement, *m.*, décision, *f.*

adjudicate [ə'dʒu:dikeit], *v.t.* Adjuger; décider, prononcer. **adjudication,** *n.* Jugement, *m.*; décision, *f.*, arrêt, *m.* **adjudicator,** *n.* Juge, *m.*, arbitre, *m.*

adjunct ['ædʒʌŋkt], *a.* Adjoint, accessoire.—*n.* Accessoire; adjoint; (*Gram.*) complément, *m.* **adjunction,** *n.* Adjonction, *f.* **adjunctive,** *a.* Accessoire.—*n.* Chose jointe, addition, *f.* **adjunctively,** *adv.* Par addition.

adjuration [ædʒu'reiʃən], *n.* Adjuration, *f.* **adjure,** *v.t.* Adjurer.

adjust [ə'dʒʌst], *v.t.* Ajuster, régler, arranger. **adjustable,** *a.* Réglable. **adjuster,** *n.* Ajusteur, metteur au point, *m.* **adjustment,** *n.* Ajustement, accommodement, arrangement, accord, *m.*; mise au point, *f.*, réglage, *m.*

adjutancy ['ædʒutənsi], *n.* Grade, *m.*, *or* fonctions, *f.pl.*, de capitaine adjudant major. **adjutant,** *n.* Capitaine adjudant major (dans un bataillon); le major de la garnison; (*Orn.*) marabout, *m.* **adjuvant,** *n.* Aide, *m.*, auxiliaire, *m.*; (*Med.*) adjuvant, *m.*

admeasurement [əd'meʒəmənt], *n.* Mesurage, *m.*; dimension, *f.*

administer [əd'ministə], *v.t.* Administrer, gérer, régir; faire prêter (an oath).—*v.i.* Subvenir, pourvoir (à). **administrate,** *v.t.* Administrer; régir. **administration** [ədminis'treiʃən], *n.* Administration, *f.*, gestion (of an estate etc.), *f.*, gouvernement, *m.* **administrative** [əd'ministrətiv], *a.* Administratif. **administratively,** *adv.* Administrativement. **administrator,** *n.* Administrateur, *m.*; (*Law*) curateur, *m.* **administratorship,** *n.* Fonctions d'administrateur, *f.pl.*; (*Law*) curatelle, *f.* **administratrix,** *n.* Administratrice, *f.*; (*Law*) curatrice, *f.*

admirable ['ædmərəbl], *a.* Admirable. **admirably,** *adv.* Admirablement, à ravir, à merveille.

admiral ['ædmərəl], *n.* Amiral; vaisseau amiral (flag-ship), *m. Rear-admiral,* contre-amiral; *vice-admiral,* vice-amiral. **admiralship,** *n.* Amiralat, *m.* **admiralty,** *n.* Amirauté, *f.*; Ministère de la Marine (in France), *m. Board of Admiralty,* conseil d'amirauté, *m.*; *Court of Admiralty,* tribunal maritime, *m. First Lord of the Admiralty,* ministre de la marine, *m.*

admiration [ædmi'reiʃən], *n.* Admiration, *f.*; étonnement, *m. To admiration,* à ravir.

admire [əd'maiə], *v.t.* Admirer; aimer; s'étonner de.—*v.i.* S'étonner. **admirer,** *n.* Admirateur, *m.*, admiratrice, *f.*; soupirant, *m.* **admiring,** *a.* Admiratif, d'admiration. **admiringly,** *adv.* Avec admiration.

admissibility [ədmisi'biliti], *n.* Admissibilité, *f.*; (*Law*) recevabilité, *f.* **admissible,** *a.* Admissible; (*Law*) recevable. **admissibly,** *adv.* D'une manière admissible. **admission** [əd'miʃən], *n.* Admission, entrée, *f.*; accès; aveu, *m.*, concession, *f.*; adjonction, *f. Admission ticket,* billet d'entrée, *m.*; *free admission,* entrée libre, *f.*; *on his own admission,* de son propre aveu.

admit [əd'mit], *v.t.* Admettre, laisser entrer; avouer, reconnaître; s'adjoindre; souffrir, tolérer.—*v.i. To admit of,* comporter, permettre; souffrir. **admittable,** *a.* Admissible. **admittance,** *n.* Accès, *m.*; admission, entrée, *f. No admittance,* on n'entre pas, défense d'entrer. **admittedly,** *adv.* De l'aveu général. *Admittedly she is ugly but I like her all the same,* il est vrai qu'elle est laide mais je l'aime quand même.

admix [əd′miks], *v.t.* Mêler, mélanger.—*v.i.* Se mélanger. **admixtion** or **admixture,** *n.* Mélange, *m.*

admonish [əd′mɔniʃ], *v.t.* Avertir, exhorter; reprendre, réprimander, admonester. **admonisher** or **admonitor,** *n.* Admoniteur, *m.*, admonitrice, *f.*

admonishment [əd′mɔniʃmənt] or **admonition** [ædmə′niʃən], *n.* Admonition, *f.*, avertissement, *m.*; remontrance, réprimande, *f.* **admonitive** or **admonitory,** *a.* D'avertissement; de remontrances.

adnate [′ædneit], *a.* (*Bot.*) Adné.

ado [ə′du:], *n.* Bruit, fracas, *m.*, façons, cérémonies, *f.pl.*, embarras, *m.*, peine, difficulté, *f.* *Much ado about nothing,* beaucoup de bruit pour rien; *to make no more ado,* ne faire ni une ni deux; *without any more ado,* sans plus de façons.

adolescence [ædo′lesəns] or **adolescency,** *n.* Adolescence, *f.* **adolescent,** *a.* and *n.* Adolescent, *m.*, adolescente, *f.*

Adolphus [ə′dɔlfəs]. Adolphe, *m.*

Adonis [ə′dounis], *n.* Adonis, *m.* **adonize** [′ædənaiz], *v.t.* Adoniser.—*v.i.* S'adoniser.

adopt [ə′dɔpt], *v.t.* Adopter. **adoptable,** *a.* Adoptable. **adopted** or **adoptive,** *a.* Adoptif, adopté, d'adoption. **adopter,** *n.* (*Law*) Adoptant, *m.* **adoption,** *n.* Adoption, *f.*

adorable [ə′dɔ:rəbl], *a.* Adorable. **adorableness,** *n.* Nature adorable, *f.* **adorably,** *adv.* D'une manière adorable, adorablement.

adoration [ædo′reiʃən], *n.* Adoration, *f.* **adore,** *v.t.* Adorer. **adorer,** *n.* Adorateur, *m.*, adoratrice, *f.* **adoringly,** *adv.* Avec adoration.

adorn [ə′dɔ:n], *v.t.* Orner; parer, embellir; (*fig.*) faire l'ornement de. *To adorn oneself,* se parer. **adornment,** *n.* Ornement, *m.*, parure, *f.*; ornementation, *f.*

adown [ə′daun] [DOWN (3)].

adrenal [ə′dri:nəl], *a.* Surrénal.—*n.pl.* Capsules surrénales, *f.pl.*

Adrian [′eidriən]. Adrien, *m.*

Adrianople [eidriə′noupl]. Andrinople, *f.*

Adriatic [eidri′ætik]. La mer Adriatique, *f.*, l'Adriatique, *f.*

adrift [ə′drift], *adv.* En or à la dérive; à l'abandon. *To go adrift,* aller à la dérive, (*fig.*) se laisser aller. *To turn oneself adrift from,* rompre avec; *to turn adrift,* laisser aller en dérive, abandonner.

adroit [ə′drɔit], *a.* Adroit, habile. **adroitly,** *adv.* Adroitement. **adroitness,** *n.* Adresse, dextérité, *f.*

adscititious [ædsi′tiʃəs], *a.* Surajouté, emprunté.

adscript [′ædskript], *a.* Adscrit.

adulate [′ædjuleit], *v.t.* Aduler. **adulation** [ædju′leiʃən], *n.* Adulation, *f.* **adulator,** *n.* Adulateur, *m.*, adulatrice, *f.* **adulatory,** *a.* Adulateur.

adult [ə′dʌlt or ′ædʌlt], *a.* and *n.* Adulte.

adulterate [ə′dʌltəreit], *v.t.* Adultérer, frelater, falsifier, sophistiquer; (*fig.*) altérer, corrompre.—*a.* Frelaté, falsifié, faux; adultéré.

adulteration [ədʌltə′reiʃən], *n.* Falsification, sophistication, *f.*, frelatage, *m.* **adulterer,** *n.* Frelateur, falsificateur, *m.* **adulterer,** *n.* Adultère, *m.* **adulteress,** *n.* (Femme)

adultère, *f.* **adulterine,** *a.* Adultérin; faux, contrefait. **adulterous,** *a.* Adultère; (*fig.*) altéré, faux. **adulterously,** *adv.* Par l'adultère. **adultery,** *n.* Adultère, *m.*

adumbrate [ə′dʌmbreit], *v.t.* Ébaucher, esquisser; faire pressentir.

adumbration [ædəm′breiʃən], *n.* Ébauche, esquisse, *f.*, pressentiment, *m.*, signes précurseurs, *m.pl.*

adust [ə′dʌst], *a.* Aduste, brûlé.

advance [əd′vɑ:ns], *v.t.* Avancer, faire avancer; élever, hausser, augmenter.—*v.i.* Avancer, s'avancer, se porter en avant. *To advance (in the service etc.),* arriver.—*n.* Mouvement en avant, *m.*; avance, *f.* (de fonds); avancement, progrès, *m.* *Any advance?* (*at auction*) qui dit mieux? *In advance,* d'avance; *to make advances,* faire des avances, faire les premiers pas; *to pay in advance,* payer d'avance. **advance-guard,** *n.* Avant-garde, *f.* **advance-sheets,** *n.pl.* (*Print.*) Bonnes feuilles, *f.pl.* **advanced,** *a.* Avancé. **advancement,** *n.* Avancement, progrès, *m.*; (*Comm.*) avance, *f.* **advancer,** *n.* Personne qui avance, *f.*

advantage [əd′vɑ:ntidʒ], *n.* Avantage, *m.*; profit, intérêt, *m.* *Advantage in, out,* (*Ten.*) avantage dedans, dehors. *To have the advantage,* avoir le dessus; *to his* or *her advantage,* à son avantage; *to show off to advantage,* faire valoir; *to take advantage of,* profiter de; *to take advantage of someone's kindness,* abuser de la bonté de quelqu'un; *to take unfair advantage of,* abuser de; *to the best advantage,* le plus avantageusement possible; *to turn to advantage,* mettre à profit, tirer parti de; *you have the advantage of me,* à qui ai-je l'honneur de parler?—*v.t.* Avantager, favoriser; servir à. **advantageous** [ædvən′teidʒəs], *a.* Avantageux (à or de). **advantageously,** *adv.* Avantageusement. **advantageousness,** *n.* Avantage, *m.*, utilité, *f.*

advent [′ædvənt], *n.* Venue, *f.*; (*Eccles.*) l'Avent, *m.* **Adventist,** *n.* Adventiste.

adventitious [ædven′tiʃəs], *a.* Adventice, fortuit. **adventitiously,** *adv.* Fortuitement.

adventure [əd′ventʃə], *n.* Aventure, *f.*, entreprise hasardeuse, *f.*; (*Comm.*) pacotille, *f.*—*v.t.* Aventurer, hasarder.—*v.i.* S'aventurer, se hasarder. **adventurer,** *n.* Aventurier, *m.* **adventuress,** *n.* Aventurière, *f.* **adventurous,** *a.* Aventureux, hardi. **adventurously,** *adv.* Aventureusement. **adventurousness,** *n.* Hardiesse, *f.*, esprit aventureux, *m.*

adverb [′ædvə:b], *n.* Adverbe, *m.* **adverbial,** *a.* Adverbial. **adverbially,** *adv.* Adverbialement.

adversary [′ædvəsəri], *n.* Adversaire, *m.*

adversative [əd′və:sətiv], *a.* Adversatif.

adverse [′ædvə:s], *a.* Adverse, contraire (à); défavorable. **adversely,** *adv.* D'une manière hostile, malheureusement. **adverseness,** *n.* Opposition; hostilité, *f.*

adversity [əd′və:siti], *n.* Adversité, *f.*

advert [əd′və:t], *v.i.* Faire allusion (à); parler (de). **advertence** or **advertency,** *n.* Attention, *f.*

advertise [′ædvətaiz], *v.t.* Annoncer, faire annoncer, afficher, faire de la publicité pour. **advertisement** [əd′və:tizmənt], *n.* Annonce (newspaper), publicité, *f.*, réclame (puff), *f.*;

avis, *m.* *Classified advertisements*, petites annonces, *f.pl.*

advertiser ['ædvətaize], *n.* Personne qui fait des annonces, *f.*; journal d'annonces, *m.* **advertising,** *n.* Publicité, réclame, *f.* *Advertising agency*, agence de publicité, *f.*

advice [əd'vais], *n.* Avis, conseil, *m.* *If you take my advice*, si vous m'en croyez; *piece of advice*, conseil, *m.*; *to take advice*, prendre conseil (de), consulter (un médecin etc.); *to take (a person's) advice*, suivre le conseil de. *Letter of advice*, (*Comm.*) lettre d'avis, *f.* **advice-boat,** *n.* Aviso, *m.*

advisable [əd'vaizəbl], *a.* Judicieux, convenable (pour *or* de); à conseiller, opportun. **advisableness** *or* **advisability,** *n.* Convenance, utilité, opportunité, *f.*

advise [əd'vaiz], *v.t.* Conseiller; donner avis (de); prévenir (de); annoncer. *Be advised by me*, suivez mon conseil, croyez-m'en; *ill-advised*, mal avisé; *to advise someone to do something*, conseiller à quelqu'un de faire quelque chose; *to keep someone constantly advised of*, tenir quelqu'un au courant de.— *v.i.* Délibérer, prendre conseil, consulter. **advisedly,** *adv.* Avec réflexion, de propos délibéré. **advisedness, n.* Prudence, circonspection, opportunité, *f.* **adviser,** *n.* Conseiller, *m.* **advisory,** *a.* Consultatif.

advocacy ['ædvəkəsi], *n.* Profession d'avocat, *f.*; défense, *f.*, plaidoyer, *m.* **advocate,** *n.* Avocat, défenseur; intercesseur, *m.*—*v.t.* Défendre, plaider; soutenir, appuyer, préconiser.

advowee [ædvau'i:], *n.* Collateur, *m.*, celui qui possède le droit suivant, *m.*

advowson [əd'vauzən], *n.* Droit de présenter à un bénéfice vacant; patronage, *m.*, collation, *f.*

adynamia [ædi'neimiə], *n.* (*Med.*) Adynamie, *f.*

adynamic [ædai'næmik], *a.* Adynamique.

adze [ædz], *n.* Herminette, doloire; aissette, *f.* —*v.t.* Entailler à l'herminette, doler.

Aegean [i:'dʒi:ən]. La mer Égée, *f.*

Aegeus ['i:dʒju:s]. Égée, *m.*

Aegina [i:'dʒainə]. Égine, *f.*

aegis ['i:dʒis], *n.* Égide, *f.*

Aegisthus [i:'dʒisθəs]. Égisthe, *m.*

Aeneas [i:'ni:əs]. Énée, *m.*

Aeneid ['i:ni:id], *n.* L'Énéide, *f.*

Aeolia [i:'ouliə]. L'Éolie, *f.*

aeolian [i:'ouliən], *a.* Éolien. *Aeolian harp*, harpe éolienne, *f.*

aeolic [i:'ɔlik], *a.* Éolique.

aeolipyle [i:'ɔlipail], *n.* Éolipile *or* éolipyle, *m.*

Aeolus ['i:ɔləs]. Éole, *m.*

aeon ['i:ən], *n.* Éternité, *f.*, éon, *m.*

aerate ['ɛəreit], *v.t.* Aérer; gazéifier. **aeration** [ɛə'reiʃən], *n.* Aération, *f.*

aerial ['ɛəriəl], *a.* Aérien.—*n.* Antenne, *f.*

aerie, aery, eyrie, *or* **eyry** ['ɛəri, 'iəri], *n.* Aire, *f.*

aeriform ['ɛərifɔ:m], *a.* Aériforme. **aerify,** *v.t.* Remplir d'air. **aerobatics** [ɛəro'bætiks], *n.pl.* Acrobaties aériennes, *f.pl.* **aerodrome** [ɛəro'droum], *n.* Aérodrome, *m.* **aerodynamic,** *a.* Aérodynamique. **aerodynamics,** *n.* Aérodynamique, *f.* **aero-engine** ['ɛəroendʒin], *n.* Aéromoteur, *m.*

aerofoil ['ɛərofɔil], *n.* Plan a profil d'aile, *m.*; voilure, *f.*

aerogram ['ɛərogræm], *n.* Radiogramme, *m.*; télégramme livré par avion, *m.* **aerograph,** *n.* Aérographe, *m.*

aerolite *or* **aerolith** ['ɛərolait, 'ɛəroliθ], *n.* Aérolithe, bolide, *m.*

aeronaut ['ɛərɔnɔ:t], *n.* Aéronaute. **aeronautic,** *a.* Aéronautique. **aeronautics,** *n.* Aéronautique, *f.*

aeroplane ['ɛəroplein], *n.* Aéroplane, avion, *m.* **aerostat,** *n.* Aérostat, *m.* **aerostatic,** *a.* Aérostatique. **aerostatics,** *n.* Aérostatique, *f.* **aerostation,** *n.* Aérostation, *f.*

aeruginous [iə'ru:dʒinəs], *a.* Érugineux.

Aeschylus [i:skiləs]. Eschyle, *m.*

Aesculapius [i:skju'leipiəs]. Esculape, *m.*

Aesop ['i:sɔp]. Ésope, *m.*

aesthete ['i:sθi:t], *n.* Esthète.

aesthetic [i:s'θetik] *or* **aesthetical,** *a.* Esthétique. **aesthetically,** *adv.* Esthétiquement. **aestheticism,** *n.* Esthétisme, *m.* **aesthetics,** *n.* Esthétique, *f.*

aestival [i:s'taivəl], *a.* Estival.

aether [ETHER].

afar [ə'fɑ:], *adv.* Loin, de loin, au loin. *Afar off*, au loin.

affability [æfə'biliti] *or* **affableness,** *n.* Affabilité, *f.*

affable ['æfəbl], *a.* Affable, doux, gracieux. **affably,** *adv.* Affablement, avec affabilité.

affair [ə'fɛə], *n.* Affaire, *f.*; affaire de cœur; (*fam.*) chose, *f.* *What a state of affairs!* C'est du propre!

affect [ə'fekt], *v.t.* Affecter; intéresser, toucher, émouvoir.—*n.* Phénomène affectif, *m.*

affectation [æfek'teiʃən] *or* **affectedness,** *n.* Affectation, *f.* **affected,** *a.* Disposé (pour etc.); affecté, précieux; maniéré, prétentieux (of style). **affectedly,** *adv.* Avec affectation. **affecting,** *a.* Touchant, émouvant, attendrissant. **affectingly,** *adv.* D'une manière touchante.

affection [ə'fekʃən], *n.* Affection, *f.*, amour, *m.*; goût, attachement, penchant, *m.*; maladie, *f.* **affectionate,** *a.* Affectueux, affectionné. **affectionately,** *adv.* Affectueusement. *Yours affectionately* (*between relatives or very intimate friends*), croyez à mes sentiments très affectueux, or votre affectionné.

affiance [ə'faiəns], *v.t.* Fiancer.—*n.* Fiançailles, *f.pl.* **affianced,** *a.* Fiancé, *m.*, fiancée, *f.*

affidavit [æfi'deivit], *n.* Déclaration par écrit sous serment, attestation, *f.*

affiliate [ə'filieit], *v.t.* Affilier; (*Law*) adopter (comme fils); attribuer, rattacher (à). *Affiliated firm*, filiale, *f.* **affiliation,** *n.* Affiliation; (*Law*) adoption (comme fils), *f.*

affinity [ə'finiti], *n.* Affinité, *f.*

affirm [ə'fə:m], *v.t.* Affirmer. **affirmable,** *a.* Qu'on peut affirmer.

affirmation [æfə'meiʃən], *n.* Affirmation, *f.* **affirmative** [ə'fə:mətiv], *a.* Affirmatif.—*n.* Affirmative, *f.* *In the affirmative*, affirmativement. **affirmatively,** *adv.* Affirmativement.

affirmer, *n.* Personne qui affirme, *f.*

affix (1) ['æfiks], *n.* Affixe, *m.*

affix (2) [ə'fiks], *v.t.* Apposer, attacher (à).

afflation [ə'fleiʃən], *n.* Action de souffler, *f.* **afflatus,** *n.* Souffle, *m.*, inspiration, *f.*

afflict [ə'flikt], *v.t.* Affliger (de); tourmenter. **afflicting,** *a.* Affligeant. **affliction,** *n.* Affliction, *f.*; calamité, *f.*, malheur, *m.* **afflictive,** *a.* Affligeant. **afflictively,** *adv.* D'une manière affligeante.

affluence ['æfluəns], *n.* Opulence, affluence, *f.*; abondance, *f.*, concours (de personnes etc.), *m.* **affluent,** *a.* Opulent, riche; affluent.—*n.* Affluent, *m.*

afflux ['æflʌks], *n.* Afflux, *m.*

afford [ə'fɔːd], *v.t.* Donner, fournir, accorder; avoir les moyens de, pouvoir. *He could not afford me a minute's interview,* il n'a pu me donner un moment d'entretien; *I cannot afford it,* mes moyens ne me le permettent pas; *I cannot afford the time,* je ne puis pas trouver le temps.

afforest [ə'fɔrist], *v.t.* Boiser; reboiser. **afforestation** [əfɔris'teiʃən], *n.* Boisement; reboisement, *m.*

affranchise [ə'fræntʃaiz], *v.t.* Affranchir. **affranchisement** [-tʃizmənt], *n.* Affranchissement, *m.*

affray [ə'frei], *n.* Bagarre, échauffourée, *f.*

affright [ə'frait], *v.t.* Effrayer.—*n.* Effroi, *m.*, épouvante, *f.* **affrightedly,** *adv.* Avec effroi.

affront [ə'frʌnt], *n.* Affront, *m.*, insulte, injure, *f.*, outrage, *m.* *To put an affront on,* faire un affront à.—*v.t.* Affronter, offenser, insulter; *rencontrer. **affronter,** *n.* Personne qui affronte, *f.*; insulteur, *m.*

affusion [ə'fjuːʒən], *n.* (*Med.*) Affusion, *f.*

Afghanistan [æf'gænistɑːn]. L'Afghanistan, *m.*

afield [ə'fiːld], *adv.* Aux champs, à la campagne. *To go far afield,* aller très loin.

afire [ə'faiə], *adv.* En feu.

aflame [ə'fleim], *adv.* En flammes.

afloat [ə'flout], *adv.* À flot; (*fig.*) en circulation. *To set a ship afloat,* mettre un vaisseau à l'eau.

afoot [ə'fut], *adv.* À pied; en marche, en route; (*fig.*) sur pied; en train. *There's something afoot,* il se prépare quelque chose.

afore [ə'fɔː], *adv.* Précédemment, auparavant; par devant. **aforementioned,** *a.* Mentionné plus haut, susdit, précité. **aforesaid,** *a.* Susdit, ledit, *m.*, ladite, *f.*, susnommé. **aforethought,** *a. With malice aforethought,* avec intention criminelle.

afraid [ə'freid], *a.* Effrayé, pris de peur. *I am afraid not,* je crains que non; *I am afraid she's gone,* je crains bien qu'elle ne soit partie; *to be afraid of,* avoir peur de.

afreet or **afrete** ['æfriːt], *n.* Afrite, *m.*

afresh [ə'freʃ], *adv.* De nouveau, de plus belle.

Africa ['æfrikə]. L'Afrique, *f.*

African ['æfrikən], *a.* Africain, d'Afrique.—*n.* Africain, *m.*, Africaine, *f.*

Afrikander, *n.* Natif de l'Afrique du sud et de souche hollandaise, Afrikander, *m.*

aft [ɑːft], *adv.* (*Naut.*) À l'arrière.—*a.* Arrière, de l'arrière.

after ['ɑːftə], *prep.* Après; sur, à la suite de; selon, d'après. *After all,* après tout, aussi bien; *after it was done,* après coup; *one after another,* à la suite l'un de l'autre. *What are you after?* Que cherchez-vous? *After Raphael,* d'après Raphaël.—*adv.* Après, d'après, ensuite. *Soon after,* bientôt après. —*a.* Subséquent, ultérieur, futur; arrière.— *conj.* Après que. **after-ages,** *n.pl.* Postérité,

f. **afterbirth,** *n.* Délivre, *m.*; (*Law*) naissance posthume, *f.* **afterclap,** *n.* Contre-coup, *m.* **aftercrop,** *n.* Seconde récolte, *f.*; regain, *m.* **after-effects,** *n.pl.* Suites, *f.pl.*, répercussion, *f.*; reliquat, *m.* (d'une maladie). **after-game,** *n.* Revanche, *f.* **afterglow,** *n.* Derniers reflets, *m.pl.*; incandescence résiduelle, *f.* **after-grass,** *n.* Regain, *m.* **after-life,** *n.* Suite de la vie, *f. In after-life,* plus tard dans la vie. **aftermath,** *n.* Regain, *m.*; (*fig.*) suites, *f.pl. The aftermath of war,* les répercussions de la guerre, *f.pl.* **afternoon,** *n.* Après-midi, *m.* or *f.* **after-pains,** *n.pl.* Douleurs qui suivent l'accouchement, *f.pl.* **afterpiece,** *n.* Divertissement, *m.* **afterthought** [-θɔːt], *n.* Arrière-pensée, réflexion après coup, *f.* **afterward** [-wəd] or **afterwards,** *adv.* Après, ensuite, plus tard. **afterwit,** *n.* Esprit de l'escalier, *m.*

aga ['eigə, 'ɑːgə], *n.* (*Turkish*) Aga, *m.*

again [ə'gein], *adv.* Encore; encore une fois, de nouveau. *Again and again,* maintes et maintes fois, à plusieurs reprises; *as large again,* deux fois aussi grand; *as much again,* encore autant; *never again,* jamais plus; *then again,* d'un autre côté; *to find again,* retrouver; *to see again,* revoir.

against [ə'geinst], *prep.* Contre; vis-à-vis; vers; pour. *As against,* comparé à; *against my return,* en prévision de mon retour; *against that,* en revanche, par contre; (*fam.*) *he is up against it,* il a la déveine; il est dans la purée; *over against,* vis à vis de, en face de.

agami ['ægəmi], *n.* (*Orn.*) Agami, oiseau trompette, *m.*

agamous ['ægəməs], *a.* (*Bot.*) Agame.

agape (1) [ə'geip], *adv.* Bouché bée. **agape** (2) ['ægəpi], *n.* (*pl.* **agapae**) Agape, *f.*

agaric ['ægərik], *n.* (*Bot.*) Agaric, *m.*

agate ['ægeit], *n.* Agate, *f.*

Agatha ['ægəθə]. Agathe, *f.*

agave [ə'geivi], *n.* (*Bot.*) Agave, agavé, *m.*

age [eidʒ], *n.* Âge, *m.*; époque, *f. Of age,* majeur; *to come of age,* atteindre sa majorité; *old age,* la vieillesse; *to be of an age to,* être d'âge (à); *under age,* mineur. *Golden age,* âge d'or; *Middle Ages,* moyen âge; *Stone Age,* âge de pierre.—*v.i.*, *v.t.* Vieillir. **aged,** *a.* Vieux, âgé. *Middle-aged,* entre deux âges; *the aged,* les vieillards, *m.pl.* **ageless,** *a.* Toujours jeune.

agency ['eidʒensi], *n.* Action, entremise; (*Comm.*) agence, *f. Through your agency,* par votre intermédiaire. *Travel agency,* agence de voyages, *f.*

agenda [ə'dʒendə], *n.* Ordre du jour; agenda, *m.*

agent ['eidʒənt], *n.* Représentant, agent, mandataire, *m. I am a free agent,* j'ai mon libre arbitre.

Agesilaus [ədʒesi'leiəs]. Agésilas, *m.*

agglomerate [ə'glɔməreit], *v.t.* Agglomérer. —*v.i.* S'agglomérer.—*a.* Aggloméré. **agglomeration,** *n.* Agglomération, *f.*

agglutinate [ə'gluːtineit], *v.t.* Agglutiner.— *v.i.* S'agglutiner. **agglutination,** *n.* Agglutination, *f.* **agglutinative,** *a.* Agglutinatif.

aggrandize ['ægrəndaiz], *v.t.* Agrandir. **aggrandizement** [ə'grændizmənt], *n.* Agrandissement, *m.*

aggravate ['ægrəveit], *v.t.* Aggraver; exagérer; (*colloq.*) agacer, pousser à bout, exaspérer. **aggravation,** *n.* Aggravation; circonstance aggravante, *f.*, agacement, *m.*
aggregate ['ægrigeit], *v.t.* Rassembler.—*a.* Collectif, global, réuni.—*n.* Masse, *f.*; ensemble, *m.*, somme totale, *f.*; (*Chem. etc.*) agrégat, *m.* *In the aggregate,* en somme, dans l'ensemble. **aggregately,** *adv.* En masse, collectivement. **aggregation,** *n.* Agrégation, *f.*, assemblage, *m.* **aggregative,** *a.* Agrégatif.
aggression [ə'greʃən], *n.* Agression, *f.*
aggressive [ə'gresiv], *a.* Agressif. **aggressiveness,** *n.* Caractère agressif, *m.* **aggressor,** *n.* Agresseur, *m.*
aggrieve [ə'griːv], *v.t.* Chagriner, affliger; blesser, léser.
aghast [ə'gɑːst], *a.* Consterné, ébahi, médusé, tout pantois.
agile ['ædʒail], *a.* Agile, leste. **agility** [ə'dʒiliti], *n.* Agilité, *f.*
Agincourt ['ædʒinkɔːt]. Azincourt, *m.*
agio ['ædʒio], *n.* Prix du change, agio, *m.*
agiotage ['ædʒətidʒ], *n.* Agiotage, *m.*
agitate ['ædʒiteit], *v.t.* Agiter, exciter; remuer, troubler; faire de l'agitation. **agitation,** *n.* Agitation; discussion, *f.*, examen, *m.* **agitator,** *n.* Agitateur; meneur, *m.*
Aglaia [ə'glaiə]. Aglaé, *f.*
aglet ['æglit] or **aiglet,** *n.* Aiguillette, *f.*; chaton, *m.* (de coudre, saule, etc.).
aglow [ə'glou], *a.* Enflammé, resplendissant.
agnail ['ægneil], *n.* Envie, *f.*
agnate ['ægneit], *a.* and *n.* Agnat, *m.* **agnatic,** *a.* Agnatique. **agnation,** *n.* Agnation, *f.*
Agnes ['ægnəs]. Agnès, *f.*
agnomen [æg'noumən], *n.* Surnom, *m.*
agnostic [æg'nɔstik], *a.* and *n.* Agnosticiste, *m.* **agnosticism,** *n.* Agnosticisme, *m.*
ago [ə'gou], *adv.* Passé, il y a. *How long ago is it?* combien de temps y a-t-il? *not long ago,* il n'y a pas longtemps; *two days ago,* il y a deux jours.
agog [ə'gɔg], *adv.* Excité, impatient, empressé; en train, en l'air. *To be all agog,* avoir la tête montée.
agoing [ə'gouiŋ], *adv.* En train, en mouvement.
agonize ['ægənaiz], *v.i.* Souffrir l'agonie, être au supplice.—*v.t.* Torturer, mettre au supplice. **agonizing,** *a.* Atroce, déchirant. **agonizingly,** *adv.* Avec angoisse. **agony,** *n.* Douleur, angoisse, *f.*, paroxysme, *m.* *To suffer agonies,* être au supplice.
agora ['ægərə], *n.* (*Gr. Ant.*) Agora, *f.*
agouti [ə'guːti], *n.* Agouti (rodent), *m.*
agrarian [ə'greəriən], *a.* Agraire.
agree [ə'griː], *v.i.* S'accorder (à or avec); être d'accord; consentir (à); convenir (de); être conforme (à). *I agree with you there,* je suis de votre avis là-dessus; *wine does not agree with me,* le vin ne me réussit pas.—*v.t.* Faire accorder (un compte). **agreeable,** *a.* Agréable, aimable; conforme (à); consentant. *I am agreeable,* je veux bien. **agreeableness,** *n.* Agrément, *m.*, amabilité, *f.*; conformité, *f.* **agreeably,** *adv.* Agréablement; conformément (à). **agreed,** *a.* Convenu, d'accord. *Are you agreed?* êtes-vous d'accord? *It's agreed,* c'est entendu, c'est convenu; *that is*

agreed on by all, tout le monde en convient. **agreement,** *n.* Accord, *m.*; convention, *f.*, contrat, pacte, marché, *m.*; conformité, *f.* *To come to an agreement,* se mettre d'accord; *do you confirm the agreement?* confirmez-vous l'accord?
agricultural [ægri'kʌltʃurəl], *a.* Agricole, d'agriculture. *Agricultural college,* école d'agriculture, *f.*
agriculture ['ægrikʌltʃə], *n.* Agriculture, *f.* **agriculturist,** *n.* Agriculteur, agronome, *m.*
agrimony ['ægriməni], *n.* Aigremoine, *f.* *Hemp agrimony,* eupatoire, *f.*; chanvre d'eau, *m.*
agronomy [ə'grɔnəmi], *n.* Agronomie, *f.*
aground [ə'graund], *adv.* Échoué; à terre. *To run aground,* s'échouer, échouer; *to run (a ship) aground,* échouer, faire échouer.
ague ['eigjuː], *n.* Fièvre intermittente, *f.* **aguish,** *a.* Fiévreux, fébrile; paludéen.
ah! [ɑː], *int.* Ah! hélas!
aha! [ɑ'hɑː], *int.* Ah ah!
ahead [ə'hed], *adv.* En avant; (*fig.*) en tête. *Go ahead!* en avant! Continue! Vas-y! *to get ahead of,* gagner l'avant de, devancer; *to look ahead,* penser à l'avenir.
ahem! [ə'hem], *int.* Hom! hem!
ahoy! [ə'hɔi], *int.* Ho! holà! *Ship ahoy!* ohé du navire!
ahull [ə'hʌl], *adv.* À sec de voiles, à la cape sèche.
ai ['ɑːiː], *n.* Aï (sloth), paresseux, *m.*
aid [eid], *v.t.* Aider, assister; secourir. *To aid each other,* s'entr'aider.—*n.* Aide, assistance, *f.*; secours, concours; subside, *m.* *With the aid of,* à l'aide de.
aide-de-camp ['eiddə'kɑ̃], *n.* Aide de camp, *m.*
aider ['eidə], *n.* Aide, *m.f.* **aidless,** *a.* Sans aide, sans secours.
aigrette ['eigret], *n.* Aigrette, *f.*
aiguille ['eigwiːl], *n.* Aiguille, *f.* (of mountain).
ail [eil], *v.t.* Faire mal à; chagriner. *What ails him?* qu'est-ce qu'il a?—*v.i.* Être souffrant.
aileron ['eilərən], *n.* Aileron, *m.*
ailing ['eiliŋ], *a.* Souffrant, indisposé, mal portant.
ailment, *n.* Mal, malaise, *m.*, indisposition, *f.*
aim [eim], *v.t.* Viser; pointer, lancer (a blow etc.).—*v.i.* Viser (à); aspirer (à); avoir pour but (de).—*n.* Point de mire, but, objet, dessein, *m.*; visée, *f.* *To miss one's aim,* manquer son coup; *to take aim at,* viser, coucher en joue. **aimless,** *a.* Sans but, sans objet.
ain't [eint] (*pop.*) = *am not, is not, are not.*
air [ɛə], *n.* Air, *m.*; vent, *m.*, brise, *f.*; (*fig.*) mine, expression, *f.* *Breath of air,* souffle de vent, *m.*, *foul air,* air vicié; *fresh air,* air pur; *in the air,* en l'air; *in the open air,* en plein air; *it's all in the air,* il n'y a rien de décidé; *there's something in the air,* il se trame quelque chose; *to build castles in the air,* faire des châteaux en Espagne; *to give oneself airs,* se donner des airs; *to give oneself an air of,* se donner un air de; *to take the air or to go out in the open air,* prendre l'air; *on the air,* qui radiodiffuse *or* radiodiffusé.—*v.t.* Aérer, donner de l'air à, mettre à l'air; sécher. *This linen must be aired,* il faut mettre ce linge à l'air; *to air a room,* aérer une pièce; *to air oneself,* prendre l'air. **air-balloon,** *n.* Ballon aérostatique, *m.* **air-bladder,** *n.* Vessie natatoire, *f.* **airborne,** *a.* (*Mil.*)

Aéroporté (of troops). **air-bump,** n. Trou d'air, m. **air-conditioned,** a. Climatisé. **air-conditioning,** n. Climatisation, f. **air-cooling,** n. Refroidissement par air, m. **aircraft,** n. Avion, m.; les avions, m.pl. **air-crew,** n. Équipage, m. (d'avion). **air-display,** n. Meeting aérien, m. **airfield,** n. Terrain d'aviation, m. **air-force,** n. Aviation militaire, f. **air-gun,** n. Fusil à vent, m. **air-hole,** n. Aspirail; (of a furnace) évent, m. **air-hostess,** n. Hôtesse de l'air, f. **air-inlet,** n. Prise d'air, f. **airless,** a. Renfermé, privé d'air. **airlift,** n. Pont aérien, m. **air-line,** n. Ligne aérienne, f. **air-liner,** n. Avion de ligne, m. **air-lock,** n. Écluse à air, f., sas, m.; (in pipe) bouchon d'air, m., poche d'air, f. **air-mail,** n. Poste aérienne, f. **airman,** n. Aviateur, m. **air-mattress,** n. Matelas à air, m. **airplane** [AEROPLANE]. **air-pocket,** n. (Av.) Trou d'air, m. **airport,** n. Aéroport, m. **air-pump,** n. Machine pneumatique, pompe à air, f. **air-scoop,** n. (Av.) Prise d'air, f. **air-shaft,** n. Puits d'aérage, m. **airship,** n. Dirigeable, m. **airsickness,** n. Mal de l'air, m. **airstrip,** n. Terrain d'atterrissage, m. **airtight,** a. Imperméable à l'air, hermétique. **airworthy,** a. Navigable. **airily,** adv. Allègrement, légèrement. **airiness,** n. Situation aérée; (fig.) légèreté, vivacité, désinvolture, f. **airing,** n. Aérage, m., ventilation, exposition à l'air, f., éventage, m.; promenade, f. To take an airing, prendre l'air, faire une promenade. **airy,** a. Ouvert à l'air; aérien, aéré; (fig.) léger, dégagé, gai, enjoué, insouciant. Airy words, paroles en l'air, f.pl.

aisle [ail], n. Bas-côté, m., nef latérale, f. **aisled,** a. À bas-côtés.

ait [eit], n. Îlot, m.

aitch [eitʃ], n. La lettre 'h'. To drop one's aitches, ne pas aspirer les h; ne pas appartenir aux hautes classes.

aitchbone ['eitʃboun], n. Culotte, f., or tranche, f., dans la culotte (de bœuf).

ajar [ə'dʒɑ:], a. Entr'ouvert, entrebâillé.

akimbo [ə'kimbou], adv. Appuyé sur la hanche. With one's arms akimbo, les poings sur les hanches.

akin [ə'kin], a. Allié (à); parent (de); (fig.) qui a rapport (avec).

alabaster ['æləbɑ:stə], n. Albâtre, m.—a. D'albâtre.

alack! [ə'læk], int. Hélas!

alacrity [ə'lækriti], n. Alacrité, f., empressement, m., promptitude, f.

Alan, Allan or **Allen** ['ælən]. Alain, m.

alarm [ə'lɑ:m], n. Alarme, alerte, f.; (Fenc.); appel, m. (du pied); réveil (clock), m. (Theat.) Alarms and excursions, alertes et échauffourées, f.pl.; false alarm, fausse alerte; to give the alarm, donner l'éveil; to take alarm, s'alarmer.—v.t. Alarmer; effrayer, faire peur à. Don't be alarmed, ne craignez rien, ne vous alarmez pas. **alarm-bell,** n. Cloche d'alarme, f., tocsin, m. **alarm-clock,** n. Réveille-matin, m. **alarm-gun,** n. Canon d'alarme, m. **alarming,** a. Alarmant. **alarmingly,** adv. D'une manière alarmante. **alarmist,** n. Alarmiste, m. or f. **alarum,** n. Réveille-matin, m.

alas! [ə'lɑ:s], int. Hélas!

alb ['ælb], n. Aube (priest's vestment), f.

Alba ['ælbə]. Albe, f.

Albania [æl'beiniə]. L'Albanie, f. **Albanian,** a. and n. Albanais.

albatross ['ælbətrɔs], n. Albatros, m.

albeit [ɔ:l'bi:it], conj. Quoique, bien que (and subj.).

albescent [æl'besənt], a. Blanchissant, pâlissant. **albinism,** n. Albinisme, m. **albino** [æl'bi:nou], n. Albinos, m. or f.

album ['ælbəm], n. Album, m.

albumen [æl'bju:men], n. Albumen, m.; blanc d'œuf, m.; albumine, f. **albumin,** n. Albumine, f. **albuminoid,** a. and n. Albuminoïde, m. **albuminous,** a. Albumineux.

albuminuria [ælbjumin'juəriə], n. Albuminurie, f.

alburnum [æl'bə:nəm], n. Aubier, m.

alcaic [æl'keiik], a. Alcaïque.

alchemic [æl'kemik] or **alchemical,** a. Alchimique. **alchemically,** adv. Par un procédé alchimique.

alchemist ['ælkəmist], n. Alchimiste, m. **alchemistic** or **alchemistical,** a. D'alchimiste, alchimique. **alchemy,** n. Alchimie, f.

Alcibiades [ælsi'baiədi:z]. Alcibiade, m.

alcohol ['ælkəhɔl], n. Alcool, m. **alcoholate,** n. Alcoolat, m. **alcoholic,** a. and n. Alcoolique. **alcoholism,** n. Alcoolisme, m. **alcoholization,** n. Alcoolisation, f. **alcoholize,** v.t. Alcooliser. **alcoholometer,** n. Alcoolomètre, alcoomètre, m.

alcoran ['ælkɔrɑ:n, ælkɔ'rɑ:n], n. Le Coran or le Koran.

alcove ['ælkouv], n. Alcôve; niche, f., enfoncement, m.; (Hort.) berceau, m.

alcyon [HALCYON].

alder ['ɔ:ldə], n. Aune, vergne, m. Alder-grove, aunaie, f.

alderman ['ɔ:ldəmən], n. Conseiller municipal, alderman, échevin, m.

Alderney ['ɔ:ldəni]. Aurigny, m.

ale [eil], n. Ale, bière, f. Pale ale, bière blonde, f., pale-ale, m.; brown ale, bière brune, f. **ale-house,** n. Taverne, f. *ale-wife,** n. Cabaretière, f.

alee [ə'li:], adv. (Naut.) Sous le vent.

alembic [ə'lembik], n. Alambic, m.

Aleppo [ə'lepou]. Alep, m.

alert [ə'lə:t], a. Alerte, vigilant, éveillé.—n. Alerte, f. On the alert, sur le qui-vive. **alertness,** n. Vigilance, promptitude, prestesse, f.

Alexander [ælig'zɑ:ndə]. Alexandre, m.

Alexandretta [æligzɑ:n'dretə]. Alexandrette, f.

Alexandria [ælig'zɑ:ndriə]. Alexandrie, f. **alexandrine** [ælig'zændrin], n. (Pros.) Alexandrin, m.

alexipharmic [əleksi'fɑ:mik], a. Alexipharmaque, antivénéneux.

alfresco [æl'freskou], adv. En plein air.

alga ['ælgə], n. (pl. **algae** ['ældʒi]) (Bot.) Algue, f.

algebra ['ældʒəbrə], n. Algèbre, f. **algebraic** [ældʒə'breiik] or **algebraical,** a. Algébrique. **algebraically,** adv. Algébriquement. **algebraist,** n. Algébriste, m.

Algeria [æl'dʒiəriə]. L'Algérie, f. **Algerian,** a. and n. Algérien.

Algiers [æl'dʒiəz]. Alger, m.

alguazil [ælgwɑ'zil], n. Alguazil, m.

alias ['eiliæs], *n.* Nom d'emprunt *or* de rechange, *m.*—*adv.* Dit, autrement nommé, alias.
alibi ['ælibai], *n.* Alibi, *m.*
alidad ['ælidæd] *or* **alidade** [-deid], *n.* Alidade, *f.*
alien ['eiliən], *a.* Étranger (à); éloigné (de). —*n.* Étranger, *m.*, étrangère, *f.* **alienability,** *n.* Aliénabilité, *f.* **alienable,** *a.* Aliénable. **alienate,** *v.t.* Aliéner (de). **alienation,** *n.* Aliénation, *f.* **alienator,** *n.* Aliénateur, *m.*, aliénatrice, *f.* **alienee,** *n.* Aliénataire. **alienism,** *n.* Aliénisme, *m.* **alienist,** *n.* Aliéniste, *m.* or *f.*
aliform ['eilifɔ:m], *a.* Aliforme.
alight (1) [ə'lait], *a.* Allumé, embrasé. *The house is alight,* le feu est à la maison; *to set alight,* mettre le feu à.
alight (2) [ə'lait], *v.i.* Descendre; mettre pied à terre; s'abattre (of birds etc.); atterrir (of airmen) *or* amerrir (sur l'eau). **alighting,** *n.* Atterrissage *or* amerrissage, *m.*
align [ALINE].
alike [ə'laik], *adv.* Également; de même, de la même manière; à la fois.—*a.* Semblable, pareil. *To be alike,* se ressembler.
aliment ['ælimənt], *n.* Aliment, *m.* **alimental** [æli'mentəl], *a.* Nutritif. **alimentally,** *adv.* D'une manière nutritive. **alimentary,** *a.* Alimentaire. *Alimentary endowment,* pension alimentaire, *f.* **alimentation,** *n.* Alimentation, *f.*
alimony ['æliməni], *n.* Pension alimentaire, *f.*
aline *or* **align** [ə'lain], *v.t.* Aligner; dressser, dégauchir.—*v.i.* S'aligner. **alinement** *or* **alignment,** *n.* Alignement, *m.* *Out of alignment,* désaligné.
aliquot ['ælikwɔt], *a.* Aliquote.
alive [ə'laiv], *a.* En vie, vivant; vif, éveillé; au monde, de ce monde; animé, sensible (à). *Dead or alive,* mort ou vif; *look alive!* remuez-vous un peu! *man alive!* grand Dieu! *more dead than alive,* plus mort que vif; *no man alive,* personne au monde; *the best man alive,* le meilleur homme du monde; *to be alive with,* grouiller de, fourmiller de; *to be quite alive to the gravity of the situation,* comprendre toute la gravité de la situation; *to burn, bury,* or *flay alive,* brûler, enterrer, *or* écorcher vif; *to keep alive,* entretenir, aviver; *while alive,* de son vivant.
alkalescence [ælkə'lesəns], *n.* Alcalescence, *f.* **alkalescent,** *a.* Alcalescent. **alkali,** *n.* Alcali, *m.* **alkalify,** *v.t.* Alcaliser.—*v.i.* S'alcaliser. **alkalimetry,** *n.* Alcalimétrie, *f.* **alkaline,** *a.* Alcalin.—*n.* Substance alcaline *f.* **alkalization,** *n.* Alcalisation, *f.* **alkalize,** *v.t.* Alcaliser.
alkanet ['ælkənet], *n.* Orcanète, buglosse, *f.*
alkoran [ALCORAN].
all [ɔ:l], *a.* Tout, tous. *All hail,* salut! *all of you,* vous tous; *all the way,* tout le long du chemin; *all together,* tous (toutes) à la fois, ensemble; *for all that,* malgré cela; *it is all the same to me,* cela m'est égal; *one and all,* tous sans exception; *to go on all fours,* marcher à quatre pattes; *with all speed,* au plus vite, à toute vitesse.—*adv.* Tout, entièrement. *All at once,* tout à coup (suddenly), tout d'un coup (all at the same time); *all right,* très bien, c'est bien entendu; *all the better,* tant mieux; *fifteen all,* (Ten.)

quinze à, *or* quinze partout; *I am all for leaving,* je ne demande qu'à partir; *I don't know at all,* je n'en sais rien; *it's all right,* tout va bien; *not at all,* point du tout; *nothing at all,* rien du tout.—*n.* and *pron.* Tout, *m.* *Above all,* surtout; *all but,* presque; *all's well,* tout va bien; *if that be all,* s'il ne tient qu'à cela, si ce n'est que cela; *if that's all,* s'il ne tient qu'à cela; *my all,* tout mon avoir; *that is all,* voilà tout, c'est tout; *to stake one's all,* jouer son tout. **all-fours,** *n.* (*Cards*) Impériale, *f.* **all-powerful,** *a.* Tout-puissant. **all-round,** *a.* Complet, sur toute la ligne. **all-rounder,** *n.* Homme universel, *m.*
Allah ['ælɑ]. Allah, *m.*
allay [ə'lei], *v.t.* Apaiser, adoucir, calmer. **allayment,** *n.* Apaisement, adoucissement, *m.*
allegation [ælə'geiʃən], *n.* Allégation, *f.*
allege [ə'ledʒ], *v.t.* Alléguer, prétendre (*that, que*).
allegiance [ə'li:dʒəns], *f.* Fidélité; obéissance, *f.* *Oath of allegiance,* serment de fidélité, *m.*
allegorical [ælə'gɔrikəl], *a.* Allégorique. **allegorically,** *adv.* Allégoriquement. **allegorist,** *n.* Allégoriste, *m.* **allegorize,** *v.t.* Allégoriser.—*v.i.* Faire des allégories. **allegory** ['æləgəri], *n.* Allégorie, *f.*
allelujah [æli'lu:jə], *n.* and *int.* Alléluia, *m.*
allergic [ə'lə:dʒik], *a.* (*Med.*) Allergique. **allergy** ['ælədʒi], *n.* Allergie, *f.*
alleviate [ə'li:vieit], *v.t.* Alléger, soulager, adoucir. **alleviation,** *n.* Allégement, adoucissement, soulagement, *m.*
alley (1) ['æli], *n.* (In a town) ruelle, *f.*, (garden) allée, *f.* *Blind alley,* impasse, *f.*, cul de sac, *m.*
alley (2) [ALLY (2)].
All Fools' Day [ɔ:l'fu:lzdei], *n.* Le 1er avril.
alliaceous [æli'eiʃəs], *a.* (*Bot.*) Alliacé.
alliance [ə'laiəns], *n.* Alliance, *f.* *To enter into an alliance* (*with*), s'allier (avec). **allied,** *a.* Allié; parent, voisin (de).
alligation [æli'geiʃən], *n.* (*Arith.*) Alliage, *m.*, règle d'alliage, *f.*
alligator ['æligeitə], *n.* Alligator, caïman, *m.* *Alligator-pear* (*avocado*), avocat, *m.*
alliteration [əlitə'reiʃən], *n.* Allitération, *f.* **alliterative,** *a.* Allitératif.
allocate ['æləkeit], *v.t.* Allouer, assigner. **allocation,** *n.* Allocation, *f.*
allocution [ælo'kju:ʃən], *n.* Allocution, *f.*
allodial [ə'loudiəl], *a.* Allodial. **allodiality,** *n.* Allodialisme, *m.* **allodium,** *n.* Franc-alleu, *m.*
allonge [ə'lɔndʒ], *n.* Allonge; (*Fenc.*) botte, *f.*
allopathic [ælo'pæθik], *a.* Allopathique. **allopathically,** *adv.* Allopathiquement. **allopathist** [ə'lɔpəθist], *n.* Allopathe, *m.* **allopathy,** *n.* Allopathie, *f.*
allot [ə'lɔt], *v.t.* Assigner, donner en partage; répartir. **allotment,** *n.* Partage, lot, lotissement, *m.*, portion; distribution, *f.*; lopin de terre, jardin ouvrier, *m.* *Allotment letter,* lettre d'allocation, *f.*
allotropic [ælo'trɔpik], *a.* Allotropique. **allotropism,** *n.* Allotropisme, *m.* **allotropy** [ə'lɔtrəpi], *n.* Allotropie, *f.*
allow [ə'lau], *v.t.* Permettre, autoriser; accorder, allouer; admettre, reconnaître. *Allowing for,* eu égard à; *allow me,* permettez-moi, permettez; *I will not allow it,* je ne le

permettrai pas; *to allow for,* tenir compte de; *to allow oneself to,* se laisser; *to allow someone to do something,* permettre à quelqu'un de faire quelque chose. **allowable,** *a.* Permis, admissible, légitime. **allowance,** *n.* Pension, rente, *f.*; allocation; ration; remise, réduction; indulgence, indemnité, *f. Short allowance,* petite ration, ration réduite; *to be on short allowance,* être rationné; *to make allowance for,* avoir égard à, tenir compte de; *to put on short allowance,* rationner; *trade allowance,* remise, réduction, *f.,* rabais, *m.*
alloy (1) [ə'lɔi], *n.* Alliage, mélange, *m. There is no joy without alloy,* il n'y a pas de bonheur sans mélange.
alloy (2) [ə'lɔi], *v.t.* Allier; (*fig.*) altérer, diminuer, corrompre.
All Saints' Day [ɔ:l'seintsdei], *n.* (Jour de) la Toussaint, *m.* **All Souls' Day,** *n.* Jour des morts, *m.*
allspice ['ɔ:lspais], *n.* Piment, *m.,* poivron, *m.*
allude [ə'lju:d], *v.i.* Faire allusion (à).
allure [ə'ljuə], *v.t.* Amorcer, attirer, séduire, inviter (à). **allurement,** *n.* Amorce, *f.,* appât, charme, attrait, *m.* **alluring,** *a.* Attrayant, séduisant. **alluringly,** *adv.* D'une manière séduisante.
allusion [ə'lju:ʒən], *n.* Allusion, *f. In allusion to,* par allusion à. **allusive,** *a.* Allusif, plein d'allusions. **allusively,** *adv.* Par allusion.
alluvia [ə'lju:viə], *n.pl.* Terres d'alluvion, *f.pl.,* alluvion, *f.* **alluvial,** *a.* Alluvial, d'alluvion. **alluvium,** *n.* Alluvion, *f.*
ally (1) [ə'lai], *v.t.* Allier.—*v.i.* S'allier (à *or* avec. ['ælai], *n.* Alié, confédéré, *m.*
ally (2) [æli], *n.,* or **ally taw.** Calot, *m.,* grosse bille, *f.*
almagest ['ælmədʒest], *n.* Almageste, *m.*
almanac ['ɔ:lmənæk], *n.* Almanach, *m.*
almightiness [ɔ:l'maitinis], *n.* Toute-puissance, *f.* **almighty,** *a.* Tout-puissant. —*n.* Tout-Puissant, *m.*
almond ['ɑ:mənd], *n.* Amande, *f. Almond furnace,* fourneau d'affineur, *m.*; *burnt almond,* praline, *f.* **almond-tree,** *n.* Amandier, *m.* **almond-willow,** *n.* Saule blanc, *m.*
almoner ['ælmənə], *n.* Aumônier, *m.* **almonry,** *n.* Aumônerie, *f.*
almost ['ɔ:lmoust], *adv.* Presque, à peu près. *I almost fell,* j'ai failli tomber.
alms [ɑ:mz], *n.* Aumône, *f. To give alms,* faire l'aumône. **alms-deed,** *n.* Œuvre de charité, *f.* **alms-giving,** *n.* L'aumône, *f.* **alms-house,** *n.* Maison de retraite, *f.,* asile, *m.* **almsman,** *n.* Vieillard hospitalisé, *m.*
aloe ['ælou], *n.* Aloès, *m. Bitter aloes,* amer d'aloès, *m.* **aloetic** [ælo'etik], *a.* Aloétique. —*n.* Médicament aloétique, *m.*
aloft [ə'lɔft], *adv.* En haut, en l'air; (*Naut.*) dans la mâture.
alone [ə'loun], *a.* Seul, solitaire. *All alone,* tout seul; *he alone did it,* lui seul le fit; *let me alone,* laissez-moi tranquille; *let alone,* (*colloq.*) sans compter, à plus forte raison.
along [ə'lɔŋ], *adv.* Le long de. *All along* (time), tout le temps; (place) tout le long du chemin; *along with,* avec; *come along,* venez donc; *get along with you,* allez-vous-en, allez vous promener. **alongside,** *adv.* Bord à bord; bord à quai.—*prep.* À côté de.
aloof [ə'lu:f], *adv.* Au loin, (*Naut.*) au large; éloigné, à l'écart. *To keep aloof,* se tenir à

l'écart.—*a.* À l'écart, distant. **aloofness,** *n.* Attitude distante, *f.*
aloud [ə'laud], *adv.* À haute voix, haut.
alpaca [æl'pækə], *n.* Alpaga (fabric); alpaca (animal), *m.*
alpenstock ['ælpənstɔk], *n.* Bâton ferré, *m.*
alpha ['ælfə], *n.* Alpha; (*fig.*) commencement, *m.*
alphabet ['ælfəbet], *n.* Alphabet; abécédaire (child's book), *m.*
alphabetic [ælfə'betik] or **alphabetical,** *a.* Alphabétique. **alphabetically,** *adv.* Alphabétiquement.
Alpheus [æl'fi:əs]. Alphée, *m.*
Alphonso [æl'fɔnzou]. Alphonse, *m.*
alpine ['ælpain], *a.* Alpin; des Alpes, alpestre. **alpinist,** *n.* Alpiniste.
Alps [ælps]. Les Alpes, *f.pl.*
already [ɔ:l'redi], *adv.* Déjà.
Alsatian [æl'seiʃən], *n.* (dog) Chien-loup, *m.* —*a.* and *n.* Alsacien (de l'Alsace).
also ['ɔ:lsou], *adv.* Aussi, également. **also-ran,** *n.* Concurrent non placé, *m.*; non-valeur, *f.*
altar ['ɔ:ltə], *n.* Autel, *m. High altar,* maître-autel, *m.* **altar-cloth,** *n.* Nappe d'autel, *f.* **altar-piece,** *n.* Tableau d'autel, *m.,* retable, *m.* **altar-screen,** *n.* Retable, *m.*
alter ['ɔ:ltə], *v.t.* Changer, modifier; retoucher, corriger. *To alter one's mind,* changer d'avis or d'idée.—*v.i.* Changer, se changer. **alterable,** *a.* Variable.
alteration [ɔ:ltə'reiʃən], *n.* Changement, *m.,* modification, *f.*
alterative [ɔ:l'tərətiv], *a.* and *n.* (*Med.*) Altératif, altérant, *m.*
altercate ['ɔ:ltəkeit], *v.i.* Avoir une querelle, se quereller. **altercation,** *n.* Altercation, *f.,* dispute, *f.*
alternate (1) [ɔ:l'tə:nit], *a.* Alternatif; alternant; (*Geom.* etc.) alterne. *Alternate rhymes,* rimes croisées, *f.pl.*
alternate (2) ['ɔ:ltəneit], *v.t.* Alterner, faire alternativement.—*v.i.* Alterner; se succéder. *Alternating current,* courant alternatif, *m.* **alternately,** *adv.* Alternativement, tour à tour; comme autre solution.
alternation [ɔ:ltə'neiʃən], *n.* (*Geol.*) Alternance, *f.*
alternative [ɔ:l'tə:nətiv], *a.* Alternatif.—*n.* Alternative, *f.*; autre solution, *f. There is no alternative,* il n'y a pas le choix or pas d'autre solution. **alternatively,** *adv.* Alternativement, tour à tour. **alternator,** *n.* (*Elec.*) Alternateur, *m.*
although [ɔ:l'ðou], *conj.* Quoique, bien que (and *subj.*).
altimeter [æl'timitə], *n.* Altimètre, *m.*
altitude ['æltitju:d], *n.* Altitude, élévation, hauteur, *f.*
alto ['æltou], *n.* Alto, *m.*
altogether [ɔ:ltə'geðə], *adv.* Tout à fait, entièrement.
alto-relievo [æltouri'li:vou], *n.* Haut-relief, *m.*
altruism ['æltruizm], *n.* Altruisme, *m.* **altruist,** *n.* Altruiste. **altruistic,** *a.* Altruiste.
alum ['æləm], *n.* Alun, *m.* **alum-pit,** *n.* Alunière, *f.* **alum-works,** *n.* Fabrique d'alun, *f.*
alumina [æ'lju:minə], *n.* Alumine, *f.*
aluminium [ælju'minjəm], *n.* or (*Am.*) **aluminum** [æ'lu:minəm], *n.* Aluminium, *m.* **aluminous,** *a.* Alumineux.

alumnus [ə'lʌmnəs], *n.* (*pl.* **alumni**) Gradué d'une université).

alveolar ['æl'viːolə], *a.* Alvéolaire. **alveolus**, *n.* (*pl.* **alveoli**) Alvéole, *m.*

alvine ['ælvain], *a.* (*Med.*) Alvin.

always ['ɔːlwəz], *adv.* Toujours.

am [æm], *1st sing. pres. indic.* (Je) suis [BE].

amain [ə'mein], *adv.* Avec force, de toutes ses forces; (*Naut.*) tout, tout ensemble.

amalgam [ə'mælgəm], *n.* Amalgame, *m.* **amalgamate**, *v.t.* Amalgamer; fusionner (of companies).—*v.i.* S'amalgamer; fusionner (of companies). **amalgamation**, *n.* Amalgamation, *f.*; (*fig.*) amalgame, fusionnement, *m.*

amanuensis [əmænju'ensis], *n.* (*pl.* **amanuenses**) Secrétaire, *m.*

amaranth ['æmərænθ], *n.* Amarante, *f.* **amaranthine**, *a.* Amarante, d'amarante.

Amaryllis [æmə'rilis], *n.* Amaryllis, *f.*

amass [ə'mæs], *v.t.* Amasser.

amateur [æmə'tə: *or* 'æmətjuːə], *n.* Amateur, *m.* **amateurish**, *a.* D'amateur. **amateurism**, *n.* (*spt.*) Amateurisme, *m.*

amativeness ['æmətivnis], *n.* Amativité, *f.*

amatorial [æmə'tɔːriəl], *a.* D'amour.

amatory ['æmətəri], *a.* D'amour, amoureux.

amaurosis [æmɔː'rousis], *n.* Amaurose, goutte sereine, *f.*

amaze [ə'meiz], *v.t.* Étonner, confondre, stupéfier. *To be amazed*, s'étonner. **amazedly**, *adv.* Avec étonnement. **amazement** *or* **amazedness**, *n.* Étonnement, *m.*, stupeur, *f.*, stupéfaction, *f.* **amazing**, *a.* Étonnant, (*fam.*) renversant. **amazingly**, *adv.* Étonnamment.

Amazon ['æməzən]. L'Amazone, *m.*

amazon ['æməzən], *n.* Amazone, *f.* **amazonian** [æmə'zouniən], *a.* D'amazone; (*fig.*) comme une amazone, hardi.

ambages [æm'beidʒiːz], *n.pl.* Ambages, *f.pl.*, détours, *m.pl.*

ambassador [æm'bæsədə], *n.* Ambassadeur, *m.* **ambassadorial** [-'dɔːriəl], *a.* D'ambassadeur. **ambassadress**, *n.* Ambassadrice, *f.*

amber ['æmbə], *n.* Ambre, *m.*—*a.* D'ambre. *Amber light* (traffic), feu orange, *m.* **amber-coloured**, *a.* Ambré. **ambergris**, *n.* Ambre gris, *m.*

ambidexter [æmbi'dekstə], *a.* and *n.* Ambidextre. **ambidexterity**, *n.* Ambidextérité, *f.* **ambidextrous**, *a.* Ambidextre.

ambient ['æmbiənt], *a.* Ambiant.

ambiguity [æmbi'gjuːiti] *or* **ambiguousness**, *n.* Ambiguïté; équivoque, *f.* **ambiguous** [æm'bigjuəs], *a.* Ambigu; équivoque; douteux. **ambiguously**, *adv.* Ambigument, d'une manière équivoque.

ambit ['æmbit], *n.* Tour, circuit, *m.*; (*fig.*) étendue, portée, *f.*

ambition [æm'biʃən], *n.* Ambition, *f.* **ambitious**, *a.* Ambitieux. *To be ambitious of*, ambitionner. **ambitiously**, *adv.* Ambitieusement.

ambivalence [æmbi'veiləns], *n.* Ambivalence, *f.* **ambivalent**, *a.* Ambivalent.

amble [æmbl], *v.i.* Aller (à) l'amble (of horse); (*fig.*) trottiner, aller son chemin, déambuler. *To make a horse amble*, mettre un cheval à l'amble.—*n.* Amble, *m.*

ambler, *n.* Cheval *or* bidet d'amble, *m.*

amblyopia [æmbli'oupiə], *n.* Amblyopie, *f.*

Ambrose ['æmbrouz]. Ambroise, *m.*

ambrosia [æm'brouziə], *n.* Ambroisie, *f.* **ambrosial**, *a.* D'ambroisie.

ambs-ace ['æmzeis], *n.* Beset, ambesas, *m.*

ambulance ['æmbjuləns], *n.* Ambulance, *f.*; hôpital militaire, *m.* **ambulance-man**, *n.* Ambulancier, *m.* **ambulance-nurse**, *n.* Ambulancière, *f.* **ambulant**, *a.* Ambulant. **ambulate**, *v.i.* Déambuler. **ambulation**, *n.* Déambulation, *f.* **ambulatory**, *a.* Ambulatoire.—*n.* Bas-côté, préau, déambulatoire, *m.*

ambuscade [æmbəs'keid], *n.* Embuscade, *f.* *To lay an ambuscade for*, dresser une embuscade à.—*v.t.* Embusquer; mettre en embuscade.

ambush ['æmbuʃ], *n.* Embuscade, *f.*, guet-apens, *m.* *To lie in ambush*, se tenir en embuscade.—*v.t.* Embusquer.—*v.i.* S'embusquer.

Amelia [ə'miːliə]. Amélie, *f.*

ameliorate [ə'miːliəreit], *v.t.* Améliorer.—*v.i.* S'améliorer. **amelioration**, *n.* Amélioration, *f.* **ameliorative**, *a.* Améliorant, améliorateur. **ameliorator**, *a.* Amendement, engrais, *m.*

amen [ɑː'men], *int.* Amen, ainsi soit-il.

amenable [ə'miːnəbl], *a.* Responsable, comptable; docile, soumis, sujet (à). *To make someone amenable to reason*, faire entendre raison à quelqu'un. **amenability** *or* **amenableness**, *n.* Responsabilité; soumission, docilité, *f.*

amend [ə'mend], *v.t.* Amender, corriger; réformer.—*v.i.* S'amender, se corriger. **amendable**, *a.* Amendable. **amendment**, *n.* Modification, *f.*, amendement, *m.*, amélioration, *f.* **amends**, *n.pl.* Dédommagement, *m.*, compensation, réparation, *f.* *To make amends for*, dédommager de, faire réparation de.

amenity [ə'miːniti *or* ə'meniti,], *n.* Aménité, *f.*, agrément, *m.*

amentaceous [æmen'teiʃəs], *a.* Amentacé.

amerce [ə'məːs], *v.t.* Condamner à l'amende. **amercement**, *n.* Amende, *f.*

America [ə'merikə]. L'Amérique, *f.* *North America*, L'Amérique du Nord; *South America*, L'Amérique du Sud.

American [ə'merikən], *a.* Américain.—*n.* Américain, *m.*, Américaine, *f.* **Americanism**, *n.* Américanisme, *m.* **Americanize**, *v.t.* Américaniser, naturaliser américain.

amethyst ['æməθist], *n.* Améthyste, *f.* **amethystine** [æmə'θistain], *a.* D'améthyste.

amiability [eimjə'biliti] *or* **amiableness**, *n.* Amabilité, *f.* **amiable** ['eimjəbl], *a.* Aimable. **amiably**, *adv.* Aimablement, avec amabilité.

amianthus [æmi'ænθəs] *or* **amiant**, *n.* (*Min.*) Amiante, *m.*

amicability [æmikə'biliti] *or* **amicableness**, *n.* Nature amicale; concorde, *f.* **amicable**, *a.* Amical. *Amicable settlement*, arrangement à l'amiable, *m.* **amicably**, *adv.* Amicalement; à l'amiable.

amice ['æmis], *n.* Amict, *m.*, aumuce, *f.*

amid [ə'mid] *or* **amidst**, *prep.* Au milieu de; parmi. **amidships**, *adv.* (*Naut.*) Par le travers. *Helm amidships!* droite la barre! *or* zéro la barre!

amiss [ə'mis], *adv.* Mal, en mauvaise part; (unseasonably) mal à propos. *To do amiss,*

mal faire; *do not take amiss what I am going to tell you,* ne prenez pas en mauvaise part ce que je vais vous dire; *nothing comes amiss to him,* il s'arrange de tout.
amity ['æmiti], *n.* Amitié, *f.*
ammeter ['æmitə], *n.* Ampèremètre, *m.*
ammonia [ə'mouniə], *n.* Ammoniaque, *f.* **ammoniac** or **ammoniacal,** *a.* Ammoniac, ammoniacal. *Gum ammoniac,* gomme ammoniaque, *f.*
ammonite ['æmənait], *n.* Ammonite, *f.*
ammonium [ə'mouniəm], *n.* Ammonium, *m.*
ammunition [æmju'niʃən], *n.* Munitions de guerre; cartouches, *f.pl. Ammunition bread,* pain de munition, *m.*; *a round of ammunition,* une cartouche. **ammunition-wagon,** *n.* Caisson, *m.* **ammunition-pouch,** *n.* Cartouchière, giberne, *f.*
amnesia [æm'ni:ziə], *n.* Amnésie, *f.* **amnesic,** *a.* Amnésique.
amnesty ['æmnəsti], *n.* Amnistie, *f.*—*v.t.* Amnistier.
amnion ['æmniən], *n.* (*Anat.*) Amnios, *m.*
amniotic [-'ɔtik], *a.* Amniotique.
amoeba [ə'mi:bə], *n.* (*pl.* **-ae, -as**) Amibe, *f.* **amoebaean,** *a.* Amibien. **amoeboid,** *a.* Amiboïde.
amok [AMUCK].
amomum [ə'mouməm], *n.* Amome, *m.*
among [ə'mʌŋ] or **amongst,** *prep.* Entre, parmi; au milieu de, chez, avec. *Among other things,* entre autres choses; *among the French,* chez les Français; *from among,* d'entre, du milieu de; *one among a thousand,* un sur mille.
amoral [æ'mɔrəl], *a.* Amoral. **amoralism,** *n.* Amoralisme, *m.*
amorous ['æmərəs], *a.* Amoureux; porté à l'amour. **amorously,** *adv.* Amoureusement. **amorousness,** *n.* Tempérament amoureux, *m.*, tendance à l'amour, *f.*
amorphous [ə'mɔ:fəs], *a.* Amorphe. **amorphousness** or **amorphism,** *n.* Amorphie, *f.*
amortization [əmɔ:ti'zeiʃən] or **amortizement,** *n.* Amortissement, *m.* **amortize,** *v.t.* Amortir.
amount [ə'maunt], *n.* Montant, total, *m.*, somme, *f.*; quantité, *f.*; (*fig.*) valeur, *f.*; résultat, *m. To the amount of,* jusqu'à concurrence de. *Have you the right amount?* avez-vous votre compte?—*v.i.* S'élever, se monter (à); revenir (à), se réduire (à). *His argument amounts to this,* son argument se réduit à ceci; *that amounts to the same thing,* cela revient au même.
amour [ə'muə], *n.* Intrigue amoureuse, *f.*
ampere ['æmpεə], *n.* (*Elec.*) Ampère, *m.*
amphibia [æm'fibiə], *n.pl.* Amphibiens, *m.pl.* **amphibian,** *n.* Amphibie, *m.* **amphibious,** *a.* Amphibie. **amphibiousness,** *n.* Nature amphibie, *f.*
amphibological [æmfibɔ'lɔdʒikəl], *a.* Amphibologique. **amphibologically,** *adv.* Amphibologiquement. **amphibology** [-'bɔlədʒi], *n.* Amphibologie, *f.*
amphibrach ['æmfibræk], *n.* (*Pros.*) Amphibraque, *m.*
amphictyon [æm'fiktjən], *n.* Amphictyon, *m.* **amphictyonic** [-ti'ɔnik], *a.* Amphictyonique. **amphictyony,** *n.* Amphictyonie, *f.*
amphioxus [æmfi'ɔksəs], *n.* (*Ichth.*) Amphioxus, *m.*

amphisbaena [æmfis'bi:nə], *n.* Amphisbène, *m.*
amphitheatre [æmfi'θi:ətə], *n.* Amphithéâtre, *m.*
amphitheatrical [-θi'ætrikəl], *a.* Amphithéâtral, d'amphithéâtre.
Amphitryon [æm'fitriən]. Amphitryon, *m.*
amphora ['æmfərə], *n.* Amphore, *f.*
ample [æmpl], *a.* Ample, large, abondant, copieux; très suffisant. **ampleness,** *n.* Ampleur; grandeur, *f.*
amplification, *n.* Amplification, *f.*
amplifier ['æmplifaiə], *n.* (*Rad. Tel.*) Amplificateur, *m.*
amplify ['æmplifai], *v.t.* Amplifier; exagérer.
amplitude, *n.* Amplitude, étendue, largeur, *f.*
amply, *adv.* Amplement.
ampoule ['æmpu:l], *n.* (*Med.*) Ampoule, *f.*
ampulla [æm'pulə], *n.* (*Bot.*) Ampoule, *f.*
amputate ['æmpjuteit], *v.t.* Amputer. **amputation,** *n.* Amputation, *f.*
amuck [ə'mʌk] or **amock** or **amok,** *adv.* To *run amuck,* devenir fou furieux.
amulet ['æmjulit], *n.* Amulette, *f.*
amuse [ə'mju:z], *v.t.* Amuser, divertir. *To be amused at,* s'amuser *or* se divertir de. **amusement,** *n.* Amusement, divertissement, *m. Amusement park,* parc d'attractions, *m.* **amusing,** *a.* Amusant, divertissant. **amusingly,** *adv.* D'une manière amusante.
Amy ['eimi]. Aimée, *f.*
amygdalic [æmig'dælik], *a.* (*Chem.*) Amygdalin, fait d'amandes. **amygdalin,** *n.* Amygdalin, *m.* **amygdaloid,** *a.* and *n.* Amygdaloïde, *f.*
amylaceous [æmi'leiʃəs], *a.* (*Chem.*) Amylacé. **amyl,** *n.* Amyle, *m.* **amylene** [-'li:n], *n.* Amylène, *m.* **amyloid,** *a.* and *n.* Amyloïde, *f.*
an [æn], *indef. art.* Un, *m.*, une, *f.*—**conj.* Si.
ana ['ɑ:nə], *n.* Ana, *m.*
anabaptism [ænə'bæptizm], *n.* Anabaptisme, *m.* **anabaptist,** *n.* Anabaptiste, *m.* or *f.* **anabaptist** or **anabaptistical,** *a.* Des anabaptistes.
anachronism [ə'nækrənizm], *n.* Anachronisme, *m.*
anachronistic [-'nistik], *a.* Anachronique.
anacoluthon [ænəkə'lju:θɔn], *n.* Anacoluthe, *f.*
anaconda [ænə'kɔndə], *n.* Anaconda, eunecte, *m.*
Anacreon [ə'nækriən]. Anacréon, *m.*
Anacreontic [ænækri'ɔntik], *a.* Anacréontique. —*n.* Poème anacréontique, *m.*
anaemia [ə'ni:miə], *n.* Anémie, *f.* **anaemic,** *a.* Anémique.
anaesthesia [ænəs'θi:ziə], *n.* Anesthésie, *f.*
anaesthetic [-'θetik], *a.* and *n.* Anesthésique, *m.*
anaesthetist [ə'ni:sθətist], *n.* Anesthésiste.
anaesthetize [ə'ni:sθətaiz], *v.t.* Anesthésier.
anaglyph ['ænəglif], *n.* Anaglyphe, *m.* **anaglyphic** or **anaglyptic,** *a.* Anaglyptique.
anagoge or **anagogy** [ænə'goudʒi], *n.* Anagogie, *f.* **anagogical,** *a.* Anagogique.
anagram ['ænəgræm], *n.* Anagramme, *f.* **anagrammatical** [-grə'mætikəl], *a.* Anagrammatique. **anagrammatically,** *adv.* Par anagramme.
anagrammatist [-'græmətist], *n.* Anagrammatiste, *m.* **anagrammatize,** *v.t., v.i.* Anagrammatiser.
anal ['einəl], *a.* (*Anat.*) Anal.

analects ['ænəlekts] or **analecta**, *n.pl.* Analectes, *m.pl.*

analeptic [ænə'leptik], *a.* and *n.* Analeptique, *m.*

analgesia [ænæl'dʒi:ziə], *n.* Analgésie, analgie, *f.*

analogical [ænə'lɔdʒikəl], *a.* Analogique. **analogically**, *adv.* Analogiquement.

analogism [ə'nælədʒizm], *n.* (*Phil.*) Analogisme, *m.* **analogist**, *n.* Personne qui fait des analogies, *f.* **analogize**, *v.t.* Expliquer analogiquement.

analogous [ə'næləgəs], *a.* Analogue. **analogously**, *adv.* D'une manière analogue. **analogy** [ə'nælədʒi], *n.* Analogie, *f.*

analysable ['ænəlaizəbl], *a.* Analysable. **analyse**, *v.t.* Analyser, faire l'analyse de. **analyser**, *n.* Analyste, analyseur, *m.* **analysis** [ə'nælisis], *n.* Analyse, *f.* **analyst** ['ænəlist], *n.* Analyste, *m.* **analytic** or **analytical**, *a.* Analytique. **analytically**, *adv.* Analytiquement. **analytics**, *n.* Art de l'analyse, *m.*

anamorphosis [ænə'mɔ:fəsis], *n.* Anamorphose, *f.*; dégénérescence, *f.*

ananas [ə'neinəs, æ'nɑ:nəs] or **anana** [ə'nɑ:nə], *n.* Ananas, *m.*

anandrous [ə'nændrəs], *a.* (*Bot.*) Anandraire, anandre.

anapaest ['ænəpi:st], *n.* Anapeste, *m.* **anapaestic**, *a.* Anapestique.—*n.* Vers anapestique, *m.*

anaphora [ə'næfərə], *n.* Anaphore, *f.*

anarchic [ə'nɑ:kik] or **anarchical**, *a.* Anarchique. **anarchically**, *adv.* Anarchiquement. **anarchism** ['ænəkizm], *n.* Anarchisme, *m.* **anarchist**, *a.* and *n.* Anarchiste. **anarchy**, *n.* Anarchie, *f.*

anasarca ['ænə'sɑ:kə], *n.* (*Path.*) Anasarque, *f.* **anasarcous**, *a.* Hydropique.

Anastasius [ænə'steiʃiəs]. Anastase, *m.*

anastomose [ə'næstəmouz], *v.i.* S'anastomoser. **anastomosis**, *n.* Anastomose, *m.*

anastrophe [ə'næstrɔfi], *n.* (*Gram.*) Anastrophe, *f.*

anathema [ə'næθəmə], *n.* Anathème, *m.* **anathematize**, *v.t.* Anathématiser, frapper d'anathème; maudire.

Anatolia [ænə'touliə]. L'Anatolie, *f.*

anatomical [ænə'tɔmikəl], *a.* Anatomique. **anatomically**, *adv.* Anatomiquement. **anatomist** [ə'nætəmist], *n.* Anatomiste, *m.* **anatomize**, *v.t.* Anatomiser. **anatomy**, *n.* Anatomie, *f.*

ancestor ['ænsəstə], *n.* Aïeul, *m.* **ancestors**, *n.pl.* Ancêtres, pères, aïeux, *m.pl.*

ancestral [æn'sestrəl], *a.* D'ancêtres, de ses ancêtres; héréditaire.

ancestry ['ænsəstri], *n.* Ancêtres, *m.pl.*; race, origine, naissance, *f.*, lignage, *m.*

Anchises [æn'kaisi:z]. Anchise, *m.*

anchor ['æŋkə], *n.* Ancre, *f. Best bower anchor*, seconde ancre; *foul anchor*, ancre surjalée; *kedge anchor*, ancre à empenneler, ancre de toue; *sheet-anchor*, maîtresse ancre, (*fig.*) ancre de miséricorde; *small bower anchor*, ancre d'affourche; *spare anchor*, ancre de rechange; *to let go* (or *drop*) *the anchor*, mouiller l'ancre; *to ride at anchor*, être à l'ancre; *to weigh anchor*, lever l'ancre.—*v.i.* Ancrer, s'ancrer, jeter l'ancre, mouiller; (*fig.*) se fixer.—*v.t.* Mouiller, ancrer. **anchorage**,

n. Mouillage, ancrage, *m.*; retraite, *f.* (d'anachorète).

anchoret ['æŋkəret] or **anchorite**, *n.* Anachorète, ermite, *m.* **anchoretic**, *a.* Anachorétique.

anchovy [æn'tʃouvi or 'æntʃəvi], *n.* Anchois, *m. Anchovy sauce*, sauce aux anchois, *f.*

anchylose ['æŋkilouz], *v.i.* S'ankyloser.—*v.t.* Ankyloser.

anchylosis [æŋki'lousis], *n.* Ankylose, *f.*

ancient (1) ['einʃənt], *a.* Ancien; antique. *The ancient world*, le monde antique, *m.*—*n.* Ancien. *The Ancient of Days*, l'Ancien des jours, l'Éternel, *m.*

***ancient** (2) ['einʃənt], *n.* Enseigne, *m.*; (*Navy*) pavillon, *m.*, enseigne, *f.*

anciently ['einʃəntli], *adv.* Anciennement. **ancientness** or ***ancientry**, *n.* Ancienneté, *f.*

ancillary [æn'siləri], *a.* Ancillaire, subordonné, auxiliaire.

ancon ['æŋkən], *n.* (*pl.* **ancones**) (*Anat.*) Ancon, *m.*

Ancona [æn'kounə]. Ancône, *f.*

and [ænd], *conj.* Et. *And so on*, et ainsi de suite; *better and better*, de mieux en mieux; *carriage and pair*, voiture à deux chevaux, *f.*; *go and see*, allez voir.

Andalusia [ændə'lu:ziə]. L'Andalousie, *f.*

Andes ['ændi:z]. Les Andes, *f.pl.*

andiron ['ændaiən], *n.* Landier; chenet, *m.*

Andorra [æn'dɔrə]. Andorre, *f.*

Andrew ['ændru:]. André, *m.*

androgyne ['ændrədʒin], *n.* Androgyne, hermaphrodite, *m.* **androgynous** [æn'drɔdʒinəs], *a.* (*Bot.*) Androgyne; (*Zool.*) hermaphrodite.

Andromache [æn'drʌməki]. Andromaque, *f.*

Andromeda [æn'drɔmədə]. Andromède, *f.*

anecdote ['ænəkdout], *n.* Anecdote, *f.* **anecdotal**, *a.* Anecdotique. **anecdotist**, *n.* Anecdotier, *m.*

anemograph [ə'nemogræf], *n.* Anémographe, *m.*

anemometer [ænə'mɔmitəl], *n.* Anémomètre, *m.* **anemometry**, *n.* Anémométrie, *f.*

anemone [ə'neməni], *n.* Anémone, *f.*

anemoscope [ə'nemoskoup], *n.* Anémoscope, *m.*

***anent** [ə'nent], *prep.* Touchant, sur, à propos de.

aneroid ['ænərɔid], *a.* and *n.* Anéroïde, *m.*

aneurism ['ænjurizm], *n.* Anévrisme, *m.* **aneurismal** [ænju'rizməl], *a.* Anévrismal.

anew [ə'nju:], *adv.* De nouveau.

anfractuose [æn'fræktjuous] or **anfractuous**, *a.* Anfractueux.

anfractuosity [-'ɔsiti], *n.* Anfractuosité, *f.*

angel ['eindʒəl], *n.* Ange; angelot (coin), *m. Guardian angel*, ange gardien. **angel-fish**, *n.* Ange de mer, *m.* **angel-water**, *n.* Eau de Portugal, *f.* **angel-winged**, *a.* Aux ailes d'ange.

Angela ['ændʒələ]. Angèle, *f.*

angelic [æn'dʒelik] or **angelical**, *a.* Angélique. **angelica**, *n.* Angélique, *f.* **angelically**, *adv.* Angéliquement. **angelicalness**, *n.* Nature angélique, *f.* **angelolatry** [eindʒəl'ɔlətri], *n.* Angélolâtrie, *f.*

angelus ['ændʒələs], *n.* Angélus, *m.*

Angelus ['ændʒələs]. Ange, *m.*

anger ['æŋgə], *n.* Colère, *f.*; emportement, *m.*; courroux, *m. To provoke someone to anger*;

exciter la colère de quelqu'un.—*v.t.* Fâcher, irriter, mettre en colère.

angina [æn'dʒainə], *n.* (*Path.*) Angine, *f.* *Angina pectoris,* angine de poitrine.

angiospermous [ændʒio'spə:məs], *a.* (*Bot.*) Angiosperme. **angiosperms,** *n.pl.* Angiospermes, *m.pl.*

angle (1) [æŋgl], *n.* Angle; coin, *m. Acute angle,* angle aigu; *obtuse angle,* angle obtus; *right angle,* angle droit; *straight angle,* angle plat. **angled,** *a.* À angles. *Right-angled,* rectangulaire.

angle (2) [æŋgl], *v.i.* Pêcher à la ligne. *To angle for,* pêcher. **angler,** *n.* Pêcheur à la ligne, *m.*; (*Ichth.*) baudroie, lophie pêcheuse, *f.*; crapaud de mer, *m.*

Anglican ['æŋglikən], *a.* Anglican.—*n.* Anglican, *m.*, anglicane, *f.*

anglice ['æŋglisi:], *adv.* En anglais. **Anglicism,** *n.* Anglicisme, *m.* **Anglicize,** *v.t.* Angliciser.

angling ['æŋgliŋ], *n.* Pêche à la ligne, *f.*

Anglomania [æŋglo'meiniə], *n.* Anglomanie, *f.*

Anglophil(e) [-fil], *n.* Anglophile.

Anglophobe [-foub], *n.* Anglophobe.

Anglophobia [-'foubiə], *n.* Anglophobie, *f.*

Anglo-Saxon, *a.* Anglo-saxon.—*n.* Anglo-Saxon, *m.*

angola [æŋ'goulə] or **angora,** *n.* Angora, *m.*

angostura [æŋgɔs'tuərə], *n.* Angusture, *f.*

angrily ['æŋgrili], *adv.* En colère, avec colère.

angry, *a.* En colère, fâché, irrité (contre *or* de), courroucé. *These people are very angry,* ces gens sont très fâchés; *they are angry with him,* ils lui en veulent; *to be angry with,* être en colère contre, en vouloir à; *to get angry,* se mettre en colère, se fâcher.

anguine ['æŋgwin], *a.* Anguiforme.

anguish ['æŋgwiʃ], *n.* Angoisse, douleur, *f.* —*v.t.* Angoisser, navrer de douleur.

angular ['æŋgjulə], *a.* Angulaire, angulé; anguleux; maigre, décharné.

angularity [æŋgju'læriti], *n.* Angularité, *f.*

angularly ['æŋgjuləli], *adv.* Angulairement. **angulate,** *a.* Angulé. **angulous,** *a.* (*Bot.*) Anguleux.

angustifoliate [æŋgʌsti'fouliət], *a.* (*Bot.*) Angustifolié.

anhelation [ænhi'leiʃən], *n.* Anhélation, *f.*

anhydrous [æn'haidrəs], *a.* (*Chem.*) Anhydre.

anil ['ænil], *n.* Anil, *m.*

anile ['ænail], *a.* De vieille femme, débile.

aniline ['ænilain], *n.* (*Chem.*) Aniline, *f.*

anility [ə'niliti], *n.* Seconde enfance, *f.*, radotage, *m.*

animadversion [æniməd'və:ʃən], *n.* Animadversion, censure, critique, *f.* **animadvert,** *v.i.* *To animadvert upon,* critiquer, censurer.

animal ['æniməl], *a.* and *n.* Animal, *m. Animal kingdom,* règne animal, *m.*; *animal spirits,* verve, *f.*, entrain, *m.*, vivacité, *f.*

animalcular [æni'mælkjulə], *a.* Animalculaire.

animalcule [-kjul], *n.* (*pl.* **animalcules** or **animalcula**) Animalcule, *m.*

animalism ['æniməlizm] or **animality** [-'mæliti], *n.* Animalité, *f.*

animalization [æniməlai'zeiʃən], *n.* Animalisation, *f.* **animalize,** *v.t.* Animaliser.

animate ['ænimeit], *v.t.* Animer (de).—*a.*

Animé. **animated,** *a.* Animé, vif. **animatedly,** *adv.* Vivement. **animating,** *a.* Qui anime, qui ranime. **animation,** *n.* Animation, vivacité, vie, *f.* **animative,** *a.* Animateur. **animator,** *n.* Animateur, *m.*

animism ['ænimizm], *n.* Animisme, *m.* **animist,** *n.* Animiste, *m.*

animosity [æni'mɔsiti], *n.* Animosité, *f.*

animus ['æniməs], *n.* Animosité, hostilité, *f.*; esprit (de), *m.*

anise ['ænis], *n.* Anis, *m.* **aniseed,** *n.* Graine d'anis, *f.*

anisette [æni'zet], *n.* Anisette, *f.*

ankle [æŋkl], *n.* Cheville du pied, *f. To sprain one's ankle,* se fouler la cheville. **ankle-bone,** *n.* Astragale, *m.* **ankle-deep,** *adv.* Jusqu'aux chevilles. **ankle-joint,** *n.* Cheville, *f.*; (*Mil.* etc.) guêtron, *m.*

Anna ['ænə]. Anne, *f.*

annalist ['ænəlist], *n.* Annaliste, *m.* **annals,** *n.pl.* Annales, *f.pl.*

annates ['æneitz], *n.pl.* Annate, *f.*

anneal [ə'ni:l], *v.t.* Détremper; adoucir (steel etc.), recuire (glass). **annealing,** *n.* Recuite, *f.*

annelid ['ænəlid], *n.* (*Zool.*) Annélide, *m.*

annex (1) [ə'neks], *v.t.* Annexer, joindre (à).

annex (2) ['æneks], *n.* Annexe, *f.* **annexation,** *n.* Annexation, *f.* **annexed,** *a.* Ci-joint, annexé.

annihilate [ə'naiileit], *v.t.* Anéantir, annihiler.

annihilation [-'leiʃən], *n.* Anéantissement, *m.*, annihilation, *f.* **annihilationist,** *n.* Annihilationniste, *m.* **annihilator,** *n.* Annihilateur, *m.*

anniversary [æni'və:səri], *a.* and *n.* Anniversaire, *m.*

Anno Domini ['ænou'dɔminai] or **A.D.** [ei'di:]. L'an du Seigneur; l'an de grâce; ap. J.-C.

annotate ['æneoteit], *v.t.* Annoter. **annotation,** *n.* Annotation, *f.* **annotator,** *n.* Annotateur, *m.*, annotatrice, *f.*

announce [ə'nauns], *v.t.* Annoncer, proclamer. **announcement,** *n.* Annonce, *f.*, avis, *m.*; lettre de faire-part, *f.*

announcer [ə'naunsə], *n.* Annonciateur; (*Theat.*) compère, *m.*, commère, *f.*, (*Rad.* *Tel.*) speaker, *m.*

annoy [ə'nɔi], *v.t.* (Inconvenience) Gêner; incommoder, ennuyer, importuner, (vex) contrarier, tracasser. *I am much annoyed,* je suis très ennuyé. **annoyance,** *n.* Ennui, désagrément, chagrin, *m.*; contrariété, *f.* **annoying,** *a.* Ennuyeux, contrariant, vexant. **annoyingly,** *adv.* Ennuyeusement.

annual ['ænjuəl], *a.* Annuel.—*n.* Annuaire, *m.*; plante annuelle, *f.* **annually,** *adv.* Annuellement, tous les ans.

annuitant [ə'nju:itənt], *n.* Bénéficiaire d'une pension *or* d'une rente viagère.

annuity [ə'nju:iti], *n.* Annuité, rente annuelle, pension, *f. Life annuity,* rente viagère, *f.*; *to buy up an annuity,* amortir une rente; *to redeem an annuity,* racheter une rente.

annul [ə'nʌl], *v.t.* Annuler.

annular ['ænjulə], *a.* Annulaire. **annulate** or **annulated,** *a.* (*Zool.* etc.) Annelé.

annulet, *n.* Annelet, filet, *m.*

annulment [ə'nʌlmənt], *n.* Annulation, *f.* *Decree of annulment,* décret abolitif, *m.*

annulus ['ænjuləs], *n.* Anneau, *m.*, bague, *f.* (de champignon).
annunciate [ə'nʌnʃieit], *v.t.* Annoncer. **annunciation,** *n.* Annonce, proclamation, *f.*, avis, *m.*; (*Eccles.*) l'Annonciation, *f.* **annunciator,** *n.* Annonciateur, *m.*
anode ['ænoud], *n.* (*Elec.*) Anode, *f.*
anodyne ['ænədain], *a.* Anodin, calmant.—*n.* (Remède) anodin, *m.*
anoint [ə'nɔint], *v.t.* Oindre. **anointed,** *a.* Oint. *The Lord's Anointed,* l'Oint du Seigneur, *m.*
anomalistic [ənɔmə'listik], *a.* (*Astron.*) Anomalistique.
anomalous [æ'nɔmələs], *a.* Anomal, irrégulier. **anomalously,** *adv.* Irrégulièrement. **anomaly,** *n.* Anomalie, *f.*
anon [ə'nɔn], *adv.* Tout à l'heure, bientôt; à l'instant.
anonymity [æno'nimiti], *n.* Anonymat, *m.*
anonymous [ə'nɔniməs], *a.* Anonyme. **anonymously,** *adv.* Anonymement. **anonymousness,** *n.* [ANONYMITY].
anosmia [ə'nozmiə], *n.* Anosmie, *f.*
another [ə'nʌðə], *a.* and *pron.* Autre, un autre; encore un. *One after another,* l'un après l'autre; *one another,* l'un l'autre, les uns les autres; *one way or another,* d'une manière ou d'une autre; *that is another thing,* c'est tout autre chose; *to help one another,* s'entr'aider.
anserine ['ænsərain], *a.* Ansérin.
answer ['ɑ:nsə], *v.t.* Répondre; répondre à; satisfaire, suffire à. *To answer the purpose,* convenir; *to answer several purposes,* servir à plusieurs usages.—*v.i.* Faire réponse; répondre (de *or* pour); raisonner; réussir. *That did not answer,* cela n'a pas réussi; *they will answer for him* or *for his honesty,* ils répondront de lui; *we have a lot to answer for,* nous sommes responsables de beaucoup de choses. —*n.* Réponse, *f.*; solution, *f.* (d'un problème). *Awaiting an answer,* en attendant le plaisir de vous lire; in, *answer to your letter,* en réponse à votre lettre. **answerable,** *a.* Susceptible de réponse; (for) responsable (de). **answerably,** *adv.* Conformément (à). **answerer,** *n.* Répondant, *m.*
ant [ænt], *n.* Fourmi, *f.* **ant-eater,** *n.* Fourmilier, *m.* **ant-hill,** *n.* Fourmilière, *f.* **antlion,** *n.* Fourmi-lion, *m.*
Antaeus [æn'ti:əs]. Antée, *m.*
antagonism [æn'tægənizm], *n.* Antagonisme, *m.*, opposition, *f.* **antagonist,** *n.* Antagoniste, *m.* **antagonistic,** *a.* Opposé (à); antagonique. **antagonize,** *v.t.* Eveiller l'antagonisme (de).
Antarctic [ænt'ɑ:ktik], *a.* and *n.* Antarctique, *m.*
antecedence [ænti'si:dəns], *n.* Antériorité, *f.* **antecedent,** *a.* and *n.* Antécédent, *m.* **antecendently,** *adv.* Antécédemment.
ante-chamber ['æntitʃeimbə], *n.* Antichambre, *f.*
ante-chapel ['æntitʃæpəl], *n.* Avant-corps de chapelle, *m.*
antediluvian [æntidi'lu:viən], *a.* and *n.* Antédiluvien, *m.*
antelope ['æntiloup], *n.* Antilope, *f.*
ante-meridiem [æntimə'ridiəm], *adv.* (*abbr.* **a.m.** [ei'em]). Avant midi. **antemundane,** *a.* Antérieur à la création.

ante-natal ['ænti'neitəl], *a.* Prénatal.
antenna [æn'tenə], *n.* (*pl.* **antennae**) Antenne, *f.*
antenuptial [ænti'nʌpʃəl], *a.* Anténuptial.
antepenult [æntipi'nʌlt] or **antepenultimate,** *a.* and *n.* Antépénultième, *f.*
anterior [æn'tiəriə], *a.* Antérieur. **anteriority** [æntiəri'ɔriti], *n.* Antériorité, *f.* **anteriorly,** *adv.* Antérieurement.
anteroom ['æntirum], *n.* Antichambre, *f.*
anthelion [æn'θi:liən], *n.* (*Meteor.*) Anthélie, *f.*
anthelmintic [ænθel'mintik], *a.* and *n.* (*Med.*) Anthelmintique, *m.*
anthem ['ænθəm], *n.* Antienne, *f.*; hymne, *m.* *National anthem,* hymne national, *m.*
anther ['ænθə], *n.* (*Bot.*) Anthère, *f.* **antheridium,** *n.* Anthéridie, *f.* **antheriferous,** *a.* Anthérifère.
anthological [ænθə'lɔdʒikəl], *a.* D'anthologie. **anthology,** *n.* Anthologie, chrestomathie, *f.*
Anthony ['æntəni]. Antoine, *m.* **Anthony's fire** ['æntəniz'faiə], *n.* (*fam.*) Feu Saint Antoine, érysipèle, *m.*
anthracite ['ænθrəsait], *n.* Anthracite, *m.* **anthracitic** or **anthracitous,** *a.* Anthraciteux.
anthrax ['ænθræks], *n.* (*Med.*) Anthrax, *m.*
anthropography [ænθrə'pɔgrəfi], *n.* Anthropographie, *f.*
anthropoid ['ænθrəpɔid], *a.* and *n.* Anthropoïde, *m.*
anthropological [ænθrɔpə'lɔdʒikəl], *a.* Anthropologique.
anthropologist [-'pɔlədʒist], *n.* Anthropologiste, anthropologue, *m.* **anthropology,** *n.* Anthropologie, *f.* **anthropometry,** *n.* Anthropométrie, *f.*
anthropomorphism [-'mɔ:fizm], *n.* Anthropomorphisme, *m.* **anthropomorphist,** *n.* Anthropomorphiste, *m.* **anthropomorphous,** *a.* Anthropomorphe.
anthropophagous [-'pɔfəgəs], *a.* Anthropophage. **anthropophagy,** *n.* Anthropophagie, *f.*
anti-aircraft [ænti'ɛəkrɑ:ft], *a.* Contre-avion, antiaérien.
antibiotic [æntibai'ɔtik], *a.* and *n.* Antibiotique, *m.*
antic ['æntik], *n.* Bouffonnerie, farce, *f.* *To play antics,* faire des singeries.
Antichrist ['æntikraist], *n.* Antéchrist, *m.*
antichristian [-'kristʃən], *a.* and *n.* Antichrétien, *m.* **antichristianism,** *n.* Antichristianisme, *m.*
anticipate [æn'tisipeit], *v.t.* Anticiper; prévenir, devancer; s'attendre à, prévoir, envisager; jouir d'avance de; se promettre. *Do you anticipate any difficulty?* vous attendez-vous à quelque difficulté? **anticipation,** *n.* Anticipation, *f.*; avant-goût, *m.*; attente, *f. By anticipation,* par anticipation, d'avance. **anticipator,** *n.* Personne qui anticipe, *f.* **anticipatory,** *a.* Par anticipation.
anticlerical [ænti'klerikəl], *a.* and *n.* Anticlérical, *m.* **anticlericalism,** *n.* Anticléricalisme, *m.*
anti-climax [ænti'klaimæks], *n.* Anticlimax, *m.*
anticlinal [ænti'klainəl], *a.* and *n.* (*Geol.*) Anticlinal, *m.*
anti-clockwise [COUNTER-CLOCKWISE].

anti-constitutional [æntikɔnsti'tju:ʃənəl], *a.* Anticonstitutionnel.
anticyclone [ænti'saikloun], *n.* Anticyclone, *m.*
anti-dazzle ['æntidæzl], *a.* Anti-aveuglant. *Anti-dazzle car lights*, phares-code, *m.pl.*
antidotal ['æntidoutəl], *a.* Qui sert d'antidote. **antidote**, *n.* Antidote, contre-poison, *m.*
anti-freeze [ænti'fri:z], *n.* Anti-gel, *m.*
Antigone [æn'tigəni]. Antigone, *f.*
Antilles [æn'tili:z]. Les Antilles, *f.pl.* *Greater Antilles*, les Grandes Antilles; *Lesser Antilles*, les Petites Antilles.
antilogarithm [ænti'lɔgəriðəm], *n.* Cologarithme, *m.*
antilogy [æn'tilədʒi], *n.* Antilogie, *f.*
antimacassar [æntimə'kæsə], *n.* Têtière, *f.*, voilette de chaise, *f.*, dossier, *m.*
antimonial [ænti'mouniəl], *a.* Antimonial. *Antimonial wine*, vin émétique, *m.* **antimoniate**, *n.* Antimoniate, *m.* **antimonic,** *a.* Antimonié. **antimonious,** *a.* Antimonieux.
antimony ['æntiməni], *n.* Antimoine, *m.*
anti-national [ænti'næʃənəl], *a.* Antinational.
antinomy [æn'tinəmi], *n.* Antinomie, *f.*
Antioch ['æntiɔk]. Antioche, *f.*
antipathetic [æntipə'θetik] or **antipathetical,** *a.* Antipathique. **antipathetically,** *adv.* Par antipathie.
antipathy [æn'tipəθi], *n.* Antipathie, *f.*, aversion, *f.*
antiphlogistic [æntiflə'dʒistik], *a.* and *n.* Antiphlogistique, *m.*
antiphonal [æn'tifənəl], *a.* En contre-chant.
antiphonary [æn'tifənəri], *n.* Antiphonaire, *m.* **antiphony,** *n.* Contre-chant, *m.*
antiphrasis [æn'tifrəsis], *n.* Antiphrase, *f.*
antipodal [æn'tipədəl], *a.* Antipodal. **antipodes** [æn'tipədi:z], *n.* Antipodes, *m.pl.*
anti-pope ['æntipoup], *n.* Antipape, *m.*
antipyretic ['æntipai'retik], *a.* Antipyrétique.
antiquarian [ænti'kweəriən], *a.* D'antiquaire; archéologique.—*n.* Antiquaire, *m.* **antiquarianism,** *n.* Goût des antiquités, *m.*; métier d'antiquaire, *m.*
antiquary ['æntikwəri], *n.* Archéologue; antiquaire, *m.* **antiquated.** *a.* Vieilli, vétuste; suranné, démodé.
antique [æn'ti:k], *a.* Antique, ancien.—*n.* The antique, l'antique, *m.* *An antique*, un objet antique, une antiquité; *antique shop*, magasin d'antiquités, *m.*
antiquity [æn'tikwiti], *n.* Antiquité, *f.*; ancienneté, *f.*
antirrhinum [ænti'rainəm], *n.* Antirrhine, *f.*
antiscorbutic [æntiskɔ:'bju:tik], *a.* and *n.* Antiscorbutique, *m.*
antiseptic [ænti'septik], *a.* and *n.* Antiseptique, *m.*
anti-slavery [ænti'sleivəri], *a.* Antiesclavagiste.
antisocial [ænti'souʃəl], *a.* Antisocial.
antistrophe [æn'tistrəfi], *n.* Antistrophe, *f.*
anti-tank [ænti'tænk], *a.* Anti-chars.
antithesis [æn'tiθəsis], *n.* Antithèse, *f.*
antithetic [-'θetik] or **antithetical,** *a.* Antithétique.
antitoxin [ænti'tɔksin], *n.* (*Med.*) Antitoxine, *f.*
antitype ['æntitaip], *n.* Antitype, *m.*
antler ['æntlə], *n.* Andouiller, bois (de cerf), *m.*
Antoninus [æntə'nainəs]. Antonin, *m.*

Antonius [æn'touniəs]. Antoine, *m.*
antonomasia [æntənə'meiziə], *n.* Antonomase, *f.*
Antony ['æntəni]. Antoine, *m.*
antonym ['æntənim], *n.* (*Gram.*) Antonyme, contraire, *m.* **antonymy,** *n.* Antonymie, *f.*
Antwerp ['æntwə:p]. Anvers, *m.*
anus ['einəs], *n.* (*Anat.*) Anus, *m.*
anvil ['ænvil], *n.* Enclume, *f.* *Two-beaked anvil*, bigorne, *f.*; *on the anvil*, (*fig.*) sur le métier, en préparation. **anvil-block,** *n.* Billot d'enclume, *m.*
anxiety [æŋ'zaiəti], *n.* Anxiété, inquiétude, sollicitude, *f.*; désir, *m.* **anxious** ['aŋkʃəs], *a.* Inquiet, soucieux, plein de sollicitude (pour); désireux (de). *To be anxious about*, être en peine de *or* inquiet sur; *to be anxious to*, désirer vivement (de), tenir à. **anxiously,** *adv.* Anxieusement, avec anxiété, avec inquiétude.
any ['eni], *a.* and *pron.* Du, de la, etc.; en; aucun; quelque; n'importe lequel. *Any better*, mieux; *any further*, plus loin; *any man*, tout homme; *any more*, encore, davantage; *any of them*, quelqu'un d'entre eux; *any others*, d'autres; *at any rate*, en tout cas; *have you any?* en avez-vous? *have you any wine?* avez-vous du vin? *I do not know any of your judges*, je ne connais aucun de vos juges; *I doubt if any of them*, je doute qu'aucun d'entre eux; *I have hardly any*, je n'en ai guère; *I haven't any*, je n'en ai pas; *not any more*, pas davantage; *not on any account*, pour rien au monde; *scarcely any*, presque pas.
anybody ['enibɔdi] or **anyone,** *pron.* Quelqu'un, chacun, qui que ce soit, n'importe qui, tout le monde. *Anybody can do it*, tout le monde peut faire cela; *I didn't see anybody*, je n'ai vu personne; *like anybody else*, comme un autre. **anyhow,** *adv.* De toute façon, de quelque manière que ce soit, en tout cas, quand même. *To do something anyhow*, faire quelque chose tant bien que mal. **anything,** *pron.* Quelque chose, *m.*, quoi que ce soit, n'importe quoi. *Anything but*, rien moins que; *as anything*, comme tout; *do anything you like*, faites tout ce qui vous plaira; *it's as easy as anything*, c'est facile comme tout; *not to say anything*, ne rien dire; *to work like anything*, travailler avec acharnement; *worth anything*, de quelque valeur. **anyway,** *adv.* [ANYHOW]. **anywhere,** *adv.* Quelque part, dans quelque endroit que ce soit, n'importe où. *Anywhere else*, autre part; *not anywhere*, nulle part.
aorist ['eiərist], *a.* and *n.* (*Gram.*) Aoriste, *m.*
aorta [ei'ɔ:tə], *n.* Aorte, *f.* **aortic,** *a.* Aortique.
apace [ə'peis], *adv.* Vite, à grands pas.
apanage ['æpənidʒ], *n.* Apanage, *m.*
apart [ə'pɑ:t], *adv.* À part; de côté, séparément. *Apart from the fact that*, hormis que . . ., outre que . . .; *apart from that all is well*, à part cela tout va bien; *joking apart*, plaisanterie à part; *to come apart*, se défaire.
apartheid [ə'pɑ:theit], *n.* (*In S. Africa*) Ségrégation, *f.*
apartment [ə'pɑ:tmənt], *n.* Chambre; pièce (d'un appartement), *f.*; logement, *m.*; (*pl.*) un appartement, *m.*
apathetic [æpə'θetik], *a.* Apathique. **apathy** ['æpəθi], *n.* Apathie, *f.*

ape [eip], *n.* Singe, *m.*, guenon, *f. Barbary ape*, magot, *m.*—*v.t.* Singer.
apeak [ə'pi:k], *adv.* (*Naut.*) À pic.
Apennines ['æpənainz]. Les Apennins, *m.pl.*
apepsy [ə'pepsi], *n.* Apepsie, *f.*
aperient [ə'piəriənt], **aperitive** [ə'peritiv], *a.* and *n.* Laxatif, *m.*
aperture ['æpətjə], *n.* Ouverture, *f.*; orifice, *m.*
apery ['eipəri], *n.* Singerie, *f.*
apetalous [ə'petələs], *a.* (*Bot.*) Apétale.
apex ['eipeks], *n.* (*pl.* **apices** or **apexes**) Sommet, *m.*, pointe, *f.*
aphaeresis [ə'fiərəsis], *n.* (*Gram.*) Aphérèse, *f.*
aphasia [æ'feiziə], *n.* Aphasie, *f.* **aphasic**, *a.* Aphasique.
aphelion [ə'fi:liən], *n.* (*Astron.*) Aphélie, *m.* or *f.*
aphesis ['æfəsis], *n.* Aphérèse, *f.*
aphis ['æfis], *n.* (*pl.* **aphides**) Aphidé, aphidien, *m.*
aphonia [ə'founiə] or **aphony**, *n.* Aphonie, *f.*
aphorism ['æfərizm], *n.* Aphorisme, *m.* **aphoristic** [æfə'ristik], *a.* Aphoristique. **aphoristically**, *adv.* Par aphorisme.
aphrodisiac [æfro'diziæk], *a.* Aphrodisiaque. —*n.* Aphrodisiaque, *m.*
aphthae ['æfθi], *n.pl.* (*Path.*) Aphte, *m.*
aphyllous [ə'filəs], *a.* (*Bot.*) Aphylle.
apiary ['eipiəri], *n.* Rucher, *m.* **apiculture**, *n.* Apiculture, *f.* **apiculturist** or **apiarist**, *n.* Apiculteur, *m.*
apiece [ə'pi:s], *adv.* La pièce; par tête, par personne, chacun.
apish ['eipiʃ], *a.* De singe, simiesque. *Apish trick*, singerie, *f.* **apishly**, *adv.* En singe. **apishness**, *n.* Singerie, sottise, *f.*
aplanatic [æplə'nætik], *a.* (*Opt.*) Aplanétique.
aplomb [ə'plɔ̃], *n.* Aplomb, *m.*, sang-froid, *m.*
apnoea [æp'ni:ə], *n.* (*Med.*) Apnée, *f.*
apocalypse [ə'pɔkəlips], *n.* Apocalypse, *f.* **apocalyptic** [-'liptik] or **apocalyptical**, *a.* Apocalyptique. **apocalyptically**, *adv.* D'une manière apocalyptique.
apocope [ə'pɔkəpi], *n.* (*Gram.*) Apocope, *f.*
apocrypha [ə'pɔkrifə], *n.pl.* Les Apocryphes, *m.pl.* **apocryphal**, *a.* Apocryphe.
apod ['æpɔd], *n.* (*Zool.*) Apode, *m.* **apodal**, *a.* Apode.
apodictic [æpə'diktik], **apodeictic** [æpə'daiktik], *a.* Apodictique.
apodosis [ə'pɔdəsis], *n.* (*Gram. etc.*) Apodose, *f.*
apogee ['æpədʒi:], *n.* Apogée, *m.*
Apollo [ə'pɔlou]. Apollon, *m.*
apologetic [əpɔlə'dʒetik] or **apologetical**, *a.* Apologétique. **apologetically**, *adv.* En forme d'apologie. **apologetics**, *n.pl.* Apologétique, *f.*
apologia [æpə'loudʒiə], *n.* Apologie; justification, *f.*
apologist [ə'pɔlədʒist], *n.* Apologiste, *m.*
apologize [ə'pɔlədʒaiz], *v.i.* S'excuser, faire des excuses (de or auprès de). *I apologized to him*, je lui ai fait mes excuses; *to apologize for someone*, faire des excuses pour quelqu'un.
apologue ['æpəlɔg], *n.* Apologue, *m.*
apology [ə'pɔlədʒi], *n.* Apologie, *f.*; excuses, *f. pl. To make an apology for*, faire des excuses or s'excuser de.
apophthegm ['æpəθem], *n.* Apophtegme, *m.*

apophthegmatical [æpəθeg'mætikəl], *a.* En forme d'apophtegme.
apoplectic [æpə'plektik], *a.* Apoplectique. *Apoplectic stroke*, coup de sang, *m.*, attaque d'apoplexie, *f.* **apoplexy**, *n.* Apoplexie, *f. A fit of apoplexy*, coup de sang, *m.*; congestion cérébrale, *f.*
apostasy [ə'pɔstəsi], *n.* Apostasie, *f.* **apostate**, *a.* and *n.* Apostat, *m.*
apostatical [æpɔs'tætikəl], *a.* Apostat. **apostatize**, *v.i.* Apostasier, abjurer.
apostle [ə'pɔsl], *n.* Apôtre, *m. The Acts of the Apostles*, les Actes des Apôtres, *m.pl. The Apostles' Creed*, le Symbole des Apôtres, *m.* **apostleship**, *n.* Apostolat, *m.*
apostolic [æpəs'tɔlik] or **apostolical**, *a.* Apostolique. **apostolically**, *adv.* Apostoliquement.
apostrophe [ə'pɔstrəfi], *n.* Apostrophe, *f.* **apostrophize**, *v.t.* Apostropher.
apothecary [ə'pɔθikəri], *n.* Apothicaire, *m.*; pharmacien, *m.*
apotheosis [əpɔθi'ousis], *n.* Apothéose, *f.* **apotheosize** [ə'pɔθiosaiz], *v.t.* Apothéoser.
appal [ə'pɔ:l], *v.t.* Épouvanter, consterner. **appalling**, *a.* Épouvantable, effrayant. **appallingly**, *adv.* Épouvantablement.
appanage [APANAGE].
apparatus [æpə'reitəs], *n.* Appareil, dispositif, *m.*
apparel [ə'pærəl], *v.t.* Vêtir; parer; (*Naut.*) équiper.—*n.* Habillement, vêtement; (*Naut.*) équipement, *m. Wearing apparel*, effets d'habillement, *m.pl.*
apparent [ə'pærənt], *a.* Évident, manifeste, apparent. *Heir apparent*, héritier présomptif, *m.* **apparently**, *adv.* En apparence, apparemment. *He is apparently right*, il semble avoir raison.
apparition [æpə'riʃən], *n.* Apparition, *f.*
apparitor [ə'pæritə], *n.* Appariteur, *m.*
appeal [ə'pi:l], *v.i.* Appeler, en appeler (de), faire appel (à); (*Law*) se pourvoir en cassation, réclamer (contre or à); (*fig.*) attirer, séduire. *That doesn't appeal to me*, cela ne me dit rien.—*n.* Appel; attrait, *m. Appeal to arbitration*, recours à l'arbitrage, *m.*; *Court of Appeal*, cour de cassation, *f.*; *without appeal*, en dernier ressort. **appealable**, *a.* Appelable, sujet à appel. **appealing**, *a.* Suppliant, attrayant, séduisant. **appealingly**, *adv.* En suppliant, de façon séduisante.
appear [ə'piə], *v.i.* Paraître; apparaître; se montrer, se présenter (à). *It appears*, il paraît; *it would appear*, il paraîtrait; *to appear on the stage*, entrer en scène. **appearance**, *n.* Apparition; apparence, figure, mine, *f.*, air, aspect, *m.*; (*Law*) comparution, *f. At first appearance*, au premier abord, au premier coup d'œil; *for the sake of appearance, in order to keep up appearances*, pour sauver les apparences; *to all appearances*, selon toute apparence; *to judge by appearances*, juger sur l'apparence; *to make one's first appearance*, faire son début, débuter; *to put in an appearance*, faire acte de présence.
appeasable [ə'pi:zəbl], *a.* Qu'on peut apaiser. **appease**, *v.t.* Apaiser, pacifier. **appeasement**, *n.* Apaisement, *m.*, adoucissement, *m.*; conciliation, *f.*
appellant [ə'pelənt], *a.* and *n.* (*Law*) Appelant, *m.*, appelante, *f.* **appellate**, *a.* D'appel.

appellation [æpə'leiʃən], n. Nom, m., appellation, dénomination, f. **appellative,** a.
Appellatif.—n. Nom commun.
append [ə'pend], v.t. Apposer, attacher (à).
appendage, n. Accessoire, apanage, m.
appendant, a. Accessoire, attaché, annexé (à).
appendicitis [əpendi'saitis], n. Appendicite, f.
appendicle, n. Appendicule, m. **appendi-
cular,** a. Appendiculaire. **appendix,** n.
(pl. **appendixes** or **appendices**) Appendice, m.
apperception [æpə'sepʃən], n. (Phil.) Aperception, f.
appertain [æpə'tein], v.i. Appartenir (à).
appetence ['æpətəns] or **appetency,** n. Appétence, envie, f. **appetent,** a. Avide (de).
appetite, n. Appétit; (fig.) désir, m., soif, f.
To give an appetite to, mettre en appétit.
appetize, v.t. Mettre en appétit. **appetizer,**
n. Apéritif, m. **appetizing,** a. Appétissant.
Appian ['æpiən]. Appien, m. The Appian Way,
la Voie Appienne, f.
applaud [ə'plɔːd], v.t. Applaudir.—v.i. Applaudir (à). **applause** [ə'plɔːz], n. Applaudissements, m.pl.
apple [æpl], n. Pomme, f. Apple of the eye,
prunelle, f. **apple-cart,** n. To upset someone's apple-cart, bouleverser les plans de
quelqu'un. **apple-pie,** n. Tourte aux
pommes, f. Apple-pie bed, lit en portefeuille,
m.; apple-pie order, ordre parfait, m. **apple-
sauce,** n. Compote de pommes, f. **apple-
tart,** n. Tarte aux pommes, f. **apple-tree,** n.
Pommier, m.
appliance [ə'plaiəns], n. Instrument, appareil,
dispositif, m.
applicability [æplikə'biliti] or **applicable-
ness,** n. Applicabilité, f.
applicable ['æplikəbl], a. Applicable.
applicant ['æplikənt], n. Postulant, candidat;
(Law) demandeur, m., demanderesse, f.
application, n. Application; sollicitation,
demande, f. For external application, usage
externe; on application, sur demande; to
make application to, s'adresser à, faire une
demande à.
applied [ə'plaid], a. Appliqué. Applied mathematics, mathématiques appliquées, f.pl.
apply [ə'plai], v.t. Appliquer (à). To apply the
brake, freiner; serrer le frein.—v.i. S'adresser
(à); s'appliquer, être applicable. To apply
for a situation, solliciter un poste; to apply
oneself, s'appliquer, se mettre (à); to apply to,
s'adresser à or chez.
appoint [ə'pɔint], v.t. Arrêter, désigner, fixer;
nommer; installer, équiper. At the appointed
hour, à l'heure convenue; a well-appointed
house, une maison bien installée. **appointee,**
n. Fonctionnaire nommé, m. **appointment,**
n. Nomination, f.; décret, arrêt; établissement; emploi, m.; rendez-vous, m.; convocation, f. By appointment to, (fournisseur)
breveté de; to make an appointment with,
donner un rendez-vous à.
apportion [ə'pɔːʃən], v.t. Partager, répartir,
assigner. **apportionment,** n. Répartition, f.,
partage, m.
appose [ə'pouz], v.t. Apposer.
apposite ['æpəzit], a. Juste; à propos;
approprié, convenable (à). **appositely,** adv.
Convenablement, justement, à propos. **appositeness,** n. À-propos, m., opportunité, f.

apposition [æpə'ziʃən], n. Apposition, f.
appraisable [ə'preizəbl], a. Évaluable. **appraise,** v.t. Priser, évaluer, estimer. **appraisement, appraisal,** n. Évaluation,
estimation; expertise, f. **appraiser,** n.
Commissaire-priseur, expert, m.
appreciable [ə'priːʃiəbl], a. Appréciable,
sensible. **appreciably,** adv. Sensiblement.
appreciate, v.t. Apprécier, estimer. He
does not appreciate it, il n'en fait pas de cas;
I fully appreciate (the fact) that . . ., je me
rends clairement compte que . . . .—v.i.
(Comm. etc.) Augmenter de valeur. **appreciation,** n. Appréciation, f.; hausse de
valeur, f. **appreciative,** a. Appréciateur.
appreciatively, adv. Favorablement.
apprehend [æpri'hend], v.t. Comprendre;
prendre, saisir, arrêter, appréhender; craindre. **apprehensible,** a. Appréhensible.
apprehension, n. Appréhension; arrestation, prise de corps; crainte, inquiétude, f.
To be dull of apprehension, avoir l'esprit
lourd; to be under some apprehension, avoir
des craintes. **apprehensive,** a. Intelligent,
prompt à saisir; appréhensif, inquiet. To be
apprehensive of, appréhender, craindre.
apprehensively, adv. Avec intelligence;
avec crainte. **apprehensiveness,** n. Appréhension, crainte; intelligence, f.
apprentice [ə'prentis], n. Apprenti, m., apprentie, f. To place as apprentice to, mettre
en apprentissage chez.—v.t. Mettre en
apprentissage. **apprenticeship,** n. Apprentissage, m.
apprise [ə'praiz], v.t. Prévenir; informer,
instruire.
approach [ə'proutʃ], n. Approche, f.; abord,
accès; rapprochement, m.; (Math.) approximation, f. To be easy of approach, être d'un
abord facile; to make approaches, faire des
avances.—v.i. Approcher, s'approcher.—v.t.
Approcher de, s'approcher de, aborder; (fig.)
pressentir, tâter (quelqu'un). **approach-
ability,** n. Accessibilité, f. **approachable,**
a. Abordable, accessible, approchable.
approaching, a. Approchant, prochain.
approbation [æprə'beiʃən], n. Approbation, f.
On approbation, à condition, à l'essai.
approbatory, a. Approbateur.
appropriate (1) [ə'proupriət], a. Approprié;
propre, convenable (à).
appropriate (2) [ə'prouprieit], v.t. Approprier, affecter (à); s'approprier; s'emparer de.
appropriately, adv. À juste titre; convenablement. **appropriateness,** n. Convenance,
f., à-propos, m., justesse, f. **appropriation,** n. Application, destination, appropriation, affectation, attribution, f., emploi,
crédit (budgétaire), m. **appropriator,** n.
Qui s'approprie, usurpateur.
approvable [ə'pruːvəbl], a. Digne d'approbation. **approval,** n. Approbation, f. On
approval, à condition. **approve,** v.t. Approuver; *essayer, éprouver; trouver bon
(que, with subj.). I don't approve of that, cela
ne me plait pas; to approve oneself, se montrer. **approver,** n. Approbateur, m.,
approbatrice, f.; *(Law) dénonciateur de ses
complices, m. **approving,** a. Approbateur,
approbatif. **approvingly,** adv. Avec approbation, d'un air approbateur.

approximate (1) [ə'prɔksimeit], *v.t.* Rapprocher.—*v.i.* Se rapprocher (de).
approximate (2) [ə'prɔksimət], *a.* Approximatif. **approximately,** *adv.* Approximativement, à peu près.
approximation [-'meiʃən], *n.* Approximation, *f.*; rapprochement, *m.*
approximative [ə'prɔksimeitiv], *a.* Approximatif. **approximatively,** *adv.* [APPROXIMATELY].
appulse [ə'pʌls], *n.* Choc, *m.*; (*Astron.*) rencontre, approche, *f.*
appurtenance [ə'pə:tənəns], *n.* Appartenance, dépendance, *f.*; (*pl.*) accessoires, *m.pl.* **appurtenant,** *a.* Appartenant (à), dépendant (de).
apricot ['eiprikɔt], *n.* Abricot, *m.* **apricot-tree,** *n.* Abricotier, *m.*
April ['eipril], *n.* Avril, *m.* *April shower,* giboulée de mars, *f.*; *to make an April fool of,* donner un poisson d'avril à.
apron ['eiprən], *n.* Tablier, *m.*; (*Artill.*) couvre-lumière, *m.*; (*Naut.*) contre-étrave, *f.* (*Av.*) aire de manœuvre or d'atterrissage, *f.* **apron-stage,** *n.* Avant-scène, *f.* **apron-string,** *n.* Cordon de tablier, *m.* *To be tied to one's mother's apron-strings,* être pendu aux jupons de sa mère.
apse [æps] or **apsis,** *n.* (*pl.* **apses** ['æpsiz] or **apsides** [æp'saidiz]) Abside, *f.*; (*Astron.*) apside, *f.* **apsidal,** *a.* Absidal, apsidal.
apt [æpt], *a.* Sujet, enclin, porté (à); propre, convenable (à); capable; (word) juste.
apterous ['æptərəs], *a.* Aptère. **apteryx,** *n.* Aptéryx, *m.*, kiwi, *m.*
aptitude ['æptitju:d] or **aptness,** *n.* Aptitude, disposition, *f.* **aptly,** *adv.* À propos; convenablement.
Apulia [ə'pju:liə]. La Pouille, L'Apulie, *f.*
aqua ['ækwə], *n.* Eau, *f.* **aqua-fortis,** *n.* Eauforte, *f.*
aquamarine [ækwəmə'ri:n], *n.* Aigue-marine, *f.*
aqua-regia [-'ri:dʒiə], *n.* Eau régale, *f.*
aquarelle, *n.* Aquarelle, *f.*
aquarium [ə'kwɛəriəm], *n.* Aquarium, *m.* **Aquarius,** *n.* (*Astron.*) Le Verseau, *m.*
aquatic [ə'kwɔtik or ə'kwætik], *a.* Aquatique.— *n.* Plante aquatique, *f.* **aquatics** or *aquatic sports.* Sports nautiques, *m.pl.*
aquatint ['ækwətint], *n.* (*Engr.*) Aquatinte, *f.*
aquavitae [-'vaiti:], *n.* Eau de vie, *f.*
aqueduct ['ækwidʌkt], *n.* Aqueduc, *m.*
aqueous ['eikwiəs], *a.* Aqueux. **aqueousness,** *n.* Aquosité, *f.* **aquiferous,** *a.* Aquifère.
aquiline ['ækwilain], *a.* Aquilin, d'aigle.
Aquinas [ə'kwainəs]. *St. Thomas Aquinas,* Saint Thomas d'Aquin.
aquosity [ə'kwɔsiti], *n.* Aquosité, *f.*
Arab ['ærəb], *a.* and *n.* Arabe. *Street Arab,* gamin, petit va-nu-pieds, *m.* **arabesque,** *a.* and *n.* Arabesque, *f.* **Arabia,** *n.* L'Arabie, *f.* *Arabia Petraea,* l'Arabie Pétrée. *Saudi Arabia,* l'Arabie Séoudite.
Arabian [ə'reibiən], *a.* and *n.* Arabe. *The Arabian Nights,* les Mille et une Nuits.
arabic ['ærəbik], *a.* Arabe, arabique. *Arabic figures,* chiffres arabes, *m.pl.*—*n.* Arabe (language), *m.* **arabist,** *n.* Arabisant, *m.*
arable ['ærəbl], *a.* Arable, labourable.
arachnid [ə'ræknid], *n.* (*Zool.*) Arachnide, *m.* **arachnidous** or **arachnidean,** *a.* Arachnéen. **arachnoid,** *n.* Arachnoïde, *f.*

araeometer [æri'ɔmitə], *n.* Aréomètre, *m.* **araeometry,** *n.* Aréométrie, *f.*
Aramaean [ærə'mi:ən], *a.* and *n.* Araméen, *m.*
araneiform [ærə'ni:ifɔ:m], *a.* Aranéiforme.
araucaria [ærɔ:'kɛəriə], *n.* (*Bot.*) Araucaria, *m.*
arbalest ['ɑ:bəlest], *n.* Arbalète, *f.*
arbiter ['ɑ:bitə], *n.* Arbitre, *m.* **arbitral,** *a.* Arbitral.
arbitrament [ɑ:'bitrəmənt], *n.* Arbitrage, *m.*, arbitration, *f.*; jugement, *m.*, décision, *f.*
arbitrarily, *adv.* Arbitrairement. **arbitrariness,** *n.* L'arbitraire, *m.* **arbitrary** ['ɑ:bitrəri], *a.* Arbitraire. **arbitrate,** *v.t.*, *v.i.* Arbitrer, décider.
arbitration [-'treiʃən], *n.* Arbitrage, *m.* *Board of arbitration,* conseil de prud'hommes, *m.* **arbitrator,** *n.* Arbitre, *m.* **arbitress,** *n.* Arbitre, *f.*
arbor ['ɑ:bə], *n.* Arbre, *m.* *Arbor vitae* ['vaiti:], thuya, *m.*
arboreal [ɑ:'bɔ:riəl], *a.* Arboricole; d'arbre(s). **arboreous** or **arborous,** *a.* D'arbre, arborescent.
arborescence [ɑ:bə'resəns], *n.* Arborescence, *f.* **arborescent,** *a.* Arborescent.
arboriculture ['ɑ:bɔrikʌltʃə], *n.* Arboriculture, *f.*
arboriculturist [-'kʌltʃərist], *n.* Arboriculteur, *m.*
arborization [ɑ:bɔrai'zeiʃən], *n.* Arborisation, *f.*
arbour ['ɑ:bə], *n.* Berceau, *m.*, tonnelle, *f.*
arbutus [ɑ:'bju:təs], *n.* Arbousier, *m.*
arc [ɑ:k], *n.* Arc, *m.* *Arc-lamp,* lampe à arc, *f.* —*v.i.* To arc (*over*), lancer des étincelles.
arcade [ɑ:'keid], *n.* Arcade, *f.*; passage, *m.*
Arcadia [ɑ:'keidiə]. L'Arcadie, *f.*
arcadian [ɑ:'keidiən], *a.* De l'Arcadie.
arcanum [ɑ:'keinəm], *n.* (*pl.* **arcana**) Arcane, mystère, *m.*
arch (1) [ɑ:tʃ], *n.* Arche, *f.*; arc, cintre, *m.*, voûte, *f.* *Court of Arches,* cour archiépiscopale, *f.*; *pointed arch,* ogive, *f.*; *triumphal arch,* arc de triomphe, *m.*—*v.t.* Voûter, cintrer, arquer. **arch-buttress,** ‹. Arc-boutant, *m.* **arched** [ɑ:tʃd], *a.* Voûté, cintré, arqué. **arch-stone,** *n.* Voussoir, *m.*, clé de voûte, *f.* **archway,** *n.* Voûte, *f.*, passage (sous une voûte); portail, *m.* **archwise,** *adv.* En forme de voûte.
arch (2) [ɑ:tʃ], *a.* Moqueur, malin, espiègle; grand, maître, archi-, insigne, fieffé. *An arch glance,* un coup d'œil espiègle. **arch-fiend,** *n.* Chef des démons, *m.* **arch-foe,** *n.* Grand ennemi, ennemi juré, *m.* **arch-heresy,** *n.* Hérésie principale, *f.* **arch-heretic,** *n.* Hérésiarque, *m.* **arch-hypocrite,** *n.* Grand hypocrite, *m.* **arch-priest,** *n.* Archiprêtre, *m.* **arch-prophet,** *n.* Grand prophète, *m.*
archaeological [ɑ:kiə'lɔdʒikəl], *n.* Archéologique. **archaeologist,** *n.* Archéologue, *m.* **archaeology** [ɑ:ki'ɔlədʒi], *n.* Archéologie, *f.*
archaic [ɑ:'keiik], *a.* Archaïque.
archaism ['ɑ:keiizm], *n.* Archaïsme, *m.* **archaist,** *n.* Archaïste.
archangel ['ɑ:keindʒəl], *n.* Archange, *m.* **archangelic** [ɑ:kæn'dʒelik], *a.* Archangélique.
archbishop ['ɑ:tʃ'biʃəp], *n.* Archevêque, *m.* **archbishopric,** *n.* Archevêché, *m.* **archdeacon,** *n.* Archidiacre, *m.* **archdeaconry,** *n.* Archidiaconat (office), *m.*; archidiaconé

(part of diocese), *m.* **archducal,** *a.* Archiducal. **archduchess,** *n.* Archiduchesse, *f.* **archduchy,** *n.* Archiduché, *m.* **archduke,** *n.* Archiduc, *m.*
archer ['ɑ:tʃə], *n.* Archer, *m.*; (*Astron.*) Sagittaire, *m.* **archery,** *n.* Tir à l'arc, *m.*
archetypal ['ɑ:kitaipəl], *a.* Original.
archetype ['ɑ:kitaip], *n.* Archétype; étalon, (measure), *m.*
archidiaconal [ɑ:kidi'ækənəl], *a.* D'archidiacre.
archiepiscopacy [ɑ:kiə'piskəpəsi], *n.* Archiépiscopat, *m.* **archiepiscopal,** *a.* Archiépiscopal.
archimandrite [ɑ:ki'mændrait], *n.* Archimandrite, *m.*
Archimedes [ɑ:ki'mi:di:z]. Archimède, *m.*
archipelago [ɑ:ki'peləgou], *n.* Archipel, *m.*
architect ['ɑ:kitekt], *n.* Architecte; (*fig.*) artisan, *m.*
architectonic [-'tɔnik], *a.* Architectonique. **architectonics,** *n.pl.* Architectonique, *f.*
architectural [-'tektʃurəl], *a.* Architectural.
architecture ['ɑ:kitektʃə], *n.* Architecture, *f.* *Gothic architecture,* architecture ogivale, *f.*
architrave ['ɑ:kitreiv], *n.* Architrave, *f.*
archives ['ɑ:kaivz], *n.pl.* Archives, *f.pl.* **archivist,** *n.* Archiviste, *m.* or *f.*
archivolt ['ɑ:kivɔlt], *n.* (*Arch.*) Archivolte, *f.*
archly ['ɑ:tʃli], *adv.* Avec espièglerie, d'un air malin. **archness,** *n.* Malice, espièglerie, *f.*
archon ['ɑ:kən], *n.* Archonte, *m.* **archonship,** *n.* Archontat, *m.*
archway [ARCH (1)].
Arctic ['ɑ:ktik], *a.* Arctique. *The Arctic Circle,* le cercle polaire arctique, *m.*; *the Arctic Ocean,* l'océan (glacial) arctique, *m.*
arcuate ['ɑ:kjueit], *a.* En forme d'arc, arqué. **arcuation,** *n.* Arcure, *f.*
ardency ['ɑ:dənsi], *n.* Ardeur, *f.* **ardent,** *a.* Ardent. *Ardent spirits,* spiritueux, *m.pl.,* liqueurs alcooliques, *f.pl.* **ardently,** *adv.* Ardemment, avec ardeur. **ardour,** *n.* Ardeur, *f.*
arduous ['ɑ:djuəs], *a.* Ardu, rude, pénible, difficile. **arduously,** *adv.* Difficilement, péniblement. **arduousness,** *n.* Difficulté, *f.*
are, *pl. pres. indic.* [BE].
area ['ɛəriə], *n.* Étendue, *f.*; aire, surface, superficie; courette d'entrée, *f.* (devant la maison). *Area steps,* escalier de service, *m. Postal area,* zone postale, *f.*
areca [ə'ri:kə], *n.* Arec, *m.* **areca-nut,** *n.* Noix d'arec, *f.* **areca-nut-tree,** *n.* Aréquier, *m.*
arena [ə'ri:nə], *n.* Arène, *f.*
arenaceous [æri'neiʃəs], *a.* Arénacé. **arenaria,** *n.* Arénaire, *f.* **arenose,** *a.* Aréneux, sablonneux.
aren't [ɑ:nt] (*colloq.*)=are not; (*vulg.*)=am not.
areola [ə'ri:ələ], *n.* (*pl.* **areolae**) (*Anat.*) Aréole, *f.* **areolar,** *a.* Aréolaire. **areolate,** *a.* Aréolé.
areometer [ARAEOMETER].
Areopagite [æri:'ɔpəgait], *n.* Aréopagite, *m.* **Areopagus,** *n.* Aréopage, *m.*
Arethusa [ærə'θju:zə]. Aréthuse, *f.*
argent ['ɑ:dʒənt], *a.* Argenté.—*n.* (*Her.*) Argent, *m.*
argentiferous [-'tifərəs], *a.* Argentifère.
argentine ['ɑ:dʒəntain], *a.* Argentin.

Argentine ['ɑ:dʒəntain], **the.** La République Argentine *or* l'Argentine, *f.*
argil ['ɑ:dʒil], *n.* Argile, *f.* **argillaceous,** *a.* Argilacé, argileux. **argilliferous,** *a.* Argilifère.
argol ['ɑ:gɔl], *n.* Tartre brut, *m.*
Argolis ['ɑ:gəlis]. L'Argolide, *f.*
argon ['ɑ:gən], *n.* (*Chem.*) Argon, *m.*
argonaut ['ɑ:gənɔ:t], *n.* Argonaute, *m.*
argosy ['ɑ:gəsi], *n.* Caraque;. *flotte, *f.*
argot ['ɑ:gou], *n.* Argot, *m.*
argotic [ɑ:'gɔtik], *a.* Argotique.
arguable ['ɑ:gjuəbl], *a.* Soutenable, discutable. **argue** ['ɑ:gju:], *v.i.* Argumenter (contre), raisonner (sur), discuter (avec); (*Law*) plaider. *Don't argue!* pas de raisonnements!—*v.t.* Discuter; soutenir, prétendre; (*fig.*) dénoter, indiquer, accuser. *To argue well for,* faire foi de, être garant de. *To argue the toss,* disputailler.
argument ['ɑ:gjumənt], *n.* Argument, raisonnement, *m.*; discussion, dispute, *f.*; thèse, *f. For argument's sake,* à titre d'exemple.
argumentation [-mən'teiʃən], *n.* Argumentation, *f.*
argumentative [-'mentətiv], *a.* Raisonneur; disposé à argumenter. *Don't be argumentative!* pas tant de raisons! **argumentatively,** *adv.* Par raisonnement. **argumentativeness,** *n.* Esprit raisonneur, *m.*; disposition à argumenter, *f.*
Argus ['ɑ:gəs], *n.* Argus, *m.*
argute [ɑ:'gju:t], *a.* Fin, subtil.
aria ['ɑ:riə], *n.* Aria, *f.*
Arian ['ɛəriən], *a. and n.* Arien, *m.,* arienne, *f.* **Arianism,** *n.* Arianisme, *m.*
arid ['ærid], *a.* Aride. **aridity** [ə'riditi] or **aridness,** *n.* Aridité, *f.*
Aries ['ɛərii:z], *n.* (*Astron.*) Le Bélier, *m.*
arietta [æri'etə], *n.* Ariette, *f.*
aright [ə'rait], *adv.* Correctement; bien.
arise [ə'raiz], *v.i.* (*past* **arose,** *p.p.* **arisen**) Se lever; s'élever; survenir, se présenter; provenir, résulter (de). *A cry arose,* un cri se fit entendre; *if the question arises,* le cas échéant.
Aristides [æris'taidi:z]. Aristide, *m.*
aristocracy [æris'tɔkrəsi], *n.* Aristocratie, *f.*
aristocrat ['æristəkræt], *n.* Aristocrate. **aristocratic** or **aristocratical,** *a.* Aristocratique. **aristocratically,** *adv.* Aristocratiquement.
Aristophanes [æris'tɔfəni:z]. Aristophane, *m.*
Aristotelian [ærist'ti:liən], *a. and n.* Aristotélicien, *m.,* aristotélicienne, *f.* **Aristotelianism,** *n.* Aristotélisme, *m.*
Aristotle ['æristɔtl]. Aristote, *m.*
arithmetic [ə'riθmətik], *n.* Arithmétique, *f.,* calcul, *m. Mental arithmetic,* calcul mental.
arithmetical [æriθ'metikəl], *a.* Arithmétique. **arithmetically,** *adv.* Arithmétiquement.
arithmetician [æriθmə'tiʃən], *n.* Arithméticien, *m.* **arithmometer,** *n.* Arithmomètre, *m.*
ark [ɑ:k], *n.* Arche, *f. Noah's ark,* l'arche de Noé, *f.; the ark of the covenant, the ark of the Lord,* l'arche d'alliance, *f.*
arm [ɑ:m], *n.* Bras, *m.*; arme (weapon), *f.*; (*pl.*) (*Her.*) armes, armoiries, *f.pl. Arm in arm,* bras dessus bras dessous; *at arm's length,* à distance; *with arms folded,* les bras

croisés; *within arm's reach*, à portée du bras; *with open arms*, à bras ouverts. *Man-at-arms*, homme d'armes, *m.*; *present arms!* présentez armes! *to arms!* aux armes! *under arms*, sous les armes.—*v.t.* Armer; donner des armes à.—*v.i.* Armer; s'armer (de); prendre les armes. **arm-band,** *n.* Brassard, *m.* **arm-chair,** *n.* Fauteuil, *m.* **armhole,** *n.* Emmanchure, entournure, *f.*

armada [ɑːˈmeidə *or* ɑːˈmɑːdə], *n.* Armada, *f.*

armadillo [ɑːməˈdilou], *n.* Tatou, *m.*

armament [ˈɑːməmənt], *n.* Armement, *m.*, armée, flotte, *f. Armaments race*, course aux armements, *f.*

armature [ˈɑːmətjuə], *n.* Armature, *f.*, induit, *m.*

Armenia [ɑːˈmiːniə]. L'Arménie, *f.*

armful [ˈɑːmful], *n.* Brassée, *f.*

armilla [ɑːˈmilə], *n.* Armille, *f.* **armillary,** *a. Armillary sphere*, (*Astron.*) Sphère armillaire, *f.*

armistice [ˈɑːmistis], *n.* Armistice, *m.*

armless [ˈɑːmlis], *a.* Sans bras. Brassard; bracelet; petit bras (de mer), *m.* **armlet,** *n.*

armorial [ɑːˈmɔːriəl], *a.* Armorial. *Armorial bearings*, armoiries, *f.pl.*

armorist [ˈɑːmərist], *n.* Armoriste, *m.*

armour [ˈɑːmə], *n.* Armure, *f.*; les blindés, *m.pl.*—*v.t.* Cuirasser, blinder. **armoured,** *a.* Cuirassé, blindé. *Armoured cruiser*, croiseur cuirassé, *m.*; *armoured train*, train blindé, *m.*; *light armoured car*, auto-mitrailleuse, *f.* **armourer,** *n.* Armurier, *m.* **armour-plate,** *n.* Plaque de blindage, *f.* **armour-plated,** *a.* Cuirassé, blindé. **armoury,** *n.* Arsenal, *m.*; salle d'armes, *f.*; armurerie, *f.*

armpit [ˈɑːmpit], *n.* Aisselle, *f.*

army [ˈɑːmi], *n.* Armée; (*fig.*) foule, multitude, *f. Army corps*, corps d'armée, *m.*; *army list*, les cadres, *m.pl.*, annuaire militaire, *m.*; *standing army*, armée permanente, *f. The Salvation Army*, l'Armée du Salut; *to join the army*, se faire soldat, s'enrôler, s'engager.

arnica [ˈɑːnikə], *n.* Arnica, *f.*

Arnold [ˈɑːnəld]. Arnaud, *m.*

aroma [əˈroumə], *n.* Arome *or* arôme, *m.*; bouquet (of wine), *m.*

aromatic [ærəˈmætik], *a.* Aromatique. **aromatization,** *n.* Aromatisation, *f.* **aromatize** [əˈroumətaiz], *v.t.* Aromatiser.

arose, *past* [ARISE].

around [əˈraund], *prep.* Autour de; (*colloq.*) environ, vers, à peu près.—*adv.* Autour, à l'entour, aux alentours. *All around*, tout autour.

arouse [əˈrauz], *v.t.* Réveiller, éveiller; exciter, provoquer.

arpeggio [ɑːˈpedʒ(i)ou], *n.* (*Mus.*) Arpège, *m.*

arquebus [HARQUEBUS].

arrack [ˈærək], *n.* Arack, *m.*

arraign [əˈrein], *v.t.* Accuser, poursuivre en justice, attaquer. **arraignment,** *n.* Mise en accusation, *f.*

arrange [əˈreindʒ], *v.t.* Arranger, régler, disposer, distribuer; organiser. **arrangement,** *n.* Arrangement, *m.*, disposition, organisation, *f.*, dispositif, *m.*; (*colloq.*) affaire, *f.*, machin, *m. To make arrangements*, faire des préparatifs (pour), s'arranger (avec). *Price by arrangement*, prix à débattre.

arrant [ˈærənt], *a.* Insigne, achevé, fieffé. *An*

arrant knave, un fier coquin. **arrantly,** *adv.* Notoirement, impudemment.

arras [ˈærəs], *n.* Tentures, tapisseries, *f.pl.*

array [əˈrei], *v.t.* Ranger, déployer; revêtir, parer.—*n.* Ordre, rang; étalage; appareil, *m. In battle array*, en ordre de bataille.

arrear [əˈriə], *n.* Arriéré; (*pl.*) arrérages, *m.pl. To be in arrears*, être en retard, avoir de l'arriéré.

arrest [əˈrest], *v.t.* Arrêter; fixer; suspendre.— *n.* Arrestation, prise de corps, *f.*; arrêt, *m.*, suspension, *f. Close arrest*, arrêts forcés, *m.pl.*; *open arrest*, arrêts simples, *m.pl.*; *to put under arrest*, mettre aux arrêts. ***arrestation** or **arrestment,** *n.* Arrestation, *f.*, arrêt, *m.*; saisie, *f.* **arresting,** *a.* Frappant, qui arrête l'attention.

arris [ˈæris], *n.* Arête vive, *f.*

arrival [əˈraivəl], *n.* Arrivée, *f.*; arrivage (of goods etc.), *m. Arrival platform*, quai d'arrivée, débarcadère, *m. New arrival*, nouveau venu, *m.*; *to await arrival* (on letters), ne pas faire suivre. **arrive,** *v.i.* Arriver (à); parvenir (à). **arrivist,** *n.* Arriviste.

arrogance [ˈærəgəns], *n.* Arrogance, *f.* **arrogant,** *a.* Arrogant. **arrogantly,** *adv.* Arrogamment.

arrogate [ˈærogeit], *v.t.* Attribuer injustement. *To arrogate to oneself*, s'arroger. **arrogation,** *n.* Prétention, usurpation, *f.*

arrow [ˈærou], *n.* Flèche, *f.*; (*fig.*) trait, *m. Shower of arrows*, grêle de flèches, *f.*; *to shoot an arrow*, lancer une flèche.—*v.t.* Indiquer par des flèches. **arrow-grass,** *n.* Triglochin, *m.* **arrow-head,** *n.* Pointe de flèche, sagittaire (plant), *f.* **arrow-maker,** *n.* Fléchier, *m.* **arrow-root,** *n.* Arrow-root, *m.* **arrow-shaped,** *a.* Sagitté.

arse [ɑːs], *n.* (*vulg.*) Cul, derrière, *m.*

arsenal [ˈɑːsənəl], *n.* Arsenal, *m.*

arsenic [ˈɑːsənik], *n.* Arsenic, *m.*—*a.* [ɑːˈsenik] Arsénique.

arsenical [ɑːˈsenikəl], *a.* Arsenical. **arsenious** [ɑːˈsiːniəs], *a.* Arsénieux. **arsenite,** *n.* Arsénite, *m.*

arsis [ˈɑːsis], *n.* (*Pros.*) Arsis, *f.*, temps fort, *m.*

arson [ˈɑːsən], *n.* Incendie volontaire, *m.*

art (1) [ɑːt], *n.* Art, *m.*; adresse, habileté, *f. Arts and crafts*, arts et métiers; *art for art's sake*, l'art pour l'art; *the noble art*, la boxe, *f.*; *Art Union*, société des amis des arts, *f.*; *faculty of arts*, faculté des lettres, *f.*; *fine arts*, beaux-arts, *m.pl.*; *school of art*, école de dessin, académie, *f.*; *work of art*, œuvre d'art, *f.* (*Cine.*) *Art director*, décorateur, *m.*

*art (2), *2nd sing. pres. indic.* [BE].

Artemisia [ɑːtəˈmiʃiə]. Artémise, *f.*

arterial [ɑːˈtiəriəl], *a.* Artériel. *Arterial road*, route à grande circulation, *f.* **arterialization,** *n.* Artérialisation, *f.* **arterialize,** *v.t.* Artérialiser.

arteritis [ɑːtəˈraitis], *n.* Artérite, *f.* **arteriotomy,** *n.* Artériotomie, *f.*

artery [ˈɑːtəri], *n.* Artère, *f.*

artesian [ɑːˈtiːʒən], *a.* Artésien. *Artesian well*, puits artésien, *m.*

artful [ˈɑːtful], *a.* Rusé, fin, artificieux. **artfully,** *adv.* Avec artifice, artificieusement, adroitement. **artfulness,** *n.* Ruse, finesse, *f.*, artifice, *m.*

arthritic [ɑːˈθritik], *a.* Arthritique.

arthritis [ɑːˈθraitis], *n.* Arthrite, *f.*

artichoke ['ɑːtitʃouk], *n.* *Chinese artichoke*, crosne, *m.* (du Japon); *globe artichoke*, artichaut, *m.*; *Jerusalem artichoke*, topinambour, *m.*

article ['ɑːtikl], *n.* Article; objet, *m.*; clause, stipulation, *f.*, statut, *m.* *Article of luggage*, colis, *m.*; *article of clothing*, pièce d'habillement, *f.*; *articles of war*, code militaire, *m.*, règlements militaires, *m.pl.*; *definite article*, (*Gram.*) article défini, *m.*—*v.t.* Engager par contrat; placer (chez un avoué) comme clerc. *Articled clerk*, clerc d'avoué, *m.*

articular [ɑːˈtikjulə], *a.* Articulaire. **articulate** [-leit], *v.t.*, *v.i.* Articuler; énoncer, parler distinctement.—*a.* [-lit] Articulé. **articulately**, *adv.* Distinctement; article par article. **articulation**, *n.* Articulation, *f.*

artifice ['ɑːtifis], *n.* Artifice, *m.*, ruse, finesse, *f.*

artificer [ɑːˈtifisə], *n.* Artisan, ouvrier; mécanicien, *m.*

artificial [ɑːtiˈfiʃəl], *a.* Artificiel; faux; factice. *Artificial manure*, engrais chimiques, *m.pl.* *Artificial limbs*, appareil prothétique, *m.*

artificiality [ɑːtifiʃiˈæliti], *n.* Nature artificielle, *f.* **artificially**, *adv.* Artificiellement.

artillerist [ɑːˈtilərist], *n.* Artilleur, *m.* **artillery**, *n.* Artillerie, *f.* *Artillery practice*, écoles à feu, *f.pl.*; *heavy artillery*, artillerie lourde. **artilleryman**, *n.* Artilleur, *m.*

artisan [ɑːtiˈzæn], *n.* Artisan, ouvrier, *m.*

artist ['ɑːtist], *n.* Artiste. *He is an artist*, il est peintre. **artistic**, *a.* Artistique. **artistically**, *adv.* Artistement, avec art. **artistry**, *n.* Habileté de touche *or* de style, *f.*

artless ['ɑːtlis], *a.* Ingénu, naïf; sans art, naturel. **artlessly**, *adv.* Ingénument, naïvement; sans art. **artlessness**, *n.* Naïveté, simplicité, *f.*

arty ['ɑːti], *a.* (*fam.*) Qui fait parade de goûts artistiques; prétentieux.

arum ['ɛərəm], *n.* (*Bot.*) Arum, *m.*

aruspex [HARUSPEX].

as [æz], *conj.* Comme; en tant que; tel que; à titre de; aussi . . . que; à mesure que; en, pour; parce que, etc. *As big as*, aussi gros que; *as for*, quant à, pour; *as for him*, quant à lui; *as he advanced*, à mesure qu'il avançait; *as he was walking*, comme il marchait; *as if*, comme si; *as it were*, pour ainsi dire; *as much as*, autant que, tant que; *as cold as charity*, froid comme le marbre; *as though*, comme si; *as yet*, jusqu'à présent, encore; *as you were*, (*Mil.*) Au temps! *be that as it may*, quoi qu'il en soit; *do as you wish*, faites comme vous voudrez; *great man as he is*, tout grand homme qu'il est; *rich as she is*, toute riche qu'elle est; *she was dressed as a page*, elle était habillée en page; *that's as may be*, c'est selon; *to act as . . .*, agir en. . . .

asafoetida [æsəˈfiːtidə], *n.* Assafœtida, *f.*

asbestos [æzˈbestɔs], *n.* Asbeste, amiante, *m.*

ascarides [æsˈkæridiːz], *n.pl.* Ascarides, *m.pl.*

ascend [əˈsend], *v.i.* Monter (à *or* sur); remonter; s'élever (of mountains etc.).—*v.t.* Monter; gravir, faire l'ascension de; remonter (a river). **ascendancy**, *n.* Ascendant, *m.*; supériorité, influence, *f.* **ascendant**, *a.* Ascendant; supérieur.—*n.* Ascendant, *m.*; supériorité, *f.*; dessus, *m.* *His star is in the ascendant*, son étoile monte.

ascending, *a.* Ascendant; montant. *Ascending scale*, gamme ascendante, *f.*

ascension, *n.* Ascension, *f.* *Ascension-day*, jour de l'Ascension, *m.* **ascensional**, *a.* Ascensionnel. **ascent**, *n.* Ascension; élévation, montée, pente, *f.*

ascertain [æsəˈtein], *v.t.* S'assurer, s'informer de, constater, vérifier. **ascertainable**, *a.* Vérifiable. **ascertainment**, *n.* Constatation, vérification, *f.*

ascetic [əˈsetik], *a.* Ascétique.—*n.* Ascète, ascétique, *m.* **asceticism**, *n.* Ascétisme, *m.*

ascidium [əˈsidiəm] or **ascidian**, *n.* Ascidie, *f.*

asclepiad [æsˈkliːpiæd], *n.* Asclépiade, *m.*

ascribable [əˈskraibəbl], *a.* Attribuable, imputable. **ascribe**, *v.t.* Attribuer, imputer (à). **ascription**, *n.* Imputation, attribution, *f.*

aseptic [æˈseptik], *a.* and *n.* Aseptique, *m.*

asexual [əˈseksjuəl], *a.* Asexué, asexuel.

ash (1) [æʃ], *n.* Frêne (tree); bâton, *m.* *Mountain-ash*, sorbier, *m.*—*a.* De frêne.

ash (2) [æʃ], *n.* Cendre, *f.*; cendres, *f.pl.*

ashamed [əˈʃeimd], *a.* Honteux, confus. *I am ashamed of you*, vous me faites rougir; *to be ashamed of*, avoir honte de.

ash-bin, -pit, *n.* Cendrier, *m.* (de foyer).

ashcan ['æʃkæn], *n.* (*Am.*) Boîte à ordures, *f.*

ash-coloured, *a.* Cendre.

ashen (1) [æʃn], *a.* De frêne.

ashen (2) [æʃn], *a.* Cendré, gris pâle, terreux.

ash-grove, *n.* Frênaie, *f.*

ashlar ['æʃlə], *n.* Moellon, *m.*, pierre de taille, *f.*

ashore [əˈʃɔː], *adv.* À terre; (of a ship) échoué. *To go ashore*, débarquer; *to run ashore*, s'échouer, faire côte.

ashtray, *n.* Cendrier, *m.* (de fumeur).

Ash-Wednesday, *n.* Mercredi des Cendres, *m.*

ashy ['æʃi], *a.* Cendré; gris pâle. *Ashy-pale*, pâle comme la mort.

Asia ['eiʃə]. L'Asie, *f.* **Asia Minor**, l'Asie-Mineure.

Asiatic [eiʃiˈætik] or **Asian**, *a.* and *n.* Asiatique.

aside [əˈsaid], *adv.* De côté; (*Theat.*) à part; à l'écart. *Setting that aside*, à part cela, sans compter cela; *to turn aside*, se détourner.—*n.* (*Theat.*) Aparté, *m.*

asinine ['æsinain], *a.* D'âne; sot.

ask [ɑːsk], *v.t.* Demander, prier (de); inviter (à); s'informer, se renseigner; interroger; poser (une question). *To ask in*, prier d'entrer; *to ask him for something*, lui demander quelque chose; *to ask someone to dinner*, inviter quelqu'un à dîner; *to ask someone to do something*, demander à quelqu'un de faire quelque chose; *to ask to see*, demander à voir.

askance [əˈskæns], *adv.* De travers, obliquement, du coin de l'œil.

askew [əˈskjuː], *adv.* De côté, de biais.

aslant [əˈslɑːnt], *adv.* Obliquement, de biais, de côté, en travers.

asleep [əˈsliːp], *a.* Endormi. *To be asleep*, dormir; *to fall asleep*, s'endormir.

aslope [əˈsloup], *adv.* En pente.

Asmodeus [æsmoˈdiːəs], *n.* Asmodée, *m.*

asp (1) [æsp] or **aspic** (1), *n.* Aspic, *m.*

asp (2) [æsp] or **aspen**, *n.* Tremble, *m.* *Aspen-grove*, tremblaie, *f.*

asparagus [əsˈpærəgəs], *n.* Les (*or* des) asperges, *f.pl.* *A stick of asparagus*, une

asperge; *asparagus bed*, aspergière, aspergerie, *f.*; *asparagus-tip*, pointe d'asperge, *f.*; *bundle of asparagus*, botte d'asperges, *f.*
aspect ['æspekt], *n.* Aspect, *m.*; exposition, *f.* *To have a southern aspect*, être exposé au midi.
aspen, *n.* [ASP (2)].—*a.* De tremble.
asperges [ə'spəːdʒiːz], *n.* Aspergès, *m.*
aspergillum [-'dʒiləm], *n.* Goupillon, *m.* **aspergillus**, *n.* (*Biol.*) Aspergille, *f.*
asperity [æs'periti], *n.* Aspérité, âpreté, rudesse, sévérité, *f.*
asperse [æs'pəːs], *v.t.* Diffamer, calomnier; asperger (sprinkle). **aspersion**, *n.* Calomnie, *f.*; aspersion, *f.* (sprinkling). *To cast aspersions on*, répandre des calomnies sur.
aspersorium [-'səːriəm], *n.* Bénitier (portatif), *m.*
asphalt ['æsfælt], *n.* Asphalte, *m.*—*a.* D'asphalte.—*v.t.* Asphalter, bitumer.
asphodel ['æsfədel], *n.* (*Bot.*) Asphodèle, *m.*
asphyxia [æs'fiksiə] or **asphyxy**, *n.* Asphyxie, *f.* **asphyxiate**, *v.t.* Asphyxier.
aspic (1) [ASP (1)].
aspic (2) ['æspik]. *n.* Aspic (savoury dish), *m.*
aspidistra [æspi'distrə], *n.* Aspidistra, *m.*
aspirant [ə'spaiərənt], *n.* Aspirant, *m.*, aspirante, *f.*, candidat, *m.*, candidate, *f.*
aspirate ['æspəreit], *v.t.* Aspirer.—*a.* [-rit] Aspiré.—*n.* (Lettre) aspirée, *f.* **aspiration**, *n.* Aspiration, *f.* **aspirative**, *a.* Aspiratif. **aspirator**, *n.* Aspirateur, *m.*
aspire [ə'spaiə], *v.i.* Aspirer (à), ambitionner. **aspiring**, *a.* Ambitieux.
aspirin ['æspirin], *n.* Aspirine, *f.*
asquint [ə'skwint], *adv.* De travers, en louchant.
ass [æs], *n.* Âne, *m.* *Asses' bridge*, pont aux ânes, *m.*; *he is a silly ass*, il est bête à manger du foin; *she-ass*, ânesse, *f.*; *to make an ass of oneself*, agir sottement, se faire moquer de soi; *young ass*, ânon, *m.*
assafoetida [ASAFOETIDA].
assagai or **assegai** ['æsəgai], *n.* Zagaie, *f.*
assail [ə'seil], *v.t.* Assaillir, attaquer. **assailable**, *a.* Attaquable. **assailant**, *n.* Assaillant, *m.*
assassin [ə'sæsin], *n.* Assassin (politique), *m.* **assassinate**, *v.t.* Assassiner. **assassination**, *n.* Assassinat, *m.* **assassinator**, *n.* Assassin, *m.*
assault [ə'səːlt], *n.* Assaut, *m.*, attaque brusquée; (*Law*) tentative de voie de fait, *f.* *Assault and battery*, voies de fait, *f.pl.*; *indecent assault*, outrage aux mœurs, *m.*—*v.t.* Assaillir, attaquer. *To be assaulted*, être victime d'une agression *or* d'une tentative de viol. **assaulter**, *n.* Assaillant, *m.*
assay [ə'sei], *n.* Épreuve, vérification, *f.*; essai, *m.* *Assay balance*, trébuchet, *m.*, balance d'essai, *f.*; *assay office*, bureau de garantie, *m.*—*v.t.* Essayer, titrer, faire l'essai de. **assayer**, *n.* Essayeur, *m.*
assegai [ASSAGAI].
assemblage [ə'semblidʒ], *n.* Assemblage, *m.* **assemble**, *v.t.* Assembler, réunir.—*v.i.* S'assembler, se réunir. **assembly**, *n.* Assemblée, réunion, *f.*; assemblage, *m.* (of a machine). *Assembly-room*, salle des fêtes, *f.*; *assembly line*, chaîne de montage, *f.*; *National Assembly*, Assemblée Nationale, *f.*; *unlawful assembly*, attroupement, *m.*
assent [ə'sent], *v.i.* Donner son assentiment

(à), admettre.—*n.* Assentiment, consentement, *m.*, sanction, *f.* **assentient**, *a.* and *n.* Approbateur, *m.*, approbatrice, *f.* **assentingly**, *adv.* Avec approbation.
assert [ə'səːt], *v.t.* Affirmer, prétendre, soutenir; revendiquer, faire valoir (one's rights etc.). **assertion**, *n.* Assertion, revendication, *f.* **assertive**, *a.* Assertif. **assertively**, *adv.* D'un ton péremptoire. **assertor**, *n.* Personne qui affirme, *f.*, défenseur, *m.*
assess [ə'ses], *v.t.* Répartir, fixer; imposer; évaluer. **assessable**, *a.* Imposable. **assessed**, *a.* Taxé, imposé, fixé. *Assessed taxes*, impôts directs, *m.pl.* **assessment**, *n.* Imposition, répartition, assiette; évaluation, *f.* **assessor**, *n.* Assesseur; répartiteur, *m.*
asset ['æset], *n.* Avoir; avantage, *m.* **assets** ['æsets], *n.pl.* Actif, *m.*, dettes actives, *f.pl. Assets and liabilities*, actif et passif, *m. Personal assets*, biens meubles, *m.pl.*; *real assets*, biens immobiliers, *m.pl.*
asseverate [ə'sevəreit], *v.t.* Affirmer solennellement. **asseveration**, *n.* Affirmation, *f.* (solennelle).
assiduity [æsi'djuːiti], *n.* Assiduité, *f.*
assiduous [ə'sidjuəs], *a.* Assidu. **assiduously**, *adv.* Assidûment.
assign [ə'sain], *v.t.* Assigner, attribuer; transférer (à).—*n.* (*Law*) Ayant droit, *m.* **assignable**, *a.* Assignable, transférable.
assignation [æsig'neiʃən], *n.* Attribution, assignation, cession, *f.*, transfert, *m.*; rendez-vous, *m.*
assignee [æsi'niː], *n.* Cessionnaire; syndic (de faillite), *m.* **assignment** [ə'sainmənt], *n.* Attribution, assignation, *f.*, transfert, *m.*, cession de biens, *f.* **assignor**, *n.* Cédant, *m.*
assimilable [ə'similəbl], *a.* Assimilable. **assimilate**, *v.t.* Assimiler.—*v.i.* S'assimiler. **assimilation**, *n.* Assimilation, *f.* **assimilative**, *a.* Assimilatif, assimilateur.
assist [ə'sist], *v.t.* Aider. *To assist each other*, s'entr'aider. **assistance**, *n.* Assistance, aide, *f.*; secours, concours, *m. To come to someone's assistance*, venir au secours de quelqu'un. **assistant**, *a.* Qui aide, auxiliaire. —*n.* Aide; adjoint, *m.*; (in a shop) commis, *m. Assistant examiner*, examinateur adjoint, *m.*; *assistant manager*, sous-directeur, *m.*
assize [ə'saiz], *n.* (*usu. in pl.*) Assises, *f.pl. Court of assizes*, cour d'assises, *f.*
associable [ə'souʃiəbl], *a.* Sociable.
associate [ə'souʃieit], *v.t.* Associer (avec *or* à). —*v.i.* S'associer (avec *or* à). *To associate with*, fréquenter.—*n.* [-iit] Associé; complice, *m.*—*a.* Associé.
association [əsousi'eiʃən], *n.* Association, *f.*; souvenir, *m.*
assonance ['æsənəns], *n.* Assonance, *f.* **assonant**, *a.* Assonant.
assort [ə'səːt], *v.t.* Assortir. **assorted**, *a.* Assorti. **assortment**, *n.* Assortiment, *m.*; classification, *f.*
assuage [ə'sweidʒ], *v.t.* Adoucir, apaiser, calmer, soulager.—*v.i.* S'apaiser, se calmer. **assuagement**, *n.* Adoucissement, *m.* **assuasive**, *a.* Adoucissant.
assume [ə'sjuːm], *v.t.* Prendre sur soi, s'arroger, s'attribuer; assumer (une responsabilité); supposer, présumer; se permettre, se donner; simuler, affecter. *He was assumed to be dead*, on le supposait mort; *under an*

assumed name, sous un nom supposé.
assuming, *a.* Arrogant, présomptueux, prétentieux. *Assuming that* . . ., mettons que . . ., en supposant que . . . (with *subj.*).
assumpsit, *n.* (*Law*) Promesse verbale, *f.*, pseudo-contrat, *m.*
assumption [ə'sʌmpʃən], *n.* Supposition; prétention; assomption (de la Sainte Vierge), *f.* **assumptive,** *a.* Qu'on peut admettre; présomptueux.
assurable [ə'ʃuərəbl], *a.* Assurable. **assurance,** *n.* Assurance, *f.* **assure,** *v.t.* Assurer. *You may rest assured that*, vous pouvez tenir pour certain que. **assuredly,** *adv.* Assurément, à coup sûr. **assuredness,** *n.* Certitude, *f.*; confiance, *f.* **assurer,** *n.* Assureur, *m.*
Assyria [ə'siriə]. L'Assyrie, *f.*
Assyrian [ə'siriən], *a.* and *n.* Assyrien, *m.* **Assyriology,** *n.* Assyriologie, *f.* **Assyriologist** [-'ɔlədʒist], *n.* Assyriologue.
astatic [ə'stætik], *a.* Astatique.
aster ['æstə], *n.* (*Bot.*, *Biol.*) Aster, *m.*
asterias [ə'stiəriæs], *n.* Astérie, *f.*
asterisk ['æstərisk], *n.* Astérisque, *m.* **asterism,** *n.* Astérisme, *m.*
astern [əs'tə:n], *adv.* (*Naut.*) À l'arrière, sur l'arrière. *To go astern*, culer; *to leave astern*, laisser à l'arrière.
asteroid ['æstərɔid], *n.* Astéroïde, *m.*
asthenia [æs'θi:niə], *n.* Asthénie, *f.* **asthenic** [æs'θenik], *a.* Asthénique.
asthma ['æsθmə], *n.* Asthme, *m.* **asthmatic** [æsθ'mætik], *a.* Asthmatique.
astigmatic [æstig'mætik], *a.* Astigmate.
astigmatism [ə'stigmətizm], *n.* Astigmatisme, *m.*
astir [ə'stə:], *a.* En mouvement, agité, en émoi, debout.
astonish [ə'stɔniʃ], *v.t.* Étonner. *I am astonished at what you tell me*, je suis étonné de ce que vous me dites. *I am astonished that*, cela m'étonne que. **astonishing,** *a.* Étonnant. **astonishingly,** *adv.* Étonnamment. **astonishment,** *n.* Étonnement, *m.* *To strike with astonishment*, frapper d'étonnement.
astound [ə'staund], *v.t.* Étonner, ébahir, étourdir. **astounding,** *a.* Renversant, abasourdissant.
astraddle [ə'strædl], *adv.* À califourchon.
Astraea [æs'tri:ə]. Astrée, *f.*
astragal ['æstrəgəl], *n.* (*Arch.*) Astragale, *m.*
astrakhan [æstrə'kæn], *n.* Astracan, astrakan, *m.*
astral ['æstrəl], *a.* Astral.
astray [ə'strei], *adv.* Égaré, (*fig.*) dévoyé. *To go astray*, s'égarer; *to lead astray*, égarer; débaucher.
astrict [ə'strikt], *v.t.* Resserrer, comprimer. **astriction,** *n.* Contrainte, *f.*; (*Med.*) constriction, *f.*
astride [ə'straid], *adv.* À califourchon. *Astride upon*, à cheval sur.
astringe [ə'strindʒ], *v.t.* Resserrer. **astringency,** *f.* Astringence, *f.* **astringent,** *a.* and *n.* Astringent, *m.*
astrolabe ['æstrəleib], *n.* Astrolabe, *m.*
astrologer [ə'strɔlədʒə], *n.* Astrologue, *m.*
astrologic [æstrə'lɔdʒik] or **astrological,** *a.* Astrologique. **astrologically,** *adv.* Astrologiquement.
astrology [ə'strɔlədʒi], *n.* Astrologie, *f.*

astronaut ['æstrənɔ:t], *n.* Astronaute, *m.*
astronautics, *n.* Astronautique, *f.*
astronomer [ə'strɔnəmə], *n.* Astronome, *m.*
astronomic [æstrə'nɔmik] or **astronomical,** *a.* Astronomique. **astronomically,** *adv.* Astronomiquement.
astronomy [ə'strɔnəmi], *n.* Astronomie, *f.*
Asturias [æs'tjuəriæs]. Les Asturies, *f.pl.*
astute [ə'stju:t], *a.* Fin, avisé; rusé, astucieux. **astutely,** *adv.* Astucieusement, avec ruse. **astuteness,** *n.* Astuce, *f.*, sagacité, *f.*
Asuncion [ɑːsuːnsi'ɔn, -θi'ɔn]. L'Assomption, *f.*
asunder [ə'sʌndə], *adv.* En deux, éloigné l'un de l'autre.
asylum [ə'sailəm], *n.* Asile, refuge; hospice, *m.* *Lunatic asylum*, hospice d'aliénés, *m.*; *political asylum*, droit d'asile, *m.*
asymmetrical [æsi'metrikəl], *a.* Asymétrique. **asymmetry,** *n.* [æ'simitri], *n.* Asymétrie, *f.*
asymptote ['æsimptout], *n.* (*Geom.*) Asymptote, *f.*
asymptotic [-'tɔtik] or **asymptotical,** *a.* Asymptotique.
asyndeton [ə'sindətən], *n.* (*Rhet.*) Asyndète, *m.*
at [æt], *prep.* À, en, dans; contre; après. *At a loss*, à perte; (*fig.*) embarrassé; *at first*, d'abord; *at hand*, sous la main; *at his request*, sur sa demande; *at home*, chez soi; *at last*, enfin; *at least*, du moins; *at my brother's*, chez mon frère; *at night*, le soir, la nuit; *at once*, tout de suite, à la fois; *at peace*, en paix; *at school*, à l'école; *at sea*, en mer; *at the same time*, en même temps; *at the top*, en haut; *at work*, à l'ouvrage; *to be always at someone*, harceler quelqu'un de querelles; *to be at one*, être d'accord; *to be hard at it*, travailler ferme; *to look at*, regarder; *what are you at?* que faites-vous? *what is he at?* qu'est-ce qu'il fait? *while we are at it*, pendant que nous y sommes.
ataraxia [ætə'ræksiə] or **ataraxy** ['ætəræksi], *n.* Ataraxie, *f.*
atavism ['ætəvizm], *n.* Atavisme, *m.* **atavistic** [ætə'vistik], *a.* Atavique.
ate [etj], *past* [EAT].
Athanasian [æθə'neiʃiən], *a.* Athanasien. *The Athanasian Creed*, le Symbole de Saint Athanase.
atheism ['eiθiizm], *n.* Athéisme, *m.* **atheist,** *n.* Athée. **atheistic** [eiθi'istik] or **atheistical,** *a.* Athée, athéistique. **atheistically,** *adv.* En athée.
athenaeum [æθə'ni:əm], *n.* Athénée, *m.*
Athenian [ə'θi:njən], *a.* and *n.* Athénien, *m.*
Athens ['æθənz]. Athènes, *f.*
athermanous [ə'θə:mənəs], *a.* Athermique.
athirst [ə'θə:st], *a.* Altéré, assoiffé.
athlete ['æθli:t], *n.* Athlète, *m.* *Athlete's foot*, pied de l'athlète, *m.*
athletic [æθ'letik], *a.* Athlétique. **athletically,** *adv.* Athlétiquement. **athleticism,** *n.* Athlétisme, *m.* **athletics,** *n.* L'athlétisme, *m.*, les sports (athlétiques), *m.pl.*
athwart [ə'θwɔ:t], *adv.* De travers.—*prep.* À travers; (*Naut.*) en travers de, par le travers de.
a-tilt [ə'tilt], *adv.* Incliné; la lance en arrêt. *To run a-tilt against*, rompre une lance avec.
Atlantean [ætlæn'ti:ən], *a.* (*Force*) comme celle d'Atlas. **Atlantes,** *n.pl.* (*Arch.*)

Atlante, *m.* **Atlantic** [ət'læntik], *a.* Atlantique. *The Atlantic coast,* le littoral atlantique.—*n.* L'(Océan) Atlantique, *m.*
atlas ['ætləs], *n.* Atlas, *m.*
atmolysis [æt'mɔlisis], *n.* Atmolyse, *f.* **atmometer,** *n.* Atmomètre, *m.*
atmosphere ['ætməsfiə], *n.* Atmosphère, *f.* (*Cine.*) *Atmosphere noise,* bruit d'ambiance, *m.* **atmospheric** [ætməs'ferik] or **atmospherical,** *a.* Atmosphérique. **atmospherics,** *n.pl.* (*Rad.*) Parasites, *m.pl.*
atoll [ə'tɔl], *n.* Atoll, attoll, *m.*
atom ['ætəm], *n.* Atome, *m.* *Atom bomb,* bombe atomique, *f.*; *not an atom of truth,* pas une parcelle de vérité. **atomic** [ə'tɔmik] or **atomical,** *a.* Atomique. *Atomic energy,* énergie atomique, *f.*; *atomic weight,* poids atomique, *m.* **atomicity** [ætə'misiti], *n.* Atomicité, *f.* **atomism,** *n.* Atomisme, *m.* **atomist,** *n.* Atomiste, *m.* **atomize,** *v.t.* Réduire en atomes *or* en poudre, pulvériser, vaporiser. **atomizer,** *n.* Pulvérisateur, *m.*
atonable [ə'tounəbl], *a.* Expiable.
atone, *v.i., v.t.* Expier; racheter. **atonement,** *n.* Expiation, réparation, *f.* *In atonement for his crimes,* en expiation de ses crimes.
atonic [ə'tɔnik], *a.* Atonique; (*Gram.*) atone.
atony ['ætəni], *n.* Atonie, *f.*
atop [ə'tɔp], *adv.* Au sommet, en haut.
atrabiliar [ætrə'biliə] or **atrabilious,** *a.* Atrabilaire, atrabilieux. **atrabiliousness,** *n.* Atrabile, *f.*
Atreus ['eitrius]. Atrée, *m.*
a-trip [ə'trip], *adv.* (*Naut.*) Dérapée (of anchor), *f.*; guindées (of topsails), *f.pl.*
atrium ['eitriəm], *n.* Atrium, *m.*
atrocious [ə'trouʃəs], *a.* Atroce. **atrociously,** *adv.* Atrocement. *Atrociously bad,* exécrable. **atrociousness** or **atrocity** [ə'trɔsiti], *n.* Atrocité, *f.*
atrophy ['ætrəfi], *n.* Atrophie, *f.*—*v.t.* Atrophier.—*v.i.* S'atrophier.
atropine ['ætrəpain], *n.* (*Chem.*) Atropine, *f.* **atropism,** *n.* Atropisme, *m.*
attach [ə'tætʃ], *v.t.* Attacher, lier (à); (*Law*) saisir. *To attach credence to,* ajouter foi à.—*v.i.* S'attacher. *No blame attaches to him,* aucun blâme ne lui est imputable. **attachable,** *a.* Qu'on peut attacher. **attaché** [ə'tæʃei], *n.* Attaché, *m.* **attaché-case,** *n.* Mallette, *f.* **attachment,** *n.* Attachement, *m.*; affection, *f.*; (*Law*) saisie-arrêt, *f.*
attack [ə'tæk], *v.t.* Attaquer; s'attaquer (à).— *n.* Attaque, *f.,* accès, *m.,* assaut, *m.* *An attack of fever,* un accès de fièvre; *an attack of nerves,* une crise de nerfs. **attackable,** *a.* Attaquable. **attacker,** *n.* Agresseur, *m.*
attain [ə'tein], *v.t.* Atteindre, parvenir à. **attainable,** *a.* Qu'on peut atteindre. **attainableness,** *n.* Possibilité d'atteindre, *f.* **attainder** [ə'teində], *n.* Mise hors la loi, *f.* **attainment** [ə'teinmənt], *n.* Acquisition, *f.*; talent, *m.*; (*pl.*) connaissances, *f.pl.*
attaint [ə'teint], *v.t.* Accuser; condamner, frapper de mort civile; flétrir, dégrader.
attar ['ætə], *n.* Essence, huile essentielle, *f.* *Attar of roses,* essence de roses, *f.*
attemper [ə'tempə], *v.t.* Tempérer, modérer.
attempt [ə'tempt], *v.t.* Tenter, essayer, tâcher (de).—*n.* Tentative, *f.,* essai, effort, *m.*; attentat, *m.* *An attempt on someone's life,* un attentat contre la vie de quelqu'un;

first attempt, coup d'essai, *m.*; *to make the attempt,* tenter le coup. **attempt*able,** *a.* Qui peut être essayé *or* tenté.
attend [ə'tend], *v.t.* S'occuper de; soigner (un malade); accompagner, servir, suivre; assister, être présent (à). *To attend a lecture,* assister à une conférence; *to attend school,* aller à l'école; *to attend the lectures on chemistry,* suivre le cours de chimie.—*v.i.* Faire attention, écouter, prêter l'oreille (à); assister, être présent (à); servir; avoir égard (à); veiller, vaquer, s'appliquer (à). *I shall attend,* j'y serai, je m'y trouverai; *to attend to one's business,* vaquer à ses affaires; *to attend upon,* servir; *you are not attending,* vous ne faites pas attention. **attendance,** *n.* Service, *m.*; assistance (à une réunion); présence, *f.*; fréquentation, *f.* (scolaire); soins (pour un malade), *m.pl.*; (*Med.*) visites, *f.pl.* *To be in attendance on,* être de service auprès de; *to dance attendance,* faire antichambre *or* le pied de grue. **attendant,** *a.* Qui suit, qui accompagne, qui dépend (de).—*n.* Assistant, aide, *m.*; serviteur, domestique; gardien, *m.*; (*Theat.*) ouvreuse, *f.*; (*pl.*) suite, *f.,* personnel, cortège, *m.*
attention [ə'tenʃən], *n.* Attention, *f.*; (*pl.*) prévenances, *f.pl.,* soins, *m.pl.* *All attention,* tout oreilles; *attention!* [-ʃʌn] (*Mil.*) *garde-à-vous!* attention! *to call someone's attention,* faire remarquer à; *to pay attention,* faire attention, avoir égard (à); *to turn one's attention to,* s'occuper de. **attentive,** *a.* Attentif (à), assidu (auprès de), prévenant (pour). **attentively,** *adv.* Attentivement. **attentiveness,** *n.* Attention, prévenance, *f.*
attenuant [ə'tenjuənt], *a. and n.* Atténuant. **attenuate,** *v.t.* Atténuer. **attenuated,** *a.* Atténué, *a.* **attenuation,** *n.* Atténuation, *f.*; amaigrissement, *m.*
attest [ə'test], *v.t.* Attester. *Attested copy,* copie certifiée, *f.* **attestation** [ætes'teiʃən], *n.* Attestation, *f.* **attestor,** *n.* Certificateur, *m.*
attic ['ætik], *n.* Mansarde, *f.,* grenier, *m.* *Attic window,* fenêtre en mansarde, *f.*; *to live in the attics,* loger sous les toits. **Attic** ['ætik], *a.* Attique. *Attic wit,* sel attique, *m.* **Attica.** L'Attique, *f.* **Atticism** [-'sizm], *n.* Atticisme, *m.* **Atticist,** *n.* Atticiste. **Atticize,** *v.i.* Affecter l'atticisme.
attire [ə'taiə], *v.t.* Vêtir, parer.—*n.* Vêtements, *m.pl.,* costume, *m.*; parure, *f.,* atours *m pl.*; ramure, *f.* (of stag).
attitude ['ætitju:d], *n.* Attitude, pose, *f.* *Attitude of mind,* manière de penser, *f.* **attitudinize** [-'tju:dinaiz], *v.i.* Poser; se donner des airs.
attorney [ə'tɔ:ni], *n.* Avoué; mandataire, *m.* *Attorney-general,* procureur-général, *m.*; *power of attorney,* procuration, *f.,* pouvoirs, *m.pl.* **attorneyship,** *n.* Charge d'avoué *or* de procureur; procuration, *f.*
attract [ə'trækt], *v.t.* Attirer. *I am most attracted to him,* il ne me plaît pas. **attractability,** *n.* Propriété d'être attiré, *f.* **attractable,** *a.* Attirable. **attractile,** *a.* Attracteur, attractif. **attractingly,** *adv.* Par attraction. **attraction,** *n.* Attraction; séduction, *f.*; (*pl.*) attraits, appas, *m.pl.* *The great attraction* (of a show), le clou. **attractive,** *a.* Attrayant, séduisant; attractif (of a magnet etc.).

Attractive price, prix intéressant, *m.* **attractively,** *adv.* D'une manière attrayante.
attractiveness, *n.* Attrait, charme, *m.*
attractivity, *n.* (*Phys.*) Attractivité, *f.*
attributable [ə'tribjutəbl], *a.* Attribuable, imputable.
attribute (1) [ə'tribjut], *v.t.* Attribuer, imputer (à).
attribute (2) ['ætribju:t], *n.* Attribut, *m.*, qualité, *f.*
attribution [ætri'bju:ʃən], *n.* Attribution, *f.*; éloge, *m.*
attributive [ə'tribjutiv], *a.* Attributif.
attrition [ə'triʃən], *n.* Attrition, *f. War of attrition*, guerre d'usure, *f.*
attune [ə'tju:n], *v.t.* Accorder.
auburn ['ɔ:bən], *a.* Châtain roux.
auction ['ɔ:kʃən], *n.* Enchère, *f.*, vente à la criée, vente aux enchères, *f. Auction-room*, salle des ventes, *f.*; *to put up for auction*, mettre aux enchères; *to sell by auction*, vendre aux enchères *or* à la criée.—*v.t.* Mettre aux enchères; vendre aux enchères.
auctioneer [-'niə], *n.* Commissaire-priseur; crieur (at markets), *m.*
audacious [ɔ:'deiʃəs], *a.* Audacieux. **audaciously,** *adv.* Audacieusement. **audaciousness** or **audacity** [ɔ:'dæsiti], *n.* Audace, *f.*, hardiesse, *f.*
audible ['ɔ:dibl], *a.* Qu'on peut entendre, distinct, intelligible. *He was scarcely audible*, on l'entendait à peine. **audibleness** *or* **audibility** [-'biliti], *n.* Perceptibilité, *f.* **audibly,** *adv.* De manière à être entendu, distinctement.
audience ['ɔ:diəns], *n.* Audience, *f.*; assistance, *f.*, public, *m.*, assistants, auditeurs, *m.pl.* **audience-chamber,** *n.* Salle d'audience, *f.*
audio-frequency ['ɔ:djo'fri:kwənsi], *n.* Audio-fréquence, *f.*
audiometer [ɔ:di'ɔmitə], *n.* Audiomètre, *m.*
audiophone, *n.* Audiophone, *m.*
audio-visual ['ɔ:djo'vizjuəl], *a.* Audio-visuel. *Audio-visual media*, moyens audio-visuels, *m.pl.*
audit ['ɔ:dit], *v.t.* Apurer, vérifier (des comptes).—*n.* Apurement, *m.*, vérification de comptes, *f. Audit office*, cour des comptes, *f.* **audit-house** *or* **-room,** *n.* Sacristie, *f.* **audition,** *n.* Audition, *f.*—*v.t.* (*fam.*) Auditionner. **auditor,** *n.* Vérificateur, censeur; expert comptable, *m.* **auditorium,** *n.* (*Theat.*) La salle, *f.*; vaisseau (d'église); parloir (de couvent), *m.*; (*Am.*) salle de conférence, *f.* **auditory,** *n.* Auditoire, *m.*, salle du tribunal, assemblée, *f.*—*a.* Auditif.
Augean [ɔ:'dʒi:ən], *a.* D'Augias, d'une grande saleté. *The Augean stables*, les écuries d'Augias, *f.pl.*
auger ['ɔ:gə], *n.* Tarière, rouanne, *f. Auger-bit*, mèche à bois, queue de cochon, *f.*; *auger-hole*, trou de tarière, *m.*; *screw-auger*, tarière à filet, *f.*
aught [ɔ:t], *n.* Quelque chose; quoi que ce soit, *m. For aught I know*, pour autant que je sache.
augment (1) [ɔ:g'ment], *v.t.* Augmenter, accroître.—*v.i.* S'augmenter, s'accroître.
augment (2) ['ɔ:gmənt], *n.* Accroissement; (*Gram.*) augment, *m.* **augmentation,** *n.*

Augmentation, *f.* **augmentative,** *a.* Augmentatif.
augur ['ɔ:gə], *v.t., v.i.* Augurer, présager. *To augur well for someone*, s'annoncer bien pour quelqu'un.—*n.* Augure, *m.*
augural ['ɔ:gjuərəl], *a.* Augural. **augury,** *n.* Augure, *m. Of good augury*, de bon augure.
august [ɔ:'gʌst], *a.* Auguste, imposant.
August ['ɔ:gəst], *n.* Août (month), *m. In August*, en août, au mois d'août.
Augustan [ɔ:'gʌstən], *a.* D'Auguste. *Augustan confession*, confession d'Augsbourg, *f.*
Augustin [ɔ:'gʌstin], *n.* Augustin, *m.* **Augustinian** [-'tiniən], *a.* Augustin.
Augustus [ɔ:'gʌstəs]. Auguste, *m.*
auk [ɔ:k], *n.* (*Orn.*) Pingouin, *m.*
auld [ɑ:ld], *a.* (*Sc.*)=old. *Auld lang Syne*, le bon vieux temps.
aulic ['ɔ:lik], *a.* Aulique.
Aulus Gellius ['ɔ:ləs dʒeliəs]. Aulu-Gelle, *m.*
aunt [ɑ:nt], *n.* Tante, *f. Great-aunt*, grand-tante. **auntie,** *n.* (*colloq.*) Tata, *f.*
aura ['ɔ:rə], *n.* Exhalaison, *f.*, effluve, *m.*
aural ['ɔ:rəl], *a.* De l'oreille. *Aural surgeon*, auriste, *m.*
aureate ['ɔ:riət], *a.* D'or, doré.
Aurelia [ɔ:'ri:liə]. Aurélie, *f.*
aurelia [ɔ:'ri:liə], *n.* Chrysalide, nymphe, *f.*
Aurelian [ɔ:'ri:liən]. Aurélien, *m.*
Aurelius [ɔ:'ri:liəs]. Aurélius, *m.* **Marcus Aurelius,** Marc-Aurèle, *m.*
auricle ['ɔ:rikl], *n.* Auricule, *f.*, pavillon de l'oreille, *m.*, oreillette (of the heart), *f.*
auricula [ɔ:'rikjulə], *n.* Auricule; oreille d'ours, *f.* **auricular,** *a.* Auriculaire.
auriferous [ɔ:'rifərəs], *a.* Aurifère.
aurist ['ɔ:rist], *n.* Auriste, *m.*
Aurora [ɔ:'rɔ:rə], *n.* Aurore, *f. Aurora Borealis*, aurore boréale. **auroral,** *a.* De l'aurore.
aurum ['ɔ:rəm], *n.* (*Chem.*) Or, *m.* **aurous,** *a.* D'or.
auscultation [ɔ:skəl'teiʃən], *n.* Auscultation, *f.*
auspice ['ɔ:spis], *n.* (*usu. in pl.*) Auspice, *m.* *Under the auspices of*, sous les auspices de.
auspicious [ɔ:'spiʃəs], *a.* De bon augure, propice, favorable. **auspiciously,** *adv.* Sous d'heureux auspices. **auspiciousness,** *n.* Aspect favorable, *m.*, heureux auspices, *m.pl.*
auster ['ɔ:stə], *n.* Auster, autan, vent du midi, *m.*
austere [ɔ:s'tiə], *a.* Austère; âpre. *To lead an austere life*, vivre en ascète. **austerely,** *adv.* Austèrement. **austereness** *or* **austerity** [ɔ:s'teriti], *n.* Austérité, *f.*
austral ['ɔ:strəl], *a.* Austral.
Australasia [ɔ:strə'leiʃiə]. L'Australasie, *f.*
Australia [ɔ:s'treiliə]. L'Australie, *f.*
Australian [ɔ:s'treiliən], *a.* and *n.* Australien, *m.*, Australienne, *f.*
Austria ['ɔ:striə]. L'Autriche, *f.*
Austrian [ɔ:'striən], *a.* and *n.* Autrichien, *m.*, Autrichienne, *f.*
authentic [ɔ:'θentik] *or* **authentical,** *a.* Authentique. **authentically,** *adv.* Authentiquement. **authenticate,** *v.t.* Authentiquer, constater, établir l'authenticité de, valider, homologuer. **authenticated,** *a.* Authentique, avéré. **authentication,** *n.*

Preuve d'authenticité, *f.* **authenticity** [ɔ:θen'tisiti], *n.* Authenticité, *f.*
author ['ɔ:θə], *n.* Auteur, *m.* **authoress,** *n.* Femme auteur, femme écrivain, *f.*
authoritarian [ɔ:θɔri'teəriən], *a.* and *n.* Autoritaire.
authoritative [ɔ:'θɔritətiv], *a.* D'autorité, revêtu d'autorité; impérieux. **authoritatively,** *adv.* Avec autorité, en maître. **authoritativeness,** *n.* Air *or* ton d'autorité, *m.* **authority,** *n.* Autorité, *f.*; autorisation, *f.*, mandat, *m.*; source, *f. The authorities,* les autorités, *f.pl.*, l'administration, *f.*; *to be an authority on something,* faire autorité en matière de quelque chose; *to exercise authority over,* exercer une autorité sur; *to have on good authority,* tenir de bonne source.
authorization [-rai'zeiʃən], *n.* Autorisation, *f.*
authorize ['ɔ:θəraiz], *v.t.* Autoriser. *To authorize someone to do something,* autoriser quelqu'un à faire quelque chose. **authorized,** *a.* Autorisé. *To be authorized to act,* avoir qualité pour agir.
authorship ['ɔ:θəʃip], *n.* Profession *or* qualité d'auteur; (*colloq.*) paternité, *f. The authorship is unknown,* l'auteur est inconnu.
autobiographer [ɔ:təbai'ɔgrəfə], *n.* Autobiographe.
autobiographic [ɔ:təbaiə'græfik] or **autobiographical,** *a.* Autobiographique.
autobiography [-bai'ɔgrəfi], *n.* Autobiographie, *f.*
autobus, *n.* (*Am.*) [BUS].
***autocar** ['ɔ:tɔkɑ:], *n.* Automobile, *f.*
autochthon [ɔ:'tɔkθən], *n.* (*pl.* **autochthones**) Autochtone, *m.* **autochthonous,** *a.* Autochtone.
autoclave ['ɔ:təkleiv], *n.* Autoclave, *m.*
autocracy [ɔ:'tɔkrəsi], *n.* Autocratie, *f.*
autocrat ['ɔ:təkræt], *n.* Autocrate, *m.*
autocratic [ɔ:tə'krætik] or **autocratical,** *a.* Autocratique. **autocratically,** *adv.* Autocratiquement.
auto-cycle ['ɔ:tosaikl], *n.* Cyclomoteur, *m.*
auto-da-fé [ɔ:toudɑ:'fei], *n.* (*pl.* **autos-da-fé**) Autodafé, *m.*
autogenous [ɔ:'tɔdʒənəs], *a.* Autogène.
autograph ['ɔ:təgræf, -ɑ:f], *n.* Autographe, *m.*—*v.t.* Signer, autographier.
autographic [-'græfik] or **autographical,** *a.* Autographe.
autography [ɔ:'tɔgrəfi], *n.* Autographie; collection d'autographes, *f.*
autogyro [ɔ:to'dʒairou], *n.* Autogyre, *m.*
automatic [ɔ:tə'mætik] or **automatical,** *a.* Automatique. *Automatic* (*pistol*), automatique, *m.* **automatically,** *adv.* Automatiquement; machinalement. **automation,** *n.* Automation, *f.*
automatism [ɔ:'tɔmətizm], *n.* Automatisme, *m.* **automatize,** *v.t.* Automatiser. **automaton,** *n.* (*pl.* **automata**) Automate, *m.*
automobile [ɔ:'tomobi:l], *n.* (*Am.*) Automobile, auto, voiture, *f.* **automobilism,** *n.* Automobilisme, *m.* **automobilist,** *n.* Automobiliste.
autonomous [ɔ:'tɔnəməs], *a.* Autonome.
autonomy, *n.* Autonomie, *f.*
autoplasty ['ɔ:təplæsti], *n.* Autoplastie, *f.*
autopsy ['ɔ:təpsi, ɔ:'tɔpsi], *n.* Autopsie, *f.*
auto-suggestion ['ɔ:tosə'dʒestʃən], *n.* Auto-suggestion, *f.*

auto-type ['ɔ:totaip], *n.* Fac-similé, *m.*, reproduction, *f.*
autumn ['ɔ:təm], *n.* Automne, *m.* or *f.*
autumnal [ɔ:'tʌmnəl], *a.* Automnal, d'automne.
auxiliary [ɔ:g'ziljəri], *a.* and *n.* Auxiliaire, *m.*
avail [ə'veil], *v.t.*, *v.i.* Profiter, servir. *To avail oneself of,* se servir de.—*n.* Service, avantage, *m.*, utilité, *f. Of what avail is it?* à quoi sert de? à quoi bon? *to be of no avail,* ne servir à rien. **available,** *a.* Disponible, valable. **availableness** or **availability,** *n.* Disponibilité, validité, *f.* **availably,** *adv.* Utilement, avec profit.
avalanche ['ævəlɑ:nʃ], *n.* Avalanche, *f.*
avarice ['ævəris], *n.* Avarice, *f.*
avaricious [ævə'riʃəs], *a.* Avare, avaricieux. **avariciously,** *adv.* Avec avarice, en avare.
avast [ə'vɑ:st], *int.* (*Naut.*) Tiens bon!
avatar ['ævətɑ:], *n.* Avatar, *m.*
***avaunt** [ə'vɔ:nt], *int.* Va-t-en! arrière!
ave ['eivi], *n.* Ave, *m. Ave Maria,* ave Maria, *m.*
avenge [ə'venʒ], *v.t.* Venger. *To avenge oneself,* se venger (de *or* sur). **avenger,** *n.* Vengeur, *m.*, vengeresse, *f.* **avenging,** *a.* Vengeur, *m.*, vengeresse.—*n.* Vengeance, *f.*
avens ['ævənz], *n.* (*Bot.*) Benoîte, *f.*
Aventine ['ævəntain]. Aventin. *Aventine Hill,* Le Mont Aventin, *m.*
avenue ['ævənju:], *n.* Avenue, *f.*; boulevard, *m.*; voie d'accès, *f.*
aver [ə'və:], *v.t.* Affirmer.
average ['ævəridʒ], *n.* Moyenne, *f.*, prix moyen, terme moyen, *m.*; mercuriale (des grains); (*Naut.*) avarie, *f. Above the average,* au-dessus du commun; *on an average,* en moyenne. *Free of average,* franc d'avarie; *general averages,* avaries communes; *particular averages,* avaries particulières; *petty averages,* menues avaries; *average-stater,* expert en avaries, *m.*—*a.* Commun, moyen. *The average Frenchman,* le Français moyen; *of average height,* de taille moyenne.—*v.t.* Établir la moyenne de; atteindre une moyenne de.—*v.i.* Revenir terme moyen à, donner une moyenne de.
averment [ə'və:mənt], *n.* Affirmation, *f.*
averse [ə'və:s], *a.* Opposé (à), ennemi (de). *I am averse to,* il me répugne de. **aversely,** *adv.* À contre-cœur. **averseness** or **aversion,** *n.* Répugnance, aversion, *f. It is his pet aversion,* c'est sa bête noire.
avert [ə'və:t], *v.t.* Détourner, écarter. **avertible,** *a.* Capable d'être détourné.
aviary ['eiviəri], *n.* Volière, *f.*
aviation [eivi'eiʃən], *n.* Aviation, *f.*
aviator ['eivieitə], *n.* Aviateur, pilote, *m.*, aviatrice, *f.*
avid ['ævid], *a.* Avide. **avidity,** *n.* Avidité, *f.* **avidly,** *adv.* Avec avidité, avidement.
avocado [ævə'kɑ:dou] *n.* (*pear*) Poire d'avocat, *f.*, avocat, *m.*
avocation [ævə'keiʃən], *n.* Distraction; occupation, *f.*; métier, *m.*
avoid [ə'vɔid], *v.t.* Éviter. *To avoid doing something,* éviter de faire quelque chose.—**v.i.* Se retirer, s'esquiver. **avoidable,** *a.* Évitable. **avoidance,** *n.* Action d'éviter, *f.*
avoirdupois [ævədə'pɔiz], *n.* Poids du commerce, *m.*
avouch [ə'vautʃ], *v.t.* Affirmer, déclarer.

avow [ə'vauɪ], *v.t.* Avouer, confesser, déclarer. **avowable**, *a.* Avouable. **avowal**, *n.* Aveu, *m.* **avowedly**, *adv.* De son propre aveu, ouvertement.
avulsion [ə'vʌlʃən], *n.* Avulsion, *f.*, arrachement, *m.*
avuncular [ə'vʌŋkjulə], *a.* Avunculaire.
await [ə'weit], *v.t.* Attendre. *Awaiting your reply*, dans l'attente de votre réponse.
awake [ə'weik], *v.t.* Éveiller, réveiller.—*v.i.* S'éveiller, se réveiller.—*a.* Éveillé; attentif. *To be awake to*, se rendre compte de; *wide awake*, bien éveillé. **awaken**, *v.t.* (*past* **awoke**, *p.p.* **awakened**) Éveiller, réveiller. **awakening**, *n.* Réveil, *m.* *A rude awakening*, un fâcheux réveil.
award [ə'wɔ:d], *v.t.* Décerner, adjuger.—*n.* Décision, *f.*, jugement arbitral, *m.*, sentence, *f.*; (*sch.*) récompense, *f.*
aware [ə'wɛə], *a.* Qui sait; instruit. *To be aware of*, savoir, avoir connaissance de; *not to be aware of*, ignorer; *not that I am aware of*, pas que je sache. **awareness**, *n.* Conscience, *f.*
awash [ə'wɔʃ], *adv.* (*Naut.*) À fleur d'eau. *The street was awash*, la rue était inondée.
away [ə'wei], *adv.* Absent; loin, au loin. *Away with you*, allez-vous-en! *far away*, au loin; *right away*, partez! en route! immédiatement; *they are all away*, ils sont tous absents; *to drive away*, chasser; *to go away*, s'en aller; *to send away*, renvoyer; *to talk away*, parler toujours; *to take away*, enlever.
awe [ɔ:], *n.* Crainte, terreur, *f.*, respect, *m.*; aube (of a wheel), *f.* *To strike with awe*, frapper de terreur, terrifier; *to stand in awe of*, craindre, redouter.—*v.t.* Inspirer du respect à; imposer à. **awe-inspiring**, *a.* Terrifiant, imposant. **aweless**, *a.* Sans crainte. **awestruck**, *a.* Frappé de terreur, terrifié.
aweather [ə'weðə], *adv.* (*Naut.*) Au vent.
aweigh [ə'wei], *adv.* (*Naut.*) Dérapée (anchor).
awful ['ɔ:ful], *a.* Terrible, redoutable, effroyable; solennel, imposant. *What awful weather!* quel temps affreux! **awfully**, *adv.* Horriblement, terriblement; (*fam.*) diablement. *It was awfully dull*, c'était d'une tristesse mortelle; *thanks awfully*, merci mille fois. **awfulness**, *n.* Caractère terrible, *m.*; solennité, *f.*
awhile [ə'wail], *adv.* Pendant quelque temps; un instant, un peu. *Wait awhile*, attendez un peu.
awkward ['ɔ:kwəd], *a.* Gauche, maladroit; malencontreux, fâcheux, embarrassant. *An awkward situation*, une situation fâcheuse; *an awkward customer*, un homme difficile; *the awkward age*, l'âge ingrat, *m.*; (*Mil.*) *the awkward squad*, le peloton des arriérés, *m.* **awkwardly**, *adv.* Gauchement, maladroitement; mal à propos. **awkwardness**, *n.* Gaucherie, maladresse, *f.*; embarras, *m.*; inconvénient, *m.*
awl [ɔ:l], *n.* Alène, *f.*; poinçon, *m.* **awl-shaped**, *a.* En alène.
awn [ɔ:n], *n.* (*Bot.*) Barbe, arête, *f.* **awned**, *a.* À barbes.
awning ['ɔ:niŋ], *n.* Tente, banne, bâche, *f.*; marquise, *f.* (outside theatre etc.); (*Naut.*) tendelet, *m.* *Rain-awning*, taud, *m.*
awoke, *past* [AWAKEN].

awry [ə'rai], *a.* and *adv.* De travers.
axe [æks], *n.* Hache, cognée, *f.* *To have an axe to grind*, servir ses intérêts personnels.
axial ['æksiəl], *a.* Axial.
axil ['æksil], *n.* (*Bot.*) Aisselle, *f.* **axillar** or **axillary**, *a.* Axillaire.
axiom ['æksiəm], *n.* Axiome, *m.* **axiomatic** [æksiɔ'mætik] or **axiomatical**, *a.* Axiomatique; évident.
axis ['æksis], *n.* (*pl.* **axes**) Axe, *m.*
axle [æksl], *n.* Arbre, essieu, *m.* (*Motor.*) *Back* or *rear axle*, pont arrière, *m.* **axle-box**, *n.* Boîte d'essieu, *f.* **axle-tree**, *n.* Essieu, *m.*
axminster ['æksminstə], *n.* Tapis de haute laine, *m.*
ay or **aye** (1) [ai], *adv.* Oui, c'est vrai. *Aye, aye!* (*Naut.*) bon quart!—*n.* Affirmation, *f.*, oui, *m.* (*pl.*) *The ayes have it*, les voix pour l'emportent; *ayes and noes*, voix pour et contre, *f.pl.*
*aye (2) [ei], *adv.* Toujours. *For aye*, à jamais, pour toujours.
azalea [ə'zeiliə], *n.* (*Bot.*) Azalée, *f.*
azarole ['æzərɔl], *n.* (*Bot.*) Azerole, *f.*
azimuth ['æziməθ], *n.* (*Astron.*) Azimut, *m.*
Azores [ə'zɔ:z]. Les Açores, *f.pl.*
azote [ə'zout], *n.* (*Chem.*) Azote, *m.*
azotic [ə'zɔtik], *a.* Azotique.
Aztec ['æztek], *a.* and *n.* Aztèque.
azure ['æʒə or 'eiʒə], *a.* Azur, *m.* *Azure stone*, lazulite, *f.*, lapis lazuli, *m.*—*a.* D'azur.—*v.t.* Azurer. **azured**, *a.* Azuré. **azurine**, *a.* Azurin.—*n.* Azurine, *f.*; pierre d'azur, *f.*
azurite, *n.* (*Min.*) Azurite, *f.*
azygous ['æzigəs], *a.* (*Physiol.*) Azygos.
azyme ['æzim], *n.* Pain azyme, *m.* **azymous**, *a.* Azyme.

B

B, b [bi:], *n.* La seconde lettre de l'alphabet, *m.*; (*Mus.*) si, *m.* *B flat*, si bémol; *B natural*, si bécarre; *he doesn't know a B from a bull's foot*, il ne sait ni A ni B.
baa [ba:], *v.i.* Bêler.—*n.* Bêlement, *m.*
babble [bæbl], *v.i.* Babiller; gazouiller, jaser; (*fig.*) murmurer (of a stream).—*n.* Babil, caquet; (*fig.*) murmure, *m.*, jaserie, *f.* **babbler**, *n.* Babillard, *m.*, babillarde, *f.* **babbling**, *a.* Babillard, bavard.
babe [beib], *n.* Enfant nouveau-né, petit enfant, *m.*
Babel ['beibəl], *n.* Babel, *f.* *A Babel of conversation*, un brouhaha de conversation.
baboon [bə'bu:n], *n.* Babouin, *m.*
baby ['beibi], *n.* Bébé, *m.* *Baby grand (piano)*, piano à demi-queue, *m.*; *baby-faced*, à figure poupine; *cry baby*, pleurard; *baby linen*, layette, *f.* **babyhood**, *n.* Première enfance, *f.* **babyish**, *a.* Enfantin, de petit enfant.
Babylon ['bæbilən]. Babylone, *f.*
Babylonian [bæbi'lounian], **Babylonic** [-'lɔnik] or **Babylonish**, *a.* Babylonien.—*n.* Babylonien, *m.*, Babylonienne, *f.*
baccalaureate [bækə'lɔ:riət], *n.* Baccalauréat, *m.*
baccarat ['bækərə], *n.* Baccara, *m.*
bacchanal ['bækənəl] or **bacchanalian** [bækə'neiliən], *a.* Bachique.—*n.* Ivrogne, buveur, *m.* **bacchanalia** or **bacchanals**, *n.pl.* Bacchanales, *f.pl.*

bacchant ['bækənt], *n.* Prêtre *or* adorateur de Bacchus, *m.*
bacchante [bə'kænti], *n.* Bacchante, *f.*
bacchic ['bækik], *a.* Bachique.
bacchius [bə'kaiəs], *n.* (*Pros.*) Bacchius, *m.*
bacciferous [bæk'sifərəs], *a.* (*Bot.*) Baccifère.
baccy ['bæki] (*colloq.*) [TOBACCO].
bachelor ['bætʃələ], *n.* Célibataire, garçon; bachelier (of arts), *m. Bachelor of Science*, bachelier *or* licencié ès sciences, *m.* **bachelor-hood** or **bachelorship**, *n.* Célibat, *m.*
bacillus [bə'siləs], *n.* (*pl.* **bacilli**) Bacille, *m.*
back [bæk], *n.* Dos, *m.*, reins, *m.pl.*; envers, *m.* (of fabric); verso, *m.* (of page etc.); fond, *m.* (of a room etc.); (*Ftb.*) arrière, *m.*; revers, *m.* (of a hill etc.); derrière, *m.* (of a house etc.). *At the back of*, derrière; *at the back of the house*, derrière la maison; *back of a chair*, dos *or* dossier de chaise, *m.*; *back of a chimney*, fond de cheminée, *m.*; *back of the hand*, revers de la main, *m.*; *back of the stage*, fond de la scène, *m.*; *back to back*, dos à dos; *behind his back*, par derrière, derrière son dos; *on the back of* (a letter etc.), au verso; *slung across the back*, en bandoulière; *the fifth floor back*, le cinquième sur la cour; *as soon as I get back*, dès mon retour; *to break someone's back*, casser les reins à quelqu'un; *to break the back of the work*, faire le plus dur du travail; *to fall on one's back*, tomber à la renverse *or* sur le dos; *to put one's back into something*, se donner entièrement à quelque chose; *to set or get a man's back up*, irriter quelqu'un; *to turn one's back on someone*, tourner le dos à quelqu'un; *when his back is turned*, quand il a le dos tourné.—*adv.* En arrière; de retour, rentré. *A few years back*, il y a quelques années; *to be back*, être de retour; *to call back*, rappeler; *to come back*, revenir; *to fall back upon*, recourir à, se replier sur; *to give back*, rendre; *to go back*, retourner, rebrousser chemin; *to send back*, renvoyer; *to trace the matter further back*, pour prendre la chose de plus haut.—*a.* Arrière, de derrière. *A back street*, une petite rue.—*v.t.* Soutenir, appuyer; endosser (a bill etc.); (*Betting*) jouer (un cheval); (*Naut.*) coiffer, masquer; empenneler (anchors); faire reculer; financer. *To back up*, appuyer, recommander, venir à l'aide de.—*v.i.* Reculer; aller en arrière, aller à reculons. *The car was backing*, l'auto faisait marche arrière; *to back out of*, se dédire *or* se tirer de.
back-bencher, *n.* Membre du Parlement sans portefeuille, *m.* **backbite**, *v.t.* Médire de, calomnier. **backbiter**, *n.* Médisant, détracteur, calomniateur, *m.* **backbiting**, *n.* Médisance, *f.* **backbone**, *n.* Épine dorsale, *f. To have no backbone*, manquer de caractère; *to the backbone*, jusqu'à la moelle des os. **back-chat**, *n.* Impertinence, *f.* **back-date**, *v.t.* Antidater. **back-door**, *n.* Porte de derrière, *f.* **backer**, *n.* Partisan, second; parieur pour, *m.* **back-fire**, *v.i.* (*Motor.*) Pétarader. **back-firing**, *n.* Retours de flamme, *m.pl.* **backgammon**, *n.* Trictrac, *m.* **back-garden**, *n.* Jardin de derrière, *m.* **background**, *n.* Arrière-plan, fond, *m.* (*Theat., Cine., Rad.*) *Background noise*, bruit de fond, *m.* **back-hand**, *n.* Coup de revers, *m.*, revers, *m. On the back-hand*, en revers. **back-handed**, *a.* Donné avec le revers de la main. *Back-handed answer*, riposte inattendue, *f.*; *back-handed compliment*, compliment équivoque, *m.* **back-kitchen**, *n.* Arrière-cuisine, *f.* **backing**, *n.* Mouvement en arrière, recul; (of the wind) renversement, *m.* **back-lash**, *n.* Contre-coup, *m.* **back-number**, *n.* Vieux numéro, *m.* (of newspaper; (*fig.*) ci-devant, *m.* (person). **back-pressure**, *n.* Contre-pression, *f.* **back-room**, *n.* Chambre de derrière, *f.* **back-scratching**, *n.* (*fam.*) Flagornerie, *f.*; flatterie mutuelle, *f.* **back-seat**, *n.* Siège de derrière, *m. To take a back seat*, (*fig.*) s'effacer. **backside**, *n.* (*pop.*) Derrière, *m.* **backsight**, *n.* Hausse (of fire-arms), *f.* **backslide**, *v.i.* Apostasier, retomber. **backslider**, *n.* Apostat; relaps, *m.* **back-sliding**, *n.* Récidive, rechute, *f.* **backstage**, *adv.* Derrière la scène; dans les coulisses. **backstairs**, *n.* Escalier de service, *m. Backstairs influence*, influence secrète; (*colloq.*) piston, *m.* **backstays**, *n.pl.* (*Naut.*) Galhaubans, *m.pl.* **backstitch**, *n.* Arrière-point, *m.* **back-stroke**, *n.* Coup de revers, *m.*; sur le dos, *f.* **backward** ['bækwəd], *a.* Arriéré; en retard; en arrière; lent, tardif, peu empressé. *To be backward* (in studies), être fort peu avancé. *Backward and forward motion*, mouvement de va-et-vient, *m.* **backwards** ['bækwədz] *or* **backward**, *adv.* À reculons; en arrière; à la renverse; à rebours. *To fall backward*, tomber à la renverse; *to lean backwards*, se pencher en arrière; *to walk backwards and forwards*, se promener de long en large. **backwardation** [bækwə'deiʃən], *n.* Déport, *m.* **backwardness**, *n.* État arriéré, retard, *m.*, lenteur, *f.* **backwater**, *n.* Eau arrêtée, *f.* **backway**, *n.* Sentier détourné, *m.* **backwoodsman**, *n.* Défricheur de forêts, *m.* (*Am.*); coureur des bois, *m.* **back-yard**, *n.* Cour de derrière, *f.*
bacon ['beikən], *n.* Lard, *m. To save one's bacon*, sauver sa peau, se tirer d'affaire.
bacterial [bæk'tiəriəl], *a.* Bactérien. **bactericidal**, *a.* Bactéricide. **bacteriological**, *a.* Bactériologique. **bacteriologist**, *n.* Bactériologiste, bactériologue. **bacteriology** [bæktiəri'ɔlədʒi], *n.* Bactériologie, *f.* **bacterium**, *n.* (*pl.* **bacteria**) Bactérie, *f.*
bad [bæd], *a.* (*comp.* **worse**, *superl.* **worst**) Mauvais; méchant (wicked); gâté (of food etc.); malade (of health); triste, malheureux, fâcheux (unfortunate). *Bad cold*, gros rhume, *m.*; *bad money*, fausse monnaie, *f.*; *he is a bad lot*, c'est un vilain personnage; *it's a bad business*, c'est une triste affaire; *it's not so bad*, ce n'est pas mal du tout; *that is too bad*, c'est trop fort; *to be in a bad way*, être en mauvais état; *to go bad*, se gâter; *to go from bad to worse*, aller de mal en pis; *to go to the bad*, tourner mal; *to have a bad finger etc.*, avoir mal au doigt etc. **bad-tempered**, *a.* Qui a mauvais caractère; de mauvaise humeur, grincheux.
bade, *past* [BID].
Baden ['baːdn], Bade, *m.*
badge [bædʒ], *n.* Insigne, *m.*; plaque, *f.*; (*Army*) écusson, *m.*; brassard, signe distinctif, *m.*
badger ['bædʒə], *n.* Blaireau, *m.*—*v.t.* Harceler. **badger-legged**, *a.* Boiteux.
badly ['bædli], *adv.* (*comp.* **worse**, *superl.*

worst) Mal; grièvement, fort, beaucoup. *Badly dressed,* mal mis; *to be badly off,* être dans le gêne; *to be badly in need of,* avoir grand besoin de; *to come off badly,* mal réussir. **badness,** *n.* Méchanceté, *f.*; mauvais état, *m.*

badminton ['bædmintən], *n.* Volant au filet, *m.*, badminton, *m.*

baffle (1) [bæfl], *v.t.* Déjouer, dérouter, rendre inutile; déconcerter, confondre.

baffle (2), *n.* Déflecteur, *m.*, chicane, *f.*; écran, *m.* (of loud-speaker).

bag [bæg], *n.* Sac, *m.*; bourse, *f.* (money); cornet (of paper), *m. In the bag,* dans le sac; *travelling-bag,* sac de voyage, *m.*; *game-bag,* gibecière, *f.*; *with bag and baggage,* avec armes et bagage.—*v.t.* Mettre en sac; tuer, abattre (du gibier); (*colloq.*) s'emparer de, accaparer; (*slang*) chiper, voler.—*v.i.* Bouffer, gonfler (of trousers). **bagful,** *n.* Sachée *f.*, sac plein, *m.* **bagman,** *n.* Commis-voyageur, *m.*

bagatelle [bægə'tel], *n.* Bagatelle, *f.*; (*Mus.*) petite pièce, *f.*; *trou-madame, *m.*

baggage ['bægidʒ], *n.* (chiefly *Am.*) Bagage, *m. To pack up bag and baggage,* plier bagage. (*colloq.*) *A saucy baggage,* une délurée. **baggage-wagon,** *n.* Fourgon, *m.*

baggy ['bægi], *a.* Déformé (of trousers).

***bagnio** ['bænjou], *n.* Maison close, *f.*; bagne, *m.*

bagpipe ['bægpaip], *n.* Cornemuse, *f.* **bag-piper,** *n.* Joueur de cornemuse, *m.*

bail (1) [beil], *n.* Caution, liberté sous caution, *f. On bail,* sous caution; *to bail out, to find bail for,* fournir caution pour.—*v.t.* Donner caution pour. **bail-bond,** *n.* Caution, *f.*

bail (2) or **bale** (1) [beil], *v.t.* Vider l'eau d'(un bateau); écoper.

bailiff ['beilif], *n.* Huissier; garde de commerce; bailli; (*Channel Isles*) chef-magistrat, *m. Farm bailiff,* régisseur, *m.* **bailiwick,** *n.* Bailliage, *m.*

bairn [bɛən], *n.* (*Sc. colloq.*) Enfant.

bait [beit], *v.t.* Amorcer (a hook); donner à manger à, faire reposer (a horse); faire combattre (bulls); (*fig.*) harceler, tourmenter.— *v.i.* Se rafraîchir (on a journey).—*n.* Amorce, *f.*; appât, leurre, *m. To take the bait,* mordre à l'hameçon.

baize [beiz], *n.* Serge, *f. Green baize,* tapis vert, *m.*

bake [beik], *v.t.* Cuire au four, faire cuire.— *v.i.* Cuire au four, boulanger; (*fig.*) brûler. **bakehouse,** *n.* Fournil, *m.*, boulangerie, *f.* **baker,** *n.* Boulanger, *m.*, boulangère, *f. Baker's man,* mitron, *m.*; *baker's shop,* boulangerie, *f.* **bakery,** *n.* Boulangerie, *f.* **baking,** *n.* Cuisson, *f.*; fournée (batch), *f. Baking-powder,* poudre remplaçant le levain, *f.*

bakelite ['beikəlait], *n.* Bakélite, *f.*

Balaclava helmet [bælə'klɑːvə 'helmit], *n.* Passe-montagne, *m.*

balance ['bæləns], *n.* Balance, *f.*; équilibre; balancier (of watch), *m. Balance of an account,* solde de compte, *m.*; *the balance of power,* l'équilibre politique, *m.*; *to hang in the balance,* rester en balance; *to keep one's balance,* se tenir en équilibre; *to lose one's balance,* perdre l'équilibre; *to strike a balance,* établir une balance, arrêter un compte, établir un bilan.—*v.t.* Balancer; peser. *To balance up,* arrêter, régler.—*v.i.* Se balancer; (*fig.*)

hésiter. **balancer,** *n.* Personne qui balance, *f.* **balance-sheet,** *n.* Bilan, *m.* **balance-weight,** *n.* Contre-poids, *m.* **balance-wheel,** *n.* Balancier (of watch); volant régulateur (of engine), *m.* **balancing,** *n.* Balancement, *m. Balancing aerial,* antenne de compensation, *f.*

balcony ['bælkəni], *n.* Balcon, *m.*

bald [bɔːld], *a.* Chauve; (*fig.*) plat, sec, nu (of style etc.).

baldachin ['bɔːldəkin], *n.* Baldaquin, *m.*

balderdash ['bɔːldədæʃ], *n.* Bêtises, *f.pl.*; balivernes, *f.pl.*; fatras, *m.*

bald-head ['bɔːldhəd] or **bald-pate,** *n.* Tête chauve, *f.* **bald-headed,** *a.* À tête chauve. *To go at it bald-headed,* y aller tête baissée. **baldly,** *adv.* Pauvrement, platement, sèchement. **baldness,** *n.* Calvitie; (*fig.*) platitude, sécheresse, pauvreté, *f.*

baldric ['bɔːldrik], *n.* Baudrier, *m.*

bale (1) [BAIL (2)].

bale (2) [beil], *n.* Balle, *f.*, ballot, *m.*—*v.t.* Emballer.—*v.i. To bale out,* (*Av.*) sauter en parachute.

bale (3) [beil], *n.* Calamité, douleur, *f.* **baleful,** *a.* Sinistre, funeste. **balefully,** *adv.* D'une manière funeste.

Balearic [bæli'ærik] **Islands.** Les Îles Baléares, *f.*

balk or **baulk** [bɔːk], *n.* Poutre, bille, *f.*; (*Billiards*) ligne de départ, *f.*—*v.t.* Frustrer, contrarier, déjouer.—*v.i.* Se dérober (horse). *To balk at something,* reculer devant quelque chose.

Balkans ['bɔːlkənz], **the.** Les Balkans, les États Balkaniques, *m.pl.*

ball (1) [bɔːl], *n.* Balle; boule (snow); pelote, *f.*, peloton (wool, string); boulet (cannon), *m.*; (*Billiards*) bille; (*Cook.*) boulette, *f.*; (filled with air) ballon, *m. Ball of the eye,* prunelle, *f.*; *ball of thread,* peloton de fil, *m.*—*v.t.* Agglomérer, pelotonner.—*v.i.* S'agglomérer (of snow). **ball-bearings,** *n.* Roulements à billes, *m.pl.* **ball-cartridge,** *n.* Cartouche à balle, *f.* **ball-cock** or **-valve,** *n.* Robinet à flotteur, *m.* **ball-joint,** *n.* Joint-sphérique, *m.* **ball-point,** *n. Ball-point pen,* stylo à bille, *m.*

ball (2) [bɔːl], *n.* Bal, *m.* **ball-room,** *n.* Salle de bal, *f. Fancy-dress ball,* bal masqué, *m.*

ballad ['bæləd], *n.* (*Mus.*) Romance, *f.*; ballade, *f.* *ballad-monger, *n.* Chansonnier, *m.* *ballad-singer, *n.* Chanteur des rues, *m.*

ballade [bæ'lɑːd], *n.* (*Lit.*) Ballade, *f.*

ballast ['bæləst], *n.* Lest, *m.*; (*Rail.*) ballast, *m. In ballast,* sur lest.—*v.t.* Lester; (*Rail.*) ensabler, empierrer. **ballast-heaver,** *n.* Délesteur, *m.* **ballast-hole,** *n.* Ballastière, *f.* **ballaster,** *n.* Terrassier, *m.* **ballasting,** *n.* (*Rail.*) Ensablement, empierrement; (*Naut.*) lestage, *m.*

ballerina [bælə'riːnə], *n.* Ballerine, *f.*

ballet ['bælei], *n.* Ballet, *m.*, ballet-girl, *f.*; (*Chorus*) figurante, *f.* **ballet-master,** *n.* Directeur des ballets, *m.* **ballet-skirt,** *n.* Tutu, *m.*

ballista [bə'listə], *n.* (*pl.* **ballistae** or **ballistas**) Baliste, *f.* **ballistics,** *n.* Balistique, *f.*

balloon [bə'luːn], *n.* Ballon, aérostat, *m.*—*v.i.* Se ballonner; monter en ballon.—*v.t.* (*Med.*) Ballonner.

ballot ['bælət], *n.* Boule, *f.*; bulletin, scrutin, *m. By ballot,* au scrutin; *second ballot,* second tour de scrutin, ballottage, *m.—v.i.* Voter au scrutin. **ballot-box,** *n.* Urne électorale, *f.* **balloting,** *n.* Vote au scrutin, *m.* **ballot-paper,** *n.* Bulletin de vote, *m.*

bally ['bæli], *a.* (*pop.*) Fichu. *The whole bally lot,* tout le saint-frusquin. **ballyhoo,** *n.* (*pop.*) Grosse réclame, *f.*, battage, *m.*

balm [ba:m], *n.* Baume, *m.*; mélisse, *f.—v.t.* Parfumer. **balmy,** *a.* Embaumé, parfumé; (*pop.*) fou, toqué.

balsam ['bɔːlsəm], *n.* Baume, *m.*

balsamic [bɔl'sæmik] or **balsamous** ['bɔːl-səməs], *a.* Balsamique. **balsamine,** *n.* Balsamine, *f.* **balsam-tree,** *n.* Balsamier, baumier, *m.*

Baltic ['bɔːltik], *n.* La Baltique, *f.*

baluster ['bæləstə], *n.* Balustre, *m.*, rampe (of a staircase), *f.* **balustered,** *a.* À balustres.

balustrade [bæləs'treid], *n.* Balustrade, *f.*

bamboo [bæm'buː], *n.* Bambou, *m.*

bamboozle [bæm'buːzl], *v.t.* (*colloq.*) Tromper, duper, enjôler. **bamboozlement,** *n.* Enjôlement, *m.*, duperie, *f.*

ban [bæn], *n.* Ban, *m.*; interdiction, *f.*; (*Eccles.*) interdit, *m. Bans of marriage* [BANNS]; *under the ban,* au ban.—*v.t.* Anathématiser, interdire, proscrire.

banal ['beinəl], *a.* Banal.

banality [bə'næliti], *n.* Banalité, *f.*

banana [bə'nɑːnə], *n.* Banane, *f.* **banana-tree,** *n.* Bananier, *m.*

banco ['bæŋkou], *a.* and *n.* Banco, *m.*, monnaie de banque, *f.*

band (1) [bænd], *n.* Bande, *f.*, lien; ruban, *m.*; raie, *f.* (*Rad.*) *Frequency band,* bande de fréquence.—*v.t.* Bander; liguer, réunir en troupe; baguer (a pigeon).—*v.i.* Se liguer.

band (2) [bænd], *n.* Bande, troupe (*Mil.*) musique, *f.*; orchestre, *m. Brass band,* fanfare, *f. Brass and reed band,* harmonie, *f.* **bandmaster,** *n.* Chef de musique, *m.* **bandsman,** *n.* Musicien, *m.* **bandstand,** *n.* Kiosque à musique, *m.* **band-waggon,** *n. To jump on the band-waggon,* se ranger du bon côté.

bandage ['bændidʒ], *n.* Bandeau; (*Surg.*) bandage, *m.* **bandage-maker,** *n.* Bandagiste, *m.*

bandanna or **bandana** [bæn'dænə], *n.* Foulard de soie de couleur (à pois jaunes ou blancs), *m.*

bandbox ['bændbɔks], *n.* Carton, *m.* (de modiste).

bandelet ['bændələt], *n.* Bandelette, *f.*

banderole ['bændərol], *n.* Banderole, bannière, *f.*

bandit ['bændit], *n.* (*pl.* **bandits** or **banditti,** [bæn'diti]) Bandit, *m.* **banditry,** *n.* Brigandage, *m.*

bandog ['bændɔg], *n.* Chien de garde, *m.*

bandoleer or **bandolier** [bændə'liə], *n.* Bandoulière, *f.*

bandy ['bændi], *v.t.* Renvoyer; échanger; se renvoyer. *To bandy words,* se renvoyer des paroles.—*v.i.* Se disputer.—*n.* Crosse, *f.—a.* Tortu. *Bandy leg,* jambe tortue, *f.* **bandy-legged,** *a.* Bancal.

bane [bein], *n.* Poison; (*fig.*) fléau, *m.* **baneberry,** *n.* Herbe de saint Christophe, *f.*

baneful, *a.* Pernicieux, funeste, nuisible. **banefully,** *adv.* Nuisiblement, funestement.

bang [bæŋ], *n.* Coup, grand bruit, *m.*, détonation, *f.—v.t.* Frapper violemment, taper. *To bang a door,* claquer une porte; *to bang one's fist on,* cogner du poing.—*int.* Pan! paf! boum!

bangle ['bæŋgl], *n.* Porte-bonheur, bracelet, *m.*

banian [BANYAN].

banish ['bæniʃ], *v.t.* Bannir, exiler. **banishment,** *n.* Bannissement, exil, *m.*

banister [BALUSTER].

banjo ['bændʒou], *n.* (*pl.* **banjos** or **banjoes**) Banjo, *m.*; (*Motor.*) carter du différentiel, *m.*

bank (1) [bæŋk], *n.* Rivage, bord, *m.*; berge, rive, *f.*; terrasse, *f.*, remblai, talus, *m.*; banc (de sable, de gazon, etc.), *m.*; digue, *f.*; carreau (of coal-mine), *m.*; (*Av.*) virage incliné, *m.* —*v.t.* Terrasser, remblayer. *Banked corner,* virage relevé. **banking** (1), *n.* Relèvement; remblai (of road), *m.*

bank (2) [bæŋk], *n.* (*Comm.*) Banque, *f. Branch bank,* banque à succursale, *f.*; *savings-bank,* caisse d'épargne, *f.—v.t.* Encaisser (de l'argent). *To bank with,* avoir pour banquier. **bank-book,** *n.* Livret de banque, *m.* **bank-clerk,** *n.* Commis de banque, *m.* **banker,** *n.* Banquier, *m.* **banking** (2), *n.* La banque, *f. Banking house,* maison de banque, *f.* **bank-note,** *n.* Billet de banque, *m.* **bank-rupt,** *a.* Failli, en faillite, en banqueroute; (*fig.*) ruiné.—*v.t.* Mettre en faillite, ruiner.— *n.* Banqueroutier, *m.*, banqueroutière, *f.*; failli, *m.*, faillie, *f. To be bankrupt,* être en faillite; *to become* or *go bankrupt,* faire faillite. **bankruptcy,** *n.* Banqueroute, faillite, *f. Court of bankruptcy,* tribunal des faillites, *m.*

banner ['bænə], *n.* Bannière, *f.* **bannered,** *a.* Garni de bannières. **banneret,** *n.* Banneret, *m.*

bannock ['bænək], *n.* (Grosse) galette d'avoine, d'orge, de farine de pois, *f.*

banns [bænz], *n.pl. Banns of marriage,* bans de mariage, *m.pl.*

banquet ['bæŋkwət], *n.* Banquet; *festin, m.* —*v.i.* Donner un banquet à.—*v.i.* Banqueter, festiner, festoyer. **banqueting-room,** *n.* Salle de banquet, *f.*

banquette [bæŋ'ket], *n.* (*Fort.*) Banquette, *f.*

banshee ['bænshiː], *n.* (*Ireland*) Fée (dont l'apparition annonce une mort), *f.*

bantam ['bæntəm], *n.* Coq (de) Bantam, *m. Bantam-weight,* (*Box.*) poids bantam, *m.*

banter ['bæntə], *v.t.* Railler, badiner.—*n.* Badinage, *m.*, raillerie, *f.* **banterer,** *n.* Railleur, *m.*, railleuse, *f.*

bantling ['bæntliŋ], *n.* Poupon, bambin, marmot, *m.*

banyan ['bænjən], *a.* and *n.* Commerçant (indien), *m.*; robe de chambre, *f.*

baptism ['bæptizm], *n.* Baptême, *m.* **baptismal** [bæp'tizməl], *a.* Baptismal. **baptist,** *n.* Baptiste, *m.* **baptistery,** *n.* Baptistère, *m.*

baptize [bæp'taiz], *v.t.* Baptiser.

bar [ba:], *n.* Barre, *f.*; (*Law etc.*) barreau, parquet, *m.*; (*fig.*) barrière, *f.*; obstacle, empêchement, *m.*; buvette, *f.*, comptoir, bar (in public-houses); (*Law*) banc des accusés, *m.*; (*Mus.*) mesure, *f.*; (*Meteor.*) bar; (*Ichth.*) bar. *Cross-bar,* barre transversale, *f.*; *bar iron,* fer en barres, *m.*; *horizontal bar,* poutre horizontale, *f.*; *parallel bars*, barres parallèles, *f.pl.*; *prisoner at the bar*, accusé, *m.*; *to be called to the bar*, être inscrit au tableau, être reçu avocat.—*v.t.* Barrer, empêcher; exclure; interdire, défendre. *To bar the door against*, barrer la porte contre, exclure.—*prep.* (*colloq.*) [BARRING].

barb (1) [bɑːb], *n.* Barbe, *f.*; barbillon, dardillon (of hook), *m.*; pointe (of an arrow etc.), *f.*; barbe, arête (of corn etc.), *f.*

barb (2) [bɑːb], *n.* Barbe, cheval de Barbarie, *m.*

barb (3) [bɑːb], *v.t.* Armer (an arrow etc.).

Barbadoes [bɑːˈbeidouz]. La Barbade, *f.*

barbarian [bɑːˈbɛəriən], *a.* and *n.* Barbare.

barbaric [bɑːˈbærik], *a.* Barbare. **barbarism** [ˈbɑːbərizm], *n.* Barbarie, *f.*; (*Gram.*) barbarisme, *m.* **barbarity** [bɑːˈbæriti], *n.* Barbarie, cruauté, *f.* **barbarize** [ˈbɑːbəraiz], *v.t.* Barbariser. **barbarous** [ˈbɑːbərəs], *a.* Barbare. **barbarousness**, *n.* Barbarie, *f.*

Barbarossa [bɑːbəˈrɔsə]. Barberousse, *m.*

barbate [ˈbɑːbeit], *a.* (*Bot.*) Barbelé, barbu.

barbecue [ˈbɑːbəkjuː], *n.* Grand gril (pour rôtir un animal entier); animal rôti entier, *m.*; grande fête, *f.*, *or* grand pique-nique, *m.*, en plein air.—*v.t.* Rôtir (un animal) tout entier.

barbed [bɑːbd], *a.* Barbelé; (*fig.*) acéré. *Barbed wire*, fil-de-fer barbelé.

barbel [ˈbɑːbəl], *n.* (*Ichth.*) Barbeau, *m.*

barber [ˈbɑːbə], *n.* Barbier, coiffeur, *m.* *Barber's block*, tête à perruque, *f.* **barber-surgeon**, *n.* Chirurgien barbier, *m.*

barberry [ˈbɑːbəri], *n.* Épine-vinette, *f.*

barbican [ˈbɑːbikən], *n.* Barbacane, *f.*

barbitone [ˈbɑːbitoun], *n.* Véronal, *m.* **barbiturate**, *n.* Barbiturate, barbiturique, *m.*

barcarole [ˈbɑːkəroul], *n.* Barcarolle, *f.*

Barcelona [bɑːsəˈlounə]. Barcelone, *f.*

bard [bɑːd], *n.* Barde, trouvère, *m.* **bardic** *or* **bardish**, *a.* De barde. **bardism**, *n.* Bardisme, *m.*

bare [bɛə], *a.* Nu, découvert; (*fig.*) seul, simple; pauvre. *The bare necessities*, le strict nécessaire, *m.*—*v.t.* Découvrir, dépouiller; mettre à nu; tirer (swords) du fourreau. **bareback**, *adv.* À dos nu. *To ride bareback*, monter un cheval à poil. **bareboned**, *a.* Décharné. **barefaced**, *a.* À visage découvert; éhonté, sans déguisement. **barefacedly**, *adv.* Ouvertement, sans déguisement, effrontément. **barefacedness**, *n.* Effronterie, *f.* **barefoot**, *a.* Nu-pieds; les pieds nus. **bareheaded**, *a.* Nu-tête, la tête nue. **barelegged**, *a.* Nu-jambes, les jambes nues. **barely**, *adv.* À peine; tout juste, simplement, seulement; pauvrement, chétivement. **bareness**, *n.* Nudité; pauvreté, misère, *f.*, dénûment, *m.*

bargain [ˈbɑːgin], *n.* Marché, *m.*, affaire; occasion, *f.* *Into the bargain*, par-dessus le marché; *it is a bargain*, c'est convenu, marché conclu; *to get the best of the bargain*, avoir la meilleure part; *to make a good bargain*, faire une bonne affaire; *to strike a bargain*, conclure un marché.—*v.i.* Marchander, faire marché. *I did not bargain for that*, je ne m'attendais pas à cela. **bargainer**, *n.* Personne qui marchande, *f.*

barge [bɑːdʒ], *n.* Bateau plat, chaland, *m.*; allège, péniche, *f.*—*v.i. To barge into*, se

heurter contre, bousculer. **barge-board**, *n.* Bordure de pignon, *f.* **bargee** [bɑːˈdʒiː] *or* **bargeman**, *n.* Batelier, *m.* **barge-master**, *n.* Patron de barque, *m.* **barge-pole**, *n.* Gaffe, *f.* *I wouldn't touch it with a barge-pole*, je n'en veux à aucun prix.

barilla [bəˈrilə], *n.* Barille, *f.*

baritone [ˈbæritoun], *a.* De baryton.—*n.* Baryton, *m.*

bark (1) [bɑːk], *n.* Écorce, *f.*; tan, *m. Peruvian bark*, quinquina, *m.*—*v.t.* Écorcer, décortiquer. **barkpit**, *n.* Fosse à tan, *f.*

bark (2) [bɑːk], *n.* Aboiement, *m. His bark is worse than his bite*, il n'est pas si méchant qu'il en a l'air.—*v.i.* Aboyer.

bark (3) *or* **barque** [bɑːk], *n.* Trois-mâts, *m.*

barker (1) [ˈbɑːkə], *n.* Écorceur, *m.*

barker (2) [ˈbɑːkə], *n.* Aboyeur, *m.* **barking**, *n.* Aboiement, *m.*

bark-mill [ˈbɑːkmil], *n.* Moulin à tan, *m.*

barky, *a.* Couvert d'écorce.

barley [ˈbɑːli], *n.* Orge, *f. Pearl barley*, orge perlé, *m.*; *peeled* or *hulled barley*, orge mondé, *m.* **barley-corn**, *n.* Grain d'orge, *m.* **barley-sugar**, *n.* Sucre d'orge, *m.* **barley-water**, *n.* Tisane d'orge, *f.*

barm [bɑːm], *n.* Levure, *f.* (de bière).

barmaid [ˈbɑːmeid], *n.* Fille de comptoir, *f.* **barman**, *n.* Garçon de comptoir, *m.*

barmy [ˈbɑːmi], *a.* [BALMY].

barn [bɑːn], *n.* Grange, *f.*; (*Am.*) étable, *f. Barn-door fowls*, oiseaux de basse-cour, *m.pl.*, volaille, *f.*; *barn floor*, aire de grange, *f.*; *barn owl*, effraie, *f.*; *barn-stormer*, acteur ambulant, cabotin, *m.*

Barnabas [ˈbɑːnəbəs], **Barnaby** [ˈbɑːnəbi]. Barnabé, *m.*

barnacle [ˈbɑːnəkl], *n.* Barnache (goose), *f.*; balane, anatife (shell-fish), *m.*; (*pl.*, *colloq.*) besicles, *f.pl.*

barnacles [ˈbɑːnəklz], *n.pl.* Morailles, *f.pl.* (for restive horses).

barometer [bəˈrɔmitə], *n.* Baromètre, *m.* **barometric** [bæroˈmetrik] *or* **barometrical**, *a.* Barométrique.

baron [ˈbærən], *n.* Baron, *m. Baron of beef*, double aloyau, *m.* **baronage**, *n.* Baronnage, *m.*; baronnie, *f.* **baroness**, *n.* Baronne, *f.*

baronet [ˈbærənet], *n.* Baronnet, *m.* **baronetage**, *n.* Corps des baronnets, *m.* **baronetcy**, *n.* Dignité de baronnet, *f.*

baronial [bəˈrouniəl], *a.* Baronnial, seigneurial. **barony** [ˈbærəni], *n.* Baronnie, *f.*

baroque [bəˈrɔk], *a.* and *n.* Baroque, *m.*

barouche [bəˈruːʃ], *n.* Calèche, *f.*

barrack (1) [ˈbærək], *n.* (*usu. in pl.*) Caserne, *f.*; (for cavalry) quartier, *m. Barrack master*, adjudant de casernement, *m.*; *barrack room*, chambrée, *f.*; *confined to barracks*, consigné.

barrack (2), *v.t.*, *v.i.* Huer.

barrage [ˈbæridʒ *or* ˈbærɑːʒ], *n.* Barrage, *m.*

barrator [ˈbærətə], *n.* Personne or marin coupable de baraterie. **barratrous**, *a.* Entaché de baraterie. **barratry**, *n.* Baraterie, malversation, *f.*

barrel [ˈbærəl], *n.* Baril, *m.*; gonne, caque (of herrings etc.), *f.*; corps (of pump); cylindre, tambour (of machine); canon (of gun); barillet (of clock), *m.*—*v.t.* Embariller, entonner, mettre en baril, encaquer. **barrel-bellied**, *a.* À gros ventre, pansu, ventru. **barrelled**, *a.* Entonné, encaqué; à baril; à

cylindre (of machines); à canon (of fire-arms); bombé (of roads). *Double-barrelled gun*, fusil à deux coups, *m.* **barrel-organ,** *n.* Orgue mécanique; orgue de Barbarie, *m.*
barren ['bærən], *a.* Stérile; infertile (of ground). **barrenly,** *adv.* Stérilement. **barrenness,** *n.* Stérilité, *f.*
barricade [bæri'keid], *n.* Barricade, *f.*—*v.t.* Barricader. **barricading,** *n.* Action de barricader, *f.*; barricades, *f.pl.*
barrier ['bæriə], *n.* Barrière, *f.*
barring ['bɑːriŋ] or **bar,** *prep. Barring a few*, hormis quelques-uns, sauf. *Barring a few*, hormis quelques-uns, à quelques-uns près; *barring mistakes*, sauf erreur.
barrister ['bæristə], *n.* Avocat, *m.*
barrow (1) ['bærou], *n.* or *wheel-barrow.* Brouette, *f. Hand-barrow*, brancard, *m.*, civière, *f.* **barrowful** or **barrow-load,** *n.* Brouettée, *f.* **barrow-man** or **barrow-boy,** *n.* (*fam.*) Marchand des quatre saisons, *m.*
barrow (2) ['bærou], *n.* Tumulus, tertre (funéraire), *m.*; terrier, *m.*
barrow (3) ['bærou], *n.* Robe de flanelle sans manches, *f.* (for infants).
bartender [BARMAN].
barter ['bɑːtə], *n.* Échange, troc; trafic, *m.*—*v.t.* Troquer, échanger.—*v.i.* Échanger, faire échange. **barterer,** *n.* Troqueur, *m.*, tro-queuse, *f.*
Bartholomew [bɑː'θɔləmju]. Barthélemy, *m.*
baryta [bə'raitə], *n.* Baryte, *f.*
barytone [BARITONE].
basalt [bə'sɔːlt], *n.* Basalte, *m.* **basaltic,** *a.* Basaltique.
bascule ['bæskjuːl], *n.* Bascule, *f.* **bascule-bridge,** *n.* Pont-levis, pont à bascule, *m.*
base (1) [beis], *a.* Bas, vil, indigne, mépri-sable; illégitime (of a child); de mauvais aloi; non précieux, de peu de valeur (of all metals, except gold and silver); faux (of coins). **base-born,** *a.* Bâtard. **base-minded,** *a.* Qui a l'âme basse. **basely,** *adv.* Bassement, lâchement, vilement. **baseness,** *n.* Bassesse, lâcheté, *f.*
base (2) [beis], *n.* Base, *f.*, fondement; fond, *m.*; (*Mus.*) basse, *f.*; barres (prisoners' base), *f.pl.*—*v.t.* Fonder (sur); asseoir (l'impôt). **baseball,** *n.* (*spt.*) Base-ball, *m.* **baseless,** *a.* Sans fondement. **basement,** *n.* Soubasse-ment; sous-sol, rez-de-chaussée anglais, *m.*
bash [bæʃ], *v.t.* (*colloq.*) Frapper, cogner.—*n.* Coup (violent). (*pop.*) *To have a bash at something*, tenter l'aventure.
***bashaw** [PACHA].
bashful ['bæʃful], *a.* Timide, intimidé. **bash-fully,** *adv.* Timidement, en rougissant. **bashfulness,** *n.* Timidité, fausse honte, *f.*
basic ['beisik], *a.* (*Chem.*) Basique; de base. *Basic slag*, scories de déphosphoration, *f.pl. Basic English*, anglais de base or élémentaire, *m.*; *basic pay*, salaire de base, *m.* **basicity,** *n.* Basicité, *f.*
basil (1) ['bæzil], *n.* Basilic (herb), *m.*
basil (2) ['bæzil], *n.* Basane (leather), *f.*
basilic [bə'zilik] or **basilical,** *a.* (*Anat.*) Basilique. **basilica,** *n.* Basilique, *f.* **basili-con** or **basilicum,** *n.* (*Pharm.*) Basilicon, basilicum, *m.*
basilisk ['bæzilisk], *n.* Basilic, *m.*
basin ['beisən], *n.* Bassin; bol, *m.*; cuvette, *f.* **basinful,** *n.* Pleine cuvette, *f.*

basis ['beisis], *n.* (*pl.* **bases**) Base, *f.*, fonde-ment, *m. Basis of a tax*, assiette d'un impôt, *f.*
bask [bɑːsk], *v.i.* Se chauffer; s'étendre (devant le feu, au soleil, etc.). *To bask in the sun*, prendre un bain de soleil.
basket ['bɑːskit], *n.* Panier, *m.*, corbeille, *f.*; bourriche (for fish or game); hotte, *f.* **basket-ball,** *n.* (*spt.*) Basket-ball, *m.*; (*fam.*) basket, *m. Basket-ball player*, basketeur, *m.* **basketful,** *n.* Plein panier, *m.* **basket-hilt,** *n.* Poignée en coquille, *f. Basket-hilted sword*, épée à poignée en coquille, *f.* **basket-maker,** *n.* Vannier, *m.* **basket-work,** *n.* Vannerie, *f.*; clayonnage, *m.*
Basle [bɑːl]. Bâle.
bas-relief [bɑːrə'liːf], *n.* Bas-relief, *m.*
bass (1) [beis], *n.* Basse; basse-taille, *f. Double bass*, contre-basse, *f.* **bass-voice,** *n.* Voix de basse, *f.*
bass (2) [bæs], *n.* Tille, *f.*, filasse, *f.* **bass-wood,** *n.* Tilleul d'Amérique, *m.*
bass (3) [bæs], *n.* (*Ichth.*) Bar, *m.*; perche, *f.*
basset (1) ['bæsit], *n.* Bassette (card game), *f.*
basset (2) ['bæsit], *n.* Basset, *m.*
bassinet [bæsi'net], *n.* Bercelonnette, *f.*, moïse, *m.*
bassoon [bə'suːn], *n.* Basson, *m.* **bassoonist,** *n.* Basson, *m.*
basso-relievo [BAS-RELIEF].
bast [bæst], *n.* [BASS (2)].
bastard ['bæstəd], *a.* Bâtard; (*fig.*) faux.—*n.* Bâtard, *m.*, bâtarde, *f.*; (*Law*) enfant naturel, *m.*; (*pop.*) salaud, *m.* **bastardize,** *v.t.* Déclarer bâtard. **bastardy,** *n.* Bâtardise, *f.*
baste [beist], *v.t.* Arroser (la viande); (*fig.*) bâtonner; (*Needlework*) bâtir.
bastinado [bæsti'neidou], *v.t.* Bâtonner.—*n.* Bastonnade, *f.*
bastion ['bæstiən], *n.* Bastion, *m.*
bat (1) [bæt], *n.* (*Cricket*) Batte, *f. Off his own bat*, par ses propres efforts.—*v.i.* Être au guichet.
bat (2) [bæt], *n.* Chauve-souris, *f. Batwing burner*, bec à papillon, *m.*
bat (3) [bɑː, bæt], *n.* Bât, *m.* **bat-horse,** *n.* Cheval de bât, *m.*
bat (4) [bæt], *n.* (*fam.*) Pas, *m.*, allure, *f. At a rare bat*, à toute allure.
bat (5) [bæt], *v.t.* (*fam.*) *Without batting an eyelid*, sans sourciller.
batata [bə'tɑːtə], *n.* Patate, *f.*
Batavian [bə'teiviən], *a.* Batave.—*n.* Batave.
batch [bætʃ], *n.* Fournée (of bread); (*fig.*) troupe, bande, *f.*; tas, *m.*; lot, *m.*
bate [beit], *v.t.* Rabattre, rabaisser. *He would not bate a shilling*, il n'en rabattrait pas d'un shilling; *with bated breath*, en retenant son souffle; en baissant la voix.
bath [bɑːθ], *n.* Bain, *m.*; baignoire (utensil), *f. Shower-bath*, douche, douche en pluie, *f.*; *hip-bath*, *sitz-bath*, bain de siège, *m.*; *tepid bath*, bain tiède, *m.*; *the Order of the Bath*, l'Ordre du Bain, *m.*; *vapour bath*, bain de vapeur, *m.*—*v.t.* Donner un bain à, baigner. —*v.i.* Prendre un bain. **bath-chair,** *n.* Voiture de malade, *f.*; fauteuil roulant, *m.* **bath-gown,** *n.* Peignoir de bain, *m.* **bath-heater,** *n.* Chauffe-bain, *m.* **bath-keeper** or **-attendant,** *n.* Baigneur, *m.*, baigneuse, *f.* **bathrobe,** *n.* (*Am.*) Robe de chambre, *f.* **bath-room,** *n.* Salle de bain(s), *f.* **bath-towel,** *n.* Serviette de bain, *f.*

bathe [beið], v.t. Baigner; tremper, mouiller. *To bathe a wound*, bassiner une plaie.—v.i. Se baigner.—n. Baignade, f. *To go for a bathe*, aller se baigner. **bather**, n. Baigneur, m., baigneuse, f.

bathing ['beiðiŋ], n. Baignade, f.; bains, m.pl. *Sea-bathing*, bains de mer, m.pl. **bathing-box**, n. Cabine de bain, f. **bathing-cap**, n. Bonnet de bain, m. **bathing-costume**, n. Costume de bain, maillot, m. **bathing-drawers** or **bathing-trunks**, n.pl. Caleçon de bain, m. **bathing-dress**, n. Costume de bain, m. **bathing-establishment**, n. Établissement de bains, m. **bathing-place**, n. Baignade, f. **bathing-resort**, n. Station balnéaire, f.

bathos ['beiθɔs], n. Pathos, m., enflure, f.; anticlimax, m.

bathymetry [bæ'θimətri], n. Bathométrie, f. bathymétrie, f. **bathyscaph**, n. Bathyscaphe, m.

bating ['beitiŋ], prep. (rare) Sauf, hormis.

batman ['bætmən], n. Ordonnance, brosseur, m.

baton ['bætən] or **batoon**, n. Bâton, m.

Batrachia [bə'treikiə], n.pl. Batraciens, m.pl. **batrachian**, a. Des batraciens.

batsman ['bætsmən], n. (Cricket) Batteur, m.

battalion [bə'tæliən], n. Bataillon, m.

batten (1) ['bætən], n. Volige, latte, f.—v.t. Fermer; engraisser; (Carp.) voliger. *To batten down the hatches*, condamner les panneaux.

batten (2) ['bætən], v.i. S'engraisser (de).

batter (1) ['bætə], v.t. Battre en brèche; battre; délabrer, ébranler, démolir. *To batter down*, abattre, renverser, battre en ruine.—n. Pâte, f.

batter (2) ['bætə], v.i. (Arch.) Avoir du fruit. —n. Fruit, m. (of wall).

battered ['bætəd], a. Délabré. *A battered face*, un visage meurtri.

battering ['bætəriŋ], n. Action de battre, f. **battering-ram**, n. Bélier, m. **battering-train**, n. Artillerie de siège, f.

battery ['bætəri], n. Batterie; (Elec.) pile, batterie, f., accumulateur, m.; action de battre en brèche, f.; (Law) voies de fait, f.pl. *Field battery*, batterie de campagne.

battle [bætl], n. Bataille, f., combat, m. *Battle array*, ordre de bataille, m.; *killed in battle*, mort à la guerre; *pitched battle*, bataille rangée; *to do battle for, against, someone*, combattre pour, contre, quelqu'un; *to give battle*, livrer bataille.—v.i. Lutter, combattre; (colloq.) batailler. **battle-axe**, n. Hache d'armes, f. **battle-cruiser**, n. Croiseur de bataille, m. **battle-dress**, n. Tenue de campagne, f. **battle-field**, n. Champ de bataille, m.

battledore ['bætldɔ:], n. Raquette, f. (au jeu de volant); battoir, m. *Battledore and shuttle-cock*, jeu de volant, m.

battlement ['bætlmənt], n. Créneau, m.—v.t. Créneler.

battleship ['bætlʃip], n. Cuirassé, m.

batty ['bæti], a. (pop.) Toqué, timbré.

bauble [bɔ:bl], n. Babiole, fanfreluche, f. *Fool's bauble*, marotte, f.

baulk [BALK].

bauxite ['bɔ:ksait], n. Bauxite, f.

Bavaria [bə'vɛəriə]. La Bavière, f. **Bavarian**, a. and n. Bavarois.

bavin ['bævin], n. Bourrée, f., cotret, m.

bawbee [bɔ:'bi:], n. (Sc.) Sou, m.

bawd [bɔ:d], n. Proxénète, f. **bawdiness**, n. Obscénité, impudicité, f. **bawdy**, a. Obscène, paillard. *Bawdy house*, lieu de débauche, bouge, m.

bawl [bɔ:l], v.i. Crier, brailler.—v.t. (pop.) Gueuler.—n. Cri, braillement, m.

bay (1) [bei], n. (Bot.) Baie, f.; laurier, m. **bay-leaf**, n. Feuille de laurier, f. (for cooking). **bay-tree**, n. Laurier, m.

bay (2) [bei], n. Baie, f., golfe (inlet of sea etc.), m. *Bay salt*, sel gris, gros sel, m.

bay (3) [bei], n. Écluse, f., bief, m.

bay (4) [bei], n. (Arch.) Baie, f. *Bay of joists*, travée, f. **bay-window**, n. Fenêtre en saillie or à baie, f.

bay (5) [bei], n. Abois, m.pl. *The stag stands at bay*, le cerf est aux abois; *to hold at bay*, tenir en échec.—v.i. Aboyer. *To bay (at) the moon*, aboyer à la lune.

bay (6) [bei], a. (Of a horse) bai. *Dark bay*, bai brun; *light bay*, bai clair.

bayadere [ba:jə'dɛə], n. Bayadère (dancing-girl), f.

bayonet ['beiənit], n. Baïonnette, f. *Bayonet charge*, charge à la baïonnette, f.—v.t. Tuer or percer à coups de baïonnette.

bazaar [bə'za:], n. Bazar, m.; vente de charité, f.

bazooka [bə'zu:kə], n. Bazooka, f.

bdellium ['dɛliəm], n. (Bot.) Bdellium, m.

be [bi:], v.i. (past was, pl. were, p.p. been) Être; exister; subsister; y avoir, se trouver; avoir; faire; devoir, falloir. *Are those his friends?* sont-ce là ses amis? *as it were*, pour ainsi dire; *be it so*, soit; *be that as it may*, quoi qu'il en soit; *had it not been for*, n'eût été; *he is asleep*, il dort; *how cold your hands are!* comme vous avez les mains froides! *how is it that . . .?* comment se fait-il que . . .? *if it were not for*, sans, n'était que; *if I were you*, à votre place; *if that is the same to you*, si cela vous est égal; *is it to be wondered at if . . .?* faut-il s'étonner si . . .? *it is no matter*, il n'importe, n'importe; *it is ten*, il est dix heures; *it is to be hoped that*, il faut espérer que; *it is warm, cold*, or *fine*, il fait chaud, froid or beau; *it were to be wished that*, il serait à désirer que; *I was to*, je devais; *my hands are cold*, j'ai froid aux mains; *nobody is to know it*, il faut que personne ne le sache; *that is nothing to me*, cela ne me fait rien; *that is not to be seen*, cela ne se voit pas; *there is or there are*, il y a, il est; *the title is to descend to his heir*, le titre doit passer à son héritier; *to be a witness*, servir de témoin; *to be better*, valoir mieux, se porter mieux; *to be cold, warm, thirsty*, or *hungry*, avoir froid, chaud, soif, or faim; *to be mistaken*, se tromper; *to be right*, avoir raison; *to be twenty years old*, avoir vingt ans; *to be very well*, se porter très bien; *to be wrong*, avoir tort; *union is strength*, l'union fait la force; *what is the matter?* qu'est-ce qu'il y a? qu'y a-t-il? *why is it that . . .?* pourquoi faut-il que . . .? *you would take him to be forty*, vous lui donneriez quarante ans.

beach [bi:tʃ], n. Plage, grève, f., rivage, m.— v.t. Échouer. **beach-comber**, n. Vague qui déferle, f.; (fam.) pilleur de plage, m. **beach-head**, n. (Mil.) Tête de pont, f.

beacon ['bi:kən], *n.* Phare, tanal, *m.*; balise, *f.*—*v.t.* Baliser, éclairer. **beaconage**, *n.* Droits de balise, *m.pl.*

bead [bi:d], *n.* Grain (de chapelet, de bracelet, de collier, etc.); globule, *m.*; baguette, monture, *f.*; (*Metal.*) cordon de soudure, *m.* *String of beads*, collier, chapelet, *m.*; *to tell one's beads*, défiler *or* égrener son chapelet; *to thread beads*, enfiler des perles.—*v.i.* Perler. **bead-roll**, *n.* Liste de ceux pour qui on doit prier, *f.* **beadsman**, *n.* Personne chargée de prier pour une autre; (vieillard) hospitalisé, *m.* **bead-tree**, *n.* Mélie, *f.*, azédarac, *m.* **beady-eyed**, *a.* Aux yeux en vrille.

beadle [bi:dl], *n.* Bedeau; appariteur, *m.* **beadledom**, *n.* Fonctionnarisme, *m.*; paperasserie, *f.*

beagle [bi:gl], *n.* Chien briquet, bigle, *m.*

beak [bi:k], *n.* Bec, *m.*; bigorne (of anvil), *f.*; (*Naut.*) éperon, (*slang*) juge (police court magistrate), *m.* **beakful**, *n.* Becquée, *f.*

beaker ['bi:kə], *n.* Gobelet, *m.*, coupe, *f.*

beam [bi:m], *n.* Poutre, *f.*; timon (of a plough, carriage, etc.); balancier (of engine); fléau (of scales); rayon (light); (*Naut.*) bau (of anchor), *m.*; large sourire (of delight etc.), *m.* *Breadth of beam*, largeur, *f.*; *cross-beam*, traverse, *f.*; *on her beam-ends*, sur le côté; (*fig.*) *to be on one's beam-ends*, être à bout de ressources. (*Elec.*) *Electron beam*, faisceau électronique, *m.*—*v.i.* Rayonner.—*v.t.* Lancer *or* darder (des rayons). **beam-tree**, *n.* Alisier blanc, *m.* **beaming**, *n.* Rayonnement, *m.*—*a.* Rayonnant, radieux. **beamless**, *a.* Sans rayon, sans éclat, terne. **beamy**, *a.* Rayonnant, brillant; massif.

bean [bi:n], *n.* Fève, *f.*; haricot, *m.*; grain, *m.* (de café). *Broad bean*, grosse fève, *f.*; *French beans*, haricots verts, *m.pl.*; *horse bean*, féverole, *f.*; (*pop.*) *I haven't got a bean*, je n'ai pas le sou; *kidney bean*, haricot blanc, *m.* *To be full of beans*, être plein d'entrain. **beanfeast** *or* **beano**, *n.* Régal, *m.*, (*pop.*) bombe, *f.* **beanstalk**, *n.* Tige de haricot, *f.*

bear (1) [beə], *n.* Ours, *m.*, ourse, *f.*; (*St. Exch.*) joueur à la baisse, baissier, *m. Great Bear*, Grande Ourse; *polar bear*, ours blanc. **bear-baiting**, *n.* Combat d'ours et de chiens, *m.* **bearberry**, *n.* Raisin d'ours, *m.* **bearbind** *or* **bear-bine**, *n.* Liseron des haies, *m.* **bear-garden**, *n.* Lieu pour les combats d'ours, *m.* *It was a regular bear-garden*, on y faisait un tapage épouvantable. **bear'sear**, *n.* (*Bot.*) Oreille d'ours, *f.* **bearish** *or* **bear-like**, *a.* D'ours; brutal, grossier. **bear-leader**, *n.* Montreur d'ours; (*sch.*) cornac, *m.* (d'un élève). **bearskin**, *n.* (*Mil.*) Bonnet d'ours.

bear (2) [beə], *v.t.* (*past* **bore**, *p.p.* **borne**) Porter, soutenir; endurer, supporter, souffrir, subir; avoir, produire (fruit etc.); enfanter; donner naissance à; y tenir; remporter. *To bear away*, emporter, remporter, (*Naut.*) porter; *to bear down*, entraîner, (*Naut.*) courir, arriver (sur); *to bear fruit*, porter fruit; *to bear off*, emporter, enlever, remporter; *to bear oneself*, se comporter, se conduire; *to bear out*, maintenir, soutenir; *to bear sway*, dominer, régner; *bear the charges*, payer les frais; *to bear witness*, témoigner; *to bring to bear upon*, porter sur, mettre en jeu, braquer (a telescope

etc.) sur; *you will bear me out when I say that* . . ., vous direz avec moi que. . . .—*v.i.* Endurer, souffrir; porter, peser; avoir rapport (à); appuyer; porter (sur); rapporter. *Bear with me a little*, un peu de patience; *how does the land bear?* comment relève-t-on la terre? *to bear off the land*, (*Naut.*) courir au large; *to bear towards*, se diriger sur *or* vers; *to bear up*, tenir bon, ne pas se laisser abattre; *to bear upon*, porter sur; *to bear upon* (a question), avoir trait à; *to bear with*, supporter, endurer.

bearable, *a.* Supportable.

beard [biəd], *n.* Barbe, *f.*, (*Bot.*) arête, barbe, *f.*—*v.t.* Braver, défier, prendre par la barbe. **bearded**, *a.* Barbu, à barbe. **beardless**, *a.* Imberbe. *Beardless boy*, blanc-bec, *m.*

bearer ['beərə], *n.* Porteur, *m.*, porteuse, *f.*; (*Arch.*) support, *m. Payable to bearer*, payable au porteur; *stretcher-bearer*, brancardier, *m.*; *to be a good bearer*, être de bon rapport (of trees etc.). **bearing**, *n.* Rapport; maintien, port, *m.*, conduite, relation, *f.*, aspect, *m.*, portée; face, *f.*; (*Arch.*) support; (*Mech.*) coussinet; (*Naut.*) gisement, relèvement, *m.*; (*pl.*, *Her.*) armoiries, *f.pl.* *Ball-bearings*, coussinets à billes, *m.pl.*; *his arrogance is beyond all bearing*, son arrogance est insupportable; *to lose one's bearings*, perdre le nord; *to take one's bearings*, s'orienter; *with ball-bearings*, monté sur billes. **bearing-cloth**, *n.* Robe de baptême, *f.* **bearing-rein**, *n.* Fausse rêne, *f.* **bearing-surface**, *n.* Surface d'appui, *f.*

beast [bi:st], *n.* Bête, *f.*; (*fig.*) animal, cochon, *m. Beast of burden*, bête de somme, *f.*; *to make a beast of oneself*, s'abrutir; *wild beast*, bête sauvage, *f.* **beastings** [BEESTINGS]. **beastliness**, *n.* Saleté, saloperie, *f.* **beastly**, *a.* Bestial; sale, malpropre, dégoûtant.—*adv.* (*colloq.*) Terriblement.

beat [bi:t], *v.t.* (*past* **beat**, *p.p.* **beaten**) Battre; frapper; piler, broyer; l'emporter sur; fouetter (of rain, snow, etc.); se frapper (la poitrine etc.); se frayer (un chemin etc.). *Beat it!* fiche-moi le camp! *can you beat it?* y a-t-il plus fort que ça? *that beats all*, cela dépasse tout; *to beat about*, chercher de tous côtés, (*fig.*) se torturer l'esprit; *to beat about the bush*, tourner autour du pot; *to beat a retreat*, battre en retraite; *to beat a wood*, battre un bois; *to beat back* or *off*, repousser; *to beat black and blue*, meurtrir; *to beat down*, abattre, diminuer; *to beat in*, enfoncer, faire entrer de force; *to beat into*, faire entrer; *to beat out*, aplatir, faire sortir; *to beat the alarm*, battre la générale; *to beat the country*, battre le pays; *to beat the reveille*, battre le réveil *or* la diane; *to beat time*, battre la mesure; *to beat to death*, assommer; *to beat up*, battre, rebattre (game), (eggs etc.), rosser.—*v.i.* Battre; être agité. *To beat about*, (*Naut.*) louvoyer; *to beat against*, se battre contre; *to beat out to sea*, gagner le large; *to beat up for soldiers*, recruter des soldats.—*n.* Coup, battement; son; itinéraire, *m.*; ronde (of policemen), *f.*, parcours (of postmen etc.), *m.*; (*Hunt.*) battue, *f.*; (*Mus.*) mesure, *f.*, temps, *m. Beat of the drum*, batterie de tambour, *f.* **beaten**, *a.* Battu. *Off the beaten track*, hors des sentiers battus. **beater**, *n.* Batteur; (*spt.*) rabatteur, *m.*; batte,

f., batteur (instrument), *m.* **beating,** *n.* Battement, *m.*; rossée, correction, *f.*; coups, *m.pl.*; batterie, *f.*; roulement (of drums etc.), *m.* [*see also* **whisk**]
beatific [biːəˈtifik], *a.* Béatifique. **beatification** [biːætifiˈkeiʃən], *n.* Béatification, *f.* **beatify** [biːˈætifai], *v.t.* Béatifier. **beatitude,** *n.* Béatitude, félicité, *f.*
Beatrice or **Beatrix** [ˈbiːətriːks]. Béatrice, *f.*
beau [bou], *n.* (*pl.* **beaux**) Petit-maître; prétendant (lover), *m.* **beau-ideal,** *n.* Idéal, type achevé, *m.* **beauish** [ˈbouiʃ], *a.* Pimpant, élégant.
beauteous [ˈbjuːtiəs], *a.* (*poet.*) Beau. **beauteously,** *adv.* Avec beauté. **beauteousness,** *n.* Beauté, *f.* **beautician** [bjuːˈtiʃən], *n.* (*Am.*) [BEAUTY-SPECIALIST]. **beautifier** [ˈbjuːtifaiə], *n.* Personne *or* chose qui embellit, *f.* **beautiful,** *a.* Très beau; (*colloq.*) magnifique. **beautifully,** *adv.* Admirablement. **beautify,** *v.t.* Embellir, orner.—*v.i.* S'embellir. **beauty,** *n.* Beauté (person and attribute), *f.* **beauty-parlour,** *n.* Institut de beauté, *m.* **beauty-specialist,** *n.* Spécialiste en produits de beauté. **beauty-spot,** *n.* Mouche, *f.*, grain de beauté, *m.*; site pittoresque, *m.*
beaver [ˈbiːvə], *n.* Castor; chapeau de castor, *m.*; visière (of a helmet), *f.*
becalm [biˈkɑːm], *v.t.* *Apaiser, calmer; (*Naut.*) abriter. *To be becalmed,* être abrité, être surpris par un calme.
because [biˈkɔːz], *conj.* Parce que. *Because of,* à cause de.
beccafico [bekəˈfiːkou], *n.* Becfigue, *m.*
bechamel [ˈbeʃəmel], *n.* (*Cook.*) Béchamelle, *f.*, sauce Béchamel, *f.*
bechance [biˈtʃɑːns], *v.i.* Arriver.—*adv.* Par hasard.
beck (1) [bek], *n.* Signe (de doigt etc.), *m.* *To be at the beck and call of,* être aux ordres de.—*v.i.* Faire signe (du doigt etc).
beck (2) [bek], *n.* Ruisseau, *m.*
beckon [ˈbekən], *v.i.* Faire signe (à).—*v.t.* Faire signe à, appeler.
becloud [biˈklaud], *v.t.* Couvrir de nuages, voiler.
become [biˈkʌm], *v.i.* (*past* **became,** *p.p.* **become**) Devenir, commencer à être. *To become accustomed to,* s'accoutumer à; *to become interested in someone,* s'intéresser à quelqu'un; *to become known,* se faire connaître; *what will become of me?* que deviendrai-je?—*v.t.* Aller bien à, convenir à, être propre à; être digne de. *It all becomes,* il sied mal. **becoming,** *a.* Bienséant, convenable, qui va bien, attrayant. **becomingly,** *adv.* Avec bienséance, convenablement, avec grâce. **becomingness,** *n.* Convenance, bienséance, *f.*
bed [bed], *n.* Lit, *m.*; couche, *f.*; (*Mach.*) banc, *m.*, table, fondation; (*Geol.*) assise, *f.*, gisement; encaissement (of roads); parterre, *m.*, plate-bande (for flowers); (*Naut.*) souille, *f.*; carré, *m.* *As you make your bed so you must lie,* comme on fait son lit on se couche; *bed and board,* pension, *f.*; *bed of a river,* lit de rivière, *m.*; *double-bedded,* à deux lits; *in bed,* au lit; *to be brought to bed of,* accoucher de; *to be (ill) in bed,* être alité; *to go to bed,* se coucher; *to keep one's bed,* garder le lit; *to lie in bed,* se tenir au lit; *to sleep in separate beds,*

faire lit à part; *to take to one's bed,* s'aliter; *to turn down the bed,* faire la couverture.—*v.t.* Coucher, mettre au lit; loger, fixer, enfoncer; parquer (oysters).—*v.i.* Coucher, se coucher; cohabiter. **bed-book,** *n.* [BEDSIDE]. **bedchamber** *n.* [BEDROOM]. **bedclothes,** *n.pl.* Les draps et les couvertures, *m.pl.*, literie, *f.* **bedding,** *n.* Literie, *f.*; litière (for animals), *f.* *Bedding-out of plants,* dépotage de plantes, *m.* **bedfellow,** *n.* Camarade de lit, *m.* **bed-hangings,** *n.pl.* Rideaux de lit, *m.pl.*, tenture de lit, *f.* **bed-pan,** *n.* Bassin de lit, *m.* **bed-plate,** *n.* (*Civ. Eng.*) Plaque de fondation, *f.*, socle, *m.* **bedpost,** *n.* Colonne de lit, *f.* **bedridden,** *a.* Alité. **bedroom,** *n.* Chambre à coucher, *f.* **bedside,** *n.* Ruelle, *f.*, chevet, *m.*, bord du lit, *m.* *Bedside book,* livre de chevet; *good bedside manner* (of doctor), bonne manière professionnelle, *f.* **bed-sitter,** *n.* (*fam.*) [SITTING-ROOM]. **bed-sore,** *n.* Escarre, *f.* **bed-spread,** *n.* Couvre-lit, *m.*, dessus de lit, *m.* **bedstead,** *n.* Lit, bois de lit, *m.*; couchette, *f.* **bedtime,** *n.* L'heure du coucher *or* de se mettre au lit, *f.* **bed-warmer,** *n.* Chauffe-lit, *m.*
bedabble [biˈdæbl], *v.t.* Asperger, éclabousser, souiller. **bedarken,** *v.t.* Assombrir, obscurcir.
bedaub [biˈdɔːb], *v.t.* Barbouiller.
bedazzle [biˈdæzl], *v.t.* Éblouir.
bedeck [biˈdək], *v.t.* Parer (de).
bedel [ˈbiːdl], *n.* Appariteur, *m.*
bedevil [biˈdevəl], *v.t.* Faire enrager, taquiner; mettre la confusion dans; ensorceler. **bedew,** *v.t.* Arroser, baigner (de); humecter de rosée.
***bedight** [biˈdait], *v.t.* Parer, orner (de).
bedim [biˈdim], *v.t.* Obscurcir.
bedizen [biˈdaizn], *v.t.* Attifer, parer.
Bedlam [ˈbedləm], *n.* Bedlam (hôpital des fous), *m.*, Charenton (at Paris); *fou, m.*, folle, *f.*; (*fig.*) tintamarre, *m.* **bedlamite,** *n.* Fou, *m.*, folle, *f.*
bedraggle [biˈdrægl], *v.t.* Crotter, traîner dans la boue. **bedrench,** *v.t.* Tremper.
bee [biː], *n.* Abeille; (*Am.*) réunion pour travailler etc., *f.* *To have a bee in one's bonnet,* avoir une araignée dans le plafond. **bee-bread,** *n.* Pollen, *m.* **bee-eater,** *n.* Guêpier, *m.* **beehive,** *n.* Ruche, *f.* **bee-keeping,** *n.* Apiculture, *f.* **bee-line,** *n.* Ligne droite, *f.* *In a bee-line,* à vol d'oiseau; *to make a bee-line for,* se diriger tout droit vers. **bee-master** or **-keeper,** *n.* Éleveur d'abeilles, *m.*, apiculteur, *m.* **beeswax,** *n.* Cire jaune, *f.*
beech [biːtʃ], *n.* Hêtre, *m.* *Plantation of beeches,* hêtraie, *f.* **beech-martin,** *n.* Fouine, *f.* **beech-mast,** *n.* Faînes, *f.pl.* **beech-nut,** *n.* Faîne, *f.* **beech-oil,** *n.* Huile de faîne, *f.*
beef [biːf], *n.* Bœuf (meat); (*pl.* **beeves**) bœuf (ox), *m.* **beef-eater,** *n.* Mangeur de bœuf; hallebardier (de la garde royale), *m.* **beef-steak,** *n.* Bifteck, *m.* **beef-tea,** *n.* Bouillon de bœuf, *m.* **beefy,** *a.* (*colloq.*) Musclé, solide.
Beelzebub [biˈelzəbʌb]. Belzébuth, *m.*
been, *p.p.* [BE].
beer [biə], *n.* Bière, *f.* *Glass of beer,* bock, *m.*, chope, *f.*; *life is not all beer and skittles,* tout n'est pas rose dans ce monde; *to think no*

small beer of oneself, se croire le premier moutardier du pape. **beer-barrel,** *n.* Tonneau à bière, *m.* **beer-engine,** *n.* Pompe à bière, *f.* **beer-garden,** *n.* Café en plein air, *m.,* guinguette, *f.* **beerhouse** or **beershop,** *n.* Taverne, brasserie, *f.,* cabaret, *m.* **beerhouse-keeper,** *n.* Cabaretier, *m.,* cabaretière, *f.*

beestings ['biːstiŋz] or ***beest** [biːst], *n.pl.* Amouille, *f.*

beet [biːt], *n.* Betterave, *f.* **beetroot,** *n.* Betterave rouge, *f.* **beet-sugar,** *n.* Sucre de betterave, *m.*

beetle (1) [biːtl], *n.* Coléoptère, *m.,* scarabée, escarbot, *m.*

beetle (2) [biːtl], *n.* Maillet, *m.,* mailloche, *f.;* batte, *f.,* battoir, *m.* (of laundress); (pavior's) hie, demoiselle, *f.;* mouton (for a pile-driver), *m.*

beetle (3) [biːtl], *v.i.* Surplomber, avancer, faire saillie. *Beetling crags,* rochers menaçants. **beetle-browed,** *a.* Au front bombé, aux sourcils épais.

beetroot ['biːtruːt], *n.* [BEET].

befall [bi'fɔːl], *v.t., v.i.* (*past* **befell,** *p.p.* **befallen**) Arriver, survenir (à).

befit [bi'fit], *v.t.* Convenir à. **befitting,** *a.* Convenable à.

befog [bi'fɔg], *v.t.* Envelopper de brouillard; (*fig.*) obscurcir (l'esprit).

befool [bi'fuːl], *v.t.* Duper, tromper.

before [bi'fɔː], *adv.* Avant (of time, order, etc.); auparavant, préalablement, en avant; plus haut; jusqu'alors, naguère, jusqu'ici. *As before,* comme par le passé; *the evening before,* la veille au soir.—*prep.* Devant (of place); avant (of time etc.); (*Law*) par-devant. *Before going there,* avant d'y aller.—*conj.* Avant que (*with subj.*); plutôt que, avant de. **beforehand,** *adv.* À l'avance, d'avance. *To be beforehand with somebody,* prendre les devants sur quelqu'un. **before-time,** *adv.* Autrefois, jadis.

befoul [bi'faul], *v.t.* Salir, souiller. **befriend,** *v.t.* Seconder, aider, protéger, secourir.

befringe [bi'frindʒ], *v.t.* Franger, garnir d'une frange.

beg [beg], *v.t.* Mendier; demander (à), prier (de). *To beg the question,* faire une pétition de principe.—*v.i.* Mendier; prier (de). *I beg to inform you,* j'ai l'honneur de vous informer. *To go begging,* ne trouver personne qui en veut; (to a dog) *beg!* fais le beau!

beget [bi'get], *v.t.* (*past* **begot,** *p.p.* **begotten**) Engendrer; (*fig.*) produire, causer. **begetter,** *n.* Père, auteur, *m.*

beggar ['begə], *n.* Mendiant, *m.,* mendiante, *f.;* gueux, *m.,* gueuse, *f.*—*v.t.* Appauvrir, ruiner; (*fig.*) épuiser. *Beggar my neighbour,* bataille (cards), *f.; beggars can't be choosers,* ne choisit pas qui emprunte; *poor beggar,* pauvre diable, *m.* **beggarly,** *a.* Chétif, pauvre, misérable.—*adv.* Misérablement, chétivement. **beggary,** *n.* Mendicité, misère, *f.*

begin [bi'gin], *v.t.* (*past* **began,** *p.p.* **begun**) Commencer; entamer, débuter; se mettre à. *To begin writing,* se mettre à écrire.—*v.i.* Commencer. *Begin afresh,* recommencez; *to begin by doing something,* commencer par faire quelque chose. **beginner,** *n.* Commençant; débutant, *m.* **beginning,** *n.* Commencement, début, *m.,* origine, *f.*

begird [bi'gəːd], *v.t.* (*p.p.* **begirt**) Ceindre, entourer (de).

begone! [bi'gɔn], *int.* Va-t'en! allez-vous-en!

begonia [bi'gounjə], *n.* (*Bot.*) Bégonia, *m.*

begotten, *p.p.* [BEGET].

begrime [bi'graim], *v.t.* Barbouiller, souiller, noircir.

begrudge [bi'grʌdʒ], *v.t.* Envier; refuser (à). **begrudgingly,** *adv.* À contre-cœur, en rechignant.

beguile [bi'gail], *v.t.* Tromper, séduire; (*fig.*) passer (le temps). **beguilement,** *n.* Séduction, tromperie, *f.* **beguiler,** *n.* Trompeur, séducteur, *m.,* trompeuse, séductrice, *f.*

begun, *p.p.* [BEGIN].

behalf [bi'hɑːf], *n.* Faveur, part, *f. In behalf of,* en faveur de; *on behalf of,* au nom de, (*Comm.*) au profit de; *they are not anxious on my behalf,* ils ne s'inquiètent pas à mon sujet.

behave [bi'heiv], *v.i.* Se comporter, se conduire. *Behave yourself!* tiens-toi bien! *well behaved,* qui se conduit bien, sage.

behaviour [bi'heivjə], *n.* Conduite, tenue, *f.;* comportement, *m.;* manières, *f.pl.* **behaviourism,** *n.* (*Phil.*) Behaviourisme, *m.*

behead [bi'hed], *v.t.* Décapiter. **beheading,** *r.* Décapitation, décollation (of St. John the Baptist), *f.*

beheld, *past* and *p.p.* [BEHOLD].

behemoth ['biːhəmɔθ, bə'hiːmɔθ], *n.* Béhémoth, monstre, *m.*

behest [bi'hest], *n.* Commandement, ordre, *m.;* injonction, *f.*

behind [bi'haind], *adv.* Derrière, par derrière, en arrière.—*prep.* Derrière, en arrière de; après, en retard de. *Behind the times,* en retard sur son siècle; *behind time,* en retard.—*n.* (*colloq.*) Derrière, *m.* **behindhand,** *a.* En arrière, en retard. *Behindhand with* or *in,* en reste de.

behold [bi'hould], *v.t.* (*past* and *p.p.* **beheld**) Voir, regarder.—*int.* Voyez! voici! voilà! **beholden,** *a.* Redevable (à). **beholder,** *n.* Spectateur, témoin, assistant, *m.*

behoof [bi'huːf], *n.* Avantage, profit, *m.* **behove,** *v.i. impers.* Incomber à. *It behoves,* il faut, il importe, il convient; *it behoves him to,* il lui appartient de.

beige [beiʒ], *a.* and *n.* Beige, *m.*

being ['biːiŋ], *n.* Être, *m.;* existence, *f. In being,* existant, vivant.—*pres.p.* [BE] Étant. *For the time being,* pour le moment.

Beirut [bei'ruːt], *n.* Beyrouth, *m.*

belabour [bi'leibə], *v.t.* Rosser, rouer de coups.

belated [bi'leitid], *a.* Attardé; tardif.

belay [bi'lei], *v.t.* (*Naut.*) Amarrer, tourner sur un taquet. **belaying-cleat,** *n.* Taquet, *m.* **belaying-pin,** *n.* Cabillot, *m.*

belch [beltʃ], *v.t.* Roter, éructer. *To belch forth,* vomir; *to belch out flames,* vomir des flammes.—*n.* Rot, *m.,* éructation, *f.*

beldam ['beldəm] or ***beldame,** *n.* Vieille sorcière, *f.,* mégère, *f.*

beleaguer [bi'liːgə], *v.t.* Assiéger, investir. **beleaguering,** *n.* Assiégement, *m.*

belee [bi'liː], *v.t.* (*Naut.*) Faire dériver, jeter sous le vent.

belfry ['belfri], *n.* Clocher, beffroi, *m. To have* or *be bats in the belfry,* (*fam.*) être toqué.

Belgian ['beldʒən], *a.* Belge, de Belgique.—*n.* Belge.

Belgium ['beldʒiəm, -ʒəm]. La Belgique, *f.*

belie [bi'lai], *v.t.* Démentir, donner un démenti à.

belief [bi'li:f], *n.* Croyance, foi, créance, *f.*; credo, *m.* *To be past all belief*, être incroyable; *to the best of one's belief*, autant qu'on le sache. **believable**, *a.* Croyable. **believe**, *v.i.* Croire (en *or* à). *I believe not*, je crois que non, je ne le crois pas; *I believe so*, je crois que oui, je le crois; *to believe in fairies*, croire aux fées; *to believe in God*, croire en Dieu. —*v.t.* Croire. *I believe you*, je vous crois, je crois bien; *I can scarcely believe my eyes*, j'en crois à peine mes yeux; *if you are to be believed*, à vous en croire; *it is a mere make-believe*, c'est un simple subterfuge; *to make believe*, faire semblant de; *to make someone believe*, faire croire à quelqu'un. **believer**, *n.* Croyant, *m.*, croyante, *f.* **believingly**, *adv.* Avec foi.

*****belike** [bi'laik], *adv.* Apparemment, peut-être.

belittle [bi'litl], *v.t.* Rabaisser, amoindrir, déprécier.

bell [bel], *n.* Cloche, clochette, *f.*; grelot (on horses etc.), *m.*; sonnette (house-bell), *f.*; timbre (on clocks, cycles, etc.), *m.*; (*Arch.*) vase, *m.*, corbeille, *f.* *Bell of a flower*, calice d'une fleur, *m.*; *chime of bells*, carillon, *m.*; *electric bell*, sonnette électrique, *f.*; *is that the first bell?* est-ce le premier coup? (*Naut.*) *three bells*, trois coups (de cloche); *to bear the bell*, être le premier, l'emporter (sur les autres); *to ring the bell*, sonner.—*v.t. To bell the cat*, attacher le grelot.—*v.i.* Bramer (of deer). **bell-boy**, *n.* (*Am.*) Chasseur, groom, *m.* **bell-buoy**, *n.* Bouée sonore, *f.* **bell-flower**, *n.* Campanule, clochette, *f.* **bell-founder**, *n.* Fondeur de cloches, *m.* **bell-foundry**, *n.* Fonderie de cloches, *f.* **bell-glass**, *n.* Cloche (de jardin), *f.* **bell-hanger**, *n.* Poseur de sonnettes, *m.* **bell-man**, *n.* Crieur public, *m.* **bell-metal**, *n.* Métal de cloche, *m.* **bell-pull**, *n.* Cordon de sonnette, *m.* **bell-push**, *n.* Bouton, *m.* **bell-ringer**, *n.* Sonneur, *m.* **bell-rope**, *n.* Corde de cloche, *f.*, cordon de sonnette, *m.* **bell-shaped**, *a.* En forme de cloche. **bell-tower**, *n.* Campanile; clocher, *m.* **bell-wether**, *n.* Sonnailler, *m.*; meneur (du troupeau), *m.*

belladonna [belə'dɔnə], *n.* Belladone, *f.*

belle [bel], *n.* Belle, beauté, *f.* **belles-lettres**, *n.* Belles-lettres, *f.pl.*

bellicose ['belikous], *a.* Belliqueux. **bellicosity**, *n.* Caractère belliqueux, *m.*

belligerency [bi'lidʒərənsi], *n.* Belligérance, *f.* **belligerent**, *a. and n.* Belligérant, *m.*

bellow ['belou], *v.i.* Beugler; mugir (of the sea).—*n.* Beuglement, *m.*; (*fig.*) hurlement, *m.*

bellows ['belouz], *n.pl.* Soufflet, *m.* *A pair of bellows*, un soufflet.

belly ['beli], *n.* Ventre, *m.*—*v.i.* Bomber, s'enfler, se gonfler. **belly-ache**, *n.* Mal au ventre, mal à l'estomac, *m.*—*v.i.* (*pop.*) Ronchonner. **belly-band**, *n.* Sous-ventrière, *f.* **belly-flop**, *n.* (*fam.*) Plat-ventre, *m.* **bellyful**, *n.* (*slang*) Ventrée, *f.* *I had my bellyful of it*, j'en ai eu tout mon soûl, j'en ai eu assez.

belong [bi'lɔŋ], *v.i.* Appartenir, être (à); faire partie (de). *This book belongs to me*, ce livre est à moi. *Things that belong together*, choses qui vont ensemble, qui font partie du même tout. **belongings**, *n.pl.* Effets, *m.pl.*, affaires, *f.pl.*

beloved [bi'lʌvd, -'lʌvid], *a.* Cher, chéri, bien-aimé.

below [bi'lou], *prep.* Sous, au-dessous de; en aval de.—*adv.* Au-dessous, dessous, en bas. *Here below*, ici-bas; *see below*, voir ci-dessous *or* ci-après.

Belshazzar [bel'ʃæzə]. Balthasar, *m.*

belt [belt], *n.* Ceinture, *f.*; ceinturon; baudrier, *m.*; (*Mach.*) courroie; (*Astron.*) bande, *f.* *Green belt*, zone verte, *f.*; *to hit below the belt*, frapper déloyalement.—*v.t.* Ceindre, entourer; fustiger. **belt-driven**, *a.* Mû par courroie. **belting**, *n.* Ceinture, *f.*; rossée, raclée, *f.*

belvedere [belvə'diə], *n.* Belvédère, *m.*

bemire [bi'maiə], *v.t.* Embourber, crotter; couvrir de boue.

bemoan [bi'moun], *v.t.* Pleurer, déplorer.—*v.i.* Gémir (sur).

bemuse [bi'mju:z], *v.t.* Stupéfier, obnubiler, hébéter.

ben [ben], *n.* Mont, pic (montagne en Écosse), *m.*—*prep. and adv.* (*Sc.*) À l'intérieur (de).

bench [bentʃ], *n.* Banc; gradin, *m.*; banquette, *f.*; (*Carp. etc.*) établi; banc, siège, parquet; tribunal, *m.*, cour, magistrature, *f. Court of King's Bench*, cour du Banc du roi; *to be raised to the bench*, être nommé juge *or* évêque.—*v.t.* Garnir de bancs. **bench-mark**, *n.* Repère, *m.* **bencher**, *n.* Doyen d'une *Inn of Court.*

bend [bend], *v.t.* (*past and p.p.* bent (1)) Plier; courber, faire plier; tourner, incliner, tendre (a bow); fléchir (the knee); (*fig.*) appliquer, diriger; (*Naut.*) frapper (une manœuvre), enverguer (une voile). *On bended knees*, à genoux; *to bend a cable*, étalinguer un câble; *to bend all one's endeavours*, appliquer tous ses efforts (à); *to bend down*, courber; *to bend one's brows*, froncer le sourcil, rider le front; *to bend round*, recourber.—*v.i.* Plier, ployer; se courber, se pencher, s'incliner; s'appliquer (à); tourner; fléchir; surplomber, faire saillie (to overhang). *To bend forward*, se pencher en avant.—*n.* Courbure, *f.*; pli; détour; coude, *m.*; (*Motor.*) tournant, virage, *m.*; (*Naut.*) nœud, ajut, *m.* (*pop.*) *Round the bend*, fou, timbré; *to go on the bend*, faire la bringue.

beneaped [bi'ni:pt], *a.* Echoué par morte-eau.

beneath [bi'ni:θ], *prep.* Sous, au-dessous de. *Beneath contempt*, extrêmement méprisable; *to marry beneath one*, faire une mésalliance. —*adv.* Au-dessous, en bas.

benedick ['benidik] *or* **benedict**, *n.* Nouveau marié, *m. To turn benedick*, se marier.

Benedict ['benidikt]. Benoît, *m.*

Benedictine [beni'diktain], *n.* Bénédictin, *m.*

benedictine [beni'dikti:n], *n.* Bénédictine (liqueur), *f.*—*a.* De l'ordre de saint Benoît; bénédictin.

benediction [beni'dikʃən], *n.* Bénédiction, *f.* **benedictory**, *a.* De bénédiction.

benefaction [beni'fækʃən], *n.* Bienfait, *m.* **benefactor**, *n.* Bienfaiteur, *m.* **benefactress**, *n.* Bienfaitrice, *f.*

benefice ['benifis], *n.* Bénéfice, *m.* **beneficed,** *a.* Pourvu d'un bénéfice. *Beneficed clergyman,* bénéficier, *m.* **beneficence** [bə'nefisəns], *n.* Bienfaisance, *f.* **beneficent,** *a.* Bienfaisant. **beneficently,** *adv.* Avec bienfaisance. **beneficial** [beni'fiʃəl], *a.* Salutaire, avantageux. **beneficially,** *adv.* Avantageusement. **beneficiary,** *n.* and *a.* Bénéficiaire, *m.*

benefit ['benifit], *n.* Bienfait, profit, avantage; bénéfice, *m.*; indemnité, *f.* (unemployment etc.); (*Theat.*) représentation à bénéfice, *f.*, (*spt.*) match à bénéfice, *m.* *For the benefit of,* au profit de, dans l'intérêt de; *to derive benefit from,* profiter de; *to give someone the benefit of the doubt,* accorder à quelqu'un le bénéfice du doute.—*v.t.* Faire du bien à.—*v.i.* Profiter; se trouver bien (de), gagner (à). **benefit society,** *n.* Société de secours mutuels, *f.*

Benelux ['benilʌks], *n.* Bénélux, *m.*

benevolence [bə'nevələns], *n.* Bienveillance, bonté, bienfaisance, *f.* **benevolent,** *a.* Bienveillant, bienfaisant. **benevolently,** *adv.* Avec bienfaisance, bénévolement.

Bengal [ben'gɔ:l]. Le Bengale, *m.* **The Bay of Bengal,** le golfe du Bengale.

Bengal-light [bengɔ:l'lait], *n.* Feu de Bengale, *m.*

Bengali or **Bengalee** [ben'gɔ:li], *n.* Bengali.

benighted [bi'naitid], *a.* Anuité, surpris par la nuit; (*fig.*) plongé dans les ténèbres, ignorant, aveugle.

benign [bi'nain], *a.* Bénin, *m.*, bénigne, *f.*, bienfaisant, doux, affable. **benignant** [bi'nignənt], *a.* Bon, bienveillant. **benignity,** *n.* Bénignité, *f.* **benignly** [bi'nainli], *adv.* Bénignement.

benison ['benizn], *n.* Bénédiction, *f.*

benjamin ['bendʒəmin], *n.* (*Bot.*) Benjoin, *m.*

bennet ['benət], *n.* Benoîte (herbe), *f.*

bent (1), *past* and *p.p.* [BEND].

bent (2) [bent], *n.* Penchant, *m.*, disposition, tendance, *f.* *To the top of his bent,* à cœur joie.—*a.* Courbé, plié; faussé. *Bent on,* déterminé *or* résolu à (le faire).

bent (3) [bent] *or* **bentgrass,** *n.* Agrostide, *f.*

benumb [bi'nʌm], *v.t.* Engourdir. *To be benumbed with cold,* ne pas se sentir de froid, être transi. **benumbment,** *n.* Engourdissement, *m.*

benzedrine ['benzidri:n], *n.* Benzedrine, *f.*

benzene or **benzine** ['benzi:n], *n.* Benzine, *f.* **benzoic,** *a.* (*Chem.*) Benzoïque. **benzoin** ['benzɔin], *n.* Benjoin, *m.* **benzoline,** *n.* Essence minérale, *f.*

beplaster [bi'plɑ:stə], *v.t.* Plâtrer.

bequeath [bi'kwi:θ], *v.t.* Léguer. **bequeathment,** *n.* Action de léguer, *f.*; legs, *m.* **bequest,** *n.* Legs, *m.*

berate [bi'reit], *v.t.* Morigéner, réprimander.

Berber ['bə:bə], *a.* and *n.* Berbère, *m.* or *f.*

berberry [BARBERRY].

bereave [bi'ri:v], *v.t.* (*past* **bereft,** *p.p.* **bereaved**) Priver (de). *The bereaved,* la famille du mort, les affligés. **bereavement,** *n.* Privation, perte, *f.*; deuil, *m.*

beret ['berei, 'berit], *n.* Béret, *m.*

bergamot ['bə:gəmɔt], *n.* Bergamote (orange), *f.*; bergamote, crassane (pear), *f.*

ɔerlin [bə:'lin], *n.* *Berline (carriage), *f.* *Berlin warehouse,* magasin de laine à broder et à tricoter, *m.*; *Berlin wool,* laine fine, *f.*

ɔerm [bə:m], *n.* Berme, *f.*

Bermudas [bə:'mju:dəz]. Les (Îles) Bermudes, *f.pl.*

Bern(e) [bə:n]. Berne, *f.*

Bernardine ['bə:nədin], *n.* Bernardin, *m.*, bernardine, *f.*

berry ['beri], *n.* Baie, *f.* *Coffee in the berry,* café en grain, *m.*—*v.i.* Porter des baies.

berserk ['bə:sə:k], *n.* Berserk, *m.* *To go berserk,* devenir fou furieux.

berth [bə:θ], *n.* Mouillage, port d'amarrage, évitage, *m.*; poste à quai, évitée, *f.*; lit, *m.*, couchette; poste, place, *f.*, emploi, *m.* *To give a wide berth to,* éviter.—*v.i.* Mouiller, venir à quai.—*v.t.* Amarrer à quai.

Bertha ['bə:θə]. Berthe, *f.*

beryl ['beril], *n.* (*Min.*) Béryl, *m.* **berylline,** *a.* De béryl. **beryllium** [bə'riliəm], *n.* Béryllium, *m.*

beseech [bi'si:tʃ], *v.t.* (*past* and *p.p.* **besought** [bi'sɔ:t]) Supplier, implorer. **beseeching,** *a.* Suppliant. **beseechingly,** *adv.* En suppliant.

beseem [bi'si:m], *v.i.* Convenir. **beseeming,** *a.* Convenable, seyant. **beseemingly,** *adv.* Convenablement.

beset [bi'set], *v.t.* (*past* and *p.p.* **beset**) Obséder, entourer, embarrasser, serrer de près, assaillir. **besetment,** *n.* Encerclement; point faible, défaut, *m.* **besetting,** *a.* Habituel, obsesseur.

***beshrew** [bi'ʃru:], *v.t.* (*only in imprecation*) Maudit soit!

beside [bi'said], *prep.* À côté de, auprès de; hors, hormis, excepté. *To be beside oneself,* être hors de soi; *beside the question, the mark,* hors du sujet, hors de propos. **besides,** *prep.* Outre, hors, hormis, excepté, sans compter. —*adv.* D'ailleurs, du reste, en outre, encore, de plus.

besiege [bi'si:dʒ], *v.t.* Assiéger. **besieged,** *n.* Assiégé, *m.* **besieger,** *n.* Assiégeant, *m.* **besieging,** *a.* Assiégeant.

besmear [bi'smiə], *v.t.* Barbouiller; souiller.

besmirch, *v.t.* Tacher, salir.

besom ['bi:zəm], *n.* Balai, *m.*

besot [bi'sɔt], *v.t.* Assoter, abrutir. **besotted,** *a.* Abruti; infatué. **besottedly,** *adv.* Sottement.

besought, *past* and *p.p.* [BESEECH].

bespangle [bi'spæŋgl], *v.t.* Orner de paillettes, passementer. *Bespangled with,* étincelant de.

bespatter [bi'spætə], *v.t.* Éclabousser, couvrir de boue.

bespeak [bi'spi:k], *v.t.* (*past* **bespoke,** *p.p.* **bespoken**) Commander; retenir; annoncer, dénoter, accuser. *To bespeak a coat,* commander un habit; *to bespeak a place,* retenir une place.

bespeckle [bi'spekl], *v.t.* Tacheter, moucheter.

bespectacled [bi'spektəkld], *a.* Portant des lunettes.

besprinkle [bi'spriŋkl], *v.t.* Arroser.

Bessarabia [besə'reibiə]. La Bessarabie, *f.*

best [best], *a.* Le meilleur, le mieux. *At best,* au mieux, tout au plus; *best man* (at weddings), garçon d'honneur, *m.*; *for the best,* pour le mieux, au mieux; *in one's best clothes,* endimanché; *the best man on earth,* le meilleur homme du monde; *the best of every-thing,* ce qu'il y a de meilleur; *the best of it is that,* le meilleur est que; *the best of the way,* la plus grande partie du chemin; *to act for the best*, faire *or* agir pour le mieux; *to do one's best*, faire tout son possible, faire de son mieux; *to have the best of it*, avoir le dessus; *to know best*, savoir mieux que personne; *to look one's best*, paraître à son avantage; *to make the best of a bad job*, faire bonne mine à mauvais jeu; *to make the best of it*, en prendre son parti, tirer le meilleur parti; *to the best of my belief*, autant que je sache; *to the best of one's ability*, de son mieux.—*adv.* Mieux, le mieux; *one had best*, mieux vaudrait, mieux vaut.—*v.t.* L'emporter sur.

best-seller, *n.* Livre (*or* auteur) à succès *or* à gros tirage, *m.*

bestain [bi'stein], *v.t.* Tacher.

bestial ['bestiəl], *a.* Bestial, de bête. **bestiality** [-'æliti], *n.* Bestialité, *f.* **bestialize**, *v.t.* Bestialiser, abrutir. **bestially**, *adv.* Bestialement. **bestiary**, *n.* Bestiaire, *m.*

bestir [bi'stə:], *v.t.* Remuer, mettre en mouvement. *To bestir oneself*, se remuer, s'empresser.

bestow [bi'stou], *v.t.* Donner, accorder. *To bestow a kindness on someone*, rendre un service à quelqu'un. **bestowal** or **bestowment**, *n.* Dispensation, *f.*

bestrew [bi'stru:], *v.t.* (*p.p.* **bestrewn** or **bestrewed**) Joncher (de), parsemer (de).

bestride [bi'straid], *v.t.* (*past* **bestrode**, *p.p.* **bestridden**) Enjamber, enfourcher (a horse); être à cheval sur.

bestud [bi'stʌd], *v.t.* Semer (de), parsemer (de).

bet [bet], *n.* Pari, *m.*, gageure, *f. To lay a bet*, parier.—*v.t., v.i.* Parier. *To bet on a horse*, jouer un cheval. *You bet!* (*colloq.*) que pariez-vous? pour sûr!

betake [bi'teik], *v.t.* (*past* **betook**, *p.p.* **betaken**) *To betake oneself to*, se mettre à, s'en aller à, avoir recours à.

Bethany ['beθəni]. Béthanie, *f.*

bethink [bi'θiŋk], *v.t.* (*past* and *p.p.* **bethought**) S'aviser (de). *To bethink oneself of*, se rappeler.

Bethlehem ['beθlihem, -liəm]. Bethléem, *m.*

betide [bi'taid], *v.t.* Arriver à, advenir à. *Woe betide you*, malheur à vous.—*v.i.* Arriver, advenir.

*betime or **betimes** [bi'taimz], *adv.* De bonne heure.

betoken [bi'toukn], *v.t.* Annoncer, présager, dénoter.

beton ['betən], *n.* Béton, *m.*

betony ['betəni], *n.* Bétoine, *f.*

betray [bi'trei], *v.t.* Trahir; tromper; révéler; faire tomber, entraîner. *To betray into error*, induire en erreur. **betrayal**, *n.* Trahison, perfidie, *f.*; révélation, *f.* **betrayer**, *n.* Traître, *m.*, traîtresse, *f.*

betroth [bi'trouð], *v.t.* Fiancer. **betrothed**, *a.* and *n.* Fiancé, *m.*, fiancée, *f.* **betrothal**, *n.* Fiançailles, *f.pl.*

better (1) ['betə], *a.* Meilleur. *My better half*, ma chère moitié; *the better the day, the better the deed*, à bon jour, bonne œuvre; *to be the better for*, se trouver bien de; *to get the better of*, avoir le dessus de, l'emporter sur. —*adv.* Mieux. *Better late than never*, mieux vaut tard que jamais; *better and better*, de mieux en mieux; *for better for worse*, vaille que vaille; *for the better*, en mieux; *I had*

better go, je ferais mieux de partir; *nothing could be better*, c'est on ne peut mieux; *so much the better!* tant mieux! *to be better worth*, valoir mieux; *to get better*, aller mieux, se porter mieux; *to grow better*, se porter mieux; *to think better of*, se raviser de; *to think the better of him*, l'estimer davantage.— *n.* Supérieur, *m.*—*v.t.* Améliorer, avancer. *To better oneself*, améliorer sa position. **betterment**, *n.* Amélioration, *f.*

better (2) ['betə] or ***bettor**, *n.* Parieur, *m.*

betting ['betiŋ], *n.* Paris, *m.pl. Betting man*, parieur, *m. The betting is ten to one*, la cote est à dix contre un. ***bettor** [BETTER (2)].

Betty ['beti]. Babette, *f.*

*betumbled [bi'tʌmbld], *a.* En désordre.

between [bi'twi:n], *prep.* Entre. *Between now and tomorrow*, d'ici à demain; *between us*, between ourselves, entre nous; *between us two*, *three, etc.*, à nous deux, à nous trois, etc.; *between whiles*, dans les intervalles, de temps en temps; *between wind and water*, à fleur d'eau. **between-decks**, *n.* (*Naut.*) Entrepont, *m.* ***betwixt**, *prep.* Entre. *Betwixt and between*, entre les deux.

bevel ['bevəl], *a.* De biais, en biseau.—*n.* Fausse équerre (tool), *f.*—*v.t.* Tailler en biseau.—*v.i.* Aller en biais, biaiser. **bevelgear**, *n.* Engrenage conique, *m.* **bevelwheel**, *n.* Roue d'angle, *f.*, pignon conique, *m.* **bevelling** or **bevelment**, *n.* Coupe en biais, *f.*, biseau, *m.*

beverage ['bevəridʒ], *n.* Breuvage, *m.*, boisson, *f.*

bevy ['bevi], *n.* Volée; troupe, compagnie, *f. Bevy of quails*, volée de cailles, *f.*; *bevy of young girls*, troupe de jeunes filles, *f.*

bewail [bi'weil], *v.t.* Pleurer, lamenter.—*v.i.* Se lamenter. **bewailing**, *n.* Lamentation, *f.*

beware [bi'wɛə], *v.i.* Se garder (de), prendre garde (à); se méfier (de). *Beware of pickpockets*, attention aux pickpockets; *beware of the dog*, prenez garde au chien.

bewhiskered [bi'wiskəd], *a.* Qui a des favoris.

bewilder [bi'wildə], *v.t.* Égarer, embarrasser, confondre, effarer, désorienter, dérouter. **bewildering**, *a.* Déroutant, ahurissant. **bewilderment**, *n.* Égarement, *m.*

bewitch [bi'witʃ], *v.t.* Ensorceler, enchanter. **bewitching**, *a.* Enchanteur, séduisant. **bewitchingly**, *adv.* D'une manière séduisante, à ravir. **bewitchment**, *n.* Ensorcellement, *m.*

*bewray [bi'rei], *v.t.* Déceler, trahir.

bey [bei], *n.* Bey, *m.* **beylic**, *n.* Beylik, *m.*

beyond [bi'jɔnd], *prep.* Par delà, au delà de; au-dessus de; outre, hors de. *Beautiful beyond description*, beau à ravir; *beyond measure*, outre mesure; *beyond one's reach*, hors de sa portée; *this is beyond me*, cela me dépasse, je n'y comprends rien; *to go beyond*, aller plus loin que.—*adv.* Là-bas.—*n.* Au-delà, *m. The back of beyond*, le bout du monde.

bezel [bezl], *n.* Chaton (of a ring), *m.*; biseau, *m.* (of a stone).

biangular [bai'æŋgjulə], *a.* À deux angles.

biannual [bai'ænjuəl], *a.* Semestriel (half-yearly); biennal (two-yearly).

bias ['baiəs], *n.* Biais, *m.*, pente, *f.*; penchant,

parti pris, préjugé, *m.—v.t.* Décentrer (a bowl); faire pencher; prévenir; influencer.—*a.* and *adv.* De biais, de travers. **biased,** *a.* Décentré; partial, prédisposé.

biaxial [bai'æksjəl], *a.* Biaxe, à deux axes.

bib [bib], *n.* Bavette, *f.*; tacaud, *m.* (fish).—*v.i.*, *v.t.* Boire (trop). **bibber,** *n.* Buveur.

bible [baibl], *n.* Bible, *f.* *Bible Society*, société biblique, *f.* **biblical** ['biblikəl], *a.* Biblique.

bibliographer [bibli'ɔgrəfə], *n.* Bibliographe, *m.* **bibliographical** [-'græfikəl], *a.* Bibliographique. **bibliography** [bibli'ɔgrəfi], *n.* Bibliographie, *f.* **bibliomancy** ['biblio mænsi], *n.* Bibliomancie, *f.* **bibliomania** [biblio'meiniə], *n.* Bibliomanie, *f.* **bibliomaniac,** *n.* Bibliomane, *m.* **bibliophile,** *n.* Bibliophile, *m.* **bibliopole** or **bibliopolist,** *n.* Libraire, *m.*

bibulous ['bibjuləs], *a.* Spongieux, absorbant; (personne) qui boit, buveur.

bicameral [bai'kæmərəl], *a.* Bicaméral.

bicarbonate [bai'kɑːbənit], *n.* Bicarbonate, *m.*

bice [bais], *n.* Bleu de cobalt, *m.*

bicentenary [baisen'tiːnəri], *a.* and *n.* Bicentenaire, *m.*

bicephalous [bai'sefələs], *a.* Bicéphale, à deux têtes.

biceps ['baiseps], *n.* (*Anat.*) Biceps, *m.*

bicker ['bikə], *v.i.* Se quereller, se chamailler. **bickerer,** *n.* Querelleur, chamailleur, *m.* **bickering,** *n.* Bisbille, *f.*, querelles, *f.pl.*

bicolour(ed) ['baikʌlə(d)], *a.* Bicolore; (*Cine.*) bichrome.

bicycle ['baisikl], *n.* Bicyclette, *f.*; (*pop.*) vélo, *m.*, bécane, *f.* *Bicycle ride*, promenade à bicyclette, *f.*; *bicycle stand*, support à bicyclette, *m.—v.i.* Faire de la bicyclette; aller à bicyclette. **bicyclist,** *n.* Cycliste.

bid [bid], *v.t.* (*past* **bade**, *p.p.* **bidden** or **bid**) Ordonner, dire, commander (de); inviter (à); offrir, enchérir. *To bid good-bye to*, dire adieu à, faire ses adieux à; *to bid two hearts*, demander deux cœurs. **bid,** *n.* Enchère, *f.* *To make a bid for power*, viser au pouvoir. *No bid!* (at cards) Parole! **bidder,** *n.* Enchérisseur, acheteur, *m.* *To the highest bidder*, au plus offrant et dernier enchérisseur. **bidding,** *n.* Commandement, ordre, *m.*; invitation, prière, *f.*, enchères, *f.pl.*

bide [baid], *a.* Endurer, attendre. *To bide one's time*, attendre le bon moment.—*v.i.* Demeurer, rester, habiter. *To bide at home*, rester chez soi.

biennial [bai'eniəl], *a.* Biennal; (*Bot.*) bisannuel. **biennially,** *adv.* Tous les deux ans, en deux ans.

bier [biə], *n.* Civière, *f.*, corbillard, *m.*

biff [bif], *n.* (*pop.*) Gnon, *m.—v.t.* Flanquer un gnon à.

*biffin ['bifin], *n.* Pomme à cuire (du Norfolk); pomme cuite au four et tapée, *f.*

bifid ['baifid], *a.* (*Bot.*) Bifide. **biflorate,** *a.* Biflore. **bifocal,** *a.* (*Opt.*) Bifocal. **bifurcate,** *v.i.* Se bifurquer. **bifurcated,** *a.* Bifurqué. **bifurcation,** *n.* Bifurcation, *f.*

big [big], *a.* Gros; grand, vaste; enceinte, grosse; pleine (of animals); (*fig.*) fier, hautain, fanfaron. *Big with child*, grosse (d'enfant); *to grow bigger*, grossir; *to look big*, faire l'important; *to talk big*, le prendre de haut. **bigness,** *n.* Grosseur, grandeur, *f.*

bigamist ['bigəmist], *n.* Bigame. **bigamous,** *a.* Bigame. **bigamy,** *n.* Bigamie, *f.*

bight [bait], *n.* Crique, anse, *f.*; (*Naut.*) boucle (of rope), *f.* *The Great Australian Bight*, la Grande Baie Australienne.

bigot ['bigət], *n.* Bigot, cagot, *m.*, fanatique. **bigoted,** *a.* Bigot, sectaire. **bigotry,** *n.* Bigoterie, cagoterie, *f.*, bigotisme, sectarisme, fanatisme, *m.*

bigwig ['bigwig], *n.* (*fam.*) Gros bonnet, *m.*

bike [baik], *n.* (*colloq.*) Vélo, *m.*, bécane, *f.*

bikini [bi'kiːni], *n.* (*Cost.*) Bikini, *m.*

*bilander ['bailəndə], *n.* (*Naut.*) Bélandre, *f.*

bilateral [bai'lætərəl], *a.* Bilatéral.

bilberry ['bilbəri], *n.* (*Bot.*) Airelle, *f.*

*bilbo ['bilbou], *n.* Rapière, *f.*; (*Naut.*, *pl.* **bilboes**) fers, *m.pl.*

bile [bail], *n.* Bile, *f.*

bilge [bildʒ], *n.* (*Naut.*) Sentine, *f.*, petits fonds (of a ship), *m.pl.*; (*colloq.*) idioties, bêtises, *f.pl.—v.i.* Faire eau.—*v.t.* Crever, défoncer. **bilge-pump,** *n.* Pompe de cale, *f* **bilgewater,** *n.* Eau de la cale, *f.*

biliary ['biliəri], *a.* Biliaire.

bilingual [bai'lingwəl], *a.* Bilingue. **bilinguist,** *n.* Personne bilingue, *f.*

bilious ['biljəs], *a.* Bilieux. *Bilious attack*, embarras gastrique, *m.* **biliousness,** *n.* Affection bilieuse; crise hépatique, *f.*

bilk [bilk], *v.t.* Flouer, filouter, frustrer.

bill (1) [bil], *n.* Bec d'oiseau, *m.—v.i.* Se becqueter. (*fam.*) *To bill and coo*, s'aimer comme deux tourtereaux.

bill (2) [bil], *n.* Hallebarde, *f.* **bill-hook,** *n.* Serpe, *f.*, vouge, *m.*

bill (3) [bil], *n.* Mémoire, compte, *m.*; facture (invoice), note (at hotels etc.), addition (at restaurants); (*Comm.*) note, *f.*; billet, effet, *m.*; (*Banking*) lettre de change, *f.*; (*Parl.*) projet de loi; (*Engl.*) bill, *m.*; affiche, *f.*, placard, *m.* *Bill at sight*, billet à vue, *m.*; *bill of exchange*, lettre de change, traite, *f.*; *bill of fare*, menu, *m.*, carte, *f.*; *bill of health*, patente de santé, *f.*; *bill of lading*, connaissement, *m.*; *bill of parcels*, facture, *f.*; *bill of rights*, déclaration des droits, *f.*; *bill of sale*, lettre de vente, *f.*, acte de propriété, *m.*; *bill of store*, bulletin d'approvisionnement, *m.*; *bill on demand*, billet à présentation, *m.*; *bill payable to bearer*, billet au porteur, *m.*; *bills of mortality*, registre mortuaire, *m.*; *handbill*, affiche, *f.*, placard, *m.*; *long-dated bill*, billet à longue échéance, *m.*; *stick no bills!* défense d'afficher! (*fam.*) *that will fill the bill*, cela fera l'affaire; *the expiration of a bill*, l'échéance d'un effet, *f.*; *to back a bill*, endosser un effet; *to discount a bill*, escompter un billet *or* un effet; *to draw a bill on*, faire traite sur, tirer sur; *to find a true bill*, prononcer la mise en accusation (de); *to take up a bill*, acquitter un billet, payer un billet; *to throw out the bill*, repousser le projet; *tradesman's bill*, mémoire de fournisseur, *m.*, facture, *f.* **bill-board,** *n.* Panneau d'affichage *m.*; (*Am.*) affiche, *f.* **bill-book,** *n.* Carnet d'échéances, *m.* **bill-broker,** *n.* Courtier de change, escompteur, *m.* **bill-case,** *n.* Porte-valeurs, porte-feuille à effets, *m.* **billfile,** *n.* Pique-notes, *m.* **bill-fold,** *n.* (*Am.*) Porte-billets, *m.* **bill-head,** *n.* Tête de facture, *f.* **bill-poster** or **bill-sticker,** *n.* Afficheur, colleur d'affiches, *m.*

bill (4) [bil], *v.t.* Afficher, mettre à l'affiche. **billing,** *n.* Affichage, *m. The actress got top billing,* l'actrice a fait tête d'affiche.
billet ['bilit], *n.* Bûche, *f.*; (*Mil.*) billet de logement, *m.*; (*Her.*) billette, *f.*—*v.t., v.i.* Loger. **billet-doux,** *n.* (*pl.* billets-doux) Billet-doux, *m.* **billeting-officer,** *n.* Chef de cantonnement, *m.* **billeting-party,** *n.* (Détachement de) cantonnement, *m.*
billiard ['biljəd], *a.* De billard. **billiard-ball,** *n.* Bille, *f.* **billiard-cloth,** *n.* Tapis, *m.* **billiard-cue,** *n.* Queue de billard, *f.* **billiard-marker,** *n.* Garçon de billard, *m.* **billiard-room,** *n.* Salle de billard, *f.* **billiard-table,** *n.* Billard, *m.* **billiards,** *n.pl.* Billard, *m.sing. To play a game of billiards,* faire une partie de billard.
billingsgate ['biliŋzgət], *n.* Langage de poissarde, *m.*
billion ['biliən], *n.* Billion, *m.* (since 1948); (*Am.*) milliard, *m.*
billow ['bilou], *n.* Grande vague, lame, *f.*—*v.i.* S'élever en vagues, rouler. **billowy,** *a.* Houleux.
billycock ['bilikɔk], *n.* (*fam.*) (Chapeau) melon, *m.*
billy-goat ['biligout], *n.* Bouc, *m.*
Bimana ['baimənə, 'bimənə], *n.pl.* (*Zool.*) Bimanes, *m.pl.* **bimanous,** *a.* Bimane.
bimetallism [bai'metəlizm], *n.* Bimétallisme, *m.*
bi-monthly [bai'mʌnθli], *a.* Bimensuel.
bin [bin], *n.* Huche, *f.*, bac, *m.*; coffre, *m.*—*v.t.* Ranger, empiler (bottles).
binary ['bainəri], *a.* Binaire.
bind [baind], *v.t.* (*past* and *p.p.* **bound**) Lier; obliger; resserrer; border (shoes etc.); garrotter, serrer; rendre constipé; relier (books). *Bound in boards,* cartonné; *I'll be bound,* j'en réponds; *that is bound to happen,* cela ne peut manquer d'arriver; *to be bound over,* être tenu de comparaître; *to be bound to,* être tenu de; *to bind a boy apprentice to,* mettre un garçon en apprentissage chez; *to bind a carpet,* border un tapis; *to bind a wound,* bander une blessure; *to bind down,* lier, astreindre (à); *to bind to,* engager à.— *v.i.* Se lier, durcir; (*pop.*) ronchonner.—*n.* (*Mus.*) Liaison, *f.*; (*Mech.*) blocage, *m.* (*pop.*) *That's a bind,* quelle scie! **binder,** *n.* Lieur; relieur, *m.*; bande, attache, *f.* **bindery,** *n.* Atelier de reliure, *m.* **binding,** *n.* Reliure, *f.*; bandeau, galon, *m.*, bordure, *f. Cloth binding,* reliure en toile, *f.*—*a.* Obligatoire; (*Med.*) astringent. **bindweed,** *n.* Liseron, *m.*
binge [bindʒ], *n.* (*pop.*) Bombe, *f. To be on the binge,* faire la bombe.
binnacle ['binəkl], *n.* (*Naut.*) Habitacle, *m.*
binocle ['binəkl], *n.* Binocle, *m.* **binocular** [bi'nɔkjulə], *a.* Binoculaire. **binoculars,** *n.pl.* Jumelles, *f.pl.*
binomial [bai'noumiəl], *a.* (*Alg.*) Binôme.
biochemical [baio'kemikəl], *a.* Biochimique. **biochemistry,** *n.* Biochimie, *f.*
biogenesis [baio'dʒenəsis], *n.* Biogénèse, *f.* **biogenetic** [baiodʒə'netik], *a.* Biogénétique.
biographer [bai'ɔgrəfə], *n.* Biographe, *m.* **biographic** or **biographical** [baiə'græfikl], *a.* Biographique.
biography [bai'ɔgrəfi], *n.* Biographie, *f.*
biologic [baio'lɔdʒik] or **biological,** *a.* Biologique. **biologist,** *n.* Biologiste, biologue, *m.*
biology [bai'ɔlədʒi], *n.* Biologie, *f.*

bipartite [bai'pɑːtait], *a.* Biparti, bipartite.
biped, *n.* Bipède, *m.* **bipedal** ['baipedl], *a.* Bipède, *m.* **biplane,** *n.* Biplan, *m.* **bipod,** *n.* Bipied, *m.*
biquadratic [baikwɔ'drætik], *a.* (*Alg.*) Bicarré.
birch [bəːtʃ], *n.* Bouleau, *m.*; verges, *f.pl. Silver birch,* bouleau blanc.—*v.t.* Battre à coups de verges, fouetter. **birchen,** *a.* De bouleau. **birching,** *n.* Coups de verges, *m.pl.* **birch-rod,** *n.* Verges, *f.pl.* **birch-tree,** *n.* Bouleau, *m.*
bird [bəːd], *n.* Oiseau, *m.*; (*fig.*) type, *m.*; (*pop.*) femme, fille, poule, *f. Little bird,* oiselet, *m. A bird in the hand is worth two in the bush,* un bon tiens vaut mieux que deux tu l'auras; *to give an actor the bird,* siffler, huer, un acteur; *to kill two birds with one stone,* faire d'une pierre deux coups. **bird-cage,** *n.* Cage d'oiseau, *f.* **bird-call,** *n.* Appeau, pipeau, *m.* **bird-catcher,** *n.* Oiseleur, *m.* **bird-fancier,** *n.* Amateur d'oiseaux, *m.*, aviculteur, *m.* **bird-lime,** *n.* Glu, *f.* **bird's-eye view,** *n.* Vue à vol d'oiseau, *f.* **bird's-nest,** *n.* Nid d'oiseau, *m. To go bird's-nesting,* aller dénicher des oiseaux.
biretta [bi'retə], *n.* Barrette, *f.*
birth [bəːθ], *n.* Naissance, *f.*; enfantement, *m.*; (*fig.*) origine, source, *f. By birth,* de naissance; *to give birth to,* donner le jour à, (animals) mettre bas; (*fig.*) donner lieu à. **birth-certificate,** *n.* Acte de naissance, *m.* **birth-control,** *n.* Limitation des naissances, *f.* **birthday,** *n.* Anniversaire, *m.* **birthplace,** *n.* Lieu de naissance, pays natal, *m.* **birth-rate,** *n.* Natalité, *f.* **birth-right,** *n.* Droit d'aînesse, *m.*
bis [bis], *adv.* Bis.
Biscay ['biskei]. La Biscaye, *f. The Bay of Biscay,* Le Golfe de Gascogne, *m.*
biscuit ['biskit], *n.* Biscuit, *m.*; petit four, petit gâteau, *m. That takes the biscuit!* ça, c'est fort! ça, c'est le bouquet!
bisect [bai'sekt], *v.t.* Couper en deux. **bisection,** *n.* Bissection, *f.*
bisexual [bai'seksjuəl], *a.* Bissexué, bissexuel.
bishop ['biʃəp], *n.* Évêque; (chess) fou, *m. Bishop's palace,* évêché, *m.* **bishopric,** *n.* Évêché, *m.*
bisk [bisk], *n.* Bisque, *f.*
bismuth ['bizməθ], *n.* Bismuth, *m.*
bison [baisn], *n.* Bison, *m.*
bissextile [bi'sekstail], *a.* Bissextil.—*n.* Année bissextile, *f.*
bistort ['bistɔːt], *n.* (*Bot.*) Bistorte, *f.*
bistoury ['bisturi], *n.* Bistouri, *m.*
bistre ['bistə], *n.* Bistre, *m.*
bisulphite [bai'sʌlfait], *n.* Bisulfite, *m.*
bit (1) [bit], *n.* Morceau, *m.*; (coin) pièce, *f.*; (*colloq.*) brin, bout, peu, *m.*; mèche (tool); (*Naut.*) bitte, *f. A bit older,* un peu plus vieux; *a good bit older,* beaucoup plus vieux; *bit by bit,* peu à peu; *every bit of it,* entièrement, tout à fait; *I don't care a bit,* ça m'est bien égal; *not a bit of it!* pas le moins du monde, pas du tout; *to do one's bit,* y mettre du sien.
bit (2) [bit], *n.* Mors (of bridle), *m. To champ at the bit,* mâcher son mors; *to take the bit between one's teeth,* prendre le mors aux dents, s'emballer.
bit (3), *past* [BITE].

bitch [bitʃ], *n.* Chienne, *f.*; femelle (in compounds), *f.*; (abusively) catin, *f.*, garce, *f.*
bite [bait], *n.* Morsure; piqûre, *f.*; coup de dent, *m.*, bouchée; (fishing) touche, *f.*; (*Print.*) larron, *m. Without bite or sip*, sans boire ni manger.—*v.t.* (*past* bit (3), *p.p.* **bitten**) Mordre; piquer; ronger; (*fig.*) attraper, pincer, couper (of the wind). *Once bitten twice shy*, chat échaudé craint l'eau froide; *to bite back an answer*, ravaler une réplique; *to bite off*, déchirer avec les dents, enlever d'un coup de dent; *to bite off more than one can chew*, tenter quelque chose au-dessus de ses forces; *to bite one's lips*, se mordre les lèvres; *to bite one's nails*, se ronger les ongles; (*fig.*) *to bite someone's head off*, rembarrer quelqu'un; *to bite the bit*, ronger le frein (of horses); *to bite the dust*, mordre la poussière; *what's biting you?* quelle mouche te pique?—*v.i.* Mordre. *Are the fish biting?* le poisson mord-il? *to bite* (to take the bait), mordre à l'hameçon. **biter**, *n.* Personne qui mord, *f.*; (*fig.*) trompeur, *m. It is a case of the biter bit*, c'est le trompeur trompé.
biting, *a.* Mordant, piquant; coupant (of the wind). **bitingly**, *adv.* D'une manière mordante.
bitter ['bitə], *a.* Amer, acerbe; (*fig.*) acharné, mordant, aigre, piquant, rigoureux.—*n.* Amer, *m.*; (*fam.*) bière amère, *f.* **bitterly**, *adv.* Avec amertume; amèrement. *Bitterly disappointed*, cruellement déçu. **bitterness**, *n.* Amertume, aigreur, âpreté, *f.* **bitters**, *n.pl.* Amers, *m.pl. To drink bitters*, (*colloq.*) prendre des apéritifs. **bitter-sweet**, *a.* Aigre-doux.—*n.* La douce-amère, *f.*
bittern ['bitə:n], *n.* Butor, *m.*
bitumen [bi'tju:mən], *n.* Bitume, *m.* **bituminization**, *n.* Bitumage, *m.* **bituminize**, *v.t.* Bituminer. **bituminous**, *a.* Bitumineux, bitumeux.
bivalve ['baivælv], *a.* and *n.* Bivalve. **bivalved** or **bivalvular**, *a.* Bivalvulaire.
bivouac ['bivuæk], *n.* Bivouac, *m.*—*v.i.* Bivouaquer.
bi-weekly [bai'wi:kly], *a.* and *adv.* (De) tous les quinze jours; toutes les deux semaines; deux fois par semaine, semi-hebdomadaire.
blab [blæb], *v.i.* Jaser, bavarder; divulguer un secret.—*v.t.* Conter, divulguer.—*n.* Bavard, jaseur, *m.*; bavarde, jaseuse, *f.*
black [blæk], *a.* Noir; (*fig.*) obscur, sombre, triste; (*Print.*) gothique. *A black eye*, un œil poché; *as black as a tinker*, noir comme une taupe; *things look black*, les choses prennent une mauvaise allure; *to beat black and blue*, rouer de coups; *to be black and blue*, être tout meurtri; *to look black at*, faire mauvais visage à; *the Black Death*, la Peste Noire.—*v.t.* Noircir; cirer (boots).—*n.* Noir, *m.*; (*pl.*) flocons de suie, *m.pl. Dressed in black*, habillé de noir; *in black and white*, en toutes lettres, par écrit; *ivory-black*, noir d'ivoire, *m.*; *lamp-black*, noir de fumée, *m.*; *the blacks*, les noirs, (*pej.*) les nègres, *m.pl.*; *to put up a black*, faire une gaffe. **blackamoor**, *n.* (*pej.*) Noir, *m.* **black-ball**, *n.* Boule noire, *f.*—*v.t.* Rejeter au scrutin. **black-beetle**, *n.* Cafard, *m.*, blatte, *f.* **blackberry**, *n.* Mûre, mûre sauvage, *f.* **blackberry-bush**, *n.* Mûrier des haies, *m.* **blackbird**, *n.* Merle, *m.* **blackboard**, *n.* Tableau noir, *m.* **blackcap**, *n.*

Fauvette à tête noire, *f.* **blackcock**, *n.* Petit coq de bruyère, tétras, *m.* **blackcurrant**, *n.* Cassis, *m.* **blackguard** ['blægɑ:d], *n.* Polisson, gredin, vaurien, *m.* **blackguardism**, *n.* Polissonnerie, *f.* **blackguardly**, *a.* Sale, canaille. **blackhead**, *n.* Point noir, *m.* **black-hole**, *n.* Cachot, *m.*
blacklead, *n.* Mine de plomb, *f.*
blackleg, *n.* (*Gambling*) Escroc, *m.*; (*Strikes*) renard, jaune, *m.*
black-letter, *n.* Caractère gothique, *m.*
blackmail, *n.* Chantage, *m.*—*v.t.* Faire chanter. **blackmailer**, *n.* Maître-chanteur, *m.*
black-market, *n.* Marché noir, *m.* **blackout**, *n.* Extinction des lumières, *f.*; black-out, *m. To have a black-out*, tomber faible, tomber en syncope. **black-pudding**, *n.* Boudin, *m.* **black sheep**, *n.* Brebis galeuse, *f.* **blacksmith**, *n.* Forgeron, *m. Blacksmith's shop*, forge, *f.* **blackthorn**, *n.* Épine noire, *f.*
blacken, *v.t.*, *v.i.* Noircir. **blacking**, *n.* Cirage (footwear); noircissement, *m.* **blackish**, *a.* Noirâtre. **blackly**, *adv.* En noir, avec noirceur. **blackness**, *n.* Noirceur, *f.*
bladder ['blædə], *n.* Vessie; (*Bot.*) vésicule, *f.* **bladderwort**, *n.* Utriculaire, *f.* **bladderwrack**, *n.* Raisin de mer, *m.*
blade [bleid], *n.* Lame (of cutting instruments), *f.*; brin (of grass), *m.*; pelle (of an oar), *f.*; branche d'hélice (of propeller), *f.*; (*fig.*) gaillard, *m. Old blade*, vieux routier; *young blade*, jeune luron. **blade-bone**, *n.* Omoplate, *f.* **bladed**, *a.* À lame. *Double-bladed*, à deux lames.
blain [blein], *n.* Pustule, *f.*
blamable or **blameable** ['bleiməbl], *a.* Blâmable. **blame**, *n.* Blâme, *m.*; faute, *f. To lay the blame on*, rejeter le blâme sur; *to take the blame*, supporter le blâme.—*v.t.* Blâmer, s'en prendre à; censurer, reprocher. *One can't blame him for it*, on ne peut lui en vouloir; *she can't be blamed*, on ne saurait la blâmer; *to blame something on someone*, imputer quelque chose à quelqu'un; *you have only yourself to blame*, vous l'avez voulu. **blameless**, *a.* Innocent, sans tache. **blamelessly**, *adv.* Irréprochablement. **blamelessness**, *n.* Innocence, *f.* **blameworthy**, *a.* [BLAMABLE].
blanch [blɑ:ntʃ], *v.t.* Blanchir; pâlir; faire pâlir; (of almonds) monder.—*v.i.* Blanchir; pâlir.
blancmange [blə'mɒnʒ], *n.* Blanc-manger, *m.*
bland [blænd], *a.* Doux, aimable, affable. **blandish** ['blændiʃ], *v.t.* Caresser, flatter, cajoler. **blandishment**, *n.* Flatterie, *f.* **blandness**, *n.* Douceur, affabilité, *f.*
blank [blæŋk], *a.* Blanc, en blanc; (*fig.*) vide, confus, déconcerté; profond, absolu; (*Arch.*) faux; fausse (of ammunition), *f. To fire with blank cartridge*, tirer à blanc. *Blank verse*, vers blancs, *m.pl.*—*n.* Blanc; (*Lotteries*) billet blanc; flan (de métal); (*fig.*) vide, *m.*, lacune, *f. In blank*, en blanc; (*fig.*) *to draw a blank*, échouer, faire chou blanc. **blankly**, *adv.* Avec confusion. **blankness**, *n.* Air confus, *m.*, confusion, *f.*; vide, néant, *m.*
blanket ['blæŋkit], *n.* Couverture, *f.*; (*Print.*) blanchet, *m. A wet blanket*, un rabat-joie, *m.*—*v.t.* Mettre une couverture autour de;

(*Naut.*) déventer, manger le vent à. **blanketing**, *n.* Couvertures, *f.pl.*
blare [blɛə], *v.i.* Sonner (comme une trompette), cuivrer.—*v.t.* Faire retentir.—*n.* Sonnerie, *f.*
blarney ['blɑːni], *n.* Eau bénite de cour, flagornerie, *f.*—*v.t.* Enjôler, flagorner; payer en monnaie de singe.
blasé ['blɑːzi], *a.* Blasé.
blaspheme [blæs'fiːm], *v.t.*, *v.i.* Blasphémer. **blasphemer**, *n.* Blasphémateur, *m.*
blasphemous ['blæsfəməs], *a.* Blasphématoire. **blasphemously**, *adv.* Avec blasphème. **blasphemy**, *n.* Blasphème, *m.*
blast [blɑːst], *n.* Vent, coup de vent; air; son (d'un instrument à vent), *m.*; explosion, *f.*; (*fig.*) souffle destructeur *or* pestilentiel.—*v.t.* Flétrir, brûler; détruire, ruiner; faire sauter. —*int.* Sacrebleu! **blasted**, *a.* Sacré.—*adv.* Rudement. **blast-engine**, *n.* Machine-soufflante, *f.* **blast-furnace**, *n.* Haut fourneau, *m.* **blasting**, *a.* Destructeur.—*n.* Coup de mine, sautage, *m.*, explosion, *f.* *By blasting*, au moyen de la mine. **blast-pipe**, *n.* Tuyau d'échappement, *m.*; tuyère, *f.*
blastema [blæs'tiːmə], *n.* Blastème, *m.*
blastoderm ['blæstodəːm], *n.* Blastoderme, *m.*
blatancy ['bleitənsi], *n.* Caractère criard, *m.*; vulgarité criarde, *f.* **blatant** ['bleitənt], *a.* Bruyant, criard. **blatantly**, *adv.* Avec une vulgarité criarde.
blather [BLETHER].
blaze [bleiz], *n.* Flamme; flambée, *f.*; feu, *m.*; (*fig.*) éclat, *m.*; étoile (on a horse), *f.* *Go to blazes!* allez au diable! *what the blazes . . .?* que diable . . .?—*v.i.* Être en flammes; flamber, brûler; étinceler (of jewels).—*v.t.* Répandre, crier par-dessus les toits (abroad); marquer (trees). *To blaze a trail*, se frayer un chemin. **blazer**, *n.* (*Cost.*) Veston de sport de flanelle; blazer, *m.* **blazing**, *a.* Flambant; enflammé, embrasé; (*fig.*) brillant; effroyable, insigne, infernal.
blazon ['bleizən], *n.* Blason, *m.*; proclamation, divulgation, *f.*—*v.t.* Blasonner; faire briller; proclamer, publier. *To blazon abroad*, crier par-dessus les toits. **blazonry**, *n.* Blasonnement, *m.*; science héraldique, *f.*
bleach [bliːtʃ], *v.t.*, *v.i.* Blanchir; (*Hairdressing*) oxygéner.—*n.* Agent de blanchiment, *m.*; (*Hairdressing*) oxygénée, *f.* **bleaching**, *n.* Blanchiment, *m.* **bleaching-liquid**, *n.* Eau de Javel, *f.* **bleaching-powder**, *n.* Poudre à blanchir, *f.*
bleak (1) [bliːk], *n.* Ablette (fish), *f.*
bleak [bliːk], *a.* Ouvert, sans abri; froid; désert; morne, triste. **bleakly**, *adv.* Froidement; d'un air morne. **bleakness**, *n.* Exposition découverte, *f.*; froidure, *f.*, froid, *m.*; tristesse, *f.*; aspect morne, *m.*
blear [bliə] *or* **bleary**, *a.* Larmoyant, trouble. —*v.t.* Rendre trouble. **blear-eyed** *or* **bleary-eyed**, *a.* Qui a les yeux larmoyants.
bleat [bliːt], *v.i.* Bêler.—*n.* Bêlement, *m.*
bleb [bleb], *n.* Ampoule, cloche, *f.*
bleed [bliːd], *v.i.* (*past and p.p.* bled) Saigner; pleurer (of vines etc.). *My nose is bleeding*, je saigne du nez.—*v.t.* Saigner; (*colloq.*) gruger, débourser. **bleeding**, *a.* Saignant.— *n.* Saignement, *m.*; (*Surg.*) saignée, *f.*
blemish ['blemiʃ], *v.t.* Tacher, flétrir, ternir. —*n.* Tache, flétrissure, *f.*, défaut, *m.*, tare, *f.*

blench [blentʃ], *v.i.* Sourciller.
blend [blend], *v.t.* Mêler, mélanger; réunir, fondre, marier.—*v.i.* Se fondre, se marier (à *or* avec).—*n.* Mélange, *m.*
blende [blend], *n.* (*Min.*) Blende, *f.*
blennorrhoea [blenɔ'riːə], *n.* Blennorrhée, *f.*
blenny ['bleni], *n.* (*Ichth.*) Baveuse, blennie, *f.*
bless [bles], *v.t.* Bénir; rendre heureux, faire le bonheur de, favoriser, réjouir. *Bless my heart or my soul*, mon dieu! sapristi! *God bless you!* Dieu vous bénisse! *to bless with*, douer de.
blessed [blest, 'blesid], *a.* Béni, saint; bienheureux, heureux; (*slang*) fichu. *The blessed Virgin*, la sainte Vierge; *to be blessed with*, avoir le bonheur d'avoir, jouir de.
blessedness ['blesidnis], *n.* Béatitude, félicité, *f.*, bonheur, *m.* *Single blessedness*, célibat, *m.*
blessing, *n.* Bénédiction, *f.*; bonheur, bienfait, bien, *m.*; grâce, *f.*, bénédicité, *m.* *To ask a blessing*, dire le bénédicité.
blest [BLESSED]. *Well, I'm blest*, eh bien! par exemple!
blether ['bleðə] *or* **blather**, *n.* Sottises, bêtises, *f.pl.*—*v.i.* Dire des inepties.
blight [blait], *v.t.* Flétrir (of the wind); brouir (of the sun); nieller (fungi); (*fig.*) frustrer, détruire.—*n.* Brouissure (of flowers and fruit); nielle, rouille (of corn etc.); (*fig.*) flétrissure, tache, *f.*
blighter ['blaitə], *n.* (*pop.*) Type, individu. *m.*; bon à rien, *m.*
Blighty ['blaiti], *n.* (*Mil. pop.*) L'Angleterre, *f.*, le foyer, *m.*
blimey ['blaimi], *int.* Zut, alors!
blind [blaind], *a.* Aveugle; obscur. *Blind alley*, cul-de-sac, *m.*, impasse, *f.*; *blind in one eye*, borgne; *blind person*, un(e) aveugle; *blind side*, côté faible, *m.*; *stone-blind*, complètement aveugle; *struck blind*, frappé de cécité; *to turn a blind eye to*, feindre de ne pas voir.—*n.* Store (for window); abat-jour, *m.*; banne (shop-blind); jalousie (Venetian); persienne (outside), *f.*; (*fig.*) voile, masque, prétexte, *m.* *The blind*, les aveugles.—*v.t.* Aveugler; (*fig.*) éblouir. **blindfold**, *v.t.* Bander les yeux à.—*a.* Les yeux bandés. **blindly**, *adv.* Aveuglément. **blind-man's buff**, *n.* Colin-maillard, *m.* **blindness**, *n.* Cécité, *f.*; aveuglement, *m.*; (*fig.*) ignorance, *f.*
blink [bliŋk], *v.i.* Clignoter, cligner des yeux; vaciller (of light).—*v.t.* Fermer les yeux sur, refuser de voir.—*n.* Clignotement, *m.*
blinker, *n.* Personne qui cligne des yeux; œillère (for horses), *f.* **blinkered**, *a.* (of person) porte des œillères (of horse); aux vues étroites (of person). **blinking**, *a.* Clignotant; (*pop.*) sacré.—*n.* Clignotement, *m.*
bliss [blis], *n.* Félicité, béatitude, *f.* **blissful**, *a.* Bienheureux. **blissfully**, *adv.* Heureusement. **blissfulness**, *n.* Félicité, béatitude, *f.*
blister ['blistə], *n.* Ampoule, bulle, *f.*; (*Med.*) vésicatoire, *m.*; cloque, *f.* (on paint).—*v.t.* Appliquer un vésicatoire à, faire venir des ampoules à.—*v.i.* S'élever en ampoules, se couvrir d'ampoules; (of paint) se cloquer.
blithe [blaið] *or* **blithesome**, *a.* Gai, joyeux. **blithely**, *adv.* Joyeusement, gaiement.
blithering ['bliðəriŋ], *a.* (*fam.*) *A blithering idiot*, un parfait crétin, *m.*
blitz [blits], *n.* Bombardement aérien, *m.* (Second World War).

blizzard ['blizəd], *n.* Tempête de neige, *f.*
bloat [blout], *v.t.* Gonfler, bouffir, boursoufler
enfler.—*v.i.* S'enfler.
bloater ['bloutə], *n.* Hareng saur; (*colloq.*)
gendarme, *m.*
blob [blɔb], *n.* Goutte (d'eau), *f.*; pâté (d'encre),
m.; (*fam.*) bévue, *f.*—*v.i.* Couler, faire des
pâtés (of a pen).
block [blɔk], *n.* Bloc, *m.*, bille, *f.*; billot, *m.*;
(*Wood-engr.*) gravure sur bois, planche; forme
(for hat); (*Naut.*) poulie, *f.*; (*Stereotyp.*)
cliché, *m.*; (*fig.*) obstacle, encombrement, *m.*
Barber's block, tête à perruque, *f.*; *block of
houses,* pâté de maisons, *m.*, îlot, *m.*; *stumbling-
block,* pierre d'achoppement, *f.*; *traffic block,*
arrêt de circulation, encombrement de voitures, embouteillage, *m.*—*v.t.* Bloquer. *To
block up,* fermer, boucher. *To block someone's
way,* barrer le passage à quelqu'un.
blockade [blɔ'keid], *n.* Blocus, *m.* *To raise
the blockade,* lever le blocus.—*v.t.* Bloquer.
blockade-runner, *n.* Forceur de blocus, *m.*
block-capitals, *n.pl.* Capitales d'imprimerie,
f.pl.
blockhead ['blɔkhed], *n.* Bête, *f.*, imbécile,
sot, *m.*, sotte, *f.* **blockheaded,** *a.* Sot,
stupide.
blockhouse, *n.* Blockhaus, *m.*
blocking, *n.* Encombrement, *m.*
blockish, *a.* Stupide.
blockmaker, *n.* Poulier, *m.*
block-tin, *n.* Étain en saumons, *m.*
bloke [blouk], *n.* (*pop.*) Type, *m.*
blond(e) [blɔnd], *a.* and *n.* Blond, *m.*, blonde, *f.*
blood [blʌd], *n.* Sang, *m.*; (*fig.*) parenté, *f.*;
tempérament, *m.*; race (of a horse); tête
chaude, *f.*, brave, *m.* *Blue-blooded,* de sang
illustre; *his blood is up,* il a la tête montée;
hot-blooded, de sang ardent; *in cold blood,* de
sang froid; *it runs in the blood,* c'est dans le
sang; *one cannot get blood out of a stone,* on
ne saurait tirer de l'huile d'un mur; *that
makes one's blood run cold,* cela vous glace le
sang; *to cause bad blood,* faire faire du mauvais
sang; *to draw blood,* faire saigner.—*a.* De
sang.—*v.t.* Saigner; (*fig.*) exaspérer, échauffer; initier à la chasse *or* à la guerre.
blood-bank, *n.* Banque de sang, *f.* **blood-
coloured,** *a.* Couleur de sang. **blood-
curdling,** *a.* À vous tourner les sangs.
blood-donor, *n.* Donneur (-euse) de sang,
m.(f.). **blood-group,** *n.* Groupe sanguin, *m.*
blood-heat, *n.* Température du sang, *f.*
blood-horse, *n.* (Cheval) pur sang, *m.*
bloodhound, *n.* Limier, *m.* **blood-letting,**
n. Saignée, *f.* **blood-money,** *n.* Prix du
sang, *m.* **blood-orange,** *n.* Sanguine, *f.*
blood-poisoning, *n.* Empoisonnement du
sang, *m.* **blood-red,** *a.* Rouge (comme du)
sang. **bloodshed,** *n.* Effusion de sang, *f.*
bloodshot, *a.* Injecté de sang. **blood-stain,**
n. Tache de sang, *f.* **blood-sucker,** *n.*
Sangsue, *f.* **bloodthirsty,** *a.* Sanguinaire,
altéré de sang. **blood-vessel,** *n.* Vaisseau
sanguin, *m.* **bloodily,** *adv.* D'une manière
sanglante. **bloodless,** *a.* Exsangue; pâle;
inanimé. *Bloodless victory,* victoire non
sanglante *or* sans effusion de sang, *f.*
bloody ['blʌdi], *a.* Sanglant, ensanglanté, sanguinaire; (*vulg.*) satané, foutu. **bloody-
minded,** *a.* (*pop.*) Têtu, pas commode,
hargneux.

bloom [blu:m], *n.* Fleur, *f.*; duvet, velouté (on
fruit), *m.*; (*Metal.*) loupe, *f.* *In bloom,* en
fleur.—*v.i.* Fleurir; (*fig.*) être éclatant.
bloomer, *n.* (*pop.*) Bévue, *f.*; (*pl.*) culotte
bouffante, *f.* **blooming,** *n.* Floraison, *f.*—*a.*
Fleurissant, (*pop.*) sacré, satané.
blossom ['blɔsəm], *n.* Fleur, *f.*—*v.i.* Fleurir,
être en fleur. *To blossom out,* s'épanouir.
blossoming, *n.* Floraison, *f.*
blot [blɔt], *n.* Tache, *f.*; pâté (of ink), *m.*—*v.t.*
Tacher, salir, souiller, barbouiller; faire un
pâté sur; sécher (with blotting-paper). *To
blot out,* rayer, effacer.—*v.i.* Boire (of paper).
blotter, *n.* Buvard, *m.* **blotting-pad,** *n.*
Sous-main, *m.* **blotting-paper,** *n.* Papier
buvard, *m.*
blotch [blɔtʃ], *n.* Pustule, tache, *f.*—*v.t.*
Couvrir de pustules *or* de taches; marbrer.
blotchy, *a.* Tacheté.
blotto ['blɔtou], *a.* (*pop.*) Complètement soûl.
blouse [blauz], *n.* Blouse; chemisette, *f.*,
corsage, chemisier, *m.*
blow [blou], *n.* Coup, *m.* *A blow with a stick,* un
coup de bâton; *a fly-blow,* chiure de mouche,
f.; *at a single blow,* d'un seul coup; *to come to
blows,* en venir aux mains; *without striking
a blow,* sans coup férir.—*v.i.* (past *blew,* *p.p.*
blown) Scuffler; faire du vent; s'épanouir
(of flowers); sauter (of a fuse); claquer (of an
electric bulb). *It is blowing,* il fait du vent;
it is blowing great guns, il fait une tempête à
tout casser; *to blow about,* voler çà et là; *to
blow off* (of a hat etc.), s'envoler; *to blow
over,* passer, se dissiper; *to blow up,* sauter,
éclater, crever.—*v.t.* Souffler; sonner (of
wind instruments); essouffler (a horse); faire
sauter (a fuse). *To blow away,* chasser,
dissiper; *to blow hot and cold,* souffler le froid
et le chaud; *to blow one's nose,* se moucher;
to blow one's own trumpet, chanter ses propres
louanges; *to blow out,* souffler, éteindre (une
lumière), faire sauter (la cervelle); gonfler
(les joues); *to blow someone a kiss,* envoyer un
baiser à quelqu'un; *to blow someone up,* faire
une scène à quelqu'un, donner un savon à
quelqu'un; *to blow up,* faire sauter; gonfler
(un pneu); *you be blowed!* allez au diable!
allez vous promener! **blow-fly,** *n.* Mouche
à viande, *f.* **blow-lamp,** *n.* Chalumeau, *m.*
blow-out, *n.* Bombance, ripaille, *f.* **blow-
pipe,** *n.* Chalumeau, *m.* **blower,** *n.* Souffleur; tablier; rideau de cheminée, *m.*;
trappe, *f.*; (*pop.*) téléphone, *m.* **blowy,** *a.*
(*colloq.*) Venteux.
blowzy ['blauzi], *a.* Rougeaud, joufflu, rubicond; ébouriffé.
blubber (1) ['blʌbə], *n.* Graisse de baleine, *f.*
blubber (2) ['blʌbə] *or* **blub,** *v.i.* Pleurer
comme un veau.
blubber-lipped, *a.* Lippu.
bludgeon ['blʌdʒən], *n.* Gourdin, casse-tête,
m.; trique, matraque, *f.*—*v.t.* Asséner un
coup de gourdin à, matraquer.
blue [blu:], *n.* Bleu. *A blue funk,* une peur
bleue; *Blue Peter,* signal de départ, *m.*; *once
in a blue moon,* dans la semaine des quatre
jeudis; *to look blue,* faire la grimace; *to talk
till one is blue in the face,* avoir beau parler.—*n.*
Bleu, *m.*; azur, *m.* *Dark blue,* bleu foncé;
light blue, bleu clair; *navy blue,* bleu marine;
out of the blue, à l'improviste; *Prussian blue,*
bleu de Prusse; *sky-blue,* bleu de ciel, bleu

d'azur; *washing blue*, bleu d'empois, *m.*; (*pl.*) *The Blues*, la garde à cheval, *f.*; (*Mus.*) les blues, *m.pl.*; *to have a fit of the blues*, avoir le cafard.—*v.t.* Bleuir; passer au bleu; gaspiller (money). **blue-bag,** *n.* Sachet à bleu, *m.*
blue-bell, *n.* Jacinthe des prés, *f.*
bluebottle, *n.* Bluet (plant), *m.*; mouche bleue (fly), *f.*
blue-book, *n.* Livre jaune, *m.*
blue-devils, *n.pl.* Maladie noire *f.*; papillons noirs, *m.pl.*
blue-eyed, *a.* Aux yeux bleus.
bluejacket, *n.* Marin, matelot, *m.*
blue-pill, *n.* Pilule mercurielle, *f.*
blue-print, *n.* Dessin négatif, *m.*; (*fam.*) bleu, projet, *m.*
blue-ribbon or **-riband,** *n.* La distinction la plus haute, *f.*; (of teetotalers) ruban que portent les buveurs d'eau, *m.*
bluestocking, *n.* Bas bleu, *m.*, femme savante, *f.*
blueness, *n.* Couleur bleue, *f.*
bluff [blʌf], *a.* Escarpé, accore; (of persons) brusque.—*n.* À-pic, *m.*, falaise, *f.*, escarpement; (pretence) bluff, *m.* *To call someone's bluff*, relever un défi.—*v.t.* Bluffer. **bluffness,** *n.* Rudesse, brusquerie, *f.*
bluish ['bluːiʃ], *a.* Bleuâtre.
blunder ['blʌndə], *n.* Bévue, grosse faute, étourderie, balourdise, *f.*—*v.i.* Faire une bévue.—*v.t.* Embrouiller. *To blunder a thing out*, laisser échapper une chose; *to blunder upon*, découvrir par hasard.
blunderbuss ['blʌndəbʌs], *n.* Tromblon, *m.*
blunderer ['blʌndərə], *n.* Maladroit, *m.*, maladroite, *f.*, étourdi, *m.*, étourdie, *f.*
blunderhead, *n.* Brouillon, *m.*, brouillonne, *f.*
blundering, *a.* Maladroit. **blunderingly,** *adv.* Étourdiment, en étourdi.
blunt [blʌnt], *a.* Émoussé, épointé; (fig.) brusque, brutal, bourru.—*v.t.* Émousser, épointer; (fig.) amortir. **bluntly,** *adv.* Brusquement, carrément; de but en blanc. **bluntness,** *n.* État émoussé, *m.*; brusquerie, *f.*
blur [bləː], *n.* Tache, *f.*, barbouillage, *m.*; brouillard, *m.*—*v.t.* Tacher, barbouiller; (fig.) brouiller.
blurb [bləːb], *n.* Puff d'un éditeur, *m.*; annonce sur un couvre-livre, *f.*
blurt [bləːt], *v.t.* Dire à l'étourdie. *To blurt out*, laisser échapper.
blush [blʌʃ], *v.i.* Rougir. *To blush to the roots of one's hair*, rougir jusqu'aux oreilles.—*n.* Rougeur, *f.* *At the first blush*, au premier abord; *to put to the blush*, faire rougir. **blushing,** *a.* Rougissant.
bluster ['blʌstə], *v.i.* Tempêter, crier (contre), fanfaronner.—*n.* Fracas, tapage, *m.*, fanfaronnade, fureur (of storms), *f.* *Why all this bluster?* pourquoi tout cet emportement? **blusterer,** *n.* Fanfaron, bravache, *m.* **blustering,** *a.* Orageux; bruyant; bravache, fanfaron. **blusteringly,** *adv.* En tempêtant, d'un air bravache.
bo [bou], *int.* *He wouldn't say bo to a goose*, c'est un nigaud, il est extrêmement timide.
boa ['bouə], *n.* Boa, *m.* **boa-constrictor,** *n.* Boa constricteur, *m.*
boar [boː], *n.* Verrat, *m.* *Wild boar*, sanglier, *m.* **boar-hound,** *n.* Chien de sanglier, *m.*, vautre, *m.*

board [boːd], *n.* Planche, *f.*; ais, écriteau, *m.*; table, pension, nourriture, *f.*; conseil, *m.*, administration, *f.*; (*Bookb.*) carton, cartonnage; (*Tailors*) établi; (*Naut.*) bord, *m.*; (*Chess*) échiquier, *m.*; (*pl.*) le théâtre, la scène, les planches, *f.pl. Above board*, cartes sur table; *board and lodging*, le gîte et le couvert; *board meeting*, réunion de comité, *f.*; *board of directors*, conseil d'administration, *m.*; *board of examiners*, jury d'examen, *m.*; *Board of Trade*, ministère du commerce, *m.*; *on board*, à bord; *on board one's ship*, à son bord; *to bind in boards*, cartonner; *to go on board*, aller à bord, s'embarquer; *to let go by the board*, négliger; *to put out to board*, mettre en pension; *to sweep the board* (in gambling), faire tapis net.—*v.t.* Planchéier; nourrir; (*Naut.*) aller à bord de, aborder, prendre à l'abordage. *To board out*, mettre en pension.—*v.i.* Être or se mettre en pension. **board-room,** *n.* Chambre du conseil, *f.*
board-wages, *n.pl.* Indemnité de nourriture, *f.*
boarder, *n.* Pensionnaire; interne.
boarding, *n.* Planchéiage, plancher, *m.*; table, nourriture, pension, *f.*; (*Bookb.*) cartonnage; (*Naut.*) abordage, *m.*
boarding-house, *n.* Pension de famille, *f.*
boarding-school, *n.* Pensionnat, *m.*, internat, *m.*
boast [boust], *v.i.* Se vanter, se glorifier.—*v.t.* Être fier de posséder, posséder.—*n.* Vanterie, *f.* *To make a boast of*, se vanter de. **boaster,** *n.* Vantard, *m.* **boastful,** *a.* Vantard. **boasting,** *n.* Vantardise, *f.* **boastingly,** *adv.* Avec vantardise.
boat [bout], *n.* Bateau, canot, *m.*, barque, *f.*; embarcation, *f. Lifeboat*, canot de sauvetage, *m.*; *long-boat*, chaloupe, *f.*; *sauce-boat*, saucière, *f.*; *steam-boat*, bateau à vapeur, *m.*; *to be in the same boat*, être dans le même cas; *to burn one's boats*, brûler ses vaisseaux; *to miss the boat*, (fig.) manquer le coche.—*v.t.* Transporter par bateau. *To boat the oars*, rentrer les avirons.—*v.i.* Se promener en bateau. **boat-deck,** *n.* Pont d'embarcation, *m.* **boat-hook,** *n.* Gaffe, *f.* **boat-house,** *n.* Garage (à bateaux), *m.* **boat-keeper,** *n.* Gardien de garage, *m.* **boat-load,** *n.* Batelée, *f.* **boatman,** *n.* Batelier, *m.*
boater ['boutə], *n.* (Hat) Canotier, *m.*
boating, *n.* Canotage, *m.*
boatswain [bousn], *n.* Maître d'équipage, *m.* *Boatswain's mate*, second maître, *m.*
boat-train, *n.* Train du bateau, *m.*
bob [bob], *n.* Perruque ronde; lentille (of a pendulum), *f.*; secousse, *f.*; coup, *m.*, tape, *f.* (blow); refrain (of a song), *m.*; petite révérence, *f.*; (*slang*) shilling, *m.*—*v.t.* Écourter (the tail); secouer, ballotter, balancer. *To bob a curtsy*, faire une petite révérence.—*v.i.* Pendiller, osciller, s'agiter. *To bob up*, revenir à la surface. **bob-sleigh,** *n.* Bobsleigh, *m.*
bobstay, *n.* (*Naut.*) Sous-barbe, *f.* **bobtail,** *n. Rag, tag, and bobtail*, racaille, canaille, *f.*
bobtailed, *a.* À queue écourtée. **bobwig,** *n.* Perruque ronde, *f.*
bobbin ['bobin], *n.* Bobine, *f.*; fuseau, *m.*
bobby ['bobi], *n.* (*colloq.*) Agent (de police), *m.*
bode [boud], *v.t.*, *v.i.* Présager. *To bode well* (ill), être de bon (mauvais) augure.
bodice ['bodis], *n.* Corsage, *m.*

bodied ['bɔdid], *a.* À corps. *Able-bodied seaman*, matelot, *m.*, de première classe; *full-bodied wine*, vin corsé, *m.* **bodiless,** *a.* Sans corps.

bodily ['bɔdili], *a.* Corporel, matériel.—*adv.* Corporellement; entièrement, en masse.

boding ['boudiŋ], *n.* Présage, pressentiment, *m.*

bodkin ['bɔdkin], *n.* Poinçon; passe-lacet, *m.*; (*Print.*) pointe, *f.*

body ['bɔdi], *n.* Corps; fond; cœur, centre; gros (main body of an army), *m.*; bande, troupe, *f.*; nef (of a church); personne, *f.*; sève (of wine), *f.*; carrosserie (of a vehicle), *f.*; corsage (of a dress), *m. Body and soul*, corps et âme; *examining body*, jury d'examen, *m.*; *dead body*, corps mort, cadavre, *m.*; *in a body*, en masse; *public body*, corporation, *f.*; *somebody*, quelqu'un; *to have body*, être corsé (of wine); *to keep body and soul together*, vivre tout juste.

body-guard, *n.* Garde du corps.

body-linen, *n.* Linge de corps, *m.*

body-snatcher, *n.* Déterreur de cadavres, *m.*

body-work, *n.* Carrosserie, *f.*

boffin ['bɔfin], *n.* (*fam.*) Savant, inventeur, *m.*

bog [bɔg], *n.* Marécage, *m.*, fondrière, *f.*; (*pl.*, *vulg.*) latrines, *f.pl.*—*v.t.* Embourber. *To get bogged*, s'embourber. **bog-trotter,** *n.* Habitant des marais, *m.*, (*colloq.*) Irlandais.

bogey ['bougi], *n.* (*Golf*) La normale du parcours; [BOGY].

boggle [bɔgl], *v.i.* Hésiter (à); reculer (devant). **boggler** ['bɔglə], *n.* Peureux, *m.*, peureuse, *f.*

boggy ['bɔgi], *a.* Marécageux.

bogie ['bougi], *n.* (*Rail.*) Bogie, *m.* **bogie-coach,** *n.* Wagon à bogie, *m.* **bogie-truck,** *n.* Plateforme à bogie, *f.*

bogus ['bougəs], *a.* Faux, simulé. *Bogus concern*, affaire véreuse, *f.*

bogy or **bogey** ['bougi], *n.* Croque-mitaine, épouvantail, *m.* **bog(e)y-man,** *n.* Le Père-Fouettard, *m.*

Bohemia [bo'hi:mjə]. La Bohême, *f.* **Bohemian.** Bohémien; bohème, *m.*—*a.* Bohémien, *m.*, bohémienne, *f.*

boil [bɔil], *v.i.* Bouillir; bouillonner. *To boil away*, se réduire à rien; (*fig.*) *to boil down to*, se réduire à; *to boil over*, déborder, s'en aller, se sauver; *to boil up*, monter; *to make the blood boil*, faire bouillonner le sang.—*v.t.* Faire bouillir; faire cuire à l'eau.—*n.* (*Med.*) Furoncle, clou, *m. To come to the boil*, (of water) commencer à bouillir; *to go off the boil*, cesser de bouillir.

boiled, *a.* Bouilli, cuit à l'eau. *A* (*lightly*) *boiled egg*, un œuf à la coque; *boiled beef*, (bœuf) bouilli, *m.*

boiler, *n.* Chaudière, *f.*; réservoir à eau chaude, *m.*; raffineur (de sucre), *m.* **boiler-house,** *n.* Salle des chaudières, *f.* **boiler-maker,** *n.* Chaudronnier, fabricant de chaudières, *m.* **boiler-plate,** *n.* Tôle pour chaudière, *f.* **boiler-suit,** *n.* Bleus, *m.pl.*

boiling, *n.* Bouillonnement, *m. The whole boiling* (lot), toute la boutique.—*a.* En ébullition. *Boiling hot*, tout bouillant. **boiling-point,** *n.* Point d'ébullition, *m.*

boisterous ['bɔistərəs], *a.* Orageux, violent; bruyant, turbulent. **boisterously,** *adv.*

Impétueusement, violemment, bruyamment. **boisterousness,** *n.* Impétuosité, turbulence; violence, *f.*

bold [bould], *a.* Hardi; audacieux, téméraire; impudent, effronté; saillant, net; à pic, escarpé. *As bold as brass*, avec un front d'airain; *to make* (so) *bold* (as) *to*, prendre la liberté de, se permettre de; *to put a bold face on it*, payer d'audace. **bold-faced,** *a.* Impudent, effronté. **boldly,** *adv.* Hardiment, intrépidement; impudemment; à pic. **boldness,** *n.* Hardiesse, audace; assurance, impudence, effronterie, *f.*

bole [boul], *n.* Tronc, fût (of a tree); (*Min.*) bol, *m.*

Bolivia [bə'livjə]. La Bolivie, *f.*

boll [boul], *n.* Capsule (du cotonnier), *f.*

bollard ['bɔləd], *n.* (*Naut.*) Pieu d'amarrage, corps-mort, *m.*; bitte de plat-bord, *f.*

Bologna [bə'lounjə]. Bologne, *f.*

Bolshevik ['bɔlʃivik], *a.* and *n.* Bolchevik. **Bolshevism,** *n.* Bolchevisme, *m.*

bolster ['boulstə], *n.* Traversin; coussin; (*Naut.*) coussin de ferrure, *m.*—*v.t.* Mettre un traversin sous; (*fig.*) appuyer, soutenir. *To bolster up*, rembourrer; (*fig.*) soutenir.

bolt [boult], *n.* Verrou; pêne; (thunder) éclair; (*Tech.*) boulon, *m.*, cheville, *f.*; (*fig.*) trait, *m.*, flèche; fuite, *f. A bolt from the blue*, un événement imprévu, un coup de foudre; *bolt upright*, tout droit, droit comme un I; *he has shot his bolt*, (*fig.*) il est à bout de ressources; *to draw a bolt*, tirer un verrou; *to make a bolt for it*, décamper, filer.—*v.t.* Verrouiller; fermer au verrou; bluter (to sift); gober, avaler (to swallow). *To bolt in*, enfermer au verrou.—*v.i.* Décamper, filer, prendre la clef des champs; s'emporter, s'emballer, prendre le mors aux dents (of a horse). **bolt-rope,** *n.* (*Naut.*) Ralingue, *f.* **bolter,** *n.* Bluteau, tamis, *m.* **bolting,** *n.* Verrouillement (of doors); blutage (sifting), *m.* **bolting-cloth,** *n.* Étamine, *f.*

bolus ['boulǝs], *n.* Bol, *m.*, (grosse) pilule, *f.*

bomb [bɔm], *n.* Bombe, *f. Atom bomb*, bombe atomique, *f.*—*v.t.* Bombarder. **bomb-crater,** *n.* Entonnoir, *m.* **bomb-proof,** *a.* À l'épreuve des bombes. **bombshell,** *n.* Bombe, *f.*, obus, *m. This news came as a bombshell to us*, cette nouvelle nous tomba des nues. **bomber,** *n.* Avion de bombardement, *m.*; bombardier, *m.* **bombing,** *n.* Bombardement, *m.*

bombard [bɔm'ba:d], *v.t.* Bombarder. **bombardier** [bɔmbə'diə], *n.* Bombardier, *m.* **bombardment** [bɔm'ba:dmənt], *n.* Bombardement, *m.*

bombasine [bʌm-, bɔmbə'zi:n], *n.* Bombasin, *m.*, alépine, *f.*

bombast ['bɔm-, 'bʌmbæst], *n.* Emphase, enflure, *f.*, boursouflage, *m.*

bombastic [bɔm'bæstik], *a.* Enflé, ampoulé, emphatique.

bona fide ['bounə'faidi], *a.* Sérieux, de bonne foi.—*adv.* Sérieusement, de bonne foi.

bon-bon ['bɔnbɔn], *n.* Bonbon, *f.*

bond [bɔnd], *n.* Lien, *m.*; liaison, *f.*; engagement, *m.*; obligation, *f.*; (*Fin.*) bon, *m.*; (*fig.*, *pl.*) la prison, les chaînes, (*f.pl. Defence bond*, bon de la défense nationale; *in bond*, à l'entrepôt; *in bond to*, en transit pour; *in bonds*, dans les fers; *matrimonial bond*, lien

conjugal; *Treasury bond*, bon du Trésor.—
v.t. Entreposer; liaisonner. *Bonded goods*,
marchandises entreposées, *f.pl.*
bondage, *n.* Esclavage, *m.*, servitude, *f.*
bonder, *n.* Entrepositaire, *m.* or *f.*
bond-holder, *n.* Obligataire, porteur d'obligation, *m.*
bondman or **bondsman**, *n.* (*pl.* **bondmen** or
bondsmen) Serf, esclave, *m.* **bondwoman**
or **bondswoman**, *n.* Esclave, *f.*
bone [boun], *n.* Os, *m.*; arête (of fish); baleine
(of whale); ivoire (of teeth), *f.*; (*pl.*) ossements, *m.pl.*; (*fam.*) dés, *m.pl.*; (*Mus.*)
cliquettes, *f.pl.* *Bone of contention*, pomme
de discorde, *f.*; *he makes no bones about that,*
il ne fait ni une ni deux; *not to make old
bones*, mourir jeune; *to have a bone to pick
with someone*, avoir maille à partir avec
quelqu'un; *to feel it in one's bones*, pressentir;
to make no bones about doing, ne pas hésiter
à faire; *what is bred in the bone will out in the
flesh*, la caque sent toujours le hareng.—*v.t.*
Désosser; (*slang*) chiper. **bone-black**, *n.*
Noir animal, *m.* **bone-setter**, *n.* Rebouteur,
m. **bone-shaker**, *n.* (*fam.*) (Of vehicle)
Vieux clou, *m.* **boneless**, *a.* Sans os.
bonehead, *n.* (*Am.*) Nigaud.
bonfire ['bɔnfaiə], *n.* Feu de joie *or* de jardin,
m.
bonnet ['bɔnit], *n.* Chapeau (woman's);
bonnet (Scotsman's), *m.*; (*Fort. etc.*) bonnette, *f.*; (*Motor.*) capot, *m.* **bonnet-maker**,
n. Modiste, *f.*
bonny ['bɔni], *a.* Gentil, joli, joyeux, gai.
bonus ['bounəs], *n.* Boni, *m.*; prime, *f.*
bony ['bouni], *a.* Osseux; plein d'arêtes (of
fish).
boo [bu:], *v.t.*, *v.i.* Huer.—*n.* Huée, *f.*—*int.*
Hou! **booing**, *n.* Huées, *f.pl.*
boob [bu:b], *n.* (*colloq.*) Gaffe, *f.*
booby ['bu:bi], *n.* Nigaud, benêt, *m.*; fou
(bird), *m.* **booby-trap**, *n.* Attrape-niais, *m.*;
(*Mil.*) mine-piège, *f.*
boodle [bu:dl], *n.* (*pop.*) Argent, fric, pèze,
m.; (*Am.*) caisse noire, *f.*
book [buk], *n.* Livre, livret; registre; (exercise-
book) cahier; (old book) bouquin, *m.* *Bank
book*, carnet de banque, *m.*; *book of tickets*,
carnet de tickets, *m.* *By book-post*, comme
imprimés, sous bande; *notebook*, carnet, *m.*;
that doesn't suit my book, cela ne me va pas;
to be in someone's good books, être bien dans
les papiers de quelqu'un; *to bring to book*,
demander compte à, faire le procès à; *to keep
books*, tenir des livres.—*v.t.* Prendre son
billet; retenir, réserver; porter au compte de,
enregistrer, inscrire. *To book a seat*, retenir
une place; *to book through to*, prendre un
billet direct pour.
bookbinder, *n.* Relieur, *m.* **bookbinding**, *n.*
Reliure, *f.*
book-case, *n.* Bibliothèque, *f.*, corps de
bibliothèque, *m.*
book-ends, *n.pl.* Serre-livres, *m.inv.*
bookie, *n.* [BOOKMAKER].
booking, *n.* Enregistrement (of parcels etc.),
m.; location (of tickets); réservation (of seats),
f. **booking-office**, *n.* Bureau d'enregistrement; guichet, *m.* *Parcel booking-office*,
bureau de messagerie, *m.*
bookish, *a.* Studieux, attaché aux livres;
livresque (style).

book-keeper, *n.* Teneur de livres, *m.* **book-
keeping**, *n.* Comptabilité, tenue des livres, *f.*
book-learned, *a.* Savant, lettré.
booklet, *n.* Livret, opuscule, *m.*
booklover, *n.* Bibliophile, *m.*
bookmaker, *n.* Faiseur de livres; (*Racing etc.*)
parieur de profession, bookmaker, *m.*
bookman, *n.* Savant, *m.*
bookmark or **book-marker**, *n.* Signet, *m.*
book-muslin, *n.* Organdi, *m.*
bookseller, *n.* Libraire, *m.* *Bookseller and
publisher*, libraire-éditeur, *m.*; *second-hand
bookseller*, marchand de livres d'occasion,
bouquiniste, *m.*
bookshelf, *n.* Rayon (de bibliothèque), *m.*
book-shop or **book-store**, *n.* Librairie, *f.*
book-slide or **book-rest**, *n.* Porte-livres, *m.*
book-stall, *n.* (*Rail.*) Bibliothèque, *f.*, étalage
de livres, *m.*
bookworm, *n.* Lépisme (mite), anobion, *m.*;
(*fig.*) dévoreur de livres, *m.*
boom (1) [bu:m], *n.* (*Naut.*) Bout-dehors, *m.*;
chaîne (in harbours etc.), *f.*; (*Cine.*) perche, *f.*
boom (2) [bu:m], *n.* Grondement, retentissement, *m.*; (*fig.*) grande (et rapide) hausse (in
business etc.), *f.*, boom, *m.*; vogue, *f.*—*v.i.*
Gronder, retentir; (*Naut.*) voguer rapidement; aller à toutes voiles; (*Comm.*) être en
hausse, prospérer.—*v.t.* Faire valoir; faire
une grosse publicité pour.
boomerang ['bu:məræŋ], *n.* Boumerang, *m.*
boon [bu:n], *n.* Bienfait, *m.*, faveur, *f.*; bien,
avantage, *m.* *It will be a great boon*, ce sera
un grand avantage.—*a.* Gai, joyeux. *Boon
companion*, gai compagnon, joyeux compère, *m.*
boor [buə], *n.* Rustre, *m.* **boorish**, *a.* Rustre,
grossier. **boorishly**, *adv.* Grossièrement.
boorishness, *n.* Rusticité, grossièreté, *f.*
boose etc. [BOOZE].
boost [bu:st], *v.t.* (*Am.*) Pousser par derrière;
lancer; (*Elec.*) survolter.—*n.* *To give someone
a boost*, faire de la réclame pour quelqu'un;
encourager quelqu'un. **booster**, *a.* and *n.*
(*Elec.*) Survolteur, *m.*
boot (1) [bu:t], *n.* Chaussure, bottine, botte
(high boot), *f.*; brodequin (for women etc.);
brodequin (for torture); coffre (in a car), *m.*
Elastic-sided boots, bottines à élastiques; *to
get the boot*, être saqué; *top-boots*, bottes à
revers; *to put on one's boots*, se chausser;
Wellington or *riding boots*, bottes à l'écuyère.
—*v.t.* (*fam.*) *To boot someone out*, flanquer
quelqu'un à la porte. **boot-black**, *n.* Cireur,
m. **boot-hook** or **boot-jack**, *n.* Tire-botte,
m. **boot-lace**, *n.* Lacet, *m.* **bootlegging**, *n.*
(*Am.*) Contrebande de l'alcool, *f.* **bootmaker**, *n.* Cordonnier, marchand de
souliers, *m.* **boot-polish**, *n.* Cirage, *m.*;
crème à chaussures, *f.* **boot-tree**, *n.* Embauchoir, *m.* **booted**, *a.* Botté. **bootee**, *n.*
Bottine d'enfant, *f.* **boots**, *n.* Décrotteur
(servant), *m.*
boot (2) [bu:t], *n.* (*Used only in*) *To boot*, en
sus, par-dessus le marché.—*v.t. impers.* Servir, profiter (à). *What boots it?* à quoi
sert?
***bootless**, *a.* Inutile, vain.
booth [bu:ð], *n.* Baraque, tente, *f.*; cabine, *f.*
booty ['bu:ti], *n.* Butin, *m.*
booze ['bu:z], *n.* Boisson alcoolique, *f.* *On the
booze*, en ribote.—*v.i.* Boire à l'excès.

boozer, *n.* Pochard, poivrot, *m.* **boozy,** *a.* Gris, en ribote, soûlard.

bo-peep [bou'piːp], *n.* Cache-cache, *m.*

boracic [bə'ræsik], *a.* Borique. *Boracic powder,* poudre boriquée, *f.*

borage ['bɔridʒ], *n.* Bourrache, *f.*

borax ['bɔːræks], *n.* Borax, *m.*

border ['bɔːdə], *n.* Bord, *m.*; bordé, *m.*, bordure (edging); frontière (of a country), *f.*; (*Gard.*) parterre, *m.*, platebande, *f. Border town,* ville frontière, *f.—v.t.* Border.—*v.i.* Aboutir, toucher (à); avoisiner. *That borders upon licence,* (*colloq.*) cela frise la licence; *to border on sixty,* approcher de la soixantaine. **borderer,** *n.* Habitant de la frontière, *m.* **bordering,** *a.* Contigu, voisin. **borderland,** *n.* Pays frontière, *m.*, confins, *m.pl.*, marche, *f.*

border-line, *n.* Ligne de démarcation, *f.—a.* Indéterminé. *Border-line case,* cas limite, *m.*

bore (1) [bɔː], *v.t.* Percer, forer, aléser; sonder, creuser; (*fig.*) ennuyer, importuner, assommer, embêter. *To be bored stiff,* s'ennuyer à mourir.—*v.i.* Percer.—*n.* Trou; calibre, *m.*, âme (of a gun), sonde (of a mine etc.), *f.*; (*fig.*) (person) fâcheux, raseur; (thing) ennui, *m.*, scie, *f.*; mascaret (in a tidal river), *m.* **boredom,** *n.* Ennui, *m.*

bore-hole, *n.* Trou de sonde, *m.*

borer ['bɔːrə], *n.* Alésoir, perceur, *m.*; tarière, *f.*, fleuret, perçoir (instrument), *m.* **boring,** *n.* Sondage, forage, alésage, *m.—a.* Ennuyeux, assommant.

bore (2), *past* [BEAR (2)].

boreal ['bɔːriəl], *a.* Boréal. **boreas,** *n.* Borée, *m.*

born [bɔːn], *a.* Né. *He was born in* . . ., il était né *or* il naquit en . . . (if dead); *I was born in,* je suis né en; *low born,* de basse naissance; *Scotsman born and bred,* un vrai Écossais d'Écosse; *she is a born musician,* elle est musicienne née; *to be born,* naître.

borne, *p.p.* [BEAR (2)]. *Borne down,* écrasé.

boron ['bɔːrɔn], *n.* (*Chem.*) Bore, *m.*

borough ['bʌrə], *n.* Bourg, *m.*, ville, *f. Rotten borough,* bourg pourri.

borrow ['bɔrou], *v.t.* Emprunter (à). *I borrowed money from him,* je lui ai emprunté de l'argent. **borrower,** *n.* Emprunteur, *m.*, emprunteuse, *f.* **borrowing,** *n.* Emprunt, *m.*

boscage ['bɔskidʒ], *n.* Bocage, *m.*

bosh [bɔʃ], *n.* Blague, farce, *f.*, bêtises, *f.pl.*, galimatias, *m.*

bosky ['bɔski], *a.* Boisé.

bosom ['buzəm], *n.* Sein; (*fig.*) cœur, *m. Bosom friend,* ami de cœur, *m.*; *in the bosom of,* au sein de.

Bosphorus ['bɔsfərəs], *n.* Le Bosphore, *m.*

boss (1) [bɔs], *n.* Bosse, *f.*; moyeu (of a wheel), *m.*

boss (2) [bɔs], *n.* Patron, chef, contremaître, *m.* —*v.t.* Diriger, contrôler; régenter. **bossiness,** *n.* Autoritarisme, *m.* **bossy,** *a.* (*fam.*) Autoritaire.

boss-eyed, *a.* (*pop.*) Louche.

bosun [BOATSWAIN].

botanic [bo'tænik], *a.* **botanical,** *a.* Botanique.

botanist ['bɔtənist], *n.* Botaniste.

botanize, *v.i.* Botaniser, herboriser.

botany, *n.* Botanique, *f.*

botch [bɔtʃ], *n.* Pustule, *f.*; (*fig.*) ravaudage, replâtrage, *m.*, mauvaise besogne, *f.—v.t.*

Ravauder, replâtrer, saveter. **botcher,** *n.* Ravaudeur, *m.*, ravaudeuse, *f.*, bousilleur, *m.*

both [bouθ], *a.* and *pron.* Tous les deux, tous deux, l'un et l'autre. *Both of us,* nous deux; *both the men,* les deux hommes; *on both sides,* des deux côtés.—*conj.* Tant, à la fois. *Both for you and him,* tant pour vous que pour lui; *both men and women,* les hommes aussi bien que les femmes; *both you and I,* (et) vous et moi.

bother ['bɔðə], *v.t.* Ennuyer, tracasser; (*colloq.*) embêter. *Don't bother me,* laissez-moi tranquille; *I can't be bothered,* ça m'embête.—*n.* Ennui, tracas, embêtement, *m.* **botheration,** *int.* Quel ennui! **bothered,** *a.* Inquiet, ennuyé. **bothersome,** *a.* Importun.

bottle [bɔtl], *n.* Bouteille, *f.*; flacon, *m.*; biberon (of baby), *m.*; (hot water) bouillotte, *f.*; (stone) cruchon, *m.*; botte (of hay), *f.—v.t.* Mettre en bouteille. *To bottle up one's feelings,* étouffer ses sentiments. **bottle-fed,** *a.* Élevé au biberon. **bottle-holder,** *n.* (*Box.*) Second, *m.* **bottle-neck,** *n.* Goulot; embouteillage (of traffic), *m.* **bottle-nosed,** *a.* À gros nez. **bottled,** *a.* En bouteilles; (*pop.*) ivre. *Bottled cider,* cidre bouché. **bottler,** *n.* Metteur en bouteilles, *m.* **bottling,** *n.* Mise en bouteilles, *f.*

bottom ['bɔtəm], *n.* Fond; bas; dessous, pied, *m.*; derrière, *m.*; base; (*Naut.*) carène, *f.*; navire, bâtiment, *m. At bottom,* au fond; *bottom dollar,* dernier sou; (*fam.*) *bottoms up!* cul sec *! from top to bottom,* de haut en bas; *to be at the bottom of,* être l'âme de (quelque intrigue etc.); *to get to the bottom of,* aller au fond de; *to probe to the bottom,* examiner à fond; *to put bottom on a ball,* (*spt.*) faire un rétro; *to sink to the bottom,* couler à fond; *to touch bottom* (of ship), talonner.—*v.t.* Asseoir, baser, fonder; mettre un fond. **-bottomed,** *a.* À fond. *Flat-bottomed,* à fond plat. **bottomless,** *a.* Sans fond. *Bottomless pit,* l'enfer, *m.*

bottomry, *n.* **bottomry-loan,** *n.* Prêt à la grosse aventure, *m.*

boudoir ['buːdwɑː], *n.* Boudoir, *m.*

bough [bau], *n.* Branche, *f.*, rameau, *m.*

bought [bɔːt], *past* and *p.p.* [BUY]. **bought-book,** *n.* Livre d'achat, *m.*

bougie ['buːʒi], *n.* (*Surg.*) Bougie, *f.*

boulder ['bouldə], *n.* Grosse pierre, roche arrondie, *f.*, bloc, *m. Boulder wall,* moraine, *f.*

boulevard ['bulvɑː], *n.* Boulevard, *m.*

bounce [bauns], *v.i.* Sauter; (re)bondir; se vanter, poser. *The cheque bounced,* c'était un chèque sans provision.—*n.* Saut, (re)bond, *m.*; vanterie, *f.*

bouncer, *n.* Fanfaron, hâbleur, vantard, *m.*

bouncing, *a.* (*colloq.*) Gros, éclatant.

bound (1) [baund], *v.i.* Bondir, sauter.—*n.* Bond, saut, *m. At a bound,* d'un saut, d'un bond.

bound (2) [baund], *n.* Borne; limite, *f. Out of bounds,* (*spt.*) hors jeu, *m.—v.t.* Borner, limiter; (*fig.*) contenir.

bound (3) [baund], *a.* Tenu (de *or* à); redevable (de). *I feel bound to say,* je dois vous dire.

bound (4) [baund], *a.* (*Naut.*) Allant (à), en partance (pour). *Homeward bound,* revenant

à son port d'attache; *where are you bound?*
où allez-vous?
bound (5), *past* and *p.p.* [BIND].
boundary ['baundəri], *n.* Limite, borne, frontière, *f.*
bounden ['baundən], *a.* Obligatoire, impérieux. *It is your bounden duty*, c'est votre
devoir sacré.
bounder ['baundə], *n.* (*fam.*) Épateur, *m.*
boundless ['baundlis], *a.* Sans bornes;
illimité. **boundlessness**, *n.* Étendue immense, infinité, *f.*
bounteous ['bauntiəs], *a.* Libéral, généreux,
bienfaisant; abondant. **bounteously**, *adv.*
Libéralement, généreusement. **bounteous-
ness** or **bountifulness**, *n.* Libéralité, munificence, générosité, bonté, *f.* **bountiful**, *a.*
Généreux, libéral; abondant. **bountifully**,
adv. Généreusement, abondamment.
bounty, *n.* Bonté, générosité, libéralité; gratification, *f.*, don, *m.*; (*Comm.*) prime, subvention, *f.*
bouquet ['bukei], *n.* Bouquet, *m.*
bourne or **bourn** (1) [bɔːn], *n.* Borne, *f.*,
frontière, limite, *f.*; terme, but, *m.*
*****bourn** (2) [bɔːn], *n.* Ruisseau, *m.*
bout [baut], *n.* Tour, *m.*, partie, *f.*; accès, *m.*,
crise, *f.*; (*Box.*) assaut, *m.*; (*Fenc.*) passe, *f.*
At one bout, d'un seul coup; *second bout*,
reprise, *f.*
bovine ['bouvain], *a.* Bovin.
bow (1) [bau], *v.t.* Courber, plier, fléchir,
incliner. *To bow down*, courber, baisser,
accabler; *to bow out*, éconduire.—*v.i.* Se
courber, s'incliner; saluer; se plier, se soumettre (à); s'affaisser, être brisé (de douleur).
I bow to your decision, je me rends à votre
décision; *to bow down*, se prosterner, s'humilier; *to bow to someone*, s'incliner devant
quelqu'un; *to make one's bow* (before leaving),
tirer sa révérence.—*n.* Salut, *m.*, révérence,
f.
bow (2) [bau], *n.* (*Naut.*) Avant, bossoir, *m.*;
(*Row.*) rameur à l'avant, le huit. **bow-side**,
n. Tribord, *m.*
bow (3) [bou], *n.* Arc; archet (of a violin);
arçon (of a saddle); nœud (of ribbons), *m.*
To have more than one string to one's bow,
avoir plusieurs cordes à son arc. **bow-
legged**, *a.* À jambes arquées, bancal. **bow-
shot**, *n.* Portée de trait, *f.* **bowstring**,
n. Corde d'arc, *f.* **bow-tie**, *n.* Nœud carré,
m. **bow-window**, *n.* Fenêtre en saillie, *f.*
bowdlerize ['baudləraiz], *v.t.* Expurger,
émasculer (un livre).
bowels ['bauəlz], *n.pl.* Entrailles, *f.pl.*, intestins, boyaux, *m.pl.*; (*fig.*) sein, *m.*; compassion, pitié, *f.*
bower (1) ['bauə], *n.* Berceau de verdure, *m.*,
tonnelle, *f.*; *****boudoir, *m.*
bower (2) ['bauə], *a.* (*Naut.*) *Bower anchor*,
ancre de bossoir, *f.*
bowery, *a.* Touffu, ombragé.
bowie-knife ['bui'naif], *n.* Couteau-poignard,
m.
bowl [boul], *n.* Bol, vase, *m.*, coupe, *f.*; jatte,
f.; fourneau (of a pipe), *m.*; boule (spherical
body), *f.*; boules, *f.pl.* *To play* (at) *bowls*,
jouer aux boules.—*v.t.* Rouler, faire rouler.
—*v.i.* (*Cricket*) Servir la balle. *To bowl along*,
rouler rapidement; *to bowl out*, renverser (le
guichet de); *to bowl over*, renverser (les

quilles); (*fig.*) déconcerter, renverser. **bowler**, *n.* Joueur de boule; (*Cricket*) lanceur,
m. **bowler(-hat)**, *n.* Chapeau melon, *m.*
bowling-alley, *n.* Jeu de boules, *m.*; (*Am.*)
quillier, *m.* **bowling-green**, *n.* Jeu de boules,
boulingrin, *m.*
bowline ['boulin, 'boulain], *n.* (*Naut.*)
Bouline, *f.*
bowman ['boumən], *n.* Archer, *m.*
bowsprit ['bousprit], *n.* (*Naut.*) Beaupré, *m.*
bow-wow ['bau'wau], *n.* (*fam.*) Toutou, *m.*—
int. Ouâ-ouâ!
box (1) [bɔks], *n.* Boîte, *f.*; (small) coffret, *m.*;
(large) coffre, *m.*, caisse, *f.*; compartiment,
cabinet particulier (at a restaurant etc.), *m.*;
malle; (*Theat.*) loge, *f.*; siège (on a carriage);
moyeu (of a wheel), *m.*; stalle (in a stable), *f.*;
maisonnette, *f.*, pied-à-terre (country-house);
(*Print.*) cassetin; buis (tree), *m.* *Cardboard
box*, carton, *m.*; *Christmas-box*, étrennes, *f.pl.*;
hat-box, étui *or* carton à chapeau, *m.*; *hunting-
box*, pavillon de chasse, *m.*; *money-box*, tire-
lire, *f.*; *sentry-box*, guérite, *f.*; *signal-box*,
cabine d'aiguillage, *f.*; *snuff-box*, tabatière, *f.*;
strong-box, coffre fort, *m.*; *to be in the wrong
box*, se tromper, se fourvoyer; *witness box*,
barre des témoins, *f.*—*v.t.* Enfermer dans une
boîte, emboîter, encaisser. *To box the compass*, savoir la rose des vents; revenir à son
point de départ. **boxed-in**, *a.* Encaissé.
box-keeper, *n.* (*Theat.*) Ouvreuse de loges,
f. **box-office**, *n.* Bureau de location, *m.*
box-pleat, *n.* Pli creux, *m.* **box-seat**, *n.*
Siège de cocher, *m.* **box-spanner**, *n.* Clef
à douille, *f.*
box (2) [bɔks], *v.i.* Boxer.—*v.t.* Souffleter,
gifler.—*n.* Soufflet, *m.* *Box on the ear*,
soufflet, *m.*, gifle, *f.* **boxer**, *n.* Boxeur,
pugiliste, *m.* **boxing**, *n.* La boxe, *f.* *Boxing-
gloves*, gants de boxe, *m.pl.*; *boxing-match*,
match de boxe, *m.*
boy [bɔi], *n.* Garçon, petit garçon, garçonnet;
(son) fils; (*fam.* and *dial.*) gars, *m.* *Bad boy*,
mauvais sujet, *m.*; *boys will be boys*, il faut
que jeunesse se passe; *cabin-boy*, mousse, *m.*;
French boy, jeune Français; *mere boy*, gamin,
m.; *old boy!* mon vieux, *m.*; (of a school)
ancien élève, *m.*; (*fam.*) *one of the boys*, un
joyeux vivant; *schoolboy*, écolier, élève,
collégien, lycéen, *m.*
boycott ['bɔikɔt], *v.t.* Boycotter. **boycotting**,
n. Boycottage, *m.*
boyhood, *n.* Enfance, adolescence, *f.*
boyish or **boylike**, *a.* Puéril; d'enfant, enfantin.
boy scout, *n.* (Jeune) éclaireur, scout, *m.*
bra [brɑː], *n.* (*pop.*) [BRASSIÈRE].
brace [breis], *n.* Couple (of game); paire (of
pistols); laisse (of greyhounds), *f.*; (*Arch.*)
tirant; brassard (of arms), *m.*; (*Carp.*) ancre,
moise, *f.*; vilebrequin (tool), *m.*; (*Print.*)
accolade, *f.*; (*Mach.*) attache, *f.*, entretoise, *f.*;
(*Naut.*) bras (of a yard), *m.*; soupente (of a
coach), *f.*; (*pl.*) bretelles, *f.pl.*—*v.t.* Lier,
serrer, attacher; bander; ancrer, armer,
entretoiser; (*fig.*) fortifier, tonifier; (*Naut.*)
brasser. *To brace someone up*, retremper,
remonter quelqu'un. **bracelet**, *n.* Bracelet,
m. **bracing**, *a.* Fortifiant, tonifiant.—*n.*
Ancrage, armement, entretoisement, *m.*
brach [brætʃ], *n.* Braque, *m.*
brachial ['breikiəl], *a.* (*Anat.*) Brachial.

brachycephalic [brækise'fælik], *a.* Brachycéphale.

bracken ['brækən], *n.* Fougère, *f.* (arborescente).

bracket ['brækit], *n.* Console, applique, *f.*, tasseau, *m.*; (brace) accolade, *f.*; bras (for a lamp etc.); (*Print.*) crochet, *m.*, parenthèse, *f.* *Between brackets*, entre crochets, entre parenthèses.—*v.t.* (*Print.*) Encadrer, réunir (des mots) par une accolade; classer *ex aequo.*

brackish ['brækiʃ], *a.* Saumâtre.

brad [bræd], *n.* Pointe, *f.* **bradawl**, *n.* Poinçon, *m.*, alêne plate, *f.*

bradshaw ['brædʃɔ:], *n.* Indicateur des chemins de fer, *m.*

brae [brei], *n.* (*Sc.*) Colline, côte, *f.*

brag [bræg], *v.i.* Se vanter, fanfaronner.—*n.* Fanfaronnade, vanterie, *f.*

braggadocio [brægə'douʃiou], *n.* Bravache, *m.*

braggart ['brægət], *n.* Fanfaron, *m.*

braggingly, *adv.* En fanfaron.

Brahmin ['brɑ:min], *n.* Brahmane, brame, *m.*

Brahminism ['brɑ:minizm], *n.* Brahmanisme, *m.*

braid [breid], *n.* Tresse; soutache, ganse, *f.*; lacet; galon, *m.*—*v.t.* Tresser, natter, soutacher.

braille [breil], *n.* Braille, *m.*

brails [breilz], *n.pl.* (*Naut.*) Cargue, *f. To brail up*, carguer.

brain [brein], *n.* Cerveau (organ), *m.*; cervelle (substance), *f.*; (*fig.*) jugement, esprit, *m.*; tête, *f. To blow one's brains out*, se faire sauter la cervelle; *to have something on the brain*, avoir l'obsession de quelque chose, être hanté par la pensée de quelque chose; *to pick someone's brains*, exploiter l'intelligence de quelqu'un; *to puzzle* or *rack one's brains*, se creuser la tête; *water on the brain*, hydrocéphale, *f.*—*v.t.* Faire sauter la cervelle à, casser la tête à. **brain-fag**, *n.* Épuisement cérébral, *m.* **brain-fever**, *n.* Fièvre cérébrale, *f.* **brain-sick**, *a.* Malade du cerveau. **brain-wave**, *n.* (*fam.*) Trouvaille, *f.* **brainwork**, *n.* Travail intellectuel, *m.* **brainless**, *a.* Sans cervelle; stupide. **brainy**, *a.* Intelligent.

braise [breiz], *v.t.* Braiser. *Braised chicken*, poulet à la casserole, *m.*

brake (1) [breik], *n.* Fourré, hallier, *m.*, fougère (thicket), *f.*

brake (2) [breik], *n.* Frein; brisoir (tool), *m.*; brimbale, *f.* (of a pump); (*Agric.*) herse, *f. Air-brake*, frein à air, *m.*; *emergency brake*, frein de secours, *m.*; *hand-brake*, frein à main; *rim-brake*, frein sur jante. *To put on the brake*, serrer le frein.—*v.t.*, *v.i.* Freiner. **brake-block**, *n.* Patin or sabot de frein, *m.* **brakes-man**, *n.* Serre-frein, *m.* **braking**, *n.* Freinage, *m.*

bramble [bræmbl], *n.* Ronce, *f.*

bran [bræn], *n.* Son, *m.*

branch [brɑ:ntʃ], *n.* Branche, *f.*, rameau, *m.*; succursale (of public establishments), *f.*; (*Rail.*) embranchement, *m.*—*v.i.* Pousser des branches. *To branch off*, s'embrancher, bifurquer; *to branch out*, se ramifier. **branchless**, *a.* Sans branches. **branchy**, *a.* Branchu, à branches.

branchia ['bræŋkiə], **branchiae** ['bræŋkii:], *n.pl.* Branchies, ouïes, *f.pl.*

brand [brænd], *n.* Brandon, tison; fer chaud,

stigmate, *m.*; flétrissure (of infamy); (*Comm.*) marque, *f.*—*v.t.* Marquer au fer chaud; flétrir; (*fig.*) stigmatiser (de). **brand-new**, *a.* Tout flambant neuf. **branding-iron**, *n.* Fer à marquer, *m.*

brandish ['brændiʃ], *v.t.* Brandir.

brandy ['brændi], *n.* Eau-de-vie, *f.*, cognac, *m.* *Liqueur brandy*, fine champagne, *f. Brandy and soda*, fine à l'eau, *f.* **brandied**, *a.* Mêlé d'eau-de-vie.

brandy-snap, *n.* Biscotte au gingembre, *f.*

brash [bræʃ], *a.* Effronté, présomptueux.

brass [brɑ:s], *n.* Cuivre jaune, laiton; (*fig.*) toupet, *m.*, effronterie, *f.*; (*slang*) de la braise, du fric (cash). *As bold as brass*, avec un front d'airain; *brass band*, fanfare, *f.*; *to get down to brass tacks*, en venir aux faits. **brassfoundry**, *n.* Fonderie de cuivre jaune, *f.* **brass-hat**, *n.* (*fam.*) Officier d'état-major, *m.* **brass-wire**, *n.* Fil de laiton, *m.* **brassy**, *a.* D'airain; (*fig.*) effronté.

brassière ['bræsjɛ:ə], *n.* Soutien-gorge, *m.*

brat [bræt], *n.* Marmot, *m.*, bambin, *m.*

bravado [brə'vɑ:dou], *n.* Bravade, *f.*

brave [breiv], *a.* Courageux, brave, vaillant; (*fig.*) fameux, excellent.—*n.* Brave, *m.*—*v.t.* Braver, défier. **bravely**, *adv.* Courageusement, bravement.

bravery ['breivəri], *n.* Bravoure, *f.*, courage, *m.*

bravo ['brɑ:vou], *n.* Bravo, *m.*—*int.* [brɑ:'vou] Bravo!

bravura [brə'vuərə], *n.* Bravoure, *f.*

brawl [brɔ:l], *n.* Dispute, rixe, querelle, *f.*; bruit, tapage, *m.*—*v.i.* Brailler, clabauder, disputer; (*fig.*) murmurer. **brawler**, *n.* Tapageur; braillard, querelleur, *m.* **brawling**, *a.* Tapageur.—*n.* Braillement, *m.*

brawn [brɔ:n], *n.* Pâté de cochon, fromage d'Italie, *m.*; (*fig.*) partie charnue, *f.*, muscles, *m.pl.* **brawniness**, *n.* Force musculaire, *f.* **brawny**, *a.* Charnu, musculeux.

bray (1) [brei], *v.t.* Broyer, piler.

bray (2) [brei], *v.i.* Braire (of asses etc.); (*fig.*) résonner, retentir.—*n.* Braiment, *m.*

braze [breiz], *v.t.* Souder; braser. **brazen**, *a.* D'airain; (*fig.*) effronté, impudent.—*v.t. To brazen it out*, payer d'effronterie. **brazenfaced**, *a.* À front d'airain; effronté.

brazier (1) ['breiziə], *n.* Chaudronnier, *m.* **brazing**, *n.* Brasage, *f.* **brazingly**, *adv.* Effrontément.

brazier (2) ['breiziə], *n.* Brasero (coal-pan), *m.*

Brazil [brə'zil], *n.* Le Brésil, *m.* **brazil-nut**, *n.* Noix du Brésil, *f.* **Brazilian**, *a.* and *n.* Brésilien, *m.*, Brésilienne, *f.*

breach [bri:tʃ], *n.* Brèche, rupture; (*fig.*) violation, infraction, *f. Breach of promise*, manque de parole, *m.*, rupture de promesse de mariage, *f.*; *breach of the peace*, attentat contre l'ordre public, *m.*; *breach of trust*, abus de confiance, *m.*—*v.t.* Battre en brèche.

bread [bred], *n.* Pain, *m. A loaf of bread*, un pain, une miche; *bread and butter letter*, lettre de remerciement, *f.*; *brown bread*, pain bis; *daily bread*, pain quotidien; *new bread*, pain tendre or frais; *on bread and water*, au pain et à l'eau; *slice of bread and butter*, tartine de beurre, *f.*; *stale bread*, pain rassis; *to be in want of bread*, manquer de pain; *to get one's bread*, gagner son pain. **breadcrumb**, *n.* Miette, *f.*; *pl.* (*Cook.*) chapelure, *f.*, gratin, *m.*

bread-fruit, *n.* Fruit à pain, *m.* **bread-fruit-tree,** *n.* Jaquier, arbre à pain, *m.* **bread-stuffs,** *n.pl.* Farines, *f.pl.* **bread-winner,** *n.* Soutien de famille, *m.*, gagne-pain, *m. inv.*

breadth [bredθ], *n.* Largeur, *f.*

break [breik], *v.t.* (*past* broke, *p.p.* broken) Rompre; briser; casser; violer, enfreindre; faire faire faillite à, ruiner; battre (flax etc.); déferler (flag); défricher (new ground); (*fig.*) faire part de, communiquer (news); amortir (a shock). *To break in,* enfoncer, défoncer; *to break in a horse,* rompre, dresser un cheval; *to break into,* envahir, se jeter dans; *to break into a trot,* prendre le trot; *to break in upon,* envahir, (*fig.*) interrompre; *to break of a bad habit,* corriger d'une mauvaise habitude; *to break off,* rompre, interrompre, arrêter; détacher; *to break one's arm* or *one's neck,* se casser un bras *or* le cou; *to break one's fall,* amortir sa chute; *to break one's journey,* s'arrêter en route, faire étape (land), faire escale (sea); *to break one's word,* manquer de parole; *to break open a door,* enfoncer une porte; *to break someone's heart,* briser le cœur à quelqu'un; *to break step,* rompre le pas; *to break the bank,* (at play) faire sauter la banque; *to break the silence,* rompre le silence; *to break through,* se frayer un passage à travers; *to break through the sound barrier,* franchir le mur du son; *to break up,* mettre en pièces, démolir, démembrer; (*fig.*) dissoudre, lever (a camp etc.); *to break upon the wheel,* rouer.

v.i. Rompre, se rompre, casser, se casser, se briser; éclater (of a storm etc.); (*Comm.*) faire faillite; sauter (of a bank); poindre (of daybreak); crever (of an abscess); déferler (of a wave); décliner, s'affaiblir, se casser (of one's constitution); changer (of the weather); faire faux bond (of ball). *To break away,* se détacher; (*Mil.*) rompre les rangs; (*Box.*) cesser le corps-à-corps. *Break!* séparez! *to break down,* s'abattre, se délabrer, s'effondrer, s'écrouler, avoir une panne (of vehicles), défaillir, s'altérer (of health), fondre en larmes; *to break in,* envahir, pénétrer, entrer dans; *to break into,* entamer; éclater en; *to break loose,* s'échapper, s'évader, (*fig.*) s'émanciper; *to break off,* rompre, s'arrêter; *to break out,* éclater, se déclarer (of diseases), jaillir, paraître, s'échapper, (*fig.*) s'abandonner (à); *to break up,* se disperser, entrer en vacances (of schools etc.), changer, se gâter (of weather); *to break with,* rompre avec.

n. Rupture, brisure, fracture; trouée, fente; (*fig.*) lacune, interruption, *f.*; changement (of the weather); arrêt (of a journey), *m.*; (*sch.*) récréation, *f.*; (*Print.*) alinéa, *m.*; brouille (between friends); (*Billiards*) série, *f. Break of continuity,* solution de continuité, *f.*; *break of day,* point du jour, *m.*, aube, *f.*, (*poet.*) aurore, *f.*; *without a break,* sans interruption, non interrompu.

breakable, *a.* Fragile.—*n.pl.* Objets fragiles, *m.pl.*

breakage, *n.* Rupture, cassure, *f.*; (*Comm.*) casse, *f.*

breakdown, *n.* (*Rail.*) Accident, *m.*; (*Motor.*) panne, *f.*; (*fig.*) débâcle, *f.*, insuccès, *m. Nervous breakdown,* épuisement nerveux, *m.*, crise de dépression nerveuse, *f.*

breaker, *n.* Infracteur, briseur; violateur,

transgresseur; dompteur (tamer); dresseur (trainer); concasseur (machine); (*Naut.*) baril de galère (keg); brisant (of the sea), *m.*

breakfast ['brekfəst], *n.* (Petit) déjeuner, *m. Breakfast-time,* heure du déjeuner, *f.*; *continental breakfast,* petit déjeuner léger, *m.*; *English breakfast,* petit déjeuner substantiel, *m.*—*v.i.* Déjeuner.

breaking, *n.* Rupture; mue (of the voice); (*fig.*) violation; (*Comm.*) banqueroute, faillite, *f.*; (abscess) aboutissement, *m.* **breaking-point,** *n.* Point de rupture, *m.* **breaking-up,** *n.*, or **break-up,** *n.* Dissolution, *f.*; (*sch.*) départ en vacances, *m.*

break-neck, *a.* Casse-cou, *m. Break-neck speed,* vitesse vertigineuse, *f.*

breakwater, *n.* Brise-lames, *m.*, digue, jetée, *f.*

bream (1) [bri:m], *n.* (*Ichth.*) Brème, *f. Black bream,* vieille de mer, *f.*; *sea-bream,* dorade bilunée, *f.*, pagel, rousseau, *m.*

bream (2) [bri:m], *v.t.* (*Naut.*) Chauffer (a ship).

breast [brest], *n.* Sein, *m.*, poitrine, *f.*; (*fig.*) cœur, *m.*, âme, conscience, *f.*; poitrail (of a horse); blanc (of a fowl), *m.*; revers (of a coat), *m.pl. At the breast,* à la mamelle (of a child); *to make a clean breast of it,* tout avouer, confesser.—*v.t.* Lutter contre, affronter.

breast-bone, *n.* Sternum, *m.*

breast-deep, *a.* and *adv.* Jusqu'à la poitrine.

breast-high, *a.* and *adv.* À hauteur d'appui.

breast-pin, *n.* Épingle de cravate, *f.*

breastplate, *n.* Cuirasse, *f.*, plastron; pectoral, *m.*

breast-stroke, *n.* Brasse (sur le ventre), *f.*

breastsummer or **bressummer,** *n.* (*Build.*) Sommier, poitrail, *m.*

breastwork, *n.* Parapet; (*Naut.*) fronteau, *m.*

breath [breθ], *n.* Haleine, respiration, *f.*, souffle, *m.*; (*fig.*) vie, existence, *f. All in one breath,* tout d'une haleine; *last breath,* dernier soupir, *m.*; *shortness of breath,* haleine courte, *f.*; *there is not a breath of wind,* il n'y a pas un souffle de vent; *to be out of breath,* être hors d'haleine or tout essoufflé; *to catch one's breath,* avoir un sursaut; *to get out of breath,* se mettre hors d'haleine, perdre haleine; *to hold one's breath,* retenir son haleine; *to take* or *draw breath,* reprendre haleine, respirer; *to take one's breath away,* couper la respiration à, (*fig.*) interdire, déconcerter; *you are wasting your breath,* taisez-vous, vous perdez votre temps.

breathable ['bri:ðəbl], *a.* Respirable.

breathe [bri:ð], *v.i.* Respirer; souffler, reprendre haleine.—*v.t.* Respirer, souffler. *To breathe in,* aspirer; *to breathe one's last,* rendre le dernier soupir; *to breathe out,* exhaler, pousser. **breather,** *n.* (*fam.*) *To have a breather,* souffler un peu; prendre un peu l'air. **breathing,** *a.* Pour respirer; (*fig.*) qui respire, vivant.—*n.* Respiration; (*Gram.*) aspiration, *f.* **breathing-space,** *n.* Temps de respirer, relâche, répit, *m.*

breathless ['breθləs], *a.* Hors d'haleine, essoufflé, haletant. **breathlessly,** *adv.* En haletant. **breathlessness,** *n.* Manque de souffle, *m.* **breath-taking,** *a.* (*fam.*) À vous couper le souffle.

bred, *p.p.* [BREED].

breech [briːtʃ], *n.* *Derrière, *m.*; culasse (of fire-arms), *f.—v.t.* Culotter, mettre une culasse à. **breech-block,** *n.* (*Artill.*) Culasse mobile, *f.* **breech-loader,** *n.* Fusil se chargeant par la culasse, *m.* **breeches,** *n.pl.* Culotte, *f.* *To wear the breeches,* (*fig.*) porter la culotte. **breeches-buoy,** *n.* Bouée culotte, *f.* **breeching,** *n.* Avaloire, *f.*; (*Naut.*) brague, *m.*

breed [briːd], *v.t.* (*past* and *p.p.* **bred**) Élever; faire naître. *Ill-bred,* mal élevé; *thoroughbred,* pur-sang; *well-bred,* bien élevé.—*v.i.* Multiplier, se reproduire.—*n.* Race, *f.* **breeder,** *n.* Éleveur, *m.* **breeding,** *n.* Élevage (of cattle etc.), *m.*; reproduction; éducation, *f.* *Good breeding,* politesse, *f.*, savoir-vivre, *m.*

breeze (1) [briːz], *n.* Braise de houille, *f.*

breeze (2) [briːz], *n.* (Forte) brise, *f.*, vent assez fort, *m.* **breeziness,** *n.* Jovialité, *f.* **breezy,** *a.* Frais; jovial. **breeze-block,** *n.* (*Build.*) Parpaing, *m.*

Bren-gun ['brenˈgʌn], *n.* Fusil mitrailleur, *m.*

bressummer [BREASTSUMMER].

brethren ['breðrən], *n.pl.* Frères, *m.pl.*

Breton ['bretən], *a.* and *n.* Breton, -onne.

breve [briːv], *n.* (*Mus.*) Brève, *f.*

brevet ['brevit], *n.* Brevet, *m.—a.* À brevet. *Brevet rank,* grade honoraire, *m.—v.t.* Breveter.

breviary ['briːviəri], *n.* Bréviaire, *m.*

brevier [brəˈviə], *n.* (*Print.*) Corps sept et demi, *f.*

brevity ['breviti], *n.* Brièveté, concision, *f.*

brew [bruː], *v.t.* Brasser; (*fig.*) tramer, machiner.—*v.i.* Faire de la bière; (*fig.*) se préparer, se tramer, couver.—*n.* [BREWING]. *Brew of tea,* infusion de thé, *f.* **brewer,** *n.* Brasseur, *m.* **brewery,** *n.* Brasserie, *f.* **brewing,** *n.* Brassage; brassin, *m.*, cuvée, *f.*

briar [BRIER].

bribe [braib], *n.* Présent (dans le but de corrompre); (*fam.*) pot-de-vin, *m.—v.t.* Gagner, corrompre, acheter, soudoyer. **briber,** *n.* Corrupteur, *m.*, corruptrice, *f.* **bribery,** *n.* Corruption, *f.*

brick [brik], *n.* Brique, *f.*; (*fig.*) brave garçon, bon enfant, *m.* *To drop a brick,* faire une gaffe.—*a.* De briques, en briques.—*v.t.* Garnir en briques, briqueter. **brickbat,** *n.* Briqueton, *m.* (*fig.*) *To hurl brickbats at,* lapider. **brick-dust,** *n.* Poussière de brique, *f.* **brick-field,** *n.* Briqueterie, *f.* **brick-kiln,** *n.* Four à briques, *m.* **bricklayer,** *n.* Maçon en briques, briqueteur, *m.* **brickwork,** *n.* Briquetage, *m.*

bridal [braidl], *a.* Nuptial, de noces.—*n.* Fête nuptiale, noce, *f.* **bride,** *n.* Nouvelle mariée, mariée; fiancée, future, prétendue, *f.* **bridecake,** *n.* Gâteau de noce, *m.* **bridegroom,** *n.* Nouveau marié, marié; fiancé, futur, *m.* *The bride and bridegroom,* les futurs conjoints; les nouveaux mariés, *m.pl.* **bridesmaid,** *n.* Demoiselle d'honneur, *f.*

*bridewell ['braidwəl], *n.* Maison de correction, *f.*

bridge [bridʒ], *n.* Pont, *m.*; passerelle (on a steamer etc.), *f.*; chevalet (of stringed instruments), dos (of the nose); (*Engl.*) bridge (game), *m.* *Suspension-bridge,* pont suspendu, *m.*; *swing bridge,* pont tournant, *m.—v.t.* Jeter un pont sur; (*fig.*) combler (une lacune).

bridge-head, *n.* Tête de pont, *f.*, point d'appui, *m.*

Bridget ['bridʒit]. Brigitte, *f.*

bridle [braidl], *n.* Bride, *f.*; (*fig.*) frein, *m.*; (*Naut.*) branches, *f.pl.—v.t.* Brider; (*fig.*) mettre un frein à, contenir.—*v.i.* Redresser la tête; se rebiffer. *To bridle up,* se rengorger. **bridle-path,** *n.* Piste cavalière, *f.*

bridoon [briˈduːn], *n.* Bridon, *m.*

brief [briːf], *a.* Bref, court, de courte durée; (*fig.*) concis.—*n.* Abrégé; dossier, *m.* *I hold no brief for him,* ce n'est pas mon affaire de le défendre.—*v.t.* Confier une cause à; donner des instructions à. **brief-case,** *n.* Serviette, *f.* **briefing,** *n.* Directives, *f.pl.* **briefless,** *a.* Sans cause (of a lawyer). **briefly,** *adv.* Brièvement, en peu de mots. **briefness,** *n.* Brièveté, concision, *f.*

brier ['braiə], *n.* Bruyère, *f.*; églantier, *m.*; (*pl.*) ronces, *f.pl.* *Sweet brier,* églantier odorant, *m.* **brier-pipe,** *n.* Pipe en bois de bruyère, *f.* **briery,** *a.* Plein de ronces.

brig [brig], *n.* (*Naut.*) Brick, *m.*

brigade [briˈgeid], *n.* Brigade, *f.* *One of the old brigade,* un vieux de la vieille.—*v.t.* Former en brigades.

brigadier [brigəˈdiə], *n.* Général de brigade, *m.*

brigand ['brigənd], *n.* Brigand, *m.* **brigandage,** *n.* Brigandage, *m.*

brigantine ['brigəntiːn], *n.* Brigantin, *m.*

bright [brait], *a.* Brillant; poli; clair, lumineux; éclatant, vif; (*fig.*) joyeux, beau, intelligent. *Brighter days,* des jours plus heureux, *m.pl.*; *to see the bright side of things,* voir tout en rose.

brighten, *v.t.* Faire briller; éclaircir, égayer; polir; (*fig.*) illustrer, embellir; dégourdir. *To brighten up,* éclaircir, (*fig.*) égayer.—*v.i.* S'éclaircir; briller, étinceler. *To brighten up,* se dérider, s'épanouir (of the face), s'éclaircir (of the weather).

brightly, *adv.* Brillamment, avec éclat.

brightness, *n.* Brillant, *m.*; clarté, *f.*; éclat, *m.*; (*fig.*) joie, vivacité, intelligence, *f.*

Bright's disease ['braits diˈziːz], *n.* Maladie de Bright, néphrite chronique, *f.*

brill [bril], *n.* (*Ichth.*) Barbue, *f.*

brilliance ['briljəns] or **brilliancy,** *n.* Brillant, lustre, éclat, *m.*

brilliant, *a.* Brillant, éclatant.—*n.* Brillant (diamond), *m.* **brilliantly,** *adv.* Brillamment, avec éclat.

brim [brim], *n.* Bord, *m.—v.t.* Remplir jusqu'au bord.—*v.i.* Être plein jusqu'au bord. *Brimming over,* débordant. **brimful,** *a.* Rempli jusqu'au bord, tout plein. *Brimful of tears,* gros de larmes. **brimless,** *a.* Sans bords.

brimstone ['brimstən], *n.* Soufre, *m.*

brindle(d) ['brindl(d)], *a.* Tacheté, bringé.

brine [brain], *n.* Saumure, *f.*

bring [briŋ], *v.t.* (*past* and *p.p.* **brought**) Apporter (in general of things); amener (in general of people and animals); conduire; porter (to carry); transporter; réduire (to reduce); (*fig.*) mettre. *To bring about,* amener, causer, opérer, provoquer; *to bring along,* apporter, amener; *to bring away,* emporter, emmener (of persons); *to bring back,* rapporter, ramener; (*fig.*) rappeler; *to bring down,* descendre, amener en bas, abattre;

humilier, rabaisser; *to bring down the house*, faire crouler la salle; *to bring forth*, produire, mettre au monde, mettre bas; *to bring forward*, amener, avancer, (*Book-keeping*) reporter; *to bring in*, faire entrer, introduire, rapporter (money, interest); *to bring into fashion*, mettre à la mode; *to bring into play*, mettre en œuvre; *to bring into question*, mettre en question; *to bring nearer*, rapprocher; *to bring off*, tirer d'affaire, sauver, renflouer; conduire à bien, réussir; *to bring on*, amener, occasionner; *to bring oneself to do something*, se résoudre à faire quelque chose; *to bring out*, faire sortir, faire paraître, publier, représenter sur la scène; *to bring over*, amener, faire passer; convertir, attirer; *to bring round*, amener, ramener; rappeler à la vie; *to bring to*, (*Naut.*) mettre en panne, arrêter; *to bring to again*, faire reprendre connaissance à; *to bring together*, réunir, assembler, réconcilier, raccommoder; *to bring to perfection*, perfectionner; *to bring under*, soumettre, assujettir; *to bring up*, nourrir, élever; monter; vomir (to vomit); *to bring up the rear*, fermer la marche; *to bring word to*, prévenir; *brought forward*, à reporter.

brink [briŋk], *n.* Bord, penchant, *m. On the brink of ruin*, à deux doigts de sa perte.

briny ['braini], *a.* Saumâtre, salé; (*fig.*) amer.

briony [BRYONY].

brisk [brisk], *a.* Vif; (*fig.*) animé, actif, gai, frais, dispos. *At a brisk pace*, à vive allure. **briskly**, *adv.* Vivement. **briskness**, *n.* Vivacité; activité, *f.*

brisket ['briskit], *n.* Poitrine (butcher's meat), *f.*

bristle ['brisl], *n.* Soie, *f.*; poil raide, *m.—v.i.* Se hérisser (de); se raidir (contre). **bristly** or **bristling**, *a.* Hérissé (de); (*Bot.*) poilu.

Britain ['britən]. La Grande-Bretagne, *f.*

Britannia metal [bri'tænjə 'metl]. Métal anglais, *m.* **Britannic**, *a.* Britannique.

British ['britiʃ], *a.* Britannique. *The British Isles*, Les Îles Britanniques, *f.pl. The British*, (*usu. in French*) Les Anglais, les Britanniques, *m.pl.*

Briton ['britən], *n.* Breton (de la Grande-Bretagne).

Brittany ['britəni]. La Bretagne, *f.*

brittle [britl], *a.* Fragile, cassant. **brittleness**, *n.* Fragilité, *f.*

broach [broutʃ], *n.* Broche, *f.—v.t.* Embrocher; mettre (a cask) en perce; introduire, entamer (a subject).—*v.i. To broach to*, (*Naut.*) faire chapelle, venir en travers.

broad [brɔ:d], *a.* Large, grand, gros, vaste; (*fig.*) libre, grossier, hardi; peu voilé (of hints); prononcé (accent). *As broad as it is long*, tout un, bonnet blanc et blanc bonnet; *broad bean*, grosse fève; *Broad Church*, Église libérale, *f.*; *broad daylight*, plein jour, *m.*; *broad grin*, gros rire, *m.*; *six feet broad*, large de six pieds, qui a six pieds de large.

broad-brimmed, *a.* À larges bords.

broadcast, *a.* À la volée; radiodiffusé.—*v.t.* Semer (du grain) à la volée; répandre (une nouvelle); radiodiffuser.—*n.* Émission, *f.* **broadcaster**, *n.* Speaker, *m.*, speakerine, *f.* **broadcasting**, *n.* Radiodiffusion, *f. Broadcasting station*, poste émetteur, *m.*

broad-cloth, *n.* Drap (noir) fin, *m.*

broaden, *v.t.* Élargir.—*v.i.* S'élargir, s'étendre.

broadly, *a.* Largement. *Broadly speaking*, généralement parlant. **broad-minded**, *a.* Tolérant, à l'esprit large. **broadness**, *n.* Largeur; (*fig.*) grossièreté, *f.* **broadsheet**, *n.* (*Lit.*) Placard, *m.* **broadshouldered**, *a.* Aux larges épaules.

broadside ['brɔ:dsaid], *n.* (*Naut.*) Côté, flanc, *m.*; bordée, *f.*; (*Print.*) in plano, *m. To fire a broadside*, tirer une bordée.—*adv. Broadside on*, par le travers.

broadsword ['brɔ:dsɔ:d], *n.* Sabre, *m.*

brocade [bro'keid], *n.* Brocart, *m.* **brocaded**, *a.* De brocart.

brocket ['brɔkit], *n.* Daguet, *m.*

brogue [broug], *n.* Accent irlandais, *m.*; brogue (shoe), *f.*

broil (1) [brɔil], *n.* Querelle, *f.*, tumulte, *m.*

broil (2) [brɔil], *v.t.* Griller.—*v.i.* Se griller. —*n.* Viande grillée, *f.*

broiler ['brɔilə], *n.* Poulet à rôtir; gril, *m.*; rôtisserie, *f.*

broiling, *a.* Brûlant.

broke, *past* [BREAK].—*a. To be broke*, (*fam.*) être à sec, être fauché.

broken ['broukən], *a.* Cassé, brisé, rompu; (*fig.*) navré; entrecoupé, décousu (of language etc.); accidenté (of country); interrompu (of sleep); délabré (of health). *Broken meat*, restes de viande, rogatons, *m.pl.*; *broken sleep*, sommeil interrompu, *m.*; *broken voice*, voix entrecoupée, *f.*; *to speak broken English*, écorcher l'anglais. **broken-backed**, *a.* Qui a les reins cassés. **broken-hearted**, *a.* Qui a le cœur brisé. *To die broken-hearted*, mourir de chagrin. **brokenly**, *adv.* Par morceaux; sans suite. **broken-winded**, *a.* Poussif.

broker ['broukə], *n.* Courtier; (second-hand goods) brocanteur, *m. Ship-broker*, courtier maritime, *m.*; *stockbroker*, agent de change, *m.* **brokerage**, *n.* Courtage, *m.*

brolly ['brɔli], *n.* (*fam.*) Parapluie, pépin, *m.*

bromide ['broumaid], *n.* Bromure, *m.*

bromine ['broumi:n, -ain], *n.* Brome, *m.*

bronchia ['brɔŋkiə], *n.pl.* Bronches, *f.pl.* **bronchial**, *a.* Bronchial.

bronchitis [brɔŋ'kaitis], *n.* Bronchite, *f.*

bronchotomy, *n.* Bronchotomie, *f.*

bronco ['brɔŋkou], *n.* (*Am.*) Cheval (non dressé), *m.*

bronze [brɔnz], *n.* Bronze, *m.—v.t.* Bronzer. **bronzed**, *a.* Bronzé, basané.

brooch [broutʃ], *n.* Broche, *f.*

brood [bru:d], *v.i.* Couver. *To brood over*, rêver à, ruminer.—*n.* Couvée, *f.* **brooder**, *n.* Couveuse, *f.* **broody**, *a.* Couveuse (hen); distrait (person).

brook (1) [bruk], *n.* Ruisseau, *m.*

brook (2) [bruk], *v.t.* (*always neg.*) (Ne pas) souffrir; avaler, digérer.

brooklet ['bruklit], *n.* Petit ruisseau, ruisselet, *m.*

broom [bru:m], *n.* Balai; genêt (plant), *m. A new broom always sweeps clean*, il n'est rien tel que balai neuf. **broom-stick**, *n.* Manche à balai, *m.* **broomy**, *a.* Couvert de genêts.

broth [brɔ:θ], *n.* Bouillon, potage, *m.*

brothel [brɔθl], *n.* (*vulg.*) Bordel, *m.*; maison mal famée, *f.*, bouge, lupanar, *m.*

brother ['brʌðə], *n.* (*pl.* **brothers**, *rhet.* **brethren**) Frère; (fellow worker) confrère, *m. Brother-in-law*, beau-frère, *m.*; *brother in* *arms*, compagnon d'armes, *m.*; *elder brother*, frère aîné; *foster-brother*, frère de lait; *younger brother*, frère cadet. **brotherhood**, *n.* Fraternité; confrérie, confraternité, *f.* **brotherly**, *a.* Fraternel.

brougham [bru:m], *n.* Coupé, *m.*

brought [brɔ:t], *past* and *p.p.* [BRING].

brow [brau], *n.* Sourcil; (*fig.*) front; sommet, *m.* *To knit the brow*, froncer le sourcil; *to smooth one's brow*, se dérider.

browbeat, *v.t.* Intimider, rudoyer.

brown [braun], *a.* Brun; sombre, rembruni; châtain (of the hair); (*Cook.*) rissolé. *Brown bread*, pain bis, *m.*; *brown paper*, papier d'emballage, *m.*; *brown shoes*, chaussures jaunes, *f.pl.*; *brown study*, rêverie, *f.*; *brown sugar*, sucre brut, *m.—n.* Brun.—*v.t.* Brunir; (*Cook.*) rissoler, faire dorer. (*fam.*) *To be browned off*, être découragé, en avoir marre. —*v.i.* Se brunir.

Brownie ['brauni], *n.* Jeannette, *f.* (junior girl scout).

browning, *n.* (*Cook.*) Caramel, *m.*

brownish, *a.* Brunâtre.

browse [brauz], *v.i.* Brouter; (*colloq.*) butiner.

bruin ['bru:in], *n.* Ours, *m.*; (*fam.*) l'Ours Martin, *m.*

bruise [bru:z], *v.t.* Meurtrir, contusionner; écraser, froisser.—*n.* Meurtrissure, contusion, *f.* **bruiser**, *n.* Boxeur, *m.*

bruit [bru:t], *n.* Bruit, *m.—v.t.* Ébruiter, faire courir le bruit (que).

brumal ['bru:məl], *a.* D'hiver, brumal.

brummagem ['brʌmədʒəm], *a.* (=Birmingham), (*colloq.*) de camelote, en toc.

brunette [bru:'net], *a.* and *n.* Brune, *f.*

brunt [brʌnt], *n.* Choc, *m.*, violence, fureur, *f.* *Brunt of battle*, le plus fort de la bataille, *m.*; *to bear the brunt of*, faire tous les frais de.

brush [brʌʃ], *n.* Brosse, *f.*; balai; pinceau, *m.*; (*fig.*) escarmouche, brossée; queue (of a fox); (*Elec.*) traînée lumineuse, *f.* *Scrubbing-brush*, brosse dure, *f.—v.t.* Brosser; balayer; (*fig.*) effleurer, raser. *To brush one's hair*, se brosser les cheveux; *to brush away*, enlever (avec la brosse), essuyer (tears); *to brush past*, frôler, passer rapidement auprès de; *to brush up*, donner un coup de brosse à, repasser, se remettre à (a subject etc.).

brusher, *n.* Brosseur, *m.*, brosseuse, *f.*

brushing, *n.* Brossée, *f.*; brossage, *m.*

brush-maker, *n.* Brossier, *m.*

brush-off, *n.* (*fam.*) Coup de balai, *m.*

brushwood, *n.* Broussailles, *f.pl.*, fourré, *m.*

brusque [brusk], *a.* Brusque. **brusqueness**, *n.* Brusquerie, *f.* **brusquely**, *adv.* Avec brusquerie.

Brussels [brʌslz], *n.* Bruxelles. *Brussels sprouts*, choux de Bruxelles, *m.pl.*

brutal [bru:tl], *a.* Brutal, cruel, inhumain.

brutality [bru:'tæliti], *n.* Brutalité, cruauté, *f.*

brutalize, *v.t.* Abrutir.

brutally, *adv.* Brutalement.

brute, *n.* Animal, *m.*, brute, bête, *f.*, brutal, *m.—a.* Brut, insensible, privé de raison; sauvage; brutal (of animals). *Brute force*, vive force, *f.*; *the brute creation*, l'espèce animale, *f.*

brutish, *a.* Abruti, de bête, brutal, grossier.

brutishly, *adv.* Brutalement, en brute.

brutishness, *n.* Brutalité, bestialité, *f.*

bryony [braiəni], *n.* (*Bot.*) Bryone, *f.*

bubble [bʌbl], *n.* Bulle; (*fig.*) chimère, illusion, *f.* *Bubble and squeak*, pommes de terre frites aux choux; *bubble company* or *scheme*, affaire véreuse, duperie, *f.—v.i.* Bouillonner. *To bubble over*, déborder; *to bubble up*, bouillonner, pétiller (of wine). **bubbly**, *a.* Plein de bulles, pétillant.—*n.* (*pop.*) (Vin de) champagne, *m.*

bubo ['bju:bou], *n.* Bubon, *m.* **bubonic**, *a.* Bubonique.

buccaneer [bʌkə'niə], *n.* Boucanier, flibustier, *m.*

buck [bʌk], *n.* Daim; chevreuil; mâle (of the hare or rabbit); (*fig.*) gaillard, beau, élégant, *m.* *To pass the buck to someone*, (*fam.*) passer la décision à quelqu'un.—*v.i.* Faire le saut de mouton. *To buck up*, se ragaillardir.—*v.t.* (*fam.*) *To buck someone up*, ravigoter, regonfler quelqu'un. **buckbean**, *n.* Ménianthe trifolié, trèfle d'eau, *m.* **buck-shot**, *n.* Chevrotine, *f.* **buckskin**, *n.* Peau de daim, *f.*

bucket ['bʌkit], *n.* Seau; baquet; auget (of a water-wheel); piston (of a pump); godet (of a dredger), *m.* *To kick the bucket*, (*slang*) sauter le pas, casser sa pipe. **bucketful**, *n.* Plein seau, *m.*

buckle [bʌkl], *n.* Boucle, agrafe, *f.—v.t.* Boucler, agrafer. *To buckle on*, endosser.— *v.i.* Se boucler; se courber. *To buckle to*, s'appliquer (à). **buckler**, *n.* Bouclier, *m.*

buckram ['bʌkrəm], *n.* Bougran, *m.*; (*fig.*) raideur, *f.* *Man in buckram*, homme de carton, être imaginaire, *m.*; *buckram style*, style compassé, *m.*

buckshee ['bʌkʃi:], *a.* (*pop.*) Gratuit, à l'œil. —*adv.* Gratis.

buckthorn ['bʌkθɔ:n], *n.* (*Bot.*) Nerprun, *m.*

buckwheat ['bʌkwi:t], *n.* Sarrasin, blé noir, *m.*

bucolic [bju:'kɔlik], *a.* Bucolique.—*n.* Poème bucolique, *m.*

bud [bʌd], *n.* Bourgeon, bouton; (*fig.*) germe, *m.* *To nip in the bud*, tuer dans l'œuf.—*v.i.* Bourgeonner. *A budding poet*, un poète en herbe, *m.—v.t.* Écussonner.

Buddha ['budə], *n.* Bouddha, *m.* **Buddhism**, *n.* Bouddhisme, *m.* **Buddhist**, *n.* Bouddhiste.

budge [bʌdʒ], *v.i.* Bouger, se remuer.—*v.t.* Bouger.

budgerigar [bʌdʒəri'gɑ:], *n.* (*Orn.*) Perruche inséparable, *f.*

budget ['bʌdʒit], *n.* Sac; (*Fin.*) budget, *m.— v.t. To budget for*, porter au budget.

buff [bʌf], *n.* Buffle, *m.*, peau de buffle, *f.*; couleur chamois, *f.—v.t.* Polir au buffle.—*a.* De couleur chamois.

buffalo ['bʌfəlou], *n.* Buffle, *m.*

buffer ['bʌfə], *n.* Tampon, amortisseur, *m.* *Buffer state*, état tampon, *m.*; *old buffer*, (*colloq.*) vieux copain; vieux ganache.

buffer-stop, *n.* (*Rail.*) Butoir, heurtoir; (*Motor.*) amortisseur, *m.*

buffet ['bʌfit], *n.* Buffet (sideboard); soufflet, coup de poing; ['bufei] buffet (refreshment room), *m.* *Cold buffet*, assiette anglaise, *f.— v.i.* Se battre à coups de poing; lutter (contre).—*v.t.* Frapper à coups de poing, souffleter. *Buffeted by the waves*, battu des vagues.

buffoon [bʌ'fu:n], *n.* Bouffon, *m.* **buffoonery**, *a.* Bouffonnerie, *f.*

bug [bʌg], *n.* Punaise, *f.*

bugaboo ['bʌgəbu:], or **bugbear** ['bʌgbɛə], *n.* Chose qui fait peur, *f.*, épouvantail, croquemitaine, *m.*; (*fig.*) bête noire, *f.*, cauchemar, *m.*

bugger ['bʌgə], *n.* (*Law*) Pédéraste, *m.*: (*indec.*) bougre, *m.*

buggy ['bʌgi], *n.* Boghei, boguet, *m.*

bugle [bju:gl], *n.* Cor de chasse; (*Mil.*) clairon, *m.*; bugle (plant), *f.* **bugler**, *n.* Clairon, *m.*

bugloss ['bju:glɔs], *n.* (*Bot.*) Buglosse, *f.*

buhl [bu:l], *n.* Boulle, *m.*, marqueterie de Boulle, *f.*

build [bild], *v.t.* (*past* and *p.p.* **built**) Bâtir, faire bâtir, construire; (*fig.*) édifier, fonder, baser. *To build on,* (*fig.*) compter sur, se fonder sur; *to build up,* élever, murer, affermir (health).—*n.* Construction; forme, carrure, taille, *f.* **builder**, *n.* Constructeur, entrepreneur de bâtiments, *m.* **building**, *n.* Construction, *f.*; édifice, bâtiment, *m.* *Building contractor,* entrepreneur, *m.*; *building materials,* matériaux de construction, *m.pl.*; *building society,* société immobilière, *f.*

bulb [bʌlb], *n.* Bulbe, oignon, *m.*; cuvette (of thermometers); poire (of indiarubber); (*Elec.*) ampoule, lampe, *f.* **bulbous**, *a.* Bulbeux.

bulbul ['bulbul], *n.* Rossignol iranien, *m.*

Bulgaria [bʌl'gɛəriə]. La Bulgarie, *f.*

Bulgarian [bʌl'gɛəriən], *a.* and *n.* Bulgare.

bulge [bʌldʒ], *n.* Bombement, *m.*, bosse, *f.*—*v.t.*, *v.i.* Faire saillie, bomber. **bulging**, *a.* Bombé.

bulimy ['bju:limi], *n.* Boulimie, *f.*

bulk [bʌlk], *n.* Volume, *m.*, grosseur; masse, *f.*, gros, *m.*; (*Naut.*) charge, *f.* *Bulk buying,* achat massif, *m.*; *in bulk,* en bloc, en gros; *laden in bulk,* chargé en grenier; *to break bulk,* commencer le déchargement, rompre charge.—*v.t.* Entasser en masse.—*v.i. To bulk large,* occuper une place importante. **bulkhead**, *n.*, Cloison étanche, *f.* **bulkiness**, *n.* Grosseur, *f.*; volume, *m.* **bulky**, *a.* Gros, encombrant.

bull [bul], *n.* Taureau, *m.*; bulle, *f.* (Pope's); (*St. Exch.*) joueur à la hausse, haussier, *m.*; mouche, *f.*, mille, *m.* (= bull's-eye); bévue, naïveté, *f.* (= Irish bull). *To take the bull by the horns,* prendre le taureau par les cornes. —*v.i.* (*St. Exch.*) Jouer à la hausse. **bull-baiting**, *n.* Combat de chiens contre un taureau, *m.* **bull-calf**, *n.* Jeune taureau; (*fig.*) benêt, *m.*

bulldog, *n.* Bouledogue, *m.* **bulldoze**, *v.t.* Intimider. **bulldozer**, *n.* (*Civ. Eng.*) Bull-dozer, *m.*

bullet ['bulit], *n.* Balle, *f.* (de fusil, de revolver). **bullet-proof**, *a.* À l'épreuve des balles.

bulletin ['bulətin], *n.* Bulletin, communiqué, *m.*

bullfight, *n.* Course de taureaux, *f.* **bull-fighter**, *n.* Toréador, *m.*

bullfinch ['bulfintʃ], *n.* (*Orn.*) Bouvreuil, *m.*; (*spt.*) haie vive, sur talus, *f.*

bullhead, *n.* (*Ichth.*) Chabot, meunier, *m.*

bullion ['buljən], *n.* Or *or* argent en lingots, *m.* Stock *of* bullion, encaisse métallique, *f.*

bullock ['bulək], *n.* Bœuf, bouvillon, *m.*

bull's-eye, *n.* Centre, noir (of a target), *m.*; œil-de-bœuf (window), *m.*; (*Naut.*) margouillet; hublot, *m.* *Bull's-eye lantern,* lanterne sourde, *f.*; *to score a bull's-eye,* taper

dans le mille, faire mouche. **bull-terrier**, *n.* Bull-terrier, *m.*

bully ['buli], *n.* Matamore, bravache, *m.*; brute, *f.*; (*sch.*) brimeur; souteneur (ponce), *m.*; engagement (*Hockey*), *m.* *Bully beef,* (*Mil. slang*) conserve de bœuf, *f.*, singe, *m.*— *v.t.* Malmener, intimider.—*v.i.* Faire le fendant *or* le matamore. *To bully off* (*Hockey*), engager.—*a.* (*Am.*) Épatant. **bullying**, *a.* Fendant, brutal.—*n.* Intimidation, brutalité, *f.*

bulrush ['bulrʌʃ], *n.* (*Bot.*) Jonc, *m.*

bulwark ['bulwək], *n.* Rempart, *m.*; (*Naut.*) pavois, *m.*

bum [bʌm], *n.* (*fam.*) Derrière, (*Vulg.*) cul, *m.*; (*Am.*) fainéant, flemmard, *m.*

bum bailiff), *n.* Huissier, recors, *m.*

bumboat, *n.* Bateau de provisions, *m.*

bumble-bee ['bʌmblbi:], *n.* Bourdon, *m.*

bumf [bʌmf], *n.* (*pop.*) Papier, *m.*; paperasses, *f.pl.*; torche-cul, *m.*

bumkin ['bʌmkin], *n.* (*Naut.*) Porte-lof, boutdehors, *m.*

bummaree [bʌmə'ri:], *n.* Revendeur de poisson (*or* demi-gros), *m.*

bump [bʌmp], *n.* Bosse, *f.*; heurt, cahot, coup, choc, *m.*—*v.t.* Frapper, cogner. (*fam.*) *To bump off,* assassiner.—*v.i.* Se cogner, heurter. **bumper**, *n.* Rasade, *f.*, rougebord, *m.*; (*Motor.*) pare-choc, *m.* **bumping**, *n.* Heurtement, *m.* **bumpy**, *a.* Cahoteux (road).

bumpkin ['bʌmpkin], *n.* Rustre, lourdaud, *m.*

bumptious ['bʌmpʃəs], *a.* Présomptueux, suffisant. **bumptiously**, *adv.* D'un air présomptueux. **bumptiousness**, *n.* Suffisance, *f.*

bun [bʌn], *n.* Petit pain rond au lait; chignon (hair), *m.*

bunch [bʌntʃ], *n.* Botte, *f.* (d'asperges, oignons, radis, etc.); bouquet, *m.*, gerbe, *f.* (de fleurs); grappe, *f.* (de raisin); houppe, *f.* (de plumes); régime, *m.* (de bananes); trousseau, *m.* (de clefs); (*fam.*) groupe, *m.*, bande, *f.*—*v.t.* Lier, botteler. *To bunch up,* retrousser.—*v.i.* Se grouper, se tasser.

bundle [bʌndl], *n.* Paquet, baluchon; ballot; tas; liasse; fagot (de bois etc.), *m.* *Bundle of asparagus,* botte d'asperges, *f.*; *bundle of papers,* liasse de papiers, *f.*—*v.t.* Empaqueter. *To bundle out,* jeter à la porte, fourrer dehors.

bung [bʌŋ], *n.* Bondon, tampon, *m.*—*v.t.* Bondonner, boucher; (*pop.*) lancer. **bunghole**, *n.* Bonde, *f.*

bungalow ['bʌŋgəlou], *n.* Maison sans étage, *f.*

bungle [bʌŋgl], *v.t.* Bousiller, gâcher, rater.— *v.i.* S'y prendre gauchement, faire de la mauvaise besogne.—*n.* Bousillage; gâchis, *m.* **bungler**, *n.* Maladroit, savetier, bousilleur, *m.* **bungling**, *a.* Maladroit, gauche.—*n.* Bousillage, gâchis, *m.*

bunion ['bʌnjən], *n.* Oignon (on the foot), *m.*

bunk (1) [bʌŋk], *n.* (*Naut.*) Couchette, *f.*

bunk (2) [bʌŋk], *v.i.* (*slang*) Filer, décamper. *To do a bunk* = to bunk.

bunker ['bʌŋkə], *n.* Soute (for coal), *f.*; banquette (golf), *f.*

bunkum ['bʌŋkəm], *n.* (*slang*) Blague, *f.*; bêtises, *f.pl.*

bunny ['bʌni], *n.* (*colloq.*) Lapin, *m.*

bunt [bʌnt], *n.* (*Naut.*) Fond de voile, *m.*

bunt-line, *n.* Cargue-fond, *f.*

bunting [′bʌntiŋ], n. Étamine, f.; (fig.) drapeaux, pavillons, m.pl.; (Orn.) bruant, m.
buoy [bɔi], n. Bouée, f. Bell-buoy, bouée sonore, f.; life-buoy, bouée de sauvetage; light-buoy, bouée lumineuse, f.; mooring buoy, corps mort, m.—v.t. To buoy up, soutenir sur l'eau, (fig.) soutenir, encourager; to buoy out, baliser. **buoy-rope,** n. Orin, m.
buoyancy, n. Légèreté, f.; élan, entrain, allant, m.; vivacité, animation, f. **buoyant,** a. Léger, flottant; animé, vif.
bur [bə:], n. Capsule épineuse, f.; (colloq.) crampon, m. (person).
burble [bə:bl], v.i. Murmurer, bafouiller.—n. Murmure, m.
burbot [′bə:bət], n. (Ichth.) Lotte commune, f.
burden [bə:dn], n. Fardeau, m.; charge, f.; poids; refrain (of a song), m. Beast of burden, bête de somme, f.; the burden of years, le poids des années; to be a burden to or. on, être à charge à.—v.t. Charger. **burdensome,** a. Onéreux; ennuyeux.
burdock [′bə:dɔk], n. (Bot.) Bardane, f.
bureau [bjuə′rou], n. Bureau, m. Information bureau, bureau de renseignements, m.
bureaucracy [bjuə′rɔkrəsi], n. Bureaucratie, f.
bureaucrat [′bjuərokræt], n. Bureaucrate, m.
bureaucratic [bjuəro′krætik], a. Bureaucratique.
burgess [′bə:dʒis], n. Bourgeois, citoyen, électeur, m.
burgh [′bʌrə], n. (Sc.) Bourg, m.
burgher [′bə:gə], n. Bourgeois; citoyen, m.
burglar [′bə:glə], n. Cambrioleur, m.
burglariously [bə:′glɛəriəsli], adv. Avec effraction.
burglary [′bə:gləri], n. Vol avec effraction, m.; cambriolage, m. **burgle,** v.t., v.i. Cambrioler.
burgomaster [′bə:gomɑ:stə], n. Bourgmestre, m.
Burgundian [bə:′gʌndjən], a. and n. Bourguignon, m., Bourguignonne, f.
Burgundy [′bə:gəndi]. La Bourgogne, f.; (wine) vin de Bourgogne, bourgogne, m.
burial [′beriəl], n. Enterrement, m., obsèques, f.pl.; inhumation, f. Christian burial, sépulture en terre sainte, f. **burial-ground,** n. Cimetière, m. **burial-place,** n. Lieu de sépulture, m. **burial-service,** n. Office des morts, m.
burin [′bjuərin], n. Burin, m.
burke [bə:k], v.t. Étrangler; (fig.) étouffer.
burl [bə:l], v.t. Noper, énouer, épincer (cloth).
burlesque [bə:′lesk], a. and n. Burlesque, m.—v.t. Parodier, travestir.
burliness [′be:linəs], n. Grosseur, corpulence; emphase, f. **burly,** a. De forte carrure.
Burma(h) [′bə:mə]. La Birmanie, f.
Burmese [bə:′mi:z], a. and n. Birman, m., Birmane, f.
burn [bə:n], v.t. (past and p.p. **burnt** or **burned**) Brûler; cuire (bricks etc.); incendier. To burn alive, brûler vif; to burn down, brûler, consumer, détruire par le feu; to burn to the ground, brûler de fond en comble; to burn one's fingers, se brûler les doigts; to burn to ashes, réduire en cendres; to burn up, brûler entièrement, consumer; to make the fire burn, achever le feu.—v.i. Brûler; (fig.) brûler, être impatient de. To burn away or out, se consumer; to burn with, brûler de.—n. Brûlure, f. **burner,** n. Brûleur; bec (of gas

etc.), m. Bunsen burner, bec Bunsen, m.
burning, n. Brûlure; combustion, cautérisation, f.; incendie, m.; fournée (lot); cuite (of bricks etc.), f.—a. En feu; brûlant, ardent. To smell something burning, sentir quelque chose qui brûle. **burning-glass,** n. Verre ardent, m. **burnt,** a. Brûlé, carbonisé. **burnt-offering,** n. Holocauste, m.
burnet [′bə:nit], n. (Bot.) Pimprenelle des prés, f.
burnish [′bə:niʃ], v.t. Brunir, polir; (Phot.) satiner.—v.i. Prendre du brillant. **burnisher,** n. Brunisseur, m., brunisseuse, f.; brunissoir (tool), m. **burnishing,** n. Brunissage; (Phot.) satinage, m.
burnous [bə:′nu:s], n. Burnous, m.
burr [bə:], n. Meule (of stag's horn); (Geol.) pierre meulière, f.; (Phon.) roulement (de l'r); grasseyement, m., barbe, ébarbure (of metal), f.; [BUR].
burrow [′bʌrou], n. Terrier, trou, m.—v.i. Se terrer; (fig.) se cacher.—v.t. Creuser.
bursar [′bə:sə], n. Économe, intendant; trésorier; boursier, m. **bursarship,** n. Économat, m. **bursary,** n. Bourse (d'études), f.; bureau de l'économe, m.
burst [bə:st], v.t. (past and p.p. **burst**) Crever; faire éclater; fendre; rompre. To burst open a door, enfoncer une porte.—v.i. Crever, éclater; sauter; percer, jaillir; s'élancer; éclore (of buds). To burst into tears, fondre en larmes; to burst out laughing, éclater de rire.—n. Éclat, éclatement, m., explosion; rupture, hernie, f.; (fig.) mouvement, accès, m. Burst of laughter, éclat de rire, m.; burst (of speed), élan, emballage, m. **bursting,** n. Éclatement, m., explosion, f.; crevaison, f.; (fig.) rupture, f.
burthen [′bə:ðən] [BURDEN].
bury [′beri], v.t. (past and p.p. **buried**) Enterrer, ensevelir, (fig.) enfoncer, plonger; cacher. **burying,** (fig.) n. [BURIAL].
bus [bʌs], n. Autobus, (fam.) bus, m. To miss the bus, manquer l'autobus, (fig.) laisser échapper une occasion, manquer le coche. **bus-conductor,** n. Receveur (d'autobus), m. **bus-driver,** n. Conducteur, chauffeur (d'autobus), m. **busman,** n. Conducteur d'autobus, m. To take a busman's holiday, faire du métier en guise de congé.
busby [′bʌzbi], n. Colback, m. (de hussard).
bush [buʃ], n. Buisson; bouchon (signboard), m.; fourré, m., terre inculte, f.; (Australia) brousse, f.; bague, douille (métallique), f. Good wine needs no bush, à bon vin point d'enseigne; to beat about the bush, tourner autour du pot.—v.t. Baguer.
bush-fighting, n. Combat sous bois, m. **bush-ranger,** n. Broussard, m. **bushiness,** n. État touffu, m.; épaisseur, f. **bushy,** a. Buissonneux; touffu.
bushel [′buʃl], n. Boisseau, m.
busily [′bizili], adv. Activement; avec empressement; d'un air affairé.
business [′biznis], n. Affaire, occupation, f.; devoir; état, métier, m. (trade); affaires, f.pl., commerce, m.; clientèle (connection), f. Business hours, heures d'ouverture, f.pl.; business man, homme d'affaires; go about your business, allez vous promener; in business, en affaires, dans les affaires, dans le commerce; it's none of your business, cela ne vous regarde

pas; *line of business*, genre de commerce, *m.*; *mind your own business!* mêlez-vous *or* occupez-vous de vos affaires! *on business*, pour affaires; *the business end of a revolver*, la gueule d'un revolver; *to attend to one's business*, être à ses affaires; *to do a great deal of business*, faire de bonnes affaires; *to do business with*, être en affaires avec; *to give up business*, se retirer des affaires; *to make it one's business to*, prendre sur soi de; *to mean business*, ne pas plaisanter, avoir des intentions sérieuses; *to settle a business*, arranger une affaire; *to set up in business*, s'établir, débuter; *what business had you there?* qu'alliez-vous faire dans cette galère? *what business is that of yours?* est-ce que cela vous regarde? *you have no business here*, vous n'avez que faire ici.

businesslike, *a.* Pratique, régulier, méthodique; franc, droit, sérieux.

busk [bʌsk], *n.* Busc, *m.* (de corset).

busker ['bʌskə], *n.* (*Theat.*) Cabotin, *m.*

buskin ['bʌskin], *n.* Brodequin, (*fig.*) cothurne, *m.*, tragédie, *f.* **buskined,** *a.* En brodequins; (*fig.*) en cothurnes, tragique.

*buss [bʌs], *n.* Gros baiser, *m.*—*v.t.* Embrasser.

bust (1) [bʌst], *n.* (*Sculp.*) Buste, *m.*; gorge, *f.* (de femme); (*Art*) bosse, *f.* *From the bust*, d'après la bosse.

bust (2) [bʌst], *v.t.* (*pop.*) Casser, rompre, crever; (*Mil.*) rétrograder.—*n.* *To go bust*, faire faillite; *to have a bust-up with someone*, se brouiller avec quelqu'un, rompre avec quelqu'un.

bustard ['bʌstəd]. *n.* (*Orn.*) Outarde, *f.*

bustle [bʌsl], *n.* Mouvement; remue-ménage, bruit, *m.*, confusion, activité, agitation; tournure (of a dress), *f.*—*v.i.* Se remuer, s'empresser.

bustling ['bʌsliŋ], *a.* Empressé, affairé, remuant; bruyant.

busy ['bizi], *a.* Affairé, occupé, empressé, en mouvement, diligent. *Busy street*, rue mouvementée, *f.* *To be busy doing . . .*, être occupé à faire. . . .—*v.r.* *To busy oneself*, s'occuper. **busybody,** *n.* Officieux, *m.*, officieuse, *f.*

but [bʌt], *conj.* Mais . . ., que . . .; sauf que; qui ne. *But that*, sans que; *it cannot but be accounted natural*, on ne peut que le considérer comme naturel; *there is not one of them but knows it*, il n'y en a pas un qui ne le sache; *to do nothing but*, ne faire que.—*adv.* Ne . . . que; seulement. *All but*, presque; *but that*, si ce n'était que; *but yesterday*, pas plus tard qu'hier; *I should have died, but for him*, sans lui, je serais mort; *the last but one*, l'avant-dernier; *there is but you who*, il n'y a que vous qui.—*prep.* Sans, excepté, à part. *But for his entreaties*, sans ses supplications.

butane ['bju:tein], *n.* (*Chem.*) Butane, *m.*

butcher ['butʃə], *n.* Boucher, *m.* *Butcher's meat*, viande de boucherie, *f.*; *butcher's shop*, boucherie, *f.*—*v.t.* Égorger, massacrer. **butcher-bird,** *n.* Pie-grièche grise, *f.* **butcher knife,** *n.* (*Am.*) [CARVING KNIFE].

butchery, *n.* Boucherie; tuerie, *f.*, massacre, carnage, *m.*

butler ['bʌtlə], *n.* Maître d'hôtel; *sommelier, *m.* *Butler's tray*, plateau à découper, *m.*

butment [ABUTMENT].

butt [bʌt], *n.* Bout; coup de tête (by an animal),

m.; crosse (of a rifle); masse (of a cue), *f.*; (*fig.*) point de mire, *m.*; cible; butte, (*Mil.*) barrique (cask), *f.*; tonneau (for rainwater), *m.*; (*Fenc.*) botte, *f.*; plastron (person), *m.*—*v.i.* Cosser, frapper de la tête (of animals).

butt-end, *n.* Gros-bout, *m.*, crosse, *f.* *With the butt-end*, à coups de crosse. **butt-plate,** *n.* Plaque de couche, *f.* (of rifle etc.).

butter ['bʌtə], *n.* Beurre, *m.* *To look as if butter would not melt in one's mouth*, faire la sainte nitouche; *melted butter*, beurre noir, *m.*—*v.t.* Beurrer. (*fam.*) *To butter someone up*, flatter quelqu'un. *Buttered eggs*, œufs brouillés (au beurre), *m.pl.*

buttercup, *n.* Bouton d'or, *m.*

butter-dish, *n.* Beurrier, *m.*

butterfly, *n.* Papillon, *m.*

buttermilk, *n.* Petit-lait, *m.*

butter-scotch, *n.* Caramel au beurre, *m.*

butterwort, *n.* Grassette, *f.*

buttery, *a.* De beurre, graisseux.—*n.* Dépense, *f.*

buttock ['bʌtək], *n.* Fesse; croupe (de cheval); culotte (de bœuf); (*Naut.*) arcasse, *f.*

button [bʌtn], *n.* Bouton, *m.*—*v.t.* Boutonner. —*v.i.* Se boutonner.

buttonhole, *n.* Boutonnière, *f.*—*v.t.* Accrocher (quelqu'un).

button-hook, *n.* Tire-bouton, *m.*

buttons, *n.* (*colloq.*) Chasseur (d'hôtel), groom, *m.*

buttress ['bʌtris], *n.* Contrefort, éperon, *m.* *Flying-buttress*, arc-boutant, *m.*—*v.t.* Arc-bouter.

butty ['bʌti], *n.* (*Mining*) Camarade; chef d'équipe, porion, *m.*

buxom ['bʌksəm], *a.* Plein de santé et d'entrain; (femme) rondelette et fraîche, aux formes rebondies. **buxomness,** *n.* Ampleur de formes, *f.*

buy [bai], *v.t.* (*past and p.p.* **bought**, bɔːt) Acheter; prendre (ticket); corrompre, gagner (to bribe). *To buy and sell*, brocanter; *to buy off or back*, racheter; *to buy in*, acheter; *to buy up*, accaparer.—*n.* (*Am. and fam.*) Achat, *m.* *A good buy*, un bon placement. **buyer,** *n.* Acheteur, acquéreur, *m.* **buying,** *n.* Achat, *m.* *Buying in*, rachat, *m.*; *buying up*, accaparement, *m.*

buzz [bʌz], *v.i.* Bourdonner. *To buzz off* (*fam.*), décamper.—*n.* Bourdonnement; brouhaha (of conversation), *m.* **buzzer,** *n.* Sirène, trompe, *f.*, vibreur, appel vibré, *m.*

buzzard ['bʌzəd], *n.* (*Orn.*) Buse, *f.*

by [bai], *prep.* Par; de; à; sur; près de, auprès de, à côté de; en (with participles). *By all means*, par tous les moyens possibles; mais certainement; *by chance*, par hasard; *by day*, durant la journée; *by doing that*, en faisant cela; *by far*, de beaucoup; *by force*, de force; *by night*, de nuit; *by no means*, nullement; *by measure*, à la mesure; *by my watch*, à ma montre; *by oneself*, tout seul; *by seven o'clock*, avant sept heures; *by sight*, de vue; *by that means*, par ce moyen; *by the day*, pour la journée, à la journée; *by the end of the day*, à la fin du jour; *by tomorrow*, d'ici à demain; *by trade*, de son métier; *by train*, par le train, en chemin de fer; *by turn*, tour à tour; *he was by me*, il était à côté de moi; *I know him by his walk*, je le reconnais à son pas; *longer by two feet*, plus long de deux pieds; *loved by all*, aimé de tous; *one by one*, un à un; *to judge by*, juger d'après; *two feet by six*, deux pieds sur six.—*adv.* Près; passé. *By and by*, tout à l'heure; *by and large*, à tout prendre; *by the by(e)*, en passant, à propos; *close by*, tout près; *to put money by*, mettre de l'argent de côté.

bye [bai], *n.* (*Cricket*) Balle passée, *f.*

bye-bye ['baibai], *n.* (*Childish*) Dodo, *m.* *To go to bye-byes*, aller faire dodo.—*int.* (*colloq.*) Adieu!

by-election, *n.* Élection partielle, *f.*

bygone, *a.* Passé, d'autrefois. **bygones**, *n.pl.* Le passé, *m.* *Let bygones be bygones*, ce qui est passé est passé.

by-law, *n.* Règlement local, *m.*

byname, *n.* Sobriquet, surnom, *m.*

by-pass, *n.* Bec-allumeur, *m.*; route d'évitement, déviation, *f.*—*v.t.* Contourner, éviter (a town).

by-path, by-road, or **by-way**, *n.* Sentier, chemin détourné, *m.*

by-play, *n.* Jeu de scène, jeu muet, *m.*

by-product, *n.* Sous-produit, *m.*

byre ['baiə], *n.* Étable à vaches, *f.*

Byronic [bai'rɔnik], *a.* Byronien. **Byronism,** *n.* Byronisme, *m.*

bystander, *n.* Spectateur, assistant, *m.*

by-street, *n.* Rue de traverse, *f.*, rue détournée, *f.*

byword, *n.* Dicton, proverbe, *m.*; (*fig.*) risée, *f.* *To have become a byword*, être passé en proverbe.

Byzantian [bi'zæntien] or **Byzantine,** *a.* Byzantin.

Byzantium [bai'zæntiəm]. Byzance, *f.*

C

C, c [si:]. Troisième lettre de l'alphabet, *m.*; (*Mus.*) ut, do, *m.*; clef d'ut, *f.*

cab [kæb], *n.* Fiacre, *m.*, voiture de place, *f.*; taxi, *m.*; guérite, *f.* **cab-stand** or **cab-rank,** *n.* Station de voitures, *f.*

cabal [kə'bæl], *n.* Cabale, *f.*—*v.i.* Cabaler.

cabaret ['kæbərei], *n.* Attractions, *f.pl.* (in a restaurant or dance-hall).

cabbage ['kæbidʒ], *n.* Chou, *m.* *Cabbage lettuce*, laitue pommée, *f.* **cabbage-butter-fly** or **cabbage-white**, *n.* Piéride du chou, *f.* **cabbage-stump**, *n.* Trognon de chou, *m.*

cabbala ['kæbələ], *n.* Cabale, *f.* **cabbalist,** *n.* Cabaliste. **cabbalistic** or **cabbalistical** [kæbə'listikl], *a.* Cabalistique.

cabby ['kæbi], *n.* (*colloq.*) Cocher, *m.*

caber ['keibə], *n.* Tronc de mélèze, *m.*

cabin ['kæbin], *n.* Cabine, chambre (for officers etc.); (*Av.*) carlingue; cabane, case, hutte, *f.* *Cabin passenger*, passager de première classe, *m.*; *chief cabin*, grande chambre; *fore cabin*, chambre d'avant.—*v.i.* Loger à l'étroit.—*v.t.* Enfermer dans une cabane; emprisonner. **cabin-boy,** *n.* Mousse, *m.*

cabined, *a.* Emprisonné, enfermé, à l'étroit.

cabinet ['kæbinit], *n.* Meuble à tiroirs; cabinet, *m.*; ministère, *m.* *Cabinet council*, conseil de cabinet, *m.*; *cabinet size*, (*Phot.*) format album, *m.* **cabinet-maker,** *n.* Ébéniste, *m.* **cabinet-making,** *n.* Ébénis-

terie, *f.* **cabinet-minister,** *n.* Ministre d'État, *m.*

cable [keibl], *n.* Câble, *m.*; câblogramme, *m.* *Cable length*, encâblure, *f.*; *cable railway*, funiculaire, *m.*; *cable stitch* (*Knitting*), point natté, *m.*—*v.t.* Câbler, télégraphier. **cablegram,** *n.* Câblogramme, *m.*

cabman ['kæbmən], *n.*(*pl.* **cabmen**) Cocher, *m.*

caboodle [kə'bu:dl], *n.* (*pop.*) *The whole caboodle*, tout le bazar.

caboose [kə'bu:s], *n.* (*Naut.*) Cuisine, cambuse, *f.*

ca' canny ['kɑ:'kæni], *int.* (*Sc.*) Travaillez doucement, mollement.—*a.* *Ca' canny strike*, grève perlée, *f.*

cacao [kə'kɑ:ou], *n.* Cacao; cacaotier (tree), *m.*

cache [kæʃ], *n.* Cache, cachette, *f.*—*v.t.* Mettre dans une cache.

cachectic [kə'kektik], *a.* Cachectique. **cachexy,** *n.* Cachexie, *f.*

cachinnation [kæki'neiʃən], *n.* Gros (*or* fou) rire, *m.*

cachou [kə'ʃu:], *n.* Cachou, *m.*

cackle [kækl], *n.* Caquet, *m.* (*pop.*) *Cut your cackle!* en voilà assez!—*v.i.* Caqueter; (*fig.*) ricaner, glousser; (of geese) cacarder. **cackler,** *n.* Poule qui caquette, *f.*; caqueteur, *m.*, caqueteuse, *f.* **cackling,** *n.* Caquetage, *m.*

cacophony [kə'kɔfəni], *n.* Cacophonie, *f.*

cactus ['kæktəs], *n.* Cactus, *m.*

cad [kæd], *n.* Goujat, *m.*; canaille, *f.*

cadastral [kə'dæstrəl], *a.* Cadastral. **cadastre,** *n.* Cadastre, *m.*

cadaveric [kə'dæverik], *a.* (*Med.*) Cadavérique. **cadaverous,** *a.* Cadavéreux.

caddie ['kædi], *n.* (*Golf*) Cadet, *m.*—*v.i.* Servir de cadet.

caddis ['kædis], *n.* Cadis, *m.* (wool fabric); phrygane, *f.* (insect).

caddish ['kædiʃ], *a.* Voyou, de goujat.

caddy ['kædi], *n.* Boîte à thé, *f.*

cade [keid], *n.* Caque, *f.*, baril, *m.* (of herring); (*Bot.*) cade, *m.*

cadence ['keidəns], *n.* Cadence, *f.*

cadet [kə'det], *n.* Cadet, *m.*; élève d'une école militaire *or* d'une école navale, *m.* **cadetship,** *n.* Brevet de cadet, *m.*

cadge [kædʒ], *v.t.*, *v.i.* Colporter; quémander; écornifler. **cadger,** *n.* Colporteur; quémandeur; écornifleur, *m.*

Cadiz ['keidiz]. Cadix.

Cadmean [kæd'mi:ən] or **Cadmian,** *a.* Cadméen.

cadre ['kɑ:də], *n.* Cadre, *m.*

caduceus [kə'dju:siəs], *n.* Caducée, *m.*

caducity [kə'dju:siti], *n.* Caducité, *f.*

caducous [kə'dju:kəs], *a.* Caduc, *m.*, caduque, *f.*

caecal ['si:kəl], *a.* Cæcal. **caecum,** *n.* Cæcum, *m.*

Caesar ['si:zə]. César, *m.*

Caesarean (1) [si:'zɛəriən], *a.* Césarien, -ienne.

Caesarean (2) [si:zə'riən], *a.* (*Surg.*) *Caesarean operation*, césarienne, *f.*

caesium [si:'ziəm], *n.* Cæsium, césium, *m.*

caesura [si:'zjuərə], *n.* Césure, *f.*

café ['kæfei], *n.* Café-restaurant, *m.*

cage [keidʒ], *n.* Cage, *f.*—*v.t.* Mettre en cage.

Cain [kein]. Caïn, *m.* *To raise Cain*, faire une scène, faire un chahut monstre.

cairn [kɛən], *n.* Cairn, mont-joie, *m.*

Cairo ['kaiərou]. Le Caire, *m.*

caisson ['keisən], *n.* Caisson, bâtardeau, *m.*
***caitiff** ['keitif], *n.* Misérable, lâche, *m.*
cajole [kə'dʒoul], *v.t.* Cajoler, enjôler.
cajoler, *n.* Cajoleur, *m.*, cajoleuse, *f.*
cajolery, *n.* Cajolerie, *f.*
cake [keik], *n.* Gâteau; morceau (of soap), *m.*, tablette (of chocolate etc.), *f.*; tourteau (of oilseed etc.); pain (of wax), *m.*; masse, croûte (concreted matter), *f.—v.i.* Se cailler, se prendre, se coller, faire croûte. *Caked with mud,* plaqué de boue.
calabash ['kæləbæʃ], *n.* Calebasse, gourde, *f.*
calabash-tree, *n.* Calebassier, *m.*
calamine ['kæləmain], *n.* Calamine, *f.*
calamitous [kə'læmitəs], *a.* Calamiteux, désastreux, funeste. **calamitously,** *adv.* Désastreusement. **calamity,** *n.* Calamité, *f.*, désastre, malheur, *m.*
calamus ['kæləməs], *n.* Roseau, rotin, *m.*
calash [kə'læʃ], *n.* Calèche, *f.*
calcareous [kæl'kɛəriəs], *a.* Calcaire.
calceolaria [kælsiə'lɛəriə], *n.* (*Bot.*) Calcéolaire, *f.*
calcic ['kælsik], *a.* Calcique. **calcify,** *v.t.* Calcifier.—*v.i.* Se calcifier.
calcine ['kælsin *or* -sain], *v.t.* Calciner.—*v.i.* Se calciner. **calcination,** *n.* Calcination, *f.*
calcite, *n.* Calcite, *f.* **calcium,** *n.* Calcium, *m. Calcium carbide,* carbure de calcium, *m.*
calc-spar ['kælkspɑ:], *n.* Spath calcaire, *m.*
calc-tuff, *n.* Tuf calcaire, *m.*
calculable ['kælkjuləbl], *a.* Calculable. **calculate,** *v.t.* Calculer; adapter; (*Am.*) penser, croire.—*v.i.* Compter (sur). **calculated,** *a.* (*colloq.*) Adapté, propre (à). *Calculated insolence,* insolence délibérée, *f.* **calculating-machine,** *n.* Machine à calculer, *f.* **calculation** [-'leiʃən], *n.* Calcul, compte, *m.*; (*pl.*) prévisions, *f.pl.* **calculative,** *a.* De calcul. **calculator,** *n.* Calculateur, *m.*
calculous ['kælkjuləs], *a.* Calculeux.
calculus ['kælkjuləs], *n.* (*Med.*) Calcul, *m.*; (*Math.*) calcul infinitésimal, *m.*
caldron [CAULDRON].
Caledonia [kæli'douniə]. La Calédonie, *f.* **New Caledonia,** La Nouvelle Calédonie, *f.*
Caledonian [kæli'douniən], *a.* Calédonien.—*n.* Calédonien, *m.*, Calédonienne, *f.*
calefacient [kæli'feiʃənt], *a.* Réchauffant. **calefaction,** *n.* Caléfaction, *f.* **calefactive** *or* **calefactory,** *a.* Qui chauffe. **calefactory,** *n.* Caléfacteur, *m.* **calefy,** *v.t.* Échauffer.—*v.i.* S'échauffer.
calendar ['kæləndə], *n.* Calendrier, *m.*; (*Law*) liste, *f. Calendar month,* mois solaire, *m.*—*v.t.* Classer, cataloguer.
calender ['kæləndə], *n.* Calandre, *f.—v.t.* Calandrer. **calendering,** *n.* Calandrage, *m.*
calends ['kæləndz], *n.pl.* Calendes, *f.pl.*
calf [kɑ:f], *n.* (*pl.* **calves**) Veau; mollet (of the leg), *m. Calf binding,* (*Bookb.*) reliure en veau, *f.; calf bound,* relié en veau; *calf's sweetbread,* ris de veau, *m.; fatted calf,* veau gras; *with calf,* pleine (of cows).
calf-love, *n.* Passion romantique de jeunesse, *f.*
calibre ['kælibə], *n.* Calibre, (*Tech.*) compas, *m.* **calibrate,** *v.t.* Calibrer, graduer; étalonner. **calibration,** *n.* Calibrage, *m.*
calico ['kælikou], *n.* Calicot, *m. Printed calico,* indienne, toile peinte, *f.* **calico-printer,** *n.* Imprimeur d'indiennes, *m.*
California [kæli'fɔ:niə]. La Californie, *f.*

calipash ['kælipæʃ], *n.* Sous-carapace (gélatineuse), *f.* **calipee,** *n.* Partie gélatineuse sous le ventre (de la tortue).
caliph ['keilif], *n.* Calife, *m.* **caliphate** ['kælifeit], *n.* Califat, *m.*
Calixtus [kə'likstəs]. Calixte, *m.*
calk (1) [kɔ:k], *v.t.* Ferrer à glace (a horse etc.).
calk (2) [CAULK].
calkin ['kælkin], *n.* Crampon, *m.*
calking-iron ['kɔ:kiŋaiən], *n.* Ferrure à glace, *f.*
call [kɔ:l], *n.* Appel, cri, *m.*; voix, *f.*; (*Naut.*) sifflet, *m.*; (*fig.*) obligation, nécessité, *f.*, devoir, *m.*; demande, invitation; vocation; visite *f.*; coup de téléphone, *m.*; appel de fonds, *m. At anybody's call,* aux ordres de tout le monde; *at call,* à vue; *bird-call,* appeau, *m.; call to order,* appel à l'ordre, *m.; to have a close call,* l'échapper belle; *to pay someone a call,* rendre visite à quelqu'un, passer chez quelqu'un; *you have no call to,* vous n'avez pas le droit de; *within call,* à portée de voix.
 v.i. Appeler, crier; venir *or* aller (chez), faire visite (à); (*Naut.*) toucher (à). *To call again* (to come), repasser chez, revenir; *to call at,* passer par, s'arrêter à (of trains etc.), faire escale (of ships); *to call on,* inviter, exhorter (à), prier, conjurer (de); rendre visite à; *to call out,* crier au secours; *to call upon,* sommer; passer chez. (*Rad.*) *This is London calling,* ici Londres.
 v.t. Appeler; nommer, qualifier (de); convoquer; rappeler. *To be called Peter,* s'appeler Pierre; *to call a taxi,* faire venir un taxi; *to call aside,* prendre à part; *to call back,* rappeler; *to call down,* appeler, faire tomber, attirer; *to call for,* demander, exiger, aller prendre; *to call forth,* produire, faire naître; *to call in,* faire rentrer; *to call in a doctor,* faire venir un médecin; *to call in money,* retirer de la monnaie de la circulation; *to call in question,* mettre en doute; *to call into action,* mettre en action; *to call into play,* mettre en jeu; *to call names,* injurier, dire des sottises; *to call off,* rappeler, rompre, décommander; *to call out,* appeler, crier, appeler en duel; (*Mil.*) appeler sous les drapeaux, mobiliser; donner un ordre de grève; *to call over the coals,* blâmer, gronder; *to call the roll,* faire l'appel; *to call together,* assembler, réunir; *to call to mind,* se rappeler; *to call to order,* rappeler à l'ordre; *to call to witness,* prendre à témoin; *to call up,* faire monter, réveiller, faire lever, mobiliser; (*fig.*) évoquer, (*Law*) appeler, citer.
call-box, *n.* Cabine téléphonique, *f.*
call-boy ['kɔ:lbɔi], *n.* (*Theat.*) Avertisseur, *m.*
caller, *n.* Visiteur, *m.* (*Teleph.*) celui, celle qui appelle.
calligraphic [kæli'græfik], *a.* Calligraphique.
calligraphy [kə'ligrəfi], *n.* Calligraphie, *f.*
calling, *n.* Appel, *m.*; profession, vocation, *f.*, métier, état, *m.*
callipers ['kælipəz], *n.* Compas de calibre, *m.*
calliper-square, *n.* Pied à coulisse, *m.*
callisthenics [kælis'θeniks], *n.pl.* Callisthénie, *f.*
callosity [kə'lɔsiti], *n.* Callosité, *f.*
callous ['kæləs], *a.* Calleux, endurci; insensible. **callously,** *adv.* Durement, impitoyablement. **callousness,** *n.* Insensibilité, *f.*, endurcissement, *m.*

callow ['kælou], *a.* Sans plume; (*fig.*) jeune, novice, blanc-bec.

call-sign, *n.* (*Rad. Teleg.*) Indicatif d'appel, *m.*

call-up, *n.* (*Mil.*) Appel sous les drapeaux, *m.*

callus ['kæləs], *n.* Cal, calus, *m.*, callosité, *f.*

calm [kɑːm], *a.* Calme. *To get calm,* se calmer.—*n.* Calme, *m.*—*v.t.* Calmer, apaiser.

calmly, *adv.* Avec calme, tranquillement.

calmness, *n.* Calme, *m.*, tranquillité, *f.*

calomel ['kæləmel], *n.* Calomel, *m.*

caloric [kə'lɔrik], *n.* Calorique, *m.*—*a.* De calorique.

calorie, *n.* Calorie, *f.*

calorific [kælə'rifik], *a.* Calorifique. **calorimeter,** *n.* Calorimètre, *m.* **calorimetry,** *n.* Calorimétrie, *f.*

caltrop ['kæltrɔp], *n.* Chausse-trape, *f.*; (*Bot.*) chardon étoilé, *m.*

calumet ['kæljumet], *n.* Calumet, *m.*

calumniate [kə'lʌmnieit], *v.t.* Calomnier. **calumniation,** *n.* Calomnie, *f.* **calumniator,** *n.* Calomniateur, *m.* **calumniatory** or **calumnious,** *a.* Calomnieux. **calumniously,** *adv.* Calomnieusement.

calumny ['kæləmni], *n.* Calomnie, *f.*

calvary ['kælvəri], *n.* Calvaire, *m.*; chemin de la croix, *m.*

calve [kɑːv], *v.i.* Vêler. **calves,** *n.pl.* [CALF].

Calvinism ['kælvinizm], *n.* Calvinisme, *m.* **Calvinist,** *n.* Calviniste, *m.* or *f.*

calyx ['keiliks or 'kæliks], *n.* Calice, *m.*

cam [kæm], *n.* (*Mech.*) Came, *f.* **cam-shaft,** *n.* Arbre à cames, *m.*

camarilla [kæmə'rilə], *n.* Camarilla, *f.*

camber ['kæmbə], *v.t.* Cambrer.—*v.i.* Se cambrer.—*n.* Cambrure, *f.*

cambist ['kæmbist], *n.* (*Fin.*) Changeur, cambiste, *m.*

Cambodia [kæm'boudiə]. Le Cambodge, *m.*

cambric ['keimbrik], *n.* Batiste, *f.* *Cambric muslin,* percale, *f.*

came (1), *past* [COME].

came (2) [keim], *n.* Plomb à vitraux, *m.*

camel ['kæməl], *n.* Chameau, *m.*, chamelle, *f.* **camel-backed,** *a.* À dos de chameau, bossu. **camel-driver** or **cameleer,** *n.* Chamelier, *m.* **camel's-hair,** *n.* Poil de chameau, *m.* *Camel's-hair brush,* pinceau, *m.*

camellia or **camelia** [kə'miːljə], *n.* Camélia, *m.*

*camelopard** [kə'meləpɑːd or 'kæmiləpɑːd], *n.* Girafe, *f.*, caméléopard, *m.*

cameo ['kæmiou], *n.* Camée, *m.*

camera ['kæmərə], *n.* Appareil (photographique), *m.* *Camera lucida,* chambre claire, *f.*; *camera obscura,* chambre noire, *f.*; *hand camera,* appareil à main, *m.* **camera-man,** *n.* Photographe, *m.* (of newspapers); (*Cine. Tel.*) opérateur, cameraman, *m.*

cami-knickers [kæmi'nikəz], *n.pl.* Chemise-culotte, *f.*

camisole ['kæmisoul], *n.* Cache-corset, *m.*

camlet ['kæmlit], *n.* (*Tex.*) Camelot, *m.*

camomile ['kæməmail], *n.* Camomille, *f.*

camouflage ['kæmuflɑːʒ], *n.* Camouflage, *m.*—*v.t.* Camoufler.

camp [kæmp], *n.* Camp, *m.* *To break up a camp,* lever un camp; *to pitch a camp,* asseoir un camp.—*v.i.* Camper. **camp-bed,** *n.* Lit de camp, *m.* **camp-stool,** *n.* Pliant, *m.*

campaign [kæm'pein], *n.* Campagne, *f.*—*v.i.*

Faire campagne. **campaigner,** *n.* Vieux soldat, *m.*

campanile [kæmpə'niːli], *n.* Campanile, *m.*

campanula [kəm'pænjulə], *n.* (*Bot.*) Campanule, *f.* **campanulate,** *a.* Campanulé.

campeachy wood [kæm'piːtʃi wud], *n.* Bois de campêche, *m.*

camper, *n.* Campeur, *m.*, campeuse, *f.*

camphor ['kæmfə], *n.* Camphre, *m.* **camphorated,** *a.* Camphré.

camping, *n.* (*Mil.*) Campement; camping, *m.* *To go camping,* faire du camping. **camping-ground,** *n.* Terrain de camping, *m.*

campion ['kæmpjən], *n.* (*Bot.*) Lychnis, compagnon, *m.*

campus ['kæmpəs], *n.* (*Am.*) Terrains d'un collège ou d'une université, *m.pl.*

can (1) [kæn], *n.* Pot, broc, bidon, *m.*; boîte en fer blanc, *f.*—*v.t.* Mettre en boîte. **can-opener,** *n.* Ouvre-boîte, *m.*

can (2) [kæn], *v.aux.* (*negative* **cannot,** *past* and *subj.* **could**) Pouvoir (to be able); savoir (to know how to). *Can I?* puis-je? *can it be true?* est-il possible que . . .? *he can read,* il sait lire; *I can do it,* je peux *or* je sais le faire; *that cannot be,* cela ne se peut pas; *you can but try,* vous pouvez toujours essayer.

Canada ['kænədə]. Le Canada.

Canadian [kə'neidiən], *a.* and *n.* Canadien.

canal [kə'næl], *n.* Canal, *m.*

canaliculate [kænə'likjulət] or **canaliculated,** *a.* (*Physiol.*) Strié, canaliculé.

canalization [kænəlai'zeifən], *n.* Canalisation, *f.*

canalize ['kænəlaiz], *v.t.* Canaliser.

Canary [kə'neəri] **Islands.** Les Îles Canaries, *f.pl.*

canary [kə'neəri], *n.* *Vin des Canaries (wine); (*Orn.*) serin, *m.*, serine, *f.* **canary-grass,** *n.* Alpiste, *m.* **canary-seed,** *n.* Millet, *m.*

canasta [kə'næstə], *n.* (*Cards*) Canasta, *f.*

cancel ['kænsəl], *v.t.* Annuler; effacer, biffer, rayer; oblitérer (un timbre); décommander; (*Comm.*) résilier.—*n.* (*Print.*) Feuillet refait, *m.* **cancellated,** *a.* (*Nat. Hist.*) Réticulé, cellulaire. **cancellation,** *n.* Annulation, *f.*; résiliation, *f.*, oblitération, *f.*

cancer ['kænsə], *n.* Cancer, *m.* **canceration,** *n.* Ulcération cancéreuse, *f.* **cancerous,** *a.* Cancéreux.

cancriform ['kæŋkrifɔːm], *a.* Cancériforme.

candelabrum [kændi'leibrəm] or **candelabra,** *n.* (*pl.* **candelabra** or **candelabras**) Candélabre, *m.*

candid ['kændid], *a.* Sincère, franc, ingénu.

candidate ['kændidit], *n.* Aspirant, candidat, *m.* **candidature,** *n.* Candidature, *f.*

candidly, *adv.* Franchement, de bonne foi.

candidness, *n.* Candeur, sincérité, bonne foi, *f.*

candied ['kændid], *a.* Candi. *Candied-peel,* écorce (de citron) confite (au sucre), *f.*

candle [kændl], *n.* Chandelle; bougie; (*fig.*) lumière, *f.* *Of 100 candle-power,* de cent bougies; *she couldn't hold a candle to you,* elle n'est rien à côté de vous; *the game is not worth the candle,* le jeu ne vaut pas la chandelle; *to burn the candle at both ends,* (*fig.*) brûler la chandelle par les deux bouts; *wax candle,* bougie.—*v.t.* Mirer (des œufs).

candle-end, *n.* Bout de chandelle, *m.*

candle-grease, n. Suif, m. **candle-light,** n. Lumière de la chandelle, f. *By candle-light,* à la chandelle.
Candlemas ['kændlməs], n. La Chandeleur, f.
candlestick, n. Chandelier, m. *Bedroom candlestick,* bougeoir, m.
candour ['kændə], n. Franchise, sincérité, bonne foi, f.
candy ['kændi], n. Candi, m.; (*Am.*) bonbons, m.pl.—v.t. Faire candir.—v.i. Se candir. **candy-striped,** a. Pékiné.
candytuft, n. (*Bot.*) Ibéride, f.
cane [kein], n. Canne, f.; jonc, m., tige (of an umbrella etc.), f.; (*Agric.*) cep, m.—v.t. Donner des coups de canne à. **cane-chair,** n. Chaise cannée, f. **cane-mill,** n. Moulin pour broyer les cannes à sucre, m. **cane-sugar,** n. Sucre de canne, m. **cane-trash,** n. Bagasse, f. **caning,** n. Coups de canne, m.pl., râclée, f.
canicular [kə'nikjulə], a. Caniculaire.
canine ['kænain], a. Canin, de chien.—n. Canine, œillère (tooth), f.
canister ['kænistə], n. Boîte en fer blanc; boîte à thé, f. **canister-shot,* n. Mitraille, f.
canker ['kæŋkə], n. Chancre; (*fig.*) ver rongeur; fléau, m.—v.t. Ronger; (*fig.*) corrompre, empoisonner.—v.i. Se ronger; (*fig.*) se gangrener, se corrompre. **canker-bit,* a. Gangrène. **canker-worm,** n. Ver rongeur, m. **cankered,** a. Rongé, gangrené.
cankerous, a. Chancreux.
canned [kænd], a. Conservé en boîtes (of fruit etc.); (*fam.*) enregistré, de conserve (of music); (*pop.*) enivré, soûl. **canning,** n. Mise en conserve, f.
cannery ['kænəri], n. Conserverie, f.
cannibal ['kænibəl], n. Cannibale, anthropophage, m. or f. **cannibalism,** n. Cannibalisme, m.
cannily ['kænili], adv. Prudemment.
cannon ['kænən], n. Canon; (*Billiards*) carambolage, m.—v.i. Caramboler. **cannon-ball,** n. Boulet de canon, m. **cannon-bone,** n. Canon (of a horse), m. **cannon-fodder,** n. Chair à canon, f. **cannon-shot,** n. Coup de canon, m. *Within cannon-shot,* à portée de canon. **cannonade,** n. Canonnade, f.—v.t. Canonner.
cannot [CAN (2)].
cannula ['kænjulə], n. (*Surg.*) Canule; (*Chem.*) burette, f.
cannular ['kænjulə], a. Tubuleux, tubulaire.
canny ['kæni], a. (*Sc.*) Prudent, avisé, rusé. *To play canny,* jouer un jeu d'attente.
canoe [kə'nu:], n. Canot, m. *Canadian canoe,* canoë canadien; *Rob-Roy canoe,* périssoire, f.; *Indian canoe,* pirogue, f.; *to paddle one's own canoe,* se tirer d'affaire tout seul.—v.i. Faire du canoë *or* de la périssoire.
canoeist, n. Canoëiste.
canon ['kænən], n. Chanoine; canon (rule), m.; (*Print.*) corps 40 *or* 44. *Canon law,* droit canon, m. **canoness,** n. Chanoinesse, f.
canonical [kə'nɔnikl], a. Canonique.—n.pl. Vêtements sacerdotaux, m.pl. **canonically,** adv. Canoniquement. **canonicalness,** n. Canonicité, f. **canonicate,** n. Canonicat, m.
canonist ['kænənist], n. Canoniste, m.
canonization [kænənai'zeiʃən], n. Canonisation, f.
canonize ['kænənaiz], v.t. Canoniser.

canonry, n. Canonicat, m.
cañon [CANYON].
canoodle [kə'nu:dl], v.i. (*pop.*) Se faire des mamours.
canopy ['kænəpi], n. Dais; (*Arch.*) baldaquin, m.; voûte (of heaven), f. *Canopy bed,* lit à baldaquin, m.—v.t. Couvrir d'un dais.
cant (1) [kænt], n. Cant, langage hypocrite, m.; afféterie; hypocrisie, cafarderie, f.; jargon, argot, m.—v.i. Parler avec afféterie *or* avec affectation.
cant (2) [kænt], n. (*Arch.*) Pan coupé, m.—v.t. Pousser, jeter de côté, incliner, renverser; biseauter.
can't [kɑ:nt] [*abbrev. of* CANNOT].
Cantabrigian [kæntə'bridʒiən] or (*colloq.*) Cantab ['kæntæb], a. De Cambridge.—n. Étudiant de Cambridge, m.
cantaloup ['kæntəlu:p], n. Cantaloup, m.
cantankerous [kæn'tæŋkərəs], a. Acariâtre, revêche, bourru. **cantankerousness,** n. Humeur acariâtre, f.
cantata [kæn'tɑ:tə], n. Cantate, f.
canteen [kæn'ti:n], n. Cantine, f., restaurant, m.; bidon (tin), m. *Canteen of cutlery,* ménagère, f.
canter ['kæntə], n. Petit galop, m. *To win in a canter,* gagner facilement, arriver dans un fauteuil.—v.i. Aller au petit galop.
canterbury ['kæntəbəri], n. Casier à musique, m.
Canterbury-bell, n. (*Hort.*) Campanule, f.
cantharis ['kænθəris], n. (*pl.* cantharides [kæn'θæridi:z]) Cantharide, f.
canticle ['kæntikl], n. Cantique, m. (*pl.*) *The Canticles,* le Cantique des cantiques.
cantilever ['kæntiliːvə], n. (*Arch.*) Encorbellement, modillon, m.
canting ['kæntiŋ], a. Hypocrite, cagot, cafard; (*Her.*) parlant. **cantingly,** adv. Avec hypocrisie; avec affectation.
cantle [kæntl], n. Morceau, m.; parcelle, f., troussequin (of a saddle), m.
canto ['kæntou], n. Chant, m.
canton ['kæntən], n. Canton, m.—v.t. Diviser en cantons; (*Mil.*) [kæn'tu:n], cantonner. **cantonment,** n. Cantonnement, m.
canula [CANNULA].
canvas ['kænvəs], n. Toile, f.; tableau, m., peinture; voile, voile à voiles (sail-cloth), f. *Canvas village,* village de toile, m.; *under canvas,* sous la tente. **canvas-work,** n. Tapisserie au canevas, f.
canvass ['kænvəs], n. Débat, m., discussion; sollicitation de suffrages; (*Comm.*) sollicitation de commandes, f.—v.t. Agiter, discuter; solliciter.—v.i. Solliciter des suffrages; solliciter des commandes, faire la place.
canvasser, n. Agent électoral; (*Comm.*) représentant, m. **canvassing,** n. Propagande électorale, f.; (*Comm.*) prospection, f., (*fam.*) porte à porte, m. inv.
cany ['keini], a. Plein de roseaux; de jonc.
canyon ['kænjən], n. Gorge, f., défilé, m.
caoutchouc ['kautʃu:k], n. Caoutchouc, m.
cap [kæp], n. Bonnet (woman's), m.; (*Universities*) toque; casquette (man's peaked cap); barrette (a cardinal's); (*Fire-arms*) capsule, amorce, f.; chapeau (of a lens etc.); capuchon (of fountain-pen), m.; (*Naut.*) chouquet; (*Horol.*) recouvrement, m., cuvette (of a watch), f. *Cap and bells,* marotte, f.; *cap in*

hand, le bonnet à la main; *skull cap*, calotte, *f.*; *if the cap fits, wear it!* À bon entendeur, salut; *to get one's cap*, (*Ftb.*) être choisi comme joueur de l'équipe première *or* internationale, gagner sa cape; *to set one's cap at*, chercher à captiver.—*v.t.* Coiffer, couvrir; saluer, se découvrir devant; (*fig.*) couronner, surpasser. *To cap a joke*, renchérir sur un bon mot. **capped**, *a.* Coiffé; couronné.

capability [keipə'biliti], *n.* Capacité, *f.*
capable, *a.* Capable; susceptible (de); compétent.
capacious [kə'peiʃəs], *a.* Ample, vaste, spacieux. **capaciousness**, *n.* Capacité, étendue, *f.* **capacitate**, *v.t.* Rendre capable de, donner pouvoir à.
capacity [kə'pæsiti], *n.* Capacité, *f. In the capacity of*, en qualité de.
cap-à-pie [kæpə'pi:], *adv.* De pied en cap.
caparison [kə'pærizn], *n.* Caparaçon, *m.*—*v.t.* Caparaçonner.
cape (1) [keip], *n.* Cap, promontoire, *m.*
cape (2) [keip], *n.* Pèlerine, cape (mantle), *f.*; (*Ch.*) camail, *m.*
caper (1) ['keipə], *n.* Bond, entrechat, *m. To cut a caper*, faire un entrechat.—*v.i.* Cabrioler; faire des entrechats, bondir, sauter.
caper (2) ['keipə], *n.* (*Bot.*) Câpre, *f. Caper sauce*, sauce aux câpres, *f.*
capercaillie *or* **capercailzie** [kæpe'keilji], *n.* Coq de bruyère, grand tétras, *m.*
Capernaum [kə'pə:niəm]. Capharnaüm, *m.*
capias ['keipiæs], *n.* (*Law*) Prise de corps, *f.*, mandat d'arrêt, *m.*
capillarity [kæpi'læriti], *n.* Capillarité, *f.*
capillary [kə'piləri], *a.* Capillaire. *The capillaries*, les vaisseaux capillaires, *m.pl.*
capital ['kæpitl], *n.* Capital, *m.*, capitaux, *m.pl.*; capitale (town), *f.*; (*Comm.*) fonds, *m.*; (*Arch.*) chapiteau, *m.*; (*Print.*) majuscule, capitale, *f. To make capital out of*, exploiter. —*a.* Capital, essentiel; (*colloq.*) excellent, parfait; (*Print.*) majuscule. *Capital fellow*, excellent garçon; *capital ship*, cuirassé, *m.*; *that's capital*, c'est parfait. **capitalism**, *n.* Capitalisme, *m.* **capitalist**, *n.* Capitaliste, *m. or f.* **capitalization** [-əlaizeiʃən], *n.* Capitalisation, *f.* **capitalize** [-laiz], *v.t.* Capitaliser. **capitally**, *adv.* Principalement; admirablement, à merveille.
capitation [kæpi'teiʃən], *n.* Capitation, *f. Capitation grant*, allocation de tant par tête, *f.*
capitol ['kæpitɔl], *n.* Capitole, *m.*
Capitoline [kə'pitəlain] **Hill.** Le Mont Capitolin, *m.*
capitular [kə'pitjulə], *a.* Capitulaire. **capitularly**, *adv.* Capitulairement. **capitulary**, *n.* Capitulaire, *m.* **capitulate**, *v.i.* Capituler.
capitulation [kəpitju'leiʃən], *n.* Capitulation, *f.*
capon ['keipən], *n.* Chapon, *m.* **caponize**, *v.t.* Chaponner.
caponiere [kæpə'niə], *n.* (*Fort.*) Cáponnière, *f.*
capot [kə'pɔt], *n.* (*Cards etc.*) Capot, *m.*—*v.t.* Faire capot.
capote [kə'pout], *n.* Manteau à capuchon, *m.*
caprice [kə'pri:s], *n.* Caprice, *m.*
capricious [kə'priʃəs], *a.* Capricieux. **capriciously**, *adv.* Capricieusement. **capriciousness**, *n.* Caractère capricieux, *m.*, humeur fantasque, *f.*, *or* inégale.

Capricorn ['kæprikɔ:n], *n.* Capricorne, *m. The Tropic of Capricorn*, le tropique du Capricorne.
caprification [kæprifi'keiʃən], *n.* Caprification, *f.*
capsicum ['kæpsikəm], *n.* (*Bot.*) Piment, *m.*
capsize [kæp'saiz], *v.i.* Chavirer (boat); capoter (motor).—*v.t.* Faire chavirer.
capstan ['kæpstən], *n.* Cabestan, *m. To man the capstan*, armer le cabestan.
capsular ['kæpsjulə], *a.* Capsulaire. **capsule**, *n.* Capsule, *f.*
captain ['kæptin], *n.* Capitaine, *m. Captain of a gun*, chef de pièce, *m.*; (*Naut.*) *captain of a top*, chef de hune; *captain of the watch*, chef de quart, *m.*—*v.t.* (*spt.*) Être capitaine de (a team). **captaincy** *or* **captainship**, *n.* Grade de capitaine, capitainat, *m.*; commandement, *m.* (of team).
captation [kæp'teiʃən], *n.* (*Law*) Captation, *f.*
caption ['kæpʃən], *n.* Prise de corps, arrestation; saisie (of things), *f.*; en-tête (of chapters etc.), *m.*; légende (of photographs etc.), *f.*; (*Cine.*) sous-titre, *m.*
captious ['kæpʃəs], *a.* Insidieux, chicaneur. **captiousness**, *n.* Disposition à la critique, *f.*; esprit de chicane; sophisme, *m.*
captivate ['kæptiveit], *v.t.* Captiver; charmer, séduire. **captivating**, *a.* Enchanteur, séduisant. **captivation**, *n.* Assujettissement, *m.*; séduction, *f.*
captive ['kæptiv], *n.* Captif, *m.*, captive, *f.*, prisonnier, *m.*, prisonnière, *f.*—*a.* Captif.
captivity [kæp'tiviti], *n.* Captivité, *f.*
captor ['kæptə], *n.* Capteur; auteur d'une prise; (*Navy*) vaisseau prenant; (*Mil.*) auteur d'une capture, *m.*
capture ['kæptʃə], *n.* Capture; prise, arrestation, *f.*—*v.t.* Capturer, prendre, arrêter; (*Rad.*) capter.
Capua ['kæpjuə]. Capoue, *f.*
capuchin ['kæpjutʃin], *n.* Capucin, *m.*, capucine, *f.*; mante à capuchon (woman's hood), *f.*
car [kɑ:], *n.* (*Lit.*) Char, chariot, *m.*; nacelle (of a balloon), *f.*; (*Motor.*) auto, voiture, *f.*; (*Rail.*) wagon; (*Tramway*) tramway, *m. Car licence* (*Motor.*), carte grise, *f.*; *dining-car*, wagon-restaurant, *m.*; *sleeping-car*, wagon-lit, *m.* **carful** *or* **car-load**, *n.* Voiturée, *f.*
car-park, *n.* Stationnement pour autos, *m.*
carabine ['kærəbain], *n.* [CARBINE].
caracol ['kærəkɔl] *or* **caracole**, *n.* Caracole, *f.*; (*Arch.*) escalier en spirale, *m.*—*v.i.* Caracoler.
caramel ['kærəmel], *n.* Caramel, *m.*
carapace ['kærəpeis], *n.* Carapace, *f.*
carat ['kærət], *n.* Carat, *m.*
caravan [kærə'væn *or* 'kærəvæn], *n.* Caravane, *f.*; roulotte; (*Motor.*) caravane, *f.*—*v.i.* Voyager en caravane. **carava(n)ning**, *n.* Voyage en caravane, *m.*
caravanserai [kærə'vænsərai], *n.* Caravansérail, *m.*
caravel [kærə'vel] *or* **carvel**, *n.* Caravelle, *f.*
caraway ['kærəwei], *n.* (*Bot.*) Carvi, cumin des prés, *m. Caraway seed*, graine de carvi, *f.*
carbide ['kɑ:baid], *n.* Carbure, *m.*
carbine ['kɑ:bain] *or* **carabine**, *n.* Carabine, *f.*
carbineer [kɑ:bi'niə], *n.* *or* **carabineer**, *n.* Carabinier, *m.*

carbohydrate [ka:bou'haidreit], *n.* Hydrate de carbone, *m.*

carbolic [ka:'bɔlik], *a.* Phénique. *Carbolic acid*, acide phénique, phénol, *m.*

carbon ['ka:bən], *n.* (*Chem.*) Carbone; (*Elec.*) charbon, *m. Carbon copy*, double au papier carbone, *m.*; *carbon paper*, papier carbone, *m.* **carbonate**, *n.* Carbonate, *m.*

carbonic [ka:'bɔnik], *a.* Carbonique.

carboniferous [ka:bə'nifərəs], *a.* Carbonifère.

carbonization [-nai'zeiʃən], *n.* Carbonisation, *f.*

carbonize ['ka:bənaiz], *v.t.* Carboniser.

carboy ['ka:bɔi], *n.* Tourie, bonbonne, *f.*

carbuncle ['ka:bʌŋkl], *n.* Escarboucle, *f.*; (*Med.*) charbon, furoncle, anthrax, *m.* **carbuncled**, *a.* Garni d'escarboucles; bourgeonné (of the nose). **carbuncular**, *a.* (*Med.*) Charbonneux.

carburation [ka:bju'reiʃən], *n.* Carburation, *f.*

carburet ['ka:buret] or **carburate** [-reit], *v.t.* Carburer. **carburetted**, *a.* Carburé.

carburettor [ka:bju'retə], *n.* Carburateur, *m.*

carcajou ['ka:kəʒu:], *n.* Carcajou, *m.*

carcanet ['ka:kənet], *n.* Parure, *f.*; collier de pierreries, *m.*

carcase or **carcass** ['ka:kəs], *n.* Carcasse, *f.*; cadavre, corps mort, *m.*

carcinoma [ka:si'noumə], *n.* (*Med.*) Carcinome, *m.* **carcinomatous**, *a.* Carcinomateux.

card [ka:d], *n.* Carte à jouer; fiche, *f.*, billet de faire-part, *m.*; (*Manuf.*) carde; (*Naut.*) rose des vents, *f.*; (*fam.*) original, drôle de type, *m. It is on the cards*, c'est fort probable; *to lay* or *put one's cards on the table*, mettre cartes sur table; *to throw up one's cards*, désespérer; *visiting card*, carte de visite, *f.*—*v.t.* Carder. **cardboard**, *n.* Carton, *m.* **card-case**, *n.* Carnet de visites, étui à cartes, *m.* **card-index**, *n.* Fichier, *m.*—*v.t.* Encarter. **card-player**, *n.* Joueur de cartes, *m.* **card-sharper**, *n.* Grec, fileur de cartes, *m.* **card-table**, *n.* Table de jeu, *f.* **carder**, *n.* Cardeur, *m.*; cardeuse (machine), *f.* **carding**, *n.* Cardage, *m.* *Carding house*, carderie, *f.*

cardamine ['ka:dəmain], *n.* (*Bot.*) Cardamine, *f.*

cardamom ['ka:dəmɔm], *n.* (*Bot.*) Cardamome, *m.*

cardiac ['ka:diæk], *a.* Cardiaque.—*n.* Cardiaque, *m.*

cardialgic [ka:di'ældʒik], *a.* Cardialgique.

cardigan ['ka:digən], *n.* Gilet de tricot (à manches), *m.*

cardinal ['ka:dinl], *n.* Cardinal, *m.*—*a.* Cardinal, principal, fondamental. *Cardinal bird*, cardinal, *m.*; *cardinal flower*, cardinale, *f.*; *cardinal points*, points cardinaux, *m.pl.* **cardinalate** or **cardinalship**, *n.* Cardinalat, *m.*

cardiogram ['ka:diogræm], *n.* (*Med.*) Cardiogramme, *m.* **cardiograph**, *n.* Cardiographe, *m.* **cardiologist** [-di'ɔlədʒist], *n.* (*Med.*) Cardiologue, *m.* **cardiology**, *n.* Cardiologie, *f.*

care [keə], *n.* Soin; souci, *m.*, sollicitude; précaution, attention, *f. Care of*, aux bons soins de, chez; *take care he does not touch you*, prenez garde qu'il ne vous touche; *take care of yourself*, soignez-vous bien; *take great care not to do it*, gardez-vous bien de le faire; *to put under the care of*, confier aux soins de; *to take care not to*, se garder de; *to take care of*, avoir soin de, s'occuper de; *to take care to*, avoir soin de (with infinit.); *to the care of*, aux soins de; *with care*, avec soin; fragile (on parcels etc.).—*v.i.* Se soucier, s'inquiéter (de). *I couldn't care less!* je m'en fiche! *I don't care!* cela m'est égal, je m'en moque! *I don't care for it*, je n'y tiens pas; *to care for*, tenir à; *what do I care?* qu'est-ce que cela me fait? **carefree**, *a.* Libre de soucis; insouciant. **caretaker**, *n.* Gardien, concierge; (*sch.*) dépensier, *m.* (*Pol.*) *Caretaker government*, gouvernement chargé d'expédier les affaires courantes, *m.* **care-worn**, *a.* Usé par le chagrin *or* les soucis.

careen [kə'ri:n], *v.t.* Mettre en carène, caréner.—*v.i.* Donner de la bande. **careening**, *n.* Carénage, *m.*

career [kə'riə], *n.* Carrière, course, *f. Careers master*, orienteur professionnel, *m.*; *in full career*, en pleine course.—*v.i.* Courir rapidement. *To career over*, parcourir. **careerist**, *n.* Arriviste.

careful ['keəful], *a.* Soigneux, attentif; prudent, économe, ménager; plein de soucis, soucieux. *Be careful!* prenez garde! faites attention! **carefully**, *adv.* Soigneusement, avec soin, attentivement. **carefulness**, *n.* Attention, *f.*; soin, *m.*

careless, *a.* Insouciant, nonchalant; négligent (de), indifférent (à). **carelessly**, *adv.* Avec insouciance, nonchalamment, négligemment. **carelessness**, *n.* Insouciance, nonchalance; négligence, *f.*, manque de soin, *m.*, indifférence, inattention, étourderie, *f.*

caress [kə'res], *n.* Caresse, *f.*—*v.t.* Caresser.

caret ['kærət], *n.* Signe d'omission, renvoi, *m.*

cargo ['ka:gou], *n.* Cargaison, *f.*, chargement, *m.* **cargo-boat**, *n.* Vapeur de charge, cargo, *m.*

Caribbean [kæri'bi:ən] **Sea.** La mer des Antilles, *f.pl.*

Caribbee ['kæribi:] **Islands.** Les Antilles, les (îles) Caraïbes, *f.pl.*

caribou ['kæribu:], *n.* Caribou, *m.*

caricature [kærikə'tjuə *or* 'kærikətjə], *n.* Caricature, charge, *f.*—*v.t.* Caricaturer, faire la charge de.

caricaturist [kærikə'tjuərist], *n.* Caricaturiste, *m.*

caries ['kɛərii:z], *n.* Carie, *f.* **carious**, *a.* Carié, gâté. *To become carious*, se carier.

carillon [kə'riljən], *n.* Carillon, *m.*

carking ['ka:kiŋ], *a.* Cuisant (of care); rongeur.

carman ['ka:mən], *n.* (*pl.* **carmen**) Charretier, *m.*; camionneur; livreur, *m.*

Carmelite ['ka:məlait], *n.* Carme, *m. Carmelite nun*, carmélite, *f.*—*a.* De carme, de carmélite.

carminative ['ka:minətiv], *a. and n.* Carminatif.

carmine ['ka:main], *n. and a.* Carmin, *m.*

carnage ['ka:nidʒ], *n.* Carnage, *m.*

carnal [ka:nl], *a.* Charnel. *Carnal knowledge*, connaissance charnelle, *f.* **carnality**, *n.* Sensualité, *f.* **carnally**, *adv.* Charnellement. **carnal-minded**, *a.* Sensuel, charnel; mondain. **carnal-mindedness**, *n.* Sensualité, *f.*

carnation [kɑ:'neiʃən], *n.* Œillet (des fleuristes); incarnat *m.*, carnation, *f.*
carnelian [CORNELIAN].
carney, *v.t.* [CARNY].
carnification [kɑ:nifi'keiʃən], *n.* Carnification, *f.*
carnify ['kɑ:nifai], *v.i.* Se carnifier.
carnival ['kɑ:nivl], *n.* Carnaval, *m.*
Carnivora [kɑ:'nivərə], *n.pl.* Carnassiers, *m.pl.* **carnivorous,** *a.* Carnivore, carnassier.
carny or **carney** ['kɑ:ni], *v.t.* Pateliner, cajoler. **carnying,** *a.* Patelin.—*n.* Patelinage, *m.*
carob ['kærəb], *n.* Caroube, *f.*; caroubier (tree), *m.*
carol ['kærəl], *n.* Chanson, *f.*, chant, *m.* A *Christmas carol,* un noël, *m.*—*v.i.* Chanter; (of lark) grisoller.
Carolingian [kæro'lindʒiən], *a.* Carolingien, carlovingien.
carotid [kə'rɔtid], *a.* (*Anat.*) Carotide, carotidien.—*n.* Carotide, *f.*
carousal [kə'rauzəl] or **carouse,** *n.* Orgie, débauche, ripaille, *f.*; festin, *m.* **carouse,** *v.i.* Boire, faire la fête. **carouser,** *n.* Grand buveur, fêtard, *m.*
carp (1) [kɑ:p], *n.* Carpe, *f. Young carp,* carpillon, carpeau, *m.*
carp (2) [kɑ:p]. *v.i.* Critiquer, chicaner (sur). *To carp at,* chicaner sur, censurer, épiloguer sur. **carper,** *n.* Gloseur, épilogueur; ronchonneur, *m.* **carping,** *a.* Chicanier, pointilleux. **carpingly,** *adv.* En glosant; malignement.
carpal ['kɑ:pəl], *a.* (*Anat.*) Carpien.
Carpathians [kɑ:'peiθiənz]. Les Carpathes, *m.pl.*
carpenter ['kɑ:pəntə], *n.* Menuisier, charpentier, *m.*—*v.i.* Faire de la charpenterie.
carpentry, *n.* Grosse menuiserie, charpenterie, *f.*
carpet ['kɑ:pit], *n.* Tapis, *m. Carpet broom,* balai de jonc, *m.*; *carpet knight,* héros de salon, *m.*; *Wilton* or *pile carpet,* moquette, *f.* —*v.t.* Garnir de tapis, tapisser. ***carpet-bag,** *n.* Sac de nuit, *m.* **carpet-slippers,** *n.* Confortables, *m.pl.* **carpet-sweeper,** *n.* Balai mécanique, *m.*
carpus ['kɑ:pəs], *n.* (*Anat.*) Carpe, *m.*
carriage ['kæridʒ], *n.* Voiture, *f.*; équipage; (*Rail.*) wagon, *m.*, voiture, *f.*; transport; port, factage (of parcels etc.); affût (of cannon), *m.*; (*Comm.*) frais de transport, *m.pl.*; (*fig.*) maintien, *m.*, tenue, démarche, conduite, *f. Carriage and four,* voiture à quatre chevaux, *f.*; *carriage and pair,* voiture à deux chevaux, *f.*; *carriage entrance,* porte cochère, *f.*; *carriage forward,* en port dû; *carriage free,* franc de port; *carriage horse,* cheval d'attelage, *m.*; *carriage paid,* port payé; *carriage road,* route carrossable, grand-route, chaussée (of streets), *f.*; *carriage-works,* carrosserie, *f.*; *to change carriages,* changer de voiture *or* de wagon; *to keep one's carriage,* avoir équipage.
carriageable, *a.* Charretier (of roads); carrossable.
carriageway, *n. Dual carriageway,* route à double circulation, *f.*
carrier ['kæriə], *n.* Commissionnaire de roulage, *m.*, camionneur; porteur, messager; (*Cycl.*) porte-bagages, *m. Aircraft-carrier,* porte-avions, *m.inv.*; *carrier-bag,* grand sac

en papier, *m.*; *carrier pigeon,* pigeon voyageur, *m.*; *carrier-wave,* (*Rad.*) onde porteuse, *f.*
carrion ['kæriən], *n.* Charogne, *f.*—*a.* De charogne. **carrion-crow,** *n.* Corbeau, *m.*, corbine, *f.*
carronade [kærə'neid], *n.* (*Naut.*) Caronade, *f.*
carrot ['kærət], *n.* Carotte, *f. Carrot soup,* soupe aux carottes, *f.* **carroty,** *a.* Couleur de carotte; (*colloq.*) roux.
carry ['kæri], *v.t.* Porter; emporter; rapporter (of dogs); mener, conduire, entraîner; faire voter, adopter; (*Arith.*) retenir; (*Law*) citer, traduire. *Carried forward,* à reporter, report; *he carries everything before him,* tout cède devant lui; *to carry about,* mener partout; *to carry away,* emporter, enlever, emmener, entraîner, ravir en extase; *to carry back,* rapporter; *to carry coals to Newcastle,* porter de l'eau à la rivière; *to carry down,* descendre; *to carry forth,* sortir; *to carry forward,* (*Comm.*) reporter; *to carry in,* rentrer; *to carry it off,* s'en tirer, réussir; *to carry off,* emporter, enlever, remporter; *to carry on,* poursuivre, continuer; faire gérer, exercer, (*colloq.*) faire des siennes; *to carry oneself,* se tenir, se conduire; *to carry out,* porter dehors; mettre à exécution; *to carry over,* transporter, (*Comm.*) reporter; *to carry the day,* remporter la victoire, l'emporter; *to carry through,* mener à bonne fin; *to carry to and fro,* porter çà et là; *to carry up,* porter en haut, monter. —*v.i.* Porter (of gun, voice, etc.).
carrying, *n.* Transport, port, *m. Carrying of arms,* port d'armes, *m.*; *carrying out,* mise à exécution, *f.*; **carryings-on,** *n.pl.* Conduite choquante, *f.*; scandale, *m.*
cart [kɑ:t], *n.* Charrette, *f.*; (*Mil.*) fourgon, *m.*; carriole (of peasants), *f.*; *Tip-cart,* tombereau, banneau, *m.*; (*pop.*) *to be in the cart,* être aux choux; *to put the cart before the horse,* mettre la charrue avant les bœufs.—*v.t.* Charrier, transporter, voiturer; (*fig.*) trimbaler. *To cart away,* enlever, emporter. **cart-horse,** *n.* Cheval de trait, *m.* **cartload,** *n.* Charretée, *f.* **cart-road,** *n.* Chemin de charroi, *m.*, route charretière, *f.* **cartshed,** *n.* Hangar, *m.* **cart-wheel,** *n.* Roue de charrette, *f. To turn cart-wheels,* faire la roue. **cartwright,** *n.* Charron, *m.* **cartage,** *n.* Charriage, transport, *m.* **carter,** *n.* Charretier, roulier, voiturier, *m.*
carte [kɑ:t], *n.* Carte, *f.*; menu, *m.* **carte blanche,** *n.* Carte blanche, *f.* **carte-de-visite,** *n.* Carte, *f.*; photographie, *f.* (on a small card).
cartel ['kɑ:təl], *n.* Cartel, *m.* **cartel-ship,** *n.* Cartel, bâtiment parlementaire, *m.*
Cartesian [kɑ:'ti:ziən], *a.* and *n.* Cartésien.
Carthage ['kɑ:θidʒ]. Carthage, *f.*
Carthaginian [kɑ:θə'dʒiniən], *a.* Carthaginois.—*n.* Carthaginois, *m.*, Carthaginoise, *f.*
Carthusian [kɑ:'θju:ziən], *a.* and *n.* (*Eccles.*) Chartreux; (*sch.*) élève de Charterhouse.
cartilage ['kɑ:tilidʒ], *n.* Cartilage, *m.*
cartilaginous [kɑ:ti'lædʒinəs], *a.* Cartilagineux.
cartography [kɑ:'tɔgrəfi], *n.* Cartographie, *f.* **cartographer,** *n.* Cartographe. **cartomancy** ['kɑ:tomænsi], *n.* Cartomancie, *f.*
carton ['kɑ:tən], *n.* Carton, *m.*; petite boîte en carton, *f.*

cartoon [kɑ:'tu:n], *n.* Carton, *m.*; caricature, *f.* (politique); (*Cine.*) dessin animé, *m.*
cartoonist, *n.* Caricaturiste; (*Cine.*) auteur de dessins animés, *m.*
cartouch [kɑ:'tu:ʃ], *n.* (*Arch.*) Cartouche, *m.*
cartridge ['kɑ:tridʒ], *n.* Cartouche, *f.*; (*Artill.*) gargousse, *f.* *Blank cartridge*, cartouche à blanc, *f.*; *to fire with blank cartridge*, tirer à blanc. **cartridge-belt**, *n.* Ceinture cartouchière, *f.* **cartridge-factory**, *n.* Cartoucherie, *f.* **cartridge-paper**, *n.* (*Ind.*) Papier à cartouche, *m.* **cartridge-pouch**, *n.* Cartouchière, giberne, *f.*
caruncle ['kærəŋkl] or [kə'rʌŋkl], *n.* Caroncule, *f.*
carve [kɑ:v], *v.t.* Sculpter, tailler; graver, ciseler; couper, dépecer, découper (meat etc.). *To carve out a career for oneself*, se faire *or* se tailler une carrière. **carver**, *n.* Découpeur, *m.*; (*Art*) sculpteur, graveur, ciseleur, *m.*
carvel [CARAVEL]. **carvel-built**, *a.* (Bateau) à francs bords.
carving, *n.* Découpage (of meat), *m.*; (*Art*) sculpture, gravure, ciselure, boiserie (woodcarving), *f.* **carving-knife**, *n.* Couteau à découper, *m.*
caryatid [kæri'ætid], *n.* Cariatide, *f.*
cascade [kæs'keid], *n.* Cascade, *f.*—*v.i.* Tomber en cascade, cascader.
case (1) [keis], *n.* Cas, état, *m.*; condition, question; (*Law*) cause, affaire, plainte, *f.*; (*Med.*) malade, blessé, *m.* *As the case may be*, selon les circonstances; *case in point*, exemple à l'appui, *m.*; *famous law-case*, cause célèbre, *f.*; *if that is the case*, s'il en est ainsi; *in any case*, en tout cas, quand même; *in case*, dans le cas où; *in such a case*, en pareil cas; *in that case*, dans ce cas, cela étant; *it is a very hard case*, cela est rude, c'est dur; *should the case occur*, le cas échéant; *such being the case*, cela étant; *that alters the case*, c'est une autre affaire, c'est une autre paire de manches; *that is the case*, il s'agit de cela.
case (2) [keis], *n.* Étui, fourreau, *m.*; caisse (for packing); boîte (of a watch), *f.*; écrin (for jewels); (*Organ*) buffet, *m.*; (*Print.*) casse; vitrine (show-case), *f.* (*Print.*) *Lower case*, bas de casse, *m.*; *upper case*, haut de casse, *m.*—*v.t.* Enfermer; emballer; envelopper, encaisser; revêtir (a building); ferrer (with iron).
cased [keist], *a.* Encaissé; (*Navy*) blindé, cuirassé. *Double cased* (silver- or gold-cased), à double boîte. **case-harden**, *v.t.* Cémenter, aciérer. (*fig.*) *A case-hardened man*, un homme endurci (dans le crime). **case-history**, *n.* Dossier médical, *m.* **case-law**, *n.* Les précédents, *m.pl.*; jurisprudence, *f.* **case-shot**, *n.* Mitraille, *f.*
casein ['keisiin], *n.* (*Chem.*) Caséine, *f.*
casemate ['keismeit], *n.* Casemate, *f.*—*v.t.* Casemater.
casement ['keismənt], *n.* Châssis de fenêtre, *m.* **casement-window**, *n.* Fenêtre à deux battants (s'ouvrant à l'extérieur), *f.*
cash [kæʃ], *n.* Argent, numéraire, *m.*; espèces (change), *f.pl.* *Cash balance*, encaisse, *f.*; *cash down*, argent comptant, *m.*; *cash on account*, acompte, *m.*; *cash on delivery*, contre remboursement; *to be in cash*, être en fonds;

to pay cash, payer en espèces, payer comptant; *to sell for cash*, vendre au comptant.—*v.t.* Toucher, encaisser (a cheque, a postal order); escompter (a bill); changer (a banknote). *To cash in on*, tirer profit de. **cashaccount**, *n.* Compte de caisse, *m.* **cashbook**, *n.* Livre de caisse, *m.* **cash-box**, *n.* Caisse, *f.* **cash-desk**, *n.* Caisse, *f.* **cashkeeper**, *n.* Caissier, *m.*
cashew [kə'ʃu:] or **cashew-nut**, *n.* Noix d'acajou, *f.* **cashew-tree**, *n.* Anacardier, *m.*
cashier (1) [kæ'ʃiə], *n.* Caissier, *m.* *Pay at the cashier's desk*, payez à la caisse.
cashier (2) [kə'ʃiə], *v.t.* (*Mil.*) Casser, dégrader.
cashmere ['kæʃmiə], *n.* Cachemire, *m.*
cash-register, *n.* Caisse enregistreuse, *f.*
casing ['keisiŋ], *n.* Revêtement; chambranle, *m.*; enveloppe, couverture, *f.*
casino [kə'si:nou], *n.* Casino, *m.*
cask [kɑ:sk], *n.* Fût, baril, *m.*, barrique, *f.*, tonneau, *m.* *To taste of the cask*, sentir le fût.—*v.t.* Mettre en baril, en tonneau *or* en barrique, enfutailler.
casket ['kɑ:skit], *n.* Écrin, *m.*, cassette, *f.*
Caspian ['kæspiən], **The.** La mer Caspienne, *f.*
cassation [kə'seiʃən], *n.* Cassation, *f.*
cassava [kə'sɑ:və], *n.* (*Bot.*) Cassave, *f.*; manioc, *m.*
casserole ['kæsəroul], *n.* Casserole, *f.*; ragoût, *m.*
cassette [kæ'set], *n.* (*Phot.*) Chargeur, *m.*
cassia ['kæsiə], *n.* (*Bot.*) Casse, *f.*
cassock ['kæsək], *n.* Soutane, *f.* **cassocked**, *a.* En soutane.
cassowary ['kæsəwəri], *n.* (*Orn.*) Casoar, *m.*
cast (1) [kɑ:st], *v.t.* (*past and p.p.* **cast**) Jeter; laisser tomber; dépouiller (of trees and animals); changer (of reptiles); (*fig.*) se décharger, déverser; (*Metal.*) couler, fondre; (*Theat.*) distribuer les rôles; (*Print.*) clicher; (*Foundry*) mouler; (*Arith.*) calculer; lancer (a fishing-line). *Cast-off clothes*, vêtements de rebut, *m.pl.*, défroque, *f.*; *to be cast away*, faire naufrage; *to cast about for*, considérer, chercher; *to cast a glance at*, jeter un regard sur; *to cast a horoscope*, faire, tirer, un horoscope; *to cast anchor*, jeter l'ancre; *to cast a shoe*, se déferrer (of horses); *to cast aside*, mettre de côté, rejeter; *to cast away*, jeter, renoncer à; *to cast down*, jeter par terre, abattre, décourager, baisser (of the eyes); *to cast lots*, tirer au sort; *to cast off*, rejeter, repousser, abandonner; (*Naut.*) démarrer; *to cast out*, chasser; *to cast up*, additionner; vomir (food).—*v.i.* Se jeter; se déjeter (of wood); (*Metal.*) se couler; (*Naut.*) abattre.
cast (2) [kɑ:st], *n.* Coup; jet (throw); lancer (of fishing-line); moule, *m.*; (*Metal.*) fonte, *f.*, creux, *m.*; (*Theat.*) distribution des rôles, *f.*, rôles, acteurs, *m.pl.*; (*fig.*) nuance, trempe, expression, tournure, *f.*; air, caractère, *m.*; (*Sculp.*) statuette, figure, *f.*, plâtre, *m.*; (*Agric.*) volée, *f.*; dépouille (of insect), *f.*; déjection (of worm), *f.* *At one cast*, d'un seul jet; *to have a cast in the eye*, loucher; (*Metal.*) *to take a cast of*, mouler.—*a.* Fondu.
caster, *n.* (*Metal.*) Fondeur, *m.* **casting**, *n.* (*Metal.*) Coulée, *f.*, fonte, *f.*, moulage, *m.*; pièce fondue, *f.*; (*Print.*) clichage, *m.*; (*Arith.*) calcul, *m.*; (*Naut.*) abattée, *f.*; pêche au

lancer, *f.*; (*Theat.*) distribution des rôles, *f.*—
a. Casting vote, voix prépondérante, *f.*
cast-iron, *n.* Fonte, *f.*—*a.* En fonte; (*fig.*) de
fer, rigide.
cast-net, *n.* Épervier, *m.*
castanet [kæstə'net], *n.* Castagnette, *f.*
castaway ['kɑ:stəwei], *a.* Rejeté.—*n.* Naufragé, *m.*
caste [kɑ:st], *n.* Caste, *f.* *To lose caste*,
déchoir, déroger.
castellated ['kæsteleitid], *a.* Crénelé; qui a
l'aspect d'un château-fort.
castigate ['kæstigeit], *v.t.* Châtier, punir;
critiquer sévèrement. **castigation,** *n.*
Châtiment, *m.*, correction, discipline, *f.*
castigator, *n.* Châtieur, critique, *m.*
castigatory, *a.* Qui corrige, qui châtie.
Castile [kæs'ti:l]. La Castille, *f.*
castle [kɑ:sl], *n.* Château, château fort, *m.*;
(*Chess*) tour, *f.* *Castles in the air*, châteaux
en Espagne.—*v.i.* (*Chess*) Roquer. **castled,**
a. Qui a un château (of a town, a hill).
castle-nut, *n.* Écrou crénelé, *m.*
castor ['kɑ:stə], *n.* Roulette (on furniture);
poivrière, *f.*; *castor (beaver); *chapeau de
castor, *m.*; (*pl.*) (pair of) *castors*, huilier, *m.*
castor-oil, *n.* Huile de ricin, *f.* **castor-
sugar,** *n.* Sucre en poudre, *m.*
castrate [kæs'treit], *v.t.* Châtrer. **castration,**
n. Castration, *f.* **castrato** (*It.*), *n.* Castrat, *m.*
casual ['kæʒjuəl], *a.* Fortuit, accidentel,
casuel, de passage; insouciant. *A casual
labourer*, un homme à l'heure. **casually,**
adv. Fortuitement, par hasard, en passant;
avec désinvolture, négligemment. **casualness,** *n.* Insouciance, désinvolture, indifférence, *f.* **casualty,** *n.* Accident (de personne), *m.*; (*Mil.*) pertes, *f.pl.* *Casualty
ward*, salle des accidentés, *f.*; *return of
casualties*, liste des morts et des blessés, *f.*
casuist ['kæʒjuist], *n.* Casuiste, *m.* **casuistic**
[kæʒju'istik] or **casuistical,** *a.* De casuiste,
casuistique. **casuistically,** *adv.* En casuiste.
casuistry ['kæʒjuistri], *n.* Casuistique, *f.*
cat [kæt], *n.* Chat, *m.*, chatte, *f.*; (*Mil.*, *Navy*)
fouet, martinet (à neuf queues); (*Naut.*)
capon (of a ship), *m.* *An* (old) *cat*, (*colloq.*)
une (vieille) chipie. *Like a cat on hot bricks*,
comme chat sur braise; *to let the cat out of
the bag*, éventer la mèche, découvrir le pot
aux roses; *to live a cat-and-dog life*, s'accorder
comme chien et chat; *tom-cat*, matou, *m.*;
when candles are away all cats are grey, la nuit
tous les chats sont gris; *when the cat's away
the mice will play*, le chat parti, les souris
dansent.—*v.t.* Caponner (an anchor).
cat-block, *n.* (*Naut.*) Poulie de capon, *f.* **cat-
burglar,** *n.* Cambrioleur acrobate, *m.*,
monte-en-l'air, *m.inv.* **catcall,** *n.* Sifflet, *m.*
cat-fish, *n.* Chat marin, *m.* **catgut,** *n.*
Corde en boyau, *f.* *Catgut-scraper*, râcleur,
m. **cat-head,** *n.* (*Naut.*) Bossoir, *m.* **catlike,**
a. Comme un chat, de chat. **catling,** *n.*
Chaton, *m.* **cat-o'-nine-tails,** *n.* Martinet,
chat à neuf queues, *m.* **cat's-cradle,** *n.* Jeu
du berceau, *m.* **cat's-eye,** *n.* (*Min.*) Œil-de-
chat, *m.*; catadioptre, *m.*; (*Motor.*) cataphote,
m. **cat's-foot,** *n.* Pied-de-chat, lierre terrestre, *m.* **cat's-paw,** *n.* Vent léger, *m.*,
risée, *f.* *To be someone's cat's-paw*, tirer les
marrons du feu pour quelqu'un. **cat's-tail,**
n. (*Bot.*) Massette, *f.*

cattiness or **cattishness,** *n.* Méchanceté,
sournoiserie, *f.* **cattish** or **catty,** *a.* Méchant,
sournois, rosse.
catabolism [kə'tæbəlizm], *n.* (*Biol.*) Catabolisme, *m.*
catachresis [kætə'kri:sis], *n.* Catachrèse, *f.*
catachrestical [kætə'krestikl], *a.* De catachrèse.
cataclysm ['kætəklizm], *n.* Cataclysme, *m.*
cataclysmal or **cataclysmic,** *a.* Cataclysmique.
catacombs ['kætəku:mz], *n.pl.* Catacombes,
f.pl.
catadioptric [kætədai'ɔptrik], *a.* Catadioptrique.
catafalque ['kætəfælk] or **catafalco,** *n.* Catafalque, *m.*; char (funèbre), *m.*
catalepsy ['kætəlepsi], *n.* Catalepsie, *f.* **cataleptic,** *a.* and *n.* Cataleptique.
catalogue ['kætəlɔg], *n.* Catalogue, *m.*, liste, *f.*,
répertoire, *m.*—*v.t.* Cataloguer.
Catalonia [kætə'lounia]. La Catalogne, *f.*
catalyse ['kætəlaiz], *v.t.* Catalyser. **catalyst,**
n. Catalyseur, *m.*
cataplasm ['kætəplæzm], *n.* Cataplasme,
m.
catapult ['kætəpʌlt], *n.* Catapulte, *f.*; lance-
pierre, *m.* (toy).—*v.t.* Catapulter. **catapult-
ing,** *n.* Catapultage, *m.*
cataract ['kætərækt], *n.* Cataracte, *f.*
catarrh [kə'tɑ:], *n.* Catarrhe, *m.* **catarrhal,**
a. Catarrhal.
catastrophe [kə'tæstrəfi], *n.* Catastrophe, *f.*;
désastre, *m.*; (*Theat.*) dénouement, *m.* **catastrophic, -ical,** *a.* Catastrophique.
catch [kætʃ], *v.t.* (*past* and *p.p.* **caught** [kɔ:t])
Attraper, prendre, saisir; (*colloq.*) pincer;
surprendre, découvrir; frapper (the eye etc.);
gagner, ne pas manquer (a train etc.). *Her
eye caught mine*, nos yeux se rencontrèrent;
if I catch you at it, si je vous y prends; *to
catch a cold*, s'enrhumer; *to catch fire*, prendre
feu, s'allumer; *to catch hold of*, saisir,
s'accrocher à; *to catch it*, en avoir, en
recevoir; *to catch on*, avoir du succès, réussir;
comprendre; *to catch someone a blow*, flanquer
un coup à quelqu'un; *to catch someone crying*,
surprendre quelqu'un à pleurer; *to catch up*,
atteindre, rattraper; saisir.—*v.i.* S'accrocher
(à), s'engager (dans), prendre, se prendre
(à).—*n.* Prise; attrape; (*fig.*) aubaine, belle
affaire, *f.*; jeu de mots, attrape-nigaud;
loquet, crochet d'arrêt; cliquet (of a wheel);
crampon (of a door); mentonnet (of a latch);
(*Mus.*) air à reprises, *m.* *She is a good catch*,
elle a de la fortune; *fair catch*, (*Ftb.*) arrêt de
volée, *m.*; *good catch*, (*Row.*) bonne attaque, *f.*;
(*Fishing*) bonne pêche, bonne prise, *f.*; *there's
a catch in it*, c'est une attrape.
catch-as-catch-can, *n.* (*spt.*) Lutte libre, *f.*,
catch, *m.*
catch-fly, *n.* Silène, *m.* **catch-penny,** *n.*
Attrape-nigaud, *m.*—*a.* D'attrape, de réclame, de boutique. **catch-phrase** or
catch-word, *n.* Mot de ralliement, *m.*;
rengaine, *f.*; (*Print.*) mot-souche, *m.*; (*Theat.*)
réplique, *f.* **catching,** *n.* Prise, capture, *f.*
—*a.* Contagieux. **catchment,** *n.* Prise
d'eau, captation, *f.* *Catchment area*, surface
de captation des eaux, *f.*, bassin de réception,
m. **catchy,** *a.* (Question) insidieuse; (air)
facile à retenir.

catechism ['kætəkizm], *n.* Catéchisme, *m.*
catechist, *n.* Catéchiste, *m.* **catechize,** *v.t.*
Catéchiser.
catechumen [kætə'kju:mən], *n.* Catéchumène.
categorical [kætə'gɔrikəl], *a.* Catégorique.
categorically, *adv.* Catégoriquement.
category ['kætəgɔri], *n.* Catégorie, *f.*
catenarian [kæti'neəriən] or **catenary**
[kə'ti:nəri], *a.* (*Geom., Math.*) En chaînette.
catenate ['kætineit], *v.t.* Enchaîner, lier.
catenation [kæti'neiʃən], *n.* Enchaînement, *m.*
cater ['keitə], *v.i.* Pourvoir (à). **caterer,** *n.*
Pourvoyeur, *m.*, pourvoyeuse, *f.*, fournisseur,
traiteur, *m.*
caterpillar ['kætəpilə], *n.* (*Ent.*) Chenille, *f.*
Caterpillar (proprietary mark) *tractor,* tracteur à chenilles, *m.,* auto-chenille, *f.*
caterwaul ['kætəwɔ:l], *v.i.* Miauler, crier
comme un chat, faire du tintamarre. **caterwauling,** *n.* Sabbat des chats, tintamarre, *m.*
catgut, cat-head, etc. [CAT].
catharsis [kə'θɑ:sis], *n.* Catharsis, *f.*; purgation, *f.* **cathartic,** *a.* and *n.* Cathartique.
cathedral [kə'θi:drəl], *n.* Cathédrale, *f.*
Cathedral town, ville épiscopale, *f.*
Catherine wheel ['kæθərin hwi:l] (*Fireworks*)
Soleil, *m.*
catheter ['kæθətə], *n.* (*Surg.*) Cathéter, *m.*
cathode ['kæθoud], *n.* Cathode, *f.,* électrode
négative, *f.* *Cathode rays,* rayons cathodiques, *m.pl.*; *cathode-ray tube,* oscillographe
cathodique, *m.* **cathodic,** *a.* Cathodique.
catholic ['kæθəlik], *a.* Universel, tolérant,
éclectique; catholique.—*n.* A (*Roman*) *Catholic,* un catholique (romain).
catholicism [kə'θɔlisizm], *n.* Catholicisme,
m.
catholicity [kæθə'lisiti], *n.* Catholicité; largeur
d'esprit, tolérance, *f.* **catholicly,** *adv.*
Catholiquement, en bon catholique.
catholicon [kə'θɔlikən], *n.* Panacée, *f.*
catkin ['kætkin], *n.* (*Bot.*) Chaton, *m.*
cat-mint ['kætmint], *n.* (*Bot.*) Cataire (plant), *f.*
catoptric [kə'tɔptrik], *a.* Catoptrique.
catoptrics, *n.pl.* Catoptrique, *f.*
catsup [KETCHUP].
cattiness etc. [CAT].
cattle [kætl], *n.* Bétail, *m.,* bestiaux, *m.pl.*
Cattle drover, bouvier, *m.*; *cattle market,*
marché aux bestiaux, *m.*; *cattle plague,* peste
bovine, *f.*; *cattle shed,* étable, *f.*; *cattle show,*
concours d'élevage, comice agricole, *m.*;
cattle truck, wagon à bestiaux, *m.*; *horned
cattle,* bêtes à cornes, *f.pl.*
Caucasus ['kɔ:kəsəs], The. Le Caucase, *m.*
caucus ['kɔ:kəs], *n.* (*U.S.*) Comité électoral, *m.*
caudal [kɔ:dl], *a.* Caudal.
caught, *past* and *p.p.* [CATCH].
caul [kɔ:l], *n.* Réseau, filet, *m.*; coiffe d'enfant, *f.*
cauldron ['kɔ:ldrən], *n.* Chaudron, *m.,*
chaudière, *f.*
cauliflower ['kɔliflauə], *n.* Chou-fleur, *m.*
cauline ['kɔ:lain], *a.* (*Bot.*) Caulinaire.
caulk [kɔ:k] or **calk,** *v.t.* Calfater; ferrer à
glace (horses). **caulker** or **calker,** *n.* Calfat,
m. **caulking,** *n.* Calfatage, *m.*
causal [kɔ:zl], *a.* Causal, causatif. **causality**
[kɔ:'zæliti], *n.* (*Phil.*) Causalité, *f.,* rapport
de cause à effet, *m.* **causally,** *adv.* Suivant
l'ordre des causes. **causation** [kɔ:'zeiʃən], *n.*
Causation, *f.*

causative ['kɔ:zətiv], *a.* Causatif.
cause [kɔ:z], *n.* Raison, cause, *f.,* motif, **sujet,**
m. *There is cause to believe,* il y a lieu de
croire; *to give cause for,* justifier; *to make
common cause with,* faire cause commune
avec; *to plead someone's cause,* plaider la cause
de quelqu'un; *to show cause,* exposer ses
raisons.—*v.t.* Causer, être cause de; occasionner, faire naître, provoquer (an accident).
To cause a thing to be done, faire faire une
chose; *to cause sorrow,* donner du chagrin;
to cause to be punished, faire punir. **causeless,** *a.* Sans cause, sans motif, sans sujet.
causelessly, *adv.* Sans cause. **causelessness,** *n.* Absence de motifs, *f.*
causeway ['kɔ:zwei], *n.* Chaussée, *f.*
caustic ['kɔ:stik], *a.* Caustique, corrosif; (*fig.*)
mordant, sarcastique.—*n.* Caustique, *m.*
cauterization [kɔ:tərai'zeiʃən], *n.* Cautérisation, *f.* **cauterize,** *v.t.* Cautériser. **cauterizing,** *n.* Cautérisation, *f.*
cautery ['kɔ:təri], *n.* Cautère, *m.*
caution ['kɔ:ʃən], *n.* Avis (warning), *m.*; précaution, prévoyance, prudence, circonspection; caution, garantie, *f.* (*fam.*) *He is a
caution,* c'est un drôle de type.—*v.t.* Avertir,
aviser (de), mettre en garde (contre); réprimander. **caution-money,** *n.* Cautionnement, *m.,* garantie, *f.* **cautionary,** *a.*
D'avertissement, de précaution, pour avertir.
Cautionary tale, conte moral, *m.* **cautious,** *a.*
Circonspect, prudent, en garde. **cautiously,**
adv. Avec précaution, prudemment, avec
circonspection. **cautiousness,** *n.* Circonspection, prudence, *f.*
cavalcade [kævəl'keid], *n.* Cavalcade, *f.*
cavalier [kævə'liə], *n.* Cavalier, *m.*—*a.* Cavalier, désinvolte. **cavalierly,** *adv.* Cavalièrement.
cavalry ['kævəlri], *n.* Cavalerie, *f.* **cavalryman,** *n.* Cavalier, *m.*
cavatina [kævə'ti:nə], *n.* Cavatine, *f.*
cave (1) [keiv], *n.* Caverne, *f.,* antre, souterrain, *m.* *Cave art,* peintures rupestres, *f.pl.*;
cave dwellers, hommes des cavernes, *m.pl.*—
v.t. Creuser.—*v.i.* *To cave in,* céder, se
soumettre, s'affaisser, s'effondrer (of buildings).
cave (2) ['keivi], *int.* (*sch.*) Attention! *To keep
cave,* faire le guet.
caveat ['keiviæt], *n.* (*Law*) Opposition, *f.*
cavern ['kævən], *n.* Caverne, *f.* **cavernous,**
a. Caverneux.
caviare [kævi'ɑ:], *n.* Caviar, *m.*
cavil ['kævil], *v.i.* Chicaner (sur).—*n.* Argutie,
chicane, *f.* **caviller,** *n.* Chicanier, *m.*
cavilling, *a.* Chicaneur, *n.* Chicanerie, *f.*
cavillingly, *adv.* Par esprit de chicane.
cavity ['kæviti], *n.* Cavité, *f.*
cavort [kə'vɔ:t], *v.i.* Cabrioler.
cavy ['keivi], *n.* Cobaye, *m.*
caw [kɔ:], *v.i.* Croasser. **cawing,** *n.* Croassement, *m.*
cayenne [kei'en] or **Cayenne pepper,** *n.*
Poivre rouge, *m.*
cayman ['keimən], *n.* Caïman, *m.*
cease [si:s], *v.i.* Cesser, discontinuer; (*fig.*)
mourir. *To cease doing something,* cesser de
faire quelque chose.—*v.t.* Cesser; faire cesser.
Cease fire! cessez le feu!—*n. Without cease,*
sans cesse. **ceaseless,** *a.* Incessant, continuel. **ceaselessly,** *adv.* Sans cesse,

continuellement. **ceasing,** *n.* Cessation, *f.*
Without ceasing, sans discontinuer.
Cecilia [sə'siliə]. Cécile, *f.*
cecity ['sesiti], *n.* Cécité, *f.*
cedar ['si:də], *n.* Cèdre, *m. Cedar wood,* bois
de cèdre, *m.*
cede [si:d], *v.t., v.i. (Law)* Céder.
cedilla [sə'dilə], *n. (Gram.)* Cédille, *f.*
ceil [si:l], *v.t.* Plafonner. **ceiling,** *n.* Plafond,
m.
celandine ['seləndain], *n. (Bot.)* Chélidoine,
éclaire, *f.*
celebrant ['selibrənt], *n.* Célébrant, *m.*
celebrate ['seləbreit], *v.t.* Célébrer, fêter.
celebrated, *a.* Célèbre, fameux.
celebration [selə'breiʃən], *n.* Célébration, *f.*
celebrator, *n.* Célébrateur, *m.*
celebrity [sə'lebriti], *n.* Célébrité, *f. All the
celebrities were there,* toutes les célébrités y
étaient.
celerity [sə'leriti], *n.* Célérité, vitesse, *f.*
celery ['seləri], *n.* Céleri, *m. Bundle of celery,*
botte de céleri, *f.; turnip-rooted celery,* céleri-
rave, *m.*
celestial [sə'lestjəl], *a.* Céleste.—*n.* Habitant
du ciel, esprit céleste, *m. The Celestials,* les
Chinois, *m.pl.* **celestially,** *adv.* D'une
manière céleste, célestement.
celibacy ['selibəsi], *n.* Célibat, *m.*
celibate ['selibit], *n.* and *a.* Célibataire.
cell [sel], *n.* Cellule, case; alvéole (of bees), *f.*;
compartiment; cachot, *m.; (Elec.)* élément,
m., pile, *f.* **celled,** *a.* Cellulé, à cellules.
cellar ['selə], *n.* Cave, *f.*; cellier, caveau, *m.*
cellarage, *n.* Caves, *f.pl.*; emmagasinage,
m. **cellarer,** *n.* Cellérier, *m.*
cellaret [selə'ret], *n.* Cave à liqueurs, *f.*
'cello ['tʃelou], *n.* (*abbv. of* violoncello) Violoncelle, *m.*
cellophane ['seləfein], *n.* Cellophane, *f.*
cellular ['seljulə], *a.* Cellulaire. **celluloid,**
n. Celluloïd, celluloïde, *m.* **cellulose,** *n.*
Cellulose, *f.*
cellulosity [selju'lɔsiti], *n.* Cellulosité, *f.*
Celt [kelt, selt], *n.* Celte. **Celtic,** *a.* Celtique.
cement [si'ment], *n.* Ciment, *m.*—*v.t.* Cimenter; *(fig.)* consolider, fortifier.—*v.i.* Se réunir.
cementation, *n. (Metal.)* Cémentation, *f.*
cement-mixer, *n.* Bétonnière, *f.*
cemetery ['semətri], *n.* Cimetière, *m.*
cenobite [CŒNOBITE].
cenotaph ['senotæf *or* -ta:f], *n.* Cénotaphe, *m.*
cense [sens], *v.t.* Encenser. **censer,** *n.* Encensoir, *m.*
censor ['sensə], *n.* Censeur, *m. Board of
censors,* commission de censure, *f.*—*v.t.* Soumettre à des coupures; censurer; interdire.
censorial [sen'sɔ:riəl], *a.* Censorial, sévère.
censorious [sen'sɔ:riəs], *a.* Critique, disposé
à blâmer et à condamner, hargneux. **cen-
soriously,** *adv.* En critique, sévèrement.
censoriousness, *n.* Disposition à la censure; manie de critiquer, *f.*
censorship ['sensəʃip], *n.* Censure, *f.*;
fonctions de censeur, *f.pl.*
censurable ['senʃurəbl], *a.* Censurable,
blâmable. **censure,** *n.* Censure, critique, *f.*,
blâme, *m. Vote of censure,* vote de blâme,
m.—*v.t.* Censurer, critiquer, blâmer. **censurer,** *n.* Censeur, critique, *m.*
census ['sensəs], *n.* Recensement, *m.*
cent [sent], *n.* Cent; sou (coin), *m. I haven't*

got a cent, je n'ai pas le sou; *ten per cent,*
dix pour cent.
centaur ['sentɔ:], *n.* Centaure, *m.*
centaury ['sentɔ:ri] *or* **centaurea** [sentɔ:'riə],
n. (Bot.) Centaurée, *f.*
centenarian [senti'nɛəriən], *n.* Centenaire.
centenary [sen'ti:nəri], *a.* Centenaire.—*n.*
Centième anniversaire, centenaire, *m.*
centennial [sen'tenjəl], *a.* De cent ans,
séculaire.
center, *n. (Am.)* [CENTRE].
centesimal, *a.* Centésimal.—*n.* Centième, *m.*
centering ['sentəriŋ], *n. (Arch.)* Centre, *m.*
centigrade ['sentigreid], *a.* Centigrade.
centigram, *n.* Centigramme, *m.* **centilitre,**
n. Centilitre, *m.* **centimetre,** *n.* Centimètre, *m.*
centipede ['sentipi:d], *n.* Scolopendre, *f.*,
mille-pattes, *m.* **centipede-ladder,** *n.*
(Naut.) Échelle de perroquet, *f.*
cento ['sentou], *n. (Mus., Lit.)* Centon, *m.*
central ['sentrəl], *a.* Central. *Central heating,*
chauffage central, *m.* **centralism,** *n.* Centralisme, *m.* **centralist,** *n.* Centraliste.
centrality [sen'træliti], *n.* Centralité, *f.*
centralization [sentrəlai'zeiʃən], *n.* Centralisation, *f.*
centralize ['sentrəlaiz], *v.t.* Centraliser.
centre ['sentə], *n.* Centre; milieu; *(fig.)*
foyer, *m. Centre of gravity,* centre de
gravité.—*v.t.* Placer au centre; *(Phot.)*
centrer; concentrer.—*v.i.* Faire centre, être
placé au centre; se concentrer.
centre-bit, *n.* Mèche anglaise, *f.*
centre-forward, *n. (Ftb.)* Avant-centre, *m.*
centre-half, *n. (Ftb.)* Demi-centre, *m.*
centric *or* **centrical,** *a.* Central, placé au
milieu. **centrically,** *adv.* Dans une position
centrale.
centricity [sen'trisiti], *n.* Position centrale, *f.*,
état central, *m.*
centrifugal [sen'trifjugl], *a.* Centrifuge.
Centrifugal force, force centrifuge, *f.*
centripetal, *a.* Centripète.
centuple ['sentjupl], *a.* Centuple.—*n.* Centuple, *m.*—*v.t.* Centupler.
centurion [sen'tjuəriən], *n.* Centurion, *(Bibl.)*
centenier, *m.*
century ['sentʃuri], *n.* Siècle, *m.*; *(Cricket)*
centaine, *f.* (de points). *In the twentieth
century,* au vingtième siècle.
cephalalgy [sefə'læIdʒi], *n.* Céphalalgie, *f.*,
mal de tête, *m.*
cephalic [se'fælik], *a.* Céphalique.
ceramic [sə'ræmik], *a.* Céramique. **ceramics,** *n.pl.* La céramique, *f.* **ceramist,** *n.*
Céramiste, *m.*
Cerberus ['sə:bərəs], *n.* Cerbère, *m.*
cere [siə], *v.t.* Cirer, enduire de cire.—*n.*
(Orn.) Cire, *f.* (of the bill).
cereal ['siəriəl], *a.* and *n.* Céréale, *f. Cereals,*
céréales en flocons, *f.pl.*, flocons d'avoine,
m.pl.
cerebellum [seri'beləm], *n.* Cervelet, *m.*
cerebellar, *a.* Cérébelleux.
cerebral ['serəbrəl], *a.* Cérébral. **cerebra-
tion,** *n.* Cérébration, *f.*
cerebro-spinal [serebro'spainl], *a.* (fever).
(Méningite) cérébro-spinale.
cerecloth ['siəklɔ:θ], *n.* Toile d'embaumement, *f.* **cerement,** *n.* Linceul, suaire
d'embaumement, *m.*

ceremonial [seri'mouniəl], *a.* De cérémonie. —*n.* Cérémonie, étiquette, *f.*, cérémonial, *m.* **ceremonialism**, *n.* Cérémonialisme, *m.* **ceremonially**, *adv.* Suivant les cérémonies, rituellement. **ceremonious**, *a.* Cérémonieux. **ceremoniously**, *adv.* Cérémonieusement. **ceremoniousness**, *n.* Manières cérémonieuses, *f.pl.*

ceremony ['serimǝni], *n.* Cérémonie, solennité, *f.*, cérémonial, *m. To stand on ceremony*, faire des façons; *without ceremony*, sans façon, sans cérémonie.

cerise [sǝ'ri:z], *a.* and *n.* Cerise, *m.*

cert [sǝ:t], *n.* [CERTAINTY].

certain ['sǝ:tin], *a.* Certain, sûr, assuré (ascertained). *A certain thing*, (something) une certaine chose, (a positive thing) une chose certaine; *for certain*, pour sûr, à coup sûr; *one thing is certain, that* . . ., ce qu'il y a de certain, c'est que . . .; *to make certain of something*, s'assurer de quelque chose. **certainly**, *adv.* Certainement. *Certainly not!* non, par exemple! **certainty**, *n.* Certitude, chose certaine, *f. To a certainty*, à coup sûr; *to bet on a certainty*, parier à coup sûr; *a dead cert(ainty)*, une certitude absolue, un gagnant sûr.

certifiable ['sǝ:tifaiǝbl], *a.* Qu'on peut certifier. *She is certifiable*, elle est folle à lier.

certificate (1) [sǝ:'tifikit], *n.* Certificat; diplôme, brevet; concordat (in bankruptcy); acte (of birth, marriage or death); extrait (copy of a register), *m. Certificate of registration*, permis de séjour, *m.*; *doctor's certificate*, attestation de médecin, *f.*

certificate (2) [sǝ:'tifikeit], *v.t.* Certifier. **certificated**, *a.* Diplômé, breveté.

certify ['sǝ:tifai], *v.t.* Certifier; notifier, donner avis à. *To certify to something*, attester quelque chose.

certiorari [sǝ:tiɔ:'reǝrai], *n.* (*Law*) Acceptation d'un appel *a minima*, *f.*

certitude ['sǝ:titju:d], *n.* Certitude, *f.*

cerulean [si'ru:liǝn], *a.* Céruléen, bleu, azuré.

cerumen [si'ru:mǝn], *n.* Cérumen, *m.* **ceruminous**, *a.* Cérumineux.

ceruse ['siǝru:s], *n.* Céruse, *f.*, blanc de céruse, *m.*

cerusite ['siǝru:sait], *n.* Cérusite, *f.*

cervical ['sǝ:vikǝl], *a.* (*Anat.*) Cervical.

cessation [se'seiʃǝn], *n.* Cessation, suspension, *f.*

cession ['seʃǝn], *n.* Cession, *f.* **cessionary**, *a.* Cessionnaire.—*n.* (*Law*) L'ayant cause.

cesspit ['sespit] or **cesspool**, *n.* Puisard, *m.*, fosse d'aisances; (*fig.*) sentine, *f.*

cestus ['sestǝs], *n.* Ceste, *m.*

cetacean [si'teiʃǝn], *n.* Cétacé, *m.* **cetaceous**, *a.* Cétacé.

Ceylon [si'lɔn]. Ceylan, *f.* **Ceylonese**, *a.* and *n.* Cingalais, *m.*, Cingalaise, *f.*

chafe [tʃeif], *v.t.* Échauffer, irriter; érailler (a cable).—*v.i.* Frotter; s'user, s'érailler (of cables); s'irriter; s'enflammer. *To chafe at*, s'irriter contre.—*n.* Irritation, *f.* **chafer**, *n.* Hanneton (insect); réchaud (dish), *m.* **chafery**, *n.* (*Metal.*) Chaufferie, *f.* **chafingdish**, *n.* Réchaud, *m.* (de table).

chaff [tʃɑ:f], *n.* Menue paille, paille hachée; (*colloq.*) plaisanterie, raillerie, blague, *f.*—*v.t.* Blaguer, taquiner, se moquer de. *You are only chaffing me*, ce n'est qu'une blague ce

que vous me dites là. **chaff-cutter**, *n.* Hache-paille, *m.* **chaffy**, *a.* De paille, plein de paille.

chaffer ['tʃæfǝ], *v.i.* Marchander.

chaffinch ['tʃæfintʃ], *n.* (*Orn.*) Pinson, *m.*

chagrin [ʃæ'gri:n], *n.* Chagrin; dépit, *m.*—*v.t.* Chagriner, vexer.

chain [tʃein], *n.* Chaîne; chaînée, *f. Gunter's chain*, chaîne d'arpenteur, *f.*—*v.t.* Enchaîner, attacher avec une chaîne *or* des chaînes; retenir par une chaîne. **chain-armour**, *n.* Cotte de mailles, *f.* **chain-bridge**, *n.* Pont suspendu, *m.* **chain-gang**, *n.* Chaîne de galériens, *f.* **chain-maker**, *n.* Chaînetier, *m.* **chain-pump**, *n.* Pompe à chapelet, *f.*, chapelet, *m.* **chain-reaction**, *n.* Réaction en chaîne, *f.* **chain-shot**, *n.* Boulet ramé, *m.* **chain-stitch**, *n.* Point de chaînette, *m.* **chain-store**, *n.* Succursale de grand magasin, *f.* **chain-work**, *n.* Travail à la chaîne, *m.* **chainless**, *a.* Sans chaîne; (*Cycl.*) acatène.

chair [tʃeǝ], *n.* Chaise, *f.*; siège, *m.*; chaire (of a professor), *f.*; fauteuil (of the chairman or president of an assembly), *m.*; (*fig.*) président; (*Rail.*) coussinet, chair, *m. Arm-chair*, fauteuil, *m.*; *bath-chair*, voiture de malade, *f. chair! chair!* à l'ordre! à l'ordre! *deck-chair*, chaise longue, *f.*, transat(lantique), *m.*; *rocking-chair*, fauteuil à bascule, *m.*; *sedan-chair*, chaise à porteurs, *f.*; *to be in the chair*, présider, occuper le fauteuil; *to leave the chair*, lever la séance; *with* . . . *in the chair*, sous la présidence de. . . .—*v.t.* Porter en triomphe; élire président. **chair-maker**, *n.* Fabricant de chaises, *m.* **chairman**, *n.* Président; *porteur de chaise, *m.* **chairmanship**, *n.* Présidence, *f.*

chaise [ʃeiz], *n.* Chaise de poste, *f.*

Chalcedon ['kælsidǝn]. Chalcédoine, *f.*

chalcedony [kæl'sedoni], *n.* Calcédoine, *f.*

chalcographer [kæl'kɔgrǝfǝ], *n.* Chalcographe, *m.* **chalcography**, *n.* Chalcographie, *f.*

Chaldea [kæl'di:ǝ]. La Chaldée, *f.*

chaldron ['tʃɔ:ldrǝn], *n.* Mesure de douze sacs (de charbon) *or* trente-six boisseaux, *f.* (à Londres).

chalice ['tʃælis], *n.* Calice, *m.*, coupe, *f.* **chaliced**, *a.* À calice.

chalk [tʃɔ:k], *n.* Craie, *f.*, calcaire, *m.*; crayon (for drawing), *m. By a long chalk*, à beaucoup près.—*v.t.* Blanchir avec de la craie; marquer *or* écrire à la craie; (*Agric.*) marner. *To chalk out*, tracer. **chalk-drawing**, *n.* Pastel, *m.* **chalkiness**, *n.* Nature crayeuse, *f.* **chalk-pit**, *n.* Carrière de craie, *f.* **chalk-stone**, *n.* (*Path.*) Concrétion calcaire, *f.* **chalky**, *a.* Crayeux, crétacé, calcaire.

challenge ['tʃælindʒ], *n.* Défi, cartel, *m.*; (*fig.*) provocation, prétention, demande; (*Law*) récusation, *f.*; (*Mil.*) qui-vive, *f.*; sommation, *f.*; (*spt.*) challenge, *m. To send a challenge to*, envoyer ses témoins à.—*v.t.* Défier; provoquer en duel; contester; (*Law*) récuser; (*Mil.*) crier qui vive à; (*Naut.*) héler. **challenger**, *n.* Auteur d'un cartel; provocateur, agresseur, champion, *m.*; (*spt.*) challenger, lanceur d'un challenge, *m.*; (*Law*) personne qui récuse un juré, *f.*; récusant, *m.* **challenging**, *a.* Provocateur, -trice; hardi.

chalybeate [kǝ'libiǝt], *a.* Ferrugineux.

chamade [ʃə'mɑːd], *n.* Chamade, *f.*
chamber ['tʃeimbə], *n.* Chambre; salle, pièce, *f.*, cabinet, *m.*; (*Artill.*) âme, *f.*; (*pl.*) bureaux, *m.pl.*, étude, *f. Chamber counsel*, avocat consultant, *m.*; *Chamber of Commerce*, chambre de commerce, *f.*; *in chambers*, en référé (of judges).—*v.t.* Enfermer dans une chambre, chambrer. **chambered**, *a.* Evidé; chambré. *Six-chambered revolver*, revolver à six coups, *m.* **chamberful**, *a.* Chambrée, chambre pleine, *f.* **chamberlain**, *n.* Chambellan; camérier (of the pope), *m.* **chamber-concert**, *n.* Concert de musique de chambre, *m.* **chamber-maid**, *n.* Femme de chambre, *f.* **chamber-music**, *n.* Musique de chambre, *f.* **chamber(-pot)**, *n.* Pot de chambre; vase de nuit, *m.*
chameleon [kə'miːljən], *n.* Caméléon, *m.*
chamfer ['tʃæmfə], *n.* Chanfrein, *m.*—*v.t.* Chanfreiner, biseauter.
chamois ['ʃæmwɑː], *n.* Chamois, *m.*
chamois-leather [ʃæmi'leðə], *n.* Chamois, *m.*, peau de chamois, *f.*
chamomile ['kæməmail] [CAMOMILE].
champ [tʃæmp], *v.t.* Ronger, mâcher. *To champ the bit*, ronger le frein.—*v.i.* Ronger son frein.—*n.* (*pop.*) [CHAMPION].
champagne [ʃæm'pein], *n.* Vin de Champagne, *m.*
*****champaign** ['tʃæmpein], *n.* Campagne, *f.*, pays ouvert, *m.*, rase campagne, *f.*—*a.* De campagne.
champignon [tʃæm'pinjən], *n.* Faux mousseron, *m.*, *Agaricus oreades.*
champion ['tʃæmpiən], *n.* Champion; (*Engl.*) recordman, *m.*—*v.t.* Soutenir, défendre. *To champion someone's cause*, prendre fait et cause pour quelqu'un. **championship**, *n.* Championnat, *m.*
chance [tʃɑːns], *n.* Chance, *f.*, hasard, sort; coup du sort, *m. By chance*, par hasard, fortuitement; *the main chance*, son intérêt propre, le solide, *m.*; *give him a chance*, prenez-le à l'essai, agissez loyalement envers lui; *now it is your chance!* vous avez la partie belle; *to leave nothing to chance*, ne rien abandonner au hasard; *to take one's chance of*, courir la chance de; *to take no chances*, ne rien hasarder.—*v.i.* Arriver par hasard, venir à. *I'll chance it*, arrive que pourra; *to chance it*, risquer le paquet; *to chance to meet*, *to chance upon*, rencontrer par hasard.—*a.* Accidentel, de hasard. **chance-medley**, *n.* (*Law*) Homicide involontaire, *m.*, *or* en légitime défense. **chancy**, *a.* (*colloq.*) Chanceux, risqué.
chancel ['tʃɑːnsəl], *n.* Sanctuaire, chœur, *m.*
chancellery ['tʃɑːnsələri], *n.* Chancellerie, *f.*
chancellor ['tʃɑːnsələ], *n.* Chancelier, *m. Chancellor of the Exchequer*, ministre des finances, *m.*; *Lord Chancellor*, grand chancelier, président de la Chambre des Lords, *m.* **chancellorship**, *n.* Charge *or* dignité de chancelier, *f.* **chancery**, *n.* Cour de la chancellerie, *f.*
chancre ['ʃæŋkə], *n.* Chancre, *m.* **chancrous** ['ʃæŋkrəs], *a.* Chancreux.
chandelier [ʃændi'liə], *n.* Lustre, *m.*
chandler ['tʃɑːndlə], *n.* Marchand *or* fabricant de chandelles, droguiste; marchand de couleurs, *m. Corn-chandler*, marchand de blé,

m.; *ship-chandler*, approvisionneur de navires, *m.* **chandlery**, *n.* Épiceries, *f.pl.*
change [tʃeindʒ], *n.* Changement, *m.*; phase (of moon), *f.*; monnaie (cash), *f.*; (*colloq.*) linge blanc, *m. A change of linen*, du linge blanc, du linge de rechange, *m.*; *a little change*, une petite distraction; *change of front*, revirement, *m.*; *change of horses*, relais, *m.*; *change of life*, retour d'âge, *m.*; *changes of life*, vicissitudes, *f.pl.*; *for a change*, pour changer; *I have no change*, je n'ai pas de monnaie; *on change*, à la Bourse; *small change*, petite monnaie; *to be a gainer or loser by the change*, gagner *or* perdre au change; *to ring the changes on*, rabâcher, broder des variations sur.—*v.t.* Changer; modifier; donner la monnaie de. *To change carriages, trains*, (*Rail.*) changer de wagon, de train; *all change!* tout le monde descend!—*v.i.* Changer (de); se renouveler (of the moon). *To change for the better*, s'améliorer; *to change up* or *down*, (*Motor.*) passer les vitesses. **changeable**, *a.* Changeant, variable, inconstant. **changeableness** or **changeability**, *n.* Caractère variable, *m.*; inconstance, *f.* **changeably**, *adv.* D'une manière variable. **changeful**, *a.* Inconstant, changeant. **changeless**, *a.* Immuable, constant, invariable.
changeling ['tʃeindʒliŋ], *n.* Enfant substitué, *m.*
changer, *n.* Changeur, *m.*
changing, *n.* Changement, *m. Changing of the guard*, relève de la garde, *f.* **changing-room**, *n.* Vestiaire, *m.*
channel ['tʃænl], *n.* Canal; lit (of rivers), *m.*; passe (of harbours), *f.*; (*Naut.*) détroit, *m.*; (*fig.*) voie, *f.*, moyen, *m.*, entremise, *f. St. George's Channel*, le canal St. Georges, *m.*; *the Channel Islands*, les îles Anglo-normandes, *f.pl.*; *the English Channel*, la Manche, *f.*—*v.t.* Creuser; (*Arch.*) canneler; évider.
chant [tʃɑːnt], *n.* Chant, plain-chant, *m.*—*v.t.*, *v.i.* Chanter, réciter en chantant. *To chant the praises of*, chanter les louanges de; (*fam.*) *to chant a horse*, maquignonner un cheval. **chanter**, *n.* Chantre, *m.*; chalumeau, *m.* (of bag-pipe). **chantress**, *n.* Choriste, chanteuse, *f.*
chanticleer [tʃænti'kliə], *n.* (*Lit.*) Chantecler, le coq, *m.*
chantry ['tʃɑːntri], *n.* Chantrerie, *f.*
chanty ['ʃɑːnti, 'ʃænti], *n.* Chanson de bord, *f.*
chaos ['keiɔs], *n.* Chaos, *m.*
chaotic [kei'ɔtik], *a.* Chaotique.
chap (1) [tʃæp], *v.t.* Gercer.—*v.i.* Gercer, se gercer.—*n.* Gerçure, crevasse (on the hands etc.), *f.* **chappy**, *a.* Plein de gerçures.
chap (2) [tʃæp], *n.* Garçon, gaillard, type, *m. Old chap*, (*colloq.*) mon vieux.
chap (3) [tʃæp] or **chop**, *n.* Mâchoire, bouche; bajoue (of pigs), *f.* **chap-fallen**, *a.* (*fam.*) Penaud, abattu, consterné.
chape [tʃeip], *n.* Chape, bouterolle, attache, *f.*
chapel ['tʃæpəl], *n.* Chapelle, *f.*; (par opposition à *church*) temple (dissident), *m.*; (*Print.*) atelier, *m.* (*sch.*) *To keep a chapel*, être présent à un office. *Chapel of ease*, (église) succursale, *f.*
chaperon ['ʃæpəroun], *n.* Chaperon, *m.*—*v.t.* Chaperonner.
chaplain ['tʃæplin], *n.* Aumônier, *m.* **chaplaincy** or **chaplainship**, *n.* Aumônerie, *f.*

chaplet ['tʃæplit], *n.* Chapelet, *m.*, guirlande, *f.*
*chapman ['tʃæpmən], *n.* Colporteur, *m.*
chapter ['tʃæptə], *n.* Chapitre, *m. A chapter of accidents*, une succession de mésaventures; *to give chapter and verse*, citer ses références, mettre les points sur les i; *to the end of the chapter*, à la fin des fins.
chapter-house, *n.* Chapitre, *m.*
char (1) [tʃɑː], *v.t.* Carboniser.—*v.i.* Se carboniser.
char (2) [tʃɑː], *n.* (*Ichth.*) Ombre chevalier, *m.*
char (3) [tʃɑː] or **chare,** *v.i.* Faire des ménages; aller en journée.—*n.* (*pop. abbr. of* CHARWOMAN). Femme de ménage, *f.*
charring (1) ['tʃɑːriŋ], *n.* Carbonisation, *f.*, flambage, *m.*
charring (2) ['tʃɑːriŋ], *n.* Travail de ménage *or* ouvrage à la journée; jour de travail, *m.*
char-a-banc ['ʃærəbæŋ], *n.* Autocar, car, *m.*
character ['kæriktə], *n.* Caractère; (*Theat.*) rôle, personnage; genre, *m.*, nature, qualité, réputation, description, *f.*; certificat (de moralité); (*fig.*) personnage, type, *m. A man of bad character*, un homme de mauvaise réputation, *m.*; *a bad character*, un mauvais sujet, *m.*; *a character actor*, un acteur de genre; *he is quite a character*, c'est un vrai original; *I do not like books of that character*, je n'aime pas les livres de ce genre; *in character*, dans son rôle, à sa place, dans le vrai; *in his character of*, en sa qualité de; *out of character*, déplacé, qui jure avec; *printed in roman characters*, imprimé en caractères romains; *she has lots of character*, elle a beaucoup de caractère; *to give a bad character to*, donner un mauvais certificat à; *to go for a character*, aller aux renseignements (of servants).
characteristic [kæriktə'ristik], *a.* Caractéristique. (*Med.*) *Characteristic symptom*, symptôme diacritique, *m.*—*n.* Trait caractéristique, *m.*; (*Gram., Math.*) caractéristique, *f.* **characteristically,** *adv.* D'une manière caractéristique.
characterize ['kæriktəraiz], *v.t.* Caractériser. **characterization,** *n.* Action de caractériser, *f.* **characterless,** *a.* Sans caractère.
charade [ʃə'rɑːd], *n.* Charade, *f.*
charcoal ['tʃɑːkoul], *n.* Charbon de bois, *m. Animal charcoal*, noir animal, *m.*; *charcoal drawing*, dessin au fusain, *m.* **charcoal-burner,** *n.* Charbonnier, *m.* **charcoal-furnace,** *n.* Carbonisateur, *m.*
chare [CHAR (3)].
chard [tʃɑːd], *n.* Carde, *f.*
charge [tʃɑːdʒ], *v.t.* Charger, accuser (de); faire payer; prendre, demander, percevoir, compter; (*fig.*) adjurer; ordonner à. (*Elec.*) *To charge a battery*, (re)charger un accumulateur; *to charge the enemy*, charger l'ennemi; *to charge to someone's account*, mettre sur le compte de.—*v.i.* (*Mil.*) Charger, faire une charge.—*n.* Charge, *f.*; prix (price), *m.*; garde, *f.*; soin; ordre, commandement; (*Law*) acte d'accusation, *m.*, accusation, *f.*; mandement (of a bishop); office, *m.*, fonctions, *f.pl.*; résumé (of a judge), *m.*; (*pl.*) frais, dépens, *m.pl.*; fournée (of kiln), *f. Bursting charge*, charge d'explosif; *free of charge*, gratis, franco; *in charge of*, à la charge de, sous la garde de; commis à la garde de; *list of charges*, tarif, *m.*; *the officer in charge*, l'officier

commandant; *to bring a charge against*, porter une accusation contre, accuser; *to give in charge*, faire arrêter; *to take charge of*, se charger de. **chargeable,** *a.* À charge (à); accusable (de); imposable; grevé (de).
charger, *n.* Grand plat; cheval de bataille, *m.*, *or* d'armes; (*Elec.*) chargeur, *m.*; (*Ind.*) chargeuse (of hopper etc.), *f.* **charging,** *n.* Chargement, *m. Battery charging*, (re)charge des accumulateurs, *f.*
charily ['tʃɛərili], *adv.* Avec précaution, avec circonspection; frugalement; à contre-cœur.
chariness, *n.* Précaution, prudence, circonspection, *f.*
chariot ['tʃæriət], *n.* Char, chariot, *m. Chariot-race*, course de chars, *f.*
charioteer [tʃæriə'tiə], *n.* Conducteur de chariot; (*Astron.*) cocher, *m.*
charitable ['tʃæritəbl], *a.* De bienfaisance; de charité; charitable. **charitably,** *adv.* Charitablement. **charity,** *n.* Charité, bienveillance; aumône, bienfaisance (alms); œuvre de bienfaisance, *f. Charity begins at home*, charité bien ordonnée commence par soi-même; *charity school*, école gratuite, *f.* orphelinat, *m.*; *out of charity*, par pure charité; *to ask for charity*, demander l'aumône.
charlady, *n.* [CHARWOMAN].
charlatan ['ʃɑːlətən], *n.* Charlatan, *m.*
charlatanic [ʃɑːlə'tænik], *a.* Charlatanesque, de charlatan. **charlatanism** or **charlatanry,** *n.* Charlatanerie, *f.*, charlatanisme, *m.*
Charles's Wain ['tʃɑːlziz'wein], *n.* (*Astron.*) Le Grand Chariot, *m.*, la Grande Ourse, *f.*
charlock ['tʃɑːlək], *n.* Moutarde des champs, *f. Joint-podded charlock*, ravenelle, *f.*
charm [tʃɑːm], *n.* Charme, *m.*; breloque (trinket), *f.*, porte-bonheur, *m. inv.*; (*pl.*) attraits, appâts, *m.pl.*—*v.t.* Charmer, enchanter. *You bear a charmed life*, votre vie est sous un charme. **charmer,** *n.* Enchanteur, *m.*, enchanteresse, *f.*, charmeur, *m.*, charmeuse, *f.* **charming,** *a.* Enchanteur, charmant; joli, délicieux, ravissant. **charmingly,** *adv.* D'une manière charmante, à ravir. **charmless,** *a.* Sans charme.
charnel ['tʃɑːnəl], *a.* De charnier. **charnel-house,** *n.* Charnier, ossuaire, *m.*
chart [tʃɑːt], *n.* Carte marine, *f.*; graphique, *m.*—*v.t.* Porter sur une carte. **chart-room,** *n.* Chambre des cartes, *f.* (*Med.*) *Temperature chart*, feuille de température, *f.*
charter ['tʃɑːtə], *n.* Charte, *f.*, acte; (*fig.*) privilège, *m. On charter*, loué, affrété.—*v.t.* Instituer par une charte, établir par un acte; (*Comm.*) fréter, affréter. *Chartered accountant*, expert comptable, *m.* **charter-party,** *n.* Charte-partie, *f.* **charter-plane,** *n.* Avion-taxi, *m.*
charterer, *n.* Affréteur, *m.* **chartism,** *n.* Chartisme, *m.* **chartist,** *n.* Chartiste, *m.*
charwoman ['tʃɑːwumən] *n.* Femme de journée, femme de ménage, *f.* **char-work,** *n.* Ouvrage à la journée, *m.*
chary ['tʃɛəri], *a.* Prudent, économe; circonspect, soigneux.
Charybdis [kə'ribdis]. Charybde, *f.*
chase [tʃeis], *n.* Chasse; poursuite; volée (of cannon), *f.*; (*Print.*) châssis, *m.*—*v.t.* Chasser, poursuivre, donner la chasse à; (*Metal.*) ciseler. *To chase away*, chasser. **chaser,** *n.*

Chasseur; ciseleur; (*Navy*) vaisseau chasseur; avion de chasse, *m.*; (*fam.*) poussecafé, *m. inv.* **chasing,** *n.* Ciselure, *f.*
chasm ['kæzəm], *n.* Abîme; chasme; vide énorme, *m.*, brèche, fissure, *f.*
chassis ['ʃæsi], *n.* (*Motor.*) Châssis, *m.*
chaste [tʃeist], *a.* Chaste, pudique; pur (of language); de bon goût (of taste). **chastely,** *adv.* Chastement, pudiquement. **chasteness,** *n.* Pureté, *f.*
chasten [tʃeisn], *v.t.* Châtier; corriger; assagir; purifier. **chastening,** *n.* Châtiment, *m.*, purifier. **chastening,** *n.* Châtiment, *m.*, correction, *f.*
chastise [tʃæs'taiz], *v.t.* Châtier. **chastisement** ['tʃæstizmənt], *n.* Châtiment, *m.*
chastity ['tʃæstiti], *n.* Chasteté, pureté, *f.*
chasuble ['tʃæzjubl], *n.* Chasuble, *f.*
chat [tʃæt], *n.* Causerie; (*colloq.*) causette, *f.*, entretien, *m.* *To have a chat,* faire la causette, tailler des bavettes (avec).—*v.i.* Causer, bavarder; (*colloq.*) faire la causette.
chatoyant [ʃə'tɔiənt], *a.* Chatoyant.
chattel [tʃætl], *n.* Bien meuble, *m.*; (*pl.*) objets mobiliers, *m.pl.* *Goods and chattels,* biens et effets, *m.pl.*
chatter ['tʃætə], *v.i.* Jaser, bavarder; jacasser (of monkeys etc.); babiller; claquer (of the teeth).—*n.* Caquetage, *m.*, jaserie, *f.* **chatterbox,** *n.* Moulin à paroles, *m.* **chatterer,** *n.* Jaseur, babillard, *m.*, babillarde, *f.* **chattering,** *n.* Jaserie, *f.*; babil, caquetage; claquement (of the teeth), *m.*; (*Eng.*) broutement, *m.*
chattiness, *n.* Loquacité, *f.* **chatty,** *a.* Causeur, bavard.
chauffeur ['ʃoufə, ʃou'fə:], *n.* Chauffeur, *m.*
chauvinism ['ʃouvinizəm], *n.* Chauvinisme, *m.* **chauvinistic,** *a.* Chauvin, chauviniste.
chaw [tʃɔ:], *v.t.* Mâcher; chiquer.—*n.* Chique (quid), *f.*
cheap [tʃi:p], *a.* À bon marché; à bon compte; peu coûteux; de peu de valeur. *Dirt cheap,* pour rien, à vil prix; *on the cheap,* à peu de frais, à bas prix; *to feel cheap,* être honteux; *to hold cheap,* faire bon marché de. **cheapjack,** *n.* Camelot, *m.* **cheapen,** *v.t.* Diminuer la valeur de, faire baisser le prix de. *To cheapen oneself,* se déprécier. **cheaper,** *a.* À meilleur marché, à meilleur compte, moins coûteux. **cheaply,** *adv.* À bon marché, à bon compte. **cheapness,** *n.* Bon marché, bas prix, *m.*; basse qualité, *f.*
cheat [tʃi:t], *n.* Fourberie, tromperie, *f.*; fourbe, trompeur, *m.*, trompeuse (person), *f.*; (*Cards* etc.) tricheur, *m.*, tricheuse, *f.*—*v.t.* Tromper, duper, friponner; (*Cards* etc.) tricher. **cheating,** *n.* Tromperie, friponnerie, filouterie; (*Cards* etc.) tricherie, *f.*
check [tʃek], *v.t.* Réprimer; arrêter, mettre obstacle à; contenir, modérer; (*Comm.*) vérifier; enregistrer (luggage etc.); (*Chess*) faire échec à.—*n.* Échec, obstacle; frein, *m.*; (*Theat.*) contremarque, *f.*; contrôle, *m.*, vérification, *f.*; (*Comm.*) mandat, bon, *m.*; (*Am.*) [CHEQUE, BILL (3)]; carreau, damier (pattern), *m.*; (*Chess*) échec, *m.* *Luggage check,* bulletin de bagages, *m.* *To hold in check,* tenir en échec; *to keep a check on,* contrôler. *Check cloth,* étoffe à carreaux, étoffe en damier, *f.* **check-book,** *n.* (*Am.*) [CHEQUE-BOOK]. **check-rail,** *n.* Contre-rail, *m.* **check-taker,** *n.* Contrôleur, receveur

de contre-marques, *m.* **checkers** [CHEQUERS].
checking, *n.* Répression; vérification, *f.*; contrôle, *m.*; enregistrement (of luggage), *m.*
checkmate ['tʃekmeit], *n.* Échec et mat, *m.*—*v.t.* Faire échec et mat à, mater.
cheek [tʃi:k], *n.* Joue; bajoue (of a pig); (*fig.*) impudence, *f.*, front, toupet, *m.*; jumelle (of a press), *f.* *Cheek by jowl,* côte à côte.—*v.t.* Narguer. **cheek-bone,** *n.* Pommette, *f.* *With high cheek-bones,* aux pommettes saillantes. **cheekinesss,** *n.* Effronterie, *f.* **cheeky,** *a.* Impudent, effronté.
cheep [tʃi:p], *n.* Piaulement, *m.*—*v.i.* Piauler.
cheer [tʃiə], *n.* Chère (food etc.); gaieté, *f.*, courage, *m.*; acclamation, *f.*, applaudissement, hourra, vivat, *m.* *To be of good cheer,* avoir bon espoir.—*v.t.* Égayer, réjouir, consoler, animer; applaudir, acclamer.—*v.i.* Se réjouir; applaudir, crier vivat, pousser des applaudissements. *Cheer up!* courage! *to cheer up,* se ranimer, prendre courage; *cheers!* à la vôtre! **cheerful,** *a.* Joyeux, gai; riant (of prospect etc.). **cheerfully,** *adv.* Gaiement, joyeusement, de bon cœur. **cheerfulness,** *n.* Gaieté, allégresse, bonne humeur, *f.* **cheerily,** *adv.* Gaiement. **cheering,** *n.* Applaudissements, vivats, hourras, *m.pl.*—*a.* Consolant, réjouissant, encourageant. **cheerio,** *int.* (*fam.*) (*Good-bye*) À bientôt! (*when drinking*) à votre santé! **cheery,** *a.* Gai, joyeux, réjoui.
cheese [tʃi:z], *n.* Fromage, *m.*; marc de pommes, *f.* *Cream cheese,* fromage blanc, *m.* *Green cheese,* fromage à la pie. *Hard cheese!* (*fam.*) pas de chance! **cheesecake,** *n.* Talmouse, *f.* **cheese-cloth,** *n.* (*Am.*) [MUSLIN]. **cheesemonger,** *n.* Marchand de fromage, *m.* **cheese-paring,** *n.* Pelure, croûte (de fromage), *f.*; (*fig.*) économie de bouts de chandelle, *f.* **cheese-rennet,** *n.* Caille-lait, *m.*, présure, *f.* **cheese-straws,** *n.pl.* Craquelins au fromage, *m.pl.* **cheese-taster,** *n.* Sonde à fromage, *f.* **cheesy,** *a.* Caséeux; qui sent le fromage.
cheetah or **chetah** ['tʃi:tə], *n.* Guépard, *m.*
chef [ʃef], *n.* Chef (cuisinier), *m.*
chemical ['kemikəl], *a.* Chimique. **chemically,** *adv.* Chimiquement. **chemicals,** *n.pl.* Produits chimiques, *m.pl.* **chemico-physical,** *a.* Chemico-physique.
chemise [ʃi'mi:z], *n.* Chemise de femme, *f.*
chemist ['kemist], *n.* (Scientist) Chimiste; (druggist) pharmacien, *m.* *Chemist's shop,* pharmacie, *f.* **chemistry,** *n.* Chimie, *f.*, chimisme, *m.* *Chemistry of the blood,* le chimisme du sang. **chemotherapy,** *n.* Chimiothérapie, *f.*
cheque [tʃek], *n.* Chèque, *m.* *Crossed, open cheque,* chèque barré, non barré. **chequebook,** *n.* Carnet de chèques, *m.*
chequer ['tʃekə], *v.t.* Quadriller; guillocher; diaprer. **chequer-board,** *n.* (*Am.*) Échiquier, damier, *m.* **chequered,** *a.* À carreaux; (*fig.*) accidenté, varié. *A chequered career,* une carrière pleine de vicissitudes.
chequers, *n.pl.* (*Am.*) Jeu de dames, *m.*; (*Tex.*) quadrillage, *m.*
cherish ['tʃeriʃ], *v.t.* Chérir; soigner; nourrir, entretenir (hopes etc.).
cheroot [ʃə'ru:t], *n.* Cigare à bouts coupés, *m.*

cherry ['tʃeri], *n.* Cerise, *f. Black-heart cherry*, guigne noire, *f.*; *to make two bites at a cherry*, agir maladroitement; *white-heart cherry*, bigarreau, *m.—a.* De cerise, cerise (*inv.*), vermeil. **cherry-cheeked,** *a.* Aux joues vermeilles. **cherry-garden** or **-orchard,** *n.* Cerisaie, *f.* **cherry-laurel**, *n.* Laurier-cerise, *m.* **cherry-pie,** *n.* Tourte aux cerises, *f.*; (*Bot., fam.*) héliotrope, *m.* **cherry-stone,** *n.* Noyau de cerise, *m.* **cherry-tree,** *n.* Cerisier, *m.*

cherub ['tʃerəb], *n.* (*pl.* **cherubs; cherubim,** biblical) Chérubin, *m.* **cherubic** [tʃə'ruːbik], *a.* De chérubin, angélique.

chervil ['tʃəːvil], *n.* (*Bot.*) Cerfeuil, *m.*

chess [tʃes], *n.* Échecs, *m.pl.* **chess-board,** *n.* Échiquier, *m.* **chessman,** *n.* Pièce, *f. A set of chessmen*, un jeu d'échecs, *m.* **chess-player,** *n.* Joueur d'échecs, *m.*

chest [tʃest], *n.* Coffre, *m.*, caisse, boîte; poitrine (of the body), *f.*; poitrail (of a horse); (*Mil.*) caisson, *m. Chest of drawers*, commode, *f. To get something off one's chest*, raconter ce qu'on a sur le cœur.—*v.t.* Encoffrer, encaisser. **chest-complaint,** *n.* Maladie de poitrine, *f.* **chest-protector,** *n.* Plastron hygiénique, *m.* **chested,** *a.* À poitrine; à poitrail (of horses). *Broad-chested*, à large poitrine; au poitrail large (of horses). **chesty,** *a.* (*fam.*) Délicat des bronches.

chesterfield ['tʃestəfiːld], *n.* Pardessus, *m.*

chestnut ['tʃesnʌt], *n.* Marron, *m.*; châtaigne, *f. That's a chestnut,* (*fig.*) c'est connu! vieille histoire! *f.*, vieux conte! *m.—a.* Châtain, marron (colour); alezan (of horses). **chestnut-tree,** *n.* Châtaignier (Spanish chestnut); marronnier d'Inde (horse-chestnut), *m. Chestnut grove*, châtaigneraie, *f.*

cheval-glass [ʃe'væl 'glɑːs], *n.* Psyché, *f.*

chevalier [ʃevə'liə], *n.* Chevalier, *m.*

cheverel ['tʃevərəl], *n.* Chevreau (leather), *m.*

chevron ['ʃevrɔn], *n.* (*Mil.*) Chevron, *m.*

chevy ['tʃevi] or **chivy** or **chivvy** ['tʃivi], *v.t.* Chasser, poursuivre.

chew [tʃuː], *v.t.* Mâcher. (*fig.*) *To chew over something*, méditer sur, ruminer quelque chose. *To chew the cud*, ruminer; *to chew tobacco*, chiquer. **chewer,** *n.* Mâcheur, *m.* **chewing-gum,** *n.* Chewing-gum, *m.*; gomme à mâcher, *f.*

chiaroscuro [kjarɔ'skuːro], *n.* (*Paint.*) Clairobscur, *m.*

chicane [ʃi'kein], *n.* Chicane, *f.—v.i.* Chicaner. **chicaner,** *n.* Chicaneur, *m.*, chicaneuse, *f.* **chicanery,** *n.* Chicanerie, chicane, *f.*

chick [tʃik], *n.* Poussin, *m.*; (*fig.*) poulet, *m.*, poulette, *f.* **chick-pea,** *n.* Pois chiche, *m.* **chickweed,** *n.* Mouron des oiseaux, *m.* **chickabiddy,** *n.* (*colloq.*) Coco(t)te, *f.* **chicken,** *n.* Poussin; poulet, *m. Don't count your chickens before they are hatched,* (*fig.*) il ne faut pas vendre la peau de l'ours avant de l'avoir tué; *he's no chicken,* ce n'est plus un enfant, tant s'en faut. **chicken-hearted,** *a.* Peureux, poltron. *A chicken-hearted fellow*, une poule mouillée, *f.* **chicken-pox,** *n.* Varicelle, *f.* **chicken-run,** *n.* Poulailler, *m.*

chicle [tʃikl], *n.* Chiclé, *m.*

chicory ['tʃikəri], *n.* (*short for* broad-leaved chicory). Chicorée, endive, *f.*, (*usu. pl.*) des endives, *f.pl.*

chide [tʃaid], *v.t.* Gronder, blâmer, réprimander.—*v.i.* Gronder, murmurer. **chiding,** *n.* Gronderie, *f.* **chidingly,** *adv.* En grondant.

chief [tʃiːf], *n.* Chef, *m.*; partie principale, *f.* (*fam.*) *The chief*, le patron, *m.—a.* Principal, premier, en chef. **chiefdom,** *n.* Souveraineté, suprématie, *f.* **chiefless,** *a.* Sans chef. **chiefly,** *adv.* Surtout, principalement. **chieftain,** *n.* Chef de clan, *m.*

chiff-chaff ['tʃiftʃæf], *n.* Pouillot véloce, *m.*

chiffon ['ʃifɔn], *n.* Chiffon, *m.*

chiffonier [ʃifə'niə], *n.* Chiffonnier, *m.*

chilblain ['tʃilblein], *n.* Engelure, *f.*

child [tʃaild], *n.* (*pl.* **children** ['tʃildrən]) Enfant. *A burnt child dreads the fire*, chat échaudé craint l'eau froide; *from a child*, dès l'enfance; *to be a good child*, être sage; *to be a naughty child*, être méchant; *with child*, enceinte, grosse.—*n. used as a. Child psychology*, psychologie infantile, *f.* **child-bearing,** *n.* Grossesse, *f.*; travail d'enfant, *m.* **child-bed,** *n.* Couches, *f.pl.* **child-birth,** *n.* Enfantement, *m.* **child's-play,** *n.* Jeu d'enfant, enfantillage, *m. It is mere child's-play*, c'est facile comme tout. **childhood,** *n.* Enfance, *f. In second childhood*, tombé en enfance. **childish,** *a.* Enfantin; puéril. *To grow childish,* tomber en enfance. **childishly,** *adv.* Puérilement, comme un enfant. **childishness,** *n.* Puérilité, *f.*; enfantillage, *m.*; seconde enfance, *f.* **childless,** *a.* Sans enfant. **childlike,** *a.* Comme un enfant, en enfant.

Chile ['tʃili]. Le Chili, *m.*

chill [tʃil], *n.* Froid; refroidissement, frisson, *m. To cast a chill over*, jeter un froid sur; *to catch a chill*, prendre froid, attraper un refroidissement; *to take the chill off*, faire tiédir, dégourdir.—*a.* Froid; glacé.—*v.t.* Refroidir; (*fig.*) glacer, faire frissonner; décourager. *Chilled meat*, viande frigorifiée, *f.* **chilliness,** *n.* Froid, frisson, *m.*; froideur, fraîcheur, *f.* **chilly,** *a.* Un peu froid (of things); frileux (of persons). *It's getting chilly this evening,* il commence à faire frisquet ce soir.

chilli ['tʃili], *n.* Piment, *m.*

Chiltern Hundreds ['tʃiltən 'hʌndridz] Communes de Chiltern, *f.pl. To accept the Chiltern Hundreds*, donner sa démission de membre de la Chambre des Communes.

chime [tʃaim], *n.* Carillon, *m.*; (*fig.*) accord de sons, son harmonieux, *m.—v.t.* Carillonner, mettre en mouvement.—*v.i.* Carillonner; s'accorder (avec). (*fig.*) *To chime in*, intervenir, placer son mot.

chimera [kai'miərə], *n.* Chimère, *f.* **chimerical** [ki'merikəl], *a.* Chimérique. **chimerically,** *adv.* Chimériquement.

chimney ['tʃimni], *n.* Cheminée, *f. Chimney ornaments*, garniture de cheminée, *f.* **chimney-corner,** *n.* Coin du feu, *m.* **chimney-flue,** *n.* Tuyau de cheminée, *m.* **chimney-piece,** *n.* Chambranle *or* manteau de cheminée, *m.*; (*colloq.*) tablette de cheminée, *f.* **chimney-pot,** *n.* Tuyau de cheminée, pot de cheminée, *m. Chimney-pot hat*, chapeau haut de forme, (*colloq.*) tuyau de poêle, *m.* **chimney-stack,** *n.* Corps de cheminée, *m.* **chimney-sweep** or **chimney-sweeper,** *n.* Ramoneur, *m.* **chimney-sweeping,** *n.* Ramonage, *m.*

chimpanzee [tʃimpæn'ziː], *n.* Chimpanzé, *m.*
chin [tʃin], *n.* Menton, *m.* (*fam.*) *Chin up!* courage!—*v.t.* To chin the bar, (*Gymn.*) toucher la barre avec le menton (en faisant une traction). **chin-strap**, *n.* Jugulaire, mentonnière, *f.* **chin-wagging**, *n.* Jabotage, bavardage, *m.*
China [tʃainə]. La Chine, *f.*
china [tʃainə], *n.* Porcelaine, *f.* *China painter*, peintre sur porcelaine, *m.*; *china shop*, magasin de porcelaine *m.* **china-aster**, *n.* Reine marguerite, *f.* **china-clay**, *n.* Argile à porcelaine, *f.*, kaolin, *m.* **chinaware**, *n.* Vaisselle de porcelaine, *f.*
*****chin-cough** [tʃinkɔf], *n.* Coqueluche, *f.*
chine [tʃain], *n.* Échine (of pork), *f.*; (*Geol.*) ravine, ravinée, *f.*
Chinese [tʃai'niːz], *a.* Chinois, de Chine. *Chinese lantern*, lanterne vénitienne, *f.*; *Chinese white*, blanc de Chine, *m.*—*n.* Chinois, *m.*, chinoise, *f.*; chinois (language), *m.*
Chink [tʃiŋk], *n.* (*pop.*) Chinois, *m.*
chink [tʃiŋk], *n.* Crevasse, fente, lézarde, *f.*; son, tintement, *m.*; (*slang*) argent, *m.*—*v.t.* Crevasser, faire crevasser; faire sonner.—*v.i.* Se fendiller, se crevasser; sonner.
chintz [tʃints], *n.* (*Tex.*) Indienne, *f.*
chip [tʃip], *n.* Copeau, fragment, éclat, *m.*; (*Cards*) jeton, *m.* *To be a chip of the old block*, chasser de race, être bien le fils de son père; *to have a chip on one's shoulder*, chercher noise à tout le monde. *n.pl.* (*Naut., fam.*) *Chips* or *chippy*, charpentier, *m.*; *fried chips*, des pommes de terre frites.—*v.t.* Tailler, hacher, ébrécher, écorner; faire un croc-en-jambe à; railler. (*Golf.*) *To chip the ball*, jouer un chip-shot.—*v.i.* S'écorner, s'ébrécher, s'éclater; s'écailler (of china etc.). *To chip in*, y mettre du sien; (*Cards*) miser; *to chip off*, s'écailler. **chipping**, *n.* Fragment, éclat, *m.*; chapelure (of bread); écaille (of china etc.), *f.*
chipmunk [tʃipmʌŋk], *n.* (*Zool.*) Tamias, écureuil d'Amérique, *m.*
chiragra [kaiə'rægrə], *n.* Chiragre, *f.*
chiromancy [kaiərɔmænsi], *n.* Chiromancie, *f.*
chiropodist [ki'rɔpədist], *n.* Pédicure, *m.* **chiropody**, *n.* Chirurgie pédicure, *f.*
chirp [tʃəːp], *v.i.* Pépier, chanter, gazouiller; grisoller (of larks); crier (of insects).—*n.* Gazouillement, pépiement, chant; cri (of insects), *m.* **chirping**, *n.* Pépiement, gazouillement, ramage; cri (of insects), *m.* **chirpiness**, *n.* Humeur gaie, *f.* **chirpy**, *a.* (*colloq.*) Gai, réjoui; bavard.
chirr [tʃəː], *v.i.* Striduler.—*n.* Stridulation, *f.*
chirrup [tʃirəp], *v.i.* [CHIRP].
chisel [tʃizl], *n.* Ciseau, *m.* *Cold chisel*, ciseau à froid, *m.* *Engraver's chisel*, burin, *m.*—*v.t.* Ciseler; (*slang*) filouter. **chiselling**, *n.* Ciselure; (*slang*) filouterie, escroquerie, *f.*
chit [tʃit], *n.* Marmot, bambin, mioche, *m.*; billet (note), permis, *m.* *Chit of a girl*, gamine, *f.*
chitchat [tʃittʃæt], *n.* Caquet, babillage, *m.*, bavardages, *m.pl.*
chitin [kaitin], *n.* Chitine, *f.*
chitterlings [tʃitəliŋz], *n.pl.* Andouilles, *f.pl.*
chivalrous [ʃivəlrəs], *a.* Chevaleresque. **chivalry**, *n.* Chevalerie, *f.*
chives [tʃaivz], *n.pl.* Ciboulette, *f.*

chivy or **chivvy** [CHEVY].
chlamys [klæmis], *n.* Chlamyde, *f.*
chlorate [klɔːreit], *n.* (*Chem.*) Chlorate, *m.* **chloric**, *a.* Chlorique. **chloride** [klɔːraid], *n.* Chlorure, *m.* *Chloride of lime*, chlorure de chaux, (*colloq.*) chlore, *m.*
chlorinate [klɔːrineit], *v.t.* Verduniser (drinking-water).
chlorination [klɔːri'neiʃən], *n.* Verdunisation, *f.*
chlorine [klɔːriːn], *n.* Chlore, *m.*
chloroform [klɔrəfɔːm], *n.* Chloroforme, *m.* —*v t.* Chloroformer.
chlorometer [klɔ'rɔmitə], *n.* Chloromètre, *m.*
chloromycetin [klɔrɔmai'siːtin], *n.* Chloromycétine, *f.*
chlorophyll [klɔːrəfil], *n.* Chlorophylle, *f.*
chlorosis [klə'rousis], *n.* (*Path.*) Chlorose, *f.*
chlorotic [klɔ'rɔtik], *a.* Chlorotique.
chlorous [klɔːrəs], *a.* Chloreux.
choc-ice [tʃɔkais], *n.* Chocolat glacé, *m.*
chock [tʃɔk], *n.* (*Naut. and Av.*) Cale, *f.*, clef, *f.* —*v.t.* Caler. *Chocked up with*, bondé de. **chock-full** or (*fam.*) **chock-a-block**, *a.* Plein comme un œuf; comble.
chocolate [tʃɔkəlit], *n.* Chocolat, *m.* *Chocolate factory*, chocolaterie, *f.* **chocolate-maker**, *n.* Chocolatier, *m.*
choice [tʃɔis], *n.* Choix, *m.*; élite, fleur, *f.*; assortiment, *m.* *For choice*, de préférence; *Hobson's choice*, choix forcé, à prendre ou à laisser; *of one's own choice*, de son propre gré; *to have no choice but to*, ne pas avoir d'autre choix que de.—*a.* Choisi; de choix; d'élite; recherché; fin (of wines); prudent, économe (de). **choiceless**, *a.* Qui n'a pas de choix. **choicely**, *adv.* Avec choix, avec grand soin. **choiceness**, *n.* Qualité recherchée, excellence, rareté, *f.*
choir [kwaiə], *n.* Chœur, *m. Male voice choir*, orphéon, *m.* **choir-boy**, *n.* Enfant de chœur, *m.* **choir-master**, *n.* Maître de chapelle, *m.* **choir-organ**, *n.* Orgue d'accompagnement, *m.* **choir-school**, *n.* Maîtrise, *f.* **choir-screen**, *n.* Jubé, *m.*
choke [tʃouk], *v.t.* Étouffer, suffoquer; engorger, boucher.—*v.i.* S'engorger, se boucher. *To choke back*, refouler; *to choke off someone*, (*fam.*) décourager quelqu'un.— *n.* Étranglement (of voice); foin (d'artichaut), (*Motor.*) starter, *m.* **choke-damp**, *n.* Air vicié, *m.*; mofette, *f.* **choke-pear**, *n.* Poire d'angoisse, *f.* **choker**, *n.* Foulard, *m.*; cravate, *f.*; collier court, *m.* (pearls etc.). **choking**, *n.* Étouffement, *m.*, suffocation, *f.*, engorgement (of things), *m.*—*a.* Étouffant. **choky**, *a.* Étouffant, suffoquant.
choler [kɔlə], *n.* Colère, bile, *f.*
choleric [kɔlərik], *a.* Colérique, irascible.
cholera [kɔlərə], *n.* Choléra, *m. Cholera morbus*, choléra morbus, *m.*
choleraic [kɔlə'reiik], *a.* Cholérique.
cholerine [kɔləriːn], *n.* Cholérine, *f.*, faux choléra, *m.*
cholesterine [kɔ'lestərin], *n.* (*Chem.*) Cholestérine, *f.*
choose [tʃuːz], *v.t.* (*past* **chose** [tʃouz], *p.p.* **chosen**) Choisir; élire; préférer; vouloir; se décider (à). *As you choose*, comme vous voudrez; *to choose rather*, aimer mieux; *I choose to do it*, il me plaît de le faire; *the*

chosen people, les élus. **chooser,** *n.* Personne qui choisit, *f.* **choosing,** *n.* Choix, *m.* **choosy,** *a.* (*fam.*) Difficile.

chop [tʃɔp], *v.t.* Couper en morceaux, hacher; trafiquer, troquer, échanger (to barter); (*Ten.*) couper (a ball). *To chop down,* abattre; *to chop logic,* ergoter, disputailler; *to chop off,* trancher, couper; *to chop up,* hacher menu. —*v.i.* Trafiquer, troquer; (*Naut.*) tourner, changer (of the wind); clapoter (of the sea). *To chop and change,* (*fig.*) girouetter.—*n.* Tranche; côtelette (de mouton), *f.*; clapotis, *m.* (of sea); (*colloq., pl.*) gueule, *f. Mutton chop,* côtelette de mouton au naturel, *f.*; *to lick one's chops,* se lécher les babouines. **chop-fallen** [CHAP-FALLEN]. **chop-house,** *n.* Restaurant, *m.* **chopstick,** *n.* Baguette, *f.,* bâtonnet, *m.* **chopper,** *n.* Ccuperet, *m.* **chopping,** *n.* Coupe, action de couper, *f.*; troc, *m.* (*Naut.*) clapotage, *m. Chopping and changing,* tergiversation, *f.,* girouetteries, *f.pl.* **chopping-block,** *n.* Hachoir, billot, *m.* **choppy,** *a.* Crevassé; haché; clapoteux (of the sea).

choral ['kɔ:rəl], *a.* Choral, en chœur, de chœur. *Choral society,* (société) chorale, *f.* **chorale** [kɔ'rɑ:l], *n.* Choral, *m.*

chord [kɔ:d], *n.* Corde, *f.*; (*Mus.*) accord, *m.*—*v.t.* Mettre des cordes à.

choreographer [kɔri'ɔgrəfə], *n.* Chorégraphe, *m.*

choreographic [-'græfic], *a.* Chorégraphique.

choreography [kɔri'ɔgrəfi], *n.* Chorégraphie, *f.*

chores [tʃɔ:z], *n.pl.* Corvées domestiques, *f.pl. To do the chores,* faire le ménage.

choriamb ['kɔriæmb] or **choriambus,** *n.* (*Pros.*) Choriambe, *m.*

chorister ['kɔristə], *n.* Choriste; enfant de chœur, *m.*

chortle [tʃɔ:tl], *v.i.* Glousser de joie; rire d'un petit rire étouffé.

chorus ['kɔ:rəs], *n.* Chœur; refrain, *m.*—*v.t., v.i.* Reprendre en chœur. **chorus-girl,** *n.* Choriste; girl, *f.*

chose, *past,* **chosen,** *p.p.* [CHOOSE].

chough [tʃʌf], *n.* Crave, *m.,* choucas, *m.*

chouse [tʃaus], *v.t.* Filouter, duper.

chow or **chow-chow** ['tʃau'tʃau], *n.* Chow-chow, chien chinois, *m.*

chrism [krizm], *n.* Chrême, *m.*

Christ [kraist]. Le Christ, *m.*

christen [krisn], *v.t.* Baptiser. **Christendom,** *n.* Chrétienté, *f.* **christening,** *n.* Baptême, *m.*

Christian ['kristjən], *a. and n.* Chrétien, *m.,* chrétienne, *f. Christian name,* nom de baptême, prénom, *m.*

Christianity [kristi'æniti], *n.* Christianisme, *m.*

Christianize ['kristjənaiz], *v.t.* Christianiser. **Christianlike,** *a.* Chrétien. **Christianly,** *adv.* Chrétiennement, en chrétien.

Christina [kris'ti:nə]. Christine, *f.*

Christmas ['krisməs], *n.* Noël, *m.,* la fête de Noël, *f. Christmas carol,* chant de Noël, *m.*; *Christmas Eve,* la veille de Noël, *f.*; *Christmas holidays,* vacances de Noël, *f.pl.* **Christmas-box,** *n.* Étrennes, *f.pl.* **Christmas-pudding,** *n.* Pudding de Noël, *m.*

Christopher ['kristəfə]. Christophe, *m.*

chromatic [kro'mætik], *a.* Chromatique.

chrome [kroum], *n.* Bichromate de potasse, *m. Chrome leather,* cuir chromé, *m.*

chromium ['kroumiəm], *n.* Chrome, *m. Chromium-plated,* chromé; *chromium-plating,* chromage, *m.*

chromogen ['kroumɔdʒən], *n.* Chromogène, *m.* **chromolithograph** [kroumɔ'laiθɔgrɑ:f], **chromolithography** [-'θɔgrəfi], *n.* Chromolithographie, *f.* **chromosome** ['kroumɔsoum], *n.* Chromosome, *m.* **chromosphere** ['kroumɔsfiə], *n.* Chromosphère, *f.* **chromotype** ['kroumɔtaip], *n.* **chromotypography** [kroumɔtai'pɔgrəfi], *n.* Chromotypographie, *f.*

chronic ['krɔnik], *a.* Chronique; continuel. *A chronic invalid,* un(e) (malade) chronique.

chronicle ['krɔnikl], *n.* Chronique, *f.*—*v.t.* Faire la chronique de, enregistrer; (*fig.*) raconter. *To chronicle small beer,* raconter des choses insignifiantes. **chronicler,** *n.* Chroniqueur, *m.*

chronogram ['krɔnəgræm], *n.* Chronogramme, *m.*

chronologer [krə'nɔlədʒə] or **chronologist,** *a.* Chronologiste, *m.*

chronological [krɔnə'lɔdʒikəl], *a.* Chronologique. **chronologically,** *adv.* Chronologiquement.

chronology [krə'nɔlədʒi], *n.* Chronologie, *f.*

chronometer [krə'nɔmitə], *n.* Chronomètre, *m.*

chrysalis ['krisəlis], *n.* Chrysalide, *f.*

chrysanthemum [kri'zænθiməm], *n.* Chrysanthème, *m.*

chrysolite ['krisəlait], *n.* Chrysolithe, *f.*

chub [tʃʌb], *n.* (*Ichth.*) Chabot, chevesne, *m.*

chubby ['tʃʌbi], *a.* Joufflu; potelé (of the hands).

chuck (1) [tʃʌk], *n.* Gloussement, *m.*—*v.i.* Glousser.

chuck (2) [tʃʌk], *n.* Petite tape sous le menton, *f.*; poulet (term of endearment), *m.,* poulette, *f.*—*v.t.* Donner des petits coups sous le menton à; jeter. (*pop.*) *To chuck out,* flanquer à la porte; *to chuck someone,* plaquer quelqu'un; *to chuck up,* abandonner. **chuck-farthing,** *n.* Fossette, *f.,* or jeu de bouchon, *m.*

chuck (3) [tʃʌk], *n.* Mandrin (on a lathe), paleron (of beef), *m.*

chuckle [tʃʌkl], *v.i.* Rire tout bas, rire sous cape (de).—*n.* Rire étouffé, gloussement, *m.*

chug [tʃʌg], *n. Chug of the engine,* souffle du moteur, *m.*—*v.i. To chug off,* partir en soufflant.

chum [tʃʌm], *n.* Camarade de chambre, intime, copain, *m.*—*v.i.* Être camarades de chambre. *To chum with,* être bien avec, s'accorder avec. **chummy,** *a.* Intime.

chump [tʃʌmp], *n.* Tronçon (de bois), *m.*; (*colloq.*) idiot, *m. Chump chop,* côtelette de gigot, *f.*; *chump end,* bas de gigot, *m.*; *off one's chump,* loufoque.

chunk [tʃʌŋk], *n.* Gros morceau (of bread), tronçon (of wood), *m.*; quignon (of bread), *m.*

church [tʃə:tʃ], *n.* Église, *f.*; (*Protestant*) temple; office (time), *m. Church clerk,* chantre, *m.*—*v.t.* Célébrer l'office des relevailles. *To be churched,* faire ses relevailles. **church-goer,** *n.* Qui va à l'église, pratiquant, *m.* **churching,** *n.* Relevailles, *f.pl.* **churchman,** *n.* (*pl.* **churchmen**) Homme d'église; ecclésiastique; anglican, *m.* **church-**

rate, *n.* Impôt au profit de l'Eglise, denier du culte, *m.* **church-service,** *n.* Office (time); service divin; paroissien (book), *m.*
churchwarden, *n.* Marguillier, *m.*; pipe hollandaise, *f.* **churchyard,** *n.* Cimetière, *m. A churchyard cough,* toux qui sent le sapin, *f.*
churl [tʃə:l], *n.* Rustre, manant, ladre, *m.* **churlish,** *a.* Grossier, rude, ladre. **churlishly,** *adv.* Grossièrement. **churlishness,** *n.* Grossièreté, *f.*
churn [tʃə:n], *n.* Baratte, *f. Milk churn* (on railway), bidon à lait, *m.*—*v.i.* Baratter.—*v.t.* Battre. **churning,** *n.* Barattage, *m.*
chute [ʃu:t], *n.* Glissière, piste (de luges), *f.*; couloir, plan incliné, *m.*
chutney [ˈtʃʌtni], *n.* Chutney, *m.*
chyle [kail], *n.* Chyle, *m.* **chylification,** *n.* Chylification, *f.* **chyliferous** [-ˈlifərəs], *a.* Chylifère. **chylify,** *v.t.* Chylifier.
chyme [kaim], *n.* Chyme, *m.* **chymification,** *n.* Chymification, *f.*
chymify [ˈkaimifai], *v.t.* Chymifier.
ciborium [siˈbɔ:riəm], *n.* Ciboire, *m.*
cicada [siˈkɑ:də], *n.* Cigale, *f.*
cicatrix [ˈsikətriks] or **cicatrice,** *n. (pl.* **cicatrices** [sikəˈtraisi:z]). Cicatrice, *f.* **cicatrization,** *n.* Cicatrisation, *f.* **cicatrize,** *v.t.* Cicatriser.—*v.i.* Se cicatriser.
Cicero [ˈsisərou]. Cicéron, *m.*
cicerone [tʃitʃəˈrouni], *n. (pl.* **ciceroni)** Cicérone, guide, *m.*
cider [ˈsaidə], *n.* Cidre, *m. New cider,* cidre doux. **cider-apple,** *n.* Pomme à cidre, *f.* **cider-brandy,** *n.* Calvados, *m.* **cider-cup,** *n.* Boisson glacée au cidre, *f.* **ciderkin,** *n.* Boisson de cidre, *f.*, petit cidre, *m.* **cider-press,** *n.* Pressoir à cidre, *m.*
cigar [siˈgɑ:], *n.* Cigare, *m.* **cigar-box,** *n.* Boîte à cigares, *f.* **cigar-case,** *n.* Porte-cigares; étui à cigares, *m.* **cigar-cutter,** *n.* Coupe-cigares, *m.* **cigar-holder,** *n.* Fumecigare, *m.* **cigar-maker,** *n.* Cigarière, *f.*
cigarette [sigəˈret], *n.* Cigarette, *f.* **cigarette-case,** *n.* Porte-cigarettes, *m. inv.*; étui à cigarettes, *m.* **cigarette-end,** *n.* Bout de cigarette, (*pop.*) mégot, *m.* **cigaretteholder,** *n.* Fume-cigarette, *m.* **cigarettepaper,** *n.* Papier à cigarettes, *m.*
ciliated [ˈsilieitid], *a.* (*Bot.*) Cilié. **ciliform,** *a.* Ciliforme.
cimeter [SCIMITAR].
cinch [sintʃ], *n.* (*Am.*) Sangle, *f.* (saddle-girth); (*pop.*) certitude, *f.*—*v.t.* Sangler.
cinchona [sinˈkounə], *n.* (*Bot.*) Quinquina, *m.*
cincture [ˈsiŋktʃə], *n.* (*poet.*) Ceinture, *f.*; (*Arch.*) filet, *m.*, moulure, *f.*
cinder [ˈsində], *n.* Cendre, *f.*; (*pl.*) escarbilles (of coal), *f.pl.*; fraisil (of a forge), *m.*, scories, *f.pl.* (of volcano). **cinder-track,** *n.* Piste cendrée, *f.*
Cinderella [sindəˈrelə]. Cendrillon, *f.*
cine-camera [siniˈkæmərə], *n.* Camera, caméra, *f.*
cinema [ˈsinimə], *n.* Cinéma, *m.* **cinemagoer,** *n.* Fervent(e), habitué(e) du cinéma.
cinematograph [siniˈmætəgrɑ:f], *n.* Cinématographe, *m.* **cinematographic,** *a.* Cinématographique. **cinematography,** *n.* Cinématographie, *f.* **cinemicrography,** *n.* Microcinématographie, *f.* **cineradiography,** *n.* Cinéradiographie, *f.*

cineraria [sinəˈrɛəriə], *n.* Cinéraire, *f.*
cinerary [ˈsinərəri], *a.* Cinéraire. **cineration** [-ˈreiʃən], *n.* Incinération, *f.*
cinnabar [ˈsinəbɑ:], *n.* Cinabre, *m.*, vermillon, *m.*
cinnamon [ˈsinəmən], *n.* Cannelle, *f.*
cinque [siŋk], *n.* Cinq (at cards), *m. Cinque Ports,* cinq ports, *m.pl.*
cinque-foil [ˈsiŋkfɔil], *n.* Quintefeuille, *f.*
cipher [ˈsaifə], *n.* Zéro; chiffre; (*fig.*) homme nul, *m.*, nullité, *f.*; monogramme, *m. He is a mere cipher,* c'est un vrai zéro; *in cipher,* en langage chiffré, en chiffre.—*v.i.* Chiffrer; écrire en chiffre.—*v.i.* Chiffrer; calculer. **cipher-key,** *n.* Clé de chiffre, *f.* **ciphering,** *n.* Calcul, *m.*, arithmétique, *f.* **cipheringbook,** *n.* Cahier d'arithmétique, *m.*
Circe [ˈsə:si]. Circé, *f.*
circean [sə'si:ən], *a.* De Circé; enchanteur.
circinate [ˈsə:sineit], *a.* (*Bot.*) Circinal.
circle [sə:kl], *n.* Cercle, *m.*; (*fig.*) coterie, *f.*, milieu, *m.* (*Log.*) cercle vicieux, *m. All your circle,* les vôtres, *pl.*; *to come full circle,* compléter son orbite, être révolu.—*v.t.* Entourer (de).—*v.i.* Se mouvoir autour (de), tournoyer.
circled [sə:kld], *a.* Circulaire, en forme de cercle.
circlet [ˈsə:klit], *n.* Petit cercle, anneau, *m.*
circling [ˈsə:kliŋ], *a.* Circulaire, tournoyant, environnant.
circuit [ˈsə:kit], *n.* Rotation, révolution, *f.*, tour; circuit, *m.*, circonférence, enceinte; tournée (of the judges etc.), *f.*; (*Elec.*) circuit, *m. Branch-circuit,* dérivation, *f.*, branchement, *m.*; *on circuit,* en tournée. **circuitbreaker,** *n.* Disjoncteur, *m.*
circuitous [sə:ˈkjuːitəs], *a.* Détourné, sinueux. **circuitously,** *adv.* D'une manière détournée, par des détours.
circular [ˈsə:kjulə], *a.* Circulaire. *Circular note,* billet circulaire, *m.*; *circular railway,* chemin de fer de ceinture, *m.*—*n.* Circulaire, *f.*, bulletin, *m. Court circular,* la Cour au jour le jour; la chronique mondaine. *f.*
circularity [sə:kjuˈlæriti], *n.* Forme circulaire, *f.*
circularize, *v.t.* (*fam.*) Circulariser, prospecter.
circularly [ˈsə:kjuləli], *adv.* Circulairement; en cercle.
circulate [ˈsə:kjuleit], *v.t.* Mettre en circulation, faire circuler, faire courir, répandre.—*v.i.* Circuler. **circulating,** *a.* Circulant. *Circulating decimal,* fraction périodique, *f.*; *circulating library,* bibliothèque circulante, *f.*; *circulating medium,* agent monétaire, *m.* **circulation,** *n.* Circulation, *f.*; tirage (of newspapers), *m.*
circulatory [ˈsə:kjulətəri], *a.* Circulaire, circulatoire.
circumambient [sə:kəmˈæmbiənt], *a.* Environnant, ambiant.
circumcise [ˈsə:kəmsaiz], *v.t.* Circoncire. **circumcision** [sə:kəmˈsiʒən], *n.* Circoncision, *f.*
circumference [sə:ˈkʌmfərəns], *n.* Circonférence, périphérie, *f.*
circumferential [sə:kəmfəˈrenʃəl], *a.* Circonférentiel.
circumflex [ˈsə:kəmfleks], *a.* (*Gram.*) Circonflexe.—*n.* Accent circonflexe, *m.*

circumfuse [sə:kəm′fju:z], *v.t.* Répandre autour. **circumfusion,** *n.* Dispersion alentour, *f.*

circumjacent [sə:kəm′dʒeisənt], *a.* Circonvoisin.

circumlocution [sə:kəmlə′kju:ʃən], *n.* Circonlocution, *f.*

circumnavigable [sə:kəm′nævigəbl], *a.* Dont on peut faire le tour par eau. **circumnavigate,** *v.t.* Naviguer autour de, faire le tour de par eau. **circumnavigation,** *n.* Circumnavigation, *f.*, périple, *m.*

circumscribe [′sə:kəmskraib], *v.t.* Circonscrire; limiter, restreindre.

circumscription [sə:kəm′skripʃən], *n.* Circonscription, restriction; périphérie, *f.* **circumscriptive,** *a.* Circonscrit. **circumscriptively,** *adv.* D'une manière circonscrite.

circumspect [′sə:kəmspekt], *a.* Circonspect. **circumspection,** *n.* Circonspection, *f.* **circumspective,** *a.* Circonspect. **circumspectly,** *adv.* Avec circonspection.

circumstance [′sə:kəmstæns], *n.* Circonstance, *f.*; état, *m.*; (*pl.*) moyens, *m.pl.*, position, *f.* *Extenuating circumstances,* circonstances atténuantes; *in straitened circumstances,* dans la gêne; *in* or *under the circumstances,* dans ces circonstances, puisqu'il en est ainsi; *to be in easy circumstances,* être dans l'aisance; *under any circumstances,* dans quelques circonstances que ce soit; *under no circumstances,* en aucun cas, sous aucun prétexte.—*v.t.* Placer. *As I was circumstanced,* dans la position où je me trouvais. **circumstantial** [sə:kəm′stænʃəl], *a.* Circonstancié, minutieux, détaillé; indirect (of evidence). **circumstantially,** *adv.* En détail. **circumstantiate,** *v.t.* Circonstancier, confirmer, établir.

circumvallation [sə:kəmvə′leiʃən], *n.* Circonvallation, *f.*

circumvent [sə:kəm′vent], *v.t.* Circonvenir. *To circumvent the law,* tourner la loi. **circumvention,** *n.* Circonvention, *f.* **circumvolution** [sə:kəmvə′lju:ʃən], *n.* Circonvolution, *f.*

circus [′sə:kəs], *n.* Cirque; rond-point (of streets), *m.*

cirrhosis [si′rousis], *n.* (*Med.*) Cirrhose, *f.*

cirrus [′sirəs], *n.* (*Bot.*) Cirre, *m.*, vrille, *f.*; cirrus (cloud), *m.* **cirrose** or **cirrous,** *a.* Cirreux.

cisalpine [sis′ælpain], *a.* Cisalpin.

cissy [′sisi], *n.* [SISSY].

Cistercian [sis′tə:ʃən], *n.* and *a.* Cistercien, de l'ordre de Citeaux.

cistern [′sistən], *n.* Citerne, *f.*, réservoir, *m.*; (*fig.*) cuvette (of a barometer), bâche (for pumps and steam engines), *f.*

cistus [′sistəs], *n.* (*Bot.*) Ciste, *m.*

*cit [sit], *n.* Bourgeois, citadin; parvenu, *m.*

citadel [′sitədl], *n.* Citadelle, *f.*

citation [sai′teiʃən], *n.* Citation, *f.* **cite,** *v.t.* Citer; sommer (de).

cithara [′siθərə], *n.* Cithare, *f.*

citizen [′sitizn], *n.* Citoyen, bourgeois; habitant, *m.*, habitante, *f.* *Fellow-citizen,* concitoyen, *m.* **citizenlike,** *a.* Bourgeois, en bourgeois. **citizenship,** *n.* Droit de cité, droit de bourgeoisie, *m.*, nationalité, *f.* *Good citizenship,* civisme, *m.*

citrate [′sitreit], *n.* (*Chem.*) Citrate, *m.* **citric,** *a.* Citrique. **citrine,** *a.* Citrin. **citron,** *n.* Cédrat, *m.* **citron-tree,** *n.* Cédratier, *m.*

city [′siti], *n.* Ville; cité, *f.* *City article,* bulletin financier, *m.*, revue de la Bourse, *f.*; *the City,* la Cité (de Londres). **city-hall,** *n.* Hôtel de ville, *m.*

civet [′sivit], *n.* Civette, *f.*

civic [′sivik], *a.* Civique. *Civic centre,* centre administratif, *m.*

civil [′sivil], *a.* Civil; municipal; honnête, poli. *Civil servant,* fonctionnaire, *m.*; *Civil Service examination,* concours d'admission aux emplois civils, *m.*; *civil war,* guerre civile, *f.*; *in the Civil Service,* dans l'administration. **civilian** [si′viljən], *n.* Bourgeois, civil, *m.* **civility,** *n.* Civilité, politesse, *f.* **civilization** [sivilai′zeiʃən], *n.* Civilisation, *f.* **civilize** [′sivilaiz], *v.t.* Civiliser. **civilizer,** *n.* Civilisateur, *m.*, civilisatrice, *f.* **civilly,** *adv.* Civilement, poliment. **civvies,** *n.pl.* (*pop.*) Vêtements civils, *m.pl.* *In civvies,* en civil. **civvy,** *n.* (*pop.*) Civil.—*a.* *Civvy Street,* le civil, la vie de pékin.

clack [klæk], *v.i.* Claquer; cliqueter, caqueter. —*v.t.* Faire claquer.—*n.* Claquement; claquet (of a mill); (*fig.*) caquet, *m.* **clack-valve,** *n.* Clapet, *m.*

clad, *past* and *p.p.* [CLOTHE].

claim [kleim], *v.t.* Demander, réclamer, prétendre à, revendiquer.—*n.* Demande, prétention, *f.*; titre, droit, *m.*; (*Law*) réclamation; (*Mining*) concession, *f.* *To lay claim to,* élever des prétentions à; *to put in a claim,* faire une réclamation. **claimable,** *a.* Qu'on peut réclamer, réclamable. **claimant,** *n.* Réclamateur, prétendant, *m.*; (*Law*) demandeur, *m.*, demanderesse, *f.*, partie requérante, *f. Rightful claimant,* ayant droit, *m.*

clairvoyance [klɛə′vɔiəns], *n.* Voyance, *f.*, don de double vue, *m.* **clairvoyant,** *n.* Voyant, *m.*, voyante, *f.*—*a.* Clairvoyant; doué de double vue.

clam (1) [klæm], *n.* Peigne (bivalve), *m.*, palourde, *f.*

*clam (2) [klæm], *v.t.* Engluer.—*v.i.* S'attacher (sur), adhérer (à).

clamber [′klæmbə], *v.i.* Grimper (sur or à.)

clamminess [′klæminis], *n.* Viscosité, moiteur (of the hands), *f.* **clammy,** *a.* Visqueux, gluant, pâteux; moite (of the hands).

clamorous [′klæmərəs], *a.* Bruyant; criard. **clamorously,** *adv.* Bruyamment, à grands cris. **clamour,** *n.* Clameur, *f.*, bruit, *m.*— *v.i.* Crier, vociférer. *To clamour against,* crier (contre); *to clamour for,* demander à grands cris.

clamp [klæmp], *n.* Crampon, *m.*; (*Carp.*) serre-joints; valet (on a bench), *m.*; mordache, *f.* (of vice); (*Agric.*) silo, tas, *m.*—*v.t.* Cramponner, serrer, pincer; mettre en silo, entasser.

clan [klæn], *n.* Clan, *m.*; clique, coterie, *f.* **clannish,** *a.* De clan, étroitement uni. **clanship,** *n.* Esprit de famille, esprit de corps, *m.*; système du clan, *m. To claim clanship with,* se dire du même clan que. **clansman,** *n.* Membre d'un clan, *m.*

clandestine [klæn′destin], *a.* Clandestin. **clandestinely,** *adv.* Clandestinement. **clandestineness,** *n.* Clandestinité, *f.*

clang [klæŋ], *n.* Cliquetis, bruit, son métallique, *m.*—*v.i.* Résonner.—*v.t.* Faire résonner. **clanger,** *n.* (*fam.*) *To drop a clanger,* faire une gaffe, faire une boulette. **clangorous** ['klæŋgərəs], *a.* Aigu, perçant, résonnant.

clank [klæŋk], *n.* Cliquetis, son métallique, son fêlé, *m.*—*v.i.* Résonner.—*v.t.* Faire résonner.

clap [klæp], *n.* Coup, *m.*; claque, *f.*; battement de mains; coup (of thunder), *m.*; (*vulg.*) (*Med.*) blennorragie, *f.*—*v.t.* Claquer, frapper, battre (the hands, wings, etc.); applaudir. *To clap one's sides,* se battre les flancs; *to clap to,* fermer avec bruit; *to clap up,* enfermer, claquemurer, (*fig.*) bâcler; *to clap down,* poser vivement; *to clap the handcuffs on,* appliquer les menottes à.—*v.i.* Claquer des mains, battre des mains; applaudir. **clap-trap,** *n.* Coup de théâtre, *m.*; chose à effet, réclame, *f.*; boniment, *m.*—*a.* À effet, à sensation. **clapper,** *n.* Applaudisseur, *m.*, (hired) claqueur, *m.*; battant (of a bell); claquet (of a mill), *m.*; (*pl.*) claquette, *f.* **clapper-claw,** *v.t.* Se battre du bec et des ongles; (*fig.*) gronder, injurier, vilipender. **clapping,** *n.* Battement des mains, *m.*, applaudissements, *m.pl.*

Clare or **Clara** ['klɛərə]. Claire, *f.*

claret ['klærət], *n.* Vin rouge de Bordeaux, *m.* **claret-colour,** *n.* Grenat, *m.*

clarification [klærifi'keiʃən], *n.* Clarification, *f.*

clarify ['klærifai], *v.i.* Se clarifier.—*v.t.* Clarifier.

clarinet [klæri'net], *n.* Clarinette, *f.*

clarion ['klæriən], *n.* Clairon, *m.*

Clarissa [klə'risə]. Clarisse, *f.*

clarity ['klæriti], *n.* Clarté, *f.*

clary ['klɛəri], *n.* (*Bot.*) Toute-bonne, *f.*

clash [klæʃ], *v.i.* Résonner, se heurter, s'entrechoquer; (*fig.*) être aux prises *or* en conflit (avec), s'opposer.—*v.t.* Faire résonner (en frappant); choquer, heurter.—*n.* Fracas, choc, conflit; cliquetis (of weapons etc.), *m.*; opposition, *f.*

clasp [klɑːsp], *n.* Fermoir, *m.*; agrafe, *f.*; (*fig.*) embrassade, *m.*, étreinte, *f.*—*v.t.* Fermer avec un fermoir, agrafer; serrer, presser, joindre. *With clasped hands,* les mains jointes. **clasp-knife,** *n.* Couteau de poche, *m.*

class [klɑːs], *n.* Classe, *f.*; (*sch.*) cours; genre, *m.*, catégorie, *f.*, cote, *f.* (of a ship). *First-class player*; joueur de premier ordre; *first-class ticket,* billet de première classe, *m.*—*v.t.* Classer. **classmate,** *n.* Camarade de classe, *m.* **classroom,** *n.* Salle de classe, classe, *f.* **classing,** *n.* Classement, *m.* **classy,** *a.* (*fam.*) Bon genre.

classic ['klæsik], *n.* Classique, *m.* *To study classics,* faire ses humanités, *f.pl.* **classic** or **classical,** *a.* Classique. **classically,** *adv.* D'une manière classique. **classicist,** *n.* Humaniste; classique, *m.*

classification [klæsifi'keiʃən], *n.* Classification, *f.*

classify ['klæsifai], *v.t.* Classifier.

clatter ['klætə], *n.* Bruit, tapage, fracas, tintamarre, *m.*—*v.i.* Faire du bruit, claquer, retentir; résonner; (of stork) craqueter.—*v.t.* Faire résonner.

Claudia ['klɔːdiə]. Claude, *f.*

Claudius ['klɔːdiəs]. Claude, *m.*

clause [klɔːz], *n.* Clause, *f.*; article; (*Gram.*) membre de phrase, *m.*, proposition, *f.*

claustral ['klɔːstrəl], *a.* Claustral.

claustrophobia [klɔːstrə'foubiə], *n.* Claustrophobie, *f.*

clavate ['kleiveit], *a.* (*Bot.*) Clavé.

claviform ['klævifɔːm], *a.* Claviforme.

clavicle ['klævikl], *n.* (*Anat.*) Clavicule, *f.*

claw [klɔː], *n.* Griffe, *f.*; (*Zool. etc.*) serre; pince (of crabs), *f.*; valet (on a bench); pied de biche (of a hammer), *m.*—*v.t.* Griffer, déchirer avec les griffes; déchirer; égratigner; (*fig.*) railler, gronder, gratter, chatouiller. **clawed,** *a.* (*Zool.*) Armé de griffes, unguifère. **clawless,** *a.* Sans griffe. **claw-hammer,** *n.* Marteau à dent, *m.*

clay [klei], *n.* Argile, terre glaise, glaise, *f.* *Baked clay,* terre cuite, *f.*; *clay pipe,* pipe en terre, *f.*; (*fig.*) *feet of clay,* pieds d'argile, *m.pl.*—*v.t.* (*Agric.*) Glaiser; terrer (sugar). **clay-pigeon,** *n.* Pigeon artificiel, *m.* **clay-pit,** *n.* Glaisière, *f.* **clay-slate,** *n.* Schiste argileux, *m.* **clay-soil,** *n.* Sol argileux, *m.* **clayey** ['kleii], *a.* Argileux.

claymore ['kleimɔː], *n.* (*Sc.*) Claymore, *f.*

clean [kliːn], *a.* Propre, pur; blanc (of linen); ciré (of shoes); (*Print.*) peu chargé (of proofs); (*fig.*) net, droit. *Clean bill of health,* patente nette, *f.*; *to make a clean breast of it,* avouer complètement; *to show a clean pair of heels,* disparaître, tourner les talons.—*adv.* Entièrement, tout à fait, droit, raide.—*v.t.* Nettoyer, laver, purifier; décrotter, cirer (shoes); vider (fish); éplucher (vegetables); écurer (sewers, canals, etc.); dégraisser (cloth etc.). *To clean out,* nettoyer; (*fig.*) plumer (a person); *to clean up,* nettoyer. **cleanable,** *a.* Nettoyable. **cleaner,** *n.* Nettoyeur, *m.*, nettoyeuse, *f.*; décrotteur (of boots); dégraisseur (of clothes); écureur (of sewers), *m.* **cleaning,** *n.* Nettoyage, nettoiement; curage (of sewers, canals, etc.); dégraissage (of clothes), *m.* *French cleaning,* nettoyage à sec.

cleanliness ['klenlinis], *n.* Propreté; netteté, *f.*

cleanly (1) ['klenli], *a.* Propre; (*fig.*) pur.

cleanly (2) ['kliːnli], *adv.* Proprement, nettement.

cleanness ['kliːnnis], *n.* Propreté, pureté; (*fig.*) netteté, justesse, innocence, *f.*

cleansable ['klenzəbl], *a.* Nettoyable.

cleanse [klenz], *v.t.* Nettoyer; curer (sewers etc.); assainir; (*fig.*) purifier. *To cleanse the blood,* purifier le sang. **cleanser,** *n.* Chose qui nettoie, *f.*, détersif; cureur (of sewers, canals, etc.), *m.* **cleansing,** *n.* Nettoiement, nettoyage, *m.*; (*fig.*) purification, *f.*; curage (of sewers, canals, etc.), *m.*

clear [kliə], *a.* Clair; net, lucide, sûr; innocent, sans tache. *All clear!* (*Naut.*) paré! (*Mil.*) fin de l'alerte; (*sch.*) rien à craindre. *Clear of,* exempt de; *in the clear,* libre, dégagé; *to get clear,* se tirer d'affaire; *to get clear of,* se débarrasser de, échapper à; *to keep clear of,* ne pas se heurter contre, ne pas se frotter à, éviter; *to make clear,* rendre clair; *to steer clear of,* éviter.—*adv.* Clair.—*v.t.* Éclaircir; clarifier (liquids); faire évacuer (a room etc.); déblayer (rubbish etc.); gagner (a profit etc.); (*Agric.*) défricher; (*fig.*) se justifier, se disculper (one's character); acquitter, innocenter; (*Customs*) passer, faire passer; (*Mil.*) balayer; (*Naut.*) parer, dégager. *The streets were cleared by the musketry fire*, les rues furent balayées par la fusillade; *to clear a cape*, doubler un cap; *to clear a good deal of money*, gagner beaucoup d'argent; *to clear a hedge* (of horse etc.), franchir une haie; *to clear away*, déblayer (obstructions); *to clear for action*, (*Naut.*) faire branle-bas de combat; *to clear from*, dégager de, débarrasser de; *to clear of*, purger de, acquitter de; *to clear off*, solder (wares); *to clear one's brow*, se dérider le front; *to clear oneself*, se réhabiliter, faire reconnaître son innocence; *to clear the customs*, acquitter les droits de douane; *to clear the table*, desservir. —*v.i.* S'éclaircir, se rasséréner; se libérer, se débarrasser. *It is clearing up*, le temps s'éclaircit; *to clear off*, s'en aller, filer, décamper; *to clear out*, se retirer; *to clear up*, s'éclaircir, se rasséréner (weather).

clear-cut, *a.* Net, d'une grande netteté. **clear-headed**, *a.* À l'esprit clair. **clear-sighted**, *a.* Clairvoyant. **clear-sighted-ness**, *n.* Clairvoyance, *f.* **clear-starch**, *v.t.* Blanchir à neuf. **clear-starcher**, *n.* Blanchisseur de fin, *m.* (*f.* blanchisseuse). **clear-starching**, *n.* Blanchissage de fin, *m.*

clearance, *n.* Dégagement; déblaiement (rubbish); (*Naut.*) congé, *m.*; dédouanement, *m.* *Clearance sale*, solde, *m.*, liquidation, *f.*; *clearance inwards*, déclaration d'entrée, *f.*; *mine clearance*, déminage, *m.*; *wheel clearance* (*Motor.*) débattement des roues, *m.*

clearing, *n.* Éclaircissement, débrouillement, *m.*; justification, *f.*; (*Comm.*) acquittement; défrichement (land), *m.*; levée (letter boxes); éclaircie (in woods), *f.*; déblaiement (rubbish), *m.* *Clearing bill*, certificat de déclaration d'entrée, *m.*; *clearing out*, enlèvement, *m.*; *clearing up*, éclaircissement, *m.* **clearing-house**, *n.* (*Rail.*) Bureau de liquidation, *m.*; (*Bank.*) chambre de compensation, *f.*; banque de virement, *f.*

clearly, *adv.* Nettement, clairement, évidemment. **clearness**, *n.* Clarté, netteté, pureté, *f.*

cleat [kli:t], *n.* (*Naut.*) Taquet, *m.*

cleavable ['kli:vəbl], *a.* Clivable, qui peut se fendre. **cleavage**, *n.* Fendage, clivage, *m.*; fissure, scission, *f.*

cleave (1) [kli:v], *v.t.* (*past* **clove** (1), **cleft** (1); *p.p.* **cloven**, **cleft** (1)) Fendre, diviser, se fendre. *In a cleft stick*, (*fig.*) dans une impasse. **cleaver**, *n.* Fendeur (person); couperet, fendoir (instrument), *m.* **cleavers**, *n.* (*Bot.*) Gaillet, caille-lait, *m.* **cleaving**, *n.* (*Min.*) Clivage, *m.*

cleave (2) [kli:v], *v.i.* (*past* **cleaved**, ***clave**) Coller, se coller, s'attacher.

clef [klef], *n.* (*Mus.*) Clef, *f.*

cleft (2) [kleft], *n.* Fente, fissure, crevasse, *f.*

cleg [kleg], *n.* Taon, *m.*

clematis ['klemətis], *n.* (*Bot.*) Clématite, *f.*

clemency ['klemənsi], *n.* Clémence; douceur (of the weather), *f.* **clement**, *a.* Doux, clément.

Clement ['klemənt]. Clément, *m.*

Clementina [klemən'ti:nə]. Clémentine, *f.*

clementine ['klementain], *n.* (*Bot.*) Clémentine, *f.*

clench [klenʃ], *v.t.* River (nails etc.); serrer (the fist). **clencher** [CLINCHER].

Cleopatra [kliə'pætrə]. Cléopâtre, *f.*

clepsydra ['klepsidrə], *n.* Clepsydre, *f.*

clerestory ['kliəstəri], *n.* (*Arch.*) Claire-voie, *f.*

clergy ['klə:dʒi], *n.* Clergé, *m.* **clergyman**, *n.* (*pl.* **clergymen**) Ecclésiastique; (*R.-C. Ch.*) prêtre, abbé, curé; (*Protestant*) ministre, pasteur, *m.*

cleric ['klerik], *n.* Ecclésiastique, prêtre, *m.* **clerical**, *a.* Clérical. *Clerical error*, faute de copiste, *f.* **clericalism**, *n.* Cléricalisme, *m.* **clerically**, *adv.* Cléricalement.

clerk [klɑːk], *n.* (*Law*) Clerc; (*Eccles.*) ecclésiastique; (*Comm.*) commis; (*Civil Service*) employé, comptable; (*Law*) greffier, *m.* *Chief clerk*, chef de bureau, *m.*; (*Turf*) *clerk of the course*, commissaire de la piste, *m.*; *clerk of works*, conducteur des travaux, *m.*; *female clerk*, commise, *f.*; *lawyer's clerk*, clerc d'avoué, *m.*; *managing clerk*, premier commis, *m.* **clerkship**, *n.* Place de clerc, place de commis, *f.*

clever ['klevə], *a.* Adroit, habile, (*colloq.*) malin; intelligent; convenable; bien fait, bien exécuté; (*dial.*) bon, obligeant, aimable. *To be clever at*, être fort en. **cleverly**, *adv.* Habilement, adroitement, avec adresse. **cleverness**, *n.* Habileté, dextérité, adresse, ingéniosité; intelligence, *f.*

clew [klu:], *n.* Pelote de fil, *f.*; (*Naut.*) point de voile, *m.*, araignée de hamac, *f.* *Ariadne's clew*, le fil d'Ariane, *m.*—*v.t.* Carguer.

cliché ['kli:ʃei], *n.* (*Print.* and *fig.*) Cliché, *m.*

click [klik], *v.i.* Faire tic-tac, cliqueter; (*pop.*) se plaire du premier coup (of two people). —*v.t.* (*Mil.*) *To click one's heels*, faire claquer ses talons.—*n.* Petit bruit sec, clic; cliquetis; (*Tech.*) cliquet, *m.*; détente, *f.*; déclic, *m.* *Click reel*, moulinet à cliquet, *m.*

client ['klaiənt], *n.* Client, *m.*, cliente, *f.*

clientele [kli:ɑ̃'tel], *n.* Clientèle, *f.*

cliff [klif], *n.* Falaise, *f.*; rocher escarpé, *m.* **cliffy**, *a.* À falaises, escarpé, à pic.

climacteric [klai'mæktərik], *a.* Climatérique. —*n.* Climatérique, *f.*

climactic [klai'mæktik], *a.* En série ascendante; arrivé à son apogée.

climate ['klaimit], *n.* Climat, *m.* **climatic**, *a.* Climatique; climatologique.

climax ['klaimæks], *n.* Gradation, *f.*; (*fig.*) comble, *m.*, apogée, *m.*

climb [klaim], *v.i.* Grimper; monter (sur); (*fig.*) s'élever. *To climb down*, (*fig.*) reculer, en rabattre, rabattre de ses prétentions.—*v.t.* Escalader, gravir, monter, grimper à, faire l'ascension de, varapper.—*n.* Ascension, montée, *f.* *Stiff climb*, ascension raide, *f.*

climber ['klaimə], *n.* Grimpeur, *m.*; ascensionniste, alpiniste, *m.* or *f.* (mountain-climber); (*Bot.*) plante grimpante, *f.* *Social climber*, arriviste, *m.* or *f.*

clime [klaim], *n.* (*poet.*) Climat; pays, *m.*

clinch [klinʃ], *v.t.* River (nails); (*Naut.*) étalinguer; conclure. *To clinch an argument*, confirmer un argument.—*n.* (*Naut.*) Nœud de bouline, *m.*; étalingure, *f.*; (*Box.*) corps à corps, *m.* **clincher**, *n.* (*fig.*) Mot sans réplique, *m.* *To give someone a clincher*, river son clou à quelqu'un; (*Cycl.*) *clincher tyre*, pneu à talons, *m.*

cling [kliŋ], *v.i.* (*past* and *p.p.* **clung**) Se cramponner, s'attacher, s'accrocher (à); coller (à) (of dresses). *A drowning man clings to any*

thing, un homme qui se noie se raccroche à tout; *to cling together*, se tenir ensemble, se tenir embrasssés. **clingstone**, *n.* (*Bot.*) Pavie, alberge, *f.*
clinic ['klinik], *a.* and *n.* Clinique, *f.* **clinical**, *a.* Clinique. **clinically**, *adv.* D'une manière clinique.
clink [kliŋk], *n.* Tintement, cliquetis, *m.*; (*pop.*) prison, cellule, *f.*—*v.i.* Tinter.—*v.t.* Faire tinter, faire résonner. *To clink glasses*, trinquer. **clinker**, *n.* Brique vitrifiée, *f.*; mâchefer, *m.*, scories, *f.pl.* **clinker-built**, *a.* Bordé à clins (of boats). **clinking**, *n.* Cliquetis, tintement, *m.*
clip [klip], *v.t.* Couper (with scissors), tailler; tondre (dogs and horses); écourter (to abridge); rogner (coins); écorcher, estropier (words); contrôler, poinçonner (tickets).—*n.* Tonte, *f.*; pince-notes, *m.*, agrafe, attache, *f.*; (*Cycl.*) pince-pantalons, *m.*; (*Mil.*) chargeur (for cartridges), *m.*; (*pop.*) taloche, *f.* (on ear etc.). **clipper**, *n.* Rogneur, *m.*, rogneuse, *f.*; (*Naut.*) fin voilier, *m.*; tondeuse (instrument), *f.* **clippers**, *n.pl.* Tondeuse, *f.* **clipper-built**, *a.* (*Naut.*) Construit en clipper. **clippie**, *n.* (*pop.*) Receveuse d'autobus, *f.* **clippings**, *n.pl.* Rognures, *f.pl.*
clique [kli:k], *n.* Coterie, *f.* **cliquish**, *a.* Attaché aux intérêts de sa coterie.
cloak [klouk], *n.* Manteau; (*fig.*) voile, masque, prétexte, *m.* *Cloak-and-dagger story*, roman de cape et d'épée, *m.*—*v.t.* Couvrir d'un manteau, (*fig.*) masquer, voiler, cacher. **cloak-room**, *n.* (*Rail.*) Consigne, *f.*, (*Theat.*) vestiaire, *m.* *Ladies' cloak-room*, vestiaire de dames.
cloche [klɔʃ], *n.* (*Hort.*) Cloche, *f.*
clock [klɔk], *n.* (Large) Horloge; (small) pendule, *f.*; coin (of stockings), *m.* *Alarm clock*, réveille-matin, *m.*; *Dutch clock*, coucou, *m.*; *eight-day clock*, horloge qui marche huit jours, huitaine, *f.*; *it is one o'clock*, il est une heure; *to work round the clock*, travailler vingt-quatre heures sur vingt-quatre, par équipes; *travelling clock*, pendulette, *f.*; *what o'clock is it?* quelle heure est-il?—*v.i.* (*Ind.*) *To clock in, out*, pointer à l'arrivée, au départ. **clockmaker**, *n.* Horloger, *m.* **clock-making**, *n.* Horlogerie, *f.* **clock-tower**, *n.* Tour d'horloge, *f.* **clockwise**, *adv.* Dans le sens des aiguilles d'une montre.
clockwork, *n.* Mouvement, mécanisme, *m.*, horlogerie, *f.*; rouages, *m.pl.*; (*fig.*) travail régulier, bien ajusté, *m.* *As regular as clockwork*, réglé comme du papier à musique; *like clockwork*, comme sur des roulettes.—*a.* Mécanique.
clod [klɔd], *n.* Motte de terre, *f.*; morceau, *m.*; talon de collier (of beef), *m.* **cloddy**, *a.* Plein de mottes. **clodhopper**, *n.* Rustre; manant, lourdaud, *m.*
clog [klɔg], *n.* Entraves (for an animal), *f.pl.*; socques; claquettes, *f.pl.* (for ladies); gros brodequins à semelle de bois, *m.pl.*; (*fig.*) empêchement, embarras, *m.*, entrave, *f.*—*v.t.* Entraver (an animal); (*fig.*) embarrasser, obstruer, encombrer, encrasser.—*v.i.* Se boucher, s'obstruer.
cloister ['klɔistə], *n.* Cloître, *m.*—*v.t.* Cloîtrer. **cloistered**, *a.* Cloîtré; claustral (of things).
close (1) [klouz], *v.t.* Fermer (to shut); clore, terminer, conclure (to terminate); serrer

(the ranks); lever (a sitting); (*fig.*) renfermer. *To close in*, enfermer; *to close up*, fermer, boucher.—*v.i.* Se fermer; clore, se terminer, conclure, finir; (*Mil.*) en venir aux mains; se cicatriser (of a wound). *To close up*, se serrer, s'obturer; *to close with*, conclure un marché, s'arranger avec (to come to an arrangement), prendre corps à corps (to grapple with).—*n.* Fin, conclusion, clôture; (*Mus.*) pause, cadence, *f.*; (*Wrestling*) corps-à-corps, *m.* *To bring to a close*, terminer; *to draw to a close*, tirer à sa fin.
close (2) [klous], *a.* Clos, bien fermé; compact, étroit, serré (avaricious, tight); lourd (of the weather), renfermé (of the air); concis (of style); (*fig.*) retiré, mystérieux, discret; attentif, appliqué. *Close at hand*, tout proche; *close season*, temps prohibé, *m.* (for shooting etc.); *close to*, près de; *in close confinement*, au secret; *it is very close!* on étouffe! *it was a close shave!* nous l'avons échappé belle! *to come to close quarters*, en venir aux mains.—*adv.* Près, de près; étroitement, hermétiquement, bien. *Close at his heels*, sur ses talons; *close by*, tout près; *close to one another*, tout près les uns des autres; *close to the ground*, à fleur de terre, à ras de terre; *to be close upon*, serrer de près.
close-fisted, *a.* Avare, pingre, serré.
close-hauled, *a.* (*Naut.*) Au plus près.
closely ['klousli], *adv.* De près; étroitement; secrètement; (*Mus.*) pause, cadence, *f.*; (*Wrestling*) tivement. *To observe closely*, veiller de près, ne pas perdre de vue.
closeness, *n.* Proximité; exactitude, *f.*; manque d'air, *m.*; lourdeur (of the weather), *f.*; air renfermé, *m.*; discrétion, réserve; intimité; vigueur (of pursuit), *f.*
close-reefed, *a.* (*Naut.*) Au bas ris.
close-set, *a.* Rapproché, serré.
close-stool ['klous stu:l], *n.* Chaise percée, *f.*
closet ['klɔzit], *n.* Cabinet; boudoir, *m.*; garde-robe, armoire, *f.* *Water-closet*, cabinet d'aisances, *m.*, W.C., *m.*—*v.t.* Enfermer dans un cabinet. *To be closeted with*, être en tête-à-tête avec.
close-up, *n.* (*Cine.*) Gros plan, *m.*
closing ['klouziŋ], *n.* Clôture, fermeture (of shops); fin, conclusion, *f.*—*a.* De clôture; dernier, final.
closure ['klouʒə], *n.* Clôture, fermeture, *f.*
clot [klɔt], *n.* Grumeau, caillot, *m.*; (*fam.*) imbécile, idiot, *m.*—*v.i.* Se cailler, se figer, se grumeler. **clottish**, *a.* (*fam.*) Imbécile. **clotty** ['klɔti], *a.* Grumeleux.
cloth [klɔ:θ], *n.* Drap (woollen or gold or silver tissue), *m.*; toile (linen tissue); nappe, *f.*, tapis (cover for a table), *m.* *Table-cloth*, nappe, *f.*, tapis (woollen), *m.*; *the cloth*, (*fig.*) le clergé; *to lay the cloth*, mettre le couvert; *to remove the cloth*, desservir. **cloth-trade**, *n.* Draperie, *f.*, commerce de draps, *m.* **cloth-worker**, *n.* Ouvrier drapier, *m.*
clothe [klouð], *v.t.* (*past and p.p.* **clad**, **clothed**) Habiller, vêtir, revêtir, couvrir (de).
clothes [klouðz], *n.pl.* Habits, vêtements, *m.pl.*, hardes, *f.pl.* *Bed-clothes*, draps et couvertures, *m.pl.*; *in plain clothes*, en civil, en bourgeois; *long-clothes*, maillot anglais (of baby), *m.*; *old clothes*, vieux habits, *m.pl.*; *old-clothes-man*, fripier, marchand d'habits,

m.; *to put on, to take off, one's clothes,* s'habiller, se déshabiller. **clothes-basket,** *n.* Panier à linge, *m.* **clothes-brush,** *n.* Brosse à habits, *f.* **clothes-horse,** *n.* Séchoir, *m.* **clothes-line,** *n.* Corde à linge, *f.* **clothes-pin,** *n.* Fichoir, *m.*; pince à linge, *f.*
clothier ['klouðiə], *n.* Fabricant de draps, drapier, *m. Ready-made clothier,* marchand de confections, *m.*
clothing, *n.* Vêtement, habillement, *m.*; vêtements, *m.pl.*
Clotilda [klə'tildə]. Clotilde, *f.*
cloud [klaud], *n.* Nuage, *m.*; (*poet.*) nue; (*fig.*) nuée; veine, tache (in marble etc.), *f. To be under a cloud,* être mal vu du monde; *to fall from the clouds,* tomber des nues; *every cloud has a silver lining,* après la pluie le beau temps.—*v.t.* Couvrir de nuages; obscurcir, voiler; (*fig.*) assombrir, répandre un nuage sur.—*v.i.* Se couvrir de nuages; se couvrir, s'obscurcir; se rembrunir (of the brow). **cloudburst,** *n.* Trombe, rafale de pluie, *f.* **cloud-capped,** *a.* Couronné de nuages, qui se perd dans les nues. **cloud-castle,** *n.* Château en Espagne, *m.* **cloud-compelling,** *a.* Qui amasse des nuages. **cloud-cuckoo-land,** *n.* Pays de cocagne, *m.* **cloudily,** *adv.* Avec des nuages; (*fig.*) obscurément. **cloudiness,** *n.* État nuageux, *m.*; obscurité; (*fig.*) tristesse, *f.* **cloudless,** *a.* Sans nuage. **cloudy,** *a.* Nuageux, couvert; nébuleux; trouble (of liquids); (*fig.*) ténébreux, sombre. *Cloudy weather,* temps couvert, *m.*; *it is getting cloudy,* le temps se couvre.
clough [klʌf], *n.* Ravin, *m.*, gorge, *f.*
clout [klaut], *n.* Morceau, *m.*, pièce, *f.*, torchon, linge, *m.*; gifle, tape, taloche, *f.*—*v.t.* Rapetasser, rapiécer; réparer; taper, souffleter; clouter, ferrer (a clog). **clout-nail,** *n.* Clou caboche, *m.*
clove (1) [CLEAVE].
clove (2) [klouv], *n.* Clou de girofle, *m. Clove of garlic,* gousse d'ail, *f.*; *oil of cloves,* essence de girofle, *f.* **clove-hitch,** *n.* (*Naut.*) Deux demi-clefs à capeler, *f.pt.* **clove-tree,** *n.* Giroflier, *m.*
cloven [klouvn], *a.* Fendu; fourchu. *To show the cloven foot,* laisser voir le bout de l'oreille. **cloven-footed** [-'futid] or **cloven-hoofed** [-'huːft], *a.* Qui a le pied fourchu.
clover ['klouvə], *n.* Trèfle, *m. Sweet clover,* mélilot, *m. To be in clover,* être comme un coq en pâte. **clovered,** *a.* Couvert de trèfle.
clown [klaun], *n.* Rustre, manant, *m.*; (*Theat.*) bouffon, paillasse, pitre, clown [kluːn], *m.* **clownish,** *a.* De paysan, rustre, grossier. **clownishly,** *adv.* En rustre, grossièrement. **clownishness,** *n.* Rusticité, grossièreté, rudesse, *f.*, tour de paillasse, *m.*
cloy [klɔi], *v.t.* Écœurer, rassasier (to glut).
cloying, *n.* Affadissement, *m.*, satiété, *f.*
club [klʌb], *n.* Massue, *f.*; (*Golf*) (for hitting ball) club, *m.*; crosse, *f.*; cercle, club, *m.*, association, *f.*; (*Cards*) trèfle, *m.*—*v.t.* Frapper avec une massue, renverser; mettre la crosse en l'air (of a rifle).—*v.i.* Se cotiser, s'associer. **club-foot,** *n.* Pied bot, *m.* **club-footed,** *a.* Pied bot. **club-headed,** *a.* À grosse tête. **club-house,** *n.* Cercle; pavillon (golf etc.), *m.* **club-law,** *n.* Loi du bâton *or* du plus fort, *f.* **club-man,** *n.* Habitué des clubs, clubman, *m.* **club-room,** *n.* Salle de

réunion, *f.* **club-shaped,** *a.* En forme de massue; claviforme.
cluck [klʌk], *v.i.* Glousser. **clucking,** *n.* Gloussement, *m.*
clue [kluː], *n.* Fil, indice, signe, *m.*, idée, *f.*; (*Theat.*) fin de réplique, *f.*; définition, *f.* (of crossword). *To give a clue to,* mettre sur la voie, mettre sur la piste, donner un indice de; (*fam.*) *to have no clue,* ne pas en avoir la moindre idée. **clueless,** *a.* (*fam.*) *To be clueless,* ne savoir rien de rien.
clump [klʌmp], *n.* Masse, *f.*, gros bloc; (*fig.*) groupe, *m. Clump of trees,* massif *or* groupe d'arbres, bouquet d'arbres, *m.*—*v.i.* Se grouper, se masser. (*fam.*) *To clump about,* marcher lourdement.—*v.t.* Grouper.
clumsily ['klʌmzili], *adv.* Gauchement, maladroitement; grossièrement. **clumsiness,** *n.* Gaucherie, maladresse, *f.* **clumsy,** *a.* Gauche, maladroit, disgracieux, lourd, mal fait (of things).
clunch [klʌnʃ], *n.* Argile schisteuse, *f.*
clung, *past* and *p.p.* [CLING].
cluster ['klʌstə], *n.* Grappe (of grapes), *f.*; bouquet (of flowers); groupe, massif (of trees); régime (of bananas); nœud (of diamonds); pâté (of houses); essaim (of bees), *m.*—*v.i.* Se former en grappes; se grouper, s'attrouper; se rassembler; se pelotonner (of bees).—*v.t.* Rassembler (en groupes), grouper. (*Arch.*) *Clustered column,* colonne en faisceau, *f.*
clutch [klʌtʃ], *v.t.* Saisir, empoigner; (*Motor.*) embrayer. *To clutch at a straw,* s'accrocher à tout.—*n.* Griffe, serre, étreinte, *f.*; (*Mach.*) manchon d'accouplement, *m.*; (*Motor.*) embrayage, cône d'embrayage et de débrayage, *m.*; couvée (of eggs), *f.* (*Motor.*) *Automatic clutch,* autodébrayage, embrayage automatique, *m.*; *to fall into someone's clutches,* tomber sous la patte de quelqu'un; *to engage the clutch,* (*Motor.*) embrayer.
clutch-pedal, *n.* Pédale d'embrayage, *f.*
clutch-shaft, *n.* Arbre primaire, *m.*
clutter ['klʌtə], *n.* Fracas, tapage, vacarme, *m.*; encombrement, *m.*, désordre, *m.*—*v.i.* Faire du bruit, du désordre.—*v.t. To clutter up,* encombrer.
clyster ['klistə], *n.* Clystère, *m.* **clyster-pipe,** *n.* Clysoir, *m.*
Clytemnestra [klaitem'nestrə]. Clytemnestre, *f.*
coach [koutʃ], *n.* Voiture, *f.*, carrosse, *m.*; (*Rail.*) voiture, *f.*, wagon, *m.*; autocar, car, *m.*; (*sch.*) répétiteur, *m.*; (*spt.*) entraîneur, instructeur, *m.*; (*Naut.*) chambre du conseil, *f. A coach and six,* un carrosse à six chevaux. —*v.t.* Voiturer; donner des leçons particulières à; entraîner. *To coach up,* (*fig.*) préparer aux examens.—*v.i.* Aller en voiture.
coach-box, *n.* Siège du cocher, *m.* **coach-builder,** *n.* Carrossier, *m.* **coach-door,** *n.* Portière, *f.* **coachful, coach-load,** *n.* Carrossée, voiture pleine, *f.* **coach-hire,** *n.* Prix de la voiture, *m.* **coach-house,** *n.* Remise, *f.* **coaching,** *n.* (*spt.*) Entraînement (d'équipe), *m.*; (*sch.*) répétitions, *f.pl.* **coachman,** *n.* (*pl.* **coachmen**) Cocher, *m.* **coach-office,** *n.* Bureau de location (de places), *m.* **coachwork,** *n.* Carrosserie, *f.*
coadjutor [kou'ædʒutə], *n.* Coadjuteur, aide, collègue, collaborateur, *m.*

coadunate [kou'ædjuneit], *a.* (*Bot.*) Coadné.
coagulable [kou'ægjuləbl], *a.* Coagulable.
coagulate, *v.i.* Se coaguler.—*v.t.* Coaguler.
coagulation, *n.* Coagulation, *f.* **coagulative,** *a.* Coagulant.
coal [koul], *n.* Charbon, *m.*; houille, *f. Live coal,* charbon ardent; *small coal,* charbon menu. *Brown coal,* lignite, *m.*; (*Mining*) *coal face,* taille, *f.*; (*Elec.*) *white coal,* houille blanche, *f. To call* or *haul the coals,* trouver à redire à, donner un savon à; *to carry coals to Newcastle,* porter de l'eau à la rivière; *to heap coals of fire on someone's head,* amasser des charbons ardents sur la tête de quelqu'un.—*v.t.* Charbonner.—*v.i.* Faire son charbon (of steamers). **coal-barge,** *n.* Chaland à charbon, *m.* **coal-bed,** *n.* Couche de houille, *f.* **coal-black,** *a.* Noir comme du charbon. **coal-box,** *n.* Boîte à charbon, *f.* **coal-bunker,** *n.* Soute à charbon, *f.* **coal-cellar,** *n.* Cave à charbon, *f.* **coal-dust,** *n.* Poussier (de charbon), *m.* **coal-field,** *n.* Bassin houiller, *m.* **coal-heaver,** *n.* Porteur de charbon, *m.* **coal-hole,** *n.* Trou à charbon; (*Naut.*) charbonnier, *m.* **coal-man,** *n.* Charbonnier, *m.* **coal-measure,** *n.* Gisement houiller, *m.*, formation houillère, *f.* **coal-merchant,** *n.* Marchand de charbon, *m.* **coal-mine,** *n.* Mine de charbon, houillère, *f.* **coal-mining,** *n.* Exploitation de la houille, *f.*—*a.* Houiller. **coal-miner,** *n.* Mineur, *m.* **coal-mouse,** *n.* (*Orn.*) Mésange noire, *f.* **coal-scuttle,** *n.* Seau à charbon, *m.* **coal-seam,** *n.* Couche de houille, *f.* **coal-tar,** *n.* Goudron de houille, coaltar, *m.* **coal-wharf,** *n.* Dépôt de houille, *m.* **coaly,** *a.* Houilleux.
coalesce [kouə'les], *v.i.* S'unir, se fondre, fusionner; (*Chem.*) se combiner. **coalescence,** *n.* Union, coalescence, adhésion, *f.* **coalescent,** *a.* Coalescent.
coalition [kouə'liʃən], *n.* Coalition, *f.*
coamings ['kouminʒ], *n.pl.* (*Naut.*) Hiloire, *f.*
coaptation [kouæp'teiʃən], *n.* (*Surg.*) Coaptation, réduction, *f.*
coarctate [kou'ɑːkteit], *a.* Coarcté, resserré.
coarctation, *n.* Coarctation, *f.*
coarse [kɔːs], *a.* Gros, grossier, brut (of sugar etc.); grossier, vulgaire. **coarse-grained,** *a.* À gros grains (of tissues etc.), à gros fil (of wood). **coarsely,** *adv.* Grossièrement.—*v.t.* Rendre plus grossier.—*v.i.* Devenir plus grossier. **coarseness,** *n.* Grossièreté, *f.*; rudesse, grosseur, *f.*
coast [koust], *n.* Côte, plage, *f.*, rivage, littoral, *m. The coast is clear,* vous pouvez passer, il n'y a plus personne.—*v.i.* Côtoyer, suivre la côte; caboter (to trade); continuer sur son lancé, en roue libre (*Cycl.*), au débrayé (*Motor.*); planer (of bird).—*v.t.* Côtoyer, longer la côte de. *To coast along,* côtoyer. **coast-guard,** *n.* Garde-côte, *m.* **coast-line,** *n.* Littoral, *m.* **coastal,** *a.* Côtier. **coaster,** *n.* Caboteur, *m.*; dessous de carafe, *m.* **coaster brake,** *n.* Frein à contre-pédalage, *m.* **coasting,** *n.* Navigation côtière, *f.*, cabotage, *m.*; (*Cycl.*) descente (de côte) en roue libre, *f.* **coastwise,** *adv.* Le long de la côte.
coat [kout], *n.* Habit; enduit (of tar), *m.*; peau (of snakes); robe (of some animals); (*Mil.*) tunique; (*Paint.*) couche; (*Anat.*) paroi;

(*Naut.*) braie, *f. Coat of mail,* cotte de mailles, *f.*; *cut your coat according to your cloth,* selon ta bourse gouverne ta bouche; *double-breasted coat,* veston croisé; *to turn one's coat,* tourner casaque.—*v.t.* Revêtir; enduire (de); (*Naut.*) garnir.
coat-hanger, *n.* Cintre, *m.*; porte-vêtements, *m. inv.*
coating, *n.* Étoffe pour habits, *f.*; enduit, *m.*, couche, *f. Rough coating,* crépi, *m.*
coat-peg, *n.* Patère, *f.* **coat-rack,** *n.* Porte-manteau, *m.* **coat-tails,** *n.* Basques, *f.pl.*
coax [kouks], *v.t.* Amadouer, cajoler, flatter. *To coax someone into doing something,* faire faire quelque chose à quelqu'un à force de cajoleries. **coaxing,** *n.* Cajolerie, *f.*, enjôlement, *m.*
co-axial [kou'æksiəl], *a.* Coaxial.
cob [kɔb], *n.* Bidet, (cheval) goussant, *m.*; balle (of maize), *f.*, or épi, *m.*; torchis, *m.*; (*pl.*) gaillette, *f.* **cobnut,** *n.* Grosse noisette, aveline, *f.*
cobalt ['koubɔːlt], *n.* Cobalt, *m.*
cobble [kɔbl], *v.t.* Carreler; saveter, rapetasser, raccommoder; paver en cailloutis.—*n.* Galet rond, pavé (for paving), *m.*
cobbler ['kɔblə], *n.* Savetier, cordonnier, *m. Cobbler's wax,* poix de cordonnier, *f.* **cobbling,** *n.* Raccommodage de souliers, *m.*
coble [koubl], *n.* Bateau de pêche à fond plat, *m.*
cobra ['koubrə], *n.* Cobra, cobra-capello, *m.*
cobweb ['kɔbweb], *n.* Toile d'araignée, *f.*
cocaine [ko'kein], *n.* Cocaïne, *f.* **cocaine-addict,** *n.* Cocaïnomane, *m.* or *f.* **cocainize,** *v.t.* Cocaïniser. **cocainism,** *n.* Cocaïnisme, *m.*
coccyx ['kɔksiks], *n.* Coccyx, *m.*
Cochin-China ['kɔtʃin'tʃainə]. La Cochinchine, *f.*
cochineal ['kɔtʃiniːl], *n.* Cochenille, *f.*
cochlea ['kɔkliə], *n.* (*Anat.*) Limaçon, *m.*
cochleariform or **cochleate,** *a.* En forme de vis, en spirale. **cochlearia** [kɔkli'eəriə], *n.* Cochléaria, *f.*
cock [kɔk], *n.* Coq; mâle (of small birds); robinet (tap); chien (of fire-arms); tas, *m.*, meulon (of hay), *m. At full cock,* armé (of weapons); *at half cock,* au cran de repos; *black-cock,* coq de bruyère, tétras, *m.*; *blow-off cock,* robinet de vidange, *m.*; *cock-and-bull story,* coq-à-l'âne, *m.*, conte à dormir debout, *m.*; *cock of the walk,* coq du village, *m.*; *old cock!* (*colloq.*) mon vieux! *the Gallic cock,* le coq gaulois; *to live like a fighting cock,* vivre comme un coq en pâte.—*v.t.* Relever; retrousser; mettre (one's hat) de côté; armer, dresser (fire-arms); mettre (hay) en meulons. *Cocked hat,* chapeau à cornes, *m.* **cock-a-doodle-doo,** *n.* Coquerico, cocorico, *m.* **cock-a-hoop,** *a.* Fier comme un coq, triomphant. **cockboat,** *n.* Coquet, petit bateau, *m.* **cockchafer,** *n.* Hanneton, *m.* **cock-crow,** *n.* Chant du coq, *m.* **cock-eyed,** *a.* De biais, de travers. **cock-fight,** *n.* Combat de coqs, *m.* **cock-horse,** *n.* (*Childish*) Dada, *m. A-cock-horse,* à dada sur mon bidet. **cockloft,** *n.* Grenier, *m.* **cock-pit,** *n.* Arène des combats de coqs, *f.*; (*Naut.*) poste des blessés, *m.*; (*Av.*) carlingue, *f.* **cockroach,** *n.* Blatte, *f.*, cafard, *m.* **cockscomb,** *n.* Crête de coq; (*Bot.*)

célosie à crête, amarante des jardiniers, *f.*; [COXCOMB]. **cockspur,** *n.* Ergot de coq, *m.*

cocksure, *a.* Sûr et certain; outrecuidant.

cocksureness, *n.* Assurance, outrecuidance, *f.* **cocktail,** *n.* Demi-sang (horse); staphylin (insect); cocktail, *m.* *Cocktail party,* cocktail, *m.* **cocky,** *a.* Effronté, suffisant, qui fait l'important.

cockade [kə'keid], *n.* Cocarde, *f.*

cockatoo [kɔkə'tu:], *n.* Kakatoès, cacatois, *m.*

cockatrice ['kɔkətrais], *n.* Basilic, *m.*

cockchafer [COCK].

cocker ['kɔkə], *v.t.* Choyer, dorloter.—*n.* Cocker (dog), *m.*

cockerel ['kɔkərəl], *n.* Jeune coq, *m.*

cocket ['kɔkət], *n.* Acquit à caution, *m.*

cockle [kɔkl], *n.* Bucarde; nielle, ivraie (corn-cockle), *f. Hot cockles* (game), la main chaude; *to warm the cockles of someone's heart,* réchauffer quelqu'un, réjouir quelqu'un.—*v.t.* Froncer. **cockle-shell,** *n.* Bucarde, *f.*; coquille de noix, *f.* (boat).

cockney ['kɔkni], *n. and a.* Natif de Londres, *m. Cockney accent,* accent faubourien, *m.*

cockroach, cockspur [COCK].

coco ['koukou], *n.* Coco, *m.* **coco-nut,** *n.* Coco, *m.*, noix de coco, *f. Coco-nut matting,* nattes en fibres de coco, *f.pl.* **coco-nut-tree,** *n.* Cocotier, *m.*

cocoa ['koukou], *n.* Cacao, *m.* **cocoa-nibs,** *n.pl.* Cacao en grains, *m.* **cocoa-nut,** etc. [COCO].

cocoon [kə'ku:n], *n.* Cocon, *m.*—*v.i.* Filer un cocon.

cod (1) [kɔd], *n.* Morue, *f.*; cabillaud (fresh cod), *m.* **cod-liver oil,** *n.* Huile de foie de morue, *f.*

cod (2) [kɔd], *n.* Cosse (pod), *f.*; (*Anat.*) scrotum, *m.*

cod (3) [kɔd], *v.t.* (*fam.*) Tromper.—*n.* Attrape, *f.*

coddle [kɔdl], *v.t.* Mitonner; dorloter, choyer.

code [koud], *n.* Code, *m.*; chiffre, *m. Highway code,* code de la route, *m.*—*v.t.* Codifier, coder; mettre en chiffre, chiffrer.

codger ['kɔdʒə], *n.* Bonhomme, original, *m.*

codicil ['kɔdisil], *n.* Codicille, *m.*

codification [koudifi'keiʃən], *n.* Codification, *f.*

codify ['koudifai], *v.t.* Codifier.

codling (1) ['kɔdliŋ], *n.* Pomme à cuire, *f.*

codling (2) ['kɔdliŋ], *n.* Petite morue (fish), *f.*

co-education ['kouedju:'keiʃən], *n.* Enseignement mixte, *m.* **co-educational,** *a.* (*sch.*) Mixte.

coefficient [kouə'fiʃənt], *n.* Coefficient, *m.*

coemption [kou'empʃən], *n.* Coemption, *f.*; achat réciproque, *m.*

coeliac ['si:liæk], *a.* (*Anat.*) Cœliaque.

coenobite ['si:nəbait], *n.* Cénobite, *m.*

coenobitic [si:nə'bitik], *a.* Cénobitique.

coequal [kou'i:kwəl], *a.* Égal. **coequality** [-'kwɔliti], *n.* Égalité, *f.*

coerce [kou'ə:s], *v.t.* Forcer, contraindre, réprimer. **coercible,** *a.* Coercible.

coercion [kou'ə:ʃən], *n.* Coercition, contrainte, *f.*

coercive [kou'ə:siv], *a.* Coercitif. **coercively,** *adv.* Par coercition.

coessential [kouə'senʃəl], *a.* De même essence.

coeternal ['koui'tə:nl], *a.* (*Theol.*) Coéternel. **coeternally,** *adv.* De toute éternité.

coeval [kou'i:vəl], *a.* Contemporain, du même âge (que).

coexist [kouig'zist], *v.t.* Coexister. **coexistence,** *n.* Coexistence, *f.* **coexistent,** *a.* Coexistant.

co-extensive ['kouiks'tensiv], *a.* De même étendue, de même durée.

coffee ['kɔfi], *n.* Café, *m. Coffee and rolls,* café complet, *m.*; *coffee roaster,* brûloir à café, *m.*; *coffee with milk, white coffee,* café au lait, *m.* **coffee-bean,** *n.* Grain de café, *m.* **coffee-cup,** *n.* Tasse à café, *f.* **coffee-grounds,** *n.pl.* Marc de café, *m.* **coffee-house,** *n.* Café, *m. Coffee-house keeper,* cafetier, *m.* **coffee-mill** or **-grinder,** *n.* Moulin à café, *m.* **coffee-pot,** *n.* Cafetière, *f.* **coffee-room,** *n.* Salle à manger (of hotel), *f.* **coffee-shrub, coffee-tree,** *n.* Caféier, cafier, *m.* **coffee-stall,** *n.* Café-roulotte, *m.* (qui s'installe la nuit dans les rues passantes).

coffer ['kɔfə], *n.* Coffre, *m.*; caisson; sas, *m.*

coffer-dam, *n.* Bâtardeau, *m.*

coffin ['kɔfin], *n.* Cercueil, *m.*, bière, *f.*—*v.t.* Enfermer dans un cercueil.

cog (1) [kɔg], *n.* Dent, *f.*—*v.t.* Garnir de dents, denter. **cog-wheel,** *n.* Roue d'engrenage, *f.* **cogged,** *a.* Denté, à dents.

cog (2) [kɔg], *v.t.* Cajoler, enjôler; piper (dice). —*v.i.* Tricher aux dés, faire des cajoleries.

cogency ['koudʒənsi], *n.* Force, puissance, *f.* **cogent,** *a.* Puissant, fort, valable, convaincant. **cogently,** *adv.* Avec force; de façon probante.

cogitate ['kɔdʒiteit], *v.i.* Méditer, penser.—*v.t.* Penser à, ruminer sur.

cogitation [kɔdʒi'teiʃən], *n.* Réflexion, pensée, méditation, *f.* **cogitative,** *a.* Pensif, réfléchi.

cognate ['kɔgneit], *a.* De la même famille; analogue.—*n.* (*Law*) Cognat, *m.* **cognation,** *n.* Analogie, parenté; (*Law*) cognation, *f.*

cognition [kɔg'niʃən], *n.* Connaissance, cognition, *f.*

cognitive ['kɔgnitiv], *a.* Cognitif.

cognizable ['kɔgnizəbl], *a.* Connaissable; (*Law*) ['kɔnizəbl], du ressort (de), de la compétence (de).

cognizance ['kɔgnizəns], *n.* Connaissance, *f.*; (*Her.*) insigne, *m.*; (*Law*) ['kɔnizns], juridiction, compétence, *f. To take cognizance of,* prendre connaissance de.

cognizant ['kɔgnizənt], *a.* Instruit; (*Law*) ['kɔniznt], compétent.

cognomen [kɔg'noumən], *n.* Surnom; nom de guerre, sobriquet, *m.*

cognovit [kɔg'nouvit], *n.* (*Law*) Aveu écrit (du défendeur), *m.*

cohabit [kou'hæbit], *v.i.* Cohabiter. **cohabitation** [-'teiʃən], *n.* Cohabitation, *f.*

coheir ['kou'ɛə], *n.* Cohéritier, *m.*

coheiress ['kou'ɛəris], *n.* Cohéritière, *f.*

coherence [kou'hiərəns] or **coherency,** *n.* Cohésion, cohérence, *f.* **coherent,** *a.* Cohérent, adhérent; conséquent; qui a de la suite dans les idées. **coherently,** *adv.* D'une manière cohérente.

cohesion [kou'hi:ʒən], *n.* Cohésion, *f.*

cohesive [kou'hi:siv], *a.* Cohésif. **cohesively,** *adv.* Cohésivement. **cohesiveness,** *n.* Cohésion, *f.*

cohort ['kouhɔːt], *n.* Cohorte, *f.*
***coif** [kɔif], *n.* Coiffe, calotte, *f.—v.t.* Coiffer. **coiffure**, *n.* Coiffure, *f.*
coign [kɔin], *n.* [*see* VANTAGE].
coil [kɔil], *n.* Rouleau (of hair etc.); repli (of serpents), *m.*; (*Naut.*) glène; (*Elec.*) bobine, *f.*; (*fig.*) *tapage, tumulte, *m.* *Induction coil*, bobine d'induction, *f.*; *this mortal coil*, le tumulte de ce monde.—*v.t.* Replier, rouler, enrouler; (*Naut.*) gléner, lover, rouer.—*v.i.* Se replier, s'enrouler.
coin [kɔin], *n.* Pièce de monnaie, *f.*, argent monnayé (money), *m.*; encoignure (corner), *f.*; coin (die); (*Arch.*) dé, *m.* *Base* or *counterfeit coin*, fausse monnaie; *to pay someone back in his own coin*, rendre à quelqu'un la monnaie de sa pièce.—*v.t.* Battre, frapper, monnayer; forger, fabriquer, inventer. *Co·ned money*, argent monnayé, *m.*; *to coin (into) money*, monnayer; *to coin money*, battre monnaie, (*fig.*) amasser de l'or, s'enrichir; *to coin words*, forger des mots. **coinage**, *n.* Monnayage, *m.*, monnaie; (*fig.*) invention, fabrication, *f.*
coincide [kouin'said], *v.i.* S'accorder, coïncider (avec).
coincidence [kou'insidəns], *n.* Coïncidence, conformité; rencontre, *f.*, accord, *m.* **coincident**, *a.* Coïncident, d'accord (avec). **coincidental**, *a.* De coïncidence.
coiner ['kɔinə], *n.* Monnayeur; faux monnayeur, *m.* **coining-press**, *n.* Balancier, *m.*
coition [kou'iʃən], *n.* Coït, *m.*, copulation; conjonction, *f.* (of the moon).
coke [kouk], *n.* Coke, *m.—v.t.* Convertir en coke.
colander ['kʌləndə], *n.* Passoire, *f.*
colchicum ['kɔlkikəm], *n.* (*Bot.*) Colchique, *m.*
colcothar ['kɔlkeθɑː], *n.* (*Chem.*) Colcotar, *m.*
cold [kould], *a.* Froid. *It is cold*, il fait froid; *to be cold* (of people), avoir froid; *that leaves me cold*, cela me laisse froid; *the water is cold*, l'eau est froide; *to get cold*, se refroidir; *to give the cold shoulder to* or *to cold shoulder*, se montrer distant à, tourner le dos à; *to have someone cold*, avoir quelqu'un à sa merci; *to throw cold water on*, décourager, doucher.—*n.* Froid; rhume (illness), refroidissement; frisson (cold feeling), *m.* *In cold blood*, de sang froid; *to have a cold*, être enrhumé; *to take* or *catch cold*, s'enrhumer. **cold-blooded**, *a.* Insensible; sans pitié; prémédité; à sang froid (of animals). **cold-bloodedness**, *n.* Sang-froid, *m.* **cold-chisel**, *n.* Ciseau à froid, *m.* **cold-drawn**, *a.* Étiré à froid. **cold-hearted**, *a.* Froid, insensible. **coldish**, *a.* Un peu froid, frais. **coldly**, *adv.* Froidement. **coldness**, *n.* Froid, *m.*, froideur, *f.* **cold-press**, *v.t.* Satiner à froid. **cold-short**, *a.* Cassant à froid (of metals). **cold steel**, *n.* L'arme blanche, *f.* **cold storage**, *n.* Conservation par le froid, *f.* *Cold storage trade*, industrie frigorifique, *f.*
cole [koul], *n.* Chou marin, *m.* **cole-rape**, *n.* Rave, *f.* **cole-seed**, *n.* (Graine, *f.*, de) colza, *m.*
colic ['kɔlik], *n.* Colique, *f.*
Coliseum [COLOSSEUM].
collaborate [kə'læbəreit], *v.i.* Collaborer (avec). **collaboration**, *n.* Collaboration, *f.* **collaborator**, *n.* Collaborateur, *m.*

collapse [kə'læps], *v.i.* S'affaisser, s'écrouler, s'effondrer; se dégonfler (of balloons); (*fig.*) s'écrouler.—*n.* Affaissement, écroulement, *m.*, débâcle, *f.*; dégonflement (of balloons), *m.* **collapsible**, *a.* Pliant, démontable.
collar ['kɔlə], *n.* Collier (of dog, horse, order); col (of a shirt); collet (of a coat), *m.*; collerette (for ladies); (*Arch.*) ceinture, *f.*; roulade (of meat), *f.* *Against the collar*, à contre-cœur; *detachable collar*, faux col, *m.*; *to seize by the collar*, saisir *or* prendre au collet; *to slip the collar*, s'échapper, devenir libre.—*v.t.* Mettre un collier à; colleter, saisir, prendre au collet; (*Cook.*) rouler. *Collared head*, fromage de tête, *m.* **collar-bone**, *n.* Clavicule, *f.* **collar-stud**, *n.* Bouton de col (de chemise), *m.*
collate [kə'leit], *v.t.* Collationner, comparer; nommer (to a living).
collateral [kə'lætərəl], *a.* Collatéral, indirect, accessoire.—*n.* (*Law*) Collatéral, *m.*; (*Am.*) caution (for loan), *f.* **collaterally**, *adv.* En ligne collatérale; collatéralement.
collation [kə'leiʃən], *n.* Collation, comparaison, *f.*; don, présent, *m.*; collation, *f.*, repas froid, *m.*
colleague ['kɔliːg], *n.* Collègue, confrère, *m.*
collect (1) [kə'lekt], *v.t.* Recueillir; ramasser, rassembler; collectionner; percevoir, encaisser (taxes); recouvrer (debts); quêter (charity); faire la levée des (lettres). *To collect oneself*, se recueillir, se remettre.—*v.i.* S'amasser.
collect (2) ['kɔlikt], *n.* Collecte; (courte) prière, *f.*
collected [kə'lektid], *a.* Rassemblé; (*fig.*) recueilli, calme, tranquille. **collectedly**, *adv.* Avec recueillement. **collectedness**, *n.* Recueillement; calme, sang-froid, *m.*
collection [kə'lekʃn], *n.* Collection, *f.*; assemblage, rassemblement, *m.*; compilation, *f.*, amas, *m.*; collecte, quête (for charity); (*Postal*) levée, *f.*; encaissement (of bills etc.), *m.*; perception (of taxes), *f.* **collective**, *a.* Collectif. **collectively**, *adv.* Collectivement. **collectivism**, *n.* Collectivisme, *m.* **collectivist**, *n.* Collectiviste.
collectivity [kɔlek'tiviti], *n.* Collectivité, *f.*
collector [kə'lektə], *n.* Collecteur; collectionneur; percepteur (of taxes); quêteur (for charity); receveur (of customs), *m.* **collectorship**, *n.* Charge de percepteur *or* de receveur; perception, recette, *f.*
colleen ['kɔliːn], *n.* (*Irish*) Jeune fille, *f.*
college ['kɔlidʒ], *n.* Collège d'Université, *m.*; école, *f. College of priests*, séminaire, *m.*
collegial [kɔ'liːdʒiəl], **collegiate**, *a.* De collège; collégial.
collet ['kɔlit], *n.* Douille, bague, *f.*; sertissure, *f.* (de pierre précieuse), chaton, *m.*
collide [kə'laid], *v.i.* Se heurter, entrer en collision; s'entrechoquer.
collier ['kɔliə], *n.* Mineur; (*Naut.*) (bateau) charbonnier, *m.*
colliery ['kɔljəri], *n.* Houillère, mine de charbon, *f.*
collimation [kɔli'meiʃən], *n.* Collimation, *f.*
collimator ['kɔlimeitə], *n.* Collimateur, *m.*
collision [kə'liʒən], *n.* Collision, *f.*, choc, *m.*; (*Naut.*) abordage; (*Rail.*) tamponnement, *m.* *To come into collision with*, heurter contre, rencontrer, (*Naut.*) s'aborder.

collocate   come

collocate ['kɔləkeit], *v.t.* Placer; (*Law*) colloquer. **collocation**, *n.* Placement, *m.*; place; (*Law*) collocation, *f.*

collodion [kə'loudiən], *n.* Collodion, *m.* **collodioned**, *a.* Collodionné.

colloid ['kɔlɔid], *a.* Colloïdal.—*n.* Colloïde, *f.*

collop ['kɔləp], *n.* Tranche de viande, *f.*

colloquial [kə'loukwiəl], *a.* De la conversation, familier. *Colloquial French*, français parlé, *m.* **colloquialism**, *n.* Expression familière, *f.* **colloquially**, *adv.* En style familier.

colloquy ['kɔləkwi], *n.* Colloque, entretien, *m.*

collotype ['kɔlətaip], *n.* Phototypie, *f.*

*****collude** [kə'lu:d], *v.i.* Être d'intelligence. **collusion**, *n.* Collusion, connivence, entente secrète, *f.* **collusive**, *a.* Collusoire.

collyrium [kə'liriəm], *n.* (*Pharm.*) Collyre, *m.*

collywobbles ['kɔliwɔbəlz], *n.* (*colloq.*) Mal au ventre, *m.*, borborygmes, *m.pl.*

colocynth ['kɔləsinθ], *n.* (*Bot.*) Coloquinte, *f.*

Colombia [kə'lʌmbiə]. La Colombie, *f.*

colon ['koulən], *n.* (*Anat.*) Colon, *m.*; (*Gram.*) deux points, *m.pl.*; (*Print.*) comma, *m.*

colonel [kə:nl], *n.* Colonel, *m.* **colonelcy** or **colonelship**, *n.* Grade de colonel, *m.*

colonial [kə'lounjəl], *a.* Colonial. **colonialism**, *n.* Colonialisme, *m.* **colonist** ['kɔlənist], *n.* Colon, *m.* **colonization**, *n.* Colonisation, *f.* **colonize** ['kɔlənaiz], *v.t.* Coloniser.

colonnade [kɔlə'neid], *n.* Colonnade, *f.*

colony ['kɔləni], *n.* Colonie, *f.*

colophon ['kɔləfən], *n.* (*Print.*) *Colophon, explicit . . . ; cy finit . . . , m.;* fin d'un livre, *f.*

colophony [kə'lɔfəni], *n.* Colophane, *f.*

Colorado-beetle [kɔlə'rɑ:dou'bi:tl], *n.* Doryphore, *m.*

color, *n.* (*Am.*) [COLOUR].

coloration [kʌlə'reiʃən], *n.* Coloration, *f.*

colorimeter [kɔlə'rimitə], *n.* Colorimètre, *m.*

colossal [kə'lɔsl], *a.* Colossal.

Colosseum [kɔlə'si:əm], *n.* Colisée, *m.*

colossus [kə'lɔsəs], *n.* (*pl.* **colossi** or **colossuses**) Colosse, *m.*

colour ['kʌlə], *n.* Couleur, *f.*; (*fig.*) prétexte, *m.*, apparence, *f.*; (*Paint.*) coloris; (*House-painting*) badigeon, *m.*, couche de peinture, *f.*; (*pl.*) (*Mil.*) drapeau; (*Navy*) pavillon, *m.*; (*spt.*) couleurs (of team etc.), *f.pl. Is this colour fast?* est-ce bon teint? *to be off colour,* être pâle, n'être pas bien en train; *to change colour,* changer de couleur; *to hoist the colours,* hisser le pavillon; *to lend colour to,* rendre vraisemblable, colorer; *to show oneself in one's true colours,* se révéler tel qu'on est, sous son vrai jour; *to strike one's colours,* amener son pavillon; *trooping the colour,* cérémonie du drapeau, *f.; with the colours flying; with the colours,* sous les drapeaux.—*v.t.* Colorer; colorier, enluminer (engravings etc.); badigeonner (walls etc.); culotter (a pipe).—*v.i.* Rougir (of persons); se colorer (of things); se culotter (of pipes). **colour-blind**, *a.* Daltonien. **colour-blindness**, *n.* Daltonisme, *m.* **colour-sergeant**, *n.* Sergent-fourrier, sergent-chef, *m.* **colourable**, *a.* Plausible, spécieux. **colourably**, *adv.* Plausiblement. **coloured**, *a.* Coloré; colorié, enluminé; de couleur (of half-breeds etc.). *Highly coloured,* exagéré. **colourful**, *a.* Coloré, pittoresque. **colouring**, *n.* Coloris, *m.*; couleur, *f.*;

(*House-painting*) badigeonnage; (*fig.*) prétexte, *m.* **colouring-matter**, *n.* Matière colorante, *f.* **colourist**, *n.* Coloriste, *m.* **colourless**, *a.* Sans couleur, incolore; terne, pâle (of style).

colporteur ['kɔlpɔ:tə, kɔlpɔ:'tə:], *n.* Colporteur, *m.* (of Bibles). **colportage**, *n.* Colportage, *m.*

colt [koult], *n.* Poulain; (*fig.*) novice, *m.* **coltish**, *a.* Jeunet; folâtre. **colt's-foot**, *n.* (*Bot.*) Pas-d'âne, *m.*

colubrine ['kɔljubrain], *a.* Colubrin; (*fig.*) rusé comme un serpent.

columbarium [kɔləm'beəriəm], *n.* (*pl.* **columbaria**) Colombaire, *m.*; colombier, *m.*

Columbia [kə'lʌmbiə]. *British Columbia,* la Colombie britannique, [COLOMBIA].

columbine ['kɔləmbain], *n.* (*Bot.*) Colombine; aquilégie, ancolie, *f.*

Columbus [kə'lʌmbəs]. Colomb, *m.*

column ['kɔləm], *n.* Colonne, *f. Agony column* (*spec. in* The Times), annonces personnelles, *f.pl.*; (*Pol.*) *fifth column,* cinquième colonne; (*Journ.*) *sports column,* rubrique sportive, *f.*

columnar [kə'lʌmnə], *a.* En colonne.

columned ['kɔləmd], *a.* À colonnes. **columnist**, *n.* (*Am.*) Journaliste (qui a sa rubrique à lui), *m.*

colure [kə'luə], *n.* Colure, *m.*

colza ['kɔlzə], *n.* (*Bot.*) Colza, *m.*

coma (1) ['koumə], *n.* Coma, *m.*, léthargie, *f.*; assoupissement, *m.*

coma (2) ['koumə], *n.* (*pl.* **comae**) (*Astron.*) Chevelure, *f.*; (*Bot.*) barbe, chevelure, *f.*

comatose ['koumətous], *a.* (*Med.*) Comateux.

comb [koum], *n.* Peigne, *m.*; étrille (for horses); crête (of a cock), *f.*; rayon (of honey), *m. Large tooth-comb,* démêloir, *m.; small comb,* peigne fin, *m.*—*v.t.* Peigner; étriller (a horse). *To comb one's hair,* se peigner; *to comb out,* démêler; (*fig.*) éplucher, nettoyer. **comb-case**, *n.* Étui à peigne, *m.*

comber ['koumə], *n.* Peigneur, *m.*, peigneuse (machine), *f.*; vague déferlante, *f.* **combing**, *n.* Action de peigner, *f.*, coup de peigne, *m.*; (*Tech.*) peignage, *m.*, (*pl.*) démêlures, *f.pl.* **combless**, *a.* Sans crête.

combat ['kɔm-, 'kʌmbət], *n.* Lutte, *f.*; combat, *m.*—*v.t., v.i.* Combattre. **combatant**, *n.* Combattant, *m.* **combative**, *a.* Combatif, agressif. **combativeness**, *n.* Combativité, *f.*

combination [kɔmbi'neiʃən], *n.* Combinaison; association, ligue, coalition, *f.*; concours (de circonstances), *m.* **combine** [kəm'bain], *v.t.* Combiner; réunir, coaliser; allier, liguer.—*v.i.* Se combiner; se coaliser (avec); se liguer, s'allier, s'unir (à); se syndiquer. *Combined movement,* mouvement d'ensemble, *m.*—*n.* ['kɔmbain] (*Comm.*) Cartel, *m.*; (or **combine-harvester**) moissonneuse-batteuse, *f.*

combustible [kəm'bʌstibl], *a.* Combustible. **combustibility**, *n.* Combustibilité, *f.* **combustion** [kəm'bʌstʃən], *n.* Combustion, *f.*, embrasement, *m. Internal combustion engine,* moteur à explosion, *m.* **combustion-chamber**, *n.* (*Motor.*) Chambre d'explosion, *f.*

come [kʌm], *v.i.* (*past* **came** [keim], *p.p.* **come**) Venir; arriver, parvenir; se présenter, advenir, se faire; devenir. *Come in!* entrez!

[90]

come on! allons! marchons! venez; *come what may*, advienne que pourra; *how comes it that*, comment se fait-il que; *I shall come and see you tomorrow*, je viendrai vous voir demain; *just come out*, vient de paraître (of books); *the time to come*, l'avenir; *to come about*, arriver, survenir; *to come across*, trouver, rencontrer par hasard; traverser (la rue etc.); *to come after*, venir après, suivre, venir chercher; *to come again*, revenir; *to come against*, heurter, frapper; *to come apart or asunder*, se détacher, se briser; *to come at*, arriver à, atteindre, parvenir à; se jeter sur; *to come away*, partir, s'en aller; *to come back*, revenir; *to come between*, intervenir, s'interposer entre; *to come by*, passer par, acquérir, se procurer; *to come down*, descendre, baisser (of prices), s'écrouler (of a building); *to come for*, venir pour, venir chercher; *to come forward*, s'avancer, avancer, se présenter; *to come home*, rentrer, revenir, *(fig.)* porter coup; *to come in*, entrer, arriver, monter (of the tide), *(fig.)* devenir la mode; *to come in again*, rentrer; *to come in and out*, entrer et sortir; *to come in for*, entrer pour, entrer pour chercher, y être pour; *to come into*, entrer (dans *or* en), hériter de; consentir, se joindre à; *to come nearer*, s'approcher (de); *to come next*, suivre; *to come of*, résulter de, provenir de, venir de, en être, en résulter; *to come off*, se détacher, s'enlever, réussir, avoir lieu, *(fig.)* s'en tirer; *to come on*, s'avancer, survenir, avoir lieu; *(spt.)* faire des progrès, venir en forme; *to come out*, sortir, se déclarer, tomber (of the hair), débuter, se montrer, paraître (of the stars etc.), s'effacer, disparaître (of stains), se tirer d'affaire, s'en tirer (from a difficulty); *to come out again*, ressortir; *to come out with*, lâcher, dire, laisser échapper; *to come over*, venir de loin, arriver d'outre-mer; *to come round*, venir, arriver, se remettre, se rétablir, revenir à soi (of health), *(fig.)* consentir; *to come to*, venir à, se remettre, revenir à soi, reprendre connaissance; *to come together*, venir ensemble, se réunir; *to come to terms*, en venir à un arrangement, tomber d'accord; *to come to the same thing*, revenir au même; *to come under*, être compris sous, subir, être soumis à; *to come up*, monter, s'élever, pousser (of plants); *to come upon*, tomber sur, surprendre, rencontrer par hasard; *to come up to*, atteindre; *where does he come from?* d'où vient-il?

come-back, *n.* Retour, *m.*; revanche, *f.*; réplique, *f.* **come-down**, *n.* *(fam.)* Humiliation, débâcle, *f.*

comedian [kə'miːdiən], *n.* Comédien, *m.*, comédienne, *f.*, comique; auteur comique, *m.*

comedy ['kɔmidi], *n.* Comédie, *f.* *Musical comedy*, opérette, *f.*

comeliness ['kʌmlinis], *n.* Aspect gracieux, *m.*; agréments, *m.pl.* **comely**, *a.* Avenant; *bienséant, convenable, digne.

comer ['kʌmə], *n.* Venant; venu, *m.*, venue, *f.* *First comer*, premier venu; *new-comer*, nouveau venu (*pl.* nouveaux venus); *open to all comers*, ouvert à tous; à tout venant.

comestible [kə'mestəbl], *a.* Comestible.—*n.* Comestible, *m.*

comet ['kɔmit], *n.* Comète, *f.* **cometary**, *a.* Cométaire.

comfit ['kʌmfit], *n.* Fruit confit, *m.*; sucrerie, *f.*

comfort ['kʌmfət], *n.* Réconfort, *m.*, consolation, *f.*; soulagement; bien-être, agrément, confort, *m.*; aise(s); aisance, *f.* *To be of good comfort*, prendre courage; *to like one's comforts*, aimer ses aises; *to live in comfort*, vivre dans l'aisance; *to take comfort*, se consoler. —*v.t.* Réconforter, soulager; consoler; encourager. **comfortable**, *a.* À son aise, dans l'aisance; agréable, confortable, consolant (of things). *To make comfortable*, mettre à son aise; *to make oneself comfortable*, se mettre à son aise, prendre ses aises. **comfortably**, *adv.* À son aise, bien, confortablement, commodément. *To be comfortably off*, jouir d'une honnête aisance. **comforter**, *n.* Consolateur (Holy Ghost), *m.*; consolatrice, *f.*; cache-nez de laine (scarf), *m.*; *(Am.)* édredon, couvre-pieds, *m.*; tétine, sucette (of baby), *f.* **comfortless**, *a.* Sans consolation; désolé, triste, inconsolable; incommode. **comfortlessly**, *adv.* Incommodément, mal, *(fig.)* inconsolablement, tristement. **comfortlessness**, *n.* Incommodité, gêne, *f.*, malaise, *m.* **comfort station**, *n.* *(Am.)* Toilette, *f.*

comfy ['kʌmfi], *a.* *(fam.)* [COMFORTABLE].

comfrey ['kʌmfri], *n.* *(Bot.)* Consoude, *f.*

comic ['kɔmik] *or* **comical**, *a.* Comique, drôle. **comic**, *n.* Magazine, journal illustré pour enfants, *m.*; *(Theat.)* comédien, comique, *m.* **comically**, *adv.* Comiquement. **comicalness** *or* **comicality**, *n.* Caractère comique, *m.*, comique, *m.*

coming ['kʌmiŋ], *n.* Venue; arrivée; approche, *f. Coming in*, entrée, *f.* *(pl.)* *Comings and goings*, allées et venues, *f.pl.*; *to be long in coming*, se faire attendre.—*a.* Qui arrive, qui vient, arrivant; à venir; prochain. *A coming man*, un homme d'avenir; *I am coming*, j'arrive!

comity ['kɔmiti], *n.* Politesse, courtoisie, *f.* *The comity of nations*, le bon accord entre les nations, *m.*

comma ['kɔmə], *n.* Virgule, *f.*; *(Mus.)* comma, *m.* *In commas*, entre guillemets; *inverted commas*, guillemets, *m.pl.*

command [kə'maːnd], *n.* Ordre, commandement; pouvoir, empire, *m.*; région, troupe sous les ordres d'un officier; autorité, *f.* *At command*, à sa disposition; *command of the sea*, maîtrise de la mer, *f.*; *to be at someone's command*, être aux ordres de quelqu'un; *to give the word of command*, commander; *to have a good command of a language*, bien posséder une langue; *to take command of*, prendre le commandement de.—*v.t.* Commander; avoir à sa disposition, posséder; inspirer (respect). *To command a view of*, donner sur, dominer; *yours to command*, (servant to master) votre très dévoué serviteur.

commandant ['kɔməndænt], *n.* Commandant, *m.*

commandeer [kɔmən'diə], *v.t.* Réquisitionner.

commander [kə'maːndə], *n.* Commandant; commandeur (of knighthood); *(Navy)* capitaine de frégate etc., *m.* *Commander-in-chief*, généralissime, commandant en chef, *m.* **commanding**, *a.* Commandant; imposant (prominent); qui domine (overlooking); impérieux, d'autorité (authoritative); *(Naut.)* maniable (breeze). *Commanding officer*, officier commandant, *m.* **commandingly,** *adv.* Impérieusement, avec autorité. **commandment,** *n.* Commandement (divin), *m.*

commando, *n.* (*Mil.*) Corps franc, commando, *m.*

commemorate [kə'meməreit], *v.t.* Célébrer, solenniser; commémorer.

commemoration [kəmemə'reiʃən], *n.* Célébration, commémoration, *f.*; souvenir, *m.*, mémoire, *f.*

commemorative [kə'memərətiv], *a.* Commémoratif.

commence [kə'mens], *v.t.* Commencer, intenter (an action). *To commence one's duties,* entrer en fonctions.—*v.i.* Commencer, devenir, débuter comme, se mettre à. **commencement,** *n.* Commencement, début, *m.*, origine, *f.*; jour de la remise solennelle des grades (dans certaines universités), *m.*

commend [kə'mend], *v.t.* Confier (à); recommander; louer, faire l'éloge de. **commendable,** *a.* Louable, recommandable. **commendableness,** *n.* Mérite, *m.* **commendably,** *adv.* D'une manière louable.

commendam [ko'mendəm], *n.* (*Eccles.*) Commende, *f.*, bénéfice par intérim, *m. To give in commendam,* commender.

commendation [kɔmən'deiʃən], *n.* Éloge, *m.*, louange, recommandation, *f. Worthy of the highest commendation,* digne des plus grands éloges.

commendatory [kə'mendətəri], *a.* De recommandation, élogieux; commendataire (abbé).

commensal [kə'mensəl], *n.* Commensal, *m.* **commensalism,** *n.* Commensalisme, *m.* **commensality** [kɔmen'sæliti], *n.* Commensalité, *f.*

commensurability [kəmenʃərə'biliti], *n.* Commensurabilité, *f.*

commensurable [kə'menʃərəbl], *a.* Commensurable. **commensurate,** *a.* Proportionné. **commensurately,** *adv.* Proportionnellement.

comment (1) ['kɔment], *n.* Commentaire, *m.*, explication, appréciation, *f.*; observation, *f.* **comment** (2) [kɔ'ment], *v.i.* Commenter.

commentary ['kɔməntəri], *n.* Commentaire, *m.*; (*sch.*) explication de texte, lecture expliquée, *f. Running commentary,* radio-reportage, *m.* (of a match). **commentator,** *n.* Commentateur, radio-reporter, *m.*

commerce ['kɔmə:s], *n.* Commerce, *m.*

commercial [kə'mə:ʃəl], *a.* Commercial, de commerce; commerçant (of towns etc.); industriel. *Commercial broker,* courtier de commerce, *m.*; *commercial law,* droit commercial, *m.*; *commercial traveller,* commis voyageur, *m.*; *commercial treaty,* traité de commerce, *m.*—*n.* (*Tel.*) Film publicitaire, *m.* **commercialize,** *v.t.* Commercialiser. **commercially,** *adv.* Commercialement.

commination [kɔmi'neiʃən], *n.* Menaces, *f.pl.*; (*Eccles.*) commination, *f.* **comminatory** *a.* Comminatoire.

commingle [kə'miŋgl], *v.t.* Mêler ensemble, mêler, confondre.—*v.i.* Se mêler ensemble *or* avec; se fondre (dans *or* en).

comminute ['kɔminju:t], *v.t.* Pulvériser, broyer.

comminution [kɔmi'nju:ʃən], *n.* Pulvérisation, *f.*; morcellement, *m.*

commiserate [kə'mizəreit], *v.t., v.i.* Plaindre, compatir à, avoir pitié de. **commiseration,** *n.* Commisération, compassion, *f.*

commissar [kɔmi'sɑ:], *n.* Commissaire, *m.* **commissariat** [kɔmi'sɛəriət], *n.* Commissariat, *m.*, intendance (militaire *or* maritime), *f.*

commissary ['kɔmisəri], *n.* Commissaire, intendant, *m.* **commissaryship,** *n.* Commissariat, *m.*

commission [kə'miʃən], *n.* Commission; perpétration, *f.*; (*Mil.*) brevet; (*Law*) mandat, *m. Commission agent,* commissionnaire, *m.*; *commission of a crime,* perpétration d'un crime, *f.*; *in commission,* (*Navy*) en armement, en service; *on commission,* en commission, sur commande; *sin of commission,* péché de commission, *m.*; *to get one's commission,* être nommé officier; *to throw up one's commission,* donner sa démission.—*v.t.* Charger, commissionner, autoriser. *Commissioned officer,* officier, *m.*; *non-commissioned officer* (*N.C.O.*), sous-officier, *m.* **commissionaire,** *n.* Portier (of a big store); chasseur (of an hotel); commissionnaire, *m.* **commissioner,** *n.* Commissaire, *m. Chief commissioner of police,* préfet de police, *m.*; *commissioner in bankruptcy,* juge-commissaire de faillite, *m.*

commissure ['kɔmisjuə], *n.* (*Anat.*) Commissure, *f.*

commit [kə'mit], *v.t.* Commettre, faire; confier, livrer, consigner; engager, lier; envoyer en prison. (*Parl.*) *To commit* (a Bill), renvoyer à une commission; *to commit a crime,* commettre, perpétrer un crime; *to commit for trial,* renvoyer aux assises; *to commit oneself,* se compromettre; *to commit to memory,* apprendre par cœur. **commitment, committal,** *n.* (*Law*) Emprisonnement, mandat de dépôt; (*Parl.*) renvoi à une commission, *m.*

committee [kə'miti], *n.* Comité, *m.*; (*Parliament*) commission, *f. Committee meeting,* comité, *m.*, réunion de comité, *f.*; *committee room,* salle de commission, *f.*; *executive committee,* bureau (of an association), *m.*; *select committee,* commission d'enquête, *f.*; *to go into committee,* se former en comité (of the House of Commons). **committee-man,** *n.* Membre du comité, *m.*

commode [kə'moud], *n.* Commode, *f. Night commode,* chaise percée, *f.* **commodious,** *a.* Spacieux. **commodiously,** *adv.* Spacieusement.

commodity [kə'mɔditi], *n.* Marchandise, denrée, *f.*, produit, *m.*

commodore ['kɔmədɔ:], *n.* (*Navy*) Chef de division, *m. Air-commodore,* général de brigade, *m.*

common ['kɔmən], *a.* Commun; ordinaire; vulgaire; du commun; courant (of prices); (*fig.*) trivial; (*Mil.*) simple. *Common law,* droit coutumier, *m.*; *common people,* menu peuple, *m.*; *Common Prayer* (Book of), liturgie anglicane, *f.*; *common sailor,* simple matelot, *m.*; *common sense,* sens commun, *m.* —*n.* Commune, *f.*; communal, *m.*, (*pl.*) communaux, *m.pl.*; (*Law*) vaine pâture, *f.*; bruyère, lande, *f. Common council,* conseil municipal, *m.*; *common councillor,* conseiller municipal, *m.*; *common room,* (*sch.*) salle des professeurs, *f.*; *Court of Common Pleas,* cour des plaids communs, *f.*, les Plaids communs, *m.pl.*; *House of Commons*, Chambre des Communes, *f.*; *in common*, en commun; *out of the common*, anormal, peu usuel, rare; *to be on short commons*, faire maigre chère; *to have nothing in common with*, n'avoir rien de commun avec; *to live in common*, faire maison commune.—*v.i.* Manger en commun.

commonable ['kɔmənəbl], *a.* Du domaine public, pour lequel le droit de vaine pâture est admis.

commonage ['kɔmənidʒ], *n.* Droit de vaine pâture; droit d'usage, *m.*

commonalty ['kɔmənlti], *n.* Le commun des hommes; le Tiers-État, *m.*

commoner ['kɔmənə], *n.* Bourgeois, roturier, *m.*; (*Law*) usager d'une servitude *or* du droit de vaine pâture, *f.*; (*Univ.*) étudiant ordinaire, *m.*; membre de la Chambre des Communes.

commonly ['kɔmənli], *adv.* Ordinairement, communément. *Very commonly*, très souvent.

commonness, *n.* Généralité, fréquence, *f.*

commonplace ['kɔmənpleis], *a.* Banal, commun, trivial.—*n.* Lieu commun, *m.*, banalité, *f.*

commonweal ['kɔmənwi:l], *n.* Le bien public, *m.*

commonwealth ['kɔmənwelθ], *n.* La chose publique, *f.*, l'État, *m. The Commonwealth of England*, la République d'Angleterre (1649–60); *the* (*British*) *Commonwealth*, le Commonwealth britannique, *m.*

commotion [kə'mouʃən], *n.* Secousse, agitation, *f.*, tumulte, *m.*

communal ['kɔmjunəl], *a.* Communal.

commune (1) [kə'mju:n], *v.i.* Parler, converser, s'entretenir (avec). *To commune with oneself*, rentrer en soi-même.

commune (2) ['kɔmju:n], *n.* Commune, *f.*

communicable [kə'mju:nikəbl], *a.* Communicable, qui peut se communiquer.

communicant, *n.* Informateur; communiant, *m.*, communiante, *f.* **communicate**, *v.t.* Communiquer, faire connaître, faire part de.—*v.i.* Communiquer, se communiquer; correspondre; (*Eccles.*) communier. **communication** [kɔmju:ni'kei ʃən], *n.* Communication, *f.*; communiqué, *m. Communication cord*, corde de secours, *f.* **communicative**, *a.* Communicatif, expansif. **communicativeness**, *n.* Caractère communicatif, *m.*

communion [kə'mju:njən], *n.* (*Eccles.*) Communion, *f.*; communication, *f.*; commerce, *m.*, relations, *f.pl. Communion cup*, calice, *m.* **communion-service**, *n.* Office du saint sacrement, *m.*, la communion, *f.* **communion-table**, *n.* Sainte table, *f.*

communiqué [kə'mju:nikei], *n.* Communiqué, *m.*

Communism ['kɔmjunizm], *n.* Communisme, *m.* **Communist**, *a.* and *n.* Communiste. **communistic**, *a.* Communiste.

community [kə'mju:niti], *n.* Communauté, société, *f.*, le public; solidarité, identité, *f. Community singing*, chants, hymnes, etc. chantés par toute l'assemblée; *community spirit*, esprit communautaire, *m.*

commutability [kɔmju:tə'biliti], *n.* Permutabilité; (*Law*) commuabilité, *f.* **commutable**, *a.* Permutable, échangeable; (*Law*) commuable.

commutation [kɔmju'teiʃen], *n.* Commutation, *f.*, échange, *m.* **commutative** [kə'mju:tətiv], *a.* Commutatif.

commutator ['kɔmjuteitə], *n.* Commutateur, *m.*

commute [kə'mju:t], *v.t.* Changer; (*Law*) commuer.—*v.i.* Aller de son lieu de résidence à son lieu de travail et vice-versa. **commuter**, *n.* Personne qui fait ce voyage tous les jours, *f.*

Como ['koumou]. Côme, *f.*

Comoro ['kɔmərou] **Islands**, Les Comores, *f.pl.*

comose ['koumous], *a.* Chevelu.

compact (1) ['kɔmpækt], *n.* Pacte, contrat, *m.*, convention, *f.*; poudrier (de dame), *m.*

compact (2) [kəm'pækt], *a.* Compact, serré, bien lié, uni; concis.—*v.t.* Rendre compact, unir. **compactly**, *adv.* D'une manière compacte; avec concision (of style).

compactness, *n.* (*Phys.*) Compacité; concision (of style), *f.*

companion [kəm'pænjən], *n.* Compagnon, *m.*, compagne, *f.*; dame *or* demoiselle de compagnie (to a lady), *f.*; pendant (of furniture), *m.*; nécessaire, *m.* (à ouvrage); petite encyclopédie, *f.*; (*Naut.*) capot d'échelle, *m. Companion ladder*, (*Naut.*) échelle de dunette, *f.*; *companion-way*, escalier des cabines, *m.* **companionable**, *a.* Sociable, d'un commerce facile. **companionableness**, *n.* Sociabilité, *f.* **companionably**, *a.* Sociablement. **companionship**, *n.* Camaraderie; compagnie, société, *f.*

company ['kʌmpəni], *n.* Compagnie; société, corporation, *f.*; monde, *m.*, assemblée, *f.*; assistance; troupe (of actors), *f.*; bande (of birds), *f.*, (*Naut.*) équipage, *m.*; (*Mil.*) compagnie, *f. Joint-stock company*, société par actions; *request the company of . . . at dinner etc.*, prient . . . de leur faire le plaisir de venir dîner, etc.; *the company*, l'administration, *f.*; *to be good company*, être un compagnon agréable; *to go into company*, aller dans le monde; *to keep bad company*, fréquenter la mauvaise compagnie; *to keep company*, voir du monde; *to keep company with*, fréquenter, tenir compagnie à, faire la cour à (to court); *to part company*, se séparer; *to sail in company*, (*Naut.*) naviguer de conserve; *two's company, three's company*, deux c'est bien, trois c'est un de trop; *we have company today*, nous avons du monde aujourd'hui.

comparable ['kɔmpərəbl], *a.* Comparable.

comparative [kəm'pærətiv], *a.* Comparatif; comparé (of philology etc.).—*n.* Comparatif, *m.* **comparatively**, *adv.* Comparativement, relativement.

compare [kəm'pɛə], *v.t.* Comparer; confronter; rapprocher (accounts etc.); vérifier. *Compared with*, en comparaison de, auprès de; *to compare notes*, échanger des idées.—*v.i.* Rivaliser.—*n.* (*poet.*) Comparaison, *f.*

comparison [kəm'pærisən], *n.* Comparaison, *f. Beyond comparison*, sans comparaison; *in comparison with*, auprès de, en comparaison de.

compartment [kəm'pɑ:tmənt], *n.* Compartiment, *m.*, subdivision, *f.*

compass ['kʌmpəs], *n.* Compas; circuit, tour, cercle, *m.*; boussole; portée (reach); étendue (of the voice), *f. A pair of compasses*, un compas; *pocket compass*, boussole de poche, *f.*; *mariner's compass*, compas de mer, *m.*; *the points of the compass*, les aires de vent, *f.pl.*; *to keep within compass*, retenir dans de justes bornes, garder les convenances, se tenir dans de justes limites; *within compass*, avec modération, sans exagération.—*v.t.* Faire le tour de, entourer; venir à bout de, atteindre, accomplir. *To compass about*, environner, assiéger; *to compass someone's ruin*, comploter la ruine de quelqu'un. **compass-card**, *n.* Rose des vents, *f.* **compass-needle**, *n.* Aiguille de boussole, *f.* **compass-saw**, *n.* Scie à guichet, *f.*

compassion [kəm'pæʃən], *n.* Compassion, pitié, *f.* **compassionate**, *a.* Compatissant. **compassionately**, *adv.* Avec compassion.

compatibility [kəm'pætibiliti], *n.* Compatibilité, *f.*

compatible [kəm'pætəbl], *a.* Compatible (avec).

compatriot [kəm'pætriət], *n.* Compatriote, *m.* or *f.*

compeer [kɔm'piə], *n.* Égal, pair; compagnon, *m.*, compagne, *f.*, compère, *m.*

compel [kəm'pel], *v.t.* Contraindre, forcer (de), obliger (à or de).

compelling, *a.* Compulsif, irrésistible.

compendious [kəm'pendiəs], *a.* Raccourci, abrégé, succinct. **compendiously**, *adv.* En abrégé, en raccourci. **compendium**, *n.* Abrégé, précis, *m.*; pochette, *f.* (of notepaper).

compensate ['kɔmpənseit], *v.t.* Dédommager (de); compenser.—*v.i.* *To compensate for*, remplacer, racheter.

compensation [kɔmpən'seiʃən], *n.* Dédommagement, *m.*, indemnité; compensation, *f.* **compensation-balance**, *n.* Balancier compensateur, *m.*

compensative [kəm'pensətiv], **compensatory** or **compensating**, *a.* Compensateur.

compete [kəm'piːt], *v.i.* Concourir (pour), faire concurrence (à); disputer; rivaliser. *To compete for*, concourir pour; *to compete with each other*, se faire concurrence.

competence ['kɔmpətəns] or **competency**, *n.* Capacité, aptitude; (*Law*) compétence, *f.*, titres, *m.pl.*; (*fig.*) aisance (fortune), *f.* *To have a competence*, avoir de quoi vivre. **competent**, *a.* Compétent (pour), capable (de); suffisant (pour). *To be competent to fill*, être capable de remplir. **competently**, *adv.* Avec compétence; d'une manière capable; suffisamment.

competition [kɔmpə'tiʃən], *n.* (*Comm.*) Concurrence, *f.*; concours (for a prize), *m.* *To come into competition with*, être en concurrence avec; *to offer for competition*, mettre au concours.

competitive [kəm'petitiv], *a.* De concurrence, de concours; qui a l'esprit de concurrence. *Competitive examination*, concours, *m.*

competitor [kəm'petitə], *n.* Compétiteur; (*Comm.*) concurrent, *m.*

compilation [kɔmpi'leiʃən], *n.* Compilation, *f.*; recueil, *m.*

compile [kəm'pail], *v.t.* Compiler, composer, recueillir. **compiler**, *n.* Compilateur, *m.*

complacence [kəm'pleisəns] or **complacency**, *n.* Satisfaction, *f.*, contentement (de soi-même), *m.*, suffisance, *f.* **complacent**, *a.*

Suffisant, de suffisance. **complacently**, *adv.* Avec un air (un ton) suffisant.

complain [kəm'plein], *v.i.* Se plaindre (de); porter plainte; (*fig.*) pleurer. **complainant**, **complainer**, *n.* Plaignant, réclameur, *m.* **complaint**, *n.* Plainte, *f.*, grief, *m.*; maladie, *f.*, mal (illness), *m.*; (*Admin.*) réclamation, *f.* *Cause of complaint*, sujet de plainte, *m.*; *to lodge a complaint*, porter plainte.

complaisance [kəm'pleizəns], *n.* Complaisance, *f.* **complaisant**, *a.* Complaisant. **complaisantly**, *adv.* Avec complaisance, avec obligeance.

complement ['kɔmplimənt], *n.* Complément (of verb, angle, etc.); le plein (of coal); l'effectif, *m.* *Full complement*, (*Navy*, *Mil.*) effectif complet, *m.* **complementary** [kɔmpli'mentəri], *a.* Complémentaire.

complete [kəm'pliːt], *a.* Complet, entier; accompli, parfait, achevé; (*fig.*) au comble. —*v.t.* Compléter, achever; (*fig.*) accomplir, combler; remplir (a form). **completely**, *adv.* Complètement. **completeness**, *n.* État complet, *m.*, perfection, *f.*

completion [kəm'pliːʃən], *n.* Achèvement, accomplissement, *m.*, perfection, *f.* (*Law*) *Occupation on completion*, entrée en jouissance à la signature de l'acte, *f.*

complex ['kɔmpleks], *a.* Complexe, compliqué.—*n.* (*Psych.*) Un ensemble (système, état d'esprit) complexe; un complexe.

complexion [kəm'plekʃən], *n.* Teint, *m.*, couleur, *f.*; aspect, caractère, *m.* *Light-complexioned*, au teint clair; *to put a different complexion upon*, présenter sous un autre jour.

complexity [kəm'pleksiti], *n.* Complexité, nature complexe, *f.* **complexly**, *adv.* D'une manière complexe.

compliance [kəm'plaiəns], *n.* Acquiescement, *m.* *In compliance with*, conformément à. **compliant**, *a.* Soumis, souple; complaisant, accommodant. **compliantly**, *adv.* Avec complaisance, servilement.

complicate ['kɔmplikeit], *v.t.* Compliquer; embrouiller. *To complicate matters*, pour compliquer l'affaire. **complicated**, *a.* Compliqué. *To become complicated*, se compliquer.

complication [-'keiʃən], *n.* Complication, *f.*

complicity [kəm'plisiti], *n.* Complicité, *f.*

compliment ['kɔmplimənt], *n.* Compliment, *m.*; (*pl.*) salutations, *f.pl.*, hommages, *m.pl.* (to a lady). *Compliments of the season*, souhaits de bonne année, *m.pl.*; *to pay a compliment*, faire un compliment; *to return the compliment*, répondre de la même manière; *with the author's compliments*, hommage de l'auteur, *m.*—*v.t.* [-'ment] Complimenter, féliciter, faire ses compliments à. **complimentary** [-'mentəri], *a.* Flatteur; en hommage; en l'honneur de (dinner). *Complimentary ticket*, billet de faveur, *m.*

complin(e) ['kɔmplin], *n.* (*Eccles.*) Complies, *f.pl.*

complot ['kɔmplɔt], *n.* Complot, *m.*—*v.i.*, *v.t.* [kəm'plɔt] Comploter.

comply [kəm'plai], *v.i.* Se soumettre, se conformer; accéder (à); remplir, observer, obéir (à) (to fulfil).

component [kəm'pounənt], *a.* Constituant, composant. *Component parts*, éléments constitutifs, *m.pl.*—*n.* (*Mech.*) Composant, *m.*, composante, partie constituante, *f.*

comport [kəm'pɔːt], *v.i.* S'accorder (avec). *To comport oneself,* se comporter. **comportment**, *n.* Conduite, *f.*, comportement, *m.*
compos mentis ['kɔmpɔs'mentis]. (*Law*) Sain d'esprit. *Non compos,* aliéné.
compose [kəm'pouz], *v.t.* Composer; écrire; rédiger, arranger; calmer, apaiser, tranquilliser. *To compose oneself,* se calmer; *to compose one's features,* se composer le visage. **composed**, *a.* Composé; calme, tranquille. **composedly** [-'pouzidli], *adv.* Tranquillement, avec calme. **composedness** [-'pouzidnis], *n.* Calme, *m.*, tranquillité, *f.* **composer**, *n.* Auteur; (*Mus.*) compositeur, *m.* **composing**, *a.* (*Pharm.*) Calmant. *Composing draught,* potion calmante, *f.*—*n.* Composition, *f.* **composing-room**, *n.* (*Print.*) Atelier de composition, *m.* **composing-stick**, *n.* Composteur, *m.*
composite ['kɔmpəzait, -zit], *a.* Composé; (*Arch.*) composite. *Composite candle,* bougie stéarique, *f.*
composition [kɔmpə'ziʃən], *n.* Composition; *f.*; (*Comm.*) atermoiement, arrangement, *m.*; (*Law*) transaction; (*Print.*) pâte à rouleaux, *f.*; (*sch.*) rédaction, *f. French composition,* thème français, *m.* **compositor** [kəm'pɔzitə], *n.* (*Print.*) Compositeur, *m.*
compost ['kɔmpɔst], *n.* Compost, terreau, *m.*
composure [kəm'pouʒə], *n.* Calme, *m.*, tranquillité, *f.*; sang-froid, *m.*
compote ['kɔmpout], *n.* Compote, *f.*
compound (1) ['kɔmpaund], *n.* Composé, *m.*; composition; (*East Ind.*) enceinte fortifiée (autour d'une habitation), *f.*—*a.* Composé. *Compound interest,* intérêts composés, *m.pl.*; *compound number,* nombre complexe, *m.*
compound (2) [kəm'paund], *v.t.* Composer; mêler, combiner; (*Comm.*) atermoyer; arranger. *To compound a felony,* entrer en composition avec le coupable (en vue de restitution).—*v.i.* S'arranger, s'atermoyer, transiger, entrer en arrangement (avec); (of horse) faiblir, flancher. *To compound with one's creditors,* s'arranger, faire un concordat avec ses créanciers.
compoundable [kəm'paundəbl], *a.* Qui peut être composé. **compounder**, *n.* (*Law*) Compositeur à l'amiable, *m.* **compounding**, *n.* Composition, *f.*
comprehend [kɔmpri'hend], *v.t.* Comprendre, se rendre compte (de). **comprehensible**, *a.* Compréhensible, intelligible. **comprehensibly**, *adv.* Intelligiblement. **comprehension**, *n.* Compréhension, intelligence, portée, *f.* **comprehensive**, *a.* Étendu, compréhensif. *Comprehensive study,* étude d'ensemble, *f.* **comprehensively**, *adv.* Largement, de façon complète. **comprehensiveness**, *n.* Étendue, portée; compréhensivité, *f.*
compress ['kompres], *n.* Compresse, *f.*—*v.t.* [kəm'pres] Comprimer; (*fig.*) resserrer.
compressibility [kəmpresi'biliti], *n.* Compressibilité, *f.* **compressible** [kəm'presəbl], *a.* Compressible, comprimable. **compression**, *n.* Compression; concision, *f.*, refoulement, *m.* **compressive**, *a.* Compressif. **compressor**, *n.* Compresseur, *m.*; frein, *m.*
comprise [kəm'praiz], *v.t.* Contenir, renfermer, comprendre, comporter.
compromise ['kɔmprəmaiz], *n.* Compromis,

arrangement, accommodement, *m.*, transaction, *f.*, moyen terme, *m. To have no spirit of compromise,* être intransigeant.—*v.t.* Compromettre; arranger. *To compromise oneself,* se compromettre.—*v.i.* Transiger, composer. **compromising**, *a.* Compromettant.
comptroller [CONTROLLER].
compulsion [kəm'pʌlʃən], *n.* Contrainte, *f. To act under compulsion,* agir par contrainte. **compulsive, compulsory**, *a.* Forcé, obligatoire, coercitif. **compulsively** or **compulsorily**, *adv.* Par force, par contrainte; forcément. *Compulsorily retired,* mis à la retraite d'office.
compunction [kəm'pʌŋkʃən], *n.* Componction, *f.*, vif remords, *m. Without any compunction,* sans scrupule.
compurgation [kɔmpəː'geiʃən], *n.* (*Law*) Témoignage justificateur (pour l'accusé), *m.*
computable [kəm'pjuːtəbl], *a.* Calculable.
computation [kɔmpju'teiʃən], *n.* Supputation, *f.*, compte, calcul, *m.*
compute [kəm'pjuːt], *v.t.* Calculer, supputer, compter, estimer. **computer**, *n.* Machine à calculer, *f.*
comrade ['kɔmreid], *n.* Camarade, compagnon, *m.* **comradeship**, *n.* Camaraderie, *f.*
con (1) [kɔn], *adv.* and *n.* Contre, *m.*
con (2) [kɔn], *v.t.* Apprendre; étudier; (*Naut.*) gouverner. *To con over,* repasser; répéter.
concatenate [kɔn'kætineit], *v.t.* Enchaîner, lier. **concatenation** [-'neiʃən], *n.* Enchaînement, *m.*, concaténation, *f.*
concave ['kɔnkeiv], *a.* Concave, creux. **concaveness** or **concavity** [kɔn'kæviti], *n.* Concavité, *f.* **concavo-concave**, *a.* Concavo-concave. **concavo-convex**, *a.* Concavo-convexe.
conceal [kən'siːl], *v.t.* Cacher; (*fig.*) dissimuler; celer or céler (à); (*Law*) receler or recéler, ne pas divulguer. **concealable**, *a.* Qu'on peut cacher. **concealed**, *a.* Caché, dissimulé, invisible, masqué (turning). **concealer**, *n.* (*Law*) Receleur, *m.* **concealment**, *n.* Action de cacher; dissimulation, *f.*; secret, mystère, *m.*; retraite, cachette, *f.*; (*Law*) recèlement, *m. Concealment of birth,* dissimulation de naissance, *f.*; *in concealment,* en secret, en cachette; *to keep in concealment,* tenir caché, se tenir caché.
concede [kən'siːd], *v.t.* Concéder, accorder, admettre. *To concede the point,* tomber d'accord sur le point, être d'accord.—*v.i.* Faire des concessions.
conceit [kən'siːt], *n.* *Trait d'esprit, *m.*; *opinion, *f.*; suffisance, vanité, *f. To be out of conceit with,* être dégoûté de; *without conceit,* sans vanité. **conceited**, *a.* Suffisant, vaniteux, enflé de vanité, infatué de soi-même. **conceitedly**, *adv.* Avec suffisance, avec vanité. **conceitedness**, *n.* Vanité, suffisance, *f.*
conceivable [kən'siːvəbl], *a.* Concevable, imaginable. **conceivably**, *adv.* D'une manière concevable. *That may conceivably be true,* il est concevable que ce soit vrai.
conceive, *v.t.* Concevoir; imaginer, se mettre dans la tête, croire, penser. *To conceive oneself,* s'imaginer, se croire.—*v.i.* Concevoir, devenir enceinte (of women).

concentrate ['kɔnsəntreit], *v.t.* Concentrer. —*v.i.* Se concentrer. *To concentrate on,* concentrer son attention sur . . . .

concentration [kɔnsən'treiʃən], *n.* Concentration, *f.* Concentration camp, camp de concentration, *m.*

concentre [kən'sentə], *v.t.* Concentrer, réunir en un centre.—*v.i.* Se concentrer.

concentric or **concentrical**, *a.* Concentrique.

concept ['kɔnsept], *n.* Concept, *m.*, idée générale, *f.* **conception** [kən'sepʃən], *n.* Conception, idée, *f.*; projet, dessein, *m.* **conceptual**, *a.* Conceptuel.

concern [kən'sə:n], *n.* Intérêt; soin, souci, *m.*, anxiété, *f.*; (*Comm.*) entreprise, *f.*, établissement, *m.*, maison, *f.*; (*fig.*) affaire, *f.* *That's my concern,* c'est mon affaire; *that's no concern of yours,* cela ne vous regarde pas. —*v.t.* Concerner, regarder; intéresser; inquiéter. *As concerns . . .,* quant à . . .; *it concerns me to know,* il m'importe de savoir; *that does not concern you,* cela ne vous regarde pas; *to all whom it may concern,* à tous ceux à qui il appartiendra; *those concerned,* les intéressés; *to be concerned about,* être inquiet de; *to concern oneself about,* s'intéresser à, s'occuper de, s'inquiéter de. **concernedly,** *adv.* Avec inquiétude. **concerning,** *prep.* Touchant, concernant, en ce qui concerne, à l'égard de. **concernment,** *n.* Intérêt, *m.*; interposition; anxiété, sollicitude, inquiétude, *f.*

concert (1) [kən'sə:t], *v.t.* Concerter.—*v.i.* Se concerter.

concert (2) ['kɔnsət], *n.* Concert; accord, *m.* *In concert,* à l'unisson; d'accord. **concert-hall,** *n.* Salle de concert, *f.* **concert-pitch,** *n.* Diapason de concert, *m.*; (*fig.*) pleine forme, *f.*

concerted [kən'se:tid], *a.* Concerté; (*Mus.*) d'ensemble.

concertina [kɔnsə'ti:nə], *n.* Accordéon hexagonal, concertina, *m.*—*v.i.* Se fermer en accordéon.

concerto [kən'tʃə:tou], *n.* (*Mus.*) Concerto, *m.*

concession [kən'seʃən], *n.* Concession, *f.*

concessionary [kən'seʃnəri], *a.* Concessionnaire. **concessive,** *a.* Concessif. **concessively,** *adv.* Par concession.

conch [kɔŋk], *n.* Conque, *f.* **concha**, *n.* (*Anat.*) Conque, *f.* **conchiferous** [-'kifərəs], *a.* Conchifère. **conchoid**, *n.* Conchoïde, *f.* **conchoidal** [-'kɔidl], *a.* Conchoïdal. **conchologist** [-'kɔlədʒist], *n.* Conchyliologiste, *m.* **conchology**, *n.* Conchyliologie, *f.*

conchy or **conchie** ['kɔntʃi], *n.* (*pop.*) Objecteur de conscience, *m.*

conciliate [kən'silieit], *v.t.* Concilier. **conciliation** [-'eiʃən], *n.* Conciliation, *f.* **conciliator** [-'silieitə], *n.* Conciliateur, *m.*, conciliatrice, *f.* **conciliatory**, *a.* Conciliant, conciliatoire.

concise [kən'sais], *a.* Concis. **concisely,** *adv.* Avec concision, succinctement. **conciseness,** *n.* Concision, *f.* **concision** [-'siʒən], *n.* Concision, *f.*

conclave ['kɔnkleiv], *n.* Conclave, *m.*; assemblée, réunion, *f.* (à huis clos).

conclude [kən'klu:d], *v.t.* Conclure; terminer; achever, finir; juger, estimer.—*v.i.* Conclure (de); se terminer (par *or* en), finir (par). **concluding,** *a.* Final, dernier. **conclusion,**

n. Conclusion, fin; décision, *f.*, jugement, *m.* *In conclusion,* pour conclure, en fin de compte; *to come to a conclusion,* se terminer, en venir à une conclusion; (*colloq.*) *to try conclusions with,* se mesurer avec. **conclusive,** *a.* Concluant, final; décisif, conclusif. **conclusively,** *adv.* D'une manière concluante. **conclusiveness,** *n.* Caractère péremptoire, caractère concluant, *m.*

concoct [kən'kɔkt], *v.t.* Mêler, confectionner; imaginer, inventer, préparer; combiner, machiner (un plan, etc.), tramer (un complot). **concoction,** *n.* Confection (d'un plat); potion; (*fig.*) machination (plotting), *f.*

concomitance [kən'kɔmitəns], *n.* Concomitance, *f.* **concomitant,** *a.* Concomitant, qui accompagne.—*n.* Accessoire, *m.* **concomitantly,** *adv.* Par concomitance, en compagnie avec d'autres.

concord (1) ['kɔnkɔ:d], *n.* Concorde, harmonie, *f.*; (*Mus.*) accord, *m.*; (*Gram.*) concordance, *f.*

concord (2) [kən'kɔ:d], *v.i.* Concorder, s'accorder.

concordance [kən'kɔ:dəns], *n.* Concordance, *f.*; lexique (to an author etc.), *m.* **concordancy,** *n.* Concordance, *f.*, accord, *m.* **concordant,** *a.* D'accord, concordant.

concordat [kən'kɔ:dæt], *n.* Concordat, *m.*

concourse ['kɔŋkɔ:s], *n.* Concours, *m.*, affluence, foule; réunion, *f.*

concrescence [kən'kresəns], *n.* Concrétion, *f.*

concrete ['kɔnkri:t], *n.* Béton, *m.*; bétonnage, *m.* *Reinforced concrete,* béton armé.—*a.* Concret.—*v.i.* [-'kri:t] Devenir concret, se condenser, se solidifier.—*v.t.* Bétonner. **concrete-mixer,** *n.* Bétonnière, *f.* **concretely,** *adv.* D'une manière concrète. **concreteness,** *n.* État concret, *m.* **concretion,** *n.* Concrétion, *f.*

concubinage [kən'kju:binidʒ], *n.* Concubinage, *m.*

concubine ['kɔŋkjubain], *n.* Concubine, *f.*

concupiscence [kən'kju:pisəns], *n.* Concupiscence, *f.* **concupiscent,** *a.* Lascif, libidineux.

concur [kən'kə:], *v.i.* S'accorder, être d'accord (avec); concourir (en *or* à).

concurrence [kən'kʌrəns], *n.* Concours; assentiment, *m.*; (*Law*) conflit (of rights), *m.* **concurrent,** *a.* Qui concourt, qui s'accorde, concourant. (*Law*) *Concurrent rights,* droits opposés, *m.pl.* **concurrently,** *adv.* Concurremment.

concuss [kən'kʌs], *v.t.* (*Med.*) Commotionner; secouer; (*fig.*) intimider.

concussion [kən'kʌʃən], *n.* Secousse, *f.*; ébranlement, choc, *m.* *Concussion of the brain,* commotion cérébrale, *f.* **concussion-fuse,** *n.* Fusée percutante, *f.* **concussive,** *a.* Qui ébranle.

condemn [kən'dem], *v.t.* Condamner (à); déclarer coupable; censurer, blâmer (to blame for). **condemnable** [kən'demnəbl], *a.* Condamnable. **condemnation** [-'neiʃən], *n.* Condamnation, censure, *f.*, blâme, *m.* **condemnatory,** *a.* Condamnatoire.

condensability [kən'densəbiliti], *n.* Condensabilité, *f.* **condensable,** *a.* Condensable. **condensation** [kɔnden'seiʃən], *n.* Condensation, *f.*

condense [kən'dens], *v.t.* Condenser; (*fig.*)

resserrer, abréger; concentrer. *Condensed milk*, lait condensé, *m.*—*v.i.* Se condenser; (*fig.*) se resserrer. **condenser,** *n.* Condenseur; (*Phys.*) condensateur, *m.* **condensing,** *n.* Condensation, *f.*

condescend [kɔndə'send], *v.i.* Condescendre, s'abaisser, daigner (à). *To condescend to someone*, traiter quelqu'un de haut en bas, user de condescendance envers quelqu'un. **condescending,** *a.* Condescendant. **condescendingly,** *adv.* Avec condescendance, de haut en bas. **condescension,** *n.* Condescendance, *f.*; acte de condescendance, *m.*

condign [kɔn'dain], *a.* Mérité, juste. **condignly,** *adv.* Justement.

condiment ['kɔndimənt], *n.* Assaisonnement, condiment, *m.*

condition [kɔn'diʃən], *n.* Condition, *f.*, état, *m.* *In a condition to*, en état de; *in good condition*, en bon état; *on condition that*, à condition que; *out of condition*, en mauvais état.—*v.t.* Conditionner. **conditional,** *a.* Conditionnel.—*n.* (*Gram.*) Conditionnel, *m.* **conditionally,** *adv.* Conditionnellement. **conditioned,** *a.* Conditionné; de condition, de rang; (*Psych.*) qui dépend d'un état antérieur. *Conditioned reflex*, réflexe conditionné, *m.*; *well conditioned*, bien conditionné, en bon état.

condolatory [kɔn'doulətəri], *a.* De condoléance.

condole [kɔn'doul], *v.i.* Prendre part à la douleur (de), exprimer ses condoléances. *To condole with*, faire ses compliments de condoléance à. **condolence,** *n.* Condoléance, *f.*

condonation [kɔndo'neiʃən], *n.* Pardon, *m.*; indulgence, *f.*

condone [kɔn'doun], *v.t.* Excuser, pardonner, racheter.

condor ['kɔndə], *n.* Condor, *m.*

conduce [kɔn'dju:s], *v.i.* Contribuer (à); conduire, tendre (à). **conducive** *a.* Qui contribue (à). *To be conducive to*, contribuer à, être favorable à. **conduciveness,** *n.* Utilité, propriété de contribuer (à), *f.*

conduct ['kɔndəkt], *n.* Conduite; direction, *f.* *Safe conduct*, sauf-conduit, *m.*—*v.t.* [kɔn'dʌkt] Conduire (à); diriger, mener. *Conducted tour*, excursion accompagnée, *f.*; *to conduct an orchestra*, diriger un orchestre; *to conduct oneself*, se conduire, se comporter. **conduct-sheet,** *n.* (*Mil.*) Feuille des punitions, *f.* **conducting,** *a.* Conducteur. **conduction,** *n.* (*Phys.*) Conduction, *f.* **conductive,** *a.* Conducteur. **conductivity,** *n.* Conductivité, *f.* **conductor,** *n.* Receveur (of an omnibus); (*Am.*) (*Rail.*) chef de train, *m.*; (*Mus.*) chef d'orchestre, *m.*; (*Phys.*) conducteur, *m.* *Lightning-conductor*, paratonnerre, *m.*; *non-conductor*, non-conducteur, *m.* **conductress,** *n.* Receveuse, *f.* (of a bus).

conduit ['kʌn-, 'kɔndit], *n.* Conduit; tuyau, *m.*; canalisation, *f.*

conduplicate [kɔn'dju:plikeit], *a.* (*Bot.*) Conduplicatif.

condyle ['kɔndil], *n.* (*Anat.*) Condyle, *m.* **condylar,** *a.* Condylien. **condyloid,** *a.* Condyloïde.

cone [koun], *n.* Cône; (*Bot.*) strobile, *m.*, pomme de pin, *f.* *Ice-cream cone*, cornet de glace, *m.* **cone-shaped,** *a.* Conique.

coney [CONY].

confabulate [kɔn'fæbjuleit], *v.i.* Causer, s'entretenir familièrement avec. **confabulation,** *n.* (*fam.* confab) Causerie, *f.*, entretien familier, *m.*

confection [kɔn'fekʃən], *n.* Confection, *f.*, friandise, *f.* **confectioner,** *n.* Confiseur, *m.*, confiseuse, *f.* **confectionery,** *n.* Confiserie, *f.*, bonbons, *m.pl.*

confederacy [kɔn'fedərəsi], *n.* Confédération (of States); ligue (of conspirators); association illégale, *f.* **confederate** [-reit], *v.t.* Confédérer.—*v.i.* Se confédérer (avec).—*a.* [-rət] Confédéré; ligué, allié (à *or* avec); de confédéré.—*n.* Confédéré, complice, *m.* **confederation** [-'reiʃən], *n.* Confédération, *f.*

confer [kɔn'fə:], *v.t.* Conférer, accorder. *To confer an honour upon*, faire un grand honneur à; *to confer upon*, conférer à.—*v.i.* Conférer (de).

conference ['kɔnfərəns], *n.* Conférence, *f.*, entretien, *m.*; congrès, *m.* *Press conference*, conférence de presse, *f.*

conferment, *n.* Collation, *f.*; octroi, *m.*

confess [kɔn'fes], *v.t.* Confesser, avouer; reconnaître, admettre.—*v.i.* Se confesser; (*Law*) faire des aveux. **confessed,** *a.* Reconnu, confessé, avoué. **confessedly** [-'fesidli], *adv.* De son propre aveu; de l'aveu de tous. **confession,** *n.* Confession, *f.*, aveu, *m.* *A frank confession is good for the soul*, rien ne soulage comme un aveu sincère; *to go to confession*, aller à confesse; *to hear someone's confession*, confesser quelqu'un. **confessional,** *n.* Confessionnal, *m.*—*a.* Confessionnel. **confessor,** *n.* Confesseur, *m.* *Father-confessor*, directeur, *m.*

confetti [kɔn'feti], *n.* Confetti, *m.*

confidant ['kɔnfidænt], *n.* Confident, *m.* **confidante,** *n.* Confidente, *f.*

confide [kɔn'faid], *v.t.* Confier (à), charger (de).—*v.i.* Se confier, se fier (à), avoir confiance (en).

confidence ['kɔnfidəns], *n.* Confiance; hardiesse, assurance; confidence (secret), *f.* *In confidence*, confidentiellement; *motion of no confidence*, motion de défiance, *f.*; *to have every confidence that* . . ., avoir l'assurance que . . .; *to put confidence in*, avoir confiance en; *to take into one's confidence*, se confier à, mettre dans le secret. **confidence-trick,** *n.* Vol à l'américaine, *m.*

confident ['kɔnfidənt], *a.* Confiant, certain, sûr; assuré. **confidential** [-'denʃəl], *a.* De confiance (of persons); confidentiel; intime. *Confidential secretary*, secrétaire particulier (-ière); *this is strictly confidential*, ceci est strictement entre nous. **confidentially,** *adv.* De confiance; confidentiellement. **confidently,** *adv.* Avec confiance; positivement.

confiding [kɔn'faidiŋ], *a.* Confiant, peu soupçonneux. **confidingly,** *adv.* D'un air confiant.

configuration [kɔnfigju'reiʃən], *n.* Configuration, *f.*

confine [kɔn'fain], *v.t.* Confiner, enfermer, emprisonner; resserrer, retenir; restreindre, limiter, borner. *Confined space*, espace restreint, *m.*; *to be confined* (of woman), faire ses couches, accoucher; *to be confined to one's room*, garder la chambre; *to confine oneself to*, se limiter *or* se borner à.—*n.* ['kɔnfain] (*usu. in pl.*) Confins, *m.pl.*; (*fig.*) limite, borne, *f.*

confinement, *n.* Emprisonnement, *m.*, détention, *f.*; (*Mil.*) arrêts, *m.pl.*; accouchement, *m.*, couches (of women), *f.pl. In close confinement*, au secret; *solitary confinement*, emprisonnement cellulaire, *m.*, réclusion, *f.*
confirm [kən'fəːm], *v.t.* Affermir; confirmer; fortifier, valider; (*Law*) homologuer. (*Eccles.*) *To be confirmed*, recevoir la confirmation.
confirmation [kɔnfə'meiʃən], *n.* Confirmation, *f.*, affermissement, *m. In confirmation of*, à l'appui de.
confirmative [kən'fəːmətiv] or **confirmatory**, *a.* Confirmatif, qui confirme, en confirmation de. **confirmed**, *a.* Invétéré, fieffé, incorrigible, endurci.
confiscate ['kɔnfiskeit], *v.t.* Confisquer. **confiscation**, *n.* Confiscation, *f.*
confiscator ['kɔnfiskeitə], *n.* Confiscateur, *m.*
confiscatory [kən'fiskətəri], *a.* Confiscant, de confiscation.
confiteor [kən'fitiɔː], *n.* Confiteor, *m.*
conflagration [kɔnflə'greiʃən], *n.* Conflagration, *f.*, incendie, *m.*
conflict (1) ['kɔnflikt], *n.* Conflit, entrechoquement, *m.*; (*fig.*) lutte, contradiction, *f.*
conflict (2) [kən'flikt], *v.i.* S'entrechoquer, lutter (contre); être en conflit, en contradiction (avec). **conflicting**, *a.* En conflit, contradictoire.
confluence ['kɔnfluəns], *n.* Confluent; concours, *m.*, (*Path.*) confluence, *f.* **confluent**, *a.* Confluent, qui conflue. *To be confluent*, confluer; se confondre.
conform [kən'fɔːm], *v.t.* Conformer.—*v.i.* Se conformer. **conformable**, *a.* Conforme (à), d'accord (avec). **conformably**, *adv.* Conformément (à).
conformation [kɔnfɔː'meiʃən], *n.* Conformation, *f.*
conformist [kən'fɔːmist], *n.* Conformiste, *m.*
conformity, *n.* Conformité, *f. In conformity with*, conformément (à).
confound [kən'faund], *v.t.* Confondre; (*fig.*) bouleverser, renverser; embarrasser, troubler. *Confound him!* que le diable l'emporte! *confound it!* zut! **confounded**, *a.* Maudit, sacré. **confoundedly**, *adv.* Terriblement, furieusement, diablement.
confraternity [kɔnfrə'təːniti], *n.* Confrérie, confraternité, *f.* **confrère**, *n.* Confrère, *m.*
confront [kən'frʌnt], *v.t.* Confronter; affronter, attaquer de front, faire face à, tenir tête à. **confrontation** [-'teiʃən], *n.* Confrontation, *f.*
confuse [kən'fjuːz], *v.t.* Rendre confus, mêler, embrouiller; (*fig.*) déconcerter; troubler. **confused**, *a.* Confus; embrouillé. **confusedly**, *adv.* Confusément. **confusedness**, *n.* Confusion, *f.* **confusing**, *a.* Qui prête à confusion. **confusion**, *n.* Confusion, *f.*, désordre, *m.*; (*fig.*) honte, *f.*, embarras, *m. Confusion worse confounded*, le comble de la confusion.
confutation [kɔnfju'teiʃən], *n.* Réfutation, *f.*
confute [kən'fjuːt], *v.t.* Réfuter.
congeal [kən'dʒiːl], *v.i.* Se congeler, se geler, se figer.—*v.t.* Congeler, glacer, geler, figer, cailler. **congealable**, *a.* Congelable. **congealment** or **congelation** [kɔndʒi'leiʃən], *n.* Congélation, *f.*
congener ['kɔndʒinə], *a.* and *n.* Congénère, *m.*

congeneric [kɔndʒi'nerik], *a.* Congénère.
congenial [kən'dʒiːniəl], *a.* De la même nature; sympathique (à *or* avec); qui convient (à). *A congenial task*, une tâche agréable; *congenial to the language*, dans le génie de la langue. **congeniality** [-'æliti], *n.* Affinité, conformité, sympathie, *f.*; caractère agréable, *m.*
congenital [kən'dʒenitl], *a.* Congénital. **congenitally**, *adv.* De naissance.
conger ['kɔŋgə], *n.* (*Ichth.*) Congre, *m.*, anguille de mer, *f.*
congeries [kɔn'dʒiərii:z], *n.* Masse informe, *f.*, amas, entassement, *m.*
congest [kən'dʒest], *v.t.* Entasser; engorger. *To become congested*, se congestionner, s'engorger; s'embouteiller (of traffic). **congested**, *a.* (*Path.*) Congestionné; embouteillé (of traffic). **congestion**, *n.* Amoncellement, amas, *m.*; (*Path.*) congestion, *f.*; encombrement, *m.* (of traffic). **congestive**, *a.* Congestif.
conglobate ['kɔnglobeit], *v.t., v.i.* (Se) mettre en boule.—*a.* Conglobé, en forme de globe.
conglomerate [kən'glɔməreit], *v.t., v.i.* (Se) conglomérer.—*a.* [-rit] Congloméré, en grappe.—*n.* (*Geol.*) Conglomérat, poudingue, *m.*
conglomeration [kɔnglɔmə'reiʃən], *n.* Conglomération, *f.*
conglutinate [kən'gluːtineit], *v.t., v.i.* (Se) conglutiner. **conglutination**, *n.* Conglutination, *f.* **conglutinative**, *a.* Conglutinant.
Congo ['kɔŋgou]. Le Congo, *m.* **Congolese**, *a.* and *n.* Congolais, *m.*, congolaise, *f.*
congratulate [kən'grætjuleit], *v.t.* Féliciter. *I congratulate you*, (je vous en fais tous) mes compliments; *to congratulate oneself on*, se féliciter de. **congratulation** [-'leiʃən], *n.* Félicitation, *f.*, compliment, *m.* **congratulator**, *n.* Personne qui félicite, *f.*, congratulateur, *m.* (*Path.*) congratulation, *f.*; **congratulatory** [kɔn'grætjulətəri], *a.* De félicitation.
congregate ['kɔŋgrigeit], *v.t.* Rassembler, réunir.—*v.i.* Se rassembler, s'assembler (chez), se rendre (à *or* dans). **congregation** [-'geiʃən], *n.* Congrégation, *f.*, fidèles (in a church), *pl.*; assemblée, réunion, *f.*, auditoire, *m.*, assistance, *f.*; amas, assemblage (of things), *m.* **congregational**, *a.* En assemblée. **congregationalist**, *n.* Congrégationaliste, *m.* or *f.*
congress ['kɔŋgres], *n.* Congrès, *m.*
congressional [kɔn'greʃənl], *a.* Congressionnel. **congressman**, *n.* Congressiste, *m.*; (*U.S.*) Membre du Congrès, *m.*
congruence ['kɔŋgruəns], *n.* Accord, *m.*, conformité, convenance, *f.*; (*Math.*) congruence, *f.* **congruent**, *a.* Convenable, conforme (à); (*Math.*) congruent. **congruity** [kən'gruːiti], *n.* Convenance, conformité, *f.*; (*Theol.*) congruité, *f.*
congruous ['kɔŋgruəs], *a.* Convenable, conforme (à); congruent. **congruously**, *adv.* Convenablement, congrûment.
conic ['kɔnik] or **conical**, *a.* Conique. **conically**, *adv.* En forme de cône. **conics**, *n.pl.* (*Geom.*) Sections coniques, *f.pl.*
conifer ['kounifə], *n.* Conifère, *m.*
coniferous [kou'nifərəs], *a.* Conifère.
conine ['kounin], *n.* Cicutine, *f.* (poison).

conjectural [kən'dʒektʃərəl], *a.* Conjectural, de conjecture. **conjecturally,** *adv.* Conjecturalement. **conjecture,** *v.t., v.i.* Conjecturer.—*n.* Conjecture, *f.*

conjoin [kən'dʒɔin], *v.t.* Joindre, conjoindre, unir.—*v.i.* Se joindre, s'unir (à).

conjoint ['kɔndʒɔint], *a.* Lié, uni, conjoint. **conjointly,** *adv.* Conjointement, ensemble.

conjugal ['kɔndʒugəl], *a.* Conjugal. **conjugally,** *adv.* Conjugalement.

conjugate ['kɔndʒugeit], *v.t.* Conjuguer. *To be conjugated,* se conjuguer. **conjugation** [-geiʃən], *n.* Conjugaison, *f.*

conjunct [kən'dʒʌŋkt], *a.* Réuni, conjoint, associé. **conjunction,** *n.* Conjonction, *f.* *In conjunction with,* conjointement avec.

conjunctiva [kɔndʒʌŋk'taivə], *n.* (*Anat.*) Conjonctive, *f.*

conjunctive [kən'dʒʌŋktiv], *a.* (*Gram.*) Conjonctif.

conjunctivitis, *n.* (*Path.*) Conjonctivite, *f.*

conjunctly, *adv.* Conjointement.

conjuncture, *n.* Conjoncture; occasion, rencontre, *f.*; concours de circonstances, *m.*

conjuration [kɔndʒu'reiʃən], *n.* Conjuration, prière, adjuration; évocation, sorcellerie, *f.*

conjure (1) [kən'dʒuə], *v.t.* Conjurer, adjurer; faire une conjuration avec.

conjure (2) ['kʌndʒə], *v.t.* Ensorceler; escamoter. *A name to conjure with,* un nom tout-puissant; *to conjure away,* exorciser; *to conjure up,* évoquer.—*v.i.* Faire de la sorcellerie; escamoter.

conjurer or **conjuror** ['kʌndʒərə], *n.* Escamoteur, prestidigitateur, illusionniste, *m.* **conjuring,** *n.* Prestidigitation, *f.*, escamotage, *m.* *Conjuring trick,* tour de prestidigitation *or* de passe-passe, *m.*; *conjuring up,* évocation, *f.*

conk [kɔŋk], *v.i.* *To conk out* (of engine etc.), caler.

conker ['kɔŋkə], *n.* (*fam.*) Marron d'Inde, *m.*

connate ['kɔneit], *a.* Né en même temps, inné.

connect [kə'nekt], *v.t.* Lier, relier, joindre, rattacher, unir (à); accoupler, embrayer, mettre en communication.—*v.i.* Se lier, se relier, se joindre; faire correspondance (of trains). **connected,** *a.* Joint, uni, lié; suivi, cohérent; en relations. *Connected by telephone,* relié par le téléphone; *to be connected with,* être joint à, se rattacher à, se rapporter à; *well connected,* de bonne famille. **connecting-pipe,** *n.* Raccordement, *m.* **connecting-rod,** *n.* Bielle, *f.* **connective,** *a.* Connectif; conjonctif.—*n.* (*Gram.*) Liaison, conjonction, *f.*; (*Bot.*) connectif, *m.* **connectively,** *adv.* Conjointement. **connexion** or **connection,** *n.* Connexion, liaison, suite, *f.*; rapport, *m.*; relations (intercourse); (*f.pl. Rail.*) correspondance, *f.*; (*Elec.*) contact, *m.*; (*Comm.*) clientèle, *f.*; parenté, famille, *f.*; (*pl.*) parents, *m.pl. In connexion with,* à propos de; *in this connexion,* à cet égard; *to run in connexion with,* être en correspondance avec (of trains).

conning-tower, *n.* (*Naut.*) Tourelle, *f.*, de commandement (of ship); kiosque, capot, *m.* (of submarine).

connivance [kə'naivəns], *n.* Connivence, *f.* **connive,** *v.i.* *To connive at,* fermer les yeux sur, être de connivence dans.

connoisseur [kɔnə'sə:], *n.* Connaisseur, *m.*

connote [kə'nout], *v.t.* Signifier, vouloir dire.

connotation [kɔno'teiʃən], *n.* Signification, connotation, (*Log.*) compréhension, *f.* **connotative** [kə'noutətiv], *a.* Connotatif, compréhensif.

connubial [kə'nju:biəl], *a.* Du mariage, conjugal.

conoid ['kounɔid], *n.* Conoïde, *m.* **conoidal,** *a.* Conoïde.

conquer ['kɔŋkə], *v.t.* Vaincre, dompter; conquérir.—*v.i.* Vaincre, remporter la victoire. **conquerable,** *a.* Qui peut être vaincu, domptable. **conquering,** *a.* Conquérant; victorieux. **conqueror,** *n.* Vainqueur, conquérant, *m.*

conquest ['kɔŋkwest], *n.* Conquête, *f.*

consanguine [kən'sæŋgwin] or **consanguineous** [kɔnsæŋ'gwiniəs], *a.* Consanguin. **consanguinity,** *n.* Consanguinité, parenté, *f.*

conscience ['kɔnʃəns], *n.* Conscience, *f. Conscience money,* restitution anonyme, *f.* (of income tax etc.); *in all conscience,* en bonne conscience; *point of conscience,* cas de conscience, *m.* **conscience-stricken,** *a.* Atteint de remords. **conscienceless,** *a.* Sans scrupule.

conscientious [kɔnʃi'enʃəs], *a.* Consciencieux; de conscience. *Conscientious objector,* objecteur de conscience, *m.* **conscientiously,** *adv.* Consciencieusement. **conscientiousness,** *n.* Conscience, *f.*, sentiment de justice, *m.*, droiture, *f.*

conscious ['kɔnʃəs], *a.* Conscient, qui a conscience *or* le sentiment (de); qui a sa connaissance; dont on a conscience (of things). *To be conscious,* avoir sa connaissance; *to be conscious of,* avoir conscience de. **consciously,** *adv.* Sciemment, avec connaissance de soi-même, en parfaite connaissance. **consciousness,** *n.* Conscience; connaissance, *f. To lose consciousness,* s'évanouir, perdre connaissance; *to regain consciousness,* reprendre connaissance.

conscript (1) ['kɔnskript], *a.* Conscrit.—*n.* Conscrit, *m.*

conscript (2) [kən'skript], *v.t.* Enrôler (par la conscription).

conscription [kən'skripʃən], *n.* Conscription, *f.*

consecrate ['kɔnsikreit], *v.t.* Consacrer (a church); bénir (the bread); sacrer (a bishop or king); canoniser (saints). *Consecrated bread,* pain bénit, *m.*; *consecrated ground,* terre sainte, *f.* **consecration** ['-kreiʃən], *n.* Consécration; canonisation, *f.*; sacre (of a king, bishop, etc.), *m.*

consecrator ['kɔnsikreitə], *n.* Consacrant, *m.* **consecratory,** *a.* Sacramentel.

consectary [kən'sektəri], *n.* Conséquence, *f.*, corollaire, *m.*

consecution [kɔnsə'kju:ʃən], *n.* Succession, consécution, *f.*; (*Gram.*) concordance, *f.*

consecutive [kən'sekjutiv], *a.* Consécutif, qui suit. *Five consecutive pages,* cinq pages de suite. **consecutively,** *adv.* Consécutivement, de suite, d'affilée; par ordre de date.

consensus [kən'sensəs], *n.* Assentiment général; consensus, *m.*, unanimité, *f.*

consent [kən'sent], *v.i.* Consentir (à).—*n.* Consentement; accord, *m. By common consent,* d'un commun accord; *by mutual consent,* de gré à gré; *the age of consent,* l'âge nubile, *m.*

consentaneous [konsen'teiniəs], *a.* Conforme (à), d'accord (avec). **consentaneously,** *adv.* Conformément, d'accord. **consentaneousness,** *n.* Accord, *m.*, conformité, *f.*

consentient [kən'senʃənt], *a.* Consentant, du même sentiment, d'accord; consentant (à).

consequence ['kɔnsikwəns], *n.* Conséquence, suite, *f.*, effet, *m.*; importance, *f. In consequence,* par conséquent; *in consequence of,* par suite de; *it is of no consequence,* cela ne fait rien; *of what consequence is it to you?* que vous importe? *the consequence is that,* il s'ensuit que, il en résulte que; *to take the consequences,* subir les conséquences. **consequent,** *a.* Résultant, par suite (de); (*Log.*) conséquent. *Consequent upon,* qui est la conséquence de.—*n.* Conséquent, *m.* **consequential** [-'kwenʃəl], *a.* Conséquent, logique; (*fig.*) suffisant, important (of persons). **consequentiality,** *n.* Justesse de raisonnement, logique; (*fig.*) suffisance, *f.*, air d'importance, *m.* **consequentially,** *adv.* Indirectement; (*fig.*) avec suffisance, d'un air important.

consequently ['kɔnsikwəntli], *adv.* and *conj.* Par conséquent.

conservancy [kən'sə:vənsi], *n.* Conservation, protection (d'un site), *f. Conservancy (board),* commission de conservation, *f.*

conservation [kɔnsə'veiʃən], *n.* Conservation, *f.*

conservatism [kən'sə:vətizm], *n.* Conservatisme, torysme, *m.* **conservative,** *a.* and *n.* Conservateur, *m. At a conservative estimate,* au bas mot, *m.* **conservator,** *n.* Conservateur, *m.*, conservatrice, *f.* **conservatory,** *n.* Conservatoire (for arts and music), *m.*; (*Hort.*) serre, *f.*—*a.* Conservateur.

conserve [kən'sə:v], *n.* Conserve, *f.*; (*pl.*) confitures, *f.pl.*—*v.t.* Conserver.

consider [kən'sidə], *v.t.* Considérer, examiner; avoir égard à; estimer, tenir (pour), regarder (comme). *All things considered,* tout bien considéré, à tout prendre; *considered opinion,* opinion réfléchie, *f.*; *consider yourself lucky,* estimez-vous heureux.—*v.i.* Considérer, songer, réfléchir (à). **considerable,** *a.* Considérable, grand, important. **considerably,** *adv.* Considérablement.

considerate [kən'sidərit], *a.* *Réfléchi, modéré, indulgent; attentif, plein d'égards; prévenant. *It is very considerate of you to,* c'est très aimable à vous de. **considerately,** *adv.* *D'une manière réfléchie; avec indulgence, avec bonté, avec égards. **considerateness,** *n.* *Caractère réfléchi, *m.*; attentions, *f.pl.*, prudence, discrétion, délicatesse, *f.*

consideration [kənsidə'reiʃən], *n.* Considération, *f.*, examen, *m.*, égards, *m.pl.*; récompense, *f.*, dédommagement, équivalent, *m.*; importance, *f. In consideration of,* en considération de; *for a consideration,* contre rémunération; *on further consideration,* réflexion faite; *out of consideration for,* par égard pour; *to be under consideration,* être en délibération; *to take into consideration,* prendre en considération, tenir compte de; *under no consideration,* sous aucun compte. **considering,** *prep.* (*colloq.*) Eu égard à; vu que, attendu que, étant donné que.

consign [kən'sain], *v.t.* Consigner, livrer,

confier (à); (*Comm.*) envoyer, expédier, faire une consignation de. *To consign to the grave,* déposer dans le tombeau.

consignee [kɔnsai'ni:], *n.* Consignataire, destinataire.

consignor [kən'sainə], *n.* Consignateur, expéditeur, *m.*

consignment [kən'sainmənt], *n.* Expédition, *f.*, envoi, *m. Consignment note,* lettre de consignation, *f.*; *to send on consignment,* envoyer en consignation, en dépôt (permanent).

consist [kən'sist], *v.i.* Consister (en). *To consist of,* se composer (de); *to consist in,* consister (en or à); *to consist with,* s'accorder avec. **consistence** or **consistency,** *n.* Consistance, suite, *f.*, esprit de suite; accord, *m.*, harmonie; stabilité, solidité, *f.* **consistent,** *a.* Ayant de la consistance, consistant; compatible (avec), conséquent. **consistently,** *adv.* D'une manière conséquente, conséquemment; conformément (à).

consistorial [kɔnsis'tɔ:riəl], *a.* Consistorial. **consistory** [kən'sistəri], *n.* Consistoire, *m.*

consolable [kən'souləbl], *a.* Consolable.

consolation [kɔnsə'leiʃən], *n.* Consolation, *f. Consolation prize,* prix de consolation, *m.* **consolatory** [kən'sɔlətəri], *a.* Consolant; de consolation.

console (1) ['kɔnsoul], *n.* Console (bracket etc.), *f.*

console (2) [kən'soul], *v.t.* Consoler (de).

consoling, *a.* Consolant, consolateur.

consolidate [kən'sɔlideit], *v.t.* Consolider.— *v.i.* Se consolider. *Consolidated funds* or *consols,* consolidés, *m.pl.* **consolidation** [-'deiʃən], *n.* Consolidation, *f.* **consolidator,** *n.* Raffermisseur, *m.*

consonance ['kɔnsənəns], *n.* Consonance, *f.*, accord, *m.*, harmonie, conformité, *f. In consonance with,* en conformité avec. **consonant,** *a.* Consonant, conforme (à), d'accord (avec).—*n.* (*Gram.*) Consonne, *f.* **consonantal** [-'næntl], *a.* Consonantique. **consonantly,** *adv.* D'accord avec.

consort (1) ['kɔnsɔ:t], *n.* Compagnon, *m.*, compagne, *f.*; époux, *m.*, épouse; (*Naut.*) conserve, *f.*; *Prince Consort,* prince consort, *m.*

consort (2) [kən'sɔ:t], *v.i.* S'associer (à). *To consort with,* fréquenter.

conspectus [kən'spektəs], *n.* Vue générale, *f.*, tableau synoptique, *m.*

conspicuous [kən'spikjuəs], *a.* Bien visible, en vue, en évidence; remarquable, éminent, frappant, marquant. *To be conspicuous by one's absence,* briller par son absence; *to make oneself conspicuous,* se mettre en évidence, attirer les regards. **conspicuously,** *adv.* Visiblement, manifestement, éminemment. **conspicuousness,** *n.* Caractère insigne, *m.*, position éminente, *f.*; voyant, éclat, *m.*

conspiracy [kən'spirəsi], *n.* Conspiration, conjuration, *f.* **conspirator,** *n.* Conspirateur; conjuré, *m.* **conspiratress,** *n.* Conspiratrice, *f.* **conspire** [-'spaiə], *v.i.* Conspirer, comploter (contre); (*fig.*) concourir, se réunir (pour). **conspiringly,** *adv.* Par conspiration.

conspue [kən'spju:], *v.t.* Conspuer.

constable ['kʌnstəbl], *n.* *Connétable; gouverneur (of castle); gardien de la paix,

agent de police, *m. Chief constable*, commissaire de police, *m.*; *to outrun the constable*, faire des extravagances, s'endetter.
constabulary [kən'stæbjuləri], *n.* Police; (*County*) gendarmerie, *f.*
constancy ['kɔnstənsi], *n.* Constance, fermeté, fidélité, *f.*; régularité, *f.* **constant**, *a.* Stable, constant, fidèle; continuel, continu.—*n.* (*Math. etc.*) Constante, *f.* **constantly**, *adv.* Constamment, invariablement.
Constantina [kɔnstən'tainə]. Constantine, *f.* **Constantine** ['kɔnstəntain]. Constantin, *m.*
constellate ['kɔnstəleit], *v.t.* Consteller. **constellation** [-'leiʃən], *n.* Constellation, *f.*
consternation [kɔnstə'neiʃən], *n.* Consternation, *f.*, atterrement, *m. In consternation*, atterré.
constipate ['kɔnstipeit], *v.t.* Constiper. **constipating**, *a.* Constipant. **constipation** [-'peiʃən], *n.* Constipation, *f.*
constituency [kən'stitjuənsi], *n.* Circonscription électorale, *f.*, électeurs, *m.pl. My constituency*, mes commettants, mes électeurs, *m.pl.* **constituent**, *a.* Constituant; essentiel, élémentaire.—*n.* Constituant, *m.*; partie constituante, *f.*, élément commettant; (*Polit.*) commettant, électeur, *m.*
constitute ['kɔnstitjuːt], *v.t.* Constituer, faire. **constitution** [-'tjuːʃən], *n.* Constitution, *f.*, tempérament, *m.*; (*pl.*) (*Hist.*) arrêts, *m.pl.* **constitutional**, *a.* Constitutionnel.—*n.* Promenade de santé, *f. To take one's constitutional*, faire sa petite promenade, prendre l'air. **constitutionalist**, *n.* Constitutionnel, *m.* **constitutionality** [-'næliti], *n.* Constitutionnalité, *f.* **constitutionally**, *adv.* Constitutionnellement; par tempérament.
constitutive ['kɔnstitjuːtiv], *a.* Constitutif.
constrain [kən'strein], *v.t.* Contraindre, forcer; retenir, comprimer, enfermer; gêner. *In a constrained manner*, d'un air gêné, *m.* **constrainedly**, *adv.* Par contrainte; d'un air gêné. **constraint**, *n.* Contrainte, gêne, *f. Without constraint*, à cœur ouvert, *m.*
constrict [kən'strikt], *v.t.* Resserrer, étrangler; brider. **constriction**, *n.* Resserrement, étranglement, *m.*; (*Med.*) strangulation, *f.* **constrictor**, *n.* (*Anat.*) Constricteur; boa constricteur, *m.*
constringent [kən'strindʒənt], *a.* Constringent, qui resserre.
construct [kən'strʌkt], *v.t.* Construire, bâtir. **constructor**, *m.* Constructeur, *m.* **construction**, *n.* Construction, *f.*; édifice, bâtiment, *m.*; (*fig.*) interprétation, *f.*, sens, *m. To put a wrong construction on everything*, interpréter tout en mal; *to put the best construction on*, donner l'interprétation la plus favorable à; *under construction*, en construction; *what construction do you put upon his conduct?* comment expliquez-vous sa conduite? **constructional**, *a.* De construction. *Constructional engineering*, construction mécanique, *f.* **constructive**, *a.* Constructif; implicite, par induction. **constructively**, *adv.* Par interprétation, par induction.
construe [kɔn'struː, kən'struː], *v.t.* Traduire mot-à-mot, analyser; (*fig.*) expliquer, interpréter. *Preposition construed with the ablative*, préposition qui gouverne l'ablatif.
consubstantial [kɔnsəb'stænʃəl], *a.* Consubstantiel (à). **consubstantiality** [-stænʃi'æliti],

n. Consubstantialité, *f.* **consubstantially**, *adv.* Consubstantiellement. **consubstantiate**, *v.t.* Unir en une seule et même substance. **consubstantiation** [-'eiʃən], *n.* Consubstantiation, impanation, *f.*
consuetudinary [kɔnswi'tjuːdinəri], *a.* and *n.* Coutumier, *m.*
consul ['kɔnsəl], *n.* Consul, *m. Consul-general*, consul général. **consular** ['kɔnsjulə], *a.* Consulaire. **consulate** or **consulship**, *n.* Consulat, *m.*
consult [kən'sʌlt], *v.t.* Consulter.—*v.i.* Délibérer, se consulter. **consultant**, *n.* Médecin consultant, *m.* **consultation** [kɔnsəl'teiʃən], *n.* Consultation, délibération, *f.* **consulting**, *a.* Consultant. *Consulting engineer*, ingénieur conseil, *m. Consulting room*, cabinet de consultation, *m.*
consumable [kən'sjuːməbl], *a.* Consumable; qu'on peut consommer.—*n.pl.* Les aliments, *m.pl.* **consume**, *v.t.* Consumer, dissiper, dévorer, gaspiller, perdre; consommer (*to use*). *To be consumed* (*with*), être dévoré (de), brûler (de).—*v.i.* Se consumer. **consumer**, *n.* Consommateur; abonné (*of gas etc.*), *m. Consumer goods*, biens de consommation, *m.pl.* **consuming**, *a.* Consumant, dévorant.
consummate (1) ['kɔnsəmeit], *v.t.* Consommer, achever, accomplir.
consummate (2) [kən'sʌmət], *a.* Consommé, complet, achevé, fieffé. **consummately**, *adv.* Parfaitement, complètement. **consummation** [kɔnsʌ'meiʃən], *n.* Consommation, fin, *f.*, accomplissement; (*fig.*) comble, *m. It is the consummation of my hopes*, c'est le comble de mes désirs.
consumption [kən'sampʃən], *n.* Consommation; destruction; phtisie, consomption, *f. To be in a consumption*, être poitrinaire; *to die of consumption*, mourir de la poitrine *or* de phtisie. **consumptive**, *a.* Destructif; poitrinaire, phtisique, tuberculeux. **consumptiveness**, *n.* Prédisposition à la tuberculose, *f.*
contact ['kɔntækt], *n.* Contact, rapport, *m.* (*Elec.*) *Contact breaker*, interrupteur, *m.*; *contact lenses*, verres de contact, *m.pl.*; *to bring into contact*, mettre en rapport; *to come into contact with*, se mettre en rapport avec; (*Elec.*) *to make* (*break*) *contact*, établir (rompre) le contact.—*v.t.* Contacter, mettre en relation avec, entrer en contact avec.
contagion [kən'teidʒən], *n.* Contagion, *f.* **contagious**, *a.* Contagieux. **contagiousness**, *n.* Nature contagieuse, *f.*
contain [kən'tein], *v.t.* Contenir; retenir, renfermer. *To contain oneself*, se contenir, se maîtriser. **containable**, *a.* Qui peut être contenu. **container**, *n.* Récipient, réservoir, *m.*; (*Comm.*) boîte, *f.*; cadre (de déménagement), *m.*
contaminate [kən'tæmineit], *v.t.* Souiller, contaminer. **contamination** [-'neiʃən], *n.* Souillure, contamination, *f.*
contango [kən'tæŋgou], *n.* (*St. Exch.*) Intérêt de report, *m.*
*****contemn** [kən'tem], *v.t.* Mépriser, dédaigner.
contemplate ['kɔntəmpleit], *v.t.* Contempler; méditer, projeter, avoir en vue; prévoir, espérer. *To contemplate doing something*, songer à faire quelque chose.—*v.i.* Songer,

méditer. **contemplation** [-ˈpleiʃən], *n.* Contemplation; pensée, méditation, vue, *f.*; projet, *m. It was in contemplation to,* il était question de; *to have in contemplation,* avoir en vue de, se proposer de. **contemplative** [ˈkɔntəmpleitiv *or* kɔnˈtem plətiv], *a.* Contemplatif; pensif. **contemplatively,** *adv.* Contemplativement. **contemplator** [ˈkɔntempleitə], *n.* Contemplateur, *m.*, contemplatrice, *f.* **contemporaneity** [kɔntempərəˈniːiti], *n.* Contemporanéité, *f.* **contemporaneous** [-ˈreiniəs], *a.* Contemporain. **contemporary** [-ˈtempərəri], *a.* Contemporain.—*n.* Contemporain, *m.*, contemporaine, *f.*; confrère (of newspapers), *m.* **contempt** [kənˈtempt], *n.* Mépris, dédain, *m. Beneath contempt,* plus que méprisable; *contempt of court,* refus de comparaître, *m.*, contumace; désobéissance aux ordres de la cour, *f.*, outrage aux magistrats, *m.*; *in contempt of,* en *or* au mépris de; *to fall into contempt,* tomber dans le mépris; *to feel contempt for,* avoir du mépris pour, tenir en mépris. **contemptible,** *a.* Méprisable, à dédaigner. **contemptibleness,** *n.* Caractère méprisable, *m.* **contemptibly,** *adv.* D'une manière méprisable. **contemptuous,** *a.* Méprisant, de mépris, dédaigneux. **contemptuously,** *adv.* Avec mépris, dédaigneusement. **contemptuousness,** *n.* Caractère méprisant, mépris, *m.* **contend** [kənˈtend], *v.i.* Lutter, combattre (contre *or* pour); contester; soutenir, affirmer, prétendre (que); se disputer un prix etc. *To contend for,* combattre pour, concourir pour, se disputer. **contender,** *n.* Compétiteur, concurrent, *m.* **contending,** *a.* En lutte, opposé, rival. *The contending parties,* les belligérants, les contestants, *m.pl.* **content** (1) [kənˈtent], *n.* Contentement, *m.*; *(pl.)* votes pour (in the House of Lords), *m.pl. Non-contents,* votes contre, *m.pl.*; *to one's heart's content,* à cœur joie.—*a.* [kənˈtent] Content, satisfait. *I am content,* je consens, je veux bien; *to be content with,* se contenter de. —*v.t.* Contenter, satisfaire. *To content oneself with,* se borner à. **contented,** *a.* Satisfait, content (de). **contentedly,** *adv.* Content, avec contentement, sans se plaindre. **contentedness,** *n.* Contentement, *m.* **content** (2) [ˈkɔntent], *n.* Contenu, *m.*; *(Chem.)* teneur, *f. Table of contents,* table des matières, *f.*; *the contents of a litre,* le contenu d'un litre, *m.* **contention** [kənˈtenʃən], *n.* Dispute, lutte, *f.*, débat, *m.*; rivalité, émulation; affirmation, prétention, *f. Bone of contention,* pomme de discorde, *f.*, sujet de contestation, *m.*, cause de litige, *f.* **contentious,** *a.* Contentieux, litigieux, disputeur, querelleur. **contentiously,** *adv.* En chicanant, contentieusement. **contentiousness,** *n.* Humeur querelleuse, *f.*, esprit litigieux, *m.* **contentment** [kənˈtentmənt], *n.* Contentement, *m. Contentment is beyond riches,* contentement passe richesse. **conterminous** [kənˈtɔːminəs], *a.* Limitrophe, voisin (de); attenant (à). **contest** (1) [ˈkɔntest], *n.* Lutte, *f.*, combat; concours, *m.*, épreuve, *f.* **contest** (2) [kənˈtest], *v.t.* Contester, disputer.

(Parl.) To contest a seat, disputer un siège; *to contest a will,* attaquer un testament.—*v.i.* Contester, se disputer, lutter. **contestable,** *a.* Contestable. **contestant,** *n.* Contestant, compétiteur, concurrent, *m.* **contestation** [-ˈteiʃən], *n.* Contestation, *f.* **context** [ˈkɔntekst], *n.* Contexte, *m. In this context,* à ce sujet. **contexture** [kənˈtekstjə], *n.* Contexture, *f.* **contiguity** [kɔntiˈgjuːiti], *n.* Contiguïté, proximité, *f.* **contiguous** [kənˈtigjuəs], *a.* Contigu, attenant (à). **contiguously,** *adv.* En contiguïté. **contiguousness,** *n.* Contiguïté, *f.* **continence** [ˈkɔntinəns] *or* **continency,** *n.* Continence, chasteté; *(fig.)* retenue, modération, *f.* **continent** (1), *a.* Continent, chaste; *(fig.)* modéré, retenu. **continently,** *adv.* Avec continence, chastement, *(fig.)* avec retenue, avec modération. **continent** (2) [ˈkɔntinənt], *n.* Continent, *m. The Continent,* l'Europe (continentale), *f.* **continental** [-ˈnentl], *a.* and *n.* Continental. **contingence** [kənˈtindʒəns] *or* **contingency,** *n.* Éventualité, *f*, cas imprévu, cas fortuit, *m.* **contingent,** *a.* Contingent, fortuit, imprévu; aléatoire. *To be contingent upon,* dépendre de.—*n. (Mil.)* Contingent; événement fortuit, *m.* **contingently,** *adv.* Éventuellement, fortuitement, par accident. **continual** [kənˈtinjuəl], *a.* Continuel; *(Law)* continu. **continually,** *adv.* Continuellement; *(Law)* continûment. **continuance** [kənˈtinjuəns], *n.* Continuation, durée, *f.*; séjour (in a place), *m.*; *(Law)* ajournement, *m.* **continuate,** *a.* Continu, ininterrompu, *(Law)* continuel. **continuation** [-ˈeiʃən], *n.* Continuation, *f.*, prolongement, *m.*; suite, durée, *f.*; *(St. Exch.)* report, *m.* **continuator,** *n.* Continuateur, *m.* **continue** [kənˈtinjuː], *v.t.* Continuer; prolonger; reprendre; conserver, perpétuer, maintenir. *To continue (on) one's way,* reprendre son chemin; se remettre en route; *to continue to do something,* continuer à faire quelque chose.—*v.i.* Continuer; se prolonger, demeurer, rester (dans); être toujours, durer. **continued,** *a.* Continu, soutenu, suivi; à suivre (of articles). *To be continued in our next,* la suite au prochain numéro, à suivre. **continuity** [kɔntiˈnjuːiti], *n.* Continuité, *f.* **continuity-girl,** *n. (Cine.)* Script-girl, *f.* **continuity shot,** *n. (Cine.)* Raccord, *m.* **continuous** [kənˈtinjuəs], *a.* Continu. **continuously,** *adv.* Continûment, sans interruption. **continuum,** *n.* Continu, *m.* **contort** [kənˈtɔːt], *v.t.* Tordre, contourner, défigurer. **contorted,** *a.* Tordu, contourné, défiguré. **contortion,** *n.* Contorsion; *(Anat.)* luxation, *f.* **contortionist,** *n.* Contorsionniste, *m.* **contour** [ˈkɔntuə], *n.* Contour, tracé (de niveau), *m.* **contour-lines,** *n.pl.* Courbes de niveau, *f.pl.* **contour-map,** *n.* Carte hypsométrique, *f.* **contra** [ˈkɔntrə], *prep.* Contre; *(Comm.)* d'autre part. *Per contra,* par contre, en compensation. **contraband** [ˈkɔntrabænd], *a.* De contrebande. *Contraband goods,* marchandises de

contrebande, *f.pl.*—*n.* Contrebande, *f.* *Contraband of war,* la contrebande de guerre, *f.*
contrabandist, *n.* Contrebandier, *m.*
contrabass ['kɔntrə'beis], *n.* Contrebasse (à cordes), *f.*
contraception [kɔntrə'sepʃən], *n.* Procédés anticonceptionnels, *m.pl.*
contraceptive, *n.* Procédé *or* appareil anticonceptionnel, *m.*—*a.* Anticonceptionnel.
contract [kən'trækt], *v.t.* Contracter (all senses); abréger, raccourcir; (*fig.*) resserrer; rider, froncer (the eyebrows etc.); prendre (a habit).—*v.i.* Se contracter, se resserrer, se rétrécir, se rider; (*Comm.*) traiter (pour), contracter, s'engager (à), entreprendre, soumissionner. *To contract for,* traiter pour; *to contract out of something,* renoncer à, se dégager de, quelquechose par contrat.—*n.* ['kɔntrækt] Contrat; pacte, *m.*, convention; adjudication, entreprise à forfait, soumission (for public works); promesse (of marriage), *f.* *Breach of contract,* rupture de contrat, *f.*; *by contract,* à forfait, par contrat; *by private contract,* de gré à gré, à l'amiable; *conditions of contract,* cahier des charges, *m.*; *to enter into a contract,* passer un contrat; *to put out to contract,* mettre à l'entreprise; *to put up to contract,* mettre en adjudication. **contractedness,** *n.* Rétrécissement, resserrement, *m.* **contractibility** [-i'biliti] *or* **contractibleness,** *n.* Contractilité, faculté de se contracter, *f.*
contractible [-'træktəbl], *a.* Contractile, susceptible de contraction. **contractile** [-'træktail], *a.* Contractile.
contractility [kɔntræk'tiliti], *n.* Force contractive, contractilité, *f.*
contraction [kən'trækʃən], *n.* Contraction, *f.*, rétrécissement; raccourcissement; retrait (of metals), *m.*; (*Math.*) abréviation, *f.*
contractor [kən'træktə], *n.* Contractant, *m.*, contractante, *f.*; entrepreneur (builder); fournisseur (for the army or navy); adjudicataire (granter), *m.*
contradict [kɔntrə'dikt], *v.t.* Contredire, démentir; *To contradict oneself,* se démentir; (*colloq.*) se couper. **contradictor,** *n.* Contradicteur, *m.* **contradiction,** *n.* Contradiction, *f.*, incompatibilité, *f.*, démenti (denial), *m.* **contradictious,** *n.* Raisonneur, ergoteur. **contradictiousness,** *n.* Esprit de contradiction, *m.* **contradictorily,** *adv.* Contradictoirement. **contradictoriness,** *n.* Nature contradictoire, *f.* **contradictory,** *a.* Contradictoire.
contradistinction [kɔntrədis'tiŋkʃən], *n.* Opposition, *f.*, contraste, *m.* *In contradistinction to,* par contraste avec.
contradistinguish [kɔntrədis'tiŋgwish], *v.t.* Distinguer (de); contraster (avec).
contraindicate [kɔntrə'indikeit], *v.t.* Contre-indiquer. **contraindicant** *or* **contraindication,** *n.* Contre-indication, *f.*
contralto [kən'træltou], *n.* (*Mus.*) Contralto, contralte, *m.*
contraption [kən'træpʃən], *n.* (*fam.*) Machin, truc, *m.*
contrapuntal [kɔntrə'pʌntl], *a.* En contrepoint.
contrariety [kɔntrə'raiəti], *n.* Contrariété, opposition, *f.* **contrarily** ['kɔntrərili], *adv.* Contrairement, en sens contraire. **contrariness,** *n.* Esprit de contrariété, de contradiction.

contrariwise ['kɔntrəriwaiz], *adv.* Au contraire; en sens opposé.
contrary ['kɔntrəri], *a.* Contraire, opposé; (*fam.*) [kən'treəri] (of person) qui aime à contrarier, pervers, revêche.—*n.* Contraire, *m.* *On the contrary,* au contraire; *quite the contrary,* tout le contraire, bien au contraire; *to the contrary,* contre, en sens contraire.—*adv.* Contrairement (à); à l'encontre (de), au rebours (de).
contrast ['kɔntraːst], *n.* Contraste, *m.* *To stand in contrast,* faire contraste.—*v.t.* [kən'træst] *or* [kən'traːst] Faire contraster; mettre en contraste.—*v.i.* Contraster, faire contraste.
contrate ['kɔntreit], *a.* (Roue) à dents (*or* cliquets) perpendiculaires au champ.
contravallation [kɔntrəvə'leiʃən], *n.* (*Fort.*) Contrevallation, *f.*
contravene [kɔntrə'viːn], *v.t.* Contrevenir à, enfreindre. **contravener,** *n.* Contrevenant, *m.* **contravention** [-'venʃən], *n.* Contravention, infraction, *f.* *In contravention of,* en violation de, *f.*
contribute [kən'tribjuːt], *v.t.* Contribuer, payer.—*v.i.* Contribuer (à); concourir, collaborer (à).
contribution [kɔntri'bjuːʃən], *n.* Contribution, *f.*, cotisation, *f.*, article (in a journal etc.), *m.*
contributive [kən'tribjutiv], *a.* Qui contribue, contributif. *To be contributive to,* contribuer à. **contributor,** *n.* Contribuant, *m.*, personne qui contribue, *f.*; (*Journ.*) collaborateur, *m.* *To be a contributor to,* contribuer à. **contributory,** *a.* Contribuant.
contrite ['kɔntrait], *a.* Contrit, pénitent. **contritely,** *adv.* Avec contrition. **contriteness,** *n.* **contrition** [-'triʃən], *n.* Contrition, pénitence, *f.*
contrivable [kɔn'traivəbl], *a.* Possible à faire, à arranger *or* à combiner. **contrivance,** *n.* Invention; combinaison, idée, *f.*; artifice, dispositif, moyen, (*fam.*) truc, *m.* **contrive,** *v.t.* Inventer, imaginer; pratiquer, ménager.—*v.i.* S'arranger de manière (à), s'arranger (pour), trouver moyen (de); parvenir (à), venir à bout (de). **contriver,** *n.* Inventeur, *m.*, inventrice, *f.* **contriving,** *a.* Ingénieux.
control [kən'troul], *n.* Autorité (supérieure), haute main, maîtrise; surveillance, *f.*; (*Tech.*) commande, *f.* *Control signals,* signalisation routière, *f.*; (*Mil.*) *control of fire,* conduite du feu, *f.*; (*Motor.*) *controls,* les leviers de commande, *m.pl.*; *out of control* (of ship, aeroplane), désemparé; *remote control,* commande à distance, télécommande, *f.*; *to lose control of oneself,* n'être plus maître de soi; *under control* (of a horse etc.), bien en main; (*Rad.*) *volume control,* contrôle de volume, *m.*—*v.t.* Diriger, régler; gouverner, commander; maîtriser, réprimer. *To control oneself,* se dominer, se retenir. **controllable,** *a.* Vérifiable; gouvernable. **controller,** *n.* Contrôleur, *m.*
controversial [kɔntrə'vəːʃəl], *a.* Sujet à controverse, polémique. **controversialist,** *n.* Controversiste, *m.*
controversy [kɔntrə'vəːsi], *n.* Controverse, polémique, *f.*; différend, *m.*
controvert ['kɔntrəvəːt], *v.t.* Controverser, disputer. **controvertible,** *a.* Sujet à controverse, controversable.

contumacious [kɔntju'meiʃəs], *a.* Obstiné, récalcitrant, opiniâtre; (*Law*) contumace. **contumaciously**, *adv.* Obstinément; (*Law*) par contumace. **contumaciousness** or **contumacy** ['kɔntjuməsi], *n.* Obstination, opiniâtreté; (*Law*) contumace, *f.*

contumelious [kɔntju'miːliəs], *a.* Injurieux, outrageant, méprisant. **contumeliously**, *adv.* Injurieusement, outrageusement.

contumely ['kɔntjuməli], *n.* Injure, *f.*, outrage, *m.*, honte, *f.*

contuse [kən'tjuːz], *v.t.* Contusionner, meurtrir. **contusion**, *n.* Contusion, meurtrissure, *f.*

conundrum [kə'nʌndrəm], *n.* Énigme, devinette, *f.*

convalesce [kɔnvə'les], *v.i.* Être en convalescence. **convalescence**, *n.* Convalescence, *f.* **convalescent**, *a.* Convalescent. *Convalescent home*, maison de convalescence, *f.—n.* Convalescent, *m.*, convalescente, *f.*

convection [kən'vekʃən], *n.* Convection, *f. Convection heater*, appareil de chauffage à convection, *m.*

convenable [kən'viːnəbl], *a.* Qui peut être convoqué.

convene [kən'viːn], *v.t.* Convoquer, réunir, assembler.—*v.i.* S'assembler, se réunir. **convener**, *n.* Personne qui convoque, *f.*

convenience [kən'viːniəns], *n.* Commodité, convenance, *f.*; objet de commodité, *m. All modern conveniences* (*mod. con.*), tout confort; *at your convenience*, sans vous déranger; *at your earliest convenience*, dès que vous le pourrez; *marriage of convenience*, mariage de convenance, *m.*; (*public*) *convenience*, chalet de nécessité, lieu d'aisances, *m.* **convenient**, *a.* Commode, convenable. *If it is convenient to you*, si cela ne vous dérange pas; *if you could make it convenient to*, si vous pouvez vous arranger de manière que (with subjunctive) *or* de manière à (with infinitive). **conveniently**, *adv.* Commodément, convenablement, sans inconvénient; sans se gêner.

convent ['kɔnvənt], *n.* Couvent, *m.*

conventicle [kən'ventikl], *n.* Conventicule, *m.*

convention [kən'venʃən], *n.* Convention, *f.*, pacte, *m.*; assemblée, *f.*; (*pl.*) convenances, *f.pl.* **conventional**, *a.* Conventionnel, de convention; ordinaire. *Conventional signs*, les indications sur une carte d'état-major. **conventionalism**, *n.* Conventionalisme, respect des convenances, *m.*; phrase de convention, *f.*, usage de convention, *m.*

conventionality [kənvenʃə'næliti], *n.* Caractère conventionnel, *m.*; les conventions (artistiques, sociales, etc.), *f.pl.* **conventionally**, *adv.* Par convention; sans originalité; ordinairement.

conventual [kən'ventjuəl], *a.* Conventuel.—*n.* Conventuel, religieux, *m.*, religieuse, *f.*

converge [kən'vɜːdʒ], *v.i.* Converger. **convergence**, *n.* Convergence, *f.* **convergent**, **converging**, *a.* Convergent.

conversable [kən'vɜːsəbl], *a.* De bonne conversation, sociable. **conversableness**, *n.* Amabilité, sociabilité, *f.* **conversably**, *adv.* D'une manière sociable.

conversant ['kɔnvəːsənt], *a.* Versé (dans); familier (avec). *Conversant with*, versé dans, au fait de, au courant de.

conversation [kɔnvə'seiʃən], *n.* Conversation, *f.*, entretien, *m. Conversation piece*, tableau de genre, *m.*; (*Law*) *criminal conversation*, adultère, *m.*; *earnest conversation*, entretien sérieux; *private conversation*, entretien particulier; *to carry on a conversation*, causer, s'entretenir; *to change the conversation*, changer de sujet. **conversational**, *a.* De conversation. *A man of great conversational powers*, un brillant causeur, *m.* **conversationalist**, *n.* Causeur.

conversazione [kɔnvəsætsi'ouni], *n.* Réunion (littéraire, artistique, *or* scientifique), *f.*

converse (1) [kən'vɜːs], *v.i.* Causer, converser, s'entretenir.

converse (2) ['kɔnvəːs], *n.* Entretien, *m.*, conversation; (*Log.*) converse; (*Math.*) réciproque, *f.—a.* (*Math.*) Réciproque.

conversely [kən'vɜːsli], *adv.* Réciproquement.

conversion [kən'vɜːʃən], *n.* Conversion, *f.*, changement, *m.*

convert (1) [kən'vɜːt], *v.t.* Convertir, transformer; faire servir.

convert (2) ['kɔnvəːt], *n.* Converti, *m.*, convertie, *f. To become a convert*, se convertir.

converter [kən'vɜːtə], *n.* Convertisseur, *m.* **convertibility** [-'biliti], *n.* Convertibilité, *f.* **convertible** [-'vəːtəbl], *a.* Convertible (of things); convertissable (of persons); (*Motor.*) décapotable. **convertibly**, *adv.* Réciproquement.

convex [kən'veks *or* 'kɔnveks] (*attributively*), *a.* Convexe.—*n.* ['kɔnveks] Corps convexe, *m.* **convexity**, *n.* Convexité, *f.* **convexly**, *adv.* De forme convexe. **convexo-concave**, *a.* Convexo-concave.

convey [kən'vei], *v.t.* Transporter (goods etc.); porter, conduire, mener, amener; transmettre (sounds etc.); présenter (thanks etc.); donner (ideas etc.); communiquer (news etc.); céder (property etc.). *That conveys nothing to me*, cela ne me dit rien; *to convey one's meaning*, traduire sa pensée; *to convey to posterity*, transmettre à la postérité. **conveyable**, *a.* Transportable, portable; exprimable; (*Law*) transférable. **conveyance**, *n.* Transport, *m.*; transmission, *f.*; véhicule, *m.*; (*Law*) cession, *f.*, transfert, *m. Means of conveyance*, moyens de transport, *m.pl.*; *public conveyance*, transports publics, *m.pl.* **conveyancer**, *n.* Notaire, *m.* **conveyancing**, *n.* Notariat, *m.*

conveyer or **conveyor**, *n.* Personne qui transporte, qui transmet, etc., *f.*; porteur, voiturier, *m.*; (appareil) transporteur, conducteur (électrique), *m. Conveyor belt*, bande transporteuse; chaîne de montage, *f.*

convict (1) [kən'vikt], *v.t.* Condamner, déclarer coupable; convaincre (of error etc.).

convict (2) ['kɔnvikt], *n.* Forçat, *galérien, *déporté, *m. Convict prison*, bagne, *m.*

conviction [kən'vikʃən], *n.* Conviction, persuasion; (*Law*) condamnation, *f. To carry conviction*, emporter conviction.

convince [kən'vins], *v.t.* Convaincre, persuader. **convincing**, *a.* Convaincant, persuasif. **convincingly**, *adv.* D'une manière convaincante.

convivial [kən'viviəl], *a.* Digne de bons convives, joyeux, jovial. **conviviality** [-'æliti], *n.* Franche gaieté, *f.*; (*pl.*) joyeux repas, *m.pl.*

convocation [kɔnvəˈkeiʃən], *n.* Convocation; (*Eccles.*) assemblée, *f.*, synode, *m.*
convoke [kənˈvouk], *v.t.* Convoquer, assembler.
convolute [ˈkɔnvəljuːt] or **convoluted**, *a.* (*Bot.*) Convoluté. **convolution** [-ˈljuːʃən], *n.* Circonvolution, *f.*, enroulement, *m.*
convolve [kənˈvɔlv], *v.t.* Rouler, enrouler.
convolvulus [kənˈvɔlvjuləs], *n.* (*pl.* **convolvuli**) Volubilis, liseron, *m.*, belle-de-jour, *f.*
convoy (1) [kənˈvɔi], *v.t.* Convoyer, escorter.
convoy (2) [ˈkɔnvɔi], *n.* Convoi, *m.*, escorte, *f.* *To sail in convoy*, naviguer en convoi.
convoy-ship, *n.* (Bâtiment) convoyeur, bâtiment d'escorte, *m.*, escorte, *f.*
convulse [kənˈvʌls], *v.t.* Convulser, donner des convulsions à; (*fig.*) ébranler, bouleverser. **convulsed**, *a.* Crispé, convulsé, bouleversé. *To be convulsed with laughter*, se tordre de rire. **convulsion**, *n.* Convulsion, *f.*; (*fig.*) commotion, *f.* *Fit of convulsions*, accès de convulsions, *m.*; *to be seized with convulsions*, tomber en convulsions. **convulsionary**, *a.* Convulsionnaire. **convulsive**, *a.* Convulsif. **convulsively**, *adv.* Convulsivement.
cony or **coney** [ˈkouni], *n.* Lapin. *m.*
coo [kuː], *v.i.* Roucouler. *To bill and coo*, faire les tourtereaux. **cooing**, *n.* Roucoulement, *m.*
cooey [ˈkuːiː], *n.* Cri, appel, *m.* (of Australian bushmen).
cook [kuk], *n.* Cuisinier, *m.*, cuisinière, *f.*; (*Naut.*) coq, *m.* *Cook-house*, (*Mil.*) cuisine, *f.*; *cook-shop*, gargote, *f.*; *head cook*, chef, *m.*— *v.i.* Cuire; faire la cuisine, cuisiner.—*v.t.* Cuire, faire cuire; apprêter; falsifier (accounts); (*fig.*) arranger. *To cook someone's goose*, contrecarrer quelqu'un. **cooker**, *n.* Cuisinière (stove), *f.*; fruit à cuire, *m. Pressure cooker*, marmite autoclave, cocotte-minute, *f.* **cookery**, *n.* Cuisine, *f.* (art). **cookery-book**, *n.* Livre de cuisine, *m.*
cookie [ˈkuki], *n.* (*Sc.*) Petit pain au lait, *m.*; (*Am.*) galette, *f.*
cooking [ˈkukiŋ], *n.* Cuisine; cuisson, *f.*
cool [kuːl], *a.* Frais, (*fig.*) calme, tranquille; hardi, peu gêné. *As cool as a cucumber*, avec un sang-froid inébranlable; *how cool that man is*, comme cet homme est sans gêne *or* a de l'aplomb; *it is cool*, il fait frais; '*keep in a cool place*', tenir au frais; *to give someone a cool reception*, donner un accueil très froid à quelqu'un; *to grow cool*, se refroidir; *to keep cool*, garder son sang-froid.—*n.* Frais, *m.*, fraîcheur, *f. In the cool*, au frais.—*v.t.* Rafraîchir; refroidir; (*fig.*) calmer, modérer. *To cool one's heels*, croquer le marmot.—*v.i.* Se refroidir; refroidir. *To cool down*, se rafraîchir; se calmer, s'apaiser. **cooler**, *n.* Rafraîchissoir, réfrigérant; (*Med.*) rafraîchissant, *m.*; (*Motor.*) radiateur, *m.*; (*pop.*) prison, cellule, *f.* **cool-headed**, *a.* De sang-froid.
cooling, *a.* Rafraîchissant, calmant. *Cooling tower*, refroidisseur, *m.*—*n.* Rafraîchissement; (*Motor. etc.*) refroidissement, *m.* **coolish**, *a.* Un peu frais, frisquet.
coolly [ˈkuːlli], *adv.* Fraîchement; (*fig.*) froidement, de sang-froid, tranquillement, sans gêne. **coolness**, *n.* Fraîcheur, *f.*, frais, *m.*; (*fig.*) froideur (indifference), *f.*; sang-froid; toupet, sans-gêne (impudence), *m.*

coolie [ˈkuːli], *n.* Portefaix indigène, coolie, *m.*
coon (1) [kuːn], *n.* (*Am.*) [RACCOON]. *He's a gone coon*, c'en est fait de lui.
coon (2) [kuːn], *n.* (*Am. slang, pej.*) Noir, *m.*, noire, *f.*
coop [kuːp], *n.* Cage à poules, mue, *f.*—*v.t.* Mettre en mue. *To coop up*, enfermer étroitement, claquemurer.
cooper [ˈkuːpə], *n.* Tonnelier, *m.*—*v.t.* Réparer. **cooperage**, *n.* Tonnellerie, *f.*
co-operate [kouˈɔpəreit], *v.i.* Coopérer, concourir (à). **co-operation** [-ˈreiʃən], *n.* Coopération, *f.*; concours, *m.* **co-operative**, *a.* Coopérant, coopératif. *Co-operative Society*, (société) coopérative, *f.*; *co-operative stores*, magasins de société coopérative, *m.pl.* **co-operator**, *n.* Coopérateur, *m.*, -trice, *f.* **co-opt** [kouˈɔpt], *v.t.* Coopter. **co-optation**, *n.* Cooptation, *f.*
co-ordinate [kouˈɔːdineit], *v.t.* Coordonner.— *a.* [kouˈɔːdinit] Du même rang, égal; (*Math.*) coordonné.—*n.* (*pl.*) Coordonnées, *f.pl.* **co-ordinately**, *adv.* Également, au même rang. **co-ordination** [-ˈneiʃən], *n.* Égalité de rang, coordination, *f.*
coot [kuːt], *n.* (*Orn.*) Foulque, *f.*
cop [kɔp], *n.* Cime, *f.*, sommet, *m.*; huppe, aigrette (of birds), *f.*; (*slang*) flic, *m.*—*v.t.* (*colloq.*) Attraper, pincer. *To cop it*, attiger; recevoir un savon.
copaiba [kɔˈpeibə] or **copaiva**, *n.* Copahu, *m.*
copal [ˈkoupəl], *n.* Copal, *m.*
coparcenary [kouˈpɑːsənəri], *n.* (*Law*) Succession par indivis, *f.* **coparcener**, *n.* Propriétaire indivis, *m.*, propriétaire indivise, *f.*
copartner [kouˈpɑːtnə], *n.* Associé, *m.* **co-partnership**, *n.* Société en nom collectif, *f.*
cope (1) [koup], *n.* Chaperon, *m.*, chape (sacerdotal vestment); (*fig.*) voûte des cieux, *f.* **cope-maker**, *n.* Chapier, *m.*—*v.t.* Couvrir, chaperonner.
cope (2) [koup], *v.i.* Se débrouiller. *To cope with*, tenir tête à; venir à bout de.
Copenhagen [koupənˈheigən]. Copenhague, *f.*
coper [ˈkoupə], *n.* [HORSE-COPER].
copier [ˈkɔpiə] or **copyist**, *n.* Copiste; (*fig.*) imitateur, *m.*
copilot [kouˈpailət], *n.* Pilote de relève, copilote, *m.*
coping [ˈkoupiŋ], *n.* Faîte (of a building); couronnement (of a wall), *m.* **coping-stone**, *n.* Chaperon; couronnement, *m.*
copious [ˈkoupiəs], *a.* Abondant, copieux. **copiously**, *adv.* Copieusement, abondamment. **copiousness**, *n.* Abondance, *f.*
copper [ˈkɔpə], *n.* Cuivre (rouge), *m.*; lessiveuse, chaudière (boiler), *f.*, chaudron (small boiler), *m.*; batterie de cuisine, *f.*; (*slang*) flic (policeman), *m.*, (*pl.*) petite monnaie, *f.*; (*St. Exch.*) valeurs cuprifères, *f.pl.*— *a.* De cuivre, en cuivre.—*v.t.* Cuivrer; (*Naut.*) doubler en cuivre. **copper beech**, *n.* Hêtre rouge, *m.* **copper-bottomed**, *a.* Doublé en cuivre, à fond de cuivre. **copper-coloured**, **copper-hued**, *a.* Cuivré. **copper-plate**, *n.* Cuivre plané, *m.*; taille-douce, *f. Copper-plate engraving*, gravure en taille-douce, *f.*; *copper-plate handwriting*, écriture moulée *or* calligraphiée, *f.* **copper-smith**, *n.* Chaudronnier, *m.* **copper-wire**, *n.* Dinanderie, *f.*

copper-wire, *n.* Fil de cuivre, *m.* **coppery,** *a.* Cuivreux.

copperas ['kɔpərəs], *n.* Couperose, *f.*; sulfate de fer, *m.*

coppice ['kɔpis] or **copse,** *n.* Taillis, *m. Coppice with standards,* taillis sous futaie. **copse,** *v.t.* Conserver en taillis.

copra ['kɔprə], *n.* Copra, *m.*

coprophagous [ko'prɔfəgəs], *a.* (*Ent.*) Coprophage.

co-proprietor [kouprə'praiətə], *n.* Co-propriétaire, *m.*

copse [kɔps], *n.* [COPPICE].

Copt [kɔpt], *n.* Copte, *m.* **Coptic,** *n.* Copte (language), *m.*—*a.* Copte.

copula ['kɔpjulə], *n.* Copule, *f.* **copulate,** *v.i.* S'accoupler. **copulation** [-'leiʃən], *n.* Copulation, *f.* **copulative,** *a.* (*Gram.*) Copulatif.—*n.* Copulative, *f.*

copy ['kɔpi], *n.* Copie, *f.*; exemple (for writing); exemplaire (of printed books); numéro (newspaper); modèle (for drawing), *m. Review copy,* exemplaire de service de presse, *m.*; *rough copy,* brouillon, *m.*; *to make a fair copy of,* mettre au net; *top copy,* original, *m.*; *true copy,* copie conforme, *f.*—*v.t.* Copier; imiter. *To copy out,* transcrire; *to copy some-one,* se modeler sur quelqu'un. **copy-book,** *n.* Cahier d'écriture, *m. To blot one's copy-book* (*fig.*), ternir sa réputation. **copy-cat,** *n.* (*fam.*) Imitateur, singe, *m.* **copyhold,** *n.* Tenure en vertu de copie du rôle de la cour seigneuriale, *f.* **copyholder,** *n.* Tenancier par copyhold, *m.*; (*Print.*) teneur de copie, *m.* **copying-book,** *n.* Copie-lettres, *f.* **copying-clerk,** *n.* Expéditionnaire, *m.* **copying-ink,** *n.* Encre à copier, *f.* **copying-press,** *n.* Presse à copier, *f.* **copyist** [COPIER]. **copyright,** *n.* Droits d'auteur, *m.pl.*; propriété littéraire, *f. This is copyright,* reproduction interdite; *copyright reserved,* tous droits réservés.

coquet [ko'ket], *v.i.* Faire des coquetteries (à); faire la coquette (avec). **coquet** or **coquette,** *n.* Coquette, *f.*

coquetry ['koukətri], *n.* Coquetterie, *f.*

coquettish [ko'ketiʃ], *a.* Coquet, en coquette; provocant (smile). **coquettishly,** *adv.* D'un air provocant.

coracle ['kɔrəkl], *n.* Bateau de pêche (en toile or cuir sur bâti d'osier), *m.*

coracoid ['kɔrəkɔid], *a.* Coracoïde.

Coral ['kɔrəl] **Sea.** La mer de Corail, *f.*

coral ['kɔrəl], *n.* Corail; hochet de corail (rattle), *m.*; œufs de homard, *m.pl.*—*a.* De corail. **coral-fisher,** *n.* Corailleur, *m.* **coral-fishing** or **coral-fishery,** *n.* Pêche du corail, *f.* **coral-reef,** *n.* Récif de corail, *m.* **coralliform,** *a.* Coralliforme. **coral-line,** *a.* Corallin.

corbeil ['kɔ:bəl], *n.* (*Arch.* and *Fort.*) Corbeille, *f.*

corbel ['kɔ:bəl], *n.* (*Arch.*) Corbeau, *m.* **corbelling,** *n.* Encorbellement, *m.*

cord [kɔ:d], *n.* Corde, *f.*, cordon; cordage, *m.*, ganse, *f.*; (*fig.*) lien, *m. Spinal cord,* cordon médullaire, *m.*—*v.t.* Corder. **cord-maker,** *n.* Cordier, *m.* **cord-wood,** *n.* Bois de stère, *m.* **cordage,** *n.* Cordage, *m.* **corded,** *a.* Cordé, à côtes (of silk); à cordes (of tyres).

cordate ['kɔ:deit] or **cordated,** *a.* (*Bot.*) Cordé.

cordelier [kɔ:də'liə], *n.* Cordelier, *m.*

cordial ['kɔ:diəl], *a.* Cordial.—*n.* Cordial, *m.*, liqueur, *f.*

cordiality [kɔ:di'æliti], *n.* Cordialité, *f.*

cordially ['kɔ:diəli], *adv.* Cordialement.

cordiform ['kɔ:difɔ:m], *a.* Cordiforme.

Cordilleras [kɔ:di'ljɛərəz]. Les Cordillères, *f.pl.*

cordon ['kɔ:dən], *n.* Cordon, *m. Cordon* (*tree*), arbre en fuseau; cordon, *m.*—*v.t. To cordon off,* isoler par un cordon (de police).

Cordova ['kɔ:dəvə]. Cordoue, *f.* **Cordovan,** *a.* and *n.* Cordouan, de Cordoue.

corduroy ['kɔ:djurɔi], *n.* Velours à côtes, *m. Corduroy road,* chaussée formée de troncs d'arbres jetés en travers, *f.*; chemin de rondins, *m.*; *corduroys* or *corduroy trousers,* pantalon de velours à côtes, *m.*

core [kɔ:], *n.* Cœur; noyau (of a casting); (*fig.*) milieu, centre, *m.*; (*Naut.*) âme (of a rope), *f.*; trognon (apple), *m. Rotten to the core,* pourri jusqu'à la moelle; *to touch to the core,* toucher profondément.—*v.t.* Vider (une pomme); creuser, évider (un moule).

co-regent [kou'ri:dʒənt], *n.* Corégent, *m.*

co-religionist [kouri'lidʒənist], *n.* Coreligionnaire, *m.* and *f.*

co-respondent ['kouris'pɔndənt], *n.* Complice, co-défendeur, *m.* (en adultère).

corf [kɔ:f], *n.* Manne, *f.*, wagonnet, *m.*

Corfu ['kɔ:fju:]. Corfou (isle), *f.*; (town), *m.*

corgy, corgi ['kɔ:gi], *n.* Basset gallois, *m.*

coriaceous [kɔri'eiʃəs], *a.* Coriacé.

coriander [kɔri'ændə], *n.* (*Bot.*) Coriandre, *f.*

Corinth ['kɔrinθ]. Corinthe, *f.*

Corinthian [kɔ'rinθiən], *a.* Corinthien.—*n.* *Viveur; amateur de sports, yachtsman, etc.

co-rival [CORRIVAL].

Coriolanus [kɔriə'leinəs]. Coriolan, *m.*

cork [kɔ:k], *n.* Liège; bouchon (for bottles etc.), *m.*—*v.t.* Boucher. **corkage,** *n.* Droit de débouchage, *m.* **cork-cutter,** *n.* Bouchonnier, *m.* **corkscrew,** *n.* Tire-bouchon, *m. Corkscrew staircase,* escalier en limaçon or en colimaçon, *m.* **cork-tipped,** *a.* À bouts de liège (of cigarettes). **cork-tree, cork-oak,** *n.* Chêne-liège, *m.* **corker,** *n.* (*pop.*) Mensonge, *m.*; homme excellent, type épatant, *m.* **corking,** *n.* Bouchage, *m.* **corky,** *a.* De liège, subéreux; qui sent le bouchon (wine).

corm [kɔ:m], *n.* (*Bot.*) Bulbe, *m.*

cormorant ['kɔ:mərənt], *n.* Cormoran; (*fig.*) rapace, affameur, *m.*

corn [kɔ:n], *n.* Grain, *m.*; céréales, *f.pl.*; blés, *m.pl.*; (*Am.*) maïs, *m.*; cor (on the foot), *m. Ear of corn,* épi de blé, *m.*; *Indian corn,* maïs, *m.*; *soft corn,* œil de perdrix, *m.*—*v.t.* Saler (beef); grener (gunpowder). **corn-chandler,** *n.* Blatier, marchand de blé, *m.* **corn-cockle,** *n.* Nielle, *f.* **corn-crake,** *n.* Râle de genêt, *m.* **corn-crops,** *n.pl.* Céréales, *f.pl.* **corn-cure,** *n.* Coricide, *m.*, remède contre les cors, *m.* **corn-cutter,** *n.* Pédicure, *m.* **corn-dealer,** *n.* Marchand de grains, *m.* **corn-exchange,** *n.* Halle aux blés, *f.* **corn-factor,** *n.* Facteur de la halle aux blés, *m.* **cornfield,** *n.* Champ de blé, *m.* **cornflakes,** *n.pl.* Paillettes de maïs, *f.pl.* **corn-flour,** *n.* Farine de maïs, *f.* **corn-flower,** *n.* Bluet, *m.* **corn-laws,** *n.pl.* Lois sur les céréales, *f.pl.* **corn-merchant,** *n.* Négociant en

grains, *m.* **corn-poppy,** *n.* Coquelicot, *m.*
corn-stack, *n.* Meule de blé, *f.* **corn-**
trade, *n.* Commerce des grains, *m.*
cornea [ˈkɔːniə], *n.* (*Anat.*) Cornée, *f.*
corned beef, *n.* Bœuf salé, *m.* (de conserve).
cornel [ˈkɔːnəl], *n.* Cornouille, *f.* **cornel-**
tree, *n.* Cornouiller, *m.*
cornelian [kɔːˈniːliən], *n.* (*Min.*) Cornaline, *f.*
corneous [ˈkɔːniəs], *a.* Corné.
corner [ˈkɔːnə], *n.* Coin, angle, *m.*; encoignure; (*Tech.*) cornière, *f.*; (*fig.*) monopole, accaparement, *m.* *Blind corner,* tournant (*or virage*) masqué; *corner kick,* (*Ftb.*)
corner [kɔrˈnɛr], *m.*; *corner house,* maison du
coin *or* qui fait le coin, *f.*; *corner seat,* place
de coin, *f.*; *corner tooth,* incisive externe, *f.*;
in the corner, au coin; *round the corner,* au
coin de la rue; tout près; *to drive into a corner,*
pousser dans un coin *or* au bout; mettre au
pied du mur; *to take a corner,* prendre un
virage, virer.—*v.t.* (*Comm.*) Accaparer; (*fig.*)
pousser dans un coin, acculer.—*v.i.* Prendre
un virage, virer.
cornered, *a.* À coins, à angles.
corner-stone, *n.* Pierre angulaire, *f.*
cornerwise, *adv.* Diagonalement.
cornet [ˈkɔːnit], *n.* Cornet (à pistons), *m.*;
oublie, *f.*, plaisir, *m.*; cornette, *f.* (of nun);
*étendard, porte-étendard, *m.*
cornice [ˈkɔːnis], *n.* Corniche, *f.*
corniferous [kɔːˈnifərəs], *a.* Qui contient de
la pierre de corne.
corniform [ˈkɔːnifɔːm], *a.* Corniforme.
Cornish [ˈkɔːniʃ], *a.* De Cornouailles, cornouail-
lais.—*n.* Le cornique, *m.* (the language).
*cornopean** [kɔːˈnoupiən], *n.* Cornet à
pistons, *m.*
cornucopia [kɔːnjuˈkoupjə], *n.* Corne
d'abondance, *f.*
Cornwall [ˈkɔːnwəl]. Cornouailles, *f.*
corny [ˈkɔːni], *a.* Abondant en grains; (*colloq.*)
pas très drôle (of a joke), banal, sentimental
(of music).
corolla [kəˈrɔlə], *n.* (*Bot.*) Corolle, *f.*
corollary [kəˈrɔləri], *n.* Corollaire, *m.*
corona [kəˈrounə], *n.* Couronne, *f.*; (*Arch.*)
larmier, *m.*; (*Bot. etc.*) couronne, *f.*; halo, *m.*
(of sun, moon).
coronach [ˈkɔrənæx], *n.* (*Sc.*) Chant funèbre,
m.
coronal [ˈkɔrənəl], *n.* Guirlande; (*fig.*)
couronne, *f.*—*a.* (*Anat.*) Coronal. **coronary,**
a. De couronne; (*Anat.*) coronaire. **corona-**
tion [-ˈneiʃən], *n.* Couronnement, sacre,
m.
coroner [ˈkɔrənə], *n.* Coroner, *m.*
coronet [ˈkɔrənit], *n.* (Petite) couronne, *f.*
coroneted, *a.* Couronné.
coronoid [ˈkɔrənɔid], *a.* (*Anat.*) Coronoïde.
corozo [kəˈrouzou], *n.* Corozo, ivoire végétal,
m.
corporal (1) [ˈkɔːpərəl], *n.* Caporal (of
infantry); brigadier (of cavalry), *m.*
corporal (2) [ˈkɔːpərəl], *a.* Corporel.—*n.*
(*R.-C. Ch.*) Corporal, *m.* **corporality**
[kɔːpəˈræliti], *n.* (*Theol.*) Matérialité, *f.*
corporally, *adv.* Corporellement.
corporate [ˈkɔːpərit], *a.* Érigé en corporation; de corporation. *Corporate name,* raison
sociale, *f.* **corporately,** *adv.* Collectivement.
corporation [kɔːpəˈreiʃən], *n.* Corporation, *f.*;

corps constitué, *m.*; société, *f.*; conseil municipal, *m.*, municipalité (of a town), *f.*; (*facet.*)
bedaine, *f.*
corporative [ˈkɔːpərətiv], *a.* Collectif,
corporatif.
corporeal [kɔːˈpɔːriəl], *a.* Corporel, matériel.
corporeally, *adv.* Corporellement, matériellement. **corporeity** [-ˈriːiti], *n.* Cor-
poréité, *f.*
corposant [ˈkɔːpəzənt], *n.* Feu de Saint-
Elme, *m.*
corps [kɔː], *n.inv.* Corps, *m.*, formation, *f.*
Army corps, corps d'armée, *m.*
corpse [kɔːps], *n.* Cadavre, corps mort, *m.*
corpulence [ˈkɔːpjuləns] *or* **corpulency,** *n.*
Corpulence, *f.*, embonpoint, *m.* **corpulent,**
a. Corpulent, gros, gras.
Corpus Christi [ˈkɔːpəs ˈkristi]. La Fête-
Dieu, *f.* **Corpus delicti** [diˈliktai], *n.* (*Law*)
Le corps du délit, *m.*
corpuscle [ˈkɔːpʌsl], *n.* Corpuscule, globule,
m.; molécule, *f.* **corpuscular** [kɔːˈpʌskju-
lə], *a.* Corpusculaire.
corral [kɔˈræl], *n.* Corral, *m.*—*v.t.* Renfermer
(dans un corral).
correct [kəˈrekt], *a.* Correct, exact, juste;
(*fig.*) convenable, en règle; pur, bon (of
style); bien élevé (of person); comme il faut.
All's correct, tout est en règle; c'est parfait;
it's the correct thing to, il est de rigueur de.—
v.t. Corriger, rectifier, reprendre; punir;
contrebalancer. *To correct oneself,* se corriger,
se reprendre; *to stand corrected,* reconnaître
son erreur, avouer qu'on a tort. **correction,**
n. Correction, *f.*; punition, *f.* *Subject to* or
under correction, sauf correction. **correc-**
tional, *a.* Correctionnel. **corrective,** *a.*
De correction, correctif.—*n.* Correctif, *m.*
correctly, *adv.* Correctement, exactement,
justement, juste; convenablement, régulièrement. **correctness,** *n.* Exactitude, justesse,
correction; pureté (of style); fidélité (of a
copy), *f.* **corrector,** *n.* Correcteur, *m.*
correlate [ˈkɔrileit], *v.i.* Correspondre, être
corrélatif.—*v.t.* Mettre en corrélation. **cor-**
relation [-ˈleiʃən]. Corrélation, *f.* **correla-**
tive [-ˈrelətiv], *a.* Corrélatif.—*n.* Corrélatif,
m. **correlatively,** *adv.* Corrélativement,
d'une manière corrélative. **correlativeness,**
n. Caractère corrélatif, *m.*
correspond [kɔrisˈpɔnd], *v.i.* Correspondre
(à *or* avec), répondre (à); s'accorder (avec);
être conforme (à). **correspondence,** *n.*
Correspondance, *f.*, rapport, *m.*, relations,
f.pl. Correspondence course, cours par correspondance, *m.* **correspondent,** *n.* Correspondant, conforme, qui se rapporte (à).—*n.*
Correspondant, *m.* **correspondently,** *adv.*
D'une manière correspondante, conformément (à). **corresponding,** *a.* Correspondant (à). **correspondingly,** *adv.* Également.
corridor [ˈkɔridɔː], *n.* Corridor; couloir;
passage, *m.*, galerie, *f.*; (*Fort.*) chemin
couvert, *m. Corridor carriage,* wagon à
couloir, *m.*; *corridor train,* train à couloir, *m.*
corrigible [ˈkɔridʒəbl], *a.* Corrigible.
corrival [kɔˈraivəl], *n.* Rival, compétiteur, *m.*
corrivalry, *n.* Rivalité, *f.*
corroborant [kəˈrɔbərənt], *a.* (*Med.*) Corroborant.—*n.* Corroborant, *m.*
corroborate [kəˈrɔbəreit], *v.t.* Corroborer,
confirmer. **corroboration** [-ˈreiʃən], *n.*

Corroboration, confirmation, *f. In corroboration of,* à l'appui de. **corroborative** [-'rɔbərətiv], *a.* Corroboratif.—*n.* (*Med.*) Corroboratif, *m.*
corroboree [kə'rɔbəri:], *n.* Danse indigène d'Australie, *f.*
corrode [kə'roud], *v.t.* Corroder, ronger; (*fig.*) miner, détruire.—*v.i.* Se corroder. **corroding**, *a.* Corrodant. **corrosion**, *n.* Corrosion; (*fig.*) destruction, *f.* **corrosive**, *a.* Corrosif; (*fig.*) rongeur. *Corrosive care,* souci rongeur, *m.*—*n.* Corrosif, *m.* **corrosively**, *adv.* Comme un corrosif. **corrosiveness**, *n.* Nature corrosive, *f.*, mordant, *m.*; (*fig.*) acrimonie, *f.*
corrugate ['kɔrugeit], *v.t.* Rider, plisser, froncer; onduler. *Corrugated iron,* tôle ondulée, *f.*; *corrugated cardboard,* carton ondulé, *m.*—*v.i.* Se plisser, se froncer, se rider. **corrugation**, *n.* Corrugation, *f.*; (*fig.*) plissement, froncement, *m.*
corrupt [kə'rʌpt], *v.t.* Corrompre.—*v.i.* Se corrompre.—*a.* Corrompu, dépravé, vicié. *Corrupt practices,* tractations malhonnêtes, *f.pl.,* faits de corruption électorale, *m.pl. To become corrupt,* se corrompre, se dépraver. **corrupter**, *n.* Corrupteur, *m.,* corruptrice, *f.* **corruptibility**, *n.* Corruptibilité, *f.* **corruptible**, *a.* Corruptible, vénal. **corrupting**, *a.* Corrupteur. **corruption**, *n.* Corruption; (*fig.*) altération (of texts etc.), *f.* **corruptive**, *a.* Corruptif. **corruptly**, *adv.* Par corruption. **corruptness**, *n.* Corruption, vénalité, *f.*
corsage ['kɔ:sidʒ], *n.* Corsage, *m.*
corsair ['kɔ:sɛə], *n.* Corsaire, *m.*
corset ['kɔ:sit], *n.* Corset, *m.*—*v.t.* Corseter. **corset-maker**, *n.* Corsetier, *m.,* corsetière, *f.*
Corsica ['kɔ:sikə]. La Corse, *f.*
Corsican ['kɔ:sikən], *a.* and *n.* Corse.
corslet ['kɔ:slit], *n.* Corselet, *m.*
cortège [kɔ:'teiʒ], *n.* Cortège (funèbre), *m.,* procession, *f.*; suite, *f.*
Cortes ['kɔ:tez], *n.pl.* Les Cortès, *f.pl.*
cortical ['kɔ:tikəl], *a.* Cortical. **corticate**, *a.* Cortiqueux. **corticiferous** [-'sifərəs], *a.* Corticifère. **corticiform** [-'tisifɔ:m], *a.* Corticiforme.
corticin ['kɔ:tisin], *n.* Corticine, *f.*
cortisone ['kɔ:tizoun], *n.* Cortisone, *f.*
corundum [kə'rʌndəm], *n.* Corindon, *m.*
Corunna [kə'rʌnə]. La Corogne, *f.*
coruscant [kɔ'rʌskənt], *a.* Scintillant, brillant.
coruscate ['kɔrəskeit], *v.i.* Scintiller, briller. **coruscation** [kɔrəs'keiʃən], *n.* Coruscation, *f.*; (*fig.*) éclat, éclair, *m.*
corvette [kɔ:'vet], *n.* (*Naut.*) Corvette, *f.*
corybant ['kɔribænt], *n.* Corybante, *m.* **corybantic** [-'bæntik], *a.* Corybantique.
corymb ['kɔrim], *n.* (*Bot.*) Corymbe, *f.* **corymbose** [kɔ'rimbous], *a.* Corymbé, corymbeux. **corymbiferous** [-'bifərəs], *a.* Corymbifère. **corymbiform** [kɔ'rimbifɔ:m], *a.* Corymbiforme.
corypheus [kɔri'fi:əs], *n.* Coryphée, *m.*
coryza [kə'raizə], *n.* Coryza, rhume de cerveau, *m.*
cos [kɔs] or **cos-lettuce**, *n.* (Laitue) romaine, *f.*
cosecant [kou'sekənt], *n.* (*Geom.*) Cosécante, *f.*
cosh [kɔʃ], *n.* Matraque, *f.*—*v.t.* Matraquer.
cosignatory [kou'signətəri], *n.* Cosignataire, *m.*
cosily ['kouzili], *adv.* À l'aise, bien au chaud, douillettement.

cosine ['kousain], *n.* (*Geom.*) Cosinus, *m.*
cosiness ['kouzinis], *n.* Confortable, *m.*
cosmetic [kɔz'metik], *a.* Cosmétique.—*n.* Cosmétique, *m.*
cosmic ['kɔzmik] or **cosmical**, *a.* Cosmique. *Cosmic rays,* rayons cosmiques, *m.pl.* **cosmically**, *adv.* Cosmiquement; avec le soleil (à son lever *or* à son coucher).
cosmogonic [kɔzmo'gɔnik], *a.* Cosmogonique.
cosmogony [kɔz'mɔgəni], *n.* Cosmogonie, *f.*
cosmographer, *n.* Cosmographe, *m.*
cosmographic [kɔzmo'græfik] or **cosmographical**, *a.* Cosmographique.
cosmography [kɔz'mɔgrəfi], *n.* Cosmographie, *f.*
cosmological [kɔzmo'lɔdʒikəl], *a.* Cosmologique. **cosmology** [-'mɔlədʒi], *n.* Cosmologie, *f.*
cosmopolite [kɔz'mɔpəlait], *n.* Cosmopolite, *m.* **cosmopolitan** [kɔzmo'pɔlitən], *a.* and *n.* Cosmopolite. **cosmopolitanism**, *n.* Cosmopolitisme, *m.*
cosmos ['kɔzmɔs], *n.* Cosmos, *m.*
Cossack ['kɔsæk], *n.* and *a.* Cosaque, *m.*
cosset ['kɔsit], *v.t.* Mitonner, dorloter, choyer.—*n.* *Agneau favori; favori, *m.,* favorite, *f.*
cost [kɔst], *n.* Prix; frais, *m.,* dépense, *f.* (*Comm.*) coût, *m.*; (*Law pl.*), dépens, *m.pl. At any cost, at all costs,* à tout prix, coûte que coûte; *cost of living,* coût de la vie, *m.; cost price,* prix coûtant; *net cost,* prix de revient, *m.; to carry costs,* (*Law*) entraîner les dépens; *to count the cost,* regarder à la dépense; *to one's cost,* à ses dépens; *what is the cost?* quel en est le prix?—*v.i.* (*past* and *p.p.* **cost**) Coûter. *Cost what it may,* coûte que coûte; *it costs me* (*pain*) *to find fault with you,* il m'en coûte de vous blâmer; *to cost dearly,* coûter cher.—*v.t.* (*Ind.*) Évaluer le coût de; établir le prix de revient de.
costal ['kɔstəl], *a.* (*Anat.*) Costal.
costard ['kɔstəd], *n.* (Grosse) pomme à côtes, *f.*
coster ['kɔstə] or **costermonger** [-'mʌŋgə], *n.* Marchand des quatre saisons, *m.*
costive ['kɔstiv], *a.* Constipé; (*colloq.*) pingre. **costiveness**, *n.* Constipation, *f.*; manque de facilité, *m.*
costliness ['kɔstlinis], *n.* Haut prix, prix élevé, *m.,* grande dépense; somptuosité, richesse, *f.* **costly**, *a.* Coûteux, de prix; somptueux, précieux, de luxe.
costmary ['kɔstmɛəri], *n.* (*Bot.*) Balsamite, *f.*
costume ['kɔstju:m], *n.* Costume, *m.*
costumer [kɔs'tju:mə] or **costumier** [kɔs'tju:miə], *n.* Costumier, *m.*
cosy ['kouzi], *a.* Chaud, confortable, douillet; à l'aise; commode et petit (of apartments).—*n.* Couvre-théière (tea-cosy), *m.*
cot (1) [kɔt], *n.* Cabane, chaumière, *f.*; bercail, parc (for sheep), *m.*
cot (2) [kɔt], *n.* Petit lit (bed), lit d'enfant; lit de campement; (*Naut.*) cadre; hamac à l'anglaise, *m. Basket cot,* moïse, *m.*
cotangent [kou'tændʒənt], *n.* Cotangente, *f.*
cotenant [kou'tenənt], *n.* Colocataire, *m.*
coterie ['koutəri], *n.* Coterie, clique, *f.*
cothurnus [kɔ'θə:nəs], *n.* Cothurne, *m.*
cottage ['kɔtidʒ], *n.* Chaumière; petite maison, villa, *f. Cottage hospital,* petit hôpital à la

campagne; *cottage piano*, piano droit, *m.*; *Swiss cottage*, chalet, *m.* **cottager,** *n.* Paysan, *m.*, paysanne, *f.* **cottar** or **cottier,** *n.* Ouvrier agricole (locataire de cottage); valet (de ferme), *m.* **cotter** ['kɔtə], *n.* (*Tech.*) Clavette, *f.*—*v.t.* Claveter, goupiller.

cotton [kɔtn], *n.* Coton, *m.*; cotonnade; percale, percaline, *f.* *Absorbent cotton*, coton hydrophile; *darning-cotton*, coton plat, à repriser; *knitting-cotton*, coton à tricoter, *m.*; *printed cotton*, Indienne, *f.*; *reel of cotton*, bobine de coton, *f.*; *sewing-cotton*, fil d'Écosse, *m.*—*v.t.* Cotonner.—*v.i.* Se cotonner; (*fig.*) être intimement lié (avec). *To cotton on to something*, s'accommoder à quelque chose; comprendre quelque chose; *to cotton to*, prendre en amitié. **cotton-cloth,** *n.* Toile de coton, *f.*, cotonnade, *f.* **cotton-gin,** *n.* Machine à égrener le coton, *f.* **cotton-goods,** *n.pl.* Cotonnade, *f.* **cotton-manufacture,** *n.* Industrie cotonnière, *f.* **cotton-mill,** *n.* Filature de coton, *f.* **cotton-plant** or **cotton-tree,** *n.* Cotonnier, *m.* **cotton-spinning,** *n.* Filage du coton, *m.* **cotton-velvet,** *n.* Velours de coton, *m.* **cotton-waste,** *n.* Déchets de coton, *m.pl.* **cotton-wool,** *n.* Ouate, *f.* *Absorbent cotton-wool*, ouate hydrophile, *f.* **cottony,** *a.* Cotonneux.

cotyle ['kɔtili:], *n.* Cotyle, *f.* **cotyledon** [kɔti'li:dən], *n.* (*Bot.*) Cotylédon, *m.* **cotyledonous,** *a.* Cotylédoné.

couch (1) [kautʃ], *n.* Canapé, divan, *m.*; lit de repos (sick-bed), *m.*—*v.i.* Se coucher, s'étendre, se baisser; se tapir.—*v.t.* Coucher, étendre; (*fig.*) rédiger, exprimer, mettre par écrit; cacher; (*Surg.*) abaisser (cataract); tenir en arrêt (a lance). **couchant,** *a.* (*Her.*) Couché, accroupi, tapi.

couch (2) [kuːtʃ] or **couch-grass** ['kuːtʃgraːs], *n.* Chiendent, *m.*

cougar ['kuːgə], *n.* Couguar, puma, *m.*

cough [kɔːf] or (*more usual*) [kɔf], *n.* Toux, *f.* *Whooping-cough*, coqueluche, *f.* *To have a cough*, tousser.—*v.i.* Tousser. *To cough up*, expectorer; (*pop.*, *fig.*) cracher (to pay). **cough-drop** or **cough-lozenge,** *n.* Pastille pour la toux, pâte pectorale, *f.* **coughing,** *n.* Toux, *f.* *Fit of coughing*, quinte de toux, *f.*

could [kud], *past* [CAN (2)].

coulee, coulie [kuː'liː], *n.* Coulée (de lave), *f.*

couloir ['kuːlwaː], *n.* Couloir, ravin, *m.*

coulomb ['kuːləm], *n.* Ampère-seconde, coulomb, *m.*

coulter ['koultə], *n.* Coutre, *m.*

council ['kaunsil], *n.* Conseil; (*Eccles.*) concile, *m.* *Cabinet council*, conseil des ministres, *m.* *County council*, conseil général; *borough* or *town council*, conseil municipal, *m.* **council-board,** *n.* Table du conseil, *f.* **council-chamber,** *n.* Chambre du conseil, *f.* **councillor** or **councilman,** *n.* Conseiller, conseiller municipal, *m.* *County councillor*, conseiller général, *m.*

counsel ['kaunsəl], *n.* Conseil, avis, *m.*; délibération, *f.*; dessein; avocat, défenseur (lawyer), *m.* *Keep your own counsel*, n'en parlez à personne; *to keep one's counsel*, garder le secret; *to take counsel's opinion*, consulter un avocat.—*v.t.* Conseiller; recommander. **counsellor,** *n.* Conseiller; conseiller d'ambassade; avocat, *m.*

count (1) [kaunt], *n.* Comte (foreign title corresponding to earl), *m.*

count (2) [kaunt], *n.* Calcul, compte, total, *m.*; (*Law*) chef d'accusation, *m.* *To lose count*, perdre le compte.—*v.t.* Compter, (*fig.*) regarder, considérer (to esteem, consider, etc.), imputer (to place to account); dépouiller (a ballot-box). *To count on, upon*, compter sur; *he hardly counts*, il ne compte guère; *the House was counted out*, on a ajourné la Chambre (faute du quorum de 40); *to be counted out* (of boxer), rester sur le plancher, (*fam.*) être compté dehors.

countdown ['kauntdaun], *n.* Compte à rebours, *m.*

countenance ['kauntinəns], *n.* Figure, mine, *f.*, air, *m.*; (*fig.*) contenance; protection, approbation, *f.*, appui, *m.* *To be out of countenance, to lose countenance*, perdre contenance, être décontenancé; *to change countenance*, changer de visage; *to give countenance to*, favoriser, encourager; *to keep one's countenance*, garder son sérieux; *to put out of countenance*, décontenancer.—*v.t.* Appuyer, encourager, favoriser; soutenir, défendre.

counter ['kauntə], *n.* Calculateur; compteur (instrument); (*Cards etc.*) jeton; comptoir (in a shop), *m.*; guichets, *m.pl.*, caisse, *f.* (bank); zinc, *m.* (café); (*Box.*, *Fenc.*) contre, *m.*; (*Mus.*) haute-contre, *f.*; poitrail, *m.* (of horse); contrefort, *m.* (of boot). *To sell under the counter*, vendre sous le comptoir.—*adv.* Contre, contrairement (à), à l'encontre (de). *To run counter to*, aller à l'encontre de.—*v.i.*, *v.t.* Parer; contrer.

counteract [kauntər'ækt], *v.t.* Contrecarrer, contre-balancer, neutraliser. **counteraction,** *n.* Action contraire, *f.*, mouvement opposé, *m.*, opposition, résistance, *f.* **counter-attack,** *n.* (*Mil.*) Contre-attaque, *f.*

counter-attraction ['kauntərə'trækʃən], *n.* Attraction opposée, *f.* **counterbalance,** *n.* Contrepoids, *m.*—*v.t.* Contre-balancer.

counterblast, *n.* Réplique, riposte, *f.*

counter-brace, *v.t.* (*Naut.*) Contre-brasser.

countercharge, *n.* Contre-accusation, *f.*

countercheck, *n.* Obstacle, *m.*, censure, réprimande, *f.*—*v.t.* Opposer, réprimer, contrecarrer. **counter-claim,** *n.* (*Law*) Demande reconventionnelle, *f.* **counter-clockwise,** *adv.* Dans le sens contraire des aiguilles d'une montre; en tournant vers la gauche; en dévissant. **counter-current,** *n.* Contre-courant, *m.* **counter-deed,** *n.* Contre-lettre, *f.* **counter-demonstration,** *n.* Contre-manifestation, *f.* **counterdraw,** *v.t.* Contre-tirer. **counter-espionage,** *n.* Contre-espionnage, *m.* **counter-evidence,** *n.* Témoignage contraire, *m.*

counterfeit ['kauntəfiːt], *a.* Contrefait, imité; faux.—*n.* Contrefaçon; fausse pièce, fausse monnaie; imitation, *f.*—*v.t.* Contrefaire, imiter; feindre.—*v.i.* Feindre.

counterfoil ['kauntəfɔil], *n.* Talon (de registre), *m.*, souche, *f.* **counterfort,** *n.* Contrefort, *m.* **counter-fugue,** *n.* (*Mus.*) Contre-fugue, *f.* **counterguard,** *n.* (*Fort.*) Contre-garde, *f.* **counter-indication,** *n.* Contre-indication, *f.*

countermand [kauntə'maːnd], *v.t.* Contremander. *Unless countermanded*, sauf contre-ordre.—*n.* Contremandement, *m.*

counter-march, *n.* Contremarche, *f.—v.i.* Contremarcher.

countermark, *n.* Contremarque, *f.—v.t.* Contremarquer.

counter-measure, *n.* Contre-mesure, *f.*

counter-mine, *n.* Contre-mine, *f.—v.t.* Contre-miner; (*fig.*) opposer, déjouer, combattre.

counter-movement, *n.* Mouvement opposé, *m.*

countermure, *n.* (*Fort.*) Contremur, *m.—v.t.* Contre-murer.

counter-offensive, *n.* Contre-offensive, *f.*

counterpane ['kauntəpein], *n.* Couvre-pied, couvre-lit, *m.,* courtepointe, *f.*

counterpart ['kauntəpɑːt], *n.* Contre-partie, *f.*; pendant; (*Law*) double, *m.* *To be the counterpart of,* faire pendant à.

counterplot, *n.* Contre-ruse, *f.*

counterpoint ['kauntəpɔint], *n.* (*Mus.*) Contre-point, *m.* **counterpoise,** *n.* Contre-poids, *m.—v.t.* Contre-balancer. **counter-poison,** *n.* Contrepoison, *m.* **counter-pressure,** *n.* Pression contraire, *f.* **counter-project,** *n.* Contre-projet, *m.* **counter-proof,** *n.* Contre-épreuve, *f.* **counter-proposal,** *n.* Contre-proposition, *f.* **counter-reformation,** *n.* Contre-réforme, *f.*

counter-revolution ['kauntə revə'luːʃən], *n.* Contre-révolution, *f.* **counter-revolutionary,** *a.* and *n.,* or **counter-revolutionist,** *n.* Contre-révolutionnaire.

counterscarp ['kauntəskɑːp], *n.* (*Fort.*) Contrescarpe, *f.*

counterseal, *v.t.* Contre-sceller.—*n.* Contresceau, contre-scel, *m.* **countershaft,** *n.* (*Mach.*) Transmission intermédiaire, *f.*

countersign ['kauntəsain], *v.t.* Contre-signer.—*n.* (*Mil.*) Mot de ralliement, *m.,* consigne, *f.*

counter-signature, *n.* Contreseing, *m.*

countersink, *v.t.* Fraiser, noyer.

counter-stroke, *n.* Retour offensif, *m.*

counter-tenor, *n.* (*Mus.*) Haute-contre, *f.*

countervail ['kauntəveil], *v.t.* Contre-balancer, compenser.

counter-view, *n.* Contraste; point de vue opposé, *m.*

counter-weight, *n.* Contrepoids, *m.*

counterwork ['kauntəwəːk], *v.t.* Contre-miner, déjouer, contrecarrer. **counter-works,** *n.pl.* (*Fort.*) Contre-attaques, *f.pl.*

countess ['kauntis], *n.* Comtesse, *f.*

counting ['kauntiŋ], *n.* Compte; dépouillement (of a ballot-box), *m.* **counting-house,** *n.* Bureau, comptoir, *m.,* caisse, *f.* **countless,** *a.* Innombrable, sans nombre.

countrified ['kʌntrifaid], *a.* (Devenu) campagnard *or* provincial.

country ['kʌntri], *n.* Pays, *m.*; contrée; région; campagne (opposed to town); province (opposed to capital); patrie (fatherland), *f.* *Across country,* à travers champs; *country gentleman or squire,* gentilhomme campagnard, gentilhomme de province, *m.,* (*fam.*) hobereau, *m.*; *country girl,* (jeune) villageoise *or* paysanne, *f.*; *country life,* vie à la campagne, vie de province, *f.*; *country town,* ville de province, *f.*; *in open country,* en rase campagne; *in the country,* à la campagne; *wine of the country,* vin du pays, *m.* **country-box,** *n.* Pied-à-terre, *m.* **country-dance,** *n.*

Contredanse, *f.,* danse rustique, *f.* **country-dancing,** *n.* Danses folkloriques, *f.pl.* **country-house, country-seat,** *n.* Maison de campagne, *f.*; château, *m.* **countryman,** *n.* Paysan, campagnard, homme de la campagne, *m.* **Fellow-countryman,** compatriote, (*fam.*) pays, *m.* **countryside,** *n.* Campagne, *f.*; pays d'alentour; paysage, *m.* **countrywoman,** *n.* Paysanne, *f.*

county ['kaunti], *n.* Comté, *m.* *County council,* conseil général, *m.*; *county court,* tribunal de première instance, *m.*; *county rate,* impôt départemental, *m.*; *county town,* chef-lieu, *m.*

coup [kuː], *n.* Coup (d'audace), *m.*; (*Billiards*) fausse blouse, *f.* *To bring off a coup,* réussir un coup.

couple [kʌpl], *n.* Couple, *f.*; couple (a male and female), *m.*; (*Carp.*) moise, *f.* *A happy young couple,* un jeune ménage heureux, *m.*; *newly married couple,* nouveaux mariés, *m.pl.* —*v.i.* S'accoupler.—*v.t.* Coupler, accoupler; attacher deux à deux, atteler; joindre.

couplet, *n.* Couplet, distique, *m.,* strophe, *f.*

coupling, *n.* Accouplement, *m.* **coupling-bar** *or* **-rod,** *n.* Bielle, *f.* **coupling-chain,** *n.* Chaîne d'attelage, *f.*

coupon ['kuːpɔ̃] or ['kuːpɔn], *n.* Coupon, *m.*; (*Polit.*) recommandation donnée par le chef de son parti à un candidat, *f.* *Bread coupons,* tickets de pain, *m.pl.*; *clothing coupons,* points textiles, *m.pl.*; *international reply coupon,* coupon-réponse international, *m.*; *petrol coupons,* bons d'essence, *m.pl.*

courage ['kʌridʒ], *n.* Courage, *m.* *To pluck up courage,* s'enhardir, s'armer de courage.

courageous [kə'reidʒəs], *a.* Courageux.

courageously, *adv.* Courageusement.

courageousness, *n.* Courage, *m.*

courier ['kuriə], *n.* Courrier, *m.*

course [kɔːs], *n.* Cours, *m.*; carrière, voie, suite, succession, *f.*; parcours (of a stream), lit (of a river), *m.*; genre (of life); service (at a meal); courant (duration), *m.*; (*Racing*) champ, terrain de course; hippodrome, *m.*; (*Build.*) assise, *f.*; (*Agric.*) assolement; (*Mining*) filon, *m.*; (*Naut.*) route, *f.*; tour (turn), *m.*; (*Med., pl.*) règles, *f.pl.* *First course,* entrée, *f.*; *in course of formation,* en train de se constituer, en voie de formation; *in course of time,* avec le temps; *in due course,* en temps voulu; *in the course of,* dans le cours de, (*of time*) dans le courant de; *of course,* naturellement, bien entendu; *that is a matter of course,* cela va sans dire; *to take its course,* prendre son cours; *to take a course of treatment,* suivre un traitement; *the right course,* la bonne voie, *f.*; *water-course,* cours d'eau, *m.—v.t.* Courir; faire courir; chasser (le lièvre).—*v.i.* Courir; circuler (of the blood).

courser ['kɔːsə], *n.* Coureur, coursier, cheval de course, *m.* **coursing,** *n.* Chasse au lévrier, *f.*; course de lévriers après un lièvre (artificiel), *f.,* coursing, *m.*

court [kɔːt], *n.* Cour, *f.*; tribunal, *m.*; impasse, *f.,* passage (small street), *m.*; (*Ten.*) court, *m.* *Back court,* cour de derrière, *f.*; *court of appeal,* cour d'appel; *criminal court,* cour de justice criminelle; *in open court,* en plein tribunal; *to go to court,* aller à la cour; *to pay court to,* faire sa cour à; *to settle out of court,* arranger à l'amiable. *Grass court,*

court sur gazon; *hard court*, court dur.—*v.t.*
Faire sa cour à, courtiser; chercher, rechercher, aller au-devant de; briguer. *To court
disaster*, courir à un échec; *to court inquiries*,
être prêt à donner tous les renseignements.
court-card, *n.* Figure, *f.* **court-day**, *n.*
Jour d'audience, *m.* **court-dress**, *n.* Habit
de cour, *m.*, robe de cour, *f.* **court-hand**, *n.*
Grosse (écriture), *f.* **court-house**, *n.* Palais
de justice, *m.* **court-martial**, *n.* Conseil de
guerre, *m.*—*v.t.* Faire passer en conseil de
guerre. **court-plaster**, *n.* Taffetas d'Angleterre, *m.* **courtyard**, *n.* Cour, *f.* (de maison).
courteous ['kɔːtiəs], *a.* Courtois, poli.
courteously, *adv.* Courtoisement, poliment.
courteousness, *n.* Courtoisie, politesse, *f.*
courtesan ['kɔːtizən *or* kɔːti'zæn], *n.* Courtisane, *f.*
courtesy ['kɔːtəsi], *n.* Courtoisie, politesse, *f.*
[CURTSY].
courtier ['kɔːtiə], *n.* Courtisan, homme de
cour, *m.*
courtliness ['kɔːtlinis], *n.* Élégance, politesse,
f. **courtly**, *a.* Poli, élégant, courtois.
courtship ['kɔːtʃip], *n.* Cour, *f.*
cousin [kʌzn], *n.* Cousin, *m.*, cousine, *f.*
Country cousin, provincial, cousin de province, *m.*; *first cousin*, cousin germain, *m.*,
cousine germaine, *f.*; *first cousin once removed*,
oncle, tante, neveu *or* nièce à la mode de
Bretagne; *second cousin*, cousin issu *or* cousine
issue de germains.
cousinly ['kʌznli], *a.* De bon cousinage.
cove [kouv], *n.* Anse, crique, *f.*; (*Arch.*) voûte,
f.; (*slang*) type, individu, *m.*—*v.t.* (*Arch.*)
Voûter, cintrer. **coved**, *a.* À voussures,
cintré. **coving**, *n.* Voussure, *f.*
covenant ['kʌvənənt], *n.* Convention, *f.*,
pacte, contrat; (*Engl. Hist.*) Covenant, *m.*;
(*Bibl.*) alliance, *f.* *To enter into a covenant*,
s'engager par contrat (à).—*v.i.* Convenir (de),
s'engager (à).—*v.t.* Stipuler par contrat.
covenanter, *n.* Partie contractante, *f.*;
(*Engl. Hist.*) [kʌvə'næntə], (*colloq.*) covenantaire, *m.*
Coventry ['kɔvəntri], *n.* (*colloq.*) *To send to
Coventry*, mettre en quarantaine, frapper
d'ostracisme.
cover ['kʌvə], *v.t.* Couvrir; voiler, déguiser;
cacher; couver (of birds); saillir (of animals);
combler (a deficit etc.); tenir la rubrique de
(of a journalist). *To be covered*, (*Comm.*)
·être à couvert; *to cover one's expenses*, couvrir
ses dépenses; *to cover off* (*Mil.*), couvrir; *to
cover one's tracks*, dépister ses poursuivants;
to cover up, couvrir entièrement; dissimuler
(the truth etc.). *To cover distances*, parcourir
du pays.—*n.* Couverture; cloche (of a dish
etc.); enveloppe (of a letter etc.); housse (of
a chair), *f.*; couvercle (of a saucepan etc.);
couvert (for game), *m.*; (*Bot.*) involucre, *m.*;
(*fig.*) voile, masque, *m.*, prétention, *f.*; abri,
m.; (*Naut.*) protection, *f.* *To take cover*, se
cacher; *under cover*, à couvert; *under cover of*,
sous la protection de, à la faveur de, (*fig.*)
sous l'apparence de; *under cover of a tree*, à
l'abri d'un arbre; *under separate cover*,
(*Comm.*) sous pli séparé. **cover-charge**, *n.*
Couvert, *m.* **coverage**, *n.* Champ d'application, *m.* *Newspaper coverage*, informations,
f.pl., étendue d'un reportage, *f.* **covering**, *n.*
Couverture; enveloppe; housse (of chairs), *f.*;

vêtement, *m.*, habits (clothing), *m.pl.* *Covering letter*, lettre d'envoi, *f.* **coverlet**, *n.*
Couvre-pied, couvre-lit, *m.*
covert ['kʌvɔːt], *n.* Couvert, abri; gîte, *m.*,
tanière, *f.*; fourré, *m.* *Tail-coverts* (of bird),
plumes tectrices de la queue, *f.pl.*—*a.* Couvert, caché, voilé, secret; insidieux; (*Law*)
en puissance de mari. **covert-way**, *n.*
(*Fort.*) Chemin couvert, *m.* **covertly**, *adv.*
Secrètement, en cachette. **coverture**, *n.*
*Abri; (*Law*) état de la femme en puissance
de mari, *m.*
covet ['kʌvit], *v.t.* Convoiter, ambitionner;
désirer ardemment. **covetable**, *a.* Convoitable. **covetous**, *a.* Avide, avaricieux,
cupide. **covetously**, *adv.* Avec convoitise,
avidement. **covetousness**, *n.* Convoitise,
cupidité, *f.*
covey ['kʌvi], *n.* Compagnie (of partridges), *f.*
cow (1) [kau], *n.* Vache, *f.*; femelle (elephant,
whale, seal, etc.), *f.* *Milch cow*, vache laitière,
f.; (*fig.*) *till the cows come home*, jusqu'à la
semaine des quatre jeudis. **cow-bane**, *n.*
(*Bot.*) Cicutaire aquatique, *f.* **cow-berry**, *n.*
Myrtille rouge; airelle, *f.* **cowboy**, *n.* Jeune
vacher; (*Am.*) cowboy, *m.* **cow-catcher**, *n.*
(*Rail.*) Chasse-bestiaux, *m.* **cow-dung**, *n.*
Bouse de vache, *f.* **cowherd**, *n.* Vacher,
m., vachère, *f.* **cowhide**, *n.* Peau de vache,
f. **cow-house** *or* **-shed**, *n.* Vacherie, étable
à vaches, *f.* **cow-keeper**, *n.* Nourrisseur, *m.*
cow-parsley, *n.* Cerfeuil sauvage, *m.* **cow-
pat**, *n.* Bouse de vache, *f.* **cow-parsnip**, *n.*
Berce, *f.* **cowpox**, *n.* Vaccine, *f.* **cow-
wheat**, *n.* (*Bot.*) Mélampyre, blé de vache,
m.
cow (2) [kau], *v.t.* Intimider, dompter.
coward ['kauəd], *n.* Lâche, poltron, *m.*,
poltronne, *f.* **cowardice** *or* **cowardliness**,
n. Couardise, poltronnerie, lâcheté, *f.*
cowardly, *a.* Couard, lâche, poltron.—*adv.*
Lâchement, en poltron, en lâche.
cower ['kauə], *v.i.* S'accroupir, se blottir,
se tapir.
cowl [kaul], *n.* Capuchon; (*Naut.*, *Av.*) capot,
m.; tabouret (for chimneys), *m.* *Penitent's
cowl*, cagoule, *f.* **cowling**, *n.* Capuchonnement, *m.* (chimney); capot, capotage, *m.*
(engine).
cowry *or* **cowrie** ['kauri], *n.* Cauris, *m.*
(money); porcelaine, *f.* (shell).
cowslip ['kauslip], *n.* Primevère, *f.*, coucou, *m.*
cox [kɔks], *v.t.* Diriger, gouverner.—*n.*
[COXSWAIN].
coxcomb ['kɔkskoum], *n.* Petit-maître, freluquet, fat, *m.*
coxcombical [kɔks'koumikl], *a.* Fat, plein de
fatuité.
coxcombry, *n.* Fatuité, *f.*
coxswain [kɔksn], *n.* Patron de chaloupe, *m.*;
(*Row.*) barreur, *m.*
coy [kɔi], *a.* Timide, réservé. **coyly**, *adv.*
Timidement, avec réserve. **coyness**, *n.*
Timidité, réserve, *f.*
coyote [kɔi'jout], *n.* Loup de prairie, coyote,
m.
coz [kʌz] [short for COUSIN].
cozen [kʌzn], *v.t.* Duper, tromper. **cozen-
age**, *n.* Fourberie, tromperie, *f.* **cozener**, *n.*
Fourbe, trompeur, *m.*
crab [kræb], *n.* Crabe, cancre, *m.*; (*Astron.*)
Cancer, *m.*, Écrevisse, *f.*; (*Mach.*) chèvre, *f.*;

(*Naut.*) cabestan volant, *m.* *To catch a crab*, (*Row.*) attaquer en sifflet, faire une embardée. **crab-apple,** *n.* Pomme sauvage, *f.* **crab-tree,** *n.* Pommier sauvage, *m.*
crabbed ['kræbid], *a.* Acariâtre, revêche, bourru; dur, noueux (of a cudgel); illisible (of writing). *Crabbed look,* mine rechignée, *f.* **crabbedly,** *adv.* D'une manière bourrue, durement, rudement. **crabbedness,** *n.* Humeur acariâtre, âpreté, rudesse, *f.* **crab-wise,** *adv.* Comme un crabe, de biais.
crack [kræk], *v.t.* Fendre; fêler (crockery etc.); gercer (the skin etc.); casser (nuts etc.); faire claquer (a whip); faire sauter (a bottle of wine); faire, lâcher (a joke); (*fig.*) rompre, briser. *To crack a crib*, (slang) cambrioler une maison; *to crack up*, (slang) se vanter de, vanter, prôner.—*v.i.* Se fendre, se lézarder; se gercer (of the skin etc.); claquer (of a whip); se fêler (of glass etc.); muer (of the voice). *To crack up*, s'effondrer, craquer; *to get cracking*, (*fam.*) s'y mettre.—*n.* Fente, crevasse, fissure; détonation (of fire-arms); lézarde, fêlure (in glass), *f.*; craquement (noise), *m.*; claquement (of a whip), *m.*; mue (of the voice); hâblerie (boast), *f.* *Crack of doom*, le jugement dernier; *to have a crack at something*, tenter l'aventure.—*a.* Fameux, d'élite. *To be a crack shot*, être un fin tireur; *a crack player*, un champion, un as, *m.* **crack-brained,** *a.* Timbré, fou. *Crack-brained fellow*, cerveau fêlé, *m.* **cracked,** *a.* Fendu, fêlé; (*fig.*) timbré. *To be a little cracked*, avoir un grain de folie. **cracker,** *n.* Vantard, craqueur; pétard (firework); (*Am.*) biscuit, *m.* *Christmas-crackers*, diablotins, *m.pl.*, papillottes à pétard, *f.pl.*; *nut-crackers*, casse-noix, *m.inv.* **crackers,** *a.* (*pop.*) Timbré, fou.
cracking, *n.* Craquement; claquement (of a whip), *m.* **cracksman,** *n.* Cambrioleur, *m.*
crackle ['krækl], *v.i.* Pétiller, craqueter, crépiter. **crackling,** *n.* Pétillement, crépitement; (*fig.*) rissolé (of roast pork), *m.* **crackled,** *a.* Fendillé; craquelé.
cracknel ['kræknl], *n.* Craquelin, *m.*, croquignole, *f.*
Cracow ['krækou]. Cracovie, *f.*
cradle [kreidl], *n.* Berceau, *m.*; (*Naut.*) ber, *m.* *From the cradle*, dès le berceau; *in the cradle*, au berceau.—*v.t.* Coucher dans un berceau, bercer; endormir (to lull). **cradle-song,** *n.* Berceuse, *f.*
craft [krɑːft], *n.* Métier (trade), *m.*; artifice, *m.*; ruse, astuce (cunning); (*Naut.*) embarcation, *f.*, bâtiment, *m.* *Small craft*, petits bateaux, canots, *m.pl.*; *the Craft*, la franc-maçonnerie, *f.* **craftily,** *adv.* Sournoisement, avec ruse. **craftiness,** *n.* Artifice, *m.*, ruse, astuce, *f.* **craftsman,** *n.* Artisan; artiste dans son métier, *m.* **craftsmanship,** *n.* Habileté technique, *f.*, exécution, *f.* *Good craftsmanship*, métier parfait, *m.*; exécution de main de maître, *f.*; *bad craftsmanship*, travail mal fait, *m.* **crafty,** *a.* Rusé, astucieux.
crag [kræg], *n.* Rocher escarpé, rocher à pic, *m.*, pointe de rocher, *f.*; (*Geol.*) crag, *m.* **cragged,** *a.* Rocailleux, escarpé, abrupt. **craggedness** or **cragginess,** *n.* Nature rocailleuse, anfractuosité, *f.* **craggy,** *a.* Rocailleux, escarpé, abrupt.
crake [kreik], *n.* (*Orn.*) Râle, *m.* *Spotted crake*, râle marouette.

cram [kræm], *v.t.* Fourrer, remplir, bourrer; entasser; farcir; préparer, chauffer (students). *To cram poultry*, gaver *or* empâter de la volaille.—*v.i.* Se bourrer, se gaver, s'empiffrer; (*fig.*) en conter, blaguer. *To cram into* (*a car*), s'entasser dans (une auto).—*n.* (slang) Colle, blague, *f.* *What a cram!* quelle colle! **crammer,** *n.* Répétiteur, préparateur, *m.*; (*colloq.*) colleur, chauffeur. *A crammer's*, (*fam.*) une boîte à bachot, *f.*
crambo ['kræmbou], *n.* Corbillon, jeu des bouts rimés, *m.* *Dumb crambo*, charade mimée, *f.*
cramp [kræmp], *n.* Crampe, *f.*; (*Tech.*) crampon, serre-joint, *m.*; (*fig.*) gêne, entrave, *f.* *To be seized with cramp*, être pris d'une crampe, avoir des crampes.—*v.t.* Cramponner; serrer; resserrer; donner la crampe à; (*fig.*) gêner, entraver, restreindre. **cramp-fish,** *n.* Torpille, *f.* **cramp-iron,** *n.* Crampon, *m.* **cramped,** *a.* Gêné. *A cramped style*, un style dur or serré; *cramped writing*, des pattes de mouche, *f.pl.*; *to be cramped* (*for space*), être très à l'étroit.
cranage ['kreinidʒ], *n.* Droit de grue, *m.*
cranberry ['krænbəri], *n.* (*Bot.*) Canneberge, *f.*
crane [krein], *n.* (*Orn., Tech.*) Grue, *f.* *Salvage crane*, grue dépanneuse, *f.*; *steam crane*, grue à vapeur; *swinging, revolving crane*, grue pivotante, *f.*; *travelling crane*, grue mobile or roulante, *f.*—*v.t.* Allonger, tendre (the neck). **crane-fly,** *n.* Tipule, *f.* **crane's-bill,** *n.* Bec-de-grue (plant), *m.*
cranial ['kreiniəl], *a.* Crânien.
craniology [kreini'ɔlɔdʒi], *n.* Cranologie or craniologie, *f.* **craniometry,** *n.* Craniométrie, *f.*
cranium ['kreiniəm], *n.* Crâne, *m.*
crank [kræŋk], *n.* Manivelle, *f.*; coude; pédalier (of a bicycle), *m.*; (*fig.*) dada, *m.*, marotte (a crotchet), *f.*; maniaque, excentrique, original (person), *m.*—*a.* (*Eng.*) Détraqué; (*Naut.*) qui a le côté faible.—*v.t.* Couder (a shaft). *To crank up a car*, mettre en route une auto à la manivelle. **crank-arm,** *n.* Manivelle, *f.*, bras de manivelle, *m.* **crank-case,** *n.* Carter (on a bicycle etc.), *m.* **crank-pin,** *n.* Bouton de manivelle, *m.* **crankshaft,** *n.* Arbre de manivelle, *m.*; (*Motor.*) vilebrequin, *m.* **cranky,** *a.* Capricieux, fantasque; impatient; maussade.
crankle ['kræŋkl], *v.i.* Serpenter, faire des détours, aller en zigzag.—*n.* Détour, zigzag, *m.*
cranny ['kræni], *n.* Crevasse, fente, lézarde, fissure, *f.* **crannied,** *a.* Crevassé, lézardé.
crape [kreip], *n.* Crêpe, *m.* *Crape band*, brassard noir, *m.* *Crape rubber*, crêpe de caoutchouc, *m.*—*v.t.* Garnir de crêpe; friser, crêper (hair).
crapulent ['kræpjulənt] or **crapulous,** *a.* Crapuleux.
crash (1) [kræʃ], *v.i.* Faire un grand fracas, éclater, retentir; se tamponner (of two cars etc.). *To crash down*, tomber avec fracas; *to crash into*, (*Motor.*) tamponner; *to crash-land* (*Av.*), atterrir brutalement; faire un crash.—*v.t.* Fracasser, briser.—*n.* Fracas, grand bruit, *m.*; (*fig.*) débâcle, ruine; faillite, banqueroute, *f.* **crash-helmet,** *n.* Serre-tête, *m.inv.* **crashing,** *a.* (*fam.*) *A crashing*

bore, un véritable assommoir. **crash-landing,** *n.* (*Av.*) Atterrissage brutal; crash, *m.*
crash (2) [kræʃ], *n.* Grosse toile, *f.* (for towels etc.).
crasis ['kreisis], *n.* (*Gram.*) Crase, *f.*
crass [kræs], *a.* Crasse, grossier, stupide. **crassly,** *adv.* Stupidement. **crassness,** *n.* Épaisseur, *f.*
crate [kreit], *n.* *Harasse, caisse à claire-voie, *f.*—*v.t.* Emballer. **crating,** *n.* Emballage, *m.*
crater ['kreitə], *n.* Cratère, *m.*
cravat [krə'væt], *n.* Cravate, *f.*
crave [kreiv], *v.t.* Implorer, solliciter, demander avec instance; (*fig.*) soupirer après. *We crave reference to* . . ., nous vous prions de vous reporter à . . . .
craving, *n.* Désir ardent, besoin impérieux, *m.*
craven [kreivn], *a.* and *n.* Lâche, poltron.
craw [krɔː], *n.* Jabot (of a bird), *m.*
crawfish, *n.* [CRAYFISH].
crawl [krɔːl], *v.i.* Ramper, se traîner; se glisser, s'insinuer (dans). *To crawl up,* grimper *or* monter à quatre pattes; *to crawl with,* grouiller de.—*n.* Mouvement traînant, *m.*; (*Swim.*) nage rampée, *f.*, crawl, *m.*; parc à poisson, vivier (fish-pond), *m.* **crawler,** *n.* Reptile; taxi en maraude, maraudeur; nageur de crawl, *m.*; (*pl.*) (*Cost.*) barboteuse, *f.*
crawling, *a.* Rampant; grouillant, fourmillant (de).
crayfish ['kreifiʃ] *or* **crawfish** ['krɔːfiʃ], *n.* Écrevisse, *f.* (in fresh water); sea-crayfish (*or* spiny lobster), langouste, *f.*
crayon ['kreiən], *n.* Crayon, pastel, fusain, *m.*—*v.t.* Crayonner, dessiner au pastel; (*fig.*) dessiner, esquisser.
craze [kreiz], *v.t.* Fendiller, craqueler (pottery); frapper de folie, rendre fou.—*n.* Folie; (*fig.*) folle idée, passion folle, *f.*; engouement, *m.*, toquade, *f.* **crazed,** *a.* Fou, dément; craquelé (china). **crazily,** *adv.* Follement.
craziness, *n.* Délabrement, *f.*; démence, folie, *f.* **crazy,** *a.* Délabré, en mauvais état, hors de service; fou, toqué. *Crazy paving,* dallage en pierres plates irrégulières, *m.*; *to be crazy about,* être fou de.
creak [kriːk], *v.i.* Crier, craquer, grincer.—*n.* or **creaking,** *n.* Cri, grincement, *m.*—*a.* Qui crie, qui craque.
cream [kriːm], *n.* Crème, *f.* *Whipped cream,* crème fouettée; *with cream,* à la crème. —*v.i.* Crémer, mousser. **cream-cheese,** *n.* Fromage à la crème, *m.* **cream-colour(ed),** *a.* Crème. **cream-jug,** *n.* Pot à crème, *m.* **cream-laid,** *a.* Vergé blanc, *m.* **creamer,** *n.* Crémeuse; écrémeuse centrifuge, *f.* **creamery,** *n.* Crémerie, *f.* **creamy,** *a.* Crémeux; de crème.
crease [kriːs], *n.* Pli, faux pli, *m.*; (*Cricket*) ligne de limite, *f.*—*v.t.* Faire des plis à, plisser, chiffonner, friper.—*v.i.* Se plisser; se friper.
create [kri'eit], *v.t.* Créer, faire naître; produire, engendrer, occasionner, causer; constituer, faire.—*v.i.* (*fam.*) Faire une scène, faire du tapage. **creation,** *n.* Création; nature, *f.*, univers, *m.*; dernière mode, *f.* **creative,** *a.* Créateur. **creativeness,** *n.* Puissance créatrice, *f.* **creator,** *n.* Créateur, *m.*
creature ['kriːtʃə], *n.* Créature, personne, *f.*, être, *m.*; animal, *m.* *A wretched creature,*

un(e) misérable; *creature comforts,* aises; *f.pl.,* bonne chère, *f.*
crèche [kreiʃ], *n.* Crèche, *f.*
credence ['kriːdəns], *n.* Créance, croyance, foi; (*Eccles. etc.*) crédence, *f.* *To give credence to,* ajouter foi à. **credence-table,** *n.* Crédence, *f.*
credentials [kri'denʃəlz], *n.pl.* Lettres de créance, *f.pl.*; pouvoirs, *m.pl.*; certificat, *m.*; papiers d'identité, *m.pl.*
credibility [kredi'biliti] *or* **credibleness,** *n.* Crédibilité, *f.*
credible ['kredibl], *a.* Croyable, digne de foi. **credibly,** *adv.* D'une manière digne de foi. *To be credibly informed,* tenir de bonne source.
credit ['kredit], *n.* Croyance, foi, *f.*; (*fig.*) influence, réputation, *f.*; mérite, honneur, *m.*; (*Comm.*) crédit, *m.* *I gave you credit for more sense,* je vous croyais plus de jugement; *on credit,* à crédit; *to do credit to,* faire honneur à; *to give credit,* vendre à crédit; *to give credit to,* ajouter foi à; *to take (the) credit for,* s'attribuer le mérite de; *worthy of credit,* digne de foi. *Letter of credit,* lettre de crédit, *f.*—*v.t.* Ajouter foi à, croire à; faire honneur à; (*Comm.*) faire crédit à (*Book-keeping*) créditer, porter au crédit de. *To credit someone with a quality,* attribuer, prêter une qualité à quelqu'un. **creditable,** *a.* Honorable, estimable, digne d'éloge. **creditableness,** *n.* Crédit, honneur, *m.* **creditably,** *adv.* Honorablement. **creditor,** *n.* Créancier, *m.*, créancière, *f.*; (*Book-keeping*) créditeur, avoir, *m.*
credulity [krə'djuːliti] *or* **credulousness** ['kredjuləsnis], *n.* Crédulité, *f.*
credulous ['kredjuləs], *a.* Crédule.
creed [kriːd], *n.* Credo, *m.*, symbole; (*fig.*) culte, *m.*, secte, *f.*; profession de foi, *f.*; croyance, foi, *f.* *The Apostles' Creed,* le symbole des Apôtres, *m.*
creek [kriːk], *n.* Crique, anse, *f.*; (*Am.*) petit cours d'eau, *m.* *creeky,* *a.* Plein de criques.
creel [kriːl], *n.* Panier de pêche, *m.*
creep [kriːp], *v.i.* (*past* and *p.p.* **crept**) Se traîner, ramper, se glisser. *To creep into,* se glisser dans, s'insinuer dans; *to creep on,* s'avancer peu à peu, s'avancer en rampant; *to creep out,* sortir doucement, sortir à l'improviste; *to creep over,* se glisser pardessus; *to creep up,* monter doucement; *to feel one's flesh creep,* avoir la chair de poule.
creeper, *n.* Reptile; grimpereau, *m.*, échelette, *f.* (bird) plante grimpante (plant), *f.*
creep-hole, *n.* Trou, *m.*, échappatoire, *f.*
creeping, *n.* Fourmillement (sensation), *m.* —*a.* Rampant, grimpant, qui fait frissonner. **creepingly,** *adv.* En rampant, lentement.
creeps, *n.pl.* *To give someone the creeps,* donner la chair de poule à quelqu'un.
creepy, *a.* Horrifique, qui donne la chair de poule; rampant.
cremate [krə'meit], *v.t.* Incinérer. **cremation,** *n.* Crémation, incinération, *f.*
crematorium [kremə'tɔːriəm], *n.* Crématorium, *m.*
crematory ['kremətri], *a.* Crématoire.
Cremona [kri'mounə]. Crémone, *f.*—*n.* Violon de Crémone; crémone, *m.*
crenate ['kriːneit] *or* **crenated,** *a.* (*Bot.*) Crénelé.
crenature ['kriːnətʃə *or* 'kre-], *n.* Crénelure, *f.*

crenellate ['krenəleit], *v.t.* Créneler. **crenellation,** *n.* Crénelure, *f.*
creole ['kri:oul], *a.* and *n.* Créole.
creosote ['kri:əsout], *n.* Créosote, *f.*
crêpe [kreip], *n.* Crêpe blanc (*or* clair), *m.*
crepitate ['krepiteit], *v.i.* Crépiter. **crepitant,** *a.* Crépitant. **crepitation,** *n.* Crépitation, *f.*, crépitement, *m.*
crept [krept], *past* and *p.p.* [CREEP].
crepuscular [krə'pʌskjulə], *a.* Crépusculaire.
crescendo [kri'ʃendou], *adv.* (*Mus.*) Crescendo.
crescent ['kresənt], *a.* Croissant.—*n.* Croissant, *m.*, demi-lune, *f.*; rue en demi-cercle, *f.* *The crescent moon,* le croissant de la lune *or* la lune à son croissant.
cress [kres], *n.* Cresson, *m.* *Water-cress;* cresson de fontaine. **cress-bed,** *n.* Cressonnière, *f.*
cresset ['kresət], *n.* Fanal, *m.*; torchère, *f.*
crest [krest], *n.* Cimier, *m.*; crête (of a cock or ridge), huppe (of a bird); aigrette (of a peacock), *f.*; (*Her.*) écusson, *m.*; armoiries, *f.pl.*—*v.t.* Orner d'un cimier; (*fig.*) surmonter. **crested,** *a.* Orné d'un cimier, à crête; huppé, à aigrette. **crestfallen,** *a.* Abattu, découragé, l'oreille basse. **crestless,** *a.* Sans crête, sans cimier; de basse naissance.
Cretan ['kri:tən], *a.* Crétois, -oise, Candiote(s).
Crete [kri:t]. La Crète, la Candie, *f.*
cretic ['kri:tik], *a.* (*Pros.*) Crétique.
cretin ['kretin, 'kri:tin], *n.* Crétin, *m.* **cretinism,** *n.* Crétinisme, *m.* **cretinize,** *v.t.* Crétiniser. **cretinous,** *a.* Crétineux, *m.*, crétineuse, *f.*
crevasse [krə'væs], *n.* Crevasse, *f.* (on a glacier).—*v.i.* Se crevasser.
crevice ['krevis], *n.* Crevasse, lézarde, fente, *f.* (in a wall); fissure, *f.* (in rock).—*v.t.* Crevasser, lézarder, fissurer.
crew (1) [kru:], *n.* Bande, troupe, *f.*; (*Naut.*) équipage, *m.*; (*Row.*) équipe, *f.* *Gun crew,* les servants, *m.pl. What a crew!* (*fig.*) Quelle engeance!
crew (2), *past* [CROW (2)].
crewel ['kru:əl], *n.* Laine à broder, *f.* **crewelwork,** *n.* Broderie, *f.*
crib [krib], *n.* Lit d'enfant, *m.*; crèche, mangeoire (in a cow-house etc.), *f.*; cabane, hutte, chaumière (cottage), *f.*; coffre, *m.*, huche (box), *f.*; (*colloq.*) traduction d'un auteur, *f.*; livre de corrigés, *m.* (*slang*) *To crack a crib,* cambrioler.—*v.t.* Chiper; copier (sur); *claquemurer.
crick [krik], *n.* Crampe, *f.*, effort, torticolis, *m.* —*v.t. To crick one's neck,* se donner le torticolis.
cricket ['krikit], *n.* Grillon, *m.*; cricket (game), *m.* (*colloq.*) *That's not cricket,* ça ne se fait pas, ce n'est pas loyal. **cricket-ball,** *n.* Balle de cricket, *f.* **cricketer,** *n.* Joueur de cricket, *m.* **cricket-field,** *n.* Terrain de cricket, *m.*
crier ['kraiə], *n.* Crieur; huissier (of a court), *m.*
Crimea [krai'mi:ə]. La Crimée, *f.*
Crimean [krai'mi:ən], *a.* Criméen, -éenne. *The Crimean War,* la guerre de Crimée.
crime [kraim], *n.* Crime, *m.*; criminalité, *f. To charge with a crime,* accuser d'un crime.
crimeless, *a.* Innocent. **criminal** ['kri

minl], *a.* and *n.* Criminel, *m.* **criminality** [-'næliti], *n.* Criminalité, *f.* **criminally,** *adv.* Criminellement. **criminate,** *v.t.* Incriminer. **crimination** [-'neiʃən], *n.* Incrimination, *f.*
criminative ['kriminətiv] *or* **criminatory,** *a.* Criminatoire. **criminologist,** *n.* Criminaliste, *m.* **criminology,** *n.* Criminologie, *f.*
crimp (1) [krimp], *v.t.* Gaufrer; friser, boucler (the hair). **crimper,** *n.* Gaufreur, friseur, *m.* **crimping,** *n.* Frisure, *f.*, crêpage; gaufrage, *m.* **crimping-iron,** *n.* Fer à friser *or* à gaufrer, *m.*
crimp (2) [krimp], *n.* Racoleur (for the army etc.), *m.*—*v.t.* Racoler.
crimson [krimzn], *a.* and *n.* Cramoisi; pourpre, *m.*—*v.t.* Teindre en cramoisi.—*v.i.* Devenir cramoisi.
crinal [krainl], *a.* Capillaire, de la chevelure.
cringe [krindʒ], *v.i.* Faire des courbettes; se tapir, s'humilier, ramper. *To cringe to,* faire le chien couchant auprès de.—*n.* Courbette, *f.*
cringing, *n.* Basse servilité, bassesse, *f.*—*a.* Craintif; obséquieux.
cringle [kringl], *n.* (*Naut.*) Patte de bouline, *f.*
crinkle [kriŋkl], *v.i.* Serpenter, aller en zigzag; se recourber.—*v.t.* Froisser; former en zigzag; rendre inégal.—*n.* Sinuosité, inégalité, *f.*; pli, *m.*; fronce, *f.* **crinkling,** *n.* Plissage, froissement, *m.* **crinkly,** *a.* Ratatiné.
crinoid ['krainɔid, 'krinoid], *n.* Crinoïde, *m.*
crinoline ['krinəli:n], *n.* Crinoline, *f.*
cripple [kripl], *n.* Boiteux, *m.*, boiteuse, *f.*; estropié, *m.*, estropiée, *f.*—*v.t.* Estropier; rendre perclus *or* infirme, (*fig.*) paralyser; mettre hors de combat; (*Naut.*) avarier. **crippled,** *a.* Estropié; perclus (de).
crisis ['kraisis], *n.* (*pl.* **crises**) Crise, *f.*; dénouement, *m.*
crisp [krisp], *a.* Cassant, croquant, croustillant (of pastry etc.); crépu, frisé (of hair); nerveux; tranchant.—*n.* (*Potato-*) *crisps,* frites, *f.pl.*—*v.t.* Friser (the hair etc.); crêper (stuffs).—*v.i.* Se crêper.
crisping-iron, *n.* Fer à friser, *m.*
crisply, *adv. To answer crisply,* répondre d'un ton tranchant.
crispness, *n.* Qualité de ce qui est croquant *or* cassant, *f.*; frisure, *f.*; netteté (of style etc.), *f.*
crispy, *a.* Crépu (hair); croquant, cassant (of pastry etc.); vif, frisquet (air).
criss-cross ['kriskrɔs], *a.* Entrecroisé.—*n.* Entrecroisement, *m.*—*v.t.* Entrecroiser.—*v.i.* S'entrecroiser.
criterion [krai'tiəriən], *n.* Critérium, *m.*
critic ['kritik], *n.* Critique; censeur, *m. Dramatic critic,* soiriste, *m.* **critical,** *a.* Critique, (*fig.*) difficile, délicat. *Critical affair,* affaire délicate, *f.* **critically,** *adv.* D'une manière critique; en critique, avec soin. *Critically ill,* dangereusement malade.
criticalness, *n.* Caractère critique, *m.*, délicatesse d'appréciation, *f.*
criticism ['kritisizm], *n.* Critique, appréciation, censure, *f.*
criticizable [kriti'saizəbl], *a.* Critiquable.
criticize ['kritisaiz], *v.t.* Critiquer, faire la critique de, censurer.—*v.i.* Faire de la critique.
critique [kri'ti:k], *n.* Critique, *f.*

croak [krouk], *v.i.* Coasser (of frogs); croasser (of rooks); (*fig.*) gronder, grogner, (*slang*) crever, claquer (to die).—*n.* Coassement (of frogs); croassement (of rooks); (*fig.*) grognement, *m.* **croaker,** *n.* Grognon; (*fig.*) faiseur de jérémiades, pessimiste, *m.* **croaky,** *a.* Enroué, rauque.

Croatia [krou'eiʃə]. La Croatie, *f.* **Croatian,** *a.* and *n.* Croate; le croate, *m.* (language).

croceate ['krousiət] or **croceous,** *a.* Safrané, jaune safran.

crochet ['krouʃei], *n.* Ouvrage au crochet, *m.* —*v.t., v.i.* Broder au crochet.

crock [krɔk], *n.* Cruche, *f.*; pot de terre, *m.* (*fam.*) Old crock, vieux clou, tacot (bicycle, car, etc.); vieux débris, croulant (person), *m.* —*v.t.* To crock one's leg, s'abîmer la jambe. **crockery** or **crockery-ware,** *n.* Faïence, vaisselle, *f.*

crocodile ['krɔkədail], *n.* Crocodile, *m.*; (*fig.*) procession, *f.* Crocodile tears, larmes de crocodile, *f.pl.*

crocus ['kroukəs], *n.* Safran, crocus, *m.*; rouge d'Angleterre (powder), *m.*

Croesus ['kri:səs]. Crésus, *m.*

croft [krɔft], *n.* Petit clos, *m.*, petite ferme, *f.*; pré, *m.* **crofter,** *n.* Petit cultivateur, *m.*

cromlech ['krɔmlek], *n.* Cromlech, *m.*

cromorne [krə'mɔ:n], *n.* (*Mus.*) Cromorne, *m.*

crone [kroun], *n.* Vieille femme, vieille, *f.*

crony ['krouni], *n.* Vieux camarade; copain, *m.*, compère, *m.*, commère, *f.*

crook [kruk], *n.* Courbure; houlette (of a shepherd), *f.*; crosse (of a bishop), *f.*; (*fig.*) détour, *m.*; (*slang*) escroc, *m.* By hook or by crook, d'une manière ou d'une autre, par un moyen ou par un autre.—*v.t.* Courber; (*fig.*) pervertir, appliquer mal à propos.—*v.i.* Se courber. **crook-backed,** *a.* Bossu, *m.*, bossue, *f.*, voûté. **crook-kneed,** *a.* Bancal. **crook-neck,** *n.* (*Am.*) Gourde, calebasse, *f.*

crooked ['krukid], *a.* Courbé, crochu, tortueux; tortu (twisted); de travers; (*fig.*) tortueux; malhonnête; [krukt] (having a crook), à béquille. **crookedly,** *adv.* Tortueusement, de travers. **crookedness,** *n.* Nature tortueuse; difformité, *f.*; (*fig.*) travers, *m.*, perversité, *f.*

croon [kru:n], *v.i.* Chantonner, chanter à voix basse, fredonner.

crooner, *n.* Fredonneur, *m.*, -euse, *f.*, chanteur de charme, *m.*

crop [krɔp], *n.* Récolte, moisson; cueillette (of fruit), *f.*; jabot (of a bird), *m.*; coupe, *f.* (of hair). Eton crop, coiffure à la garçonne, *f.*; hunting-crop, fouet (de chasse), *m.*; neck and crop, entièrement, complètement; second crop, regain, *m.*—*v.t.* Tondre, couper; écourter (horses); brouter (of animals).—*v.i.* Donner une récolte. To crop out, (Geol.) affleurer; to crop up, se présenter, surgir. **crop-eared,** *a.* Essorillé, courtaud (of horses etc.). **cropper,** *n.* To come a cropper, faire une culbute, (*fam.*) se casser le nez, (*fig.*) faire fiasco. **cropping,** *n.* Action de couper; action de brouter; exploitation d'un champ, *f.* **cropping-out,** *n.* (Geol.) Affleurement, *m.*

crosier ['krouziə or 'krouzjə], *n.* Crosse (of a bishop), *f.* **crosiered,** *a.* Crossé.

cross [krɔs], *n.* Croix, *f.*; carrefour (of roads

etc.), *m.*; (*fig.*) revers, malheur, *m.*, traverse, contrariété, *f.*; croisement (of breeds), *m.* Criss-cross, croisé, en croix; sign of the cross, signe de la croix, *m.*; to bear one's cross, (*fig.*) porter sa croix.—*a.* En travers, de travers; fâcheux, contraire; maussade, de mauvaise humeur, vexé, fâché. Cross answer, réponse de travers, *f.*; cross woman, femme de mauvaise humeur, *f.*

v.t.—Croiser; marquer d'une croix, faire une croix à; barrer (a cheque); (*fig.*) franchir; contrarier, contrecarrer. To cross again, repasser; to cross a threshold, franchir un seuil; to cross each other, se croiser, s'entrecroiser; to cross off or out, effacer, rayer, biffer; to cross one's mind, se présenter à l'esprit; to cross oneself, faire le signe de la croix, se signer; to cross over (sea, river), traverser, passer.

v.i.—Être mis en travers; faire la traversée; se croiser (of letters).—*prep.* À travers.

cross-action, *n.* Procès en reconvention, *m.* **cross-armed,** *a.* Les bras croisés. **cross-arrow,** *n.* Carreau, *m.* **crossbar,** *n.* Traverse; (*Ftb.*) barre de but, *f.* **cross-beam,** *n.* Traverse, *f.* **cross-bearer,** *n.* Porte-croix, *m.* **cross-bencher,** *n.* Membre du Centre, *m.* **cross-bones,** *n.pl.* Os en croix, *m.pl.* Skull and cross-bones (on flag), tête de mort et tibias. **crossbow,** *n.* Arbalète, *f.* **crossbow-man,** *n.* Arbalétrier, *m.* **cross-breed,** *n.* Race croisée, *f.*; métis, *m.*, -isse, *f.*—*v.t.* Croiser. **cross-breeding,** *n.* Croisement, *m.* **cross-bun,** *n.* Petit pain marqué d'une croix (fait pour le Vendredi-Saint), *m.* **cross-check,** *n.* Recoupement, *m.*—*v.t.* Recouper, faire des recoupements. **cross-country,** *a.* À travers champs. (Racing) Cross-country running, cross, *m.* **cross-current,** *n.* Renvoi de courant, *m.* **cross-cut,** *v.t.* Couper en travers, de biais. **cross-examination,** *n.* Contre-interrogatoire, *m.* **cross-examine,** *v.t.* Interroger; (*Law*) contre-interroger. **cross-eyed,** *a.* Affecté de strabisme, louche. **cross-fire,** *n.* Feu croisé, *m.* **cross-grained,** *a.* Aux fibres irrégulières (of wood); (*fig.*) revêche, acariâtre. To be cross-grained, avoir l'esprit à rebours. **cross-hatch,** *v.t.* (*Engr.*) Contre-hacher. **cross-hatching,** *n.* Contre-hachure, *f.* **crossing,** *n.* Passage d'un trottoir à l'autre (of streets), *m.*; traversée (by sea), *f.*; passage; carrefour, croisement (of streets); croisement (of animals); (*fig.*) travers, *m.*, contrariété, *f.* **cross-jack,** *n.* Voile barrée, fortune (in a sloop), *f.* **cross-keys,** *n.* Clefs en sautoir, *f.pl.* **cross-legged,** *a.* Les jambes croisées. **crosslet,** *n.* (*Her.*) Croisette, *f.* **crossly,** *adv.* En travers, de travers; avec mauvaise humeur; contrairement. **crossness,** *n.* Mauvaise humeur, méchanceté, *f.* **cross-patch,** *n.* Grognon, *m.* **cross-path,** *n.* Chemin de traverse, *m.* **cross-piece,** *n.* Traverse, entretoise, *f.* **cross-purpose,** *n.* Opposition, contradiction, *f.*, malentendu, *m.* To be at cross-purposes, se contrecarrer. **cross-question,** *v.t.* [CROSS-EXAMINE].—*n.* Contre-examen, *m.* **cross-reference,** *n.* Renvoi, *m.*—*v.t.* Établir les renvois de (book). **cross-road,** *n.* Chemin de traverse, *m.* **cross-roads,** *n.pl.* Carrefour, *m.* **cross-section,** *n.* Coupe en travers, *f.*; (*Geom.*)

section droite, *f.*; (*fig.*) échantillonnage, *m.*
cross-shaped, *a.* En forme de croix, cruciforme. **cross-summons,** *n.* Contre-
citation, *f.* **cross-talk,** *n.* Répliques, *f.pl.*;
interférence (entre circuits téléphoniques), *f.*
cross-trees, *n.pl.* (*Naut.*) Barres, *f.pl.* **cross-
voting,** *n.* Votes éparpillés, *m.pl.* **cross-
wind,** *n.* Vent contraire, *m.* **crossways** or
crosswise, *adv.* En travers; en croix, en
forme de croix, en sautoir. **cross-word
(puzzle),** *n.* Mots croisés, *m.pl.*
crotch [krɔtʃ], *n.* Fourche (of tree), *f.*; fourchet, *m.* (of trousers).
crotchet [′krɔtʃit], *n.* Lubie, *f.*, caprice, *m.*,
boutade, marotte; (*Mus.*) noire, *f.* **crotchety,**
a. Sujet aux lubies, capricieux, d'humeur
difficile.
croton [′kroutən], *n.* (*Bot.*) Croton, *m.*
crouch [krautʃ], *v.i.* Se tapir, se blottir; (*fig.*)
faire le chien couchant (auprès de). **crouching,** *a.* Accroupi, tapi.
croup (1) [kru:p], *n.* Croupe (of animals), *f.*;
croupion (of birds), *m.*
croup (2) [kru:p], *n.* (*Path.*) Croup, *m.*
croupier [′kru:piə], *n.* Croupier, *m.*
crow (1) [krou], *n.* Corneille, *f.* *As the crow
flies,* à vol d'oiseau; *to have a crow to pluck
with someone,* avoir maille à partir avec
quelqu'un. **crow-bar,** *n.* Pince, *f.*; levier, *m.*
crowfoot or **crow's-foot,** *n.* (*Naut.*)
Araignée, *f.*; patte d'oie, *f.* (near the eye);
(*Mil.*) chausse-trappe, *f.*; (*Bot.*) bouton d'or,
m. **crow-keeper** or **-scarer,** *n.* Épouvantail, *m.* **crow's nest,** *n.* (*Naut.*) Hune, *f.*
crow (2) [krou], *v.i.* (*past* **crew, crowed,** *p.p.*
crowed) Chanter (of cocks). *To crow over,*
chanter victoire sur.—*n.* Chant du coq, *m.*
crowd [kraud], *n.* Foule, cohue, *f.*, rassemblement, *m.* *The crowd,* (*Theat.*) les figurants,
m.pl.—*v.t.* Serrer, encombrer; presser. *To
be crowded with,* regorger de; *to crowd sail,*
forcer de voiles, faire force de voiles; *to crowd
with,* remplir de.—*v.i.* Se presser en foule, se
serrer. *To crowd in,* arriver en foule; *to
crowd out,* sortir en foule; *to crowd round,* se
presser, entourer en foule. **crowded,** *a.*
Serré; encombré, bondé (de).
crown [kraun], *n.* Couronne, *f.*; crête, *f.*,
sommet; écu (piece of money), *m.*; collet (of
a cap etc.); fond (of a hat), *m.*; flèche (of an
anchor), *f.*; clef de voûte, *f.* (of an arch);
axe, *m.* (of road). *Crown prince,* prince
héritier, *m.*; *crown prosecutor,* procureur
général, *m.*; *on his coming to the crown,* à
son avènement au trône.—*v.t.* Couronner;
combler; (*Draughts*) damer. *To crown all,*
pour comble de malheur.
crown-colony, *n.* Colonie de la couronne,
f.
crowning, *n.* Couronnement; (*fig.*) comble,
accomplissement, *m.*—*a.* Dernier, final,
suprême. *As a crowning misfortune,* pour
comble de malheur.
crown-land, *n.* Domaine de la couronne, *m.*
crown-wheel, *n.* (*Horol.*) Roue de champ;
(*Motor.*) couronne, *f.*
crown-work, *n.* (*Fort.*) Ouvrage à couronne,
m., couronne, *f.*
crozier [CROSIER].
crucial [′kru:ʃəl], *a.* Crucial; (*fig.*) définitif,
décisif. *Crucial test,* épreuve décisive, *f.*
crucible [′kru:sibl], *n.* Creuset, *m.*

cruciferous [kru:′sifərəs], *a.* and *n.* (*Bot.*)
Crucifère, *f.*
crucifix [′kru:sifiks], *n.* Crucifix, *m.* **crucifixion** [kru:si′fikʃən], *n.* Crucifiement, *m.*,
crucifixion, *f.* **cruciform,** *a.* Cruciforme.
crucify, *v.t.* Crucifier.
crude [kru:d], *a.* Cru; (*fig.*) informe, indigeste; grossier, imparfait, fruste (person,
manners). *Crude oil,* mazout, *m.*, huile
brute, *f.*; *crude salt,* gros sel, *m.* **crudely,**
adv. Crûment. **crudeness** or **crudity,** *n.*
Crudité, nature informe, *f.*
cruel [′kru:əl], *a.* Cruel. **cruelly,** *adv.*
Cruellement. **cruelty,** *n.* Cruauté, inhumanité, *f.*; acte inhumain, *m.*; (*Law*) mauvais
traitements, sévices, *m.pl.*
cruet [′kru:it], *n.* Burette, *f.* **cruet-stand,** *n.*
Huilier, *m.*, ménagère, *f.*
cruise [kru:z], *n.* Croisière, course, *f. On a
cruise,* en croisière.—*v.i.* Croiser, faire la
course; marauder (of taxi). **cruiser,** *n.*
Croiseur, *m.* *Battle-cruiser,* croiseur de
bataille, *m.*
crumb [krʌm], *n.* Mie; miette, *f. A crumb,*
une miette; *the crumb,* la mie; *a crumb of
comfort,* un brin de consolation.—*v.t.* Émietter; (fry in bread-crumbs) paner. **crumb-
brush,** *n.* Brosse à miettes, *f.* **crumb-tray,**
n. Ramasse-miettes, *m.*
crumby [′krʌmi], *a.* Qui a beaucoup de mie;
(*slang*) mauvais, moche, tocard.
crumble [krʌmbl], *v.t.* Émietter; (*fig.*) pulvériser, broyer, réduire en poussière.—*v.i.*
S'émietter; tomber en poussière. *To crumble
down,* tomber en ruine, s'écrouler, s'ébouler
(of earth). **crumbling,** *n.* Éboulement, *m.*;
émiettement, *m.*—*a.* Croulant, qui s'éboule.
crumbly, *a.* Friable.
crump [krʌmp], *a.* Cassant.—*n.* Coup violent,
m.; chute, *f.*
crumpet [′krʌmpit], *n.* Petite crêpe, crêpe
bretonne (for tea), *f.*
crumple [krʌmpl], *v.t.* Chiffonner, froisser.
—*v.i.* Se rider, se chiffonner, se ratatiner.
To crumple up (of persons), s'effondrer.
crunch [krʌnʃ], *v.t.* Croquer; broyer, écraser.
—*v.i.* (footsteps in snow, sand) Crisser,
s'écraser.—*n.* Coup de dent; grincement, *m.*;
crissement, *m.*
crupper [′krʌpə], *n.* Croupe; croupière, *f.*
crural [′kruərəl], *a.* (*Anat.*) Crural.
crusade [kru:′seid], *n.* Croisade, *f.*—*v.i.* To
crusade (against), lancer une croisade (contre).
crusader, *n.* Croisé, *m.*
*****cruse** [kru:z], *n.* Cruche, *f.*
crush [krʌʃ], *n.* Écrasement, choc, *m.*; foule,
cohue, *f.*; soirée, *f.* (*slang*) *To have a crush
on somebody,* avoir un béguin pour quelqu'un.
—*v.t.* Écraser, broyer; bocarder (to pound
or stamp); froisser (of a dress); (*fig.*) accabler,
opprimer, étouffer, anéantir. *To crush in,*
enfoncer; *to crush out,* exprimer; *to crush a
rebellion,* écraser or étouffer une rébellion.—
v.i. S'écraser. **crush-hat,** *n.* Claque, *m.*
crusher, *n.* Écraseur, concasseur, *m.* **crushing,** *n.* Broiement, écrasement, *m.*—*a.*
Écrasant; (*fig.*) foudroyant. **crushing-
machine,** *n.* Machine à broyer, *f.*; (*Metal.*)
bocard; (*Agric.*) concasseur, *m.*
crust [krʌst], *n.* Croûte, *f.*, croûton, *m.*; (*Geol.*)
écorce, *f.*, dépôt, *m.* (in wine). *To earn one's
crust,* gagner sa croûte.—*v.t.* Couvrir d'une

croûte, encroûter.—*v.i.* Se couvrir d'une croûte, s'encroûter. **crustily,** *adv.* D'une manière morose, d'un ton bourru, avec humeur. **crustiness,** *n.* Humeur maussade, mauvaise humeur, *f.* **crusty,** *a.* Qui a beaucoup de croûte, couvert d'une croûte; (*fig.*) bourru, morose, maussade, hargneux. **Crustacea** [krʌsˈteiʃiə], *n.pl.* Crustacés, *m.pl.* **crustaceous,** *a.* Crustacé.

crutch [krʌtʃ], *n.* Béquille, *f.*; fourche, *f.* (trousers). *On crutches,* avec des béquilles. —*v.t.* Étayer, étançonner.

crux [krʌks], *n.* Point difficile, nœud (d'une question), *m.*; crise, *f.*

cry [krai], *n.* Cri, *m. In full cry,* donnant de la voix (of hounds); *it's a far cry,* il y a loin; *the cries of London,* les cris de Londres; *to have a good cry,* pleurer tout son content.— *v.i.* Crier; s'écrier; pleurer (to weep). *To cry aloud,* élever la voix; *to cry bitterly,* pleurer à chaudes larmes; *to cry for,* réclamer; *to cry off,* quitter la partie, refuser de procéder; *to cry out,* s'écrier, se plaindre bruyamment; *to cry out against,* se récrier contre.—*v.t.* Crier. *To cry down,* décrier, blâmer; *to cry up,* exalter, prôner, vanter. **cry-baby,** *n.* Pleurard, pleurnicheur, *m.* **crying,** *n.* Cri, *m.,* cris, *m.pl.*; larmes (weeping), *f.pl.*—*a.* Criant; qui pleure. *A crying shame,* une vraie honte, un scandale.

crypt [kript], *n.* Crypte, *f.* **cryptic,** *a.* Secret, occulte; énigmatique. **cryptically,** *adv.* Secrètement, à mots couverts.

cryptogam, *n.* (*Bot.*) Cryptogame, *f.*

cryptogamous [kripˈtɔgəməs], *a.* Cryptogame.

cryptogram, *n.* Cryptogramme, *m.* **cryptography,** *n.* Cryptographie, *f.*

crystal [kristl], *n.* Cristal, *m.*; boule de cristal, *f.*—*a.* De cristal. *Crystal clear,* clair comme le jour. **crystal-gazer,** *n.* Voyant, *m.,* voyante, *f.* **crystal-gazing,** *n.* Divination par la boule de cristal, *f.* **crystal-set,** *n.* Poste à galène, *m.*

crystalline [ˈkristəlain], *a.* Cristallin, limpide. *Crystalline lens,* cristallin (of the eye), *m.*

crystallization [kristəlaiˈzeiʃən], *n.* Cristallisation, *f.*

crystallize [ˈkristəlaiz], *v.t.* Cristalliser.—*v.i.* Se cristalliser. *Crystallized fruits,* fruits glacés, fruits candis, *m.pl.*

crystallographic [kristəloˈgræfik], *a.* Cristallographique.

crystallography [kristəˈlɔgrəfi], *n.* Cristallographie, *f.*

crystalloid [ˈkristəlɔid], *a.* and *n.* Cristalloïde, *f.*

cub [kʌb], *n.* Petit (of a wild beast); ourson (of a bear); lionceau (of a lion); louveteau (of a wolf); renardeau (of a fox), *m.*; (*fig.*) blanc-bec; louveteau (boy-scout), *m. An unlicked cub,* un ours mal léché.—*v.i., v.t.* Mettre bas.

Cuba [ˈkjuːbə]. Cuba. **Cuban,** *a.* and *n.* Cubain, *m.,* cubaine, *f.*

cubage [ˈkjuːbidʒ] or **cubature,** *n.* Cubage, *m.*

cubby-hole [ˈkʌbiˈhoul], *n.* Retraite, cachette, *f.*; placard, *m.*; niche, *f.* (beside dash-board of car).

cube [kjuːb], *n.* Cube, *m. Cube root,* racine cubique, *f.*—*v.t.* Cuber. **cubic** or **cubical,** *a.* Cubique, cube. **cubiform,** *a.* Cubique, en cube. **cubism,** *n.* (*Paint.*) Cubisme, *m.*

cubeb [ˈkjuːbeb], *n.* (*Bot.*) Cubèbe, *m.*

cubicle [ˈkjuːbikl], *n.* Compartiment, box (de dortoir), *m.*; cabine, *f.* (in public baths; at tailor's for fitting).

cubit [ˈkjuːbit], *n.* Coudée, *f.* **cubital,** *a.* Cubital.

cuboid [ˈkjuːbɔid], *a.* and *n.* Cuboïde, *m.*

cuckold [ˈkʌkəld], *n.* Mari trompé, (*colloq.*) cocu, *m.*—*v.t.* Faire cocu, tromper. **cuckoldom, cuckoldry,** *n.* Cocuage, *m.*

cuckoo [ˈkuku:], *n.* Coucou, *m.*—*a.* (*fig.*) Niais; toqué. **cuckoo-clock,** *n.* Coucou, *m.* **cuckoo-flower,** *n.* Cresson des prés, *m.,* cardamine, *f.* **cuckoo-pint,** *n.* Pied-de-veau, arum, *m.* **cuckoo-spit,** *n.* Crachat de coucou, *m.*

cucullate [ˈkjuːkəleit] or **cucullated,** *a.* Encapuchonné.

cucumber [ˈkjuːkʌmbə], *n.* Concombre, *m. As cool as a cucumber,* avec un sang-froid imperturbable. **cucumber-frame,** *n.* Châssis à concombre, *m.*

cucurbit [kjuːˈkəːbit], *n.* Cucurbite, *f.* **cucurbitaceous** [-ˈteiʃəs], *a.* Cucurbitacé.

cud [kʌd], *n.* Bol alimentaire, *m.*; panse, *f.*; chique (de tabac), *f. To chew the cud,* ruminer.

cudbear [ˈkʌdbɛə], *n.* Teinture d'orseille, *f.*

cuddle [kʌdl], *v.t.* Serrer (tendrement) dans ses bras; étreindre.—*v.i.* S'étreindre (amoureusement); se blottir; se peloter. **cuddling,** *n.* Pelotage, *m.* **cuddlesome, cuddly,** *a.* Qu'on peut serrer dans ses bras.

cuddy [ˈkʌdi], *n.* (*Naut.*) Petite cabine, *f.,* rouf, *m.*; placard, buffet, *m.*

cudgel [ˈkʌdʒəl], *n.* Bâton, gourdin, *m.,* trique, *f. To take up the cudgels for,* prendre fait et cause pour.—*v.t.* Bâtonner. *To be cudgelled,* recevoir des coups de bâton; *to cudgel one's brains,* se casser la tête. **cudgel-proof,** *a.* À l'épreuve du gourdin. **cudgelling,** *n.* Coups de bâton, *m.pl.,* volée de coups, *f.*

cue [kjuː], *n.* Queue de billard; (*Theat.*) réplique, *f.,* rôle, *m.*; (*fig.*) avis, mot, indice, *m.*; veine (mood), *f. To give him the cue,* lui donner la réplique, lui faire la leçon; *to miss-cue,* faire fausse queue; *to take one's cue from,* se régler sur, prendre exemple sur. **cue-rack,** *n.* Porte-queues, *m.*

cuff [kʌf], *n.* Soufflet, calotter, battre.—*n.* Calotte, taloche, *f.*; manchette (of a sleeve), *f.*; parement (of a coat); poignet (of a gown), *m.*

cuff-link, *n.* Bouton de manchette, *m.*

cuirass [kwiˈræs], *n.* Cuirasse, *f.* **cuirassier** [kwiˈræsiə], *n.* Cuirassier, *m.*

culinary [ˈkjuːlinəri], *a.* De cuisine, culinaire.

cull [kʌl], *v.t.* Recueillir, cueillir; (*fig.*) choisir.

cullender [ˈkʌlində] [COLANDER].

culm [kʌlm], *n.* (*Bot.*) Chaume, *m.,* tige, *f.*; (*Min.*) (poussier d') anthracite, *m.*

culmiferous [kʌlˈmifərəs], *a.* (*Bot.*) Culmifère.

culminate [ˈkʌlmineit], *v.i.* Se terminer (en), finir (par); (*Astron.*) culminer, passer au méridien. **culmination** [-ˈneiʃən], *n.* Point culminant, apogée, *m.*; (*Astron.*) culmination, *f.*

culpability [kʌlpəˈbiliti] or **culpableness,** *n.* Culpabilité, *f.*

culpable ['kʌlpəbl], _a._ Coupable. **culpably,** _adv._ D'une manière coupable.

culprit ['kʌlprit], _n._ Accusé, _m._, accusée, _f._; inculpé, _m._, inculpée, _f._; coupable, _m._ or _f._

cult [kʌlt], _n._ Culte, _m._

cultivable ['kʌltivəbl], _a._ Cultivable. **cultivate,** _v.t._ Cultiver. **cultivation** [-'veiʃən], _n._ Culture, _f._ _Intensive cultivation,_ culture intensive; _under cultivation,_ en culture. **cultivator,** _n._ Cultivateur, extirpateur, _m._

cultriform ['kʌltrifɔ:m], _a._ Cultriforme. **cultrirostral,** _a._ (_Orn._) Cultrirostre.

cultural ['kʌltʃərəl], _a._ Agricole, cultural; culturel. _Cultural exchanges,_ échanges culturels, _m.pl._; _Cultural Attaché,_ attaché culturel, _m._

culture ['kʌltʃə], _n._ Culture, _f._; (_Biol._) culture; (_fig._) instruction, éducation, _f._, savoir, _m._ **cultured,** _a._ Cultivé. **culturist,** _n._ Cultivateur, éleveur; partisan de la culture générale (de l'esprit), _m._

culverin ['kʌlvərin], _n._ Couleuvrine, _f._

culvert ['kʌlvə:t], _n._ Ponceau, petit aqueduc, canal (d'amenée), _m._

cumber ['kʌmbə], _v.t._ Embarrasser, encombrer, gêner (de).—_n._ Embarras, obstacle, _m._ **cumbersome** or **cumbrous,** _a._ Embarrassant, gênant, difficile à manier. **cumbersomely,** _adv._ D'une manière embarrassante, lourdement, maladroitement. **cumbersomeness** or **cumbrousness,** _n._ Embarras, _m._, lourdeur, _f._

cumin ['kʌmin], _n._ Cumin, _m._

cummerbund [kʌmə'bʌnd], _n._ (Large) ceinture d'étoffe drapée, _f._

cumulate ['kju:mjuleit], _v.t._ Accumuler, cumuler. **cumulation** [-'leiʃən], _n._ Accumulation, _f._; cumul, _m._; (_Law_) cumulation, _f._

cumulative ['kju:mjulətiv], _a._ Cumulatif. **cumulatively,** _adv._ Cumulativement.

cumulus, _n._ Cumulus, _m._

cuneate ['kjuniit], _a._ En forme de coin, cunéaire. **cuneiform** ['kjuniifɔ:m], _a._ Cunéiforme.

cunning ['kʌniŋ], _n._ Finesse, ruse, astuce; adresse, _f._—_a._ Fin, rusé, adroit, astucieux. **cunningly,** _adv._ Avec finesse, adroitement, avec art, ingénieusement; par ruse. **cunningness,** _n._ Ruse, finesse, _f._

cup [kʌp], _n._ Tasse, coupe, _f._; gobelet, (_Paint._) godet, _m._; (_Bot. etc._) calice, _m._; (_Med._) ventouse, _f._—_v.t._ (_Med._) Appliquer des ventouses à, ventouser. _In one's cups,_ ivre, pris de vin; _it's just my cup of tea,_ voilà ce qu'il me faut; _it's not my cup of tea,_ ce n'est pas le genre de chose que j'apprécie; _it's another cup of tea,_ c'est une autre histoire; _the stirrup cup,_ le coup de l'étrier, _m._ **cup-and-ball,** _n._ Bilboquet, _m._ **cupbearer,** _n._ Échanson, _m._ **cup-final,** _n._ (_Ftb._) Finale de la coupe, _f._ **cupful,** _n._ Tasse, pleine tasse, _f._ **cup-tie,** _n._ (_Ftb._) Match de coupe, _m._

cupboard ['kʌbəd], _n._ Armoire (for clothes etc.), _f._; placard (in a wall), _m._ _Cupboard love,_ amour intéressé, _m._

cupel ['kju:pəl], _n._ Coupelle, _f._—_v.t._ Coupeller. **cupellation,** _n._ Coupellation, _f._

Cupid ['kju:pid], _n._ Cupidon, _m._

cupidity [kju'piditi], _n._ Cupidité, _f._

cupola ['kju:pələ], _n._ Coupole, _f._; (_Metal._) cubilot, _m._

cupping ['kʌpiŋ], _n._ Application de ventouses, _f._ **cupping-glass,** _n._ Ventouse, _f._

cupreous ['kju:priəs], _a._ Cuivreux.

cupro-nickel [kjuprou'nikl], _n._ Cupro-nickel, _m._

cupulate ['kju:pjulət], _a._ (_Bot._) Muni d'une cupule, cupulé. **cupule,** _n._ Cupule, _f._

cur [kə:], _n._ Chien bâtard, chien errant; chien hargneux, _m._; (_fig._) malotru, _m._, vilaine bête, _f._

curable ['kjuərəbl], _a._ Guérissable, curable. **curableness,** _n._ Curabilité, _f._

curaçao or **curaçoa** [kjuərə'sou], _n._ Curaçao (liqueur), _m._

curacy ['kjuərəsi], _n._ Vicariat, _m._

curare [kju'rɑ:ri] or ['kju:rəri], _n._ Curare, _m._ **curarize** ['kju:rəraiz], _v.t._ Curariser.

curate ['kjuərət], _n._ Vicaire, desservant, _m._

curative ['kjuərətiv], _a._ Curatif.—_n._ Remède, _m._

curator [kjuə'reitə], _n._ Administrateur; conservateur (of a museum); (_Law_) curateur, _m._ **curatorship,** _n._ (_Law_) Curatelle, _f._

curb [kə:b], _n._ Gourmette, _f._; (_fig._) frein, _m._; [KERB].—_v.t._ Mettre la gourmette à, gourmer; (_fig._) réprimer, contenir, brider; freiner. _One must curb one's instincts,_ il faut freiner ses passions. **curb-bit,** _n._ Mors à gourmette, _m._ **curbless,** _a._ Effréné, sans frein.

curcuma ['kə:kjumə], _n._ (_Bot._) Curcuma, _m._

curd [kə:d], _n._ Caillé, lait caillé, _m._; caillebotte; caillette, _f._—_v.t._ Cailler, figer. **curdle,** _v.t._ Cailler, figer.—_v.i._ Se cailler, se figer; (_poet._) se glacer. **curdling,** _n._ Caillage (lait), _m._ _A blood-curdling cry,_ un cri qui vous glace le sang. **curdy,** _a._ Caillé, figé.

cure [kjuə], _n._ Guérison, _f._; remède, _m._; (_Eccles._) cure, _f._ _Cure of souls,_ charge d'âmes, _f._; _to take a cure,_ faire une cure, suivre un traitement.—_v.t._ Guérir; sécher (hay etc.); mariner (fish etc.); saler (meat, skins, etc.); (_fig._) remédier à, corriger. **cureless,** _a._ Incurable. **curing,** _n._ Guérison, _f._ salaison, _f._

curfew ['kə:fju:], _n._ Couvre-feu, _m._ **curfew-bell,** _n._ Le couvre-feu, _m._

curio ['kjuəriou], _n._ Curiosité, _f._, objet rare, _m._; bibelot, _m._

curiosity [kjuəri'ɔsiti], _n._ Curiosité, _f._ _Dealer in curiosities,_ marchand de curiosités, antiquaire, _m._; _old curiosities,_ objets or bibelots anciens, _m.pl._; _out of curiosity,_ par curiosité. **curiosity-shop,** _n._ Magasin d'antiquités, _m._ **curious,** _a._ Curieux; (_fig._) remarquable, pas ordinaire, surprenant, singulier. **curiously,** _adv._ Curieusement. _Curiously enough,_ par une singulière coïncidence. **curiousness,** _n._ Curieux, _m._, singularité, _f._

curl [kə:l], _n._ Boucle (of hair); moue (of lips); spirale (of smoke); ondulation, _f._—_v.t._ Boucler, friser, (_fig._) faire onduler.—_v.i._ Friser; se replier, s'entortiller (of serpents etc.); s'entrelacer (of vines etc.); tourbillonner (of smoke); onduler, ondoyer, moutonner (of waves). _To curl up,_ s'enrouler, se pelotonner (of cats); se recroqueviller (of leaves etc.), se relever (of lip). **curl-cloud,** _n._ Cirrus, _m._ **curl-paper,** _n._ Papillote, _f._ **curled,** _a._ Crépu, frisé. **curling,** _n._ Frisure, ondulation (of waves), _f._; jeu de palets, _m._ **curling-irons** or **curling-tongs,** _n.pl._ Fer à friser, _m._ **curly,** _a._ Frisé, bouclé. _Curly-headed,_ à la tête bouclée, aux cheveux frisés.

curlew ['kəːljuː], *n.* (*Orn.*) Courlis, *m.*
curlew-jack, *n.* Turlu, *m.*
curmudgeon [kəːˈmʌdʒən], *n.* Ladre, pingre; bourru, *m.*
currant ['kʌrənt], *n.* Groseille (à grappes), *f.* *Black currant,* cassis, *m.*; (*dried*) *currants,* raisins de Corinthe, *m.pl.*; *red currants,* groseilles rouges, *f.pl.*; *red currant jelly,* gelée de groseilles, *f.*; *white currants,* groseilles blanches, *f.pl.* **currant-bush,** *n.* Groseillier, *m.*
currency ['kʌrənsi], *n.* Circulation (of money etc.), *f.*, cours; crédit, *m.*, vogue, *f.* *Foreign currency,* devises étrangères, *f.pl.*; *hard currency,* devises fortes, *f.*; *legal currency,* monnaie légale, *f.*; *metallic currency,* numéraire, *m.*; *paper currency,* papier-monnaie, *m.*; *to give currency to,* donner cours à.
current, *a.* Courant; actuel; admis, reçu. *Current events,* actualités, *f.pl.*; *current price,* prix courant, *m.*; *to be* or *pass current,* avoir cours, être admis.—*n.* Courant; cours d'eau, *m.* (*Elec.*) *Direct current,* courant continu.
currently, *adv.* Couramment; généralement. *It is currently reported that,* on prétend que, le bruit court que.
curricle ['kʌrikl], *n.* Cabriolet à deux roues et deux chevaux, *m.*
curriculum [kəˈrikjuləm], *n.* (*sch.*) Programme, plan d'études, *m.*
currier ['kʌriə], *n.* Corroyeur, *m.*
currish ['kʌriʃ], *a.* Hargneux, de chien. **currishly,** *adv.* D'une manière hargneuse *or* vile.
curry ['kʌri], *v.t.* Corroyer (leather); étriller (a horse); (*fig.*) rosser; (*Cook.*) apprêter au cari. *To curry favour with,* s'efforcer d'obtenir les bonnes grâces de. *Curried rice,* riz au cari, *m.*—*n.* Cari, *m.* **curry-comb,** *n.* Étrille, *f.* **curry-powder,** *n.* Cari, *m.*
curse [kəːs], *n.* Malédiction, imprécation, *f.*; (*fig.*) fléau, malheur, *m.*—*v.t.* Maudire; (*fig.*) affliger.—*v.i.* Proférer des malédictions, jurer; (*colloq.*) sacrer. *Curse (it)!* malédiction! *To be cursed with,* être affligé de, avoir pour son malheur; *to curse and swear,* jurer et blasphémer.
cursed ['kəːsid], *a.* Maudit, exécrable. **cursedly,** *adv.* Abominablement; terriblement. **cursing,** *n.* Malédiction, *f.*
*cursitor ['kəːsitə], *n.* Greffier de la Cour de Chancellerie, *m.*
cursive ['kəːsiv], *a.* Cursif.—*n.* Cursive, *f.*
cursor ['kəːsə], *n.* Curseur, *m.* (de règle à calcul.)
cursorily ['kəːsərili], *adv.* Rapidement, à la hâte, superficiellement. **cursoriness,** *n.* Rapidité, *f.*, caractère superficiel, *m.* (d'un examen, etc.). **cursory,** *a.* Rapide, superficiel; général. *At a cursory glance,* d'un regard superficiel.
curt [kəːt], *a.* Brusque, bref, sec; (*fig.*) cassant. **curtly,** *adv.* Brusquement, sèchement.
curtail [kəːˈteil], *v.t.* Retrancher, amoindrir, diminuer; raccourcir, abréger; restreindre (expenses); enlever (rights etc.). **curtailment,** *n.* Raccourcissement, *m.*, diminution, restriction, réduction, *f.*
curtain [kəːtn], *n.* Rideau, *m.*; (*Fort.*) courtine, *f.*; (*Theat.*) rideau, *m.*, toile, *f.* *The Iron Curtain,* le rideau de fer; *to raise, to lower*

the *curtain,* lever, baisser le rideau (de scène); *the curtain drops, falls,* le rideau tombe.—*v.t.* Garnir de rideaux; (*fig.*) envelopper, voiler. *To curtain off,* séparer par des rideaux. **curtain-call,** *n.* (*Theat.*) Rappel, *m.* *To take a curtain call,* être rappelé (devant le rideau). **curtain-hook,** *n.* Patère à embrasse, *f.* **curtain-lecture,** *n.* Semonce conjugale, *f.*, sermon d'alcôve, *m.* **curtain-raiser,** *n.* Lever de rideau, *m.* **curtain-rod,** *n.* Tringle à rideau, *f.*
curtsy, curtsey ['kəːtsi], *n.* Révérence.—*v.i.* Faire la révérence.
curule ['kjuəruːl], *a.* (*Rom. Ant.*) Curule. *Curule chair,* chaise curule.
curvation [kəːˈveiʃən], *n.* Courbure, *f.*
curvature ['kəːvətjə *or* 'kəːvətʃə], *n.* Courbure, sphéricité; (*Med.*) déviation, *f.*
curve [kəːv], *n.* Courbe, *f.*—*v.t.* Courber; cintrer.—*v.i.* Se courber, devenir courbe, décrire une courbe.
curvet [kəːˈvet], *v.i.* Faire des courbettes; sauter, gambader.—*n.* Courbette, *f.*
curvicaudate [kəːviˈkɔːdət], *a.* Curvicaude. **curvifoliate,** *a.* Curvifolié. **curvilinear,** *a.* Curviligne. **curvirostral,** *a.* Curvirostre.
cushat ['kuʃət], *n.* (*Sc.*) Pigeon ramier, *m.* (ringdove).
cushion ['kuʃən], *n.* Coussin; matelas (of a steam engine); coussinet (of a pump etc.), *m.*; (tampon) amortisseur, *m.*; (*Billiards*) bande, *f.* *Off the cushion,* par la bande.—*v.t.* Faire asseoir sur un coussin; garnir de coussins; amortir; (*Billiards*) acculer à la bande. **cushioned,** *a.* Garni de coussins; rembourré. **cushioning,** *n.* Amortissement (des chocs), *m.*
cushy ['kuʃi], *a.* (*slang*) Pépère, de tout repos.
cusp [kʌsp], *n.* Corne du croissant, pointe; (*Bot.*) cuspide, *f.*; (*Arch.*) lobe, *m.* **cuspid, cuspidate, cuspidated,** *or* **cuspidal,** *a.* Pointu, cuspidé, *f.*; (*Bot. etc.*) terminé en pointe; canine (tooth).
cuss [kʌs], *n.* (*slang*) Vaurien, chenapan, *m.* *He's a queer cuss,* c'est un drôle de type; *it isn't worth a tinker's cuss,* ça ne vaut pas un pet de lapin. **cussedness,** *n.* Perversité, méchanceté, *f.*, esprit de contradiction, *m.*
custard ['kʌstəd], *n.* Crème (au lait), *f.* *Baked custard,* œufs au lait, *m.pl.*, flan, *m.*; *caramel custard,* crème renversée, *f.*
custodian [kʌsˈtoudiən], *n.* Gardien; conservateur, *m.*
custody ['kʌstədi], *n.* Garde; prison, détention, *f.* *In close custody,* au secret; *in custody,* en état d'arrestation; *in safe custody,* en lieu sûr; *to commit to someone's custody,* confier à la garde de quelqu'un; *to give into custody,* faire arrêter.
custom ['kʌstəm], *n.* Coutume, habitude, *f.*, usage, *m.*; pratique (of a shop), *f.*; achalandage (of a store), *m.*; (*pl.*) douane, *f.*; droits (taxes), *m.pl.* (*U.S.*) *Custom-made suits,* complets (faits) sur mesure; *custom-built furniture,* meubles à façon, *m.pl.*; *to clear the customs,* passer (quelque chose) en douane. **custom-house,** *n.* Douane, *f.* *Custom-house bonds,* acquits à caution, *m.pl.* **customs-duty,** *n.* Droit de douane, *m.* **customs-officer,** *n.* Douanier, *m.* **customarily,** *adv.* Ordinairement, habituellement, d'habitude. **customariness,** *n.*

Habitude, fréquence, *f.* **customary,** *a.*
Ordinaire, d'usage, reçu, accoutumé; (*Law*)
coutumier.

customer, *n.* Chaland, client, *m.*; pratique, *f.*;
(*colloq.*) individu, particulier, *m.* *Queer
customer,* drôle de type, *m.*; *to know one's
customers,* connaître son monde; *ugly customer,* mauvais coucheur, *m.* [CUSS].

cut [kʌt], *n.* Coup (cut, blow, stroke, etc.),
m.; morceau (piece cut off), *m.*; coupure
(place cut open); coupe (of clothes, hair,
playing-cards); taille (shape); façon, tournure
(figure); (*Engr.*) gravure, planche, *f.*; chemin
de traverse (short way), *m.*; (*Ten. etc.*) coup
tranchant, *m.* *A good cut,* une bonne coupe
(of clothes); *crew cut,* cheveux (coupés) en
brosse, *m.*; *to be a cut above someone,* être
supérieur à quelqu'un; *to make a short cut,*
couper au plus court; *to draw cuts,* tirer à la
courte paille; *to take the short cut,* prendre le
raccourci; *to take one's cut,* prendre sa part
(of profits).

v.t.—(*past* and *p.p.* **cut**) Couper, trancher;
tailler (cut out); fendre (cleave); découper
(carve, cut out, etc.); rogner; se couper (the
nails); piquer, percer (to prick, hurt, etc.);
faire semblant de ne pas voir, rompre avec,
laisser (an acquaintance) là; faire (one's
teeth etc.). *To cut across,* couper en travers,
se mettre en travers (of plans); *to cut a
figure,* faire figure; *to cut a loaf,* entamer un
pain; *to cut along,* filer, jouer des jambes; *to
cut capers,* faire des siennes; *to cut down,*
abattre, rogner, abréger, réduire; *to cut it
fine,* réduire au minimum; arriver de justesse;
faire tout juste; *to cut off,* couper, trancher,
tailler, supprimer, retrancher, extirper, élider,
intercepter, empêcher; (*Av.*) *to cut off the
engine,* couper les gaz; *to cut off with a
shilling,* déshériter; *to cut one's stick,* filer,
déguerpir; *to cut one's teeth,* faire ses dents;
to cut one's way, se frayer un chemin; *to cut
out,* tailler, couper, découper, ôter, priver,
retrancher, (*fig.*) surpasser, éclipser; *to be
cut out for,* (*fig.*) être taillé pour; *to have one's
work cut out,* avoir du pain sur la planche;
to cut out work for, tailler de la besogne à;
to cut short, abréger, interrompre, couper la
parole à; *to cut small,* hacher, rapetisser; *to
cut (someone),* rompre avec, planter là, laisser
là, ne pas saluer, faire comme si on ne connaissait pas; *to cut to pieces,* écharper, tailler en
morceaux; *to cut to the heart,* fendre le cœur
à; *to cut up,* couper, écharper, disséquer,
découper, éreinter (of a reviewer); *to be cut
up,* (*fig.*) être blessé; avoir de la peine.—*v.i.*
Couper; se couper; percer (of the teeth). *That
cuts both ways,* c'est un argument à deux
tranchants; *to cut and come again,* revenir au
plat; *to cut away,* filer, se sauver, déguerpir.
a.—Coupé. *Cut and dried,* tout prêt, tout
fait.

cut-off, *n.* (*Steam-engine*) Fin de l'admission, *f.*
cut-out, *n.* Découpe, *f.*; (*Elec.*) coupe-
circuit, *m.* **cut-price,** *n.* Prix réduit, *m.*
cutpurse, *n.* Coupeur de bourse, *m.* **cutter,**
n. Coupeur; coupoir (tool); (*Naut.*) cutter,
cotre, *m.*; (*Tech.*) fraise, *f.* **cut-throat,** *n.*
Coupe-jarret, *m.* *Cut-throat place,* coupe-
gorge, *m.*

cutting [ˈkʌtiŋ], *n.* Incision; tranchée, excavation, voie encaissée; taille, rognure (piece);

coupe (of wood, cards, hair, etc.); (*Hort.*)
bouture, *f.*; (*Viniculture*) sarment, *m.* *Newspaper cutting,* coupure de journal, *f.*—*a.* Incisif; (*fig.*) piquant, tranchant, mordant.
cutting-out, *n.* Découpage, *m.*, coupe, *f.*
cutting-up, *n.* Dépècement, *m.*; (*fig.*)
éreintement (of a book), *m.*

cutaneous [kjuˈteiniəs], *a.* Cutané.

cutch [kʌtʃ], *n.* Cachou, *m.*

cute [kjuːt], *a.* Rusé, fin; (*Am.*) attirant,
délicieux (of child, girl); plaisant; ingénieux,
amusant (of thing, gadget).

cuticle [ˈkjuːtikl], *n.* Cuticule; (*Bot.*) pellicule,
f., épiderme, *m.* **cuticular,** *a.* Cuticuleux,
épidermique.

cutlass [ˈkʌtləs], *n.* (*Naut.*) Sabre d'abordage,
m.

cutler [ˈkʌtlə], *n.* Coutelier, *m.* **cutlery,** *n.*
Coutellerie, *f.*

cutlet [ˈkʌtlət], *n.* Côtelette; escalope, *f.*

cuttle [ˈkʌtl] or **cuttle-fish,** *n.* Seiche, *f.*
Cuttle-fish bone, os de sèche, *m.*

cutty [ˈkʌti], *a.* Court. *Cutty pipe,* brûle-
gueule, *m.*

cutwater [ˈkʌtwɔːtə], *n.* Taille-mer, *m.*

cwm [kuːm], *n.* (*Welsh*) Vallon; cirque, *m.*

cyanide [ˈsaiənaid], *n.* Cyanure, *m.*

Cyclades [ˈsiklədiːz]. Les Cyclades, *f.pl.*

cyclamen [ˈsikləmen], *n.* Cyclamen, *m.*

cycle [saikl], *n.* Cycle, *m.*; bicyclette (bicycle),
f., vélo, *m.* *Cycle of the moon,* cycle lunaire;
cycle of the sun, cycle solaire; *cycle-racing
track,* vélodrome, *m.*; *cycle cover,* culasse, *f.*;
the Arthurian cycle, le cycle d'Arthur, le
cycle breton.—*v.i.* Faire de la bicyclette, aller
à bicyclette.

cyclic [ˈsaiklik], *a.* Cyclique. **cycling,** *n.*
Cyclisme, *m.*—*a.* De cycliste. **cyclist,** *n.*
Cycliste. **cyclo-cross,** *n.* Cyclo-cross, *m.*
cyclograph, *n.* Cyclographe, *m.* **cycloid,**
n. Cycloïde, roulette, *f.* **cycloidal,** *a.*
Cycloïdal.

cyclometer [saiˈklɔmitə], *n.* Compteur
kilométrique, *m.*

cyclone [ˈsaikloun], *n.* Cyclone, *m.*

cyclonic [saiˈklɔnik], *a.* Cyclonal, cyclonique.

cyclopaedia [ENCYCLOPAEDIA].

cyclopean [saiklouˈpiːən, saiˈkloupiən], *a.*
Cyclopéen.

cyclops [ˈsaiklɔps], *n.* Cyclope, *m.*

cyclostyle [ˈsaikləstail], *n.* Autocopiste (à
stencils), *m.*

cyclotron [ˈsaiklɔtrɔn], *n.* Cyclotron, *m.*

cygnet [ˈsignət], *n.* Jeune cygne, *m.*

cylinder [ˈsilində], *n.* Cylindre; (*Tech.*) tambour; corps de pompe (of a pump), *m.*
cylinder-head, *n.* Culasse, *f.*

cylindrical [siˈlindrikl], *a.* Cylindrique.
cylindriform, *a.* Cylindriforme.
cylindroid [ˈsilindrɔid], *a.* Cylindroïde.

cyma [ˈsaimə], *n.* (*Arch.*) Cimaise, *f.*; (*Bot.*)
cyme, *f.*

cymatium [saiˈmætiəm], *n.* (*Arch.*) Cimaise, *f.*

cymbal [ˈsimbəl], *n.* Cymbale, *f.* **cymbalist**
or **cymbal-player,** *n.* Cymbalier, *m.*

Cymric [ˈkimrik], *a.* Kymrique, gallois.

cynic [ˈsinik], *n.* Cynique; railleur; sceptique.
cynical, *a.* Cynique. **cynically,** *adv.*
Cyniquement.

cynicism [ˈsinisizm], *n.* Cynisme, *m.*

cynocephalus [sainoˈsefələs], *n.* Cynocéphale,
m.

cynosure ['sainəʃuə], *n.* (*Astron.*) Cynosure, Petite Ourse, *f.*; (*fig.*) point d'attraction, point de mire, *m.* *The cynosure of all eyes*, le point de mire de tous les regards, *m.*

cypress ['saiprəs], *n.* Cyprès, *m.* **cypress-grove,** *n.* Cyprière, *f.* **cypress-tree,** *n.* Cyprès, *m.* **cypress-wood,** *n.* Cyprès, bois de cyprès, *m.*

Cyprian ['sipriən], *a.* and *n.* Cypriote.

cyprine ['saiprin], *n.* (*Ichth.*) Cyprin, *m.*

Cypriot ['sipriət], *n.* Cypriote.

cypripedium [sipri'pi:diəm], *n.* (*Bot.*) Cypripède, *m.*

Cyprus ['saiprəs]. Chypre, *f.*

Cyrenaic [sairə'neiik], *a.* and *n.* Cyrénaïque.

Cyrenaica [sairə'neiikə]. La Cyrénaïque, *f.*

Cyrillic [si'rilik], *a.* Cyrillien, cyrillique.

cyst [sist], *n.* (*Anat. etc.*) Kyste, *m.* **cystic,** *a.* Cystique.

cystitis [sis'taitis], *n.* (*Path.*) Cystite, *f.*

cystocele ['sistousi:l], *n.* Cystocèle, *f.*

Cythera [si'θiərə]. Cythère, *f.*

czar etc. [TSAR].

Czech [tʃek], *a.* and *n.* Tchèque. **Czecho-slovak,** *a.* and *n.* Tchécoslovaque. **Czecho-slovakia,** *n.* Tchécoslovaquie, *f.*

D

D, d [di:]. Quatrième lettre de l'alphabet, *m.*; (*Mus.*) ré, *m.*; *abbr. of denarius* = penny, *m.* 6*d.,* sixpence.

dab [dæb], *n.* Coup léger, *m.*, tape, *f.*; éclaboussure, tache, *f.*; (*slang*) expert, adepte; petit morceau (a bit), *m.*; (*Ichth.*) limande, *f.* *To be a dab (hand) at,* s'entendre à, être au fait de.—*v.t.* Toucher légèrement; éponger à petits coups.

dabble [dæbl], *v.t.* Humecter; éclabousser. —*v.i.* Barboter, patauger. *To dabble in,* se mêler de, faire (quelque chose) en amateur.

dabbler ['dæblə], *n.* Un qui se mêle de . . ., qui fait l'amateur.

dabchick ['dæbtʃik], *n.* (*Orn.*) Petit grèbe, castagneux, *m.*

dabster ['dæbstə], *n.* (*slang*) *He is a dabster at it,* c'est un malin, il s'y connaît.

dace [deis], *n.* (*Ichth.*) Vandoise, *f.*, dard, *m.*

dachshund ['dækshund], *n.* Basset allemand, *m.*

Dacia ['deiʃiə]. La Dacie, *f.*

dactyl ['dæktil], *n.* Dactyle, *m.*

dactylic [dæk'tilik], *a.* Dactylique.

dactylography [dækti'lɔgrəfi], *n.* Dactylo-graphie, *f.*

dad [dæd] *or* **daddy** ['dædi], *n.* Papa, *m.* **daddy-long-legs,** *n.* Tipule, *f.*, maringouin, *m.* (crane-fly); (*U.S.*) faucheux, *m.*, araignée des champs, *f.*

dado ['deidou], *n.* (*Arch.*) Dé, fût vertical; lambris (on walls), *m.*

Daedalus ['di:dələs]. Dédale, *m.*

daffodil ['dæfədil], *n.* Jonquille, *f.*, narcisse des prés, *m.* *Chequered daffodil,* fritillaire, *f.*

daft [dɑ:ft], *a.* Niais, sot, à moitié fou.

dagger ['dægə], *n.* Poignard, *m.*, dague, *f.*; (*Print.*) obèle, *m.* *At daggers drawn,* à couteaux tirés; *to look daggers at,* lancer des regards furibonds à.

daggle [dægl], *v.i.* Se crotter, se traîner dans la boue.—*v.t.* Crotter, traîner dans la boue.

daggle-tail [DRAGGLE].

dago ['deigou], *n.* (*pej.*) Italien, *m.*, -ienne, *f.*

daguerreotype [də'gerotaip], *n.* Daguerréo-type, *m.*—*v.t.* Daguerréotyper. **daguerreo-typism,** *n.* Daguerréotypie, *f.*

dahlia ['deiliə], *n.* (*Bot.*) Dahlia, *m.* *Blue dahlia,* (*fig.*) un merle blanc.

Dail Eireann [dɔil'ɛərən], *n.* (*Irish*) Parlement de la République Irlandaise, *m.*

daily ['deili], *a.* Journalier, quotidien; (*Astron.*) diurne.—*n.* Un (journal) quotidien, *m.*; femme de ménage, *f.*—*adv.* Journellement, tous les jours; de jour en jour.

daintily ['deintili], *adv.* Délicatement; avec délicatesse. **daintiness,** *n.* Délicatesse, *f.*, goût difficile, *m.* **dainty,** *a.* Friand; délicat, difficile.—*n.* Friandise, *f.*

dairy ['dɛəri], *n.* Laiterie, *f.* **dairy-butter,** *n.* Beurre fermier, *m.* **dairy-farm,** *n.* Ferme laitière, *f.* **dairy-farming,** *n.* L'industrie laitière, *f.* **dairy-man,** *n.* Nourrisseur; crémier, *m.* **dairy-produce,** *n.* Produits laitiers, *m.pl.*

dais [deis, 'deiis], *n.* Estrade, *f.*

daisy ['deizi], *n.* Marguerite, pâquerette, *f.* *To push up the daisies,* être mort et enterré. **daisy-chain,** *n.* Guirlande de marguerites, *f.* **daisy-cutter,** *n.* Cheval (*or* balle) qui rase le gazon.

dale [deil], *n.* Vallon, *m.*; vallée, *f.* *Up hill and down dale,* par monts et par vaux. **dalesman,** *n.* Habitant des vallées, *m.*

dalliance ['dæliəns], *n.* Folâtrerie, *f.*; badinage, *m.*; caresses, *f.pl.* **dally,** *v.i.* Folâtrer, perdre son temps; tarder, différer; (*fig.*) s'amuser, badiner (avec).

Dalmatia [dæl'meiʃiə]. La Dalmatie, *f.*

dam (1) [dæm], *n.* Mère (of animals), *f.*

dam (2) [dæm], *n.* Digue (of a canal), *f.*; barrage, batardeau (of a river), *m.*—*v.t.* Diguer, barrer, endiguer.

damage ['dæmidʒ], *n.* Dommage; tort, dégât; (*fig.*) préjudice, détriment, *m.*; (*Comm.*) avarie, *f.*; (*pl.*) (*Law*) dommages-intérêts, *m.pl.* *War damages,* dommages de guerre, *m.pl.*; (*fam.*) *what's the damage?* c'est combien?—*v.t.* Endommager; avarier (in transport); (*fig.*) faire tort à, nuire à, compromettre.—*v.i.* S'endommager. **damageable,** *a.* Pouvant s'endommager, avariable. **damaging,** *a.* Nuisible, préjudiciable (à).

damascene [dæmə'si:n], *n.* Prune de Damas, *f.*—*v.t.* Damasquiner. **damascening,** *n.* Damasquinerie, *f.*, damasquinage, *m.*; damasquinure (ornament), *f.*

damask ['dæməsk], *n.* Damas, damassé, *m.* *Damask rose,* rose incarnat, *f.* **damasking,** *n.* Damassure, *f.* **damask-worker,** *n.* Damasseur, *m.* **damassin,** *n.* Damassin, *m.*

dame [deim], *n.* (*poet.*) Dame; (*sch.*)*maîtresse d'école, *f.*; titre donné aux femmes membres de certains ordres anglais; comique travesti en femme dans une 'pantomime'. **dame-school,** *n.* École enfantine dirigée par une femme, *f.*

damn [dæm], *v.t.* Damner; (*fig.*) condamner, désapprouver; (*Theat.*) siffler (as a mark of disapprobation).—*int.* Sacrebleu! *Damn all,* rien du tout; *he is doing damn all,* il n'en fiche pas une datte.

damnable ['dæmnəbl], *a.* Damnable, maudit, odieux. **damnably,** *adv.* Odieusement, abominablement, diablement.

damnation [dæm'neiʃən], *n.* Damnation, *f.—int.* Zut! Sacrebleu!

damnatory ['dæmnətəri], *a.* Condamnatoire.

damned [dæmd], *a.* Damné, maudit, exécrable.

damning ['dæmiŋ], *a.* Écrasant (of evidence).

Damocles ['dæməkli:z]. Damoclès, *m.*

***damosel,** *n.* [DAMSEL].

damp [dæmp], *n.* Humidité; (*fig.*) tristesse, *f.,* froid, abattement, *m.* *Choke-damp,* mofette, *f.—a.* Humide; moite; (*fig.*) triste, abattu.— *v.t.* Rendre humide; humecter; étouffer (a fire); (*fig.*) décourager, abattre, refroidir. *To damp the spirits of,* décourager. **dampen,** *v.t.* Humecter; abattre, refroidir. **damper,** *n.* Éteignoir; registre (of a chimney); (*Piano*) étouffoir, *m.,* pédale douce, sourdine, *f.;* (*fig.*) rabat-joie, *m.* *To put a damper on,* jeter un voile de tristesse sur. **damping,** *n.* Humectation, *f.;* amortissement, *m.* **dampish,** *a.* Un peu humide, moite. **dampness,** *n.* Humidité, moiteur, *f.*

***damsel** ['dæmzəl], *n.* Jeune fille, demoiselle, *f.* **damsel-fly,** *n.* Demoiselle, *f.*

damson ['dæmzən], *n.* Prune de Damas, *f.* **damson-tree,** *n.* Prunier de Damas, *m.*

dance [dɑ:ns], *n.* Danse, *f.* (waltz etc.); soirée dansante, *f.,* bal, *m.* *Dance hostess,* entraîneuse, *f.; dance music,* musique de danse, *f.; dance of death,* danse macabre, *f.; to give a dance,* donner un bal; *to lead (someone) a dance,* en faire voir de toutes les couleurs (à quelqu'un); *to lead the dance,* mener la danse.—*v.i.* Danser.—*v.t.* Danser; faire danser. *To dance attendance,* faire le pied de grue, faire antichambre. **dance-hall,** *n.* Dancing, *m.* **dancer,** *n.* Danseur, *m.,* danseuse, *f.* **dancing,** *n.* Danse, *f.—a.* De danse. **dancing-master,** *n.* Maître de danse, *m.* **dancing-room,** *n.* Salle de danse, *f.* **dancing-school,** *n.* École de danse, *f.*

dandelion ['dændilaiən], *n.* (*Bot.*) Pissenlit, *m.* *Dandelion clock,* boule de pissenlit, *f.*

dander ['dændə], *n.* (*colloq.*) Irritation, mauvaise humeur, *f.* *He got my dander up,* il m'a exaspéré; *it got (raised) my dander up,* cela m'a fait monter la moutarde au nez.

dandify ['dændifai], *v.t.* Adoniser.

dandle [dændl], *v.t.* Dorloter, bercer. *I dandled him on my knee,* je l'ai fait sauter sur mes genoux.

dandruff ['dændrəf], *n.* Pellicules, *f.pl.*

dandy ['dændi], *n.* Dandy, élégant, petit-maître, gandin, *m.—a.* De dandy, élégant; (*Am.*) épatant, excellent. **dandyism,** *n.* Dandysme, *m.*

Dane [dein], *n.* Danois, *m.,* Danoise, *f.* *A great Dane,* un (chien) danois.

danewort ['deinwə:t], *n.* (*Bot.*) Hièble, yèble, sureau, *m.*

danger ['deindʒə], *n.* Danger, péril, *m.* *In danger of falling,* en danger de tomber. **dangerous,** *a.* Dangereux. *On dangerous ground* (*fig.*), sur un terrain brûlant. **dangerously,** *adv.* Dangereusement.

dangle [dæŋgl], *v.i.* Pendiller, brimbaler, baller. *To dangle after,* être à la traîne, être pendu aux basques (d'un homme), être pendu aux jupes (d'une femme).—*v.t.*

Laisser pendre, balancer, agiter. **dangler,** *n.* Godelureau, soupirant, *m.* **dangling,** *a.* Ballant.

Danish ['deiniʃ], *a.* Danois.—*n.* Danois (language), *m.*

dank [dæŋk], *a.* Humide et froid.

Danube ['dænju:b]. Le Danube, *m.*

Danubian [dæ'nju:biən], *a.* Danubien.

Danzig ['dæntsig]. Dantzig, *m.* **Danziger** ['dæntsigə], *a.* and *n.* Dantzikois (*fem.* -oise).

dap [dæp], *v.i.* Pêcher à la trembleuse.—*v.t.* Faire trembloter, faire sauter *or* rebondir.

daphne ['dæfni], *n.* (*Bot.*) Daphné, *m.*

dapper ['dæpə], *a.* Petit et vif, pimpant; soigné (of a man).

dapping ['dæpiŋ], *n.* Pêche à la trembleuse, *f.*

dapple [dæpl] *or* **dappled,** *a.* Pommelé, truité, miroité.—*v.t.* Tacheter, pommeler.— *v.i.* Se pommeler, se tacheter.—*n.* Tache; couleur panachée, *f.* **dapple-grey,** *n.* Gris pommelé, *m.*

dare [dɛə], *v.i.* (*3rd sing. pres.* he **dare**; *past* **durst** *or* **dared**) Oser. *How dare you!* vous avez cette audace! Quelle impudence! *I dare say that,* j'ose dire que, je parie que; *I dare say!* sans doute; je le crois bien; *to dare to do,* oser faire.—*v.t.* Défier, mettre au défi, braver; affronter, provoquer. *If you dare me to do it,* si vous me défiez de le faire. **dare-devil,** *a.* and *n.m.* Casse-cou, risque-tout, téméraire. **daring,** *a.* Audacieux, hardi, casse-cou.—*n.* Hardiesse, audace, *f.* **daringly,** *adv.* Audacieusement, hardiment.

dark [dɑ:k], *n.* Ténèbres, *f.pl.,* obscurité, *f.* *After dark,* à la nuit close; *to keep somebody in the dark,* laisser quelqu'un dans l'ignorance (de).—*a.* Obscur, sombre, noir; foncé (of tints); brun, basané (of the complexion); (*fig.*) caché, secret, mystérieux. *Dark horse,* cheval de course dont on ne connaît pas la forme, (*fig.*) personne dont on ne peut prévoir les réactions, mystère (of a man); *dark lantern,* lanterne sourde, *f.; the Dark Ages,* le haut moyen-âge, *m.; it is dark,* il fait sombre, il fait nuit; *it is growing dark,* il commence à faire nuit, la nuit tombe, le jour baisse; *to see only the dark side (of something),* voir tout en noir. **dark-room,** *n.* (*Phot.*) Chambre noire, *f.* **darken,** *v.t.* Obscurcir; brunir (the complexion); assombrir (colours in painting); (*fig.*) troubler. *I shall never darken his doors again,* je ne remettrai plus les pieds chez lui.—*v.i.* S'obscurcir; se rembrunir, s'assombrir. **darkening,** *n.* Obscurcissement, rembrunissement; assourdissement (of colours), assombrissement, *m.* **darkish,** *a.* Un peu sombre; noirâtre; un peu brun. **darkling,** *a.* (*Lit.*) Obscur, sombre, assombri; (*now rare*) dans l'obscurité. **darkly,** *adv.* Obscurément; sourdement; dans les ténèbres; d'un air menaçant; d'une façon mystérieuse. **darkness,** *n.* Obscurité, *f.,* ténèbres, *f.pl.,* teinte foncée (of colours), *f.,* teint brun (of the complexion), *m.* **darksome,** *a.* (*Lit.*) Sombre. **darky,** *n.* (*pej.*) Moricaud, nègre, *m.;* (*slang*) la nuit; lanterne sourde, *f.*

darling ['dɑ:liŋ], *n.* Chéri, *m.,* chérie, *f.,* mignon, *m.,* mignonne, *f.,* bien-aimé, *m.,* bien-aimée, *f.,* idole, *f.* *My darling,* (*colloq.*)

mon ange, mon chou, *m.*, ma chérie, *f.—a.* Chéri, favori, bien-aimé; adorable.
darn (1) [dɑːn], *adv.* and *int.* (*Am. slang*) (*euph.* for DAMN) *It was darn good of you,* c'était rudement chic de votre part.
darn (2) [dɑːn], *n.* Reprise, *f.—v.t.* Repriser, faire des reprises à. **darning,** *n.* Reprise, *f.* **darning-cotton,** *n.* Coton à repriser, *m.* **darning-needle,** *n.* Aiguille à repriser, *f.* **darning-wool,** *n.* Laine à repriser, *f.*
darnel [ˈdɑːnəl], *n.* (*Bot.*) Ivraie, *f.*
dart [dɑːt], *n.* Dard, trait, *m.*, fléchette, *f.*; élan soudain, *m.*; (*Dress.*) pince, *f.—v.t.* Darder, lancer (contre).—*v.i.* Se lancer, s'élancer (sur). *To dart off,* partir comme un trait; *to dart out,* surgir.
dartre [ˈdɑːtə], *n.* (*Med.*) Dartre, *f.*
Darwinian [dɑːˈwiniən], *a.* Darwinien.
Darwinism [ˈdɑːwinizm], *n.* Darwinisme, *m.* **Darwinist,** *n.* Darwiniste.
dash [dæʃ], *n.* Choc, coup, *m.*, attaque subite, *f.*, coup de main, *m.*; impétuosité, *f.*, entrain, cran, *m.*; élan soudain, *m.*; tiret, *m.*; trait (with a pen), *m.*; (*fig.*) soupçon, *m.*, teinte (small quantity), *f.*, grain, *m.*, pointe, *f.*, filet (of liquid), *m. A dash of vinegar,* un filet de vinaigre; *to cut a dash,* mener grand train, faire de l'effet; *to make a dash at,* se précipiter sur.—*v.t.* Jeter, précipiter; heurter, briser; déconcerter; abattre. *To dash away,* jeter, repousser; *to dash down,* précipiter, renverser; *to dash in pieces,* briser en morceaux; *to dash off,* ébaucher, esquisser, faire en un clin d'œil.—*v.i.* Se heurter, se briser; se précipiter, se lancer (contre); jaillir. *To dash off,* (*fig.*) filer, partir en vitesse; *to dash through,* s'élancer à travers.—*int.* Zut! **dash-board,** *n.* Garde-boue, *m.inv.*; (*Motor.*) tableau de bord, *m.* **dashing,** *a.* Fougueux, brillant, superbe; pimpant, élégant.
dastard [ˈdæstəd], *n.* Un lâche ignoble. **dastardly** or **dastard,** *a.* Lâche, d'une lâcheté ignoble. **dastardliness,** *n.* Lâcheté, *f.*, acte d'une lâcheté ignoble, *m.*
data [ˈdeitə], *n.pl.* Données, *f.pl.*
date (1) [deit], *n.* Date, échéance, *f.*, millésime (on coins etc.), *m.*; (*Am. pop.*) rendez-vous, *m. It's a date,* c'est entendu. *At long date,* à longue échéance; *blind date,* rendez-vous entre inconnus; *dated* or *under date of,* en date de, à la date de; *out of date,* suranné, vieilli, démodé, (*Comm.*) périmé (overdue); *up to date,* à la page, au goût du jour; à jour.—*v.t.* Dater. —*v.i.* Dater (de). *To date from* or *to date back to,* remonter à, dater de. **date-line,** *n.* Ligne de changement de date, *f.* **date-stamp,** *n.* Timbre dateur, *m.* **dateless,** *a.* Sans date. **dating,** *n.* Datation, *f.*
date (2) [deit], *n.* Datte (fruit), *f.* **date-palm,** *n.* Dattier, *m.*
dated [ˈdeitid], *a.* Daté, en date; démodé, suranné. *A letter dated April 2nd,* une lettre datée du 2 avril.
dative [ˈdeitiv], *a.* and *n.m.* Datif.
datum [ˈdeitəm], *n.* (*pl.* **data**) Donnée, *f.*
datura [dæˈtjuərə], *n.* (*Bot.*) Datura, *m.*
daub [dɔːb], *v.t.* Barbouiller, enduire, peinturlurer; (*fig.*) surcharger, déguiser (de).—*n.* Barbouillage, peinturlurage; (*Build.*) torchis, *m.*; (*Paint.*) croûte, *f.* **dauber,** *n.* Barbouilleur, *m.*
daughter [ˈdɔːtə], *n.* Fille, *f.* **daughter-in-law,**
n. Belle-fille, bru, *f.* **daughterly,** *a.* Filial. —*adv.* En fille, filialement.
daunt [dɔːnt], *v.t.* Effrayer, intimider, décourager. **dauntless,** *a.* Intrépide. **dauntlessly,** *adv.* Avec intrépidité. **dauntlessness,** *n.* Intrépidité, *f.*
dauphin [ˈdɔːfin], *n.* Dauphin, *m.* **dauphiness,** *n.* Dauphine, *f.*
davenport [ˈdævənpɔːt], *n.* (Petit) bureaupupitre, secrétaire, *m.*; (*Am.*) canapé, divan, *m.*
David [ˈdeivid]. David, *m.*
davit [ˈdævit], *n.* (*Naut.*) Bossoir, *m.*
Davy Jones [ˈdeiviˈdʒounz]. L'Océan, *m. Davy Jones's locker,* le fond de la mer.
Davy-lamp [ˈdeiviˈlæmp], *n.* Lampe de sûreté, *f.*
daw [dɔː], *n.* (*Orn.*) *Jack-daw,* choucas, *m.*
dawdle [dɔːdl], *v.i.* Flâner, muser, baguenauder.—*v.t. To dawdle away one's time,* gaspiller le temps. **dawdler,** *n.* Flâneur, musard, *m.*
dawn [dɔːn], *n.* Aube, *f.*, point du jour, *m.*; aurore, *f.—v.i.* Poindre, paraître, luire; (*fig.*) naître, percer. **dawning,** *a.* Naissant.—*n.* [DAWN].
day [dei], *n.* Jour, *m.*; journée (of work etc.); (*fig.*) bataille, victoire, *f.*; (*pl.*) temps, *m.*, jours, *m.pl. All day* (*long*), toute la journée; *any day,* n'importe quel jour; *at the present day,* de nos jours; *better days,* des jours meilleurs; *broad day,* plein jour; *by day,* le jour, de jour; *by the day,* à la journée; *day after day* or *day by day,* de jour en jour; *day in day out,* à longueur de journée; *day off,* jour de congé (of clerk); *day out,* jour de sortie (of servant); *every day,* tous les jours; *every second day* or *every other day,* tous les deux jours; *from day to day,* d'un jour à l'autre; *from this day,* à partir d'aujourd'hui; *good day,* bonjour; *in former days,* autrefois, jadis; *in the days of,* au temps de, du temps de; *in the days of old,* au temps jadis; *of former days,* d'autrefois; *of the present day,* actuel, contemporain; *sufficient unto the day is the evil thereof,* à chaque jour suffit sa peine; *the better the day the better the deed,* bon jour, bonne œuvre; *the day after,* le lendemain; *the day after tomorrow,* après-demain; *the day before,* la veille; *the day before that on which,* la veille du jour où; *the day before yesterday,* avant-hier; *the day of the month,* le quantième du mois; *these days,* de nos jours; *this day,* aujourd'hui, ce jour-ci; *this day,* or *today,* fortnight, d'aujourd'hui en quinze; *this day last year,* l'an dernier à pareil jour; *this day* or *today week,* d'aujourd'hui en huit; *those were the days,* c'était le bon temps; *to call it a day,* cesser, s'en tenir là; *to carry the day,* remporter la victoire, (*Law*) avoir gain de cause; *today,* aujourd'hui; *to have had its day,* avoir fait son temps; *two days after,* le surlendemain; *two days before,* l'avantveille, *f.*
day-boarder, *n.* Demi-pensionnaire, *m.* or *f.* **day-book,** *n.* Journal, *m.* **day-boy, daygirl,** *n.* Externe, *m.* or *f.* **day-break,** *n.* Point du jour, *m.*, aube, *f.* **day-dream,** *n.* Rêverie, *f.* **daylight,** *n.* Lumière du jour, *f. Broad daylight,* grand jour; *by daylight,* de jour; *in broad daylight,* au grand jour, en plein jour. **day-star,** *n.* Étoile du matin, *f.*; soleil,

m. **day's work,** *n.* Ouvrage d'un jour, *m.*; journée, *f. It's all in the day's work,* il faut s'attendre à ça, cela n'a rien d'anormal. **day-work,** *n.* Travail à la journée, *m.* **day-time,** *n.* Journée (from sunrise to sunset), *f.*

daze [deiz], *v.t.* Éblouir; hébéter.—*n.* (*Min.*) Mica, *m.*; étourdissement, *m.*, stupéfaction, *f. In a daze,* hébété.

dazzle [dæzl], *v.t.* Éblouir, aveugler.—*v.i.* S'éblouir. **dazzling,** *a.* Éblouissant. **dazzlingly,** *adv.* D'une manière éblouissante.

deacon ['di:kən], *n.* Diacre, *m.* **deaconess,** *n.* Diaconesse, *f.* **deaconry** or **deaconship,** *n.* Diaconat, *m.*

dead [ded], *a.* Mort; inanimé; inerte, insensible; éventé (of liquor); amorti, sans flamme (of fire); sourd (of sound); mat (of colours); debout (of the wind); plat (of a calm); au rebut (of letters). *Dead as a doornail* or *dead as mutton,* mort et bien mort; *dead beat,* éreinté, épuisé; *dead calm,* calme plat, *m.*; *dead coal,* charbon éteint, *m.*; *dead drunk,* ivre-mort; *dead ground,* (*Mil.*) terrain mort, *m.*; *dead letter,* lettre morte (inoperative), *f.,* lettre tombée au rebut, *f.*; *dead-letter office,* bureau des rebuts, *m.*; *dead lift,* (*fig.*) dernière extrémité, *f.,* état désespéré, *m.*; *dead loss,* perte sèche, *f.*; (*fig.*) (of person) crétin; *dead march,* marche funèbre, *f.*; *dead men,* (*fig.*) bouteilles vides, *f.pl.*; *dead reckoning,* (*Naut.*) route estimée, *f.*; *by dead reckoning,* à l'estime; *the Dead Sea,* la Mer Morte, *f.*; *dead sleep,* profond sommeil, *m.*; *dead shot,* fin tireur, *m.,* qui fait mouche à tout coup; *dead stop,* halte subite, *f.*; *dead time of the year* or *dead season,* morte-saison, *f.*; *dead wall,* muraille pleine or sans baies, *f.,* mur blanc, *m.*; *dead water,* remous du sillage, *m.*; *dead weight,* poids mort, *m.*; *money lying dead,* argent qui dort, *m.*; *to a dead certainty,* à coup sûr; *to come to a dead stop,* s'arrêter net; être acculé.—*n.* Cœur (winter), fort, *m. At dead of night,* dans le silence or au plus profond de la nuit. *The dead,* les morts, *m.pl.*

dead-beat, *n.* (*Am. slang*) Chevalier d'industrie, *m.* **dead-end,** *n.* Cul-de-sac, *m.*; impasse, *f.* **dead-eye,** *n.* (*Naut.*) Cap de mouton, *m.,* moque, *f.* **dead-house,** *n.* Morgue, *f.* **dead-lights,** *n.* Faux sabords, *m.pl.,* frise des sabords, *f.* **deadlock,** *n.* Situation sans issue; impasse, *f. To be at a deadlock,* être acculé or bloqué, se trouver dans une impasse. **dead-nettle,** *n.* Ortie blanche, *f.* **deadpan,** *a.* Sans expression.

deaden [dedn], *v.t.* Amortir; émousser (to blunt); éventer (liquor); matir, amatir (gold and silver); assourdir (sounds). **deadliness,** *n.* Nature mortelle, *f.* **deadly,** *a.* Mortel, à mort; comme la mort; acharné, meurtrier. *Deadly dull,* profondément triste, triste à pleurer, assommant; *deadly nightshade,* (*Bot.*) belladonne, *f.*; *in deadly earnest,* tout à fait sérieux.—*adv.* Mortellement. **deadness,** *n.* Mort, *f.*; (*fig.*) engourdissement, *m.,* stagnation, froideur, *f.*; évent (of liquor), *m.*

deaf [def], *a.* Sourd; (*fig.*) insensible. *Deaf and dumb,* sourd-muet; *deaf as a post,* sourd comme un pot; *to turn a deaf ear to,* rester sourd à, faire la sourde oreille à. **deaf-mute,** *n.* Sourd-muet, *m.,* sourde-muette, *f.*

deafen [defn], *v.t.* Rendre sourd, assourdir. **deafening,** *a.* Assourdissant. **deafly,** *adv.* Mal, imparfaitement (of hearing). **deafness,** *n.* Surdité, *f.*

deal [di:l], *n.* Quantité; (*Cards*) donne, *f.*; affaire, *f.,* marché, *m.*; bois blanc, bois (de sapin), *m. A good deal to do,* beaucoup or fort à faire; *a great deal, a good deal,* beaucoup (de); *by a good deal,* à beaucoup près; *it's a deal!* tope là! *it's your deal,* c'est à vous de donner (les cartes); *new deal,* nouvelle donne, *f.*; (*U.S.*) *the New Deal* (policy), le New Deal, *m.*; *to do a deal with someone,* conclure un marché avec quelqu'un.—*v.t.* (*past* and *p.p.* dealt [delt]) Distribuer; répartir; (*Cards*) donner; porter, asséner (blows).—*v.i.* Agir, traiter, en user (avec); se servir chez (a shop); (*Comm.*) faire le commerce, s'occuper, se mêler (de). *I know how to deal with that boy,* je sais comment il faut traiter ce garçon; *I'll deal with it,* j'en fais mon affaire; *to deal well by someone,* en user bien avec quelqu'un; *to deal with someone,* (*Comm.*) se fournir chez quelqu'un; *to deal with a matter,* connaître d'une question; *to have to deal with,* avoir affaire à.

dealer, *n.* Marchand; donneur (at cards). *Double dealer,* fourbe, *m.* **dealing,** *n.* Conduite, manière d'agir, *f.*; procédé, *m.,* affaire, *f.*; (*pl.*) affaires, relations, *f.pl.,* rapports, *m.pl. Double dealing,* duplicité, *f.*

dean [di:n], *n.* Doyen, *m.* **deanery,** *n.* Rang, *m.,* résidence, paroisse d'un doyen anglican. *f.* **deanship,** *n.* Doyenné; décanat; doyennat, *m.* (of professor).

dear [diə], *a.* Cher; précieux; (*fig.*) joli, gentil, charmant. *Dear Mr. Jones,* (in letters) cher Monsieur; *Dear Sir,* Monsieur. *To get dear, dearer,* renchérir; *to run for dear life,* se sauver à toutes jambes.—*adv.* Cher; chèrement, beaucoup.—*n.* Cher; cher ami, *m.*; chère; chère amie, *f.*—*int. Oh dear!* Mon Dieu! **dearly,** *adv.* Chèrement, cher; tendrement. **dearly-bought,** *a.* Payé cher, coûteux. **dearness,** *n.* Cherté; (*fig.*) tendresse, *f.*

dearth [də:θ], *n.* Disette, *f.*

death [deθ], *n.* Mort, *f.*; (*poet.*) trépas; (*Law*) décès, *m. At death's-door,* à deux doigts de la mort; *at the point of death,* à l'agonie; *it will be the death of me,* j'en mourrai; *that child will be the death of me,* cet enfant me fera mourir; *to beat to death,* assommer de coups; *to be frozen to death,* mourir de froid; *to be sick unto death,* être malade à en mourir; *to catch one's death,* attraper la (sa) mort; *to die a natural death,* mourir de sa belle mort; *to drink oneself to death,* se tuer à force de boire; *to frighten to death,* faire mourir de frayeur; *to put to death,* mettre à mort.

death-bed, *n.* Lit de mort, *m.* **death-blow,** *n.* Coup mortel; coup de grâce, *m.*; (*fig.*) ruine complète, *f.* **death-dealing,** *a.* Meurtrier. **death-duties,** *n.pl.* Droits de succession, *m.pl.* **deathless,** *a.* Impérissable. **death-like,** *a.* Semblable à la mort, de mort; cadavéreux. **deathly,** *a.* Comme la mort, de mort. **death-mask,** *n.* Masque mortuaire, *m.* **death's-head,** *n.* Tête de mort, *f.* **death-rate,** *n.* Taux de mortalité, *m.* **death-rattle,** *n.* Râle, *m.* **death-throes,** *n.* Agonie, *f. To be in one's death-throes,* agoniser.

death-trap, *n.* Endroit, croisement très dangereux, *m.* **death-warrant,** *n.* Ordre d'exécution, *m.* **death-watch,** *n.* Veillée (des morts); (*Ent.*) horloge de la mort, *f.* **death-wound,** *n.* Blessure mortelle, *f.*

deb [deb], *n.* (*fam.*) [DÉBUTANTE].

débâcle, debacle [dei-, di'bɑ:kl], *n.* Débâcle, *f.*

debar [di'bɑ:], *v.t.* Exclure, priver (de).

debark (1) [di:bɑ:k], *v.t.* Écorcer, arracher l'écorce (d'un arbre).

debark (2) [DISEMBARK].

debase [di'beis], *v.t.* Avilir, abaisser; abâtardir; (*Chem.*) adultérer, falsifier; (*Coin.*) altérer, déprécier. **debasement,** *n.* Abaissement, avilissement, *m.*, dégradation; (*Coin.*) altération, dépréciation, *f.* **debasing,** *a.* Avilissant.

debatable [di'beitəbl], *a.* Contestable, sujet à contestation. **debate,** *n.* Débats, *m.pl.*, réunion contradictoire, *f.*; discussion, délibération, dispute, *f.*—*v.t.* Débattre, discuter, disputer.—*v.i.* Délibérer (sur); contester (avec). *To debate with oneself,* délibérer. **debater,** *n.* Personne qui discute, *f.*; orateur parlementaire; argumentateur, *m.* **debating-society,** *n.* Association qui organise des réunions contradictoires, *f.*

debauch [di'bɔ:tʃ], *n.* Débauche, *f.*—*v.t.* Débaucher, corrompre, pervertir. **debauchee** [debɔ:'tʃi:], *n.* Libertin, débauché, *m.*

debaucher [di'bɔ:tʃə], *n.* Débaucheur, *m.*, débaucheuse, *f.*, corrupteur, *m.*, corruptrice, *f.* **debauchery,** *n.* Débauche, *f.*

debenture [di'bentʃə], *n.* Obligation, *f.*; certificat de drawback (at the customs), *m.* **debenture-holder,** *n.* Porteur d'obligations, *m.* **debenture-stock,** *n.* Obligations sans garantie, *f. pl.*

debilitate [di'biliteit], *v.t.* Débiliter, affaiblir, anémier.

debilitation [-'teiʃən], *n.* Débilitation, *f.*, affaiblissement, *m.*

debility, *n.* Débilité, faiblesse, *f.*

debit ['debit], *n.* Débit, *m. To carry to someone's debit,* porter au débit de quelqu'un.—*v.t.* Débiter (de), passer au débit (de). **debit-balance,** *n.* Solde débiteur, *m.* **debit-side,** *n.* Débit, doit, *m.*

debonair [debə'nɛə], *a.* Jovial; de caractère enjoué; élégant.

debouch [di'bu:ʃ], *v.i.* Déboucher. **debouchment,** *n.* Débouchement, *m.* **debouchure,** *n.* Embouchure, *f.*; col, *m.* (in mountainous country).

débris, debris ['debri:], *n.* Débris, *m.pl.*

debt [det], *n.* Dette, *f.*; dette, *f.*; créance, *f. Bad debt,* mauvaise créance, *f.; book debts,* actif, *m.; deeply in debt,* accablé de dettes; *I am in your debt,* je suis votre débiteur; *in debt,* endetté; *national debt,* dette publique; *out of debt out of danger,* qui ne doit rien ne craint rien; *to be in debt to,* être débiteur de; *to discharge a debt,* acquitter une dette; *to pay the debt of nature,* payer son tribut à la nature; *to run* or *get into debt,* faire des dettes, s'endetter.

debtor, *n.* Débiteur, *m.*, débitrice, *f.*; (*Book-keeping*) doit, *m. Debtor and creditor account,* compte par doit et avoir, *m.*

debunk [di'bʌŋk], *v.t.* (*fam.*) Jeter à bas de sa couchette; (*fig.*) renverser de son piédestal,

déboulonner (a person); **dégonfler** (propaganda).

débutante ['deibjutɑ:t], *n.* Débutante, *f.* (at court).

decade ['dekəd, 'dekeid], *n.* Décade, *f.*; décennie, *f.*

decadence ['dekədəns], *n.* Décadence, *f.* **decadent,** *a.* Décadent.

decagon ['dekəgən], *n.* Décagone, *m.*

decagram(me), *n.* Décagramme, *m.*

decagynous [də'kædʒinəs], *a.* (*Bot.*) Décagyne.

decahedron [dekə'hi:drən], *n.* Décaèdre, *m.*

decalcification [di:kælsifi'keiʃən], *n.* Décalcification, *f.* **decalcify,** *v.t.* Décalcifier.

decalitre ['dekəli:tə], *n.* Décalitre, *m.*

decalogue ['dekələg], *n.* Décalogue, *m.*

Decameron [di'kæmərən], *n.* Décaméron, *m.*

decametre ['dekəmi:tə], *n.* Décamètre, *m.*

decamp [di'kæmp], *v.i.* Décamper; lever le camp.

decanal [di'keinəl], *a.* Décanal; du côté du doyen, du côté S. du chœur.

decant [di'kænt], *v.t.* Décanter, verser.

decantation [di:kæn'teiʃən], *n.* Décantation, *f.*

decanter [di'kæntə], *n.* Carafe, *f. Small decanter,* carafon, *m.*

decapitate [di'kæpiteit], *v.t.* Décapiter.

decapitation [-'teiʃən], *n.* Décapitation, *f.*

decapod ['dekəpəd], *n.* Décapode, *m.*

decarbonize [di:'kɑ:bənaiz], *v.t.* Décarboniser. **decarburation,** *n.* Décarburation, *f.*

decarburize [di:'kɑ:bjuraiz], *v.t.* Décarburer.

decasyllabic [dekəsi'læbik], *a.* Décasyllabe, décasyllabique. **decasyllable** [-'siləbl], *n.* Décasyllabe, *m.*

decay [di'kei], *n.* Décadence, *f.*; déclin, délabrement, dépérissement, *m.*; pourriture, décomposition; ruine, *f. Decay of teeth,* dental decay, carie des dents, *f.; to fall into decay,* tomber en ruine *or* en décadence, se délabrer.—*v.i.* Tomber en décadence, se délabrer; dépérir (of plants); se gâter (of fruit); se carier (of teeth etc.); s'user (to wear out).

decease [di'si:s], *n.* (*Law*) Décès, *m.*—*v.i.* Décéder. **deceased,** *a.* Décédé, feu.—*n.* Défunt, *m.*, défunte, *f.*

deceit [di'si:t], *n.* Supercherie, fourberie, tromperie, ruse; (*Law*) fraude, *f.* **deceitful,** *a.* Trompeur; décevant (of things). **deceitfully,** *adv.* Frauduleusement. **deceitfulness,** *n.* Caractère trompeur, *m.*, fausseté, *f.*

deceivable [di'si:vəbl], *a.* Facile à tromper.

deceive, *v.t.* Décevoir; tromper, abuser. *To deceive oneself,* s'abuser, se tromper, se faire illusion. **deceiver,** *n.* Imposteur, trompeur, *m.*, trompeuse, *f.*

decelerate [di:'seləreit], *v.t.*, *v.i.* Ralentir. **deceleration,** *n.* Décélération, *f.,*; ralentissement, *m.*

December [di'sembə], *n.* Décembre, *m.*

decemvir [di'semvə:], *n.* Décemvir, *m.* **decemvirate,** *n.* Décemvirat, *m.*

decency ['di:sənsi], *n.* Bienséance, *f.*, convenances, *f.pl.*; décence (modesty), *f.*; honnêteté, *f.*

decennial [di'senjəl], *a.* Décennal.

decent ['di:sənt], *a.* Bienséant, décent, honnête; propre, convenable; aimable, gentil; (*colloq.*) passable, modéré. *A decent chap,* un chic type. **decently,** *adv.* Décemment; convenablement; passablement.

decentralization [di:sentrəlai′zeiʃən], *n.* Décentralisation, *f.*, régionalisme, *m.*

decentralize [di:′sentrəlaiz], *v.t.* Décentraliser.

deception [di′sepʃən], *n.* Tromperie, fraude, duperie, *f.* **deceptive,** *a.* Décevant, trompeur, mensonger, déceptif. **deceptively,** *adv.* Trompeusement. **deceptiveness,** *n.* Caractère trompeur, *m.*

decern [di′sɔːn], *v.t.* (*Sc. Law*) Décerner.

dechristianize [di:′kristiənaiz], *v.t.* Déchristianiser.

decibel [′desibel], *n.* Décibel, *m.*

decide [di′said], *v.t.* Décider; décider de.—*v.i.* Décider; se décider; se prononcer (pour). *To decide on something,* se décider à quelque chose; *to decide to do something,* se décider à, se résoudre à, décider de faire quelque chose. **decided,** *a.* Décidé, prononcé; positif, bien arrêté; ferme, résolu. **decidedly,** *adv.* Décidément; positivement, certainement, résolument.

deciduous [di′sidjuəs], *a.* (*Bot.*) À feuillage caduc.

decigram [′desigræm], *n.* Décigramme, *m.*

decilitre, *n.* Décilitre, *m.*

decimal [′desiməl], *a.* Décimal. *Decimal point,* virgule, *f.*—*n.* Décimale, fraction décimale, *f.* *Recurring decimal,* fraction périodique, *f.*; *to four places of decimals,* jusqu'à la quatrième décimale.

decimate [′desimeit], *v.t.* Décimer. **decimation,** *n.* Décimation, *f.*

decipher [di′saifə], *v.t.* Déchiffrer. **decipherable,** *a.* Déchiffrable. **decipherer,** *n.* Déchiffreur, *m.* **decipherment,** *n.* Déchiffrement, *m.*

decision [di′siʒən], *n.* Décision; (*fig.*) résolution, fermeté, *f.*; (*Law*) jugement, *m.* *To come to a decision,* prendre une décision, prendre un parti, se décider.

decisive [di′saisiv], *a.* Décisif; concluant. **decisively,** *adv.* Décisivement, d'une manière décisive. **decisiveness,** *n.* Caractère décisif, *m.*

decivilize [di:′sivilaiz], *v.t.* Déciviliser.

deck (1) [dek], *n.* (*Naut.*) Pont; tillac (merchant ships); plan (of aeroplane); tablier, *m.* (of bridge). *Between decks,* entrepont, *m.*; *fore-deck,* gaillard d'avant, *m.*; *hurricane-deck,* pont de manœuvre; *lower deck,* pont inférieur; *quarter-deck,* gaillard d'arrière, *m.*; *to clear the decks,* faire branle-bas.—*v.t.* Ponter, couvrir d'un pont. **deck-chair,** *n.* Transatlantique, *m.* **deck-hand,** *n.* Matelot de pont, *m.* **decker** (1), *n.* Vaisseau ponté, *m.* *Three-decker,* vaisseau à trois ponts, *m.* (*Motor.*) *Single-decker* (bus), autobus sans impériale, *m.*; *double-decker* (bus), autobus à impériale, *m.*; *three-decker* (sandwich), sandwich double (avec trois tranches de pain), *m.*

deck (2) [dek], *v.t.* Parer (de); orner, embellir. *To deck oneself out,* s'endimancher. **decker** (2), *n.* Personne qui pare, *f.* **decking,** *n.* Ornement, *m.*

declaim [di′kleim], *v.i., v.t.* Déclamer (contre). **declaimer,** *n.* Déclamateur, *m.*

declamation [deklə′meiʃən], *n.* Déclamation, *f.*

declamatory [di′klæmətəri], *a.* Déclamatoire.

declaration [deklə′reiʃən], *n.* Déclaration; proclamation, *f.*

declarative [di′klærətiv], *a.* Explicatif; (*Law*) déclaratif. **declaratory,** *a.* Déclaratif, énonciatif; (*Law*) déclaratoire.

declare [di′kleə], *v.t.* Déclarer; (*Cards*) appeler; (*fig.*) annoncer, affirmer, proclamer. *To declare oneself guilty,* s'avouer coupable; *to declare war on,* déclarer la guerre à.—*v.i.* Se déclarer, se prononcer (pour). *I declare!* ah, par exemple! ma parole! *to declare off,* quitter la partie, y renoncer, tirer son épingle du jeu.

declaredly [di′klɛəridli], *adv.* Formellement, ouvertement. **declarer,** *n.* Déclarateur, *m.* -trice, *f.*; (*Cards*) déclarant, *m.*, -ante, *f.*

declension [di′klenʃən], *n.* (*rare*) Décadence, *f.*; déclin, *m.*; (*Gram.*) déclinaison, *f.*

declinable [di′klainəbl], *a.* Déclinable.

declination [dekli′neiʃən], *n.* Déclin, *m.*; (*Astron.*) déclinaison, *f.*

decline [di′klain], *v.t.* Pencher, incliner; s'écarter; refuser, s'excuser; éviter; (*Gram.*) décliner.—*v.i.* Pencher; décliner; dévier, baisser (of price). *To decline from,* dévier de.—*n.* Déclin, *m.*, décadence; (*Path.*) maladie de langueur, phtisie, *f.* *To be in a decline, to go into a decline,* (*Med.*) être atteint de consomption.

declinometer [dekli′nɔmitə], *n.* Déclinomètre, *m.*

declivity [di′kliviti], *n.* Déclivité, pente, *f.*

declivous [di′klaivəs], *a.* En pente, déclive.

declutch [di:′klʌtʃ] *v.i.* Débrayer.

decoct [di′kɔkt], *v.t.* Faire bouillir; (*rare*) digérer. **decoction,** *n.* Décoction, *f.*

decode [di:′koud], *v.t.* Déchiffrer, traduire en clair. **decoding,** *n.* Déchiffrage, déchiffrement, *m.*

decoherer [di:ko′hiərə], *n.* (*Teleg.*) Décohéreur, *m.*

decoke [di′kouk], *v.t.* [DECARBONIZE].

decomplex [di:′kɔmpleks], *a.* Composé d'idées complexes.

decomposable [di:kəm′pouzəbl], *a.* Décomposable. **decompose,** *v.t.* Décomposer.—*v.i.* Se décomposer.

decomposite [di:′kɔmpəzait], *a.* Surcomposé. **decomposition** [di:kɔmpə′ziʃən], *n.* Décomposition, *f.*

decompress [di:kəm′pres], *v.t.* Décomprimer.

decompression [di:kəm′preʃən], *n.* Décompression, *f.* *Decompression chamber,* sas de décompression, *m.*

decontaminate [di:kən′tæmineit], *v.t.* Désinfecter.

decontrol [di:kən′troul], *v.t.* Détaxer, rendre libre de nouveau, libérer (prices, rents etc.).—*n.* Libération, *f.* (of prices, rents, etc.).

décor [dei′kɔ:], *n.* (*Theat.*) Décor, *m.*

decorate [′dekəreit], *v.t.* Décorer, orner, embellir. **decoration** [-′reiʃən], *n.* Décoration, *f.*; ornement, embellissement, *m.*; médaille, *f.* **decorative,** *a.* De décoration, décoratif. **decorator,** *n.* Décorateur, peintre en bâtiment, *m.*

decorous [′dekərəs *or* di:′kɔːrəs], *a.* Bienséant, convenable. **decorously,** *adv.* Convenablement, avec bienséance, comme il faut.

decorticate [di:′kɔ:tikeit], *v.t.* Décortiquer. **decortication,** *n.* Décortication, *f.*

decorum [di′kɔːrəm], *n.* Bienséance, *f.*, décorum, *m.*, convenances, *f.pl.*

decouple [di:'kʌpl], *v.t.* Découpler.
decoy [di'kɔi], *v.t.* Leurrer, attirer dans un piège, amorcer.—*n.* Leurre; piège, *m.*; oiseau de leurre, *m.* **decoy-duck,** *n.* Appeau, appelant, *m.*
decrease (1) ['di:kri:s], *n.* Décroissement, *m.*; décroissance, diminution; décrue (of water), *f.*; (*Comm.*) déchet, *m.*, baisse, *f.*
decrease (2) [di'kri:s], *v.i.* Diminuer; décroître.—*v.t.* Faire décroître, diminuer, amoindrir. **decreasingly,** *adv.* De moins en moins.
decree [di'kri:], *n.* Décret; (*Law*) arrêt, jugement, *m.*—*v.t.* Arrêter, décréter; décerner (decoration). *Decree nisi,* jugement provisoire, *m.*
decrement ['dekrimənt], *n.* Décroissement; décours, *m.*
decrepit [di'krepit], *a.* Décrépit, caduc, *m.*, caduque, *f.*; qui tombe en ruine.
decrepitate [di'krepiteit], *v.t.* Calciner (un sel), faire décrépiter.—*v.i.* Décrépiter.
decrepitation [dikrepi'teiʃən], *n.* Décrépitation, *f.*
decrepitude [di'krepitju:d], *n.* Décrépitude, vieillesse, *f.*
decrescent [di'kresənt], *a.* Décroissant.
decretal [di'kri:təl], *n.* Décrétale, *f.*; recueil de décrétales, *m.* **decretalist,** *n.* Décrétaliste, *m.*
decrial [di'kraiəl], *n.* (*rare*) Décri, dénigrement, *m.*
decry [di'krai], *v.t.* Décrier, dénigrer.
decubitus [di:'kju:bitəs], *n.* (*Path.*) Décubitus, *m.*; eschare, *f.*
decumbent [di'kʌmbənt], *a.* (*Bot.*) Couché.
decuple ['dekjupl], *a.* Décuple.—*v.t.* Décupler.
decurion [də'kjuəriən], *n.* Décurion, *m.*
decussate [di'kʌseit] or **decussated,** *a.* (*Bot.*) Décussé. **decussation,** *n.* Décussation, *f.*
dedicate ['dedikeit], *v.t.* Dédier (à); consacrer (à). **dedicated,** *a.* Dédié, consacré (à). **dedication** [-'keiʃən], *n.* Dédicace, *f.* **dedicator,** *n.* Dédicateur, *m.* **dedicatory** [-'keitəri], *a.* Dédicatoire.
deduce [di'dju:s], *v.t.* Déduire, inférer, conclure (de), tirer des conséquences (de). **deducible,** *a.* Qu'on peut déduire.
deduct [di'dʌkt], *v.t.* Déduire, rabattre, retrancher. **deduction,** *n.* Déduction; conséquence, conclusion; (*Comm.*) remise, *f.* **deductive,** *a.* Déductif. *Deductive reasoning,* raisonnement par déduction, *m.* **deductively,** *adv.* Par déduction.
deed [di:d], *n.* Action, *f.*; fait, exploit; (*Law*) titre, acte, contrat, *m.* *Private deed,* acte sous seing privé, *m.* **deed-box,** *n.* Coffret à documents, *m.* **deed-poll,** *n.* Acte unilatéral, *m.*
deem [di:m], *v.t.* Juger; penser, croire, estimer; considérer *or* regarder comme. *To be deemed,* être réputé, passer (pour); *to deem it prudent,* penser qu'il est prudent de; *to deem it right,* juger convenable de.
deep [di:p], *a.* Profond; extrême; foncé (of colour); grave (of sound); grand (of mourning); (*fig.*) rusé, fin. *Deep mourning,* grand deuil, *m.*; *deep sea lead,* grande sonde, *f.*; *this well is thirty feet deep,* ce puits a trente pieds de profondeur *or* est profond de trente pieds *or* a une profondeur de trente pieds; *to*

go deep into, traiter à fond; *to go off the deep end,* (*fig.*) s'emporter, s'emballer; *two or three deep,* (*Mil.*) sur deux ou sur trois rangs.—*n.* (*poet.*) Océan; abîme, *m.*
deep-drawn *or* **deep-fetched,** *a.* Long, profond (oï sighs). **deep-freeze,** *n.* Réfrigérateur à basse température, *m.* **deep-laid,** *a.* Ténébreux, secret. **deep-read,** *a.* Érudit. **deep-rooted,** *a.*, **deep-seated,** *a.* Profond, enraciné. **deep-toned,** *a.* Aux tons graves, *m.pl.*
deepen, *v.t.* Approfondir; assombrir, obscurcir; rendre (colour) plus foncé, rendre (sound) plus grave.—*v.i.* S'assombrir, devenir plus profond *or* plus foncé. **deepening,** *n.* Approfondissement, *m.* **deeply,** *adv.* Profondément; extrêmement; fortement (of colour); gravement (of sound); (*fig.*) avec ruse. **deepness,** *n.* Profondeur; (*fig.*) ruse, *f.*
deer [diə], *n. collect.* Les cervidés, *m.pl. Fallow deer,* daim, *m.*, daine, *f.*; *red deer,* cerf, *m.* **deerskin,** *n.* Peau de daim, *f. Deerskin shoes,* chaussures de daim, *f.pl.* **deer-stalker,** *n.* Chasseur de cerf à l'affût, *m.*; casquette de chasse, *f.* (spéciale pour cette chasse). **deer-stalking,** *n.* Chasse au cerf à l'affût, *f.*
deface [di'feis], *v.t.* Défigurer; mutiler; gâter; effacer (to erase); lacérer (to tear off). **defacement,** *n.* Dégradation; mutilation, *f.*
defalcate [di'fælkeit], *v.t.* Défalquer.—*v.i.* Détourner des fonds.
defalcation [di:fæl'keiʃən], *n.* Défalcation, *f.*; détournement de fonds, *m.*
defamation [defə'meiʃən], *n.* Diffamation, *f.*
defamatory [di'fæmətəri], *a.* Diffamatoire, diffamant.
defame [di'feim], *v.t.* Diffamer. **defamer,** *n.* Diffamateur, *m.*; Zoïle, *m.*
default [di'fɔ:lt], *n.* Défaut, manque, *m.*; (*Law*) contumace, *f. In default of,* à défaut de; *to suffer default,* (*Law*) faire défaut; *to win by default,* gagner par forfait.—*v.i.* Faire défaut, manquer (à). **defaulter,** *n.* Délinquant, *m.*, délinquante, *f.*; (*Mil.*) réfractaire; consigné; (*Law*) défaillant, *m.*, défaillante, *f.*; concussionnaire (of public money), *m.*
defeasance [di'fi:zəns], *n.* (*Law*) Abrogation, annulation; contre-lettre, *f.* **defeasible,** *a.* Annulable.
defeat [di'fi:t], *n.* Défaite, déroute, *f.*—*v.t.* Battre, mettre en déroute, vaincre; mettre en minorité (the Government); faire échouer; (*fig.*) annuler, déjouer, frustrer. *To defeat one's own ends,* aller contre ses propres intentions. **defeatism,** *n.* Défaitisme, *m.*
defeatist [di'fi:tist], *a.* and *n.* Défaitiste.
defecate ['defəkeit], *v.i, v.t.* Déféquer; purifier, clarifier. **defecation,** *n.* Défécation, *f.*
defect [di'fekt], *n.* Défaut, *m.*; défectuosité, imperfection, *f.*; (*Law*) vice, *m.* **defection,**—*n.* Défection; (*Relig.*) apostasie, *f.* **defective,** *a.* Défectueux, imparfait, en défaut, en mauvais état; (*Law*) vicieux; (*Gram.*) défectif. **defectively,** *adv.* Défectueusement. **defectiveness,** *n.* Imperfection, défectuosité, *f.*
defence [di'fens], *n.* Défense, *f. Civil Defence* (=*C.D.*), défense passive, *f.*; *in defence of,* pour la défense de. **defenceless,** *a.* Sans défense.

[127]

defend [di'fend], *v.t.* Défendre (de), protéger (contre). **defendable,** *a.* Défendable. **defendant,** *n.* Défendeur, *m.*, défenderesse, *f.*, accusé, *m.*, accusée, *f.* **defender,** *n.* Défenseur, *m.* **defensible,** *a.* Défendable; (*fig.*) soutenable, justifiable. **defensive,** *a.* Défensif.—*n.* Défensive, *f.* *On the defensive,* sur la défensive. **defensively,** *adv.* Défensivement.

defer [di'fə:], *v.t.* Différer, remettre, renvoyer; (*Mil.*) ajourner, mettre en sursis.—*v.i.* Différer; déférer (à). *To defer to someone's judgment,* en déférer à quelqu'un.

deference ['defərəns], *n.* Déférence, *f.* *Out of deference to,* par déférence pour; *with all due deference to you,* sauf votre respect.

deferent ['defərənt], *a.* Déférent. (*Anat.*) *Deferent duct,* canal déférent, *m.*

deferential [defə'renʃəl], *a.* De déférence, plein de déférence, respectueux. **deferentially,** *adv.* Avec déférence, avec respect.

deferment [di'fə:mənt], *n.* (*Mil.*) Sursis, *m.* (d'appel); ajournement, *m.*

defiance [di'faiəns], *n.* Défi, *m.* *In defiance of,* au mépris de; *to set at defiance,* défier, braver. **defiant,** *a.* De défi, provocant; défiant. *A defiant gesture,* un geste de défi, *m.* **defiantly,** *adv.* D'un air de défi.

deficiency [di'fiʃənsi], *n.* Défaut, *m.*; carence, insuffisance, imperfection, *f.*, manque, *m.*; faiblesse, *f.*; déficit, *m.* **deficient,** *a.* Défectueux; imparfait; insuffisant; faible. *He is deficient in those qualities,* ces qualités lui manquent; *mentally deficient,* à petite mentalité, déficient; *to be deficient in,* manquer de.

deficit ['defisit], *n.* Déficit, *m.*

defile (1) ['di:fail], *n.* Défilé, *m.*

defile (2) [di'fail], *v.i.* Défiler.

defile (3) [di'fail], *v.t.* Souiller; salir; déshonorer; déflorer, débaucher. **defilement,** *n.* Souillure, *f.*

definable [di'fainəbl], *a.* Définissable. **define,** *v.t.* Définir; déterminer.

definite ['definit], *a.* Déterminé; net, clair; arrêté; (*Gram.*) défini. *Give me a definite answer,* répondez-moi nettement. **definitely,** *adv.* Nettement, d'une manière déterminée. **definiteness,** *n.* Caractère déterminé, *m.*

definition [defi'niʃən], *n.* Définition; (*Opt.*) netteté, clarté, précision, *f.*

definitive [di'finitiv], *a.* Définitif.—*n.* Définitif, déterminatif, *m.* **definitively,** *adv.* Définitivement, en définitive. **definitiveness,** *n.* Caractère définitif, *m.*

deflagrate ['defləgreit], *v.t.* (*Chem.*) Faire flamber.—*v.i.* Flamber. **deflagration,** *n.* Déflagration, *f.*

deflate [di'fleit], *v.t.* Dégonfler. *Your tyres are deflated,* vos pneus sont dégonflés. **deflation,** *n.* Dégonflement, *m.*, érosion par le vent, *f.*; déflation monétaire, *f.* **deflationary,** *a.* De déflation.

deflect [di'flekt], *v.t.* Faire dévier, détourner. —*v.i.* Dévier; décliner (of the magnetic needle). **deflection,** *n.* Déviation; déclinaison (of the needle), *f.* **deflector,** *n.* (*Motor.*) Déflecteur, *m.*

defloration [di:flɔ'reiʃən], *n.* Défloration, *f.*

deflower [di'flauə], *v.t.* Déflorer; (*fig.*) flétrir.

defoliate [di:'foulieit], *v.t.* Défeuiller. **defoliation,** *n.* Défoliation, défeuillaison, *f.*

deforest [di:'fɔrist], *v.t.* Déboiser.

deforestation [di:fɔris'teiʃən], *n.* Déboisement, *m.*

deform [di'fɔ:m], *v.t.* Déformer, défigurer. **deformation,** *n.* Déformation, *f.*, défigurement, *m.* **deformed,** *a.* Difforme. **deformedly,** *adv.* D'une manière difforme. **deformity,** *n.* Difformité, infirmité; laideur, *f.*

defraud [di'frɔ:d], *v.t.* Frauder, faire du tort à; (*fig.*) priver (de). **defrauder,** *n.* Fraudeur, *m.*, fraudeuse, *f.*

defray [di'frei], *v.t.* Défrayer; payer; couvrir (to make up expenses etc.). ***defrayal,*** **defrayment,** *n.* Défrayement, remboursement, *m.*

deft [deft], *a.* Adroit, habile. **deftly,** *adv.* Adroitement, lestement. **deftness,** *n.* Adresse, habileté, *f.*

defunct [di'fʌŋkt], *a.* Défunt, trépassé, mort, décédé.—*n.* Défunt, *m.*, défunte, *f.*

defy [di'fai], *v.t.* Défier, braver, mettre au défi (quelqu'un de faire quelque chose). *To defy description,* défier toute description.

degeneracy [di'dʒenərəsi] or **degeneration** [didʒenə'reiʃən], *n.* Dégénérescence, *f.*; abâtardissement, *m.*

degenerate (1) [di'dʒenərət], *a.* and *n.* Dégénéré, abâtardi.

degenerate (2) [di'dʒenəreit], *v.i.* Dégénérer, s'abâtardir (dans *or* en).

deglutition [di:glu'tiʃən], *n.* Déglutition, *f.*

degradation [degrə'deiʃən], *n.* Dégradation, *f.*; (*fig.*) avilissement, *m.*

degrade [di'greid], *v.t.* Dégrader; (*fig.*) avilir, ravaler. **degraded,** *a.* Dégradé. **degrading,** *a.* Dégradant, avilissant. **degradingly,** *adv.* D'une manière avilissante.

degree [di'gri:], *n.* Degré, *m.*; marche, *f.*, échelon; rang, ordre, *m.*; qualité, condition; (*Arith.*) tranche, *f.*; (*Univ.*) grade, *m.* *By degrees,* par degrés, peu à peu, graduellement; *to a certain degree,* jusqu'à un certain point; *to a degree,* au plus haut point, à l'extrême; *to put a prisoner through the third degree,* passer un prisonnier à tabac; *to such a degree that,* à tel point que; *to take one's degree in law,* faire son droit; *university degree,* grade universitaire, *m.*

dehisce [di'his], *v.i.* (*Bot.*) S'ouvrir, être déhiscent. **dehiscence,** *n.* Déhiscence, *f.*

dehumanize [di:'hju:mənaiz], *v.t.* Déshumaniser.

dehydrate [di:'haidreit], *v.t.* Déshydrater. *Dehydrated eggs,* œufs en poudre, *m.pl.* **dehydration,** *n.* Déshydratation, *f.*

de-ice [di:'ais], *v.t.*, *v.i.* Dégivrer. **de-icer,** *n.* Dégivreur, *m.* **de-icing,** *n.* Dégivrage, *m.*

deicide ['di:isaid], *n.* Déicide, *m.*

deification [di:ifi'keiʃən], *n.* Déification, *f.* **deify,** *v.t.* Déifier.

deign [dein], *v.i.* Daigner.—*v.t.* Daigner, accorder.

deism ['di:izm], *n.* Déisme, *m.* **deist,** *n.* Déiste, *m.* **deistic** [di:'istik], *a.* De déiste.

deity ['di:iti], *n.* Divinité, *f.*; (*Myth.*) déité, *f.*

deject [di'dʒekt], *v.t.* Abattre, décourager. **dejected,** *a.* Abattu, triste, déprimé. **dejectedly,** *adv.* Tristement, d'un air abattu. **dejectedness** or **dejection,** *n.* Abattement, découragement, *m.*; (*Med.*) évacuation, déjection, *f.*

dekko ['dekou], *n.* (*slang*) Regard, coup d'œil, *m.*

delate [di'leit], *v.t.* Dénoncer.

delay [di'lei], *n.* Délai, retard, *m.*; (*pl.*) lenteurs, *f.pl.* *Without delay*, sans délai, tout de suite.—*v.t.* Différer, retarder; remettre, ajourner.—*v.i.* Tarder, s'arrêter. *Delayed action bomb*, bombe à retardement, *f.*

del credere [del'kredəri], *n.* (*Comm.*) Ducroire, *m.*

dele ['di:li], *n.* (*Print.*) Deleatur, *m.*—*v.t.* Marquer d'un deleatur.

delectable [di'lektəbl], *a.* Délectable.

delectability [dilektə'biliti], *n.* Délectabilité, *f.* **delectably**, *adv.* Délectablement, d'une manière délectable.

delectation [dilek'teiʃən], *n.* Délectation, *f.*

delegacy ['deligəsi], *n.* Délégation, *f.*, autorité déléguée, *f.*

delegate (1) ['deligit], *a.* Délégué.—*n.* Délégué, *m.*

delegate (2) ['deligeit], *v.t.* Déléguer. **delegation**, *n.* Délégation, *f.* **delegator**, *n.* (*Law*) Délégant, délégateur, *m.*

delete [də'li:t], *v.t.* Effacer, rayer, biffer.

deleterious [deli'tiəriəs], *a.* Délétère, nuisible.

deletion [di'li:ʃən], *n.* Rature, *f.*, grattage, *m.*; suppression (of words etc.), *f.*

delf [delf], *n.* Faïence de Delft, *f.*

deliberate (1) [di'libərit], *a.* Délibéré, prémédité, calculé; réfléchi, avisé.

deliberate (2) [də'libəreit], *v.i.* Délibérer. *To deliberate upon*, délibérer sur.

deliberately, *adv.* De propos délibéré, à dessein; lentement. **deliberateness**, *n.* Délibération, réflexion, circonspection, prudence, *f.*; lenteur prudente, *f.*; intention marquée, *f.* **deliberation** [-'reiʃən], *n.* Délibération, *f.*, débat, *m.*; réflexion, circonspection, *f.* **deliberative**, *a.* Délibératif; délibérant (of an assembly). **deliberatively**, *adv.* Par délibération.

delicacy ['delikəsi], *n.* Délicatesse; friandise (a dainty), *f.* **delicate**, *a.* Délicat. *Delicate feelings*, sentiments de délicatesse, *m.pl.* **delicately**, *adv.* Délicatement, avec délicatesse; (*fig.*) discrètement. **delicateness**, *n.* Délicatesse, *f.*

delicious [di'liʃəs], *a.* Délicieux. **deliciously**, *adv.* Délicieusement. **deliciousness**, *n.* Goût délicieux, *m.*; délices, *f.pl.*

delict ['di:likt], *n.* (*Law*) Délit, *m.*, offense, *f.* *Flagrant delict*, flagrant délit, *m.*

delight [di'lait], *n.* Délices, *f.pl.*, plaisir, *m.* *This garden is my delight*, ce jardin fait mes délices; *to the great delight of*, au grand plaisir de.—*v.t.* Plaire à, faire les délices de, réjouir, enchanter, charmer. *To be delighted to*, être enchanté de.—*v.i.* Se plaire. *To delight in*, se plaire à, se faire un plaisir de, trouver son bonheur à. **delightedly**, *adv.* Avec joie, avec enchantement. **delightful**, *a.* Délicieux; charmant (of a person); ravissant. **delightfulness**, *n.* Charme, *m.*, délices, *f.pl.*

delimit [di'limit], *v.t.* Délimiter. **delimitation**, *n.* Délimitation, *f.*

delineate [di'linieit], *v.t.* Esquisser, dessiner, tracer, peindre; (*fig.*) décrire. **delineation**, *n.* Délinéation; esquisse, peinture; (*fig.*) description, *f.* **delineator**, *n.* Dessinateur; peintre, *m.*

delinquency [di'liŋkwənsi], *n.* Délit, *m.*, faute, délinquance, *f.* *Juvenile delinquency*, délinquance juvénile, *f.* **delinquent**, *n.* Contrevenant, délinquant, *m.* *Juvenile delinquent*, jeune délinquant, *m.*

deliquesce [deli'kwes], *v.i.* Tomber en déliquescence. **deliquescence**, *n.* Déliquescence, *f.* **deliquescent**, *a.* Déliquescent.

deliquium [di'likwiəm], *n.* (*Chem.*) Deliquium, *m.*; (*Path.*) syncope, *f.*

delirious [di'liriəs], *a.* En délire, dans le délire; de délire; délirant. *To become delirious*, entrer en délire; *to be delirious*, avoir le délire, délirer. **deliriously**, *adv.* Frénétiquement. *Deliriously happy*, fou de joie. **deliriousness**, *n.* Délire, *m.* **delirium**, *n.* Délire; (*fig.*) transport de joie, *m.* *Delirium tremens*, delirium tremens, *m.*

delitescence [di:li'tesəns], *n.* Délitescence, *f.* **delitescent**, *a.* Délitescent.

deliver [di'livə], *v.t.* Délivrer, sauver; faire remettre, rendre, apporter, distribuer (letters etc.); remettre (a letter, a parcel, etc.); livrer (goods or a place); prononcer (a speech); (faire) accoucher (a woman). *To be delivered of a child*, accoucher d'un enfant; *to deliver a message*, remettre un message à; *to deliver from*, délivrer de, sauver de; *to deliver oneself up to*, se livrer à; *to deliver the goods*, livrer la marchandise; (*fig.*) tenir ses engagements; *to deliver up*, livrer, rendre. **deliverable**, *a.* (*Comm.*) Livrable. **deliverance**, *n.* Délivrance, *f.*; accouchement (of a woman), *m.* **deliverer**, *n.* Libérateur, *m.*, libératrice, *f.*, sauveur, *m.* **delivery**, *n.* Délivrance, remise, *f.*; débit, *m.*, diction (of a speech); livraison (of goods); distribution (of letters), *f.*; accouchement (of a woman), *m.* *Payment on delivery*, payement à la livraison, *m.*, livraison contre remboursement, *f.*; *sale for future delivery*, vente à terme, *f.* **delivery-van**, *n.* Camion de livraison, *m.*; camionnette, *f.*

dell [del], *n.* Vallon, *m.*

delouse [di:'laus], *v.t.* Ôter les poux de, épouiller.

Delphi ['delfai]. Delphes, *f.*

delphin ['delfin], *a.* Du Dauphin (de France).

delphinium [del'finiəm], *n.* Delphinium, *m.*, delphinette, *f.*

delta ['deltə], *n.* Delta, *m.*

deltoid ['deltoid], *a.* (*Anat.*) Deltoïde.

delude [di'lju:d], *v.t.* Tromper, abuser, duper. *To delude oneself*, se faire illusion, s'abuser. **deluder**, *n.* Trompeur, imposteur, *m.*

deluding, *a.* Mensonger, illusoire, trompeur.

deluge ['delju:dʒ], *n.* Déluge, *m.*—*v.t.* Inonder.

delusion [di'lju:ʒən], *n.* Illusion, erreur, *f.* *A fond delusion*, une douce illusion; *to labour under a delusion*, s'abuser, être dans l'erreur. **delusive** or **delusory**, *a.* Illusoire, trompeur. **delusiveness**, *n.* Caractère illusoire, *m.*

delve [delv], *v.t.*, *v.i.* Bêcher, creuser; (*fig.*) sonder, pénétrer. *To delve into one's pocket*, fouiller dans sa poche.

demagnetize [di:'mægnətaiz], *v.t.* Démagnétiser. **demagnetization** [-'zeiʃən], *n.* Démagnétisation, *f.*

demagogue ['deməgɔg], *n.* Démagogue, *m.*

demagogic [demə'gɔdʒik] or [-'gɔgik], *a.* Démagogique. **demagogy**, *n.* Démagogie, *f.*

*demain [DEMESNE].

demand [di'mɑːnd], *n.* Demande, réclamation, requête, *f. In full of all demands,* pour solde de tout compte; *in great demand,* très demandé, très recherché; *in little demand,* peu demandé; *on demand,* sur demande; *à vue, sur présentation; demand draft,* traite à vue, *f.; supply and demand,* l'offre et la demande, *f.—v.t.* Demander; réclamer; exiger, requérir. **demandable,** *a.* Exigible. **demandant,** *n.* (*Law*) Demandeur, *m.,* demanderesse, *f.* **demander,** *n.* Demandeur; preneur, acheteur, *m.*

demarcation [diːmɑː'keiʃən], *n.* Démarcation, *f. Line of demarcation,* ligne de démarcation, *f.*

dematerialize [diːmə'tiəriəlaiz], *v.t., v.i.* (Se) dématérialiser.

demean [di'miːn], *v.t.* *Conduire, comporter. *To demean oneself,* se comporter, se conduire; (*colloq.*) s'abaisser, se dégrader. **demeanour,** *n.* Conduite, *f.,* maintien, *m.;* tenue, *f.,* air, *m.*

dement [di'ment], *v.t.* Rendre fou. **demented,** *a.* Fou, dément.

demerit [diː'merit], *n.* Démérite, *m.*

demesne [di'miːn *or* -'mein], *n.* Domaine, *m.,* possession, *f.;* terres, *f.pl.,* propriété, *f.*

demi ['demi], *prep.* Demi, à demi. **demidevil,** *n.* Demi-démon, *m.* **demigod,** *n.* Demi-dieu, *m.* **demijohn,** *n.* Damejeanne, bonbonne, *f.*

demilitarization [diːmilitərai'zeiʃən], *n.* Démilitarisation, *f.* **demilitarize,** *v.t.* Démilitariser.

demilune ['demiluːn], *n.* (*Fort.*) Demi-lune, *f.*

demisable [di'maizəbl], *a.* (*Law*) Qui peut être légué *or* loué à bail. **demise,** *n.* Décès, *m.,* mort, *f.; (Law)* transmission de propriété par testament *or* bail, *f.—v.t.* Léguer; céder à bail.

demi-semiquaver ['demi'semi'kweivə], *n.* (*Mus.*) Triple croche, *f.*

*demiss [di'mis], *a.* Servile. **demission,** *n.* Démission, abdication, *f.;* *dégradation, *f.*

demister [diː'mistə], *n.* (*Motor.*) Appareil antibuée, *m.*

demit [di'mit], *v.i.* Démissionner.—*v.t. To demit office,* résigner ses fonctions.

demitone ['demitoun], *n.* Demi-ton, *m.*

demiurge ['demiə:dʒ], *n.* Démiurge, *m.*

demob (*fam.*) [DEMOBILIZATION].

demobilization ['diːmoubilai'zeiʃən], *n.* Démobilisation, *f.* **demobilize** [-'moubilaiz], *v.t.* Démobiliser. (*Mil. slang*) *To be demobbed,* être démobilisé.

democracy [di'mɔkrəsi], *n.* Démocratie, *f.*

democrat ['deməkræt], *n.* Démocrate, *m.*

democratic [-'krætik], *a.* Démocratique.

democratically, *adv.* Démocratiquement.

democratize [di'mɔkrətaiz], *v.t.* Démocratiser.

democratization [-tai'zeiʃən], *n.* Démocratisation, *f.*

Democritus [de'mɔkritəs]. Démocrite, *m.*

demographer [di'mɔgrəfə], *n.* Démographe.

demographic [demo'græfik], *a.* Démographique.

demography [di'mɔgrəfi], *n,* Démographie, *f.*

demolish [di'mɔliʃ], *v.t.* Démolir. **demolisher,** *n.* Démolisseur.

demolition [demə'liʃən], *n.* Démolition, *f.*

demon ['diːmən], *n.* Démon, diable, mauvais génie, *m.*

demoniac [di'mouniæk], *a.* and *n.* Démoniaque.

demoniacal [diːmə'naiəkl], *a.* Démoniaque.

demonic [di'mɔnik], *a.* Démoniaque, diabolique; génial.

demonology [diːmə'nɔlədʒi], *n.* Démonographie, démonologie, *f.* **demonolatry,** *n.* Démonolâtrie, *f.*

demonstrable [di'mɔnstrəbl], *a.* Démontrable. **demonstrably,** *adv.* Par la démonstration, démonstrativement.

demonstrate ['demənstreit], *v.t.* Démontrer, constater.—*v.i.* (*Polit.*) Faire une manifestation, manifester. **demonstration** [-'treiʃən], *n.* Démonstration, *f.;* (*Polit.*) manifestation, *f.;* (*pl.*) témoignages, *m.pl. Demonstrations of affection,* témoignages de tendresse, *m.pl.*

demonstrative [di'mɔnstrətiv], *a.* Démonstratif. **demonstratively,** *adv.* Démonstrativement. **demonstrator,** *n.* Démonstrateur, *m.;* (*Polit.*) manifestant, *m.*

demoralization [dimɔrəlai'zeiʃən], *n.* Démoralisation, *f.*

demoralize [di'mɔrəlaiz], *v.t.* Démoraliser; dépraver, corrompre.

Demos ['diːmɔs], *n.* Le peuple.

Demosthenes [də'mɔsθəniːz]. Démosthène, *m.*

demotic [di'mɔtik], *a.* Démotique.

demote [di'mout], *v.t.* (*Mil.*) Réduire à un grade inférieur, rétrograder.

demotion [di'mouʃ(ə)n], *n.* Réduction à un grade inférieur, *f.*

demulcent [di'mʌlsənt], *a.* Adoucissant, émollient.

demur [di'mə:], *n.* Hésitation, objection, *f.— v.i.* Hésiter, temporiser; (*Law*) produire une exception. *To demur to,* faire objection à, s'opposer à.

demure [di'mjuə], *a.* Réservé, posé, grave; d'une modestie affectée. **demurely,** *adv.* D'un air posé; avec une modestie affectée. **demureness,** *n.* Gravité, *f.;* air posé, *m.;* airs de sainte nitouche, *m.pl.*

demurrage [di'mʌridʒ], *n.* (*Naut.*) Surestarie, indemnité pour détention de marchandises, *f.*

demurrer [di'mʌrə], *n.* (*Law*) Question préjudicielle, *f.,* moyen dilatoire, *m.,* exception péremptoire, *f.*

demy [di'mai], *n.* Coquille (of paper), *f.;* (*Oxford Univ.*) boursier, *m.* (of Magdalen College).

den [den], *n.* Antre; repaire (of thieves etc.). *m.;* loge (in menageries), *f.;* (*fig.*) bouge, taudis, *m.;* (*colloq.*) cabinet de travail, *m.,* turne, *f.*

denary ['diːnəri], *a.* Décimal, dénaire.

denationalization [diːnæʃənəlai'zeiʃən], *n.* Dénationalisation, *f.*

denationalize [diː'næʃənəlaiz], *v.t.* Dénationaliser.

denaturalization [diːnætʃərəlai'zeiʃən], *n.* Dénaturalisation, *f.*

denaturalize [diː'nætʃərəlaiz], *v.t.* Dénaturaliser.

denature [diː'neitʃə], *v.t.* Dénaturer.

denazification [diːnɑːtsifi'keiʃ(ə)n], *n.* Dénazification, *f.*

denazify [diː'nɑːtsifai], *v.t.* Dénazifier.

dendrite ['dendrait], *n.* Dendrite, *f.* **dendritic** [-'dritik], *a.* Dendritique. **dendroid**, *a.* Dendroïde. **dendrology** [-'drɔlǝdʒi], *n.* Dendrologie, *f.*

dene [di:n], *n.* Vallon, *m.*; dune, *f.*

denegation [di:nǝ'geiʃǝn], *n.* *Dénégation, *f.*

dengue ['deŋgi], *n.* (*Med.*) Dengue, *f.*

deniable [di'naiǝbl], *a.* Niable. **denial**, *n.* Déni, *m.*, dénégation, *f.*; reniement (of St. Peter), *m.* *Flat denial*, dénégation formelle, *f.*

denier (1) [di'naiǝ], *n.* Dénégateur, *m.*, -trice, *f.*

denier (2) ['deniǝ], *n.* (*Hosiery*) Denier, *m.* *A 15-denier stocking*, un bas 15 deniers.

denigrate ['di:nigreit], *v.t.* Noircir, dénigrer. **denigration**, *n.* Dénigrement, *m.*, calomnie, médisance, *f.* **denigrator**, *n.* Dénigreur, *m.*

denims ['denimz], *n.pl.* (*Mil.*) Tenue de corvée, *f.*

denitrify [di'naitrifai], *v.t.* Dénitrifier.

denizen ['denizn], *n.* Citoyen, habitant; étranger qui a obtenu les petites lettres de naturalisation en Angleterre, *m.*—*v.t.* *Donner droit de cité à. **denizenship**, *n.* *Demi-naturalisation, *f.*

Denmark ['denma:k]. Le Danemark, *m.*

Dennis ['denis]. Denis, *m.*

denominate [di'nɔmineit], *v.t.* Nommer, appeler; dénommer. **denomination** [-'neiʃǝn], *n.* Dénomination, *f.*; communion, *f.*, culte, *m.*, secte, *f.* *Fractions of same denomination*, fractions de même dénominateur, *f.pl.*; *money of small denominations*, petite monnaie, *f.*; coupures, *f.pl.* **denominational**, *a.* Confessionnel (of schools). **denominative** [di'nɔminǝtiv], *a.* Dénominatif. **denominator**, *n.* Dénominateur, *m.* *Common denominator*, dénominateur commun.

denotation [di:no'teiʃǝn], *n.* Indication; désignation; signification (d'un mot); (*Log.*) extension, *f.*

denote [di'nout], *v.t.* Dénoter, marquer, indiquer; signifier, vouloir dire; (*Log.*) s'étendre à.

dénouement [dei'numã:], *n.* Dénouement, *m.*

denounce [di'nauns], *v.t.* Dénoncer; déclarer. **denouncement**, *n.* Dénonciation, déclaration, *f.* **denouncer**, *n.* Dénonciateur, *m.*, -trice, *f.*

dense [dens], *a.* Dense, épais; compact; stupide, bête. **densely**, *adv.* En masse, en foule compacte. **density**, *n.* Densité, épaisseur, *f.*

dent (1) [dent], *n.* Renfoncement, *m.*, bosselure; entaille, coche, *f.*—*v.t.* Bosseler, cabosser; ébrécher; faire une entaille sur; marquer.

dent (2) [dent], *n.* Dent (tooth, cog), *f.*

dental [dentl], *a.* Dentaire; (*Gram.*) dental. —*n.* (*Gram.*) Dentale, *f.* *Dental surgeon*, chirurgien dentiste, *m.* **dentary**, *a.* Dentaire, des dents. **dentate** or **dentated**, *a.* (*Bot.* etc.) Denté, dentelé. **denticle**, *n.* (*Arch.*) Denticule, *m.* **denticulate** [-'tikju lǝt] or **denticulated**, *a.* (*Arch.*) Dentelé; (*Bot.*) denticulé. **denticulation** [-'leiʃǝn], *n.* Denteleure, *f.* **dentiform**, *a.* Dentiforme. **dentifrice**, *n.* Dentrifrice, *m.*

dentine ['denti:n], *n.* Dentine, *f.* **dentist**, *n.* Dentiste, chirurgien dentiste, *m.* **dentistry**, *n.* Art du dentiste, *m.*, dentisterie, *f.* **dentition** [-'tiʃen], *n.* Dentition, *f.*

denture ['dentʃǝ], *n.* Denture, *f.*; dentier, *m.*; (*fam.*) râtelier, *m.*

denudate ['di:njudeit] or **denude** [di'nju:d], *v.t.* Dénuder; (*fig.*) dénuer, dépouiller, dégarnir. **denudation**, *n.* Dénudation, *f.*

denunciation [dinʌnsi'eiʃǝn], *n.* Dénonciation, délation; condamnation, *f.* **denunciator** [di'nʌnsieitǝ], *n.* Dénonciateur, *m.*, -trice, *f.*

deny [di'nai], *v.t.* Nier, démentir; (*Law*) dénier, renier; refuser; rejeter, renoncer à. *He is not to be denied*, il le veut à tout prix; *not to be denied*, incontestable; *to deny doing* or *having done something*, nier avoir fait quelque chose; *to deny oneself*, faire abnégation de soi-même; *to deny oneself something*, se priver de quelque chose; *to deny one's door*, faire dire qu'on n'est pas chez soi, faire défendre sa porte (à); *to deny something to someone*, refuser quelque chose à quelqu'un.

deobstruent [di'ɔbstruǝnt], *a.* (*Med.*) Désobstruant, désobstructif.

deodorant [di:'oudǝrǝnt], *n.* [DEODORIZER], **deodorization** [di:oudǝrai'zeiʃǝn], *n.* Désodorisation, *f.* **deodorize** [-'oudǝraiz], *v.t.* Désodoriser, désinfecter. **deodorizer**, *n.* Désinfectant, désodorisant, *m.* **deodorizing**, *a.* Désinfectant, désinfecteur.

deontology [di:ɔn'tɔlǝdʒi], *n.* Déontologie, *f.*

deoxidization [di:ɔksidai'zeiʃǝn], *n.* Désoxydation, *f.*

deoxidize [di'ɔksidaiz], *v.t.* Désoxyder.

depart [di'pa:t], *v.i.* Partir, s'en aller, se retirer, s'éloigner; (*fig.*) se départir; mourir, trépasser. *To depart from one's duty*, s'écarter de son devoir.—*v.t.* Quitter. *To depart this life*, mourir, quitter ce monde.

departed [di'pa:tid], *a.* Mort, défunt; passé, évanoui.—*n.* *The departed*, le défunt, *m.*, les trépassés, *m.pl.*

department [di'pa:tmǝnt], *n.* Département, service, *m.*; (*Polit.*) bureau, *m.*, direction; (*Comm.*) division, partie, *f.*, comptoir (in a shop), *m.* *Department store*, grand magasin, *m.*; *intelligence department*, service des renseignements, *m.*; *manager of a department*, (*Comm.*) chef de service, *m.*

departmental [di:pa:t'mentl], *a.* Départemental.

departure [di'pa:tʃǝ], *n.* Départ; éloignement; écart, *m.*, déviation, *f.*; (*fig.*) mort, *f.*, trépas, *m.* *A new departure*, une nouvelle orientation; un nouvel usage. *To take one's departure*, s'en aller, prendre congé.

depauperize [di:'pɔ:pǝraiz], *v.t.* Tirer de l'indigence; abolir le paupérisme dans.

depend [di'pend], *v.i.* Dépendre (de); se confier (à), compter (sur), se reposer (sur). *Depend upon it*, soyez-en sûr, comptez-y, croyez-le bien; *it all depends*, cela dépend. **dependable**, *a.* Digne de confiance; sûr. **dependant**, *n.* Protégé; pensionnaire, *m.* **dependence**, *n.* Dépendance; confiance, *f.* *No dependence can be placed on what he says*, il est impossible de se fier à ce qu'il dit. **dependency**, *n.* Dépendance, *f.* *Foreign dependency*, possession à l'étranger, *f.* **dependent**, *a.* Dépendant; (*Law*) relevant (de); à la charge de; (*Gram.*) subordonné. *Dependent relatives*, parents à charge, *m.pl.*

depict [di'pikt], *v.t.* Peindre, dépeindre, décrire.
depiction [di'pikʃ(ə)n], *n.* Peinture, description, *f.*
depilate ['depileit], *v.t.* Dépiler. **depilation,** *n.* Dépilation, *f.*, dépilage, *m.* **depilatory** [di'pilətəri], *a.* Dépilatif, dépilatoire.—*n.* Dépilatoire, *m.*
deplenish [di'pleniʃ], *v.t.* Dégarnir; vider, désemplir.
deplete [di'pli:t], *v.t.* Amoindrir, épuiser. **depletion,** *n.* Épuisement, *m.*
deplorable [di'plɔ:rəbl], *a.* Déplorable; pitoyable (contemptible). **deplorableness,** *n.* État déplorable, *m.* **deplorably,** *adv.* Déplorablement; pitoyablement. **deplore,** *v.t.* Déplorer.—*v.i.* Se lamenter.
deploy [di'plɔi], *v.t.* (*Mil.*) Déployer.—*v.i.* Se déployer. **deployment,** *n.* Déploiement, *m.*
deplumation [di:plu'meiʃən], *n.* Mue, *f.*
deplume [di'plu:m], *v.t.* Déplumer.
depolarization [di:poulərai'zeiʃən], *n.* Dépolarisation, *f.*
depolarize [di:'pouləraiz], *v.t.* Dépolariser.
depone [di'poun], *v.i.* (*Law*) Déposer (de *or* sur). **deponent,** *n.* Déposant; (*Gram.*) déponent, *m.*
depopulate [di:'pɔpjuleit], *v.t.* Dépeupler.—*v.i.* Se dépeupler. **depopulation** [-'leiʃən], *n.* Dépeuplement, *m.*, dépopulation, *f.*
deport [di'pɔ:t], *v.t.* Déporter, expulser. **To deport oneself,** se comporter, se conduire.
deportation [di:pɔ:'teiʃən], *n.* Déportation, *f.*, expulsion, *f.*
deportment [di'pɔ:tmənt], *n.* Tenue, conduite, *f.*, manières, *f.pl.*
deposal [di'pouzl], *n.* Déposition, *f.*
depose [di'pouz], *v.t. and v.i.* Déposer (de). **To depose from,** déposer de; **to depose to** (a fact), déposer sur *or* de.
deposit [di'pɔzit], *n.* Dépôt; (*Banking*) versement, *m.*; gage, nantissement, *m.*, arrhes, *f.pl.*, caution, *f.*; (*Geol.*) gisement, gîte, *m.*; (*pl.*) alluvions, apports, *m.pl. Deposit account,* compte de dépôt de fonds, *m.*—*v.t.* Déposer; verser. **depositary,** *n.* Dépositaire, *m.*
deposition [di:pə'ziʃən], *n.* Déposition, *f.*; dépôt, *m.*
depositor [di'pɔzitə], *n.* (*Banking*) Déposant, *m.*, -ante, *f.*; (*Comm.*) dépositeur, *m.*, -trice, *f.*
depository, *n.* Dépôt; (*colloq.*) dépositaire, *m.* garde-meubles (furniture); répertoire (book), *m.*
depot ['depou *or* di'pou], *n.* Dépôt, *m.*; (*Am.*) ['di:pou], gare, *f. Depot ship,* ravitailleur, *m.*
depravation [di:prə'veiʃən], *n.* Dépravation, *f.*
deprave [di'preiv], *v.t.* Dépraver, corrompre. **depraved,** *a.* Dépravé, corrompu. *To become depraved,* se dépraver, se corrompre.
depravity [di'præviti], *n.* Dépravation; corruption, *f.*
deprecate ['deprikeit], *v.t.* *Détourner par la prière, conjurer; désapprouver, désavouer, s'opposer à. *I strongly deprecate his interfering,* je m'oppose fortement à ce qu'il intervienne. **deprecatingly,** *adv.* Avec désapprobation; d'un air de protestation. **deprecation** [-'keiʃən], *n.* Déprécation; désapprobation, *f.*, désaveu, *m.* **deprecative** ['deprikeitiv] *or* **deprecatory,** *a.* De déprécation, d'excuse; qui devance les reproches.

depreciate [di'pri:ʃieit], *v.t.* Déprécier.—*v.i.* Se déprécier, perdre de sa valeur. **depreciation** [-'eiʃən], *n.* Dépréciation, *f.* **depreciator** [-'pri:ʃieitə], *n.* Dépréciateur, *m.*; dénigreur, *m.* **depreciatory,** *a.* Dépréciatif; péjoratif.
depredate ['deprideit], *v.t.* Piller, saccager, ravager.—*v.i.* Commettre des déprédations. **depredation** [-'deiʃən], *n.* Déprédation, *f.*, pillage, *m.*
depredator ['deprideitə], *n.* Pillard, déprédateur, *m.*
depredatory ['deprideitəri *or* di'predətri], *a.* (Acte) de déprédation.
depress [di'pres], *v.t.* Baisser, abaisser; abattre, faire languir; accabler, décourager; incliner (to sink). **depressed,** *a.* Abattu; bas (low). *Depressed area,* région de chômage (involontaire), *f.* **depression,** *n.* Abaissement, *m.*; dépression, *f.*; (*Meteor.*) zone dépressionnaire, *f.*, enfoncement, creux; (*fig.*) abattement, découragement, *m.*; (*Comm.*) crise, *f.* **depressor,** *n.* (*Anat.*) Abaisseur, *m.*
deprivation [depri'veiʃən], *n.* Privation; perte, *f.*
deprive [di'praiv], *v.t.* Priver (de); déposséder.
depth [depθ], *n.* Profondeur, *f.*; enfoncement (recess), *m.*; hauteur (of a flounce etc.), *f.*; cœur, fort (of the seasons), *m.*; vigueur (of colouring, *f.*; (*Print.*) corps (of letters), *m.*; épaisseur (thickness), *f.*; (*Naut.*) creux (of the hold), *m.*; chute (of a sail), *f.*; (*fig.*) comble (of suffering etc.), *m. Depth of winter,* cœur de l'hiver, *m.*; *in the depths,* au fond; *in the lowest depths of,* au fin fond de; *to get out of one's depth,* to go beyond one's depth, perdre pied, (*fig.*) parler de ce qu'on ignore.—*n.pl.* (*Lit.*) The depths, l'abîme, le gouffre, *m.* **depth-charge,** *n.* Grenade sous-marine, *f.*
depurate ['depjureit], *v.t.* Dépurer.—*a.* Dépuré. **depuration** [-'reiʃən], *n.* Dépuration, *f.* **depurative** [-'pjuərətiv], *a. and n.* Dépuratif, *m.*
deputation [depju'teiʃən], *n.* Députation, délégation, *f.*
depute [di'pju:t], *v.t.* Députer, déléguer.
deputize ['depjutaiz], *v.i.* Remplacer quelqu'un; remplir une suppléance; doubler (un acteur).
deputy ['depjuti], *n.* Député, délégué; adjoint (assistant), *m.*; représentant, *m.* **deputy-chairman,** *n.* Vice-président, *m.* **deputy-governor,** *n.* Sous-gouverneur, *m.* **deputy-judge,** *n.* Juge suppléant, *m.* **deputy-manager,** *n.* Sous-directeur, *m.* **deputy-mayor,** *n.* Adjoint au maire, adjoint, *m.*
deracinate [di'ræsineit], *v.t.* Déraciner, extirper.
deracination [diræsi'neiʃ(ə)n], *n.* Déracinement, *m.*, extirpation, *f.*
derail [di'reil], *v.t.* (*Rail.*) Dérailler. **derailment,** *n.* Déraillement, *m.*
derange [di'reindʒ], *v.t.* Déranger; déranger le cerveau de, troubler l'esprit de. *To be deranged,* avoir le cerveau dérangé. **derangement,** *n.* Dérangement, *m.*; dérangement du cerveau, *m.*, aliénation mentale, *f.*
deration [di:'ræʃ(ə)n], *v.t.* Dérationner. **derationing,** *n.* Mise en vente libre, *f.*

Derby ['dɑːbi]. Le Derby (d'Epsom); chapeau melon, *m.*
derelict ['derilikt], *a.* Délaissé, abandonné.— *n.* Vaisseau abandonné; (*Law*) objet abandonné, *m.*, épave,*f.* **dereliction** [-'likʃən], *n.* Abandon, *m.*; négligence, *f.*, oubli, *m.* (of a duty). *Dereliction of duty*, manquement au devoir, *m.*
derequisition [diːrekwi'ziʃ(ə)n], *v.t.* Déréquisitionner.—*n.* Déréquisition, *f.*
derestrict [diːre'strikt], *v.t.* (*Administration*) Libérer. *To derestrict a road*, libérer une route de toute limitation de vitesse.
deride [di'raid], *v.t.* Tourner en dérision, se moquer de, se rire de. **deridingly**, *adv.* Par dérision.
derision [di'riʒən], *n.* Dérision, moquerie, *f.*; objet de dérision, *m.* **derisive** [-'raisiv], *a.* Dérisoire, moqueur. **derisively**, *adv.* Par dérision, d'un air moqueur. **derisory**, *a.* Dérisoire.
derivable [di'raivəbl], *a.* Qu'on peut faire dériver; qu'on peut déduire.
derivation [deri'veiʃən], *n.* Dérivation; origine, *f.*
derivative [di'rivətiv], *a.* Dérivé; influencé par; (*Med.*) dérivatif.—*n.* (*Gram.*) Dérivé; (*Mus.*) accord dérivé; (*Med.*) dérivatif, *m.* **derivatively**, *adv.* Par dérivation.
derive [di'raiv], *v.t.* Dériver; (*Gram.*) faire dériver; (*fig.*) recueillir, tirer (de).—*v.i.* Venir, dériver (de); descendre (de).
derm [dəːm], *n.* Derme, *m.* **dermatitis**, *n.* (*Med.*) Dermite, dermatite, *f.* **dermatologist**, *n.* Dermatologiste, dermatologue, *m.* **dermatology**, *n.* Dermatologie, *f.*
dermic ['dəːmik], *a.* Dermique.
derogate ['derogeit], *v.t.* Déprécier.—*v.i.* Déroger. *To derogate from*, déroger à. **derogation** [-'geiʃən], *n.* Dérogation, *f.* **derogatory** [di'rɔgətəri], *a.* Dérogatoire, dérogeant (à).
derrick ['derik], *n.* Grue, *f.*; derrick, *m.* **derrick-boom**, *n.* Mât de charge, *m.*
derring-do ['deriŋ'duː], *n.* Audace, *f.* *Deeds of derring-do*, hauts faits, *m.pl.*
dervish ['dəːviʃ], *n.* Derviche, *m.*
descant (1) ['deskænt], *n.* *Chant, déchant, *m.*, mélodie; variation; (*fig.*) dissertation, paraphrase, *f.*
descant (2) [dis'kænt], *v.i.* Discourir, disserter, faire des discours (sur).
descend [di'send], *v.i.* Descendre, tomber; s'abaisser (to lower oneself). *To be descended from*, descendre de, tirer son origine de; *to descend upon*, tomber sur, passer à (of inheritance). **descendant**, *n.* Descendant, *m.*, -ante, *f.*; (*pl.*) descendance, postérité, *f.* **descendent**, *a.* Descendant, qui descend, provenant (de).
descent [di'sent], *n.* Descente; chute, pente; descendance, naissance, origine (of lineage), *f.*
describable [dis'kraibəbl], *a.* Descriptible.
describe, *v.t.* Décrire, dépeindre, peindre. **describer**, *n.* Descripteur, narrateur, *m.*
description [dis'kripʃən], *n.* Description; désignation (of a person), *f.*; (*Law*) signalement, *m.*; (*colloq.*) qualité, sorte, espèce, *f.* *Beyond description*, indescriptible. **descriptive**, *a.* Descriptif. *Descriptive catalogue*, catalogue raisonné.

descry [dis'krai], *v.t.* Découvrir, apercevoir; aviser; reconnaître.
desecrate ['desəkreit], *v.t.* Profaner, violer (une sépulture). **desecration**, *n.* Profanation, *f.* **desecrator**, *n.* Profanateur, *m.*, -trice, *f.*
desert (1) [di'zəːt], *n.* Mérite, *m.*; mérites, *m.pl.* *According to one's deserts*, selon ses mérites.
desert (2) ['dezət], *a.* Désert, solitaire.—*n.* Désert, *m.*, solitude, *f.*
desert (3) [di'zəːt], *v.t.* Abandonner, déserter. —*v.i.* (*Mil.*) Déserter. **deserted**, *a.* Abandonné, désert. **deserter**, *n.* Déserteur; transfuge, *m.* **desertion**, *n.* Désertion, *f.*, abandon, *m.*
deserve [di'zəːv], *v.t.* Mériter, être digne de. **deservedly**, *adv.* À bon droit, justement, à juste titre. **deserving**, *a.* De mérite, méritoire; méritant. *Deserving case*, cas digne d'intérêt, *m.*
deshabille ['dezæbiːl] *or* desə'biːl], *n.* Déshabillé, *m.*
desiccate ['desikeit], *v.t.* Dessécher.—*v.i.* Se dessécher.
desiccated ['desikeitid], *a.* Desséché.
desiccation [desi'keiʃən], *n.* Dessiccation, *f.* **desiccative**, *a.* and *n.* Dessiccatif, *m.*
desiderate [di'zidəreit], *v.t.* Sentir le besoin de, réclamer.
desideratum [dizidə'reitəm], *n.* (*pl.* **desiderata**) Desideratum, *m.*
design [di'zain], *n.* Dessein, projet, *m.*, intention, disposition, *f.*; dessin (drawing), (*Manuf.*) modèle, *m.*; plan, *m.*, ébauche, représentation, *f.* *By design*, à dessein; *Dior's latest designs*, les dernières créations de Dior, *f.pl.*; *to have designs upon*, avoir des desseins sur.—*v.t.* Avoir le dessein de, projeter, se proposer de; dessiner; faire le plan de; destiner (à); créer, inventer. **designedly**, *adv.* À dessein, avec intention, de propos délibéré. **designer**, *n.* Inventeur; auteur; architecte; dessinateur (draughtsman), *m.* **designing**, *a.* Artificieux, intrigant.—*n.* Dessin, *m.*, création, *f.*
designate (1) ['dezigneit], *v.t.* Désigner, nommer.
designate (2) ['dezignət], *a.* Désigné, nommé. **designation** [dezig'neiʃən], *n.* Désignation, *f.*
desirability [dizaiərə'biliti], *n.* Caractère désirable, *m.*
desirable [di'zaiərəbl], *a.* Désirable, à desirer, à souhaiter, agréable. **desirableness**, *n.* Caractère désirable; avantage, *m.* **desirably**, *adv.* D'une manière désirable, agréablement; avantageusement.
desire [di'zaiə], *n.* Désir, *m.*, envie; prière, demande, *f.* *By desire*, sur demande, à la demande (de); *to have a desire to*, avoir envie de, désirer.—*v.t.* Désirer, souhaiter; prier, charger (de). *That leaves a lot to be desired*, cela laisse beaucoup à désirer. **desireless**, *a.* Exempt de désirs.
desirous, *a.* Qui désire; désireux (de), empressé (à). *To be desirous of*, avoir envie de, désirer.
desist [di'zist], *v.i.* Se désister, cesser (de), renoncer (à). **desistance**, *n.* Désistement, *m.*
desk [desk], *n.* Pupitre (in school); bureau (in office), *m.*; caisse (in a shop); chaire (of

lecturer), *f.*; lutrin (for music or lectern), *m.*
Cash desk, caisse, *f.*; *pedestal desk*, bureau
ministre, *m.*; *roll-top desk*, bureau américain,
m.
desolate (1) ['desəlit], *a.* Désolé, inhabité,
solitaire, dévasté.
desolate (2) ['desəleit], *v.t.* Désoler; dévaster,
ravager, dépeupler. **desolately,** *adv.* D'une
manière désolée. **desolation** [-'leiʃən], *n.*
Désolation, *f.* *Abomination of desolation*,
l'abomination de la désolation, *f.*
desolator ['desəleitə], *n.* Désolateur, *m.*,
-trice, *f.*
despair [dis'pɛə], *n.* Désespoir, *m. In despair*,
au désespoir; *to drive to despair*, réduire au
désespoir, désespérer.—*v.i.* Désespérer (de),
se désespérer. **despairing,** *a.* Désespéré.
despairingly, *adv.* Désespérément.
despatch [DISPATCH].
desperado [despə'reidou, -'ra:dou], *n.* Désespéré, cerveau brûlé, forcené, risque-tout, *m.*
desperate ['despərit], *a.* Désespéré; dont on
désespère; furieux, forcené; à outrance,
acharné, terrible. *Desperate fight*, combat
acharné, *m.* **desperately,** *adv.* Désespérément; (*fig.*) à l'excès, excessivement,
éperdument. **desperateness,** *n.* Nature
désespérée; fureur, *f.*, acharnement, *m.*
desperation [-'reiʃən], *n.* Désespoir, *m.*;
fureur, *f.*, acharnement, *m.*
despicable ['despikəbl], *a.* Méprisable.
despicableness, *n.* Caractère méprisable,
m., abjection, *f.* **despicably,** *adv.* Bassement, d'une manière méprisable.
despise [dis'paiz], *v.t.* Mépriser, dédaigner.
despiser, *n.* Contempteur, *m.* **despisingly,**
adv. Avec mépris.
despite [dis'pait], *n.* (*Lit.*) Dépit, *m.*—*prep.* En
dépit de, malgré.
despoil [dis'pɔil], *v.t.* Dépouiller, piller,
spolier. **despoiler,** *n.* Spoliateur, *m.*,
-trice, *f.*
despoliation [dispouli'eiʃən], *n.* Spoliation, *f.*
despond [dis'pɔnd], *v.i.* Se décourager, se
laisser abattre; désespérer (de).—*n. The
slough of despond*, l'abîme du désespoir, *m.*
despondency, *n.* Abattement, désespoir,
découragement, *m.* **despondent,** *a.* Découragé, abattu. **despondently** or **despond-
ingly,** *adv.* Avec abattement, d'un air abattu.
despot ['despɔt], *m.* Despote, *m.* **despotic**
[-'pɔtik] or **despotical,** *a.* Despotique.
despotically, *adv.* Despotiquement, en
despote.
despotism ['despətizm], *n.* Despotisme, *m.*
desquamate ['deskwæmeit], *v.t.* Desquamer.
desquamation, *n.* Desquamation, *f.*
dessert [di'zə:t], *n.* Dessert, *m. At dessert*,
au dessert.—*a.* De dessert. **dessert-dish,** *n.*
Compotier, *m.* **dessert-knife,** *n.* Couteau à
dessert, *m.* **dessert-service,** *n.* Un service
de dessert, *m.*
destination [desti'neiʃən], *n.* Destination, *f.*
destine ['destin], *v.t.* Destiner, désigner, fixer
(à). **destiny,** *n.* Destin, *m.*, destinée, *f.*
destitute ['destitju:t], *a.* Dépourvu, destitué,
privé, dénué (de); indigent. **destitution**
[-'tju:ʃən], *n.* Dénuement, abandon, *m.*,
indigence, *f.*
destroy [dis'trɔi], *v.t.* Détruire, exterminer,
ruiner, perdre; anéantir. *Ambition destroyed
him*, c'est l'ambition qui l'a perdu. **destroyer,**

n. Destructeur; (*Naut.*) contre-torpilleur,
destroyer, *m.* **destroying,** *a.* Destructeur,
destructif.
destructible [dis'trʌktəbl], *a.* Destructible.
destruction [dis'trʌkʃən], *n.* Destruction, *f.*,
anéantissement, *m.*; ruine, *f.* **destructive,** *a.*
Destructeur, destructif (de); funeste, fatal
(à). *Destructive distillation*, (*Chem.*) distillation sèche, *f.* **destructively,** *adv.* D'une
manière destructive. **destructiveness,** *n.*
Caractère destructeur, *m.*, nature destructive, *f.*
desuetude ['dezwitju:d], *n.* Désuétude, *f.*
desultorily ['desəltərili], *adv.* À bâtons rompus, sans suite, d'une manière décousue.
desultoriness, *n.* Décousu, *m.* **desultory,**
a. À bâtons rompus, décousu, sans suite.
detach [di'tætʃ], *v.t.* Détacher (de); isoler,
séparer; dételer (of wagons). *To become
detached*, se détacher. **detachable,** *a.*
Démontable, détachable. **detached,** *a.*
Détaché, isolé, entouré de jardins (of houses);
désintéressé (of opinions); indifférent (of
attitude). **detachment,** *n.* Détachement,
m.
detail (1) ['di:teil], *n.* Détail, *m. In detail*,
minutieusement, en détail.
detail (2) [di'teil], *v.t.* Détailler, expliquer en
détail; (*Mil.*) désigner (pour), affecter (à).
detailed, *a.* Détaillé; circonstancié (of an
account).
detain [di'tein], *v.t.* Retenir; détenir; arrêter;
(*Law*) empêcher.
detainee [ditei'ni:], *n.* Détenu, *m.*
detainer [di'teinə], *n.* Personne qui retient, *f.*,
détenteur, *m.*, détention illégale (d'un objet),
f., maintien (d'un accusé) en prison, *m. Writ
of detainer*, ordre de surseoir à l'élargissement,
m.
detect [di'tekt], *v.t.* Découvrir; apercevoir,
détecter. **detectable,** *a.* Discernable, qu'on
peut découvrir. **detection,** *n.* Découverte, *f.*
detective, *n.* Agent de la (police de) sûreté,
policier, détective, *m. A detective novel*, un
roman policier. **detector,** *n.* Découvreur;
(*Tech.*) détecteur, *m.*
detent [di'tent], *n.* Détente, *f.* **detention,** *n.*
Action de retenir, *f.*; retard, *m.*; (*Law*)
détention, *f.*; (*sch.*) consigne, *f. Detention
barracks*, prison militaire, *f.*
deter [di'tə:], *v.t.* Détourner, empêcher (de);
dissuader (de).
detergent [di'tə:dʒənt], *a. and n.* Détersif,
détergent, *m.*
deteriorate [di'tiəriəreit], *v.i.* Se détériorer.—
v.t. Détériorer. **deterioration** [-'reiʃən], *n.*
Détérioration, *f.*; dépérissement, *m.* (of
machinery).
determinable [di'tə:minəbl], *a.* Déterminable. **determinant,** *n.* (*Math.*) Déterminant,
m. **determinate,** *a.* Déterminé, établi, fixé;
définitif, décisif. **determinately,** *adv.* De
façon décisive; définitivement. **determination** [-'neiʃən], *n.* Détermination, décision, *f.*;
conviction, résolution; (*Law*) expiration, *f.*
determinative [di'tə:minətiv], *a.* Déterminatif; (*Law*) déterminant.
determine [di'tə:min], *v.t.* Déterminer,
décider, fixer; régler, constater.—*v.i.* Se
déterminer, se décider, résoudre; (*Law*) finir,
expirer, se terminer. **determined,** *a.*
Résolu, convaincu, obstiné. **determinedly,**

adv. Résolument. **determinism,** *n.* Déterminisme, *m.* **determinist,** *n.* Déterministe. **deterrent** [di'terənt], *a.* Préventif.—*n.* Arme préventive, *f.*

detersive [di'tə:siv], *a.* and *n.* Détersif, *m.*

detest [di'test], *v.t.* Détester. **detestable,** *a.* Détestable; (*fig.*) odieux, atroce. **detestably,** *adv.* Détestablement.

detestation [di:tes'teiʃən], *n.* Détestation, *f.* *To hold in detestation,* avoir en horreur, exécrer.

dethrone [di'θroun], *v.t.* Détrôner. **dethronement,** *n.* Détrônement, *m.*

detonate ['di:- *or* 'detəneit], *v.i.* Détoner.—*v.t.* Faire détoner. **detonating,** *a.* À détonation, fulminant. *Detonating bulb,* larme batavique, *f.* *Detonating powder,* poudre fulminante, *f.* **detonation** [-'neiʃən], *n.* Détonation, *f.*

detonator ['detəneitə], *n.* Détonateur, *m.*

detour ['deituə *or* di'tuə], *n.* Détour, *m.*

detract [di'trækt], *v.t.* Enlever, ôter (à); dénigrer, rabattre.—*v.i.* Déroger (à). **detractingly,** *adv.* Par détraction, par dénigrement. **detraction,** *n.* Détraction, *f.*, dénigrement, *m.* **detractive** or **detractory,** *a.* Détracteur. **detractor,** *n.* Détracteur, *m.*

detrain [di'trein], *v.t.*, *v.i.* Débarquer d'un train.

detriment ['detrimənt], *n.* Détriment, préjudice, dommage, *m.* **detrimental** [-'mentl], *a.* Préjudiciable, nuisible (à). **detrimentally,** *adv.* D'une manière préjudiciable.

detrition [di'triʃən], *n.* Détrition, *f.*, frottement, *m.*

detritus [di'traitəs], *n.* Détritus, débris, *m.*

*detrude [di'tru:d], *v.t.* Précipiter, repousser.

*detruncate [di'trʌŋkeit], *v.t.* Tronquer, écourter, couper.

deuce [dju:s], *n.* (*Cards*) Deux, *m.*; (*Ten.*) à deux; à égalité; (*colloq.*) diable, diantre, *m.* *Deuce again,* à deux encore, (or) avantage détruit; *what the deuce are you doing?* que diable faites-vous?—*int.* Diable! diantre!

deuterocanonical [dju:tərokə'nɔnikl], *a.* Deutérocanonique.

Deuteronomy [dju:tə'ronəmi], *n.* Deutéronome, *m.*

devaluation [di:vælju'eiʃən], *n.* Dévaluation, *f.* **devalue** [di:'vælju], **devaluate** [di:'væljueit], *v.t.* Dévaluer, déprécier.

devastate ['devəsteit], *v.t.* Dévaster. **devastating,** *a.* Dévastateur. **devastation** [-'teiʃən], *n.* Dévastation, *f.*

develop [di'veləp], *v.t.* Développer; (*Med.*) contracter, faire; amplifier (argument); (*Phot.*) révéler, exploiter (of resources); développer. **developer,** *n.* (*Phot.*) Révélateur, *m.* **developing** or **development,** *n.* Développement, *m.*; exploitation, *f.*; ampleur, *f.*; fait nouveau, *m.* *Development theory,* théorie de l'évolution, *f.*

*devest [di'vest], *v.t.* (*Law*) Aliéner (as a right).

deviate ['di:vieit], *v.i.* Dévier, se dévier; s'écarter (de). **deviation** [-'eiʃən], *n.* Déviation, *f.*, écart, *m.* **deviationism,** *n.* Déviationnisme, *m.* (from a political dogma). **deviationist,** *n.* Déviationniste, *m.* or *f.*

device [di'vais], *n.* Dessein, expédient, moyen, stratagème, *m.*; invention, *f.*, dis-

positif, mécanisme, *m.*; devise (motto), *f.*; (*fam.*) truc, *m.* *To leave someone to his own devices,* livrer quelqu'un à lui-même.

devil [devl], *n.* Diable, démon, *m.*; (*colloq.*) nègre (d'un écrivain ou d'un avocat); (*pl.*) *blue devils,* mélancolie, *f.*, ennui, *m.* (*fam.*) *Be a devil,* laissez-vous tenter; *dare-devil,* téméraire, audacieux; *devil's-bit scabious,* mors du diable, *m.*; *printer's devil,* jeune apprenti imprimeur, *m.*; *she-devil,* diablesse, *f.*; *talk of the devil and his horns will appear,* quand on parle du loup, on en voit la queue; *the devil!* ah diable! *the devil is in him,* il a le diable au corps; *the devil on two sticks,* le diable boiteux; *the devil take,* (que) le diable emporte; *there is the devil to pay,* c'est le diable à confesser; *to give the devil his due,* rendre justice au diable; *to play the very devil,* faire le diable à quatre; *what the devil!* que diable!—*v.t.* Griller et poivrer.—*v.i.* Faire, être le nègre (d'un écrivain). **devilfish,** *n.* Poulpe, *m.*, pieuvre, *f.* **devil-may-care,** *a.* and *n.* Étourdi. **devil-worship,** *n.* Culte du diable, *m.*

devilish, *a.* Maudit, diabolique, de diable. **devilishly,** *adv.* Diaboliquement, diablement, en diable, rudement. **devilishness,** *n.* Caractère diabolique, *m.* **devilment,** **devilry,** *n.* Diablerie, *f.*

devious ['di:viəs], *a.* Détourné, tortueux, écarté, de travers; (*fig.*) errant, vagabond, faux. **deviously,** *adv.* En déviant; (*fig.*) à tort. **deviousness,** *n.* Détours, *m.pl.*, tortuosité, *f.* (of thought, speech).

devisable [di'vaizəbl], *a.* Imaginable; (*Law*) disponible (of property).

devise [di'vaiz], *n.* Disposition testamentaire, *f.*, legs, *m.*—*v.t.* Imaginer, inventer, trouver; tramer, machiner; (*Law*) disposer par testament, léguer.—*v.i.* Projeter.

devisee [devi'zi *or* divai'zi:], *n.* Légataire, *m.*

deviser [di'vaizə], *n.* Inventeur, *m.* **devising,** *n.* Invention, *f.*

devisor [devi'zɔ: *or* di'vaizə], *n.* (*Law*) Testateur, *m.*, -trice, *f.*

devitalize [di:'vaitəlaiz], *v.t.* Dévitaliser.

devoid [di'vɔid], *a.* Exempt, dénué, dépourvu (de). *Devoid of,* sans.

devolution [di:və'lu:ʃən], *n.* Dévolution, *f.*; (*Biol.*) dégénération, *f.*; (*Law*) déchéance, *f.*; (*Polit.*) délégation, *f.*

devolve [di'vɔlv], *v.t.* Rouler; transférer, transmettre; déléguer.—*v.i.* Échoir, revenir; (*Law*) être dévolu (à). *It devolves upon me to,* c'est à moi de.

Devonian [di'vouniən], *a.* and *n.* (*Geol.*) Dévonien, *m.*

Devonshire ['devnʃə] **cream,** *n.* Crème caillée, *f.*

devote [di'vout], *v.t.* Dévouer, consacrer (à); livrer (à). **devoted,** *a.* Dévoué, consacré, voué; prédestiné; maudit (accursed). **devotedly,** *adv.* Avec dévouement. **devotedness,** *n.* Dévouement, *m.* **devotee** [devo'ti:], *n.* Dévot, *m.*, -vote, *f.*; fanatique, passionné, *m.* **devotion,** *n.* Dévotion, *f.*; (*pl.*) prières, *f.pl.*; dévouement, *m.*

devotional [di'vouʃənəl], *a.* Religieux, porté à la dévotion, de dévotion (of things).

devour [di'vauə], *v.t.* Dévorer. **devouring,** *a.* Dévorant, destructeur. **devouringly,** *adv.* En dévorant.

devout [di'vaut], *a.* Dévot, pieux, fervent. **devoutly,** *adv.* Dévotement; sincèrement. **devoutness,** *n.* Dévotion, piété, *f.*
dew [dju:], *n.* Rosée, *f.*—*v.t.* Humecter de rosée; mouiller, arroser. **dewberry,** *n.* Mûre de haie, *f.* **dew-claw,** *n.* Ergot, *m.* (of dogs). **dewdrop,** *n.* Goutte de rosée, *f.* **dewlap,** *n.* Fanon, *m.* (of cow). **dew-sprinkled,** *a.* Couvert de rosée. **dew-worm,** *n.* Lombric, ver de terre, *m.* **dewy,** *a.* De rosée; couvert de rosée.
dexter ['dekstə], *a.* Droit; (*Her.*) dextre.
dexterity [deks'teriti] or **dexterousness,** *n.* Dextérité, adresse, *f.*
dexterous ['dekstrəs], *a.* Adroit; habile. **dexterously,** *adv.* Adroitement, habilement.
dextrin ['dekstrin], *n.* (*Chem.*) Dextrine, *f.*
dextrorse [deks'trɔ:s], *a.* and *adv.* Dextrorsum (*inv.*).
dextrose ['dekstrous], *n.* Dextrose, *m.* or *f.*
dey [dei], *n.* Dey, *m.*
dhow [dau], *n.* (*Naut.*) Boutre, *m.* (Arab vessel).
diabase ['daiəbeis], *n.* Diabase, *f.*
diabetes [daiə'bi:ti:z], *n. sing.* and *pl.* Diabète, *m.* **diabetic** [-'betik], *a.* and *n.* Diabétique.
diabolic [daiə'bɔlik] or **diabolical,** *a.* Diabolique. **diabolically,** *adv.* Diaboliquement.
diabolism [dai'æbəlizm], *n.* Satanisme, *m.*; magie noire, *f.* **diabolo,** *n.* Diabolo, *m.*
diachylon [dai'ækilən] or **diachylum,** *n.* Diachylum, diachylon, *m.*
diaconal [dai'ækənəl], *a.* Diaconal.
diacritical [daiə'kritikl], *a.* Diacritique.
diadelphous [daiə'delfəs], *a.* (*Bot.*) Diadelphe.
diadem ['daiədem], *n.* Diadème, *m.* **diademed,** *a.* Ceint d'un diadème.
diaeresis [dai'iərəsis], *n.* (*pl.* **-ses**) Tréma, *m.*, diérèse, *f.*
diagnose [daiəg'nouz], *v.t.* Diagnostiquer.
diagnosis [daiəg'nousis], *n.* Diagnose, *f.*; diagnostic, *m.* **diagnostic** [-'nɔstik], *a.* Diagnostique.—*n.* Signe diagnostique, symptôme, *m.* **diagnostics,** *n.* Diagnose, *f.*
diagonal [dai'ægənəl], *a.* Diagonal.—*n.* Diagonale, *f.* **diagonally,** *adv.* Diagonalement.
diagram ['daiəgræm], *n.* Diagramme, graphique, tracé, schéma, *m.*, épure, *f.* **diagrammatic** [-grə'mætik], *a.* Schématique.
dial ['daiəl], *n.* Cadran, *m.* *Miner's dial,* boussole de mineur, *f.*; *sun-dial,* cadran solaire, *m.*; (*pop.*) tête, gueule, *f.*—*v.t.* (*Teleph.*) Composer (un numéro).—*v.i.* Faire marcher le tabulateur, appeler à l'automatique. **dial-plate,** *n.* Cadran, *m.* **dial-work,** *n.* Cadrature, *f.*
dialect ['daiəlekt], *n.* Dialecte, patois; (*fig.*) langage, *m.* **dialectic** [-'lektik] or **dialectical,** *a.* Dialectique. **dialectically,** *adv.* Dialectiquement. **dialectician** [-'tiʃən], *n.* Dialecticien, *m.*
dialectics [daiə'lektiks], *n.pl.* Dialectique, *f.*
dialogic [daiə'lɔdʒik], *a.* Dialogique.
dialogist [dai'ælədʒist], *n.* Interlocuteur; auteur de dialogues, *m.* **dialogize,** *v.t.* Dialoguer.
dialogue ['daiəlɔg], *n.* Dialogue; entretien, *m.*
dialyse ['daiəlaiz], *v.t.* Dialyser.
dialyser [daiə'laizə], *n.* Dialyseur, *m.*

dialysis [dai'ælisis], *n.* Dialyse, *f.*
diamagnetic [daiəmæg'netik], *a.* Diamagnétique. **diamagnetism** [-'mægnətizm], *n.* Diamagnétisme, *m.*
diamantiferous [daiəmæn'tifərəs], *a.* Diamantifère.
diameter [dai'æmitə], *n.* Diamètre, *m.* **diametral** or **diametrical** [-ə'metrikl], *a.* Diamétral. **diametrally** or **diametrically,** *adv.* Diamétralement.
diamond ['daiəmənd], *n.* Diamant; (*Cards*) carreau, *m.*; (*Print.*) corps quatre, *m.* *A rough diamond,* un homme qui cache ses qualités sous des dehors rudes, une rude écorce; *black diamonds,* la houille; *cut diamond,* diamant taillé; *diamond cut diamond,* fin contre fin; *diamond of the first water,* diamant de première eau; *set of diamonds,* garniture de diamants, *f.* **diamond-cutter,** *n.* Lapidaire, *m.* **diamond-dust,** *n.* Égrisée, *f.* **diamond-shaped,** *a.* En losange, taillé en losange.
Diana [dai'ænə]. (*Myth.*) Diane, *f.*; (*Lit.*) chasseresse, *f.*
diandrous [dai'ændrəs], *a.* (*Bot.*) Diandre.
diapason [daiə'peizən], *n.* Diapason, *m.*
diaper ['daiəpə], *n.* Linge ouvré, linge damassé, *m.*; serviette hygiénique, couche (of baby), *f.*; (*Arch.*) panneau à losanges, *m.*—*v.t.* Ouvrir, damasser. **diapered,** *a.* Ouvré, gaufré; découpé en losanges.
diaphanous [dai'æfənəs], *a.* Diaphane.
diaphoretic [daiəfo'retik], *a.* and *n.* Diaphorétique.
diaphragm ['daiəfræm], *n.* Diaphragme, *m.*; membrane, cloison, *f.* *Diaphragm of a telephone,* membrane vibrante d'un téléphone. **diaphragmatic** [-fræg'mætik], *a.* Diaphragmatique.
diaphysis [dai'æfisis], *n.* Diaphyse, *f.*
diarist ['daiərist], *n.* Auteur d'un journal (particulier), *m.*
diarize [daiə'raiz], *v.i.* Tenir un journal.
diarrhoea [daiə'ri:ə], *n.* Diarrhée, *f.* **diarrhoeic,** *a.* Diarrhéique.
diarthrosis [daiɑ:'θrousis], *n.* Diarthrose, *f.*
diary ['daiəri], *n.* Journal (particulier); agenda, *m.*
diastase ['daiəsteiz], *n.* (*Chem.*) Diastase, *f.* **diastasic,** *a.* Diastasique. **diastasis,** *n.* (*Surg.*) Diastase, *f.* **diastema,** *n.* Diastème, *m.*
diastole [dai'æstəli], *n.* (*Physiol.*) Diastole, *f.*
diastyle, *n.* (*Arch.*) Diastyle, *m.*
diatessaron [daiə'tesərən], *n.* (*Mus.*) Intervalle de quarte; accord des quatre évangélistes, *m.*
diathermancy [daiə'θə:mənsi], *n.* Diathermanéité, *f.* **diathermanous,** *a.* Diathermane. **diathermy,** *n.* Diathermie, *f.*
diathesis [dai'æθəsis], *n.* Diathèse, *f.*
diatonic [daiə'tɔnik], *a.* (*Mus.*) Diatonique.
diatribe ['daiətraib], *n.* Diatribe, *f.*
dibble [dibl], *n.* Plantoir, *m.*—*v.t.* Planter au plantoir.
dibs [dibz], *n.pl.* (Jeu d') osselets, *m.pl.*; (*pop.*) galette, *f.*, pognon, *m.*
dice [dais], *n.pl.* Dés, *m.pl.*—*v.i.* Jouer aux dés. **dice-box,** *n.* Cornet à dés, *m.* **dicer,** *n.* Joueur aux dés, *m.*
dichotomous [dai'kɔtəməs], *a.* (*Bot.*) Dichotome, dichotomique. **dichotomy,** *n.* Dichotomie, *f.*

dichroic [dai'krouik], *a.* Dichroïque.
dichroism ['daikroizm], *n.* Dichroïsme, *m.*
dichromatic [-'mætik], *a.* Dichromatique.
dickens ['dikinz], *int.* Diantre! *What the dickens!* que diable!
dicker ['dikə], *v.i., v.t.* (*Am.*) Marchander.
dicky ['diki], *n.* (*colloq.*) Âne, baudet, *m.*; siège de derrière; (*Motor.*) spider, *m.*; plastron (mobile) (shirt-front), *m.—a.* (*fam.*) Défectueux, peu sûr. *A dicky heart,* un cœur défectueux. **dicky-bird,** *n.* Petit oiseau, *m.*
dicotyledon [daikɔti'li:dən], *n.* (*Bot.*) Dicotylédone, *f.* **dicotyledonous,** *a.* Dicotylédone.
dicrotic [dai'krɔtik], *a.* Dicrote (pulse).
dictaphone ['diktəfoun], *n.* Dictaphone, *m.,* machine à dicter, *f.*
dictate (1) [dik'teit], *v.t.* Dicter.—*v.i.* Commander (à).
dictate (2) ['dikteit], *n.* Précepte, ordre, *m.*; (*fig.*) inspiration, voix, *f.* **dictation** [-'teiʃən], *n.* Dictée, *f.*; (*fig.*) acte autoritaire, *m. From his dictation,* sous sa dictée. **dictator,** *n.* Dictateur, *m.* **dictatorial** [-tə'tɔ:riəl] or **dictatory,** *a.* Dictatorial, de dictateur; impérieux, arrogant; autoritaire, magistral. **dictatorially,** *adv.* Dictatorialement. **dictatorship,** *n.* Dictature, *f.*
diction ['dikʃən], *n.* Diction, *f.*; débit, *m.* **dictionary,** *n.* Dictionnaire, *m. A walking dictionary,* un dictionnaire ambulant, un puits de science.
dictum ['diktəm], *n.* (*pl.* **dictums** or **dicta**) Dire, dicton, *m.*; opinion personnelle d'un juge, *f.*
did, *past* [DO].
didactic [di'dæktik] or **didactical,** *a.* Didactique. **didactically,** *adv.* Didactiquement.
didacticism [dai'dæktisizm], *n.* Didactique, *f.*
diddle [didl], *v.t.* (*colloq.*) Duper, rouler; *He diddled me out of a thousand francs,* il m'a roulé de mille francs.
didelphian [dai'delfiən], **didelphic,** or **didelphous,** *a.* Didelphe.
Dido ['daidou]. (*Lit.*) Didon, *f.*
didymous ['didiməs], *a.* (*Bot.*) Didyme.
didynamia [daidi'næmiə], *n.pl.* (*Bot.*) Didynamie, *f.*
die (1) [dai], *n.* (*pl.* **dies** [daiz]) Coin (for stamping); (*pl.* **dice**) dé (à jouer), *m.*; (*fig.*) chance, *f.,* hasard, *m. A cast of the die,* un coup de dé; *the die is cast,* le sort en est jeté. **die-sinker,** *n.* Graveur en creux, *m.* **die-sinking,** *n.* Gravure en creux, *f.*
die (2) [dai], *v.i.* (*past* **died**; *pres.p.* **dying**; *p.p.* **died**) Mourir; (*fig.*) s'éteindre, se perdre, cesser; crever (of animals). *He died yesterday,* il est mort hier; *to be dying,* se mourir; *to die a natural death,* mourir de sa belle mort; *to die away,* s'affaiblir, s'éteindre, se mourir; *to die broken-hearted,* mourir de chagrin; *to die down,* s'apaiser, se calmer; *to die of,* mourir de; *to die out,* s'éteindre, disparaître, s'oublier.
die-hard ['daihɑ:d], *n.* (*Mil.*) Un (régiment) qui meurt et ne se rend pas; (*Polit.*) un conservateur enragé, un ultra, un intransigeant.
dielectric [daii'lektrik], *a. and n.* Diélectrique, *m.*
Diesel [di:zl], *a.* (*Eng.*) Diesel. *Diesel engine,* moteur diesel, *m.*

diesis ['daiisis], *n.* (*Mus.*) Dièse, *m.*
dies non [daiiz'nɔn], *n.* (*Law*) Jour férié, *m.*
diet ['daiət], *n.* Régime, *m.*; diète, nourriture; diète (assembly), *f. To be on a diet,* être au régime.—*v.t.* Mettre à la diète, mettre au régime.—*v.i.* Faire diète, être au régime. **dietary,** *n.* Diète, *f.,* régime alimentaire, *m.* —*a.* De diète. **dietetic** [-'tetik] or **dietetical,** *a.* Diététique. **dietetics,** *n.pl.* Diététique, *f.* **dietine,** *n.* Diétine, *f.*
differ ['difə], *v.i.* Différer (de); n'être pas d'accord, se quereller (avec). *To agree to differ,* garder chacun son opinion.
difference ['difərəns], *n.* Différence; dispute (quarrel), *f.*; différend (discrepancy), *m.*; divergence, *f.,* écart, *m. It makes no difference,* cela ne fait rien, c'est la même chose; *to pay the difference,* faire l'appoint; *to split the difference,* partager le différend, (*colloq.*) couper la poire en deux; *to tell the difference between,* faire la différence entre, distinguer. —*v.t.* Différencier. **different,** *a.* Différent, divers, divergent, autre.
differential [difə'renʃəl], *a.* Différentiel.—*n.* (*Tech.*) Différentiel, *m.*; (*Math.*) différentielle, *f.*
differentiate [difə'renʃieit], *v.t.* Différencier, distinguer; (*Math.*) différentier. **differentiation,** *n.* Différenciation; (*Math.*) différentiation, *f.* **differently,** *adv.* Différemment, autrement.
difficult ['difikəlt], *a.* Difficile; malaisé. *It was difficult for him to,* il avait de la difficulté à. **difficulty,** *n.* Difficulté; peine, *f.,* embarras, *m.*; (*pl.*) embarras pécuniaire, *m. To be in a difficulty,* être dans l'embarras; *to be in difficulties,* être dans la gêne, être gêné; *to make difficulties,* soulever des objections, faire des difficultés; *with difficulty,* avec peine; *without difficulty,* sans peine.
diffidence ['difidəns], *n.* Défiance (de soi), modestie, timidité, *f.* **diffident,** *a.* Timide, hésitant. **diffidently,** *adv.* Avec hésitation, timidement.
diffluence ['difluəns], *n.* Diffluence, *f.* **diffluent,** *n.* Diffluent, *m.*
difformed [di'fɔ:md], *a.* (*Bot.*) De forme anormale.
diffract [di'frækt], *v.t.* Diffracter. **diffraction,** *n.* Diffraction, *f.* **diffractive,** *a.* Diffractif.
diffuse (1) [di'fju:s], *a.* Répandu, étendu; diffus, verbeux (of style).
diffuse (2) [di'fju:z], *v.t.* Répandre.
diffused [di'fju:zd], *a.* Répandu, irrégulier; (*Opt.*) diffus. *Diffused lighting,* éclairage indirect, *m.,* lumière diffuse, *f.*; *to be diffused,* se répandre. **diffusedly** [-'fju:zidli] or **diffusely** [-'fju:sli], *adv.* Diffusément. **diffuseness,** *n.* Verbosité, diffusion; abondance, *f.* **diffusion,** *n.* Diffusion, dispersion; propagation, *f.* **diffusive,** *a.* Qui se répand; abondant, diffus (of style). **diffusively,** *adv.* Au loin, dans toutes les directions.
dig [dig], *v.t.* (*past* and *p.p.* **dug** (1) or ***digged**) Creuser; bêcher; piocher; fouir, fouiller. *To dig open,* ouvrir; *to dig out,* extraire, déterrer; *to dig through,* percer, transpercer; *to dig up,* déterrer, arracher.—*v.i.* Bêcher, piocher; creuser la terre; faire des fouilles. (*Mil.*) *To dig in,* se retrancher.—*n.* Coup (de bêche), (de coude); (*colloq.*) coup de patte, *m.*

digest (1) [di'dʒest], *v.t.* Rédiger, élaborer, digérer; (*Chem.*) faire digérer; digérer (food etc.).—*v.i.* Digérer.

digest (2) ['daidʒest], *n.* Sommaire, abrégé (of a science), *m.*; recueil (de lois), *m.*

digester [di'dʒestə], *n.* (*Chem.*) Digesteur, *m.*; marmite de Papin, *f.* **digestible,** *a.* Digestible. **digestion,** *n.* Digestion, *f.* **digestive,** *a.* and *n.* Digestif, *m.*

digger ['digə], *n.* Personne qui bêche, *f.*, terrassier; chercheur d'or, mineur; fouilleur (for remains etc.); (*pop.*) Australien, *m.* **digging,** *n.* Fouille, *f.*, creusement, déblai; terrassement (of trenches), *m.*; (*pl.*) mines d'or, *f.pl.*, placers, *m.pl.*; (*pop.*) (*abbr.* **digs**) Logement, garni, *m. He lives in diggings* (or *digs*), il loge en garni.

*dight [dait], *v.t.* Parer, apprêter.—*a.* Orné, paré.

digit ['didʒit], *n.* Doigt (mesure de 20 millimètres); (*Arith.*) chiffre, *m.* **digital,** *a.* Digital. **digitaliform** [-'tælifɔːm], *a.* Digitiforme.

digitaline ['didʒitəlin], *n.* (*Chem.*) Digitaline, *f.*

digitalis [didʒi'teilis], *n.* Digitale, *f.* **digitate** or **digitated,** *a.* Digité. **digitigrade,** *n.* (*Zool.*) Digitigrade, *m.*

diglyph ['daiglif], *n.* (*Arch.*) Diglyphe, *m.*

dignified ['dignifaid], *a.* Plein de dignité, digne; noble, fier, solennel. **dignify,** *v.t.* Honorer, élever, illustrer; décorer (de). **dignitary,** *n.* Dignitaire, *m.* **dignity,** *n.* Dignité, *f. It is beneath his dignity to talk to us,* il ne saurait s'abaisser jusqu'à parler avec nous; *to stand on one's dignity,* se tenir sur son quant-à-soi.

digraph ['daigrɑːf], *n.* Digramme, *m.*

digress [dai'gres or di'gres], *v.i.* Faire une digression; s'écarter (de); s'égarer (dans). **digression,** *n.* Digression, *f.* **digressive,** *a.* De digression. **digressively,** *adv.* Par digression.

digynous ['daidʒinəs], *a.* (*Bot.*) Digyne.

dihedron [dai'hiːdrən], **dihedral,** *n.* and *a.* Dièdre, *m.*

dike [daik], *n.* Digue, *f.*, fossé; (mines) filon stérile, *m.*; (*Geol.*) veine de basalte, *f.*—*v.t.* Endiguer.

*dilacerate [dai'læsəreit], *v.t.* Dilacérer, déchirer.

dilapidate [di'læpideit], *v.t.* Délabrer, dilapider.—*v.i.* Se délabrer, tomber en ruine. **dilapidated,** *a.* Délabré. **dilapidation,** *n.* Délabrement, *m.*, dilapidation, *f.*; (*pl.*) (*Law*) detériorations, dégradations, *f.pl.* **dilapidator,** *n.* Dilapidateur, *m.*, -trice, *f.*

dilatability [dileitə'biliti or dai-], *n.* Dilatabilité, *f.* **dilatable,** *a.* Dilatable. **dilatation** or **dilation,** *n.* Dilatation, *f.* **dilate,** *v.t.* Dilater, élargir, étendre.—*v.i.* Se dilater; (*fig.*) s'étendre (to descant). **dilator,** *n.* (*Anat.*) Dilatateur, *m.*

dilatoriness ['dilətərinis], *n.* Lenteur, négligence, *f.* **dilatory,** *a.* Négligent, lent, (*Law*) dilatoire.

dilemma [di'lemə or dai'lemə], *n.* Dilemme, *m.*; alternative, *f.*; (*fig.*) embarras, *m. On the horns of a dilemma,* enfermé dans un dilemme.

dilettante [dili'tænti], *n.* (*pl.* **dilettanti**) Amateur des beaux arts, dilettante, *m.* **dilettantism,** *n.* Dilettantisme, *m.*

diligence ['dilidʒəns], *n.* Diligence, assiduité, *f.*, soin, *m.*; diligence (coach) ['diliʒɑ̃ns], *f.* **diligent,** *a.* Diligent, appliqué. **diligently,** *adv.* Diligemment, avec application.

dill [dil], *n.* Aneth (plant), *m.*

dilly-dally ['dili'dæli], *v.i.* Lanterner, barguigner. **dilly-dallying,** *n.* Lanternerie, *f.*, barguignage, *m.*

*diluent ['diljuənt], *a.* Délayant, diluant.

dilute [dai- or di'ljuːt], *v.t.* Délayer; diluer; étendre d'eau; couper (wine); (*fig.*) affaiblir. —*a.* Dilué, mitigé. **dilution** or **diluting,** *n.* Dilution (of liquids), *f.*; délayement or délayage (act); (*fig.*) affaiblissement, *m.*

diluvial [di'ljuːviəl or dai'ljuːviəl] or **diluvian,** *a.* Diluvial, diluvien. **diluvium,** *n.* Diluvium, *m.*

dim [dim], *a.* Obscur, obscurci, trouble; sombre, blafard; terne, pâle, faible (of light); incertain, indécis, vague. *To be dim-sighted,* avoir la vue trouble; *to grow dim,* s'obscurcir; (*colloq.*) *to take a dim view of,* avoir mauvaise opinion de.—*v.t.* Obscurcir; offusquer; atténuer; ternir; éclipser. (*Motor.*) *To dim the headlights,* baisser les phares.—*v.i.* S'obscurcir; se tenir.

dime [daim], *n.* (*Am.*) Un dizième de dollar, *m.*, dîme, *f.*

dimension [di'menʃən or dai-], *n.* Dimension, proportion, étendue, cote, *f.*—*v.t.* Calculer les dimensions; coter.

dimensional [dai'menʃənəl], *a.* Dimensionnel. *Three dimensional,* à trois dimensions; (*Cine.*) *three-dimensional* (*3-D*) *film,* film en relief, *m.*; *3-D system,* procédé stéréoscopique, *m.*

diminish [di'miniʃ], *v.t.* Diminuer, amoindrir; abaisser (to lower the height of).—*v.i.* Diminuer. **diminishing,** *a.* Qui diminue. **diminishingly,** *adv.* Avec dénigrement. **diminution** [dimi'njuːʃən], *n.* Diminution, *f.* **diminutive** [di'minjutiv], *a.* Petit, diminutif, minuscule.—*n.* Diminutif, *m.* **diminutively,** *adv.* En petit. **diminutiveness,** *n.* Petitesse, exiguïté, *f.*

dimissory [di'misəri], *a.* Dimissorial; (*Eccles.*) dimissoire.

dimity ['dimiti], *n.* Basin, coton rayé, *m.*

dimly ['dimli], *adv.* Obscurément, indistinctement, faiblement, à peine; sans éclat. *Dimly lighted,* peu éclairé. **dimness,** *n.* Obscurcissement, *m.*; obscurité; faiblesse (of sight), *f.*; aspect terne, *m.*; manque d'éclat, *m.*

dimorphous [dai'mɔːfəs], *a.* Dimorphe. **dimorphism,** *n.* Dimorphisme, *m.*, dimorphie, *f.*

dimple [dimpl], *n.* Fossette, *f.* (on chin); ride, *f.* (on water).—*v.t.* Former des fossettes dans; rider.—*v.i.* Se former en fossettes; (*fig.*) se rider (of water etc.).

din [din], *n.* Vacarme, tapage, fracas; cliquetis (of arms etc.), *m.*—*v.t.* Étourdir, assourdir; corner (to repeat).

dine [dain], *v.i.* Dîner (de). *To dine out,* dîner en ville, dîner dehors; *to dine with Duke Humphrey,* dîner par cœur.—*v.t.* Donner à dîner à. **diner,** *n.* Dîneur, *m.*

ding-dong ['diŋ'dɔŋ], *n.* Tintement des cloches, *m.*—*adv.* Digue-dong.

dinghy ['diŋgi], *n.* (*Naut.*) Youyou, canot, *m.*

dinginess ['dindʒinis], *n.* Couleur terne, *f.*; aspect sale or défraîchi, *m.*

dingle [diŋgl], *n.* Vallon boise, *m.*
dingo ['diŋgou], *n.* Dingo, *m.*
dingy ['dindʒi], *a.* Terne; sale; défraîchi; (*colloq.*) crasseux, miteux.
dining ['dainiŋ], *n.* Action de dîner, *f.* **dining-car**, *n.* Wagon-restaurant, *m.* **dining-hall**, *n.* Réfectoire, *m.* **dining-room**, *n.* Salle à manger, *f.* **dining-rooms**, *n.pl.* Restaurant *m.* **dining-table**, *n.* Table de salle à manger, *f.*
dinner ['dinə], *n.* Dîner, *m.* **dinner-bell**, *n.* Cloche du dîner, *f.* **dinner-jacket**, *n.* Smoking, *m.* **dinner-party**, *n.* (Grand) dîner; les invités, les convives, *m.pl.* **dinner-service, dinner-set**, *n.* Service de table, *m.* **dinner-time**, *n.* Heure du dîner, *f.* **dinner-wagon**, *n.* Servante, *f.* (furniture).
dinornis [dai'nɔːnis], *n.* Dinornis, *m.*
dinosaur, dinosaurian [-nə'sɔːriən], *n.* Dinosaurien, *m.*
dinotherium [-'θiəriəm], *n.* Dinothérium, *m.*
dint (1) [dint], *n.* Force, *f.*, pouvoir, *m.* By *dint of*, à force de.
dint (2) [DENT] (1)].
diocesan [dai'ɔsisən], *a.* Diocésain.—*n.* Évêque diocésain, *m.*
diocese ['daiəsis], *n.* Diocèse, *m.*
Diogenes [dai'ɔdʒəniːz]. Diogène, *m.*
dionaea [daio'niːə], *n.* (*Bot.*) Dionée, *f.*
Dionysius [daiə'naisiəs]. (*Greek Hist.*) Denys, *m.*
Dionysus [daiə'naisəs]. (*Myth.*) Dionysos, *m.*
diopter [dai'ɔptə], *n.* Dioptre, *m.*; dioptrie, *f.* **dioptric**, *a.* Dioptrique. **dioptrics**, *n.pl.* Dioptrique, *f.*
diorama [daiə'rɑːmə], *n.* Diorama, *m.* **dioramic** [daiə'ræmik], *a.* Dioramique.
diorite ['daiərait], *n.* Diorite, *f.*
dioxide [dai'ɔksaid], *n.* (*Chem.*) Bioxyde, *m.*
dip [dip], *v.t.* Plonger (dans); tremper, mouiller; faire biaiser (to slant); saluer (a flag); baisser (head-lights); (*fig.*) puiser (dans).—*v.i.* Plonger; tremper (dans); incliner (of the needle); (*Mining etc.*) s'incliner. *To dip into*, s'engager dans, feuilleter, parcourir (a book).—*n.* Plongeon, *m.*, baignade, *f.*, inclinaison (of the needle); chandelle à la baguette (candle); dépression (of the horizon), *f.* *To take a dip*, prendre un bain (de mer).
dip-stick, *n.* (*Motor.*) Réglette-jauge, *f.*
diphtheria [dif'θiəriə], *n.* Diphtérie, *f.*
diphthong ['difθɔŋ], *n.* Diphtongue, *f.*
diphthongization [difθɔŋgai'zeiʃən], *n.* Diphtongaison, *f.*
diphthongize ['difθɔŋgaiz], *v.t.* Diphtonguer.
diploma [di'ploumə], *n.* Diplôme, *m.*
diplomacy [di'ploumǝsi], *n.* Diplomatie, *f.*
diplomat ['diplomæt] or **diplomatist** [-'ploumətist], *n.* Diplomate, *m.* **diplomatic** [-'mætik], *a.* Diplomatique. **diplomatically**, *adv.* Diplomatiquement; avec tact. **diplomatics**, *n.pl.* Diplomatique, *f.*
dipody ['daipədi], *n.* Dipodie, *f.*
dipper ['dipə], *n.* Plongeur, *m.*; cuillère à pot, *f.*; merle d'eau (bird), *m.* **dipping**, *n.* Plongement, *m.*, plongée, immersion, *f.*; (*Mining*) inclinaison, *f.* *Dipping needle*, aiguille d'inclinaison, *f.*; *dipping net*, épuisette, *f.*
dippy ['dipi], *a.* (*pop.*) Timbré, dingue.
dipsomania [dipso'meiniə], *n.* Dipsomanie, *f.*
dipsomaniac, *n.* Dipsomane, *m.*

Diptera ['diptərə] or **dipterans**, *n.pl.* (*Ent.*) Diptères, *m.pl.* **dipterous**, *a.* Diptère.
diptych ['diptik], *n.* (*Rom. Ant.*) Diptyque, *m.*
dire ['daiə], *a.* Terrible; affreux; cruel.
direct [di'rekt or dai-], *a.* Direct, droit; exprès, positif, clair. *Direct taxes*, contributions directes, *f.pl.*—*adv.* (*colloq.*) Directement, droit.—*v.t.* Diriger; ordonner, charger (de); indiquer, donner des renseignements à. *To direct a letter*, adresser une lettre; *to direct attention to*, appeler l'attention de . . . à.
direction [di'rekʃən or dai-], *n.* Direction, *f.*; ordre, *m.*, instruction, *f.*; sens, côté, *m.*; adresse (of a letter), *f.* *In all directions*, de tous côtés; *in every direction*, dans tous les sens. **directive**, *a.* Qui dirige, dirigeant.— *n.* Directive, *f.* **directly**, *adv.* Directement, immédiatement; (*colloq.*) ['drekli] tout de suite, immédiatement (of time); aussitôt que (as soon as). **directness**, *n.* Mouvement direct, *m.*; direction en droite ligne; (*fig.*) droiture, *f.* **director**, *n.* Directeur, administrateur, gérant; (*Cine.*) metteur en scène, réalisateur; guide; régent (of the Bank of France), *m.* **directorate**, *n.* Conseil d'administration, *m.*, direction, *f.* **directorial** [-'tɔːriəl], *a.* Directorial, de directeur. **directorship**, *n.* Directorat; poste de directeur, *m.*
directory [di'rektəri], *n.* Directoire; (*Postal*) annuaire, *m.* **directress**, *n.* Directrice, *f.*
direful ['daiəful], *a.* Terrible, affreux, désastreux; cruel. **direfully**, *adv.* Terriblement, affreusement, cruellement. **direfulness**, *n.* Horreur, *f.*
dirge [dəːdʒ], *n.* Chant funèbre, *m.*
dirigible ['diridʒəbl], *a.* Dirigeable.—*n.* (Ballon) dirigeable, *m.*
dirk [dəːk], *n.* Poignard, *m.*
dirt [dəːt], *n.* Saleté; crasse; boue, crotte, fange; ordure, *f.* *Tò eat dirt*, (*fig.*) s'humilier, se rétracter; *to treat like dirt*, traiter comme le dernier des derniers.—*v.t.* Salir; souiller; crotter. **dirtily**, *adv.* Salement; (*fig.*) vilainement, bassement. **dirtiness**, *n.* Saleté, malpropreté; (*fig.*) bassesse, vilenie, *f.* **dirty**, *a.* Sale, malpropre, crasseux, crotté; immonde; (*fig.*) bas, vilain; mauvais (of weather). *Dirty action*, action sale, *f.*; *dirty fellow*, saligaud, *m.*; *dirty trick*, vilain tour, *m.*; *dirty work*, saleté, *f.*—*v.t.* Salir, crotter; (*fig.*) souiller.
disability [disə'biliti], *n.* Incapacité, impuissance, *f.*
disable [dis'eibl], *v.t.* Rendre incapable, mettre hors d'état (de); mettre hors de service; (*Mil.*) mettre hors de combat; (*Law*) rendre inhabile (à); désemparer. **disabled**, *a.* Hors d'état; hors de service; (*Mil.*) hors de combat; (*Navy*) désemparé. *Disabled ex-service men*, mutilés de guerre, *m.pl.* **disablement**, *n.* Mise hors de combat; invalidité, *f.*
disabuse [disə'bjuːz], *v.t.* Désabuser (de).
disaccord [disə'kɔːd], *n.* Désaccord, *m.*—*v.i.* Être en désaccord (avec).
disaccustom [disə'kʌstəm], *v.t.* Désaccoutumer, déshabituer.
disadvantage [disəd'vɑːntidʒ], *n.* Désavantage, inconvénient, *m.*; perte (loss), *f.* *At a disadvantage*, au désavantage, à son désavantage, au dépourvu; *to be under a disadvantage*, avoir le désavantage (de).—*v.t.*

Désavantager. **disadvantageous** [disædvən-'teidʒəs], a. Désavantageux (à). **disadvantageously**, adv. Désavantageusement. **disaffect** [disə'fekt], v.t. Aliéner, désaffectionner. **disaffected**, a. Mal disposé (pour), mécontent, dissident. **disaffection**, n. Désaffection, f., mécontentement, m. **disaffiliate** [disə'filieit], v.t. Désaffilier. **disaffiliation** [disəfili'eiʃən], n. Désaffiliation, f. **disaffirm** [disə'fə:m], v.t. (Law) Annuler, casser. **disaggregate** [dis'ægrəgeit], v.t. Désagréger. **disagree** [disə'gri:], v.i. Différer, ne pas s'accorder, être en désaccord (avec); se brouiller, se quereller. My dinner disagreed with me, mon dîner m'a fait mal. **disagreeable**, a. Désagréable; fâcheux. **disagreeableness**, n. Désagrément, m., nature désagréable, f. **disagreeably**, adv. Désagréablement. **disagreement**, n. Différence, f., désaccord, m.; différend, m.; brouille, f. **disallow** [disə'lau], v.t. Désapprouver; ne pas admettre, refuser, désavouer, défendre. **disallowable**, a. Défendu, interdit, qui n'est pas permis. **disallowance**, n. Rejet, m., désapprobation, f. **disappear** [disə'piə], v.i. Disparaître; s'amuir (of a vowel). **disappearance**, n. Disparition, f.; amuissement, m. **disappoint** [disə'point], v.t. Désappointer, décevoir, manquer de parole à, tromper dans son attente; frustrer (de); (fig.) déconcerter, déjouer. He was disappointed in love, il a eu des chagrins d'amour. **disappointing**, a. Décevant. **disappointment**, n. Désappointement, m.; déception, f.; contretemps, mécompte, m., contrariété, f. **disapprobation** [disæpro'beiʃən] or **disapproval** [disə'pru:vəl], n. Désapprobation, f. **disapprobatory** [dis'æprobeitəri] or **disapproving**, a. Désapprobateur. **disapprove** [disə'pru:v], v.t. Désapprouver.— v.i. To disapprove of, désapprouver. **disapprovingly**, adv. Avec désapprobation. **disarm** [dis'a:m], v.t. Désarmer; (fig.) détourner.—v.i. Se désarmer. **disarmament**, n. Désarmement, m. **disarming**, a. Désarmant. **disarrange** [disə'reindʒ], v.t. Déranger. **disarrangement**, n. Dérangement, désordre, m. **disarray** [disə'rei], v.i. Mettre en désarroi or en désordre.—n. Désarroi, désordre, m. **disarticulate** [disa:'tikjuleit], v.t. Désarticuler; démembrer. **disassemble** [disə'sembl], v.t. Démonter, désassembler (a machine). **disaster** [di'za:stə], n. Désastre, malheur, m. **disastrous**, a. Désastreux. **disastrously**, adv. Désastreusement. **disastrousness**, n. Nature désastreuse, f. **disavow** [disə'vau], v.t. Désavouer. **disavowal**, n. Désaveu; reniement, m. **disband** [dis'bænd], v.t. Licencier, congédier; disperser.—v.i. Se débander, se disperser, être licencié. **disbanding** or **disbandment**, n. Licenciement, m. **disbar** [dis'ba:], v.t. Rayer du tableau des avocats. **disbelief** [disbi'li:f], n. Incrédulité, f. **disbelieve** [disbi'li:v], v.t. Ne pas croire,

refuser de croire. To disbelieve every word of, ne pas croire un seul mot de. **disbeliever**, n. Incrédule. **disbench** [dis'bentʃ], v.t. (Law) Rayer du tableau des avocats-doyens. **disbranch** [dis'bra:nʃ], v.t. Ébrancher. **disbud** [dis'bʌd], v.t. Ébourgeonner. **disbudding**, n. Ébourgeonnement, m. **disburden** [dis'bə:dən], v.t. Décharger (de); (fig.) débarrasser, soulager (de). To disburden one's heart to, ouvrir son cœur à. **disburse** [dis'bə:s], v.t. Débourser. **disbursement**, n. Déboursement; paiement, m.; dépense, f.; (pl.) déboursés, m.pl.; (Comm.) débours, m.pl. **disburser**, n. Personne qui débourse, f. **disc** [DISK]. **discard** [dis'ka:d], v.t. Mettre de côté; congédier; écarter; exclure, éliminer; (Cards) faire son écart, écarter, se défausser.—n. (Cards) Écart, m., défausse, f.; (Ind.) pièce de rebut, f. **discern** [di'zə:n or di'sə:n], v.t. Discerner, distinguer. **discernible**, a. Perceptible, visible. **discernibly**, adv. Visiblement. **discerning**, a. Judicieux, éclairé, attentif. **discerningly**, adv. Avec discernement. **discernment**, n. Discernement, jugement, m. **discharge** [dis'tʃa:dʒ], n. Déchargement, m.; décharge (of fire-arms etc.), f.; décochement (of arrows), m.; mise en liberté, f., élargissement (from prison); accomplissement (of a duty), m.; réhabilitation (of bankrupt), f.; quittance (payment), f.; renvoi, congé (of a servant); (Mil.) congé définitif, m., réforme, f.; (Med.) écoulement, m., suppuration, f. Discharge pipe, tuyau de décharge, m.—v.t. Décharger; congédier, renvoyer (a servant); libérer, élargir (from confinement); acquitter, payer (a debt); décocher, lancer (arrows); décharger (fire-arms); s'acquitter de, remplir (a duty); (Mil., Navy) congédier; (Law) quitter.—v.i. Suppurer (of a wound etc.). **discharger**, n. (Elec.) Excitateur, éclateur, m. **disciple** [di'saipl], n. Disciple, m. **discipleship**, n. État, m., or qualité, f., de disciple. **disciplinable** ['disiplinəbl], a. Disciplinable. **disciplinarian** [-'neəriən], a. Disciplinaire, qui se fait obéir.—n. Personne rigide pour la discipline, f. To be a good disciplinarian, savoir se faire obéir. **disciplinary** ['disiplinəri], a. Disciplinaire. **discipline** ['disiplin], n. Discipline, f.—v.t. Discipliner, former; punir. **disclaim** [dis'kleim], v.t. Désavouer, renier, nier, répudier; (Law) se désister, renoncer à. **disclaimer**, n. Désaveu, désistement, m. **disclose** [dis'klouz], v.t. Découvrir, révéler, divulguer; (fig.) mettre au jour, faire voir. **disclosure**, n. Révélation, découverte, divulgation, f. **discobolus** [dis'kɔbələs], n. (Ant.) Discobole, m. **discoid** ['diskɔid] or **discoidal** [dis'kɔidəl], a. Discoïde, discoïdal. **discoloration** [diskʌlə'reiʃən], n. Décoloration, f. **discolour** [dis'kʌlə], v.t. Décolorer. **discomfit** [dis'kʌmfit], v.t. Défaire; décontenancer, contrarier. **discomfiture**, n. Défaite, déroute, déconvenue, f.

discomfort [dis'kʌmfət], *n.* Incommodité, *f.*, inconfort, malaise, *m.*; gêne, *f.*—*v.t.* Affliger, chagriner, incommoder, gêner, inquiéter.

discommend [diskə'mend], *v.t.* Blâmer, censurer.

discommode [diskə'moud], *v.t.* Incommoder. **discommodious,** *a.* Incommode.

*****discommon** [dis'kɔmən], *v.t.* Révoquer le droit de vaine pâture *or* le droit de vente (aux étudiants).

discompose [diskəm'pouz], *v.t.* Déranger, troubler, agiter; irriter, chagriner; défaire (the features). **discomposure,** *n.* Trouble, désordre, *m.*, agitation, *f.*

disconcert [diskən'səːt], *v.t.* Déconcerter, troubler. **disconcerting,** *a.* Déconcertant, troublant. **disconcertment,** *n.* Embarras, trouble, *m.*

disconnect [diskə'nekt], *v.t.* Désunir, séparer; (*Mach.*) désembrayer; couper la communication. **disconnected,** *a.* Débrayé; déconnecté; (*fig.*) décousu. **disconnexion,** *n.* Désunion, séparation, *f.*

disconsolate [dis'kɔnsələt], *a.* Inconsolable, désolé; triste, morne (of scenery). **disconsolately,** *adv.* Inconsolablement, tristement. **disconsolateness,** *n.* Désolation, *f.*

discontent [diskən'tent], *a.* Mécontent.— *n.* Mécontentement, *m.*—*v.t.* Mécontenter. **discontented,** *a.* Mécontent (de). **discontentedly,** *adv.* Avec mécontentement, à contre-cœur. **discontentedness** or **discontentment,** *n.* Mécontentement, *m.*

discontinuance [diskən'tinjuəns] or *****discontinuation** [-'eiʃən], *n.* Discontinuation, cessation, *f.* **discontinue** [-'tinju:], *v.t.* Discontinuer; cesser de prendre, se désabonner à (a newspaper etc.).—*v.i.* Discontinuer, s'interrompre.

discontinuity [diskɔnti'nju:iti], *n.* Discontinuité, *f.* **discontinuous** [-'tinjuəs], *a.* Discontinu.

discord ['diskɔːd], *n.* Discorde, désunion; (*Mus.*) dissonance, *f.* *To sow discord,* semer la discorde. **discordance,** *n.* Discordance, *f.* **discordant** [-'kɔːdənt], *a.* Discordant; (*fig.*) en désaccord. **discordantly,** *adv.* Sans accord, d'une manière discordante.

discount (1) ['diskaunt], *n.* Escompte; rabais, *m.*; (*Arith.*) règle d'escompte, *f.* *At a discount,* au rabais, en baisse; (*fig.*) en défaveur.

discount (2) [dis'kaunt], *v.t.* Escompter, faire l'escompte de; (*fig.*) décompter, rabattre.— *v.i.* Faire l'escompte. **discountable,** *a.* Escomptable.

discountenance [dis'kauntənəns], *v.t.* Décontenancer, décourager, recevoir froidement.

discounter [dis'kauntə], *n.* Escompteur, *m.* **discounting,** *n.* Escompte, *m.*

discourage [dis'kʌridʒ], *v.t.* Décourager, détourner. **discouragement,** *n.* Découragement, *m.*, désapprobation, *f.* **discouraging,** *a.* Décourageant.

discourse (1) ['diskɔːs], *n.* Discours, entretien; (*fig.*) langage, propos, *m.*

discourse (2) [dis'kɔːs], *v.i.* Discourir, s'entretenir, traiter (de).—*****v.t.* Faire entendre.

discourteous [dis'kə:tiəs], *a.* Impoli, discourtois. **discourteously,** *adv.* Impoliment, brusquement. **discourtesy,** *n.* Impolitesse, *f.*, manque de courtoisie, *m.*

discover [dis'kʌvə], *v.t.* Découvrir, trouver;

révéler, montrer, faire voir. **discoverable,** *a.* Qu'on peut découvrir; visible, apparent. **discoverer,** *n.* Découvreur, *m.* **discovery,** *n.* Découverte, *f.*

discredit [dis'kredit], *n.* Doute, discrédit, *m.*, déconsidération, *f.*; déshonneur, *m.*, honte, *f.* —*v.t.* Ne pas croire; déshonorer, discréditer. **discreditable,** *a.* Peu honorable; déshonorant; honteux. **discreditably,** *adv.* D'une maniére peu honorable.

discreet [dis'kri:t], *a.* Discret, prudent, circonspect, sage. **discreetly,** *adv.* Discrètement, sagement, prudemment. **discreetness,** *n.* Discrétion, *f.*

discrepancy [dis'krepənsi], *n.* Désaccord, *m.*, contradiction, *f.* **discrepant,** *a.* Différent, opposé; en contradiction (avec).

discrete [dis'kri:t], *a.* Discontinu; (*Math.*) discret.

discretion [dis'kreʃən], *n.* Discrétion, prudence, sagesse, *f.*; jugement, discernement, *m.* *To surrender at discretion,* se rendre à discrétion; *to use one's own discretion,* faire ce que l'on juge à propos; *years of discretion,* l'âge de raison, *m.* **discretionally,** *adv.* À discrétion. **discretionary,** *a.* Discrétionnaire. *Discretionary power,* (*Law*) pouvoir discrétionnaire, *m.*

discretive [dis'kri:tiv], *a.* Disjonctif, distinct. **discretively,** *adv.* D'une manière disjonctive.

discriminate [dis'krimineit], *v.t.* Discriminer, distinguer, séparer, discerner (de).—*v.i.* Faire des distinctions.—*a.* [-'kriminit] Judicieux. **discriminately,** *adv.* Avec discernement. **discriminating, discriminative, discriminatory,** *a.* Discriminatoire, distinctif; judicieux, de bon jugement.

discrimination [-'neiʃən], *n.* Discrimination, *f.*, discernement, jugement, *m.*; distinction, marque distinctive, *f.* *Without discrimination,* sans discernement.

discrown [dis'kraun], *v.t.* Découronner, priver de la couronne, déposer.

disculpate [dis'kʌlpeit], *v.t.* Disculper, justifier.

discursive [dis'kə:siv], *a.* Décousu, sans suite, discursif. **discursively,** *adv.* D'une manière décousue; en passant d'une idée à une autre.

discus ['diskəs], *n.* (*Ant.*) Disque, *m.*

discuss [dis'kʌs], *v.t.* Discuter, débattre, **discussible,** *a.* Discutable. **discussion,** *n.* Discussion, *f.*, débat; examen, *m.* *Under discussion,* en discussion.

disdain [dis'dein], *n.* Dédain, mépris, *m.*— *v.t.* Dédaigner, mépriser. **disdainful,** *a.* Dédaigneux, méprisant. **disdainfully,** *adv.* Dédaigneusement. **disdainfulness,** *n.* Dédain, *m.*

disease [di'zi:z], *n.* Maladie, *f.*, mal; (*fig.*) vice, *m.* *Foot-and-mouth disease,* fièvre aphteuse, *f.* **diseased,** *a.* Malade; (*fig.*) dérangé, malsain, morbide.

disembark [disəm'ba:k], *v.t., v.i.* Débarquer. **disembarkation** [disemba:'keiʃən], *n.* Débarquement, *m.*

disembodied [disəm'bɔdid], *a.* Désincarné; (*Mil.*) désincorporé. **disembodiment,** *n.* Désincarnation, *f.*; (*Mil.*) licenciement, *m.* **disembody,** *v.t.* Dépouiller du corps; (*Mil.*) désincorporer.

disembogue [disəm'boug], v.i. Déboucher (of river); débouquer (of ship).—v.t. Décharger, déverser.
disembowel [disəm'bauəl], v.t. Éventrer, arracher les entrailles à.
disembroil [disəm'brɔil], v.t. Débrouiller.
disenable [disə'neibl], v.t. Rendre incapable (de), paralyser.
disenchant [disən'tʃɑ:nt], v.t. Désenchanter. **disenchantment**, n. Désenchantement, m.
disencumber [disən'kʌmbə], v.t. Débarrasser (de), désencombrer. **disencumbrance**, n. Débarras, m.
disendow [disən'dau], v.t. Priver (une église etc.) de ses biens. **disendowment**, n. Sécularisation des biens (de l'Église), f.
disengage [disən'geidʒ], v.t. Dégager, débarrasser; détacher; (Tech.) débrayer.—v.i. Se dégager; (Fenc.) dégager. **disengaged**, a. Dégagé; libre; inoccupé. **disengagement**, n. Dégagement, détachement, m., rupture de fiançailles, f.
disentangle [disən'tæŋgl], v.t. Démêler, débrouiller; débarrasser (de); (colloq.) dépêtrer (de). **disentanglement**, n. Débrouillement; dégagement, démêlement, dénouement, m.
disenthral [disən'θrɔ:l], v.t. Affranchir, tirer d'esclavage. **disenthralment**, n. Affranchissement, m.
disentitle [disən'taitl], v.t. Faire perdre son droit à, ôter le droit à.
disentomb [disən'tu:m], v.t. Exhumer.
disestablish [disis'tæbliʃ], v.t. Séparer (l'Église de l'État). **disestablishment**, n. Séparation de l'Église et de l'État, f.
disfavour [dis'feivə], n. Défaveur, f. To be in great disfavour with, être très mal vu de; to fall into disfavour, tomber en défaveur. —v.t. Voir avec défaveur, désapprouver; décourager.
disfiguration [disfigju'reiʃən] or **disfigurement** [dis'figəmənt], n. Action de défigurer; difformité, f. **disfigure** [-'figə], v.t. Défigurer, enlaidir, gâter.
disfranchise [dis'fræntʃaiz], v.t. Priver de ses privilèges électoraux, priver du droit de vote.
disfranchisement [dis'fræntʃizmənt], n. Privation or perte de privilèges électoraux, f.
disgorge [dis'gɔ:dʒ], v.t. Dégorger, rendre, vomir.—v.i. Rendre gorge. **disgorger**, n. Dégorgeoir, m. (for fish).
disgrace [dis'greis], n. Disgrâce, honte, f., déshonneur, m. To be in disgrace, être dans la disgrâce, être en pénitence (of a child); to be the disgrace of, être la honte de, faire la honte de; to the disgrace of, à la honte de.— v.t. Disgracier; déshonorer, avilir. **disgraceful**, a. Honteux; déshonorant, ignoble. **disgracefully**, adv. Honteusement. **disgracefulness**, n. Honte, ignominie, f., déshonneur, m.
disgracious [dis'greiʃəs], a. Disgracieux, déplaisant.
disgruntle [dis'grʌntl], v.t. Contrarier, agacer, mécontenter.
disgruntled [dis'grʌntld], a. Mécontent; de mauvaise humeur.
disguisable [dis'gaizəbl], a. Déguisable. **disguise**, n. Déguisement, travestissement; (fig.) masque, voile, m. In disguise, déguisé. —v.t. Déguiser, travestir; (fig.) cacher,

voiler, masquer, contrefaire. **disguised**, a. Déguisé; (slang) gris, ivre. **disguisement** [DISGUISE]. **disguising**, n. Déguisement, m. There is no disguising that . . ., il faut avouer que. . . .
disgust [dis'gʌst], n. Dégoût, m., aversion, f.; ennui, m.—v.t. Dégoûter (de); écœurer. **disgustedly**, adv. Avec dégoût. **disgusting**, a. Dégoûtant, repoussant, écœurant. **disgustingly**, adv. D'une manière dégoûtante.
dish [diʃ], n. (pl. dishes) Plat (utensil); mets (food), m.; (pl.) vaisselle; (Phot.) cuvette, f. Made-up dish, plat apprêté, m.; to wash the dishes, laver la vaisselle; vegetable-dish, légumier, m.—v.t. Dresser, servir, apprêter; (colloq.) enfoncer, ruiner, flamber. To dish up, dresser, servir. **dish-cloth** or *dishclout, n. Torchon, m. **dish-cover**, n. Couvercle (de plat), m., cloche, f. **dishwater**, n. Eau de vaisselle, lavure, f.
dishabille [disæ'bi:l], n. Déshabillé, m.
dishabituate [dishə'bitjueit], v.t. Déshabituer.
disharmonious [dishɑ:'mouniəs], a. Discordant. **disharmonize**, v.t. Rendre discordant. **disharmony**, n. Inharmonie, f.; désaccord, m.
dishearten [dis'hɑ:tən], v.t. Décourager, abattre; détourner (de). **disheartening**, a. Décourageant.
*disherison [dis'herisən], n. (Law) Exhérédation, f. *disherit, v.t. Déshériter.
dishevel [di'ʃevəl], v.t. Mettre (les cheveux) en désordre, ébouriffer. **dishevelled**, a. Les cheveux ébouriffés; dépeigné, ébouriffé.
dishonest [dis'ɔnist], a. Malhonnête. **dishonestly**, adv. Malhonnêtement. **dishonesty**, n. Improbité, malhonnêteté, f.
dishonour [dis'ɔnə], n. Déshonneur, m.—v.t. Déshonorer; avilir; (Comm.) laisser protester (un effet). Dishonoured bill, effet protesté; dishonoured cheque, chèque impayé, m. **dishonourable**, a. Sans honneur; déshonorant, honteux (of things). **dishonourably**, adv. Malhonnêtement.
dishorn [dis'hɔ:n], v.t. Décorner.
disillusion [disi'lju:ʒən], v.t. Désillusionner.— n., or **disillusionment**. Désillusionnement. m.
disinclination [disinkli'neiʃən], n. Éloignement, m.; aversion, répugnance, f. **disincline** [-'klain], v.t. Éloigner (de); mal disposer. **disinclined**, a. Peu disposé.
disincorporate [disin kɔ:pəreit], v.t. Désincorporer; priver des privilèges d'une corporation; dissoudre (une société).
disinfect [disin'fekt], v.t. Désinfecter. **disinfectant**, n. Désinfectant, m. **disinfection**, n. Désinfection, f. **disinfector**, n. Désinfecteur, m.
disingenuous [disin'dʒenjuəs], a. Sans franchise, de mauvaise foi, dissimulé, peu sincère. **disingenuously**, adv. Sans candeur, de mauvaise foi, faussement. **disingenuousness**, n. Dissimulation, mauvaise foi, fausseté, f.
disinherit [disin'herit], v.t. Déshériter; (Law) exhéréder. **disinheritance**, n. Déshéritement, m.
disintegrable [dis'intəgrəbl], a. Susceptible de se désagréger. **disintegrate**, v.t. Désagréger; désintégrer.—v.i. Se désagréger, se

désintégrer. **disintegration,** *n.* Désagrégation; désintégration, *f.* **disintegrator,** *n.* Broyeur, concasseur, *m.*

disinter [disin'tə:], *v.t.* Déterrer, exhumer.

disinterested [dis'intrestid], *a.* Désintéressé. **disinterestedly,** *adv.* Avec désintéressement. **disinterestedness,** *n.* Désintéressement, *m.*

disinterment [disin'tə:mənt], *n.* Exhumation, *f.*

disjoin [dis'dʒɔin], *v.t.* Déjoindre, disjoindre, désunir.

disjoint [dis'dʒɔint], *v.t.* Désarticuler, disloquer, démonter, démembrer. **disjointed,** *a.* Désarticulé, disloqué, démembré, démonté; (*fig.*) décousu, sans suite (of style etc.). **disjointedly,** *adv.* D'une manière décousue *or* incohérente. **disjointedness,** *n.* Le décousu, *m.*, l'incohérence, *f.* (of a speech).

disjunct [dis'dʒʌŋkt], *a.* Disjoint, séparé. **disjunction,** *n.* Disjonction, séparation, *f.* **disjunctive,** *a.* Disjonctif.—*n.* (*Gram.*) Disjonctive, *f.* **disjunctively,** *adv.* Séparément.

disk [disk], *n.* Disque, *m.* (*Mil.*) *Identity disk,* plaque d'identité, *f.*; (*Med.*) *slipped disk,* hernie discale, *f.* **disk-harrow,** *n.* Pulvérisateur, *m.* **disk-jockey,** *n.* (*Rad.*) Présentateur, *m.*, présentatrice, *f.*, du disque des auditeurs. **disk-wheel,** *n.* Roue pleine, *f.*

dislike [dis'laik], *v.t.* Ne pas aimer; avoir du dégoût pour. *Not to dislike,* ne pas trouver mauvais, aimer assez; *to be disliked,* n'être pas aimé (de), être mal vu (de).—*n.* Aversion, *f.*; dégoût, *m.* *Likes and dislikes,* goûts et antipathies, *m.pl.*; *to take a dislike to,* prendre en aversion *or* en grippe, se dégoûter de.

dislocate [dislo'keit], *v.t.* Disloquer, démettre; déboîter (a bone etc.) **dislocation,** *n.* Dislocation; luxation, *f.*; déboîtement, *m.*; désorganisation (of traffic), *f.*

dislodge [dis'lɔdʒ], *v.t.* Déloger; déplacer; (*Hunt.*) débucher.

disloyal [dis'lɔiəl], *a.* Infidèle, perfide, déloyal. **disloyally,** *adv.* Infidèlement, perfidement, déloyalement. **disloyalty,** *n.* Défection (de), infidélité (à), déloyauté, perfidie, *f.*

dismal ['dizməl], *a.* Sans gaîté, sombre, morne, triste. **dismally,** *adv.* Lugubrement, tristement. **dismalness,** *n.* État sombre, *m.*; tristesse, *f.*

dismantle [dis'mæntl], *v.t.* Dévêtir; démonter (a machine); (*Mil.*) démanteler; (*Navy*) désarmer; (*fig.*) dépouiller. **dismantlement** *or* **dismantling,** *n.* Démantèlement; désarmement; démontage, *m.*

dismast [dis'ma:st], *v.t.* Démâter. **dismasting,** *n.* Démâtage, *m.*

dismay [dis'mei], *n.* Effroi, *m.*, terreur, épouvante, consternation, *f.*--*v.t.* Effarer, épouvanter, consterner.

dismember [dis'membə], *v.t.* Démembrer. **dismembering** *or* **dismemberment,** *n.* Démembrement, *m.*

dismiss [dis'mis], *v.t.* Renvoyer (de); congédier; mettre à la porte; destituer, quitter (a subject etc.); rejeter (an appeal etc.); bannir, chasser (thoughts etc.). *Let us dismiss the subject,* n'en parlons plus; *to dismiss from one's mind,* bannir de son esprit. (*Mil.*)

Dismiss! Rompez!—*n. To sound the dismiss,* sonner la breloque. **dismissal,** *n.* Renvoi; congé, *m.*; destitution, *f.*; (*Law*) acquittement, *m.* **dismissible,** *a.* Amovible, renvoyable.

dismount [dis'maunt], *v.t.* Démonter, désarçonner, faire descendre.—*v.i.* Descendre de cheval, mettre pied à terre.

disobedience [diso'bi:diəns], *n.* Désobéissance, *f.* **disobedient,** *a.* Désobéissant. **disobediently,** *adv.* En désobéissant. **disobey** [diso'bei], *v.t.* Désobéir à.

disoblige [diso'blaidʒ], *v.t.* Désobliger. **disobliging,** *a.* Désobligeant. **disobligingly,** *adv.* Désobligeamment, d'une manière désobligeante. **disobligingness,** *n.* Désobligeance, *f.*

disorder [dis'ɔ:də], *n.* Désordre, dérèglement, *m.*; indisposition, maladie (illness), *f.*; dérangement, trouble, tumulte, *m.*—*v.t.* Mettre en désordre, déranger; troubler; rendre malade (to make ill), indisposer. **disordered,** *a.* En désordre, dérangé, déréglé; malade. **disorderly,** *a.* En désordre, déréglé; immoral, vicieux; tumultueux, turbulent. *Disorderly house,* maison de débauche, *f.*

disorganization [disɔ:gəni'zeiʃən *or* -nai'zeiʃən], *n.* Désorganisation, *f.*

disorganize [dis'ɔ:gənaiz], *v.t.* Désorganiser.

disorientate [dis'ɔ:riənteit], *v.t.* Désorienter.

disown [dis'oun], *v.t.* Désavouer, nier, renier.

disparage [dis'pæridʒ], *v.t.* Déprécier, ravaler, dénigrer. **disparagement,** *n.* Dénigrement, déshonneur, reproche, *m.*; honte, *f.*, mépris, tort, *m.* *Without disparagement to you,* sans vouloir vous faire tort. **disparaging,** *a.* Dénigrant, désavantageux, injurieux. **disparagingly,** *adv.* Par dénigrement; avec mépris.

disparate ['dispərit], *a.* Disparate. **disparates,** *n.pl.* Disparates, choses disparates, *f.pl.* **disparity** [-'pæriti], *n.* Disparité, inégalité, *f.*

dispart [dis'pa:t], *v.t.* Diviser, séparer.—*v.i.* Se diviser, se séparer.

dispassionate [dis'pæʃənət], *a.* Sans passion, calme; impartial. **dispassionately,** *adv.* Sans passion, avec calme; sans parti pris.

dispatch [dis'pætʃ], *v.t.* Dépêcher, expédier; achever. *He dispatched the wounded tiger,* il acheva la tigre blessé.—*n.* Dépêche, expédition, *f.*, envoi, *m.*; diligence, promptitude, *f.* *Dispatch-money,* prime pour vive expédition, *f.*; *dispatch-rider,* estafette, *f.*; *dispatch case,* portefeuille de voyage, *m.*; *to use all dispatch,* user de diligence; *mentioned in dispatches,* cité à l'ordre du jour. **dispatcher,** *n.* Expéditeur, *m.*, -trice, *f.*

dispel [dis'pel], *v.t.* Dissiper, chasser.

dispensable [dis'pensəbl], *a.* Dont on peut se dispenser *or* se passer.

dispensary [dis'pensəri], *n.* Dispensaire, *m.*; pharmacie, *f.*

dispensation [dispən'seiʃən], *n.* Dispensation; dispense, *f.*; (*fig.*) bienfait, don, *m.*, calamité, épreuve (de la Providence), *f.*

dispensatory [dis'pensətəri], *a.* Qui peut accorder des dispenses.—*n.* Pharmacopée, *f.*

dispense [dis'pens], *v.t.* Distribuer, dispenser, administrer; (*Pharm.*) préparer (medicine).

Dispensing chemist, pharmacien d'ordonnances, *m. To dispense with*, se passer de. **dispenser**, *n.* Dispensateur, *m.*, -trice, *f.*

dispeople [dis'piːpl], *v.t.* Dépeupler.

dispersal [DISPERSION].

disperse [dis'pəːs], *v.t.* Disperser; dissiper; répandre, disséminer.—*v.i.* Se disperser, s'éparpiller, s'égailler.—*n. (Mil.)* Berloque, breloque (bugle-sound), *f.* **dispersedly**, *adv.* Çà et là, sporadiquement. **dispersion** or **dispersal**, *n.* Dispersion, *f.*

dispirit [dis'pirit], *v.t.* Décourager, abattre. **dispirited**, *a.* Découragé, abattu. **dispiritedness**, *n.* Abattement, découragement, *m.* **dispiriting**, *a.* Décourageant.

dispiteous [dis'pitjəs], *a.* Impitoyable. **dispiteously**, *adv.* Impitoyablement.

displace [dis'pleis], *v.t.* Déplacer; destituer (from a post). *(Polit.) Displaced persons*, personnes déplacées, *f.pl.* **displacement**, *n.* Déplacement, *m.*

display [dis'plei], *n.* Exposition, parade, manifestation, *f.*; *(fig.)* étalage; faste; déploiement (of troops), *m. To make a display of*, faire parade *or* faire étalage de.—*v.t.* Montrer, exposer, étaler; faire parade de; *(fig.)* manifester; *(Mil.)* déployer. *(Print.) Words displayed in bold type*, mots en vedette, *m.pl.*

displease [dis'pliːz], *v.t.* Déplaire à; mécontenter, contrarier, fâcher, vexer. **displeased**, *a.* Mécontent, offensé (de). **displeasing**, *a.* Désagréable, offensant.

displeasure [dis'pleʒə], *n.* Déplaisir, chagrin; courroux, *m. To incur someone's displeasure*, s'attirer le courroux de quelqu'un.

displume [dis'pluːm], *v.t.* Déplumer.

disport [dis'pɔːt], *v.t. To disport oneself*, s'amuser, se divertir.—*v.i.* Se divertir, s'amuser, s'ébattre.—*n.* Divertissement, *m.*, ébats, *m.pl.*

disposable [dis'pouzəbl], *a.* Disponible. **disposal**, *n.* Disposition; vente, cession (sale), *f. To have at one's disposal*, avoir à sa disposition.

dispose [dis'pouz], *v.t.* Disposer; porter (the mind). *Disposed to think*, porté à croire; *ill-disposed*, mal intentionné; *to dispose of*, céder, vendre, se défaire de, se débarrasser de; *to dispose of one's time*, employer son temps; *to dispose of someone*, se défaire de quelqu'un; *to be disposed of*, à vendre, à céder; *to be disposed of by private contract*, à vendre à l'amiable; *well-disposed*, bien intentionné. **disposedly**, *adv.* D'un air compassé. **disposer**, *n.* Dispensateur; arbitre, *m.* D'un ton de reproche.

disposition [dispə'ziʃən], *n.* Disposition, *f.*; caractère, naturel, *m.*; inclination, *f.*

dispossess [dispə'zes], *v.t.* Déposséder (de); *(Law)* exproprier. **dispossession**, *n.* Dépossession; expropriation, *f.* **dispossessor*, *n.* Spoliateur, *m.*

dispraise [dis'preiz], *v.t.* Déprécier, blâmer. —*n.* Blâme, dénigrement, *m.* **dispraisingly*, *adv.* D'un ton de reproche.

disproof [dis'pruːf], *n.* Réfutation, *f.*

disproportion [disprə'pɔːʃən], *n.* Disproportion; disconvenance (of age), *f.*—*v.t.* Mal proportionner, disproportionner. **disproportionate**, *a.* Disproportionné. **disproportionately**, *adv.* D'une manière

disproportionnée; sans symétrie. **disproportionateness**, *n.* Disproportion, *f.*, caractère disproportionné, *m.*

disprove [dis'pruːv], *v.t.* Réfuter.

disputable ['dispjuːtəbl], *a.* Discutable, contestable. **disputant** or **disputer** [-'pjuːtə], *n.* Disputeur, *m.* **disputation** [-'teiʃən], *n.* Dispute, discussion, contestation, *f.*, débat, *m.* **disputatious**, *a.* Disputeur; *(colloq.)* disputailleur, batailleur.

dispute [dis'pjuːt], *n.* Différend, *m.*, discussion, *f.*; conflit, *m. Beyond dispute*, sans contredit, incontestable, incontestablement; *trade dispute*, conflit du travail, *m.*—*v.t.* Disputer, discuter; contester.—*v.i.* Disputer, discuter, raisonner.

disqualification [diskwɔlifi'keiʃən], *n.* Incapacité, *f.*; *(Law)* cause d'incapacité, *f.*

disqualify [dis'kwɔlifai], *v.t.* Rendre incapable (de); disqualifier.

disquiet [dis'kwaiət], *n.* Inquiétude, *f.*—*v.t.* Inquiéter. **disquietous**, *a.* Inquiet. **disquietude** or **disquietness**, *n.* Inquiétude, agitation, anxiété, *f.*

disquisition [diskwi'ziʃən], *n.* Recherches, *f.pl.*, investigation, *f.*, examen, *m.*; dissertation, *f.*

disregard [disri'gɑːd], *n.* Insouciance, indifférence, *f. In disregard of*, au mépris de. —*v.t.* Négliger, regarder avec indifférence, faire peu de cas de. **disregardful**, *a.* Insouciant, négligent (de).

disrelish [dis'reliʃ], *n.* Dégoût, *m.*, aversion, *f.*—*v.t.* Avoir du dégoût pour, trouver mauvais.

disrepair [disri'pɛə], *n.* Délabrement, *m. To be in disrepair*, être en mauvais état; *to fall into disrepair*, se délabrer.

disreputable [dis'repjutəbl], *a.* De mauvaise réputation, mal famé; compromettant, déshonorant (of things). **disreputably**, *adv.* D'une manière peu honorable. **disrepute** [-ri'pjuːt], *n.* Discrédit, déshonneur, *m.*; mauvaise réputation, *f. To bring into disrepute*, faire tomber en discrédit; *to fall into disrepute*, tomber en discrédit.

disrespect [disris'pekt], *n.* Manque de respect, irrespect, *m.* **disrespectful**, *a.* Irrespectueux. *To be disrespectful to*, manquer de respect à. **disrespectfully**, *adv.* Peu respectueusement, sans respect.

disrobe [dis'roub], *v.t.* Déshabiller, dévêtir; dépouiller (de).—*v.i.* Se déshabiller, se dépouiller (de).

disroot [dis'ruːt], *v.t.* Déraciner.

disrupt [dis'rʌpt], *v.t.* Rompre. **disruption**, *n.* Rupture, dislocation; scission, *f.* **disruptive**, *a.* Disruptif.

dissatisfaction [dissætis'fækʃən], *n.* Mécontentement, *m.*, insatisfaction, *f.*

dissatisfied [dis'sætisfaid], *a.* Mécontent (de). **dissatisfy**, *v.t.* Mécontenter.

dissect [di'sekt], *v.t.* Disséquer. **dissection**, *n.* Dissection, *f.* **dissector**, *n.* Disséqueur, dissecteur, *m.*

disseize [dis'siːz], *v.t.* *(Law)* Déposséder (illégalement).

disseizee [dissi'ziː], *n.* Partie dépossédée illégalement, *f.* **disseizin**, *n.* Dépossession illégale, *f.*

dissemble [di'sembl], *v.i.* Dissimuler, feindre; faire l'hypocrite.—*v.t.* Dissimuler, déguiser, cacher. **dissembler,** *n.* Dissimulateur, hypocrite, *m.* **dissembling,** *n.* Dissimulation, *f.* **dissemblingly,** *adv.* En dissimulant.

disseminate [di'semineit], *v.t.* Disséminer, répandre, propager, faire circuler (news). **dissemination,** *n.* Dissémination, propagation, *f.* **disseminator,** *n.* Propagateur, semeur, *m.*

dissension [di'senʃən], *n.* Dissension, *f.* *To sow dissension,* semer la zizanie.

dissent [di'sent], *n.* Dissentiment, *m.*; (*Relig.*) dissidence, *f.*—*v.i.* Différer (de); différer de sentiment (avec); différer de l'Église établie. **dissenter,** *n.* Dissident, *m.,* dissidente, *f.,* non-conformiste. **dissentient,** *a.* Dissident, opposé. *Without a dissentient voice,* à l'unanimité.—*n.* Opposant, *m.,* -ante, *f.*

dissepiment [di'sepimənt], *n.* (*Bot.*) Cloison, *f.*

dissert [di'sə:t] or ***dissertate** ['disəteit], *v.i.* Disserter. **dissertation** [-'teiʃən], *n.* Dissertation, *f.*

dissertator ['disəteitə], *n.* Dissertateur, *m.*

disserve [di'sə:v], *v.t.* Desservir. **disservice,** *n.* Mauvais service, *m.*

dissever [di'sevə], *v.t.* Séparer (de); arracher (de). **disseverance,** *n.* Séparation, division, *f.*

dissidence ['disidəns], *n.* Dissidence, *f.* **dissident,** *a.* Dissident.—*n.* Dissident, *m.,* -dente, *f.*

dissimilar [di'similə], *a.* Dissemblable (à); différent (de). **dissimilarity** [-'læriti], *n.* Dissemblance, *f.*

dissimulate [di'simjuleit], *v.t.* Dissimuler. **dissimulation,** *n.* Dissimulation, *f.* **dissimulator,** *n.* Dissimulateur, *m.,* -trice, *f.*

dissipate ['disipeit], *v.t.* Dissiper.—*v.i.* Se dissiper. **dissipated,** *a.* Dissipé. **dissipation,** *n.* Dissipation (*fig.*) distraction, *f.*

dissociate [di'souʃieit], *v.t.* Désassocier, dissocier. **dissociation,** *n.* Dissociation, *f.*

dissolubility [disɔljuˈbiliti], *n.* Dissolubilité, solubilité, *f.*

dissoluble ['disɔljubl], *a.* Dissoluble.

dissolute ['disɔlju:t], *a.* Dissolu. **dissolutely,** *adv.* Dissolument. **dissoluteness,** *n.* Dérèglement, *m.,* débauche, *f.* **dissolution** [-'lju:ʃən], *n.* Dissolution; suppression (of monasteries etc.), *f.*

dissolvable [di'zɔlvəbl], *a.* Soluble, dissoluble.

dissolve [di'zɔlv], *v.t.* Dissoudre; désunir, séparer; détruire, supprimer; résoudre (a doubt etc.). *The partnership is dissolved,* l'association est dissoute.—*v.i.* Se dissoudre; se séparer. *To dissolve into tears,* fondre en larmes.—*n.* (*Cine.*) Fondu enchaîné, *m.* **dissolvent,** *a.* and *n.* Dissolvant, *m.* **dissolver,** *n.* Dissolvant, *m.*

dissonance ['disənəns], *n.* Dissonance; discordance, *f.* **dissonant,** *a.* Dissonant, discordant.

dissuade [di'sweid], *v.t.* Dissuader (de), détourner (de). **dissuader,** *n.* Personne qui dissuade, *f.* **dissuasion,** *n.* Dissuasion, *f.* **dissuasive,** *a.* Dissuasif.

dissyllabic [DISYLLABIC].

distaff ['distɑ:f], *n.* Quenouille, *f.* *The distaff side,* le côté maternel, *m.*

distance ['distəns], *n.* Distance, *f.*; éloignement, lointain, *m.,* perspective, *f.*; trajet (journey), *m.*; (*fig.*) réserve, *f.*; (*Mus.*) intervalle, *m.* *At a distance,* de loin; *in the distance,* dans le lointain; *to keep at a distance,* tenir à distance; *to keep one's distance* or *to keep oneself at a distance,* se tenir à distance. —*v.t.* Distancer, laisser en arrière. **distant** ['distənt], *a.* Éloigné, lointain; (*fig.*) réservé, froid. *A distant likeness,* une faible ressemblance; *a distant relation,* un parent éloigné; *he is very distant,* il est très réservé; *in the distant future,* dans un avenir lointain. **distantly,** *adv.* De loin; d'une manière éloignée; (*fig.*) avec réserve; froidement.

distaste [dis'teist], *n.* Dégoût, *m.,* aversion, répugnance (pour), *f.* **distasteful,** *a.* Désagréable, offensant, antipathique (à). **distastefulness,** *n.* Aversion, répugnance, *f.*

distemper [dis'tempə], *n.* Maladie (in dogs), *f.*; (*fig.*) désordre, *m.*; (*Paint.*) détrempe, *f.*—*v.t.* Déranger, troubler; détremper, peindre en détrempe. **distempered,** *a.* Dérangé, troublé; peint en détrempe. **distempering,** *n.* Peinture en détrempe, *f.*

distend [dis'tend], *v.t.* Étendre; dilater, enfler, gonfler; (*Med.*) distendre.—*v.i.* Se détendre, se gonfler. **distensible,** *a.* Dilatable. **distension,** *n.* (*Med.*) Distension, *f.,* ballonnement, *m.*

distich ['distik], *n.* Distique, *m.*

distil [dis'til], *v.t.* Distiller; faire tomber goutte à goutte; (*fig.*) extraire (de).—*v.i.* Distiller; tomber goutte à goutte, couler lentement.

distillation [disti'leiʃən], *n.* Distillation, *f.*

distillatory [dis'tilətəri], *a.* Distillatoire. **distiller,** *n.* Distillateur, *m.* **distillery,** *n.* Distillerie, *f.* **distilling,** *n.* Distillation, *f.*

distinct [dis'tiŋkt], *a.* Distinct; exprès, clair, net. *As distinct from,* à la différence de. **distinction,** *n.* Distinction; (*sch.*) mention, *f.* **distinctive,** *a.* Distinctif. **distinctively,** *adv.* D'une manière distinctive. **distinctiveness,** *n.* Caractère distinctif, *m.* **distinctly,** *adv.* Distinctement, clairement, nettement; (*fig.*) indéniablement. **distinctness,** *n.* Clarté, netteté, *f.*

distinguish [dis'tiŋgwiʃ], *v.t.* Distinguer (de). *To distinguish oneself,* se distinguer, se signaler.—*v.i.* Établir une distinction (entre). **distinguishable,** *a.* Que l'on peut distinguer, perceptible. **distinguished,** *a.* Distingué. *A distinguished foreigner,* un étranger de distinction; *a distinguished man,* un homme éminent. **distinguisher,** *n.* Observateur judicieux, *m.* **distinguishing,** *a.* Distinctif. **distinguishingly,** *adv.* Avec distinction, avec discernement; spécialement.

distort [dis'tɔ:t], *v.t.* Tordre, contourner; décomposer (one's features); (*fig.*) torturer, défigurer, fausser. **distorted,** *a.* Tordu, décomposé; déformé; (*fig.*) torturé, faussé. **distorting,** *a.* Déformant. **distortion,** *n.* Contorsion, altération, déformation, *f.*

distract [dis'trækt], *v.t.* Distraire, détourner (de); tourmenter, troubler; bouleverser, rendre fou. **distracted,** *a.* Bouleversé, fou, insensé, hors de soi. **distractedly,** *adv.* Follement, éperdument. **distractedness** or **distraction,** *n.* Distraction, *f.,* trouble, *m.,* confusion; démence, folie, *f.* *To drive to distraction,* mettre hors de soi, faire perdre la tête à; *to love to distraction,* aimer à la folie.

distracting, *a.* Atroce, déchirant, affolant. *Distracting cares*, soucis dévorants, *m.pl.*
distrain [dis'trein], *v.t.* Saisir.—*v.i.* Opérer une saisie. **distrainable**, *a.* Saisissable. *Not distrainable*, insaisissable. **distrainor**, *n.* Huissier, *m.* **distraint**, *n.* Saisie-arrêt, *f.*
distraught [dis'trɔːt], *a.* Affolé, éperdu.
distress [dis'tres], *n.* Détresse, affliction, peine, *f.*, chagrin, *m.*; misère (poverty), *f.*; épuisement, *m.*; (*Law*) saisie, *f.* *Signal of distress*, signal de détresse, *m.*; *to fall into distress*, tomber dans la misère.—*v.t.* Affliger, désoler; inquiéter; (*Law*) saisir. **distressed**, *a.* Affligé, malheureux; épuisé; dans la misère (poor). **distressful**, *a.* Affligeant; de détresse; malheureux. **distressfully**, *adv.* Cruellement. **distressing**, *a.* Affligeant, désolant; douloureux, pénible.
distributable [dis'tribjutəbl], *a.* Distribuable, répartissable. **distribute**, *v.t.* Distribuer; répartir (to allot); répandre. **distribution** [-'bjuːʃən], *n.* Distribution, répartition, *f.* **distributive** [-'tribjutiv], *a.* Distributif.—*n.* Mot distributif, *m.* **distributively**, *adv.* Distributivement, un à un.
distributor, *n.* Distributeur, *m.*, -trice, *f.*; concessionnaire (for cars etc.), *m.*; (*Tech.*) distributeur, *m.*
district ['distrikt], *n.* Contrée, région, *f.*, arrondissement, district, *m.*; quartier (of a town), *m.*; (*Postal*) circonscription du bureau, *f.*, secteur, *m.* **district nurse**, *n.* Infirmière visiteuse, *f.*
distrust [dis'trʌst], *n.* Défiance; méfiance, *f.*, doute, soupçon, *m.*—*v.t.* Se défier de, se méfier de. **distrustful**, *a.* Défiant; méfiant, soupçonneux. **distrustfully**, *adv.* Avec méfiance. **distrustfulness**, *n.* Caractère méfiant, *m.*
disturb [dis'təːb], *v.t.* Troubler; déranger. **disturbance**, *n.* Trouble, *m.*; confusion, émeute, *f.*; bruit, tapage, *m.*; perturbation, *f.*; désordre, *m.* **disturber**, *n.* Perturbateur, *m.*, perturbatrice, *f.* **disturbing**, *a.* Perturbateur; fâcheux (news etc).
distyle ['daistail], *n.* (*Arch.*) Distyle, *m.*
disunion [dis'juːniən], *n.* Désunion, *f.*
disunite [disju'nait], *v.t.* Désunir, séparer.—*v.i.* Se désunir, se séparer (de).
disuse (1) [dis'juːs], *n.* Désuétude, *f.*; (*Law*) non-usage, *m.* *To fall into disuse*, tomber en désuétude.
disuse (2) [dis'juːz], *v.t.* Cesser de se servir de; *déshabituer. **disused**, *a.* Hors d'usage; inusité, vieilli, désuet (of words).
disyllabic [disi'læbik], *a.* Dissyllabe.
disyllable [di'siləbl], *n.* Dissyllabe, *m.*
ditch [ditʃ], *n.* Fossé, *m.* *To die in the last ditch*, résister jusqu'à la dernière extrémité. —*v.t.* Entourer d'un fossé, verser dans le fossé; (*pop.*) abandonner. *When he lost his money, she ditched him*, dès qu'il perdit son argent, elle l'abandonna. *To ditch an aeroplane*, faire un atterrissage forcé dans la mer. —*v.i.* Creuser un fossé. **ditcher**, *n.* Qui creuse ou qui cure les fossés. *Last-ditcher*, qui résiste jusqu'à la fin.
dither ['diðə], *n.* *To be all of a dither*, être tout agité, être tout tremblant.—*v.i.* Trembler, trembloter, hésiter, s'agiter sans but.
dithery ['diðəri], *a.* (*fam.*) Tremblotant.

dithyramb ['diθiræmb, -ræm], *n.* Dithyrambe, *m.* **dithyrambic** [-'ræmbik], *a.* Dithyrambique.
dittany ['ditəni], *n.* (*Bot.*) Dictame, *m.*, fraxinelle, *f.*
ditto ['ditou], *adv.* Idem; (*Comm.*) dito.
dittology [di'tɔlədʒi], *n.* Dittologie, *f.*
ditty ['diti], *n.* Chanson, chansonnette, *f.*
ditty-bag, *n.* (*Naut.*) Nécessaire (de marin), *m.*
diuretic [daiju'retik], *a.* and *n.* Diurétique, *m.*
diurnal [dai'əːnəl], *a.* Journalier, du jour; (*Med.*) quotidien; (*Astron.*) diurne. **diurnally**, *adv.* Journellement, chaque jour.
divagate ['daivəgeit], *v.i.* Divaguer. **divagation** [-'geiʃən], *n.* Divagation, *f.*
divan [di'væn], *n.* Divan, *m.*
divaricate [di'værikeit *or* dai-], *v.i.* Diverger, se séparer, se partager en deux, bifurquer.—*a.* [-kit] Divariqué. **divarication** [-'keiʃən], *n.* Séparation, division en deux branches, *f.*
dive [daiv], *v.i.* Plonger, faire un plongeon. *To dive into*, sonder, approfondir, examiner à fond; se précipiter dans.—*n.* Plongeon, *m.*; (*Navy*) plongée (of a submarine), *f.*; (*pop.* esp. *Am.*) cabaret, *m.*, boîte de nuit, *f.* **dive-bombing**, *n.* (*Av.*) Bombardement en piqué, *m.* **diver**, *n.* Plongeur; scaphandrier; plongeon (bird), *m.*
diverge [dai'vəːdʒ], *v.i.* Diverger (de). **divergence** *or* **divergency**, *n.* Divergence, *f.* **divergent**, *a.* Divergent.
divers ['daivəz], *a.* Divers; plusieurs.—*n.* Quelques-uns, *m.pl.*
diverse [dai'vəːs], *a.* Divers, varié. **diversely**, *adv.* Diversement. **diversification** [-ifi'keiʃən], *n.* Changement, *m.*, variation, *f.*
diversify [dai'vəːsifai], *v.t.* Diversifier, varier (colours etc.).
diversion [dai'vəːʃən], *n.* Divertissement, amusement, *m.*; diversion, distraction, *f.*; détournement, *m.*, dérivation, *f.* **diversionary**, *a.* (*Mil.*) Destiné à faire diversion. *Diversionary tactics*, tactique de diversion, *f.*
diversity, *n.* Diversité, variété, *f.*
divert [dai'vəːt], *v.t.* Divertir, réjouir, récréer; distraire, détourner (de), dévier. **diverting**, *a.* Divertissant, amusant.
divest [di'vest *or* dai'-], *v.t.* Dépouiller (de). *To divest oneself of*, se dépouiller de, se dévêtir de. **divestiture**, *n.* (*Law*) Dessaisissement, *m.*, dépossession, *f.*
dividable [di'vaidəbl], *a.* Divisible. **divide**, *v.t.* Diviser; séparer; partager, distribuer; (*Parl.*) faire aller aux voix. *Divide!* aux voix! —*v.i.* Se diviser, se partager; (*Parl.*) aller aux voix. *Opinion was divided*, les avis étaient partagés.
dividend ['dividend], *n.* Dividende, *m.*
divider [di'vaidə], *n.* Personne qui divise, *f.*; (*pl.*) compas à pointes sèches, *m.*
divination [divi'neiʃən], *n.* Divination; prédiction, *f.* **divinatory**, *a.* Divinatoire.
divine [di'vain], *a.* Divin; (*fam.*) adorable, parfait.—*n.* Théologien, ecclésiastique, *m.*—*v.t.* Deviner, pressentir. **divinely**, *adv.* Divinement. **divineness**, *n.* Divinité, *f.* **diviner**, *n.* Devin, *m.*, devineresse, *f.* *Water-diviner*, sourcier, *m.* **divining-rod**, *n.* Baguette divinatoire, *f.*

diving ['daiviŋ], n. Plongement, m., action de plonger, f. **diving-bell**, n. Cloche à plongeur, f. **diving-board**, n. Plongeoir, m. **diving-suit**, n. Scaphandre, m.

divinity [di'viniti], n. Divinité; théologie, f.; (sch.) enseignement religieux, m. *Student in divinity*, étudiant en théologie, m.

divisibility [divizi'biliti], n. Divisibilité, f.

divisible [di'vizibl], a. Divisible.

division [di'viʒən], n. Division, f., partage, m.; scission, f.; vote, m. *Compound division*, (Arith.) division des nombres complexes, f.; *parliamentary division* (or *constituency*), circonscription électorale, f.; *simple division*, division des nombres entiers, division à un chiffre; *on a division*, (Parl.) en allant aux voix; *without a division*, sans vote.

divisional [di'viʒənl], a. (Mil.) Divisionnaire.

divisor [di'vaizə], n. (Math.) Diviseur, m.

divorce [di'vɔːs], n. Divorce, m.; séparation, désunion, f. *To sue for a divorce*, plaider en divorce.—v.t. Séparer, divorcer avec.—v.i. Se séparer (de). **divorcee**, n. Divorcé, m., -ée, f. *divorcement**, n. Divorce, m.

divorcer, n. Personne qui divorce; cause de divorce, f.

divot ['divət], n. (Golf) Motte de gazon, f.

divulge [dai'vʌldʒ or di'-], v.t. Divulguer, publier. **divulgence, divulgation**, or **divulgement**, n. Divulgation, f. **divulger**, n. Divulgateur, m.

dizziness ['dizinis], n. Vertige, étourdissement, m. **dizzy**, a. Étourdi, pris d'étourdissement; vertigineux (of a height). *To make dizzy*, donner le vertige à.

do (1) [duː], v.t. (2nd sing. **doest** ['duːist]; aux. **dost** [dʌst]; 3rd sing. **does** [dʌz], *doth** [dʌθ]; past **did, didst**; p.p. **done** [dʌn]; negative **don't** [dount], **didn't, doesn't** [dʌznt]) Faire; rendre (service, justice, etc.); finir (to finish); (Cook.) cuire, faire cuire; mettre dedans, duper (to cheat). *Can you do this up* (repair)? pouvez-vous remettre ceci en état? *do as you propose*, veuillez faire ce que vous proposez; *done!* tope là! c'est entendu! *done for*, flambé, perdu; *done to a turn*, cuit à point; *he is done for*, c'en est fait de lui, il est perdu; *it can't be done*, pas moyen; *it is done, but badly*, ce n'est ni fait ni à faire; *overdone*, trop cuit (of meat); *please do your utmost*, veuillez faire votre possible; *such things are not done*, ces choses-là ne se font pas; *to be done up*, n'en pouvoir plus, être éreinté; *to be doing well*, faire de bonnes affaires, réussir; *to do again* or *to do over again*, refaire; *to do evil*, faire le mal; *to do good*, faire le bien; *to do him good*, lui faire du bien; *to do it again*, recommencer; *to do nothing*, ne rien faire; *to do nothing of the sort*, n'en faire rien; *to do over*, enduire (de), couvrir (de); *to do right*, faire bien; *to do up*, empaqueter, emballer, remettre en état, remettre à neuf; *to do wrong*, faire mal; *to have nothing to do with*, n'avoir que faire de; *to have something to do with*, y être pour quelque chose; *underdone*, saignant (of meat); *well done!* bravo! très bien! *well-done*, bien cuit (of meat); *what is done cannot be undone*, à chose faite point de remède; *what is to be done?* que faire? *what would you have me do?* que voulez-vous que je fasse?

v.i.—Se porter, se trouver, se sentir, être;

se conduire (of one's health); aller, convenir (to suit); suffire (to suffice); finir (to finish); se mêler (à). *Do as I do*, faites comme moi; *has he done?* a-t-il fini? *have done!* finissez! assez! *how do you do?* comment vous portez-vous? comment allez-vous? *I have done*, j'ai fini; *nothing to do with*, rien à voir avec; *that will do*, c'est bien comme cela, cela suffit; *that will never do*, cela n'ira jamais; *to do away with*, supprimer, se défaire de, faire disparaître; *to do by*, agir envers, en agir avec; *to do for*, tuer; *to do without*, se passer de; *to have done with*, ne plus se mêler avec, en finir avec, en avoir assez de; *to have to do with*, avoir affaire à, avoir affaire de, avoir à démêler avec; *will that do?* cela fera-t-il l'affaire? cela vous va-t-il? est-ce bien comme cela?

v.aux.—*Do be quiet!* taisez-vous donc! *do you like her?—do I!* l'aimez-vous?—si je l'aime! *do you think so?* le croyez-vous? *he knows better than I do*, il le sait mieux que moi; *I do but follow*, je ne fais que suivre; *what does he say?* que dit-il?

n.—Duperie, escroquerie (cheat), f.; soirée, réception; (Mil.) affaire, f. **do-nothing**, n. Fainéant, m.

do (2) [dou], n. (Mus.) Do, ut, m.

doc (pop.) [DOCTOR].

docile ['dousail], a. Docile. **docility** [-'siliti], n. Docilité, f.

dock (1) [dɔk], v.t. Écourter; (fig.) retrancher, rabattre; rogner (accounts etc.); (Naut.) mettre dans le bassin; (Comm., Navy) faire entrer aux docks; garer (on rivers).

dock (2) [dɔk], n. Bassin, dock, m.; patience (plant), f.; banc des accusés (in a court), m. *Dry-dock*, bassin de radoub, m.; *floating-dock*, bassin à flot, m. **dock-dues**, n.pl. Droits de bassin, m.pl. **docker**, n. Déchargeur, docker, m. **dock-gate**, n. Vanne de bassin, f. **dock-yard**, n. Arsenal de marine, chantier de construction, m.

docket ['dɔkit], n. Étiquette, fiche, f.; (Law) registre des jugements rendus, m.—v.t. Étiqueter; enregistrer.

doctor ['dɔktə], n. Docteur, médecin, m. *Doctors' Commons*, Collège des docteurs en droit civil, m.; *doctor of divinity*, docteur en théologie; *doctor of laws*, docteur en droit; *doctor of medicine*, docteur en médecine, docteur-médecin; *doctor of science*, docteur ès sciences.—v.t. Soigner, droguer; (fig.) altérer, changer, fausser; frelater (wine). **doctoral**, a. Doctoral. **doctorate**, n. Doctorat, m. **doctorship**, n. Doctorat, m. *doctress**, n. Doctoresse, femme-médecin, f.

doctrinaire [dɔktri'nɛə], a. Doctrinaire.

doctrinal [dɔk'trainl or 'dɔktrinəl], a. Doctrinal; dogmatique.

doctrine ['dɔktrin], n. Doctrine, f.

document ['dɔkjumənt], n. Document, titre, m.; pièce, f., écrit, m.—v.t. Munir de documents, munir des papiers nécessaires. **documental** [dɔkju'mentəl] or **documentary**, a. De documents; justificatif, authentique. **documentary**, a. (Cine.) Documentaire (film). *Documentary evidence*, preuve authentique, f.—n. (Cine.) Documentaire, m.

documentation [-'teiʃən], n. Documentation, f.

dodder ['dɔdə], *n.* (*Bot.*) Cuscute, *f.*—*v.i.* Marcher d'un pas tremblant. **dodderer,** *n.* Gâteux, croulant, *m.* **doddering, doddery,** *a.* Tremblotant, branlant.

dodecagon [dou'dekəgən], *n.* Dodécagone, *m.*

dodecahedral [doudekə'hi:drəl], *a.* Dodécaédrique. **dodecahedron,** *n.* Dodécaèdre, *m.*

dodge [dɔdʒ], *v.i.* Se jeter de côté, s'esquiver; (*fig.*) ruser, faire des détours.—*v.t.* Éviter; esquiver; dépister. *To dodge the issue,* prendre par la venelle.—*n.* Tour, détour, *m.,* (*Ftb.*) esquive, évite; ruse, ficelle, *f.* **dodgems,** *n.pl.* Autos tamponneuses, autos scooter, *f.pl.* **dodger,** *n.* Rusé, malin, finaud, *m.,* finaude, *f. An artful dodger,* un fin matois, un rusé compère, un roublard.

dodo ['doudou], *n.* (*Orn.*) Dronte, *m.*; (*colloq.*) vieille perruque, rombière, *f.*

doe [dou], *n.* Daine, *f. Doe rabbit,* lapine, *f.*

doer ['du:ə], *n.* Faiseur; auteur, *m.*

does [dʌz], (*archaic*) **doeth** ['du:əθ], *3rd sing.* [DO].

doff [dɔf], *v.t.* Tirer, enlever, ôter.

dog [dɔg], *n.* Chien; chenet (andiron); chien de fusil; valet (on a bench), *m.*; (*facet.*) coquin, gaillard, *m.* **Bulldog,** bouledogue, *m.*; *cunning dog,* rusé coquin; *give a dog a bad name and hang him,* qui veut noyer son chien l'accuse de la rage; *house-dog,* chien de garde; *lap-dog,* bichon, *m.*; *let sleeping dogs lie,* ne réveillons pas le chien qui dort; *lucky dog!* quel veinard! *old dog,* vieux routier, vieux farceur, *m.*; *sad dog,* triste sujet, *m.*; *to go to the dogs,* prendre le chemin de l'hôpital; *to lead a dog's life,* mener une vie de chien; *watch-dog,* chien de garde.—*v.t.* Suivre à la piste; harceler, guetter, épier. *To dog someone's footsteps,* être toujours aux trousses de quelqu'un.

dogate ['dougeit], *n.* Dogat, *m.*

dogberry, *n.* Cornouille, *f.* **dog-biscuit,** *n.* Biscuit pour chiens, *m.* **dog-cart,** *n.* Dogcart, *m.,* charrette anglaise, *f.* **dog-collar,** *n.* Collier; (*fam.*) col romain, *m.* **dog-days,** *n.pl.* Canicule, *f. To be in the dog-days,* être dans la canicule.

doge [doudʒ], *n.* Doge, *m.*

dog-faced, *a.* À face de chien.

dog-fight, *n.* Combat de chiens, *m.*; duel aérien, *m.*

dog-fish, *n.* Roussette, *f.,* chien de mer, cagnot, milandre, squale, *m.*

dogged ['dɔgid], *a.* Obstiné; acharné. **doggedly,** *adv.* Avec acharnement, obstinément; résolument. **doggedness,** *n.* Obstination, *f.,* acharnement, *m.*

dogger ['dɔgə], *n.* (*Naut.*) Dogre, *m.*

doggerel ['dɔgərəl], *n.* Vers burlesques, vers de mirliton, *m.pl.*—*a.* Sans mesure; burlesque.

doggie, *n.* (*Childish*) Tou-tou, *m.* **doggish,** *a.* De chien.

doggo ['dɔgou], *adv. To lie doggo,* se tenir coi.

dog-hole, *n.* Niche de chien, *f.*; (*fig.*) taudis, chenil, *m.* **dog-kennel,** *n.* Chenil, *m.* **dog-Latin,** *n.* Latin de cuisine, *m.*

dogma ['dɔgmə], *n.* Dogme, *m.* **dogmatic** or **dogmatical** [-'mætikəl], *a.* Dogmatique. **dogmatically,** *adv.* Dogmatiquement. **dogmaticalness,** *n.* Caractère dogmatique, *m.*

dogmatism ['dɔgmətizm], *n.* Dogmatisme, *m.* **dogmatist,** *n.* Dogmatiste, *m.* **dogmatize,** *v.i.* Dogmatiser.

dog-rose, *n.* Églantier (brier), *m.*; églantine (flower), *f.*

dog('s)-ear, *n.* Corne, *f.,* pli au coin d'une page, *m.*—*v.t.* Faire des cornes aux pages. **dog-show,** *n.* Exposition canine, *f.*

dog-star, *n.* La Canicule, *f.,* Sirius, *m.* **dog-tired,** *a.* Exténué, mort de fatigue. **dog-vane,** *n.* (*Naut.*) Penon, *m.*

dog-violet, *n.* Violette des chiens, *f.*

dogwood ['dɔgwud], *n.* Cornouiller, *m.*

doily ['dɔili], *n.* Serviette de dessert, *f.,* dessous de lampe etc., *m.*

doing ['du:iŋ], *n.* (*usu. in pl.*) Faits, *m.pl.*; actions, *f.pl.,* exploits, *m.pl. That requires some doing,* ce n'est pas fait en un tour de main; *underhand doing,* menées secrètes, *f.pl.*

doldrums ['dɔldrəmz], *n.pl.* (*Naut.*) La Zone des calmes. (*fig.*) *He is in the doldrums,* il a le cafard.

dole (1) [doul], *n.* Aumône, *f.,* partage, don, *m.*; allocation de chômage, *f. To be on the dole,* être à la charge de l'assistance publique. —*v.t. To dole out,* distribuer, répartir avec parcimonie.

***dole** (2) [doul], *n.* Chagrin, *m.,* tristesse, lamentation, *f.* **doleful,** *a.* Plaintif, triste, lugubre, malheureux. **dolefully,** *adv.* Tristement, plaintivement, douloureusement. **dolefulness,** *n.* Tristesse, *f.*

dolerite ['dɔlərait], *n.* Dolérite, *f.*

dolichocephal [dɔlikou'sefl], *n.* Dolichocéphale, *m.* or *f.* **dolichocephalic,** *a.* Dolichocéphale.

doll [dɔl], *n.* Poupée, *f.*; (*Am. pop.*) jeune fille, *f. Doll's house,* maison de poupée, *f.*; *to play with a doll,* jouer à la poupée.—*v.t. To doll oneself up,* se pomponner, s'endimancher.

dollar ['dɔlə], *n.* Dollar, *m.*

dollop ['dɔləp], *n.* (*fam.*) Gros morceau, *m.*

dolman ['dɔlmən], *n.* Dolman (cloak), *m.*

dolmen ['dɔlmen], *n.* Dolmen, *m.* (tablestone).

dolomite ['dɔləmait], *n.* Dolomie, dolomite, *f.*

dolorous ['dɔlərəs], *a.* (*poet.*) Douloureux.

dolphin ['dɔlfin], *n.* Dauphin, *m.*; patte d'oie, *f.* (near a bridge); (*Naut.*) baderne (of mast), *f.*; bouée (de corps-mort), *f.*

dolt [doult], *n.* Lourdaud, sot, butor, *m.* **doltish,** *a.* Sot, stupide, lourdaud. **doltishly,** *adv.* Sottement, en lourdaud. **doltishness,** *n.* Sottise, stupidité, *f.*

domain [do'mein], *n.* Domaine, *m.* **domanial,** *a.* Domanial.

dome [doum], *n.* Dôme, *m.*; (*fig.*) édifice, *m. Domes of silence* (for chairs), dômes du silence, *m.pl.*; (*colloq.*) crâne, *m.* **domed,** *a.* À dôme; en forme de dôme.

Domesday Book ['du:mzdeibuk], *n.* Grand cadastre d'Angleterre (fait par Guillaume le Conquérant), *m.*

domestic [də'mestik], *a.* De famille, casanier; domestique (of animals). *Domestic agency,* bureau de placement, *m.*—*n.* Domestique, *m.* or *f.,* servante, *f.* **domestically,** *adv.* Dans son intérieur. **domesticate,** *v.t.* Domestiquer, apprivoiser; (*fig.*) rendre casanier; accoutumer à la vie domestique. **domesticated,** *a.* Casanier (of persons); apprivoisé (of animals). *To become domesticated,* se

domestiquer. **domestication** [-'keiʃən], *n.* Domestication, *f.*, apprivoisement, *m.* **domesticity** [domes'tisiti], *n.* Domesticité, *f.*
domicile ['dɔmisail *or* -sil], *n.* Domicile, *m.* **domicile** *or* **domiciliate**, *v.t.* Établir. *To become domiciled*, se domicilier. **domiciled,** *a.* Domicilié.
domiciliary [dɔmi'siliəri], *a.* Domiciliaire. **domiciliation** [-'eiʃən], *n.* Domiciliation, *f.*
dominance ['dɔminəns], *n.* Dominance, *f.* **dominant,** *a.* Dominant.—*n.* (*Mus.*) Dominante, *f.* **dominate,** *v.i.* Dominer; prévaloir, prédominer.—*v.t.* Dominer sur. **domination** [-'neiʃən], *n.* Domination, *f.* **dominator,** *n.* Dominateur, *m.*
domineer [dɔmi'niə], *v.i.* Dominer (sur). *To domineer over,* tyranniser, régenter. **domineering,** *a.* Impérieux, autoritaire, tyrannique.
dominical [do'minikəl], *a.* Dominical.—*n.* Dominicale, *f.*
Dominica [də'minikə]. La Dominique, *f.*
Dominican [do'minikən], *a.* and *n.* Dominicain, *m. Dominican nun,* Dominicaine, *f. The Dominican Republic,* la République Dominicaine.
dominie ['dɔmini], *n.* (*Sc.*) Magister, pédagogue, maître d'école, *m.*
dominion [do'miniən], *n.* Domination, autorité, *f.*, pouvoir; empire, *m.*; (*pl.*) états, *m.pl.*, possessions, *f.pl.*, dominions (britanniques), *m.pl.*
domino ['dɔminou], *n.* Domino (hood, game), *m. In a domino,* en domino; *to play at dominoes,* jouer aux dominos.
don (1) [dɔn], *n.* Don (title); (*fig.*) grand seigneur; (*Univ.*) professeur d'université, *m.* **don** (2) [dɔn], *v.t.* Mettre, endosser.
donate [do'neit], *v.t.* Donner, faire un don de. **donation** [-'neiʃən], *n.* Donation, *f.*, don, *m.*
donative ['dounətiv], *n.* Don, présent, *m.*, largesse, *f.*
done [dʌn], *p.p.* [DO].
donee [do'ni:], *n.* (*Law*) Donataire.
donga ['dɔŋgə], *n.* (*S. African*) Ravin, *m.*
donkey ['dɔŋki], *n.* Âne, baudet, *m.*, bourrique, *f. Donkey feed-pump,* cheval alimentaire, *m.*; *donkey ride,* promenade à dos d'âne, *f.*; *for donkey's years,* depuis une éternité; *riding (on) a donkey,* monté sur un âne; *to ride a donkey,* aller à dos d'âne; *to talk the hind leg off a donkey,* jaser comme une pie borgne. **donkey-boy,** *n.* Ânier, *m.* **donkey-engine,** *n.* Petit-cheval, *m.* **donkey-race,** *n.* Course d'ânes, *f.* **donkey-work,** *n.* Travail de routine, *m.*
donnish ['dɔniʃ], *a.* Pédant, gourmé; à l'allure, d'allure académique.
donor ['dounə], *n.* Donateur, *m.*, donatrice, *f.*; donneur, *m.*, donneuse, *f. Blood donor,* donneur de sang, *m.*
do-nothing; **don't** [dount], *neg.* [DO].
doodah ['du:dɑ:], *n.* (*fam.*) Machin, truc, *m. To be all of a doodah,* avoir le trac.
doodle [du:dl], *v.i.* Faire de petits dessins, griffonner.—*n.* Petit dessin, griffonnage, *m.* **doodle-bug,** *n.* (*fam.*) Bombe volante, *f.*
doom [du:m], *v.t.* Condamner (à); (*fig.*) destiner, vouer (à); (*poet.*) juger.—*n.* Jugement, *m.*; destin funeste, sort malheureux, *m.*; perte, ruine, *f. Crack of doom,* (*fig.*) le

jugement dernier. **doomsday,** *n.* Jour du jugement dernier, *m. To put off till doomsday,* remettre à l'an quarante. **Doomsday Book** [DOMESDAY BOOK].
door [dɔ:], *n.* Porte; portière (of a vehicle), *f.*; (*Steam-engine*) registre, *m. At death's door,* aux portes du tombeau, à la mort; *back-door,* porte de derrière; *carriage-door,* porte cochère; *folding-doors,* porte à deux battants, porte brisée; *he lives next door,* il demeure à côté; *house door,* porte de maison; *indoors,* à la maison, chez soi; *next door to,* à côté de; *out of doors,* dehors, en plein air; *street door,* porte d'entrée; *the fault lies at his door,* la faute en est à lui; *to close one's door against,* fermer sa porte à; *to lay it at some-one's door,* s'en prendre à quelqu'un de; *to lie at the door of,* être imputable à; *to turn out of doors,* mettre à la porte; *with, behind, closed doors,* à huis clos.
door-bell, *n.* Sonnette, *f.* **door-case** *or* **door-frame,** *n.* Châssis de porte, *m.* **door-handle,** *n.* Poignée de porte, *f.* **door-keeper,** *n.* Concierge, portier (of a house); gardien (of public places); (*Parl.*) huissier, *m.* **door-knob,** *n.* Poignée (ronde) de porte, *f.* **doorman,** *n.* Portier, *m.* **door-mat,** *n.* Paillasson, *m. I'll never be a door-mat,* je ne me laisserai jamais marcher dessus. **door-nail,** *n.* Clou de porte, *m. Dead as a door-nail,* bien mort. **door-plate,** *n.* Plaque, *f.* **door-post,** *n.* Montant de porte, *m.* **door-scraper,** *n.* Décrottoir, *m.* **door-spring,** *n.* Ferme-porte, *m.* **door-step,** *n.* Seuil de la porte, pas de (la) porte, *m.* **door-way,** *n.* Entrée (de porte), porte, *f.*
dope [doup], *n.* Liquide visqueux (used for food or as a lubricant), enduit, *m.* (of car, aeroplane); pâte (d'opium); drogue, narcotique, *f.*; (*fam.*) (faux) renseignements, *m.pl.*; idiot, imbécile, *m.*—*v.t.* Enduire, laquer; droguer, doper. **dope-fiend,** *n.* Toxicomane. **dop(e)y** ['doupi], *a.* Hébété, drogué; abruti.
dor [dɔ:], *n.* Insecte bourdonnant, *m. Dor-bee,* bourdon, frelon, *m.*; *dor-beetle,* bousier; hanneton, *m.*
dorado [do'rɑ:dou], *n.* Dorade, *f.*
Dorian ['dɔriən], *a.* and *n.* Dorien, *m.*
Doric ['dɔrik], *a.* and *n.* Dorique, *m.*
dormancy ['dɔ:mənsi], *n.* Repos, *m.* **dormant,** *a.* Dormant; assoupi; (*Her.*) endormi; qui dort, mort (of capital); commanditaire (of partners). *To lie dormant,* sommeiller, dormir (of capital etc.).
dormer ['dɔ:mə] *or* **dormer-window,** *n.* Lucarne, *f.*
dormitive ['dɔ:mitiv], *a.* Dormitif, soporifique. **dormitory,** *n.* Dortoir, *m.*
dormouse ['dɔ:maus], *n.* (*pl.* **dormice**) Loir, *m.*
Dorothy ['dɔrəθi]. Dorothée, *f.*
dorsal ['dɔ:səl], *a.* Dorsal. **dorsibranchiate,** *n.* Dorsibranche, *m.*
dory ['dɔ:ri], *n.* Doris, *m.* (small fishing boat); youyou, *m.* (*John*) *dory,* poisson Saint-Pierre, zée forgeron, *m.*; dorée, *f.*
dose [dous], *n.* Dose, *f.*—*v.t.* Médicamenter; administrer, faire prendre un médicament à; proportionner; doser. **dosimetric** [dɔsi'metrik], *a.* Dosimétrique.
doss [dɔs], *n.* (*pop.*) Lit, *m.*—*v.i. To doss down,* se coucher. **doss-house,** *n.* Asile de nuit, *m.*

dossal ['dɔsəl], *n.* Tenture de fond de chœur, *f.*

dossier ['dɔsjei], *n.* Dossier, *m.*; documents, *m.pl.*

dossil ['dɔsil], *n.* (*Surg.*) Bourdonnet, *m.*

dost [dʌst] [DO].

dot [dɔt], *n.* Point, *m.* *To pay on the dot*, payer recta.—*v.t.* Marquer d'un point, marquer avec des points; (*Paint.*) pointiller; (*Mus.*) pointer. *To dot one's I's*, mettre les points sur les i; *the dotted line*, le pointillé; *cut, tear along the dotted line*, détacher suivant le pointillé; *to sign on the dotted line*, accepter toutes les conditions, consentir à tout (of transaction). *To dot someone one*, flanquer une beigne à quelqu'un.—*v.i.* (*colloq.*) Clopiner.

dotage ['doutidʒ], *n.* Seconde enfance, *f.*, radotage, *m.*

dotal ['doutəl], *a.* Dotal.

dotard ['doutəd], *n.* Radoteur, *m.*

dote [dout], *v.i.* Radoter; raffoler (de). *To dote on*, aimer à la folie, raffoler de. **dotingly**, *adv.* À la folie, avec extravagance.

dotterel ['dɔtərəl], *n.* (*Orn.*) Guignard, *m.*

dotty ['dɔti], *a.* Gâteux, en enfance; dingue.

double [dʌbl], *a.* Double, en deux; à double tour (of locks); (*fig.*) faux. *Bent double*, voûté; *double chin*, double menton, *m.*; *double Dutch*, baragouin, *m.*; *double entry*, tenue des livres en partie double, *f.*; *to grow double*, se voûter, être courbé presque en deux.—*n.* Double; pendant; (*Mil.*) pas de course, *m.*; (*Hunt.*) ruse, *f.* *Double or quits*, quitte ou double; *my double*, mon pendant, mon sosie.—*adv.* Double; au double. *Double as big as*, deux fois plus grand que. *Double that*, le double de cela; *to fold double*, plier en deux.—*v.t.* Doubler; plier en deux, faire un pli à; serrer, fermer (fists). *He was doubled up with pain*, il se tordait de douleur; *to be doubled up with laughter*, se tordre de rire.—*v.i.* Doubler; faire des détours, user de ruse, biaiser. *To double back*, revenir sur ses pas.

double-barrelled, *a.* À deux coups (of firearms); à charnière (of a surname). **double-bass**, *n.* Contre-basse, *f.*

double-bed, *n.* Grand lit, lit à deux places. **double-bedded**, *a.* À deux lits (of a room).

double-breasted, *a.* Croisé. *Double-breasted suit*, complet avec veston croisé, *m.* **double-cross**, *v.t.* Duper, tromper. **double-dealer**, *n.* Trompeur, fourbe, *m.*; quelqu'un qui joue un double jeu. **double-dealing**, *n.* Duplicité, fourberie, *f.*, double jeu, *m.* **double-decker**, *n.* Autobus à impériale, *m.* **double-dye**, *v.t.* Teindre deux fois. **double-dyed**, *a.* Bon teint; (*fig.*) fieffé, endurci. *Double-dyed villain*, un fieffé coquin. **double-entendre** ['du:blɑ̃'tɑ̃:dr], *n.* Mot à double entente, *m.* **double-faced**, *a.* Trompeur, fourbe. **double-fault**, *v.i.* (*Ten.*) Faire une double faute. **double-jointed**, *a.* Désossé, désarticulé. **double-lock**, *v.t.* Fermer à double tour. **double-quick**, *a.* *In double-quick time*, en moins de deux, en moins de rien. **double-room**, *n.* Chambre pour deux personnes, *f.* **double-tongued**, *a.* Dissimulé, fourbe.

doubleness, *n.* État double, *m.*, duplicité, *f.*

doubler, *n.* Personne qui double, *f.*; (*Manuf.*) doubleur, *m.*, doubleuse, *f.*

doublet ['dʌblit], *n.* *Pourpoint; doublet (of words); coup double, doublé (two shots); (*pl.*) (at dice) doublet, *m.*

doubloon [dʌb'lu:n], *n.* Doublon, *m.*

doubly ['dʌbli], *adv.* Doublement.

doubt [daut], *n.* Doute, *m.*; hésitation, appréhension, *f.* *Beyond a doubt*, sans aucun doute; *beyond all doubt*, hors de doute, indubitable; *no doubt that*, sans doute que; *to be in doubt*, être en doute.—*v.i.* Douter; soupçonner; craindre, hésiter.—*v.t.* Douter de. **doubter**, *n.* Douteur, sceptique, *m.*

doubtful, *a.* Douteux, incertain; indécis. *Doubtful company*, compagnie louche, *f.*; *to be doubtful of*, douter de. **doubtfully**, *adv.* D'une manière douteuse; avec indécision, d'une manière ambiguë. **doubtfulness**, *n.* Incertitude; ambiguïté, *f.* **doubtingly**, *adv.* D'une manière douteuse. **doubtless**, *adv.* Sans doute, indubitablement, assurément. **doubtlessly**, *adv.* Incontestablement, sans doute.

***douceur** [du:'sə:], *n.* Gratification, *f.*, présent, pot-de-vin, *m.*

douche [du:ʃ], *n.* Bock, irrigateur, *m.*

dough [dou], *n.* Pâte, *f.*; (*pop.*) argent, *m.*, galette, *f.* **dough-nut**, *n.* Pet de nonne, *m.*

doughy ['doui], *a.* Pâteux, mou.

doughty ['dauti], *a.* Vaillant, preux.

dour ['duə], *a.* (*Sc.*) Austère et froid; obstiné.

douse [daus], *v.t.* Plonger dans l'eau; éteindre.—*v.i.* Tomber dans l'eau; être plongé dans l'eau (de force).

dove [dʌv], *n.* Colombe, *f.*; pigeon, *m.* *Ring-dove*, ramier, *m.*; *rock-dove*, biset, *m.* **dove-colour**, *n.* Gorge-de-pigeon, *m.* **dove-coloured**, *a.* Couleur gorge-de-pigeon. **dove-cot(e)** or **dove-house**, *n.* Colombier, *m.*

Dover ['douvə]. Douvres, *m.* *The Straits of Dover*, le Pas-de-Calais, *m.*

dovetail ['dʌvteil], *n.* Queue d'aronde, *f.*—*v.t.* Assembler en queue d'aronde; réunir, joindre (parfaitement).

dowager ['dauədʒə], *n.* Douairière; (*fig.*) dame âgée, *f.* *The Dowager Marchioness of . . .*, la Marquise douairière de . . . .

dowdy ['daudi], *a.f.* Gauche et mal mise, mal fagotée.—*n. An old dowdy*, une rombière, *f.*

dowel ['dauəl], *n.* (*Carp.*) Goujon, *m.*; cheville en bois, *f.*—*v.t.* Assembler avec des goujons.

dower ['dauə], *n.* Douaire, *m.*, don, *m.*—*v.t.* Doter (de). ***dowered**, *a.* Doté; (*fig.*) favorisé de la nature. **dowerless**, *a.* Sans dot.

dowlas ['dauləs], *n.* Toile commune, *f.*

down (1) [daun], *n.* Duvet; (*Bot.*) coton, *m.*, fleur, *f.* *Down bed*, lit de plume, *m.*

down (2) [daun], *n.* Dune, *f.* *The Downs*, les hautes plaines crayeuses; les dunes, *f.pl.*

down (3) [daun], *adv.* En bas; à bas; bas, à terre; en aval (down stream); tombé, apaisé (of the wind); couché (of the sun); couchée (of the moon); pas remonté (of clocks); à plat (tyre); en baisse (of prices); (*fig.*) sur le déclin, en défaveur. *Down at heel*, éculé (of shoe), râpé (of person); *down in the mouth*, découragé, abattu, penaud; *down with!* à bas! *down with it!* avalez ça! *to be down on one's luck*, (*colloq.*) n'avoir pas de chance; (*slang*) être dans la débine; *to go down*, aller en aval,

descendre; *up and down*, çà et là, de haut en bas.—*prep.* En bas de; vers le bas de. *Down stream*, en aval.—*a.* Abattu.—*v.t.* Abattre; mettre bas.—*n.* (*fam.*) *To have a down on someone*, avoir une dent contre quelqu'un. **downcast**, *a.* Abattu; baissé (of eyes). **downfall**, *n.* Chute; (*fig.*) débâcle, *f.* **downfallen**, *a.* Tombé; déchu, ruiné. **downgrade**, *n.* Descente, *f.* *On the down-grade*, sur le déclin. **downhearted**, *a.* Découragé. **downhill**, *a.* Incliné; en pente.—*adv.* En descendant. **downpour**, *n.* Averse, pluie torrentielle, *f.*
downright, *a.* Direct; franc; véritable, vrai. —*adv.* Net, tout droit, tout à fait, complètement. **downstairs**, *adv.* En bas (de l'escalier). *To be downstairs*, être en bas, être au rez-de-chaussée; *to go downstairs*, descendre. **downtrodden**, *a.* Foulé aux pieds, opprimé.
downward, *a.* De haut en bas, qui descend, descendant, incliné. *Downward course*, chute, *f.* **downward** or **downwards**, *adv.* En bas, en descendant; en aval.
downy ['dauni], *a.* De duvet, duveteux; couvert de duvet (of fruit); (*slang*) rusé.
dowry ['dauri], *n.* Dot, *f.*, douaire, apport dotal, *m.*
dowser ['dausə], *n.* Sourcier, *m.* **dowsing-rod**, *n.* Baguette de sourcier, *f.*
doxology [dɔk'sɔlədʒi], *n.* Doxologie, *f.*
doyen ['dɔijən], *n.* Doyen, *m.*
doyly [DOILY].
doze [douz], *v.i.* S'assoupir, s'endormir, sommeiller, être assoupi. *To doze over one's work*, s'endormir sur son ouvrage.—*n.* Petit somme, *m.* *To have a doze*, faire un somme.
dozy, *a.* Assoupi.
dozen [dʌzn], *n.* Douzaine, *f.* *Baker's dozen*, treize à la douzaine; *daily dozen*, exercices physiques, *m.pl.*; *to talk nineteen to the dozen*, être un vrai moulin à paroles.
drab [dræb], *a.* Gris sale, brun terne; (*fig.*) terne, décoloré.—*n.* Étoffe de couleur terne, (écrue or beige); (*fig.*) (woman) une traînée; une souillon, *f.*
drabble [dræbl], *v.t.* Traîner dans la boue, crotter.—*v.i.* Patauger.
dracaena [drə'siːnə], *n.* (*Bot.*) Dracéna, *m.*
drachm [dræm], *n.* Drachme, *f.*
Draco ['dreikou]. Dracon, *m.* **draconian** [drə'kouniən] or **draconic** [-'kɔnik], *a.* Draconien.
draff [dræf], *n.* Rebut, *m.*; lavasse, lie, *f.*
draft [drɑːft], *v.t.* Dessiner, rédiger; (*Mil.*) détacher.—*n.* Dessin (sketch); brouillon (document), *m.*; (*Comm.*) traite, *f.*; (*Mil.*) détachement, *m.* *Draft amendment*, projet d'amendement, *m.* [DRAUGHT].
drag [dræg], *v.t.* Traîner, tirer; (*Naut.*) draguer. *To drag about*, traîner; *to drag away from*, entraîner, arracher de; *to drag on*, entraîner; (*fig.*) traîner en longueur; *to drag out*, faire sortir de force; *to drag the anchor*, chasser sur son ancre.—*v.i.* Se traîner; traîner; (*Naut.*) chasser (of the anchor).—*n.* Chose qu'on traîne (et qui résiste); herse; drague; gaffe, *f.*; grappin; patin, sabot (of brake); drag (coach à quatre chevaux), *m.*; (*Hunt.*) voie artificielle, *f.*, drag, *m.*; résistance à l'avance; traînance, *f.*; (*Billiards*) rétro; (*fig.*) poids mort, *m.* *To be a drag*

upon, être à charge à; *to put on the drag*, enrayer. **drag-net**, *n.* Seine, *f.*, chalut, *m.*
draggle [drægl], *v.t.* Traîner dans la boue, traîner par terre.—*v.i.* Se crotter. **draggle-tailed**, *a.* (Woman) dont les jupes traînent; négligée, malpropre.
dragoman ['drægoumən], *n.* Drogman, *m.*
dragon ['drægən], *n.* Dragon; (*Astron.*) Dragon, *m.* **dragonet**, *n.* Petit dragon, *m.*; (*Ichth.*) doucet, savary, *m.* **dragon-fly**, *n.* Demoiselle, libellule, *f.*, agrion, *m.* **dragonish**, *a.* En forme de dragon; de dragon. **dragon-like**, *a.* En dragon, comme un dragon. **dragon's blood**, *n.* Sang-dragon, *m.* **dragon-tree**, *n.* Dragonnier, *m.*
dragoon [drə'guːn], *n.* (*Mil.*) Dragon, *m.*—*v.t.* Livrer aux dragonnades; (*fig.*) forcer par des mesures violentes.
drain [drein], *v.t.* Faire écouler; (*Cook.*) égoutter; dessécher, assécher; drainer; (*fig.*) épuiser; vider (a glass etc.).—*v.i.* S'écouler. —*n.* Tranchée, *f.*, égout; (*Agric.*) drain, fossé d'écoulement; (*fig.*) épuisement, *m.* **drain-cock**, *n.* Robinet purgeur, *m.* **drain-pipe**, *n.* Tuyau d'écoulement, *m.*
drainage, *n.* Écoulement; (*Agric.*) drainage; (*Mining*) dessèchement, *m.* **draining**, *n.* Écoulement, drainage, *m.* **draining-board**, *n.* Égouttoir, *m.*
drake [dreik], *n.* Canard, *m.*; pierre plate (capable de ricocher), *f.*; (*Ent.*) éphémère vulgaire, *m.* *Wild drake*, malart, *m.* *To play ducks and drakes*, faire des ricochets; *to play ducks and drakes with one's money*, jeter l'argent par les fenêtres.
dram [dræm], *n.* (*Pharm.*) Drachme; goutte (drink), *f.* **dram-shop**, *n.* Débit de spiritueux, *m.*
drama ['drɑːmə], *n.* Drame, *m.*; (*fig.*) théâtre, *m.*
dramatic [drə'mætik] or **dramatical**, *a.* Dramatique. *Dramatic art*, l'art dramatique; *dramatic critic*, critique théâtral, *m.* **dramatis personae**, *n.pl.* (*Theat.*) Personnages, *m.pl.*
dramatist ['drɑːmətist or dræmətist], *n.* Auteur dramatique, dramaturge, *m.* **dramatize**, *v.t.* Dramatiser.
drank, *past* [DRINK].
drape [dreip], *v.t.* Draper, tendre (de).—*n.* (*Am.*) Rideau, *m.* **draper**, *n.* Drapier, *m.* *Linen-draper*, marchand de nouveautés, *m.*, marchande de nouveautés, *f.*; *woollen-draper*, marchand de drap, *m.* **drapery**, *n.* Draperie, *f.* *Linen drapery*, nouveautés, *f.pl.*; *woollen drapery*, étoffes de laine, *f.pl.*
drastic ['dræstik], *a.* Énergique, radical; brutal.—*n.* and *a.* (*Med.*) Drastique, *m.*
drat [dræt], *int.* Nom de nom! sacristi!
draught [drɑːft], *n.* Tirage; trait, *m.*; action de tirer, *f.*; courant d'air; coup (of drink); dessin (drawing); coup de filet (of fish); tirant (depth of water), *m.*; (*Med.*) potion, *f.*; (*pl.*) jeu de dames (game), *m.* [DRAFT]. *At one draught*, d'un trait, d'un seul coup; *draught beer*, bière à la pression, *f.*; *in long draughts*, à grands traits; *rough draught*, brouillon, *m.* **draught-board**, *n.* Damier, *m.* **draught-horse**, *n.* Cheval de trait, *m.*
draughtsman, *n.* Dessinateur, *m.*; pion (du jeu de dames), *m.* **draughty**, *a.* Plein de courants d'air.

draw [drɔː], *v.t.* (*past* **drew** [druː]; *p.p.* **drawn**) Tirer; traîner; dessiner (a picture etc.); dresser (maps etc.); toucher (rations, salary, etc.); arracher (teeth); vider (poultry); étirer (wire); puiser (water etc.); (*fig.*) attirer (à *or* sur); entraîner (dans *or* à). *To draw a blank*, faire chou blanc; *to draw a bow*, tendre un arc; *to draw a game*, faire partie nulle; *to draw along*, traîner; *to draw aside*, tirer à l'écart; *to draw a sigh*, pousser un soupir; *to draw away*, entraîner, (*fig.*) détourner; *to draw back*, tirer en arrière, retirer; *to draw breath*, respirer; *to draw down*, tirer en bas, faire descendre; *to draw forth*, tirer en avant, faire sortir, susciter, provoquer; *to draw in*, rentrer, réduire; *to draw information*, puiser des renseignements; *to draw in one's horns*, rabattre ses prétentions; *to draw lots for*, tirer au sort; *to draw nearer*, approcher; *to draw off*, soutirer, tirer, ôter, (*fig.*) détourner (de); *to draw on*, tirer, mettre, (*fig.*) attirer; *to draw out*, tirer, arracher, faire avancer, (*fig.*) prolonger; *to draw the long bow*, exagérer, dire des gasconnades; *to draw up*, tirer en haut, (*Mil.*) ranger, (*Law*) dresser, rédiger (deeds etc.), (*Navy*) aligner; *to draw up contracts*, rédiger des contrats; *to draw water*, puiser de l'eau; *what salary does he draw?* quels appointements touche-t-il?

v.i.—Tirer; se rétrécir, se contracter; tirer l'épée, dégainer; dessiner (with a pencil); s'infuser (of tea); porter (of sails); (*spt.*) faire partie nulle *or* match nul. *To draw back*, se retirer, reculer, s'en dédire; *to draw in*, diminuer, baisser (of the day); *to draw near*, s'approcher; *to draw off*, se retirer; *to draw on*, s'avancer; *to draw oneself up*, se ranger; *to draw to a close*, tirer à sa fin; *to draw together*, se rassembler, se réunir; *to draw up*, s'arrêter, se ranger; *to draw up with*, arriver à la hauteur de.

n.—Tirage (au sort), étirage (of metal), *m.*; attraction; (*spt.*) partie nulle, *f.*; geste ultra-rapide du tireur (de revolver), *m. To be quick on the draw*, être prompt à la riposte.

drawback ['drɔːbæk], *n.* Mécompte, désavantage, inconvénient, *m.*; (*Customs*) drawback, *m. It is a great drawback*, c'est un grand inconvénient. **drawbridge**, *n.* Pont-levis, *m.* **draw-net**, *n.* [DRAG-NET]. **draw-plate**, *n.* Filière, *f.* **draw-well**, *n.* Puits à poulie, *m.*
drawer (1) ['drɔːə], *n.* Tireur, *m.*, tireuse (of a bill), *f.*; puiseur (of water).
drawer (2) [drɔː], *n.* Tiroir (furniture); (*pl.*) caleçon, *m. Chest of drawers*, commode, *f.*; *pair of drawers*, pantalon (de femme), *m.*
drawing ['drɔːiŋ], *n.* Tirage; dessin (sketch), *m. Freehand drawing*, dessin à main levée, *m.* **drawing-board**, *n.* Planche à dessin, *f.* **drawing-book**, *n.* Cahier de dessin, *m.* **drawing-pen**, *n.* Tire-ligne, *m.* **drawing-pin**, *n.* Punaise (pour le dessin), *f.*
drawing-room, *n.* Salon, *m.*; (*Court*) réception, *f. Drawing-room suite*, ameublement de salon, *m.*; *there was a drawing-room today*, il y a eu réception à la cour aujourd'hui; *to hold a drawing-room*, recevoir.
drawl [drɔːl], *v.i.* Parler d'une voix traînante. —*n.* Voix traînante, *f.* **drawling**, *a.* Traînant; qui traîne ses paroles.
drawn [drɔːn], *a.* Indécis, égal (of a battle etc.); tiré, nu (of a sword). *A drawn battle*,

bataille indécise, *f.*; *a drawn game*, partie nulle, *f.*; *with drawn swords*, sabre au clair.
dray [drei], *n.* Camion, haquet, *m.* **dray-horse**, *n.* Cheval de trait, *m.* **drayman**, *n.* Camionneur, haquetier, livreur, *m.*
dread [dred], *n.* Terreur, crainte, *f. In dread of*, de crainte de; *to be in dread of*, redouter, craindre.—*a.* Redoutable, terrible; auguste, imposant.—*v.t.* Craindre, redouter. **dreadful**, *a.* Affreux, terrible, épouvantable. **dreadfully**, *adv.* Terriblement, affreusement, horriblement. *dreadless, a.* Sans peur, intrépide. *dreadlessness, n.* Intrépidité, *f.* **dreadnought**, *n.* Paletot-pilote, drap fort, *m.*; (*Navy*) (cuirassé du genre) dreadnought, *m.*
dream [driːm], *n.* Songe, rêve, *m. Day-dream*, rêverie, *f.*—*v.i.* (*past* and *p.p.* **dreamed** [driːmd] or **dreamt** [dremt]) Rêver; (*fig.*) s'imaginer. *To dream of*, rêver à, rêver. *I shouldn't dream of doing it!* jamais je ne m'aviserais de faire cela!—*v.t.* Rêver. *To dream away one's time*, passer son temps à rêver. **dreamer**, *n.* Rêveur, *m.*, rêveuse, *f.*; (*fig.*) visionnaire, *m.* **dreamland**, *n.* Le pays des rêves, *m.* **dreamless**, *a.* Sans rêve. **dreamlessly**, *adv.* Sans rêve. **dreamy**, *a.* Rêveur, songeur; chimérique, visionnaire.
drear [driə] or **dreary** ['driəri], *a.* Triste, morne, lugubre. **drearily**, *adv.* Tristement, lugubrement. **dreariness**, *n.* Tristesse, *f.*, aspect morne, *m.*
dredge (1) [dredʒ], *n.* Drague, *f.*—*v.t.*, *v.i.* Draguer. **dredger** (1), *n.* Pêcheur à la drague; dragueur (boat), *m.* **dredging**, *n.* Dragage, *m.*
dredge (2) [dredʒ], *v.t.* Saupoudrer (de farine etc.). **dredger** (2), *n.* Saupoudreuse, *f.*
dreggy ['dregi], *a.* Plein de lie. **dregs**, *n. pl.* Lie, *f. To the dregs*, jusqu'à la lie.
drench [drentʃ], *v.t.* Tremper, mouiller (de); noyer (de); (*Vet.*) donner un breuvage à.—*n.* (*Vet.*) Breuvage, *m.* **drencher**, *n.* Personne qui donne des breuvages; averse (of rain), *f.*
Dresden ['drezdən], Dresde, *f.*
dress [dres], *v.t.* Habiller, vêtir, parer, orner; panser (a wound etc.); (*Agric.*) donner une façon à; apprêter (food etc.); (*Manuf.*) apprêter; (*Mil.*) aligner; (*Navy*) pavoiser. *Badly dressed*, mal mis, *m.*, mal mise, *f.*; *to dress oneself*, s'habiller, faire sa toilette; *to dress one's hair*, se coiffer; *to dress out*, parer, orner, attifer, (*fig.*) donner une fausse apparence à; *well dressed*, bien mis, *m.*, bien mise, *f.*
v.i.—S'habiller; se mettre; se vêtir (de); faire sa toilette; (*Mil.*) s'aligner. *Right dress!* (*Mil.*) à droite alignement!
n.—Habillement, *m.*; robe (of a woman); mise, toilette; (*Mil.*) tenue, *f.*; (*Court etc.*) grand costume, *m. Dress clothes*, habit de soirée, *m.*; *dress goods*, vêtements pour femmes et enfants, *m. pl.*; *dress rehearsal*, répétition générale, *f.*; *evening dress*, tenue de soirée, *f.*; *full dress*, grande toilette, (*Mil.*) grande tenue, *f.*; *low-necked dress*, robe décolletée, *f.*
dress-circle, *n.* (*Theat.*) Fauteuils de balcon, *m. pl.* **dress-coat**, *n.* Habit (noir), frac, *m.* **dressmaker**, *n.* Couturière, *f.* **dressmaking**, *n.* Confections pour dames, *f. pl.*, couture, *f.* **dress-preserver**, *n.* Sous-bras, *m.*
dresser, *n.* Personne qui habille, *f.*, habilleur,

m.; (*Manuf.*) apprêteur, *m.*, apprêteuse, *f.*; dressoir (in a kitchen); externe des hôpitaux, *m.*

dressing, *n.* Toilette, *f.*, habillement; pansement (of a wound etc.); (*Cook.*) assaisonnement; (*Manuf.*) apprêt; corroyage (of skins), *m.*; (*Agric.*) façon, *f.* (of a field); fumure, *f.*, engrais, *m.*; (*Mil.*) alignement (of troops); (*Naut.*) pavoisement (of ship), *m.* (*Cook.*) *French dressing,* vinaigrette, *f.*; (*Agr.*) *top dressing,* fumure superficielle, *f.* **dressing-case,** *n.* Mallette de toilette, *f.* **dressing-down,** *n.* Râclée, *f.* **dressing-gown,** *n.* Robe de chambre, *f.*, peignoir, *m.* **dressing-room,** *n.* Cabinet de toilette, *m.*; (*Theat.*) loge (d'acteur), *f.* **dressing-station,** *n.* (*Mil.*) Poste de secours, *m.* **dressing-table,** *n.* Coiffeuse, table de toilette, *f.*

dressy, *a.* Qui aime la toilette, élégant, chic, coquette (person); habillée (gown).

drew, *past* [DRAW].

dribble [dribl], *v.i.* Tomber goutte à goutte, dégoutter; baver; (*Ftb.*) dribbler.—*v.t.* Laisser dégoutter, laisser tomber goutte à goutte; (*Ftb.*) conduire (le ballon) du bout du pied, dribbler. **driblet,** *n.* Chiquette, *f. In driblets,* petit à petit.

dried, *p.p.* [DRY]; **drier,** *n.* [DRYER].

drift [drift], *n.* Monceau (de neige etc.); tourbillon, *m.*, rafale, *f.*; objet flottant, *m.*; (*fig.*) tendance, *f.*, but, objet, *m.*; (*Naut.*) dérive, *f.*; (*Geol.*) diluvium, *m.*, terrains de transport, *m.pl.*; (*S. African*) gué, *m.* *Drift-ice,* glaces flottantes, *f.pl.*; *drift-wood,* bois flottant, *m.*—*v.t.* Chasser, pousser; amonceler, entasser.—*v.i.* Dériver, aller à la dérive, flotter; s'amonceler, s'amasser. **drifter,** *n.* (*Naut.*) Chalutier, *m.*

drill [dril], *n.* Foret, *m.*, mèche, *f.*; (*Agric.*) semoir en lignes; sillon (furrow); (*Mil.*) exercice, *m.*, manœuvre, *f.* (*Dentist's*) drill, fraise, *f.*; hand-drill, tamponnoir, *m.*; drille, *f.*; *pneumatic drill,* foreuse pneumatique, *f.*—*v.t.* Forer, percer; (*Agric.*) semer par sillons; (*Mil.*) faire faire l'exercice à.—*v.i.* (*Mil.*) Faire l'exercice. **drill-ground,** *n.* Terrain de manœuvre, *m.* **drill-sergeant,** *n.* Sergent instructeur, *m.*

drilling, *n.* Forage, *f.*; (*Dent.*) fraisage; (*Agric.*) semis par lignes; (*Mil.*) exercice, *m.*, manœuvres, *f.pl.* **drilling-machine,** *n.* Machine à percer, foreuse, *f.*

drily or **dryly,** *adv.* Sèchement.

drink [driŋk], *n.* Boisson, *f.* (*fig.*) ivresse (drunkenness), *f. To be the worse for drink,* être ivre; *to give someone a drink,* donner à boire à quelqu'un; *to have a drink,* se désaltérer, boire un coup; *to take to drink,* s'adonner à la boisson.—*v.t.* (*past* **drank,** *p.p.* **drunk**) Boire. *To drink in,* imbiber, absorber; *to drink like a fish,* boire comme un trou; *to drink off,* boire d'un coup or d'un trait; *to drink to,* boire à la santé de.

drinkable, *a.* Buvable, potable.

drinker, *n.* Buveur, *m.*, buveuse, *f.*; ivrogne, *m.*, ivrognesse, *f. Hard drinker,* buveur intrépide, *m.*

drinking, *a.* Adonné à la boisson; potable; de boire, à boire.—*n.* Le boire, *m.*; la boisson, ivrognerie, *f.*, l'alcoolisme, *m.* **drinking-bout,** *n.* Soûlerie, *f.* **drinking-fountain,** *n.* Fontaine publique, *f.* **drinking-song,** *n.*

Chanson bachique, chanson à boire, *f.* **drinking-trough,** *n.* Abreuvoir, *m.* **drinking-water,** *n.* Eau potable, *f.*

drink-money, *n.* Pourboire, *m.* **drink-offering,** *n.* Libation, *f.*

drip [drip], *v.i.* Dégoutter, tomber goutte à goutte. *To be dripping wet,* être tout trempé; *to be dripping with blood,* ruisseler de sang.—*v.t.* Faire dégoutter, laisser tomber goutte à goutte.—*n.* Goutte, *f.*; égout; (*Arch.*) larmier, *m.*; (*slang*) nouille (of a person), *f.* **drip-moulding,** *n.* Jet d'eau (of window), *m.*

dripping, *n.* Graisse de rôti, *f.*; (*pl.*) gouttes, *f.pl.* **dripping-pan,** *n.* Lèchefrite, *f.*

dripstone, *n.* (*Arch.*) Larmier, *m.*

drive [draiv], *v.t.* (*past* **drove,** *p.p.* **driven**) Pousser; chasser; enfoncer, planter (a nail etc.); mener, conduire (cars, horses, etc.); percer (a tunnel etc.); porter, forcer, contraindre, réduire (à); faire marcher (a machine); (*Naut.*) pousser à la dérive, dériver; rabattre (game-birds). *To drive a bargain,* conclure un marché; *to drive away,* chasser, éloigner, renvoyer; *to drive back,* repousser, refouler; *to drive in,* faire entrer, enfoncer; *to drive mad,* rendre fou; *to drive off,* renvoyer, chasser; *to drive on,* pousser, entraîner, exciter (à); *to drive out,* faire sortir, chasser.—*v.i.* Aller (à); se diriger, courir (à or sur); conduire; aller en voiture; (*Naut.*) aller à la dérive. (*Motor.*) *Can you drive?* Savez-vous conduire? *Drive on!* en route! *to drive about,* se promener en voiture; *to drive against,* pousser vers, s'élancer contre; *to drive at,* tendre à, vouloir en venir à; *to drive by,* passer (en voiture); *to drive faster,* aller plus vite; *to drive off,* partir or s'en aller en voiture; *to drive on,* s'avancer, presser les chevaux; *to drive out,* sortir (en voiture); *to drive up,* arriver (en voiture).

n.—Promenade or course en voiture; promenade pour les voitures, grande avenue or allée (place), *f.*; (*Ten., Cricket*) coup droit, drive, *m.*, balle longue et appuyée, *f.*; (*Golf*) crossée de départ, *f.*; (*Hunt.*) battue, *f.*; (*Mech.*) commande, transmission, *f.*, entraînement, *m.*; (*fig.*) énergie entreprenante, *f. He has got drive,* il est plein d'énergie et d'initiative.

drivel [drivl], *n.* Bave, *f. This is mere drivel,* c'est tout simplement du bavardage.—*v.i.* Baver; (*fig.*) radoter. **driveller,** *n.* Radoteur, *m.*, radoteuse, *f.*

driven [drivn] [DRIVE].

driver ['draivə], *n.* Personne qui conduit, *f.*; cocher (a carriage); conducteur (of cattle etc.); voiturier (of a cart); driver (*esp.* in races of 'trot attelé'), *m.*; (*Rail.*) mécanicien; (*Motor. etc.*) chauffeur, conducteur, *m.*

driving ['draiviŋ], *n.* Action de conduire, *f.*; percement (of tunnels), *m.*—*a.* Qui pousse, qui conduit; moteur. **driving-band** or **driving-belt,** *n.* Courroie, *f.* (de transmission). **driving-box,** *n.* Siège de cocher, *m.* **driving-chain,** *n.* Chaîne de transmission, *f.* **driving-licence,** *n.* Permis de conduire, *m.* **driving-shaft,** *n.* Arbre moteur, *m.* **driving-test,** *n.* Examen pour permis de conduire, *m.* **driving-wheel,** *n.* Roue motrice, *f.*

drizzle [drizl], *v.i.* Bruiner, tomber en petites gouttes, crachiner.—*n.* Bruine, pluie fine, *f.*, crachin, *m.* **drizzly,** *a.* De bruine.

droll [droul], *a.* Plaisant, drôle. *Droll fellow,* drôle de corps, *m.*; *droll thing,* drôlerie, drôle de chose, *f.*—**n.* Plaisant, farceur, *m.* **drollery,** *n.* Plaisanterie, drôlerie, farce, *f.* **drollish,** *a.* Assez drôle, un peu drôle.
dromedary ['drʌmədəri *or* 'drɔm-], *n.* Dromadaire, *m.*
drone [droun], *n.* (*Ent.*) Faux-bourdon; (*fig.*) frelon; fainéant (person); bourdonnement (sound), *m.*—*v.i.* Bourdonner; (*fig.*) vivre dans la fainéantise. *To drone out,* bourdonner, chantonner, psalmodier. **droning,** *a.* Bourdonnant.—*n.* Bourdonnement, *m.*
drool [druːl], *v.i.* [DRIVEL].
droop [druːp], *v.i.* Languir, se pencher, tomber, pencher; (*fig.*) s'affaiblir, faiblir.—*v.t.* Laisser tomber, laisser pendre. **drooping,** *a.* Languissant, abattu; baissé, penché.—*n.* Abattement, *m.*, langueur, *f.* **droopingly,** *adv.* Languissamment.
drop [drɔp], *n.* Goutte; chute (fall); bascule (of gallows); pendant, *m.*, pendeloque (for the ear etc.), *f.*; pastille (sweetmeat); (*Naut.*) chute (of the principal square sails), *f.* *A drop in the ocean,* une goutte d'eau dans la mer.—*v.t.* Laisser tomber; jeter (the anchor); faire (a curtsy); sauter (a stitch); déposer (quelqu'un) quelque part; glisser, laisser échapper (to utter); quitter, abandonner (to desist). *Can I drop you somewhere?* Puis-je vous déposer quelque part? *to drop a brick,* faire une gaffe; *to drop a letter into the post,* jeter une lettre à la poste; *to drop anchor,* jeter l'ancre; *to drop an acquaintance,* cesser de voir quelqu'un.—*v.i.* Tomber goutte à goutte; dégoutter (de); tomber; échapper (slip). *To drop astern,* culer; *to drop away,* s'en aller l'un après l'autre; *to drop behind,* se laisser dépasser, rester en arrière; *to drop down,* tomber par terre; *to drop in,* entrer en passant; *to drop off,* tomber, se détacher, s'en aller, s'endormir, mourir, (*Comm.*) diminuer; *to drop out,* tomber dehors, se retirer, rester en arrière; *to drop with fatigue,* tomber de fatigue.
drop-hammer, *n.* Mouton, *m.* **drop-keel,** *n.* (Quille de) dérive, *f.* **drop-kick,** *n.* (*Rugby*) Coup (de pied) tombé, *m.* **drop-lamp,** *n.* Suspension, *f.*
droplet, *n.* Gouttelette, *f.*
drop-out, *n.* (*Rugby*) Coup de renvoi, *m.*
dropper, *n.* Compte-gouttes, *m.*; (*Fishing*) bout de ligne, *m.*
droppings, *n.pl.* Fientes (d'oiseaux), *f.pl.* **dropping-tube,** *n.* Pipette, *f.*
drop-scene, *n.* Rideau (de fin d'acte), *m.*; (*fig.*) scène décisive, rupture, *f.*
dropsical ['drɔpsikəl], *a.* Hydropique.
drop-stroke or **-shot,** *n.* (*Ten.*) Volée amortie, *f.*
dropsy ['drɔpsi], *n.* Hydropisie, *f.*
dropwort ['drɔpwəːt], *n.* (*Bot.*) Filipendule, *f.*
drosera ['drɔsərə], *n.* (*Bot.*) Drosère, *f.*, droséra, *m.*
dross [drɔs], *n.* Scorie, crasse, *f.*; (*fig.*) rebut, déchet, *m.* **drossy,** *a.* Plein de scories; (*fig.*) impur, sans valeur.
drought [draut], *n.* Sécheresse, *f.* *Official drought,* sécheresse (officiellement) déclarée. **droughtiness,** *n.* Sécheresse, *f.* **droughty,** *a.* Sec, aride; (*fig.*) altéré.
drove (1) [drouv], *n.* Troupeau (en marche),

m.; (*fig.*) foule, troupe (en marche), *f.* *In droves,* en foule. **drover,** *n.* Conducteur de bestiaux, bouvier, *m.*
drove (2) [drouv], *past* [DRIVE].
drown [draun], *v.t.* Noyer; (*fig.*) submerger, absorber; étouffer (noise). *A drowned man,* un noyé; *to be drowned,* être noyé; *to drown oneself* or *be drowned in,* être plongé dans.—*v.i.* Se noyer. **drowning,** *a.* Qui se noie.—*n.* Case of drowning, noyade, *f.*; *death by drowning,* asphyxie par submersion, *f.*; *he saved the child from drowning,* il sauva l'enfant qui se noyait.
drowsily ['drauzili], *adv.* Comme endormi; (*fig.*) avec indolence, sans énergie. **drowsiness,** *n.* Assoupissement, *m.* **drowsy,** *a.* Assoupi; somnolent; lourd, stupide.
drub [drʌb], *v.t.* Rosser, battre. **drubbing,** *n.* Volée, *f.* (de coups).
drudge [drʌdʒ], *n.* Homme (*or* femme) de peine, souffre-douleur, *m.*—*v.i.* Travailler sans relâche, peiner. **drudgery,** *n.* Travail pénible, *m.*; corvée, vile besogne, *f.* **drudgingly,** *adv.* Péniblement, laborieusement.
drug [drʌg], *n.* Drogue, *f.* *Drug in* or *on the market,* rossignol, *m.*—*v.t.* Droguer; (*fig.*) empoisonner. **drug-addict, drug-fiend,** *n.* Toxicomane. **drug-store,** *n.* (*Am.*) Pharmacie, *f.*
drugget ['drʌgət], *n.* Droguet, *m.*
druggist, *n.* (*Am.*) Pharmacien, *m.*
druid ['druːid], *n.* Druide, *m.*
drum [drʌm], *n.* Tambour, *m.*; caisse, *f.*; tympan (of the ear), *m.* *Big drum,* grosse caisse; *kettle-drum,* timbale, *f.*; *muffled drum,* tambour voilé.—*v.i.* Battre du tambour (sur); tambouriner; (*fig.*) tinter. *To drum into the ears,* corner aux oreilles.—*v.t.* (*Mil.*) *To drum out,* chasser ignominieusement, dégrader; *to drum up one's partisans,* battre le rappel (de ses partisans).
drum-major, *n.* Tambour-major, *m.*
drummer, *n.* Tambour, *m.*; (*Am. slang*) commis-voyageur, *m.* **drumming,** *n.* Bruit de tambour, tambourinage, *m.*
drum-stick, *n.* Baguette de tambour, *f.*; pilon, *m.*; cuisse (of a fowl), *f.*
drunk [drʌŋk], *a.* Ivre, gris, soûl. *Dead drunk,* ivre-mort. **drunkard,** *n.* Ivrogne, *m.*, ivrognesse, *f.* **drunken,** *a.* Ivre; d'ivresse, d'ivrogne. **drunkenly,** *adv.* En ivrogne. **drunkenness,** *n.* Ivresse; ivrognerie, *f.*
drupaceous [druː'peiʃəs], *a.* (*Bot.*) Drupacé. **drupel,** *n.* Drupéole, *m.*
dry [drai], *a.* Sec, desséché, à sec; aride; altéré, qui a soif; (*fig.*) piquant, caustique; ennuyeux. *Dry as tinder,* sec comme de l'amadou, comme de l'étoupe; *dry goods,* étoffes, *f.pl.*, tissus, *m.pl.*; *dry toast,* rôtie sans beurre, *f.*; *to be dry,* avoir soif, être altéré; faire sec (of the weather).—*v.t.* (*past* and *p.p.* **dried** [draid]) Sécher; mettre à sec; dessécher. *To dry one's eyes,* s'essuyer les yeux; *to dry one's tears,* sécher, essuyer ses larmes; *to dry up,* sécher, dessécher. *Dried eggs,* œufs en poudre, *m.pl.*—*v.i.* Sécher. *To dry up,* tarir; se taire. **dry-beat,** *v.t.* Battre à tour de bras, rosser. **dry-cleaning,** *n.* Nettoyage à sec, *m.* **dry-dock,** *n.* Bassin de radoub, *m.*, cale sèche, *f.*
dryad ['draiəd], *n.* Dryade, *f.*
dryas ['draiəs], *n.* (*Bot.*) Dryade, *f.*

dryer or **drier,** *n.* Siccatif, dessiccatif, séchoir, *m.*

dry-eyed, *a.* Les yeux secs, sans larmes.

drying, *n.* Dessèchement, *m.*, dessiccation, *f.* —*a.* Qui sèche, siccatif. **drying-room,** *n.* Séchoir; étendage, *m.*

dryness, *n.* Sécheresse, aridité, *f.*

dry-nurse, *n.* Sevreuse, nourrice sèche, *f. To dry-nurse,* élever au biberon. **dry-rot,** *n.* Pourriture sèche, *f.* **dry-rub,** *v.t.* Frotter à sec. **drysalter,** *n.* Marchand de salaisons; marchand de produits chimiques, *m.* **dry-shod,** *a.* and *adv.* À pied sec. **dry-stove,** *n.* Étuve, *f.*

dual ['dju:əl], *a.* Double; (*Gram.*) duel, au duel. *Dual carriage-way,* route à double circulation, *f.*—*n.* Duel, *m.* **dualism,** *n.* Dualisme, *m.* **dualist,** *n.* Dualiste. **duality** [-'æliti], *n.* Dualité, *f.*

dub [dʌb], *v.t.* Armer chevalier; (*colloq.*) qualifier, baptiser; (*Cine.*) doubler (a film). *Dubbed version,* version doublée, *f.*

dubbin ['dʌbin], **dubbing** (1) ['dʌbiŋ], *n.* Dégras, *m.*

dubbing (2), *n.* (*Cine.*) Doublage, *m.* (of a film).

dubiety [dju:baiəti], *n.* Doute, *m.*, incertitude; indécision, *f.*

dubious ['dju:biəs], *a.* Douteux, incertain; louche, équivoque. **dubiously,** *adv.* Douteusement. **dubiousness,** *n.* Doute, *m.*, incertitude, *f.*; caractère équivoque, *m.*

ducal ['dju:kəl], *a.* Ducal.

duchess ['dʌtʃis], *n.* Duchesse, *f.*

duchy ['dʌtʃi], *n.* Duché, *m.*

duck [dʌk], *n.* Cane, *f.*; canard, *m.*; toile à voile (canvas), *f.*, (*pl.*) pantalon blanc; plongeon (dip), *m.*; (*Box.*) esquive, *f.*; chou, poulet, *m.*, poulette (term of endearment), *f. To make a duck,* (*Cricket*) faire chou-blanc, ne pas marquer un point; *to play ducks and drakes,* faire des ricochets; *to play ducks and drakes with one's money,* jeter l'argent par les fenêtres; *wild duck,* canard sauvage.—*v.t.* Plonger dans l'eau; (*Naut.*) donner la cale à; baisser subitement (the head).—*v.i.* Plonger; faire le plongeon; baisser la tête subitement (pour éviter un coup); (*Box.*) esquiver; (*Mil.*) saluer (bullets). **duckbill,** *n.* Ornithorynque, *m.* **duck-board,** *n.* (*Mil.*) Caillebotis, *m.* **duck-gun,** *n.* Canardière, *f.*

ducking, *n.* Plongeon; (*Naut.*) baptême de la ligne, *m.*

duckling, *n.* Caneton, *m.*

duck-shooting, *n.* Chasse aux canards, *f.* **duck-weed,** *n.* Lentille d'eau, *f.*

ducky ['dʌki], *n.* (*fam.*) Petit chat; petit chou, *m.*

duct [dʌkt], *n.* Conduit; (*Anat.*) vaisseau, canal, *m.*

ductile ['dʌktil], *a.* Ductile; (*fig.*) docile, souple.

ductility [dʌk'tiliti], *n.* Ductilité; souplesse, *f.*

dud [dʌd], *a.* and *n.* (*pop.*) Mauvais, mal fait, raté.

dude [dju:d], *n.* Gommeux, *m.* (*U.S.*) *Dude ranch,* ferme pour touristes, *f.*

dudgeon (1) ['dʌdʒən], *n.* Colère, *f.*, ressentiment, *m. In high dudgeon,* fort en colère; *to take in dudgeon,* prendre en mauvaise part, s'offenser de.

duds [dʌdz], *n.pl.* (*colloq.*) Nippes, frusques, *f.pl.*

due [dju:], *a.* Dû; convenable, propre, juste; (*Comm.*) échu, arrivé à l'échéance; (*fig.*) requis, voulu. *Due to,* par suite de, à cause de; *due to and from,* les créances et les dettes; *in due form,* dans les formes voulues, en règle, dans les règles; *in due time,* au moment voulu; *in due time and place,* en temps et lieu; *I am due for a haircut,* j'ai besoin de me faire couper les cheveux; *the train is due at eight o'clock,* le train doit arriver à huit heures [OVERDUE]; *to fall due,* échoir.—*n.* Dû; (*pl.*) droit, impôt, *m.*, redevance, *f. The falling due,* l'échéance, *f.*; *to give someone his due,* donner à quelqu'un ce qui lui est dû, rendre justice à quelqu'un; *to give the devil his due,* rendre justice au diable, ne pas peindre le diable plus noir qu'il n'est; *town dues,* octroi, *m.*—*adv.* Droit, directement. *Just walk on due north,* continuez droit au nord.

duel ['dju:əl], *n.* Duel, *m.*, (*fig.*) lutte, contestation, *f. To fight a duel,* se battre en duel.

duelling, *n.* Le duel, *m.* **duellist,** *n.* Duelliste, *m.*

duenna [dju:enə], *n.* Duègne, *f.*

duet [dju:et], *n.* Duo, *m.*

duffel, duffle [dʌfl], *n.* Molleton, *m.*

duffer ['dʌfə], *n.* Maladroit; godiche, *m.*

dug (1) [dʌg], *past* and *p.p.* [DIG].

dug (2) [dʌg], *n.* Pis, trayon (of animals), *m.*

dug-out, *n.* Abri-caverne, *m. Dug-out canoe,* pirogue, *f.*

duke [dju:k], *n.* Duc, *m.* **dukedom,** *n.* Duché, *m.*; dignité de duc, *f.*

dulcet ['dʌlsət], *a.* Doux, harmonieux. **dulcify,** *v.t.* Dulcifier. **dulcifying.** *a.* Dulcifiant.

dulcimer ['dʌlsimə], *n.* Tympanon, *m.*

dull [dʌl], *a.* Lourd, hébété, stupide (of persons); lourd, gris, sombre (of the weather); sourd (of sound); triste (melancholy); émoussé (blunt); terne, peu brillant (of colour); (*Comm.*) calme, plat; (*fig.*) ennuyeux. *A dull fire,* un triste feu; *as dull as ditch-water,* ennuyeux comme la pluie; *dull of hearing,* qui entend mal, dur d'oreille; *dull season,* morte-saison, *f.*; *to be dull,* être ennuyeux ou assommant (boring); *to feel dull,* s'ennuyer.—*v.t.* Hébéter; émousser (to blunt); ternir (tarnish); engourdir (to numb). —*v.i.* S'hébéter, s'engourdir, s'émousser.

dullard ['dʌləd], *n.* Âne, *m.* (of person), cancre, lourdaud, *m.*

dull-brained, *a.* À l'esprit lourd, obtus. **dull-browed,** *a.* Au visage terne; peu intelligent. **dull-eyed,** *a.* Au regard terne.

dullish, *a.* Un peu lourd; sans beaucoup d'éclat, quelque peu terne.

dullness, *n.* Lenteur, *f.*; assoupissement, ennui; fil émoussé (of blade); manque d'éclat, *m.*, ternissure; faiblesse (of sounds), *f.*

dull-sighted, *a.* À la vue faible. **dull-witted,** *a.* Lourd, stupide.

dully, *adv.* Lourdement, tristement.

duly ['dju:li], *adv.* Dûment, exactement, justement; convenablement. *I have duly received your favour of,* j'ai bien reçu votre honorée du.

dumb [dʌm], *a.* Muet, réduit au silence; (*Am.*) stupide, bête, bouché. *To strike dumb,* rendre muet.

dumb-bells, *n.pl.* Haltères, *m.pl.*

dumbfound [dʌm'faund], *v.t.* Confondre, abasourdir, interdire.

dumbly, *adv.* Sans rien dire, en silence.
dumbness, *n.* Mutisme, (*fig.*) silence, *m.*
dumb-show, *n.* Pantomime, *f.*, jeu muet, *m.*
dumb-waiter, *n.* Desserte, *f.*
dummy ['dʌmi], *n.* Muet, *m.*, muette, *f.* mannequin, objet factice, imité, faux; (*fig.*) homme de paille; (*Cards*) mort, *m.* *To play dummy,* faire le mort.
dump [dʌmp], *v.t.* Déposer, mettre en dépôt, décharger, déverser; (*Australia*) mettre (la laine) en balles.—*n.* Coup sourd; tas; dépôt; dépotoir; jeton, palet, *m.*; (*pop.*) lieu, endroit, *m.* **dumping,** *n.* Inondation du marché par des produits vendus au-dessous de leur valeur, *f.*; dumping, bourrage du marché, *m.*; versage, versement, *m.* **dumping-cart** or **dumper,** *n.* Camion à bascule, *m.* **dumping-ground,** *n.* Décharge, *f.*; dépotoir, *m.*
*****dumpish** ['dʌmpiʃ], *a.* Déprimé; maussade.
*****dumpishness,** *n.* Tristesse, mélancolie, *f.*
dumpling ['dʌmpliŋ], *n.* Pâte cuite, *f.*
dumps, *n.pl.* Tristesse, humeur noire, *f.* *To be* (*down*) *in the dumps,* être triste comme un bonnet de nuit.
dumpy ['dʌmpi], *a.* Trapu, gros et court, boulot.—*n.* Pouf (humpty); tom-pouce, en-cas (umbrella), *m.*
dun (1) [dʌn], *a.* Brun foncé; bai (of horses). —*n.* (*Ent.*) Subimago, *m.*
dun (2) [dʌn], *n.* Créancier importun, *m.*—*v.t.* Importuner; (*fam.*) tanner.
dunce [dʌns], *n.* Ignorant, âne, sot, *m.*, ignorante, ganache, *f.* *Dunce's cap,* bonnet d'âne, *m.*
dunderhead ['dʌndəhed], *n.* Imbécile, *m.*
dune [dju:n], *n.* Dune, *f.*
dung [dʌŋ], *n.* Fiente; crotte (of mice, sheep, rabbits, etc.), *f.*; crottin (of horses), *m.*; bouse (of cattle), *f.*; fumées (of stags), *f.pl.*; (*Agric.*) fumier, *m.*—*v.t.* Fumer.—*v.i.* Fienter.
dung-cart, *n.* Tombereau à fumier, *m.*
dunghill, *n.* Fumier, *m.* **dungy,** *a.* De fumier.
dungarees [dʌŋgə'ri:z], *n.pl.* Combinaison, *f.*, bleus, *m.pl.*
dungeon ['dʌndʒən], *n.* Cachot, *m.*
dunk [dʌŋk], *v.t.* (*Am.*) Tremper (du pain, un croissant, etc.) dans son café, etc.; faire la trempette.
Dunkirk ['dʌnkə:k]. Dunkerque, *m.*
dunlin ['dʌnlin], *n.* (*Orn.*) Bécasseau, *m.*, alouette de mer, *f.*
dunnage ['dʌnidʒ], *n.* (*Naut.*) Fardage, *m.*
dunning ['dʌnin], *n.* Importunité; salaison (curing of cod-fish), *f.*
dunnock ['dʌnək], *n.* (*Orn.*) Fauvette d'hiver, *f.*
duo ['dju:ou], *n.* Duo, *m.* **duodecimal,** *a.* Duodécimal. **duodecimals,** *n.pl.* (*Arith.*) Multiplication des nombres complexes, *f.*
duodecimo, *n.* (*Print.*) In-douze, *m.*
duodenal [dju:o'di:nl], *a.* (*Anat.*) Duodénal. *Duodenal ulcer,* ulcère au duodénum, *m.*
duodenum [dju:o'di:nəm], *n.* Duodénum, *m.*
dupe [dju:p], *n.* Dupe, *f.*—*v.t.* Duper, trom-per; (*colloq.*) flouer. *****dupery,** *n.* Duperie, *f.*
dupion ['dju:pjən], *n.* Doupion, *m.*
duple [dju:pl], *a.* Double. **duplex,** *a.* Duplex.
duplicate (1) ['dju:plikət], *a.* Double.—*n.* Double, duplicata, *m.*; (pawnbroker's) recon-naissance, *f.* *In duplicate,* en double.

duplicate (2) ['dju:plikeit], *v.t.* Doubler; copier. **duplication** [-'keiʃən], *n.* Duplica-tion, *f.* **duplicator,** *n.* Duplicateur, *m.*
duplicity [dju:'plisiti], *n.* Duplicité, mauvaise foi, dissimulation, *f.*
durability [djuərə'biliti] or **durableness,** *n.* Solidité, durabilité, *f.* **durable,** *a.* Durable. **durably,** *adv.* D'une manière durable.
duramen [dju:'reimən], *n.* Cœur de bois, *m.*
durance ['djuərəns], *n.* Captivité, *f.* *To be in durance vile,* être dans un vil cachot.
duration [djuə'reiʃən], *n.* Durée, *f.* *For the duration,* pour la durée (de la guerre).
duress [djuə'res], *n.* Emprisonnement, *m.*; (*Law*) contrainte, *f.* *Under duress,* à son corps défendant.
during ['djuəriŋ], *prep.* Pendant, durant.
*****durst** [də:st], *past* [DARE].
dusk [dʌsk], *n.* Crépuscule, *m.*; obscurité; teinte sombre (colour), *f.* *In the dusk of the evening, at dusk,* à la brune, à la nuit tom-bante, entre chien et loup.—*a.* Obscur, sombre. **duskily,** *adv.* Obscurément.
duskiness, *n.* Obscurité, teinte sombre, *f.*
dusky, *a.* Foncé, sombre; noiraud, noirâtre.
dust [dʌst], *n.* Poussière; poudre, *f.*; balayures (sweepings), *f.pl.*; (*colloq.*) tapage, bruit, *m.*, commotion, *f.*; (*fig.*) cendres des morts, *f.pl.*; condition basse et misérable, *f.* *Coal-dust,* poussier de charbon, *m.*; *sawdust,* sciure, *f.*; *to grind into dust,* réduire en poussière; *to kick up a dust,* (*fig.*) faire du tapage; *to throw dust in someone's eyes,* jeter de la poudre aux yeux de quelqu'un; *to trample in the dust,* fouler aux pieds.—*v.t.* Épousseter; couvrir de poussière, saupoudrer (de). (*fam.*) *To dust someone's jacket,* étriller quelqu'un.
dust-bin, *n.* Boîte à ordures, poubelle, *f.*
dust-cart, *n.* Tombereau, *m.*
duster, *n.* Torchon, chiffon (à meubles), *m.*
dust-hole, *n.* Trou aux ordures, *m.*
dustiness, *n.* État poudreux; état poussiéreux, *m.*
dust-jacket, *n.* Jaquette, *f.*, couvre-livre, *m.* (of book).
dustman, *n.* Boueur, (*fam.*) boueux, *m.*
dustpan, *n.* Pelle à poussière, *f.*
dusty, *a.* Poussiéreux, couvert de poussière; poudreux. (*fam.*) *That's not so dusty,* ce n'est pas mal du tout.
Dutch [dʌtʃ], *a.* Hollandais, de Hollande.—*n.* Hollandais (language), *m.* **Dutchman,** *n.* Hollandais, *m.* **Dutch-oven,** *n.* Rôtissoire, *f.* **Dutchwoman,** *n.* Hollandaise, *f.*
duteous ['dju:tiəs], *a.* [DUTIFUL].
dutiable ['dju:tiəbl], *a.* Soumis aux droits de douane.
dutiful ['dju:tiful], *a.* Obéissant, soumis, res-pectueux. **dutifully,** *adv.* Avec soumission, respectueusement. **dutifulness,** *n.* Sou-mission, déférence, *f.*
duty ['dju:ti], *n.* (*pl.* **duties**) Devoir; (*Customs*) droit; (*Mil.* etc.) service, *m.* *Duty covered by orders,* service commandé; *duty-free,* sans droits de douane; *in duty bound,* engagé d'honneur; *on duty,* de service, de garde, en faction (of sentinels); *to come off duty,* des-cendre de service; *to do duty for,* servir de, prendre la place de; *to do one's duty,* faire son devoir; *to enter upon one's duties,* entrer en fonctions.

duumvir [dju:'ʌmvə:], *n.* Duumvir, *m.*
duumvirate, *n.* Duumvirat, *m.*
*****dwale** [dweil], *n.* (*Bot.*) Belladone, douce-amère, *f.*
dwarf [dwɔ:f], *n.* and *a.* Nain, *m.*, naine, *f.*—*v.t.* Rapetisser; (*Hort.*) rabougrir.—*v.i.* Se rapetisser, se rabougrir. **dwarfish**, *a.* De nain; insignifiant, petit. **dwarfishly**, *adv.* En nain. **dwarfishness**, *n.* Taille de nain, petitesse, *f.*
dwell [dwel], *v.i.* (*past* and *p.p.* dwelt) De-meurer, habiter; rester. *To dwell on*, appuyer sur, peser sur, insister sur.
dweller, *n.* Habitant, *m.*, habitante, *f. Cave-dweller*, troglodyte.
dwelling, *n.* Habitation, demeure, *f.* **dwelling-house**, *n.* Maison d'habitation, *f.* **dwelling-place**, *n.* Résidence, *f.*; (*Law*) domicile, *m.*
dwindle [dwindl], *v.i.* Diminuer, s'amoin-drir; dépérir, dégénérer; se réduire (à).
dye [dai], *v.t.* Teindre.—*v.i.* Teindre, se teindre. *To dye black*, teindre en noir; *dyed in the wool*, bon teint, (*fig.*) enragé, convaincu, fanatique.—*n.* Teinture, teinte; matière tinc-toriale; couleur, nuance, *f.*; (*fig.*) caractère, *m.*, nature, qualité; noirceur, *f. A crime of so deep a dye*, un crime aussi noir; *a villain of the deepest dye*, un coquin fieffé [DOUBLE].
dye-bath, **dye-beck**, *n.* Cuve, *f.* (de tein-turier). **dye-house**, *n.* Teinturerie, *f.*
dyeing ['daiiŋ], *n.* Teinture, *f.*
dyer ['daiə], *n.* Teinturier, *m.*, teinturière, *f.*
dyer's-broom, *n.* Genestrolle, *f.* **dyer's-weed**, *n.* Réséda des teinturiers, *m.*, gaude, *f.*
dye-stuff, *n.* Teinture, matière tinctoriale, *f.* **dye-wood**, *n.* Bois de teinture; bois tinc-torial, *m.* **dye-works**, *n.pl.* Teinturerie, *f.sing.*
dying ['daiiŋ], *a.* Mourant, moribond; de la mort (of things); suprême, dernier. *Dying man*, mourant, moribond; *dying words*, der-niers mots, dernières paroles; *to be dying*, se mourir, être à la mort, être mourant. **dying-bed**, *n.* Lit de mort, *m.*
dyke [DIKE].
dynamic [dai'næmik] or **dynamical**, *a.* Dynamique. **dynamically**, *adv.* Dyna-miquement. **dynamics**, *n.pl.* Dynamique, *f.sing.*
dynamism ['dainəmizm], *n.* Dynamisme, *m.* **dynamist**, *n.* Dynamiste, *m.*
dynamite ['dainəmait], *n.* Dynamite, *f.*—*v.t.* Dynamiter. **dynamiter**, *n.* Dynamiteur, *m.*
dynamo ['dainəmou], *n.* Dynamo, *f.* **dynamograph**, *n.* Dynamographe, *m.*
dynamometer [dainə'mɔmitə], *n.* Dynamo-mètre, *m.* **dynamometric** [-'metrik], *a.* Dynamométrique.
dynast ['dainæst], *n.* Dynaste, *m.* **dynastic** [-'næstik], *a.* Dynastique.
dynasty ['dinəsti], *n.* Dynastie, *f.*
dyne [dain], *n.* (*Phys.*) Dyne, *f.*
dysenteric [disn'terik], *a.* Dysentérique.
dysentery ['disntri], *n.* Dysenterie, *f.*
dyspepsia [dis'pepsiə] or **dyspepsy**, *n.* Dys-pepsie, *f.* **dyspeptic**, *a.* Dyspepsique, dyspeptique.
dyspnoea [disp'ni:ə], *n.* Dyspnée, *f.* **dyspnoic** [-'nouik], *a.* Dyspnéique.
dysuria [di'sjuəriə] or **dysury**, *n.* Dysurie, *f.* **dysuric** [di'sjuərik], *a.* Dysurique.

E

E, e [i:], cinquième lettre de l'alphabet, *m.*; (*Mus.*) mi, *m.*
each [i:tʃ], *a.* Chaque.—*pron.* Chacun, *m.*, chacune, *f. Each one*, chacun, *m.*, chacune, *f.*; *each other*, l'un l'autre, les uns les autres; *for each other*, l'un pour l'autre, les uns pour les autres; *of each other*, l'un de l'autre, les uns des autres.
eager ['i:gə], *a.* Vif, ardent (à); impatient (de); avide, désireux; empressé (à *or* de). **eagerly**, *adv.* Ardemment; impatiemment; avec empressement. **eagerness**, *n.* Ardeur, impétuosité, *f.*; empressement, *m.*; impa-tience; avidité, *f.*
eagle [i:gl], *n.* Aigle, *m.* or *f. Golden eagle*, aigle royal. **eagle-eyed**, *a.* Aux yeux d'aigle. **eagle-owl**, *n.* Grand-duc, *m.* **eagle-stone**, *n.* (*Min.*) Aétite, pierre d'aigle, *f.* **eagle-winged**, *a.* Aux ailes d'aigle.
eaglet, *n.* Aiglon, *m.*
eagre ['i:gə], *n.* Mascaret, *m.*
*****ean** [YEAN].
ear [iə], *n.* Oreille, *f.*; épi (of corn), *m.*; anse (of a vessel), *f. Over head and ears in love*, follement amoureux; *to be all ears*, être tout oreilles, tout ouïe; *to have a good ear* (*for music*), avoir de l'oreille; *to prick up one's ears*, dresser les oreilles; *to set by the ears*, mettre aux prises, brouiller; *to turn a deaf ear*, faire la sourde oreille; *up to the ears*, jusqu'au cou, complètement.—*v.i.* Monter en épi.
ear-ache ['iereik], *n.* Mal d'oreille, *m.*
ear-drop, *n.* Pendant d'oreille, *m.* **ear-drum**, *n.* Tympan, tambour de l'oreille, *m.*
eared, *a.* Qui a des oreilles; (*Bot.*) épié. *Full-eared*, à épis pleins (of corn); *long-eared*, aux longues oreilles.
earl [ə:l], *n.* Comte, *m.* **earl-marshal**, *n.* Comte-maréchal, *m.*
earldom, *n.* Comté, *m.*
earless ['iələs], *a.* Sans oreilles.
earliest ['ə:liəst], *a.* Premier; le plus ancien. *At the earliest*, au plus tôt. **earliness**, *n.* Heure peu avancée, heure prématurée, *f.*; diligence; précocité (of fruits), *f.*
early, *a.* Matinal; matineux (of persons); premier, ancien; prématuré, précoce, hâtif (of fruit etc.). *Early age*, âge tendre, bas âge, *m.*; *early ages*, premiers âges, anciens temps, *m.pl.*; *early Church*, Église primitive, *f.*; *to be an early riser*, être matineux.—*adv.* De bonne heure, de bon matin, de grand matin; tôt; dans les premiers jours de. *Early on*, tout de suite, dès les premiers temps, tout au début.
ear-mark, *v.t.* Marquer à l'oreille (sheep); faire une marque au coin de (a bill); (*fig.*) réserver, mettre de côté. **ear-phones**, *n.pl.* Casque, *m.* **ear-ring**, *n.* Boucle d'oreille, *f.* **ear-shaped**, *a.* En forme d'oreille. **ear-splitting**, *a.* Assourdissant, à vous fendre les oreilles. **ear-trumpet**, *n.* Cornet acoustique, *m.* **ear-wax**, *n.* Cérumen, *m.*
earn [ə:n], *v.t.* Gagner, acquérir; (*fig.*) mériter, valoir. **earnings** ['ə:niŋz], *n.pl.* Gain; fruit du travail, *m.*
earnest ['ə:nist], *a.* Sérieux, empressé, sincère.—*n.* Gage, *m.*, garantie, *f.*; arrhes, *f.pl.*; denier à Dieu; (*fig.*) avant-goût, *m. Are you in earnest?* parlez-vous sérieusement?

in good earnest, très sérieusement; *to be in earnest,* être sérieux.

earnestly, *adv.* Sérieusement, avec empressement.

earnest-money, *n.* Arrhes, *f.pl.*

earnestness, *n.* Ardeur, *f.*, empressement, *m.*; sérieux, *m.*, conviction, *f.*

ear-piercing, *a.* Perçant, déchirant (of sound).

ear-shot, *n.* *Within ear-shot,* à portée de voix.

earth [əːθ], *n.* Terre, *f.*; terrier (of a fox etc.), *m.* *Down to earth* (of person), terre à terre; *made earth,* terre rapportée, *f.*; *mother earth,* mère commune, *f.*; *nothing on earth,* rien au monde.—*v.t.* Enterrer, enfouir, couvrir de terre; (*Elec.*) pourvoir d'un fil de terre, joindre à la terre. *To earth oneself,* se terrer; *to earth up,* butter.—*v.i.* Se terrer. **earth-bag,** *n.* Sac de terre, *m.* **earth-bank,** *n.* Levée de terre, *f.* **earth-board,** *n.* Versoir, *m.* **earthborn,** *a.* Né de la terre.—*n.* Terriens, *m.pl.* **earth-bound,** *a.* Retenu par la terre; (*fig.*) attaché aux biens terrestres. **earthbred,** *a.* De basse naissance; vil, abject. **earthen,** *a.* De terre. **earthenware,** *n.* Poterie, vaisselle de terre, faïence, *f.*—*a.* De faïence.

earthliness [ˈəːθlinis], *n.* Mondanité, *f.*, attachement aux biens terrestres, *m.* **earthling,** *n.* Mortel, *m.* **earthly,** *a.* Terrestre. *For no earthly reason,* sans la moindre raison. —*n.* (*pop.*) *He hasn't an earthly,* il n'a pas l'ombre d'une chance. **earthly-minded,** *a.* Mondain. **earthy,** *a.* De terre, terreux; terre à terre.

earth-nut, *n.* Gland de terre, *m.*; (*sometimes*) truffe, *f.*

earthquake, *n.* Tremblement de terre, *m.* **earth-shaking,** *a.* Qui fait trembler la terre. **earthward,** *adv.* Vers la terre. **earthwork,** *n.* Terrassement, *m.*; (*Fort.*) ouvrage en terre, *m.* **earthworm,** *n.* Ver de terre, *m.*

earwig, *n.* Perce-oreille, *m.*

ease [iːz], *n.* Aisance, aise; facilité; tranquillité, *f.*, repos, *m.*; (*fig.*) soulagement (of pain), *m.* *At ease,* à l'aise; *stand at ease!* (*Mil.*) en place, repos! *to take one's ease,* se mettre à l'aise, prendre ses aises; *with ease,* avec facilité; *with the greatest of ease,* avec la plus grande facilité.—*v.t.* Soulager, adoucir, mettre à l'aise; (*fig.*) tranquilliser, calmer; (*Naut.*) filer. (*Row.*) *Ease all!* Stoppe (partout)! (*Naut.*) *Ease her!* doucement!—*v.i.* *To ease up,* se relâcher; ralentir. ***easeful,** *a.* Tranquille, paisible.

easel [iːzl], *n.* Chevalet, *m.*

easement [ˈiːzmənt], *n.* Soulagement, *m.*

easily [ˈiːzili], *adv.* Facilement, largement, sans peine; aisément, à l'aise. **easiness,** *n.* Aisance; facilité; douceur, *f.*

east [iːst], *n.* Est, orient; levant, *m.* *East Indiaman,* navire des Indes orientales, *m.* *Far East,* Extrême-Orient, *m.*; *Middle East,* Moyen-Orient, *m.*; *Near East,* Proche-Orient.—*a.* D'est, de l'est, d'orient; oriental. *East wind,* vent d'est, *m.*

Easter [ˈiːstə], *n.* Pâques, *m.*; (*Jewish*) pâque, *f.* *Easter Day,* jour de Pâques, *m.*; *Easter Eve,* le samedi saint; *m.*; *Easter Monday,* le lundi de Pâques, *m.* *To do one's Easter duty,* faire ses pâques.

easterly [ˈiːstəli], *a.* D'est. *In an easterly*

direction, vers l'est, en direction de l'est.— *adv.* Vers l'orient, vers l'est, à l'est.

eastern [ˈiːstən], *a.* D'est, d'orient, oriental. *Eastern Question,* la question d'Orient; *Great Eastern Railway,* Chemin de fer de l'Est, *m.*

eastward, *adv.* À l'est, vers l'est, vers l'orient.

easy [ˈiːzi], *a.* Facile; aisé; confortable; débonnaire, accommodant; tranquille; libre, naturel (of style); à l'aise; dans l'aisance. *As easy as winking,* simple comme bonjour; *by easy stages,* par petites étapes; *easy chair,* fauteuil, *m.*; *easy of belief,* crédule; *free and easy,* désinvolte, sans cérémonie; *I am easy in my mind,* j'ai l'esprit tranquille, je suis sans inquiétude; *I am quite easy on that score,* je suis tranquille là-dessus; *it is as easy as possible,* c'est aussi facile que possible; *to make oneself easy about,* se tranquilliser sur; *to take it easy,* en prendre à son aise; se la couler douce.—*adv.* Doucement. (*Row.*) *Easy!* En douce! *Easy all!* Stoppe (partout)! *To pull easy,* tirer en douce, mollir.—*v.i.* Cesser (de ramer); stopper.

easy-going, *a.* Accommodant, complaisant, peu exigeant.

eat [iːt], *v.t.* (*past* **ate** [eit, et], *p.p.* **eaten** [iːtn]) Manger; ronger (to corrode). *To eat a good dinner,* faire un bon dîner; *to eat away,* consumer, ronger; *to eat one's heart out,* ronger le cœur; *to eat one's words,* ravaler ses paroles; *to eat up,* manger, achever de manger; (*fam.*) *what's eating you?* quelle mouche vous pique?—*v.i.* Manger. *Rust eats into iron,* la rouille ronge le fer. **eatable,** *a.* Mangeable, bon à manger, comestible.—*n.* Comestible, *m.*; (*pl.*) vivres, *m.pl.* **eater,** *n.* Mangeur, *m.*, mangeuse, *f.* **eating,** *n.* Action de manger, *f.*; manger, *m.* *Eating and drinking,* le boire et le manger, *m.*; *this makes good eating,* c'est bon à manger; *to be fond of good eating,* aimer la bonne chère.—*a.* Dévorant, rongeur; au couteau (of apples); à croquer (of chocolate). **eating-house,** *n.* Restaurant, *m.* *Eating-house-keeper,* restaurateur, traiteur, *m.* **eats,** *n.pl.* (*slang*) Boustifaille, *f.*

eaves [iːvz], *n.* Égout, *m.* (or avance, *f.*) du toit; gouttières, *f.pl.* **eavesdrop,** *v.i.* Écouter aux portes. **eavesdropper,** *n.* Écouteur aux portes, *m.*

ebb [eb], *v.i.* Baisser; décliner, refluer, se retirer. *To ebb and flow,* monter et baisser. —*n.* Reflux; (*Naut.*) jusant; (*fig.*) déclin, *m.*, décadence, *f.* *At a low ebb,* très bas; *ebb tide,* marée descendante, *f.*; *the ebb and flow,* le flux et le reflux, *m.* **ebb-tide,** *n.* Jusant, *m.* **ebbing,** *n.* Qui reflue; sur le déclin.

***ebon** [ˈebən], *a.* D'ébène; (*fig.*) noir.

ebonize [ˈebənaiz], *v.t.* Ébéner.

ebony [ˈebəni], *n.* Ébène, *f.*, bois d'ébène, *m.* —*a.* D'ébène. **ebony-tree,** *n.* Ébénier, *m.*

ebriety [iˈbraiəti], *n.* Ébriété, *f.*

ebrious [ˈiːbriəs], *a.* En état d'ébriété.

Ebro [ˈiːbrou]. L'Èbre, *m.*

ebullience [iˈbʌliəns] or **ebulliency,** *n.* Ébullition, effervescence, *f.* **ebullient,** *a.* En ébullition, bouillonnant.

ebullition [ebəˈliʃən], *n.* Ébullition; (*fig.*) effervescence, *f.*, transport, accès, *m.*

eccentric [ikˈsentrik], *a.* Excentrique; désaxé; (*fig.*) original, singulier.—*n.* Excentrique, *m.*

eccentrically, *adv.* Excentriquement.

eccentricity [eksen'trisiti], *n.* Excentricité, *f.*
ecchymosis [eki'mousis], *n.* (*Path.*) Ecchymose, *f.*
ecclesia [i'kli:ziə], *n.* Ecclésie, *f.* *ecclesiast, *n.* Ecclésiaste, *m.*
ecclesiarch [ə'kli:zia:k], *n.* Ecclésiarque, *m.*
Ecclesiastes [əkli:zi'æsti:z]. L'Ecclésiaste, *m.*
ecclesiastic [əkli:zi'æstik], *a.* Ecclésiastique.
—*n.* Ecclésiastique, *m.* **ecclesiastical**, *a.* Ecclésiastique. **ecclesiastically**, *adv.* Ecclésiastiquement.
echelon ['eʃəlɔn], *n.* (*Mil.*) Échelon, *m.*—*v.t.* Échelonner.
echinus [ə'kainəs], *n.* (*Conch.*) Oursin, hérisson de mer, *m.*; (*Arch.*) échine, *f.*
echo ['ekou], *n.* Écho, *m. To cheer to the echo,* applaudir à tout rompre.—*v.t.* Répéter en écho, répercuter; (*fig.*) répéter.—*v.i.* Faire écho; retentir, résonner (de). **echoless**, *a.* Sans écho.
éclair [e'kle:ə], *n.* Éclair, *m.*
éclat ['eiklɑ:], *n.* Éclat, *m.*; gloire, *f.*
eclectic [ek'lektik], *a.* Éclectique.—*n.* Éclectique, *m.* **eclecticism**, *n.* Éclectisme *m.*
eclipse [i'klips], *n.* Éclipse, *f.*—*v.t.* Éclipser; (*fig.*) surpasser, exceller.—*v.i.* S'éclipser.
ecliptic [i'kliptik], *n.* Écliptique, *f.*—*a.* Écliptique, de l'écliptique.
eclogue ['eklɔg], *n.* Églogue, *f.*
economic [i:kə'nɔmik] or **economical**, *a.* Économique (of things); économe, ménager (of persons). **economically**, *adv.* Économiquement. **economics**, *n.pl.* Économie politique, *f.*
economist [i'kɔnəmist], *n.* Économiste, *m. Political economist,* économiste, *m.* **economize**, *v.t.* Économiser.—*v.i.* User d'économie. **economizer**, *n.* Personne économe, *f.*; (*Mach.*) économiseur, *m.* **economy**, *n.* Économie, *f.*; système, *m. Planned economy,* économie planifiée, *f.*
ecstasy ['ekstəsi], *n.* Extase, *f.*, transport, *m.*
ecstatic [eks'tætik] or **ecstatical**, *a.* Extatique, d'extase. **ecstatically**, *adv.* Extatiquement; avec ravissement.
ectocyst ['ektosist], *n.* Ectocyste, *m.* **ectoderm**, *n.* Ectoderme, *m.* **ectoplasm**, *n.* Ectoplasme, exoplasme, *m.*
ectozoon [ektou'zouɔn], *n.* Ectozoaire, *m.*
ectropium [ek'tropiəm], *n.* Ectropion, *m.*
Ecuador [ekwə'dɔ:]. La République de l'Équateur, *f.*
ecumenical [œCUMENICAL].
eczema ['ekzimə], *n.* Eczéma, *m.* **eczematous** [-'zi:mətəs], *a.* Eczémateux.
edacious [i'deiʃəs], *a.* Vorace.
edacity [i'dæsiti], *n.* Voracité, *f.*
eddy ['edi], *n.* Remous (of water); tourbillon (of wind), *m.*—*v.i.* Tourbillonner.
edema [œDEMA].
Eden ['i:dən], *n.* Éden, *m.*
edentate [i'denteit], *a.* and *n.* (*Zool.*) Édenté, *m.*
edge [edʒ], *n.* Bord (rim); fil, tranchant (of sharp instruments), *m.*; lisière (of a wood etc.), *f.*; cordon (of a coin), *m.*; angle (of a prism), *m.*; tranche (of a book), *f. To be on edge,* avoir les nerfs en pelote; *to have the edge on,* être supérieur à; *to put to the edge of the sword,* passer au fil de l'épée; *to set one's teeth on edge,* agacer les dents; *to take off the*

edge, émousser; *to take the edge off one's appetite,* étourdir la faim; *with gilt edges,* doré sur tranche; *words with an edge,* paroles caustiques, *f.pl.*—*v.t.* Affiler, aiguiser; border (to border); (*Carp.*) abattre les angles à; (*fig.*) exaspérer, aiguillonner, pousser, exciter.—*v.i. To edge away,* (*Naut.*) s'éloigner graduellement; *to edge in,* glisser, couler; s'insérer. **edged**, *a.* Tranchant; bordé. *Gilt-edged,* doré sur tranche; de tout repos (of stock); *two-edged,* à deux tranchants. **edgeless**, *a.* Émoussé. **edge-tool**, *n.* Instrument tranchant, *m. Edge-tool maker,* taillandier, *m.*; *edge-tool trade,* taillanderie, *f.* **edgeways** or **edgewise**, *adv.* De côté, de champ. *Can I get a word in edgeways?* Pourrais-je placer mon mot?
edginess, *n.* Nervosité, *f.* **edging**, *n.* Bordure, *f.* **edgy**, *a.* Aux arêtes vives aux contours secs; (*fig.*) anguleux, énervé.
edible ['edibl], *a.* Comestible, bon à manger. —*n.* Comestible.
edict ['i:dikt], *n.* Édit, *m.*
edification [edifi'keiʃən], *n.* Édification, *f.*
edifice ['edifis], *n.* Édifice, *m.*
edify ['edifai], *v.t.* Édifier. **edifying**, *a.* Édifiant.
Edinburgh ['edinbrə; *Scot.* 'embrou]. Édimbourg, *m.*
edit ['edit], *v.t.* Éditer, être éditeur de; rédiger, diriger; préparer une édition de.
edition [i'diʃən], *n.* Édition, *f. School edition,* édition classique.
editor ['editə], *n.* Compilateur, annotateur, auteur d'une édition critique; (*newspapers*) rédacteur en chef, directeur, *m. News editor,* rédacteur au service des informations.
editorial [edi'tɔ:riəl], *a.* D'éditeur, de rédacteur.—*n.* Article de fond, *m.* **editorship**, *n.* Travail de compilation, d'annotation, *m.*; direction (d'un journal), *f.*
Edmund ['edmənd]. Edmond, *m.*
educate ['edjukeit], *v.t.* Élever; faire l'éducation de, instruire. **educated**, *a.* Instruit, lettré.
education [edju'keiʃən], *n.* Éducation, *f.*; enseignement, *m.*; instruction, *f. Adult* or *further education,* enseignement post-scolaire; *general education,* instruction générale; *Ministry of Education,* Ministère de l'Éducation Nationale, *m.* **educational**, *a.* D'éducation, scolaire.
educator ['edjukeitə], *n.* Éducateur, *m.*; éducatrice, *f.*
educe [i'dju:s], *v.t.* Tirer, faire sortir, extraire.
eduction [i'dʌkʃən], *n.* Éduction, émission; décharge, *f.*
edulcorate [i'dʌlkəreit], *v.t.* (*Pharm.*) Édulcorer. **edulcoration**, *n.* Édulcoration, *f.*
Edward ['edwəd]. Édouard, *m.*
eel [i:l], *n.* Anguille, *f.* **eel-fishing**, *n.* Pêche à l'anguille, *f.* **eel-pie**, *n.* Pâté d'anguille, *m.* **eel-pout**, *n.* Lotte, *f.*
eerie ['iəri], *a.* Étrange, mystérieux, qui fait peur. **eeriness**, *n.* Étrangeté surnaturelle, *f.*
efface [i'feis], *v.t.* Effacer. **effaceable**, *a.* Effaçable. **effacement**, *n.* Effaçage, effacement, *m.*
effect [i'fekt], *n.* Effet, *m.*; (*pl.*) effets, biens, *m.pl. For effect,* pour faire de l'effet; *in effect,* en effet; *of no effect,* sans effet, inutile, (*Law*)

nul et non avenu; *to carry into effect*, accomplir, èxécuter, mettre à effet; *to give effect to*, rendre valide, mettre à exécution; *to have an effect on*, produire un effet sur; *to no effect*, en vain, sans résultat; *to take effect*, faire son effet, opérer, (*Law*) entrer en vigueur; *without effect*, sans effet, sans résultat.—*v.t.* Effectuer, exécuter, accomplir. **effective,** *a.* Effectif; efficace. **effectively,** *adv.* Effectivement; efficacement. **effectiveness,** *n.* Efficacité, *f.* **effectless,** *a.* Sans effet, inutile. **effectual,** *a.* Efficace. **effectually,** *adv.* Efficacement.

effeminacy [i'feminəsi] or **effeminateness,** *n.* Mollesse, nature efféminée, *f.* **effeminate,** *a.* Efféminé. **effeminately,** *adv.* D'une manière efféminée. **effeminize,** *v.t.* Efféminer, amollir.

effervesce [efə:'ves], *v.i.* Être en effervescence; entrer en effervescence; mousser (of beverages). **effervescence,** *n.* Effervescence, *f.* **effervescent** or **effervescing,** *a.* Effervescent; mousseux; gazeux (of aerated waters).

effete [i'fi:t], *a.* Usé; stérile, épuisé, caduc.

efficacious [efi'keiʃəs], *a.* Efficace. **efficaciously,** *adv.* Efficacement.

efficacy ['efikəsi], *n.* Efficacité, *f.*

efficiency [i'fiʃənsi], *n.* Efficacité; bonne condition, *f.*; (*Mach.*) rendement, effet utile, *m.* **efficient,** *a.* (*Phil.*) Efficient; efficace (of remedies); capable, compétent, utile (of persons). **efficiently,** *adv.* Efficacement.

effigy ['efidʒi], *n.* Effigie, *f.*

effloresce [eflɔ:'res], *v.i.* S'effleurir. **efflorescence,** *n.* Efflorescence; (*Bot.*) fleuraison, floraison, *f.* **efflorescent,** *a.* Efflorescent; (*Bot.*) fleurissant.

effluence ['efluəns], *n.* Effluence, *f.* **effluent,** *a.* Effluent.—*n.* Cours d'eau dérivé, *m.*

effluvium [i'flu:viəm], *n.* (*pl.* **effluvia**) Exhalaison, *f.*, effluve, *m.*

efflux ['eflʌks], *n.* Effusion, effluxion, *f.*, efflux, *m.*

effort ['efət], *n.* Effort, *m.*; (*colloq.*) ouvrage, *m.* *It is a great effort for me*, il m'en coûte beaucoup de; *to use every effort*, faire tous ses efforts pour. **effortless,** *a.* Sans effort.

effrontery [i'frʌntəri], *n.* Effronterie, *f.*

effulge [i'fʌldʒ], *v.i.* Resplendir. **effulgence,** *n.* Splendeur, *f.*, éclat, *m.* **effulgent,** *a.* Resplendissant, éclatant.

effuse [i'fju:z], *v.t.* Répandre, verser.—*v.i.* Émaner, se répandre; (*Med.*) s'épancher. **effusion,** *n.* Effusion, *f.*, épanchement, *m.* **effusive,** *a.* Expansif; (*fig.*) excessif, exubérant. **effusively,** *adv.* Avec effusion. **effusiveness,** *n.* Effusion, *f.*

eft [eft], *n.* Salamandre, *f.*, triton, *m.*

egad! [i'gæd], *int.* Ma foi!

Egeria [ə'dʒiəriə]. Égérie, *f.*

egg [eg], *n.* Œuf; (*Arch.*) ove, *m.* *Addled egg*, œuf couvi; *boiled egg*, œuf à la coque; *fried egg*, œuf sur le plat; *hard-boiled egg*, œuf dur; *new-laid egg*, œuf frais; *poached eggs*, œufs pochés; *scrambled eggs*, œufs brouillés; *to lay eggs*, pondre; *yolk of egg*, jaune d'œuf, *m.* (*fam.*) *Good egg*, brave type; à la bonne heure.—*v.t.* Pousser (à). **egg-cup,** *n.* Coquetier, *m.* **egg-dealer,** *n.* Coquetier, marchand d'œufs, *m.* **egg-flip,** *n.* Lait de

poule, *m.* **egg-plant,** *n.* Aubergine, *f.* **egg-shaped,** *a.* En forme d'œuf, ovoïde. **egg-shell,** *n.* Coquille d'œuf, *f.* **egg-whisk,** *n.* Fouet à blancs, *m.*; bat-œufs, *m.inv.*

eglantine ['egləntain], *n.* Églantier, *m.*; églantine (flower), *f.*

*eglogue [ECLOGUE].

ego ['egou], *n.* Le moi, *m.* **egocentric,** *n.* Égocentrique.

egoism ['egouizm], *n.* Égoïsme, *m.* **egoist,** *n.* Égoïste, *m.* **egotism,** *n.* Égotisme, culte du moi, *m.* **egotist,** *n.* Égotiste. **egotistic** [-ə'tistik] or **egotistical,** *a.* Égotiste. **egotize,** *v.i.* Parler trop de soi, tout rapporter à soi.

egregious [i'gri:dʒəs], *a.* Insigne, énorme; fameux. **egregiously,** *adv.* D'une manière insigne. **egregiousness,** *n.* Énormité, *f.*

egress ['i:gres] or **egression** [i'greʃən], *n.* Sortie, issue, *f.*

egret ['i:grət], *n.* Aigrette, *f.*

Egypt ['i:dʒipt]. L'Égypte, *f.* *Lower Egypt*, la Basse Égypte; *Upper Egypt*, la Haute Égypte. **Egyptian** [i'dʒipʃən], *a.* and *n.* Égyptien, *m.*, Égyptienne, *f.*

eh! [ei], *int.* Eh! hé! hein!

eider ['aidə] or **eider-duck,** *n.* Eider, *m.* **eiderdown** ['aidədaun], *n.* Édredon, *m.*

eight [eit], *a.* Huit.—*n.* (*Row.*) Un huit (de couple *or* de pointe). **eighteen,** *a.* Dix-huit. **eighteenth,** *a.* Dix-huitième; dix-huit. **eightfold,** *a.* Octuple; huit fois plus grand. **eighth,** *a.* Huitième; huit (of monarchs etc.).—*n.* (*Mus.*) Octave, *f.* **eighthly,** *adv.* Huitièmement, en huitième lieu. **eightieth,** *a.* Quatre-vingtième. **eight-score,** *a.* Huit vingtaines, *f.pl.*, cent soixante. **eighty,** *a.* Quatre-vingts. *Eighty-one*, quatre-vingt-un; *page eighty*, page quatre-vingt.

Eire ['ɛərə]. L'Irlande, *f.*

eisteddfod [ais'teðvəd], *n.* (*Welsh*) Assemblée (de bardes), *f.*, jeux floraux, *m.pl.*

either ['aiðə], *pron.* L'un ou l'autre, *m.*, l'une ou l'autre, *f.*; l'un d'eux, *m.*, l'une d'elles, *f.*; (*used negatively*) ni l'un ni l'autre, *m. sing.*, ni l'une ni l'autre, *f.* *I do not expect either of them*, je n'attends ni l'un ni l'autre; *on either side*, de chaque côté.—*conj.* Ou, soit. *Either he knows it or you do*, ou bien il le sait, ou vous le savez; *either he or his friend*, soit lui, soit son ami.—*adv.* Non plus. *I don't either*, moi non plus.

ejaculate [i'dʒækjuleit], *v.t.* Pousser (un cri). —*v.i.* S'écrier; éjaculer. **ejaculation,** *n.* Cri, *m.*, exclamation, *f.*; éjaculation, *f.* **ejaculatory,** *a.* Éjaculatoire; (*Anat.*) éjaculateur.

eject [i'dʒekt], *v.t.* Rejeter; émettre (flames); chasser, expulser, (*Law*) évincer. **ejection** or **ejectment,** *n.* Expulsion, éjection, *f.* (*Law*) éviction, *f.* **ejector,** *n.* Auteur d'une expulsion, *m.*—*a.* (*Av.*) *Ejector seat*, siège éjecteur, *m.*

eke [i:k], *v.t.* *To eke out*, allonger; suppléer à, augmenter; ménager. *To eke out a living*, se faire une maigre pitance.

eke [i:k], **adv.* Aussi.

elaborate (1) [i'læbərət], *a.* Élaboré, soigné, fini; compliqué. **elaborate** (2) [i'læbəreit], *v.t.* Élaborer. **elaborately,** *adv.* Laborieusement, avec soin,

soigneusement. **elaborateness,** *n.* Fini, *m.*; complication, *f.*
elaboration [ilæbə'reiʃən], *n.* Élaboration, *f.*
elaeometer [eli'ɔmitə], *n.* Élaïomètre, *m.*
elapse [i'læps], *v.i.* S'écouler.
elastic [i'læstik], *a.* Élastique. *Elastic band,* élastique, *m.—n.* Élastique, *m.* **elastically,** *adv.* D'une manière élastique.
elasticity [elæs'tisiti], *n.* Élasticité, *f.*
elate [i'leit], *v.t.* Élever, exalter, transporter. **elated,** *a.* Transporté, exalté. **elatedly,** *adv.* Avec joie; avec orgueil.
elater ['elətə:], *n.* (*Ent.*) Élater, élatère, *m.*
elaterite [i'lætərait], *n.* Élatérite, *f.*
elaterium [elə'tiəriəm], *n.* (*Bot.*) Élatérion, concombre sauvage, *m.*
elation [i'leiʃən], *n.* Transport de joie, *m.*, exaltation, ivresse, *f.*
Elba ['elbə]. L'île d'Elbe, *f.*
Elbe [elb], **the,** L'Elbe, *m.*
elbow ['elbou], *n.* Coude, *m.* *At one's elbow,* à côté de soi; *out at elbows,* percé au coude, déguenillé; *to lean one's elbow on,* s'accouder sur; (*fig.*) *to lift one's elbow,* hausser le coude; *up to the elbows,* jusqu'au coude.—*v.t.* Coudoyer, pousser du coude. *To elbow one's way out,* se frayer un chemin avec le coude. **elbow-grease,** *n.* Huile de bras, *f.* **elbow-room,** *n.* Coudées franches, *f.pl.*
*****eld** [eld], *n.* Vieillesse, *f.*; (*fig.*) le temps jadis, *m.*
elder (1) ['eldə], *n.* Sureau, *m.* **elder-berry,** *n.* Baie de sureau, *f.* **elder-flower,** *n.* Fleur de sureau, *f.* **elder-wine,** *n.* Vin de sureau, *m.*
elder (2) ['eldə], *a.* Aîné, plus âgé; plus ancien.—*n.* Aîné; ancien, *m.* **elderly,** *a.* D'un certain âge. **eldership,** *n.* Aînesse; ancienneté, *f.* **eldest,** *a.* Le plus âgé, l'aîné.
Eleanor ['elinə]. Éléonore, *f.*
elecampane [elikæm'pein], *n.* (*Bot.*) Aunée, *f.*
elect [i'lekt], *a.* Élu, choisi, nommé. *The president elect,* le futur président.—*n.* Élu, *m.* (*pl.*) *The elect,* les élus, *m.pl.—v.t.* Élire, nommer, choisir; (*fig.*) se décider à. **election,** *n.* Élection, *f.* *General election,* élections générales, *f.pl.*
electioneer [ilekʃə'niə], *v.i.* Solliciter des votes, travailler les électeurs. **electioneering,** *n.* Manœuvres électorales, *f.pl. Election-(eering) agent,* agent électoral, *m.*
elective [i'lektiv], *a.* Électif; électoral. **electively,** *adv.* Par choix, par élection. **elector,** *n.* Électeur, votant, *m.* **electoral,** *a.* Électoral, d'électeur. **electorate,** *n.* Électorat, *m.*; les électeurs, les votants, *m.pl.*
electric [i'lektrik] or **electrical,** *a.* Électrique. *Electrical engineer,* ingénieur électricien, *m.*; *electric bell,* sonnette électrique, *f.*; *electric eel,* gymnote, *m.*; *electric shock,* secousse électrique, *f.* **electrically,** *adv.* Électriquement.
electrician [elek'triʃən or ilek-], *n.* Électricien, *m.*
electricity [ilek'trisiti], *n.* Électricité, *f.*
electrification [i'lektrifi'keiʃən], *n.* Électrisation; électrification, *f.* **electrifier,** *n.* Électriseur, *m.* **electrify,** *v.t.* Électriser; électrifier. **electrifying,** *a.* Électrisant (of speech etc.).
electro [i'lektrou] [ELECTROTYPE].
electrochemistry [i'lektrou'kemistri], *n.* Électrochimie, *f.*

electrocute [i'lektrokju:t], *v.t.* Électrocuter.
electrocution [ilektro'kju:ʃən], *n.* Électrocution, *f.*
electrode [i'lektroud], *n.* Électrode, *f.*
electro-dynamic ['ilektroudai'næmik], *a.* Électrodynamique.
electro-dynamics, *n.pl.* Électrodynamique, *f.*
electrolier [ilektrou'liə], *n.* Lustre électrique, *m.*
electrolyse [i'lektrolaiz], *v.t.* Électrolyser. **electrolyte,** *n.* Électrolyte, *m.*
electrolysis [ilek'trɔlisis], *n.* Électrolyse, *f.*
electro-magnet [i'lektrou'mægnit], *n.* Électro-aimant, *m.* **electro-magnetic,** *a.* Électromagnétique. **electro-metallurgy,** *n.* Électrométallurgie, *f.*
electrometer [ilek'trɔmitə], *n.* Électromètre, *m.*
electron [i'lektrɔn], *n.* Électron, *m.* **electronic,** *a.* Électronique. **electronics,** *n.* Électronique, *f.*
electro-negative [i'lektrou'negətiv], *a.* Électronégatif.
electrophorus [i:lek'trɔfərəs], *n.* Électrophore, *m.* **electro-plate,** *n.* Argenture électrique, *f.—v.t.* Plaquer, argenter. **electro-plating,** *n.* Plaqué, *m.*, argenture, *f.* **electro-positive,** *a.* Électropositif.
electroscope [i'lektrɔskoup], *n.* Électroscope, *m.* **electrostatic,** *a.* Électrostatique. **electrotherapeutic,** *a.* Électrothérapeutique. **electrotherapy,** *n.* Électrothérapie, *f.* **electro-thermancy,** *n.* Électrothermie, *f.*
electrotype [i'lektroutaip], *n.* Électrotype; (*Print.*) galvano, *m.—v.t.* Électrotyper. **electrotyping,** *n.* Galvanoplastie, *f.*
electuary [i'lektjuəri], *n.* (*Pharm.*) Électuaire, *m.*
eleemosynary [elii:'mɔsinəri], *a.* De charité; d'aumône.—*n.* Personne qui vit d'aumône, *f.*
elegance ['eligəns], *n.* Élégance, *f.* **elegant,** *a.* Élégant, chic.—*n.* Élégant, beau, *m.* **elegantly,** *adv.* Élégamment.
elegiac [eli'dʒaiək], *a.* Élégiaque.—*n.* Vers élégiaque, *m.*
elegist ['elidʒist], *n.* Poète élégiaque, *m.* **elegy,** *n.* Élégie, *f.*
element ['elimənt], *n.* Élément; facteur, *m.*; (*Chem.*) corps simple, *m.*; (*pl.*) rudiments, *m.pl.*; connaissances premières, *f.pl. In one's element,* dans son élément. **elemental** [-'mentəl], *a.* Élémentaire. **elementary,** *a.* Élémentaire. *Elementary school,* école primaire, *f. Elementary chemistry,* rudiments de chimie, *m.pl.*
elephant ['elifənt], *n.* Éléphant, *m.* *White elephant,* (*fig.*) objet inutile et encombrant, *m.* **elephant-driver,** *n.* Cornac, *m.* **elephantiasis** [-'taiəsis], *n.* Éléphantiasis, *f.*
elephantine [eli'fæntain], *a.* Éléphantin, d'éléphant; (*fam.*) éléphantesque.
elevate ['eliveit], *v.t.* Élever; hausser, exalter, enfler, exciter. **elevated,** *a.* Élevé; (*colloq.*) gris (tipsy). **elevation,** *n.* Élévation; hauteur, altitude, *f. Front elevation,* façade, *f.* **elevator,** *n.* (*Anat.* etc.) Élévateur, *m.*; (*Am.*) ascenseur (lift), *m.*; (*Av.*) gouvernail d'altitude, *m.* **elevatory** ['eliveitəri], *a.* Qui peut élever.—*n.* (*Surg.*) Élévatoire, *m.*

eleven [i'levn], *a.* Onze. *The eleven,* les apôtres, *m.pl.*; (*spt.*) le onze, *m.* **elevenses,** *n.pl.* (*colloq.*) Thé ou café de onze heures, *m.*
eleventh, *a.* Onzième; onze (of kings etc.). *The eleventh of May,* le onze mai; *at the eleventh hour,* au dernier moment.
elf [elf], *n.* (*pl.* **elves** [elvz]). Esprit follet, lutin, elfe, *m.* **elf-child,** *n.* Enfant substitué, *m.* **elfin,** *a.* Des lutins, des elfes.—*n.* Gamin, bambin, *m.* **elfish** or **elvish,** *a.* Des lutins, des elfes; espiègle. **elf-lock,** *n.* Mèche de cheveux tordus *or* emmêlés (comme par les lutins), *f.*
elicit [i'lisit], *v.t.* Faire sortir, tirer (de); déduire, découvrir, faire avouer (à); arracher; provoquer.
elide [i'laid], *v.t.* (*Gram.*) Élider.—*v.i.* S'élider.
eligibility [elidʒi'biliti], *n.* Éligibilité, *f.*
eligible ['elidʒəbl], *a.* Éligible; convenable (pour); avantageux (à *or* pour); acceptable. *Eligible match,* un parti avantageux. **eligibly,** *adv.* Convenablement, avantageusement.
Elijah [i'laidʒə]. Élie.
eliminate [i'limineit], *v.t.* Éliminer, enlever, supprimer. **eliminating,** *a.* Éliminateur, éliminatoire. **elimination,** *n.* Élimination, *f.*
Elisha ['ilaiʃə]. Élisée.
elision [i'liʒən], *n.* Élision, *f.*
élite [ei'li:t], *n.* Élite, *f.*
elixir [i'liksə], *n.* Élixir, *m.*
Elizabeth [i'lizəbəθ]. Élisabeth, *f.* **Elizabethan,** *a.* Élisabéthain.
elk [elk], *n.* (*Zool.*) Élan, *m.*
ell [el], *n.* Aune, *f.* (measure). *Give him an inch and he'll take an ell,* donnez-lui un pied et il en prendra quatre.
Ellen ['elən]. Hélène, *f.*
ellipse ['lips], *n.* (*Geom.*) Ellipse, *f.* **ellipsis,** *n.* (*pl.* **ellipses**) (*Gram.*) Ellipse, *f.* **ellipsoid,** *n.* Ellipsoïde, *m.* **elliptic** or **elliptical,** *a.* Elliptique. **elliptically,** *adv.* Elliptiquement; (*Gram.*) par ellipse; (*Geom.*) en forme d'ellipse. **ellipticity,** *n.* Ellipticité, *f.*
elm [elm], *n.* Orme, *m.* *Wych-elm,* orme blanc; *young-elm,* ormeau, *m.* **elm-grove,** *n.* Ormaie, *f.* **elm-sapling,** *n.* Ormille, *f.*
elocution [elə'kju:ʃən], *n.* Élocution, diction, *f.* **elocutionist,** *n.* Déclamateur; professeur de diction, *m.*
elongate ['i:lɔŋgeit], *v.t.* Allonger, prolonger, étendre. **elongated,** *a.* Allongé. **elongation,** *n.* Allongement, prolongement; éloignement, *m.*; (*Surg.*) élongation, *f.*
elope [i'loup], *v.i.* S'enfuir (avec un amant). *To elope with,* se faire enlever par. **elopement,** *n.* Fuite, *f.*, enlèvement, *m.*
eloquence ['elokwəns], *n.* Éloquence, *f.* **eloquent,** *a.* Éloquent. **eloquently,** *adv.* Éloquemment.
else [els], *adv.* Autrement, ou bien, ailleurs.—*a.* Autre. *Anything else,* n'importe quoi d'autre; *anywhere else,* n'importe où ailleurs; *everybody else,* tout autre; *everything else,* toute autre chose, tout le reste; *everywhere else,* partout ailleurs; *nobody else,* aucun autre, personne d'autre; *nothing else,* rien d'autre; *nowhere else,* nulle part ailleurs, en aucun autre pays; *someone* (*somebody*) *else,* quelqu'un d'autre; *something else,* autre chose, *f.*;

somewhere else, autre part, ailleurs; *what else?* quoi encore? quoi de plus? *where else?* où encore? *who else?* qui encore?
elsewhere, *adv.* Ailleurs, autre part.
Elsie ['elsi]. Élise, *f.*
elucidate [i'lju:sideit], *v.t.* Expliquer, éclaircir, élucider. **elucidation,** *n.* Éclaircissement, *m.*, élucidation, explication, *f.*
elude [i'lju:d], *v.t.* Éluder, éviter, échapper à. **elusion,** *n.* Subterfuge, *m.*, réponse évasive; dérobade, *f.* **elusive,** *a.* Évasif, artificieux (answer); fuyant, insaisissable (person). **elusively,** *adv.* Évasivement.
elver ['elvə], *n.* (*Ichth.*) Civelle, *f.*
elvish [ELFISH].
Elysian [i'liziən], *a.* Élyséen. *Elysian fields,* Champs Élysées, *m.pl.* **Elysium,** *n.* Élysée, *m.*
elytron ['elitrən], *n.* (*pl.* **elytra**) Élytre, *m.*
emaciate [i'meiʃieit], *v.i.* Maigrir, s'amaigrir.—*v.t.* Amaigrir. **emaciated,** *a.* Amaigri, maigre, décharné; (*Bot.*) étiolé. **emaciation,** *n.* Amaigrissement, *m.* maigreur, *f.*; (*Bot.*) étiolement, *m.*
emanate ['eməneit], *v.i.* Émaner. **emanation,** *n.* Émanation, *f.*
emancipate [i'mænsipeit], *v.t.* Affranchir, émanciper (de). **emancipated,** *a.* Émancipé, affranchi. **emancipation,** *n.* Affranchissement, *m.*, émancipation, *f.*
emasculate [i'mæskjuleit], *v.t.* Châtrer; (*fig.*) affaiblir, énerver, efféminer.—*a.* [-lət] Châtré; (*fig.*) efféminé, lâche. **emasculation,** *n.* Castration; émasculation; (*fig.*) mollesse, *f.*
embalm [im'ba:m], *v.t.* Embaumer. **embalmer,** *n.* Embaumeur, *m.* **embalming,** *n.* Embaumement, *m.*
embank [im'bæŋk], *v.t.* Endiguer, remblayer; encaisser (a canal etc.). **embankment,** *n.* Levée, *f.*; terrassement, talus, *m.*; (*Rail.*) remblai, *m.*; (*river, canal*) berge, *f.*, quai, *m.*
embarcation [EMBARKATION].
embargo [im'ba:gou], *n.* Embargo, *m.*—*v.t.* Mettre l'embargo sur; défendre, interdire.
embark [im'ba:k], *v.t.* Embarquer.—*v.i.* S'embarquer (sur); (*fig.*) s'engager (dans).
embarkation [emba:'keiʃən], *n.* Embarquement, *m.*
embarrass [im'bærəs], *v.t.* Embarrasser; gêner; déconcerter. **embarrassed,** *a.* Embarrassé, gêné. **embarrassing,** *a.* Embarrassant. **embarrassingly,** *adv.* D'une manière embarrassante. **embarrassment,** *n.* Embarras, *m.*; (*fig.*) perplexité, *f.*; dérangement (in one's business etc.), *m.*, gêne (in money matters), *f.*
embassy ['embəsi], *n.* Ambassade, *f.*
embattle [im'bætl], *v.t.* (*Arch.*) Créneler. **embattled,** *a.* Crénelé. **embattlement** [BATTLEMENT].
embed [im'bed], *v.t.* Enfoncer, coucher (dans); encastrer, enrober.
embellish [im'beliʃ], *v.t.* Embellir, orner (avec). **embellishment,** *n.* Embellissement, ornement, *m.*; (*Mus. pl.*) fioritures, *f.pl.*
ember (1) ['embə], *n.* Braise, cendre ardente, *f.*
ember (2) ['embə], *n.* *Anniversaire, *m.* **Ember-days,** *n.* Les Quatre-Temps, *m.pl.* **ember-goose,** *n.* (*Orn.*) Plongeon glacial, *m.* **Ember-week,** *n.* Semaine des Quatre-Temps, *f.*

embezzle [im'bezl], *v.t.* Détourner; s'approprier frauduleusement. **embezzlement**, *n.* Détournement, *m.* **embezzler**, *n.* Détourneur (de fonds), *m.*

embitter [im'bitə], *v.t.* Rendre amer; (*fig.*) abreuver d'amertume, empoisonner; aigrir, envenimer. **embittered**, *a.* Aigri.

emblazon [im'bleizn], *v.t.* Blasonner (de); (*fig.*) publier, proclamer. **emblazoner**, *n.* Peintre d'armoiries, héraut, *m.* **emblazonry**, *n.* Blason, *m.*, armoiries, *f.pl.*

emblem ['embləm], *n.* Emblème, *m.*; (*Her.*) devise, *f.* **emblematic** [-'mætik] or **emblematical**, *a.* Emblématique. **emblematically**, *adv.* D'une manière emblématique. **emblematize** [em'blemətaiz], *v.t.* Représenter par emblèmes; symboliser.

emblements ['emblimənts], *n.* (*Law*) (Produits des) emblavures; récoltes sur pied, *f.pl.*

embodiment [im'bɔdimənt], *n.* Incarnation; personnification; (*Mil.*) incorporation, *f.* **embody**, *v.t.* Incarner, revêtir d'un corps; (*Mil.* etc.) incorporer (dans); (*fig.*) personnifier. *To embody a clause in a Bill*, incorporer une clause, *or* un article, dans un projet de loi.

embolden [im'bouldn], *v.t.* Enhardir.

embolic [em'bɔlik], *a.* Embolique.

embolism ['embəlizm], *n.* (*Chronol.*) Embolisme, temps intercalé, *m.*; (*Path.*) embolie, *f.*

emboss [im'bɔs], *v.t.* Bosseler, relever en bosse; gaufrer (paper); (*Sculp.*) travailler en bosse, repousser. **embossing**, *n.* Bosselage; gaufrage, *m.* **embossment**, *n.* Relief, *m.*; bosselure, *f.*

embrace [im'breis], *n.* Embrassement, *m.*, étreinte, *f.*—*v.t.* Embrasser, étreindre; (*fig.*) saisir, accepter; comprendre, renfermer. *To embrace the opportunity*, saisir, *or* profiter de, l'occasion. **embracement**, *n.* Embrassement, *m.*, étreinte, *f.*

embrasure [im'breiʒə], *n.* Embrasure, *f.*

embrocation [embrə'keiʃən], *n.* Embrocation, *f.*

embroider [im'brɔidə], *v.t.* Broder. **embroiderer**, *n.* Brodeur, *m.*, brodeuse, *f.* **embroidery**, *n.* Broderie, *f.* **embroidery-frame**, *n.* Métier à broder, tambour, *m.*

embroil [im'brɔil], *v.t.* Brouiller, embrouiller. **embroilment**, *n.* Embrouillement, *m.*, brouille, *f.*; (*fig.*) désordre, *m.*, confusion, *f.*

embryo ['embriou], *n.* Embryon, germe, *m.* *In embryo*, à l'état embryonnaire, en embryon.—*a.* D'embryon, à l'état d'embryon, en germe, en herbe.

embryogeny [embri'ɔdʒəni], *n.* Embryogénie, *f.*

embryological [embriə'lɔdʒikəl], *a.* Embryologique. **embryologist**, *n.* Embryologiste, *m.*

embryology [embri'ɔlədʒi], *n.* Embryologie, *f.* **embryonic**, *a.* Embryonnaire.

emend [i'mend], *v.t.* Corriger; (*Law*) émender.

emendation [i:men'deiʃən], *n.* Correction, émendation, *f.*

emendator ['i:məndeitə], *n.* Correcteur, *m.*

emerald ['emərəld], *n.* Émeraude, *f.* *Emerald Isle*, L'île d'émeraude (l'Irlande), *f.*

emerge [i'mə:dʒ], *v.i.* Surgir; déboucher, sortir (de); ressortir; (*Geol. etc.*) émerger. **emergence**, *n.* Action de surgir; (*Opt.*) émergence, *f.* **emergency**, *n.* Circonstance critique; conjoncture; crise, *f.*, cas imprévu, *m. In case of emergency*, en cas d'urgence. *Emergency exit*, sortie de secours, *f.*; (*Med.*) *emergency operation*, opération à chaud, *f.* **emergent**, *a.* Qui s'élève; (*Phys.*) émergent.

emeritus [i'meritəs], *a.* Émérite.

emersion [i'mə:ʃən], *n.* Émersion, *f.*

emery ['eməri], *n.* Émeri, *m. Emery cloth*, toile d'émeri, *f.*

emetic [i'metik], *n.* Émétique, *m.*—*a.* Émétique.

emigrant ['emigrənt], *n.* Émigrant, *m.*, émigrante, *f.*; (*Fr. Hist.*) émigré, *m.*, émigrée, *f.* —*a.* Émigrant. **emigrate**, *v.i.* Émigrer. **emigration**, *n.* Émigration, *f.*

Emily ['emili]. Émilie, *f.*

eminence ['eminəns] or **eminency**, *n.* Éminence, élévation; colline, *f.*, sommet, *m.*; (*fig.*) grandeur, distinction, célébrité, *f. His Eminence*, son Éminence (title of cardinal). **eminent**, *a.* Éminent; distingué, illustre. **eminently**, *adv.* Éminemment, au suprême degré, par excellence.

emir [e'miə], *n.* Émir.

emissary ['emisəri], *n.* Émissaire, messager, *m.*—*a.* D'émissaire.

emission [i'miʃən], *n.* Émission, *f.* **emissive**, *a.* Émissif.

emit [i'mit], *v.t.* Jeter; exhaler, dégager; (*Fin.*) émettre.

emmet ['emit], *n.* Fourmi, *f.*

emollient [i'mɔliənt], *a. and n.* Émollient, *m.*

emolument [i'mɔljumənt], *n.* (*usu. pl.*) Émoluments, *m.pl.*, rémunération, *f.*; (*fig.*) profit, gain, *m.*

emotion [i'mouʃən], *n.* Émotion, *f.* **emotional**, *a.* Porté à l'émotion, émotif. **emotionalism**, *n.* Émotivité, *f.*; appel aux émotions, *m.* **emotive**, *a.* Émouvant, émotif.

empale [IMPALE].

empanel [im'pænl], *v.t.* Inscrire sur la liste du jury.

empathy ['empəθi], *n.* Pénétration par sympathie, *f.*

emperor ['empərə], *n.* Empereur, *m. Emperor-moth*, paon de nuit, *m.*; saturnie, *f.*

emphasis ['emfəsis], *n.* (*pl.* **emphases**) Force, énergie, emphase, *f.*; accent, *m. To lay emphasis upon, to put emphasis on*, appuyer sur. **emphasize**, *v.t.* Appuyer sur; prononcer avec force, accentuer, souligner. **emphatic** [im'fætik] or **emphatical**, *a.* Fort, énergique; expressif; accentué, emphatique; (*fig.*) positif, décidé. **emphatically**, *adv.* Expressivement; avec force, énergiquement; carrément, positivement.

emphractic [em'fræktik], *a.* Emphractique.

emphysema [emfi'si:mə], *n.* (*Med.*) Emphysème, *m.* **emphysematous** [-'si:mətəs], *a.* Emphysémateux.

empire ['empaiə], *n.* Empire, *m.* (*Rom. Hist.*) *The Lower Empire*, le Bas Empire, *m.*

empiric [em'pirik], *n.* Empirique; charlatan, *m.* **empiric** or **empirical**, *a.* Empirique, guidé par l'expérience. **empirically**, *adv.* Empiriquement, en empirique. **empiricism**, *n.* Empirisme, *m.* **empiricist,** *n.* Empiriste, *m.*

emplacement [im'pleismənt], *n.* (*Mil.*) Emplacement, *m.* (of a gun).

employ [im'plɔi], *v.t.* Employer; se servir de, mettre en usage. *To employ oneself in,* s'employer à, s'occuper à; *to employ work-men,* employer des ouvriers.—*n.* Emploi, *m.*; charge, occupation, *f. To be in someone's employ,* être au service de quelqu'un. **em-ployable,** *a.* Que l'on peut employer, employable. **employee,** *n.* Employé, *m.,* employée, *f.* **employer,** *n.* Patron, *m.,* patronne, *f.*; employeur, *m.* **employment,** *n.* Emploi, *m.,* occupation, *f. Employment agency,* bureau de placement, *m.*; *full employ-ment,* plein emploi; *out of employment,* sans travail; *to be in search of employment,* chercher un emploi.

emporium [em'pɔ:riəm], *n.* Entrepôt, *m.*; (*fam.*) grand magasin, *m.*

empower [em'pauə], *v.t.* Autoriser (à), donner plein pouvoir à, mettre à même (de). *I empower you to act for me,* je vous autorise à agir pour moi.

empress ['empres], *n.* Impératrice, *f.*

emptier ['emptiə], *n.* Videur, *m.,* videuse, *f.* **emptiness,** *n.* Vide, *m.*; (*fig.*) vanité, nullité, *f.,* néant, *m.*

emption ['empʃən], *n.* Emption, *f.,* achat, *m.*

empty ['empti], *a.* Vide, à vide; désert (of streets etc.); (*fig.*) vain, stérile. *Empty threats,* menaces en l'air, *f.pl.*—*n.* Caisse *or* bouteille vide, *f.*—*v.t.* Vider, décharger.—*v.i.* Se vider; se décharger, se jeter (dans).

empty-handed, *a.* Les mains vides, (*fam.*) bredouille. **empty-headed,** *a.* Ignorant, à tête vide.

empyreal [em'piriəl] *or* **empyrean** [empi-'ri:ən], *a.* and *n.* Empyrée, *m.*

emu ['i:mju:], *n.* (*Orn.*) Émeu, *m.*

emulate ['emjuleit], *v.t.* Rivaliser avec; imiter. *To emulate someone's example,* imiter quel-qu'un. **emulation,** *n.* Émulation, rivalité, *f. In emulation of each other,* à l'envi l'un de l'autre. **emulative,** *a.* Émulateur. **emu-lator,** *n.* Émule, *m.*

emulgent [i'mʌldʒənt], *a.* (*Physiol.*) Émul-gent.

emulous ['emjuləs], *a.* Rival; avide, désireux (de). **emulously,** *adv.* Avec émulation, à l'envi.

emulsification [imʌlsifi'keiʃən], *n.* Émul-sionnement, *m.* **emulsify,** *v.t.* Émulsionner.

emulsion [i'mʌlʃən], *n.* Émulsion, *f.* **emul-sive,** *a.* Émulsif.

emunctory [i'mʌŋktəri], *n.* (*Anat.*) Émonc-toire, *m.*

enable [i'neibl], *v.t.* Mettre à même (de); mettre en état (de); permettre (de).

enact [i'nækt], *v.t.* Ordonner, arrêter; rendre (a law); jouer, faire (a part). *A terrible tragedy was enacted,* un drame horrible s'est déroulé. **enactment,** *n.* Promulgation; loi, ordonnance, *f.,* décret, acte législatif, *m.* **enactor,** *n.* Auteur, *m.*

enamel [i'næml], *n.* Émail, *m.*—*v.t.* Émailler (de).—*v.i.* Peindre en émail. **enamel-painting,** *n.* Peinture sur émail, *f.* **enamel-work,** *n.* Émaillure, *f.*

enamelled, *a.* En émail. **enameller** *or* **enamellist,** *n.* Émailleur, peintre en émail, *m.* **enamelling,** *n.* Émaillure, *f.*; émaillage, *m.*

enamour [i'næmə], *v.t.* (*used now only n p.p.*) Rendre amoureux. *To be enamoured of,* être épris de.

encage [in'keidʒ], *v.t.* Encager, mettre en cage.

encamp [in'kæmp], *v.i.* Camper.—*v.t.* Camper, faire camper. **encampment,** *n.* Campement, *m.*

encase [in'keis], *v.t.* Encaisser, enfermer; revêtir (de). **encasement,** *n.* Revêtement, *m.*

encaustic [en'kɔ:stik], *a.* and *n.* Encaustique, *f. Encaustic pavement,* carrelage encausti-que, *m.*

enceinte [ã:'sẽ:t], *n.* (*Fort.*) Enceinte, *f.*

encephalon [en'sefələn], *n.* (*Anat.*) Encéphale, *m.*

enchain [in'tʃein], *v.t.* Enchaîner.

enchant [in'tʃɑ:nt], *v.t.* Enchanter; (*fig.*) charmer, ravir (de). **enchanter,** *n.* En-chanteur, *m.* **enchanting,** *a.* Enchanteur, ravissant, charmant. **enchantingly,** *adv.* À ravir, d'une manière ravissante. **enchant-ment,** *n.* Enchantement, charme, *m.,* fasci-nation, *f.* **enchantress,** *n.* Enchanteresse, *f.*

enchase [in'tʃeis], *v.t.* Enchâsser.

encircle [in'sə:kl], *v.t.* Ceindre, entourer (de), encercler. **encircling,** *a.* and *n.* (D')en-cerclement, *m.*

enclave [en'kleiv], *n.* Enclave, *f.*—*v.t.* En-claver.

enclitic [en'klitik], *a.* and *n.* (*Gram.*) Encli-tique, *f.*

enclose [in'klouz], *v.t.* Enclore, clore; clôturer (a field); entourer, environner; contenir; renfermer, mettre sous enveloppe, envoyer avec; envoyer sous le même pli (letters etc.). **enclosed,** *a.* Entouré, environné; inclus, ci-inclus, sous ce pli (of parcels, letters, etc.). *Enclosed please find . . . ,* Veuillez trouver ci-inclus . . . . **enclosure,** *n.* Action de clore, clôture; enceinte (space enclosed), *f.*; pesage, *m.* (at a race meeting); chose incluse, *f.,* contenu (thing enclosed), *m. The enclosures were missing,* les pièces jointes manquaient.

encomiast [en'koumiæst], *n.* Panégyriste, louangeur, *m.*

encomiastic [enkoumi'æstik], *a.* Élogieux, d'éloges. **encomium,** *n.* Éloge, *m.,* louange, *f.*

encompass [in'kʌmpəs], *v.t.* Entourer, en-vironner; embrasser, renfermer.

encore [ɔŋ'kɔ:], *n.* and *int.* Bis.—*v.t.* Bisser.

encounter [in'kauntə], *n.* Rencontre, *f.*; combat, *m.,* lutte, dispute, *f.*—*v.t.* Rencon-trer, aborder; (*fig.*) éprouver, essuyer.

encourage [in'kʌridʒ], *v.t.* Encourager. *To encourage someone to do something,* encourager quelqu'un à faire quelque chose.

encouragement, *n.* Encouragement, *m.*

encouraging, *a.* Encourageant. **encourag-ingly,** *adv.* D'une manière encourageante.

encrimson [en'krimzən], *v.t.* Empourprer.

encroach [in'kroutʃ], *v.i.* Empiéter (sur); abuser (de). **encroachingly,** *adv.* En empiétant. **encroachment,** *n.* Empiéte-ment, *m.,* usurpation, *f.*

encrust [in'krʌst], *v.t.* Incruster; encroûter (de).

encumber [in'kʌmbə], *v.t.* Encombrer, accabler, embarrasser (de); grever (an estate). *An encumbered estate*, un domaine grevé d'hypothèques. **encumbrance,** *n.* Encombrement, embarras, *m.*; hypothèque, *f. Without encumbrances*, sans charges.

encyclical [en'siklikl], *a.* and *n.* Encyclique, *f.*

encyclopaedia [ensaiklə'pi:diə], *n.* Encyclopédie, *f.* **encyclopaedic** or **encyclopaedical,** *a.* Encyclopédique. **encyclopaedist,** *n.* Encyclopédiste, *m.*

encysted [in'sistid], *a.* Enkysté. *To become encysted*, s'enkyster.

end [end], *n.* Fin; extrémité, *f.*, bout; but, objet, *m.*; (*fig.*) dessein, *m.*, issue, *f. Approaching end*, fin prochaine; *at an end*, fini, terminé, épuisé, apaisé; *at the end of two months*, au bout de deux mois; *big end*, (*Motor.*) tête de bielle, *f.*; *by the end of*, avant la fin de; *dead end*, cul-de-sac, *m.*, impasse, *f.*; *end to end*, bout à bout; *from end to end*, d'un bout à l'autre; *in the end*, à la fin, au bout du compte; *no end of*, (*colloq.*) force; *odd end*, reste, *m.*; *on end*, debout, d'affilée; *the end crowns all*, la fin couronne l'œuvre; *the ends of the earth*, le bout du monde; *there's an end of it*, c'est fini, voilà tout! *there's no end to it*, cela n'en finit pas; *three days on end*, trois jours de suite; *to attain one's ends*, parvenir à son but; *to be at a loose end*, se trouver sans avoir rien à faire; *to be at an end*, être arrivé à sa fin; *to be at one's wit's end*, y perdre son latin; *to beat all ends up*, battre à plate couture; *to come to a bad end*, faire une mauvaise fin; *to draw to an end*, tirer *or* toucher à sa fin; *to get hold of the wrong end of the stick*, mal comprendre; *to go off the deep end*, (*pop.*) se mettre en colère, s'emporter comme une soupe au lait; *to keep one's end up*, tenir bon; *to make an end of*, achever, en finir avec; *to make both ends meet*, joindre les deux bouts; *to make one's hair stand on end*, faire dresser les cheveux sur la tête; *to put an end to*, mettre fin à, tuer; *to serve one's end*, tendre à son but; *to the end that*, afin que.—*v.t.* Finir, terminer, achever.—*v.i.* Finir, se terminer (en); conclure, cesser (de parler etc.); aboutir, se réduire (à). *Never ending*, qui n'en finit pas, sans fin; *to end by doing something*, finir par faire quelque chose. **end-paper,** *n.* Garde, *f.* **end-piece,** *n.* Bout, *m.*

endanger [in'deindʒə], *v.t.* Mettre en danger, compromettre, risquer, hasarder.

endear [in'diə], *v.t.* Rendre cher (à). **endearing,** *a.* Tendre, affectueux; qui inspire l'affection. **endearment,** *n.* Attrait, charme, *m.*; (*pl.*) caresses, *f.pl.*; mots tendres, *m.pl.*

endeavour [in'devə], *n.* Effort, *m.*, tentative, *f. To use every endeavour*, faire tous ses efforts (pour).—*v.i.* Tâcher, essayer, tenter (de), chercher (à).

endecagon etc. [HENDECAGON].

endemic [en'demik], *a.* Endémique. *Endemic disease*, endémie, *f.*, mal, *m.*, maladie, *f.*, endémique.

ending ['endiŋ], *n.* Fin, conclusion; (*Gram.*) terminaison, désinence, *f.*

endive ['endiv], *n.* Chicorée, *f.* (salad). *Curled endive*, chicorée frisée.

endless ['endlis], *a.* Sans fin; éternel, perpétuel, interminable. *Endless screw*, vis sans fin, *f.* **endlessly,** *adv.* À l'infini, sans cesse. **endlessness,** *n.* Perpétuité, infinité, *f.*

endocardiac [endou'ka:diæk], *a.* Endocardiaque. **endocarditis** [-'daitis], *n.* Endocardite, *f.* **endocardium,** *n.* Endocarde, *m.* **endocarp,** *n.* Endocarpe, *m.* **endocrane,** *n.* Endocrâne, *m.* **endocrine,** *a.* Endocrine. **endocrinology,** *n.* Endocrinologie, *f.* **endoderm,** *n.* Endoderme, *m.* **endogamy,** *n.* Endogamie, *f.* **endogenous** [-'dɔdʒənəs], *a.* and *n.* Endogène, *m.* **endometritis,** *n.* Endométrite, *f.* **endoparasite** [-'pærəsait], *n.* Endoparasite, *m.* **endoplasm,** *n.* Endoplasme, *m.* **endoplast,** *n.* Endoplaste, *m.* **endopleura,** *n.* Endoplèvre, *f.*

endorse [in'dɔ:s], *v.t.* Endosser; viser (passports); (*fig.*) sanctionner, appuyer, approuver. **endorsee,** *n.* (*Comm.*) Porteur, *m.* **endorsement,** *n.* Suscription, *f.*; (*Comm.*) endos, endossement (endorsing); visa (of passports), *m.*; (*fig.*) sanction, approbation, *f.* **endorser,** *n.* (*Comm.*) Endosseur, *m.*

endosmose [en'dɔzmous], **endosmosis** [-'mousis], *n.* (*Phys.*) Endosmose, *f.* **endosmotic** [-'mɔtik], *a.* Endosmotique. **endosperm,** *n.* Endosperme, *m.* **endospermic,** *a.* Endospermé. **endospore,** *n.* Endospore, *m.*

endow [en'dau], *v.t.* Doter (de); (*fig.*) douer (de). **endowment,** *n.* Dotation, *f. Endowment fund*, caisse de dotation, *f.*

endue [in'dju:], *v.t.* Revêtir (quelqu'un de pouvoirs spéciaux); douer (de).

endurable [in'djuərəbl], *a.* Supportable, endurable. **endurance,** *n.* Endurance; souffrance, patience, résistance, *f. Beyond endurance*, insupportable; *endurance test*, essai de durée, *m.*, (*spt.*) épreuve d'endurance, *f.*

endure [in'djuə], *v.t.* Supporter, souffrir, souffrir patiemment; endurer.—*v.i.* Durer; endurer, souffrir. **enduring,** *a.* Endurant, qui endure, patient; durable, qui dure (lasting). **enduringly,** *adv.* Patiemment; d'une manière durable.

endways ['endweiz] or **endwise** [-waiz], *adv.* Debout, de champ; bout à bout (end to end).

enema [i'ni:mə, 'enimə], *n.* Enéma, irrigateur (instrument); lavement (action), *m.*

enemy ['enəmi], *n.* Ennemi, *m.*, ennemie, *f.* —*a. Enemy action*, bombardement(s), tir, torpillage(s) ennemi(s), *m.*

energetic [enə'dʒetik], *a.* Énergique. **energetically,** *adv.* Énergiquement. **energize,** *v.t.* Donner de l'énergie à.

energumen [enə'gju:mən], *n.* Énergumène, *m.*

energy ['enədʒi], *n.* Énergie, *f.*

enervate ['enə:veit], *v.t.* Affaiblir, amollir aveulir, énerver. **enervation,** *n.* Affaiblissement, amollissement, aveulissement, *m.*; mollesse, *f.*

enfeeble [in'fi:bl], *v.t.* Affaiblir. **enfeeblement,** *n.* Affaiblissement, *m.*

enfeoff [in'fef], *v.t.* Inféoder; investir. **enfeoffment,** *n.* Inféodation, *f.*

enfilade [enfi'leid], *n.* Enfilade, *f. Enfilade fire*, tir d'enfilade, *m.*—*v.t.* (*Mil.*) Enfiler, tirer en enfilade sur. **enfilading,** *n.* Enfilade, *m.*

enfold [in'fould], *v.t.* Envelopper.

enforce [in'fɔːs], *v.t.* Donner de la force à; faire respecter, faire observer; faire exécuter; forcer, contraindre; (*fig.*) appuyer. **enforcedly,** *adv.* Forcément, de force. **enforcement,** *n.* Mise en vigueur, exécution, *f.*

enfranchise [in'fræntʃaiz], *v.t.* Affranchir (a slave); admettre au suffrage; donner le droit de vote à, donner le droit de cité à. **enfranchisement,** *n.* Affranchissement, *m.*; admission au suffrage, au droit de cité, *f.*

engage [in'geidʒ], *v.t.* Engager; retenir, prendre (to take); louer (to hire); arrêter (a bargain); occuper (attention etc.); inviter (for dancing etc.); (*Mach.*) engrener, mettre en prise; (*fig.*) en venir aux mains avec. *To engage attention,* attirer l'attention avec, avoir l'attention de; *to engage in conversation,* entrer en conversation avec.—*v.i.* S'engager, s'obliger (à); livrer combat, en venir aux mains. *To engage in* (an enterprise), s'embarquer dans. **engaged,** *a.* Fiancé (to marry); occupé (not at leisure); pas libre (of telephone, lavatory); aux prises, aux mains (fighting); (*Arch.*) engagé; (*Mach.*) engrené; en prise. **engagement,** *n.* Engagement, *m.*; occupation; invitation, *f.*; fiançailles, *f.pl.*; combat, *m. Not to keep an engagement,* manquer à un engagement; *to have an engagement,* être pris; *to make an engagement,* prendre un rendez-vous. **engaging,** *a.* Engageant, attrayant. **engagingly,** *adv.* D'une manière engageante.

engender [in'dʒendə], *v.t.* Engendrer, faire naître, causer, produire.—*v.i.* S'engendrer.

engine ['endʒin], *n.* Machine, *f.*, moteur, *m.*; (*Rail.*) locomotive, *f.*; (*fig.* and *rare*) instrument, moyen, agent, *m. A ten-horse-power engine,* un moteur de dix chevaux; *fire-engine,* pompe à incendie, *f.*; *high-pressure engine,* machine à haute pression; *steam-engine,* machine à vapeur; *to stop the engine,* couper l'allumage. **engine-driver,** *n.* (*Rail.*) Mécanicien, *m.* **engine-house,** *n.* Atelier, *m.,* remise, *f.*; dépôt de pompes à incendie (fire), *m.* **engine-man,** *n.* Mécanicien, *m.* **engine-room,** *n.* Chambre des machines, *f.* **engine-shed,** *n.* (*Rail.*) Dépôt des machines, *m.* **engine-trouble,** *n.* Panne de moteur, *f.* **engine-turned,** *a.* Guilloché. **engine-turning,** *n.* Guillochage, *m.*

engineer [endʒi'niə], *n.* Ingénieur; (*Am.*) [ENGINE-DRIVER]; (*Manuf.*) constructeur-mécanicien; (*Mil.*) soldat du génie; (*pl.*) le génie, *m. Civil engineer,* ingénieur civil; *corps of engineers,* (*Mil.*) le Génie; *mining engineer,* ingénieur des mines; *sound engineer,* ingénieur du son.—*v.t.* (*colloq.*) Arranger, machiner. **engineering,** *n.* Art de l'ingénieur, *m. Civil engineering,* génie civil, *m.*; *electrical engineering,* technique électrique, *f. Engineering college,* école des arts et métiers, *f.*

England ['inglənd]. L'Angleterre, *f.* **New England,** la Nouvelle-Angleterre, *f.*

English ['ingliʃ], *a.* Anglais; à l'anglaise, de l'Angleterre. *English girl,* jeune Anglaise, *f.* —*n.* Anglais, *m.*; les Anglais, *m.pl.*; anglais (language), *m.*; (*Print.*) saint-augustin, *m. In plain English,* en bon anglais; *Old English,* gothique (printing), *f. The English Channel,* la Manche, *f.*—*v.t.* Rendre en anglais. **English-built,** *a.* De construction anglaise.

Englishman, *n.* Anglais, *m.* **English-speaking,** *a.* De langue anglaise, anglophone. **Englishwoman,** *n.* Anglaise, *f.*

engorge [in'gɔːdʒ], *v.t.* Dévorer, engloutir.

*engraft [in'grɑːft], *v.t.* Greffer.

engrain [in'grein], *v.t.* Teindre en couleurs solides [INGRAIN].

engrave [in'greiv], *v.t.* Graver. **engraver,** *n.* Graveur, *m.* **engraving,** *n.* Gravure, *f. Copperplate engraving,* taille-douce, *f.*; *dealer in engravings,* marchand d'estampes, *m.*; *line-engraving,* gravure au trait, *f.*; *steel-engraving,* gravure sur acier, *f.*; *stroke-engraving,* gravure au burin, *f.*; *wood-engraving,* gravure sur bois, *f.*

engross [in'grous], *v.t.* Grossoyer (to copy); accaparer (to forestall); s'emparer de, absorber, occuper (to occupy). *Engrossed by,* préoccupé de, plongé dans. **engrosser,** *n.* *Accapareur; copiste d'actes, *m.* **engrossment,** *n.* Action de grossoyer, *f.*; accaparement (forestalling), *m.*

engulf [in'gʌlf], *v.t.* Engouffrer; (*fig.*) engloutir.

enhance [in'hɑːns], *v.t.* Enchérir, renchérir; (*fig.*) rehausser, relever, mettre en valeur, en relief; souligner. **enhancement,** *n.* *Enchérissement, renchérissement, *m.*; hausse, *f.*; (*fig.*) rehaussement, embellissement, *m.*

enigma [i'nigmə], *n.* Énigme, *f.* **enigmatic** [enig'mætik] or **enigmatical,** *a.* Énigmatique, obscur, mystérieux. **enigmatically,** *adv.* Énigmatiquement, obscurément.

enigmatist [i'nigmətist], *n.* Faiseur d'énigmes, *m.* **enigmatize,** *v.t.* Énigmatiser.

enjoin [in'dʒɔin], *v.t.* Enjoindre; prescrire (à). ***enjoinment,** *n.* Injonction, *f.*

enjoy [in'dʒɔi], *v.t.* Jouir de, posséder; goûter, aimer, trouver bon. *Did you enjoy yourself?* vous êtes-vous bien amusé? *I enjoyed that very much,* j'ai trouvé cela très bon (of food etc.), très bien (of other things), cela m'a beaucoup plu; *to enjoy good health,* jouir d'une bonne santé; *to enjoy oneself,* s'amuser, se divertir.

enjoyable, *a.* Agréable, dont on peut jouir.

enjoyment, *n.* Jouissance (de), *f.*; plaisir, *m.*

enkindle [in'kindl], *v.t.* Enflammer; (*fig.*) exciter.

enlace [in'leis], *v.t.* Enlacer.

enlarge [in'lɑːdʒ], *v.t.* Agrandir, étendre, dilater; (*dial.*) élargir (to set free).—*v.i.* Grandir, s'agrandir; se développer. *To enlarge upon,* s'étendre sur. **enlargement,** *n.* Agrandissement (also Phot.), *m.*; extension, *f.*; augmentation, *f.*; élargissement (from prison), *m.*; (*Path.*) dilatation; hypertrophie (of the heart), *f.* **enlarger,** *n.* (*Phot.*) Agrandisseur, *m.*

enlighten [in'laitn], *v.t.* Éclairer, illuminer. **enlightenment,** *n.* Éclaircissement, *m.*; lumières, *f.pl.*

enlist [in'list], *v.t.* Enrôler, engager.—*v.i.* S'engager, s'enrôler. **enlistment,** *n.* Engagement, enrôlement, *m.*

enliven [in'laivn], *v.t.* Égayer, animer. **enlivening,** *a.* Qui anime, qui égaye.

enmesh [in'meʃ], *v.t.* Prendre dans (*or* comme dans) un filet.

enmity ['enmiti], *n.* Inimitié; animosité, haine, hostilité, *f. At enmity with,* ennemi de.

enneagon ['eniəgən], *n.* Ennéagone, *m.*
enneagonal [-'ægənl], *a.* Ennéagone,
ennéagonal. **enneagynous,** *a.* (*Bot.*)
Ennéagyne.
enneandrous [eni'ændrəs], *a.* Ennéandre.
enneapetalous [-'petələs], *a.* Ennéapétale.
ennoble [i'noubl], *v.t.* Anoblir; (*fig.*) ennoblir. **ennoblement,** *n.* Anoblissement;
(*fig.*) ennoblissement, *m.*
enormity [i'nɔːmiti] or **enormousness,** *n.*
Énormité, *f.* **enormous,** *a.* Énorme; (*fig.*)
atroce, monstrueux; anormal. **enormously,**
adv. Énormément.
enough [i'nʌf], *a.* and *adv.* Assez. *Curiously
enough* ..., chose curieuse ...; *large enough,*
assez grand; *more than enough,* plus qu'il
n'en faut; *that's enough,* c'en est assez, en
voilà assez, cela suffit; *to be enough,* suffire,
être suffisant.
enquire [INQUIRE].
enrage [in'reidʒ], *v.t.* Faire enrager; irriter,
exaspérer, rendre furieux.
enrapture [in'ræptʃə], *v.t.* Transporter, ravir.
enrich [in'ritʃ], *v.t.* Enrichir. **enrichment,** *n.*
Enrichissement, *m.*
enring [en'riŋ], *v.t.* (*poet.*) Entourer.
enrobe [in'roub], *v.t.* Vêtir, revêtir.
enrol [in'roul], *v.t.* Enrôler, enregistrer,
inscrire.—*v.i.* S'enrôler, se faire inscrire.
enrolment, *n.* Enrôlement, enregistrement,
m., inscription, *f.*
ensanguined [in'sæŋgwind], *a.* Ensanglanté.
ensconce [in'skɔns], *v.t.* Cacher. *To ensconce
oneself,* se cacher (dans), se blottir; se rencogner; se pelotonner.
enshrine [in'ʃrain], *v.t.* Enchâsser (dans);
conserver.
enshroud [in'ʃraud], *v.t.* Mettre dans un
linceul; (*fig.*) couvrir, cacher; voiler.
ensiform ['ensifɔːm], *a.* Ensiforme, xiphoïde.
ensign ['ensain; (*R. Navy*) 'ensin or 'ensən], *n.*
Enseigne, *f.*, drapeau; (*Navy*) pavillon de
poupe; (*Mil.*) porte-drapeau (person), *m.*
ensign-bearer, *n.* Porte-drapeau, *m.*
ensigncy, *n.* Grade d'enseigne, *m.*
ensilage ['ensilidʒ], *n.* Ensilage; fourrage
ensiloté, *m.*
enslave [in'sleiv], *v.t.* Réduire à l'esclavage;
asservir; (*fig.*) captiver. **enslavement,** *n.*
Asservissement, *m.*
ensnare [in'snɛə], *v.t.* Prendre au piège;
(*fig.*) attraper, enjôler, séduire.
ensue [in'sjuː], *v.i.* S'ensuivre. **ensuing,** *a.*
Suivant; prochain.
ensure [in'ʃuə], *v.t.* Assurer; garantir.
entablature [en'tæblətʃə], *n.* Entablement, *m.*
entail [en'teil], *v.t.* Substituer (à); (*fig.*)
entraîner, imposer. *Entailed estate,* bien substitué, *m.*—*n.* Substitution, *f.* **entailment,**
n. Substitution, *f.*
entangle [in'tæŋgl], *v.t.* Emmêler; enchevêtrer; empêtrer (one's feet); engager; (*fig.*)
embrouiller, embarrasser. **entanglement,**
n. Embrouillement, embarras, *m.* *Wire
entanglement,* réseaux de fil de fer, *m.pl.*
entasis ['entəsis], *n.* (*Arch.*) Renflement (très
léger) d'une colonne, *m.*
enter ['entə], *v.t.* Entrer dans, pénétrer;
inscrire (names etc.); enregistrer (parcels);
(*Law*) intenter (an action); (*Book-keeping*)
porter. *To enter a profession,* embrasser une
carrière; *to enter one's name,* s'inscrire; *to*

enter the army, entrer dans l'armée, se faire
soldat; *to enter the Church,* entrer dans les
ordres; *to enter the navy,* entrer dans la
marine, se faire marin.—*v.i.* Entrer; s'engager (dans). *To enter for,* se présenter à,
s'engager pour; *to enter into,* entrer dans,
prendre part à; *to enter upon,* aborder,
commencer, débuter dans; *to enter upon an
office,* entrer en fonctions. **entering,** *n.*
Entrée, *f.* *On entering,* à son entrée.
enteric [en'terik], *a.* Entérique. *Enteric fever,*
la fièvre typhoïde, *f.*
enteritis [entə'raitis], *n.* Entérite, *f.*
enterocolitis, *n.* Entérocolite, *f.*
enterotomy [entə'rɔtəmi], *n.* Entérotomie, *f.*
enterprise ['entəpraiz], *n.* Entreprise,
hardiesse, *f.*; caractère entreprenant, esprit
d'entreprise, *m.* *Free enterprise,* libre entreprise, *f.*; *to show enterprise,* faire preuve d'un
esprit d'entreprise. **enterpriser,** *n.* Homme
entreprenant, *m.* **enterprising,** *a.* Entreprenant, qui a l'esprit d'entreprise, plein
d'initiative.
entertain [entə'tein], *v.t.* Recevoir (to receive);
divertir, régaler, amuser (to amuse); avoir,
concevoir (an idea etc.); nourrir (vain hopes
etc.); accepter, accueillir (a proposal). *To
entertain someone to dinner,* donner à dîner à
quelqu'un.—*v.i.* Recevoir (guests). *Do you
entertain a great deal?* Recevez-vous beaucoup? **entertainer,** *n.* Personne qui divertit
or qui amuse, *f.*; (*Theat.* etc.) diseur, *m.*,
diseuse, *f.*, comique; hôte, *m.*, hôtesse, *f.*
entertaining, *a.* Amusant, divertissant.
entertainingly, *adv.* Agréablement, d'une
manière divertissante. **entertainment,** *n.*
Hospitalité, *f.*; accueil (reception), *m.*;
festin, repas, *m.*, fête, *f.*; divertissement,
spectacle, amusement (amusement), *m.*
Entertainment tax, taxe sur les spectacles, *f.*
enthrall [in'θrɔːl], *v.t.* Asservir, assujettir;
(*fig.*) captiver, ravir.
enthrone [in'θroun], *v.t.* Mettre sur le trône;
introniser (a bishop). **enthronement,** *n.*
Intronisation, *f.*
enthuse [in'θjuːz], *v.i.* *To enthuse over,*
s'enthousiasmer de or pour.
enthusiasm [in'θjuːziæzm], *n.* Enthousiasme,
m. **enthusiast,** *n.* Enthousiaste.
enthusiastic [inθjuːzi'æstik] or **enthusiastical**
a. Enthousiaste. **enthusiastically,** *adv.*
Avec enthousiasme, en enthousiaste.
enthymeme ['enθimiːm], *n.* (*Log.*) Enthymème, *m.*
entice [in'tais], *v.t.* Attirer; entraîner (dans);
séduire (à). *To entice away,* entraîner au
loin, enlever; *to entice into,* entraîner dans.
enticement, *n.* Appât, charme, *m.*; tentation, séduction, *f.* **enticer,** *n.* Tentateur,
séducteur, *m.*, séductrice, *f.* **enticing,** *a.*
Séduisant, attrayant, tentant. **enticingly,**
adv. D'une manière séduisante or attrayante.
entire [in'taiə], *a.* Entier, complet. *Entire
horse,* cheval entier. **entirely,** *adv.* Entièrement, complètement, tout entier. **entirety,**
n. Totalité, *f.*; le tout, *m.*; intégrité, *f.* *In its
entirety,* en entier.
entitle [in'taitl], *v.t.* Intituler, appeler; donner droit à. *To be entitled to,* avoir droit à,
être en droit de.
entity ['entiti], *n.* Entité, *f.*, être de raison,
m.

entoil [en'tɔil], *v.t.* Prendre dans des filets; prendre au piège.

entomb [in'tu:m], *v.t.* Ensevelir. **entombment,** *n.* Ensevelissement, *m.*, mise au tombeau, sépulture, *f.*

entomological [entəmə'lɔdʒikəl], *a.* Entomologique. **entomologist** [-'mɔlədʒist], *n.* Entomologiste, *m.* **entomology,** *n.* Entomologie, *f.*

entozoology [entɔzou'ɔlədʒi], *n.* Entozoologie, *f.* **entozoon** [-'zouən], *n.* (*pl.* **entozoa**) Entozoaire, *m.*

entrails ['entreilz], *n.pl.* Entrailles, *f.pl.*

entrain [in'trein], *v.t.* and *v.i.* (S')embarquer en chemin de fer.

entrammel [in'træməl], *v.t.* Entraver, empêtrer.

entrance (1) ['entrəns], *n.* Entrée, *f.*; commencement, début (beginning), *m.*; (*fig.*) initiation, *f.* *Disguised entrance,* (*Mil.*) entrée en chicane, *f.*; *entrance money,* prix d'entrée, *m.* **entrance-fee,** *n.* Entrée, *f.* **entrance-hall,** *n.* Vestibule, *m.*

entrance (2) [in'tra:ns], *v.t.* Extasier, ravir. **entrancement,** *n.* Extase, *f.* **entrancing,** *a.* Prenant; ravissant; d'un charme profond; d'une beauté captivante.

entrant ['entrənt], *n.* Inscrit (in a competition), *m.*; inscrite, *f.*; débutant (in a new profession), *m.*, débutante, *f.*

entrap [in'træp], *v.t.* Prendre au piège, attraper (dans).

entreat [in'tri:t], *v.t.* Supplier, prier instamment (de). **entreaty,** *n.* Prière; supplication; (*pl.*) sollicitation, *f.*, instances, *f.pl.*

entrench [in'trentʃ], *v.t.* Retrancher.—*v.i.* Faire des tranchées. *To entrench upon,* empiéter sur, enfreindre. **entrenching-tool,** *n.* Pelle-bêche, *f.* **entrenchment,** *n.* Retranchement, *m.*

entrust [in'trʌst], *v.t.* Charger (de).

entry ['entri], *n.* Entrée, *f.*; inscription (registration), *f.*; (*Book-keeping*) écriture, *f.*, article, *m.*; (*Customs*) déclaration d'entrée; (*Law*) prise de possession, *f.* *By double entry,* en partie double; *by single entry,* en partie simple; *no entry,* sens interdit, passage interdit; *to make an entry against,* (*Comm.*) débiter.

entwine [in'twain], *v.t.* Enlacer, entrelacer, entortiller.—*v.i.* S'enlacer, s'entrelacer, s'entortiller.

enumerate [i'nju:məreit], *v.t.* Énumérer, dénombrer. **enumeration,** *n.* Énumération, *f.*

enunciate [i'nʌnʃieit], *v.t.* Énoncer; prononcer.—*v.i.* Articuler. **enunciation** [-'eiʃən], *n.* Énonciation, *f.*; (*Geom.*) énoncé, *m.*; articulation, *f.*

enunciative [i'nʌnʃiətiv], *a.* Énonciatif. **enunciatively,** *adv.* D'une manière énonciative.

envelop [in'veləp], *v.t.* Envelopper (de *or* dans).

envelope ['enviloup, 'ɔnvəloup], *n.* Enveloppe, *f.* *In an envelope,* sous enveloppe; *in the same envelope,* sous le même pli.

envelopment [en'veləpmənt], *n.* Enveloppement, *m.*

envenom [in'venəm], *v.t.* Envenimer; exaspérer (to embitter).

enviable ['enviəbl], *a.* Digne d'envie, enviable. **enviably,** *adv.* D'une manière

enviable. **envious,** *a.* Envieux (de). *With envious eyes,* d'un œil d'envie. **enviously,** *adv.* Avec envie, par envie.

environ [in'vaiərən], *v.t.* Environner (de). **environment,** *n.* Milieu, entourage, environnement, *m.*

environs [in'vaiərənz *or* 'environz], *n.pl.* Environs, *m.pl.*

envisage [in'vizidʒ], *v.t.* Envisager.

envoy ['envɔi], *n.* Envoyé; (*Pros.*) envoi, *m.*

envy ['envi], *n.* Envie, *f.* *Green with envy,* dévoré d'envie.—*v.t.* Envier, porter envie à.

enwrap [in'ræp], *v.t.* Envelopper.

enzootic [enzo'ɔtik], *a.* Enzootique.—*n.* Enzootie, *f.*

enzyme ['enzaim], *n.* Enzyme, diastase, zymase, *f.*

eocene ['i:osi:n], *a.* and *n.* (*Geol.*) Éocène, *m.*

Eolian, Eolic, etc. [ÆOLIAN].

eolith ['i:oliθ], *n.* Éolithe, *m.*

epact ['i:pækt], *n.* (*Astron.*) Épacte, *f.*

epanalepsis [epənə'lepsis], *n.* Épanalepse, *f.*

epanorthosis [epənɔ:'θousis], *n.* Épanorthose, *f.*

epaulement [i'pɔ:lmənt], *n.* (*Fort.*) Épaulement, *m.*

epaulet(te) ['epɔ:let], *n.* Épaulette, *f.*

epenthesis [e'penθisis], *n.* (*pl.* **epentheses**) Épenthèse, *f.*

epenthetic [epen'θetik], *a.* Épenthétique.

epergne [i'pɔ:n], *n.* Surtout de table, *m.*

ephemera [i'femərə], *n.* (*pl.* **ephemerae**) Éphémère, *m.* **ephemeral** *or* **ephemeric,** *a.* Éphémère. **ephemerally,** *adv.* Éphémèrement. **ephemeris,** *n.* (*pl.* **ephemerides** [ifə'meridi:z]) Éphémérides, *f.pl.*

Ephesus ['efisəs]. Éphèse, *f.*

ephod ['efɔd], *n.* Éphod, *m.*

ephor ['efə], *n.* Éphore, *m.*

epic ['epik], *a.* Épique; (*fig.*) légendaire.—*n.* Épopée, *f.*, poème épique, *m.*

epicarp ['epika:p], *n.* (*Bot.*) Épicarpe, *m.*

epicene ['episi:n], *a.* (*Gram.*) Épicène.

epichirema [epikai'ri:mə], *n.* Épichérème, *m.*

epicranium [epi'kreiniəm], *n.* Épicrâne, *m.*

epicure ['epikjuə], *n.* Gourmet, gastronome, *m.* **Epicurus** [epi'kjuərəs]. Épicure, *m.*

Epicurean [epikju'ri:ən], *a.* D'Épicure, épicurien.—*n.* Épicurien, *m.* **Epicureanism** *or* **epicurism,** *n.* Épicurisme, *m.*

epicycle ['episaikl], *n.* Épicycle, *m.*

epidemic (1) [epi'demik] *or* **epidemical,** *a.* Épidémique. **epidemic** (2), *n.* Épidémie, *f.* **epidemically,** *adv.* Épidémiquement.

epidermis [epi'də:mis], *n.* Épiderme, *m.* **epidermal** *or* **epidermic,** *a.* Épidermique. **epidermoid,** *a.* Épidermoïde.

epidiascope [epidaiə'skoup], *n.* Lanterne magique, *f.*, projecteur, *m.*

epigastric, *a.* Épigastrique. **epigastrium** [epi'gæstriəm], *n.* (*Anat.*) Épigastre, *m.*

epigenesis [epi'dʒenisis], *n.* Épigénèse, *f.*

epigenetic [epidʒə'netik] *or* **epigenous** [ə'pidʒənəs], *a.* (*Bot.*) Épigénéique.

epiglottic [epi'glɔtik], *a.* Épiglottique. **epiglottis,** *n.* Épiglotte, *f.*

epigram ['epigræm], *n.* Épigramme, *f.* **epigrammatic** [-grə'mætik] *or* **epigrammatical,** *c.* Épigrammatique, mordant.

epigrammatically, *adv.* Épigrammatiquement. **epigrammatist** [-'græmətist], *n.* Épigrammatiste, *m.*

epigraph ['epigræf], *n.* Épigraphe, *f.* **epigraphic,** *a.* Épigraphique.

epigraphist [i'pigrəfist], *n.* Épigraphiste, *m.*

epigynous [i'pidʒinəs], *a.* (*Bot.*) Épigyne.

epilepsy ['epilepsi], *n.* Épilepsie, *f.* **epileptic,** *a.* and *n.* Épileptique. *Epileptic fit,* attaque d'épilepsie, *f.* **epileptoid,** *a.* Épileptiforme.

epilogize [e'pilədʒaiz], *v.i.* Composer, déclamer, dire un épilogue.

epilogue ['epilɔg], *n.* Épilogue, *m.*

Epiphany [i'pifəni], *n.* Épiphanie, fête des Rois, *f.*

epiphyllous [epi'filəs], *a.* (*Bot.*) Épiphylle.

epiphyte ['epifait], *n.* (*Bot.*) Épiphyte, *f.* **epiphytal, epiphytic** [-'fitik], *a.* Épiphytique.

epiploic [epi'plouik], *a.* (*Anat.*) Épiploïque.

epiploon [e'piplouən], *n.* Épiploon, *m.*

epirhizous [epi'raizəs], *a.* (*Bot.*) Épirrhize.

Epirus [ə'paiərəs]. Épire, *f.*

episcopacy [i'piskəpəsi], *n.* Épiscopat; épiscopalisme, *m.* **episcopal,** *a.* Épiscopal. *Episcopal palace,* évêché, palais de l'évêque, *m.*; *episcopal see,* évêché, *m.* **episcopalian** [-'peiliən], *a.* and *n.* Épiscopalien, *m.* **episcopally,** *adv.* Épiscopalement. **episcopate,** *n.* Épiscopat, *m.*

episode ['episoud], *n.* Épisode, *m.* **episodic** [-'sɔdik] or **episodical,** *a.* Épisodique. **episodically,** *adv.* Épisodiquement.

epispastic [epi'spæstik], *a.* and *n.* (*Med.*) Épispastique, *m.*

episperm ['epispə:m], *n.* (*Bot.*) Épisperme, *m.* **epispermic,** *a.* Épispermatique.

epistemology [episti:'mɔlədʒi], *n.* Épistémologie, *f.*

epistle [i'pisl], *n.* Épître, *f.*

epistolarian [i'pistə'leəriən], *a.* and *n.* Épistolier, *m.*, épistolière, *f.* **epistolary** [i'pistələri], *a.* Épistolaire. *epistolize, v.i.* Écrire des lettres.

epistolographic [epistəlou'græfik], *a.* Épistolographique.

epistolography [epistə'lɔgrəfi], *n.* Épistolographie, *f.*

epistyle ['epistail], *n.* (*Arch.*) Épistyle, *m.*, architrave, *f.*

epitaph ['epita:f], *n.* Épitaphe, *f.*

epithalamium [epiθə'leimiəm], *n.* Épithalame, *m.*

epithelial [epi'θi:liəl], *a.* Épithélial. **epithelium,** *n.* Épithélium, *m.*

epithet ['epiθet], *n.* Épithète, *f.* **epithetic** [epi'θetik], *a.* Épithétique.

epitome [i'pitəmi], *n.* Épitomé, abrégé, précis, *m.* **epitomist,** *n.* Auteur d'un épitomé, abréviateur, *m.* **epitomize,** *v.t.* Faire un abrégé de, abréger; être une image en petit de.

epizootic [epizo'ɔtik], *a.* Épizootique. *Epizootic disease,* épizootie, *f.*

epoch ['i:pɔk], *n.* Époque, *f.*

epochal ['epɔkl] or **epoch-making,** *a.* Qui fait époque, historique, inoubliable.

epode ['epoud], *n.* Épode, *f.*

eponym ['epənim], *n.* Éponyme, *m.*

eponymic [epo'nimik] or **eponymous** [e'pɔniməs], *a.* Éponymique.

epopee ['epopi:] or **epopoeia,** *n.* Épopée, *f.*

epsom salts ['epsəm sɔ:lts], *n.* Sulfate de magnésie, *m.*, sels anglais, sels d'Epsom, *m.pl.*

equability [ekwə'biliti], *n.* Uniformité, égalité, *f.*

equable ['ekwəbl], *a.* Uniforme, égal. *Equable temperament,* humeur égale, *f.* **equably,** *adv.* Également, uniformément; d'une voix égale, sans hausser le ton.

equal ['i:kwəl], *a.* Égal; (*fig.*) impartial, juste. *Equal to,* de force à; *equal to the task,* à la hauteur de la tâche; *on equal terms,* à conditions égales; *to be equal to a journey,* être de force à entreprendre un voyage; *to be equal to* (*something*), en avoir la force, en avoir les moyens.—*n.* Égal, *m.*, égale, *f.*; (*pl.*) pareils, égaux, *m.pl.*—*v.t.* Égaler, être égal à.

equality [i'kwɔliti], *n.* Égalité, *f.*

equalization [i:kwəlai'zeiʃən], *n.* Égalisation, péréquation, *f.* **equalize,** *v.t.* Égaliser; compenser.—*v.i.* (*Ftb.*) Égaliser. **equally,** *adv.* Également, pareillement.

equanimity [i:kwə'nimiti], *n.* Égalité d'âme, équanimité, *f. To recover one's equanimity,* retrouver son calme. *equanimous,* *a.* D'un caractère égal.

equate [i'kweit], *v.t.* Égaliser; égaler; mettre en parallèle; mettre en équation.

equation [i'kweiʃən], *n.* Équation, *f.*

equator [i'kweitə], *n.* Équateur, *m.*

equatorial [ekwə'tɔ:riəl], *a.* Équatorial, de l'équateur.

equerry ['ekwəri], *n.* Écuyer, *m.*

equestrian [i'kwestriən], *a.* Équestre.—*n.* Cavalier, *m.*; (*Circus*) écuyer, *m.*, écuyère, *f.*

equiangular [i:kwi'æŋgjulə], *a.* Équiangle. **equidifferent** [-'difərənt], *a.* Équidifférent. **equidistance,** *n.* Équidistance, *f.* **equidistant,** *a.* Équidistant. **equidistantly,** *adv.* À égale distance.

equilateral [i:kwi'lætərəl], *a.* Équilatéral.

equilibrate [i:kwi'laibreit or i:'kwilibreit], *v.t.* Équilibrer, contrebalancer.—*v.i.* S'équilibrer.

equilibration [i:kwili'breiʃən or i:kwilai-], *n.* Équilibration, action d'équilibrer, *f.*

equilibrist [i:'kwilibrist or i:kwi'laibrist], *n.* Équilibriste; danseur de corde, *m.*

equilibrium [i:kwi'libriəm], *n.* Équilibre, *m. To keep one's equilibrium,* garder l'équilibre; *to remain in equilibrium,* se tenir en équilibre.

equine ['i:kwain, 'ekwain], *a.* Du cheval, équin.

equinoctial [i:kwi'nɔkʃl], *a.* Équinoxial, d'équinoxe. *Equinoctial gales,* tempêtes d'équinoxe, *f.pl.*; *equinoctial tides,* grandes marées, marées d'équinoxe, *f.pl.*—*n.* Ligne équinoxiale, *f.* **equinoctially,** *adv.* Dans la direction de la ligne équinoxiale.

equinox ['i:kwinɔks], *n.* Équinoxe, *m.*

equip [i'kwip], *v.t.* Équiper; (*Tech.*) outiller.

equipage ['ekwipidʒ], *n.* Appareil, équipage; équipement, *m.*

equipment [i'kwipmənt], *n.* Équipement, matériel, outillage; (*Mil.*) grand équipement; fourniment (leather straps etc.), *m.*

equipoise ['i:kwipɔiz], *n.* Équilibre, *m.*

equipollence [i:kwi'pɔləns] or **equipollency,** n. Équipollence, f. **equipollent,** a. Équipollent.

equiponderant, a. De même poids; se faisant équilibre.

equipotential [i:kwipo'tenʃəl], a. Équipotentiel, de potentiel constant.

equisetum [ekwi'si:təm], n. (Bot.) Équisetum, m.; queue de cheval, f.

equitable ['ekwitəbl], a. Équitable, juste. **equitableness,** n. Équité, f. **equitably,** adv. Équitablement.

equitation [ekwi'teiʃən], n. Équitation, f.

equity ['ekwiti], n. Équité, justice, f.

equivalence [i'kwivələns], n. Équivalence, égalité de valeur, égalité de force, f. **equivalent,** a. Équivalent (à). To be equivalent to, être équivalent à, équivaloir à.—n. Équivalent, m. **equivalently,** adv. D'une manière équivalente.

equivocal [i'kwivəkl], a. Équivoque, ambigu. **equivocality,** n. Équivoque, nature équivoque, ambiguïté, f. **equivocally,** adv. D'une manière équivoque. **equivocate,** v.i. User d'équivoque, équivoquer. **equivocation** [-'keiʃən], n. Équivoque, f. **equivocator,** n. Personne qui use d'équivoque, f.

era ['iərə], n. Ère, f. Christian era, ère chrétienne; to mark an era, faire époque.

eradiate [i'reidieit], v.i. Rayonner. **eradiation,** n. Radiation, f., rayonnement, m.

eradicable [i'rædikəbl], a. Déracinable, extirpable. **eradicate,** v.t. Déraciner; (fig.) extirper, exterminer. **eradication** [-'keiʃən], n. Éradication, extermination, extirpation, f., déracinement, m.

erasable [i'reizəbl], a. Effaçable.

erase [i'reiz], v.t. Raturer, effacer, rayer. **erasement,** n. Grattage, effacement, m. **eraser,** n. Grattoir, m., gomme à effacer, f. **erasure,** n. Grattage, m., rature, f.

Erasmus [i'ræzməs]. Érasme, m.

***ere** [ɛə], adv., conj., and prep. Avant, avant que; plutôt que (rather than). Ere long, avant peu; ere now, avant aujourd'hui, déjà; erewhile, naguère.

erect [i'rekt], a. Debout, droit, élevé.—v.t. Ériger, dresser; (Geom.) élever; (fig.) établir, fonder, monter, installer. **erectile,** a. Érectile. **erection,** n. Action de dresser, construction, érection, élévation; (fig.) fondation, f., établissement, montage, m.; installation, f. **erectness,** n. Posture droite, f. **erector,** n. Constructeur; (fig.) fondateur; (Anat.) muscle-érecteur, m.

***eremite** ['erimait], n. Ermite, m. **eremitic** [eri'mitik], a. Érémitique.

erethism ['erəθizm], n. Éréthisme, m.

erg [ə:g] or **ergon,** n. Erg, m.

ergo ['ə:gou], adv. Ergo, donc, par conséquent.

ergot ['ə:gɔt], n. Ergot, m. **ergotine,** n. Ergotine, f. **ergotism,** n. Ergotisme, m.

Erie ['iəri], **Lake,** Le lac Érié.

Erin ['erin], n. L'Irlande; la verte Erin, f.

eristic [ə'ristik], a. and n. Éristique, f.

ermine ['ə:min], n. Hermine, f.—a. D'hermine. **ermined,** a. Revêtu d'hermine.

erne [ə:n], n. Orfraie, f., pygargue, aigle des mers, m.

erode [i'roud], v.t. Éroder, ronger. **erosion,** n. Érosion, f. **erosive,** a. Érosif.

erotic [i'rɔtik], a. Érotique.—n. Poème érotique, m. **eroticism, erotism,** n. Érotisme, m. **erotomania** [-o'meiniə], n. Érotomanie, f. **erotomaniac,** n. Érotomane, érotomaniaque, m. or f.

erpetology [HERPETOLOGY].

err [ə:], v.i. Errer, s'écarter, s'égarer (de); (fig.) se tromper, faire erreur; être dans l'erreur. To err from the straight and narrow (path), s'écarter du droit chemin; to err on the side of modesty, pécher par modestie.

errancy ['erənsi], n. État d'erreur, m., errements, m.pl.

errand ['erənd], n. Message, m., commission, course, f. On an errand, en course; to go on an errand, aller faire une commission. **errand-boy,** n. Garçon de courses; petit commissionnaire; saute-ruisseau (in a lawyer's office), chasseur (in a restaurant), m.

errant ['erənt], a. Errant. Knight errant, chevalier errant, m. **errantry,** n. Vie errante, f.

erratic [i'rætik], a. Erratique; errant, excentrique; fantaisiste; d'une marche irrégulière; inégal; intermittent.—n. (Geol.) Bloc erratique, m. **erratically,** adv. Sans règle, sans ordre.

erratum [i'reitəm], n. (pl. **errata**) Erratum, m., errata, m.pl.

erroneous [i'rouniəs], a. Erroné, faux. **erroneously,** adv. À faux, à tort. **erroneousness,** n. Erreur, fausseté, f.

error ['erə], n. Erreur, faute, f., écart, m. Error in direction, écart latéral, m.; errors excepted, sauf erreur ou omission; in error, dans l'erreur, par erreur.

Erse [ə:s], a. and n. Erse, gaélique, m.

***erst** [ə:st], adv. Autrefois, jadis. **erstwhile,** a. (poet.) D'antan.

erubescence [eru'besəns], n. Érubescence, rougeur, f. **erubescent,** a. Érubescent, rougeâtre.

eructation [i:rʌk'teiʃən], n. Éructation, f.

erudite ['erudait], a. Érudit, savant.—n. Érudit, m.

erudition [eru'diʃən], n. Érudition, f.

erupt [i'rʌpt], v.i. Faire éruption (of volcano); percer (of teeth).

eruption [i'rʌpʃən], n. Éruption, f. **eruptive,** a. Éruptif.

eryngium [e'rindʒiəm], n. (Bot.) Érynge, f.

erysipelas [eri'sipiləs], n. Érysipèle, érésipèle, m.

erysipelatous [erisi'pelətəs], a. Érysipélateux.

erythema [eri'θi:mə], n. Érythème, m.

escalade [eskə'leid], n. Escalade, f.—v.t. Escalader.

escalator ['eskəleitə], n. Escalier roulant, m.

escallop [is'kɔləp] [SCALLOP].

escapade [eskə'peid], n. Escapade; frasque, fredaine, f.

escape [is'keip], n. Évasion; fuite (of gas), f.; échappement (of blinds), m.; (fig.) délivrance, f. Escape of gas, fuite de gaz; escape of steam, échappement de la vapeur, m.; fire-escape, échelle de sauvetage, f.; there is no escape from it, il n'y a pas moyen d'y échapper; to have a narrow escape, l'échapper belle; to make good one's escape, s'échapper, s'evader (from prison).—*v.t.* Échapper à; éviter. *To escape one's memory*, sortir de la mémoire.—*v.i.* Échapper, s'échapper; s'évader (from prison). **escapement,** *n.* Échappement, *m.* (of clock); déversoir, *m.* (for water). **escapism,** *n.* Littérature d'évasion, *f.* **escapist,** *a.* D'évasion (of art, *esp.* literature).

escarp [is'kɑ:p], *v.t.* (*Fort.*) Escarper.—*n.* Escarpe, *f.* **escarpment,** *n.* Escarpement, talus, *m.*

eschalot [SHALLOT].

eschatological [eskətə'lɔdʒikl], *a.* Eschatologique. **eschatology** [-'tɔlədʒi], *n.* Eschatologie, *f.*

escheat [is'tʃi:t], *n.* Déshérence, *f.*; bien en déshérence, *m. Right of escheat,* droit d'aubaine, *m.*—*v.t.* Confisquer (une succession); faire échoir à.—*v.i.* Tomber en déshérence, échoir (à). **escheatable,** *a.* Susceptible de déshérence. **escheatment,** *n.* Déshérence; dévolution (d'un héritage) à l'État, *f.*

eschew [is'tʃu:], *v.t.* Éviter; renoncer à.

escort (1) [is'kɔ:t], *v.t.* Escorter.

escort (2) ['eskɔ:t], *n.* Escorte, *f.*; cavalier, *m.*

escritoire [eskri'twɑ:], *n.* *Écritoire, *f.*; secrétaire, bureau, *m.*

esculent ['eskjulənt], *a.* Esculent, comestible.

escutcheon [is'kʌtʃən], *n.* Écusson, *m.* **escutcheoned,** *a.* Orné d'écussons, écussonné.

Eskimo ['eskimou], *n. and a.* Esquimau, *m.,* esquimaude, femme esquimau, *f.*

esoteric [eso'terik] or **esoterical,** *a.* Ésotérique. **esoterism,** *n.* Ésotérisme, *m.*

espalier [is'pæljə], *n.* Espalier, *m. To grow on an espalier,* venir en espalier.

esparto [es'pɑ:tou], *n.* Sparte, alfa, *m.*

especial [is'peʃəl], *a.* Spécial, particulier. **especially,** *adv.* Spécialement, surtout, particulièrement.

Esperantist [espə'ræntist], *a. and n.* Espérantiste. **Esperanto,** *n.* Esperanto, *m.*

espial [is'paiəl], *n.* Regards indiscrets, *m.pl.,* espionnage, *m.*; *espion, *m.*

espionage ['espiənidʒ or -'nɑ:ʒ], *n.* Espionnage, *m.*

esplanade [esplə'neid], *n.* Esplanade, promenade, *f.*

espousal [is'pauzl], *n.* Adoption, adhésion, *f.*; (*pl.*) épousailles, *f.pl.* **espouse,** *v.t.* Épouser; (*fig.*) adopter, embrasser.

espy [is'pai], *v.t.* Apercevoir, aviser, voir, découvrir; épier, observer, surveiller (to watch).

esquire [is'kwaiə], *n.* Écuyer, *m.* (A complimentary adjunct to the names of professional men in the addresses of letters etc., e.g. *Herbert W. Meredith, Esq.* Monsieur Herbert W. Meredith.)

essay ['esei], *n.* Essai, *m.,* épreuve, *f.*; effort, *m.,* tentative, *f.*; (*sch.*) composition, dissertation, *f.*—*v.t.* [ə'sei] Essayer (de). **essayist,** *n.* Essayiste.

essence ['esəns], *n.* Essence, *f.*

essential [i'senʃəl], *a.* Essentiel.—*n.* (*also pl.*) Essentiel, *m.* **essentiality** [isenʃi'æliti], *n.* Essentialité, *f.* **essentially** [i'senʃəli], *adv.* Essentiellement.

essentialness, *n.* Extrême importance, *f.,* le fait d'être essentiel, *m.*

establish [is'tæbliʃ], *v.t.* Établir, fonder; constituer; (*fig.*) confirmer; prouver. *To establish one's innocence,* prouver son innocence; *to establish oneself,* s'établir; *to establish touch,* prendre contact. **established,** *a.* Établi, institué; solide; convenu, reçu (agreed). *Established in 1760,* maison fondée en 1760. **establishment,** *n.* Établissement, *m.*; maison, *f.,* train de maison, *m.*; Église établie, *f.*; institution, création, installation, *f.*; (*Mil.*) effectif, *m.*; (*fig.*) affermissement, *m.,* confirmation, *f. Branch establishment,* succursale, *f.*; *establishment charges,* frais généraux, *m.pl.* (*Mil.*) *On a peace establishment,* (effectifs militaires) sur le pied de paix; *on a war establishment,* (effectifs) sur le pied de guerre; *the Establishment,* L'Église (établie, anglicane), *f.*; les personnes influentes, *f.pl.*

estate [is'teit], *n.* État, rang (condition), *m.*; propriété, terre, *f.,* bien, domaine (property), *m.*; succession, (of a deceased person), *f.*; état (body politic), *m.*; (*Bankruptcy*) actif, *m. Life estate,* biens en viager, *m.pl.*; *personal estate,* biens mobiliers; *the Third Estate,* le Tiers-État, *m.* **estate-agent,** *n.* Agent d'affaires, agent immobilier, courtier en immeubles, gérant, *m.* **estate duty,** *n.* Droits de succession, *m.pl.* **estate-office,** *n.* Bureau de gérance de propriétés, *m.*

esteem [is'ti:m], *n.* Estime, considération, *f.* —*v.t.* Estimer, regarder comme. *To esteem oneself lucky,* s'estimer heureux; (*Comm.*) *your esteemed favour,* votre honorée.

estimable ['estiməbl], *a.* Dont on peut estimer la valeur, estimable, digne d'estime. *Not very estimable,* peu recommandable.

estimate (1) ['estimət], *n.* Évaluation, *f.,* calcul, devis, *m.*; (*fig.*) appréciation, opinion, *f.,* jugement, *m. Rough estimate,* devis approximatif.

estimate (2) ['estimeit], *v.t.* Estimer, apprécier; évaluer, calculer. **estimation** [-'meiʃən], *n.* Estimation, opinion, estime, *f.,* jugement, *m.* **estimative,** *a.* Estimatif. **estimator,** *n.* Estimateur, *m.*

estival ['estivl], *a.* Estival, d'été. **estivation** [-'veiʃən], *n.* Estivation, *f.*

Estonia [es'tounia]. L'Estonie, *f.*

estop [es'tɔp], *v.t.* (*Law*) Empêcher, exclure, opposer une fin de non-recevoir. **estoppage** or **estoppel,** *n.* Exception, fin de non-recevoir, *f.*

estovers [es'touvəz], *n.pl.* (*Law*) Affouage, droit au bois, *m.*; pension alimentaire, *f.*

estrange [is'treindʒ], *v.t.* Aliéner, éloigner (de). **estrangement,** *n.* Aliénation, *f.,* éloignement, *m.,* brouille, *f.*

estray [is'trei], *n.* (*Law*) Bête épave, *f.*

estreat [is'tri:t], *n.* (*Law*) Extrait authentique, *m.*—*v.i.* Faire un extrait de (*esp.* of penalties).

estuary ['estjuəri], *n.* Estuaire, *m.*

et cetera [et'setrə] (abbr. **etc.**) Et caetera, *m.*

etch [etʃ], *v.t.* Graver à l'eau-forte. **etcher,** *n.* Graveur à l'eau-forte, aquafortiste, *m.* **etching,** *n.* Gravure à l'eau-forte, eau-forte, *f.* **etching-needle,** *n.* Pointe à graver, *f.*

eternal [i'tə:nl], *a.* Éternel.—*n.* Éternel, *m.* **eternally,** *adv.* Éternellement. **eternity,** *n.*

Éternité, *f.* **eternize,** *v.t.* Éterniser, rendre éternel.

etesian [i'ti:ʒiən], *a.* Étésien.

ethane ['eθein], *n.* Éthane, *m.*

ether ['i:θə], *n.* Éther, *m.*

ethereal [i'θiəriəl] or ***ethereous,*** *a.* Éthéré; céleste; (*Chem.*) volatil. *Ethereal oil,* huile essentielle, *f.*; *ethereal salt,* éther composé, *m.* **etherealize,** *v.t.* Rendre éthéré; mettre au-dessus des contingences de ce monde (of passion etc.). **etherify,** *v.t.* Éthérifier. **etherism,** *n.* Éthérisme, *m.* **etherization,** *n.* Éthérisation, *f.* **etherize,** *v.t.* Éthériser. **etheromania,** *n.* Éthéromanie, *f.*

ethic ['eθik] or ***ethical,*** *a.* Éthique; moral. **ethically,** *adv.* Suivant les principes de l'éthique *or* de la morale. **ethics,** *n.pl.* Morale, éthique, *f.sing.*

Ethiopia [i:θi'oupiə]. L'Éthiopie, *f.* **Ethiopian,** *a.* and *n.* Éthiopien, *m.*, Éthiopienne, *f.* **Ethiopic** [i:θi'ɔpik], *a.* Éthiopique.

ethmoid ['eθmɔid], *n.* (*Anat.*) Os ethmoïde, l'ethmoïde, *m.*

ethnic ['eθnik] or ***ethnical,*** *a.* Ethnique. **ethnographer** [-'nɔgrəfə], *n.* Ethnographe, *m.* **ethnographic** [-nə'græfik], *a.* Ethnographique.

ethnography [eθ'nɔgrəfi], *n.* Ethnographie, *f.* **ethnological** [eθno'lɔdʒikl], *a.* Ethnologique. **ethnologist** [-'nɔlədʒist], *n.* Ethnologue, ethnologiste, *m.* **ethnology,** *n.* Ethnologie, *f.*

ethology [i:'θɔlədʒi], *n.* Éthologie, *f.*

ethyl ['eθil], *n.* Éthyle, *m.*

etiolate ['i:tiəleit], *v.t.* Étioler.—*v.i.* S'étioler. **etiolated,** *a.* Étiolé. **etiolation** [-'leiʃən], *n.* Étiolement, *m.*

etiologist [i:ti'ɔlədʒist], *n.* Étiologiste. **etiology,** *n.* Étiologie, *f.*

etiquette ['etiket], *n.* Étiquette, *f.*, convenances, *f.pl.*, cérémonial de cour, protocole, *m.*

Etna ['etnə]. L'Etna, *m. Mount Etna,* le mont Etna, l'Etna.

Etruria [i'truəriə]. L'Étrurie, *f.*

Etruscan [i'trʌskən], *a.* and *n.* Étrusque.

etymological [etimə'lɔdʒikl], *a.* Étymologique. **etymologically,** *adv.* Étymologiquement. **etymologist** [-'mɔlədʒist], *n.* Étymologiste, *m.* **etymology,** *n.* Étymologie, *f.*

eucalyptus [ju:kə'liptəs], *n.* (*Bot.*) Eucalyptus, *m.*

eucharist ['ju:kərist], *n.* Eucharistie, *f.* **eucharistic,** *a.* Eucharistique.

euchology [ju:'kɔlədʒi], *n.* Eucologe, *m.*

Euclid ['ju:klid], *n.* Euclide; géométrie (euclidienne), *f.*

eudemonism [ju:'di:mənizm], *n.* Eudémonisme, *m.* **eudemonist,** *n.* Eudémoniste. **eudiometer** [ju:di'ɔmitə], *n.* Eudiomètre, *m.* **eudiometric** [-'metrik] or ***eudiometrical,*** *a.* Eudiométrique. **eudiometry,** *n.* Eudiométrie, *f.*

eugenics [ju:'dʒeniks], *n.* Eugénique, *f.*

eulogist ['ju:lədʒist], *n.* Panégyriste, *m.* **eulogistic** [ju:lə'dʒistik], *a.* Élogieux. **eulogium** [ju:'loudʒiəm] or ***eulogy*** ['ju:lədʒi], *n.* Éloge, panégyrique, *m.* **eulogize** ['ju:lədʒaiz], *v.t.* Louer, faire l'éloge de.

eunuch ['ju:nək], *n.* Eunuque, *m.*

eupepsia [ju:'pepsiə], *n.* Eupepsie, *f.* **eupeptic,** *a.* Eupeptique.

euphemism ['ju:fimizm], *n.* Euphémisme, *m.* **euphemistic** [-'mistik], *a.* Euphémique. **euphemistically,** *adv.* Euphémiquement.

euphonic [ju:'fɔnik], **euphonical** or **euphonious** [ju:'founiəs], *a.* Euphonique; (*fig.*) mélodieux, harmonieux, agréable à l'oreille. **euphoniously,** *adv.* Euphoniquement, mélodieusement, harmonieusement.

euphony ['ju:fəni], *n.* Euphonie, *f. For the sake of euphony,* par euphonie.

euphorbia [ju:'fɔ:biə], *n.* Euphorbe, *f. Euphorbiaceous plant,* euphorbiacée, *f.*

euphoria [ju:'fouriə], *n.* Euphorie, *f.*

euphoric [ju:'fourik], *a.* Euphorique.

euphrasy ['ju:frəsi], *n.* (*Bot.*) Eufraise, *f.*

Euphrates [ju:'freiti:z]. L'Euphrate, *m.*

euphuism ['ju:fjuizm], *n.* Style précieux, *m.*, préciosité, *f.* **euphuist,** *n.* Précieux, *m.*, précieuse, *f.* **euphuistic** [ju:fju'istik], *a.* Précieux, affecté (of style).

Eurasian [juə'reiʃən], *n.* and *a.* Eurasien, *m.*, -ienne, *f.*

Euripides [juə'ripidi:z]. Euripide, *m.*

Europa [juə'roupə]. (*Myth.*) Europe, *f.*

Europe ['juərəp]. L'Europe, *f.*

European [juərə'pi:ən], *a.* Européen.—*n.* Européen, *m.*, Européenne, *f.* **Europeanize,** *v.t.* Européaniser.

euthanasia [ju:θə'neiziə], *n.* Euthanasie, *f.*

Euxine ['ju:ksain]. Le Pont-Euxin, *m.*

evacuant [i'vækjuent], *a.* and *n.* Évacuant, *m.* **evacuate,** *v.t.* Évacuer. **evacuation** [-'eiʃən], *n.* Évacuation, *f.* **evacuative,** *a.* Évacuatif. **evacuee,** *n.* Évacué, *m.*; évacuée, *f.*

evade [i'veid], *v.t.* Éluder, esquiver, éviter, se soustraire à; échapper à, déjouer, tourner (la loi).

evaluate [i'væljueit], *v.t.* Évaluer. **evaluation** [-'eiʃən], *n.* Évaluation, *f.*

evanescence [i:və'nesəns], *n.* Disparition; (*fig.*) instabilité, *f.*, état éphémère, *m.* **evanescent,** *a.* Fugitif, éphémère.

evangelical [i:væn'dʒelikl], *a.* Évangélique. **evangelically,** *adv.* Évangéliquement.

evangelism [i'vændʒəlizm], *n.* Évangélisme, *m.*; prédication de l'Évangile, *f.* **evangelist,** *n.* Évangéliste, *m. St. John Evangelist,* Saint-Jean l'Évangéliste. **evangelization,** *n.* Évangélisation, *f.* **evangelize,** *v.t.* Évangéliser.

evaporable [i'væpərəbl], *a.* Évaporable. **evaporate,** *v.i.* S'évaporer.—*v.t.* Faire évaporer. **evaporation** [-'reiʃən], *n.* Évaporation, *f.* **evaporative,** *a.* Évaporatif. **evaporimeter,** *n.* Évaporimètre, *m.*

evasion [i'veiʒən], *n.* Moyen évasif; subterfuge, *m.*; faux-fuyant, *m.*; échappatoire, défaite, *f.* **evasive,** *a.* Évasif. **evasively,** *adv.* Évasivement. **evasiveness,** *n.* Caractère évasif (d'une déclaration, etc.), *m.*

Eve [i:v]. Ève, *f.*

eve [i:v], *n.* Veille, *f.*; *soir, *m.* (*Lit.*) *At eve,* le soir; *Christmas Eve,* la veille de Noël; *on the eve of,* à la veille de.

even (1) [i:vn], *n.* (*poet.*) Soir, *m.* **evensong,** chant du soir, *m.*, vêpres, *m.pl.* **eventide,** soir, crépuscule, *m.*

even (2) [i:vn], *a.* Égal; régulier (of breathing, pulse); uni (smooth); de niveau (avec), au niveau (de), à fleur (de) (level with); pair (of number). *Even money, even sum,* compte rond; *even money,* paris égaux; *even reckoning makes lasting friends,* les bons comptes font les bons amis; (*Law*) *of even date,* de même date; *to be even with,* être quitte avec, rendre la pareille à; *to make it even,* arrondir (une somme); *to make even,* araser, aplanir.—*adv.* Même, aussi bien; précisément. *Even as,* comme; *even as . . . so,* de même que . . . de même; *even now,* à l'instant même; *even so,* quand même; *even though,* quand même.— *v.t.* Égaler, égaliser; niveler, aplanir. (*fam.*) *To even things up,* égaliser les choses. **even-handed,** *a.* Impartial, équitable. **even-handedness,** *n.* Impartialité, *f.* **even-numbered,** *a.* Qui porte un numéro pair; pair. **even-tempered,** *a.* Calme, placide, égal.

evening [′i:vniŋ], *n.* Soir, *m.*; soirée, *f.*; (*fig.*) déclin, *m.* *A pleasant evening,* une soirée charmante; *evening star,* étoile du soir, *f.*; *good evening!* bonsoir! *in the evening,* le soir; *last evening,* hier (au) soir; *the evening after tomorrow,* après-demain soir; *the evening before, the previous evening,* la veille au soir; *the next evening,* le lendemain soir; *tomorrow evening,* demain soir; *to spend the evening at home,* passer la soirée à la maison, chez soi.— *a.* Du soir. *Evening dress,* tenue de soirée, *f.*; *evening party, evening performance,* soirée, *f.*

evening-primrose, *n.* (*Bot.*) Herbe aux ânes, *f.*

evenly [′i:vnli], *adv.* Également; de niveau; (*fig.*) impartialement. *Evenly matched,* de force égale. **evenness,** *n.* Égalité; régularité; sérénité, *f.*, calme, *m.*, impartialité, *f.*

event [i′vent], *n.* Événement, *m.*; issue, *f.*; dénouement (of a poem, a play, etc.), *m.*; (*spt.*) épreuve, *f.* *At all events,* en tout cas, dans tous les cas; *in the event of his coming,* au cas où il viendrait. **eventful,** *a.* Plein d'événements, mouvementé.

eventual [i′ventjuəl], *a.* Éventuel, aléatoire; final, définitif. **eventuality,** *n.* Éventualité, *f.* **eventually,** *adv.* En définitive, finalement, à la fin, par la suite. **eventuate,** *v.i.* Se terminer, aboutir; (*fig.*) arriver (of event).

ever [′evə], *adv.* Toujours; jamais. *.As soon as ever he had done it,* aussitôt qu'il l'eut fait; *be it ever so little,* si peu que ce soit; *ever after,* à tout jamais; *ever and anon,* de temps en temps; *ever since,* depuis; *ever so little,* tant soit peu; *ever so long,* un temps infini; *ever so many,* je ne sais combien; *for ever,* à jamais; *for ever and ever,* à tout jamais, dans tous les siècles des siècles; *if I have ever . . . ,* si j'ai jamais . . .; *if there ever was one,* s'il en fut jamais; *scarcely ever, hardly ever,* presque jamais; *wine for ever!* vive le vin!

evergreen, *a.* Toujours vert.—*n.* Arbre toujours vert, arbre à feuilles persistantes, *m.* *Evergreens,* plantes vertes, *f.pl.* **everlasting,** *a.* Éternel, perpétuel, immortel; durable, inusable (cloth).—*n.* Éternité, *f.*; l'éternel, *m.*; immortelle (plant), *f.* **everlastingly,** *adv.* Éternellement. **everlastingness,** *n.* Éternité, durée perpétuelle, *f.* **ever-living,** *a.* Immortel.

evermore, *adv.* Toujours; éternellement. *For evermore,* à jamais.

ever-sharp, *a.* (Porte-mine) à mine pointue. —*n.* Porte-mine, stylo-mine, *m.*

eversion [i′və:ʃən], *n.* Renversement, *m.* *Eversion of the eyelids,* ectropion, éraillement, *m.*

every [′evri], *a.* Chaque, tout, tous les. *Every day,* tous les jours, chaque jour; *every inch a king,* un roi jusqu'au bout des ongles; *every little helps,* tout fait nombre; *every man for himself,* chacun pour soi, sauve qui peut! *every now and then,* de temps à autre; *every one,* chacun, *m.*, chacune, *f.*, tous, *pl.*; *every one of them,* tous sans exception; *every other combatant,* un combattant sur deux; *every other day,* tous les deux jours; *it's all true, every word of it,* c'est vrai, absolument vrai; c'est la vérité, mot pour mot.

everyday, *a.* Journalier, quotidien; ordinaire, banal; de tous le jours.

everyone or **everybody,** *n.* Tout le monde; n'importe qui; le premier venu. *Everybody's business,* les affaires de tout le monde; *everybody that,* tous ceux qui; (*fam.*) *everybody that is anybody,* tout le gratin.

everything, *n.* Tout, *m.* *Everything comes to him who waits,* tout vient à point à qui sait attendre.

everyway, *adv.* Sous tous les rapports; de toutes les manières, de toute manière.

everywhere, *adv.* Partout. *Everywhere he went,* partout où il est allé.

evict [i′vikt], *v.t.* Évincer, expulser. **eviction,** *n.* Éviction, expulsion, dépossession, *f.*

evidence [′evidəns], *n.* Évidence; preuve, *f.*, témoignage (proof); témoin (witness), *m.* *Evidence for the prisoner,* les témoins à décharge; *evidence for the prosecution,* témoins à charge; *to be in evidence,* être en évidence; *to give evidence,* déposer; *to give evidence of,* faire voir, faire preuve de or donner la preuve de; *to turn King's evidence,* dénoncer ses complices (après promesse de pardon).—*v.t.* Montrer, manifester, prouver, démontrer.

evident, *a.* Évident, visible. **evidential** [-′denʃəl], *a.* D'évidence, indicateur. **evidently,** *adv.* Évidemment, manifestement.

evil [i:vl], *a.* Mauvais; malheureux, de malheur; malfaisant, malin, méchant (of spirits etc.). *The evil eye,* le mauvais œil; *the evil spirit,* l'esprit malin.—*n.* Mal; malheur, *m.*, calamité, *f.* *Evil be to him that evil thinks,* honni soit qui mal y pense; *king's evil,* écrouelles, *f.pl.*; *sufficient unto the day is the evil thereof,* à chaque jour suffit sa peine; *to choose the lesser of two evils,* choisir le moindre entre deux maux.—*adv.* Mal. **evil-disposed,** *a.* Malveillant. **evil-doer,** *n.* Malfaiteur, méchant, *m.*, méchante, *f.* **evil-looking,** *a.* De mauvaise mine, vilain. **evil-minded,** *a.* Mal intentionné. **evil-smelling,** *a.* Nauséabond. **evil-speaking,** *n.* Médisance, *f.*

evilness, *n.* Méchanceté, *f.*

evince [i′vins], *v.t.* Montrer, manifester, démontrer, dénoter, témoigner.

eviscerate [i′visəreit], *v.t.* Éventrer, éviscérer. **evisceration** [-′reiʃən], *n.* Éviscération, *f.*

evocation [evo′keiʃən], *n.* Évocation, *f.* **evocative** [i′vɔkətiv], *a.* Évocateur.

evoke [i′vouk], *v.t.* Évoquer; susciter.

evolution [iːvəˈluːʃən *or* evəˈljuːʃən], *n.* Évolution, *f.*; (*Geom.*) développement, *m.*; (*Math.*) extraction des racines, *f.*; (*Phys.*) dégagement (de chaleur), *m.* **evolutionary,** *a.* Évolutif. **evolutionism,** *n.* Évolutionnisme, *m.* **evolutionist,** *n.* Évolutionniste. **evolve** [iˈvɔlv], *v.t.* Dérouler; développer; (*Chem.*) dégager.—*v.i.* Se dérouler; se développer; (*Chem.*) se dégager.

evulsion [iˈvʌlʃən], *n.* Arrachement, *m.*

ewe [juː], *n.* Brebis, *f.* **ewe-lamb,** *n.* Agnelle, *f.*; (*fig.*) trésor, *m.* **ewe-neck,** *n.* Encolure de cerf (of horse), *f.*

ewer [ˈjuə], *n.* Aiguière, *f.*, broc, *m.*

ex- [eks], *pref.* Ancien, ex-. *Ex-schoolmaster,* ancien professeur, *m.*

exacerbate [igˈzæsəbeit], *v.t.* Exaspérer; aggraver; (*Med.*) rendre plus aigu. **exacerbation,** *n.* Exaspération, aggravation; (*Med.*) exacerbation, *f.*

exact [igˈzækt], *v.t.* Exiger, extorquer.—*v.i.* Commettre des exactions.—*a.* Exact, précis. **exacting,** *a.* Exigeant. **exaction,** *n.* Action d'exiger, exaction, *f.* **exactitude** *or* **exactness,** *n.* Exactitude, *f.* **exactly,** *adv.* Exactement, précisément, au juste; juste. **exactor,** *n.* Exacteur, extorqueur, *m.*

exaggerate [igˈzædʒəreit], *v.t.* Exagérer. **exaggeration** [-ˈreiʃən], *n.* Exagération, *f.* **exaggerative,** *a.* Exagérant, exagératif. **exaggerator,** *n.* Exagérateur, *m.*

exalt [igˈzɔːlt], *v.t.* Exalter, élever; (*fig.*) louer. **exaltation** [egzɔːlˈteiʃən], *n.* Exaltation, élévation, *f.* **exalted,** *a.* Exalté; élevé. *Exalted personage,* haut personnage, *m.* **exaltedness,** *n.* Élévation, *f.*; caractère élevé, *m.*

exam [igˈzæm], *n.* (*sch.*) [EXAMINATION].

examination [igzæmiˈneiʃən], *n.* Examen, *m.*; inspection, vérification, *f.*; (*Law*) interrogatoire (of prisoners), *m.*; audition (of witnesses), *f.* *Competitive examination,* concours, *m.*; *customs examination,* visite de la douane, *f.*; *examination paper,* épreuve, *f.*, questions d'examen, *f.pl.*; *on or after examination,* après examen; *post mortem examination,* autopsie, *f.*; *to pass an examination,* réussir à un examen; *to sit* (*for*) *an examination,* passer un examen; *viva voce examination,* oral examination, épreuves orales, *f.pl.*; *written examination,* épreuves écrites, *f.pl.*

examine [igˈzæmin], *v.t.* Examiner; visiter; vérifier; viser (a passport); compulser (documents etc.); (*Law*) interroger.

examinee [igzæmiˈniː], *n.* Candidat, *m.*

examiner [igˈzæminə], *n.* Examinateur; (*Law*) juge d'instruction, *m.*

example [igˈzɑːmpl], *n.* Exemple, *m.* *For example,* par exemple; *to set an example,* donner l'exemple.

exanimate [egˈzænimət], *a.* Inanimé; (*fig.*) abattu.

exarch [ˈeksɑːk], *n.* Exarque, *m.* **exarchate,** *n.* Exarchat, *m.*

exasperate [igˈzɑːspəreit], *v.t.* Exaspérer; irriter, aigrir. **exasperation** [-ˈreiʃən], *n.* Exaspération, irritation, *f.*

excavate [ˈekskəveit], *v.t.* Creuser, excaver. **excavation** [-ˈveiʃən], *n.* Excavation, *f.*; fouilles, *f.pl.*, tranchée, *f.* **excavator,** *n.* Piocheuse-défonceuse, *f.*

exceed [ikˈsiːd], *v.t.* Excéder, dépasser; (*fig.*)

surpasser. **exceeding,** *a.* Grand, extrême. —*adv.* Excessivement. **exceedingly,** *adv.* Très, fort, extrêmement.

excel [ikˈsel], *v.t.* Surpasser, l'emporter sur. —*v.i.* Exceller, se distinguer (à).

excellence [ˈeksələns], *n.* Excellence, perfection, supériorité, *f.*; mérite, *m.* **excellency,** *n.* *His Excellency,* Son Excellence, *f.* **excellent,** *a.* Excellent. **excellently,** *adv.* Excellemment, parfaitement.

except [ikˈsept], *v.t.* Excepter; exclure (de).— *v.i.* Faire des objections (à). *To except against,* récuser.—*prep.* Excepté, à l'exception de, hors, sauf.—*conj.* À moins que, à moins de. **excepting,** *prep.* Excepté, hormis, à l'exception de. **exception,** *n.* Exception; objection, *f.* *By way of exception,* par exception; *to take exception to,* se formaliser de, (*Law*) s'opposer à, récuser; *without exception,* sans exception; *with this exception,* à cette exception près. **exceptionable,** *a.* Blâmable, à critiquer. **exceptional,** *a.* Exceptionnel. **exceptionally,** *adv.* Exceptionnellement.

excerpt [ˈeksəːpt], *n.* Extrait, *m.*, citation, *f.*, passage; emprunt (à un texte), *m.*

excess [ikˈses], *n.* Excès; surpoids, excédent (of weight), *m.* *Excess fare,* supplément, *m.*; *excess luggage,* excédent de bagages, *m.*; *to excess,* à l'excès. **excessive,** *a.* Excessif, extrême; immodéré. **excessively,** *adv.* Excessivement, à l'excès.

exchange [iksˈtʃeindʒ], *n.* Échange, troc, *m.*; (*Comm.*) change, *m.*; Bourse (edifice), *f.* *Bill of exchange,* lettre de change, *f.*; *corn exchange,* halle aux blés, *f.*; *exchange of prisoners,* échange de prisonniers, *m.*; (*Comm.*) *foreign exchange,* devises étrangères, *f.pl.*; *in exchange for,* en échange de; *rate of exchange,* taux du change, *m.*; *telephone exchange,* central téléphonique, *m.*; *to be a loser* or *gainer by the exchange,* perdre or gagner au change.—*v.t.* Échanger, changer (contre or pour).—*v.i.* Faire un échange. **exchange-broker,** *n.* Courtier de change, *m.* **exchange-office,** *n.* Bureau de change, *m.* **exchanger,** *n.* Banquier qui fait le change, *m.*

exchequer [iksˈtʃekə], *n.* Trésor; Ministère des Finances, l'Échiquier, *m. Chancellor of the Exchequer,* Ministre des Finances, *m.*; *Exchequer bill,* bon du Trésor, *m.*

excisable [ekˈsaizəbl], *a.* Imposable; sujet aux droits de l'accise. **excise,** *n.* (*England*) Excise, *f.*; (*France*) contributions indirectes, *f.pl.*, régie, *f.*—*v.t.* Soumettre à l'accise, imposer; (*Surg.*) exciser. **excise-bond,** *n.* Acquit à caution, *m.* **excise-duty,** *n.* Droit de régie, *m.* **excise-man,** *n.* Préposé or employé de la régie, *m.*

excision [ekˈsiʒən], *n.* (*Surg.*) Excision, *f.*

excitability [iksaitəˈbiliti], *n.* Excitabilité; émotivité, *f.*

excitable [ikˈsaitəbl], *a.* Excitable, irritable; émotif, impressionnable.

excitant [ˈeksitənt], *a.* Excitant.—*n.* (*Med.*) Stimulant, *m.* **excitation** [-ˈteiʃən], *n.* Excitation, *f.*

excite [ikˈsait], *v.t.* Exciter; irriter; animer, émouvoir, passionner; (*fig.*) provoquer, porter (à). **excitedly,** *adv.* D'une manière agitée. **excitement,** *n.* Émoi, *m.*, surexcitation, *f.*; motif d'excitation, *m.*; émotion, agitation, *f. In great excitement*, tout hors de soi. **exciter**, *n.* Excitateur, instigateur, *m.*, excitatrice, instigatrice, *f.* (*Elec.*) *Exciter coil*, bobine d'induction, *f.* **exciting**, *a.* Émouvant, passionnant, palpitant; (*Med.*) excitant. **exclaim** [iks′kleim], *v.i.* S'écrier, crier; se récrier, s'exclamer. *To exclaim against*, se récrier contre. **exclamation** [-′meiʃən], *n.* Exclamation, *f.*, cri, *m. Note of exclamation, exclamation mark*, point d'exclamation, *m.* **exclamative** [eks′klæmətiv], **exclamatory** [iks′klæmətəri], *a.* Exclamatif, d'exclamation. **exclamatively, exclamatorily**, *adv.* Exclamativement. **exclude** [iks′klu:d], *v.t.* Exclure (de), empêcher d'entrer (of air, draught, etc.); ne pas admettre; proscrire. *To exclude someone from the sacraments*, refuser les sacrements à quelqu'un. **excluding**, *prep.* Sans compter. **exclusion**, *n.* Exclusion, *f.* **exclusionist**, *n.* Personne exclusive, *f.* **exclusive**, *a.* Exclusif. *A very exclusive club*, un cercle très fermé; *exclusive* (*of*), à l'exclusion de, non compris; *to be mutually exclusive*, s'exclure; *to have exclusive rights in* or *the exclusive rights of*, avoir l'exclusivité de. **exclusively**, *adv.* Exclusivement. *Exclusively of*, à l'exclusion de. **exclusiveness**, *n.* Caractère exclusif, *m.*, nature exclusive, *f.* **exclusivism**, *n.* Exclusivisme, *m.* **excogitate** [eks′kɔdʒiteit], *v.t.* Inventer, imaginer, combiner; machiner (of plot). **excogitation** [-′teiʃən], *n.* Longue réflexion, invention, *f.* **excommunicate** [ekskə′mju:nikeit], *v.t.* Excommunier. **excommunication** [-′keiʃən], *n.* Excommunication, *f.* **excoriate** [eks′kɔ:rieit], *v.t.* Écorcher; (*Surg.*) excorier. **excoriation** [-′eiʃən], *n.* Écorchure; (*Surg.*) excoriation, *f.* **excrement** [′ekskrimənt], *n.* Excrément, *m.* **excremental** [-′mentl] or **excrementitious** [-′tiʃəs], *a.* Excrémenteux, excrémentiel, excrémentitiel. **excrescence** [eks′kresəns] or **excrescency**, *n.* Excroissance, *f.*; bourrelet, *m.*, loupe, *f.* (on tree trunk). **excrescent**, *a.* Qui forme une excroissance; (*fig.*) superflu. **excreta** [iks′kri:tə], *n.pl.* Excréta, *m.pl.* **excrete**, *v.t.* Excréter. **excretion** [iks′kri:ʃən], *n.* Excrétion, *f.* **excretive** or **excretory**, *n.* Excrétoire, excréteur. **excruciate** [iks′kru:ʃieit], *v.t.* Tourmenter, torturer, mettre au supplice. **excruciating**, *a.* Atroce, affreux, horrible. **excruciatingly**, *adv.* (*esp.* in) *excruciatingly funny*, tordant, à pouffer de rire. **excruciation** [-′eiʃən], *n.* Tourment atroce, *m.*, affreuse torture, *f.* **exculpate** [′ekskʌlpeit], *v.t.* Disculper, justifier. **exculpation** [-′peiʃən], *n.* Justification, disculpation, *f.* **exculpatory** [eks′kʌlpətəri], *a.* Qui disculpe; justificatif. **excursion** [eks′kə:ʃən], *n.* Excursion, randonnée, promenade, *f.*, petit voyage, *m.*; (*fig.*) digression, *f. Excursion ticket*, billet d'excursion, *m.*; *excursion train*, train de plaisir, *m.*; *to be on an excursion*, être en excursion; *to make an excursion*, faire une excursion. **excursionist**, *n.* Excursionniste,

touriste. **excursionize**, *v.i.* Excursionner; faire des excursions. **excursive** [eks′kə:siv], *a.* Errant, vagabond; (*fig.*) décousu, digressif (of style). **excursively**, *adv.* À bâtons rompus, sans plan. **excursiveness**, *n.* Tendance à s'écarter de son sujet, *f.* **excusable** [iks′kju:zəbl], *a.* Excusable. **excusably**, *adv.* Excusablement. *He was excusably angry*, sa colère était justifiée. **excusatory**, *a.* D'excuse, justificatif. **excuse** (1) [iks′kju:s], *n.* Excuse, *f.*; prétexte, *m. By way of excuse*, en guise d'excuse; *to find an excuse*, chercher des excuses; *to make excuses*, s'excuser. **excuse** (2) [iks′kju:z], *v.t.* Excuser, pardonner; dispenser de, faire remise de. *Excuse me!* excusez! pardon! *excuse the expression*, passez-moi ce mot; *have me excused*, faites-moi excuser; (*sch.*) *may I be excused?* est-ce que je peux sortir? (*Mil., Navy*) *to be excused a fatigue*, être exempté d'une corvée; *to be excused from duty, to be on the excused list*, être exempt de service; *to excuse oneself for*, s'excuser de. **exeat** [′eksiæt], *n.* Exeat, *m.* **execrable** [′eksikrəbl], *a.* Exécrable. **execrably**, *adv.* Exécrablement. **execrate** [′eksikreit], *v.t.* Exécrer, détester, maudire. **execration** [-′kreiʃən], *n.* Exécration, *f.* **execratory**, *a.* Exécratoire. **executable** [′eksikjutəbl], *a.* Exécutable, faisable. **execute** [′eksikju:t], *v.t.* Exécuter, faire, accomplir; remplir (an order). *To execute a criminal*, exécuter un criminel; *to execute a deed*, signer un contrat. **execution** [-′kju:ʃən], *n.* Exécution, *f.*; accomplissement, *m.*; (*Law*) saisie-exécution, *f.*; supplice, *m. In the execution of one's duty*, dans l'exercice de ses fonctions; *to carry into execution, to put into execution*, mettre à exécution; *to do great execution*, causer des ravages, *n.* Bourreau; exécuteur des hautes œuvres, *m.* **executive** [ig′zekjutiv], *a.* Exécutif. *Executive committee* (of an association), le bureau, *m.*; (*Mil.*) *executive duties*, service de détail, *m.*; (*Am.*) *executive order*, décret-loi, *m.*; *executive word of command*, commandement d'exécution, *m.*—*n.* Pouvoir exécutif, *m.*; (*Comm.*) directeur, chef de service, *m.* **executor** [ig′zekjutə], *n.* Exécuteur testamentaire, *m.* **executory** [ig′zekjutri], *a.* and *n.* (*Law*) Exécutoire. **executrix**, *n.* Exécutrice testamentaire, *f.* **exegesis** [eksi′dʒi:sis], *n.* Exégèse, *f.* **exegete** [′eksidʒi:t], *n.* Exégète, *m.* **exegetical** [-′dʒetikl], *a.* Exégétique. **exemplar** [ig′zemplə], *n.* Modèle, exemplaire, *m.* **exemplarily**, *adv.* Exemplairement. **exemplariness, exemplarity**, *n.* Nature exemplaire, *f.* **exemplary**, *a.* Exemplaire; modèle. *An exemplary mother*, une mère modèle. **exemplification** [igzemplifi′keiʃən], *n.* Démonstration; (*Law*) ampliation, *f.* **exemplify** [ig′zemplifai], *v.t.* Démontrer par des exemples; donner un exemple de; (*Law*) faire une ampliation de. **exempt** [ig′zempt or eg′zemt], *v.t.* Exempter (de).—*a.* Exempt. **exemption,** *n.* Exemption, *f.*

exequatur [eksi'kweitə], *n.* Exequatur, *m.*

exequies ['eksikwiz], *n.pl.* Obsèques, *f.pl.*

exercisable ['eksəsaizəbl], *a.* Susceptible d'être exercé.

exercise ['eksəsaiz], *n.* Exercice; (*sch.*) thème, devoir, *m.* *Breathing exercises,* gymnastique respiratoire, *f.*—*v.t.* Exercer. *To exercise a dog,* promener un chien, donner de l'exercice à un chien.—*v.i.* S'exercer; (*Mil.*) faire l'exercice. **exercise-book,** *n.* Cahier de devoirs, *m.* **exerciser,** *n.* Exerçant; (*Gym.*) exerciseur, *m.* **exercitation,** *n.* Exercice, *m.*, pratique, *f.*; (*sch.*) dissertation, *f.*, discours *or* exercice oratoire, *m.*

exergue [eg'zə:g], *n.* Exergue, *m.*

exert [ig'zə:t], *v.t.* Déployer, employer; faire usage de, mettre en œuvre; exercer (of influence, pressure, etc.). *To exert oneself,* faire des efforts (pour), s'efforcer (de), se remuer, se donner de la peine; *to exert oneself to the utmost,* faire tous ses efforts. **exertion,** *n.* Effort, *m.*; contention (d'esprit), *f.*; exercice, emploi, *m.* *It is an exertion for him to speak,* c'est pour lui un effort pénible de parler.

exeunt ['eksiənt]. (*Theat.*) Ils sortent.

exfoliate [eks'foulieit], *v.t.* Exfolier; déliter (of stone).—*v.i.* S'exfolier; se déliter. **exfoliation** [-'eiʃən], *n.* Exfoliation, *f.*; délitation, desquamation (of scaly skin), *f.*

exhalation [eksə'leiʃən], *n.* Exhalaison; exhalation, évaporation; expiration, *f.*, souffle, *m.*

exhale [eks'heil], *v.t.* Exhaler, émettre.—*v.i.* S'exhaler.

exhaust [ig'zɔ:st], *v.t.* Épuiser. *To exhaust a vessel of the air contained therein,* faire le vide dans un récipient; *to exhaust someone's patience,* mettre quelqu'un à bout.—*v.i.* S'échapper.—*n.* Échappement, *m.* **exhaust-box,** *n.* (*Motor.*) Pot d'échappement, silencieux, *m.* **exhaust-pipe,** *n.* (*Motor.*) Tuyau d'échappement, *m.* **exhaust-valve,** *n.* Soupape d'échappement, *f.*

exhausted, *a.* Épuisé. **exhauster,** *n.* Personne qui épuise; chose qui épuise, *f.* **exhaustible,** *a.* Épuisable. **exhausting,** *a.* Épuisant; (*fam.*) éreintant.

exhaustion [ig'zɔ:stʃən], *n.* Épuisement, *m.* **exhaustive,** *a.* Qui épuise; (*fig.*) complet, plein, exhaustif, *m.*, -ive, *f.* **exhaustively,** *adv.* À fond, complètement.

exhibit [ig'zibit], *v.t.* Montrer; faire voir; exposer; (*fig.*) exhiber, offrir.—*n.* Objet exposé, *m.*; (*Law*) pièce à conviction, *f.*

exhibition [eksi'biʃən], *n.* Exposition; représentation, *f.*, spectacle, *m.*; (*Univ.*) bourse; (*Law*) exhibition, *f.* *To make an exhibition of oneself,* se donner en spectacle. **exhibitioner,** *n.* (*Univ.*) Boursier, *m.* **exhibitionism,** *n.* Exhibitionnisme, *m.* **exhibitionist,** *n.* Exhibitionniste.

exhibitor [eg'zibitə], *n.* Exposant (at a public exhibition), *m.*; exploitant (of a cinema), *m.*

exhilarate [ig'ziləreit], *v.t.* Réjouir, égayer; ragaillardir, ranimer, revivifier. **exhilarating,** *a.* Qui égaye, réjouissant, divertissant, vivifiant. **exhilaration** [-'reiʃən], *n.* Réjouissance, hilarité, gaieté, joie de vivre, *f.*

exhort [ig'zɔ:t], *v.t.* Exhorter (à).—*v.i.* Faire des exhortations. **exhortation** [-'teiʃən], *n.* Exhortation, *f.* **exhortative,** *a.* Exhortatif. **exhortatory,** *a.* Exhortatoire.

exhumation [eksju:'meiʃən], *n.* Exhumation, *f.* **exhume** [eks'hju:m *or* ig'zju:m], *v.t.* Exhumer, déterrer.

exigence ['eksidʒəns] *or* **exigency,** *n.* Exigence, nécessité, *f.*; besoin, *m.*; situation critique, extrémité, *f.* **exigent,** *a.* Urgent, pressant. *Exigent of,* qui requiert, qui réclame.

exiguity [eksi'gju:iti], *n.* Exiguïté, petitesse, *f.* **exiguous** [eg'zigjuəs], *a.* Exigu, très petit.

exile ['eksail], *n.* Exil, *m.*; exilé *m.*, exilée (person), *f.* *To drive into exile,* exiler, bannir.—*v.t.* Exiler.

exility [eg'ziliti], *n.* Petitesse; ténuité; subtilité, *f.*

exist [ig'zist], *v.i.* Exister. **existence,** *n.* Existence, *f.*; être, *m.* *To be in existence,* exister; *to come into existence,* naître. **existent** *or* **existing,** *a.* Existant, qui existe, actuel. **existentialism,** *n.* Existentialisme, *m.* **existentialist,** *n.* Existentialiste.

exit ['eksit], *n.* Sortie, *f.*; (*Theat.*) il (elle) sort. *To make one's exit,* sortir, s'en aller, (*fig.*) mourir.

exodus ['eksədəs], *n.* Exode, *m.*

exogamous [ek'sɔgəməs], *a.* Exogame. **exogamy,** *n.* Exogamie, *f.*

exogenous [ek'sɔdʒənəs], *a.* (*Bot.*) Exogène.

exonerate [ig'zɔnəreit], *v.t.* Décharger, dispenser, exempter, exonérer, justifier. **exoneration** [-'reiʃən], *n.* Décharge, justification, exemption, exonération, *f.* **exonerative,** *a.* Qui décharge, qui exonère.

exophthalmia [eksɔf'θælmiə], *n.* Exophtalmie, *f.* **exophthalmic,** *a.* Exophtalmique. **exophthalmus,** *n.* Exophtalmie, *f.*

exorbitance [egz'ɔ:bitəns], *n.* Excès, *m.*, énormité, *f.* **exorbitant,** *a.* Exorbitant, excessif, exagéré. **exorbitantly,** *adv.* Excessivement.

exorcism ['eksɔ:sizəm], *n.* Exorcisme, *m.* **exorcist,** *n.* Exorciste, *m.* **exorcize** ['eksɔ:saiz], *v.t.* Exorciser. **exorcizer,** *n.* Exorciste, *m.*

exordial [eg'zɔ:diəl], *a.* Liminaire; servant d'introduction. **exordium,** *n.* Exorde, *m.*

exoskeleton [eksou'skelətən], *n.* Exosquelette, *m.*

exosmose ['eksozmouz], *n.* Exosmose, *f.* **exosmotic** [-'mɔtik], *a.* Exosmotique.

exoteric [eksou'terik], *a.* Exotérique; populaire; (pour le) public.

exotic [eg'zɔtik], *a.* Exotique.—*n.* Plante exotique, *f.* **exotically,** *adv.* Exotiquement.

expand [iks'pænd], *v.t.* Étendre, déployer, faire épanouir; amplifier; dilater (gas); détendre (steam).—*v.i.* Se dilater; s'épanouir, s'étendre, se déployer; se développer. **expandable,** *a.* Extensible. **expanse,** *n.* Étendue, *f.* **expansibility** *or* **expansiveness,** *n.* Expansibilité, *f.* **expansible,** *a.* Expansible. **expansion,** *n.* Expansion; dilatation; détente; extension, étendue (area), *f.*; épanouissement (opening), *m.* **expansion-gear,** *n.* Appareil de détente, *m.* **expansionist,** *n.* Expansionniste. **expansive,** *a.* Expansif.

expatiate [eks'peiʃieit], *v.i.* S'étendre (sur). **expatiation** [-'eiʃən], *n.* Long discours, *m.*

expatriate [eks'peitrieit], *v.t.* Expatrier, bannir. *To expatriate oneself*, s'expatrier; renoncer à sa nationalité. **expatriation** [-'eiʃən], *n.* Expatriation, *f.*; renoncement à sa nationalité, *m.*

expect [iks'pekt], *v.t.* Attendre; s'attendre à, compter sur (things); espérer, croire, penser. *He is expected to make a speech*, on compte sur lui pour prononcer un discours; *he is not expected to live*, on ne compte pas le sauver; *I expect a great deal of pleasure*, je me promets beaucoup de plaisir; *she is expecting*, elle attend un bébé; *that must be expected*, il faut s'y attendre; *to know what to expect*, savoir à quoi s'en tenir; *you are expected*, on compte sur vous; *you are expected at two*, on vous attend à deux heures. **expectance** or **expectancy**, *n.* Attente; espérance, *f.*; (*Law*) expectative, *f.* **expectant**, *a.* Expectant. *She is an expectant mother*, elle attend un enfant.—*n.* Personne qui est dans l'expectative, *f.* **expectantly** or **expectingly**, *adv.* Dans l'attente. **expectation** [-'teiʃən], *n.* Attente, espérance; expectative, *f.*; probabilité, *f. Beyond one's expectations*, au delà de ses espérances; *he always lives in expectation*, il vit toujours dans l'expectative; *in expectation of*, dans l'attente de; *to answer one's expectations*, répondre à ses espérances. **expecter**, *n.* Personne qui attend *or* qui espère, *f.*

expectorant [eks'pektərənt], *a.* Expectorant. —*n.* Expectorant, *m.* **expectorate**, *v.t., v.i.* Expectorer. **expectoration** [-'reiʃən], *n.* Expectoration, *f.* **expectorative**, *a.* Expectorant.

expedience [iks'pi:diəns] or **expediency**, *n.* Convenance, utilité, opportunité, *f. The doctrine of expedience*, opportunisme, *m.* **expedient**, *a.* Convenable, à propos, utile, opportun.—*n.* Expédient, *m. To resort to expedients*, user d'expédients. **expediently**, *adv.* Convenablement, à propos.

expedite ['ekspədait], *v.t.* Expédier, hâter; activer, accélerer. **expedition** [-'diʃən], *n.* Expédition; promptitude, diligence, hâte, *f. On an expedition*, en expédition. **expeditionary**, *a.* (*Mil.*) Expéditionnaire.

expeditious [ekspi'diʃəs], *a.* Expéditif, prompt. **expeditiously**, *adv.* Promptement. **expeditiousness**, *n.* Promptitude, *f.*

expel [iks'pel], *v.t.* Expulser, chasser, faire sortir; (*sch.*) renvoyer. **expelling**, *a.* Expulseur.—*n.* Expulsion, *f.*

expend [iks'pend], *v.t.* Dépenser; (*fig.*) employer; épuiser; consacrer. **expenditure**, *n.* Dépense, *f.*, dépenses, *f.pl.*; (*fig.*) sacrifice, *m.*

expense [iks'pens], *n.* Dépense, *f.*; dépens; frais, *m.pl. At* (*a*) *great expense*, à grands frais; *at any expense*, à tout prix; *at the expense of*, aux frais de, aux dépens de; *at the expense of one's life*, au prix de sa vie; *free of expense*, sans frais, franco; *incidental expenses*, faux frais; *petty expenses*, menus frais; *to clear one's expenses*, faire ses frais; *to go to expense*, faire des frais; *to pay its expenses*, couvrir les frais (of a thing); *to put to expense*, occasionner des frais à. **expensive**, *a.* Dispendieux, coûteux, cher (of things); dépensier (person). *An expensive victory*, une victoire coûteuse, *f.*; *that is expensive*, cela coûte cher. **expensively**, *adv.* À grands

frais. **expensiveness**, *n.* Dépense, *f.*; prix élevé, *m.*; prodigalité (of a person), *f.*

experience [eks'piəriəns], *n.* Connaissance acquise (par soi-même), expérience; épreuve (personnelle), *f.*; sentiment, *m. To have a delightful experience*, éprouver une sensation délicieuse; *to know from experience*, savoir pour l'avoir éprouvé.—*v.t.* Éprouver, faire l'expérience de. **experienced**, *a.* Éprouvé, expérimenté. **experiential** [ekspiːəri'enʃəl], *a.* Fondé sur l'expérience; empirique.

experiment [eks'perimənt], *n.* Expérience, *f.* (de laboratoire); essai, *m.*—*v.t., v.i.* Expérimenter. **experimental** [-'mentəl], *a.* Expérimental; d'essai. **experimentally**, *adv.* Par expérience, expérimentalement. **experimentation**, *n.* Expérimentation, *f.* **experimenter**, *n.* Expérimentateur, *m.*

expert (1) [eks'pəːt], *a.* Expert, habile. **expert** (2) ['ekspəːt], *n.* Technicien, expert, *m.*

expertly [eks'pəːtli], *adv.* Habilement. **expertness**, *n.* Habileté, adresse, expertise, *f.*

expiable ['ekspiəbl], *a.* Que l'on peut expier, expiable.

expiate ['ekspieit], *v.t.* Expier. **expiation** [-'eiʃən], *n.* Expiation, *f.*

expiatory ['ekspjətri], *a.* Piaculaire, expiatoire.

expiration [ekspi'reiʃən], *n.* Expiration; fin, *f.*, terme (end), *m.*; déchéance (of insurance policy), *f.*

expire [eks'paiə], *v.i.* Expirer, mourir, rendre l'âme; prendre fin. **expiring**, *a.* Expirant. **expiry**, *n.* Expiration, *f.*; terme, *m.*; fin, échéance, *f.*

explain [iks'plein], *v.t.* Expliquer. *To explain away*, donner une explication satisfaisante de.—*v.i.* S'expliquer. **explainable**, *a.* Explicable. **explainer**, *n.* Explicateur, *m.*

explanation [eksplə'neiʃən], *n.* Explication, *f.*; éclaircissement, *m.*

explanatory [iks'plænətri], *a.* Explicatif.

expletive [eks'pli:tiv], *a.* Explétif.—*n.* Explétif; (*colloq.*) juron, *m.*

explicable ['eksplikəbl], *a.* Explicable. **explicative** or **explicatory**, *a.* Explicatif.

explicate ['eksplikeit], *v.t.* (*Log.*) Développer; (*Lit.*) expliquer, dégager le sens exact (d'un passage). **explication**, *n.* (*Log.*) Développement, *m.*, interprétation, *f.*; (*Lit.*) explication, élucidation (d'un texte), *f.*

explicit [iks'plisit], *a.* Explicite, formel; franc. **explicitly**, *adv.* Explicitement. **explicitness**, *n.* Caractère explicite, *m.*; franchise, *f.*

explode [iks'ploud], *v.t.* Faire éclater; faire sauter (a mine); (*fig.*) démontrer la fausseté (d'une théorie), discréditer. *Exploded theory*, théorie abandonnée.—*v.i.* Éclater, sauter, faire explosion. *To explode with laughter*, éclater de rire. **exploder**, *n.* Détonateur, *m.*; personne qui renverse (une doctrine), *f.*

exploit (1) ['eksplɔit], *n.* Exploit, haut fait; fait d'armes, *m.*

exploit (2) [iks'plɔit], *v.t.* Exploiter. **exploitable**, *a.* Exploitable. **exploitation** [-'teiʃən], *n.* Exploitation, *f.* **exploiter**, *n.* Exploiteur, *m.*, -teuse, *f.*

explorable [eks'plo:rəbl], *a.* Qui peut être exploré, explorable. **exploration** [-'reiʃən], *n.* Exploration, *f.*; (*fig.*) examen, *m.*;

recherche, *f.* **exploratory,** *a.* Explorateur, d'exploration.
explore [eks'plɔ:], *v.t.* Explorer; (*fig.*) examiner, sonder. **explorer,** *n.* Explorateur, *m.*
explosion [iks'plouʒən], *n.* Explosion, *f.* **explosive** [-'plousiv], *a.* Explosif, explosible. *Explosive consonant,* (*Gram.*) consonne explosive, *f.—n.* Explosif, *m. High explosive,* explosif brisant, *m.* **explosiveness,** *n.* Explosibilité, *f.*
exponent [eks'pounənt], *n.* (*Math.*) Exposant; (*fig.*) représentant; interprète; protagoniste, *m.* **exponential** [-'nenʃəl], *a.* (*Math.*) Exponentiel.
export (1) ['ekspɔ:t], *n.* Exportation; marchandise exportée, *f. Export duty,* droit de sortie, *m.; export trade,* commerce d'exportation, *m.*
export (2) [eks'pɔ:t], *v.t.* Exporter. **exportation** [-'teiʃən], *n.* Exportation, sortie, *f.* **exporter,** *n.* Exportateur, *m.*
expose [iks'pouz], *v.t.* Exposer; (*fig.*) révéler, découvrir, démasquer, dénoncer; (*Comm.*) étaler (goods). *To expose a fraud,* démasquer une fraude; *to expose oneself,* s'exposer, s'afficher, (*Law*) commettre un outrage public à la pudeur; *to expose oneself to ridicule,* se rendre ridicule. **exposition** [-'ziʃən], *n.* Exposition, *f.,* exposé, *m.* **expositor** [-'pɔzitə], *n.* Interprète, commentateur, *m.*
expostulate [iks'pɔstjuleit], *v.i.* Faire des remontrances (à). **expostulation** [-'leiʃən], *n.* Remontrance, *f.* **expostulatory,** *a.* De remontrance.
exposure [iks'pouʒə], *n.* Exposition (aux intempéries, à un danger), *f.;* abandon (of a baby); étalage (of goods); éclat, esclandre, *m.;* (*Phot.*) pose, exposition, *f. Double exposure,* surimpression, *f.; exposure meter,* pose-mètre, *m.; to die of exposure,* mourir de froid.
expound [iks'paund], *v.t.* Expliquer, exposer, interpréter. **expounder,** *n.* Interprète, *m.* **expounding,** *n.* Exposition, explication, *f.*
express [iks'pres], *a.* Exprès; formel, explicite. *By express delivery,* par exprès; *express image,* image exacte; *express train,* train express, *m.—n.* Exprès (messenger); express, train express, *m.—v.t.* Exprimer; expédier par grande vitesse; émettre.
expressible [eks'presibl], *a.* Exprimable. **expression** [eks'preʃən], *n.* Expression, manifestation, *f. Past expression,* au-delà de toute expression, inexprimable; *with expression,* avec expression. **expressionism,** *n.* Expressionnisme, *m.* **expressionless,** *a.* Sans expression; impassible. **expressive,** *a.* Expressif. *To be expressive of,* exprimer. **expressively,** *adv.* D'une manière expressive. **expressiveness,** *n.* Force d'expression, énergie, *f.* **expressly,** *adv.* Expressément, directement, formellement; exprès.
expropriate [eks'prouprieit], *v.t.* Exproprier. **expropriation** [-'eiʃən], *n.* Expropriation, *f.*
expulsion [eks'pʌlʃən], *n.* Expulsion, *f. Expulsion order,* décret d'expulsion, *m.,* interdiction de séjour, *f.* **expulsive,** *a.* Expulsif.
expunge [eks'pʌndʒ], *v.t.* Effacer, biffer.
expurgate ['ekspə:geit], *v.t.* Corriger, expurger (a book). **expurgation** [-'geiʃən], *n.* Épuration, expurgation, *f.*

expurgatory [eks'pə:gətəri], *a.* (*R.-C.*) *Expurgatory index,* index expurgatoire, *m.*
exquisite ['ekskwizit], *a.* Exquis; vif, extrême (of pain); raffiné, délicat. *Exquisite malice,* malice consommée, *f.—*n.* Élégant, petit-maître, dandy, *m.* **exquisitely,** *adv.* D'une manière exquise; parfaitement; vivement, extrêmement. **exquisiteness,** *n.* Nature exquise, perfection; violence (of grief, pain, etc.), *f.*
exsanguine [eks'sæŋgwin], *a.* Exsangue.
exscind [ek'sind], *v.t.* Exciser.
ex-service man [eks'sə:vismən], *n.* Ancien combattant, *m.*
exsiccation [eksi'keiʃən], *n.* Dessèchement; assèchement, *m.*
extant [ek'stænt], *a.* Qui existe encore; subsistant.
extemporaneous [ekstempə'reiniəs] or **extemporary** [-'tempərəri], *a.* Improvisé, impromptu. **extemporaneously,** *adv.* D'abondance, sans préparation.
extempore [eks'tempəri], *a.* Improvisé.—*adv.* Impromptu, sans préparation, par improvisation. *To speak extempore,* improviser (un discours). **extemporization** [-rai'zeiʃən], *n.* Improvisation, *f.* **extemporize** [-'tempər aiz], *v.t.* Improviser. **extemporizer,** *n.* Improvisateur, *m.,* -trice *f.*
extend [iks'tend], *v.t.* Étendre; prolonger; tendre (to hold out); (*spt.*) pousser (a horse, a ship); (*Law*) évaluer; saisir (property). *To extend a welcome,* souhaiter la bienvenue.—*v.i.* S'étendre; se prolonger (of time); se propager (to spread). **extensibility,** *n.* Extensibilité, *f.* **extensible,** *a.* Extensible. **extension,** *n.* Extension; étendue, prolongation (of time), *f.;* (*Teleph.*) poste, *m.;* annexe, *f.* (of building). **extensive,** *a.* Étendu, vaste; ample, spacieux. **extensively,** *adv.* D'une manière étendue; bien, très, au loin. **extensiveness,** *n.* Étendue, *f.* **extensor,** *n.* (*Anat.*) Extenseur, muscle extenseur, *m.*
extent [iks'tent], *n.* Étendue, *f.;* (*fig.*) degré, point, *m.;* (*Law*) évaluation; saisie (of property), *f. To a certain extent,* jusqu'à un certain point; *to a great extent,* dans une large mesure; *to the extent of,* jusqu'à.
extenuate [eks'tenjueit], *v.t.* *Exténuer; atténuer, amoindrir. **extenuating,** *a.* (*Law*) Atténuant. **extenuation** [-'eiʃən], *n.* Exténuation; (*Law*) atténuation, *f.*
exterior [eks'tiəriə], *a.* Extérieur, en dehors. (*Geom.*) *Exterior angle,* angle externe, *m.—n.* Extérieur, *m.* **exteriorly,** *adv.* Extérieurement.
exterminate [eks'tə:mineit], *v.t.* Exterminer; extirper. **extermination** [-'neiʃən], *n.* Extermination; extirpation, *f.* **exterminator,** *n.* Exterminateur, *m.,* -trice, *f.* **exterminatory,** *a.* Exterminateur.
extern [eks'tə:n], *n.* Externe, *m.*
external [eks'tə:nl], *a.* Extérieur, externe (of students etc.). **externalize,** *v.t.* Extérioriser. **externally,** *adv.* Extérieurement, au dehors, à l'extérieur. **externals,** *n.pl.* Dehors, *m.pl.,* l'extérieur, *m.,* formes extérieures, *f.pl.*
exterritoriality [eksteritɔ:ri'æliti], *n.* Exterritorialité, *f.*
extinct [iks'tiŋkt], *a.* Éteint; disparu, qui

n'existe plus (of animals etc.); aboli, tombé en désuétude. **extinction,** *n.* Extinction, *f.* **extinguish** [iks'tiŋgwiʃ], *v.t.* Éteindre; faire cesser; (*fig.*) éclipser, surpasser en splendeur. **extinguishable,** *a.* Qu'on peut éteindre, extinguible. **extinguisher,** *n.* *Éteignoir (thing), *m.*; éteigneur, *m.* (man); extincteur, *m.* (apparatus). **extinguishing,** *a.* Extincteur. **extinguishment,** *n.* Extinction, *f.* **extirpate** ['ekstə:peit], *v.t.* Extirper, exterminer; détruire. **extirpation** [-'peiʃən], *n.* Action d'extirper; extirpation, *f.* **extirpator,** *n.* Extirpateur, *m.*, -trice, *f.* **extol** [iks'toul], *v.t.* Exalter, prôner, vanter. *The minister extolled him to the skies,* le ministre le portait aux nues. **extort** [iks'tɔ:t], *v.t.* Extorquer, arracher. *To extort an answer,* arracher une réponse; *to extort a promise from,* arracher une promesse à. **extortion,** *n.* Extorsion, *f.* **extortionate** [iks'tɔ:ʃnit], *a.* Extorsionnaire, exorbitant. **extortioner,** *n.* Extorqueur, exacteur, *m.* **extra** ['ekstrə], *a.* En sus; supplémentaire, extraordinaire. *Extra charge,* prix en sus, supplément, *m.*; *no extra charges,* pas de frais supplémentaires.—*n.* Supplément; (*Cine.*) figurant, *m.*, -ante, *f.*—*adv.* En sus, de plus. *Extra strong,* extra-solide. **extract** (1) ['ekstrækt], *n.* Extrait; concentré (of meat etc.), *m.* **extract** (2) [iks'trækt], *v t.* Extraire, tirer (de); arracher (teeth) à. *To have a tooth extracted,* se faire arracher une dent. **extraction,** *n.* Extraction, origine, *f.* **extractive,** *a.* and *n.* Extractif, *m.* **extractor,** *n.* Arracheur, extracteur, *m.*; pince, *f.* **extradite** ['ekstrədait], *v.t.* Extrader. **extraditable,** *a.* Qui justifie l'extradition (of offence); passible d'extradition (of person). **extradition** [-'diʃən], *n.* Extradition, *f.* **extrados** [eks'treidɔs], *n.* (*Arch.*) Extrados, *m.* **extra-judicial** [ekstrədʒu:'diʃəl], *a.* Extrajudiciaire; extralégal. **extra-judicially,** *adv.* Extrajudiciairement. **extramundane** [ekstrə'mʌndein], *a.* Au delà du monde matériel; extra-terrestre. **extraneous** [eks'treinjəs], *a.* Étranger (à); extérieur, non-essentiel. **extraordinarily** [iks'trɔ:dnrili], *a.* Extraordinairement. **extraordinariness,** *n.* Caractère extraordinaire, *m.*, rareté, singularité, *f.* **extraordinary,** *a.* Extraordinaire, hors ligne, rare. *Ambassador extraordinary,* ambassadeur extraordinaire, *m.*; *extraordinary meeting,* assemblée d'urgence, *f.* **extra-parochial** [ekstrəpə'roukiəl], *a.* Qui n'est pas de la paroisse. **extrapolate** [ekstrəpə'leit], *v.i.* Extrapoler. **extrapolation,** *n.* Extrapolation, *f.* **extravagance** [iks'trævəgəns], *n.* Extravagance; prodigalité, *f.*, folles dépenses, *f.pl.,* gaspillage, *m.* **extravagant,** *a.* Extravagant (unreasonable); prodigue, dépensier, dispendieux, exorbitant (of things).—*n.* Prodigue, extravagant, *m.*, -ante, *f.* **extravagantly,** *adv.* D'une manière extravagante; prodigalement; excessivement, follement. **extravaganza** [ekstrævə'gænzə], *n.* (*Lit.* and *Mus.*) Œuvre fantaisiste et bouffonne, *f.* **extravagate** [iks'trævəgeit], *v.i.* S'écarter; s'égarer, divaguer; extravaguer.

extravasated [ekstrævə'seitid], *a.* (*Med.*) Extravasé. *To be extravasated,* s'extravaser. **extravasation** [-'seiʃən], *n.* Extravasation or extravasion, *f.*; épanchement, *m.* **extravert** [EXTROVERT]. **extreme** [iks'tri:m], *a.* Extrême. *Extreme case,* cas exceptionnel, *m.*; *extreme views,* opinions extrémistes, *f.pl.*—*n.* Extrémité, *f.*; extrême, *m. Extremes meet,* les extrêmes se touchent; *in the extreme,* à l'extrême; *to carry to extremes,* pousser à l'extrême, outrer les choses. **extremely,** *adv.* Extrêmement, au dernier degré. **extremist,** *n.* Extrémiste; ultra, *m.* **extremity** [-'tremiti], *n.* Extrémité, *f.*, extrême, *m.*; cas extrême, bout, *m.*, fin, *f.*, comble, *m. The extremities,* les extrémités, *f.pl.; to drive to extremities,* pousser à bout. **extricable** ['ekstrikəbl], *a.* Qu'on peut dégager. **extricate,** *v.t.* Débarrasser, dégager, tirer (de). *To extricate oneself,* se tirer d'affaire. **extrication** [-'keiʃən], *n.* Débarrassement, *m.*, délivrance, *f.* **extrinsic** [eks'trinsik], *a.* Extrinsèque. **extrinsically,** *adv.* Extrinsèquement. **extrovert** ['ekstrəvə:t], *n.* Extroverti, *m.*, -ie, *f.* **extrude** [eks'tru:d], *v.t.* Expulser, refouler. **extrusion** [-'tru:ʒən], *n.* Expulsion, *f.* **exuberance** [ig'zju:brəns], *n.* Exubérance, surabondance, *f.* **exuberant,** *a.* Exubérant, surabondan . **exuberantly,** *adv.* Avec exubérance. **exuberate,** *v.i.* Déborder, surabonder. **exudation** [eksju:'deiʃən], *n.* Exsudation, *f.* **exude** [ek'sju:d], *v.i.* Exsuder.—*v.t.* Faire exsuder. **exulcerate** [ig'zʌlsəreit], *v.t.* Exulcérer. **exulceration** [-'reiʃən], *n.* Exulcération; (*fig.*) exaspération, *f.* **exult** [ig'zʌlt], *v.i.* Se réjouir, exulter (de). *Our neighbours exulted over our defeats,* nos voisins se réjouissaient de nos défaites. **exultant,** *a.* Joyeux, triomphant. **exultation** [-'teiʃən], *n.* Triomphe, *m.*, exultation, *f.* **exultingly,** *adv.* D'un air de triomphe. **exuviae** [ig'zju:vii:], *n.pl.* Dépouilles, *f.pl.*; (*Zool.*) dépouille, *f.*; (*Geol.*) débris organiques, *m.pl.* **exuviate,** *v.t.* Se dépouiller de. **eyas** ['aiəs], *n.* Jeune faucon; *(*fig.*) blanc-bec, *m.*

eye [ai], *n.* Œil (*pl.* yeux); trou (of a needle); (*Naut.*) œillet; lit (of the wind); (*Bot.*) œil, bouton, *m.*; porte (catch for a hook); (*fig.*) vue, *f.*; regard, *m. Before one's eyes,* sous les yeux de; *black eye,* œil poché; *blind in one eye,* borgne; (*Mil.*) *eyes front!* fixe! *eyes right!* tête à droite! *farther than the eye can reach,* à perte de vue; *in the twinkling of an eye,* en un clin d'œil; *practised eye,* œil exercé; (*pop.*) *that's all my eye,* c'est de la blague! *there was not a dry eye in the room,* tous les yeux étaient mouillés de larmes; *the tears stood in his eyes,* il avait les larmes aux yeux; *to cast down one's eyes,* baisser les yeux; *to cast one's eyes over,* jeter un coup d'œil sur; *to cry one's eyes out,* s'épuiser de larmes; *to give someone the glad eye,* faire de l'œil à quelqu'un; *to have an eye to,* avoir l'œil à, veiller à; *to have in one's eye,* avoir en vue; (*spt.*) *to have one's eye in,* avoir la balle dans l'œil, avoir l'œil exercé; *to keep an eye on,* surveiller, ne pas perdre de vue; *to open someone's eyes,* ouvrir, dessiller les yeux à

quelqu'un; *to open one's eyes wide*, écarquiller les yeux; (*pop.*) *to pipe one's eye*, pleurnicher; *to please the eye*, flatter le regard; *to shut one's eyes to*, fermer les yeux sur; *to strike the eye*, frapper les yeux; *with one's own eyes*, de ses propres yeux; *with tears in one's eyes*, les larmes aux yeux.—*v.t.* Regarder, observer, suivre des yeux; lorgner; toiser.
eyeball, *n.* Bulbe de l'œil, *m.* **eyebright,** *n.* (*Bot.*) Eufraise, *f.* **eyebrow,** *n.* Sourcil, *m.* *To knit the eyebrows*, froncer les sourcils; *to raise an eyebrow*, (*fig.*) sourciller.
eyed [aid], *a.* *Blue-eyed*, aux yeux bleus; *dull-eyed*, au regard sombre; *in the kingdom of the blind the one-eyed is King*, au royaume des aveugles les borgnes sont rois.
eye-glance, *n.* Coup d'œil, *m.*, œillade, *f.*, regard, *m.* **eyeglass,** *n.* (Single) monocle, *m.* *Double eyeglass*, lorgnon, pince-nez, *m.* **eye-hole,** *n.* Orbite; petit judas, *m.* **eyelash,** *n.* Cil, *m.*
eyeless, *a.* Sans yeux; aveugle.
eyelet or **eyelet-hole,** *n.* Œillet, *m.*
eyelid, *n.* Paupière, *f.* **eye-opener,** *n.* Révélation, surprise, *f.* **eye-piece,** *n.* (*Opt.*) Oculaire, *m.* **eye-reach,** *n.* Portée de la vue, *f.* **eye-salve,** *n.* Collyre, *m.* **eye-shade,** *n.* Garde-vue, *m.* **eyesight,** *n.* Vue, *f.* **eyesore,** *n.* Chose qui blesse l'œil, *f.*, objet d'aversion, *m.*, bête noire, *f.* **eye-tooth,** *n.* Dent œillère, *f.* **eye-wash,** *n.* (*Pharm.*) Collyre liquide, *m.*; (*pop.*) boniments, *m.pl.*, bourrage de crâne, *m.* **eye-witness,** *n.* Témoin oculaire, *m.*
eyot [AIT].
eyre [ɛə], *n.* Tournée (of judges), *f.* *Justice in eyre*, juge qui va en tournée, juge ambulant, *m.*
eyry [AERIE].
Ezekiel [e'zi:kiəl]. Ézéchiel, *m.*
Ezra ['ezrə]. Esdras, *m.*

F

F, f [ef], *n.* Sixième lettre de l'alphabet; (*Mus.*) fa, *m.* *F sharp*, fa dièse, *m.*
Fabian ['feibiən], *a.* Fabien; (*fig.*) temporisateur.
fable [feibl], *n.* Fable, *f.*, conte, *m.*—*v.i.* Feindre.—*v.t.* Imaginer, inventer, prétendre; (*fig.*) en conter, mentir. **fabled,** *a.* Inventé, fabuleux.
fabric ['fæbrik], *n.* Construction, *f.*; édifice, ouvrage, *m.*; étoffe, *f.*, tissu, *m.*; (*fig.*) système, *m.*
fabricate ['fæbrikeit], *v.t.* Fabriquer, inventer, contrefaire. **fabrication** [-'keiʃən], *n.* Fabrication, invention, *f.*
fabricator ['fæbrikeitə], *n.* *Constructeur, fabricateur, *m.*, -trice, *f.*, inventeur, *m.*
fabulist ['fæbjulist], *n.* Fabuliste, *m.* **fabulous,** *a.* Fabuleux. **fabulously,** *adv.* Fabuleusement. **fabulousness,** *n.* Caractère fabuleux, *m.*
façade [fə'sɑ:d], *n.* Façade; (*Fort.*) courtine (haute) muraille, *f.* *He put on a façade of politeness*, il feignait la politesse.
face [feis], *n.* Figure, *f.*; visage, *m.*; face, surface (chiefly of things), *f.*; (*fig.*) apparence,

f., état, aspect, *m.*; mine, physionomie; hardiesse, *f.*, front (impudence), *m.*; façade, *f.*, devant (front), *m.*; grimace (wry face), *f.*; facette (of a diamond), *f.*; cadran (of a watch), *m.*; (*Print.*) œil, *m.* *Before one's face*, sous les yeux de; *face to face*, vis-à-vis; *he had the face to assert*, il eut l'audace d'affirmer; *on the face of it*, à première vue; *to laugh in someone's face*, rire au nez de quelqu'un; *to lose face*, perdre contenance, essuyer une humiliation; *to make faces at*, faire des grimaces à; *to pull a long face*, (*colloq.*) faire une tête; *to put a good face on a bad business*, faire bonne mine à mauvais jeu; *to save face*, sauver la face, sauver les apparences; *to set one's face against*, s'opposer à; *to show one's face*, se montrer, se présenter, paraître; *to shut the door in someone's face*, fermer la porte au nez de quelqu'un; *to slap someone's face*, donner un soufflet à quelqu'un; *to tell to one's face*, dire en face; *to wash one's face*, se laver la figure, se débarbouiller. **face-cloth, face-flannel,** *n.* Gant de toilette, *m.* **face-lifting,** *n.* Ridectomie, *f.*, lifting, *m.* **face-powder,** *n.* Poudre de riz, *f.* **face-towel,** *n.* Serviette de toilette, *f.* **face-value,** *n.* Valeur nominale, *f.*
v.t.—Faire face à, affronter, braver; envisager; mettre un revers à, mettre des parements à, parer (garments); revêtir (a wall etc.); donner sur, être exposé à (of houses etc.). *Faced with silk*, à revers de soie; *to face a thing out*, soutenir une assertion, persister dans sa conduite *or* dans son entreprise; *to face down*, confondre par son effronterie; *to face out*, braver, payer d'audace; *to face the music*, (*fig.*) tenir tête à la meute (des critiques), affronter la tempête (des reproches).
v.i.—Prendre un faux dehors; (*Mil.*) faire front. *Face about!* volte-face! demi-tour! *Right face!* À droite, droite.
faced, *a.* À visage, à figure. *Double-faced*, à deux visages; *full-faced*, qui a la figure pleine.
facer, *n.* Coup (de poing) en plein visage, *m.*; (*fig.*) obstacle imprévu et soudain, *m.*
facet ['fæsit], *n.* Facette, *f.*—*v.t.* Facetter. **faceted,** *a.* À facettes. **faceting,** *n.* Facettage, *m.*
facetiae [fə'si:ʃii:], *n.pl.* Facéties, *f.pl.*
facetious [fə'si:ʃəs], *a.* Facétieux. **facetiously,** *adv.* Facétieusement. **facetiousness,** *n.* Caractère facétieux, *m.*, plaisanterie, *f.*
facial ['feiʃəl], *a.* Facial.
facies ['feiʃii:z], *n.* Face, *f.*; (*Nat. Hist. etc.*) aspect de la flore *or* de la faune, faciès, *m.*
facile ['fæsail], *a.* Facile; complaisant. **facileness** or **facility** [fə'siliti], *n.* Facilité, *f.*
facilitate [fə'siliteit], *v.t.* Faciliter. **facilitation** [-'teiʃən], *n.* Action de faciliter, facilité, *f.*
facing ['feisiŋ], *n.* Parement (of garments); revers, retroussis; parement, revêtement (of structures); (*Mil.*) changement de front, *m.*
facsimile [fæk'simili], *n.* Fac-similé, *m.* *In facsimile*, fac-similaire.—*v.t.* Fac-similer.
fact [fækt], *n.* Fait, *m.* *As a matter of fact* or *in fact*, en effet, de fait, effectivement, à vrai dire, à la vérité; *in point of fact*, au fait; *matter-of-fact man*, homme positif, *m.*
faction ['fækʃən], *n.* Faction; (*fig.*) discorde, dissension, *f.* **factious,** *a.* Factieux.

factiously, *adv.* D'une manière factieuse, en factieux. **factiousness,** *n.* Esprit factieux, *m.*
factitious [fæk'tiʃəs], *a.* Factice, artificiel, faux. **factitiously,** *adv.* Facticement.
factitive ['fæktitiv], *a.* (*Gram.*) Factitif.
factor ['fæktə], *n.* Agent; facteur, *m.* **factorage,** *n.* (*Comm.*) Courtage, *m.*; commission, *f.* **factorise,** *v.t.* (*Math.*) Décomposer en facteurs. **factory,** *n.* Usine, fabrique, filature, *f.*; atelier; (*Foreign trade*) comptoir, *m.*, factorerie, *f.*
factotum [fæk'toutəm], *n.* Factotum; (*Print.*) passe-partout, *m.*
factual ['fæktjuəl], *a.* Effectif, réel, positif.
facula ['fækjulə], *n.* (*pl.* **faculae**) (*Astron.*) Facule, *f.*
facultative ['fækəlteitiv], *a.* Facultatif; contingent.
faculty ['fækəlti], *n.* Faculté, *f.*, pouvoir, talent, *m.*; (*fig.*) moyens, *m.pl.*, puissance, *f.* *Faculty of law*, faculté de droit; *to be in possession of all one's faculties*, jouir de toutes ses facultés.
fad [fæd], *n.* Marotte, toquade, manie, *f.* **faddist,** *n.* Personne qui a une marotte, *f.*; maniaque, *m.* **faddy,** *a.* Capricieux, maniaque.
fade [feid], *v.i.* Se faner, se flétrir; s'évanouir; disparaître, périr, se passer.—*n.* (*Cine.*) Fondu, *m.* *Fade in*, ouverture en fondu, *f.*; *fade out*, fondu au noir, *m.*—*v.t.* Flétrir, faire flétrir. **fading,** *a.* Qui se fane, qui se flétrit; mourant, languissant.—*n.* Flétrissure, *f.*; affaiblissement, *m.*, disparition, atténuation, *f.* (de la lumière, du son).
faecal ['fiːkəl], *a.* Fécal.
faeces ['fiːsiz], *n.pl.* Matière fécale, *f.* sing.; (*Med.*) fèces, *f.pl.*
fag [fæg], *v.i.* Travailler dur, piocher (à); (*fig.*) se fatiguer.—*v.t.* Forcer à piocher; fatiguer, éreinter. *Fagged out,* éreinté.—*n.* (*sch.*) Jeune élève au service d'un grand, *m.*; fatigue, peine, corvée, *f.*; (*pop.*) cigarette, *f.* **fag-end,** *n.* (*Naut.*) Bout (of a rope), *m.*; (*pop.*) mégot (of cigarette), *m.*; queue (of winter), *f.*; (*pl.*) bribes, *f.pl.* (of conversation).
faggot ['fægət], *n.* Fagot, *m.*; bourrée, *f.* (of small branches); (*Fort.*) fascine, *f.*; *(Mil.)* passe-volant, *m.*; (*Cook.*) attignole, crépinette, *f.*—*v.t.* Lier ensemble, fagoter.
fail [feil], *v.i.* Faillir; manquer (to miss); échouer (not to succeed); faiblir; (*Comm.*) faire faillite. *I shall not fail to come,* je ne manquerai pas de venir; *I shall not fail to do it,* je n'y manquerai pas; *my sight is failing,* ma vue commence à baisser; *words fail me,* les paroles me manquent.—*v.t.* Manquer à, faire défaut à; abandonner (to desert).—*n.* Manque, *m.*, faute, *f.*, insuccès, *m. Without fail,* sans faute. **failing,** *n.* Défaut, *m.*, faute; faiblesse; (*Comm.*) faillite, *f.*—*a.* Faiblissant, défaillant, manquant.—*prep.* À défaut de.
failure ['feiljə], *n.* Manque, défaut (want); affaiblissement (of strength etc.); insuccès, *m.*, affaire manquée, *f.*, fiasco, *m.*; chute (of a play etc.); (*Comm.*) faillite, *f. He is a failure,* c'est un raté.
fain [fein], *a.* (*Lit.*) Bienheureux; trop heureux; obligé de se contenter de.—*adv.* Avec plaisir, volontiers. *I fain would come, but . . . ,*

je viendrais volontiers, mais . . . , je serais fort heureux de venir, mais. . . .
faint [feint], *a.* Faible, défaillant; affaibli; languissant; abattu, découragé; timide, mou, léger, faible. *Faint blue,* bleu pâle; *I haven't the faintest idea,* je n'en ai pas la moindre idée; *faint praise,* éloges tièdes, *m.pl.*; *to feel faint,* se sentir mal; *to grow fainter,* s'affaiblir. —*v.i.* S'évanouir, défaillir; perdre courage, faiblir. *To faint away,* s'évanouir, se trouver mal, perdre connaissance.—*n.* Évanouissement, *m.*, défaillance, syncope, *f. In a dead faint,* évanoui. **faint-hearted,** *a.* Timide, sans courage, découragé. *To get faint-hearted,* perdre courage. **faint-heartedly,** *adv.* Lâchement, pusillanimement. **faint-heartedness,** *n.* Pusillanimité, timidité, lâcheté, *f.* **fainting,** *n.* Évanouissement, *m.*, défaillance, syncope, *f.*—*a.* Défaillant. *In a fainting fit,* sans connaissance, évanoui. **faintish,** *a.* Un peu faible, défaillant. **faintly,** *adv.* Faiblement; d'une voix éteinte; mollement. **faintness,** *n.* Faiblesse, *f.*
fair [fɛə], *a.* Beau; propice, agréable; bon, favorable (of the wind); clair (clear), blond, blanc (of the complexion etc.); juste, équitable (just); légitime, permis (allowed); (*fig.*) assez bon, passable; (*Comm.*) courant. *At set fair,* au beau fixe; *fair and square,* honorable; *fair enough,* d'accord; *fair play,* franc jeu, jeu loyal; *fair price,* juste prix, prix raisonnable, *m.*; *that is not fair* (at games), cela n'est pas de jeu; *to be a fair judge,* être un bon juge; *to be in a fair way,* être en train de; *to bid fair to,* promettre de; *to make a fair copy,* mettre au net.—*adv.* Bien; de bonne foi, honorablement. *Fair and square,* en plein milieu; (*fig.*) loyalement, carrément; *he charged fair for the goods,* il vendait les marchandises à un prix raisonnable.—*n.* Foire (market); *belle femme, belle, *f. The fair,* le beau sexe. **fair-complexioned,** *a.* Blond, à peau blanche. **fair-dealing,** *n.* Loyauté, bonne foi, *f.*—*a.* De bonne foi; loyal, honnête. **fair-haired,** *a.* Aux cheveux blonds. **fair-minded,** *a.* Équitable, impartial.
fairing ['fɛəriŋ], *n.* (*Av.*) Profilage, carénage, *m.*; entoilage, *m.*; (*Naut.*) effilement, *m.*
fairish, *a.* Assez bon, passable; plutôt blond (hair). **fairly,** *adv.* Bien; loyalement, ouvertement, franchement; doucement; parfaitement; avec impartialité; avec justesse; honnêtement, de bonne foi; passablement, assez. **fairness,** *n.* Beauté; couleur blonde (of the hair); blancheur (of the complexion); équité, probité, honnêteté, impartialité, bonne foi, *f.*
fairway ['fɛəwei], *n.* Chenal, *m.*, passe, *f.*; (*Ten.*) le milieu du court; (*Golf*) parcours normal, *m.*
fairy ['fɛəri], *n.* Fée, *f.*—*a.* Des fées, féerique. *Fairy rose,* rose pompon, *f.* **fairy-land,** *n.* Royaume des fées, *m.*, féerie, *f.* **fairy-light,** *n.* Lampion, *m.* **fairy-like,** *a.* Comme une fée. **fairy-ring,** *n.* Cercle des fées, *m.* **fairy-tale,** *n.* Conte de fées, *m.*
faith [feiθ], *n.* Foi, croyance; (*fig.*) fidélité, *f. In faith!* ma foi! *in good faith,* de bonne foi; *to die in the faith,* mourir en religion; *to put faith in,* avoir foi en.—*int.* Ma foi! en vérité! **faithful,** *a.* Fidèle.—*n.* Fidèle; (*pl.*) les fidèles, *m.pl.*; (*Mohammedan*) les croyants,

m.pl. **faithfully,** *adv.* Fidèlement, loyalement. *To promise faithfully,* promettre formellement; *yours faithfully* (to unknown person on business), veuillez agréer mes salutations distinguées. **faithfulness,** *n.* Fidélité, *f.* **faith-healing,** *n.* Guérison par le moyen de la prière et de la suggestion, *f.* **faithless,** *a.* Sans foi, infidèle. **faithlessness,** *n.* Infidélité; déloyauté, *f.*

fake [feik], *v.t., v.i.* Truquer, maquiller, dissimuler (les tares), maquignonner (of horses). *To fake a story,* inventer une histoire.—*n.* (Tout) objet truqué, *m.* **faker,** *n.* Truqueur, maquilleur, *m.* **faking,** *n.* Trucage, maquillage, *m.*

fakir [fə'kiə], *n.* Fakir, *m.*

falcate ['fælkeit], **falcated,** *a.* Falciforme.

falchion ['fɔ:lʃən], *n.* *Cimeterre, *m.*; (*Archaeol.*) fauchon, *m.*

falcon ['fɔ:lkən], *n.* Faucon, *m.* **falconer,** *n.* Fauconnier, *m.* **falconet,** *n.* Fauconneau, *m.* **falconry,** *n.* Fauconnerie, *f.*

faldstool ['fɔ:ldstu:l], *n.* Prie-Dieu (of king); siège-pliant, *m.* (of a bishop).

fall [fɔ:l], *v.i.* (*past* fell; *p.p.* **fallen**) Tomber, choir; s'abaisser, descendre; succomber, périr, mourir; se jeter; baisser, diminuer; en venir; incomber (à); s'allonger (of face). *To fall away,* maigrir, dépérir, déserter; *to fall away from,* abandonner, quitter; *to fall back,* tomber en arrière; (*Mil.*) reculer, se replier; *to fall back upon,* se replier sur; *to fall between two stools,* être assis entre deux chaises; *to fall down,* tomber par terre, se prosterner, s'écrouler; *to fall due,* échoir; *to fall for,* tomber amoureux de; *to fall for it,* s'y laisser prendre; *to fall foul of,* se brouiller avec, se prendre de querelle avec; *to fall ill,* tomber malade; *to fall in,* s'écrouler, (*Mil.*) se mettre en rangs, s'aligner; *fall in!* Rassemblement! *to fall into,* se conformer à; *to fall in with,* rencontrer, s'accorder avec; *to fall off,* tomber, diminuer; *to fall out,* tomber, se brouiller, arriver, advenir (of things); (*Mil.*) *fall out!* Rompez vos rangs! *to fall out with,* se brouiller avec; *to fall short,* faire défaut (de), s'en falloir, manquer; *to fall through,* échouer, tomber dans l'eau; *to fall to,* échoir à, se mettre à; *to fall to blows,* en venir aux coups; *to fall under,* être compris sous, tomber sous; *to fall upon,* tomber sur, fondre sur, attaquer, incomber à, être à la charge de.—*v.t.* [FELL (3)].

n.—Chute; chute des feuilles, *f.*, (*Am.*) automne, *m.*; tombée (of night); baisse (in price); quantité tombée (of rain, of snow, etc.), *f.*; éboulement (of earth), *m.*; chute, *f.*, cascade, cataracte (of rivers etc.), *f.*; décrue (of waters); pente (slope); diminution (decrease); voilette (veil), *f. There has been a fall of snow,* il est tombé de la neige; *to break a fall,* amortir une chute; *to meet with a fall,* faire une chute, tomber; *to speculate on a fall,* (*Comm.*) jouer à la baisse.

fallacious [fə'leiʃəs], *a.* Trompeur, fallacieux, illusoire. **fallaciously,** *adv.* Fallacieusement. **fallaciousness,** *n.* Caractère trompeur, *m.*, fausseté, *f.*

fallacy ['fæləsi], *n.* Fausseté, illusion, *f.*; sophisme, *m.*

fallen, *p.p.* [FALL].

fallibility [fæli'biliti], *n.* Faillibilité, *f.*

fallible ['fæləbl], *a.* Faillible.

falling ['fɔ:liŋ], *n.* Chute, *f. Falling away,* amaigrissement, dépérissement, *m.*; défection, *f.*; *falling aback,* (*Naut.*) abattée, *f.*; *falling in,* effondrement, écroulement, éboulement (of earth), *m.*; *falling off,* chute, diminution, baisse; défection, apostasie; (*Naut.*) abattée, *f.*; *falling out,* brouillerie; rupture, *f.*; *falling star,* étoile filante, *f.* **falling-sickness,** *n.* Épilepsie, *f.*

fall-out, *n.* Retombées radioactives, *f.pl.*

fallow ['fælou], *a.* En jachère; (*fig.*) inculte; fauve (of deer etc.). *Fallow finch,* cul-blanc, motteux, *m.*; *to let lie fallow,* laisser en friche; *to lie fallow,* être en friche.—*n.* Jachère, friche, *f.*—*v.t.* Jachérer, défricher.

fall-pipe, *n.* Descente d'eau, *f.*

false [fɔ:ls], *a.* Faux, perfide, déloyal; infidèle; feint, prétendu, simulé; illégal (of imprisonment). *False bottom,* double fond, *m.*; *false start,* faux départ, *m.*; *false teeth,* fausses dents, *f.pl.*; *to play false,* tromper. **falsehearted,** *a.* Perfide, trompeur. **falseheartedness,** *n.* Perfidie, *f.* **falsehood,** *n.* Mensonge, *m.*; le faux, *m.* **falsely,** *adv.* Faussement. **falseness** or **falsity,** *n.* Fausseté; perfidie, *f. The falseness of a report,* la fausseté d'une nouvelle.

falsetto [fɔ:l'setou], *n.* (*Mus.*) Voix de fausset, *f.*, fausset, *m.*

falsification [fɔ:lsifi'keiʃən], *n.* Falsification, *f.*

falsifier ['fɔ:lsifaiə], *n.* Falsificateur; faussaire; faux monnayeur (of coin), *m.*

falsify ['fɔ:lsifai], *v.t.* Falsifier; fausser; réfuter; prouver la fausseté de (to disprove).

falsity [FALSENESS].

falter ['fɔ:ltə], *v.i.* Hésiter, bégayer; trembler, chanceler. **faltering,** *n.* Hésitation, *f.* **falteringly,** *adv.* Avec hésitation, en tremblant.

fame [feim], *n.* Renom, *m.*, réputation, gloire, renommée, *f. House of ill-fame,* maison de tolérance, *f.*, lieu mal-famé, *m.* **famed,** *a.* Renommé, fameux, célèbre. **fameless,** *a.* Sans renom.

familiar [fə'miljə], *a.* Familier, intime; de la famille. *To be familiar with,* être familier avec, connaître; *to grow familiar,* se familiariser; *to make oneself familiar with,* se familiariser avec.—*n.* Ami intime; démon, esprit familier; (*Inquisition*) familier, *m.*

familiarity [fəmili'æriti], *n.* Familiarité, *f. Familiarity breeds contempt,* la familiarité engendre le mépris.

familiarize [fə'miljəraiz], *v.t.* Familiariser.

familiarly, *adv.* Familièrement, sans cérémonie.

family ['fæmili], *n.* Famille, *f.*—*a.* De famille, de la famille. *To be in the family way,* être enceinte. **family-tree,** *n.* Arbre généalogique, *m.*

famine ['fæmin], *n.* Famine, disette, *f.*

famish ['fæmiʃ], *v.t.* Affamer, faire mourir de faim.—*v.i.* Être affamé; mourir de faim. **famished,** *a.* Affamé.

famous ['feiməs], *a.* Fameux, célèbre, renommé (pour). **famously,** *adv.* Avec une grande renommée; fameusement; (*fig.*) furieusement, prodigieusement; à merveille.

fan [fæn], *n.* Éventail; ventilateur, *m.*; aile (of propeller), *f.*; gouvernail (of a windmill), soufflet (of bellows); (*Agric.*) *van, tarare, *m.*;

(*colloq.*) admirateur enthousiaste d'un artiste *or* d'un sport, fervent, fanatique, *m.*—*v.t.* Éventer; souffler (a fire); (*Agric.*) vanner; (*fig.*) exciter, activer.—*v.i.* To fan out, se déployer en éventail. **fancase,** *n.* Étui à éventail, *m.* **fan-light,** *n.* Vasistas, *m.* **fanlike,** *a.* En éventail. **fan-mail,** *n.* Courrier des admirateurs, *m.* **fanmaker,** *n.* Éventailliste, *m.* **fanner,** *n.* Vanneur; tarare, ventilateur, *m.* **fan-palm,** *n.* Palmieréventail, *m.* **fan-shaped,** *a.* En éventail. **fantail,** *n.* Pigeon-paon; (*Gas*) bec-éventail, *m.* **fantailed,** *a.* A queue d'aronde. **fanvaulting,** *n.* Réseau en éventail, *m.*

fanatic [fə'nætik] or **fanatical,** *a.* Fanatique.— *n.* Fanatique. **fanatically,** *adv.* D'une manière fanatique, avec fanatisme. **fanaticism,** *n.* Fanatisme, *m.* **fanaticize,** *v.t.* Fanatiser.

fancied ['fænsid], *a.* Imaginaire, imaginé, supposé. (*Turf*) A fancied horse, un cheval bien coté. **fancier,** *n.* Amateur (de). **fanciful,** *a.* Fantaisiste, fantasque, capricieux; fantastique (of things). **fancifully,** *adv.* Fantasquement, capricieusement. **fancifulness,** *n.* Caractère fantastique *or* fantasque, *m.*, bizarrerie, *f.* **fancy,** *n.* Fantaisie, imagination; idée, pensée, *f.*, caprice, goût (pour), *m.*, envie (de), *f.* To take a fancy to, prendre du goût pour; to take a fancy to a place, affectionner un endroit; to take a fancy to someone, prendre quelqu'un en affection. —*a.* De fantaisie; costumé (of a ball). *Fancy price,* prix de fantaisie, *m.*—*v.t.* S'imaginer, penser, se figurer; aimer, avoir du goût pour. To fancy oneself, s'en faire accroire; to fancy one's tennis, se croire bon joueur de tennis. —*v.i.* S'imaginer, se figurer, croire. *Just fancy!* figurez-vous! **fancy-cakes,** *n.* Gâteaux à la crème, *m.pl.* **fancy-dress,** *n.* Travesti, *m.* *Fancy-dress ball,* bal costumé, *m.* **fancy-framed,** *a.* Créé par l'imagination, imaginaire. **fancy-free,** *a.* Le cœur libre. **fancy-goods,** *n.* Objets de fantaisie, *m.pl.*; étoffes de fantaisie, nouveautés, *f.pl.* **fancy-sick,** *a.* Qui a l'imagination malade. **fancy-work,** *n.* Broderie, *f.*, ouvrage de dames, *m.*

fane [fein], *n.* Temple, édifice sacré, *m.*

fanfare ['fænfeə], *n.* Fanfare, *f.*

fanfaronade [fænfæro'neid], *n.* Fanfaronnade, *f.*

fang [fæŋ], *n.* Croc (of dogs); crochet (of reptiles), *m.*; racine (of teeth), *f.*; boutoir, *m.*, défense, *f.* (of boars); (*fig.*) griffe, serre, *f.* **fanged,** *a.* Armé de dents, crocs, *or* défenses. **fangless,** *a.* Sans crocs, sans dents; (*fig.*) édenté.

fanon ['fænən], *n.* (*R.-C. Ch. etc.*) Fanon, *m.*

fantasia [fæntə'ziə *or* fæn'teiziə], *n.* (*Mus.*) Fantaisie, *f.*

fantasm etc. [PHANTASM].

fantastic [fæn'tæstik] or **fantastical,** *a.* Fantastique, bizarre; fantasque, capricieux (of persons).—*n.* Personne fantasque, *f.* **fantastically,** *adv.* D'une manière fantastique, fantastiquement, fantasquement. **fantasticalness,** *n.* Fantaisie, bizarrerie, *f.*; caractère fantasque, *m.*

fantasy ['fæntəsi], *n.* Fantaisie, *f.*

far [fɑː], *a.* (*comp.* **farther, further;** *superl.* **farthest, furthest**) Lointain, éloigné, reculé. *The Far East,* l'extrême Orient, *m.*; *the far*

side, le côté droit.—*adv.* Loin, au loin; bien, fort, beaucoup. *As far as,* aussi loin que, jusqu'à; *as far as I know,* (autant) que je sache; *as far as the eye can reach* [EYE]; *by far,* de beaucoup; *far and near,* de près et de loin; *far and wide,* de tous côtés; *far be it from me to,* loin de moi la pensée de; *far between,* à de longs intervalles, de loin en loin; *far from,* loin de; *far from it,* loin de là, tant s'en faut; *far inferior,* bien inférieur; *far off,* au loin; *how far?* jusqu'où? jusqu'à quel point? combien de distance? *how far is it to* . . .? combien y a-t-il d'ici à . . .? *in so far as,* en tant que; *so far as to,* jusqu'à; *so far so good,* c'est très bien jusqu'ici; *the day was far spent,* la journée était fort avancée; *thus far,* jusqu'ici; *to go too far,* aller trop loin. **faraway,** *a.* Rêveur, perdu (look); lointain. **farfamed,** *a.* Célèbre, renommé au loin. **farfetched,** *a.* Recherché; tiré par les cheveux, forcé, affecté. **far-flung,** *a.* Vaste. **fargone,** *a.* Avancé; (*fam.*) amoureux. **far-off,** *a.* Lointain, reculé. **far-reaching,** *a.* D'une grande portée. **far-seeing** or **far-sighted,** *a.* Clairvoyant, prévoyant, avisé, prescient; qui a la vue longue, presbyte. **far-sightedness,** *n.* Presbytie; (*fig.*) clairvoyance, prévoyance, prescience, *f.*

faradaic [færə'deiik], *a.* Faradique. **faradization** [-dai'zeifən], *n.* Faradisation, *f.*

farandole [færən'doul], *n.* Farandole (a dance), *f.*

farce [fɑːs], *n.* Farce, *f.*—*v.t.* Farcir.

farcical ['fɑːsikəl], *a.* Burlesque; (*fig.*) drôle, risible, bouffon, absurde, grotesque. **farcically,** *adv.* Burlesquement; drôlement.

farcin ['fɑːsin] or **farcy,** *n.* (*Vet.*) Farcin, *m.* *Affected with farcin,* farcineux.

fare [feə], *v.i.* Aller; se porter, être, se trouver; manger, se nourrir, vivre. *To fare badly,* se trouver mal, faire mauvaise chère; *to fare well,* faire bonne chère.—*n.* Prix de la course; prix de la place, *m.*, place; course (in a cab etc.), *f.*; voyageur (person), client, *m.*; chère, nourriture, *f.*, menu (food), *m.* *Bill of fare,* menu, *m.*, carte du jour, *f.*; *excess fare,* supplément, *m.*; *fares, please!* places, s'il vous plaît; *full fare,* place entière, *f.*; *here is my fare,* voici le prix de ma place; *return fare,* l'aller et retour; *single fare,* billet simple, *m.*

farewell ['feəwel *or* feə'wel], *n.* Adieu, *m.* *To bid farewell to,* faire ses adieux à.—*a.* D'adieu.—*int.* Adieu, bon voyage.

farina [fə'rainə], *n.* Farine, *f.*; (*Bot.*) pollen, *m.*

farinaceous [færi'neifəs], *a.* Farineux, fariné.

farinose ['færinouz], *a.* Farineux.

farm [fɑːm], *n.* Ferme, *f.*—*v.t.* Affermer, prendre à ferme; cultiver, exploiter. *To farm out,* donner à ferme. **farm-bailiff,** *n.* Régisseur, *m.* **farm-buildings,** *n.pl.* Bâtiments de ferme, *m.pl.*, dépendances de ferme, *f.pl.* **farm-equipment,** *n.* Matériel agricole, *m.* **farm-hand,** *n.* Valet de ferme, *m.* **farm-labourer,** *n.* Ouvrier agricole, *m.* **farm-servant,** *n.* Valet de ferme, *m.*, fille de ferme, *f.* **farm-yard,** *n.* Basse-cour, *f.*

farmer, *n.* Cultivateur; fermier (tenant-farmer); métayer (produce-sharing farmer), *m.* **farmer-general,** *n.* (*Hist.*) Fermier-général, *m.* **farm-house,** *n.* Ferme, *f.*

farming, *n.* Agriculture, culture, exploitation agricole, *f.* *General farming,* polyculture, *f.*; *mechanized farming,* motoculture, *f.* **farmstead,** *n.* Ferme, *f.*

faro ['fɛərou], *n.* Pharaon (game), *m.*

Faroe ['fɛərou] **Islands.** Les îles Féroé, *f.pl.*

farrago [fə'reigou], *n.* Fatras, farrago, *m.*

farrier ['færiə], *n.* Maréchal ferrant, *m.*

farrow ['færou], *n.* Portée, cochonnée, *f.—v.t.* Mettre bas (of pigs).—*v.i.* Cochonner.

fart [fɑːt], *n.* (*vulg.*) Pet, *m.—v.i.* Péter.

farther ['fɑːðə], *a.* Ultérieur, plus éloigné; autre, encore un. *Farther end,* extrémité, *f.,* fond, *m.—adv.* Plus loin, au delà (de); en outre, davantage, de plus. **farthermore,** *adv.* De plus. **farthest,** *a.* Le plus éloigné.—*adv.* and *n.* Le plus loin. *At farthest,* au plus tard (of time), au plus (of quantity).

farthing ['fɑːðiŋ], *n.* Farthing, liard, *m.* *Not to be worth a farthing,* n'avoir pas *or* ne pas valoir un rouge liard.

farthingale ['fɑːðiŋgeil], *n.* Vertugadin, *m.*

fasces ['fæsiːz], *n.pl.* (*Rom. Ant.*) Faisceaux, *m.pl.*

fascia ['fæʃiə], *n.* (*pl.* **fasciae**) (*Anat.*) Fascia, *m.*; (*Arch.*) fasce, *f.* **fascial,** *a.* Fascial.

fasciated, *a.* Fascié. **fasciation** [-'eiʃən], *n.* (*Bot.*) Fasciation, *f.*

fascicle ['fæsikl] or **fascicule,** *n.* Fascicule, *m.*

fascicular [fə'sikjulə], **fasciculate,** or **fasciculated,** *a.* Fasciculé.

fascinate ['fæsineit], *v.t.* Fasciner; charmer, séduire. **fascinating,** *a.* Fascinateur, enchanteur, séduisant. *Fascinating look,* regard fascinateur, *m.* **fascination** [-'neiʃən], *n.* Fascination, séduction, *f.,* charme, *m.*

fascine [fə'siːn], *n.* Fascine, *f.* *To line with fascines,* (*Fort.*) fasciner.

fascism ['fæʃizm], *n.* Fascisme, *m.* **fascist,** *a.* and *n.* Fasciste.

fash [fæʃ], *n.* (*Sc.*) Ennui, tracas, *m.—v.t.* Ennuyer. *To fash oneself,* se tracasser.

fashion ['fæʃən], *n.* Façon, forme; manière (way); la mode, *f.*; le grand monde, *m.*; (*fig.*) goût, style, *m.* *In a fashion, after a fashion,* tant bien que mal, tel quel; *in fashion,* à la mode; *in the English fashion,* à l'anglaise; *in the French fashion,* à la française; *it is the fashion,* c'est la mode; *out of fashion,* passé de mode, démodé; *people of fashion,* gens à la mode, *m.pl.*; *to be in fashion,* être à la mode; *to bring into fashion,* mettre à la mode; *to come into fashion,* devenir à la mode; *to go out of fashion,* passer de mode; *to set the fashion,* donner le ton.—*v.t.* Façonner, former. **fashion-magazine,** *n.* Journal de modes, *m.* **fashion-plate,** *n.* Gravure de mode, *f.*

fashionable ['fæʃnəbl], *a.* À la mode, élégant, de luxe, de bon ton, (*fam.*) chic. *Fashionable man,* élégant, homme du monde, *m.*; *fashionable woman,* élégante; *fashionable world,* le beau monde. **fashionableness,** *n.* Élégance, distinction, *f.* **fashionably,** *adv.* À la mode, élégamment.

fast (1) [fɑːst], *n.* Jeûne, *m.—v.i.* Jeûner, faire maigre. **fast-day,** *n.* Jour de jeûne; jour maigre (Friday), *m.* **faster,** *n.* Jeûneur, *m.,* -euse, *f.* **fasting,** *n.* Jeûne, *m.—a.* De jeûne. **fast(ing)-day,** *n.* Jour de jeûne, jour maigre, *m.*

fast (2) [fɑːst], *a.* Ferme, fixe, solide (firm); fidèle, constant (faithful); profond (of sleep); bon teint (of colours); serré (of knots); (*Naut.*) amarré (made fast); bien fermé (of doors); vite, rapide (quick); en avance (of clocks etc.); (*fig.*) dissolu. *Fast train,* train rapide, *m.*; *to make fast,* attacher, fixer, assujettir, fermer (doors, windows), (*Navy*) amarrer.—*adv.* Ferme, fortement (firm); vite, rapidement (quickly); fort (of raining); profondément (of someone asleep). *To hold fast,* tenir bon; *to live fast,* être un viveur; *to play fast and loose,* jouer double jeu; *to stand fast,* s'arrêter, montrer du courage, ne pas broncher; *to stick fast,* bien tenir, ne pas lâcher.

fasten [fɑːsn], *v.t.* Attacher, fixer; lier; fermer (windows, doors, etc.). *To fasten down,* assujettir; *to fasten up,* attacher; *to fasten (something) upon (someone),* imputer à, mettre sur le dos de.—*v.i.* S'attacher (à); s'acharner (à); se fermer. **fastener** or **fastening,** *n.* Attache; agrafe (of dress); fermeture; espagnolette (of windows), *f.*

fasti ['fæstai], *n.pl.* (*Rom. Ant.*) Fastes, *m.pl.*

fastidious [fæs'tidiəs], *a.* Difficile; dédaigneux; délicat; exigeant. **fastidiously,** *adv.* Dédaigneusement, d'un air de dégoût. **fastidiousness,** *n.* Goût difficile, *m.*

fastigiate [fæs'tidʒieit], *a.* (*Bot.*) Fastigié.

fastness ['fɑːstnis], *n.* Fermeté, sûreté; rapidité, vitesse, *f.*; place forte (stronghold); liberté d'allures; légèreté de conduite, *f.*

fat [fæt], *a.* Gras; gros (of persons); (*fig.*) riche, fertile. *A fat living,* un gros bénéfice; *fat as a pig,* gras comme un cochon; *fat stroke,* le plein (d'une lettre). *Fat-head,* nigaud, idiot, *m.—n.* Gras, *m.*; graisse; (*fig.*) substance, *f.* *The fat was in the fire,* le feu était au pot; *to live on the fat of the land,* faire bonne chère; *to make fat,* engraisser; *to run to fat, to put on fat,* prendre de l'embonpoint. —*v.t.* Engraisser. **fats,** *n.pl.* Matières grasses, *f.pl.*

fatal ['feitəl], *a.* Fatal, funeste; mortel. **fatalism,** *n.* Fatalisme, *m.* **fatalist,** *n.* Fataliste. **fatality** [fə'tæliti], *n.* Fatalité, *f.*; accident mortel, *m.* **fatally,** *adv.* Fatalement, funestement. **fate,** *n.* Destin, sort, *m.* *The Fates,* les Parques, *f.pl.* **fated,** *a.* Destiné. *It was fated to be,* c'était écrit. **fateful,** *a.* Fatal.

father ['fɑːðə], *n.* Père, *m.*; (*pl.*) pères, ancêtres, aïeux, *m.pl.* *Father-in-law,* beau-père, *m.*; *godfather,* parrain, *m.*; *grandfather,* grand-père, *m.*; *Holy Father,* Saint-Père, *m.*; *like father like son,* tel père tel fils; *stepfather,* beau-père, *m.*; *the early fathers,* les Pères de l'Église, *m.pl.—v.t.* Servir de père à, adopter; engendrer. *To father upon,* attribuer à. **fatherhood,** *n.* Paternité, *f.* **fatherland,** *n.* Pays natal, *m.,* patrie, *f.* **father-lasher,** *n.* (*Ichth.*) Cotte-chabot, scorpion de mer, *m.* **fatherless,** *a.* Orphelin de père, sans père. **fatherliness,** *n.* Amour paternel, *m.* **fatherly,** *a.* Paternel, de père.—*adv.* Paternellement, en père.

fathom ['fæðəm], *n.* Toise; (*Naut.*) brasse (=6 pieds=1 m. 829); (*fig.*) portée, profondeur, *f.—v.t.* Sonder; (*fig.*) approfondir, pénétrer. **fathomless,** *a.* Sans fond; (*fig.*) impénétrable, incompréhensible.

*fatidic [fə'tidik], *a.* Fatidique.
fatigue [fə'ti:g], *n.* Fatigue, (*Mil.*) corvée, *f.* *Fatigue dress*, tenue de corvée, *f.*, treillis, *m.*; *fatigue party*, corvée, *f.*; *to be worn out with fatigue*, n'en pouvoir plus de fatigue; *to stand fatigue*, supporter la fatigue.—*v.t.* Fatiguer, lasser. **fatiguing**, *a.* Fatigant.—*pres.p.* Fatiguant.
fatling ['fætliŋ], *n.* Bête grasse, *f.* **fatness**, *n.* Graisse, *f.*; embonpoint (of persons), *m.*; (*fig.*) fertilité, abondance, *f.*
fatted ['fætid], *a.* Engraissé; gras. *The fatted calf*, le veau gras.
fatten [fætn], *v.t.* Engraisser; (*fig.*) enrichir. —*v.i.* (*fig.*) *To fatten on*, s'engraisser de, s'enrichir de. **fattener**, *n.* Engraisseur, *m.*, -euse, *f.* **fattening**, *a.* Engraissant.—*n.* Engraissement, *m.*
fattiness ['fætinis], *n.* Nature graisseuse, *f.* **fattish**, *a.* Un peu gras. **fatty**, *a.* Graisseux. *n.* (*pop.*) Grosse personne, *f.*
fatuity [fə'tju:iti] or **fatuousness** ['fætjuəsnis], *n.* Imbécillité, sottise, fatuité, *f.*
fatuous ['fætjuəs], *a.* Sot; béat.
fauces ['fɔːsiz], *n.pl.* (*Anat.*) Gosier, *m.*
faucet ['fɔːsit], *n.* Cannelle, cannette, *f.*; fausset; (*Am.*) robinet, *m.*
fault [fɔːlt], *n.* Faute, *f.*; défaut, vice, *m.*; (*Geol.*) faille, *f.* *A fault confessed is half redressed*, péché avoué est à demi pardonné; *at fault*, en défaut; (*Ten.*) *double fault*, double faute, *f.*; *to a fault*, à l'excès, même trop; *to find fault with*, trouver à redire à, blâmer, critiquer; *whose fault is it?* à qui la faute?
fault-finder, *n.* Personne qui trouve toujours à redire, *f.*, censeur, épilogueur, *m.* **fault-finding**, *n.* Critique, censure, *f.*—*a.* Épilogueur. **faultily**, *adv.* D'une manière fautive, défectueusement. **faultiness**, *n.* Défauts, *m.pl.*; imperfections, *f.pl.*; imperfection, *f.* **faultless**, *a.* Sans défaut, sans faute, impeccable. **faultlessly**, *adv.* Irréprochablement. **faultlessness**, *n.* Perfection, *f.* **faulty**, *a.* Fautif, blâmable, défectueux.
faun [fɔːn], *n.* Faune, *m.*
fauna ['fɔːnə], *n.* Faune, *f.* *Fauna and flora*, la faune et la flore.
favour ['feivə], *n.* Faveur, *f.*, bonnes grâces, *f.pl.*; bienfait, *m.*, bonté; grâce (permission), *f.*; couleurs, faveurs (ribbons), *f.pl.*; (*Comm.*) honorée, estimée, estimée lettre, *f.* *By favour of*, à la faveur de; *in his favour*, en sa faveur; *to ask a favour of*, demander une faveur à; *to be in favour with*, être dans les bonnes grâces de; *to do me the favour of*, me faire le plaisir de; *to fall out of favour*, perdre sa popularité; *to find favour with*, trouver grâce auprès de; *to get into favour with*, se faire aimer de; *your favour of the 3rd instant*, votre honorée du trois courant.—*v.t.* Favoriser, gratifier, honorer (de). **favourable**, *a.* Favorable, propice. **favourableness**, *n.* Caractère favorable, *m.*, bienveillance, *f.* **favourably**, *adv.* Favorablement. **favoured**, *a.* Favorisé. *Ill-favoured*, laid, de mauvaise mine; *well-favoured*, de bonne mine.
favourite ['feivərit], *n.* Favori, *m.*, -ite, *f.* *To be a great favourite*, être très aimé de, plaire beaucoup à, être très populaire.—*a.* Favori, bien-aimé, préféré. **favouritism**, *n.* Favoritisme, *m.*

fawn [fɔːn], *n.* Faon, *m.*; (*fig.*) ***caresse servile, basse flatterie, *f.*—*v.i.* Faonner (of animals). *To fawn upon*, caresser, flatter, câliner.
fawner, *n.* Flatteur servile, adulateur, *m.*
fawning, *n.* Caresse, flatterie, câlinerie, *f.* —*a.* Flatteur, servile. **fawningly**, *adv.* En caressant, d'une manière caressante, par flagornerie.
fay (1) [fei], *n.* Fée, *f.*
*fay (2) [fei], *n.* Foi, *f.* *By my fay*, par ma foi.
*fay (3) [fei], *v.t.* Joindre; affleurer.
fealty ['fiːəlti], *n.* Fidélité, constance, loyauté, *f.*
fear [fiə], *n.* Crainte, peur, terreur; inquiétude, *f.*, souci; respect, *m.* *For fear of*, de peur de, de crainte de; *for fear that*, de peur que (with subjunctive); *no fear!* il n'y a pas de danger! *there is no fear*, il n'y a rien à craindre; *to be in fear of*, avoir peur de, craindre; *to go in fear of one's life*, craindre pour sa vie.—*v.t.* Craindre, redouter, avoir peur de.—*v.i.* Craindre, avoir peur. *Never fear!* soyez sans crainte! rassurez-vous! **fearful**, *a.* *Qui a peur, craintif, timide; terrible, affreux, effrayant. *To be fearful of*, craindre, redouter. **fearfully**, *adv.* Craintivement, avec crainte; terriblement, d'une manière effrayante. **fearfulness**, *n.* Crainte, terreur, *f.*, effroi, *m.* **fearless**, *a.* Sans peur, intrépide, sans crainte. **fearlessly**, *adv.* Sans crainte, avec intrépidité. **fearlessness**, *n.* Intrépidité, *f.* **fearsome**, *a.* Effrayant, redoutable, terrifiant.
feasibility [fiːzi'biliti], *n.* Possibilité, praticabilité, *f.*
feasible ['fiːzəbl], *a.* Faisable, praticable.
feast [fiːst], *n.* Festin, *m.*; fête, *f.*; régal, *m.* *Enough is as good as a feast*, contentement passe richesse; *movable feast*, fête mobile, *f.*—*v.t.* Fêter, régaler, festoyer. *To feast one's eyes on*, se repaître de.—*v.i.* Faire festin, festiner, se régaler. **feaster**, *n.* Donneur de festins; amateur de bonne chère, *m.* **feasting**, *n.* Festin, régal, *m.*
feat [fiːt], *n.* Exploit, fait, haut fait, *m.*, action, *f.*; tour de force, *m.*—*a.* Habile; élégant, coquet.
feather ['feðə], *n.* Plume; penne (of a bird's wing and tail), *f.*; épi (of hair); (*Mil.*) plumet, *m.* *A feather in one's cap*, une distinction; *birds of a feather*, gens de même farine; *birds of a feather flock together*, qui se ressemble s'assemble; *in full feather*, en grande toilette; *to be in high feather*, être de bonne humeur, plein d'entrain; *to show the white feather*, manquer de courage, (*colloq.*) saigner du nez. —*v.t.* Orner d'une plume; donner des ailes à; mettre (an oar) à plat. *To feather one's nest*, faire sa pelote, mettre du foin dans ses bottes. (*Row.*) *Feather!* Les pelles à plat! *To feather along the water*, plumer. **feather-bed**, *n.* Lit de plume, *m.* **feather-brain**, *n.* Tête de linotte, *f.*, étourdi, *m.* **feather-duster**, *n.* Plumeau, *m.* **feather-edged**, *a.* À biseau. **feathergrass**, *n.* Stipe empennée, *f.* **feather-weight**, *n.* (*Box.*) Poids plume, *m.*
feathered, *a.* Garni de plumes, emplumé; empenné (of arrows); (*fig.*) ailé, rapide. **featherless**, *a.* Sans plumes. **feathery**, *a.* Garni de plumes, plumeux; (*fig.*) léger comme une plume.
feature ['fiːtʃə], *n.* Trait, *m.*; (*pl.*) physionomie, *f.*, visage, *m.*; figure, *f.*; (*fig.*) signe,

point, caractère, *m.*, spécialité, *f.* (*Cine.*) *Feature film,* grand film, *m.*; *redeeming feature,* beau côté, *m.*—*v.t.* Caractériser; représenter; (in a film) tenir le rôle de; mettre en vedette. *Hard-featured,* aux traits durs; *ill-featured,* laid. **featureless,** *a.* Sans traits bien marqués; sans caractère.

febrifuge ['febrifjuːdʒ], *a.* and *n.* Fébrifuge, *m.*

febrile ['fiːbrail], *a.* Fébrile.

February ['februəri], *n.* Février, *m.*

fecal [FAECAL].

feck [fek], *n.* (*Sc.*) Force, vigueur; valeur, quantité, *f.* **feckless,** *a.* Faible, veule, mesquin; étourdi, irréfléchi. **fecklessly,** *adv.* Avec veulerie; maladroitement. **fecklessness,** *n.* Veulerie; incapacité, *f.*

feckly, *adv.* Pour la plupart; presque.

fecula ['fekjulə], *n.* Fécule, *f.*, amidon, *m.* **feculence** ['fekjuləns], *n.* Féculence, *f.*, manque de limpidité, *m.*, fétidité, *f.* **feculent,** *a.* Féculent, trouble, plein de dépôt, fétide.

fecund ['fekənd], *a.* Fécond. **fecundate,** *v.t.* Féconder. **fecundation** [-'deiʃən], *n.* Fécondation, *f.*

fecundity [fə'kʌnditi], *n.* Fécondité, *f.*

fed, *past* [FEED].

federal ['fedərəl], *a.* and *n.* Fédéral, *m.* **federalism,** *n.* Fédéralisme, *m.* **federalist,** *n.* Fédéraliste.

federate (1) ['fedərit], *a.* Fédéré.

federate (2) ['fedəreit], *v.t.* Fédérer.—*v.i.* Se fédérer.

federation [fedə'reiʃən], *n.* Fédération, *f.* **federative,** *a.* Fédératif.

fee [fiː], *n.* Honoraires, *m.pl.*, salaire; (*Eccles.* etc.) droit; (*colloq.*) pourboire, *m.*, gratification, *f.*; (*Feud.*) fief, *m.*; propriété héréditaire, *f.* *Registration fee,* droit d'inscription, *m.* *Surplice fees,* casuel, *m.*—*v.t.* Payer; payer des honoraires à; graisser la patte à. **fee-simple,** *n.* Propriété libre, *f.* **fee-splitting,** *n.* (*Med.*) Dichotomie, *f.*

feeble ['fiːbl], *a.* Faible; débile. *To grow feeble,* s'affaiblir. **feeble-minded,** *a.* Faible d'esprit. **feebleness,** *n.* Faiblesse, *f.* **feebly,** *adv.* Faiblement.

feed [fiːd], *n.* Nourriture; pâture, *f.*, pâturage (for cattle), *m.*; (*Motor. etc.*) alimentation, *f.* *Feed of oats,* picotin d'avoine, *m.*; *to be off one's feed,* perdre l'appétit.—*v.t.* (*past* and *p.p.* **fed**) Nourrir; donner à manger à; paître, faire paître (cattle); nourrir (de); (*fig.*) alimenter; (*Ftb.*) servir, donner du jeu à. *He fed him with the hope of liberty,* il le reput de l'espérance de la liberté; (*pop.*) *to be fed up,* en avoir marre, en avoir plein le dos.—*v.i.* Se nourrir; paître, manger (of animals). *To feed upon,* se nourrir de, se repaître de, (*fig.*) se bercer de. **feed-back,** *n.* (*Rad.*) Rétroaction, *f.* **feed-pump,** *n.* Pompe alimentaire, *f.*

feeder, *n.* Nourrisseur, *m.*; mangeur, convive; affluent (tributary) (*Tech.*) appareil d'alimentation, *m.*; trémie (mill), *f.*; (*colloq.*) bavette (bib), *f.* **feeding,** *n.* Nourriture; pâture (for cattle), *f.* **feeding bottle,** *n.* Biberon, *m.*

feel [fiːl], *v.t.* (*past* and *p.p.* **felt**) Tâter, toucher, sentir; éprouver, ressentir; se ressentir de. *To feel one's way,* avancer à tâtons, (*fig.*) y aller avec précaution; *to feel*

someone's *pulse,* tâter le pouls à quelqu'un; *to feel the cold,* être sensible au froid; (*Mil.*) *to feel the enemy,* tâter l'ennemi; *feel your right!* appuyez à droite!—*v.i.* Sentir, se sentir; se trouver. *To feel cold,* avoir froid; *to feel for,* avoir de la sympathie pour; *to feel ill,* se sentir malade; *to feel like doing something,* avoir envie de faire quelque chose; *to feel rough,* être dur au toucher; *to feel soft,* être doux au toucher.—*n.* Toucher; attouchement; tact, *m.* **feeler,** *n.* Antenne (of an insect); moustache (of a cat), *f.*; (*fig.*) ballon d'essai, *m.* **feeling,** *n.* Toucher; sentiment, *m.*, sensibilité, émotion, *f.* *Feeling of cold* or *of warmth,* sensation de froid or de chaleur, *f.*; *ill-feeling,* rancune, *f.*; *to have no feelings,* n'avoir pas de sensibilité; *to hurt someone's feelings,* blesser les sentiments de quelqu'un. —*a.* Tendre, touchant; sensible. *He spoke in a most feeling manner,* il parla de la manière la plus touchante. **feelingly,** *adv.* D'une manière touchante, sensiblement, avec émotion, avec chaleur.

feet, *n.pl.* [FOOT].

feign [fein], *v.t.* Feindre, simuler.—*v.i.* Feindre, dissimuler, faire semblant (de).

feigned [feind], *a.* Feint, simulé. **feignedly** ['feinidli] or **feigningly,** *adv.* Avec feinte. **feigning,** *n.* Feinte, simulation, *f.*

feint [feint], *n.* Feinte, *f.*—*v.i.* Feinter.

feldspar ['feldspaː], *n.* Feldspath, *m.* **feldspathic** [-'spæθik], *a.* Feldspathique.

felicitate [fə'lisiteit], *v.t.* Féliciter; *rendre heureux. **felicitation** [-'teiʃən], *n.* Félicitation, *f.* **felicitous,** *a.* Heureux, bien trouvé. **felicitously,** *adv.* Heureusement. **felicity,** *n.* Félicité, *f.*, bonheur, *m.*

felid ['fiːlid], *n.* Félidé, *m.*

feline ['fiːlain], *a.* Félin, de chat.

fell (1) [fel], *n.* Peau (de bête), fourrure, toison, *f.* **fellmonger,** *n.* Pelletier, peaussier, *m.*

fell (2) [fel], *a.* Impitoyable, féroce, cruel.

fell (3) [fel], *v.t.* Abattre, assommer, terrasser. **feller,** *n.* Abatteur, *m.*

fell (4) [fel], *n.* Montagne, colline rocheuse, *f.*

fell (5), *past* [FALL].

felloe ['felou], *n.* Jante, *f.*

fellow ['felou], *n.* Compagnon, camarade, confrère; associé, membre; (*Univ.*) membre de la Corporation d'un Collège universitaire; semblable, pendant, pareil (of things); (*colloq.*) garçon, gaillard; individu, type, mec, *m.* *Bedfellow,* camarade de lit, *m.*; *fine fellow,* beau gars, *m.*; *good fellow,* brave type, *m.*; *good-for-nothing fellow,* mauvais sujet, *m.*; *here is the fellow to this picture,* voici le pendant de ce tableau; *old fellow,* vieux bonhomme, *m.*; *queer fellow,* drôle de type, *m.*; *schoolfellow,* camarade de collège, (*colloq.*) copain, *m.*; *these shoes are not fellows,* ces souliers ne sont pas pareils.—*v.t.* S'accorder avec, s'assortir avec. **fellow-citizen,** *n.* Concitoyen, *m.*, concitoyenne, *f.* **fellow-countryman,** *n.* Compatriote, *m.* **fellow-creature, fellow-being,** *n.* Semblable, *m.* **fellow-feeling,** *n.* Sympathie, *f.* **fellow-prisoner,** *n.* Compagnon de prison, *m.*

fellowship ['felouʃip], *n.* Société, association, *f.*; (*Univ.*) titre de 'fellow', *m.*; bourse de recherche, *f.* *Good fellowship,* bonne camaraderie, *f.*

fellow-soldier, *n.* Frère d'armes, camarade de régiment, *m.* **fellow-student**, *n.* Condisciple, *m.* **fellow-sufferer**, *n.* Compagnon d'infortune, *m.* **fellow-townsman**, *n.* Concitoyen, *m.* **fellow-traveller**, *n.* Compagnon de voyage; (*Polit.*) sympathisant communiste, communisant, *m.* **fellow-worker**, *n.* Compagnon; collaborateur, *m.*, -trice, *f.*

felly [FELLOE].

felo-de-se ['fi:loudi:'si:], *n.* (*pl.* **felones-de-se**) Qui s'est tué (*or* a tenté de se tuer) étant de sang-froid; meurtrier de soi; suicide, *m.*

felon ['felən], *n.* Criminel; (*Med.*) panaris (whitlow), *m.*—*a.* Félon, traître; cruel. **felonious** [fə'louniəs], *a.* Criminel; scélérat. **feloniously**, *adv.* Avec une intention criminelle. **felony**, *n.* Crime, *m.*

felt (1) [felt], *n.* Feutre, chapeau de feutre, *m. Roofing felt*, carton bitumé, *m.*; *soft felt hat*, chapeau mou, *m.*—*v.t.* Feutrer. **felting**, *n.* Feutrage, *m.* **felty**, *a.* Feutré.

felt (2), *past* [FEEL].

felucca [fə'lʌkə], *n.* Felouque, *f.*

female ['fi:meil], *a.* Féminin, de femme, des femmes; femelle (of animals). *A female friend*, une amie.—*n.* Femme; jeune personne; femelle (of animals), *f.*

feme covert [fem 'kʌvət], *n.* (*Law*) Femme en puissance de mari, *f.* **feme sole**, *n.* Femme non mariée, célibataire *or* veuve, *f.*

feminality [femi'næliti] *or* **femineity** [-'ni:iti], *or* **femininity**, *n.* Féminéité, *f.*

feminine ['feminin], *a.* Féminin. *In the feminine gender*, (*Gram.*) au féminin. **femininely**, *adv.* En femme. **feminism**, *n.* Féminisme, *m.* **feminist**, *n.* Féministe. **feminization** [-'zeiʃən], *n.* Féminisation, *f.* **feminize**, *v.t.* Féminiser.

femoral ['femərəl], *a.* Fémoral.

femur ['fi:mə], *n.* (*Med.*) Fémur, *m.*

fen [fen], *n.* Marais, marécage, *m.*

fence [fens], *n.* Clôture, enceinte; palissade, barrière; (*Turf*) haie; escrime (art of fencing); (*fig.*) défense, *f.*; (*slang*) receleur (of stolen goods), *m. To sit on the fence*, (*fig.*) ne pas s'engager, ménager la chèvre et le chou.—*v.t.* Enclore, mettre une clôture à, palissader; (*fig.*) protéger, défendre. *To fence in*, enclore. —*v.i.* Faire des armes, tirer des armes; parer. ***fenceless**, *a.* Ouvert; (*fig.*) sans défense.

fencer ['fensə], *n.* Escrimeur, tireur (d'armes), *m.*; cheval bon sauteur de haies, *m.* ***fencibles**, *n.pl.* Miliciens (soldats pour la défense du territoire, lesquels ne peuvent être envoyés à l'étranger), *m.pl.* **fencing**, *n.* Escrime; enceinte, clôture, *f.* **fencing-master**, *n.* Maître d'armes, maître d'escrime, *m.* **fencing-match**, *n.* Assaut d'armes, *m.* **fencing-school**, *n.* Salle d'armes, *f.*

fend [fend], *v.t.* Se garder (de); détourner. *To fend off*, parer.—*v.i.* *To fend for oneself*, se débrouiller, veiller à ses intérêts.

fender ['fendə], *n.* Garde-feu, *m.*; (*Naut.*) défense, *f.*; (*Motor.*) aile, *f.*

fennel [fenl], *n.* (*Bot.*) Fenouil, *m.*

fenny ['feni], *a.* Marécageux, des marais.

fenugreek ['fenju:gri:k], *n.* (*Bot.*) Fenugrec, *m.*

feoff [fef], *v.t.* Investir d'un fief, donner l'investiture à; (*fig.*) douer. **feoffee**, *n.* Personne investie d'un héritage foncier, *f.*

feoffment, *n.* Inféodation; investiture d'un héritage foncier, *f.*

feracious [fə'reiʃəs], *a.* Fertile, fécond.

feracity [fə'ræsiti], *n.* Fertilité, *f.*

feral ['fiərəl], *a.* Sauvage.

feretory ['feritri], *n.* Châsse, *f.*

ferial ['fiəriəl], *a.* Férial; férié.

ferment (1) ['fə:mənt], *n.* Ferment, *m.*; fermentation, *f.*

ferment (2) [fə:'ment], *v.i.* Fermenter.—*v.t.* Faire fermenter; (*fig.*) exciter. **fermentable**, *a.* Fermentable. **fermentation** [-'teiʃən], *n.* Fermentation, *f.* **fermentative**, *a.* Fermentatif; de fermentation.

fern [fə:n], *n.* Fougère, *f.* **fern-brake**, **fernery**, *n.* Fougeraie, *f.* **fern-owl**, *n.* Engoulevent, *m.* **fern-stand**, *n.* Jardinière à fougères, *f.* **ferny**, *a.* Plein de fougères, couvert de fougères.

ferocious [fə'rouʃəs], *a.* Féroce. **ferociously**, *adv.* Avec férocité, d'une manière féroce. **ferociousness** *or* **ferocity** [fə'rɔsiti], *n.* Férocité, *f.*

ferreous ['feriəs], *a.* Ferrugineux.

ferret ['ferit], *n.* Furet, *m.*; padou (tape), *m.* —*v.t.* Fureter. *To ferret out*, dépister, dénicher.—*v.i.* Chasser au furet, fureter. **ferreter**, *n.* Fureteur, *m.*

ferric ['ferik], *a.* Ferrique.

ferriferous [fe'rifərəs], *a.* Ferrifère. **ferro-concrete**, *n.* Béton armé, *m.* **ferrocyanide**, *n.* Ferrocyanure, *m.*

ferruginous [fə'ru:dʒinəs], *a.* Ferrugineux.

ferrule ['feru:l], *n.* Virole (ring), *f.*; ['ferəl] bout (ferré), embout, *m.* (of umbrella, stick).

ferry ['feri], *v.t.* Passer en bac. *To ferry over*, passer.—*n.* Bac, passage, *m. Aerial ferry*, pont transbordeur, *m.*; *air-ferry*, avion transbordeur, *m.* **ferry-boat**, *n.* Bac, bateau transbordeur de trains, *m.* **ferryman**, *n.* Passeur; (*poet.*) nocher, *m.*

fertile ['fə:tail], *a.* Fertile, fécond. **fertility** [-'tiliti] *or* **fertileness**, *n.* Fertilité, fécondité, *f.*

fertilization [fə:tilai'zeiʃən], *n.* Fertilisation, *f.*

fertilize, *v.t.* Fertiliser. **fertilizer**, *n.* Fertilisant, engrais, *m.*

ferula ['ferulə], *n.* Sceptre impérial (of the Eastern empire), *m.*; (*Bot.*) férule, *f.*

ferule ['feru:l], *n.* Férule, *f.*

fervency ['fə:vənsi], *n.* Ardeur, ferveur, *f.* **fervent**, *a.* Ardent, fervent, vif. **fervently**, *adv.* Ardemment, avec ferveur.

fervid ['fə:vid], *a.* Ardent, passionné; chaud, brûlant. **fervidly**, *adv.* Avec chaleur, ardemment. **fervidness** *or* **fervour**, *n.* Ferveur, ardeur, chaleur, *f.*

fescennine ['fesənain], *a.* (*Rom. Ant.*) Fescennin.

fescue ['feskju:], *n.* (*sch.*) Baguette (pointer), *f.* **fescue-grass**, *n.* Fétuque, *f.*

fesse [fes], *n.* (*Her.*) Fasce, *f.* **fessy**, *a.* Fascé.

festal ['festəl], *a.* De fête. **festally**, *adv.* Joyeusement.

fester ['festə], *v.i.* S'ulcérer; (*fig.*) se corrompre, s'envenimer.—*n.* Abcès, *m.*, pustule, *f.*

festival ['festivəl], *a.* De fête, de festin, joyeux, gai.—*n.* Fête, *f.*; (*Mus.*, *Theat.*) festival, *m.* **festive**, *a.* De fête, de festin, joyeux.

festivity [fes'tiviti], *n.* Fête, *f.*; réjouissances, *f.pl.*

festoon [fes'tu:n], *n.* Feston, *m.*—*v.t.* Festonner (de).—*v.i.* Pendre en festons.

fetch [fetʃ], *v.t.* Chercher, aller chercher; apporter (bring); amener (persons etc.); puiser, tirer (to draw); prendre, reprendre (one's breath); amorcer (a pump); pousser (a sigh); porter, asséner (a blow); rapporter, valoir (a price). *These goods fetch a great deal*, cette marchandise rapporte beaucoup; *this repair will fetch about twenty pounds*, cette réparation ira chercher dans les vingt livres; *to come and fetch*, aller chercher; *to fetch away*, emporter, emmener; *to fetch back*, rapporter, ramener; *to fetch down*, faire descendre, descendre, rabattre; *to fetch in*, faire entrer; *to fetch off*, enlever, emporter, emmener; *to fetch out*, faire sortir, emporter; *to fetch up*, faire monter, monter; vomir; s'arrêter.—*v.i.* Se mouvoir.—*n.* Ruse, *f.*; tour, stratagème, *m.*; (*Naut.*) virage, *m.* **fetcher**, *n.* Chercheur, *m.*, -euse, *f.*, rapporteur (of dogs), *m.* **fetching**, *a.* Séduisant, attrayant.

fête [feit], *n.* Fête, *f.*—*v.t.* Fêter.

fetid ['fi:tid], *a.* Fétide. **fetidity** [fe'tiditi] or **fetidness**, *n.* Fétidité, *f.*

fetish ['fi:tiʃ] or ['fetiʃ], *n.* Fétiche, *m.* **fetishism**, *n.* Fétichisme, *m.*

fetlock ['fetlɔk], *n.* Fanon (du cheval), *m.* **fetlock-joint**, *n.* Boulet, *m.*

fetter ['fetə], *v.t.* Entraver, enchaîner. *To fetter a horse*, entraver un cheval. **fetterless**, *a.* Sans entraves, sans fers, libre. **fetterlock**, *n.* Entrave, *f.* **fetters**, *n.pl.* (*fig.*) Fers, *m.pl.*, chaînes; entraves (for a horse), *f.pl.*

fettle [fetl], *v.t.* Arranger, préparer.—*v.i.* Être occupé à ranger.—*n.* Bon état, *m.*

fetus [FOETUS].

feu [fju:], *n.* (*Sc.*) Bail perpétuel moyennant une certaine redevance, *m.*—*v.t.* Accorder un tel bail.

feud (1) [fju:d], *n.* Querelle, inimitié (de clans); vendetta, *f.*

feud (2) [fju:d], *n.* Fief, *m.* **feudal**, *a.* Féodal. **feudalism**, *n.* Féodalité, *f.*, système féodal, *m.* **feudalist**, *n.* Feudiste, *m.* **feudality** [fju:'dæliti], *n.* Féodalité, *f.* **feudatory** ['fju:dətəri], *a.* and *n.* Feudataire, vassal.

fever ['fi:və], *n.* Fièvre, *f.* *To be in a fever*, avoir la fièvre; *trench-fever*, fièvre des tranchées, *f.*—*v.t.* Donner la fièvre à.—*v.i.* Avoir la fièvre. **fever-hospital**, *n.* Hôpital de fiévreux, *m.* **fever-stricken**, *a.* Atteint de la fièvre.

feverfew ['fi:vəfju:], *n.* (*Bot.*) Pyrexie, *f.*; pyrèthre, *m.*, matricaire, *f.*

feverish, *a.* Fiévreux; (*fig.*) fébrile. **feverishly**, *adv.* Fébrilement. **feverishness**, *n.* État fiévreux, *m.*

few [fju:], *a.* Peu de. *A few*, quelques; *every few days*, à quelques jours d'intervalle, tous les deux ou trois jours; *few and far between*, rares et espacés; *few people think thus*, peu de gens pensent ainsi; *give me a few pears*, donnez-moi quelques poires; *one of the few good ministers*, un des rares bons ministres.—*n.* Peu de gens, *m.pl.*, peu de personnes, *f.pl.* *A few*, quelques-uns, *m.pl.*, quelques-unes, *f.pl.*; *a good few*, un bon nombre; *not a few*, assez nombreux. **fewer**, *a.* Moins (de); moins nombreux. **fewest**, *a.* Le moins de. **fewness**, *n.* Petit nombre, *m.*

fey [fei], *a.* Voué à la mort; de l'autre monde.

fez [fez], *n.* Fez, *m.*

fiancé [fjã'se], *n.* (*fem.* **-ée**) Fiancé, *m.*, fiancée, *f.*

fiasco [fi'æskou], *n.* Fiasco, four, *m.* *To be a fiasco*, faire fiasco or four.

fiat ['faiət], *n.* Autorisation, *f.*; ordre, commandement, décret, *m.*

fib [fib], *n.* Petit mensonge, *m.*—*v.i.* Mentir, dire des contes. **fibber**, *n.* Menteur, *m.*, -euse, *f.*, faiseur de contes, *m.*, -euse, *f.*

fibre ['faibə], *n.* Fibre, *f.* **fibril**, *n.* Fibrille, *f.* **fibrillar**, *a.* Fibrillaire. **fibrillation** [-ri'leiʃən], *n.* Fibrillation, *f.* **fibrillous**, *a.* Fibrilleux. **fibrin**, *n.* Fibrine, *f.* **fibrinous**, *a.* Fibrineux.

fibroma [fai'broumə], *n.* Fibrome, *m.*

fibrositis [faibrə'saitis], *n.* (*Med.*) Cellulite, *f.* **fibrous** ['faibrəs], *a.* Fibreux.

fibula ['fibjulə], *n.* (*Anat.*) Péroné, *m.*; (*Ant.*) fibule, *f.*

fickle [fikl], *a.* Volage, inconstant. *A fickle light*, une lumière incertaine. **fickleness**, *n.* Inconstance, légèreté, *f.*

fictile ['fiktil], *a.* Plastique; céramique.

fiction ['fikʃən], *n.* Fiction, *f.* *What he says is pure fiction*, ce qu'il dit c'est de pure invention. *Works of fiction*, ouvrages d'imagination, romans, *m.pl.* **fictional**, *a.* De romans.

fictionize, *v.t.* Romancer.

fictitious [-'tiʃəs], *a.* Fictif, imaginaire; (*fig.*) faux, factice. **fictitiously**, *adv.* Fictivement. **fictitiousness**, *n.* Caractère fictif, *m.* **fictive**, *a.* Fictif.

fid [fid], *n.* (*Naut.*) Épissoir (for splicing), *m.*; clef (of a mast), *f.*; coin, *m.*, cale, *f.*; tas, *m.*

fiddle [fidl], *n.* Violon; (*pej.*) crincrin, *m.*; (*pop.*) resquille, combine, *f.* *It's not honest, it's a fiddle*, ce n'est pas honnête, c'est une resquille; *to play second fiddle to*, (*fig.*) faire second violon à, jouer le second rôle.—*v.i.* Jouer du violon; (*fig.*) baguenauder, niaiser (to trifle); (*pop.*) faire la combine, resquiller. *To be always fiddling*, perdre son temps à des riens.—*v.t.* Jouer (un air) sur le violon. **fiddle-bow**, *n.* Archet, *m.* **fiddle-de-dee**, *int.* Turlututu; tatata! **fiddle-faddle**, *n.* Fadaises, niaiseries, sornettes, *f.pl.*—*a.* Niais. **fiddle-stick**, *n.* Archet de violon, *m.* **fiddlesticks!** *int.* Bah! quelle blague! **fiddle-string**, *n.* Corde de violon, *f.*

fiddler ['fidlə], *n.* Joueur de violon; (*pej.*) violoneux; ménétrier, *m.* **fiddling** ['fidliŋ], *n.* Raclage (of violin), *m.*; (*fig.*) niaiserie, *f.*; tripotage, baguenaudage, *m.*—*a.* Frivole, musard, insignifiant.

fidei-commissary ['faidiai-'kɔmisəri], *a.* (*Law*) Fidéicommissaire. **fidei-commission**, *n.* Fidéicommis, *m.*

fidelity [fi'deliti], *n.* Fidélité, *f.*

fidget ['fidʒit], *n.* Agitation, *f.*, crispations, *f.pl.*; être remuant (person), *m.* *It gives me the fidgets*, cela me donne des crispations; *what a fidget you are!* comme vous êtes énervé!—*v.i.* Se remuer, se tourmenter, s'agiter. **fidgety**, *a.* Remuant, agité; ennuyeux (troublesome).

fidibus ['faidibəs], *n.* Papillote, allumette de papier, *f.*

fiducial [fi'dju:ʃəl], *a.* Fiduciel. **fiducially**, *adv.* Fiduciairement. **fiduciary**, *a.* and *n.* Fiduciaire, *m.*

fie! [fai], *int.* Fi! fi donc! *Fie upon* . . .!
fi de . . .!

fief [fi:f], *n.* Fief, *m.*

field [fi:ld], *n.* Champ, *m.*; pré (meadow), *m.*;
(*Mil.*) campagne, *f.*; champ de bataille, *m.*,
bataille, *f.*; banc (of ice), *m.*; (*Turf etc.*)
courants, *m.pl.* *Battle-field*, champ de
bataille, *m.*; *field of fire*, champ de tir, *m.*;
in the field, en campagne, aux champs; *in the
open field*, en plein champ; *in the scientific
field*, dans le domaine des sciences; *on the
field*, sur le terrain (duelling); *to take the field*,
(*Mil.*) se mettre en campagne.—*v.i.* (*Cricket*)
Tenir le champ.—*v.t.* (*Cricket*) Arrêter (a
ball); réunir (a team). **field-artillery**, *n.*
Artillerie de campagne, *f.* **field-battery**, *n.*
Batterie de campagne, *f.* **field-day**, *n.* (*Mil.*)
Jour de revue *or* de manœuvres; (*fig.*) grand
jour, jour de grand succès, *m.* **field-dressing**,
n. (*Mil.*) Pansement individuel, *m.* **fieldfare**, *n.* Litorne, tourdelle, *f.* **field-glass**, *n.*
Jumelle, lorgnette, *f.* **field-gun**, *n.* Pièce de
campagne, *f.* **field-hospital**, *n.* Hôpital de
campagne, *m.*, ambulance, *f.* **field-marshal**,
n. Maréchal, *m.* **field-mouse**, *n.* Mulot, *m.*
field-officer, *n.* Officier supérieur, *m.*
field-piece, *n.* Pièce de campagne, *f.* **field-
sports**, *n.pl.* Exercices de plein air, *m.pl.*,
chasse et pêche, *f.* **field-surgeon**, *n.*
Chirurgien d'ambulance, *m.* **field-survey**,
n. Service géographique, *m.* **field-work**, *n.*
Travaux pratiques, *m.pl.* **field-works**, *n.pl.*
(*Mil.*) Ouvrages de campagne, *m.pl.*

fiend [fi:nd], *n.* Démon, *m.* **fiendish**, *a.*
Diabolique, infernal. **fiendishness**, *n.*
Méchanceté infernale, *f.*

fierce [fiə:s], *a.* Violent, brutal, féroce,
farouche, furieux. **fiercely**, *adv.* Férocement, furieusement. **fierceness**, *n.* Violence,
fureur, brutalité, *f.*; (*fig.*) acharnement, *m.*,
ardeur, impétuosité, *f.*

fieriness ['faiərinis], *n.* Fougue, ardeur, *f.*,
emportement, *m.* **fiery**, *a.* De feu; enflammé, de flamme; (terrain) très sec; (*fig.*)
ardent, fougueux, bouillant.

fife [faif], *n.* Fifre, *m.*—*v.i.* Jouer du fifre.
fifer, *n.* Fifre, *m.* **fiferail**, *n.* (*Naut.*)
Râtelier, *m.*

fifteen [fif'ti:n], *a.* and *n.* Quinze, *m.* **fifteenth**, *a.* and *n.* Quinzième, *m.*; quinze (of
the days of the month etc.). **fifteenthly**, *adv.*
Quinzièmement.

fifth [fifθ], *a.* Cinquième; cinq (of the days of
the month etc.). *Charles the Fifth*, Charles-
Quint; *Pope Sixtus the Fifth*, le pape Sixte-
Quint. *Fifth form*, la (classe de) seconde.—*n.*
Cinquième, *m.*; (*Mus.*) quinte, *f.* **fifthly**,
adv. Cinquièmement.

fiftieth ['fiftiiθ], *a.* and *n.* Cinquantième, *m.*

fifty, *a.* and *n.* Cinquante, *m.* *About fifty*,
une cinquantaine; *fifty-one*, cinquante et un;
to go fifty-fifty with, se mettre de moitié avec.
fiftyfold, *a.* Cinquante fois.

fig [fig], *n.* Figue, *f.*; figuier (tree), *m.* *A fig
for!* foin de! fi de! *in full fig*, en grande
toilette, (*Mil.*) en grande tenue; *not to care a
fig for*, se moquer de, (*pop.*) se ficher pas mal
de. **fig-eater**, *n.* Bec-figue (bird), *m.* **fig-
leaf**, *n.* Feuille de figuier, *f.* **fig-marigold**,
n. Ficoïde, *f.* **fig-tree**, *n.* Figuier, *m.* **figwort**, *n.* Scrofulaire; ficaire, *f.*

fight [fait], *v.i.* (*past* and *p.p.* **fought** [fɔ:t]) Se
battre; combattre (avec); (*fig.*) lutter. *To
fight shy of*, se méfier de, éviter.—*v.t.* Se
battre avec, combattre; livrer (a battle). *To
fight a duel*, se battre en duel; *to fight a
question*, débattre une question; *to fight it out*,
lutter jusqu'au bout; *to fight off*, repousser;
to fight one's way, se frayer un chemin; *to
fight the battles of one's country*, combattre
pour son pays.—*n.* Combat, *m.*, bataille,
action; (*fig.*) lutte, *f.* *Free fight*, bagarre,
mêlée générale, *f.*; *in the thick of the fight*, au
fort de la bataille; *to have a fight*, se battre;
to show fight, to be full of fight, montrer les
dents. **fighter**, *n.* Combattant; (*pej.*) batailleur, ferrailleur, *m.*; (*Av.*) chasseur, *m.* *Prize-
fighter*, boxeur de profession, *m.*; *prize-
fighting*, boxe professionnelle, *f.*; match de
boxe (pour un prix), *m.* **fighting**, *n.* Combat,
m.; rixe, lutte, *f.* *Fighting line*, ligne de
combat, *f.* **fighting-men**, *n.pl.* Combattants, hommes disponibles, *m.pl.* **fighting-
top**, *n.* (*Navy*) Hune militaire, *f.*

figment ['figmənt], *n.* Fiction, invention,
f.

figurable ['figjuərəbl], *a.* Figurable.

figurant ['figjuərənt], *n.* (*Theat.*) Figurant, *m.*,
-ante, *f.*

figuration [figjuə'reiʃən], *n.* Configuration, *f.*,
contour, *m.*, silhouette, *f.* (of thing); représentation figurative, allégorie, *f.*; ornementation (of embroidery), *f.*; (*Mus.*) contrepoint
fleuri, *m.*

figurative ['figjuərətiv], *a.* Figuré; figuratif,
allégorique, métaphorique. *In a figurative
sense*, au figuré. **figuratively**, *adv.* Au
figuré; figurativement. **figurativeness**, *n.*
Caractère métaphorique, *m.*

figure ['figə], *n.* Figure; taille, tournure (of
a person), *f.*; personnage, *m.*, personnalité, *f.*;
dessin (on stuffs); (*Arith.*) chiffre, *m.* *Academical figure*, académie, *f.*; *figure of speech*,
façon de parler, *f.*; *fine figure*, belle taille, *f.*;
lay figure, mannequin, *m.*; *to cut a figure*,
faire figure; *to reach three figures*, monter à
cent.—*v.t.* Figurer, former; façonner; (*fig.*)
imaginer. *To figure out*, calculer.—*v.i.*
Figurer. *To figure out*, se chiffrer; *to figure to
oneself*, se figurer, s'imaginer. **figured**, *a.*
À dessin. **figure-drawing**, *n.* Dessin de
figure, *m.* **figure-head**, *n.* (*Naut.*) Figure
de proue, *f.*, buste; (*fig.*) homme de paille,
prête-nom, *m.* **figure-skating**, *n.* Patinage
de fantaisie; tracé des figures sur la glace, *m.*
figurine, *n.* Figurine, *f.*

Fiji ['fi:dʒi:]. *The Fiji Islands*, les îles Fidji *or*
Viti, *f.pl.*

filament ['filəmənt], *n.* Filament, *m.* **filamentous** [-'mentəs], *a.* Filamenteux.

filbert ['filbə:t], *n.* Aveline, grosse noisette, *f.*
filbert-tree, *n.* Avelinier, *m.*

filch [filtʃ], *v.t.* Escamoter, filouter, chiper.
filcher, *n.* Filou, chipeur, *m.*

file [fail], *n.* Lime (tool), *f.*; liasse, *f.*, dossier,
classeur (of papers), *m.*; liste (list); collection
(of newspapers); (*Mil.*) file; (*Theat.* etc.)
queue, *f.* *Card-index file*, fichier, *m.*; *cunning
old file*, vieux finaud, *m.*; *in Indian file*, en
file indienne; *in single file*, un à un; *rat-tail
file*, queue de rat, *f.*; *to stand in file*, faire
queue.—*v.t.* Limer; affiler; mettre en liasse;
(*Law*) déposer (a petition etc.). *To file away*,
classer.—*v.i.* (*Mil.*) Marcher à la file. *To file*

off, défiler; *to file out*, sortir à la file. **file-cutter**, *n*. Tailleur de limes, *m*. **file-leader**, *n*. Chef de file, *m*. **filer**, *n*. Limeur, *m*.
filial ['filiəl], *a*. Filial. **filiality** [fili'æliti], *n*. Filialité, *f*. **filially**, *adv*. Filialement. **filiation** [-'eiʃən], *n*. Filiation, *f*.
filibuster ['filibʌstə], *n*. Flibustier, *m*.—*v.i.* Faire le flibustier, flibuster. (*Polit*.) *Filibustering tactics*, manœuvres obstructives, *f.pl.*
filiform ['filifɔ:m], *a*. Filiforme.
filigree ['filigri:] or ***filigrane**, *n*. Filigrane, *m*.—*v.t.* Filigraner. **filigreed**, *a*. À filigrane.
filing ['failin], *n*. Limure, *f*.; mise en liasse, *f*., classement, *m*. *Filing off*, défilé, *m*., défilade, *f*. **filing-cabinet**, *n*. Cartonnier, classeur, *m*. **filings**, *n.pl*. Limaille, *f.sing*.
fill [fil], *v.t.* Emplir, remplir; combler (fill up), boucher; bourrer (to stuff); occuper; rassasier. *To fill a pipe*, bourrer une pipe; *to fill a post*, occuper un poste; *to fill a tooth*, plomber une dent; *to fill in*, remplir, insérer (insert); *to fill the bill*, faire l'affaire; *to fill up*, remplir, combler, compléter; *to fill up the time by*, employer le temps à; *the wind fills the sails*, le vent gonfle les voiles.—*v.i.* Se remplir, s'emplir. *To fill out*, se gonfler, s'enfler, prendre de l'embonpoint (to get stout).—*n*. Suffisance, *f*.; (*colloq*.) *One's fill*, tout son soûl. **filler**, *n*. Remplisseur, *m*.
fillet ['filit], *n*. Bandeau; filet (of meat or fish), *m*. *Fillet of beef*, filet de bœuf, *m*.; *fillet of veal*, rouelle de veau, *f*.—*v.t.* Ceindre d'un bandeau; détacher les filets de. *Filleted sole*, filet de sole, *m*.
filling ['filin], *n*. Action de remplir, remplissage; chargement (of waggon etc.); bourrage (of pipe); gonflement (of balloon); remblayage (of ditch); plombage (of teeth), *m*. —*a*. Qui remplit; rassasiant. **filling-station**, *n*. Poste d'essence, *m*.
fillip ['filip], *n*. Chiquenaude, *f*., (*fig*.) coup de fouet, *m*.—*v.t.* Donner une chiquenaude à; (*fig*.) encourager.
fillister ['filistə], *n*. Bouvet, *m*. (tool).
filly ['fili], *n*. Pouliche; (*fig*.) jeune fille pleine d'entrain, *f*.
film [film], *n*. Taie (over the eyes), pellicule; (*Anat*.) tunique, *f*.; (*fig*.) nuage, voile, *m*.; (*Phot*.) couche sensible, *f*.; (*Cine*.) film, *m*. *Film club, film society*, ciné-club, *m*.; *film director*, cinéaste, metteur en scène, *m*.; *film fan*, amateur de cinéma, cinéphile, *m*.; *film library*, cinémathèque, *f*.; *film star*, vedette de cinéma, *f*.; *serial film*, film à épisodes, *m*.; *talking film*, film parlant, *m*.—*v.t.* Couvrir d'une tunique, d'une pellicule, etc.; filmer, mettre à l'écran.—*v.i.* Tourner un film. *To film well*, être photogénique. **film-script**, *n*. Scénario, script, *m*. **film-strip**, *n*. Film fixe, *m*.
filmic, *a*. Qui appartient au cinéma, à l'écran, filmique. **filmy**, *a*. Couvert d'une pellicule, d'un voile léger.
filter ['filtə], *n*. Filtre, *m*.—*v.t.* Filtrer. **filtering**, *a*. Filtrant. **filtering-machine**, *n*. Filtre, *m*. **filter-tip**, *n*. Bout filtrant, *m*. (of cigarette).
filth [filθ], *n*. Ordure, saleté; (*fig*.) corruption, *f*. **filthily**, *adv*. Salement. **filthiness**, *n*. Saleté, *f*. **filthy**, *a*. Sale, immonde; (*fig*.) obscène, infect.

filtrate ['filtreit], *v.t.* Filtrer. **filtration** [-'treiʃən], *n*. Filtration, *f*.
fimbriate ['fimbriat], *a*. (*Bot*.) Fimbrié, frangé, bordé.—*v.t.* [-eit] Franger, border.
fin [fin], *n*. Nageoire, *f*.; aileron, *m*. (of shark); (*Naut., Av*.) dérive, *f*.; (*Motor*.) ailette, *f*. (of radiator).
finable ['fainəbl], *a*. Passible d'amende.
final [fainl], *a*. Final, dernier, définitif, décisif.—*n*. (*spt*.) Finale, *f*.; (*pl*.) (*Univ*.) examen final, *m*.
finale [fi'na:li], *n*. (*Mus*.) Finale, *m*.
finalist ['fainəlist], *n*. (*spt*.) Finaliste. **finality**, *n*. Caractère décisif, *m*.; (*Phil*.) finalité, *f*.
finally ['fainəli], *adv*. Enfin, finalement, définitivement, en dernier lieu.
finance [fi'næns] or [fai-], *n*. Finance, *f*.; (*pl*.) finances, *f.pl*. *High finance*, la haute finance, *f*.; *his finances are in a bad way*, ses fonds sont bas. **financial** [fi'nænʃəl], *a*. Financier. **financially**, *adv*. En matière de finances.
financier [fi'nænsiə], *n*. Financier, *m*.
finch [fintʃ], *n*. (*Orn*.) Pinson, *m*. *Thistle* (or *yellow*) *finch*, chardonneret, *m*.
find [faind], *v.t.* (*past* and *p.p.* **found**) Trouver; découvrir, constater, estimer; (*Law*) déclarer (guilty); rendre, prononcer (a verdict); (*fig*.) pourvoir. *To find again*, retrouver; *to find fault with*, trouver à redire à; *to find in*, pourvoir de; *to find it necessary to*, se voir obligé de; *to find oneself in*, se fournir de, se pourvoir de; *to find out*, trouver, découvrir, inventer; démasquer; *to find out about*, se renseigner sur; découvrir la vérité de.—*n*. Découverte, trouvaille, *f*. **findable**, *a*. Trouvable. **finder**, *n*. Trouveur, *m*., -euse, *f*. **finding**, *n*. (*Law*) Conclusion, *f*., verdict, *m*.; découverte, *f*. *Findings is keepings*, ce qui est bon à prendre est bon à garder.
fine (1) [fain], *n*. Amende, *f*.—*v.t.* Mettre à l'amende; condamner (quelqu'un) à une amende de.
fine (2) [fain], *a*. Fin, pur; raffiné, délicat; rusé, subtil; beau (handsome); (*fig*.) bon, excellent, accompli; (*colloq*.) joli, fameux. *Fine feathers make fine birds*, la belle plume fait le bel oiseau; *it is fine*, il fait beau (of the weather); *not to put too fine a point on it*, pour ne pas mâcher les mots; *that is all very fine, but . . .*, tout cela est très joli, mais . . . .—*adv*. *To cut it fine*, arriver de justesse.—*v.t.* Affiner (to refine); coller, clarifier (wine).—*int*. À la bonne heure! **fine arts**, *n.pl*. Beaux arts, *m.pl*. **fine-draw**, *v.t.* Faire une reprise perdue à.—*v.i.* Rentraire. **fine-drawer**, Rentrayeur, *m*., -euse, *f*. **fine-drawing**, *n*. Reprises perdues, *f.pl*. **fine-drawn**, *a*. Filé fin; (*fig*.) subtil; (*spt*.) très entraîné. **finely**, *adv*. Fin, délicatement, subtilement; élégamment; (*colloq*.) bien; (*iron*.) joliment. **fineness**, *n*. Finesse, délicatesse; élégance, subtilité, *f*., titre, *m*. (of gold). **finer**, *n*. Affineur, *m*. **finery**, *n*. Parure, *f*., beaux habits, *m.pl*. **fine-spoken**, *a*. Beau parleur, *m*. **fine-spun**, *a*. Filé fin; (*fig*.) subtil.
finesse [fi'nes], *n*. Finesse; finasserie, *f*.—*v.i.* User de finesse; (*Whist etc*.) finasser.
finger ['fingə], *n*. Doigt, *m*.; (*fig*.) main, *f*. *He has a finger in every pie*, il fourre son nez partout; *he will not lift a finger to help you*, ne remuera pas le petit doigt pour vous

aider; *to blow on one's fingers*, souffler dans ses doigts; *to have at one's finger-tips*, savoir sur le bout du doigt; *to keep one's fingers crossed*, toucher du bois; *to point with one's finger*, montrer du doigt *or* au doigt.—*v.t.* Toucher, manier. *To finger a piece of music*, doigter un morceau de musique.—*v.i.* (*Mus.*) Doigter. **finger-biscuit,** *n.* Langue-de-chat, *f.* **finger-board,** *n.* Manche (of a violin), clavier (of piano), *m.* **finger-bowl** or **-glass,** *n.* Rince-bouche, rince-doigts, *m.* **fingered,** *a. Light-fingered gentry*, gens aux doigts crochus, *m.pl.* **fingering,** *n.* Maniement; ouvrage délicat; (*Mus.*) doigté, *m.* **fingerling,** *n.* Saumoneau, parr, *m.* **finger-nail,** *n.* Ongle de la main, *m.* **finger-post,** *n.* Poteau indicateur *m.* **finger-print,** *n.* Empreinte digitale, *f.* **finger-stall,** *n.* Doigtier, *m.*

finial ['finial], *n.* (*Arch.*) Fleuron, épi, *m.*

finical ['finikəl], **finicking,** or (*colloq.*) **finicky,** *a.* Précieux, affété, méticuleux. **finically,** *adv.* Précieusement, avec afféterie. **finicalness,** *n.* Afféterie, *f.*

fining ['fainiŋ], *n.* (*Metal.*) Affinage, *m.*; clarification, *f.*; collage (of wine), *m.* **fining-forge,** *n.* Forge d'affinage, *f.* **fining-pot,** *n.* Creuset, *m.*

finis ['fainis], *n.* Fin, *f.* (of a book).

finish ['finiʃ], *v.t.* Finir, terminer; achever, consommer; (*Tech.*) usiner. *To finish off*, mettre la dernière main à; expédier (wounded animal).—*v.i.* Cesser, finir, prendre fin. *To finish third* (in race), arriver troisième.—*n.* Fini, *m.*; (*fig.*) fin, *f.*; (*spt.*) arrivée, *f.* **finished,** *a.* Fini; (*fig.*) parfait, soigné. **finisher,** *n.* Personne qui finit, *f.*, fini finisseur, *m.*, -euse, *f.*; (*fig.*) le coup de grâce, *m.* **finishing,** *a.* Qui complète; dernier. (*spt.*) *Finishing* line, ligne d'arrivée, *f.*; *finishing school*, école de perfectionnement (pour jeunes filles), *f.*; *finishing stroke*, dernière main, *f.*, coup de grâce, *m.*

finite ['fainait], *a.* Fini; borné. **finitely,** *adv.* Dans de certaines limites. **finiteness,** *n.* Caractère fini, *m.*

Finland ['finlənd]. La Finlande, *f.*

finless ['finlis], *a.* Sans nageoires. **finlike,** *a.* En forme de nageoire. **finned,** *a.* À nageoires. **finny,** *a.* Qui a des nageoires, à nageoires. *The finny tribe*, la race qui habite les eaux, *f.*, les poissons, *m.pl.*

Finn [fin], *n.* Finlandais, *m.*, -aise, *f.*, Finnois, *m.*, -oise, *f.* **Finnish,** *a.* Finlandais, *m.*, -aise, *f.*—*n.* Le finnois, *m.* (language).

finnan ['finən], *n.* Aiglefin fumé, *m.*

fiord [fjɔ:d], *n.* Fiord, *m.*

fiorin ['faiərin], *n.* (*Bot.*) Agrostide (grass), *f.*

fir [fə:], *n.* Sapin; bois de sapin, *m.* **fir-cone,** *n.* Pomme de pin, *f.* **fir-grove,** *n.* Sapinière, *f.* **fir-tree,** *n.* Sapin, *m.*

fire [faiə], *n.* Feu, incendie (house etc. on fire), *m.*; (*fig.*) fougue, ardeur, *f.* *Blue fire*, feu de Bengale, *m.*; (*Theat.*) gros effets, *m.pl.*; *cross fire*, feu croisé, *m.*; *enfilade fire*, feu d'enfilade, *m.*; *fire!* au feu! *he will never set the Thames on fire*, il n'a pas inventé la poudre; *heavy fire*, feu nourri, *m.*; *long-range fire*, tir à longue portée, *m.*; *open fire*, feu dans la cheminée; *running fire*, feu roulant, *m.*; *St. Anthony's fire*, érysipèle, *m.*; *to add fuel to the fire*, jeter de l'huile sur le feu; *to be on fire*, être en feu, en flammes; *to be under fire*,

essuyer le feu; *to catch fire*, prendre feu; *to cease fire*, cesser le feu; *to go through fire and water for*, se jeter au feu pour; *to hang fire*, faire long feu; *to make a fire*, faire du feu; *to miss fire*, rater; *to put out a fire*, éteindre un feu *or* un incendie; *to put to fire and sword*, mettre à feu et à sang; *to set on fire, to set fire to*, mettre le feu à; *to take fire*, s'enflammer, (*fig.*) se mettre en colère.—*v.t.* Mettre le feu à; embraser, incendier, enflammer; tirer, décharger (fire-arms); (*pop.*) renvoyer, mettre à la porte. *To fire off*, tirer, décharger; *to fire with*, enflammer de.—*v.i.* Prendre feu; s'enflammer; tirer, faire feu (sur); (*Motor.*) donner (of engine); *fire!* (*Mil.*) feu! faites feu! *fire away*, commencez! (*colloq.*) vas-y! *to fire at*, faire feu sur; *to fire up*, s'enflammer, prendre feu, s'emporter.

fire-alarm, *n.* Avertisseur d'incendie, *m.* **fire-arms,** *n.pl.* Armes à feu, *f.pl.* **fire-ball,** *n.* Pot à feu, *m.*; (*Meteor.*) globe de feu, bolide, *m.* **fire-balloon,** *n.* Montgolfière, *f.* **fire-box,** *n.* Foyer, *m.* **fire-brand,** *n.* Tison, *m.*; (*fig.*) boutefeu, brandon (de discorde), *m.* **fire-brick,** *n.* Brique réfractaire, *f.* **fire-brigade,** *n.* (Corps de) sapeurs pompiers, *m.* **fire-bucket,** *n.* Seau à incendie, *m.* **fire-clay,** *n.* Argile réfractaire, *f.* **fire-control,** *n.* (*Mil.*) Direction du tir, *f.* **firecracker,** *n.* Pétard, *m.* **firecrest,** *n.* Roitelet à moustache, roitelet à triple bandeau, *m.* **fire-damp,** *n.* (Feu) grisou, *m.* **fire-dog,** *n.* Chenet, *m.* **fire-eater,** *n.* Mangeur de feu, *m.* **fire-engine,** *n.* Pompe à incendie, *f.* **fire-escape,** *n.* Échelle de sauvetage, *f.* **fire-extinguisher,** *n.* Extincteur, *m.* **fire-fly,** *n.* Lampyre, *m.*, luciole, *f.* **fire-grate,** *n.* Grille, *f.* **fire-guard,** *n.* Garde-feu, *m.* **fire-insurance,** *n.* Assurance contre l'incendie, *f.* **fire-irons,** *n.* Garniture de foyer, *f.* **fire-lighter,** *n.* Allume-feu, *m.* **firelock,** *n.* Mousquet, fusil à pierre, *m.* **fireman,** *n.* Pompier; (*Naut.*) chauffeur, *m.* **fire-office,** *n.* Bureau d'assurance contre l'incendie, *m.* **fireplace,** *n.* Cheminée, *f.*, foyer, âtre, *m.* **fire-plug,** *n.* Bouche d'incendie, *f.* **fire-policy,** *n.* Police d'assurance contre l'incendie, *f.* **fireproof,** *a.* À l'épreuve du feu, incombustible, ignifuge. **fire-screen,** *n.* Écran, *m.* **fire-ship,** *n.* Brûlot, *m.* **fireside,** *n.* Coin du feu; (*fig.*) foyer domestique, *m.* **fire-station,** *n.* Poste de pompiers, *m.* **fire-step,** *n.* Banquette de tir, *f.* **firewood,** *n.* Bois de chauffage, *m.* **fireworks,** *n.pl.* Feu d'artifice, *m.* *To let off fireworks*, tirer un feu d'artifice; (*fig.*) faire un discours à gros effets. **fire-worship,** *n.* Culte du feu, *m.* **fire-worshipper,** *n.* Adorateur du feu, guèbre, *m.* or *f.*

firing, *n.* Action d'incendier, *f.*; chauffage (heating), *m.*; cuisson (of pottery etc.), *f.*; combustible (fuel); (*Mil.*) feu, tir, *m.*, fusillade, *f.* *Quick firing*, feu rapide, *m.* **firing-line,** *n.* Ligne de feu, *f.* **firing-party, firing squad,** *n.* Peloton d'exécution, *m.*

firkin ['fə:kin], *n.* Quartaut; barillet (of butter), *m.*

firm (1) [fə:m], *a.* Ferme, solide, constant. *To stand firm*, tenir ferme, tenir bon.

firm (2) [fə:m], *n.* Maison de commerce, raison sociale, firme, *f.* *Signature of the firm*, signature sociale, *f.*

firmament ['fə:məmənt], *n.* Firmament, *m.*
firman ['fə:mən], *n.* Firman, *m.*
firmly ['fə:mli], *adv.* Fermement, solidement; constamment. **firmness**, *n.* Fermeté, solidité, *f.*
firn [fə:n], *n.* Névé, *m.*
first [fə:st], *a.* Premier; unième. *At first sight*, à première vue; *he was the very first to complain*, il s'est plaint tout le premier; *in the first place*, en premier lieu; *the first that comes*, le premier venu, *m.*; *to be first in the field*, prendre les devants; *twenty-first*, vingt et unième.—*n.* (Le) premier, (la) première; début, commencement, *m.*—*adv.* Premièrement, d'abord, au commencement; pour la première fois. *At first*, d'abord; *first and last*, d'un bout à l'autre; *first catch your hare*, il ne faut pas vendre la peau de l'ours avant de l'avoir tué; *first of all*, en premier lieu, tout d'abord; *first or last*, tôt ou tard; *first thing*, en premier lieu, avant tout; *from the first*, dès l'abord; *to arrive first*, arriver le premier. **first-aid**, *n.* Premiers secours, *m.pl.* *First-aid post*, poste de secours, *m.* **first-born**, *a.* Premier-né, aîné. **first-class** or **first-rate**, *a.* De premier ordre; de premier choix; (*colloq.*) de première force. *First-class compartment*, compartiment de première classe, *m.* **first-fruits**, *n.pl.* Prémices, *f.pl.* **first-hand**, *a.* De première main, *n.* **firstling**, *n.* Premier-né, *m.* (lamb). **firstly**, *adv.* Premièrement.
firth [fə:θ], *n.* (*Sc.*) Estuaire, *m.*
fisc [fisk], *n.* Fisc, *m.* **fiscal**, *a.* Fiscal.—*n.* (*Spain and Portugal*) Procureur du roi; (*Scotland*) procureur fiscal, *m.* **fiscally**, *adv.* Fiscalement.
fish [fiʃ], *n.* Poisson, *m.*; (*Card-games*) fiche; (*Naut.*) traversière; jumelle, *f.* *A pretty kettle of fish*, un beau gâchis, une jolie affaire; *a queer fish*, un drôle de type, *m.*; *neither fish nor fowl*, ni chair ni poisson; *to be like a fish out of water*, être comme un poisson sur la paille; *to have other fish to fry*, avoir d'autres chiens à fouetter.—*v.i.* Pêcher. *To fish for*, pêcher, (*fig.*) rechercher, quêter; *to fish for compliments*, quêter des compliments; *to fish in troubled waters*, pêcher en eau trouble; *to go fishing*, aller à la pêche.—*v.t.* Pêcher; fouiller dans; (*Naut.*) traverser (the anchor), jumeler (a mast). **fish-bone**, *n.* Arête, *f.* **fish-farming**, *n.* Pisciculture, *f.* **fish-hook**, *n.* Hameçon, *m.* **fish-kettle**, *n.* Poissonnière, *f.* **fish-knife**, *n.* Couteau à poisson, *m.* **fish-market**, *n.* Marché au poisson, *m.* **fishmonger**, *n.* Marchand de poisson, *m.* **fish-plate**, *n.* Éclisse, *f.*, couvre-joint, *m.* **fish-slice**, *n.* Truelle à poisson, *f.* **fish-wife** or **fish-woman**, *n.* Marchande de poisson, *f.*
fisher or **fisherman**, *n.* Pêcheur, *m.* **fishery**, *n.* Pêche; pêcherie, *f.* *Herring-fishery*, pêche aux harengs, *f.*; *the fisheries of Newfoundland*, les pêcheries de Terre-Neuve, *f.pl.*
fishiness, *n.* Goût de poisson *m.*; (*slang*) caractère louche, *m.*
fishing, *n.* Pêche, *f.* *To go fishing*, aller à la pêche. *Mackerel fishing*, pêche au maquereau. **fishing-boat**, *n.* Bateau de pêche, *m.* **fishing-line**, *n.* Ligne de pêche, *f.* **fishing-rod**, *n.* Canne à pêche, *f.* **fishing-tackle**, *n.* Attirail de pêche, *m.*
fishlike, *a.* Comme un poisson.

fishy, *a.* De poisson, poissonneux; qui sent le poisson; (*slang*) louche, véreux.
fissile ['fisail], *a.* Fissile; (*Phys.*) fissible.
fission ['fiʃ(ə)n], *n.* (*Biol.*) Fissiparité; (*Phys.*) fission, désintégration, *f.* *Nuclear fission*, fission nucléaire, *f.*
fissiparity [fisi'pæriti], *n.* Fissiparité, *f.*
fissiparous [fi'sipərəs], *a.* Fissipare. **fissiped** ['fisiped], *a.* Fissipède.
fissure ['fiʃə], *n.* Fissure, fente, *f.*—*v.t.* Faire des fentes à. *To become fissured*, se fissurer.
fist [fist], *n.* Poing, *m.* **fisted**, *a.* Au poing. *Close-fisted*, serré, avare, dur à la détente. **fistful**, *n.* Poignée, *f.* **fisticuffs**, *n.pl.* Coups de poing, *m.pl.*
fistula ['fistjulə], *n.* Fistule, *f.* **fistular**, **fistulous**, *a.* Fistuleux, fistulaire.
fit (1) [fit], *n.* Accès (of rage etc.), *m.*; attaque (of illness); attaque de nerfs, convulsion, *f.*; (*fig.*) caprice, *m.* *By fits and starts*, à bâtons rompus, par sauts et par bonds, par boutades; *to go into fits of laughter*, être pris d'un fou rire; *to throw a fit*, tomber en convulsions.
fit (2) [fit], *a.* Propre, bon, convenable (à); juste, à propos; capable (de); en bonne santé, en forme. *Fit for use*, en état de servir; *fit to drink*, buvable, potable; *fit to eat*, bon à manger, mangeable; *to keep fit*, rester en forme, se tenir en haleine; *to think fit*, juger convenable, juger bon.—*n.* Ajustement (of clothes), *m.*; (*fig.*) coupe, forme, *f.* *They are a first-rate fit*, ils vont à ravir.—*v.t.* Convenir à; aller à (of clothes); faire aller à, habiller, chausser; adapter, accommoder, ajuster; préparer. *Let him whom the cap fits wear it*, qui se sent morveux qu'il se mouche; *that coat fits you well*, cet habit vous va bien; *to fit on*, essayer; monter; *to fit out*, équiper, monter, donner un trousseau à, armer (a ship); *to fit up*, arranger, monter, meubler.—*v.i.* Convenir; s'adapter (à), s'ajuster (à); aller bien (of clothes). *To fit in with*, s'accorder avec, être en harmonie avec.
fitchew ['fitʃu:], *n.* Putois, *m.*
fitful ['fitful], *a.* Agité; capricieux; irrégulier, saccadé. **fitfully**, *adv.* Par boutades; irrégulièrement.
fitly ['fitli], *adv.* À propos, convenablement, justement. **fitness**, *n.* Convenance, aptitude (à), *f.*; à-propos, *m.* *Physical fitness*, santé physique, bonne forme, *f.* **fitted**, *a.* Fait (pour). *Fitted carpet*, tapis ajusté, *m.* **fitter**, *n.* Ajusteur, *m.*; (*Dress.*) essayeur, *m.*
fitting ['fitin], *a.* Convenable, à propos, juste. *Easy fitting* (garment), où l'on est à l'aise.—*n.* Ajustement, essayage, *m.*, (*pl.*) garniture, *f.*, ferrures, fournitures, *f.pl.* *Fitting in*, emboîtement, *m.*; *fitting out*, (*Navy*) armement, (*Mil.*) équipement, *m.* **fittingly**, *adv.* Convenablement.
five [faiv], *a.* and *n.* Cinq, *m.* **fivefold**, *adv.* Cinq fois; quintuple. **fiver**, *n.* (*fam.*) Billet de cinq livres, *m.* **fives**, *n.pl.* Balle au mur (game), *f.* **fives-court**, *n.* Cour de balle au mur, *f.* **fivestones**, *n.pl.* Osselets, *m.pl.*
fix [fiks], *v.t.* Fixer, attacher, arrêter, établir; (*colloq.*) réparer. *Fix bayonets!* baïonnet·e au canon! *to fix bayonets*, mettre la baïonnette au canon; *to fix oneself*, s'établir, se fixer; *to fix up*, arranger, régler.—*v.i.* Se fixer. *To fix upon*, s'arrêter à, choisir.—*n.* Difficulté, impasse, *f.*, embarras, *m.* *To be in a fix*,

(colloq.) être dans le pétrin. **fixable,** a. Fixable.

fixation [fik'seiʃən], n. Fixation, f. **fixative,** a. Fixatif, fixateur. **fixed** [fikst], a. Fixe, fixé. *Fixed price,* prix marqué, prix fixe, m. **fixedly** ['fiksidli], adv. Fixement. **fixedness** or **fixity,** n. Fixité, f. **fixer,** n. Fixateur, m. **fixing,** n. Fixage, m., fixation, f. **fix-solution,** n. Fixateur, m.

fixture ['fikstʃə], n. Meuble à demeure, m., agencements fixes, m.pl.; match, engagement, m. (prévu, annoncé). *List of fixtures,* programme, m.

fizgig ['fizgig], n. Jeune (fille) évaporée; toupie d'Allemagne, f.

fizz [fiz] or **fizzle** [fizl], v.i. Siffler, pétiller.—n. Sifflement, pétillement, m.; (pop.) champagne. m. (pop.) *To fizzle out,* ne pas aboutir, avorter. **fizzy,** a. Gazeux (lemonade etc.), mousseux (wine).

flabbergast ['flæbəgɑːst], v.t. (slang) Épater, abasourdir. *To be flabbergasted,* être épaté, rester baba, éberlué.

flabbiness ['flæbinis], n. Flaccidité, f. **flabby,** a. Flasque; mollasse (of person).

flaccid ['flæksid], a. Flasque, mou. **flaccidity** [-'siditi] or **flaccidness,** n. Flaccidité, f.

flag (1) [flæg], v.i. Pendre mollement; se relâcher, faiblir, languir; s'affaisser.

flag (2) [flæg], n. Drapeau, m.; (Naut.) pavillon, m.; iris (plant), m.; carreau, m., dalle (stone), f. *Battalion flag,* fanion, m.; *bearer of a flag of truce,* parlementaire, m.; *flag of truce,* drapeau blanc, drapeau parlementaire, m.; *to strike the flag,* amener son pavillon, amener. —v.t. Paver, daller; orner de drapeaux, pavoiser. **flag-day,** n. Jour de quête, m. **flag-officer,** n. Chef d'escadre, m. **flag-ship,** n. Vaisseau amiral, m. **flagstaff,** n. Mât de pavillon, m.; hampe du drapeau, f. **flagstone,** n. Dalle, f. **flag-waver,** n. (fam.) Chauvin, m. **flag-waving,** n. (fam.) Chauvinisme, esprit cocardier, m.

flagellant ['flædʒələnt], n. Flagellant, m. **flagellate** ['flædʒəleit], v.t. Flageller.—a. [-lət], Flagellé. **flagellation** [-'leiʃən], n. Flagellation, f. **flagelliform** [-'dʒelifɔːm], a. Flagelliforme.

flageolet [flædʒo'let], n. Flageolet, m.

flagging (1) ['flægiŋ], a. Pendant, qui pend; qui s'affaiblit; languissant.—n. Relâchement, m.

flagging (2) ['flægiŋ], n. Dallage (paving), m.

flagitious [flə'dʒiʃəs], a. Scélérat, infâme, abominable. **flagitiously,** adv. D'une manière infâme. **flagitiousness,** n. Scélératesse, infamie, f.

flagon ['flægən], n. Flacon, m.; burette (in a church), f.

flagrancy ['fleigrənsi], n. Énormité, notoriété, f. **flagrant,** a. Flagrant, notoire, énorme. **flagrantly,** adv. D'une manière flagrante or scandaleuse.

flail [fleil], n. Fléau, m.

flair [fleə], n. Perspicacité, f., flair, m.; aptitude (à), f. *To have a flair for languages,* avoir le don des langues.

flak [flæk], n. (fam.) Tir contre-avions, m.

flake [fleik], n. Flocon, m.; écaille; étincelle, flammèche, f.—v.t. Former en flocons,

écailler.—v.i. S'écailler. **flaky,** a. Floconneux, en flocons; écaillé; feuilleté (of pastry). *Flaky paste,* pâte feuilletée, f.

flam [flæm], n. (slang) Sornette, blague, f., conte, m.—v.t. Amuser avec des sornettes.

flamboyance [flæm'bɔiəns], n. Qualité flamboyante, f. **flamboyant,** a. Flamboyant.

flame [fleim], n. Flamme, f.; feu, m. *An old flame,* une ancienne passion, f.; *to burst into flames,* s'enflammer brusquement.—v.i. Flamber, jeter de la flamme; s'enflammer, flamboyer. *To flame up,* (fig.) s'emporter. **flame-coloured,** a. Couleur de feu, ponceau. **flameless,** a. Sans flamme. **flamelet,** n. Flammette, f. **flame-thrower,** n. Lance-flammes, m. **flaming,** a. Flamboyant, flambant; en feu; (fig.) violent, ardent; (pop.) sacré, satané. **flamingly,** adv. Avec ardeur, avec véhémence. **flamy,** a. De flamme.

flamen ['fleimən], n. Flamine, m.

flamingo [flə'miŋgou], n. (Orn.) Flamant, m.

flan [flæn], n. Flan, m., tarte aux fruits, f.

Flanders ['flɑːndəz], La Flandre, f.

flange [flændʒ], n. Bride, f., rebord (of a tube etc.); (Tech.) boudin (of wheels), m.; (Motor.) ailette, collerette, f.—v.t. Brider, rabattre.

flank [flæŋk], n. Flanc; côté, m. (Mil.) *Flank-march,* marche de flanc, f.; *flank-movement,* mouvement tournant, m.—v.t. Flanquer (de); (Mil.) prendre en flanc.—v.i. Border, toucher (à). **flanker,** n. (Mil.) Flanqueur, flanc-garde, m.; (Fort.) ouvrage flanquant, m. **flanking,** n. Flanquement, m.—a. *Flanking fire,* feu de flanquement, m.

flannel [flænl], n. Flanelle, f.; (pl.) pantalon de flanelle, m.—a. De flanelle.

flannelette, n. Flanelle de coton, finette, f.

flap [flæp], v.t. Frapper légèrement; battre, agiter. *To flap its wings,* battre des ailes.—v.i. Battre légèrement; pendre, pendiller; (fig. and pop.) s'agiter sans but, s'affoler.—n. Battement, coup (d'aile); claquement (of sail); petit coup (de la main), m., tape, f.; battant (of a table etc.); bord, bord rabattu (of a hat), m.; patte (of a pocket), f.; pan (of a coat); bout (of the ear), m.; oreille (of a shoe), f.; rabat (of envelope); (fig. and pop.) affolement, m. **flapdoodle,** n. Fatras, m., blague, f. **flap-eared,** a. Aux oreilles pendantes. **flapjack,** n. Crêpe, f.

flapper ['flæpə], n. (Orn.) Jeune canard sauvage, halbran; perdreau, m.; (fig.) jeune fille qui n'a pas encore fait ses débuts, gamine, f.

flapping, n. Battement d'ailes, clapotement (of sail), m.

flare [fleə], v.i. Flamboyer, lancer des lueurs inégales; (fig.) briller d'un vif éclat; s'évaser (of skirt). *To flare up,* se mettre en colère, s'emporter.—n. Flamme, vive clarté, f.; (Av.) brûlot; évasement, godet (of skirt), m.

flare-up, n. Flambée, f.

flaring, a. Étincelant, éblouissant.

flash [flæʃ], n. Éclair, éclat, jet de lumière; (fig.) trait, m., lueur, saillie, f.; (Mil.) écusson, m. *Flash in the pan,* feu de paille, m.; *flash of lightning,* éclair, m.; *flash of the eye,* vif coup d'œil, m.; *flash of wit,* trait d'esprit, m.—v.i. Luire, éclater, étinceler; passer comme un éclair. *To flash with,* briller de, étinceler de.—v.t. Faire jaillir, jeter, lancer.—a. Faux (of coins etc.); d'argot (of words). **flash-back**, *n.* (*Cine.*) Retour en arrière, *m.* **flashiness**, *n.* Ton tapageur, faux brillant, *m.* **flashing**, *n.* Éclair, éclat, flamboiement; clignotement (of signal), *m.* **flashlamp**, *n.* Lampe de poche, *f.* **flash-light**, *n.* (*Phot.*) Flash, *m.* **flashy**, *a.* Voyant, clinquant, tapageur; superficiel. **flask** [flɑːsk], *n.* Flacon, *m.*, gourde, *f. Powder-flask*, poire à poudre, *f.* **flasket** ['flɑːskit], *n.* Corbeille, *f.* **flat** [flæt], *a.* Plat; uni, plane, égal; étendu (on the ground); épaté (of the nose); éventé (of wine etc.); (*Comm.*) languissant; (*Mus.*) bémol; grave (of sound); (*fig.*) net, clair; fade, insipide (of taste); abattu, attristé; (*Paint.*) mat, embu. *To fall flat* (of story, joke), tomber à plat, manquer son effet; *to fall flat on the ground*, tomber de tout son long; *to get flat*, s'aplatir, s'éventer (of wine etc.); *to lay flat*, coucher à plat, renverser, terrasser; *to lie flat*, être étendu à terre.—*n.* Surface plane, *f.*; terrain plat; étage (in a house), appartement, *m.*; (*Mus.*) bémol; (*Theat.*) châssis, *m.*, paroi, *f.* (*Naut.*) *In the flats*, à fond de cale, *m.*—*v.t.* Aplatir.—*v.i.* S'aplatir. **flat-footed**, *a.* Pied plat; (*slang*) résolu. **flat-iron**, *n.* Fer à repasser, *m.* **flatly**, *adv.* À plat; (*fig.*) nettement, clairement, péremptoirement. **flatness**, *n.* Aplatissement, *m.*; égalité, *f.*; évent (of wine etc.), *m.*; gravité (of sound); (*fig.*) insipidité, platitude, *f.* **flat-racing**, *n.* Le plat, *m.* **flat-rate**, *n.* Taux uniforme, *m.*

flatten [flætn], *v.t.* Aplatir, aplanir; éventer (liquor); amortir (colours); (*Metal.*) laminer; (*fig.*) abattre, attrister; (*Mus.*) rendre grave. —*v.i.* S'aplatir, s'aplanir; s'éventer. **flattening**, *n.* Aplatissement, aplanissement; (*Metal.*) laminage, *m.* **flatting-mill**, *n.* Laminoir, *m.* **flattish**, *a.* Un peu plat. **flatter** ['flætə], *v.t.* Flatter. *To flatter oneself*, se flatter (de). **flatterer**, *n.* Flatteur, *m.*, -euse, *f.* **flattering**, *a.* Flatteur. **flatteringly**, *adv.* D'une manière flatteuse, flatteusement. **flattery**, *n.* Flatterie, *f.* **flatulence** ['flætjuləns] or **flatulency**, *n.* Flatuosité; flatulence, *f.*; (*fig.*) vide, creux, *m.* **flatulent**, *a.* Flatueux; (*fig.*) ampoulé, gonflé, creux.

flaunt [flɔːnt], *v.i.* Se pavaner, parader, flotter.—*v.t.* Faire parade de, étaler, déployer; afficher.—*n.* Étalage, *m.*, vaine parure, parade, *f.* **flaunting**, *a.* Éclatant, voyant, vaniteux.

flautist ['flɔːtist], *n.* Joueur de flûte, flûtiste, *m.* **flavour** ['fleivə], *n.* Saveur, *f.*; goût, fumet (of meat); arome (of tea, coffee, etc.); bouquet (of wine), *m.*—*v.t.* Donner du goût, un arome, un parfum, etc. à, assaisonner (de), aromatiser. **flavoured**, *a.* Savoureux. **flavouring**, *n.* Assaisonnement, *m.* **flavourless**, *a.* Sans saveur, fade.

flaw [flɔː], *n.* Défaut, *m.*; fêlure; brèche, fente; paille (in precious stones), *f.*; (*Naut.*) grain, *m.*; (*Law*) nullité, *f.*, pour vice de forme.— *v.t.* Fêler, gercer. **flawless**, *a.* Parfait, sans défaut. **flawlessness**, *n.* Perfection, *f.* **flawy**, *a.* Défectueux.

flax [flæks], *n.* Lin, *m.*—*a.* De lin. **flax-comb**, *n.* Séran, *m.* **flax-dresser**, *n.* Séranceur, *m.* **flax-dressing**, *n.* Sérançage, *m.* **flaxen**, *a.*

De lin; blond filasse (of the hair). **flax-field**, *n.* Linière, *f.* **flay** [flei], *v.t.* Écorcher, dépouiller; (*pop.*) rosser. **flayer**, *n.* Écorcheur, *m.* **flaying**, *n.* Écorchement, *m.* **flea** [fliː], *n.* Puce, *f. To send away with a flea in one's ear*, mettre la puce à l'oreille. **flea-bane**, *n.* (*Bot.*) Pulicaire, *f.* **flea-bite**, *n.* Morsure de puce; (*fig.*) bagatelle, *f.*, rien, petit mal, *m.* **flea-bitten**, *a.* Mangé des puces, (of horse's coat) moucheté.

fleam [fliːm], *n.* (*Vet.*) Flamme, *f.* **fleck** [flek], *n.* Tache, moucheture, marque, *f.* —*v.t.* Moucheter, tacheter (de).

fled, *past* [FLEE].

fledge [fledʒ], *v.t.* Garnir de plumes. **fledged**, *a.* Couvert de plumes. *Full-fledged*, en état de voler. **fledgeling**, *n.* Oisillon; béjaune, *m.*

flee [fliː], *v.i.* (*past* and *p.p.* **fled**) S'enfuir, prendre la fuite, se réfugier.—*v.t.* Fuir, éviter.

fleece [fliːs], *n.* Toison, *f.*; (*Tex.*) nappe, *f.*, molleton, *m.* · *Golden fleece*, toison d'or.—*v.t.* Tondre; (*fig.*) écorcher, plumer, gruger. **fleecy**, *a.* Laineux, (*fig.*) floconneux, moutonneux. *Fleecy clouds*, nuages moutonnés, *m.pl.*

fleer [fliə], *v.i.* Se moquer (de).—*v.t.* Se moquer de, railler.—*n.* Raillerie, grimace, *f.*

fleet (1) [fliːt], *n.* Flotte, *f. The Home Fleet*, la flotte métropolitaine.

fleet (2) [fliːt], *a.* Vite, rapide, leste, léger à la course.—*v.i.* Passer rapidement; s'envoler, s'enfuir. **fleeting**, *a.* Fugitif, fugace, éphémère, passager. **fleetingly**, *adv.* D'une manière passagère. **fleetly**, *adv.* Vite, rapidement. **fleetness**, *n.* Rapidité, vitesse, *f.*

Fleming ['flemiŋ], *n.* Flamand, *m.*, Flamande, *f.* **Flemish**, *a.* Flamand.

flench [flenʃ] or **flense** or **flinch** (1), *v.t.* Enlever la graisse (d'une baleine); dépouiller (un phoque).

flesh [fleʃ], *n.* Chair; viande (meat), *f.*; (*Paint.*) chairs, *f.pl. In the flesh*, en chair et en os, en vie; *neither fish, flesh, nor fowl*, ni chair ni poisson; *to make one's flesh creep*, donner la chair de poule à; *to pick up flesh*, reprendre de l'embonpoint; *to put on flesh*, s'empâtir, prendre de l'embonpoint.—*v.t.* Assouvir (a passion); essayer (a sword); (*Hunt.*) acharner; écharner (hides). **flesh-brush**, *n.* Brosse à friction, *f.* **flesh-colour**, *n.* Couleur (de) chair, *f.* **flesh-coloured**, *a.* Couleur de chair, incarnat. **flesh-day**, *n.* Jour gras, *m.* **flesh-fly**, *n.* Mouche à viande, *f.* **flesh-hook**, *n.* Croc, *m.* **fleshiness**, *n.* État charnu, embonpoint, *m.* **fleshless**, *a.* Décharné. **fleshliness**, *n.* Appétits charnels, *m.pl.* **fleshly**, *a.* De la chair, charnel; sensuel. **flesh-pot**, *n.* Potée de viande, *f. The flesh-pots of Egypt*, les bonnes choses, *f.pl.* **flesh-tint**, *n.* Teinte de chair, *f.*; (*Paint.*) (*pl.*) carnations, chairs, *f.pl.* **flesh-wound**, *n.* Blessure superficielle, blessure en séton, *f.* **fleshy**, *a.* Charnu.

flew, *past* [FLY (2)].

flews [fluːz], *n.pl.* Babines, *f.pl.* (of a deep-mouthed hound).

flex (1) [fleks], *n.* Fil électrique (for movable electric lamps, etc.), *m.*

flex (2) [fleks], *v.t.* Fléchir.

flexibility [fleksi'biliti], n. Flexibilité, f.
flexible ['fleksibl], a. Flexible, souple. **flexion,** n. Courbure, flexion, f. **flexional,** a. Flexionnel. *Flexional ending*, désinence, m. **flexor,** n. (*Anat.*) Muscle fléchisseur, m. **flexuose** or **flexuous,** a. Flexueux. **flexure,** n. Flexion, courbure, flexure, f. *Flexure fault*, pli-faille, m.
flick [flik], n. Petit coup (de fouet, de torchon), m.; chiquenaude, f.; (pl.) (pop.) le ciné, m. *With a flick of the wrist*, d'un revers de main. —v.t. Effleurer; donner une chiquenaude à, un coup sec à.
flicker ['flikə], v.i. Trembloter, vaciller (of a light); se trémousser, battre des ailes (of birds); ciller (of eyelids), cligner, clignoter. **flickering,** n. Trémoussement; clignement, clignotement, m.; vacillation, f.—a. Vacillant, tremblotant, clignotant.
flier [FLYER].
flight [flait], n. Vol, m., volée (of birds etc.), f.; fuite, f.; trajectoire, f. (of bullets); (fig.) élan, m., envolée, f., essor, transport, m.; saillie, f. (of wit); cours (of time), m.; (*Av.*) escadrille, ligne, f. *At a single flight*, d'un coup d'aile; *flight number*, numéro de vol, m.; *flight of stairs*, escalier, m.; *flight of steps*, perron, m.; *in flight*, en déroute, (*Av.*) en plein vol; *to put to flight*, mettre en fuite; *to take flight*, prendre la fuite. **flightiness,** n. Légèreté, étourderie, f. **flight-lieutenant,** n. Capitaine aviateur, m. **flighty,** a. Étourdi, léger; volage.
flimsiness ['flimzinis], n. Légèreté, f., manque de consistance or de solidité, m.; (fig.) faiblesse, mesquinerie, f. **flimsy,** a. Mollasse, faible, léger, sans consistance, sans solidité. *Flimsy excuse*, faible prétexte, m.—n. (*Australia*) Aérogramme, m.
flinch (1) [FLENCH].
flinch (2) [flintʃ], v.i. Reculer, fléchir, broncher, s'écarter (de), céder. *Without flinching*, sans sourciller.
fling [fliŋ], v.t. (past and p.p. **flung** [flʌŋ]) Jeter, lancer. *To fling away*, prodiguer, jeter par la fenêtre (of money), rejeter, repousser; *to fling down*, jeter à terre, abattre; *to fling off*, rejeter; *to fling open*, ouvrir brusquement; *to fling out*, jeter dehors; *to fling up*, jeter en l'air, abandonner.—v.i. Ruer, taper (of horses); (fig.) s'emporter, regimber.—n. Coup (lancé), m.; ruade, f. (of horse); pas seul, m. (Highland dance); (fig.) essai, m., tentative, f.; trait, coup de patte, m., raillerie, f. *To have a fling at*, donner un coup de patte à; essayer; *to have one's fling*, jeter sa gourme, faire des fredaines; s'en donner à cœur joie.
flint [flint], n. Silex, m., pierre à briquet, pierre à fusil; (fig.) roche, dureté, f. **Flint and steel*, briquet, m.; *to skin a flint*, faire des économies de bouts de chandelle. **flintglass,** n. Flint-glass, m. **flint-lock,** a. Fusil à pierre, m. **flinty,** a. Caillouteux; siliceux; (fig.) dur, insensible, de pierre.
flip [flip], v.t. Donner une chiquenaude, un petit coup à.—n. Petit coup, m., chiquenaude, f.; flip (beverage), m.
flippancy ['flipənsi], n. Ton léger, m., légèreté, f.; bavardage, m. **flippant,** a. Léger, désinvolte, délié, cavalier (of manners, air); irrévérencieux. **flippantly,** adv. Légèrement; cavalièrement, d'un petit ton dégagé.
flipper ['flipə], n. Nageoire, f.

flirt [flə:t], v.i. (of woman) Faire la coquette, coqueter; flirter; (of man) conter fleurette, faire le galant.—v.t. Jeter, lancer.—n. Coquette, f. **flirtation** [-'teiʃən], n. Coquetterie, f.; flirt, m. **flirtatious,** a. Coquette; flirteur.
flit [flit], v.i. Fuir, voltiger; (*Sc.*) déménager, changer de demeure. *To flit away*, s'en aller; *to flit by*, passer légèrement; passer rapidement.—n. *To do a moonlight flit*, déménager à la cloche de bois.
flitch [flitʃ], n. Flèche de lard, f., dosse, f. (of wood).
flitter-mouse ['flitəmaus], n. Chauve-souris, f.
flitting ['flitiŋ], n. Départ, déménagement (change of residence), m.—a. Fugitif, rapide.
float [flout], v.i. Flotter, surnager. *To float on one's back*, faire la planche.—v.t. Faire flotter, (fig.) mettre à flot, lancer. *To float a company*, former une société.—n. Masse flottante, f.; train (of wood); flotteur, m.; charrette basse, f., char (in a carnival), m. *Float gauge*, indicateur à flotteur, m. **floatboard,** n. Aube, f.
floatable, a. Flottable.
floatage ['floutidʒ], n. Flottage, m. **floater,** n. Flotteur, m., personne qui fait la planche; (fig.) personne qui forme une compagnie, f.; électeur incertain, indépendant, influençable.
floating, a. Flottant. *Floating battery*, batterie flottante, f.; *floating bridge*, pont flottant, m.; *floating capital*, fonds de roulement, m.; *floating dock*, bassin à flot, m.—n. Mise à flot, f.; lancement (of a ship etc.), m.
flocculent ['flɔkjulənt], a. (*Bot.*) Floconneux.
flock [flɔk], n. Troupeau, m.; bande, troupe, f.; ouailles (clergyman's congregation), f.pl.; flocon, m., bourre (of wool etc.), f.; (*Chem.*) flocons, m.pl., précipité, m.—v.i. S'attrouper, s'assembler, accourir en foule; aller par bandes (of birds). *Birds of a feather flock together*, qui se ressemble s'assemble. **flockbed,** n. Matelas de bourre, m. **flock-paper,** n. Papier velouté, m.
floe [flou], n. Nappe de glaçons flottants, f., banc de glaces, m.; banquise, f.
flog [flɔg], v.t. Fouetter, flageller, fustiger; (pop.) vendre, bazarder. *To flog a dead horse*, chercher à ressusciter un mort. **flogger,** n. Fouetteur, m. **flogging,** n. Le fouet, m., les verges, f.pl.; flagellation, fustigation, f. *To get a flogging*, être fouetté, recevoir le fouet.
flood [flʌd], n. Déluge, m.; inondation, crue, f.; (fig.) cours d'eau, torrent, fleuve, flot, m.; marée, f. *At the flood*, à marée haute; *flood of tears*, torrent de larmes, m.—v.t. Inonder, submerger, noyer. *To flood the carburettor*, noyer le carburateur. *To flood with*, inonder de. **flood-gate,** n. Écluse, f. **flood-light,** n. Lumière à grands flots, f.; projecteur, m.—v.t. Illuminer (un monument) avec des projecteurs, embraser. **flood-tide,** n. Marée montante, f., flot, flux, m.
flooding, n. Inondation, f.; (*Med.*) perte de sang, f.
floor [flɔ:], n. Plancher; carreau, parquet (pavement); étage (story), m.; aire (of a barn), f.; tablier (of a bridge), m.; (*Naut.*) varangue, f.; fond, m. *Inlaid floor*, parquet, m.; *on the first floor*, au premier; *on the ground floor*, au rez-de-chaussée; *to take the floor*, prendre la parole; (slang) *to wipe the*

floor with, battre à plate couture.—*v.t.* Planchéier, parqueter; (*fig.*) jeter par terre, terrasser; réduire au silence, désarçonner; (*sch.*) refuser (un candidat). **floor-cloth**, *n.* Serpillière, *f.*; linoléum, *m.* **floor-timber**, *n.* (*Naut.*) Varangue, *f.* **floor-walker**, *n.* (*Am.*) [SHOP-WALKER].

flooring, *n.* Plancher, parquet; parquetage, planchéiage (process), *m.*

flop [flɔp], *int.* Plouf!—*n.* Coup mat, choc sourd, *m.* (comme d'un corps qui tombe à l'eau); (*Theat.*) four, fiasco, *m.*—*v.i.* Tomber en faisant floc ou plouf; (*fig.*) faire fiasco.

floppy ['flɔpi], *a.* Flasque, mou.

Flora ['flɔːrə]. Flore, *f.*

flora ['flɔːrə], *n.* Flore, *f.* **floral**, *a.* Floral. *Floral games*, jeux floraux, *m.pl.*

Florence ['flɔrəns]. Florence, *f.*

Florentine ['flɔrəntain], *a.* and *n.* Florentin.

florescence [flɔ'resəns], *n.* (*Bot.*) Fleuraison, *f.* **floret**, *n.* Fleurette, *f.*, fleuron, *m.*

floriculture ['flɔːrikʌltʃə], *n.* Floriculture, *f.*

florid ['flɔrid], *a.* Fleuri, vermeil.

Florida ['flɔridə]. La Floride, *f.*

floridity [flɔ'riditi] or **floridness**, *n.* Teint *or* style fleuri, *m.* **floridly**, *adv.* D'une manière fleurie.

floriferous [flɔ'rifərəs], *a.* Florifère. **floriform**, *a.* Floriforme.

florilegium [flɔri'liːdʒiəm], *n.* Florilège, *m.*

florin ['flɔrin], *n.* Florin, *m.*

florist ['flɔrist], *n.* Fleuriste.

floscule ['flɔskjul], *n.* Fleurette, *f.*, fleuron, *m.* **flosculous** ['flɔskjuləs], *a.* (*Bot.*) Flosculeux.

floss [flɔs], *n.* Bourre (of silk), *f.*; (*Metal.*) floss, *m.*; (*Bot.*) duvet, *m.* **floss-silk**, *n.* Floche, filoselle, bourre de soie, *f.*

flotation [flo'teiʃən], *n.* Flottement, *m.*

flotilla [flo'tilə], *n.* Flottille, *f.*

flotsam ['flɔtsəm], *n.* Épave flottante, *f.* *Flotsam and jetsam*, débris flottants, *m.pl.*, épaves, *f.pl.*

flounce [flauns], *n.* Volant (de robe), *m.*, secousse, *f.*; coup de queue, *m.*—*v.t.* Garnir de volants.—*v.i.* (*fig.*) Se démener, se débattre. *To flounce out*, sortir bruyamment.

flounder (1) ['flaundə], *n.* (*Ichth.*) Flet, petit flétan, *m.*

flounder (2) ['flaundə], *v.i.* Se débattre; patauger.

flour ['flauə], *n.* Farine, fécule (of potatoes etc.), *f.*—*v.t.* Convertir en farine; enfariner, saupoudrer de farine. **flour-bin**, *n.* Farinière, huche, maie; boîte à farine (for kitchen), *f.* **flour-dredger**, *n.* Saupoudroir à farine, *m.* **flour-merchant**, *n.* Marchand de farines, *m.* **flour-mill**, *n.* Moulin, *m.*, minoterie, *f.*

flourish ['flʌriʃ], *n.* Éclat, embellissement, *m.*; fleur de rhétorique, *f.*; trait de plume, parafe; geste large; panache (in manners, attitude); moulinet, tour, *m.*; (*Mus.*) fioriture, *f.*, prélude, *m.*; fanfare (of trumpets), *f. With a great flourish of trumpets*, à son de trompe. —*v.t.* Fleurir, orner de fioritures; orner de traits de plume, parafer; faire faire le moulinet à; brandir (a sword etc.).—*v.i.* Fleurir; venir bien (of plants); prospérer, être florissant; faire des traits de plume; (*Mus.*) faire des fioritures, sonner une fanfare; s'exprimer en style fleuri. **flourishing**, *a.* Florissant.

—*n.* Brandissement (d'épée etc.), *m.*; fanfare, *f.* **flourishingly**, *adv.* D'une manière florissante.

floury ['flauəri], *a.* Farineux; enfariné; couvert de farine.

flout [flaut], *v.t.* Railler, narguer; se moquer de, se rire de.—*n.* Moquerie, raillerie, *f.* **flouting**, *n.* Moquerie, raillerie, *f.*

flow [flou], *v.i.* S'écouler, couler; monter, fluer (of the tide); (*fig.*) découler (de). *To flow back*, refluer; *to flow down*, couler, descendre; *to flow from*, découler de, provenir de, venir de; *to flow in*, affluer, arriver en foule; *to flow over*, déborder.—*n.* Écoulement; flux, *m.*; coulée, *f.*; (*fig.*) épanchement, *m.*; abondance, facilité (of speech), *f. Back flow*, refoulement, *m.*; *ebb and flow*, flux et reflux, *m.*

flower ['flauə], *n.* Fleur; (*fig.*) élite, *f.*; (*Print.*) fleuron, *m.* *Wild flower*, fleur des champs, fleur sauvage, *f.*—*v.i.* Fleurir, être en fleur.— *v.t.* Orner de fleurs; ouvrager. **flower-bed**, *n.* Plate-bande, *f.*, parterre, *m.* **flower-garden**, *n.* Jardin d'agrément, *m.* **flower-pot**, *n.* Pot à fleurs; pot de fleurs, *m.* **flower-show**, *n.* Exposition horticole, *f.* **flower-stand**, *n.* Jardinière, *f.* **flower-work**, *n.* Ouvrage à fleurs, *m.*; fleurons, *m.pl.*

flower-de-luce, *n.* Fleur de lis, *f.*; iris des marais, *m.*

flowered, *a.* Figuré, à fleurs; fleuri. *Double flowered*, à fleurs doubles. **floweret**, *n.* Fleurette, *f.* **flowerless**, *a.* Sans fleurs. **flowery**, *a.* De fleurs, plein de fleurs, fleuri.

flowing ['flouin], *a.* Coulant; (*fig.*) débordant; naturel.—*n.* Cours, écoulement, *m.* **flowingly**, *adv.* D'une manière coulante, aisée, facile.

flown [floun], *a.* Envolé. *High-flown*, gonflé, ampoulé, outré (of style).

fluctuate ['flʌktjueit], *v.i.* Balancer, flotter, osciller, varier. **fluctuating** or **fluctuant**, *a.* Flottant; incertain; variable, changeant. **fluctuation** [-'eiʃən], *n.* Fluctuation, *f.*; (*fig.*) balancement, doute, *m.*

flu [fluː], *n.* (*colloq.*) [INFLUENZA].

flue [fluː], *n.* Tuyau de cheminée; carneau (of a furnace), *m.*, peluche, *f.*; tramail, *m.* (net); patte, *f.* (of anchor).

fluency ['fluːənsi], *n.* Facilité, *f.* (of speech). **fluent**, *a.* Coulant, courant; facile, disert. *To speak fluent French*, parler le français couramment. **fluently**, *adv.* Couramment, facilement, avec facilité.

fluff [flʌf], *n.* Duvet, *m.*, peluches, *f.pl.*—*v.t.* Ébouriffer (hair); (*colloq.*) manquer, rater. *To fluff one's lines*, hésiter, se tromper, bafouiller (en jouant la comédie). **fluffy**, *a.* Duveteux, plein de duvet.

fluid ['fluːid], *a.* and *n.* Fluide, liquide, *m.* *Fluid diet*, diète liquide, *f.* **fluidity** [-'iditi], *n.* Fluidité, *f.*

fluke [fluːk], *n.* Patte (d'ancre), *f.*; carrelet (fish), *m.*; (*fig.*) coup de raccroc, *m. By a fluke*, par raccroc. **fluky**, *a.* De raccroc; incertain, hasardeux.

flummery ['flʌməri], *n.* Bouillie, *f.*; (*fig.*) fadaises, sornettes, *f.pl.*

flummox ['flʌməks], *v.t.* Déconcerter, embarrasser; (*sch.*) coller. *No need to get flummoxed*, il n'y a pas de quoi perdre la tête.

flung, *past* and *p.p.* [FLING].

flunk [flʌŋk], *v.t.* (*Am.*) Recaler.—*v.i.* Se faire recaler (à un examen).

flunkey ['flʌŋki], *n.* Laquais; (*colloq.*) flagorneur, sycophante, pied plat, *m.*

fluor ['fluːɔ:] or **fluor-spar**, *n.* Fluorine, *f.* **fluorine**, *n.* Fluor, *m.*

fluorescein [fluə'resiin], *n.* Fluorescéine, *f.* **fluorescence**, *n.* Fluorescence, *f.* **fluorescent**, *a.* Fluorescent. **fluoroscopy** [-'rɔskɔpi], *n.* Fluoroscopie, *f.*

flurry ['flʌri], *n.* Agitation, *f.*, désordre, émoi; coup de vent, grain, *m.*, rafale, *f.* *In a flurry*, en émoi.—*v.t.* Agiter, ahurir. *Don't get flurried*, ne vous troublez pas; ne perdez pas la tête.

flush [flʌʃ], *n.* Rougeur, *f.*; transport, accès, *m.*; chasse d'eau; pousse (de feuilles), *f.*; (*Cards*) floch, flush, *m.* *In the first flush of youth*, dans la première fraîcheur de la jeunesse.—*v.t.* Faire rougir, rougir, colorer; laver à grande eau; actionner la chasse d'eau; (*Hunt.*) lever, faire lever, faire partir; affleurer; (*fig.*) animer, exciter.—*v.i.* Rougir; partir tout à coup.—*a.* Frais, plein de vigueur; à fleur, au ras (level). *Flush with the ground*, à ras de terre; *to be flush of money*, être bien pourvu d'argent, être en fonds. **flushing**, *n.* Rougeur, *f.*; chasse, *f.* (of w.c., sewer); nettoiement à grande eau, *m.* **flushness**, *n.* Abondance, prospérité, *f.*

fluster ['flʌstə], *v.t.* Déconcerter, agiter, ahurir.—*n.* Agitation, *f.* *In a fluster*, en émoi.

flute [fluːt], *n.* Flûte; (*Arch.*) cannelure, *f.*— *v.t.* (*Arch.*) Canneler; tuyauter, gaufrer.—*v.i.* Jouer de la flûte. **flute-player** or **flutist**, *n.* Joueur de flûte, flûtiste, *m.*

fluted, *a.* Cannelé; tuyauté, gaufré. **fluting**, *n.* (*Arch.*) Cannelure, *f.* **fluty**, *a.* Flûté.

flutter ['flʌtə], *n.* Trémoussement, émoi, *m.*; agitation; palpitation, *f.*; battement d'ailes, *m.* *I'm all of a flutter*, je suis tout agité *or* tout en émoi; *to have a flutter*, parier; tenter sa chance (à la loterie, aux courses); *to put in a flutter*, mettre en émoi.—*v.t.* Mettre en désordre, agiter, ahurir.—*v.i.* Battre des ailes; se trémousser, s'agiter; palpiter, battre irrégulièrement (of the pulse).

fluvial ['fluːviəl], *a.* Fluvial. **fluviatic** [-'ætik] or **fluviatile**, *a.* Fluviatile. **fluvio-marine**, *a.* Fluviomarin. **fluviometer** [-'ɔmitə], *n.* Fluviomètre, *m.*

flux [flʌks], *n.* Flux, courant, *m.*; (*Path.*) dysenterie, *f.*, (*Metal.*) fondant, *m.*—*v.t.* Fondre; (*Med.*) purger. **fluxion**, *n.* Écoulement, *m.*; (*Math.*) flux continuel, déplacement continuel, *m.*

fly (1) [flai], *n.* (*pl.* **flies**) Mouche; (*pl.* **flys**) voiture de louage, *f.*, fiacre, *m.* *Horse-fly*, taon, *m.*; *Spanish fly*, cantharide, *f.*; *the fly on the coach-wheel*, la mouche du coche; *there's a fly in the ointment*, il y a un cheveu; *to rise to the fly*, mordre à l'hameçon, gober la mouche; *wet fly*, mouche noyée. **fly-bane**, *n.* Silène, attrape-mouche, *m.* **fly-bitten**, *a.* Piqué des mouches. **fly-blow**, *n.* Œufs de mouche, *m.pl.* **fly-blown**, *a.* Couvert d'œufs de mouches; (*fig.*) gâté, corrompu. **fly-catcher**, *n.* Attrapeur de mouches; (*fig.*) nigaud, *m.*; gobe-mouches (bird), *m.* **fly-fishing**, *n.* Pêche à la mouche, *f.* **fly-leaf**, *n.* Feuillet de garde, *m.* **fly-paper**, *n.* Papier tue-mouches, *m.* **fly-trap**, *n.* Dionée (plant), *f.*, attrape-mouche, *m.* **fly-weight**, *n.* Poids mouche, *m.*

fly (2) [flai], *v.i.* (*past* **flew** [fluː], *p.p.* **flown** [floun]) Voler, s'envoler, se sauver, prendre la fuite, fuir, s'enfuir. *To fly asunder*, éclater, se briser; *to fly at*, s'élancer sur; *to fly away*, s'envoler, s'enfuir; *to fly back*, faire ressort; *to fly for refuge*, se réfugier; *to fly from justice*, se soustraire à la justice; *to fly in pieces*, éclater, se briser, voler en éclats; *to fly in the face of*, braver; *to fly into a passion*, s'emporter, se mettre en colère; *to fly open*, s'ouvrir subitement; *to fly up*, monter, voler (of sparks); *to fly over*, survoler; *to let fly*, lancer; (*fig.*) s'emporter, éclater (in anger).—*v.t.* Faire voler; fuir, éviter. *To fly a flag*, battre un pavillon; *to fly a kite*, faire voler un cerf-volant; *to fly one's country*, quitter son pays.—*a.* (*pop.*) Malin. **fly-half**, *n.* (*Rugby*) Demi d'ouverture, *m.* **fly-over**, *n.* Enjambement, *m.* **fly-past**, *n.* Défilé aérien, *m.* **fly-sheet**, *n.* Feuille volante, *f.* **fly-wheel**, *n.* Volant, *m.*

flyer, *n.* Aviateur, *m.*, -trice, *f.*; oiseau, insecte qui vole, *m.* **flying**, *a.* Volant. *Flying camp*, camp volant, *m.*; *flying colours*, enseignes déployées, *f.pl.*; *to come off with flying colours*, s'en tirer avec honneur; *flying squad*, brigade mobile, *f.*; *flying start*, (*spt.*) départ lancé; *the Flying Dutchman*, le Vaisseau fantôme.—*n.* Vol, *m.*; aviation, *f.* **flying-boat**, *n.* Hydravion à coque, *m.* **flying-bomb**, *n.* Bombe volante, *f.* **flying-buttress**, *n.* Arc-boutant, *m.* **flying-fish**, *n.* Poisson volant, *m.* **flying-ground**, *n.* Aérodrome, champ d'aviation, *m.*

foal [foul], *n.* Poulain, *m.*, pouliche, *f.* *Foal of the ass*, ânon, *m.*; *in foal*, pleine.—*v.i.* Pouliner, mettre bas.

foam [foum], *n.* Écume; bave; mousse, *f.*—*v.i.* Écumer; moutonner (of the sea); baver (of animals). *To foam with rage* or *to foam at the mouth*, écumer de rage. **foaming**, *a.* Écumant. **foamy**, *a.* Écumeux; mousseux.

fob [fɔb], *n.* Gousset (de pantalon), *m.*—*v.t.* Duper, tromper, filouter. *To fob off*, transférer (à); (*fam.*) *to fob someone off with something*, refiler quelque chose à quelqu'un.

focal ['foukəl], *a.* Focal, du foyer. *Focal plane*, plan focal, *m.* **focalization** [-lai'zeiʃən], *n.* Mise au point, *f.*

fo'c'sle ['foukəsl] [FORECASTLE].

focus ['foukəs], *n.* (*pl.* **foci** ['fousai] or **focuses** ['foukəsiz]) Foyer, *m.* *In focus*, au point; *the focus of a mirror*, le foyer d'un miroir.—*v.t.* Mettre au point; concentrer. **focusing**, *n.* Mise au point, *f.* **focusing-cloth**, *n.* Voile noir pour mise au point, *m.* **focusing-screen**, *n.* Verre dépoli, *m.*

fodder ['fɔdə], *n.* Fourrage, *m.*, pâture, *f.* *Cannon-fodder*, chair à canon, *f.*—*v.t.* Nourrir, affourager. **foddering**, *n.* Affouragement, *m.*

foe [fou], *n.* Ennemi, adversaire, *m.*

foetus ['fiːtəs], *n.* Foetus, embryon, *m.*

fog [fɔg], *n.* Brouillard, *m.*; (*Phot.*) voile, *m.*; (*fig.*) obscurité, confusion, perplexité, *f.* *Sea fog*, brume, *f.*—*v.t.* Assombrir; (*fig.*) embarrasser, embrouiller. **fog-bound**, *a.* Enveloppé de brouillard; arrêté par le brouillard. **fog-horn,** n. Trompe de brume, sirène, f. **fog-signal,** n. Signal de brume, m.

foggily, adv. Obscurément. **fogginess,** n. État brumeux, m.; (*fig.*) obscurité, perplexité, f. **foggy,** a. Brumeux; (*fig.*) sombre, obscur. *It is foggy,* il fait du brouillard.

fogy, fogey ['fougi], n. Ganache, vieille perruque, f.

foible [fɔibl], n. Faible, point faible, m.; (*pl.*) faiblesses, f.pl.

foil [fɔil], n. Feuille de métal, f.; tain (for a mirror), m.; défaite, f., échec (check); contraste, repoussoir (set off), (*Fenc.*) fleuret, m. *To act as a foil to,* faire ressortir, servir de repoussoir à.—*v.t.* Déjouer, faire échouer; frustrer; (*Hunt.*) dépister. **foiling,** n. (*Hunt.*) Foulées, f.pl.

foin [fɔin], n. (*Fenc.*) Botte, f.—*v.i.* Porter une botte.—*v.t.* Frapper de la pointe.

foist [fɔist], v.t. Fourrer; intercaler, glisser. *To foist upon,* imposer à, faire avaler à.

fold [fould], v.t. Plier, ployer; envelopper; serrer. *To fold a letter,* plier une lettre; (*Cook.*) *to fold in,* incorporer (whipped cream, stiffened white of egg); *to fold one's arms,* croiser les bras; *to fold sheep,* parquer des moutons.—n. Pli, repli; bourrelet (of fat), m.; (*Geol.*) plissement, m.; parc (for sheep); troupeau (flock), m.; battant (of a door), m.; feuille (of a screen), f. *A hundredfold,* centuple; *sheep-fold,* bergerie, f., bercail, m.; *threefold,* triple; *twofold,* double.

folder ['fouldə], n. Plieur, m., plieuse, f.; plioir (tool), m.; chemise (for documents), f.; dépliant, prospectus, m.; (*pl.*) pince-nez, m. **folding,** n. Pliage; parcage, m.—a. Pliant; brisé, à deux battants (of doors). **folding-bed,** n. Lit pliant, m. **folding-chair,** n. Chaise pliante, f. **folding-doors,** n.pl. Porte à deux battants, f. **folding-machine,** n. Plieuse, f. **folding-screen,** n. Paravent, m. **foldless,** a. Sans plis.

foliaceous [fouli'eiʃəs], a. (*Bot.*) Foliacé.

foliage ['fouljidʒ], n. Feuillage, m., frondaison, f.—*v.t.* Orner de feuillage. **foliar,** a. Foliaire. **foliate,** v.t. Battre en feuilles; étamer (a mirror); (*Arch.*) orner de feuilles. —a. Feuillé; garni de feuilles; feuillu. **foliation** [-i'eiʃən], n. Foliation, f.

folio ['fouliou], n. In-folio, m.; page, f., folio, m.—*v.t.* Paginer.

folk [fouk], n., or **folks,** n.pl. Gens, personnes, f.pl., monde, m. *Good kind of folk,* de bonnes gens; *these little folk,* ce petit monde; *my folks,* les miens; *your folks,* les vôtres. **folk-dancing,** n. Danses folkloriques, f.pl. **folk-lore,** n. Folklore, m., légendes, traditions, superstitions populaires, f.pl. **folklorist,** n. Folkloriste, m. **folk-song,** n. Chanson populaire, f. **folksy** ['fouksi], a. (*Am.*) Sociable.

follicle ['fɔlikl], n. Follicule, m. **follicular** [-'likjulə], a. **folliculous,** a. Folliculeux.

follow ['fɔlou], v.t. Suivre; poursuivre; observer, imiter; s'attacher à, exercer. *To follow a profession,* exercer une profession; *to follow up,* suivre de près; (*fig.*) exploiter.—*v.i.* S'ensuivre, résulter. *As follows,* ainsi qu'il suit, comme suit; *it follows that,* il s'ensuit que.—n. (*Billiards*) Coulé, m. **follower,** n. Suivant; partisan; compagnon;

(*colloq.*) amoureux, m. **following,** a. Suivant, de suite. *The year following,* l'année suivante, f.—n. Suite, f., gens, m.pl.; parti, m. **follow-my-leader,** n. Jeu de la queue leu leu, m.

folly ['fɔli], n. Folie, sottise, bêtise, f.; édifice inutile, m., folie, f. *An act of folly,* une folie.

foment [fo'ment], v.t. Fomenter. **fomentation** [-'teiʃən], n. Fomentation, f. **fomenter,** n. Fomentateur; fauteur, m.

fond [fɔnd], a. Aimant, affectueux, tendre; passionné (pour); fou (de); indulgent, bon (pour); doux, cher (of hopes); vain, sot, insensé. *To be fond of,* aimer, affectionner, tenir à, être friand de; *to be passionately fond of,* aimer à la folie, être fou de.

fondle [fɔndl], v.t. Câliner, caresser.

fondly ['fɔndli], adv. Tendrement; naïvement. **fondness,** n. Tendresse, tendresse aveugle; affection; inclination, f., penchant, goût, m.

font [fɔnt], n. Fonts baptismaux, m.pl.; bénitier, m.; (*Print.*) [FOUNT.]

fontanel [fɔntə'nel], n. (*Anat.*) Fontanelle, f.

food [fu:d], n. Nourriture, f., aliment, m.; vivres, m.pl.; denrées (all except meat), f.pl.; pâture (for animals), f. *Articles of food,* **food-stuffs,** comestibles, m.pl.; *food and drink,* le boire et le manger; *food control,* ravitaillement, m.; *food for thought,* matière à réflexion, f.; *food-poisoning,* intoxication alimentaire, f.; *he gave me some food,* il m'a donné à manger.

fool [fu:l], n. Sot, bête; insensé, imbécile, niais, m.; dupe, f.; fou (jester), m.; (*Cook.*) marmelade à la crème, f. *Not such a fool,* pas si bête; *to make a fool of,* se moquer de, se ficher de; *to make a fool of oneself,* se rendre ridicule, se faire moquer de soi; *to play the fool,* faire la bête.—*v.t.* Duper; (*colloq.*) se moquer de. *To fool away,* gaspiller. *You don't fool me,* je ne suis pas dupe.—*v.i.* Faire la bête. *You are fooling,* vous plaisantez; vous blaguez. **Fool's-cap,** n. Bonnet d'âne, m.; **foolscap,** n. Papier écolier, m. **fool's-parsley,** n. (*Bot.*) Petite ciguë, f.

foolery, n. Folie, sottise; niaiserie, f. **foolhardily,** adv. Témérairement. **foolhardiness,** n. Témérité, audace, f. **foolhardy,** a. Téméraire.

fooling, n. Niaiserie, bouffonnerie, plaisanterie, f. **foolish,** a. Sot, insensé, bête, ridicule. *To make someone look foolish,* décontenancer quelqu'un. **foolishly,** adv. Follement, sottement, bêtement; imprudemment. **foolishness,** n. Folie, sottise, f.

foolproof, a. À l'épreuve des imbéciles, indéréglable. **fool-trap,** n. Attrape-nigaud, m.

foot [fut], n. (*pl.* **feet** [fi:t]) Pied, m.; patte (of insects etc.); jambe (of compasses); pied (of a pillar), f.; bas (of a page), m.; fond (of a sail), m.; (*Mil.*) infanterie, f. *At foot,* ci-dessous, ci-après; *foot by foot,* pied à pied; *forefoot,* pied de devant; *my foot!* mon œil! *on foot,* à pied; *to find one's feet,* s'acclimater, voler de ses propres ailes; (*fig.*) *to have cold feet,* saigner du nez, caner; *to put one's best foot foremost,* partir du bon pied; *to put one's foot down,* faire acte d'autorité, interdire quelque chose; *to put one's foot in it,* mettre les pieds dans le plat; *to set foot on,* mettre le pied sur; *to set on foot,* mettre en train, mettre sur pied; *to trample under foot,* fouler aux pieds, piétiner.—*v.t.* Fouler (the ground etc.); mettre un pied à, rempiéter (a stocking

etc.); remonter (boots etc.); payer (a bill).—
v.i. Marcher, aller à pied; danser. *To foot it,*
y aller à pied. **foot-and-mouth disease,** *n.*
Fièvre aphteuse; (*fam.*) cocotte, *f.*
football, *n.* Ballon; football (game), *m.* **footballer,** *n.* Footballeur, joueur de football,
m. **football-match,** *n.* Match de football,
m. **foot-bath,** *n.* Bain de pieds, *m.* **foot-
board,** *n.* Marchepied, *m.*, (*Mus.*) pédale, *f.*
foot-brake, *n.* Frein à pied, *m.* **foot-bridge,**
n. Passerelle, *f.*
footed, *a.* Broad-footed, au pied large; *four-
footed,* à quatre pattes. **footer,** *n.* (*fam.*)
Football, *m.* **footfall,** *n.* Pas, bruit de pas, *m.*
foot-fault, *n.* Faute de pied, *f.*—*v.i.* Faire
une faute de pied. **foot-guards,** *n.pl.* Gardes
à pied, *m.pl.* **foot-hills,** *n.pl.* Vallonnements,
m.pl., collines basses, *f.pl.* **foothold,** *n.*
Prise pour le pied, *f.*; (*fig.*) point d'appui, *m.*
To get a foothold, prendre pied; *to lose one's
foothold,* perdre pied.
footing ['futiŋ], *n.* Pied, point d'appui;
établissement, *m.*; position, *f.*, conditions de
vie, *f.pl.*; admission, *f.*; rempiétage (of
stockings); remontage (of boots), *m.*; (*Arch.*)
base, *f.* *He missed his footing,* le pied lui
manqua; *on an equal footing,* sur un pied
d'égalité; *on a war footing,* sur le pied de
guerre; *on the same footing as,* sur le même
pied que; *to gain* or *get a footing,* prendre
pied; *to pay one's footing,* payer sa bienvenue;
we could not meet on the same footing as before,
nos rapports ne pourraient pas être les
mêmes qu'auparavant.
footlights, *n.pl.* (*Theat.*) Rampe, *f.sing.*
footman, *n.* Laquais, valet de pied, *m.*
footnote, *n.* Note au bas de la page, apostille, *f.*
footpace, *n.* Pas, *m.* *At a footpace,* au pas.
footpad, *n.* Voleur de grand chemin, *m.*
foot-passenger, *n.* Piéton, *m.* **foot-path,** *n.*
Sentier; trottoir (in streets); accotement, *m.*,
banquette, *f.*, bas-côté (by roadside), *m.*
footplate, *n.* Plate-forme de la locomotive, *f.*
foot-print, *n.* Empreinte du pied, *f.*
foot-race, *n.* Course à pied, *f.* **foot-rest,** *n.*
(*Cycl.*) Repose-pied, cale-pied(s), *m.inv.*
foot-rope, *n.* (*Naut.*) Marchepied, *m.*,
ralingue de bordure, *f.* **foot-rot,** *n.* (*Vet.*)
Fourchet, *m.* **foot-rule,** *n.* Pied-de-roi, *m.*
foot-slogger, *n.* Pousse-cailloux, biffin, *m.*
foot-soldier, *n.* Fantassin, *m.*
footsore ['futsɔː], *a.* Qui a mal aux pieds.
foot-stalk, *n.* (*Bot.*) Pétiole, *m.* **foot-starter,** *n.*
Démarreur à pédale, à kick; kick, *m.* **foot-
step,** *n.* Pas, *m.*; trace, *f.*; vestige; (*Print.*)
marchepied, *m.* (*fig.*) *To follow in someone's
footsteps,* marcher sur les traces de quelqu'un.
footstool, *n.* Tabouret, *m.*
foot-warmer, *n.* Chaufferette, *f.*, chauffe-
pieds, *m.*; (*Rail.*) bouillotte, *f.* **footway,** *n.*
Trottoir, *m.* **footwear,** *n.* Chaussures, *f.pl.*
foot-work, *n.* (*spt.*) Jeu de pieds, de jambes,
m.
foozle [fu:zl], *n.* (*Golf*) Coup raté; (*fam.*)
travail bousillé, *m.*—*v.t.* (*Golf*) Rater (un
coup); (*fam.*) bousiller, louper.
fop [fɔp], *n.* Fat, *m.* **fopling,** *n.* Petit fat, *m.*
foppery, *n.* Affectation, fatuité, *f.* **foppish,**
a. Affecté, sot, fat. **foppishly,** *adv.* Avec
affectation, en fat. **foppishness,** *n.* Fatuité,
prétention, *f.*
for [fɔː], *prep.* Pour, par; de, à, vers; pendant;

depuis; en place de, en lieu de; en faveur de;
à cause de, pour le compte de; malgré; pour
avoir; pour que (with subj.). *As for me,* quant
à moi, pour moi; *but for,* sans, n'eût été; *for
all that,* pour autant, malgré cela; *for aught
we know,* autant qu'on sache, autant que nous
sachions; *for example,* par exemple; *for more
than a month past,* depuis plus d'un mois; *for
oneself,* pour son compte; *for pity's sake,* par
pitié; *for the present,* pour le présent, pour le
moment, quant à présent; *for your sake,* pour
l'amour de vous; *had it not been for him,*
sans lui; *had it not been for his courage,* n'eût
été son courage, s'il n'avait pas été aussi
courageux; *he is going away for a week,* il part
pour une semaine; *I have been here for a
week,* je suis ici depuis une semaine; *I was
there for a week,* j'y ai été (pendant) une
semaine; *in exchange for,* en échange de; *it
is not for you to,* ce n'est pas à vous de; *there
is something to be said for and against,* il y a
du pour et du contre; *what for?* pourquoi
(faire)? *what's that for?* à quoi sert cela?
word for word, mot à mot.—*conj.* Car.
forage ['fɔridʒ], *n.* Fourrage, *m.*—*v.i.* Fourrager. *To forage for grass,* fourrager au vert;
to forage for hay, fourrager au sec. **forage-
cap,** *n.* Bonnet de police, calot, *m.* **forager,**
n. Fourrageur, *m.* **forage-wa(g)gon,** *n.*
Fourragère, *f.* **foraging,** *n.* Fourragement,
m.
*forasmuch [fɔrəz'mʌtʃ], *conj.* Forasmuch as,
d'autant que, attendu que, vu que.
foray ['fɔrei], *n.* Incursion, razzia, *f.*, raid, *m.*
—*v.t.* Fourrager, ravager, piller.
forbade, *past* [FORBID].
forbear (1) ['fɔːbɛə], *n.* Aïeul, ancêtre, *m.* *Our
forbears,* nos pères.
forbear (2) [fɔː'bɛə], *v.t.* (*past* **forbore,** *p.p.*
forborne) Cesser; épargner, supporter.—*v.i.*
S'abstenir, s'empêcher, se garder (de). **forbearance,** *n.* Patience; indulgence, *f.*,
ménagement, *m.* **forbearingly,** *adv.* Avec
patience, avec indulgence.
forbid [fə'bid], *v.t.* (*past* **forbad, forbade,**
p.p. **forbidden**) Défendre, interdire (de);
empêcher (de). *God forbid!* à Dieu ne plaise!
he is forbidden to, il lui est défendu de;
smoking forbidden, défense de fumer; *to forbid
someone to,* défendre à quelqu'un de; *to forbid
someone something,* défendre quelque chose à
quelqu'un. **forbiddance,** *n.* Interdiction,
défense, *f.* **forbidding,** *a.* Rebutant, repoussant; rébarbatif. **forbiddingly,** *adv.* D'un
air rébarbatif.
force [fɔːs], *n.* Force; violence, *f.*; efficacité;
valeur, *f.*; (*Mil.*, *pl.*) forces, *f.pl.*, armée, *f.*
By sheer force, de vive force; *in force,* (*Law*)
en vigueur, (*Mil.*) en force; *land and sea
forces,* forces de terre et de mer, *f.pl.*; *naval
forces,* unités navales, *f.pl.*; *to come into force,*
entrer en vigueur.—*v.t.* Forcer, obliger, contraindre (à or de); violenter, violer; (*Mil.*)
emporter d'assaut, chasser, pousser. *To
force a passage,* forcer un passage; *to force
back,* repousser, faire reculer; *to force down,*
faire descendre; *to force in,* enfoncer; *to force
on,* imposer à; *to force one's way into,* entrer
de force dans; *to force one's way through,*
s'ouvrir un chemin; *to force open,* forcer; *to
force out,* chasser, faire sortir, pousser dehors.
forced, *a.* Forcé, contraint; guindé (of

style). *Forced landing*, atterrissage forcé, *m.*; *forced vegetables*, *fruit*, primeurs, *f.pl.* **forcedly,** *adv.* De force. **forceful,** etc. [FORCIBLE]. **forceless,** *a.* Sans force. **forcemeat,** *n.* Farce, *f.*, hachis, *m.* *Forcemeat ball*, boulette de viande hachée, *f.*; quenelle, *f.* **forceps** ['fɔːseps], *n.pl.* (*Surg.*) Pince, *f.*, forceps, *m.sing.* **force-pump** *or* **forcing-pump,** *n.* Pompe foulante, *f.* **forcer,** *n.* Personne qui force, *f.*; piston foulant, *m.* **forcible** ['fɔːsibl], *a.* Fort; énergique; forcé; (*Law*) par force. **forcibleness,** *n.* Force; violence, *f.* **forcibly,** *adv.* Par force; fortement; emphatiquement. **forcing,** *n.* (*Hort.*) L'action de forcer, *f.* **forcing-house,** *n.* Serre chaude, *f.* **ford** [fɔːd], *n.* Gué, *m.*—*v.t.* Passer à gué, traverser à gué, guéer. **fordable,** *a.* Guéable. **fore** (1) [fɔː], *int.* (*Golf*) Gare devant! **fore** (2) [fɔː], *a.* Antérieur; de devant; (*Naut.*) de misaine. *Fore and aft*, (*Naut.*) de l'avant à l'arrière; *the fore-part*, la partie antérieure, le devant.—*adv.* D'avance; (*Naut.*) de l'avant. **fore-cabin,** *n.* Cabine d'avant, *f.* *Fore-cabin passenger*, passager de seconde classe, *m.* **fore-carriage,** *n.* Avant-train, *m.* **fore-cited,** *a.* Précité. **fore-court,** *n.* Avant-cour, *f.* **fore-deck,** *n.* Gaillard d'avant, *m.* **fore-edge,** *n.* (*Bookb.*) Gouttière, *f.* (of a book). **fore-end,** *n.* Partie de devant, partie antérieure, *f.*; fût (of a rifle), *m.* **fore-foot,** *n.* Pied de devant, *m.* **fore-mentioned,** *a.* Précité, ci-dessus; (*Law*) susmentionné. **fore-part,** *n.* Devant, avant, *m.* **fore-quarters,** *n.pl.* Avant-main (of a horse), *m.* **fore-reach,** *v.t.* (*Naut.*) Gagner sur. **fore-sail,** *n.* Voile de misaine, *f.* **fore-topmast,** *n.* Petit mât de hune, *m.* **fore-yard,** *n.* Vergue de misaine, *f.* [FORE-COURT].

forearm ['fɔːrɑːm], *n.* Avant-bras, *m.*—*v.t.* [fɔːr'ɑːm], Prémunir. **forebode** [fɔː'boud], *v.t.* Présager, prédire; pressentir. **foreboding,** *n.* Mauvais augure, mauvais présage, pressentiment (de malheur), *m.* **forecast** ['fɔːkɑːst], *n.* Prévoyance, prévision, *f.*; pronostic; calcul, projet, *m.* *Weather forecast*, prévisions météorologiques, *f.pl.*— *v.t.* Prévoir; pronostiquer; projeter, calculer. **forecastle** ['fɔːkɑːsl, fouksl], *n.* Gaillard d'avant, *m.*, plage avant, *f.*; (in merchant ship) poste de l'équipage, *m.* **forecastle-deck,** *n.* Pont de gaillard, *m.* **foreclose** [fɔː'klouz], *v.t.* Forclore, exclure. **foreclosure,** *n.* Forclusion, saisie, *f.* **foredoom** [fɔː'duːm], *v.t.* Condamner par avance; prédire. **forefather** ['fɔːfɑːðə], *n.* Aïeul, ancêtre, *m.*; (*pl.*) aïeux, ancêtres, *m.pl.* **forefinger** ['fɔːfiŋgə], *n.* Index, *m.* **forefront** ['fɔːfrʌnt], *n.* Façade, *f.*, devant, *m.* *In the forefront*, (*Mil.*) en première ligne; au premier rang. **foregather** [fɔː'gæðə], *v.i.* S'assembler, se réunir. *To foregather with*, fréquenter. **forego** (1) [fɔː'gou], *v.t.* Précéder, aller devant. **foregoing,** *a.* Précédent, antérieur. *In the foregoing part*, dans ce qui précède; *the foregoing day*, le jour précédent, *m.* **foregone,** *a.* Passé; prévu, résolu, pris d'avance. *It was a foregone conclusion*, l'issue ne fut jamais douteuse.

forego (2) [FORGO]. **foreground** ['fɔːgraund], *n.* Premier plan; (*Mil.*) avant-terrain, *m.* **forehand** ['fɔːhænd], *n.* Avant-main, *m.* (*Ten.*) *Forehand stroke*, coup d'avant-main, coup droit, *m.*; *forehand court*, côté droit du court, *m.* **forehead** ['fɔrid], *n.* Front, *m.* **foreign** ['fɔrin], *a.* Étranger. *Foreign grown*, de provenance étrangère; *Foreign Office*, ministère des affaires étrangères, *m.*; *in foreign parts*, à l'étranger, dans les pays étrangers; *that is foreign to his nature*, cela lui répugne, cela est incompatible avec son caractère. **foreign-built,** *a.* De construction étrangère. **foreigner,** *n.* Étranger, *m.* **forejudge** [fɔː'dʒʌdʒ], *v.t.* Préjuger. **foreknow** [fɔː'nou], *v.t.* Savoir d'avance; prévoir. **foreknowledge** [fɔː'nɔlidʒ], *n.* Prescience, prévision, *f.* **forel** ['fɔrəl], *n.* Parchemin (for the cover of books), *m.* **foreland** ['fɔːlənd], *n.* Promontoire, cap, *m.* **foreleg** ['fɔːleg], *n.* Patte de devant, *f.* **forelock** ['fɔːlɔk], *n.* Goupille, *f.*; cheveux de devant, *m.pl.*; mèche de devant, *f.*; toupet, *m.* *To take time by the forelock*, saisir l'occasion aux cheveux, par les cheveux. **foreman** ['fɔːmən], *n.* (pl. **foremen**) Chef (of a jury); contremaître; chef d'atelier *or* d'équipe; brigadier, *m. Works foreman*, conducteur, contremaître, des travaux, *m.*; *printer's foreman*, prote, *m.* **foremast** ['fɔːmɑːst], *n.* Mât de misaine, *m.* **foremost** ['fɔːmoust], *a.* Premier; le plus avancé de tous; en tête, au premier rang. *First and foremost*, tout d'abord. **forenamed** ['fɔːneimd], *a.* Susnommé, susdit. **forenoon** ['fɔːnuːn], *n.* Matin, *m.*, matinée, *f.* *In the forenoon*, dans la matinée. **forensic** [fɔ'rensik], *a.* De barreau, de palais. *Forensic medicine*, médecine légale, *f.* **foreordain** ['fɔːrɔː'dein], *v.t.* Préordonner, prédestiner. ***forerun** [fɔː'rʌn], *v.t.* Précéder, devancer; présager. **forerunner** [fɔː'rʌnə], *n.* Avant-coureur, précurseur, *m.*; (*fig.*) symptôme, *m.* **foresee** [fɔː'siː], *v.t.* (*past* **foresaw,** *p.p.* **foreseen**) Prévoir. **foreseeable,** *a.* ·Prévisible. **foreshadow** [fɔː'ʃædou], *v.t.* Préfigurer; annoncer.—*n.* Type, symbole, *m.* **foreshore** ['fɔːʃɔː], *n.* Plage; partie du littoral qui est découverte à marée basse, *f.*, (*Law*) laisse de mer, *f.* **foreshorten** [fɔː'ʃɔːtn], *v.t.* (*Paint.*) Dessiner en raccourci. **foreshortened,** *a.* Présenté en raccourci. **foreshortening,** *n.* Raccourci, *m.* **foreshow** [fɔː'ʃou], *v.t.* Prédire, présager. **foresight** ['fɔːsait], *n.* Prévoyance, *f.*; guidon (of a fire-arm), *m.* *Lack of foresight*, imprévoyance, *f.* **foreskin** ['fɔːskin], *n.* (*Anat.*) Prépuce, *m.* **foreskirt** ['fɔːskəːt], *n.* Pan du devant, *m.* **forest** ['fɔrist], *n.* Forêt, *f.*—*a.* De forêt, forestier. **forest-born,** *a.* Sauvage; né dans une forêt. **forested,** *a.* Couvert de forêts, boisé. **forester,** *n.* Habitant d'une forêt, garde forestier, *m.* **forest-laws,** *n.* Lois forestières, *f.pl.* **forest-ranger,** *n.* Garde forestier, *m.* **forestry,** *n.* Sylviculture, *f.*

School of forestry, forestry school, école forestière, *f.* **forest-tree,** *n.* Arbre de haute futaie, *m.*

forestall [fɔː'stɔːl], *v.t.* Anticiper, prévenir, devancer; *(*Comm.*) accaparer. **forestaller,** *n.* Accapareur, celui qui devance, *m.* **forestalling,** *n.* Accaparement, *m.*

foretaste ['fɔːteist], *n.* Avant-goût, *m.*; anticipation, *f.*—*v.t.* [-'teist] Goûter par avance, avoir un avant-goût de.

foretell [fɔː'tel], *v.t.* Prédire. **foreteller,** *n.* Prophète, *m.* **foretelling,** *n.* Prédiction, *f.*

forethought ['fɔːθɔːt], *n.* Prévoyance, prescience; préméditation; prévenance, *f.*

foretoken [fɔː'toukn], *v.t.* Présager, pronostiquer.—*n.* Présage, signe avant-coureur; pronostic, *m.*

foretooth ['fɔːtuːθ], *n.* (*pl.* **foreteeth**) Dent de devant, incisive, *f.*

foretop ['fɔːtɔp], *n.* (*Naut.*) Hune de misaine, *f.*

forewarn [fɔː'wɔːn], *v.t.* Prévenir, avertir.

forewheel ['fɔːhwiːl], *n.* Roue de devant, *f.*; train de devant, *m.*

forewoman ['fɔːwumən], *n.* Première (ouvrière), contremaîtresse; présidente (of jury), *f.*

foreword ['fɔːwəːd], *n.* Préface, *f.*; avant-propos, *m.*

forfeit ['fɔːfit], *n.* Amende (fine), forfaiture, confiscation, *f.*; (*Games*) gage, *m.*; (*fig.*) peine (penalty), *f.*, (*spt.*) forfait; dédit, *m. To play at forfeits,* jouer aux gages, jouer aux petits jeux; *forfeit clause (of contract),* clause de dédit, *f.*—*a.* Confisqué; (*fig.*) perdu.—*v.t.* Forfaire (à); confisquer; perdre, être passible d'une amende de. *To forfeit one's word,* manquer à sa parole; *to forfeit one's rights,* perdre ses droits, être déchu de ses droits. **forfeitable,** *a.* Confiscable, sujet à confiscation. **forfeiture,** *n.* Forfaiture, confiscation; perte, déchéance, *f.*; (*Comm.*) dédit, *m.*

forfend [fɔː'fend], *v.t.* Garder de, détourner. *God forfend that,* Dieu me garde de; à Dieu ne plaise!

forgather [FOREGATHER].

forge [fɔːdʒ], *n.* Forge, *f.*—*v.t.* Forger; contrefaire (money etc.), fabriquer (a document etc.); (*fig.*) forger (une excuse); faire un faux en.—*v.i.* Commettre un faux. *To forge ahead,* (*Naut.*) courir de l'avant; pousser de l'avant; dépasser (les concurrents). **forger,** *n.* Faussaire; faux-monnayeur, *m.* **forgery,** *n.* Falsification, *f.*; contrefaçon; supposition, *f.*; faux, crime de faux, *m.* **forging,** *n.* Forgeage, *m.*; pièce forgée, *f.*

forget [fə'get], *v.t., v.i.* (*past* **forgot,** *p.p.* **forgotten**) Oublier. *To forget oneself,* s'oublier; *to forget to do something,* oublier de faire quelque chose.

forgetful, *a.* Oublieux. *To be forgetful of,* négliger, oublier. **forgetfulness,** *n.* Oubli, manque de mémoire, *m.*; négligence, *f.*

forget-me-not, *n.* Myosotis, *m.*

forgive [fə'giv], *v.t.* Pardonner, faire grâce de, faire remise de, remettre; pardonner à, faire grâce à. *To forgive something,* pardonner quelque chose à; *to forgive someone,* pardonner à quelqu'un de. **forgiveness,** *n.* Pardon, *m.*; indulgence, clémence, grâce, remise (of a debt), *f.*; (*Theol.*) rémission, *f.*

forgiver, *n.* Personne qui pardonne, *f.* **forgiving,** *a.* Clément, généreux, miséricordieux.

forgo [fɔː'gou], *v.t.* Renoncer à, s'abstenir de, se refuser à.

forgot, *past,* **forgotten,** *p.p.* [FORGET].

fork [fɔːk], *n.* Fourchette; fourche; bifurcation (of roads); pointe (of an arrow etc.), *f.*; zigzag (of lightning), *m.*—*v.i.* Fourcher; bifurquer.—*v.t.* Enlever avec une fourche. *To fork out money,* (*colloq.*) débourser, payer. **forked,** *a.* Fourchu; (*Bot.*) bifurqué. *Forked lightning,* éclair en zigzag, *m.*; (*Mil.*) foudres (badge), *f.pl.* **forkedly,** *adv.* En fourche.

forlorn [fə'lɔːn], *a.* Abandonné, désespéré, délaissé, solitaire; perdu. *Forlorn hope,* (*Mil.*) enfants perdus, *m.pl.*; troupes sacrifiées, *f.pl.*; entreprise désespérée, *f.*; *forlorn appearance,* air triste, *m.*, mine désolée, *f.* **forlornness,** *n.* Délaissement, abandon; état désespéré, *m.,* misère, *f.*

form [fɔːm], *n.* Forme, figure; formalité, cérémonie; tournure (of expression), *f.*; banc (seat), *m.*; (*sch.*) classe, *f.*; gîte (of a hare), *m.*; formule, *f.*, imprimé (printed form), *m.*; (*Print.*) forme, *f. In bad form,* de mauvais goût; de mauvaise humeur; *in due form,* dans les formes, en bonne forme; (*sch.*) *in the sixth form,* (in France), en première; *form-room,* (salle de) classe, *f.*—*v.t.* Former, faire; composer, constituer; façonner. *To form an idea of,* se faire une idée de; *to form part of,* faire partie de.—*v.i.* Se former, prendre forme; se gîter (of hares). (*Mil.*) *Form fours, right!* À droite par quatre, droite! *to form up,* se ranger.

formal ['fɔːməl], *a.* Formel, de forme; pointilleux, minutieux; affecté, cérémonieux, formaliste. **formalism,** *n.* Formalisme, *m.* **formalist,** *n.* Formaliste, *m.* **formality** [-'mæliti], *n.* Formalité, cérémonie; affectation, *f.*; formalisme, *m.*

formalin ['fɔːməlin], *n.* Formaline, *f.*

formalize ['fɔːməlaiz], *v.t.* Donner une forme à. **formally,** *adv.* Avec formalité, en forme, formellement.

format ['fɔːmæt], *n.* Format, *m.*; dimensions, *f.pl.* (of book, page, etc.).

formation [fɔː'meiʃən], *n.* Formation, *f.*; ordre, *m. Close formation,* (*Mil.*) ordre serré, *m.*

formative ['fɔːmətiv], *a.* Formatif, formateur; plastique. *Formative arts,* arts plastiques, *m.pl. Formative years,* les années de formation, *f.pl.,* l'enfance, *f.*

forme (*Print.*) [FORM].

former ['fɔːmə], *a.* Précédent, passé; ancien; premier (first of two).—*pron.* Celui-là, celle-là. *n.*—Gabarit, calibre, moule, *m. Sixth-former,* élève de sixième (équivalent de la 'première' des lycées français). **formerly,** *adv.* Autrefois, auparavant; jadis, anciennement.

formic ['fɔːmik], *a.* Formique. **formication,** *n.* (*Med.*) Fourmillement, *m.*

formidable ['fɔːmidəbl], *a.* Formidable, redoutable. **formidableness,** *n.* Nature formidable, *f.* **formidably,** *adv.* D'une manière formidable, formidablement.

formless ['fɔːmlis], *a.* Informe, sans forme. **formlessness,** *n.* Absence de forme, *f.*

Formosa [fɔː'mousə]. Formose, *f.*

formula ['fɔ:mjulə], *n.* (*pl.* **formulae**)
Formule, *f.* **formulary,** *n.* Formulaire, *m.*
formulate, *v.t.* Formuler. **formulation,** *n.*
Formulation, *f.*
fornicate ['fɔ:nikeit], *v.i.* Forniquer.
fornication ['fɔ:nikeiʃən], *n.* Fornication, *f.*
fornicator ['fɔ:nikeitə], *n.* Fornicateur, *m.*
forrel ['fɔrəl], *n.* [FOREL].
forsake [fə'seik], *v.t.* (*past* **forsook,** *p.p.* **forsaken**) Délaisser, abandonner. *To forsake a vice,* se corriger d'un vice; *to forsake one's colours,* quitter les drapeaux, déserter; *to forsake one's religion,* apostasier. **forsaking,** *n.* Délaissement, abandon, *m.,* apostasie, *f.*
forsooth [fə'su:θ], *adv.* En vérité, ma foi.
***forspent** [fɔ:'spent], *a.* Épuisé.
forswear [fə'swɛə], *v.t.* (*past* **forswore,** *p.p.* **forsworn**) Abjurer, répudier. *To forswear oneself,* se parjurer.—*v.i.* Se parjurer. ***forswearer,** *n.* Parjure, *m.* **forswearing,** *n.* Abjuration, répudiation, *f.* **forsworn,** *a.* Parjure.
forsythia [fɔ:'saiθiə], *n.* Forsythie, *f.*
fort [fɔ:t], *n.* Fort, *m.,* forteresse, *f.*
fortalice ['fɔ:təlis], *n.* Fortin, *m.*
forte (1) [fɔ:t], *n.* Fort, *m.* *It is not my forte,* ça n'est pas mon fort.
forte (2) ['fɔ:ti], *adv.* (*Mus.*) Fortet.
forth [fɔ:θ], *adv.* En avant; hors, dehors, au dehors; au loin. *And so forth,* et ainsi de suite; *from this day forth,* à partir d'aujourd'hui; *to hold forth,* disserter; *to set forth,* énoncer, formuler; se mettre en route.
forthcoming [-'kʌmiŋ], *a.* Tout prêt, prêt à paraître; prochain, à venir; (*fam.*) prêt à parler. **forthright** ['fɔ:θrait], *a.* Franc, carré, net, brutal.—*adv.* [fɔ:θ'rait]. Tout de suite; nettement. **forthwith** [-'wið], *adv.* Incontinent, aussitôt, sur-le-champ, tout de suite.
fortieth ['fɔ:tiiθ], *a.* Quarantième.
fortifiable ['fɔ:tifaiəbl], *a.* Fortifiable.
fortification [fɔ:tifi'keiʃən], *n.* Fortification, *f.*
fortify ['fɔ:tifai], *v.t.* Fortifier; munir (de), armer (de); remonter (wine). *Fortified town,* place forte, *f.* **fortifying,** *a.* (*fig.*) Réconfortant, fortifiant, remontant.
fortitude ['fɔ:titju:d], *n.* Force d'âme, *f.,* courage, *m.*
fortnight ['fɔ:tnait], *n.* Quinze jours, *m.pl.,* quinzaine, *f.* *A fortnight ago,* il y a quinze jours; *a fortnight ago yesterday,* il y a eu hier quinze jours; *today fortnight,* d'aujourd'hui en quinze; *to adjourn for a fortnight,* remettre à quinzaine. **fortnightly,** *adv.* Tous les quinze jours.—*a.* Bimensuel.
fortress ['fɔ:tris], *n.* Forteresse, place forte, *f.*; camp retranché, *m.*
fortuitous [fɔ:'tjuitəs], *a.* Fortuit. **fortuitously,** *adv.* Fortuitement, par hasard.
fortunate ['fɔ:tʃnit *or* 'fɔ:tjunət], *a.* Heureux, fortuné. **fortunately,** *adv.* Heureusement, par bonheur.
fortune ['fɔ:tʃən], *n.* Fortune, *f.,* sort (lot), destin, *m.* *By good fortune,* par bonheur, par bonne fortune; *fortune is blind,* le sort est aveugle; *good fortune,* bonne chance, bonne fortune; *people of fortune,* les gens riches, *m.pl.*; *the fortune of war,* le sort des armes; *to tell fortunes,* dire la bonne aventure; *to have one's fortune told,* se faire dire la bonne aventure; *to make a fortune,* faire fortune; *to seek*

one's fortune, chercher fortune. **fortune-hunter,** *n.* Aventurier, *m.,* coureur de dots, *m.* **fortune-teller,** *n.* Diseur de bonne aventure, *m.* **fortune-telling,** *n.* La bonne aventure, *f.*
forty ['fɔ:ti], *a.* Quarante. *About forty,* une quarantaine, *f.*; *forty winks,* un petit somme, *m.*; *she is in her forties,* elle a passé la quarantaine; *she must be nearly forty,* elle doit friser la quarantaine; *the forty-hour week,* la semaine des quarante heures; *in the forties,* dans les années quarante. **forty-one,** *a.* and *n.* Quarante et un, *m.*
forum ['fɔ:rəm], *n.* Forum, *m.*
forward ['fɔ:wəd], *a.* Avancé, en avant; (*fig.*) empressé (de), prompt (à), ardent (à); précoce (of fruit etc.); impertinent, présomptueux.—*n.* (*Ftb.*) Avant, *m.* *Centre-forward,* avant-centre, *m.*—*adv.* En avant; en évidence. *From this day forward,* dorénavant; *from that time forward,* depuis ce temps-là; *to push oneself forward,* se mettre en évidence, se pousser en avant.—*v.t.* Avancer, hâter, activer; faire pousser; (*Comm.*) envoyer, transmettre, expédier; faire suivre (letters). *Forward!* en avant! *please forward!* prière de faire suivre! *to forward the views of,* seconder les intentions de. **forwarder,** *n.* Promoteur, *m.* **forwarding,** *n.* Expédition, *f.* *Forwarding agent,* commissionnaire expéditeur, *m.* **forwardly,** *adv.* Avec empressement; effrontément, hardiment. **forwardness,** *n.* Empressement; avancement, progrès, *m.*; précocité (of fruit etc.); assurance, hardiesse; effronterie, *f.*
fossa ['fɔsə], *n.* (*pl.* **fossae** ['fɔsi:]) (*Anat.*) Fosse, *f.*
fosse [fɔs], *n.* Fossé, *m.* **fosse-way,** *n.* Route militaire exécutée par les Romains en Angleterre, *f.*
fossil ['fɔsil], *a.* and *n.* Fossile, *m.* **fossiliferous** [-'lifərəs], *a.* Fossilifère. **fossilization** [-lai'zeiʃən], *n.* Fossilisation, *f.* **fossilize,** *v.t.* Fossiliser. *To become fossilized,* se fossiliser.
fossorial [fɔ'sɔ:riəl], *a.* (*Zool.*) Fouisseur.
foster ['fɔstə], *v.t.* Élever, nourrir; (*fig.*) favoriser, encourager. **foster-brother,** *n.* Frère de lait, *m.* **foster-child** *or* **fosterling** *n.* Nourrisson, *m.* **foster-father,** *n.* Père nourricier, *m.* **foster-mother,** *n.* Mère nourricière, *f.* **foster-sister,** *n.* Sœur de lait, *f.*
fostering, *n.* Nourriture, *f.*; protection, *f.*; soins, *m.pl.*—*a.* Bienfaisant, protecteur.
fother ['fɔðə], *v.t.* (*Naut.*) Aveugler, boucher. *To fother a leak,* aveugler une voie d'eau.
fought [fɔ:t], *past* and *p.p.* [FIGHT].
foul [faul], *a.* Sale, malpropre, immonde, souillé, trouble, bourbeux (water); impur (spirit); fétide, infect, malsain (air); grossier, obscène (language); engagé (screw), encrassé (engine); (*fig.*) mauvais, atroce, noir, odieux; (*Print.*) chargé. *Foul deed,* infamie, *f.,* acte criminel, *m.*; *foul stomach,* estomac chargé; *by fair means or foul,* de gré ou de force; *foul air,* air vicié, *m.*; *foul breath,* mauvaise haleine, *f.*; *foul language,* langage grossier, *m.*; *foul play,* jeu déloyal, *m.,* trahison, *f.,* vilain tour, *m.*; *to meet with foul play,* être victime d'un guet-apens, être assassiné; *foul weather,* gros temps, *m.*; *foul wind,* (*Naut.*) vent contraire,

m.; *to run foul of*, aborder, se heurter à, (*fig.*) déchirer à belles dents.—*n.* (*spt.*) Coup bas, déloyal, interdit, *m.*; (*Naut.*) collision, *f.*; (*Billiards*) fausse-queue, *f.*—*v.t.* Salir, souiller, troubler; encrasser (fire-arms); (*Naut.*) aborder; s'engager (of ropes). **foul-faced,** *a.* Laid, hideux. **foul-mouthed,** *a.* Grossier. **foully,** *adv.* Salement, vilainement, honteusement. **foulness,** *n.* Saleté, impureté; turpitude, noirceur, *f.*

foumart ['fuːmɑːt], *n.* Putois, *m.*

found (1) [faund], *past* and *p.p.* [FIND].

found (2) [faund], *v.t.* Fonder, poser les fondements de, établir; fondre, mouler (to cast).

foundation [faun'deiʃən], *n.* Fondement, *m.*, fondation, *f.*, établissement, *m.*; création, (*fig.*) base, source, *f.* (*sch.*) To be on the *foundation*, être boursier; *to lay the foundations of*, poser les fondements de.

foundationer, *n.* Boursier, *m.*

foundation-garment, *n.* Gaine, *f.*

foundation-stone, *n.* Première pierre, *f.*

founder (1) ['faundə], *n.* Fondateur, auteur; (*Metal.*) fondeur, *m.*

founder (2) ['faundə], *n.* Courbature, fourbure (of horse), *f.*—*v.t.* Surmener (un cheval), rendre (un cheval) fourbu.—*v.i.* (*Naut.*) Couler à fond, sombrer, couler bas; broncher (of a horse); (*fig.*) échouer. **foundered,** *a.* Courbatu, fourbu (of a horse); sombré, coulé à fond (of ships). *Foundered at sea*, sombré en mer. **foundering,** *n.* Engloutissement, *m.*, submersion (of ship), *f.*; écroulement, effondrement (of ground, building, horse), *m.*

foundling ['faundliŋ], *n.* Enfant trouvé, *m.*

foundress ['faundris], *n.* Fondatrice, *f.*

foundry ['faundri], *n.* Fonderie, *f.*

fount [faunt], *n.* Fontaine, (*fig.*) cause, *f.*, principe, *m.*, source, *f.*; (*Print.*) fonte, *f.* *A fount of knowledge*, un puits de science.

fountain ['fauntin], *n.* Fontaine, source, *f.*; jet d'eau, *m.* **fountain-head,** *n.* Source, origine, *f.* **fountain-pen,** *n.* Porte-plume réservoir; stylo, *m.*

fountainless, *a.* Sans fontaine, sans eau.

four [fɔː], *a.* and *n.* Quatre. *Carriage and four*, voiture à quatre chevaux, *f.*; *on all fours*, à quatre pattes. **four-angled,** *a.* À quatre angles. **four-cornered,** *a.* À quatre coins. **four-engined,** *a.* (*Av.*) Quadrimoteur. **four-flusher,** *n.* (*Am.*) Bluffeur, vantard, *m.* **four-fold,** *a.* Quatre fois, quatre fois autant, quadruple. **four-footed,** *a.* Quadrupède, à quatre pieds. **four-in-hand,** *adv.* À grandes guides, à quatre chevaux. *To drive four-in-hand*, conduire à grandes guides. **four-master,** *n.* Quatre-mâts, *m. inv.* **four-poster,** *n.* Lit à colonnes, *m.* ***fourscore,** *a.* and *n.* Quatre-vingts, *m.* *Fourscore and ten*, quatre-vingt-dix. **four-seater,** *n.* Voiture à quatre places, *f.* **foursome,** *n.* (*Golf*) Partie double, *f.* **foursquare,** *a.* Carré; quadrangulaire. **four-wheeled,** *a.* À quatre roues. **four-wheeler,** *n.* Voiture à quatre roues, *f.*

fourteen ['fɔː'tiːn], *a.* Quatorze. **fourteenth,** *a.* Quatorzième; quatorze (of kings and dates).

fourth [fɔːθ], *a.* Quatrième; quatre (of kings and dates). *The fourth part*, la quatrième

partie, le quart.—*n.* Quart, *m.*; (*Mus.*) quarte, *f.* **fourthly,** *adv.* Quatrièmement.

fowl [faul], *n.* Oiseau de basse-cour; oiseau volatile (bird), *m.*, poule (hen), *f.*; (*Cook.*) volaille, *f.* *Wild fowl*, gibier d'eau, *m.*—*v.i.* Chasser aux oiseaux. **fowler,** *n.* Oiseleur, *m.* **fowl-house,** *n.* Poulailler, *m.* **fowling,** *n.* Chasse aux oiseaux sauvages, *f.* **fowling-piece,** *n.* Fusil de chasse, *m.*

fox [fɔks], *n.* (*pl.* **foxes**) Renard; (*fig.*) rusé, matois, *m.* *A sly fox*, un rusé compère, *m.*; *young fox*, renardeau, *m.*—*v.t.* Tacher, piquer (of book leaves); mystifier, tromper.—*v.i.* Feindre, ruser, user de feintes, renarder. *To fox about, around*, fureter partout. **fox-brush,** *n.* Queue de renard, *f.* **fox-cub,** *n.* Jeune renard, renardeau, *m.* **fox-evil** or **fox's-evil,** *n.* (*Path.*) Alopécie, pelade, *f.* **foxglove,** *n.* Digitale, *f.* **fox-hole,** *n.* Renardière, *f.*; (*Mil.*) niche-abri, *f.* **fox-hound,** *n.* Chien pour la chasse au renard, *m.* **fox-hunt** or **fox-hunting,** *n.* Chasse au renard, *f.* **fox-hunter,** *n.* Chasseur au renard, *m.* **foxlike,** *a.* De renard, rusé. **foxtail,** *n.* Queue-de-renard (plant), *f.* **fox-terrier,** *n.* Fox, *m.* **fox-trap,** *n.* Piège à renard, traquenard, *m.* **foxtrot,** *n.* Fox-trot, *m.* (dance).

foxed [fɔkst], *a.* Taché de roux; piqué (paper, beer). **foxy,** *a.* De renard, rusé; roux (red).

foyer ['fɔiei], *n.* (*Theat.*) Foyer, *m.*

fraction ['frækʃən], *n.* Fraction, *f.* *Vulgar fraction*, fraction ordinaire. **fractional** or **fractionary,** *a.* Fractionnaire.

fractious ['frækʃəs], *a.* Revêche, maussade, hargneux, de mauvaise humeur; récalcitrant. **fractiously,** *adv.* De mauvaise humeur. **fractiousness,** *n.* Humeur querelleuse, maussaderie, *f.*

fracture ['fræktʃə], *n.* Fracture, cassure, *f.*—*v.t.* Casser, rompre; (*Surg.*) fracturer.—*v.i.* Se fracturer, se rompre.

fragile ['frædʒail] (*rarely* ·dʒil), *a.* Fragile. **fragility** [fræ'dʒiliti], *n.* Fragilité, *f.*

fragment ['frægmənt], *n.* Fragment, éclat, débris, *m. Chosen fragments of an author*, morceaux choisis d'un auteur, *m.pl.*—*v.t.* Réduire en morceaux. **fragmentary,** *a.* Composé de fragments; fragmentaire.

fragrance ['freigrəns] or **fragrancy,** *n.* Odeur suave, *f.*, parfum, *m.* **fragrant,** *a.* Odoriférant, parfumé, au doux parfum, qui sent bon. **fragrantly,** *adv.* Avec un parfum agréable.

frail [freil], *a.* Frêle, fragile, faible.—*n.* Cabas, panier d'emballage, *m.* **frailness** or **frailty,** *n.* Faiblesse, fragilité, *f.*

frame [freim], *n.* Charpente, *f.*; châssis (of a window etc.), *m.*; chambranle (of a door), *m.*; caisse (of a carriage), *f.*; (*Shipbuilding*) membrure, *f.*, couple; (*Av.*) fuselage, *m.*; (*fig.*) forme, *f.*, système, *m.*; organisation, *f.*; cadre (of pictures etc.), *m.*; métier (for embroidering etc.), *m.*; (*Cine., Tel.*) image, *f.*; (*Phot.*) châssis-presse (for printing), *m.*; disposition (of mind), *f.*; (of umbrella) monture, *f.* (*Math.*) *Frame of reference*, système de coordonnées, *m.*; (*Cine.*) frame-by-frame exposure, tournage image par image, *m.*; *eighteen frames per second*, dix-huit images par seconde.—*v.t.* Former, construire; régler (sur); encadrer; (*Cine., Tel.*) cadrer; imaginer, inventer; exprimer; faire. *To frame an innocent man*,

monter une cabale contre un homme innocent. **frame-up,** *n.* (*fam.*) Coup monté,
m.
framer, *n.* Encadreur; (*fig.*) auteur (d'un
projet), *m.* **framing,** *n.* Encadrement (of
pictures), *m.*; conception, *f.* (d'une idée, d'un
plan); (*Cine.*, *Tel.*) cadrage, *m.*
framework, *n.* Charpente, *f.*; châssis, fuselage
(of an aeroplane), *m.*
France [frɑːns]. La France, *f.*
Frances ['frɑːnsis]. Françoise, *f.*
franchise ['fræntʃaiz], *n.* Franchise, *f.*, droit
de vote, *m.*, immunité, *f.*, privilège, *m.*
Francis ['frɑːnsis]. François, Francis, *m.*
Franciscan [fræn'siskən], *a.* and *n.* Franciscain, *m.* *Franciscan nun,* Franciscaine, *f.*
francophile ['fræŋkofail], *a.* and *n.* Francophile, *m.* **francophobe,** *a.* and *n.* Francophobe, *m.*
frangible ['frændʒibl], *a.* Fragile, cassant.
frangipani [frændʒi'pɑːni], *n.* Frangipanier
(tree), *m.*; (*Cook.*) frangipane, *f.*
Frank [fræŋk], *n.* Franc, *m.*, Franque, *f.*—
prop. n. François, *m.*
frank [fræŋk], *a.* Franc, sincère, libéral; libre.
—*v.t.* Affranchir.
Frankfort ['fræŋkfɔːt], **Frankfurt** ['fræŋkfət].
Francfort, *m.*
frankincense ['fræŋkinsens], *n.* Encens, *m.*
Frankish ['fræŋkiʃ], *a.* Franc, *m.*, franque, *f.*
franklin ['fræŋklin], *n.* Propriétaire libre,
franc-tenancier, *m.*
frankly ['fræŋkli], *adv.* Franchement. **frankness,** *n.* Franchise, sincérité, *f.*
frantic ['fræntik], *a.* Frénétique, fou, forcené,
furieux. *Frantic with joy,* ivre de joie.
frantically, *adv.* Follement, avec frénésie,
en furieux.
frap [fræp], *v.t.* (*Naut.*) Aiguilleter, brider.
To frap a tackle, aiguilleter un palan.
frass [fræs], *n.* (*Ent.*) Chîures, *f.pl.* (of larvae).
fraternal [frə'tɜːnəl], *a.* Fraternel. **fraternally,** *adv.* Fraternellement, en frère.
fraternity, *n.* Fraternité, confrérie, *f.*
fraternization [frætə:nai'zeiʃən], *n.* Fraternisation, *f.*
fraternize ['frætənaiz], *v.i.* Fraterniser (avec).
fratricidal [frætri'saidl], *a.* Fratricide.
fratricide, *n.* Fratricide, *m.*
fraud [frɔːd] or **fraudulence,** *n.* Fraude,
supercherie, *f.*, dol, *m.*; imposteur, *m.* *That
man is a perfect fraud,* impossible de se fier
à cet homme; *pious fraud,* pieux mensonge,
m. **fraudulent,** *a.* Frauduleux, dolosif, de
mauvaise foi. *Fraudulent conversion,* carambouillage, *m.* **fraudulently,** *adv.* Frauduleusement; en fraude.
fraught [frɔːt], *a.* Rempli, gros, plein (de);
riche, fertile (en). *Fraught with events,* gros
d'événements; *fraught with misfortunes,* fertile
en malheurs.
fraxinella [fræksi'nelə], *n.* (*Bot.*) Fraxinelle, *f.*,
dictame, *m.*
fray [frei], *n.* Échauffourée, mêlée, bagarre;
*éraillure, *f.* *In the thick of the fray,* au plus
fort de la mêlée.—*v.t.* Érailler, effilocher.
Frayed cuffs, manchettes usées, effilochées,
f.pl.—*v.i.* S'érailler. **fraying,** *n.* Éraillure, *f.*
frazzle [fræzl], *n.* (*pop.*) *Worn to a frazzle,*
usé jusqu'à la corde.
freak [friːk], *n.* Boutade, *f.*, caprice *m.*;
bizarrerie, *f.*; être (*or* chose) à part, monstre,
m.; bigarrure, *f.* *Freak of nature,* caprice de la
nature, *m.*; *by a freak of chance, of fortune,* par
un coup du (de) hasard, par un jeu du hasard;
he is a freak, c'est un drôle de type.—*v.t.*
Bigarrer, tacheter (de). **freakish,** *a.* Bizarre,
fantasque, capricieux. **freakishly,** *adv.*
Capricieusement. **freakishness,** *n.* Boutade,
bizarrerie, humeur capricieuse, *f.*
freckle [frekl], *n.* Éphélide, tache de rousseur,
tache de son, *f.*—*v.t.* Tacheter. **freckled** or
***freckly,** *a.* Plein de taches de rousseur;
taché de son; tacheté, tavelé; truité.
Frederick ['fredrik]. Frédéric, *m.*
free [friː], *a.* Libre, indépendant; exempt;
sincère, franc; gratuit, volontaire; aisé,
dégagé, sans gêne. *Delivered free,* rendu
franco à domicile; *fancy-free,* qui a le cœur
libre; *free and easy,* sans façon, sans gêne; *free
copy,* spécimen, *m.*; *free fight,* mêlée générale,
f.; *free from,* exempt de; *free hand,* liberté
(d'agir), carte blanche, *f.*; *free on board,*
franco à bord; *free on rail,* franco en gare; *free
ticket,* billet de faveur, *m.*; *free wheel,* roue
libre, *f.*; *free will,* libre arbitre, franc arbitre,
m.; *of his own free will,* de son plein gré; *to
make free with,* ne pas se gêner avec, user
librement de; *to sail free,* avoir du largue; *to
set free,* mettre en liberté.—*adv.* Gratis;
franco.—*v.t.* Délivrer, libérer; lever l'hypothèque sur; déshypothéquer; mettre en vente
libre; affranchir, exempter; dégager. *To free
oneself,* s'affranchir.
freeboard, *n.* Accastillage, *m.* **freebooter,** *n.*
Maraudeur; flibustier, *m.* **freeborn,** *a.* Né
libre. **freedman,** *n.* Affranchi, *m.*
freedom, *n.* Liberté (de); indépendance, *f.*;
aisance, *f.*, sans-gêne, *m.*; bourgeoisie (of a
city), *f.*; droit de cité, *m.*; libre usage, *m.*
Freedom of speech, le franc-parler.
freehand, *n.* (*Drawing*) Le dessin à main
levée, *m.* **free-hearted,** *a.* Libre, libéral,
généreux. **freehold,** *n.* Propriété foncière
libre, *f.*, franc-alleu, *m.* **free-holder,** *n.*
Propriétaire foncier; *franc tenancier, *m.*
freelance, *n.* Journaliste, acteur indépendant,
sans contrat.
freely, *adv.* Librement, franchement, sans
contrainte, gratuitement, volontiers; copieusement, libéralement.
freeman, *n.* Citoyen, homme libre, *m.*
freemason, *n.* Franc-maçon, *m.* **freemasonry,** *n.* Franc-maçonnerie, *f.*
free-minded, *a.* Sans souci.
freeness, *n.* Sincérité, candeur, générosité,
libéralité, *f.*
free-spoken, *a.* Qui a son franc-parler.
freestone, *n.* Pierre de taille, *f.*
freestyle, *n.* Nage libre, *f.*
freethinker, *n.* Esprit fort, libre penseur,
m.
free-trade, *n.* Libre-échange, *m.* *Free-trade
area,* zone de libre-échange, *f.* **free-trader,**
n. Libre-échangiste, *m.*
free-wheel, *v.i.* Faire roue libre.
freeze [friːz], *v.t.* (*past* **froze**, *p.p.* **frozen**)
Geler; (*Fin.*) bloquer (prices, wages).—*v.i.*
Glacer, se geler, se glacer. *It is freezing,* il
gèle.—*n.* Gel, *m.* **freezer,** *n.* Sorbetière, *f.*
freezing, *n.* Congélation, *f.*; (*Fin.*) blocage,
m.—*a.* Glacial. **freezing-mixture,** *n.*
Mélange réfrigérant, *m.* **freezing-point,** *n.*
Point de congélation, *m.*

Freiburg ['fraibə:g]. Fribourg-en-Brisgau, *m.*
freight [freit], *n.* Cargaison, *f.*, chargement;
fret (cost), *m.* *Freight car* (*Am.*), wagon de
marchandises, *m.*; (*Av.*) *freight plane*, avion
de transport, *m.*—*v.t.* Fréter, affréter (de).
freighter, *n.* Affréteur, *m.*; cargo, vapeur
de charge, *m.* **freighting,** *n.* Affrètement, *m.*
French [frentʃ], *a.* Français. *After the French
fashion*, à la française; *French ambassador*,
ambassadeur de France, *m.*; *French beans*,
haricots verts, *m.pl.*; *French chalk*, talc, *m.*,
pierre de savon, *f.*; *French cleaning*, nettoyage
à sec (de grande classe), *m.*; *French cleaner*,
teinturier-dégraisseur; *French dressing*, vinaigrette, *f.*; *French horn*, cor d'harmonie, *m.*;
French lesson, leçon de français, *f.*; *French
master* or *teacher*, professeur de français, *m.*;
French loaf, flûte, *f.*; *French plums*, prunes
d'Agen, *f.pl.*; *French polish*, vernis au tampon, *m.*; *French roll*, petit pain, *m.*; *French
toast*, tranche de pain frite, *f.*, canapé, *m.*;
French whiting, blanc d'argent, *m.*; *French
window*, porte-fenêtre, *f.*; *to take French
leave*, décamper sans mot dire, filer à
l'anglaise.—*n.* Français (language), *m.* *The
French*, les Français, *m.pl.* **Frenchman,** *n.*
Français, *m.* **Frenchwoman,** *n.* Française, *f.*
Frenchify, *v.t.* Franciser. *To become Frenchified*, se franciser. **Frenchy,** *a.* (*fam.*) À
la française, qui a un petit air français.—*n.*
Français.
frenum ['fri:nʌm], *n.* Filet, frein (de la
langue), *m.*
frenzied ['frenzid], *a.* Forcené, délirant.
frenzy ['frenzi], *n.* Frénésie, *f.*; égarement
d'esprit, délire, *m.*
frequence ['fri:kwəns] or **frequency,** *n.* Fréquence; répétition fréquente, *f.* (*Rad.*)
Carrier frequency, fréquence fondamentale,
f.; *high, low frequency*, haute, basse fréquence;
high-frequency current, courant à haute fréquence; (*Med.*) courant alto-fréquent; *very
high frequency* or *V.H.F.*, modulation de
fréquence, *f.*
frequent (1) ['fri:kwənt], *a.* Fréquent, très
répandu; rapide (pulse).
frequent (2) [fri'kwent], *v.t.* Fréquenter;
hanter. **frequentation** [-'teiʃən], *n.* Fréquentation, *f.*
frequentative [fri'kwentətiv], *n.* (*Gram.*)
Fréquentatif, *m.* **frequenter,** *n.* Familier,
habitué, *m.* **frequently,** *adv.* Fréquemment,
souvent.
fresco ['freskou], *n.* Fresque, *f.* *Fresco painting*, peinture à fresque, *f.*; *to paint in fresco*,
peindre à fresque.
fresh [freʃ], *a.* Frais; récent, nouveau; (*fig.*)
fougueux, vigoureux; novice, vert; original;
(*slang*) gai (tipsy), impertinent, qui fait le
malin; entreprenant (with girls). *Fresh air*,
air pur (not stuffy), air frais (not overheated);
fresh as a daisy, frais comme une rose; *fresh
complexion*, un teint frais, *m.*; *fresh paragraph*,
nouveau paragraphe, à la ligne; *fresh water*, de
l'eau douce (not salt), de l'eau fraîche (fresh-
drawn), *f.*; *he is fresh from college*, il est frais
émoulu de l'Université; *is there anything
fresh?* y a-t-il du nouveau?—*adv.* Nouvellement. *Fresh-cut*, fraîchement coupé; *fresh-
shaven*, rasé de frais. **freshen,** *v.t.* Rafraîchir.—*v.i.* Se rafraîchir. *The wind freshens*,
le vent fraîchit. **freshet,** *n.* Courant d'eau

douce, *m.*; crue, *f.* **freshly,** *adv.* Fraîchement; récemment, nouvellement, depuis peu.
freshman or (*colloq.*) **fresher,** *n.* Étudiant
de première année, bizuth, *m.* **freshness,** *n.*
Fraîcheur; (*fig.*) nouveauté; naïveté, *f.*
freshwater, *a.* D'eau douce *or* de rivière.
Freshwater sailors, marins d'eau douce,
m.pl.
fret [fret], *n.* Fermentation; (*fig.*) agitation de
l'âme; irritation; (*Mus.*) touche, touchette
(of guitar etc.); (*Arch.*) grecque, *f.*—*v.t.* User
par le frottement, frotter (contre); ronger,
écorcher (to gall); chagriner, irriter, agiter;
découper, ciseler.—*v.i.* Se chagriner, se
fâcher, s'inquiéter; se tourmenter; s'user,
s'érailler; se frotter. *To fret inwardly*, ronger
son frein.
fretful, *a.* Chagrin, de mauvaise humeur,
maussade; agité, inquiet. **fretfully,** *adv.*
Avec chagrin, de mauvaise humeur. **fretfulness,** *n.* Mauvaise humeur, irritation, *f.*
fretsaw, *n.* Scie à découper, *f.*
fretting, *n.* Tracas, *m.*—*a.* Chagrinant, inquiétant.
fretwork, *n.* Ouvrage à claire-voie; travail
ajouré, bois découpé, découpage, *m.*; (*Arch.*)
grecque, *f.*
Freudian ['frɔidiən], *a.* Freudien.
friability [fraiə'biliti] or **friableness,** *n.*
Friabilité, *f.* **friable,** *a.* Friable.
friar ['fraiə], *n.* Moine, *m.* *Black Friars*,
Dominicains, frères prêcheurs, *m.pl.*; *Grey
Friars*, Franciscains, frères mineurs, Mino-
rites; *White Friars*, Carmes. *Friar's balsam*,
baume de benjoin, *m.* **friar-like** or **friarly,**
a. De moine. **friary,** *n.* Monastère, couvent,
m.
fribble [fribl], *n.* Un rien qui vaille, un
baguenaudier, *m.*—*v.i.* Baguenauder, niaiser.
Fribourg ['fribuə]. Fribourg (Suisse), *m.*
fricassee [frikə'si:], *n.* Fricassée, gibelotte, *f.*
—*v.t.* Fricasser; mettre en gibelotte.
fricative ['frikətiv], *n.* Fricative, *f.*—*a.* Fricatif.
friction ['frikʃən], *n.* Frottement, *m.*; (*Med.*)
friction, *f.* **friction-clutch,** *n.* Embrayage
à friction, *m.* **friction-tube,** *n.* Étoupille, *f.*
Friday ['fraid(e)i], *n.* Vendredi, *m.* *Good
Friday*, vendredi saint, *m.*
fridge [fridʒ], *n.* (*fam.*) Frigidaire, *m.* (trade
mark).
fried, *past* and *p.p.* [FRY].
friend [frend], *n.* Ami, *m.*, amie, *f.*; Quaker,
m., Quakeresse, *f.* *A friend in need is a friend
indeed*, c'est dans le besoin qu'on connaît ses
amis; *bosom friend*, ami de cœur, ami intime,
m.; *like a friend*, en ami, comme un ami;
short reckonings make long friends, les bons
comptes font les bons amis; *the best of friends
must part*, il n'est si bonne compagnie qui ne
se sépare; *to make friends with*, se lier avec.
friendless, *a.* Sans ami, délaissé, abandonné. **friendliness,** *n.* Bienveillance, *f.*
friendly, *a.* D'ami, amical; ami (de), bien
disposé, favorable (à), bienveillant (pour).
Friendly society, société de secours mutuel, *f.*;
in a friendly way, en ami; *to be on friendly
terms*, être au mieux ensemble. *The Friendly
Islands*, les îles des Amis, *f.pl.* **friendship,** *n.*
Amitié, *f.*
Friesland ['fri:zlənd]. La Frise, *f.*
frieze [fri:z], *n.* Frise, *f.*—*a.* De frise.

frigate ['frigit], *n.* Frégate, *f.* *Frigate bird*, frégate, *f.* **frigatoon**, *n.* Frégaton, *m.*

fright [frait], *n.* Effroi, *m.*, épouvante, frayeur, *f.* *To give someone a fright*, faire peur à quelqu'un; *to take fright*, s'effrayer; *what a fright she is!* *she looks a fright*, elle est mise à faire peur. **frighten**, *v.t.* Épouvanter, effrayer, faire peur à. **frightful**, *a.* Épouvantable, effroyable, affreux. **frightfully**, *adv.* Effroyablement, affreusement. **frightfulness**, *n.* Horreur, frayeur, *f.*

frigid ['fridʒid], *a.* Froid, glacial. *Frigid zone*, zone glaciale, *f.*; *frigid politeness*, politesse glaciale, *f.*

frigidity [fri'dʒiditi] or **frigidness**, *n.* Frigidité, froideur, *f.* **frigidly**, *adv.* Froidement.

frigorific [frigɔ'rifik], *a.* Frigorifique.

frill [fril], *n.* Volant, *m.*, ruche, *f.*, jabot (de chemise), *m.* (*pl.*) *Without frills*, simplement, sans façons.—*v.t.* Plisser, froncer; rucher, tuyauter.

fringe [frindʒ], *n.* Frange, *f.*; bord, *m.*; bordure, *f.* (*Grecian*) *fringe*, cheveux à la chien, *m.pl.*; effilé, *m.*, effiloche, effiloque, *f.*; *on the fringe of*, en marge de; *the outer fringe* (*of a city*), la grande banlieue; (*fam.*) *the fringe*, les représentations hors festival, *f.pl.* —*v.t.* Franger, border. **fringy**, *a.* À frange, orné de franges.

frippery ['fripəri], *n.* Friperie, *f.*

frisk [frisk], *n.* Gambade, *f.*—*v.i.* Sautiller, gambader, frétiller, folâtrer. **friskiness**, *n.* Folâtrerie, gaieté, vivacité, *f.* **frisky**, *a.* Vif, enjoué, folâtre; animé, fringant (of horses).

frit [frit], *n.* (*Glass*) Fritte, *f.*

frith [friθ] or **firth**, *n.* Estuaire, *m.* (of a river); terrain boisé ou couvert de taillis; *breuil, *m.*

fritillary [fri'tiləri], *n.* Fritillaire, *f.*, damier, *m.*

fritter ['fritə], *n.* Beignet, *m.* *Apple fritters*, beignets aux pommes, *m.pl.*—*v.t.* Couper en morceaux, morceler. *To fritter away* (*one's time or money*), gaspiller, dissiper.

frivolity [fri'vɔliti], *n.* Frivolité, *f.*

frivolous ['frivələs], *a.* Frivole. **frivolously**, *adv.* D'une manière frivole. **frivolousness**, *n.* Frivolité, *f.*

frizz [friz] or **frizzle** [frizl], *v.t.* Friser, crêper.—*v.i.* Frisotter (of hair); poncer (leather).—*n.* Boucle de cheveux crêpés, *f.*; frisure, *f.* **frizzy**, *a.* Frisottant, crêpé; trop frisé (of permanent waving).

fro [frou], *adv.* En s'éloignant. *To go to and fro*, aller et venir; *to walk to and fro*, se promener de long en large.

frock [frɔk], *n.* Robe d'enfant, robe, *f.*; (monk's) froc, *m.*; (workman's) blouse, *f.* (sailor's) jersey, maillot, *m.* **frock-coat**, *n.* Redingote, *f.* **frocked**, *a.* En froc.

frog [frɔg], *n.* Grenouille, *f.*; fourchette (in a horse's foot), *f.*; (*Mil.*) porte-épée, portebaïonnette, *m.*, bélière, *f.*; (*Med.*) aphte, *m.* *Frogs and loops*, brandebourgs, *m.pl.*; *to have a frog in one's throat*, avoir un chat dans la gorge. **frog-eater**, *n.* Mangeur de grenouilles; (*pej.*) Français. **frogged**, *a.* Orné de brandebourgs. **froggy**, *a.* [FROGEATER]. **frogman**, *n.* Homme-grenouille, *m.* **frog-point**, *n.* (*Rail.*) Pointe de cœur, *f.*; (cœur de) croisement, *m.* **frog-spawn**, *n.* Œufs de grenouille, *m.pl.*

frolic ['frɔlik], *n.* Espièglerie, *f.*, ébats, *m.pl.*, gambades, *f.pl.*—*v.i.* Folâtrer, gambader. **frolicsome**, *a.* Folâtre, espiègle. **frolicsomely**, *adv.* Joyeusement, gaiement. **frolicsomeness**, *n.* Folâtrerie, gaieté, espièglerie, *f.*

from [frɔm], *prep.* De; depuis, dès, à partir de; par (for the sake of); d'après (according to); par suite de, en conséquence de (on account of); de la part de (on the part of). *As from*, à partir de (of date); *down from*, à bas de, en bas de, du haut de; *from above*, d'en haut; *from afar*, de loin; *from age to age*, de siècle en siècle; *from amidst*, du milieu de; *from among*, d'entre; *from behind*, de derrière; *from beneath*, d'en bas; *from beyond*, d'au delà; *from hence*, d'ici; *from his ʌhildhood*, dès l'enfance; *from his manner*, à en juger par son air; *from home*, de chez moi, sorti, absent; *from it*, en, de cela, de là; *from me*, de ma part; *from me to you*, de moi à vous; *from nature*, d'après nature; *from the midst of*, du sein de; *from thence*, de là; *from . . . till*, depuis . . . jusqu'à; *from under*, de dessous; *from within*, de dedans; *from without*, de dehors; *from you*, de votre part; *to come from England*, venir d'Angleterre.

frond [frɔnd], *n.* (*Bot.*) Fronde, *f.* (of ferns); feuille, *f.* (of palm-tree). **frondescence**, *n.* Feuillaison, frondaison, *f.* **frondiferous** [-'difərəs], **frondose** or **frondous**, *a.* (*Bot.*) Feuillu, feuillé.

front [frʌnt], *n.* Devant, *m.*; face, façade (of a building), *f.*; audace, *f.*, front, (*fam.*) toupet (cheek, impudence), *m.*; passe (bonnet), tige (of a boot), *f.*; plastron, devant de chemise (shirt-front), *m.* *At the front*, au front; *in front of*, devant, en face de, en avant de; *sea-front*, digue, esplanade, *f.*; *shop-front*, devanture de magasin, *f.*; *to come to the front*, faire figure, se faire remarquer; *to show a bold front*, faire bonne contenance.—*v.t.* Faire face à; s'opposer à; donner sur; orner d'une façade.—*v.i.* Faire face (à), être vis-à-vis (de). (*Mil.*) *Left front!* À gauche, gauche!—*a.* De devant, d'avant, premier.

frontage, *n.* Façade, devanture (of a shop), *f.* **frontal**, *a.* and *n.* Frontal, *m.* **fronted**, *a.* À façade; qui a un front.

front-bench, *n.* (*Parl.*) Première banquette, *f.* **front-door**, *n.* Porte d'entrée, *f.* **frontroom**, *n.* Chambre, pièce, sur le devant, *f.*; pièce où l'on reçoit, *f.* **front-view**, *n.* Vue de face, *f.* **front-wheel**, *n.* Roue avant, *f.*

frontier ['frʌntjə], *n.* and *a.* Frontière, *f.*; (*Am.*) limite ouest des territoires habités. *Frontier town*, ville frontière, *f.* **frontierguard**, *n.* Garde-frontière, *m.*, gardes-frontière, *m.pl.* **fronting**, *a.* En face de, vis-à-vis de. **frontispiece**, *n.* Frontispice, *m.* **frontlet**, *n.* Fronteau, bandeau, *m.*

frost [frɔːst or frɔst], *n.* Gelée, *f.*, gel, *m.*; (of a play) four, fiasco, *m.* *Glazed frost*, verglas, *m.*; *ground frost*, gelée blanche, *f.*; *hoar-frost*, givre, *m.*—*v.t.* Glacer; (*fig.*) blanchir; damasquiner; craqueler, dépolir, givrer (glass). **frost-bite**, *n.* Gelure, froidure, *f.* **frost-bitten**, *a.* Gelé. **frost-bound**, *a.* Retenu par les glaces. **frosted**, *a.* Givré, dépoli (glass). **frostily**, *adv.* Froidement, avec une froideur glaciale. **frostiness**, *n.* Froid glacial, *m.* **frosty**, *a.* De gelée; glacé;

(*fig.*) froid. *It is a frosty morning*, il gèle ce matin.

froth [frɔːθ *or* frɔθ], *n.* Écume; mousse (on liquor), *f.—v.i.* Écumer; mousser.—*v.t.* Faire mousser. **frothily**, *adv.* Avec de l'écume; (*fig.*) avec futilité, en bavardant. **frothy**, *a.* Écumeux; écumant; mousseux; (*fig.*) vain, frivole.

*froward ['frɔːəd], *a.* Revêche, obstiné, opiniâtre, rebelle. ***frowardly**, *adv.* Opiniâtrement, obstinément. ***frowardness**, *n.* Humeur revêche; obstination, indocilité, *f.*

frown [fraun], *n.* Froncement de sourcil; regard courroucé, *m. The frowns of fortune*, les revers de la fortune, *m.pl.—v.i.* Froncer les sourcils, se renfrogner; être contraire (à). (*fig.*) *To frown upon*, désapprouver. **frowning**, *a.* Rechigné, renfrogné; (*fig.*) menaçant. **frowningly**, *adv.* D'un air sombre; (*fig.*) d'un air menaçant.

frowst [fraust], *v.i.* (*fam.*) Se renfermer chez soi. **frowsty**, *a.* Qui sent le renfermé.

frowzy ['frauzi], *a.* Sale, malpropre; qui sent le renfermé.

frozen [frouzn], *a.* Glacé, gelé; (*Fin.*) gelé, bloqué.

fructiferous [frʌk'tifərəs], *a.* Fructifère. **fructification** [-i'keiʃən], *n.* Fructification, *f.* **fructiform**, *a.* Fructiforme.

fructify ['frʌktifai], *v.i.* Fructifier.—*v.t.* Fertiliser, féconder.

fructose ['frʌktouz], *n.* Fructose, *m.*

frugal [fruːgl], *a.* Frugal, économe, ménager. **frugality** [-'gæliti], *n.* Économie, frugalité, *f.* **frugally**, *adv.* Frugalement, avec économie.

frugivorous [fruː'dʒivərəs], *a.* Frugivore.

fruit [fruːt], *n.* Fruit, *m.*; fruits, *m.pl.*; (*fig.*) avantage, profit, *m. First fruits*, prémices, *f.pl.*; *I eat lots of fruit*, je mange beaucoup de fruits; (*fig.*) *to bear fruit*, porter fruit, être couronné de succès.—*a.* À fruit, de fruit, fruitier.—*v.i.* Produire du fruit. **fruit-basket**, *n.* Panier à fruit, *m.* **fruit-cake**, *n.* Cake, *m.* **fruit-tree**, *n.* Arbre fruitier, *m.*

fruiterer, *n.* Fruitier, *m.*, fruitière, *f.* **fruitful**, *a.* Fertile; (*fig.*) fécond. **fruitfully**, *adv.* Fertilement, abondamment. **fruitfulness**, *n.* Fertilité; (*fig.*) fécondité, *f.*

fruition [fruː'iʃən], *n.* Jouissance, réalisation, *f.* **fruitless**, *a.* Stérile; (*fig.*) infructueux, inutile. **fruitlessly**, *adv.* Inutilement, vainement. **fruity**, *a.* Fruité; corsé.

frumentaceous [fruːmən'teiʃəs], *a.* (*Bot.*) Frumentacé.

frumenty ['fruːmənti], *n.* Bouillie (de farine de froment), *f.*

frump [frʌmp], *n.* Femme désagréable et mal habillée, (*fam.*) vieille sorcière, *f. What a lot of frumps they looked!* comme elles étaient attifées!

frustrate [frʌs'treit], *v.t.* Frustrer, rendre inutile, déjouer; (*Law*) annuler. **frustration** [-'treiʃən], *n.* Frustration, *f.*, insuccès, *m.*, renversement, *m.*

frustum ['frʌstəm], *n.* (*pl.* **frusta**) Tronc (of cone), *m.*

frutescent [fruː'tesənt], *a.* Frutescent.

fry [frai], *n.* Fretin, frai (small fish), *m.*; (*Cook.*) friture, fressure, *f. Small fry*, menu fretin, *m.—v.t.* (*past and p.p.* **fried**) Frire, faire frire, sauter. *Fried eggs*, œufs au plat,

m.pl.; *fried potatoes*, pommes de terre frites, *f.pl.*; *he has other fish to fry*, il a bien d'autres chats à fouetter.—*v.i.* Frire. **frying-pan**, *n.* Poêle à frire, *f. To fall out of the frying-pan into the fire*, tomber de Charybde en Scylla.

fuchsia ['fjuːʃə], *n.* Fuchsia, *m.*

fucus ['fjuːkəs], *n.* (*pl.* **fuci**) Fucus, varech, *m.*

fuddle [fʌdl], *v.t.* Griser; hébéter.—*v.i.* Se griser. **fuddled**, *a.* À moitié gris.

fudge [fʌdʒ], *int.* Bah!—*n.* Travail bâclé, *m.*; bourde, blague, faribole, *f.*; (sweet) fondant américain, *m.—v.t.* Bâcler, bousiller, donner le coup de pouce à (un compte).

fuel ['fjuəl], *n.* Combustible; (*fig.*) aliment, *m. To add fuel to*, alimenter; *to add fuel to the fire*, verser de l'huile sur le feu. **fuel-oil**, *n.* Mazout, *m.*

fug [fʌg], *n.* Remugle, *m.* **fuggy**, *a.* Qui sent le renfermé.

fugacious [fjuː'geiʃəs], *a.* Fugace, fugitif, passager; (*Bot.*) caduc, -uque, éphémère.

fugitive ['fjuːdʒitiv], *a.* Fugitif; fuyard, passager.—*n.* Fugitif, transfuge, déserteur; (*Mil.*) fuyard, *m.* **fugitiveness**, *n.* Nature fugitive, inconstance, instabilité, *f.*

fugue [fjuːg], *n.* (*Mus.*) Fugue, *f.*

fulcrum ['fʌlkrəm], *n.* (*pl.* **fulcra**) Point d'appui, *m.*

fulfil [ful'fil], *v.t.* Accomplir, réaliser, exécuter; combler, satisfaire. *To fulfil oneself*, remplir sa destinée. **fulfilment** *or* **fulfilling**, *n.* Exécution, *f.*, accomplissement, *m.*

*fulgency ['fʌldʒənsi], *n.* Resplendissement, *m.*, splendeur, *f.* ***fulgent**, *a.* Resplendissant, éclatant.

fulgurate ['fʌlgjureit], *v.i.* Fulgurer. **fulguration** [fʌlgə'reiʃən], *n.* Fulguration, *f.* **fulgurite**, *n.* Fulgurite, *m.*

fuliginous [fjuː'lidʒinəs], *a.* Fuligineux.

full (1) [ful], *a.* Plein, rempli; comble, replet, gras; entier, complet, tout; ample; (*fig.*) repu, accablé, surchargé (de); abondant. *At full speed*, à toute vitesse; *fill full*, remplissez jusqu'aux bords; *full meal*, un repas copieux, *m.*; *full moon*, pleine lune, *f.*; *full stop*, point, *m.*; *full supply*, ample provision, *f.*; *full up!* (of bus etc.) Complet! *in full light*, en pleine lumière.—*adv.* Tout à fait, entièrement, complètement; au moins; parfaitement, bien. *Full in one's face*, en plein visage; *to know full well*, savoir parfaitement.—*n.* Plein; comble, *m.*, satiété, mesure complète, *f.*; soûl, *m. At its full* (of the moon), dans son plein; *in full*, en toutes lettres; intégralement; *in full of all demands*, (*Comm.*) pour solde de tout compte; *to give a passage in full*, citer un passage en entier; *to the full*, entièrement. **full-back**, *n.* (*Ftb.*) Arrière, *m.* **full-blooded**, *a.* Pur sang (of horse); (*fig.*) robuste; sanguin. **full-blown**, *a.* Épanoui; (*fig.*) dans tout son éclat. **full-bodied**, *a.* Gros, replet; corsé (of wine). **full-dress**, *n.* Grande toilette; (*Mil. etc.*) grande tenue, *f.* **full-faced**, *a.* Au visage plein. **full-fed**, *a.* Bien nourri. **full-grown**, *a.* Adulte. **full-length**, *a.* En pied (of portraits). **full-sized**, *a.* En grand; de grand format (of paper). **full-steam**, *adv.* À toute vapeur. **full-tilt**, *adv.* Au grand galop, à toute bride. *To run full-tilt against*, donner tête baissée contre. **fully**, *adv.* Pleinement, entièrement, tout à fait; parfaitement, bien, au moins.

full (2) [ful], *v.t.* Fouler (cloth). **fuller,** *n.* Foulon, *m.* **fuller's-earth,** *n.* Terre à foulon, *f.* **fullery** or **fulling-mill,** *n.* Moulin à foulon, *m.* **fulling,** *n.* Foulage, *m.*

fullness ['fulnis], *n.* Plénitude, *f.,* plein, *m.,* abondance; ampleur, *f.;* volume; trop plein (excessive fullness), *m. In the fullness of time,* quand les temps furent révolus.

fulmar ['fulmə], *n.* (*Orn.*) Fulmar, *m.*

fulminant ['fʌlminənt], *a.* and *n.* Fulminant.

fulminate (1) ['fʌlmineit], *v.t., v.i.* Fulminer.

fulminate (2) ['fʌlminət], *n.* Fulminate, *m.*

fulminating, *a.* Fulminant. **fulmination** [-'neiʃən], *n.* Fulmination, *f.* **fulminatory,** *a.* Fulminatoire. **fulminic** [-'minik], *a.* Fulminique.

fulsome ['fulsəm], *a.* Excessif, écœurant, servile; gonflé (of style). **fulsomely,** *adv.* D'une manière dégoûtante. **fulsomeness,** *n.* Servilité, grossièreté, *f.*

fumble [fʌmbl], *v.i.* Farfouiller; tâtonner. —*v.t.* Manier maladroitement. *To fumble along,* aller à tâtons. **fumbler,** *n.* Maladroit, *m.* **fumblingly,** *adv.* Gauchement, en tâtonnant.

fume [fju:m], *n.* Fumée, vapeur; (*fig.*) colère, *f.*—*v.i.* Fumer, jeter de la fumée; s'exhaler; (*fig.*) s'échauffer, être en colère, rager. *To fret and fume,* se faire du mauvais sang, se tourmenter.—*v.t.* Fumer. **fumed,** *a.* Fumé. *Fumed oak,* chêne patiné. **fuming,** *a.* (*Chem.*) Fumant; (*fig.*) bouillonnant de colère. **fumingly,** *adv.* En colère, avec rage.

***fumet** ['fju:mit], *n.* (*Hunt.*) Fumées (of a stag), *f.pl.*

fumigate ['fju:migeit], *v.t.* Fumiger; désinfecter.—*v.i.* Faire des fumigations. **fumigation** [-'geiʃən], *n.* Fumigation, désinfection, *f.* **fumigator,** *n.* Fumigateur, *m.;* boîte fumigatoire, *f.*

fumitory ['fju:mitəri], *n.* (*Bot.*) Fumeterre, *f.*

fun [fʌn], *n.* Amusement, *m.,* plaisanterie, drôlerie, *f. For fun,* pour rire; *he is full of fun,* il a le mot pour rire; (*fig.*) *now the fun will start,* voilà la danse qui va commencer; *to have good fun,* se bien amuser; *to make fun of,* tourner en ridicule, se moquer de. **funfair** ['fʌnfɛə], *n.* Fête foraine, *f.*

funambulist [fju:'næmbjulist], *n.* (*Ant.*) Funambule, danseur de corde, *m.*

function ['fʌŋkʃən], *n.* Fonction, *f.,* métier, emploi, *m.;* cérémonie, réception, *f.*—*v.i.* Fonctionner, marcher. **functional,** *a.* Fonctionnel. **functionary,** *n.* Fonctionnaire, *m.* **functionate,** *v.i.* [FUNCTION].

fund [fʌnd], *n.* Fonds, *m.;* caisse, *f. Regimental fund,* masse, *f.; sinking fund,* caisse d'amortissement, *f.; the public funds,* les fonds publics, *m.pl.; old-age pension fund,* caisse des retraites pour la vieillesse, *f.; to be in funds,* être en fonds.—*v.t.* Placer, mettre dans les fonds publics, inscrire sur le grand-livre. **funded,** *a.* Consolidé; en rentes. **fund-holder,** *n.* Rentier, *m.*

fundament ['fʌndəmənt], *n.* Fondement; siège; (*Anat.*) anus, *m.* **fundamental** [-'mentl], *a.* Fondamental.—*n.pl.* Principe fondamental, *m.* **fundamentally,** *adv.* Fondamentalement, essentiellement.

funeral ['fju:nərəl], *a.* Funèbre, funéraire. *Funeral honours,* honneurs funèbres, *m.pl.; funeral oration,* oraison funèbre, *f.; funeral service,* office des morts, *m.*—*n.* Enterrement, convoi funèbre, *m.;* funérailles, obsèques, *f.pl.* (*fam.*) *That's your funeral,* ça c'est votre affaire. **funereal** [-'niəriəl], *a.* Funèbre; lugubre, sépulcral.

fungicide ['fʌndʒisaid], *a.* and *n.* Fongicide, *m.*

fungoid ['fʌŋgɔid], *a.* Fongiforme. **fungous,** *a.* Fongueux. **fungus,** *n.* (*pl.* **fungi** ['fʌndʒai]) Champignon; (*Med.*) fongus, *m.*

funicle ['fju:nikl], *n.* (*Bot.*) Funicule, *m.* **funicular** [-'nikjulə], *a.* Funiculaire. *Funicular railway,* funiculaire, *m.* **funiform,** *a.* Funiforme.

funk [fʌŋk], *n.* Peur; (*slang*) frousse, *f.*—*v.t.* Éviter, avoir peur de. *To be in a funk,* avoir le trac; *to put in a funk,* donner la frousse à. **funky,** *a.* Froussard.

funnel [fʌnl], *n.* Entonnoir; tuyau, *m.;* cheminée (on steamers), *f.*

funny ['fʌni], *a.* Amusant, drôle, facétieux, comique; bizarre. *Funny-bone,* le petit juif, *m.; to feel all funny,* se sentir tout chose.

fur [fə:], *n.* Fourrure, *f.;* gibier à poil, *m.;* (*fig.*) dépôt, tartre, *m.,* incrustation, *f. To make the fur fly,* se battre avec acharnement. —*v.t.* Fourrer, garnir de fourrure.—*v.i.* S'incruster, s'encrasser (of the tongue). **fur-lined,** *a.* Doublé de fourrure. **fur-trade,** *n.* Pelleterie, *f.*

furbelow ['fə:bilou], *n.* Falbala, *m.*

furbish ['fə:biʃ], *v.t.* Fourbir. **furbisher,** *n.* Fourbisseur, *m.*

furcation [fə:'keiʃən], *n.* Bifurcation, *f.*

furfur ['fə:fə], *n.* Furfur, *m.* **furfuraceous** [-fju'reiʃəs], *a.* Furfuracé.

furious ['fjuəriəs], *a.* Furieux, acharné. **furiously,** *adv.* Avec fureur, avec acharnement, en furieux. **furiousness,** *n.* Furie, fureur, *f.,* acharnement, *m.*

furl [fə:l], *v.t.* (*Naut.*) Ferler, serrer. **furling-line,** *n.* Raban de ferlage, *m.*

furlong ['fə:lɔŋ], *n.* Furlong (la huitième partie d'un mille anglais, 201 mètres), *m.*

furlough ['fə:lou], *n.* (*Mil.*) Congé, *m. On furlough,* en congé.

furnace ['fə:nis], *n.* Fournaise, *f.;* fourneau (of a forge); foyer (of an engine), *m. Blast-furnace,* haut fourneau, *m.*

furnish ['fə:niʃ], *v.t.* Fournir, garnir, pourvoir (de); meubler. *Furnished flat,* appartement meublé; *furnished room,* chambre garnie, *f.* **furnisher,** *n.* Fournisseur, marchand de meubles, *m.* **furnishing,** *n.* Ameublement, *m.,* garniture, *f.*

furniture ['fə:nitʃə], *n.* Meubles, *m.pl.* mobilier, ameublement; équipement, matériel; équipage, *m.;* (*Print.*) garniture, *f. A piece of furniture,* un meuble, *m. A full set of furniture,* un mobilier complet, *m. Second-hand-furniture dealer,* brocanteur, *m.* **furniture-remover,** *n.* Déménageur, *m.* **furniture-van,** *n.* Voiture de déménagement, *f.;* tapissière, *f.* **furniture-warehouse,** *n.* Garde-meuble, *m.*

furred [fə:d], *a.* Fourré; chargé (of the tongue); incrusté (of kettle etc.).

furrier ['fʌriə], *n.* Fourreur, pelletier, *m.*

furrow ['fʌrou], *n.* Sillon, *m.;* ride; rainure, *f.* —*v.t.* Sillonner, rider (the face); faire des rainures à.

furry ['fə:ri], *a.* Fourré, couvert de fourrures,

further ['fə:ðə], *a.* Plus éloigné, ultérieur; autre, nouveau. *Further obligation*, surcroît d'obligation, *m.*—*adv.* Plus loin; de plus, encore; ultérieurement; au delà. *To go further into something*, entrer plus avant dans quelque chose.—*v.t.* Avancer; faciliter, favoriser, seconder; servir. **furtherance**, *n.* Avancement; progrès, *m.* **furthermore**, *adv.* De plus, en outre, d'ailleurs. **furthermost furthest**, *a.* Le plus éloigné; le plus reculé. *The furthest end*, le fond, le bout, *m.* [FARTHEST].

furtive ['fə:tiv], *a.* Furtif. **furtively**, *adv.* Furtivement, à la dérobée.

furuncle ['fjurəŋkl], *n.* (*Path.*) Furoncle, *m.*

fury ['fjuəri], *n.* Furie, fureur, *f.*; acharnement, *m.*

furze [fə:z], *n.* Ajonc, jonc marin; genêt épineux, *m.* **furze-bush**, *n.* Buisson d'ajonc, *m.* **furzy**, *a.* Plein d'ajoncs.

fusarole ['fju:zəroul], *n.* (*Arch.*) Fusarolle, *f.*

fuscous ['fʌskəs], *a.* Brun foncé, bistre.

fuse [fju:z], *v.t.* Fondre, liquéfier.—*v.i.* Se fondre. *The light has fused*, les plombs ont sauté.—*n.* Mèche, fusée, *f.*; (*Elec.*) fusible, plomb, *m.* *Delay-action fuse*, fusée à retard; *percussion fuse*, fusée percutante; *safety fuse*, mèche de sûreté, *f.*; *time-fuse*, fusée fusante, fusée à temps, *f.* *The fuse has gone*, le plomb a sauté. **fuse-wire**, *n.* Fil fusible, *m.*

fusee [fju:'zi:], *n.* Fusée, *f.*; allumette-tison, *f.*

fuselage ['fju:zilɑ:ʒ *or* -lidʒ], *n.* Fuselage, *m.*

fusel oil ['fju:zl'ɔil], *n.* Huile de fusel, *f.*, fusel, *m.*; huile de pomme de terre, *f.*, alcool amylique, *m.*

fusibility [fju:zi'biliti], *n.* Fusibilité, *f.* **fusible** ['fju:zibl], *a.* Fusible.

fusilier [fju:zi'liə], *n.* Fusilier, *m.* **fusillade**, *n.* Fusillade, *f.*

fusion ['fju:ʒən], *n.* Fusion, *f.* **fusionism**, *n.* Fusionnisme, *m.* **fusionist**, *a. and n.* Fusionniste.

fuss [fʌs], *n.* Fracas, bruit, embarras, *m.*, façons, *f.pl.* *To make a fuss*, faire des embarras, faire des façons; *to make a fuss of someone*, être aux petits soins pour quelqu'un. **fussily**, *adv.* Avec embarras. **fussiness**, *n.* Air or ton d'importance, *m.* **fuss-pot**, *n.* (*fam.*) Tâtillon, *m.* **fussy**, *a.* Qui fait des embarras; affairé.

fustian ['fʌstjən], *n.* Futaine, *f.*; (*fig.*) galimatias, *m.*—*a.* De futaine; (*fig.*) boursouflé, ampoulé.

fustic ['fʌstik], *n.* Fustet, bois jaune, *m.*

fustigate ['fʌstigeit], *v.t.* Fustiger, battre à coups de bâton. **fustigation** [-'geiʃən], *n.* Fustigation, *f.*

fustiness ['fʌstinis], *n.* Odeur de moisi, *f.* **fusty**, *a.* Qui sent le renfermé, le moisi.

futile ['fju:tail], *a.* Futile, vain, frivole. **futility** [-'tiliti], *n.* Futilité, *f.*

futtock ['fʌtək], *n.* (*Naut.*) Genou-allonge, *m.*, allonge, *f.* *Futtock shrouds*, haubans de revers, *m.pl.*, gambes de hune, *f.pl.*

future ['fju:tʃə], *a.* Futur, à venir.—*n.* Avenir; (*Gram.*) futur, *m.* *For the future*, *in the future*, à l'avenir; *he has a future*, il ira loin; *in the near future*, dans un proche avenir; *verb in the future*, verbe au futur, *m.*

futurism, *n.* Futurisme, *m.* **futuristic**, *a.* Futuriste.

futurity [fju:'tjuəriti], *n.* Avenir, *m.*

fuze [FUSE].

fuzz [fʌz], *v.i.* S'en aller en peluche, en duvet. —*n.* Bourre, *f.*, duvet, *m.* (on blankets); flou, *m.* (of a photograph). **fuzzball**, *n.* Vesse-de-loup, *f.* **fuzzy**, *a.* Duveteux, floconneux; bouffant, moutonné (hair); flou (photograph).

fy! [FIE!].

G

G, g [dʒi:], septième lettre de l'alphabet; (*Mus.*) sol, *m.*

gab [gæb], *n.* Faconde, *f.*, bagout, *m.* *To have the gift of the gab*, (*colloq.*) avoir la langue bien pendue.

gabardine [GABERDINE].

gabble [gæbl], *v.i.* Parler très vite, bredouiller (à force de parler vite); caqueter, jacasser. —*n.* Bredouillement; caquet, *m.*

gaberdine ['gæbədin], *n.* Gabardine, *f.*

gabion ['geibiən], *n.* (*Fort.*) Gabion, *m.* *To cover with gabions*, gabionner.

gable [geibl], *n.* Pignon, gable, *m.* *Small gable*, gablet, *m.* **gable-end**, *n.* Pignon, *m.*

Gaboon [gə'bu:n]. Le Gabon, *m.*

gaby ['geibi], *n.* Niais, nigaud, *m.*

gad [gæd], *n.* (*Mining*) Coin d'acier, *m.*; *pointe, f.*—*v.i.* Courir çà et là, battre le pavé. *To gad about*, courir la prétantaine.

gadfly, *n.* Taon, *m.*

gadget ['gædʒit], *n.* (*slang*) Instrument, accessoire; truc, machin, *m.*

Gaelic ['geilik], ʌ. and *n.* Gaélique, *m.*

gaff [gæf], *n.* Gaffe, *f.* *To blow the gaff*, (*slang*) vendre la mèche.—*v.t.* Gaffer (a fish).

gaffer ['gæfə], *n.* Compère, vieux bonhomme, *m.*, contremaître; patron, *m.*

gag [gæg], *n.* Bâillon, *m.*; (*Theat.*) plaisanterie, *f.*; (*Cine.*) gag, *m.*—*v.t.* Bâillonner.—*v.i.* (*Theat.*) Faire la balançoire, cascader. **gagger**, *n.* Bâillonneur, *m.* **gagging**, *n.* Bâillonnement, *m.*

gaga ['gægə], *a.* (*colloq.*) Gaga.

gage [geidʒ], *n.* Gage, *m.*, assurance, *f.*—*v.t.* Mettre en gage.

gaggle [gægl], *n.* Troupeau d'oies, *m.*; troupe (of women etc.), *f.*—*v.i.* Crier comme une oie, cacarder.

gaiety ['geiəti], *n.* Gaieté, *f.*; éclat, *m.* **gaily**, *adv.* Gaiement, joyeusement; avec éclat, d'une manière pimpante.

gain [gein], *n.* Gain, profit, avantage, *m.*—*v.t.* Gagner, acquérir, obtenir, se faire; remporter (a victory); atteindre. *He had nothing to gain by it*, il n'eut aucun profit à en retirer; *to gain ground*, gagner du terrain; *to gain over*, attirer à soi, se faire (des amis); *to gain time*, gagner du temps.—*v.i.* L'emporter (sur); avancer (of watches etc.). *To gain upon*, gagner sur, empiéter sur. **gainer**, *n.* Gagnant, *m.*, bénéficiaire, *m.* or *f.* *To be a gainer by*, gagner à. **gainful**, *a.* Profitable, lucratif, avantageux. **gainfully**, *adv.* Utilement, avec profit. **gainfulness**, *n.* Avantage, profit, gain, *m.* **gainings**, *n.pl.* Gains, profits, *m.pl.* **gainless**, *a.* Inutile, sans profit.

gainsay ['geinsei], *v.t.* Contredire. **gainsayer**, *n.* Contradicteur, *m.* **gainsaying**, *n.* Contradiction, *f.*, démenti, *m.*

gait [geit], *n.* Démarche, allure, *f.*

gaiter ['geitə], *n.* Guêtre, *f.*

gaitered, *a.* Guêtré.

gala ['geilə *or* 'gɑ:lə], *n.* Gala, *m.* **gala-day**, *n.* Jour de fête, *m.* **gala-night**, *n.* Soirée de gala, *f.*

galactic [gə'læktik], *a.* Galactique. **galacto-meter**, *n.* Pèse-lait, *m.* **galactophagist**, *n.*, **galactophagous**, *a.* Galactophage. **galactose**, *n.* Galactose, *f.*

galantine ['gælənti:n], *n.* Galantine, *f.*

Galatea [gælə'ti:ə]. Galatée, *f.*

Galatia [gə'leiʃiə]. La Galatie, *f.*

Galatian, *a.* and *n.* Galate.

galaxy ['gæləksi], *n.* Voie lactée, galaxie, *f.*; (*fig.*) assemblage brillant, *m.*, constellation, *f.*

gale [geil], *n.* Coup de vent, *m.*, tempête, *f.* *To blow a gale*, souffler en tempête.

galea ['geiliə], *n.* (*Bot.*, *Orn.*) Casque, *m.*

galeate ['gælieit] *or* **galeated** [-'eitid], *a.* (*Bot.*) Casqué.

galena [gə'li:nə], *n.* (*Min.*) Galène, *f.*

Galicia [gə'liʃiə]. La Galicie (Poland); La Galice (Spain), *f.*

Galilean [gæli'li:ən], *a.* and *n.* Galiléen, *m.*, -éenne, *f.*

Galilee ['gælili:]. La Galilée, *f.*

Galileo [gæli'li:ou]. Galilée, *m.*

galingale ['gæliŋgeil], *n.* (*Bot.*) Souchet odorant, *m.*

gall [gɔ:l], *n.* Fiel, *m.*; écorchure (sore); noix de galle, galle (on trees etc.), *f.*; (*fig.*) rancune, *f.*, chagrin, *m.*—*v.t.* Écorcher; (*fig.*) fâcher, irriter, vexer. **gall-bladder**, *n.* Vésicule du fiel, *f.* **gall-nut**, *n.* Noix de galle, *f.* **gall-stone**, *n.* Calcul biliaire, *m.*

gallant ['gælənt], *a.* Brave, intrépide; [gə'lænt], galant.—*n.* Brave; preux, *m.*; [gə'lænt], galant, homme galant; amant, *m.*

gallantly ['gæləntli], *adv.* Bravement, courageusement; galamment. **gallantry**, *n.* Vaillance, bravoure; galanterie, intrigue amoureuse, *f.*

galleon ['gæliən], *n.* Galion, *m.*

gallery ['gæləri], *n.* Galerie, *f.*; (*Theat.*) balcon, *m.* Art gallery, musée, *m.*; *public gallery*, (*Parl.*) tribune publique, *f.*; *to play to the gallery*, jouer pour la galerie.

galley ['gæli], *n.* Galère (*Naut.*) cuisine; (*Print.*) galée, *f.* **galley-proof**, *n.* Épreuve en placard, *f.* **galley-slave**, *n.* Galérien, *m.*

galliard ['gæliəd], *n.* Gaillarde (dance), *f.*

Gallic ['gælik], *a.* Gaulois, *gallique. **Gallican**, *a.* Gallican. **Gallicanism**, *n.* Gallicanisme, *m.* **Gallicism**, *n.* Gallicisme, *m.*

gallic ['gælik], *a.* (*Chem.*) Gallique.

galligaskins [gæli'gæskinz], *n.* *Grègues, *f.pl.*

gallimaufry [gæli'mɔ:fri], *n.* Salmigondis, *m.*, galimafrée, *f.*

gallinaceous [gæli'neiʃəs], *a.* (*Orn.*) Gallinacé.

galling ['gɔ:liŋ], *a.* Irritant, vexant.

galliot ['gæliət], *n.* Galiote, *f.*

gallipot ['gælipɔt], *n.* Petit pot (à pommade), *m.*

gallivant [gæli'vænt], *v.i.* Courir çà et là (avec des femmes).

gallomania [gælo'meiniə], *n.* Gallomanie, *f.* **gallomaniac**, *n.* Gallomane, *m.*

gallon ['gælən], *n.* Gallon (quatre litres et demi), *m.*

galloon [gə'lu:n], *ń.* Galon, *m.* *To bind with*

galloon, galonner, border de galon. **gallooned**, *a.* Galonné.

gallop ['gæləp], *n.* Galop, *m.* *Full gallop*, grand galop; *hand gallop*, petit galop.—*v.i.* Galoper, aller au galop. *To gallop off*, partir au galop. **galloper**, *n.* Cheval qui galope, *m.*; (*Mil.*) officier d'ordonnance, *m.* *Galloping consumption*, phtisie galopante, *f.*

galloway ['gælowei], *n.* Poney du Galloway, *m.*; bœuf ou vache de la race de Galloway.

gallows ['gæylouz], *n.* Potence, *f.*; (*Gym.*) portique, *m.* **gallows-bird**, *n.* Gibier de potence, *m.*

galop ['gæləp], *n.* (*Dance*) Galop, *m.*—*v.i.* Danser un galop.

galore [gə'lɔ:], *n.* and *adv.* À foison; à gogo.

galosh [gə'lɔʃ], *n.* Caoutchouc (rubber over-shoe), *m.*

galvanic [gæl'vænik], *a.* Galvanique.

galvanism ['gælvənizm], *n.* Galvanisme, *m.* **galvanization** [-'zeiʃən], *n.* Galvanisation, *f.* **galvanize** [-naiz], *v.t.* Galvaniser. **galvanometer** [-'nɔmitə], *n.* Galvano-mètre, *m.* **galvanoplasty**, *n.* Galvano-plastie, *f.*

gam [gæm], *n.* Troupeau de baleines, *m.*; réunion, *f.*, échange de visites, *m.* (entre chasseurs de baleines).—*v.i.* Se réunir en troupe.

gambet ['gæmbət], *n.* (*Orn.*) Gambette, *m.*

Gambia ['gæmbiə]. La Gambie, *f.*

gambit ['gæmbit], *n.* (*Chess*) Gambit, *m.*

gamble [gæmbl], *v.i.* Jouer de l'argent. *He gambled away his money*, il perdit son argent au jeu. **gambler**, *n.* Joueur, *m.* **gambling**, *n.* Jeu, *m.* **gambling-house**, *n.* Maison de jeu, *f.* **gambling-table**, *n.* Table de jeu, *f.*

gamboge [gæm'boudʒ], *n.* Gomme-gutte, *f.*

gambol [gæmbl], *n.* Gambade, *f.*; ébats, *m.pl.*—*v.i.* Gambader, faire des gambades, folâtrer.

gambrel-roof ['gæmbrəlru:f], *n.* Toit en croupe, *m.*

game (1) [geim], *n.* Jeu, *m.*, partie, *f.*; (*pl.*) (*sch.*) sport, *m.* *A game of tennis*, une partie de tennis, *f.*; *drawn game*, partie nulle; *the game is up* (*fig.*), la partie est jouée; *to be on one's game*, être bien en forme; *to give up the game*, quitter la partie; *to make game of*, se moquer de; (*fig.*) *to play the game*, jouer franc jeu; (*fam.*) *what's your game?* Où voulez-vous en venir?—*v.i.* Jouer de l'argent.—*a.* Estro-pié (of leg, arm, etc.); courageux. *To be game for anything*, être prêt à tout. **game-ball**, *n.* (*spt.*) Balle décisive, *f.*

game (2) [geim], *n.* Gibier, *m.* *Small game*, menu gibier. **game-bag**, *n.* Carnassière, *f.* **game-cock**, *n.* Coq de combat, *m.* **game-keeper**, *n.* Garde-chasse, *m.* **game-laws**, *n.pl.* Lois sur la chasse, *f.pl.* **game-licence**, *n.* Permis de chasse, *m.* **game-preserve**, *n.* Parc à gibier, *m.*

gamesome ['geimsəm], *a.* Enjoué. **game-somely**, *adv.* Gaiement. **gamesomeness**, *n.* Enjouement, *m.*

gamester ['geimstə], *n.* Joueur, *m.*

gamete ['gæmi:t], *n.* Gamète, *m.*

gaming [GAMBLING].

gamma-rays ['gæməreiz], *n.pl.* (*Phys.*) Rayons gamma, *m.pl.*

*gammer** ['gæmə], *n.* Commère, bonne femme, *f.*

gammon ['gæmən], *n.* Quartier de lard fumé; (*Backgammon*) tric-trac, *m.*; (*colloq.*) blague, *f.*—*v.t.* Saler et fumer (bacon); (*colloq.*) blaguer, mettre dedans; (*Naut.*) lier; (*Backgammon*) battre. **gammoning,** *n.* (*Naut.*) Liure, *f.*

gamp [gæmp], *n.* (*colloq.*) Riflard (umbrella), *m.*

gamut ['gæmət], *n.* (*Mus.*) Gamme, *f.*

gamy ['geimi], *a.* (*Cook.*) Faisandé, avancé.

gander ['gændə], *n.* Jars, *m.*

gang (1) [gæŋ], *n.* Bande, troupe, brigade, équipe (of workmen), *f.*—*v.i.* (*pop.*) To gang up on someone, attaquer quelqu'un; to gang up with, faire bande avec. **ganger,** *n.* Chef d'équipe; cantonnier, *m.*

gang (2) [gæŋ], *v.i.* (*Sc.*, past and *p.p.* **gaed**) Aller.

Ganges ['gændʒiːz]. Le Gange, *m.*

gangling ['gæŋgliŋ], *a.* Dégingandé, trop grand pour son âge.

ganglion ['gæŋgliən], *n.* (*pl.* **ganglia**) Ganglion, *m.*

gang-plank [GANGWAY].

gangrene ['gæŋgriːn], *n.* Gangrène, *f.* —*v.t.* Gangrener.—*v.i.* Se gangrener. **gangrened,** *a.* Gangrené. **gangrenous,** *a.* Gangreneux.

gangster ['gæŋstə], *n.* Gangster, bandit, *m.*

gangway ['gæŋwei], *n.* Passage, *m.*; (*Naut.*) passerelle (pour débarquer); coupée, *f. Gangway!* Laissez passer, s'il vous plaît!

gannet ['gænit], *n.* Fou (bird), *m.*

gantry ['gæntri], *n.* Chantier, *m.* (for a barrel); portique, pont roulant, *m.* (of a crane).

Ganymede ['gænimiːd]. Ganymède, *m.*

gaol [JAIL].

gap [gæp], *n.* Brèche, ouverture, *f.*, passage, trou, *m.*; lacune (in a book); trouée (in a forest), *f. To fill a gap,* remplir une lacune; *to stop a gap,* boucher un trou. (*fam.*) *To bridge the gap,* faire la soudure.—*v.t.* Ébrécher. **gap-toothed,** *a.* Aux dents écartées.

gape [geip], *v.i.* Bâiller; s'ouvrir, s'entr'ouvrir (of doors etc.); (*fig.*) bayer, avoir la bouche béante. *To gape at,* regarder bouche bée.—*n.* Bâillement, *m.* **gaper,** *n.* Bâilleur; bayeur, *m.* **gaping,** *a.* Béant.—*n.* Bâillement, *m.*

garage [gə'raːʒ *or* gə'raːdʒ], *n.* Garage, *m.*—*v.t.* Garer.

garb [gaːb], *n.* Costume, habit, habillement, *m.*, dehors, *m.pl.*—*v.t.* (*Rhet.*) Vêtir.

garbage ['gaːbidʒ], *n.* Entrailles, issues; ordures, *f.pl.* **garbage-can,** *n.* (*Am.*) Boîte à ordures, *f.* [see **dust-**]

garble [gaːbl], *v.t.* Mutiler, tronquer (a quotation etc.), altérer. **garbler,** *n.* Mutilateur, faussaire, *m.*

garboard ['gaːbɔːd], *n.* (*Naut.*) Gabord, *m.* **garboard-strake,** *n.* Virure de gabord, *f.*

garden [gaːdn], *n.* Jardin, *m.*—*v.i.* Jardiner. **garden-chair,** *n.* Chaise de jardin, *f.* **gardener,** *n.* Jardinier, *m.* **garden-flower,** *n.* Fleur de jardin, *f.* **garden-mould,** *n.* Terreau, *m.* **garden-party,** *n.* Réception en plein air; garden-party, *f.* **garden-produce,** *n.* Denrées potagères, *f.pl.* **garden-warbler,** *n.* (*Orn.*) Fauvette des jardins, *f.*

gardenia [gaː'diːnjə], *n.* Gardénia, *m.*

gardening, *n.* Jardinage, *m.*

garfish ['gaːfiʃ], *n.* Aiguille de mer, orphie, *f.*

gargle [gaːgl], *v.i.* Se gargariser.—*n.* Gargarisme, *m.*

gargoyle ['gaːgɔil], *n.* Gargouille, *f.*

garish ['geəriʃ], *a.* Éclatant, voyant. **garishness,** *n.* Excès d'éclat; luxe criard, *m.*

garland ['gaːlənd], *n.* Guirlande, *f.*—*v.t.* Enguirlander.

garlic ['gaːlik], *n.* Ail, *m. Clove of garlic,* gousse d'ail, *f.*

garment ['gaːmənt], *n.* Vêtement, *m.*

garner ['gaːnə], *n.* Grenier, *m.*—*v.t.* Mettre en grenier, engranger; (*fig.*) amasser, entasser.

garnet ['gaːnit], *n.* Grenat; (*Naut.*) bredindin, *m.*

garnish ['gaːniʃ], *v.t.* Garnir, orner de; (*Law*) appeler en justice.—*n.* Garniture, *f.* **garnishee** [-'ʃiː], *n.* (*Law*) Saisie-arrêt, *f.* **garnishment,** *n.* Garniture, parure, *f.*, ornement, embellissement, *m.*; (*Law*) citation, *f.* **garniture,** *n.* Garniture, *f.*; embellissement, *m.*

garran [GARRON].

garret ['gærət], *n.* Galetas, *m.*, mansarde, soupente, *f.* **garreteer** [-'tiə], *n.* Habitant d'un galetas; (*fig.*) pauvre écrivain, *m.*

garrison ['gærisən], *n.* Garnison, *f. Garrison artillery,* artillerie de place, *f.*; *garrison town,* ville de garnison, *f.*—*v.t.* Mettre garnison dans; mettre en garnison. **garrisoned,** *a.* De garnison. *To be garrisoned at,* être en garnison à.

garron ['gærən], *n.* Bidet d'Irlande *or* d'Écosse, *m.*

garrot ['gærət], *n.* (*Surg.*) Garrot, *m.*

garrotte [gə'rɔt], *n.* Garrotte, *f.*—*v.t.* Garrotter.

garrulity [gə'ruːliti], *n.* Garrulité, loquacité, *f.*

garrulous ['gæruləs], *a.* Babillard, loquace.

garter ['gaːtə], *n.* Jarretière, *f.*; (*Am.*) supportchaussette, *m.*—*v.t.* Attacher des jarretières à, lier avec une jarretière.

garth [gaːθ], *n.* Enclos, clos, *m.*; cour gazonnée (entourée par un cloître), *f.*

gas (1) *abbr.* for [GASOLENE]. **gas-station,** *n.* (*Am.*) Poste d'essence, *m.*

gas (2) [gæs], *n.* (*pl.* **gases**) Gaz, *m. Laughing gas,* gaz hilarant, *m.*—*v.t.* Gazer; intoxiquer par un gaz. **gas-bomb,** *n.* Bombe asphyxiante, *f.* **gas-burner,** *n.* Bec de gaz, *m.* **gas-chamber,** *n.* Chambre à gaz, *f.* **gas-cooker,** *n.* Réchaud à gaz, four à gaz, *m.* **gas-engine,** *n.* Moteur à gaz, *m.* **gas-fire,** *n.* Radiateur à gaz, *m.* **gas-fitter,** *n.* Gazier, *m.* **gas-holder** (reservoir *or* tank), *n.* Gazomètre, *m.* **gas-light,** *n.* Gaz, bec de gaz, *m.* **gas-lighter,** *n.* Allumoir, *m.* **gas-lighting,** *n.* Éclairage au gaz, *m.* **gas-main,** *n.* Conduite de gaz, *f.* **gas-man,** *n.* Gazier, *m.* **gas-mask,** *n.* Masque à gaz, *m.* **gas-meter,** *n.* Compteur à gaz, *m.* **gas-oil,** *n.* Gaz-oil, *m.* **gas-pipe,** *n.* Tuyau de gaz, *m.* **gas-stove,** *n.* Fourneau à gaz, *m.* **gas-tar,** *n.* Goudron de houille, coaltar, *m.* **gas-works,** *n.pl.* Usine à gaz, *f.*

gascon ['gæskən], *a.* and *n.* Gascon.

gasconade [gæskə'neid], *n.* Gasconnade, *f.*—*v.i.* Dire des gasconnades.

Gascony ['gæskəni]. La Gascogne, *f.*

gaselier [gæsə'liə], *n.* Lustre à gaz, *m.*

gaseous ['geisiəs], *a.* Gazeux. **gassed,** *a.* Gazé; intoxiqué par le gaz.

gash [gæʃ], n. Balafre, estafilade, entaille, f. v.t. Balafrer, taillader.

gasiform ['gæsifɔːm], a. Gazéiforme. **gasify,** v.t. Gazéifier.

gasket ['gæskit], n. (*Naut.*) Garcette, f., raban de ferlage, m.; (*Steam-eng.*) garniture, f.

gasogene ['gæsodʒiːn], n. Gazogène, m.

gasolene or **gasoline** ['gæsəliːn], n. Gazolène, gazoléine, gazoline; (*Am.*) essence, f.

gasometer [GAS-HOLDER].

gasp [gɑːsp], v.i. Respirer avec peine. To gasp for breath, haleter.—n. Respiration haletante, f.; sursaut (de surprise), soupir convulsif, m. At one's last gasp, à son dernier soupir.

gasper ['gɑːspə], n. (*pop.*) Cigarette, f.

gasping, n. Respiration haletante, f.—a. Respirant avec peine, haletant.

gasteropod ['gæstərəpɔd], n. Gastéropode, m.

gastralgia [gæsˈtrældʒiə], n. Gastralgie, f. **gastric,** a. Gastrique. **gastritis** [-ˈtraitis], n. Gastrite, f. **gastro-enteritis,** n. Gastro-entérite, f.

gastronome ['gæstrənoum] or **gastronomist** [gæsˈtrɔnəmist], n. Gastronome, m. **gastronomic** [-ˈnɔmik], a. Gastronomique. **gastronomy** [-ˈtrɔnəmi], n. Gastronomie, f. **gastro-vascular,** a. Gastro-vasculaire.

gat [gæt], n. Chenal, m., (*Naut.*) passe, f. (entre des bancs de sable).

gate [geit], n. Porte, grande porte, porte cochère, f.; barrière (turnpike-gate); grille (iron gate), f.; (*spt.*) le public (payant), les entrées, la recette.—v.t. (*Univ.*) Consigner. **gate-bill,** n. (*Oxf., Camb.*) Amendes pour rentrée tardive, f.pl. **gate-crash,** v.i. Resquiller. **gate-crasher,** n. Intrus, resquilleur, m. **gate-house,** n. Maison du gardien, f. (in park); corps-de-garde, m. (of castle). **gate-keeper,** n. Portier; (*Rail.*) garde-barrière, m. **gate-money,** n. Entrées, f.pl. **gate-post,** n. Montant de porte, m. **gateway,** n. Porte, porte cochère, f.; portail (large doorway); guichet (small), m.

gather ['gæðə], v.t. Ramasser; assembler, rassembler; recueillir (to collect); cueillir (fruits etc.); prendre, contracter (a habit etc.); (*fig.*) conclure, inférer (de); (*Dress.*) froncer. To gather strength, se rétablir, s'affermir; to gather in taxes, percevoir les impôts.—v.i. Se rassembler, se réunir, s'assembler; s'amasser; grandir, croître; (*Path.*) former un abcès.—n. Pli, froncis, m. **gatherer,** n. Personné qui cueille, f., cueilleur; percepteur (of taxes); vendangeur (of grapes); (*Bookb.*) assembleur, m. **gathering,** n. Rassemblement, m.; assemblée, réunion; perception (of taxes); récolte, cueillette (of fruit etc.), f.; (*Dress.*) froncis; (*Med.*) abcès; (*Print.*) assemblage, m.

gattorugine [BLENNY].

gaud [gɔːd], n. Ornement voyant, m.; parure un peu criarde; babiole, f. **gaudily,** adv. Fastueusement, avec éclat. **gaudiness,** n. Faste, m., ostentation, f., éclat clinquant, faux brillant, m. **gaudy,** a. Voyant, éclatant; fastueux, de mauvais goût.—n. (*Univ.*) Banquet anniversaire, m.

gauffer [GOFFER].

gauge [geidʒ], v.t. Jauger, mesurer; (*fig.*) juger.—n. Jauge, mesure, f.; calibre, m.; (*Naut.*) tirant d'eau, m.; (*Rail.*) voie, f. Narrow gauge, à voie étroite. **gauger,** n.

Jaugeur, m. **gauging,** n. Jaugeage, calibrage, m. **gauging-rod,** n. Jauge, f.

Gaul [gɔːl]. La Gaule, f. **Gaulish,** a. Gaulois. —n. Le gaulois. The Gauls, les Gaulois, m.pl.

Gaullism ['goulizm], n. Gaullisme, m. **Gaullist,** a. and n. Gaulliste.

gaunt [gɔːnt], a. Maigre, décharné; lugubre.

gauntlet ['gɔːntlit], n. Gantelet, m. To run the gauntlet, passer par les baguettes; to take up the gauntlet, ramasser le gant; to throw down the gauntlet to, jeter le gant à.

gauze [gɔːz], n. Gaze, f. **gauzy,** a. Diaphane.

gave, past [GIVE].

gavel [gævl], n. Marteau de président, m.

gavelkind ['gævlkaind], n. Partage égal (des terres), m.

gawk [gɔːk], n. Sot, maladroit, m. **gawky,** a. Dégingandé. Gawky fellow, grand maladroit, empoté, m.

gay [gei], a. Gai, réjoui, joyeux; pimpant, brillant. As gay as a lark, gai comme pinson; to lead a gay life, mener une vie de plaisirs. **gayety** [GAIETY]. **gayly** [GAILY].

gaze [geiz], v.i. Regarder fixement.—n. Regard fixe or attentif, m. **gazer,** n. Contemplateur, spectateur, m.

gazebo [gəˈziːbou], n. Kiosque de jardin; belvédère; balcon, m.

gazelle [gəˈzel], n. Gazelle, f.

gazette [gəˈzet], n. Gazette, f.; bulletin officiel, m. London Gazette, Journal officiel du gouvernement anglais, m.—v.t. Publier or annoncer dans le Journal officiel. He is not yet gazetted, sa nomination n'est pas encore officielle. **gazetteer** [-ˈtiə], n. Dictionnaire géographique, m.; gazetier, m.

gean [dʒiːn], n. Cerise sauvage, merise, f. **gean-tree,** n. Merisier, m.

gear [giə], n. Appareil, accoutrement, attirail, m.; effets, m.pl.; harnais (of a horse), m.; (*Naut.*) apparaux, m.pl., drisse, f.; (*Mach.*) engrenage; (*Cycl.*) développement, m.; (*Motor.*) vitesse, f.; (*fig.*) marchandises, f.pl., biens, m.pl. (*Motor.*) Bottom, first or low gear, première, f.; in gear, embrayé, en marche; neutral gear, point mort, m.; in top gear, en prise; out of gear, débrayé, détraqué; (*fig.*) engrené.—v.i. S'embrayer, s'engrener. —v.t. Embrayer, engrener. **gear-box,** n. Boîte de changement de vitesse, f. **gear-case,** n. Carter, garde-chaîne, m. **gear-lever,** n. Levier des vitesses, m. **gear-wheel,** n. Pignon, braquet, m.

gearing, n. Engrenage, m.

gee [dʒiː], int. Hue! Gee up, hue! **gee-gee,** n. Dada, m.

geese, pl. [GOOSE].

geezer ['giːzə], n. Old geezer, vieux bonhomme, m.

Gehenna [giˈhenə], n. Géhenne, f.

gelatinate [dʒəˈlætineit] or **gelatinize,** v.i. Se gélatinifier.—v.t. Gélatinifier.

gelatine ['dʒelətiːn], n. Gélatine, f. Explosive gelatine, plastic, m.

gelatiniform [dʒeləˈtinifɔːm], a. Gélatiniforme.

gelatinization [dʒəlætinaiˈzeiʃən], n. Gélatinisation, f. **gelatinous,** a. Gélatineux.

geld [geld], v.t. Châtrer. **gelder,** n. Châtreur, m. **gelding,** n. Cheval hongre, m.; castration, f.

gelose ['dʒelouz], n. (Chem.) Gélose, f.
gem [dʒem], n. Pierre précieuse, f., joyau; bourgeon (bud), m.; (fig.) bijou (de), m.; (sch.) perle, f.—v.i. Bourgeonner. **gemmed**, a. Orné, parsemé (de).
geminate ['dʒemineit], a. Géminé. **gemination**, n. Gémination, f.
Gemini ['dʒeminai], n.pl. (Astron.) Gémeaux, m.pl.
gemmiferous [dʒə'mifərəs], a. Gemmifère. **gemmiform**, a. Gemmiforme. **gemmule**, n. Gemmule, f.
gender ['dʒendə], n. Genre, m.
gene [dʒi:n], n. Gène, m.
genealogical [dʒi:niə'lɔdʒikl], a. Généalogique.
genealogist [dʒi:ni'ælədʒist], n. Généalogiste, m. **genealogy** [-'ælədʒi], n. Généalogie, f.
general ['dʒenərəl], a. Général, commun, ordinaire; d'ensemble, de public. Attorney-General, procureur général, m.; for general use, à l'usage de tout le monde; general agent, agent d'affaires, m.; general (servant), bonne à tout faire, f.; general staff, état-major général, m.; in general, en général; in general, la masse du public.—n. Général, m.; le public, le vulgaire, m.; (Mil.) générale (drum-call), f.; Lieutenant-General, général de division, m.; Major-General, général de brigade, m.
generalissimo [dʒenərə'lisimou], n. Généralissime, m.
generality [dʒenə'ræliti], n. Généralité; la plupart, f.
generalization [dʒenərəlai'zeiʃən], n. Généralisation, f. **generalize**, v.t. Généraliser.
generally, adv. En général, ordinairement, généralement.
generalship ['dʒenərəlʃip], n. Généralat; (fig.) talent de général, m., stratégie, f.
generant ['dʒenərənt], a. and n. Générateur, m., génératrice, f. **generate**, v.t. Produire, engendrer. **generation** [-'reiʃən], n. Génération, famille; production, f.; âge, m. **generative**, a. Génératif, générateur. **generator**, n. Générateur, m. Electricity generator, génératrice, f. **generatrix**, n. (Math.) Génératrice, f.
generic [dʒə'nerik] or **generical**, a. Générique.
generosity [dʒenə'rɔsiti], n. Générosité, magnanimité, libéralité, f. **generous**, a. Généreux; (fig.) abondant, riche (en). **generously**, adv. Généreusement.
Genesis ['dʒenəsis]. (Bibl.) La Genèse, f.
genesis ['dʒenəsis], n. Genèse, f.; (Math.) génération, f.
genet ['dʒenət], n. Genette, f.
genetic [dʒə'netik], a. Génétique. **genetics**, n. Génétique, f.
Geneva [dʒə'ni:və]. Genève, f. **The Lake of Geneva**, le lac Léman, le lac de Genève, m.
geneva [dʒə'ni:və], n. Genévrette, f. (wine); genièvre, m. (spirit).
Genevese [dʒenə'vi:z], a. Genevois.
genial ['dʒi:niəl], a. Doux, réconfortant; bienveillant, bon; généreux; cordial, joyeux. **geniality** [-'æliti] or **genialness**, n. Bonne humeur, nature sympathique, gaieté, f., entrain, m. **genially**, adv. Avec bonté, d'un air affable.
genie ['dʒi:ni], n. (Myth.) Génie, djinn, m.

genital ['dʒenitl], a. Génital.—n.pl. Parties génitales, f.pl.
genitive ['dʒenitiv], n. (Gram.) Génitif, m.
genius ['dʒi:niəs], n. Génie, m.; (fig.) disposition naturelle, f. To have a genius for, avoir le don, le génie, de.
Genoa ['dʒenoə]. Gênes, f.
genocide ['dʒenəsaid], n. Génocide, m.
Genoese [dʒeno'i:z], a. Génois.
gent [GENTLEMAN].
genteel [dʒen'ti:l], a. (now iron.) De bon ton, comme il faut, distingué. **genteelly**, adv. Comme il faut, bien, bourgeoisement.
genteelness, n. Élégance, f., bon ton, m.
gentian ['dʒenʃən], n. Gentiane, f. **gentianella** [dʒenʃə'nelə], n. Gentianelle, f.
Gentile ['dʒentail], a. and n. Gentil, m.
gentility [dʒen'tiliti], n. Bon ton, m., distinction; *politesse, élégance, f.; (collect.) la bonne société.
gentle [dʒentl], a. Doux, aimable; paisible; modéré (of slopes etc.); *bien né, noble. Gentle reader, ami lecteur, m.; of gentle birth, bien né.
gentlefolk or **gentlefolks**, n.pl. Personnes de bon ton, f.pl., gens comme il faut, gens bien élevés, m.pl.
gentleman ['dʒentlmən], n. (pl. gentlemen) Monsieur; homme de bon ton, homme comme il faut, galant homme, homme d'honneur; homme bien né. A perfect gentleman, un homme très comme il faut; a young gentleman, un jeune homme, m.; (Law) gentleman of independent means, homme sans profession, rentier, m.; gentlemen's agreement, engagement sur parole, m.; Gentlemen (on public convenience), hommes, m.pl.; gentlemen's (size in) gloves, gants d'homme, m.pl.; this gentleman, ce monsieur, m.; those gentlemen, ces messieurs, m.pl.; to play the fine gentleman, faire le monsieur. **gentleman-in-waiting**, n. Gentilhomme de service, m. **gentleman-like** or **gentlemanly**, a. Distingué, de bon ton, comme il faut, bien élevé; honorable, délicat. **gentlemanliness**, n. Bon ton, m., distinction, f., savoir-vivre, m.
gentleness, n. Douceur, bonté, f.
gentlewoman, n. (pl. gentlewomen) Dame or jeune fille de condition or de bonne famille, f.
gently, adv. Doucement.
gentry ['dʒentri], n. Personnes de distinction, f.pl.; haute bourgeoisie; petite noblesse, f.; (iron.) gens, m.pl.
genuflect ['dʒenjuflekt], v.i. Faire une génuflexion. **genuflexion** [dʒenju'flekʃən], n. Génuflexion, f.
genuine ['dʒenjuin], a. Pur, vrai, véritable, authentique, naturel; sincère. **genuinely**, adv. Purement, sincèrement, authentiquement. **genuineness**, n. Authenticité, vérité, sincérité, f.
genus ['dʒenəs or 'dʒi:nəs], n. (pl. genera ['dʒenərə]) Genre, m.
geocentric [dʒi:ou'sentrik], a. Géocentrique.
geode [dʒi:oud], n. Géode, f.
geodesic [dʒi:ou'desik], a. Géodésique. **geodesy** [-'ɔdəsi], n. Géodésie, f.
geodynamic [dʒi:oudai'næmik], a. Géodynamique.
Geoffrey ['dʒefri]. Geoffroi, m.

geogeny [dʒi'ɔdʒəni], *n.* Géogénie, *f.*
geognosy [dʒi'ɔgnəsi], *n.* Géognosie, *f.*
geographer [dʒi'ɔgrəfə], *n.* Géographe, *m.*
geographical [-ə'græfikl], *a.* Géographique.
geographically, *adv.* Géographiquement.
geography [dʒi'ɔgrəfi], *n.* Géographie, *f.*
geological [dʒi:ɔ'lɔdʒikl], *a.* Géologique.
geologically, *adv.* Géologiquement. **geologist** [-'ɔlədʒist], *n.* Géologue, *m.* **geology**, *n.* Géologie, *f.*
geomancy [dʒio'mænsi], *n.* Géomance, géomancie, *f.*
geometer [dʒi:'ɔmitə] or **geometrician** [dʒi:ɔmə'triʃən], *n.* Géomètre, *m.* **geometric** [-'metrik] or **geometrical**, *a.* Géométrique, géométral. **geometrically**, *adv.* Géométriquement, *géométralement. **geometrize**, *v.i.* Géométriser. **geometry**, *n.* Géométrie, *f.*
geophysical [dʒi:ɔ'fizikl], *a.* Géophysique. **geophysics**, *n.* Physique du globe, géophysique, *f.*
George [dʒɔ:dʒ]. Georges, *m.*; (*Av. slang*) pilote automatique, *m.* *By George!* Sapristi! **Georgia** ['dʒɔ:dʒiə]. La Géorgie, *f.* **Georgian**, *a.* and *n.* Géorgien; du règne des quatre rois Georges.
Georgics ['dʒɔ:dʒiks], *n.pl.* Géorgiques, *f.pl.*
Georgina [dʒɔ:'dʒi:nə]. Georgina, Georgette, *f.*
geranium [dʒə'reiniəm], *n.* (*Bot.*) Géranium, *m.*
gerfalcon ['dʒɜ:fɔ:kən], *n.* (*Orn.*) Gerfaut, *m.*
germ [dʒɜ:m], *n.* Germe, *m.*; (*fam.*) microbe pathogène, *m.*
German (1) ['dʒɜ:mən], *a.* and *n.* Allemand, *m.*, Allemande, *f.*; allemand (language), *m.* *German measles*, rubéole, *f.*; *German silver*, maillechort, *m.*
german (2) ['dʒɜ:mən], *a.* Germain, parent, proche; pertinent, qui a rapport (à). *A cousin german*, un cousin germain.
germander [dʒɜ:'mændə], *n.* Germandrée, *f.*
germane [GERMAN (2)].
Germania [dʒɜ:'meiniə]. La Germanie, *f.*
Germanic [dʒɜ:'mænik], *a.* Germanique. **Germanism** ['dʒɜ:mənizm], *n.* Germanisme, *m.* **Germanize**, *v.t., v.i.* Germaniser.
Germanus [dʒɜ:'meinəs]. Germain, *m.*
Germany ['dʒɜ:məni]. L'Allemagne, *f.*
germen ['dʒɜ:mən], *n.* Germe, *m.*
germicidal ['dʒɜ:misaidl], *a.* Microbicide.
germinal ['dʒɜ:minl], *a.* Germinal, de germe. **germinate**, *v.t.* Germer; pousser, bourgeonner.—*v.t.* Faire germer. **germination** [-'neiʃən], *n.* Germination, *f.* **germinative**, *a.* Germinatif.
gerontocracy [dʒerɔn'tɔkrəsi], *n.* Gérontocratie, *f.*
gerrymander ['gerimændə], *v.t.* (*Am.*) Découper arbitrairement les circonscriptions électorales; manigancer, truquer (une élection, une affaire). **gerrymandering**, *n.* Truquage électoral, *m.*; manigances, *f.pl.*
gerund ['dʒerənd], *n.* (*Gram.*) Gérondif, substantif verbal, *m.* **gerundive** [dʒə'rʌndiv], *a.* Du gérondif.—*n.* Adjectif verbal, *m.*
Gervase [dʒə:'veiz]. Gervais, *m.*
gestation [dʒes'teiʃən], *n.* Gestation, *f.* **gestatory** ['dʒestətəri], *a.* Gestatoire.
gesticulate [dʒes'tikjuleit], *v.i.* Gesticuler. **gesticulation** [-'leiʃən], *n.* Gesticulation, *f.*

gesticulator, *n.* Gesticulateur, *m.* **gesticulatory**, *a.* Gesticulaire.
gesture ['dʒestʃə], *n.* Geste; mouvement expressif, *m.*, action, *f.*—*v.i.* Gesticuler.—*v.t.* Accompagner de gestes.
get [get], *v.t.* (*past* and *p.p.* got) (Se) procurer, acquérir, obtenir; recevoir (to receive); remporter (to gain); gagner (to earn); avoir; apprendre (to learn); acheter (to buy); arriver à, atteindre (to reach); aller chercher (to fetch); trouver (to find); faire se faire, (to induce, make, cause, etc.); attraper, s'attirer (to catch etc.). *He got him to draw up a prescription*, il lui fit écrire une ordonnance; *he got it here*, il l'a obtenu ici; *he's got measles*, il a attrapé la rougeole; *that's all I've got to say*, voilà tout ce que j'ai à dire; *to get a footing*, s'établir; *to get a move on*, (*fam.*) se dépêcher; *to get all one can out of them*, les exploiter de son mieux; *to get by heart*, apprendre par cœur; *to get friends*, se faire des amis; *to get hold of*, s'emparer de, saisir, obtenir, trouver, influencer; *to get the better of*, l'emporter sur.—*v.i.* Se mettre (en); devenir, se faire (to become); aller (to go). *Get on with it!* allez donc! *get out! get out of it!* va-t'en! allez-vous-en! *it was getting late*, il se faisait tard; *to get about*, sortir, prendre de l'exercice; *to get about again*, reprendre ses occupations; *to get above*, surpasser, se mettre au-dessus de; *to get across*, traverser; *to get ahead*, passer devant, faire des progrès, prospérer, réussir; *to get along*, s'avancer, cheminer, faire marcher; *to get around*, se répandre, s'ébruiter; *to get at*, arriver à, parvenir à; suborner, attaquer; atteindre; *to get away*, s'en aller, se sauver, échapper (à), enlever, ôter; *to get away with something*, s'en tirer; *to get back*, revenir, regagner, recouvrer; *to get behind*, rester en arrière, être en retard (de ses payements); *to get beyond*, dépasser; *to get by*, passer, se tirer (de); *to get clear*, se tirer (de); *to get down*, descendre, faire descendre; avaler (to swallow); abattre; se mettre; *to get drunk*, s'enivrer; *to get forward*, avancer, faire avancer; *to get free*, s'échapper, se dégager; *to get from*, tirer, arracher; se tirer, s'échapper de; *to get home*, arriver, arriver chez soi; *to get in*, entrer, s'insinuer, rentrer, se glisser dans; faire entrer; *to get in debt*, faire des dettes; *to get into*, se mettre en, entrer dans, monter dans, tomber dans; *to get into a dispute*, s'engager dans une querelle; *to get into Parliament*, être élu (député); *to get killed*, se faire tuer; *to get loose*, s'échapper; *to get made* or *done*, faire faire; *to get married*, se marier; *to get near*, approcher, s'approcher (de); *to get off*, se tirer, s'en tirer, s'échapper, se sauver; descendre; ôter, enlever; s'ôter; *to get old*, vieillir; *to get on*, avancer, réussir, faire des progrès, cheminer; faire avancer; mettre; monter sur; *to get oneself up*, se faire beau, s'endimancher; *to get out*, sortir, s'en tirer; faire sortir, tirer, enlever; *to get over*, passer, passer à travers, surmonter, vaincre, se consoler de, se remettre de, venir à bout de; *to get over it*, se remettre; *to get ready*, apprêter, se préparer; *to get rich*, s'enrichir; *to get rid of*, se débarrasser de; *to get round (someone)*, enjôler; *to get taken in*, se laisser attraper; *to get through*, passer par, parcourir, venir à

bout de, se tirer de; *to get tired*, se lasser, se fatiguer; *to get to*, arriver à, atteindre; *to get together*, assembler, réunir, se réunir; *to get to sleep*, s'endormir; *to get under*, se mettre au-dessous de, passer sous; *to get up*, se lever, organiser, exciter, monter, faire monter, lever, préparer, arranger, blanchir (linen), (*colloq.*) se mettre au courant de; *to get up again*, relever, ramasser, se relever; *to get upon*, monter sur; *to get well again*, se rétablir; *to get well paid*, se faire bien payer; *to get wet*, se mouiller; *to get young again*, rajeunir; *what is he getting at?* où veut-il en venir?

get-away, *n.* Fuite, *f.*; départ, *m.*

getting, *n.* Acquisition, *f.*, gain, *m.* **getting-up**, *n.* Lever, *m.*; organisation, *f.* (d'une fête); montage, *m.* (d'une pièce); préparation, *f.* (d'un examen); maquillage, *m.*; (*Naut.*) gréage, *m.*

get-up, *n.* (*colloq.*) Toilette, *f.*; affublement, *m.*

gewgaw ['gju:gɔ:], *n.* Babiole, bagatelle, *f.*, colifichet, *m.*

geyser ['gi:zə], *n.* Chauffe-bain, *m.*; (*Geol.*) geyser, *m.*

Ghana ['gɑːnə]. Le Ghana, *m.*

ghastliness ['gɑːstlinis], *n.* Pâleur, *f.*; aspect effrayant, *m.* **ghastly**, *a.* Pâle, pâle comme la mort; horrible, affreux.

Ghent [gent]. Gand, *m.*

gherkin ['gəːkin], *n.* Cornichon, *m.*

ghetto ['getou], *n.* Ghetto, *m.*

ghillie [GILLIE].

ghost [goust], *n.* Revenant, fantôme, spectre; esprit, *m.*, âme, ombre, *f.*; (*pej.*) nègre, *m.* (écrivain qui fait le travail d'un autre). *Not the ghost of a chance*, pas la moindre chance; *the Holy Ghost*, le Saint-Esprit; *to give up the ghost*, rendre l'âme.—*v.i.* Servir de nègre (à), prêter sa plume (à). **ghostlike**, *a.* De fantôme, spectral, pâle comme un spectre. **ghostly**, *a.* Spirituel; de spectre. **ghost-story**, *n.* Histoire de revenants, *f.*

ghoul [gu:l], *n.* Goule, *f.* **ghoulish**, *a.* De goule.

ghyll [GILL (2)].

giant ['dʒaiənt], *n.* Géant, *m.*—*a.* De géant. **giantess**, *n.* Géante, *f.* **giant-like**, *a.* Gigantesque, de géant.

*****gib** [gib], *n.* Vieux chat, vieux matou, *m.*; (*Engin.*) contre-clavette, *f.*

gibber ['dʒibə], *v.i.* Baragouiner. **gibberish**, *n.* Baragouin, charabia, *m.*

gibbet ['dʒibit], *n.* Potence, *f.*, gibet, *m.*—*v.t.* Attacher au gibet, pendre à une potence; (*fig.*) pilorier.

gibbon ['gibən], *n.* Gibbon (ape), *m.*

gibbous ['gibəs] or **gibbose**, *a.* Gibbeux.

gibbosity [gi'bɔsiti], *n.* Gibbosité, *f.*

gibe [dʒaib], *v.i.* Railler, se moquer (de).—*v.t.* Se moquer de, railler.—*n.* Sarcasme, *m.*; raillerie, moquerie, *f.* **giber**, *n.* Railleur, *m.* **gibingly**, *adv.* D'un air moqueur, ironiquement.

giblets ['dʒiblits], *n.pl.* Abatis, *m.pl.*

Gibraltar [dʒi'brɔːltə]. Gibraltar, *m.*

giddily ['gidili], *adv.* Étourdiment, à l'étourdie. **giddiness**, *n.* Vertige, étourdissement, *m.*; (*fig.*) étourderie, humeur folâtre, *f.* **giddy**, *a.* Étourdi; (*fig.*) écervelé, volage; vertigineux, qui donne le vertige. *I feel*

giddy, la tête me tourne; *that makes me feel giddy*, cela me donne le vertige; *to play the giddy goat*, faire l'imbécile.

Gideon ['gidiən]. Gédéon, *m.*

gift [gift], *n.* Don, présent, cadeau; (*fig.*) talent, *m.* (*Law*) *Deed of gift*, donation entre vifs, *f.*; *Christmas gifts*, étrennes, *f.pl.*; (*fam.*) *it's a gift*, c'est facile à faire; *one must not look a gift horse in the mouth*, à cheval donné on ne regarde pas la bride; *to have the gift of the gab*, (*colloq.*) avoir la langue bien pendue.—*v.t.* Douer, doter (de). **gifted**, *a.* Doué de, de talent, apte.

gig [gig], *n.* Cabriolet, *m.*; yole, *f.*; (*Tech.*) laineuse, *f.*

gigantic [dʒai'gæntik], *a.* Gigantesque, de géant.

gigantism ['dʒaigəntizm], *n.* Gigantisme, *m.*

giggle [gigl], *v.i.* Rire nerveusement, rire tout bas, un peu bêtement.—*n.* Ricanement, petit rire bête, *m.*

gild [gild], *v.t.* Dorer; (*fig.*) embellir. *To gild the pill*, dorer la pilule. **gilder**, *n.* Doreur, *m.* **gilding**, *n.* Dorure, *f.*, (*fig.*) clinquant, *m.*

Gilead ['giliæd]. Galaad, *m.*

Giles [dʒailz]. Gilles, *m.*

gill (1) [gil], *n.* (*usu. in pl.*) Ouïes (of fish), *f.pl.*; (*pl.* **gills**), caroncules, *f.pl.* (of birds); (*slang*) bajoues, *f.pl.* (of a man); lamelles, *f.pl.* (of mushroom); ailettes, *f.pl.* (of radiator).

gill (2) [gil], *n.* Ravin boisé; ruisseau (du ravin), *m.*; peigne, *m.* (for hemp).

gill (3) [dʒil], *n.* Treize centilitres, *m.pl.*, (*colloq.*) canon, *m.*

gillie ['gili], *n.* (*Highlands*) Serviteur, *m.* (of a sportsman).

gillyflower ['dʒiliflauə], *n.* Giroflée, *f.*

gilt [gilt], *n.* Dorure, *f.*—*a.* Doré. **gilt-edged**, *a.* Doré sur tranche. *Gilt-edged securities*, valeurs de tout repos, *f.pl.* **gilthead**, *n.* Daurade, *f.* **gilt-silver**, *n.* Vermeil, *m.*

gimbal [dʒimbl], *n.* (*usu. pl.*) Balancier, *m.*; suspension à la Cardan, *f.*

gimcrack ['dʒimkræk], *n.* Pacotille, camelote, *f.*

gimlet ['gimlit], *n.* Vrille, *f.*

gimmick ['gimik], *n.* Caractéristique personnelle, *f.*; machin; tour (trick), *m.* *To cultivate a gimmick*, se donner un petit genre.

gimp [gimp], *n.* Galon, *m.*, ganse, *f.*

gin [dʒin], *n.* Trébuchet, piège; genièvre, gin (liquor), *m.*; chèvre (windlass), *f.*; (*Tech.*) machine à égrener, *f.*—*v.t.* Égrener; (*fig.*) prendre au trébuchet. **gin-palace**, *n.* Débit de spiritueux, *m.*

ginger ['dʒindʒə], *n.* Gingembre, *m.*; (*fam.*) poil de carotte, *m.* (red-haired person).—*v.t.* (*colloq.*) *To ginger up*, activer, émoustiller. **ginger-ale**, *n.* Limonade gazeuse, *f.* **ginger-beer** or **ginger-pop**, *n.* Bière au gingembre, *f.* **gingerbread**, *n.* Pain d'épice, *m.* **ginger-haired**, *a.* Roux, rouquin. **gingerly**, *adv.* Tout doucement, délicatement.

gingham ['giŋəm], *n.* Étoffe de coton, imprimée ordinairement de carreaux, *f.*

gingival [dʒin'dʒaivl], *a.* Gingival.

gingle [JINGLE].

ginning ['dʒiniŋ], *n.* Égrenage, *m.*

gipsy ['dʒipsi], *n.* Bohémien, tzigane, *m.*, bohémienne, *f.* **gipsy-moth**, *n.* Zigzag, *m.* **gipsy-table**, *n.* Guéridon, *m.*

giraffe | glaze

giraffe [dʒi'rɑːf], *n.* Girafe, *f.*
gird [gəːd], *v.t.* (*past* and *p.p.* **girt**) Ceindre (de); entourer, environner (de); lier; se revêtir de; vêtir (de); sangler (a horse). *To gird up one's loins*, se ceindre les reins.—*v.i. To gird at*, railler.—*n.* Raillerie, *f.*, sarcasme, *m.*
girder ['gəːdə], *n.* Poutre, solive, traverse, *f.*
girdle [gəːdl], *n.* Ceinture, *f.*; ceinturon, *m.*; (=suspender-belt) porte-jarretelles, *m.*; [= GRID-IRON, *Sc.*].—*v.t.* Ceinturer. **girdle-belt,** *n.* Ceinturon, *m.* **girdle-maker,** *n.* Ceinturier, *m.*
girkin [GHERKIN].
girl [gəːl], *n.* Fille, jeune fille; jeune personne, *f.* **girlhood,** *n.* Jeunesse, *f.* (d'une femme). **girlish,** *a.* De jeune fille. **girlishly,** *adv.* En jeune fille.
girt [gəːt], *past* and *p.p.* [GIRD].
girth [gəːθ], *n.* Sangle, *f.*, tour, *m.*, circonférence, *f. In girth*, de tour.
girt-line ['gəːtlain], *n.* (*Naut.*) Cartahu, *m.*
gist [dʒist], *n.* Fond, fin mot; point principal, *m.*, substance, *f.* (of a talk); (*Law*) motif principal, *m.*
give [giv], *v.t.* (*past* **gave**, *p.p.* **given**) Donner; livrer, rendre, accorder; faire (an answer, credit, one's compliments, one's love etc.); remettre, transmettre; appliquer (to apply); porter (a blow etc.); pousser (a groan etc.); sonner (a sound); prononcer (a verdict etc.). *Give and take*, donnant donnant; *give the devil his due*, à chacun son dû; *give way,* (*Naut.*) nage partout! *I'll give it him!* je lui réglerai son compte! *to be given to* (drink etc.), se livrer à, être porté à; *to give a description of*, décrire; *to give a present*, faire un cadeau; *to give a shriek*, jeter un cri de terreur; *to give away*, donner; trahir; *to give away the bride*, conduire la fiancée à l'autel; *to give back again*, rendre; *to give battle*, livrer bataille; *to give ear*, être attentif, prêter l'oreille (à); *to give forth*, publier; *to give ground*, reculer; *to give in*, céder, donner, rendre; *to give in charge*, faire arrêter; *to give judgment*, rendre *or* prononcer un jugement; *to give oneself up*, se rendre, se constituer prisonnier; *to give oneself up to*, se rendre, se livrer, s'abandonner (à); *to give one's mind to*, s'adonner à; *to give out*, émettre, annoncer, distribuer; *to give over*, abandonner, céder, laisser, quitter; *to give place*, céder, faire place (à); *to give quarter to*, faire quartier à; *to give the slip*, se dérober, s'échapper; *to give up*, abandonner, renoncer à, rendre, céder, se dessaisir de, quitter, donner sa langue aux chats (of riddles); *to give warning or notice to*, donner congé *or* donner son congé à (a servant etc.); *to give way*, céder, se relâcher, reculer, plier, s'abandonner (à).—*v.i.* Céder; plier (to bend); prêter (to stretch). *To give in*, céder, plier, s'affaisser; *to give out*, être à bout, s'épuiser; (*colloq.*) *to give over*, cesser. —*n.* Élasticité, *f.*
given, *a.* Adonné, porté, disposé (à); donné. *Given these difficulties*, étant donné ces difficultés; *in a given time*, dans un temps donné.
giver, *n.* Donneur, dispensateur, *m.*
giving, *n.* Action de donner, *f.*, don, *m.*
gizzard ['gizəd], *n.* Gésier, *m.*
glacial ['gleifəl], *a.* Glacial, glaciaire. **glacier** ['glæsiə], *n.* Glacier, *m.*

glacis ['glæsis], *n.* (*Fort.*) Glacis, *m.*
glad [glæd], *a.* Content, aise, bien aise; heureux (de). *They would be only too glad*, ils ne demanderaient pas mieux que de; *we are very glad to see you*, nous sommes très contents de vous voir; *you will be glad to hear*, vous apprendrez avec plaisir. **gladden,** *v.t.* Réjouir.
glade [gleid], *n.* Clairière, percée, *f.*
gladiator ['glædieitə], *n.* Gladiateur, *m.* **gladiatorial** [-'tɔːriəl], *a.* Gladiatorial, gladiatoire.
gladiolus ['glædiələs, glædi'ouləs], *n.* (*pl.* **gladioli** [glædi'oulai]) Glaïeul, *m.*
gladly ['glædli], *adv.* Volontiers, avec plaisir. **gladness** or ***gladsomeness,** *n.* Joie, gaieté, *f.*, plaisir, *m.* **gladsome,** *a.* (*poet.*) Joyeux, gai.
***gladstone** ['glædstən] or **gladstone-bag,** *n.* Sac de voyage, *m.*
glair [glɛə], *n.* Glaire, *f.*—*v.t.* Glairer. **glaireous** or **glairy,** *a.* Glaireux.
glamorous ['glæmərəs], *a.* Charmeur, ensorcelant.
glamour ['glæmə], *n.* Charme, prestige, éclat, *m.*
glance [glɑːns], *n.* Ricochet, coup en biais; regard, coup d'œil, *m.*; (*fig.*) éclair, trait de lumière, *m.*—*v.i.* Jeter un coup d'œil (sur); briller, étinceler. *To glance off*, ricocher; *to glance over*, parcourir.
gland [glænd], *n.* (*Anat.*) Glande, *f.*
glanders ['glændəz], *n.pl.* Morve, *f.*
glandiferous [glæn'difərəs], *a.* Glandifère.
glandiform ['glændifɔːm], *a.* Glandiforme.
glandular or **glandulous,** *a.* Glandulaire, glanduleux. **glanduliferous** [-dju'lifərəs], *a.* Glandifère.
glans [glænz], *n.* Gland, *m.*
glare [glɛə], *n.* Éclat, *m.*, lumière éblouissante, lueur, *f.*; regard irrité, farouche, *m.*—*v.i.* Éblouir; luire, briller; regarder d'un air furieux. **glaring,** *a.* Voyant, éblouissant, criant, éclatant; choquant; manifeste, notoire. **glaringly,** *adv.* Manifestement, d'une manière patente.
glass [glɑːs], *n.* (*pl.* **glasses**) Verre, *m.*; vitre (window), *f.*; châssis, *m.* (in garden); (*pl.*) lunettes; jumelles (field-glasses), *f.pl. Cut glass*, cristal taillé, *m.*; *eyeglass*, monocle, lorgnon, *m.*; *glass case*, vitrine, *f.*; *glass door*, porte vitrée, *f.*; *glass of wine*, verre de vin, *m.*; *glass, with care!* fragile! *hour-glass*, sablier, *m.*; *looking-glass*, miroir, *m.*; *magnifying glass*, loupe, *f.*; *plate glass*, glace, *f.*; *stained glass*, vitraux, *m.pl.*; (*weather-*)*glass*, baromètre, *m.*; *window-glass*, verre à vitre, *m.*—*a.* De verre.
glass-blower, *n.* Souffleur, verrier, *m.*
glass-blowing, *n.* Soufflage de verre, *m.*
glass-furnace, *n.* Four de verrerie, *m.*
glass-house, *n.* Verrerie, *f.*; (*pop.*) prison militaire, *f.* **glass-maker,** *n.* Verrier, *m.*
glass-roof, *n.* Verrière, *f.* **glass-ware,** *n.* Verrerie, *f.* **glassworks,** *n.* Verrerie, manufacture de verre, *f.* **glassy,** *a.* Vitreux, transparent. *Glassy stare*, regard fixe, *m.*
glaucescence [glɔː'sesəns], *n.* Glaucescence, *f.* **glaucescent,** *a.* Glaucescent.
glaucoma [glɔː'koumə], *n.* (*Path.*) Glaucome, *m.*
glaucous ['glɔːkəs], *a.* Glauque.
glaze [gleiz], *v.t.* Vitrer; vernir, vernisser (to

varnish); glacer (pastry etc.); lustrer (linen etc.). **glazier,** *n.* Vitrier, *m.* **glazing,** *n.* Vitrage (of windows); vernissage, glaçage; vernis (glaze), *m.*

gleam [gli:m], *n.* Rayon, *m.*, lueur, *f.*, trait de lumière, *m.*—*v.i.* Briller, luire (de). **gleaming,** *a.* Rayonnant, miroitant, luisant.

glean [gli:n], *v.t.* Glaner; grappiller (grapes). **gleaner,** *n.* Glaneur, grappilleur, *m.* **gleaning,** *n.* Glanage, *m.*, glanure, *f.*; grappillage, *m.*

glebe [gli:b], *n.* Glèbe, terre, *f.*, sol, *m.* **glebeland,** *n.* Terre d'église, *f.*, clos du presbytère, *m.*

glee [gli:], *n.* Joie, gaieté; (*Mus.*) chant à plusieurs voix (sans accompagnement), *m.* *In high glee,* débordant de joie. **gleeful,** *a.* Joyeux, gai. **gleefully,** *adv.* Gaiement, joyeusement.

gleet [gli:t], *n.* (*Path.*) Écoulement, *m.*

glen [glen], *n.* Vallon, ravin, *m.*

glib [glib] *a.* Coulant, glissant, délié, volubile. *A glib tongue,* une langue bien pendue. **glibly,** *adv.* Avec volubilité; doucereusement. **glibness,** *n.* Volubilité, facilité, faconde, *f.*; spéciosité, *f.*

glide [glaid], *v.i.* Couler, glisser; se glisser (dans).—*n.* Glissade, *f.*; (*Av.*) vol plané, *m.* **glider,** *n.* (*Av.*) Planeur, *m.* **glidingly,** *adv.* Doucement, en glissant, en planant.

glimmer ['glimə], *n.* Lueur, *f.*, faible rayon, *m.* *A glimmer of hope,* un rayon *or* une lueur d'espoir; *to turn down the gas to a glimmer,* mettre le gaz en veilleuse.—*v.i.* Entre-luire, luire faiblement; poindre (of the dawn). **glimmering,** *n.* Faible lueur; (*fig.*) légère apparence, *f.*—*a.* Faible, vacillant.

glimpse, *n.* Échappée de lumière, *f.*; coup d'œil, *m.*, vue rapide, *f.* *To catch a glimpse of,* entrevoir.

glint, *n.* Trait de lumière, *m.*, lueur, *f.*—*v.i.* Luire par moments.

glisten ['glisn], *v.i.* **glister** ['glistə], *v.i.* **glitter** ['glitə], *v.i.* Briller, reluire, scintiller, étinceler, chatoyer.—*n.* Éclat, lustre, *m.* **glittering,** *a.* Brillant, luisant, étincelant. **glitteringly,** *adv.* Avec éclat.

gloaming ['gloumiŋ], *n.* Crépuscule, *m.* *In the gloaming,* à la brune, entre chien et loup.

gloat [glout], *v.i.* Dévorer *or* couver des yeux; (*fig.*) se régaler (to gloat over). **gloatingly,** *adv.* Avec une satisfaction méchante.

global [gloubl], *a.* Global. *Global war,* guerre mondiale, *f.*, conflit mondial, *m.*

globate ['gloubeit] *or* **globated,** *a.* Sphérique.

globe [gloub], *n.* Globe, *m.*—*v.i.*, *v.t.* Arrondir. **globe-flower,** *n.* Trolle d'Europe, *m.* **globe-shaped,** *a.* En forme de globe. **globe-trotter,** *n.* Globe-trotter, *m.*

globose [glo'bous], **globous** ['gloubəs], *or* **globular** ['glɔbjulə], *a.* Globuleux, sphérique; (*Bot.*) globeux.

globosity [glo'bɔsiti], *n.* Sphéricité, *f.*

globule ['glɔbju:l], *n.* Globule, *m.*

globulin ['glɔbjulin], *n.* Globuline, *f.*

glomerule ['glɔmərɔ:l], *n.* Glomérule, *m.*

gloom [glu:m] *or* **gloominess,** *n.* Obscurité, *f.*, ténèbres, *f.pl.*; (*fig.*) tristesse, *f.* *To cast or throw a gloom over,* assombrir, attrister.—*v.i.* Être obscur; être sombre; s'attrister.—*v.t.* Assombrir; (*fig.*) attrister. **gloomily,** *adv.* Obscurément; d'un air triste, lugubrement. **gloomy,** *a.* Sombre, obscur; morne; triste,

mélancolique. *Gloomy weather,* temps sombre, *m.*

glorification [glɔ:rifi'keiʃən], *n.* Glorification; réjouissance, *f.*

glorify ['glɔ:rifai], *v.t.* Glorifier. **glorious,** *a.* Glorieux; illustre, splendide, magnifique, superbe. **gloriously,** *adv.* Glorieusement, avec gloire.

glory ['glɔ:ri], *n.* Gloire; (*Paint.*) auréole, *f.*—*v.i.* Se glorifier (de).

glory-hole ['glɔ:rihoul], *n.* (*fam.*) Capharnaüm, *m.*

gloss [glɔs], *n.* Lustre; luisant, apprêt, *m.*; (*fig.*) glose, *f.*, commentaire, *m.*—*v.i.* Gloser, interpréter; lustrer, apprêter, donner de l'éclat à. *To gloss over,* farder, glisser sur, pallier.

glossarist ['glɔsərist], *n.* Glossateur, *m.* **glossary** ['glɔsəri], *n.* Glossaire, *m.*

glossiness ['glɔsinis], *n.* Lustre, brillant, glacé, *m.*

glossographer [glɔ'sɔgrəfə], *n.* Glossographe, *m.* **glossography,** *n.* Glossographie, *f.*

glossy ['glɔsi], *a.* Lustré, brillant, luisant.

glottal [glɔtl], *a.* Glottique. (*Phon.*) *Glottal stop,* coup de glotte, *m.*

glottis ['glɔtis], *n.* (*Anat.*) Glotte, *f.*

glove [glʌv], *n.* Gant, *m.*—*v.t.* Ganter. **glover,** *n.* Gantier, *m.* **glove-stretcher,** *n.* Baguette à gants, *f.* **glove-trade,** *n.* Ganterie, *f.*

glow [glou], *v.i.* Brûler (de); briller; (*fig.*) s'échauffer, s'enflammer.—*n.* Lueur rouge, *f.*; (*fig.*) feu, éclat, *m.*, splendeur, *f.*; teint vermeil, rouge, *m.* *To be in a glow,* sentir une douce chaleur (par tout le corps); *to put in a glow,* allumer le sang à, embraser.

glower ['glauə], *v.i.* (at) Regarder d'un air maussade *or* sévère.

glowing, *a.* Incandescent, embrasé; ardent, animé; chaleureux. *To speak in glowing terms of,* dire merveille de. **glowingly,** *adv.* Vivement, chaleureusement.

glow-worm, *n.* Ver luisant, *m.*, luciole, *f.*

gloxinia [glɔk'siniə], *n.* (*Bot.*) Gloxinie, *f.*

gloze [glouz], *v.i.* Gloser. *To gloze over,* pallier.

glucose ['glu:kous], *n.* Glucose, *f.* or *m.*

glue [glu:], *n.* Colle-forte, *f.*—*v.t.* Coller. **glue-pot,** *n.* Pot à colle, *m.* **gluey** *or* ***gluish,** *a.* Gluant, poisseux.

glum [glʌm], *a.* Renfrogné, maussade, de mauvaise humeur, morne.

glume [glu:m], *n.* (*Bot.*) Glume, *f.*

glut [glʌt], *v.t.* Gorger, rassasier; (*fig.*) repaître (the eyes); assouvir (one's wrath); encombrer, engorger (the market). *To glut oneself,* se gorger (de).—*n.* Surabondance, *f.*, excès, *m.*, pléthore, *f.*

gluten ['glu:tən], *n.* Gluten, *m.* **glutinative,** *a.* Glutinatif. **glutinosity** [-'nɔsiti] *or* **glutinousness,** *n.* Glutinosité, *f.* **glutinous,** *a.* Glutineux.

glutton [glʌtn], *n.* Gourmand, goinfre, *m.* *A glutton for work,* un bœuf pour le travail, un bourreau de travail. *To eat like a glutton,* Manger en glouton. **gluttonous,** *a.* Gourmand, glouton, goulu, vorace. **gluttonously,** *adv.* En glouton, goulument. **gluttonize,** *v.i.* Gloutonnerie, *n.*

glycerine ['glisəri:n], *n.* Glycérine, *f.*

glycogen ['glaikoudʒən], *n.* Glycogène, *m.*

glycol ['glaikɔl], *n.* Glycol, *m.*
glyph [glif], *n.* (*Arch.*) Glyphe, *m.*
glyptics ['gliptiks], *n.pl.* Glyptique, *f.*
gnarled [nɑːld] or **gnarly**, *a.* Noueux, plein de nœuds.
gnash [næʃ], *v.t.* Grincer.—*v.i.* Grincer des dents. **gnashing,** *n.* Grincement, *m.*
gnat [næt], *n.* Cousin, moucheron, *m.* **gnat-snapper,** *n.* Gobe-mouches, *m.*
gnaw [nɔː], *v.t.* Ronger. **gnawer,** *n.* Rongeur, *m.* **gnawing,** *n.* Rongement, *m.* —*a.* Rongeant, rongeur.
gneiss [nais], *n.* (*Min.*) Gneiss, *m.*
gnome [noum], *n.* Gnome, *m.*, gnomide, *f.* **gnomic,** *a.* Gnomique.
gnomon ['noumɔn], *n.* Gnomon, *m.*
gnomonics [nou'mɔniks], *n.pl.* Gnomonique, *f.*
gnosis ['nousis], *n.* Gnose, *f.*
gnostic ['nɔstik], *n.* Gnostique, *m.* **gnosticism,** *n.* Gnosticisme, *m.*
gnu [nuː], *n.* Gnou, *m.*
go [gou], *v.i.* (*past* **went,** *p.p.* **gone**) Aller, se rendre; marcher, passer; s'en aller, partir (to leave); disparaître (to disappear); devenir (to become); mener (to lead); contribuer (à); être sur le point de, se mettre (à). *Go ahead!* en avant! *go it!* allez donc! allez-y! *I do it, but it goes against the grain,* je le fais, mais c'est à contre-cœur; *to go about,* aller çà et là, entreprendre, (*Naut.*) virer de bord; (*Mil.*) faire demi-tour; *to go abroad,* voyager, aller à l'étranger; *to go against,* aller contre, s'opposer à, être contraire à; *to go ahead,* aller de l'avant; *to go along,* poursuivre son chemin, marcher, s'en aller; *to go ashore,* débarquer, aborder, échouer; *to go aside,* se mettre de côté; *to go astray,* s'égarer; *to go away,* s'en aller, partir; *to go back,* retourner, s'en retourner, reculer; *to go backward,* aller à reculons, reculer; *to go backwards and forwards,* aller et venir; *to go between,* s'interposer, s'entremettre; *to go beyond,* aller au delà, dépasser; *to go by,* passer, passer devant, se régler sur, s'écouler (of time); *to go down,* descendre, se coucher (of sun), tomber, baisser, rétrograder, (*Naut.*) couler à fond, sombrer; *to go far,* aller loin; *to go for,* aller chercher, passer pour, se jeter sur, sauter dessus; *to go for nothing,* ne compter pour rien, ne pas compter; *to go forth,* sortir; *to go forward,* avancer; *to go from,* quitter, s'écarter de, se départir de; *to go halves with,* être de moitié avec; *to go in,* entrer; *to go in for,* se présenter à, concourir pour, se décider pour, tenter, essayer, entreprendre (to attempt); *to go into mourning,* se mettre en deuil; *to go near,* approcher; *to go off,* partir (of gun), s'en aller, se vendre, s'écouler (of goods); *to go on,* aller, avancer, continuer, se passer, poursuivre, se conduire; *to go on ahead,* prendre les devants; *to go one's own way,* aller son chemin; *to go out,* sortir, aller dans le monde, s'éteindre; *to go out of one's way to,* se donner bien de la peine pour; *to go out of (the way),* se détourner de; *to go over,* passer, traverser, parcourir; *to go places* (*colloq.*), sortir, s'avancer; *to go round,* faire un détour; *to go the whole hog, to go through with it,* aller jusqu'au bout; *to go through,* passer par, traverser, fendre, subir, souffrir, parcourir; *to go together,* marcher ensemble, s'accorder; *to go to sleep,* s'endormir; *to go*

up, monter; *to go up and down,* courir çà et là, monter et descendre; *to go up a river,* remonter un fleuve; *to go up for an examination,* subir un examen; *to go upon,* se fonder sur; *to go up to,* aborder, accoster; *to go with,* aller avec, accompagner; *to go ₐwithout,* se passer de; *to let go,* lâcher prise; *where are you going?* où allez-vous? *who goes there?* qui vive?
    n.—Mode, vogue, *f.*; (*fig.*) entrain, *m.*, énergie, *f.*; coup, essai, accès, *m. At one go,* d'un coup; *it is no go,* ça ne passe pas! pas moyen! *to be all the go,* faire fureur; *to be always on the go,* avoir toujours le pied en l'air; *to have a go* (*try*), essayer un coup; *to have plenty of go,* être plein d'entrain or d'énergie. **go-ahead,** *a.* Entreprenant. **go-between,** *n.* (*pej.*) Intermédiaire; entremetteur, *m.,* entremetteuse, *f.* **go-by,** *n.* Action d'éluder; (*fig.*) défaite, *f.*, détour, artifice, *m. To give the go-by to,* passer sans saluer, planter là; y renoncer. ***go-cart,** *n.* Chariot d'enfant, *m.*, trotteuse, *f.* **go-getter,** *n.* Homme d'affaires énergique; arriviste, *m.* **go-slow,** *a.* Go-slow policy, grève de lenteur, *f.*
goad [goud], *n.* Aiguillon, *m.*—*v.t.* Aiguillonner; (*fig.*) exciter, stimuler, pousser.
goal [goul], *n.* But; terme, *m. To score a goal,* marquer un but. **goal-keeper,** *n.,* or **goalie** (*fam.*) (*Ftb.*) Gardien de but, *m.* **goal-post,** *n.* Montant de but, *m.*
goat [gout], *n.* Chèvre, *f. Goat skin,* peau de chèvre, *f.*; *he-goat,* bouc, *m.*; *she-goat,* chèvre, *f. To act the goat, the giddy goat,* faire l'imbécile. **goatherd,** *n.* Chevrier, *m.*
goatsucker, *n.* Engoulevent (bird), *m.*
goatee [gou'tiː], *n.* Barbiche, *f.*
goatish, *a.* De bouc, lascif. **goat's-beard,** *n.* Salsifis sauvage, *m.*, barbe-de-bouc, *f.*
gobble [gɔbl], *v.t.* Gober, avaler.—*v.i.* Glouglouter (of turkeys).
gobbler ['gɔblə], *n.* Glouton, goulu; dindon, *m.*
goblet ['gɔblit], *n.* Gobelet, *m.*
goblin ['gɔblin], *n.* Lutin, *m.*
gobo ['goubou], *n.* (*Cine.*) Écran opaque, *m.*
goby ['goubi], *n.* (*Ichth.*) Gobie, *m.*
God [gɔd], *n.* Dieu, *m. God forbid!* à Dieu ne plaise! *God helps those who help themselves,* aide-toi, le ciel t'aidera; *God tempers the wind to the shorn lamb,* à brebis tondue Dieu mesure le vent; *would to God!* plût à Dieu! **godchild,** *n.* Filleul, *m.*, filleule, *f.* **god-daughter,** *n.* Filleule, *f.* **goddess,** *n.* Déesse, *f.* **godfather,** *n.* Parrain, *m.* **godhead,** *n.* Divinité, *f.* **godless,** *a.* Athée, impie. **godlessness,** *n.* Impiété, *f.* **godlike,** *a.* Divin. **godliness,** *n.* Piété, *f.* **godly,** *a.* Pieux, dévot. **godmother,** *n.* Marraine, *f.* **godsend,** *n.* Aubaine, trouvaille, *f.* **godship,** *n.* Divinité, *f.* **godson,** *n.* Filleul, *m.* **godspeed,** *n.* Succès, *m.* **Godward(s),** *adv.* Envers Dieu.
Godfrey ['gɔdfri], Godefroi, *m.*
godown [go'daun], *n.* (*East Indies*) Comptoir, entrepôt, *m.*
godwit ['gɔdwit], *n.* (*Orn.*) Barge, *f.*
goer ['gouə], *n.* Marcheur, *m.*, marcheuse, *f. Comers and goers,* allants et venants, *m.pl.*; *theatre-goer,* habitué du théâtre, *m.*
goffer ['gɔfə], *v.t.* Gaufrer.—*n.* Godron, tuyauté, *m.*

goggle [gɔgl], *v.i.*   Rouler de gros yeux. *Goggle eyes*, des yeux en boules de loto, *m.pl.* **goggle-eyed**, *a.*   Aux gros yeux à fleur de tête. **goggles**, *n.pl.*   Lunettes (protectrices), *f.pl.*

going ['gouiŋ], *n.*   Marche, démarche, allée, *f.*, départ, *m.*   *Going back*, retour, *m.*; (*sch.*) rentrée, *f.*; *going in*, entrée, *f.*; *going out*, sortie, *f.*; *goings-on*, faits et gestes, *m.pl.*, manège, *m.*; *I have heard all about your goings-on*, j'ai eu de vos nouvelles.

goitre ['gɔitə], *n.*   (*Med.*) Goitre, *m.* **goitrous**, *a.* Goitreux.

gold [gould], *n.*   Or, *m.*   *As good as gold*, sage comme une image.—*a.* D'or, en or.   *A gold ring*, un anneau d'or *or* une bague en or. **gold-beater**, *n.*   Batteur d'or, *m.*   *Gold-beater's skin*, baudruche, *f.* **gold-digger**, *n.* Chercheur d'or, *m.*; (*pop.*) femme entretenue, *f.* **gold-drawer**, *n.*   Tireur d'or, *m.* **gold-dust**, *n.*   Poudre d'or, *f.* **gold-fields**, *n.pl.* Placer, *m.* **goldfinch**, *n.*   Chardonneret, *m.* **goldfish**, *n.*   Poisson rouge, *m.* **gold-leaf**, *n.* Or en feuilles, *m.* **gold-lettered**, *a.*   En lettres d'or. **gold-plate**, *n.*   Vaisselle d'or, *f.* **goldsmith**, *n.*   Orfèvre, *m.*   *Goldsmith's work*, orfèvrerie, *f.* **gold-standard**, *n.* Étalon or, *m.* **gold-thread**, *n.*   Fil d'or, *m.* **gold-worked**, *a.*   Broché d'or.

Gold Coast ['gould 'koust]. La Côte de l'Or, *f.* (Ghana).

golden, *a.*   D'or.   *Golden wedding*, noces d'or, *f.pl.* **golden-chain**, *n.*   Faux-ébénier, *m.* **golden-rod**, *n.*   Verge d'or, *f.* **golden syrup**, *n.*   Mélasse raffinée, *f.*

Golden Horn ['gouldən 'hɔːn].   La Corne d'or, *f.*

golf [gɔlf *or* gɔf], *n.*   Golf, *m.* **golf-club**, *n.* Club de golf, *m.* (building and instrument). **golf-course** *or* **golf-links**, *n.*   Terrain de golf, *m.* **golfer**, *n.*   Joueur de golf, golfeur, *m.*

golliwog ['gɔliwɔg] *or* **gollywog**, (*pej.*)   *n.* Poupée d'étoffe (noire), *f.*

golly ['gɔli], *int.*   Ciel!

golosh [GALOSH].

gomerel ['gɔmərəl], *n.*   (*Sc.*) Niais, idiot, *m.*

Gomorrah [gə'mɔrə].   Gomorrhe, *f.*

gonad ['gɔnæd], *n.*   Gonade, *f.*

gondola ['gɔndələ], *n.*   Gondole; nacelle (de ballon), *f.* **gondolier** [-'liə], *n.*   Gondolier, *m.*

gone [gɔːn, gɔn], *a.*   Allé, parti; perdu, disparu; passé, écoulé; adjugé (at auctions). *Far gone*, avancé; *going, going, gone!* une fois, deux fois, adjugé! (*fam.*) *gone in the head*, timbré; *he is gone*, il s'en est allé, il est mort; *his money is all gone*, il a dépensé tout son argent; *in days gone by*, au temps jadis; (*fam.*) *to be gone on someone*, être épris de quelqu'un.

goner, *n.*   (*pop.*) Homme mort, *m.*   *He's a goner*, il est fichu.

gonfalon ['gɔnfələn] *or* **gonfanon**, *n.*   Gonfalon, gonfanon, *m.* **gonfalonier**, *n.*   Gonfalonier, *m.*

gong [gɔŋ], *n.*   Gong; timbre (of clock), *m.*; (*pop.*) décoration militaire, *f.*—*v.t.*   (*fam.*) Sommer un conducteur de s'arrêter pour une contravention au code.

gongorism ['gɔŋgorizm], *n.*   (*Lit.*) Gongorisme, *m.*

goniometer [gɔni'ɔmitə], *n.*   Goniomètre, *m.* **goniometry**, *n.*   Goniométrie, *f.*

gonorrhoea [gɔnə'riːə], *n.*   Blennoragie, *f.*

good [gud], *a.*   (*comp.* **better,** *superl.* **best**) Bon; de bien, honnête; convenable, avantageux; valide, solide; (*colloq.*) sage.   *A good deal*, beaucoup; *as good as*, presque, comme, aussi bon que; *be so good as to*, veuillez; *good day!* bonjour! *good evening!* bonsoir! *good for you!* bravo! *good humour*, bonne humeur, *f.*, enjouement, *m.*; *good luck*, bonheur, *m.*, bonne chance, *f.*; *good morning!* bonjour! *good nature*, bonté, bonhomie, humanité, complaisance, *f.*, bon naturel, *m.*; *good night*, bonsoir! bonne nuit! *good to eat*, bon à manger; *in good earnest*, tout de bon, sérieusement; *it is as good as done*, c'est une affaire faite; *it is as good as yours*, il vaut bien le vôtre; *it's no good*, cela ne vaut rien, c'est inutile; *it's no good your asking*, vous avez beau le demander; *that's a good one!* en voilà une bonne! *that's as good as saying*, autant dire que; *to be as good as gold*, être sage comme une image (of children); *to be good*, être sage (of children); *to be good at*, être fort en, exceller à, être expert à; *to make good*, exécuter, compenser, indemniser; assurer; accomplir; prospérer; racheter son passé; *to stand good*, être valide; *very good*, *I'll do it*, c'est bien, je vais le faire.—*n.*   Bien, bon, avantage, profit, *m.*   *For good (and all)*, pour (tout) de bon; *good and evil*, le bien et le mal; *it's no good complaining*, inutile de se plaindre; *much good may it do you!* grand bien vous fasse! *so much to the good*, c'est toujours autant de gagné; *to come to no good*, n'aboutir à rien; *to do no good*, ne faire rien qui vaille; *what's the good of?* à quoi bon? (*pl.*) Meubles, effets, biens, *m.pl.*, marchandises, *f.pl.*; *goods manager*, directeur des messageries, *m.*; *goods station*, gare de marchandises, *f.*; *goods train*, train de marchandises, *m.*; *the goods department*, les messageries, *f.pl.*—*adv.* Bien.   *As good*, aussi bien; *very good*, fort bien.—*int.* Bon! bien! c'est très bien!

good-breeding, *n.*   Politesse, *f.*, savoir-vivre, *m.* **good-bye!** *int.*   Adieu!   *Good-bye for the present*, au revoir. **good-class**, *a.*   Bien élevé, de bonne famille; de choix.   *A good-class shop*, une boutique de choix. **good-conduct**, *a.*   De bonne moralité.   *A good-conduct certificate*, certificat de moralité, *m.* **good-fellowship**, *n.*   Camaraderie, *f.* **good-for-nothing**, *n.*   Vaurien, *m.* **Good Friday**, *n.*   Vendredi saint, *m.* **good-humoured**, *a.* De bonne humeur, enjoué, gai. **goodliness**, *n.*   Beauté, grâce, belle apparence, *f.* **good-looking**, *a.*   Beau, joli. **goodly**, *a.* Beau, bon, considérable, gros. ***goodman**, *n.* Maître (de la maison), *m.* **good-natured**, *a.* D'un bon naturel, bon, bienveillant. **goodness**, *n.*   Bonté; probité, *f.*   *Goodness knows*, Dieu sait! *goodness knows how*, Dieu sait comme; *thank goodness!* Dieu merci! ***goodwife**, *n.*   Maîtresse de maison, *f.* **goodwill**, *n.*   Bienveillance, bonne volonté, complaisation, bonté; (*Comm.*) clientèle, *f.*; achalandage, *m.* **goody**, *n.*   Sucrerie, *f.*, bonbon, *m.*—*int.* (*Am.*) Bon! excellent! **goody-goody**, *n.*   (*fam.*) Petit saint, *m.*   *To be a goody-goody*, faire sa Sophie (of a girl).

goof [guːf], *n.*   (*Am.*) Grand dadais, sot, *m.*

goosander [guː'sændə], *n.*   (*Orn.*) Grand harle, harle lièvre, *m.*

goose [guːs], *n.* (*pl.* **geese** [giːs]) Oie, *f.*; (*fig.*) imbécile, nigaud; (*Tailor's*, *pl.* **gooses**) carreau, *m.* *Goose*(*-note*), couac, *m.*; *a green goose*, un oison; *to go on a wild-goose chase*, chercher midi à quatorze heures. **gooseberry** ['guzbəri], *n.* Groseille à maquereau, *f.* **gooseberry-bush**, *n.* Groseillier, *m.* **goose-flesh**, *n.* Chair de poule, *f.* **goose-grass**, *n.* Grateron, *m.* **goose-neck**, *n.* Col de cygne, *m.* **goose-quill**, *n.* Plume d'oie, *f.* **goose-step**, *n.* Pas de l'oie, *m.*

gorcock ['gɔːkɔk], *n.* Coq de bruyère, *m.* **gorcrow**, *n.* Corneille noire, *f.*

Gordian ['gɔːdiən], *a.* Gordien. *Gordian knot*, nœud gordien, *m.*

gore [gɔː], *n.* Sang, sang caillé; (*Dress.*) soufflet, godet, *m.*—*v.t.* Donner un coup de corne à. *Gored skirt*, jupe à panneaux, *f.*

gorge [gɔːdʒ], *n.* Gorge, *f.*; gosier, *m.* *It makes my gorge rise*, cela me soulève le cœur, cela me dégoûte.—*v.t.* Gorger, avaler, rassasier. —*v.i.* Se gorger (de).

gorgeous ['gɔːdʒəs], *a.* Magnifique, splendide, fastueux. **gorgeously**, *adv.* Superbement, magnifiquement. **gorgeousness**, *n.* Magnificence, splendeur, *f.*

gorget ['gɔːdʒit], *n.* (*Surg.*) Gorgeret, *m.*; (*Mil.*) hausse-col, *m.*

Gorgon ['gɔːgən]. Gorgone, *f.*

gorilla [gɔ'rilə], *n.* Gorille, *m.*

goring ['gɔːriŋ], *n.* Coup de corne, *m.*; blessure, *f.*

gormand ['gɔːmənd], *a.* Gourmand. **gormandize** [-daiz], *v.i.* Bâfrer. **gormandizer**, *n.* Goinfre, *m.* **gormandizing**, *n.* Gourmandise, *f.*

gorse [gɔːs], *n.* Ajonc, *m.*

gory ['gɔːri], *a.* Sanglant, couvert de sang.

gosh! [gɔʃ], *int.* Mince alors!

goshawk ['gɔshɔːk], *n.* (*Orn.*) Autour, *m.*

gosling ['gɔzliŋ], *n.* Oison; *chaton, *m.*

gospel ['gɔspəl], *n.* Évangile, *m.* *To take as gospel* (*truth*), prendre pour argent comptant, accepter comme parole d'évangile. **gospeller**, *n.* *Hot gospeller*, Évangéliste zélé, *m.*

gossamer ['gɔsəmə], *n.* Fil de la Vierge, *m.*

gossip ['gɔsip], *n.* Commère, *f.*, causeur, *m.*, -euse, *f.*; causerie, *f.*, commérage, (*colloq.*) potin, *m.*—*v.i.* Bavarder, faire des commérages. **gossiping**, *n.* Commérage, *m.*, (*colloq.*) potins, *m.pl.* **gossip-writer**, *n.* (*Journ.*) Échotier, *m.* **gossipy**, *a.* Anecdotique (of style); familier, potinier.

got [gɔt], *past* and *p.p.* (GET).

Goth [gɔθ], *n.* Goth, *m.*; (*fig.*) barbare, *m.*

gotha ['goutə], *n.* Gotha, avion de bombardement allemand (1914–1918 war), *m.*

Gothic ['gɔθik], *a.* Gothique, ogival. **Gothicism**, *n.* Style gothique, *m.*; (*fig.*) barbarie, rudesse, *f.* **Gothicize**, *v.t.* Ramener à la barbarie.

gouge [gaudʒ], *n.* Gouge, *f.*—*v.t.* Gouger. *To gouge out*, arracher (an eye etc.).

gourd ['guəd], *n.* Gourde, calebasse, *f.* **gourd-plant**, *n.* Calebassier, *m.*

gout [gaut], *n.* Goutte, *f.*, **gouty**, *a.* Goutteux.

govern ['gʌvən], *v.t.* Gouverner, régir, diriger. *To govern oneself*, être maître de soi, se gouverner. **governable**, *a.* Docile, gouvernable. **governance**, *n.* Gouvernement, *m.*, administration, *f.* **governess**, *n.*

Institutrice, gouvernante, *f.* **governing**, *n.* Gouvernement, *m.*, administration, *f.* *Governing classes*, classes dirigeantes, *f.pl.* **government**, *n.* Gouvernement, *m.*, administration, *f.*, régime, *m.* **governmental** [-'mentl], *a.* Gouvernemental. **governor**, *n.* Gouverneur, gouvernant; directeur (of an institution); (*Mech.*) régulateur; (*slang*) maître, patron, *m.*, (*sch. slang*) père, *m.* **governor-general**, *n.* Gouverneur général, *m.* **governorship**, *n.* Gouvernement, *m.*; fonctions de Gouverneur, *f.pl.*

gowan [gauən], *n.* (*Sc.*) Pâquerette, *f.*

gown [gaun], *n.* Robe, *f.* *Dressing-gown*, peignoir, *m.*; *morning-gown*, robe de chambre, *f.*; *night-gown*, chemise de nuit, *f.*—*v.t.* Revêtir d'une robe, habiller. **gowned**, *a.* En robe. **gownsman**, *n.* (*pl.* **gownsmen**) Homme de robe, *m.*; (*pl.*) gens de robe, étudiants, *m.pl.*

grab [græb], *v.t.* Empoigner, saisir (d'un geste brusque).—*n.* (*Civ. Eng.*) Excavateur, *m.*, pelle automatique, *f.*

grabble [græbl], *v.i.* Chercher à tâtons.

grace [greis], *n.* Grâce; faveur, *f.*; pardon; (*Mus.*) agrément, *m.*; bénédicité (before meal), *m.*; grâces (after meal), *f.pl.*; (*pl.*) (*Myth.*) Grâces, *f.pl. Her grace*, madame la duchesse; *his grace*, monsieur le duc, monseigneur l'archevêque; *to have the grace to*, avoir la politesse, la bonne grâce, de; *with a good grace*, de bonne grâce.—*v.t.* Orner, embellir: illustrer, honorer (de).

graceful, *a.* Gracieux, bien fait, élégant. **gracefully**, *adv.* Gracieusement, élégamment. **gracefulness**, *n.* Grâce, *f.*

graceless, *a.* Sans grâce; dépravé.

grace-note, *n.* (*Mus.*) Note d'agrément, *f.*

gracile ['græsil], *a.* Grêle, mince, menu, petit.

gracility [grə'siliti], *n.* Gracilité, ténuité, petitesse, *f.*

gracious ['greiʃəs], *a.* Gracieux (pour or envers); clément, bon, favorable, agréable, bénin. *Good gracious!* bonté divine! **graciously**, *adv.* Gracieusement, avec bonté, favorablement. *To be graciously pleased to*, daigner. **graciousness**, *n.* Bonté, grâce, condescendance, *f.pl.*

gradation [grə'deiʃən], *n.* Gradation, *f.*

gradatory ['greidətəri], *a.* Graduel, par degrés.

grade [greid], *n.* Grade; degré, rang, *m.*—*v.t.* Classer; calibrer; graduer. **grading**, *n.* Classement; calibrage, *m.*; graduation, *f.*

gradient ['greidiənt], *n.* (*Rail.*) Rampe, inclinaison, *f.*

gradual ['grædjuəl], *a.* Graduel, par degrés, gradué. **gradually**, *adv.* Graduellement, par degrés, peu à peu. **graduate** [-ət], *n.* Gradué; (*Chem.*) verre gradué, *m.*—*v.t.* [-eit]. Graduer.—*v.i.* Être reçu à un examen d'enseignement supérieur. **graduation** [-'eiʃən], *n.* Graduation; (*Univ.*) remise d'un diplôme, *f.*

graecism ['griːsizm], *n.* Hellénisme, *m.* **graecize**, *v.t.* Gréciser.

graffito [græ'fiːtou], *n.* (*pl.* **graffiti**) Graffite, graffito, *m.*, (*pl.*) graffites, graffiti, *m.pl.*

graft [grɑːft], *v.t.* Greffer, enter (sur).—*n.* Greffe, *f.*; (*colloq.*) corruption, *f.*, rabiot, *m.* **grafter**, *n.* Greffeur. **grafting**, *n.* Greffe, *f.* **grafting-knife**, *n.* Greffoir, *m.*

grail [greil], *n.* *The Holy Grail*, le Saint-Graal.

grain [grein], *n.* Grain, *m.*; céréales, *f.pl.*; fil (of marble etc.), *m.*; fibres (of wood), *f.pl.*; (*weight*) 0·065 gramme, *m.*; (*pl.*) drêche (brewer's grains), *f.* *Against the grain*, contre le fil, (*fig.*) à contre-cœur, à rebrousse-poil. —*v.t.* Grener, greneler, granuler (leather). **grained, grainy,** *a.* Grenu; grenelé. *Coarse-grained*, à gros grain, à gros poil. **grainer,** *n.* Peintre spécialisé dans l'imitation du bois, *m.* **graining,** *n.* Peinture, *f.*, *or décor*, *m.*, imitant le bois.

grallae ['græli] or **grallatores** [grælə'tɔːriːz], *n.pl.* (*Orn.*) *Gralles, échassiers, *m.pl.* **grallatory,** *a.* Grallipède. **grallic,** *a.* Des échassiers.

gram or **gramme** [græm], *n.* Gramme, *m.*

graminaceous [græmi'neiʃəs] or **graminivorous** [-'nivərəs], *a.* Herbivore. **gramineous** [grə'miniəs], *a.* (*Bot.*) Graminée (*only used in fem.*).

graminifolious [græmini'fouliəs], *a.* Graminiforme.

grammar ['græmə], *n.* Grammaire, *f.* *That is bad grammar*, ce n'est pas grammatical.

grammarian [grə'mɛəriən], *n.* Grammairien, *m.*

grammar-school, *n.* Lycée, collège, *m.*

grammatical, *a.* Grammatical; de grammaire. **grammatically,** *adv.* Grammaticalement. **grammaticize,** *v.t.* Rendre grammatical.

gramophone ['græməfoun], *n.* Gramophone; phonographe, *m.*

grampus ['græmpəs], *n.* Épaulard, *m.*

Granada [grə'nɑːdə]. Grenade, *f.*

granadilla [grænə'dilə], *n.* Grenadille, fleur de la passion, *f.*

granary ['grænəri], *n.* Grenier, *m.*

grand [grænd], *a.* Grand, magnifique, sublime, grandiose. *Grand* (*piano*), piano à queue, *m.* *Grand vizier*, grand vizir, *m.* **grandad, grand-dad,** *n.* (*colloq.*) Grandpapa, *m.* *grandam, n. Grand-mère; (*fig.*) vieille, *f.* **grandchild,** *n.* (*pl.* **grandchildren**) Petit-fils, *m.*, petite-fille, *f.* **granddaughter,** *n.* Petite-fille, *f.* **grandfather** or **grandsire,** *n.* Grand-père, *m.* **grandmother,** *n.* Grand-mère, *f.* *That's teaching your grandmother to suck eggs*, c'est Gros-Jean qui en remontre à son curé. **grand-nephew,** *n.* Petit-neveu, *m.* **grandniece,** *n.* Petite-nièce, *f.* **grandson,** *n.* Petit-fils, *m.*

grandee [græn'diː], *n.* Grand d'Espagne, *m.*

grandeur ['grændjə], *n.* Grandeur, *f.*, éclat, *m.*, splendeur, *f.*

grandiloquence [græn'diləkwəns], *n.* Langage pompeux, *m.*; emphase, grandiloquence, *f.* **grandiloquent** or *grandiloquous, a.* Pompeux, enflé, grandiloquent.

grandly, *adv.* Grandement, magnifiquement, avec éclat.

grandstand ['grændstænd], *n.* Tribune, *f.*

grange [greindʒ], *n.* *Grange, *f.*; manoir (avec ferme), *m.* **granger,** *n.* Régisseur, *m.*

granite ['grænit], *n.* Granit, *m.*

granivorous [grə'nivərəs], *a.* Granivore.

granny ['græni], *n.* (*colloq.*) Bonne-maman, *f.*; (*Naut.*) nœud de vache, *m.*

grant [grɑːnt], *v.t.* Accorder, concéder; convenir, avouer, supposer, admettre; (*Law*) octroyer. *God grant it!* Dieu le veuille! *granted!* soit! *granted that it be so*, supposé que cela soit; *to grant a pardon*, accorder une grâce; *to take for granted*, être persuadé, penser (que); se croire permis (de).—*n.* (*Law*) Don, *m.*, cession, donation, *f.*; aide, subvention, bourse; concession, *f.* **grantee** [grɑːn'tiː], *n.* Concessionnaire; impétrant. **grantor,** *n.* Donateur.

granular ['grænjulə] or *granulary, a.* En grains; granulé, granuleux, granulaire. **granulate,** *v.t.* Grener, granuler.—*v.i.* Se granuler. **granulation** [-'leiʃən], *n.* Granulation, *f.* **granule,** *n.* Granule, *m.* **granulous,** *a.* Granuleux.

grape [greip], *n.* Grain de raisin, *m.*; (*pl.*) raisins, *m.pl.* *A bunch of grapes*, une grappe de raisin. **grape-fruit,** *n.* Pamplemousse, *m.* **grape-gatherer,** *n.* Vendangeur, *m.*, -euse, *f.* **grape-gathering,** *n.* Vendange, *f.* **grape-grower,** *n.* Viticulteur, *m.* **grape-hyacinth,** *n.* Muscari, *m.* **grape-shot,** *n.* Mitraille, *f.* **grape-stone,** *n.* Pépin de raisin, *m.* **grape-vine,** *n.* Treille, *f.*; (*fig.*) source de canards, *f.*

graph [græf, grɑːf], *n.* (*Math.*) Courbe, *f.*; graphique, diagramme, *m.*—*v.t.* Graphiquer, tracer (une courbe). **graphic** ['græfik], *a.* Graphique, pittoresque. **graphically,** *adv.* Graphiquement, pittoresquement. **graph-paper,** *n.* Papier quadrillé, *m.*

graphite ['græfait], *n.* Graphite, *m.*

graphologist [græ'fɔlədʒist], *n.* Graphologue.

graphology, *n.* Graphologie, *f.* **graphometer,** *n.* Graphomètre, *m.*

grapnel ['græpnəl], *n.* Grappin, *m.*

grapple ['græpl], *n.* Grappin, *m.*; lutte, *f.*, combat de lutteurs, *m.*—*v.t.* Accrocher; grappiner; saisir à bras le corps.—*v.i.* En venir aux prises; lutter (contre); (*Navy*) en venir à l'abordage; (*fig.*) manier. *To grapple with*, en venir aux prises avec; *to grapple with a subject*, s'attaquer à un sujet. **grappling-irons,** *n.pl.* Grappins d'abordage, *m.pl.*

*grapy ['greipi], a. De raisin.

grasp [grɑːsp], *v.t.* Empoigner, saisir, prendre avec la main; serrer, tenir; embrasser; tâcher d'atteindre, vouloir se saisir de. *Grasp all, lose all*, qui trop embrasse, mal étreint; *to grasp at*, tâcher de saisir, s'accrocher à.—*n.* Prise, étreinte, poignée; (*fig.*) portée, *f.*, pouvoir, *m.*; appréhension, connaissance, *f.* *To lose one's grasp*, lâcher prise; *within one's grasp*, à la portée de la main. **grasper,** *n.* Personne qui empoigne, *f.*; homme avide, *m.* **grasping,** *a.* Avide, cupide, avare.

grass [grɑːs], *n.* Herbe, *f.*; gazon, herbage, *m.* —*v.t.* Mettre en herbe, gazonner. *To put or turn out to grass*, mettre au vert.—*v.i.* (*slang*) Dénoncer quelqu'un à la police. **grass-blade,** *n.* Brin d'herbe, *m.* **grass-brush,** *n.* Brosse en chiendent, *f.* **grass-covered,** *a.* Couvert d'herbe. **grasshopper,** *n.* Sauterelle, *f.* **grassiness,** *n.* État herbu, *m.* **grass-land,** *n.* Prairie, *f.* **grass-plot,** *n.* Pelouse, *f.*, carré de gazon, *m.* **grass-snake,** *n.* Couleuvre (à collier), *f.* **grass-widow,** *n.* (*fam.*) Femme dont le mari est absent; demi-veuve, *f.* **grassy**, *a.* Herbeux, couvert de gazon, verdoyant.

grate (1) [greit], *n.* Grille, *f.*; foyer (fireplace), *m.*

grate (2) [greit], *v.t.* Râper; frotter.—*v.i.* Crisser (sur *or* contre). *To grate the teeth*, grincer des dents *or* les dents; *to grate upon*, écorcher, (*fig.*) choquer, agacer.

grated ['greitid], *a.* Grillé. *Grated window*, fenêtre grillée, *f.*

grateful ['greitful], *a.* Reconnaissant; (*fig.*) agréable. *To be grateful to him for it*, lui en savoir gré. **gratefully**, *adv.* Avec reconnaissance; (*fig.*) agréablement. **gratefulness**, *n.* Gratitude, reconnaissance, *f.*; (*fig.*) agrément, *m.*

grater ['greitə], *n.* Râpe, *f.*

gratification [grætifi'keiʃən], *n.* Satisfaction, *f.*; contentement, plaisir, *m.*; gratification, récompense, *f.*

gratify ['grætifai], *v.t.* Contenter, satisfaire, faire plaisir à; récompenser. **gratifying**, *a.* Agréable; (*fig.*) flatteur.

grating ['greitiŋ], *n.* Grille, *f.*, grillage; grincement, son discordant, *m.*; chapelure (of bread), *f.*; (*Naut.*) caillebotis, *m.*—*a.* Grinçant, discordant, choquant, désagréable. **gratingly**, *adv.* D'une manière discordante, désagréablement.

gratis ['greitis], *adv.* Gratuitement, gratis, pour rien.—*a.* Gratis, gratuit.

gratitude ['grætitju:d], *n.* Gratitude, reconnaissance, *f.*

gratuitous [grə'tju:itəs], *a.* Gratuit; (*fig.*) volontaire; bénévole. *Gratuitous assumption*, supposition gratuite, *f.* **gratuitously**, *adv.* Gratuitement; (*fig.*) sans motif, sans raison suffisante. **gratuity**, *n.* Don, présent, *m.*, gratification, *f.*; pourboire, *m.*; (*Mil.*) prime de demobilisation, *f.*

gravamen [grə'veimən], *n.* (*pl.* **gravamina**) Grief; fondement (d'une accusation), *m.*

grave (1) [greiv], *n.* Tombe, fosse, *f.*; tombeau, *m.* **grave-clothes**, *n.pl.* Linceul, *m.* **grave-digger**, *n.* Fossoyeur, *m.* **gravedigging**, *n.* Fossoyage, *m.* **graveless**, *a.* Sans sépulture. **gravestone**, *n.* Pierre sépulcrale, tombe, *f.* **graveyard**, *n.* Cimetière, *m.*

grave (2) [greiv], *a.* Grave, sérieux. **gravely**, *adv.* Gravement, sérieusement.

grave (3) [greiv], *v.t.* Graver, tailler, ciseler. *To grave a ship*, espalmer un navire.

gravel [grævl], *n.* Gravier, sable, *m.*; (*Med.*) gravelle, *f.*—*v.t.* Sabler, couvrir de gravier; *(fig.)* embarrasser. **gravel-pit**, *n.* Sablière, *f.* **gravel-walk**, *n.* Allée sablée, *f.*

gravelly, *a.* Graveleux, plein de sable.

graven [greivn], *a.* Gravé, taillé, ciselé. *A graven image*, une image taillée.

graveness [GRAVITY] (1).

graver ['greivə], *n.* Graveur; burin (instrument), *m.*; (*Naut.*) espalmeur, *m.*

graves (1) [grɑːv], *n.* Vin de Graves, *m.*

graves (2) [greivz] [GREAVES].

gravid ['grævid], *a.* Grosse, enceinte.

graving ['greiviŋ], *n.* Gravure; (*Naut.*) action d'espalmer, *f.* **graving-dock**, *n.* Bassin de radoub, *m.* **graving-tool**, *n.* Burin, *m.*

gravitate ['græviteit], *v.i.* Graviter. **gravitation** [-'teiʃən], *n.* Gravitation, *f.*

gravity (1) ['græviti], *n.* Gravité, *f.*, caractère sérieux, *m.*; air sérieux, *m.*

gravity (2) ['græviti], *n.* Gravité, pesanteur, *f.* *Specific gravity*, poids spécifique, *m.*

gravy ['greivi], *n.* Jus, *m.* (de viande); sauce, *f.* **gravy-beef**, *n.* Pot-au-feu (dans le gîte), *m.* **gravy-boat**, *n.* Saucière, *f.*

gray [GREY].

grayling ['greiliŋ], *n.* (*Ichth.*) Ombre, *m.*

graze [greiz], *v.t.* Effleurer, raser, frôler; érafler, écorcher (the skin); faire paître, mener paître (cattle etc.).—*v.i.* Paître, brouter.—*n.* Écorchure, éraflure, *f.* **grazier**, *n.* Éleveur, *m.* **grazing-ground** or **grazing-land**, *n.* Pâturage, *m.*

grease [griːs], *n.* Graisse, *f.*—*v.t.* Graisser. *To grease someone's palm*, graisser la patte à quelqu'un. **grease-band**, *n.* Bande enduite de glu horticole, *f.* **grease-box**, *n.* Boîte à huile, *f.* **grease-gun**, *n.* Pompe à graisse, *f.* **grease-paint**, *n.* Fard, *m.*

greaser, *n.* Graisseur, *m.*

greasiness ['griːzinis], *n.* Onctuosité, *f.*, état graisseux, *m.* **greasing**, *n.* Graissage, *m.*, lubrification, *f.*

greasy ['griːzi], *a.* Gras, graisseux, taché de graisse; (*fig.*) onctueux. *Greasy pole*, mât de cocagne, *m.*

great [greit], *a.* Grand; considérable; important, principal; gros (de). *A great deal* (*of*), *a great many* (*of*), beaucoup (de); *a great man*, un grand homme; *great cry, little wool*, grand bruit, petite besogne; *great with child*, enceinte; *it's no great thing*, ce n'est pas grand'chose; *the great*, les grands, *m.pl.* **great-aunt**, *n.* Grand-tante, *f.* **great-granddaughter**, *n.* Arrière-petite-fille, *f.* **great-grandfather**, *n.* Bisaïeul, *m.* **great-grandmother**, *n.* Bisaïeule, *f.* **great-grandparents**, *n.pl.* Arrière-grands-parents, *m.pl.* **great-grandson**, *n.* Arrière-petit-fils, *m.* **great-nephew**, *n.* Petit-neveu, *m.* **great-niece**, *n.* Petite-nièce, *f.* **great-uncle**, *n.* Grand-oncle, *m.*

great-coat, *n.* Pardessus, *m.*; (*Mil.*) capote, *f.*

greathearted, *a.* Courageux, au cœur noble.

greatly, *adv.* Grandement, fort, beaucoup, de beaucoup.

greatness, *n.* Grandeur; sublimité; intensité, force, énormité, *f.*

greave [griːv], *n.* Jambière, *f.*; jambart, *m.*

greaves [griːvz], *n.pl.* Cretons, *m.pl.*

grebe [griːb], *n.* (*Orn.*) Grèbe, *f.*

Grecian ['griːʃən], *a.* Grec, *m.*, grecque, *f.*, de Grèce.—*n.* Helléniste, *m.* **grecque**, *n.* Grecque, *f.*

Greece [griːs]. La Grèce, *f.*

greed [griːd], *n.* Cupidité, avidité, *f.* **greedily**, *adv.* Avidement, avec avidité. **greediness**, *n.* Cupidité, avidité; gourmandise, gloutonnerie, *f.* **greedy**, *a.* Cupide, avide; glouton, vorace.

Greek [griːk], *a.* Grec, *m.*, grecque, *f.*, de Grèce.—*n.* Grec, *m.*, Grecque, *f.*; grec (language), *m.* *Greek fire*, feu grégeois; *it is all Greek to me*, c'est de l'hébreu pour moi.

green [griːn], *a.* Vert; (*fig.*) frais, nouveau, neuf, récent; jeune, novice; peu cuit (of meat). *Bottle-green*, vert bouteille; *emerald-green*, vert émeraude; *green old age*, verte vieillesse, *f.*; *green-room*, (*Theat.*) foyer, *m.*; *not as green as all that*, (slang) pas si bête que cela; *sea-green*, vert de mer; *to have green fingers*, être excellent jardinier.—*n.* Vert, *m.*; verdure, *f.*; pelouse, *f.*, gazon, *m.*; (*pl.*)

légumes verts, choux, *m.pl.*, herbes potagères, *f.pl.* **greenback,** *n.* Billet de banque des États-Unis, *m.* **green-bone,** *n.* (*Ichth.*) Orphie, *f.* **green-cloth,** *n.* Tapis vert, *m.* **green-eyed,** *a.* Aux yeux verts. **greenfinch,** *n.* Verdier, *m.* **green-fly,** *n.* Puceron, *m.* **greengage,** *n.* Reine-claude, *f.* **greengrocer,** *n.* Fruitier, *m.*, -tière, *f.*, marchand de légumes, *m.* **greenhorn,** *n.* Blanc-bec, niais, *m.* **greenhouse,** *n.* Serre, *f.* **greenshank,** *n.* Chevalier à pieds verts, *m.* **greensickness,** *n.* Chlorose, *f.*, pâles couleurs, *f.pl.* **greensward,** *n.* Pelouse, *f.*, gazon, *m.* **greenwood,** *n.* Bois, *m.*, forêt, *f.*

greenery, *n.* Verdure, *f.* **greenish,** *a.* Verdâtre. **greenly,** *adv.* Nouvellement, prématurément; en novice. **greenness,** *n.* Verdure; fraîcheur; verdeur (unripeness); (*fig.*) simplicité, inexpérience, *f.*

Greenland ['gri:nlənd]. (*Geog.*) Le Groenland, *m.*

greet [gri:t], *v.t.* Saluer, accueillir.—*v.i.* (*Sc.*) Pleurer. **greeting,** *n.* Salutation, *f.*, salut, *m.*; (*pl.*) compliments, *m.pl.*; (*Sc.*) larmes, *f.pl.*

gregarious [grə'gɛəriəs], *a.* Grégaire.'
Gregorian [grə'gɔːriən¹], *a.* Grégorien.
Gregory ['gregəri]. Grégoire, *m.*
grenade [grə'neid], *n.* Grenade, *f.* Hand grenade, grenade à main, *f.*
grenadier [grenə'diə], *n.* Grenadier, *m.*
grenadine ['grenədi:n], *n.* Grenadine, *f.*
grew [gru:], *past* [GROW].
grey [grei], *a.* Gris. Grey matter, intelligence, matière cérébrale, *f.*; iron-grey, gris de fer; the grey mare is the better horse, c'est elle qui porte la culotte; to turn grey, grisonner.
grey-beard, *n.* Barbe grise, *f.*; vieillard, barbon, *m.* **greybearded,** *a.* À la barbe grise.
grey-eyed, *a.* Aux yeux gris.
grey-haired, *a.* Aux cheveux gris.
grey-headed, *a.* À la tête grise.
greyhound, *n.* Lévrier, *m.*
greyish, *a.* Grisâtre. **greyishness,** *n.* Teinte grisâtre, *f.*
greyness, *n.* Gris, *m.*
greywacke ['greiwækə], *n.* Grauwacke, *f.*
grice [grais], *n.* Cochon de lait, *m.*
grid [grid], *n.* Gril, *m.* **griddle,** *n.* Gril; (*Mining*) tamis, *m.*
gridelin ['gridəlin], *n.* Gris de lin, *m.*
gridiron ['gridaiən], *n.* Gril, *m.*
grief [gri:f], *n.* Douleur, tristesse, peine, affliction, *f.*; chagrin, déplaisir, *m.* To come to grief, faire fiasco, finir mal, tomber (de cheval, de bicyclette). **grievance,** *n.* Grief, *m.*; injustice, *f.*
grieve [gri:v], *v.t.* Chagriner, attrister, affliger, faire de la peine à.—*v.i.* Se chagriner, s'affliger. **grieving,** *n.* Doléance, *f.* **grievingly,** *adv.* Avec douleur, avec chagrin. **grievous,** *a.* Lourd, douloureux, grave, affligeant; énorme, atroce. **grievously,** *adv.* Grièvement, cruellement, douloureusement. **grievousness,** *n.* Gravité, énormité, *f.*
griffin ['grifin] or **griffon,** *n.* Griffon, *m.*; (*Ang.-Ind.*) nouveau venu.
grig [grig], *n.* Équille, *f.*, lançon, *m.*; grillon, *m.* Merry as a grig, gai comme un pinson.
grill [gril], *v.t.* Griller, faire griller; (*pop.*)

questionner sans arrêt. The superintendent grilled the suspect, le commissaire cuisina le suspect.—*n.* Gril, *m.*; grillade; viande grillée, *f.*
grillage ['grilidʒ], *n.* Grillage, *m.*
grille [gril], *n.* Grille; (*Motor.*) calandre, *f.*
grilse [grils], *n.* Saumoneau, *m.*
grim [grim], *a.* Farouche, féroce; lugubre, effrayant, menaçant; sinistre, sardonique. **grim-faced,** *a.* À la mine féroce.
grimace [gri'meis], *n.* Grimace, *f.*; (*pl.*) grimacerie, *f.*—*v.i.* Grimacer. **grimacing,** *a.* Grimacier.
grimalkin [gri'mælkin], *n.* Vieux chat, *m.*
grime [graim], *n.* Saleté, noirceur, *f.*, noir, *m.* —*v.t.* Salir, noircir. **grimily,** *adv.* Salement. **griminess,** *n.* Saleté, noirceur, *f.*
grimly ['grimli], *adv.* D'un air farouche, sinistre. **grimness,** *n.* Air renfrogné, aspect effrayant, air farouche, *m.*
grimy ['graimi], *a.* Sale, noirci, encrassé.
grin [grin], *n.* Grimace, *f.*, rire, ricanement, *m.* A hideous grin, un affreux sourire, *m.*—*v.i.* Rire en montrant les dents, ricaner, grimacer.
grinning, *n.* Ricanement, *m.*—*a.* Grimacier.
grind [graind], *v.t.* (*past* and *p.p.* **ground**) Moudre; broyer; aiguiser, émoudre, repasser (knives etc.); roder (a valve); grincer (teeth); (*fig.*) opprimer, fouler, écraser.—*v.i.* Moudre; se broyer, se moudre; grincer (of the teeth). To grind away (sch. slang) piocher, bûcher. **grinder,** *n.* Repasseur, émouleur; broyeur, *m.*; molaire, dent molaire, *f.* Organ-grinder, joueur d'orgue, *m.* **grinding,** *n.* Broiement, *m.*, mouture, *f.*; grincement (of the teeth); repassage (of knives); polissage (of stone etc.), *m.*; (*fig.*) oppression, *f.* **grindstone,** *n.* Meule, *f.* (*fam.*) To keep one's nose to the grindstone, travailler sans répit.
grip (1) [grip], *n.* Prise, étreinte, *f.*, serrement, *m.*; valise (bag); poignée (handle), *f.* To get a grip of the situation, prendre la situation bien en main; to lose one's grip, lâcher prise, (*fig.*) commencer à manquer de poigne.—*v.t.* Empoigner, saisir, serrer.
grip (2) [grip], *n.* Petit fossé, *m.*, rigole, *f.*
gripe [graip], *v.t.* Saisir; opprimer; donner la colique à, donner des tranchées à; (*Naut.*) saisir, amarrer.—*v.i.* Avoir la colique; (*Naut.*) serrer le vent de trop près.—*n.* Saisine, *f.*; (*n.pl.*) colique, *f.*, tranchées, *f.pl.* **griping,** *n.* Colique, *f.*, tranchées, *f.pl.*—*a.* De colique; (*fig.*) cuisant, affreux; avare, rapace (of a miser). **gripingly,** *adv.* Avec des tranchées.
gripper ['gripə], *n.* (*Print.*) Pince, *f.*
griskin ['griskin], *n.* Grillade de porc, *f.*
grisly ['grizli], *a.* Hideux, affreux, horrible.
grist [grist], *n.* Blé à moudre, *m.*, mouture, *f.*; (*fig.*) gain, profit, *m.* To bring grist to the mill, faire venir l'eau au moulin, mettre du beurre dans les épinards.
gristle ['grisl], *n.* Cartilage, *m.* **gristly,** *a.* Cartilagineux.
grit [grit], *n.* Grès, sable, *m.*; (*pl.*) gruau d'avoine (groats), *m.*; (*fig.*) courage, *m.*, endurance, *f.* To have grit, (*fig.*) avoir du cran or du cœur. **gritstone,** *n.* Grès dur, *m.* Millstone grit, grès à meule, *m.* **grittiness,** *n.* État graveleux, *m.* **gritty,** *a.* Graveleux, plein de gravier; grumeleux (of fruit).

grizzle [grizl], *n.* Grison, gris, *m.*; *perruque, *f.*—*v.i.* Grogner, grognonner; pleurnicher. **grizzled,** *a.* Grison, grisonnant, grisâtre. **grizzly,** *a.* Grisâtre. *Grizzly bear*, ours gris d'Amérique, *m.*
groan [groun], *n.* Gémissement, grognement, *m. To give a groan*, pousser un gémissement. —*v.i.* Gémir, grogner.
grot [grout], *n.* (Ancienne) pièce de 4 pence. **groats** [GRIT].
grocer ['grousə], *n.* Épicier, *m.* **groceries,** *n.pl.* Articles d'épicerie, *m.pl.* **grocery,** *n.* Épicerie, *f.*
grog [grɔg], *n.* Grog, *m.* **grog-blossom,** *n.* Bourgeon, *m.* (on nose). **grog-shop,** *n.* Cabaret, débit de liqueurs, bistro, *m.*
groggy, *a.* Gris, pochard; titubant; aux jambes faibles (of a horse); qui tient à peine debout (boxer).
grogram ['grɔgrəm], *n.* ((*Fr.*) gros grain). Tissu grossier de soie et laine, *m.*
groin [grɔin], *n.* Aine; (*Arch.*) arête, *f.* **groined,** *a.* *Groined roof*, voûte d'arête, *f.*
gromwell ['grɔmwəl], *n.* (*Bot.*) Grémil, *m.*
groom [gru:m], *n.* Palefrenier, valet d'écurie; valet, *m.*—*v.t.* Panser. *Well-groomed man*, homme bien soigné, *m.* **grooming,** *n.* Pansage, *m.* **groomsman,** *n.* Garçon d'honneur, *m.*
groove [gru:v], *n.* Rainure, rayure, cannelure; (*fig.*) ornière (rut), *f. Always in the same groove*, toujours dans la même routine.—*v.t.* Creuser, canneler, faire une rainure à.
grope [group], *v.i.* Tâtonner. *To grope about*, aller à tâtons; *to grope for*, chercher à tâtons; *to grope in*, entrer à tâtons. **gropingly,** *adv.* À tâtons.
grosbeak ['grousbi:k], *n.* (*Orn.*) Gros-bec, *m.*
gross [grous], *a.* Gros; grossier, rude; (*Comm.*) brut; (*fig.*) flagrant, énorme. *Gross weight*, poids brut, *m.*—*n.* Gros, *m.*, douze douzaines, *f.pl.*, grosse; masse, *f. In the gross*, en gros. **grossly,** *adv.* Grossièrement; d'une manière flagrante. **grossness,** *n.* Grossièreté; énormité, *f.*
grot [grɔt] or **grotto,** *n.* Grotte, *f.*
grotesque [gro'tesk], *a.* Grotesque. **grotesquely,** *adv.* Grotesquement. **grotesqueness,** *n.* Grotesque, *m.*
grouch [grautʃ] [GROUSE (2)].
ground (1) [graund], *p.p.* [GRIND] and *a.* Broyé, moulu; aiguisé (sharpened). *Ground glass*, verre dépoli, *m.*; *ground rice*, farine de riz, *f.*
ground (2) [graund], *n.* Terre, *f.*; terrain (plot); sol (soil); pays, territoire (land), *m.*; (*pl.*) jardins, terrains, *m.pl.*, parc; sédiment, marc de café; fond (of pictures, coloured fabrics, etc.); (*fig.*) fondement, sujet, motif, principe, *m.*, cause, raison, *f. Ground for suspicion*, matière à soupçon, *f.*; *the ground of accusation*, chef d'accusation, *m.*; *to be on sure ground*, être bien fondé, être sûr de son fait; *to be under ground*, être sous terre; *to burn to the ground*, brûler de fond en comble; *to fall to the ground*, tomber par terre, se réduire à rien; *to gain ground*, gagner du terrain; *to keep one's ground*, tenir bon; *to lose ground*, perdre du terrain, lâcher pied; *to take ground*, (*Naut.*) échouer; *to touch ground*, talonner.—*v.t.* Fonder, baser, établir,

appuyer (sur); (*Mil.*) reposer. *Ground arms!* reposez armes!—*v.i.* Échouer, talonner.
ground-ash, *n.* Plant de frêne, *m.* **ground-bait,** *n.* Amorce de fond (in fishing), *f.* **ground-bass,** *n.* (*Mus.*) Basse contrainte, *f.* **ground-floor,** *n.* Rez-de-chaussée, *m.* **ground-game,** *n.* Gibier à poil, *m.* **ground-ivy,** *n.* Lierre terrestre, *m.*, herbe de Saint Jean, *f.* **ground-line,** *n.* Ligne de fond, *f.* **ground-plan,** *n.* Plan de fondation, *m.* **ground-plot,** *n.* Terrain à bâtir, *m.* **ground-rent,** *n.* Rente foncière, *f.* **ground-sheet,** *n.* Tapis de sol, *m.* **ground-staff,** *n.* (*Av.*) Personnel rampant, *m.* **ground-swell,** *n.* Houle, lame de fond, *f.* **groundwork,** *n.* Fond, fondement, *m.*, base, *f.*; (*Paint.*) plan, canevas, *m.*
grounded, *a.* Fondé, établi. *Well-grounded*, bien fondé. **groundedly,** *adv.* Sur de bons principes, solidement. **grounding,** *n.* *To have a good grounding in*, connaître bien les éléments de. **groundless,** *a.* and **groundlessly,** *adv.* Sans fondement. **groundlessness,** *n.* Manque de fondement, *m.*, frivolité, *f.* **groundling,** *n.* Homme sans culture, *m.*; (*Ichth.*) loche épineuse, *f.*; poisson de fond, *m.*
groundsel ['graundsəl], *n.* (*Bot.*) Seneçon, *m.*
group [gru:p], *n.* Groupe, peloton, *m. To form a group or groups*, se grouper.—*v.t.* Grouper. **group-captain,** *n.* Colonel d'aviation, *m.* **grouping,** *n.* Groupement, *m.*
grouse (1) [graus], *n.* Tétras. *Wood grouse or great grouse*, coq de bruyère, *m.*
grouse (2) [graus], *v.i.* (slang) Grogner, murmurer, grincher.—*n. To have a grouse against*, avoir un grief contre; *to like a good grouse*, aimer à rogner.
grout [graut], *n.* Mortier liquide, coulis, *m.* (*pl*) sédiment, *m.*, lie, *f.*—*v.t.* Remplir de coulis; jointoyer; fouiller (with the snout). **grouting,** *n.* Jointoiement au mortier liquide, *m.*
grove [grouv], *n.* Bocage, bosquet, *m. Oak-grove*, chênaie, *f.*
grovel [grɔvl], *v.i.* Ramper, se vautrer. **groveller,** *n.* Être abject, être rampant, *m.* **grovelling,** *a.* Rampant, abject, vil.—*n.* Bassesse, *f.*
grow [grou], *v.i.* (past **grew** [gru:]) *p.p.* **grown**) Croître, pousser, s'accroître, augmenter, se développer; devenir, se faire (to become); naître, germer; parvenir. *To grow again*, repousser, recroître; *to grow better*, s'améliorer, se remettre, se porter mieux; *to grow big*, grossir; *to grow cold*, se refroidir; *to grow confused*, se troubler; *to grow fainter and fainter*, s'affaiblir de plus en plus; *to grow fat*, engraisser; *to grow grey*, grisonner; *to grow hot*, s'échauffer; *to grow into*, devenir, passer en; *to grow into fashion*, venir à la mode; *to grow in years*, vieillir, se faire vieux; *to grow lean*, maigrir; *to grow less*, diminuer; *to grow old*, vieillir; *to grow out of favour*, perdre les bonnes grâces; *to grow out of use*, passer, vieillir; *to grow poor*, s'appauvrir; *to grow rich*, s'enrichir; *to grow sleepy*, s'assoupir; *to grow ugly*, enlaidir; *to grow up*, croître, grandir, arriver à maturité; *to grow worse*, empirer, aller plus mal; *to grow young again*, rajeunir.—*v.t.* Cultiver; faire pousser, laisser pousser.
grower, *n.* Cultivateur, producteur, *m.*

growing, *a.* Croissant.—*n.* Croissance; culture, *f.*

growl [graul], *v.i.* Grogner, gronder.—*n.* Grognement, grondement, *m.*

grown [groun], *a.* Fait. *English-grown,* de provenance anglaise; *full-grown,* qui a pris toute sa croissance; *full-grown girl,* grande fille; *grown man,* homme fait, *m.* **grown-up,** *a.* Fait, grand.—*n.* Adulte. *The grown-ups,* les grands, *m.pl.,* les grandes personnes, *f.pl.*

growth [grouθ], *n.* Croissance, *f.,* accroissement; produit, cru, *m.,* récolte (produce), *f.;* (*fig.*) progrès, développement, *m.*

groyne [groin], *n.* Épi (on foreshore), *m.*

grub [grʌb], *n.* Larve, *f.,* ver blanc, *m.;* (*slang*) mangeaille, nourriture, *f.*—*v.t.* Défricher, fouiller. *To grub up,* arracher, extirper.—*v.i.* Bêcher, creuser; (*slang*) manger. **grub-axe** or **grub-hoe,** *n.* Hoyau, *m.* **grubbing-up,** *n.* Essartement, *m.* **grubby,** *a.* Véreux; (*fig.*) sale, mal peigné.

grudge [grʌdʒ], *n.* Rancune, animosité, *f.,* mauvais vouloir, *m. To have a grudge against,* avoir une dent contre, en vouloir à.—*v.t.* Donner à contre-cœur.—*v.i.* Envier à, regarder avec envie. **grudgingly,** *adv.* À contre-cœur; de mauvaise grâce.

gruel ['gru:əl], *n.* Gruau, *m.*

gruesome ['gru:səm], *a.* Macabre, horrible, lugubre, terrifiant.

gruff [grʌf], *a.* Bourru, brusque, rude, rébarbatif. **gruffly,** *adv.* D'un air renfrogné; rudement. **gruffness,** *n.* Rudesse, brusquerie, *f.,* ton bourru, *m.*

grumble ['grʌmbl], *v.i.* Murmurer, se plaindre, grogner, grommeler (contre *or* de).

grumbler ['grʌmblə], *n.* Grondeur, grogneur, grognon, *m.* **grumbling,** *n.* Murmure, grognement, *m.* **grumblingly,** *adv.* En grommelant.

grume [gru:m], *n.* Grumeau, caillot, *m.*

grumous ['gru:məs], *a.* Grumeleux; épais.

grumpiness ['grʌmpinis], *n.* Mauvaise humeur, maussaderie, *f.* **grumpy,** *a.* Bourru, morose, bougon.

Grundy (Mrs.) ['misiz'grʌndi]. *Not to care what Mrs. Grundy says,* se moquer du qu'en dira-t-on. **grundyism,** *n.* Pruderie, pudibonderie, *f.*

grunt [grʌnt], *v.i.* Grogner.—*n.* Grognement, *m.* **grunter,** *n.* Grogneur; cochon, *m.* **grunting,** *n.* Grognement, *m.* **gruntingly,** *adv.* En grognant.

gruntling, *n.* Petit cochon, goret, *m.*

guaiacum ['gwaiəkəm], *n.* Gaïac, *m.*

guano ['gwɑ:nou], *n.* Guano, *m.*

guarantee [gærən'ti:], *n.* Garant, *m.,* caution, garantie, *f.*—*v.t.* Garantir. **guarantor,** *n.* Garant, *m.*

guaranty [GUARANTEE].

guard [gɑ:d], *n.* Garde; défense, protection, *f.;* garde, *m.* (person); (*Rail.*) conducteur, chef de train, *m.;* chaîne en sautoir (for a watch), *f.;* onglet (for mounting), *m. Advance guard,* avant-garde, *f.; guard's van,* (*Rail.*) fourgon, *m.;* (*Mil.*) *Home Guard,* milice, *f.; life-guard,* garde du corps, *m.; on guard,* de garde, en faction; *rear-guard,* arrière-garde, *f.; to be on one's guard,* se tenir sur ses gardes; *to be caught off one's guard,* être pris au dépourvu; *to come off guard,* descendre la garde; *to mount guard,* monter la garde.—

v.t. Garder, défendre, protéger, veiller sur. *To guard (oneself) against,* se prémunir contre.—*v.i.* Se garder, se tenir sur ses gardes; se prémunir (contre).

guarded, *a.* Prudent, circonspect; réservé. **guardedly,** *adv.* Avec circonspection, avec réserve. **guardedness,** *n.* Circonspection, réserve, *f.*

guard-house, *n.* Corps de garde, poste, *m.* **guard-iron,** *n.* (*Rail.*) Chasse-pierres, *m.* **guard-room,** *n.* Corps de garde, *m.,* salle de police, *f.* **guardship,** *n.* Stationnaire, *m.* **guardsman,** *n.* (*pl.* **guardsmen**) Garde, *m.*

guardian, *n.* Gardien; tuteur (of minors); (*Law*) curateur; (*Poor Law*) administrateur (de la taxe des pauvres), *m.*—*a.* Gardien, tutélaire. *Guardian angel,* ange gardien. **guardianship,** *n.* Tutelle, protection, défense, *f.*

Guatemala [gwætə'mɑ:lə]. Le Guatemala. **Guatemalan,** *a.* and *n.* Guatémaltèque. Guatémalien.

guava ['gwɑ:və], *n.* Goyave, *f.* **guava-tree,** *n.* Goyavier, *m.*

gudgeon ['gʌdʒən], *n.* Goujon; (*Mech.*) tourillon, *m.;* (*fig.*) dupe, *f.,* jocrisse, *m.*

guelder-rose ['geldərouz], *n.* (*Bot.*) Boule de neige, *f.,* obier, *m.*

guerdon ['gə:dən], *n.* (*Lit.*) Récompense, *f.*—*v.t.* Récompenser.

Guernsey ['gə:nzi]. Guernesey.

guerrilla [gə'rilə], *n.* (*Mil.*) Guérilla, *f.;* guérillero, *m.*

guess [ges], *v.t., v.i.* Deviner, conjecturer; (*Am. colloq.*) supposer, croire.—*n.* Conjecture, *f. At a rough guess,* à peu près; *I give you three guesses,* je vous le donne en trois; *to make a good guess,* deviner juste.

guesser, *n.* Devineur, *m. To be a good* or *a bad guesser,* deviner juste *or* mai.

guess-work, *n.* Conjecture, *f.*

guest [gest], *n.* Invité, convive; hôte, *m. Paying guest,* pensionnaire. **guest-chamber,** *n.* Chambre d'amis, *f.* **guest-house,** *n.* Pension de famille, *f.*

guest-rope [ges'roup] or **guest-warp,** *n.* (*Naut.*) Faux-bras, *m.*

guffaw [gə'fɔ:], *n.* Gros rire, *m.*—*v.i.* Pouffer de rire, s'esclaffer.

Guiana [gi'ɑ:nə]. La Guyane, *f.* **Guianese,** *a.* and *n.* Guyanais, *m.,* -aise, *f.*

guidance ['gaidəns], *n.* Conduite, direction, gouverne, *f. I tell you that for your guidance,* je vous dis cela pour votre gouverne.

guide [gaid], *n.* Guide, conducteur, *m.;* glissière (slide), *f. Girl Guide,* éclaireuse, *f.*—*v.t.* Conduire, guider; diriger, gouverner. *Guided missile,* (*Mil.*) engin téléguidé, *m.* **guide-book,** *n.* Guide, *m.* **guideless,** *a.* Sans guide. **guide-post,** *n.* Poteau indicateur, *m.;* (*fig.*) point de repère, *m.* **guiding,** *a.* Directeur.

guild [gild], *n.* Corporation, *f.;* corps de métier, *m.,* guilde, *f.* **guildhall,** *n.* Hôtel de ville, *m.*

guilder ['gildə], *n.* Florin (Dutch coin), *m.*

guile [gail], *n.* Astuce, *f.,* artifice, *m.* **guileful,** *a.* Astucieux. **guilefully,** *adv.* Astucieusement. **guilefulness,** *n.* Artifice, *m.* **guileless,** *a.* Simple, ingénu, sans artifice; franc, sincère. **guilelessness,** *n.* Simplicité, naïveté, sincérité, franchise, *f.*

guillemot ['gilimɔt], *n.* (*Orn.*) Guillemot, *m.*
guilloche [gi'louʃ], *n.* Guillochis, *m. To decorate with guilloche*, guillocher.
guillotine [gilə'ti:n], *n.* Guillotine, *f.—v.t.* Guillotiner.
guilt [gilt], *n.* *Crime, m.*; culpabilité, *f.*
guiltily, *adv.* Criminellement. **guiltiness,** *n.* Culpabilité, *f.* **guiltless,** *a.* Innocent. *To hold guiltless*, tenir pour innocent. **guiltlessly,** *adv.* Innocemment. **guiltlessness,** *n.* Innocence, *f.* **guilty,** *a.* Coupable. *The guilty party*, le coupable; *to find guilty*, (*Law*) déclarer coupable; *to plead guilty*, s'avouer coupable.
Guinea ['gini]. La Guinée, *f.*
guinea ['gini], *n.* Guinée, *f.* **guinea-fowl** or **guinea-hen,** *n.* Pintade, *f.* **guinea-pepper,** *n.* Poivre de Guinée, *m.* **guinea-pig,** *n.* Cochon d'Inde, cobaye, *m.*
guise [gaiz], *n.* Guise, façon, apparence, *f.*; costume, *m.*, dehors, *m.pl.* **guiser,** *n.* Masque, *m.*
guitar [gi'ta:], *n.* Guitare, *f.* **guitarist,** *n.* Guitariste.
gulch [gʌltʃ], *n.* (*Am.*) Ravin, *m.*
gules [gju:lz], *n.* (*Her.*) Gueules, *m.pl.*
gulf [gʌlf], *n.* Golfe, *m.*, baie, *f.*; (*fig.*) gouffre, abîme, *m.* **gulfy,** *a.* Plein de golfes.
gull [gʌl], *n.* Mouette, *f.*, goéland; (*fig.*) gogo, jobard, *m.*; *duperie, f.—v.t.* Duper, flouer.
gullet ['gʌlit], *n.* Gosier, *m.*
gullibility ['gʌli'biliti], *n.* Crédulité, *f.* **gullible** ['gʌləbl], *a.* Crédule, facile à duper.
gully ['gʌli], *n.* Ravin, *m.* **gully-hole,** *n.* Bouche d'égout, *f.—v.t.* Raviner.
gulp [gʌlp], *v.t.* Avaler, gober.—*v.i.* Essayer d'avaler.—*n.* Goulée, gorgée, *f.*, trait, *m. At a gulp*, d'un trait.
gum (1) [gʌm], *n.* Gomme, *f. Gum arabic*, gomme arabique, *f.—v.t.* Gommer.
gum (2) [gʌm], *n.* (*Anat.*) Gencive, *f.*
gumboil, *n.* Abcès aux gencives, *m.*; fluxion (à la joue), *f.*
gum-boots, *n.pl.* Bottes de caoutchouc, *f.pl.*
gumminess, *n.* Viscosité, *f.*
gumming, *n.* Gommage, *m.* **gummy** or **gummous,** *a.* Gommeux.
gumption ['gʌmpʃən], *n.* (*colloq.*) Sens pratique, *m.*, jugeotte, *f. To have gumption*, être débrouillard.
gum-tree, *n.* Gommier, *m.* (*fig.*) *Up a gum-tree*, dans le pétrin.
gun [gʌn], *n.* Canon, *m.*; pièce d'artillerie, *f.*, bouche à feu; (*pl.*) artillerie, *f.*; fusil (non rayé); (*Am.*) revolver, *m. Big gun*, (*colloq.*) gros-bonnet, *m.*; *field-gun*, pièce de campagne, *f.*; *heavy guns*, grosse artillerie, *f.*; *machine-gun*, mitrailleuse, *f.*; *quick-firing gun*, canon à tir rapide, *m.*; *rifled gun*, canon rayé, *m.*; (*fig.*) *to be going great guns*, aller tambour battant; *to stick to one's guns*, ne pas en démordre. **gun-barrel,** *n.* Canon de fusil, *m.* **gunboat,** *n.* Canonnière, *f.* **gun-carriage,** *n.* Affût (de canon), *m.* **gun-cotton,** *n.* Fulmicoton, coton poudre, *m.* **gun-deck,** *n.* Batterie, *f.* **gun-drill,** *n.* Exercice du canon, *m.* **gun-licence,** *n.* Port d'armes, *m.* **gun-maker,** *n.* Armurier, *m.* **gun-pit,** *n.* Emplacement de pièce, *m.* **gun-port,** *n.* Sabord, *m.* **gunpowder,** *n.* Poudre à canon, *f. The Gunpowder Plot*, la conspiration des poudres, *f.* **gun-running,**

n. Contrebande d'armes, *f.* **gunshot,** *n.* Portée de fusil (range), *f.*; coup de canon (discharge); coup de feu (wound), *m.* **gun-smith,** *n.* Armurier, *m.* *gunstick, n.* Baguette (de fusil), *f.*; (*Artill.*) refouloir, *m.* **gun-stock,** *n.* Fût (de fusil), *m.*
gunnel [GUNWALE].
gunner, *n.* Canonnier, servant, artilleur, *m.* **gunnery,** *n.* Artillerie, *f.*; tir au canon, *m.*
gunter ['gʌntə] or **Gunter's-chain,** *n.* Chaîne d'arpentage, *f.*
gunwale [gunl], *n.* (*Naut.*) Plat-bord, *m.*
gurgle [gə:gl], *v.i.* Faire glouglou; gargouiller. **gurgling,** *a.* Glouglou, gargouillement, *m.*
gurnard ['gə:nəd] or **gurnet,** *n.* (*Ichth.*) Grondin, *m. Red gurnard*, rouget, *m.*; *sapphirine gurnard*, pernon, *m.*; *yellow gurnard*, doucet, *m.*
gush [gʌʃ], *n.* Jaillissement, *m.*; effusion, *f.*, jet, flot; épanchement, débordement (of feelings), *m.—v.i.* Jaillir, ruisseler; (*fig.*) être sentimental à l'excès, s'attendrir (sur). *To gush out*, jaillir. **gusher,** *n.* (*Min.*) Puits jaillissant, *m.* **gushing,** *a.* Bouillonnant; expansif, empressé.
gusset ['gʌsit], *n.* Gousset, soufflet (of garment), *m.*
gust (1) [gʌst], *n.* Coup de vent, *m.*, bouffée, rafale, *f.*; (*fig.*) transport, accès, *m.* **gusty,** *a.* Orageux, venteux.
gust (2) [gʌst], *n.* Goût, *m.—*gust.t.* Goûter. **gustation** [-'teiʃən], *n.* Gustation, *f.*
gusto ['gʌstou], *n.* Goût, *m.*; (*fig.*) délectation, *f. With great gusto*, avec beaucoup de plaisir, beaucoup de verve, de brio.
gut [gʌt], *n.* Boyau, intestin, *m.*; corde à boyau (catgut), *f.*; (*pl.*) intestins, *m.pl.*, ventre, *m.*, panse, *f.*; (*fam.*) courage, cran, *m.—v.t.* Éventrer, vider; (*fig.*) détruire. *The house was entirely gutted*, il ne restait plus que les quatre murs. **gutless,** *a.* (*pop.*) Mollasse, qui manque de cran.
gutta ['gʌtə], *n.* (*pl.* **guttae**) Goutte, *f.*
gutta-percha [gʌtə'pə:tʃə], *n.* Gutta percha, *m.*
gutta-serena, *n.* Goutte sereine, *f.*
gutter ['gʌtə], *n.* Gouttière (on a house), *f.*; ruisseau (in the street); caniveau (in a road); (*fig.*) sillon, *m.*, cannelure, *f.—v.t.* Sillonner, canneler.—*v.i.* Couler. *The candle gutters*, la chandelle coule. **gutter-pipe,** *n.* Tuyau de descente, *m.* **guttersnipe,** *n.* Gamin, voyou, *m.*
guttiferous [gə'tifərəs], *a.* (*Bot.*) Guttifère.
guttiform ['gʌtifɔ:m], *a.* Guttiforme.
gutting ['gʌtiŋ], *n.* Vidage (of fish), *m.*
guttle [gʌtl], *v.i.* Bâfrer.—*v.t.* Dévorer.
guttural ['gʌtərəl], *a.* Guttural.—*n.* Gutturale, *f.*
guy [gai], *n.* Effigie de Guy Fawkes, *f.*; (*fig.*) épouvantail, *m.*; (*Naut.*) corde soutien, *f.*, guide, *m.*; type, individu, *m. To look like a guy*, être mal fagoté.—*v.t.* Se moquer de, travestir. **guy-rope,** *n.* Cordon de tente, *m.*; corde de contre-appui, *f.*
guzzle [gʌzl], *v.t., v.i.* Boire *or* manger avidement; bouffer (of food), lamper (of drink).
guzzler ['gʌzlə], *n.* (*colloq.*) Sac à vin, bâfreur.
gybe [dʒaib], *v.t., v.i.* (*Naut.*) Gambiller.
gym [dʒim], *n.* [GYMNASIUM].
gymkhana [dʒim'ka:nə], *n.* Gymkhana, *m.*
gymnasium [dʒim'neiziəm], *n.* Gymnase, *m.*

gymnast ['dʒimnæst], *n.* Gymnaste, *m.*
gymnastic [-'næstik], *a.* Gymnastique.
gymnastics, *n.pl.* Gymnastique, *f.* **gymnic,**
a. Gymnique. **gymnosophist** [-'nɔsəfist],
n. Gymnosophiste, *m.* **gymnosophy,** *n.*
Gymnosophie, *f.* **gymnosperm,** *n.* (*Bot.*)
Gymnosperme, *f.*
gymnotus [dʒim'noutəs], *n.* (*pl.* **gymnoti**)
Gymnote, *m.*
gynaecium [dʒaini'siːəm], *n.* Gynécée, *f.*
gynaecological, *a.* Gynécologique. **gynae-**
cologist, *n.* Gynécologue, *m.* **gynaecology,**
n. Gynécologie, *f.*
gynandria [dʒai'nændriə], *n.pl.* (*Bot.*) Gynandrie, *f.* **gynandrous,** *a.* Gynandre.
*****gynarchy** ['dʒainɑːki], *n.* Gynécocratie, *f.*
gypseous ['dʒipsiəs], *a.* Gypseux. **gypsum**
['dʒipsəm], *n.* Gypse, *m.*
gypsy [GIPSY].
gyrate [dʒai'reit], *v.i.* Tournoyer. **gyration**
[-reiʃən], *n.* Mouvement giratoire, *m.*
gyratory ['dʒairətəri], *a.* Giratoire. **gyre,** *n.*
Cercle, *m.* **gyromancy,** *n.* Gyromancie, *f.*
gyroscope, *n.* Gyroscope, *m.* **gyroscopic,**
a. Gyroscopique.
*****gyve** [dʒaiv], *v.t.* Enchaîner.—*n.pl.* Fers,
m.pl., chaînes, *f.pl.*

H

H, h [eitʃ], huitième lettre de l'alphabet, *m.* or *f.*
ha! [hɑː], *int.* Ha!
haar [hɑːr], *n.* (*Sc.*) Brume glaciale (venant
de l'Est), *f.*
habeas corpus ['heibiəs 'kɔːpəs], *n.* Habeas
corpus, *m.* (loi sur la liberté individuelle).
haberdasher ['hæbədæʃə], *n.* Mercier,
chemisier, *m.* **haberdashery,** *n.* Mercerie,
chemiserie, *f.*
habergeon ['hæbədʒən], *n.* Haubergeon, *m.*
*****habiliment** [hə'bilimənt], *n.* Habillement,
apprêt; (*pl.*) attirail, *m.*
habit ['hæbit], *n.* Habitude, coutume, *f.*; (*pl.*)
mœurs, *f.pl.* *Habit of the body,* disposition
habituelle, *f.*, tempérament, *m.*; *riding-habit,*
habit de cheval, *m.*, amazone, *f.*; *to be in the
habit of,* avoir coutume de; *to get into the
habit of,* prendre l'habitude de.—*v.t.* Vêtir.
habitable ['hæbitəbl], *a.* Habitable.
(*C*) **habitant** ['hæbitənt], *n.* Habitant (in
Canada and Louisiana); Canadien *or* Américain français, *m.*
habitat ['hæbitæt], *n.* Habitat, *m.*
habitation [hæbi'teiʃən], *n.* Habitation, demeure, *f.*
habitual [hə'bitjuəl], *a.* Habituel. **habitu-**
ally, *adv.* Habituellement, d'habitude.
habituate, *v.t.* Habituer, accoutumer. *To
habituate oneself,* s'habituer. **habitude**
['hæbitjuːd], *n.* Habitude, coutume, *f.*
hack (1) [hæk], *v.t.* Hacher, couper, tailler en
pièces; ébrécher; (*fig.*) massacrer, écorcher;
donner (exprès) un coup de pied sur la
jambe.—*v.i.* Avoir une toux sèche.
hack (2) [hæk], *n.* Cheval de louage, *m.*; rosse
(sorry horse), *f.*; fiacre, *m.*, voiture de louage,
f.; (*fig.*) écrivassier à gages, *m.*
hack (3) [hæk], *n.* Pic de mineur, *m.*; entaille;
gerçure, *f.*; (*Ftb.*) coup de pied sur le tibia, *m.*
hackle ['hækl], *n.* Séran, sérançoir, *m.*; filasse,

soie écrue, *f.*; camail (of poultry), *m.* (*fig.*)
His hackles are rising, il se dresse sur ses
ergots.—*v.t.* Sérancer; déchirer. **hackling-**
machine, *n.* Peigneuse, *f.*
hackney ['hækni], *n.* Cheval de louage, *m.*—
v.t. Avilir par l'usage, user. **hackney-**
carriage, *n.* Fiacre, *m.* **hackneyed,** *a.*
Banal, rebattu. *Hackneyed phrase,* cliché, *m.*
had [hæd] [HAVE].
haddock ['hædək], *n.* (*Ichth.*) Aiglefin, *m.*
Hades ['heidiːz], *n.* Les Enfers, *m.pl.*
haematite ['hemətait], *n.* Hématite, *f.* **haema-**
tocele, *n.* Hématocèle, *f.* **haematosis,** *n.*
Hématose, *f.*
haematuria [hiːmə'tjuəriə], *n.* Hématurie, *f.*
haemoglobin, *n.* Hémoglobine, *f.*
haemophilia, *n.* Hémophilie, *f.*
haemorrhage ['heməridʒ], *n.* Hémorrhagie, *f.*
haemorrhoidal [-'rɔidl], *a.* Hémorroïdal.
haemorrhoids ['hemərɔidz], *n.pl.* Hémorroïdes, *f.pl.*
haemostasia [hiːmɔs'tæziə], *n.* Hémostase,
hémostasie, *f.*
haft [hɑːft], *n.* Manche, *m.*, poignée, *f.*—*v.t.*
Emmancher.
hag [hæg], *n.* Vieille sorcière; (*pop.*) vieille fée,
vieille peau, *f.* **hag-ridden,** *a.* Tourmenté
par le cauchemar.
haggard ['hægəd], *a.* Hagard, farouche, égaré.
haggardly, *adv.* D'un air hagard.
haggis ['hægis], *n.* (*Sc.*) Hachis de foie, cœur,
mou, etc., mêlés à de la farine d'avoine, des
oignons, de la graisse de bœuf, le tout enfermé et cuit dans un estomac de mouton.
haggish ['hægiʃ], *a.* De sorcière, difforme,
hideux.
haggle [hægl], *v.i.* Marchander, barguigner.
haggler ['hæglə], *n.* Barguigneur, marchandeur, *m.*
hagiographer [hædʒi'ɔgrəfə *or* hægi'ɔgrəfə], *n.*
Hagiographe, *m.* **hagiography** *or* **hagio-**
logy, *n.* Hagiographie, *f.*
Hague (The) [ðə'heig]. (*Geog.*) La Haye, *f.*
ha-ha ['hɑːhɑː], *n.* Saut de loup, haha, *m.*
hail (1) [heil], *n.* Grêle, *f.*—*v.i.* Grêler. **hail-**
stone, *n.* Grêlon, *m.* **hailstorm,** *n.* Tempête de grêle, *f.*
hail (2) [heil], *n.* Salut, appel, *m. He is hail-
fellow-well-met with him,* il le traite de pair
à compagnon; *within hail,* à portée de la voix.
—*int.* Salut! salut à vous!—*v.t.* Saluer;
(*Naut.*) héler. *To hail a taxi,* héler *or* appeler
un taxi; *to hail from,* venir de.
hair [heə], *n.* Cheveu (a single hair); *m.*;
cheveux, *m.pl.,* chevelure (head of hair), *f.*;
poil (on the body, on animals, etc.), crin
(horsehair), *m.*; soies (bristles), *f.pl.* *Head
of hair,* cheveux, *m.pl.,* chevelure, *f.*; *not
worth a hair,* d'aucune valeur; *to a hair,*
exactement; *to do one's hair,* se coiffer; *to
dress someone's hair,* coiffer quelqu'un; *to
have one's hair cut,* se faire couper les
cheveux; *to make one's hair stand on end,*
faire dresser les cheveux; *to split hairs,*
chicaner sur les mots, épiloguer, couper un
cheveu en quatre; *to tear one's hair,* s'arracher
les cheveux. **hairbreadth,** *n.* [HAIR'S-
BREADTH]. **hair-brush,** *n.* Brosse à cheveux,
f. **haircloth,** *n.* Étoffe de crin, *f.* **hair-cut,**
n. Coupe de cheveux, *f.* **hairdresser,** *n.*
Coiffeur, *m.* **haired,** *a.* *Red-haired,* aux
cheveux roux. **hair-grip,** *n.* Pince-guiches,

m., barrette, *f.* **hairiness,** *n.* Nature velue, *f.*
hairless, *a.* Chauve, sans cheveux; sans poil (of animals). **hair-net,** *n.* Résille, *f.* **hair-oil,** *n.* Huile capillaire, *f.* **hair-pencil,** *n.* Pinceau, *m.* **hairpin,** *n.* Épingle à cheveux, *f.* **hair-raising,** *a.* Horrifique, effrayant, à vous faire dresser les cheveux. **hair's-breadth,** *n.* Épaisseur d'un cheveu, *f.* To have a hair's-breadth escape, l'échapper belle. **hair-shirt,** *n.* Haire, *f.*, cilice, *m.* **hair-sieve,** *n.* Tamis de crin, *m.* **hair-space,** *n.* (*Print.*) Espace d'un point, *f.* **hair-splitting,** *n.* Ergotage, coupage de cheveux en quatre, *m.* **hair-spring,** *n.* Ressort spiral, *m.* **hair-trigger,** *n.* Double détente, *f.*
hairy, *a.* Velu, chevelu, poilu; hirsute.
hake [heik], *n.* (*Ichth.*) Merluche, *f.*, (*fam.*) colin, *m.*
halberd ['hælbəd], *n.* Hallebarde, *f.* **halberdier** [-'diə], *n.* Hallebardier, *m.*
halcyon ['hælsiən], *n.* Alcyon, *m.*—*a.* Halcyon days, jours heureux, jours calmes, *m.pl.*
hale (1) [heil], *a.* Robuste, sain, vigoureux, bien portant. To be hale and hearty, avoir bon pied, bon œil.
hale (2) [heil], *v.t.* Haler, tirer, traîner.
half [hɑːf], *a.* and *n.* (*pl.* **halves** [hɑːvz]) Moitié, *f.*, demi, *m.*, demie, *f.* Half a loaf, la moitié d'un pain; half and half, moitié de l'un, moitié de l'autre, (*fam.*) moitié moitié; half an hour, une demi-heure, *f.*; half as much, la moitié moins; half as much again, la moitié plus; my better half, ma chère moitié, *f.*; (*pop.*) not half! Tu parles! Beaucoup! one hour and a half, une heure et demie; to divide in halves, partager en deux, diviser en deux parties égales; to do things by halves, faire les choses à demi; to go halves with, être de moitié avec; too long by half, trop long de moitié; too much by half, moitié de trop—*adv.* À demi, à moitié. **half-back,** *n.* (*Ftb.*) Demi, *m.* (*Rugby*) Scrum half(-back), demi de mêlée. **half-baked,** *a.* À moitié cuit; (*pop.*) niais. **half-binding,** *n.* Demi-reliure, *f.* **half-bound,** *a.* En demi-reliure. **half-breed, half-caste,** *n.* Métis, *m.*, -isse, *f.* **half-brother,** *n.* Demi-frère, frère utérin, frère consanguin, *m.* **half-circle,** *n.* Demi-cercle, *m.* **half-crown,** *n.* Demi-couronne, *f.* **half-dead,** *a.* À moitié mort. **half-done,** *a.* À moitié fait; à moitié cuit (of meat). **half-empty,** *a.* À moitié vide. **half-fare,** *n.* Demi-place, *f.*, demi-tarif, *m.* **half-finished,** *a.* À moitié fait; imparfait. **half-hearted,** *a.* Tiède, mesquin, peu généreux. **half-holiday,** *n.* Demi-congé, *m.* **half-length,** *n.* Demi-longueur, *f.*—*a.* En buste. **half-mast,** *n.* At half-mast, à mi-mât. Flag at half-mast, pavillon en berne, *m.* **half-moon,** *n.* Demi-lune, *f.* **half-mourning,** *n.* Demi-deuil, *m.* **half-pay,** *n.* Demi-solde, *f.* Officer on half-pay, officier en demi solde, *m.*
halfpenny ['heipni], *n.* (*pl.* **halfpence** ['heipəns]) Demi-penny, *m.*
half-pint, *n.* Demi-pinte, *f.*, quart de litre, *m.* **half-price,** *n.* Moitié prix, *m.*; demi-place (fare), *f.* **half-sister,** *n.* Demi-sœur, sœur consanguine, sœur utérine, *f.* **half-timbered,** *a.* Half-timbered house, maison en colombage, *f.* **half-time,** *n.* (*Ftb.*) La mi-temps, *f.* Half-time work, travail à mi-temps, *m.* **half-title,**

n. (*Print.*) Faux titre, *m.* **half-tone,** *n.* Demi-teinte, *f.*; similigravure (engraving), *f.* **half-track,** *n.* Autochenille, *f.* **half-volley,** *n.* Demi-volée, *f.* **half-way,** *adv.* À mi-chemin. Half-way up the hill, à mi-côte; to meet someone half-way, couper la poire en deux, faire la moitié des avances. **half-witted,** *a.* Niais, sot, idiot. **half-(year),** *n.* Semestre, *m.* **half-yearly,** *adv.* Semestriel, tous les six mois.
halibut ['hælibət], *n.* (*Ichth.*) Flétan, *m.*
halieutic [hæli'juːtik], *a.* Halieutique. **halieutics,** *n.pl.* Halieutique, *f.*
halitosis [hæli'tousis], *n.* (*Med.*) Mauvaise haleine, *f.*
halituous [hə'litjuəs], *a.* Halitueux, moite.
hall [hɔːl], *n.* Salle, *f.*; vestibule (entrance-hall), château, manoir (seat), *m.*; (*Univ.*) maison, fondation universitaire, *f.*; réfectoire (dining-hall), *m.*; hôtel de ville (town hall), *m.* Hall porter, concierge, *m.* **hall-mark,** *n.* Poinçon de contrôle, *m.* (on gold and silver ware); (*fig.*) cachet, *m.*, empreinte, *f.*—*v.t.* Contrôler, poinçonner. **hall-marking,** *n.* Contrôlage, *m.*, poinçonnage, *m.* **hall-stand,** *n.* Porte-habits, *m.inv.*
hallelujah [hæli'luːjə], *n.* Alléluia, *m.*
halliard [HALYARD].
hallo [hə'lou], *n.* Huée, *f.*, cri, *m.*—*v.i.* Crier, huer.—*int.* Holà! hé!
halloo [hæ'luː], *int.* (*Hunt.*) Taïaut!—*v.i.* Crier taïaut; crier.
hallow ['hælou], *v.t.* Sanctifier, consacrer.
Hallowe'en [hælou'iːn], *n.* (*Sc., Am.*) La veille de la Toussaint, *f.* **Hallowmas,** *n.* La Toussaint, *f.*
hallucinate [hə'ljuːsineit], *v.t.* Halluciner. **hallucination** [-'neifən], *n.* Hallucination; (*fig.*) déception, illusion, *f.* **hallucinatory,** *a.* Hallucinatoire.
hallway ['hɔːlwei], *n.* (*Am.*) Vestibule, *m.*
halo ['heilou], *n.* (*Astron.*) Halo, cercle lumineux, *m.*; (*Paint etc.*) auréole, *f.*
halogen ['hælodʒən], *n.* Halogène, *m.* **halogenous** [hə'lɔdʒənəs], *a.* Halogène. **haloid,** *a.* and *n.* Haloïde, *m.*
halt [hɔːlt], *n.* Halte, *f.*; arrêt; clochement, *m.*—*a.* Boiteux, estropié.—*v.i.* Faire halte; boiter; (*fig.*) hésiter, balancer.—*int.* Halte-là! **halting-place,** *n.* (*Mil.*) Étape, *f.*
halter ['hɔːltə], *n.* Licou, *m.*, longe, *f.* (for horses); corde (for hanging), *f.*—*v.t.* Mettre le licou à; mettre la corde au cou à.
halve [hɑːv], *v.t.* Diviser en deux, partager en deux.
halyard ['hæljəd], *n.* Drisse, *f.*
ham [hæm], *n.* Jambon; *jarret (of a person), *m.*; (*Theat.*) navet (of play), *m.*—*v.t.* An actor who hams his part, un comédien qui joue comme un pied. **ham-fisted,** *a.* (*fam.*) Maladroit, brutal.
hamadryad [hæmə'draiæd], *n.* Hamadryade, *f.*
hamlet ['hæmlit], *n.* Hameau, *m.*
hammer ['hæmə], *n.* Marteau, *m.* (for fire-arms), *m.* Hammer and tongs, avec fureur, avec violence; to bring under the hammer, mettre aux enchères.—*v.t.* Marteler, forger; enfoncer. To hammer out a line, marteler un vers.—*v.i.* Marteler; travailler avec le marteau. To hammer at, s'attaquer à, harceler (someone). **hammer-cloth,** *n.*

Housse, *f.* (of driver's seat). **hammerer** or **hammerman**, *n.* Marteleur, frappeur, *m.* **hammer-head (shark)**, *n.* Requin marteau, *m.*

hammering, *n.* Martelage, *m.* *To give one's opponent a good hammering*, cogner dur sur son adversaire.

hammock ['hæmək], *n.* Hamac, *m.*

hamper (1) ['hæmpə], *n.* Panier, mannequin, *m.*, manne, *f.* *Fish hamper*, bourriche, *f.*

hamper (2) ['hæmpə], *v.t.* Empêtrer, embarrasser, gêner.

hamster ['hæmstə], *n.* Hamster, *m.*

hamstring ['hæmstriŋ], *n.* Tendon du jarret, *m.*—*v.t.* (*past* and *p.p.* **hamstrung**) Couper le jarret à; (*fig.*) couper les moyens à.

hand [hænd], *n.* Main, *f.*; palme (measure of four inches), *f.*; signature, écriture (writing), *f.*; (*Cards*) jeu, *m.*, partie, *f.*; aiguille (of a watch etc.), *f.*; ouvrier, bras, homme, employé, *m.*; part, *f.*, côté (side), *m.*; entremise, *f.*, moyen, intermédiaire, doigt (of God), *m.* *At first hand*, de première main; *at hand*, sous la main; *bound hand and foot*, pieds et poings liés; *by hand*, à la main; *cash in hand*, espèces en caisse, *f.pl.*; *from hand to hand*, de main en main; *hands off!* à bas les mains! *hands off the Queen*, ne touchez pas à la Reine! *hand to hand*, corps à corps; *in hand*, en main, en train, (*Comm.*) en caisse; *off-hand*, sur-le-champ, tout de suite, brusque, brusquement, cavalièrement; *on all hands*, de tous côtés; *on each hand*, de chaque côté; *on hand*, en main, (*Comm.*) en magasin; *on one's hands*, sur les bras; *on the other hand*, de l'autre côté, d'autre part, par contre; *out of hand*, fini, achevé, indiscipliné; *second-hand*, d'occasion; *sword in hand*, l'épée à la main; *they are hand and glove together*, ils sont comme les deux doigts de la main; *to give or lend a hand to*, donner un coup de main à; *to be a good hand at*, savoir s'y prendre; *to be an old hand*, n'être pas novice, s'y connaître; *to bring up by hand*, élever au biberon; *to carry matters with a high hand*, mener les choses rondement; *to change hands*, changer de main; *to get one's hand in*, se faire la main; *to get the upper hand*, prendre le dessus; *to have a hand in*, être pour quelque chose dans, tremper dans; *to have no hand in*, n'être pour rien dans; *to have one's hands full*, avoir des affaires par-dessus les bras; *to keep in hand*, tenir en bride; *to lay hands on*, s'emparer de; *to lay violent hands on oneself*, attenter à ses jours; *to live from hand to mouth*, vivre au jour le jour; *to play into each other's hands*, s'entendre comme larrons en foire; *to set one's hand to*, mettre la main à; *to shake hands with*, serrer la main à; *to show one's hand*, découvrir son jeu; *to take a hand*, faire une partie; *with both hands*, à deux mains.

v.t.—Passer, donner, remettre; donner la main à; conduire, guider. *To hand about or round*, faire passer de main en main, faire circuler; *to hand down*, transmettre, aider à descendre; *to hand over*, remettre, céder.

handbag, *n.* Sac à main, *m.* **handbarrow**, *n.* Civière, *f.* **hand-basket**, *n.* Panier, *m.* **hand-bell**, *n.* Sonnette, clochette, *f.* **handbill**, *n.* Affiche (poster), *f.*, prospectus, *m.*; annonce, feuille volante, *f.* **handbook**, *n.* Manuel; guide, *m.* **hand-cart**, *n.* Voiture

à bras, *f.* **handcuff**, *n.* Menotte, *f.*—*v.t.* Mettre les menottes à. **handful**, *n.* Poignée, *f.*; (*fig.*) petit nombre, peu, *m.* *That child is quite a handful*, c'est un enfant terrible. **hand-gallop**, *n.* Petit galop, *m.* **hand-grenade**, *n.* Grenade, *f.* **hand-loom**, *n.* Métier à main, à domicile, *m.* **handmaid**, *n.* Servante, *f.* **handmill**, *n.* Moulin à bras, *m.* **hand-picked**, *a.* Triés sur le volet (of soldiers etc.). **handrail**, *n.* Garde-fou, *m.*, rampe, main courante, *f.* **hand-reading**, *n.* Chiromancie, *f.* **hand-saw**, *n.* Scie à main, *f.* **handshake**, *n.* Poignée de main, *f.*, serrement de main, *m.* **hand-spike**, *n.* Anspect, *m.* **hand-trolley**, *n.* Bard, *m.* **hand-vice**, *n.* Étau à main, *m.* **handwriting**, *n.* Écriture, *f.*

handicap ['hændikæp], *n.* Handicap, désavantage; rendement, *m.*—*v.t.* Handicaper. **handicapped**, *a.* Désavantagé; (*spt.*) handicapé. **handicapper**, *n.* Handicapeur, *m.*

handicraft ['hændikrɑ:ft], *n.* Métier, travail manuel, *m.* **handicraftsman**, *n.* Artisan, *m.*

handily ['hændili], *adv.* Adroitement; commodément. **handiness**, *n.* Adresse, dextérité; commodité, *f.*

handiwork ['hændiwə:k], *n.* Ouvrage, travail manuel, *m.*

handkerchief ['hæŋkətʃif], *n.* Mouchoir (de poche); foulard (for the neck), *m.*

handle [hændl], *n.* Manche, *m.*; poignée (of a sword etc.), *f.*; bouton (of a door), *m.*; anse (of a jug), *f.*; brimbale (of a pump); queue (of a frying-pan); manivelle (of a printing-press), *f.*; bras (of a wheelbarrow), *m.* *A handle to one's name*, un titre; *starting handle*, (*Motor.*) manivelle de mise en marche, *f.*; (*fam.*) *to fly off the handle*, s'emporter, sortir de ses gonds; *to give a handle to*, donner prise à.—*v.t.* Manier; toucher à, manipuler; brasser.

handle-bar, *n.* Guidon (of a bicycle), *m.* (*pop.*) *A handle-bar moustache*, moustaches raides, *f.pl.*

handling, *n.* Maniement, traitement, *m.*

handsel ['hænsəl], *n.* Étrenne, *f.*; (*fig.*) avant-goût, *m.*, arrhes, *f.pl.*—*v.t.* Étrenner; inaugurer.

handsome ['hænsəm], *a.* Beau, bien fait, élégant; (*fig.*) gracieux, généreux, comme il faut, flatteur. **handsomely**, *adv.* Joliment, élégamment; généreusement, avec grâce. **handsomeness**, *n.* Beauté, élégance, grâce; générosité, *f.*

hand-spike, handwriting [HAND].

handy ['hændi], *a.* Adroit, habile; commode; à portée de la main. *Handy-girl*, petite main; *handy-man*, ouvrier adroit pour tout, homme à tout faire, bon bricoleur, *m.*

handy-dandy, *n.* Dans quelle main la pierre (game), *m.*

hang [hæŋ], *v.t.* (*past* and *p.p.* **hanged** or **hung**; en général, **hanged** s'emploie en parlant du supplice). Pendre, suspendre; accrocher (à); tendre, tapisser (de); laisser pendre, pencher, baisser (the head etc.); poser (doors etc.). *Hang it!* fichtre! diable! *go and be hanged*, va-t'en au diable! *to hang fire*, faire long feu (of fire-arms), (*fig.*) vaciller, hésiter; *to hang the rudder*, monter le gouvernail.—*v.i.* Pendre, être suspendu; s'accrocher, se pendre, s'attacher (à); baisser, se pencher (à); pendiller (to swing); (*fig.*) rester, reposer (sur). *To hang about*, rôder autour de; *to hang back*, reculer, hésiter; *to hang by a thread*, ne tenir qu'à un fil; *to hang down*, pendre, être suspendu (à), pencher, s'incliner; *to hang in doubt*, être en suspens; *to hang over*, être suspendu sur, surplomber, menacer; *to hang together*, tenir, se tenir, s'accorder (of arguments etc.), faire la paire. **hang-dog,** *n.* Pendard, *m.* *Hang-dog look*, mine patibulaire, *f.*, air en dessous, *m.* **hanger,** *n.* Croc, crochet; coutelas, couteau de chasse, *m.* **hanger-on,** *n.* Dépendant, parasite, *m.* **hanging,** *n.* Suspension, pendaison, corde, tenture; pose (of paper etc.), *f.*; collage, *m.*; (*pl.*) tapisserie, tenture, *f.*—*a.* Suspendu. *Hanging matter*, cas pendable, *m.* **hangman,** *n.* Bourreau, *m.* **hang-nail** [AGNAIL]. **hang-over,** *n.* (*pop.*) *To have a hang-over*, avoir la gueule de bois.

hangar ['hæŋə], *n.* (*Av.*) Hangar, *m.*

hank [hæŋk], *n.* Poignée, *f.*, écheveau, *m.*; (*Naut.*) rocambeau, anneau de bois, *m.*

hanker ['hæŋkə], *v.i.* Désirer ardemment. *To hanker after*, soupirer après. **hankering,** *n.* Grande envie, *f.*, vif désir, *m.*

hanky-panky ['hæŋki'pæŋki], *n.* Tour de passe-passe, *m.*, supercherie, *f.*

Hansard ['hænsɑːd], *n.* Compte rendu officiel des débats parlementaires anglais, *m.*

Hanse [hæns]. Hanse, *f.*

Hanseatic [hænsi'ætik], *a.* Hanséatique.

hansom ['hænsəm], *n.* Cabriolet, hansom, cab, *m.*

*hap [hæp], *n.* Hasard, sort, *m.*—*v.i.* Arriver par hasard.—*v.t.* (*Sc.*) Couvrir, envelopper.

haphazard, *n.* Hasard, sort, accident, *m.* *At, by haphazard*, au petit bonheur.—*a.* Au petit bonheur, fortuit.

hapless, *a.* Infortuné, malheureux. **haplessly,** *adv.* Malheureusement. **haply,** *adv.* Par hasard; peut-être.

happen [hæpn], *v.i.* Arriver, advenir, se passer; se trouver par hasard. *A man happened to pass*, un homme vint à passer; *as if nothing had happened*, comme si de rien n'était; *happen what may!* advienne que pourra! *he happened to hear*, il apprit par hasard; *if he happened to come*, si par hasard il arrivait; *if it happens again*, si cela se reproduit; *if you happen to be in need of*, s'il se trouve que vous ayez besoin; *you don't happen to have . . . ?* vous n'auriez pas par hasard . . . ?

happily ['hæpili], *adv.* Heureusement, par bonheur. **happiness,** *n.* Bonheur, *m.* **happy,** *a.* Heureux, joyeux, content. **happy-go-lucky,** *a.* Sans souci.

harangue [hə'ræŋ], *n.* Harangue, *f.*—*v.t.* Haranguer.—*v.i.* Prononcer une harangue. **haranguer,** *n.* Harangueur, *m.*

harass ['hærəs], *v.t.* Harasser, harceler.

harbinger ['hɑːbindʒə], *n.* Avant-coureur, précurseur, annonciateur, *m.*

harbour ['hɑːbə], *n.* Port, havre; (*fig.*) refuge, asile, gîte, *m.*—*v.t.* Héberger, recéler, donner asile à; (*fig.*) entretenir, nourrir. *How can you harbour such a thought?* comment pouvez-vous entretenir une pareille idée?—*v.i.* Se réfugier. **harbour-dues,** *n.pl.* Droits de mouillage, *m.pl.* **harbour-installations,**

Installations portuaires, *f.pl.* **harbour-master,** *n.* Capitaine du port, *m.*

harbourage, *n.* Refuge, *m.*; hospitalité, *f.*

harbourer, *n.* Personne qui donne asile (à), *f.*

hard [hɑːd], *a.* Dur, ferme; (*fig.*) malaisé, difficile; pénible, rude, rigoureux; dur à la détente (stingy). *Hard and fast rule*, règle rigoureuse et immuable, *f.*; *hard frost*, forte gelée, *f.*; *hard labour*, travaux forcés, *m.pl.*; *hard of belief*, incrédule; *hard of hearing*, dur d'oreille; *hard luck*, manque de chance, *m.*, pas de chance! *hard to deal with*, intraitable; *hard to please*, difficile à contenter; *hard up*, à sec, à court (d'argent); *hard water*, de l'eau dure; *hard words*, duretés, *f.pl.*; *in hard cash*, en espèces sonnantes; *to be a hard drinker*, boire sec; *to be hard on someone*, être sévère envers quelqu'un.—*n.* Tabac en barre, *m.*; (*Naut.*) cale, *f.*; (*pl.*) déchets (de chanvre etc.), *m.pl.*—*adv.* Dur, rudement, péniblement; fort, ferme. *Hard-a-port!* tribord tout! *hard by*, tout près, auprès de; *he looked hard at*, il regarda fixement; *to work hard*, travailler dur. **hard-bitten,** *a.* (*fig.*) Tenace, dur (of people). **hard-boiled,** *a.* Dur (egg); (*fig.*) dur, peu sentimental, réaliste. **hard-earned,** *a.* Péniblement gagné, qui a coûté de la peine. **hard-featured,** *a.* Aux traits durs. **hard-fought,** *a.* Acharné, opiniâtre. **hard-hearted,** *a.* Dur, insensible, inflexible, inhumain. **hard-hitting,** *a.* (*fig.*) *A hard-hitting speech*, discours combatif. **hard-mouthed,** *a.* Qui a la bouche dure (of a horse); (*fig.*) qui a la dent dure. **hard-pressed,** *a.* Aux abois. **hard-tack,** *n.* Biscuit de mer, *m.*; (*fam.*) galette, *f.* **hard-wearing,** *a.* Durable. **hard-won,** *a.* Gagné au prix de grands efforts. **hard-working,** *a.* Laborieux.

harden [hɑːdn], *v.t.* Durcir, rendre dur, tremper (steel); (*fig.*) endurcir (à).—*v.i.* Durcir, s'endurcir, devenir dur. **hardening,** *n.* Durcissement, *m.*; (*fig.*) endurcissement, *m.*; trempe (of steel), *f.*

hardihood ['hɑːdihud], *n.* Hardiesse, audace, intrépidité, *f.*

hardily ['hɑːdili], *adv.* Durement, hardiment. **hardiness,** *n.* Hardiesse, *f.*; tempérament robuste, *m.*; (*fig.*) effronterie, assurance, *f.*

hardly ['hɑːdli], *adv.* Difficilement, à peine, guère (scarcely); durement, rudement, mal. *Hardly ever*, presque jamais.

hardness ['hɑːdnis], *n.* Dureté, fermeté, solidité; rigueur, difficulté; brutalité; crudité (of water), *f.*

hardship ['hɑːdʃip], *n.* Fatigue, peine, privation, *f.*; (*pl.*) épreuves, souffrances, *f.pl.*

hardware ['hɑːdwɛə], *n.* Quincaillerie, *f.* **hardwareman,** *n.* Quincaillier, *m.*

hardy ['hɑːdi], *a.* Hardi, courageux; dur; vigoureux; fort, robuste; de pleine terre (of plants).

hare [hɛə], *n.* Lièvre, *m.* *Jugged hare*, civet de lièvre, *m.*; *to run with the hare and hunt with the hounds*, ménager la chèvre et le chou; *young hare*, levraut, *m.*—*v.i.* Courir à toute vitesse. *To hare off*, se sauver à toutes jambes. **harebell,** *n.* Campanule, *f.* **hare-brained,** *a.* Écervelé, étourdi. **hare-lip,** *n.* Bec-de-lièvre, *m.* **hare's-foot,** *n.* (*Bot.*) Pied-de-lièvre, *m.*

harem, hareem [hɑːˈriːm], *n.* Harem, *m.*

hark [hɑːk], *v.i.* Écouter, prêter l'oreille. *To hark back*, prendre le contre-pied (of hounds); ramener la conversation sur le sujet; revenir à ses moutons.—*int.* Écoutez!

harken [HEARKEN].

harl [hɑːl], *n.* Filaments du chanvre *or* du lin, *m.pl.*; filasse, *f.*

harlequin [ˈhɑːlikwin], *n.* Arlequin, *m.*

harlot [ˈhɑːlət], *n.* Prostituée, courtisane; (*pop.*) fille, *f.*

harlotry [ˈhɑːlətri], *n.* Prostitution, *f.*

harm [hɑːm], *n.* Tort, dommage, mal, *m. Out of harm's way*, en sûreté; hors d'état de nuire; *there is no harm in him*, il n'y entend pas malice; *there is no harm in that*, il n'y a pas de mal à cela.—*v.t.* Nuire à, faire du mal à. **harmful**, *a.* Nuisible, malfaisant. **harmfully**, *adv.* D'une manière nuisible. **harmfulness**, *n.* Nocivité, *f.* **harmless**, *a.* Innocent, inoffensif; sain et sauf, sans aucun mal; hors d'état de nuire. *To hold harmless*, protéger, mettre à couvert. **harmlessly**, *adv.* Innocemment; sans aucun mal.

harmonic [hɑːˈmɔnik], *a.* Harmonique; harmonieux.—*n.pl.* Harmonique, *f.* **harmonica**, *n.* Harmonica, *m.* **harmonious** [-ˈmouniəs], *a.* Harmonieux; mélodieux. **harmoniously**, *adv.* Harmonieusement; (*fig.*) en bon accord.

harmonist [ˈhɑːmənist], *n.* Harmoniste, *m.*

harmonium [hɑːˈmouniəm], *n.* Harmonium, *m.*

harmonize [ˈhɑːmənaiz], *v.t.* Rendre harmonieux, accorder; harmoniser; (*fig.*) mettre d'accord.—*v.i.* S'harmoniser, être en harmonie (avec); (*fig.*) s'accorder. **harmonizer**, *n.* Harmoniste, *m.* **harmony**, *n.* Harmonie, *f.*; accord, *m.*

harness [ˈhɑːnis], *n.* Harnais, harnachement, *m. To die in harness*, mourir sous le harnais, mourir debout.—*v.t.* Harnacher; atteler (to a carriage); *armer; aménager (a stream, to produce electricity). **harness-maker**, *n.* Sellier; bourrelier, *m.* **harness-making**, *n.* Sellerie, bourrellerie, *f.*

harp [hɑːp], *n.* Harpe, *f. Jew's-harp*, guimbarde, *f.*—*v.i.* Jouer de la harpe. *To harp on one string*, rabâcher toujours la même chose. **harper**, *n.* Ménestrel, *m.* **harpist**, *n.* Harpiste, *m.*

harpoon [hɑːˈpuːn], *n.* Harpon, *m.*—*v.t.* Harponner. **harpooner**, *n.* Harponneur, *m.*

harpsichord [ˈhɑːpsikɔːd], *n.* Clavecin, *m.*

harpy [ˈhɑːpi], *n.* Harpie, *f.*

harquebus [ˈhɑːkwibʌs], *n.* Arquebuse, *f.* **harquebusade** [-ˈseid], *n.* Arquebusade, *f.* **harquebusier** [-ˈsiə], *n.* Arquebusier, *m.*

harridan [ˈhæridən], *n.* Chipie, mégère, *f.*

harrier [ˈhæriə], *n.* Braque (dog); busard (bird), *m.*; (*spt.*) coureur de cross, *m.*

Harriet [ˈhæriət]. Henriette, *f.*

harrow [ˈhærou], *n.* Herse, *f.*—*v.t.* Herser; (*fig.*) déchirer, torturer. **harrowing**, *n.* Hersage, *m.*; (*fig.*) déchirement, *m.*—*a.* Déchirant, navrant.

Harry [ˈhæri]. Henri. *To play old Harry with*, détraquer, en faire voir de grises à.

harry [ˈhæri], *v.t.* Harceler; piller, dévaster.

harsh [hɑːʃ], *a.* Âpre, rude, aigre, dur; discordant. **harshly**, *adv.* Durement, sévèrement, aigrement. **harshness**, *n.* Âpreté, aigreur, rudesse, sévérité; discordance, *f.*

harslet [HASLET].

hart [hɑːt], *n.* Cerf, *m. Hart of ten*, dix-cors, *m.*

hartshorn [ˈhɑːtshɔːn], *n.* Essence de corne de cerf, ammoniaque liquide, *f.*

hart's-tongue, *n.* Scolopendre, langue-de-cerf, *f.*

harum-scarum [ˈhɛərəmˈskɛərəm], *a.* Écervelé, étourdi.—*n.* Étourdi, hurluberlu, *m.*

harvest [ˈhɑːvist], *n.* Moisson (of corn); récolte (of fruits etc.), *f. Harvest moon*, lune de la moisson, *f.*; *to get in the harvest*, faire la moisson.—*v.t.* Moissonner; récolter. **harvest-bug**, *n.* Rouget, trombidion, aoûtat, lepte, *m.* **harvester**, *n.* Moissonneur, *m.*; moissonneuse (machine), *f.* **harvest-home**, *n.* Fin de la moisson; fête de la moisson, *f.* **harvestman**, *n.* Moissonneur, *m.* **harvest-mouse**, *n.* Souris des moissons, *f.*

has [hæz], *3rd sing. pres.* [HAVE].

has-been [ˈhæːzbiːn], *n.* (*fam.*) Homme fini, raté, *m.*

hash [hæʃ], *n.* Hachis, *m. To make a hash of*, (*fig.*) gâcher, faire un joli gâchis de; *to settle someone's hash*, régler son compte à quelqu'un.—*v.t.* Hacher, hacher menu, (*fig.*) plagier.

hashish [ˈhæʃiʃ], *n.* Hachisch, *m.*

haslet [ˈhæzlit], *n.* Fressure, *f.*

hasp [hæsp *or* hɑːsp], *n.* Loquet, *m.*; espagnolette, *f.*—*v.t.* Fermer au loquet.

hassock [ˈhæsək], *n.* Coussin, *m.* (for knees or feet).

hast [hæst], *2nd sing. pres.* [HAVE].

haste [heist], *n.* Hâte, précipitation, *f.*, emportement, *m.*; diligence, *f. In great haste*, en grande hâte, très pressé; *in haste*, à la hâte; *more haste less speed*, hâtez-vous lentement; *to make haste*, se hâter, se dépêcher.—*v.t.* Hâter, dépêcher, presser; avancer, accélérer. —*v.i.* Se hâter, se dépêcher, se presser, s'empresser. *To haste away*, se hâter de fuir, s'en aller précipitamment; *to haste back*, revenir à la hâte; *to haste up*, accourir.

hasten [HASTE, *v.*].

hastily, *adv.* À la hâte; brusquement; avec emportement. **hastiness**, *n.* Hâte, précipitation, *f.*; emportement, *m.*, vivacité, *f.* **hastings**, *n.pl.* Fruits *or* légumes précoces *or* hâtifs, *m.pl. Green hastings*, pois hâtifs, *m.pl.*

hasty, *a.* Rapide, précipité; inconsidéré, vif, emporté. *To be hasty*, avoir la tête près du bonnet. **hasty-pudding**, *n.* Bouillie au lait, *f.*

hat [hæt], *n.* Chapeau, *m. Bowler-hat*, chapeau melon, *m.*; *felt hat*, feutre, *m.*; *hats off!* chapeau bas! *soft felt hat*, chapeau mou, *m.*; *straw hat*, chapeau de paille, canotier, *m.*; *top-hat*, chapeau haut de forme, *m.*; *to keep under one's hat*, garder pour soi; *to talk through one's hat*, dire des sottises. **hatband**, *n.* Ruban de chapeau; bourdalou (with buckle); crêpe (mourning), *m.* **hatbox**, *n.* Carton, *m.*, *or* boîte, *f.*, à chapeau. **hat-brush**, *n.* Brosse à chapeau, *f.* **hatless**, *a.* Tête nue (of men), en cheveux (of women). **hat-maker**, *n.* Chapelier, *m.* **hat-making**, *n.* Chapellerie, *f.* **hat-peg**, *n.* Patère, *f.* **hat-stand**, *n.* Porte-chapeaux, *m. inv.* **hatter**, *n.* Chapelier, *m.* **hat-trade**, *n.* Chapellerie, *f.* **hat-trick**, *n.* (*spt.*) Trois buts (etc.) marqués l'un après l'autre par le même joueur, trois succès consécutifs.

hatch [hætʃ], *n.* Couvée (of chickens); éclosion (of eggs); porte coupée (door); (*Naut.*) écoutille, *f.*; (*pl.* **hatches**) panneaux des écoutilles, *m.pl.*—*v.t.* Couver (to incubate); faire éclore; (*fig.*) tramer, produire; hacher (of drawing). *Don't count your chickens before they are hatched*, ne vendez pas la peau de l'ours avant de l'avoir mis à terre.—*v.i.* Éclore.

*hatchel ['hætʃəl] [HACKLE].
hatchery ['hætʃəri], *n.* Établissement de pisciculture, *m.*
hatchet ['hætʃit], *n.* Cognée, hachette, hache, *f. To bury the hatchet*, se réconcilier, faire la paix; *to take up the hatchet*, faire la guerre.
hatchet-face, *n.* Figure en lame de couteau, *f.*
hatching ['hætʃiŋ], *n.* Hachure (engraving); éclosion (of eggs), *f.*
hatchment ['hætʃmənt], *n.* (*Her.*) Écusson funéraire, *m.*
hatchway ['hætʃwei], *n.* (*Naut.*) Écoutille, *f.*
hate [heit], *n.* Haine, *f.*—*v.t.* Haïr, détester, avoir en horreur. *I hate to be in the way*, je suis désolé d'être de trop. **hateful**, *a.* Odieux, détestable. **hatefully**, *adv.* Odieusement. **hatefulness**, *n.* Odieux, *m.* **hater**, *n.* Ennemi, *m. To be a good hater*, savoir haïr.
*hath [HAS].
hatred ['heitrid], *n.* Haine, *f.*
hauberk ['hɔːbəːk], *n.* Haubert, *m.*
haugh [hɑːx], *n.* (*Sc.*) Pré baignant, *m.*
haughtily ['hɔːtili], *adv.* Hautainement, avec arrogance. **haughtiness**, *n.* Arrogance, *f.*
haughty, *a.* Hautain, arrogant.
haul [hɔːl], *n.* Tirage, remorquage; coup de filet, *m. At a haul*, d'un coup de filet.—*v.t.* Tirer, remorquer, haler; charrier, transporter. *To haul down*, amener; *to haul in*, (*Naut.*) haler à bord; *to haul out* or *up*, hisser; *to haul over the coals*, réprimander, gronder.
haulage ['hɔːlidʒ], *n.* Camionnage, roulage; remorquage, *m.*
haulier ['hɔːlje], *n.* Hercheur; camionneur, *m.*
haulm [hɔːm], *n.* Fanes, *f.pl.*; chaume, *m.*
haunch [hɔːntʃ], *n.* Hanche, *f.* (of animal); quartier, cuissot, *m.* (of venison); (*pl.* **haunches**) l'arrière-train, *m.* (of horse).
haunt [hɔːnt], *n.* Lieu que l'on fréquente, *m.*; retraite, *f.*, rendez-vous; repaire (of thieves etc.), *m.*—*v.t.* Hanter, fréquenter, visiter; (*fig.*) obséder, tourmenter. *That house is haunted*, il y a des revenants dans cette maison. **haunter**, *n.* Personne qui hante, *f.*, habitué, visiteur habituel, *m.* **haunting**, *a.* Obsédant (of memory), hallucinant.
*hautboy ['ouboi], *n.* Hautbois, *m.*
Havana [hə'vænə]. La Havane, *f.*
have [hæv], *v.t.* and *aux.* (*2nd sing.* ***hast** [hæst], *3rd sing.* **has** [hæz], ***hath**; *past* **had**, *2nd sing.* ***hadst**; *p.p.* **had**) Avoir, tenir, posséder; contenir; prendre; faire. *Had all the soldiers fought*, si tous les soldats avaient combattu; *had he known*, s'il avait su; *had it not been for the filial respect*, n'eût été or sans le respect filial; *he will have it so*, il veut que ce soit ainsi; *he will not have me do that*, il ne veut pas que je le fasse; *I had as lief*, j'aime autant; *I had rather*, j'aimerais mieux; *I have it*, j'y suis; *I have to be at the office at 4 o'clock*, il faut que je sois au bureau à quatre heures; *I'll have him back again*, je le

ferai revenir: *let him have that book*, donnez-lui ce livre; *she will not have him*, elle ne veut pas de lui; *this may be had at . . .*, cela s'obtient chez . . .; *to have a care*, prendre garde (de); *to have breakfast*, déjeuner; *to have from*, tenir de; *to have in*, faire entrer; *to have it out with someone*, s'expliquer avec quelqu'un; *to have nothing for it but to*, être réduit à; *to have on*, avoir, porter (to wear), (*slang*) attraper, mettre dedans; *to have pleasure*, avoir du plaisir; *to have something done*, faire faire quelque chose; *to have to do with*, avoir affaire à; *to have up*, faire monter; (*pop.*) citer en justice; *what will you have?* que voulez-vous? (*slang*) *you've had it*, vous voilà refait.
haven [heivn], *n.* Havre, port; (*fig.*) asile, *m.*
haversack ['hævəsæk], *n.* (*Mil.*) Musette, *f.*; havresac, *m.*
having ['hæviŋ], *n.* Avoir, *m.*; possession, fortune, *f.*, biens, *m.pl.*
havoc ['hævək], *n.* Dégât, ravage, *m. To make havoc of*, *to play havoc with*, faire de grands ravages dans.
haw (1) [hɔː], *n.* Paupière or membrane nictitante, *f.* (of animal). **hawfinch**, *n.* Gros-bec or dur-bec, *m.*
haw (2) [hɔː], *n.* Cenelle, *f.*
haw (3) [hɔː], *int.* (*Am.*) Dia! (to a horse).
Hawaii [hɑː'waiiː]. Hawaï.
haw-haw ['hɔː'hɔː], *n.* Gros rire bête, *m.*; prononciation prétentieuse, *f.*
hawk [hɔːk], *n.* Faucon, *m.*—*v.t.* Chasser au faucon; colporter; graillonner, cracher. **hawker**, *n.* Colporteur, (*colloq.*) mercanti, camelot, *m.*; fauconnier, *m.* **hawk-eyed**, *a.* Aux yeux d'aigle. **hawking**, *n.* Fauconnerie, *f.*; colportage, *m.*; graillonnement, *m.*
hawk-moth, *n.* Sphinx, *m.*
hawse [hɔːz], *n.* (*Naut.*) Affour, *m.* **hawse-hole**, *n.* Écubier, *m.*
hawser ['hɔːzə], *n.* Haussière, *f.*, grelin, *m.*
hawthorn ['hɔːθɔːn], *n.* Aubépine, *f.*
hay [hei], *n.* Foin, *m.* (*fam.*) *To hit the hay*, se coucher, se bâcher. *To make hay*, faire les foins; (*fig.*) *to make hay of*, mettre en désordre, détruire; *to make hay while the sun shines*, battre le fer pendant qu'il est chaud. **haycock**, *n.* Meulon de foin, *m.* **hay-fever**, *n.* Rhume des foins, *m.* **hay-harvest**, *n.* Fenaison, *f.* **hayloft**, *n.* Fenil, *m.* **haymaker**, *n.* Faneur, *m.*, faneuse (woman or machine), *f.* **hay-making**, *n.* Fenaison, *f.* **hay-market**, *n.* Marché aux foins, *m.* **hayrack**, *n.* Râtelier d'écurie, *m.* **hay-rake**, *n.* Râteau, fauchet, *m.* **hayrick** or **haystack**, *n.* Meule de foin, *f.* **haywire**, *a.* (*fam.*) Excédé. *To go haywire*, perdre son sens commun.
hazard ['hæzəd], *n.* Hasard, *m.*; (*Cards*) chance, *f. At all hazards*, à tout hasard; *to run the hazard*, courir le risque (de).—*v.t.* Hasarder, risquer.—*v.i.* Se hasarder, s'aventurer. **hazardous**, *a.* Hasardeux. **hazardously**, *adv.* Hasardeusement.
haze [heiz], *n.* Petite brume, *f.* (*fig.*) obscurité, *f.*
hazel [heizl], *n.* Noisetier, coudrier, *m.* Noisette, *f.* **hazel-copse**, *n.* Coudraie, *f.* **hazel-eyed**, *a.* Aux yeux couleur de noisette. **hazel-nut**, *n.* Noisette, *f.*
hazily ['heizili], *adv.* Indistinctement, nébuleusement.

haziness, *n.* État brumeux, *m.*; imprécision, incertitude, *f.*
hazy ['heizi], *a.* Brumeux; (*fig.*) nébuleux, vaporeux; estompé, flou. *To have hazy notions,* avoir des idées vagues.
he [hi:], *pron.* Il, celui, lui. *He and I,* lui et moi; *he that* or *he who,* celui qui. **he-,** *pref.* Mâle. **he-elephant,** *n.* Éléphant mâle, *m.* **he-goat,** *n.* Bouc, *m.* **he-man,** *n.* (*pop.*) Homme viril, beau mâle, *m.*
head [hed], *n.* Tête, *f.*; chef, avant, *m.*; proue (of a ship), *f.*; haut bout (of a table); chevet (of a bedstead); fond (of a barrel), *m.*; colonne, chute (of water), *f.*; pièces (of game), *f.pl.*; source (of a river); pointe (of an arrow), *f.*; fer (of an axe, spear, etc.), *m.*; pomme (of a cane); hure (of a wild boar), *f.*; bois (of a stag), *m.*; (*fig.*) sujet, chapitre, article, *m.*; source, origine, *f. A head* or *per head,* par tête or par personne; *at the head of,* en tête de; *at the head of the table,* au haut bout de la table; *five head of game,* cinq pièces de gibier; *from head to foot,* des pieds à la tête; *head foremost,* la tête la première; *head (on beer),* mousse, *f.,* faux-col, *m.; head over heels,* en faisant la culbute; *heads or tails,* pile ou face; *head to wind,* cap au vent; *he is head and shoulders taller than you,* il vous dépasse de la tête et des épaules; *not to be able to make head or tail of,* n'y rien comprendre, ne pas s'y reconnaître; *on this head,* sur ce chapitre, sur ce point; *the wine goes to his head,* le vin lui monte à la tête; *to be hot-headed,* avoir la tête près du bonnet; *to be over head and ears in debt,* avoir des dettes par-dessus la tête; *to come to a head,* aboutir; suppurer; mûrir; *to eye from head to foot,* toiser; *to gather head,* gagner de la force; *to give his head to,* lâcher la bride à; *to lay or put heads together,* s'entendre (pour); *to make head against,* tenir tête à; *to run in one's head,* trotter dans la tête; *to take it into one's head to,* se mettre dans la tête de; *to trouble one's head about,* s'inquiéter de.
v.t.—Se mettre à la tête de; conduire, diriger; façonner la tête de (nails etc.); (*Ftb.*) jouer (le ballon) de la tête.—*v.i. To head for,* (*Naut.*) mettre le cap sur; (*fam.*) se diriger vers, s'avancer vers.—*a.* Premier, principal, en chef.
headache, *n.* Mal de tête, *m.,* migraine, *f.* **headband,** *n.* Bandeau, *m.*; (*Bookb.*) tranche-file, *f.* **head-cheese,** *n.* (*Am.*) Fromage de tête, *m.* **head-dress,** *n.* Coiffure, *f.* **head-gear,** *n.* Garniture de tête, coiffure, *f.*; (*Mining*) chevalement (of pit-head), *m.* **head-land,** *n.* Cap, *m.,* pointe, *f.,* promontoire, *m.*; (*Agric.*) tournière, *f.* **head-light,** *n.* (*Motor.*) Phare, *m.* **headline,** *n.* (*Print.*) Ligne de tête, *f.,* en-tête, *m.*; (in newspapers) titre, sous-titre, *m.* **headmaster,** *n.* Principal, directeur, proviseur, *m.* **head-mistress,** *n.* Directrice, *f.* **head-money,** *n.* Capitation, *f.* **head office,** *n.* Bureau central, *m.* **head-on,** *a.* and *adv.* De front. *Head-on collision,* collision frontale, *f.* **head-piece,** *n.* Casque, *m.*; (*colloq.*) tête, caboche, *f.* **head-phone,** *n.* (*Teleph.*) Casque, *m.* **head-quarters,** *n.pl.* Quartier général, *m. Head-quarters staff,* état-major général, *m.* **head-rest,** *n.* Appui-tête, *m.* **head-room,** *n.* Tirant d'air, *m.* **head-rope,** *n.* Longe, *f.* **head-shrinker,**

n. Réducteur de têtes (of Indian tribes); (*Am. slang*) psychiatre, *m.* **headsman,** *n.* Bourreau, *m.* **headstall,** *n.* Têtière, *f.* **headstone,** *n.* (*Arch.*) Pierre angulaire; pierre tombale, *f.* **headstrong,** *a.* Opiniâtre, obstiné, entêté. **headway,** *n.* Progrès, *m. To make headway,* avancer, progresser. **headwind,** *n.* Vent debout, *m.* **head-work,** *n.* Travail de tête, *m.*
headed, *a.* À tête. *Gold-headed,* à pomme d'or. **header,** *n.* Chef, ouvrier qui façonne les têtes (of nails); entêteur (of pins), *m.*; (*Build.*) boutisse (brick), *f.*; (*Ftb.*) coup de tête, *m.* (*Swim.*) *To take a header,* piquer une tête. **headiness,** *n.* Emportement, *m.,* impétuosité, précipitation; nature capiteuse (of drink), *f.* **heading,** *n.* Titre, en-tête, *m.,* tête de lettre, *f.*; fond (of a cask), *m.*; (*Ftb.*) jeu de tête, *m.*; (*Mining*) avancée, galerie d'avancement, *f.* **headless,** *a.* Sans tête, sans chef. **headlong,** *adv.* La tête la première; (*fig.*) à corps perdu, tête baissée, précipitamment.—*a.* Précipité, impétueux, irréfléchi, inconsidéré. **headmost,** *a.* tête, en tête. **headship,** *n.* Direction, primauté, *f.* **heady,** *a.* Capiteux (of drink); emporté, violent.
heal [hi:l], *v.t.* Guérir; cicatriser; (*fig.*) apaiser. *Heal-all,* panacée, *f.*—*v.i.* Guérir, se guérir; se cicatriser. **healer,** *n.* Guérisseur, *m.,* -euse, *f.*; remède, *m.* **healing,** *a.* Curatif; (*fig.*) salutaire, doux, calmant. *The healing art,* l'art de guérir, *m.*—*n.* Guérison, *f.*
health [helθ], *n.* Santé, *f.*; salubrité (of a place), *f.*; toast, *m. National Health Service,* sécurité sociale; *in good health,* en bonne santé, bien portant; *in bad health,* mal portant, malade; *to drink someone's health,* boire à la santé de quelqu'un; *bill of health,* patente de santé, *f.* **healthful,** *a.* Sain, salubre, salutaire. **healthfully,** *adv.* En bonne santé; salutairement. **healthfulness,** *n.* Santé; salubrité, *f.* **healthily,** *adv.* En santé; sainement. **healthiness,** *n.* Santé, salubrité, *f.* **healthy,** *a.* Bien portant, en santé; sain, salubre, salutaire.
heap [hi:p], *n.* Tas, monceau, amas, *m.* (*pop.*) *To be knocked all of a heap,* en rester stupéfait. —*v.t.* Entasser, amonceler, accumuler. *To heap insults on,* charger d'injures; *to heap the measure,* combler la mesure; *to heap up,* entasser, amonceler, amasser.
hear [hiə], *v.t.* (*past* and *p.p.* **heard** [hə:d]) Entendre; entendre dire; écouter (to listen); (*fig.*) apprendre. *Hear him!* écoutez-le donc! *to hear out,* écouter jusqu'au bout; *to hear it said,* entendre dire.—*v.i.* Entendre; entendre parler; écouter; recevoir des nouvelles, avoir des nouvelles (de). *Hear! hear!* très bien! bravo! *I never heard of such a thing!* on n'a jamais vu chose pareille! *let us hear from you,* donnez-nous de vos nouvelles; *to hear of,* entendre parler de, avoir des nouvelles de.
hearer, *n.* Auditeur, assistant, *m.*
hearing, *n.* Ouïe (the sense); audition (of witnesses); (*Law*) audience, enquête (of a petition etc.), *f.* *Hard of hearing,* dur d'oreille; *he said it in my hearing,* il l'a dit devant moi; *he was condemned without a hearing,* il fut condamné sans avoir pu plaider sa cause; *to get a hearing,* obtenir audience; *to give a hearing,* donner audience à, écouter; *within*

hearing, à portée de la voix; *out of hearing*, hors de portée de la voix.
hearken [hɑːkn], *v.i.* Écouter.
hearsay ['hiəsei], *n.* Ouï-dire, *m.* *To know from hearsay*, savoir par ouï-dire.
hearse [həːs], *n.* Corbillard, *m.* *Hearse-cloth*, drap mortuaire, *m.*—**v.t.* Ensevelir.
heart [hɑːt], *n.* Cœur; (*fig.*) courage; fond, centre, *m.*; (*Naut.*) moque, *f.* *At heart*, au fond; *by heart*, par cœur; (*fig.*, *poet.*) *heart of oak*, les vaisseaux, *hearts of oak*, les marins de la marine anglaise, *m.pl.*; *heart to heart talk*, conversation intime, *f.*; *in one's heart of hearts*, au plus profond de son cœur; *queen of hearts*, dame de cœur (in cards), *f.*; *to be out of heart*, être découragé; *to break one's heart*, avoir le cœur brisé; *to break the heart of*, briser le cœur de; *to do one's heart good*, réjouir le cœur; *to have at heart*, avoir à cœur de; *to have one's heart in one's mouth*, avoir la gorge serrée; *to have one's heart in one's boots*, avoir une peur bleue; *to have the heart to*, avoir le courage de; *to keep a good heart*, faire contre mauvaise fortune bon cœur; *to lay to heart*, se graver dans le cœur; *to lose heart*, perdre courage; *to lose one's heart to*, s'éprendre de; *to one's heart's content*, à cœur joie; *to put in good heart*, donner du cœur à, rendre le courage à; *to set one's heart on*, vouloir absolument avoir, avoir à cœur; *to take heart*, prendre courage; *to take to heart*, prendre à cœur; *to wear one's heart upon one's sleeve*, agir et parler à cœur ouvert; *with all my heart*, de tout mon cœur; *with open heart*, à cœur ouvert.
heartache, *n.* Douleur de cœur, *f.*, chagrin, *m.* **heart-attack**, *n.* Crise cardiaque, *f.* **heart-break**, *n.* Crève-cœur, *m.* **heartbreaking**, *n.* Déchirement de cœur, *m.*—*a.* Qui fend le cœur, navrant. **heart-broken**, *a.* Qui a le cœur brisé. **heartburn**, *n.* Brûlures d'estomac, aigreurs, *f.pl.* **heartburning**, *n.* Aigreur, animosité, rancune, *f.* **heart-disease**, *n.* Maladie de cœur, *f.* **heart-failure**, *n.* Arrêt du cœur, *m.* **heartfelt**, *a.* Qui vient du cœur. **heart-rending**, *a.* À fendre le cœur, navrant. **heartsearching**, *a.* Qui sonde le cœur.—*n.* Hésitations, *f.pl.*; scrupule, *m.* **heart's-ease**, *n.* Pensée sauvage, *f.* **heart-sick**, *a.* Qui a la mort dans l'âme; navré; soucieux. **heartsore**, *n.* Crève-cœur, *m.* **heart-strings**, *n.pl.* Fibre du cœur, *f.* *A tug at one's heartstrings*, un serrement de cœur. **heart-struck**, *a.* Frappé au cœur, consterné. **heart-whole**, *a.* Le cœur libre, non amoureux; sincère. **hearted**, *a.* *Broken-hearted*, qui a le cœur brisé; *hard-hearted*, le cœur dur; *heavy-hearted*, le cœur gros; *light-hearted*, le cœur gai; *stout-hearted*, courageux; *tender-hearted*, tendre. **hearten**, *v.t.* Encourager, animer. **heartily**, *adv.* Cordialement, de bon cœur; de bon appétit (of eating). **heartiness**, *n.* Cordialité; vigueur (of the appetite), *f.* **heartless**, *a.* Sans cœur, sans pitié; lâche. **heartlessly**, *adv.* Sans cœur, cruellement; lâchement. **heartlessness**, *n.* Insensibilité, cruauté, *f.*, manque de pitié; *manque de courage, *m.* **hearty**, *a.* Sincère, cordial; robuste, vigoureux; abondant, bon (of meals); qui a bon appétit (of eaters). *To be hale and hearty*, avoir bon pied, bon œil.

hearth [hɑːθ], *n.* Âtre, foyer, *m.* **hearthbrush**, *n.* Balai de cheminée, *m.* **hearthrug**, *n.* Tapis de foyer, *m.* **hearthstone**, *n.* Pierre de cheminée, *f.*; blanc d'Espagne, *m.*
heat [hiːt], *n.* Chaleur; (*fig.*) ardeur; colère (anger), *f.*; (*Racing*) série, épreuve, *f.* *On heat*, en chaleur, en rut (of animals). *The deciding heat* (in a race), la belle, *f.*; *to get into a heat*, s'animer, s'enflammer, s'emporter.—*v.t.* Chauffer, échauffer, enflammer.—*v.i.* S'échauffer. **heated**, *a.* Chaud; échauffé; animé. **heater**, *n.* Personne qui chauffe, *f.*; appareil de chauffage; fer chaud, fer à chauffer, *m.* **heating**, *n.* Chauffage, *m.* **heat-wave**, *n.* Vague de chaleur, *f.*
heath [hiːθ], *n.* Bruyère, lande; brande (plant), *f.* **heath-cock**, *n.* Petit coq de bruyère, tétras, *m.*
heathen [hiːðn], *a.* and *n.* Païen, *m.*, -enne, *f.* **heathendom**, *n.* Le monde païen, le paganisme, *m.* **heathenish** ['hiːðəniʃ], *a.* Païen; (*fig.*) barbare, sauvage. **heathenishly**, *adv.* En païen. **heathenism**, *n.* Paganisme, *m.*
heather ['heðə], *n.* Bruyère, brande, *f.* **heathery** or **heathy** ['hiːθi], *a.* Plein de bruyères.
heave [hiːv], *n.* Effort, *m.* (pour soulever), secousse, *f.*; soulèvement (rising), *m.*—*v.t.* (*past* **heaved, hove** [houv], *p.p.* **heaved**) Lever; élever; soulever; jeter, lancer; pousser (a sigh). (*Naut.*) *To heave the ship ahead*, virer de l'avant.—*v.i.* Se soulever; palpiter, battre (of the bosom, heart, etc.); avoir des haut-le-cœur, faire des efforts pour vomir. (*Naut.*) *To heave in sight*, apparaître; *to heave to*, se mettre en panne; *to heave up*, déraper.
heaven [hevn], *n.* Ciel, *m.*, cieux, *m.pl.* *Good heavens!* juste ciel! *to be in the seventh heaven of delight*, être aux anges; *to move heaven and earth*, remuer ciel et terre, faire des efforts inouïs. **heaven-born** or **heaven-bred**, *a.* Divin, céleste. **heavenly**, *a.* Céleste, divin.—*adv.* D'une manière céleste, divinement. **heaven-sent**, *a.* Providentiel.
heaver ['hiːvə], *n.* Porteur, portefaix, *m.* *Coal-heaver*, porteur de charbon, *m.*
heavily ['hevili], *adv.* Pesamment, lourdement; fortement, fort, avec acharnement; tristement, d'un air abattu. **heaviness**, *n.* Pesanteur, lourdeur, *f.*, poids, *m.*; (*fig.*) tristesse, *f.*, abattement; mauvais état (of roads etc.), *m.*
heavy (1) ['hevi], *a.* Lourd, pesant; (*fig.*) grave; gros (of the sea etc.); pénible, ennuyeux; accablé, morne, triste; difficile, mauvais (of roads etc.); fort, profond. *Heavy cavalry*, la grosse cavalerie; *heavy cold*, gros rhume, *m.*; *heavy day*, journée chargée, *f.*; *heavy eyes*, yeux battus; *heavy father*, (*Theat.*) père noble; (*Mil.*) *heavy fire*, feu intense, *m.*; *heavy road*, mauvais chemin, *m.*; *heavy smoker*, gros fumeur; *heavy task*, tâche difficile, *f.*; *to hang* or *lie heavy on*, peser sur, être à charge à. **heavy-gaited**, *a.* À pas pesants. **heavy-handed**, *a.* À la main lourde, gauche. **heavy-headed**, *a.* Stupide, lourd. **heavy-hearted**, *a.* Le cœur gros, accablé. **heavy-laden**, *a.* Qui porte un lourd fardeau. **heavy-weight**, *n.* (*Box.*)

Poids lourd, *m. Light heavy-weight*, poids mi-lourd, *m.*
heavy (2) ['hi:vi], *a.* Poussif (horse).
hebdomadal [heb'dɔmədl] or **hebdomadary**, *a.* Hebdomadaire. **hebdomadally**, *adv.* Hebdomadairement.
hebetate ['hebəteit], *v.t.* Hébéter.
Hebraic [hi:'breiik], *a.* Hébraïque. **Hebraically**, *adv.* Hébraïquement.
Hebraism ['hi:breiizm], *n.* Hébraïsme, *m.* **Hebraist**, *n.* Hébraïste, hébraïsant, *m.*
Hebrew ['hi:bru:], *n.* Hébreu, Juif, *m.*, Juive, *f.*; hébreu (language), *m.—a.* Hébreu, *m.*; hébraïque, *f.*
hecatomb ['hekətəm, -tu:m], *n.* Hécatombe, *f.*
heckle [hekl], *v.t.* Embarrasser de questions, harasser (at public meetings).
heckler ['heklə], *n.* Questionneur acharné, interrupteur, *m.* **heckling**, *n.* Série de questions agaçantes, *f.*
hectic ['hektik] or ***hectical**, *a.* Hectique; agité, fiévreux.
hectogram ['hektogræm], *n.* Hectogramme, hecto, *m.* **hectolitre**, *n.* Hectolitre, *m.* **hectometre**, *n.* Hectomètre, *m.*
hector ['hektə], *n.* Fanfaron, matamore, *m.—v.i.* Faire le fendant.—*v.t.* Rudoyer. **hectoring**, *a.* Impérieux, esbroufeur.
hedge [hedʒ], *n.* Haie, *f.—a.* De bas-étage, interlope. *Hedge-lawyer*, avocat marron, *m.* —*v.t.* Entourer d'une haie. *To hedge a bet*, parier pour et contre; *to hedge in*, enfermer. —*v.i.* Se cacher; parier pour et contre; (*fig.*) éviter de se compromettre. **hedge-bill** or **hedging-bill**, *n.* Serpe, *f.*, croissant, *m.* **hedgehog**, *n.* Hérisson, *m.* **hedge-hop**, *v.i.* Voler en rase-mottes. **hedge-hyssop**, *n.* Gratiole, *f.* **hedgerow**, *n.* Bordure de haies, *f.* **hedge-school**, *n.* École en plein air; école buissonnière, *f.* **hedge-sparrow**, *n.* Mouchet, *m.*, fauvette d'hiver, *f.*
hedonism ['hi:dənizm], *n.* Hédonisme, *m.* **hedonist**, *n.* Hédoniste.
heed [hi:d], *n.* Attention, *f*, soin, *m. To give heed*, faire attention (à); *to take heed*, prendre garde.—*v.t.* Faire attention à, prendre garde à, écouter. **heedful**, *a.* Attentif, vigilant, circonspect. **heedfully**, *adv.* Attentivement. **heedfulness**, *n.* Attention, vigilance, *f.*, soin, *m.* **heedless**, *a.* Étourdi, inattentif, insouciant. **heedlessly**, *adv.* Négligemment; inconsidérément, étourdiment. **heedlessness**, *n.* Inattention, insouciance, étourderie, *f.*
heel [hi:l], *n.* Talon; (*fig.*) pied (of a mast etc.), *m.*; (*Naut.*) gîte, bande (slant), *f.*; éperon, ergot, *m.* (of cock); (*Am. slang*) personne méprisable, *f. To be at the heels of*, être sur les talons de, être aux trousses de; *to be down at heel*, être percé aux talons, traîner la savate; *to cool one's heels*, faire antichambre, faire le pied de grue; *to go head over heels*, faire la culbute; *to show one's heels*, prendre la fuite; *to take to one's heels*, prendre ses jambes à son cou; *to tread upon someone's heels*, marcher sur les talons de quelqu'un.— *v.i.* Danser, tourner. *To heel out*, (*Rugby*) talonner; *to heel over*, (*Naut.*) donner de la bande; *to heel to port*, (*Naut.*) plier sur bâbord.—*v.t.* Mettre un talon à.
heel-piece, *n.* Talon, *m.*
heel-tap, *n.* Fond de verre, *m.*

hefty ['hefti], *a.* (*fam.*) Solide, costaud.
hegemony ['hi:dʒeməni or hi:'geməni], *n.* Hégémonie, *f.*
heifer ['hefə], *n.* Génisse, *f.*
heigh-ho! ['hei'hou], *int.* Ah! (expressing disappointment, regret).
height [hait], *n.* Hauteur, élévation; taille, stature, *f.*; (*fig.*) comble, faîte, apogée, *m. The height of presumption*, le comble de la présomption. *The height of summer*, le cœur, le fort de l'été. **heighten**, *v.t.* Rehausser, relever, (*fig.*) accroître, augmenter; renchérir.
heinous ['heinəs], *a.* Atroce. **heinously**, *adv.* Atrocement, d'une manière atroce. **heinousness**, *n.* Atrocité, énormité, *f.*
heir [ɛə], *n.* Héritier. *Heir-apparent*, héritier présomptif, *m.* **heir-at-law**, *n.* Héritier légitime, *m.* **heirdom**, *n.* Droit de succession, *m.* **heiress**, *n.* Héritière, *f.* **heirless**, *a.* Sans héritier. **heirloom**, *n.* Meuble de famille, *m.* **heirship**, *n.* Hérédité, qualité d'héritier, *f.*
held, *past* [HOLD].
Helen ['helin]. (*Myth.*) Hélène, *f.*
Helena ['helinə]. (*Hist.*) Hélène, *f.*
heliacal [hi:'laiəkəl] or ***heliac** ['hi:liæk], *a.* Héliaque.
helianthemum [hi:li'ænθəməm], *n.* Hélianthème, *m.* **helianthus**, *n.* Hélianthe, *m.*
helical ['helikl], **helicoid** ['helikɔid], **helicoidal**, *a.* Hélicoïdal.
helicopter ['helikɔptə], *n.* Hélicoptère, *m.*
heliocentric [hi:lio'sentrik], *a.* Héliocentrique.
heliograph, *n.* Héliographe, *m.*
heliography [hi:li'ɔgrəfi], *n.* Héliographie, *f.*
heliogravure ['hi:liogrəvuə], *n.* Héliogravure, *f.*
helioscope, *n.* Hélioscope, *m.*
heliotherapy, *n.* Héliothérapie, *f.*
heliotrope ['hi:liətroup], *n.* Héliotrope, *m.* **heliotropic**, *a.* Héliotropique. **heliotropism**, *n.* Héliotropisme, *m.*
helium ['hi:liəm], *n.* (*Chem.*) Hélium, *m.*
helix ['hi:liks], *n.* (*pl.* **helices**) Hélice, *f.*; (*Anat.*) hélix, *m.*; (*Arch.*) spirale, volute, *f.*
hell [hel], *n.* Enfer, *m.*; (*fig.*) tripot (gambling), *m. A hell of a noise*, un bruit d'enfer; *a hell upon earth*, une vraie galère, *f.*; *to raise hell*, (*fam.*) faire un malheur, faire une scène; *to work like hell*, travailler dur. **hell-born**, *a.* Sorti de l'enfer, infernal. **hell-cat**, *n.* Furie, sorcière infernale, *f.* **hell-hound**, *n.* Chien de l'enfer, suppôt de Satan, *m.* **hellish**, *a.* Infernal, d'enfer. **hellishly**, *adv.* Infernalement. **hellishness**, *n.* Caractère infernal, *m.*
hellebore ['helibɔ:], *n.* Ellébore, *m.*
Hellene [he'li:n], *n.* Hellène, *m.*; hellène, *f.*
Hellenic [-'li:nik], *a.* Hellénique.
Hellenism ['helənizm], *n.* Hellénisme, *m.* **Hellenist**, *n.* Helléniste, *m.*
hello [he'lou], *int.* Holà! allô! (on telephone); tiens! (surprise).
helm [helm], *n.* Gouvernail, timon, *m.*, barre (tiller), *f.*; heaume (helmet), *m. Man at the helm*, l'homme de barre, *m.*; *to be at the helm*, tenir la barre, tenir le gouvernail. **helmsman**, *n.* Timonier, *m.*
helmet ['helmit], *n.* Casque, *m.*
helot ['helət], *n.* Ilote, *m.* **helotism**, *n.* Ilotisme, *m.*

help [help], *n.* Secours, *m.*; aide, assistance, *f.*; remède (remedy), *m.* *Help!* à l'aide! au secours! *there's no help for it*, il le faut bien, il n'y a rien à y faire; *to cry for help*, crier au secours; *with the help of*, au moyen de; *with the help of God*, Dieu aidant.—*v.t.* Aider, secourir, assister; servir (at table); empêcher (prevent); éviter (avoid). *God help you!* Dieu te vienne en aide! *God helps those who help themselves* [GOD]; *help yourself* (at meal), servez-vous; *how can I help it?* que voulez-vous que j'y fasse? *how can it be helped?* qu'y faire? *I can't help it*, je n'y puis rien; *I cannot help saying*, je ne puis m'empêcher de dire; *that won't help us much*, cela ne nous servira pas à grand'chose; *to help down*, aider à descendre; *to help forward*, aider à avancer; *to help oneself*, se servir (de), prendre; *to help out*, aider à sortir, tirer d'embarras; *to help over*, aider à surmonter; *to help up*, aider à monter.—*v.i.* Aider, servir, contribuer. **helper,** *n.* Aide, *m.* **helpful,** *a.* Utile; secourable. **helping,** *a.* Utile. *To lend a helping hand*, donner un coup de main.—*n.* Portion (of food served), *f.* **helpless,** *a.* Faible, impuissant; sans ressource, sans appui. **helplessly,** *adv.* Faiblement; sans ressource. **helplessness,** *n.* Faiblesse, impuissance, *f.* **helpmate** or **helpmeet,** *n.* Aide, compagnon, *m.*, compagne; *(fig.)* épouse, *f.* **help-yourself,** *a.* *Help-yourself service*, libre-service, *m.* (in shop or restaurant).

helter-skelter ['heltə 'skeltə], *adv.* Pêle-mêle; en désordre, en pagaille.

helve [helv], *n.* Manche, *m.* *To throw the helve after the hatchet*, jeter le manche après la cognée.—*v.t.* Emmancher (une hache). **helved,** *a.* À manche, emmanché.

Helvetia [hel'vi:ʃə]. L'Helvétie, *f.* **Helvetian,** *n.* Helvétien. *m.*, Helvétienne, *f.* **Helvetic** [-'vetik], *a.* Helvétique.

hem (1) [hem], *n.* Ourlet, bord, *m.*—*v.t.* Ourler, border. *To hem in*, enfermer, entourer, cerner. **hem-stitch,** *n.* Ourlet à jour, *m.*—*v.t.* Ourler à jour.

hem (2) [hem], *int.* Hem!—*v.i.* Faire hem. *To hem and haw*, ânonner.

hematite [HAEMATITE].

hematocele, etc. [HAEMATO-].

hemicycle ['hemisaikl], *n.* Hémicycle, *m.*

hemiplegia [hemi'pli:dʒiə], *n.* Hémiplégie, *f.*

hemipter [hi'miptə] or **hemipteron,** *n.* *(Ent.)* Hémiptère, *m.*

hemisphere ['hemisfiə], *n.* Hémisphère, *m.* **hemispheric** [-'sferik] or **hemispherical,** *a.* Hémisphérique.

hemistich ['hemistik], *n.* Hémistiche, *m.*

hemlock ['hemlɔk], *n.* Ciguë, *f.*

hemorrhage, etc. [HAEMORRHAGE].

hemp [hemp], *n.* *(Bot.)* Chanvre, *m.*; *(fig.)* corde, *f.* **hemp-comb,** *n.* Séran, *m.* **hemp-dresser,** *n.* Séranceur, chanvrier, *m.* **hemp-field,** *n.* Chènevière, *f.* **hemp-nettle,** *n.* *(Bot.)* Galéopsis, *m.* **hemp-seed,** *n.* Chènevis, *m.*

hempen, *a.* De chanvre.

hen [hen], *n.* Poule; femelle (of birds), *f.* **hen-bane,** *n.* *(Bot.)* Jusquiame, *f.* **hen-coop,** *n.* Cage à poulets, *f.* **hen-house,** *n.* Poulailler, *m.* **hen-pecked,** *a.* Gouverné par sa femme,

qui se laisse mener par le bout du nez. **hen-roost,** *n.* Juchoir, *m.*

hence [hens], *adv.* D'ici; de là, ainsi (for this reason); désormais (of time). *A week hence,* dans huit jours.

henceforth or **henceforward,** *adv.* Désormais, dorénavant, à l'avenir.

henchman ['hentʃmən], *n.* Écuyer, valet; *(fig.)* partisan, satellite, acolyte, *m.*

hendecagon [hen'dekəgən], *n.* Hendécagone, *m.* **hendecasyllable** [-'siləbl], *n.* Hendécasyllabe, *m.*

Henry ['henri]. Henri, *m.*

hepatic [hi'pætik], *a.* Hépatique. **hepatica,** *n.* *(pl.* **hepaticae)** Hépatique, *f.*

hepatite ['hepətait], *n.* *(Min.)* Hépatite, *f.* **hepatitis** [-'taitis], *n.* *(Path.)* Hépatite, *f.* **hepatization** [-'zeiʃən], *n.* Hépatisation, *f.*

hepatocele ['hepətosi:l], *n.* Hépatocèle, *f.*

heptagon ['heptəgən], *n.* Heptagone, *m.* **heptagonal** [-'tægənəl], *a.* Heptagonal.

heptaphyllous [heptə'filəs], *a.* *(Bot.)* Heptaphylle.

heptarchy ['heptɑ:ki], *n.* Heptarchie, *f.*

her [hə:], *pers. pron.* Elle, la, lui.—*poss. a.* Son, sa, ses.—*pron.* Celle, *f.*

herald ['herəld], *n.* Héraut, *m.*; *(fig.)* avant-coureur, précurseur, *m.*—*v.t.* Annoncer. *To herald in*, introduire, annoncer (the seasons).

heraldic [hi'rældik], *a.* Héraldique.

heraldry ['herəldri], *n.* Science héraldique, *f.*, blason, *m.* *Canting heraldry*, armes parlantes, *f.pl.* *Book of heraldry*, armorial, *m.*

herb [hə:b], *n.* Herbe, *f.* *Pot-herbs,* herbes potagères, *f.pl.*; *sweet herbs*, fines herbes, *f.pl.* **herb-shop,** *n.* Herboristerie, boutique d'herboriste, *f.*

herbaceous [hə:'beiʃəs], *a.* Herbacé.

herbage ['hə:bidʒ], *n.* Herbage, *m.* **herbal,** *n.* Herbier, *m.*—*a.* Des herbes. **herbalist,** *n.* Herboriste. **herbarium** [-'bɛəriəm], *n.* *(pl.* **herbaria)** Herbier, *m.* **herbescent** [-'besənt], *a.* Herbeux.

herbivore ['hə:bivɔ:], *n.* Herbivore, *m.* **herbivorous** [-'bivərəs], *a.* Herbivore. **herborization,** *n.* Herborisation, *f.* **herborize,** *v.i.* Herboriser. **herbous,** *a.* Herbeux, herbu.

Herculean [hə:'kju:liən or hə:kju'li:ən], *a.* Herculéen, d'Hercule.

Hercules ['hə:kjuli:z]. Hercule, *m.*

herd [hə:d], *n.* Troupeau, *m.*, troupe, *f.* *The common herd*, le commun, *m.*, la foule, *f.*—*v.i.* Vivre en troupeau, s'attrouper, s'associer.—*v.t.* Garder, surveiller; rassembler en troupeau. **herdsman,** *n.* *(pl.* **herdsmen)** Bouvier, *m.*

here [hiə], *adv.* Ici; voici, que voici. *From here to there*, d'ici là; *here!* présent! venez ici! tenez! *here and there*, çà et là; *here below*, ici-bas; *here goes!* allons-y! *here he comes*, le voici qui vient; *here's for you*, voici quelque chose pour vous; *here's my point*, voici le point où je veux en venir; *here's to you*, à votre santé; *here they are*, les voici; *I am here*, me voici; *it is neither here nor there*, cela ne fait rien à l'affaire; *see here!* tenez! *the little boy here*, le petit garçon que voici; *this one here*, celui-ci.

hereabout [hiərə'baut] or **hereabouts,** *adv.* Près d'ici, par ici, ici près. **hereafter,** *adv.* Ci-après; désormais, dorénavant; dans la vie

à venir.—*n.* L'au-delà, *m.*, la vie future, *f.*
hereat [-'æt], *adv.* À ceci, de ceci. **hereby,**
adv. Par ce moyen, par ceci, par là; (*Law*)
par ces présentes; tout près. **herein** [-'in],
adv. En ceci, ici, ci-inclus. **hereinafter,**
adv. Ci-après. **hereof** [-'ɔv], *adv.* De ceci,
de là, d'où. **hereon,** *adv.* Là-dessus, sur
ceci. **hereto** [-'tu:], *adv.* Jusqu'à présent,
jusqu'à ce point; à ceci. **heretofore,** *adv.*
Jadis, jusqu'ici. **hereunto** [hiərʌn'tu:],
adv. À ceci. **hereupon,** *adv.* Là-dessus.
herewith, *adv.* Avec ceci, ci-joint.
hereditament [heri'ditəmənt], *n.* Bien, *m.*
(dont on hérite).
hereditarily [hi'reditərili], *adv.* Héréditairement. **hereditary,** *a.* Héréditaire. **heredity,**
n. Hérédité, *f.*
heresiarch ['herəsiɑ:k], *n.* Hérésiarque, *m.*
heresy ['herəsi], *n.* Hérésie, *f.* **heretic,** *n.*
Hérétique, *m.* or *f.*
heretical [hi'retikəl], *a.* Hérétique.
heritable ['heritəbl], *a.* Héréditaire, dont on
peut hériter. **heritage,** *n.* Héritage, *m.*
heritor, *n.* Héritier, *m.* **heritrix,** *n.*
Héritière, *f.*
hermaphrodite [hə:'mæfrodait], *n.* Hermaphrodite, *m.* **hermaphroditism,** *n.* Hermaphrodisme, *m.*
hermeneutic [hə:mə'nju:tik], *a.* Herméneutique.—*n.* Herméneutique, *f.*
hermetic [hə:'metik], *a.* Hermétique. **hermetically,** *adv.* Hermétiquement.
hermit ['hə:mit], *n.* Ermite, *m.* **hermitage,**
n. Ermitage, *m.* **hermit-crab,** *n.* Bernard
l'ermite, *m.* **hermitical** [-'mitikəl], *a.*
D'ermite.
hernia ['hə:niə], *n.* Hernie, *f.* **hernial,**
herniary, *a.* Herniaire.
hero ['hiərou], *n.* (*pl.* **heroes**) Héros, *m.* **hero-
worship,** *n.* Culte des héros, *m.*
Herod ['herəd]. Hérode, *m.* *To out-Herod
Herod,* Tempêter, fanfaronner.
heroic [hi'rouik] or **heroical,** *a.* Héroïque.
heroically, *adv.* Héroïquement. **heroicomic** or **heroicomical,** *a.* Héroïcomique.
heroics, *n.* Grandiloquence, *f.*
heroin [hi'rouin or 'heroin], *n.* Héroïne, *f.*
heroine ['heroin], *n.* Héroïne, *f.*
heroism, *n.* Héroïsme, *m.*
heron ['herən], *n.* Héron, *m.* **heronry,** *n.*
Héronnière, *f.*
herpes ['hə:pi:z], *n.* Herpès, *m.*; dartre, *f.*
herpetic [-'petik], *a.* Herpétique. **herpetology** [-tɔlədʒi], *n.* Herpétologie, *f.*
herring ['heriŋ], *n.* Hareng, *m.* *Red herring,*
hareng saur, *m.*; (*fig.*) diversion, *f. To draw
a red herring across the path,* hucher à dépister
les chiens; (*fig.*) faire dévier la conversation;
chercher à donner le change. **herring-bone,**
n. Arête de hareng, *f.*; (*Dress.*) point de
chausson, *m.*; (*Arch.*) pierres d'assises angu-
laires, *f.pl.* **herring-fishery,** *n.* Harengaison,
f. **herring-gull,** *n.* Goéland argenté, *m.*
hers [hə:z], *pron.* Le sien, *m.*, la sienne, *f.*, les
siens, *m.pl.*, les siennes, *f.pl. A friend of hers,*
un de ses amis, *m.*, une de ses amies, *f.*
herse [hə:s], *n.* (*Fort.*) Herse, *f.*
herself [hə:'self], *pron.* Elle-même, elle; se.
By herself, toute seule.
hesitancy ['hezitənsi], *n.* Hésitation, indécision, *f.* **hesitant,** *a.* Hésitant. **hesitate,** *v.i.*
Hésiter. *To hesitate to do something,* hésiter

à faire quelque chose. **hesitatingly,** *adv.*
En hésitant. **hesitation** [-'teiʃən], *n.* Hésitation, *f.*
Hessian ['heʃən, 'hesiən], *a.* and *n.* Hessois;
(*Tex.*) toile d'emballage, *f.* *Hessian boots,*
bottes à la Souvarof, *f.pl.*
heteroclite ['hetərəklait], *a.* Hétéroclite.—*n.*
Mot hétéroclite, *m.* **heteroclitic** [-'klitik] or
heteroclitical, *a.* Hétéroclite.
heterodox ['hetərədɔks], *a.* Hétérodoxe.
heterodoxy, *n.* Hétérodoxie, *f.*
heterodyne ['hetərodain], *a.* and *n.* (*Rad.*)
Hétérodyne, *m.*
heterogeneity [hetərodʒə'ni:iti] or **hetero-
geneousness** [-'dʒi:niəsnis], *n.* Hétérogénéité, *f.*
heterogeneous [hetəro'dʒi:niəs], *a.* Hétérogène.
heteroscian [hetə'rɔʃiən], *a.* and *n.* Hétéro-
scien, *m.*
heterosexual [hetərə'seksjuəl], *a.* Hétéro-
sexuel.
hew [hju:], *v.t.* (*p.p.* **hewn**) Tailler, couper.
Hewn stone, pierre taillée, *f.*; *to hew coal,*
piquer la houille; *to hew down,* abattre.
hewer, *n.* Tailleur (of stone); piqueur (of
coal); fendeur de bois (of wood), *m.* **hewing,**
n. Coupe, taille, *f.*, équarrissage, *m.*
hexachord ['heksəkɔ:d], *n.* Hexacorde, *m.*
hexagon ['heksəgən], *n.* Hexagone, *m.* **hexagonal** [hek'sægənəl], *a.* Hexagone.
hexahedral [heksə'hi:drəl], *a.* Hexaèdre.
hexahedron [heksə'hi:drən], *n.* Hexaèdre,
m.
hexameter [hek'sæmitə], *n.* Hexamètre, *m.*
hexandrous [hek'sændrəs], *a.* (*Bot.*) Hexan-
dre.
hey! [hei], *int.* Hé! hein!
heyday ['heidei], *n.* Beaux jours, *m.pl.*; (*fig.*)
printemps, matin, *m.*
Hezekiah [hezə'kaiə]. Ézéchias, *m.*
hi! [hai], *int.* Hé! ohé! holà!
hiatus [hai'eitəs], *n.* Hiatus, *m.*; (*fig.*) lacune,
f.
hibernate ['haibəneit], *v.i.* Hiverner, hiberner.
hibernating, *a.* Hibernant. **hibernation**
[-'neiʃən], *n.* Hibernation, *f.*
Hibernian [hai'bə:niən], *a.* and *n.* Irlandais,
m., Irlandaise, *f.* **hibernianism,** *n.* Idiotisme
irlandais, *m.*
hibiscus [hi'biskəs], *n.* (*Bot.*) Ketmie, *f.*
hiccough, hiccup ['hikʌp], *n.* Hoquet, *m.*—
v.i. Avoir le hoquet, hoqueter.
hickory ['hikəri], *n.* Hickory, noyer blanc
d'Amérique, *m.*
hidden [hidn], *a.* Caché, secret; (*fig.*) occulte,
mystérieux.
hide (1) [haid], *n.* Peau, *f.*, cuir, *m.* **hide-
bound,** *a.* Dont la peau adhère aux muscles;
(*fig.*) dur, intraitable, bigot, étroit; relié en
peau (book).
hide (2) [haid], *v.t.* (*past* **hid,** *p.p.* **hid,**
hidden) Cacher; enfouir (in the ground).
Hide-and-seek, cache-cache, *m.*—*v.i.* Se
cacher, se tenir caché, se fourrer.
hideous ['hidiəs], *a.* Hideux, affreux. **hideously,** *adv.* Hideusement. **hideousness,**
n. Caractère hideux, *m.*, laideur, horreur, *f.*
hiding (1) ['haidiŋ], *n.* (*colloq.*) Rossée, raclée,
f. To give someone a good hiding, tanner le
cuir à quelqu'un.

hiding (2) [ˈhaidiŋ], *a.* Qui cache; qui se cache.—*n. In hiding,* caché. **hiding-place,** *n.* Cachette, *f.*
hie [hai], *v.i.* Se hâter, courir, se rendre (à).
hierarchal [haiəˈrɑːkəl], **hierarchic** or **hierarchical,** *a.* Hiérarchique. **hierarchically,** *adv.* Hiérarchiquement.
hierarchy [ˈhaiərɑːki], *n.* Hiérarchie, *f.*
hieratic [haiəˈrætik], *a.* Hiératique.
hieroglyph [ˈhaiərəglif], *n.* Hiéroglyphe, *m.* **hieroglyphic** or **hieroglyphical** [-ˈglifikəl], *a.* Hiéroglyphique. **hieroglyphically,** *adv.* Par hiéroglyphes. **hierophant,** *n.* Hiérophante, *m.*
higgle [higl], *v.i.* Marchander.
higgledy-piggledy [ˈhigldiˈpigldi], *adv.* Pêlemêle, en vrac, en pagaille.
high [hai], *a.* Haut, élevé, haut placé; (*fig.*) grand; sublime, important; fier, altier, prétentieux; fort, puissant, violent, vif; saillant (of cheek-bones); cher (of prices); faisandé (of game); avancé (of meat). *From on high,* d'en haut; *high and dry,* à sec; *high and low,* de haut en bas; les grands et les petits; *high and mighty manner,* air de grand seigneur, *m.*; *higher and higher,* de plus en plus haut; *high days and holidays,* les jours de fête, *m.pl.*; *high life,* le grand monde, *m.*; *High Mass,* grand-messe, *f.*; *high mind,* esprit élevé; *high noon,* plein midi, *m.*; *high price,* prix élevé, *m.*; *high road,* grand chemin, *m.*, grand-route, *f.*; *high speed,* grande vitesse; *high street,* grand-rue, *f.*; *high water,* haute marée, *f.*; *high-water mark,* niveau des hautes eaux, *m.*; *on high,* en haut; *six feet high,* haut de six pieds; *the High Church,* la haute Église anglicane, *f.*; *the Most High,* le Très-Haut, *m.*; *it is high time,* il est grand temps; *to leave someone high and dry,* laisser tomber quelqu'un; *to speak of someone in high terms,* parler de quelqu'un en termes flatteurs; *with a high hand,* haut la main.—*adv.* Haut, en haut, hautement; grandement; fort, fortement. *To aim high,* (*fig.*) avoir de hautes visées; *to play high,* jouer gros jeu; *to run high,* s'échauffer (feelings), être grosse (sea).
highball [ˈhaibɔːl], *n.* (*Am.*) Verre de whisky à l'eau à la glace, *f.*, whisky-soda, *m.*
high-born, *a.* De haute naissance. **highclass,** *a.* De premier ordre. **high-coloured,** *a.* Haut en couleur, d'une couleur éclatante. **high-crowned,** *a.* Haut de forme (hat); en dos d'âne (road). **high-flier,** *n.* Personne ambitieuse, *f.*; enthousiaste, *m.* **high-flown,** *a.* Orgueilleux, enflé; ampoulé (of style); outré. **high-flying,** *a.* Au vol élevé; (*fig.*) extravagant, ambitieux. **high-frequency,** *a.* À haute fréquence. **high-grade,** *a.* À haute teneur. *High-grade petrol,* supercarburant, *m.* **high-handed,** *a.* Arbitraire, tyrannique. **high-lows,** *n.pl.* Bottines lacées, *f.pl.* **highmettled,** *a.* Plein de feu, fougueux. **highminded,** *a.* *Altier; magnanime. **highmindedness,** *n.* Magnanimité, noblesse d'âme, *f.* **high-pitched,** *a.* Aigu (of sound). **high-powered,** *a.* De haute puissance. **high-pressure,** *a.* À haute pression. **highpriest,** *n.* Grand-prêtre, *m.* **high-sounding,** *a.* Pompeux; ronflant (of style). **highspeed,** *a.* À grande vitesse. (*Cine.*) *Highspeed cinematography,* prise de vues en

accéléré, *f.* **high-spirited,** *a.* Fougueux, plein de courage, plein de cœur.
highbrow [ˈhaibrau], *a.* and *n.* (*fam.*) Intellectuel.
higher [ˈhaiə], *a.* Plus haut, plus élevé; supérieur. *Higher education,* instruction supérieure. **highest,** *a.* Le plus haut, le plus élevé. *At the highest,* au comble. **highlight,** *n.* Point culminant, (*fam.*) clou, *m.*
highly, *adv.* Hautement; fortement, fort; fort bien, éminemment. *Highly blamable,* fort blâmable; *highly strung,* nerveux; *to speak highly of,* parler en termes flatteurs de.
highfalutin [haifəˈluːtin], *a.* (*fam.*) Ampoulé (of style).
highland [ˈhailənd], *a.* Des montagnes; de la Haute Écosse. **highlander,** *n.* Montagnard de l'Écosse, *m.* **highlands,** *n.pl.* Pays montagneux, *m.*; **The Highlands,** hautes terres de l'Écosse, *f.pl.*, la Haute Écosse.
Highness [ˈhainis], *n.* Altesse (title), *f.* **highness,** *n.* Hauteur; élévation, *f.*
highway [ˈhaiwei], *n.* Grand chemin, *m.*, grande route, *f.* *Highway robbery,* vol sur le grand chemin, *m.* **highwayman,** *n.* Voleur de grand chemin, *m.*
hike [haik], *v.i.* Aller à pied, vagabonder; faire des excursions à pied sac au dos et camper. **hiker,** *n.* Touriste à pied et campeur. **hiking,** *n.* Excursions à pied, *f.pl.*
hilarious [hiˈlɛəriəs], *a.* Gai, joyeux. **hilarity** [hiˈlæriti], *n.* Hilarité, *f.*
Hilary [ˈhiləri]. Hilaire, *m.*
hill [hil], *n.* Colline, montagne, *f.*, coteau, *m.*, butte, *f.*; côte, *f.* *Up hill and down dale,* par monts et par vaux. *Sharp hill,* montée (or descente) rapide, *f.*—*v.t.* Remblayer; butter.
hilliness, *n.* Nature montueuse, *f.*
hillock [ˈhilək], *n.* Monticule, *m.*, butte, *f.*
hill-side, *n.* Flanc de coteau, *m.* **hilly,** *a.* Montueux, montagneux, accidenté.
hilt [hilt], *n.* Poignée, garde, *f.* *Up to the hilt,* jusqu'à la garde, complètement.
hilum [ˈhailəm], *n.* (*Bot.*) Hile, *m.*
him [him], *pron.* Le, lui; (*dem.*) celui. **himself,** *pron.* Lui-même, lui, soi-même; (*reflexive*) se. *By himself,* tout seul; *he thinks himself,* il se croit.
hind (1) [haind], *n.* Biche (deer), *f.*
hind (2) [haind], *n.* Valet de ferme (farmservant); (*fig.*) paysan, rustre, *m.*
hind (3) [haind] or **hinder** (1) [ˈhaində], *a.* De derrière, postérieur, arrière. *Hind legs,* jambes de derrière, *f.pl.*; *hind quarters* (of horse), arrière-main, *f.* **hindmost** or **hindermost,** *a.* Dernier. *The Devil take the hindmost,* chacun pour soi.
hinder (2) [ˈhaində], *v.t.* Empêcher; gêner; embarrasser, retarder. *Frost hinders the growth of plants,* le froid retarde la croissance des plantes. **hinderer,** *n.* Personne qui empêche; chose qui empêche, *f.* **hindrance,** *n.* Empêchement, obstacle, *m.*
Hindi [ˈhindi], *n.* L'hindî, *m.* (language).
Hindu [hinˈduː], *a.* and *n.* Hindou. **Hinduism,** *n.* L'hindouisme, *m.* **Hindustan.** L'Hindoustan, *m.* **Hindustani,** *n.* L'hindoustani, *m.* (language).
hinge [hindʒ], *n.* Gond, *m.*; paumelle, *f.*; charnière (butt-hinge), *f.*; (*fig.*) pivot, *m.* *To be off the hinges,* (*fig.*) être en confusion;

to come off the hinges, sortir de ses gonds.—*v.t.* Garnir de gonds.—*v.i.* Tourner (sur).

hinny [ˈhini], *n.* Bardot, *m.* (mule).—*v.i.* Hennir.

hint [hint], *n.* Insinuation, allusion, *f.*, mots couverts, *m.pl.*; (*fig.*) soupçon, *m.*; conseils, *m.pl.* *Broad hint*, allusion évidente, *f.*; *he understood the hint*, il comprit à demi-mot; *to drop a hint*, donner à entendre (que); *to take the hint*, comprendre à demi-mot.—*v.i.* Donner à entendre (à), insinuer, suggérer; faire allusion (à), indiquer.

hinterland [ˈhintəlænd], *n.* Arrière-pays, hinterland, *m.*

hip [hip], *n.* Hanche, *f.*; fruit de l'églantine, *m.* *To smite hip and thigh*, détruire complètement, anéantir.—*v.t.* Déhancher; (*fig.*) attrister.

hip-bath, *n.* Bain de siège, *m.* **hip-bone**, *n.* Os iliaque, *m.* **hip-joint**, *n.* Articulation coxale, *f.* **hip-roof**, *n.* Croupe, *f.*

hippic [ˈhipik], *a.* Hippique.

hippocampus [hipoˈkæmpəs], *n.* Hippocampe, *m.* **hippocras**, *n.* Hypocras, *m.*

Hippocrates [hiˈpɔkrətiːz]. Hippocrate, *m.*

hippocratic [hipoˈkrætik], *a.* Hippocratique.

hippodrome [ˈhipodroum], *n.* Hippodrome, *m.*

hippophagist [hiˈpɔfədʒist], *n.* Hippophage, *m.*

hippopotamus [ˈhipouˈpɔtəməs], *n.* (*pl.* **hippopotami** or **-muses**) Hippopotame, *m.*

hire [ˈhaiə], *n.* Louage, prix de louage; salaire, *m.*, gages, *m.pl.* *For hire*, à louer, libre (taxi); *on hire*, de louage.—*v.t.* Louer, prendre à louage; engager, employer; (*fig.*) soudoyer, acheter (to bribe). *To hire oneself out*, se louer. **hire-purchase**, *n.* Vente à tempérament, location-vente, *f.*

hired [ˈhaiəd], *a.* De louage; (*fig.*) mercenaire. **hireling**, *a.* and *n.* Mercenaire, *m.*

hirer [ˈhaiərə], *n.* Personne qui loue, *f.*, loueur, *m.* **hiring**, *n.* Louage, *m.*

hirsute [ˈhəːsjuːt], *a.* Velu, hirsute.

his [hiz], *a.* Son, sa, ses.—*pron.* Le sien, *m.*, la sienne, *f.*, les siens, *m.pl.*, les siennes, *f.pl.* *A friend of his*, un de ses amis; *it is his*, c'est à lui; *those lips of his*, ses lèvres.

Hispanic [hisˈpænik], *a.* Hispanique.

hispid [ˈhispid], *a.* (*Bot.*) Hispide.

hiss [his], *v.i.*, *v.t.* Siffler. *To hiss at a play*, siffler une pièce.—*n.* Sifflement; sifflet, *m.* **hissing**, *n.* Sifflement, *m.*—*a.* Sifflant.

hist! [hist], *int.* Chut! Pst!

histological [histɔˈlɔdʒikəl], *a.* Histologique. **histology** [hisˈtɔlədʒi], *n.* Histologie, *f.*

historian [hisˈtɔːriən], *n.* Historien, *m.*

historic [-ˈtɔrik] or **historical**, *a.* Historique. **historically**, *adv.* Historiquement.

historiographer [-ˈɔgrəfə], *n.* Historiographe, *m.*

history [ˈhistəri], *n.* Histoire, *f.*

histrion [ˈhistriən], *n.* Comédien; *histrion, *m.*

histrionic [histriˈɔnik] or **histrionical**, *a.* Histrionique, d'histrion. **histrionically**, *adv.* En histrion. **histrionics**, *n.pl.* Cabotinage, *m.*

hit [hit], *v.t.* (*past* and *p.p.* **hit**) Frapper, heurter; atteindre (a mark); donner (a blow); toucher. *Hit or miss*, vaille que vaille; *to hit back*, rendre coup pour coup; *to hit it off well together*, s'accorder bien; *to hit the nail on the head*, mettre le doigt dessus; *to hit* upon, trouver, tomber sur, se heurter contre; *you have hit him*, (*fig.*) vous avez touché la corde, vous l'avez piqué au vif; *you have hit it*, (*fig.*) vous y êtes, vous avez mis le doigt dessus.—*v.i.* Frapper, heurter (contre).—*n.* Coup, coup au but, *m.*; chance, trouvaille; (*fig.*) idée, invention, *f.*; (*Theat.*) succès, *m.* *Happy hit*, remarque à propos, *f.*; *lucky hit*, coup heureux, *m.*; *to make* or *be a hit*, réussir.

hit-and-run, *a.* *Hit-and-run driver*, chauffard, *m.*

hitch [hitʃ], *v.i.* S'accrocher; clocher, sauter à cloche-pied; s'entretailler, se coupler (of horses).—*v.t.* Accrocher, attacher; (*Naut.*) nouer, amarrer. (*pop.*) *To be hitched up*, être marié.—*n.* Accroc, obstacle, *m.*; anicroche, entrave, *f.*; empêchement; (*Naut.*) nœud, *m.* *Clove-hitch*, deux demi-clefs, *f.pl.*; *half-hitch*, demi-clef, *f.*; *technical hitch*, (*Rad. etc.*) incident technique, *m.*; *there's a hitch somewhere*, il y a quelque chose qui cloche; *without a hitch*, sans accroc.

hitch-hike, *v.i.* Faire de l'auto-stop. **hitch-hiker**, *n.* Auto-stoppeur. **hitch-hiking**, *n.* Auto-stop, *m.*

hither [ˈhiðə], *adv.* Ici. *Hither and thither*, çà et là.—*a.* Le plus rapproché. **hithermost**, *a.* Le plus proche. **hitherto**, *adv.* Jusqu'ici. **hitherward** or **hitherwards**, *adv.* De ce côté, par-ci.

Hitlerism [ˈhitlərizm], *n.* Hitlérisme, *m.*

hitter [ˈhitə], *n.* Frappeur, cogneur, *m.*

hive [haiv], *n.* Ruche, *f.*; (*fig.*) essaim (swarm), *m.*—*v.t.* Mettre dans une ruche.—*v.i.* Vivre ensemble. *To hive off*, essaimer.

hives [haivz], *n.* Varicelle pustuleuse, *f.*

ho! or **hoa!** [hou], *int.* Hé! ho! (to express surprise, to call attention, to stop (horses)). (*Naut.*) *Westward ho!* En route pour l'Ouest! *Land ho!* Terre! Terre en vue!

hoar [hɔː], *a.* Blanc; (*fig.*) blanchi, gris. **hoar-frost**, *n.* Gelée blanche, *f.*, givre, (*Lit.*) frimas, *m.*

hoard [hɔːd], *n.* Monceau, amas (secret); magot, trésor, *m.*—*v.t.* Amasser, accumuler, entasser.—*v.i.* Thésauriser, amasser. **hoarder**, *n.* Thésauriseur, accapareur, *m.* **hoarding**, *n.* Accumulation; clôture en planches, *f.*, panneau-réclame, *m.*, (screen of boards) palissade, *f.*

hoariness [ˈhɔːrinis], *n.* Blancheur; vieillesse, *f.*

hoarse [hɔːs], *a.* Enroué, rauque. *Hoarse throat*, enrouement, *m.*; *to get hoarse*, s'enrouer. **hoarsely**, *adv.* D'une voix enrouée; avec un son rauque. **hoarseness**, *n.* Enrouement, *m.*; son rauque, *m.*

hoary [ˈhɔːri], *a.* Blanc; blanchi, chenu, aux cheveux gris *or* blancs; vénérable. **hoary-headed**, *a.* Aux cheveux gris.

hoax [houks], *n.* Mystification, mauvaise plaisanterie, attrape, *f.*; mauvais tour (trick); canard (false news), *m.*—*v.t.* Mystifier, attraper. **hoaxer**, *n.* Mystificateur, *m.*

hob [hɔb], *n.* Plaque (of a fire-grate), *f.*; rustre, manant (peasant); (*Myth.*) lutin, *m.*

hobble [ˈhɔbl], *v.i.* Clocher, clopiner; aller clopin clopant.—*v.t.* Entraver; (*fig.*) mettre dans l'embarras.—*n.* Clochement, *m.*, difficulté, *f.*, embarras, *m.*; entrave, *f.* *To get into a hobble*, se mettre dans le pétrin. **hobble-skirt**, *n.* Jupe fourreau, *f.*

hobbledehoy [hɔbldi'hɔi], *n.* Grand dadais, *m.*
hobby ['hɔbi], *n.* *Bidet; (*fig.*) dada, *m.*,
marotte (favourite pursuit), distraction, *f.*;
hobereau (bird), *m.* **hobby-horse,** *n.* Cheval
de bois, dada, *m.*; marotte (favourite pursuit),
f. (*fig.*) *To ride one's pet hobby-horse,* enfourcher son dada.
hobgoblin [hɔb'gɔblin], *n.* Lutin, *m.*
hobnail ['hɔbneil], *n.* Clou à grosse tête, *m.*,
caboche, *f.*; (*fig.*) rustre, manant, *m.* **hob-**
nailed, *a.* Garni de clous à grosse tête,
ferré.
hobnob ['hɔbnɔb], *v.i.* Trinquer ensemble,
choquer le verre (avec). *To hobnob with,* être
de pair à compagnon avec.
hobo ['houbou], *n.* (*Am.*) Chemineau, *m.*
Hobson's choice [CHOICE].
hock [hɔk], *n.* Jarret (of a horse); vin du Rhin
(wine), *m.*; (*pop.*) gage, *m.* (*pop.*) *In hock,*
au clou.
hockey ['hɔki], *n.* Hockey, *m.* **hockey-stick,**
n. Crosse de hockey, *f.*
hocus ['houkəs], *v.t.* Attraper, filouter, duper.
—*n.* Narcotique, *m.*; boisson soporifique, *f.*
hocus-pocus, *n.* Tour de passe-passe, *m.*,
filouterie, *f.*—*v.i.* Faire des tours de passe-
passe.—*v.t.* Mystifier.
hod [hɔd], *n.* Oiseau, *m.*, auge, *f.* (de maçon);
seau à charbon, *m.*
Hodge [hɔdʒ] (*corrupt. of* Roger). *Friend
Hodge,* Jacques Bonhomme.
hodman ['hɔdmən], *n.* (*pl.* **hodmen**) Aide-
maçon, *m.*
hodometer [hɔ'dɔmitə], *n.* Odomètre, *m.*
hoe [hou], *n.* Houe, binette, *f.* *Dutch hoe,*
sarcleur, *m.*—*v.t.*, *v.i.* Houer; biner, sarcler.
hoeing, *n.* Sarclage, *m.*
hog [hɔg], *n.* Cochon; goret; (*Comm.*) porc,
pourceau, *m.*; (*fam.*) glouton, *m.* *To go the
whole hog,* aller jusqu'au bout.—*v.t.* (*Naut.*)
Goreter; (*pop.*) saisir avidement, garder pour
soi.—*v.i.* S'arquer. **hog-back,** *n.* Dos d'âne,
m. **hoggish,** *a.* De cochon; grossier. **hog-**
gishly, *adv.* En cochon; grossièrement.
hoggishness, *n.* Cochonnerie; gloutonnerie,
grossièreté, *f.* **hog-wash,** *n.* Eaux grasses,
f.pl., lavasse, *f.*
Hogmanay [hɔgmə'nei], *n.* (*Sc.*) La Saint-
Sylvestre (New Year's Eve).
hogshead ['hɔgzhed], *n.* Muid, *m.*; barrique
(cask), *f.*, de 240 litres.
hoick, hoik ['hɔik], *v.t.* Arracher d'un coup
sec; (*Av.*) redresser, cabrer (an aeroplane).
hoicks, *int.* [YOICKS].
hoiden [HOYDEN].
hoist [hɔist], *v.t.* Hisser; guinder (with a
winch); lever; arborer (a flag). *Hoist with
one's own petard,* pris à son propre piège.—*n.*
Grue, *f.*, treuil, palan, *m.* **hoisting,** *n.*
Levage, hissage, guindage, *m.*
hoity-toity ['hɔiti'tɔiti], *int.* Allons donc!
Tatata!—*a.* Écervelé; susceptible; qui se
donne des airs.
hokum ['houkəm], *n.* Boniments, *m.pl.*; drame
et jeu sans valeur, *m.*
hold [hould], *n.* Prise, *f.*; appui, soutien
(support), *m.*; garde (custody); place forte
(fortress); (*fig.*) habitation, demeure, *f.*;
(*Naut.*) cale, *f.*; (*Mus.*) point d'orgue, *m.* *To
get* or *take hold of,* prendre, saisir, s'accrocher à, s'emparer de, trouver, découvrir; *to
have a hold on,* avoir prise sur; *to keep hold

of, retenir, ne pas abandonner; *to let go one's
hold,* lâcher prise.—*v.t.* (*past and p.p.* **held**)
Tenir, retenir; arrêter; détenir; garder, maintenir; occuper, avoir; contenir (to contain);
tenir pour, regarder comme; célébrer. *Hold!
tenez! arrêtez! hold the line,* (*Teleph.*) ne
quittez pas; *to hold a bet,* parier; *to hold a
conversation with . . . .,* s'entretenir avec . . .;
to hold back, retenir, cacher, ne pas produire;
to hold down, retenir, baisser; *to hold fast,*
tenir ferme, tenir bon; *to hold forth,* tendre,
avancer, offrir, promettre; *to hold in,* retenir;
to hold in place, tenir en place; *to hold off,*
tenir à distance; *to hold one's breath,* retenir
son haleine; *to hold oneself,* se tenir, se
regarder (comme); *to hold oneself in,* se contenir, se retenir; *to hold one's own,* se maintenir, tenir pied, tenir tête (à); *to hold one's
tongue* or *one's peace,* se taire; *to hold out,*
tendre, offrir, promettre; *to hold over,*
remettre, ajourner; *to hold the enemy,* immobiliser l'ennemi; *to hold together,* tenir
ensemble; *to hold up,* lever, soulever, soutenir, maintenir; cesser, arrêter, retarder.—*v.i.*
Tenir; se maintenir, durer; supporter, endurer; s'attacher, adhérer (à); rester,
demeurer; s'arrêter; être vrai, se trouver
vrai. *Hold hard,* arrêtez! halte-là! *hold on,*
arrêtez! (*Teleph.*) ne quittez pas! *hold tight!*
Tenez-vous bien! Ne lâchez pas! *to hold
aloof,* se tenir à l'écart; *to hold back,* se tenir en
arrière, hésiter; *to hold fast,* tenir ferme, tenir
bon, s'accrocher; *to hold forth,* haranguer,
pérorer; *to hold good,* être vrai, ne pas se
démentir, être valable; *to hold on,* s'accrocher
à; tenir bon, persévérer, poursuivre; *to hold
out,* tenir bon, tenir tête (à); durer; *to hold up,*
se soutenir, cesser (of the rain), s'éclaircir (of
the weather); *to hold with,* prendre parti pour,
être du parti de.
hold-all, *n.* Enveloppe de voyage, *f.* **holder,**
n. Personne qui tient, *f.*; (*spt.*) tenant, *m.*,
locataire, tenancier, *m.*; poignée, anse,
manche, *f.*, porte-; (*Fin.*) porteur, possesseur, titulaire, *m.* **holdfast,** *n.* Crampon;
(*Tech.*) valet, *m.* **holding,** *n.* Possession,
tenure, *f.*; terre affermée, ferme, *f.* **hold-up,**
n. Arrêt de la circulation, *m.*; panne, *f.*;
hold-up, *m.*
hole [houl], *n.* Trou; antre, *m.*, caverne, *f.*;
orifice, *m.*, ouverture, *f.* *A dead and alive
hole,* un trou perdu; *a large hole in the profits,*
une grande brèche dans les profits; *full of
holes,* plein de trous; *rabbit hole,* terrier de
lapin, *m.*; *to be put in a hole,* être dans une
impasse; *to make a hole in a pie,* faire une
brèche à un pâté; *with a hole in it,* troué.—*v.t.*
Trouer, pratiquer un trou dans; (*Billiards*)
blouser, bloquer; (*Golf.*) envoyer dans le
trou. **hole-and-corner,** *a.* Secret, clandestin.
holiday ['hɔlidei], *n.* Fête, *f.*, jour de fête, jour
férié, *m.*; (*sch.* etc.) congé, jour de congé, *m.*,
(*pl.*) vacances, *f.pl.* *Bank-holiday,* fête légale;
holidays with pay, congé payé; *to be on holiday,* être en congé, en vacance(s).—*a.* De
fête, de congé; de vacances. **holiday-**
maker, *n.* Fêteur, excursionniste, villégia-
teur, *m.*
holily ['houlili], *adv.* Saintement. **holiness,**
n. Sainteté, *f.* *His Holiness,* Sa Sainteté (the
Pope).

Holland ['hɔlənd]. La Hollande, *f.*
holland ['hɔlənd], *n.* Toile de Hollande, *f.* *Brown holland*, toile écrue, *f.* **hollands,** *n.* Genièvre de Hollande, *m.*
hollo or **holloa,** etc. [HALLO].
hollow ['hɔlou], *a.* Creux; vide; sourd (of sound); (*fig.*) faux, perfide, trompeur. *He was beaten hollow*, il fut battu à plate couture. —*n.* Creux, *m.*, cavité, anfractuosité, *f.*; basfond, *m.*—*v.t.* Creuser, évider. **holloweyed,** *a.* Aux yeux creux. **hollow-ground,** *a.* Évidé (of razors). **hollow-hearted,** *a.* Faux, dissimulé, trompeur. **hollowness,** *n.* Creux, *m.*; (*fig.*) faussété, perfidie, *f.*
holly ['hɔli], *n.* Houx, *m.* **holly-grove,** *n.* Houssaie, *f.* **hollyhock,** *n.* Rose trémière, passe-rose, *f.*
holm [houm], *n.* Îlot, *m.*; yeuse (tree), *f.* **holm-oak,** *n.* Yeuse, *f.*
holocaust ['hɔlokɔːst], *n.* Holocauste, *m.*
holograph ['hɔlogræf], *n.* Document *or* testament olographe, *m.*
holothurian [hɔlo'θjuəriən], *n.* Holothurie, *f.*
holster ['houlstə], *n.* Fonte; sacoche, *f.*; étui, *m.* (de revolver).
holus-bolus ['houləs'bouləs], *adv.* D'un coup, d'un trait.
holy ['houli], *a.* Saint, sacré; bénit. *Holy alliance*, sainte-alliance, *f.*; *Holy Ghost*, le Saint-Esprit; *Holy Land*, Terre Sainte, *f.*; *holy water*, eau bénite, *f.*; *Holy Week*, la semaine sainte, *f.*; *holy writ*, les saintes écritures, *f.pl.*—*n.* *The Holy of Holies*, le saint des saints, *m.*
homage ['hɔmidʒ], *n.* Hommage, *m.*
home [houm], *n.* Foyer domestique, chez-soi; logis, *m.*, maison, *f.*, intérieur, *m.*; (*fig.*) demeure, *f.*, asile; pays, *m.*, patrie (native land), *f.* *At home*, chez soi, à la maison; *at home day*, jour de réception, *m.*; *away from home*, absent, en voyage; *from home*, sorti, absent; *Home Fleet*, la flotte métropolitaine, *f.*; *Home Office*, Ministère de l'Intérieur, *m.*; *home rule*, autonomie, indépendance législative, *f.*; *the ideal home exhibition*, l'exposition des arts ménagers, *f.*; *there is no place like home*, il n'y a pas de petit chez-soi; *to be back home*, être de retour; *to come home*, rentrer, revenir chez soi, retourner dans son pays; *to feel oneself at home*, se sentir à son aise; *to have a home of one's own*, avoir un chez-soi; *to make oneself at home*, se mettre à son aise, faire comme chez soi, ne pas se gêner.—*a.* De la maison, domestique; indigène, de l'intérieur; (*fig.*) direct, qui porte coup.—*adv.* Chez soi, au logis, à la maison; dans son pays; (*fig.*) directement, droit au but. *To bring home to*, faire admettre à; *to come home to*, toucher au vif; *to strike home*, porter (coup).—*v.i.* Revenir au colombier (of pigeon). *Homing pigeon*, pigeon voyageur, *m.*
home-brewed, *a.* (Bière) brassée à la maison.
home-coming, *n.* Retour au foyer, *m.*
home-grown, *a.* Indigène; du crû (of wines). **homeland,** *n.* Patrie, *f.*; pays natal, *m.* **home-made,** *a.* Fait à la maison. *Homemade bread*, pain de ménage, *m.* **home-sick,** *a.* Qui a le mal du pays, nostalgique. **homesickness,** *n.* Mal du pays, *m.*, nostalgie, *f.* **homespun,** *a.* Fait à la maison, de ménage; (*fig.*) sans façon, simple, rustique. **homestead,** *n.* Manoir, *m.*, ferme, *f.*

homeliness, *n.* Caractère domestique, *m.*; simplicité; rusticité, *f.* **homely,** *a.* Du ménage; simple, sans façon; (*Am.*) dépourvu de beauté, laid.
Homer ['houmə]. Homère, *m.*
homeward or **homewards,** *adv.* Vers la maison; vers son pays, de retour. **homeward-bound,** *a.* (*Naut.*) Retournant au port; retournant au pays.
homework, *n.* Devoirs, *m.pl.*
homicidal [hɔmi'saidl], *a.* Homicide, meurtrier. **homicide,** *n.* Homicide, *m.* *Justifiable homicide*, homicide par légitime défense, *m.*
homily ['hɔmili], *n.* Homélie, *f.*
homocentric [hɔmo'sentrik], *a.* Homocentrique.
homoeopath ['houmiopæθ], *n.* Homéopathe, *m.* **homoeopathic** [-'pæθik], *a.* Homéopathique. **homoeopathy,** *n.* Homéopathie, *f.*
homogeneity [hɔmədʒi'niːiti] or **homogeneousness,** *n.* Homogénéité, *f.* **homogeneous** [hɔmə'dʒiːniəs] or **homogeneal,** *a.* Homogène.
homologate [ho'mɔləgeit], *v.t.* Homologuer. **homologation** [homɔlə'geiʃən], *n.* Homologation, *f.* **homologous** [-'mɔləgəs], *a.* Homologue.
homonym ['hɔmənim], *n.* Homonyme, *m.* **homonymous** [ho'mɔniməs], *a.* Homonyme. **homonymy** [ho'mɔnimi], *n.* Homonymie, *f.*
homosexual [hɔmo'seksjuəl], *a.* and *n.* Homosexuel.
hone [houn], *n.* Pierre à rasoir, pierre à repasser, *f.*—*v.t.* Repasser.
honest ['ɔnist], *a.* Honnête, loyal, probe, de bonne foi, sincère. *Honest man*, homme de bien, honnête homme, *m.*; *the honest truth*, la pure vérité. **honestly,** *adv.* Honnêtement, avec probité, de bonne foi, sincèrement. **honesty,** *n.* Honnêteté, probité, bonne foi, sincérité, loyauté; (*fig.*) chasteté, vertu; (*Bot.*) lunaire, monnaie du pape, *f.*
honey ['hʌni], *n.* Miel, *m.*; (*fig.*) chérie, *f.*, ange, *m.*—*v.t.* Mettre du miel dans, sucrer avec du miel. **honey-bag,** *n.* Sac à miel, *m.* **honey-bee,** *n.* Abeille, mouche à miel, *f.* **honey-buzzard,** *n.* (Buse) bondrée, *f.* **honeycomb,** *n.* Rayon de miel, *m.* *Honeycomb towel*, serviette nid d'abeilles, *f.* **honeycombed,** *a.* Alvéolé, percé de trous. **honeydew,** *n.* Miellée, *f.* **honeymoon,** *n.* Lune de miel, *f.*, voyage de noces, *m.* **honeymooner,** *n.* Nouveau marié. **honeymouthed,** *a.* Doucereux, mielleux. **honeysuckle,** *n.* Chèvrefeuille, *m.*
honeyed, *a.* Emmiellé; doux, miellé, mielleux.
honk [hɔŋk], *n.* (*Motor.*) Cornement, *m.*—*v.i.* (*Motor.*) Corner.
honorarium [ɔnə'rɛəriəm], *n.* Honoraires, *m.pl.*
honorary ['ɔnərəri], *a.* Honoraire.
honorific [ɔnə'rifik], *a.* Honorifique.
honour ['ɔnə], *n.* Honneur, *m.*; (*fig.*) dignité, estime, *f. Honour to whom honour is due*, à tout seigneur tout honneur; *in honour of*, en l'honneur de, à la gloire de; *on one's honour*, sur l'honneur, foi d'homme d'honneur; *seat of honour*, la place d'honneur, *f.*; *there is honour among thieves*, les loups ne se mangent pas entre eux; *word of honour*, parole

d'honneur, *f.*—*v.t.* Honorer (de); faire honneur à, faire bon accueil à (a bill). **honourable**, *a.* Honorable, d'honneur. *The Right Honourable*, le très honorable. **honourableness**, *n.* Caractère honorable, honneur, *m.* **honourably**, *adv.* Honorablement. **honoured**, *a.* Honoré. **honourer**, *n.* Personne qui honore, *f.*

hooch [huːtʃ], *n.* (*Am.*) Gnole, *f.*; boissons fortes, *f.pl.*

hood [hud], *n.* Capuchon, *m.*; capuche, capeline, *f.* (for women); chaperon, *m.*, coiffe, *f.*; capote, *f.* (of vehicles); capot, *m.* (of boats); épitòge, *f.* (on acad. gown).—*v.t.* Encapuchonner; couvrir; chaperonner (hawk). **hoodwink**, *v.t.* Bander les yeux à; (*fig.*) en imposer à, tromper.

hoodlum ['huːdləm], *n.* Chenapan, voyou, *m.*

hoodoo ['huːduː], *n.* Vaudou; porteur de malheur; malheur, *m.*

hoof [huːf *or* huf], *n.* Sabot, *m.* *To pad the hoof*, (*slang*) battre le pavé.—*v.t.* *To hoof it*, (*fam.*) aller à pied. **hoof-bound**, *a.* (*Vet.*) Encastelé. **hoofed**, *a.* À sabot, ongulé. **hoof-mark**, *n.* Trace de sabot, *f.*

hook [huk], *n.* Crochet, croc; hameçon (for fishing), *m.*, amorce; faucille (sickle), *f.* *By hook or by crook*, d'une manière ou d'une autre, coûte que coûte; *he's fallen for her, hook, line and sinker*, il est vraiment mordu; *hook and eye*, agrafe et porte, *f.*; (*Box.*) *left hook*, crochet du gauche, *m.*; *on his own hook*, (*slang*) pour son propre compte; *to sling one's hook*, (*fam.*) décamper.—*v.t.* Accrocher; agrafer; courber; prendre à l'hameçon, attraper. *To hook it*, (*slang*) filer, déguerpir; (*Golf*) *to hook the ball*, faire un coup tiré.

hookah ['hukə], *n.* Narghileh, *m.*

hooked [hukt], *a.* Crochu, recourbé; aquilin (of the nose).

hookedness ['hukidnis], *n.* Forme crochue, *f.*

hooker, *n.* (*Naut.*) Hourque, *f.*; (*Rugby*) talonneur, *m.*

hook-nose, *n.* Nez aquilin, *m.* **hook-nosed**, *a.* Au nez aquilin.

hookworm ['hukwəːm], *n.* Ankylostome, *m.*

hooligan ['huːligən], *n.* Voyou, *m.* **hooliganism**, *n.* Voyouterie, *f.*

hoop [huːp], *n.* Cercle; cerceau, *m.*; huppe (of birds); jante (of a wheel), *f.*; panier (of dress), *m.*; (*Croquet*) arceau, *m.*; [WHOOP]. *To bowl a hoop*, conduire un cerceau.—*v.t.* Cercler; garnir (a wheel) de jantes; (*fig.*) entourer.

hooper, *n.* Tonnelier, *m.*

hooping-cough [WHOOP].

hoop-iron, *n.* Feuillard, *m.*

hoop-la, *n.* Jeu des anneaux, *m.*

hoopoe ['huːpou], *n.* (*Orn.*) Huppe, *f.*

Hoosier ['huːziə], *n.* Habitant de l'Indiana, *m.*

hoot [huːt], *v.i.* Huer; (*Motor.*) klaxonner.—*v.t.* Huer, poursuivre de huées; siffler (a play). *To hoot at*, huer.—*n.* *or* **hooting**, *n.* Huée, vocifération, *f.*, huées, *f.pl.* **hooter**, *n.* (*colloq.*) Sirène d'usine *or* d'une automobile, *f.*, klaxon, *m.*

hop [hɔp], *n.* Saut, sautillement; houblon (plant), *m.*; bal populaire, *m.* *Caught on the hop*, pris au pied levé; *Hop o' my Thumb*, le Petit Poucet; *hop, skip* (or *step*) *and jump*, triple saut, *m.*—*v.i.* Sauter, sautiller; (*fig.*) danser. (*pop.*) *To hop it*, ficher le camp; *to hop on one leg*, sauter à cloche-pied.

hop-bine, *n.* Sarment de houblon, *m.* **hopgarden** *or* **hop-field**, *n.* Houblonnière, *f.* **hop-picking**, *n.* Cueillette du houblon, *f.* **hop-pole**, *m.* Échalas, *m.* **hopscotch**, *n.* Marelle, *f.*

hope [houp], *n.* Espérance, *f.*, espoir, *m.*, attente, *f.* *Cape of Good Hope*, le cap de Bonne Espérance; *forlorn hope* [FORLORN]; *in the hope of*, dans l'attente que; *it is his last hope*, c'est sa planche de salut; *to pin or set one's hopes on doing something*, nourrir l'espoir de faire quelque chose.—*v.t.* Espérer, s'attendre à.—*v.i.* Espérer. *I do hope*, j'espère bien; *I hope that*, j'aime à croire que; *I hope to see him*, j'espère le voir; *to hope against hope*, espérer contre toute espérance; *we must hope for the best*, il ne faut pas désespérer.

hopeful, *a.* Plein d'espérance; qui promet beaucoup; encourageant. *To be hopeful that*, avoir bon espoir que.—*n.* (*iron.*) *The young hopeful*, l'espoir de la famille, *m.* **hopefully**, *adv.* Avec espoir, avec confiance. **hopefulness**, *n.* Bon espoir, *m.*, confiance, *f.*

hopeless, *a.* (Effort) vain, impuissant; (excuse) non valable; (difficulté) inextricable; (douleur) inconsolable; (mal) irrémédiable, incurable; (négociation) inutile, sans issue possible; (personne) perdue, incorrigible, décourageante; (situation) désespérée. **hopelessly**, *adv.* Sans espoir. *Hopelessly in love*, amoureux sans retour. **hopelessness**, *n.* Désespoir, état désespéré, *m.*

hopper, *n.* Sauteur, *m.*, personne qui sautille; trémie (of a mill), *f.*; (*Agric.*) semoir, *m.*

hopping, *n.* Action de sauter à cloche-pied; cueillette du houblon, *f.*

horal ['hɔːrəl] *or* **horary**, *a.* Horaire.

horde [hɔːd], *n.* Horde, *f.*

horehound ['hɔːhaund], *n.* Marrube, *m.*

horizon [hə'raizən], *n.* Horizon, *m.* *On the horizon*, à l'horizon.

horizontal [hɔri'zɔntl], *a.* Horizontal. **horizontally**, *adv.* Horizontalement.

hormone ['hɔːmoun], *n.* Hormone, *f.*

horn [hɔːn], *n.* Corne, *f.*; bois (of a stag), *m.*; coupe (cup); (*Ent.*) antenne, *f.*; (*Mus.*) cor, cornet, *m.*; *French horn*, cor d'harmonie, *m.*; *hunting horn*, cor de chasse, *m.*; *horn of plenty*, corne d'abondance, *f.*; *to blow the horn*, sonner du cor, (*Motor.*) corner; *to draw in one's horns*, rentrer ses cornes, réprimer son ardeur; *to shed its horns* (of a stag), muer.—*a.* De corne. **hornbeam**, *n.* Charme (tree), *m.* **horn-beetle**, *n.* Cerf-volant, *m.* **hornbill**, *n.* (*Orn.*) Calao, *m.* **horn-blower**, *n.* Sonneur (de trompe), *m.* ***hornbook**, *n.* Abécédaire, *m.* **horn-fish**, *n.* Orphie, *f.* **hornpipe**, *n.* Cornemuse; danse des matelots, *f.* **hornwork**, *n.* (*Fort.*) Ouvrage à corne, *m.*

horned, *a.* Cornu, à cornes. **horned-owl**, *n.* Duc, *m.* **horny**, *a.* De corne; calleux, comme la corne.

hornet ['hɔːnit], *n.* Frelon, *m.* *To bring a hornets' nest about one's ears*, tomber dans un guêpier.

horography [hə'rɔgrəfi], *n.* Horographie, *f.*

horological [hɔrə'lɔdʒikəl], *a.* D'horloge, d'horlogerie.

horology [hə'rɔlədʒi], *n.* Horlogerie, *f.*

horoscope ['hɔrəskoup], *n.* Horoscope, *m.*

horrent ['hɔrənt], *a.* (*Poet.*) Hérissé.

horrible ['hɔribl], *a.* Horrible, affreux, atroce. **horribleness,** *n.* Caractère affreux, *m.*, horreur, *f.* **horribly,** *adv.* Horriblement, affreusement.

horrid ['hɔrid], *a.* Affreux, horrible. **horridly,** *adv.* Affreusement. **horridness,** *n.* Horreur, *f.*, caractère horrible, *m.* **horrific,** *a.* Horrifique. **horrify,** *v.t.* Horrifier, faire horreur à.

horripilation [hɔripi'leiʃən], *n.* (*Med.*) Horripilation, *f.*

horror ['hɔrə], *n.* Horreur, *f.* *I have a horror of hypocrites,* j'ai toujours en horreur les hypocrites. **horror-stricken** or **horror-struck,** *a.* Frappé d'horreur.

horse [hɔːs], *n.* Cheval, *m.*, chevaux, *m.pl.*; (*Mil.*) cavalerie, *f.*; (*Tech.*) chevalet, séchoir, *m.*; (*Naut.*) marche-pied, *m. Change of horses,* relais, *m.*; *it is a good horse that never stumbles,* il n'est si bon cheval qui ne bronche; *led horse,* cheval de main, *m.*; *master of the horse,* grand écuyer, *m.*; *spare* or *extra horse,* cheval de rechange, *m.*; *that's a horse of another colour,* c'est une autre paire de manches; *to flog a dead horse,* chercher à ressusciter un mort; *to get on horseback,* monter en selle; *to put the cart before the horse,* mettre la charrue devant les bœufs; *to ride on horseback,* aller à cheval; *to ride the high horse, to get on one's high horse,* monter sur ses grands chevaux; *to send a horse to grass,* mettre un cheval au vert; *to take horse,* monter à cheval; *towel-horse,* porte-serviettes, *m.*; *vaulting horse,* cheval d'arçons, *m.*; *white horses,* (*Naut.*) moutons, *m.pl.*; *wild horses wouldn't make me do that,* rien au monde ne me ferait faire cela.—*v.t.* Mettre sur un cheval; fournir un cheval *or* des chevaux à.

horse-artillery, *n.* Artillerie à cheval, *f.* **horseback,** *n.* Dos de cheval, *m. On horseback,* à cheval. **horse-bean,** *n.* Féverole, *f.* **horse-blanket** or **horse-rug,** *n.* Couverture de cheval, *f.* **horseblock,** *n.* Montoir, *m.* **horse-box,** *n.* Wagon-écurie, *m.*; fourgon pour le transport des chevaux, *m.* **horse-boy,** *n.* Garçon d'écurie, *m.* **horse-breaker,** *n.* Dresseur de chevaux, *m.* **horse-chestnut,** *n.* Marron d'Inde; marronnier d'Inde (tree), *m.* **horse-cloth,** *n.* Housse, *f.* **horse-dealer** or **horse-coper,** *n.* Marchand de chevaux, maquignon, *m.* **horse-doctor,** *n.* Vétérinaire, *m.* **horse-drawn,** *a.* Attelé; à traction chevaline. **horse-fair,** *n.* Foire aux chevaux, *f.* **horse-flesh,** *n.* Viande de cheval, *f.* **horse-fly,** *n.* Taon, *m.* **Horse Guards,** *n.pl.* (*England*) Gardes à cheval, *m.pl.*; garde du corps, *f.* **horsehair,** *n.* Crin de cheval, crin, *m.* **horse-laugh,** *n.* Gros rire, rire bruyant, *m.* **horse-leech,** *n.* Grosse sangsue, *f.*; (*fig.*) vétérinaire, *m.* **horse-mackerel,** *n.* Maquereau bâtard, saurel, *m.* **horseman,** *n.* (*pl.* **horsemen**) Cavalier; écuyer, *m. To be a good horseman,* être bon écuyer. **horsemanship,** *n.* Équitation, *f.*; manège, *m.* **horse-pistol,** *n.* Pistolet d'arçon, *m.* **horse-play,** *n.* Jeu de mains, *m.* **horse-pond,** *n.* Abreuvoir, *m.* **horse-power,** *n.* Cheval-vapeur, *m. A ten horse-power car,* (*fam.*) une dix chevaux. **horse-race,** *n.* Course de chevaux, *f.* **horse-radish,** *n.* Raifort, *m.* **horseshoe,** *n.* Fer de cheval; fer à cheval, *m.*; (*pl.*) ferrure, *f.*—*a.* En fer à

cheval. **horseshoeing,** *n.* Ferrage des chevaux, *m.* **horse-show,** *n.* Exposition de chevaux, *f.*, concours hippique, *m.* **horse-soldier,** *n.* Cavalier, *m.* **horse-tail,** *n.* Queue-de-cheval, *f.* **horsewhip,** *n.* Cravache (riding-whip), *f.*—*v.t.* Cravacher. **horse-woman,** *n.* Cavalière, écuyère, *f.*

horsy ['hɔːsi], *a.* (*fam.*) Hippomane.

hortatory ['hɔːtətəri], *a.* Exhortatoire, d'exhortation.

horticultural [hɔːti'kʌltʃərəl], *a.* D'horticulture, horticole, horticultural.

horticulture ['hɔːtikʌltʃə], *n.* Horticulture, *f.* **horticulturist** [-'kʌltʃərist], *n.* Horticulteur, *m.*

hose [houz], *n.* Bas, *m.pl.*; tuyau d'arrosage, boyau (pipe), *m.*; (*Naut.*) manche à eau, *f.*

hosier ['houʒə], *n.* Bonnetier (et chemisier), *m.* **hosiery,** *n.* Bonneterie, *f.*

hospice ['hɔspis], *n.* Hospice, *m.*

hospitable ['hɔspitəbl], *a.* Hospitalier. **hospitably,** *adv.* Avec hospitalité.

hospital, *n.* Hôpital, *m.*, infirmerie, *f.*; hospice, *m. Hospital attendant,* infirmier, *m.*; *hospital nurse,* infirmière, *f.*; *hospital ship,* vaisseau-hôpital, *m.*; *hospital train,* train sanitaire, *m.*

hospitality [hɔspi'tæliti], *n.* Hospitalité, *f.*

host [houst], *n.* Hôte; hôtelier, aubergiste, *m.*; armée, foule, multitude; (*R.-C. Ch.*) hostie, *f. He who reckons without his host must reckon twice,* qui compte sans son hôte à deux fois à compter.

hostage ['hɔstidʒ], *n.* Otage, *m.*

hostel ['hɔstəl], *n.* Hôtel or foyer pour les étudiants etc., *m. Youth hostel,* auberge de la jeunesse, *f.* **hostelry,** *n.* Auberge, hôtellerie, *f.*

hostess ['houstis or 'houstes], *n.* Hôtesse, *f.*

hostile ['hɔstail], *a.* Hostile, ennemi; (*fig.*) opposé, contraire (à). **hostilely,** *adv.* Hostilement, d'une manière hostile.

hostility [hɔs'tiliti], *n.* Hostilité, *f.*

hostler [OSTLER].

hot [hɔt], *a.* Chaud, ardent; bouillant (boiling); brûlant, piquant, épicé (to the taste); (*fig.*) vif, violent, échauffé. *All hot,* tout chaud; *boiling hot,* tout bouillant; *hot as a pepper-corn,* vif comme la poudre; *hot fire,* feu vif; *hot springs,* thermes, *m.pl.*, station thermale, *f.*; *to be burning hot,* brûler, être brûlant; *to be hot* (of persons), avoir chaud, (of weather) faire chaud, (of things) être chaud; *to be hot on the trail,* poursuivre de près; *to grow hot,* s'échauffer; *to make hot,* faire chauffer, réchauffer; *to make it too hot for someone,* rendre la vie intenable à quelqu'un. **hotbed,** *n.* Couche, *f. Hotbed of treason,* foyer de trahison, *m.* **hot-blooded,** *a.* Excitable, ardent, passionné. **hot-headed,** *a.* Violent, fougueux, emporté, impétueux. **hot-house,** *n.* Serre chaude, *f.* **hot-plate,** *n.* Réchaud, *m.* **hot-press,** *v.t.* Presser à chaud; catir (cloth); satiner (paper).

hotchpot ['hɔtʃpɔt], *n.* (*Law*) Ensemble des biens et valeurs composant une succession, *m.*

hotchpotch ['hɔtʃpɔtʃ], *n.* Hochepot, salmigondis, *m.*, macédoine, *f.*

hotel [ho'tel], *n.* Hôtel, *m.* **hotel-keeper,** *n.* Hôtelier, *m.*, hôtelière, *f.*

hotly, *adv.* Avec chaleur, chaudement, vivement; avec acharnement. **hotness,** *n.* Chaleur; (*fig.*) passion, violence, *f.*

hot-water bottle, *n.* Bouillotte, *f.*

hough [hɔk], *n.* Jarret (of animals), *m.—v.t.* Couper les jarrets à.

hound [haund], *n.* Chien de chasse, chien courant, *m. Pack of hounds,* meute, *f. To run with the hare and hunt with the hounds,* ménager la chèvre et le chou.—*v.t.* Chasser au chien courant; (*fig.*) traquer; exciter. **hound-fish,** *n.* Chien de mer, *m.* **hound's-tongue,** *n.* Langue-de-chien (plant), *f.*

hour [ˈauə], *n.* Heure, *f. An hour ago,* il y a une heure; *an hour and a half,* une heure et demie; *a quarter of an hour,* un quart d'heure; *at the eleventh hour,* au dernier moment; *by the hour,* à l'heure; *half an hour,* une demi-heure; *in a lucky hour,* dans un bon moment or un moment heureux; *to keep bad hours,* rentrer tard; *within an hour,* dans une heure. **hour-glass,** *n.* Sablier, *m.* **hour-hand,** *n.* Petite aiguille, *f.*

hourly [ˈauəli], *a.* Continuel, d'heure en heure à l'heure.—*adv.* D'heure en heure.

house (1) [haus], *n.* Maison, *f.,* logis, *m.,* demeure, habitation, *f.*; ménage (household), *m.*; famille (family); (*Parl.*) chambre, *f.*; (*Theat.*) salle, *f. A country-house,* une maison de campagne; *a man's house is his castle,* charbonnier est maître chez soi; *a nobleman's house,* un hôtel; *a religious house,* une maison religieuse, un couvent, un monastère; *at one's house,* chez soi; *house full,* (*Theat.*) salle comble; *house of cards,* château de cartes, *m.*; *on the house* (of drink etc.), aux frais du cafetier; *public house,* café, *m.,* brasserie, *f.*; *the House of Commons,* la Chambre des Communes; *the House of Lords,* la Chambre des Lords; *the Houses of Parliament,* le Parlement, *m.*; (*Theat.*) *to bring the house down,* avoir un succès fou; *to have neither house nor home,* n'avoir ni feu ni lieu; *to keep a good house,* tenir bonne table; *to keep house,* tenir maison; *to keep open house,* tenir table ouverte; *to keep* (*to*) *the house,* garder la maison; *to move house,* déménager; *to set up house,* entrer en ménage.

house (2) [hauz], *v.t.* Loger, recevoir chez soi, héberger; garer (a vehicle); rentrer (corn etc.); faire rentrer (cattle etc.).

house-agent, *n.* Agent de location, *m.* **house-breaker,** *n.* Cambrioleur; démolisseur, *m.* **house-breaking,** *n.* Vol avec effraction, cambriolage, *m.*; démolition, *f.* **house-charge,** *n.* Couvert, *m.* **house-dog,** *n.* Chien de garde, *m.* **house-fly,** *n.* Mouche domestique, *f.* **household,** *n.* Maison, *f.,* ménage, *m.,* famille, *f.—a.* De ménage, domestique. *Household gods,* pénates, dieux domestiques, *m.pl.*; *household goods,* meubles, *m.pl.,* mobilier, *m.*; *household utensils,* ustensiles de ménage, *m.pl.*; *household word,* mot d'usage courant, mot dans toutes les bouches, *m.* **householder,** *n.* Chef de famille, chef de maison, *m.* **housekeeper,** *n.* Femme de charge, ménagère, *f.*; concierge, *m.* or *f.* **housekeeping,** *n.* Ménage, *m.*; économie domestique, *f. To start housekeeping,* entrer en ménage. **house-leek,** *n.* (*Bot.*) Joubarbe, *f.* **housemaid,** *n.* Bonne à tout faire, femme de chambre, *f.* **house-painter,** *n.* Peintre en bâtiments, *m.* **house-party,** *n.* Invités qui passent quelques jours à un château, etc. **house-porter,** *n.* Portier,

concierge, *m.* **house-proud,** *a.* (Trop) fier de son chez-soi. **house-rent,** *n.* Loyer, *m.* **house-room,** *n.* Place, *f.,* logement, *m.* **house-sparrow,** *n.* Moineau, *m.* **house-steward,** *n.* Maître d'hôtel, *m.* **house-surgeon,** *n.* Interne en chirurgie, *m.* **house-top,** *n.* Faîte, toit, *m. To proclaim from the house-tops,* crier par-dessus les toits. **house-warming,** *n.* Pendaison de la crémaillère, *f.*

houseful, *n.* Maisonnée; (*Theat.*) salle comble, *f.*

houseless, *a.* Qui n'a point de demeure; sans asile, sans abri.

housewife (1) [ˈhauswaif], *n.* Ménagère, maîtresse de maison, *f.*

housewife (2) [ˈhʌzif], *n.* Trousse (needlecase), *f.*

housewifery [ˈhauswifri], *n.* Économie domestique, *f.*

housework, *n.* Travaux ménagers, *m.pl. To do the housework,* faire le ménage.

housing [ˈhauziŋ], *n.* Logement, *m.*; rentrée, *f.,* rentrage, *m.*; enchâssure; (*pl.*) housse, *f.* (de cheval); caparaçon, *m.*

hovel [hɔvl or hʌvl], *n.* Appentis, *m.,* bicoque, *f.,* taudis, *m.,* masure, *f.*

hover [ˈhɔvə or ˈhʌvə], *v.i.* Planer; hésiter. *To hover about,* errer, rôder.

how [hau], *adv.* Comment, de quelle façon; combien; comme, que. *How amiable virtue is,* que la vertu est aimable; *how beautiful!* comme or que c'est beau! *how far,* jusqu'où, jusqu'à quel point; *how far have we got with?* où en sommes-nous de? *how heartily,* avec quel zèle; *how I wish I could!* si seulement je pouvais! *how is it that?* comment se fait-il que? *how is that?* comment ça? *how kind you are!* comme or que vous êtes bon! *how large,* de quelle grandeur; *how long have you been here?* depuis quand êtes-vous ici? *how many,* combien; *how much,* combien; *how now!* qu'est-ce donc! *how often?* combien de fois? *how old are you?* quel âge avez-vous? *how very much,* combien, à quel degré; *to know how to do something,* savoir faire quelque chose; *you see how I love you,* vous voyez combien je vous aime.

howbeit [hauˈbiːit], *adv.* Néanmoins, quoi qu'il en soit.

however, *conj.* Cependant, pourtant, du reste, d'ailleurs, toutefois.—*adv.* De quelque manière que; quelque . . . que. *However he may do it,* de quelque manière qu'il le fasse; *however important it may be,* si important qu'il soit; *however little,* si peu que ce soit; *however rich he may be,* quelque riche qu'il soit, tout riche qu'il est; *however that may be,* quoi qu'il en soit; *however wisely,* quelque sagement que.

howitzer [ˈhauitsə], *n.* Obusier, *m.*

howl [haul], *n.* Hurlement, cri; mugissement, *m.—v.i.* Hurler, crier; mugir. *To howl at,* hurler or crier contre or après. **howler,** *n.* Bévue, bourde énorme, *f.* **howling,** *n.* Hurlement; cri; (*fig.*) mugissement, *m.—a.* Hurlant; plein de hurlements; énorme. *A howling success,* un succès fou.

howlet [ˈhaulit], *n.* Hulotte, *f.*

howsoever, *adv.* De quelque manière que.

hoy (1) [hɔi], *n.* (*Naut.*) Heu, vaisseau côtier, *m.*

hoy! (2) [hɔi], *int.* Hé! holà!

hoyden [hɔidn], *n.* Garçon manqué, *m.* (of a girl).—*v.i.* Garçonner, jouer. **hoydenish,** *a.* Garçonnière, *f.*

hub [hʌb], *n.* Moyeu, *m.*; (*fig.*) centre, pivot, *m.* **hub-cap,** *n.* (*Motor.*) Enjoliveur, *m.*

hubble-bubble ['hʌbl'bʌbl], *n.* Narguilé à eau; gargouillement (d'eau), *m.*

hubbub ['hʌbʌb], *n.* Vacarme, brouhaha, tintamarre, *m.*

hubby ['hʌbi], *n.* (*pop.*) Mari, *m.*

huckaback ['hʌkəbæk], *n.* Grosse toile ouvrée, *f.*

huckleberry ['hʌklbəri], *n.* (*Bot.*) Airelle, *f.*

huckster ['hʌkstə], *n.* Revendeur, regrattier, *m.*—*v.i.* Revendre en détail. **huckstering,** *n.* Regratterie, *f.*; marchandage, *m.*

huddle [hʌdl], *v.t.* Entasser pêle-mêle, (*fig.*) brouiller, confondre ensemble; bâcler (to perform hastily). *To be huddled up,* être entassé, blotti (dans un coin).—*v.i.* Se mêler, se coudoyer, se presser; (*fig.*) se confondre. —*n.* Tas confus, fouillis, méli-mélo, ramassis, *m. To go into a huddle,* conférer ensemble, entrer en conclave.

hue (1) [hju:], *n.* Couleur, teinte, nuance, *f.*

hue (2) [hju:], *n.* Huée, clameur, *f. To raise a hue and cry after,* crier haro sur, crier tollé contre.

huff [hʌf], *n.* Emportement, accès de colère, *m. To be in a huff,* être fâché.—*v.t.* Froisser; (*Draughts*) souffler.—*v.i.* Se gonfler, s'enfler, se mettre en colère, pester (contre). **huffily** or **huffishly,** *adv.* Avec arrogance, avec humeur. **huffiness** or **huffishness,** *n.* Arrogance, humeur, pétulance, *f.* **huffish** or **huffy,** *a.* Fanfaron; arrogant, fier; vexé, de mauvaise humeur.

hug [hʌg], *v.t.* Embrasser, étreindre, serrer dans ses bras; (*Naut.*) serrer, raser (the coast); étouffer (of a bear). *To hug the land,* serrer la côte; *to hug the wind,* (*Naut.*) pincer le vent.—*n.* Embrassement, *m.*, étreinte, *f.*

huge [hju:dʒ], *a.* Vaste, immense, énorme; formidable. **hugely,** *adv.* Énormément, immensément, extrêmement. **hugeness,** *n.* Grandeur énorme, immensité, *f.*

hugger-mugger ['hʌgə'mʌgə], *n.* Désordre, *m.*, confusion, *f. In hugger-mugger fashion,* négligemment.—*adv.* Négligemment, en désordre.

Huguenot ['hju:gənɔt *or* -nou], *n.* Huguenot, *m.*

hulk [hʌlk], *n.* Carcasse (of a ship), *f.*, ponton, *m.*; (*pl.*) bagne, *m. To send to the hulks,* envoyer sur les pontons *or* au bagne. **hulking,** *a.* Gros, lourd. *Hulking fellow,* gros pataud, *m.*

hull [hʌl], *n.* Coque (of a ship); cosse, gousse (of peas, beans, etc.); écale (of nuts), *f.*—*v.t.* Percer la coque de (a ship), mettre (a ship) à sec; écaler (nuts); écosser (beans); décortiquer (rice etc.).

hullabaloo [hʌləbə'lu:], *n.* Vacarme, tintamarre, *m.*

hullo [HELLO].

hum [hʌm], *v.i., v.t.* Fredonner (of men), bourdonner (of bees); ronfler. *To hum and ha(w),* bredouiller, hésiter, faire une réponse évasive, tourner autour du pot; *to make things hum,* mener rondement les choses.—*n.* Bourdonnement, ronflement, brouhaha (of conversation), *m.*

human ['hju:mən], *a.* Humain. *Human being,* être humain, *m.*; (*pl.*) les humains, *m.pl.*

humane [hju:'mein], *a.* Humain, compatissant, bienfaisant. **humanely,** *adv.* Humainement, avec humanité.

humanist ['hju:mənist], *n.* Humaniste, *m.* or *f.*

humanitarian [hju:mæni'tɛəriən], *a.* and *n.* Humanitaire, *m.*

humanity [hju:'mæniti], *n.* Humanité, *f.*

humanization [-'zeiʃən], *n.* Humanisation, *f.*

humanize ['hju:mənaiz], *v.t.* Humaniser. *To become humanized,* s'humaniser.

humanly, *adv.* Humainement.

humble [hʌmbl], *a.* Humble; modeste.—*v.t.* Humilier, abaisser, mortifier. **humble-bee,** *n.* Bourdon, *m.* **humble-pie,** *n. To eat humble-pie,* s'humilier, filer doux, avaler un affront.

humbleness, *n.* Humilité, modestie, *f.* **humbly,** *adv.* Humblement, avec humilité; modestement.

humbug ['hʌmbʌg], *n.* Blague, farce, tromperie, *f.*, charlatanisme, *m.*, (*slang*) fumisterie, *f.*; hâbleur, blagueur, farceur, charlatan, (*slang*) fumiste, *m. That's all humbug,* tout ça c'est de la blague.—*v.t.* Blaguer, tromper, conter des sornettes à.—*v.i.* Faire le charlatan.

humdrum ['hʌmdrʌm], *a.* Monotone, ennuyeux, assommant, fatigant. *Humdrum daily life,* le train-train journalier, *m.*

humectation [hju:mek'teiʃən], *n.* Humectation, *f.*

humeral ['hju:mərəl], *a.* (*Anat.*) Huméral.

humerus, *n.* Humérus, *m.*

humic ['hju:mik], *a.* (*Chem.*) Humique.

humid ['hju:mid], *a.* Humide. **humidity** [-'miditi], *n.* Humidité, *f.*

humiliate [hju:'milieit], *v.t.* Humilier, abaisser. **humiliating,** *a.* Humiliant. **humiliation** [-'eiʃən], *n.* Humiliation, *f.* **humility** [-'militi], *n.* Humilité, *f.*

humming ['hʌmiŋ], *n.* Bourdonnement, fredonnement, *m.*; (*fig.*) murmure, *m.* **humming-bird,** *n.* Oiseau-mouche, colibri, *m.* **humming-top,** *n.* Toupie d'Allemagne, *f.*

hummock ['hʌmək], *n.* Mamelon, monticule, tertre, *m.*

humoral ['hju:mərəl], *a.* (*Med.*) Humoral. **humoralism,** *n.* Humorisme, *m.* **humoralist,** *n.* Humoriste, *m.*

humorist ['hju:mərist], *n.* Humoriste, *m.*, personne spirituelle, *f.* **humorous,** *a.* Humoristique; plaisant, drôle, comique. **humorously,** *adv.* Plaisamment, drôlement, comiquement. **humorousness,** *n.* Badinage, *m.*, drôlerie, *f.*, caractère fantasque, *m.*

humour ['hju:mə], *n.* Humeur, disposition, *f.*; humour, *m. In a humour for,* en train de, en humeur de; *to be in a good* or *bad humour,* être de bonne *or* de mauvaise humeur; *to put in a good humour,* mettre en bonne humeur. —*v.t.* Complaire à, laisser faire, ménager, se prêter à. **humoured,** *a. Good-humoured,* d'un caractère aimable. **humourless,** *a.* Sans esprit, sans caractère. **humoursome,** *a.* Pétulant, fantasque, capricieux.

hump [hʌmp], *n.* Bosse, *f. To have the hump,* (*slang*) être maussade, broyer du noir. **humpback,** *n.* Bossu, *m.* **humpbacked,** *a.* Bossu.

humph! [mf], *int.* Hum, hum! (expressing doubt, disapproval).

humus ['hju:məs], *n.* (*Hort.*) Humus, *m.*

hunch [hʌntʃ], *n.* Gros morceau (of bread, cheese); bosse (on the back), *f.* *To have a hunch that . . .*, soupçonner que . . . .—*v.t.* Arrondir (son dos); se voûter. **hunchback,** *n.* Bossu, *m.*, bossue, *f.* **hunchbacked,** *a.* Bossu.

hundred ['hʌndrəd], *a.* Cent. *Two hundred men,* deux cents hommes; *two hundred and one men,* deux cent un hommes.—*n.* Cent, *m.*; centaine, *f.*; canton, district, *m.* *In hundreds,* par centaines. **hundredfold,** *a.* and *n.* Centuple, *m.* **hundredth,** *a.* and *n.* Centième, *m.* **hundredweight,** *n.* Quintal, *m.*, cinquante kilos, *m.pl.*

hung, *p.p.* [HANG].

Hungarian [hʌŋ'gɛəriən], *a.* Hongrois.—*n.* Hongrois, *m.*, Hongroise, *f.*; hongrois (language), *m.* **Hungary.** La Hongrie, *f.*

hunger ['hʌŋgə], *n.* Faim, *f.*; (*fig.*) ardent désir (de), *m.* *Hunger is the best sauce,* il n'est sauce que d'appétit; *hunger will break through stone walls,* la faim chasse le loup hors du bois; *to feel a keen pang of hunger,* sentir vivement la faim.—*v.i.* Avoir faim; être affamé (de). *To hunger after,* être affamé (de), soupirer après. **hunger-march,** *n.* Marche de la faim, *f.* **hunger-strike,** *n.* Grève de la faim, *f.*

hungered, *a.* Qui a faim, affamé. **hungrily,** *adv.* Avidement. **hungry,** *a.* Affamé, qui a faim; maigre (of soils etc.). *A hungry man is an angry man,* ventre affamé n'a pas d'oreilles; *to be as hungry as a hunter,* avoir une faim de loup; *to be hungry,* avoir faim; *to feed the hungry,* nourrir ceux qui ont faim.

hunk [hʌŋk], *n.* Gros morceau (of cake, cheese), *m.*

hunkers ['hʌŋkəz], *n.pl.* (*dial.*) *On one's hunkers,* accroupi.

hunks [hʌŋks], *n.* Ladre, grippe-sou, *m.*

hunt [hʌnt], *v.t.* Chasser à courre; (*fig.*) poursuivre, chercher. *To hunt down,* traquer, mettre aux abois; *to hunt out,* dénicher, dépister; *to hunt up,* chercher.—*v.i.* Chasser au chien courant, aller à la chasse.—*n.* Chasse à courre; meute (pack of hounds), *f.* **hunter,** *n.* Chasseur; cheval de chasse, *m.*; montre à savonnette, *f.* **hunting,** *n.* Chasse; (*fig.*) recherche, poursuite, *f.* *Fox-hunting,* chasse au renard. **hunting-ground,** *n.* Terrain de chasse, *m.* *It is his happy hunting-ground,* c'est là qu'il est dans son élément. **hunting-horn,** *n.* Cor de chasse, *m.* **hunting-lodge** or **hunting-seat,** *n.* Rendez-vous or pavillon de chasse, *m.* **huntress,** *n.* Chasseuse; (*poet.*) chasseresse, *f.* **huntsman,** *n.* (*pl.* **huntsmen**) Veneur, piqueur, *m.* **huntsmanship,** *n.* La vénerie, *f.*

hurdle [hə:dl], *n.* Claie, *f.*—*v.t.* (*spt.*) Sauter. **hurdle-race,** *n.* Course de haies, *f.*

hurdy-gurdy ['hə:digə:di], *n.* Vielle, *f.*; orgue de Barbarie, *m.*

hurl [hə:l], *v.t.* Lancer (avec force), précipiter, jeter. *To hurl reproaches at,* accabler de reproches. **hurler,** *n.* Lanceur, *m.* **hurling,** *n.* Lancement, *m.*; le hockey irlandais, *m.*

hurley, *n.* Le hockey irlandais.

hurly-burly ['hə:libə:li], *n.* Tintamarre, brouhaha, tohu-bohu, *m.*

hurrah [hu'ra:], **hurray** [hu'rei], *n.* Hourra, *m.*—*v.i.* Pousser des hourras.

hurricane ['hʌrikən], *n.* Ouragan, *m.*, tempête, *f.* **hurricane-deck,** *n.* Pont-promenade, *m.* **hurricane-lamp,** *n.* Lanterne-tempête, *f.*

hurried ['hʌrid], *a.* Précipité, pressé; fait à la hâte. **hurriedly,** *adv.* Précipitamment, à la hâte.

hurry ['hʌri], *n.* Hâte, précipitation, *f.*; (*fig.*) tumulte, *m.*, confusion, *f.* *Done in a hurry,* fait à la hâte, fait avec précipitation; (*fam.*) *he won't do that in a hurry,* il ne fera pas ça de sitôt; *in no hurry to,* peu empressé de; *there is no hurry,* rien ne presse; *to be in a hurry;* être pressé.—*v.t.* Hâter, presser, précipiter; accélérer, faire dépêcher. *To hurry away,* emmener or entraîner précipitamment; *to hurry back,* ramener en toute hâte; *to hurry in,* faire entrer précipitamment; *to hurry on,* presser, pousser, entraîner; *to hurry up,* hâter, dépêcher.—*v.i.* Se hâter, se dépêcher, se presser; presser le pas. *To hurry away,* s'en aller à la hâte; *to hurry back,* revenir à la hâte; *to hurry down,* descendre à la hâte; *to hurry in,* entrer précipitamment; *to hurry on,* se hâter, se presser; (*Row.*) *to hurry on the stroke,* attaquer trop tôt; *to hurry over,* faire à la hâte, expédier; *to hurry up,* se hâter, se dépêcher.

hurt [hə:t], *n.* Mal, *m.*, blessure, *f.*; (*fig.*) tort, dommage, *m.*—*v.t.* (*past and p.p.* **hurt**) Faire mal à, (*fig.*) nuire à, offenser, blesser, choquer. *To hurt oneself,* se faire du mal; *to hurt someone's feelings,* blesser les sentiments de quelqu'un.—*v.i.* Faire du mal; faire mal. *It does not hurt,* cela ne fait pas de mal; *it hurts,* cela fait mal.

hurtful, *a.* Nuisible (à); (*fig.*) préjudiciable (à). **hurtfully,** *adv.* D'une manière nuisible, pernicieusement.

hurtle [hə:tl], *v.i.* Se précipiter; se heurter. —*v.t.* Lancer, projeter.

hurtleberry ['hə:tlbəri], *n.* (*Bot.*) Airelle, *f.*

hurtless ['hə:tlis], *a.* Inoffensif; sans blessure. **hurtlessly,** *adv.* Sans aucun mal.

husband ['hʌzbənd], *n.* Mari, époux, *m.* *As husband and wife,* maritalement; *ship's husband,* gérant à bord, *m.*—*v.t.* Ménager, économiser. **husbandman,** *n.* (*pl.* **husbandmen**) Laboureur, cultivateur, *m.* **husbandry,** *n.* Agriculture, industrie agricole; économie, frugalité, *f.*

hush [hʌʃ], *n.* Silence, calme, *m.*—*int.* Chut! paix!—*v.t.* Taire, faire taire, imposer silence à; (*fig.*) calmer, apaiser. *To hush up,* étouffer, supprimer.—*v.i.* Se taire, faire silence. **hush-hush,** *a.* Secret. **hush-money,** *n.* Prix du silence, *m.*

hushaby ['hʌʃəbai], *int.* Dodo!

husk [hʌsk], *n.* Cosse, gousse (of peas etc.), *f.*; brou, *m.*; écale (of a nut), *f.*; balle, enveloppe, pellicule (of grain), *f.*—*v.t.* Écosser (peas etc.); éplucher (maize); écaler (nuts); monder (barley etc.). **husked,** *a.* À cosse; écossé; mondé. *Husked barley,* orge mondé, *m.*

huskiness ['hʌskinis], *n.* Enrouement (of the voice), *m.* **husky,** *a.* Cossu; rauque, enroué (of the voice); (*colloq.*) costaud, fort.—*n.* Chien esquimau, *m.*

hussar [hu'za:], *n.* Hussard, *m.*

hussy ['hʌsi], *n.* Friponne, coquine, *f.*

hustings ['hʌstiŋz], *n.pl.* (Before 1872)

Estrade (pour haranguer les électeurs), assemblée électorale, *f.*
hustle [hʌsl], *v.t.* Bousculer, presser, pousser. —*v.i.* Se presser, se dépêcher.—*n.* Bousculade, hâte, *f.* **hustler,** *n.* Débrouillard; remueur d'affaires; type dynamique, *m.*
huswife [HOUSEWIFE (2)].
hut [hʌt], *n.* Hutte, cabane; (*Mil.*) baraque, *f.*; (*pl.*) baraquements, *m.pl.* **hutted,** *a. Hutted camp,* baraquement, *m.*
hutch [hʌtʃ], *n.* Huche, *f.*; clapier (for rabbits); pétrin (kneading-trough), *m.*
hutment [ˈhʌtmənt], *n.* Baraquement, *m.*
huzza! [huˈza:], *int.* Hourra!
hyacinth [ˈhaiəsinθ], *n.* (*Bot.*) Jacinthe, *f.*
hyaline [ˈhaiəlain], *a.* Hyalin, diaphane.
hybrid [ˈhaibrid], *a.* and *n.* Hybride, *m.*
hydra [ˈhaidrə], *n.* Hydre, *f.*
hydragogue [ˈhaidrəgɔg], *n.* (*Med.*) Hydragogue, *m.*
hydrangea [haiˈdrændʒiə], *n.* (*Bot.*) Hortensia, *m.*
hydrant [ˈhaidrənt], *n.* Prise d'eau, *f. Fire hydrant,* bouche d'incendie, *f.*
hydrate [ˈhaidreit], *n.* (*Chem.*) Hydrate, *m.* **hydration,** *n.* Hydratation, *f.*
hydraulic [haiˈdrɔ:lik], *a.* Hydraulique. **hydraulics,** *n.pl.* Hydraulique, *f.*
hydride [ˈhaidraid], *n.* (*Chem.*) Hydrure, *m.*
hydrocarbon, *n.* Hydrocarbure, *m.* **hydrocele,** *n.* Hydrocèle, *f.* **hydrocephalus,** *n.* Hydrocéphalie, *f.* **hydrochlorate,** *n.* Hydrochlorate, *m.* **hydrochloric,** *a.* (Acide) chlorhydrique. **hydrodynamic** [-ˈnæmik], *a.* Hydrodynamique. **hydrodynamics,** *n.pl.* Hydrodynamique, *f.* **hydro-electric,** *a.* Hydro-électrique.
hydrogen [ˈhaidrədʒen], *n.* Hydrogène, *m. Hydrogen bomb* or (*fam.*) *H-bomb,* bombe à hydrogène, bombe H, *f.* **hydrogenated,** *a.* Hydrogéné. **hydrogenize,** *v.t.* Hydrogéner.
hydrographer [haiˈdrɔgrəfə], *n.* Hydrographe, *m.*
hydrographic [haidroˈgræfik], *a.* Hydrographique. **hydrography,** *n.* Hydrographie, *f.*
hydrology, *n.* Hydrologie, *f.*
hydrolysis [haiˈdrɔlisis], *n.* Hydrolyse, *f.*
hydromel [ˈhaidrəmel], *n.* Hydromel, *m.*
hydrometer [haiˈdrɔmitə], *n.* Hydromètre, *m.* **hydrometric,** *a.* Hydrométrique. **hydrometry,** *n.* Hydrométrie, *f.* **hydrophobia** [-ˈfoubiə], *n.* Hydrophobie, rage, *f.* **hydrophobic,** *a.* Hydrophobe. **hydropic** [-ˈdrɔpik], *a.* Hydropique.
hydroplane [ˈhaidroplein], *n.* Hydroplane, hydravion, *m.* **hydropneumatic** [-njuˈmæ tik], *a.* Hydropneumatique. **hydrostatic** [-ˈstætik] or **hydrostatical,** *a.* Hydrostatique. **hydrostatics,** *n.pl.* Hydrostatique, *f.* **hydrosulphuric** [-sʌlˈfjuərik], *a.* Sulphydrique. **hydrotherapeutics** [-θerəˈpju:tiks], *n.pl.* Hydrothérapie, *f.*
hyena [haiˈi:nə], *n.* Hyène, *f.*
hygiene [ˈhaidʒi:n], *n.* Hygiène, *f.* **hygienic** [haiˈdʒi:nik] or **hygienical,** *a.* Hygiénique. **hygienically,** *adv.* Hygiéniquement.
hygrology [haiˈgrɔlədʒi], *n.* Hygrologie, *f.*
hygrometer, *n.* Hygromètre, *m.* **hygrometric** [-ˈmetrik] or **hygrometrical,** *a.* Hygrométrique. **hygrometry,** *n.* Hygrométrie, *f.*

hylozoic [hailoˈzouik], *a.* Hylozoïque. **hylozoism,** *n.* Hylozoïsme, *m.*
hymen [ˈhaimən], *n.* Hymen, hyménée, *m.*
hymeneal [-ˈni:əl] or **hymenean,** *a.* De l'hymen, de l'hyménée, nuptial.—*n.* Chant d'hyménée, *m.*
Hymenoptera [haiməˈnɔptərə], *n.pl.* (*Ent.*) Hyménoptères, *m.pl.* **hymenopteral** or **hymenopterous,** *a.* Hyménoptère.
hymn [him], *n.* (*Eccles.*) Hymne, *m.* or *f.,* cantique, *m.*—*v.t.* Célébrer par des hymnes. —*v.i.* Chanter des hymnes. **hymn-book** or **hymnal,** *n.* Recueil d'hymnes, hymnaire, *m.*
hyoid [ˈhaiɔid], *a. Hyoid bone,* l'os hyoïde, *m.*
hypaethral [haiˈpi:θrəl], *a.* Hypèthre.
hyperbaton [haiˈpɔ:bətən], *n.* Hyperbate, *f.*
hyperbola [haiˈpɔ:bələ], *n.* (*Geom.*) Hyperbole, *f.*
hyperbole [haiˈpɔ:bəli], *n.* (*Gram.*) Hyperbole, *f.* **hyperbolic** [-ˈbɔlik] or **hyperbolical,** *a.* Hyperbolique. **hyperbolically,** *adv.* Hyperboliquement. **hyperbolist,** *n.* Faiseur d'hyperboles, *m.* **hyperbolize,** *v.t.* Exagérer. —*v.i.* User de l'hyperbole. **hyperborean** [-ˈbɔ:riən], *a.* Hyperboréen, hyperborée.
hypercritic, *n.* Hypercritique, *m.* **hypercritical,** *a.* Critique à l'excès. *To be hypercritical,* épiloguer, ergoter. **hypercriticism,** *n.* Critique exagérée, *f.* **hypersensitive,** *a.* Hypersensible, hypersensitif.
hypertrophied [haiˈpɔ:trəfaid], *a.* Hypertrophié. **hypertrophy** [haiˈpɔ:trəfi], *n.* Hypertrophie, *f.*
hyphen [ˈhaifən], *n.* Trait d'union, *m.* **hyphenate,** *v.t.* Mettre un trait d'union à.
hypnosis [hipˈnousis], *n.* Hypnose, *f.* **hypnotic** [hipˈnɔtik], *a.* and *n.* Hypnotique, *m.*
hypnotism [ˈhipnətizm], *n.* Hypnotisme, *m.* **hypnotist,** *n.* Hypnotiste. **hypnotize,** *v.t.* Hypnotiser.
hypochondria [haipəˈkɔndriə], *n.* Hypocondrie, *f.* **hypochondriac** [haipəˈkɔn driæk], *a.* and *n.* Hypocondriaque, *m.*
hypocrisy [hiˈpɔkrisi], *n.* Hypocrisie, *f.*
hypocrite [ˈhipəkrit], *n.* Hypocrite, *m.* or *f.* **hypocritical** [-ˈkritikl], *a.* Hypocrite. **hypocritically,** *adv.* Hypocritement, en hypocrite.
hypoderm [ˈhaipədə:m], *n.* Hypoderme, *m.* **hypodermic,** *a.* Hypodermique.
hypogastric [haipəˈgæstrik], *a.* Hypogastrique.
hypogastrium [haipəˈgæstriəm], *n.* (*Anat.*) Hypogastre, *m.*
hypogeous [-pɔˈdʒi:əs], *a.* Hypogé. **hypogeum** [-ˈdʒi:əm], *n.* Hypogée, *m.* **hypoglossal** [-ˈglɔsəl], *a.* Hypoglosse. *Hypoglossal nerve,* hypoglosse, *m.*
hypophosphate [haipoˈfɔsfeit], *n.* Hypophosphate, *m.*
hypostasis [haiˈpɔstəsis], *n.* Hypostase, *f.* **hypostatic** [-ˈstætik] or **hypostatical,** *a.* Hypostatique. **hyposulphite** [-ˈsʌlfait], *n.* Hyposulfite, *m.*
hypotenuse [haiˈpɔtənju:z], *n.* (*Geom.*) Hypoténuse, *f.*
hypothec [haiˈpɔθek], *n.* Hypothèque, *f.* **hypothecary,** *a.* Hypothécaire. **hypothecate** [-ˈpɔθikeit], *v.t.* Hypothéquer. **hypothesis,** *n.* Hypothèse, *f.*

hypothetic [haipə'θetik] or **hypothetical**, *a.* Hypothétique. **hypothetically**, *adv.* Hypothétiquement.
hypsometer [hip'sɔmitə], *n.* Hypsomètre, *m.* **hypsometry**, *n.* Hypsométrie, *f.*
hyson [haisn], *n.* Thé vert (de Chine), *m.*
hyssop ['hisəp], *n.* (*Bot.*) Hysope, *f.*
hysteria [his'tiəriə], *n.*, or **hysterics** [-'teriks], *n.pl.* Crise de nerfs, attaque de nerfs, *f.* **hysteric** or **hysterical**, *a.* Hystérique.
hysterotomy [histə'rɔtəmi], *n.* Hystérotomie, *f.*

I

I, i [ai]. Neuvième lettre de l'alphabet, *m.*
I [ai], *pron.* Je, moi. *I*, moi; *I speak*, je parle; *it is I*, c'est moi; *it is I who am speaking*, c'est moi qui parle.
iamb ['aiæmb] or **iambus** [ai'æmbəs], *n.* Iambe, *m.* **iambic**, *a.* Iambique.—*n.* Iambe, *m.*
Iberian [ai'biəriən], *a.* and *n.* Ibérien, *m.*, Ibérienne, *f.*
ibex ['aibeks], *n.* Bouquetin, *m.*
ibis ['aibis], *n.* (*Orn.*) Ibis, *m.*
ice [ais], *n.* Glace, *f.* *Ice age*, période glaciaire, *f.*; *to break the ice*, rompre la glace, faire les premières avances; *to cut no ice*, ne faire aucune impression.—*v.t.* Glacer (cakes); frapper (wine).—*v.i.* (*Av.*) *To ice up*, givrer.
ice-axe, *n.* Piolet, *m.* **ice-bank**, *n.* Banquise, *f.* **iceberg**, *n.* Iceberg, gros bloc de glace, *m.* **ice-bound**, *a.* Pris dans *or* bloqué par les glaces. **ice-box**, *n.* Glacière, *f.* **ice-breaker**, *n.* Brise-glace, *m.* **ice-cream**, *n.* Glace, *f.* **ice-field**, *n.* Champ de glace, *m.* **ice-floe**, *n.* Banc de glaces flottantes, *m.* **ice-hockey**, *n.* Hockey sur glace, *m.* **ice-house**, *n.* Glacière, *f.* **ice-plant**, *n.* Ficoïde cristalline, *f.* **ice-rink**, *n.* Salle de patinage, *f.*
iced, *a.* Glacé; frappé (of wine etc.). *Iced lolly*, sucette, *f.*
Iceland ['aislənd]. L'Islande, *f.* **Icelander**, *n.* Islandais, *m.*, Islandaise, *f.*
Icelandic [ais'lændik], *a.* Islandais, d'Islande.
ichneumon [ik'nju:mən], *n.* Ichneumon, rat d'Égypte, *m.*
ichnographic [ikno'græfik] or **ichnographical**, *a.* Ichnographique. **ichnography** [ik'nɔgrəfi], *n.* Ichnographie, *f.*
ichor ['aikə or 'ikə], *n.* Ichor, *m.* **ichorous**, *a.* Ichoreux.
ichthyological [ikθiə'lɔdʒikl], *a.* Ichtyologique. **ichthyologist**, *n.* Ichtyologiste, *m.* **ichthyology** [-'ɔlədʒi], *n.* Ichtyologie, *f.* **ichthyophagist**, *n.* ichthyophagous, *a.* Ichtyophage. **ichthyosaurus** [-'sɔːrəs], *n.* Ichtyosaure, *m.*
icicle ['aisikl], *n.* Petit glaçon, *m.* **icily**, *adv.* Froidement, **iciness**, *n.* Froid glacial, *m.*
icing, *n.* Glacé; frappage (of wine), *m.*
icon ['aikɔn], *n.* Icone, *f.*
iconoclasm, *n.* Iconoclasme, *m.*
iconoclast [ai'kɔnəklæst], *n.* Iconoclaste, *m.* **iconographer** [-'nɔgrəfə], *n.* Iconographe. **iconography**, *n.* Iconographie, *f.* **iconolater** [-'nɔlətə], *n.* Iconolâtre, *m.* **iconolatry**, *n.* Iconolâtrie, *f.* **iconology**, *n.* Iconologie, *f.* **iconostasis**, *n.* Iconostase, *f.*
icosahedron [aikosə'hiːdrən], *n.* Icosaèdre, *m.*

icterical [ik'terikl], *a.* Ictérique.
icterus ['iktərəs], *n.* Ictère, *m.*, jaunisse, *f.*
icy ['aisi], *a.* Glacé, glacial. *Icy road*, route verglacée, *f.*
idea [ai'diːə], *n.* Idée, *f.* *A general idea*, idée d'ensemble, *f.*; *the idea!* par exemple! a-t-on idée? *to get ideas into one's head*, se faire des idées; *to have an idea of*, avoir *or* se faire une idée de; *to have no idea that*, ne pas se douter que. **ideal**, *a.* and *n.* Idéal, *m.* *Ideal beauty*, le beau idéal, *m.* **idealism**, *n.* Idéalisme, *m.* **idealist**, *n.* Idéaliste, *m.* **ideality** [-'æliti], *n.* Idéalité, *f.* **idealization** [-'zeiʃən], *n.* Idéalisation, *f.* **idealize**, *v.t.* Idéaliser. **ideally**, *adv.* En idée, idéalement.
identical [ai'dentikl], *a.* Identique, même. **identically**, *adv.* Identiquement.
identification [aidentifi'keiʃən], *n.* Identification, *f.*
identify [ai'dentifai], *v.t.* Identifier (avec); constater l'identité de, reconnaître. *To identify oneself*, s'identifier.
identity [ai'dentiti], *n.* Identité, *f.* *Identity card*, carte d'identité, *f.*; *identity disk*, (*Mil.*) plaque d'identité, *f.*
ideographic [aidio'græfik], *a.* Idéographique. **ideography** [-'ɔgrəfi], *n.* Idéographie, *f.*
ideological [-'lɔdʒikl], *a.* Idéologique. **ideologist**, *n.* Idéologue, *m.* **ideology** [-'ɔlədʒi], *n.* Idéologie, *f.*
ides [aidz], *n.pl.* Ides, *f.pl.*
idiocy ['idiəsi], *n.* Idiotie, *f.*
idiom ['idiəm], *n.* Idiome; idiotisme, *m.* **idiomatic** [-'mætik] or **idiomatical**, *a.* Idiomatique; qui est de la langue familière *or* courante. *Idiomatic expression*, idiotisme, *m.* **idiomatically**, *adv.* D'une manière idiomatique.
idiopathic [idio'pæθik], *a.* Idiopathique. **idiopathy** [-'ɔpəθi], *n.* Idiopathie, *f.*
idiosyncrasy [idio'siŋkrəsi], *n.* Idiosyncrasie, *f.*
idiot ['idiət], *n.* Idiot, *m.*, idiote, *f.*; imbécile, *m. or f.* **idiotic** [-'ɔtik] or **idiotical**, *a.* Idiot, d'imbécile; stupide, bête.
idle [aidl], *a.* Oisif, paresseux, indolent (lazy); désœuvré (at leisure); en chômage (person out of work), en repos (of a machine etc.); (*fig.*) inutile, vain, frivole. *Idle fellow*, fainéant, paresseux, *m.*; *idle hours*, heures de loisir, *f.pl.*, moments perdus, *m.pl.*; *idle tale*, conte à dormir debout, conte en l'air, *m.*; *idle talk*, balivernes, *f.pl.*; *idle words*, paroles en l'air, *f.pl.*—*v.i.* Ne rien faire, faire le paresseux, fainéanter; (*Motor.*) tourner au ralenti.—*v.t.* Perdre, gaspiller, passer dans la paresse. *To idle away one's time*, perdre son temps. **idleness**, *n.* Paresse; oisiveté; inutilité, *f.*; désœuvrement, *m.* **idler**, *n.* Oisif, fainéant, paresseux, *m.* **idly**, *adv.* Dans l'oisiveté, en paresseux; inutilement, vainement, follement.
idol ['aidəl], *n.* Idole, *f.* **idol-worship**, *n.* Culte des idoles, *m.*
idolater [-'dɔlətə], *n.* Idolâtre, *m.* **idolatress**, *n.* Femme idolâtre, *f.* **idolatrous**, *a.* Idolâtre. **idolatrously**, *adv.* Avec idolâtrie. **idolatry**, *n.* Idolâtrie, *f.*
idolize ['aidəlaiz], *v.t.* Idolâtrer. **idolizing**, *a.* Idolâtre.—*n.* Idolâtrie, *f.*
idyll ['aidil or 'idil], *n.* Idylle, *f.*
idyllic [ai'dilik or i'dilik], *a.* Idyllique.

if [if], *conj.* Si, quand, quand même. *As if,* comme si; *even if,* même si, quand même; *even if it were so,* quand cela serait; *I wonder if he will come,* je me demande s'il viendra; *if anything, I am paying more than was agreed between us,* s'il y a une différence, je vous paye plus que le prix convenu entre nous; *if ever there was one,* s'il en fut jamais; *if I were you,* à votre place; *if necessary,* s'il le faut, au besoin; *if not,* sinon, si ce n'est; *if only,* si seulement; ne fût-ce que . . .; *if possible,* si cela est possible, s'il se peut; *if so,* s'il en est ainsi; *if there is any difference,* s'il y a une différence; *to look as if,* avoir l'air de; *we will buy it if it costs us double,* nous l'achèterons, quand même il nous coûterait le double.

igloo ['iglu:], *n.* Hutte de neige, *f.* (des Esquimaux); igloo, *m.*

igneous ['igniəs], *a.* Igné.

ignis fatuus ['ignis 'fætuəs], *n.* (*pl.* **ignes fatui**) Feu follet, *m.*

ignite [ig'nait], *v.t.* Allumer; mettre en feu. —*v.i.* Prendre feu, s'allumer. **ignitible,** *a.* Inflammable. **ignition** [-'niʃən], *n.* Ignition, *f.*; (*Motor.*) allumage, *m.* *Ignition key,* clé de contact, *f.*

ignoble [ig'noubl], *a.* Plébéien, roturier; bas, vil, ignoble. **ignobleness,** *n.* Ignobilité, *f.* **ignobly,** *adv.* Ignoblement; d'une manière ignoble. *Ignobly born,* de basse naissance.

ignominious [igno'miniəs], *a.* Ignominieux; (*Law*) infamant. **ignominiously,** *adv.* Ignominieusement; (*Law*) d'une manière infamante.

ignominy ['ignəmini], *n.* Ignominie; (*Law*) infamie, *f.*

ignoramus [ignə'reiməs], *n.* Ignorant, ignare, *m.*, (*fam.*) âne bâté, *m.*

ignorance ['ignərəns], *n.* Ignorance, *f.* **ignorant,** *a.* Ignorant. *Not to be ignorant of,* savoir bien; *to be ignorant of,* ignorer. **ignorantly,** *adv.* Par ignorance; avec ignorance.

ignore [ig'nɔ:], *v.t.* Feindre d'ignorer, vouloir ignorer; ne tenir aucun compte de; ne pas vouloir reconnaître (une personne); (*Law*) déclarer qu'il n'y a pas lieu à poursuivre; rendre un non-lieu.

iguana [i'gwa:nə], *n.* Iguane, *m.*

ikon [ICON].

ileum ['iliəm], *n.* Iléon, iléum, *m.* **ileus,** *n.* Iléus, *m.*

ilex ['aileks], *n.* (*Bot.*) Yeuse, *f.*

iliac ['iliæk], *a.* (*Anat.*) Iliaque. *Iliac passion,* passion iliaque, *f.*, coliques de miserere, *f.pl.*

Iliad ['iliəd], *n.* Iliade, *f.*

ilium ['iliəm], *n.* (*Anat.*) Ilion, ilium, *m.*

ilk [ilk], *a.* (*Sc.*) Même. *Of that ilk,* de la localité du même nom.

ill [il], *a.* Mauvais, méchant; malade, souffrant (of the health). *It's an ill wind that blows nobody any good,* à quelque chose malheur est bon; *to fall ill,* tomber malade; *to take it ill,* trouver mauvais, prendre mal.—*n.* Mal, *m. To speak ill of . . .,* dire du mal de . . . .—*adv.* Mal; peu. *Ill able to,* peu capable de; *ill at ease,* mal à l'aise; *it ill becomes you,* il vous sied mal. **ill-advised,** *a.* Malavisé; impolitique. **ill-affected,** *a.* Mal intentionné. **ill-bred,** *a.* Mal élevé. **ill-considered,** *a.* Irréfléchi, peu considéré. **ill-contrived,** *a.* Mal imaginé. **ill-deserved,**

a. Peu mérité. **ill-disposed,** *a.* Mal intentionné, mal disposé (envers), peu disposé (à). **ill-doing,** *n.* Mal, *m.,* mauvaise action, *f.* **ill-fated,** *a.* Infortuné, malheureux. **ill-favoured,** *a.* De mauvaise mine, laid. **ill-featured,** *a.* Laid. **ill-feeling,** *n.* Ressentiment, *m.* **ill-founded** or **ill-grounded,** *a.* Mal fondé, sans fondement. **ill-gotten,** *a.* Mal acquis. *Ill-gotten gains seldom prosper,* bien mal acquis ne profite jamais. **ill-health,** *n.* Mauvaise santé, *f.* **ill-informed,** *a.* Mal renseigné. **ill-judged,** *a.* Malavisé, imprudent. **ill-mannered,** *a.* Malappris. **ill-meaning,** *a.* Mal intentionné. **ill-minded,** *a.* Mal disposé. **ill-nature,** *n.* Méchanceté, *f.* **ill-natured,** *a.* Méchant, d'un mauvais naturel. **ill-naturedly,** *adv.* Méchamment. **ill-omened,** *a.* De mauvais augure. **ill-qualified,** *a.* Peu capable, peu qualifié. **ill-sounding,** *a.* Malsonnant, inharmonieux. **ill-starred,** *a.* Né sous une mauvaise étoile, de mauvais augure, malheureux. **ill-tempered,** *a.* Maussade, de mauvaise humeur. **ill-timed,** *a.* Déplacé, intempestif, mal à propos. **ill-treat** or **ill-use,** *v.t.* Maltraiter. **ill-will,** *n.* Mauvais vouloir, *m.*; inimitié, rancune, *f. I bear him no ill-will,* je ne lui en veux pas.

illegal [i'li:gəl], *a.* Illégal; illicite. **illegality** [-'gæliti], *n.* Illégalité, *f.* **illegalize,** *v.t.* Rendre illégal. **illegally,** *adv.* Illégalement.

illegibility [iledʒi'biliti], *n.* Illisibilité, *f.* **illegible** [i'ledʒibl], *a.* Illisible. **illegibly,** *adv.* Illisiblement.

illegitimacy [ilə'dʒitiməsi], *n.* Illégitimité, *f.* **illegitimate** [-'dʒitimit], *a.* Illégitime, non autorisé; naturel (of children). **illegitimately,** *adv.* Illégitimement.

illiberal [i'libərəl], *a.* Illibéral, peu généreux; borné, étroit. **illiberality,** *n.* Illibéralité, *f.,* manque de générosité, *m.*; petitesse, *f.* **illiberally,** *adv.* Sans libéralité; sans générosité.

illicit [i'lisit], *a.* Illicite. **illicitly,** *adv.* Illicitement. **illicitness,** *n.* Nature illicite, *f.*

illimitable [i'limitəbl], *a.* Illimitable. **illimitably,** *adv.* D'une manière illimitable. **illimitedness,** *n.* Nature illimitée, infinité, *f.*

illiteracy [i'litərəsi], *n.* Analphabétisme; manque d'instruction, *m.*

illiterate [i'litərət], *a. and n.* Illettré, analphabète.

illness ['ilnis], *n.* Maladie, indisposition, *f.*

illogical [i'lɔdʒikl], *a.* Illogique, peu logique. **illogically,** *adv.* Illogiquement, peu logiquement.

illude [i'lju:d], *v.t.* Tromper.

illume [i'lju:m], *v.t.* Illuminer, éclairer.

illuminant [i'lju:minənt], *a.* Illuminant.—*n.* Illuminant, *m.,* lumière, *f.* **illuminate** [-neit], *v.t.* Illuminer, éclairer; enluminer (to decorate).

illuminati [ilju:mi'neitai], *n.pl.* Illuminés, *m.pl.* **illuminating,** *a.* Qui éclaire.—*n.* Enluminure, *f.* **illumination** [-'neiʃən], *n.* Illumination; enluminure (of books etc.), *f.* **illuminative,** *a.* Illuminatif. **illuminator** or **illuminer,** *n.* Illuminateur; (*Paint.*) enlumineur, *m.,* enlumineuse, *f.* **illumine,** *v.t.* Illuminer, éclairer.

illusion [i'lu:ʒən *or* i'lju:ʒən], *n.* Illusion, *f.* *Optical illusion*, illusion d'optique, *f.* **illusionist**, *n.* Illusionniste. **illusive** *or* **illusory**, *a.* Illusoire. **illusively**, *adv.* Illusoirement. **illusiveness**, *n.* Caractère illusoire, *m.*

illustrate ['iləstreit], *v.t.* Illustrer; (*fig.*) éclaircir, élucider, expliquer; orner, embellir. **illustration** [-'treiʃən], *n.* Illustration; explication, *f.*; éclaircissement, exemple, *m.*; gravure, *f.* *A noble illustration*, une preuve éclatante, *f.*; *by way of illustration*, à titre d'exemple.

illustrative [i'lʌstrətiv], *a.* Qui éclaircit, explicatif. **illustratively**, *adv.* Pour servir d'explication.

illustrator ['iləstreitə], *n.* Illustrateur; interprète, commentateur, *m.*

illustrious [i'lʌstriəs], *a.* Illustre, célèbre, glorieux. **illustriously**, *adv.* D'une manière illustre; avec éclat. **illustriousness**, *n.* Éclat, *m.*, gloire, éminence, *f.*

I'm [I AM].

image ['imidʒ], *n.* Image, *f.*; (*fig.*) portrait, *m.*; idole, *f.* *He is the image of his father*, il est le portrait de son père.—*v.t.* Représenter par une image; (*fig.*) figurer, peindre, se figurer, s'imaginer. **image-breaker**, *n.* Iconoclaste, *m.* **image-worship**, *n.* Culte des idoles, *m.*

imagery, *n.* Images, idoles, *f.pl.*; langage figuré, *m.*; figure de rhétorique, *f.*

imaginable [i'mædʒinəbl], *a.* Imaginable. **imaginary**, *a.* Imaginaire. **imagination** [-'neiʃən], *n.* Imagination, *f.*; conception, idée, *f.* *It's your imagination!* vous l'avez rêvé! **imaginative**, *a.* Imaginatif. **imagine**, *v.t.* Imaginer, se faire une idée de; s'imaginer, se figurer. *Just imagine* . . ., figurez-vous un peu . . .; *you can imagine how surprised I was!* pensez si je fus surpris! **imaginer**, *n.* Imaginateur, *m.* **imagining**, *n.* Imagination, conception, *f.*

imago [i'meigou], *n.* (*pl.* **imagines** [i'mædʒi ni:z]) (*Ent.*) Imago, *f.*, insecte parfait, *m.*

imbecile ['imbisail *or* 'imbisi:l], *a.* and *n.* Imbécile. **imbecility** [-'siliti], *n.* Imbécillité, *f.*

imbed [EMBED].

imbibe [im'baib], *v.t.* Imbiber, absorber; (*fig.*) puiser, prendre. **imbiber**, *n.* Buveur, absorbant, *m.*

imbricated ['imbrikeitid], *a.* (*Bot. etc.*) Imbriqué. **imbrication** [-'keiʃən], *n.* Imbrication, *f.* **imbricative**, *a.* Imbricatif.

imbroglio [im'brouliou], *n.* Imbroglio, *m.*

imbrue [im'bru:], *v.t.* Tremper (dans).

imbrute [im'bru:t], *v.t.* Abrutir.—*v.i.* S'abrutir.

imbue [im'bju:], *v.t.* Imprégner, teindre; (*fig.*) pénétrer, douer (de). **imbued**, *a.* Imbu, pénétré (de).

imitable ['imitəbl], *a.* Imitable.

imitate ['imiteit], *v.t.* Imiter. **imitation** [-'teiʃən], *n.* Imitation; (*Comm.*) contrefaçon, *f.*; (*Paint.*) pastiche, *m.* (*Comm.*) *Beware of imitations*, méfiez-vous des contrefaçons; *imitation leather*, cuir artificiel, *m.* **imitative**, *a.* Imitatif, imitateur. **imitator**, *n.* Imitateur, *m.*, imitatrice, *f.*; (*Comm.*) contrefacteur, *m.*

immaculate [i'mækjulit], *a.* Sans tache, immaculé. **immaculately**, *adv.* Sans tache, sans défaut; irréprochablement. **immaculateness**, *n.* Pureté sans tache, *f.*; impeccabilité (of dress), *f.*

immanence ['imənəns], *n.* Immanence, *f.* **immanent**, *a.* Immanent.

immaterial [imə'tiəriəl], *a.* Immatériel; indifférent, peu important. *It is immaterial*, peu importe, cela n'a pas d'importance. **immaterialism**, *n.* Immatérialisme, *m.* **immaterialist**, *n.* Immatérialiste, *m.* **immateriality** [-'æliti], *n.* Immatérialité, *f.* **immaterialize** [-'tiəriəlaiz], *v.t.* Immatérialiser. **immaterially**, *adv.* Immatériellement.

immature [imə'tjuə], *a.* Pas mûr; pas mûri; prématuré. **immaturely**, *adv.* Prématurément, avant la maturité. **immatureness** *or* **immaturity**, *n.* Immaturité, *f.*

immeasurable [i'meʒərəbl], *a.* Immense, infini; incommensurable. **immeasurably**, *adv.* Outre mesure, immensément, infiniment.

immediacy [i'mi:djəsi], *n.* Imminence, *f.*; caractère immédiat, *m.*

immediate [i'mi:djət], *a.* Immédiat; urgent, très pressé (on letters). *In the immediate future*, dans l'immédiat. **immediately**, *adv.* Immédiatement, tout de suite, sur-le-champ. —*conj.* Aussitôt que, dès que. **immediateness**, *n.* Caractère immédiat, *m.*; promptitude, *f.*

immemorial [imi'mɔ:riəl], *a.* Immémorial. *From time immemorial*, de temps immémorial. **immemorially**, *adv.* De temps immémorial.

immense [i'mens], *a.* Immense. **immensely**, *adv.* Immensément. **immensity**, *n.* Immensité, *f.*

immerse [i'mə:s], *v.t.* Plonger, immerger, enfoncer. **immersion**, *n.* Immersion, *f.* *Immersion heater*, chauffe-liquides électrique, *m.*

immigrant ['imigrənt], *a.* and *n.* Immigrant, *m.* **immigrate**, *v.i.* Immigrer. **immigration** [-'greiʃən], *n.* Immigration, *f.*

imminence ['iminəns], *n.* Imminence, *f.* **imminent**, *a.* Imminent. **imminently**, *adv.* Sur le point d'arriver.

immiscibility [imisi'biliti], *n.* Immiscibilité, *f.* **immiscible**, *a.* Immiscible.

immobile [i'moubail], *a.* Fixe; immobile. **immobility** [imo'biliti], *n.* Immobilité, *f.* **immobilization** [imoubilai'zeiʃən], *n.* Immobilisation, *f.* **immobilize** [i'moubilaiz], *v.t.* Immobiliser.

immoderate [i'mɔdərit], *a.* Immodéré, excessif. **immoderately**, *adv.* Immodérément. **immoderation** [-'eiʃən], *n.* Immodération, *f.*, excès, *m.*

immodest [i'mɔdist], *a.* Immodeste, peu modeste, impudique. **immodestly**, *adv.* Immodestement, sans modestie, impudiquement. **immodesty**, *n.* Immodestie, impudeur, impudicité, *f.*

immolate ['iməleit], *v.t.* Immoler. **immolation** [-'leiʃən], *n.* Immolation, *f.*; sacrifice, *m.* **immolator**, *n.* Immolateur, *m.*

immoral [i'mɔrəl], *a.* Immoral; dissolu. **immorality** [-'æliti], *n.* Immoralité, *f.* **immorally**, *adv.* Immoralement.

immortal [i'mɔːtl], *a.* Immortel. **immortality** [-'tæliti], *n.* Immortalité, *f.* **immortalization** [-təlai'zeiʃən], *n.* Action d'immortaliser, *f.* **immortalize** [i'mɔːtəlaiz], *v.t.* Immortaliser, rendre immortel. **immortally,** *adv.* Immortellement.
immortelle, *n.* (*Bot.*) Immortelle, *f.*
immovability [imu:və'biliti] or **immovableness,** *n.* Immuabilité, fixité, *f.*
immovable [i'mu:vəbl], *a.* Fixe, immuable, inébranlable; (*Law*) immeuble. **immovably,** *adv.* D'une manière fixe, inébranlablement, immuablement; (*fig.*) avec insensibilité.
immune [i'mju:n], *a.* À l'abri (de), immunisé, vacciné (contre).
immunity [i'mju:niti], *n.* Immunité, exemption, *f.* **immunization,** *n.* (*Med.*) Immunisation, *f.* **immunize,** *v.t.* (*Med.*) Immuniser.
immure [i'mjuə], *v.t.* Entourer de murs; enfermer (dans); cloîtrer.
immutability [imju:tə'biliti], *n.* Immutabilité, *f.* **immutable,** *a.* Immuable. **immutably,** *adv.* Immuablement.
imp [imp], *n.* Diablotin, petit démon; petit diable (urchin), *m.*
impact (1) ['impækt], *n.* Choc, impact, *m.*, collision, *f.*
impact (2) [im'pækt], *v.t.* Serrer, encastrer.
impair (1) [im'pɛə], *v.t.* Altérer, diminuer, affaiblir, détériorer. **impairment,** *n.* Altération, détérioration, diminution, *f.*
impair (2) [im'pɛə], *a.* Impair.
impale [im'peil], *v.t.* Empaler; (*Her.*) séparer par un pal. **impalement,** *n.* Empalement, *m.*; (*Her.*) ecu tiercé en pal, *m.*
impalpability [impælpə'biliti], *n.* Impalpabilité, *f.*
impalpable [im'pælpəbl], *a.* Impalpable; intangible.
impanate [im'peinət], *a.* (*R.-C. Ch.*) Impané.
impanation [impə'neiʃən], *n.* Impanation, *f.*
impanel [EMPANEL].
imparisyllabic [impærisi'læbik], *a.* Imparisyllabique.
imparity [im'pæriti], *n.* Imparité, inégalité, *f.*
impart [im'pɑːt], *v.t.* Accorder, donner, faire part à; communiquer, instruire de.
impartial [im'pɑːʃl], *a.* Impartial, désintéressé. *An impartial friend,* un tiers désintéressé, *m.* **impartiality** [-i'æliti], *n.* Impartialité, *f.* **impartially,** *adv.* Impartialement.
impassable [im'pɑːsəbl], *a.* Impraticable, infranchissable.
impassibility [impæsi'biliti] or **impassibleness,** *n.* Impassibilité, *f.* **impassible,** *a.* Impassible.
impassion [im'pæʃən], *v.t.* Passionner, enflammer. **impassioned,** *a.* Passionné.
impassive [im'pæsiv], *a.* Impassible, insensible. **impassively,** *adv.* Impassiblement. **impassiveness,** *n.* Impassibilité, *f.*
impaste [im'peist], *v.t.* Pétrir; couvrir d'une couche de pâte; (*Paint.*) empâter. **impasto,** *n.* (*Paint.*) Empâtement, *m.* **impastoed,** *a.* Peint en pleine pâte.
impatience [im'peiʃəns], *n.* Impatience, *f.* **impatient,** *a.* Impatient; (*fig.*) emporté. *To get impatient,* s'impatienter. **impatiently,** *adv.* Impatiemment.
impeach [im'piːtʃ], *v.t.* Mettre en accusation,

accuser; attaquer; (*Law*) récuser (un témoin). **impeachable,** *a.* Accusable, attaquable. **impeacher,** *n.* Accusateur, *m.* **impeachment,** *n.* Mise en accusation; accusation, *f.*
impeccability [impekə'biliti], *n.* Impeccabilité, *f.* **impeccable** [-'pekəbl], *a.* Impeccable. **impeccably,** *adv.* Impeccablement.
impecuniosity [impikju:ni'ɔsiti], *n.* Manque de moyens, *m.*, pauvreté, *f.* **impecunious** [impi'kju:niəs], *a.* Besogneux.
impedance [im'pi:dəns], *n.* (*Elec.*) Impédance, *f.*
impede [im'pi:d], *v.t.* Empêcher; retarder, gêner. **impediment** [-'pedimənt], *n.* Empêchement, obstacle, *m.*; (*fig.*) difficulté, *f.*, embarras, *m.* *Impediment in the speech,* défaut de prononciation, *m.*; *to throw impediments in the way,* mettre des bâtons dans les roues. **impedimenta,** *n.pl.* Impedimenta, bagages, *m.pl.*
impel [im'pel], *v.t.* Pousser (à); forcer (de). **impellent,** *a.* and *n.* Moteur, *m.* **impelling,** *a.* Impulsif, moteur.
impend [im'pend], *v.i.* Être suspendu sur, menacer; être imminent; s'approcher. **impendence** or **impendency,** *n.* Imminence, *f.* **impendent** or **impending,** *a.* Imminent, menaçant.
impenetrability [impenitrə'biliti] or **impenetrableness,** *n.* Impénétrabilité, *f.* **impenetrable** [-'penitrəbl], *a.* Impénétrable; (*fig.*) inaccessible, insensible. **impenetrably,** *adv.* Impénétrablement.
impenitence [im'penitəns] or **impenitency,** *n.* Impénitence, *f.* **impenitent,** *a.* Impénitent. **impenitently,** *adv.* Dans l'impénitence.
impennate [im'penət], *a.* Sans plumes; sans ailes, aptère.
imperative [im'perətiv], *a.* Impératif; (*fig.*) obligatoire.—*n.* Impératif, *m.* *In the imperative,* à l'impératif. **imperatively,** *adv.* Impérativement.
imperceptible [impə'septibl], *a.* Imperceptible, insensible. **imperceptibleness** or **imperceptibility,** *n.* Imperceptibilité, *f.* **imperceptibly,** *adv.* Imperceptiblement, insensiblement.
imperfect [im'pə:fikt], *a.* Imparfait; incomplet. *a.* and *n.* (*Gram.*) Imparfait, *m.* **imperfection** [-'fekʃən], *n.* Imperfection, *f.* **imperfectly,** *adv.* Imparfaitement. **imperfectness,** *n.* État imparfait, *m.*
imperforate [im'pə:fərit], *a.* Imperforé; non-perforé (stamp). **imperforation** [-'reiʃən], *n.* Imperforation, *f.*
imperial [im'piəriəl], *a.* Impérial; (*fig.*) souverain, princier; grand jésus (of paper).—*n.* Impériale (beard etc.), *f.* **imperialism,** *n.* Impérialisme, colonialisme, *m.* **imperialist,** *a.* Impérialiste.—*n.* Impérialiste, *m.*; (*pl.*) impériaux (soldiers of the Emperor), *m.pl.* **imperialistic,** *a.* Colonialiste. **imperially,** *adv.* Impérialement; en empereur.
imperil [im'peril], *v.t.* Mettre en danger, hasarder, risquer.
imperious [im'piəriəs], *a.* Impérieux. **imperiously,** *adv.* Impérieusement. **imperiousness,** *n.* Caractère impérieux, *m.*; arrogance, hauteur, *f.*

imperishable [im′periʃəbl], *a.* Impérissable. **imperishableness,** *n.* Caractère impérissable, *m.* **imperishably,** *adv.* Impérissablement.

impermanence [im′pəːmənəns], *n.* Impermanence, *f.* **impermanent,** *a.* Impermanent, transitoire.

impermeability [impəːmiə′biliti], *n.* Imperméabilité, *f.* **impermeable** [-′pəːmiəbl], *a.* Imperméable.

impersonal [im′pəːsənəl], *a.* Impersonnel. **impersonality** [-pəːsə′næliti], *n.* Impersonnalité, *f.* **impersonally,** *adv.* Impersonnellement.

impersonate [im′pəːsəneit], *v.t.* Personnifier; (*Theat.*) représenter, jouer le rôle de. **impersonation** [-′neiʃən], *n.* Personnification; (*Theat.*) représentation, création, *f.,* rôle, *m.* **impersonator,** *n.* Personnificateur, *m.,* -trice, *f.*; imitateur, *m,* -trice, *f.*

impertinence [im′pəːtinəns], *n.* Impertinence, insolence, *f.* **impertinent,** *a.* Impertinent, insolent; hors de propos. *Impertinent person,* impertinent, *m.,* impertinente, *f.,* insolent, *m.,* insolente, *f.* **impertinently,** *adv.* D'un ton insolent; hors de propos, mal à propos.

imperturbability [impətəːbə′biliti], *n.* Imperturbabilité, *f.* **imperturbable** [-′təːbəbl], *a.* Imperturbable. **imperturbably,** *adv.* Imperturbablement.

impervious [im′pəːviəs], *a.* Imperméable, impénétrable; (*fig.*) inaccessible. **imperviously,** *adv.* D'une manière impénétrable. **imperviousness,** *n.* Imperméabilité, impénétrabilité, *f.*

impetigo [impi′taigou], *n.* (*Med.*) Impétigo, *m.*

impetrate [′impitreit], *v.t.* Impétrer, obtenir. **impetration** [-′treiʃən], *n.* Impétration, *f.*

impetuosity [impetju′ɔsiti] or **impetuousness** [im′petjuəsnis], *n.* Impétuosité, *f.* **impetuous** [-′petjuəs], *a.* Impétueux. **impetuously,** *adv.* Impétueusement.

impetus [′impitəs], *n.* Impulsion, vitesse acquise, *f.*; élan, essor, *m.*

impiety [im′paiəti], *n.* Impiété, *f.*

impinge [im′pindʒ], *v.i.* Se heurter (à or contre); empiéter (sur). **impingement,** *n.* Heurt; empiètement, *m.*

impious [′impiəs], *a.* Impie. **impiously,** *adv.* En impie, avec impiété.

impish [′impiʃ], *a.* Espiègle, malicieux. **impishness,** *n.* Espièglerie, *f.*

implacability [implækə′biliti], *n.* Implacabilité; haine implacable, *f.* **implacable,** *a.* Implacable, acharné. **implacably,** *adv.* Implacablement.

implant [im′plɑːnt], *v.t.* Implanter; (*fig.*) imprimer, inculquer.

implausible [im′plɔːzibl], *a.* Peu plausible, peu vraisemblable. **implausibly,** *adv.* Peu plausiblement.

implement (1) [′implimənt], *n.* Outil; instrument; ustensile, *m.*; (*pl.*) attirail, *m.* *Flint implement,* outil de pierre, *m.*

implement (2) [′impliment], *v.t.* Exécuter; accomplir; mettre en œuvre. **implementation** or **implementing,** *n.* Exécution, mise en œuvre, *f.*

implicate [′implikeit], *v.t.* Impliquer. **implication** [-′keiʃən], *n.* Implication, *f.* *By implication,* implicitement.

implicit [im′plisit], *a.* Implicite; (*fig.*) aveugle. *Implicit obedience,* obéissance absolue, *f.* **implicitly,** *adv.* Implicitement. **implicitness,** *n.* Caractère implicite, *m.*; (*fig.*) foi implicite, confiance aveugle, *f.*

implied [im′plaid], *a.* Implicite, tacite, qui va sans dire. **impliedly,** *adv.* Implicitement; tacitement.

implore [im′plɔː], *v.t.* Implorer, conjurer, supplier (de). **imploring,** *a.* Suppliant. **imploringly,** *adv.* Instamment, d'un ton de supplication.

imply [im′plai], *v.t.* Impliquer, signifier, vouloir dire; donner à entendre (to hint).

impolicy [im′pɔlisi], *n.* Mauvaise politique; inopportunité, inconvenance, *f.*

impolite [impə′lait], *a.* Impoli. **impolitely,** *adv.* Impoliment. **impoliteness,** *n.* Impolitesse, *f.*

impolitic [im′pɔlitik], *a.* Impolitique; imprudent. **impoliticly,** *adv.* Impolitiquement.

imponderability [impɔndərə′biliti] or **imponderousness,** *n.* Impondérabilité, *f.* **imponderable** [-′pɔndərəbl] or **imponderous,** *a.* Impondérable.

import (1) [′impɔːt], *n.* Portée, signification, *f.,* sens, *m.*; importance, valeur, *f.*; (*Comm.*) importation, *f.* *Import duty,* droit d'entrée, *m.*

import (2) [im′pɔːt], *v.t.* Importer; introduire; signifier, vouloir dire, indiquer. **importable,** *a.* Importable.

importance [im′pɔːtəns], *n.* Importance, *f.* **important,** *a.* Important. *It is important that* . . . , il importe que . . . . **importantly,** *adv.* Avec importance, d'une manière importante. **importation** [-′teiʃən] or **importing,** *n.* Importation, *f.* **importer,** *n.* Importateur, *m.*

importunate [im′pɔːtjunit], *a.* Importun; pressant. **importunately,** *adv.* Importunément, avec importunité.

importune [im′pɔːtjuːn], *v.t.* Importuner. **importunity** [-′tjuːniti], *a.* Importunité, *f.*

impose [im′pouz], *v.t.* Imposer.—*v.i.* En imposer (à). *To impose upon,* en imposer à, tromper, en faire accroire à. **imposing,** *a.* Imposant.—*n.* (*Print.*) Imposition, *f.* **imposing-stone,** *n.* (*Print.*) Marbre, *m.*

imposition [impə′ziʃən], *n.* Impôt (tax), *m.*; imposture (deceit), supercherie, *f.*; (*sch.*) pensum, *m.*

impossibility [impɔsi′biliti], *n.* Impossibilité, *f.*; chose impossible, *f.*

impossible [im′pɔsəbl], *a.* Impossible. *It is impossible for me,* il m'est impossible de, il n'y a pas moyen de.—*n.* L'impossible, *m.* *No one is expected to do the impossible,* à l'impossible nul n'est tenu.

impost [′impoust], *n.* Impôt; (*Arch.*) imposte, *f.*

impostor [im′pɔstə], *n.* Imposteur, *m.* **imposture,** *n.* Imposture, tromperie, *f.*

impotence [′impətəns] or **impotency,** *n.* Impuissance, *f.* **impotent,** *a.* Impuissant; faible; (*Path.*) impotent, perclus. **impotently,** *adv.* Sans force; en vain.

impound [im′paund], *v.t.* Mettre en fourrière; (*fig.*) enfermer, emprisonner.

impoverish [im′pɔvəriʃ], *v.t.* Appauvrir. **impoverishment,** *n.* Appauvrissement, *m.*

impracticability [impræktikə'biliti] or **impracticableness**, *a.* Impraticabilité, impossibilité, *f.* **impracticable** [-'præktikəbl], *a.* Impraticable; intraitable (of persons). **impracticably**, *adv.* D'une manière impraticable. **imprecate** ['imprəkeit], *v.t.* Faire des imprécations contre, maudire. **imprecation** [-'keiʃən], *n.* Imprécation, *f. A fierce imprecation*, un gros juron, *m.* **imprecatory**, *a.* Imprécatoire. **imprecise** [impri'sais], *a.* Imprécis. **imprecision**, *n.* Imprécision, *f.* **impregnable** [im'pregnəbl], *a.* Imprenable; inexpugnable; (*fig.*) inébranlable. **impregnably**, *adv.* De manière à être imprenable. **impregnate** [im'pregneit], *v.t.* Imprégner (de); féconder. **impregnated**, *a.* Imprégné (de); fécondé. **impregnation** [-'neiʃən], *n.* Fécondation, imprégnation, *f.* **impresario** [imprə'zɑːriou], *n.* Imprésario, *m.* **imprescriptibility** [imprəskripti'biliti], *n.* Imprescriptibilité, *f.* **imprescriptible** [-'skriptibl], *a.* Imprescriptible. **impress** (1) [im'pres], *v.t.* Imprimer (à); empreindre; (*fig.*) graver à (to effect); pénétrer (de); impressionner, imposer à (de); (*Mil.*) réquisitionner. **impress** (2) ['impres], *n.* Impression, empreinte, *f.* **impressibility** [-i'biliti], *n.* Sensibilité, *f.* **impressible** [-'presibl], *a.* Impressionnable, sensible. **impression**, *n.* Impression, empreinte; (*fig.*) idée, *f.*; (*Print.*) foulage, *m. My impression is that*, j'ai dans l'idée que; *proof impression*, épreuve avant la lettre, *f.*; *to be under the impression that . . .*, avoir l'impression que. . . . **impressionable**, *a.* Impressionnable. **impressionism**, *n.* (*Paint.*) Impressionnisme, *m.* **impressionist**, *n.* Impressionniste. **impressionistic**, *a.* Impressionniste. **impressive**, *a.* Impressionnant, frappant, touchant, émouvant. **impressively**, *adv.* De manière à faire impression; d'une manière touchante *or* pénétrante. **impressiveness**, *n.* Force, puissance, grandeur, nature touchante, nature pénétrante, *f.* **impressment**, *n.* Réquisition (de vivres), *f.*; presse (of sailors), *f.* **imprest** ['imprest], *n.* Avance de fonds, *m.* **imprimatur** [impri'meitə], *n.* Imprimatur, *m.*; (*fig.*) sanction, approbation, *f.* **imprint** (1) [im'print], *v.t.* Imprimer, empreindre. **imprint** (2) ['imprint], *n.* Empreinte, *f.*; nom de l'imprimeur *or* de l'éditeur (en tête *or* à la fin), *m.* **imprison** [im'prizn], *v.t.* Emprisonner, mettre en prison, enfermer. **imprisonment**, *n.* Emprisonnement, *m.*, détention, *f. A year's imprisonment*, un an de prison; *false imprisonment*, détention illégale, *f.* **improbability** [imprɔbə'biliti], *n.* Improbabilité; invraisemblance, *f.* **improbable** [im'prɔbəbl], *a.* Improbable, invraisemblable. **improbably**, *adv.* Invraisemblablement. **improbity** [im'proubiti], *n.* Improbité, *f.* **impromptu** [im'promptjuː], *a.* Impromptu, improvisé.—*adv.* Par improvisation, sans préparation, impromptu.—*n.* Impromptu, *m.* **improper** [im'prɔpə], *a.* Inconvenant, peu convenable (à); malséant, peu propre (à),

impropre (of language), inexact. *He is an improper person for that employment*, il convient peu à cet emploi; *improper character*, personne de mauvaise réputation, *f.*; *improper fraction*, nombre fractionnaire, *m.* **improperly**, *adv.* D'une manière peu convenable; à tort, improprement, mal à propos. **impropriate** [im'prouprieit], *v.t.* Approprier; (*Eccles.*) séculariser.—*a.* [-ət] Sécularisé. **impropriation** [-'eiʃən], *n.* Sécularisation, *f.*; bénéfice sécularisé, *m.* **impropriator** [-'prouprieitə], *n.* Possesseur d'un bénéfice sécularisé, *m.* **impropriety** [impro'praiəti], *n.* Inconvenance (of conduct); impropriété (of language), *f.* **improvable** [im'pruːvəbl], *a.* Susceptible d'amélioration, amendable, perfectible. **improve** [im'pruːv], *v.t.* Améliorer, perfectionner (an invention etc.); faire des progrès à, faire avancer; utiliser, profiter de; bonifier (land etc.); embellir (to embellish); faire valoir, exploiter (to cultivate).—*v.i.* S'améliorer; se perfectionner; se bonifier (of wine etc.); faire des progrès, avancer; s'embellir; (*Comm.*) hausser, augmenter de prix. *To have improved*, avoir fait des progrès, être embelli (in looks); *to improve on acquaintance*, gagner à être connu; *to improve the shining hour*, pour s'occuper; *to improve upon*, améliorer, perfectionner, surpasser, ajouter à. **improvement**, *n.* Amélioration, *f.*; perfectionnement; progrès, avancement (in learning), *m.*; instruction, *f.*; emploi (use), *m.*; application pratique, *f. There is room for improvement*, cela laisse à désirer; *to be an improvement on*, surpasser, valoir mieux que. **improver**, *n.* Personne qui améliore *or* qui utilise, *f.*; réformateur, *m.*, réformatrice, *f.*; (*Dress.*) apprentie, *f.* **improving**, *a.* Améliorant; instructif, édifiant. **improvidence** [im'prɔvidəns], *n.* Imprévoyance, *f.* **improvident**, *a.* Imprévoyant. **improvidently**, *adv.* Avec imprévoyance, sans prévoyance. **improvisation** [imprəvai'zeiʃən], *n.* Improvisation, *f.* **improvisator** [-prəvai'zeitə], **improviser**, *n.* Improvisateur, *m.* **improvisatrice** [improviːzɑː'triːtʃei], *n.* (*pl.* **improvisatrici**) Improvisatrice, *f.* **improvise** ['imprəvaiz], *v.t.* Improviser. **imprudence** [im'pruːdəns], *n.* Imprudence, *f.* **imprudent**, *a.* Imprudent. *An imprudent act*, une imprudence. **imprudently**, *adv.* Imprudemment. **impuberal** [im'pjuːbərəl], *a.* Impubère. **impuberty**, *n.* Impuberté, enfance, *f.* **impudence** ['impjudəns], *n.* Impudence, effronterie, *f.* **impudent**, *a.* Impudent, effronté. *An impudent person*, un(e) insolent(e). **impudently**, *adv.* Impudemment, effrontément. **impugn** [im'pjuːn], *v.t.* Attaquer, contester; (*fig.*) mettre en doute; (*Law*) récuser. **impugner** (an invention etc.), Antagoniste, *m.* **impugnment**, *n.* (*Law*) Récusation, *f.* **impulse** ['impʌls] or **impulsion** [-'pʌlʃən], *n.* Impulsion, *f.*, mouvement; (*fig.*) motif, élan, *m. Sudden impulse*, coup de tête, *m.* **impulsive** [im'pʌlsiv], *a.* Impulsif, primesautier. **impulsively**, *adv.* Par impulsion, par un mouvement involontaire. **impulsiveness**, *n.* Caractère impulsif, *m.*

impunity [im'pju:niti], *n.* Impunité, *f.* With *impunity*, impunément.

impure [im'pjuə], *a.* Impur; impudique. **impurely**, *adv.* Impurement; impudiquement. **impurity**, *n.* Impureté; impudicité, *f.*

imputable [im'pju:təbl], *a.* Imputable.

imputation [-'teiʃən], *n.* Imputation, accusation, *f.* *Have you heard any imputation to the contrary?* avez-vous reçu avis du contraire? **imputative**, *a.* Imputatif. **imputatively**, *adv.* Par imputation. **impute**, *v.t.* Imputer, attribuer (à).

in [in], *prep.* En, dans; à; par; pour; sur; avec, chez, parmi (among). *At six o'clock in the evening,* à six heures du soir; *he will do it in one hour,* il fera cela en une heure; *he will start in one hour,* il partira dans une heure; *in a black coat,* en habit noir; *in a carriage,* en voiture; *in a fog,* par le brouillard; *in another light,* sous un autre jour; *in bed,* au lit; *in black and white,* par écrit; *in blank,* en blanc; *in doing that,* en faisant cela; *in England,* en Angleterre; *in for a penny, in for a pound,* le vin est tiré, il faut le boire; *in good health,* en bonne santé; *in his country,* dans son pays; *in January (February etc.),* en janvier, au mois de janvier (février etc.); *in Japan,* au Japon; *in Paris,* à Paris; *in self-defence,* pour sa propre défense; *in spite of,* malgré; *in spring,* au printemps; *in summer (autumn, winter),* en été (automne, hiver); *in that,* vu que, puisque; *in that case,* dans ce cas; *in the accusative,* au cas régime; *in the air,* dans l'air, en l'air; *in the City,* dans la cité; *in the class-room,* dans la classe; *in the country,* à la campagne (out of town); *in the distance,* au loin; *in the English way,* à l'anglaise; *in the fashion,* à la mode; *in the morning,* le matin; *in the name of,* au nom de; *in the sun,* au soleil; *in the U.S.A.,* aux États-Unis; *in town,* en ville; *in vino veritas,* bu n'a point de secrets; *never in his life,* jamais de sa vie; *one in ten,* un sur dix; *the way in which,* la manière dont; *they came in bands,* ils sont venus par bandes; *to be clothed in,* être vêtu de; *you must expect that in children,* il faut s'attendre à cela chez les enfants.—*adv.* Dedans, au dedans, rentré; chez soi, à la maison, y (at home); élu (elected); au pouvoir (in power). *All in,* tout compris; (*fam.*) éreinté; *I am in for six months of it,* j'en ai pour six mois à m'ennuyer; *I have had my coals in,* j'ai fait ma provision de charbon; *is my brother in?* mon frère est-il à la maison, est-il chez lui, y est-il? *my hand is in,* je suis en train; *my luck is in,* je suis en veine; *put it in,* mettez-le dedans; *the first in,* le premier arrivé; *the Conservatives are in now,* les conservateurs sont au pouvoir à present; *the harvest is in,* la moisson est rentrée; *thrown in,* pardessus; *to be in for it,* être dedans, y être; *to come in,* entrer; *to have in,* faire entrer, faire provision de, se procurer (things); *to take in,* rentrer (harvest); duper (to cheat); mettre dedans.—*n.* To *know all the ins and outs of a matter,* connaître les tenants et les aboutissants d'une affaire.

inability [inə'biliti], *n.* Impuissance, incapacité, *f.*

inaccessibility [inæksesi'biliti] or **inaccessibleness**, *n.* Inaccessibilité, *f.* **inaccessible**

[-'sesibl], *a.* Inaccessible; inaccostable, inabordable (à).

inaccuracy [i'nækjurəsi], *n.* Inexactitude, *f.* **inaccurate**, *a.* Inexact. **inaccurately**, *adv.* Inexactement.

inaction [i'nækʃən], *n.* Inaction, inertie, *f.* **inactive**, *a.* Inactif; inerte (of things). **inactively**, *adv.* Inactivement. **inactivity** [-'tiviti], *n.* Inactivité, *f.*

inadequacy [i'nædikwəsi] or **inadequateness**, *n.* Insuffisance, imperfection, *f.* **inadequate**, *a.* Insuffisant; imparfait, défectueux, incomplet. **inadequately**, *adv.* Insuffisamment.

inadmissibility [inədmisi'biliti], *n.* Inadmissibilité, *f.* **inadmissible** [-'misibl], *a.* Inadmissible.

inadvertence [inəd'və:təns] or **inadvertency**, *n.* Inadvertance, *f.* **inadvertent**, *a.* Négligent, inattentif. **inadvertently**, *adv.* Par inadvertance.

inalienability [ineiliənə'biliti] or **inalienableness**, *n.* Inaliénabilité, *f.*

inalienable [in'eiliənəbl], *a.* Inaliénable; inséparable. **inalienably**, *adv.* D'une manière inaliénable.

inalterability [inɔ:ltərə'biliti], *n.* Inaltérabilité, *f.* **inalterable** [-'ɔ:ltərəbl], *a.* Inaltérable.

inane [i'nein], *a.* Vide; (*fig.*) inepte, absurde. **inanimate** [i'nænimit], *a.* Inanimé; mort. **inanition** [inæ'niʃən], *n.* Inanition, *f.*

inanity [i'næniti], *n.* Inanité, *f.*

inapplicability [inəplikə'biliti], *n.* Inapplicabilité, *f.*

inapplicable [i'næplikəbl], *a.* Inapplicable. **inapplication** [-'keiʃən], *n.* Inapplication, *f.* **inapposite** [i'næpəzit], *a.* Peu approprié, inapplicable, mal à propos, sans rapport.

inappreciable [inə'pri:ʃəbl], *a.* Inappréciable, insensible. **inappreciably**, *adv.* Inappréciablement.

inapprehensible [inæpri'hensibl], *a.* Incompréhensible, inintelligible. **inapprehensive**, *a.* Insouciant; sans crainte.

inapproachable [inə'proutʃəbl], *a.* Inaccessible, inabordable.

inappropriate [inə'proupriit], *a.* Peu propre, qui ne convient pas.

inapt [i'næpt], *a.* Inapte, impropre, peu propre (à). **inaptitude** or **inaptness**, *n.* Inaptitude, *f.* **inaptly**, *adv.* Mal, improprement.

inarch [i'nɑ:tʃ], *v.t.* (*Hort.*) Greffer par rapprochement. **inarching**, *n.* Greffage, *m.*

inarticulate [inɑ:'tikjulit], *a.* Inarticulé. **inarticulately**, *adv.* D'une manière inarticulée, indistinctement. **inarticulateness**, *n.* Défaut d'articulation, *m.*

inartistic [inɑ:'tistik], *a.* Peu artistique.

inasmuch [inəz'mʌtʃ], *adv.* Vu que, attendu que, d'autant que.

inattention [inə'tenʃən], *n.* Inattention; distraction; négligence, *f.* **inattentive**, *a.* Inattentif, distrait; négligent. **inattentively**, *adv.* Sans attention, négligemment.

inaudibility [inɔ:di'biliti], *n.* Imperceptibilité, insaisissabilité, *f.* **inaudible** [i'nɔ:dibl], *a.* Imperceptible, qu'on ne peut entendre. **inaudibly**, *adv.* À ne pouvoir être entendu.

inaugural [i'nɔ:gjurəl], *a.* Inaugural, d'inauguration. **inaugurate**, *v.t.* Inaugurer.

inauguration [-'reiʃən], *n.* Inauguration, *f.*
inauguratory, *a.* D'inauguration.
inauspicious [inɔː'spiʃəs], *a.* Malheureux, peu propice. **inauspiciously,** *adv.* Sous de mauvais auspices. **inauspiciousness,** *n.* Mauvais auspices, *m.pl.*
inbeing ['inbiːiŋ], *n.* Existence inhérente, nature essentielle, *f.*
inboard ['inbɔːd], *adv.* (*Naut.*) Dans la cale d'un vaisseau.—*prep.* En abord de.
inborn ['inbɔːn], **inbred** ['inbred], *a.* Inné, naturel.
inbreeding [in'briːdiŋ], *n.* Consanguinité, *f.*; croisement consanguin, *m.*
incalculable [in'kælkjuləbl], *a.* Incalculable. **incalculably,** *adv.* Incalculablement.
incandescence [inkæn'desəns], *n.* Incandescence, *f.* **incandescent,** *a.* Incandescent. *Incandescent burner,* bec Auer, *m.*; *incandescent lamp,* lampe à incandescence, *f.*
incantation [inkæn'teiʃən], *n.* Incantation, *f.*, charme, *m.*
incantatory [in'kæntətəri], *a.* Incantatoire.
incapability [inkeipə'biliti], *n.* Incapacité, *f.* **incapable** [-'keipəbl], *a.* Incapable (de); peu susceptible (de).
incapacitate [inkə'pæsiteit], *v.i.* Rendre incapable (de). **incapacitation** [-'teiʃən], *n.* Incapacité; (*Law*) privation de capacité légale, *f.* **incapacity** [-'pæsiti], *n.* Incapacité, *f.*
incarcerate [in'kɑːsəreit], *v.t.* Incarcérer, mettre en prison. **incarceration** [-'reiʃən], *n.* Incarcération, *f.*
incarnate (1) [in'kɑːnit], *a.* Incarné. *A devil incarnate,* un diable incarné.
incarnate (2) [in'kɑːneit], *v.t.* Revêtir de chair, incarner. **incarnation** [-'neiʃən], *n.* Incarnation, *f.*
incautious [in'kɔːʃəs], *a.* Imprévoyant, inconsidéré, imprudent. **incautiously,** *adv.* Imprudemment, inconsidérément; par mégarde. **incautiousness,** *n.* Imprudence, négligence, *f.*
incendiarism [in'sendjərizm], *n.* Crime d'incendie, *m.* **incendiary,** *a.* and *n.* Incendiaire. *Incendiary bomb,* bombe incendiaire, *f.*
incense ['insens], *n.* Encens, *m.*—*v.t.* ['insens] Encenser; [in'sens] irriter, exaspérer (contre); provoquer. **incense-breathing,** *a.* (*poet.*) Embaumé.
incentive [in'sentiv], *n.* Motif, stimulant, encouragement, *m.*—*a.* Excitant, stimulant.
inception [in'sepʃən], *n.* Commencement, *m.* **inceptive,** *a.* Initial; (*Gram.*) inchoatif.
incertitude [in'sɔːtitjuːd], *n.* Incertitude, *f.*
incessant [in'sesənt], *a.* Incessant; continuel. **incessantly,** *adv.* Sans cesse, sans relâche, continuellement.
incest ['insest], *n.* Inceste, *m.*
incestuous [in'sestjuəs], *a.* Incestueux. **incestuously,** *adv.* Incestueusement. **incestuousness,** *n.* État incestueux, *m.*
inch [intʃ], *n.* Pouce (2·539 centimètres), *m.* *By inches* (of dying), peu à peu, à petit feu; *every inch,* jusqu'au bout des ongles; *he did not yield an inch,* il n'a pas reculé d'une semelle; *inch by inch,* pied à pied; *within an inch of,* à deux doigts de.
inchoate ['inkouit], *a.* Commencé, incomplet, rudimentaire.—**v.t.* [-eit] Commencer. **inchoately,** *adv.* À l'état rudimentaire.

inchoation [-'eiʃən], *n.* ʋCommencement, *m.*
inchoative [in'kouətiv], *a.* (*Gram.*) Inchoatif.
incidence ['insidəns], *n.* Incidence, *f.*
incident, *a.* Qui arrive; particulier, qui appartient (à).—*n.* Incident, événement, *m.*; (*pl.*) péripéties, *f.pl.* **incidental** [-'dentl], *a.* Fortuit, accidentel; accessoire. *Incidental expenses,* faux frais, *m.pl.*; (*Theat.*) *incidental music,* musique de scène, *f.*—*n.* Chose fortuite, *f.* **incidentally,** *adv.* Fortuitement, par hasard, incidemment; soit dit en passant.
incinerate [in'sinəreit], *v.t.* Incinérer. **incineration,** *n.* Incinération, *f.* **incinerator,** *n.* Incinérateur, *m.*
incipience [in'sipiəns], *n.* Commencement, *m.* **incipient,** *a.* Naissant, qui commence, premier.
incise [in'saiz], *v.t.* Inciser, graver. **incised,** *a.* Incisé. **incision** [-'siʒən], *n.* Incision, *f.* **incisive** [-'saisiv], *a.* Incisif. **incisor** [-'saizə], *n.* (Dent) incisive, *f.*
incitant [in'saitənt], *a.* and *n.* Incitant, *m.* **incitation** [-si'teiʃən], *n.* Incitation, *f.* **incite** [in'sait], *v.t.* Inciter, exciter, stimuler; encourager, porter (à).
incitement [in'saitmənt], *n.* Encouragement, *m.*, excitation, *f.*, motif, stimulant, *m.*; (*Med.*) incitation, *f.* **inciter,** *n.* Instigateur, incitateur, *m.*
incivility [insi'viliti], *n.* Incivilité, malhonnêteté, impolitesse, *f.*
inclemency [in'klemənsi], *n.* Inclémence, *f.*; intempérie, *f.pl.*, rigueur (of the weather etc.), *f.* **inclement,** *a.* Inclément; rigoureux.
inclinable [in'klainəbl], *a.* Enclin, porté, tendant (à).
inclination [inkli'neiʃən], *n.* Inclinaison, pente; inclination (of the head or body), *f.*; penchant, goût (liking), *m.* *From inclination,* par inclination, par goût.
incline (1) ['inklain], *n.* Pente, *f.*, plan incliné, *m.*; (*Rail.*) rampe, *f.*
incline (2) [in'klain], *v.t.* Incliner, (faire) pencher; (*fig.*) porter, disposer (à).—*v.i.* Incliner, s'incliner, pencher; (*fig.*) être porté, être disposé (à); tirer (sur) (of colours). *To incline to the right,* (*Mil.*) appuyer à droite. *Left incline,* oblique à gauche, (marche)! **inclined,** *a.* Incliné; enclin (à); porté, disposé (à). *I am that way inclined,* je suis porté à cela; *if you feel inclined,* si le cœur vous en dit; *inclined plane,* plan incliné, *m.*
include [in'kluːd], *v.t.* Comprendre, comporter, renfermer. **included,** *a.* Compris, y compris. *Not included,* sans compter; *this room included,* y compris cette chambre. **including,** *a.* or *adv.* Comprenant, y compris. *Including the ladies,* y compris les dames, les dames comprises.
inclusion [in'kluːʒən], *n.* Inclusion, *f.*
inclusive [in'kluːsiv], *a.* Inclusif; qui renferme, qui comprend. *Inclusive of,* y compris; *inclusive terms,* tout compris, sans suppléments. **inclusively,** *adv.* Inclusivement.
incoercible [inkou'əːsibl], *a.* (*Phys.*) Incoercible.
incog [in'kɔg], *adv.* (*colloq.*)=**incognito** [in'kɔgnitou], *adv.* Incognito.
incoherence [inkou'hiərəns], **incoherency,** or **incohesion** [-'hiːʒən], *n.* Incohérence, *f.* **incoherent,** *a.* Incohérent. **incoherently,**

adv. Sans cohérence, d'une manière incohérente.

incombustibility [inkəmbʌsti'biliti] or **incombustibleness,** *n.* Incombustibilité, *f.* **incombustible** [-'bʌstibl], *a.* Incombustible.

income ['inkʌm], *n.* Revenu, *m. Private income,* rente, *f.*, rentes, *f.pl.* **income-tax,** *n.* Impôt sur le revenu, *m.*

incomer ['inkʌmə], *n.* Personne qui entre, *f.*; intrus, *m.* **incoming,** *a.* Nouveau, entrant. —*n.pl.* Revenus, *m.pl.*

incommensurability [inkəmenʃərə'biliti], *n.* Incommensurabilité, *f.* **incommensurable** [-'menʃərəbl], *a.* Incommensurable. **incommensurate,** *a.* Incommensurable, disproportionné.

incommode [inkə'moud], *v.t.* Incommoder, gêner, déranger. **incommodious,** *a.* Incommode. **incommodiously,** *adv.* Incommodément. **incommodiousness** or **incommodity** [inkə'mɔditi], *n.* Incommodité, *f.*

incommunicability [inkəmju:nikə'biliti], *n.* Incommunicabilité, *f.* **incommunicable** [-'mju:nikəbl], *a.* Incommunicable, peu communicatif. **incommunicative,** *a.* Peu communicatif, insociable.

incommutability [inkəmju:tə'biliti], *n.* Incommutabilité, *f.* **incommutable** [-'mju:təbl], *a.* Incommuable; (*Law*) incommutable.

incomparable [in'kɔmpərəbl], *a.* Incomparable. **incomparably,** *adv.* Incomparablement.

incompatibility [inkəmpæti'biliti], *n.* Incompatibilité, *f.* **incompatible** [-'pætibl], *a.* Incompatible. **incompatibly,** *adv.* Incompatiblement.

incompetence [in'kɔmpitəns] or **incompetency,** *n.* Incompétence, insuffisance; (*Law*) incapacité, *f.* **incompetent,** *a.* Incompétent, incapable, insuffisant. **incompetently,** *adv.* Incompétemment.

incomplete [inkəm'pli:t], *a.* Imparfait, inachevé, incomplet. **incompletely,** *adv.* Incomplètement, imparfaitement. **incompleteness,** *n.* État incomplet, *m.*, imperfection, *f.*

incomprehensibility [inkɔmprihensi'biliti] or **incomprehensibleness,** *n.* Incompréhensibilité, *f.* **incomprehensible** [-'hensibl], *a.* Incompréhensible. **incomprehensibly,** *adv.* Incompréhensiblement. **incomprehensive,** *a.* Peu étendu, borné.

incompressibility [inkəmpresi'biliti], *n.* Incompressibilité, *f.* **incompressible** [-'presibl], *a.* Incompressible.

inconceivable [inkən'si:vəbl], *a.* Inconcevable. **inconceivableness,** *n.* Nature inconcevable, *f.* **inconceivably,** *adv.* D'une manière inconcevable.

inconclusive [inkən'klu:siv], *a.* Qui n'est pas concluant, inconcluant. **inconclusively,** *adv.* D'une manière peu concluante, sans conclure. **inconclusiveness,** *n.* Nature peu concluante, *f.*

incondensable [inkən'densəbl], *a.* Non condensable.

incondite [in'kɔndit], *a.* Mal fait, inachevé, informe, cru.

inconformity [inkən'fɔːmiti], *n.* Manque de conformité, manque d'accord, *m.*

incongruity [inkɔŋ'gruːiti], *a.* Désaccord, *m.*, incongruité; inconvenance, *f.*

incongruous [in'kɔŋgruəs], *a.* Incongru, inconvenant, impropre; (*fig.*) disparate, hétéroclite. **incongruously,** *adv.* Incongrûment; mal à propos.

inconsequence [in'kɔnsikwəns], *n.* Inconséquence; fausse déduction, *f.* **inconsequent,** *a.* Inconséquent. **inconsequential** [-'kwenʃəl], *a.* Illogique, mal déduit; sans importance. **inconsequentially** or **inconsequently,** *adv.* Inconséquemment, illogiquement.

inconsiderable [inkən'sidərəbl], *a.* Peu considérable, petit, insignifiant; de peu d'importance. **inconsiderableness,** *n.* Manque d'importance, *m.*

inconsiderate [inkən'sidərət], *a.* Inconsidéré, irréfléchi; sans égards pour les autres. **inconsiderately,** *adv.* Inconsidérément, sans réflexion. *To behave inconsiderately (towards),* manquer d'égards (envers). **inconsiderateness** or **inconsideration** [-'reiʃən], *n.* Irréflexion, inconsidération, imprudence, *f.*

inconsistency [inkən'sistənsi] or **inconsistence,** *n.* Inconséquence; inconsistance, incompatibilité, contradiction, *f.* **inconsistent,** *a.* Incompatible (avec), contradictoire (à); inconséquent, manquant de suite. **inconsistently,** *adv.* Inconséquemment; illogiquement.

inconsolable [inkən'souləbl], *a.* Inconsolable (de). **inconsolably,** *adv.* Inconsolablement.

inconsonance [in'kɔnsənəns], *n.* Discordance, *f.*, manque d'harmonie, *m.* **inconsonant,** *a.* Discordant; peu conforme.

inconspicuous [inkən'spikjuəs], *a.* Peu apparent, peu remarquable, mal défini. **inconspicuousness,** *n.* Caractère peu remarquable, *m.*

inconstancy [in'kɔnstənsi], *n.* Inconstance, *f.*; caractère changeant, *m.* **inconstant,** *a.* Inconstant, volage, changeant. **inconstantly,** *adv.* Inconstamment.

incontestable [inkən'testəbl], *a.* Incontestable, irrécusable. **incontestably,** *adv.* Incontestablement, sans contredit. **incontested,** *a.* Incontesté.

incontinence [in'kɔntinəns] or **incontinency,** *n.* Incontinence, *f.* **incontinent,** *a.* Incontinent. **incontinently,** *adv.* *Avec incontinence; immédiatement, aussitôt, sur-le-champ.

incontrovertible [inkɔntrə'vəːtibl], *a.* Incontestable, indisputable. **incontrovertibly,** *adv.* Incontestablement, sans contredit.

inconvenience [inkən'viːniəns] or **inconveniency,** *n.* Inconvénient, *m.*, incommodité, *f.*; embarras, dérangement, ennui, *m.*; difficulté, *f. To put to great inconvenience,* donner beaucoup de dérangement à. **inconvenience,** *v.t.* Déranger, incommoder, gêner. **inconvenient,** *a.* Incommode, gênant, malcommode. *If it is inconvenient to you,* si cela vous gêne; *you come at an inconvenient time,* vous venez dans un mauvais moment. **inconveniently,** *adv.* Incommodément, mal.

inconvertible [inkən'vəːtibl], *a.* Non convertible, inconvertible.

inconvincible [inkən'vinsibl], *a.* Qu'on ne peut convaincre.

incorporate [in'kɔ:pəreit], *v.t.* Incorporer, former en société.—*v.i.* S'incorporer. **incorporated,** *a.* Incorporé. **incorporation** [-'reiʃən], *n.* Incorporation, *f.*
incorporeal [inkɔ:'pɔ:riəl], *a.* Incorporel, immatériel. **incorporeally,** *adv.* D'une manière incorporelle, immatériellement. **incorporeity** [-'ri:iti], *n.* Incorporalité, immatérialité, *f.*
incorrect [inkə'rekt], *a.* Incorrect, inexact. **incorrectly,** *adv.* Incorrectement; inexactement. **incorrectness,** *n.* Incorrection; inexactitude, *f.*
incorrigibility [inkɔridʒi'biliti] or **incorrigibleness,** *n.* Incorrigibilité, *f.*
incorrigible [in'kɔridʒibl], *a.* Incorrigible. **incorrigibly,** *adv.* Incorrigiblement.
incorrupt [inkə'rʌpt] or **incorrupted,** *a.* Incorrompu, pur, intègre. **incorruptibility** [-i'biliti] or **incorruptibleness,** *n.* Incorruptibilité, intégrité, *f.* **incorruptible** [-'rʌptibl], *a.* Incorruptible. **incorruption,** *n.* Incorruption, intégrité, *f.* **incorruptive,** *a.* Incorruptible. **incorruptness,** *n.* Incorruptibilité, pureté, intégrité, *f.*
incrassate [in'kræseit], *v.t.* Épaissir; s'épaissir. —*a.* [-sit] Épaissi. **incrassation** [-'seiʃən], *n.* Épaississement, *f.*
increase (1) [in'kri:s], *v.t.* Augmenter, agrandir, accroître.—*v.i.* Croître, s'accroître; augmenter, s'accentuer.
increase (2) ['inkri:s], *n.* Augmentation (of prices), *f.*, accroissement (of speed), surcroît (of work); (*fig.*) produit, *m.*; crue (of rivers), *f.* **increasing,** *a.* Croissant. *To go on increasing,* aller toujours croissant. **increasingly,** *adv.* De plus en plus.
incredibility [inkredi'biliti] or **incredibleness,** *n.* Caractère incroyable, *m.*; incrédibilité, *f.*
incredible [in'kredibl], *a.* Incroyable. **incredibly,** *adv.* Incroyablement, d'une manière incroyable.
incredulity [inkrə'dju:liti], *n.* Incrédulité, *f.*
incredulous [in'kredjuləs], *a.* Incrédule. **incredulousness,** *n.* Incrédulité, *f.*
increment ['inkrimənt], *n.* Augmentation, *f.*; produit, *m.*; plus-value, *f.*; quantité différentielle, *f.*
incriminate [in'krimineit], *v.t.* Incriminer. **incriminating,** *a.* Tendant à incriminer, (pièces) à conviction (of articles). **incriminatory,** *a.* Tendant à incriminer.
incrust [ENCRUST].
incrustation [inkrʌs'teiʃən], *n.* Incrustation, *f.*
incubate ['inkjubeit], *v.t.* Couver. **incubation** [-'beiʃən], *n.* Incubation, *f.*
incubator ['inkjubeitə], *n.* Couveuse artificielle, *f.*
incubus ['iŋkjubəs], *n.* Incube, cauchemar; (*fig.*) grand poids, *m.*
inculcate ['inkʌlkeit], *v.t.* Inculquer (à). **inculcation** [-'keiʃən], *n.* Action d'inculquer, *f.*, enseignement, *m.*
inculpate ['inkʌlpeit], *v.t.* Inculper, incriminer. **inculpation** [-'peiʃən], *n.* Inculpation, *f.* **inculpatory,** *a.* Qui tend à incriminer.
incumbency [in'kʌmbənsi], *n.* Charge; possession d'un bénéfice, *f.* **incumbent,** *a.* Couché, posé, appuyé (sur); enjoint, imposé, obligatoire. *To be incumbent on,* incomber à; *to feel it incumbent on one to do* . . ., se faire un devoir de . . . .—*n.* Titulaire, bénéficier, *m.*
incunabulum [inkju'næbjuləm], *n.* (*pl.* **incunabula**) Incunable, *m.*
incur [in'kə:], *v.t.* Encourir (censure), s'attirer (anger), s'exposer à; contracter, faire (debts).
incurability [inkjuərə'biliti] or **incurableness** *n.* Incurabilité, *f.* **incurable** [in'kjuərəbl], *a.* Incurable, inguérissable.—*n.* Incurable, *m.* *Hospital for incurables,* les Incurables, *m.pl.* **incurably,** *adv.* Incurablement, sans remède.
incuriosity [inkjuəri'ɔsiti], *n.* Incuriosité, *f.*
incurious [in'kjuəriəs], *a.* Peu curieux, sans curiosité, incurieux. **incuriously,** *adv.* Sans curiosité, incurieusement.
incursion [in'kə:ʃən], *n.* Incursion, irruption, *f.*
incurvate (1) [in'kə:veit], *v.t.* Courber.
incurvate (2) [in'kə:vit], *a.* or **incurved,** *a.* Courbé. **incurvation** [-'veiʃən], *n.* Courbure, *f.*
incurve [in'kə:v], *v.t.* Courber.
incuse [in'kju:z], *v.t.* Frapper en creux.
indebted [in'detid], *a.* Endetté; redevable (de). *Indebted for,* redevable de; *indebted to,* redevable à. **indebtedness,** *n.* Dette, obligation, *f.*
indecency [in'di:sənsi], *n.* Indécence, action indécente, *f.*, propos indécent, *m.* **indecent,** *a.* Indécent. **indecently,** *adv.* Indécemment.
indeciduous [indi'sidjuəs], *a.* (*Bot.*) Persistant.
indecipherable [indi'saifərəbl], *a.* Indéchiffrable.
indecision [indi'siʒən], *n.* Indécision, irrésolution, *f.* **indecisive** [-'saisiv], *a.* Peu décisif, indécis. **indecisively,** *adv.* D'une manière indécise. **indecisiveness,** *n.* État indécis, *m.*
indeclinable [indi'klainəbl], *a.* Indéclinable.
indecomposable [indi:kəm'pouzəbl], *a.* Indécomposable; (*Chem.*) simple.
indecorous [indi'kɔ:rəs *or* in'dekərəs], *a.* Inconvenant. **indecorously,** *adv.* D'une manière inconvenante. **indecorousness** or **indecorum** [indi'kɔ:rəm], *n.* Manque de décorum, *m.*, malséance, inconvenance, *f.*
indeed [in'di:d], *adv.* En effet, en vérité; vraiment; il est vrai, à dire vrai, à la vérité. *Indeed!* vraiment! allons donc! comment! *Yes indeed!* mais certainement!
indefatigable [indi'fætigəbl], *a.* Infatigable. **indefatigably,** *adv.* Infatigablement, sans se fatiguer.
indefeasibility [indifi:zi'biliti], *n.* Inaliénabilité, imprescriptibilité, *f.* **indefeasible** [-'fi:zibl], *a.* Inaliénable, imprescriptible.
indefectibility [indifekti'biliti], *n.* Indéfectibilité, *f.*
indefectible [indi'fektibl], *a.* Indéfectible.
indefensible [indi'fensibl], *a.* Indéfendable, inexcusable; insoutenable. **indefensibly,** *adv.* D'une manière inexcusable.
indefinable [indi'fainəbl], *a.* Indéfinissable.
indefinite [in'definit], *a.* Indéfini, vague. *Indefinite leave,* congé illimité, *m.* **indefinitely,** *adv.* Indéfiniment, vaguement. **indefiniteness,** *n.* Nature indéfinie, *f.*
indelible [in'delibl], *a.* Indélébile, ineffaçable. *Indelible pencil,* crayon à copier, *m.* **indelibly,** *adv.* D'une manière indélébile, ineffaçablement.

indelicacy [in'delikəsi], *n.* Indélicatesse, grossièreté, inconvenance, *f.*
indelicate [in'delikit], *a.* Indélicat, grossier, inconvenant. **indelicately,** *adv.* D'une manière indélicate, indélicatement.
indemnification [indemnifi'keiʃən], *n.* Indemnisation, *f.*, dédommagement, *m.*
indemnify [in'demnifai], *v.t.* Dédommager, indemniser (de); garantir (contre).
indemnity [in'demniti], *n.* Dédommagement, *m.*; indemnité; garantie, *f.* *Act of Indemnity,* bill d'indemnité, *m.*
indemonstrable [indi'mɔnstrəbl *or* in'de mɔnstrəbl], *a.* Qu'on ne peut démontrer, indémontrable.
indent [in'dent], *v.t.* Denteler; ébrécher, échancrer; (*Print.*) renfoncer; bosseler; empreindre.—*v.i.* To indent for, passer une commande pour, réquisitionner.—*n.* Dentelure, bosselure; empreinte (stamp), *f.*; (*Bank*) ordre d'achat, *m.*; (*Mil.*) ordre de réquisition, *m.* **indented,** *a.* Dentelé; échancré.
indentation [-'teiʃən], *n.* Dentelure; échancrure, *f.*
indention, *n.* (*Print.*) Renfoncement, *m.*
indenture [in'dentʃə], *n.* Titre; contrat; (*esp. pl.*) contrat d'apprentissage, *m.*—*v.t.* Mettre en apprentissage.
independence [indi'pendəns] *or* **independency,** *n.* Indépendance, *f.* **independent,** *a.* Indépendant; libre. *An independent gentleman, a man of independent means,* un rentier, *m.*; *independent firing,* (*Mil.*) feu à volonté, *m.*; *independent school,* école libre, *f.*; *to be independent,* vivre dans l'indépendance.—*n.* Indépendant, *m.* **independently,** *adv.* Indépendamment, sans tenir compte (de); dans l'indépendance.
indescribable [indi'skraibəbl], *a.* Indicible, indescriptible. **indescribably,** *adv.* Indescriptiblement, indiciblement.
indestructibility [indistrʌkti'biliti], *a.* Indestructibilité, *f.* **indestructible** [-'strʌktibl], *a.* Indestructible.
indeterminable [indi'tə:minəbl], *a.* Qu'on ne saurait déterminer; (*Math.*) indéterminable. **indeterminably,** *adv.* D'une manière indéterminable. **indeterminate,** *a.* Indéterminé; imprécis. **indeterminately,** *adv.* D'une manière indéterminée. **indetermination** [-'neiʃən], *n.* Indétermination, indécision, *f.*
index ['indeks], *n.* (*pl.* **indexes** ['indeksiz] *or* **indices** ['indisi:z]) Indice, signe, indicateur, *m.*; index, *m.* (of books); aiguille (hand of a watch etc.), *f.*; (*Anat.*) index, doigt indicateur; (*Math.*) exposant, *m.* *Index expurgatorius,* index expurgatoire, index, *m.*—*v.t.* Dresser la table alphabétique de.
India ['indjə]. L'Inde, *f.*
Indiaman ['indjəmən], *n.* Navire des Indes orientales, *m.*
Indian ['indjən], *a.* Indien; des Indiens; de l'Inde, des Indes. *Indian corn,* maïs, *m.*; *Indian ink,* encre de Chine, *f.*; *Indian summer,* été de la Saint-Martin, *m.*; *in Indian file,* en file indienne, (*fam.*) à la queue leu leu.—*n.* Indien, *m.*, Indienne, *f.* *Red Indian,* peau-rouge, *m.* or *f.*
India paper, *n.* Papier de Chine *or* du Japon, *m.*
india-rubber, *n.* Caoutchouc, *m.*, gomme

élastique, *f.* *India-rubber band,* élastique, *m.*; *india-rubber stamp,* timbre en caoutchouc, *m.*
indicate ['indikeit], *v.t.* Indiquer. **indication** [-'keiʃən], *n.* Indication, *f.*, signe, indice, *m.*
indicative [in'dikətiv], *a.* and *n.* Indicatif, *m.* *Indicative mood,* mode indicatif, *m.*; *in the indicative,* à l'indicatif.
indicator ['indikeitə], *n.* Indicateur; (*Anat.*) muscle indicateur, *m.* **indicatory,** *a.* Qui indique, indicateur; indicatif.
indict [in'dait], *v.t.* Inculper, traduire en justice, mettre en accusation. **indictable,** *a.* Attaquable en justice.
indiction [in'dikʃən], *n.* (*Rom. Ant.*) Indiction, *f.*
indictment [in'daitmənt], *n.* Accusation; mise en accusation, *f.* *Bill of indictment,* acte d'accusation, *m.*
Indies ['indiz] (the). Les Indes, *f.pl.* *The West Indies,* les Antilles, *f.pl.*
indifference [in'difrəns], *n.* Indifférence, apathie; médiocrité, *f.* **indifferent,** *a.* Indifférent; impartial; passable, médiocre. **indifferently,** *adv.* Indifféremment; ni bien ni mal, passablement, médiocrement.
indigence ['indidʒəns], *n.* Indigence, *f.* **indigent,** *a.* Nécessiteux, indigent.
indigenous [in'didʒinəs], *a.* Du pays, indigène.
indigested [indi'dʒestid], *a.* Indigeste, non digéré; (*fig.*) informe. **indigestible,** *a.* Indigeste, difficile à digérer. **indigestion,** *n.* Indigestion, dyspepsie, *f.*
indignant [in'dignənt], *a.* Indigné (de); plein d'indignation. **indignantly,** *adv.* Avec indignation. **indignation** [-'neiʃən], *n.* Indignation, *f.* *To give vent to one's indignation,* faire éclater son indignation.
indignity [in'digniti], *n.* Indignité, *f.*; outrage, affront, *m.*
indigo ['indigou], *n.* Indigo, *m.* **indigo-plant,** *n.* Indigotier, *m.*
indirect [indi'rekt], *a.* Indirect; (*fig.*) oblique, détourné, insidieux. *Indirect fire,* tir indirect, *m.*; (*Gram.*) *indirect speech,* discours indirect, *m.*; *indirect taxes,* contributions indirectes, *f.pl.* *indirection,* *n.* Obliquité, *f.* *By indirection,* par des moyens détournés. **indirectly,** *adv.* Indirectement. **indirectness,** *n.* Manque de droiture, *m.*
indiscernible [indi'sə:nibl], *a.* Imperceptible.
indisciplinable [in'disiplinəbl], *a.* Indisciplinable. **indiscipline,** *n.* Indiscipline, *f.*
indiscreet [indis'kri:t], *a.* Indiscret, peu judicieux, irréfléchi, imprudent. **indiscreetly,** *adv.* Indiscrètement. **indiscreetness** *or* **indiscretion** [-'kreʃən], *n.* Indiscrétion, imprudence, *f.*
indiscriminate [indis'kriminit], *a.* Confus, indistinct, sans distinction; sans discernement, aveugle. **indiscriminately,** *adv.* Sans distinction, à tort et à travers, au hasard, aveuglément. **indiscriminating,** *a.* Qui ne fait pas de distinction, aveugle. **indiscrimination** [-'neiʃən], *n.* Manque de discernement, *m.*
indispensable [indis'pensəbl], *a.* Indispensable, de première nécessité, nécessaire. **indispensableness,** *n.* Indispensabilité, *f.* **indispensably,** *adv.* Indispensablement.
indispose [indis'pouz], *v.t.* Indisposer (contre), déranger, détourner, éloigner (de). **indisposed,** *a.* Souffrant. **indisposition**

[-pə'ziʃən], n. Indisposition, f.; dérangement, malaise, m.

indisputable [indis'pju:təbl], a. Incontestable, indiscutable. **indisputableness** or **indisputability** [-'biliti], n. Incontestabilité, indiscutabilité, f. **indisputably**, adv. Incontestablement, sans contredit, sans conteste.

indissolubility [indisɔlju'biliti], n. Indissolubilité, f.

indissoluble [indi'sɔljubl], a. Indissoluble. **indissolubly**, adv. Indissolublement.

indistinct [indis'tiŋkt], a. Indistinct, confus, imprécis, peu précis, vague. **indistinctly**, adv. Indistinctement, confusément, vaguement. **indistinctness** or **indistinction**, n. Confusion, obscurité, f.; manque de netteté, m.

indistinguishable [indis'tiŋgwiʃəbl], a. Indistinct, imperceptible, insaisissable, qu'on ne peut distinguer.

indite [in'dait], v.t. Rédiger. ***inditement**, n. Rédaction, f.

individual [indi'vidjuəl], a. Individuel, isolé; original; seul, unique.—n. Individu, particulier, m. A private individual, un simple particulier, m. **individualism**, n. Individualisme, m. **individualist**, n. Individualiste. **individuality** [-'æliti], n. Individualité, personnalité, f. **individualization** [-əlai'zeiʃən], n. Individualisation, f. **individualize** [-'vidjuəlaiz], v.t. Individualiser; singulariser. **individually**, adv. Individuellement.

indivisibility [indivizi'biliti], n. Indivisibilité, f. **indivisible** [-'vizibl], a. Indivisible. **indivisibly**, adv. Indivisiblement.

Indo-China ['indou'tʃainə]. L'Indo-Chine, f. **Indo-Chinese**, a. and n. Indochinois.

indocile [in'dousail], a. Indocile. **indocility** [-'siliti], n. Indocilité, f.

indoctrinate [in'dɔktrineit], v.t. Instruire; circonvenir, endoctriner. **indoctrination** [-'neiʃən], n. Instruction, f.; endoctrinement, m. **indoctrinator**, n. Endoctrineur, m.

Indo-European ['indoujuərə'pi:ən], a. Indoeuropéen.

indolence ['indələns], n. Indolence, paresse, f. **indolent**, a. Indolent, paresseux. **indolently**, adv. Indolemment, nonchalamment.

indomitable [in'dɔmitəbl], a. Indomptable. **indomitably**, adv. Indomptablement.

Indonesia ['indou'ni:ziə]. L'Indonésie, f.; (former) Indes néerlandaises, f.pl. **Indonesian** [indou'ni:ziən], a. and n. Indonésien,-ne, m. Indonésienne, f.

indoor ['indɔ:], a. Intérieur, interne. Indoor games, jeux de société, m.pl. **indoors** [in'dɔ:z], adv. À la maison, au dedans. Indoors and out, au dedans et au dehors. To stay indoors, garder la maison, ne pas sortir.

indorse [ENDORSE].

indraught ['indrɑ:ft], n. Appel d'air; courant remontant (of a river), m.

indubitable [in'ʤu:bitəbl], a. Indubitable, incontestable. **indubitably**, adv. Indubitablement.

induce [in'dju:s], v.t. Porter, persuader, engager, décider, induire, pousser (à); amener, causer, produire, faire naître. Induced current, courant induit, m.; to induce the belief, donner lieu de penser. **inducement**, n. Raison, tentation, f., motif, mobile,

encouragement, m. **inducer**, n. Instigateur, séducteur, m. ***inducible**, a. Qu'on peut induire, causer.

induct [in'dʌkt], v.t. Mettre en possession, installer (a clergyman, civil servant, etc.). **inductance** [in'dʌktəns], n. (Elec.) Inductance, f.; coefficient de self-induction, m. Inductance coil, bobine de self-induction; (fam.) self, f. **inductile** [in'dʌktail], a. Inductile. **inductility** [-'tiliti], n. Inductilité, f. **induction** [in'dʌkʃən], n. Installation; induction, f. **induction-coil**, n. Bobine d'induction, f. **inductive**, a. Qui amène; par induction; inductif. **inductively**, adv. Par induction. **inductor**, n. (Elec.) Inducteur, m.

indue [ENDUE].

indulge [in'dʌlʤ], v.t. Contenter, satisfaire; avoir trop d'indulgence pour; (fig.) flatter, caresser (a hope etc.). To indulge oneself, s'écouter; to indulge someone with, permettre à quelqu'un. He is indulged in everything, on lui passe toutes ses fantaisies.—v.i. Se laisser aller, se livrer à, s'abandonner (à). To indulge in, se livrer à, se laisser aller à. **indulgence**, n. Faveur, f., plaisir, agrément, m.; (R.-C. Ch.) indulgence, f. **indulgent**, a. Indulgent, facile, complaisant. **indulgently**, adv. Avec douceur, avec indulgence.

indult [in'dʌlt], n. (R.-C. Ch.) Indult, m.

indurate ['indjuəreit], v.t. Durcir, indurer; (fig.) endurcir.—v.i. Durcir, s'endurcir.—a. [-rət] Endurci, induré. **induration** [-'reiʃən], n. Durcissement, endurcissement, m., induration, f., tissu induré, m.

Indus ['indəs]. L'Indus, le Sind, m.

industrial [in'dʌstriəl], a. Industriel, de l'industrie. Industrial disease, maladie du travail, f. **industrialism**, n. Industrialisme, m. **industrialist**, n. Chef industriel, industrialiste, m. **industrialize**, v.t. Industrialiser. **industrious**, a. Travailleur; actif, diligent, laborieux; empressé. **industriously**, adv. Laborieusement, assidûment, diligemment.

industry ['indəstri], n. Travail, m., diligence, activité; assiduité, f.; (fig.) empressement, m.; industrie (manufacture), f.

indwell [in'dwel], v.i., v.t. (past and p.p. **indwelt**) Habiter.

indweller ['indwelə], n. Habitant, m., habitante, f.

indwelling ['indweliŋ], a. Dans l'âme, intérieur, intime.

inebriant [i'ni:briənt] or **inebriating**, a. Enivrant.

inebriate [i'ni:brieit], v.t. Enivrer.—a. [-ət] Enivré.—n. Ivrogne, m. **inebriation** [-'eiʃən] or **inebriety** [-'braiəti], n. Ivresse, ébriété, f.; ivrognerie, f.; alcoolisme, m.

inedible [in'edibl], a. Immangeable; non comestible.

inedited [in'editid], a. Inédit; sans notes.

ineffability [inefə'biliti] or **ineffableness**, n. Ineffabilité, f.

ineffable [i'nefəbl], a. Ineffable. **ineffably**, adv. Ineffablement.

ineffaceable [ini'feisəbl], a. Ineffaçable, indélébile. **ineffaceably**, adv. Ineffaçablement, d'une manière ineffaçable.

ineffective [ini'fektiv], a. Inefficace, sans effet. **ineffectiveness**, n. Inefficacité, f.; manque d'effet, m. **ineffectual** [-'fektjuəl], *a.* Inefficace, inutile, vain; incapable. **ineffectually,** *adv.* Inutilement, sans effet. **ineffectualness,** *n.* Inefficacité, *f.* **inefficacious** [inefi'keiʃəs], *a.* Inefficace. **inefficaciously,** *adv.* Inefficacement. **inefficacy** [i'nefikəsi], *n.* Inefficacité, *f.* **inefficiency** [ini'fiʃənsi], *n.* Inefficacité, incapacité, incompétence, *f.* **inefficient,** *a.* Inefficace; incapable. **inefficiently,** *adv.* Inefficacement, maladroitement, d'une manière incompétente.

inelastic [inə'læstik], *a.* Sans élasticité; sans souplesse; raide; qui ne se prête pas. **inelasticity** [-elæs'tisiti], *n.* Manque d'élasticité, *m.*

inelegance [i'neligəns], *a.* Inélégance, *f.* **inelegant,** *a.* Sans élégance, inélégant; sans goût, grossier. **inelegantly,** *adv.* Sans élégance, inélégamment.

ineligibility [inelidʒi'biliti], *n.* Inéligibilité, *f.*; manque d'attrait, *m.* **ineligible,** *a.* Inéligible; peu propre (à).

ineluctable [inə'lʌktəbl], *a.* Inéluctable, inévitable. **ineluctably,** *adv.* Inéluctablement, inévitablement.

inept [i'nept], *a.* Inepte, sot, absurde, peu propre, inutile (à); (*Law*) nul, de nul effet (of document). **ineptitude** or **ineptness,** *n.* Ineptie; inaptitude, *f.* **ineptly,** *adv.* Ineptement, sottement.

inequality [ini'kwɔliti], *n.* Inégalité, disparité, *f.*

inequitable [in'ekwitəbl], *a.* Peu équitable, injuste. **inequitably,** *adv.* Injustement.

ineradicable [ini'rædikəbl], *a.* Qu'on ne peut extirper, indéracinable.

inert [i'nəːt], *a.* Inerte.

inertia [i'nəːʃə], *n.* Inertie, force d'inertie, inactivité, *f.* **inertly,** *adv.* D'une manière inerte, lourdement. **inertness,** *n.* Inertie, *f.*

inestimable [in'estiməbl], *a.* Inestimable; incalculable. **inestimably,** *adv.* D'une manière inestimable.

inevitability [inevitə'biliti] or **inevitableness** [in'evitəblnis], *n.* Caractère inévitable, *m.* **inevitable,** *a.* Inévitable; fatal. **inevitably,** *adv.* Inévitablement.

inexact [inig'zækt], *a.* Inexact. **inexactitude, inexactness,** *n.* Inexactitude, *f.*

inexcusable [iniks'kjuːzəbl], *a.* Inexcusable, sans excuse. **inexcusableness,** *n.* Caractère inexcusable (of insult etc.), *m.* **inexcusably,** *adv.* Inexcusablement.

inexecutable [inik'sekjutəbl], *a.* Inexécutable. **inexecution** [-eksi'kjuːʃən], *n.* Inexécution, *f.*

inexhausted [inig'zɔːstid], *a.* Inépuisé. **inexhaustible,** *a.* Inépuisable. **inexhaustibleness,** *n.* Nature inépuisable, *f.* **inexhaustibly,** *adv.* Inépuisablement. **inexhaustive,** *a.* Inépuisable.

inexistence [inig'zistəns], *n.* Non-existence, *f.* **inexistent,** *a.* Non-existant.

inexorability [ineksərə'biliti] or **inexorableness,** *n.* Caractère inexorable, *m.*, inflexibilité, *f.*

inexorable [in'eksərəbl], *a.* Inexorable, inflexible. **inexorably,** *adv.* Inexorablement.

inexpedience [iniks'piːdiəns] or **inexpediency,** *n.* Inopportunité, *f.* **inexpedient,** *a.* Inopportun, mal à propos. *To deem it inexpedient to,* ne pas juger à propos de.

inexpediently, *adv.* Inopportunément, mal à propos.

inexpensive [iniks'pensiv], *a.* Peu coûteux, bon marché. **inexpensively,** *adv.* À peu de frais, à bon marché.

inexperience [iniks'piəriəns], *n.* Inexpérience, *f.* **inexperienced,** *a.* Inexpérimenté, sans expérience.

inexpert [ineks'pəːt], *a.* Inexpérimenté, maladroit, inhabile. **inexpertly,** *adv.* Maladroitement.

inexpiable [i'nekspiəbl], *a.* Inexpiable. **inexpiably,** *adv.* D'une manière inexpiable.

inexplicable [i'neksplikəbl], *a.* Inexplicable. **inexplicably,** *adv.* D'une manière inexplicable.

inexplicit [iniks'plisit], *a.* Peu explicite, obscur.

inexplorable [iniks'plɔːrəbl], *a.* Qu'on ne peut explorer.

inexplosive [iniks'plousiv], *a.* Inexplosible.

inexpressible [iniks'presibl], *a.* Inexprimable, indicible. **inexpressibly,** *adv.* D'une manière inexprimable. **inexpressive,** *a.* Sans expression, inexpressif.

inexpugnable [iniks'pʌgnəbl], *a.* Imprenable, inexpugnable.

inextensible [iniks'tensibl], *a.* Inextensible.

inextinguishable [iniks'tiŋgwiʃəbl], *a.* Inextinguible.

inextricable [i'nekstrikəbl], *a.* Inextricable, qu'on ne peut pas débrouiller. **inextricableness,** *n.* Nature inextricable, *f.* **inextricably,** *adv.* D'une manière inextricable.

infallibility [infæli'biliti] or **infallibleness,** *n.* Infaillibilité, *f.*

infallible [in'fælibl], *a.* Infaillible, immanquable. **infallibly,** *adv.* Infailliblement, immanquablement.

infamous ['infəməs], *a.* Infâme; (*Law*) infamant. **infamously,** *adv.* D'une manière infâme. **infamy** or **infamousness,** *n.* Infamie, *f.*

infancy ['infənsi], *n.* Première enfance, *f.*, bas âge, *m.*; (*Law*) minorité, *f.* **infant,** *n.* Enfant en bas âge, petit enfant; (*Law*) mineur, *m.*, mineure, *f.*—*a.* En bas âge, dans l'enfance, petit; (*fig.*) naissant, qui commence. *Infant colony,* colonie naissante, *f.* **infant-like,** *a.* Enfantin, comme un enfant. **infant-school,** *n.* École maternelle, *f.*

infanta [in'fæntə], *n.* Infante (of Spain), *f.*

infante [in'fænti], *n.* Infant (of Spain), *m.*

infanticide [in'fæntisaid], *n.* Infanticide, *m.*

infantile ['infəntail], *a.* Enfantin, d'enfant. *Infantile paralysis,* paralysie infantile, *f.*

infantilism, *n.* (*Med.*) Infantilisme, *m.*

infantry ['infəntri], *n.* Infanterie, *f. Infantry of the line,* infanterie de ligne; *light infantry,* infanterie légère; *motorized infantry,* infanterie motorisée; *mounted infantry,* infanterie montée, *f.* **infantryman,** *n.* Fantassin, *m.*

infatuate [in'fætjueit], *v.t.* Infatuer, entêter, tourner la tête à, engouer, affoler. *To become infatuated with,* s'engouer de, aimer à la folie. **infatuation,** *n.* [-'eiʃən], *n.* Engouement, *m.*; passion violente; infatuation, *f.*; (*fam.*) toquade, *f.*

*infeasible [in'fiːzibl], *a.* Impraticable.

infect [in'fekt], *v.t.* Infecter (de); (*Law*) entacher; (*Phon.*) modifier (a vowel). **infection,** *n.* Infection, contagion, *f.* **infectious,**

a. Infect; contagieux, infectieux. **infectiousness,** *n.* Nature contagieuse, contagion, *f.* **infective,** *a.* Contagieux.

infelicitous [infi'lisitəs], *a.* Malheureux; mal trouvé. **infelicity,** *n.* Infélicité, *f.*, malheur, *m.*

infer [in'fə:], *v.t.* Inférer, déduire de; (*fig.*) supposer. *I infer from that* . . ., je suppose par cela . . . .

inferable [in'fə:rəbl], *a.* Qu'on peut inférer, à inférer.

inference ['infərəns], *n.* Conséquence, conclusion, déduction, *f.* **inferential** [-'renʃəl], *a.* Déductif. **inferentially,** *adv.* Par déduction.

inferior [in'fiəriə], *a.* Inférieur; subordonné. —*n.* Inférieur, *m.*

inferiority [infiəri'ɔriti], *n.* Infériorité, *f.*

infernal [in'fə:nəl], *a.* Infernal, d'enfer, de l'enfer; (*fig.*) diabolique, détestable. *Infernal machine,* machine infernale, *f.* **infernally,** *adv.* Infernalement.

inferno, *n.* L'enfer; brasier, *m.*

infertile [in'fə:tail], *a.* Stérile, infertile. **infertility** [-'tiliti], *n.* Infertilité, stérilité, *f.* **infertilizable** [-ti'laizəbl], *a.* Infertilisable.

infest [in'fest], *v.t.* Infester.

infeudation [infju'deiʃən], *n.* Inféodation, *f.*

infibulate [in'fibjuleit], *v.t.* Infibuler. **infibulation,** *n.* Infibulation, *f.*

infidel ['infidəl], *a.* and *n.* Infidèle, mécréant, *m.*, -ante, *f.*; incrédule. **infidelity** [-'deliti], *n.* Infidélité; déloyauté (of servant), *f.*

infield ['infi:ld], *n.* Terres avoisinant le corps de ferme; (*Sc.*) terres de labour, *f.pl.*; (*Am. base-ball*) le terrain (à l'intérieur des bases); (*Cricket*) terrain proche des 'guichets', *m.* **infieldsman,** *n.* (*pl.* **-men**) Joueur placé près des 'guichets', *m.*

infighting ['infaitiŋ], *n.* (*Box.*) Le corps à corps, *m.*

infiltrate ['infiltreit], *v.i.* S'infiltrer (dans); pénétrer.—*v.t.* Pénétrer, incruster. **infiltration** [-'treiʃən], *n.* Infiltration; incrustation, *f.*; (*Pol.*) noyautage, *m.*

infinite ['infinit], *a.* Infini, illimité, sans bornes.—*n.* Infini, *m.* **infinitely,** *adv.* Infiniment, à l'infini; fort. **infinitesimal** [-'tesiməl], *a.* Infinitésimal.

infinitive [in'finitiv], *a.* and *n.* Infinitif, *m.* **infinitude,** *n.* Infinité, *f.* **infinity** or **infiniteness,** *n.* Infinité; immensité, *f. To infinity,* à l'infini.

infirm [in'fə:m], *a.* Infirme, faible; maladif; (*fig.*) inconstant, irrésolu; (*Law*) invalide (document). *Infirm of purpose,* irrésolu, velléitaire. **infirmary,** *n.* Hôpital, *m.*, infirmerie, *f.* **infirmity** or **infirmness,** *n.* Infirmité, faiblesse, *f.*

infix (1) [in'fiks], *v.t.* Fixer, implanter; (*fig.*) inculquer, graver; (*Philol.*) infixer.

infix (2) ['infiks], *n.* Infixe, *m.*

inflame [in'fleim], *v.t.* Enflammer; (*fig.*) exciter, irriter.—*v.i.* S'enflammer.

inflammability [inflæmə'biliti] or **inflammableness,** *n.* Inflammabilité, *f.* **inflammable,** *a.* Inflammable.

inflammation [inflə'meiʃən], *n.* Inflammation, *f. Inflammation of the chest,* fluxion de poitrine, pleurésie, *f.*; *inflammation of the lungs,* pneumonie, *f.*

inflammatory [in'flæmətri], *a.* Inflammatoire; (*fig.*) incendiaire. *Inflammatory speeches,* discours incendiaires, *m.pl.*

inflatable [in'fleitəbl], *a.* Gonflable. **inflate** [in'fleit], *v.t.* Enfler, gonfler. **inflated,** *a.* Enflé, gonflé; exagéré; ampoulé, boursouflé (of style).

inflation [in'fleiʃən], *n.* Enflure, *f.*, gonflement, *m.*; inflation (monétaire), *f.*

inflect [in'flekt], *v.t.* Fléchir; varier, moduler (the voice); (*Mus.*) altérer (a note); (*Gram.*) conjuguer (verbs). **inflection,** *n.* Inflexion, modulation, *f.*

inflexibility [infleksi'biliti] or **inflexibleness** [in'fleksiblnis], *n.* Inflexibilité, *f.* **inflexible** [in'fleksibl], *a.* Inflexible. **inflexibly,** *adv.* Inflexiblement.

inflexion [INFLECTION].

inflict [in'flikt], *v.t.* Infliger, imposer, faire subir; faire (pain); donner (blow); occasionner (à). **infliction,** *n.* Infliction; (*fig.*) peine, *f.*, châtiment, *m.*, vexation, *f. It is a real infliction,* c'est une vraie bénédiction! **inflictive,** *a.* Inflictif.

inflorescence [inflɔ'resəns], *n.* (*Bot.*) Inflorescence, floraison, *f.*

influence ['influəns], *n.* Influence (sur), *f.*, empire, *m. He was under the influence,* il avait bu.—*v.t.* Influencer; influer (sur). *Influenced by,* soumis à l'influence de. **influential** [-'enʃəl], *a.* Influent, qui a de l'influence. **influentially,** *adv.* Avec influence; par influence; (*Elec.*) par induction.

influenza [influ'enzə], *n.* Influenza, grippe, *f.*

influx ['inflʌks] or **influxion** [in'flʌkʃən], *n.* Affluence; entrée, invasion; pénétration; embouchure, *f.*

inform [in'fɔ:m], *v.t.* Informer, instruire, renseigner, avertir; faire savoir à; animer, inspirer. *To inform against,* dénoncer; *to inform oneself,* s'instruire, s'informer de; *to inform someone with certain principles,* inculquer certains principes à quelqu'un.—*v.i.* Dénoncer.

informal [in'fɔ:məl], *a.* En dehors des règles or des formes reçues, sans cérémonie, simple; officieux. **informality** [-'mæliti], *n.* Vice de forme; manque de cérémonie, *m.*; simplicité, *f.* **informally,** *adv.* Irrégulièrement; sans cérémonie; sans façon; en petit comité; officieusement.

informant [in'fɔ:mənt], *n.* Correspondant, *m.*, personne qui informe, *f.*; informateur, *m.*

information [infə'meiʃən], *n.* Renseignement, *m.*, renseignements, *m.pl.*; avis, *m.*, nouvelle, *f.*; savoir, *m.*; (*Law*) dénonciation; enquête, *f. Appetite for information,* vif désir de savoir, *m.*; *information bureau,* bureau de renseignements, *m.*; *piece of information,* renseignement, *m.*, indication, *f.*; *to get information on,* se procurer des renseignements sur; *to lay an information against,* dénoncer; *to seek information,* aller aux renseignements.

informative [in'fɔ:mətiv], *a.* Instructif; éducatif.

informed [in'fɔ:md], *a.* Au courant, renseigné.

informer [in'fɔ:mə], *n.* Délateur, dénonciateur; (*colloq.*) mouchard, *m.*

infraction [in'frækʃən], *a.* Infraction, contravention, *f.*

infra dig [infrə'dig], *a.* Au-dessous de sa dignité.

infrangible [in'frændʒibl], *a.* Infrangible; incassable; inviolable.

infra-red [infrə'red], a. Infra-rouge.
infrequency [in'fri:kwənsi] or **infrequence**, n. Rareté, f. **infrequent**, a. Rare. **infrequently**, adv. Rarement.
infringe [in'frindʒ], v.t. Enfreindre, violer, transgresser. To infringe upon, empiéter (sur). **infringement**, n. Infraction, violation, f., empiètement (sur), m., atteinte (à); contrefaçon (of a patent), f. **infringer**, n. Infracteur; contrefacteur (of a patent), m.
infuriate [in'fjuərieit], v.t. Rendre furieux. **infuriated**, a. Furieux, en fureur.
infuse [in'fju:z], v.t. Infuser; faire infuser; macérer; verser, introduire; (fig.) inspirer (à), pénétrer. To be infused, s'infuser. **infusibility** [-i'biliti], n. Infusibilité, f.
infusible [in'fju:zibl], a. Infusible; (fig.) qu'on peut inspirer or faire entrer.
infusion [in'fju:ʒən], n. Infusion, f.
infusive [in'fju:siv], a. Infusible.
infusoria [infju:'sɔ:riə], n.pl. (Zool.) Infusoires, m.pl.
ingathering ['ingæðəriŋ], n. Moisson, rentrée de la moisson, f.
ingenious [in'dʒi:niəs], a. Ingénieux, habile. **ingeniously**, adv. Ingénieusement; spirituellement. **ingeniousness** or **ingenuity** [indʒi'nju:iti], n. Ingéniosité, habileté, f.
ingenuous [in'dʒenjuəs], a. Franc, sincère; naïf; candide. **ingenuously**, adv. Ingénument, naïvement. **ingenuousness**, n. Ingénuité, naïveté, f.
ingle [ingl], n. Feu; foyer, m. **ingle-nook**, n. Coin du feu, m.
inglorious [in'glɔ:riəs], a. Obscur; inconnu; déshonorant, honteux. **ingloriously**, a. Sans gloire; honteusement, avec déshonneur. **ingloriousness**, n. Absence d'éclat, obscurité, ignominie, f.
ingoer ['ingouə], n. Entrant, m. **ingoing**, n. Entrée, f.—a. Entrant, nouveau. Ingoing tenant, nouveau locataire, m.
ingot ['ingət], n. Lingot, m. **ingot-mould**, n. Lingotière, f.
ingraft [in'grɑ:ft], v.t. [ENGRAFT].
ingrain [in'grein], v.t. [ENGRAIN]. **ingrained**, a. Encrassé; (fig.) enraciné, invétéré.
***ingrate** [in'greit], a. and n. (Lit.) Ingrat, m., ingrate, f.
ingratiate [in'greiʃieit], v.t. Insinuer (dans). To ingratiate oneself with, s'insinuer dans les bonnes grâces de, se faire bien voir de quelqu'un. **ingratiating**, a. Insinuant; engageant. **ingratiatingly**, adv. D'une manière insinuante, (fam.) d'un air patelin; d'une manière engageante, d'un air engageant.
ingratitude [in'grætitju:d], n. Ingratitude, f. I reaped nothing but ingratitude, je n'ai été payé(e) que d'ingratitude.
ingredient [in'gri:diənt], n. Ingrédient; élément, m.
ingress ['ingres], n. Entrée, f.; (Astron.) ingression; admission (of gas etc.), f.
ingrowing ['ingrouiŋ], a. Incarné (nail). **ingrown**, a. Incarné; (fig.) invétéré.
ingulf [in'gʌlf], v.t. Engloutir.
ingurgitate [in'gə:dʒiteit], v.t. Ingurgiter. **ingurgitation** [-'teiʃən], n. Ingurgitation, f.
inhabit [in'hæbit], v.t. Habiter; habiter (dans). **inhabitable**, a. Habitable. **inhabitance** or ***inhabitancy**, n. Habitation, résidence,

f. **inhabitant**, n. Habitant, m., habitante, f.
inhabitation [-'teiʃən], n. Habitation, f.
inhabited, a. Habité.
inhalant [in'heilənt], n. (Produit employé pour l') inhalation, f.
inhalation [inhə'leiʃən], n. Inhalation; inspiration, f.
inhale [in'heil], v.t. Aspirer; respirer, humer. —v.i. Avaler la fumée (of cigarette). **inhaler**, n. Personne qui respire or qui avale la fumée de sa cigarette, f.; respirateur; masque respiratoire, m. Atomizer inhaler, inhalateur pulvérisateur, m.
inharmonic [inhɑ:'mɔnik], a. Peu harmonieux, discordant. **inharmonious** [-'mouniəs], a. Sans harmonie, discordant, peu musical. **inharmoniously**, adv. Sans harmonie. **inharmoniousness**, n. Manque d'harmonie, f.
inhere [in'hiə], v.i. Être inhérent (à). **inherence**, n. Inhérence, f. **inherent**, a. Inhérent, naturel (à). **inherently**, adv. Par inhérence. To be inherently generous, être né généreux.
inherit [in'herit], v.t. Hériter (de).—v.i. Hériter, recueillir une succession. **inheritable**, a. Héréditaire. **inheritably**, adv. En héritage, par voie d'héritage. **inheritance**, n. Héritage, patrimoine, m.; hérédité, succession, f. **inheritor**, n. Héritier, m. **inheritress**, n. Héritière, f.
inhesion [in'hi:ʒən], n. Inhérence, f.
inhibit [in'hibit], v.t. Arrêter, empêcher, interdire; frapper (un prêtre) d'interdit, mettre (un prêtre) en interdit. **inhibition** [-'biʃən], n. Interdiction, défense, f.; (Psych.) inhibition, f. **inhibitive, inhibitory**, a. Inhibitoire.
inhospitable [in'hɔspitəbl], a. Inhospitalier. **inhospitableness** or **inhospitality** [-'tæliti], n. Inhospitalité, f. **inhospitably**, adv. Inhospitalièrement.
inhuman [in'hju:mən], a. Inhumain, barbare; dénaturé; cruel, insensible. **inhumanity** [-'mæniti], n. Inhumanité, barbarie; brutalité, f. **inhumanly**, adv. Inhumainement, avec inhumanité.
inhumation [inhju'meiʃən], n. Inhumation, f., enterrement, m.
inhume [in'hju:m], v.t. Inhumer, enterrer.
inimical [i'nimikəl], a. Hostile, ennemi; contraire (à). **inimically**, adv. Hostilement, en ennemi.
inimitability [inimitə'biliti], n. Caractère inimitable, m.
inimitable [i'nimitəbl], a. Inimitable. **inimitably**, adv. D'une manière inimitable.
iniquitous [i'nikwitəs], a. Inique, injuste.
iniquity, n. Iniquité, f.
initial [i'niʃəl], a. Initial; premier. (Print.) Initial letter, lettrine, f.—n. Initiale, f.—v.t. Mettre ses initiales à; parafer; viser. **initially**, adv. Au commencement.
initiate [i'niʃieit], v.t. Initier (à or dans); amorcer, commencer, lancer.—v.i. Prendre l'initiative.—a. and n. Initié, -ée. **initiation** [-'eiʃən], n. Initiation, f.
initiative [i'niʃiətiv], a. Initiateur.—n. Initiative, f. He has no initiative, il n'a aucune initiative, il ne s'avise jamais de rien; to take the initiative, prendre l'initiative. **initiator**, n. Initiateur; lanceur, m.

inject [in'dʒekt], *v.t.* Injecter; faire une piqûre.

injection [in'dʒekʃən], *n.* Injection; (*Med.*) piqûre, *f. Injection cock*, robinet d'injection, *m.*; *rectal injection*, lavement, *m.* **injector**, *n.* Injecteur, *m.*

injudicious [indʒu'diʃəs], *a.* Peu judicieux, malavisé, imprudent, inconsidéré. **injudiciously**, *adv.* Peu judicieusement, imprudemment. **injudiciousness**, *n.* Caractère peu judicieux, *m.*; imprudence (of an action), *f.*

injunction [in'dʒʌŋkʃən], *n.* Injonction; recommandation, *f.*, commandement, (*Law*) arrêt de sursis, *m.*

injure ['indʒə], *v.t.* Nuire à, faire tort à, léser; endommager (to damage), (*Comm.*) avarier; faire mal à, blesser; porter préjudice à. *To injure one's health*, altérer sa santé, se faire du mal. **injured**, *a.* Offensé; blessé. *The injured*, les blessés, les accidentés, *m.pl.*; *the injured party*, l'offensé, *m.* **injurer**, *n.* Personne qui nuit, *f.*; auteur d'un tort, *m.*

injurious [in'dʒuəriəs], *a.* Nuisible, préjudiciable (à). **injuriously**, *adv.* À tort. **injuriousness**, *n.* Nocivité, *f.*; caractère nuisible, *m.*

injury ['indʒəri], *n.* Tort, mal, préjudice; dégât, dommage (to goods), *m.*, (*Med.*) lésion, blessure, *f.*; (*Naut.*) avaries, *f.pl. To the injury of*, au détriment de.

injustice [in'dʒʌstis], *n.* Injustice, *f.*

ink [iŋk], *n.* Encre, *f. Copying-ink*, encre communicative, *f.*; *Indian ink*, encre de Chine; *in red ink*, à l'encre rouge; *marking-ink*, encre à marquer le linge; *printing-ink*, encre d'imprimerie.—*v.t.* Tacher or barbouiller d'encre; (*Print.*) encrer, toucher. *To ink in a drawing*, repasser un dessin à l'encre. **ink-bag**, *n.* Poche or glande à encre, *f.* **ink-bottle**, *n.* Bouteille à encre, *f.* **ink-fish**, *n.* Seiche, *f.*, calmar, *m.* **inkhorn**, *n.* Encrier, *m.*; écritoire, *f.* **inkpot**, *n.* Encrier, *m.* **inkstand**, *n.* Grand encrier, encrier de bureau, *m.* **ink-trough**, *n.* (*Print.*) Encrier, *m.* **ink-well**, *n.* Encrier (pour table percée), *m.*

inker, *n.* (*Print.*) Toucheur, rouleau-toucheur, *m.* **inkiness**, *n.* Noirceur d'encre, *f.* **inking-pad**, *n.* Tampon à impression, tampon encreur, *m.* **inking-roller** [INKER]. **inky**, *a.* D'encre; taché d'encre; noir comme de l'encre.

inkling ['iŋkliŋ], *n.* Soupçon, vent (d'une affaire), *m.*

inlaid [in'leid], *a.* Incrusté, marqueté. *Inlaid work*, marqueterie, *f.*, ouvrage en marqueterie, *m.*

inland ['inlənd], *a.* Intérieur, de l'intérieur. *Inland revenue*, contributions directes et indirectes, *f.pl.*; *an inland telegram*, un télégramme pour l'intérieur, *m.*—*n.* Intérieur (d'un pays), *m.*

inlay (1) ['inlei], *n.* Marqueterie, incrustation, *f.*

inlay (2) [in'lei], *v.t.* (*past and p.p.* **inlaid**) Marqueter, incruster. **inlayer**, *n.* Marqueteur, *m.* **inlaying**, *n.* Marqueterie, incrustation, *f.*; encartage, *m.* (of books).

inlet ['inlit], *n.* Entrée, *f.*, passage, *m.*, voie, *f.*; petit bras de mer, *m.*; valve; soupape d'admission, *f.*

inmate ['inmeit], *n.* Habitant, *m.*, locataire, *m.* (of a house); interne, pensionnaire, *m.* (in an asylum).

inmost ['inmoust], *a.* Le plus profond, le plus secret.

inn [in], *n.* Auberge, *f.*; hôtel, *m.*; hôtellerie, *f. Inn of court*, école de droit, *f.*; *to put up at an inn*, descendre à une auberge, à l'hôtel. **innkeeper**, *n.* Aubergiste, hôtelier, *m.* **inn-yard**, *n.* Cour d'auberge, *f.*

innards ['inədz], *n.pl.* (*pop.*) Entrailles, *f.pl.*, intestins, *m.pl.*

innate [i'neit], *a.* Inné, infus; foncier. **innateness**, *n.* (*Phil.*) Innéité, *f.*

innavigable [i'nævigəbl], *a.* Innavigable.

inner ['inə], *a.* Intérieur, de l'intérieur; (*fig.*) interne, secret. *Inner court*, arrière-cour, *f.*; *inner ear* (*Anat.*), oreille interne, *f.*; *inner harbour*, arrière-port, *m.*; *inner meaning*, sens profond, *m.* **innermost**, *a.* Le plus intérieur, le plus reculé.

innings ['iniŋs], *n.pl.* (*Law*) Relais de mer, *m.pl.*; tour (at cricket), *m.*

innocence ['inəsəns], *n.* Innocence, *f.* **innocent**, *a.* Innocent; permis, légitime.—*n.* Innocent; (*fig.*) idiot, *m.*, idiote, *f.* **innocently**, *adv.* Innocemment.

innocuous [i'nɔkjuəs], *a.* Qui ne fait point de mal, innocent, inoffensif. **innocuously**, *adv.* Innocemment, sans nuire. **innocuousness**, *n.* Innocuité, *f.*

innominate [i'nɔminit], *a.* (*Anat.*) Innominé; (*Law*) innomé, innommé. *Innominate bone*, os innominé, os iliaque, *m.*

innovate ['inoveit], *v.i.* Innover. **innovating**, *a.* Novateur. **innovation** [-'veiʃən], *n.* Innovation, *f.*, changement, *m.* **innovator** ['inoveitə], *n.* Innovateur (-trice), novateur (-trice).

innoxious [i'nɔkʃəs], *a.* Inoffensif. **innoxiousness**, *n.* Innocuité, *f.*

innuendo [inju'endou], *n.* Insinuation, allusion malveillante, *f.*, mot couvert, *m.*

innumerable [i'nju:mərəbl], *a.* Innombrable, sans nombre. **innumerably**, *adv.* Sans nombre, innombrablement.

inobservable [inəb'zə:vəbl], *a.* Inobservable. **inobservance** or **inobservation** [-'veiʃən], *n.* Inobservance, inobservation, *f.*

inoculate [i'nɔkjuleit], *v.t.* Inoculer, vacciner; (*Hort.*) écussonner. **inoculation**, *n.* Inoculation, *f.*, vaccin, *m.*, vaccination, *f.*; (*Hort.*) greffe en écusson, *f.*

inoculator [i'nɔkjuleitə], *n.* Inoculateur, *m.*, inoculatrice, *f.*; (*Hort.*) greffeur en écusson, *m.*

inodorous [in'oudərəs], *a.* Inodore.

inoffensive [ino'fensiv], *a.* Inoffensif, innocent. **inoffensively**, *adv.* Innocemment, inoffensivement. **inoffensiveness**, *n.* Caractère inoffensif, *m.*, innocence, *f.*

inofficious [ino'fiʃəs], *a.* (*Law*) Inofficieux, inopérant.

inoperable [in'ɔpərəbl], *a.* Inopérable.

inoperative [in'ɔpərətiv], *a.* (*Law*) Inopérant, sans effet.

inopportune [in'ɔpətju:n], *a.* Inopportun, intempestif, mal à propos. **inopportunely**, *adv.* Inopportunément, à contre-temps, mal à propos. **inopportuneness**, **inopportunity**, *n.* Inopportunité, *f.*

inordinate [i'nɔ:dinit], *a.* Désordonné, démesuré, immodéré. **inordinately**, *adv.*

D'une manière désordonnée; démesurément, immodérément. **inordinateness,** *n.* Nature démesurée, *f.*; excès, *m.*
inorganic [inɔː'gænik], *a.* Inorganique. **inorganically,** *adv.* D'une manière inorganique.
inosculate [i'nɔskjuleit], *v.i.* S'anastomoser, s'unir.—*v.t.* Aboucher, unir. **inosculation** [-'leiʃən], *n.* Inosculation, anastomose, *f.*
input ['input], *n.* Puissance absorbée, puissance d'alimentation, consommation, *f.*
inquest ['inkwest], *n.* Enquête, *f.* (after sudden death). *To hold an inquest on,* faire une enquête en présence du corps. **The Last Inquest,* le Jugement dernier.
inquietude [in'kwaiətjuːd], *n.* Inquiétude, *f.*, malaise, *m.*
inquire [in'kwaiə], *v.t.* Demander. *To inquire one's way,* demander son chemin.—*v.i.* S'enquérir, s'informer (de); s'adresser (à *or* chez); examiner. *He inquired after your health,* il a demandé des nouvelles de votre santé; *inquire within,* s'adresser ici; *I will inquire,* je m'en informerai; *to inquire after,* demander des nouvelles de; *to inquire into,* s'informer de. **inquirer,** *n.* Investigateur, *m.*, investigatrice, *f.* **inquiring,** *a.* Investigateur, scrutateur, curieux. *He is of an inquiring disposition,* il est d'un tempérament curieux. **inquiringly,** *adv.* D'un air *or* d'un regard interrogateur. **inquiry,** *n.* Demande, investigation, recherche, *f.*; (*pl.*) informations, *f.pl.*, renseignements, *m.pl.*, (*Law*) enquête, *f. Court of inquiry,* commission d'enquête, *f.*; *inquiry office,* bureau de renseignements, *m.*; *on inquiry,* renseignements pris; *to make inquiries about,* prendre des renseignements sur, s'informer de; *without inquiry,* sans prendre de renseignements.
inquisition [inkwi'ziʃən], *n.* Recherche, investigation; (*R.-C. Ch.*) inquisition; (*Law*) enquête, perquisition, *f.* **inquisitional,** *a.* Inquisitorial.
inquisitive [in'kwizitiv], *a.* Curieux. **inquisitively,** *adv.* Avec curiosité. **inquisitiveness,** *n.* Curiosité, *f.* **inquisitor,** *n.* Inquisiteur; enquêteur, *m.* **inquisitorial** [-'tɔːriəl], *a.* Inquisitorial.
inroad ['inroud], *n.* Incursion, irruption, invasion, *f.*; (*fig.*) empiétement (sur), *m. To make inroads upon,* entamer, ébrécher (one's capital, fortune).
inrush ['inrʌʃ], *n.* Irruption, entrée soudaine, *f.*
insalubrious [insə'ljuːbriəs], *a.* Insalubre. **insalubrity,** *n.* Insalubrité, *f.*
insane [in'sein], *a.* Fou, aliéné; dérangé; (*fig.*) insensé. *To become insane,* perdre la raison, tomber en démence. **insanely,** *adv.* Comme un fou, follement.
insanitary [in'sænitəri], *a.* Insalubre, peu hygiénique; malsain.
insanity [in'sæniti] *or* **insaneness,** *n.* Folie, démence, *f.*
insatiability [inseiʃə'biliti] *or* **insatiableness,** *n.* Insatiabilité, *f.* **insatiable,** *a.* Insatiable. **insatiably,** *adv.* Insatiablement. **insatiate,** *a.* Insatiable; inassouvi. **insatiately,** *adv.* Insatiablement.
inscribe [in'skraib], *v.t.* Inscrire; dédier (à). **inscriber,** *n.* Personne qui inscrit, *f.*; auteur d'une dédicace, *m.*

inscription [in'skripʃən], *n.* Inscription, *f.*; titre (title), *m.*; dédicace (dedication), *f.* **inscriptive,** *a.* (Caractère, style) d'inscription.
inscrutability [inskruːtə'biliti] *or* **inscrutableness,** *n.* Impénétrabilité, inscrutabilité, *f.*
inscrutable [in'skruːtəbl], *a.* Inscrutable, impénétrable. **inscrutably,** *adv.* Impénétrablement, inscrutablement.
insect ['insekt], *n.* Insecte, *m.*
insecticide [in'sektisaid], *a.* and *n.* Insecticide, *m.*
Insectivora [insek'tivərə], *n.pl.* Insectivores, *m.pl.*
insectivore [in'sektivɔː], *n.* Insectivore, *m.*
insectivorous [insek'tivərəs], *a.* Insectivore.
insectocution, *n.* (*Am.*) Électrocution des insectes, *f.* **insectocutor,** *n.* Appareil pour électrocuter les insectes, *m.*
insecure [insi'kjuə], *a.* En danger; chanceux, hasardeux; peu sûr, peu sclide, mal assuré. **insecurely,** *adv.* Sans sûreté, en danger. **insecurity,** *n.* Manque de sûreté; danger, péril, *m.*; incertitude, *f.*
inseminate [in'semineit], *v.t.* Féconder artificiellement.
insemination [insemi'neiʃən], *n.* Insémination, *f. Artificial insemination,* insémination, fécondation artificielle, *f.*
insensate [in'sensət], *a.* Insensible; insensé.
insensibility [insensi'biliti], *n.* Insensibilité, *f.*; évanouissement, *m.*, perte de connaissance, syncope, *f.* **insensibilize,** *v.t.* Insensibiliser.
insensible [in'sensibl], *a.* (Unfeeling) Insensible; imperceptible; insignifiant; (unconscious) inconscient; sans connaissance; indifférent. **insensibly,** *adv.* Insensiblement, peu à peu. **insensitive,** *a.* Insensible. **insensitiveness,** *n.* Insensibilité, *f.* **insentient** [in'senʃiənt], *a.* Insensible.
inseparability [insepərə'biliti] *or* **inseparableness,** *n.* Inséparabilité, *f.*
inseparable [in'sepərəbl], *a.* Inséparable. **inseparably,** *adv.* Inséparablement. **inseparate,** *a.* Uni; indivisible.
insert (1) ['insəːt], *n.* (*Print.*) Insertion, *f.*; pièce intercalée *or* rapportée, *f.*; raccord, *m.*; (*Cine.*) scène-raccord, *f.*; pastille (of clutch-plate), *f.*; entre-rondelle, *f.* (of washer); encartage (on a page), *m.*
insert (2) [in'səːt], *v.t.* Insérer, faire insérer (dans).
insertion [in'səːʃən], *n.* Insertion; intercalation, interpolation, *f.*; entre-deux (of lace), *m.*; incrustation (of lace), *f.*; (*Eng.*) garniture, *f. Insertion joint,* joint à bague (de garniture), *m.*
inset ['inset], *n.* Encart; hors-texte, *m.*—*v.t.* Encarter; insérer en cartouche.
inshore [in'ʃɔː], *adv.* and *a.* Près du rivage.
inshrine [ENSHRINE].
inside [in'said], *n.* Dedans, intérieur, *m.*; estomac, *m.*; entrailles, *f.pl. I am having trouble with my inside,* j'ai l'estomac dérangé; *inside out,* à l'envers, à fond; *to turn inside out,* retourner, (*fig.*) mettre sens dessus dessous.—*a.* Intérieur, d'intérieur, de l'intérieur. *Inside drive car,* conduite intérieure, *f.*—*adv.* À l'intérieur, en dedans.—*prep.* En, dans, à l'intérieur de.

insidious [in'sidiəs], *a.* Insidieux, captieux, perfide. **insidiously,** *adv.* Insidieusement. **insidiousness,** *n.* Nature insidieuse; astuce, *f.*

insight ['insait], *n.* Perspicacité, pénétration, *f.*; aperçu, *m.*

insignia [in'signiə], *n.pl.* Insignes, *m.pl.*

insignificance [insig'nifikəns], *n.* Insignifiance, futilité, *f.*, peu d'importance, *m.* **insignificant,** *a.* Insignifiant, de peu d'importance, de rien.

insincere [insin'siə], *a.* Peu sincère, dissimulé, faux, hypocrite. **insincerely,** *adv.* Sans sincérité, de mauvaise foi, hypocritement. **insincerity** [-'seriti], *n.* Manque de sincérité, *m.*, dissimulation, hypocrisie, fausseté, *f.*

insinuate [in'sinjueit], *v.t.* Insinuer, glisser (dans); donner à entendre.—*v.i.* S'insinuer, se glisser (dans). **insinuating,** *a.* Insinuant. **insinuatingly,** *adv.* D'une manière insinuante *or* câline. **insinuation** [-'eiʃən], *n.* Insinuation, *f.*

insinuative [in'sinjuətiv], *a.* Insinuant.

insipid [in'sipid], *a.* Insipide, fade. **insipidity** [-'piditi] *or* **insipidness,** *n.* Insipidité, fadeur, *f.* **insipidly,** *adv.* Insipidement, fadement.

insist [in'sist], *v.i.* Insister (sur *or* à); persister; exiger, vouloir absolument. **insistence** *or* **insistency,** *n.* Insistance, *f.* **insistent,** *a.* Insistant, qui insiste.

insnare [ENSNARE].

insobriety [inso'braiəti], *n.* Intempérance, *f.*

insociable [UNSOCIABLE].

*insolate ['insoleit], *v.t.* Exposer au soleil. *insolation [-'leiʃən], *n.* Exposition au soleil, *f.*, ensoleillement, *m.*; insolation, *f.*, coup de soleil, *m.*

insolence ['insoləns], *n.* Insolence, *f.*; effronterie, *f.* **insolent,** *a.* Insolent. **insolently,** *adv.* Insolemment, avec insolence.

insolubility [insolju'biliti] *or* **insolubleness,** *n.* Insolubilité, *f.*; indissolubilité, *f.* **insoluble** [in'soljubl], *a.* Insoluble; indissoluble.

insolvable [in'solvəbl], *a.* Qu'on ne peut pas payer, insoluble.

insolvency [in'solvənsi], *n.* Insolvabilité, faillite, *f.* **insolvent,** *a.* Insolvable, en faillite. *To become insolvent,* faire faillit:.—*n.* Débiteur, *m.*, débitrice, *f.*; (*Comm.*) failli(-e).

insomnia [in'somniə], *n.* Insomnie, *f.*

insomuch [inso'mʌtʃ], *adv.* Au point (que), à un tel point (que), tellement (que).

inspect [in'spekt], *v.t.* Inspecter, examiner, visiter.

inspection [in'spekʃən], *n.* Inspection, revue, *f.*, contrôle, examen, *m.*; surveillance, *f.* *Kit inspection,* revue de petit équipement, *f.*; *on closer inspection,* en y regardant de plus près; *to inspect a regiment,* passer un régiment en revue. **inspector,** *n.* Inspecteur, vérificateur (of weights and measures), *m.* **inspectorship,** *n.* Inspectorat, *m.*

inspiration [inspi'reiʃən], *n.* Inspiration, *f.*; encouragement, *m.*

inspiratory [in'spaiərətəri], *a.* Inspirateur.

inspire [in'spaiə], *v.t.* Inspirer, souffler (dans); animer (de). *To be inspired with,* être inspiré de.—*v.i.* Aspirer. **inspirer,** *n.* Inspirateur, *m.* **inspiring,** *a.* Inspirateur; qui donne du

courage; qui élève l'esprit; noble et stimulant (of a speech).

inspirit [in'spirit], *v.t.* Animer, encourager.

inspissate [in'spiseit], *v.t.* Épaissir. **inspissation** [-'seiʃən], *n.* Épaississement, *m.*

inst. ['instənt] = INSTANT, *a.*

instability [instə'biliti], *n.* Instabilité, *f.*

install [in'stɔ:l], *v.t.* Installer; monter, poser (an apparatus, a machine). *To install oneself,* s'installer. **installation** [instə'leiʃən], *n.* Installation, *f.*; montage, *m.*, pose, *f.* (of machine, equipment).

instalment [in'stɔ:lmənt], *n.* Installation, *f.*; (*Comm.*) acompte, paiement à compte, versement partiel, *m.*; fascicule, *m.* (of a publication); épisode, *m.* (of serial).

instance ['instəns], *n.* Requête, demande, *f.*, instances, *f.pl.*; exemple, *m.*, occasion, circonstance, *f.*, cas, *m.* *At the instance of,* à la demande de; *for instance,* par exemple; *in the first instance,* tout d'abord, en premier lieu; *in the present instance,* dans le cas actuel *or* dans la circonstance qui nous occupe; *in this particular instance,* dans le cas actuel, (*Law*) dans l'espèce.—*v.t.* Citer pour exemple. **instancy,** *n.* Instance (of request), imminence, urgence, *f.*

instant ['instənt], *a.* Instant, pressant, immédiat; courant (of the month). *The 15th instant* or *the 15th inst.,* le 15 courant.—*n.* Instant, moment, *m.* *The instant that . . . ,* aussitôt que, dès que; *this instant,* à l'instant, tout de suite. **instantaneous** [-'teiniəs], *a.* Instantané. **instantaneously,** *adv.* Instantanément. **instantaneousness,** *n.* Instantanéité, *f.*

instanter [in'stæntə], *adv.* (*fam.*) Immédiatement, sans délai, séance tenante. **instantly,** *adv.* À l'instant; tout de suite; sur-le-champ; *instamment, avec instance (urgently).

instate [in'steit], *v.t.* (*Law*) Établir, installer.

instead [in'sted], *adv.* À la place. *Instead of,* au lieu de; *to be instead of,* tenir lieu de, remplacer.

instep ['instep], *n.* Cou-de-pied, *m.* *I have a high instep,* j'ai le pied cambré.

instigate ['instigeit], *v.t.* Exciter, inciter, pousser (à). **instigation** [-'geiʃən], *n.* Instigation, *f.*

instigator ['instigeitə], *n.* Instigateur, *m.*, instigatrice, *f.*

instil [in'stil], *v.t.* Instiller; (*fig.*) inculquer lentement, inspirer (à). **instillation** [-'leiʃən], *n.* Instillation, *f.*, versage goutte à goutte, *m.*; (*fig.*) inspiration, *f.* **instiller,** *n.* Personne qui instille, qui fait pénétrer, *f.*

instinct (1) ['instiŋkt], *n.* Instinct, *m.* *By instinct,* par instinct.

instinct (2) [in'stiŋkt], *a.* Animé, plein; pétri (de). *Instinct with life,* respirant la vie.

instinctive [in'stiŋktiv], *a.* Instinctif; (*fig.*) spontané. **instinctively,** *adv.* D'instinct, instinctivement.

institute ['institju:t], *n.* Institut; *principe, précepte, *m.*, loi, *f.* *Evening institute,* cours du soir (pour adultes), *m.pl.*—*v.t.* Instituer, établir, fonder; intenter (a lawsuit); investir (an ecclesiastic). *To institute proceedings against,* intenter un procès à.

institution [insti'tju:ʃən], *n.* Institution, *f.*, établissement, *m.*, investiture (of an ecclesiastic), *f.* *Charitable institution,* établissement de bienfaisance, hospice, *m.*; *this has* *become an institution*, c'est passé dans les mœurs. **institutor**, *n.* Fondateur, *m.*, fondatrice, *f.*

instruct [in'strʌkt], *v.t.* Instruire, enseigner; donner des instructions à, charger (de).

instruction [in'strʌkʃən], *n.* Instruction, *f.*, enseignement, *m. Driving instruction*, leçons de conduite, *f.pl.*; *I have had my instructions*, j'ai reçu une consigne. **instructional**, *a.* D'instruction. **instructive**, *a.* Instructif. **instructively**, *adv.* D'une manière instructive. **instructor**, *n.* (*Mil.*) Instructeur; précepteur, moniteur, *m. Driving instructor*, professeur de conduite, *m.* **instructress**, *n.* Préceptrice, monitrice, *f.*

instrument ['instrumənt], *n.* Instrument; (*Law*) acte, contrat, écrit, *m.*; (*fig.*) agent, moyen, *m.—v.t.* (*Mus.*) Instrumenter. **instrumental** [-'mentl], *a.* Instrumental; (*Mus.*) d'instruments. *To be instrumental in*, contribuer à, être pour quelque chose dans. **instrumentalist**, *n.* Instrumentiste, *m.* and *f.* **instrumentality** [-men'tæliti], *n.* Concours, moyen, *m.*, action, *f.* **instrumentally** [-'mentəli], *adv.* Comme instrument; (*Mus.*) par des instruments. **instrumentation** [-'teiʃən], *n.* (*Mus.*) Instrumentation, *f.* [INSTRUMENTALITY].

insubmersibility [insʌbmə:si'biliti], *n.* Insubmersibilité, *f.* **insubmersible**, *a.* Insubmersible.

insubordinate [insə'bɔ:dinət], *a.* Insubordonné, mutin (of soldier etc.); indocile. **insubordination**, *n.* Insubordination; insoumission; indocilité, *f.*

insubstantial [insəb'stænʃəl], *a.* Qui manque de substance.

insufferable [in'sʌfərəbl], *a.* Insupportable, intolérable. **insufferably**, *adv.* Insupportablement, intolérablement.

insufficiency [insə'fiʃənsi], *n.* Insuffisance, *f.* **insufficient**, *a.* Insuffisant. **insufficiently**, *adv.* Insuffisamment.

insufflate ['insʌfleit], *v.t.* Insuffler; gonfler. **insufflation** [insə'fleiʃən], *n.* Insufflation, *f.* **insufflator**, *n.* (*Med.*) Insufflateur, *m.*

insular ['insjulə], *a.* Insulaire; (*fig.*) borné, étroit, rétréci. **insularism** ['insjulərizm], **insularity** [-'læriti], *n.* Insularité, *f.*

insulate [-leit], *v.t.* Isoler; calorifuger. **insulated**, *a.* Isolé; calorifugé; frigorifique. **insulation** [-'leiʃən], *n.* Isolement, *m.*; (*Phys.*) isolation, *f.* **insulator**, *n.* Isolateur, isoloir, isolant, godet de support (of wire, piano), *m.*

insulin ['insjulin], *n.* Insuline, *f.*

insult (1) [in'sʌlt], *v.t.* Insulter, faire insulte à, injurier.—*v.i.* Triompher (sur); insulter (à).

insult (2) ['insʌlt], *n.* Insulte, injure, *f.*, affront, *m. To offer an insult to*, faire un affront à. **insulting**, *a.* Insultant, outrageux, injurieux. **insultingly**, *adv.* Insolemment, injurieusement, d'une manière insultante.

insuperability [insju:pərə'biliti], *n.* Nature insurmontable, *f.* **insuperable** [in'sju:pərəbl], *a.* Insurmontable, invincible. **insuperably**, *adv.* D'une manière insurmontable.

insupportable [insə'pɔ:təbl], *a.* Insupportable, intolérable. **insupportableness**, *n.* Nature insupportable, *f.* **insupportably**, *adv.* Insupportablement, intolérablement.

insuppressible [insə'presibl], *à.* Irrépressible, irrésistible, inextinguible (of laughter).

insurable [in'ʃuərəbl], *a.* Qu'on peut assurer, assurable. **insurance** [in'ʃuərəns], *n.* Assurance, *f. Fire-insurance*, assurance contre l'incendie; *insurance broker*, courtier d'assurances, *m.*; *insurance company*, compagnie d'assurances, *f.*; *insurance office*, bureau d'assurances, *m.*; *insurance policy*, police d'assurance, *f.*; *insurance premium*, prime d'assurance, *f.*; *life-insurance*, assurance sur la vie; *marine insurance company*, compagnie d'assurances maritimes, *f.*

insure [in'ʃuə], *v.t.* Assurer, faire assurer; (*fig.*) garantir. **insured**, *n.* Assuré, *m.*, assurée, *f.* **insurer**, *n.* Assureur, *m.*

insurgent [in'sə:dʒənt], *a.* and *n.* Insurgé, *m.*

insurmountable [insə'mauntəbl], *a.* Insurmontable, infranchissable. **insurmountably**, *adv.* Insurmontablement.

insurrection [insə'rekʃən], *n.* Insurrection, *f.*, soulèvement, *m. To rise in insurrection*, s'insurger, se soulever. **insurrectional**, **insurrectionary**, *a.* Insurrectionnel. **insurrectionist**, *n.* Émeutier, insurgé, rebelle, *m.*

insusceptibility [insəsepti'biliti], *n.* Manque de susceptibilité, *m.*, insensibilité (à), non-susceptibilité, *f.* **insusceptible** [-'septibl], *a.* Qui n'est pas susceptible (de), insensible (à).

insweep ['inswi:p], *n.* (*Motor.*) Étranglement, *m.* (of chassis).

intact [in'tækt], *a.* Intact, indemne.

intaglio [in'ta:liou], *n.* Intaille, *f.*

intake ['inteik], *n.* Prise, *f.*, appel (of air, steam), *m.*, adduction, admission, amenée, arrivée, *f. Intake valve*, soupape d'admission, *f.*

intangibility [intændʒi'biliti] or **intangibleness**, *n.* Intangibilité, *f.* **intangible** [in'tændʒibl], *a.* Intangible. **intangibly**, *adv.* D'une manière intangible.

integer ['intədʒə], *n.* Entier, nombre entier, *m.*

integral ['intəgrəl], *a.* Intégral; (*Chem.*) intégrant. *Integral calculus*, calcul intégral.—*n.* Totalité, *f.*, tout, *m.*; (*Math.*) intégrale, *f.* **integrality** [-'græliti], *n.* Intégralité, *f.* **integrally**, *adv.* Intégralement. **integrant**, *a.* Intégrant.

integrate ['intəgreit], *v.t.* Compléter, rendre entier; (*Math.*) intégrer. **integration** [-'greiʃən], *n.* Intégration, *f.* **integrator**, *n.* (*Math.*) Intégrateur, *m. Surface integrator*, planimètre, *m.*

integrity [in'tegriti], *n.* Intégrité, probité, rectitude; pureté, *f. In its integrity*, en entier (of text, etc.).

integument [in'tegjumənt], *n.* Tégument, *m.*

intellect ['intilekt], *n.* Intelligence, *f.*, esprit, entendement, *m.* **intellection** [-'lekʃən], *n.* Appréhension, compréhension, *f.* **intellective**, *a.* Intellectif. **intellectual**, *a.* Intellectuel; intelligent.—*n.* Intellectuel, *m.*, -elle, *f.* **intellectually**, *adv.* Intellectuellement, d'une manière intellectuelle; par l'intelligence.

intelligence [in'telidʒəns], *n.* Intelligence, *f.*, esprit, *m.*; renseignement, avis, *m.*, renseignements, *m.pl.*, nouvelle (information), *f.*; accord (concord), *m. Intelligence department*, service des renseignements, *m.*; *Intelligence*

Service, Deuxième Bureau, *m.*; *latest intelligence*, dernières nouvelles; *shipping intelligence*, nouvelles maritimes, *f.pl.* *intelligencer, n.* Messager, agent secret, espion, *m.* **intelligent**, *a.* Intelligent. **intelligently**, *adv.* Intelligemment, avec intelligence. **intelligentsia**, *n.* Les intellectuels, *m.pl.*, l'intelligentsia, *f.*
intelligibility [intelidʒi'biliti] or **intelligibleness**, *n.* Intelligibilité, clarté, *f.*
intelligible [in'telidʒibl], *a.* Intelligible. **intelligibly**, *adv.* Intelligiblement.
intemperance [in'tempərəns], *n.* Intempérance, *f.*; alcoolisme, *m.* **intemperate**, *a.* Démesuré, immodéré, excessif; intempérant; violent, emporté, peu mesuré (of language); adonné à la boisson, buveur, buveuse. **intemperately**, *adv.* Avec excès, immodérément. **intemperateness**, *n.* Intempérance, *f.*
intend [in'tend], *v.t.* Se proposer de, avoir l'intention de, compter, vouloir; destiner (à); vouloir dire. **intendant**, *n.* Intendant, *m.* **intended**, *a.* Projeté; intentionnel, prémédité, futur (spouse). *To be intended for*, être destiné à.—*n.* (*colloq.*) Prétendu, futur, *m.*, prétendue, future, *f.* **intendedly**, *adv.* À dessein. **intending**, *a.* *Intending purchasers*, acheteurs éventuels, *m.pl.*
intense [in'tens], *a.* Intense, véhément; (*fig.*) opiniâtre, acharné; très sérieux; vif, fort, aigu (pain etc.). **intensely**, *adv.* Avec intensité, vivement, fortement. **intenseness** or **intensity**, *n.* Intensité; force, violence, *f.* **intensifier**, *n.* (*Phot.*) Renforçateur, *m.* **intensify**, *v.t.* Rendre plus vif, intensifier; (*Phot.*) renforcer. **intensive**, *a.* Intensif. *Intensive culture*, culture intensive, *f.* **intensively**, *adv.* Intensivement.
intent [in'tent], *a.* Attentif, tout entier (à); absorbé (par); déterminé (à); fixe, profond (of look, expression).—*n.* Dessein, but, objet; sens, *m.*, intention, portée, *f.* *To all intents and purposes*, en fait, à tous égards, virtuellement; *to the intent that*, afin que; *with intent*, de propos délibéré.
intention [in'tenʃən], *n.* Intention, *f.*; dessein, but, *m.* *With the best of intentions*, dans la meilleure intention. **intentional**, *a.* Intentionnel, d'intention, fait à dessein. **intentionally**, *adv.* Avec intention, à dessein, exprès. **intentioned**, *a.* Intentionné (only used with *bien*, *mal*, or *mieux*).
intently [in'tentli], *adv.* Attentivement. **intentness**, *n.* Attention, force d'application, *f.*
inter [in'tə:], *v.t.* Enterrer, inhumer, ensevelir.
interact [intər'ækt], *v.i.* Réagir l'un sur l'autre. **interacting**, *a.* À action conjuguée, réciproque. **interaction**, *n.* Action réciproque, interaction, *f.*
interagent [intər'eidʒənt], *n.* Intermédiaire, *m.*
interallied [intər'ælaid], *a.* Interallié.
interbreed [intə'bri:d], *v.t.* Croiser, entrecroiser (of races, strains, etc.).—*v.i.* Se reproduire par croisement. **interbreeding**, *n.* Croisement, *m.*; mariage consanguin, *m.*
intercalary [in'tə:kələri] or **intercalar**, *a.* Intercalaire. **intercalate**, *v.t.* Intercaler. **intercalation** [-'leiʃən], *n.* Intercalation, *f.*
intercede [intə'si:d], *v.t.* Intercéder (auprès de). **interceder**, *n.* Intercesseur, *m.* **interceding**, *n.* Intercession, *f.*

intercept (1) [intə'sept], *v.t.* Intercepter; arrêter, dérober (the sight); (*fig.*) surprendre.
intercept (2) ['intəsept], *n.* Segment de droite, *m.* **interception**, *n.* Interception, *f.* **interceptor** [-'septə], *n.* Siphon, *m.* (d'égout); intercepteur, *m.*
intercession [intə'seʃən], *n.* Intercession, *f.* **intercessor**, *n.* Intercesseur, *m.*
interchange (1) [intə'tʃeindʒ], *v.t.* Échanger.
interchange (2) ['intətʃeindʒ], *n.* Échange, *m.*, succession, *f.*; (*fig.*) variété, *f.* **interchangeable** [·'tʃeindʒəbl], *a.* Interchangeable, permutable. **interchangeably**, *adv.* Alternativement.
intercolumnar [intəkə'lʌmnə], *a.* (*Arch.*) (Espace) entre des colonnes; (*Anat.*) intercolumnaire.
intercolumniation [intəkəlʌmni'eiʃən], *n.* (*Arch.*) Entre-colonne, entre-colonnement, *m.*
intercommunicate [intəkə'mju:nikeit], *v.i.* Communiquer entre soi. **intercommunication** [-'keiʃən], *n.* Communication réciproque, *f.*; (*pop.*) (*abbr.* intercom). Téléphone intérieur; interphone, *m.*
interconnected [intəkə'nektid], *a.* (Pièces, salles) communiquant entre elles; conjugué (of controls), communicant; en rapport.
intercontinental [intəkɔnti'nentl], *a.* Intercontinental.
intercostal [intə'kɔstl], *a.* Intercostal.
intercourse ['intəkɔ:s], *n.* Commerce, *m.*, relations, *f.pl.*, rapports, *m.pl.*
intercross [intə'krɔs], *v.t.* Entrecroiser, entrelacer.—*v.t.* S'entrecroiser, s'entrelacer [INTERBREED].
interdepartmental [intədi:pɑ:t'mentl], *a.* Commun à plusieurs services.
interdepend [intədi'pend], *v.i.* Être solidaires, dépendre l'un de l'autre, les uns des autres. **interdependence**, *n.* Interdépendance, solidarité, *f.*; enchaînement, *m.*; interpénétration, *f.* **interdependent**, *a.* Solidaire, interdépendant.
interdict (1) [intə'dikt], *v.t.* Interdire, interdire à, défendre à, défendre.
interdict (2) ['intədikt] or **interdiction** [-'dikʃən], *n.* Interdit *m.*, défense, interdiction, *f. To lay a priest under an interdict*, mettre un prêtre en interdit, frapper un prêtre d'interdiction; *to raise*, *to remove the interdict*, lever l'interdit, l'interdiction. **interdictory**, *a.* D'interdiction.
interest ['intərest], *v.t.* Intéresser. *To be interested in*, s'intéresser à.—*n.* Intérêt, *m.*; protection, *f.*, crédit, *m.* *At high interest*, à de gros intérêts; *at interest*, à intérêt; *compound interest*, intérêt composé, *m.*; *simple interest*, intérêt simple, *m.*; *to bear interest*, porter intérêt; *to give one's interest to*, accorder sa protection à; *to have an interest in*, avoir des intérêts dans; *to have interest with*, avoir du crédit auprès de; *to put out to interest*, placer à intérêt; *to repay with interest*, rendre avec usure. **interested**, *a.* Intéressé. **interesting**, *a.* Intéressant. **interestingly**, *adv.* D'une manière intéressante.
interfere [intə'fiə], *v.i.* Intervenir, se mêler (de); s'entre-tailler, se couper (of horses). *To interfere with*, se mêler de, gêner, contrarier, déranger, entraver, nuire à. **interference**, *n.* Intervention; ingérence, *f.*; (*Opt.*) interférence, *f.*; (*Rad.*) brouillage, *m.*,

parasites, *m.pl.* **interfering,** *a.* Gênant; qui se mêle de tout (of person).
interfused [intə'fju:zd], *a.* Mêlé, parsemé.
intergradation [:intəgrə'deiʃən], *n.* Rapprochement graduel, *m.*
interim ['intərim], *n.* Intérim, intervalle, *m. Ad interim,* par intérim; *in the interim,* sur ces entrefaites, en attendant; (*Law*) *interim order,* avant faire droit, *m.*—*a.* Provisoire, intérimaire.
interior [in'tiəriə], *a.* and *n.* Intérieur, *m. Interior angle,* angle interne, *m.*
interjacent [intə'dʒeisənt], *a.* Intermédiaire.
interject [intə'dʒekt], *v.t.* Intercaler; interjecter; observer, faire observer, s'écrier, protester (in conversation). **interjection** [-'dʒekʃən], *n.* Interjection, *f.* **interjectional,** *a.* Interjectif.
interknit (1) [intə'nit], *v.t.* Entrecroiser, entrelacer.—*v.i.* S'entrecroiser, s'entrelacer.
interknit (2) [intə'nit], *a.* Entrecroisé, entrelacé.
interlace [intə'leis], *v.t.* Entrelacer. **interlacing,** *n.* Entrelacement, *m.*
interlard [intə'lɑ:d], *v.t.* Entrelarder (de). **interlarding,** *n.* Entrelardement, *m.*
interleaf ['intəli:f], *n.* Feuillet intercalé, feuillet blanc, *m.*
interleave [intə'li:v], *v.t.* Interfolier (de).
interline [intə'lain], *v.t.* Interligner; écrire entre les lignes; poser une doublure intermédiaire (à un manteau etc.). **interlineal** [-'liniəl], **interlinear,** *a.* Interlinéaire. **interlineation** [-'eiʃən], *n.* Intercalation, *f.*
interlink [intə'liŋk], *v.t.* Lier ensemble, enchaîner; rattacher, relier.
interlock [intə'lɔk], *v.t.* Enclencher, emboîter; synchroniser, rendre solidaires (of recording apparatus).—*v.i.* S'accrocher, s'enclencher, s'emboîter, s'engrener.
interlocution [intələ'kju:ʃən], *n.* Interlocution, discussion, *f.,* dialogue, *m.* **interlocutor** [-'lɔkjutə], *n.* Interlocuteur; (*Sc. law*) jugement interlocutoire, *m.* **interlocutory,** *a.* En forme de dialogue; (*Law*) interlocutoire. *Interlocutory judgment,* arrêt interlocutoire, *m.*
interloper ['intəloupə], *n.* Intrus, *m.,* intruse, *f.;* (*Comm.*) courtier marron; navire interlope, *m.*
interlude ['intəlu:d], *n.* Intermède, *m.*
interlunar [intə'lu:nə] or *interlunary,* *a.* Interlunaire.
intermarriage [intə'mæridʒ], *n.* Mariage entre parents, *m.,* alliance, *f.* **intermarry,** *v.i.* Se marier entre parents; se marier les uns avec les autres.
intermaxillary [intə'mæksiləri], *a.* Intermaxillaire.
intermeddle [intə'medl], *v.i.* Se mêler (de), s'immiscer (dans). **intermeddler,** *n.* Personne qui se mêle des affaires d'autrui, *f.,* officieux, *m.,* officieuse, *f.* **intermeddling,** *n.* Intervention officieuse, *f.*
intermediary [intə'mi:diəri], *a.* and *n.* Intermédiaire, *m.*
intermediate [inte'mi:diət], *a.* Intermédiaire, moyen. **intermediately,** *adv.* D'une manière intermédiaire. **intermedium,** *n.* Intermédiaire, *m.*
interment [in'tə:mənt], *n.* Enterrement, *m.,* inhumation, *f.*

interminable [in'tə:minəbl], *a.* Interminable. **interminably,** *adv.* D'une manière interminable.
intermingle [intə'miŋgl], *v.t.* Entremêler.—*v.i.* S'entremêler.
intermission [intə'miʃən], *n.* Intermission, *f.* relâche, intervalle; (*Cine.*) entr'acte, *m.*
intermit [-'mit], *v.t.* Interrompre, cesser.—*v.i.* Cesser, s'arrêter. **intermittent,** *a.* Intermittent. **intermittently,** *adv.* Par intervalles, par intermittence.
intermix [intə'miks], *v.t.* Entremêler.—*v.i.* S'entremêler. **intermixture,** *n.* Mélange, *m.*
intermundane [intə'mʌndein], *a.* Entre les mondes.
intermuscular [intə'mʌskjulə], *a.* Intermusculaire.
intern [in'tə:n], *v.t.* Interner.
internal [in'tə:nl], *a.* Interne, intérieur; intrinsèque, intime. **internally,** *adv.* Intérieurement.
international [intə'næʃənl], *a.* International.—*n.* (Joueur) international, *m.* **internationalism,** *n.* Internationalisme, *m.* **internationalization,** *n.* Internationalisation, *f.* **internationalize,** *v.t.* Internationaliser.
internecine [intə'ni:sain], *a.* De carnage réciproque, meurtrier.
internee [intə:ni:], *n.* Interné, *m.,* internée, *f.*
internment [in'tə:nmənt], *n.* Internement, *m. Internment camp,* camp de concentration, camp de prisonniers, *m.*
internode ['intənoud], *n.* (*Bot.*) Entrenœud, *m.*
internuncio [intə'nʌnʃiou], *n.* Internonce (of the pope), *m.*
interoceanic [intərouʃi'ænik], *a.* Interocéanique.
interosseous [intə'rɔsiəs], *a.* Interosseux.
interpellate [in'tə:pəleit], *v.t.* (*Fr. Parl.*) Interpeller. **interpellation** [-'ləiʃən], *n.* Interpellation, *f.* **interpellator,** *n.* Interpellateur, *m.*
interpenetrate [intə'penitreit], *v.t.* Pénétrer dans les moindres recoins, envahir.—*v.i.* Se pénétrer réciproquement. **interpenetration,** *n.* Interpénétration (politique, etc.); pénétration réciproque, *f.* **interphone** ['intəfoun], *n.* Téléphone intérieur; téléphone reliant des bureaux, des services, *m.*
interplanetary [intə'plænətəri], *a.* Interplanétaire.
interplay ['intəplei], *n.* Effet produit par la juxtaposition, l'accumulation, etc., des couleurs, des sons, *m.,* réaction, *f.*
interpolate [in'tə:poleit], *v.t.* Interpoler; intercaler. **interpolation** [-'leiʃən], *n.* Interpolation; intercalation, *f.* **interpolator,** *n.* Interpolateur, *m.*
interpose [intə'pouz], *v.t.* Interposer; offrir sa médiation.—*v.i.* S'interposer, intervenir. **interposition** [-tə:pə'ziʃən], *n.* Interposition; intervention, médiation, *f.*
interpret [in'tə:prit], *v.t.* Interpréter; expliquer. **interpretable,** *a.* Qui peut s'interpréter, explicable. **interpretation** [-'teiʃən], *n.* Interprétation, *f.* **interpretative** [-'tə:pritətiv], *a.* Interprétatif. **interpretatively,** *adv.* Par interprétation. **interpreter,** *n.* Interprète, truchement, *m.* **interpretership,** *n.* Interprétariat, *m.*

interracial [intə'reiʃəl], *a.* Interracial; commun à plusieurs races; qui divise les races.
interregnum [intə'regnəm], *n.* Interrègne, *m.* **interrex,** *n.* Interroi, régent, *m.*
interrogate [in'terəgeit], *v.t.* Interroger, questionner. **interrogation** [-'geiʃən], *n.* Interrogation, question, *f.* **interrogative** [-'rɔgətiv], *a.* Interrogatif, interrogateur.—*n.* (*Gram.*) Mot interrogatif, *m.* **interrogatively,** *adv.* Interrogativement. **interrogatory** [-'rɔgətəri], *n.* Interrogations, *f.pl.*; série de questions, *f.*—*a.* Interrogatif.
interrupt [intə'rʌpt], *v.t.* Interrompre. **interruptedly,** *adv.* Avec des interruptions; de façon peu suivie. **interrupter,** *n.* Interrupteur, *m.*, interruptrice, *f.* **interruption** [-'rʌpʃən], *n.* Interruption, *f.*; (*fig.*) obstacle, *m.*
intersect [intə'sekt], *v.t.* Entrecouper; (*Geom.*) couper.—*v.i.* (*Geom.*) Se couper, se croiser, s'entrecroiser. **intersection** [-'sekʃən], *n.* Intersection, *f.*
interspace ['intəspeis], *n.* Intervalle; espacement, *m.*
intersperse [intə'spə:s], *v.t.* Entremêler (de); parsemer (de).
interstellar [intə'stelə], *a.* (*Astron.*) Interstellaire.
interstice [in'tə:stis], *n.* Interstice; intervalle, *m.*
intertropical [intə'trɔpikl], *a.* Intertropical.
intertwine [intə'twain], *v.t.* Entrelacer.—*v.i.* S'entrelacer.
interval ['intəvəl], *n.* Intervalle, *m.*, battement (between two trains); (*Theat.*) entr'acte, *m.*; (*Ftb.*) mi-temps, *f.* *At intervals,* par intervalles; *at long intervals,* à de longs intervalles, de loin en loin.
intervene [intə'vi:n], *v.i.* Intervenir, s'interposer; survenir, arriver (of circumstances); s'écouler (of time). **intervening,** *a.* Intervenant (of persons); intermédiaire (of space, places, time, etc.). *Intervening party,* intervenant, *m.*, intervenante, *f.* **intervention** [-'venʃən], *n.* Intervention; interposition, (action of things), *f.*
interview ['intəvju:], *n.* Entrevue; (*Journ.*) interview, *f.*—*v.t.* Avoir une entrevue avec; (*Journ.*) interviewer. **interviewer,** *n.* Interviewer, *m.*
interweave [intə'wi:v], *v.t.* (*past* **interwove** [-'wouv), *p.p.* **interwoven**) Entrelacer; entremêler. *Interwoven with golden threads,* broché d'or, tissé d'or. **interweaving,** *n.* Entrelacement, entremêlement, *m.*
interworking [intə'wə:kiŋ], *n.* Action réciproque, *f.*
interwreathed [intə'ri:ðd], *a.* Tressé en guirlande.
intestacy [in'testəsi], *n.* État de celui qui meurt intestat, *m.* **intestate,** *a.* Intestat. *Heir of one that dies intestate,* héritier ab intestat, *m.*—*n.* Intestat.
intestinal [in'testinl], *a.* Intestinal.
intestine [in'testin], *a.* and *n.* Intestin, *m.* *Intestine war,* guerre intestine, *f.*
intimacy ['intiməsi], *n.* Intimité, *f.*
intimate (1) ['intimit], *a.* Intime, lié. *Intimate knowledge,* connaissance approfondie, *f.*—*n.* Familier, ami intime, *m.*, amie intime, *f.*
intimate (2) ['intimeit], *v.t.* Donner à entendre; intimer (à). **intimately,** *adv.* Intimement.

intimation [inti'meiʃən], *n.* Avis, *m.*, indication; prémonition, *f.*
intimidate [in'timideit], *v.t.* Intimider. **intimidation** [-'deiʃən], *n.* Intimidation, *f.*
into ['intu], *prep.* Dans, en, à, entre; (*Math.*) par, multiplié par.
intolerable [in'tɔlərəbl], *a.* Intolérable, insupportable. **intolerableness,** *n.* Intolérabilité, *f.* **intolerably,** *adv.* Intolérablement, insupportablement. **intolerance,** *n.* Intolérance, *f.* **intolerant,** *a.* Intolérant. *Intolerant of,* incapable de supporter. **intolerantly,** *adv.* Avec intolérance. **intoleration** [-'reiʃən], *n.* Intolérantisme, *m.*
intonate ['intoneit], *v.t.* Psalmodier; entonner. **intonation** [-'neiʃən], *n.* Intonation, *f.* **intone** [in'toun], *v.t.*, *v.i.* Psalmodier; entonner.
intoxicant [in'tɔksikənt], *n.* Boisson alcoolique, *f.* **intoxicate** [in'tɔksikeit], *v.t.* Enivrer (de). **intoxicated,** *a.* Ivre; (*fig.*) enivré (de). **intoxicating,** *a.* Enivrant. *Intoxicating liquors,* boissons alcooliques, *f.pl.* **intoxication** [-'keiʃən], *n.* Ivresse, *f.*; (*fig.*) enivrement, *m.*
intractability [intræktə'biliti] or **intractableness,** *n.* Naturel intraitable, *m.*, indocilité, *f.* **intractable** [in'træktəbl], *a.* Intraitable, indocile, obstiné; insoluble (of problem). **intractably,** *adv.* D'une manière intraitable; d'une manière butée.
intradermic [intrə'də:mik], *a.* Intradermique.
intrados [in'treidɔs], *n.* (*Arch.*) Intrados, *m.*
intransigent [in'trænsidʒənt], *a.* Intransigeant. **intransigence,** *n.* Intransigeance, *f.*
intransitive [in'trænsitiv], *a.* Intransitif. **intransitively,** *adv.* Intransitivement.
intransmissibility [intrænzmisi'biliti], *n.* Intransmissibilité, *f.* **intransmissible,** *a.* Intransmissible.
intransmutable [intrænz'mju:təbl], *a.* Nontransmuable.
intransparency [intrænz'pɛərənsi or -'pærənsi], *n.* Opacité, *f.*
intrant ['intrənt], *n.* Inscrit (for a race); débutant (in a profession), *m.*
intravenous [intrə'vi:nəs], *a.* Endo-veineux, intraveineux. *Intravenous injection,* piqûre intraveineuse, *f.*
intrench [ENTRENCH].
intrepid [in'trepid], *a.* Intrépide. **intrepidity** [-'piditi], *n.* Intrépidité, *f.* **intrepidly,** *adv.* Intrépidement, avec intrépidité, *f.*
intricacy ['intrikəsi] or **intricateness,** *n.* Embrouillement, embarras, *m.*; complication, *f.*, dédale, *m.* **intricate,** *a.* Embrouillé; embarrassé; obscur; compliqué. **intricately,** *adv.* D'une manière embrouillée.
intrigue [in'tri:g], *n.* Intrigue, *f.*—*v.i.* Intriguer. **intriguer,** *n.* Intrigant, *m.*, intrigante, *f.* **intriguing,** *a.* Intrigant, qui excite la curiosité.—*n.* Intrigues, machinations, *f.pl.*—*pres.p.* Intriguant. **intriguingly,** *adv.* Par intrigue; en intriguant.
intrinsic [in'trinsik] or **intrinsical,** *a.* Intrinsèque. **intrinsically,** *adv.* Intrinsèquement.
introduce [intrə'dju:s], *v.t.* Introduire, faire entrer; présenter (persons to one another), faire connaître (à). *Introduce your friend to me,* faites-moi connaître votre ami; *to introduce oneself,* s'introduire, se présenter.

introducer, *n.* Introducteur, *m.* **introduction** [-'dʌkʃən], *n.* Introduction; présentation; recommandation (by letter), *f.*; avant-propos, *m.* (of book). **introductive**, *a.* Qui sert d'introduction à. **introductory**, *a.* Introductoire, d'introduction, préliminaire; qui sert d'introduction (à).

introit [in'trouit], *n.* Introït, *m.*

intromission [intro'miʃən], *n.* Admission, intromission, *f.* **intromit** [-'mit], *v.t.* Admettre.—*v.i.* (*Sc. Law*) S'ingérer, s'introduire.

introspection [intro'spekʃən], *n.* Introspection, *f.* **introspective**, *a.* Introspectif; qui s'analyse.

introversion [intro'vəːʃən], *n.* Recueillement, *m.*, retour sur soi-même, *m.*; retournement; entropion (of eyelid), *m.*

introvert (1) ['introvəːt], *n.* Introverti.

introvert (2) [intro'vəːt], *v.t.* Tourner en dedans. *Introverted rhymes*, rimes embrassées, *f.pl.*

intrude [in'truːd], *v.i.* S'introduire, se faufiler, se fourrer. *To intrude on*, importuner, déranger, abuser de; *to intrude oneself*, se présenter sans être invité, être un intrus, faire intrusion.—*v.t.* Introduire, imposer, fourrer. **intruder**, *n.* Importun, *m.*, importune, *f.*, intrus, *m.*, intruse, *f.*

intrusion [in'truːʒən], *n.* Intrusion, importunité; (*fig.*) usurpation, *f.*, empiètement, *m. Why this intrusion?* pourquoi m'importuner ainsi?

intrusive [in'truːsiv], *a.* Importun; indiscret; (*Geol.*) injecté, d'intrusion. **intrusively**, *adv.* D'une manière importune. **intrusiveness**, *n.* Importunité; indiscrétion, *f.*

intrust [ENTRUST].

intubate [intju'beit], *v.t.* (*Vet.*) Tuber. **intubation**, *n.* Tubage, *m.*

intuition [intju'iʃən], *n.* Intuition, *f.* **intuitive** [-'tjuːitiv], *a.* Intuitif, d'intuition. **intuitively**, *adv.* Par intuition, intuitivement.

intumescence [intju'mesəns], *n.* Intumescence, enflure, *f.*

intussusception [intəsə'sepʃən], *n.* Intussusception, *f.*

inula ['injulə], *n.* (*Bot.*) Inule, aunée, *f.*

inundate ['inʌndeit], *v.t.* Inonder (de). *Inundated with*, (*fig.*) inondé, débordé (de). **inundation** [-'deiʃən], *n.* Inondation, *f.*, débordement, *m.*

inure [i'njuə], *v.t.* Habituer, accoutumer, endurcir, aguerrir, rompre; (*Law*) entrer en vigueur. *To inure to war*, aguerrir. **inurement**, *n.* Accoutumance, habitude, *f.*, endurcissement, *m.*

inutility [inju'tiliti], *n.* Inutilité, *f.*

invade [in'veid], *v.t.* Envahir; (*fig.*) empiéter sur, porter atteinte à. **invader**, *n.* Envahisseur, *m.* **invading**, *a.* Envahissant; d'invasion.

invalid (1) [in'vælid], *a.* (*Law*) Invalide, de nul effet.

invalid (2) ['invəliːd *or* 'invəlid], *a.* Malade, infirme.—*n.* Malade, *m.* and *f.*, personne malade, *f. He is a helpless invalid*, il est impotent.—*v.t.* Rendre malade *or* infirme. *To invalid (a man) out of the army*, réformer, mettre à la réforme.—*v.i.* (*Mil.*) Être réformé, se faire réformer; se faire porter malade.

invalidate [in'vælideit], *v.t.* Invalider, casser,

déclarer de nul effet. **invalidation**, *n.* (*Law*) Invalidation; cassation (of judgment), *f.*

invalidity [invə'liditi], *n.* Invalidité, faiblesse, *f.*

invalidly [in'vælidli], *adv.* Illégalement.

invaluable [in'væljuəbl], *a.* Inestimable, sans prix. **invaluableness**, *n.* Valeur inestimable, *f.* **invaluably**, *adv.* D'une manière inestimable.

invariability [invɛəriə'biliti] *or* **invariableness**, *n.* Invariabilité, *f.*

invariable [in'vɛəriəbl], *a.* Invariable, constant, uniforme. **invariably**, *adv.* Invariablement, immanquablement; constamment, uniformément.

invasion [in'veiʒən], *n.* Invasion, *f.*, envahissement, *m.*; (*fig.*) violation, atteinte, *f.*

invective [in'vektiv], *a.* Invectif, injurieux, satirique.—*n.* Invective, *f.*

inveigh [in'vei], *v.i.* Invectiver (contre). **inveigher**, *n.* Personne qui se répand en invectives, *f.*

inveigle [in'viːgl, in'veigl], *v.t.* Séduire, attirer, entraîner. **inveiglement**, *n.* Séduction, *f.* **inveigler**, *n.* Séducteur, *m.*, -trice, *f.*

invent [in'vent], *v.t.* Inventer. **invention**, *n.* Invention, *f.* **inventive**, *a.* Inventif. **inventor**, *n.* Inventeur, *m.*

inventory ['invəntri], *n.* Inventaire, *m.*—*v.t.* Inventorier, inscrire dans un inventaire.

inventress [in'ventris], *n.* Inventrice, *f.*

Inverness [invə'nes], *n. Inverness cape*, macfarlane, *m.*

inverse [in'vəːs], *a.* Inverse. **inversely**, *adv.* En sens inverse, en raison inverse, inversement.

inversion [in'vəːʃən], *n.* Inversion, *f.*; (*fig.*) renversement, *m.*

invert (1) [in'vəːt], *a.* (*Chem.*) Inverti (of sugar).—*n.* (*Psych.*) Inverti, *m.*

invert (2) [in'vəːt], *v.t.* Tourner sens dessus dessous, renverser; (*fig.*) intervertir. **inverted**, *a.* Renversé, inverse; interverti (of order of things). **invertedly**, *adv.* Dans un ordre renversé, en sens inverse.

invertebrate [in'vəːtibrit], *a. and n.* Invertébré, *m.*

invest [in'vest], *v.t.* Vêtir, revêtir (de); (*Mil.*) investir, bloquer; investir, placer (money).

investigate [in'vestigeit], *v.t.* Rechercher, examiner; enquêter sur. **investigation** [-'geiʃən], *n.* Investigation, recherche, enquête; étude, *f. For investigation*, aux fins d'enquête. **investigative** *or* **investigatory**, *a.* Investigateur. **investigator**, *n.* Investigateur, *m.*, investigatrice, *f. Private investigator*, détective privé, *m.*

investiture [in'vestitʃə], *n.* Investiture; remise de décorations, *f.* **investive**, *a.* Qui revêt; qui investit. **investment**, *n.* Placement (of money); (*Mil.*) investissement, *m.* **investor**, *n.* Personne qui place ses fonds, *f. Small investor*, petit rentier, *m.*

inveteracy [in'vetərəsi] *or* **inveterateness**, *a.* Caractère invétéré; acharnement, *m.* **inveterate**, *a.* Invétéré, enraciné; acharné. *To grow inveterate*, s'invétérer, s'enraciner. **inveterately**, *adv.* D'une manière invétérée.

invidious [in'vidiəs], *a.* Odieux; désagréable; ingrat (of task), vexatoire. *Invidious comparison*, comparaison désobligeante, *f.* **invidiously**, *adv.* Odieusement. **invidiousness**,

n. Odieux, *m.*; injustice, *f.*; caractère blessant, *m.* (of a thing).
invigilate [in'vidʒileit], *v.i.* Surveiller les candidats (à un examen). **invigilator**, *n.* Surveillant, *m.*, -ante, *f.*
invigorate [in'vigəreit], *v.t.* Fortifier; donner de la vigueur à. **invigorating**, *a.* Fortifiant, vivifiant, tonifiant. **invigoration** [-'reiʃən], *n.* Action de fortifier, *f.*
invincibility [invinsi'biliti] or **invincibleness**, *n.* Nature invincible, *f.*
invincible [in'vinsibl], *a.* Invincible. **invincibly**, *adv.* Invinciblement.
inviolability [invaiələ'biliti] or **inviolableness**, *n.* Inviolabilité, *f.*
inviolable [in'vaiələbl], *a.* Inviolable. **inviolably**, *adv.* Inviolablement. **inviolate**, *a.* Inviolé, pur, intact.
invisibility [invizi'biliti] or **invisibleness**, *n.* Invisibilité, *f.*
invisible [in'vizibl], *a.* Invisible. **invisibly**, *adv.* Invisiblement.
invitation [invi'teiʃən], *n.* Invitation, *f.*
invitatory [in'vaitətəri], *a.* D'invitation, invitatoire.
invite [in'vait], *v.t.* Inviter, engager (à); (*fig.*) appeler, provoquer. **inviter**, *n.* Personne qui invite, *f.*, hôte, *m.*, hôtesse, *f.* **inviting**, *a.* Attrayant, appétissant, tentant. **invitingly**, *adv.* D'une manière attrayante. **invitingness**, *n.* Attrait, *m.*
invocation [invo'keiʃən], *n.* Invocation, *f.* *Church* (*placed*) *under the invocation of St. Paul*, église placée sous le vocable de saint Paul.
invocatory [in'vɔkətəri], *a.* Invocatoire.
invoice ['invɔis], *n.* Facture, *f. Invoice book*, livre, journal d'achats, *m.*; *as per invoice*, suivant la facture; *to make out an invoice*, établir, faire, une facture.—*v.t.* Facturer. **invoice-clerk**, *n.* Facturier, *m.*
invoke [in'vouk], *v.t.* Invoquer. **invoker**, *n.* Invocateur, *m.*, -trice, *f.*
involucral [invə'lju:krəl], **involucrate**, *a.* (*Bot.*) Involucré.
involucre ['invəlju:kə], **involucrum** [invo'lju:krəm], *n.* Involucre, *m.*, collerette, *f.*; fane, *f.*
involuntarily [in'vɔləntərili], *adv.* Involontairement. **involuntariness**, *n.* Caractère involontaire, *m.* **involuntary**, *a.* Involontaire.
involute ['invəlju:t], *n.* (*Geom.*) Développante, *f.* **involuted** or **involutive**, *a.* (*Bot.*) Involutif. **involution** [-'lju:ʃən], *n.* Enchevêtrement, *m.*, complication; (*Bot. etc.*) involution, *f.*
involve [in'vɔlv], *v.t.* Envelopper (to envelop); comporter, compromettre, impliquer, entraîner, engager (to entail); comprendre, renfermer (to comprise); embarrasser, entortiller (to entangle). *That involves expense*, cela entraîne de la dépense; *to be involved in debts*, être endetté; *to involve in difficulties*, plonger dans des difficultés; *to involve oneself in trouble*, s'attirer des ennuis; *to involve oneself in debt*, s'endetter. **involved**, *a.* Embrouillé, entortillé, compliqué. **involvement**, *n.* Embarras pécuniaire, *m.*; difficulté, gêne, *f.*; complication; implication, *f.*
invulnerability [invʌlnərə'biliti] or **invulnerableness**, *n.* Invulnérabilité, *f.*

invulnerable [in'vʌlnərəbl], *a.* Invulnérable. **invulnerably**, *adv.* Invulnérablement.
inward ['inwəd], *a.* Intérieur, interne. **inward** or **inwards**, *adv.* En dedans, intérieurement. **inwardly**, *adv.* Intérieurement, intimement. **inwardness**, *n.* Caractère intérieur, sens intime, *m.*
inweave [in'wi:v], *v.t.* (*past* **inwove**, *p.p.* **inwoven**) Enlacer, tisser, brocher.
inwrap [ENWRAP].
inwrought [in'rɔ:t], *a.* Brodé (dessins), broché (de).
iodic [ai'ɔdik], *a.* Iodique.
iodide ['aiodaid], *n.* Iodure, *m.*
iodiferous [aio'difərəs], *a.* Iodifère.
iodine ['aiodain or 'aiədi:n], *n.* Iode, *m.* **iodize**, *v.t.* Ioder.
iodoform [ai'oudəfɔ:m], *n.* Iodoforme, *m.*
ion ['aiən], *n.* Ion, *m.*
Ionia [ai'ouniə]. L'Ionie, *f.*
Ionian [ai'ouniən], *a.* and *n.* Ionien, *m.*, -ienne, *f.*
Ionic [ai'ɔnik], *a.* Ionique. *Ionic order*, (*Arch.*) ordre ionique, *m.*
ionization [aiənai'zeiʃən], *n.* Ionisation, *f.* **ionize**, *v.t.* Ioniser.—*v.i.* S'ioniser.
ionosphere [ai'ɔnəsfi:ə], *n.* Ionosphère, *f.*
iota [ai'outə], *n.* Iota; rien, *m. Iota subscript*, iota souscrit, *m.* **iotacism**, *n.* Iotacisme, *m.*
ipecacuanha [ipikækju'ænə], *n.* Ipécacuana, (*colloq.*) ipéca, *m.*
Iphigenia [ifidʒi'naiə]. Iphigénie, *f.*
Iran [i:'rɑ:n]. L'Iran, *m.*
Iranian [ai'reiniən], *a.* and *n.* Iranien, *m.*, -ienne, *f.*
Iraq, Irak [i:'rɑ:k]. L'Irak, *m.* **Iraqi, Iraquian**, *a.* and *n.* Irakien, *m.*, -ienne, *f.*
irascibility [iræsi'biliti], *n.* Irascibilité, *f.*
irascible [i'ræsibl], *a.* Irascible.
irate [ai'reit], *a.* Courroucé, irrité.
ire ['aiə], *n.* Colère, *f.*, courroux, *m.* **ireful**, *a.* Courroucé, furieux. **irefully**, *adv.* Avec colère.
Ireland ['aiələnd]. L'Irlande, *f.*
Irene [ai'ri:n, ai'ri:ni]. Irène, *f.*
iridescence [iri'desəns], *n.* Iridescence, irisation, *f.*; aspect irisé, *m.* **iridescent**, *a.* Iridescent, irisé; chatoyant.
iridium [aiə'ridiəm], *n.* Iridium, *m.*
iris ['aiəris], *n.* (*pl.* **irises**) Iris, *m.* **iris-root**, *n.* Racine d'iris, *f.*
irisated or **irised**, *a.* Irisé, chatoyant.
irisation [-'seiʃən], *n.* Irisation, *f.*
Irish ['aiəriʃ], *a.* and *n.* Irlandais, *m.*, -aise, *f. Irish bull*, grosse et naïve contradiction verbale; *the Irish Sea*, la mer d'Irlande, *f.* **Irishism**, *n.* Locution irlandaise, *f.* **Irishman**, *n.* Irlandais, *m.* **Irishwoman**, *n.* Irlandaise, *f.*
irk [ə:k], *v.t.* Peiner, affliger; ennuyer. *It irks me to have to do it*, il m'en coûte d'avoir à le faire. **irksome**, *a.* Pénible, ennuyeux, ingrat. **irksomely**, *adv.* D'une manière ennuyeuse. **irksomeness**, *n.* Caractère (*or* genre) fastidieux, ingrat, *m.*
iron ['aiən], *n.* Fer; (*Tech.*) ferrement, *m. Angle-iron*, fer cornier, *m.*, cornière, *f.*; *cast iron*, fonte, *f.*; *corrugated iron*, tôle ondulée, *f.*; *flat-iron*, fer à repasser, *m.*; *galvanized iron*, fer galvanisé, *m.*; *hoop iron*, (fer) feuillard, *m.*; *in irons*, aux fers; *Iron Age*, âge de fer, *m.*;

iron ration, vivres de réserve, *m.pl.*; *old iron*, ferraille, *f.*; *pig iron*, gueuse, *f.*; *sheet-iron*, tôle, *f.*; *to have many irons in the fire*, avoir beaucoup d'affaires sur les bras, courir deux lièvres à la fois; *to rule with a rod of iron*, gouverner d'une main de fer; *wrought iron*, fer forgé, *m.—a.* De fer, en fer.—*v.t.* Repasser (linen etc.); mettre les fers à (to shackle); garnir de fer. **iron-bound,** *a.* Cerclé de fer, garni de fer. *Iron-bound shore*, côte à pic, *f.* **iron-clad,** *a.* Cuirassé, blindé.—*n.* Cuirassé, *m.* **iron-filings,** *n.pl.* Limaille de fer, *f.* **iron-founder,** *n.* Fondeur en fer, *m.* **iron-foundry,** *n.* Fonderie de fer, *f.* **iron-grey,** *a.* Gris de fer. **iron-hearted,** *a.* Au cœur de fer. **iron-master,** *n.* Maître de forge, métallurgiste, *m.* **iron-mill,** *n.* Usine métallurgique, fonderie; aciérie, *f.* **ironmonger,** *n.* Quincaillier, *m.* **ironmongery,** *n.* Quincaillerie, *f.* **iron-mould,** *n.* Tache de rouille, *f.* **iron-ore,** *n.* Minerai de fer, *m.* **ironside,** *n.* Côte-de-fer, *f.* **iron-stand,** *n.* Porte-fer (à repasser), *m.* **iron-stone,** *n.* Minerai de fer, *m.* **iron-wire,** *n.* Fil de fer, *m.* **iron-wood,** *n.* Bois de fer, *m.* **iron-work,** *n.* Serrurerie; ferrure, *f.*, ferrures, *f.pl.*, ferrements, *m.pl.*, ouvrage en fer, *m.* **iron-works,** *n.pl.* Forges, *f.pl.*; usine métallurgique, *f.*

ironer, *n.* Repasseuse, *f.*

ironic [aiə′rɔnik] or **ironical,** *a.* Ironique. **ironically,** *adv.* Ironiquement.

ironing, *n.* Repassage, *m.—a.* À repasser. **ironing-board,** *n.* Planche à repasser, *f.*

irony (1) [′aiərəni], *n.* Ironie, *f.*

irony (2) [′aiəni], *a.* De fer.

irradiance [i′reidiəns], *n.* Rayonnement; éclat, *m.*

irradiate [i′reidieit], *v.t.* Rayonner sur; éclairer.—*v.i.* Rayonner. **irradiation** [-di′ei ʃən], *n.* Irradiation, *f.*; (*fig.*) éclat, *m.*, splendeur; illumination, *f.* (of spirit).

irrational [i′ræʃənl], *a.* Irraisonnable, déraisonnable; (*Math.*) irrationnel. **irrationality** [iræʃə′næliti], *n.* Déraison, *f.*, caractère irrationnel, *m.*; (*fig.*) absurdité, *f.* **irrationally,** *adv.* Sans raison, irrationnellement, déraisonnablement.

irreclaimable [irə′kleiməbl], *a.* Incorrigible, invétéré. **irreclaimably,** *adv.* Incorrigiblement.

irrecognizable etc. [UNRECOGNIZABLE].

irreconcilability [irekənsailə′biliti] or **irreconcilableness,** *n.* Nature irréconciliable; incompatibilité, *f.*

irreconcilable [irekən′sailəbl], *a.* Irréconciliable (avec); incompatible (avec); implacable; inconciliable. **irreconcilably,** *adv.* Irréconciliablement; d'une manière inconciliable.

irrecoverable [iri′kʌvərəbl], *a.* Irrécouvrable; irréparable. **irrecoverableness,** *n.* Nature irréparable; perte sans ressource, *f.* **irrecoverably,** *adv.* Irréparablement, irrémédiablement.

irredeemable [iri′di:məbl], *a.* Irrachetable; non amortissable (of bonds, shares); irrémédiable. **irredeemably,** *adv.* Sans recours; définitivement; totalement.

irreducible [iri′dju:sibl], *a.* Irréductible. **irreducibility** [-dju:si′biliti] or **irreducibleness,** *n.* Irréductibilité, *f.*

irreformable [iri′fɔ:məbl], *a.* Inaltérable, irréformable.

irrefragability [irefrəgə′biliti] or **irrefragableness,** *n.* Nature irréfragable, *f.*

irrefragable [i′refrəgəbl], *a.* Irréfragable, irréfutable. **irrefragably,** *adv.* Irréfragablement.

irrefutability [irəfju:tə′biliti], *n.* Caractère irréfutable, *m.*

irrefutable [i′refjutəbl], *a.* Irréfutable. **irrefutably,** *adv.* D'une manière irréfutable.

irregular [i′regjulə], *a.* Irrégulier, anormal; déréglé, désordonné, vicieux. *Irregular household*, faux ménage; (*Law*) *irregular document*, document informe, *m.—n.* Soldat d'un corps de troupes irrégulières, *m.* **irregularity** [-′læriti], *n.* Irrégularité, *f.*, dérèglement, *m.*; conduite déréglée, *f.* **irregularly,** *adv.* Irrégulièrement.

irrelative [i′relətiv], *a.* Sans liaison, sans rapport.

irrelevance [i′reləvəns] or **irrelevancy** [i′reləvənsi], *n.* Manque d'à propos, *m.*, inconséquence, *f.* **irrelevant,** *a.* Hors de propos, non pertinent; inapplicable (à). **irrelevantly,** *adv.* Sans rapport, mal à propos.

irrelievable [iri′li:vəbl], *a.* Qu'on ne peut soulager; sans remède.

irreligion [iri′lidʒən], *n.* Irréligion, *f.* **irreligious,** *a.* Irréligieux. **irreligiously,** *adv.* Irréligieusement. **irreligiousness,** *n.* Irréligion, *f.*

irremediable [iri′mi:diəbl], *a.* Irrémédiable, sans remède. **irremediableness,** *n.* Nature irrémédiable, *f.* **irremediably,** *adv.* Irrémédiablement.

irremissible [iri′misibl], *a.* Irrémissible, impardonnable. **irremissibleness,** *n.* Nature irrémissible or impardonnable, *f.*

irremovability [irimu:və′biliti], *n.* Fermeté inébranlable; inamovibilité, *f.* **irremovable** [-′mu:vəbl], *a.* Inébranlable, immuable; inamovible; invincible (difficulty). **irremovably,** *adv.* Immuablement, inébranlablement.

irreparability [irepərə′biliti], *n.* Nature irréparable, *f.*

irreparable [i′repərəbl], *a.* Irréparable. **irreparably,** *adv.* Irréparablement, sans remède.

irrepealability [irəpi:lə′biliti], *n.* Irrévocabilité, *f.* **irrepealable** [-′pi:ləbl], *a.* Irrévocable. **irrepealably,** *adv.* Irrévocablement.

irreplaceable [iri′pleisəbl], *a.* Irremplaçable.

irreprehensible [ireprə′hensibl], *a.* Irrépréhensible, exempt de blâme. **irreprehensibly,** *adv.* D'une manière irrépréhensible.

irrepressible [iri′presibl], *a.* Irrépressible; inextinguible (of laughter).

irreproachable [iri′proutʃəbl], *a.* Irréprochable, sans tache. **irreproachableness,** *n.* Nature irréprochable, *f.* **irreproachably,** *adv.* Irréprochablement.

irreprovable [iri′pru:vəbl], *a.* Irrépréhensible. **irreprovably,** *adv.* D'une manière irrépréhensible.

irresistibility [irizisti′biliti] or **irresistibleness,** *n.* Irrésistibilité, *f.* **irresistible** [-′zistibl], *a.* Irrésistible. **irresistibly,** *adv.* Irrésistiblement.

irresoluble [i′rezəljubl], *a.* Insoluble.

irresolute [i'rezolju:t], *a.* Irrésolu, indécis. **irresolutely**, *adv.* Irrésolument, avec hésitation. **irresolution** [-'lu:ʃən] or **irresoluteness**, *n.* Irrésolution, hésitation, indécision, *f.*; manque de décision, *m.*

irresolvability [irizɔlvə'biliti], *n.* Insolubilité; irréductibilité, *f.* **irresolvable**, *a.* Insoluble; irréductible, indécomposable.

irrespective [iris'pektiv], *a.* Indépendant (de), sans égard (pour). *Irrespective of*, indépendamment de. **irrespectively**, *adv.* Indépendamment (de), sans égard (pour).

irrespirable [i'respirəbl], *a.* Irrespirable.

irresponsibility [irispɔnsi'biliti], *n.* Irresponsabilité, étourderie, *f.*; manque de sérieux, *m.* **irresponsible** [-'pɔnsibl], *a.* Irresponsable; irréfléchi, étourdi, évaporé; brouillon. **irresponsive**, *a.* Froid, réservé, apathique. **irresponsiveness**, *n.* Froideur, indifférence, *f.*

irretrievable [iri'tri:vəbl], *a.* Irréparable, irrémédiable. **irretrievably**, *adv.* Irréparablement.

irreverence [i'revərəns], *n.* Irrévérence, *f.*, manque de respect, *m.* **irreverent**, *a.* Irrévérent, irrévérencieux. **irreverently**, *adv.* Irrévéremment, avec irrévérence.

irreversible [iri'və:sibl], *a.* Irrévocable. **irreversibly**, *adv.* Irrévocablement.

irrevocability [irevəkə'biliti] or **irrevocableness**, *n.* Irrévocabilité, *f.* **irrevocable** [i'revəkəbl], *a.* Irrévocable. **irrevocably**, *adv.* Irrévocablement.

irrigable ['irigəbl], *a.* Irrigable. **irrigate**, *v.t.* Arroser, irriguer. **irrigation** [iri'geiʃən], *n.* Arrosage, arrosement, *m.*, irrigation, *f.*

irritability [iritə'biliti], *n.* Irritabilité, *f.* **irritable** ['iritəbl], *a.* Irritable. **irritant**, *a.* and *n.* Irritant, *m.* **irritate**, *v.t.* Irriter. *To be irritated*, s'irriter. **irritation** [iri'teifən], *n.* Irritation, *f.*; (*Biol.*) stimulation (of organ), *f.*

irruption [i'rʌpʃən], *n.* Irruption, *f.* **irruptive**, *a.* Qui fait irruption.

is, *3rd sing. indic. pres.* [BE].

Isabel ['izəbel] or **Isabella** [izə'belə]. Isabelle, *f.*

isabel ['izəbel], *a. inv.* Isabelle (colour).

Isaiah [ai'zaiə]. Isaïe, *m.*

ischium ['iskiəm], *n.* (*Anat.*) Ischion, *m.*

ischuretic [iskjuə'retik], *a.* Ischurétique.

ischuria [is'kjuəriə], *n.* (*Path.*) Ischurie, *f.*

Ishmael ['iʃmeil]. Ismaël, *m.* **Ishmaelite** ['iʃməlait], *n.* Ismaélite; (*fig.*) paria, révolté.

isinglass ['aizinɡlɑ:s], *n.* Colle de poisson; gélatine, *f. Bengal isinglass*, agar-agar, *m.*; (*fam.*) mica, *m.*

Islam ['izlɑ:m]. Islam, *m.* **Islamic** [-'læmik], *a.* Islamique. **Islamism**, *n.* Islamisme, *m.* **Islamite**, *n.* Islamite, *m.*

island ['ailənd], *n.* Île, *f.*; refuge, *m.* (in street). **islander**, *n.* Insulaire, *m.* or *f.*

isle [ail], *n.* Île, *f. Fair-Isle* (*stitch, knitting*), (point, tricot) Jacquard, *m.* **islet**, *n.* Îlot, *m.*

isobar ['aisobɑ:], *n.* Isobare, *f.*

isochromatic [aisoukro'mætik], *a.* Isochromatique.

isochronal [ai'sɔkrənəl] or **isochronous**, *a.* Isochrone. **isochronism**, *n.* Isochronisme, *m.*

isoclinal [aisou'klainl], *a.* Isoclinal.

isodynamic [aisoudai'næmik], *a.* Isodynamique, isodyname.

isolate ['aisəleit], *v.t.* Isoler. **isolated**, *a.* Isolé, seul. **isolation** [-'leiʃən], *n.* Isolement, *m. Isolation ward*, service des contagieux, *m.* **isolationist**, *a.* and *n.* Isolationniste.

Isolde [i'zɔldə]. Iseu(l)t, Yseu(l)t, *f.*

isomeric [aiso'merik], *a.* Isomère.

isosceles [ai'sɔsəli:z], *a.* Isocèle, isoscèle.

isotherm ['aisoθə:m], *n.* Isotherme, *f.* **isothermal** [-'θə:ml], *a.* Isotherme.

isotonic [aiso'tɔnik], *a.* Isotonique.

isotropic [aiso'trɔpik], *a.* Isotrope. **isotropism** [-'sɔtrəpizm], *n.* Isotropie, *f.*

Israel ['izreiəl]. Israël, *m.*; l'état d'Israël; (*Bibl.*) le royaume d'Israël, *m. To go to Israel*, aller en Israël. **Israeli**, *n.* and *a.* Israélien, *m.* **Israelite** ['izrəlait or 'izreiəlait], *n.* Israélite, *m.* or *f.* **Israelitic** [-'litik] or **Israelitish** [-'laitiʃ], *a.* Israélite.

issue ['isju: or 'iʃju:], *n.* Issue, sortie (egress), *f.*; écoulement (of water etc.), *m.*; distribution (sending out); émission (of bank-notes, stamps); expédition (of orders etc.); parution, publication, impression (of books etc.), *f.*; événement, résultat (result), *m.*; enfants, *m.pl.*, famille, postérité (progeny) (*Law*) question, *f.*, point, *m.*; (*Med.*) cautère (en pleine suppuration), *m. At issue*, en question, en litige; *to die without issue*, mourir sans enfants; *to join* or *take issue*, discuter, différer d'opinion (avec).—*v.t.* Publier; expédier, distribuer; mettre en circulation, émettre (bank-notes); faire délivrer (tickets); (*Law*) donner, lancer. *To issue a writ*, lancer un mandat.—*v.i.* Sortir, jaillir (de); (*fig.*) émaner, provenir; découler (de); terminer, se terminer, déboucher (dans); (*Mil.*) faire une sortie, déboucher.

isthmian [is'θmiən], *a. Isthmian games*, jeux isthmiques, *m.pl.*

isthmus ['isməs], *n.* Isthme, *m.*

it [it], *pron.* Il, *m.*, elle, *f.*; (*accusative*) le, *m.*, la, *f.*; (*dative*) lui; (*impers.*) il, ce, cela. *At it*, in it, to it, y; *for it*, en, y, pour cela; *from it*, en; *if it be so*, s'il en est ainsi; *I have heard it said*, je l'ai entendu dire; *it is I who said it*, c'est moi qui l'ai dit; *it is over*, c'est fini; *it is raining*, il pleut; *it is said*, on dit; *it is supposed*, on croit; *it is they who said it*, ce sont eux qui l'ont dit; *it must be*, il le faut; *of it*, en; *she's got 'it'*, elle a de ça; *that's it*, c'est ça; *that's not it*, ce n'est pas cela; *that's the truth of it*, c'est là la vérité, telle est la vérité.

it (2) [it], *n.* (*Italian*). *Gin and it*, gin vermouth, *m.*

Italian [i'tæliən], *a.* and *n.* Italien, *m.*, -ienne, *f.*; italien (language), *m.* **Italianize**, *v.t.* Italianiser.

italic [i'tælik], *a.* Italique.—*n.* (*pl.*) Italiques, *m.pl.* **italicize** [-saiz], *v.t.* Mettre or imprimer en italiques.

Italy ['itəli]. L'Italie, *f.*

itch [itʃ], *n.* Démangeaison; gale (disease), *f.* —*v.i.* Démanger. *My fingers are itching to*, les doigts me démangent de. **itching**, *n.* Démangeaison, *f.* **itchy**, *a.* Galeux.

item ['aitəm], *n.* Article; détail, *m.*, rubrique, *f. Item of news*, nouvelle, *f.*; *items on the agenda*, questions à l'ordre du jour, *f.pl.*— *adv.* Item, de plus.

itemize ['aitəmaiz], *v.t.* Détailler (an account).
iterant ['itərənt], *a.* Qui répète, itératif.
iterate ['itəreit], *v.t.* Réitérer, répéter.
iteration [itə'reiʃən], *n.* Itération, répétition, *f.*
iterative, *a.* Itératif. **iteratively,** *adv.* Itérativement.
Ithaca ['iθəkə]. Ithaque, *f.*
itineracy [i'tinərəsi] or **itinerancy,** *n.* Vie ambulante, *f.*, vagabondage, *m.* **itinerant,** *a.* Ambulant. **itinerary,** *n.* Itinéraire, *m.*
its [its], *poss.a.* Son, *m.*, sa, *f.*; ses, *m.pl.* **itself,** *pron.* Lui, elle, soi, lui-même, *m.*, elle-même, *f.*; soi-même, *m.*; (*reflexive*) se. *To go of itself,* aller tout seul; *virtue itself,* la vertu même.
Ivanhoe ['aivənhou]. Ivanhoé, *m.*
ivied ['aivid], *a.* Couvert de lierre.
ivory ['aivəri], *n.* Ivoire, *m.*—*a.* D'ivoire. *The Ivory Coast,* la Côte d'Ivoire, *f.* **ivory-black,** *n.* Noir d'ivoire, *m.* **ivory-nut,** *n.* Corozo, *m.* **ivory paper,** *a.* Bristol, *m.* **ivory-turner,** *n.* Tourneur en ivoire, *m.* **ivory-worker,** *n.* Sculpteur sur ivoire, ivoirier, *m.*
ivy ['aivi], *n.* Lierre, *m. Ground ivy,* lierre terrestre, *m.*, herbe de Saint-Jean, *f.* **ivy-berry,** *n.* Baie de lierre, *f.* **ivy-leaved,** *a.* À feuilles de lierre. **ivy-mantled,** *a.* Couvert de lierre.
izard ['izəd], *n.* Isard, *m.*

J

J, j [dʒei]. Dixième lettre de l'alphabet, *m.*
jab [dʒæb], *v.t.* Frapper de la (or comme avec une) pointe; (*Box.*) donner un coup sec à.—*n.* Coup de pointe, coup sec, *m.*; (*Med.*) piqûre, *f.*
jabber ['dʒæbə], *v.i.* Jaboter, jacasser; baragouiner.—*n.* Bavardage, baragouinage, baragouin, *m.* **jabberer,** *n.* Bredouilleur, *m.*, bredouilleuse, *f.*, baragouineur, *m.*, baragouineuse, *f.* **jabbering,** *n.*=jabber, *m.*
jacinth ['dʒæsinθ], *n.* Jacinthe, *f.*
Jack [dʒæk]. Jean, Jeannot, *m.*
jack [dʒæk], *n.* Tourne-broche (spit); brocheton (small pike), *m.*; chèvre, *f.*, chevalet, *m.* (for sawing timber); cric (lifting jack); pavillon (flag); matelot (sailor); (*Cards*) valet; (*Bowls*) cochonnet, *m.*; (*Archaeol.*) broc en cuir, *m. Boot-jack,* tire-botte, *m.*; *hydraulic jack,* vérin, *m.; Jack Ketch,* le bourreau, *m.; jack of all trades,* homme de tous les métiers, Maître Jacques, homme à tout faire, *m.; jack o' lantern,* feu follet, *m.*—*v.t. To jack up,* soulever avec un cric, avec un vérin. **jack-by-the-hedge,** *n.* Alliaire, *f.* **jack-in-office,** *n.* Fonctionnaire insolent, *m.* **jack-in-the-box,** *n.* Boîte à surprise, *f.*, diable à ressort, *m.* **jack-knife,** *n.* Couteau de poche, *m. Jack-knife dive,* (plongeon en) saut de carpe, *m.* **jack-pudding,** *n.* Paillasse, bouffon, *m.* **jack-snipe,** *n.* Bécassine, *f.* **jack-tar,** *n.* Marin, *m.* **jack-towel,** *n.* Essuie-mains (sur rouleau), *m.*
jackal ['dʒækɔ:l], *n.* Chacal, *m.*
jackanapes ['dʒækəneips], *n.* Singe; fat, freluquet, *m.*
jackass ['dʒækæs], *n.* Âne, baudet, bourriquet, *m.*; (*fig.*) idiot, *m.*, bourrique, *f.*

jackdaw ['dʒækdɔ:], *n.* Choucas, *m.*, corneille des clochers, *f.*
jacket ['dʒækit], *n.* Jaquette, veste, *f.*; vestor, *m.*; (*Mil.*) dolman, *m.*; vareuse; (*Tech.*) chemise, enveloppe, *f. Potatoes cooked in their jackets,* pommes de terre en robe de chambre, *f.pl.*
Jacob ['dʒeikəb]. Jacob, *m. Jacob's ladder,* l'échelle de Jacob, *f.* **Jacob's staff** ['dʒeikəbz 'staːf], *n.* (*Bot.*) Molène commune, *f.*; bouillon-blanc, *m.*; (*Astron.*) astrolabe, *m.*
Jacobin ['dʒækəbin], *n.* Jacobin, *m.* **Jacobinic** or **Jacobinical** [-'binikəl], *a.* Jacobin; de jacobin.
Jacobite, *n.* Jacobite, partisan des Stuarts, *m.*
jaconet ['dʒækənet], *n.* Jaconas, *m.*
Jacquard loom ['dʒækɑːd'luːm], *n.* Métier Jacquard, jacquard, *m.*
jade [dʒeid], *n.* Rosse, haridelle; (*fig.*) coquine, friponne (woman), *f.*; (*Min.*) jade, *m.*—*v.t.* Surmener, harasser, éreinter. **jaded,** *a.* Surmené, excédé de fatigue, éreinté.
Jaffa ['dʒæfə]. (*anc.*) Joppé; (*mod.*) Jaffa.
jag [dʒæg], *n.* Dent de scie, dentelure; (*fig.*) brèche, *f.*; (*slang*) une Jaguar (car).—*v.t.* Ébrécher, denteler.
jagged ['dʒægid] or **jaggy,** *a.* Dentelé, ébréché. *Jagged rocks,* rochers déchiquetés, aux arêtes vives; *jagged wound,* plaie mâchée.
jaggedness, *n.* Dentelure, *f.*
jaguar ['dʒægjuə], *n.* Jaguar, *m.*
jail [dʒeil], *n.* Prison, geôle, *f.* **jail-bird,** *n.* Gibier de potence, *m.* **jail-book,** *n.* Livre d'écrou, *m.* **jail-delivery,** *n.* Levée d'écrou, *f.* **jailer,** *n.* Geôlier, *m.*
jalopy [dʒə'lɔpi], *n.* (*pop.*) (*Motor.*) Carriole, bagnole, *f.*
jam [dʒæm], *n.* Confitures, *f.pl.*; presse, foule, *f.*; encombrement, embouteillage, *m.* (of traffic); embâcle, *m.* (on a river).—*v.t.* Serrer, presser, bloquer; (*Rad.*) brouiller.—*v.i.* Se coincer. **jamming,** *n.* Coincement, calage, enrayage, *m.*; brouillage, *m.* **jam-pot,** *n.* Pot à confitures, *m.*
Jamaica [dʒə'meikə]. La Jamaïque, *f.* **Jamaican,** *a.* and *n.* Jamaïquain, -e.
jamb [dʒæm], *n.* Jambage, montant, chambranle, *m.*
jamboree [dʒæmbə'riː], *n.* (*Am. slang*) Fête bruyante, tapageuse; grande réunion des éclaireurs, jamboree, *m.*
James [dʒeimz]. Jacques, *m.*
Jane [dʒein]. Jeanne, *f.*; (*Austral.*) femme, *f.* **Janet** ['dʒænət]. Jeannette, Jeanneton, *f.*
jangle [dʒæŋgl], *v.i.* *Se quereller, faire un bruit de ferraille.—*v.t.* Choquer avec bruit, (*fig.*) exaspérer, agacer (of nerves).
janitor ['dʒænitə], *n.* Portier, concierge, *m.*
janizary ['dʒænizəri] or **janissary,** *n.* Janissaire, *m.*
jankers ['dʒænkəz], *n.* (*Mil. pop.*) Piquet des punis, *m.*
Jansenism ['dʒænsənizm], *n.* Jansénisme, *m.* **Jansenist,** *n.* Janséniste, *m.*
January ['dʒænjuəri], *n.* Janvier, *m.*
Jap [dʒæp], *a.* and *n.* (*fam.*) Japonais, -aise, *m. Jap silk,* pongée (du Japon), *m.*
Japan (1) [dʒə'pæn]. Le Japon, *m.* **Japanese** [-'niːz], *a.* and *n.* Japonais, *m.*, Japonaise, *f.*; japonais (language), *m.*
japan (2) [dʒə'pæn], *n.* Laque, vernis, *m. Japan earth,* terre du Japon, *f.*—*v.t.* Laquer;

vernir. **japanner**, *n.* Vernisseur, laqueur, *m.*
japanning, *n.* Vernissage, *f.*
jape [dʒeip], *n.* Plaisanterie, badinerie, *f.*
japonica [dʒə'pɔnikə], *n.* (*Bot.*) Cognassier du Japon, *m.*; rose du Japon, *f.*
jar (1) [dʒɑ:], *v.i.* Être discordant (of a musical instrument); être contraire à, heurter, choquer, s'entre-choquer (to clash); jurer (of colours); (*fig.*) se disputer, se heurter, se quereller (to quarrel). *Their interests jar, leurs intérêts sont contraires.*—*v.t.* Remuer, secouer; faire trembler; ébranler.—*n.* Son discordant, *m.*; choc, *m.*, secousse; querelle; contestation (dispute), *f. Family jars*, disputes de famille, *f.pl.*; *on the jar*, entr'ouvert, entrebâillé.
jar (2) [dʒɑ:], *n.* Jarre, cruche (vessel), *f.*, bocal (glass), *m. Leyden jar*, bouteille de Leyde, *f.*
jargon ['dʒɑ:gən], *n.* Jargon; (*Min.*) zircon, jargon, *m.*
jarring ['dʒɑ:riŋ], *n.* Son discordant (harsh sound), *m.*; discorde, *f.*, querelles, *f.pl.*; contestation (dispute), *f.*—*a.* Discordant; en conflit; jurant (avec).
jarvey ['dʒɑ:vi], *n.* Cocher de fiacre, *m.*; (*fam.*) automédon, *m.*
jasmine ['dʒæsmin], *n.* Jasmin, *m.*
jasper ['dʒæspə], *n.* Jaspe, *m.*
jaundice ['dʒɔ:ndis], *n.* Jaunisse, *f.* **jaundiced**, *a.* Qui a la jaunisse; (*fig.*) prévenu (contre).
jaunt [dʒɔ:nt], *n.* Petite promenade *or* excursion, *f.*—*v.i.* Errer çà et là; faire une petite promenade *or* excursion. **jauntily**, *adv.* Avec insouciance, légèrement, avec enjouement; prétentieusement, avec affectation. **jauntiness**, *n.* Légèreté, *f.*, enjouement, *m.*
jaunting-car, *n.* Char à bancs irlandais, *m.*
jaunty, *a.* Léger, enjoué, sémillant.
javelin ['dʒævəlin], *n.* Javeline, *f.*, javelot, *m.*
jaw [dʒɔ:], *n.* Mâchoire; (*abusive*) bouche, gueule, *f.*; (*fam.*) sermon, *m.*, réprimande, *f.* (*vulg.*) caquet, bavardage, *m.*; (*fig., pl.*) portes, *f.pl.*; bras, *m.pl.*, étreintes, *f.pl.*—*a.* and *n.* Molaire, *f.*—*v.t.* (*vulg.*) Crier après; sermonner.—*v.i.* (*vulg.*) Gueuler; bavarder. **jawbone**, *n.* Mâchoire, *f.*
jay [dʒei], *n.* Geai, *m.*; (*colloq.*) idiot, *m.* **jaywalk**, *v.i.* Marcher le nez en l'air. **jaywalker**, *n.* Piéton distrait, *m.*
jazz [dʒæz], *n.* Jazz, *m. Jazz-band*, jazz-band, *m.*—*v.t.* To *jazz up*, animer, émoustiller.
jazzy, *a.* Discordant (sound); tapageur (colour).
jealous ['dʒeləs], *a.* Jaloux. **jealously**, *adv.* Jalousement; par jalousie. **jealousy** or ***jealousness**, *n.* Jalousie, *f.*
jean [dʒi:n], *n.* Coutil, treillis, *m.*; (*pl.*) (*Am.*) pantalon (de coutil, *m.*), blue jeans, *m.pl.*
jeep [dʒi:p], *n.* Jeep, *f.*
jeer [dʒiə], *n.* Raillerie, moquerie, huée, *f.*, brocard, *m.*—*v.i.* Railler (de), se moquer (de), goguenarder.—*v.t.* Railler, huer, se moquer de. **jeerer**, *n.* Railleur, *m.*, railleuse, *f.*; moqueur, *m.*, moqueuse, *f.* **jeering**, *a.* Railleur, moqueur, goguenard.—*n.* Raillerie, moquerie, *f.* **jeeringly**, *adv.* En raillant, d'un ton moqueur.
jehu ['dʒi:hju:], *n.* Cocher (qui conduit trop vite), automédon, *m.*

jejune [dʒə'dʒu:n], *a.* Vide, à jeun, maigre; sec, aride, stérile. **jejuneness**, *n.* Aridité, pauvreté, stérilité, *f.*
jellied ['dʒelid], *a.* En gelée.
jelly ['dʒeli], *n.* Gelée, *f.* **jelly-bag**, *n.* Chausse à filtrer, *f.* **jelly-fish**, *n.* Méduse, *f.* **jellymould**, *n.* Moule à gelées, *m.* **jellypowder**, *n.* (*Cook.*) Gélatine en poudre, *f.*
jemmy ['dʒemi], *n.* (*slang*) Pince-monseigneur, *f.*, monseigneur, *m.*
jennet ['dʒenit], *n.* Genet (d'Espagne), *m.*
jenny ['dʒeni], *n.* Métier à filer, *m.*
jeopardize ['dʒepədaiz], *v.t.* Hasarder, risquer, mettre en danger. **jeopardy**, *n.* Danger, hasard, *m.*
jerboa (2) [dʒə:'buə], *n.* Gerboise, *f.*
jeremiad [dʒeri'maiəd], *n.* Jérémiade, *f.*
Jeremiah [dʒeri'maiə]. Jérémie, *m.*
Jericho ['dʒerikou]. Jéricho, *m.*
jerk [dʒə:k], *n.* Saccade, secousse, *f.*; (*Am.*) (*pop.*) déplombé, *m.*—*v.t.* Donner une poussée à; jeter, lancer. *To jerk out*, dire d'un ton sec. **jerked-beef**, *n.* Bœuf salé et séché au soleil, *m.* **jerkily**, *adv.* Par saccades.
jerky, *a.* Saccadé; irrégulier.
jerkin ['dʒə:kin], *n.* Pourpoint, justaucorps; paletot (de cuir), *m.*
Jerome ['dʒerəm]. Jérôme, *m.*
jerque [dʒə:k], *v.t.* Visiter (un navire). *Jerque note* = CLEARING BILL.
Jerry ['dʒeri], *n.* (*pej.*) Fritz, boche; (*pop.*) pot de chambre, *m.*
jerry-built ['dʒeribilt], *a.* Mal bâti. *That's a jerry-built house*, c'est un vrai château de cartes que cette maison-là, une bâtisse en carton. **jerrycan**, *n.* Jerrycan, bidon à essence, *m.*
jersey ['dʒə:zi], *n.* Vareuse de laine, *f.*, maillot, tricot, jersey, chandail, *m.*
Jerusalem [dʒə'ru:sələm]. Jérusalem, *f.* [ARTICHOKE].
jess [dʒes], *n.* (*Hawking*) Jet, *m.* (strap or ribbon tied round each leg).
jessamine [JASMINE].
jest [dʒest], *n.* Plaisanterie, facétie, *f.*, bon mot, mot pour rire, *m.*; risée (laughing-stock), *f. In jest*, en plaisantant, pour rire.—*v.i.* Plaisanter (de *or* avec), badiner (sur), railler de. **jest-book**, *n.* Recueil de bons mots, *m.* **jester**, *n.* Plaisant, railleur, *m.*; bouffon, fou, *m.* **jesting**, *a.* De plaisanterie, pour rire, badin.—*n.* Raillerie, plaisanterie, *f.*, badinage, *m.* **jestingly**, *adv.* En plaisantant, pour rire.
Jesuit ['dʒezjuit], *n.* Jésuite, *m. Jesuits' bark*, quinquina, *m.* **Jesuitic** [-'itik] or **Jesuitical**, *a.* Jésuitique. **Jesuitically**, *adv.* Jésuitiquement, en jésuite. **Jesuitism**, *n.* Jésuitisme, *m.*
Jesus ['dʒi:zəs]. Jésus, *m.*
jet [dʒet], *n.* Jet, jet d'eau; gicleur, *m.*; (*Min.*) jais, *m. Gas-jet*, bec, *m.*; *jet engine*, turboréacteur, *m.*; *jet plane*, avion à réaction, *m.*—*v.i.* S'élancer; gicler; *jet pavaner (to strut).
jet-black, *a.* Noir comme du jais. **jet-pipe**, *n.* Tuyère, *f.* (of jet plane). **jet-propelled**, *a.* À réaction.
jetsam ['dʒetsəm], *n.* Marchandise jetée à la mer, *f.*
jettison ['dʒetisən], *n.* Jet à la mer, *m.*—*v.t.* Jeter par-dessus bord.
jetty (1) ['dʒeti], *a.* Noir comme du jais.

jetty (2) ['dʒeti], n. Jetée, f. **jetty-head**, n. Musoir, m.

Jew [dʒuː], n. Juif, m. **jew's-harp**, n. Guimbarde, f.; (*Naut.*) cigale (d'ancre), f.

jewel ['dʒuːəl], n. Joyau, bijou, m., pierre précieuse, f.; (*pl.*) pierreries, f.pl.; rubis (of watch), m.pl. *She's a jewel*, (*fig.*) c'est une perle.—*v.t.* Orner de bijoux, parer de pierreries; (*Horol.*) monter sur rubis. **jewel-case**, n. Écrin, m. **jeweller**, n. Joaillier, bijoutier, m. **jewelry** or **jewellery**, n. Joaillerie, bijouterie, f.

Jewess ['dʒuːis], n. Juive, f. **Jewish**, a. Juif, des Juifs. **Jewry**, n. Juiverie, f.

Jezebel ['dʒezəbəl]. Jézabel, f.—n. Mégère, f.; femme éhontée; vieille femme fardée, f.

jib (1) [dʒib], n. (*Naut.*) Foc, m. *Flying jib*, clin-foc, m. **jib-boom**, n. Bâton de foc, bout-dehors de foc, m.

jib (2) [dʒib], v.i. Reculer, se dérober; regimber.

jibe [GIBE].

jiffy ['dʒifi], n. *In a jiffy*, en un clin d'œil, en un tournemain, m.

jig [dʒig], n. Gigue (dance), f., gabarit, m.—v.i. Danser la gigue.

jigger ['dʒigə], n. (*Naut.*) Tapecul, m.; (*Mining*) crible, m.; (*Billiards*) appui-queue, m.

jig-saw ['dʒigsɔː], n. Scie à chantourner, f. *Jig-saw puzzle*, puzzle, jeu de patience, m.

jilt [dʒilt], n. Coquette, f.—v.t. Faire la coquette à l'égard de, planter là; duper, tromper, jouer.

jimp [dʒimp], a. (*Sc.*) Svelte, mince, élégant (person), trop juste (weight, measure).

jingle ['dʒiŋgl], n. Tintement (of bells); cliquetis (of glasses, metals, etc.), m.; (*Austral.*) carriole, f.—v.i. Tinter (of bells etc.); s'entrechoquer (of glasses etc.).—v.t. Faire tinter, faire cliqueter.

jingo ['dʒiŋgou], n. Chauvin, m. *By jingo!* nom d'une pipe! par exemple! **jingoism**, n. Chauvinisme, m.

jink [dʒiŋk], (*Sc.*), v.i. S'esquiver.—v.t. Esquiver.—n. (*Ftb.*) Évite, esquive, f.pl. *To have high jinks*, s'amuser, s'ébattre, folâtrer; s'en donner à cœur joie.

jinx [dʒiŋks], n. Porte-guigne, m.

jitters ['dʒitəz], n.pl. (*slang*) Trouille, frousse, f. *To give the jitters*, flanquer la trouille.

jiu-jitsu [JU-JITSU].

Joan [dʒoun]. Jeanne, f. *Joan of Arc*, Jeanne d'Arc.

job [dʒɔb], n. Travail, ouvrage, m.; tâche, pièce, f.; besogne, chose à faire, f., affaire, f.; emploi, m.; (*Print.*) ouvrage de ville; (*Polit.*) tripotage, coup, m. *By the job*, à forfait, à la tâche, à la pièce (among workmen); *he has got a good job*, il a trouvé une bonne place; *it is a bad job for him*, c'est bien malheureux pour lui; *it is a good job*, c'est une belle affaire; *job hand* or *jobman*, bricoleur, m.; *job lot*, solde, m., occasion, f.; *that's just the job*, cela fait juste l'affaire.—v.t. Louer; tripoter.—v.i. Travailler à la tâche; agioter, spéculer (in stocks and shares); louer des chevaux *or* des voitures. **jobmaster**, n. Loueur de voitures, m. **job-printer**, n. Imprimeur de circulaires, de prix-courants, etc., m. **job-work**, n. Travail aux pièces, m.; (*Print.*) ouvrages de ville, m.pl.

jobber ['dʒɔbə], n. Ouvrier à la tâche; agioteur, coulissier (in stocks and shares); faiseur, exploiteur, m. **jobbery**, n. Tripotage, m., intrigue (politique), f. **jobbing**, n. Ouvrage à la tâche; agiotage; (*Print.*) ouvrage de ville; tripotage, m. **jobbing-gardener**, n. Jardinier à la journée, f.

jockey ['dʒɔki], n. Jockey, m.—v.t. Duper, tromper.—v.i. Manœuvrer.

jocose [dʒo'kous], a. Plaisant, jovial. **jocosely**, adv. En plaisantant, en badinant. **jocoseness**, n. Humeur joviale, f.

jocular ['dʒɔkjulə], a. Plaisant, facétieux. **jocularity**, n. Jovialité, jocosité, f. **jocularly**, adv. Facétieusement.

jocund ['dʒɔkənd], a. Joyeux, enjoué, gai. **jocundly**, adv. Joyeusement, gaiement. **jocundness**, n. Gaieté, f., enjouement, m.

jodhpurs ['dʒɔdpuːəz], n.pl. Pantalon d'équitation, m.

joey ['dʒoui], n. (*Austral.*) Jeune kangourou, m.

jog [dʒɔg], v.t. Pousser d'un coup de coude; secouer, cahoter; (*fig.*) rafraîchir (la mémoire). —v.i. Se mouvoir; marcher lentement. *To be jogging*, s'en aller, se mettre en route; *to jog along*, aller doucement, aller son petit bonhomme de chemin, aller cahin-caha.—n. Secousse légère, f., cahot; coup de coude; petit trot, m.

jogger ['dʒɔgə], n. *Memory jogger*, pense-bête, m.

joggle [dʒɔgl], v.t. Secouer légèrement. **joggle-joint**, n. Joint à goujon, m.

jog-trot, n. Petit trot, (*fig.*) train-train, m.

John [dʒɔn]. Jean, m. *Johnnie*, (*colloq.*) Jeannot. *John Bull*, John Bull; *John Lackland*, Jean sans Terre.

John Dory [DORY].

Johnny cake ['dʒɔni'keik], n. (*Am.*) Galette de farine de maïs, f. (*Mil.*) *Johnny Newcome*, *Johnny Raw*, bleu, m.

join [dʒɔin], v.t. Joindre, unir; associer (à); rejoindre (to overtake); relier (roads etc.). *He joined me in Paris*, il m'a rejoint à Paris; *to join battle*, en venir aux mains; *to join forces with*, se joindre à, s'atteler avec; *to join issue*, différer d'opinion avec; *to join the army*, s'engager; *will you join our party?* voulez-vous être des nôtres?—v.i. Se joindre, s'unir; s'inscrire, s'enrôler; s'associer; prendre part (à); se toucher. *He joined in the plan*, il fut de l'entreprise. **joiner**, n. Menuisier, m. **joinery**, n. Menuiserie, f. **joining**, n. Action de joindre; jonction; union, f., assemblage, m.

joint [dʒɔint], n. Jointure, f., joint; nœud (knot), m., pièce, grosse pièce (of meat); phalange (finger-joint); charnière (hinge); soudure, f.; (*Geol.*) joint, m., diaclase, f.; cassure, f.; (*Anat.*) articulation, f.; (*Bot.*) nœud, m.; (*slang*) boîte; maison interlope ou louche, f. *A cut from the joint*, une tranche de rôti; *out of joint*, disloqué, démis, (*fig.*) dérangé; *to put one's arm out of joint*, se démettre le bras; *universal joint*, joint universel, m.—v.t. Couper aux jointures; joindre, rapporter (to join).—a. Commun, en commun, ensemble, réuni. *With joint consent*, d'un commun accord. **joint-guardian**, n. Cotuteur, m. **joint-heir**, n. Cohéritier, m. **joint letter**, n. Lettre collective, f. **joint-pin**, n. Goupille, f. **joint-stock**, n. Capital,

fonds commun, *m.* *Joint-stock bank,* banque par actions, *f.* **joint-stock company,** *n.* Société anonyme, *f.*

jointed, *a.* Articulé, jointé; séparé. **jointer** or **jointing-plane,** *n.* Varlope, *f.* **jointly,** *adv.* Conjointement; de concert.

jointure, *n.* Douaire, *m.*

joist [dʒɔist], *n.* Solive, poutre, poutrelle, *f.*

joke [dʒouk], *n.* Bon mot, mot pour rire, *m.*, plaisanterie, (*fam.*) blague, *f.* *A practical joke,* un mauvais tour, *m.*, une mystification, *f.*; *in joke,* pour rire, en plaisantant; *not to know how to take a joke,* entendre mal la plaisanterie; *that's no joke,* cela n'est pas drôle; *to carry a joke too far,* pousser trop loin la plaisanterie; *to crack a joke,* dire un bon mot; *to crack one's joke,* avoir le mot pour rire; *what a good joke!* la bonne plaisanterie! or (*colloq.*) en voilà une bonne!—*v.t.* Plaisanter sur, railler de.—*v.i.* Plaisanter, badiner; rire de. **joker,** *n.* Plaisant, farceur; joker (at cards), *m.* **joking,** *a.* With a *joking expression,* d'un air de plaisanterie.—*n.* Plaisanterie, farce, *f.* *Joking apart,* plaisanterie à part. **jokingly,** *adv.* En plaisantant, pour rire.

jollification [dʒɔlifi'keiʃən], *n.* Partie de plaisir, *f.* *To have a jollification,* faire la noce.

jollily ['dʒɔlili], *adv.* Joyeusement, gaillardement. **jolliness** or **jollity,** *n.* Joie, gaieté, *f.* **jolly,** *a.* Gai, joyeux, gaillard, réjoui. **jollyboat,** *n.* Petit canot, *m.*

jolt [dʒoult], *n.* Cahot, choc, *m.*—*v.t.* Cahoter. —*v.i.* Faire des cahots. **jolting,** *n.* Cahotage, *m.*

Jonah ['dʒounə]. Jonas, *m.*; guignard; porte-malheur, *m.*

jonquil ['dʒɔŋkwil], *n.* (*Bot.*) Jonquille, *f.*

Jordan ['dʒɔ:dən]. Le Jourdain, *m.* (river), la Jordanie, *f.* (country). *Jordan almond,* amande de Malaga, *f.* **jordan** ['dʒɔ:dən], *n.* (*vulg.*) Pot de chambre, *m.*

joss [dʒɔs], *n.* Idole chinoise, *f.* **joss-house,** *n.* Pagode chinoise, *f.* **joss-stick,** *n.* Bâtonnet du culte, *m.*; bâton d'encens, *m.*

jostle [dʒɔsl], *v.i.* Jouer des coudes.—*v.t.* Pousser, bousculer; (*spt.*) gêner, serrer (un concurrent).

jot [dʒɔt], *n.* Iota, brin, *m.* *Not a jot,* pas un iota, rien du tout.—*v.t.* Noter. *To jot down,* noter, prendre note de.

jottings ['dʒɔtiŋz], *n.pl.* Notes, *f.pl.*

joule [dʒu:l], *n.* Joule, *m.*

journal ['dʒə:nəl], *n.* Journal, *m.*; publication (newspaper), *f.*; (*Comm.*) livre-journal, *m.* **journalese,** *n.* Style de journaliste, *m.* **journalism,** *n.* Journalisme, *m.* **journalist,** *n.* Journaliste; publiciste, *m.* **journalize,** *v.t.* Insérer dans un journal; écrire dans les journaux; (*Book-keeping*) porter au journal. —*v.i.* Tenir un journal.

journey ['dʒə:ni], *n.* Voyage (by land or through life); trajet (distance), *m.*; *journée (a day's work), *f.* *A pleasant journey to you!* bon voyage! *by slow journeys,* à petites journées; *on the journey,* en route; *to take, to undertake, to make, a journey, to go on a journey,* faire un voyage.—*v.i.* Voyager. **journey-bated,** *a.* Harassé de fatigue.

journeying, *n.* Voyage, *m.*

journeyman, *n.* (*pl.* **journeymen**) Garçon, compagnon, ouvrier; homme de peine, *m.*;

horloge (électrique) distributrice, *f.* *Journeyman carpenter,* compagnon charpentier, *m.*; *journey tailor,* garçon tailleur, *m.*

journeywork, *n.* Ouvrage à la journée, *m.*

joust [dʒu:st, dʒaust], *n.* Joute, *f.*—*v.t.* Jouter.

Jove [dʒouv]. Jupiter, *m.* *By Jove!* bigre! mâtin!

jovial ['dʒouviəl], *a.* Joyeux, gai. **joviality** [-'æliti], *n.* Humeur joviale, jovialité, *f.* **jovially,** *adv.* Jovialement, joyeusement. **jovialness,** *n.* Humeur joviale, *f.*

Jovian ['dʒouviən], *a.* De Jupiter.

jowl [dʒaul], *n.* Joue; hure (of salmon), *f.* *Cheek by jowl,* côte à côte.

joy [dʒɔi], *n.* Joie, *f.* *To leap for joy,* sauter de joie; *to wish someone joy,* féliciter quelqu'un; (*iron.*) *I wish you joy,* je vous en souhaite!— *v.i.* Se réjouir (de *or* avec). **joy-ride,** *n.* Balade en auto, *f.* **joy-stick,** *n.* (*Av.*) Levier de commande, (*fam.*) manche à balai, *m.* **joyful,** *a.* Joyeux. **joyfully,** *adv.* Joyeusement. **joyfulness,** *n.* Allégresse, joie, *f.* **joyless,** *a.* Sans joie, triste. **joylessly,** *adv.* Sans joie, tristement. **joylessness,** *n.* Tristesse, *f.* **joyous,** *a.* Joyeux. **joyously,** *adv.* Joyeusement. **joyousness,** *n.* Allégresse, *f.*

jube ['dʒu:bi:], *n.* (*Arch.*) Jubé, *m.*

jubilant ['dʒu:bilənt], *a.* Réjoui; jubilant. **jubilate,** *v.i.* Exulter, se réjouir; (*fam.*) jubiler, être dans la jubilation. **jubilation** [-'leiʃən, *n.* Réjouissances de triomphe, *f.pl.*, jubilation, *f.*; triomphe, *m.*

jubilee ['dʒu:bili:], *n.* Jubilé, *m.*; (*fig.*) jubilation, allégresse, *f.* *Jubilee celebrations,* fêtes jubilaires, *f.pl.*

Judaea [dʒu'di:ə]. La Judée, *f.*

Judaic [dʒu:'deiik] or **Judaical,** *a.* Judaïque. **Judaically,** *adv.* Judaïquement.

Judaism ['dʒu:deiizm], *n.* Judaïsme, *m.* **Judaize,** *v.i.* Judaïser.—*v.t.* Donner une interprétation judaïque à. **Judaizing,** *a.* Judaïsant.

Judas ['dʒu:dəs]. Judas, *m.*—*a.* De judas (sandy or carroty). *Judas kiss,* baiser de Judas, *m.* *Judas (-trap, -door),* judas (in a door), *m.* **Judas-tree,** *n.* Gainier commun, arbre de Judée, *m.*

judge [dʒʌdʒ], *n.* Juge, arbitre; (*fig.*) connaisseur, *m.* *To be a judge of,* se connaître à or en, s'y connaître.—*v.t.* Juger; discerner, décider, considérer. *Judging from,* à en juger par; *to judge for oneself,* juger par soi-même. **judgeship,** *n.* Fonctions de juge, *f.pl.*; dignité de juge, *f.* **judgment,** *n.* Jugement, *m.*; arrêt, *m.*, sentence, *f.*; (*fig.*) avis, sens, *m.*, opinion, *f.* *To have a correct judgment,* avoir l'esprit juste. **Judgment Day,** *n.* Jour du jugement; jugement dernier, *m.* **judgment-hall,** *n.* (*Lit.*) Salle de justice, *f.*; (*Bibl.*) prétoire, *m.* **judgment-seat,** *n.* Tribunal, *m.*

judicature ['dʒu:dikətʃə], *n.* Judicature justice; cour de justice, *f.* **judicial** [dʒu:'diʃəl], *a.* Judiciaire, juridique. *Judicial separation,* séparation de corps et de biens, *f.* **judicially,** *adv.* Judiciairement, juridiquement. **judiciary** ['dʒu:'diʃəri], *a.* Judiciaire.—*n.* L'ordre judiciaire, *m.*; la judicature, *f.*

judicious [dʒu:'diʃəs], *a.* Judicieux, sage, prudent. **judiciously,** *adv.* Judicieusement. **judiciousness,** *n.* Jugement, *m.*, sagesse, *f.*, bon sens, *m.*

judo ['dʒu:dou], *n.* Jiu-jitsu, (*fam.*) judo, *m.*

jug [dʒʌg], *n.* Broc, *m.*; crucne, *f.* *Jug of water*, pot d'eau, *m.*; *water jug*, pot à eau, *m.* —*v.t.* Faire un civet de (hare). *Jugged hare*, civet de lièvre, *m.*

juggle [dʒʌgl], *v.i.* Faire des tours de passe-passe; *(fig.)* escamoter.—*v.t.* Jouer, duper, escamoter; en imposer à.—*n.* Jonglerie, *f.*; escamotage, tour de passe-passe, *m.* **juggler,** *n.* Jongleur; escamoteur; *(fig.)* charlatan, *m.* **jugglery** or **juggling,** *n.* Jonglerie, *f.*, escamotage, *n.* **jugglingly,** *adv.* Par jonglerie.

Jugoslav [juːgəˈslɑːv], *etc.* [YUGOSLAV].

jugular [ˈdʒuːg- or ˈdʒʌgjulə], *a.* and *n.* Jugulaire, *f.*

jugulate [ˈdʒʌgjuleit], *v.t.* Étrangler, égorger; *(fig.)* juguler (a disease).

juice [dʒuːs], *n.* Jus; suc, *m.*, sève (sap), *f.*; *(pop.)* essence, *f.*, jus, *m.* **juiceless,** *a.* Sans jus. **juiciness,** *n.* Abondance de jus *or* de suc, *f.* **juicy,** *a.* Plein de jus, juteux; succulent; savoureux (of story, report, etc.).

ju-jitsu [dʒuːˈdʒitsu], *n.* Jiu-jitsu, *m.*

jujube [ˈdʒuːdʒuːb], *n.* Jujube, *m.* **jujube-tree,** *n.* Jujubier, *m.*

jukebox [ˈdʒuːkbɔks], *n.* Phonographe à sous, *m.*

julep [ˈdʒuːləp], *n.* Julep, *m.*

Julian [ˈdʒuːliən], *n.* Julien, *m.*—*a.* Julien.

Juliet [ˈdʒuːljət], *n.* Juliette, *f.*

July [dʒuːˈlai], *n.* Juillet, *m.*

jumble [dʒʌmbl], *v.t.* Jeter pêle-mêle, mêler ensemble, confondre, brouiller.—*v.i.* Se mêler confusément, se brouiller.—*n.* Pêle-mêle, brouillamini, méli-mélo, *m.*, confusion, *f.* *Jumble-sale*, vente de charité, *f.*

jump [dʒʌmp], *n.* Saut, bond; sursaut; obstacle (à sauter), *m.* *High jump*, saut en hauteur; *long jump*, saut en longueur; *running jump*, saut avec élan; *standing jump*, saut sans élan.—*v.i.* Sauter; *(colloq.)* se rencontrer, s'accorder (to agree); se jeter, se précipiter (sur). *Great wits jump together*, les grands esprits se rencontrent; *to jump at*, accepter avec empressement, se jeter sur; *to jump on to it*, (Row.) se lancer sur la barre de pied; *to jump out of*, sauter hors de; *to jump out of bed*, sauter à bas du lit; *to jump over*, sauter par dessus; *to jump to a conclusion*, conclure sans réflexion; *to jump up*, se lever vivement. —*v.t.* Sauter, franchir d'un bond; sauter de; faire sauter. *(fam.)* *To jump the queue*, resquiller (dans une queue). **jumper,** *n.* Sauteur, *m.*, sauteuse, *f.*; chandail, jersey, jumper, *m.* **jumpiness,** *n.* Nervosité, *f.* **jumping,** *n.* Saut, *m.*—*a.* Sauteur. **jumping-jack,** *n.* Pantin, *m.* **jumpy,** *a.* Nerveux; saccadé.

junction [ˈdʒʌŋkʃən], *n.* Jonction, *f.*; *(Rail.)* embranchement, *m.* **juncture,** *n.* Jointure, *f.*; moment critique, *m.*, conjoncture (critical time), *f.*

June [dʒuːn], *n.* Juin, *m.*

jungle [dʒʌŋgl], *n.* Jungle, brousse, *f.*; fourré, *m.*

junior [ˈdʒuːniə], *a.* Jeune, cadet. *Junior classes*, classes inférieures, *f.pl.*; *junior clerk*, second clerc, *m.* *Smith Junior*, *Smith Jr.*, Smith fils.—*n.* Cadet, inférieur en âge, *m.*

juniper [ˈdʒuːnipə], *n.* Genièvre, *m.* **juniper-berry,** *n.* Baie de genièvre, *f.* **juniper-tree,** *n.* Genévrier, genièvre, *m.*

junk [dʒʌŋk], *n.* Jonque (ship), *f.*; vieux cordage (old cordage), *m.*; objets de rebut, *m.pl.*; bœuf salé (salt beef), *m.* **junk-heap,** *n.* Dépotoir, *m.* **junk-ring,** *n.* Couronne de piston, *f.* **junk-shop,** *n.* Friperie, *f.*

junket [ˈdʒʌŋkit], *n.* Jonchée (cheese), *f.*, lait caillé, caillebotte, *m.*, talmouse (cake); partie fine, *f.*—*v.i.* Se régaler, festoyer, faire ripaille. —*v.t.* Régaler. **junketing,** *n.* Bombance, *f.*

junta [ˈdʒʌntə] or **junto,** *n.* Junte; *(fig.)* faction, cabale, *f.*, camarilla, *f.*

juridical [dʒuəˈridikl], *a.* Juridique. **juridically,** *adv.* Juridiquement.

jurisconsult [dʒuərisˈkɔnsʌlt], *n.* Jurisconsulte, *m.*

jurisdiction [dʒuərisˈdikʃən], *n.* Juridiction, compétence, *f.* **jurisdictional,** *a.* Juridictionnel. **jurisprudence** [-ˈpruːdəns], *n.* Jurisprudence, *f.*

jurist [ˈdʒuərist], *n.* Juriste, *m.*

juror [ˈdʒuərə], *n.* Juré, *m.*

jury [ˈdʒuəri], *n.* Jury, *m.* *Foreman of the jury*, chef du jury, *m.*; *gentlemen of the jury*, messieurs les jurés; *grand jury*, jury d'accusation; *jury process*, convocation de jury, *f.*; *petty jury*, jury de jugement, *m.* **jury-box,** *n.* Banc du jury, *m.* **juryman,** *n.* Juré, *m.* **jury-mast** [ˈdʒuərimɑːst], *n.* Mât de fortune, *m.*

just [dʒʌst], *a.* Juste, équitable.—*adv.* Juste, justement, précisément; tout, tout juste, seulement, un peu. *Except just one*, à l'exception d'un seul; *he had just arrived*, il venait d'arriver; *he has just gone out*, il vient de sortir; *I have just seen him*, je viens de le voir; *it is just like him*, c'est bien de lui; *it was just the thing to do*, cela venait bien à propos pour; *just as*, au moment où, tout comme; *just at present*, en ce moment; *just by*, tout près; *just consider*, voyez donc, considérez donc; *just in time*, juste à temps; *just let us see*, voyons un peu; *just now*, à l'instant; *just out*, vient de paraître (of books); *just so*, précisément, parfaitement; *they have just the same opinion as you*, ils ont précisément la même opinion que vous.

justice [ˈdʒʌstis], *n.* Justice, *f.*; juge (magistrate), *m.* *Justice of the Peace*, juge de paix, *m.*; *Lord Chief Justice*, premier juge, *m.*; *to do justice to*, faire justice à; *(fig.)* faire honneur à (a dinner etc.). **justiceship,** *n.* Dignité de juge, magistrature, *f.* **justiciable,** *a.* Justiciable. **justiciar** [-ˈtiʃiə:], *n.* Grand justicier, *m.* **justiciary,** *a.* Juridique.—*n.* Justicier, *m.* *High court of justiciary*, cour d'appel (en Écosse), *f.*

justifiable [dʒʌstiˈfaiəbl], *a.* Justifiable, légitime, permis. **justifiableness,** *n.* Caractère justifiable, *m.* **justifiably,** *adv.* D'une manière justifiable, légitimement.

justification [dʒʌstifiˈkeiʃən], *n.* Justification, *f.* **justificative** [dʒʌstifikeitiv] or **justificatory,** *a.* Justificatif.

justifier [ˈdʒʌstifaiə], *n.* Justificateur, *m.*

justify [ˈdʒʌstifai], *v.t.* Justifier, autoriser, permettre; *(Print.)* justifier, parangonner. *To be justified in*, être autorisé à, être fondé à; *to feel justified in*, se croire autorisé à, croire devoir.

justly [ˈdʒʌstli], *adv.* Exactement, justement; à bon droit, à bon titre, avec justice. **justness,** *n.* Justice (equity); justesse, exactitude (accuracy), *f.*

jut [dʒʌt], *v.i.* Avancer, faire saillie. *To jut out*, faire saillie, se projeter.—*n.* Saillie, *f.*

jute [dʒuːt], *n.* Jute, *m.*

jutting ['dʒʌtiŋ], *a.* En saillie, saillant.—*n.* Saillie, *f.*

juvenile ['dʒuːvənail], *a.* Jeune; juvénile, de jeunesse, de la jeunesse. *Juvenile ball*, bal d'enfants, *m.*; *juvenile delinquency*, délinquance juvénile, *f.*; *juvenile delinquents* or *offenders*, jeunes délinquants, délinquants mineurs, *m.pl.*—*n.* Jeune, *m.* or *f.*; adolescent, *m.*, -ente, *f.* **juvenility** [-'niliti], *n.* Jeunesse, juvénilité, *f.*

juxtalinear [dʒʌkstə'liniə], *a.* Juxtalinéaire.

juxtapose [dʒʌkstə'pouz], *v.t.* Juxtaposer.

juxtaposition [-pə'ziʃən], *n.* Juxtaposition, *f. In juxtaposition*, juxtaposé, à côté l'un de l'autre.

K

K, k [kei]. Onzième lettre de l'alphabet, *m.*

Kaffir ['kæfə]. Cafre, *m.*

kailyard ['keiljɑːd], *n.* Jardin potager, *m.*

kale [keil] or **kail**, *n.* (*Sc.*) Chou, *m. Sea-kale*, chou marin, *m.*

kaleidoscope [kə'laidəskoup], *n.* Kaléidoscope, *m.* **kaleidoscopic**, *a.* Kaléidoscopique.

kali ['keili], *n.* (*Bot.*) Kali, *m.*

kangaroo [kæŋgə'ruː], *n.* Kangourou, *m.* **kangaroo-bear**, *n.* Koala, *m.*

Kantian ['kɑːntiən], *a.* Kantien, de Kant.

kaolin ['keiəlin], *n.* (*Min.*) Kaolin, *m.*

Kashmir [kæʃ'miə]. Le Cachemire, *m.*

Katharine ['kæθərin]. Catherine, *f.*

keck [kek], *v.i.* Avoir des haut-le-cœur; avoir envie de vomir.

keckle [kekl], *v.t.* (*Naut.*) Fourrer (un câble).

kedge [kedʒ], *n.* Ancre à jet, ancre toueuse, *f.* —*v.t.* Touer, haler (a ship).—*v.i.* Se touer. **kedging**, *n.* Halage, touage, *m.*, touée, *f.*

keel [kiːl], *n.* Quille; carène, *f.*, chaland charbonnier, *m.*; (*Sc.*) ocre rouge, *m. On an even keel*, de niveau, d'aplomb.—*v.t.* Faire chavirer.—*v.i.* Se tourner la quille en l'air, chavirer. ***keelage**, *n.* Droit de mouillage, *m.* **keel-haul**, *v.t.* Donner la cale humide à. **keel-hauling**, *n.* Cale humide, *f.*

keeling ['kiːliŋ], *n.* (*Sc.*) Morue franche, *f.*, cabillaud, *m.*

keelson [KELSON].

keen [kiːn], *a.* Affilé, aigu, acéré, aiguisé; (*fig.*) vif, ardent, âpre; acharné; poignant, amer, mordant (bitter); pénétrant, perçant, piquant (piercing); grand, dévorant (of the appetite). *Keen as mustard*, brûlant de zèle; *keen competition*, concurrence acharnée; *keen prices*, prix très étudiés.—*n.* (*Irish*) Lamentation funèbre, *f.* (en veillant un mort).—*v.i.* Lamenter. **keen-edged**, *a.* Bien affilé. **keen-eyed**, *a.* Au regard perçant. **keenly**, *adv.* Vivement, ardemment, âprement. **keenness**, *n.* Finesse (of edge); (*fig.*) subtilité, *f.*; vivacité, ardeur, *f.*, empressement, *m.*; mordant, *m.* (of troops); âpreté, aigreur, *f.* (of cold). **keen-sighted**, *a.* Aux yeux perçants; perspicace. **keen-witted**, *a.* À l'esprit vif, perspicace; à l'esprit délié.

keep [kiːp], *v.t.* (*past* and *p.p.* **kept** [kept]) Tenir, retenir, garder; maintenir, conserver (to preserve); avoir (fowls etc.); entretenir (to support); nourrir (to board); avoir à son service; (*fig.*) observer; célébrer, fêter (to celebrate); garantir, protéger (to protect); remplir; continuer (to continue). *Her father keeps her at home*, son père la garde auprès de lui; *keep it up!* allez-y! tenez bon! *to keep a birthday*, célébrer un anniversaire; *to keep bad company*, fréquenter des gens de mauvaise compagnie; *to keep a promise*, remplir, tenir, une promesse; *to keep a secret*, garder un secret; *to keep a servant*, avoir une domestique; *to keep at home*, faire rester à la maison; *to keep at it*, continuer, s'entêter (à un travail); *to keep at someone*, harceler quelqu'un; *to keep away*, éloigner, tenir éloigné; *to keep back*, retenir, garder, tenir en réserve, retarder; *to keep bad hours*, se coucher à des heures indues; *to keep company with*, fréquenter, courtiser, faire la cour à; *to keep down*, tenir en bas, modérer, comprimer, tenir dans l'abaissement, (*Comm.*) maintenir bas; *to keep down a meal*, ne pas rendre, ne pas vomir (un repas), garder (un repas); *to keep from*, préserver de, détourner de, empêcher de; *to keep good hours*, se coucher de bonne heure; *to keep house*, tenir la maison, tenir le ménage; *to keep in*, tenir enfermé, retenir, (*sch.*) mettre en retenue, consigner; *to keep in view*, ne pas perdre de vue; *to keep off*, éloigner, tenir éloigné, détourner; *to keep someone on* (of employee), garder; *to keep on*, nourrir de; continuer; *to keep one's bed*, garder le lit; *to keep one's ground*, tenir bon, tenir ferme, ne pas lâcher pied; *to keep one's hand in*, s'entretenir la main; *to keep one's word*, tenir sa parole; *to keep open house*, tenir table ouverte; *to keep order*, maintenir le bon ordre; *to keep out*, ne pas admettre, faire rester dehors, écarter, éloigner; *to keep pace with*, aller de pair avec, se tenir au courant de; *to keep someone waiting*, faire faire le pied de grue à quelqu'un; *to keep something to oneself*, garder quelque chose pour soi; *to keep the pot boiling*, faire bouillir la marmite, faire aller le pot-au-feu; *to keep to*, s'en tenir à; *to keep to it*, faire travailler, faire marcher; *to keep under*, tenir dessous, contenir, retenir; *to keep up*, tenir levé, soutenir, continuer, entretenir, faire veiller.—*v.i.* Se tenir; rester, demeurer (to stay); se diriger, aller (to go); se garder, se conserver (to last); (*fig.*) se garder, se maintenir. *He keeps on singing from morning till night*, il est toujours à chanter du matin au soir; *to keep in touch with*, rester en contact avec; *keep off the grass!* ne marchez pas sur l'herbe! *keep there!* restez là! *meat does not keep well*, la viande ne se garde pas; *to keep away*, se tenir éloigné, rester éloigné; *to keep back*, se tenir en arrière, se tenir à l'écart; *to keep* (doing, saying, telling, etc.), ne pas cesser de; *to keep down*, rester en bas, rester baissé, (*Comm.*) se maintenir bas; *to keep from*, s'abstenir de, se tenir de; *to keep in*, rester dedans, garder la maison; *to keep in with*, rester bien avec; *to keep it up*, aller toujours; s'en donner; *to keep off*, s'éloigner. (*Naut.*) tenir le large; *to keep on*, avancer, continuer de, aller toujours, aller son train; *to keep oneself up*, se tenir levé, se soutenir, se maintenir, ne pas se coucher; *to keep out,* se tenir dehors, ne pas entrer; ne pas approcher; *to keep out of the way,* se tenir à l'écart; *to keep quiet,* rester coi; *to keep silent,* se taire; *to keep to,* s'en tenir à, tenir ferme à; *to keep to one's word,* tenir sa parole; *to keep up,* continuer; *to keep up with,* aller de pair avec.

    n.—Donjon, réduit (stronghold), *m.*; nourriture, *f.*, entretien (support); état, *m.*, condition (condition), *f.* *The keep of a horse,* l'entretien d'un cheval.

keeper ['kiːpə], *n.* Garde; gardien; surveillant (watchman), *m.* *Gamekeeper,* garde-chasse, *m.*; *keeper of a museum,* conservateur d'un musée, *m.*; *Keeper of the Great Seal,* Garde des Sceaux, *m.* **keeping,** *n.* Garde, surveillance; conservation; *(fig.)* harmonie, *f.*, unisson, *m.* *In keeping,* en harmonie avec; *in safe keeping,* sous bonne garde; *in perfect keeping with,* en parfait accord avec. **keeps,** *n.* *(fam.)* *For keeps,* pour toujours, définitivement. **keepsake,** *n.* Souvenir, *m.*

keg [keg], *n.* Caque, *f.* (of herring), petit baril, tonnelet, *m.*

kelp [kelp], *n.* Varech, *m.*; soude de varech, *f.*

kelpie ['kelpi], *n.* Esprit des eaux, *m.*; *(Austral.)* chien métis, *m.*

kelson ['kelsən], *n.* Contre-quille, carlingue, *f.*

kelt [kelt], *n.* Charognard, ravalé, *m.*

ken [ken], *n.* Vue; portée, *f.* *It's beyond my ken,* c'est plus que je ne saurais dire; cela me dépasse.—*v.t.* Apercevoir, savoir.

kennel [kenl], *n.* Chenil, *m.*; niche, *f.*; terrier (of a fox); trou (of wild beasts); ruisseau (gutter), *m.*; *(fig.)* meute (pack of hounds, wolves), *f.*—*v.i.* Se coucher, se loger (of a dog).—*v.t.* Mettre dans un chenil.

kentledge ['kentlidʒ], *n.* *(Naut.)* Gueuse, *f.*

kept [kept], *a.* Entretenu, *p.p.* [KEEP].

kerb [kəːb], *n.* Bordure de trottoir, margelle (of a well), *f.* **kerb-stone,** *n.* Bordure (de trottoir), *f.*, parement, *m.*

kerchief ['kəːtʃif], *n.* Fichu, *m.*

kerf [kəːf], *n.* Trait de scie, trait de chalumeau, *m.*; bout coupé, *m.*, surface de coupe, *f.*

kermes ['kəːmiːz], *n.* Kermès, *m.*

kern [kəːn], *n.* Fantassin irlandais, *m.*; *(Print.)* crénage, *m.*

kernel ['kəːnl], *n.* Graine, amande, *f.*, pignon (of pine-cone), *m.*; noyau (in stone-fruit), pépin (pulpy fruit), *m.*; *(fig.)* fond, essentiel, *m.*, noix, *f.*—*v.i.* Se former en grain.

kerosene ['kerosiːn], *n.* Kérosène, *m.*, kérosine, *f.*, pétrole lampant, *m.*

kersey ['kəːzi], *n.* Gros drap (à côtes), *m.* **kerseymere,** *n.* Casimir, *m.* [CASHMERE].

kestrel ['kestrəl], *n.* Crécerelle, *f.*, émouchet, *m.*

ketch [ketʃ], *n.* *(Naut.)* Quaiche, *f.*, ketch, *m.*; dundee, dindet, *m.*

ketchup ['ketʃəp], *n.* Sauce relevée, *f.*

kettle [ketl], *n.* Bouilloire, *f.*; chaudron (cooking kettle), *m.*; gamelle de campement (camp-kettle), *m.* *A pretty kettle of fish,* un beau gâchis; *tea-kettle,* bouilloire, *f.* **kettle-drum,** *n.* Timbale, *m.*

key [kiː], *n.* Clef, clé, *f.*; *(Arith. etc.)* corrigé, *m.*; *(Mus.)* ton, *m.*; touche (on a piano etc.), *f.* *To have the key of the street,* avoir la clef des champs; *under lock and key,* sous clef; *with a key,* à clef.—*v.t.* *(Mus.)* Accorder. *(fam.)*

To key up, surexciter, tendre. **key-board,** *n.* Clavier, *m.* **keyhole,** *n.* Trou de la serrure, *m.* **key-industry,** *n.* Industrie de base, industrie clef, *f.* **key-money,** *n.* Denier à Dieu, *m.* **key-note,** *n.* Tonique, *f.*; *(fig.)* idée maîtresse, *f.* **key-plate,** *n.* Entrée de clé, *f.*, trou de la serrure, *m.* **key-ring,** *n.* Anneau brisé, *m.* **key-stone,** *n.* Clef de voûte, *f.*

keyless, *a.* Sans clef; à remontoir (of watches).

khaki ['kɑːki], *n.* Kaki, *m.*

khan [kɑːn], *n.* Kan, khan, *m.*

kibe [kaib], *n.* Engelure, gerçure, *f.*

kibosh ['kaibɔʃ, 'kibɔʃ], *n.* Bêtises, *f.pl.*, des blagues, *f.pl.* *To put the kibosh on something,* mettre fin à, bousiller quelque chose.

kick [kik], *n.* Coup de pied; recul (recoil), *m.*; ruade (animals), *f.*; *(fig.)* vigueur, énergie, *f.* *(Ftb.)* *Free kick,* coup franc, *m.*; *to get a kick out of,* prendre grand plaisir à.—*v.t.* Donner un coup de pied à; frapper *or* pousser du pied; *(Ftb.)* botter. *To kick down,* renverser d'un coup de pied; *to kick one's heels,* faire le pied de grue; *to kick out,* chasser à coups de pied; *to kick up a row,* faire du tapage, faire de la poussière.—*v.i.* Donner des coups de pied; ruer, regimber (animals); reculer (fire-arms). *Alive and kicking,* plein de vie; *to kick at,* regimber contre.

kicker, *n.* Personne qui donne des coups de pied, *f.*; rueur, *m.*, rueuse, *f.* **kicking,** *n.* Coups de pied, *m.pl.*; ruades (animals), *f.pl.* **kicking-strap,** *n.* Plate-longe (for horses), *f.*

kick-off, *n.* *(Ftb.)* Coup d'envoi, *m.* **kick-out,** *n.* Coup de renvoi, *m.* (donné aux 22 m.).

kickshaw ['kikʃɔː], *n.* Colifichet, *m.*, bagatelle, *f.*; *(Cook.)* friandise, *f.*

kid [kid], *n.* Chevreau, *m.*; *(Naut.)* gamelle, *f.*; fagot (faggot); *(colloq.)* enfant, mioche, gosse, *m.*; *(slang)* blague, *f.*—*a.* De chevreau. *Kid gloves,* gants de chevreau, *m.pl.*; *to handle with kid gloves,* ménager.—*v.t.* *(fam.)* En conter à, faire accroire à. *No kidding!* sans blague!—*v.i.* Chevroter, mettre bas (of the goat). **kidder,** *n.* Blagueur, carolleur, *m.*

kidnap ['kidnæp], *v.t.* Enlever (un homme, une femme, un enfant), kidnapper. **kidnapper,** *n.* Auteur d'enlèvement, ravisseur, *m.*

kidney ['kidni], *n.* Rein; rognon (of animals), *m.*; *(fig.)* trempe, sorte (sort), *f.*, acabit, *m.* *A man of my kidney (colloq.),* un homme de ma sorte, de ma trempe. **kidney-bean,** *n.* Haricot nain; haricot d'Espagne (scarlet runner), *m.* **kidney-potato,** *n.* Vitelotte, *f.* **kidney-shaped,** *a.* Réniforme. **kidney-vetch,** *n.* Vulnéraire, *f.*

kilderkin ['kildəkin], *n.* Demi-baril, *m.* (environ 75 litres).

kill [kil], *v.t.* Tuer; faire mourir; abattre (to slaughter). *Killed on the spot,* tué sur place, tué net; *to kill by inches,* faire mourir à petit feu; *to kill oneself,* se tuer; *to kill time,* tuer le temps; *to kill two birds with one stone,* faire d'une pierre deux coups.—*n.* *(Hunt.)* Mise à mort, *f.*; pièces abattues, *f.pl.*; le tableau, *m.*

killer, *n.* Tueur, *m.*

killick ['kilik], *n.* *(Naut.)* Grosse pierre, *f.* (pour amarrer une barque); petite ancre, *f.*; insigne de matelot de première classe, *m.*

killing, *n.* Tuerie, boucherie, *f.*, massacre, *m.*

—*a.* Mortel; assommant, écrasant (of work); (*fam.*) crevant, tordant; tueur, meurtrier (of looks etc.).

kill-joy, *n.* Rabat-joie, trouble-fête, *m.*

kiln [kiln], *n.* Four, *m.* *Brick-kiln,* four à briques; *lime-kiln,* four à chaux. **kiln-dry,** *v.t.* (*past* and *p.p.* **kiln-dried**) Sécher au four.

kilocycle ['kiləsaikl], *n.* Kilocycle, *m.*

kilogramme [-græm], *n.* Kilogramme, *m.*

kilometre ['kiləmiːtə], *n.* Kilomètre, *m.* **kilometric** [-'metrik], *a.* Kilométrique.

kilowatt [-wɔt], *n.* Kilowatt, *m.*

kilt [kilt], *n.* Jupon (de montagnard écossais), kilt, *m.*

kin [kin], *n.* Parenté, *f.*; parent, *m.*, parente, *f.*, allié, *m.*, alliée, *f.* *Next of kin,* le plus proche parent, *m.*; la famille, *f.*

kind [kaind], *a.* Bon, bienveillant, bienfaisant; obligeant, complaisant (obliging). *A kind word,* une parole d'affection; *my kind regards to him,* faites-lui toutes mes amitiés; *will you be so kind as to,* voulez-vous avoir la bonté de. —*n.* Genre, *m.,* sorte, espèce, *f.* *In kind,* en nature; *nothing of the kind,* rien de la sorte, rien de pareil.

kindergarten ['kindəgɑːtn], *n.* Jardin d'enfants, *m.*; école maternelle, *f.*

kindhearted ['kaind'hɑːtid], *a.* Bon, bienveillant. **kindheartedness,** *n.* Bonté de cœur, *f.*

kindle [kindl], *v.t.* Allumer, enflammer; (*fig.*) éveiller, réveiller, exciter.—*v.i.* S'allumer, s'enflammer. **kindling(-wood), kindlings,** *n.* Petit bois, *m.*; bois d'allumage, *m.*

kindliness ['kaindlinis], *n.* Bienveillance, bienfaisance, douceur, bonté, *f.* **kindly,** *a.* Bon, bienveillant, favorable, doux.—*adv.* Avec bienveillance; avec bonté; complaisamment.

kindness ['kaindnis], *n.* Bienveillance, bonté; complaisance, douceur, *f.*; bienfait, *m.* *Act of kindness,* acte de bienveillance, *m.*

kindred ['kindrid], *n.* Parenté, *f.*; parents, *m.pl.*—*a.* De même nature, de la même famille.

*****kine** [kain], *pl.* [COW (1)].

kinema ['kinimə] etc. [CINEMA].

king [kiŋ], *n.* Roi, *m.*; (*Draughts*) dame, *f.* *King's Bench,* cour du banc du roi, *f.*; *king's evidence,* témoin de la couronne, *m.*; *king's evil,* écrouelles, *f.pl.*; *king's yellow,* orpiment, *m.*—*v.t.* (*Draughts*) Damer.

king-at-arms, *n.* Roi d'armes, *m.*

kingcraft, *n.* Art de régner, *m.*

king-cup, *n.* Bouton d'or, *m.*

kingdom [kiŋdəm], *n.* Royaume, *m.*; (*fig.*) empire, *m.*; (*Nat. Hist.*) règne, *m.* *United Kingdom,* Royaume-Uni, *m.* **kingdom come** (*colloq.*) Le ciel, l'autre monde, *m.* *To send someone to kingdom come,* expédier quelqu'un dans l'autre monde, envoyer quelqu'un ad patres.

kingfisher, *n.* Martin-pêcheur, *m.*

kingless, *a.* Sans roi.

kinglet, *n.* Roitelet, *m.*

kinglike, *adv.* En roi; comme un roi, royalement.

kingling, *n.* Roitelet, *m.*

kingly, *a.* De roi, royal.—*adv.* En roi.

king-pin, *n.* Cheville ouvrière; (*games*) quille du milieu, *f.*; (*fam.*) gros bonnet, *m.*

king-post, *n.* Poinçon; (*Av.*) pylône, *m.*

kingship, *n.* Royauté, *f.*

kink [kiŋk], *n.* Nœud, *m.*, boucle; vrille, *f.*; faux pli, *m.*; (*Naut.*) coque, *f.* (of rope); torticolis, *m.*; (*colloq.*) point faible, défaut, *m.*—*v.i.* Se nouer, se tortiller, vriller. **kinky,** *a.* Bouché (of material); bossué, bosselé; en vrilles.

kino ['kainou], *n.* Kino, *m.*

kinsfolk ['kinzfouk], *n.* Parents, alliés, *m.pl.*

kinsman, *n.* Parent, allié, *m.* **kinswoman,** *n.* Parente, alliée, *f.*

kiosk ['kiːɔsk], *n.* Kiosque, *m.*

kip [kip], *v.i.* (*pop.*) To *kip down,* se coucher, se pieuter.

kipper ['kipə], *n.* Hareng doux, légèrement salé et fumé, *m.*

kirk [kəːk], *n.* Église d'Écosse, *f.*

kirsch(wasser) ['kiəʃvɑːsə], *n.* Kirsch, *m.*

*****kirtle** [kəːtl], *n.* Jupe, *f.* (for women); tunique, *f.* (for men).

kiss [kis], *n.* Baiser, *m.*—*v.t.* Embrasser. *To kiss each other,* s'embrasser; *to kiss hands,* baiser la main (du roi *or* de la reine); *to kiss one's hand to,* envoyer un baiser à; *to kiss the dust,* mordre la poussière. **kisser,** *n.* (*slang*) Bouche, *f.* **kissing,** *n.* Baisement (of the Pope's slipper), *m.*; baisers, embrassements, *m.pl.* *Kissing of hands,* baisemain, *m.* **kissing-crust,** *n.* Baisure, *f.* **kissing-gate,** *n.* Portillon à chicanes, *m.*

kit [kit], *n.* Petit équipement, fourniment, *m.,* effets, *m.pl.*; trousse, *f.*; outils (of a workman), *m.pl.*; petit chat (cat), *m.* **kit-bag,** *n.* Sac (d'ordonnance), *m.*; musette, *f.*

kitchen ['kitʃin], *n.* Cuisine, *f.* **kitchener,** *n.* Fourneau de cuisine; cuisinier (in monastery), *m.* **kitchenette,** *n.* Petite cuisine, *f.* **kitchen-garden,** *n.* Jardin potager, *m.* **kitchen-maid,** *n.* Fille de cuisine, *f.* **kitchen-range,** *n.* Cuisinière (anglaise), *f.,* fourneau de cuisine, *m.* **kitchen-utensils,** *n.pl.* Batterie de cuisine, *f.* **kitchen-wench,** *n.* Laveuse de vaisselle, *f.*

kite [kait], *n.* Milan (bird); cerf-volant (toy); (*fig.*) vautour (rapacious person), *m.* *To fly a kite,* enlever un cerf-volant; (*Comm.*) maintenir son crédit au moyen de billets de complaisance. **kite-flying,** *n.* (*Comm.*) Billets de complaisance, *m.pl.*

kith [kiθ], *n.* Parenté, *f.*; parents, proches, *m.pl.* *Kith and kin,* parents et amis, *m.pl.*

kitten [kitn], *n.* Chaton, petit chat, *m.*—*v.i.* Avoir des petits. **kittenish,** *a.* De petit chat; (*fig.*) (of a girl) folâtre, coquette, féline, chatte.

kittiwake ['kitiweik], *n.* Mouette tridactyle, *f.*

kitty ['kiti], *n.* (*Cards*) Poule, cagnotte, *f.*

kiwi ['kiːwi], *n.* Kiwi, *m.*

klaxon ['klæksən], *n.* Klaxon, *m.*

kleptomania [klepto'meiniə], *n.* Kleptomanie, *f.* **kleptomaniac,** *n.* and *a.* Kleptomane.

knack [næk], *n.* Adresse, *f.,* tour de main, talent, chic, *m.*

knacker ['nækə], *n.* Équarrisseur; entrepreneur de démolitions, *m.* *Knacker's yard,* écorcherie, *f.*

knag [næg], *n.* Nœud, *m.*; cheville, *f.* **knaggy,** *a.* Noueux; (*fig.*) hargneux.

knap [næp], *n.* Éminence, colline, *f.*

knapsack ['næpsæk], *n.* Havresac, *m.*

knave [neiv], *n.* Fripon, coquin; (*Cards*) valet, *m.* **knavery,** *n.* Friponnerie, coquinerie;

malice (waggishness), f. **knavish,** a. Fripon, de fripon, de fourbe; malin, malicieux (waggish). *Knavish trick,* friponnerie, f. **knavishly,** adv. En fripon; malicieusement, avec malice (waggishly). **knavishness,** n. Friponnerie, f.
knead [ni:d], v.t. Pétrir. **kneading,** n. Pétrissage, m. **kneading-trough,** n. Pétrin, m.
knee [ni:], n. Genou, m.; (*Naut.*) courbe, f.; (*Tech.*) coude, m. *Broken knees* (of horses), couronnement, m.; *down on your knees!* à genoux! *on one's knees,* à genoux; *to break the knees of* (horses), couronner; *to bring someone to his knees,* mettre quelqu'un à genoux, forcer quelqu'un à capituler. **kneebreeches,** n.pl. Culotte courte, f. **knee-cap** or **-piece,** n. Genouillère (pad); (*Anat.*) rotule, f. **knee-deep,** a. À la hauteur du genou, jusqu'aux genoux. **knee-joint,** n. Joint du genou, m., articulation du genou, f. **knee-jointed,** a. (*Bot.*) Géniculé. **kneepad,** n. Genouillère, f.
kneel [ni:l], v.i. (*past* and p.p. **knelt** [nelt]) S'agenouiller. *To kneel down,* se mettre à genoux, s'agenouiller. **kneeling,** n. Action de s'agenouiller; génuflexion, f.—a. À genoux, agenouillé. **kneeling-chair,** n. Prie-Dieu, m. **kneeling-stool,** n. Agenouilloir, m.
knell [nel], n. Glas, m.—v.i. Tinter.
knew, past [KNOW].
knickerbocker ['nikəbɔkə], n. (pl.) Culotte bouffante, f.
knickers ['nikəz], n. Culotte (de femme), f.
knick-knack ['niknæk], n. Brimborion, m., babiole, f.; colifichet, bibelot, m.
knife [naif], n. (pl. **knives** [naivz]) Couteau; (*Tech.*) coupoir; (*Surg.*) scalpel, bistouri, m. *Carving-knife,* couteau à découper; *clasp-knife,* couteau pliant; *clasp-knife with lock-back,* couteau à cran d'arrêt; *dessert-knife,* couteau à dessert; *knife and fork,* couvert, m.; *knife basket,* panier à couteaux, m.; *paper-knife,* coupe-papier, m.; *pen-knife,* canif, m.; *pruning-knife,* serpette, f.; *table-knife,* couteau de table; *to have one's knife in,* poursuivre avec acharnement; *war to the knife,* guerre à outrance, f.—v.t. Frapper à coup de couteau, poignarder; (*fig.*) dégommer (a politician etc.). **knife-blade,** n. Lame de couteau, f. **knife-board,** n. Planche à couteaux, f. **knife-grinder,** n. Rémouleur, repasseur de couteaux, m. **knife-handle,** n. Manche de couteau, m. **knife-rest,** n. Porte-couteau, m.
knight [nait], n. Chevalier; (*Chess*) cavalier, m. *Knight of the shears,* tailleur, m.; *knight of the shire,* représentant d'un comté, m.—v.t. Créer chevalier. **knight-errant,** n. Chevalier errant, m. **knight-errantry,** n. Chevalerie errante, f. **knighthood,** n. Chevalerie, f. **knightliness,** n. Caractère chevaleresque, m. **knightly,** a. Chevaleresque, de chevalier.
knit [nit], n. Tricot; (ensemble des) mailles, m. *Of a fine knit,* à mailles fines, serrées.—v.t. Tricoter; froncer (the brows); (*fig.*) joindre, attacher, lier. *A well-knit body,* un corps bien bâti. **knitter,** n. Tricoteur, m. **knitting,** a. Tricot, m. **knitting-machine,** n. Tricoteuse, f. **knitting-needle,** n. Aiguille à tricoter, f.
knittle [nitl], n. (*Naut.*) Raban, m.
knob [nɔb], n. Bosse, f.; bouton (of a door);

nœud ('in wood), m. **knobbed,** a. Noueux.
knobby, a. Plein de nœuds, noueux.
knock [nɔk], v.t. Frapper, heurter, cogner. *To knock about,* bousculer, malmener; *to knock down,* renverser, assommer, adjuger (at sales); *to knock in,* enfoncer; *to knock off,* faire sauter, achever (to get through); *to knock off a good deal of work,* abattre de l'ouvrage; *to knock out,* faire sortir (à force de coups), faire sauter; (*Box.*) *to knock someone out,* knock-outer, mettre quelqu'un knock-out; *to knock up,* monter, réveiller (en frappant à la porte) (to awake); éreinter (to fatigue).—v.i. Frapper, heurter, cogner; se heurter, se cogner. *To knock about,* rouler sa bosse, aller de par le monde; (*Naut.*) bourlinguer; *to knock off,* faire la pause, cesser le travail; *to knock on,* (*Ftb.*) faire un en-avant; *to knock over,* renverser; *to knock under,* se rendre, se soumettre; *the engine is knocking,* le moteur cogne.—n. Coup, choc; cognement, m. *There is a knock at the door,* on frappe à la porte; *to hear a knock,* entendre frapper. **knock-about,** a. Bruyant, violent. *Knock-about comic,* clown, m. **knock-kneed,** a. Cagneux. **knock-out,** n. Coup de grâce, m.; (*Box.*) knock-out, m. *It was a knock-out,* ça a été formidable, renversant; *knock-out contest,* (*spt.*) éliminatoire, f. **knock-up,** n. (*spt.*) *To have a knock-up,* faire des balles.
knocker, n. Personne qui frappe, f.; heurtoir, marteau (on a door), m. **knocking,** n. Coups, m.pl.
knoll (1) [noul], n. Monticule, tertre, m., butte, f.
knoll (2) [noul], v.t. Sonner, tinter.—v.i. Sonner.
knot [nɔt], n. Nœud; groupe (group of persons etc.), m.; (*fig.*) difficulté, f., embarras, m.; (*Orn.*) canut, m. *Sword-knot,* dragonne, f.; *to make twelve knots,* filer douze nœuds.—v.t. Nouer; lier; (*fig.*) embrouiller.—v.i. Faire des nœuds; se nouer. **knotted,** a. Noueux.
knotgrass, n. Renouée, f. **knotless,** a. Sans nœuds. **knottiness,** n. Abondance de nœuds, f.; (*fig.*) embrouillement, m., complexité, f. **knotty,** a. Noueux; (*fig.*) dur (hard); embrouillé, difficile, compliqué (intricate), épineux.
knout [naut], n. Knout, m.—v.t. Knouter, donner le knout.
know [nou], v.t. (*past* **knew** [nju:], p.p. **known** [noun]) Savoir, apprendre (to learn); connaître (to be acquainted with); reconnaître (to recognize). *He has even been known to,* on l'a même vu; *he knows all about it,* il sait tout, il s'y connaît; *he knows what he is about,* il est sûr de son fait; *I have known it to happen,* j'ai vu cela se produire; *I know a good thing when I see it,* je m'y connais; *I know better,* je m'en garderai bien; *I know how to deal with him,* je sais comment il faut le prendre; *not that I know,* pas que je sache; *not to know one from the other,* ne pouvoir distinguer l'un de l'autre; *to know by heart,* savoir par cœur; *to know by sight,* connaître de vue; *to know how to read and write,* savoir lire et écrire; *to know of,* connaître, avoir connaissance de; *to know one's lesson,* savoir sa leçon; *to know someone,* connaître quelqu'un; *to know something,* savoir quelque

chose; *to know two languages*, posséder deux langues; *to let someone know something*, faire savoir, faire connaître, faire part de quelque chose à quelqu'un; *to make known*, faire connaître, signaler, démasquer; *to make one-self known*, se faire connaître; *you ought to have known better*, vous n'auriez pas dû vous y laisser prendre; *you ought to know better at your age*, vous devriez être plus raisonnable à votre âge; *you wouldn't know her from a French girl*, on la prendait pour une jeune Française.—*n.* *To be in the know*, connaître le dessous des cartes, être dans le secret. **know-all,** *n.* *He is a know-all*, il a la science infuse, il sait toujours tout; il a des lumières sur tout. **know-how,** *n.* Savoir-faire, *m.*
knowing, *a.* Intelligent, instruit; fin, malin. *A knowing fellow*, un rusé compère; *a knowing smile*, un sourire entendu. **knowingly,** *adv.* Sciemment; avec ruse, avec finesse (cunningly), habilement; d'un air entendu.
knowledge ['nɔlidʒ], *n.* Connaissance, science, *f.*; savoir, *m.*; lumières, connaissances, *f.pl.* *Not to my knowledge*, pas que je sache; *to his knowledge*, à sa connaissance; *without my knowledge*, à mon insu. **knowledgeable,** *a.* Bien informé; intelligent; (*fam.*) à la page, au courant.
knuckle [nʌkl], *n.* Jointure, articulation du doigt, *f.*; jarret (of meat), *m.* *To rap over the knuckles*, donner sur les doigts à.—*v.i.* *To knuckle down*, caler la bille la main à terre (at marbles); céder, mettre les pouces; *to knuckle under*, se soumettre, mettre les pouces. **knuckle-bone,** *n.pl.* Osselet, *m.* **knuckled,** *a.* Articulé. **knuckle-duster,** *n.* Coup de poing américain, *m.* **knuckle-joint,** *n.* Joint articulé, *m.*
knur [nəː], *n.* Nœud de bois, *m.* (dans un tronc); balle (dure), *f.* (pour jouer au knur and spell, sorte de hockey).
knurl [nəːl], *n.* Molette, *f.*
Kodak ['koudæk], *n.* Kodak, *m.* (reg. trade name).
Koran [ko'raːn], *n.* Coran, *m.*
Korea [ko'riːə]. La Corée, *f.*
Korean, *a.* and *n.* Coréen, *m.*, -éenne, *f.*
kosher ['koufə], *a.* Cachir, cacher (*fem.* -ère) (meat).
kotow ['kou'tau], *v.i.* Se prosterner (à la chinoise); faire des courbettes.
kudos ['kjuːdɔs], *n.* (*colloq.*) Gloriole, *f.*
kulak ['kuːlæk], *n.* Koulak, *m.*
kyanize ['kaiənaiz], *v.t.* Injecter de cyanure.
ky, kye [kai], *n.pl.* (*Sc.*) Vaches, *f.pl.*
kyle [kail], *n.* (*Sc.*) Passe, *f.*, pertuis, *m.*
kylie ['kaili], *n.* (*Austral.*) Boomerang, *m.*

L

L, l [el]. Douzième lettre de l'alphabet, *m.*
la! (1) [laː], *int.* (*dial.*) Là! voyez donc! tenez!
la (2) [laː], *n.* (*Mus.*) La, *m.*
laager ['laːgə], *n.* (*S. Afr.*) Campement, *m.*
lab [læb], *n.* (*fam.*) Labo, *m.*
label [leibl], *n.* Étiquette, *f.*; (*Law*) codicille, *m.*, queue (of a deed), *f.*; (*Arch.*) larmier, *m.*; (*Her.*) lambel, *m.*; (*Ind.*) label, *m.*—*v.t.* Étiqueter; (*fig.*) désigner sous le nom de.

labellum [lə'beləm], *n.* (*Bot.*) Labelle, *m.*
labial ['leibiəl], *a.* Labial.—*n.* (*Gram.*) Labiale, *f.* **labialize,** *v.t.* Labialiser. **labiate,** *a.* (*Bot.*) Labié.
laboratory [lə'bɔrətəri or 'læbərətəri], *n.* Laboratoire, *m.*
laborious [lə'bɔːriəs], *a.* Laborieux, pénible. **laboriously,** *adv.* Laborieusement, péniblement. **laboriousness,** *n.* Labeur, *m.*, difficulté, *f.*
labour ['leibə], *n.* Travail, labeur, *m.*, peine, *f.*; ouvrage (piece of work), *m.*; travail d'enfant (travail), *m.* *Hard labour*, travaux forcés, *m.pl.*; *manual labour*, main-d'œuvre, *f.*; *the Labour Party*, le parti travailliste; *the labour question*, la question ouvrière; *the labours of Hercules*, les travaux d'Hercule, *m.pl.*; *to be in labour*, être en travail (d'enfant); *to have one's labour for one's pains*, en être pour sa peine; *to lose one's labour*, perdre sa peine.—*v.t.* Travailler; *labourer (to till); (fig.) pousser, poursuivre, élaborer, travailler.—*v.i.* Travailler, se donner de la peine; souffrir; être en mal d'enfant; chercher (à), tâcher, s'efforcer (de). *To labour under a delusion*, être dans l'erreur; *to labour under a disease*, souffrir d'une maladie.
laboured, *a.* Laborieux, pénible.
labourer, *n.* Manœuvre, homme de peine, *m.* *Bricklayer's or mason's labourer*, aide-maçon, *m.*; *day-labourer*, journalier, *m.*
labour-exchange, *n.* Bureau de placement (municipal *or* d'État), *m.*
labouring, *a.* Qui travaille; laborieux. *Labouring class*, classe ouvrière, *f.*
labour-saving, *a.* *Labour-saving device*, économiseur de travail, *m.*
Labrador ['læbrədɔː], *n.* Le Labrador; chien de Terre-Neuve. *Golden labrador*, terre-neuve doré, *m.*
laburnum [lə'bəːnəm], *n.* Faux ébénier; cytise, *m.*
labyrinth ['læbirinθ], *n.* Labyrinthe, *m.* **labyrinthian** [-'rinθiən], *a.* De labyrinthe.
lac [læk], *n.* Gomme-laque, laque (résine), *f.*; lack, *m.* *Lac of rupees*, lack de roupies, *m.*
lace [leis], *n.* Dentelle, *f.*, point; passement, galon; lacet (a string); ruban, cordon (tape), *m.* *Boot-lace*, lacet de bottine, *m.*; *Brussels lace*, point de Bruxelles, *m.*; *gold-lace*, galon d'or; *silver-lace*, galon d'argent, *m.*; *corset-lace, stays-lace*, lacet de corset, *m.*—*v.t.* Lacer (to fasten); garnir de dentelle, galonner (to adorn with lace); (*fig.*) orner, (*Naut.*) transfiler (sails); mettre de l'eau-de-vie dans (coffee etc.). **lace-frame,** *n.* Métier à dentelle, *m.* **lace-hole,** *n.* Œillet, *m.* **lace-maker or lace-manufacturer,** *n.* Fabricant de dentelles, passementier, *m.*; dentellière, *f.* **lace-manufacture,** *n.* Fabrication de dentelles, passementerie, *f.* **lace-pillow,** *n.* Coussin, coussinet (à dentelle), *m.*; tambour, *m.* **lace-trade,** *n.* Commerce des dentelles, *m.*; passementerie, *f.* **lace-work,** *n.* Dentelles, *f.pl.*; passementerie, *f.*
Lacedaemon [læsi'diːmən]. Lacédémone, Sparte, *f.* **Lacedaemonian,** *a.* and *n.* Lacédémonien, -ienne, Spartiate.
lacerate ['læsəreit], *v.t.* Déchirer, lacérer.—*a.* [-rət] Déchiré; (*Bot.*) lacéré. **laceration** [-'reifən], *n.* Déchirure, lacération, *f.*
lacertoid [lə'səːtɔid], *a.* Lacertiforme.

lachrymal ['lækriməl], *a.* Lacrymal. ***lachrymary***, *a.* **lachrymatory**, *a.* and *n.* Lacrymatoire, *m.* *Lachrymatory shell*, obus lacrymogène, *m.* **lachrymose**, *a.* Larmoyant.

laciniate [lə'siniət] or **laciniated**, *a.* (*Bot.*) Lacinié.

lacing ['leisiŋ], *n.* Lacement, *m.*; (*Naut.*) transfilage, *m.*

lack [læk], *n.* Manque, besoin, défaut, *m.* *For lack of*, faute de; *there was no lack of food*, on ne manquait pas d'aliments.—*v.t.* Manquer de—*v.i.* Manquer.

lackadaisical [lækə'deizikəl], *a.* Minaudier, affecté; apathique, nonchalant (par affectation). **lackadaisy!** or **lack-a-day!** *int.* Hélas.

lackey ['læki], *n.* Laquais, *m.*; (*fam.*) larbin, *m.*

lacking, *a.* Vide (de), manquant (de). (*colloq.*) *He is a bit lacking*, il est un peu simple; *information is lacking*, les renseignements font défaut. **lackland**, *a.* Sans terre. **lacklustre**, *a.* Sans éclat, sans brillant; morne.

laconic [lə'kɔnik], *a.* Laconique. **laconically**, *adv.* Laconiquement.

laconicism [lə'kɔnisizm], **laconism**, *n.* Laconisme, *m.*

lacquer ['lækə], *n.* Laque, *m.*—*v.t.* Laquer. **lacquering**, *n.* Vernissure en laque, *f.*; laquage, vernissage; émaillage, *m.*

lacrosse [lə'krɔs], *n.* (*spt.*) Crosse canadienne, *f.*

lactate ['lækteit], *n.* (*Chem.*) Lactate, *m.* **lactation** [-'teiʃən], *n.* Lactation, *f.* **lacteal**, *a.* Lacté; laiteux. *Lacteal fever*, fièvre de lait, *f.* **lacteous**, *a.* Laiteux. **lactescence** [-'tesəns], *n.* Lactescence, *f.* **lactescent**, *a.* Lactescent. **lactic**, *a.* Lactique. **lactiferous** [-'tifərəs], *a.* Lactifère. **lactiform**, *a.* Lactiforme. **lactometer** [-'tɔmitə], *n.* Lactomètre, galactomètre, *m.* **lactose**, *n.* Lactose, *f.*

lacuna [lə'kjuːnə], *n.* (*pl.* **lacunae**) Lacune, *f.* **lacunary**, *a.* Lacunaire.

lacustrine [lə'kʌstriːn], *a.* Lacustre. (*Archaeol.*) *Lacustrine dwellings*, cité lacustre, *f.*

lacy ['leisi], *a.* De dentelle.

lad [læd], *n.* Garçon, jeune homme; gaillard, *m.* *Well, my lad*, eh bien, mon garçon, *or* mon brave!

ladder ['lædə], *n.* Échelle, *f.* *Rope-ladder*, échelle de corde, *f.*; *scaling-ladder*, échelle de siège, *f.*; *step-ladder*, échelle double, *f.*; escabeau, *m.*; *Jacob's ladder*, (*Naut.*) échelle de revers, *f.*; démaillage (in stocking), *m.* —*v.t.* Démailler (un bas). **ladder-proof**, *a.* Indémaillable (of stockings).

lade [leid], *v.t.* (*p.p.* **laden**) Charger (de); puiser, jeter (water). *Heavily laden*, lourdement chargé.

la-di-da ['laːdiːˈdɑː], *a.* (*fam.*) Affecté (of voice etc.).

ladies, *pl.* [LADY].

lading ['leidiŋ], *n.* Chargement, *m.* *Bill of lading*, connaissement, *m.*

ladle [leidl], *n.* Cuiller à pot, cuiller à potage, louche; aube, palette (of a water-wheel), *f.* *Soup ladle*, louche, *f.—v.t.* Vider, puiser. *To ladle out*, servir à la louche, (*fig.*) débiter. **ladleful**, *n.* Cuillerée, *f.*

lady ['leidi], *n.* (*pl.* **ladies**) Dame, *f.* *Ladies!* mesdames! mesdemoiselles! *Ladies* (on public

convenience), femmes, *f.pl.*; *ladies' compartment*, dames seules; *my lady*, madame la comtesse, madame la vicomtesse, etc.; *she is quite a lady*, c'est une femme très comme il faut; *young lady*, demoiselle, *f.* **ladies' man**, *n.* Coqueluche des dames, *m.* **lady-bird**, **lady-bug**, or **lady-cow**, *n.* Coccinelle, bête à bon Dieu, *f.* **lady-chapel**, *n.* Chapelle de la Vierge, *f.* **Lady-day**, *n.* Fête de l'Annonciation, *f.* **lady-killer**, *n.* Bourreau des cœurs, *m.*, coqueluche des dames, *f.*, lovelace, homme à bonnes fortunes, *m.* **lady-like**, *a.* De dame, comme il faut, qui a l'air distingué. **lady-love**, *n.* La dame de ses pensées, *f.* **lady's-bedstraw**, *n.* (*Bot.*) Gaillet, *m.* **lady's-maid**, *n.* Femme de chambre, *f.* **lady's-mantle**, *n.* (*Bot.*) Alchémille, *f.* **lady's-seal**, *n.* Sceau de Notre Dame, *m.* **lady's-slipper**, *n.* Sabot de la Vierge *or* Notre-Dame, *m.* **lady's-smock**, *n.* Cardamine, *f.*, cresson des prés, *m.*

ladyship, *n.* Madame, *f.* *Her Ladyship* or *Your Ladyship*, madame la comtesse, madame la vicomtesse, etc.

Laertes [lei'əːtiːz]. Laërte, *m.*

lag (1) [læg], *v.i.* Rester en arrière, se traîner; traîner (of things).—*n.* Retard, *m.* **laggard** ['lægəd] or **lagger**, *n.* Traînard, lambin, *m.*

lag (2) [læg], *v.t.* Envelopper, garnir.—*n.* Latte, *f.* (used for lagging). *Wooden lags*, lattis, *m. sing.* **lagging**, *n.* Enveloppe (de chaudière), chemise, *f.*

lag (3) [læg], *n.* Repris de justice; forçat, *m.* *He is an old lag*, c'est un vieux cheval de retour.

lager ['laːgə], *n.* Bière blonde (allemande), *f.*

lagoon [lə'guːn], *n.* Lagune, *f.*; lagon (in an atoll), *m.*

lagopus [lə'goupəs], *n.* Lagopède, *m.*

laic ['leiik], *a.* and *n.* Laïque, *m.* **laicization** [-sai'zeiʃən], *n.* Laïcisation, *f.* **laicize** ['leiisaiz], *v.t.* Laïciser.

laid [leid], *a.* Vergé (of paper). *Cream-laid*, vergé blanc.

lair [lɛə], *n.* Repaire, antre, *m.*; tanière, *f.*; liteau (of a wolf), *m.*; bauge (of a boar), *f.*; abri, enclos (for cattle), *m.*

laird [lɛəd], *n.* (*Sc.*) Propriétaire, châtelain, *m.*

laity ['leiiti], *n.* Laïques, *m.pl.*

lake (1) [leik], *n.* Lac, *m.* *Lake School, Lake Poets*, école lakiste, *f.*; *the Lake District*, la région des Lacs (N.W. England). **lake-dwelling**, *n.* Habitation lacustre, *f.* **lakelet**, *n.* Petit lac, *m.* **lake-like**, *a.* En forme de lac, comme un lac.

lake (2) [leik], *n.* Laque (colour), *f.*

lam [læm], *v.i.*, *v.t.* (*slang*) Étriller, passer à tabac, rosser.

lama (1) ['laːmə]. [LLAMA].

lama (2) ['laːmə], *n.* (*Buddhist Relig.*) The *Grand Lama*, le grand Lama. **lamasery** ['laːməzəri], *n.* Lamaserie, *f.*, couvent, monastère de lamas, *m.*

lamb [læm], *n.* Agneau, *m.* *God tempers the wind to the shorn lamb*, à brebis tondue Dieu mesure le vent; *with lamb*, pleine (of ewes). —*v.i.* Agneler. **lambkin**, *n.* Agnelet, petit agneau, *m.* **lamb-like**, *a.* Doux comme un agneau. **lamb's-lettuce**, *n.* Mâche, valérianelle, *f.* **lamb's-skin**, *n.* Peau d'agneau, *f.* **lamb's-wool**, *n.* Laine d'agneau, agneline, *f.*

lambent ['læmbənt], *a.* Qui effleure; qui rayonne doucement. **lambitive,** *a.* À lécher (medicine).

lame [leim], *a.* Boiteux, estropié (crippled); (*fig.*) défectueux, imparfait. *A lame excuse,* une piètre excuse; *a lame man,* un estropié, un boiteux, *m.*; *lame verses,* des vers boiteux, *m.pl.*; *to walk lame,* boiter, clocher.—*v.t.* Estropier. **lamely,** *adv.* En boitant, en clochant; (*fig.*) imparfaitement, mal. **lameness,** *n.* Claudication, *f.*; clochement, boitement, *m.*; (*fig.*) imperfection, faiblesse (of an excuse), *f.*

lamella [lə'melə], *n.* (*pl.* **lamellae**) Lamelle, *f.*

lamellar ['læmələ], **lamellate, lamellated,** or **lamellose,** *a.* Lamellé, lamelleux. **lamellibranch** [lə'melibrænk], *n.* Lamellibranche, *m.* **lamellibranchiate** [-'brænkiət], *a.* Lamellibranche. **lamellicorn,** *n.* Lamellicorne, *m.* **lamelliferous** [læme'lifərəs], *a.* Lamellifère. **lamelliform,** *a.* Lamelliforme. **lamellirostral,** *a.* Lamellirostre.

lament [lə'ment], *v.i.* Se lamenter, pleurer. *To lament for,* pleurer; *to lament over,* se lamenter sur, gémir de, s'affliger de.—*v.t.* Déplorer, se lamenter sur, pleurer; s'affliger de.—*n.* Lamentation, complainte, *f.*

lamentable ['læməntəbl], *a.* Lamentable, pitoyable, déplorable. **lamentably,** *adv.* Lamentablement, déplorablement.

lamentation [læmən'teifən], *n.* Lamentation, jérémiade, *f.*; (*Art*) Piéta, Piété, *f.*

lamented [lə'mentid], *a.* Regretté (the late).

lamenter, *n.* Personne qui se lamente, *f.*

lamenting, *a.* Qui se lamente.—*n.* Lamentation, *f.*

lamia ['leimiə], *n.* Lamie, *f.*

lamina ['læminə], *n.* (*pl.* **laminae**) Lame, *f.*

Lammas ['læməs], *n.* (*Sc.*) Le premier août, *m.*

lamp [læmp], *n.* Lampe; lanterne (for a carriage etc.); (*fig.*) lumière, *f.* *Arc lamp,* lampe à arc, *f.*; *argand lamp,* lampe d'Argand, *f.*, quinquet, *m.*; *ceiling-lamp,* plafonnier, *m.*; *floor-lamp,* lampadaire, *m.*; *illumination-lamp,* lampion, *m.*; *incandescent lamp,* lampe à incandescence, *f.*; *safety lamp,* lampe de sûreté, *f.*; *spirit-lamp,* lampe à alcool, *f.*; *street-lamp,* réverbère, *m.* **lamp-black,** *n.* Noir de fumée, *m.* **lamp-bracket,** *n.* Porte-lanterne, porte-phare, *m.*; applique, *f.* **lamplight,** *n.* Lumière de la lampe, *f.* **lamplighter,** *n.* Allumeur, *m.* **lampmaker, lamp-man,** *n.* Lampiste, *m.* **lamppost,** *n.* Lampadaire, *m.*; (*colloq.*) asperge (montée) (tall person), *f.*; réverbère, *m.* *To hang at the lamp-post,* mettre à la lanterne. **lamp-room,** *n.* Lampisterie, *f.* **lampshade,** *n.* Abat-jour, *m.* **lamp-stand,** *n.* Pied de lampe, *m.*

lampas ['læmpəs], *n.* (*Vet.* and *Text.*) Lampas, *m.*

lampoon [læm'puːn], *n.* Pasquinade, satire, *f.*, libelle, *m.*—*v.t.* Écrire un libelle *or* une satire contre. **lampooner,** *n.* Libelliste, *m.*

lamprey ['læmpri], *n.* Lamproie, *f.*

lanate ['leinət], *a.* Laineux.

lance [laːns], *n.* Lance, *f.*—*v.t.* Percer d'un coup de lance; (*Surg.*) donner un coup de lancette à, percer; déchausser (the gums).

lance-corporal ['laːns'kɔːpərəl], *n.* Soldat de première classe, caporal suppléant, *m.*

lanceolate ['laːnsiolət] or **lanceolated,** *a.* (*Bot.*) Lancéolé.

lancer ['laːnsə], *n.* Lancier, *m.*; (*pl.*) lanciers (a dance), *m.pl.*

lancet ['laːnsit], *n.* Lancette, *f.*; (*Dent.*) déchaussoir, *m.*; (*Arch.*) ogive, *f.* **lancet-shaped,** *a.* En ogive.

lancinate ['laːnsineit], *v.t.* Lanciner. **lancination** [-'neifən], *n.* Lancination, *f.*

land [lænd], *n.* Terre, *f.*; pays (country); (*Law*) bien-fonds, terrain (piece of land), *m.*; (*Agric.*) planche, *f.*; (*Mach.*) cordon (of piston), *m.*; cloison (of rifle), *f.* *Back to the land!* le retour à la terre; *distant lands,* pays lointains, *m.pl.*; *Holy Land,* la Terre Sainte; *native land,* patrie, *f.*; *promised land,* terre promise, *f.*; *to make land,* (*Naut.*) aborder, atterrir; *to see how the land lies,* sonder le terrain.—*v.i.* Débarquer (à *or* sur), aborder, prendre terre; (*fig.*) arriver, tomber (by chance); (*Av.*) atterrir; amérir. (*fig.*) *To land on one's feet,* retomber sur ses pattes.—*v.t.* Mettre à terre, prendre (a fish); débarquer, faire mettre à terre; amener (à). *To land a prize,* remporter un prix; *to land someone a blow,* flanquer un coup à quelqu'un. **land-agent,** *n.* Agent immobilier, *m.* **landfall,** *n.* Atterrissage, *m.* *To make a landfall,* arriver en vue de terre. **landholder,** *n.* Propriétaire foncier, *m.* **landjobber,** *n.* Spéculateur sur les biens fonciers, *m.* **landlady,** *n.* Propriétaire (of houses), maîtresse (of a lodging-house); aubergiste, hôtesse (of an inn), *f.* **landlocked,** *a.* Enfermé entre des terres. **landlord,** *n.* Propriétaire; hôte, hôtelier, aubergiste (of an inn), *m.* **landlubber,** *n.* Marin d'eau douce, *m.* **landmark,** *n.* Borne, limite, *f.*; signal, point de repère, *m.*; (*Naut.*) amers, *m.pl.* **land-office,** *n.* Bureau du cadastre, *m.* **landowner,** *n.* Propriétaire foncier, *m.* **landrail,** *n.* Râle de genêt, *m.* **landscape,** *n.* Paysage, *m.*; vue, *f.* **landscape-garden,** *n.* Jardin paysager; jardin à l'anglaise, *m.* **landscape-gardener,** *n.* Dessinateur de jardins, jardinier paysagiste, *m.* **landscape-painter,** *n.* Paysagiste, *m.* **landslide** or **landslip,** *n.* Éboulement de terre, *m.* **landsman,** *n.* (*pl.* **landsmen**) Homme à terre, terrien, *m.* **land-surveyor,** *n.* Arpenteur, *m.* **land-tax,** *n.* Impôt foncier, *m.* **landward,** *adv.* Du côté de la terre, vers la terre. **land-wind,** *n.* Vent de terre, *m.*

landau ['lændou], *n.* Landau, *m.*

landed, *a.* Foncier; territorial; de bien-fonds. *Landed property,* propriété foncière, *f.*; bien-fonds, *m.*

landing, *n.* Palier, carré (at the top of a staircase); (*Naut.*) débarquement; (*Av.*) atterrissage, *m.* *Forced landing,* atterrissage forcé. **landing-barge, landing-craft,** *n.* Péniche de débarquement, *f.* **landing-ground,** *n.* Terrain d'atterrissage, *m.* **landing-net,** *n.* Épuisette, *f.* **landing-place** or **landing-stage,** *n.* Débarcadère, *m.* **landing-strip,** *n.* Piste d'atterrissage, *f.*

landless, *a.* Sans terre.

lane [lein], *n.* Ruelle, *f.*, passage; (*country*) chemin vicinal, *m.*; (*spt.*) piste individuelle, *f.*
*langrage ['læŋgridʒ], *n.* (*Naut.*) Mitraille, *f.*
language ['læŋgwidʒ], *n.* Langage, *m.*, langue, expression, *f.* *Classical languages*, langues mortes; *modern languages*, langues vivantes; *to use bad language*, dire des grossièretés.
languid ['læŋgwid], *a.* Languissant, faible; mou. **languidly**, *adv.* Languissamment, faiblement; mollement. **languidness**, *n.* Langueur, faiblesse; mollesse, *f.*
languish ['læŋgwiʃ], *v.i.* Languir. **languishing**, *a.* Languissant, langoureux. *Languishing looks*, regards langoureux, *m.pl.* **languishingly**, *adv.* Languissamment, langoureusement.
languor ['læŋgə], *n.* Langueur, *f.* **languorous**, *a.* Langoureux.
laniard [LANYARD].
laniferous [lə'nifərəs] or **lanigerous**, *a.* Lanifère, lanigère.
lank [læŋk], *a.* Efflanqué; maigre; décharné; fluet, grêle. *To grow lank*, s'amaigrir. **lankness**, *n.* Maigreur; *mollesse, *f.* **lanky**, *a.* Grand et maigre, long et mince; dégingandé; efflanqué. *Lanky fellow*, grand flandrin, *m.*
lanner ['lænə], *n.* (*Orn.*) Lanier, *m.* **lanneret**, *n.* Laneret, *m.*
lansquenet ['lɑːnskənet], *n.* Lansquenet, *m.*
lantern ['læntən], *n.* Lanterne, *f.*; (*Mil.*) falot; (*Naut.*) fanal, phare, *m.* *Chinese lantern*, lanterne vénitienne, *f.*; *dark lantern*, lanterne sourde; *magic lantern*, lanterne magique; *signalling lantern*, lanterne-signal, *f.* **lantern-jaws**, *n.pl.* Joues creuses, *f.pl.*
lantern-slide, *n.* Vue sur verre, projection, *f.*
*lanuginous [lə'njuːdʒinəs], *a.* Lanugineux.
lanyard ['lænjəd], *n.* (*Naut.*) Aiguillette, ride, *f.*; (*Artill.*) (cordon) tire-feu, *m.*
Laos ['laouz]. Laos, *m.*
Laotian ['laouʃən], *a. and n.* Laotien, *m.*, -ienne, *f.*
lap [læp], *n.* Pan, *m.*, basque, *f.* (of a coat); giron, *m.*; (*fig.*) genoux, *m.pl.*; sein; (*Arch.*) recouvrement; (*Racing*) tour de piste, *m.* *In my lap*, sur mes genoux; *in the lap of*, au sein de.—*v.t.* Envelopper, plier (to wrap); laper (to lick). (*spt.*) *He lapped the other competitors*, il a pris un tour aux autres concurrents; *to lap up*, laper, avaler; (*fig.*) gober.—*v.i.* Laper; se replier, retomber; clapoter (of waves). *To lap over*, recouvrir. **lap-dog**, *n.* Bichon, petit chien, chien de manchon, *m.* **lap-joint**, *n.* (*Naut.*) Clin, *m.* **lapwork**, *n.* Ouvrage à clin, *m.*
lapel [lə'pel], *n.* Revers (d'habit), *m.*
lapidary ['læpidəri], *a. and n.* Lapidaire, *m.* *Lapidary style*, style lapidaire, *m.* **lapidate**, *v.t.* Lapider. **lapidation** [-'deiʃən], *n.* Lapidation, *f.* **lapidescence**, *n.* Pétrification, *f.* **lapidific**, *a.* Lapidifique.
lapidify [lə'pidifai], *v.t.* Lapidifier.—*v.i.* Se lapidifier, se pétrifier.
lapis-lazuli ['læpis'læzjulai], *n.* Lapis, lapis-lazuli; outremer, *m.*
Lapland ['læplənd]. La Laponie, *f.* **Laplander** ['læpləndə], *n.* Lapon, *m.*, Lapone, *f.*
Lapp [læp], *a. and n.* Lapon, Lapone; le lapon (language).
lappet ['læpit], *n.* Pan; revers (of coat); rabat (of priest); cache-entrée (of lock), *m.* *Ear-lappet*, oreillette, *f.* (of cap).

lapping ['læpiŋ], *n.* Lapement, *m.*; recouvrement, *m.*
lapse [læps], *n.* Cours, *m.*, marche, *f.*, laps (of time), *m.*; dévolution (of a living etc.); chute (of water); faute, erreur (fault), *f.*; manquement, écart, manque (deviation), *m.* *Lapse of memory*, absence (de mémoire), *f.*; *lapse of the tongue*, lapsus linguae, *m.*—*v.i.* S'écouler; tomber, déchoir; devenir périmé; faillir, manquer (à). *The right of presentation lapses to the king*, le droit de patronage passe au roi. **lapsed**, *a.* Déchu; périmé; caduc (of contract, will).
lapwing ['læpwiŋ], *n.* Vanneau, *m.*
*larboard (1) ['lɑːbəd], *a.* (*Naut.*) Bâbord, *inv.*
*larboard (2) ['lɑːbɔːd], *a.* (*Naut.*) Bâbord, *inv.*
larceny ['lɑːsəni], *n.* Larcin, vol, *m.*
larch [lɑːtʃ], *n.* (*Bot.*) Mélèze, *m.*
lard [lɑːd], *n.* Saindoux, *m.*; panne; graisse de porc; (*Pharm.*) axonge, *f.*—*v.t.* Larder (de).
larder ['lɑːdə], *n.* Garde-manger, *m.*
larding-pin, *n.* Lardoire, *f.*
lares ['lɛəriːz], *n.pl.* Lares, dieux lares, *m.pl.*
large [lɑːdʒ], *a.* Grand, gros; étendu, considérable; fort. *As large as life*, grandeur nature; *at large*, en liberté, libre, en général; *large sum*, forte somme; *to go* or *sail large*, (*Naut.*) aller ou courir largue; *to grow large*, grossir, grandir; *to set a prisoner at large*, relâcher, relaxer, élargir un prisonnier. **large-handed**, *a.* (*fig.*) Généreux, libéral. **large-hearted**, *a.* Généreux, magnanime. **largely**, *adv.* Amplement, largement, grandement; abondamment; au long, en grande partie. **largeness**, *n.* Grandeur, étendue, ampleur, *f.*
largess(e) ['lɑːdʒes], *n.* Largesse, libéralité, *f.*
lariat ['læriət], *n.* Corde à piquet, *f.* (for horses); lasso, *m.*
lark [lɑːk], *n.* Alouette; (*Cook.*) mauviette; (*fig.*) escapade, farce; (*slang*) rigolade, *f.* *To lark, to have a lark*, faire des farces, s'amuser, rigoler.
larkspur, *n.* Pied-d'alouette, *m.*
larrikin ['lærikin], *n.* Gamin des rues, voyou, *m.*
larrup ['lærəp], *v.t.* (*pop.*) Rosser.
larva ['lɑːvə], *n.* (*pl.* **larvae**) Larve, *f.*
laryngeal [lə'rindʒiəl], *a.* Laryngé, laryngien.
laryngitis [lærin'dʒaitis], *n.* Laryngite, *f.*
laryngology [-'gɔlədʒi], *n.* Laryngologie, *f.*
laryngotomy ['lærinks], *n.* Laryngotomie, *f.*
larynx ['lærinks], *n.* (*pl.* **larynges**) Larynx, *m.*
lascar ['læskə], *n.* Matelot indien, *m.*
lascivious [lə'siviəs], *a.* Lascif. **lasciviously**, *adv.* Lascivement. **lasciviousness**, *n.* Lasciveté, *f.*
lash [læʃ], *n.* Mèche (cord at end of whip), *f.*; coup de fouet; (*fig.*) coup, trait, sarcasme, *m.* *Eyelash* [EYE]; *to be under the lash*, être exposé aux coups de la critique.—*v.t.* Cingler, fouetter, battre; châtier; lier, attacher (to tie); (*Naut.*) amarrer, saisir. *Insults which lash him into a fury*, les insultes qui excitent sa fureur.—*v.i.* Fouetter, battre (contre). *To lash out at someone*, lancer des critiques cinglantes contre quelqu'un. **lasher**, *n.* Fouetteur, *m.*; (*Naut.*) corde d'amarrage, *f.*; barrage (weir), *m.* **lashing**, *a.* Cinglant, fouettant.—*n.* Coups de fouet, *m.pl.*; (*Naut.*)

ligne d'amarrage, *f.*—*n.pl.* (*fam.*) Des tas, des tonnes; en veux-tu, en voilà.
lass [læs], *n.* (*Sc.*) Jeune fille, *f.* **lassie,** *n.* Fillette, *f.*
lassitude ['læsitjuːd], *n.* Lassitude, *f.*
lasso [lə'suː or 'læsou], *n.* Lasso, *m.*—*v.t.* Prendre au lasso.
last (1) [lɑːst], *a.* Dernier, passé. *I have been waiting for you for the last two hours,* il y a deux heures que je vous attends; *I have not been to Paris for the last ten years,* il y a dix ans que je ne suis allé à Paris; *last but not least,* le dernier (nommé), mais non le moindre; *last but one,* avant-dernier; *last night,* hier soir; *last week,* la semaine dernière; *on one's last legs,* à bout de ressources; *the last time,* la dernière fois; *this day last week,* il y a aujourd'hui huit jours; *this day last year,* il y a aujourd'hui un an.—*n.* Bout, *m.,* fin, *f. At last,* à la fin, enfin; *to breathe one's last,* rendre le dernier soupir; *to the last,* jusqu'au bout, jusqu'à la fin, jusqu'au dernier moment; *we have not heard the last of it,* on n'a pas fini d'en entendre parler, tout n'est pas dit.—*adv.* Pour la dernière fois. *He spoke last,* il a parlé le dernier.—*v.i.* Durer. *To last out,* surpasser en durée; *to last over,* durer jusqu'à.
last (2) [lɑːst], *n.* Forme (for shoes), *f.*—*v.t.* Mettre sur la forme. **last-maker,** *n.* Formier, *m.*
lasting (1), *a.* Durable, permanent. **lastingly,** *adv.* D'une manière durable. **lastingness,** *n.* Durabilité, *f.* **lastly,** *adv.* En dernier lieu, enfin.
lasting (2), *n.* Mise sur la forme, *f.*
latch [lætʃ], *n.* Loquet, *m.,* clenche, *f.*—*v.t.* Fermer au loquet. *On the latch,* fermé au loquet. **latchkey,** *n.* Passe-partout, *m.,* clef de la maison, *f.*
latchet ['lætʃit], *n.* Cordon de soulier, *m.*
late [leit], *a.* Tard; en retard; tardif (of fruit, vegetables, etc.); avancé (of time); ancien, ex- (former); feu (dead); récent, dernier (recent). *Of late years,* dans ces dernières années, *f.pl.; the late king,* feu le roi; *the latest posterity,* la postérité la plus reculée; *to be late,* être en retard.—*adv.* Tard; sur la fin; récemment, depuis peu. *At latest,* au plus tard; *better late than never,* mieux vaut tard que jamais; *late of London,* dernièrement domicilié à Londres; *of late,* dernièrement, récemment, depuis peu; *to be getting late,* (*impers.*) se faire tard; *very late,* à une heure avancée. **lately,** *adv.* Dernièrement, récemment; il y a peu de temps, depuis peu. **lateness,** *n.* Retard, *m.;* heure avancée, *f.;* temps avancé, *m.;* tardiveté, *f.* **later,** *a.* Postérieur, ultérieur.—*adv.* Plus tard. **latest,** *a.* Dernier. *At the latest,* au plus tard.
latecomer, *n.* Retardataire.
lateen-sail [lə'tiːn seil], *n.* Voile latine, *f.*
latent ['leitənt], *a.* Caché, secret, latent.
lateral ['lætərəl], *a.* De côté, latéral. **laterally,** *adv.* Latéralement, de côté.
Lateran ['lætərən]. Latran, *m. St. John Lateran,* Saint-Jean de Latran; *the Lateran councils,* les conciles du Latran, *m.pl.*
lath [lɑːθ], *n.* Latte, *f.*—*v.t.* Latter. **lathy,** *a.* Aussi mince qu'une latte, sec, décharné.
lathe [leið], *n.* Tour, *m.*—*v.t.* Tourner.
lather ['læðə], *n.* Mousse; (*fig.*) écume, *f.*—*v.t.*

Couvrir *or* enduire de mousse, savonner; (*colloq.*) rosser, battre, fouetter.—*v.i.* Mousser.
Latin ['lætin], *a.* and *n.* Latin. **Latin-American,** *a.* and *n.* Latino-américain, *m.,* -aine, *f.* **Latinism,** *n.* Latinisme, *m.*
Latinist, *n.* Latiniste, *m.* **Latinity** [-'tiniti], *n.* Latinité, *f.* **Latinize,** *v.t.* Latiniser.
latish ['leitiʃ], *a.* Un peu tard, un peu en retard.—*adv.* Un peu tard.
latitude ['lætitjuːd], *n.* Latitude; étendue (breadth), *f.*
latitudinal [læti'tjuːdinəl], *a.* Latitudinal.
latitudinarian [-'neəriən], *a.* and *n.* Latitudinaire, tolérantiste, *m.*
latria ['lætriə], *n.* Latrie, *f.*
latrine [lə'triːn], *n.* Latrine, *f.;* (camp) latrines; (*Mil., pl.*) feuillées, *f.pl.;* (*Naut.*) poulaines (for seamen); bouteilles (for officers), *f.pl.*
latten ['lætən], *n.* Fer-blanc, laiton, métal laminé, *m.* **latten-brass,** *n.* Cuivre laminé, *m.*
latter ['lætə], *a.* Dernier; moderne, récent. *Latter-Day Saints,* Mormons, *m.pl.; the latter,* ce dernier, ces derniers, celui-ci, ceux-ci, *m.,* cette dernière, ces dernières, celle-ci, celles-ci, *f.; the latter end,* la fin.
lattergrass, *n.* Regain, *m.*
latterly, *adv.* Depuis peu, dernièrement.
lattice ['lætis], *n.* Treillis, treillage, *m. Lattice (-window),* fenêtre treillissée, *f.*—*v.t.* Treillisser. **lattice-work,** *n.* Treillis, treillage, *m.*
Latvia ['lætviə]. La Lettonie, *f.* **Latvian,** *a.* and *n.* Letton, *m.,* Lettone, *f.;* Lettonien, *m.,* Lettonienne, *f.; n. only,* Lette, *m.* or *f.*
laud [lɔːd], *v.t.* Louer, célébrer. *To laud to the skies,* élever jusqu'aux nues.—*n.* Louange, *f.* Lauds, (*R.-C. Ch.*) laudes, *f.pl.* **laudable,** *a.* Louable, digne de louanges. **laudableness,** *n.* Qualité louable, *f.;* mérite, *m.*
laudably, *adv.* Louablement, d'une manière louable.
laudanum ['lɔːdnəm], *n.* Laudanum, *m. Containing laudanum,* laudanisé.
laudatory ['lɔːdətəri], *a.* Laudatif, louangeur.
lauder ['lɔːdə], *n.* Louangeur, panégyriste, *m.*
laugh [lɑːf], *n.* Rire, *m.,* risée (of derision), *f. Loud laugh,* gros rire, éclat de rire, *m.; to be good for a laugh,* faire rire, être amusant; *to burst into a laugh,* éclater de rire; *to force a laugh,* rire du bout des dents *or* des lèvres; *to have a good laugh at,* se bien moquer de, rire beaucoup de.—*v.i.* Rire. *Laugh today and cry tomorrow,* tel qui rit vendredi dimanche pleurera; *he who laughs last laughs longest,* rira bien qui rira le dernier; *he will laugh on the wrong side of his face,* je lui ferai passer son envie de rire; *to burst out laughing,* éclater de rire, partir d'un éclat de rire; *to laugh at,* se moquer de, se rire de, se jouer de; *to laugh down,* tourner en ridicule; *to laugh in one's sleeve,* rire dans sa barbe; *to laugh in someone's face,* rire au nez de quelqu'un.
laughable, *a.* Risible. **laugher,** *n.* Rieur, *m.,* rieuse, *f.* **laughing,** *a.* Rieur, enjoué, qui aime à rire. *It is no laughing matter,* il n'y a pas de quoi rire.—*n.* Rires, *m.pl.* **laughing-gas,** *n.* Gaz hilarant, *m.* **laughing-stock,** *n.* Risée, *f.,* objet de risée, *m.* **laughingly,** *adv.* En riant. **laughter,** *n.* Rire, *m.,* rires, *m.pl.;*

risée, moquerie, *f. Burst of laughter,* éclat de rire, *m.; to break out into laughter,* éclater de rire; (*fam.*) *to split one's sides with laughter,* se tordre de rire.

Launcelot ['lɑːns-, 'lɔːnslət]. Lancelot, *m.*

launch [lɔːntʃ], *v.t.* Lancer; mettre à la mer. *To launch an attack,* déclencher une attaque. —*v.i.* Se lancer, se jeter. *To launch forth* or *out into,* se lancer dans, se répandre en.—*n.* Lancement, *m.,* mise à l'eau; chaloupe (boat), vedette, *f.* **launching,** *n.* (*Naut.*) Mise à l'eau, *f.,* lancement, *m.*

launder ['lɔːndə], *n.* (*Mining*) Caniveau, *m.,* auge, *f.*—*v.t.* Blanchir; lessiver (of linen). **launderette,** *n.* Laverie automatique, *f.* **laundering,** *n.* Blanchissage, *m.* **laundress,** *n.* Blanchisseuse, *f.* **laundry,** *n.* Buanderie; blanchisserie, *f.,* linge à blanchir, *m. Fine laundry,* blanchisserie de fin.

Laura ['lɔːrə]. Laure, *f.*

laureate ['lɔːriət], *a.* Couronné de lauriers, lauréat. *Poet Laureate,* poète lauréat, *m.*

laurel ['lɔrəl], *n.* Laurier, *m. Laurel wreath,* couronne de laurier, *f.* **laurelled,** *a.* Couronné de laurier. **laurustinus** [-'əstainəs] or **laurestine,** *n.* Laurier-thym, *m.*

Laurence ['lɔrəns]. Laurent, *m.,* Laurence, *f.*

lava ['lɑːvə], *n.* Lave, *f.*

lavatory ['lævət(ə)ri], *n.* Water-closet, *m.,* les lavabos, *m.pl.,* les water, *m.pl.*

lave [leiv], *v.t.* (*Lit.*) Laver, baigner.—*v.i.* Se laver, se baigner.

lavender ['lævəndə], *n.* Lavande, *f.* **lavender-cotton,** *n.* (*Bot.*) Santoline, *f.* **lavender-water,** *n.* Eau de lavande, *f.*

laver ['leivə], *n.* *Aiguière, *f.*; algue comestible, *f.*

lavish ['læviʃ], *a.* Prodigue.—*v.t.* Prodiguer. **lavisher,** *n.* Prodigue, *m.* **lavishly,** *adv.* Prodigalement, avec prodigalité. **lavishness,** *n.* Prodigalité, *f.*

law [lɔː], *n.* Loi, *f.*; droit, *m. Air-law,* le droit aérien; *civil law,* droit civil; *commercial law,* droit commercial; *common law,* droit coutumier; *criminal law,* droit criminel; *ecclesiastical law,* droit canon; *international law,* droit international; *law case,* cause civile, *f.*; *law costs* or *expenses,* frais de procédure, *m.pl.*; *Law Courts,* Palais de Justice, *m.,* les tribunaux, *m.pl.*; *law of nations,* droit des gens; *maritime law,* droit maritime; *military law,* code militaire, code de justice militaire, *m.,* législation militaire, *f.*; *point of law,* question de droit, *f.*; *Roman law,* droit romain; *to be at law,* être en procès; *to enforce the law,* appliquer la loi; (*fam.*) *to have the law on someone,* faire un procès à quelqu'un; *to go to law with,* citer en justice, intenter un procès à; *to quash a judgment on a point of law,* casser un jugement pour vice de forme; *to study law,* étudier le droit, faire son droit; *to take the law into one's own hands,* se faire justice à soi-même.

law-abiding, *a.* Soumis aux lois, ami de l'ordre, pacifique. **law-book,** *n.* Livre de droit, *m.* **law-breaker,** *n.* Transgresseur de la loi, *m.* **lawgiver,** *n.* Législateur, *m.* **law-list,** *n.* Annuaire judiciaire, *m.* **law-maker,** *n.* Législateur, *m.* **law-student,** *n.* Étudiant en droit, *m.* **lawsuit,** *n.* Procès, *m.* **law-writer,** *n.* Expéditionnaire, *m.*

lawful, *a.* Légitime, licite, permis. **lawfully,**

adv. Légitimement. **lawfulness,** *n.* Légitimité, *f.*

lawless, *a.* Sans loi; (*fig.*) sans frein, déréglé. **lawlessly,** *adv.* Sans loi; illégalement. **lawlessness,** *n.* Désordre, *m.,* licence, *f.*

lawn [lɔːn], *n.* Pelouse, *f.*; linon (linen), *m.* (*fam.*) *The lawn,* l'épiscopat, *m.* **lawn-mower,** *n.* Tondeuse de gazon, *f.* **lawn-tennis,** *n.* Tennis sur gazon; tennis, *m.*

lawny, *a.* Uni comme une pelouse; fait de linon.

lawyer ['lɔːjə], *n.* Homme de loi; avocat; avoué (solicitor), *m.*; notaire (notary); jurisconsulte (jurist), *m.* **lawyer-like,** *a.* En homme de loi.

lax [læks], *a.* Lâche, mou, flasque; (*fig.*) relâché, négligent.

laxation [læk'seiʃən], *n.* Relâchement, *m.*

laxative ['læksətiv], *a.* and *n.* Laxatif, *m.*

laxity or **laxness,** *n.* Relâchement, *m.*; flaccidité, *f.*; manque d'exactitude, *m.* **laxly,** *adv.* Mollement; sans exactitude.

lay (1) [lei], *past* [LIE].

lay (2) [lei], *v.t.* (*past* and *p.p.* **laid**) Placer, mettre, poser; coucher, étendre (to stretch); faire (a wager); parier (a bet); pondre (eggs); tendre, dresser (a snare); abattre (the dust); calmer, apaiser (to calm). *He lays all the blame on me,* il en rejette toute la faute sur moi; *to lay a fault on,* imputer une faute à; *to lay a gun,* pointer un canon; *to lay aside,* mettre de côté, abandonner; *to lay before,* soumettre à, mettre sous les yeux de, exposer à; *to lay by,* mettre de côté; *to lay claim to,* prétendre à, revendiquer; *to lay down,* mettre bas, déposer (les armes), poser (a principle), quitter, abandonner (to give up), expliquer (the law), coucher; *to lay down one's life for,* donner sa vie pour; *to lay hold of,* s'emparer de, saisir; *to lay in,* faire provision de, se procurer; (*fam.*) *to lay off someone,* laisser quelqu'un tranquille; *to lay on,* appliquer, imposer, poser; (*fam.*) arranger, organiser; *to lay oneself down,* se coucher, s'étendre; *to lay open,* ouvrir, mettre à nu, exposer; *to lay out,* arranger, dépenser, débourser, ensevelir (a corpse), planter, disposer (a garden etc.), tracer; agencer; *to lay over,* étendre, couvrir, incruster; *to lay siege to,* assiéger; *to lay snares for,* tendre des pièges à; *to lay to heart,* prendre à cœur; *to lay up,* mettre de côté, amasser, faire garder la chambre à, (*Naut.*) désarmer; *to lay waste,* dévaster.—*v.i.* Pondre. (*fam.*) *To lay off,* cesser; (*Naut.*) *to lay to,* être à la cape.

lay (3) [lei], *n.* Lai, *m.,* chanson, *f.,* chant, *m.,* genre d'affaires, *m.,* spécialité, *f.,* (*Naut.*) part, *f.* (de pêche). (*Print.*) *Lay-mark,* repère, *m.*

lay (4) [lei], *a.* Lai, laïque. *Lay brother,* frère convers, *m.*; *lay figure,* mannequin, *m.*

lay-by ['leibai], *n.* Espace réservé au stationnement sur les bas-côtés des grandes routes, *m.*

lay-clerk ['lei'klɑːk], *n.* Chantre, *m.*

lay-days (*Naut.*) [*see* LYING].

layer ['leiə], *n.* Couche, *f.,* lit (a stratum), *m.*; (*Geol.*) assise, *f.*; (*Hort.*) marcotte, *f.*; provin (of vine), *m.*; pondeuse (hen), *f.*; (*Artill.*) pointeur, *m.*

laying ['leiiŋ], *n.* Mise, pose, *f.,* posage, *m.*; ponte (of eggs), *f. Laying out,* arrangement, *m.*, disposition, *f.*; ensevelissement (of a corpse), *m.*

layman ['leimən], *n.* (*pl.* **laymen**) Laïque, profane, séculier, *m.*

lay-out ['leiaut], *n.* Dessin, tracé, *m.*; disposition, *f.*, agencement, *m.*

lazaretto [læzə'retou], *n.* Lazaret, *m.*

Lazarus ['læzərəs]. Lazare, *m.*

laze [leiz], *v.t.*, *v.i.* To laze about, baguenauder; to laze away one's time, fainéanter.

lazily ['leizili], *adv.* Lentement; en paresseux, paresseusement; indolemment. **laziness**, *n.* Paresse, oisiveté, *f.* **lazy**, *a.* Paresseux, indolent. Lazy fellow, fainéant, *m.* **lazybones**, *n.* Fainéant, paresseux, *m.*

lazzarone [lætsə'rounei], *n.* (*pl.* **lazzaroni**) Lazarone, *m.*

lea [li:], *n.* (*poet.*) Prairie; jachère, *f.*

leach [li:tʃ], *v.t.* Filtrer. **leach-tub**, *n.* Baquet pour lessiver, *m.*

lead (1) [led], *n.* Plomb (metal), *m.*; (*Naut.*) sonde; (*Print.*) entre-ligne, interligne; mine de plomb (for pencils), *f.*; (*pl.*) plombs, toits, *m.pl.*, toiture, *f.* Blacklead, mine de plomb, *f.*, graphite, *m.*; lead colic, colique saturnine, *f.*; lead-shot, grenaille de plomb, *f.*; petit plomb, *m.*; red lead, minium, *m.*; to heave the lead, jeter la sonde; white lead, blanc de céruse, *m.*—*v.t.* Plomber, couvrir de plomb; (*Print.*) interligner. **leaded**, *a.* Plombé; (*Print.*) interligné. Leaded lights, fenêtres à vitres enchâssées dans des plombs, *f.pl.* **leaden**, *a.* De plomb; (*fig.*) lourd; couvert (of the sky). **lead-pencil**, *n.* Crayon à la mine de plomb, *m.* **lead-wire**, *n.* Fil de plomb, *m.* **lead-work**, *n.* Plombage, *m.* **lead-works**, *n.pl.* Plomberie, *f.*

lead (2) [li:d], *v.t.* (*past and p.p.* **led** [led]) Mener, guider, conduire; porter, faire, induire (à); entraîner (à or dans). Leading his troops, à la tête de ses troupes; the causes that led up to, les causes qui ont amené; to lead about, mener partout; to lead astray, égarer, détourner, (*fig.*) dévergonder; to lead back, ramener, reconduire; to lead in, introduire; to lead into, entraîner dans; to lead on, conduire, entraîner; pousser, inciter; to lead out, faire sortir, emmener; to lead out of the way, égarer; to lead someone a dog's life, faire une vie de chien à quelqu'un; to lead someone to believe, faire croire à quelqu'un, porter quelqu'un à croire; to lead the way, montrer le chemin, marcher en tête; to lead up to, amener.—*v.i.* Conduire, mener; (*games*) jouer le premier, avoir la main, débuter; (*Mil.*) ouvrir la marche. To lead off, débuter, partir le premier.—*n.* Conduite, direction, *f.*, commandement, *m.*, préséance, *f.*, pas, *m.*; laisse (for dog), *f.*; (*billiards*) acquit, *m.*; (*cards*) main, *f.*; (*games*) début, *m.*, ouverture, *f.*; (*Theat.*) premier rôle, *m.*, vedette, *f.*; (*Elec.*) conducteur, *m.*, connexion, *f.* It's your lead, c'est à vous la main; to be in the lead, être en première place; to have the lead, avoir la main (at cards); to keep a dog on a lead, garder un chien en laisse; to take the lead, marcher en avant, dominer, présider.

leader ['li:də], *n.* Conducteur, guide, chef, meneur, premier; (*Journ.*) article de fond, éditorial, leader; cheval de volée (horse); (*Polit.*) chef de parti, leader, *m.*; (*Hort.*) pousse principale, *f.*; (*Print.*) point conducteur, *m.*; (*Cine.*) amorce, *f.* **leadership**, *n.* Conduite, direction, *f.*; qualités de chef, *f.pl.*

leader-writer, *n.* Éditorialiste, *m.*

leading, *a.* Premier, principal, chef, grand. Leading article, article de fond, *m.*; leading man, chef, *m.*, notabilité, *f.*; (*Theat.*) premier rôle, jeune premier, *m.*; leading question, question insidieuse, *f.*; he is one of the leading lights, c'est une des autorités en la matière.—*n.* Conduite, direction, *f.* **leading-strings**, *n.* Lisière, *f.*

leadsman ['ledzmən], *n.* (*Naut.*) Sondeur, *m.*

leaf [li:f], *n.* (*pl.* **leaves** [li:vz]) Feuille, *f.*; feuillet (of a book etc.), battant (of a door), *m.*; rallonge, *f.*, battant, *m.* (of a table). To take a leaf out of someone's book, suivre l'exemple de quelqu'un; to turn over a new leaf, (*fig.*) changer de conduite; to turn over the leaves of, feuilleter.—*v.i.* Pousser des feuilles. **leaf-gold**, *n.* Or en feuilles, *m.* **leaf-mould**, *n.* Terreau, *m.* **leaf-stalk**, *n.* Pétiole, *m.*

leafage, *n.* Feuillage, *m.*

leafless, *a.* Sans feuilles, effeuillé.

leaflet, *n.* Feuillet, imprimé, prospectus, *m.*; (*Bot.*) foliole, *f.*

leafy, *a.* Feuillu, couvert de feuilles.

league [li:g], *n.* Ligue; lieue (3 miles), *f.* The League of Nations, la Société des Nations; the seven-league boots, les bottes de sept lieues, *f.pl.*; to be in league with, être d'intelligence avec.—*v.i.* Se liguer. **leaguer**, *n.* Confédéré, ligueur.

leak [li:k], *n.* Fuite, perte d'eau; infiltration; (*Naut.*) voie d'eau, *f.* To spring a leak, (*Naut.*) faire eau.—*v.i.* Fuir, couler, faire eau; prendre l'eau (of shoes). To leak out, transpirer, s'éventer. **leakage**, *n.* Coulage, *m.*; fuite, perte, voie d'eau, *f.* **leaky**, *a.* Qui coule, qui fuit; (*Naut.*) qui fait eau; qui prend l'eau (shoe).

lean (1) [li:n], *a.* and *n.* Maigre, *m.* To grow, to get lean, maigrir; to make lean, amaigrir. **leanness**, *n.* Maigreur, *f.*

lean (2) [li:n], *v.i.* (*past and p.p.* **leaned** or **leant** [lent]) S'appuyer, s'incliner, se pencher; pencher, incliner (to slope). To lean back against, s'adosser à; to lean on, s'appuyer sur; to lean on one's elbow, s'accouder; to lean out, se pencher au dehors.—*v.t.* Appuyer, faire pencher, incliner. **leaning**, *n.* Penchant, *m.*, (*fig.*) tendance, *f.*—*a.* Penché. **lean-to**, *n.* Appentis, *m.*

leap [li:p], *n.* Saut, bond, *m.* By leaps and bounds, par sauts et par bonds; to take a leap (in the dark), faire un saut (dans l'inconnu). —*v.t.* Sauter, franchir.—*v.i.* Sauter, bondir; s'élancer, se précipiter; jaillir (of flames). To leap for joy, sauter de joie. **leap-frog**, *n.* Saute-mouton, *m.* **leap-year**, *n.* Année bissextile, *f.*

leaper, *n.* Sauteur, *m.*, sauteuse, *f.*

leaping, *a.* Qui saute, qui fait des sauts. **leaping-board**, *n.* Tremplin, *m.*

learn [lə:n], *v.t.* (*past and p.p.* **learned** or **learnt**) Apprendre. To learn one's lesson, se le tenir pour dit.—*v.i.* Apprendre, s'instruire.

learned ['lə:nid], *a.* Savant, instruit, lettré, érudit. Learned in the law, versé dans le droit; *learned man*, savant, *m.*; *learned profession*, profession libérale, *f.* **learnedly**, *adv.* Savamment.

learner, *n.* Élève, commençant, apprenti, *m.*, personne qui apprend, *f.* *Learner driver*, élève chauffeur.

learning, *n.* Science, instruction, *f.*, savoir, *m.*, connaissances, *f.pl.*; érudition, *f.* *Polite learning*, belles-lettres, *f.pl.*

lease [li:s], *n.* Bail, *m.* *A new lease of life*, un regain de vie; *long lease*, bail à long terme; *on a lease*, à bail.—*v.t.* Louer, donner à bail; prendre à bail. **leasehold**, *n.* Tenure par bail, *f.*—*a.* À bail. **leaseholder**, *n.* Locataire à bail, *m.* or *f.* **lease-lend**, *n.* Prêt-bail, *m.inv.*

leash [li:ʃ], *n.* Laisse, *f.*, (*Hunt.*) harde de trois (chiens), *f.*, (*fig.*) un trio, *m.* *To hold in* or *on the leash*, tenir en laisse.—*v.t.* Mener en laisse, attacher, tenir en laisse.

least [li:st], *a.* Le moindre, le plus petit.—*adv.* Le moins. *At least*, au moins, du moins; *at the least*, pour le moins; *not in the least*, point du tout, nullement, pas le moins du monde; *to say the least (of it)*, pour ne pas dire plus, au bas mot. **leastways, leastwise**, *adv.* Du moins, en tout cas.

leather ['leðə], *n.* Cuir, *m.* *Upper leather*, empeigne, *f.*—*v.t.* (*colloq.*) Étriller, rosser. **leather-dresser**, *n.* Peaussier, mégissier, *m.* **leather-seller**, *n.* Marchand de cuir, *m.*

leatherette, *n.* Simili-cuir, *m.*; toile cuir, *f.* **leathering**, *n.* (*fam.*) Râclée, rossée, *f.* **leathern**, *a.* De cuir, de peau. **leathery**, *a.* Comme du cuir, coriace.

leave [li:v], *n.* Permission, *f.*, congé; adieu, *m.* *By someone's leave*, avec la permission de quelqu'un; *extension of leave*, prolongation de congé, *f.*; *on leave*, en congé (one month at least), en permission (less than a month); *sick leave*, congé de convalescence, *m.*; *to give leave*, donner la permission de, permettre à; *to take French leave*, filer à l'anglaise; *to take leave of*, prendre congé de, faire ses adieux à; *with your leave*, avec votre permission.—*v.t.* (*past and p.p.* **left** [left]) Laisser; quitter, abandonner (to depart from); partir de; s'en remettre (à); cesser (de). *He had no choice left*, il n'avait plus le choix; *he left London*, il partit de Londres; *he left the house*, il quitta la maison, il sortit de la maison; *he left the pen on the table*, il laissa le stylo sur la table; *I had nothing left to dispose of*, il ne me restait rien que je pusse vendre; *I have nothing left*, il ne me reste rien; *I leave that to you*, je m'en rapporte à vous; *leave it to me*, laissez-moi faire, je m'en charge; *leave well alone*, le mieux est l'ennemi du bien; *on leaving*, au sortir (de); *to be left*, rester; *to be left till called for*, poste restante (of letters), *f.*; *to be left without*, rester sans; *to have got some left*, en avoir de reste, avoir encore; *to leave about*, laisser traîner; *to leave alone*, laisser tranquille; *to leave no stone unturned*, remuer ciel et terre; *to leave off*, quitter, cesser, discontinuer; mettre (clothes etc.) au rebut; *to leave off a dress*, cesser de porter un habit; *to leave out*, supprimer, omettre, oublier; *to leave word*, faire dire à; laisser un message, faire faire la commission (à).—*v.i.* Partir, quitter; cesser. *To leave off*,

cesser, s'arrêter, en rester là. **leave-taking**, *n.* Adieux, *m.pl.*

leaved [li:vd], *a.* À feuilles; à battants (of doors).

leaven [levn], *n.* Levain, *m.*—*v.t.* Faire lever. **leavened**, *a.* Qui contient du levain. *Leavened bread*, pain levé, *m.*

leavings ['li:viŋz], *n.pl.* Restes, *m.pl.*

Lebanese ['lebəni:z], *a. and n.* Libanais, -e.

Lebanon ['lebənən]. Le Liban, *m.*

lecher ['letʃə], *n.* Libertin, *m.* **lecherous**, *a.* Lascif, libertin, lubrique. **lecherously**, *adv.* Lascivement, lubriquement, en libertin. **lecherousness** or **lechery**, *n.* Lasciveté, *f.*, libertinage, *m.*

lectern ['lektən], *n.* Lutrin, *m.*

lector ['lektə], *n.* (*Eccles.*) Lecteur, *m.*

lecture ['lektʃə], *n.* Conférence (sur), leçon (de), *f.*; (*fig.*) sermon, *m.*, semonce, *f.* *Course of lectures*, cours, *m.*; *to give a lecture*, faire une conférence.—*v.t.* Faire un cours à; (*fig.*) sermonner, semoncer.—*v.i.* Faire un cours (de), faire une conférence (sur); (*fig.*) faire un sermon, sermonner. **lecture-room**, *n.* Salle de conférences, *f.*

lecturer, *n.* Conférencier; maître de conférences, *m.* *Assistant-lecturer, part-time, temporary, lecturer*, chargé de cours, *m.* **lectureship**, *n.* Maîtrise de conférences, *f.*

led [led], *past and p.p.* [LEAD (2)]. *Led horse*, cheval de main, *m.*

ledge [ledʒ], *n.* Rebord, bord, *m.*; saillie, *f.*, banc de récifs, *m.*; (*Arch.*) saillie, *f.*

ledger ['ledʒə], *n.* Grand livre, *m.*; registre; (*Build.*) moise, filière, *f.* (of scaffolding); dalle, *f.* (of tomb); chevet, *m.* (of mine). **ledger-line**, *n.* Ligne de fond (in fishing), *f.*

lee [li:], *n.* (*Naut.*) Côté sous le vent, *m.*—*a.* Sous le vent. *Lee shore*, terre sous le vent, *f.*; *lee side*, côté sous le vent. **lee-gauge**, *n.* Dessous du vent, *m.*; (*fig.*) marge, *f.*; retard, *m.*

leech [li:tʃ], *n.* Sangsue, *f.*; *mire, médecin (doctor), *m.*; (*Naut.*) chute (of a sail), *f.*; (*fig.*) importun, collant, *m.*—*v.t.* Mettre des sangsues à; *soigner, médeciner. **leech-lines**, *n.pl.* Cargues-boulines, *f.pl.* **leech-rope**, *n.* Ralingue de chute, *f.*

*****leechcraft**, *n.* Art de guérir, *m.*; médecine, *f.*

leek [li:k], *n.* Poireau, *m.* *Stone leek*, ciboule, *f.*

leer ['liə], *n.* Œillade, *f.*; regard de côté, regard malicieux or polisson, *m.*—*v.i.* Lorgner. *To leer at*, regarder de côté or du coin de l'œil.

leeringly, *adv.* En regardant de côté d'un air polisson or moqueur. **leery**, *a.* Malin, rusé. *To be leery of*, se méfier de; soupçonner.

lees [li:z], *n.pl.* Lie, *f.*

leeward ['lu:əd], *a. and adv.* (*Naut.*) Sous le vent.

Leeward ['lu:əd] **Islands.** Les Îles sous le vent, *f.pl.*

lee-way ['li:wei], *n.* Dérive, *f.*; (*fig.*) marge, *f.*

left (1) [left], *past and p.p.* [LEAVE]. *Left-overs*, restes, *m.pl.* (of food).

left (2) [left], *a.* Gauche. *Eyes left!* (*Mil.*) tête (à) gauche! *left turn*, (*Mil.*) à gauche, gauche.—*n.* Gauche, *f.* *On the left*, à gauche; (*Polit.*) *the Left*, la gauche. **left-handed**, *a.* Gaucher; à gauche (of screws); (*fig.*) gauche. *Left-handed marriage*, mariage de la main gauche, mariage morganatique, *m.* **left-handedness**, *n.* Usage habituel de la main gauche, *m.* **left-hander,** *n.* Gaucher, -ère; (*fam.*) coup de la main gauche, *m.* **left-wing.** *a.* and *n.* **left-winger,** *n.* (*Polit.*) De la gauche.

leg [leg], *n.* Jambe; patte (of birds, insects, etc.); tige (of boots); cuisse (of poultry), *f.*; pied (of furniture); gigot (of mutton); trumeau (of beef), *m.*; branche (of compasses), *f. Blackleg* [BLACK]; *he has not a leg to stand upon,* il ne sait plus sur quel pied danser; *leg-of-mutton sleeves,* manches à gigot, *f.pl.*; on one leg, à cloche-pied; *to be on one's last legs,* tirer vers sa fin, être aux abois; *to be on one's legs,* être sur pied, être debout; *to give one a leg up,* aider à monter; *to have sea-legs,* avoir le pied marin; *to pull someone's leg,* se moquer de quelqu'un; (*pop.*) faire marcher; *to put one's best leg foremost,* se trémousser de son mieux; *to set on his legs again,* remettre sur pied; *shake your legs,* (*fam.*) dépêchez-vous; grouillez-vous; *wooden leg,* jambe de bois, *f.*, (*fam.*) pilon, *m.*
leg-bail, *n.* Fuite, *f.* **leg-guard,** *n.* Jambière, *f.* **leg-pull,** *n.* (*fam.*) Blague, *f.*
leg-rest, *n.* Appui pour la jambe, *m.*
legacy ['legəsi], *n.* Legs, *m. To come into a legacy,* faire un héritage, hériter; *to leave a legacy to,* faire un legs à. **legacy-duty,** *n.* Droits de succession, *m.pl.*
legal [li:gl], *a.* Légal, de loi, de droit, judiciaire, juridique. *To be legal tender,* avoir cours (of money).
legality [li'gæliti], *n.* Légalité, *f.*
legalization ['li:gəlai'zeiʃən], *n.* Légalisation, *f.*
legalize ['li:gəlaiz], *v.t.* Légaliser, (*fig.*) autoriser, régulariser. **legally,** *adv.* Légalement.
legate (1) ['legit], *n.* Légat, *m.*
legate (2) [le'geit], *v.t.* Léguer.
legatee [legə'ti:], *n.* Légataire, *m. General* or *residuary legatee,* légataire universel.
legation [li'geiʃən], *n.* Légation, *f.*
legator [le'geitə], *n.* Testateur, *m.*, testatrice, *f.*
legatory ['legətəri], *n.* Légataire, *m.*
legend ['ledʒənd], *n.* Légende, *f.* **legendary,** *a.* Légendaire, fabuleux. **legendry,** *n.* La légende (in general); recueil de légendes, *m.*
legerdemain [ledʒədə'mein], *n.* Tour de passe-passe, escamotage, *m.*; prestidigitation, *f.*
leger-line [ledʒə'lain], *n.* (*Mus.*) Ligne postiche *or* supplémentaire *f.*
legged [legd *or* legid], *a.* À jambes, à pieds. *Four-legged,* à quatre pattes; *two-legged,* à deux jambes, bipède. **leggings,** *n.pl.* Jambières, guêtres, *f.pl.*; leggings, *m.pl.* **leggy,** *a.* À longues jambes, dégingandé.
Leghorn [lə'gɔ:n]. Livourne. *Leghorn hat,* chapeau de paille d'Italie, *m.*; leghorn (fowl), *m. or f.*
legibility [ledʒi'biliti] *or* **legibleness** ['ledʒi blnis], *n.* Lisibilité, netteté d'écriture, *f.*, caractère lisible, *m.*
legible ['ledʒibl], *a.* Lisible. **legibly,** *adv.* Lisiblement.
legion ['li:dʒən], *n.* Légion, *f. The Foreign Legion,* la Légion (étrangère); *the American, the British Legion,* l'Association américaine, britannique, des Anciens Combattants; *their name is legion,* ils sont sans nombre, innombrables. **legionary,** *a.* De légion.—*n.* Légionnaire, *m.*

legislate ['ledʒisleit], *v.t.* Légitérer, faire des lois. **legislation** [-'leiʃən], *n.* Législation, *f.*
legislative ['ledʒislətiv], *a.* Législatif. **legislator,** *n.* Législateur, *m.* **legislature,** *n.* Corps (*or* pouvoir) législatif, *m.*
legist ['li:dʒist], *n.* Légiste, *m.*
legitimacy [lə'dʒitiməsi], *n.* Légitimité, *f.*
legitimate [lə'dʒitimət], *a.* Légitime; juste, correct, exact.—*v.t.* [-meit] Légitimer.
legitimately, *adv.* Légitimement, à bon droit. **legitimation** [-'meiʃən], *n.* Légitimation; légalisation (of currency), *f.* **legitimist,** *n.* Légitimiste, *m.* or *f.* **legitimize,** *v.t.* Légitimer.
legume ['legju:m] *or* **legumen** [lə'gju:mən], *n.* Légume, *m.*
leguminous [lə'gju:minəs], *a.* Légumineux. *Leguminous plant,* une légumineuse, *f.*
leister ['li:stə], *n.* Trident, *m.*—*v.t.* Pêcher au trident.
leisure ['leʒə], *n.* Loisir, *m.*; commodité, *f. At leisure,* de loisir; *at one's leisure,* à loisir; à tête reposée; à ses moments perdus; *to be at leisure,* être libre, avoir du loisir; *you are at leisure to come or not,* il vous est loisible de venir ou non; *you can do it in your leisure hours,* vous pouvez le faire à vos moments perdus. **leisured,** *a.* Désœuvré; de loisir (of life). *Leisured life,* vie oisive; *the leisured class* or *classes,* les oisifs. **leisureliness,** *n.* Absence de hâte, lenteur, *f.* **leisurely,** *adv.* À loisir.—*a.* Fait à loisir; mesuré, sans hâte.
lemma ['lemə], *n.* (*Math.*) Lemme, *m.*
lemon ['lemən], *n.* Citron, limon, *m. The answer is a lemon,* (*fam.*) bernique! des dattes! des nèfles! **lemonade,** *n.* Limonade, *f.*
lemon-grass, *n.* Jonc odorant, *m.* **lemon-peel,** *n.* Écorce de citron, *f.* **lemon-plant,** *n.* Verveine citronnelle, *f.* **lemon sole,** *n.* Sole limande, *f.* **lemon squash,** *n.* Citronnade, *f.* **lemon-squeezer,** *n.* Presse-citrons, *m.inv.* **lemon-tree,** *n.* Citronnier, *m.*
lemur ['li:mə *or* 'lemə], *n.* Lémur, maki, *m.* **lemurian, lemurid,** *n.* Lémurien, *m.* **lemures** ['lemjuəri:z], *n.pl.* (*Rom. Ant.*) Lémures, *m.pl.*
lend [lend], *v.t.* (*past* and *p.p.* **lent** (1)) Prêter; (*fig.*) donner. *To lend a hand to,* aider, donner la main à; donner un coup de main à; *to lend against securities,* prêter sur gages. **lender,** *n.* Prêteur, *m.*, prêteuse, *f.* **lending,** *n.* Prêt, *m. Lending library,* bibliothèque de prêt, *f.*; cabinet de lecture, *m.*
length [leŋθ], *n.* Longueur; étendue; pièce (piece), *f.*; degré, point (degree), *m.*; durée (of time), *f. At full length,* tout au long (not abridged), en toutes lettres (of writing), tout de son long (of persons); *at great length,* fort au long, longuement; *at length,* enfin; tout au long; *full length,* en pied, grandeur nature; *half length,* en buste; *over the length and breadth of the land,* par tout le pays; (*fam.*) en long et en large; *the whole length,* toute la pièce (of silks etc.); *to fall full length,* tomber de tout son long; *to go the length of thinking,* aller jusqu'à penser; *to go the whole length,* aller jusqu'au bout; *to go to great lengths,* aller bien loin; *to such lengths,* si loin; *two feet in length,* deux pieds de longueur, de long.
lengthen ['leŋθən], *v.t.* Allonger, étendre; rallonger (to piece); prolonger (time). *To*

lengthen out, étendre, prolonger.—*v.i.* S'allonger, devenir plus long, s'étendre; se prolonger (of time); croître, grandir, (*colloq.*) rallonger (of days etc.).
lengthening, *n.* Allongement, *m.*; prolongation (of time), *f.*; accroissement (of days); rallongement (piecing), *m.* **lengthily**, *adv* Longuement; tout au long. **lengthiness**, *n.* Longueur; prolixité (of a speech), *f.* **lengthways** or **lengthwise**, *adv.* En longueur, en long; dans le sens de la longueur. **lengthy**, *a.* Un peu long, ennuyeux, prolixe. *A lengthy report*, un long compte-rendu.
leniency ['li:niənsi], *n.* Douceur, clémence, indulgence (pour), *f.* **lenient**, *a.* Doux, indulgent (à, envers, or pour); (*Med.*) lénitif.
leniently, *adv.* Avec douceur, avec indulgence.
lenitive ['lenitiv], *a.* and *n.* (*Med.*) Lénitif, calmant, *m.* **lenity**, *n.* Douceur, indulgence, clémence, *f.*
leno ['li:nou], *n.* Tarlatane, *f.*
lens [lenz], *n.* (*pl.* **lenses**) (*Opt.*) Lentille, loupe, *f.*; verre (de lunette), verre grossissant, *m.*, (*Phot.*) objectif, *m.* (*Phot.*) *Front, back lens*, système antérieur, postérieur (of lens); *single, landscape lens*, objectif simple; *compound lens*, objectif composé. **lens-hood**, *n.* Parasoleil, *m.*
lent (1), *past* and *p.p.* [LEND].
Lent (2) [lent], *n.* Carême, *m. Lent term*, (*sch.*) le second trimestre. *Mid-Lent*, la mi-carême, *f.*; *to keep Lent*, faire carême. **Lenten**, *a.* De carême. **Lent-lily**, *n.* Narcisse des prés, *m.*
lenticular [len'tikjulə], *a.* Lenticulaire; lenticulé.
lentiform ['lentifɔ:m], *a.* Lentiforme.
lentigo [len'taigou], *n.* Lentigo, *m.*; tache de rousseur, *f.*
lentil ['lentil], *n.* Lentille, *f.*
lentisk ['lentisk], *n.* Lentisque, *m.*
Leo ['li:ou], *n.* Léon, *m.*; (*Astron.*) Le Lion, *m.*
leonine ['li:ənain], *a.* De lion, léonin. *Leonine convention*, contrat léonin, *m.*
leopard ['lepəd], *n.* Léopard, *m. Can the leopard change his spots?* Il mourra dans sa peau; chassez le naturel, il revient au galop; *American leopard*, jaguar, *m.*; *hunting leopard*, guépard, *m.*; *leopard cat*, ocelot, *m.*
leper ['lepə], *n.* Lépreux, *m.* **leper-house**, *n.* Léproserie, *f.*
Lepidoptera [lepi'dɔptərə], *n.pl.* (*Ent.*) Lépidoptères, *m.pl.* **lepidopteral**, *a.* Lépidoptère.
leporine ['lepərain], *a.* De lièvre.
leprechaun [lepri'kɔ:n], *n.* (*Irish Myth.*) Farfadet, lutin, *m.*
leprosy ['leprəsi], *n.* Lèpre, *f.*
leprous ['leprəs], *a.* Lépreux.
Lesbian ['lezbiən], *n.* Lesbienne, *f.* **lesbianism**, *m.* Saphisme, *m.*
lese-majesty [li:z'mædʒəsti], *n.* Lèse-majesté, *f.*
lesion ['li:ʒən], *n.* Lésion, *f.*
less [les], *a.* Moindre, plus petit, inférieur. *To grow less*, diminuer, s'amoindrir, se rapetisser; *we have less time*, nous avons moins de temps.—*adv.* Moins. *A man less*, un homme de moins; *for less than*, à moins de; *he continued none the less*, il n'en continua pas moins; *he has less than a hundred francs left*, il lui reste moins de cent francs; *he sings less*

than I, il chante moins que moi; *less and less*, de moins en moins; *no less*, rien moins, pas moins; *so much the less*, d'autant moins; *the less . . . the more . . .*, moins . . . plus. . . .—*n.* Moins; moindre, *m.*
lessee [le'si:], *n.* Locataire à bail; (*Law*) preneur, concessionnaire, *m.*
lessen [lesn], *v.t.* Diminuer, amoindrir, rapetisser, rabaisser (to lower); ralentir (to slow down).—*v.i.* Diminuer, s'amoindrir, se rapetisser. **lessening**, *n.* Amoindrissement, *m.*, diminution, *f.*
lesser ['lesə], *a.* Moindre, plus petit; (*fig.*) inférieur. *Lesser fry*, menu fretin, *m.*; *lesser rivers*, cours d'eau secondaires, *m.pl.*
lesson [lesn], *n.* Leçon, *f. English lesson*, leçon d'anglais; *to hear the lessons*, faire réciter les leçons; *let that be a lesson to you*, que cela vous serve de leçon!—*v.t.* Faire la leçon (à).
lessor [le'sɔ:], *n.* Bailleur, *m.*, bailleresse, *f.*
lest [lest], *conj.* De peur que, de crainte que (*followed by* ne *with subjunctive*).
let (1) [let], *v.t.* (*past and p.p.* **let**) Laisser, permettre à (to permit); souffrir que (*with subjunctive*); faire (to cause); louer (a house). *Do not let me disturb you*, que je ne vous dérange pas; *he was let off with a fine*, il en fut quitte pour une amende; *house to let*, maison à louer; *I will let you off the bargain*, je vous tiens quitte du marché; *let ABC be any angle*, soit A B C un angle quelconque; *let him come*, qu'il vienne; *let him go with me*, laissez-le venir avec moi; *let me hear you directly*, que je vous entende à l'instant; *let me see*, voyons; *let no one go out of the house*, que personne ne sorte; *let that child sleep*, laissez dormir cet enfant; *let there be light!* que la lumière soit! *let us go*, allons; *let well alone*, le mieux est l'ennemi du bien; *to be let with immediate possession*, à louer présentement; *to let alone*, laisser tranquille, laisser, laisser là; *to let an opportunity slip*, laisser échapper l'occasion; *to let blood*, saigner; *to let down*, descendre, faire descendre, baisser, rabattre; *to let one-one down*, manquer de parole envers quelqu'un, faire faux bond à quelqu'un, (*fam.*) laisser tomber; *to let fall*, laisser tomber, prononcer, dire; *to let fall a remark*, faire une remarque en passant; *to let go*, lâcher, lâcher prise, laisser aller; *to let have*, donner, laisser à; *to let in*, faire entrer, ouvrir la porte à, insérer; *to let into*, admettre dans, mettre dans, laisser entrer, confier à; *to let someone into a secret*, révéler un secret à quelqu'un; *to let know*, faire savoir à, informer; *to let loose*, lâcher; *to let off*, laisser partir, laisser échapper, tirer (fire-arms), faire partir (a rocket etc.), faire grâce à; *to let oneself go*, se laisser aller; *to let out*, faire sortir, laisser sortir, élargir (clothes), laisser échapper, divulguer (a secret), louer (a house); *to let see*, faire voir; *to let slide*, ne pas s'inquiéter de; *to let the cat out of the bag*, éventer la mèche, découvrir le pot aux roses; *to let up*, faire *or* laisser monter.—*v.i.* Se louer. *To let on*, (*fam.*) moucharder.
let (2) [let], *v.t.* *Empêcher.—*n.* Empêchement; obstacle, délai, *m. Let* (ball), (*Ten.*) (balle) à remettre. *Without let or hindrance*, sans entrave, en toute liberté.
let-down ['let'daun], *n.* Déception, *f.*

lethal ['li:θəl], *a.* Mortel, fatal. *Lethal chamber,* chambre d'asphyxie (in animals' pound), chambre d'exécution (for electrocution etc.), *f.*
lethargic [lə'θɑ:dʒik] or **lethargical,** *a.* Léthargique.
lethargy ['leθədʒi], *n.* Léthargie, *f.*
Lethe ['li:θi:], *n.* Léthé, *m.* **Lethean** [li'θi:ən], *a.* Du Léthé, de l'oubli.
lethiferous [lə'θifərəs], *a.* Léthifère.
letter ['letə], *n.* Lettre, *f.*; (*pl. fig.*) belles-lettres, *f.pl. Letter of attorney,* procuration, *f.*; *letter of exchange,* lettre de change, *f.*; *letter of mark,* lettre de marque, *f.*; *letters patent,* lettres patentes, *f.pl.*; *registered letter,* lettre chargée *or* recommandée, *f.*—*v.t.* Mettre le titre à. **letter-book,** *n.* Copie de lettre, *m.* **letter-box,** *n.* Boîte aux lettres, *f.* **letter-card,** *n.* Carte-lettre, *f.* **letter-case,** *n.* Porte-lettres, *m.* **letter-clip,** *n.* Serre-papiers, *m.* **letter-paper,** *n.* Papier à lettres (grand format), *m.* **letterpress,** *n.* Impression typographique, *f.* **Letterpress printing,** la typographie, *f.* **letter-writer,** *n.* Auteur de lettres; épistolier, *m.*
lettered, *a.* Lettré, savant; (*Bookb.*) avec le titre marqué au dos. **lettering,** *n.* Titre, *m.*; lettres, *f.pl.*; caractères, *m.pl.*
letting ['letin], *n.* Louage, *m. Letting out,* location, *f.*; rallongement, agrandissement (of garment), *m.*
lettuce ['letis], *n.* Laitue, *f. Cabbage lettuce,* laitue pommée; *cos lettuce,* (laitue) romaine; *lamb's lettuce,* mâche, boursette, *f.*
let-up ['letʌp], *n.* Diminution, *f.*; adoucissement, *m. We worked three days without a let-up,* nous avons travaillé trois jours sans arrêt, sans prendre le temps de respirer.
leucocyte ['lju:kosait], *n.* Leucocyte, *m.* **leucocytosis** [-'tousis], *n.* Leucocytose, *f.*
leucoma, *n.* Leucome, *m.* **leucorrhoea** [-'ri:ə], *n.* Leucorrhée, *f.*, fleurs blanches, pertes blanches, *f.pl.*
Levant [lə'vænt], *n.* Levant, *m.*—*a.* Du Levant, levantin. **levant** [le-], *v.i.* (*fam.*) Décamper, s'enfuir.
Levantine [li'væntain], *n.* Levantin (native of the Levant), *m.*; levantine (silk), *f.*
levee ['levi], *n.* *Lever, *m.*; réception (royale), *f. A levee will be held,* il y aura réception; *to hold a levee,* recevoir (of high official).
level [levl], *a.* De niveau (avec), au niveau (de); horizontal; uni (of surface); égal (à). *Level crossing,* passage à niveau, *m.*; *level with,* au niveau de, de niveau avec, à fleur de; *to do one's level best,* faire tous ses efforts; faire, travailler de son mieux; *to have a level head,* avoir le cerveau bien équilibré.—*n.* Niveau, *m.*, surface unie, *f.*; (*Mining*) galerie, *f. At an international level,* sur un plan international; *dead level,* niveau parfaitement uni, *m.*; *difference of level,* dénivellation, *f.*; *discussions at ministerial level,* discussions à l'échelon ministériel; *on a level with,* de niveau avec; *on the level,* à plat, (*slang*) sincère, honnête, digne de confiance; *speed on the level,* vitesse en palier, *f.*—*v.t.* Aplanir, niveler, mettre de niveau; pointer (fire-arms); porter, asséner (a blow). *To level down,* abaisser au même niveau; *to level out,* niveler, égaliser; *to level up,* élever au niveau de; *to level with the dust,* raser, renverser.—

v.i. Viser, mettre en joue, pointer. **level-headed,** *a.* Équilibré, pondéré, de sens rassis. **level-headedness,** *n.* Bon sens, *m.*, pondération, *f.*, équilibre, *m.* **leveller,** *n.* Niveleur, égalitaire; rouleau compresseur, *m.* **levelling,** *n.* Nivellement; arasement; pointage (of guns), *m.* **levelling-staff,** *n.* Jalon, *m.*, mire de nivellement, *f.*
lever ['li:və], *n.* Levier, *m. Hand-lever,* manette, *f.*; *reversing lever,* levier de renversement, *m.* **lever-watch,** *n.* Montre à ancre, *f.*
leveret ['levərət], *n.* Levraut, *m.*
leviable ['leviəbl], *a.* Qui peut être levé.
leviathan [lə'vaiəθən], *n.* Léviathan, *m.*
levigate ['levigeit], *v.t.* (*Pharm.*) Pulvériser; polir. **levigation** [-'geiʃən], *n.* Pulvérisation, *f.*
levitate ['leviteit], *v.i.* Se soulever (by levitation).—*v.t.* Soulever (by levitation). **levitation,** *n.* Action de rendre léger; légèreté, *f.*
Levite ['li:vait], *n.* Lévite, *m.*
Levitical [lə'vitikəl], *a.* Lévitique, des lévites. *Levitical degree,* degré (de parenté) qui empêche le mariage, *m.* **Leviticus,** *n.* Lévitique, *m.*
levity ['leviti], *n.* Légèreté, *f.*; manque de sérieux, *m.*
levy ['levi], *n.* Levée; perception (d'impôts), *f. Levy in mass,* levée en masse, *f.*—*v.t.* Lever; imposer (a fine etc.). *To levy execution on someone's goods (and chattels),* faire une saisie-exécution sur les biens de quelqu'un.
lewd [lju:d], *a.* Impudique, lascif. **lewdly,** *adv.* Impudiquement. **lewdness,** *n.* Impudicité, *f.*
lexicographer [leksi'kɔgrəfə], *n.* Lexicographe, *m.* **lexicographic** [-'græfik], *a.* Lexicographique. **lexicography,** *n.* Lexicographie, *f.* **lexicology,** *n.* Lexicologie, *f.*
lexicon ['leksikən], *n.* Lexique, dictionnaire, *m.*
Leyden jar ['laidən'dʒɑ:], *n.* Bouteille de Leyde, *f.*
liability [laiə'biliti] *n.* Responsabilité; tendance, *f.*; danger, *m.*; (*Comm.*) (*pl.*) engagements, *m.pl.*, passif, *m. Assets and liabilities,* actif et passif; *to be unable to meet one's liabilities,* ne pas pouvoir faire face à ses engagements; *to meet one's liabilities,* faire face à ses engagements.
liable ['laiəbl], *a.* Sujet (à), exposé (à), passible (de), responsable (de).
liaison [li'eizən], *n.* Liaison, *f.*; union illicite, *f.* (*Mil.*) *Liaison officer,* agent de liaison, *m.*; *to make the liaison between two words,* faire la liaison entre deux mots.
liar ['laiə], *n.* Menteur, *m.*, menteuse, *f.*
lias ['laiəs], *n.* (*Geol.*) Liais, *m.*
libation [li'beiʃən], *n.* Libation, *f.*
libel [laibl], *n.* Libelle, écrit diffamatoire, *m.*, diffamation, *f.*; calomnie, *f. Action for libel,* procès en diffamation, *m.*; *to prosecute for libel,* poursuivre en diffamation.—*v.t.* Diffamer. **libeller,** *n.* Diffamateur, libelliste, *m.* **libelling,** *n.* Diffamation, *f.* **libellous,** *a.* Diffamatoire.
liberal ['libərəl], *a.* Libéral, généreux; prodigue, abondant, copieux, ample. *Liberal arts,* arts libéraux, *m.pl.*—*n.* (*Polit.*) Libéral, *m.* **liberalism,** *n.* Libéralisme, *m.* **liberality** [-'ræliti], *n.* Libéralité, *f.*

liberalize ['libərəlaiz], *v.t.* Rendre libéral.
liberally, *adv.* Libéralement, généreusement, largement, librement.
liberate, ['libəreit], *v.t.* Libérer, rendre libre,
élargir; délivrer (de); lâcher (a pigeon).
liberation [-'reiʃən], *n.* Mise en liberté, *f.*,
élargissement (of prisoners); affranchissement,
m.; libération, délivrance, *f.*; lâcher (of a
pigeon), *m.* **liberator** ['libəreitə], *n.* Libérateur, *m.*, libératrice, *f.*
Liberia [lai'biːəriə]. Le Libéria, *m.*
libertine ['libətin], *a.* Libertin, débauché.—*n.*
Libre-penseur; libertin, m. **libertinism,** *n.*
Libertinage, *m.*; mœurs dissolues, *f.pl.*,
débauche, dissipation, *f.*
liberty ['libəti], *n.* Liberté, *f.*; privilèges, *m.pl.*,
franchises, *f.pl.* To be at liberty, être en
liberté; *to be at liberty to,* être libre de; *to set
at liberty,* mettre en liberté; *to take liberties
with,* prendre des libertés avec; *to take the
liberty of,* se permettre de.
libidinous [li'bidinəs], *a.* Libidineux.
libido ['libidou], *n.* Libido, *f.*
Libra ['laibrə], *n.* (*Astron.*) La Balance, *f.*
librarian [lai'brɛəriən], *n.* Bibliothécaire, conservateur de bibliothèque, *m.*
library ['laibrəri], *n.* Bibliothèque, *f.* Film,
record, *library,* cinémathèque, discothèque,
f.
librate [lai'breit], *v.i.* Balancer, osciller, se
tenir en équilibre. **libration** [-'breiʃən], *n.*
Balancement, *m.*; (*Astron.*) libration, *f.*
libratory, *a.* Oscillatoire.
librettist [li'bretist], *n.* Librettiste, *m.*
libretto, *n.* Libretto, livret, *m.*
Libya ['libiə]. La Lybie, *f.*
lice [lais] (*pl.*) [LOUSE].
licence ['laisəns], *n.* Licence, liberté; permission, *f.*, permis; (*fig.*) dérèglement, *m.*;
autorisation (of a preacher), *f.*; brevet (of a
bookseller), *m.*; (*Comm.*) patente, *f.* Driving
licence, permis de conduire, *m.*; gun-licence,
port d'armes; permis de chasse, *m.*; marriage-
licence, dispense de bans, *f.* **license,** *v.t.*
Autoriser, accorder un permis à. **licensed,**
a. Autorisé; breveté; (*Comm.*) patenté.
Licensed hotel, restaurant, hôtel, restaurant
qui a la permission de vendre des boissons
alcoolisées. **licensee** [-'siː], *n.* Détenteur
de patente, patenté, *m.* **licenser,** *n.* Agent
qui accorde les autorisations; censeur (of
plays), *m.*
licentiate [lai'senʃiət], *n.* Licencié; (*Ch.*)
novice, *m.*
licentious [lai'senʃəs], *a.* Licencieux, déréglé.
licentiously, *adv.* Licencieusement. **licentiousness,** *n.* Licence, *f.*, dérèglement, *m.*
lichen ['laikən], *n.* Lichen, *m.*
lich-gate ['litʃgeit], *n.* Porche (couvert) de
cimetière, *m.*
licit ['lisit], *a.* Licite, légal, permis. **licitly,**
adv. Licitement.
lick [lik], *v.t.* Lécher; laper (to lap); (*slang*)
flanquer des coups à, rosser (to beat); battre
à plate couture. *To lick into shape,* faire
prendre tournure à; *to lick someone's boots,*
lécher les bottes à quelqu'un; *to lick up,*
laper, avaler, dévorer.—*n.* Coup de langue,
m.; la chose léchée, *f.* *I gave it a lick and a
promise,* je l'ai nettoyé à la six-quatre-deux;
we were proceeding at a terrific lick, nous
allions à bride abattue, à tombeau ouvert.

lickerish ['likəriʃ], *a.* Friand; avide; lascif.
lickerishly, *adv.* Lascivement. **lickerish-
ness,** *n.* Friandise; paillardise, *f.*
licking, *n.* (*slang*) Coups, *m.pl.*; roulée,
raclée, *f.*
lick-spittle, *n.* Parasite abject, *m.*
licorice [LIQUORICE].
lictor ['liktə], *n.* (*Rom. Ant.*) Licteur, *m.*
lid [lid], *n.* Couvercle, *m.*; paupière (of the
eye), *f.*; (*Bot.*) opercule, *m.*; (*slang*) chapeau,
m. *I dip my lid to him,* je lui tire mon
chapeau; *that puts the lid on it,* ça c'est le
comble! *with the lid off,* effréné.
lie (1) [lai], *n.* Mensonge; démenti, *m.* *To give
the lie to,* donner un démenti à; *white lie,*
mensonge pieux, *m.*—*v.i.* (*past* and *p.p.* lied)
Mentir. *To lie unblushingly,* mentir comme
un arracheur de dents.
lie (2) [lai], *v.i.* (*past* lay [lei], *p.p.* lain) Être
couché, se coucher; reposer, être, être situé,
se trouver; s'appuyer (to lean); rester (to
remain); consister (to consist); (*Law*) se
soutenir. *He lay on his death-bed,* il était sur
son lit de mort; *here lies,* ci-gît; *it lies in my
power to,* il dépend de moi de; *lie down!* (to
dog) couchez! *the difference lies in this,* la
différence consiste en ceci; *the lion lay dead,*
le lion était mort; *the town lies between two
valleys,* la ville est située or se trouve entre
deux vallées; *to let lie,* laisser là; *to lie about*
(of articles), traîner çà et là; *to lie at someone's
door,* être imputable à quelqu'un; *to lie at the
root of,* être la cause de; *to lie by,* se tenir en
réserve, être tenu en réserve; *to lie down,* se
coucher, se reposer; *to lie down under an
insult,* to take an insult lying down, ne pas
relever une insulte; *to lie heavy on,* peser sur;
to lie idle, chômer, dormir (of money); *to lie
in,* être en couches, faire ses couches; *to lie in
the way,* être un obstacle; *to lie in wait,* être,
se mettre, or se tenir en embuscade, être aux
aguets; (*fam.*) *to lie low,* se tapir, rester coi;
to lie on one's oars, cesser de travailler; *to lie
to,* (*Naut.*) être à la cape; *to lie under,* être
sujet or exposé à, être sous le poids de; *to
lie with,* dépendre de; *to lie with someone,*
coucher avec quelqu'un.—*n.* Gisement, *m.*,
position, situation, *f.* *To know the lie of the
land,* (*fig.*) savoir où en sont les choses.
lie-abed, *n.* Grand dormeur, *m.*
lie-detector, *n.* Machine à déceler le mensonge, *f.*
lief [liːf], *adv.* Volontiers. *I had* (or *I would*)
as lief, j'aimerais autant.
liege [liːdʒ], *a.* Lige.—*n.* and *a.* Lige, vassal.
liege-lord, *n.* Suzerain, *m.* **liege-man,** *n.*
Homme lige, *m.*
lie-in, *n.* Grasse matinée, *f.*
lien ['liːən], *n.* Privilège, droit (de nantissement, de rétention), *m.*
lieu [ljuː], *n.* Lieu, *m.* *In lieu of,* au lieu de, en
place de.
lieutenancy [lef'tenənsi, (*Am.*) luː'tenənsi], *n.*
Lieutenance, *f.* **lieutenant,** *n.* Lieutenant,
m. Deputy lieutenant, sous-gouverneur de
comté, *m.*; second lieutenant, sous-lieutenant,
m.; lieutenant-colonel, lieutenant-colonel, *m.*;
lieutenant-commander, (*Navy*) capitaine de
corvette, *m.*; lieutenant-general, général de
division, *m.*
life [laif], *n.* (*pl.* **lives**) Vie, *f.*; homme vivant,
m.; personne, *f.*; (*fig.*) la vie, âme, vivacité, *f.*,

entrain (spirits); mouvement, *m.*; (*Lit.*) biographie, *f.*; (*Paint. etc.*) naturel, *m.* *At that time of life*, à cet âge; *fashionable life*, beau monde, *m.*; *for life*, à vie, sa vie durant, à perpétuité; *from life*, d'après nature; *high life*, le grand monde, *m.*; *I cannot for the life of me*, je ne peux pas, dussé-je y perdre la vie; *in his* or *her life*, de son vivant; *manner of life*, manière de vivre, *f.*; *many lives were lost*, un grand nombre de personnes ont péri; *never in one's life*, jamais de sa vie; *pension for life*, pension viagère, *f.*; *picture drawn to the life*, portrait d'une ressemblance frappante, *m.*; *prime of life*, fleur de l'âge, *f.*; *single life*, célibat, *m.*; *to come to life*, s'animer; revenir à la vie; *to depart this life*, quitter cette vie, mourir; *to fly for one's life*, chercher son salut dans la fuite; *to give life to*, donner de la vie à; *to see life*, s'amuser; *to set up in life*, lancer dans la vie; *to the life*, au naturel. **life-annuity**, *n.* Rente viagère, *f.* **life-belt**, *n.* Ceinture de sauvetage, *f.* **life-blood**, *n.* (*fig.*) Le sang, *m.*, l'âme, *f.* **life-boat**, *n.* Canot de sauvetage, *m.* **life-buoy**, *n.* Bouée de sauvetage, *f.* **life-giving**, *a.* Vivifiant. **lifeguard**, *n.* Garde du corps; (*pl.*) les Gardes du corps, *m.pl.* **lifeguardsman**, *n.* Cavalier de la garde, *m.* **life-insurance**, *n.* Assurance sur la vie, *f.* **life-interest**, *n.* Usufruit, *m.*, rente viagère, *f.* **lifeless**, *a.* Sans vie, inanimé; (*fig.*) sans vigueur, sans mouvement. **lifelessly**, *adv.* Sans vie; sans vigueur. **lifelessness**, *n.* Absence de vie; absence de mouvement, *f.* **lifelike**, *a.* Comme un être vivant, d'après nature, vivant, ressemblant. **life-line**, *n.* (*Naut.*) Garde-corps, garde-fou, *m.* **life-long**, *a.* De toute la vie. **life-peer**, *n.* Pair à vie, *m.* **life-policy**, *n.* Police d'assurance sur la vie, *f.* **life-preserver**, *n.* Appareil de sauvetage; casse-tête (weapon), *m.* **life-size**, *a.* Grandeur nature. **lifetime**, *n.* Vie, *f.*, vivant, *m.* *In his lifetime*, de son vivant; *it will last a lifetime*, c'est inusable.

lift [lift], *n.* Action de lever or de soulever, *f.*, élévation, *f.*, effort; coup de main (help), *m.*; monte-charge (hoisting-machine); élévateur, ascenseur, *m.*; (*Naut.*) balancine, *f.* *To give a lift to*, donner un coup de main à, faire monter avec soi (dans sa voiture).—*v.t.* Lever, soulever, hausser, soupeser (to try the weight of); (*fig.*) élever, relever; (*Sc.* and *Irish*) voler; (*Lit.*) plagier. **lift-boy**, **lift-man**, *n.* Liftier, *m.* **lift-girl**, *n.* Liftière, *f.* **lifting**, *n.* Action de lever, *f.*; enlèvement (de bétail), *m.* **lifting-jack**, *n.* Cric, *m.*

ligament ['ligəmənt], *n.* Ligament; (*fig.*) lien, *m.* **ligamentous** [-'mentəs], *a.* Ligamenteux.

ligature ['ligətʃə], *n.* Ligature, *f.*; (*Mus.*) liaison, *f.*—*v.t.* Ligaturer.

light (1) [lait], *n.* Lumière, *f.*, jour (daylight); clair (of the moon etc.), *m.*; clarté (of the eye etc.); lueur, *f.*; feu; (*fig.*) aspect, point de vue, *m.*, lumière, *f.* *Advertising lights*, enseignes lumineuses, *f.pl.*; *by the light of*, à la lumière de, à la clarté de; *electric light*, éclairage à l'électricité; *in its true light*, sous son vrai jour; *it is light*, il fait jour, il fait clair; *light and shade*, clair-obscur, *m.*; *lights out*, (*Mil.*) l'extinction des feux; (*Av.*) *navigation lights*,

feux de bord, *m.pl.*; *not to stand in someone's light*, ne pas cacher le jour à or ne pas chercher à nuire à quelqu'un; *riding lights*, (*Naut.*) feux de position, *m.pl.*; *this picture is not in the right light*, ce tableau n'est pas bien éclairé; *to be a leading light*, (*fig.*) être une lumière; *to bring to light*, révéler, mettre au jour; *to come to light*, se manifester; *to give light to*, éclairer; *to see* (*the*) *light*, voir la lumière; *to see the red light*, flairer le danger; *to stand in one's own light*, (*fig.*) se nuire; *to switch on the light*, allumer (l'électricité); *to throw light on a subject*, jeter de la lumière sur un sujet; *traffic lights*, signaux lumineux, *m.pl.*; *will you give me a light?* voulez-vous me donner du feu?—*v.t.* (*past* and *p.p.* **lighted** or **lit**) Allumer; illuminer, éclairer (of windows etc.). *To light a candle*, allumer une chandelle; *to light the streets*, éclairer les rues; *to light up*, éclairer.—*v.i.* (*past* and *p.p.* **lighted**) *To light up*, briller, s'enflammer, s'animer, s'épanouir; *to light upon*, descendre or tomber sur; rencontrer. **lighting**, *n.* Éclairage, *m.* *Lighting-up time*, heure d'éclairage, *f.* **lightless**, *a.* Sans lumière, sans feu, éteint. **light-year**, *n.* Année-lumière, *f.*

light (2) [lait], *a.* Léger; (*fig.*) gai, frivole, léger (of morals); clair (of colour etc.); blond (of complexion). *Light artillery*, artillerie légère, *f.*; *light engine*, locomotive haut-le-pied, *f.*; *to make light of*, faire peu de cas de. **light-fingered**, *a.* Qui a les doigts crochus, fripon. **light-headed**, *a.* Qui a la tête légère, étourdi; en délire. **light-hearted**, *a.* Gai, réjoui. **light-heartedness**, *n.* Enjouement, *m.*, gaieté, *f.* **lightly**, *adv.* Légèrement, à la légère; lestement, facilement, aisément; gaiement. **light-minded**, *a.* Léger, frivole, volage, inconstant. **lightness**, *n.* Légèreté, *f.* **light-weight**, *n.* (*Box.*) Poids léger, *m.*; (*fig.*) personne de peu de poids, *f.*

lighten [laitn], *v.t.* Éclairer, illuminer; soulager, alléger (to alleviate).—*v.i.* Éclairer; faire des éclairs. **lightening**, *n.* Éclaircissement; allègement; soulagement, *m.*

lighter ['laitə], *n.* Personne qui allume, *f.*, allumeur, *m.*, allumeuse, *f.*; briquet, *m.* (for cigarettes); (*Naut.*) allège, gabare, *f.*, chaland, *m.* **lighterage**, *n.* Frais d'allège, *m.pl.* **lighterman**, *n.* Gabarier, *m.*

lighthouse ['laithaus], *n.* Phare, feu, *m.* **lighthouse-keeper**, *n.* Gardien de phare, *m.*

lightning ['laitniŋ], *n.* Éclair, *m.*, les éclairs, *m.pl.*; foudre, *f.* *Flash of lightning*, éclair, *m.*; *lightning progress*, progrès foudroyants, *m.pl.*; *like greased lightning*, aussi vite que l'éclair, en un clin d'œil; *sheet lightning*, éclairs de chaleur, *m.pl.*; *struck by lightning*, frappé de la foudre. **lightning-rod** or **lightning-conductor**, *n.* Paratonnerre, *m.*

lights [laits], *n.pl.* Mou (of animals), *m.*

lightship ['laitʃip], *n.* Bateau-feu, *m.*

lightsome ['laitsəm], *a.* Clair, éclairé; (*fig.*) gai, riant; gracieux, agile.

ligneous ['liɡniəs], *a.* Ligneux. **lignify**, *v.t.* Lignifier.—*v.i.* Se lignifier. **lignite**, *n.* Lignite, *m.*

lignum vitae ['lignəm 'vaiti:], *n.* (Bois de) gaïac, *m.*

like (1) [laik], *a.* and *prep.* Semblable, tel, pareil; même, égal, *vraisemblable. *As like as not*, bien probablement; *does this portrait look like him?* est-ce que ce portrait lui ressemble? *like master, like man*, tel maître, tel valet; *that is just like you*, c'est bien vous, je vous reconnais bien là; *that is something like!* à la bonne heure! *to be as like as two peas*, se ressembler comme deux gouttes d'eau; *to be like*, ressembler à; *to feel like doing something*, avoir envie de faire quelque chose; *to look like*, avoir l'air de, ressembler à; *to sing like a bird*, chanter comme un oiseau; *what is he like?* comment est-il?—*n.* Chose pareille, *f.*, pareil, *m.*; même chose, *f. And the like*, et autres choses pareilles; *suchlike*, choses semblables, *f.pl.*; *the likes of you*, les gens de votre sorte, les personnes comme vous; *to do the like*, en faire autant; *to give like for like*, rendre la pareille.

like (2) [laik], *v.t.* Aimer bien, trouver bon, trouver bien; vouloir, vouloir bien, désirer, plaire, être bien aise (de). *As you like*, comme il vous plaira, comme vous voudrez; *come when you like*, venez quand vous voudrez; *he will do as he likes*, (j'ai beau dire), il en fera à sa tête; *how do you like your tea?* comment prenez-vous votre thé? or comment trouvez-vous votre thé? *I do not like it at all*, il ne me plaît guère, je ne le trouve pas bon du tout; *I should like nothing better*, je ne demande pas mieux (que de); *I should like to go there*, je voudrais bien y aller; *if you like*, si vous voulez, si bon vous semble; *to like best*, aimer mieux, préférer.—*n.* Goût, *m.*; préférence, *f. Everyone has his likes and dislikes*, chacun a son goût, des goûts et des couleurs il ne faut pas disputer.

likeable ['laikəbl], *a.* Sympathique, aimable.

likelihood ['laiklihud] or **likeliness**, *n.* Probabilité, vraisemblance, *f. In all likelihood*, selon toute apparence.

likely ['laikli], *a.* Probable, vraisemblable. *He is likely to come*, il est probable qu'il viendra; *he was most likely ignorant of it*, il est très probable qu'il l'ignorait; *I am likely to call on you*, j'irai probablement vous voir; *not likely!* pas de danger! *very likely*, c'est bien possible.—*adv.* Probablement, vraisemblablement.

liken [laikn], *v.t.* Comparer (à or avec); faire ressembler (à).

likeness ['laiknis], *n.* Ressemblance; apparence, *f.*, portrait, air, *m. To have one's likeness taken*, faire faire son portrait.

likewise, *adv.* Également, pareillement, de même, aussi.

liking, *n.* Gré, goût, penchant, *m.*, inclination *f.*; amitié, *f. To have a liking for*, avoir du goût pour; *to take a liking to*, prendre goût à.

lilac ['lailək], *n.* Lilas, *m.*

liliaceous [lili'eiʃəs], *a.* Liliacé.

lilt [lilt], *v.i.* Chanter gaiement.—*n.* Chant joyeux, *m.*; forte cadence, *f.*

lily ['lili], *n.* Lis, *m.* Belladonna lily, amaryllis, *f.*; *lily of the valley*, muguet, *m.* **lily-livered**, *a.* (*fam.*) Froussard, poltron.

limb [lim], *n.* Membre (of the body); (*colloq.*) enfant terrible, *m.*; bord (edge), *m.*; grosse branche (of a tree), *f.*; (*Astron.*) limbe, *m.*

Limb of the law, suppôt de justice, représentant de la loi, flic, *m.*; *out on a limb*, sur la corde raide; *to tear limb from limb*, mettre en pièces. **limbed**, *a.* Membré.

limber (1) ['limbə], *a.* Souple, flexible; (*fig.*) agile.—*v.t.* Assouplir.—*v.i.* To limber up, se chauffer les muscles. **limberness**, *n.* Souplesse, *f.*

limber (2) ['limbə], *n.* Avant-train, *m. Limber boxes*, coffres à munitions, *m.pl.*—*v.i.* To limber up, amener l'avant-train.

limbless ['limlis], *a.* Sans membres.

limbo ['limbou], *n.* Limbes, *m.pl.*, (*fig.*) prison, *f.*; oubli, *m.*

lime (1) [laim], *n.* (*Bot.*) Lime, limette, *f.* **lime-juice**, *n.* Jus de limette, *m.* **lime-tree**, *n.* Tilleul (linden); limettier, *m.*

lime (2) [laim], *n.* Chaux; glu (for catching birds), *f.*—*v.t.* Engluer, prendre au gluau; (*fig.*) prendre dans un piège; (*Agric.*) chauler. **lime-burner**, *n.* Chaufournier, *m.* **lime-kiln**, *n.* Four à chaux, *m.* **limelight**, *n.* Lumière oxyhydrique, *f.*; (*Theat.*) les feux de la rampe, *m.pl. To be in the limelight*, être en évidence. **lime-pit**, *n.* Carrière de pierre à chaux, *f.* **limestone**, *n.* Pierre à chaux, *f.*; (*Geol.*) calcaire, *m.* **lime-water**, *n.* Eau de chaux, *f.*

limen ['limən], *n.* (*Psych.*) Seuil, *m.*

limerick ['limərik], *n.* Petit poème comique ou satirique en cinq vers, *m.*

limey ['laimi], *n.* (*Am.*) Matelot or bateau anglais; (*Austral.*) Anglais nouveau arrivé.

liminal ['liminəl], *a.* Liminaire, de seuil.

limit ['limit], *n.* Limite, borne, *f.*; (*pl.*) cadre, *m. Limits of a fortress*, limites de la garnison, *f.pl.*; (*fam.*) *that's the limit!* ça c'est le comble!—*v.t.* Limiter, borner, restreindre. *To limit the meaning of a word*, limiter le sens d'un mot. **limitable**, *a.* Qu'on peut limiter. **limitation** [-'teiʃən], *n.* Limitation, restriction; (*Law*) prescription, *f.* **limitative**, *a.* Limitatif. **limited**, *a.* Limité, borné; (*Math.*) déterminé; (*Comm.*) à responsabilité limitée, anonyme. *Limited monarchy*, monarchie constitutionnelle, *f.* **limitedly**, *adv.* Avec des limites. **limitless**, *a.* Sans limite.

limn [lim], *v.t.* *Enluminer; peindre, dessiner. **limner** ['limnə], *n.* Peintre, *m.* **limning** ['limiŋ], *n.* *Enluminure; peinture, *f.*

limousine [limu'zi:n], *n.* Limousine, *f.*

limp [limp], *a.* Mou, flasque, sans consistance. —*v.i.* Boiter. *Limping verse*, vers boiteux, *m.*; *to limp along*, aller clopin-clopant. **limpingly**, *adv.* En boitant, clopin-clopant.

limpet ['limpit], *n.* Lépas, *m.*, patelle, *f.*

limpid ['limpid], *a.* Limpide. **limpidity** [-'piditi] or **limpidness**, *n.* Limpidité, *f.*

limy ['laimi], *a.* Calcaire; gluant (viscous).

linch-pin ['lintʃpin], *n.* Esse; clavette (d'essieu), *f.*

linden ['lindən], *n.* (*Bot.*) Tilleul, *m.*

line [lain], *n.* Ligne; corde, *f.*, cordeau, *m.* (string); file, *f.*, alignement (row); trait (dash), *m.*; raie (streak), *f.*; contour (outline), *m.*; ride (wrinkle), *f.*; (*Rail.*) voie; lignée, race (family), *f.*; [PLUMB-LINE]; (*fig.*) genre (d'affaires etc.); (*Pros.*) vers; mot, petit mot (short letter), *m.*; limite (limit), *f.*; (*Naut.*) service, *m.*; (*Mil.*) haie, *f. Air-line*, ligne aérienne; *double line*, voie double, *f.*; *fighting*

line, ligne de combat; (*Teleph.*) *hold the line!* ne quittez pas! *in a line*, en ligne, aligné; *infantry of the line*, infanterie de ligne, *f.*; *it is hard lines*, c'est dur, c'est bien rude; *leading line*, article de réclame, *m.*; *line of battle*, ordre de bataille, *m.*; *line of business* or *country*, partie, *f.*, métier, *m.*; *line of fire*, ligne de tir; *line of sight*, ligne de mire, *f.*; *main line*, voie principale, grande ligne, *f.*; *not in my line*, pas de mon ressort; *send or drop me a line*, envoyez-moi un mot; *ship of the line*, vaisseau de ligne, *m.*; *single line*, (*Rail.*) voie unique, *f.*; *to come into line with the others*, se ranger avec les autres; *to draw the line somewhere*, savoir s'arrêter; *to shoot a line*, galéjer, exagérer son importance; *to toe the line*, rentrer dans l'obéissance *or* dans le rang.—*v.t.* Ligner; régler; rayer; doubler (garments); garnir (de); border (de); revêtir (walls). *To line up*, aligner, mettre en ligne. —*v.i.* Aligner; niveler.

lineage ['liniədʒ], *n.* Lignée, race, famille, *f.*

lineal ['liniəl], *a.* Linéaire; (*Genealogy*) en ligne directe, linéal. **lineally**, *adv.* En ligne directe. **lineament**, *n.* Trait, linéament, *m.* **linear**, *a.* Linéaire.

line-engraving, *n.* Taille-douce, *f.* **line-fishing**, *n.* Pêche à la ligne, *f.* **line-shooter**, *n.* Galéjeur, *m.* **line-shooting**, *n.* Galéjade, *f.*

linen ['linin], *n.* Toile, toile de lin, *f.*, lin; linge (clothes), *m. Clean linen*, linge blanc, *m.*; *dirty linen*, linge sale, *m.*; *one must not wash one's dirty linen in public*, il faut laver son linge sale en famille.—*a.* De toile. **linen-draper**, *n.* Marchand de nouveautés, de toiles, *m.* **linen-drapery**, *n.* Nouveautés, *f.pl.* **linen-fold**, *a.* (Panelling) À plis de serviette. **linen-press, linen-cupboard**, *n.* Armoire à linge, *f.* **linen-room**, *n.* Lingerie, *f.* **linen-thread** or **-yarn**, *n.* Fil de lin, *m.* **linen-warehouse**, *n.* Magasin de blanc, *m.*

liner ['lainə], *n.* (*Naut.*) Paquebot de ligne, transatlantique, *m.*; doubleur (d'habits), *m.*; (*Eng.*) chemise, *f.*, manchon, *m.*; fileteur, *m.*

linesman, *n.* (*Mil.*) Lignard, *m.* (*colloq.*); (*Ftb.*) arbitre de touche; (*Ten.*) arbitre de lignes, *m.*; (*Teleg. etc.*) poseur de lignes, surveillant de lignes, *m.*

ling [liŋ], *n.* (*Bot.*) Bruyère, *f.*; (*Ichth.*) lingue, morue (longue), *f.*

linger ['liŋgə], *v.i.* Traîner, tarder; hésiter. *To linger behind*, rester en arrière. **lingerer**, *n.* Traînard, *m.* **lingering**, *n.* Retard, *m.*, lenteur; hésitation, *f.*—*a.* Qui tarde, qui traîne, lent; languissant. *Lingering illness*, maladie de langueur, *f.* **lingeringly**, *adv.* Lentement, avec langueur; avec hésitation.

lingerie ['lɛ̃:ʒəri:], *n.* Lingerie de femme, *f.*

lingo ['liŋgou], *n.* (*slang*) Jargon, *m.*; langue, *f.*

lingua franca ['liŋgwə 'fræŋkə], *n.* Sabir, *m.*

lingual ['liŋgwəl], *a.* Lingual. **linguiform**, *a.* Linguiforme. **linguist**, *n.* Linguiste, *m.* **linguistic** [-'gwistik], *a.* Linguistique.—*n.pl.* Linguistique, *f.*

liniment ['linimənt], *n.* Liniment, *m.*

lining ['lainiŋ], *n.* Doublure; garniture (of garments), *f.*; coiffe (of a hat), *f.*; (*Build.*) revêtement, *m.*; (*fig.*) intérieur, *m.*, paroi, *f. Glazed lining*, lustrine, *f.*

link [liŋk], *n.* Chaînon, anneau, maillon, *m.*; (*Naut.*) paillon, *m.*; torche, *f.*, flambeau (torch); (*fig.*) lien, *m.*; trait d'union, *m.*; (*pl.*) lande, *f.* (*Av.*) *Air link*, liaison aérienne, *f.*; *cuff-links*, boutons de manchettes (à chaînettes), *m.pl.*; *golf-links*, terrain de golf, *m.*—*v.t.* Lier, relier (avec); enchaîner (dans); unir.—*v.i.* S'allier (à). **linkage**, *n.* (*Motor.*) Timonerie, *f.*; chaînons, *m.pl.* ***link-boy** or **-man**, *n.* Porte-flambeau, *m.* **link-motion**, *n.* Mécanisme de détente, *m.*, coulisse, *f.*

linnet ['linit], *n.* Linotte, *f.*, linot, *m.*

linoleum [li'nouljəm], *n.* Linoléum, *m.*

linotype ['lainotaip], *n.* Linotype, *f.* **linotyper** or **linotypist**, *n.* Linotypiste, *m.*

linseed ['linsi:d], *n.* Graine de lin, *f.* **linseed-meal**, *n.* Farine de (graine de) lin, *f.* **linseed-oil**, *n.* Huile de lin, *f.* **linseed-poultice**, *n.* Cataplasme de farine de lin, *m.*

linsey-woolsey ['linzi'wulzi], *n.* Tiretaine, *f.*; (*fig.*) galimatias, *m.*

*****linstock** ['linstɔk], *n.* Boute-feu, *m.*

lint [lint], *n.* Charpie, *f.*

lintel ['lintl], *n.* Linteau, *m.*

lion ['laiən], *n.* Lion, *m.*; (*fig.*) célébrité, *f. Lion's cub*, lionceau, *m.*; *the lion's share*, la part du lion; *to rush into the lion's mouth*, se mettre dans la gueule du lion. **lion-hearted**, *a.* Au cœur de lion. **lion-tamer**, *n.* Dompteur de lions,' *m.*

lioness ['laiənes], *n.* Lionne, *f.* **lionize**, *v.t.* Faire une célébrité de; visiter, montrer les curiosités de.

lip [lip], *n.* Lèvre; babine (of some beasts), *f.*; bord (of things); bec (of a jug), *m.*; (*fig.*) insolence, impertinence, *f. To keep a stiff upper lip*, tenir le coup, faire bonne contenance; *to open one's lips*, desserrer les dents. **lip-read**, *v.t.*, *v.i.* Lire sur les lèvres. **lip-salve**, *n.* Pommade pour les lèvres, *f.* **lip-service**, *n.* Paroles insincères, *f.pl. To pay lip service to*, payer de bonnes paroles. **lipstick**, *n.* Bâton de rouge, *m.*

liquation [li'kweiʃən], *n.* (*Metal.*) Liquation, *f.* **liquefaction** [likwi'fækʃən], *n.* Liquéfaction, *f.* **liquefiable**, *a.* Liquéfiable.

liquefy ['likwifai], *v.t.* Liquéfier.—*v.i.* Se liquéfier.

liquescent [li'kwesənt], *a.* Qui se liquéfie.

liqueur [li'kjuə], *n.* Liqueur, *f.*

liquid ['likwid], *a.* Liquide; doux, coulant; limpide, clair.—*n.* Liquide, *m.* **liquidate**, *v.t.* Liquider; (*pop.*) arranger. **liquidation** [-'deiʃən], *n.* Liquidation, *f.*, acquittement (of a debt), *m.* **liquidator**, *n.* Liquidateur, *m.*

liquidity [li'kwiditi], *n.* Liquidité, *f.*

liquor ['likə], *n.* (*Chem.*) Liqueur, solution, *f.*; (*Cook.*) jus, *m.*; (*Am.*) boisson alcoolique, *f. In liquor*, ivre, gris; *to be the worse for liquor*, être pris de boisson. (*Am.*) *Hard liquor*, alcool, *m.*—*v.t.* Graisser (le cuir). *To liquor up*, (*colloq.*) enivrer.—*v.i.* Boire, chopiner.

liquorice ['likəris], *n.* Réglisse, *f.*

Lisbon ['lizbən]. Lisbonne, *f.*

lisp [lisp], *v.t.*, *v.i.* Dire (θ, ð) au lieu de (s, z); (*colloq.*) susurrer, zozoter. **lisper**, *n.* Personne qui a cette défaut de prononciation.

lissom ['lisəm], *a.* Souple, leste.

list (1) [list], *n.* Liste, *f.*, rôle, tableau, *m.*; (*Naut.*) bande; lisière (selvedge of cloth), *f.*; (*Arch.*) listel, *m.*; (*pl.*) lice, arène (arena), *f. Army List*, annuaire de l'armée, *m.*; *Civil*

List, liste civile, *f.*; *list of bills for collection*, bordereau d'effets à encaisser, *m.*; *list of wines*, carte des vins, *f.*; *on the sick list*, souffrant; *retired list*, cadre de retraite, *m.*; *to enter the lists*, entrer en lice.—*v.t.* Enrôler, enregistrer, cataloguer (to enrol).—*v.i.* S'engager, s'enrôler (to enlist); (*Naut.*) donner de la bande. **list-shoe**, *n.* Chausson, *m.*

*list (2) [list], *v.i.* Vouloir, désirer (to choose); écouter (to listen). (*Impers.*) *The wind bloweth where it listeth*, le vent souffle où cela lui plaît.

listel [listl], *n.* (*Arch.*) Listel, *m.*

listen [lisn], *v.i.* Écouter. *To listen in*, capter, surprendre (une conversation); (*Rad.*) être (*or* se mettre) à l'écoute, écouter la T.S.F. *or* la radio; *to listen* (*out*) *for*, chercher à entendre; *to listen to someone*, écouter quelqu'un; *listening-post*, poste d'écoute, *m.* **listener** ['lisnə], *n.* Auditeur; (in a bad sense) écouteur, *m.* **listener-in**, *n.* Sansfiliste; auditeur.

listless ['listlis], *a.* Nonchalant, insouciant, inattentif; apathique. **listlessly**, *adv.* Nonchalamment, avec insouciance; inattentivement. **listlessness**, *n.* Nonchalance, insouciance; apathie, inertie; inattention, *f.*

lit, *past* and *p.p.* [LIGHT (1)].

litany ['litəni], *n.* Litanie, *f.*

literacy ['litərəsi], *n.* Aptitude à lire et à écrire, *f.*

literal ['litərəl], *a.* Littéral. **literal-minded**, *a.* Prosaïque.

literality [litə'ræliti] or **literalness**, *n.* Littéralité, *f.*, sens littéral, *m.* **literally**, *adv.* Littéralement, à la lettre, au pied de la lettre.

literarily ['litərərili], *adv.* Littérairement. **literary**, *a.* Littéraire; lettré (of persons). *Literary man*, littérateur, homme de lettres, *m.*

literate ['litərət], *a.* Qui sait lire et écrire.

literati [litə'reitai], *n.pl.* Hommes de lettres, littérateurs, *m.pl.*

literature ['litəritʃə], *n.* Littérature, *f.*; les œuvres littéraires, *f.pl.*; la carrière des lettres, *f.*

litharge [li'θɑːdʒ], *n.* Litharge, *f.*

lithe [laið] or **lithesome**, *a.* Pliant, flexible, souple. **litheness**, *n.* Flexibilité, souplesse, *f.*

lithium ['liθiəm], *n.* Lithium, *m.* *Lithium-bearing mineral*, minéral lithinifère, *m.*

lithograph ['liθogræf], *n.* Lithographie, *f.*—*v.t.* Lithographier.

lithographer [li'θogrəfə], *n.* Lithographe, *m.* **lithographic** ['græfik] or **lithographical**, *a.* Lithographique. **lithographically**, *adv.* Par la lithographie.

lithography [li'θogrəfi], *n.* Lithographie, *f.*

lithopone ['liθəpoun], *n.* Lithopone, *m.*

lithotome ['liθotoum], *n.* (*Surg.*) Lithotome, *m.* **lithotomic** [-'tɔmik], *a.* De *or* par la lithotomie. **lithotomy**, *n.* Lithotomie, *f.*

lithotritor ['liθətraitə], *n.* Lithotriteur, *m.*

lithotrity [li'θotriti], *n.* Lithotritie, *f.*

lithotype ['liθətaip], *n.* Lithotypographie, *f.*

Lithuania [liθju'einiə]. La Lituanie *or* Lithuanie, *f.*

litigant ['litigənt], *a.* En litige, litigant.—*n.* Plaideur, *m.* **litigate**, *v.t.* Plaider, disputer. —*v.i.* Être en procès. **litigation** [-'geiʃən], *n.*

Litige; procès, *m.* **litigious** [-'tidʒəs], *a.* Litigieux, contentieux; processif (of persons).

litigiously, *adv.* Contentieusement; en chicaneur. **litigiousness**, *n.* Esprit litigieux, *m.*; chicane, *f.*

litmus ['litməs], *n.* Tournesol, *m.* **litmus-paper**, *n.* Papier tournesol, *m.*

litotes ['laitotiːz], *n.* (*Rhet.*) Litote, *f.*

litre ['liːtə], *n.* Litre, *m.*

litter ['litə], *n.* Litière, civière (vehicle), *f.*; ordures, *f.pl.*, détritus, *m.pl.*; (*fig.*) fouillis, désordre, *m.*; portée (of animals), *f.*—*v.t.* Joncher; jeter çà et là, mettre en fouillis; (*fig.*) mettre en désordre; mettre bas (of animals); salir. *To litter down* (of horse), faire la litière à.

litter-bin ['litəbin], *n.* Boîte à ordures, *f.*

little [litl], *a.* Petit; minime, exigu; mesquin. *Little mind*, petit esprit, *m.*; *little one*, enfant, petit, petit enfant, *m.*—*n.* Peu, *m.* *To think little of*, faire peu de cas de.—*adv.* Peu, un peu, pas beaucoup, peu de chose, peu de, guère de. *A little*, un peu; *as little as possible*, le moins possible; *be it ever so little*, si peu que ce soit; *ever so little* or *however little*, tant soit peu; *little by little*, petit à petit, peu à peu; *little or none*, peu ou point; *not a little*, pas mal de. **littleness**, *n.* Petitesse, *f.*

littoral ['litərəl], *a.* and *n.* Littoral, *m.*

liturgic [li'təːdʒik] or **liturgical**, *a.* Liturgique.

liturgy ['litədʒi], *n.* Liturgie, *f.*

live (1) [liv], *v.i.* Vivre; résider, demeurer, habiter (reside); se nourrir (de); survivre. *As long as he lives*, tant qu'il vivra; *enough to live on*, de quoi vivre; *long live the Queen!* vive la Reine! *to live by*, vivre de; *to live down*, arriver à vaincre, survivre à; *to live down a scandal*, faire oublier un scandale avec le temps; *to live from hand to mouth*, vivre au jour le jour; *to live happily* or *unhappily*, faire bon or mauvais ménage; *to live happy days*, couler des jours heureux; *to live in London*, demeurer à Londres, habiter Londres; *to live one's life*, vivre (de) sa vie; *to live out of the house*, ne pas coucher à la maison; *to live upon*, vivre de, se nourrir de; *to live up to one's income*, vivre selon ses moyens; *to live up to one's reputation*, faire honneur à sa réputation; *to live well*, faire bonne chère.—*v.t.* Mener (une vie).

live (2) [laiv], *a.* En vie, vivant; ardent, allumé, vif (of coals); (*Elec.*) chargé. *Live-bait*, amorce vive, *f.*; *live cartridge*, cartouche chargée, *f.*; *live claim*, créance valable, *f.*; *live rail*, rail conducteur, *m.*; *livestock*, bétail, *m.*; *live weight*, poids utile, *m.*; *live wire*, fil sous tension, *m.*; (*fig.*) personne énergique, *f.*

lived [livd], *a.* De vie. *Long-lived*, qui vit longtemps, de longue vie; *short-lived*, d'une courte vie, passager, de courte durée.

livelihood ['laivlihud], *n.* Vie, subsistance, *f.*; gagne-pain, *m.*; moyens d'existence, *m.pl.*

liveliness ['laivlinis], *n.* Vivacité, gaieté, *f.*

livelong ['livlɔŋ], *a.* Durable, long, sans fin. *The livelong day*, toute la sainte journée.

lively ['laivli], *a.* Vif, gai, enjoué, animé; vivant (of a place).

liven [laivn], *v.t.* *To liven up*, animer, activer.

liver (1) ['livə], *n.* *Fast liver*, viveur, noceur, *m.*; *good liver*, bon vivant, *m.*; *loose liver*, débauché, *m.*

liver (2) ['livə], *n.* Foie, *m.* **liver-coloured,** *a.* Rouge foncé. **liver-complaint,** *n.* Maladie de foie, *f.* **liverwort,** *n.* Hépatique, *f.*
livered, *a.* Lily-livered, au foie blanc, peureux, poltron. **liverish,** *a.* Qui a le foie dérangé. *I feel liverish,* je me sens mal en train.
livery ['livəri], *n.* Livrée; pension (for horses), *f. Full livery,* grande livrée; *to put out at livery,* mettre en pension (horses); *undress livery,* petite livrée. **liveryman,** *n.* (*pl.* **liverymen**) Homme qui porte la livrée; (City of London) membre d'une corporation, *m.* **livery-stable,** *n.* Écurie de chevaux de louage; pension pour les chevaux, *f. Livery-stable keeper,* loueur de chevaux, *m.*
lives [laivz], *pl.* [LIFE].
livestock [LIVE (2)].
Livia ['liviə]. Livie, *f.*
livid ['livid], *a.* Livide, blême. **lividity** [-'viditi] or **lividness,** *n.* Lividité, *f.*
living ['livin], *n.* Vie, subsistance, existence, *f.*; genre de vie, *m.,* chère, *f.,* entretien, *m.*; (*Eccles.*) bénéfice, *m.,* cure, *f. For a living,* pour vivre, pour gagner sa vie; *standard of living,* niveau de vie, *m.*; *to earn one's* (or *get a) living,* gagner sa vie *or* de quoi vivre; *to work for one's living,* travailler pour gagner sa vie.—*a.* En vie, vivant; vif. *Living force,* force vive, *f.*; *living or dead,* mort ou vif; *living wage,* salaire minimum, *m.*; *the living,* les vivants, *m.pl.*; *we didn't see a living soul,* nous n'avons pas vu âme qui vive; *while living,* de son vivant. **living-room,** *n.* Salle de séjour, *f.*
Livy ['livi]. Tite-Live, *m.*
lixiviate [lik'sivieit], *v.t.* Lixivier, lessiver. **lixiviation** [-'eiʃən], *n.* Lixiviation, *f.* **lixivium,** *n.* Lessive, *f.*
lizard ['lizəd], *n.* Lézard, *m.*
llama ['lɑːmə], *n.* Lama, *m.*
lo! [lou], *int.* Voici, voilà, voyez, regardez. *Lo and behold!* voilà que!
loach [loutʃ], *n.* (*Ichth.*) Loche, *f.*
load [loud], *n.* Charge, *f.,* fardeau; (*fig.*) poids; chargement, *m.,* charretée (cartful), *f. He gives way under the load,* il succombe sous le poids; *peak load* (*Elec.*), charge maximum, *f.*; *to take a load off someone's mind,* soulager l'esprit à quelqu'un.—*v.t.* Charger; (*fig.*) combler, accabler (de). *Loaded stick,* canne plombée, *f.*; (*pop.*) *to be loaded* (of person), être soûl; *to load a man with insults,* accabler un homme d'injures; *to load dice,* piper des dés; *to load wine,* frelater du vin. **load-line,** *n.* Ligne de charge, *f.* **load-shedding,** *n.* (*Elec.*) Délestage, *m.* **loadstone,** *n.* Aimant naturel, *m.*
loader, *n.* Chargeur, *m.* **loading,** *n.* Chargement, *m.*; charge (of fire-arms), *f.*
loaf [louf], *n.* (*pl.* **loaves**) Pain (long), *m.*; miche (round), *f.*; (*vulg.*) caboche, *f.* (intelligence). *Cottage loaf,* pain de ménage.—*v.i.* Flâner, fainéanter. *To loaf about town,* battre le pavé; *to loaf one's time away,* gaspiller son temps. **loafer,** *n.* Fainéant, badaud, batteur de pavé, *m.* **loaf-sugar,** *n.* Sucre en pain, *m.*
loam [loum], *n.* Terre grasse (argile, sable et humus), *f.*; torchis, *m.*—*v.t.* Enduire de torchis. **loamy,** *a.* Glaiseux, gras.
loan [loun], *n.* Emprunt; prêt (de), *m. I had obliged him with a loan,* je lui avais rendu un service d'argent; *loan society,* société de crédit, *f.*; *on loan to,* (*Mil.*) détaché auprès de; à titre de prêt; *to raise a loan,* faire un emprunt.—*v.t.* Prêter.
loan-word, *n.* Mot d'emprunt, *m.*
loath [louθ], *a.* Fâché, peiné. *Nothing loath,* très volontiers; *to be loath to,* être fâché de, faire à contre-cœur.
loathe [louð], *v.t.* Détester; avoir de l'aversion pour. *I loathe meat,* la viande me répugne.
loathing ['louðiŋ], *adv.* Dégoût, *m.,* aversion, répugnance, *f.* **loathingly,** *adv.* À contrecœur, avec répugnance. **loathly** or **loathsome,** *a.* Dégoûtant, odieux. **loathsomeness,** *n.* Qualité dégoûtante, *f.*
lob [lɔb], *n.* *Rustre, lourdaud, butor, *m.*; (*Ten.*) lob, *m.,* chandelle, *f.*; (*Cricket*) balle lente bôlée en dessous.—*v.t.* (*Ten.*) Jouer en chandelle, lober; (*Cricket*) bôler en dessous.
lobar ['loubə], *a.* Lobaire.
lobby ['lɔbi], *n.* Couloir, *m.*; salle d'attente (waiting-room), *f.*; (*Theat.*) entrée, *f.*—*v.i.* (*Polit.*) Faire les couloirs. **lobbyist,** *n.* Parlementaire intrigant, *m.*
lobe [loub], *n.* Lobe, *m.* **lobed,** *a.* Lobé. **lobelet,** *n.* Lobiole, *m.*
lobelia [lou'biːliə], *n.* Lobélie, *f.*
lobster ['lɔbstə], *n.* Homard, *m. Norway lobster,* langoustine, *f.*; *spiny lobster,* langouste, *f.* **lobster-pot,** *n.* Casier à homards, *m.*
lobular ['lɔbjulə], *a.* Lobulaire. **lobule,** *n.* Lobule, *m.*
lob-worm ['lɔbwəːm], *n.* Arénicole des pêcheurs, *f.*
local ['loukəl], *a.* Local, régional; topographique; (on addresses) en ville.—*n.* (*pop.*) *The local,* le bistro du coin, *m.* **locality** [-'kæliti], *n.* Localité, situation; résidence, *f.*
localization [loukəlai'zeiʃən], *n.* Localisation, *f.* **localize,** *v.t.* Localiser. *To become localized,* se localiser. **locally,** *adv.* Localement.
locate [lou'keit], *v.t.* Placer, établir, fixer; déterminer la place de. *To locate a battery,* repérer une batterie. **location** [-'keiʃən], *n.* Situation, *f.,* emplacement, *m.*; location, *f.*; (*Cine.*) extérieurs, *m.pl. Location by sound,* repérage par le son, *m.*; *to shoot a film on location,* tourner un film en extérieurs.
loch [lɔx], *n.* (*Sc.*) Lac, *m. Sea-loch,* fjord, bras de mer, *m.*
lochia ['lɔkiə], *n.pl.* (*Path.*) Lochies, *f.pl.* **lochial,** *a.* Lochial.
lock [lɔk], *n.* Serrure; écluse (of a canal); platine (of a fire-arm); mèche, boucle (of hair), *f.*; flocon (of wool), *m.*; (*pl.*) cheveux, *m.pl.*; boucles de cheveux, *f.pl. Arm-lock,* clef de bras, *f.* (in wrestling); *dead-lock,* impasse, *f.*; *double lock,* serrure à double tour, *f.*; *padlock,* cadenas, *m.*; *spring-lock,* serrure à ressort, *f.*; *under lock and key,* sous clef.—*v.t.* Fermer à clef; accrocher (wheels etc.); enrayer (with the drag); (*Print. etc.*) serrer, bloquer. *To double-lock,* fermer à double tour; *to lock in,* enfermer, renfermer; *to lock out,* fermer la porte à, renvoyer (workmen); fermer ses ateliers à; *to lock up,* serrer, enfermer, tenir sous clef, mettre en prison, coffrer, (*Print.*) serrer.—*v.i.* Fermer à clef, s'embloquer.
lockage ['lɔkidʒ], *n.* Écluses, *f.pl.*; péage d'écluse, *m.*

locker ['lɔkə], *n.* Armoire, *f.*; coffre, *m.*; (*Naut.*) caisson, *m.* *Davy Jones's locker*, le fond de la mer, *m.*; *locker-room*, vestiaire, *m.*; *locker's order*, passavant, *m.*
locket ['lɔkit], *n.* Porte d'écluse, *f.* **lock-jaw** ['lɔkdʒɔ:], *n.* Trisme, tétanos, *m.* **lock-keeper**, *n.* Éclusier, *m.* **lock-nut**, *n.* Contre-écrou, *m.* **lock-out**, *n.* Fermeture (of workshops), *f.*, renvoi en masse (of workmen), *m.* **locksmith**, *n.* Serrurier, *m.* **lockstitch**, *n.* Point indécousable, *m.* **lock-up**, *a.* Fermant à clef.—*n.* (*fam.*) Violon, corps de garde, *m.*; fermeture, *f.*
locomotion [loukə'mouʃən], *n.* Locomotion, *f.*
locomotive ['loukəmoutiv], *a.* Mobile, locomotif.—*n.* Locomotive, *f.*
locomotor ataxy ['loukəmoutə ə'tæksi], *n.* Ataxie locomotrice, *f.*
locum tenens ['loukəm 'ti:nenz], *n.* Remplaçant, *m.*
locus ['loukəs] (*pl.* loci ['lousai]), *n.* Emplacement, *m.*, situation, *f.*; lieu géométrique, *m.*; scène (of some event), *f.* *Locus standi*, (*Law*) droit d'ester en justice.
locust ['loukəst], *n.* Sauterelle d'Orient, *f.*, criquet, *m.*; caroubier (plant), *m.* **locust-tree**, *n.* Faux acacia, robinier, *m.*
locution [lo'kju:ʃən], *n.* Locution, *f.*
lode [loud], *n.* Filon, *m.* **lodestar**, *n.* Étoile polaire, *f.*
lodge [lɔdʒ], *n.* Loge (de concierge), *f.*; pavillon *m.*; maisonnette (de garde); tanière (of wild beasts), *f.*—*v.t.* Loger; abriter; mettre, planter, enfoncer (to put); déposer (to put down); implanter (in the heart); interjeter (an appeal); verser, coucher, abattre (wheat etc.). *To lodge a complaint*, porter plainte.— *v.i.* Loger, se loger; s'arrêter, se fixer; se coucher, verser (crops). *The ball lodged in a hillock*, la balle se logea dans un hillock. **lodge-keeper**, *n.* Concierge, *m.* **lodger**, *n.* Locataire; pensionnaire, *m.* and *f.* **lodging**, *n.* Logement; appartement; (*fig.*) gîte, abri, *m.*; *lodging allowance*, indemnité de logement, *f.*; *to let furnished lodgings*, louer en garni; *to live in furnished lodgings*, loger en garni. **lodging-house**, *n.* Hôtel garni, *m.* **lodgment**, *n.* Logement; dépôt (of cash), *m.*
loft [lɔft], *n.* Grenier, *m.*, soupente, *f.*; galerie, tribune, *f.*; pigeonnier, *m.*—*v.t.* (*Golf*) *To loft the ball*, envoyer la balle en l'air. **loftily**, *adv.* Haut, avec hauteur, pompeusement, fièrement, *n.* **loftiness**, *n.* Élévation, *f.*; hauteur, fierté, pompe; sublimité, *f.* **lofty**, *a.* Haut, élevé; fier, altier; sublime (style).
log [lɔg], *n.* Bûche, *f.*, soliveau, rondin, bloc de bois, tronc d'arbre; (*Naut.*) loch, *m.* *To heave the log*, jeter le loch; *to sleep like a log*, dormir comme une souche.—*v.t.* Noter, étalonner. **log-board**, *n.* Table de loch, *f.* **log-book**, *n.* Journal *or* livre de bord, *m.*; (*Motor.*) carnet de route, *m.* **log-cabin**, *n.* Hutte de troncs d'arbre, *f.* **log-man**, *n.* Porteur de bois; (*Am.*) bûcheron, *m.* **log-wood**, *n.* Bois de campêche, *m.*
loganberry ['lougənberi], *n.* Ronce-framboise, *f.*
logan-stone ['lougən'stoun], *n.* Rocher branlant, *m.*
logarithm ['lɔgəriθm], *n.* Logarithme, *m.*

logarithmic [-'riðmik], *a.* Logarithmique. **logarithmically**, *adv.* Au moyen des logarithmes.
logged, *a.* Stagnant, marécageux. *Waterlogged*, engagé, rempli d'eau. **logger**, *n.* (*Am.*) Bûcheron, *m.*
loggerhead ['lɔgəhed], *n.* *Sot, lourdaud, *m.* *To be at loggerheads*, être aux prises *or* à couteaux tirés; *to set at loggerheads*, brouiller, mettre la discorde entre.
logic ['lɔdʒik], *n.* Logique, *f.* **logical**, *a.* Logique, de la logique. **logically**, *adv.* Logiquement.
logician [lo'dʒiʃən], *n.* Logicien, *m.*
logistic [lo'dʒistik], *a.* Logistique. **logistics**, *n.* Logistique, *f.*
logographer [lo'gɔgrəfə], *n.* Logographe, *m.*
logomachy [lo'gɔməki], *n.* Logomachie, *f.*
loin [lɔin], *n.* Longe (of veal), *f.*; filet, *m.* (of mutton); (*pl.*) reins, lombes, *m.pl.* **loincloth**, *n.* Pagne, *m.*
loiter ['lɔitə], *v.i.* Flâner, traîner, lambiner, s'amuser en chemin. *To loiter in the woods*, flâner dans les bois.—*v.t.* Perdre, gaspiller. *To loiter away one's time*, gaspiller son temps. **loiterer**, *n.* Musard, flâneur, *m.* **loitering**, *n.* Flânerie, *f.*—*a.* Flâneur, traînard, lambin. **loiteringly**, *adv.* En paresseux.
loll [lɔl], *v.i.* S'étaler, se prélasser, se pencher; pendre (of the tongue).—*v.t.* Laisser pendre (the tongue). **lolling**, *a.* Étendu, étalé (of the tongue).
Lollard ['lɔləd], *n.* Sectateur de Wyclif, *m.*
lollipop ['lɔlipɔp], *n.* Sucre d'orge, *m.*, sucette, *f.*
lolly ['lɔli], *n.* (*fam.*) Sucette, *f.*; (*slang*) galette, *f.* (money).
Lombardy ['lʌmbədi]. La Lombardie, *f.*
lomentaceous [loumen'teiʃəs], *a.* Lomentacé.
London ['lʌndən]. Londres, *m.* *London pride*, (*Bot.*) désespoir des peintres, *m.*
Londoner ['lʌndənə], *n.* Londonien, *m.*, Londonienne, *f.*
lone [loun], *a.* Isolé, solitaire; délaissé. **loneliness**, *n.* Solitude, *f.*; isolement, *m.* **lonely**, *a.* Isolé; délaissé. **lonesome**, *a.* Solitaire. **lonesomeness**, *n.* Solitude, *f.*
long (1) [lɔŋ], *v.i.* Avoir bien envie, brûler (de), soupirer (après); (*impers.*) tarder (de). *I long to go there*, il me tarde d'y aller; *to long for*, soupirer après.
long (2) [lɔŋ], *a.* Long; étendu, prolongé, allongé. *A long face*, une triste figure; *a long figure*, un gros chiffre; *a long time*, longtemps, depuis longtemps, pendant longtemps; *death will not be long in coming*, la mort ne tardera pas à venir; *in the long run*, à la longue; *long home*, la dernière demeure, *f.*; *long range*, longue portée, *f.*; *long shot* (Cine.), plan d'ensemble, *m.*; *to be three feet long*, avoir trois pieds de long *or* être long de trois pieds. —*n.* The long and the short of, le fort et le faible de.—*adv.* Fort; longtemps, longuement; depuis longtemps; pendant longtemps; durant. *All night long*, tout le long de la nuit; *all one's life long*, toute sa vie durant; *before* or *ere long*, bientôt, avant peu, sous peu; *have you been here long?* y a-t-il longtemps que vous êtes ici? *how long have you been here?* combien de temps y a-t-il que vous êtes ici? *long ago*, il y a longtemps, depuis longtemps; *not long after*, peu de temps après,

not long before, peu de temps avant; *so long!* au revoir! à un de ces jours! *so long as,* tant que.
longanimity [lɔŋɡəˈnimiti], *n.* Longanimité, *f.*
long-bill, *n.* (*Orn.*) Bécassine, *f.* **long-boat,** *n.* Chaloupe, *f.* **longbow,** *n.* Arc, *m. To draw the longbow,* exagérer, hâbler, **gaber.* **long-dated,** *a.* À longue échéance. **long-distance,** *a.* À longue distance; de fond (of runner). **long-established,** *a.* Établi depuis longtemps. **long-forgotten,** *a.* Oublié depuis longtemps. **long-headed,** *a.* Dolichocéphale, perspicace. **long-legged,** *a.* À longues jambes. **long-lived,** *a.* Qui vit longtemps; de longue durée. **long-lost,** *a.* Perdu depuis longtemps. **long-range,** *a.* À grand rayon d'action. **long-sighted,** *a.* Clairvoyant; presbyte. *I am long-sighted,* j'ai la vue longue. **long-sightedness,** *n.* Prévoyance; presbytie, *f.* **long-standing,** *a.* De longue date; de vieille date. **long-suffering,** *n.* Longanimité, patience, *f.—a.* Endurant, patient. **long-term,** *a.* À long terme; à longue date. **long-winded,** *a.* De longue haleine; interminable, ennuyeux.
longe [LUNGE].
longer [ˈlɔŋɡə], *a.* Plus long.—*adv.* Plus longtemps; de plus, encore. *I shall wait no longer,* je n'attendrai plus.
longeval [lɔnˈdʒiːvəl] or **longaeval,** *a.* Qui vit longtemps. **longevity** [-ˈdʒeviti], *n.* Longévité, *f.*
longhand [ˈlɔŋhænd], *n.* Écriture ordinaire, *f.*
longing [ˈlɔŋiŋ], *n.* Désir ardent, *m.,* envie, *f.* **longingly,** *adv.* Avec ardeur.
longish [ˈlɔŋiʃ], *a.* Un peu long.
longitude [ˈlɔndʒitjuːd], *n.* Longitude, *f.* **longitudinal** [-ˈtjuːdinəl], *a.* Longitudinal. **longitudinally,** *adv.* Longitudinalement.
longshoreman [ˈlɔŋʃɔːmən], *n.* Pêcheur à la côte (de moules, coquillages etc.), ramasseur de varech; homme de peine (dans un port), *m.*
loo [luː], *n.* La mouche (game), *f.;* (*pop.*) les water(s), *m.pl.*
*looby [ˈluːbi], *n.* Nigaud, niais, sot, *m.*
loof [LUFF].
look [luk], *v.i.* Regarder, sembler, avoir l'air, paraître; donner sur (of a house etc.). *How does it look?* quel effet cela fait-il? *it looks like rain,* on dirait qu'il va pleuvoir; *looked for,* attendu; *look here!* dites donc! tenez! *look out!* attention! gare! *look out for squalls,* attendez-vous à des bourrasques; *look sharp,* dépêchez-vous; *our house looks out on the river,* notre maison donne sur la rivière; *to look about,* regarder autour de soi, avoir l'œil ouvert; *to look after,* avoir soin de, soigner, veiller à, s'occuper de, surveiller; *to look askance,* regarder de travers or d'un œil méfiant; *to look at,* regarder, considérer, envisager; *to look away,* détourner ses regards; *to look back,* regarder en arrière, jeter un regard rétrospectif; *to look back upon,* se souvenir de, se reporter à; *to look down upon,* regarder de haut en bas, (*fig.*) mépriser; *to look for,* chercher, rechercher, s'attendre à; *to look forward to,* attendre avec impatience, s'attendre à, espérer; *to look ill,* avoir l'air malade; *to look in,* faire une petite visite, entrer en passant, dire un petit bonjour à; *to*

look in the face, regarder en face; *to look into,* regarder dans, examiner, s'informer de; *to look like,* avoir l'air de, ressembler à; *to look on,* regarder, considérer, être spectateur (de); *to look out,* chercher, prendre garde, se défier, être sur ses gardes, avoir l'œil au guet, (*Naut.*) être en vigie; *to look out of,* regarder par; *to look out upon,* donner sur; *to look over,* jeter un coup d'œil sur, parcourir des yeux, examiner, surveiller, pardonner; *to look round,* jeter un coup d'œil en arrière, se retourner; parcourir; *to look through,* regarder à travers, parcourir; **to look to,* veiller à, prendre garde à; *to look to the north,* exposé au nord; *to look up,* regarder en haut, lever les yeux, relever la tête, (*Comm.*) être à la hausse, aller voir, chercher (quelque chose); *to look upon,* regarder, considérer; *to look up to,* respecter, considérer, mettre son espoir en; *to look very serious,* avoir la mine très grave; *to look well,* avoir l'air bien portant, avoir une belle apparence, faire bien (of things).—*n.* Regard, air, *m.,* apparence, mine, *f.;* coup d'œil, *m. By the look of him,* à le voir; *by the look of it,* à ce qu'il paraît; *good looks,* bonne mine; *he didn't get a look-in,* (*colloq.*) il n'a pas eu la moindre chance; *to give a look-in,* (*colloq.*) faire une petite visite, passer chez; *to give a look over,* jeter un coup d'œil sur; *to have a good look,* regarder bien; *to take a last look at,* jeter un dernier regard sur, regarder une dernière fois.
looker-on, *n.* Spectateur, *m.*
looking, *a.* À l'air . . .; à la mine . . . . *Good-looking,* beau; *ill-looking,* de mauvaise mine; *nice-looking,* mignon. **looking-glass,** *n.* Miroir, *m.,* glace, *f.*
look-out, *n.* Guet, *m.,* vigilance, vue, *f.;* (*Mil.*) guetteur, *m.;* (*Naut.*) vigie, *f. Look-out post,* poste de guetteur, *m.; that's my look-out,* c'est mon affaire; *to keep a look-out,* avoir l'œil au guet, être en vigie; *to keep a sharp look-out,* guetter d'un œil attentif, veiller bien.
look-see, *n.* (*colloq.*) Coup d'œil (d'inspection), *m.*
loom [luːm], *n.* Métier à tisser, *m.;* silhouette vague, *f.;* (*Naut.*) mirage, *m.,* (*Row.*) manche, *m.* (of oar); (*Orn.*) catmarin, canard sauvage, *m.—v.i.* Apparaître indistinctement, se dessiner dans le lointain. *To loom large,* paraître imminent; occuper le premier plan; *to loom up,* surgir. **looming,** *a.* Vague, estompé.
loon [luːn], *n.* Coquin, drôle, chenapan; (*Orn.*) grand plongeon, *m. Greater loon,* grèbe huppé, *m.; smaller loon,* petit grèbe or castagneux, *m.*
loony [ˈluːni], *a.* (*colloq.*) Piqué, marteau. **loony-bin,** *n.* (*fam.*) Asile d'aliénés, *m.*
loop [luːp], *n.* Boucle; bride (for a button), *f.;* (*Tech.*) tenon, *m.;* (*Av.*) looping, *m. Inverted loop,* looping à l'envers; *to loop the loop,* boucler la boucle; (*Av.*) faire un looping; *to loop up,* retrousser. **loop-hole,** *n.* Meurtrière, *f.,* créneau, *m.;* (*fig.*) échappatoire, *f.,* faux-fuyant, *m.* **loop-holed,** *a.* À meurtrières, crénelé. **loopy,** *a.* (*pop.*) Toqué, fêlé, dingo.
loose [luːs], *a.* Délié, défait; détaché, déchaîné; ample, large; branlant, qui a du jeu (shaky); qui n'est pas ferme; (*fig.*) relâché, lâche (of morals); vague, décousu, sans liaison; licencieux; libre. *He is a loose fish,* c'est un homme déréglé; *loose cash,* menue monnaie, *f.;* *to be*

[301]

at a loose end, se trouver désœuvré; *to cast loose*, larguer; *to get loose*, se détacher, branler (of teeth); *to let loose*, lâcher, mettre en liberté, donner cours à, déchaîner.—*n.* *On the loose*, dissolu, dissipé.—*v.t.* Délier, relâcher, lâcher, (*fig.*) déchaîner. **loosely,** *adv.* Librement, lâchement; négligemment; vaguement; licencieusement; d'une manière décousue, sans liaison.

loosen, *v.t.* Délier, détacher, défaire; desserrer; ébranler.—*v.i.* Se délier; se défaire; se desserrer. **looseness,** *n.* État desserré, relâchement; caractère vague; caractère lâche, *m.*; ampleur, *f.*; (*Med.*) dévoiement, cours de ventre, *m.*

loosestrife ['luːsstraif], *n.* (*Bot.*) Salicaire, *f.*

loot [luːt], *n.* Butin; pillage, *m.*—*v.t.* Piller. **looter,** *n.* Pillard, *m.*

lop [lɔp], *v.t.* Élaguer, ébrancher.—*v.i.* (*Naut.*) Clapoter. **lop-eared,** *a.* Oreillard (animal). **lopping,** *n.* Élagage, ébranchement, *m.* **lop-sided,** *a.* Qui penche trop d'un côté, déjeté.

lope [loup], *v.i.* Avancer par (petits) bonds.

loquacious [loˈkweiʃəs], *a.* Loquace. **loquacity** [-ˈkwæsiti], *n.* Loquacité, *f.*

lord [lɔːdl, *n.* Seigneur; (*fig.*) maître; (*Engl. title*) lord, *m.* *House of Lords*, Chambre des Lords, *f.*; *lords and ladies* (*Bot.*), pied-de-veau, *m.*; *Lord's Supper*, la Cène, *f.*; *my lord*, Monsieur, Milord, Monseigneur (to a prince, to a nobleman, to a bishop, etc.); *Our Lord*, notre Seigneur, *m.*; *the Lord's Prayer*, l'oraison dominicale, *f.*; *the year of our Lord*, l'an de grâce, *m.*—*v.t.* *To lord it over*, dominer, faire le maître. **lord-lieutenancy,** *n.* Vice-royauté, *f.* **lord-lieutenant,** *n.* Vice-roi, *m.* **lordliness,** *n.* Hauteur, *f.*, orgueil, *m.* **lordling,** *n.* Petit seigneur; hobereau, *m.* **lordly,** *a.* De seigneur, noble; arrogant, hautain, altier, fier.—*adv.* En seigneur; avec arrogance, avec fierté. **lordship,** *n.* Seigneurie, *f.* *Your lordship*, Monseigneur.

lore [lɔː], *n.* Savoir, *m.*; science, *f.*

lorgnette [lɔːˈnjet], *n.* Face-à-main, *m.*, lorgnette, *f.*

loris ['lɔːris], *n.* (*Zool.*) Loris, *m.*

lorry ['lɔri], *n.* Camion, *m.*

lory ['lɔːri], *n.* (*Orn.*) Lori, *m.*

lose [luːz], *v.t.* (*past* and *p.p.* **lost**) Perdre; faire perdre; égarer. *The ship was lost on the coast of Africa*, le vaisseau a péri sur la côte d'Afrique; *to be lost at sea*, périr dans un naufrage; *to lose one's temper*, s'emporter; *to lose one's way*, s'égarer; *to lose sight of*, perdre de vue; *to lose touch*, perdre le contact; *to make someone lose something*, faire perdre quelque chose à quelqu'un.—*v.i.* Perdre; (in value) perdre de (sa valeur); retarder (of clocks etc.). *To lose by*, perdre à; *to lose in people's estimation*, baisser dans l'estime publique.

loser ['luːzə], *n.* Perdant (at play), *m.* *To be a loser*, être en perte; *to be a loser by it*, y perdre; *to be a good loser*, être beau joueur.

loss [lɔs], *n.* Perte, *f.*; (*Hunt.*) défaut, *m.*; déperdition; extinction (of voice), *f.* *At a loss*, dans l'embarras, embarrassé, à perte (to sell), (*Hunt.*) en défaut; *dead loss*, perte sèche, *f.*; *to be at a loss to*, avoir de la peine à; *to be at a loss what to do*, ne savoir que faire; *to make good a loss*, réparer une perte. **lost,** *a.* Perdu; égaré (strayed); abîmé (ruined);

(*Parl.*) rejeté. (*pop.*) *Get lost!* fiche-moi le camp! *To be lost in public esteem*, être déchu dans l'estime du public.

Lot [lɔt]. Loth, *m.*

lot [lɔt], *n.* Sort, destin, *m.*, part; quantité (quantity), *f.*; tas (of persons); lot (at a sale), *m.*; (*Comm.*) partie, *f.*; (*Am.*) terrain à bâtir, *m.* *A lot of*, (*colloq.*) beaucoup de; *all the lot of you*, tous tant que vous êtes; *bad lot*, mauvais garnement, *m.*; *by lot*, au sort; *to cast in one's lot with*, partager la fortune de; *to draw or cast lots*, tirer au sort; *to fall to someone's lot*, arriver à quelqu'un, tomber en partage à quelqu'un.—*v.t.* Lotir.

loth [LOATH].

Lothario [loˈθɛəriou]. Lothaire, *m.*

lotion ['louʃən], *n.* Lotion, *f.*

lottery ['lɔtəri], *n.* Loterie, *f.* *It is all a lottery*, c'est une affaire de hasard, c'est une loterie.

lotto ['lɔtou], *n.* Loto, *m.*

lotus ['loutəs], *n.* Lotus, lotos, *m.* **lotus-eater,** *n.* Lotophage, *m.*; (*fig.*) rêveur, *m.*

loud [laud], *a.* Haut; fort, grand; éclatant, bruyant, retentissant; tapageur (noisy); criard (of colours etc.). **loudly,** *adv.* Haut, fort, hautement, à haute voix; avec grand bruit, à grands cris. **loud-mouthed,** *a.* Au verbe haut; gueulard. **loudness,** *n.* Force, *f.*, grand bruit, éclat, *m.* **loud-speaker,** *n.* (*Rad.*) Haut-parleur, *m.*

lough [lɔx], *n.* (*Irish*) Lac; bras de mer, *m.*

Louisa [luˈiːzə], **Louise** [luˈiːz]. Louise, *f.*

Louisiana [luiziˈɑːnə]. La Louisiane, *f.*

lounge [laundʒ], *v.i.* Flâner; être couché *or* étendu *or* appuyé paresseusement (sur). *To lounge away the time*, passer le temps en flânant.—*n.* Marche nonchalante, *f.*; promenoir; sofa (couch), *m.*, petit salon; hall (of hotel), *m.* *Lounge jacket*, veston, *m.*; *lounge suit*, complet veston, *m.* **lounger,** *n.* Flâneur, *m.*

lour, lower ['lauə], *v.i.* Froncer les sourcils (to frown); s'assombrir, s'obscurcir (of the weather). *The sky lours*, le temps se couvre. **louring,** *a.* Couvert, sombre; (*fig.*) menaçant. *Louring look*, air renfrogné, *m.*; *louring weather*, temps couvert, *m.* **louringly,** *adv.* D'un air renfrogné, d'une manière menaçante.

louse [laus], *n.* (*pl.* **lice**) Pou, *m.* **lousewort,** *n.* Pédiculaire, herbe aux poux, *f.* **lousily** ['lauzili], *adv.* En pouilleux. **lousiness,** *n.* État pouilleux, *m.* **lousy** ['lauzi], *a.* Pouilleux; (*fig.*) bas, vil, sale.

lout [laut], *n.* Rustre, butor, *m.* **loutish,** *a.* Rustre. **loutishly,** *adv.* En rustre.

louver, louvre ['luːvə], *n.* (*Av., Motor.*) Auvent, *m.*, persienne, *f.*; (*Naut.*) jalousie, *f.*, abat-sons, *m.* (of steeple).

lovable ['lʌvəbl], *a.* Digne d'être aimé, aimable.

lovage ['lʌvidʒ], *n.* (*Bot.*) Livèche, *f.*

love [lʌv], *v.t.* Aimer.—*n.* Amour, *m.*, affection; amitié (friendship), *f.*; ami, *m.*, amie (term of endearment), *f.*; (*Ten.*) zéro, rien. *For love*, par amour; *give my love to him*, faites-lui mes amitiés; *love fifteen*, rien à quinze; *love laughs at locksmiths*, l'amour force toutes les serrures; *my love to all*, mes amitiés à tous; *to be in love*, être amoureux; *to be in love with*, être amoureux de, être épris de; *to fall in love with*, tomber amoureux de, devenir épris de; *to make love to*, faire la cour à, conter fleurette à; *to play for love*, jouer pour rien *or* pour le plaisir de jouer. **love-affair,** *n.* Amourette, *f.* **love-apple,** *n.* Pomme d'amour (tomato), *f.* **love-birds,** *n.pl.* Inséparables, *m.pl.* **love-child,** *n.* Enfant naturel, enfant de l'amour, *m.* **love-knot,** *n.* Lacs d'amour, *m.* **love-letter,** *n.* Billet doux, *m.* **love-lies-bleeding,** *n.* (*Bot.*) Queue de renard, *f.* **love-making,** *n.* Cour, *f.* **love-match,** *n.* Mariage d'inclination, *m.* **love-potion,** *n.* Philtre, *m.* **love-song,** *n.* Chanson d'amour; romance, *f.* **love-story,** *n.* Histoire d'amour, histoire galante, *f.* **love-suit,** *n.* Cour, *f.*, assiduités, *f.pl.* **love-token,** *n.* Gage d'amour, *m.*

loveless ['lʌvlis], *a.* Sans amour.

loveliness, *n.* Amabilité; beauté, *f.*, charme, *m.*

lovelock ['lʌvlɔk], *n.* Accroche-cœur, *m.*

lovelorn, *a.* Abandonné; délaissé.

lovely, *a.* Charmant, ravissant, séduisant, gracieux.

lover ['lʌvə], *n.* Amant, *m.*, amante, *f.*, amoureux; prétendant (suitor); amateur (de), *m.*

lovesick, *a.* Malade d'amour.

loving ['lʌviŋ], *a.* Aimant, affectueux, affectionné, tendre; d'amour (of things). *Loving kindness*, bonté, miséricorde, *f.* **loving-cup,** *n.* Coupe de l'amitié, *f.* **lovingly,** *adv.* Tendrement, affectueusement.

low (1) [lou], *a.* Bas; petit; peu élevé, vulgaire; profond (of bows); (*fig.*) lent (of fever); abattu (in spirits). *At low water*, à marée basse; *in a low voice*, d'une voix faible *or* basse; *low bodice*, corsage décolleté, *m.*; *low mass*, messe basse, *f.*; *low pressure*, basse pression, *f.*; *Low Sunday*, dimanche de Quasimodo, *m.*; *low-water mark*, étiage, niveau des basses eaux, *m.*; *my funds are low*, les eaux sont basses chez moi; *to bring low*, abattre, humilier; *to lay low*, abattre, coucher par terre; *to lie low*, se tapir, se tenir coi; *to run low*, baisser.—*adv.* Bas, en bas; à voix basse; à bas prix; profondément (of bows). *To live low*, se nourrir peu. **low-born,** *a.* De basse naissance. **low-brow,** *a.* Peu intellectuel.—*n.* Philistin, *m.*, -ine, *f.* **low-built,** *a.* (*Naut.*) De bas bord. **low-class,** *a.* Inférieur, vulgaire, sans distinction. **low-crowned,** *a.* Bas de forme (of hats). **low-down,** *n.* (*fam.*) *To give the low-down on*, tuyauter sur.—*a.* (*fam.*) Bas, vil. **low-lying,** *a.* Bas. **low-minded,** *a.* D'esprit vulgaire. **low-necked,** *a.* Décolleté. **low-priced,** *a.* À bas prix, bon marché. **low-spirited,** *a.* Abattu, triste, découragé.

low (2) [lou], *v.i.* Beugler; (*Sc.*) flamber.

Low [lou] **Countries.** Les Pays-Bas, *m.pl.*

lower (1) ['louə], *a.* Plus bas, inférieur; bas. *Lower down*, plus bas; *lower end*, le bas bout, *m.*; *lower plane*, plan inférieur, *m.* **lower-class,** *n.* Peuple, *m.*

lower (2) ['louə], *v.t.* Baisser, abaisser; descendre; rabaisser, humilier, ravaler (to humiliate); diminuer, affaiblir (to diminish); amener (a flag). *To lower in the estimation of*, perdre dans l'esprit de; *to lower oneself*, s'abaisser, se ravaler.

lower (3) ['lauə] [LOUR].

lowering ['louəriŋ], *n.* Abaissement, *m.*, diminution, *f.*

lowest ['louist], *a.* Le plus bas, le dernier.

lowing ['louiŋ], *n.* Mugissement, beuglement, *m.*

***lowland** ['loulənd], *n.* Terrain bas, *m.*; plaine *f.* *The Lowlands* (of Scotland), les basses terres, *f.pl.* **lowlander,** *n.* Habitant des plaines, *m.*

lowliness ['loulinis], *n.* Humilité, *f.* **lowly,** *a.* Humble.—*adv.* Humblement.

lowness ['lounis], *n.* Situation basse, petitesse, *f.*; peu de profondeur, *m.*; faiblesse (weakness); dépression (of price), *f.*; abaissement (of temperature); abattement (of spirits), découragement, *m.*; vulgarité, petitesse; (*Mus.*) gravité, *f.* *The lowness of the price*, le bas prix.

loxodromic [lɔksə'drɔmik], *a.* Loxodromique. **loxodromics,** *n.pl.* Loxodromie, *f.*

loyal ['lɔiəl], *a.* Fidèle, loyal. *The loyal toast*, le toast au roi, à la reine. **loyalist,** *n.* Loyaliste, *m.* or *f.*; personne attachée au gouvernement, *f.* **loyally,** *adv.* Fidèlement, loyalement. **loyalty,** *n.* Fidélité, *f.*

lozenge ['lɔzindʒ], *n.* Pastille, *f.*; (*Geom., Her., etc.*) losange, *m.* **lozenged,** *a.* En losange.

lubber ['lʌbə], *n.* Lourdaud, *m.* *Land-lubber*, marin d'eau douce, *m.* **lubberly,** *a.* Maladroit, gauche.

lubricant ['lju:brikənt], *n.* Lubrifiant, *m.* **lubricate,** *v.t.* Lubrifier. **lubrication** [-'keiʃən], *n.* Lubrication, *f.*

lubricator ['lju:brikeitə], *n.* Graisseur, *m.*

lubricity [lju:'brisiti], *n.* Lubricité, *f.*

Lucan ['lu:kən]. Lucain, *m.*—*a.* De Saint Luc.

lucarne [lu'ka:n], *n.* Lucarne, *f.*

luce [lju:s], *n.* (*Ichth.*) Brochet, *m.*

lucent ['lusənt], *a.* Lumineux, luisant.

lucerne [lju:'sə:n], *n.* Luzerne, *f.*

Lucian ['lu:ʃiən]. Lucien, *m.*

lucid ['lju:sid], *a.* Lucide, lumineux; limpide, transparent. **lucidly,** *adv.* Lucidement.

lucidity [lju:'siditi] or **lucidness,** *n.* Transparence, limpidité, lucidité, *f.*

Lucifer ['lju:sifə], *n.* (*Astron.*) Lucifer, *m.*; allumette (match), *f.* **Luciferian** [-'fiəriən], *a.* De Lucifer. **luciferous** [-'sifərəs], *a.* Lucifère. **lucifugous,** *a.* Lucifuge.

luck [lʌk], *n.* Chance, fortune, *f.*, bonheur, *m.* *By good luck*, par bonheur; *by ill luck*, par malheur; *good luck*, bonne chance, *f.*; *good luck to you*, bonne chance! *ill luck*, mauvaise fortune, *f.*, malheur, *m.*; *pot-luck*, la fortune du pot, *f.*; *stroke of luck*, coup de chance, *m.*; *to be out of luck*, être en guignon; *to bring good luck*, porter bonheur; *to have a run of luck*, être en veine; *to try one's luck*, tenter sa chance; *what luck!* quelle chance! **luckily,** *adv.* Heureusement, par bonheur. **luckiness,** *n.* Bonheur, *m.* **luckless,** *a.* Malheureux, guignard. **lucky,** *a.* Heureux. *To be lucky*, avoir de la chance; (of thing) porter bonheur. **lucky-dip,** *n.* Sac à surprise, *m.*

lucrative ['lju:krətiv], *a.* Lucratif. **lucratively,** *adv.* D'une manière lucrative.

lucre ['lu:kə], *n.* Lucre, *m.*

Lucretia [lu'kri:ʃiə]. Lucrèce, *f.*

Lucretius [lu'kri:ʃiəs]. Lucrèce, *m.*

lucubration [lju:kju'breiʃən], *n.* Élucubration, *f.*

Lucy ['lu:si]. Lucie, *f.*

ludicrous ['lju:dikrəs], *a.* Plaisant, risible, comique, ridicule, grotesque. **ludicrously,** *adv.* Plaisamment, risiblement, comiquement, ridiculement. **ludicrousness,** *n.* Côté plaisant, aspect comique, *m.*
luff [lʌf], *v.i.* Lofer.—*n.* Lof, *m.*
luffer [LOUVER].
lug [lʌg], *v.t.* Traîner; tirer. *To lug away,* entraîner, enlever de force; *to lug in,* faire entrer de force; *to lug out,* tirer dehors, faire sortir, dégainer (a sword).—*n.* (*dial.* and *Sc.*) Oreille; anse, *f.,* tasseau, *m.* **lug-sail,** *n.* Voile à bourcet, *f.* **lug-worm,** *n.* Ver rouge, *m.*
luge [lju:dʒ], *n.* Luge, *f.*
luggage ['lʌgidʒ], *n.* Bagage, *m.,* bagages, *m.pl.* *Left-luggage office,* consigne, *f.* **luggage-carrier,** *n.* Porte-bagages, *m.* **luggage-receipt** or **luggage-ticket,** *n.* Bulletin de bagages, *m.* **luggage-van,** *n.* Fourgon, *m.*
lugger ['lʌgə], *n.* Lougre; chasse-marée, *m.*
lugubrious [lu:'gju:briəs], *a.* Lugubre. **lugubriously,** *adv.* Lugubrement.
Luke [lu:k]. Luc, *m.*
lukewarm ['lu:kwɔːm], *a.* Tiède; (*fig.*) peu zélé. *To get lukewarm,* s'attiédir. **lukewarmly,** *adv.* Tièdement; (*fig.*) avec peu de zèle. **lukewarmness,** *n.* Tiédeur, *f.;* (*fig.*) manque de zèle, *m.*
lull [lʌl], *v.t.* Bercer, endormir; calmer. *To lull to sleep,* endormir, inviter au sommeil; *to lull with false hopes,* bercer de vaines espérances.—*v.i.* Se calmer, s'apaiser.—*n.* Moment de calme, *m.;* (*Naut.*) accalmie, *f.*
lullaby ['lʌləbai], *n.* Berceuse, *f.*
lulling ['lʌliŋ], *a.* Endormant, calmant.
lumbago [lʌm'beigou], *n.* Lumbago, *m.* **lumbar,** *a.* (*Anat.*) Lombaire.
lumber ['lʌmbə], *n.* Vieilleries, *f.pl.;* (vieux) objets encombrants, *m.pl.,* fatras; (*Am.*) bois de charpente (timber), *m.*—*v.t.* Entasser sans ordre; remplir de fatras.—*v.i.* Se traîner lourdement. **lumberjack, lumberman,** *n.* Bûcheron, *m.* **lumber-room,** *n.* Lieu, *or* chambre de débarras, *f.*
lumbering *a.* Lourd, encombrant.
luminary ['lju:minəri], *n.* Corps lumineux, luminaire; (*fig.*) flambeau, *m.* **luminiferous** [-'nifərəs], *a.* Luminifère. **luminosity,** *n.* Luminosité, *f.* **luminous,** *a.* Lumineux. **luminously,** *adv.* Lumineusement. **luminousness,** *n.* Luminosité, *f.*
lump [lʌmp], *n.* Masse, *f.;* morceau, bloc (piece), *m.* *A lump sum,* somme globale, *f.; in the lump,* en bloc; *lump of sugar,* morceau de sucre, *m.; to have a lump in one's throat,* se sentir le cœur gros.—*v.t.* Prendre en bloc; mettre en masse; réunir ensemble; (*fam.*) encaisser. *If you don't like it you can lump it,* si ça ne vous plaît pas, c'est le même prix; *lumped together,* en bloc. **lump-sucker,** *n.* (*Ichth.*) Lompe, lièvre de mer, gros mulet, *m.* **lump-sugar,** *n.* Sucre en morceaux, *m.*
lumper, *n.* Déchargeur, débardeur, *m.* **lumpish,** *a.* Gros, lourd, pesant. **lumpishly,** *adv.* Lourdement. **lumpishness,** *n.* Lourdeur, *f.* **lumpy,** *a.* Grumeleux; couvert de bosses; (mer) clapoteuse.
lunacy ['lu:nəsi], *n.* Aliénation mentale, *f.*
lunar ['lu:nə], *a.* Lunaire; en forme de lune; de la lune. *Lunar caustic,* nitrate d'argent, *m.*
lunarian [lu:'nɛəriən], *n.* Habitant de la lune,

m. **lunary,** *a.* and *n.* Lunaire, *m.* **lunate,** *a.* En demi-lune.
lunatic ['lu:nətik], *a.* De fou, d'aliéné.—*n.* Aliéné, *m.,* aliénée, *f.;* fou, *m.,* folle, *f.* *Lunatic fringe,* les extrémistes, *m.pl.* **lunatic-asylum,** *n.* Asile d'aliénés, *m.,* *petites maisons, *f.pl.*
lunation [lu'neiʃən], *n.* Lunaison, *f.*
lunch [lʌntʃ], *n.* Déjeuner (vers midi), *m.*—*v.i.* Déjeuner. **luncheon,** *n.* Grand déjeuner, *m.* **lunch-time,** *n.* L'heure du déjeuner, *f.*
lunette [lu:'net], *n.* (*Fort.*) Lunette, *f.*
lung [lʌŋ], *n.* (*usu.* in *pl.*) Poumon; mou (of veal etc.), *m.* *Iron lung,* poumon d'acier, *m.*
lunge [lʌndʒ], *n.* (*Fenc.*) Botte, *f.,* coup droit, *m.*—*v.i.* Porter une botte, se fendre. *To lunge out at,* allonger un coup (de poing, de pied) à.
lungwort ['lʌŋwɔːt], *n.* (*Bot.*) Pulmonaire, *f.*
luniform ['lju:nifɔːm], *a.* Luniforme. **lunisolar** [-'soulə], *a.* Luni-solaire.
lunt [lʌnt], *n.* (*Artill.*) Mèche, *f.,* cordon, *m.*
lunulate ['lu:njulət], *a.* (*Bot.*) Lunulé.
lupin ['lju:pin], *n.* (*Bot.*) Lupin, *m.*
lupine ['lu:pain], *a.* De loup (wolfish).
lupus ['lju:pəs], *n.* Lupus, *m.*
lurch [ləːtʃ], *n.* Embardée, *f.,* cahot, *m.;* (*fig.*) embarras, *m.;* (*Backgammon*) bredouille, partie double, *f.* *To give a lurch* (of a ship), faire une embardée, (of a carriage) faire un cahot; *to leave in the lurch,* planter là, laisser dans l'embarras.—*v.i.* Faire une embardée (of a ship). **lurcher,** *n.* Chien de braconnier (croisé de collie et de greyhound); maraudeur, chapardeur, *m.*
lure [ljuə], *n.* Leurre, appât, piège, *m.;* (*fig.*) attrait, *m.*—*v.t.* Leurrer, attirer, séduire.
lurid ['ljuərid], *a.* Sombre, blafard, lugubre; sinistre; sensationnel, hautement coloré.
lurk [ləːk], *v.i.* Être aux aguets; se tenir caché, se cacher. **lurker,** *n.* Personne aux aguets; personne qui se cache, *f.* **lurking,** *a.* Caché, secret. **lurking-place,** *n.* Cachette, *f.*
luscious ['lʌʃəs], *a.* Délicieux, savoureux; liquoreux (of wine). **lusciously,** *adv.* Délicieusement. **lusciousness,** *n.* Nature succulente, douceur extrême; volupté, *f.*
lush [lʌʃ], *a.* Luxuriant.
lust [lʌst], *n.* Luxure, *f.;* désir lascif, *m.;* (*fig.*) convoitise, *f.*—*v.i.* Désirer immodérément. *To lust after,* convoiter. **lustful,** *a.* Lascif, sensuel, luxurieux. **lustfully,** *adv.* Avec luxure. **lustily,** *a.* Vigoureusement, de toutes ses forces. **lustiness,** *n.* Vigueur, *f.*
lustral ['lʌstrəl], *a.* Lustral. **lustration** [-'treiʃən], *n.* Lustration, *f.*
lustre (1) ['lʌstə], *n.* Brillant (gloss), lustre; (*fig.*) éclat, *m.,* splendeur, *f.* **lustreless** *or* **lack-lustre,** *a.* Terne.
lustre (2) ['lʌstə], *n.* (*Rom. Ant.*) Lustre (space of five years), *m.*
lustrous ['lʌstrəs], *a.* Brillant, lustré. **lustrousness,** *n.* Éclat, lustre, *m.*
lusty ['lʌsti], *a.* Vigoureux, robuste, fort.
lute [lju:t], *n.* Luth; (*Chem.*) lut, *m.*—*v.t.* (*Chem.*) Luter. **lute-maker,** *n.* Luthier, *f.* **lutenist,** *n.* Luthiste, *m.* and *f.*
luteic ['lju:tiik], *a.* (*Chem.*) Lutéique. **lutein,** *n.* Lutéine, *f.*
Lutetia [lu:'ti:ʃiə]. Lutèce (old name for Paris), *f.*
Lutheran ['lu:θərən], *a.* and *n.* Luthérien, *m.* **Lutheranism,** *n.* Luthéranisme, *m.*

luxate ['lʌkseit], *v.t.* Luxer. **luxation** [-'seiʃən], *n.* Luxation, *f.*
Luxembourg ['lʌksembɔːg]. Le Luxembourg (Duchy), *m.*
luxuriance [lʌg'zjuəriəns] or **luxuriancy**, *n.* Exubérance, surabondance, luxuriance, *f.* **luxuriant**, *a.* Exubérant, surabondant, luxuriant. **luxuriantly**, *adv.* En abondance, richement. **luxuriate**, *v.i.* Croître *or* vivre dans l'abondance; s'abandonner (à), nager (dans), se plaire (dans). *To luxuriate in,* se livrer avec abandon à.
luxurious [lʌg'zjuəriəs], *a.* De luxe, somptueux, luxueux. **luxuriously**, *adv.* Avec luxe, somptueusement. **luxuriousness**, *n.* Somptuosité, *f.*
luxury ['lʌkʃəri], *n.* Luxe, *m.*, exubérance, *f.*; fin morceau, régal; objet de luxe, *m.*
lycanthropy [lai'kænθrəpi], *n.* Lycanthropie, *f.*
lyceum [lai'siːəm], *n.* (*Am.*) Lycée, *m.*
lychnis ['liknis], *n.* (*Bot.*) Lychnide, *f.*, lychnis, *m.*
lycopodiaceous [laikəpoudi'eiʃəs], *a.* Lycopodiacé. **lycopodium** [-'poudiəm], *n.* Lycopode, *m.*
lyddite ['lidait], *n.* Mélinite, *f.*
Lydia ['lidiə]. Lydie, *f.*
Lydian ['lidiən], *a.* and *n.* Lydien.
lye [lai], *n.* Lessive, *f.* **lye-trough**, *n.* Baquet à lessive, *m.*
lying (1) ['laiiŋ], *n.* Mensonge, *m.*—*a.* Menteur; mensonger (of things). **lyingly**, *adv.* Mensongèrement.
lying (2), *pres.p.* [LIE (2)]. *Lying days,* (*Naut.*) jours de planche, *m.pl.* **lying-in**, *n.* Couches, *f.pl.* **lying-in** *hospital,* maison d'accouchement, *f.*, maternité, *f.*
lymph [limf], *n.* Lymphe, *f.*; vaccin, *m.* **lymphatic** [-'fætik], *a.* Lymphatique.—*n.* Vaisseau lymphatique, *m.*
lynch [lintʃ], *v.t.* Lyncher (exécuter sommairement). *Lynch law,* loi de Lynch, *f.* **lynching**, *n.* Exécution sommaire, *f.*, lynchage, *m.*
lynx [links], *n.* Lynx, *m.* **lynx-eyed**, *a.* Aux yeux de lynx.
Lyons ['laiənz]. Lyon, *m.* **The Gulf of Lyons** (common error in English for **Lions**), le Golfe du Lion, *m.*
lyre ['laiə], *n.* Lyre, *f.* **lyric** ['lirik] or **lyrical**, *a.* Lyrique.—*n.* Poème lyrique, *m.*; (*pl.*) (*Theat.*) couplets de revue, *m.pl.* **lyricism**, *n.* Lyrisme, *m.* **lyricist**, *n.* Poète lyrique; (*Theat.*) parolier, *m.* **lyrist** ['lirist], *n.* Joueur de lyre, *m.*
Lysander [lai'sændə]. Lysandre, *m.*

M

M, m [em]. Treizième lettre de l'alphabet, *m.*
ma [mɑː], *n.* (*pop.*) Maman, *f.*
ma'am [mɑːm], *n.* (*abbr.* for **madam**) (Usual form of address to Royal ladies in conversation) Madame.
mac [mæk], *n.* (*pop.*) Imperméable, imper, *m.*
macabre [mə'kɑːbr], *a.* Macabre; surnaturel.
macaco [mə'keikou], *n.* Macaque, *m.*
macadam [mə'kædəm], *n.* Macadam, *m.*

macadamization [-ai'zeiʃən], *n.* Macadamisation, *f.* **macadamize**, *v.t.* Macadamiser.
macaque [mə'kæk], *n.* Macaque, *m.*
macaroni [mækə'rouni], *n.* Macaroni; *(fig.)* fat, petit-maître, *m.*
macaronic [mækə'rɔnik], *a.* Macaronique.
macaroon [mækə'ruːn], *n.* Macaron, *m.*
macassar [mə'kæsə], *n.* Huile pour les cheveux, *f.*
macaw [mə'kɔː], *n.* Ara, *m.* **macaw-tree**, *n.* Palmier acrocome, *m.*
Maccabees ['mækəbiːz], *the.* Les Macchabées, *m.pl.*
Maccabeus [mækə'biːəs]. Macchabée, *m.*
mace [meis], *n.* Masse (staff), *f.*; macis (of the nutmeg), *m.* **mace-bearer** (or *Sc.*) **macer**, *n.* Massier, *m.*
Macedonia [mæsi'douniə]. La Macédoine, *f.*
macerate ['mæsəreit], *v.t.* Macérer. **maceration** [-'reiʃən], *n.* Macération, *f.*
Machiavelli [mækiə'veli]. Machiavel, *m.* **Machiavellian**, *a.* Machiavélique. **Machiavellism**, *a.* Machiavélisme, *m.* **Machiavellist**, *n.* Machiavéliste, *m.*
machicolation [mətʃikə'leiʃən], *n.* Mâchicoulis, *m.*
machinate ['mækineit], *v.t.* Machiner, tramer. **machination** [-'neiʃən], *n.* Machination, *f.*
machine [mə'ʃiːn], *n.* Machine, *f.*; (*fig.*) instrument, *m.*; appareil, *m.* (aeroplane); (*Polit.*) leviers de commande (d'un parti), *m.pl.* **machine-gun**, *n.* Mitrailleuse, *f.* **machine-gunner**, *n.* Mitrailleur, *m.* **machine-made**, *a.* Fait à la machine. **machine-shop**, *n.* Atelier d'usinage, *m.* **machine-tool**, *n.* Machine-outil, *m.*
machined, *a.* Usiné. **machinery**, *n.* Mécanique, *f.*, mécanisme, *m.*; machines, *f.pl.*; (*poet.*) merveilleux, *m.* **machining**, *n.* (*Print.*) Tirage à la machine, *m.* **machinist**, *n.* Machiniste, mécanicien, *m.*
mackerel ['mækərəl], *n.* Maquereau, *m.* *Mackerel breeze,* bonne brise, *f.*; *mackerel sky,* ciel pommelé, *m.* **mackerel-boat**, *n.* Maquilleur, *m.*
mackintosh ['mækintɔʃ], *n.* Imperméable, *m.*
macle, makle [mækl], *n.* (*Print.*) Maculature, bavochure, *f.*—*v.t.* Maculer, bavocher.
macrocosm ['mækrokɔzm], *n.* Macrocosme, *m.*
macropod ['mækropɔd], *a.* Macropode.
macula ['mækjulə] *or* **macule**, *n.* (*pl.* **maculae**) Macule; tache jaune (de la rétine, *f.*
maculate ['mækjuleit], *v.t.* Tacher, maculer. **maculation** [-'leiʃen], *n.* Maculage, *m.*
mad [mæd], *a.* Fou, aliéné, insensé; affolé; furieux (fierce), enragé (of animals). *Mad about, after, on,* fou de; *mad as a March hare,* fou à lier; *mad with,* furieux contre; *mad with pain,* fou de douleur; *to drive mad,* rendre fou, faire perdre la tête à; *to go mad,* devenir fou, enrager (of animals). **madcap**, *a.* Étourdi, écervelé, fou.—*n.* Fou, *m.*, folle, *f.*; écervelé, *m.*, écervelée, *f.* **madden**, *v.t.* Rendre fou; faire enrager, exaspérer. **maddening**, *a.* À rendre fou, enrageant. **madhouse**, *n.* Maison de fous, *f.* **madly**, *adv.* Follement, furieusement; en fou, à la folie. **madman**, *n.* (*pl.* **madmen**) Aliéné, fou, *m.* **madness**, *n.* Démence,

fureur, folie; rage (of animals), *f.* *To drive to madness*, rendre fou.
Madagascan, *a.* and *n.* Malgache.
Madagascar [mædə'gæskə]. Madagascar, *m.*
madam ['mædəm], *n.* Madame, *f.*
madder ['mædə], *n.* Garance, *f.* **madder-root**, *n.* Alizari, *m.*, garance, *f.*
made [meid], *a.* Fait, confectionné. *A made man*, homme dont la position est assurée; *a self-made man*, fils de ses œuvres, arrivé seul, *m.*; *(ready) made dishes*, plats préparés, *m.pl.*; *made so as to*, fait de façon à; *made up*, artificiel, fait à plaisir, inventé (of stories), maquillé (of the face).
Madeira [mə'diərə]. Madère, *f.*—*n.* Madère, *m.* (wine).
Madge [mædʒ] or **Maggie** ['mægi]. Margot, *f.*
Madonna [mə'dɔnə], *n.* Madone, *f.*
madrepore ['mædripɔ:], *n.* Madrépore, *m.*
madrigal ['mædrigəl], *n.* Madrigal, *m.*
Maecenas [mi'si:næs]. Mécène, *m.*
maelstrom ['meilstroum, -əm], *n.* (*Geog.*) Malstrom; (*fig.*) tourbillon, *m.*
magazine [mægə'zi:n], *n.* Magasin, *m.* (storeroom; also of rifle); (*Navy*) soute aux poudres, *f.*; magazine, *m.*; revue (periodical), *f.* *Powder-magazine*, poudrière, *f.*
Magdalen ['mægdəlin]. Madeleine, *f.*
Magellan [mə'gelən]. **Straits of,** Le Détroit de Magellan, *m.*
magenta [mə'dʒentə], *a.* and *n.* Magenta (colour), *m.*
maggot ['mægət], *n.* Larve, *f.*, (*colloq.*) ver, asticot, *m.*; (*fig.*) caprice, *m.*, lubie, *f.* **maggoty**, *a.* Véreux, plein de vers; (*fig.*) capricieux.
Magi ['meidʒai], *n.pl.* Mages, *m.pl.*
magian ['meidʒiən]. *a.* Des mages.—*n.* Mage, *m.* **magianism**, *n.* Magisme, *m.*
magic ['mædʒik], *n.* Magie, *f.*—*a.*, or **magical** Magique. **magically**, *adv.* Magiquement.
magician [mə'dʒiʃən], *n.* Magicien, *m.*, magicienne, *f.*; (*Am.*) prestidigitateur, *m.*
magisterial [mædʒis'tiəriəl], *a.* De maître, de magistrat; magistral. **magisterially**, *adv.* Magistralement.
magistrate ['mædʒistrit], *n.* Magistrat, *m.* *Examining magistrate*, juge d'instruction, *m.* *Police court magistrate*, juge de paix, *m.*
magistrature [mæ'dʒistrətjuə], *n.* Magistrature, *f.*
Magna-Charta ['mægnə'ka:tə], *n.* La Grande Charte, *f.* (1215).
magnanimity [mægnə'nimiti], *n.* Magnanimité, *f.* **magnanimous** [-'næniməs], *a.* Magnanime. **magnanimously**, *adv.* Magnanimement.
magnate ['mægneit], *n.* Magnat; grand; (*colloq.*) gros bonnet, *m.*
magnesia [mæg'ni:ʃə], *n.* (*Chem.*) Magnésie, *f.*; (*Pharm.*) magnésie blanche, *f.* **magnesian** [-'ni:ʃən], *a.* Magnésien. *Magnesian limestone*, dolomie, *f.*, calcaire magnésien, *m.* **magnesite** [-'ni:zait], *n.* Magnésite, *f.*
magnesium [mæg'ni:ziəm or -'ni:ʃiəm], *n.* Magnésium, *m.* *Magnesium light*, lumière magnésique, *f.*
magnet ['mægnit], *n.* Aimant, *m.* **magnetic** [-'netik] or **magnetical**, *a.* Aimanté; magnétique; (*fig.*) attractif, attirant. *Magnetic field*, champ magnétique, *m.* **magnetically**, *adv.* Par le magnétisme. **magnetism**

['mægnitizm], *n.* Magnétisme, *m.*; (*Elec.*) aimantation, *f.*; puissance attractive, *f.* *Animal magnetism*, magnétisme animal, *m.* **magnetite**, *n.* Magnétite, *f.* **magnetize**, *v.t.* Aimanter; (*fig.*) magnétiser. **magnetizer**, *n.* Magnétiseur, *m.*
magneto [mæg'ni:tou], *n.* Magnéto, *f.* **magnetometer** [-'tɔmitə], *n.* Magnétomètre, *m.*
magnetron [mæg'ni:trɔn], *n.* Magnétron, *m.*
magnification [mægnifi'keiʃən], *n.* Grossissement, *m.*; glorification, exaltation, *f.*
magnificence [mæg'nifisəns], *n.* Magnificence, *f.* **magnificent**, *a.* Magnifique, superbe. **magnificently**, *adv.* Magnifiquement. **magnifico**, *n.* Grand patricien (à Venise), *m.*
magnified ['mægnifaid], *a.* Grossi. **magnifier**, *n.* Verre grossissant, *m.*; personne qui exalte *or* exagère, *f.* **magnify**, *v.t.* Magnifier, augmenter, grossir; (*fig.*) exalter. **magnifying**, *a.* Qui grossit. *Magnifying power*, grossissement, *m.* **magnifying-glass**, *n.* Verre grossissant, *m.*, loupe, *f.*
magniloquence [mæg'nilokwəns], *n.* Emphase, *f.*; style pompeux, *m.* **magniloquent**, *a.* Emphatique; pompeux.
magnitude ['mægnitju:d], *n.* Grandeur; importance, *f.*
magnolia [mæg'noulia], *n.* (*Bot.*) Magnolia, magnolier, *m.*
magnum ['mægnəm], *n.* Magnum, *m.*
magpie ['mægpai], *n.* Pie, *f.*
maharajah [ma:hə'ra:dʒə], *n.* Maharajah, *m.*
maharanee [ma:hə'ra:ni:], *n.* Maharani, *f.*
mahogany [mə'hɔgəni], *n.* Acajou, bois d'acajou, *m.*—*a.* En *or* d'acajou.
Mahomet [MOHAMMED].
Mahometan [MOHAMMEDAN].
mahout [mə'hu:t], *n.* Cornac, *m.*
maid [meid], *n.* Fille, jeune fille; vierge (virgin); bonne, servante, domestique (servant), *f.* *Chambermaid*, fille de chambre, *f.*; *housemaid*, servante, *f.*; *kitchen-maid*, fille de cuisine, *f.*; *lady's-maid*, femme de chambre, *f.*; *maid of all work*, bonne à tout faire; *maid of honour*, demoiselle d'honneur; (*Cook.*) petite tarte; *nursery-maid* or *nurse-maid*, bonne d'enfant, *f.*; *the Maid of Orleans*, la pucelle d'Orléans; *to remain an old maid*, rester fille. **maid-servant**, *n.* Servante, *f.*
maiden [meidn], *a.* De fille, de jeune fille; virginal, de vierge; (*fig.*) pur, neuf, frais; de début (of a speech). *Maiden aunt*, tante non mariée, *f.*; *maiden lady*, demoiselle, *f.*; *maiden name*, nom de jeune fille, *m.*; *maiden speech*, premier discours d'un nouveau membre du Parlement; *maiden voyage*, premier voyage, *m.*—*n.* Jeune fille, fille, *f.* **maidenhair**, *n.* Capillaire, *m.* (plant). **maidenhead**, *n.* Virginité, *f.* **maidenhood**, *n.* Célibat, *m.* (of a girl). **maiden-like**, *a.* De jeune fille; modeste, pudique. **maidenliness**, *n.* Tenue de jeune fille; modestie de jeune fille, *f.* **maidenly**, *a.* De jeune fille; modeste, chaste.—*adv.* En jeune fille, modestement, avec pudeur.
mail (1) [meil], *n.* Mailles (armour), *f.pl.* *Coat of mail*, cotte de mailles, *f.*—*v.t.* Vêtir d'une cotte de mailles. **mailed**, *a.* À mailles. *The mailed fist*, (*fig.*) la poigne, la force (armée).

mail (2) [meil], *n.* Malle, malle-poste, *f.*; courrier, *m.*, dépêches (letters), *f.pl.*—*v.t.* (*Am.*) Mettre à la poste. **mail-bag,** *n.* Sac des dépêches, sac postal, *m.* **mail-boat** or **mail-steamer,** *n.* Paouebot-poste, *m.* **mail-coach,** *n.**Malle-poste,*f.*, wagon-poste, *m.* **mail-guard,** *n.* Courrier de la malle, *m.* **mail-order,** *n.* Commande par la poste, *f.* **mail-train,** *n.* Train-poste, *m.* **mailing-list,** *n.* Liste de correspondants, *f.*

maim [meim], *v.t.* Mutiler, estropier; (*fig.*) tronquer.

main [mein], *a.* Principal, premier; grand; important, essentiel. *By main force,* par force, de haute lutte; (*Rail.*) *main line,* grande ligne, *f.*; *main sewer,* égout collecteur, *m.*; *main street,* rue principale, *f.*; *the main body,* (*Mil.*) le gros; *the main thing,* l'essentiel, le principal, *m.*; *to have an eye to the main chance,* veiller à ses propres intérêts.—*n.* Gros, *m.*, plus grande partie, *f.*; principal océan, *m.*; force (strength), *f.*; grand conduit, tuyau; *combat de coqs (cock-fight), *m.* *In the main,* pour la plupart, en général; *to turn off* (*gas etc.*) *at the main,* or *mains,* fermer le robinet d'arrivée; *with might and main,* de toutes ses forces. **main-brace,** *n.* Grard bras, *m.* (*fig.*) *To splice the main-brace,* boire un coup. **main-deck,** *n.* Premier pont, *m.* **mainland,** *n.* Continent, *m.* **mainly,** *adv.* Principalement, surtout. **mainmast,** *n.* Grand mât, *m.* **mainsail,** *n.* Grand'voile, *f.* **mainsheet,** *n.* Grande écoute, *f.* **mainspring,** *n.* Grand ressort, ressort moteur, *m.*; (*fig.*) cheville ouvrière, *f.*, mobile, *m.* **mainstay,** *n.* Soutien, *m.*; (*fig.*) âme, *f.* **maintop,** *n.* Grande hune, *f.* **main-topmast,** *n.* Grand mât de hune, *m.* **main-yard,** *n.* Grand'vergue, *f.*

maintain [mein'tein], *v.t.* Maintenir; soutenir, alléguer, prétendre; conserver; entretenir, nourrir (to keep in food). **maintainable,** *a.* Soutenable, tenable. **maintainer,** *n.* Personne qui maintient, qui soutient, *f.*

maintenance ['meintənəns], *n.* Maintien, soutien; entretien, moyen d'existence, *m.*; (*Law*) pension alimentaire, *f.* *Maintenance grant,* bourse d'entretien, *f.*; *separate maintenance,* séparation de biens, *f.*

Mainz [maints]. Mayence, *f.*

maisonette [meizə'net], *n.* Petit appartement réparti sur deux étages, *m.*

maize [meiz], *n.* Maïs, blé de Turquie, *m.*

majestic [mə'dʒestik], *a.* Majestueux. **majestically,** *adv.* Majestueusement.

majesty ['mædʒəsti], *n.* Majesté, *f.* *His or Her Majesty,* Sa Majesté, *f.*

major ['meidʒə], *a.* Plus grand, majeur.—*n.* Commandant, chef de bataillon (of infantry); chef d'escadron (of cavalry), *m.*; (*Log.*) majeure; (*Law*) personne majeure, *f.* *Drum-major,* tambour-major; *sergeant-major,* sergent-major, adjudant, *m.* **major-domo,** *n.* Majordome, *m.* **major-general,** *n.* Général de brigade, *m.*

Majorca [mə'dʒɔːkə]. Majorque, *f.*

majority [mə'dʒɔriti], *n.* Majorité, *f.*; (*Mil.*) grade de chef de bataillon *or* d'escadron, *m.*

majorize ['meidʒəraiz], *v.i.* (*Rugby*) Transformer un essai en but.

make [meik], *v.t.* (*past* and *p.p.* **made**) Faire; créer, façonner, fabriquer, confectionner;

rendre (to render); forcer, contraindre (to oblige); amasser, gagner (money). *He is not such a fool as you make him out,* il n'est pas aussi bête que vous le représentez; *I can't make anything of it* or *I can't make head or tail of it,* je n'y comprends rien; *to make a fire,* faire du feu; *to make a fool of,* se jouer de; *to make a fortune,* faire fortune; *to make again,* refaire; *to make a great deal by,* tirer beaucoup de profit de; *to make amends for,* dédommager de; *to make a mistake,* se tromper; *to make an appointment with,* donner un rendez-vous à, prendre rendez-vous avec; *to make angry,* fâcher; *to make a noise,* faire du bruit; *to make away with,* se défaire de, gaspiller, aliéner (one's property), tuer (somebody), se suicider (oneself); *to make believe,* faire accroire à; *to make fast,* attacher, (*Naut.*) amarrer; *to make free with,* traiter sans façon(s), en user librement avec; *to make friends with,* se lier d'amitié avec; *to make fun of,* se moquer de; *to make good,* soutenir, prouver, réparer, dédommager de; *to make haste,* se dépêcher, se hâter; *to make hay while the sun shines,* battre le fer quand il est chaud, profiter des circonstances; *to make head* or *headway,* faire des progrès, avancer; *to make ill,* rendre malade; *to make it up,* se raccommoder, se réconcilier; *to make known,* faire connaître, faire savoir à; *to make land,* découvrir la terre; *to make less,* rapetisser, amoindrir; *to make light of,* faire peu de cas de; *to make love to,* courtiser, faire la cour à; *to make much of,* faire grand cas de, câliner, choyer, dorloter (a child); *to make no difference,* être sans importance; *to make nothing out of,* ne tirer aucun profit de; *to make oneself heard, understood, known, etc.,* se faire entendre, comprendre, connaître, *etc.*; *to make one's escape,* se sauver; *to make out,* comprendre, déchiffrer, distinguer, établir (to prove), dresser (a bill); *to make over to,* céder à, transmettre; *to make ready,* préparer; *to make shift with,* s'arranger de, s'accommoder de; *to make sick,* faire vomir; *to make sure,* assurer; *to make sure of,* compter sur, s'assurer de; *to make the best of,* tirer le meilleur parti de; *to make the best of a bad job,* faire contre mauvaise fortune bon cœur; *to make the most of,* profiter de, tirer le meilleur parti de, faire le plus grand cas de; *to make the mouth water,* faire venir l'eau à la bouche; *to make too free with,* prendre des libertés avec; *to make up,* compléter, combler, façonner (clothes), inventer (a story), accommoder, arranger (a quarrel), régler, établir, balancer (accounts), (*Print.*) mettre en pages; *to make up for,* suppléer à, dédommager de, rattraper (time); *to make up one's mind,* se décider, prendre son parti; *to make water,* uriner, (*Naut.*) faire eau; *to make way,* se frayer un chemin, avancer, faire des progrès.—*v.i.* Se diriger (vers); contribuer (à); faire (comme si); penser (à); monter (of the tide). *To make as if,* faire semblant de, avoir l'air de, prétendre; *to make believe,* faire semblant; *to make direct for,* se diriger sur; *to make do* (*with*), s'arranger de; *to make for,* s'avancer sur, s'élancer sur, (*Naut.*) mettre le cap sur; *to make of,* comprendre; *to make off,* décamper, filer, se sauver; *to make up,* se grimer, se maquiller; *to make up for,* suppléer à, dédommager de, compenser, racheter; *to make up to*, s'avancer vers, faire des avances à, faire la cour à.—*n.* Façon, forme, tournure; fabrication, construction, structure, *f.* **make-and-break,** *n.* (*Elec.*) Conjoncteur-disjoncteur, *m.*—*a.* Intermittent. **make-believe,** *n.* Feinte, *f.,* semblant, *m.* **makeshift,** *n.* Pis aller, expédient, moyen de fortune, *m.* **make-up,** *n.* Contexture, *f.*; maquillage, *m.* **make-weight,** *n.* Supplément; (*fig.*) remplissage, *m.*

maker ['meikə], *n.* Créateur, auteur; faiseur; (*Comm.*) fabricant, *m.* **maker-up,** *n.* (*Print.*) Metteur en pages, *m.* **making,** *n.* Création, façon, fabrication, construction; confection (of clothes); forme, *f.* **making-up,** *n.* Façon, confection (of clothes); (*Print.*) mise en pages, *f.*

malachite ['mæləkait], *n.* Malachite, *f.*

malacology [mælə'kɔlədʒi], *n.* Malacologie, *f.*

maladjusted [mælə'dʒʌstid], *a.* Inadapté. **maladjustment,** *n.* Inadaptation, *f.*

maladministration [mælədminis'treiʃən], *n.* Mauvaise administration, *f.*

maladroit ['mælədrɔit], *a.* Maladroit.

malady ['mælədi], *n.* Maladie, *f.*

Malaga ['mæləgə]. Malaga, *m.*

Malagasy [mælə'gæsi], *a.* and *n.* Malgache, *m.* and *f.*

malaise [mæ'leiz], *n.* (*Med.*) Malaise, *m.*

malander ['mæləndə], *n.* (*usu. pl.*) Malandre, *f.*

malapert ['mæləpə:t], *a.* Malappris, impertinent. **malapertness, *n.* Insolence, *f.*

malapropism ['mæləprɔpizm], *n.* Impropriété d'expression, *f.*

malaria [mə'lɛəriə], *n.* Malaria, *f.*, paludisme, *m.*

Malay [mə'lei] **Archipelago** or **Malaysia** or **Malaya.** La Malaisie, *f.*

malcontent ['mælkəntent], *a.* and *n.* Mécontent, *m.*

Maldive ['mældaiv] **Archipelago.** Les Maldives, *f.pl.*

male [meil], *a.* Mâle; masculin.—*n.* Mâle, *m.*

malediction [mæli'dikʃən], *n.* Malédiction, *f.*

malefactor ['mælifæktə], *n.* Malfaiteur, *m.*

maleficence [mə'lefisəns], *n.* Malfaisance, *f.* **maleficent,** *a.* Malfaisant. **malevolence,** *n.* Malveillance, *f.* **malevolent,** *a.* Malveillant. **malevolently,** *adv.* Avec malveillance.

malformation [mælfɔ:'meiʃən], *n.* Malformation, *f.*

malice ['mælis], *n.* Malice; malveillance, méchanceté; rancune; (*Law*) intention criminelle, *f.* *To bear malice*, vouloir du mal à, garder rancune à; *with malice prepense* or *aforethought*, avec préméditation, avec intention criminelle.

malicious [mə'liʃəs], *a.* Malicieux. **maliciously,** *adv.* Méchamment. **maliciousness,** *n.* Malice, malveillance, *f.*

malign [mə'lain], *a.* Malin, *m.*, maligne, *f.*; méchant; pernicieux.—*v.t.* Diffamer, noircir.

malignant [mə'lignənt], *a.* Malin, méchant. **malignantly,** *adv.* Malignement, méchamment.

maligner [mə'lainə], *n.* Diffamateur, détracteur, *m.*

malignity [mə'ligniti], *n.* Malignité, malveillance, *f.*

malinger [mə'liŋgə], *v.i.* (*Mil.*) Faire le malade. **malingerer,** *n.* Simulateur, faux

malade, *m.* **malingering,** *n.* Maladie feinte, *f.*

**malkin ['mɔ:kin], *n.* Maritorne, *f.*

mall [mɔ:l], *n.* Gros maillet; mail (promenade), *m.* **The Mall** [ðə'mæl]. **Pall Mall** ['pel'mel] (avenues de Londres).

mallard ['mæləd], *n.* Canard sauvage, *m.*

malleability [mæliə'biliti], *n.* Malléabilité, *f.*

malleable ['mæliəbl], *a.* Malléable.

malleolus [mə'li:oləs], *n.* (*pl.* **malleoli**) (*Anat.*) Malléole, *f.*

mallet ['mælit], *n.* Maillet, *m.*; tapette, *f.*

mallow ['mælou] or **mallows,** *n.* (*Bot.*) Mauve, *f.*

malmsey ['mɑ:mzi], *n.* Malvoisie, *f.*

malnutrition [mælnju'triʃən], *n.* Sous-alimentation, *f.*

malodorous [mæ'loudərəs], *a.* Malodorant.

malpighia [mæl'pigiə], *n.* (*Bot.*) Malpighie, *f.* **malpighian** [mæl'pigiən], *a.* De Malpighi.

malpractice [mæl'præktis], *n.* Malversation, *f.*, méfait, *m.*, incurie, *f.*

malt [mɔ:lt], *n.* Malt, *m.*—*v.t.* Malter. **malthouse,** *n.* Malterie, *f.* **malting,** *n.* Maltage, *m.* **malt-kiln,** *n.* Touraille, *f.* **maltman** or **maltster,** *n.* Malteur, *m.*

Malta ['mɔ:ltə]. Malte, *f.*

Maltese [mɔ:l'ti:z], *a.* and *n.* Maltais, *m.* *Maltese cross,* croix de Malte, *f.*

Malthusian [mæl'θju:ziən], *a.* and *n.* Malthusien.

maltreat [mæl'tri:t], *v.t.* Maltraiter. **maltreatment,** *n.* Mauvais traitement, *m.*

malvaceous [mæl'veiʃəs], *a.* (*Bot.*) Malvacé.

malversation [mælvə'seiʃən], *n.* Malversation, *f.*

mamba ['mæmbə], *n.* Mamba, *f.*

mameluke ['mæməlju:k], *n.* Mameluk, *m.*

mamilla [mæ'milə], *n.* (*Anat., Bot.*) Mamelon, *m.* **mamilliform** [mə'milifɔ:m], *a.* Mamelliforme, mamelonné.

mamma [mə'mɑ:], *n.* Maman, *f.*

mammal ['mæməl], *n.* Mammifère, *m.* **mammalia** [mə'meiliə], *n.pl.* (*Zool.*) Mammifères, *m.pl.* **mammalogy,** *n.* Mammalogie, *f.* **mammary** ['mæməri], *a.* (*Anat.*) Mammaire. **mammiferous** [-'mifərəs], *a.* Mammifère. **mammiform,** *a.* Mammiforme.

Mammon ['mæmən]. Mammon, *m.* **mammonist,** *n.* Adorateur de Mammon, *m.*

mammoth ['mæməθ], *n.* Mammouth, *m.*—*a.* (*fam.*) Énorme, géant.

Man [mæn], **Isle of.** L'île de Man, *f.*

man [mæn], *n.* (*pl.* **men**) Homme, *m.*; domestique, valet (servant); ouvrier (workman); employé (employee); garçon (porter), *m.*; (*pl.*) hommes, gens, *m.pl.*; (*Mil.*) troupes, *f.pl.*; (*Chess*) pièce, *f.*; (*Draughts*) pion, *m.* *A dead man,* un mort, *m.*; (*pop.*) une bouteille vide, *f.*; *as man to man, between man and man,* d'homme à homme; *head man,* chef, *m.*; *man about town,* boulevardier, *m.*; *man and wife,* mari et femme; *man cook,* cuisinier, *m.*; *man's estate,* âge viril, *m.*; *the man in the street,* l'homme de la rue, le grand public; *to a man,* tous jusqu'au dernier; *well, my man!* eh bien! mon brave!—*v.t.* Garnir d'hommes; servir (a gun); armer (a pump, a boat); amariner (a prize). **man-eater,** *n.* Cannibale, anthropophage, *m.* **man-handle,** *v.t.*

Manutentionner; (*fig.*) maltraiter. **man-hater,** *n.* Misanthrope, *m.* **man-hole,** *n.* Trou individuel, *m.*; trou de visite, *m.*; bouche d'accès, *f.* **man-killer,** *n.* Tueur d'hommes, *m.* **man-of-war,** *n.* Vaisseau de guerre, *m.* **man-power,** *n.* Main d'œuvre, *f.*; (*Mil.*) effectifs, *m.pl.* **man-servant,** *n.* Domestique, *m.*

manacle ['mænəkl], *v.t.* Mettre les menottes à; (*fig.*) garrotter. **manacles,** *n.pl.* Menottes, *f.pl.*

manage ['mænidʒ], *v.t.* Diriger, mener, conduire; arranger (things); gouverner, administrer, gérer; ménager (to scheme); manier, dompter (a horse etc.). *I know how to manage it,* je sais comment m'y prendre; *I shall manage it,* j'en viendrai à bout.—*v.i.* S'arranger (pour), parvenir à; venir à bout (de); trouver moyen (de). *He knows how to manage,* il sait ce qu'il a à faire. **manageable,** *a.* Traitable, maniable. *A manageable child,* un enfant docile, *m.*

management, *n.* Conduite, administration; (*Comm.*) gestion (direction), *f.*; artifice, savoir-faire (contrivance), *m.* '*Under new management*', 'changement de propriétaire'.

manager, *n.* Directeur, administrateur; majordome (of a household); (*Comm.*) gérant; (*Theat.*) régisseur, *m.*; (*spt.*) manager, *m.* *General manager,* directeur général; *sales manager,* directeur commercial, *m.*; *she is a good manager,* elle est bonne ménagère. **manageress,** *n.* Directrice, gérante, *f.* **managerial,** *a.* Directorial. **managing,** *n.* Gestion, direction, *f.*—*a.* Directeur, gérant. *Managing director,* administrateur, gérant, *m.*; *she is a managing woman,* c'est une maîtresse femme.

manatee [mænə'ti:], *n.* Lamantin, *m.*

manchineel [mæntʃi'ni:l], *n.* (*Bot.*) Mancenille, *f.* **manchineel-tree,** *n.* Mancenillier, *m.*

Manchuria [mæn'tʃuəriə]. La Mandchourie, *f.*

manciple ['mænsipl], *n.* Économe (of a college etc.), *m.*

mandamus [mæn'deiməs], *n.* (*Law*) Mandement, *m.*

mandarin ['mændərin], *n.* Mandarin, *m.* **mandarin-orange,** *n.* Mandarine, *f.*

mandatary ['mændətəri], *n.* Mandataire, *m.*

mandate ['mændeit], *n.* Commandement, mandat; ordre, *m.* **mandated,** *a.* Sous mandat. **mandatory,** *a.* and *n.* Mandataire, *m.*

mandible ['mændibl], *n.* Mandibule, *f.*

mandibular [mæn'dibjulə], *a.* Mandibulaire.

mandolin ['mændəlin], *n.* Mandoline, *f.*

mandragora [mæn'drægərə] or **mandrake** ['mændreik], *n.* (*Bot.*) Mandragore, *f.*

mandrel ['mændrəl], *n.* Mandrin, *m.*

mandrill ['mændril], *n.* Mandrill, *m.*

manducate ['mændjukeit], *v.t.* Mastiquer, mâcher.

mane [mein], *n.* Crinière, *f.* **maned,** *a.* À crinière.

manes ['meini:z], *n.pl.* Mânes, *m.pl.*

manful ['mænful], *a.* D'homme, viril. **manfully,** *adv.* En homme, virilement, vaillamment. **manfulness,** *n.* Virilité, *f.*, courage, *m.*

manganese ['mæŋgəni:z], *n.* Manganèse, *m.*

mange [meindʒ], *n.* Gale (du chien), *f.*

mangel-wurzel ['mæŋgl'wə:zl], *n.* Betterave fourragère, *f.*

manger ['meindʒə], *n.* Mangeoire, crèche, *f.* *The dog in the manger,* le chien du jardinier.

manginess ['meindʒinis], *n.* État galeux, *m.*

mangle [mæŋgl], *v.t.* Déchirer, mutiler; calandrer (linen).—*n.* Calandre, *f.* **mangler,** *n.* Calandreur, *m.* **mangling,** *n.* Calandrage, *m.*

mango ['mæŋgou], *n.* (*Bot.*) Mangue, *f.* **mango-tree,** *n.* Manguier, *m.*

mangosteen [mæŋgəs'ti:n], *n.* (*Bot.*) *Mangostan, mangoustan (tree), *m.*; mangouste (fruit), *f.*

mangrove ['mæŋgrouv], *n.* (*Bot.*) Mangle, *f.*; manglier, manguier (tree), *m.*

mangy ['meindʒi], *a.* Galeux.

manhood ['mænhud], *n.* Virilité, *f.*; âge viril, *m.*; nature humaine, *f.* *Manhood suffrage,* suffrage universel masculin, *m.*

mania ['meiniə], *n.* Folie, rage, manie, *f.*

maniac ['meiniæk], *n.* Fou furieux, *m.*, folle furieuse, *f.*, fou, *m.*, folle, *f.*; (*fig.*) maniaque, *m.*—*a.* or **maniacal** [mə'naiəkəl], *a.* Furieux, fou.

Manichaean [mæni'ki:ən], *a.* Des manichéens. **Manichaeism,** *n.* Manichéisme, *m.* **Manichee,** *n.* Manichéen, *m.*, manichéenne, *f.*

manicure ['mænikjuə], *n.* Soin des ongles, *m.* —*v.t.* Soigner les ongles. **manicurist,** *n.* Manucure, *m.* and *f.*

manifest ['mænifest], *v.t.* Manifester, témoigner, laisser voir, montrer. *To manifest a cargo,* déclarer une cargaison.—*a.* Manifeste, évident.—*n.* Manifeste, *m.*; (*Naut.*) état général de chargement, *m.* **manifestation** [-'teifən], *n.* Manifestation, *f.* **manifestly,** *adv.* Manifestement. **manifesto** [-'festou], *n.* Manifeste, *m.*

manifold ['mænifould], *a.* Divers, multiple; varié.—*n.* (*Eng.*) Tubulure, *f.*; collecteur, *m.* —*v.t.* Polycopier. **manifoldly,** *adv.* Diversement. **manifoldness,** *n.* Multiplicité, *f.*

manikin ['mænikin], *n.* Bout d'homme, mannequin, homuncule, *m.*

Manila [mə'nilə]. Manille, *f.*

manila [mə'nilə], *n.* Chanvre de Manille, *m.*

manilla [mə'nilə], *n.* Manille, *f.*

manioc ['mæniɔk], *n.* Manioc, *m.*

maniple ['mænipl], *n.* Manipule, *m.*

manipular [mə'nipjulə], *a.* Manipulaire.

manipulate [mə'nipjuleit], *v.t.* Manipuler. **manipulation** [-'leifən], *n.* Manipulation, *f.* **manipulator,** *n.* Manipulateur, *m.*

mankind [mæn'kaind], *n.* Genre humain, *m.*, l'humanité, *f.* **manlike,** *a.* D'homme, viril; mâle; hommasse (of a woman). **manliness,** *n.* Caractère viril, *m.* **manly,** *a.* D'homme, viril, mâle.

manna ['mænə], *n.* Manne, *f.*

mannequin ['mænikin], *n.* (*Dress.*) Mannequin, *m.* *Mannequin parade,* défilé de mannequins, *m.*

manner ['mænə], *n.* Manière, mode, *f.*, air; genre, *m.*, sorte, façon, espèce; coutume, habitude, *f.*; (*pl.*) mœurs, *f.pl.*, politesse, *f.* *After the manner of,* à la manière de, d'après; *all manner of things,* toutes sortes de choses, *f.pl.*; *good manners,* bonnes manières, *f.pl.*, savoir-vivre, *m.*; *in a manner of speaking,* en quelque sorte, pour ainsi dire; *in like manner,*

de même; *in the same manner as*, de même que, comme; *manners and customs*, us et coutumes, *m.* and *f.pl.*; *manners change with the times*, autres temps, autres mœurs; *the manner in which*, la manière dont; *to have no manners*, n'avoir pas de savoir-vivre; *to learn manners*, apprendre à vivre. **mannered**, *a.* Aux manières (simples etc.). *Ill-mannered*, mal élevé. **mannerism**, *n.* Air maniéré, maniérisme, *m.*; tic, *m.* **mannerist**, *n.* Maniériste, *m.* **mannerliness**, *n.* Civilité, politesse, *f.* **mannerly**, *a.* Poli.
manning ['mæniŋ], *n.* Armement, équipement, *m.*
mannish ['mæniʃ], *a.* Hommasse.
manœuvrability [mə'nu:vrəbiliti], *n.* Maniabilité, *f.* (of a car, plane). **manœuvrable**, *a.* Maniable.
manœuvre [mə'nu:və], *n.* Manœuvre, *f.*—*v.i.* Manœuvrer.—*v.t.* Faire manœuvrer, manœuvrer. **manœuvrer**, *n.* Conducteur de manœuvres, manœuvrier, *m.* **manœuvring**, *n.* Manœuvres, *f.pl.*
manometer [mə'nɔmitə], *n.* Manomètre, *m.*
manometrical [mæno'metrikəl], *a.* Manométrique.
manor ['mænə], *n.* Seigneurie, *f.* **manorhouse**, *n.* Manoir, château seigneurial, *m.*
manorial [mə'nɔ:riəl], *a.* Seigneurial.
mansard roof ['mænsəd'ru:f], *n.* Toit en mansarde, comble brisé, *m.*
manse [mæns], *n.* Presbytère, *m.*
mansion ['mænʃən], *n.* Château (in country); hôtel (particulier) (town house); (*pl.*) immeuble de rapport, *m.*; maison divisée en appartements, *f.* **mansion-house**, *n.* Château, *m.*; hôtel du lord-maire de Londres, de Dublin, etc., *m.*
manslaughter ['mænslɔ:tə], *n.* (*Law*) Homicide involontaire, *m.* **manslayer**, *n.* Meurtrier, homicide, *m.*
mansuetude ['mænswɔtju:d], *n.* Mansuétude, *f.*
mantel [mæntl] or **mantelpiece** ['mæntlpi:s], *n.* Manteau *or* dessus de cheminée, *m.*, cheminée, *f.*
mantelet ['mæntələt], *n.* Mantelet, *m.*
mantilla [mæn'tilə], *n.* Mantille, *f.*
mantis ['mæntis], *n.* (*Ent.*) Mante, *f.* *Praying mantis*, mante religieuse, *f.*
mantissa [mæn'tisə], *n.* Mantisse, *f.*
mantle [mæntl], *n.* Manteau; (*Gas*) manchon, *m.*—*v.t.* Couvrir, voiler.—*v.i.* S'étendre, se répandre. *The mantling bowl*, le bol qui se couvre d'écume.
mantling ['mæntliŋ], *n.* (*Her.*) Lambrequin, *m.*
Mantua ['mæntjuə]. Mantoue, *f.*
manual ['mænjuel], *a.* Manuel, de la main. *Manual exercise*, (*Mil.*) maniement d'armes, *m.*—*n.* Manuel (book); (*Organ*) clavier, *m.* **manually**, *adv.* Manuellement.
manufactory [mænju'fæktəri], *n.* Fabrique, usine, *f.*, ateliers, *m.pl.* **manufacture**, *n.* Manufacture, confection, fabrication, *f.*; (*pl.*) industrie, *f.*, manufacturière, *f.*, produits des manufactures, *m.pl.*—*v.t.* Manufacturer, fabriquer, confectionner.—*v.i.* Se livrer à l'industrie. **manufacturer**, *n.* Manufacturier, fabricant, industriel, *m.* **manufacturing**, *a.* Manufacturier.—*n.* Fabrication, *f.*

manumission [mænju'miʃən], *n.* Manumission, *f.*, affranchissement, *m.* **manumit**, *v.t.* Affranchir.
manure [mə'njuə], *n.* Engrais, fumier, *m.*—*v.t.* Engraisser, fumer.
manuscript ['mænjuskript], *a.* and *n.* Manuscrit, *m.*
Manx [mæŋks], *a.* De l'île de Man, mannois. *Manx cat*, chat sans queue, *m.*
many ['meni], *a.* Beaucoup (de), bien (des); nombreux; plusieurs, maint, divers. *A good many* or *a great many*, un très grand nombre de; *as many again*, deux fois autant; *as many as*, autant que, jusqu'à (before a numeral); *how many?* combien? *in many instances*, dans bien des cas; *many a*, maint, bien des; *many a time*, maintes fois; *many more*, maint autre, beaucoup d'autres; *so many*, tant, tant de; *there's many a true word spoken in jest*, on dit souvent la vérité en riant; *too many*, trop, trop de.—*n.* *The many*, la multitude, la foule, *f.* **many-coloured**, *a.* Multicolore. **many-headed**, *a.* Aux têtes nombreuses. **many-sided**, *a.* Qui a plusieurs côtés, polygone; (*fig.*) complexe.
map [mæp], *n.* Carte, carte géographique, *f.* *Map of a town*, plan d'une ville, *m.*; *map of the world*, mappemonde, *f.*; *ordnance map*, carte d'état-major, *f.*—*v.t.* Faire une carte or un plan de, tracer. —**map-maker**, *n.* Cartographe, *m.* **mapping**, *n.* Cartographie, *f.*
maple [meipl], *n.* Érable, *m.* **maple-sugar**, *n.* Sucre d'érable, *m.*
mar [ma:], *v.t.* Gâter, défigurer; (*fig.*) troubler.
marabou ['mærəbu:], *n.* Marabout (bird), *m.*
marabout ['mærəbu:t], *n.* Marabout (priest), *m.*
maraschino [mærə'ski:nou], *n.* Marasquin (liqueur), *m.*
marasmus [mə'ræzməs], *n.* Marasme, *m.*
marathon ['mærəθɔn], *n.* Marathon, *m.*
maraud [mə'rɔ:d], *v.i.* Marauder. **marauder**, *n.* Maraudeur, malandrin, *m.* **marauding**, *n.* Maraude, *f.*, maraudage, *m.*
marble [ma:bl], *n.* Marbre, *m.*; bille (toy), *f.* *Game of marbles*, jeu de billes, *m.*; *glass marble*, agate, *f.*—*a.* De marbre.—*v.t.* Marbrer. **marble-cutting**, *n.* Marbrerie, *f.* **marble-mason**, *n.* Marbrier, *m.* **marble-quarry**, *n.* Carrière de marbre; marbrière, *f.* **marble-works**, *n.pl.* Marbrerie, *f.*
marbled, *a.* Marbré. **marbling**, *n.* Marbrure, *f.*
marcasite ['ma:kəsait, -sit], *n.* Marcassite, *f.*
marcel ['ma:səl] or **marcel-wave**, *n.* Ondulation (permanente) à la Marcel, *f.*
March [ma:tʃ], *n.* (*Mil.*) Mars (month), *m. Mad as a March hare*, fou à lier.
march [ma:tʃ], *n.* (*Mil.*) Marche, *f.*; (*fig.*) progrès, *m.*; frontière (frontier), *f. Day's march*, étape, *f.*; *dead march*, marche funèbre, *f.*; *forced march*, marche forcée, *f.*; *march past*, défilé, *m.*; *quick march*, pas accéléré, *m.*; *to lead the march*, ouvrir la marche; *to steal a march on*, gagner une marche sur.—*v.i.* Marcher, se mettre en marche; (*fig.*) avancer. *Quick march!* pas accéléré, marche! *to march abreast*, marcher de front; *to march in*, entrer; *to march off*, se mettre en marche, s'en aller, (*colloq.*) plier bagage; *to march on*, marcher, avancer; *to march out*, sortir; *to*

march past, défiler devant, défiler; *to march
with*, (of land etc.), être limitrophe à.—*v.t.*
Faire marcher, mettre en marche. *To march
off*, emmener, faire décamper; *to march out*,
faire sortir.
marching ['mɑːtʃiŋ], *n.* Marche, *f.*—*a.* De
marche. *In marching order*, en tenue de
route; *marching orders*, feuille de route, *f.*;
marching regiment, régiment de ligne, *m.*;
(fig.) to give someone his marching orders,
signifier son congé à quelqu'un.
marchioness [mɑːʃə'nes], *n.* Marquise, *f.*
marchpane ['mɑːtʃpein], *n.* [MARZIPAN].
marconigram [mɑː'kouniɡræm], *n.* Dépêche
par sans-fil, *f.*
Marcus Aurelius ['mɑːkəs ɔː'riːliəs]. Marc-
Aurèle, *m.*
mare [mɛə], *n.* Jument, *f.* **mare's-nest**, *n.*
Merle blanc, *m.* **mare's-tail**, *n.* Queue de
chat (cloud); pesse d'eau (plant), *f.*
mareca [mæ'riːkə] [WIDGEON].
maremma [mə'remə], *n.* Maremme, *f.*
Margaret ['mɑːɡərit]. Marguerite, *f.*
margaric [mɑː'ɡærik], *a.* Margarique.
margarine ['mɑːɡəriːn or -dʒəriːn], *n.* Margarine, *f.*
margay ['mɑːɡei], *n.* Margay, chat-tigre, *m.*
margin ['mɑːdʒin], *n.* Marge (of paper etc.),
f.; bord (of a river, lake, etc.), *m. In the
margin*, en marge.—*v.t.* Border; mettre une
marge à. **margin-release**, *n.* Déclenche-
marge, *m.*
marginal, *a.* En marge; marginal. *Marginal
seat*, *(Polit.)* siège obtenu à une faible
majorité et âprement disputé, *m.*
margravate or **margraviate** [mɑː'ɡreiviət],
n. Margraviat, *m.* **margrave** ['mɑːɡreiv], *n.*
Margrave, *m.*
marguerite ['mɑːɡəriːt], *n.* *(Bot.)* Grande
marguerite, *f.*
Mariana Islands. Îles Mariannes, *f.pl.*
marigold ['mærigould], *n.* *(Bot.)* Souci, *m.*
marine [mə'riːn], *a.* Marin, de mer; naval.
Marine infantry, infanterie de marine, *f.*;
marine store dealer, marchand de ferrailles *or*
de chiffons, *m.*—*n.* Soldat de marine, fusilier
marin, *m.*; *(pl.)* infanterie de marine, *f. Tell
that to the marines*, allez conter cela à d'autres.
mariner ['mærinə], *n.* Marin, *m. Mariner's
card*, rose des vents, *f.*; *mariner's compass*,
boussole, *f.*
marionette [mæriə'net], *n.* Marionnette à fils, *f.*
marital ['mæritəl], *a.* Marital. **maritally**,
adv. Maritalement.
maritime ['mæritaim], *a.* Maritime.
marjoram ['mɑːdʒərəm], *n.* Marjolaine, *f.*
Mark [mɑːk]. Marc, *m.*
mark [mɑːk], *n.* Marque, *f.*, signe, *m.*; empreinte; *(fig.)* distinction, importance, *f.*;
témoignage (of esteem etc.), *m.*; *(sch.)* note, *f.*;
point, *m.*; but, blanc, *m.*, cible (target), *f.*;
marc (coin), *m.*; croix (signature), *f.*; *(spt.)*
ligne de départ, *f.*; *(Naut.)* amer, *m. He is
not up to the mark*, il n'est pas à la hauteur;
man of mark, homme marquant, *m.*; *near the
mark*, près de la vérité; *on your marks! get set!
go!* à vos marques! prêts! partez! *to be hardly
up to the mark*, laisser à désirer; *to be
quick off the mark*, démarrer vivement, avoir
la compréhension facile; *to hit the mark*,
atteindre le but; *to make one's mark*, acquérir
de la distinction, se faire un nom; *to miss one's*

mark, manquer son coup.—*v.t.* Marquer,
remarquer; *(sch.)* coter, noter; témoigner;
signaler; *(fig.)* observer, faire attention à.
Mark! remarquez bien, notez bien; *mark
my words*, faites bien attention à ce que je
dis; *(Ftb.)* mark your men! Surveillez bien *or*
marquez chacun votre adversaire! *to mark
down*, dévaloriser, baisser de prix; *to mark
out*, désigner; *to mark time*, marquer le
pas.
marked, *a.* Marqué, évident; prononcé (of
accent). *The separation became more marked*,
la scission s'accusa de plus en plus. **markedly**, *adv.* D'une façon marquée.
marker, *n.* Marqueur; jeton (counter); signet
(for a book), *m.*
market ['mɑːkit], *n.* Marché, *m.*; halle, *f.*;
débit (sale); cours (price); *(Comm.)* débouché,
m. In our market, sur notre place; *in the
market*, au marché, en vente, sur la place; *to
find a market for*, trouver un débouché *or*
des acheteurs pour.—*v.t.* Acheter au marché,
vendre au marché. *To go marketing*, aller
faire son marché. **market-day**, *n.* Jour de
marché, *m.* **market-garden**, *n.* Jardin
maraîcher, *m.* **market-gardener**, *n.*
Maraîcher, *m.* **market-gardening**, *n.*
Culture maraîchère, *f.* **market-hall**, *n.*
Marché couvert, *m.* **market-house**, *n.*
Halle, *f.* **market-place**, *n.* Marché, *m.*
market-price, *n.* Cours du marché, prix
courant, *m.* **market-town**, *n.* Ville où se
tient un marché, *f.*, bourg, *m.* **market-
woman**, *n.* Femme de la halle, marchande,
f.
marketable, *a.* De bon débit; courant (of
price). **marketeer**, *n. Black marketeer*,
trafiquant du marché noir, *m.* **marketing**,
n. Marché, *m.*; service commercial, *m.*
marking ['mɑːkiŋ], *n.* Marquage, *m.* **marking-ink**, *n.* Encre à marquer, *f.* **marking-
iron**, *n.* Fer à marquer, *m.*
marksman ['mɑːksmən], *n.* *(pl.* **marksmen)**
Bon tireur, *m.* **marksmanship**, *n.* Adresse
au tir, *f.*
marl [mɑːl], *n.* Marne, *f.*—*v.t.* Marner.
marling, *n.* Marnage, *m.* **marl-pit**, *n.*
Marnière, *f.* **marlstone**, *n.* Marne dure,
marne siliceuse, *f.* **marly**, *a.* Marneux.
marline ['mɑːlin], *n.* *(Naut.)* Merlin, *m.*
marline-spike, *n.* Épissoir, *m.*
marmalade ['mɑːməleid], *n.* Confiture
d'oranges, *f.*
Marmora ['mɑːmərə], Sea of. La Mer de
Marmara, *f.*
marmoreal [mɑː'mɔːriəl] or **marmorean**
[mɑː'mɔːriən], *a.* Marmoréen, de marbre.
marmoset [mɑːmə'zet], *n.* Ouistiti, *m.*
marmot ['mɑːmət], *n.* Marmotte, *f.*
Maronite ['mærənait], *n.* Maronite, *m.*
maroon (1) [mə'ruːn], *n.* Marron(slave), *m.*—
v.t. Abandonner dans une île déserte.
maroon (2) [mə'ruːn], *n.* and *a.* Marron
pourpré (colour), *m.*
maroon (3) [mə'ruːn], *n.* Fusée à pétard
(firework), *f.*
marplot ['mɑːplɔt], *n.* Brouillon, gaffeur, *m.*
marque [mɑːk], *n.* Lettre de marque, *f.*
marquee [mɑː'kiː], *n.* Grande tente (for
garden parties etc.), *f.*
Marquesas [mɑː'keisæs]. Les Îles Marquises,
f.pl.

marquess ['mɑːkwis] or **marquis**, *n.* Marquis, *m.* **marquessate** or **marquisate**, *n.* Marquisat, *m.*

marquetry ['mɑːkətri], *n.* Marqueterie, *f.*

marriage ['mærɪdʒ], *n.* Mariage, *m.*; noces (wedding), *f.pl. To give in marriage*, donner en mariage. **marriageable**, *a.* À marier, mariable, nubile. **marriage articles**, *n.* Contrat de mariage, *m.* **marriage-bed**, *n.* Lit nuptial, *m.* **marriage certificate**, **marriage lines**, *n.* Acte de mariage, *m.* **marriage-contract**, *n.* Contrat de mariage, *m.* **marriage-portion**, *n.* Dot, *f.*

married ['mærɪd], *a.* Marié; conjugal (of things). *Married couple*, mari et femme, *m.*; ménage, *m.*; *married life*, vie conjugale, *f.*; *married state*, mariage, *m.*; *newly married couple*, nouveaux mariés, *m.pl.*

marrow ['mærou], *n.* Moelle; (*fig.*) essence, *f. Vegetable marrow*, courgette, *f.* **marrow-bone**, *n.* Os à moelle, *m.* **marrowfat**, *n.* Pois carré, *m.* **marrowless**, *a.* Sans moelle, veule. **marrowy**, *a.* Plein de moelle.

marry ['mæri], *v.t.* Marier (to give away or to perform the ceremony); se marier avec, épouser (to take in marriage). *To marry below one's station*, se mésallier.—*v.i.* Se marier. *To marry again*, se remarier.—**int.* Vraiment, pardi!

Mars [mɑːz]. Mars, *m.*

Marseilles [mɑːˈseilz]. Marseille, *f.*

marsh [mɑːʃ], *n.* Marais, *m.* **marsh-fever**, *n.* Fièvre paludéenne, *f.* **marsh-gas**, *n.* Gaz des marais, méthane, *m.* **marsh-hen**, *n.* Poule d'eau, *f.* **marsh-land**, *n.* Pays marécageux, *m.* **marsh-mallow**, *n.* (*Bot.*) Guimauve, *f.*; bonbon à la guimauve, *m.* **marsh-marigold**, *n.* Souci d'eau, *m.* **marshy**, *a.* Marécageux.

marshal [mɑːʃl], *n.* Maréchal; (*Navy*) prévôt; (*Am.*) préfet, *m.* *Air-marshal*, général de corps d'armée aérienne, *m.*; *field-marshal*, maréchal, *m.*, (France) maréchal de France, *m.*—*v.t.* Ranger; mettre en ordre; classer; introduire (quelqu'un). ***marshalship**, *n.* Dignité de maréchal, *f.*

marsupial [mɑːˈsjuːpiəl], *a. and n.* Marsupial, *m.*

mart [mɑːt], *n.* Marché, entrepôt; débouché (outlet), *m.*

martello [mɑːˈtelou] or **martello-tower**, *n.* Tour de vigie, *f.*

marten ['mɑːtən], *n.* Martre, *f. Beech marten*, fouine, *f.*

Martha ['mɑːθə]. Marthe, *f.*

martial [mɑːʃl], *a.* Martial; de guerre, de bataille; guerrier, belliqueux. **martial law**, *n.* Loi martiale, *f.*; code militaire, *m. Martial array*, ordre de bataille, *m.* **martially**, *adv.* En guerrier, d'une manière martiale.

Martian, *a. and n.* Martien, *m.*, -ienne, *f.*

martin ['mɑːtin], *n.* Martin, martinet, *m.*

martinet (1) [mɑːtiˈnet], *n.* Officier strict sur la discipline, *m.*, (*fam.*) pète-sec, *m. To be a martinet*, mener les gens à la baguette.

martinet (2) [mɑːtiˈnet], *n.* (*Orn.*) Hirondelle de fenêtre, *f.*

martingale ['mɑːtiŋgeil], *n.* Martingale, *f.*

Martinmas ['mɑːtinmæs], *n.* La Saint-Martin, *f.*

martlet ['mɑːtlit], *n.* (*Orn.*) Martinet, *m.*; (*Her.*) merlette, *f.*

martyr ['mɑːtə], *n.* Martyr, *m.*, martyre, *f. To be a martyr to*, souffrir beaucoup de.—*v.t.* Martyriser. **martyrdom**, *n.* Martyre, *m.*

martyrize, *v.t.* (*fam.*) Faire souffrir, martyriser. **martyrologist** [-ˈrɔlədʒist], *n.* Martyrologiste, *m.* **martyrology**, *n.* Martyrologe, *m.* **martyry**, *n.* Chapelle (en l'honneur) d'un martyr, *f.*

marvel [mɑːvl], *n.* Merveille, chose merveilleuse, *f. Marvel of Peru*, belle de nuit, *f.*—*v.i.* S'émerveiller, s'étonner. *To marvel at*, s'émerveiller de.

marvellous ['mɑːv(i)ləs], *a.* Merveilleux, étonnant. **marvellously**, *adv.* À merveille. **marvellousness** ['mɑːvləsnis], *n.* Merveilleux, *m.*

Marxism ['mɑːksism], *n.* Marxisme, *m.* **Marxist**, *a. and n.* Marxiste.

Mary ['mɛəri]. Marie, *f.*

marzipan [mɑːziˈpæn], *n.* Massepain, *m.*

mascara [mæsˈkɑːrə], *n.* Cosmétique pour les cils, *m.*

mascot ['mæskət], *n.* Mascotte, *f.*

masculine ['mæskjulin], *a.* Mâle, d'homme; (*Gram.*) masculin; hommasse (of women).— *n.* Masculin, *m. In the masculine*, au masculin. **masculinely**, *adv.* Virilement, en homme. **masculinity** [-ˈliniti], *n.* Masculinité, *f.*

mash [mæʃ], *n.* Mélange, *m.*, pâte, bouillie, *f.*; mâche (for cattle), *f.*; pâtée (for dog, fowl), *f.* Bran mash, son mouillé, barbotage, *m.* (for horses).—*v.t.* Broyer; mélanger; (*Brewing*) brasser. *Mashed potatoes*, purée de pommes de terre, *f.* **mash-tub**, *n.* (*Brewing*) Cuve-matière, *f.* **mashy**, *a.* Mélangé, écrasé, broyé.

mask [mɑːsk], *n.* Masque, *m.*; (*Arch.*) mascaron; loup (woman's mask), *m.*; (*Phot.*) cache, *m.*; (*Hunt.*) tête, *f.* (of fox). *To throw off the mask*, lever le masque.—*v.t.* Masquer; déguiser. *Masked battery*, batterie masquée, *f.*—*v.i.* Se masquer. **masker**, *n.* Masque, *m.*, personne masquée, *f.*

maslin ['mæzlin], *n.* Méteil, *m.*

masochism ['mæzokizm], *n.* Masochisme, *m.* **masochist**, *a.* Masochiste.

mason ['meisən], *n.* Maçon, *m. Freemason*, franc-maçon, *m.* **masonic** [məˈsɔnik], *a.* Maçonnique.

masonry ['meisənri], *n.* Maçonnerie, *f. Free-masonry*, franc-maçonnerie, *f.*

masque [mɑːsk], *n.* (*Lit.*) Comédie-ballet, *f.* masque, *m.*

masquerade [mæskəˈreid], *n.* Mascarade, *f.* —*v.i.* Se masquer, aller en masque, faire une mascarade. *To masquerade as*, se faire passer pour, se déguiser en. **masquerader**, *n.* Masque, *m.*; (*fig.*) imposteur, *m.*

mass (1) [mæs], *n.* Masse, *f.*; amas, gros, *m.*; multitude, foule (crowd), *f. A mass of things*, une foule de choses; *the masses*, les masses, *f.pl.*, la foule, *f.*—*v.t.* Masser.—*v.i.* Se masser; s'amonceler (of clouds). **massing**, *n.* Concentration, *f.*, rassemblement, *m.* (of troops); amoncellement (of clouds), *m.*, agglomération, *f.* **mass-meeting**, *n.* Assemblée en masse, *f.*

mass (2) [mæs, mɑːs], *n.* Messe, *f. High mass*, grand'messe, *f.*; *low mass*, messe basse, *f.*; *to hear mass*, assister à la messe. **mass-book**, *n.* Livre de messe, missel, *m.*

massacre ['mæsəkə], *n.* Massacre, *m.*—*v.t.*

Massacrer. **massacrer,** *n.* Massacreur, *m.*

massage [mæ'sɑːʒ], *n.* Massage, *m.*—*v.t.* Masser. **masseur,** *n.* Masseur, *m.* **masseuse,** *n.* Masseuse, *f.*

massicot ['mæsikət], *n.* Massicot, *m.*

massive ['mæsiv] or **massy, a.* Massif. **massively,** *adv.* En masse, massivement. **massiveness,** *n.* Caractère massif, *m.*

mast [mɑːst], *n.* Mât, *m.*; (*pl.*) mâts, *m.pl.,* mâture, *f. Before the mast,* sur le gaillard d'avant; *foremast,* mât de misaine; *half-mast high,* à mi-mât; *jury-mast,* mât de fortune; *main-mast,* grand mât; *mizzen-mast,* mât d'artimon; *spare mast,* mât de rechange.— *v.t.* Mâter. **masted,** *a.* Mâté. *A three-masted ship,* un trois-mâts, *m.* **mast-head,** *n.* Tête de mât, *f.* **mastless,** *a.* Sans mât.

master ['mɑːstə], *n.* Maître, directeur, chef; (*Naut.*) patron, maître (of a merchant vessel, of a fishing boat); patron (of workmen); (*sch. etc.*) maître d'école, professeur; monsieur (title given to boys in their teens), (*fig.*) possesseur, *m. French master,* professeur de français; *headmaster* or *high master,* principal (de collège), proviseur (de lycée), *m.*; *he is a master hand at it,* il y est passé maître; *master hand,* main de maître, *f.*; *Master of Arts,* diplômé d'études supérieures de lettres, *m.*; *Master of the Horse,* Grand Écuyer, *m.*; *Master of the Mint,* directeur de la Monnaie, *m.*; *Master of the Rolls,* garde des archives, *m.*; *to be a past master in,* être passé maître en; *to be one's own master,* s'appartenir, ne dépendre que de soi; *to be thoroughly master of,* posséder à fond, savoir à fond; *to make one-self master of,* se rendre maître de.—*v.t.* Maîtriser, surmonter, dompter, vaincre; se rendre maître de; l'emporter sur.

master-builder, *n.* Entrepreneur de bâtiments, *m.* **master-key,** *n.* Passe-partout, *m.* **master-mind,** *n.* Esprit supérieur, *m.* **masterpiece,** *n.* Chef-d'œuvre, *m.* **master-string,** *n.* Corde principale, *f.* **master-stroke** or **master-touch,** *n.* Coup de maître, *m.*

masterful, *a.* De maître, impérieux, dominateur. **masterless,** *a.* Sans maître. **masterly,** *a.* De maître; magistral. **mastership,** *n.* Direction; (*Collège*) chaire; (*fig.*) autorité, habileté, supériorité, *f.* **mastery,** *n.* Empire, pouvoir, *m.*; supériorité, prééminence, maîtrise, *f. To contend for the mastery of,* le disputer à; *to get the mastery of,* maîtriser.

mastic ['mæstik], *n.* Mastic, *m.* **mastic-tree,** *n.* Lentisque, *m.*

masticate ['mæstikeit], *v.t.* Mâcher. **mastication** [-'keiʃən], *n.* Mastication, *f.* **masticatory,** *a.* and *n.* Masticatoire, *m.*

mastiff ['mæstif], *n.* Mâtin, *m.*

mastitis [mæs'taitis], *n.* Mastite, *f.*

mastodon ['mæstodon], *n.* Mastodonte, *m.*

mastoid ['mæstoid], *a.* Mastoïde. *Inflammation of the mastoid,* mastoïdite, *f.* **mastoidean** [-'toidiən], *a.* Mastoïdien.

masturbate ['mæstəːbeit], *v.i.* Se masturber. **masturbation,** *n.* Masturbation, *f.*

mat (1) [mæt], *n.* Natte, *f.*; paillasson (of straw); dessous de lampe (for lamps); (*Naut.*) paillet, *m. Door-mat,* paillasson, *m.*; *grass-mat,* rabane, *f.*; *table-mat,* dessous de plat,

rond de table, *m.*—*v.t.* Natter, tresser; couvrir de nattes or de paillassons. *Matted hair,* cheveux emmêlés, *m.pl.*

mat (2) or **matt,** *a.* Mat.

matador ['mætədɔː], *n.* Matador, *m.*

match [mætʃ], *n.* Allumette (for lighting); (*Artill.*) mèche, *f.*; pareil, pendant, égal (an equal); mariage (marriage); parti (person to be married), *m.*; lutte (contest), *f.*; match, *m.*, partie; course (in running, sailing, rowing, etc.), *f. Drawn match,* match nul, *m.*; *safety match,* allumette suédoise, *f.*; *wax match,* allumette bougie, *f. To be a bad match,* aller mal ensemble (of things); *to be a good match,* aller bien ensemble, être bien assorti; *to be a match for,* être de taille à, être de la force de; *to be more than a match for,* être trop fort pour; *to make a good match,* faire un bon mariage, épouser un bon parti; *to meet (with) one's match,* trouver à qui parler; *to strike a match,* gratter une allumette.—*v.t.* Assortir, appareiller, égaler, apparier (pairs of things); rivaliser avec; tenir tête à, se mesurer avec (to oppose). *Evenly matched,* de force égale; *to match boards,* bouveter des planches.—*v.i.* S'assortir, être pareil; convenir, s'accorder, s'harmoniser.

matchable, *a.* Comparable, pareil.

matchboarding, *n.* Planches bouvetées, *f.pl.* **match-box,** *n.* Boîte d'allumettes, *f.* **match-lock,** *n.* Fusil à mèche, *m.* **match-maker,** *n.* Marieur, *m.*, marieuse, *f.*; fabricant d'allumettes, *m.* **match-making,** *n.* Manie d'arranger des mariages; fabrication des allumettes, *f.* **match-tub,* *n.* (*Artill.*) Baril à mèches, *m.*, (*Naut.*) marmotte, *f.*

matchet ['mætʃit], *n.* Machette, *f.*

matching, *n.* Assortiment, appareillement, appariement, *m.*

matchless, *a.* Incomparable, sans pareil. **matchlessly,** *adv.* Incomparablement. **matchlessness,** *n.* Incomparabilité, *f.*

matchwood, *n.* Bois d'allumettes, *m. To reduce to matchwood,* mettre en miettes.

mate [meit], *n.* Camarade, compagnon, *m.*, compagne, *f.*; (*Naut.*) second maître (in the Navy); officier (on merchant vessel); (*Chess*) mat, *m.*—*v.t.* Égaler, assortir, apparier; tenir compagnie avec; (*Chess*) mater, faire échec et mat. **mateless,** *a.* Sans compagnon, sans compagne. **mating,** *n.* Accouplement (of animals), *m.*

maté ['mætei], *n.* Maté, *m.*

mater ['meitə], *n.* (*colloq.*) The mater, ma mère, *f.* (*Anat.*) Dura mater, dure-mère, *f.*; pia mater, pie-mère, *f.*

material [mə'tiəriəl], *a.* Matériel; essentiel, important, considérable.—*n.* Matière; étoffe, *f.*, tissu (cloth); matériel (stores), *m.*; (*pl.*) matériaux, *m.pl.*; (*Art*) fournitures, *f.pl. Raw material,* matière première, *f.* **materialism** or **materialness,** *n.* Matérialisme, *m.* **materialist,** *n.* and *a.* Matérialiste, *m.* **materialistic,** *a.* Matérialiste. **materiality** [-'æliti], *n.* Matérialité; importance, *f.* **materialize,** *v.t.* Matérialiser.—*v.i.* Se réaliser. **materially,** *adv.* Matériellement, essentiellement.

materia medica, *n.* (*Med.*) Matière médicale, *f.*

maternal [mə'tə:nl], *a.* Maternel. **maternally,** *adv.* Maternellement. **maternity,** *n.* Maternité, *f.*

matey ['meiti], *a.* (*pop.*) Amical.

mathematic [mæθə'mætik] or **mathematical,** *a.* Mathématique, des mathématiques. **mathematically,** *adv.* Mathématiquement. **mathematician** [-'tiʃən], *n.* Mathématicien, *m.*

mathematics, *n.pl.* Mathématiques, *f.pl.* *Applied mathematics,* mathématiques appliquées; *higher mathematics,* mathématiques spéciales.

maths [mæθs], *n. fam. abbr. for* [MATHEMATICS].

Matilda [mə'tildə]. Mathilde, *f.*

matinée ['mætinei], *n.* (*Theat.*) Matinée, *f.* *Matinée idol,* idole du public, *f.*

matins ['mætinz], *n.pl.* Matines, *f.pl.*

*****matrass** ['mætrəs], *n.* (*Chem.*) Matras, *m.*

matriarch ['meitriɑ:k], *n.* Matriarche, *f.*; (*fam.*) femme qui porte les chausses, *f.* **matriarchy** ['meitriɑ:ki], *n.* Matriarcat, *m.*

matricide ['mætrisaid], *n.* Matricide, *m.*

matriculate [mə'trikjuleit], *v.i.* Prendre ses inscriptions (après avoir passé l'examen d'entrée dit 'matriculation').—*v.t.* Immatriculer.

matriculation [mətrikju'leiʃən], *n.* Ancien examen de fin d'études (équivalant au baccalauréat) qui donnait le droit de s'inscrire dans une Université.

matrimonial [mætri'mouniəl], *a.* Conjugal; (*Law*) matrimonial. **matrimonially,** *adv.* Conjugalement.

matrimony ['mætriməni], *n.* Mariage, *m.*, la vie conjugale, *f.*

matrix ['meitriks], *n.* Matrice, *f.*

matron ['meitrən], *n.* Matrone, *f.*, mère de famille; infirmière en chef (of a hospital etc.); (*sch.*) intendante, *f.*

matronal, matron-like or **matronly,** *a.* De matrone; d'un âge mûr, d'un certain âge; respectable.

matter ['mætə], *n.* Matière; chose, affaire, *f.*; fond; sujet; (*Med.*) pus, *m.*; (*fig.*) importance (import), *f.* *As a matter of fact,* le fait est que; *as if nothing was the matter,* comme si de rien n'était; *a small matter,* une bagatelle; *as matters stand,* au point où en sont les choses; *in matters of,* en matière de; *matter of course,* chose toute naturelle, chose qui va sans dire, *f.*; *matter of record,* fait authentique, *m.*; *matter of taste,* affaire de goût, *f.*; *no matter how,* n'importe comment; *printed matter,* imprimés, *m.pl.*; *something must be the matter,* il faut qu'il y ait quelque chose sous jeu; *the manner and the matter,* la forme et le fond; *the matter I speak of,* le sujet dont je parle; *what is the matter?* Nothing, qu'y a-t-il? de quoi s'agit-il? Il n'y a rien; *what is the matter with you?* Nothing, qu'avez-vous? *or* qu'est-ce qui vous prend? Je n'ai rien.—*v.imp.* Importer. *It does not matter very much,* ce n'est pas grand'chose; *it does not matter whether you did it or not,* il importe peu que vous l'ayez fait ou non; *it matters,* il importe; *it matters little,* peu importe; *it matters not,* n'importe, il n'importe; *what matter?* qu'importe?

Matterhorn ['mætəhɔ:n]. Le (Mont) Cervin, *m.*

matter-of-course, *a.* Tout naturel.

matter-of-fact, *a.* Pratique, positif. **matter-of-factness,** *n.* Esprit pratique, prosaïsme, *m.*

mattery, *a.* Purulent.

Matthew ['mæθju]. Mathieu, *m.*

matting ['mætiŋ], *n.* Paillasson (of straw), *m.*; natte (of rush), *f.*

mattock ['mætək], *n.* Pioche, *f.*

mattress ['mætris], *n.* Matelas, *m.* *Spring mattress,* sommier élastique, *m.*; *wire mattress,* sommier métallique. **mattress-maker,** *n.* Matelassier, *m.*, matelassière, *f.*

maturate ['mætjuəreit], *v.t.* Mûrir, faire mûrir.—*v.i.* Mûrir. **maturation,** *f.* *n.* Maturation, *f.* **maturative,** *a.* Maturatif.

mature [mə'tjuə], *a.* Mûr, mûri.—*v.t.* Mûrir, faire mûrir.—*v.i.* Mûrir; (*Comm.*) échoir, venir à échéance. **maturely,** *adv.* Mûrement. **matureness** or **maturity,** *n.* Maturité; échéance (of bills), *f.* *To come to maturity,* venir à échéance (of bills).

matutinal [mætju'tainl], *a.* Matutinal, du matin.

Maud [mɔ:d]. Madelon, *f.*

maudlin ['mɔ:dlin], *a.* Pleurard, pleurnichard; d'une sentimentalité affectée et larmoyante; qui a le vin triste (étant gris).

maul [mɔ:l], *n.* Maillet, *m.*—*v.t.* Rosser, rouer de coups, meurtrir; déchirer, écharper. **maul-stick** ['mɔ:lstik], *n.* (*Paint.*) Appui-main, *m.*

maunder ['mɔ:ndə], *v.i.* Divaguer.

Maundy Thursday ['mɔ:ndi'θə:zdi], *n.* Jeudi saint, *m.*

Mauritius [mə'riʃəs]. L'Île Maurice, l'Île de France, *f.*

mausoleum [mɔ:sə'li:əm], *n.* Mausolée, *m.*

mauve [mouv], *a.* Mauve.

mavis [SONG-THRUSH].

maw [mɔ:], *n.* Jabot (of birds), *m.*; caillette (of ruminants), *f.* **maw-worm,** *n.* Ver intestinal, *m.*

mawkish ['mɔ:kiʃ], *a.* Fade, insipide; sottement sentimental. **mawkishness,** *n.* Fadeur, insipidité, *f.*

maxillary [mæk'siləri], *a.* (*Anat.*) Maxillaire.

maxim ['mæksim], *n.* Maxime, *f.* **maxim-monger,** *n.* Débiteur de maximes, *m.*

Maximian [mæk'simiən]. Maximien, *m.*

Maximilian [mæksi'miljən]. Maximilien, *m.*

maximize, *v.t.* Porter au maximum.

maximum ['mæksiməm], *n.* (*pl.* **maxima**) Maximum, *m.*

Maximus ['mæksiməs]. Maxime, *m.*

May [mei], *n.* Mai (month), *m.*—*v.i.* Célébrer le premier mai. *To go a-maying.* **may-blossom,** *n.* Aubépine, *f.* **may-bug,** *n.* Hanneton, *m.* **May-day,** *n.* Premier mai, *m.* **mayday,** *int.* (*Rad.*) M'aider (Signal international équivalent à S.O.S.). **may-fly,** *n.* Éphémère, *m.* **maypole,** *n.* Le mai, *m.* **May-queen,** *n.* Reine du premier mai, *f.*

may [mei], *v.aux.* (*2nd sing.* **mayest,** *****mayst,** *past* **might**) Pouvoir, être autorisé à. *He may go,* il peut sortir; *I may as well go there,* autant y aller; *it may be that,* il se peut que (*with subj.*); *it might be,* cela se pourrait; *it might happen that,* il pourrait se faire que; *it might have added to their glory,* cela aurait pu ajouter à leur gloire; *maybe,* peut-être; *may I!* puis-je! puissé-je! *may I die if . . .,* que je meure si . . .; *one might as well,* autant vaudrait; *that may be,* cela se peut; *that might be,* cela pourrait être; *you may be humiliated,* il se peut que vous soyez humilié; *you may have seen,* vous avez pu voir; *you may not have seen,* vous avez pu ne pas voir; *you might be humiliated,* il se pourrait que vous soyez humilié; *you might have gone there,* vous auriez pu y aller.

mayonnaise [meiə′neiz], *n.* Mayonnaise, *f.*

mayor [mɛə], *n.* Maire, *m.* **mayoralty,** *n.* Mairie, *f.* **mayoress,** *n.* Femme du maire, *f.*

mazard [′mæzəd], *n.* (*Bot.*) Guigne (noire), *f.*

maze [meiz], *n.* Labyrinthe, dédale; (*fig.*) embarras, *m.,* perplexité, *f.* **mazy,** *a.* Sinueux; (*fig.*) embrouillé, compliqué.

mazurka [mə′zə:kə], *n.* Mazurka, *f.* *To dance a mazurka,* mazurker.

me [mi:], *pron.* Me, moi. *Of me, from me,* de moi; *to me,* moi, à moi, me; (*fam.*) je; *me too,* moi aussi.

mead [mi:d], *n.* Hydromel; (*poet.*) pré (meadow), *m.*

meadow [′medou], *n.* Pré, *m.,* prairie, *f.* **meadow-grass,** *n.* Pâturin, *m.* **meadow-land,** *n.* Herbage, *m.* **meadow-saffron,** *n.* Colchique, *m.* **meadowsweet,** *n.* Reine des prés, herbe aux abeilles, *f.* **meadowy,** *a.* De prairie, herbu.

meagre [′mi:gə], *a.* Maigre; pauvre. **meagrely,** *adv.* Maigrement; pauvrement. **meagreness,** *n.* Maigreur; pauvreté, *f.*

meal [mi:l], *n.* Farine, *f.;* repas (repast), *m.* **meal-time,** *n.* Heure du repas, *f.* **meal-tub,** *n.* Huche à farine, *f.*

mealies, *n.pl.* Maïs, *m.* **mealiness,** *n.* Nature farineuse; (*fig.*) douceur, *f.* **mealy,** *a.* Farineux, poudreux. **mealy-mouthed,** *a.* Doucereux.

mean (1) [mi:n], *a.* Bas, méprisable, vil, abject; médiocre (of little value); mesquin, commun (low-minded); pauvre, petit, humble (humble); sordide, avare (avaricious). *A mean affair,* une affaire mesquine, *f.; a mean trick,* un vilain tour. **mean-spirited,** *a.* Lâche, à l'âme basse. *He was a mean-spirited coward,* c'était un poltron dépourvu d'honneur.

mean (2) [mi:n], *a.* Moyen. *Mean distance,* distance moyenne, *f.—n.* Milieu, *m.,* moyen terme, *m.;* (*Math.*) moyenne, *f. Golden mean,* le juste milieu, *m.*

mean (3) [mi:n], *v.t.* (*past and p.p.* **meant** [ment]) Signifier, vouloir dire, entendre; se proposer de, avoir l'intention de, vouloir (to intend); destiner (pour *or* de). *Do you mean it?* êtes-vous sérieux? parlez-vous sérieusement? *he did not mean it,* il ne l'a pas fait exprès; *that means a lot to me,* cela a beaucoup d'importance pour moi; *this was meant for you,* cela vous était destiné; *to mean business,* ne pas plaisanter, avoir des intentions sérieuses; *what does that word mean?* que veut dire ce mot? *what do you mean?* que voulez-vous dire? *without meaning it,* sans le vouloir.—*v.i.* Vouloir, entendre. *To mean well,* avoir de bonnes intentions; *to mean well towards,* vouloir le bien de.

meander [mi′ændə], *n.* Détour, méandre, *m.,* sinuosité, *f.—v.i.* Serpenter, aller en serpentant. **meandering,** *a.* Onduleux, sinueux, tortueux.

meaning [′mi:niŋ], *n.* Signification, *f.,* sens, *m.;* intention, *f.,* dessein, *m.;* pensée (thought), *f.; Double meaning,* double sens, *m.; that is not my meaning,* ce n'est pas là ce que je veux dire, ce n'est pas là ma pensée; *to know the meaning of something,* savoir ce que quelque chose veut dire; *to say something with meaning,* dire quelque chose d'un ton significatif; *what is the meaning of that?* que veut dire cela? *que signifie cela?—a.* Significatif; à intentions. *Well-meaning,* bien intentionné.

meaningful, *a.* Significatif, plein de sens.

meaningless, *a.* Qui n'a pas de sens, dénué de sens. **meaningly,** *adv.* D'un air, d'un ton, significatif.

meanly [′mi:nli], *adv.* Bassement; vilement; abjectement; pauvrement; mesquinement; chétivement, médiocrement. **meanness,** *n.* Bassesse, *f.;* pauvreté, mesquinerie; médiocrité, *f.*

means [mi:nz], *n.* Moyen, *m.,* voie, *f.;* moyens, *m.pl.,* fortune, *f.,* ressources, *f.pl. A man of private means,* un rentier, *m.; by all means,* absolument, certainement, mais oui! *by fair means,* par des voies honnêtes, honnêtement; *by fair means or foul,* n'importe comment; *by means of,* au moyen de; *by no means,* pas du tout, en aucune façon, aucunement; *by some means or other,* de manière ou d'autre; *by this means,* par ce moyen; *to live on one's means,* vivre de ses revenus.

meantime [mi:n′taim] *or* **meanwhile,** *n.* and *adv. In the meantime,* dans l'intervalle, en attendant, cependant, sur ces entrefaites.

measled [mi:zld] *or* **measly,** *a.* Atteint de rougeole; atteint de ladrerie; mesquin (mean).

measles [mi:zlz], *n.pl.* Rougeole, *f.;* ladrerie (of swine), *f. German measles,* rubéole, *f.*

measurable [′meʒərəbl], *a.* Mesurable. **measurableness,** *n.* Mesurabilité, *f.* **measurably,** *adv.* Avec mesure; modérément; sensiblement, appréciablement.

measure [′meʒə], *n.* Mesure; (*fig.*) capacité, portée, *f.;* (*Parl.*) projet de loi, *m.;* (coal) assise, *f.;* gisement, *m. Beyond measure or out of all measure,* outre mesure, sans mesure, démesurément; *in a great measure,* en grande partie; *in some measure,* en quelque sorte, jusqu'à un certain point; *the measure of my days,* le nombre de mes jours; *there is measure in everything,* il y a une limite à tout; *to get the measure of* (an opponent etc.), prendre la mesure de; *to have a coat made to measure,* faire faire un habit sur mesure; *to take legal measures,* avoir recours aux voies légales; *to take measures,* prendre des mesures; *to take someone's measure for a coat,* prendre la mesure d'un habit à quelqu'un.—*v.t.* Mesurer; arpenter (land); prendre mesure à (a person for clothes); (*fig.*) considérer, toiser, métrer. *This measures ten feet,* ceci a dix pieds de longueur; *to measure one's length* (on the ground), tomber de tout son long; *to measure other people's corn by one's own bushel,* mesurer les autres à son aune.—*v.i. To measure up to one's task,* être à la hauteur de sa tâche. **measured,** *a.* Mesuré; égal, uniforme, cadencé, scandé. *He spoke in no measured terms,* il parla en termes peu mesurés. **measureless,** *a.* Infini, illimité. **measurement,** *n.* Mesurage; arpentage (of

land), *m.*; mesure, dimension, *f.* **measurer,** *n.* Mesureur; arpenteur (of land); toiseur (of buildings), *m.* **measuring,** *n.* Mesurage, arpentage, *m.*
meat [miːt], *n.* Viande; nourriture, *f.*, aliment (food), *m. Boiled meat,* bouilli, *m.*; *meat breakfast,* déjeuner à la fourchette, *m.*; *roast meat,* rôti, *m.*; *that's meat and drink to me,* c'est ce qui me fait vivre. **meat-broth,** *n.* Bouillon gras, *m.* **meat-fly,** *n.* Mouche à viande, *f.* **meat-safe,** *n.* Garde-manger, *m.* **meat-soup,** *n.* Soupe grasse, *f.* **meaty,** *a.* Charnu; (*fig.*) plein de substance, bien rempli.
Mecca [ˈmekə]. La Mecque, *f.*
mechanic [məˈkænik], *n.* Artisan, ouvrier mécanicien, *m. Garage mechanic,* garagiste, *m.* **mechanic** or **mechanical,** *a.* Mécanique; d'ouvrier, d'artisan; machinal (done without intelligence). **mechanically,** *adv.* Mécaniquement; machinalement (without intelligence).
mechanician [mekəˈniʃən], *n.* Mécanicien, *m.*
mechanics [məˈkæniks], *n.pl.* Mécanique, *f.*
mechanism [ˈmekənizm], *n.* Mécanisme, *m.*
mechanist [ˈmekənist], *n.* Mécanicien, *m.*
mechanization [ˈmekənaiˈzeiʃən], *n.* Mécanisation, *f.* **mechanize,** *v.t.* Mécaniser. *Mechanized army,* armée motorisée, *f.*; *mechanized farming,* motoculture, *f.*
Mechlin [ˈmeklin]. Malines, *f.*
mechlin [ˈmeklin], *n.* Dentelle de Malines, *f.*
medal [medl], *n.* Médaille, *f. Medal bar,* barrette, *f.*; *medal clasp,* agrafe, *f.* **medallic** [məˈdælik], *a.* De médaille. **medallion,** *n.* Médaillon, *m.*
medallist [ˈmedəlist], *n.* Médailleur (engraver); médailliste (collector); médaillé (one rewarded), *m.*
meddle [medl], *v.i.* Se mêler (de), toucher (à), intervenir, s'immiscer (dans). **meddler,** *n.* **meddlesome** or **meddling,** *a.* Intrigant; officieux; (*colloq.*) touche-à-tout.
Medea [miˈdiːə]. Médée, *f.*
mediaeval [mediˈiːvəl], *a.* Du moyen âge, médiéval. **mediaevalist** [mediˈiːvəlist], *n.* Médiéviste.
medial [ˈmiːdiəl], *a.* Moyen; (*Gram.*) médial. **medially,** *adv.* Médialement. **median,** *a.* Médian.—*n.* (*Geom.*) Médiane, *f.* **mediant,** *n.* (*Mus.*) Médiante, *f.*
mediastinum [miːdiəsˈtainəm], *n.* (*pl.* **mediastina**) (*Anat.*) Médiastin, *m.*
mediate [ˈmiːdieit], *v.i.* S'entremettre, intervenir (en faveur de); s'interposer (dans).— *a.* [-ət] Médiat, intermédiaire. **mediately,** *adv.* Médiatement. **mediation** [-ˈeiʃən], *n.* Médiation, entremise, *f.* **mediatization** [-ətaiˈzeiʃən], *n.* Médiatisation, *f.* **mediatize** [ˈmiːdiətaiz], *v.t.* Médiatiser. **mediator,** *n.* Médiateur, *m.* **mediatorial** [-ˈtɔːriəl] or **mediatory** [ˈmiːdiətəri], *a.* Médiateur. **mediatorship,** *n.* Office de médiateur, *m.* **mediatrix** [miːdiˈeitriks], *n.* Médiatrice, *f.*
medicable [ˈmedikəbl], *a.* Curable.
medical [ˈmedikəl], *a.* Médical; de médecine (of schools etc.); en médecine (of students etc.). (*Mil.*) *The medical department,* le service de santé. *Medical jurisprudence,* médecine légale, *f.*; *medical man,* médecin, *m.*; *medical officer,* officier sanitaire, *m.*; *medical practitioner,* (médecin) praticien;

medical profession, la médecine, la Faculté, *f.*; *medical student,* étudiant en médecine, *m.*; *to take medical advice,* consulter un médecin. **medically,** *adv.* En médecine; suivant les règles de la médecine; médicalement.
medicament [meˈdikəmənt], *n.* Médicament, *m.* **medicamental** [-ˈmentl], *a.* Médicamentaire, médicamenteux.
medicaster [ˈmedikæstə], *n.* Médicastre, charlatan, *m.* **medicate,** *v.t.* Médicamenter, traiter. **medication** [-ˈkeiʃən], *n.* Médication, *f.* **medicative,** *a.* Médicateur.
medicinal [məˈdisinl], *a.* Médicinal. **medicinally,** *adv.* En médecine.
medicine [ˈmedsin], *n.* Médecine, *f.*, médicament, *m.*, purgation, *f.*; (*fig.*) remède, *m. To give someone a taste of his own medicine,* rendre la pareille à quelqu'un; (*fam.*) *to take one's medicine,* avaler la pilule. **medicine-chest,** *n.* Pharmacie, *f.* **medicine-man,** *n.* Sorcier, *m.*
Medici [ˈmeditʃi]. Médicis, *m.pl.*
medick [ˈmedik], *n.* (*Bot.*) Luzerne, *f.*
medico- [ˈmedikou], comb. form. Médico-.
medico-legal, *a.* Médico-légal.
medico [ˈmedikou], *n.* (*fam.*) Médecin, toubib, *m.*
medieval [MEDIAEVAL].
Medina [məˈdiːnə]. Médine, *f.*
mediocre [ˈmiːdioukə], *a.* Médiocre. **mediocrity** [-ˈɔkriti], *n.* Médiocrité, *f.*
meditate [ˈmediteit], *v.i.* Méditer (sur).—*v.t.* Avoir l'intention de, se proposer de, méditer, projeter. **meditated,** *a.* Médité, projeté. **meditation** [-ˈteiʃən], *n.* Méditation, *f.* **meditative** [ˈmeditətiv], *a.* Méditatif.
Mediterranean [meditəˈreiniən]. La Méditerranée, *f.*—*a.* Méditerrané; méditerranéen (pertaining to the Mediterranean). *Mediterranean Sea,* Mer Méditerranée, *f.*
medium [ˈmiːdiəm], *n.* (*pl.* **media** or **mediums**) Milieu, moyen, *m.*; voie, entremise, *f.*; (*Log.*) moyen terme, *m.*; (*Math.*) moyenne proportionnelle, *f.*; agent intermédiaire (agent); (*Spiritualism*) médium, *m. Circulating medium,* agent monétaire, *m.*; *happy medium,* juste milieu, *m.*; *through the medium of,* par l'intermédiaire de.—*a.* Moyen.
medlar [ˈmedlə], *n.* Nèfle (fruit), *f.*; néflier (tree), *m.*
medley [ˈmedli], *n.* Mélange, *m.*; confusion, *f.*; bariolage, méli-mélo, *m.*; (*Mus.*) pot pourri, *m.*—*a.* Mêlé, hétéroclite, bariolé.
medulla [miˈdʌlə], *n.* Médulle, moelle, *f.* **medullary** [miˈdʌləri], ***medullar,** *a.* Médullaire.
Medusa [miˈdjuːzə]. Méduse, *f.*
meed [miːd], *n.* Récompense, *f. To receive one's meed of praise,* recevoir sa part d'éloges.
meek [miːk], *a.* Doux, paisible, humble, soumis. **meek-eyed,** *a.* Au regard doux. **meekly,** *adv.* Avec douceur; humblement. **meekness,** *n.* Douceur; humilité, *f.*
meerschaum [ˈmiəʃɔːm], *n.* Écume de mer, *f. Meerschaum pipe,* pipe en écume de mer, *f.*
meet (1) [miːt], *v.t.* (*past* and *p.p.* **met**) Rencontrer, aller à la rencontre de; trouver, recevoir (to find); faire la connaissance de; faire face à, affronter (to face); se présenter devant (to appear before); faire honneur à (a bill); (*fig.*) satisfaire, remplir (to satisfy). *To meet death,* affronter la mort; *to meet one's*

engagements, faire face à ses engagements; *to meet the case*, faire l'affaire.—*v.i.* Se rencontrer; se voir; se réunir, s'assembler (to assemble); se joindre, se réunir (to join). *Extremes meet*, les extrêmes se touchent; *his father has met with a serious accident*, un grave accident est arrivé à son père; *to meet half-way*, se faire des concessions mutuelles; *to meet with*, rencontrer, trouver, découvrir, éprouver, subir, essuyer, recevoir; *to meet with one's death*, trouver la mort; *when shall we meet again?* quand nous reverrons-nous?—*n.* Rendez-vous de chasse, *m.*; réunion, *f.*; (*Geom.*) point d'intersection, de tangence, *m.*

meet (2) [miːt], *a.* Propre, convenable. **meetly,** *adv.* Convenablement, à propos, comme il faut. **meetness,** *n.* Convenance, propriété, *f.*

meeting ['miːtiŋ], *n.* Rencontre; entrevue (interview); assemblée, réunion, *f.*, meeting (assembly), *m.*; séance (sitting), *f.*; confluent (of rivers), *m.*; jonction (of roads), *f.* *Right of meeting*, droit de réunion, *m.* **meeting-house,** *n.* Temple (de Quakers), *m.*

megacephalic [megəsi'fælik] or **megacephalous** [-'sefələs], *a.* Mégalocéphale.

megalith ['megəliθ], *n.* Mégalithe, *m.* **megalithic** [-'liθik], *a.* Mégalithique.

megalomania [-lou'meiniə], *n.* Mégalomanie, *f.* **megalomaniac,** *n.* Mégalomane, *m.*

megalosaurus [-'sɔːrəs], *n.* Mégalosaure, *m.*

megaphone ['megəfoun], *n.* Mégaphone, *m.*

megapod ['megəpɔd], *n.* Mégapode, *m.*

megatherium [-'θiəriəm], *n.* Mégathérium, *m.*

megaton [-tʌn], *n.* Mégatonne, *f.*

megrim ['miːgrim], *n.* Migraine, *f.*, caprice, *m.*, lubie, *f.*; vertigo, *m.* (of horse); (*pl.*) dépression (nerveuse), *f.*

meiosis [mai'ousis], *n.* Litote, *f.*

melancholia [melən'kouliə], *n.* (*Med.*) Mélancolie, *f.*

melancholic, *a.* (*Med.*) Mélancolique, hypocondriaque.

melancholy ['melənkəli], *n.* Mélancolie, tristesse, *f.*—*a.* Mélancolique, triste, affligeant.

melanic [me'lænik], *a.* Mélanique.

melanism ['melənizm], *n.* Mélanisme, *m.* **melanosis** [-'nousis], *n.* Mélanose, *f.*

Melchizedek [mel'kizədek]. Melchisédech, *m.*

melilot ['melilɔt], *n.* (*Bot.*) Mélilot, *m.*

melliferous [me'lifərəs], *a.* Mellifère. **mellification** [-i'keiʃən], *n.* Mellification, *f.*

mellifluence [me'lifluəns], *n.* Douceur, *f.* **mellifluous,** *a.* Mielleux, doucereux.

mellow ['melou], *a.* Mûr, fondant (of fruit); moelleux, doux, velouté; jovial, gai; gris, entre deux vins; meuble (of land).—*v.t.* Mûrir, faire mûrir; ameublir (land); (*Paint.*) donner du moelleux à; (*fig.*) rendre mélodieux, adoucir, amollir.—*v.i.* Mûrir; prendre du moelleux; devenir meuble (of land); (*fig.*) s'adoucir, s'amollir. **mellowing,** *n.* Maturation, *f.*, adoucissement; ameublissement (of land), *m.* **mellowness,** *n.* Maturité, *f.*; velouté, moelleux, *m.*; (*fig.*) douceur, *f.*

melodeon [me'loudiən], *n.* *Mélodion; accordéon, *m.*

melodic [-'lɔdik], *a.* Mélodique.

melodious [mə'loudiəs], *a.* Mélodieux.

melodiously, *adv.* Mélodieusement. **melodiousness,** *n.* Mélodie, *f.*

melodist ['melodist], *n.* Mélodiste, *m.*

melodrama ['melədrɑːmə], *n.* Mélodrame, *m.* **melodramatic** [-drə'mætik], *a.* Mélodramatique. **melodramatically,** *adv.* Mélodramatiquement. **melodramatist** [-'dræmətist], *n.* Mélodramaturge, *m.*

melody ['melədi], *n.* Mélodie, *f.*, air; (*Mus.*) chant, thème, *m.*

melon ['melən], *n.* Melon, *m.* **melon-bed,** *n.* Melonnière, *f.* **melon-shaped,** *n.* En forme de melon.

melt [melt], *v.t.* Fondre, faire fondre; (*fig.*) attendrir, faire faiblir.—*v.i.* Fondre, se fondre; (*fig.*) fléchir, faiblir, s'attendrir. *To melt away*, fondre, disparaître; *to melt into tears*, fondre en larmes. **melter,** *n.* Fondeur, *m.*

melting, *a.* Qui fond; fondant (of fruit); étouffant (of the weather); (*fig.*) attendrissant, touchant.—*n.* Fusion, fonte, *f.*; attendrissement, *m.* **melting-point,** *n.* Point de fusion, *m.* **melting-pot,** *n.* Creuset, *m.*

member ['membə], *n.* Membre; membre du parlement, *m.* **membered,** *a.* Membré; qui a des membres. *Large-membered*, membru. **membership,** *n.* Les membres d'une société etc., *m.pl.*

membrane ['membrein], *n.* Membrane, *f.* **membraniform,** *a.* Membraniforme. **membranous** [-'breinəs], *a.* Membraneux.

memento [mə'mentou], *n.* Souvenir, mémento, *m.*

memoir ['memwɑː], *n.* Mémoire, *m.* **memoirist,** *n.* Auteur de mémoires, *m.*

memorable ['memərəbl], *a.* Mémorable. **memorably,** *adv.* D'une manière mémorable.

memorandum [memə'rændəm], *n.* (*pl.* **memoranda**) Note, *f.*, mémorandum; (*Comm.*) bordereau, *m.* *To make a memorandum of*, prendre note de, noter. **memorandum-book,** *n.* Agenda; carnet, *m.*

memorial [mi'mɔːriəl], *n.* Souvenir, mémoire; monument commémoratif, *m.*; requête, pétition, demande, *f.*; (*Diplom.*) mémorial, *m.*—*a.* Commémoratif. **memorialist,** *n.* Pétitionnaire; mémorialiste, *m.* **memorialize,** *v.t.* Présenter une requête à, pétitionner; commémorer.

memorize ['meməraiz], *v.t.* Apprendre par cœur; conserver au souvenir.

memory ['meməri], *n.* Mémoire, *f.*; (*colloq.*) souvenir, *m.* *Bad memory*, mauvaise mémoire, mémoire de lièvre, *f.*; *childhood memory*, souvenir d'enfance, *m.*; *from memory*, de mémoire; *in memory of*, en souvenir de; *this occurred within my own memory*, ceci est arrivé de mon temps; *to the best of my memory*, autant qu'il m'en souvient; *within the memory of man*, de mémoire d'homme.

mem-sahib ['memsɑːb], *n.* (*In India*) Madame, *f.* (titre de respect accordé à une Européenne mariée).

men, *pl.* [MAN.]

menace ['menəs], *n.* Menace, *f.*—*v.t.* Menacer. **menacer,** *n.* Personne qui menace, *f.* **menacing,** *a.* Menaçant. **menacingly,** *adv.* D'un air menaçant.

menagerie [mə'nædʒəri], *n.* Ménagerie, *f.*

mend [mend], *v.t.* Raccommoder, réparer; corriger, améliorer. *To mend a pen, a pencil,* tailler une plume, un crayon; *to mend one's pace*, hâter le pas; *to mend one's ways*, changer de vie, rentrer dans le bon chemin.—*v.i.* S'améliorer, se corriger, se rétablir (of health); se remettre au beau (of the weather). *My health is mending*, ma santé se rétablit; *the evil is past mending*, le mal est sans remède.—*n.* Raccommodage, *m.*; reprise, *f.* *To be on the mend*, être en train de se remettre, être en voie d'amélioration. **mendable**, *a.* Réparable; (*fig.*) corrigible.

mendacious [men'deiʃəs], *a.* Mensonger.

mendacity [men'dæsiti], *n.* Mensonge, *m.*; duplicité, *f.* *In him mendacity was almost a disease*, l'habitude de mentir était chez lui presque une maladie.

Mendelian [men'di:liən], *a.* (*Biol.*) Mendélien.

Mendelism, *n.* Mendélisme, *m.*

mender ['mendə], *n.* Raccommodeur, *m.*, -euse, *f.*

mendicant ['mendikənt], *a.* Mendiant, de mendicité. *Mendicant friar*, moine mendiant, *m.*—*n.* Mendiant, *m.*, -iante, *f.* **mendicity** [-'disiti], *n.* Mendicité, *f.*

mending ['mendiŋ], *n.* Raccommodage; ravaudage, reprisage (of stockings), *m.*; réparation, *f.* *Past mending*, sans remède, perdu.

Menelaus [mene'leiəs]. (*Gr. Lit.*) Ménélas, *m.*

menial ['mi:niəl], *a.* De domestique; (*fig.*) subalterne, servile.—*n.* Domestique; (*fig.*) valet, laquais, *m.*

meningitis [menin'dʒaitis], *n.* Méningite, *f.*

meninx ['mi:niŋks], *n.* Méninge, *f.*

meniscus [mə'niskəs], *n.* (*Opt.*) Ménisque, *m.*

menisperm ['menispə:m], *n.* (*Bot.*) Ménisperme, *m.*

menology [mə'nɔlədʒi], *n.* Ménologe, *m.*

menopause ['menopɔ:z], *n.* Ménopause, *f.*

menorrhagia, *n.* Ménorrhagie, *f.* **menorrhoea**, *n.* Ménorrhée, *f.*

menses ['mensiz], *n.pl.* Menstrues, règles, *f.pl.* **menstrual**, *a.* Menstruel. **menstruation** [-stru'eiʃən], *n.* Menstruation, *f.* **menstruum**, *n.* Dissolvant, *m.*

mensurability [menʃurə'biliti], *n.* Mensurabilité, *f.*

mensurable ['menʃurəbl], *a.* Mesurable. **mensuration** [-sju'reiʃən], *n.* Mesurage, *m.*, mesure, *f.*

mental [mentl], *a.* Mental. *A mental (case)*, un aliéné, *m.*; *mental arithmetic*, calcul mental, *m.*; *mental defective*, (enfant) déficient, anormal; *mental reservation*, restriction mentale, *f.*; *mental specialist*, médecin aliéniste, *m.* **mentality**, *n.* Mentalité, *f.*; esprit, *m.* **mentally**, *adv.* Mentalement.

menthol ['menθɔl], *n.* Menthol, *m.*

mention ['menʃən], *n.* Mention, indication, *f.* —*v.t.* Dire, faire mention de, mentionner, parler de; citer; constater (que). *Don't mention it!* il n'y a pas de quoi; *not to mention*, sans compter, sans parler de; *to be mentioned in dispatches*, (*Mil.*) être l'objet d'une citation, avoir une citation (à l'ordre du jour); *to mention an instance*, pour citer un exemple.

mentor ['mentə], *n.* Mentor, guide, *m.*

menu ['menju], *n.* Menu, *m.*, carte, *f.*

Mephistopheles [mefis'tɔfili:z]. Méphistophélès, *m.* **Mephistophelian** [mefistə'fi:liən], *a.* Méphistophélique.

mephitic [mə'fitik], *a.* Méphitique. **mephitis** [-'faitis] or **mephitism** ['mefitizm], *n.* Méphitisme, *m.*

mercantile ['mə:kəntail], *a.* Marchand, de commerce, commerçant. *In mercantile circles*, dans le commerce; *mercantile community*, classe commerçante, *f.*; *mercantile establishment*, maison de commerce, *f.*; *mercantile law*, droit commercial, *m.*; *mercantile marine*, marine marchande, *f.*; *mercantile nation*, nation commerçante, *f.*; *mercantile town*, ville de commerce, *f.* **mercantilism**, *n.* Mercantilisme, *m.*

mercenarily ['mə:sənərili], *adv.* D'une manière mercenaire, mercenairement. **mercenariness**, *n.* Vénalité, *f.* **mercenary**, *a.* Mercenaire, vénal.—*n.* Mercenaire, *m.* or *f.*

mercer ['mə:sə], *n.* *Mercier; marchand de soieries (silk mercer), *m.* **mercerize**, *v.t.* Merceriser. **mercery**, *n.* Commerce des soieries, *m.*

merchandise ['mə:tʃəndaiz], *n.* Marchandise, *f.*

merchant ['mə:tʃənt], *n.* Négociant, commerçant; marchand en gros; (*pop.*) type, individu, *m.*—*a.* Marchand; commercial. **merchantable**, *a.* Vendable; de vente facile. **merchant-like**, *a.* En négociant. **merchantman** or **merchant-ship**, *n.* Navire marchand, *m.* **merchant-seaman**, *n.* Marin de la marine marchande, *m.* **merchant-service**, *n.* Marine marchande, *f.* **merchant-tailor**, *n.* Marchand-tailleur, *m.*

merciful ['mə:siful], *a.* Miséricordieux. **mercifully**, *adv.* Miséricordieusement. **mercifulness**, *n.* Miséricorde, *f.* **merciless**, *a.* Sans pitié, impitoyable. **mercilessly**, *adv.* Impitoyablement, sans pitié.

mercurial [mə:'kjuəriəl], *a.* De Mercure; de mercure; (*fig.*) mercuriel, vif, éveillé; inconstant. **mercuriality**, *n.* Vivacité, inconstance, *f.*

mercury ['mə:kjuəri], *n.* Mercure, *m.*; mercuriale (plant), *f.* *The mercury is falling*, le baromètre baisse.

mercy ['mə:si], *n.* Miséricorde; pitié; grâce, indulgence (pardon), *f. At the mercy of*, à la merci de, au gré de; *for mercy's sake*, par grâce; *mercy!* grâce! *mercy-stroke*, coup de grâce; *recommendation to mercy*, recours en grâce, *m.*; *sisters of mercy*, sœurs de charité, *f.pl.*; *to beg for mercy*, demander grâce; *to have mercy on*, avoir pitié de; *what a mercy!* quel bonheur! **mercy-seat**, *n.* Propitiatoire, *m.*

mere (1) [miə], *n.* Lac, étang, *m.*

mere (2) [miə], *a.* Pur, simple, seul, rien que; vrai, franc. *A mere nothing*, un rien, *m.* **merely**, *adv.* Simplement, seulement, rien que, pas autre chose que.

meretricious [meri'triʃəs], *a.* D'un éclat factice (style). **meretriciousness**, *n.* Clinquant, faux brillant (style), *m.*

merganser [mə:'gænsə], *n.* (*Orn.*) Harle, *m.*

merge [mə:dʒ], *v.t.* Fondre, amalgamer, absorber.—*v.i.* Se perdre (dans). *To merge into*, se fondre dans, se perdre dans, se confondre avec. **merger**, *n.* Fusion, *f.* *Merger company*, sociétés réunies, *f.pl.*

meridian [mə'ridiən], *a.* Méridien; de midi. —*n.* Méridien; (*fig.*) apogée, *m.* *In the*

meridian of his glory, à l'apogée de sa gloire. **meridional,** *a.* and *n.* Méridional, *m.*
meringue [mə'ræŋ], *n.* Meringue, *f.*
merino [mə'ri:nou], *n.* Mérinos, *m.*
merit ['merit], *n.* Mérite, *m.*—*v.t.* Mériter. *To merit well of,* bien mériter de. **meritorious** [-'tɔ:riəs], *a.* Méritoire (of things); méritant (of persons). **meritoriously,** *adv.* D'une manière méritoire. **meritoriousness,** *n.* Mérite, *m.*
merlin ['mə:lin], *n.* Émerillon (bird), *m.*
merlon ['mə:lən], *n.* (*Fort.*) Merlon, *m.*
mermaid ['mə:meid], *n.* Sirène, *f.* **mermaid-fish,** *n.* Ange de mer, angelot, *m.* **merman,** *n.* (*Myth.*) Triton, *m.*
merrily ['merili], *adv.* Joyeusement, gaiement. **merriment,** *n.* Gaieté, réjouissance, *f.*
merry (1) ['meri], *a.* Joyeux, gai, plaisant; (*colloq.*) un peu gris. *Merry as a lark,* gai comme un pinson; **merry England,* la joyeuse Angleterre; *the more the merrier,* plus on est de fous, plus on rit; *to make merry with,* se réjouir de, se divertir de. **merry-andrew,** *n.* Paillasse, bouffon, *m.* **merry-go-round,** *n.* Chevaux de bois, *m.pl.*; manège, *m.* **merry-making,** *n.* Réjouissance, fête, *f.*, divertissement, *m.* **merrythought,** *n.* Lunette, fourchette (in a fowl's breast), *f.*
merry (2) ['meri], *n.* Merise (wild cherry), *f.*
*meseems [mi'si:mz], *v.imp.* Il me semble.
mesembryanthemum [məsembri'ænθəməm], *n.* (*Bot.*) Mésembryanthème, *m.*
mesenteric [mesen'terik], *a.* Mésentérique.
mesentery ['mesəntəri], *n.* Mésentère, *m.*
mesh [meʃ], *n.* Maille, *f.*; moule (for netting), *m.*; prise, *f.*; engrenage, *m.*—*v.t.* Prendre au filet; mailler; engrener.
mesmeric [mez'merik], *a.* Mesmérique. **mesmerism** ['mezmərizm], *n.* Mesmérisme, magnétisme animal, *m.* **mesmerize,** *v.t.* Magnétiser; hypnotiser. **mesmerizer,** *n.* Magnétiseur, *m.*
mesocarp ['mesoka:p], *n.* (*Bot.*) Mésocarpe, *m.* **mesoderm,** *n.* (*Anat.*) Mésoderme, *m.* **mesodermic** [-'də:mik], *a.* Mésodermique.
Mesopotamia [mesəpə'teimiə]. La Mésopotamie, *f.*
mess [mes], *n.* Gâchis, *m.*; saleté (dirt), *f.*; mets, plat (dish), *m.*; (*Mil.*) mess, *m.,* table (of officers), *f.*; popote, *f.* (in the field); ordinaire *m.* (of privates); plat (of seamen), *m.* *Mess allowance,* indemnité de table, *f.*; *mess fund,* fonds de l'ordinaire (de la compagnie), *m.*; *mess tin,* gamelle (individuelle), *f.*; *to be in a fine mess,* être dans de beaux draps, être dans un bel état; *to make a mess of,* gâcher; *to make a mess of it,* faire fiasco; *what a mess!* quel gâchis! *what a mess you are making!* quel gâchis vous faites là!—*v.i.* Manger; manger ensemble; faire du gâchis. *To mess about,* patauger.—*v.t.* Donner à manger à; salir (with dirt).
message ['mesidʒ], *n.* Message, *m.,* commission, *f.*
messenger ['mesəndʒə], *n.* Messager; commissionnaire; coursier (in office); (*fig.*) avant-coureur, *m. King's messenger,* courrier, messager d'État, *m.*
Messiah [mə'saiə], *n.* Messie, *m.*
messianic [mesi'ænik], *a.* Messianique.
messieurs, Messrs. ['mesəz], *n.pl.* Messieurs, *m.pl.*

Messina [me'si:nə]. Messine, *f. Straits of Messina,* le phare, le détroit, de Messine.
messmate ['mesmeit], *n.* Camarade de table, *m.*
messuage ['meswidʒ], *n.* (*Law*) Maison et ses dépendances, *f.pl.*
messy ['mesi], *a.* Sale; graisseux, salissant.
metabolic [metə'bɔlik], *a.* Métabolique. **metabolism** [mə'tæbolizm], *n.* Métabolisme, *m.*
metacarpal [metə'ka:pəl], *a.* Métacarpien. **metacarpus,** *n.* Métacarpe, *m.*
metage ['mi:tidʒ], *n.* Mesurage (de la houille etc.), *m.*
metagenesis [metə'dʒenəsis], *n.* Métagénèse, *f.*
metal [metl], *n.* Métal; cailloutis, empierrement (for roads); (*Rail.*) rail, *m. To leave the metals,* dérailler.—*v.t.* Ferrer, empierrer (a road). **metalled,** *a.* Empierré. **metallic** [mə'tælik], *a.* Métallique. **metalliferous** [-'lifərəs], *a.* Métallifère. **metalling,** *n.* Empierrement, *m.*
metallization [metəlai'zeiʃən], *n.* Métallisation, *f.* **metallize,** *v.t.* Métalliser. **metallography** [-'lɔgrəfi], *n.* Métallographie, *f.*
metalloid ['metəlɔid], *n.* Métalloïde, *m.* **metallurgic** [-'lə:dʒik] or **metallurgical,** *a.* Métallurgique.
metallurgist [me'tælədʒist or 'metələ:dʒist], *n.* Métallurgiste, *m.* **metallurgy,** *n.* Métallurgie, *f.*
metamorphic [metə'mɔ:fik], *a.* Métamorphique. **metamorphism,** *n.* Métamorphisme, *m.*
metamorphose [metə'mɔ:fouz], *v.t.* Métamorphoser.
metamorphosis [metə'mɔ:fəsis], *n.* Métamorphose, *f.*
metaphor ['metəfə], *n.* Métaphore, *f.* **metaphoric** [-'fɔrik] or **metaphorical,** *a.* Métaphorique. **metaphorically,** *adv.* Métaphoriquement.
metaphorist ['metəfərist], *n.* Métaphoriste.
metaphysical [metə'fizikl], *a.* Métaphysique. **metaphysically,** *adv.* Métaphysiquement. **metaphysician,** *n.* Métaphysicien, *m.,* -ienne, *f.* **metaphysics,** *n.pl.* Métaphysique, *f.*
metaplasm ['metəplæzm], *n.* Métaplasme, *m.*
metastasis [mə'tæstəsis], *n.* Métastase, *f.*
metatarsus [metə'ta:səs], *n.* Métatarse, *m.*
metathesis [mə'tæθəsis], *n.* Métathèse, *f.*
mete [mi:t], *v.t.* Mesurer. *To mete out,* distribuer, décerner (of rewards); assigner (of punishments). **meting,** *n.* Mesurage, *m.*; allocation, distribution, *f.*
metempsychosis [mətempsi'kousis], *n.* Métempsycose, *f.*
meteor ['mi:tiə], *n.* Météore, *m.* **meteoric** [-'ɔrik], *a.* Météorique.
meteorite ['mi:tiərait], *n.* Météorite, *m.* or *f.*
meteorological [-ə'lɔdʒikl], *a.* Météorologique. **meteorologist** [-'rɔlədʒist], *n.* Météorologiste, *m.* **meteorology,** *n.* Météorologie, *f.*
meter ['mi:tə], *n.* Mesureur; compteur (for gas), *m.* [METRE].
methane ['meθein], *n.* Gaz des marais, méthane, *m.*
*metheglin [me'θeglin], *n.* (*Wales*) Hydromel, *m.*

*methinks[miˈθiŋks], *v.imp.* (*past* **me-thought** [miˈθɔ:t]. Il me semble (que).
method [ˈmeθəd], *n.* Méthode, *f.*; procédé, *m.*; modalité, *f.*; (*fig.*) manière, *f.*, ordre, *m.* *Methods of applying a law*, modalités d'application d'une loi, *f.pl.*; *technical methods in a factory*, procédés techniques dans une usine, *m.pl.*
methodic [məˈθɔdik] or **methodical**, *a.* Méthodique. **methodically**, *adv.* Méthodiquement.
Methodism [ˈmeθədizm], *n.* Méthodisme, *m.* **Methodist**, *n.* Méthodiste, *m.* or *f.*
methodize, *v.t.* Arranger avec méthode, arranger systématiquement.
Methuselah [meˈθju:zələ]. Mathusalem, *m.*
methyl [ˈmeθil], *n.* (*Chem.*) Méthyle, *m.* **methylate**, *v.t.* Méthyler. *Methylated spirit*, alcool dénaturé, alcool à brûler, *m.*
meticulous [məˈtikjuləs], *a.* Méticuleux. **meticulousness**, *n.* Méticulosité, *f.*
metonymy [miˈtɔnimi], *n.* Métonymie, *f.*
metope [ˈmetəpi], *n.* (*Arch.*) Métope, *f.*
metre [ˈmi:tə], *n.* Mètre; (*Pros.*) vers, *m.*, mesure, *f.* **metric** [ˈmetrik], *a.* Métrique. **metrical** [ˈmetrikl], *a.* Métrique; en vers. **metrically**, *adv.* En vers.
metrician [məˈtriʃən], *n.* Métricien, *m.*
metrology [məˈtrɔlədʒi], *n.* Métrologie, *f.*
metromania [metroˈmeiniə], *n.* Métromanie, *f.* **metromaniac**, *n.* Métromane, *m.*
metronome [ˈmetronoum], *n.* Métronome, *m.*
metropolis [məˈtrɔpəlis], *n.* Capitale, métropole, *f.* **metropolitan** [-ˈpɔlitən], *a.* De la capitale, métropolitain.—*n.* Métropolitain, archevêque, *m.*
mettle [metl], *n.* Courage, cœur, *m.*; fougue, ardeur, vivacité, *f.*; caractère, tempérament, *m.* *To put someone on his mettle*, piquer quelqu'un d'honneur; *to show one's mettle*, donner sa mesure, faire ses preuves; *to try someone's mettle*, tâter le courage de quelqu'un. **mettled** or **mettlesome**, *a.* Fougueux, ardent, vif.
mew [mju:], *n.* Mouette (bird); mue, cage (cage), *f.*; miaulement (cry of a cat), *m.*; (*pl.*) écuries, *f.pl.*; impasse, ruelle (behind large town houses), *f.*—*v.t.* Enfermer (to shut up); muer (hawks etc.).—*v.i.* Miauler (of cats); muer (to moult); changer (to change). **mewing**, *n.* Miaulement (of a cat), *m.*
mewl [mju:l], *v.i.* Vagir, piailler. **mewling**, *n.* Vagissement, *m.*—*a.* Piaillard.
mews [mju:z], *n.pl.* Écuries (en ville), *f.pl.*
Mexican [ˈmeksikən], *a. and n.* Mexicain, *m.*, -aine, *f.*
Mexico [ˈmeksikou]. Le Mexique (country), *m.*; Mexico (city), *m.*
mezereon [məˈziəriən], *n.* Mézéréon, bois gentil, *m.*
mezzanine [ˈmezəni:n], *n.* (*Arch.*) Mezzanine, *f.* **mezzanine-floor**, *n.* Entresol, *m.*
mezzo-relievo [ˈmedzou rəˈli:vou], *n.* Demi-relief, *m.* **mezzo-soprano**, *n.* Mezzo-soprano, mezzo, *m.* **mezzotint** or **mezzotinto** [-ˈtintou], *n.* Mezzo-tinto, *m.*, gravure à la manière noire, *f.*
miaow [mjau], **miaul** [mjaul], *v.i.* Miauler.
miasma [maiˈæzmə], *n.* (*pl.* **miasmata** or ***miasms**) Miasme, *m.* **miasmatic** [-ˈmætik], *a.* Miasmatique.

mica [ˈmaikə], *n.* Mica, *m.* **micaceous** [-ˈkeiʃəs], *a.* Micacé. **mica-schist**, *n.* Micaschiste, *m.*
mice, *pl.* [MOUSE].
Michael [maikl]. Michel, *m.* **Michael-Angelo**. Michel-Ange, *m.* **Mick** (*diminutive of Michael*) Michel; (*pop.*) Irlandais, *m.* **Mickey** (*diminutive of Michael*). Michel. (*pop.*) *To take the mickey out of someone*, se payer la tête de quelqu'un.
Michaelmas [ˈmiklməs], *n.* La Saint-Michel, *f.* (*sch.*) *Michaelmas term*, premier trimestre.
mickle [mikl], *a.* (*Sc.*) Beaucoup de. *Many a little makes a mickle*, les petits ruisseaux font les grandes rivières.
microbe [ˈmaikroub], *n.* Microbe, *m.* **microbial** [-ˈkroubiəl], *a.* Microbien, microbique. **microbiology** [-baiˈɔlədʒi], *n.* Microbiologie, *f.*
microcephalic [maikrəsəˈfælik] or **microcephalous** [maikrəˈsefələs], *a.* Microcéphale.
microcosm [ˈmaikrəkɔzm], *n.* Microcosme, *m.* **microfilm** [maikrəˈfilm], *n.* Microfilm, *m.* **micrography** [-ˈkrɔgrəfi], *n.* Micrographie, *f.* **microgroove** [ˈmaikrəgru:v], *n.* Microsillon, *m.*
microlith [ˈmaikrəliθ], *n.* Microlithe, *m.* **micrology** [-ˈkrɔlədʒi], *n.* Micrologie, *f.* **micrometer** [-ˈkrɔmitə], *n.* Micromètre, *m.* **micron** [ˈmaikrɔn], *n.* Micron, *m.*; millième de millimètre, *m.*
microphone [ˈmaikrəfoun], *n.* Microphone, *m.*
microscope [ˈmaikrəskoup], *n.* Microscope, *m.* *Electron microscope*, microscope électronique, *m.* **microscopic** [-ˈskɔpik] or **microscopical**, *a.* Microscopique. **microscopically**, *adv.* Au microscope.
microwave [ˈmaikroweiv], *n.* Onde ultra-courte, *f.*
microzoan [maikroˈzouən], *n.* Microzoaire, *m.*
micturition [miktjuəˈriʃən], *n.* Micturition; (*fam.*) urination, *f.*
mid [mid], *a.* Du milieu, moyen.—**n.* Milieu, *m.*—*prep.* Au milieu de. **mid-air**, *n.* Milieu de l'air, haut des airs, *m.* *In mid-air*, entre ciel et terre. **mid-course**, *n.* Milieu du chemin, *m.* **midday**, *n.* Midi, *m.*—*a.* De midi. **midland**, *a.* De l'intérieur, du centre. **mid-leg**, *n.* Mi-jambe, *f.* **Mid-Lent**, *n.* Mi-carême, *f.* **midmost**, *a.* Au milieu, au centre; central. **midnight**, *n.* Minuit, *m.*—*a.* De minuit. **midrib**, *n.* (*Bot.*) Nervure médiane, *f.* **midriff**, *n.* Diaphragme, *m.* **mid-sea**, *n.* Pleine mer, *f.*; milieu de la mer, *m.* **midship**, *n.* (*Naut.*) Milieu du vaisseau, *m.* *Midship beam*, maître bau, *m.* **midshipman**, *n.* (*pl.* **midshipmen**) Aspirant de marine, *m.* **midships** [AMIDSHIPS]. **midstream**, *n.* Milieu du courant; milieu du fleuve, *m.*—*adv.* Au milieu du courant. **midsummer**, *n.* Milieu de l'été, cœur de l'été, *m.* *Midsummer Day*, la Saint-Jean. **midway**, *a.* À mi-chemin.—*adv.* À mi-chemin, à moitié chemin; à mi-côte (of a hill). **midwinter**, *n.* Fort de l'hiver, *m.*
middle [midl], *n.* Milieu, centre, *m.*; taille, ceinture, *f.* *He was up to his middle in water*, il avait de l'eau jusqu'à la ceinture; *in the middle of*, au milieu de; *middle of the road policy*, une politique modérée.—*a.* Du milieu,

du centre, central; intermédiaire, moyen. *Middle age*, âge mûr, *m.*; *Middle Ages*, Moyen Âge, *m.*; *middle class*, bourgeoisie, *f.*; *middle course*, moyen terme, *m.*; *middle distance*, second plan, *m.*; *middle watch*, (*Naut.*) petit quart, *m.*
middle-aged, *a.* Entre deux âges. **middle-man**, *n.* Intermédiaire, tiers, *m.* **middle-most**, *a.* Le plus au milieu, le plus central. **middle-sized**, *a.* De taille moyenne. **middling**, *a.* Médiocre, moyen, passable, assez bien (*of health*); (*Comm.*) bon, ordinaire. **middlingly**, *adv.* Passablement, médiocrement.
middy ['midi] (*facet.*) [MIDSHIPMAN].
midge [midʒ], *n.* Moucheron, *m.*
midget ['midʒit], *n.* Nain, nabot, *m.*
midst [midst], *n.* Milieu; (*fig.*) fort, sein, cœur, *m. In the midst of*, au sein de, dans le milieu de; *in the midst of winter*, en plein hiver.—*prep.* Au milieu de, parmi.
midwife ['midwaif], *n.* (*pl.* **midwives**) Sage-femme, accoucheuse, *f.* **midwifery** ['midwifəri], *n.* Obstétrique, *f.*
mien [miːn], *n.* Mine, *f.*, air, *m.*
miff [mif], *n.* Bouderie, fâcherie, *f.*
might (1), *past* [MAY].
might (2) [mait], *n.* Force, puissance, *f. With might and main*, de toutes ses forces. **mightily**, *adv.* Fortement, vigoureusement; grandement, extrêmement. **mightiness**, *n.* Grandeur, puissance, force, *f.* **mighty**, *d.* Fort, puissant; grand, important.—*adv.* Fort, très, extrêmement.
mignonette [minjə'net], *n.* Réséda, *m.*
migraine ['miːgrein], *n.* (*Med.*) Migraine, *f.*
migrant ['maigrənt], *n.* Émigré (*of persons*), migrateur (*of birds*), *m.*
migrate [mai'greit], *v.i.* Émigrer. *They migrated in one body*, ils émigrèrent en masse.
migration [mai'greiʃən], *n.* Migration, émigration, *f.*
migratory ['maigrətəri], *a.* Migratoire; migrateur.
mike [maik] [MICROPHONE].
mil [mil], *n.* Millième de pouce; millilitre, *m.*
Milanese [milə'niːz]. Le Milanais, *m.*
milch [miltʃ], *a.* À lait, laitière. **milch-cow**, *n.* Vache laitière, vache à lait, *f.*
mild [maild], *a.* Doux; léger (*of drink, tobacco, etc.*); bénin, modéré. *Mild climate*, climat doux *or* tempéré, *m.*; *mild efforts*, efforts faibles, *m.pl.* **milden**, *v.t.* Adoucir. —*v.i.* S'adoucir. **milder**, *a.* Plus doux; moins rigoureux.
mildew ['mildjuː], *n.* Rouille, nielle; moisissure, *f.*, mildiou, *m.*, taches d'humidité, *f.pl.* —*v.t.* Frapper de rouille, gâter par l'humidité; souiller, tacher.
mildly ['maildli], *adv.* Doucement, avec douceur; modérément. **mildness**, *n.* Douceur, *f.*
mile [mail], *n.* Mille, *m.* English mile = 1609·3 m. *Miles better*, infiniment mieux.
milestone, *n.* Borne milliaire, borne kilométrique, *f.*
mileage ['mailidʒ], *n.* Longueur kilométrique, *f.*; prix par mille, *m.*
Milesian [mai'liːzjən *or* mai'liːʒən], *a.* and *n.* Milésien, *m.*
milfoil ['milfoil], *n.* Mille-feuille, *f.*

miliary ['miliəri], *a.* Miliaire. *Miliary fever*, fièvre miliaire, *f.*
militant ['militənt], *a.* Militant.—*n.* Activiste, *m.*
militarily ['militərili], *adv.* Militairement. **militarism**, *n.* Militarisme, *m.* **militarist**, *n.* Militariste, *m.* **military**, *a.* Militaire. *Military examination*, concours d'admission aux écoles militaires, *m.*; *military law*, code (de justice) militaire, *m.*—*n.* Les militaires, *m.pl.*, la troupe, *f.*
militate ['militeit], *v.i.* Militer (contre).
militia [mi'liʃə], *n.* Milice, *f.* **militiaman**, *n.* Milicien, soldat de la milice, *m.*
milk [milk], *n.* Lait, *m. Milk and water*, lait coupé; (*fig.*) fade, insipide, sans caractère; *skim milk*, lait écrémé, *m.*; *to come home with the milk*, rentrer à la première heure, rentrer dès les chats.—*v.t.* Traire; (*fam.*) dépouiller, écorcher (quelqu'un), exploiter (quelqu'un).
milk-can, *n.* Pot au lait, *m.* **milk-diet**, *n.* Régime lacté, *m.* **milker**, *n.* Vache laitière (cow), *f.* **milk-fever**, *n.* Fièvre de lait, *f.* **milk-float**, *n.* Voiture de laitier, *f.* **milkiness**, *n.* Nature laiteuse; (*fig.*) douceur, *f.* **milk-jug**, *n.* Pot au lait, *m.* **milk-livered**, *a.* Lâche, poltron. **milkmaid**, *n.* Laitière, *f.* **milkman**, *n.* Laitier, *m.* **milk-pail**, *n.* Seau à lait, *m.* **milk-pan**, *n.* Jatte à lait, terrine à lait, *f.* **milksop**, *n.* (*colloq.*) Poule mouillée, *f.* **milk-tooth**, *n.* Dent de lait, *f.* **milk-white**, *a.* Blanc comme du lait. **milk-woman**, *n.* Laitière, *f.* **milky**, *a.* Laiteux. *Milky Way*, voie lactée, *f.*
mill [mil], *n.* Moulin, *m.*; filature, fabrique (factory), *f.*, millième (coin), *m. Cotton-mill*, filature de coton, *f.*; *rolling-mill*, laminoir, *m.*; *sawmill*, scierie, *f.*; *sugar-mill*, raffinerie, *f.*; *to bring grist to the mill*, porter de l'eau au moulin; *water-mill*, moulin à eau, *m.*; *windmill*, moulin à vent, *m.*—*v.t.* Moudre; fouler (to full); (*Coin.*) estamper; faire mousser (chocolate); (*slang*) donner une volée de coups de poing à.—*v.i.* Fourmiller, tourner en rond (of crowd).
millboard, *n.* Carton-pâte, *m.* **millboard-maker**, *n.* Cartonnier, *m.* **mill-dam**, *n.* Barrage de moulin, *m.* **milled**, *a.* Moleté, foulé (of cloth). *Double-milled*, croisé; *milled edge* (on a coin), cordon, *m.* **mill-hopper**, *n.* Trémie, *f.* **mill-horse**, *n.* Cheval de moulin, *m.* **mill-owner**, *n.* Propriétaire de moulin; chef de fabrique, usinier, industriel, filateur, *m.* **mill-pond**, *n.* Retenue, *f.*; réservoir de moulin, *m. The sea was as calm as a mill-pond*, nous avions une mer d'huile. **mill-race**, *n.* Courant de moulin, bief, biez, *m.* **millstone**, *n.* Meule de moulin, *f. Millstone grit*, pierre meulière, *f.*; *to have a millstone about one's neck*, avoir la corde au cou; *to see through a millstone*, voir au travers les murs. **millwright**, *n.* Constructeur de moulins, *m.*
millenarian [milə'neəriən], *a.* De mille ans; millénaire.—*n.* Millénaire, *m.* **millenarianism**, *n.* Millénarisme, *m.*
millenary ['milənəri], *a.* Millénaire, du millénaire.
millennial [mi'leniəl], *a.* Millénaire, du millénaire. **millennium**, *n.* Millénaire, *m.*, mille ans; les temps messianiques, *m.pl.*
millepede ['milipiːd], *n.* Mille-pieds, *m.*
millepore ['milipɔː], *n.* Millépore, *m.*

miller ['milə], *n.* Meunier, minotier, *m.* Miller's wife, meunière, *f.* **miller's-thumb,** *n.* (*Ichth.*) Meunier, chabot, *m.*

millesimal [mi'lesiml], *a.* De millième.

millet ['milət] or **millet-grass,** *n.* Millet, mil, *m. Indian millet,* sorgho, *m.*

milliard ['miliəd], *n.* Milliard, (*Am.*) billion, *m.*

*milliary ['miliəri], *a.* Milliaire.

milligram(me) ['miligræm], *n.* Milligramme, *m.* **millilitre,** *n.* Millilitre, *m.* **millimetre,** *n.* Millimètre, *m.*

milliner ['milinə], *n.* Marchande de modes; modiste, *f.* **millinery,** *n.* Modes, *f.pl.*

million ['miljən], *n.* Million, *m. The million,* la foule, *f.*, les masses, *f.pl.* **millionaire** [-'nɛə], *n.* Millionnaire, *m.* **millionary,** *a.* De millions, par millions. **millionth,** *a.* and *n.* Millionième, *m.*

milt [milt], *n.* Laite, laitance, *f.* (of fish); rate, *f.* (of mammals).—*v.t.* Féconder. **milter,** *n.* Poisson laité, mâle, *m.* **miltwort,** *n.* Doradille, *f.*

mime [maim], *n.* Mime, *m.*—*v.t.* Mimer (a scene).—*v.i.* Jouer par gestes.

mimeograph ['mimiogrɑːf], *n.* Autocopiste, *m.*

mimesis [mai'miːsis], *n.* (*Rhet.*) Mimèse, *f.*; (*Biol.*) mimétisme, *m.*

mimetic [mi'metik], *a.* D'imitation.

mimic ['mimik], *a.* Imitateur, mimique; imitatif (of animals).—*n.* Mime, imitateur, *m.*—*v.t.* Contrefaire, imiter. **mimicry,** *n.* Mimique, imitation; parodie, *f.*

miminy-piminy ['mimini-'pimini], *a.* (*fam.*) Affété, précieux, prétentieux.

mimosa [mi'mouzə], *n.* (*Bot.*) Mimosa, *m.*

mimulus ['mimjuləs], *n.* (*Bot.*) Mimule, *m.*

minaret ['minəret], *n.* Minaret, *m.*

minatory ['minətəri], *a.* Menaçant.

mince [mins], *v.t.* Hacher menu; dire du bout des lèvres. *Not to mince matters,* parler franchement.—*v.i.* Marcher à petits pas; minauder (in speaking), mignarder.—*n.* Hachis, haché, *m.*

mincemeat, *n.* Hachis, *m.*; pâte d'épices, *f.* (formée de fruits secs, hachés menu—raisins, amandes, pommes, peau d'orange confite, etc.—enrobés dans de la graisse de bœuf et aromatisés). *To make mincemeat of,* hacher menu comme chair à pâté. **mince-pie,** *n.* Tartelette au mincemeat, *f.*

mincing, *a.* Affecté, minaudier. **mincing-knife** or **mincing-machine,** *n.* Hache-viande, hachoir, *m.* **mincingly,** *adv.* Avec minauderie, avec affectation.

mind [maind], *n.* Esprit, *m.,* intelligence; envie, *f.,* désir, *m.* (inclination); opinion, pensée, idée, *f.,* avis (opinion); souvenir, *m.,* mémoire (memory), *f. A grovelling mind,* une âme de boue; *a noble mind,* une belle âme; *nobleness of mind,* noblesse d'âme, *f.; of sound mind,* sain d'esprit; *that went out of my mind,* cela m'est sorti de la tête; *time out of mind,* de temps immémorial; *to alter one's mind,* changer d'idée; *to be of the same mind,* être du même avis (que); *to be out of one's mind,* avoir perdu la raison; *to be uneasy in one's mind,* n'avoir pas l'esprit tranquille; *to bear in mind,* ne pas oublier; *to call to mind,* se rappeler, se souvenir de; *to give one's mind to,* s'adonner à, s'appliquer à; *to give someone a piece of one's mind,* dire son fait à quelqu'un, tancer vertement quelqu'un; *to go out of one's mind,* perdre la raison; *to have a good mind to, to have half a mind to,* avoir bien envie de; *to have one's mind clear about,* avoir le cœur net de; *to have something on one's mind,* avoir quelque chose qui vous préoccupe; *to know one's mind,* savoir à quoi s'en tenir; *to make up one's mind,* se décider, prendre son parti, se résigner à; *to put someone in mind of something,* rappeler quelque chose au souvenir de quelqu'un; *to set one's mind on something,* désirer ardemment quelque chose; *to speak one's mind,* dire sa pensée, dire sa façon de penser; *to tell someone your mind,* dire à quelqu'un son fait.
v.t.—Songer à, faire attention à, s'occuper de, s'inquiéter de, regarder à (to care about); se défier de, avoir peur de (to beware of); obéir à, écouter (to obey); soigner, garder (to nurse); surveiller, observer (to watch). *Do not mind it,* ne faites pas attention à cela; *I do not mind the money,* je ne regarde pas à l'argent; *I do not mind what they say,* je ne m'inquiète pas de ce qu'on dit; *I don't mind going with you,* je veux bien aller avec vous; *if you don't mind,* si cela vous est égal; *mind what you are about!* prenez garde à ce que vous faites! *mind your own business,* mêlez-vous de ce qui vous regarde; *never mind,* peu importe, tant pis; *never mind him,* ne faites pas attention à lui; *you do not mind what I say,* vous ne faites pas attention à ce que je dis.

minded, *a.* Disposé, enclin. *Feeble-minded,* qui a l'esprit faible; *high-minded,* magnanime; *if you are so minded,* si le cœur vous en dit; *low-minded,* qui a l'esprit bas, vil, commun; *sober-minded,* d'un esprit sobre, sage, raisonnable.

mindful, *a.* Attentif (à), soigneux (de); qui se souvient (de). **mindfully,** *adv.* Attentivement. **mindfulness,** *n.* Attention, *f.*

mindless, *a.* Inattentif (à); sans esprit.

mine (1) [main], *pron.poss.* Le mien, *m.,* la mienne, *f.;* les miens, *m.pl.,* les miennes, *f.pl.—a.* A moi. *A favourite of mine,* un de mes favoris; *a friend of mine,* un de mes amis, un ami à moi; *that is no fault of mine,* ce n'est pas de ma faute; *this is mine,* cela est à moi *or* m'appartient, (comes from me) est de moi.

mine (2) [main], *n.* Mine, *f.—v.t.* Miner, creuser; saper. **mine-detector,** *n.* Détecteur de mines, *m.* **mine-field,** *n.* (*Min.*) Région minière, *f.;* (*Naut.*) champ de mines, *m.* **mine-layer,** *n.* (*Navy*) Mouilleur de mines, *m.* **mine-shaft,** *n.* Puits de mine, *m.* **mine-sweeper,** *n.* (*Navy*) Dragueur de mines, *m.* **mine-thrower,** *n.* Lance-mines, *m.inv.*

miner ['mainə], *n.* Mineur, *m.*

mineral ['minərəl], *a.* and *n.* Minéral; (*Min.*) minerai, *m. Mineral rights,* droits miniers, *m.pl.; mineral waters,* eaux minérales, *f.pl.; the mineral kingdom,* le règne minéral, *m.* **mineralizable,** *a.* Minéralisable. **mineralization** [-lai'zeiʃən], *n.* Minéralisation, *f.* **mineralize,** *v.t.* Minéraliser. **mineralizing,** *a.* Minéralisateur. **mineralogical** [-'lɔdʒikl], *a.* Minéralogique. **mineralogist** [-'rælədʒist], *n.* Minéralogiste, *m.* **mineralogy,** *n.* Minéralogie, *f.*

Minerva [mi'nəːvə], (*Myth.*) Minerve, *f.*

mingle [miŋgl], *v.t.*   Mélanger, mêler; entremêler (avec).—*v.i.* Se mêler, se mélanger (avec, dans, *or* en); s'entremêler (avec *or* en). **mingling,** *n.* Mélange, *m.*

miniature ['mini(ə)tʃə], *n.* Miniature, *f.*, portrait en miniature, *m.*—*a.* En miniature. **miniature-painter,** *n.* Miniaturiste, peintre en miniature, *m.*

minify ['minifai], *v.t.* Amoindrir, réduire.

minikin ['minikin], *n.* Mignon, *m.*, mignonne (minion), *f.*; homuncule, nabot, *m.*; camion (pin), *m.*—*a.* Tout petit, mignon, affecté, minaudier.

minim ['minim], *n.* Goutte, *f.*; (*Mus.*) blanche, *f.*; pygmée, nain, *m.*, naine, *f.* (dwarf); (*Franciscan*) minime, *m.*; jambage, *m.* (in writing).

minimal ['miniməl], *a.* Minimum.

minimum ['miniməm], *n.* (*pl.* **minima**) Minimum, *m.*

mining ['mainiŋ], *n.* Exploitation des mines, *f.*, travail dans les mines, *m.*—*a.* Des mines; de mineur, minier. *A mining centre,* un centre minier, *m.*; *mining gallery,* galerie de mine, *f.*; *mining industry,* industrie minière, *f.*

minion ['minjən], *n.* *Mignon, *m.*, mignonne, *f.*; favori, *m.*, favorite, *f.*; (*Print.*) mignonne, *f.* *Minions of the law,* les recors de la justice, *m.pl.*

minister ['ministə], *n.* Ministre; (*Eccles.*) pasteur; (*fig.*) instrument, *m.* *Minister of State,* ministre d'État, *m.*; *Prime Minister,* premier ministre, *m.*—*v.t.* Administrer; donner, fournir.—*v.i.* Servir (à); (*Eccles.*) officier à, contribuer, pourvoir (à). *To minister to,* assister, venir au secours de, contribuer à, pourvoir à.

ministerial [minis'tiəriəl], *a.* De ministère, du pouvoir exécutif, ministériel. **ministerialist,** *n.* Ministériel, *m.* **ministerially,** *adv.* Ministériellement. **ministering,** *a.* Secourable. *Ministering angel,* ange secourable, *m.* **ministrant,** *n.* (*Eccles.*) Desservant, officiant, *m.* **ministration** [-'treiʃən], *n.* Ministère, *m.*, entremise, *f.*; service, *m.*

ministry ['ministri], *n.* Ministère, gouvernement; département, *m.*

*****minium** ['miniəm], *n.* Minium, *m.*

miniver ['minivə], *n.* Petit-gris, menu-vair, *m.*

mink [miŋk], *n.* Vison, *m.*

minnow ['minou], *n.* Vairon, *m.*

minor ['mainə], *a.* Moindre; de second ordre, secondaire, petit, mince; (*Mus., Geog., etc.*) mineur. *In a minor key,* en mineur; *Minor Orders,* ordres mineurs, *m.pl.*—*n.* Mineur, *m.*, mineure, *f.*

Minorca [mi'nɔːkə]. Minorque, *f.*

minority [mai'nɔriti], *n.* Minorité, *f.*

Minotaur ['minotɔː], *n.* Minotaure, *m.*

minster ['minstə], *n.* Cathédrale, église abbatiale, *f.*

minstrel ['minstrəl], *n.* Ménestrel, *m.*; (*fam.*) poète, musicien, chanteur, *m.* **minstrelsy,** *n.* Chant des ménestrels, art du ménestrel, *m.*; (*fig.*) musique, *f.*, chant, *m.*

mint (1) [mint], *n.* Menthe, *f.* *Peppermint,* menthe poivrée, *f.*

mint (2) [mint], *n.* La Monnaie, *f.*; l'hôtel des monnaies, *m.* *In mint state,* à l'état neuf; *master of the mint,* directeur de la monnaie, *m.*; *to have a mint of money,* être tout consu d'or.—*v.t.* Monnayer, frapper; (*fig.*) forger, fabriquer, inventer.

mintage, *n.* Objet monnayé; droit de monnayage, *m.* **minter,** *n.* Monnayeur, *m.* **minting,** *n.* Monnayage, *m.*

minuet [minju'et], *n.* Menuet, *m.*

minus ['mainəs], *prep.* Moins; sans (without). —*n.* Moins, *m.* (*pop.*) *He's a minus quantity,* c'est un zéro.

minute (1) [mai'njuːt *or* mi'njuːt], *a.* Menu, minuscule, très petit; minutieux. **minutely** (1), *adv.* Minutieusement; exactement; en détail. **minuteness,** *n.* Petitesse, exiguïté; exactitude, *f.*; détails minutieux, *m.pl.*

minute (2) ['minit], *n.* Minute, *f.*; instant; moment; brouillon, projet, *m.*, minute, note, *f.* *Minutes* (of a meeting), procès-verbal, compte-rendu, *m.*; *punctual to a minute,* exact à une minute près; *this minute,* à l'instant; *this very minute,* à l'instant même; *to expect someone every minute,* attendre quelqu'un d'un instant à l'autre; *to make a minute of,* prendre note de; *up to the minute,* à la dernière mode, de la dernière heure.—*v.t.* Minuter, prendre note de.

minute-book, *n.* Registre des procès-verbaux; journal, *m.* **minute-gun,** *n.* Canon de détresse, *m.* **minute-hand,** *n.* Aiguille des minutes, grande aiguille, *f.* **minutely** (2), *a.* À chaque minute; de toutes les minutes.— *adv.* À chaque minute. **minute-wheel,** *n.* Roue des minutes, *f.*

minutiae [mi'njuːʃiiː], *n.pl.* Minuties, *f.pl.*

minx [miŋks], *n.* Coquine, friponne, *f.*

miracle ['mirəkl], *n.* Miracle, *m.* *By a miracle,* par miracle. **miracle-monger,** *n.* Faiseur de miracles, *m.* **miracle-play,** *n.* Miracle, mystère, *m.*

miraculous [mi'rækjuləs], *a.* Miraculeux. **miraculously,** *adv.* Miraculeusement, par miracle. **miraculousness,** *n.* Caractère miraculeux, *m.*

mirage [mi'rɑːʒ], *n.* Mirage, *m.*

mire ['maiə], *n.* Boue, bourbe, fange, vase, *f.* *To sink in the mire,* s'enfoncer dans la boue, s'embourber.—*v.t.* Embourber. **miriness,** *n.* État boueux, *m.* **miry,** *a.* Fangeux, bourbeux

mirk [MURK].

mirror ['mirə], *n.* Miroir, *m.*, glace, *f.* *Distorting mirror,* miroir déformant, *m.*; *driving-mirror,* rétroviseur, *m.*—*v.t.* Refléter.

mirth [məːθ], *n.* Gaieté, hilarité, *f.*, rire, *m.* **mirthful,** *a.* Gai, joyeux. **mirthfully,** *adv.* Gaiement, joyeusement. **mirthfulness,** *n.* Allégresse, *f.* **mirthless,** *a.* Sans gaieté, triste. **mirthlessness,** *n.* Tristesse, *f.*, manque de gaieté, *m.*

misadventure [misəd'ventʃə], *n.* Mésaventure, *f.*, contretemps, *m.*

misalliance [misə'laiəns], *n.* Mésalliance, *f.* **misallied,** *a.* Mésallié.

misanthrope ['misənθroup] *or* **misanthropist** [-'sænθrəpist], *n.* Misanthrope, *m.* **misanthropic** *or* **misanthropical** [-an'θrɔpikl], *a.* Misanthrope; misanthropique (of things).

misanthropy [mi'sænθrəpi], *n.* Misanthropie, *f.*

misapplication [misæpli'keiʃən], *n.* Mauvaise application, *f.* **misapply** [-ə'plai], *v.t.* Mal appliquer, détourner (of funds etc.).

misapprehend [misæpri'hend], *v.t.* Comprendre mal. *He protested that he had been* *misapprehended,* il protesta qu'on l'avait mal compris. **misapprehension,** *n.* Malentendu, *m.,* méprise, *f.*

misappropriate [misə'prouprieit], *v.t.* Détourner. **misappropriation** [-'eiʃən], *n.* Détournement, mauvais emploi, *m.*

misbecome [misbi'kʌm], *v.t.* (*past* **misbecame**) Convenir mal à, messeoir à. **misbecoming,** *a.* Peu convenable, messéant. **misbecomingly,** *adv.* D'une manière inconvenante. **misbecomingness,** *n.* Inconvenance, *f.*

misbegotten [misbi'gɔtn], *a.* Illégitime, âtbard; (*fig.*) mal né, malencontreux.

misbehave [misbi'heiv], *v.i.* Se comporter mal. **misbehaviour,** *n.* Mauvaise conduite, *f.*

misbelief [misbi'li:f], *n.* Fausse croyance, *f.* **misbeliever,** *n.* Mécréant, infidèle, *m.* **misbelieving,** *a.* Mécréant, infidèle.

miscalculate [mis'kælkjuleit], *v.t.* Calculer mal. **miscalculation** [-'leiʃən], *n.* Calcul erroné, *m.*; mécompte, *m.*

miscall [mis'kɔ:l], *v.t.* Appeler à tort.

miscarriage [mis'kæridʒ], *n.* Insuccès, coup manqué, échec, *m.*; fausse couche (of a woman), *f. Miscarriage of justice,* erreur judiciaire, *f.*

miscarry [mis'kæri], *v.i.* Ne pas réussir, manquer, échouer; ne pas arriver à sa destination (not to arrive); faire une fausse couche (of women).

miscellanea [misə'leinjə], *n.pl.* Miscellanées, *m.pl.* **miscellaneous** [-'leinjəs], *a.* Varié, de toute espèce, divers; général. *Miscellaneous news,* faits divers, *m.pl.*; *miscellaneous works,* mélanges, *m.pl.* **miscellanist** [-'selənist], *n.* Auteur de mélanges, *m.*

miscellany [mi'seləni], *n.* (*pl.* **miscellanies**) Mélange, *m.*; mélanges (book), *m.pl.*

mischance [mis'tʃɑ:ns], *n.* Malheur, accident, *m.,* mésaventure, infortune, *f.*

mischief ['mistʃif], *n.* Mal, dommage, dégât, tort, *m. Out of pure mischief,* par pure méchanceté; *that child is always getting into mischief,* cet enfant n'arrête pas de faire des bêtises; *to be up to some mischief,* faire quelque mal, méditer quelque sale tour; *to do mischief,* faire du mal; *to keep someone out of mischief,* empêcher quelqu'un de faire des malices; *to make mischief between,* semer la discorde entre or parmi, brouiller; *to mean mischief,* méditer un mauvais coup. **mischief-maker,** *n.* Brouillon, *m.* **mischief-making,** *a.* Malfaisant; qui brouille les gens.

mischievous ['mistʃivəs], *a.* Méchant, malicieux; malfaisant, mauvais, nuisible (of things); espiègle (children). **mischievously,** *adv.* Méchamment. **mischievousness,** *n.* Méchanceté; espièglerie (of children), *f.*

mischoose [mis'tʃu:z], *v.t.* (*past* **mischose**, *p.p.* **mischosen**) Choisir mal.

miscibility [misi'biliti], *n.* Miscibilité, *f.*

miscible ['misibl], *a.* Miscible.

miscomputation [miskɔmpju'teiʃən], *n.* Erreur de calcul, *f.,* mécompte, *m.*

miscompute [miskəm'pju:t], *v.t.* Calculer mal.

misconceive [miskən'si:v], *v.t., v.i.* Mal concevoir, juger mal. **misconceived,** *a.* Mal conçu, faux, erroné. **misconception**

[-'sepʃən], *n.* Conception erronée, *f.*; malentendu, *m.*

misconduct (1) [mis'kɔndʌkt], *n.* Mauvaise conduite, *f.*

misconduct (2) [miskən'dʌkt], *v.t.* Conduire mal. *To misconduct oneself,* se conduire mal.

misconjecture [miskən'dʒektʃə], *n.* Fausse conjecture, *f.*—*v.t.* Conjecturer à tort.—*v.i.* Faire de fausses conjectures.

misconstruction [miskən'strʌkʃən], *n.* Fausse interprétation, *f.,* contresens, *m.* **misconstrue** [-'stru:], *v.t.* Mal interpréter; (*fig.*) traduire mal.

miscopy [mis'kɔpi], *v.t.* Copier de travers.

miscount [mis'kaunt], *v.t.* Compter mal.—*v.i.* Faire une erreur de compte.—*n.* Mécompte, *m.*

miscreant ['miskriənt], *n.* Mécréant; (*fig.*) misérable, vaurien, *m.*

mis-cue [mis'kju:], *v.i.* (*Billiards*) Faire fausse queue.—*n.* Fausse queue, *f.*

misdate [mis'deit], *v.t.* Dater mal.—*n.* Fausse date, *f.*

misdeal [mis'di:l], *v.t.* Maldonner.—*n.* Maldonne, *f.*

misdeed [mis'di:d], *n.* Méfait, *m.*

misdemean [misdə'mi:n], *v.r. To misdemean oneself,* se comporter mal. **misdemeanant,** *n.* Délinquant, *m.* **misdemeanour,** *n.* Délit, crime, *m.,* offense, *f.*

misdirect [misdai'rekt], *v.t.* Mal diriger, renseigner mal; mettre une fausse adresse à (letters etc.).

misdo [mis'du:], *v.t.* (*past* **misdid**, *p.p.* **misdone** [-'dʌn]) Malfaire.—*v.i.* Commettre des fautes. **misdoer,** *n.* Malfaiteur, *m.* **misdoing,** *n.* Méfait, *m.*

mise [mi:z], *n.* (*Hist.*) Accord, *m. The Mise of Amiens,* l'Accord d'Amiens.

misemploy [misəm'plɔi], *v.t.* Employer mal, faire un mauvais emploi de. **misemployment,** *n.* Mauvais emploi, *m.*

misentry [mis'entri], *n.* Inscription erronée, *f.*

miser ['maizə], *n.* Avare, *m.* **miser-like,** *a.* and *adv.* En avare, comme un avare.

miserable ['mizərəbl], *a.* Misérable, pitoyable, malheureux; triste, affreux; mesquin (shabby). *To make someone's life miserable,* rendre la vie dure à quelqu'un. **miserableness,** *n.* État malheureux, *m.* **miserably,** *adv.* Misérablement, malheureusement; pitoyablement, affreusement; mesquinement.

miserere [mizə'riəri], *n.* (*R.-C. Ch.*) Miséréré, *m.* **misericord,** *n.* (*Arch.*) Miséricorde, *f.*

miserliness ['maizəlinis], *n.* Avarice, *f.*

miserly ['maizəli], *a.* D'avare, avare, sordide.

misery ['mizəri], *n.* Misère, *f.*; (*fig.*) tourment, supplice, *m.*; (*fam.*) geigneur, *m.,* -euse, *f. To put out of his misery,* mettre fin aux souffrances de.

misesteem [mises'ti:m], *v.t.* Estimer à tort.—*n.* Mésestime, *f.* **misestimate** [-'estimeit], *v.t.* Estimer à tort, mal apprécier.

misfashion [mis'fæʃən], *v.t.* Former mal, mal façonner. **misfashioned,** *a.* Difforme.

*misfeasance [-'fi:zəns], *n.* (*Law*) Dommage, tort, *m.*; abus de pouvoir, *m.*

misfire [mis'faiə], *v.i.* Rater; (*Motor.*) avoir des ratés.—*n.* Raté d'allumage, *m.*; (*fig.*) faillite, *f.*

misfit ['misfit], *n.* Vêtement manqué, *m.*; inadapté, *m.* (person).

misfortune [mis'fɔːtʃən], *n.* Malheur, *m.*, infortune, *f. Misfortunes never come singly,* un malheur ne vient jamais seul.
misgive [mis'giv], *v.t. (past* **misgave,** *p.p.* **misgiven)** Inspirer des doutes *or* des craintes à. **misgiving,** *n.* Pressentiment, soupçon, doute, *m.*; inquiétude, *f.*
misgovern [mis'gʌvən], *v.t.* Gouverner mal. **misgoverned,** *a.* Mal gouverné. **misgovernment,** *n.* Mauvais gouvernement, *m.*
misguidance [mis'gaidəns], *n.* Fausse direction, *f.* **misguide,** *v.t.* Égarer, mal guider. **misguided,** *a.* Malencontreux; peu judicieux; fourvoyé, dévoyé. *Misguided enthusiasm,* enthousiasme hors de propos, *m.* **misguidedly,** *adv.* Sans jugement.
mishandle [mis'hændl], *v.t.* Manier mal, traiter mal; malmener.
mishap [mis'hæp], *n.* Contretemps, malheur, *m.*, mésaventure, *f.*
mishmash ['miʃmæʃ], *n.* Mélange, fatras, méli-mélo, *m.*
misinform [misin'fɔːm], *v.t.* Mal renseigner. **misinformation** [-fə'meiʃən], *n.* Faux renseignement, *m.* **misinformed,** *a.* Mal renseigné (sur).
misinterpret [misin'təːprit], *v.t.* Interpréter mal. **misinterpretation** [-'teiʃən], *n.* Fausse interprétation, *f.*, contresens, *m.*
misjudge [mis'dʒʌdʒ], *v.t.* Juger mal, méjuger; se tromper sur. **misjudgment,** *n.* Jugement erroné, *m.*
mislay [mis'lei], *v.t. (past and p.p.* **mislaid)** Égarer.
mislead [mis'liːd], *v.t. (past and p.p.* **misled** [mis'led])* Égarer, induire en erreur; fourvoyer; tromper. **misleader,** *n.* Trompeur, corrupteur, *m.* **misleading,** *a.* Trompeur.
mismanage [mis'mænidʒ], *v.t.* Diriger mal. —*v.i.* S'y prendre mal, s'arranger mal (pour). **mismanagement,** *n.* Mauvaise administration, *f.*
mismatch [mis'mætʃ], *v.t.* Mal assortir, mal apparier.
misname [mis'neim], *v.t.* Mal nommer.
misnomer [mis'noumə], *n.* Erreur de nom, *f.*; faux nom, *m.*, fausse désignation, *f.*
misogamist [mi'sɔgəmist], *n.* **misogamous,** *a.* Misogame.
misogynist [mi'sɔdʒinist], *n.* Misogyne, *m.* **misogynous,** *a.* Misogyne. **misogyny,** *n.* Misogynie, *f.*
misplace [mis'pɫeis], *v.t.* Mal placer; déplacer. **misplaced,** *a.* Mal placé; déplacé; hors de propos.
misprint (1) ['misprint], *n.* Faute d'impression, erreur typographique, *(fam.)* coquille, *f.*
misprint (2) [mis'print], *v.t.* Imprimer incorrectement.
misprize [mis'praiz], *v.t.* Mépriser.
mispronounce [misprə'nauns], *v.t.* Prononcer mal *or* incorrectement. **mispronunciation** [-nʌnsi'eiʃən], *n.* Prononciation incorrecte, *f.*
misproportion [misprə'pɔːʃən], *v.t.* Proportionner mal.
misquotation [miskwo'teiʃən], *n.* Fausse citation, *f.* **misquote** [-'kwout], *v.t.* Citer à faux.
misread [mis'riːd], *v.t.* Mal lire, mal interpréter.

misreckon [mis'rekən], *v.t.* Calculer mal. **misreckoning,** *n.* Calcul erroné, *m.*
misrelate [misri'leit], *v.t.* Raconter inexactement. **misrelation** [-'leiʃən], *n.* Rapport erroné, *m.*
misreport [misri'pɔːt], *v.t.* Rapporter inexactement.—*n.* Rapport inexact, *m.*
misrepresent [misrepri'zent], *v.t.* Représenter mal, dénaturer. **misrepresentation** [-teiʃən], *n.* Faux rapport, *m.*
misrule [mis'ruːl], *n.* Désordre; mauvais gouvernement, *m.*
miss (1) [mis], *n.* Mademoiselle, demoiselle, *f. Miss Helen,* Mademoiselle Hélène.
miss (2) [mis], *n.* Manque, *m.*; perte (loss), *f.*; faute, erreur, méprise (mistake), *f.*; *(Billiards* etc.) manque de touche, coup manqué, *m.* —*v.t.* Manquer; omettre, sauter (to omit); s'apercevoir de l'absence de, regretter vivement, ne plus trouver. *I miss my friend very much,* mon ami me manque beaucoup; *I missed the train,* j'ai manqué le train; *I missed you badly,* je vous ai bien regretté; *to miss fire,* rater (of a pistol etc.); *to miss one's mark,* manquer son coup; *to miss out,* passer, omettre; *to miss out a halting-place,* brûler une étape.—*v.i.* Manquer; ne pas réussir, échouer, se tromper; *(Billiards)* manquer de touche. *To be missing,* être absent, manquer (of things).
missal [misl], *n.* Missel, *m.*
missel-thrush ['misl'θrʌʃ], *n. (Orn.)* Draine, grosse grive, *f.*
misshape [mis'ʃeip], *v.t.* Défigurer, déformer. **misshapen,** *a.* Difforme.
missile ['misail], *a.* De jet, de trait.—*n.* Projectile, *m. Guided missile,* engin téléguidé, *m.*
missing ['misiŋ], *a.* Qui manque, absent, perdu, disparu. *Killed, wounded, or missing,* tués, blessés, ou disparus.
mission ['miʃən], *n.* Mission, *f.* **missionary,** *a.* Des missions.—*n.* Missionnaire, *m.* **missioner,** *n.* Missionnaire paroissial, *m.*
missis *or* **missus** ['misis], *n. (pop.) The missis,* ma femme, ma légitime; Madame, *f.*
missive ['misiv], *a. and n.* Missive, lettre, *f.*
misspell [mis'spel], *v.t. (past and p.p.* **misspelt)** Épeler mal. **misspelling,** *n.* Faute d'orthographe, *f.*
misspend [mis'spend], *v.t. (past and p.p.* **misspent)** Employer mal; gaspiller.
misstate [mis'steit], *v.t.* Rapporter incorrectement. **misstatement,** *n.* Rapport erroné, *m.*
missus [MISSIS].
mist [mist], *n.* Brume; bruine (Scotch mist), *f.*; crachin, *m.* (in Normandy); buée (on mirrors etc.), *f.*—*v.t.* Couvrir (une glace) de buée.—*v.i.* Se couvrir de buée. *The hills mist over,* les collines disparaissent sous la brume.
mist-preventive, *n. (Motor.)* Antibuée, *m.*
mistakable [mis'teikəbl], *a.* Qui prête à erreur.
mistake [mis'teik], *v.t. (past* **mistook** [-'tuk], *p.p.* **mistaken)** Se tromper de *or* sur, se méprendre à *or* sur; prendre (pour). *He mistook me for you,* il m'a pris pour vous.—*v.i.* Se tromper, se méprendre, s'abuser. *If I mistake not,* si je ne m'abuse; *to be mistaken,* se tromper, *or* être dans l'erreur.—*n.* Erreur, méprise, faute, bévue (blunder), *f. And no mistake!* c'est positif; *by mistake,* par mégarde,

par erreur; *no mistake!* sans aucun doute, à coup sûr; *to make a mistake*, se tromper, être dans l'erreur. **mistaken**, *a.* Qui se trompe; faux, erroné (of things). **mistakenly**, *adv.* Par méprise. **mistakingly**, *adv.* Par méprise.

mister, **Mr.** ['mistə], *n.* Monsieur, *m.* *Mr. Smith*, Monsieur Smith.

mistime [mis'taim], *v.t.* Faire mal à propos. **mistimed**, *a.* Inopportun.

mistiness ['mistinis], *n.* État brumeux, *m.*

mistle-thrush [MISSEL-THRUSH].

mistletoe ['misltou], *n.* Gui, *m.*

mistral ['mistrəl], *n.* Mistral, *m.*

mistranslate [mistrænz'leit *or* mistrɑːns'leit], *v.t.* Mal traduire. **mistranslation** [-'leiʃən], *n.* Traduction incorrecte, *f.*

mistress ['mistris], *n.* Maîtresse; patronne; institutrice (school), *f.* *Headmistress*, directrice, *f.*; *my mistress is not at home*, madame n'y est pas.

mistrust [mis'trʌst], *n.* Méfiance, défiance, *f.*, soupçon, *m.*—*v.t.* Se méfier de, soupçonner. **mistrustful**, *a.* Méfiant. **mistrustfully**, *adv.* Avec méfiance. **mistrustfulness**, *n.* Méfiance, *f.*

mistune [mis'tjuːn], *v.t.* Accorder mal; désaccorder.

misty ['misti], *a.* Brumeux; vaporeux (of light); (*fig.*) confus.

misunderstand [misʌndə'stænd], *v.t.* (*past and p.p.* **misunderstood**) Mal comprendre, entendre mal; se méprendre sur. **misunderstanding**, *n.* Conception erronée, *f.*; malentendu (mistake), *m.*; mésintelligence (quarrel), *f.*

misusage [mis'juːsidʒ] *or* **misuse** (1) [-'juːs], *n.* Abus, mauvais emploi, *m.*; mauvais traitements, *m.pl.*

misuse (2) [mis'juːz], *v.t.* Faire un mauvais usage de, mésuser de; maltraiter (to treat ill).

mite [mait], *n.* Mite (creature), *f.*; denier (money), *m.*; (*fig.*) rien, *m.*, obole, *f.*; (*fam.*) petit gosse, moutard, *m.* *The widow's mite*, le denier de la veuve. **mity**, *a.* Plein de mites.

mitigate ['mitigeit], *v.t.* Mitiger, adoucir, modérer. **mitigating**, *a.* Adoucissant, atténuant. *Mitigating circumstances*, circonstances atténuantes, *f.pl.* **mitigation** [-'geiʃən], *n.* Mitigation, *f.*, adoucissement, *m.*

mitre ['maitə], *n.* Mitre, *f.*; (*Carp.*) onglet, *m.*—*v.t.* Assembler à onglet. **mitred**, *a.* Orné d'une mitre, mitré; (*Carp.*) en onglet. **mitriform**, *a.* (*Bot.*) En forme de mitre.

mitten [mitn], *n.* Mitaine, *f.* (*colloq.*) *To get the mitten*, être congédié.

mittimus ['mitiməs], *n.* Mandat de dépôt, *m.*

mity [MITE].

mix [miks], *v.t.* Mêler, mélanger; couper (drinks); faire, former (de); malaxer (of cement); allier (of metals). *To mix it*, (*pop.*) en venir aux coups.—*v.i.* Se mélanger, se mêler (de); s'associer (à). *Colours which mix well*, des couleurs qui s'accordent bien; *people who mix with crooks*, des gens qui s'associent avec les escrocs. **mix up**, *v.t.* Mêler; embrouiller; confondre. *After his accident everything was mixed up*, à la suite de son accident, tout était embrouillé; *he mixed me up with my father*, il me confondait avec mon

père. **mix-up**, *n.* Confusion, *f.*, embrouillement, *m.*; (*pop.*) pagaïe, *f.*

mixed [mikst], *a.* Mélangé, mêlé (de); assorti; mixte; (*Math.*) fractionnaire, (*Chem.*) composé. *Mixed marriage*, mariage mixte, *m.*; *to join in mixed bathing*, prendre part aux bains mixtes; *to play in the mixed doubles*, jouer en double mixte. **mixedly**, *adv.* Confusément. **mixer**, *n.* (*Tech.*) Mélangeur, *m.*; (*Cine.*) opérateur du son, *m.* *He is a bad mixer*, il n'est pas sociable. **mixing**, *n.* Mélange; brassage, *m.*; préparation (in pharmacy), *f.*; (*Cine.*) mixage, *m.* **mixture**, *n.* Mélange, *m.*; (*Pharm.*) potion, mixture, *f.*

mixen ['miksən], *n.* Tas de fumier, *m.*

mizen [mizn], *n.* Artimon, *m.* **mizen-mast**, *n.* Mât d'artimon, *m.* **mizen-top**, *n.* Hune d'artimon, *f.* **mizen-topmast**, *n.* Mât (de perroquet) de fougue, *m.* **mizen-yard**, *n.* Vergue de perroquet, *f.*

mizzle [mizl], *v.i.* Bruiner; (*slang*) décamper.

mnemonic [ni'mɔnik], *a.* Mnémonique. **mnemonics**, *n.pl.* Mnémonique, *f.*

moan [moun], *n.* Gémissement, *m.*, plainte; (*fig.*) lamentation, *f.* *The moan of the wind*, le gémissement du vent.—*v.i.* Gémir; (*fig.*) se lamenter; (*pop.*) grognonner.—*v.t.* Gémir de *or* sur; se lamenter sur, pleurer, déplorer.

moanful, *a.* Lugubre, triste, lamentable. **moanfully**, *adv.* Tristement, plaintivement.

moat [mout], *n.* Fossé, *m.*, douve, *f.*—*v.t.* Entourer d'un fossé *or* de fossés.

mob [mɔb], *n.* Foule; populace, canaille, *f.*; rassemblement, attroupement, *m.* *Mob law*, la loi de la populace, *f.*; *mob psychology*, la psychologie des foules, *f.*; *riotous mob*, attroupement, rassemblement, *m.*—*v.t.* Houspiller, malmener; assiéger. **mobbish**, *a.* De la populace, populacier; tumultueux.

mob-cap, *n.* Cornette, *f.*

mobile ['moubail], *a.* Mobile.

mobility [mou'biliti], *n.* Mobilité; légèreté (inconstancy), *f.*

mobilizable [moubi'laizəbl], *a.* Mobilisable.

mobilization [moubilai'zeiʃən], *n.* Mobilisation, *f.*

mobilize ['moubilaiz], *v.t.* Mobiliser.

mobocracy [mɔ'bɔkrəsi], *n.* (*fam.*) Voyoucratie, démagogie, *f.* **mobster**, *n.* Gangster, *m.*

moccasin ['mɔkəsin], *n.* Mocassin, *m.*

Mocha ['moukə], *n.* Moka (coffee), *m.*

mock [mɔk], *v.t.* Se moquer de; narguer, tromper, contrefaire.—*v.i.* Railler. *To mock at*, se moquer de.—*a.* Dérisoire, burlesque; faux, simulé, contrefait (false). *Mock prophet*, faux prophète, *m.*

mocker, *n.* Moqueur, *m.*, -euse, *f.* **mockery**, *n.* Moquerie, raillerie; illusion, *f.*, semblant, simulacre, *m.*

mock-heroic, *a.* Héroï-comique. **mock-sun**, *n.* (*Astron.*) Parhélie, *m.* **mock-turtle**, *n.* Soupe à la tête de veau, *f.* **mock-up**, *n.* Maquette, réplique, *f.*

mocking, *n.* Moquerie, *f.* **mocking-bird**, *n.* Oiseau moqueur, *m.* **mockingly**, *adv.* En se moquant, d'un ton moqueur.

modal [moudl], *a.* Modal. **modality** [mou'dæliti], *n.* Modalité, *f.*

mode [moud], *n.* Mode, façon, manière, *f.*; (*Phil.*, *Mus.*, etc.) mode, *m.* *A mode of life*, une façon de vivre.

model [mɔdl], *n.* Modèle, *m.*; représentation, *f.*; moule (mould); mannequin; (*fig.*) plan, système, *m.* *Model aeroplane*, modèle d'avion, avion miniature, *m.*; *model husband*, mari modèle, *m.*—*v.t.* Modeler; faire *or* former d'après un modèle; (*Cloth.*) présenter des vêtements (in fashion parades). **modeller,** *n.* Modeleur, *m.* **modelling,** *n.* Modelage, *m.*

Modena [mo'deinə]. Modène, *f.* *Modena red,* pourpre foncé. **Modenese,** *a.* and *n.* Modénais, *m.*, -aise, *f.*

moderate (1) ['mɔdərit], *a.* Modéré; modique, ordinaire, passable, médiocre.

moderate (2) ['mɔdəreit]. Modérer, adoucir, tempérer.—*v.i.* Se modérer.

moderately, *adv.* Modérément, passablement; médiocrement. **moderateness,** *n.* Modération, *f.* **moderating,** *a.* Modérateur.

moderation [mɔdə'reiʃən], *n.* Modération; retenue, mesure, *f.*; (*pl.*) (*Oxford Univ.*) premier examen du B.A., *m.* *In moderation,* modérément, avec mesure, *f.*

moderator, *n.* Modérateur, *m.*, -trice, *f.*; (*Presbyterian*) président, *m.*; (*Oxford Univ.*) examinateur, *m.* **moderatorship,** *n.* Fonctions de modérateur, *f.pl.*; (*Presbyterian*) présidence, *f.*

modern ['mɔdən], *a.* and *n.* Moderne, *m.* *Modern languages,* langues vivantes, *f.pl.* **modernism,** *n.* Modernisme, *m.* **modernist,** *n.* Moderniste, *m.*

modernity [mɔ'də:niti], *n.* Modernité, *f.* **modernize,** *v.t.* Moderniser, rendre moderne; (*Arch.*) moderner. **modernness,** *n.* Nouveauté, modernité, *f.*

modest ['mɔdist], *a.* Modeste; pudique, chaste (of women); modéré (of demands etc.). **modestly,** *adv.* Modestement, avec modestie; pudiquement, chastement; modérément. **modesty,** *n.* Modestie, *f.*; pudeur, pudicité, *f.*; modération, *f.*; modicité (of expenditure). *f.*

modicum ['mɔdikəm], *n.* Petite portion, *f.*

modifiable ['mɔdifaiəbl], *a.* Modifiable.

modification [-i'keiʃən], *n.* Modification, *f.*

modificative ['mɔdifikeitiv], *a.* Modificatif.

modify, *v.t.* Modifier.—*v.i.* Se modifier.

modillion [mo'diliən], *n.* (*Arch.*) Modillon, *m.*

modish ['moudiʃ], *a.* À la mode; (of persons) faraud. **modishly,** *adv.* À la mode. **modishness,** *n.* Conformité à la mode, *f.*

modulate ['mɔdjuleit], *v.t.* Moduler. **modulating,** *a.* Modulant. **modulation** [-'leiʃən], *n.* Modulation, *f.* **modulator,** *n.* Modulateur, *m.*

module ['mɔdjul], *n.* (*Arch.*) Module, *m.*

Mogul [mou'gʌl], *n.* Mogol, *m.*

mohair ['mouhɛə], *n.* Poil de chèvre angora, mohair, *m.*

Mohammed [mo'hæməd]. Mahomet, *m.*

Mohammedan [mo'hæmədən], *a.* and *n.* Mahométan, *m.*, mahométane, *f.* **Mohammedanism,** *n.* Mahométisme, *m.*

Mohawk ['mouhɔ:k], *n.* Nom d'une tribu indienne de l'Amérique du Nord.

Mohock ['mouhɔk], *n.* (*Corruption of* MOHAWK). Bandit des rues de Londres, 18ᵉ siècle.

moiety ['mɔiəti], *n.* (*Law*) Moitié, *f.*

moil [mɔil], *v.i.* Peiner, travailler dur. *To toil and moil,* suer sang et eau.

moire [mwɑ:], *n.* Moire (silk), *f.*

moist [mɔist], *a.* Moite, humide, mouillé.

moisten [mɔisn], *v.t.* Humecter, rendre moite, mouiller, moitir (of skin), arroser (pastry). **moisture** *or* **moistness,** *n.* Moiteur, humidité, *f.*

molar ['moulə], *a.* and *n.* Molaire, *f.*

molasses [mo'læsiz], *n.pl.* Mélasse, *f.*

mole [moul], *n.* Taupe (animal); tache, *f.*, grain de beauté (on the skin); môle (pier), *m.* **mole-catcher,** *n.* Taupier, *m.* **mole-cricket,** *n.* Taupe-grillon, *m.*, courtilière, *f.* **mole-hill,** *n.* Taupinière, *f.* *To make a mountain out of a molehill,* faire d'un œuf un bœuf. **moleskin,** *n.* Peau de taupe, molesquine, *f.*, velours de coton, *m.* **mole-trap,** *n.* Taupière, *f.*

molecular [mo'lekjulə], *a.* Moléculaire.

molecule ['mɔl-, 'mouləkju:l], *n.* Molécule, *f.*

molest [mo'lest], *v.t.* Molester; vexer; inquiéter; tourmenter. **molestation** [-'teiʃən], *n.* Vexation, *f.*

mollifiable ['mɔlifaiəbl], *a.* Qu'on peut adoucir.

mollification [mɔlifi'keiʃən], *n.* Amollissement, adoucissement, *m.* **mollifier,** *n.* Adoucissant, calmant; (*Med.*) émollient, *m.*

mollify ['mɔlifai], *v.t.* Amollir; adoucir; apaiser (of anger).

mollusc ['mɔləsk], *n.* Mollusque, *m.*

mollycoddle ['mɔlikɔdl], *v.t.* Gâter, choyer, câliner (un enfant).—*n.* Enfant choyé.

molten ['moultən], *a.* Fondu, de fonte.

Moluccas [mo'lʌkəs]. (*Geog.*) Les Moluques, *f.pl.*

molybdenum [mɔlib'di:nəm], *n.* Molybdène, *m.*

moment ['moumənt], *n.* Moment, instant, *m.*; (*fig.*) importance, *f.* *At that moment,* à ce même moment; *at the present moment,* actuellement, à l'heure qu'il est; *at this moment,* en ce moment; *he stops every moment,* il s'arrête à tout moment; *in a moment,* dans un moment; *not for a moment,* pour rien au monde; *of no moment,* d'aucune importance; *the moment that,* dès que, aussitôt que; *this moment,* à l'instant; *this very moment,* à l'instant même. **momentarily,** *adv.* Momentanément, à tout moment. **momentary,** *a.* Momentané; de peu de durée, passager. **momently,** *adv.* À tout moment, d'un moment à l'autre.

momentous [mo'mentəs], *a.* Important, d'une importance capitale. **momentum,** *n.* (*Phys.*) Force vive; vitesse acquise, *f.* *To gather momentum,* acquérir de la vitesse, *f.*

monachal ['mɔnəkl], *a.* Monacal. **monachism,** *n.* Monachisme, *m.*

monad ['mɔnəd], *n.* Monade, *f.*

monadelphous [mɔnə'delfəs], *a.* (*Bot.*) Monadelphe.

monadic [mo'nædik] *or* **monadical,** *a.* Des monades.

monandria [mo'nændriə], *n.* Monandrie, *f.*

monarch ['mɔnək], *n.* Monarque, *m.*

monarchic [mə'nɑ:kik] *or* **monarchical,** *a.* Monarchique, de monarque, souverain. **monarchically,** *a.* Monarchiquement, à la manière d'une monarchie. **monarchist,** *n.* Monarchiste, *m.* **monarchize,** *v.t.* Monarchiser. **monarchy,** *n.* Monarchie, *f.*

monastery ['mɔnəstri], *n.* Monastère, *m.*

monastic [mə'næstik], *a.* Monastique. **monastically,** *adv.* En moine. **monasticism** [mo'næstisizm], *n.* Monachisme, *m.*; vie monastique, *f.*
Monday ['mʌndi], *n.* Lundi, *m.*
monetary ['mʌnətəri], *a.* Monétaire. **monetization** [-tai'zeiʃən], *n.* Monétisation, *f.* **monetize** ['mʌnətaiz], *v.t.* Monétiser.
money ['mʌni], *n.* Argent, *m.*; monnaie, *f.*, espèces (coins), *f.pl.* Copper money, monnaie de cuivre, *f.*, billon, *m.*; counterfeit money, fausse monnaie; he had his money's worth, il en a eu pour son argent; he made his money by, il s'enrichit de; made of money, cousu d'or; money article, bulletin financier, *m.*; money down or ready money, argent comptant, *m.*; public money, deniers publics, *m.pl.*; silver money, monnaie d'argent, *f.*; to fetch money, rapporter de l'argent; to make money, gagner de l'argent; to put money out to interest, placer de l'argent; to receive money, recevoir or toucher de l'argent.
money-bag, *n.* Sac à argent, *m.*, sacoche, *f.* **money-bill,** *n.* Loi de finance, *f.* **money-box,** *n.* Tirelire, *f.*; tronc, *m.* **money-broker,** *n.* Courtier de change, *m.* **money-changer,** *n.* Changeur, *m.* **moneyed,** *a.* Riche, qui a de l'argent. The moneyed interest, le parti de l'argent, *m.* **money-grubber,** *n.* Grippe-sou, *m.* **money-grubbing,** *a.* Cupide, avare. **money-lender,** *n.* Prêteur d'argent, *m.* **moneyless,** *a.* Sans argent. **money-market,** *n.* Bourse, *f.*, marché financier, *m.* **money-order,** *n.* Mandat, *m.* **money-spider,** *n.* Araignée (rouge) porte-bonheur, *f.* **money-taker,** *n.* Caissier, *m.* **money-wort,** *n.* Nummulaire, herbe aux écus, *f.*
monger ['mʌŋgə], *suf.* (*as in* FISHMONGER, IRONMONGER, etc.) Marchand, *m.*
Mongol ['mɔŋgɔl], *a.* and *n.* Mongol, *m.* **Mongolia** [mɔŋ'goulia]. La Mongolie, *f.* **Mongolian** [-'goulian], *a.* Mongol. **Mongoloid,** *a.* Mongoloïde.
mongoose [MUNGOOSE].
mongrel ['mʌŋgrəl], *a.* Métis; (*fig.*) hybride, mélangé.—*n.* Métis, *m.*, métisse, *f.*; chien métis, *m.*
moniliform [mə'nilifɔ:m], *a.* Moniliforme.
monism ['mɔnizm], *n.* Monisme, *m.* **monist,** *n.* Moniste, *m.*
monistic [mo'nistik], *a.* Monistique.
monition [mo'niʃən], *n.* Avertissement, avis, *m.*
monitive ['mɔnitiv], *a.* D'admonition. **monitor,** *n.* Moniteur, *m.*; monitor (iron-clad), *m.*—*v.t.* (Rad., Tel.) Contrôler les émissions. **monitorial** [-'tɔ:riəl], *a.* Monitorial. **monitoring,** *n.* (Rad., Tel.) Monitoring, *m.* Monitoring station, station d'écoute, *f.* **monitory,** *a.* Monitoire, d'admonition; d'avertissement. Monitory letters, lettres monitoires, *f.pl.* **monitress,** *n.* Monitrice, *f.*
monk [mʌŋk], *n.* Moine, *m.* **monk-fish,** *n.* Ange de mer, angelot, *m.*
monkery ['mʌŋkəri], *n.* Moinerie, *f.* **monkhood,** *n.* Moinerie, *f.* **monkish,** *a.* De moine, monacal. **monk's-hood,** *n.* Aconit, *m.*
monkey ['mʌŋki], *n.* Singe, *m.*; guenon, *f.*; mouton (pile-driver), *m.* The young monkey!

le gamin! to get one's monkey up, se mettre en colère.
monkey-business, *n.* Sale tour, *m.* **monkey-flower,** *n.* Mimule, *m.* **monkey-nut** [PEANUT]. **monkey-puzzle,** *n.* Araucaria, *m.* **monkey-trick,** *n.* Singerie, *f.* **monkey-wrench,** *n.* Clé anglaise, *f.*
monobasic [mɔno'beisik], *a.* Monobase.
monocarpous, *a.* Monocarpe.
monochord ['mɔnokɔ:d], *n.* Monocorde, *m.*
monochromatic [-krə'mætik], *a.* Monochrome.
monochrome, *n.* Monochrome, *m.*
monocle ['mɔnəkl], *n.* Monocle, *m.*
monoclinic [mɔno'klinik], *a.* Monoclinique.
monoclinous [mɔno'klainəs], *a.* Monocline.
monocotyledon [mɔnoukɔti'li:dən], *n.* (Bot.) Monocotylédone, *f.* **monocotyledonous,** *a.* Monocotylédone.
monocular [mo'nɔkjulə], *a.* Monoculaire.
monocycle ['mɔnəsaikl], *n.* Monocycle, *m.*
monodelphic [-'delfik], *a.* Monodelphe, monodelphien.
monodic [mo'nɔdik], *a.* Monodique.
monody ['mɔnədi], *n.* Monodie, *f.*
monœcia [mo'ni:ʃiə], *n.pl.* (Bot.) Monoecies, *f.pl.* **monœcious,** *a.* Monoïque.
monogamic [mɔnə'gæmik] or **monogamous** [mo'nɔgəməs], *a.* Monogame.
monogamist [mo'nɔgəmist], *n.* Monogame, *m.*
monogamy [mə'nɔgəmi], *n.* Monogamie, *f.*
monogenesis [mɔnə'dʒenisis], *n.* Monogénèse, *f.* **monogenetic** [-dʒi'netik], *a.* Monogénésique.
monogenism [mə'nɔdʒinizm], *n.* Monogénisme, *m.*
monogram ['mɔnəgræm], *n.* Monogramme, *m.* **monogrammatic** [-grə'mætik], *a.* Monogrammatique.
monograph ['mɔnəgrɑ:f], *n.* Monographie, *f.* **monography** [mo'nɔgrəfi], *n.* Monographie, *f.*
monolith ['mɔnəliθ], *n.* Monolithe, *m.* **monolithic,** *a.* Monolithe.
monologue ['mɔnələg], *n.* Monologue, *m.*
monomania [mɔno'meiniə], *n.* Monomanie, *f.* **monomaniac,** *n.* Monomane, *m.* or *f.*
monometallism [mɔnə'metəlizm], *n.* Monométallisme, *m.* **monometallist,** *n.* Monométalliste, *m.*
monometer [mə'nɔmitə], *n.* Monomètre, *m.*
monometric [mɔno'metrik], *a.* Monométrique.
monomial [mo'noumiəl], *a.* (Alg.) Monôme, *m.*
monopetalous [mɔnə'petələs], *a.* (Bot.) Monopétale.
monophyllous [mɔnə'filəs], *a.* Monophylle.
monoplane ['mɔnəplein], *n.* Monoplan, *m.*
monopolist [mə'nɔpəlist], *n.* Accapareur, monopolisateur, *m.* **monopolistic,** *a.* Monopolistique. **monopolize,** *v.t.* Monopoliser, accaparer. **monopoly,** *n.* Monopole, accaparement, *m.*
monopteral [mə'nɔptərəl], *a.* (Arch.) Monoptère, *m.*
monorail ['mɔnəreil], *n.* Monorail, *m.*
monosyllabic [mɔnəsi'læbik], *a.* Monosyllabe, monosyllabique. **monosyllabism** [mɔno'siləbizm], *n.* Monosyllabisme, *m.* **monosyllable** ['mɔnəsiləbl or mɔnə'siləbl], *n.* Monosyllabe, *m.*

monotheism ['mɔnoθi:izm], *n.* Monothéisme, *m.* **monotheist,** *n.* Monothéiste, *m.*

monotone ['mɔnətoun], *n.* Ton monotone, *m.*, voix monotone, *f.*

monotonous [mə'nɔtənəs], *a.* Monotone. **monotonously,** *adv.* Avec monotonie, d'une manière monotone. **monotony,** *n.* Monotonie, *f.*

monotype ['mɔnotaip], *n.* Monotype, *m.* **monotypic** [-'tipik], *a.* Monotype.

monoxide [mɔ'nɔksaid], *n.* (*Chem.*) Protoxyde, *m. Lead monoxide,* oxyde de plomb, *m.*

monsoon [mɔn'su:n], *n.* Mousson, *f.*

monster ['mɔnstə], *n.* Monstre, *m.*; (*fam.*) colosse, géant, *m.*

monstrance ['mɔnstrəns], *n.* Ostensoir, *m.*

monstrosity [mɔn'strɔsiti], *n.* Monstruosité, *f.* **monstrous** ['mɔnstrəs], *a.* Monstrueux; énorme, prodigieux. *It is a monstrous thing,* cela passe les bornes; *it is monstrous to think that . . .,* il est horrible de penser que. . . . **monstrously,** *adv.* Monstrueusement; prodigieusement, énormément. **monstrousness,** *n.* Monstruosité, *f.*

montage ['mɔntɑ:ʒ], *n.* (*Cine.*) Montage, *m.*

month [mʌnθ], *n.* Mois, *m. By the month,* au mois; *calendar month,* mois civil; *lunar month,* mois lunaire; *the day of the month,* le quantième du mois, *m.* **monthly,** *a.* Mensuel, de tous les mois. *Monthly newspaper,* revue mensuelle, *f.*; *monthly nurse,* garde d'accouchée, *f.*—*n.* (*fam.*) Revue mensuelle, *f.*; (*pl., pop.*) *monthlies,* menstrues, règles, *f.pl.*—*adv.* Mensuellement, tous les mois, par mois.

monument ['mɔnjumənt], *n.* Monument, *m.* **monumental** [-'mentl], *a.* De monument; monumental. **monumentally,** *adv.* En monument.

moo [mu:], *v.i.* Meugler, beugler.—*n.* Meuglement, *m.*

mooch [mu:tʃ], *v.i. To mooch about,* flânocher, baguenauder.—*v.t.* Chiper.

mood [mu:d], *n.* Humeur, disposition, *f.*; (*Gram.* etc.) mode, *m. To be in the mood for,* être d'humeur à, être en train de. **moodily,** *adv.* Tristement. **moodiness,** *n.* Mauvaise humeur, tristesse, *f.* **moody,** *a.* De mauvaise humeur, triste, morne, chagrin, d'humeur changeante.

moon [mu:n], *n.* Lune, *f. By the light of the moon,* au clair de la lune; *full moon,* pleine lune; *new moon,* nouvelle lune; *to believe the moon is made of green cheese,* prendre des vessies pour des lanternes.—*v.i.* Muser. *To moon about,* flâner.

moonbeam, *n.* Rayon de lune, *m.* **moon-calf,** *n.* Monstre; imbécile, idiot, *m.* **moon-fish,** *n.* Lampris tacheté, poisson-lune, *m.* **moonlight,** *n.* Clair de lune, *m. By moonlight,* au clair de lune. **moonlit,** *a.* Éclairé par la lune. **moonrise,** *n.* Lever de la lune, *m.* **moonshine,** *n.* Clair de lune, *m.*; (*fig.*) chimères, sornettes, balivernes, *f.pl.*; (*Am. slang*) boisson alcoolique de contrebande, *f.* **moonstone,** *n.* Pierre de lune, *f.* **moonstruck,** *a.* Lunatique. **moonwort,** *n.* Lunaire, *f.*

moonish, *a.* Lunatique. **moonless,** *a.* Sans lune. **moony,** *a.* En forme de lune; (*fig.*) (perdu) dans la lune, rêveur.

Moor [muə], *n.* Maure, *m.* **Moorish,** *a.* Des Maures; mauresque.

moor (1) [muə], *n.* Lande, bruyère, *f.*; marais, *m.* **moor-cock** or **moor-fowl,** *n.* Coq de bruyère, *m.* **moor-hen,** *n.* Poule d'eau, *f.* **moorland,** *n.* Lande, bruyère, *f.*, marais, *m.*

moor (2) [muə], *v.t.* Amarrer.—*v.i.* S'amarrer.

mooring ['muəriŋ], *n.* Amarrage, *m.*; (*pl.*) amarres, *f.pl.*, mouillage, *m.*

moose [mu:s], *n.* Élan du Canada, *m.*

moot [mu:t], *v.t.* Discuter, débattre, controverser.—**n.* Conférence, *f.*, débat, *m.*, parlotte, *f.*—*a.* Discutable, sujet à contestation. *Moot case* or *moot point,* question discutable, question à débattre, *f.* **mooted,** *a.* Soulevé, discuté.

mop [mɔp], *n.* Balai à laver; écouvillon; (*Naut.*) faubert, lave-pont, *m.*—*v.t.* Nettoyer avec un balai, éponger. *To mop one's face,* s'éponger la figure; (*fam.*) *to mop up a drink,* lamper une boisson. **mopping-up,** *n.* (*Mil.*) Nettoyage, *m.*

mope [moup], *v.i.* Être triste, s'ennuyer; être hébété.—*n.* Personne qui s'ennuie, personne hébétée, *f.* **moping** or **mopish,** *a.* Triste, qui s'ennuie, hébété. **mopishly,** *adv.* Tristement, dans l'abattement. **mopishness,** *n.* Tristesse, *f.*; abattement, *m.*

moral ['mɔrəl], *a.* Moral; de morale.—*n.* Morale, *f.*; moralité, *f.*; (*pl.*) mœurs, *f.pl.* **morale** [mɔ'rɑ:l], *n.* Moral, *m.* (of troops etc.). **moralist,** *n.* Moraliste, *m.*

morality [mə'ræliti], *n.* Morale; moralité, *f.* **moralization** [-lai'zeiʃən], *n.* Moralisation, *f.* **moralize** ['mɔrəlaiz], *v.i.* Moraliser. *To moralize on,* moraliser sur, faire de la morale sur.—*v.t.* Rendre moral; corriger les mœurs de; moraliser. **moralizing,** *a.* Moralisant.

morally ['nɔrəli], *adv.* Moralement, au moral, dans un sens moral. *He was morally and physically qualified for war,* il avait les qualités physiques et morales requises pour la guerre; *to live morally,* vivre selon les préceptes de la morale.

morass [mɔ'ræs], *n.* Marais, *m.*, fondrière, *f.* **morassy,** *a.* Marécageux.

moratorium [mɔrə'tɔ:riəm], *n.* Moratorium, *m.*

Moravian [mɔ'reiviən], *a.* and *n.* Morave.

morbid ['mɔ:bid], *a.* Maladif, malsain, morbide. **morbidly,** *adv.* Morbidement.

morbidity [-'biditi] or **morbidness,** *n.* État maladif, état morbide, *m.* **morbific** [-'bifik], *a.* Morbifique. **morbose,** *a.* Malsain, **morbeux.* **morbosity** [-'bɔsiti], *n.* État maladif, *m.*

mordacious [mɔ:'deiʃəs], *a.* Mordant, caustique, piquant. **mordacity** [-'dæsiti], *n.* Mordacité, *f.* **mordant,** *a.* and *n.* Mordant, *m.*

Mordecai [mɔ:di'keiai]. Mardochée, *m.*

more [mɔ:], *a.* and *adv.* Plus; plus de; plus nombreux; encore; davantage. *A great many more,* beaucoup d'autres encore; *more and more,* de plus en plus; *more haste less speed,* qui trop se hâte reste en chemin; *more or less,* plus ou moins; *more than,* plus que, plus de (followed by a number); *much more,* beaucoup plus, bien plus, bien davantage; *never more,* jamais plus, plus jamais; *no more,* pas davantage; *no more of that!* arrêtez cela! *nothing more than,* pas plus que; *once more,* encore une fois; *one more,* encore un, un de plus; *some more,* encore un peu, encore quelques-uns, davantage; *so much the more*, d'autant plus, à plus forte raison; *the more*, plus, d'autant plus, davantage; *the more that*, d'autant plus que; *the more you speak the less you will learn*, plus vous parlerez, moins vous apprendrez; *to be more frightened than hurt*, avoir plus de peur que de mal; *to be no more*, être mort, n'être plus.

moreen [mo'ri:n], *n.* Damas de laine, *m.*

morel [mo'rel], *n.* Morille (fungus); morelle (plant), *f.*

morello [mo'relou], *n.* Griotte, cerise amère (cherry), *f.* **morello-tree**, *n.* Griottier, *m.*

moreover [mɔ:'rouvə], *adv.* De plus, d'ailleurs, en outre.

Moresque [mo'resk], *a.* Moresque, mauresque.

morganatic [mɔ:gə'nætik], *a.* Morganatique.

morgue [mɔ:g], *n.* (*Lit.*) Morgue, *f.*, orgueil, *m.*; (*pop.*) dépôt mortuaire, *m.*, morgue, *f.*

moribund ['mɔribʌnd], *a.* Moribond.

morion ['mɔriən], *n.* Morion (helmet), *m.*

Mormon ['mɔ:mən], *a. and n.* Mormon, *m.* **Mormonism**, *n.* Mormonisme, *m.*

morn [mɔ:n], *n.* (*poet.*) Matin, *m.*, aurore, *f.*

morning ['mɔ:niŋ], *n.* Matin, *m.*, matinée, *f.* *All the morning*, toute la matinée; *every morning*, tous les matins; *from morning till night*, depuis le matin jusqu'au soir; *good morning*, bonjour; *in the morning*, le matin; *in the course of the morning*, dans la matinée; (*the*) *first thing in the morning*, dès la première heure; *the morning after tomorrow*, après-demain matin; *the morning before*, la veille au matin; *the morning before yesterday*, avant-hier matin; *the next morning*, le lendemain matin; *where have you been all the morning?* où avez-vous passé la matinée?— *a.* Du matin. *In morning dress*, en toilette du matin, en tenue de ville; *morning-coat*, jaquette, *f.*; *morning performance*, (*Theat.*) matinée, *f.*; *morning-room*, petit salon, *m.*

Moroccan [mə'rɔkən], *a. and n.* Marocain, *m.*, Marocaine, *f.*

Morocco [mə'rɔkou]. (*Geog.*) Le Maroc, *m.*

morocco, *n.* Maroquin (binding etc.), *m.* **morocco-leather**, *n.* Maroquin, *m.* *Morocco-leather goods*, maroquinerie, *f.*

moron ['mɔ:rən], *n.* Crétin, idiot, *m.*

morose [mə'rous], *a.* Morose. **morosely**, *adv.* Avec humeur. **moroseness** or **morosity** [mə'rɔsiti], *n.* Morosité, *f.*

Morpheus ['mɔ:fju:s]. Morphée, *f.*

morphia ['mɔ:fiə] or **morphine**, *n.* Morphine, *f.* **morphinism**, *n.* Morphinisme, *m.*

morphinomania [-finou'meiniə], *n.* Morphinomanie, *f.* **morphinomaniac**, *n.* Morphinomane, *m.*

morphogenesis [mɔ:fə'dʒenisis], *n.* Morphogénèse, *f.* **morphography** [-'fɔgrəfi], *n.* Morphographie, *f.*

morphological [mɔ:fə'lɔdʒikl], *a.* Morphologique. **morphologically**, *adv.* Morphologiquement. **morphology** [-'fɔlədʒi], *n.* Morphologie, *f.* **morphosis** [-'fousis], *n.* Morphose, *f.*

morris ['mɔris] or **morris-dance**, *n.* Danse rustique costumée (les danseurs représentant les personnages de la légende de Robin des bois), *f.* **morris-dancer**, *n.* Danseur (de cette danse), *m.*

morrow ['mɔrou], *n.* Demain, lendemain, *m.*

Good-morrow, bonjour; *on the morrow*, le lendemain; *the day after tomorrow*, après-demain; *tomorrow*, demain.

morse [mɔ:s], *n.* Morse, cheval marin, *m.*; (*Teleg.*) morse, *m.* *The Morse code*, l'alphabet morse, *m.*

morsel [mɔ:sl], *n.* Morceau, *m.*

mort [mɔ:t], *n.* (*Hunt.*) Hallali, *m.*; (*Ichth.*) saumon de trois ans, *m.*

mortal [mɔ:tl], *a.* Mortel, sujet à la mort, meurtrier, funeste (deadly); des mortels, humain (human); à outrance, à mort (of combats). *Any mortal thing*, n'importe quoi, quoi que ce soit.—*n.* Mortel, *m.*, mortelle, *f.* *A mere mortal*, up simple mortel. **mortality** [-'tæliti], *n.* Mortalité; humanité, *f.* **mortally**, *adv.* Mortellement, à mort.

mortar ['mɔ:tə], *n.* Mortier, *m.* *Trench mortar*, mortier de tranchée, *m.* **mortar-board**, *n.* Mortier, *m.*

mortgage ['mɔ:gidʒ], *n.* Hypothèque, *f.* *Mortgage charge*, affectation hypothécaire, *f.*; *mortgage deed*, contrat hypothécaire, *m.*; *to pay off a mortgage*, purger une hypothèque; *to raise a mortgage*, prendre une hypothèque. —*v.t.* Hypothéquer. **mortgagee** [-gə'dʒi:], *n.* Créancier hypothécaire, *m.* **mortgager**, *n.* Débiteur sur hypothèque, *m.*

mortician [mɔ:'tiʃən], *n.* (*Am.*) Entrepreneur de pompes funèbres, *m.*

mortiferous [mɔ:'tifərəs], *a.* Mortel, funeste, mortifère. **mortification** [-i'keiʃən], *n.* Mortification; (*Path.*) gangrène, *f.*

mortified ['mɔ:tifaid], *a.* Mortifié; (*fig.*) affligé; (*Path.*) gangrené.

mortify ['mɔ:tifai], *v.t.* Mortifier; (*Path.*) faire gangrener. *To mortify oneself*, se mortifier.—*v.i.* Se gangrener. **mortifying**, *a.* Mortifiant.

mortise ['mɔ:tis], *n.* Mortaise, *f.*—*v.t.* Mortaiser, assembler à mortaise. *Mortise and tenon*, mortaise et tenon. **mortise-chisel**, *n.* Bec-d'âne, *m.* **mortising-machine**, *n.* Mortaiseuse, *f.*

mortmain ['mɔ:tmein], *n.* (*Law*) Mainmorte, *f.*

mortuary ['mɔ:tjuəri], *n.* Morgue, *f.*, dépôt mortuaire, *m.*—*a.* Mortuaire.

mosaic [mo'zeiik], *a. and n.* Mosaïque, *f.* **mosaic-work**, *n.* Ouvrage en mosaïque, *m.*; mosaïque, *f.*

Mosaism ['mouzeiizm], *n.* Mosaïsme, *m.* **Mosaist**, *n.* Mosaïste, *m.*

moschatel [mɔskə'tel], *n.* (*Bot.*) Moscatelle, *f.*

Moscow ['mɔskou]. (*Geog.*) Moscou, *m.*

Moses ['mouziz]. Moïse, *m.*; (*pej.*) Juif, usurier, *m.* *Holy Moses!* grand Dieu!

Moslem ['mʌzlim or 'mɔzləm], *a. and n.* Musulman, *m.*

mosque [mɔsk], *n.* Mosquée, *f.*

mosquito [mɔs'ki:tou], *n.* Moustique, *m.* **mosquito-bite**, *n.* Piqûre de moustique, *f.* **mosquito-net**, *n.* Moustiquaire, *f.*

moss [mɔs], *n.* Mousse, *f.*; marais, *m.*; tourbière (bog), *f.*—*v.t.* Couvrir de mousse. **moss-clad** or **moss-grown**, *a.* Couvert de mousse, moussu. **mossiness**, *n.* État moussu, *m.* **moss-rose**, *n.* Rose moussue, *f.* **moss-trooper**, *n.* (*Engl. Hist.*) Maraudeur, bandit, *m.* (17ᵉ siècle). **mossy**, *a.* Moussu, couvert de mousse.

most [moust], *a.* Le plus; le plus grand. *Most men*, la plupart des hommes; *most people*, la plupart des gens; *the most part*, la plus grande partie, *f.*—*adv.* Le plus, plus; très, fort. *A most valuable book*, un livre des plus précieux; *most laudable efforts*, des efforts des plus louables; *most likely*, très probablement: *most vile*, très, fort, *or* bien vil; *the animals that man has most admired are* . . ., les animaux que l'homme a le plus admirés sont . . .; *to an extent which is most remarkable*, à un degré des plus remarquables.—*n.* La plupart, *f.*; le plus grand nombre, *m.* *To make the most of*, tirer le meilleur parti de, ménager.

mostly ['moustli], *adv.* Pour la plupart; le plus souvent; principalement.

mote [mout], *n.* Atome, *m.*; paille (in the eye), *f.*

motel ['moutel], *n.* Motel, *m.*

motet [mou'tet], *n.* (*Mus.*) Motet, *m.*

moth [moθ], *n.* (*pl.* **moths** [moθs]). (*Ent.*) Lépidoptère; papillon de nuit, *m.*; phalène, *f.*; artison, *m.*; teigne, mite (in clothes), *f.* **moth-balls**, *n.* Boules de naphtaline, *f.pl.* **moth-eaten**, *a.* Rongé des mites, piqué des vers; (*fam.*) suranné (of ideas). **moth-proof**, *a.* Antimite.

mother (1) ['mʌðə], *n.* Mère; bonne mère, bonne femme (familiar term of address), *f.* *Grandmother* [GRAND]; *Mother Cary's chicken*, pétrel, *m.*; *mother-in-law*, belle-mère; *stepmother*, belle-mère; *to be a mother to*, être une mère pour.—*a.* Mère; maternel; métropolitain (of churches). *Mother tongue*, langue maternelle, langue mère, *f.*; *the mother-country*, mère patrie, *f.*—*v.t.* Servir de mère à; dorloter; adopter comme son enfant; donner naissance à (quelque chose), enfanter (quelque chose).

mother (2) ['mʌðə], *n.* Moisissure (slimy substance in liquors), *f.*

mothercraft, *n.* Puériculture, *f.* **motherhood**, *n.* Maternité, *f.* **motherless**, *a.* Sans mère. **motherly**, *a.* Maternel, de mère.—*adv.* Maternellement, en mère.

mother-of-pearl, *n.* Nacre, *f.*

mother-wit, *n.* Esprit naturel, *m.*

mothery, *a.* Moisi (of liquids).

mothy ['moθi], *a.* Plein de mites.

motion ['mouʃən], *n.* Mouvement, *m.*; signe (signal), *m.*; motion (at a meeting); proposition; (*Med.*) selle, *f.* (*Cine.*) *Motion picture*, film, *m.*; *perpetual motion*, mouvement perpétuel; *the laws of motion*, les lois du mouvement, *f.pl.*; *to carry a motion*, faire adopter une motion; *to propose a motion*, faire une proposition; *to put in motion*, mettre en mouvement.—*v.t.* Faire signe (à).

motionless, *a.* Immobile.

motivate ['moutiveit], *v.t.* Motiver (une action).

motive ['moutiv], *a.* Moteur, qui fait mouvoir. *Motive power*, force motrice, *f.*—*n.* Motif, mobile, *m.*

motley ['motli], *a.* Bigarré, mêlé, mélangé, bariolé. *To put on the motley*, revêtir le costume de bouffon.

motor ['moutə], *n.* Moteur, *m.*—*v.i.* Aller, voyager en auto; conduire en auto. **motor-boat**, *n.* Canot automobile, *m.* **motor-bus**, *n.* Autobus, *m.* **motor-car**, *n.* Automobile, *f.*; (*fam.*) auto, voiture, *f.* **motor-coach**, *n.* Autocar, car, *m.* **motor-cycle**, *n.* Motocyclette, *f.* **motor-cyclist**, *n.* Motocycliste,

m. **motoring**, *n.* Automobilisme, *m.* **motorist**, *n.* Automobiliste, *m.* **motorize**, *v.t.* Motoriser. **motor-lorry**, *n.* Camion automobile, *m.* **motor-school**, *n.* Auto-école, *f.* (*pl.* auto-écoles). **motor-scooter**, *n.* Scooter, *m.* **motor-spirit**, *n.* Essence, *f.* **motorway**, *n.* Autoroute, *f.* **motory**, *a.* Moteur. *Motory muscles*, muscles moteurs, *m.pl.*

mottle [motl], *v.t.* Madrer; diaprer; marbrer. **mottled**, *a.* Pommelé, moucheté, tacheté; madré (of wood); marbré (of soap).

motto ['motou], *n.* (*pl.* **mottoes**) Devise, *f.*

mould [mould], *n.* Moisi (mouldiness), *m.*, moisissure, *f.*; terreau (earth), *m.*; moule, *m.*, forme, *f.*; (*fig.*) modèle, *m.*, trempe, *f.*; (*Naut.*) gabarit, *m.*—*v.t.* Mouler; (*fig.*) modeler, former, pétrir.—*v.i.* Moisir, se moisir (to become mouldy).

moulder (1) ['mouldə], *n.* Mouleur, *m.*

moulder (2) ['mouldə], *v.i.* Se réduire en poudre, en poussière. *To moulder away*, tomber en poussière.—*v.t.* Réduire en poussière. **mouldering**, *a.* Rongé.

mouldiness ['mouldinis], *n.* Moisissure, *f.*

moulding ['mouldiŋ], *n.* Moulure, *f.*

mouldwarp ['mouldwɔ:p], *n.* Taupe, *f.*

mouldy ['mouldi], *a.* Moisi; (*pop.*) assommant, moche; mal en train (unwell). *To get mouldy*, se moisir; *to smell mouldy*, sentir le moisi.

moult [moult], *v.i.* Muer. **moulting**, *n.* Mue, *f.*

mound [maund], *n.* Butte, *f.*, tertre (over a grave), *m.*; (*fig.*) levée, digue, *f.*, remblai, *m.*; (*Fort.*) remparts, *m.pl.* *Mound of earth*, tas de terre, *m.*—*v.t.* Fortifier par un rempart etc., faire une digue à.

mount [maunt], *n.* Mont, *m.*, montagne, *f.*; monture (horse), *f.*; (*Turf*) monte, *f.*; (*Phot.*) carton, *m.*—*v.t.* Monter, monter sur. *To mount a drawing*, monter un dessin; *to mount a play*, monter une pièce; *to mount guard*, monter la garde; *to mount the throne*, monter sur le trône.—*v.i.* Monter, s'élever; monter à cheval. *The expenditure was mounting up*, les dépenses augmentaient.

mountain ['mauntin], *n.* Montagne, *f.* *Mountain battery*, artillerie de montagne, *f.*; *to make mountains out of mole-hills*, s'en faire une montagne; *waves mountain-high*, des vagues hautes comme des montagnes.—*a.* De montagne, des montagnes, montagnard, montagneux (of scenery); (*fig.*) vaste, énorme.

mountain-ash, *n.* Sorbier des oiseaux, *m.* **mountain-dew**, *n.* Whisky (d'Écosse), *m.* **mountaineer** [-'niə], *n.* Montagnard; alpiniste, ascensionniste, *m.*—*v.i.* Faire des ascensions. **mountaineering**, *n.* Alpinisme, *m.*

mountainous ['mauntinəs], *a.* Montagneux, de montagnes; (*fig.*) énorme.

mountebank ['mauntibæŋk], *n.* Charlatan, saltimbanque, *m.*

mounted ['mauntid], *a.* Monté, à cheval; (*Phot.*) collé. *Mounted infantry, police*, infanterie, police, montée, *f.* **mounter**, *n.* (*Tech.*) Monteur, *m.*, -euse, *f.* **mounting**, *n.* Montage, *m.*, monture, *f.*; (*Phot.*) collage, *m.*; (*Artill.*) affût, affûtage, *m.*; (*Theat.*) mise à la scène, *f.*

mourn [mɔːn], *v.t.* Pleurer, déplorer.—*v.i.* Pleurer, se lamenter. *To mourn for*, pleurer. **mourner,** *n.* Personne affligée *or* qui porte le deuil, *f.*; pleureur, *m.*, -euse, *f.* (hired), personne qui suit le convoi, *f. Chief mourner*, personne qui mène le deuil, *f.*; *to be one of the mourners*, suivre le deuil, être du convoi. **mournful,** *a.* Triste, lugubre; lamentable, déplorable. **mournfully,** *adv.* Tristement, lamentablement. **mournfulness,** *n.* Tristesse, *f.*, chagrin, *m.*

mourning, *n.* Affliction, lamentation, *f.*; deuil (clothes), *m. Deep mourning*, grand deuil; *mourning band*, crêpe, brassard de deuil, *m.*; *to go into mourning for*, prendre le deuil de; *to go out of mourning*, quitter le deuil; *to wear mourning*, être en deuil.—*a.* Affligé, triste; de deuil. **mourningly,** *adv.* Tristement, lugubrement.

mouse [maus], *n.* (*pl.* **mice** [mais]) Souris, *f. Field-mouse*, mulot, *m.*; *meadow-mouse*, campagnol, *m.*—*v.i.* Chasser des souris. **mouse-coloured,** *a.* Gris (de) souris. **mouse-hole,** *n.* Trou de souris, *m.* **mouse-trap,** *n.* Souricière, *f.*

mouser ['mausə], *n.* Chasseur de souris, *m.*

moustache [mu'staːʃ], *n.* Moustache, *f.*

mousy ['mausi], *a.* Gris (of colour); timide (of persons).

mouth (1) [mauθ], *n.* (*pl.* **mouths** [mauðz]) Bouche; gueule (of ravenous beasts); embouchure (of rivers); grimace (wry face); ouverture, entrée, *f.*, orifice (opening); goulot (of a bottle), *m. By word of mouth*, de vive voix; *to be down in the mouth*, être déconcerté, être tout penaud; *to be in everyone's mouth*, être dans toutes les bouches; *to live from hand to mouth*, vivre au journe jour; *to make mouths*, faire des grimaces; *to make someone's mouth water*, faire venir l'eau à la bouche à quelqu'un; *to shut someone's mouth*, fermer la bouche à quelqu'un; *with open mouth*, la bouche béante.

mouth (2) [mauð], *v.t.* Crier; happer, saisir avec la bouche.—*v.i.* Crier; grimacer.

mouthed [mauðd], *a. Foul-mouthed*, mal embouché, grossier; *hundred-mouthed*, aux cent bouches; *mealy-mouthed*, doucereux; *wide-mouthed*, qui a la bouche large. **mouther** [-ð-], *n.* Péroreur, *m.* **mouthful** [-θ-], *n.* Bouchée; gorgée (of wine), *f. At a mouthful*, d'une seule bouchée. **mouthing** [-ð-], *n.* Déclamation, *f.* **mouthless** [-θ-], *a.* Sans bouche. **mouthy** [-ð-], *a.* (*pop.*) Braillard.

mouth-organ, *n.* Harmonica, *f.* **mouth-piece,** *n.* Embouchure, *f.*; porte-cigare, porte-cigarette; (*fig.*) interprète, porte-parole, *m.* **mouth-wash,** *n.* Dentifrice, *m.*

movable ['muːvəbl], *a.* Mobile; (*Law*) meuble.—*n.* Meuble, *m.*; (*pl.*) meubles, biens meubles, effets mobiliers, *m.pl. Movable feast*, fête mobile, *f.* **movability** *or* **movableness,** *n.* Mobilité, *f.* **movably,** *adv.* D'une manière mobile.

move [muːv], *v.t.* Remuer; déplacer; mouvoir, faire mouvoir, mettre en mouvement, faire marcher, faire aller; transporter (goods etc.); (*fig.*) émouvoir, toucher, exciter, pousser (à); proposer (that); (*Chess*) jouer. *To be moved by*, se laisser émouvoir par; *to move away*, éloigner, enlever; *to move back*, remettre à sa place, rapporter; *to move forward*, avancer;

to move heaven and earth, remuer ciel et terre; *to move out*, déloger, sortir; *to move to pity*, toucher, émouvoir.—*v.i.* Bouger, se remuer, se mouvoir, se déplacer; se mettre en mouvement, aller, partir, marcher, s'avancer; s'ébranler (of an army); déménager (to move house); faire une motion; (*Chess*) jouer. *Move on, please!* circulez, s'il vous plaît! *the troops began to move*, les troupes se mirent en marche; *to move about*, se remuer, aller çà et là; *to move aside*, s'écarter; *to move away*, s'éloigner, s'en aller; *to move back*, reculer, se reculer; *to move backward*, reculer; *to move down*, descendre; *to move in*, emménager, entrer, rentrer; *to move in the highest circles*, fréquenter le grand monde; *to move off*, s'éloigner, s'en aller, se mettre en marche; *to move on*, passer son chemin, avancer, s'avancer; *to move out*, sortir, déménager; *to move round*, se tourner, tourner; *to move up*, monter, avancer.—*n.* Mouvement; coup; (*Chess*) trait, *m.*, marche (progress), *f. Masterly move*, coup de maître, *m.*; *to be on the move*, être en mouvement, se remuer; *to get a move on*, se presser; *to get on the move*, se mettre en marche, s'ébranler; *to have the move*, jouer le premier; *to make a move*, se préparer à partir; *to play the first move*, avoir le trait; *what is to be the next move?* que va-t-on faire maintenant? *whose move is it?* à qui est-ce à jouer?

movement, *n.* Mouvement; (*Polit.*) groupe d'action, mouvement, *m.*

mover, *n.* Moteur; mobile, *m.*; force motrice, *f.*; auteur d'une motion *or* d'une proposition, *m. Prime mover*, principe moteur, *m.*, force motrice, *f.*

movie, *n.* (*Am.*) Film, *m. The movies*, le cinéma, *m.*

moving, *a.* Mouvant, mobile; (*fig.*) émouvant, attendrissant. *Moving power*, force motrice, *f.*—*n.* Mouvement, *m.*; déménagement (of furniture); déplacement (change of place), *m.* **movingly,** *adv.* D'une manière émouvante.

mow (1) [mau], *n.* Tas (de foin etc.), *m.*, meule; *moue, grimace, *f.*

mow (2) [mou], *v.t.* Faucher; couper, tondre. *To mow down*, abattre, faire tomber. **mower,** *n.* Faucheur (person), *m.*; faucheuse, tondeuse (machine), *f.* **mowing,** *n.* Fauchage, *m.*; fauchée, fauche (produce), *f.* **mowing-machine,** *n.* Faucheuse, *f.*; tondeuse (de gazon), *f.* **mowing-time,** *n.* Fauchaison, *f.*

much [mʌtʃ], *a.* Beaucoup, beaucoup de.— Beaucoup, bien, fort, très; à peu près (nearly). *As much*, autant; *he is not much given to*, il n'aime guère; *how much?* combien (de)? *much about the same*, à peu près la même chose; *much ado about nothing*, beaucoup de bruit pour rien; *much as we should like to meet you*, si grand que soit notre désir de vous satisfaire; *much more*, bien plus; *much of a muchness*, c'est bonnet blanc et blanc bonnet; *my work is too much for me*, ma besogne est au-dessus de mes forces; *nothing much*, pas grand'chose; *pretty much*, à peu près; *so much*, tant; *so much as*, tant que, autant que, même; *so much for*, voilà pour; *so much more*, d'autant plus; *so much so that*, si bien que, à tel point que; *so much the better*, tant mieux; *so much the more . . . that*, d'autant plus . . . que; *that much*, autant que

cela; *to make much of,* faire grand cas de; *too much,* trop, de trop, trop (de); *you are not much the wiser for it,* vous n'en êtes pas plus avancé, vous n'en savez pas plus long. **much-loved,** *a.* Bien-aimé.
muchness, *n.* *Much of a muchness* [MUCH].
mucilage ['mjuːsilidʒ], *n.* Mucilage, *m.*
mucilaginous [-'lædʒinəs], *a.* Mucilagineux.
muck [mʌk], *n.* Fumier (dung), *m.*; fange (mud); (*fig.*) saleté, *f.*, objet méprisable, *m.* —*v.t.* Fumer; salir (to dirty). *To muck out a stable,* nettoyer une écurie; *to muck up a job,* gâcher une besogne.—*v.i.* (*pop.*) *To muck about,* flâner; *to muck about with a girl,* tripoter une fille; *to muck in with someone,* chambrer avec quelqu'un. **mucker,** *n.* (*pop.*) Copain, *m.* **muckiness,** *n.* Saleté, ordure, *f.*
mucky, *a.* Sale, malpropre.
muckle (*Sc.*) [MICKLE].
muckrake, *v.i.* Dévoiler des scandales.
mucous ['mjuːkəs], *a.* Muqueux. *Mucous membrane,* muqueuse, *f.* **mucus,** *n.* Mucus, *m.*; mucosité, *f.*
mud [mʌd], *n.* Boue, bourbe, *(poet.)* fange; vase, *f.*, limon (slime), *m.* *Mud wall,* mur de terre, mur en torchis, *m.*; *to stick in the mud,* s'embourber.—*v.t.* Embourber, couvrir de boue; troubler (a liquid).
mud-bank, *n.* Banc de sable, de vase, *m.*
mud-cart, *n.* Tombereau, *m.* **muddily,** *adv.* Salement. **muddiness,** *n.* État boueux, état trouble, *m.* **mudguard,** *n.* Garde-boue, garde-crotte, *m.* **mudlark,** *n.* Gamin des rues, *m.* **mud-slinger,** *n.* (*fam.*) Calomniateur, *m.*, -trice, *f.*
muddle [mʌdl], *v.t.* Brouiller; troubler; gâcher. *He has muddled away all his money,* il a gaspillé tout son argent; *he has muddled the whole affair,* il a gâté toute l'affaire.—*v.i.* Faire du gâchis. *To muddle through,* se débrouiller.—*n.* Confusion, *f.*, désordre, gâchis, *m.* *All in a muddle,* tout brouillé. **muddled,** *a.* Troublé; hébété; gris (in liquor). **muddle-headed,** *a.* Stupide, brouillon. **muddler,** *n.* Brouillon, *m.*, -onne, *f.*
muddy ['mʌdi], *a.* Boueux, bourbeux; crotté, couvert de boue (splashed); terreux (complexion); nuageux (of precious stones); trouble (of wine etc.); (*Naut.*) vaseux.—*v.t.* Troubler.
muezzin [muˈezin], *n.* Muezzin, *m.*
muff [mʌf], *n.* Manchon; (*fig.*) empoté, cornichon (person), *m.*—*v.t.* (*spt.*) Rater, manquer (a catch, a shot).
muffin ['mʌfin], *n.* Muffin, *m.*, petit pain rond (pour le thé), *m.*
muffle [mʌfl], *v.t.* Emmitoufler, affubler; assourdir (a bell etc.); voiler (a drum etc.); bander (the eyes). *To muffle up,* affubler, emmitoufler.—*n.* Moufle, *f.* **muffler,** *n.* Cache-nez, *m.*; (*Box.*) gant, *m.* (*Exhaust-*) *muffler,* silencieux, *m.*
mufti ['mʌfti], *n.* Mufti, muphti, *m.* (*Mil.*) *To be in mufti,* être en civil *or* en bourgeois.
mug [mʌg], *n.* Pot, *m.*, tasse, *f.*; (*slang*) visage, nez, *m.*; gueule (mouth), *f.*; imbécile, *m.*, poire, *f.*—*v.t.*, *v.i.* (*slang*) Bûcher, piocher (un sujet). *To mug up French for an exam,* bûcher le français en vue d'un examen. **muggy,** *a.*

Humide, lourd, mou. **mugwort,** *n.* Armoise, herbe à cent goûts, *f.*
mulatto [mjuˈlætou], *n.* Mulâtre, *m.*, mulâtresse, *f.*
mulberry ['mʌlbəri], *n.* Mûre, *f.* **mulberry-bush** *or* **tree,** *n.* Mûrier, *m.*
mulch [mʌltʃ], *n.* Paillis, *m.*—*v.t.* Pailler, fumer.
mulct [mʌlkt], *n.* Amende, *f.*—*v.t.* Mettre à l'amende, frapper d'une amende (de); (*fig.*) priver de.
mule [mjuːl], *n.* Mulet, *m.*, mule, *f.* *As stubborn as a mule,* têtu comme un mulet. **mule-driver** *or* **muleteer** [mjuːlə'tiə], *n.* Muletier, *m.* **mule-jenny,** *n.* Métier à filer en fin, *m.* **mulish,** *a.* De mulet; (*fig.*) têtu, obstiné.
mull [mʌl], *n.* Gâchis, *m.*; (*Sc.*) cap, promontoire, *m.*; (*Tex.*) mousseline, *f.* *To make a mull of,* gâcher, rater.—*v.t.* Faire chauffer et épicer; (*colloq.*) gâcher, manquer, rater. (*fam.*) *To mull over,* ruminer. *Mulled wine,* vin chaud épicé.
mullein ['mʌlin], *n.* (*Bot.*) Molène, *f.* *Great mullein,* bouillon-blanc, *m.*
muller ['mʌlə], *n.* Molette (à broyer), *f.*
mullet ['mʌlit], *n.* Mulet, *m.* *Grey mullet,* muge, capiton, *m.*; *red mullet,* rouget, *m.*
mulligatawny [mʌligə'tɔːni], *n.* Potage au cari, *m.*
mulligrubs ['mʌligrʌbz], *n.pl.* Colique, *f.*, tranchées, *f.pl.*; (*colloq.*) le cafard, *m.*
mullion ['mʌlian], *n.* Meneau, *m.* **mullioned,** *a.* À meneaux.
multangular [mʌl'tæŋgjulə], *a.* Polygonal.
multarticulate [mʌltɑː'tikjulət], *n.* Multiarticulé. **multicapsular,** *a.* Multicapsulaire.
multicoloured ['mʌltikʌləd], *a.* Multicolore.
multicylinder, *a.* Polycylindrique.
multidigitate [mʌlti'didʒitət], *a.* Multidigité.
multifarious [mʌlti'fɛəriəs], *a.* Varié, divers, multiplié. **multifariously,** *adv.* Diversement, avec une grande diversité. **multifariousness,** *n.* Diversité, multiplicité, variété, *f.*
multifid ['mʌltifid], *a.* Multifide. **multiflorous** [-'flɔːrəs], *a.* Multiflore. **multifold,** *a.* Divers, varié. **multiform,** *a.* Multiforme.
multilateral [-'lætərəl], *a.* À plusieurs côtés; polygonal. **multilocular** [-'lɔkjulə], *a.* Multiloculaire. **multi-millionaire,** *n.* Milliardaire. **multiparity** [-'pæriti], *n.* Multiparité, *f.* **multiparous** [-'tipərəs], *a.* Multipare. **multiphase** [-'feiz], *a.* Multiphasé.
multiple ['mʌltipl], *a.* and *n.* Multiple, *m.* *Multiple store,* maison à succursales, *f.* **multiplex,** *a.* Multiplex. **multiplicable** [-'plikəbl], *a.* Multipliable. **multiplicand** [-pli'kænd], *n.* Multiplicande, *m.* **multiplication** [-'keiʃən], *n.* Multiplication, *f.* **multiplicative** ['mʌltiplikeitiv], *a.* Multiplicatif. **multiplicator,** *n.* Multiplicateur, *m.* **multiplicity** [-'plisiti], *n.* Multiplicité, *f.* **multiplied,** *a.* Multiplié. **multiplier,** *n.* Multiplicateur, *m.*
multiply ['mʌltiplai], *v.t.* Multiplier.—*v.i.* Multiplier, se multiplier. **multiplying,** *a.* Multipliant. **multiplying-glass,** *n.* Multipliant, verre multipliant, *m.* **multipolar** [-'poulə], *a.* Multipolaire.

multitude ['mʌltitjuːd], *n.* Multitude, *f.*
multitudinous [-'tjuːdinəs], *a.* Très nombreux, innombrable.
multivalve ['mʌltivælv], *n.* Multivalve, *f.*
multivalvular [-'vælvjulə], *a.* Multivalve.
mum (1) [mʌm], *a.* Muet. *To keep mum,* avoir la bouche close, se taire.—*int.* Bouche close! chut!
mum (2) [mʌm], *n.* (*fam.*) Maman, *f.*
mum (3) [mʌm], *v.i.* Mimer.
mumble [mʌmbl], *v.i.* Marmotter. **mumbler,** *n.* Marmotteur, *m.*; -euse, *f.* **mumblingly,** *adv.* En marmottant.
mummer ['mʌmə], *n.* Mime (acteur); (*pej.*) cabotin, *m.* **mummery,** *n.* Pantomime; mômerie, *f.*
mummification [mʌmifi'keiʃən], *n.* Momification, *f.*
mummiform ['mʌmifɔːm], *a.* En forme de momie.
mummify ['mʌmifai], *v.t.* Momifier.
mummy ['mʌmi], *n.* Momie, *f.*; (*childish*) maman, *f.* *To beat to a mummy,* rouer de coups, réduire en bouillie.
mump [mʌmp], *v.i.* *Mendier; bouder, se renfrogner; (*Prov.*) grignoter; marmotter. **mumper,** *n.* Gueux, *m.*, gueuse, *f.* **mumpish,** *a.* De mauvaise humeur, maussade. **mumps,** *n.pl.* Mauvaise humeur, *f.*; (*Med.*) oreillons, *m.pl.*
munch [mʌntʃ], *v.t., v.i.* Mâcher, croquer.
mundane ['mʌndein], *a.* Mondain. **mundaneness** or *mundanity** [-'dæniti], *n.* Mondanité, *f.*
mungoose ['mʌŋguːs], *n.* Mangouste, *f.*
municipal [mjuː'nisipl], *a.* Municipal. *Municipal law,* droit municipal *or* civil, *m.* **municipality** [-'pæliti], *n.* Municipalité, *f.* **municipally,** *adv.* Municipalement.
municipium [mjuːni'sipiəm], *n.* (*Rom. Ant.*) Municipe, *m.*
munificence [mju'nifisəns], *n.* Munificence, *f.* **munificent,** *a.* Libéral, généreux, munifique. **munificently,** *adv.* Libéralement, avec munificence.
muniment ['mjuːnimənt], *n.* Charte, *f.*, document, titre, *m.*; *fortification, *f.*, fort, *m.*; (*fig.*) défense, *f.* **muniment-room,** *n.* Archives, *f.pl.*
munition [mjuː'niʃən], *n.* (*pl.*) Munitions (de guerre), *f.pl.*—*v.t.* Approvisionner. **munition-factory,** *n.* Fabrique de munitions, *f.* **munition-ship,** *n.* Vaisseau de transport, *m.*
muraena [mjuə'riːnə], *a.* (*Ichth.*) Murène, *f.*
mural ['mjuərəl], *a.* Mural.—*n.* Peinture murale, *f.*
murder ['mɔːdə], *n.* Meurtre, homicide, *m.* *Murder!* à l'assassin! *murder will out,* la vérité se découvre toujours; *wilful murder,* meurtre avec préméditation, assassinat, *m.*—*v.t.* Assassiner, tuer; (*fig.*) massacrer, estropier, écorcher (a language etc.). *To murder a name,* estropier un nom; *to murder French,* parler français comme une vache espagnole. **murderer,** *n.* Meurtrier, assassin, *m.* **murderess,** *n.* Meurtrière, *f.* **murdering** or **murderous,** *a.* Meurtrier, assassin. **murderously,** *adv.* Par le meurtre, d'une façon sanguinaire.
murex ['mjuəreks], *n.* Murex, *m.*
muriate ['mjuəriət], *n.* Muriate, chlorure, *m.*
muriatic [-'ætik], *a.* Chlorhydrique.

murk [məːk], *n.* Ténèbres, *f.pl.*
murkiness ['məːkinis], *n.* Obscurité, *f.*
murky, *a.* Sombre, obscur, ténébreux.
murmur ['məːmə], *n.* Murmure, *m.*—*v.i.* Murmurer. **murmurer,** *n.* Murmurateur, *m.*, personne qui murmure, *f.* **murmuring,** *a.* Murmurant, murmurateur.—*n.* Murmure, *m.*, murmures, *m. pl.* **murmuringly,** *adv.* En murmurant.
murrain ['mʌrin], *n.* Épizootie, peste, *f.*
murrhine ['mʌrin], *a.* Murrhin.
muscadel [mʌskə'del] or *muscatel,** *n.* Muscat, muscatel (wine); raisin muscat; muscat royal, muscat vert (pear), *m.*—*a.* Muscat.
muscle [mʌsl], *n.* Muscle, *m.*—*a.* Musclé. *Strong-muscled,* fortement musclé.
muscovado [mʌskə'vɑːdou], *n.* Cassonade, *f.*
Muscovy. La Moscovie, *f.* *Muscovy duck,* canard musqué, *m.*
muscular ['mʌskjulə], *a.* Musculaire (of strength etc.); musculeux (of limbs etc.). **muscularity** [-'læriti], *n.* Muscularité, *f.* **musculature,** *n.* Musculature, *f.*
Muse [mjuːz], *n.* Muse, *f.*
muse [mjuːz], *v.i.* Méditer, rêver. *To muse upon,* rêver à, méditer sur.—*v.t.* Penser à, méditer.—*n.* Muse, rêverie, méditation, *f.* *In a muse,* rêveur, pensif. **muser,** *n.* Rêveur, rêvasseur, *m.*
museum [mju'ziːəm], *n.* Musée, *m.*
mush [mʌʃ], *n.* (*Am.*) Bouillie de maïs, *f.*; (*Rad. Tel.*) friture, *f.*, brouillage, *m.* **mushy,** *a.* Détrempé (food, ground); (*Rad. Tel.*) brouillé; blet (medlar).
mushroom ['mʌʃrum], *n.* Champignon; (*fig.*) parvenu (upstart), *m.* *Flap-mushroom,* cèpe, *m.*—*v.i.* Cueillir des champignons; se propager, s'étendre. **mushroom-bed,** *n.* Champignonnière, *f.* **mushroom-spawn,** *n.* Blanc de champignon, *m.*
music ['mjuːzik], *n.* Musique, *f.* *To face the music,* (*colloq.*) affronter les opposants; *to set to music,* mettre en musique.
musical, *a.* Musical; (*fig.*) harmonieux, mélodieux; qui aime la musique. *Musical instrument,* instrument de musique, *m.* **musical-box,** *n.* Boîte à musique, *f.* **musically,** *adv.* En musique, musicalement.
music-book, *n.* Cahier de musique, *m.* **music-case,** *n.* Porte-musique, *m.* **music-hall,** *n.* Music-hall, *m.* **music-lover,** *n.* Musicomane, *m.* or *f.* **music-master,** *n.* Professeur de musique, *m.* **music-room,** *n.* Salle de musique *or* de concert, *f.* **music-stand,** *n.* Pupitre à musique, *m.* **music-stool,** *n.* Tabouret de piano, *m.*
musician [mjuː'ziʃən], *n.* Musicien, *m.*, musicienne, *f.*; (*pl.*) musiciens, *m.pl.*; la musique, *f.sing.*
musicographer [mjuːzi'kɔgrəfə], *n.* Musicographe, *m.* **musicologist,** *n.* Musicologue, *m.*
musing ['mjuːziŋ], *n.* Méditation; (*pl.*) rêverie, *f.*
musk [mʌsk], *n.* Musc, *m.*—*v.t.* Musquer. **musk-deer,** *n.* Chevrotain porte-musc, musc, *m.* **muskiness,** *n.* Odeur de musc, *f.* **musk-melon,** *n.* Melon muscat, *m.* **muskox,** *n.* Bœuf musqué, *m.* **musk-rat,** *n.* Rat musqué, *m.* **musk-rose,** *n.* Rose musquée, *f.*

musk-seed, *n.* Graine d'ambrette, *f.*
musky, *a.* Musqué, parfumé de musc.
musket ['mʌskit], *n.* Fusil, mousquet, *m.*
musket-ball or **musket-shot,** *n.* Balle de
fusil, *f.* **musketeer** [-'tiə], *n.* Mousquetaire, *m.*
musketry ['mʌskitri], *n.* Mousqueterie, *f.*, tir,
m. Discharge of musketry, fusillade, *f.*; *school
of musketry,* école de tir, *f.*
musky [MUSK].
muslin ['mʌzlin], *n.* Mousseline, *f.—a.* De
mousseline. *Book muslin,* organdi, *m.*
musquash ['mʌskwɔʃ], *n.* (*Zool.*) Rat musqué;
(*Comm.*) castor du Canada, *m.*
mussel [mʌsl], *n.* Moule, *f.*
Mussulman ['mʌsəlmən], *n.* Musulman, *m.*,
musulmane, *f.—a.* Musulman, en musulman.
must (1) [mʌst], *v.i.* Falloir; devoir. *He must
have lost his way,* il se sera égaré; *I must do
it,* il faut que je le fasse; *it must be so,* il le
faut, il le faut absolument; *something must be
done,* il faut faire quelque chose; *that must be
the case,* cela doit être ainsi; *you must know,*
vous devez savoir, il faut que vous sachiez.
—n. (*fam.*) *That is a must,* il ne faut pas
manquer cela.
must (2) [mʌst], *n.* (Of wine) Moût, vin doux,
m.; (=mustiness) moisi, *m.—a.* (Of elephant,
camel) furieux.
*mustachio [MOUSTACHE].
mustang ['mʌstæŋ], *n.* Mustang, *m.*
mustard ['mʌstəd], *n.* Moutarde, *f.*; (*Bot.*)
sénévé, *m.* **mustard-bath,** *n.* Bain sinapisé,
m. **mustard-gas,** *n.* Gaz moutarde, *m.*
mustard-pot, *n.* Moutardier, *m.* **mustard-
poultice,** *n.* Sinapisme, *m.* **mustard-seed,**
n. Graine de moutarde, *f.*
muster ['mʌstə], *n.* Appel, *m.*, revue, *f.*; rassemblement, *m.*; troupe, bande, *f.*; contrôles
(list), *m.pl. To pass muster,* passer, être
acceptable.—*v.t.* Faire l'appel de; passer en
revue; réunir, rassembler, se procurer. *How
many do we muster?* combien sommes-nous?
to muster up courage, prendre son courage à
deux mains.—*v.i.* S'assembler, se réunir;
passer la revue.
muster-roll, *n.* Feuille d'appel, *f.*; contrôle;
(*Navy*) rôle d'équipage, *m. To call over the
muster-roll,* faire l'appel.
mustily ['mʌstili], *adv.* Avec un goût de
moisi; avec une odeur de renfermé. **mustiness,** *n.* Moisi; renfermé (closeness), *m.*
musty, *a.* Moisi; qui sent le renfermé
(close).
mutability [mjuːtə'biliti], *n.* Mutabilité,
instabilité, inconstance, *f.*
mutable ['mjuːtebl], *a.* Muable, inconstant.
mutation [mjuː'teiʃən], *n.* Mutation, *f.*,
changement, *m.*
mute (1) [mjuːt], *a.* Muet, *m.*, muette, *f.—n.*
Muet, *m.*, muette, *f.*; (*Mus.*) sourdine (de
violon); (*Gram.*) lettre muette, *f.*; croque-mort
(at a funeral), *m.—v.t.* Amortir (strings of a
musical instrument). **mutely,** *adv.* En
silence. **muteness,** *n.* Mutisme, silence, *m.*
mutism, *n.* Mutisme, *m.*
mute (2) [mjuːt], *n.* Fiente (of birds), *f.—v.i.*
Fienter.
mutilate ['mjuːtileit], *v.t.* Mutiler, estropier;
tronquer. **mutilated,** *a.* Mutilé. **mutilation** [-'leiʃən], *n.* Mutilation, *f.* **mutilator**

['mjuːtileitə], *n.* Mutilateur, *m.*, mutila-
trice, *f.*
mutineer [mjuːti'niə], *n.* Révolté, rebelle,
mutin, *m.*
mutinous ['mjuːtinəs], *a.* Rebelle, mutiné,
mutin. **mutinously,** *adv.* D'un air de
révolte, séditieusement. **mutiny,** *n.* Mutinerie, sédition, révolte, *f. Indian Mutiny,* la
révolte des Cipayes.—*v.i.* Se mutiner,
s'insurger, se révolter.
mutt [mʌt], *n.* (*pop.*) Nigaud, *m.*
mutter ['mʌtə], *v.t., v.i.* Marmotter.—*n.*
Marmottement; grommellement, *m.* **mutterer,** *n.* Marmotteur, *m.* **muttering,** *a.*
Marmotteur, murmurant.—*n.* Murmure,
marmottement, marmottage, *m.* **mutter-
ingly,** *adv.* En marmottant, en murmurant.
mutton [mʌtn], *n.* Mouton, *m. Leg of mutton,*
gigot, *m.* **mutton-bird,** *n.* Puffin fuligineux,
puffin à bec grêle, *m.* **mutton-chop,** *n.*
Côtelette de mouton, *f.* **mutton-headed,** *a.*
Nigaud.
mutual ['mjuːtjuəl], *a.* Mutuel, réciproque.
Mutual friend, ami commun. **mutuality**
[-'æliti], *n.* Réciprocité, mutualité, *f.*
mutually, *adv.* Mutuellement, réciproquement.
mutule ['mjuːtjuːl], *n.* (*Arch.*) Mutule, *f.*
muzzle [mʌzl], *n.* Museau (of animals), *m.*;
bouche, gueule (of cannon), *f.*; bout (of
rifles, pistols, etc.), *m.*; tuyau (of bellows),
m.; muselière (fastening for the mouth), *f.—
v.t.* Museler; bâillonner. **muzzle-loader,**
n. Arme se chargeant par la bouche, *f.*
muzzle-velocity, *n.* Vitesse à la bouche, *f.*
muzzling, *n.* Musellement, *m.*
muzzy ['mʌzi], *a.* Brouillé, confus, vague; un
peu gris.
my [mai], *poss. a.* Mon, *m.*, ma, *f.*, mes, *pl.—
int. My! my!* Par exemple!
mycetology [maisi'tɔlədʒi], *n.* Mycologie, *f.*
mycoderma [maikou'dəːmə], *n.* Mycoderme,
m. **mycological** [-'lɔdʒikl], *a.* Mycologique. **mycologist,** *n.* Mycologue, *m.*
mycology [-'kɔlədʒi], *n.* Mycologie, *f.*
mycophagist, *n.* Mycophage, *m.*
myelitis [maiə'laitis], *n.* Myélite, *f.* **myelomeningitis** [-loumenin'dʒaitis], *n.* Myélo-
méningite, *f.*
myocarditis [maiəkɑ:'daitis], *n.* Myocardite,
f. **myography** [-'ɔgrəfi], *n.* Myographie, *f.*
myological [-'lɔdʒikl], *a.* Myologique.
myology [-'ɔlədʒi], *n.* Myologie, *f.*
myope ['maioup], *n.* Myope, *m.* **myopia**
[-'oupiə] or **myopy,** *n.* Myopie, *f.* **myopic,**
a. Myope.
myosotis [maiə'soutis], *n.* (*Bot.*) Myosotis,
m.
myotomy [mai'ɔtəmi], *n.* Myotomie, *f.*
myriad ['miriəd], *n.* Myriade, *f.—a.* (*poet.*)
Innombrable. **myriametre,** *n.* Myriamètre,
m. **myriapod,** *n.* Myriapode, *m.*
myrmidon ['məːmidən], *n.* Myrmidon,
spadassin, *m.*
myrrh [məː], *n.* Myrrhe, *f.*
myrrhine [MURRHINE].
myrtiform ['məːtifɔːm], *a.* Myrtiforme.
myrtle [məːtl], *n.* Myrte, *m.* **myrtle-berry,**
n. Baie de myrte, *f.*
myself [mai'self], *pron.* Moi-même; moi. *I
consider myself,* je me crois; *I was by myself,*
j'étais tout seul.

mystagogue ['mistəgɔg], *n.* Mystagogue, *m.*
mysterious [mis'tiəriəs], *a.* Mystérieux.
mysteriously, *adv.* Mystérieusement.
mysteriousness, *n.* Mystère, *m.*, nature mystérieuse, *f.*
mystery ['mistəri], *n.* Mystère, *m.*
mystic ['mistik], *n.* (*Theol.*) Mystique; initié, magicien.—*a.* Cabalistique, ésotérique (rite); magique (formula); occulte, surnaturel (power); allégorique, emblématique (sign); (*Law, Theol.*) mystique. **mystical,** *a.* (*Theol.*) Mystique. **mystically,** *adv.* Mystiquement.
mysticism ['mistisizm], *n.* Mysticisme, *m.*, mysticité, *f.*
mystification [-fi'keiʃən], *n.* Mystification, *f.* **mystifier,** *n.* Mystificateur, *m.*, mystificatrice, *f.* **mystify** [-fai], *v.t.* Envelopper de mystère, mystifier.
mystique [miːs'tiːk], *n.* Mystique, *f.*
myth [miθ], *n.* Mythe, *m.* **mythical,** *a.* Mythique. **mythography** [-'θɔgrəfi], *n.* Mythographie, *f.* **mythological** [-'lɔdʒikl], *a.* Mythologique. **mythologically,** *adv.* D'une manière mythologique.
mythologist [mi'θɔlədʒist], *n.* Mythologue, *m.* **mythology,** *n.* Mythologie, *f.*
myxoma [mik'soumə], *n.* Myxome, *m.*
myxomatosis [miksəmə'tousis], *n.* Myxomatose, *f.*

N

N, n [en]. Quatorzième lettre de l'alphabet.
nab [næb], *v.t.* Happer, saisir, pincer.
nabob ['neibɔb], *n.* Nabab, *m.*
nacarat ['nækəræt], *n.* Nacarat, *m.*
nacre ['neikə], *n.* Nacre, *f.* **nacreous,** *a.* Nacré.
nadir ['neidiə], *n.* Nadir, *m.*
nag (1) [næg], *n.* Bidet, petit cheval, *m.*; chamaillerie, *f.*
nag (2) [næg], *v.t., v.i.* Gronder, chamailler, criailler. *To nag at* or *after,* crier après, critiquer. **nagging,** *a.* (*pers.*) Querelleur, (*pain*) agaçant.
naiad ['naiæd], *n.* Naïade, *f.*
nail [neil], *n.* Clou; ongle (of claws, fingers, or toes), *m. Hard as nails,* dur comme du fer; *one nail drives out another,* un clou chasse l'autre; *to bite one's nails,* se ronger les ongles; *to cut one's nails,* se couper *or* se tailler les ongles; *to drive in a nail,* enfoncer un clou; *to hit the nail on the head,* mettre le doigt dessus, frapper juste; *to pay on the nail,* payer comptant, payer rubis sur l'ongle; *to work tooth and nail,* s'y mettre de toutes ses forces.—*v.t.* Clouer; garnir de clous; clouter; (*fig.*) prendre au mot, river son clou à. *To nail someone* (to an argument or bargain), prendre quelqu'un au mot, y prendre quelqu'un; *to nail up,* clouer, fermer à clous, condamner (a window, a door, etc.).
nail-brush, *n.* Brosse à ongles, *f.* **nail-factory** or **nail-works,** *n.* Clouterie, *f.* **nail-file,** *n.* Lime à ongles, *f.* **nail-head,** *n.* Tête de clou, *f.* **nail-headed,** *a.* À tête de clou. **nail-scissors,** *n.pl.* Ciseaux à ongles, *m.pl.*
nailer, *n.* Cloutier, *m.* **nailery,** *n.* Clouterie, *f.* **nailing,** *n.* Clouage, clouement, *m.*

naïve [naː'iːv] or **naive** ['neiiv], *a.* Naïf, ingénu. **naïvely,** *adv.* Naïvement. **naïvety** or **naïveté,** *n.* Naïveté, *f.*
naked ['neikid], *a.* Nu, à nu; à découvert, ouvert (open to view); dégarni (unfurnished); sans défense (defenceless); évident, manifeste (evident). *Naked bond,* (*Law*) contrat sans garantie, *m.*; *naked light,* feu nu; *stark naked,* tout nu; *with the naked eye,* à l'œil nu. **nakedly,** *adv.* À nu, manifestement, ouvertement; à découvert. **nakedness,** *n.* Nudité, *f.*
namby-pamby ['næmbi 'pæmbi], *a.* Maniéré, affété, minaudier.
name [neim], *n.* Nom; (*fig.*) renom, *m.*, renommée, réputation, *f. Another name for,* synonyme de; *assumed name,* nom d'emprunt, pseudonyme, nom de guerre, *m.*; *by name,* de nom; *Christian name,* nom de baptême, prénom, petit nom, *m.*; *family name,* nom de famille, *m.*; *give a dog a bad name and hang him,* qui veut noyer son chien l'accuse de la rage; *he came in my name,* il est venu de ma part; *in name,* de nom; *in the name of,* au nom de; *maiden name,* nom de jeune fille, *m.*; *the house is in the name of,* la maison est sous le nom de; *to call names,* dire des injures à; *to give one's name,* décliner son nom; *to go by the name of,* être connu sous le nom de; *to make a name for oneself,* se faire une réputation; *to mention no names,* ne nommer personne; *what is that gentleman's name? comment s'appelle ce monsieur? what is your name?* comment vous appelez-vous?—*v.t.* Nommer, appeler; mentionner, désigner. *To be named,* s'appeler, se nommer, être appelé (of things).
named, *a.* Nommé, désigné. *Above-named,* ci-dessus mentionné. **nameless,** *a.* Sans nom, anonyme; inconnu.
namely, *adv.* À savoir, nommément, c'est-à-dire.
name-plate, *n.* Plaque, *f.* **namesake,** *n.* Homonyme, *m.*
nankeen [næn'kiːn], *n.* Nankin, *m.*
nanny ['næni], *n.* Bonne d'enfant, nurse, (*childish*) nounou, *f.* **nanny-goat,** *n.* Bique, *f.*
nap [næp], *n.* Poil (of cloth, hats, etc.); duvet (of plants); somme (sleep); napoléon (game); tuyau certain (racing), *m. Afternoon nap,* sieste, *f.*—*v.i.* Faire un somme; sommeiller; (*fig.*) s'endormir, manquer de vigilance. *To catch napping,* prendre au dépourvu; *to go nap on,* jouer son va-tout sur.
napalm ['neipaːm], *n.* Napalm, *m.*
nape [neip], *n.* Nuque, *f.*
napery ['neipəri], *n.* (*Sc.*) Linge de table, *m.*
naphtha ['næfθə], *n.* Naphte, *m.* **naphthaline,** *n.* Naphtaline, *f.* **naphthol,** *n.* Naphtol, *m.*
naphthylamine, *n.* Naphtylamine, *f.*
napiform ['neipifɔːm], *a.* Napiforme.
napkin ['næpkin], *n.* Serviette; couche (for babies), *f.* **napkin-ring,** *n.* Rond de serviette, *m.*
napless ['næplis], *a.* Sans poil; râpé. **nappiness,** *n.* État poilu, *m.* **nappy,** *a.* Capiteux (of wine etc.); poilu, velu.—*n.* (*fam.*) Couche, *f.* (for babies).
Napoleon [nə'pouljən]. Napoléon, *m.*
Napoleonic, *a.* Napoléonien, *m.*, -ienne, *f.*
narcissism, *n.* Narcissisme, *m.*

Narcissus [nɑːˈsisəs]. Narcisse, *m.*
narcissus [nɑːˈsisəs], *n.* Narcisse, *m.*
narcotic [nɑːˈkɔtik], *a.* and *n.* Narcotique, *m.*
narcotically, *adv.* Avec un effet narcotique.
narcotine [ˈnɑːkətin], *n.* Narcotine, *f.* **narcotism**, *n.* Narcotisme, *m.* **narcotize**, *v.t.* Narcotiser.
nard [nɑːd], *n.* Nard, *m.*
narghile [ˈnɑːgilei], *n.* Narguilé, *m.*
nark [nɑːk], *n.* (*pop.*) *Copper's nark*, mouchard, mouton, *m.*—*v.t. Nark it!* Fiche-moi la paix!
narked [nɑːkt], *a.* (*pop.*) En rogne.
narrate [nəˈreit], *v.t.* Raconter, narrer.
narration [nəˈreiʃən], *n.* Narration, *f.*, récit, *m.*
narrative [ˈnærətiv], *n.* Récit, narré, *m.*—*a.* Narratif. **narratively**, *adv.* Sous forme de narration.
narrator [nəˈreitə], *n.* Narrateur, *m.*
narrow [ˈnærou], *a.* Étroit, resserré; à l'étroit, gêné; rétréci, limité, borné (contracted, of confined views, etc.); de près (near). *Narrow mind*, esprit borné, *m.*; *to be in narrow circumstances*, être à l'étroit, vivre à l'étroit; *to have a narrow escape*, l'échapper belle.—*n.pl.* Détroit, pas, étranglement, *m.*—*v.t.* Rétrécir, resserrer, limiter, borner.—*v.i.* Se rétrécir, se resserrer.
narrow-brimmed, *a.* À petits bords.
narrowing, *n.* Rétrécissement, *m.* **narrowly**, *adv.* Étroitement, à l'étroit; exactement, soigneusement, scrupuleusement, attentivement; de près; mesquinement (sparingly). *We narrowly escaped being killed*, nous avons failli être tués. **narrow-minded**, *a.* À l'esprit étroit. **narrowness**, *n.* Étroitesse, *f.*, manque d'étendue, rétrécissement, *m.*; petitesse, mesquinerie (meanness), *f.*; exiguïté, pauvreté (of means etc.), *f.*
narwhal [ˈnɑːwəl], *n.* Narval, *m.*
nasal [neizl], *a.* Nasal, du nez.—*n.* (*Gram.*) Nasale, *f.* **nasality** [-ˈzæliti], *n.* Nasalité, *f.* **nasalize**, *v.t.* Nasaliser. **nasally**, *adv.* Nasalement.
nascent [ˈnæsənt], *a.* Naissant.
nastily [ˈnɑːstili], *adv.* Salement, malproprement; (*fig.*) grossièrement, vilainement. **nastiness**, *n.* Saleté, malpropreté; obscénité, grossièreté, *f.*
nasturtium [nəsˈtəːʃəm], *n.* Capucine, *f.*
nasty [ˈnɑːsti], *a.* Sale, malpropre; (*fig.*) vilain, mauvais, désagréable; obscène, dégoûtant. *Nasty boy*, vilain enfant; *nasty cold*, vilain rhume, *m.*; *nasty weather*, vilain or sale temps, *m.*; *nasty wound*, blessure grave, *f.*; *to smell nasty*, sentir mauvais; *to turn nasty*, prendre un air méchant.
natal [neitl], *a.* Natal, de naissance.
natation [nəˈteiʃən], *n.* Natation, *f.* **natatorial** [neitəˈtɔːriəl] or **natatory** [ˈneitətəri], *a.* Natatoire, nageur.
nation [ˈneiʃən], *n.* Nation, *f. Law of nations*, droit des gens, *m. The United Nations*, les Nations Unies, *f.pl.*
national [ˈnæʃənl], *a.* National. *National anthem*, hymne national, *m.*; *national debt*, dette publique, *f.*; *national insurance*, assurances sociales, *f.pl.* **nationalism**, *n.* Nationalisme, *m.* **nationalist**, *n.* Nationaliste, *m.* **nationality** [-ˈnæliti], *n.* Nationalité, *f.*

nationalization [-əlaiˈzeiʃən], *n.* Nationalisation, naturalisation, *f.* **nationalize**, *v.t.* Rendre national, nationaliser. **nationally**, *adv.* Nationalement.
native [ˈneitiv], *a.* Natif, naturel; indigène, du pays, de son pays; originaire, primitif; maternel (of language etc.). *Native genius*, le génie naturel, *m.*; *native gold*, or natif, *m.*; *native land*, patrie, terre natale, *f.*; *native place*, pays natal, *m.*; *native productions*, productions indigènes, *f.pl.*; *native soil*, sol natal, *m.*; *native tongue*, langue maternelle, *f.*—*n.* Natif (of a town etc.); habitant (of an island); naturel (of savage tribes); indigène (of plants, of non-European countries, etc.), *m.*; (*pl.*) huîtres (du pays), *f.pl. A native of England*, Anglais de naissance; *a native of Paris*, natif de Paris; *native of*, originaire de.
nativity [nəˈtiviti], *n.* Nativité; naissance, *f. Nativity play*, mystère de la Nativité, *m.*; *to cast someone's nativity*, tirer l'horoscope de.
natron [ˈneitrən], *n.* (*Min.*) Natron, natrum, *m.*
natter [ˈnætə], *v.i.* (*fam.*) Grogner; bavarder. —*n.* (*pop.*) *To have a natter*, tailler une bavette.
nattiness [ˈnætinis], *n.* (*pop.*) Élégance, *f.*
natty [ˈnæti], *a.* Pimpant, propret, coquet; adroit.
natural [ˈnætʃərəl], *a.* Naturel; réel; naïf, sans affectation, simple; (*Mus.*) bécarre; (*Paint.*) au naturel. *Natural selection*, sélection naturelle, *f.*—*n.* (*Mus.*) Bécarre, *m.* **naturalism**, *n.* Naturalisme, *m.* **naturalist**, *n.* Naturaliste, *m.* **naturalization** [-laiˈzeiʃən], *n.* Naturalisation, *f.* **naturalize**, *v.t.* Naturaliser. **naturally**, *adv.* Naturellement, au naturel. **naturalness**, *n.* Naturel; caractère naturel, *m.*; naïveté, simplicité, *f.*, manque d'affectation, *m.*
nature [ˈneitʃə], *n.* Nature, *f.*; naturel (disposition), *m. By nature*, naturellement, de nature; *from nature*, (*Paint. etc.*) d'après nature; *good nature*, bon naturel, *m.*, bonté, bonhomie, *f.*; *ill-nature*, mauvais naturel, *m.*, méchanceté, *f.*; *in the nature of things*, dans l'ordre des choses; *of a nature to*, de nature à; *something in the nature of . . .*, une espèce or sorte de . . .; *to pay the debt of nature*, payer sa dette à la nature. **natured**, *a.* De nature; de naturel. *Good-natured*, d'un bon naturel; *ill-natured*, d'un mauvais naturel, méchant. **naturedly**, *adv. Good-naturedly*, avec bonté, avec bonhomie; *ill-naturedly*, méchamment.
naught [nɔːt], *n.* Néant, rien; (*Arith.*) zéro, *m. To come to naught*, échouer, avorter, faire fiasco; *to set at naught*, mépriser, braver, défier.
naughtily [ˈnɔːtili], *adv.* Par méchanceté.
naughtiness, *n.* Méchanceté, *f.* **naughty**, *a.* Méchant. *Naughty boy!* vilain! méchant! *naughty trick*, méchanceté, *f.*, vilain tour, *m.*
nausea [ˈnɔːsiə], *n.* Nausée, *f.*; soulèvement de cœur, *m.*
nauseate [ˈnɔːsieit], *v.t.* Dégoûter.—*v.i.* Avoir des nausées, avoir du dégoût (pour).
nauseating, **nauseous**, *a.* Nauséabond, dégoûtant, écœurant. **nauseation** [-ˈeiʃən], *n.* Dégoût, *m.* **nauseously**, *adv.* D'une manière écœurante. **nauseousness**, *n.* Nature nauséabonde, *f.*
nautical [ˈnɔːtikl], *a.* Nautique; marin (of miles etc.).

nautilus ['nɔːtiləs], *n.* Nautile, argonaute, *m.*
naval [neivl], *a.* Naval; maritime; de la marine (de guerre). *Naval architect,* constructeur de vaisseaux, *m.; naval base,* port de guerre, *m.; naval forces,* armée de mer, *f.; naval officer,* officier de marine, *m.; naval station,* station navale, *f.,* port de guerre, *m.*
nave [neiv], *n.* Nef (of a church), *f.;* moyeu (of a wheel), *m.*
navel [neivl], *n.* Nombril; (*fig.*) centre, cœur, *m.* **navel-string,** *n.* Cordon ombilical, *m.* **navel-wort,** *n.* Cotylédon, *m.*
navigability [nævigə'biliti] or **navigableness,** *n.* Navigabilité, *f.* **navigable** ['nævigəbl], *a.* Navigable.
navigate ['nævigeit], *v.i.* Naviguer.—*v.t.* Naviguer sur; gouverner. *To navigate a vessel,* gouverner un navire. **navigation** [-'geiʃən], *n.* Navigation, *f. Aerial navigation,* navigation aérienne, *f.; inland navigation,* navigation intérieure. **navigation-laws,** *n.pl.* Code maritime, *m.,* législation maritime, *f.*
navigator ['nævigeitə], *n.* Navigateur, *m.*
navvy ['nævi], *n.* Terrassier, *m. Steam-navvy,* excavateur à vapeur, *m.*
navy ['neivi], *n.* Marine de guerre, *f. Merchant Navy,* marine marchande, *f.* **navy-agent,** *n.* Agent maritime, *m.* **navy blue,** *a.* and *n.* Bleu marine, *m.inv.* **navy-board,** *n.* Conseil d'amirauté, *m.* **navy-list,** *n.* Annuaire de la marine, *m.* **navy-surgeon,** *n.* Chirurgien de marine, *m.* **navy-yard,** *n.* Arsenal maritime, *m.*
nay [nei], *adv.* Non; bien plus; et même, qui plus est. *I cannot say him nay,* je ne puis le lui refuser; *to say nay,* refuser.
Nazarene [næzə'riːn], *a.* De Nazareth.—*n.* Nazaréen, *m.*
Nazarite ['næzərait], *n.* Juif dissident, *m.*
naze [neiz], *n.* Promontoire, cap, *m.*
Nazi ['nɑːtsi], *a.* and *n.* (*Polit.*) Nazi. **nazify,** *v.t.* Nazifier. **nazism,** *n.* Nazisme, *m.*
Neapolitan [niə'pɔlitən], *a.* Napolitain, de Naples.—*n.* Napolitain, *m.,* Napolitaine, *f.*
neap tide [niːp'taid], *n.* Marée de morte eau, *f.*
near [niə], *a.* Proche, rapproché; parcimonieux, chiche (parsimonious); cher (dear); exact, fidèle (faithful); de gauche (left). *Near horse,* cheval de gauche, (in team) porteur, *m.; near relation,* proche parent, *m.,* proche parente, *f.; near side,* côté du montoir, côté gauche de la route, *m.; that was a near thing!* (*fam.*) c'était moins cinq!—*adv.* Près, près de, de près, auprès de; presque, à peu près. *Nearer and nearer,* de plus en plus près; *to draw near,* s'approcher; *to draw near to,* s'approcher de.—*prep.* Près de, auprès de. *To be near one's end,* toucher à sa fin.—*v.t., v.i.* S'approcher de.
nearby, *adv., prep.,* and *a.* Tout près, tout proche.
nearly, *adv.* De près; à peu près; peu s'en faut, presque; chichement, mesquinement (parsimoniously). *He copied it as nearly as possible,* il le copia aussi exactement que possible; *he is not nearly so mean as his brother,* il n'est pas à beaucoup près aussi ladre que son frère; *he was nearly drowned,* il faillit se noyer; *he was nearly hanged,* peu s'en est fallu qu'il ne fût pendu; *it is nearly five o'clock,* il est près de cinq heures; *they*

are nearly related, ils sont très proches parents.
nearness, *n.* Proximité; exactitude; proche parenté, intimité; parcimonie, mesquinerie (parsimony), *f.*
near-sighted, *a.* Qui à la vue basse, myope.
neat (1) [niːt], *n.* Gros bétail, *m.,* vache, *f.* **neat-herd,** *n.* Bouvier, vacher, *m.* **neat's-foot-oil,** *n.* Huile de pied de bœuf, *f.* **neat's-tongue,** *n.* Langue de bœuf, *f.*
neat (2) [niːt], *a.* Propre, soigné, net, bien rangé; simple et élégant, joli; pur, sec (unadulterated); bien tourné. *A neat trick,* un tour adroit; *a neat turn of phrase,* une phrase bien tournée. **neatly,** *adv.* Proprement; nettement; d'une manière soignée; adroitement (dexterously). *An idea neatly expressed,* une idée élégamment exprimée. **neatness,** *n.* Propreté, netteté, simplicité, *f.*
nebula ['nebjulə], *n.* (*Astrol.*) Nébuleuse, *f.;* (*Med.*) taie, *f.* **nebulosity** [-'lɔsiti], *n.* Nébulosité, *f.* **nebulous,** *a.* Nébuleux. **nebulously,** *adv.* Nébuleusement.
necessaries ['nesəsəriz], *n.pl.* Le nécessaire, *m.* **necessarily,** *adv.* Nécessairement, de nécessité, forcément. **necessary,** *a.* Nécessaire. *If necessary,* s'il le faut, (*Comm.*) au besoin; *to be necessary,* falloir, être nécessaire. **necessitate** [ni'sesiteit], *v.t.* Nécessiter. **necessitation** [-'teiʃən], *n.* Obligation, contrainte, *f.*
necessitous [ni'sesitəs], *a.* Nécessiteux, dans le besoin.
necessity [ni'sesiti], *n.* Nécessité, *f.;* besoin (indigence), *m. A case of necessity,* un cas de force majeure; *from necessity,* par nécessité, par besoin; *necessity is the mother of invention,* nécessité rend ingénieux; *of necessity,* nécessairement, forcément; *to be under the necessity to,* se trouver dans la nécessité de; *to make a virtue of necessity,* faire de nécessité vertu.
neck [nek], *n.* Cou; goulot (of bottles etc.); manche (of a violin); collet (of meat), *m.;* encolure, *f.* (of a dress); langue (of land), *f. By half a neck,* (*Racing*) d'une tête; *neck and crop,* complètement; *neck and neck,* de très près, à égalité; *neck or nothing,* tout ou rien; *stiff neck,* torticolis, *m.; to break one's neck,* se casser le cou; *to get it in the neck* (*fam.*), se faire sonner les cloches; *to have a* (*brass*) *neck,* (*pop.*) avoir du culot; *to save one's neck,* sauver sa peau; *to stick out one's neck,* prendre des risques; *V neck,* décolleté pointu, en pointe; *with a low neck* (of a dress), décolleté.—*v.i.* (*slang*) Faire des mamours. **neckband,** *n.* Tour-du-cou (de chemise), *m.,* encolure, *f.* **necked,** *a.* Au cou. *Longnecked,* au long cou; *short-necked,* au cou court; *square-necked* (dress), à décolleté carré; *stiff-necked,* au cou raide, altier, arrogant. **neckerchief,** *n.* Foulard (for men), fichu (for women), *m.* **necklace,** *n.* Collier, *m.* **neck-tie,** *n.* Cravate, *f.*
necrological [nekrə'lɔdʒikl], *a.* Nécrologique. **necrologist** [ne'krɔlədʒist], *n.* Nécrologue, *m.* **necrology** [ne'krɔlədʒi], *n.* Nécrologie, *f.*
necromancer ['nekrəmænsə], *n.* Nécromancien, *m.,* nécromancienne, *f.* **necromancy,** *n.* Nécromancie, *f.* **necromantic** [-'mæntik], *a.* Nécromantique. **necrophagous**

[-'krɔfəgəs], *a.* Nécrophage. **necrophobia** [-krə'foubiə], *n.* Nécrophobie, *f.* **necropolis** [-'krɔpɔlis], *n.* Nécropole, *f.*
necrosis [ne'krousis], *n.* Nécrose, *f.*
nectar ['nektə], *n.* Nectar, *m.* **nectarean** [-'tɛəriən] or **nectareous**, *a.* De nectar.
nectarine ['nektərin], *n.* Brugnon, *m.*
nectary, *n.* (*Bot.*) Nectaire, *m.*
need [ni:d], *n.* Besoin, *m.*; nécessité; adversité; indigence, *f. If need be,* le cas échéant; *in case of need,* au besoin, en cas de besoin; *there is no need of that,* il n'y a pas besoin de cela; *to be in need,* être dans la misère; *to be in need of, to stand in need of,* or *to have need of,* avoir besoin de; *to see to the needs of,* pourvoir aux besoins de; *what need is there of that?* quel besoin y a-t-il de cela? quelle nécessité y a-t-il pour cela?—*v.t.* Avoir besoin de; exiger. *I needed no second permission,* je ne me le fis pas dire deux fois; *that needs much care,* cela exige beaucoup de soin. —*v.i.* Avoir besoin; devoir, avoir (à); (*impers.*) falloir, être nécessaire. *It needs the pen of,* il faudrait la plume de; *need he go?* Est-il obligé d'y aller? *you need not come,* vous pouvez vous dispenser de venir, inutile de venir. **needful,** *a.* Nécessaire. *The needful,* le nécessaire, *m.* **needfully,** *adv.* Nécessairement. **needfulness,** *n.* Nécessité, *f.* **needily,** *adv.* Dans le besoin. **neediness,** *n.* Indigence, nécessité, *f.*, besoin, *m.*
needle [ni:dl], *n.* Aiguille; boussole (compass), *f.*; (*Arch.*) obélisque, *m. Crochet needle,* crochet, *m.*; *darning-needle,* aiguille à repriser, *f.*; *eye of a needle,* trou d'aiguille, *m.*; *sewing-needle,* aiguille à coudre, *f.*; *to look for a needle in a haystack,* chercher une aiguille dans une botte de foin; *to thread a needle,* enfiler une aiguille.—*v.t.* (*fam.*) Irriter, agacer.—*a.* (spt.) *Needle match,* match critique et vivement contesté, *m.*
needle-case, *n.* Étui à aiguilles, *m.* **needleful,** *n.* Aiguillée, *f.* **needle-valve,** *n.* Soupape à pointeau, *f.* **needle-woman,** *n.* Couturière (à la journée), *f.* **needlework,** *n.* Ouvrage à l'aiguille, *m.*; (*sch.*) couture, *f. To do needlework,* travailler à l'aiguille.
needless ['ni:dlis], *a.* Inutile. *It is needless to say that,* il va sans dire que, inutile de dire que. **needlessly,** *adv.* Inutilement. **needlessness,** *n.* Inutilité, *f.*
needs [ni:dz], *adv.* (*used only with* must) Nécessairement, absolument, de toute nécessité. *I must needs,* il faut absolument que je (*with subj.*); *needs must when the devil drives,* nécessité n'a pas de loi.
needy ['ni:di], *a.* Indigent, nécessiteux, besogneux.
ne'er [nɛə] [NEVER].
nefarious [ni'fɛəriəs], *a.* Abominable, infâme. **nefariously,** *adv.* Abominablement.
negate [ni'geit], *v.t.* Nier; nullifier.
negation [ni'geiʃən], *n.* Négation, *f.*
negative ['negətiv], *n.* Négative, *f.*, (*Phot.*) cliché, négatif, *m. In the negative,* négativement.—*a.* Négatif.—*v.t.* Décider négativement, rejeter. **negatively,** *adv.* Négativement.
neglect [ni'glekt], *n.* Négligence, *f.*; manque d'attention; oubli, *m. From neglect,* par négligence.—*v.t.* Négliger, manquer à. **neglected,** *a.* Négligé. **neglectful,**

Négligent; oublieux (de). **neglectfully,** *adv.* Négligemment.
negligence ['neglidʒəns], *n.* Négligence, incurie, *f.*; oubli, *m.* **negligent,** *a.* Négligent; nonchalant; oublieux (de). **negligently,** *adv.* Négligemment, avec négligence. **negligible,** *a.* Négligeable.
negotiability [nigouʃiə'biliti], *n.* Négociabilité, *f.*
negotiable [ni'gouʃiəbl], *a.* Négociable.
negotiate, *v.t.* Négocier.—*v.i.* Négocier, être en négociation (avec); (*Parl.*) entreprendre des pourparlers. **negotiation** [-'eiʃən], *n.* Négociation, *f.*; (*pl.*) pourparlers, *m.pl.*
negotiator [ni'gouʃieitə], *n.* Négociateur, *m.*
Negress ['ni:gres or 'ni:gris], *n.* Négresse, *f.* (*both now pej.*).
Negro ['ni:grou], *n.* Noir, homme de couleur, *m.*; Noire, femme de couleur, *f.*
Negroid, *a.* Négroïde.
negus ['ni:gəs], *n.* Vin chaud épicé, *m.*
neigh [nei], *v.i.* Hennir.—*n.* Hennissement, *m.* **neighing,** *n.* Hennissement, *m.*
neighbour ['neibə], *n.* Voisin, *m.*, voisine, *f.*; (*Bibl.*) prochain, *m. Next-door neighbour,* plus proche voisin; *to have as a neighbour,* avoir pour voisin.—*a.* Voisin.—*v.t.* Avoisiner. **neighbourhood,** *n.* Voisinage, *m.*; alentours, environs, *m.pl.*; quartier, *m.* (*fig.*) *In the neighbourhood of a hundred,* cent environ, aux alentours de cent. **neighbouring,** *a.* Voisin, avoisinant, d'alentour. **neighbourly,** *a.* De voisin, de bon voisin; obligeant. *In a neighbourly way,* en bon voisin.
neither ['naiðə or 'ni:ðə], *a.* and *pron.* Ni l'un ni l'autre, *m.*, ni l'une ni l'autre, *f.*, ni les uns ni les autres, *m.pl.*, ni les unes ni les autres, *f.pl.*—*conj.* Ni; non plus. *Neither . . . nor,* ni . . . ni.—*adv.* Du reste, d'ailleurs.
nelumbium [ni'lʌmbiəm], *n.* (*Bot.*) Nélombo, nélumbo, *m.*
nematode ['nemətoud], *n.* Nématode, *f.*
Nemean [ni'mi:ən], *a.* Néméen, de Némée.
Nemesis ['nemisis], *n.* Némésis, *f.*; vengeance, justice distributive, *f.*
nenuphar ['nenjufɑ:], *n.* Nénuphar, *m.*
neo-Catholic [ni:ou'kæθəlik], *a.* and *n.* Néo-catholique, *m.* **neo-Catholicism** [ni:oukə'θɔlisizm], *n.* Néo-catholicisme, *m.*
neo-Christian [ni:ou'kristiən], *a.* and *n.* Néo-chrétien, *m.* **neo-Christianity** [-'æniti], *n.* Néo-christianisme, *m.*
neo-classicism, *n.* Néo-classicisme, *m.*
neolithic [ni:ə'liθik], *a.* Néolithique, *a.*
neological [ni:ə'lɔdʒikl], *a.* Néologique.
neologism [ni'ɔlədʒizm], *n.* Néologisme, *m.*
neologist, *n.* Néologue, néologiste, *m.*
neology, *n.* Néologie, *f.*
neon ['ni:ɔn], *n.* (*Chem.*) Néon, *m.*—*a. Neon light,* lampe au néon, *f.*
neophyte ['ni:əfait], *n.* Néophyte, *m.* or *f.*
neoplasm ['ni:əplæzm], *n.* Néoplasme, *m.*
Neoplatonic [ni:ouplə'tɔnik], *a.* Néoplatonique. **Neoplatonism** [-'pleitənizm], *n.* Néo-platonisme, *m.* **Neoplatonist,** *n.* Néo-platonicien, *m.*
Nepal [ni'pɔ:l]. Le Népal, *m.* **Nepalese** [nepə'li:z], *a.* and *n.* Népalais, *m.*, -aise, *f.*
nepenthe [nə'penθi], *n.* Népenthès, *m.*
nephew ['nefju or 'nevju], *n.* Neveu, *m.* *Grand-nephew, great-nephew,* petit-neveu, *m.*

nephralgia [ne'fræld3iə], *n.* Néphralgie, *f.*
nephritic [-'fritik], *a.* and *n.* Néphrétique,
m. **nephritis** [-'fraitis], *n.* Néphrite, *f.*
nepotism ['nepətizm], *n.* Népotisme, *m.*
Neptune ['neptju:n]. Neptune, *m.*
Neptunian [nep'tju:niən], *a.* Neptunien.
Neptunism ['neptjunizm], *n.* Neptunisme, *m.*
Nereid ['niəriid], *n.* Néréide, *f.*
Nero ['ni:ərou]. Néron, *m.*
neroli ['niərəli], *n.* Néroli, *m.*
nerval [nə:vl], *a.* Nerval. **nervation**
[-'veiʃən], *n.* Nervation, *f.*
nerve [nə:v], *n.* Nerf; (*fig.*) courage, sang-
froid, *m.*, audace, *f.*; (*Arch.*, *Bot.*) nervure, *f.*
(*pop.*) *He has a nerve!* il en a un toupet! *To
get on someone's nerves*, donner sur les nerfs à
quelqu'un; *to lose one's nerve*, perdre son
sang-froid.—*v.t.* Donner du nerf *or* de la
force à, fortifier. **nerve-cell**, *n.* Cellule
nerveuse, *f.* **nerved**, *a.* (*Bot.*) Nervé.
nerveless, *a.* Sans nerf; (*fig.*) sans vigueur,
sans force. **nerve-racking**, *a.* Horripilant,
énervant. **nervine**, *n.* Nervin, *m.* **nervi-
ness**, *n.* Nervosité, *f.* **nervose**, *a.* (*Bot.*)
Nervé.
nervous ['nə:vəs], *a.* (Sinewy) Nerveux;
(timid) timide, craintif. *Nervous break-down*,
dépression nerveuse, *f.*; *the nervous system*,
le système nerveux. **nervously**, *adv.*
Nerveusement, timidement. **nervousness**,
n. Inquiétude, timidité, *f.*; état nerveux, *m.*
nervure, *n.* Nervure, *f.* **nervy**, *a.* (*fam.*)
Nerveux; énervé.
nest [nest], *n.* Nid, *m.*; nichée (brood of birds),
f.; (*fig.*) repaire, *m.*; jeu, *m.*; série, *f.* *A nest
of thieves*, un repaire de voleurs; *nest of
drawers*, chiffonnier, classeur, *m.*; *nest of
shelves*, casier, *m.*; *nest of tables*, table gigogne,
f.—*v.i.* Nicher, faire un nid.—*v.t.* Emboîter.
nest-egg, *n.* Nichet; pécule, *m.* **nesting**, *a.*
Nicheur.
nestle [nesl], *v.i.* Nicher, se nicher. *To nestle
close to*, se serrer contre, se blottir.—*v.t.*
Nicher, loger; (*fig.*) chérir, choyer. **nestling**, *n.* Petit oiseau encore au nid, béjaune,
m.
Nestor ['nestə]. Nestor, *m.*
Nestorian [nes'tɔ:riən], *a.* and *n.* Nestorien,
m. **Nestorianism**, *n.* Nestorianisme, *m.*
net [net], *n.* Filet, rets; réseau (for the hair);
tulle (textile fabric), *m.* *Landing-net*,
épuisette, *f.*—*v.t.* Prendre dans un filet;
(*Hort.*) couvrir d'un filet (soft fruits etc.);
(*Ftb.*) envoyer la balle dans le filet, marquer
un but; (*Comm.*) rapporter net, produire *or*
rapporter des bénéfices. *I netted a thousand
pounds*, j'ai gagné mille livres net.—*v.i.* Faire
du filet.—*a.* Net; pur. *Net profit*, profit net,
m.
net-ball, *n.* (*spt.*) Net(-ball), *m.* **net-maker**, *n.*
Fabricant de filets, *m.* **netting**, *n.* Filet,
réseau, *m.*; pêche au filet, *f.*; (*Naut.*) bastingage, *m.* **netting-needle**, *n.* Navette, *f.*
netting-pin, *n.* Moule, *m.*
nether ['neðə], *a.* Bas, inférieur. **nether-
most**, *a.* Le plus bas.
Netherlands (the). Les Pays-Bas, *m.pl.*
nettle [netl], *n.* Ortie, *f.* *Dead nettle*, ortie
blanche.—*v.t.* Piquer, agacer, irriter. **nettle-
rash**, *n.* Urticaire, *f.* **nettle-tree**, *n.* (*Bot.*)
Micocoulier, *m.*
network, *n.* Réseau, enchevêtrement, *m.*

neuralgia [nju:'ræld3ə], *n.* Névralgie, *f.*
neuralgic, *a.* Névralgique.
neurasthenia [nju:ræs'θi:niə], *n.* Neurasthénie, *f.* **neurasthenic** [-'θenik], *a.*
Neurasthénique. **neurine**, *n.* Névrine,
neurine, *f.*
neuritis [nju:'raitis], *n.* Névrite, *f.* **neurologist**, *n.* Neurologue, *m.* **neurology**
[-'rɔlədʒi], *n.* Neurologie, *f.* **neuropatho-
logy** [-oupə'θɔlədɹi], *n.* Neuropathologie, *f.*
neuropterous [nju:'rɔptərəs], *a.* Névroptère.
neuropteran, *n.* Névroptère, *m.*
neurosis [nju:'rousis], *n.* Névrose, *f.* **neurotic**,
a. and *n.* Névrosé, neurotique. **neurotomy**,
n. Névrotomie, *f.*
neuter ['nju:tə], *a.* Neutre, asexué (bee);
châtré (cat).—*n.* Neutre, *m.*; personne neutre,
f.
neutral ['nju:trəl], *a.* and *n.* Neutre; indifférent; (*Motor.*) point-mort, *m.* **neutralist**, *a.* and *n.* Neutraliste. **neutrality**
[-'træliti], *n.* Neutralité; indifférence, *f.*
neutralization [nju:trəlai'zeiʃən], *n.* Neutralisation, *f.* **neutralize**, *v.t.* Neutraliser.
neutron ['nju:trən], *n.* Neutron, *m.*
never ['nevə], *adv.* Jamais; ne . . . jamais.
I have never seen it, je ne l'ai jamais vu; *never
a word*, pas un mot; *never in my life*, jamais
de la vie; *never mind*, peu importe! qu'à cela
ne tienne! *well, I never!* pas possible! par
exemple! *were it never so fine*, si beau que
ce soit.
never-ending, *a.* Qui ne finit point, perpétuel.
never-failing, *a.* Toujours prêt, infaillible.
nevermore [-'mɔ:], *adv.* Ne . . . jamais plus,
ne . . . plus jamais.
nevertheless, *conj.* Néanmoins, cependant,
pourtant.
new [nju:], *a.* Neuf (novel); nouveau (recent,
different); frais, récent (fresh). *A new book*,
un livre neuf (unused), un livre nouveau
(newly out), un nouveau livre (a different
one); *a new fashion*, une nouvelle mode; *a
new hat*, un chapeau neuf; *a new word*, un
mot nouveau; *a new work*, un nouvel ouvrage;
as good as new, presque neuf, comme neuf;
brand-new, flambant neuf, tout battant neuf;
new bread, pain frais, *m.*; *new guard*, (*Mil.*)
garde montante, *f.*; *new milk*, lait du jour, *m.*;
new to the trade, nouveau dans le métier; *new
vine*, du vin nouveau; *New Year*, nouvel an,
m.; *New Year's Day*, le jour de l'an, *m.*; *New
Year's Eve*, la Saint-Sylvestre; *New Year
gifts*, étrennes, *f.pl.*; *the new moon*, la nouvelle
lune; *to make as good as new*, remettre à neuf.
new-born, *a.* Nouveau-né. *New-born
daughters*, filles nouveau-nées. **new-comer**,
n. Nouveau venu, *m.*; (*sch.*) nouveau, *m.*
newel ['nju:əl], *n.* Noyau (d'escalier), *m.*
newfangled, *a.* (*fig.*) Tout flambant neuf,
d'un modernisme outré. **new-fashioned**, *a.*
De nouvelle mode, fait à la mode du jour.
new-laid, *a.* Frais (of eggs).
Newfoundland ['nju:fəndlænd *or* nju:'faund
lənd]. Terre-Neuve, *f.*—*n.* Terre-neuve
(dog), *m.*
New Guinea [nj:u'gini]. La Nouvelle-
Guinée, *f.*
newish ['nju:iʃ], *a.* Assez neuf; assez nouveau.
newly ['nju:li], *adv.* Nouvellement, fraîchement, récemment, de nouveau. **newness**, *n.*
Nouveauté; inexpérience (want of practice), *f.*

New Orleans [nju:'ɔ:liənz]. La Nouvelle-Orléans, *f.*
news [nju:z], *n.* Nouvelle, *f.*, nouvelles, *f.pl.*; (*Rad.*, *Tel.*) bulletin d'informations, *m.* *No news is good news*, point de nouvelles, bonnes nouvelles; *to be in the news*, être en vedette; *to tell a piece of news*, dire une nouvelle; *what news?* quelles nouvelles? qu'y a-t-il de nouveau? quoi de neuf? **news agency,** *n.* Agence d'informations, *f.* **news-agent,** *n.* Marchand de journaux, *m.* **news-boy,** *n.* Crieur *or* vendeur de journaux, *m.* **newscaster,** *n.* (*Tel.*) Speaker, *m.*, speakerine, *f.* **newspaper,** *n.* Journal, *m.* **news-print,** *n.* Papier-journal, *m.* **news-room,** *n.* Salle des journaux, *f.*; service des informations, *m.* (in newspaper office). **news-sheet,** *n.* Feuille, *f.* **news-stall, news-stand,** *n.* Kiosque à journaux; étalage de marchands de journaux, *m.* **news theatre,** *n.* Ciné-actualités, *m.* **newsy,** *a.* Plein de nouvelles.—*n.* (*Am.*) Vendeur de journaux, *m.*
newt [nju:t], *n.* Triton, *m.*, salamandre, *f.*
New Zealand [nju:'zi:lənd]. La Nouvelle-Zélande, *f.* **New Zealander,** *n.* Néo-Zélandais(e).
next [nekst], *a.* Voisin, le plus voisin; le plus près; de côté; prochain (of future time); suivant (of past time); premier (first after). *He came next day*, il est venu le jour suivant *or* le lendemain; *he will come next month*, il viendra le mois prochain; *I will take the next train*, je prendrai le train suivant; *Monday next*, lundi prochain; *next but one*, deuxième; *next but two*, troisième; *next door to*, très voisin de, ressemblant fort à; *next of kin*, le plus proche parent, *m.*; *next to* (place), à côté de, contigu à; *next to nothing of*, presque rien de; *next to that, the best course to follow will be . . .*, à défaut de cela, la meilleure marche à suivre sera de . . .; *the next day but one*, le surlendemain; *the next interview*, la prochaine entrevue; *the next Monday*, le lundi suivant; *the next morning*, le lendemain matin; *the next world*, l'autre monde, la vie à venir; *to know what to do next*, savoir ce qu'il faut faire ensuite.—*adv.* Après, ensuite, puis. *He came next*, il vint immédiatement après; *what next?* après? et après? ensuite?—*prep.* Next to, à côté de, après. *He sat next to me*, il était assis à côté de moi; *next to impossible*, à peu près *or* presque impossible.
next-door, *n.* La maison d'à côté.—*adv.* (D')à côté.
nexus ['neksəs], *n.* Connexion, *f.*
nib [nib], *n.* Bec (of a pen), *m.*; pointe (point), *f.* *Cocoa nibs*, fèves de cacao, *f.pl.* **nibbed,** *a.* À bec; à pointe. *Broad nibbed*, à grosse pointe; *hard-nibbed*, qui a le bec dur.
nibble [nibl], *v.t.* Mordiller, grignoter; mordre à (the bait); brouter (the grass etc.). —*n.* Grignotement, *m.*; touche, *f.* (of fish).
nibs [nibz], *n.* (*facet.*) *His nibs*, Sa Seigneurie.
nice [nais], *a.* Bon, agréable, friand; (*colloq.*) délicat, gentil, aimable, charmant, propre; exact, difficile, exigeant (fastidious). *A nice child*, un enfant gentil; *a nice critic*, un critique raffiné; *a nice dinner*, un bon dîner; *a nice distinction*, une distinction subtile;

(*fam.*) *a nice fellow!* un brave type! *a nice little wife*, une bonne petite femme; *a nice-looking man*, un bel homme; *a very nice girl*, une jeune fille bien aimable, une petite fille très sage; *how nice!* que c'est charmant! *I hear nice goings on of you*, j'en entends de belles sur votre compte; *over nice*, par trop difficile. **nicely,** *adv.* Bien, agréablement; délicatement; exactement, justement; scrupuleusement; gentiment, aimablement; joliment; d'une manière recherchée. *That will do nicely*, cela fera très bien l'affaire.
Nicene ['naisi:n *or* nai'si:n], *a.* De Nicée. *The Nicene creed*, le symbole de Nicée, *m.*
niceness ['naisnis], *n.* Goût agréable, *m.*; amabilité, gentillesse, *f.*; délicatesse; exactitude, justesse; recherche, *f.* *Niceness of taste*, délicatesse du goût, *f.*
nicety ['naisəti], *n.* Délicatesse, finesse, *f.*; soin scrupuleux, *m.*; précision; exactitude, *f.*; (*pl.* **niceties**) friandises, *f.pl.* *The niceties of a language*, les subtilités d'une langue; *to a nicety*, exactement, parfaitement, à point.
niche [nitʃ], *n.* Niche, *f.*
Nicholas ['nikələs]. Nicolas, *m.*
Nick [nik]. Nicolas. *Old Nick*, le diable.
nick [nik], *n.* Moment précis, *m.*; encoche, entaille (notch), *f.*; (*Print.*) cran, *m.* *In the nick of time*, fort à propos, à point nommé; *to come just in the nick of time*, arriver comme marée en carême; tomber à pic.—*v.t.* Faire une entaille dans, entailler; (*pop.*) pincer; carotter. *To nick it*, deviner juste.—*v.i.* (*spt.*) *To nick in*, couper.
nickel [nikl], *n.* Nickel, *m.*, pièce de nickel, *f.*; (*Am.*) pièce de cinq cents, *f.*—*v.t.* Nickeler. **nickel-plated,** *a.* Nickelé. **nickel-silver,** *n.* Maillechort, *m.* **nickel-steel,** *n.* Acier au nickel, *m.*
nick-nack [KNICK-KNACK].
nickname ['nikneim], *n.* Sobriquet, surnom, *m.*—*v.t.* Donner un sobriquet à.
nicotian [ni'kouʃiən], *n.* Nicotiane, *f.*—*a.* Nicotique.
nicotine ['nikəti:n], *n.* Nicotine, *f.* **nicotinism,** *n.* Nicotinisme, *m.*
nictate ['nikteit] *or* **nictitate** ['niktiteit], *v.i.* Ciller, cligner les yeux; (of horses) nicter. **nictation** [-'teiʃən], *n.* Nictation, nictitation, *f.* **nictitating,** *a.* Nictitant, clignotant.
nidification [nidifi'keiʃən], *n.* Nidification, construction d'un nid, *f.*
nidify ['nidifai], *v.t.* Nidifier.
niece [ni:s], *n.* Nièce, *f.* *Grand-niece*, petite-nièce, *f.*
niffy ['nifi], *a.* (*fam.*) Puant.
nifty ['nifti], *a.* (*fam.*) Pimpant.
Niger ['naidʒə]. Le Niger, *m.*
Nigeria [nai'dʒiəriə]. Nigeria, *m.* **Nigerian,** *a.* and *n.* Nigérien, *m.*, -ienne, *f.*
niggard ['nigəd], *a.* Avare, ladre.—*n.* Avare, ladre, grippe-sou, *m.* **niggardliness,** *n.* Mesquinerie, ladrerie, *f.* **niggardly,** *adv.* Avec avarice, en avare.—*a.* Mesquin, ladre, chiche.
nigger ['nigə], *n.* (*all pej.*) Nègre, moricaud, *m.*
niggle [nigl], *v.i.* Tatillonner; fignoler. **niggling,** *a.* Tatillon (of a person); fignolé (of work).

nigh [nai], *adv.* Près de; presque. *To draw nigh,* approcher, s'approcher (de); *well nigh,* presque, à peu près.—*a.* Proche, rapproché, près, près de.
night [nait], *n.* Nuit, *f.*; soir (evening), *m. A good night's rest to you!* bonne nuit! *all night,* toute la nuit; *at night,* la nuit, le soir; *eight o'clock at night,* huit heures du soir; *every night,* toutes les nuits, tous les soirs; *first night,* première, *f.*; *good night!* bonsoir! bonne nuit; *it is night,* il fait nuit; *last night,* la nuit dernière, hier (au) soir; *night after night,* plusieurs nuits de suite, tous les soirs; *the night before,* la veille (au soir); *the night before last,* avant-hier soir; *tomorrow night,* demain soir; *tonight,* ce soir, cette nuit; *to turn night into day,* faire de la nuit le jour.
night-bird, *n.* Oiseau de nuit, *m.* **night-cap,** *n.* Bonnet de nuit; (*colloq.*) grog, posset, *m.* **night-cart,** *n.* Voiture de vidange, *f.* **night-club,** *n.* Boîte de nuit, *f.* **night-dress, night-gown,** or **night-shirt,** *n.* Chemise de nuit, *f.* **night-fall,** *n.* Tombée de la nuit, *f. At nightfall,* à la nuit tombante. **nightjar,** *n.* Engoulevent, *m.* **night-light,** *n.* Veilleuse, *f.* **night-long,** *a.* De toute la nuit. **nightly,** *a.* Nocturne, de nuit.—*adv.* Chaque nuit, toutes les nuits; tous les soirs. **nightmare,** *n.* Cauchemar, *m.* **nightmarish,** *a.* Cauchemardesque. **nightshade,** *n.* Morelle, *f. Deadly nightshade,* belladone, *f.*; *woody nightshade,* douce-amère, *f.* **night-shift,** *n.* Équipe de nuit, *f.* **night-soil,** *n.* Vidanges, *f.pl.* **night-time,** *n.* Nuit, *f. In the night-time,* pendant la nuit. **night-walker,** *n.* Rôdeur de nuit; somnambule, *m.* **night-watch,** *n.* Garde de nuit, *f.* **night-watchman,** *n.* Veilleur de nuit, *m.* **night-work,** *n.* Travail de nuit, *m.* **nighty** or **nightie,** *n.* [NIGHT-DRESS].
nightingale ['naitiŋgeil], *n.* Rossignol, *m.*
nigrescent [nai'gresənt], *a.* Nigrescent; noirâtre.
nigrify ['naigrifai], *v.t.* Nigrifier.
nihilism ['naihilizm], *n.* Nihilisme, *m.* **nihilist,** *n.* Nihiliste, *m.* **nihilistic** [-'listik], *a.* Nihiliste.
nil [nil], *n.* Rien, néant, zéro, *m.*
Nile [nail], **The.** Le Nil, *m.*
nilometer [nai'lomitə], *n.* Nilomètre, *m.*
nimble [nimbl], *a.* Agile, léger, leste. **nimble-footed,** *a.* Aux pieds légers. **nimbleness,** *n.* Agilité, *f.* **nimble-witted,** *a.* À l'esprit vif *or* délié. **nimbly,** *adv.* Agilement, lestement.
nimbus ['nimbəs], *n.* Nimbe; (*Meteor.*) nimbus, *m.*
nincompoop ['ninkəmpu:p], *n.* (*prob. alterat. of* NON COMPOS) [*see* COMPOS]. Niais, sot, nigaud, *m.*
nine [nain], *a. and n.* Neuf. *A nine days' wonder,* la merveille d'un jour; *dressed up to the nines,* tiré à quatre épingles; *he is nine,* il a neuf ans; *possession is nine points of the law,* c'est la loi du premier occupant; *the Nine,* les Muses, *f.pl.*
ninefold, *a.* Neuf fois autant. **ninepins,** *n.pl.* Quilles, *f.pl.*; jeu de quilles, *m.* **nineteen,** *n.* Dix-neuf, *m. She talks nineteen to the dozen,* c'est un vrai moulin à paroles. **nineteenth,** *a. and n.* Dix-neuvième; dix-neuf (of the month), *m. The nineteenth hole* (*Golf*), la

buvette, *f.* **ninetieth,** *a. and n.* Quatre-vingt-dixième, *m.* **ninety,** *a. and n.* Quatre-vingt-dix, *m.*
ninny ['nini], *n.* Nigaud, niais, *m.*
ninth [nainθ], *a. and n.* Neuvième; neuf (of the month or of a dynasty), *m.* **ninthly,** *adv.* Neuvièmement.
nip [nip], *n.* Pincement, *m.*, pince, *f.*, serrement, *m.*; coupure, morsure; (*Hort.*) brûlure (par le froid), *f.*; (*fig.*) trait piquant; petit coup (sip), *m.*; (*Naut.*) étrive, *f.*—*v.t.* Pincer; couper; mordre; (*Hort.*) brûler (par le froid); (*fig.*) piquer; (*Naut.*) étriver. *She was nipped in the bud,* la mort la frappa au berceau; *to nip in the bud,* détruire *or* tuer dans l'œuf; *to nip off,* couper, enlever le bout de.—*v.i.* Aller vite, courir chez; boire la goutte. **nipper,** *n.* Pince, *f.*; (*colloq.*) gamin, gosse, *m.*; (*pl.*) pincettes, pinces, *f.pl.* **nipping,** *a.* Mordant, piquant; perçant (of cold). **nippy,** *a.* Preste, rapide, alerte; vif, mordant, perçant (of cold).
nipple [nipl], *n.* Mamelon, bout de sein, *m.*; tétine; cheminée (of fire-arms), *f.*; (*Motor.* etc.) raccord, *m.* **nipplewort,** *n.* Lampsane, *f.*
nirvana [niə'va:nə], *n.* Nirvâna, *m.*
nisi ['naisai], *Latin conj.* À moins que—*a. Decree (order) nisi,* arrêt provisoire, *m.*
nit [nit], *n.* Lente, *f.*; (*fam.*) nullité, *f.*, propre à rien, *m.*
nitrate ['naitreit], *n.* Nitrate, *m.* **nitre** ['naitə], *n.* Nitre, *m.* **nitre-bed,** *n.* Nitrière, *f.* **nitric,** *a.* Nitrique, azotique. **nitrify,** *v.t.* Nitrifier.
nitrogen ['naitrədʒən], *n.* Azote, *m.* **nitrogenous** [-'trɔdʒinəs], *a.* Azoté. **nitro-glycerin(e)** [naitro'glisəri:n], *n.* Nitro-glycérine, *f.* **nitrous,** *a.* Nitreux.
nitwit ['nitwit], *n.* Imbécile, *m.* or *f.*
no [nou], *a. and adv.* Non, pas, ne . . . pas de, ne . . . point de; pas un, nul, aucun. *Have you no friends?* (query) n'avez-vous pas d'amis? *have you no friends?* (reproach) n'avez-vous pas des amis? *he has no money on him,* il n'a pas d'argent sur lui; *I am no musician,* je ne suis pas du tout musicien; *no admittance,* entrée interdite; *no ball,* (*Cricket*) balle nulle; *no doubt,* sans doute; *no fear of that,* il n'y a pas de danger; *no longer,* ne . . . plus; *no matter,* n'importe; *no matter how unruly the House,* si agitée que soit la Chambre; *no more,* ne . . . plus, pas davantage; *no one,* personne, pas un; *no smoking,* défense de fumer; *no sooner said than done,* aussitôt dit, aussitôt fait; *no such thing,* il n'en est rien; *nowhere,* nulle part; *there is no avoiding it,* il n'y a pas moyen de l'éviter; *there is no means of doing it,* il n'y a pas moyen de le faire.—*n.* Non, *m. The ayes and the noes,* les voix pour et contre.
Noah ['nouə]. Noé, *m.*
nob [nɔb], *n.* (*colloq.*) Caboche, *f.*; gros bonnet, *m.*
nobble [nɔbl], *v.t.* (*fam.*) Acheter, corrompre; (*Turf*) droguer; écloper.
nobiliary [no'biliəri], *n.* Nobiliaire, *f.*
nobility [no'biliti], *n.* Noblesse, *f.*
noble [noubl], *n.* Noble, *m.*—*a.* Noble; illustre, magnifique, grand; généreux. *Noble deed,* action d'éclat, *f.* **nobleman,** *n.* Noble, gentilhomme, *m.* **nobleness,** *n.* Noblesse, *f.*

noblewoman, *n.* Femme noble, *f.* **nobly,** *adv.* Noblement; superbement.

nobody ['noubədi], *pron.* Personne, *m. I know nobody,* je ne connais personne; *nobody else,* personne d'autre; *nobody knows it,* personne ne le sait; *to be nobody,* ne pas compter; *who is there? nobody,* qui est là? personne.—*n.* Zéro, inconnu, *m.*

noctambulant [nɔk'tæmbjulənt], *a.* Noctambule. **noctambulism,** *n.* Noctambulisme, somnambulisme, *m.* **noctambulist,** *n.* Noctambule, somnambule, *m.*

noctiluca [nɔkti'luːkə], *n.* Noctiluque, *f.*

nocturnal [nɔk'təːnl], *a.* Nocturne, de nuit. **nocturnally,** *adv.* Nocturnement. **nocturne,** *n.* (*Mus.*) Nocturne, *m.*; (*Paint.*) effet de nuit, *m.*

nod [nɔd], *n.* Signe de tête, *m.*; inclination de tête, *f. The land of Nod,* le pays des rêves; *to give a nod,* faire signe que oui.—*v.i.* Faire un signe de tête; s'incliner; sommeiller (to be drowsy). *To nod to,* faire un signe de tête à.—*v.t.* Montrer par une inclination de tête. *To nod assent,* faire signe que oui. **nodding,** *a.* Penché, incliné; dodelinant. *To have a nodding acquaintance with,* connaître vaguement.

nodal [noudl], *a.* Nodal.

noddle [nɔdl], *n.* (*colloq.*) Caboche, tête, *f.*

noddy ['nɔdi], *n.* Sot, niais, *m.*

node [noud], *n.* Nœud, *m.*; (*Surg.*) nodus, *m.*

nodose [nou'dous], *a.* Noueux.

nodosity [nou'dɔsiti], *n.* Nodosité, *f.*

nodular ['nɔdjulə], *a.* Nodulaire. **nodule,** *n.* Nodule, rognon, *m.*

nog [nɔg], *n.* Cheville (de bois), *f.*—*v.t.* Cheviller.

noggin ['nɔgin], *n.* Petit pot (en étain); quart de pinte, *m.*

nohow ['nouhau], *adv.* En aucune façon, aucunement.

noise [nɔiz], *n.* Bruit; tapage, fracas, vacarme; tintement (ringing in the ears), bourdonnement (buzzing); (*fig.*) éclat, retentissement, *m. He is the big noise* (*pop.*), c'est le grand ponte; *to hold one's noise,* (*colloq.*) se taire; *to make a noise,* faire du bruit; *what a noise!* quel fracas! quel tapage!—*v.t.* Ébruiter, publier, répandre, crier sur les toits. *To be noised abroad,* se répandre au loin; *to noise abroad,* répandre au loin. **noiseless,** *a.* Sans bruit; silencieux. **noiselessly,** *adv.* Sans bruit; silencieusement. **noiselessness,** *n.* Silence, *m.* **noisily,** *adv.* Bruyamment. **noisiness,** *n.* Grand bruit; tapage, tintamarre, *m.*

noisome ['nɔisəm], *a.* Malsain, infect, nuisible. **noisomely,** *adv.* D'une manière nuisible. **noisomeness,** *n.* Nocivité; infection, *f.*

noisy ['nɔizi], *a.* Bruyant, tapageur; turbulent (of children). *To be noisy,* faire du bruit.

nomad ['noumæd], *n.* Nomade, *m.* **nomadic** [no'mædik], *a.* Nomade.

no-man's-land, *n.* Zone neutre, *f.*

nomenclator ['noumənkleitə], *n.* Nomenclateur, *m.* **nomenclature,** *n.* Nomenclature, *f.*

nominal ['nɔminl], *a.* Nominal; de nom. *Nominal roll,* état nominatif, *m.* **nominalism,** *n.* Nominalisme, *m.* **nominalist,** *n.* Nominaliste, *m.* **nominally,** *adv.* De nom; nommément, nominalement. **nominate,** *v.t.*

Nommer; désigner; présenter, proposer (a candidate etc.). **nomination** [-'neiʃən], *n.* Nomination; présentation, *f.* **nominative,** *a.* Au nominatif, nominatif.—*n.* (*Gram.*) Nominatif, sujet, *m.* **nominator,** *n.* Nominateur, *m.* **nominee** [-'niː], *n.* Personne nommée, *f.*; (*R.-C. Ch.*) nominataire, *m.* or *f.*; candidat choisi, *m.*

non-ability [nɔnə'biliti], *n.* Inhabilité, incapacité, *f.* **non-acceptance,** *n.* Non-acceptation, *f.* **non-acquaintance,** *n.* Ignorance, *f.* **non-admittance,** *n.* Refus d'admettre, *m.*

nonage ['nɔnidʒ], *n.* Minorité, *f.*

nonagenarian [nounədʒi'nɛəriən], *a.* and *n.* Nonagénaire.

non-aggression [nɔnə'greʃən], *a.* and *n.* Non-agression, *f.*

non-alcoholic [nɔnælkə'hɔlik], *a.* Non-alcoolique, sans alcool. **non-appearance,** *n.* (*Law*) Défaut (de comparution), *m.* **non-attendance,** *n.* Absence, *f.*

nonce [nɔns], *n.* Occasion, *f.*; dessein, *m. For the nonce,* pour le coup.

nonchalance ['nɔnʃələns], *n.* Nonchalance, *f.* **nonchalant,** *a.* Nonchalant. **nonchalantly,** *adv.* Nonchalamment.

non-combatant [nɔn'kʌmbətənt *or* -'kɔmbətənt], *a.* and *n.* Non-combattant, *m.* **non-commissioned** [-kə'miʃənd], *a.* Sans brevet. *Non-commissioned officer,* sous-officier. **non-committal,** *a.* Qui n'engage à rien, réservé, diplomatique. **non-completion,** *n.* Non-achèvement, *m.* **non-compliance,** *n.* Refus d'acquiescer, *m.* **non compos (mentis),** *a.* Aliéné, fou. **non-conducting,** *a.* Non-conducteur. **non-conductor,** *n.* Non-conducteur, *m.* **non-conformist,** *n.* and *a.* Dissident, non-conformiste, *m.* **nonconformity,** *n.* Dissidence, non-conformité, *f.* **non-delivery,** *n.* Non-livraison; non-réception, *f.*

nondescript ['nɔndiskript], *a.* Qu'on n'a pas décrit, indéfinissable, sans nom, quelconque. —*n.* Chose sans nom, chose indéfinissable, *f.*

none [nʌn], *pron.* Nul, *m.*, nulle, *f.*, aucun, *m.*, aucune, *f.*, pas un, *m.*, pas une, *f.*, personne, *m.*—*a.* and *adv.* Pas, point; néant (in schedules). *I have none,* je n'en ai pas; *I will have none,* je n'en veux pas; *none the less,* pas moins . . . pour cela; *none the more,* pas plus . . . pour cela.

nonentity [nɔ'nentiti], *n.* Non-existence, *f.*, néant, *m.*; (*fig.*) nullité, *f.*, zéro, *m.*

nones [nounz], *n.pl.* Nones, *f.pl.*

non-essential [nɔni'senʃəl], *a.* Qui n'est pas essentiel.

nonesuch ['nʌnsʌtʃ], *n.* Sans pareil, non-pareil.—*n.* Nonpareille (apple), *f.*

non-execution [nɔneksə'kjuːʃən], *n.* Inexécution, *f.* **non-existence,** *n.* Non-existence, *f.* **non-existent,** *a.* Qui n'existe pas.

non-ferrous, *a.* Non-ferreux.

non-inflammable, *a.* Ininflammable.

non-interference, **non-intervention,** *n.* Non-intervention, *f.*, laisser-faire, *m.*

nonius ['nouniəs], *n.* (*Astron.*) Nonius, vernier, *m.*

non-juror [nɔn'dʒuərə], *n.* Non-assermenté, *m.*, personne qui refuse de prêter serment de fidélité, *f.*

non-metallic, *a.* Non-métallique.
non-observance, *n.* Inobservation, *f.*
nonpareil [nɔnpə'rel], *a.* Nonpareil, sans égal.—*n.* (*Print. etc.*) Nonpareille, *f.*
non-payment [nɔn'peimənt], *n.* Non-payement, *m.*
non-performance, *n.* Inexécution, *f.*
nonplus (1) ['nɔnplʌs], *n.* Embarras, *m.*, perplexité, *f.* *At a nonplus*, à quia.
nonplus (2) [nɔn'plʌs], *v.t.* Embarrasser, interdire; mettre au pied du mur, mettre à quia. **nonplussed**, *a.* Embarrassé, dérouté.
non-professional [nɔnprə'feʃənl], *a.* Étranger à la profession; d'amateur.
non-residence, *n.* Non-résidence, *f.* **non-resident**, *a.* Non-résident, qui ne prend que les repas (in an hotel), externe (of a student); forain (of landlords).—*n.* Non-résident, *m.*
non-resistance, *n.* Obéissance passive; non-résistance, *f.*
nonsense ['nɔnsəns], *n.* Non-sens, *m.*; sottise, absurdité, *f.* *No nonsense!* pas de bêtises! *Nonsense!* allons donc! quelle sottise! *To talk nonsense*, dire des bêtises. **nonsensical** [-'sensikl], *a.* Vide de sens, absurde, qui n'a pas le sens commun. **nonsensically**, *adv.* Contre le sens commun, sottement, absurdement.
non-skid [nɔn'skid], *a.* Antidérapant. **non-smoker**, *n.* Non-fumeur; compartiment pour non-fumeurs, *m.*
non-stop ['nɔn'stɔp], *a. and adv.* Sans arrêt.
nonsuit ['nɔnsjuːt], *n.* (*Law*) Désistement; (jugement de) débouté; non-lieu, *m.*—*v.t.* Mettre hors de cour; débouter; rendre une ordonnance de non-lieu.
non-transferable [nɔn'trænsfərəbl], *a.* Personnel.
non-union [nɔn'juːniən], *a.* Non-syndiqué.
non-usage, *n.* Non-usage, *m.*
noodle [nuːdl], *n.* Nigaud, benêt, sot, *m.*; (*pl.*) (*Cook.*) nouilles, *f.pl.*
nook [nuk], *n.* Recoin, réduit, *m.* *Nooks and corners*, coins et recoins, *m.pl.*
noon [nuːn], *n.* Midi, *m.* *At noon*, en plein midi. **noonday**, *n.* Midi, *m.*—*a.* De midi. **noontide**, *n.* Heure de midi, *f.*, midi, *m.*
noose [nuːs], *n.* Nœud coulant, lacet, *m.*—*v.t.* Prendre au lacet, au collet, au lasso.
nopal [noupl], *n.* (*Bot.*) Nopal, *m.*
nor [nɔː], *conj.* Ni; ni . . . ne. *Neither he nor I*, ni lui ni moi; *nor could any soldier venture beyond*, aucun soldat ne pouvait d'ailleurs s'aventurer au delà; *nor I either*, ni moi non plus; *nor was he to*, et il ne devait pas non plus; *nor was this all*, et ce n'était pas tout; *nor you either*, ni vous non plus.
Nordic ['nɔːdik], *a.* Nordique.
norm [nɔːm], *n.* Norme, *f.*
normal [nɔːml], *a.* Normal. **normality**, *n.* Normalité, *f.* **normalize**, *v.t.* Normaliser. **normally**, *adv.* Normalement.
Norman ['nɔːmən], *a. and n.* Normand, *m.*, Normande, *f.* **Normandy**. La Normandie, *f.*
north [nɔːθ], *n.* Nord, septentrion, *m.*—*a.* Du nord, septentrional. *North star*, étoile polaire, *f.*; *north wind*, vent du nord, *m.*—*adv.* Au nord. **north-east**, *n.* Nord-est, *m.* **north-west**, *n.* Nord-ouest, *m.*
northerly ['nɔːðəli], *a.* Septentrional, du nord. —*adv.* Au nord, vers le nord. **northern**, *a.*

Du nord, septentrional. *Northern Ireland*, l'Irlande du nord, *f.* *Northern lights*, aurore boréale, *f.* **northerner**, *n.* Habitant du nord, *m.* **northernmost**, *a.* Le plus au nord.
northward (1) ['nɔːθwəd], *a.* Vers le nord, au nord.
northward (2) ['nɔːθwəd] or **northwards**, *adv.* Vers le nord, au nord.
Norway ['nɔːwei]. La Norvège, *f.*
Norwegian [nɔː'wiːdʒən], *a. and n.* Norvégien, *m.*, Norvégienne, *f.*; (*language*) le norvégien, *m.*
nose [nouz], *n.* Nez; museau (of animals); odorat (sense of smell); bouquet (of wine); tuyau (of bellows), *m.* *He scarcely sees what passes under his nose*, c'est à peine s'il voit ce qui se passe sous son nez; *pug-nose*, nez épaté, *m.*; *Roman nose*, nez aquilin, *m.*; *the cars were running nose to tail*, les voitures se touchaient; *the parson's nose*, le croupion; *to bleed at the nose*, saigner du nez; *to blow one's nose*, se moucher; *to blow someone's nose*, moucher quelqu'un; *to follow one's nose*, aller tout droit devant soi; *to lead by the nose*, mener par le bout du nez; *to pay through the nose*, payer un prix excessif, être salé; *to put someone's nose out of joint*, supplanter quelqu'un, mortifier quelqu'un; *to speak through one's nose*, parler du nez; *to thrust or poke one's nose into other people's business*, fourrer son nez où l'on n'a que faire; *to turn up one's nose at*, faire fi de; *turned-up nose*, nez retroussé.—*v.t.* Flairer. *To nose out*, flairer, éventer, dépister.—*v.i.* To nose about, fureter.
nose-bag, *n.* Musette mangeoire, musette (for horses etc.), *f.* **nose-band**, *n.* Muserolle (for horses etc.), *f.* **nose-bleed**, *n.* Saignement de nez, *m.* **nose-cap**, *n.* Embouchoir (for rifle), *m.* **nose-dive**, *v.i.* (*Av.*) Piquer du nez.—*n.* Piqué, *m.* **nosegay**, *n.* Bouquet, *m.* **nose-piece**, *n.* (*Tech.*) Bec, ajutage, *m.*; porte-objectifs (of microscope), *m.*
nosed, *a.* Au nez. *Flat-nosed*, au nez épaté; *snub-nosed*, qui a le nez camus. **noseless**, *a.* Sans nez.
nosography [no'sɔgrəfi], *n.* Nosographie, *f.*
nosologist, *n.* Nosologiste, *m.* **nosology**, *n.* Nosologie, *f.*
nostalgia [nɔs'tældʒə], *n.* Nostalgie, *f.*, mal du pays, *m.* **nostalgic**, *a.* Nostalgique.
nostril ['nɔstril], *n.* Narine, *f.*; naseau (of a horse etc.), *m.*
nostrum ['nɔstrəm], *n.* Panacée, *f.*, remède de charlatan, *m.*
nosy ['nouzi], *a.* (*pop.*) Fouinard.
not [nɔt], *adv.* Non; ne . . . pas, ne . . . point, pas, non pas; vraiment (expressing surprise). *Good or not*, bon ou non; *I do not see*, je ne vois pas; *I hope not*, j'espère que non; *is it not?* n'est-ce pas? *it is not any use my talking*, j'ai beau dire; *it is not so with*, il n'en est pas ainsi de; *not a little*, pas mal de; *not at all*, point du tout; *not but that*, non que, non pas que, ce n'est pas que (with subjunctive); *not even*, pas même; *not here*, pas ici; *thank you very much! not at all!* merci beaucoup! de rien *or* je vous en prie *or* il n'y a pas de quoi; *that is not in my line*, ce n'est pas de mon ressort; *why not?* pourquoi pas?
notability [nouta'biliti], *n.* Notabilité, *f.*

notable ['noutəbl], *a.* Notable, insigne; remarquable.—*n.* Notable, personnage important, *m.* **notably,** *adv.* Notamment (specially).

notarial [no'tɛəriəl], *a.* De notaire, notarial; notarié (done by a notary).

notary ['noutəri], *n.* Notaire, *m.* *Notary's business,* notariat, *m.*

notation [no'teiʃən], *n.* Notation; (*Math.*) numération écrite, *f.*

notch [nɔtʃ], *n.* Coche, encoche, entaille, brèche, *f.*; cran de mire, cran; œilleton (on tangent-sight), *m.*—*v.t.* Entailler, ébrécher. **notchboard,** *n.* Limon d'escalier, *m.*

note [nout], *n.* Note, marque, *f.*, signe, *m.*; lettre (letter), *f.*, billet, *m.*; remarque, marque (distinction), *f.*; (*Gram.*) point; (*fig.*) ton, accent, *m.* *Advice note,* lettre d'avis, *f.*; *bank-note,* billet de banque, *m.*; *credit note,* lettre de crédit, *f.*; *note of exclamation,* point d'exclamation, *m.*; *promissory note,* billet, bon, *m.*; *to take a note of,* prendre note de.—*v.t.* Noter, prendre note de; signaler, remarquer. **notebook,** *n.* Carnet, *m.* **note-case,** *n.* Portefeuille, *m.* **notepaper,** *n.* Papier à lettres, *m.*

noted, *a.* Distingué (person); célèbre (thing). **noteless,** *a.* Peu remarquable, obscur. **noteworthiness,** *n.* Importance, *f.* **noteworthy,** *a.* Remarquable, digne d'être remarqué.

nothing ['nʌθiŋ], *n.* Rien, néant, *m.* *A mere nothing,* un rien, une vétille; (*fig.*) un zéro.—*pron.* (Ne) . . . rien. *Do nothing of the kind,* gardez-vous-en bien; *good-for-nothing,* bon à rien; *next to nothing,* presque rien, rien qui vaille; *nothing at all,* rien du tout; *nothing could be easier,* rien de plus facile; *nothing doing* (pop.), rien à faire; *nothing else,* rien d'autre, pas autre chose; *nothing good,* rien de bon; *nothing if not amusing,* amusant avant tout; *nothing much,* pas grand'chose; *nothing of the kind,* rien de la sorte; *nothing venture nothing have,* qui ne risque rien n'a rien; *that is nothing to do with me,* cela ne me regarde pas; *there is nothing to boast of,* il n'y a pas de quoi se vanter; *there is nothing to laugh at,* il n'y a pas de quoi rire; *this pupil does nothing but talk,* cet élève ne fait que bavarder; *to come to nothing,* n'aboutir à rien; *to do nothing but,* ne faire que; *to go for nothing,* compter pour rien; *to make nothing of,* ne rien comprendre à, n'avoir aucune difficulté à; *worth nothing,* sans valeur, sans mérite.—*adv.* En rien, nullement, aucunement. *Nothing like as good,* loin d'être aussi bon. **nothingness,** *n.* Néant, rien, *m.*

notice ['noutis], *n.* Connaissance, observation; attention, *f.*; préavis, avis, *m.*, information; notice (article in a newspaper); (*Law*) notification, intimation, annonce (announcement in newspaper), affiche (bill), *f.* *A week's notice,* un préavis de huit jours. *At short notice,* à court délai; *at the shortest notice,* dans le plus bref délai; *biographical notice,* notice biographique, *f.*; *notice is hereby given that* . . ., vous êtes informé que . . .; *notice to pay,* avertissement, *m.*; *notice to quit,* congé, *m.*; *take notice!* avis! *to attract notice,* attirer l'attention, se faire remarquer; *to bring into notice,* faire connaître; *to come into notice,* se faire connaître; *to give notice,* donner avis,

avertir, notifier, donner congé, prévenir, (of servant) donner ses huit jours; *to take notice of,* faire attention à, remarquer, s'apercevoir de, avoir des prévenances pour; *until further notice,* jusqu'à nouvel ordre; *without a moment's notice,* immédiatement; *you are beneath our notice,* vous ne méritez pas que l'on vous réponde.—*v.t.* Prendre connaissance de, s'apercevoir de, remarquer; faire attention à; avoir des égards pour.

noticeable, *a.* Perceptible. **noticeably,** *adv.* Perceptiblement, sensiblement. **notice-board,** *n.* Écriteau; tableau (d'affichage); panneau indicateur (on roads), *m.*

notification [noutifi'keiʃən], *n.* Notification, *f.*, avis, avertissement, *m.*

notify ['noutifai], *v.t.* Faire savoir, notifier.

notion ['nouʃən], *n.* Notion, idée; prétention, *f.* *He has no notion of going away,* il n'a pas l'intention de s'en aller; *the extravagant notion they entertain of themselves,* la haute opinion qu'ils ont d'eux-mêmes. **notional,** *a.* Spéculatif; imaginaire; capricieux.

notoriety [noutə'raiəti], *n.* Notoriété, *f.*

notorious [no'tɔːriəs], *a.* Notoire, insigne (infamous). *A notorious rogue,* un fameux coquin. **notoriously,** *adv.* Notoirement. **notoriousness,** *n.* Notoriété, *f.*

notwithstanding [nɔtwið'stændiŋ], *prep.* Malgré, nonobstant, en dépit de.—*adv.* Néanmoins.

nougat ['nuːgɑː], *n.* Nougat, *m.*

nought [NAUGHT].

noun [naun], *n.* Nom, substantif, *m.* *Noun clause,* proposition substantive, *f.*; *proper noun,* nom propre, *m.*

nourish ['nʌriʃ], *v.t.* Nourrir, alimenter; (*fig.*) entretenir, encourager, fomenter. **nourishing,** *a.* Nourrissant, nutritif. **nourishment,** *n.* Nourriture, alimentation, *f.*

nous [naus], *n.* Intelligence, *f.*; sens commun, *m.*

Nova Scotia ['nouvə'skouʃə]. La Nouvelle-Écosse, *f.*

novel [nɔvl], *a.* Nouveau, original.—*n.* Roman, *m.*

novelette [nɔvə'let], *n.* Nouvelle (short), *f.*; roman rose, *m.* **novelist** or **novel-writer,** *n.* Romancier, *m.*

novelty ['nɔvəlti], *n.* Nouveauté, *f.*

November [no'vembə], *n.* Novembre, *m.*

novercal [no'vəːkl], *a.* De marâtre, *f.*

novice ['nɔvis], *n.* Novice, *m.* or *f.*

novitiate [nə'viʃiət], *n.* Noviciat, *m.*

novocaine ['nouvəkein], *n.* (*Pharm.*) Novo-caïne, *f.*

now [nau], *adv.* Maintenant, à présent, actuellement; alors, or, donc (in argument). *Before now,* déjà; *five days from now,* d'ici cinq jours; *from now on,* dès maintenant; *just now,* tout à l'heure, à l'instant; *now and then,* de temps en temps; *now . . . now,* tantôt . . . tantôt; *now or never,* c'est le cas ou jamais; *now's the time,* voici le moment; *now then, are you going to be quiet?* eh bien! allez-vous rester tranquille? *now the state of affairs was critical,* la situation était critique; *right now* (*Am.*), tout de suite, immédiatement; *till now,* jusqu'ici.

nowadays, *adv.* Aujourd'hui, de nos jours, à l'heure actuelle, par le temps qui court.

nowhere ['nouhwɛə], *adv.* Nulle part. *To be nowhere* (race, examination), être bien battu.

nowise ['nouwaiz], *adv.* En aucune manière, nullement.

noxious ['nɔkʃəs], *a.* Nuisible, malfaisant. **noxiously**, *adv.* D'une manière nuisible. **noxiousness**, *n.* Qualité nuisible, nocivité, *f.*

nozzle [nɔzl], *n.* Nez; bec, bout; (*Motor. etc.*) ajutage, *m.*; lance (de tuyau), *f.*

nub [nʌb], *n.* Petit morceau, *m.*; *bosse, *f.*; essentiel, noyau (of the matter), *m.*

nubile ['nju·bil], *a.* Nubile. **nubility** [-'biliti], *n.* Nubilité, *f.*

nuclear ['nju:kliə], *a.* Nucléaire. *Nuclear fission*, fission de l'atome, *f.*; *nuclear war*, guerre atomique, *f.* **nucleus**, *n.* Noyau, *m.*

nude [nju:d], *a.* Nu. *Nude figure*, académie, *f.* —*n.* Le nu, *m.* **nudist**, *n.* Nudiste, *m.* or *f.* *Nudist camp*, camp de nudistes, *m.* **nudity**, *n.* Nudité, *f.*

nudge [nʌdʒ], *n.* Coup de coude, *m.*—*v.t.* Donner un coup de coude à, pousser du coude.

nugatory ['nju:gətəri], *a.* Futile, frivole; nul.

nugget ['nʌgit], *n.* Pépite, *f.*

nuisance ['nju:səns], *n.* Peste, plaie, *f.*, fléau, ennui, désagrément, tourment, *m.*; ordures, *f.pl.*; (*Law*) dommage, *m.* *Commit no nuisance*, défense d'uriner; *he is a nuisance to*, c'est une peste pour; *what a nuisance!* comme c'est ennuyeux!

null [nʌl], *a.* Nul. *Null and void*, nul et non avenu.

nullification [nʌlifi'keiʃən], *n.* Annulation, *f.*

nullify ['nʌlifai], *v.t.* Infirmer, annuler.

nullity ['nʌliti], *n.* Nullité, *f.* *The sentence was treated as a nullity*, la sentence fut regardée comme nulle et non avenue.

numb [nʌm], *a.* Engourdi, transi.—*v.t.* Engourdir (par).

number ['nʌmbə], *n.* Nombre; chiffre (figure), *m.*; quantité, *f.*; numéro (of things in succession, as houses etc.), *m.*; livraison (of publications); harmonie, *f.*, vers, *m.*; (*fig.*, *pl.*) nombres, *m.pl.* *A number of*, un certain nombre de, plusieurs, une foule de (gens); *cardinal, ordinal, odd*, *or even number*, nombre cardinal, ordinal, impair, *or* pair; *days without number*, des jours innombrables; *in great numbers*, en grand nombre; *in numbers*, par livraisons (of books etc.); *one of our number*, un des nôtres; *the superiority of numbers*, l'avantage du nombre; *twelve in number*, au nombre de douze; *your number is up!* (*iron.*) tu as gagné! ton compte est bon.—*v.t.* Compter, mettre au nombre de; numéroter (things in succession). *He was numbered with the dead*, il fut mis au nombre des morts; *I number him among my friends*, je le compte parmi mes amis; *the army numbered 50,000 men*, l'armée se montait à 50.000 hommes.—*v.i.* (*Mil.*) Se numéroter.

number-board, *n.* Tableau d'affichage, *m.* **number-plate**, *n.* (*Motor.*) Plaque d'immatriculation *or* minéralogique, *f.*

numbering, *n.* Supputation, *f.*, numérotage, *m.* **numbering-machine**, *n.* Machine à numéroter, *f.* **numbering-stamp**, *n.* Numéroteur, *m.*

numberless, *a.* Sans nombre, innombrable.

numbness ['nʌmnis], *n.* Engourdissement, *m.*

numbskull [NUMSKULL].

numerable ['nju:mərəbl], *a.* Qu'on peut compter, nombrable.

numeral ['nju:mərəl], *a.* Numéral.—*n.* Lettre numérale, *f.*, chiffre, *m.* **numerally**, *adv.* Numériquement. **numerary**, *a.* Numéral.

numeration [-'reiʃən], *n.* Numération, *f.*

numerator ['nju:məreitə], *n.* Numérateur, *m.* **numerical** [-'merikl], *a.* Numérique. **numerically**, *adv.* Numériquement.

numerous ['nju:mərəs], *a.* Nombreux. **numerously**, *adv.* En grand nombre. **numerousness**, *n.* Grand nombre, *m.*; cadence, harmonie, *f.*; nombre, *m.*

numismatic [nju:miz'mætik], *a.* Numismatique. **numismatics**, *n.pl.*, or **numismatology** [-mə'tɔlədʒi], *n.* Numismatique, *f.* **numismatist** [-'mizmətist], *n.* Numismate, *m.*

nummulite ['nʌmjulait], *n.* Nummulite, *f.*

numskull ['nʌmskʌl], *n.* Benêt, idiot, *m.*

nun [nʌn], *n.* Religieuse, (*fam.*) nonne, *f.*

nunciature ['nʌnʃiətjə], *n.* Nonciature, *f.*

nuncio ['nʌnʃiou], *n.* Nonce, *m.*

nuncupative ['nʌnkjupeitiv], *a.* Nuncupatif.

nunnery ['nʌnəri], *n.* Couvent (de religieuses), *m.*

nuptial ['nʌpʃəl], *a.* Nuptial, de noces. **nuptials**, *n.pl.* Noces, *f.pl.*

nurse [nə:s], *n.* Nourrice (for infants); bonne d'enfant, *f.*; garde-malade (for the sick), *m.* or *f.*; infirmier, *m.*, infirmière, *f.* (in hospitals). *Monthly nurse*, garde (d'accouchée), *f.*; *to put out to nurse*, mettre en nourrice; *wet nurse*, nourrice, *f.*—*v.t.* Allaiter; nourrir, élever; soigner, garder (the sick); (*fig.*) entretenir, ménager, dorloter. **nurse-maid**, *n.* Bonne d'enfant, *f.*

nursery ['nə:səri], *n.* Chambre des enfants; (*Hort.*) pépinière; magnanerie (of silkworms), *f.* *Nursery rhyme*, chanson d'enfants, *f.*; *nursery tale*, conte d'enfants, *m.* **nursery-garden**, *n.* Pépinière, *f.* **nursery-maid**, *n.* Bonne d'enfant, *f.* **nursery-man**, *n.* (*pl.* -men) Pépiniériste, *m.* **nursery-school**, *n.* École maternelle, *f.* **nursey**, *n.* Nounou (childish).

nursing ['nə:siŋ], *n.* Allaitement, *m.*; soins, *m.pl.*—*a.* Nourricier. **nursing-home**, *n.* Clinique, maison de santé, *f.* **nursling**, *n.* Nourrisson, *m.*

nurture ['nə:tʃə], *n.* Nourriture; éducation, *f.*—*v.t.* Nourrir; élever.

nut [nʌt], *n.* Noix, noisette (hazel-nut), *f.*; écrou (of a screw), *m.*; (*colloq.*) tête, caboche, *f.*; (*colloq.*) élégant, petit-maître, *m.* *A poor nut*, un pauvre sot. *A nut to crack*, du fil à retordre; *lock-nut*, contre-écrou, *m.*; *to be off (dead) one's nut* or *to be nuts*, être toqué.—*v.i.* Cueillir des noisettes. *To go nutting*, aller cueillir la noisette.

nutation [nju'teiʃən], *n.* Nutation, *f.*

nut-brown, *a.* Châtain, brun. **nut-cracker**, *n.* Casse-noix (bird), *m.*; casse-noisettes, *m.* **nuthatch**, *n.* Sittelle; *f.*; pic-maçon, *m.* (bird). **nutmeg**, *n.* Muscade, *f.* **nutmeg-tree**, *n.* Muscadier, *m.* **nutshell**, *n.* Coquille de noix, *f.* *To put it in a nutshell*, se résumer en un mot. **nut-tree**, *n.* Noisetier, *m.*

nutrient ['nju:triənt], *a.* Nourrissant.

nutriment ['nju:trimənt], *n.* Nourriture, *f.*

nutrition [nju'triʃən], *n.* Nutrition; alimentation, *f.* **nutritional**, *a.* Alimentaire.

nutritious [nju'triʃəs] or **nutritive** ['njuːtritiv], *a*. Nourrissant, nutritif.

nutty, *a*. Qui a un goût de noisette; savoureux; (*pop*.) fêlé, toqué.

nux vomica [nʌks'vɔmikə], *n*. Noix vomique, *f*.

nuzzle [nʌzl], *v.i.* Fouiller (avec le groin) (of pig); fourrer son nez contre (of dog, horse, etc.); (*fig*.) se blottir contre.

nyctalopia [niktə'loupiə], *n*. Nyctalopie, *f*.

nylon ['nailɔn], *n*. Nylon, *m*.

nymph [nimf], *n*. Nymphe, *f*.

nymphaea [nim'fiːə], *n*. (*Bot*.) Nymphée, *f*.

nymphean [nim'fiːən], *a*. De nymphe.

nymphlike, *a*. Comme une nymphe.

nymphomania [-o'meiniə], *n*. Nymphomanie, *f*. **nymphomaniac,** *n*. Nymphomane, *f*.

O

O, o [ou]. Quinzième lettre de l'alphabet, *m*. *An O,* un zéro, *m*.

O, oh [ou], *int*. *O! oh! O dear!* aïe!

oaf [ouf], *n*. *Enfant de fée; idiot, imbécile (dolt), *m*. **oafish,** *a*. Stupide, idiot, lourdaud. **oafishness,** *n*. Stupidité, *f*.

oak [ouk], *n*. Chêne; bois de chêne, *m*. *Holm-oak,* yeuse, *f*., chêne vert, *m*. **oaken,** *a*. De chêne.

oak-apple, *n*. Pomme de chêne, *f*. **oak-gall,** *n*. Noix de galle, *f*. **oak-grove,** *n*. Chênaie, *c*. **oakling,** *n*. Jeune chêne, *m*. **oak-tree,** *n*. Chêne, *m*.—*a*. De chêne.

oakum ['oukəm], *n*. Étoupe, *f*. *To pick oakum,* faire de l'étoupe.

oar [ɔː], *n*. Aviron, *m*., rame, *f*., aviron de pointe, *m*. *Stroke oar,* aviron de nage, *m*.; *to unship the oars,* désarmer.—*v.i.* Ramer, tirer en pointe. **oared,** *a*. À avirons. *Eight-oared boat,* un huit de pointe, *m*. **oarsman,** *n*. (*pl*. **oarsmen**) Rameur (de pointe), *m*. **oars-manship,** *n*. Art de ramer, l'aviron, *m*.

oasis [ou'eisis], *n*. (*pl*. **oases**) Oasis, *f*.

oast [oust], *n*. Four à houblon, *m*. **oasthouse,** *n*. Sécherie à houblon, *f*.

oat [OATS].

oatcake ['outkeik], *n*. Galette d'avoine, *f*.

oaten ['outən], *a*. D'avoine.

oath [ouθ], *n*. Serment; juron, *m*. *On oath, on one's oath,* sous serment; *to break one's oath,* fausser son serment, se parjurer; *to put on his oath,* faire prêter serment à; *to rap out an oath,* lâcher un juron; *to swear an oath,* faire un serment; *to take an oath,* prêter serment; *tremendous oath,* gros juron, *m*.; *volley of oaths,* bordée de jurons, *f*. **oath-breaking,** *n*. Parjure, *m*.

oatmeal ['outmiːl], *n*. Farine d'avoine, *f*.

oats [outs], *n.pl*. Avoine, *f*.; (wild) folle avoine, *f*. *To be off one's oats,* être mal en train; *to feel one's oats,* être tout guilleret; *to sow one's wild oats,* jeter sa gourme.

obduracy ['ɔbdjurəsi], *n*. Endurcissement, entêtement, *m*.; impénitence, *f*. **obdurate,** *a*. Endurci, obstiné, opiniâtre; impénitent. **obdurately,** *adv*. Obstinément, avec endurcissement.

obedience [o'biːdjəns], *n*. Obéissance, soumission, *f*. *In obedience to,* par obéissance à; *to give obedience to,* obéir à. **obedient,** *a*. Obéissant, soumis. *Your obedient servant* (from officials), Croyez, M., à mes sentiments dévoués. **obediently,** *adv*. Avec obéissance.

obeisance [o'beisəns], *n*. Révérence, *f*., salut, *m*.; obéissance, *f*.

obelisk ['ɔbəlisk], *n*. Obélisque, *m*.; (*Print*.) croix, *f*.

obese [o'biːs], *a*. Obèse. **obeseness** or **obesity** [o'biːsiti], *n*. Obésité, *f*.

obey [o'bei], *v.t*. Obéir à; (*Law*) obtempérer à.—*v.i*. Obéir.

obfuscate ['ɔbfʌskeit], *v.t*. Offusquer, obscurcir. **obfuscation** [-'keiʃən], *n*. Offuscation, *f*.

obituary [ɔ'bitjuəri], *a*. Obituaire; nécrologique.—*n*. Nécrologie, *f*. *Obituary notice,* notice nécrologique, *f*.

object (1) ['ɔbdʒikt], *n*. Objet, *m*.; chose, matière, *f*.; (aim) but, *m*.; considération, *f*.; (*Gram*.) régime; (*colloq*.) objet effrayant, *m*., horreur, *f*. *He will not gain his object,* il n'atteindra pas son but; *money is no object,* l'argent ne compte pas; *the object aimed at,* le point de mire, *m*.; *what an object you are! comme vous voilà fait! with the object of,* dans le but de.

object (2) [ɔb'dʒekt], *v.t*. Objecter; opposer. —*v.i*. Faire objection (à); s'opposer (à); se refuser (à); répugner (à). *Do you object to having the door shut?* vous opposez-vous à ce que la porte soit fermée?

object-glass, *n*. Objectif, *m*. **object-lesson,** *n*. Leçon de choses, *f*.; exemple, modèle, *m*.

objection [ɔb'dʒekʃən], *n*. Objection, *f*.; obstacle, *m*.; (*Racing*) contestation, *f*. *Have you any objection?* vous opposez-vous? *I have a great objection to that man,* cet homme me répugne; *I have no objection,* je ne m'y oppose nullement, je le veux bien; je ne demande pas mieux; *I see no objection to,* je ne vois pas d'inconvénient à; *to raise all sorts of objections,* élever toutes sortes d'objections. **objectionable,** *a*. Déplaisant, répugnant, inadmissible. *Objectionable language,* langage répréhensible, *m*.; propos choquants, *m.pl*.

objective [ɔb'dʒektiv], *a*. Objectif. *Objective case,* régime direct, *m*.—*n*. Objectif, but; (*Gram*.) régime, *m*. **objectively,** *adv*. Objectivement. **objectiveness** or **objectivity** [-'tiviti], *n*. Objectivité, *f*.

objector [ɔb'dʒektə], *n*. Protestataire, *m*. *Conscientious objector,* objecteur de conscience, *m*.

objurgation [ɔbdʒəː'geiʃən], *n*. Objurgation, *f*. **objurgatory** [-'dʒəːgətəri], *a*. Objurgatoire.

oblate (1) ['ɔbleit], *n*. Oblat, *m*.

oblate (2) [ob'leit], *a*. (*Geom*.) Aplati (vers les pôles). **oblateness,** *n*. Aplatissement, *m*.

oblation [ɔ'bleiʃən], *n*. Oblation, offrande, *f*.

obligation [ɔbli'geiʃən], *n*. Obligation, *f*.; engagement, *m*. *To be under an obligation to,* avoir de l'obligation à; (*Comm*.) *to honour one's obligations,* faire honneur à ses engagements; *to lay under an obligation,* obliger; *under an obligation to,* dans l'obligation de, tenu de; *without obligation* (*Comm*.), sans engagement. **obligatory** [ɔ'bligətəri], *a*. Obligatoire, de rigueur.

oblige [ɔ'blaidʒ], *v.t*. Obliger; faire plaisir à; astreindre (de or à). *I shall be very much* *obliged to you*, je vous serai très obligé (de); *oblige me by not saying anything about it*, faites-moi le plaisir de n'en rien dire; *oblige me with*, ayez l'obligeance de me donner. **obligee** [ɔbli'dʒi:], *n.* (*Law*) Obligataire, *m.* or *f.* **obliger** [ɔ'blaidʒə], *n.* Personne qui oblige, *f.* **obliging**, *a.* Obligeant. **obligingly**, *adv.* Obligeamment. **obligingness**, *n.* Obligeance, *f.* **obligor** [ɔbli'gɔ:], *n.* (*Law*) Débiteur, *m.*, débitrice, *f.* **oblique** [o'bli:k], *a.* Oblique; indirect. *Oblique dealings*, procédés détournés, *m.pl.*; *oblique fire*, tir d'écharpe, *m.* **obliquely**, *adv.* Obliquement; indirectement, d'une manière détournée. *To fire obliquely*, battre (or prendre) d'écharpe. **obliqueness** or **obliquity** [-'blikwiti], *n.* Obliquité, *f.* **obliterate** [o'blitəreit], *v.t.* Effacer, oblitérer. **obliteration** [-'reiʃən], *n.* Rature, oblitération, *f.*, effaçage, *m.* **oblivion** [o'bliviən], *n.* Oubli, *m.* *Act of oblivion*, loi d'amnistie, *f.* **oblivious**, *a.* Oublieux (de). *To be totally oblivious of*, ignorer tout à fait. **oblong** ['ɔblɔŋ], *a.* Oblong.—*n.* Rectangle, *m.* **obloquy** ['ɔbləkwi], *n.* Calomnie, *f.*, reproche malveillant, blâme; déshonneur, *m.*, honte, *f.* **obnoxious** [ɔb'nɔkʃəs], *a.* Odieux, désagréable, déplaisant; *sujet, exposé (liable) (à). **obnoxiously**, *adv.* D'une manière déplaisante, odieusement. **obnoxiousness**, *n.* Caractère désagréable, *m.* **oboe** ['ouboi or 'oubou], *n.* Hautbois, *m.* **oboist**, *n.* Hautboïste, *m.* or *f.* **obolus** ['ɔbələs] or **obol** ['ɔbəl], *n.* Obole, *f.* **obscene** [ɔb'si:n], *a.* Obscène, sale. **obscenely**, *adv.* D'une manière obscène. **obsceneness** or **obscenity** [-'si:niti], *n.* Obscénité, *f.* **obscurantism** [ɔbskjuə'ræntizm], *n.* Obscurantisme, *m.* **obscurantist**, *a.* and *n.* Obscurantiste. **obscuration** [ɔbskjuə'reiʃən], *n.* Obscurcissement, *m.*; (*Astron.*) obscuration, *f.* **obscure** [ɔb'skjuə], *a.* Obscur; (*fig.*) caché.— *v.t.* Obscurcir; voiler (lights). **obscurely**, *adv.* Obscurément. **obscurity**, *n.* Obscurité, *f.* **obsequies** ['ɔbsikwiz], *n.pl.* Obsèques, *f.pl.* **obsequious** [ɔb'si:kwiəs], *a.* Obséquieux, soumis. **obsequiously**, *adv.* Obséquieusement. **obsequiousness**, *n.* Soumission obséquieuse, *f.* **observable** [ɔb'zə:vəbl], *a.* À observer, observable, sensible; remarquable. **observably**, *adv.* Sensiblement. **observance**, *n.* Observance; pratique, observation, *f. Duties more honoured in their breach than in their observance*, devoirs plus souvent négligés que remplis. **observant**, *a.* Observateur, attentif à observer. *He is very observant*, rien ne lui échappe; *we know how observant he was of his master*, on sait avec quel respect il traitait son précepteur. **observation** [-'veiʃən], *n.* Observation, *f.*; remarque, *f. Observation post*, poste d'observation, *m.*; (*Naut.*) *to take an observation*, faire le point. **observatory**, *n.* Observatoire, *m.* **observe** [ɔb'zə:v], *v.t.* Observer; remarquer, apercevoir; faire remarquer. **observer**, *n.* Observateur, *m.*, -trice, *f.* **observing**, *f.*

Observateur. **observingly**, *adv.* Attentivement. **obsess** [ɔb'ses], *v.t.* Obséder. **obsessed**, *a.* Obsédé. **obsession**, *n.* Obsession, *f.* **obsidian** [ɔb'sidiən], *n.* Obsidiane, obsidienne, *f.* **obsolescence** [ɔbsə'lesəns], *n.* État de ce qui vieillit, vieillissement, *m.* **obsolescent**, *a.* Vieillissant, qui vieillit, qui tombe en désuétude (of laws etc.). **obsolete** ['ɔbsəli:t], *a.* Vieilli, suranné; tombé en désuétude. **obsoleteness**, *n.* Désuétude, *f.* **obstacle** ['ɔbstəkl], *n.* Obstacle, empêchement, *m.*, difficulté, *f.* **obstetric** [ɔb'stetrik] or **obstetrical**, *a.* Obstétrical. **obstetrician** [-sti'triʃən], *n.* Accoucheur, *m.* **obstetrics**, *n.pl.* Obstétrique, *f.* **obstinacy** ['ɔbstinəsi] or **obstinateness**, *n.* Obstination, opiniâtreté, *f.*; entêtement (of character); acharnement (of a struggle), *m.* **obstinate**, *a.* Obstiné, opiniâtre, entêté; têtu (of children); acharné (of combats). **obstinately**, *adv.* Obstinément; opiniâtrement; avec acharnement. **obstreperous** [ɔb'strepərəs], *a.* Turbulent, tapageur; récalcitrant. **obstreperously**, *adv.* Avec turbulence; d'une manière bruyante. **obstreperousness**, *n.* Turbulence, *f.* **obstruct** [ɔb'strʌkt], *v.t.* Empêcher, mettre obstacle à, retarder; obstruer, encombrer, boucher. *A cloud obstructs the light of the sun*, un nuage intercepte la lumière du soleil; *obstruct the view*, gêner la vue. **obstruction**, *n.* Empêchement, obstacle, *m.*; (*Med., Polit.*) obstruction, *f.*; (traffic) encombrement, *m.* **obstructive**, *a.* Qui empêche, qui obstrue; (*Med.*) obstructif. **obtain** [ɔb'tein], *v.t.* Obtenir, gagner; se procurer.—*v.i.* Prévaloir, s'établir, avoir cours. **obtainable**, *a.* Qu'on peut obtenir, procurable. **obtainment**, *n.* Action d'obtenir, obtention, *f.* **obtrude** [ɔb'tru:d], *v.t.* Imposer.—*v.i.* S'introduire de force; être importun. **obtruder**, *n.* Importun, *m.* **obtrusion** [ɔb'tru:ʒən], *n.* Introduction forcée; importunité, *f.* **obtrusive**, *a.* Importun. **obtrusively**, *adv.* D'une manière importune, indiscrètement. **obtrusiveness**, *n.* Importunité, *f.* **obturate** ['ɔbtjureit], *v.t.* Obturer. **obturation** [ɔbtju'reiʃən], *n.* Obturation, *f.* **obturator** [-'reitə], *n.* Obturateur, *m.* **obtuse** [ɔb'tju:s], *a.* Obtus; émoussé; stupide. **obtusangular** or **obtusangled**, *a.* Obtusangle. **obtusely**, *adv.* D'une manière obtuse, obtusément; (*fig.*) stupidement. **obtuseness**, *n.* État émoussé, *m.*; (*fig.*) stupidité, *f.* **obverse** (1) [ɔb'və:s], *a.* Obvers, obverse; (*Bot.*) obcordé. **obverse** (2) ['ɔbvə:s], *n.* Face, *f.*, avers, obvers (of medals, coins, etc.), *m.* **obviate** ['ɔbvieit], *v.t.* Éviter, obvier à, parer à. **obvious** ['ɔbviəs], *a.* Évident, clair, qui saute aux yeux. *It is not quite so obvious as you imagine*, la chose est loin d'être aussi claire que vous l'imaginez; *it is quite obvious that he has changed his mind*, il est évident qu'il a changé d'avis; *obvious fact*, fait patent. **obviously**, *adv.* Évidemment, visiblement. **obviousness**, *n.* Évidence, clarté, *f.*

occasion [ə'keiʒən], *n.* Occasion, occurrence, rencontre; raison, cause, *f.*, sujet, motif; besoin (need), *m. For the occasion,* pour la circonstance; *on all occasions,* en toute occasion; *on another occasion,* une autre fois; *on occasion,* à l'occasion, de temps en temps, au besoin; *on the first occasion,* à la première occasion; *on the occasion of . . .,* à l'occasion de . . .; *on this occasion,* à cette occasion, dans cette circonstance; *should the occasion arise,* le cas échéant; *there is no occasion for,* il n'y a pas besoin de; *to profit by the occasion,* profiter de l'occasion; *to rise to the occasion,* se montrer à la hauteur des circonstances; *what occasion is there for so much secrecy?* quelle nécessité y a-t-il d'un si grand secret? —*v.t.* Occasionner, causer, produire. **occasional,** *a.* Occasionnel, intermittent, casuel, fortuit. *Occasional chair,* chaise volante, *f.*; *occasional poem,* poème de circonstance, *m.* **occasionally,** *adv.* Quelquefois, occasionnellement, parfois, de temps en temps.
occident ['ɔksidənt], *n.* Occident, *m.* **occidental** [-'dentl], *a.* Occidental.
occipital [ɔk'sipitl], *a.* Occipital.
occiput ['ɔksipʌt], *n.* Occiput, *m.*
occlude [ɔ'klu:d], *v.t.* Boucher, obstruer; occlure.
occult [ɔ'kʌlt], *a.* Occulte.—*v.t.* (*Astron.*) Occulter. **occultation** [-'teiʃən], *n.* Occultation, *f.* **occultly,** *adv.* Occultement. **occultness,** *n.* Secret, *m.*
occupancy ['ɔkjupənsi], *n.* Occupation, *f.* **occupant,** *n.* Occupant, habitant; locataire (tenant); titulaire (of a post), *m.* **occupation** [-'peiʃən], *n.* Occupation, *f.*; emploi, état, métier, *m.*; possession, *f.* **occupational,** *a.* Professionnel. *Occupational disease,* maladie professionnelle, *f.*; *occupational therapy,* thérapie rééducative, *f.*
occupier ['ɔkjupaiə], *n.* Occupant; locataire (tenant), habitant, *m.*, habitante, *f. First occupier,* premier occupant, *m.*
occupy ['ɔkjupai], *v.t.* Occuper; employer; habiter (a house etc.). *To be occupied in* or *with,* s'occuper de or à.
occur [ə'kə:], *v.i.* Se présenter, se rencontrer, se trouver; survenir, arriver, se produire. *An accident has occurred to me,* il m'est arrivé un accident; *a thought occurred to me,* une pensée me vint à l'esprit; *it occurred to me that,* l'idée m'est venue que; *that won't occur again,* cela n'arrivera plus.
occurrence [ə'kʌrəns], *n.* Occurrence, rencontre, *f.*, événement, *m. It is an everyday occurrence,* cela se voit tous les jours.
ocean ['ouʃən], *n.* Océan, *m. He has oceans of money,* il est tout cousu d'or.—*a.* De l'océan. **ocean-going,** *a.* De long cours. *Ocean-going steamer,* long courrier, *m.*
Oceanian [ouʃi'einiən], *a.* and *n.* Océanien.
oceanic [ouʃi'ænik], *a.* Océanique.
oceanographic [ouʃiənɔ'græfik], *a.* Océanographique. **oceanography** [-'nɔgrəfi], *n.* Océanographie, *f.*
ocellate [o'selət], *a.* Ocellé. **ocellus** [o'seləs], *n.* (*pl.* **ocelli**) Ocelle, *m.*
ocelot ['ousilɔt], *n.* Ocelot, *m.*
ochlocracy [ɔk'lɔkrəsi], *n.* Ochlocratie, *f.*
ochre ['oukə], *n.* Ocre, *f.*
ochreous ['oukriəs], *a.* Ocreux.
o'clock [CLOCK].

octagon ['ɔktəgən], *n.* Octogone, *m.* **octagonal** [-'tægənəl], *a.* Octogone, octogonal.
octahedron [ɔktə'hi:drən], *n.* Octaèdre, *m.*
octandria [ɔk'tændriə], *n.* (*Bot.*) Octandrie, *f.*
octane ['ɔktein], *n.* Octane, *m. High-octane fuel,* supercarburant, *m.*
octangular [ɔk'tæŋgjulə], *a.* Octogone.
octant ['ɔktənt], *n.* Octant, *m.*
octave ['ɔktiv], *n.* (*Mus., Eccles.*) Octave, *f.*
octavo [ɔk'teivou], *n.* In-octavo, *m.*
octennial [ɔk'tenjəl], *a.* De huit ans. **octennially,** *adv.* Tous les huit ans.
octet(te) [ɔk'tet], *n.* (*Mus.*) Octuor, *m.*
October [ɔk'toubə], *n.* Octobre, *m.*
octogenarian [ɔktoudʒi'neəriən], *a.* and *n.* Octogénaire, *m.* or *f.*
octopus ['ɔktəpəs], *n.* Pieuvre, *f.*
octoroon [ɔktə'ru:n], *n.* Octavon, *m.*
octosyllabic [ɔktosi'læbik], *a.* Octosyllabe, octosyllabique. **octosyllable** [-'siləbl], *n.* Mot octosyllabe, *m.*
octuple ['ɔktjupl], *a.* Octuple.—*v.t.* Octupler.
ocular ['ɔkjulə], *a.* Oculaire. **ocularly,** *adv.* De ses propres yeux. **oculist,** *n.* Oculiste, *m.*
odd [ɔd], *a.* Impair, de surplus, de reste, quelques (surplus); d'appoint (of money); déparié (not fellows); dépareillé (of books etc.); (*fig.*) étrange, singulier, bizarre. *Odd fish,* drôle de corps, *m.*; *odd job man,* factotum, *m.*; *odd man out,* éliminé; *odd moments,* moments perdus, *m.pl.*; *odd number,* nombre impair; *the odd game,* la belle; *thirty pounds odd,* trente et quelques livres; *to make up the odd money,* faire l'appoint. **oddity,** *n.* Bizarrerie, *f.*; original, *m.*, originale (person), *f. He is a great oddity,* c'est un original s'il en fut jamais. **odd-looking,** *a.* À la mine bizarre. **oddly,** *adv.* Étrangement, singulièrement; bizarrement. **oddments,** *n.pl.* Bric-à-brac, *m.*, fins de séries, *f.pl.* **oddness,** *n.* Singularité, *f.* **odds,** *n.pl.* Inégalité, disparité, *f.*; (*fig.*) avantage, *m.*, supériorité, *f.*; chances, *f.pl.*; dispute, querelle (quarrel), *f. It makes no odds,* cela ne fait rien; *odds and ends,* petits bouts, *m.pl.*, bric-à-brac, *m.*; (*Racing*) odds on, cote, *f.* (of a horse); *the odds are,* il y a à parier (que); *to be at odds with,* être mal avec; *to have the odds against one,* avoir toutes les chances contre soi; *to set at odds,* brouiller; *what odds is that to me?* qu'est-ce que cela me fait à moi?
ode [oud], *n.* Ode, *f.*
odeum [ou'di:əm], *n.* Odéon, *m.*
odious ['oudjəs], *a.* Odieux. **odiously,** *adv.* Odieusement, *f.*; odieux, *m.* **odiousness,** *n.* Nature odieuse, *f.*; odieux, *m.*
odium ['oudiəm], *n.* Détestation, *f. To cast odium upon,* rendre odieux.
odometer [ɔ'dɔmitə], *n.* Odomètre, *m.*
odontalgia [ɔdɔn'tældʒə], *n.* Odontalgie, *f.* **odontalgic,** *a.* Odontalgique, *m.*
odontoid [ɔ'dɔntɔid], *a.* Odontoïde. **odontology** [-'tɔlədʒi], *n.* Odontologie, *f.*
odoriferous [oudə'rifərəs], *a.* Odoriférant.
odorous ['oudərəs], *a.* Odorant. **odour,** *n.* Odeur, *f.*, parfum, *m. In bad odour,* en mauvaise odeur. **odourless,** *a.* Inodore, sans odeur.
Odyssey ['ɔdisi], *n.* Odyssée, *f.*
oecumenical [i:kju'menikl], *a.* Œcuménique.
oedema [i:'di:mə], *n.* Œdème, *m.* **oedematous,** *a.* Œdémateux.

Oedipus ['i:dipəs]. Œdipe, *m. Oedipus complex,* complexe d'Œdipe, *m.*

oenanthic [i:'nænθik], *a.* Œnanthique.

oenology [-'nɔlədʒi], *n.* Œnologie, *f.*

oenometer [-'nɔmitə], *n.* Œnomètre, *m.*

oenophilist, *n.* Œnophile, *m.*

o'er [OVER].

oesophagotomy [i:sɔfə'gɔtəmi], *n.* Œsophagotomie, *f.* **oesophagus** [i:'sɔfəgəs], *n.* (*Anat.*) Œsophage, *m.*

oestrum ['i:strəm], *n.* Œstre; (*fig.*) stimulant, *m.*

of [ɔv], *prep.* De; parmi, d'entre. *First of all,* avant tout; *it is very good of you,* c'est bien aimable à vous; *it is very stupid of you,* c'est bien sot de votre part; *of all things,* par-dessus tout; *of late,* dernièrement; *of necessity,* par nécessité; *of old,* d'autrefois, de jadis; *of oneself,* de soi-même; *on the first of July,* le premier juillet; *the best of men,* le meilleur des hommes.

off [ɔf *or* ɔ:f], *adv.* Au loin, à distance; d'ici; rompu, séparé, enlevé; fini; (of electricity etc.) fermé; (of food) qui n'est plus frais. *Day off,* jour de congé, *m.*; *fifty yards off,* à cinquante pas; *hands off!* à bas les mains! n'y touchez pas! *hats off!* chapeaux bas! *he lives two miles off,* il demeure à deux milles d'ici; *I am off,* je m'en vais, me voilà parti; *I'll go farther off,* j'irai plus loin; *off and on,* de temps à autre, par boutades, à bâtons rompus; *off goes B.,* voilà B. parti; *off* (*stage*), (*Theat.*) à la cantonade; *off with him!* emmenez-le; *off with that!* ôtez cela; *off with you!* allez-vous-en, filez; *straight off,* tout de suite; *the house is a mile off,* la maison est à un mille de distance; *the match is off,* le mariage est rompu; (*spt.*) le match n'aura pas lieu; *they're off,* les voilà partis; *to be well off,* être bien dans ses affaires; *to come off,* s'échapper, se détacher; se réaliser, réussir; *to cut off,* trancher, amputer; *to go off,* s'en aller; *to go off to sleep,* s'endormir; *to polish off* (food), avaler; *to put off,* remettre, ajourner; *to take off,* imiter, contrefaire; (*Av.*) décoller; *to tear off,* arracher; *we are but poorly off,* nous ne sommes guère à l'aise; *you come off cheap,* vous en êtes quitte à bon marché.—*a.* Le plus éloigné; hors montoir, hors main. *Off day,* jour de congé, *m.*; jour où l'on ne brille pas, *m.*; *off ground,* (game) chat perché; *off horse* (in a team), sous-verge, *m.*; *off licence,* consommation à domicile; *off side,* côté droit, hors montoir, (*Ftb.*) hors-jeu; *off time,* temps libre, *m.*; *off white,* blanc teinté.—*prep.* De, de dessus; de devant; (*Naut.*) au large de. *Off one's head,* éperdu, fou, détraqué; *off the hinges,* hors des gonds; *one must not take one's eye off one's book,* il ne faut pas ôter les yeux de dessus son livre; *take the cloth off* (the table), ôtez la nappe (de dessus la table); *the ship was off the port,* le vaisseau était au large du port; *to be off colour,* n'être pas dans son assiette; *to be off one's food,* n'avoir pas d'appétit; *to dine off boiled beef,* dîner de bouilli.

offal [ɔfl], *n.* Issues, *f.pl.*; viande de rebut, *f.*, abats, déchets, *m.pl.*; rebut, refus, *m.*

off-chance, *n.* Chance improbable, *f.*

offence [ə'fens], *n.* Attaque, agression; faute, offense, *f.*; outrage, *m.*, injure, *f.*; contravention, violation (of a law etc.), *f.*, délit, crime, *m. Capital offence,* crime capital, *m.*; *second*

offence, récidive, *f.*; *to commit an offence against,* faire outrage à, porter atteinte à; *to give offence to,* offenser, blesser; *to take offence,* s'offenser de; *weapons of offence,* armes offensives, *f.pl.*

offend [ə'fend], *v.t.* Offenser, choquer, outrager, blesser; déplaire à; violer, enfreindre, transgresser (to transgress).—*v.i.* Déplaire; commettre une offense. *To offend against,* nuire à. **offender,** *n.* Offenseur; (*Law*) contrevenant, délinquant; pécheur, *m. Old offender,* récidiviste, *m.*; *the First Offenders Act,* la loi de sursis.

offensive [ə'fensiv], *a.* Offensant, désagréable; choquant, blessant; offensif (assailant). *Offensive weapons,* armes offensives, *f.pl.*—*n.* Offensive, *f. To take the offensive,* prendre l'offensive. **offensively,** *adv.* D'une manière offensante; offensivement. **offensiveness,** *n.* Nature offensante, *f.*

offer ['ɔfə], *v.t.* Offrir, présenter, proposer à. *Offers to go,* (*Theat.*) fausse sortie; *to offer oneself* or *itself,* s'offrir, se présenter; *to offer resistance,* résister à, faire résistance à; *to offer violence,* faire violence à.—*v.i.* S'offrir, se présenter à; essayer de, vouloir (to attempt). *To offer to,* faire l'offre de, offrir de.—*n.* Offre, *f.*; propositions de mariage, *f.pl.*; tentative, *f.*, essai (attempt), *m. On offer,* à vendre.

offering, *n.* Offrande, *f.*; sacrifice, *m.*

offertory, *n.* Offertoire, *m.*

off-hand, *adv.* Au premier abord, immédiatement, sans réflexion, sur-le-champ; cavalièrement.—*a.* Brusque, sans cérémonie, dégagé, cavalier; impromptu, improvisé. **off-handed,** *a.* Sans façon, sans gêne. **off-handedness,** *n.* Sans façon, sans gêne.

office ['ɔfis], *n.* Office, emploi, ministère, *m.*, charge, *f.*, fonctions, *f.pl.*; devoir (duty), pouvoir (service), *m.*; place (place), *f.*; bureau (apartments), *m.*, agence, *f.*; cabinet (private), *m.*; étude (lawyers), *f.*; (*pl.*) offices (of a house), *m.pl.*; communs (outhouses), *m.pl. A jack in office,* un petit employé; *head office,* bureau central; *Holy Office,* le Saint-Office, *m.*, l'Inquisition, *f.*; *last offices,* derniers devoirs, *m.pl.*; *office boy,* saute-ruisseau, *m.*; *office hours,* heures de bureau, *f.pl.*; *the cares of office,* le souci des affaires, *m.*; *the Foreign Office,* le ministère des affaires étrangères; *the Home Office,* le ministère de l'intérieur; *through the good offices of . . .,* par les soins de . . .; *to be in office,* être en fonctions, être au pouvoir.

officer ['ɔfisə], *n.* Officier; fonctionnaire (of the Government); agent (of police); huissier (of a court); membre du bureau (of a society), *m. Custom-house officer,* douanier, *m.*; *field officer,* officier supérieur, *m.*; *half-pay officer,* officier en demi-solde, *m.*; *non-commissioned officer,* sous-officier, *m.*; *regimental officer,* officier de troupe; *staff officer,* officier d'état-major, *m.*—*v.t.* Fournir des officiers à.

officered, *a.* Commandé; pourvu d'officiers. *His army was badly officered,* son armée était mal commandée; *well-officered troops,* troupes bien encadrées, *f.pl.*

official [ə'fiʃl], *a.* Officiel. *Official gazette,* bulletin officiel, *m.*—*n.* Fonctionnaire; employé; (*pej.*) bureaucrate, *m.*; (*pl.*) les dirigeants, les membres du Comité, *m.pl.*

officialdom, *n.* Bureaucratie, *f.* **officialese,** *n.* Jargon administratif, *m.* **officially,** *adv.* Officiellement.

officiate [ə'fiʃieit], *v.i.* Officier, desservir; exercer ses fonctions. **officiating,** *a.* Officiant, desservant; qui exerce ses fonctions.

officinal [ə'fisinl], *a.* (*Pharm.*) Officinal.

officious [ə'fiʃəs], *a.* Officieux; importun. **officiously,** *adv.* Officieusement; importunément. **officiousness,** *n.* Zèle officieux, *m.*

offing ['ɔfiŋ], *n.* (*Naut.*) *In the offing*, au large; (*fig.*) en perspective; *the offing*, le large, *m.*, la pleine mer, *f.*

offscouring, *n.* Rebut, *m.*

offset, *n.* (*Hort.*) Rejeton, repoussoir, *m.*; (*Comm.*) compensation, *f.*; (*Arch.*) saillie, *f.*, ressaut; (*Eng.*) désaxage, décalage, *m.*—*v.t.* Compenser; (*Tech.*) désaxer, décaler.

offshoot, *n.* Rejeton, *m.*

off-shore, *adv.* Au large.

offspring, *n.* Enfants, descendants, *m.pl.*; (*fig.*) fruit, produit, *m.*

oft [ɔft], (*poet.*) [OFTEN].

often [ɔfn], *adv.* Souvent. *As often as not*, le plus souvent; *how often?* combien de fois? *too often*, trop souvent, trop de fois; *very often*, bien souvent. **oftentimes** or **oft-times,** *adv.* Souvent, mainte fois.

ogee [ou'dʒi:], *n.* Cimaise, *f.*

ogival [ou'dʒaivl], *a.* Ogival.

ogive [ou'dʒaiv], *n.* Ogive, *f.*

ogle [ougl], *v.t.* Lorgner; lancer des œillades à.—*n.* Œillade, *f.* **ogler,** *n.* Lorgneur, *m.*, lorgneuse, *f.* **ogling,** *n.* Lorgnerie, *f.*, œillades, *f.pl.*

Ogpu ['ɔgpu], *n.* (*Polit.*) Le Guépéou.

ogre ['ougə], *n.* Ogre, *m.* **ogress** ['ougres], *n.* Ogresse, *f.*

oh! [ou], *int.* Oh! hélas!

ohm [oum], *n.* (*Elec.*) Ohm, *m.*

oil [ɔil], *n.* Huile, *f.*; (*Am.*) pétrole, *m. In oils,* (*Paint.*) à l'huile. *Essential oil,* huile essentielle; *fuel oil,* mazout, *m.*; *lubricating oil,* huile de graissage; *paraffin oil,* pétrole lampant, *m.*; *to pour oil on troubled waters,* calmer la tempête; *to strike oil,* rencontrer le pétrole, (*fig.*) trouver le filon.—*v.t.* Huiler; graisser (machinery etc.); (*fig.*) délier (the tongue).

oil-bearing, *a.* Pétrolifère. **oilcake,** *n.* Tourteau, *m.* **oil-can,** *n.* Burette (for a bicycle), *f.* **oil-cloth,** *n.* Toile cirée (pour meuble), *f.* **oil-colour,** *n.* Couleur à l'huile, *f.* **oil-field,** *n.* Gisement pétrolifère, *m.* **oil-fired,** *a.* Chauffé au mazout. **oil gas,** *n.* Gaz de pétrole, *m.* **oil-hole,** *n.* Trou de graissage, *m.* **oiliness,** *n.* Onctuosité, nature huileuse, *f.* **oiling,** *n.* Huilage, graissage, *m.*; onction, *f.* **oil-king,** *n.* Roi du pétrole, *m.* **oil-lamp,** *n.* Lampe à huile *or* à pétrole, *f.* **oilman,** *n.* Pétrolier; huilier; graisseur, *m.* **oil-painting,** *n.* Peinture à l'huile, *f.* **oil-plant,** *n.* Plante oléagineuse, *f.* **oil-press,** *n.* Pressoir à huile, *m.* **oil-silk,** *n.* Taffetas gommé, *m.* **oilskin,** *n.* Toile cirée vernie, *f.* **oil-stone,** *n.* Pierre à huile, *f.* **oil-stove,** *n.* Réchaud à pétrole, *m.* **oil-tanker,** *n.* (*Naut.*) Pétrolier; (*Motor.*) camion-citerne, *m.* **oil-well,** *n.* Puits à pétrole, *m.* **oil-works,** *n.* Huilerie, *f.* **oily,** *a.* Huileux; (*fig.*) oléagineux, onctueux.

ointment ['ɔintmənt], *n.* Onguent, *m.*,

pommade, *f. Fly in the ointment,* ombre au tableau, *f.*

O.K. or **okay** [ou'kei], *a.* (*colloq.*) O.K., très bien; bon, d'accord, ça va; exact.—*v.t.* Approuver.

okapi [ou'ka:pi], *n.* Okapi, *m.*

old [ould], *a.* Vieux; âgé; ancien, antique. *An old man,* un vieillard, un vieil homme, un homme âgé; *an old woman,* une vieille femme, (*colloq.*) une vieille; *at ten years old,* à l'âge de dix ans; *how old are you?* quel âge avez-vous? *how old do you take me to be?* quel âge me donnez-vous? *I am ten years old,* j'ai dix ans; *of old,* jadis, anciennement; *old age,* la vieillesse, *f.*; *old age pension,* retraite, *f.*; *old boy* (*girl*) (of school), ancien(ne) élève; *old enough to,* en âge de, d'âge à; *old man* (*chap, boy*), mon vieux, mon brave; *old people,* vieillards, *m.pl.*, vieilles gens, *f.pl.*; *old people's home,* hospice de vieillards, *m.*; *ten years old,* âgé de dix ans; *that story is as old as the hills,* cette histoire-là est vieille comme le monde; *the good old days,* le bon vieux temps; *the oldest,* le plus âgé; *the old folks,* les vieux; *the Old Testament,* l'Ancien Testament; *the old world,* l'ancien monde, *m.*; *to be too old to,* n'avoir plus l'âge de; *to grow old,* vieillir.

old-established, *a.* Ancien, établi depuis longtemps. **old-fashioned,** *a.* À l'ancienne mode, démodé, suranné; de vieille roche (of persons). *An old-fashioned car,* une auto vieux modèle. **old-maid,** *n.* Vieille fille, *f.* **old-maidish,** *a.* De vieille fille. **old-timer,** *n.* Un vieux de la vieille. **old-world,** *a.* D'autrefois, antique.

olden, *a.* Vieux, ancien. *In olden times,* au temps jadis, du temps que Berthe filait.

oldish, *a.* Un peu vieux, vieillot.

oleaginous [ouli'ædʒinəs], *a.* Oléagineux.

oleander [ouli'ændə], *n.* (*Bot.*) Laurier-rose, oléandre, *m.*

olefiant ['oulifaiənt], *a.* Oléfiant. **oleic** [ou'li:ik], *a.* Oléique.

oleiferous [ouli'ifərəs], *a.* Oléifère.

oleomargarine [oulio'ma:gəri:n], *n.* Oléomargarine, *f.* **oleometer** [ouli'ɔmitə], *n.* Oléomètre, *m.*

olfactory [ɔl'fæktəri], *a.* Olfactif, *m.*

olibanum [ɔ'libənəm], *n.* Oliban, *m.*

oligarchic [ɔli'ga:kik] or **oligarchical,** *a.* Oligarchique.

oligarchy ['ɔliga:ki], *n.* Oligarchie, *f.*

oligist ['ɔlidʒist], *a.* and *n.* Oligiste, *m.*

olio ['ouliou], *n.* Olla podrida, *f.*, mélange, recueil, pot-pourri, *m.*, macédoine, *f.*

oliphant ['ɔlifənt], *n.* Olifant, *m.*

olivaceous [ɔli'veiʃəs], *a.* Olivacé; olivâtre.

olivary ['ɔlivəri], *a.* Olivaire.

olive ['ɔliv], *n.* Olive, *f.*, olivier (tree), *m. Beef olive,* paupiette de bœuf, *f.*; *Mount of Olives,* Mont des Oliviers, *m.*; *olive colour,* couleur olive, *f.*; *olive complexion,* teint olivâtre, *m.*; *olive green,* vert olive, *m.* **olive-branch,** *n.* Rameau d'olivier, *m.* **olive-garden, olive-grove,** *n.* Jardin d'oliviers, *m.*, olivaie, oliveraie, *f.* **olive-oil,** *n.* Huile d'olive, *f.*

Oliver ['ɔlivə], Olivier, *m.*

Olympia [o'limpiə], Olympie, *f.*

olympiad [o'limpiæd], *n.* Olympiade, *f.* **olympian,** *a.* Olympien. **olympic,** *a.*

Olympique. *The Olympic Games*, les jeux olympiques, *m.pl.*

Olympus. Olympe, *m.*

ombre ['ɔmbə], *n.* Hombre (game), *m.*

omega ['oumigə], *n.* Oméga, *m.*

omelet(te) ['ɔmǝlit], *n.* Omelette, *f.*

omen ['oumǝn], *n.* Augure, *m.* **omened**, *a.* D'augure. *Ill-omened*, de mauvais augure.

omentum [o'mentǝm], *n.* (*pl.* **omenta**) Épiploon, *m.*

ominous ['ɔminǝs], *a.* De mauvais augure, sinistre; menaçant. **ominously**, *adv.* De mauvais augure.

omissible [o'misibl], *a.* Qu'on peut omettre. **omission**, *n.* Omission, *f.* **omissive**, *a.* Qui omet, oublieux.

omit [o'mit], *v.t.* Omettre; oublier.

omnibus ['ɔmnibǝs], *n.* Omnibus, *m.* (*Motor-*) *omnibus*, autobus, *m. Omnibus edition*, œuvres en un volume, *f.pl.*

omnifarious [ɔmni'fɛǝriǝs], *a.* De toutes sortes.

omnipotence [ɔm'nipǝtǝns], *n.* Omnipotence, toute-puissance, *f.* **omnipotent**, *a.* Tout-puissant, omnipotent.—*The Omnipotent*, le Tout-Puissant, *m.* **omnipotently**, *adv.* Avec omnipotence, avec la toute-puissance.

omnipresence [ɔmni'prezǝns], *n.* Omniprésence, *f.* **omnipresent**, *a.* Omniprésent.

omniscience [ɔm'nisiǝns], *n.* Omniscience, *f.* **omniscient**, *a.* Omniscient.

omnium ['ɔmniǝm], *n.* Omnium, *m.* **omnium gatherum** [-'gæðǝrǝm], *n.* Méli-mélo, fatras (of things), ramassis (of persons), *m.*

omnivorous [ɔm'nivǝrǝs], *a.* Omnivore.

omoplate ['ɔmopleit], *n.* Omoplate, *f.*

on [ɔn], *prep.* Sur, dessus; à; de; en, dans; lors de, après. *A curse on him*, qu'il soit maudit, maudit soit-il; *a ring on the finger*, une bague au doigt; *on loss on loss*, perte sur perte; *mad on her*, amoureux d'elle; *on a fine day*, par un beau jour; *on application*, sur demande; *on approval*, après acceptation; *on arriving*, arrivé (à), parvenu (à); *on condition that*, à condition que; *on credit*, à crédit; *on entering*, en entrant; *on examination*, après examen; *on fire*, en flammes; *on foot*, à pied; *on further inquiry*, après plus amples renseignements; *on hand*, entre les mains, (*Comm.*) en magasin; *on high*, en haut; *on holiday*, en congé; *on horseback*, à cheval; *on Monday*, lundi; *on my arrival in Paris*, à mon arrivée à Paris; *on my honour*, sur mon honneur; *on my side*, de mon côté; *on penalty of death*, sous peine de mort; *on purpose*, à dessein, exprès, de parti pris; *on such an occasion*, en pareille circonstance, à une telle occasion; *on that day*, ce jour-là; *on the cheap*, bon marché; *on the committee*, membre du bureau; *on the left*, à gauche; *on the right*, à droite; *on the second of April*, le deux avril; *on the table*, sur la table; *on the way*, en chemin, chemin faisant; *on the whole*, en somme, à tout prendre; *on the wing*, au vol!; *on thy life*, au péril de ta vie; *peace was settled on favourable terms*, la paix fut conclue à des conditions favorables; *to deliberate on it*, en délibérer; *to have pity on*, avoir pitié de; *to rely on someone for help*, compter sur l'assistance de quelqu'un; *to smile on*, sourire à.—*adv.* Dessus, en avant, avant, avancé (forward); toujours (continuation); de suite (succession). *And so on*, et ainsi de suite; *far*

on in the night, bien avant dans la nuit; *he entered with his hat on*, il entra le chapeau sur la tête; *on!* en avant! *on and on*, sans cesse, interminablement; *on with the show!* que le spectacle commence; *play on*, continuez de jouer; *read on*, lisez toujours; *that's simply not on*, c'est impossible, il n'y a pas moyen; *to keep on playing*, ne pas cesser de jouer, continuer à jouer, jouer toujours; *to live on*, continuer d'exister; *to put on*, mettre; *with one's shoes, boots*, or *gloves on*, chaussé, botté, or ganté.—*a.* (*Cricket*) *The on side*, le côté gauche; *to the on*, à gauche.

onager ['ɔnǝdʒǝ], *n.* (*Zool.*) Onagre, *m.*

onanism ['ounǝnizm], *n.* Onanisme, *m.*

once [wʌns], *adv.* Une fois, une seule fois; autrefois, jadis (formerly). *All at once* (all together), tous (toutes) à la fois; (suddenly) tout à coup; *at once*, sur-le-champ, tout de suite; *once a fortnight*, tous les quinze jours; *once before*, une première fois; *once bitten twice shy*, chat échaudé craint l'eau froide; *once (and) for all*, une fois pour toutes; *once I knew how to sing*, autrefois je savais chanter; *once more*, encore une fois; *once upon a time there was*, il était une fois; *this once*, pour cette fois-ci; *when once*, quand, lorsque, une fois que. **once-over**, *n.* Coup d'œil critique, *m.*

one [wʌn], *a.* and *n.* Un, un *m.*, une, *f.*; seul, un certain, *m.* *As one man*, comme un seul homme; *at one*, uni, d'accord, réconcilié; *four ones*, quatre unités, *f.pl.*; *he has but one child*, il n'a qu'un seul enfant; *it is all one to me what he does or says*, peu m'importe ce qu'il fait ou dit; *one and all*, tous jusqu'au dernier; *one and only*, seul, unique; *one man*, un homme; *there is one Charles*, il y a un certain Charles.—*pron.* On, l'on; vous (*accusative*); celui, *m.*, celle, *f.*; quelqu'un; un homme, *m.*, une femme, *f. A good thing and a bad one*, une bonne chose et une mauvaise; **anyone** [ANY]; **everyone** [EVERY]; *every one of you*, tous tant que vous êtes; *he is one who*, c'est un homme qui; *he is the one who*, c'est celui qui; *it does one good to hear him*, cela fait du bien de l'entendre; *no one*, personne; *one another*, l'un l'autre, l'une l'autre, les uns les autres, les unes les autres; *one by one*, à un, l'un après l'autre; *one like it*, le pareil, *m.*; *one of them*, un d'eux, un d'entre eux; *one of themselves*, un des leurs; *one's*, son, sa, ses; *one sees that every day*, on voit cela or cela se voit, tous les jours; *one with another*, l'un portant l'autre; **someone** [SOME]; *that one*, celui(celle)-là; *the great ones of the earth*, les grands de la terre; *the little ones*, les petits enfants, les petits (animaux), *m.pl.*; *the one which*, celui(celle) qui or que; *the only one*, le seul, *m.*, la seule, *f.*; *this one*, celui(celle)-ci; *to talk about one thing and another*, causer de choses et d'autres; *which one?* lequel, laquelle?

one-armed, *a.* Manchot. **one-eyed**, *a.* Borgne. **one-horse**, *a.* À un cheval. (*Am.*) *A one-horse town*, un trou perdu, *m.* **one-pair**, *a.* (Appartement au) premier, *m.* **one-self**, *pron.* Soi, soi-même; (*reflexive*) se. **one-sided**, *a.* À un côté, à une face; (*fig.*) partial, unilatéral; inégal. **one-sidedness**, *n.* Partialité, *f.* **one-way**, *a.* *One-way street*, rue à sens unique, *f.*; *one-way ticket*, billet simple, *m.*

oneness, *n.* Unité, *f.*
onerous [ˈɔnərəs], *a.* Onéreux. **onerousness,** *n.* Poids, *m.*, charge, *f.*
onion [ˈʌnjən], *n.* Oignon, *m.* *Spring onion,* ciboule, *f.* *(slang) To know one's onions,* s'y connaître; connaitre son boulot. **onion-bed,** *n.* Oignonnière, *f.* **onion-sauce,** *n.* Sauce à l'oignon, *f.*
onlooker [ˈɔnlukə], *n.* Spectateur, *m.*, spectatrice, *f.*
only [ˈounli], *a.* Seul; unique. *Only child,* enfant unique.—*adv.* Seulement; rien que; uniquement; ne ... que. *He only sleeps when he is sleepy,* il ne dort que quand il a sommeil; *it only angers him the more,* cela ne fait que l'irriter davantage; *only fancy!* imaginez un peu! *only see!* voyez un peu! *only yesterday,* pas plus tard qu'hier.—*conj.* Mais.
onomatopoeia [ɔnəmætəˈpiːə], *n.* Onomatopée, *f.*
onrush [ˈɔnrʌʃ], *n.* Ruée, *f.*
onset [ˈɔnset], *n.* Assaut, *m.*, attaque, charge, *f.*; *commencement, début, *m.* *At the first onset,* d'emblée, au premier abord.
onslaught [ˈɔnslɔːt], *n.* Attaque, *f.*; assaut, *m.*
ontological [ɔntəˈlɔdʒikəl], *a.* Ontologique. **ontologist** [-ˈtɔlədʒist], *n.* Ontologiste, *m.* **ontology,** *n.* Ontologie, métaphysique, *f.*
onus [ˈounəs], *n.* Fardeau, *m.*, charge, responsabilité, obligation, *f.*
onward [ˈɔnwəd], **onwards,** *adv.* En avant. *To go onward,* avancer, s'avancer.—*a.* En avant; avancé, progressif.
onyx [ˈɔniks], *n.* Onyx, *m.*
oodles [uːdlz], *n.pl.* *(pop.)* Des tas (de), *m.pl.,* une flopée (de), *f.*
oof [uːf], *n.* *(slang)* Galette, *f.*; pognon, *m.*, braise, *f.*
oolite [ˈouolait], *n.* Oolithe, *m.* **oolitic** [-ˈlitik], *a.* Oolithique. **oology** [-ˈɔlədʒi], *n.* Oologie, *f.*
oomph [umf], *n.* *(pop.)* Sex-appeal, *m.*
ooze [uːz], *n.* Limon, *m.*, vase, *f.*; suintement; duvet, *m.* (of fabrics). *Atlantic ooze,* vase de l'Atlantique, *f.*—*v.i.* Suinter, filtrer; *(fig.)* transpirer, s'ébruiter. *A secret oozes out,* un secret s'ébruite; *his courage oozed out,* son courage s'évanouit. **oozing,** *n.* Suintement, *m.*; filtration, *f.*; *(fig.)* ébruitement, *m.* **oozy,** *a.* Vaseux, limoneux.
opacity [oˈpæsiti], *n.* Opacité, *f.*
opah [ˈoupə], *n.* Poisson-lune, *m.*
opal [oupl], *n.* Opale, *f.* **opalescence** [-əˈlesəns], *n.* Opalescence, *f.* **opalescent,** *a.* Opalescent.
opaline [ˈoupəlain], *a.* Opalin. **opalized,** *a.* Opalisé.
opaque [oˈpeik], *a.* Opaque; *(fig.)* épais. **opaqueness,** *n.* Opacité, *f.*
open [oupn], *v.t.* Ouvrir; déboucher (a bottle); pratiquer (a hole); *(fig.)* expliquer, entamer (to explain); commencer, entamer; révéler, exposer (to reveal); décacheter (a letter); défaire (a package); dessiller (the eyes); inaugurer. *To open an account,* ouvrir un compte; *to open fire,* ouvrir le feu; *to open one's legs,* écarter les jambes; *to open the pleadings,* ouvrir les débats; *to open up,* ouvrir (a street etc.); frayer (a way), entamer (to begin).—*v.i.* S'ouvrir; commencer; s'entrouvrir (to open a little). *The door opened,* la porte s'ouvrit; *these flowers are beginning to*

open, ces fleurs commencent à s'épanouir; *this door opens on the garden,* cette porte ouvre sur le jardin.
    a.—Ouvert, découvert, à découvert, nu; à ciel ouvert (roofless); franc, sincère (frank); libre (free); plein (of the air etc.); *(fig.)* manifeste, clair, visible. *Half open,* entr'ouvert; *I am open to any reasonable offer,* je suis prêt à accepter toute offre raisonnable; *I am open to argument,* je suis disposé à écouter les raisons contraires; *in the open* (air), en plein air; *in the open country,* en rase campagne; *in the open sea,* en pleine mer; *open cheque,* chèque non barré; *open credit,* crédit à découvert, *m.*; *open road,* chemin libre, *m.*; *open to,* disposé à; *open to an engagement,* libre pour un engagement; *to sleep in the open air,* coucher à la belle étoile; *wide open,* tout grand ouvert.
open-cast, *a.* À ciel ouvert. **open-eyed,** *a.* Vigilant. **open-handed,** *a.* Libéral, généreux, donnant. **open-handedness,** *n.* Libéralité, *f.* **open-hearted,** *a.* Franc, *m.*, franche, *f.* **open-heartedly,** *adv.* Franchement. **open-heartedness,** *n.* Franchise, *f.* **open-minded,** *a.* Sans parti pris, libéral, à l'esprit ouvert. **open-mouthed,** *a.* La bouche ouverte, bouche béante, bouche bée. **open-necked,** *a.* À col ouvert. **open-work,** *n.* Ouvrage à jour, ouvrage à claire-voie, *m.*
opener, *n.* Ouvreur, *m.*, ouvreuse, *f.* *Tin-opener,* ouvre-boîte, *m.* **opening,** *n.* Ouverture, embrasure, *f.*; commencement, début, *m.*; chance; éclaircie (in forests etc.); échappée (in a vein), *f.*; *(Comm.)* débouché, *m.*—*a.* Qui commence, d'inauguration; *(Med.)* laxatif. *The opening chapter,* le premier chapitre. **openly,** *adv.* Ouvertement; franchement, sans détour. **openness,** *n.* Franchise, sincérité, candeur, *f.*
opera [ˈɔpərə], *n.* Opéra, *m.* *Comic opera,* opéra bouffe. **opera-glass,** *n.* Lorgnette, *f.*; *(pl.)* jumelles, *f.pl.* **opera-hat,** *n.* Claque, *m.* **opera-house,** *n.* Opéra, *m.*
operable [ˈɔpərəbl], *a.* Opérable.
operate [ˈɔpəreit], *v.i.* Opérer, agir; *(Fin.)* spéculer. *To operate for a rise or for a fall,* jouer à la hausse or à la baisse; *to operate on someone for appendicitis,* opérer quelqu'un de l'appendicite.—*v.t.* Opérer, effectuer; faire jouer, actionner.
operatic [ɔpəˈrætik], *a.* D'opéra.
operating [ˈɔpəˈreitiŋ], *a.* Qui opère, opératif; *(Theol.)* opérant. *Operating room,* salle d'opération, *f.*; *operating surgeon,* chirurgien opérant, opérateur, *m.*; *operating theatre,* amphithéâtre, *m.* **operation** [-ˈreiʃən], *n.* Opération, action, *f.* *In full operation,* en pleine vigueur; *to come into operation,* entrer en vigueur. **operational,** *a.* *(Mil.)* De campagne, d'opérations; *(Tech.)* en état de marche.
operative [ˈɔpərətiv], *a.* Actif, efficace; manuel, ouvrier, des ouvriers.—*n.* Artisan, ouvrier, *m.* **operator,** *n.* Opérateur, *m.* *Telephone operator,* téléphoniste; *radio operator,* radio, *m.*
opercular [ɔˈpəːkjulə], *a.* *(Bot.)* Operculaire. **operculated,** *a.* Operculé. **operculiform** [ɔˈpəːkjulifɔːm], *a.* Operculiforme. **operculum,** *n.* Opercule, *m.*

operetta [ɔpə'retə], *n.* Opérette, *f.*
ophicleide ['ɔfiklaid], *n.* Ophicléide, *m.*
ophidian [o'fidiən], *a.* and *n.* Ophidien, *m.*
ophiography [ɔfi'ɔgrəfi], *n.* Ophiographie, *f.*
ophiologist, *n.* Ophiologiste, *m.* **ophiology,** *n.* Ophiologie, *f.*
ophite ['ɔfait], *n.* Ophite, *m.*
ophthalmia [ɔf'θælmiə], *n.* Ophtalmie, *f.* **ophthalmic,** *a.* Ophtalmique. **ophthalmology** [-'mɔlədʒi], *n.* Ophtalmologie, *f.* **ophthalmoscope** [-'θælmɔskoup], *n.* Ophtalmoscope, *m.* **ophthalmotomy** [-'mɔtəmi], *n.* Ophtalmotomie, *f.*
opiate ['oupiit], *n.* Opiat, *m.*—*a.* Opiacé.
opine [o'pain], *v.i.* Opiner, être d'avis, penser.
opinion [ə'pinjən], *n.* Opinion, *f.,* avis, sentiment; jugement, *m.*; idée, pensée; consultation (counsel's), *f. In my opinion,* à mon avis; *in the opinion of,* selon l'opinion de; *public opinion,* l'opinion publique; *that's a matter of opinion,* c'est une affaire d'opinion; *to be entirely of the opinion of,* être entièrement de l'avis de, abonder dans le sens de; *to be of opinion that,* être d'avis que; *to be of the opinion of,* être de l'avis de; *to give one's opinion,* donner son opinion; *to have a high opinion of,* tenir en haute estime; *to take counsel's opinion,* consulter un avocat.
opinionated or **opinionative,** *a.* Opiniâtre; plein de soi-même, imbu de ses opinions.
opinionatively, *adv.* Opiniâtrement.
opinionativeness, *n.* Opiniâtreté, *f.*
opinioned, *a.* Plein de soi-même, suffisant.
opium ['oupjəm], *n.* Opium, *m.* **opium-fiend,** *n.* Opiomane.
opodeldoc [ɔpo'deldɔk], *n.* (*Pharm.*) Opodeldoch, *m.*
opossum [o'pɔsəm], *n.* Opossum, *m.*; sarigue, *f.*
opponent [ə'pounənt], *n.* Opposant, adversaire, *m.*
opportune ['ɔpətjuːn], *a.* Opportun, à propos. *To appear at an opportune moment,* tomber bien. **opportunely,** *adv.* À propos. **opportuneness,** *n.* Opportunité, *f.*; à propos, *m.* **opportunism,** *n.* Opportunisme, *m.* **opportunist,** *n.* Opportuniste, *m.* **opportunity** [-'tjuːniti], *n.* Occasion, *f. Opportunity makes the thief,* l'occasion fait le larron; *to take the opportunity,* profiter de l'occasion; *when the opportunity occurs,* à l'occasion.
opposability [əpouzə'biliti], *n.* Opposabilité, *f.*
opposable, *a.* Opposable.
oppose [ə'pouz], *v.t.* Opposer; s'opposer à, résister à, combattre.—*v.i.* S'opposer. **opposed,** *a.* Opposé. **opposer,** *n.* Adversaire, opposant, *m.*
opposite ['ɔpəzit], *a.* Opposé; vis-à-vis, contraire (à), en face. *He is your opposite number,* (*fam.*) c'est votre homologue; *on the opposite side of the river,* de l'autre côté de la rivière; *the opposite sex,* l'autre sexe, *m.*; *the opposite way,* en sens inverse; *those opposite,* nos voisins d'en face.—*n.* L'opposé, le contrepied, *m.*—*adv.* Vis-à-vis, en face.—*prep.* En face de, vis-à-vis de. **oppositely,** *adv.* En face de, en sens opposé. **oppositeness,** *n.* Situation opposée, *f.,* état contraire, *m.*
opposition [ɔpə'ziʃən], *n.* Opposition, résistance; concurrence (competition), *f.*; obstacle, empêchement (obstacle), *m. In opposition to,* par opposition à, contrairement

à; *to be in the opposition,* être de l'opposition; *to set up in opposition,* entrer en concurrence.
oppress [ə'pres], *v.t.* Opprimer; accabler; (*Med.*) oppresser.
oppression [ə'preʃən], *n.* Oppression, *f.*; accablement, abattement, *m. Oppression of the heart,* serrement de cœur, *m.*
oppressive, *a.* Accablant, oppressif; lourd. **oppressively,** *adv.* Oppressivement, d'une manière oppressive. **oppressiveness,** *n.* Caractère oppressif, *m.,* nature accablante; lourdeur, *f.*
oppressor, *n.* Oppresseur, *m.*
opprobrious [ə'proubriəs], *a.* Infamant; injurieux. **opprobriously,** *adv.* Avec opprobre, d'une manière outrageante. **opprobriousness,** *n.* Caractère injurieux (of an illusion), *m.* **opprobrium,** *n.* Opprobre, *m.*
opt [ɔpt], *v.i.* Opter.
optative ['ɔptətiv *or* ɔp'teitiv], *a.* Optatif.
optic (1) ['ɔptik] *or* **optical,** *a.* Optique; d'optique. *Optical illusion,* illusion d'optique, *f.*
optic (2) ['ɔptik], *n.* (*slang*) Œil, *m.*
optically, *adv.* Par l'optique. **optician** [-'tiʃən], *n.* Opticien, *m.* **optics,** *n.pl.* L'optique, *f.*
optimism ['ɔptimizm], *n.* Optimisme, *m.* **optimist,** *m.* Optimiste, *m.* **optimistic,** *a.* Optimiste.
option ['ɔpʃən], *n.* Option, *f.,* choix, *m.*; (*St. Exch.*) option, *f. Option market,* marché à prime, *m.*; (*Law*) *without the option of a fine,* sans substitution d'amende. **optional,** *a.* Facultatif.
opulence ['ɔpjuləns], *n.* Opulence, *f.* **opulent,** *a.* Opulent. **opulently,** *adv.* Opulemment, avec opulence.
opuscule [ɔ'pʌskjuːl], *n.* Opuscule, *m.*
or (1) [ɔː, ɔ], *conj.* Ou; (*negatively*) ni. *Either you or he,* ou vous ou lui; *or else,* ou bien, autrement.
or (2) [ɔː], *n.* (*Her.*) Or, *m.*
orache ['ɔritʃ], *n.* (*Bot.*) Arroche, *f.*
oracle ['ɔrəkl], *n.* Oracle, *m.*
oracular [ɔ'rækjulə], *a.* D'oracle; (*fig.*) dogmatique, magistral. **oracularly,** *adv.* En oracle.
oral ['ɔːrəl], *a.* Oral.—*n.* (*fam.*) Examen oral, *m.* **orally,** *adv.* Oralement; par la bouche.
orange ['ɔrindʒ], *n.* Orange, *f.*; orangé, *m.,* couleur orange, *f.* **orangeade** [-'dʒeid], *n.* Orangeade, *f.* **orange-blossom,** *n.* Fleur d'oranger, *f.* **orange-coloured,** *a.* Couleur d'orange, orangé. **orange-house,** *n.* Orangerie, *f.* **orange-man,** *n.* Marchand d'oranges; (*Engl. Hist.*) Orangiste, *m.* **orange-peel,** *n.* Écorce d'orange, *f.* **orange-stick,** *n.* Bâtonnet, *m.* **orange-tree,** *n.* Oranger, *m.*
orangery ['ɔrindʒəri], *n.* Orangerie, *f.*
orang-outang [o'ræŋu'tæŋ], *n.* Orang-outang, *m.*
oration [o'reiʃən], *n.* Allocution, harangue, *f.,* discours, *m. Funeral oration,* oraison funèbre, *f.* **orator** ['ɔrətə], *n.* Orateur, *m.* **oratorian** [-'tɔːriən], *n.* Oratorien, *m.* **oratorical** [-'tɔrikl], *a.* Oratoire. **oratorically,** *adv.* Oratoirement.
oratorio [ɔrə'tɔːriou], *n.* Oratorio, *m.*

oratory ['ɔrətri], *n.* Art oratoire, *m.*, éloquence, *f.*; oratoire (chapel), *m.*

orb [ɔ:b], *n.* Globe; corps sphérique; orbe; (*fig.*) cercle, *m.*, révolution, période (of time), *f.* **orbed,** *a.* Rond, sphérique. **orbicular** [-'bikjulə], **orbiculate,** *a.* Orbiculaire. **orbicularly,** *adv.* Orbiculairement.

orbit ['ɔ:bit], *n.* Orbe, *m.*; (*Anat., Astron.*) orbite, *f.*; (*Polit.*) sphère d'influence, *f.* **orbital,** *a.* (*Anat.*) Orbitaire.

orc [ɔ:k], *n.* Épaulard, *m.*, orque, *f.*

orchard ['ɔ:tʃəd], *n.* Verger, *m.* **orchardist,** *n.* Pomiculteur, *m.*

orchestra ['ɔ:kistrə], *n.* Orchestre, *m.* *Orchestra stalls,* fauteuils d'orchestre, *m.pl.*

orchestral [ɔ:'kestrəl], *a.* D'orchestre, orchestral. **orchestrate,** *v.t.* Orchestrer.

orchestration [ɔ:kis'treiʃən], *n.* Orchestration, *f.*

orchid ['ɔ:kid], *n.* Orchidée, *f.*

orchil ['ɔ:tʃil] or **orchilla** [ɔ:'tʃilə], *n.* (*Bot.*) Orseille (des teinturiers), *f.*

ordain [ɔ:'dein], *v.t.* Ordonner, décréter, prescrire; établir, instituer; (*Bibl.*) élire, choisir. *He has been ordained* (*priest*), il a été ordonné prêtre, il a reçu les ordres. **ordainer,** *n.* Ordonnateur; (*Eccles.*) ordinant, *m.* **ordaining,** *a.* Ordonnateur; (*Eccles.*) ordinant.

ordeal [ɔ:'di:əl], *n.* *Ordalie; (*fig.*) dure épreuve, *f.*

order ['ɔ:də], *n.* Ordre; règlement, *m.*, règle (rule); décoration (badge); (*Mil.*) consigne; (*Law*) ordonnance, *f.*; (*Theat. etc.*) billet de faveur, *m.*; classe, *f.*, rang, *m.*, commande (for goods), *f.*; mandat (draft), *m.* *By order,* par ordre; *close order,* ordre serré, *m.*; *extended order,* ordre dispersé, *m.*; *in alphabetical order,* par ordre alphabétique; *in holy orders,* dans les ordres; *in order,* en bonne forme; *in order that,* afin que; *in order to,* afin de; *in skirmishing order,* en tirailleurs; *in very good order,* en très bon état; *law and order,* l'ordre public; *made to order,* fait sur commande; *marching order,* ordre de marche, *m.*; *mention in orders,* citation, *f.*; *money order,* mandat-poste, *m.*; *order!* à l'ordre! *Order in Council,* décret-loi, *m.*; *Order of the Bath,* Ordre du Bain, *m.*; *order of the day,* ordre du jour, *m.*; *out of order,* en mauvais état, dérangé, irrégulier, détraqué, déréglé; indisposé, malade; *postal order,* bon de poste, *m.*; *till further orders,* jusqu'à nouvel ordre; *to break an order,* manquer à la consigne; *to call to order,* rappeler à l'ordre; *to cancel an order,* lever la consigne; *to get out of order,* se détraquer; *to keep in order,* tenir dans l'ordre, tenir; *to keep order,* maintenir l'ordre; *to order,* à ordre (of cheques), sur commande (of clothes etc.); *to put in order,* mettre en ordre, mettre de l'ordre dans; *to put out of order,* déranger, mettre en désordre. **order-book,** *n.* Carnet de commandes, *m.* **order-form,** *n.* Bon de commande, *m.*; formule de commande, *f.*

v.t.—Ordonner, donner l'ordre à; régler, arranger (to regulate); diriger, conduire (to conduct); commander (clothes etc.); prescrire (medicine). *Order arms!* reposez armes! *the dinner is ordered,* le dîner est commandé; *they ordered him to be set free,* ils le firent mettre en liberté; *to be ordered to,* recevoir

l'ordre de; *to order about,* faire aller et venir; *to order a coat,* commander un habit; *to order away* or *off,* ordonner à . . . de s'en aller; *to order in,* ordonner d'entrer; *to order out,* ordonner de sortir; *to order someone to do something,* ordonner à quelqu'un de faire quelque chose.

ordering, *n.* Disposition, *f.*, arrangement, *m.*

orderliness ['ɔ:dəlinis], *n.* Bon ordre, *m.*, méthode, discipline, *f.* **orderly,** *n.* (*Mil.*) Planton, *m.* *Hospital orderly,* infirmier, *m.*; *mounted orderly,* estafette, *f.*; *officer's orderly,* ordonnance d'officier, *f.—a.* En bon ordre, méthodique, rangé. *On orderly duty,* de planton; *orderly officer,* officier de service, *m.*; *orderly room,* salle de rapport, *f.*

ordinal ['ɔ:dinl], *a.* Ordinal.—*n.* Nombre ordinal; (*Eccles.*) ordinaire de la messe, *m.*

ordinance ['ɔ:dinəns], *n.* Ordonnance, *f.*

ordinand ['ɔ:dinænd], *n.* (*Eccles.*) Ordinand, *m.*

ordinarily ['ɔ:dinərili], *adv.* Ordinairement, d'ordinaire. **ordinary,** *a.* Ordinaire; moyen. —*n.* Ordinaire, *m.*; table d'hôte, *f.* *Out of the ordinary,* exceptionnel, sortant de l'ordinaire, peu commun; *ship in ordinary,* (*Naut.*) bâtiment en réserve.

ordinate ['ɔ:dinət], *n.* (*Math.*) Ordonnée, *f.*

ordination [-'neiʃən], *n.* Ordination, *f.*

ordnance ['ɔ:dnəns], *n.* Artillerie, *f.* *Ordnance map,* carte d'état major, *f.*; *piece of ordnance,* pièce d'artillerie, bouche à feu, *f.*

ordure ['ɔ:djuə], *n.* Ordure, *f.*

ore [ɔ:], *n.* Minerai, *m.* *Iron-ore,* minerai de fer, *m.*

oread ['ɔ:riæd], *n.* Oréade, *f.*

organ ['ɔ:gən], *n.* Organe; orgue (musical instrument), *m.* *Barrel-organ,* orgue de Barbarie, *m.*; *theatre organ,* orgue de cinéma, *m.* **organ-blower,** *n.* Souffleur d'orgue, *m.* **organ-builder,** *n.* Facteur d'orgues, *m.* **organ-case,** *n.* Buffet d'orgue, *m.* **organ-loft,** *n.* Tribune d'orgue, *f.* **organ-pipe,** *n.* Tuyau d'orgue, *m.* **organ-stop,** *n.* Jeu d'orgue, *m.* **organ-tuner,** *n.* Accordeur d'orgues, *m.*

organdie ['ɔ:gəndi], *n.* (*Tex.*) Organdi, *m.*

organic [ɔ:'gænik], *a.* Organique; des organes. *Organic chemistry,* chimie organique, *f.* **organically,** *adv.* Organiquement.

organism ['ɔ:gənizm], *n.* Organisme, *m.*

organist ['ɔ:gənist], *n.* Organiste, *m.*

organization [ɔ:gənai'zeiʃən], *n.* Organisation; œuvre, *f.*; organisme, *m.* **organize** ['ɔ:gənaiz], *v.t.* Organiser; aménager. **organizer,** *n.* Organisateur, *m.* **organizing,** *n.* Organisation, *f.* *Organizing ability,* qualités d'organisation, *f.pl.*

organzine ['ɔ:gənzi:n], *n.* Organsin, *m.*

orgasm ['ɔ:gæzm], *a.* Orgasme, *m.*

orgiastic ['ɔ:dʒiæstik], *a.* Orgiaque.

orgy ['ɔ:dʒi], *n.* Orgie, *f.*

oriel ['ɔ:riəl], *n.* Fenêtre en saillie, *f.*

orient ['ɔ:riənt], *n.* Orient, *m.—a.* Levant; naissant; d'orient, oriental; (*fig.*) brillant, étincelant, éclatant; oriental [-'entl], *a.* Oriental, d'Orient.—*n.* Natif de l'Orient, oriental, *m.* **orientalism,** *n.* Orientalisme, *m.* **orientalist,** *n.* Orientaliste, *m.* **orientalize,** *v.t.* Orientaliser. **orientate,** *v.t.* Orienter. **orientation** [-'teiʃən], *n.* Orientation, *f.*

orifice ['ɔrifis], *n.* Orifice, *m.*, ouverture, *f.*

origin ['ɔridʒin], *n.* Origine, source; provenance, *f.*

original [ə'ridʒinl], *a.* Original, inédit (new); originel, originaire (earliest); primitif (of meanings etc.). *An original person,* une personne originale, un(e) original(e); *original sin,* péché originel; *the original sum,* le total premier, *m.—n.* Original, *m.* **originality** [-'næliti], *n.* Originalité, *f.* **originally,** *adv.* Originairement; originellement, dans l'origine; d'une manière originale, originalement.

originate [ə'ridʒineit], *v.t.* Faire naître, produire, donner naissance à; (*fig.*) concevoir, inventer.—*v.i.* Tirer son origine (de), avoir son origine (dans). **origination** [-'neiʃən], *n.* Génération, origine, *f.* **originator,** *n.* Initiateur, auteur, *m.*

oriole ['ɔːrioul], *n.* (*Orn.*) Loriot, *m.*

Orion [o'raiən], *n.* Orion, *m.*

orison ['ɔrizən], *n.* Oraison, prière, *f.*

Orkneys (The) ['ɔːkniz]. Les Orcades, *f.pl.*

orle ['ɔːl], *n.* (*Arch.*) Orle, *m.*

Orleans ['ɔːliənz], *n.* Orléans, *m.*; (*pl.*) pruneaux (d'Orléans), *m.pl.*

orlop ['ɔːlɔp], *n.* (*Naut.*) Faux pont, *m.*

ormolu ['ɔːmoluː], *n.* Or moulu, *m.—a.* En or moulu.

ornament ['ɔːnəmənt], *n.* Ornement, *m.—v.t.* Orner, décorer (de). **ornamental** [-'mentl], *a.* Ornemental, d'ornement; d'agrément. **ornamentally,** *adv.* Pour servir d'ornement, pour ornement. **ornamentation** [-'teiʃən], *n.* Ornementation, décoration, *f.*, embellissement, *m.*

ornate [ɔː'neit], *a.* Orné, élégant, paré. **ornately,** *adv.* Avec ornement. **ornateness,** *n.* Ornementation (exagérée), *f.*

ornithological [ɔːniθə'lɔdʒikl], *a.* Ornithologique. **ornithologist** [-'θɔlədʒist], *n.* Ornithologiste, ornithologue, *m.* **ornithology,** *n.* Ornithologie, *f.* **ornithorhyncus** [-o'riŋkəs], *n.* Ornithorynque, *m.*

orography [ɔ'rɔgrəfi], *n.* Orographie, *f.*

orologist [ɔ'rɔlədʒist], *n.* Orographe, *m.*

orotund ['ɔːrɔtand], *a.* Sonore; emphatique, ampoulé.

orphan ['ɔːfən], *n. a.* and *n.* Orphelin, *m.*, orpheline, *f. Orphan home,* orphelinat, *m.*; *war orphan,* pupille de la Nation.—*v.t.* Rendre orphelin. **orphanage,** *n.* État d'orphelin; orphelinat, *m.*

Orphean [ɔː'fiːən], *a.* D'Orphée.

Orpheus ['ɔːfiəs]. Orphée, *m.*

Orphic ['ɔːfik], *a.* Orphique; enchanteur, *m* enchanteresse, *f.*

orphrey ['ɔːfrei], *n.* Orfroi, *m.*

orpiment ['ɔːpimənt], *n.* Orpiment, *m.*

orpine ['ɔːpin], *n.* (*Bot.*) Orpin, *m.*

orrery ['ɔrəri], *n.* Planétaire, *m.*

orris ['ɔris], *n.* (*Bot.*) Iris, *m.*; passementerie, *f.* **orris-root,** *n.* Racine d'iris, *f.*

ort [ɔːt], *n.* Débris, rebut, *m.*; (*pl.*) restes, *m.pl.*

orthodox ['ɔːθədɔks], *a.* Orthodoxe. **orthodoxly,** *adv.* D'une manière orthodoxe. **orthodoxy,** *n.* Orthodoxie, *f.*

orthoepist ['ɔːθouiːpist], *n.* Personne qui prononce bien, *f.* **orthoepy,** *n.* Orthoépie, *f.*

orthographic [ɔːθə'græfik] or **orthographical,** *a.* Orthographique. **orthographically,** *adv.* Selon les règles de l'orthographe. **orthography** [-'θɔgrəfi], *n.* Orthographe, orthographie, *f.*

orthop(a)edic [ɔːθə'piːdik], *a.* Orthopédique. **orthop(a)edist** [-'piːdist], *n.* Orthopédiste, *m.*

orthop(a)edy ['ɔːθəpiːdi], *n.* Orthopédie, *f.*

ortolan ['ɔːtələn], *n.* (*Orn.*) Ortolan, *m.*

oscillate ['ɔsileit], *v.i.* Osciller; (*fig.*) balancer, vaciller. **oscillating,** *a.* Oscillant. **oscillation** [-'leiʃən], *n.* Oscillation, *f.* **oscillator,** *n.* Oscillateur, *m.*

oscillatory ['ɔsileitəri], *a.* Oscillatoire.

oscillograph [ɔ'siləgrɑːf], *n.* Oscillographe, *m.*

osculation [ɔskju'leiʃən], *n.* Osculation, *f.* **osculatory** ['ɔskjulətri], *a.* Osculateur.—*n.* (*R.-C. Ch.*) Paix, patène, *f.*

osier ['ouʒiə], *n.* Osier, *m.* **osier-bed,** *n.* Oseraie, *f.*

osmium ['ɔsmiəm], *n.* (*Chem.*) Osmium, *m.*

osmund ['ɔzmənd], *n.* (*Bot.*) Osmonde, *f.*

osprey ['ɔsprei], *n.* (*Orn.*) Orfraie, *f.*, pygargue, *m.*

osseous ['ɔsiəs], *a.* Osseux.

Ossianic [ɔsi'ænik], *a.* Ossianique.

ossicle ['ɔsikl], *n.* Ossicule, osselet, *m.* **ossification** [-fi'keiʃən], *n.* Ossification, *f.* **ossify** ['ɔsifai], *v.t.* Ossifier.—*v.i.* S'ossifier.

ossuary ['ɔsjuəri], *n.* Charnier; ossuaire, *m.*

Ostend [ɔs'tend]. Ostende.

ostensible [ɔs'tensibl], *a.* Prétendu. **ostensibly,** *adv.* En apparence.

ostensory [ɔs'tensəri], *n.* Ostensoir, *m.*

ostentation [ɔsten'teiʃən], *n.* Ostentation, *f.*, faste, étalage, *m.* **ostentatious,** *a.* Pompeux, fastueux, de parade. **ostentatiously,** *adv.* Fastueusement, avec ostentation.

osteoblast ['ɔstiəblæst], *n.* Ostéoblaste, *f.*

osteoclasis [ɔstiə'kleisis], *n.* Ostéoclasie, *f.*

osteogenesis [-'dʒenəsis], *n.* Ostéogénie, *f.*

osteography [ɔsti'ɔgrəfi], *n.* Ostéographie, *f.*

osteological [ɔstiə'lɔdʒikl], *a.* Ostéologique.

osteologist [ɔsti'ɔlədʒist], *n.* Ostéologue, *m.*

osteology [ɔsti'ɔlədʒi], *n.* Ostéologie, *f.*

osteopath ['ɔstiəpæθ], *n.* Ostéopathe, *m.*

osteopathy [ɔsti'ɔpəθi], *n.* Ostéopathie, *f.*

osteoplasty [-ə'plæsti], *n.* Ostéoplastie, *f.*

osteotomy [-'ɔtəmi], *n.* Ostéotomie, *f.*

ostler ['ɔslə], *n.* Garçon d'écurie, *m.*

ostracism ['ɔstrəsizm], *n.* Ostracisme, *m.* **ostracize,** *v.t.* Frapper d'ostracisme, exiler.

ostrich ['ɔstritʃ], *n.* Autruche, *f.* **ostrich-feather,** *n.* Plume d'autruche, *f.*

otalgia [o'tældʒə], *n.* Otalgie, *f.*

other ['ʌðə], *a.* Autre. *Every other day,* tous les deux jours; *other people,* d'autres, autrui; *the one is as bad as the other,* l'un vaut l'autre; *the other day,* l'autre jour.—*pron.* Autre; autrui. *All the others,* tous les autres; *each other,* l'un l'autre, les uns les autres; *of all others,* entre tous; *some . . . , others,* les uns..., les autres.—*adv.* Autrement.

otherwise, *adv.* Autrement; sans quoi.

otiose ['ouʃious], *a.* Superflu, oiseux.

otter ['ɔtə], *n.* Loutre, *f.*

otto ['ɔtou] [ATTAR].

Ottoman ['ɔtəmən], *a.* Ottoman.—*n.* Ottoman (Turk), *m.*; ottomane, *f.*, divan, *m.*

ought (1) [ɔːt], *v.aux.* Devoir; falloir. *It is as it ought to be,* c'est comme il faut; *that ought to do,* je pense que cela suffira; *these things ought not to be so,* il ne devrait pas en être ainsi; *you ought to do it,* vous devriez le faire; *you ought to have done this,* vous auriez dû faire ceci; *you ought to have seen*, il aurait fallu voir.

ought (2) [AUGHT].

ounce [auns], *n.* Once, *f.* (weight); (*Zool.*) once, *f.*, léopard des neiges, *m.*

our ['auə], *a.poss.* Notre, *sing.*, nos, *pl.* At or to *our place*, chez nous.

ours ['auəz], *pron.* Le nôtre, *m.*, la nôtre, *f.*, les nôtres, *pl.*; à nous. *A friend of ours*, un de nos amis; *it is ours*, c'est à nous.

ourselves, *pron.* Nous-mêmes; nous. *He is one of ourselves*, il est des nôtres; *we consider ourselves*, nous nous croyons.

ousel [OUZEL].

oust [aust], *v.t.* Évincer, déloger, débusquer.

out [aut], *adv.* Hors, dehors; sorti (out of doors); découvert, exposé (disclosed); (*Mil.*) sur pied; éteint (extinct); épuisé, fini (at an end); jusqu'au bout, jusqu'à la fin (to the end); haut, à haute voix (loudly); embarrassé, dans l'embarras (puzzled); dans l'erreur (in error); publié, paru (of books); épanoui (of flowers). *Flat out* (*pop.*), à toute vitesse; *get out of that*, va-t'en, ôte-toi de là; *hear me out*, entendez-moi jusqu'au bout; *I found you out*, je vous ai déniché, je vous ai découvert; *I was fifty pounds out of pocket by it*, j'y ai perdu cinquante livres; *I wish I were out of it*, je voudrais bien m'en être tiré; *it's her day out*, c'est son jour de sortie; *just out*, vient de paraître; *out!* dehors! (*Ten.*) faute! *out and out*, vrai, complet, achevé, fieffé; *out loud*, tout haut; *out of*, hors de, sans; *out of a job*, sans emploi; *out of ammunition*, à bout de munitions; *out of charity*, par charité; *out of danger*, hors de danger; *out of date*, suranné, démodé; *out of doors*, dehors, au grand air; *out of favour*, disgracié; *out of friendship*, par amitié; *out of hand*, sur-le-champ, tout de suite; *out of measure*, outre mesure; *out of money*, sans argent; *out of number*, innombrable, sans nombre; *out of order*, dérangé, contraire au règlement; *out of place*, déplacé; *out of print*, épuisé (of book); *out of sight*, hors de vue; *out of sight, out of mind*, loin des yeux, loin du cœur; *out of temper*, en colère, de mauvaise humeur; *out of the way*, excessif, retiré (secluded); *out of tune*, faux; *out of use*, inusité, vieilli; *out with him!* à la porte! *out with it!* dites ce que c'est! achevez! *put out*, mécontent; *seven out of ten*, sept sur dix; *she laughed right out*, elle rit tout haut; *speak out*, parlez plus haut; *the cask is out*, le tonneau est vide; *the fire is out*, le feu est éteint; *the sun is out*, il fait du soleil; *the truth must out*, il faut que la vérité sorte; *time out of mind*, de temps immémorial; *to be out in one's reckoning*, être loin de compte; *to be out of*, être sans, être à bout de, manquer de; *to be out of sorts*, être indisposé, n'être pas dans son assiette; *to be out to do something*, avoir à tâche de faire quelque chose; *to come out*, débuter; *to drink out of a glass*, boire dans un verre; *to fall out of the frying-pan into the fire*, tomber de la poêle dans la braise; *to feel out of it*, se sentir de trop; *to read out of a book*, lire dans un livre; *to squeeze out*, exprimer; *to throw out of the window*, jeter par la fenêtre; *you put me quite out*, vous me déroutez.—*a.* Externe.—*int.* Dehors! hors d'ici!—*n.* (*Print.*) Bourdon, *m. Ins and outs*, coins et recoins, *m.pl.*

outbalance [aut'bæləns], *v.t.* L'emporter sur, surpasser.

outbid, *v.t.* (*past* **-bid** or **-bade,** *p.p.* **-bidden** or **-bid**) Enchérir sur, surenchérir; surpasser. **outbidder,** *n.* Surenchérisseur, *m.*

outboard, *a. Outboard motor-boat*, hors-bord, *m.*

outbrave, *v.t.* Braver, défier.

outbreak, *n.* Éruption, *f.*, débordement, déchaînement, soulèvement, *m.*; insurrection, émeute, explosion; épidémie, *f.*; incendie (of fire), *m.*

outbuilding, *n.* Bâtiment extérieur, *m.*, dépendance, *f.*

outburst, *n.* Explosion, *f.*, transport, éclat, *m.*

outcast, *a.* Expulsé, proscrit, rejeté; sans feu ni lieu.—*n.* Proscrit, banni, expulsé, paria, *m.*

outclass, *v.t.* Surclasser.

outcome, *n.* Résultat, *m.*

outcrop, *n.* (*Geol.*) Affleurement, *m.*

outcry, *n.* Grand cri, *m.*, clameur, *f.*, tollé, *m.*

outdare, *v.t.* Surpasser en audace; braver, affronter.

outdated, *a.* Démodé.

outdistance, *v.t.* Distancer, surpasser.

outdo, *v.t.* (*past* **outdid,** *p.p.* **outdone**) Surpasser, exceller, l'emporter sur.

outdoor, *a.* En plein air; externe. *Outdoor clothes*, vêtements de ville, *m.pl.* **outdoors,** *adv.* En plein air, au dehors, hors de la maison.

outer ['autə], *a.* Extérieur, du dehors, externe. **outermost,** *a.* Le plus extérieur; le plus avancé.

outface [aut'feis], *v.t.* Affronter, braver, faire baisser les yeux à.

outfall, *n.* Embouchure, décharge, *f.*, déversoir, *m.*

outfield, *n.* (*spt.*) Terrain éloigné, *m.*

outfit, *n.* Attirail, outillage, armement, équipement; trousseau, *m. Outfit allowance*, frais d'équipement, *m.pl.* **outfitter,** *n.* Confectionneur et chemisier; (*Mil.* and *Navy*) fournisseur d'objets d'équipements, *m.*

outflank, *v.t.* Déborder, tourner.

outflow, *v.i.* S'écouler.—*n.* Sortie, *f.*, écoulement, *m.*

outfly, *v.t.* (*past* **outflew,** *p.p.* **outflown**) Dépasser au vol.

outgeneral, *v.t.* Surpasser en tactique; l'emporter sur.

outgoing, *a.* Sortant, qui sort. **outgoings,** *n.pl.* Dépenses, *f.pl.*

outgrow [aut'grou], *v.t.* (*past* **outgrew,** *p.p.* **outgrown**) Surpasser en croissance; dépasser, surpasser. *He outgrows his clothes*, ses habits deviennent trop petits.

outgrowth ['autgrouθ], *n.* Excroissance; conséquence, *f.*

out-Herod, *v.t.* Dépasser en cruauté etc. *That out-Herods Herod*, cela dépasse tout; *to out-Herod Herod*, être plus royaliste que le roi.

outhouse, *n.* Hangar, *m.*; dépendance, *f.*

outing, *n.* Excursion, sortie, promenade, *f.*

outlander, *n.* Étranger, *m.*

outlandish, *a.* Étranger; bizarre; retiré.

outlandishness, *n.* Étrangeté, *f.*

outlast, *v.t.* Durer plus longtemps que, survivre à.

outlaw, *n.* Proscrit, *m.*—*v.t.* Mettre hors la loi, proscrire. **outlawry,** *n.* Mise hors la loi, proscription, *f.*

outlay, *n.* Dépense, *f.*, débours, *m.pl.*
outlet, *n.* Issue, sortie, voie d'écoulement, *f.*; (*Comm.*) débouché, *m.*
outlier ['autliə], *n.* (*Geol.*) Massif détaché, témoin, *m.*
outline, *n.* Contour; profil, *m.*, esquisse, ébauche, *f.*; grandes lignes, *f.pl.*—*v.t.* Dessiner le contour de; esquisser.
outlive [aut'liv], *v.t.* Survivre à, vivre plus longtemps que.
outlook, *n.* Vue, perspective, *f.*
outlying, *a.* Éloigné, isolé, détaché; extra-muros (of parts of a town).
out-manœuvre [autmə'nu:və], *v.t.* Déjouer.
outmarch, *v.t.* Devancer; laisser en arrière.
outmoded, *a.* Démodé.
outnumber, *v.t.* Surpasser en nombre.
out-of-date, *a.* Démodé, dépassé.
out-of-school, *a.* Extra-scolaire (activities).
out-of-the-way, *a.* Perdu, peu fréquenté.
outpace, *v.t.* Devancer, dépasser.
out-patient, *n.* Malade externe *or* à domicile, *m.*
outplay, *v.t.* Surpasser, dominer.
outpost, *n.* Avant-poste, *m.*
outpour, *v.t.* Épancher, verser à flots. **outpouring,** *n.* Effusion, *f.*, épanchement, *m.*
output, *n.* Rendement, débit, *m.*
outrage ['autreidʒ], *n.* Outrage, *m.*, atteinte, *f. Outrage on common decency,* attentat à la pudeur, *m.*—*v.t.* Outrager. **outrageous** [-'reidʒəs], *a.* Outrageux, outrageant; furieux, violent, atroce, indigne, outré, exagéré (excessive). **outrageously,** *adv.* Outrageusement, d'une manière outrée, énormément. **outrageousness,** *n.* Nature outrageante, énormité, *f.*
outride, *v.t.* (*past* **outrode,** *p.p.* **outridden**) Dépasser, devancer à cheval. **outrider,** *n.* Piqueur, *m.*
outrigger, *n.* Portant-dehors; porte-à-faux, *m.*
outright, *adv.* Sur-le-champ, tout de suite; entièrement, complètement (completely); sans gêne, sans contrainte, net, carrément (without constraint).
outrival, *v.t.* L'emporter sur.
outrun, *v.t.* (*past* **outran,** *p.p.* **outrun**) Dépasser à la course, gagner de vitesse.
outsail, *v.t.* Dépasser à la voile; dépasser.
outsell, *v.t.* (*past and p.p.* **outsold**) Vendre plus cher que; vendre en plus grand nombre que.
outset, *n.* Début, commencement, *m. At the very outset,* dès l'origine.
outshine, *v.t.* (*past and p.p.* **outshone**) Surpasser en éclat, éclipser.
outside [aut'said], *a.* Extérieur, externe, du dehors. **The outside passengers,* les voyageurs de l'impériale, *m.pl.*—*adv.* Dehors, en dehors, à l'extérieur.—*prep.* Hors de, à l'extérieur de, en dehors de.—*n.* Dehors, extérieur, *m.*; rissolé (of roast meat), *m.*; (*Ftb.*) ailier, *m. At the outside,* tout au plus.
outsider, *n.* Étranger, qui n'a rien à faire avec, profane; intrus; (*Bank*) coulissier; (*Ftb.*) ailier; (*pl.*) le public, *m.*, les profanes, *m.pl.*; (horse) outsider, *m.*
outsit [aut'sit], *v.t.* (*past and p.p.* **outsat**) Rester (assis) plus longtemps que.
outsize [aut'saiz], *a.* De grande taille, de taille exceptionelle; hors série.
outskirts, *n.pl.* Extrémité, *f.*, bords, *m.pl.*;

lisière (of a wood), *f.*; faubourg (of a town), *m.*
outsmart, *v.t.* Rouler, surpasser en finesse.
outspan, *v.i., v.t.* Dételer.
outspoken, *a.* Franc, clair, carré. **outspokenness,** *n.* Franchise brutale, *f.*
outspread, *v.t.* (*past and p.p.* **outspread**) Étendre, déployer.
outstanding, *a.* Non payé, encore dû, à percevoir (of debts etc.); (*fig.*) suréminent; en suspens (of business).
outstare, *v.t.* Faire baisser les yeux à, déconcerter.
outstay, *v.t.* Rester plus longtemps que. *To outstay one's welcome,* s'incruster.
outstretched, *a.* Étendu, déployé, tendu.
outstrip, *v.t.* Gagner de vitesse, devancer, distancer.
outvote, *v.t.* L'emporter sur.
outwalk, *v.t.* Marcher plus vite que, devancer.
outward (1) ['autwəd], *a.* Extérieur, du dehors, externe; superficiel.
outward (2) *or* **outwards,** *adv.* À l'extérieur; au dehors, extérieurement. *An outward-bound ship,* un navire en cours de voyage *or* en partance.
outwardly, *adv.* Extérieurement, à l'extérieur, au dehors; (*fig.*) en apparence.
outwardness, *n.* Objectivité, *f.*
outwear, *v.t.* (*p.p.* **outworn**) Durer plus longtemps que.
outweigh, *v.t.* Peser plus que; l'emporter sur.
outwit, *v.t.* Surpasser en finesse, duper; mettre en défaut.
outwith, *adv.* (*Sc*) [WITHOUT, *adv.*]
outwork, *n.* (*Fort.*) Ouvrage avancé, *m.*
outworker, *n.* Ouvrier à domicile, *m.*
outworn, *a.* Usé.
ouzel [u:zl], *n.* *Merle, *m. Brook-ouzel,* râle d'eau, *m.*; *ring-ouzel,* merle à plastron, *m.*; *water-ouzel,* merle plongeur, *m.*
oval [ouvl], *a.* and *n.* Ovale, *m.*
ovarian [ou'veəriən], *a.* Ovarien. **ovariotomy** [-'ɔtəmi], *n.* Ovariotomie, *f.*
ovary ['ouvəri], *n.* Ovaire, *m.*
ovate ['ouveit], *a.* Ové.
ovation [o'veiʃən], *n.* Ovation, *f.*
oven [ʌvn], *n.* Four, *m. Dutch oven,* cuisinière, *f.*; *field oven,* four roulant, *m.*; *in a quick, slow oven,* à feu vif, doux. **ovenful,** *n.* Fournée, *f.*
over ['ouvə], *prep.* Sur; par-dessus; au-dessus de; de l'autre côté de, au-delà de (on the other side); durant, pendant (during). *He lost over a hundred pounds,* il a perdu plus de cent livres sterling; *I shall be two hours over it,* j'en ai pour deux heures; *over head and ears in debt,* criblé de dettes; *over hill and dale,* par monts et par vaux; *over the water,* de l'autre côté de l'eau; *over there,* là-bas; *the aeroplane flew over England,* l'avion survola l'Angleterre; *the water is over one's shoes,* l'eau est au-dessus des souliers; *to be all over someone,* faire l'empressé auprès de quelqu'un; *to be placed over,* être placé au-dessus de; *to watch over someone's interests,* veiller aux intérêts de quelqu'un.
　　adv.—D'un côté à l'autre; de l'autre côté; par-dessus, au-dessus; trop (too); plus de (more than); de reste (more than the quantity assigned). *All over,* partout, par tout, des pieds jusqu'à la tête; *all the world over,* par

toute la terre; *carried over*, reporté; *I have heard it over*, je l'ai entendu du commencement jusqu'à la fin; *over!* tournez! (la page); (*Cricket*) changez! (de côté); (*Teleg.*) à vous! *over again*, de nouveau, encore une fois; *over and above*, en outre, en sus; *over and over (again)*, mille fois, sans cesse, incessamment; *red all over*, tout rouge; *the milk boiled over*, le lait s'est sauvé; *there is nothing over*, il n'y a rien de reste; *to fall over*, tomber à la renverse (people), se renverser (things); *to get over*, franchir, se remettre de, *passer; *to get* or *put* (something) *over*, (*pop.*) se faire comprendre; *to give over*, cesser; *to hand over*, livrer, remettre; *to have something over*, avoir de reste; *you are splashed all over*, vous êtes couvert d'éclaboussures.

a.—Fini, terminé, fait; passé. *He is over from France*, il est rentré de France; *I am glad it is over*, je suis content que ce soit fini; *it's all over with*, c'en est fait de; *the business is not over yet*, l'affaire n'est pas encore finie; *the danger is over*, le danger est passé; *to be all over*, être fini; *to be all over with*, en être fait de; *to be nearly over*, tirer à sa fin.

over-abundance [ouvərə'bʌndens], *n.* Surabondance, *f.* **over-abundant**, *a.* Surabondant.

overact [ouvər'ækt], *v.t.* Outrer, exagérer.

overacting, *n.* Charge, *f.*

over-age, *a.* Trop vieux.

overall, *n.* Blouse, *f.*; tablier, *m.*; (*pl.*) salopette, combinaison, *f.*—*a.* Global, total. *Over-all length* (dimensions), encombrement, *m.*

over-anxious, *a.* Qui met trop de soin.

overarm ['ouvəra:m], *a.* (*Box.*) *Overarm blow*, coup croisé; (*Ten.*) *overarm service*, service par en-dessus; (*Swim.*) *overarm* (*side-stroke*), nage indienne de côté (overarm).

overawe, *v.t.* Intimider, imposer à.

overbalance, *v.t.* L'emporter sur. *To overbalance* (*oneself*), perdre l'équilibre, faire la bascule.—*n.* Excédent, *m.*, prépondérance, *f.*

overbear, *v.t.* (*past* **overbore**, *p.p.* **overborne**) Maîtriser, surmonter, renverser.

overbearing, *a.* Impérieux, arrogant, autoritaire.

overbid, *v.t.* (*past* **overbid** or **overbade**, *p.p.* **overbidden**) Enchérir sur.

overboard, *adv.* Par-dessus bord, à la mer.

overbuild, *v.t.* (*past* and *p.p.* **overbuilt**) Surcharger de bâtiments.

overburden, *v.t.* Surcharger; accabler (de).

overbuy, *v.i.* (*past* and *p.p.* **overbought**) Faire trop d'achats.

over-capitalize, *v.t.* Surcapitaliser.

overcast [ouvə'ka:st], *v.t.* (*past* and *p.p.* **overcast**) Assombrir, obscurcir; porter trop haut (to compute); (*Dress.*) surjeter.—*a.* Couvert, nuageux; (*fig.*) sombre, obscur.

over-cautious, *a.* Par trop prudent.

overcharge, *v.t.* Surcharger; faire payer trop cher; majorer; charger trop (a fire-arm).—*n.* Charge excessive, *f.*; prix excessif, *m.*; surtaxe (of taxes), *m.*

overcloud, *v.t.* Couvrir de nuages; (*fig.*) obscurcir.

overcoat, *n.* Pardessus, *m.*

overcolour, *v.t.* Colorer trop; (*fig.*) exagérer.

overcome [ouvə'kʌm], *v.t.* (*past* **overcame**, *p.p.* **overcome**) Surmonter, vaincre, accabler. *I am quite overcome*, je n'en puis plus.—*v.i.* Être victorieux, l'emporter.

over-confidence, *n.* Confiance excessive, *f.*

over-confident, *a.* Trop confiant; présomptueux, téméraire.

overcrowd, *v.t.* Encombrer à l'excès, trop remplir.

overcrowding, *n.* Surpeuplement, *m.*

overdo, *v.t.* (*past* **overdid**, *p.p.* **overdone**) Exagérer, outrer; faire trop cuire; harasser, fatiguer (to fatigue). **overdone**, *a.* Trop cuit; éreinté (exhausted); (*fig.*) exagéré, outré.

overdose, *n.* Dose trop forte, *f.*

overdraft, *n.* Découvert, *m.*

overdraw, *v.t.* (*past* **overdrew**, *p.p.* **overdrawn**) Excéder. *To overdraw one's account*, dépasser le montant de son crédit, tirer à découvert.

overdress, *v.i.* Faire trop de toilette.

overdrive, *v.t.* (*past* **overdrove**, *p.p.* **overdriven**) Surmener; (*fig.*) pousser trop loin (a joke etc.).—*n.* (*Motor.*) Vitesse surmultipliée, *f.*

overdue, *a.* En retard.

overeat [ouvər'i:t], *v.i.* Manger trop.

over-elaborate, *a.* Trop compliqué.

overestimate, *v.t.* Évaluer trop haut, surestimer.

overexcite, *v.t.* Surexciter. **overexcitement**, *n.* Surexcitation, *f.*

over-expose, *v.t.* (*Phot.*) Surexposer. **overexposure**, *n.* Surexposition, *f.*

overfamiliar, *a.* Trop familier.

overfeed, *v.t.* Nourrir trop.

overflow, *v.i.* Déborder, se déborder; regorger (de).—*v.t.* Inonder.—*n.* Inondation, *f.*, débordement, *m.*; (*fig.*) surabondance, *f.*, excès, trop-plein, *m.* **overflowing**, *a.* Qui déborde, trop plein; (*fig.*) surabondant.—*n.* Débordement, épanchement, *m.*, effusion, *f.* *The hall was filled to overflowing*, il y avait salle comble. **overflowingly**, *adv.* À l'excès; surabondamment.

over-fond, *a.* Fou (de). **over-fondness**, *n.* Tendresse excessive, *f.*

overgrow, *v.t.* (*past* **overgrew**, *p.p.* **overgrown**) Couvrir (of plants).—*v.i.* Grandir trop. **overgrown**, *a.* Couvert (with plants etc.); trop grand, énorme. **overgrowth**, *n.* Accroissement excessif, *m.*

overhand, *n.* Dessus, *m.*

overhang, *v.t.* Surplomb; porte-à-faux, *m.*—*v.t.* (*past* and *p.p.* **overhung**) Pencher sur, être suspendu sur, surplomber; (*fig.*) menacer; pencher, surplomber; faire saillie. **overhanging**, *a.* En surplomb.

overhaul [ouvə'hɔ:l], *v.t.* Examiner, revoir; réviser, vérifier, démonter; (*Naut.*) radouber; gagner, rattraper (overtake).—*n.* Examen détaillé, *m.*; réfection, révision, *f.*, démontage, *m.*

overhead, *adv.* Par-dessus la tête, en haut.—*a.* Aérien (of wires etc.). *Overhead price*, prix forfaitaire, *m.*—*n.pl.*, or **overheads**. (*Comm.*) Frais généraux, *m.pl.*

overhear, *v.t.* (*past* and *p.p.* **overheard**) Entendre par hasard.

overheat, *v.t.* Échauffer trop; surchauffer. *To overheat oneself*, s'échauffer.

over-indulge, *v.t.* Gâter, être trop indulgent pour; se laisser aller trop librement à. **over-indulgent,** *a.* Trop indulgent.

overjoyed, *a.* Transporté de joie, ravi.

overladen, *a.* Surchargé (de).

overland, *a.* Par voie de terre. *Overland route,* voie de terre, *f.*

overlap, *v.t.* Recouvrir; déborder, dépasser. —*n.* Recouvrement, *m.* **overlapping,** *n.* Recouvrement, chevauchement, *m.*

overlay, *n.* Matelas; couvre-lit, *m.*—*v.t.* (*past* and *p.p.* **overlaid**) Couvrir.

overleaf, *adv.* Au verso.

overleap, *v.t.* Sauter par-dessus, franchir.

overlighted, *a.* Trop éclairé.

overload, *v.t.* Surcharger, surmener.—*n.* Surcharge, *f.*

overlook ['ouvə'luk], *v.t.* Avoir vue sur, donner sur, dominer; surveiller (to superintend); fermer les yeux sur (to excuse); passer sur, ne pas remarquer, négliger (to pass by).

overlooker ['ouvəlukə], *n.* Surveillant, inspecteur; contremaître (in factories), *m.* **overlooking,** *n.* Surveillance, *f.*—*a.* Qui a vue (sur), donnant (sur).

overlord, *n.* Suzerain, *m.*

overlying, *a.* Superposé.

overmantel, *n.* Étagère de cheminée, *f.*

over-mastering, *a.* Irrésistible; dominateur.

overmuch, *n.* Trop, *m.*—*a.* Excessif.—*adv.* Par trop, excessivement.

*over-nice, *a.* Trop délicat, difficile.

overnight, *adv.* Durant la nuit; hier soir; du jour au lendemain.

overpass, *n.* Passage supérieur, *m.*—*v.t.* Traverser; surpasser; outrepasser; omettre; ne pas remarquer.

overpay, *v.t.* Payer trop, surpayer, payer trop cher.

overpeopled, *a.* Surpeuplé.

overplus, *n.* Surplus, excédent, *m.*

over-populate, *v.t.* Surpeupler. **over-population,** *n.* Surpeuplement, *m.*

overpower, *v.t.* Être trop fort pour, vaincre; accabler (de). **overpowering,** *a.* Accablant, écrasant. **overpoweringly,** *adv.* Excessivement.

overpraise, *v.t.* Louer à l'excès.

overprint, *n.* Surcharge; surimpression, *f.*—*v.t.* Surcharger (a stamp); surimprimer.

overprize, *v.t.* Évaluer trop, estimer trop.

overproduction, *n.* Surproduction, *f.*

overrate ['ouvə'reit], *v.t.* Estimer trop haut, faire trop de cas de; surtaxer.

overreach, *v.t.* Tromper, jouer, duper.—*v.i.* Forger (of horses). *To overreach oneself,* trop présumer de ses forces (overstrain).

override, *v.t.* (*past* **overrode,** *p.p.* **overridden**) Surmener, outrepasser.

over-ripe, *a.* Trop mûr; trop fait (of cheese).

overrule, *v.t.* Dominer, gouverner, maîtriser; (*Law*) rejeter. **overruling,** *a.* Qui gouverne, souverain.

overrun, *v.t.* (*past* **overran,** *p.p.* **overrun**) Envahir, faire une irruption dans; infester (de); (*Print.*) remanier.—*v.i.* Déborder; (*Motor.*) entraîner le moteur. **overrunning,** *n.* Envahissement, *m.*, incursion, *f.*; (*Print.*) remaniement, *m.*

oversea or **overseas,** *a. and adv.* D'outre-mer.

oversee, *v.t.* Surveiller, avoir l'œil sur. **overseer,** *n.* Surveillant; administrateur du Bureau de bienfaisance; contremaître, chef d'atelier (of a factory etc.); (*Print.*) prote, *m.*

oversensitive, *a.* Hypersensible.

*overset, *v.t.* (*past* and *p.p.* **overset**) Renverser; verser (a vehicle); faire chavirer (a boat); (*fig.*) bouleverser.—*v.i.* Se renverser; verser (of vehicles); chavirer (of boats).

oversew, *v.t.* Surjeter.

overshadow, *v.t.* Ombrager, jeter dans l'ombre; éclipser, protéger.

overshoes, *n.pl.* Caoutchoucs, *m.pl.*

overshoot, *v.t.* (*past* and *p.p.* **overshot**) Dépasser. *To overshoot the mark,* dépasser le but.—*n.* (*Av.*) Rase-mottes, *m.inv.*

overshot, *a.* En dessus. *Overshot wheel,* roue mue en dessus, *f.*

oversight, *n.* Inadvertance, *f.*, oubli, *m.*; surveillance (superintendence), *f.*

oversleep, *v.i.* (*past* and *p.p.* **overslept**) Dormir au delà de son heure. *To oversleep oneself,* dormir trop longtemps.

overspend, *v.i.* Gaspiller son argent.—*v.r.* S'épuiser. **overspending,** *n.* Gaspillage, *m.*, prodigalité, *f.* **overspent,** *a.* Épuisé, exténué, excédé.

overspread, *v.t.* (*past* and *p.p.* **overspread**) Se répandre sur, couvrir.

overstate ['ouvə'steit], *v.t.* Exagérer.

overstatement, *n.* Exagération, *f.*

overstay, *v.t.* Dépasser la durée prévue de. *He has overstayed his welcome,* il a abusé de l'hospitalité de ses hôtes.

overstep, *v.t.* Dépasser.

overstock, *n.* Surabondance, *f.*—*v.t.* Remplir trop, encombrer (de).

overstrain, *v.t.* Outrer, pousser trop loin, forcer, surmener. *To overstrain oneself,* s'éreinter.—*v.i.* Faire de trop grands efforts. —*n.* Surmenage, *m.*

overstress, *v.t.* Trop insister sur, mettre trop l'accent sur; (*Tech.*) surcharger.—*n.* Surcharge, *f.*

overstrung, *a.* *Overstrung piano,* piano oblique, *m.*

over-subscribe, *v.t.* Surpasser.

overt ['ouvə:t], *a.* Ouvert, évident, manifeste, non déguisé. *Market overt,* marché public, *m.* **overtly,** *adv.* Ouvertement, manifestement. **overtness,** *n.* Franchise, *f.*

overtake, *v.t.* (*past* **overtook,** *p.p.* **overtaken**) Atteindre, rattraper; doubler, dépasser; surprendre. *No overtaking,* défense de doubler.

overtax, *v.t.* Surtaxer, surcharger pressurer.

overthrow (1) ['ouvə'θrou], *v.t.* (*past* **overthrew,** *p.p.* **overthrown**) Renverser; bouleverser, défaire, détruire.

overthrow (2) ['ouvəθrou], *n.* Renversement, bouleversement, *m.*, défaite; ruine, destruction, *f.*

overtime, *n.* Heures supplémentaires, *f.pl. Overtime rate,* tarif heures supplémentaires.

overtire, *v.t.* Excéder de fatigue.

overtone, *n.* (*usu. pl.*) Harmoniques, *m.pl.*

overtop, *v.t.* S'élever au-dessus de, dépasser.

over-train, *v.t.* Surentraîner.—*v.i.* Se claquer.

overtrump, *v.t.* Surcouper.—*n.* Surcoupe, *f.*

overture, *n.* Ouverture; offre, *f.*

overturn, *v.t.* Renverser; bouleverser; verser (a vehicle); faire chavirer (a boat).—*v.i.* Verser. **overturning,** *n.* Renversement, bouleversement, *m.*; chavirement, *m.* (of boat); capotage, *m.* (of car, aeroplane).

overvaluation, *n.* Estimation trop élevée, *f.*

overvalue, *v.t.* Estimer trop; (*Comm.*) évaluer trop.

overweening, *a.* Présomptueux, outrecuidant.

overweight, *n.* Excédent, *m.*, surcharge, *f.*

overwhelm, *v.t.* Accabler (de); combler de (kindness etc.). **overwhelming,** *a.* Accablant, écrasant. **overwhelmingly,** *adv.* D'une manière accablante.

overwork (1) [ouvə'wə:k], *v.t.* (*past* and *p.p.* **overworked** or **overwrought**) Surcharger de travail, excéder; surmener (a horse). *To overwork oneself,* se surmener.

overwork (2) ['ouvəwə:k], *n.* Travail excessif; travail en sus (extra); surmenage, *m.*

*****overworn,** *a.* Accablé de fatigue; usé.

overwrought [-'rɔ:t], *a.* Trop travaillé, trop élaboré; excédé, surmené.

Ovid ['ɔvid]. Ovide, *m.*

oviduct ['ouvidʌkt], *n.* Oviducte, *m.*

ovine ['ouvain], *a.* Ovine.

oviparous [o'vipərəs], *a.* Ovipare. **ovipositor** [ouvi'pɔzitə], *n.* Ovipositeur, *m.* **ovoid** ['ouvɔid], *a.* Ovoïde. **ovolo,** *n.* (*Arch.*) Ove, *m. Small ovolo,* ovicule, *m.* **ovulation,** *n.* Ovulation, *f.*

owe [ou], *v.t.* Devoir; être redevable à . . . de. *You must owe it to me,* vous me devrez cela.

owing, *a.* Dû (à). *Owing to,* à cause de, grâce à, qui tient à.

owl [aul], *n.* Hibou, *m. Barn owl,* or *church owl,* or *screech owl,* or *white owl,* or *church owl,* or *screech owl,* or *white owl,* effraie or chouette des clochers, *f.*; *brown owl* or *hootowl* or *wood-owl,* chat-huant, *m., or* hulotte, *f.*; *great white owl,* harfang, *m.*; *little owl* or *sparrow owl,* chevêche, *f.* **owlet,** *n.* Jeune hibou, *m.* **owlish,** *a.* De hibou. **owl-light,** *n.* Crépuscule, *m.*

own [oun], *a.* Propre (à soi). *At his own house,* chez lui; *it is a trick of his own,* c'est un tour de sa façon; *my own,* à moi, le mien; *my own money,* mon propre argent; *my own self,* moi-même; *there is not much of his own in that book,* il n'y a pas beaucoup du sien dans ce livre; *to hold one's own,* se maintenir.—*v.t.* Posséder, être propriétaire de (to possess) réclamer (to claim); avouer, confesser, convenir de (to confess).

owner ['ounə], *n.* Propriétaire, possesseur, *m. Shipowner,* armateur, *m.*; *the rightful owner,* l'ayant droit. **ownership,** *n.* Propriété, *f.*

ox [ɔks], *n.* (*pl.* **oxen**) Bœuf, *m.* **ox-eye,** *n.* (*Bot.*) Grande marguerite, *f.*; (*Orn.*) mésangère, *f.* **ox-fly,** *n.* Taon, *m.* **ox-goad,** *n.* Aiguillon, *m.* **ox-stall,** *n.* Étable à bœufs, *m.* **ox-tail,** *n.* Queue de bœuf, *f. Ox-tail soup,* soupe à la queue de bœuf, *f.* **ox-tongue,** *n.* (*Bot.*) Langue-de-bœuf, *f.*

oxalic [ɔk'sælik], *a.* Oxalique.

oxidation [ɔksi'deiʃən], *n.* Oxydation, *f.*

oxide ['ɔvid], *n.* Oxyde, *m.*

oxidizable [ɔksi'daizəbl], *a.* Oxydable.

oxidization [ɔksidai'zeiʃən], *n.* Oxydation; calcination, *f.* **oxidize** ['ɔksidaiz], *v.t.* Oxyder; calciner.

Oxonian [ɔk'souniən], *n.* Étudiant de l'université d'Oxford, Oxfordien, Oxonien, *m.*

oxyacetylene [ɔksiə'setili:n], *a.* Oxyacétylénique.

oxygen ['ɔksidʒən], *n.* Oxygène, *m.* **oxygenate,** *v.t.* Oxygéner. **oxygenation** [-'neiʃən], *n.* Oxygénation, *f.* **oxygenize,** *v.t.* Oxygéner.

oxygenous [ɔk'sidʒənəs], *a.* D'oxygène.

oxymoron [ɔksi'mɔ:rən], *n.* Alliance de mots, *f.*

oxytone ['ɔksitoun], *n.* Oxyton, *m.*

oyer ['ɔiə], *n.* (*Law*) Audition, *f. Oyer and terminer,* audition et jugement, *m.*

oyez! [ou'jes], *int.* Oyez! écoutez! faites silence!

oyster ['ɔistə], *n.* Huître, *f. Dumb as an oyster,* muet comme une carpe. *Pearl oyster,* huître perlière. **oyster-bed,** *n.* Banc d'huîtres, *m.* **oyster-breeding,** *n.* Ostréiculture, *f.* **oyster-catcher,** *n.* Huîtrier, *m.* **oyster-farm,** *n.* Parc à huîtres, *m.*, clayère, *f.* **oyster-farming,** *n.* Industrie huîtrière, ostréicole, *f.* **oyster-fishing,** *n.* Pêche des huîtres, *f.* **oyster-man,** *n.* Écailler, *m.* **oyster-shell,** *n.* Écaille d'huître, *f.* **oyster-woman,** *n.* Écaillère, *f.*

ozocerite [ou'zɔsərait], *n.* Ozocérite, cire minérale, *f.*

ozone [ou'zoun], *n.* Ozone, *m.* **ozoniferous** [-'nifərəs], *a.* Ozonifère.

ozonize ['ouzɔnaiz], *v.t.* Ozoniser.

ozonometer [ouzɔ'nɔmitə], *n.* Ozonomètre, *m.*

P

P, p [pi:]. Seizième lettre de l'alphabet, *m. To mind one's P's and Q's,* être sur son bien-dire, mettre les points sur les i, ouvrir l'œil.

pa [pɑ:], *n.* (fam.) Papa, *m.*

pabular ['pæbjulə], *a.* Alimentaire. **pabulum,** *n.* Aliment, *m.*, nourriture, *f.*

pace [peis], *n.* Pas, *m.*; allure (of a horse), *f.*; train, *m.*; vitesse, *f. At a great pace,* à grands pas, à grand train; *at an even pace,* au train soutenu, à l'allure égale; *at a slow pace,* au petit pas; *at a smart pace,* à vive allure; *at a walking pace,* au pas; *to force the pace,* forcer le pas, l'allure, la vitesse; *to gather pace,* prendre de la vitesse; *to go the pace,* être un viveur; *to keep pace with,* marcher avec, suivre, (*fig.*) marcher de pair avec; *to make, set, the pace,* donner le pas, donner l'allure, mener le train; *to mend* or *quicken one's pace,* presser le pas; *to put a horse through its paces,* faire passer un cheval à la montre; *to put someone through his paces,* mettre quelqu'un à l'épreuve.—*v.i.* Aller au pas, marcher; (of horse) aller l'amble. *To pace up and down,* se promener de long en large.—*v.t.* Arpenter; (*spt.*) entraîner. *To pace (off) a distance,* mesurer une distance au pas.

paced, *a.* Au pas. *Easy-paced,* doux au montoir; *slow-paced,* au pas lent; *thorough-paced rascal,* un fameux coquin.

pace-maker, *n.* Entraîneur, *m.*; meneur de train, *m.* **pace-making,** *n.* Règlement de l'allure, *m.*

pacha [PASHA].

pachyderm ['pækidə:m], *n.* Pachyderme, *m.* **pachydermatous** [-'də:mətəs], *a.* Pachyderme.

pacific [pə'sifik], *a.* Pacifique, paisible.—*n.* *The Pacific* (*Ocean*), le Pacifique, l'océan Pacifique, *m.* **pacification** [pæsifi'keiʃən], *n.* Pacification, *f.* **pacificatory** [pə'sifikətəri], *a.* Pacificateur, conciliatoire. **pacifier** ['pæsifaiə], *n.* Pacificateur, *m.* **pacifism** ['pæsifizm], *n.* Pacifisme, *m.* **pacifist** ['pæsifist], *n.* Pacifiste, *m.* or *f.* **pacify** ['pæsifai], *v.t.* Pacifier, apaiser. **pacifying,** *a.* Pacificateur. **pack** [pæk], *n.* Paquet, ballot, *m.*, balle, *f.*; bât, *m.* (of mule); (*Mil.*) paquetage, havresac, sac, *m.*; meute (of hounds), *f.*; jeu (of cards); (*Naut.*) embâcle, *m.* (of ice); (*Ftb.*) pack, *m.*; (*fig.*) tas, *m.* *Pack of lies*, tas, tissu de mensonges, *m.*; *put on packs!* sac au dos! *what a pack of nonsense!* quel tas de bêtises!—*v.t.* Emballer, empaqueter, encaisser; bourrer; tasser; mettre en baril (fish, meat, etc.); encaquer (herrings); trier subrepticement (a jury etc.); entasser (persons). *The train was packed*, le train était bondé. *To pack off*, expédier.—*v.i.* Se tasser; s'assembler; se grouper. *To pack off*, plier bagage; *to pack up*, emballer, empaqueter, faire sa malle; *to send packing*, envoyer promener. **package** ['pækidʒ], *n.* Colis, paquet, *m.* **packer,** *n.* Emballeur, empaqueteur, *m.* **packet,** *n.* Paquet, *m.*; paquebot (packet boat), *m.* *To make a packet*, gagner un argent fou. **pack-horse,** *n.* Cheval de bât, *m.* **pack-ice,** *n.* Glace de banquise, *f.*, pack, *m.* **pack-saddle,** *n.* Bât, *m.* **pack-thread,** *n.* Ficelle, *f.* **packing** ['pækiŋ], *n.* Emballage, encaissement, *m.*; mise en caisse, *f.*; rembourrage, *m.*, garniture (of a piston), *f.*; manipulation, *f.* (of jury). *To do one's packing*, faire ses malles. **packing-case,** *n.* Caisse d'emballage, *f.* **packing-case-maker,** *n.* Layetier, *m.* **packing-needle,** *n.* Aiguille à emballage, *f.*, carrelet, *m.* **packing-paper,** *n.* Papier d'emballage, *m.* **pact** [pækt], *n.* Pacte, *m.* **pad** [pæd], *n.* Tampon; coussinet, bourrelet (cushion), *m.*; sellette (of a saddle), *f.*; bloc (de papier), *m.*; bourriche, *f.*; (*Fenc.*) plastron, *m.*; (*Cricket*) jambière, *f.*; *route, *f.*; chemin, *m.*; bidet, cheval de promenade (pad-nag), *m.* *Gentleman of the pad*, voleur de grand chemin; *writing-pad*, sous-main, bloc de papier, *m.*—*v.i.* Aller à pied.—*v.t.* Ouater; rembourrer. *Padded cell*, cellule matelassée, *f.*; *padded shoulders*, épaules garnies; *to pad the hoof*, aller à pied. **padding,** *n.* Ouate, bourre, *f.*; remplissage, *m.*; délayage (in literary work or speech), *m.*; cheville (in line of poetry), *f.* **paddle** [pædl], *n.* Pagaie; palette, aube (of a wheel), *f.*; nageoire (of penguin, tortoise, etc.), *f.*—*v.t.* Pagayer. *To paddle one's own canoe*, se tirer seul d'affaire.—*v.i.* Barboter (comme un canard), patauger; battre (du linge); faucher (of horse); (*Row.*) tirer en douce; trottiner (to toddle). **paddle-board,** *n.* Palette, *f.* **paddle-boat,** *n.* Bateau à aubes, *m.* **paddle-box,** *n.* Tambour, *m.* **paddle-wheel,** *n.* Roue à aubes, *f.* **paddler** ['pædlə], *n.* Pagayeur, *m.*; barboteur, *m.*; (*pl.*) (*Cost.*) barboteuse, *f.* **paddling-pool,** *n.* Grenouillère, *f.* **paddock** ['pædək], *n.* Enclos, pré, pâturage, *m.*

Paddy ['pædi], *n.* Irlandais, *m.*; Patrice, *m.* **paddy-field,** *n.* Champ de riz, *m.* **padishah** ['pɑːdiʃɑː], *n.* Padischa, *m.* **padlock** ['pædlɔk], *n.* Cadenas, *m.*—*v.t.* Cadenasser, fermer au cadenas. **padre** ['pɑːdrei], *n.* Aumônier (militaire), *m.* **Padua** ['pædjuə]. Padoue, *f.* **Paduan,** *a.* and *n.* Padouan (-ane). **paean** ['piːən], *n.* Péan, *m.* **paederast** [PEDERAST], **paederasty** [PEDERASTY]. **pagan** ['peigən], *a.* and *n.* Païen, *m.*, païenne, *f.* **paganish,** *a.* Païen. **paganism,** *n.* Paganisme, *m.* **paganize,** *v.t.* Rendre païen; paganiser. **page** [peidʒ], *n.* Page (boy), *m.*; page (of a book), *f.* *Left-hand page*, verso; *right-hand page*, recto, *m.*—*v.t.* (*Print.*) Paginer. **pageant** ['pædʒənt], *n.* Spectacle pompeux; cortège (*or* spectacle) historique, *m.* *An empty pageant*, un pur spectacle. **pageantry,** *n.* Pompe, *f.*, faste, apparat, *m.* **page-boy,** *n.* Chasseur; groom, *m.* **page-proof,** *n.* Épreuve en page, *f.* **paginal** ['pædʒinl], *a.* À la page, page à page. **pagination** or **paging** ['peidʒiŋ], *n.* (*Print.*) Pagination, *f.* **paging-machine,** *n.* Machine à numéroter, *f.* **pagoda** [pə'goudə], *n.* Pagode, *f.* **paid** [peid], *a.* Payé, acquitté; pour acquit (on receipts); affranchi (of letters). *Carriage paid*, port payé. **paid-up,** *a.* Libéré (of shares etc.). **pail** [peil], *n.* Seau, *m.*, seille, *f.* (wooden); (*Naut.*) baille, *f.* **pailful,** *n.* (Plein) seau, *m.* **pain** [pein], *n.* Douleur, *f.*, peine (care), *f.* *He has a pain in his finger*, il a mal au doigt; *in pain*, souffrant; *on pain of*, sous peine de; *shooting pain*, douleur lancinante, *f.*, élancement, *m.*; *to be in pain*, souffrir; *to give someone pain*, (physical) faire souffrir quelqu'un, (mental) faire de la peine à quelqu'un; *to have nothing for one's pains*, en être pour sa peine; *to take pains*, se donner de la peine.—*v.t.* Faire mal à, faire souffrir; (*fig.*) faire de la peine à; peiner, affliger. **pained,** *a.* Attristé, peiné. **painful,** *a.* Douloureux, pénible; (*fig.*) fâcheux. **painfully,** *adv.* Douloureusement, péniblement. **painfulness,** *n.* Douleur; peine, *f.* **pain-killer,** *n.* Anodin, antalgique, *m.* **painless,** *a.* Sans douleur, indolore. **painstaking,** *a.* Soigneux, assidu; travailleur, appliqué. *Painstaking work*, travail soigné. **paint** [peint], *n.* Couleur; peinture, *f.*; fard (for the face), *m.* *Wet paint*, peinture fraîche; *attention à la peinture!*—*v.t.* Peindre; (*fig.*) dépeindre; farder (the face). *To paint the throat*, badigeonner la gorge.—*v.i.* Peindre; se farder. *To paint white*, peindre en blanc. **paint-box,** *n.* Boîte de couleurs, *f.* **paint-brush,** *n.* Pinceau, *m.* **painter,** *n.* Peintre; peintre décorateur; câbleau, *m.*; bosse, amarre, *f.* *To cut the painter*, couper les amarres. **painting,** *n.* Peinture, *f.*; tableau (picture), *m.* **paintwork** ['peintwəːk], *n.* (*Build.*) Les peintures, *f.pl.* **pair** [pɛə], *n.* Paire, *f.*; couple (of married people etc.), *m.* *A carriage and pair*, une voiture à deux chevaux; *in pairs*, deux à deux. *Pair of stairs*, (un) étage, *m.*; *pair of steps*, escabeau, *m.*; *pair of trousers*, pantalon, *m.—v.t.* Apparier, accoupler; marier (colours); (*fig.*) assortir.—*v.i.* S'accoupler, s'apparier; (*fig.*) s'assortir.

pairing, *n.* Accouplement, appariement, *m.* **pairing-off,** *n.* (*Parl.*) Absence convenue d'un membre ministériel et d'un membre de l'opposition, *f.* **pairing-time,** *n.* Saison de l'accouplement, *f.*

pair-oar, *n.* Deux de pointe (sans barreur), *m.*

pajamas [pə'dʒɑ:məz], *n.* (*Am.*) Pyjama, *m.*

Pakistan [pɑ:ki'stɑ:n *or* pæki'stɑ:n]. Le Pakistan, *m.*

pal [pæl], *n.* (*slang*) Camarade, copain, *m.—v.i.* *To pal up with someone*, se lier d'amitié avec quelqu'un; devenir copain avec quelqu'un.

palace ['pælis], *n.* Palais, *m.* *Archbishop's palace*, archevêché, *m.*; *bishop's palace*, évêché, *m.* **palace-car,** *n.* Wagon de luxe, *m.*

paladin ['pælədin], *n.* Paladin, *m.*

palaeographer [pæli'ɔgrəfə], *n.* Paléographe.

palaeographic [-ə'græfik], *a.* Paléographique.

palaeography [pæli'ɔgrəfi], *n.* Paléographie, *f.*

palaestra [pə'li:strə], *n.* Palestre, *f.* **palaestral,** *a.* Palestrique.

palankeen *or* **palanquin** [pælən'ki:n], *n.* Palanquin, *m.*

palatable ['pælətəbl], *a.* Agréable au goût, bon; (*fig.*) agréable. **palatableness,** *n.* Saveur agréable, *f.*

palatal, *a.* (*Gram.*) Palatal.—*n.* Palatale, *f.*

palate ['pælit], *n.* Palais; (*fig.*) goût, *m.* *Cleft palate*, palais fendu; *soft palate*, voile du palais, *m.*

palatial [pə'leiʃl], *a.* Du palais, palatial; magnifique, grandiose.

palatinate [pə'lætinit], *n.* Palatinat, *m.*

palatine ['pælətain], *a. and n.* Palatin, *m.*

palaver [pə'lɑ:və], *n.* Palabre, *f.*; conférence, *f.* (with natives); verbiage, *m.*; flagornerie, *f.*; embarras, *m.pl.—v.i.* Palabrer, dire de belles paroles, faire des phrases.—*v.t.* Amadouer, flagorner.

pale [peil], *a.* Pâle, blême; (*fig.*) blafard (of light). *A pale green dress*, une robe d'un vert pâle; *pale as death*, pâle comme la mort; *to turn pale*, pâlir.—*v.t.* Pâlir, faire pâlir; entourer de palis, palissader; (*fig.*) renfermer. —*v.i.* Pâlir; (*fig.*) s'éclipser. *His story pales beside yours*, son histoire pâlit auprès de la vôtre.—*n.* Pieu, palis; pal (punishment), *m.*; limites (bounds), *f.pl.*; enceinte (enclosure), *f.*; (*fig.*) giron, sein (of the Church), *m. Beyond the pale*, au ban de la société.

pale-eyed, *a.* Aux yeux ternes.

pale-face, *n.* Blanc, *m.*, blanche, *f.* **pale-faced,** *a.* Au teint pâle.

palely, *adv.* Avec pâleur, *f.*

paleness, *n.* Pâleur, *f.*

Palermo [pə'lə:mou]. Palerme.

Palestine ['pælistain]. Palestine, *f.* **Palestinian** ['pælis'tiniən], *a. and n.* Palestin; palestinien.

palette ['pælit], *n.* Palette, *f.* **palette-knife,** *n.* Couteau à palette, *m.*

palfrey ['pɔ:lfri], *n.* Palefroi, *m.* **palfreyed,** *a.* Monté sur un palefroi.

palindrome ['pælindroum], *n.* Palindrome, *m.*

paling ['peiliŋ], *n.* Palissade, *f.*

palinode ['pælinoud], *n.* Palinodie, *f.*

palisade [pæli'seid], *n.* Palissade, *f.*; palis, *m.* —*v.t.* Palissader.

palish ['peiliʃ], *a.* Un peu pâle, pâlot.

pall [pɔ:l], *n.* Poêle; (*fig.*) drap mortuaire; pallium (of an archbishop); manteau (mantle), *m.*; voile (of smoke etc.), *m.—v.t.* Couvrir d'un manteau de parade (to cloak); envelopper; affadir, rendre insipide (to make vapid); affaiblir.—*v.i.* Devenir fade, s'affadir. *It soon palls on one*, on s'en dégoûte vite.

palladium [pə'leidiəm], *n.* Palladium, *m.*

pall-bearer, *n.* Personne qui tient un cordon du poêle, *f.*

pallet ['pælit], *n.* Grabat, *m.*, paillasse, *f.*; palette, *f.*

palliasse ['pæliæs], *n.* Paillasse, *f.*

palliate ['pælieit], *v.t.* Pallier. **palliation** [-'eiʃən], *n.* Palliation, *f.*

palliative ['pæliətiv], *a. and n.* Palliatif, *m.*

pallid ['pælid], *a.* Pâle, blême, blafard. **pallidly,** *adv.* Avec pâleur. **pallidness,** *n.* Pâleur, *f.*

pallium ['pæliəm], *n.* Pallium, *m.*

pall-mall ['pel'mel], *n.* *Mail, *m.*

pallor ['pælə], *n.* Pâleur, *f.*

pally ['pæli], *a.* (*slang*) Liant. *To be pally with someone*, être lié, être copain avec quelqu'un.

palm [pɑ:m], *n.* Paume (of the hand), *f.*; palmier (tree), *m.*; palme (branch); (*Naut.*) patte, *f. To bear the palm*, remporter la palme; *to grease someone's palm*, graisser la patte à quelqu'un; *with open palm*, la main ouverte.—*v.t.* Escamoter; manier (to handle). *To palm off a thing upon someone for*, faire passer à quelqu'un une chose pour.

palmar ['pælmə], *a.* Palmaire. **palmate,** *a.* Palmé.

palmer ['pɑ:mə], *n.* *Pèlerin (revenant de la Terre-Sainte); paumier; prestidigitateur, *m.*

palmette [pæl'met], *n.* Palmette, *f.* **palmiferous** [-'mifərəs], *a.* Palmifère.

palmiped ['pælmiped], *a. and n.* Palmipède, *m.*

palmist ['pɑ:mist], *n.* Chiromancien, *m.* **palmistry,** *n.* Chiromancie, *f.*

palm-oil, *n.* Huile de palme, *f.* **Palm Sunday,** *n.* Dimanche des Rameaux, *m.* **palm-tree,** *n.* Palmier, *m.*

palmy ['pɑ:mi], *a.* Beau, glorieux, heureux. *In the palmy days of*, dans les jours heureux de.

palp [pælp], *n.* Palpe, *f.*

palpability [pælpə'biliti], *n.* Nature palpable, *f.*

palpable ['pælpəbl], *a.* Palpable; manifeste, évident, clair. **palpably,** *adv.* Palpablement, d'une manière palpable; manifestement.

palpate [pæl'peit], *v.t.* Palper.

palpation [pæl'peiʃən], *n.* (*Med.*) Palpation, *f.*

palpebral ['pælpəbrəl], *a.* (*Anat.*) Palpébral.

palpitate ['pælpiteit], *v.i.* Palpiter. **palpitating,** *a.* Palpitant. **palpitation** [-'teiʃən], *n.* Palpitation, *f.*

palsied ['pɔ:lzid], *a.* Frappé de paralysie, paralytique. **palsy,** *n.* Paralysie, *f.*

palter ['pɔ:ltə], *v.i.* Tergiverser, biaiser, équivoquer. **palterer,** *n.* Chercheur d'équivoques, de faux-fuyants, *m.*

paltriness ['pɔ:ltrinis], *n.* Mesquinerie, *f.*; petitesse, *f.* **paltry,** *a.* Mesquin, misérable. *A paltry excuse*, une misérable excuse; *a paltry sum*, une somme insignifiante; *his verses are of the most paltry description*, vers sont des plus pitoyables.

paludal [pə'lju:dəl], *a.* Paludique; paludéen, *m.*, -enne, *f.*
paly ['peili], *a.* (*Her.*) Palé; vergeté.
Pamela ['pæmələ]. Paméla, *f.*
pampas ['pæmpəs], *n.* Pampas, *f.pl.* **pampasgrass**, *n.* Gynérion argenté, *m.*; herbe des pampas, *f.*
pamper ['pæmpə], *v.t.* Choyer, dorloter; (*fig.*) flatter, caresser.
pamphlet ['pæmflit], *n.* Brochure, *f.*; (*literary, scientific*) opuscule, *m.*; (*pej.*) pamphlet, *m.*
pamphleteer [-'tiə], *n.* Auteur de brochures; (*pej.*) pamphlétaire, *m.*—*v.i.* Écrire des brochures *or* des pamphlets.
Pan [pæn]. (Le dieu) Pan. *The pipes of Pan,* la flûte de Pan.
pan [pæn], *n.* Casserole, *f.*; poêlon, *m.*; *bassinet (of a gun), *m.*; batée, *f.* (to wash gold-bearing earth). *Flash in the pan,* feu de paille, *m.*; *frying-pan,* poêle, *f.*; *his gun flashed in the pan,* son fusil rata; *lavatory-pan,* cuvette de cabinets, *f.*; *preserving-pan,* bassine, *f.*; *warming-pan,* bassinoire, *f.* (*Cine.*) *Pan shot,* panoramique, *m.*—*v.t.* To pan out, laver (à la batée).—*v.i.* Rendre, produire. *The business did not pan out well,* l'affaire n'a pas réussi.
panacea [pænə'si:ə], *n.* Panacée, *f.*
panache [pæ'næʃ], *n.* Panache, *m.*, ostentation, *f.*
pan-Americanism [pænə'merikənizm], *n.* Pan-américanisme, *m.*
pancake ['pænkeik], *n.* Crêpe, *f.* *As flat as a pancake,* plat comme une galette; *to toss a pancake,* faire sauter une crêpe.—*v.i.* (*Av.*) *To pancake to the ground,* descendre à plat, asseoir l'appareil, (se) plaquer.
panchromatic [pænkro'mætik], *a.* (*Phot., Cine.*) Panchromatique.
pancratium [pæn'kreiʃiəm], *n.* Pancrace, *m.*
pancreas ['pænkriəs], *n.* (*Anat.*) Pancréas, *m.* **pancreatic** [-'ætik], *a.* Pancréatique.
pandects ['pændekts], *n.pl.* Pandectes, *f.pl.*
pandemic [pæn'demik], *a.* Pandémique.—*n.* Pandémie, *m.*
pandemonium [pændi'mouniəm], *n.* Pandémonium, *m.*
pander ['pændə], *n.* Entremetteur, *m.*—*v.i.* Se prêter à, se faire complaisant pour.
pane [pein], *n.* Carreau, *m.*, vitre, *f.*
panegyric [pæni'dʒirik], *n.* Panégyrique, *m.*—*a.* De panégyrique.
panegyrical, *a.* Élogieux.
panegyrist [pæni'dʒirist], *n.* Panégyriste, *m.*
panegyrize ['pænidʒiraiz], *v.t.* Louer, faire l'éloge de.—*v.i.* Faire un panégyrique.
panel [pænl], *n.* Panneau, *m.*; (*Law*) tableau, *m.*; liste (of a jury etc.), *f.*; *Instrument panel,* tableau de manœuvre, *m.*; planche de bord, *f.*—*v.t.* Diviser en panneaux; lambrisser; (*Law*) dresser une liste de. **panelled**, *a.* Lambrissé, boisé; revêtu de boiseries. *Oak-panelled,* à panneaux de chêne. **panelling**, *n.* Panneaux, *m.pl.*, lambrissage, *m.*
panel-doctor, *n.* Médecin au service des assurances sociales, *m.*
pang [pæŋ], *n.* Angoisse, vive douleur, *f.*, serrement de cœur, *m.* *To feel the pangs of hunger,* entendre crier ses entrailles.
panic ['pænik], *n.* Panique; terreur panique, *f.* —*a.* Panique.—*v.t.* Remplir de panique, affoler.—*v.i.* Être pris de panique, s'affoler.

panic-(grass), *n.* (*Bot.*) Panic, panis, *m.*
panic-stricken, *a.* Pris de panique, affolé.
panicky, *a.* (*colloq.*) Sujet à la panique, alarmiste. *Don't get panicky,* ne vous affolez pas.
panicle ['pænikl], *n.* (*Bot.*) Panicule, *f.*
paniculate [pə'nikjulət] *or* **panicled,** *a.* Panicule.
panification [pænifi'keiʃən], *n.* Panification, *f.*
panjandrum [pæn'dʒændrəm], *n.* (*colloq.*) Un gros bonnet, *m.* *Grand Panjandrum,* grand manitou, *m.*
pannage ['pænidʒ], *n.* (*Law*) Panage, *m.*
pannier ['pæniə], *n.* Panier, panier de bât, *m.*, hotte, *f.*
pannikin ['pænikin], *n.* Écuelle, *f.*, gobelet, *m.* (en fer-blanc).
panoply ['pænəpli], *n.* Panoplie, armure complète, *f.*
panorama [pænə'rɑ:mə], *n.* Panorama, *m.* **panoramic** [-'ræmik], *a.* Panoramique.
pansy ['pænzi], *n.* (*Bot.*) Pensée, *f.*; (*slang*) mignon, giton, *m.*
pant [pænt], *n.* Palpitation, *f.*, souffle pantelant, halètement, battement, *m.*—*v.i.* Haleter, palpiter, panteler, battre du flanc (animal). *To pant after,* soupirer après; *to pant for breath,* haleter, être à court de souffle. **panting**, *n.* Battement de cœur, *m.*; palpitation, *f.*, essouflement, *m.*; (*fig.*) désir ardent, *m.*—*v.t.* To pant out, dire en haletant. **pantingly**, *adv.* En palpitant, en haletant.
pantagruelian [pæntəgru'eliən], *a.* Pantagruélique. **pantagruelism** [-'gru:əlizm], *n.* Pantagruélisme, *m.* **pantagruelist**, *n.* Pantagruéliste, *m.*
pantaloon [pæntə'lu:n], *n.* Pantalon, *m.*; (*pl.*) pantalon, *m.*
pantechnicon [pæn'teknikən], *n.* Garde-meuble, *m.*; voiture de déménagement, tapissière, *f.*
pantheism ['pænθi:izm], *n.* Panthéisme, *m.* **pantheist**, *n.* Panthéiste, *m.* **pantheistic** [-'istik] *or* **pantheistical**, *a.* Panthéistique.
pantheon [-'θi:ən], *n.* Panthéon, *m.*
panther ['pænθə], *n.* Panthère, *f.*; (*Am.*) couguar, puma, *m.*
panties ['pæntiz], *n.pl.* (*colloq.*) Culotte de petit enfant, *f.*; culotte collante (of a woman).
pantile ['pæntail], *n.* Tuile faîtière *or* flamande, *f.*
pantler ['pæntlə], *n.* Panetier, *m.*
pantograph ['pæntogræf *or* -grɑ:f], *n.* Pantographe, *m.*
pantomime ['pæntəmaim], *n.* Pantomime, *f.*; spectacle traditionnel de Noël, fondé sur un conte de fée; pantomime (person), *m.* **pantomimic** [-'mimik], *a.* Pantomime. **pantomimist**, *n.* Pantomime, *m.*
pantry ['pæntri], *n.* Office, *f.*, garde-manger, *m.*
pants [pænts], *n.pl.* (*Colloq.*) Caleçon, *m.* (*Am.*) pantalon, *m.*
pap [pæp], *n.* Mamelle, *f.*; mamelon, tétin, *m.*; bouillie (food), *f.*
papa [pə'pɑː], *n.* Papa, *m.*
papacy ['peipəsi], *n.* Papauté, *f.* **papal**, *a.* Papal, du pape. *The Papal States,* Les États de l'Église *or* Pontificaux, *m.pl.*
papaverous [pə'peivərəs], *a.* (*Bot.*) De pavot. *Papaverous plant,* papavéracée, *f.*
papaw [pə'pɔː], *n.* (*Bot.*) Papaye, *f.* **papaw-tree,** *n.* Papayer, *m.*

paper ['peipə], *n.* Papier, *m.*; feuille de papier, *f.*; journal (newspaper); papier-monnaie, (*Comm.*) effet, *m.*; billets, *m.pl.*; valeurs, *f.pl.*; mémoire, *m.*, étude (article); composition (examination-paper), *f.*; (*pl.*) papiers, titres, mémoires, *m.pl.*, dossier, *m.* *Art paper,* papier couché, *m.*; *blotting-paper,* papier buvard, *m.*; *brown paper,* papier gris, *m.*; *call-up papers,* ordre d'appel, *m.*; *carbon paper,* papier carbone, *m.*; *foreign paper,* papier pelure, *m.*; *glossy paper,* papier brilant, *m.*; *imperial paper,* papier jésus, *m.*; *letter-paper* or *note-paper,* papier à lettres, *m.*; *long dated paper,* billet à longue échéance, *m.*; *printing-paper,* papier d'impression, *m.*; *public papers,* journaux, *m.pl.*, feuilles publiques, *f.pl.*; *ship's papers,* papiers de bord, *m.pl.*; *short paper,* valeur payable à vue, *f.*; *silver paper,* papier d'argent, *m.*; *tissue-paper,* papier de soie, *m.*; *tracing-paper,* papier à calquer, *m.*; *voting-paper,* bulletin de vote, *m.*; *waste paper,* papier de rebut, *m.*; *writing-paper,* papier à écrire, papier à lettres, *m.*; *to commit to paper, to put down on paper,* coucher par écrit; *the idea is excellent on paper,* l'idée est excellente en théorie; *to read a paper* (to learned society etc.), faire une communication, une conférence, un exposé; *to send in one's papers,* donner sa démission.—*a.* De papier. *A paper army,* une armée sur le papier; *paper bag,* sac en papier, *m.*; *paper blockade,* blocus ineffectif, *m.*; *paper currency,* papier-monnaie, *m.*; *paper profits,* profits fictifs, *m.pl.*; *paper work,* épreuves écrites, *f.pl.*—*v.t.* Tapisser (de papier), mettre du papier sur; empaqueter. **paper-back,** *n.* Livre broché, *m.* **paper-backed,** *a.* Broché. **paper-chase,** *n.* Rallye-papier, *m.* **paper-clamp,** *n.* Pince-notes, pince-feuilles, *m.* **paper-clip,** *n.* Attache, *f.*, trombone, *m.* (wire). **papered,** *a.* Tapissé. **paper-fastener,** *n.* Attache métallique, *f.* **paper-folder,** *n.* Plioir, *m.* **paper-hanger,** *n.* Colleur de papier, *m.* **paper-hangings,** *n.pl.* Papier peint, *m.* **paper-holder,** *n.* Serre-papiers, *m.* **paper-knife,** *n.* Coupe-papier, *m.* **paper-maker,** *n.* Fabricant de papier, *m.* **paper-making,** *n.* Fabrication du papier, papeterie, *f.* **paper-mill,** *n.* Papeterie, *f.* **paper-money,** *n.* Papier-monnaie, *m.* **paper-trade,** *n.* Papeterie, *f.* **paperweight,** *n.* Presse-papiers, *m.*

papier-mâché [pæpjei'mæʃei], *n.* Carton-pâte, *m.*

papilionaceous [pəpilio'neiʃəs], *a.* (*Bot.*) Papilionacé. *Papilionaceous plant,* papilionacée, *f.*

papilla [pə'pilə], *n.* (*Anat.*) Papille, *f.* **papillary, papillose,** *a.* Papillaire. **papilliferous** [pæpi'lifərəs], *a.* Papillifère.

papilliform [pə'pilifɔːm], *a.* Papilliforme.

papism ['peipizm], *n.* Papisme, *m.* **papist,** *n.* Papiste, *m.* **papistry,** *n.* Papisme, *m.*

pappose [pə'pous] or **pappous** ['pæpəs], *a.* (*Bot.*) Pappeux. **pappus,** *n.* (*Bot.*) Aigrette, *f.*

pappy ['pæpi], *a.* Mou, pâteux, flasque.

Papua ['pəpuːə]. Papouasie, Nouvelle-Guinée, *f.* **Papuan,** *a.* and *n.* Papou.

papula ['pæpjulə], *n.* Papule, *f.* **papuliferous** [-'lifərəs], *a.* Papulifère. **papulous,** *a.* Papuleux.

papyraceous [pæpi'reiʃəs], *a.* Papyracé.

papyrus [pə'paiərəs], *n.* (*pl.* **papyri**) Papyrus, *m.*

par [pɑː], *n.* Pair, *m.*, égalité, *f.*, (*Golf*) normale, *f.* *Above par,* au-dessus du pair; *at par,* au pair; *exchange at par,* change à la parité, *m.*; *below par,* au-dessous du pair; (*fig.*) *to feel below par,* être mal en train; *on a par with,* de pair avec.

parabasis [pə'ræbəsis], *n.* Parabase, *f.*

parable ['pærəbl], *n.* Parabole, *f.*

parabola [pə'ræbələ], *n.* Parabole, *f.* **parabolic** [pærə'bɔlik] or **-ical,** *a.* Par parabole; allégorique; (*Geom.*) parabolique. **parabolically,** *adv.* Paraboliquement.

paraboloid [pə'ræbəlɔid], *n.* Paraboloïde, *m.*

paracentesis [pærə'sentisis], *n.* Paracentèse, *f.*

parachronism [pær'ækrənizm], *n.* Parachronisme, *m.*

parachute [pærə'ʃuːt], *n.* Parachute, *m.*—*v.i.* Descendre en parachute, parachuter.—*v.t.* Parachuter. **parachuting,** *n.* Parachutage, *m.* **parachutist,** *n.* Parachutiste, *m.* or *f.*

Paraclete ['pærəkliːt], *n.* Le Paraclet, *m.*

parade [pə'reid], *n.* Parade, *f.*; étalage, *m.*; esplanade, promenade publique, *f.*; boulevard maritime, *m.*; (*Mil.*) rassemblement; exercice, *m.*; défilé, cortège, *m.*; procession, *f.* *Beauty parade,* concours de beauté, *m.*; *church parade,* rassemblement (d'une unité) pour assister à l'office, *m.*; (*fig.*) promenade des familles à la sortie de l'office, *f.*; *fashion parade,* présentation de collections, *f.*; *mannequin parade,* défilé de mannequins (in a shop), *m.*; *on parade,* à l'exercice; *parade ground,* place d'armes, *f.*, terrain de manœuvre, *m.*; *to go on parade,* parader.—*v.t.* Faire parade de; afficher; promener fièrement; (*Mil.*) rassembler, faire l'inspection de, faire défiler.—*v.i.* Faire de la parade; (*Mil.*) faire la parade; parader.

paradigm ['pærədaim], *n.* Paradigme, *m.*

paradise ['pærədais], *n.* Paradis, *m.* *Bird of paradise,* paradisier, *m.*; *earthly paradise,* paradis sur terre, *m.*; *to go to paradise,* aller en paradis; *to live in a fool's paradise,* vivre dans une fausse sécurité. **paradisiacal** [-di'zaiəkl], *a.* Paradisiaque.

paradox ['pærədɔks], *n.* Paradoxe, *m.* **paradoxical** [-'dɔksikl], *a.* Paradoxal. **paradoxically,** *adv.* D'une manière paradoxale, paradoxalement. **paradoxy,** *n.* Paradoxisme, *m.*

paraffin ['pærəfin], *n.* (*Chem.*) Paraffine, *f.*; (*colloq. instead of* paraffin oil) pétrole, *m.* *Paraffin lamp,* lampe à pétrole, *f.*; *paraffin wax,* paraffine solide, *f.*—*v.t.* Paraffiner; pétroler.

paragenesis [pærə'dʒenisis], *n.* Paragénésie, *f.*

paragon ['pærəgən], *n.* Parangon; modèle; (*fig.*) phénix (person), chef-d'œuvre, *m.*

paragraph ['pærəgraːf], *n.* Paragraphe; alinéa (break in a page), *m.*; entrefilet (in newspapers), *m.* *To begin a new paragraph,* aller à la ligne.—*v.t.* Diviser en paragraphes. **paragraphically,** *adv.* Par paragraphes.

Paraguay ['pærəgwai]. Le Paraguay, *m.* **Paraguayan,** *a.* and *n.* Paraguayen, -enne.

parakeet [pærə'kiːt], *n.* (*Orn.*) Perruche, *f.*

parallactic [pærə'læktik], *a.* Parallactique.

parallax ['pærəlæks], *n.* Parallaxe, *f.*

parallel ['pærəlel], *a.* Parallèle; (*fig.*) semblable, pareil. *To run parallel with,* être

parallèle à, aller parallèlement à, se conformer à. *Parallel connection,* accouplement parallèle, *m.*; *cells in parallel,* piles en parallèle, *f.pl.*; *dynamos out of parallel,* dynamos déphasées, *f.pl.—n.* Ligne parallèle, *f.*, parallèle, *m.*; (*fig.*) comparaison, *f. To draw a parallel between,* établir un parallèle entre; *without parallel,* sans pareil.—*v.t.* Mettre dans une ligne parallèle (à); mettre en parallèle; (*fig.*) comparer (à); être pareil (à). *Never paralleled,* qui n'a jamais eu son pareil. **parallelism,** *n.* Parallélisme, *m.*; (*fig.*) ressemblance, comparaison, *f.*, parallèle, *m.* **parallelepiped** [-'lepiped] or **parallelepipedon** [-'pipidən], *n.* Parallélépipède, *m.* **parallelogram** [-'leləgræm], *n.* Parallélogramme, *m.* **parallelly,** *adv.* Parallèlement.
paralogism [pə'rælədʒizm], *n.* Paralogisme, *m.* ***paralogize,** *v.i.* Faire un paralogisme.
paralyse ['pærəlaiz], *v.t.* Paralyser. *To be paralysed,* être frappé de paralysie; *to be paralysed in one arm,* être paralysé d'un bras; *to be paralysed with fear,* être glacé d'effroi, transi de peur.
paralysis [pə'rælisis], *n.* Paralysie, *f.* **paralytic** [pærə'litik], *a.* Paralytique.—*n.* Paralytique, *m.* or *f. Paralytic stroke,* attaque de paralysie, *f.*
parameter [pə'ræmitə], *n.* Paramètre, *m.*
paramilitary [pærə'militəri], *a.* Paramilitaire.
paramount ['pærəmaunt], *a.* Souverain, suprême, principal. *Lord paramount,* suzerain, *m.*; *paramount power,* le pays souverain, *m. Of paramount importance,* d'une suprême importance; *pleasure is paramount with him,* chez lui le plaisir l'emporte sur tout.—*n.* Souverain, seigneur, *m.* **paramountcy** [-si], *n.* Suzeraineté; primauté, *f.*
paramour ['pærəmuə], *n.* Amant, *m.*, amante, maîtresse, *f.*
paranoia [pærə'nɔiə], *n.* Paranoïa, *f.*
parapet ['pærəpit], *n.* (*Fort.*) Parapet; garde-fou, garde-corps (on bridge etc.), *m.*
paraph ['pærəf], *n.* Parafe, *m.—v.t.* Parafer.
paraphernal [pærə'fɔːnl], *a.* (*Law*) Paraphernal. **paraphernalia** [-'neiliə], *n.pl.* (*Law*) Biens paraphernaux, *m.pl.*; équipage, attirail, *m.*; ornements, atours, falbalas, *m.pl.*
paraphrase ['pærəfreiz], *n.* Paraphrase, *f.—v.t.* Paraphraser. **paraphraser,** *n.* Paraphraseur, *m.* **paraphrast** [-fræst], *n.* Paraphraste, *m.* **paraphrastic** [-'fræstik], *a.* Paraphrastique.
paraplegia [pærə'pliːdʒə], *n.* Paraplégie, *f.*
parasang ['pærəsæŋ], *n.* Parasange, *f.*
paraselene [pærəsə'liːni], *n.* (*Astron.*) Parasélène, *f.*
parasite ['pærəsait], *n.* Parasite, écornifleur, pique-assiette, *m.* **parasitic** [-'sitik] or **parasitical,** *a.* Parasite, parasitique. **parasitically,** *adv.* En parasite.
parasitism ['pærəsitizm], *n.* Parasitisme, *m.*
parasol [pærə'sɔl], *n.* Ombrelle, *f.*, parasol, *m.*
parasynthesis [pærə'sinθisis], *n.* Dérivation parasynthétique, *f.* **parasynthetic,** *a.* Parasynthétique.
paratactic [pærə'tæktik], *a.* (*Gram.*) Paratactique. **parataxis,** *n.* Parataxe, *f.*
paratrooper [pærə'truːpə], *n.* (Soldat) parachutiste, *m.*

paratroops ['pærətruːps], *n.pl.* (Soldats) parachutistes, *m.pl.*
paratyphoid [pærə'taifɔid], *n.* Paratyphoïde, *f.*
paravane ['pærəvein], *n.* Paravane, paremines, *m.*
parboil ['paːbɔil], *v.t.* Faire bouillir à demi.
parbuckle ['paːbʌkl], *n.* (*Naut.*) Trévire, *f.—v.t.* Trévirer.
Parcae ['paːsiː], *n.pl.* (*Myth.*) Parques, *f.pl.*
parcel [paːsl], *n.* Colis, paquet; lot, *m.*; (*Comm.*) partie (a part), *f.*; (*pej.*) tas, *m. Bill of parcels,* facture d'envoi, *f.*; *parcel post,* service des colis postaux, *m.*; *parcels delivery,* service de livraison (à domicile), factage, *m.*; *parcels office,* bureau des messageries, *m.*; *postal parcel,* colis postal, *m.*; *to be part and parcel of,* faire partie intégrante de; *to do up a parcel,* faire un paquet.—*v.t.* Morceler, diviser, partager; empaqueter; (*Naut.*) limander. *To parcel out,* morceler (land), parceller, partager; *to parcel up,* emballer, mettre en paquets.
parcenary ['paːsənəri], *n.* (*Law*) Succession indivise, *f.* **parcener,** *n.* Copropriétaire, cohéritier, *m.*
parch [paːtʃ], *v.t.* Brûler, dessécher (par la chaleur). *My lips are parched with thirst,* la soif m'a desséché les lèvres; *to be parched up,* être desséché; *to be parched with thirst,* être dévoré de soif.—*v.i.* Se brûler; se dessécher.
parchment ['paːtʃmənt], *n.* Parchemin, *m. Parchment paper,* papier parcheminé, *m.* **parchment-maker,** *n.* Parcheminier, *m.* **parchment-works,** *n.* Parcheminerie, *f.*
*pard [paːd], *n.* Léopard, *m.*
pardon ['paːdən], *n.* Pardon, *m.*; (*Law*) grâce, *f. General pardon,* amnistie, *f.*; *I beg your pardon!* je vous demande pardon! *I beg your pardon?* plaît-il? pardon? comment? *to ask someone's pardon for something,* demander pardon à quelqu'un de quelque chose.—*v.t.* Pardonner (quelque chose à quelqu'un), pardonner à; gracier. *Pardon me!* pardon! permettez! **pardonable,** *a.* Excusable, pardonnable (of things); digne de pardon (of persons); (*Law*) graciable. **pardonableness,** *n.* Nature pardonnable, *f.* **pardonably,** *adv.* Excusablement. ***pardoner,** *n.* Vendeur d'indulgences, *m.*
pare [pɛə], *v.t.* Peler (fruit etc.); éplucher; rogner (to clip); ébarber (paper etc.); doler (leather); parer (horse's hoof). *To pare one's nails,* se couper or se rogner les ongles.
paregoric [pæri'gɔrik], *a.* and *n.* Parégorique, *m.*
parenchyma [pə'reŋkimə], *n.* Parenchyme, *m.*
parent ['pɛərənt], *n.* Père, *m.*, mère, *f.*; (*pl.*) parents, les père et mère; (*Law*) ascendants directs, *m.pl.—a.* Mère. *Submarine parent ship,* ravitailleur de sous-marins, *m.* **parentage,** *n.* Parentage, *m.*; naissance, extraction, *f.*
parental [pə'rentl], *a.* Des parents, du père, de la mère; paternel, maternel.
parenthesis [pə'renθisis], *n.* (*pl.* **parentheses**) Parenthèse, *f. By way of parenthesis,* par parenthèse; *in parentheses,* entre parenthèses. **parenthetic** [-pærən'θetik] or **parenthetical,** *a.* Entre parenthèses. **parenthetically,** *adv.* Par parenthèse.
parenthood, *n.* Paternité, maternité, *f.*

parget ['pɑ:dʒit], *n.* Crépi, plâtre, *m.—v.t.* Crépir. **pargeting, pargetry,** *n.* Crépissage, plâtrage, *m.*; plâtres, *m.pl.*

parhelion [pɑː'hiːliən], *n.* (*pl.* **parhelia**) Parélie, parhélie, faux soleil, *m.*

pariah ['pɛəriə], *n.* Paria, *m.* **pariah-dog,** *n.* Chien métis des Indes, *m.*

Parian ['pɛəriən], *a.* De Paros.

parietal [pə'raiətl], *a.* De mur; (*Anat.*) pariétal.

paring ['pɛəriŋ], *n.* Rognage, rognement; ébarbage; dolage; épluchage, *m.* *Cheese-paring* (*fig.*), parcimonie, lésine, *f.*; (*pl.*) rognures (clippings); épluchures (of vegetables); pelures (of fruit etc.), *f.pl.*; cisaille (of metal), *f.* **paring-knife,** *n.* Tranchet, *m.*

Paris ['pæris]. Paris, *m.* *Plaster of Paris,* plâtre de Paris, plâtre de moulage, *m.*

parish ['pæriʃ], *n.* (*Eccles.*) Paroisse; (*civil*) commune, *f.* *To come on the parish,* tomber à la charge de la commune.—*a.* De la commune; communal, vicinal (of roads, rates, etc.); (*Eccles.*) de la paroisse, paroissial. *Parish church,* église paroissiale, *f.*; *parish priest,* curé du village, *m.*; *parish-pump politics,* politique de clocher, *f.*; *parish register,* registres de la paroisse, *m.pl.*; *parish relief,* secours du bureau de bienfaisance, *m.*; *parish school,* école communale, *f.*

parishioner [pə'riʃənə], *n.* Habitant de la commune; paroissien, *m.*

Parisian [pə'riziən], *a.* De Paris, parisien.—*n.* Parisien, *m.*, Parisienne, *f.*

parisyllabic [pærisi'læbik], *a.* Parisyllabe, parisyllabique.

parity ['pæriti], *n.* Parité; égalité (of rank etc.); analogie, *f.* *At parity,* à la parité, au pair.

park [pɑːk], *n.* Parc, *m.* *Car-park attendant,* gardien d'autos, *m.*; *public park,* jardin public, *m.—v.t.* Enfermer dans un parc; parquer, garer. (*colloq.*) *To park oneself,* s'installer, se planquer.—*v.i.* Stationner. **parking,** *n.* Stationnement, parcage, *m.* *No parking,* défense de stationner; *parking lights,* feux de position, *m.pl.*; *parking meter,* compteur de stationnement, *m.*; *parking place,* (parc de) stationnement, *m.* **park-keeper,** *n.* Gardien de parc, *m.*

parky ['pɑːki], *a.* (*colloq.*) Frisquet.

parlance ['pɑːləns], *n.* Parler, langage, *m.* *In common parlance,* dans le langage ordinaire; *in legal parlance,* en termes de pratique.

parley ['pɑːli], *n.* Pourparlers, *m.pl.*, négociation, *f.*, conférence, *f.* *To beat a parley,* battre la chamade.—*v.i.* Être *or* entrer en pourparlers (avec); (*Mil.*) parlementer; entamer des négociations.

parliament ['pɑːləmənt], *n.* Parlement, *m.*; (*France*) les Chambres, *f.pl.* *Act of Parliament,* loi, *f.*; *in Parliament,* au parlement; *Member of Parliament,* député, *m.*; *the two Houses of Parliament,* les deux Chambres, *f.pl.*

parliamentarian [-'tɛəriən], *n.* Parlementaire, *m.* **parliamentary** [-'mentəri], *a.* Parlementaire, du parlement. *Parliamentary election,* élection législative, *f.*; *parliamentary language,* langage parlementaire, langage courtois, *m.*; *parliamentary register,* liste électorale, *f.*

parlour ['pɑːlə], *n.* Petit salon; parloir (in convents or schools), *m.* *Bar parlour,* arrière-salle de taverne, *f.*; *beauty-parlour,* institut de beauté, *m.*; *parlour games,* petits jeux de société; *parlour tricks,* arts d'agrément, talents de société, *m.pl.* **parlour-boarder,** *n.* Élève en chambre, *m.* or *f.* **parlour-maid,** *n.* Femme de chambre, *f.* (qui sert à table).

parlous ['pɑːləs], *a.* Alarmant, dangereux, périlleux, précaire; *fin, rusé, fourbe; rude.

Parma ['pɑːmə]. Le duché de Parme; (la ville de) Parme.

Parmesan [pɑːmi'zæn], *n.* Parmesan (cheese), *m.*

Parnassian [pɑː'næsiən], *a.* Du Parnasse; (*Lit.*) Parnassien.—*n.* Parnassien, *m.* **Parnassus,** *n.* Parnasse, *m.*

parochial [pə'roukiəl], *a.* Communal; (*Eccles.*) paroissial. *Parochial spirit,* esprit de clocher, *m.* **parochialism,** *n.* Esprit de clocher, *m.* **parochially,** *adv.* Par commune; par paroisse.

parodist ['pærədist], *n.* Parodiste, pasticheur, *m.*

parody ['pærədi], *n.* Parodie, *f.* *Parody of justice,* travestissement de la justice, *m.—v.t.* Parodier.

parol ['pærəl], *n.* (*Law*) *By parol,* verbalement.

parole [pə'roul], *n.* Parole (d'honneur), *f.*; *mot d'ordre, *m.* *To be on parole,* être prisonnier sur parole; *to break one's parole,* manquer à sa parole.

paronomasia [pærənə'meiziə], *n.* Paronomase, *f.*

paronym ['pærənim], *n.* Paronyme, *m.*

paronymous [pə'rɔniməs], *a.* Paronymique. **paronymy,** *n.* Paronymie, *f.*

parotid [pə'rɔtid], *a.* and *n.* (*Anat.*) Parotide, *f.*

paroxysm ['pærəksizm], *n.* Paroxysme, accès, *m.*

paroxytone [pə'rɔksitoun], *n.* and *a.* Paroxyton, *m.*

parpen ['pɑːpən], *n.* Parpaing, *m.* *Parpen wall,* mur de parpaing, *m.*

parquet ['pɑːki or pɑː'ket], *n.* Parquet, *m.—v.t.* Parqueter. **parquet-flooring,** *n.* Parquetage, *m.* **parquetry,** *n.* Parqueterie, *f.*

parr [pɑː], *n.* Saumoneau, *m.*

parricidal [pæri'saidl], *a.* Parricide. **parricide** ['pærisaid], *n.* Parricide, *m.*

parrot ['pærət], *n.* (*Orn.*) Perroquet, *m.* *Hen parrot,* perruche, *f.*; *parrot disease,* psittacose, *f.*; *parrot-green,* céladon, *a.* and *n.*; *to repeat parrot-fashion,* répéter comme un perroquet; seriner. **parrotry,** *n.* Psittacisme, *m.*

parry ['pæri], *v.t.* Parer, détourner; (*fig.*) éluder, éviter. *To parry and thrust,* riposter; *to parry a question,* éluder une question.—*n.* Parade, *f.*

parse [pɑːz], *v.t.* Analyser (grammaticalement).

Parsee [pɑː'siː], *n.* Parsi, Guèbre, *m.*

parsimonious [pɑːsi'mouniəs], *a.* Parcimonieux; économe; pingre. **parsimoniously,** *adv.* Avec parcimonie. **parsimoniousness** or **parsimony** ['pɑːsiməni], *n.* Parcimonie, épargne; pingrerie, *f.*

parsing ['pɑːziŋ], *n.* Analyse grammaticale, *f.*

parsley ['pɑːsli], *n.* (*Bot.*) Persil, *m.*

parsnip ['pɑːsnip], *n.* (*Bot.*) Panais, *m.*

parson ['pɑːsn], *n.* Curé; (*Protestant*) pasteur, *m.* *Parson's nose* (*colloq.*), croupion (d'une volaille), *m.* **parsonage** ['pɑːsnidʒ], *n.* Presbytère, *m.*, cure, *f.*

part [pɑːt], *n.* Partie; part, portion (portion), *f.*; (*Theat.*) rôle; parti (side), *m.*; fascicule, *m.*; livraison (of a book), *f.*; endroit (place), *m.*; région (district), *f.*; quartier (quarter); (*pl.*) talent, *m.*, moyens, *m.pl.*; intelligence, *f. Do your part and do not trouble about the rest,* faites votre devoir et ne vous inquiétez pas du reste; *for my part,* quant à moi, pour moi; *for the most part,* pour la plupart; *from all parts,* de tous côtés; *good in parts,* bon en partie; *I had no part in it,* je n'y suis pour rien; *in a great part,* en grande partie; *in foreign parts,* à l'étranger; *in good part,* en bonne part; *in ill part,* en mauvaise part; *in my part of the world,* par chez moi; *in part,* en partie, partiellement; *in parts,* par fascicule (of books); *in the early part,* dans les premiers jours, au commencement; *in these parts,* dans ces parages; *machine part,* élément de machine, *m.*; *man of (good) parts,* homme de talent; *on the part of,* de la part de; *part and parcel,* partie intégrante, *f.*; *parts of speech,* parties du discours, *f.pl.*; *principal parts* (of verb), temps principaux, *m.pl.*; *single parts,* pièces détachées; *spare parts,* pièces de rechange, *f.pl.*; *that is too much presumption on your part,* c'est une trop grande présomption de votre part; *the funny part is that . . .,* ce qu'il y a de comique c'est que . . .; *the greater part,* la plupart, la plus grande partie; *to be the part of,* être du devoir de; *to form part of,* faire partie de; *to play a part,* jouer un rôle; *to sing in parts,* chanter à plusieurs voix; *to take part in,* prendre part à; *to take the part of,* prendre le parti *or* la défense de, prendre fait et cause pour.—*v.t.* Partager, diviser; fendre (a crowd); séparer (de); (*Naut.*) rompre (a cable); (*Chem.*) faire le départ de. *To part company with someone,* se séparer de quelqu'un; *to part one's hair,* se faire une raie.—*v.i.* Se séparer (de); se quitter; se rompre (of cables). *To part with,* se défaire de, se séparer de.—*a. Item taken in part exchange,* reprise *f.*; *part payment,* versement à compte, *m.*, paiement partiel, *m.*—*adv.* Partiellement, en partie. *Part one, part the other,* moitié l'un, moitié l'autre. **part-owner,** *n.* Co-propriétaire. **part-singing,** *n.* Chant en parties, *m.* **part-song,** *n.* Chanson à plusieurs voix, *f.* **part-time,** *n.* and *a.* (Emploi) à temps partiel. *To be on part time,* être en chômage partiel.

partake [pɑːˈteik], *v.t.* (*past* **partook,** *p.p.* **partaken**) Participer, prendre part (à).—*v.i. To partake of,* prendre part à, participer à; (to have something of the nature of) participer de, tenir de. *To partake of a dish,* goûter, manger un mets; *to partake of a meal,* prendre un repas. **partaker,** *n.* Participant, *m. To be a partaker of,* participer à, prendre part à.

parterre [pɑːˈtɛə], *n.* Parterre, *m.*

parthenogenesis [pɑːθənouˈdʒenisis], *n.* Parthénogénèse, *f.*

Parthia [ˈpɑːθiə]. Parthie, *f.* **Parthian,** *n.* and *a.* Parthe. *A Parthian shot,* la flèche du Parthe.

partial [ˈpɑːʃl], *a.* Partial (biased), injuste; partiel (not total). *To be partial to,* aimer, avoir un faible pour. **partiality** [-ʃiˈæliti], *n.* Partialité (bias); (*fig.*) prédilection, *f.*, goût, *m.*; affection, préférence, *f.* **partially,** *adv.*

Avec partialité, partialement (with a bias), partiellement, en partie (in part).

partible [ˈpɑːtibl], *a.* Divisible.

participant [pɑːˈtisipənt], *a.* and *n.* Participant, *m.* **participate,** *v.i.* Participer (à). *To participate of,* participer de; *to participate in,* prendre part à, participer à.—*v.t.* Participer à. **participation** [-ˈpeiʃən], *n.* Participation, *f.* **participative** [-ˈtisipeitiv], *a.* Participatif. **participator** [-ˈtisipeitə], *n.* Participant, *m.*

participial [-ˈsipiəl], *a.* De la nature du participe. **participially,** *adv.* Comme participe.

participle [ˈpɑːtisipl], *n.* Participe, *m. Past participle,* participe passé, *m.*; *present participle,* participe présent.

particle [ˈpɑːtikl], *n.* Particule, molécule, parcelle, *f.*; atome, *m.*; paillette (of metal), *f. He has not a particle of honour in him,* il n'a pas un grain d'honneur.

parti-coloured [ˈpɑːtiˈkʌləd], *a.* Bigarré, bariolé, panaché.

particular [pəˈtikjulə], *a.* Particulier, déterminé, spécial; précis, exact, minutieux, méticuleux, pointilleux, scrupuleux; difficile, exigeant (over-nice). *A particular account,* un récit détaillé; *a particular friend of mine,* un de mes amis intimes; *I am not particular to a day,* je ne regarde pas à un jour; *nothing particular,* rien de particulier; *particular in one's dress,* recherché dans sa toilette; *to be particular about it,* y tenir, y regarder de près; *to be particular in choosing,* choisir avec soin.—*n.* Particularité, *f.*, détail; (*pl.*) détails, renseignements, *m.pl.*; signalement, *m. For further particulars apply to . . .,* pour plus amples renseignements s'adresser à . . .; *further particulars,* de plus amples détails; *in every particular,* en tout point; *in particular,* particulièrement, en particulier. **particularity** [-ˈlæriti], *n.* Particularité, *f.*; détail; point circonstancié, *m.* **particularize** [-ˈtikjuləraiz], *v.t.* Particulariser, détailler minutieusement.—*v.i.* Entrer dans des détails minutieux; préciser. **particularly,** *adv.* Particulièrement; principalement, surtout.

parting [ˈpɑːtiŋ], *a.* De séparation; d'adieu; dernier. *Parting words,* paroles d'adieu, *f.pl.* —*n.* Séparation, *f.*, départ, *m.*; rupture (of cable), *f.*; raie (of hair), *f. To be at the parting of the ways,* être au carrefour.

partisan [pɑːtiˈzæn], *n.* Partisan, *m.*; bâton (quarterstaff), *m.*; pertuisane (halbert), *f. Partisan spirit,* esprit de parti, *m.*

partition [pɑːˈtiʃən], *n.* Partage (division), *m.*; cloison (in a room etc.), *f. Glass partition,* vitrage, *m.*—*v.t.* Partager, diviser; séparer par une cloison. **partition-wall,** *n.* Mur de refend, *m.*, cloison, *f.*

partitive [ˈpɑːtitiv], *a.* and *n.* Partitif, *m.* **partitively,** *adv.* Dans un sens partitif.

partly [ˈpɑːtli], *adv.* En partie, partiellement.

partner [ˈpɑːtnə], *n.* (*Comm.*) Associé, *m.*, -ée, *f.*; (*colloq.*) compagnon, *m.*, compagne, *f.*; (*Dancing*) danseur, *m.*, danseuse, *f.*, cavalier, *m.*; (*Cards, spt.*) partenaire, *m.*; (*Naut. pl.*) étambrai, *m. Sleeping* (*or dormant*) *partners,* associés commanditaires; *senior partner,* associé principal; *junior partner,* associé intéressé, *m.*—*v.t.* S'associer à; être le partenaire de (games); mener (a woman in dancing). **partnership,** *n.* Association, *f.*

To enter into partnership with, s'associer avec; *to take someone into partnership,* prendre quelqu'un comme associé.
partridge ['pɑːtridʒ], *n.* (*Orn.*) Perdrix, *f.* *Young partridge,* perdreau, *m.*
parturient [pɑːˈtjuəriənt], *a.* Prête à enfanter; en parturition. **parturition** [-ˈriʃən], *n.* Enfantement, *m.,* parturition, *f.*
party ['pɑːti], *n.* Parti (politique), *m.*; partie (of pleasure), *f.*; (*fig.*) réunion, *f.*; réception, *f.*; monde, *m.*; (*Mil.*) détachement, *m.*; troupe, *f.*; groupe, *m.*; bande, *f.*; (*colloq.*) personne, *f.,* individu, *m.* *Attacking party,* colonne d'attaque, *f.*; *birthday party,* réunion d'anniversaire, *f.*; *contracting party,* partie contractante, *f.,* contractant, *m.*; *evening party,* soirée, *f.*; *fatigue party,* corvée, *f.*; *firing party,* peloton d'exécution, *m.*; *hunting party,* partie de chasse, *f.*; *Labour Party,* parti travailliste, *m.*; *landing party,* compagnie de débarquement, *f.*; *leader of a party,* chef de parti, *m.*; *party allegiance,* fidélité à son parti, *f.*; *party dress,* toilette de soirée, *f.*; *party spirit,* esprit de parti, *m.*; *rescue party,* équipe de secours, *f.*; *storming party,* colonne d'assaut, *f.*; *third party,* tiers, *m.,* tierce personne, *f.*; *third party insurance,* assurance au tiers, *f.*; *third party risks,* risques de préjudice au. tiers, *m.pl.*; *to be a party to,* être complice de; *to be of the party,* être de la partie; *to get up a party,* faire une partie; *to give a party,* recevoir du monde, donner une soirée; *to go to a party,* aller en soirée; *will you join our party?* voulez-vous être des nôtres?
party-man, *n.* Homme de parti, *m.* **party-wall,** *n.* Mur mitoyen, *m.*
parvis ['pɑːvis], *n.* Parvis, *m.*
Paschal [pɑːskl], *a.* Pascal.
pasha ['pɑːʃə], *n.* Pacha, *m.*
pashalic ['pɑːʃəlik], *n.* Pachalik, *m.*
pasque-flower ['pæskflauə], *n.* Pulsatille, fleur de Pâques, *f.*
pasquinade [pæskwiˈneid], *n.* Pasquinade, *f.*
pass [pɑːs], *v.t.* Passer; passer par, passer devant; dépasser; devancer; faire passer; approuver (accounts); prononcer (sur); faire (a law); voter (an Act etc.); engager (one's word). *That passes my comprehension,* cela me dépasse; *to pass a candidate,* recevoir un candidat; *to pass an examination,* être reçu, réussir, à un examen; *to pass by,* passer devant *or* à côté de, omettre, oublier, ne pas faire attention à, pardonner; *to pass muster,* passer, être passable; *to pass off,* faire passer, faire accepter, faire accroire, donner en payement; *to pass over,* ˺ franchir, traverser, pardonner, omettre, glisser sur; *to pass round,* faire circuler; *to pass sentence,* prononcer le jugement; *to pass the buck,* mettre l'affaire sur le dos de quelqu'un; *to pass the censor,* être accepté par la censure; *to pass the news along,* faire circuler les nouvelles.—*v.i.* Passer, se passer, s'écouler (of time); mourir (to die); (*Exam.*) être reçu; (*Ftb.*) faire une passe; (*fig.*) arriver, avoir lieu. *Be it said in passing,* soit dit en passant; *pass!* (*Cards*) parole! *pass on!* circulez! *to be brought to pass,* arriver, s'accomplir; *to bring to pass,* accomplir, faire arriver; *to come to pass,* arriver; *to let someone pass,* livrer passage à quelqu'un; *let it pass!* passe pour cela! *to pass away,* se passer, s'évanouir, disparaître,

mourir; *to pass by,* passer devant; *to pass for,* passer pour; *to pass on,* passer son chemin, passer outre; trépasser, mourir; *to pass out,* sortir; (*fig.*) s'évanouir; *to pass over,* passer sur; *to pass through,* passer par; *words passed between them,* il y a eu quelques paroles entre eux.—*n.* Passage, défilé, *m.*; gorge, *f.,* col, *m.*; (*Rail.*) carte de circulation, *f.*; permis; (*Mil. etc.*) laissez-passer, sauf-conduit, *m.,* permission, *f.*; (*Navy*) lettres de mer, *f.pl.*; (*Ftb.*) passe, *f.*; (*Fenc.*) passe, botte, *f.*; (*Theat. etc.*) billet gratuit, *m.*; entrée libre, *f.*; (*fig.*) point, état, *m.,* extrémité, *f.* *Have things come to this pass?* les choses en sont-elles venues là? *he knows enough to get a pass,* il sait tout juste ce qu'il faut pour passer l'examen.
passable ['pɑːsəbl], *a.* Praticable; navigable (of water); passable, tolérable. **passably,** *adv.* Passablement; tolérablement.
passage ['pæsidʒ], *n.* Passage, *m.,* traversée, *f.*; (*Arch.*) couloir, corridor, *m.*; ruelle, *f.*; rapports, *m.pl.,* privautés, *f.pl.* *Passage of arms,* passe d'armes, *f.*; échange de mots vifs, *m. Bird of passage,* oiseau de passage, *m.*; *to force a passage,* s'ouvrir un passage; *to work one's passage,* gagner son passage. **passage-money,** *n.* Prix de la traversée, *m.*
passant ['pæsənt], *a.* (*Her.*) Lion passant gardant, lion léopardé, *m.*
pass-book, *n.* Livre de compte, carnet de banque, *m.* **pass-key,** *n.* Passe-partout, *m.* **pass-mark,** *n.* Moyenne, *f.* **pass-out ticket,** *n.* Contremarque de sortie, *f.*
passenger ['pæsəndʒə], *n.* Voyageur, *m.,* -euse, *f.*; passager, *m.,* -ère, *f.* (by sea or air); (*fig.*) non-valeur (in game etc.), *f.* **passenger train,** *n.* Train de voyageurs, *m.*
passer ['pɑːsə] or **passer-by,** *n.* (*pl.* **passers-by**) Passant, *m.*
passerine ['pæsərain], *a.* (*Orn.*) Des passereaux.
passible ['pæsibl], *a.* Passible.
passing ['pɑːsiŋ], *a.* Passager, éphémère, fugitif.—*adv.* Extrêmement, éminemment, fort bien.—*n.* Passage; écoulement (of time), *m.*; (*fig.*) trépas (death), *m. Passing of a Bill,* adoption d'un projet de loi, *f.* **passing-bell,** *n.* Glas, *m.* **passing-note,** *n.* Note de passage, *f.*
passion ['pæʃən], *n.* Passion; colère, *f.,* emportement, *m. In a passion,* en colère; *music is a passion with him,* la musique est sa passion; *to have a passion for doing something,* avoir la passion de, s'acharner à, faire quelque chose; *to put oneself into a passion,* se mettre en colère, s'emporter. **passionate,** *a.* Passionné, ardent; irascible, vif, emporté. **passionately,** *adv.* À la passion; à la folie, passionnément; avec colère, ardemment. **passionateness,** *n.* Caractère passionné, *m.*; véhémence, ardeur, *f.* **passion-flower,** *n.* Passiflore, fleur de la passion, *f.* **Passion play,** *n.* Mystère (de la Passion), *m.* **Passion Week,** *n.* Semaine de la Passion, *f.* **passionless,** *a.* Sans passion; impassible.
passive ['pæsiv], *a.* and *n.* Passif, *m. Verb in the passive,* verbe au passif, *m.* **passively,** *adv.* Passivement. **passivity** [-ˈsiviti] or **passiveness,** *n.* Passivité, inertie, *f.*
Passover ['pɑːsouvə], *n.* La pâque, *f.*
passport ['pɑːspɔːt], *n.* Passeport, *m. Passport photograph,* photo d'identité, *f.*

password ['pɑ:swəːd], *n.* Mot de passe; mot d'ordre, *m.*

past [pɑ:st], *a.* Passé; ancien; dernier (recent). *These past days*, ces jours derniers, *m.pl.—prep.* Au-delà de; au-dessus de; près de; sans, hors de; plus de (of age); passé (of the hour). *For some time past*, depuis quelque temps; *half-past twelve*, midi et demi; *half-past two*, deux heures et demie; *he ran past*, il passa près de là en courant; *in the past tense*, au passé; *in times past*, autrefois; *it is past ten*, il est dix heures passées; *it is ten minutes past three*, il est trois heures dix; *past a child*, qui a passé l'enfance; *past belief*, incroyable; *past cure*, incurable; *past endurance*, insupportable; *past feeling*, sans sentiment; *past remedy*, sans remède.—*n.* Passé, *m. In the past*, au temps passé; autrefois; *that's a thing of the past*, cela n'existe plus; *what is his past?* quels sont ses antécédents? **past-master**, *n.* Maître passé, passé maître, expert, *m.*

paste [peist], *n.* Colle de farine, colle (for sticking); pâte (for pastry), *f.*; stras (imitation gem), *m.—v.t.* Coller. *To paste up*, afficher. **pasteboard**, *n.* Carton, *m.—a.* De carton. **pasteboard-maker**, *n.* Cartonnier, *m.*

pastel ['pæstəl], *n.* Pastel, *m.* **pastellist**, *n.* Pastelliste, *m.*

pastern ['pæstəːn], *n.* Paturon, *m.*

pasteurize ['pæstəraiz], *v.t.* Pasteuriser (milk).

pasticcio [pæs'titʃou] or **pastiche** [pæs'tiːʃ], *n.* Pastiche, *m.*

pastille [pæs'tiːl], *n.* Pastille, *f.*

pastime ['pɑːstaim], *n.* Passe-temps, amusement, *m.*, distraction, *f.*

pastiness ['peistinis], *n.* Nature pâteuse (of bread etc.) *f.*; teint brouillé (of person), *m.*

pasting ['peistiŋ], *n.* Collage, *m.* (*fig.*) *To give someone a pasting*, flanquer une rossée à quelqu'un.

pastor ['pɑːstə], *n.* Pasteur; berger (shepherd), *m.*

pastoral ['pɑːstərəl], *a.* Pastoral.—*n.* Pastorale, églogue, *f.* **pastorally**, *adv.* Pastoralement. **pastorate**, *n.* Pastorat, *m.* **pastorless**, *a.* Sans pasteur.

pastry ['peistri], *n.* Pâtisserie, *f.* **pastrycook**, *n.* Pâtissier, *m.*

pasturable ['pɑːstjuərəbl], *a.* Pâturable. **pasturage** ['pɑːstjuərədʒ], *n.* Pâturage, *m.* **pasture**, *n.* Pâture, *f.*, herbage, *m.*; pâturage (ground), *m.—v.i.* Paître.—*v.t.* Faire paître. **pastureland**, *n.* Pâturage, *m.* **pastureless**, *a.* Sans pâture.

pasty (1) ['pæsti], *n.* Pâté, *m.*

pasty (2) ['peisti], *a.* Pâteux. *Pasty face*, visage terreux or brouillé, *m.*

pat [pæt], *n.* Petite tape; caresse; coquille, *f.*; rond de beurre, *m. Pat on the back* (*fig.*), éloge, mot d'encouragement, *m.—adv. and a.* À propos, tout juste.—*v.t.* Taper, tapoter; caresser, flatter. *To pat oneself on the back*, s'applaudir. **pat-ball**, *n.* La balle au camp (game).

patch [pætʃ], *n.* Pièce; mouche (of the face), *f.*; morceau (of land); (*Naut.*) placard (for mending a sail), *m.*; emplâtre (on wound), *m.*; échappée, *f.*, pan, *m.* (of sky); tache (of colour), *f.*; pastille (for tyre), *f. Eye-patch*, couvre-œil, *m.*; *not to be a patch on*, (slang)

n'être pas digne d'être comparé à; *to strike a bad patch*, être en déveine.—*v.t.* Rapiécer, raccommoder. *To patch up*, arranger (à la va-vite); bâcler; rabibocher (a quarrel).

patcher, *n.* Ravaudeur, *m.*, ravaudeuse, *f.*; savetier, gâcheur, *m.*

patchiness, *n.* Manque d'harmonie, manque d'unité, *m.*

patching, *n.* Rapiéçage, ravaudage, *m.*

patchwork, *n.* Ouvrage fait de pièces rapportées, mélange, *m.*, mosaïque, *f.*

patchy, *a.* Fait de pièces et de morceaux; inégal; mal fondu.

pate [peit], *n.* (*colloq.*) Caboche, tête, *f. Empty-pated, shallow-pated*, à caboche vide.

patella [pə'telə], *n.* Rotule; patelle, *f.*

paten ['pætən], *n.* Patène, *f.*

patent ['peitənt *or* 'pætənt], *n.* Lettres patentes, *f.pl.*, brevet, brevet d'invention, *m. To take out a patent*, prendre un brevet.—*a.* Breveté; (*fig.*) patent, apparent, évident.—*v.t.* Accorder des lettres patentes à; breveter. **patent leather**, *n.* Cuir verni, *m.* **patent medicine** *n.* Spécialité pharmaceutique, *f.* **patent office**, *n.* Bureau des brevets d'invention, *m.*

patentable, *a.* Brevetable. **patented**, *a.* Breveté. **patentee** [-'tiː], *n.* Breveté, *m.*, brevetée, *f.*

pater (the) ['peitə], *n.* (*colloq.*) Mon père, le paternel.

patera ['pætərə], *n.* (*pl.* **paterae**) Patère, *f.*

paterfamilias [peitəfə'miliæs], *n.* Père de famille, *m.*

paternal [pə'təːnl], *a.* Paternel. *Paternal grandfather*, aïeul paternel, *m.*; *paternal grandmother*, aïeule paternelle, *f.* **paternally**, *adv.* Paternellement. **paternity**, *n.* Paternité, *f.*

paternoster [pætə'nɔstə], *a.* Patenôtre, *f.*, pater, *m.*

path [pɑːθ], *n.* Sentier, chemin, *m.*; allée (in a garden), *f.*; (*Racing*) piste, *f.*, route, *f.*, cours, *m.*; trajectoire, *f.* (of comet, bullet). *Beaten path*, chemin battu, *m.*; *by-path*, sentier détourné, *m.* **foot-path** [FOOT]. *Path of duty*, ligne du devoir, *f.*; *path of glory*, chemin de la gloire, *m.* **pathless**, *a.* Sans chemin frayé; (*fig.*) inconnu.

pathetic [pə'θetik], *a. and n.* Pathétique, *m.* **pathetically**, *adv.* Pathétiquement.

pathfinder, *n.* Pionnier, éclaireur, *m.*

pathogenesis [pæθəo'dʒenisis], *n.* Pathogénie, *f.* **pathogenic** [pæθo'dʒenik], *a.* Pathogène; pathogénique. **pathognomonic** [-θɔgno'mɔnik], *a.* Pathognomonique.

pathological [pæθə'lɔdʒikl], *a.* Pathologique. **pathologically**, *adv.* Pathologiquement. **pathologist** [-'θɔlədʒist], *n.* Pathologiste, *m.* **pathology**, *n.* Pathologie, *f.*

pathos ['peiθɔs], *n.* Pathétique, *m.*

pathway ['pɑːθwei], *n.* Sentier; trottoir (of street); accotement (of street, road), *m.*

patience ['peiʃəns], *n.* Patience, *f.* (*Cards*) réussite. *To be out of patience*, être à bout de patience; *to get out of patience*, s'impatienter; *to have patience*, patienter, prendre patience; *to lose patience*, perdre patience; *to play patience*, faire des réussites; *to put out of patience*, impatienter, faire perdre patience à; *to tax, try, someone's patience sorely*, mettre la patience de quelqu'un à une rude épreuve.

patient, *a.* Patient, endurant.—*n.* Malade,

m. or *f.*; patient (-e); client(-e) (of doctor). **patiently,** *adv.* Patiemment.
patina ['pætinə], *n.* Patine, *f.*
patio ['pɑːtiou], *n.* Patio, *m.*
patly ['pætli], *adv.* À propos, à point. **patness,** *n.* Justesse, *f.*, à-propos, *m.*
patriarch ['peitriɑːk], *n.* Patriarche, *m.* **patriarchal** [-'ɑːk], *a.* Patriarcal. **patriarchally,** *adv.* Patriarcalement.
patriarchate ['peitriɑːkeit], *n.* Patriarcat, *m.*
patrician [pə'triʃən], *a.* and *n.* Patricien, *m.,* patricienne, *f.,* patrice, *m.* **patriciate** [-ʃiːit], *n.* Patriciat, *m.*
Patrick ['pætrik], Patrice, *m.*
patrimonial [pætri'mouniəl], *a.* Patrimonial. **patrimonially,** *adv.* Comme patrimoine.
patrimony ['pætriməni], *n.* Patrimoine, *m.*
patriot ['peitriət *or* 'pætriət], *n.* Patriote, *m.* or *f.* **patriotic** [-'ɔtik], *a.* Patriotique (of things); patriote (of persons). **patriotically,** *adv.* Patriotiquement, en patriote.
patriotism ['peitriətizm], *n.* Patriotisme, *m.*
patrol [pə'troul], *n.* Patrouille, ronde, *f.*—*v.i.* Aller en patrouille, patrouiller; faire une ronde.—*v.t.* Faire la patrouille dans. **patrol-boat,** *n.* Bateau patrouilleur, *m.* **patrol-car,** *n.* Voiture de police, *f.* **patrolman,** *n.* Patrouilleur, *m.*
patron ['peitrən], *n.* Patron; protecteur; (*Comm.*) client, *m.*; pratique, *f. Patron saint,* patron, *m.,* patronne, *f. The patrons of the cinema,* le public *or* les habitués du cinéma.
patronage ['pætrənidʒ], *n.* Patronage, *m.,* protection, *f.*
patroness ['peitrənis], *n.* Patronne, protectrice; dame patronnesse (of charities), *f.*
patronize ['pætrənaiz], *v.t.* Favoriser, protéger, patronner; fréquenter (a shop); traiter avec condescendance. **patronizer,** *n.* Protecteur, *m.,* -trice, *f.* **patronizing,** *a.* Protecteur. *Patronizing tone,* ton de condescendance, *m.* **patronizingly,** *adv.* D'un air de protection.
patronymic [pætrə'nimik], *a.* Patronymique. —*n.* Nom patronymique, *m.*
patten ['pætən], *n.* Patin, socque; (*Arch.*) soubassement, *m.*
patter (1) ['pætə], *v.i.* Frapper à petits coups, crépiter. *To patter about,* trottiner çà et là. **pattering,** *n.* Grésillement; bruit de petits coups (of feet), *m.*
patter (2) ['pætə], *n.* Bagout, boniment; caquet; parlé, *m.* (in song etc.).—*v.i.* Caqueter, babiller sans arrêt.—*v.t.* Dire vite, bredouiller; parler mal.
pattern ['pætən], *n.* Modèle (pour); patron (for cutting); échantillon (specimen or sample); dessin (design); exemple, *m. To have made to pattern,* faire faire sur modèle; *to take as a pattern,* se modeler sur. **pattern-card** *or* **pattern-book,** *n.* Carte d'échantillons, *f.* **pattern-draughtsman,** *n.* Dessinateur, *m.* **pattern-maker,** *n.* Modeleur, *m.*
patty ['pæti], *n.* Petit pâté, *m.*; bouchée (à la reine), *f.*
paucity ['pɔːsiti], *n.* Petit nombre, *m.,* petite quantité, *f.,* manque, *m.,* paucité, disette (de), *f.*
Paul [pɔːl], Paul, *m. Paul Jones* (dance), boulangère, *f.* **Paula** ['pɔːlə], Paule, *f.*
paunch [pɔːntʃ], *n.* Panse, *f.,* ventre, *m.*; (*fam.*)

bedaine, *f.*; (*Naut.*) baderne, *f.* **paunchy,** *a.* Pansu.
pauper ['pɔːpə], *n.* Indigent, *m.* **pauperism,** *n.* Paupérisme, *m.* **pauperize,** *v.t.* Réduire à l'indigence.
pause [pɔːz], *n.* Pause, *f.*; silence, moment de silence; intervalle; (*Pros.*) repos; (*Mus.*) point d'orgue, *m. Awful pause,* silence de mort, *m.*—*v.i.* Faire une pause, s'arrêter; délibérer; attendre, hésiter, réfléchir. *I pause for a reply,* j'attends votre réponse; *to pause upon,* bien considérer.
pavan ['pævən], *n.* Pavane, *f.*
pave [peiv], *v.t.* Paver (de). *To pave the way for,* frayer le chemin à *or* pour. **pavement,** *n.* Pavement, dallage, trottoir (side-walk) *m.*; (*Am.*) chaussée, *f.*; carreau (of tiles), *m.*; dalles (of flagstones), *f.pl.*; pavé (of marble etc.), *m.* **paver** or **paviour,** *n.* Paveur, *m.*
Pavia ['peiviə], Pavie, *f.*
pavilion [pə'viliən], *n.* Pavillon, *m.,* tente, *f. Chinese pavilion,* chapeau chinois, *m.*—*v.t.* Munir de pavillons *or* de tentes; abriter sous un pavillon *or* une tente.
paving ['peiviŋ], *n.* Pavage, *m.* **paving-stone,** *n.* Pavé, *m.* **paving-tile** or **paving-brick,** *n.* Carreau, *m.*
pavonine ['pævənain], *a.* Irisé, gorge-de-pigeon.
paw [pɔː], *n.* Patte; (*facet.*) main, *f.*—*v.t.* Manier, tripoter (to handle); donner des coups de griffe à, griffer (to scratch). *To paw the ground,* piaffer.—*v.i.* Trépigner.
pawkiness ['pɔːkinis], *n.* Malice, *f.*; humour de pince-sans-rire, *m.* **pawky,** *a.* Malicieux.
pawl [pɔːl], *n.* Linguet, cliquet, *m.*
pawn [pɔːn], *n.* Pion (chess); (*fig.*) gage, nantissement, *m. In pawn,* en gage; *to be someone's pawn,* être le jouet de quelqu'un; *to put in pawn,* mettre en gage; *to take out of pawn,* dégager.—*v.t.* Engager, mettre en gage. **pawnbroker,** *n.* Prêteur sur gage; (*France*) commissionnaire du mont-de-piété, *m.* **pawnshop,** *n.* Boutique de prêteur sur gage, *f.*; (*France*) mont-de-piété, *m.* **pawn-ticket,** *n.* Reconnaissance du mont-de-piété, *f.*
pawnee [-'niː], *n.* Prêteur sur gage, *m.*
pawner, *n.* Emprunteur sur gage, *m.*
pax [pæks], *n.* (*Eccles.*) Paix, *f.*—*int.* (*sch.*) Pouce!
pay [pei], *n.* Paye, paie, solde, *f.*; gages, *m.pl.*; (*Mil.*) salaire, prêt (of a private), *m. Extra pay,* haute solde, haute paye, *f.*; *full pay,* paye entière, *f.*; *half-pay,* demi-solde, *f.*; *half-pay officer,* officier en demi-solde, *m.*; *to be in the pay of,* être à la solde de; *to draw one's pay,* toucher sa solde *or* son prêt.—*v.t.* (past and *p.p.* **paid**) Payer, acquitter, s'acquitter de; rapporter (bring in); faire (compliments etc.); rendre (honour); (*Naut.*) goudronner, enduire (to pitch etc.). *Carriage not paid,* port dû; *carriage paid,* port payé; *to pay an account,* solder un compte; *to pay a person,* payer quelqu'un; *to pay a visit on,* faire une visite à; *to pay away,* dépenser; (*Naut.*) laisser filer (a rope); *to pay back,* rendre, restituer; *to pay down,* payer argent comptant; *to pay for,* payer, payer *or* acheter cher; *to pay homage to,* rendre hommage à; *to pay in,* verser; *to pay off,* payer, solder, acquitter, liquider, congédier; *to pay one's addresses to,* faire la cour à, courtiser (if to a lady), faire sa

cour à; *to pay one's way*, se suffire; *to pay out*, verser, payer; désintéresser; filer (a rope); dérouler (a film); *to pay someone something*, payer quelque chose à quelqu'un; *to pay the piper*, payer les violons, payer l'amende; *to pay up*, payer, s'exécuter; *you will pay dearly for this insolence*, cette insolence vous coûtera cher.—*v.i.* Payer; rapporter. *Pay as you earn*, retenue de l'impôt à la source, *f.*; *this does not pay*, le jeu ne vaut pas la chandelle, ça ne rapporte pas; *to pay through the nose*, payer un prix excessif. **pay-day**, *n.* Jour de paye, *m.* **pay-load**, *n.* (*Av.*) Poids utile, *m.* **paymaster**, *n.* Payeur; (*Mil.*) capitaine-trésorier, trésorier, *m.*

payable, *a.* Payable. *Payable to bearer*, au porteur; *payable to order*, à l'ordre de.

payee [pei'i:], *n.* Porteur, bénéficiaire, *m.* **payer**, *n.* Payeur, *m.* **paying**, *a.* Payant; rémunérateur, lucratif. *Paying guest*, pensionnaire, *m.*—*n.* Paiement, versement; (*Naut.*) goudronnage, *m.* *Paying stuff*, suif, *m.* **payment**, *n.* Payement, paiement, versement, *m.* *On payment*, après versement, moyennant paiement, *m.*; *payment in full of all demands*, pour solde de tout compte, *m.*; *payment on account*, acompte, *m.*

pea [pi:], *n.* Pois, *m.* *Green peas*, petits pois, *m.pl.*; *sweet pea*, pois de senteur, *m.* **pea-green**, *a.* Vert pois. **peanut**, *n.* Arachide, cacahuète, *f.* **pea-pod** or **pea-shell**, *n.* Cosse de pois, *f.* **pea-shooter**, *n.* Sarbacane, *f.* **pea-soup**, *n.* Purée de pois, *f.* **pea-souper**, *n.* Brouillard jaune, *m.*

peace [pi:s], *n.* Paix, *f.* *At peace*, en paix; *breach of the peace*, attentat contre l'ordre public, *m.*; *justice of the peace*, juge de paix, *m.*; *peace of God*, trêve de Dieu, *f.*; *peace of mind*, tranquillité d'âme, *f.* *To hold one's peace*, se taire; *to keep the peace*, ne pas troubler l'ordre public; *to make one's peace with*, se réconcilier avec. **peace-loving**, *a.* Pacifique. **peacemaker**, *n.* Pacificateur, *m.* **peace-making**, *n.* Pacification, *f.* **peace-offering**, *n.* Sacrifice de propitiation, *m.*; (*fig.*) cadeau de réconciliation, *m.*

peaceable, *a.* Pacifique. **peaceably**, *adv.* En paix; avec calme. **peaceful**, *a.* Paisible; tranquille, calme. **peacefully**, *adv.* Paisiblement, tranquillement. **peacefulness**, *n.* Tranquillité, *f.*, calme, *m.* **peaceless**, *a.* Sans paix, agité.

peach [pi:tʃ], *n.* Pêche, *f.* *A peach of a girl*, un beau brin de fille, *m.*—*v.i.* (*slang*) Moucharder. **peach-colour** or **peach-coloured**, *a.* Couleur de fleur de pêcher, *f.* **peach-stone**, *n.* Noyau de pêche, *m.* **peach-tree**, *n.* Pêcher, *m.*

peacock ['pi:kɔk], *n.* Paon, *m.* *In peacock's feathers*, paré des plumes du paon. **peacock-butterfly**, *n.* Paon de jour, *m.* **peafowl**, *n.* Paon, *m.* **pea-hen**, *n.* Paonne, *f.*

pea-jacket ['pi:dʒækit], *n.* (*Naut.*) Vareuse, *f.*

peak [pi:k], *n.* Cime (of a mountain), *f.*; pic, sommet, *m.*; visière (of a cap); pointe, *f.*, bec (point) (*Naut.*) pic, *m.*; corne, *f.* *Gaff-sail peak*, point de drisse, *m.*; (*Rail.* etc.) *peak hours*, heures de pointe, *f.pl.*; (*Elec.*) *peak load*, charge-maximum, *f.*; (*Ind.*) *peak output*, record de production, *m.*—*v.i.* S'amaigrir.—*v.t.* (*Naut.*) Apiquer. **peak-halliards**, *n.pl.* Drisses du pic, *f.pl.*

peaked, *a.* À pic, à pointe; à visière. **peaky**, *a.* À pic; (*colloq.*) malingre, pâlot.

peal [pi:l], *n.* Carillon (of bells); coup, bruit, grondement, *m.* (of cannon, thunder); éclat (of laughter), *m.*—*v.i.* Carillonner, sonner à toute volée; retentir, résonner; gronder.—*v.t.* Faire retentir, faire résonner; carillonner.

pear [pɛə], *n.* Poire, *f.*

pearl [pə:l], *n.* Perle; (*Print.*) parisienne, *f.*; (*Her.*) argent, *m.* Mother-of-pearl, nacre, *f.*; *to cast pearls before swine*, donner de la confiture aux cochons.—*v.t.*, *v.i.* Perler. **pearl-ash**, *n.* Perlasse, *f.* **pearl-barley**, *n.* Orge perlé, *m.* **pearl-diver**, *n.* Pêcheur de perles, *m.* **pearled**, *a.* Perlé, orné de perles. **pearl-fishing**, *n.* Pêche des perles, *f.* **pearl-grey**, *a.* Gris perle. **pearl-oyster**, *n.* Huître perlière, *f.* **pearl-shell**, *n.* Coquille nacrée, *f.* **pearl-white**, *n.* Blanc de perle, *m.*

pearlies, *n.pl.* Boutons de nacre, *m.pl.*; costume couvert de paillettes nacrées, *m.* **pearly**, *a.* De perle, perlé.

pear-shaped ['pɛəʃeipt], *a.* En forme de poire, piriforme.

pear-tree ['pɛətri:], *n.* Poirier, *m.*

peasant ['pezənt], *n.* Paysan, *m.*, paysanne, *f.* **peasant-like**, *a.* De paysan, rustique. **peasant-proprietor**, *n.* propriétaire exploitant, *m.* **peasantry**, *n.* Paysans, campagnards, gens de la campagne, *m.pl.*; paysannat, *m.*

pease, *pl.* [PEA]. **pease-pudding**, *n.* Purée de pois, *f.*

peat [pi:t], *n.* Tourbe, *f.* **peat-bog** or **peat-moss**, *n.* Tourbière, *f.* **peat-reek**, *n.* Fumée de tourbe, *f.*; (*Sc.* and *Irish*) whisky, *m.* **peat-worker**, *n.* Tourbier, *m.* **peaty**, *a.* Tourbeux.

pebble [pebl], *n.* Caillou, galet (on sea-shore), *m.* *You're not the only pebble on the beach*, vous n'êtes pas unique au monde. **pebble-work**, *n.* Cailloutage, *m.* **pebbly** ['pebli], *a.* Caillouteux.

peccable ['pekəbl], *a.* Peccable. **peccadillo** [pekə'dilou], *n.* Peccadille, *f.* **peccancy** ['pekənsi], *n.* État de péché; péché, *m.* **peccant**, *a.* Coupable; (*Med.*) peccant. **peccary** ['pekəri], *n.* Pécari, *m.* **peccavi** [pe'keivəi], *n.* Peccavi, *m.* *To cry peccavi*, dire son mea culpa.

peck [pek], *n.* Picotin (of oats etc.), *m.*; (*fig.*) quantité (large quantity), *f.*; coup de bec (of a bird); (*colloq.*) bécot (kiss), *m.*; (measure of capacity) 9·1 litres.—*v.t.* Becqueter, donner des coups de bec à. *A hen-pecked husband*, un mari mené par sa femme; *to peck a hole*, faire un trou à coup de bec; *to peck at*, picoter; *to peck up*, ramasser avec le bec. **pecker**, *n.* Pivert, *m.* *To keep one's pecker up*, (*slang*) ne pas perdre courage. **pecking**, *n.* Coups de bec, *m.pl.*; becquetage, *m.* **peckish**, *a.* (*colloq.*) En appétit.

pectinate ['pektinət], *a.* Pectiné. **pectoral** ['pektərəl], *a.* and *n.* Pectoral, *m.* **peculate** ['pekjuleit], *v.i.* *Malverser, se rendre coupable de péculat.—*v.t.* Détourner. **peculation** [-'leiʃən], *n.* Péculat, *m.* **peculator**, *n.* Concussionnaire, *m.*

peculiar [pi'kju:liə], *a.* Particulier, propre; singulier, bizarre.—*n.* Propriété particulière;

(*Canon law*) chapelle privilégiée, *f.* **peculiarity** [-'æriti], *n.* Singularité, particularité, *f.* **peculiarly,** *adv.* Particulièrement, singulièrement.

pecuniary [pi'kju:niəri], *a.* Pécuniaire.

pedagogic(al) [pedə'gɔdʒik(l)], *a.* Pédagogique.

pedagogue ['pedəgɔg], *n.* Pédagogue, *m.* **pedagogy,** *n.* Pédagogie, *f.*

pedal [pedl], *n.* Pédale, *f.*—*v.i.* Pédaler. **pedaller** or **pedalist,** *n.* Pédaleur, *m.* **pedal-note** or **pedal-stop,** *n.* Pédale, *f.*

pedant ['pedənt], *n.* Pédant, *m.*

pedantic [pi'dæntik], *a.* Pédant, pédantesque (of things). **pedantically,** *adv.* Pédantesquement.

pedantry ['pedəntri], *n.* Pédantisme, *m.*, pédanterie, *f.*

peddle [pedl], *v.t.* Colporter.—*v.i.* Faire le colportage; (*fig.*) s'occuper de bagatelles, niaiser. **peddler** [PEDLAR]. **peddling,** *a.* Mesquin, de peu de valeur.—*n.* Colportage, *m.*

pederast ['pedəræst], *n.* Pédéraste, *m.* **pederasty,** *n.* Pédérastie, *f.*

pedestal ['pedistl], *n.* Piédestal, socle; (*Mach.*) palier, *m.* W.C. *pedestal,* cuvette de cabinet, *f.*

pedestrian [pə'destriən], *a.* À pied, pédestre; (*fig.*) prosaïque, terre à terre.—*n.* Piéton, marcheur, *m.*

pedicel ['pedisl] or **pedicle** ['pedikl], *n.* (*Bot.*) Pédicelle, pédoncule, *m.*

pedicular [pə'dikjulə], *a.* Pédiculaire.

pediculate [pə'dikjulət], *a.* Pédiculé.

pedigree ['pedigri:], *n.* Généalogie; origine, *f.*; arbre généalogique, *m.*; certificat d'origine (of dog etc.), *m.* *Pedigree bull,* taureau de (pure) race, *m.*

pedimanous [pə'dimənəs], *a.* Pédimane.

pediment ['pedimənt], *n.* (*Arch.*) Fronton, *m.*

pedlar ['pedlə], *n.* Colporteur, *m.*, colporteuse, *f.* **pedlary,** *n.* Marchandise de colporteur, *f.*, colportage, *m.*

pedometer [pə'dɔmitə], *n.* Podomètre, *m.*

peduncle [pə'dʌŋkl], *n.* (*Bot.*) Pédoncule, *m.* **peduncular** [-'dʌŋkjulə], *a.* Pédonculaire. **pedunculate,** *a.* Pédonculé.

pee [pi:], *v.i.* (*colloq.*) Uriner, faire pipi.

peel [pi:l], *n.* Pelure; écorce (of oranges, lemons, etc.), *f.*; petite tour carrée (stronghold), *f.*; pelle de four (shovel), *f.*; (*Ichth.*) saumoneau, *m.* *Candied peel,* écorce (de citron) confite, *f.*—*v.t.* Peler; éplucher; monder (barley); (*fig.*) dépouiller, piller.—*v.i.* Se peler; s'écailler; (*colloq.*) enlever son veston; se mettre en maillot. **peelings,** *n.pl.* Épluchures, *f.pl.*

peep [pi:p], *n.* Coup d'œil, regard à la dérobée, *m.*; pointe (of day), *f.*, piaulement, pépiement (of birds), *m.* *Bo-peep,* cache-cache, *m.*; *to take a peep at,* donner un coup d'œil à, regarder furtivement.—*v.i.* Regarder à la dérobée; paraître, poindre, percer, se montrer (to appear). **peep-hole,** *n.* Judas, *m.* **peep-o'-day,** *n.* Point du jour, *m.* **peep-show,** *n.* Optique, *f.*; vues stéréoscopiques, *f.pl.*

peeper, *n.* Curieux, *m.*; poussin (chicken), *m.*; (*slang*) œil, *m.* **peeping-Tom,** *n.* Voyeur, *m.*

peer (1) [piə], *v.i.* Scruter du regard; poindre.

Peering eyes, regards scrutateurs, *m.pl.*; *to peer into,* dévisager, sonder.

peer (2) [piə], *n.* Pair; (*fig.*) égal, pareil, *m.*

peerage ['piəridʒ], *n.* Pairie, *f.*; les pairs, *m.pl.* *Life peerage,* pairie à vie, *f.*; *to raise to the peerage,* anoblir, élever à la pairie. **peeress,** *n.* Pairesse, *f.*

peerless, *a.* Incomparable; sans pareil, hors de pair. **peerlessly,** *adv.* Incomparablement. **peerlessness,** *n.* Supériorité incomparable, *f.*

peeve [pi:v], *v.t.* Fâcher, irriter. **peeved,** *a.* Fâché.

peevish, *a.* Irritable, maussade, grincheux. **peevishly,** *adv.* Maussadement, avec mauvaise humeur. **peevishness,** *n.* Maussaderie, humeur acariâtre, *f.*

peewit [PEWIT].

peg [peg], *n.* Cheville; patère (of hats etc.), *f.*; fausset (for casks), piquet (of tent), *m.*; (*colloq.*) une fine à l'eau, *f.* *Clothes-peg,* patère, *f.*; *not to stir a peg,* ne pas bouger d'une semelle; *to be a square peg in a round hole,* ne pas être à sa place; *to buy a suit off the peg,* acheter un complet tout fait; *to come down a peg,* baisser d'un cran; *to take down a peg,* rabattre le caquet à.—*v.t., v.i.* Cheviller. *To peg away,* travailler sans relâche, piocher toujours; *to peg down,* fixer avec des piquets; (*fig.*) entraver; *to peg out,* jalonner (a claim), toucher le piquet de but (croquet); (*slang*) mourir, casser sa pipe.

Pegasus ['pegəsəs], *n.* Pégase, *m.*

Peggy ['pegi]. Margot, *f.*

peg-top, *n.* Toupie, *f.*

pejorative [pi:dʒərətiv], *a.* Péjoratif.

Pekinese [pi:ki'ni:z], *a.* and *n.* Pékinois; (épagneul) pékinois, *m.*

Pelagian [pə'leidʒiən], *a.* Pélagien. **Pelagianism,** *n.* Pélagianisme, *m.*

pelagic [pə'lædʒik], *a.* Pélagique.

pelf [pelf], *n.* Gain, lucre, *m.*; richesses mal acquises, *f.pl.*

pelican ['pelikən], *n.* Pélican, *m.*

pelisse [pə'li:s], *n.* Pelisse, *f.*

pellagra [pe'lægrə], *n.* Pellagre, *f.*

pellet ['pelit], *n.* Boulette, *f.*; grain de plomb, *m.*

pellicle ['pelikl], *n.* Pellicule, *f.*

pellicular [pe'likjulə], *a.* Pelliculaire.

pellitory ['pelitəri], *n.* Pariétaire, *f.*

pell-mell ['pel'mel], *adv.* Pêle-mêle.

pellucid [pə'lju:sid], *a.* Transparent, clair, pellucide. **pellucidity** [-'siditi] or **pellucidness,** *n.* Transparence, clarté, lucidité, *f.*

pelmet ['pelmit], *n.* Lambrequin, *m.*

Peloponnese (the) [peləpə'ni:z]. Le Péloponnèse, *m.* **Peloponnesian,** *a.* and *n.* Péloponnésien.

pelota [pe'loutə], *n.* Pelote basque, *f.*

pelt (1) [pelt], *v.t.* Assaillir, battre. *Full-pelt,* ventre à terre; *the rain pelted down,* la pluie tombait à torrents; *to pelt with stones,* assaillir à coups de pierres. **pelting,** *a.* Battant (of rain).—*n.* Attaque, *f.*, assaut, *m.*; grêle (de pierres), *f.*

pelt (2) [pelt], *n.* Peau, *f.*—*v.t.* Écorcher. **pelt-monger,** *n.* Peaussier, *m.* **peltry,** *n.* Pelleterie, *f.*

pelvic ['pelvik], *a.* Pelvien. **pelvimeter** [-'vimitə], *n.* Pelvimètre, *m.* **pelvis,** *n.* Bassin, *m.*

pemmican ['pemikən], *n.* Conserve de viande, *f.*; pemmican, *m.*

pen [pen], *n.* Plume, *f.*; parc, enclos (for cattle etc.); poulailler (for poultry), *m.* *Fountain-pen*, plume à réservoir, *f.*, stylo, *m.*; *pen-and-ink drawing*, dessin à la plume, *m.*—*v.t.* Écrire; rédiger; parquer, enfermer (cattle). *To pen up*, enfermer, parquer. **pen-friend,** *n.* Correspondant, *m.*, -ante, *f.* **penful,** *n.* Plumée d'encre, *f.* **pen-holder,** *n.* Porte-plume, *m.* **penknife,** *n.* Canif, *m.* **penman,** *n.* (*pl.* **penmen**) Calligraphe; écrivain, *m.* **penmanship,** *n.* Calligraphie, *f.* **pen-name,** *n.* Nom de plume, pseudonyme, *m.* **pen-point,** *n.* Tire-ligne, *m.* **pen-wiper,** *n.* Essuie-plume, *m.*

penal [pi:nl], *a.* Pénal, passible d'une amende. *Penal servitude*, travaux forcés, *m.pl.*; *penal statute*, loi pénale, *f.*

penalize ['pi:nəlaiz], *v.t.* Attacher une peine à (a crime); infliger une peine à (a person); (*spt.*) pénaliser.

penalty ['penəlti], *n.* Peine; pénalité, amende (fine), *f.*; (*Ftb.*) penalty, *m.* *Penalty area, kick, spot,* (*Ftb.*) surface, *f.*, coup de pied, *m.*, point, *m.*, de réparation; *to pay the penalty of*, payer le forfait de.

penance ['penəns], *n.* Pénitence, *f.* *To do penance*, faire pénitence (de).

pence, *pl.* [PENNY].

pencil [pensl], *n.* Crayon; pinceau (brush); (*Opt.*) faisceau, *m.* *Lead pencil*, crayon à mine de plomb; *propelling pencil*, porte-mine, *m.*—*v.t.* Dessiner or écrire au crayon. *To pencil one's eyebrows*, se faire les sourcils. **pencil-case,** *n.* Porte-crayon, *m.* **pencil-drawing,** *n.* Dessin au crayon, *m.* **pencil-mark,** *n.* Marque au crayon, *f.* **pencil-shaped,** *a.* En forme de pinceau; (*Bot.*) pénicillé. **pencil-sharpener,** *n.* Taille-crayon, *m.*

pendant ['pendənt], *n.* Pendant, *m.*, pende-loque, *f.*; pendentif; lustre (for gas etc.), *m.*; (*Naut.*) flamme (flag), *f.* *Broad pendant*, guidon, *m.*

pendency ['pendənsi], *n.* (*Law*) Litispen-dance, *f.* **pendent,** *a.* Pendant; suspendu (hanging); en instance; en cours.

pendentive [pen'dentiv], *n.* (*Arch.*) Pendentif, *m.*; trompe, *f.*

pending ['pendiŋ], *a.* Pendant, non décidé.—*prep.* Pendant; en attendant.

pendulous ['pendjuləs], *a.* Pendant (lip).

pendulum ['pendjuləm], *n.* Pendule, balan-cier, *m.* **pendulum-bob,** *n.* Lentille de pendule, *f.* **pendulum-clock,** *n.* Pendule, *f.*

Penelope [pe'neləpi]. Pénélope, *f.* *Penelope's web*, (*fig.*) travail de Pénélope, *m.*

penetrability [penitrə'biliti], *n.* Pénétrabilité, *f.*

penetrable ['penitrəbl], *a.* Pénétrable, sensible.

penetralia [-'treiliə], *n.pl.* Sanctuaire, *m.*

penetrate, *v.t., v.i.* Pénétrer (dans).

penetrating, *a.* Pénétrant, perçant; clair-voyant, perspicace.

penetration [-'treiʃən], *n.* Pénétration, *f.*

penetrative ['penitreitiv], *a.* Pénétrant.

penguin ['peŋgwin], *n.* Manchot, *m.*

penicillate [pi'nisilət], *a.* Pénicillé. **penicilli-form** [-'silifɔ:m], *a.* Pénicilliforme.

penicillin [peni'silin], *n.* Pénicilline, *f.*

peninsula [pi'ninsjulə], *n.* Péninsule, pres-qu'île, *f.* **peninsular,** *a.* En forme de péninsule, péninsulaire. *The Peninsular War* (1808-13), la guerre d'Espagne, *f.*

penis ['pi:nis], *n.* Pénis, *m.*

penitence ['penitəns], *n.* Pénitence, *f.*, repentir, *m.* **penitent,** *a.* Pénitent, repen-tant.—*n.* Pénitent, *m.*, pénitente, *f.* **peni-tential** [-'tenʃl], *a.* De pénitence, péniten-tiel. *Penitential psalms,* psaumes de la pénitence, *m.pl.*; *penitential works,* œuvres pénitentielles, *f.pl.*—*n.* Pénitentiel, *m.* **peni-tentiary,** *a.* Pénitentiaire.—*n.* Pénitencier, *m.*, maison pénitentiaire (house of correction), *f.*; (*Am.*) prison, *f.* **penitently,** *adv.* Avec pénitence.

pennant ['penənt], *n.* (*Naut.*) Flamme, *f.*

pennate ['penət], *a.* (*Bot.*) Penné, pinné.

penniform ['penifɔ:m], *a.* Penniforme.

penniless ['penilis], *a.* Sans le sou, sans ressources.

pennon ['penən], *n.* *Pennon, *m.*; banderole, flamme, *f.*

Pennsylvania [pensil'veinjə]. La Pennsylvanie, *f.*

penny ['peni], *n.* (*pl.* **pence,** of a sum, or **pennies,** of a number of coins) Penny, *m.* *In for a penny, in for a pound*, quand le vin est tiré, il faut le boire; *it cost me a pretty penny*, on ne m'en a pas fait cadeau; *not to be worth a penny*, n'avoir pas le sou; *take care of the pence and the pounds will take care of themselves*, il n'y a pas de petites économies; (*colloq.*) *the penny's dropped!* voilà qu'il com-prend! *to turn an honest penny*, gagner honnêtement sa vie.

penny-a-liner, *n.* Journaliste à dix centimes la ligne; écrivaillon, *m.* **penny-dreadful,** *n.* Feuilleton à gros effets; roman à deux sous, *m.* **pennyroyal,** *n.* Pouliot, *m.* **penny-weight,** *n.* Un gramme et demi. **penny-wise,** *a.* Ménager de bouts de chandelle. *To be penny wise and pound foolish*, être économe dans les petites choses et prodigue dans les grandes. **pennywort,** *n.* Hydro-cotyle, *f.* **pennyworth,** *n.* Valeur de deux sous, *f.*; (*fig.*) un bon marché, *m.*

penologist [pi:'nɔlədʒist], *n.* Criminaliste, *m.* **penology,** *n.* Criminologie, *f.*

pensile ['pensail], *a.* Suspendu, pendant.

pension ['penʃən], *n.* Pension; pension de retraite, retraite (of officers etc.), *f.* *Old age pension*, retraite pour la vieillesse, *f.*, *retiring pension*, pension de retraite, *f.*; *to retire on a pension*, prendre sa retraite.—*v.t.* Pensionner. *To pension off*, mettre à la retraite; *to be pensioned off*, être mis à la retraite.

pensionable, *a.* Qui a droit à une pension.

pensionary, *n.* Pensionnaire, *m.*—*a.* Pen-sionné; de pension. **pensioner,** *n.* Pension-naire; (*Mil.*) invalide, *m.*

pensive ['pensiv], *a.* Pensif, préoccupé, rêveur. **pensively,** *adv.* D'un air pensif.

pensiveness, *n.* Air pensif, air préoccupé, *m.*

penstock ['penstɔk], *n.* Vanne, *f.*

pent [pent], *a.* Enfermé, parqué. *Pent up*, enfermé, (*fig.*) étouffé, refoulé.

pentagon ['pentəgən], *n.* Pentagone, *m.* **pentagonal** [-'tægənl], *a.* Pentagonal, pentagone. **pentamerous** [-'tæmərəs], *a.*

Pentamère. **pentameter** [-'tæmitə], *n.*
Pentamètre, *m.* **pentandria,** *n.* (*Bot.*)
Pentandrie, *f.*
Pentateuch ['pentətjuːk], *n.* Pentateuque, *m.*
pentathlon [-'tæθlən], *n.* (*spt.*) Pentathlon, *m.*
Pentecost ['pentikɔst], *n.* Pentecôte, *f.* **Pentecostal** [-'kɔstl], *a.* De la Pentecôte.
penthouse ['penthaus], *n.* Appentis, *m.*
penult [pe'nʌlt] or **penultima,** *n.* Pénultième, *f.* **penultimate,** *a.* Pénultième, avant-dernier.—*n.* (*Gram.*) Pénultième, *f.*
penumbra [pi'nʌmbrə], *n.* Pénombre, *f.*
penurious [pi'njuəriəs], *a.* Avare; ladre; pauvre (of things). **penuriously,** *adv.* Avec pénurie, parcimonieusement. **penuriousness** or **penury** ['penjuəri], *n.* Pénurie, *f.*
peony ['piːəni], *n.* Pivoine, *f.*
people [piːpl], *n.* Peuple, *m.*, nation, *f.*, habitants, gens, *m.pl.*; le vulgaire, *m.*, la foule (the crowd, the vulgar), *f.*; on, monde, *m.*, personnes (persons in general), *f.pl.* *Bad people*, de méchantes gens; *my people live in France*, mes parents demeurent en France; *old people*, les vieilles gens; *our people*, les nôtres; *people say*, on dit; *the English people*, la nation anglaise, *f.*, le peuple anglais, *m.*; (*Myth.* etc.) *the little people*, les fées, *f.pl.*; *there were a great many people in the park*, il y avait beaucoup de monde dans le parc.—*v.t.* Peupler (de).
pep [pep], *n.* (*colloq.*) Entrain, *m.*; fougue, *f.* *Full of pep*, plein de sève, plein d'allant.—*v.t. To pep up*, donner de l'entrain à.
pepper ['pepə], *n.* Poivre, *m.* *Cayenne pepper*, poivre de Cayenne, *m.*; *pepper and salt*, (Colour) poivre et sel, *m.*—*v.t.* Poivrer; (*fig.*) cribler de coups.
pepper-box or **pepper-caster,** *n.* Poivrière, *f.* **peppercorn,** *n.* Grain de poivre, *m.*; (*fig.*) bagatelle, *f.* *Peppercorn rent*, loyer nominal, *m.* **pepper-mill,** *n.* Moulin à poivre, *m.* **peppermint,** *n.* Menthe poivrée, *f.* *Peppermint drop*, pastille de menthe, *f.* **pepper plant,** *n.* Poivrier, *m.* **peppery,** *a.* Poivré; piquant; irritable.
per [pəː], *prep.* Par; le, *m.*, la, *f.*, les, *pl.*; (*Comm.*) par l'entremise de (firm of carriers etc.). *A shilling per hundred*, un shilling le cent; *as per*, (*Comm.*) suivant; *per cent*, pour cent; *per week*, par semaine; *seventy miles per hour*, soixante-dix milles à l'heure.
*peradventure [pəːrəd'ventʃə], *adv.* Par hasard, d'aventure, peut-être.
perambulate [pə'ræmbjuleit], *v.t.* Parcourir. **perambulation** [-'leiʃən], *n.* Parcours, *m.*; promenade, *f.*; inspection de limites, *f.* **perambulator,** *n.* Voiture d'enfant, *f.*; (*Cine.*) chariot, *m.* (of camera).
perceivable [pə'siːvəbl], *a.* Perceptible, sensible. **perceivably,** *adv.* Perceptiblement, sensiblement. **perceive,** *v.t.* Apercevoir; s'apercevoir de (to recognize); (*Phil.*) percevoir.
percentage [pə'sentidʒ], *n.* Pourcentage, intérêt, profit, etc., pour cent, *m.*; (*fig.*) proportion, *f.* *A percentage*, tant pour cent.
perceptibility [pəsepti'biliti], *n.* Perceptibilité, *f.* **perceptible** [-'septibl], *a.* Perceptible, sensible. **perceptibly,** *adv.* Perceptiblement, d'une manière perceptible, sensiblement.

perception [pə'sepʃən], *n.* Perception, sensibilité, découverte, observation, *f.* **perceptive,** *a.* Perceptif.
perceptivity [pəːsep'tiviti], *n.* Faculté de perception, *f.*
perch [pəːtʃ], *n.* Perche (fish), *f.*; perchoir (for fowls etc.), *m.*; perche (5½ yards), *f.* *To knock someone off his perch*, déloger or dégommer quelqu'un.—*v.t.* Percher.—*v.i.* Percher, se percher.
***perchance** [pə'tʃɑːns], *adv.* Par hasard, peut-être, par aventure.
percher ['pəːtʃə], *n.* (Oiseau) percheur, *m.*
perchloric [pə'klɔrik or pə'klɔːrik], *a.* Perchlorique. **perchloride,** *n.* Perchlorure, *m.*
percipient [pə'sipiənt], *a.* Doué de perception, percepteur.—*n.* Être intelligent or perceptif, *m.*
percolate ['pəːkəleit], *v.i.* Filtrer, s'infiltrer.— *v.t.* Filtrer, passer à travers. **percolation** [-'leiʃən], *n.* Filtration, infiltration, *f.* **percolator,** *n.* Filtre, filtre à café, *m.*; cafetière automatique, *f.*
percussion [pə'kʌʃən], *n.* Percussion, *f.* **percussion-cap,** *n.* Capsule, *f.* **percussion-fuse,** *n.* Fusée percutante, *f.* **percussion-gun,** *n.* Fusil à piston, *m.* **percussive** or **percutient** [-'kjuːʃiənt], *a.* Percutant.
perdition [pə'diʃən], *n.* Perdition, ruine, *f.*
peregrinate ['perigrineit], *v.i.* Voyager. **peregrination** [-'neiʃən], *n.* Pérégrination, *f.*, voyage à l'étranger, *m.*
peregrine ['perigrin], *n.* Faucon pèlerin, *m.*
peremptorily ['perəmptərili or pə'remptərili], *adv.* Péremptoirement, absolument, formellement. **peremptoriness,** *n.* Caractère péremptoire; ton décisif, *m.*
peremptory ['perəmptəri or pə'remptəri], *a.* Péremptoire, tranchant, absolu.
perennial [pə'reniəl], *a.* Vivace (of plants); (*fig.*) éternel; intarissable (of springs).—*n.* Plante vivace, *f.* **perenniality** [-'æliti], *n.* Pérennité, *f.* **perennially,** *adv.* Continuellement, perpétuellement.
perfect (1) ['pəːfikt], *a.* Parfait; achevé, complet, accompli. *Perfect tense*, parfait, *m.*
perfection [-'fekʃən], *n.* Perfection, *f.* *To perfection*, en perfection, dans la perfection, parfaitement. **perfectly,** *adv.* Parfaitement. **perfectness,** *n.* Perfection, *f.*
perfect (2) [pə'fekt], *v.t.* Rendre parfait, perfectionner; achever; compléter. **perfecter,** *n.* Personne qui perfectionne, qui a le souci de la perfection, *f.* **perfectibility** [-i'biliti], *n.* Perfectibilité, *f.* **perfectible** [-'fektibl], *a.* Perfectible.
perfervid [pə'fəːvid], *a.* Ardent, exalté.
perfidious [pə'fidiəs], *a.* Perfide. **perfidiously,** *adv.* Perfidement. **perfidiousness** or **perfidy** ['pəːfidi], *n.* Perfidie, *f.*
perfoliate [pə'fouliət], *a.* (*Bot.*) Perfolié.
perforate ['peːfəreit], *v.t.* Perforer, percer (d'outre en outre). **perforating-machine,** *n.* Machine à percer, *f.* **perforation** [-'reiʃən], *n.* Percement, *m.*, perforation; ouverture, *f.*, trou (hole), *m.*, dentelure (of postage-stamp), *f.* **perforative,** *a.* Perforatif.
perforce [pə'fɔːs], *adv.* Forcément, de force.
perform [pə'fɔːm], *v.t.* Exécuter, accomplir, faire, effectuer; (*Theat.*) jouer, représenter; remplir (to fulfil); (*Mus.*) exécuter. *To perform a piece of music*, exécuter un morceau

de musique; *to perform a vow*, accomplir un vœu; *to perform one's part*, remplir son rôle. —*v.i.* Jouer un rôle. *To perform on the piano*, jouer du piano.
performable, *a.* Faisable, exécutable, praticable; (*Theat.*) jouable. **performance**, *n.* Action, *f.*, accomplissement; ouvrage, *m.*, œuvre (thing done); (*Mach.*) fonctionnement; rendement, *m.*; (*Theat.*) représentation; (*Mus.*) exécution; (*spt.*) performance, *f.*; (*Circus etc.*) exercices, *m.pl. Evening performance*, (*Theat.*) soirée, *f.*; *morning performance*, matinée, *f.*; *no performance*, relâche, *m.* **performer**, *n.* (*Theat.*) Acteur, *m.*, actrice, *f.*, comédien, *m.*, comédienne, *f.*; (*Mus.*) artiste, *m.* or *f.*, exécutant, musicien, *m.* **performing**, *a. Performing dog*, chien savant, *m.*
perfume (1) ['pə:fju:m], *n.* Parfum, *m.*
perfume (2) [pə'fju:m], *v.t.* Parfumer (de).
perfumer [pə'fju:mə], *n.* Parfumeur, *m.*, parfumeuse, *f.* **perfumery**, *n.* Parfumerie, *f.*
perfunctorily [pə'fʌŋktərili], *adv.* Par manière d'acquit; négligemment, tant bien que mal.
perfunctoriness, *n.* Négligence, *f.* **perfunctory**, *a.* Négligent, fait par manière d'acquit; de pure forme.
pergola ['pə:gələ], *n.* Pergola, *f.*
perhaps [pə'hæps], *adv.* Peut-être. *Perhaps not*, peut-être que non; *perhaps so*, peut-être que oui.
peri ['piəri], *n.* Péri, *m.* or *f.*; (*colloq.*) une beauté.
perianth ['periænθ], *n.* (*Bot.*) Périanthe, *m.*
pericardium [-'ka:diəm], *n.* (*Anat.*) Péricarde, *m.*
pericarp ['perika:p], *n.* (*Bot.*) Péricarpe, *m.*
perichondrium [-'kɔndriəm], *n.* Périchondre, *m.*
Pericles ['perikli:z]. Périclès, *m.*
pericranium [-'kreiniəm], *n.* (*Anat.*) Péricrâne, *m.*
perigee ['peridʒi:], *n.* (*Astron.*) Périgée, *m.*
perigynous [pə'ridʒinəs], *a.* (*Bot.*) Périgyne, *m.*
perihelion [peri'hi:liən], *n.* (*Astron.*) Périhélie, *m.*
peril ['peril], *n.* Péril, danger, *m. At one's peril*, à ses risques et périls; *in peril of one's life*, en danger de mort. **perilous**, *a.* Périlleux, dangereux. **perilously**, *adv.* Périlleusement. **perilousness**, *n.* Nature périlleuse, *f.*, danger, *m.*
perimeter [pə'rimitə], *n.* Périmètre, *m.*
perineal [pə'riniəl], *a.* Périnéal. **perineum** [peri'ni:əm], *n.* Périnée, *m.*
period ['piəriəd], *n.* Période, *f.*, temps, espace de temps, *m.*, durée; époque (epoch); fin, *f.*, terme (end); (punctuation) point, *m.*; (*Rhet.* etc.) phrase, *f.*; (*pl.*) (*Physiol.*) menstrues, *f.pl. At a later period*, plus tard; *fair period*, (*Meteor.*) éclaircie, *f.*; *period furniture*, meubles d'époque, *m.pl.*; *the fiscal period*, l'exercice financier, *m.* **periodic** [-'ɔdik], *a.* Périodique. **periodical**, *a.* Périodique.—*n.* Périodique, ouvrage périodique, journal, magazine, *m.* **periodically**, *adv.* Périodiquement, de temps en temps.
periodicity [piəriɔ'disiti], *n.* Périodicité, *f.*
periosteal [peri'ɔstiəl], *a.* Périostéique, périostéal.
periosteum [peri'ɔstiəm], *n.* (*Anat.*) Périoste, *m.* **periostitis** [-'taitis], *n.* Périostite, *f.*

peripatetic [peripə'tetik], *a.* and *n.* Péripatéticien, *m.*; (*fig.*) (marchand) ambulant, *m.*
peripateticism [-'tetisizm], *n.* Péripatétisme, *m.*, philosophie péripatéticienne, *f.*
peripeteia [peripə'taiə], *n.* Péripétie, *f.*
peripheral [pə'rifərəl], *a.* Périphérique.
periphery, *n.* Périphérie, *f.*
periphrase ['perifreiz], *v.t., v.i.* Périphraser.
periphrasis [pə'rifrəsis], *n.* (*pl.* **periphrases**) Périphrase, *f.* **periphrastic** [-'fræstik], *a.* De périphrase, périphrastique.
periphrastically, *adv.* Par périphrase.
periplus ['periplʌs], *n.* Periple, *m.*
peripteral [pə'riptərəl], *a.* Périptère, *m.*
periscope ['periskoup], *n.* Périscope, *m.*
perish ['periʃ], *v.i.* Périr (de), mourir; dépérir. *To be perished with cold*, (*colloq.*) être tout transi de froid, être presque mort de froid; *to perish by the sword*, périr par le fer; *to perish from hunger*, mourir de faim.—*v.i.* Détériorer, gâter. **perishable**, *a.* Périssable. **perishableness**, *n.* Nature périssable *or* éphémère, *f.* **perisher**, *n.* (*colloq.*) Individu; bon à rien, *m.*
peristalsis [peri'stælsis], *n.* Péristaltisme, *m.* **peristaltic**, *a.* Péristaltique.
peristyle ['peristail], *n.* (*Arch.*) Péristyle, *m.*
peritoneum [peri'touniəm], *n.* Péritoine, *m.*
peritonitis [peritə'naitis], *n.* Péritonite, *f.*
*periwig ['periwig], *n.* Perruque, *f.*
periwinkle ['periwiŋkl], *n.* (*Bot.*) Pervenche, *f.*; (mollusc) bigorneau, vignot, *m.*
perjure ['pə:dʒə], *v.t. To perjure oneself*, se parjurer. **perjurer**, *n.* Parjure, *m.* or *f.* **perjury**, *n.* Parjure; (*Law*) faux témoignage, faux serment, *m. Wilful perjury*, parjure prémédité.
perk [pə:k], *v.i.* Se rengorger, porter le nez au vent, porter la tête haute. *To perk up*, se ranimer, se raviver; se requinquer.—*v.t. To perk up one's ears*, dresser les oreilles; *to perk up someone* (of drink etc.), ravigoter quelqu'un. **perkily**, *adv.* D'un air éveillé. **perkiness**, *n.* Air éveillé; ton guilleret, *m.*
perks [PERQUISITE].
perky, *a.* Fier, déluré; outrecuidant, suffisant.
permanency ['pə:mənənsi] *or* **permanence**, *n.* Permanence, *f.* **permanent**, *a.* Permanent; en permanence. *Permanent wave*, (ondulation) permanente, indéfrisable, *f.*; *permanent way*, (*Rail.*) la voie. **permanently**, *adv.* En permanence, d'une manière permanente.
permanganate [pə:'mæŋgənit], *n.* Permanganate, *m.*
permeability [pə:miə'biliti], *n.* Perméabilité, *f.*
permeable ['pə:miəbl], *a.* Pénétrable, perméable. **permeate**, *v.t.* Pénétrer, percer, filtrer à travers. **permeation** [-'eiʃən], *n.* Pénétration, *f.*
permissible [pə'misibl], *a.* Permis, qui peut être permis, tolérable. **permission** [-'miʃən], *n.* Permission, *f.*, permis, *m.* **permissive**, *a.* Qui permet; toléré. **permissively**, *adv.* Avec permission; par tolérance.
permit (1) [pə'mit], *v.t.* Permettre à (quelqu'un de). *As circumstances permit*, suivant les circonstances; *you are permitted to speak*, on vous permet de parler, vous avez la permission de parler.

permit (2) ['pə:mit], *n.* Permis; congé, passe-debout, *m.* *Export permit*, autorisation d'exporter, *f.*
permutable [pə'mju:təbl], *a.* Permutable.
permutation [pə:mju'teiʃən], *n.* Permutation, *f.*
permute [pə'mju:t], *v.t.* Permuter. **permuter**, *n.* Permutant, *m.*
pernicious [pə'niʃəs], *a.* Pernicieux. **perniciously**, *adv.* Pernicieusement. **perniciousness**, *n.* Nature pernicieuse, *f.*
pernickety [pə'nikiti], *a.* (*colloq.*) Vétilleux, pointilleux.
peroration [perə'reiʃən], *n.* Péroraison, *f.*
peroxide [pə'rɔksaid], *n.* Peroxyde, *m.—v.t.* Oxygéner (hair). **peroxidize**, *v.t.* Peroxyder.
perpend [pə:'pend], *v.t.* Peser, considérer.
perpendicular [pə:pən'dikjulə], *a.* Perpendiculaire.—*n.* Ligne perpendiculaire, perpendiculaire, *f.* **perpendicularity** [-'læriti], *n.* Perpendicularité, *f.* **perpendicularly**, *adv.* Perpendiculairement.
perpetrate ['pə:pitreit], *v.t.* Commettre, exécuter; (*Law*) perpétrer. *To perpetrate a crime*, commettre un crime; *to perpetrate a pun*, faire un mauvais calembour. **perpetration** [-'treiʃən], *n.* Exécution; (*Law*) perpétration, *f.* **perpetrator**, *n.* Auteur (d'un crime), coupable, criminel, *m.*
perpetual [pə'petjuəl], *a.* Perpétuel, continuel, incessant. **perpetually**, *adv.* Perpétuellement, sans cesse. **perpetuate**, *v.t.* Perpétuer. **perpetuation** [-'eiʃən], *n.* Perpétuation, *f.* **perpetuity** [-'tju:iti], *n.* Perpétuité, *f.* *In, to, for perpetuity*, à perpétuité.
perplex [pə'pleks], *v.t.* Embarrasser, embrouiller, jeter dans la perplexité. **perplexed**, *a.* Perplexe, embarrassé. **perplexedly**, *adv.* D'une manière embarrassée. **perplexing**, *a.* Embarrassant. **perplexity**, *n.* Embrouillement, embarras, *m.*, perplexité, *f.*
perquisite ['pə:kwizit], *n.* Émolument casuel, *m.*; (*pl.*) petits profits, *m.pl.* **perquisition** [-'ziʃən], *n.* Perquisition, *f.*
perry ['peri], *n.* Poiré, *m.*
persecute ['pə:sikju:t], *v.t.* Persécuter. **persecuting**, *a.* Persécuteur. **persecution** [-'kju:ʃən], *n.* Persécution, *f.* **persecutor**, *n.* Persécuteur, *m.*, persécutrice, *f.*
perseverance [pə:si'viərəns], *n.* Persévérance, *f.* **persevere** [-'viə], *v.i.* Persévérer (à *or* dans). **persevering**, *a.* Persévérant. **perseveringly**, *adv.* Avec persévérance.
Persia ['pə:ʃə]. La Perse, *f.*
Persian ['pə:ʃən], *a.* De Perse, persan. *Persian carpet*, tapis persan, *m.*; *Persian cat*, angora, *m.*; *Persian Gulf*, Golfe Persique, *m.*; *Persian wheel*, noria, *f.—n.* Persan, *m.*, Persane, *f.*; (*Ant.*) Perse, *m.*; perse (language), *m.*
persicaria [pə:si'kɛəriə], *n.* (*Bot.*) Persicaire, *f.*
persist [pə'sist], *v.i.* Persister (dans *or* à); continuer. **persistence** or **persistency**, *n.* Persistance, *f.* **persistent**, *a.* Persistant; opiniâtre. **persistently**, *adv.* Avec persistance.
person ['pə:sən], *n.* Personne, *f.*; personnage, caractère, *m.*; (*pl.*) personnes, *f.pl.*, gens, *n.pl.*, du monde. *A person*, quelqu'un, *m.*, quelqu'une, *f.*; *I know no such person*, je ne connais personne de ce nom; *in person*, en

personne; *no person*, personne; *to attend in person*, assister en personne; *to be no respecter of persons*, ne pas faire cas des personnalités; *to speak in the first person*, parler à la première personne; *young persons*, les jeunes gens.
personable, *a.* De bonne mine, beau de sa personne. **personage**, *n.* Personnage, *m.*
personal, *a.* Personnel. *Personal and real property*, biens meubles et immeubles, *m.pl.*; *personal column*, petite correspondance, *f.*; *personal remark*, personnalité, *f.* **personality** [-'næliti], *n.* Personnalité, *f.* **personalization** [-lai'zeiʃən], *n.* Personnalisation, *f.*
personalize ['pə:sənəlaiz], *v.t.* Personnaliser. **personally**, *adv.* Personnellement. **personalty**, *n.* (*Law*) Biens mobiliers, *m.pl.*
personate ['pə:səneit], *v.t.* Se faire passer pour; représenter, contrefaire, jouer le rôle de. —*a.* [-nət] (*Bot.*) Personnée, *a.f.* **personation** [-'neiʃən], *n.* Représentation; personnification, *f.* **personator**, *n.* Personne qui passe pour une autre, *f.*, imposteur, *m.*
personification [pə:sɔnifi'keiʃən], *n.* Personnification, *f.*
personified [pə:'sɔnifaid], *a.* Personnifié, en personne.
personify [pə:'sɔnifai], *v.t.* Personnifier.
personnel [pə:sə'nel], *n.* Personnel, *m.*
perspective [pə'spektiv], *a.* Perspectif, de perspective; d'optique. *Perspective glass*, verre optique, *m.—n.* Perspective; (*fig.*) vue, *f.* *To see something in its true perspective*, voir quelque chose sous son vrai jour. **perspectively**, *adv.* Selon les règles de la perspective; en perspective.
perspicacious [pə:spi'keiʃəs], *a.* Pénétrant, clairvoyant, perspicace; perçant (of the sight). **perspicacity** [-'kæsiti], *n.* Vue pénétrante; perspicacité, pénétration, sagacité, *f.*
perspicuity [pə:spi'kju:iti] or **perspicuousness** [-'spikjuəsnis], *n.* Clarté, perspicuité, netteté, *f.* **perspicuous**, *a.* Clair, net. **perspicuously**, *adv.* Nettement, avec clarté.
perspiration [pə:spi'reiʃən], *n.* Transpiration, sueur, *f.* *To be covered with perspiration*, être tout en nage *or* tout en sueur.
perspire [pə'spaiə], *v.i.* Transpirer, suer. **perspiring**, *a.* En sueur.
persuade [pə'sweid], *v.t.* Persuader (à); persuader (quelqu'un de); déterminer, décider (à). *To persuade from*, dissuader de; *to persuade oneself*, se plaire à croire. **persuasible** [-'sweizibl] or **persuadable**, *a.* Que l'on peut persuader, persuasible. **persuasion**, *n.* Persuasion; (*fig.*) opinion; (*colloq.*) croyance, religion (creed), *f.* **persuasive**, *a.* Persuasif. **persuasively**, *adv.* D'une manière persuasive. **persuasiveness**, *n.* Force persuasive; persuasion, *f.*
pert [pə:t], *a.* Mutin, hardi; impertinent, insolent (saucy).
pertain [pə:'tein], *v.i.* Appartenir, se rapporter (à).
pertinacious [pə:ti'neiʃəs], *a.* Obstiné, opiniâtre. **pertinaciously**, *adv.* Obstinément, opiniâtrement. **pertinaciousness** or **pertinacity** [-'næsiti], *n.* Obstination, opiniâtreté, *f.*, entêtement, *m.*
pertinence ['pə:tinəns] or **pertinency**, *n.* Convenance, justesse, *f.*, à-propos, *m.* **pertinent**, *a.* Pertinent, convenable, à

propos. **pertinently,** adv. Pertinemment, convenablement, à propos.
pertly ['pəːtli], adv. Impertinemment, insolemment. **pertness,** n. Impertinence, insolence, mutinerie, f.
perturb [pə'təːb], v.t. Agiter, troubler.
perturbation [pəːtə'beiʃən], n. Agitation, f., bouleversement, trouble, m.; (Astron.) perturbation, f. **perturbed,** a. Troublé, inquiet, agité. **perturber,** n. Perturbateur, m.
Peru [pə'ruː]. Le Pérou, m.
*peruke [pə'ruːk], n. Perruque, f. **perukemaker,** n. Perruquier, m.
perusal [pə'ruːzl], n. Lecture, f.; *examen, m. Worthy of perusal, digne d'être lu. **peruse,** v.t. Lire attentivement. **peruser,** n. Lecteur, m., lectrice, f.
Peruvian [pə'ruːviən], a. Péruvien, du Pérou. Peruvian bark, quinquina, m.—a. and n. Péruvien, m., Péruvienne, f.
pervade [pə'veid], v.t. Pénétrer dans, s'infiltrer dans, se répandre dans, remplir; (fig.) régner dans. **pervading,** a. All-pervading, dominant, régnant; qui se répand partout.
perverse [pə'vəːs], a. Pervers, méchant; contrariant; opiniâtre. **perversely,** adv. Avec perversité, méchamment. **perverseness** or **perversity,** n. Perversité, méchanceté, f.; esprit contrariant, m. **perversion,** n. Perversion, f.; pervertissement, m.
pervert (1) [pə'vəːt], v.t. Pervertir; fausser, dénaturer.
pervert (2) ['pəːvəːt], n. Perverti, m. **perverted,** a. Perverti. **perverter,** n. Pervertisseur, m., -euse, f., corrupteur, m., -trice, f. **pervertible,** a. Pervertissable.
pervious ['pəːviəs], a. Perméable, pénétrable; accessible. **perviousness,** n. Perméabilité; pénétrabilité, f.
pesky ['peski], a. (colloq.) Exécrable, maudit.
pessary ['pesəri], n. (Med.) Pessaire, m.
pessimism ['pesimizm], n. Pessimisme, m. **pessimist,** n. Pessimiste, m. or f. **pessimistic,** a. Pessimiste.
pest [pest], n. Peste, f.; insecte nuisible; (fig.) fléau, m. ***pest-house,** n. Lazaret, m.
pester ['pestə], v.t. Tourmenter, ennuyer, importuner. **pesterer,** n. Importun, fâcheux, m.
pestiferous [pes'tifərəs], a. Pestifère; malfaisant, pernicieux.
pestilence ['pestiləns], n. Peste, pestilence, f. **pestilent,** a. Pestilentiel, contagieux; méchant, malfaisant, pernicieux. **pestilential** [-'lenʃl], a. Pestilentiel; malfaisant, funeste, pernicieux. **pestilently,** adv. Pernicieusement.
pestle [pesl], n. Pilon, m.—v.t. Piler.
pet [pet], n. Chéri, m., chérie, f., favori, m., favorite, f.; animal familier; enfant gâté; dépit, accès d'humeur, m. To be a great pet, être très aimé; to be in a pet, être de mauvaise humeur.—a. Favori. Pet aversion, bête noire, f.; pet name, petit nom d'amitié, m.—v.t. Choyer, dorloter, gâter; (Am.) caresser, câliner.
petal [petl], n. Pétale, m. **petaliform,** a. Pétaliforme. **petaline,** a. Pétalin. **petalled,** a. À pétales, pétalé. **petaloid,** a. Pétaloïde.
petard [pə'taːd], n. Pétard, m. Hoist with his own petard, pris dans son propre traquenard.

Peter ['piːtə]. Pierre, m. (Naut.) Blue Peter, pavillon de partance, m.
peter out [piːtəraut], v.i. (colloq.) S'épuiser, mourir, disparaître; tomber à l'eau (scheme), flancher (engine).
petersham ['piːtəʃəm], n. Ratine, f.; extrafort, m.
petiolar ['petiələ], a. Pétiolaire. **petiolate,** a. Pétiolé.
petiole ['petioul], n. (Bot.) Pétiole, m.
petition [pi'tiʃən], n. Pétition, demande; supplique, prière; (Law) requête, f. Right of petition, droit de pétition, m.—v.t. Pétitionner; prier, implorer; (Law) présenter une requête à. **petitionary,** a. Suppliant, de supplication. **petitioner,** n. Pétitionnaire; suppliant, m., -ante. f.; (Law) requérant, m., -ante, f.
petrel ['petrəl], n. (Orn.) Pétrel, m. Stormy petrel, oiseau des tempêtes; (fig.) semeur de discorde, m.
petrifaction [petri'fækʃən], n. Pétrification, f. **petrifactive** [-'fæktiv], a. Pétrifiant. **petrified,** a. Pétrifié. Petrified with terror, paralysé de terreur.
petrify ['petrifai], v.t. Pétrifier.—v.i. Se pétrifier.
petrography [pe'trɔgrəfi], n. Pétrographie, f.
petroil ['petrɔil], n. Mélange, m. (d'huile et d'essence).
petrol ['petrəl], n. Essence (de pétrole), f. Petrol-can, bidon d'essence, m.; petrol station, poste d'essence, m.; petrol tank, réservoir d'essence, m.
petroleum [pi'trouliəm], n. Pétrole, m., huile depétrole, f. **petroliferous** [petro'lifərəs], a. Pétrolifère.
petrology [pe'trɔlədʒi], n. Pétrologie, f.
petrous ['petrəs], a. Pierreux.
petticoat ['petikout], n. Jupon, m. *Petticoat government, régime de cotillons, m.
pettifogger ['petifɔgə], n. Avocassier, chicaneur, m. **pettifoggery,** n. Chicane, avocasserie, f. **pettifogging,** a. Avocassier, chicaneur; chicanier (of methods etc.).
pettiness ['petinis], n. Petitesse, mesquinerie, f.
pettish ['petiʃ], a. Irritable. **pettishly,** adv. Avec humeur, avec dépit. **pettishness,** n. Mauvaise humeur, impatience, f.
pettitoes ['petitouz], n.pl. Pieds de porc, m.pl.
petty ['peti], a. Petit; mesquin, chétif; (Law) inférieur, ordinaire. Petty cash, petite monnaie, f.; petty charges, (Comm.) menus frais, m.pl.; petty jury, (Law) jury ordinaire, m.; petty offence, contravention, f.
petty-officer, n. (Navy) Officier marinier, m. The petty officers, les gradés, m.pl.
petulance ['petjuləns], n. Irritabilité, f. **petulant,** a. Irritable. **petulantly,** adv. Avec irritation, d'un ton irrité.
petunia [pi'tjuːniə], n. (Bot.) Pétunia, m.
petuntse [pə'tʌntsə], n. Pétunsé, pétunzé, m.
pew [pjuː], n. Banc d'église, m. Churchwarden's pew, banc d'œuvre, m.; (colloq.) take a pew, asseyez-vous, prenez un siège.
pewit ['piːwit], n. (Orn.) Vanneau, m.
pewter ['pjuːtə], n. Étain, potin, m.; vaisselle d'étain, f. Pewter pot, broc d'étain, m. **pewterer,** n. Potier d'étain, m.
phaeton ['feitən], n. Phaéton, m.

phagocyte ['fægosait], *n.* Phagocyte, *m.*
phagocytosis [-'tousis], *n.* Phagocytose, *f.*
phalaena [fə'liːnə], *n.* (*Ent.*) Phalène, *f.*
phalanger [fə'lændʒə], *n.* Phalanger, *m.*
phalangiform, *a.* Phalangiforme.
phalansterian [fælən'stiəriən], *a.* and *n.*
Phalanstérien, *m.*
phalanstery ['fælənstri], *n.* Phalanstère, *m.*
phalanx ['fælænks], *n.* (*pl.* (*Anat.*) **phalanxes**
['fælæŋksiz], (*Bot.* etc.) **phalanges** [fə'læn
dziːz]). Phalange, *f.*
phallic ['fælik], *a.* Phallique. **phallus** [-əs],
n. Phallus, *m.*
phanerogam ['fænərəgæm], *n.* (*Bot.*) Phanérogame, *f.* **phanerogamous** [-'rɔgəməs], *a.*
Phanérogame.
phantasm ['fæntæzm], *n.* Fantôme, *m.*,
illusion, *f.* **phantasmagoria** [-mə'gɔːriə], *n.*
Fantasmagorie, *f.* **phantasmagorical**
[-'gɔrikl], *a.* Fantasmagorique. **phan-
tasmal** [fæn'tæzml], *a.* De fantôme.
phantom, *n.* Fantôme, *m.* (*Elec.*) *Phantom
circuit*, circuit fantôme, *m.*
Pharaoh ['feərou], *n.* Pharaon, *m.*
Pharaonic [feərei'ɔnik], *a.* Pharaonique.
Pharisaic [færi'seiik] or **Pharisaical**, *a.*
Pharisaïque.
Pharisaism ['færiseiizm], *n.* Pharisaïsme, *n.*
Pharisee ['færisiː], *n.* Pharisien, *m.*, phari-
sienne, *f.*
pharmaceutic [fɑːmə'sjuːtik] or **pharmaceutical**, *a.* Pharmaceutique. **pharma-
ceutically**, *adv.* Suivant la pharmaceutique.
pharmaceutics, *n.pl.* Pharmaceutique, *f.*
pharmacological [fɑːməkə'lɔdʒikl], *a.* Pharmacologique. **pharmacologist** [-'kɔlədʒist],
n. Pharmacologue, *m.* **pharmacology**, *n.*
Pharmacologie, *f.* **pharmacopoeia** [-'piːə],
n. Pharmacopée, *f.*, codex, *m.*
pharmacy ['fɑːməsi], *n.* Pharmacie, *f.*
pharyngitis [færin'dʒaitis], *n.* Pharyngite, *f.*
pharynx ['færiŋks], *n.* Pharynx, *m.*
phase [feiz], *n.* Phase, *f.*, aspect, *m.* (*Elec.*)
Out of phase, déphasé.
phasma ['fæzmə], *n.* (*pl.* **phasmata**) (*Ent.*)
Phasme, *m.*
pheasant ['fezənt], *n.* Faisan, *m.* *Hen
pheasant*, faisane, *f.*; *pheasant shooting*, chasse
au faisan, *f.*; *young pheasant*, faisandeau, *m.*
pheasantry, *n.* Faisanderie, *f.*
phelloderm ['feloudəːm], *n.* (*Bot.*) Phelloderme, *m.* **phellogenetic** [-dʒi'netik], *a.*
Phellogène.
phenakistoscope [fenə'kistoskoup], *n.* Phénakistiscope, praxinoscope, *m.*
phenology [fiː'nɔlədʒi], *n.* Phénologie, *f.*
phenomenal [fi'nɔmənəl], *a.* Phénoménal.
phenomenalism, *n.* Phénoménalisme, *m.*
phenomenology [-'nɔlədʒi], *n.* Phénoménologie, *f.*
phenomenon [fi'nɔmənən], *n.* (*pl.* **phenomena**) Phénomène, *m.*
phenyl ['fiːnil], *n.* Phényle, *m.* *Phenyl alcohol*,
phénol, *m.*
phew [fjuː], *int.* Pouf!
phial ['faiəl], *n.* Fiole, *f.*
Philadelphia [filə'delfiə]. Philadelphie, *f.*
philander [fi'lændə], *v.i.* Conter fleurette,
flirter. **philanderer**, *n.* Flirteur, galant,
m.
philanthropic [filən'θrɔpik] or **philanthro-
pical**, *a.* Philanthropique.

philanthropist [fi'lænθrəpist], *n.* Philanthrope,
m. **philanthropy**, *n.* Philanthropie, *f.*
philatelic [filə'telik], *a.* Philatélique. **philate-
list** [fi'lætəlist], *n.* Philatéliste, *m.* or *f.*
philately [fi'lætəli], *n.* Philatélie, *f.*
philharmonic [filhɑː'mɔnik], *a.* Philharmonique.
philhellene ['filheliːn], *n.* Philhellène, *m.*
philhellenism [-'helənizm], *n.* Philhellénisme, *m.*
Philip ['filip]. Philippe, *m.*
philippic [fi'lipik], *n.* Philippique, *f.*
Philippines ['filipiːnz], **the**. Les Philippines,
f.pl.
Philistine ['filistain], *a.* and *n.* Philistin, (*fig.*)
épicier, *m.*
Philistinism ['filistinizm], *n.* Philistinisme, *m.*
philological [filə'lɔdʒikl], *a.* Philologique.
philologist [fi'lɔlədʒist], *n.* Philologue, *m.*
philology, *n.* Philologie, *f.*
philomel ['filəmel] or **philomela** [-'miːlə], *n.*
Philomèle, *f.*, le rossignol, *m.*
philosopher [fi'lɔsəfə], *n.* Philosophe; savant,
m. *Moral philosopher*, moraliste, *m.*; *natural
philosopher*, physicien, *m.*; *philosopher's stone*,
pierre philosophale, *f.* **philosophical**
[-'sɔfikl], *a.* Philosophique; philosophe,
modéré, calme (of persons). **philosophically**, *adv.* Philosophiquement; en philosophe.
philosophize [fi'lɔsəfaiz], *v.i.* Philosopher.
philosophy, *n.* Philosophie, *f.* *Moral
philosophy*, la morale, l'éthique, *f.*; *natural
philosophy*, la physique, *f.*
philotechnic [filo'teknik], *a.* Philotechnique.
philter or **philtre** ['filtə], *n.* Philtre, *m.*
phiz [fiz], *n.* Visage, *m.*; (*colloq.*) binette, *f.*
phlebitis [fli'baitis], *n.* Phlébite, *f.* **phleboto-
mize**, *v.t.* Phlébotomiser, saigner. **phlebotomy**, *n.* Phlébotomie, saignée, *f.*
phlegm [flem], *n.* Flegme, *m.*
phlegmasia [fleg'meisiə], *n.* Phlegmasie, *f.*
phlegmatic [fleg'mætik] or **phlegmatical**, *a.*
Flegmatique. **phlegmatically**, *adv.* Flegmatiquement.
phlegmy ['flemi], *a.* Flegmatique, pituiteux.
phlogisticate [flo'dʒistikeit], *v.t.* Phlogisti-
quer.
phlogiston [flo'dʒistən], *n.* Phlogistique, *m.*
phlogosis [flo'gousis], *n.* Phlogose, *f.*
phlox [flɔks], *n.* (*Bot.*) Phlox, *m.*
phlyctaena [flik'tiːnə], *n.* Phlyctène, ampoule,
f.

phobia ['foubiə], *n.* Phobie, *f.*
Phoebe ['fiːbi]. Phébé, *f.*
Phoebus ['fiːbəs]. Phébus; (*fig.*) soleil, *m.*
Phoenician [fi'niʃiən], *a.* Phénicien.—*n.*
Phénicien, *m.*, Phénicienne, *f.*
phoenix ['fiːniks], *n.* Phénix, *m.* **phoenix-
like**, *a.* and *adv.* Comme le phénix.
pholas ['fouləs], *n.* Pholade, *f.*
phone [foun], *n.* (*colloq.*) [TELEPHONE.]
phonetic [fə'netik], *a.* Phonétique. **phonetically**, *adv.* Phonétiquement. **phoneticism**,
n. Phonétisme, *m.* **phonetics**, *n.pl.* Phonétique, *f.*
phonetist ['founitist], or **phonetician** [founi
'tiʃən], *n.* Phonéticien, *m.*
phoney ['founi], *a.* (*colloq.*) Faux, factice. *The
phoney war*, la drôle de guerre, *f.*—*n.*
Charlatan, *m.*
phonic ['fɔnik], *a.* Phonique.

phonograph ['founəgræf *or* -grɑːf]. *n.* Phonographe, *m.* **phonographic**[-'græfik], *a.* Phonographique. **phonography** [-'nɔgrəfi], *n.* Phonographie, *f.* **phonology** [-'nɔlədʒi], *n.* Phonologie, *f.* **phonometer** [-'nɔmitə], *n.* Phonomètre, *m.*

phosphate ['fɔsfeit], *n.* Phosphate, *m.* **phosphide,** *n.* Phosphure, *m.* **phosphor,** *n.* Phosphore; (*Astron.*) Lucifer, *m.* **phosphorbronze,** *n.* Bronze phosphoré, *m.*

phosphoresce [fɔsfə'res], *v.i.* Être phosphorescent. **phosphorescence,** *n.* Phosphorescence, *f.* **phosphorescent,** *a.* Phosphorescent. **phosphoric** [-'fɔrik], *a.* Phosphorique.

phosphorism ['fɔsfərizm], *n.* Phosphorisme, *m.* **phosphorous** ['fɔsfərəs], *a.* Phosphoreux.

phosphorus ['fɔsfərəs], *n.* Phosphore, *m.* **phosphorus-box,** *n.* Briquet phosphorique, *m.* **phosphuretted,** *a.* Phosphuré.

photo ['foutou] [PHOTOGRAPH]. **photocopy,** *n.* Photocopie, *f.* **photo-electric,** *a.* Photoélectrique. *Photo-electric cell,* cellule photoélectrique, *f.* **photo-finish,** *n.* (*spt.*) Décision par photo, *f.*

photogenic [foutə'dʒenik], *a.* Photogénique.

photograph ['foutəgræf *or* -grɑːf], *n.* Photographie, (*colloq.*) photo, *f. To take a photograph,* prendre une photographie.—*v.t.* Photographier.—*v.i.* Faire de la photographie. *To photograph well,* être photogénique. **photographer** [fə'tɔgrəfə], *n.* Photographe, *m. Street photographer,* photostoppeur.

photographic [foutə'græfik], *a.* Photographique. **photographically,** *adv.* Photographiquement.

photography [fe'tɔgrəfi], *n.* Photographie, *f.* **photogravure** [foutogrə'vjuə], *n.* Héliogravure, photogravure, *f.* **photolithography** [-li'θɔgrəfi], *n.* Photolithographie, *f.*

photology [fou'tɔlədʒi], *n.* Photologie, *f.* **photomechanical** [-omi'kænikl], *a.* Photomécanique. **photometer** [-'tɔmitə], *n.* Photomètre, *m.* **photometric** [-o'metrik] *or* **photometrical,** *a.* Photométrique. **photometry** [-'tɔmitri], *n.* Photométrie, *f.* **photophobia** [-o'foubiə], *n.* Photophobie, *f.* **photostat** [-stæt], *n.* Appareil photostat, *m.* **photosynthesis** [-'sinθisis], *n.* Photosynthèse, *f.* **phototelegraphy** [-ti'legrəfi], *n.* Téléphotographie, *f.* **phototype** [-taip], *n.* Phototype, *m.*

phrase [freiz], *n.* Phrase, locution, expression, *f. As the phrase is,* comme on dit.—*v.t.* Exprimer, nommer; (*Mus.*) phraser. **phrase-book,** *n.* Recueil d'expressions, *m.* **phraseological** [freiziə'lɔdʒikl], *a.* Phraséologique. **phraseologist** [-'ɔlədʒist], *n.* Phraseur, *m.* **phraseology** [freizi'ɔlədʒi], *n.* Phraséologie, *f.* **phrenetic** [frə'netik], *a.* Fou, frénétique. **phrenic** ['frenik], *a.* (*Anat.*) Phrénique. **phrenological** [frenə'lɔdʒikl], *a.* Phrénologique. **phrenologist** [-'nɔlədʒist], *n.* Phrénologiste, phrénologue, *m.* **phrenology,** *n.* Phrénologie, *f.* **Phrygia** ['fridʒiə]. La Phrygie, *f.* **Phrygian,** *a.* Phrygien. **phthiriasis** [θairi'eisis], *n.* Phtiriase, *f.* **phthisical** ['tizikl], *a.* Phtisique.

phthisis ['θaisis], *n.* Phtisie, *f.* **phut** [fʌt], *adv.* (*pop.*) *To go phut,* claquer. **phylactery** [fi'læktəri], *n.* Phylactère, *m.* **phylarch** ['failɑːk], *n.* Phylarque, *m.* **phylarchy,** *n.* Phylarchie, *f.* **phyletic** [-'letik], *a.* Phylétique.

phyllite ['filait], *n.* Phyllithe, *f.* **phylloid,** *a.* Phylloïde. **phyllopodous** [-'lɔpədəs], *a.* Phyllopode.

phylloxera [filɔk'siərə], *n.* (*Ent.*) Phylloxéra, *m.*

physic ['fizik], *n.* Médecine, *f.*; (*fig.*) remède, *m.—v.t.* Médicamenter; droguer, purger. **physical,** *a.* Physique; médical. *Physical fitness,* santé physique, *f.*; *physical impossibility,* impossibilité matérielle, *f.*; *physical jerks,* exercices physiques, *m.pl.*; *physical training,* éducation physique, *f.* **physically,** *adv.* Physiquement.

physician [fi'ziʃən], *n.* Médecin, *m.* **physicism** ['fizisizm], *n.* Physicisme, *m.* **physicist,** *n.* Physicien, *m.* **physics,** *n.pl.* La physique, *f.* **physiocrat,** *n.* Physiocrate, *m.*

physiognomic [fiziɔg'nɔmik], *a.* Physionomique, physiognomonique. **physiognomist** [-'ɔgnəmist], *n.* Physionomiste, *m. or f.* **physiognomy** [fizi'ɔgnəmi *or* -'ɔnəmi], *n.* Physionomie; physiognomonie, *f.* **physiographical** [fiziə'græfikl], *a.* De la physiographie. **physiography** [-'ɔgrəfi], *n.* Physiographie, *f.* **physiological** [fiziə'lɔdʒikl], *a.* Physiologique. **physiologically,** *adv.* Par la physiologie. **physiologist** [-'ɔlədʒist], *n.* Physiologiste, *m. physiology, m.* Physiologie, *f.* **physiotherapy** [fiziə'θerəpi], *n.* Physiothérapie, *f.*

physique [fi'ziːk], *n.* Physique, *m.* **phytochemistry** [faitou'kemistri], *n.* Phytochimie, *f.* **phytography** [fai'tɔgrəfi], *n.* Phytographie, *f.* **phytology** [-'tɔlədʒi], *n.* Phytologie, *f.* **pi** [pai], *a.* (*pop.*) Pieux; béat. **piacular** [pai'ækjulə], *a.* Expiatoire, piaculaire; criminel. **pia mater** ['paiə 'meitə], *n.* (*Anat.*) Piemère, *f.*

pianist ['piənist], *n.* Pianiste, *m. or f.* **piano** ['pjænou *or* 'pjɑːnou] *or* **pianoforte** [-'fɔːti], *n.* Piano, *m. Cottage* or *upright piano,* piano droit; *grand piano,* piano à queue; *to play (on) the piano,* jouer du piano.—*adv.* Piano, doucement.

pianola [piə'noulə], *n.* Pianola, *m.* **piano-maker,** *n.* Facteur de pianos, *m.* **piano-stool,** *n.* Tabouret de piano, *m.* **piano-tuner,** *n.* Accordeur de pianos, *m.* **piastre** [pi'æstə], *n.* Piastre, *f.* **piazza** [pi'ædzə], *n.* Place, piazza, *f.* **pibroch** ['piːbrɔx], *n.* Pibroch, *m.,* air de cornemuse écossaise, *m.* **pica** ['paikə], *n.* Pie (bird), *f.*; (*Print.*) cicéro, *m.*; (*Path.*) pica, *m.* **picaresque** [pikə'resk], *a.* Picaresque. ***picaroon** [pikə'ruːn], *n.* Voleur, forban, *m.* **piccalilli** ['pikəlili], *n.* Conserves au vinaigre et à la moutarde, *f.pl.* **piccaninny** ['pikənini], (*ɲej.*) *n.* Négrillon, *m.* **piccolo** ['pikəlou], *n.* Petite flûte, *f.* **pick** (1) [pik], *n.* Pic, *m.,* pioche (tool), *f.*; picot (mason's pick), *m.*

pick (2) [pik], *v.t.* Piquer, picoter; cueillir (to gather); prendre, choisir, trier (to choose); enlever, ôter (to pull off); ronger (a bone); chercher (a quarrel); plumer (a fowl etc.); prendre dans, vider (a pocket); crocheter (a lock); éplucher (to clean). *To have a bone to pick with,* avoir maille à partir avec; *to pick a lock,* crocheter une serrure; *to pick and choose,* être difficile à satisfaire, chipoter; *to pick a quarrel with,* chercher querelle à; *to pick holes in,* critiquer, trouver à redire à; *to pick oakum,* éplucher, effiler des étoupes; *to pick off,* enlever, ôter; abattre un à un (enemy soldiers etc.); *to pick on* (*someone*), chercher querelle à, critiquer, persécuter; *to pick one's teeth* or *one's nails,* se curer les dents or les ongles; *to pick one's way,* choisir son chemin; *to pick out,* choisir, arracher; *to pick pockets,* voler à la tire; *to pick the salad,* éplucher la salade; *to pick to pieces,* déchirer à belles dents; *to pick up,* ramasser, relever, apprendre, prendre, capter (un courant, des ondes).—*v.t.* Grignoter. *To pick up again,* reprendre ses forces, se refaire; *to pick up for sides,* tirer les camps.—*n.* Choix (choice), *m. The pick of the basket* or *bunch,* la crème, la fleur, la fine fleur.

pickaback ['pikəbæk], *adv.* Sur le dos.
pickaxe ['pikæks], *n.* Pioche, *f.*
picked [pikt], *a.* D'élite, choisi. *Picked men,* hommes d'élite, hommes de choix, *m.pl.; picked troops,* troupes d'élite, *f.pl.* **picker,** *n.* Cueilleur, *m.,* -euse, *f.;* éplucheur, *m.,* -euse, *f.;* chercheur, *m.,* -euse (of quarrels), *f.*
pickerel ['pikərəl], *n.* (*Ichth.*) Brocheton, *m.*
picket ['pikit], *n.* Piquet, jalon; petit poste, *m. Inlying picket,* piquet intérieur, *m.; stable picket,* garde d'écurie, *f.; to be on picket,* être de piquet.—*v.t.* Former en piquet; guetter (of strikers etc.).
picking ['pikiŋ], *n.* Action de cueillir, d'ôter, or de choisir, *f.;* épluchage (cleaning); triage (choosing); effilage (of oakum), *m.;* (*pl.*) épluchures; (*fig.*) choses à recueillir, *f.pl.;* petits profits, *m.pl.*
pickle [pikl], *n.* Saumure, marinade, *f.;* (*pl.*) conserves au vinaigre, *f.pl. Little pickle,* petit polisson, *m.; to be in a fine pickle,* être dans de beaux draps; *to have a rod in pickle for,* la garder bonne à, apprêter une sauce à. —*v.t.* Conserver au vinaigre, mariner; saler; (*Metal.*) décaper. **pickled,** *a.* Mariné, conservé au vinaigre; (*pop.*) ivre. **pickling,** *n.* Marinage, saumurage, *m.*
picklock ['piklɔk], *n.* Crochet à serrures; crocheteur de serrures, *m.* **pick-me-up,** *n.* Cordial, remontant; (*Med.*) confortant, *m.*
pickpocket, *n.* Voleur à la tire, *m.* **pick-up,** *n.* Ramassage, *m.;* chose ramassée; reprise, *f.* (of engine, business); pick-up, *m.* (of gramophone).
picnic ['piknik], *n.* Pique-nique, *m.—v.i.* Faire un pique-nique. **picknicker,** *n.* Pique-niqueur, *m.;* -euse, *f.*
Pictish ['piktiʃ], *a.* Pictique, des Pictes.
pictorial [pik'tɔːriəl], *a.* Illustré; de peintre, pittoresque. **pictorially,** *adv.* Avec illustrations.
picture ['piktʃə], *n.* Tableau, *m.;* peinture; (*fig.*) figure, image, *f. Dark side of the picture,* revers de la médaille, *m.; he is the picture of health,* il respire la santé; *he is the very picture*

of his father, il est le portrait or la vivante image de son père; (*fam.*) *the pictures,* le cinéma; (*fig.*) *to put in the picture,* mettre au courant.—*v.t.* Peindre; (*fig.*) dépeindre, représenter, décrire. *To picture to oneself,* se figurer, se représenter.
picture-book, *n.* Livre d'images, *m.* **picture-cleaning,** *n.* Nettoyage de tableaux, *m.* **picture-frame,** *n.* Cadre, *m.* **picture-frame-maker,** *n.* Encadreur, *m.* **picture-gallery,** *n.* Galerie de tableaux, *f.,* musée de peinture, *m.* **picture-goer,** *n.* Habitué du cinéma, *m.* **picture-palace,** *n.* Cinéma, *m.* **picturesque** [-'resk], *a.* Pittoresque. **picturesquely,** *adv.* D'une manière pittoresque, pittoresquement. **picturesqueness,** *n.* Le pittoresque, *m.*
picturize ['piktʃəraiz], *v.t.* Adapter (un roman) à l'écran.
piddle [pidl], *v.t.* S'occuper de bagatelles, pignocher, niaiser; (*pop.*) uriner. **piddling,** *a.* Futile, frivole.
pidgin English ['pidʒin 'ingliʃ], *n.* Jargon commercial anglo-chinois, (*fam.*) petit nègre, *m.*
pie [pai], *n.* Pâté (of meat), *m.;* tourte (of fruit); *pie (bird), f. (colloq.) As easy as pie,* simple comme bonjour; *to eat humble pie,* avaler des couleuvres; *to have a finger in the pie,* y être pour quelque chose. **pie-crust,** *n.* Croûte de pâté, *f.* **pie-dish,** *n.* Tourtière, terrine, timbale, *f.*
piebald ['paibɔːld], *a.* Pie (of horses).
piece [piːs], *n.* Pièce (of large dimensions), *f.;* morceau (a portion, a bit, etc.); fragment, bout (fragment); (*fig.*) passage (in a book); (*Paint.*) tableau, *m. All of a piece,* tout d'une pièce, à l'avenant (de); *a piece of business,* une affaire; *a piece of furniture,* un meuble; *a piece of impertinence,* une impertinence; *a piece of news,* une nouvelle; *a piece of soap,* un morceau de savon; *a piece of wit,* un trait d'esprit; *a theatrical piece,* une pièce de théâtre; *broken piece,* fragment, tronçon, éclat, *m.; I'll give him a piece of my mind,* je lui dirai son fait; *piece of artillery,* bouche à feu, *f.; so much a piece,* chacun, par tête, la pièce; *the pieces of a machine,* les pièces d'une machine, *f.pl.; to break to pieces,* mettre en pièces, tomber en pièces; *to fly to pieces,* voler en éclats; *to go (all) to pieces,* perdre son sang-froid, tous ses moyens; *to say one's piece,* prononcer son discours; *to take to pieces,* démonter, se démonter.—*v.t.* Rapiécer, mettre une pièce à. *To piece together,* joindre, unir, coordonner.—*v.i.* Se joindre, s'unir.
piece-goods, *n.* Marchandises à la pièce, *f.pl.;* tissu en pièces, *m.* **piecemeal,** *adv.* Par morceaux, peu à peu. **piece-work,** *n.* Travail à la tâche, *m.*
pied [paid], *a.* Bariolé, bigarré; pie (of horses).
Piedmont ['piːdmɔnt]. Le Piémont, *m.*
pier [piə], *n.* Jetée, *f.;* pont (on river), *m.;* pile (of a bridge), *f.;* (*Arch.*) trumeau, pied-droit, *m.* **pier-dues,** *n.pl.* Droits de jetée, *m.pl.* **pier-glass,** *n.* Trumeau, *m.* **pier-head,** *n.* Bout de la jetée, musoir, *m.*
pierce [piːəs], *v.t.* Percer, pénétrer. *To pierce through,* transpercer; *to pierce through and through,* percer de part en part. **pierced,** *a.* À jour (of openwork). **piercer,** *n.* Perçoir,

m.; (*Mining*) épinglette, *f.*; perceur (person), *m.* **piercing,** *a.* Perçant; pénétrant. **piercingly,** *adv.* D'une manière perçante. **piercingness,** *n.* Pénétration, *f.* **pietist** ['paiətist], *n.* Piétiste, *m.* or *f.* **piety,** *n.* Piété, *f.* **piffle** [pifl], *n.* (*colloq.*) Bêtises, balivernes, futilités, *f.pl.—v.i.* Dire *or* faire des niaiseries. **piffling,** *a.* Futile.

pig [pig], *n.* Cochon, porc, pourceau; saumon (of lead), *m.*, gueuse (of iron), *f.* *Sucking-pig,* cochon de lait, *m.*; *to buy a pig in a poke,* acheter chat en poche; *to make a pig of oneself,* manger gloutonnement.—*v.t.* Cochonner, mettre bas. *To pig it,* vivre en pourceau. **pig-driver,** *n.* Porcher, *m.* **piggery,** *n.* Étable à cochons, *f.* **piggy, piglet, pigling,** *n.* Porcelet, goret, *m.* **pigheaded,** *a.* Têtu, stupide. **pigheadedness,** *n.* Opiniâtreté, *f.*, entêtement, *m.* **pig-iron,** *n.* Gueuse, *f.* **pig-nut,** *n.* Terrenoix, *f.* **pig-sticking,** *n.* Chasse au sanglier, *f.* **pigsty,** *n.* Étable à cochons, porcherie, *f.* **pigtail,** *n.* Queue (de cheveux), *f.*, tabac en corde (tobacco), *m.* **pigtailed,** *a.* À queue.

pigeon ['pidʒin], *n.* Pigeon, *m.* *Carrier-pigeon,* pigeon voyageur, *m.*; *clay pigeon,* pigeon artificiel, *m.*; (*colloq.*) *that's my pigeon,* ça c'est mon affaire; *to pluck a pigeon,* plumer un pigeon. **pigeon-fancier,** *n.* Colombophile, *m.* or *f.* **pigeon-hearted,** *a.* Timide, craintif. **pigeon-hole,** *n.* Boulin, *m.*; case (for papers etc.), *f.—v.t.* Classer, mettre au rancart. *Set of pigeon-holes,* casier, *m.*; *to be pigeon-holed,* rester dans les cartons. **pigeon-house,** *n.* Pigeonnier, colombier, *m.* **pigeon-livered,** *a.* Timide, peureux. **pigeon-shooting,** *n.* Tir aux pigeons, *m.* **pigmean** [PYGMEAN].

pigment ['pigmənt], *n.* Couleur, *f.*, pigment, *m.—v.t.* Teindre, colorer. **pigmentation,** *n.* Pigmentation, *f.* **pigmented,** *a.* Pigmenté. **pigmy** [PYGMY].

pike [paik], *n.* Pique (weapon); hampe (for colours); fourche (fork), *f.*; brochet (fish); pic (mountain), *m.*; barrière (turnpike), *f.* (*Am.*) route à grande circulation, *f.* **piked,** *a.* Pointu, en pointe. **pikeman,** *n.* Piquier, *m.* **pikestaff,** *n.* Bois de pique; bâton ferré, *m.* *Plain as a pikestaff,* clair comme de l'eau de roche.

pilaster [pi'læstə], *n.* (*Arch.*) Pilastre, *m.* **Pilate** ['pailət]. (*Bibl.*) Pilate, *m.* **Pilatus** [pi'lɑːtəs]. (*Geol.*) Le Mont Pilate, *m.*

pilau [pi'lau] or **pilaw, pilaff,** *n.* Pilau, pilaf, *m.*

pilchard ['piltʃəd], *n.* (*Ichth.*) Pilchard, *m.* *Small pilchard,* sardine, *f.*

pile [pail], *n.* Tas, monceau; (*fig.*) édifice, bâtiment; (*Build.*) pieu (stake); pilotis (for foundations), *m.*; (*Elec.*) pile, *f.*; poil (nap of cloth); faisceau (of fire-arms), *m.* *Atomic pile,* pile atomique, *f.*; *funeral pile,* bûcher, *m.*; *pile of wood,* bûcher, *m.*; *row of piles,* pilotis, *m.*; *to drive a pile,* enfoncer un pieu; *to make one's pile,* faire fortune.—*v.t.* Entasser, empiler, amonceler; mettre *or* ranger (fire-arms) en faisceau. *To pile arms,* former les faisceaux; *to pile it on,* (*colloq.*) exagérer; *to unpile arms,* rompre les faisceaux.—*v.i.* To *pile up,* s'empiler, s'entasser.

pileate ['pailiət] or **pileated** ['pailieitid], *a.* (*Bot.*) À chapeau. **pile-bridge,** *n.* Pont sur pilotis, *m.* **pile-driver** or **pile-driving-machine,** *n.* Sonnette, *f.* **pile-driving,** *n.* Enfoncement des pieux, *m.* **pile-planking,** *n.* Plancher sur pilotis, *m.*, plate-forme sur pilotis, *f.* **piles,** *n.pl.* (*Path.*) Hémorroïdes, *f.pl.* *Blind piles,* hémorroïdes sèches. **pile-work,** *n.* Pilotage, pilotis, *m.* **pilewort** ['pailwəːt], *n.* (*Bot.*) Ficaire, *f.* **pilfer** ['pilfə], *v.t.* Dérober, chiper.—*v.i.* Dérober, commettre un petit vol. **pilferage,** *n.* Chapardage, *m.* **pilferer,** *n.* Chapardeur, chipeur, *m.* **pilfering,** *n.* Petit vol, larcin, *m.* **pilgrim** ['pilgrim], *n.* Pèlerin, *m.*, pèlerine, *f.* **pilgrimage,** *n.* Pèlerinage, *m.* **piling** ['pailiŋ], *n.* Empilage; amoncellement; ouvrage en pilotis, pilotage, *m.* **pill** [pil], *n.* Pilule, *f.*; (*pop.*) balle, *f.*, ballon, *m.* *To gild the pill,* dorer la pilule; *to swallow many a bitter pill,* en avaler de dures. **pill-box,** *n.* Boîte à pilules, *f.*; (*Mil.*) réduit en béton pour une mitrailleuse, *m.*

pillage ['pilidʒ], *n.* Pillage, saccagement, *m.* —*v.t.* Saccager, piller; faire main basse sur. **pillager,** *n.* Pillard, *m.*

pillar ['pilə], *n.* Pilier, *m.*, colonne, *f.*; (*fig.*) support, soutien, *m.* *From pillar to post,* çà et là; *to send from pillar to post,* renvoyer de Caïphe à Pilate. **pillar-box,** *n.* Boîte aux lettres, *f.* **pillared,** *a.* À colonnes. **pillau** [PILAU].

pillion ['piljən], *n.* Coussinet (de cheval), *m.*; selle (de femme), *f.*; siège, *m.* (*or* selle, *f.*) arrière (on motorcycle). *To ride pillion,* monter en croupe, monter derrière. **pillory** ['piləri], *n.* Pilori, *m.—v.t.* Pilorier, mettre au pilori. **pillow** ['pilou], *n.* Oreiller; (*Tech.*) coussinet, *m.* *To smooth the pillow,* lisser l'oreiller.—*v.t.* Reposer, coucher (comme sur un oreiller); servir d'oreiller à; (*fig.*) soutenir. **pillow-case** or **pillow-slip,** *n.* Taie d'oreiller, *f.* **pilose** or **pilous** ['pailous], *a.* Poilu, velu. **pilot** ['pailət], *n.* Pilote, *m.* *Coastal pilot,* lamaneur, *m.*; *test pilot,* pilote d'essais, *m.—v.t.* Piloter, servir de pilote à; (*fig.*) conduire, diriger. **pilot-boat,** *n.* Bateau-pilote, *m.* **pilot-cloth,** *n.* Drap-pilote, *m.* **pilot-coat** or **-jacket,** *n.* Vareuse, *f.* **pilot-engine,** *n.* Machine-pilote, *f.* **pilot-fish,** *n.* Pilote, *m.* **pilot-lamp,** *n.* Lampe de contrôle, *f.* **pilot-officer,** *n.* Sous-lieutenant aviateur, *m.* **pilotage,** *n.* Droit de pilotage, pilotage, *m.* *Coastal pilotage,* lamanage, *m.* **pilotless,** *a.* Sans pilote. *Pilotless plane,* avion robot, *m.* **pilule** ['pilju:l], *n.* Pilule, *f.* **pimento** [pi'mentou], *n.* Piment, *m.* **pimp** [pimp], *n.* Entremetteur, souteneur, proxénète, *m.* **pimpernel** ['pimpənel], *n.* Pimprenelle, *f.*, mouron, *m.* *Scarlet pimpernel,* mouron rouge, *m.* **pimping** ['pimpiŋ], *a.* Petit, chétif, mesquin. **pimple** [pimpl], *n.* Bouton, *m.*, pustule, *f.*; bourgeon (in the face), *m.* **pimpled** or **pimply,** *a.* Bourgeonné, pustuleux. **pin** [pin], *n.* Épingle; cheville, clavette (peg), *f.*; essieu (of a pulley); rouleau (rolling-pin), *m.*; pivot, tourillon, *m.*; (*fig.*) rien, *m.*, bagatelle, *f.* *For two pins,* pour un peu; *not to care a* *pin for,* se soucier comme de l'an quarante de; *to be on pins and needles,* être sur des charbons ardents; *to have pins and needles in one's hand,* avoir des fourmis dans la main, avoir la main qui vous fourmille; *to hear a pin drop,* entendre voler une mouche.—*v.t.* Attacher avec une épingle, épingler, attacher; goupiller, cheviller. *To pin down,* attacher avec une épingle, clouer, fixer; *to pin down to,* lier à, tenir à; *to pin one's hopes on,* fonder tous ses espoirs sur; *to pin someone down to the facts,* obliger quelqu'un à s'en tenir aux faits; *to pin up,* trousser avec une épingle, retrousser.

pinafore ['pinəfɔ:], *n.* Tablier, *m.* (d'enfant).
pinaster [pi'næstə], *n.* (*Bot.*) Pinastre, *m.*
pin-case, *n.* Étui à épingles, *m.* **pin-cushion,** *n.* Pelote, *f.* **pin-feather,** *n.* Petite plume, *f.*
pin-feathered, *a.* Aux plumes naissantes.
pin-headed, *a.* À tête d'épingle; peu intelligent. **pin-maker,** *n.* Épinglier, fabricant d'épingles, *m.* **pin-money,** *n.* Épingles, *f.pl.*; argent de poche, *m.* **pin-point,** *v.t.* (*Mil.*) Indiquer exactement. **pin-pricks,** *n.pl.* Coups d'épingles, *m.pl.* *A policy of pin-pricks,* une politique de coups d'épingle.
pin-up (girl), *n.* Pin-up, *f.* **pin-valve,** *m.* Pointeau, *m.*
pincers ['pinsəz], *n.pl.* Pince, *f.*, tenailles, *f.pl.*
pinch [pintʃ], *n.* Pincée (of salt etc.); prise (of snuff), *f.*; (*fig.*) embarras, *m.*, difficulté, nécessité, *f.*, besoin, pinçon, *m.*, angoisse, *f.* *At a pinch,* au besoin, en cas de nécessité; *to give someone a pinch,* pincer quelqu'un; *to take a story with a pinch of salt,* prendre une histoire avec un grain de sel; *when it comes to the pinch,* au moment décisif.—*v.t.* Pincer; serrer, gêner (of clothes); serrer de près (to press hard); mettre dans la gêne, mettre à l'étroit (to straiten); (*pop.*) chiper, chaparder; arrêter, pincer (a criminal). *Pinched for money,* à court d'argent; *pinched for room,* à l'étroit; *pinched with cold,* transi de froid; *pinched with hunger,* tiré par la faim (of face); *this shoe pinches me,* ce soulier me gêne; *to pinch oneself,* se priver du nécessaire.—*v.i.* Pincer, se gêner, être dans la gêne (to live close); se priver du nécessaire (to be straitened). *To know where the shoe pinches,* savoir où le bât blesse; *to pinch and scrape,* liarder.
pinchbeck, *n.* Similor, *m.*
pinchers [PINCERS].
pinch-fist or **pinchpenny,** *n.* Grippe-sou, *m.*
pinching, *a.* Pressant, piquant (of cold).—*n.* Pincement, *m.*
Pindar ['pində]. Pindare, *m.*
Pindaric [pin'dærik], *a.* Pindarique.—*n.* Ode pindarique, *f.*
pine [pain], *n.* Pin (tree); ananas (fruit); bois de pin (wood), *m.*—*v.i.* Languir. *To pine after,* soupirer après; *to pine away,* languir, dépérir. **pineapple,** *n.* Ananas, *m.* **pine-needle,** *n.* Aiguille de pin, *f.* **pine-nut,** *n.* Pomme de pin, *f.* **pine-wood,** *n.* Pinède, *f.*
pineal ['piniəl *or* pai'ni:əl], *a.* (*Anat.*) Pinéal.
pinery, *n.* Serre à ananas, *f.*
pinetum [pai'ni:təm], *n.* Sapinière, *f.*
pinfold ['pinfould], *n.* Fourrière, *f.*
ping [piŋ], *n.* Sifflement (of a bullet), *m.*—*v.i.* Siffler, cingler. **ping-pong,** *n.* Ping-pong, tennis de table, *m.*

pinion ['pinjən], *n.* Aileron, bout d'aile, *m.*; plume (feather), *f.*; (*Tech.*) pignon, *m.*; (*pl.*) liens (pour les bras), *m.pl.* Bevel pinion, pignon d'angle.—*v.t.* Couper le bout de l'aile à; lier les bras à; lier, enchaîner. **pinioned,** *a.* Ailé; (*fig.*) les bras liés.
pink [piŋk], *n.* Œillet (flower); rose (colour), *m.*, (*fig.*) perle, fleur, crème, *f.* *In the pink of condition,* en excellente condition; (*colloq.*) *to be in the pink,* se porter à merveille.—*a.* Couleur de rose, rose. (*colloq.*) *Strike me pink,* je veux être pendu!—*v.t.* Travailler à jour, percer; découper, déchiqueter.—*v.i.* Cliqueter (of engine).
pinking, *n.* Découpure, *f.*
pinkish, *a.* Rosâtre.
pinnace ['pinəs], *n.* Pinasse, *f.*, grand canot (du capitaine), *m.*
pinnacle ['pinəkl], *n.* Pinacle; (*fig.*) faîte, sommet, *m.* *Pinnacle of glory,* faîte de la gloire, *m.*
pinner ['pinə], *n.* Coiffe, *f.*, bonnet, *m.*
pint [paint], *n.* Pinte (un demi-litre); chopine (old French measure), *f.* **pint-bottle,** *n.* Demi-litre, *m.*
pintail ['pinteil], *n.* (*Orn.*) Pilet (duck), *m.*
pintle [pintl], *n.* (*Artill.*) Cheville ouvrière, *f.*; (*Naut.*) aiguillot, *m.*
piny ['paini], *a.* Couvert de pins.
pioneer [paiə'niə], *n.* Pionnier, *m.*; (*fig.*) défricheur, *m.*—*v.i.* Frayer le chemin.—*v.t.* Servir de pionnier à.
pious ['paiəs], *a.* Pieux. **piously,** *adv.* Pieusement.
pip [pip], *n.* Pépin (of fruit); point (on cards), *m.*; pépie (in birds), *f.*; (*Rad.*) top, *m.*; (*Mil.*) étoile, *f.* (sign of rank). (*colloq.*) *To give someone the pip,* donner le cafard à quelqu'un.—*v.i.* Piauler (of birds).—*v.t.* (*colloq.*) Vaincre, battre.
pipage ['paipidʒ], *n.* Canalisation, *f.*
pipe [paip], *n.* Tuyau, conduit, *m.*; pipe (for smoking, wine, etc.), *f.*; (*Naut.*) sifflet; (*Mus.*) pipeau, chalumeau, *m.*; (*Med. etc.*) canule, *f.* *Cutty pipe,* brûle-gueule, *m.*; *main pipe,* tuyau principal, *m.*; *the pipe of peace,* le calumet de paix, *m.*—*v.i.* Jouer du chalumeau, siffler. (*pop.*) *Pipe down!* Boucle-la! (*colloq.*) *to pipe up,* se faire entendre.—*v.t.* (*Naut.*) Appeler d'un coup de sifflet; canaliser (oil etc.). *To pipe one's eye,* (*colloq.*) pleurer.
pipe-case, *n.* Étui à pipe, *m.* **pipe-clay,** *n.* Terre de pipe, craie, *f.*; (tailor's) savon à marquer, *m.* **pipe-line,** *n.* Canalisation à pétrole, *f.*, oléoduc, *m.* **pipe-major,** *n.* (*Mil.*) Cornemuse-chef, *m.* **pipe-rack,** *n.* Râtelier à pipes, *m.*
piper, *n.* Joueur de flûte etc., *m.* *To pay the piper,* payer les violons. **piping,** *n.* Tubulure, *f.*, tuyautage, *m.*, (*Naut.*) liséré, passepoil, *m.*—*a.* Qui joue du chalumeau, sifflant; criard, flûté (of the voice). *Piping hot,* (*colloq.*) tout bouillant, tout chaud.
pipit [pipit], *n.* (*Orn.*) Pipi, pipit, *m.* *Meadow-pipit,* pipit des prés, *m.*, farlouse, *f.*; *rock-pipit,* pipit de rocher; *tree-pipit,* pipit des buissons.
pipkin ['pipkin], *n.* Casserole de terre, *f.*; poêlon, *m.*
pippin ['pipin], *n.* Reinette, *f.* *Normandy pippins,* pommes tapées, *f.pl.*

[383]

pip-squeak ['pipskwiːk], *n.* (*colloq.*) Gringalet, *m.*

piquancy ['piːkənsi], *n.* Goût piquant; piquant, *m.* **piquant**, *a.* Piquant. **piquantly**, *adv.* D'une manière piquante.

pique [piːk], *n.* Pique, brouillerie, *f.*; point (punctilio), *m.* *To take a pique*, se piquer, s'offenser.—*v.t.* Piquer, offenser. *To pique oneself on*, se piquer de.

piquet [pi'kit], *n.* Piquet, *m.*; (*Mil.*) [PICKET].

piracy ['pairəsi], *n.* Piraterie; (*fig.*) contrefaçon, *f.*, plagiat, *m.*

Piraeus [pai'riːəs], **The.** Le Pirée, *m.*

pirate ['pairit], *n.* Pirate, forban, écumeur de mer; (*fig.*) contrefacteur, plagiaire, *m.*—*v.t.* Voler; (*fig.*) contrefaire, piller.—*v.i.* Pirater, exercer la piraterie; (*fig.*) faire une contrefaçon, commettre un plagiat. *Pirate bus*, autobus (privé) concurrent des grandes compagnies, *m.*

piratical [pai'rætikl], *a.* De pirate; (*fig.*) de contrefaçon. **piratically**, *adv.* En pirate; (*fig.*) en contrefaçon.

pirating ['pairətiŋ], *a.* De piraterie, de contrefaçon.—*n.* Piraterie; contrefaçon, *f.*, démarquage, *m.*

pirogue [pi'roug], *n.* Pirogue, *f.*

pirouette [piru'et], *n.* Pirouette, *f.*—*v.i.* Pirouetter.

piscatory ['piskətəri] or **piscatorial** [-'tɔːriəl], *a.* De la pêche, de pêcheur.

pisces ['pisiːz], *n.pl.* (*Astron.*) Les Poissons, *m.pl.*

piscicultural [pisi'kʌltʃərəl], *a.* Piscicole. **pisciculture** ['pisikʌltʃə], *n.* Pisciculture, *f.* **pisciculturist**, *n.* Pisciculteur, *m.* **pisciform**, *a.* Pisciforme.

piscina [pi'sainə], *n.* Piscine, *f.*

piscine ['pisain], *a.* De poisson.

piscivorous [pi'sivərəs], *a.* Piscivore.

pish! [piʃ], *int.* Bah! Pouah!

pismire ['pismaiə], *n.* Fourmi, *f.*

piss [pis], *v.i.* Pisser.—*n.* Urine, *f.* **pissabed**, *n.* (*pop.*) Pissenlit (dandelion), *m.* **pissed**, *a.* (*vulg.*) Soûl. **pisser**, *n.* Pisseur, *m.* **pissing**, *n.* Pissement, *m.*

pissasphalt ['pisæsfɔlt], *n.* Asphalte, *m.*

pistachio [pis'taːʃiou], *n.* Pistache, *f.* **pistachio-tree**, *n.* Pistachier, *m.*

pistil ['pistil], *n.* (*Bot.*) Pistil, *m.*

pistol [pistl], *n.* Pistolet, *m.* *Horse pistol*, pistolet d'arçon, *m.*—*v.t.* Tuer d'un coup de pistolet. **pistol-case**, *n.* Boîte à pistolets, *f.* **pistol-holsters**, *n.pl.* Fontes, *f.pl.* **pistol-shot**, *n.* Coup de pistolet, *m.* *Within pistol-shot*, à portée de pistolet, *f.*

pistole [pis'toul], *n.* Pistole, *f.*

piston ['pistən], *n.* Piston, *m.* **piston-head**, *n.* Tête de piston, *f.* **piston-ring**, *n.* Segment de piston, *m.* **piston-rod**, *n.* Tige de piston, *f.* **piston-stroke**, *n.* Coup de piston, *m.*

pit [pit], *n.* Fosse; (*fig.*) cavité, *f.*; (*Theat.*) parterre; (*Mining*) puits; creux (of the stomach), *m.*; aisselle (of the arm); marque, empreinte (mark), *f. Coal-pit*, mine de houille, *f.*; *rifle-pit*, trou de tirailleurs, *m.*—*v.t.* Creuser; marquer de petits creux, grêler. *To pit against*, opposer à, mettre aux prises avec; *to pit with*, marquer de.

pitapat ['pitəpæt], *n.* Palpitation de cœur, *f.*, battement, *m.*—*adv.* En palpitant, en battant.

Her heart went pitapat, le cœur lui battait; *to go pitapat*, battre, palpiter.

pit-boy, *n.* Galibot, *m.* **pit-coal**, *n.* Charbon de terre, *m.*, houille, *f.* **pitfall**, *n.* Trappe, *f.*, piège, *m.* **pit-head**, *n.* Carreau, *m.* **pitman**, *n.* (*pl.* **pitmen**) Mineur, *m.* **pit-prop**, *n.* Support de mine, *m.* **pit-saw**, *n.* Scie de long, *f.*

pitch (1) [pitʃ], *n.* Jet, lancement, *m.* (of stone, ball); (*Naut.*) tangage, *m.*; point, degré (degree), *m.*; pente, *f.*, penchant (slope), *m.*; taille, stature (stature); élévation, hauteur (elevation); épaisseur (of gear etc.), *f.*; (*Mus.*) ton, diapason, *m.*; (*Cricket*) espace entre les guichets, *m. To play pitch-and-toss*, jouer à pile ou face; *to queer someone's pitch*, bouleverser les plans de quelqu'un, contrecarrer quelqu'un.—*v.t.* Jeter, lancer; asseoir, établir, fixer (to fix); dresser (a tent); (*Mus.*) donner le ton à. *To pitch a yarn*, conter une histoire; *to pitch out of the window*, jeter par la fenêtre.—*v.i.* S'abattre (of birds); (*Naut.*) tanguer, plonger; tomber, se jeter (to fall); camper (to camp). *To pitch into*, se jeter dans, tomber sur, (*colloq.*) dire des injures à; *to pitch it strong*, parler avec beaucoup de véhémence, exagérer; *to pitch upon*, faire choix de, s'arrêter à; *to pitch upon the right person*, tomber juste sur la personne qu'il faut. **pitched**, *a.* Rangé. *Pitched battle*, bataille rangée, *f.* **pitch-farthing**, *n.* Fossette (game), *f.* **pitchfork**, *n.* Fourche, *f.*—*v.t.* (*fam.*) *To pitchfork someone into a chairmanship*, bombarder quelqu'un président. **pitching**, *n.* Plongement (of vehicles); (*Naut.*) tangage, *m.*

pitch (2) [pitʃ], *n.* Poix, *f.*; brai (coal-tar), *m. Pitch dark*, noir comme dans un four.—*v.t.* Enduire de poix, poisser.

pitch-coal, *n.* Jais, *m.*

pitcher (1) ['pitʃə], *n.* (*Baseball etc.*) Lanceur, *m.*

pitcher (2) ['pitʃə], *n.* Cruche, *f. Pitchers have ears*, les murs ont des oreilles; *the pitcher goes to the well once too often*, tant va la cruche à l'eau qu'à la fin elle se casse.

pitch-pine, *n.* Pin à trochets, pitchpin, *m.*

pitchy, *a.* Poissé, poisseux; enduit de poix; (*fig.*) noir, sombre.

piteous ['pitiəs], *a.* Piteux; pitoyable (pitiful). **piteously**, *adv.* Pitoyablement, piteusement. **piteousness**, *n.* État piteux, *m.*; tristesse, *f.*

pith [piθ], *n.* Moelle; force, vigueur, énergie; quintessence, substance, *f.*, essentiel, *m.* **pithily**, *adv.* Fortement, vigoureusement, avec énergie; avec concision. **pithiness**, *n.* Force, vigueur, énergie, concision, *f.* **pithless**, *a.* Sans moelle; (*fig.*) sans énergie, sans force. **pithy**, *a.* Plein de moelle; (*fig.*) fort, énergique, vigoureux; succinct, condensé.

pitiable ['pitiəbl], *a.* Pitoyable, à faire pitié. **pitiableness**, *n.* État pitoyable, *m.* **pitiful**, *a.* Pitoyable; compatissant (compassionate). **pitifully**, *adv.* Pitoyablement; avec compassion. **pitifulness**, *n.* État pitoyable, *m.*; pitié, compassion (pity), *f.* **pitiless**, *a.* Impitoyable, sans pitié, dur. **pitilessly**, *adv.* Impitoyablement, sans pitié. **pitilessness**, *n.* Caractère impitoyable, *m.*, cruauté, *f.*

pittance ['pitəns], *n.* Pitance, *f.*; (*fig.*) maigre salaire, *m.*

pitted ['pitid], *a.* Grêlé (with smallpox). *Pitted against*, opposé à.

pituita [pitju'aitə], *n.* Pituite, *f.*

pituitary [pi'tjuːitəri], *a.* Pituitaire.

pituitous [pi'tjuːitəs], *a.* Pituiteux.

pity ['piti], *n.* Pitié, compassion, *f.*; dommage (regret), *m. For pity's sake*, par pitié; *it is a pity*, c'est dommage; *it is a thousand pities*, c'est bien dommage; *the more's the pity*, tant pis; *to have pity on*, avoir pitié de; *to move someone to pity*, exciter la compassion de quelqu'un; *what a pity!* quel dommage!— *v.t.* Avoir pitié de, prendre en pitié, plaindre. *He is to be pitied*, il est à plaindre.

pitying, *a.* Compatissant; de pitié. **pityingly**, *adv.* Avec pitié, avec compassion.

pivot ['pivət], *n.* Pivot, *m.—v.i.* Pivoter.—*v.t.* Faire pivoter. **pivot-man**, *n.* (*Mil.*) Guide, *m.*

pivotal, *a.* Pivotal.

pixie, pixy ['piksi], *n.* Elfe, lutin, *m.*; fée, *f.*

placability [plækə'biliti], *n.* Placabilité, *f.* **placable** ['plækəbl], *a.* Facile à apaiser.

placard ['plækɑːd], *n.* Placard, *m.*, affiche, pancarte, *f.—v.t.* Afficher, placarder (de).

placate [plə'keit], *v.t.* Apaiser, concilier. **placation**, *n.* Apaisement, *m.*, conciliation, *f.* **placatory**, *a.* Conciliatoire, propitiatoire.

place [pleis], *n.* Lieu, endroit, *m.*, localité; place (situation etc.); position, *f.*, rang (rank), *m.*; demeure, résidence (dwelling), *f.*; poste, office; château, *m.*, maison (seat); ville (town), *f.*; emploi, *m.*, condition (employment), *f.*; pas, *m.*, préséance (priority), *f.*; espace (space); emplacement (for a house etc.), *m. Come to my place*, venez chez moi; *fortified place*, place forte, place de guerre, *f.*; *in high places*, en haut lieu; *in its place*, à sa place; *in one's place, in place*, en place; *in place of*, à la place de, au lieu de; *in the first place*, en premier lieu, d'abord; *in the next place*, ensuite; *Louis XI came in his time and place*, Louis XI vint en son temps et lieu; *out of a place*, sans place; *out of place*, déplacé, mal à propos, inopportun; *to change places with someone*, changer de place avec quelqu'un; *to give place to*, faire place à, céder le pas à; *to know one's place*, observer les distances; *to put someone in his place*, remettre quelqu'un à sa place; *to take place*, avoir lieu; *to take someone's place*, remplacer quelqu'un; *to three places of decimals*, à trois décimales. —*v.t.* Placer, mettre. *A placed horse*, un placé; (*colloq.*) *I can't place you*, je ne vous remets pas; (*spt.*) *to be placed third*, se classer troisième; *to place an order*, passer une commande.

place-kick, *n.* (*Ftb.*) Coup de pied placé, *m.* **place-man**, *n.* Homme en place, fonctionnaire, arriviste, *m.* **place-name**, *n.* Nom de lieu, *m.*

placenta [plə'sentə], *n.* Placenta, *m.*

placer, *n.* Placeur, *m.*; (*Gold-digging*) placer, gisement aurifère, *m.*

placet ['pleiset], *n.* (*sch.*) Assentiment, *m.*

placid ['plæsid], *a.* Placide, tranquille, calme, paisible.

placidity [plə'siditi] or **placidness**, *n.* Placidité, *f.*, calme, *m.*, tranquillité, *f.*

placidly, *adv.* Placidement, tranquillement, avec calme.

placket ['plækit], *n.* Fente (de la jupe), *f.*

plagal [pleigl], *a.* (*Mus.*) Plagal.

plagiarism ['pleidʒiərizm], *n.* Plagiat, *m.* **plagiarist** or **plagiary**, *a.* and *n.* Plagiaire, *m.* **plagiarize**, *v.t.* S'approprier par plagiat, plagier, contrefaire.—*v.i.* Commettre un plagiat.

plague [pleig], *n.* Peste; (*fig.*) plaie, *f.*, fléau, tourment, *m. He is the plague of my life*, il fait le tourment de ma vie, il est ma bête noire; *plague on!* peste de!—*v.t.* Frapper de la peste; (*fig.*) être un tourment pour, tourmenter. *To plague to death*, assommer.

plague-spot, *n.* Foyer d'infection, ulcère, *m.* **plaguily**, *adv.* (*colloq.*) Furieusement, terriblement. **plaguy**, *a.* (*colloq.*) Maudit.

plaice [pleis], *n.* Carrelet, *m.*; plie franche, *f.*

plaid [plæd], *n.* Plaid; tartan, *m.*

plain [plein], *a.* Uni, plat, plain; simple, sans façon (simple); commun, ordinaire (ordinary); sans attraits (of looks); évident, clair (evident); franc, sincère (frank); (*Cook.*) au naturel. *He used very plain language*, il parla sans détour; *in plain clothes*, en bourgeois, en civil; *in plain English*, en termes clairs; *it was all plain sailing*, toutes les difficultés avaient été aplanies; *plain as a pikestaff*, clair comme le jour; *plain truth*, franche vérité, *f.—adv.* Simplement, clairement, distinctement; franchement, nettement.—*n.* Plaine, *f.*

plain-chant or **plain-song**, *n.* Plain-chant, *m.* **plain cooking**, *n.* Cuisine bourgeoise, *f.* **plain-dealing**, *n.* Droiture, franchise, *f.—a.* Loyal, franc. **plainly**, *adv.* Bonnement; distinctement; clairement, simplement; sans déguisement, franchement. **plainness**, *n.* Simplicité; clarté; franchise, sincérité, *f.*; manque d'attraits (of looks), *m.* **plain-sewing** or **plain-work**, *n.* Travaux de simple couture, *m.pl.* **plain-speaking**, *n.* Franchise, *f.* **plain-spoken**, *a.* Franc, clair, explicite.

plaint [pleint], *n.* Plainte, *f.*

plaintiff ['pleintif], *n.* Demandeur, *m.*, demanderesse, *f.*, plaignant, *m.*, plaignante; partie civile (claiming damages), *f.*

plaintive ['pleintiv], *a.* Plaintif. **plaintively**, *adv.* Plaintivement, d'une voix plaintive. **plaintiveness**, *n.* Ton plaintif, *m.*

plait [plæt], *n.* Natte, tresse (of hair), *f.*; pli, *m.* (=pleat).—*v.t.* Tresser, natter (hair); plisser. **plaited**, *a.* Natté, à nattes, tressé, à tresses (of the hair); plissé.

plan [plæn], *n.* Plan, dessein, projet, système, *m. According to plan*, selon les prévisions.— *v.t.* Tracer un plan, faire le plan de; (*fig.*) projeter. *Planned economy*, économie dirigée, *f.*; *to plan ahead*, arranger d'avance; *to plan to do something*, se proposer de faire quelque chose.

plane (1) [plein], *a.* Plan.—*n.* (*Geom.*) Plan, *m.*, surface plane, *f.*; (*Carp.*) rabot, *m.*; (*colloq.*) avion, *m.*; (*fig.*) niveau, *m. Elevating plane* (of aeroplane), gouvernail de profondeur, *m.* —*v.t.* Raboter, aplanir. **plane-table**, *n.* Planchette, *f.*

plane (2) [plein] or **plane-tree**, *n.* Platane, *m.*

planer ['pleinə], *n.* Raboteur; (*Print.*) taquoir, *m.*

planet ['plænit], *n.* Planète, *f.* **planetarium**, *n.* Planétaire, planétarium, *m.* **planetary**, *a.* Planétaire.

plangent ['plænd3ənt], *a.* Retentissant, strident.

planimetry [plə'nimitri], *n.* Planimétrie, *f.*

planing ['pleiniŋ], *n.* Rabotage, *m.* **planing-machine,** *n.* (Machine) raboteuse, *f.*

planish ['plæniʃ], *v.t.* Dresser au marteau; polir. **planisher,** *n.* Planeur, *m.*

planisphere ['plænisfiə], *n.* Planisphère, *m.*

plank [plæŋk], *n.* Planche, *f.*, ais, madrier (thick oak plank); (*Naut.*) bordage; (*Polit.*) programme, *m.* *To walk the plank,* passer à la planche.—*v.t.* Planchéier; (*Naut.*) border. *To plank down,* (*slang*) déposer, abouler. **planking,** *n.* Planchéiage; (*Naut.*) bordage, *m.*

plankton ['plæŋktən], *n.* Plancton, *m.*

planner ['plænə], *n.* Auteur d'un plan, homme à projets, *m.* *Town-planner,* urbaniste, *m.*

planning, *n.* Tracé d'un plan, *m.*; (*Polit.*) dirigisme, *m.*, planification, *f.*; (*fig.*) conception, invention, *f.* *Family planning,* contrôle des naissances, *m.*; *town-planning,* urbanisme, *m.*

plant [plɑ:nt], *n.* Plante, *f.*, plant (young tree etc.); (*Tech.*) matériel, outillage; (*slang*) coup monté, tour, *m.*; escroquerie, *f.*; mouchard, *m.*—*v.t.* Planter; (*fig.*) poser, placer, déposer, établir. (*Hort.*) *To plant out,* repiquer.

plantain ['plæntin], *n.* Plantain, *m.*; banane des Antilles, *f.* **plantain-tree,** *n.* Bananier, *m.*

plantation [plæn'teiʃən], *n.* Plantation; colonie (colony), *f.*; (*fig.*) établissement, *m.*, fondation, *f.*

planter ['plɑ:ntə], *n.* Planteur, colon, *m.* **planting,** *n.* Plantage, *m.*, plantation, *f.* *Planting out,* repiquage, *m.* **planting-tool,** *n.* Plantoir, *m.*

plantlet ['plɑ:ntlit] or **plantule,** *n.* Plantule, *f.*

plaque [plɑ:k], *n.* Plaque, *f.*

plash [plæʃ], *n.* Mare, *f.*, flaque d'eau, *f.*; clapotement, *m.*—*v.t.* Éclabousser; entrelacer.—*v.i.* Clapoter. **plashy,** *a.* Bourbeux.

plasm [plæzm], *n.* Protoplasme, *m.* **plasma,** *n.* Plasma (du sang), *m.* **plasmatic,** *a.* Protoplasmatique.

plasmodium [plæz'moudiəm], *n.* Plasmode, plasmodie, *f.* **plasmology** [-'mɔlədʒi], *n.* Plasmologie, *f.* **plasmolysis,** *n.* Plasmolyse, *f.*

plaster ['plɑ:stə], *n.* Plâtre; (*Pharm.*) emplâtre, *m.* *Court plaster,* taffetas d'Angleterre, *m.*; *plaster of Paris,* plâtre à mouler, *m.*; *sticking plaster,* emplâtre résineux, sparadrap, *m.*—*v.t.* Plâtrer; enduire (de); (*Med.*) mettre un emplâtre à. **plasterwork,** *n.* Plâtrage, *m.*

plastered, *a.* Plâtré; (*pop.*) ivre. **plasterer,** *n.* Plâtrier, *m.* **plastering,** *n.* Plâtrage, *m.* **plastery,** *a.* Plâtreux.

plastic ['plæstik], *a.* Plastique. *Plastic surgery,* chirurgie plastique, *f.*—*n.pl.* Plastiques, *m.pl.* **plasticine** [-tisi:n], *n.* Pâte à modeler, *f.* (reg. trade name). **plasticity** [-'tisiti], *n.* Nature plastique, plasticité, *f.*

plat (1) [plæt], *n.* Petite pièce de terre, *f.*

plat (2) [PLAIT].

platan ['plætən], *n.* Platane, *m.*

Plate [pleit], **the River.** Le Rio de la Plata, *m.*

plate [pleit], *n.* Assiette; (*Metal.* and *Phot.*) plaque; vaisselle plate (gold and silver

articles); (*Tech.*) platine (of a lock), *f.*; (*Print.*) cliché, *m.*; (*Engr.*) planche, *f.* *Dinner plate,* assiette plate; *gold-plate,* vaisselle d'or, *f.*; *piece of plate,* pièce d'argenterie, *f.*; *silver-plate,* vaisselle d'argent, argenterie, *f.*; (*fig.*) *to have a lot on one's plate,* avoir du pain sur la planche.—*v.t.* Plaquer (de); dorer, argenter (to cover with gold or silver); réduire en plaques, laminer; revêtir d'armure de plaques, cuirasser, blinder; étamer (a mirror).

plateau ['plætou, plə'tou], *n.* Plateau, *m.*

plate-basket, *n.* Panier pour l'argenterie, *m.* **plated,** *a.* Plaqué. **plateful,** *n.* Assiettée, *f.* **plate-glass,** *n.* Glace sans tain, *f.* **plate-layer,** *n.* (*Rail.*) Poseur de rails, *m.*

platen ['plætən], *n.* (*Print.*) Platine, *f.*

plate-rack, *n.* Porte-assiettes, *m.* **plate-warmer,** *n.* Chauffe-assiettes, *m.*

platform ['plætfɔ:m], *n.* Terrasse, plateforme; estrade, *f.*; (*Rail.*) quai; tablier (of a bridge); (*Polit.*) programme, *m.*, profession de foi (politique), *f.* *Arrival platform,* quai d'arrivée, débarcadère, *m.*; *departure platform,* embarcadère, quai de départ, *m.*

plating ['pleitiŋ], *n.* Placage, *m.* *Armour-plating,* blindage, *m.*

platiniferous [plæti'nifərəs], *a.* Platinifère. **platinoid,** *a.* Platinoïde.

platinotype ['plætinotaip], *n.* Platinotypie, *f.* **platinum** ['plætinəm], *n.* Platine, *m.* *Platinum blonde,* blonde platinée, *f.*

platitude ['plætitju:d], *n.* Platitude, *f.* **platitudinize** [-inaiz], *v.i.* Débiter des banalités, dire des platitudes. **platitudinous,** *a.* Plat; qui débite des platitudes.

Plato ['pleitou]. Platon, *m.* **Platonic** [plə'tɔnik], *a.* Platonicien; platonique. **Platonically,** *adv.* D'une manière platonique.

Platonism ['pleitənizm], *n.* Platonisme, *m.*

platoon [plə'tu:n], *n.* (*Mil.*) Section, *f.*, *peloton, *m.* *Platoon commander,* chef de section, *m.*

platter ['plætə], *n.* Écuelle, *f.*; (*Am.*) plat, *m.*

platting ['plætiŋ], *n.* Tresse, natte, *f.*

platycephalous [plæti'sefələs], *a.* Platycéphale.

platypus ['plætipəs], *n.* Ornithor(h)ynque, *m.*

plaudit ['plɔ:dit], *n.* Applaudissement, *m.*

plausibility [plɔ:zi'biliti] or **plausibleness,** *n.* Plausibilité, *f.*

plausible ['plɔ:zibl], *a.* Plausible; captieux, enjôleur (of persons). **plausibly,** *adv.* Plausiblement, d'une manière plausible *or* spécieuse.

Plautus ['plɔ:təs]. Plaute, *m.*

play [plei], *n.* Jeu, *m.*; récréation (recreation), *f.*; essor (scope), *m.*; carrière, *f.*; badinage, *m.*; (*Mus.*) exécution, *f.*; spectacle, théâtre (playhouse), *m.*; (*Theat.*) comédie, pièce, *f.* *A play on words,* un jeu de mots; *at play,* en récréation; *by-play,* jeu de scène, *m.*; *child's-play,* jeu d'enfant, *m.*; *fair play,* franc jeu, *m.*, bonne foi, *f.*; *foul play,* jeu déloyal, *m.*, perfidie, trahison, *f.*; *in play,* pour badiner, pour rire, en plaisantant; (*spt.*) en jeu (of ball); *I will keep the enemy in play,* j'amuserai l'ennemi; *out of play,* hors jeu; *to bring into play,* mettre en jeu; *to give fair play to,* donner beau jeu à, jouer franc jeu avec; *to give full play to,* donner libre carrière à; *to have full play,* avoir libre essor *or* pleine carrière; *to have play*, avoir du jeu.—*v.i.* Jouer (à *or* sur); folâtrer (to frolic); (*Mus.*) jouer (de); briller, chatoyer (of precious stones). *It is not your turn to play*, ce n'est pas à vous à jouer; *to play against*, jouer contre; *to play at*, jouer à; *to play at sight*, jouer (un morceau) à première vue; *to play fair*, jouer franc jeu; *to play false*, jouer faux, tricher, tromper; *to play fast and loose with someone's affections*, abuser de l'affection de quelqu'un; *to play for love*, jouer pour l'honneur; *to play high*, jouer gros jeu; *to play into someone's hands*, jouer le jeu de quelqu'un; *to play low*, jouer petit jeu; *to play upon*, jouer de, toucher (the piano, organ), pincer de (the harp, guitar), se jouer de, s'amuser de, faire un tour à (to mock); *to play with*, jouer avec, se jouer de (to trifle with, to mock); *whose turn is it to play?* à qui est-ce à jouer?—*v.t.* Jouer, jouer à; faire jouer (a machine etc.); représenter, faire (a play, rôle, etc.); (*Mus.*) jouer de, toucher de, pincer de. *To play a deep game*, jouer au fin; *to play a fish*, fatiguer un poisson; *to play a game of*, faire une partie de; *to play cards*, jouer aux cartes; *to play off*, déployer, étaler; opposer; (*spt.*) rejouer un match nul; (*fam.*) *to play old Harry with*, en faire voir des vertes et des pas mûres à; *to play one's cards well*, jouer bien son jeu; (*fig.*) *to play second fiddle*, jouer un rôle de sous-fifre; *to play somebody up*, agacer quelqu'un; *to play the fool*, badiner, faire la bête; *to play truant*, faire l'école buissonnière; *to play up*, jouer de son mieux; *to play up to*, flatter, aduler; (*Theat.*) donner la réplique à; *to play with* (a person), se jouer de, se moquer de.

playable, *a.* Jouable.

play-bill, *n.* Affiche de théâtre, *f.*, programme de spectacle, *m.* **play-book**, *n.* Recueil de pièces de théâtre, *m.* **play-day**, *n.* Jour de congé, *m.*

player, *n.* Joueur, *m.*, joueuse, *f.*; (*Theat.*) acteur, *m.*, actrice, *f.*, comédien, *m.*, comédienne, *f.*; artiste, *m or f.*; (*Mus.*) exécutant, musicien, *m.*; (*spt.*) (joueur) professionnel.

playfellow or **playmate**, *n.* Camarade de jeu, *m.* or *f.* **playgoer**, *n.* Amateur de théâtre, *m.*, coureur de spectacles, *m.* **playground**, *n.* Cour de récréation, *f.* **play-hour**, *n.* Heure de récréation, *f.* **playhouse**, *n.* Salle de spectacle, *f.*, théâtre, *m.* **playlet**, *n.* Piécette, *f.* **play-night**, *n.* Jour de spectacle, *m.* **play-pen**, *n.* Parc pour enfants, *m.* play-room, *n.* Salle de récréation, *f.* **plaything**, *n.* Jouet, joujou, *m.* **playtime**, *n.* Heures de récréation, *f.pl.*, récréation, *f.* **playwright** or **playwriter**, *n.* Auteur dramatique; dramaturge, *m.*

playful, *a.* Qui aime à jouer, enjoué, folâtre, badin. **playfully**, *adv.* En badinant; avec enjouement. **playfulness**, *n.* Badinage, enjouement, *m.*

playing-card, *n.* Carte à jouer, *f.* **playing-field**, *n.* Terrain de jeux, *m.*

plea [pli:], *n.* Procès, *m.*, cause, *f.*; (*Law*) prétexte, *m.*, excuse, *f.*; exception, défense, *f.*; supplication, *f.* *Court of Common Pleas*, les plaids communs, *m.pl.*; *plea for mercy*, appel à la clémence, *m.*

pleach [pli:tʃ], *v.t.* Entrelacer, enlacer.

plead [pli:d], *v.t.* Plaider, déclarer, alléguer,

faire valoir.—*v.i.* Plaider. *To plead for*, parler en faveur de; *to plead guilty*, se déclarer coupable; *to plead not guilty*, se déclarer innocent; *to plead with*, intervenir auprès de, implorer.

pleadable, *a.* Plaidable. **pleader**, *n.* Avocat; (*fig.*) intercesseur, *m.*

pleading, *n.* Plaidoirie, *f.*; prières, *f.pl.*; (*pl.*) débats, *m.pl.* *Special pleading*, plaidoyer spécieux, *m.*—*a.* Implorant. **pleadingly**, *adv.* D'un ton suppliant.

pleasant ['plezənt], *a.* Agréable (à), charmant (pour); aimable; gai. **pleasantly**, *adv.* Agréablement, d'une manière charmante. **pleasantness**, *n.* Agrément, charme, *m.* **pleasantry**, *n.* Plaisanterie, *f.*; enjouement, *m.*

please [pli:z], *v.t.* Plaire à; faire plaisir à; charmer; contenter, satisfaire. *To be pleased*, être content, être content de, se plaire à, se faire un plaisir de, vouloir bien; *to please oneself*, se contenter, se plaire, faire comme on veut.—*v.i.* Plaire (à); (*impers.*) il plaît. *As you please*, comme il vous plaira, comme bon vous semblera, comme vous voudrez; *if I please*, si cela me plaît; (*if you*) *please*, s'il vous plaît; *I please* (*choose*) *to*, il me plaît de; *may it please the Court*, plaise à la cour; *please God*, s'il plaît à Dieu; *please lift up your hand*, veuillez lever la main, levez la main s'il vous plaît; *to be pleased to* (*do a thing*), avoir la bonté de, vouloir bien, se faire un plaisir de (faire une certaine chose); *we are pleased to think*, il nous plaît de penser; *you are pleased to say so*, cela vous plaît à dire.

pleased, *a.* Charmé, content, heureux (de); satisfait de (with things). *Pleased as Punch*, enchanté, fier comme Artaban. **pleasing**, *a.* Agréable, charmant; aimable, gracieux (of looks); riant, agréable (of things). **pleasingly**, *adv.* Agréablement. **pleasingness**, *n.* Agrément, charme, *m.*

pleasurable ['pleʒərəbl], *a.* Agréable, charmant. **pleasurably**, *adv.* Agréablement.

pleasure, *n.* Plaisir; agrément; gré, *m.*, volonté (will), *f.* *At my pleasure*, à mon gré, à mon plaisir; *at pleasure*, à volonté, à plaisir; *the pleasure is mine*, mais c'est moi qui suis enchanté; *to afford pleasure to*, faire plaisir à; *to esteem it a pleasure to*, se faire un plaisir de; *to have the pleasure of*, avoir l'avantage de; *to make a pleasure of*, mettre son plaisir à; *to request the pleasure of Mr. A's company*, prier M. A. de vouloir bien venir; *to take pleasure in*, prendre plaisir à; *what is your pleasure?* qu'y a-t-il pour votre service?—*v.i.* Se plaire (à), prendre plaisir (à). **pleasure-boat**, *n.* Bateau de plaisance, *m.* **pleasure-ground**, *n.* Parc, jardin d'agrément, *m.* **pleasure-loving**, *a.* Amoureux des plaisirs. **pleasure-seeking**, *n.* Jouisseur, *m.* **pleasure-trip**, *n.* Voyage d'agrément, *m.*

pleat [pli:t], *n.* Plissé, *m.*—*v.t.* Plisser.

plebeian [pli:'bi:ən], *a. and n.* Plébéien, *m.*, -ienne, *f.*, roturier, *m.*, -ière, *f.*

plebiscite ['plebisit], *n.* Plébiscite, *m.*

plebs [plebz], *n.*, **the**, *n.* Peuple, prolétariat, *m.*; (*Rom. Ant.*) plèbe, *f.*

pledge [pledʒ], *n.* Gage; nantissement; toast, *m.*, santé (toast), *f.*; (*Temperance*) vœu de tempérance, *m.*; (*Law*) caution, *f.*; promesse, parole d'honneur, *f.*, vœu, *m.* *To hold in*

pledge, tenir en gage; *to put in pleage,* mettre en gage, engager; *to take the pledge,* faire vœu de tempérance.—*v.t.* Engager, mettre en gage; garantir, se porter garant de (to vouch for); boire à la santé de, porter un toast à (to drink a health). *Pledged chattels,* (*Law*) biens nantis, *m.pl.* **pledgee** [-'dʒi:], *n.* Gagiste, *m.* **pledger,** *n.* Emprunteur sur gages; débiteur; garant, *m.*; personne qui boit à la santé (de), *f.*

pledget ['pledʒit], *n.* Tampon, sindon, *m.*

Pleiad ['plaiəd]. (*pl.* **Pleiades**) Pléiade, *f.*

pleistocene ['plaistəsi:n], *a.* and *n.* Pléistocène, *m.*

plenarily ['pli:nərili], *adv.* Pleinement, complètement. **plenary,** *a.* Plein, complet, entier; plénier (of indulgences). *Plenary assembly,* assemblée plénière, *f.*

plenipotentiary [plenipo'tenʃəri], *a.* and *n.* Plénipotentiaire, *m.*

plenitude ['plenitju:d], *n.* Plénitude, *f. In the plenitude of her glory,* à l'apogée de sa gloire.

plenteous ['plentiəs], *a.* Abondant. **plenteously,** *adv.* Abondamment. **plenteousness,** *n.* Abondance, *f.*

plentiful ['plentiful], *a.* Abondant. **plentifully,** *adv.* Abondamment, en abondance. **plentifulness,** *n.* Abondance, *f.*

plenty ['plenti], *n.* Abondance, *f. Horn of plenty,* corne d'abondance, *f.*; *there are plenty of them,* il y en a à foison; *there is plenty of it,* il y en a bien assez; *to have plenty of time,* avoir bien assez de temps; *to live in plenty,* vivre à l'aise.—*a.* (*colloq.*) Abondant.—*adv.* En abondance.

plenum ['pli:nəm], *n.* Plein, *m.*, pléthore, *f.*

pleonasm ['pli:ənæzm], *n.* Pléonasme, *m.* **pleonastic** [-'næstik], *a.* Pléonastique, redondant. **pleonastically,** *adv.* D'une manière pléonastique.

plesiosaurus [pli:zio'sɔ:rəs], *n.* Plésiosaure, *m.*

plethora ['pleθərə], *n.* Pléthore, *f. Plethora of wit,* surabondance d'esprit, *f.* **plethoric** [-'θərik], *a.* Pléthorique.

pleura ['pluərə], *n.* Plèvre, *f.*

pleurisy ['pluərəsi], *n.* Pleurésie, *f.* **pleuritic** [-'ritik], *a.* Pleurétique. **pleurodynia** [-o'dainiə] *n.* Pleurodynie, *f.* **pleuronectid** [-o'nektid], *n.* Pleuronecte, *m.*

plexus ['pleksəs], *n.* Plexus, *m.*

pliability [plaiə'biliti] or **pliableness,** *n.* Souplesse, flexibilité, *f.*

pliable ['plaiəbl], *a.* Pliable, pliant, flexible.

pliancy ['plaiənsi] or **pliantness,** *n.* Flexibilité, *f.* **pliant,** *a.* Pliant, flexible. **pliantly,** *adv.* Souplement; docilement.

plica ['plaikə], *n.* Pli (of skin), *m.*; plique (polonaise), *f.*

plicate ['plaikit] or **plicated,** *a.* (*Bot.*) Plicatif.

pliers ['plaiəz], *n.pl.* Pinces, *f.pl.*

plight [plait], *n.* État, *m.*, condition, *f.*; *en-gagement, gage, *m. As is the plight,* comme c'est le cas; *to be in a sorry plight,* être dans une triste condition.—*v.t.* Engager. *To plight one's troth,* engager sa foi.

plimsoll ['plimsəl], *n.* Chaussure bain de mer, *f.* (*Naut.*) *Plimsoll line,* ligne de Plimsoll, *f.*

plinth [plinθ], *n.* Plinthe, *f.*, socle, *m.*

Pliny ['plini]. Pline, *m.*

pliocene ['plaiosi:n], *a.* and *n.* (*Geol.*) Pliocène, *m.*

plod [plɔd], *v.i.* Marcher péniblement; (*fig.*)

peiner, piocher, travailler assidûment. **plodder,** *n.* Piocheur, *m.* **plodding,** *a.* Laborieux, piocheur.—*n.* Travail laborieux or pénible, *m.*

plop [plɔp], *adv.*, *n.*, and *int.* Plouf, flac, pouf, *m.*—*v.i.* Tomber en faisant plouf.

plosive ['plousiv], *a.* and *n.* (Consonne) plosive, *f.*

plot [plɔt], *n.* Complot, *m.*, conspiration, trame, *f.*; morceau, *m.*, petite pièce (de terre), *f.*, petit terrain, *m.*, intrigue (of a play etc.), *f. Building-plot,* lotissement, *m.*; *grass-plot,* pelouse, *f.*; *to lay* or *hatch a plot,* tramer un complot; *vegetable plot,* coin des légumes, *m.*—*v.i.* Comploter, conspirer.—*v.t.* Comploter, tramer; machiner; (*Surv.*) faire le plan de. *To plot a curve,* tracer une courbe; *to plot a graph,* tracer un graphique.

plotter, *n.* Conspirateur, comploteur, *m.*; abaque (device), *m.* **plotting,** *n.* Machinations, *f.pl.*, complots, *m.pl.*; (*Surv.*) action de rapporter, *f.*; tracé (of graph), *m.* **plotting-scale,** *n.* Échelle à rapporter, *f.*

plough [plau], *n.* Charrue; (*fig.*) culture, agriculture, *f.*; (*Bookb.*) rognoir; (*Carp.*) bouvet, *m. The Plough,* le Chariot, *m.*, la Grande-Ourse, *f. To put one's hand to the plough,* mettre la main à l'ouvrage.—*v.t.* Labourer, faire passer la charrue sur; creuser; (*fig.*) sillonner, fendre (waves etc.); (*slang*) refuser (à un examen). *To be ploughed in an examination,* être refusé, recalé, à un examen; *to plough through a book,* lire laborieusement un livre jusqu'au bout; *to plough up,* déterrer, détourner, soulever (avec la charrue).—*v.i.* Labourer.

ploughable ['plauəbl], *a.* Labourable.

plough-boy, *n.* Garçon de charrue, *m.* **plougher,** *n.* Laboureur, *m.* **ploughing,** *n.* Labourage, *m.* **plough-land,** *n.* Terre de labour, terre labourable, terre arable, *f.* **ploughman,** *n.* (*pl.* **ploughmen**) Laboureur; (*fig.*) rustre, paysan, *m.* **ploughshare,** *n.* Soc de charrue, *m.*

plover ['plʌvə], *n.* (*Orn.*) Pluvier, *m. Plover's eggs,* œufs de vanneau, *m.pl.*

plow [plau], *n.* (*Am.*) [PLOUGH].

pluck [plʌk], *v.t.* Arracher, tirer; cueillir (flowers, fruit, etc.), plumer (poultry); épiler (eyebrows). *To pluck away,* arracher; *to pluck down,* faire tomber; *to pluck up,* arracher, enlever, déraciner, reprendre (courage).—*n.* Cœur, courage, *m.*; fressure (of animals), *f. He gave my sleeve a pluck,* m'a tiré la manche.

pluckily, *adv.* Courageusement. **plucky,** *a.* Courageux.

plug [plʌg], *n.* Tampon, bouchon, *m.*; bonde, *f.* (of cask); cheville (peg), *f.*; effet d'eau, *m.* (of W.C.); robinet (street-plug), *m.*; (*Elec.*) prise de courant; (*Teleph.*) fiche, *f.*; chique (of tobacco), *f. Sparking plug,* bougie (d'allumage), *f.*—*v.t.* Tamponner, boucher. (*fam.*) *To plug a song,* faire une publicité fracassante à une chanson.—*v.i.* (*fam.*) *To plug away,* persévérer, bûcher; (*Elec.*) *to plug in,* établir la connexion, brancher.

plum [plʌm], *n.* Prune, *f.*; *raisin sec (raisin), *m.*; *(slang) cent mille livres sterling, *m.pl. French plum,* pruneau, *m.*; *sugar plums,* dragées, *f.pl.*; *the plum jobs, the plums,* les meilleurs postes, (*fam.*) les bons fromages,

m.pl. **plum-cake,** *n.* Gâteau aux raisins, *m.*
plum-duff, *n.* Pudding aux raisins, *m.*
plum-pudding, *n.* Plum-pudding, *m.*
plum-stone, *n.* Noyau de prune. *m.* **plum-tart,** *n.* Tourte aux prunes, *f.* **plum-tree,** *n.* Prunier, *m.*
plumage ['plu:midʒ], *n.* Plumage, *m.*
plumb [plʌm], *adv.* À plomb, d'aplomb, perpendiculairement; juste, exactement; (*Am.*) complètement.—*a.* Droit, vertical.—*v.t.* Plomber; (*Naut.*) sonder.—*n.* Plomb, *m.* **plumb-line,** *n.* Fil à plomb, m., (*Naut.*) ligne de sonde, *f.*
plumbaginous [plʌm'bædʒinəs], *a.* De plombagine. **plumbago** [-'beigou], *n.* Plombagine, *f.*
plumbean ['plʌmbiən] or **plumbeous,** *a.* De plomb.
plumber ['plʌmə], *n.* Plombier, *m.* **plumbery,** *n.* Plomberie, *f.*
plumbiferous [plʌm'bifərəs], *a.* Plombifère.
plumbing ['plʌmiŋ], *n.* Plomberie, *f.*; tuyauterie, *f.,* tuyaux, *m.pl.*; sondage (sounding), *m.*
plume [plu:m], *n.* Plume, *f.*; panache, plumet, *m.*; crinière (on a helmet); (*fig.*) palme, marque d'honneur, *f.*—*v.t.* Plumer, orner de plumes; nettoyer (of birds). *To plume oneself on,* se piquer de. **plumeless,** *a.* Sans plumes; sans panache. **plumelet,** *n.* Petite plume; plumule, *f.*
plummer-block ['plʌmə'blɔk], *n.* Palier, *m.*
plummet ['plʌmit], *n.* Plomb (de fil à plomb), *m.*
plumose ['plu:mous] or **plumous** ['plu:məs], *a.* Plumeux.
plump [plʌmp], *a.* Dodu, potelé, gras.—*adv.* Tout d'un coup; droit.—*v.t.* Engraisser; jeter brusquement. *To plump up (a pillow),* secouer, taper (un oreiller).—*v.i.* Tomber d'aplomb, tomber lourdement. *To plump for,* voter pour *or* donner tous ses votes pour (un seul candidat).
plumper, *n.* (*colloq.*) Bourde, *f.,* mensonge (lie), *m.*; (*fig.*) vote donné à un seul candidat, *m.* **plumpish,** *a.* Grasset, grassouillet. **plumply,** *adv.* Nettement, rondement. **plumpness,** *n.* Embonpoint, *m.,* rondeur, *f.*
plumy ['plu:mi], *a.* Couvert de plumes.
plunder ['plʌndə], *v.t.* Piller, dépouiller.—*n.* Butin; pillage (plundering), *m. To give up to plunder,* livrer au pillage. **plunderer,** *n.* Pillard, *m.*
plunge [plʌndʒ], *v.i.* Plonger, piquer une tête; se plonger, se précipiter, se jeter; se cabrer (horse); tanguer, piquer du nez (ship); (*slang*) jouer gros jeu. *Plunging fire,* feu plongeant, *m.*—*v.t.* Plonger, précipiter.—*n.* Action de plonger, *f.*; plongeon, *m. To take the plunge,* faire le plongeon, ne plus hésiter.
plunger ['plʌndʒə], *n.* Plongeur; (*Hydr.*) piston plongeur; (*slang*) parieur à outrance, *m.*
pluperfect [plu:'pə:fikt], *a.* and *n.* Plus-que-parfait, *m.*
plural ['pluərəl], *a.* and *n.* Pluriel, *m. Plural vote,* vote plural, *m.* **pluralism,** *n.* Cumul, *m.* **pluralist,** *n.* Ecclésiastique qui jouit de plus d'un bénéfice; cumulard, *m.* **plurality** [-'ræliti], *n.* Pluralité, *f.*; cumul, *m.*; majorité, *f.* **plurally,** *adv.* Au pluriel; par cumul.

plus [plʌs], *prep.* (*Math.*) Plus.—*a.* Positif.—*n.* Plus; signe de l'addition, *m.*—*adv.* Et davantage. **plus-fours,** *n.* Culotte bouffante, *f.,* culotte de golf, *f.*
plush [plʌʃ], *n.* Peluche, *f.* **plushes,** *n.pl.* Culotte de valet de pied, *f.* **plushy,** *a.* Pelucheux; (*colloq.*) luxueux.
Plutarch ['plu:ta:k]. Plutarque, *m.*
Pluto ['plu:tou]. Pluton, *m.*
plutocracy [plu:'tɔkrəsi], *n.* Ploutocratie, *f.*
plutocrat ['plu:tokræt], *n.* Ploutocrate, *m.* **plutocratic** [-'krætik], *a.* Ploutocratique.
plutonian [plu:'touniən], *a.* Plutonien. **plutonic** [-'tɔnik], *a.* Plutonique.
plutonism ['plu:tənizm], *n.* Plutonisme, *m.* **plutonist,** *n.* Plutoniste, *m.*
plutonium, *n.* Plutonium, *m.*
pluvial ['plu:viəl], *a.* Pluvial. **pluviometer** [-'ɔmitə], *n.* Pluviomètre, *m.* **pluvious,** *a.* Pluvieux.
ply (1) [plai], *v.t.* Manier (fortement); exercer, employer; faire, exécuter; poursuivre, presser (to urge). *To ply an oar,* manier l'aviron; *to ply someone with drink,* presser quelqu'un de boire; *to ply the oar,* faire force de rames; *to ply with questions,* presser de questions.—*v.i.* Travailler; faire le service, faire la navette. (*Naut.*) *To ply to windward,* bouliner.
ply (2) [plai], *n.* Pli, *m.* (of cloth); fil, *m.* (of wool); toron, *m.* (of rope).
plywood ['plaiwud], *n.* Contre-plaqué, *m.*
pneumatic [nju'mætik], *a.* Pneumatique. *Pneumatic drill,* pic pneumatique, *m.*; *pneumatic tyre,* pneumatique, (*colloq.*) pneu, *m.* **pneumatics,** *n.pl.* Pneumatique, *f.*
pneumatology [-ə'tɔlədʒi], *n.* Pneumatologie, *f.*
pneumonia [nju'mouniə], *n.* Pneumonie, *f.* **pneumonic** [-'mɔnik], *a.* and *n.* Pneumonique, *m.*
poach [poutʃ], *v.t.* Braconner, voler, piller (to steal); pocher (eggs); (*Ten.*) chiper (a ball). *Poached eggs,* œufs pochés, *m.pl.*—*v.i.* Braconner; s'amollir (of the ground). *To poach on someone's preserves,* marcher sur les brisées de quelqu'un. **poacher,** *n.* Braconnier, *m.* **poachiness,** *n.* Humidité (of soil), *f.* **poaching,** *n.* Braconnage, *m.* **poachy,** *a.* Humide, mou, boueux (of ground).
pochard ['poutʃəd], *n.* (*Orn.*) Milouin, *m.*
pock [pɔk], *n.* Pustule (de petite vérole), *f.* **pock-marked,** *a.* Grêlé. **pock-wood,** *n.* Gaïac, *m.*
pocket ['pɔkit], *n.* Poche, *f.*; gousset (fob), *m.*; pochette (in a notebook etc.); blouse (of a billiard table), *f. To be in pocket by,* gagner à; *to be out of pocket by,* perdre à; *to have in one's pocket,* avoir en poche; *to have someone in one's pocket,* avoir quelqu'un dans sa manche; *to pay out of one's own pocket,* payer de sa poche; *to pick pockets,* voler à la tire; *to spare someone's pocket,* ménager la bourse de quelqu'un.—*v.t.* Empocher, mettre en poche; avaler, digérer (an affront); (*Billiards*) blouser. *To pocket an insult,* avaler un affront.
pocket-book, *n.* Portefeuille, calepin, carnet, *m.* **pocketful,** *n.* Pleine poche, *f.* **pocket-handkerchief,** *n.* Mouchoir de poche, *m.* **pocket-knife,** *n.* Couteau de poche, *m.* **pocket-money,** *n.* Argent de poche, *m.*

pod [pɔd], *n.* Cosse, gousse, *f.*—*v.i.* Former des cosses.—*v.t.* Écosser. **podded**, *a.* Cossu.
podagra [pou'dægrə], *n.* Podagre, *f.*
podagric [pou'dægrik], *a.* Podagre, goutteux.
podginess ['pɔdʒinis], *n.* Embonpoint, *m.*, rondeur, *f.* **podgy**, *a.* Gras, potelé.
poem ['pouim], *n.* Poème, *m.*; poésie (short poem), *f.*
***poesy** ['pouisi], *n.* Poésie, *f.* **poet**, *n.* Poète, *m.* *Minor poet*, poète de second ordre.
poetaster [-'tæstə], *n.* Poétereau, rimailleur, *m.* **poetess**, *n.* Femme poète, *f.*
poetic [pou'etik] *or* **poetical**, *a.* Poétique. **poetically**, *adv.* Poétiquement. **poetics**, *n.pl.* Poétique, *f.*
poetize ['pouitaiz], *v.t.*, *v.i.* Poétiser. **poetry**, *n.* Poésie, *f.* *The Art of Poetry*, l'Art Poétique.
pogrom ['pɔgrəm], *n.* Pogrom(e), *m.*
poignancy ['pɔinənsi], *n.* Piquant, *m.*; nature poignante, violence,*f.* **poignant**, *a.* Piquant, vif, poignant, cuisant. **poignantly**, *adv.* D'une manière piquante *or* cuisante.
poind [pɔind], *n.* (*Sc.*) Saisie-exécution, *f.*—*v.t.* Saisir (des biens).
point [pɔint], *n.* Point (spot, place, etc.), *m.*; pointe (sharp end etc.); aiguillette (aiglet); (*Engr.*) pointe, pointe sèche; (*Print.*) pointure; (*Compass*) quart de vent, *m.*, aire de vent; (*Naut.*) garcette de ris (of a sail); queue de rat (of a cable); place (*or* jour) à droite de guichet dans son prolongement, *f.*; (*spt.*) point, *m.*; (*Rationing*) coupon, ticket; (*fig.*) question, fin, *f.*; détail, but, caractère, rapport, *m.*; qualité, *f.*; (*Rail.*) (*pl.*) aiguillage, *m.*, aiguille, *f.* *Armed at all points*, armé de toutes pièces; *at the point of*, au point de; *at the point of death*, à l'article de la mort; *Brussels point*, point de Bruxelles, *m.*; *decimal point*, virgule, *f.*; *he has his good points*, il a ses qualités; *in all points*, en tout point; *in point*, en question; *in point of*, en fait de, en matière de; *in point of fact*, en effet, à la vérité; *main point*, essentiel, point capital, *m.*; *not to the point*, hors de propos; *on the point of*, sur le point de; *point of impact*, point de chute, *m.*; *point of view*, point de vue, *m.*; *rallying-point*, point de ralliement, *m.*; *that is beside the point*, cela n'a rien à voir à l'affaire; *that is not the point*, ce n'est pas là la question, il ne s'agit pas de cela; *to come to the point*, venir au fait; *to gain one's point*, arriver à ses fins, atteindre son but; *to make a point of*, se faire un devoir de *or* une règle de; *to press one's point*, maintenir son dire; *to stretch a point*, forcer ses moyens, faire une concession; *to the point*, à propos; *to the point of cruelty*, jusqu'à la cruauté; (*Box.*) *to win on points*, gagner aux points; *up to a point*, dans une certaine mesure; *what would be the point of doing that?* à quoi bon faire cela?—*v.t.* Mettre une pointe à, aiguiser, tailler (to make pointed); signaler, indiquer, montrer du doigt (to point out); diriger (to direct); pointer (fire-arms etc.); ponctuer (to punctuate); (*Naut.*) garnir (a sail) de garcettes de ris, mettre une queue de rat à (a rope etc.); (*Build.*) jointoyer. *To point out*, signaler, faire remarquer, appeler l'attention . . . sur; *to point the finger at*, montrer du doigt.—*v.i.* Se diriger, se tourner (vers);

tomber en arrêt (of dogs). *To point at*, montrer du doigt, indiquer.
point-blank, *adv.* À bout portant; à brûle-pourpoint, carrément.—*a.* Catégorique, direct (of a denial etc.). **point-duty**, *n.* Service pour la réglementation de la circulation, *m.* *Policeman on point-duty*, agent de la circulation, *m.* **pointed**, *a.* Pointu; (*fig.*) mordant, piquant; direct (personal); (*Arch.*) ogival. **pointedly**, *adv.* Expressément; d'une manière piquante. **pointer**, *n.* Index, *m.*; ḫaguette (rod), *f.*; chien d'arrêt (dog), *m.*; (*Rail.*) aiguille, *f.* **pointing**, *n.* Pointage (of a gun etc.); (*Build.*) jointoiement, *m.*; (*Gram.*) ponctuation, *f.* **pointless**, *a.* Sans pointe; (*fig.*) insignifiant, plat. **pointsman**, *n.* (*Rail.*) Aiguilleur, *m.* **point-to-point** (race), *n.* Course au clocher, *f.*
poise [pɔiz], *n.* Poids, équilibre; aplomb; port (de tête), *m.* *At poise*, en équilibre; en suspens; *he has poise*, il a de la prestance.—*v.t.* Balancer, tenir en équilibre.
poison [pɔizn], *n.* Poison, *m.*—*v.t.* Empoisonner. *Poisoned wound*, plaie envenimée, *f.* **poison-nut**, *n.* Noix vomique, *f.*
poisoner ['pɔizənə], *n.* Empoisonneur, *m.*, empoisonneuse, *f.* **poisoning**, *n.* Empoisonnement, *m.* **poisonous**, *a.* Vénéneux (of plants); venimeux (of animals); toxique (gas); (*fig.*) empoisonné, funeste. **poisonously**, *adv.* Avec venin. **poisonousness**, *n.* Nature vénéneuse, *f.*
poke [pouk], *n.* Coup de coude *or* de poing, *m.*; *sac, *m.*; poche, *f.* *To buy a pig in a poke*, acheter chat en poche, acheter les yeux fermés.—*v.t.* Fourrer; pousser (to push); remuer, fourgonner (the fire). *To poke fun at*, se moquer de; *to poke one's nose into*, fourrer son nez dans; *to poke oneself up in a little room*, s'enfermer à l'étroit dans une petite pièce.—*v.i.* *To poke about*, tâtonner; *to poke about after*, chercher à tâtons. **poke-weed**, *n.* Raisin d'Amérique, *m.*
poker, *n.* Tisonnier; (*Tech.*) fourgon; poker (card-game), *m.* *Stiff as a poker*, raide comme un piquet. **poker-faced**, *a.* Au visage impassible. **poker-work**, *n.* Pyrogravure, *f.*
poky, *a.* (*colloq.*) Petit, mesquin.
polacca [pɔ'lækə], *n.* Polacre, polonaise, *f.*
Poland ['poulənd]. La Pologne, *f.*
polar ['poulə], *a.* Polaire. *Polar bear*, ours blanc, *m.*
polarity [pou'læriti], *n.* Polarité, *f.* **polarization** [-ərai'zeiʃən], *n.* Polarisation, *f.* **polarize**, *v.t.* Polariser.
Pole [poul], *n.* Polonais, *m.*, Polonaise, *f.*
pole [poul], *n.* Perche, *f.*, jalon; bâton (curtain pole); timon (of a carriage); balancier (for dancing); échalas (for vines etc.); mât (flag-pole etc.), *m.*; hampe (for colours), *f.*; poteau (telegraph pole), *m.*; flèche (of a mast); (*Surv.*) *perche (about 5 metres), *f.*; (*Astron.*, *Geog.*) pôle, *m.* *Greasy pole*, mât de cocagne, *m.*; *maypole*, mai, *m.*; (*pop.*) *up the pole*, timbré, piqué.—*v.t.* Faire avancer au moyen d'une perche.
poleaxe ['poulæks], *n.* Hache d'armes, *f.*; (*Naut.*) hache d'abordage, *f.*; assommoir, merlin, *m.*—*v.t.* Assommer.
polecat ['poulkæt], *n.* Putois, *m.*
polemic [pə'lemik], *a.* Polémique.—*n.* Polémiste (person), *m.*; polémique, *f.*

polemical, *a.* Polémique. **polemics,** *n.pl.* Polémique, *f.*
polemize ['pɔləmaiz], *v.i.* Polémiquer.
pole-star, *n.* Étoile polaire, *f.* **pole-vaulting,** *n.* Saut à la perche, *m.*
polianthes [pɔli'ænθi:z], *n.* (*Bot.*) Tubéreuse, *f.*
police [pə'li:s], *n.* Police, *f.* *Military* or *county police,* gendarmerie, *f.—v.t.* Policer, maintenir l'ordre dans. **police-court,** *n.* Tribunal de simple police, *m.* **police-inspector,** *n.* Officier de paix, *m.* **police-sergeant,** *n.* Brigadier de police, *m.* **police-station,** *n.* Commissariat *or* poste de police, *m.*
policed, *a.* Policé. **policing,** *n.* Police, *f.,* maintien de l'ordre, *m.*
policeman, *n.* (*pl.* **policemen**) Agent de police, sergent de ville, gardien de la paix, *m.*
policewoman, *n.* Femme agent, *f.*
policy ['pɔlisi], *n.* Politique, *f.*; système, plan, *m.,* prudence, *f.*; mode d'action, *m.*; ligne de conduite, *f.*; programme, *m.* *Foreign policy,* politique extérieure, *f.*; *insurance policy,* police d'assurance, *f.*; *public policy,* l'intérêt public, *m.* **policy-holder,** *n.* Assuré, porteur d'une police d'assurance, *m.*
poliomyelitis ['pouliɔmaiə'laitis] or (*fam.*) **polio,** *n.* Poliomyélite, *f.*
Polish ['pouliʃ], *a.* Polonais.—*n.* Le polonais, *m.*
polish ['pɔliʃ], *v.t.* Polir; vernir (furniture); cirer (shoes); astiquer (leather); (*fig.*) façonner, dégourdir. *To polish off,* se débarrasser de, finir; *to polish up one's French,* dérouiller son français.—*v.i.* Se polir.—*n.* Poli, *m.*; (*fig.*) élégance, politesse, *f.* *Floor polish,* encaustique, cire à parquet, *f.*;
polished, *a.* Poli; (*fig.*) de manières élégantes. **polisher,** *n.* Polisseur *or* polissoir (tool), *m.* *Floor polisher,* cireur de parquet, *m.*; *French polisher,* vernisseur au tampon, *m.* **polishing,** *n.* Polissage, *m.*; vernis (de meubles); cirage (of boots), *m.*
polite [pə'lait], *a.* Poli, élégant, honnête, complaisant (pour). *Polite literature,* belles-lettres, *f.pl.*; *polite society,* le beau monde, *m.* **politely,** *adv.* Poliment. **politeness,** *n.* Politesse, *f.*
politic ['pɔlitik], *a.* Politique.
political [pə'litikl], *a.* Politique. **politically,** *adv.* Politiquement. **politician** [-'tiʃən], *n.* Homme politique; (*pej.*) politicien, *m.* **politics,** *n.pl.* La politique, *f.* **polity,** *n.* Constitution politique, *f.*; régime, *m.*
polka ['pɔlkə or 'poulkə], *n.* Polka, *f.*
Poll [pɔl]. (*colloq.*) Jacquot (parrot), *m.*
poll [poul], *n.* *Tête (head); liste de personnes (register of persons); liste électorale (register of electors); élection, *f.,* scrutin, *m.*; sondage (of public opinion), *m.* *The poll is open,* le scrutin est ouvert; *to demand a poll,* demander le scrutin; *to go to the poll,* aller aux votes *or* au scrutin; *to head the poll,* venir en tête de liste.—*v.t.* Tondre (to clip); étêter (trees); faire inscrire (a vote); voter (to vote); obtenir (a certain number of votes). **polled,** *a.* Étêté. **poller,** *n.* Personne qui étête les arbres, *f.*; votant (voter), *m.* **polling,** *n.* Élection, *f.,* vote, *m.* **polling-booth,** *n.* Bureau de scrutin, *m.*
pollack ['pɔlək], *n.* (*Ichth.*) Merlan jaune, *m.* *Green pollack,* colin, *m.*

pollard ['pɔləd], *n.* Têtard, *m.*; recoupe (meal), *f.—v.t.* Étêter (trees).
pollen ['pɔlən], *n.* Pollen, *m.*
pollinate ['pɔlineit], *v.t.* Émettre du pollen sur.
pollination [pɔli'neiʃən], *n.* Pollination, *f.*
poll-tax, *n.* Capitation, *f.*
pollute [pə'lju:t], *v.t.* Polluer, souiller (de). **polluter,** *n.* Corrupteur, *m.,* -trice, *f.,* profanateur, *m.,* profanatrice, *f.* **pollution** [-'lju:ʃən], *n.* Pollution, profanation, souillure, *f.*
polo ['poulou], *n.* Polo, *m.* *Polo stick,* maillet, *m.*; *water-polo,* water-polo, *m.*
poltergeist ['pɔltəgaist], *n.* Esprit frappeur, *m.*
poltroon [pɔl'tru:n], *n.* Poltron, *m.,* poltronne, *f.* **poltroonery,** *n.* Poltronnerie, *f.*
polyandria [pɔli'ændriə], *n.* (*Bot.*) Polyandrie, *f.* **polyandrous** [-əs], *a.* Polyandre. **polyandry,** *n.* Polyandrie, *f.*
polyanthus, *n.* Primevère, *f.*
polychrome [-kroum], *a.* Polychrome. **polychromy,** *n.* Polychromie, *f.*
polygamist [-'ligəmist], *n.* Polygame, *m.* or *f.* **polygamous,** *a.* Polygame. **polygamy,** *n.* Polygamie, *f.*
polyglot ['pɔliglɔt], *a.* and *n.* Polyglotte, *f.*
polygon, *n.* Polygone, *m.* **polygonal** [-'ligənl], *a.* Polygonal.
polygraph ['pɔligræf], *n.* Polygraphe, *m.*
polyhedral [-'hi:drəl], *a.* Polyèdre. **polyhedron,** *n.* Polyèdre, *m.*
Polynesia [pɔli'ni:ziə]. La Polynésie, *f.* **Polynices** [pɔli'naisi:z]. Polynice, *m.*
polynomial [pɔli'noumiəl], *n.* (*Alg.*) Polynôme, *m.*
polyp ['pɔlip], *n.* (*Zool.*) Polypier, *m.*
polypetalous [-'petələs], *a.* (*Bot.*) Polypétale.
polypody ['pɔlipədi], *n.* (*Bot.*) Polypode, *m.* **polypous** ['pɔlipəs], *a.* (*Path.*) Polypeux, *m.* **polypus,** *n.* Polype, *m.*
polysyllabic [-si'læbik], *a.* Polysyllabique, polysyllabe. **polysyllable** [-'siləbl], *n.* Polysyllabe, *m.*
polysynthetic [-sin'θetik], *a.* Polysynthétique.
polytechnic [-'teknik], *a.* Polytechnique.—*n.* École d'arts et métiers, *f.*
polytheism [pɔli'θi:izm], *n.* Polythéisme, *m.* **polytheist,** *n.* Polythéiste, *m.* **polytheistic** [-'istik], *a.* Polythéiste.
pom [pɔm], *n.* (*colloq.*) Loulou de Poméranie, *m.*
pomace ['pʌməs], *n.* Marc de pommes, *m.*
pomade [pə'meid], **pomatum** [-'meitəm], *n.* Pommade, *f.*
pomegranate ['pɔm-, 'pʌmgrænət], *n.* Grenade, *f.* *Pomegranate syrup,* sirop de grenadine, *m.* **pomegranate-tree,** *n.* Grenadier, *m.*
Pomerania [pɔmə'reiniə]. La Poméranie, *f.*
pommel [pʌml], *v.t.* Battre, rosser.—*n.* Pommeau (of a saddle, sword, etc.), *m.* **pommelled,** *a.* À pommeau.
pomp [pɔmp], *n.* Pompe, *f.,* éclat, faste, *m.*
Pompeii [pɔm'pi:ai]. Pompéi, *f.*
Pompey ['pɔmpi]. Pompée, *m.*
pom-pom ['pɔm'pɔm], *n.* (*Mil.*) Canon-mitrailleuse, *m.*
pompon ['pɔmpɔn], *n.* Pompon, *m.*; rose-pompon, *f.*

pomposity [pɔm'pɔsiti] or **pompousness,** *n.*
Pompe, ostentation; emphase (of language),
prudhommerie, suffisance, *f.*
pompous ['pɔmpəs], *a.* Pompeux, fastueux,
prétentieux; suffisant. **pompously,** *adv.*
Pompeusement, fastueusement; avec suffisance.
ponce [pɔns], *n.* (*pop.*) Souteneur, marlou;
(*Am.*) greluchon, *m.*
pond [pɔnd], *n.* Étang, vivier, *m.*; mare (pool),
f.; abreuvoir (for cattle), *m.* **pond-weed,** *n.*
Potamot luisant, *m.*
ponder ['pɔndə], *v.t.* Peser, considérer,
réfléchir à.—*v.i.* Méditer, faire réflexion.
ponderability [-rə'biliti], *n.* Pondérabilité, *f.*
ponderable, *a.* Pondérable. **ponderation**
[-'reiʃən], *n.* Pondération, *f.* **pondering,** *n.*
Méditation, *f.* **ponderingly,** *adv.* Avec
méditation, avec réflexion.
ponderous ['pɔndərəs], *a.* Lourd, pesant.
ponderously, *adv.* Pesamment. **ponder-**
ousness, *n.* Pesanteur, *f.*
poniard ['pɔniəd], *n.* Poignard, *m.*—*v.t.* Poignarder.
pontiff ['pɔntif], *n.* Pontife; évêque, prélat, *m.*
pontifical [-'tifikl], *a.* and *n.* Pontifical, *m.*
pontifically [-'tifikəli], *adv.* Pontificalement, en pontife. **pontificals,** *n.pl.* Habits
pontificaux, *m.pl.* **pontificate,** *n.* Pontificat,
m.—*v.i.* Pontifier; (*colloq.*) faire l'important.
Pontine ['pɔntain] **Marshes (the).** Les marais
Pontins, *m.pl.*
Pontius Pilate ['pɔnʃəs'pailət]. Ponce Pilate,
m.
pontonier [pɔntə'niə], *n.* Pontonnier, *m.*
pontoon [pɔn'tuːn], *n.* Ponton, bac, *m.*;
(*Cards*) vingt-et-un. **pontoon-bridge,** *n.*
Pont de bateaux, *m.*
pony ['pouni], *n.* Poney, petit cheval, *m.*;
(*slang*) vingt-cinq livres sterling, *m.pl.* **pony-**
chaise, *n.* Chaise à poney, *f.*, panier, *m.*
poodle [puːdl], *n.* Caniche, barbet, *m.*
pooh! [puː], *int.* Bah! allons donc! **pooh-**
pooh, *v.t.* Se moquer de, tourner en ridicule.
pool [puːl], *n.* Étang, *m.*, mare; piscine, *f.* (for
swimming); (*Cards, Billiards, etc.*) poule, *f.*;
mise en commun, communauté, *f.*, pool, *m.*;
(*Comm.*) masse, *f.* *Football pool,* concours de
pronostics sur les championnats de football,
m.—*v.t.* Mettre en commun.
poop [puːp], *n.* Dunette, poupe, *f.*
poor [puːə], *a.* Pauvre, indigent; malheureux
(unhappy); méchant, triste (paltry); mauvais,
méchant (bad). *A poor excuse,* une mauvaise
excuse; *a poor man,* un homme pauvre, un
pauvre; *as poor as a church mouse,* gueux
comme un rat d'église; *poor fare,* mauvaise
chère, *f.*; *poor little fellow,* pauvre petit; *the
patient has passed a poor night,* le malade a
passé une mauvaise nuit; *the poor,* les indigents, les pauvres, *m.pl.*; *the poor fellow,* le
malheureux; *to have a poor opinion of,* avoir
une triste opinion de.
poor-box, *n.* Tronc des pauvres, *m.* **poor-**
house, *n.* Asile des indigents, *m.* **poor-law,**
n. Loi sur l'assistance publique; *f.* **poor-**
ness, *n.* Pauvreté, indigence; médiocrité;
mauvaise qualité (bad quality), *f.* **poor-rate,**
n. Taxe des pauvres, *f.* **poor-spirited,** *a.*
Pusillanime. **poor-spiritedness,** *n.* Pusillanimité, *f.*

poorly, *a.* Indisposé, souffrant.—*adv.* Pauvrement, mal, tristement.
pop [pɔp], *n.* Petit bruit vif et sec, *m.*; boisson
pétillante, *f.*, champagne, *m.*; (*Am.*) papa,
m. (*colloq.*) *My watch is in pop,* ma montre
est au clou; (*colloq.*) *the pops,* les chansons
en vogue, *f.pl.*—*v.i.* Entrer *or* sortir subitement; sauter, péter. *Off he pops,* le voilà
parti; *to pop in,* entrer subitement, entrer
pour un instant; *to pop off,* s'en aller subitement, partir à la hâte; mourir subitement; *to
pop out,* sortir subitement, s'esquiver; *to pop
up,* se lever subitement.—*v.t.* Pousser,
fourrer, *or* mettre subitement; (*slang*)
accrocher, mettre au clou. *To pop the question,* faire une demande (en mariage).—*int.*
Crac! Pan!
pop-corn, *n.* Maïs grillé et éclaté, *m.*
pope [poup], *n.* Pape; (*Greek Church*) pope, *m.*
Pope's eye, noix (de veau etc.), *f.*; *pope's
head,* tête de loup, *f.* **pope-Joan,** *n.* Nain
jaune (game), *m.*
popedom, *n.* Papauté, *f.* **popery,** *n.* Papisme,
m.
pop-eyed, *a.* Aux yeux en boules de loto, aux
yeux étonnés.
pop-gun, *n.* Canonnière, *f.*, pistolet, *m.* (toy).
*****popinjay** ['pɔpindʒei], *n.* Perroquet; papegai
(for shooting at); freluquet, fat (fop), *m.*
popish ['poupiʃ], *a.* Papiste; de papiste (of
things). **popishly,** *adv.* En papiste.
poplar ['pɔplə], *n.* (*Bot.*) Peuplier, *m.*
poplin ['pɔplin], *n.* Popeline, *f.*
poppet ['pɔpit], *n.* Poupée, marionnette, *f.*;
(*pl.*) (rowlock) *poppets,* montants de dames,
m.pl. (*colloq.*) *My poppet,* mon chéri, ma
chérie; *she's a poppet,* elle est mignonne.
popple [pɔpl], *v.i.* Clapoter, onduler; danser
(sur l'eau).
poppy ['pɔpi], *n.* Pavot (garden-poppy);
coquelicot (field-poppy), *m.* *Poppy Day,* le
onze novembre. **poppycock,** *n.* (*pop.*)
Bêtises, *f.pl.* **poppy-head,** *n.* Tête de
pavot, *f.*
pop-shop, *n.* (*slang*) Mont-de-piété, *m.*
populace ['pɔpjuləs], *n.* Populace, *f.*; peuple,
m.
popular ['pɔpjulə], *a.* Populaire; en vogue,
couru; à la portée de tous (price). *To make
oneself popular with everyone,* se faire bien
voir de tout le monde. **popularity** [-'læriti],
n. Popularité, *f.*
popularize ['pɔpjuləraiz], *v.t.* Populariser,
vulgariser; rendre populaire; mettre en
vogue. **popularly,** *adv.* Populairement.
populate ['pɔpjuleit], *v.t.* Peupler.—*v.i.* Se
peupler. **population** [-'leiʃən], *n.* Population, *f.*
populous ['pɔpjuləs], *a.* Populeux. **populous-**
ness, *n.* Densité de population, *f.*
porbeagle ['pɔːbiːgl], *n.* (*Ichth.*) Lamie long-
nez, *f.*; requin-marsouin, *m.*
porcelain ['pɔːslin], *n.* Porcelaine, *f.*
porch [pɔːtʃ], *n.* Porche; (*Phil.*) le Portique, *m.*
porcine ['pɔːsain], *a.* De porc, porcin.
porcupine ['pɔːkjupain], *n.* Porc-épic, *m.*
pore (1) [pɔː], *n.* Pore, *m.*
pore (2) [pɔː], *v.i.* Regarder avec grande attention. *To pore over,* avoir les yeux fixés sur,
dévorer (a book).
porism ['pɔːrizm], *n.* (*Geom.*) Porisme, *m.*
poristic [pɔː'ristik], *a.* Poristique.

pork [pɔːk], *n.* Porc, *m.* **pork-butcher,** *n.* Charcutier, *m.* *Pork-butcher's shop,* charcuterie, *f.* **pork-chop,** *n.* Côtelette de porc, *f.* **pork-pie,** *n.* Pâté de porc, *m.*

porker, *n.* Porc d'engrais, cochon, *m.* **porket** or **porkling,** *n.* Jeune porc, *m.*

pornographer [pɔːˈnɔgrəfə], *n.* Pornographe, *m.*

pornographic [pɔːnoˈgræfik], *a.* Pornographique. **pornography** [pɔːˈnɔgrəfi], *n.* Pornographie, *f.*

porosity [poːˈrɔsiti] or **porousness,** *n.* Porosité, *f.*

porous [ˈpɔːrəs], *a.* Poreux.

porphyritic [pɔːfiˈritik], *a.* Porphyrique. **porphyrize,** *v.t.* Porphyriser.

porphyry [ˈpɔːfiri], *n.* Porphyre, *m.*

porpoise [ˈpɔːpəs], *n.* Marsouin, *m.*

porraceous [pɔˈreiʃəs], *a.* (Couleur) vert poireau.

porridge [ˈpɔridʒ], *n.* Bouillie, *f.* *Oatmeal porridge,* bouillie d'avoine, *f.* **porringer** [ˈpɔrindʒə], *n.* Bol à bouillie, *m.*

port [pɔːt], *n.* Port (harbour); *maintien, air, *m.*, tenue (carriage), *f.*; (Steam engine) lumière, *f.*; (*Naut.*) bâbord; porto (wine), *m.*—*v.t.* Porter. *To port arms,* présenter les armes obliquement pour l'inspection; *to port the helm,* mettre la barre à bâbord. **port-admiral,** *n.* Amiral du port, *m.* **port-charges** or **port-dues,** *n.pl.* Frais de port, *m.pl.* **port-fire,** *n.* Boute-feu, *m.* **port-hole,** *n.* Sabord, *m.* **port-lid,** *n.* Mantelet de sabord, *m.*

portability [pɔːtəˈbiliti] or **portableness,** *n.* Nature portative, *f.*

portable [ˈpɔːtəbl], *a.* Portatif, transportable.

portage [ˈpɔːtidʒ], *n.* Port, transport; portage, *m.*

portal [pɔːtl], *n.* Portail, *m.*—*a. Portal vein,* veine porte, *f.*

portcullis [pɔːtˈkʌlis], *n.* Herse, sarrasine, *f.* **portcullised,** *a.* À herse.

Porte [pɔːt]. Porte, *f.* *The Sublime Porte,* la Sublime Porte, *f.*

portend [pɔːˈtend], *v.t.* Présager, augurer.

portent [ˈpɔːtənt], *n.* Présage sinistre, mauvais augure, *m.*

portentous [pɔːˈtentəs], *a.* De mauvais augure, de sinistre présage; prodigieux. **portentously,** *adv.* Sinistrement; prodigieusement.

porter [ˈpɔːtə], *n.* Commissionnaire; portefaix, portier, concierge (door-keeper); porteur (street porter); (*Rail.*) porteur; (*Comm.*) garçon de magasin; porter (liquor), *m.* *Porter's knot,* crochet de portefaix, *m.* **porterage,** *n.* Port; factage, *m.*

portfolio [pɔːtˈfouliou], *n.* Carton, *m.*; chemise, serviette, *f.*; (*Polit.*) portefeuille, *m.*

portico [ˈpɔːtikou], *n.* Portique, *m.*

portion [ˈpɔːʃən], *n.* Portion, partie, part; dot (dowry), *f.*—*v.t.* Partager, distribuer; doter (to dower). *To portion out,* répartir, distribuer. **portionless,** *a.* Sans dot.

portliness [ˈpɔːtlinis], *n.* Port majestueux, noble maintien, *m.*; corpulence, *f.* **portly,** *a.* D'un port majestueux; corpulent.

portmanteau [pɔːtˈmæntou], *n.* Valise, *f.* *Portmanteau word,* mot contracté (e.g. chortle=chuckle and snort, squarson= squire and parson), *n.*

portrait [ˈpɔːtrit], *n.* Portrait, *m.* *Full-length*

portrait, portrait en pied; *half-length portrait,* portrait en buste; *to have one's portrait taken,* faire faire son portrait. **portrait-painter,** *n.* Portraitiste, *m.*

portraiture [ˈpɔːtritʃə], *n.* Portrait, *m.*; (*fig.*) peinture, description, *f.*

portray [pɔːˈtrei], *v.t.* Peindre; (*fig.*) dépeindre, décrire. **portrayal,** *n.* Portrait, *m.*; peinture. description, *f.*

portress [ˈpɔːtris], *n.* Portière, concierge, *f.*

Portugal [ˈpɔːtʃug(ə)l]. Le Portugal, *m.* **Portuguese** [-ˈgiːz], *a.* Portugais.—*n.* Portugais, *m.*, Portugaise, *f.*; portugais (language), *m.*

pose [pouz], *v.t.* Embarrasser, confondre, fermer la bouche à; poser (a question); citer (an example); faire prendre une pose à (a model).—*v.i.* Poser (to attitudinize). *To pose as an Englishman,* se faire passer pour Anglais.—*n.* Pose, *f.* **poser** [ˈpouzə], *n.* Question embarrassante, *f.* **poseur** [pouˈzɔː], *n.* Poseur, *m.*, poseuse, *f.*

posh [pɔʃ], *a.* (*colloq.*) Chic, chouette.—*v.t. To posh oneself up,* s'attifer.

posit [ˈpɔzit], *v.t.* Poser en principe (que).

position [pəˈziʃən], *n.* Situation, position; condition, *f.*, état; principe avancé, principe; (*Naut.*) point, *m.*; (*Arith.*) fausse position, *f.* *In a false position,* dans une position fausse; *in a position to,* en état de, à même de; (*Post-office*) *position closed,* guichet fermé.—*v.t.* Placer, mettre en position. **position-finder,** *n.* Indicateur de position, *m.*

positive [ˈpɔzitiv], *a.* Positif; absolu, sûr, certain; décisif, résolu, obstiné.—*n.* Positif, *m.* **positively,** *adv.* Positivement; absolument; décisivement. **positiveness,** *n.* Nature positive, *f.*; caractère positif, *m.*

positivism, *n.* Positivisme, *m.* **positivist,** *n.* Positiviste, *m.*

posse [ˈpɔsi], *n.* Détachement (d'agents de police), *m.*; force publique (d'un comté); *cohue, foule (crowd), *f.*

possess [pəˈzes], *v.t.* Posséder; avoir; jouir de; se rendre maître de. *To be possessed by the devil,* être possédé du diable; *to be possessed of,* être en possession de, (*fig.*) être doué de; *to possess oneself,* être maître de soi; *to possess oneself of,* se rendre maître de, s'emparer de.

possession [pəˈzeʃən], *n.* Possession, *f.* *Possession is nine-tenths of the law,* possession vaut titre; *to enter into possession of,* entrer en possession de; *to put in possession,* mettre en possession; *to take possession of,* prendre possession de, entrer en jouissance de, s'emparer de.

possessive [pəˈzesiv], *a. and n.* Possessif, *m.* *A possessive mother,* une mère abusive.

possessor, *n.* Possesseur; porteur (of a bill), *m.* **possessory,** *a.* Possessoire.

posset [ˈpɔsit], *n.* Lait caillé au vin, *m.*

possibility [pɔsiˈbiliti], *n.* Possibilité, *f.*, le possible; moyen (means), *m.* *Possibilities are infinite,* le possible est immense.

possible [ˈpɔsibl], *a.* Possible. *As far as possible,* dans la mesure du possible; *as soon as possible,* le plus tôt possible; *if possible,* si possible.—*n.* (*Shooting*) *To score a possible,* faire le maximum. **possibly,** *adv.* Vraiment, en fait; peut-être. *How can I possibly help it?* comment puis-je l'éviter, dites-moi? *when I*

possibly can, I will return, je reviendrai quand je le pourrai.
possum ['pɔsəm], *n.* Opossum, *m.* *To play possum,* se tenir coi, cacher son jeu.
post [poust], *n.* Poteau (wooden); montant (of a door); emploi, *m.*; (*Mil.*) poste, *m.*; (*Post-office*) poste, *f.*, bureau de poste; (*Naut.*) étambot; papier à lettres (paper), *m.* **bed-post** [BED]; *by post,* par la poste, par le courrier; *by return of post,* par retour du courrier; *deaf as a post,* sourd comme un pot; *the last post,* (*Mil.*) la dernière relève, *f.*; *the post is gone,* la levée est faite; (*Turf*) *to be left at the post,* manquer le départ; *to win on the post,* gagner de justesse; *when is the next post out?* à quand le prochain départ?—*v.t.* Afficher; mettre à la poste, (*Mil. etc.*) poster, placer, affecter; (*Book-keeping*) porter au grand livre. *I'll keep you posted,* je vous tiendrai au courant; *to be well posted up in,* être ferré sur; *to post up,* poser, afficher (bills).—*v.i.* Voyager en poste, courir la poste. *To post off,* s'en aller en poste. **postal,** *a.* Postal. *Postal order,* mandat-poste, *m.* **post-boy,** *n.* *Postillon, courrier, *m.* **post-captain,** *n.* Capitaine de vaisseau, *m.* **post-card,** *n.* Carte postale, *f.* *Picture postcard,* carte postale illustrée, *f.* **post-chaise** or **post-coach,** *n.* Chaise de poste, *f.* **post-day,** *n.* Jour du courrier, *m.* **post-free,** *adv.* Franco. **post-haste,** *adv.* En grande hâte. *To go post-haste,* courir la poste. **post-horse,** *n.* Cheval de poste, *m.* **post-house,** *n.* Poste aux chevaux, *f.* **postman,** *n.* (*pl.* postmen) Facteur, préposé aux postes, *m.* **postmark,** *n.* Cachet de la poste, *m.*—*v.t.* Timbrer. **postmaster,** *n.* Receveur des postes; (*Mil.*) vaguemestre, *m.* *Postmaster General,* directeur général des postes, *m.* **postmistress,** *n.* Receveuse des postes, *f.* **post-office,** *n.* Bureau de poste, *m.*, poste, *f.* *General Post Office,* Grande Poste, *f.*; *post-office directory,* annuaire du téléphone, Bottin (in France), *m.*; *Post Office Savings Bank,* caisse d'épargne postale, *f.*; *to be left at the post-office till called for,* poste restante. **post-paid,** *a.* Affranchi, port payé.—*adv.* Franco.
postage, *n.* Port de lettre, port, affranchissement, *m.* *Postage due,* port supplémentaire; *to pay the postage of,* payer le port de, affranchir. **postage-stamp,** *n.* Timbre-poste, *m.*
post-communion [poust kə'mju:niən], *n.* Postcommunion, *f.*
postdate, *n.* Postdate, *f.*—*v.t.* Postdater.
postdiluvial or **postdiluvian** [-di'lu:viən], *a.* Postdiluvien.
poster ['poustə], *n.* Affiche, *f.*, placard, *m.* *Bill-poster,* colleur d'affiches, afficheur, *m.*
posterior [pɔs'tiəriə], *a.* Postérieur.—*n.* (*colloq.*) Postérieur, derrière, *m.* **posteriority** [-'ɔriti], *n.* Postériorité, *f.* **posteriors,** *n.pl.* Le postérieur, derrière, *m.* **posterity** [-'teriti], *n.* Postérité, *f.* *The remotest posterity,* la postérité la plus reculée.
postern ['poustə:n], *n.* Poterne, *f.*; porte de derrière, porte dérobée, *f.*—*a.* De derrière.
postgraduate [poust'grædjuət], *n.* Étudiant diplômé, licencié, *m.*—*a.* *Postgraduate course,* cours de troisième cycle, *m.*
posthumous ['pɔstjuməs], *a.* Posthume.

posthumously, *adv.* Après la mort, après décès.
postillion [pɔs'tiliən], *n.* Postillon, *m.*
posting ['poustiŋ], *n.* Voyage en poste; collage, affichage (of bills), *m.*; (*Book-keeping*) inscription au grand livre, mise à jour, *f.*; (*Mil.*) affectation; mise en faction, *f.*; (*Riding*) trot à l'anglaise, *m.*
postmeridian [poustmə'ridiən], *a.* De l'après-midi. **post meridiem** [*abbr.* **p.m.**, 'pi:'em], *adv.* De l'après-midi, du soir. *At four p.m.,* à 16 heures. **post-mortem,** *adv.* Après décès. *Post-mortem* (*examination*), autopsie, *f.* **post-natal** [-'neitəl], *a.* Postérieur à la naissance. **post-nuptial** [-'nʌpʃ(ə)l], *a.* Postérieur au mariage. **post-obit** [-'ɔbit], *n.* Contrat exécutoire après décès, *m.*
postponable [poust'pounəbl], *a.* Ajournable. **postpone** [-'poun], *v.t.* Ajourner, différer, remettre. **postponement,** *n.* Ajournement, *m.*, remise, *f.*
post-prandial [poust'prændiəl], *a.* D'après dîner, après le repas.
post-scoring ['poust 'skɔ:riŋ], *n.* (*Cine.*) Post-synchronisation, *f.*
postscript ['poustskript], *n.* [*abbr.* **P.S.**, 'pi:'es] Post-scriptum, *m.*
postulant ['pɔstjulənt], *n.* Postulant, *m.*, postulante, *f.*
postulate (1) ['pɔstjuleit], *v.t.* Postuler; supposer, réclamer.
postulate (2) ['pɔstjulət], *n.* Postulat, *m.* **postulation** [-'leiʃən], *n.* Postulat; (*fig.*) supposition, *f.*
posture ['pɔstʃə], *n.* Posture, pose; position, *f.*, état, *m.*—*v.t., v.i.* Poser.
post-war [poust'wɔ:], *a.* D'après guerre. *The post-war period,* l'après-guerre, *m.*
posy ['pouzi], *n.* Petit bouquet, *m.*; *devise, *f.*
pot [pɔt], *n.* Pot, *m.*; marmite, *f.* *Pots and pans,* batterie de cuisine, *f.*; *pots of money,* des mille et des cents; *the pot calls the kettle black,* la pelle se moque du fourgon; *to go to pot,* s'en aller au diable, faire fiasco; *to keep the pot boiling,* faire bouillir la marmite.—*v.t.* Empoter, mettre en pot; conserver. **pot-bellied,** *a.* Pansu, ventru. **pot-belly,** *n.* Gros ventre, *m.*, bedaine, *f.* **pot-boiler,** *n.* Œuvre, *f.*, or travail, *m.*, qui vous fait vivre. **pot-boy,** *n.* Garçon de cabaret, *m.* **pot-companion,** *n.* Camarade de bouteille, *m.* **pot-herb,** *n.* Plante potagère, *f.* **pot-hole,** *n.* (*Geol.*) Marmite torrentielle; (*Motor.*) flache, *f.* *Road full of pot-holes,* chemin plein de nids de poules. **pot-holer,** *n.* Spéléologue, *m.* **pot-holing,** *n.* Spéléologie, *f.* **pothook,** *n.* Crémaillère, *f.*; jambage (in writing), *m.* **pothouse,** *n.* Cabaret, *m.* **pot-hunter,** *n.* (*spt.*) Coureur de prix, *m.* **pot-luck,** *n.* Fortune du pot, *f.* *To take pot-luck,* partager la fortune du pot. **potman,** *n.* Garçon de cabaret, *m.* **potsherd** [-'ʃɔ:d], *n.* Tesson, *m.* **pot-shot,** *n.* Coup tiré au petit bonheur; coup tiré à petite portée, *m.* **pot-valiant,** *a.* Brave après boire.
potable ['poutəbl], *a.* Potable.
potash ['pɔtæʃ], *n.* Potasse, *f.*
potassium [pə'tæsiəm], *n.* Potassium, *m.*
potation [pə'teiʃən], *n.* Boisson, gorgée, *f.*; (*pl.*) libations, *f.pl.*
potato [pə'teitou], *n.* (*pl.* **potatoes**) Pomme de terre, *f.* *Indian potato,* igname, *f.*; *mashed*

potatoes, purée de pommes de terre, *f.*; *potato disease*, maladie des pommes de terre, *f.*; *sweet potato*, patate, *f.*

poteen [pɔ'tiːn], *n.* Whisky irlandais distillé illicitement, *m.*

potency ['poutənsi], *n.* Puissance, force, vigueur, *f. Potency of a medicine*, efficacité d'un remède, *f.* **potent**, *a.* Puissant, fort; (*fig.*) efficace, puissant. **potentate**, *n.* Potentat, *m.*

potential [pə'tenʃəl], *a.* Potentiel, latent.—*n.* (*Elec. etc.*) Potentiel. **potentiality** [-i'æliti], *n.* Virtualité, *f. Military potentialities of a country*, potentiel de guerre d'une nation, *m.*

potentilla [poutən'tilə], *a.* (*Bot.*) Potentille, *f.*

potently ['poutəntli], *adv.* Puissamment, efficacement.

potful, *n.* Potée, *f.*

pother ['pɔðə], *n.* Tumulte; bruit, vacarme, tintamarre; ennui, embarras, *m.*—*v.t.* Tourmenter, ennuyer, tracasser.

potion ['pouʃən], *n.* Potion, *f.*; breuvage, *m.*

pottage ['pɔtidʒ], *n.* Potage (épais), *m.*

potted, *a.* En pot, en terrine. *Potted meat*, conserve de viande, *f.*

potter (1) ['pɔtə], *n.* Potier, *m. Potter's clay*, argile plastique, *f.*; *potter's wheel*, tour de potier, *m.*

potter (2) ['pɔtə], *v.i.* To potter about, s'amuser à des riens, flâner.

pottery ['pɔtəri], *n.* Poterie, *f.*

potting ['pɔtiŋ], *n.* (*Hort.*) Mise en pot, *f.*—*a. Potting shed*, serre, resserre, *f.*

pottle [pɔtl], *n.* Pot (deux litres); panier (of strawberries etc.), *m.*

potty ['pɔti], *a.* (*fam.*) Insignifiant; facile; toqué; entiché.

pouch [pautʃ], *n.* Poche, *f.*, petit sac, *m.*; gibecière; blague (for tobacco), *f. Ammunition pouch*, cartouchière, giberne, *f.*; *cartridge pouch*, cartouchière, poche à cartouches, *f.*—*v.t.* Empocher; avaler (of birds).

poult [poult], *n.* Jeune volaille, *f.* **poulterer**, *n.* Marchand de volailles, *m.*

poultice ['poultis], *n.* Cataplasme, *m. Mustard poultice*, sinapisme, *m.*—*v.t.* Mettre un cataplasme à.

poultry ['poultri], *n.* Volaille, *f.* **poultry-farming**, *n.* Élevage de la volaille, *m.* **poultry-house**, *n.* Poulailler, *m.* **poultry-yard**, *n.* Basse-cour, *f.*

pounce (1) [pauns], *v.i.* Fondre (sur).—*v.t.* *Saisir avec les serres (of birds).—*n.* Griffe, serre (of birds of prey), *f.*

pounce (2) [pauns], *v.t.* Poudrer (de sandaraque); (*Drawing*) poncer.—*n.* Sandaraque, poudre de sandaraque; ponce (for drawing), *f.* **pounce-box**, *n.* Poudrier, *m.*

pound (1) [paund], *n.* Livre (avoirdupois: 453 grammes; apothecaries' weight: 373 grammes); livre sterling, *f. By the pound*, à la livre; *so much in the pound*, tant pour cent, tant par livre.

pound (2) [paund], *v.t.* Broyer, piler, concasser; (*Metal.*) bocarder; mettre (des animaux) en fourrière.—*v.i.* To pound along, marcher lourdement; *to pound away at*, cogner dur sur, frapper à coups redoublés sur.

pound (3) [paund], *n.* Fourrière (enclosure), *f.* **pound-keeper**, *n.* Gardien de fourrière, *m.*

poundage ['paundidʒ], *n.* Commission de tant par livre, *f.*; mise en fourrière, *f.*

pounder ['paundə], *n.* Pilon, *m. A twenty-four pounder*, (*Artill.*) une pièce de vingt-quatre, *f.*; (*Fishing*) un poisson de vingt-quatre livres.

pounding ['paundiŋ], *n.* Broiement; (*Metal.*) bocardage, *m.*

pour [pɔː], *v.t.* Verser; répandre. *To pour forth*, répandre, lancer, lâcher (a broadside); *to pour out*, verser, répandre, décharger, épancher.—*v.i.* Couler; se précipiter; pleuvoir à verse (of rain). *To pour down*, tomber à verse; *to pour in*, arriver en foule, entrer de tous côtés, entrer à flots.

pouring ['pɔːriŋ], *a.* Torrentiel (of rain).

pout [paut], *v.i.* Bouder, faire la moue. *To pout at*, bouder; *to pout one's lip*, faire la moue.—*n.* Bouderie, moue, *f.*; tacaud (fish), *m.* **pout-eel**, *n.* Lotte, *f.* **pouter**, *n.* Boudeur, *m.*, boudeuse, *f.*; pigeon à grosse gorge, boulant, *m.* **pouting**, *a.* Qui fait la moue; boudeur.

poverty ['pɔvəti], *n.* Pauvreté, misère, indigence, *f. To be reduced to poverty*, tomber dans la misère. **poverty-stricken**, *a.* Réduit à la misère, indigent.

powder ['paudə], *n.* Poudre, *f. Blasting powder*, poudre de mine, *f.*; *face-powder*, poudre de riz, *f.*; *gunpowder*, poudre à canon, *f.*; *it is not worth powder and shot*, le jeu ne vaut pas la chandelle; *smokeless powder*, poudre sans fumée, *f.*; *to fall to powder*, tomber en poussière; *to grind to powder*, pulvériser; (*fig.*) *to keep one's powder dry*, parer aux événements; *tooth-powder*, poudre dentifrice, *f.*; *to waste powder and shot*, jeter sa poudre aux moineaux.—*v.t.* Réduire en poudre, pulvériser; poudrer (the hair); saupoudrer (to sprinkle). *To powder one's face*, se poudrer.

powder-box, n. Poudrier, *m.*, poudrière, *f.* (for drying ink). **powder-cart**, *n.* Caisson, *m.* **powder-chest**, *n.* Caisson à poudre, *m.* **powder-compact**, *n.* Poudrier (de dame), *m.* **powdered**, *a.* Pulvérisé, en poudre; poudré (of the hair); saupoudré (sprinkled). **powder-flask** or **powder-horn**, *n.* Poire à poudre, *f.* **powder-magazine**, *n.* Poudrière; (*Navy*) soute aux poudres, *f.* **powder-mill**, *n.* Poudrerie, *f.* **powder-monkey**, *n.* Mousse gargoussier, *m.* **powder-puff**, *n.* Houppe, *f.*, pompon, *m.* **powder-room**, *n.* Toilettes pour dames, *f.pl.*

powdering, *n.* Pulvérisation, *f.*; action de poudrer les cheveux; salaison, *f.* **powdery**, *a.* Poudreux; friable.

power ['pauə], *n.* Pouvoir, *m.*; force (strength); autorité, puissance (might etc.); faculté (right etc.), *f.*; (*pl.*) facultés, *f.pl.*, talents, *m.pl. A machine of eight horse-power*, une machine de la force de huit chevaux; *balance of power*, équilibre des puissances, *m.*; *fire power*, puissance de feu, *f.*; *full powers*, pleins pouvoirs, *m.pl.*; *it is not in my power to*, je n'ai pas le pouvoir de, il n'est pas en mon pouvoir de; *the Great Powers*, les grandes puissances, *f.pl.*; *the powers that be*, les autorités constituées, *f.pl.*; *to be in power*, être au pouvoir; *to have it in one's power to*, avoir en son pouvoir de; (*Math.*) *to the fourth power*, à la puissance quatre; *to the* *utmost of one's power,* de tout son pouvoir.— *v.t.* Actionner. **power-driven** or **power-operated,** *a.* Mû, actionné, par moteur. **power-house,** *n.,* or **power-station.** Usine génératrice, station centrale, *f.* **power-loom,** *n.* Métier mécanique, *m.* **power-politics,** *n.* Politique de la force armée, *f.* **powerful,** *a.* Puissant, fort; efficace. **powerfully,** *adv.* Puissamment, fortement, efficacement. **powerfulness,** *n.* Puissance, *f.* **powerless,** *a.* Impuissant, faible; inefficace. **powerlessness,** *n.* Impuissance, *f.* **pow-wow** ['pauwau], *n.* (*Red Indians*) Devin, *m.*; assemblée, *f.*; (*fam.*) conférence, palabre, *f.*—*v.i.* (*fam.*) Discuter, palabrer.

pox [pɔks], *n.* Vérole, *f. Chicken-pox,* varicelle, *f.*; *cow-pox,* vaccine, *f.*; *small-pox,* petite vérole, variole, *f.*

practicability [præktikə'biliti] or **practicableness,** *n.* Nature praticable, possibilité, praticabilité, *f.* **practicable,** *a.* Praticable.

practical ['præktikl], *a.* Pratique. *Practical joke,* mauvaise farce, *f.* **practically,** *adv.* En pratique; à peu près, pratiquement. *Practically finished,* presque terminé; *to look at things practically,* considérer les choses sous leur aspect pratique. **practicalness,** *n.* Nature pratique, *f.*

practice ['præktis], *n.* Pratique, habitude, *f.,* usage, exercice, *m.*; clientèle (of doctors, barristers, etc.), *f.*; *artifice, *m.*, menée, intrigue, *f.*; (*Arith.*) méthode des parties aliquotes, *f. In practice,* dans la pratique; (*spt. etc.*) en forme; *practice makes perfect,* c'est en forgeant qu'on devient forgeron; *sharp practice(s),* procédés peu honnêtes, *m.pl.,* filouterie, *f.*; *target practice,* exercices de tir, tir à la cible, *m.*; *to get out of practice,* se perdre la main, se rouiller; *to make it one's practice to,* to make a practice of, se faire une habitude de; *to put into practice,* pratiquer. **practician** [-'tiʃən], *n.* Praticien, *m.*

practise ['præktis], *v.t.* Pratiquer, mettre en pratique; exercer, pratiquer (a profession etc.); (*Mus.*) étudier; s'exercer à (shot at tennis etc.). *To practise what one preaches,* prêcher d'exemple.—*v.i.* (*Mus.*) Étudier; s'exercer (à); exercer, faire de la clientèle (of doctor). *To practise upon,* en imposer à, tromper, exploiter.

practised, *a.* Exercé, expérimenté (à); versé (dans); habile. **practiser,** *n.* Personne qui pratique *or* qui met en pratique, *f.*; praticien, *m.* **practising,** *a.* Praticien, en exercice, exerçant.

practitioner [præk'tiʃənə], *n.* Praticien. *General practitioner,* médecin ordinaire, *m.*; *medical practitioner,* médecin, *m.*

praetexta [pri:'tekstə], *n.* (*Rom. Ant.*) Prétexte, *f.*

praetor ['pri:tə], *n.* (*Rom. Ant.*) Préteur, *m.* **praetorial** [-'tɔ:riəl], *a.* Prétorial. **praetorian,** *a.* and *n.* Prétorien. **praetorium,** *n.* Prétoire, *m.* **praetorship,** *n.* Préture, *f.*

pragmatic [præg'mætik] or **pragmatical,** *a.* Pragmatique; officieux; infatué de soi. **pragmatically,** *adv.* Pragmatiquement; d'un ton suffisant.

pragmatism ['prægmətizm], *n.* Pragmatisme, *m.*; pédantisme, *m.*

prairie ['preəri], *n.* Prairie, savane, *f.*

praise [preiz], *n.* Louange, *f.,* éloge, *m. Beyond*

all praise, au-dessus de tout éloge; *in praise of,* à la louange de; *to sing the praises of,* chanter les louanges de; *to speak in praise of,* faire l'éloge de.—*v.t.* Louer, faire l'éloge de; glorifier; vanter. *To praise to the skies,* porter aux nues. **praiseless,** *a.* Sans éloge. **praiseworthily,** *adv.* D'une manière louable. **praiseworthy,** *a.* Louable, digne d'éloges; méritoire.

pram [præm], *n.* Prame (ship), *f.*; (*colloq.*) voiture d'enfant; voiture à bras, *f.*

prance [prɑːns], *v.i.* (Of horse) Fringuer, caracoler. **prancing,** *n.* Action de se cabrer, *f.*—*a.* Fringant.

prang [præŋ], *v.t.* (*fam.*) (*Av.*) Bousiller.

prank [præŋk], *n.* Escapade, niche, *f.,* tour, *m. To play one's pranks,* faire des siennes; *to play pranks on,* faire des niches à, jouer des tours à. **prankish,** *a.* Badin; espiègle, malin.

prate [preit], *v.i.* Jaser, babiller, bavarder (de); dire des riens.—*v.t.* Débiter, dire sottement. **prater,** *n.* Bavard, *m.,* -arde, *f.,* babillard, *m.,* -arde, *f.* **prating,** *a.* Bavard, babillard. **pratingly,** *adv.* En bavard, en babillard.

prattle [prætl], *v.i.* Babiller, jaser, caqueter; murmurer (of brooks etc.).—*n.* Babil, caquetage, bavardage, *m.* **prattler,** *n.* Bavard, *m.,* -arde, *f.,* babillard, *m.,* -arde, *f.* **prattling,** *n.* Bavardage, caquet, *m.*; murmure, babil (of streams), *m.*

prawn [prɔːn], *n.* Crevette rouge, *f.*; bouquet, *m.*; salicoque, *f.*

praxis ['præksis], *n.* Exercice, *m.* (de grammaire).

Praxiteles [præk'sitiliːz]. Praxitèle, *m.*

pray [prei], *v.i.* Prier. *He is past praying for,* il est irrémédiablement perdu; (*fam.*) il est incorrigible; *to pray for,* prier pour, implorer; *to pray to God,* prier Dieu.—*v.t.* Prier, supplier. *I pray you,* je vous prie, je vous en prie; *pray!* de grâce! *pray be seated,* veuillez vous asseoir.

prayer [preə], *n.* Prière, supplication; (*Law*) demande, *f. The Lord's Prayer,* l'oraison dominicale, *f.*; *to say one's prayers,* faire sa prière. **prayer-book,** *n.* Livre de prières, *m.*; liturgie, *f.* **prayerful,** *a.* Porté à la prière.

praying ['preiiŋ], *n.* Prière, *f.* **prayingly,** *adv.* En priant, avec prière.

preach [priːtʃ], *v.t., v.i.* Prêcher. *To preach down,* dénigrer, prêcher contre; *to preach to the converted,* prêcher un converti; *to preach up,* prêcher, prôner. **preacher,** *n.* Prédicateur, *m.* **preachify,** *v.i.* Sermonner. **preaching,** *n.* Prédication, *f.*

preacquaint [priːə'kweint], *v.t.* Prévenir. **preacquaintance,** *n.* Connaissance préalable, *f.*

pre-adamic [priːə'dæmik] or **pre-adamitic** [-ædə'mitik], *a.* Préadamite. **pre-adamite** [-'ædəmait], *n.* Préadamite, *m.*

preadmission [priːəd'miʃən], *n.* Admission antérieure, *f.*

preadmonish [-əd'mɔniʃ], *v.t.* Avertir préalablement. **preadmonition** [-ædmə'niʃən], *n.* Avertissement, *m.*

preamble [priː'æmbl], *n.* Préambule; exposé des motifs (of an Act of Parliament), *m.*

preannounce [priːə'nauns], *v.t.* Annoncer d'avance.

preappoint [-ə'pɔint], *v.t.* Nommer d'avance.

prearrange [-ə'reindʒ], *v.t.* Arranger d'avance.
prebend ['prebənd], *n.* Prébende, *f.* **prebendal** ['prebəndəl], *a.* De prébende.
prebendary ['prebəndəri], *n.* Chanoine, prébendier, *m.*
precarious [pri'kɛəriəs], *a.* Précaire; incertain (of the weather). **precariously,** *adv.* Précairement. **precariousness,** *n.* Nature précaire, *f.*; incertitude, *f.*
precative ['prekətiv] or **precatory,** *a.* Suppliant, de prière.
precaution [pri'kɔ:ʃn], *n.* Précaution, *f.* *By way of precaution,* par précaution; *to take precautions,* prendre des précautions.—*v.t.* Précautionner (contre), mettre sur ses gardes. **precautionary,** *a.* De précaution.
precede [pri'si:d], *v.t.* Précéder; avoir le pas sur.
precedence [presidəns or pri'si:dəns], *n.* Préséance, *f.*, pas, *m.*, priorité; *supériorité (superiority), *f.* *To have* or *take precedence of* or *over,* avoir le pas sur.
precedent (1) [pri'si:dənt] or **preceding,** *a.* Précédent.
precedent (2) ['presidənt], *n.* Précédent, *m.*
precentor [pri'sentə], *n.* Premier chantre, *m.*; maître de chapelle, *m.*
precept ['pri:sept], *n.* Précepte, *m.* **preceptor** [pri'septə], *n.* Précepteur, *m.* **preceptorial** [-'tɔ:riəl], *a.* Préceptoral, de précepteur. **preceptorship,** *n.* Préceptorat, *m.* **preceptory** [-'septəri], *a.* De préceptes.—*n.* Commanderie de l'ordre du Temple, *f.* **preceptress,** *n.* Préceptrice, institutrice, *f.*
precession [pri'seʃn], *n.* Précession, *f.*
precinct ['pri:siŋkt], *n.* Limite, borne, enceinte, *f.*; (*Am.*) circonscription électorale; (*pl.*) pourtour (of cathedral), *m.*; alentours, environs, *m.pl.*
preciosity [preʃi'ɔsiti], *n.* Préciosité, *f.*
precious ['preʃəs], *a.* Précieux; affecté; (*slang*) fameux, fichu. *Precious near it,* il s'en fallut de peu.—*n.* *My precious!* mon amour! **preciously,** *adv.* Précieusement; (*slang*) fameusement, diablement. **preciousness,** *n.* Haute valeur, *f.*
precipice ['presipis], *n.* Précipice, *m.*
precipitable [pri'sipitəbl], *a.* (*Chem.*) Précipitable. **precipitance** [pri'sipitəns] or **precipitancy,** *n.* Précipitation, hâte, *f.*; empressement excessif, *m.* **precipitant,** *a.* Qui se précipite, précipité.—*n.* (*Chem.*) Précipitant, *m.* **precipitantly,** *adv.* Précipitamment.
precipitate (1) [pri'sipitit], *a.* Précipité, qui se précipite.—*n.* (*Chem.*) Précipité, *m.*
precipitate (2) [pri'sipiteit], *v.t.* Précipiter. *To be precipitated,* (*Chem.*) se précipiter.—*v.i.* Se précipiter. **precipitately,** *adv.* Précipitamment. **precipitation** [-'teiʃn], *n.* Précipitation, *f.*
precipitous [pri'sipitəs], *a.* Escarpé, abrupt. **precipitously,** *adv.* À pic, en précipice; (*fig.*) précipitamment. **precipitousness,** *n.* Précipitation, *f.*
précis ['preisi:], *n.* Précis (abstract), résumé, *m.*
precise [pri'sais], *a.* Précis, exact; formaliste, pointilleux, scrupuleux. **precisely,** *adv.* Précisément, exactement, au juste; scrupuleusement. *At 3 p.m. precisely,* à trois heures précises. **preciseness,** *n.* Précision, exactitude; formalité, *f.* **precisian** [-'siʒən], *n.*

Formaliste, *m.* **precision** [-'siʒən], *n.* Précision, exactitude, *f.* *Precision instrument,* instrument de précision, *m.*
preclude [pri'klu:d], *v.t.* Exclure; empêcher, (prevent). **preclusion** [-'klu:ʒən], *n.* Exclusion, *f.* **preclusive** [-'klusiv], *a.* Qui exclut; qui empêche. **preclusively,** *adv.* Avec exclusion.
precocious [pri'kouʃəs], *a.* Précoce. **precociously,** *adv.* Précocement. **precociousness** or **precocity** [-'kɔsiti], *n.* Précocité, *f.*
precognition [pri:kɔg'niʃn], *n.* Connaissance antérieure, *f.*; (*Sc. law*) enquête préliminaire, *f.*
preconceive [pri:kən'si:v], *v.t.* Se figurer d'avance, juger d'avance; (*Phil.*) préconcevoir. **preconceived,** *a.* Formé d'avance, (*Phil.*) préconçu. *Preconceived idea,* idée préconçue, *f.* **preconception** [-'sepʃn], *n.* Opinion préconçue, prévention, *f.*, préjugé, *m.*
preconcert [pri:kən'sə:t], *v.t.* Concerter d'avance.
preconize ['pri:kənaiz], *v.t.* Préconiser.
preconsign [pri:kən'sain], *v.t.* Consigner d'avance.
preconstitute [pri:'kɔnstitju:t], *v.t.* Constituer préalablement.
precontract [pri:kən'trækt], *v.t.* Contracter préalablement.—*n.* [-'kɔntrækt] Contrat antérieur, *m.*
precursor [pri'kə:sə], *n.* Précurseur, avant-coureur, *m.* **precursory,** *a.* Précurseur.
predate [pri:'deit], *v.t.* Antidater.
predatory ['predətəri], *a.* De rapine, de proie, pillard, rapace.
predecease [pri:di'si:s], *v.t.* Prédécéder.—*n.* Prédécès, *m.*
predecessor ['pri:disesə], *n.* Prédécesseur, devancier, *m.*
predesign [pri:di'zain], *v.t.* Désigner d'avance.
predestinate (1) [pri:'destinit], *a.* Prédestiné. **predestinate** (2) [pri:'destineit] or **predestine,** *v.t.* Prédestiner. **predestination** [-'neiʃn], *n.* Prédestination, *f.*
predetermination [pri:dətə:mi'neiʃn], *n.* Prédétermination, *f.*
predetermine [pri:di'tə:min], *v.t.* Prédéterminer, arrêter d'avance. **predetermining,** *a.* Prédéterminant.
predicable ['predikəbl], *a.* and *n.* (*Log.*) Prédicable, *m.*
predicament [pri'dikəmənt], *n.* Catégorie, *f.*, ordre; état, *m.*, position difficile, situation fâcheuse, *f.*; (*Log.*) prédicament, *m.* *You put me in a nice predicament,* vous me mettez dans une singulière position.
predicate (1) ['predikit], *n.* Prédicat, attribut, *m.*
predicate (2) ['predikeit], *v.t.* Affirmer. **predication** [-'keiʃn], *n.* Affirmation, assertion; prédication, *f.* **predicative,** *a.* Affirmatif; prédicatif.
predict [pri'dikt], *v.t.* Prédire. **predictable,** *a.* Qui peut être prédit. **prediction** [-'dikʃn], *n.* Prédiction, prévision, *f.* **predictive,** *a.* Qui prédit; prophétique. **predictor,** *n.* Personne qui prédit, *f.*, prophète, *m.*
predilection [pri:di'lekʃn], *n.* Prédilection, *f.*

prediscovery [priːdisˈkʌvəri], *n.* Découverte antérieure, *f.*

predispose [priːdisˈpouz], *v.t.* Prédisposer. *To be predisposed in favour of*, être prédisposé en faveur de. **predisposition** [-pəˈziʃən], *n.* Prédisposition, *f.*

predominance [priˈdɔminəns] or **predominancy,** *n.* Prédominance, *f.*, ascendant, *m.* **predominant,** *a.* Prédominant. **predominantly,** *adv.* D'une manière prédominante. **predominate,** *v.i.* Prédominer, prévaloir. *Slightly predominating*, quelque peu plus nombreux.

pre-elect [priːilˈlekt], *v.t.* Élire d'avance. **pre-election,** *n.* Élection antérieure, *f.—a.* Antérieur à l'élection.

pre-eminence [priːˈeminəns], *n.* Prééminence, supériorité, *f.* **pre-eminent,** *a.* Prééminent. **pre-eminently,** *adv.* D'une manière prééminente, par excellence.

pre-empt [priːˈempt], *v.t.* Préempter. **pre-emption,** *n.* Préemption, *f.*

preen [priːn], *v.t.* Lisser, nettoyer (ses plumes). *To preen oneself*, se piquer; s'attifer.

pre-engage [priːinˈgeidʒ], *v.t.* Engager d'avance. **pre-engagement,** *n.* Engagement antérieur, *m.*

pre-establish [priːisˈtæbliʃ], *v.t.* Préétablir. **pre-establishment,** *n.* Établissement antérieur, *m.*

pre-examination [priːigzæmiˈneiʃən], *n.* Examen préalable, *m.* **pre-examine,** *v.t.* Examiner préalablement.

pre-exist [priːigˈzist], *v.i.* Préexister. **pre-existence,** *n.* Préexistence, *f.* **pre-existent,** *a.* Préexistant.

prefab [ˈpriːfæb], *n.* (*colloq.*) Maison préfabriquée, *f.* **prefabricate** [-ˈfæbrikeit], *v.t.* Préfabriquer.

preface [ˈprefis], *n.* Préface, *f.*; avant-propos, *m.—v.t.* Faire une préface à; faire précéder.

prefatory [ˈprefətəri], *a.* Qui sert de préface, préliminaire, introductif.

prefect [ˈpriːfekt], *n.* Préfet, *m.*; (*sch.*) surveillant, *m.* **prefectorial** [-ˈtɔːriəl], *a.* Préfectoral. **prefecture** or ***prefectship,** *n.* Préfecture, *f.*

prefer [priˈfəː], *v.t.* Préférer, aimer mieux; présenter (to a living etc.); avancer, élever (to advance); offrir, adresser, déposer (a charge etc.). *To prefer a complaint*, formuler une plainte, déposer une plainte (contre).

preferable [ˈprefərəbl], *a.* Préférable (à). **preferably,** *adv.* Préférablement, de préférence.

preference [ˈprefərəns], *n.* Préférence; chose préférée, *f. By preference*, de préférence; *preference share*, action privilégiée, *f.* **preferential** [-ˈrenʃl], *a.* De préférence, privilégié, préférentiel.

preferment [priˈfəːmənt], *n.* Avancement, *m.*; promotion, *f.*

prefiguration [priːfigjuəˈreiʃən], *n.* Préfiguration, *f.*, symbole, *m.* **prefigurative** [-ˈfigjuˌrətiv], *a.* Symbolique, typique. **prefigure,** *v.t.* Figurer d'avance.

prefix (1) [priːˈfiks], *v.t.* Mettre en tête, mettre devant.

prefix (2) [ˈpriːfiks], *n.* (*Gram.*) Préfixe, *m.*

pregnancy [ˈpregnənsi], *n.* Grossesse; (*fig.*) fécondité, *f.* **pregnant,** *a.* Enceinte, grosse; (*fig.*) gros, plein (de), fertile, fécond (en).

pregnantly, *adv.* Avec fertilité, pleinement.

preheat [priːˈhiːt], *v.t.* Échauffer d'avance.

prehensile [priˈhensail] or **prehensory,** *a.* Préhensile. **prehension,** *n.* Préhension, *f.*

prehistoric [priːhisˈtɔrik], *a.* Préhistorique. **prehistory** [-ˈhistəri], *n.* Préhistoire, *f.*

pre-ignition [priːigˈniʃən], *n.* Auto-allumage, *m.*

prejudge [priːˈdʒʌdʒ], *v.t.* Juger d'avance, préjuger; condamner. **prejudgment,** *n.* Jugement par avance, *m.*

prejudice [ˈpredʒudis], *v.t.* Prévenir, nuire à (to injure); donner des préjugés à. *This did not prejudice me much in his favour*, cela ne me prévint pas beaucoup en sa faveur.—*n.* Prévention, *f.*, préjugé; préjudice, tort, dommage (injury), *m. To do someone a prejudice*, faire tort *or* porter préjudice à quelqu'un; *to my prejudice*, à mon détriment; *without prejudice*, sous toutes réserves; *without prejudice to*, sans préjudice de. **prejudiced,** *a.* Prévenu; à préjugés. **prejudicial** [-ˈdiʃl], *a.* Préjudiciable, nuisible (à). **prejudicially,** *adv.* D'une manière préjudiciable.

pre-knowledge [priːˈnɔlidʒ], *n.* Connaissance antérieure, *f.*

prelacy [ˈpreləsi] or **prelateship,** *n.* Prélature, *f.*, épiscopat, *m.* **prelate** [ˈprelit], *n.* Prélat, *m.* **prelatic** [-ˈlætik] or **prelatical,** *a.* De prélat.

prelection [priˈlekʃən], *n.* Conférence publique *or* devant une classe d'étudiants, *f.* **prelector,** *n.* Conférencier, *m.*

prelibation [priːlaiˈbeiʃən], *n.* Avant-goût, *m.*

preliminarily [priˈliminərili], *adv.* Préliminairement. **preliminary,** *a.* and *n.* Préliminaire, *m.*

prelude [ˈpreljuːd], *n.* Prélude, *m.—v.t.* Préluder à.—*v.i.* Préluder. **prelusive** [-ˈljuːsiv] or **prelusory,** *a.* Préliminaire, préparatoire.

premature [ˈpremətjuə], *a.* Prématuré. **prematurely,** *adv.* Prématurément. **prematureness** or **prematurity** [-ˈtjuəriti], *n.* Prématurité, *f.*

premeditate [priˈmediteit], *v.t.* Préméditer, méditer d'avance. **premeditated,** *a.* Prémédité. **premeditatedly,** *adv.* Avec préméditation. **premeditation** [-ˈteiʃən], *n.* Préméditation, *f.*

premier [ˈpriːmiə *or* ˈpremjə], *n.* Premier ministre, *m.—a.* (*colloq.*) Premier (de rang). **première** [prəˈmjɛə], *n.* (*Theat.*) Première, *f.*

premiership, *n.* Dignité de premier ministre, *f.*

premise (1) [priˈmaiz], *v.t.* Exposer d'avance, commencer par dire.—*v.i.* Commencer (par); poser des prémisses.

premise (2) [ˈpremis], *n.* (*Log.*) Prémisse, *f.* **premises** [ˈpremisiz], *n.pl.* Lieux, *m.pl.*; établissement, local, *m. Large premises*, vaste local, *m.*; *on the premises*, sur place, dans l'établissement; sur les lieux.

premium [ˈpriːmiəm], *n.* Prime, prime d'encouragement, *f.*; pas de porte, *m.*; prix, *m.*, récompense, *f. At a premium*, à prime; *high premium*, forte prime, *f.*; *to be at a premium*, faire prime.

*premonish [priˈmɔniʃ], *v.t.* Avertir d'avance, prévenir.

premonition [priːmə'niʃən], *n.* Avis préliminaire, avertissement; pressentiment, *m.* **premonitory** [-'mɔnitəri], *a.* Qui avertit d'avance, prémonitoire, précurseur.
prenatal [priː'neitl], *a.* Prénatal.
prenotion [priː'nouʃən], *n.* Prénotion, *f.*
prenuptial [priː'nʌpʃəl], *a.* Prénuptial.
preoccupancy [priː'ɔkjupənsi], *n.* Préoccupation, occupation antérieure, *f.*; droit d'occupation, *m.* **preoccupation** [-'peiʃən], *n.* Préoccupation, anticipation, absorption, *f.* **preoccupied** [-'ɔkjupaid], *a.* Préoccupé, absorbé. **preoccupy** [-'ɔkjupai], *v.t.* Occuper avant un autre; (*fig.*) préoccuper, prévenir.
preordain [priːɔː'dein], *v.t.* Ordonner *or* arranger d'avance, prédéterminer, préordonner.
prep [prep], *n.* (*sch. fam.*) Étude, *f.*; devoirs, *m.pl.*—*a.* (*fam.*) *Prep school*, école primaire indépendante, *f.*
prepaid [priː'peid], *a.* Affranchi, franc de port.—*adv.* Franco.
preparation [prepə'reiʃən], *n.* Préparation, *f.*; préparatifs, apprêts (for a journey etc.), *m.pl.*; (*sch.*) heures d'étude, *f.pl.*, la préparation aux examens, *f. To make preparations for*, faire des préparatifs *or* prendre des dispositions pour.
preparative [pri'pærətiv], *a.* Préparatoire; qui prépare.—*n.* Préparatif, apprêt, *m.*
preparatively, *adv.* D'une manière préparatoire. **preparatory**, *a.* Préparatoire. *Preparatory school*, école primaire indépendante, *f.*—*adv.* Comme préparation, préalablement. *Preparatory to*, avant de.
prepare [pri'pɛə], *v.t.* Préparer.—*v.i.* Se préparer, s'apprêter (à). **preparedly**, *adv.* Par des mesures préparatoires. **preparedness**, *n.* État de préparation, *m.* **preparer**, *n.* Préparateur, *m.*; apprêteur (of food etc.), *m.*
prepay [priː'pei], *v.t.* Payer d'avance; affranchir (letters). **prepayment**, *n.* Payement d'avance; affranchissement (of letters), *m.*
prepense [pri'pens], *a.* (*Law*) Prémédité.
preponderance [pri'pɔndərəns], *n.* Prépondérance, *f.* **preponderant**, *a.* Prépondérant.
preponderate, *v.i.* Avoir la prépondérance, l'emporter (sur). **preponderating**, *a.* Prépondérant.
preposition [prepə'ziʃən], *n.* Préposition, *f.* **prepositional**, *a.* Prépositif.
prepositive [pri'pɔzitiv], *a.* Prépositif.—*n.* Mot prépositif, prépositif, *m.*
prepossess [priːpə'zes], *v.t.* Pénétrer de; prendre possession de, prévenir. *This speech did not prepossess them in his favour*, ce discours ne les prévint pas en sa faveur.
prepossessing, *a.* Prévenant, agréable, engageant. **prepossession** [-'zeʃən], *n.* Prévention, *f.*, préjugé, *m.*
preposterous [pri'pɔstərəs], *a.* Absurde, déraisonnable. *It is preposterous*, c'est le monde renversé. **preposterously**, *adv.* Absurdement, déraisonnablement. **preposterousness**, *n.* Absurdité, déraison, *f.*
prerequisite [priː'rekwizit], *a.* Nécessaire auparavant.—*n.* Chose nécessaire auparavant, nécessité préalable, *f.*
prerogative [pri'rɔgətiv], *n.* Prérogative, *f.*
presage (1) ['presidʒ], *n.* Présage, *m.*

presage (2) [pri'seidʒ], *v.t.* Présager. *The weather presages a storm*, le temps annonce une tempête.
presbyopia [prezbi'oupiə], *n.* Presbytie, *f.* **presbyopic** [-'ɔpik], *a.* Presbyte.
presbyter ['prezbitə], *n.* (*Eccles. Hist.*) Ancien; (*Epis. Ch.*) prêtre; (*Presbyterian Ch.*) ministre presbytérien, *m.* **presbyterial** [-'tiəriəl], *a.* Presbytéral. **Presbyterian**, *a.* and *n.* Presbytérien, *m.*, Presbytérienne, *f.* **Presbyterianism**, *n.* Presbytérianisme, *m.*
presbytery ['prezbitəri], *n.* Presbytère, *m.*
prescience ['preʃəns], *n.* Prescience, *f.* **prescient**, *a.* Prescient, doué de prescience.
prescind [pri'sind], *v.t.* Couper, retrancher.—*v.i. To prescind from*, faire abstraction de.
prescribe [pri'skraib], *v.t.* Prescrire; (*Med.*) ordonner.—*v.i.* Faire la loi; (*Med.*) faire une ordonnance.
prescript ['priːskript], *n.* Précepte, *m.* **prescriptible** [pri'skriptibl], *a.* Prescriptible. **prescription**, *n.* (*Law*) Prescription; (*Med.*) ordonnance, *f.* **prescriptive**, *a.* Établi *or* acquis par prescription.
pre-selector [priːsi'lektə], *n.* (*Motor.*) Présélecteur, *m.* *Pre-selector gears*, boîte de vitesses à présélection, *f.*
presence ['prezəns], *n.* Présence, *f.*; air, maintien, *m.*, mine (mien), *f.*; personnage supérieur, *m. A dignified presence*, un air majestueux; *in presence of*, en présence de; *in such a presence*, devant une telle assemblée; *presence of mind*, présence d'esprit, *f.*; *saving your presence*, sauf votre respect. **presence-chamber**, *n.* Salle de réception, *f.*
present (1) ['prezənt], *a.* Présent; actuel; courant (of the month). *At the present moment*, à présent, actuellement; *at the present time*, à l'heure qu'il est; *in the present tense*, au présent; *to be present at*, assister à.—*n.* Présent; cadeau, don, *m. For the present*, pour le moment; *in the present*, (*Gram.*) au présent; *know all men by these presents*, à tous ceux qui ces présentes verront; *to make a present*, faire un cadeau; *to make someone a present of something*, faire cadeau de quelque chose à quelqu'un.
present (2) [pri'zent], *v.t.* Présenter, offrir (à); (*Law*) déférer (au tribunal compétent). *Present!* en joue! joue! *present arms!* présentez armes! *to present somebody with something*, faire cadeau de quelque chose à quelqu'un.
presentable [pri'zentəbl], *a.* Présentable.
presentation [prezən'teiʃən], *n.* Présentation, *f. On presentation*, à présentation; *presentation copy*, exemplaire offert par l'auteur *or* l'éditeur (of a book), *m.* **presentee** [-'tiː], *n.* Prêtre présenté à un bénéfice, collataire, *m.*
presenter [pri'zentə], *n.* Présentateur, collateur, *m. Presenter of a debutante (at court)*, marraine d'une débutante, *f.*
presentiment [pri'zentimənt], *n.* Pressentiment, *m.*
presently ['prezəntli], *adv.* Tout à l'heure, bientôt.
presentment [pri'zentmənt], *n.* Présentation, *f.*; tableau, *m.*, représentation; (*Law*) dénonciation spontanée (par le grand jury), *f.*
preservable [pri'zəːvəbl], *a.* Qu'on peut conserver. **preservation** [prezəː'veiʃən], *n.* Salut, *m.*, conservation; préservation (de), *f. In a good state of preservation*, en bon état de

conservation. **preservative** [pri'zə:vətiv], *a.*, or **preservatory**, *a.* and *n.* Préservateur, préservatif, conservateur, *m.* **preserve**, *n.* Confiture, *f.*, conserves, *f.pl.*; réserve, *f.*, parc pour la conservation du gibier, *m.*, chasse réservée, *f.—v.t.* Préserver (de); conserver; confire (fruit etc.). *Preserved fruits,* fruits confits, *m.pl.*; *preserved meat,* conserves de viande, *f.pl.*; *well-preserved person,* personne bien conservée, *f.* **preserver**, *n.* Sauveur, *m.*; conservateur, *m.*, conservatrice, *f. Life preserver,* porte-respect, *m.*
preside [pri'zaid], *v.i.* Présider (à). *To preside at a meeting,* présider à une assemblée.
presidency ['prezidənsi] or **presidentship**, *n.* Présidence, *f.*
president ['prezidənt], *n.* Président, *m.*, présidente, *f.*; *(Univ.)* recteur; *(College)* proviseur, *m.*, directrice, *f. Vice-president,* vice-président, *m.* **presidential**, *a.* Présidentiel; de président. *Presidential angel,* *(Ant.)* ange gardien, *m.*
presiding [pri'zaidiŋ], *a.* Présidant. *Mr. B. presiding,* (séance) présidée par M. B.; *presiding judge,* président, *m.*
press [pres], *v.t.* Presser; serrer, étreindre; enrôler (sailors) de force; satiner (paper); pressurer (fruit); repasser, donner un coup de fer à (a suit); *(fig.)* insister sur. *To cold-press,* satiner à froid; *to hot-press,* satiner à chaud; *to press a thing on,* imposer une chose à; *to press down,* presser, appuyer fortement sur; *to press forward,* pousser, faire avancer; *to press hard,* presser fort, serrer de près; *to press home one's advantage,* poursuivre son avantage; *to press out,* exprimer, pressurer; *to press someone to stay,* presser quelqu'un de rester; *to press the button,* appuyer sur le bouton.—*v.i.* Presser, pousser; avancer, se presser. *To press forward,* se hâter, avancer, se porter en avant; *to press on,* pousser en avant, poursuivre son chemin; *to press upon,* serrer.—*n.* Presse, pression, *f.*; pressoir (for fruit etc.), *m.*; armoire à linge, *f. Error of the press,* faute d'impression, *f.*; *in the press,* sous presse; *in time for press,* à temps pour l'impression; *press of sail,* force de voiles, *f.*; *printing-press,* presse d'imprimerie, *f.*; *(Ten.)* racket press, presse à raquette, *f.*; *the press,* le journalisme, *m.*, la presse, *f.*; *to go to press,* mettre sous presse; *to pass a proof for press,* donner le bon à tirer; *too late for press,* trop tard pour l'impression.
press-agency, *n.* Agence d'informations, *f.*
press-agent, *n.* Agent de publicité, *m.*
press-bed, *n.* Lit-armoire, *m.* **press-box**, *n. (spt.)* Stand de la presse, *m.* **press-cutting**, *n.* Coupure de journal, *f.* **press-gallery**, *n.* Tribune de la presse, *f.* **press-gang**, *n.* *(Naut.)* Presse, *f.* **pressman**, *n.* *(pl.* press-**men**) *(Print.)* Pressier; journaliste, reporter (journalist), *m.* **press-money**, *n. (Hist.)* Prime de l'engagement, *f.* **press-photo-grapher**, *n.* Photographe de la presse, *m.* **press-stud**, *n.* Bouton à pression, *m.* **press-warrant**, *n. (Hist.)* Autorisation de faire la presse, *f.* **presswork**, *n. (Print.)* Tirage, *m.*
pressed, *a.* Satiné. *Hard pressed,* serré de près; aux abois; *pressed for money,* à court d'argent; *pressed for time,* très pressé.
presser, *n.* Presseur, pressoir, *m.* **pressing**,

a. Urgent, pressant.—*n.* Action de presser, pression, *f.*; pressage (of cloth); pressurage (of fruit); satinage (of paper), *m. Pressing-roller,* rouleau à satiner, *m.*; *to require pressing,* se faire prier. **pressingly**, *adv.* D'une manière pressante, instamment.
pressure ['preʃə], *n.* Pression; tension; force, urgence, *f.*; poids (weight), *m. Blood pressure,* tension artérielle, *f. High, low,* or *mean pressure,* haute, basse, or moyenne pression, *f.*; *the pressure of business,* l'urgence des affaires, *f.*; *to act under pressure,* agir par contrainte; *to put pressure on someone,* exercer une pression sur quelqu'un. **pressure-cooker**, *n.* Autoclave; auto-cuiseur, *m.* **pressure-gauge**, *n.* Manomètre, *m.* **pressurize**, *v.t.* Pressuriser.
*****prestation** [pres'teiʃən], *n.* Prestation, redevance, *f.*
prestidigitation [prestididʒi'teiʃən], *n.* Prestidigitation, *f.* **prestidigitator** [-'didʒiteitə], *n.* Prestidigitateur, *m.*
prestige [pres'ti:ʒ], *n.* Prestige, *m.*
presto ['prestou], *adv.* Prestement; *(Mus.)* presto. *Hey presto!* passez muscade!
prestressed [pri:'strest], *a.* Précontraint (of concrete).
presumable [pri'zju:məbl], *a.* Présumable. **presumably**, *adv.* Probablement, il est à croire que.
presume [pri'zju:m], *v.t.* Présumer; supposer. —*v.i.* Présumer; se permettre, avoir l'audace (de), prendre la liberté (de). *Presume not that I am the thing I was,* n'allez pas croire que je sois ce que j'étais autrefois; *to presume upon,* présumer trop de. **presuming**, *a.* Présomptueux, indiscret. **presumingly**, *adv.* Précomptueusement.
presumption [pri'zʌmpʃən], *n.* Présomption, *f.* **presumptive**, *a.* Présumé; *(Law)* présomptif. **presumptively**, *adv.* Par présomption.
presumptuous [pri'zʌmptjuəs], *a.* Présomptueux. **presumptuously**, *adv.* Présomptueusement. **presumptuousness**, *n.* Présomption, *f.*
presuppose [pri:sə'pouz], *v.t.* Présupposer. **presupposition** [-sʌpə'ziʃən], *n.* Présupposition, *f.*
pretence [pri'tens], *n.* Prétexte, faux semblant, *m.*, simulation, feinte; prétention, *f. To make a pretence of,* faire semblant de; *under false pretences,* par moyens frauduleux; *under pretence of,* sous prétexte de; *under pretence of friendship,* sous couleur d'amitié.
pretend [pri'tend], *v.t.* Prétexter; feindre, simuler, faire semblant de; prétendre. *To pretend ignorance,* faire l'ignorant.—*v.i.* Prétendre (à); feindre (de), faire semblant (de). *To pretend to be dead,* faire le mort; *to pretend to be ill,* faire semblant d'être malade, faire le malade.
pretended, *a.* Prétendu, soi-disant, feint. *This pretended Arabic work,* ce prétendu livre arabe.
pretender, *n.* Personne qui prétend, *f.*; prétendant, *m.*, -ante, *f.*; simulateur, *m.*, -trice, *f.*
pretension, *n.* Prétention, *f. Of great pretensions,* à prétentions; *of no pretensions,* sans prétentions; *to have pretensions to,* avoir des prétentions à.

pretentious [pri'tenʃəs], *a.* Prétentieux, ambitieux. **pretentiously,** *adv.* Prétentieusement. **pretentiousness,** *n.* Air prétentieux, *m.*, prétention, *f.*

preterhuman [pri:tə'hju:mən], *a.* Surhumain.

preterit(e) ['pretərit], *n.* (*Gram.*) Prétérit, *m. In the preterite,* au prétérit.

pretermission [pri:tə'miʃən], *n.* Omission; (*Rhet.*) prétermission, prétérition, *f.*

preternatural [pri:tə'nætʃərəl], *a.* Surnaturel, contre nature. **preternaturally,** *adv.* Surnaturellement. **preternaturalness,** *n.* État surnaturel, *m.*

pretext (1) ['pri:tekst], *n.* Prétexte, faux semblant, *m. Under the pretext of,* sous prétexte de.

pretext (2) [pri'tekst], *v.t.* Prétexter.

prettify ['pritifai], *v.t.* Enjoliver. **prettily** [-tili], *adv.* Joliment, gentiment. **prettiness,** *n.* Gentillesse, élégance, *f.*, agrément, *m.*

pretty ['priti], *a.* Joli, gentil; (*colloq.*) habile; (*iron.*) beau. *A pretty fellow!* un joli garçon! *a pretty state of affairs!* nous voilà bien! *she's as pretty as a picture,* elle est jolie comme un cœur.—*adv.* Assez; passablement. *I am pretty sure of the fact,* je suis presque certain du fait; *pretty much,* presque, à peu près; *pretty near,* à peu près; *pretty nearly,* à peu de chose près; *pretty well,* assez bien; *sitting pretty,* bien placé. **pretty-pretty,** *a.* Bellot, affété.

prevail [pri'veil], *v.i.* Prévaloir, l'emporter (sur); réussir (to succeed); dominer. *Easterly winds prevail here during the month of March,* le vent d'est règne ici pendant le mois de mars; *to be prevailed on to,* se laisser persuader de, consentir à; *to prevail on,* décider (à), persuader (de), entraîner (à); *to prevail over,* prévaloir sur, l'emporter sur; *to prevail upon oneself to,* se résoudre à, se persuader de. **prevailing,** *a.* Dominant, régnant; général, répandu. *The prevailing opinion,* l'opinion générale, *f.*

prevalence ['prevələns], *n.* Influence, prédominance, *f.*; fréquence, durée (of weather, disease, etc.), *f.* **prevalent,** *a.* Régnant, dominant; général. **prevalently,** *adv.* Généralement.

prevaricate [pri'værikeit], *v.i.* Équivoquer; tergiverser, biaiser, mentir. **prevarication** [-'keiʃən], *n.* Tergiversation, *f.* **prevaricator,** *n.* Chicaneur, menteur, *m.*

prevent [pri'vent], *v.t.* Empêcher, détourner (de); prévenir, parer à. **preventable,** *a.* Qu'on peut empêcher, évitable. **preventer,** *n.* Personne *or* chose qui empêche, *f.*—*a.* (*Naut.*) Faux. *Preventer backstay,* galhauban volant, *m.*; *preventer stay,* faux étai, *m.* **prevention,** *n.* Empêchement, *m. Prevention is better than cure,* mieux vaut prévenir que guérir; *society for the prevention of cruelty to animals,* société protectrice des animaux, *f.* **preventive,** *a.* Préventif.—*n.* Préservatif, *m.* **preventively,** *adv.* Pour empêcher, préventivement.

preview ['pri:vju:], *n.* Avant-première, *f.*

previous ['pri:viəs], *a.* Antérieur, préalable. *Previous question,* (*Parl.*) question préalable; *previous to,* avant; *to be previous,* (*colloq.*) anticiper. **previously,** *adv.* Antérieurement,

préalablement, auparavant. *Previously to,* avant, avant de. **previousness,** *n.* Antériorité, priorité; (*colloq.*) anticipation, précipitation, *f.*

prevision [pri:'viʒən], *n.* Prévision, *f.*

pre-war [pri:'wɔ:], *a.* D'avant-guerre. *The pre-war period,* l'avant-guerre, *m.*—*adv.* Avant la guerre.

prey [prei], *n.* Proie, *f. Bird of prey,* oiseau de proie, *m.*; *to be a prey to,* être en proie à, être la proie de; *to fall a prey to,* devenir la proie de.—*v.i.* Faire sa proie (de). *To prey on,* miner, ronger, tourmenter, obséder (on the mind). **preyer,** *m.* Spoliateur, *m.*

Priapus [prai'eipəs]. Priape, *m.*

price [prais], *n.* Prix, *m.*; (*Turf*) cote, *f. At any price,* à tout prix, coûte que coûte; *at greatly reduced prices,* au grand rabais; *at half-price,* à moitié prix; *cost price,* prix coûtant; *fair price,* juste prix; *high price,* prix élevé; *market price,* prix courant, *m.*; *the lowest price,* le dernier prix; *to rise in price,* hausser de prix; *trade price,* prix net, *m.*; *under price,* à vil prix; (*colloq.*) *what price my chances?* quelles sont mes chances? *what price my new car?* Que pensez-vous de ma nouvelle voiture?—*v.t.* Tarifer, mettre un prix à. **price-cutting,** *n.* Rabais, *m.* **priceless,** *a.* Sans prix, inappréciable; tordant, impayable (of joke etc.). **price-list,** *n.* Tarif, *m.* **price-ramp,** *n.* Hausse exorbitante, *f.* **price-ring,** *n.* Coalition de vendeurs, *f.*

prick [prik], *n.* Piqûre; pointe, *f.*; piquant; (*fig.*) aiguillon (goad); remords, *m.*—*v.t.* Piquer; dresser (the ears); désigner, marquer (to designate); aiguillonner (to goad); (*fig.*) pousser, exciter, tourmenter de remords; (*Mus.*) noter; (*Naut.*) pointer (a chart). *To prick off,* piquer, marquer, désigner; *to prick out,* (*Hort.*) repiquer, transplanter; *to prick up the ears,* dresser les oreilles.—*v.i.* Piquer; piquer des deux. *To prick on,* s'avancer au galop, piquer des deux.

pricker, *n.* Poinçon, *m.*, pointe, *f.*; piquant, *m.*; (*Tech.*) épinglette, *f.*

pricking, *n.* Piqûre, *f.*; picotement (tingling), *m.*; (*Naut.*) pointage, *m.*—*a.* Qui pique, piquant.

prickle [prikl], *n.* Aiguillon, piquant, *m.*; épine, *f.*—*v.t.* Piquer.—*v.i.* Fourmiller.

prickleback [STICKLEBACK].

prickliness ['priklinis], *n.* Nature épineuse, *f.*

prickly, *a.* Piquant, armé d'épines, épineux, hérissé. *Prickly heat,* lichen vésiculaire, *m.*; *prickly pear,* figuier de Barbarie, *m.*, (*pop.*) raquette, *f.* **prickwood,** *n.* Fusain, *m.*

pride [praid], *n.* Orgueil, *m.*, fierté, *f.*, troupe bande (of lions), *f.* (*Bot.*) *Honest pride,* noble orgueil; *London pride,* désespoir des peintres, *m. Puffed up with pride,* bouffi d'orgueil; *to be the pride of,* faire l'orgueil de; *to take pride in,* se faire gloire de; mettre son orgueil à.—*v.r. To pride oneself on,* se piquer de, s'enorgueillir de, se vanter de.

prier ['praiə], *n.* Curieux, (*colloq.*) fureteur, *m.*

priest [pri:st], *n.* Prêtre, *m. High-priest,* grand prêtre; *parish priest,* curé, *m.* **priestcraft,** *n.* Intrigues de prêtres, *m.pl.* **priestess,** *n.* Prêtresse, *f.* **priesthood,** *n.* Prêtrise, *f.*, sacerdoce, clergé, *m.*; (*pej.*) prêtraille, *f.* **priestlike,** *a.* De prêtre. **priestliness,** *n.*

Air de prêtre, *m.* **priestly,** *a.* De prêtre, sacerdotal. **priest-ridden,** *a.* Mené par les prêtres.

prig [prig], *v.t.* (*slang*) Chiper.—*n.* Faquin, fat; pédant, collet monté, *m.* **priggish,** *a.* Suffisant, pédant. **priggishly,** *adv.* Avec suffisance. **priggishness,** *n.* Suffisance; bégueulerie, *f.*

prim [prim], *a.* Affecté, précieux, compassé, collet monté.

primacy ['praiməsi], *n.* Primatie; primauté (supremacy), *f.*

prima facie ['praimə'feiʃiei], *a.* and *adv.* De prime abord. (*Law*) *Prima facie case,* affaire qui paraît bien fondée.

primage ['praimidʒ], *n.* (*Naut.*) Chapeau, *m.*; gratification, *f.*

primal ['praiməl], *a.* Originel, primitif; principal.

primarily ['praimərili], *adv.* Dans le principe. **primary,** *a.* Primitif, premier; principal; (*Sch.*) primaire, élémentaire. (*Am.*) *Primary election* or *primary,* élection préliminaire (pour élire des candidats), *f.*; *primary materials,* denrées de première nécessité, *f. pl.*

primate ['praimit], *n.* Primat, *m.* **primate-ship,** *n.* Primatie, *f.* **primatial** [-'meiʃl], *a.* Primatial.

prime [praim], *a.* Premier, principal; de premier rang, de première qualité, excellent. *Of prime importance,* de toute première importance; *prime cost,* prix de revient, *m.*; *prime minister,* premier ministre, *m.*; (*Math.*) *prime number,* nombre premier, *m.*—*n.* Aube, *f.*, point du jour; commencement, *m.*, premiers temps, *m.pl.*; printemps (spring), *m.*; meilleure partie, fleur, élite, *f.*, choix (best part), *m.*; comble de perfection (perfection), *m.*; (*Fenc.*) prime, *f.*; (*fig.*) beauté, force, fraîcheur, fleur, première jeunesse, *f. Prime of life,* fleur de l'âge, *f.*; *to be in its prime,* être dans toute sa beauté; *to be in one's prime,* être dans la fleur de l'âge; *to be past one's prime,* avoir passé le bel âge.—*v.t.* Amorcer (fire-arms); (*Paint.*) imprimer. *To prime a pump,* amorcer une pompe; *to prime someone with information,* mettre quelqu'un au courant de l'affaire; (*pop.*) *well primed* (*with liquor*), bien parti.—*v.i.* (*Steam-eng.*) Projeter de l'eau (dans le cylindre). **primely,** *adv.* En premier lieu, primitivement; parfaitement, on ne saurait mieux. **primeness,** *n.* Excellence, *f.*

primer ['praimə], *n.* Premier livre (de lecture etc.); (*R.-C. Ch.*) livre d'heures, *m.*; (*Print.*) romain, *m.*; (*Artill.*) amorce, épinglette, *f.*

primero [pri'meərou], *n.* Prime (game), *f.*

primeval [prai'mi:vəl], *a.* Primitif, primordial.

priming ['praimiŋ], *n.* Amorçage, *m.*; amorce (of a gun), *f.*; (*Paint.*) impression; (*Steameng.*) projection de l'eau (dans le cylindre), *f.* **priming-pan,** *n.* Bassinet (of fire-arms), *m.* **priming-wire,** *n.* (*Artill.*) Épinglette, *f.*

primiparous [prai'mipərəs], *a.* Primipare.

primitive ['primitiv], *a.* Primitif.—*n.* Primitif, mot primitif, *m.* **primitively,** *adv.* Primitivement. **primitiveness,** *n.* Caractère primitif, *m.*

primly ['primli], *adv.* D'un air collet monté.

primness ['primnis], *n.* Afféterie, *f.*

primogenitor [praimou'dʒenitə], *n.* Premier ancêtre, *m.* **primogeniture,** *n.* Primogéniture, *f.* ***primogenitureship,** *n.* Droit d'aînesse, *m.*

primordial [prai'mɔ:diəl], *a.* Primordial.

primrose ['primrouz], *n.* Primevère, *f.* (*fig.*) *The primrose path,* le chemin de velours, *m.* **primrose-bed,** *n.* Lit de primevères, *m.*

primula ['primjulə], *n.* Primevère, primula, *f.*

prince [prins], *n.* Prince, *m. Prince of Wales,* Prince de Galles; (*Bot.*) *Prince's feather,* amarante, *f.* **princedom,** *n.* Principat, *m.*, principauté, *f.* **princelet** or **princeling,** *n.* Petit prince, *m.* **princelike,** *a.* Digne d'un prince; de prince. **princeliness,** *n.* Caractère de prince, *m.*; munificence de prince, *f.* **princely,** *a.* De prince, princier, digne d'un prince, royal; magnifique, riche.—*adv.* En prince, en princesse, magnifiquement. **princess,** *n.* Princesse, *f.*

principal ['prinsipl], *a.* Principal, premier, en chef. *Principal parts* (*of verb*), temps principaux, *m.pl.*—*n.* Partie principale, *f.*, chef; principal, directeur, patron; proviseur (of a lycée), *m.*; directrice, *f.*; (*Comm.*) associé principal, commettant; (*Arch.*) arbalétrier (rafter), *m. Principal and agent,* commettant et agent, *m.* **principality** [-'pæliti], *n.* Principauté, *f.* **principally,** *adv.* Principalement, surtout. **principalship,** *n.* Principalat, *m.*

principle ['prinsipl], *n.* Principe, *m. Of no principles,* sans principes; *on principle,* par principe; *to be a man of principle,* avoir des principes. **principled,** *a.* Qui a des principes. *High-principled,* qui a des principes; *low-principled,* qui a de mauvais principes.

prink [priŋk], *v.t.* Attifer.—*v.i.* S'attifer; (of bird) se lisser les plumes.

print [print], *v.t.* Imprimer; faire une empreinte sur; (*Phot.* etc.) tirer. *Printed by,* imprimé par, imprimerie de (on books); *printed matter,* imprimés, *m.pl.*—*v.i.* Imprimer; se faire imprimer.—*n.* Empreinte (mark), impression, trace, marque, *f.*; imprimé (printed book), *m.*; estampe, gravure (engraving), *f.*; journal, *m.*, feuille (newspaper), *f.*; moule (mould), *m.*; indienne, colonnade (stuff), *f.*; (*Phot.*) épreuve, *f.*; (*Print.*) caractère, *m. Close print,* impression serrée, *f.*; *in print,* imprimé, disponible; *this book is out of print,* l'édition de ce livre est épuisée; *to appear in print,* se faire imprimer. **printable,** *a.* Imprimable. **printer,** *n.* Imprimeur, typographe, *m. Letterpress printer,* imprimeur typographe, *m.*; *lithographic printer,* imprimeur lithographe; *printer's error,* coquille, *f.*; *printer's ink,* encre d'imprimerie, *f.*; *printer's reader,* correcteur d'épreuves, *m.*

printing, *n.* Impression; imprimerie (the art etc.), *f. Printing off,* tirage, *m.*; *printing process,* procédé de tirage, *m.* **printing-frame,** *n.* (*Phot.*) Châssis-presse, *m.* **printing-house,** *n.* Imprimerie, *f.* **printing-machine,** *n.* Presse mécanique, machine à imprimer; (*Phot. Cine.*) tireuse, *f.* **printing-office,** *n.* Imprimerie, *f.* **printing-paper,** *n.* Papier d'impression, *m.* **printing-press,** *n.* Presse à imprimer, *f.*

printless, *a.* Qui ne laisse point d'empreinte.

print-seller, *n.* Marchand d'estampes, *m.*
print-shop, *n.* Magasin d'estampes, *m.*
print-works, *n.* Imprimerie d'étoffes, *f.*
prior (1) ['praiə], *a.* Antérieur.—*adv.* Antérieurement (à), avant.
prior (2) ['praiə], *n.* Prieur, *m.* **prioress**, *n.* Prieure, *f.*
priority [prai'ɔriti], *n.* Priorité, *f.* *To have* or *take priority over*, avoir la préséance sur, primer.
priorship ['praiəʃip], *n.* Prieuré, *m.* **priory**, *n.* Prieuré, *m.*
prise [praiz], *n.* Levier, *m.*—*v.t.* *To prise open*, ouvrir avec un levier; *to prise up*, soulever à l'aide d'un levier; forcer à l'aide d'un levier.
prism [prizm], *n.* Prisme, *m.* **prismatic** [-'mætik] or **prismatical**, *a.* Prismatique. **prismatically**, *adv.* En forme de prisme.
prison [prizn], *n.* Prison, *f.* *Out of prison*, hors de prison; *to be in prison*, être en prison; *to break out of prison*, s'évader; *to take out of prison*, retirer de prison.—*v.t.* (*poet.*) Emprisonner; captiver.
prison-break, *n.* Évasion de prison, *f.* **prison-breaker**, *n.* Évadé de prison, *m.*
prisoner, *n.* Prisonnier, *m.*, prisonnière, *f.* (*Law*) *Prisoner* (*at the bar*), accusé, prévenu, *m.*; *to be kept a close prisoner*, rester étroitement enfermé; *to take prisoner*, faire prisonnier; *witness for the prisoner*, témoin à décharge, *m.*
prisoner's-base, *n.* Les barres (game), *f.pl.*
prison-house, *n.* Prison, *f.* **prison-van**, *n.* Voiture cellulaire, *f.* **prison-yard**, *n.* Préau de prison, *m.*
pristine ['pristain], *a.* Primitif, premier, de jeunesse.
***prithee!** ['priði], *int.* De grâce! je vous en prie!
privacy ['praivəsi or 'privəsi], *n.* Retraite, solitude, intimité, *f.* *In privacy*, dans son intérieur, en son particulier.
private ['praivit], *a.* Particulier, personnel, privé; caché, retiré, confidentiel, secret, clandestin; de famille; bourgeois, civil, de ville (of dress); (*Law*) à huis clos. *A private staircase*, escalier dérobé, *m.*; *he has private means*, il a de la fortune personnelle; *marked private*, marquée 'personnelle' (of a letter); *private agreement*, acte sous seing privé, *m.*; *private boarding house*, pension bourgeoise, *f.*; *private car*, voiture particulière, *f.*; *private education*, enseignement par un précepteur, *m.*; *private individual*, simple particulier, *m.*; *private lessons*, leçons particulières, répétitions, *f.pl.*; *private life*, vie privée, *f.*; *private lodgings*, maison meublée, *f.*; (*Polit.*) *private member*, simple député, *m.*; *private parts*, parties (honteuses), *f.pl.*; *private property*, propriété privée, *f.*; *private pupil*, élève particulier, *m.*; *private room*, cabinet particulier, *m.*; *private school*, école libre, *f.*; *private soldier*, simple soldat, *m.*; *private tutor*, précepteur, *m.*; *they live in a very private way*, ils mènent une vie très retirée.—*n.* (*Mil.*) Simple soldat, *m.* *In private*, en particulier, en bourgeois, dans la vie privée, (*Law*) à huis clos.
privateer [praivə'tiə], *n.* Corsaire, *m.*—*v.i.* Faire une course. **privateering**, *n.* La course, *f.*
privately ['praivitli], *adv.* En particulier; en

secret; de gré à gré (of sales); en bourgeois, en rentier (of living); (*Law*) à huis clos.
privation [prai'veiʃən], *n.* Privation; perte, absence, *f.*
privative ['privətiv], *a.* Qui prive, négatif; (*Gram.*) privatif.—*n.* Négation, *f.*; (*Gram.*) privatif, *m.* **privatively**, *adv.* Négativement.
privet ['privit], *n.* (*Bot.*) Troène, *m.*
privilege ['privilidʒ], *n.* Privilège, *m.*, (*Law*) immunité, *f.*—*v.t.* Privilégier. **privileged**, *a.* Privilégié.
privily ['privili], *adv.* Secrètement, en secret.
privity ['priviti], *n.* (*Law*) Lien, *m.*, obligation, *f.*; connaissance, *f.*
privy ['privi], *a.* Privé, secret; caché, dérobé, retiré. *Keeper of the privy purse*, trésorier du roi, *m.*; *privy chamber*, chambre du conseil, *f.*; *privy Council*, conseil privé, *m.*; *Privy Councillor*, conseiller privé, *m.*; *privy purse*, cassette particulière (du roi), *f.*; *privy seal*, petit sceau, *m.*; *privy to*, qui a connaissance de.—*n.* Cabinet d'aisance, *m.*, cabinets, lieux d'aisance, *m.pl.*; (*Law*) ayant droit, ayant cause, *m.*
prize (1) [PRISE].
prize (2) [praiz], *n.* Prise, capture (things taken), *f.*; prix (reward); lot (in a lottery), *m.*; (*fig.*) bonne fortune, aubaine, *f.* *It is a lawful prize*, c'est de bonne prise; *prize bull*, taureau primé; *the vessel returned to port with her prize*, le vaisseau rentra au port avec sa prise; *to win a prize*, remporter un prix.—*v.t.* Priser, évaluer, estimer.
prize-court, *n.* Tribunal des prises, *m.* **prize-essay**, *n.* Composition couronnée, *f.* **prize-fight**, *n.* Assaut de pugilat, *m.* **prize-fighter**, *n.* Pugiliste, boxeur de profession, *m.* **prize-fighting**, *n.* La boxe professionnelle, *f.* **prize-giving**, *n.* Distribution des prix, *f.* **prize-list**, *n.* Palmarès, *m.* **prize-man**, *n.* Lauréat, *m.* **prize-medal**, *n.* Médaille d'honneur, *f.* **prize-money**, *n.* Part de prise, *f.*; prix en espèces, *m.* **prize-winner**, *n.* Lauréat, gagnant, *m.* **prize-winning**, *a.* Primé.
pro (1) [prou], *prep.* Pour. *Pro and con*, pour et contre, le pour et le contre; *pro-British*, anglophile; *pro rata*, au pro rata.
pro (2) [prou], *n.* (*spt. colloq.*) Professionnel, *m.*, -elle, *f.*
probability [prɔbə'biliti], *n.* Probabilité, vraisemblance, *f.* *In all probability*, selon toute apparence. **probable** ['prɔbəbl], *a.* Probable; vraisemblable. **probably**, *adv.* Probablement.
probate ['proubeit], *n.* Vérification, validation, homologation (d'un testament), *f.* **probate-duty**, *n.* Droits de succession, *m.pl.*
probation [prə'beiʃən], *n.* Probation, épreuve, *f.*; (*Univ. etc.*) examen, stage, *m.* *On probation*, à l'essai; stagiaire; (*Law*) sous surveillance de la police; *probation officer*, surveillant des condamnés mis en liberté surveillée, *m.* **probationary** [-'beiʃənəri], *a.* D'épreuve; de probation. **probationer**, *n.* Aspirant, stagiaire; novice, *m.*
probe [proub], *n.* Sonde, *f.*, stylet, *m.*; (*Am. colloq.*) enquête, *f.*—*v.t.* Sonder; (*fig.*) approfondir, examiner à fond.
probe-scissors, *n.pl.* Ciseaux boutonnés, *m.pl.*
probing, *a.* Pénétrant (of question).

probity ['prɔbiti], *n.* Probité, *f.*
problem ['prɔbləm], *n.* Problème, *m. Problem child*, enfant difficile, *m. or f.*; *problem play*, (*Theat.*) pièce à thèse, *f.* **problematic** [-'mætik] or **problematical**, *a.* Problématique. **problematically**, *adv.* Problématiquement.
proboscis [prə'bɔsis], *n.* (*pl.* **proboscides**) Trompe, *f.*, (*facet.*) nez, *m.*
procedural [prə'si:dʒərəl], *a.* De procédure.
procedure [prə'si:dʒə], *n.* Procédé, *m.*, procédure, *f. The rules of procedure*, le règlement intérieur (d'une assemblée), *m.*
proceed [prə'si:d], *v.i.* Procéder, avancer, marcher, continuer son chemin; provenir (de); continuer, se mettre (à); se rendre, aller (à un lieu). *They have threatened to proceed against him*, on a menacé de lui intenter un procès; *things are proceeding quite normally*, les choses vont leur train; *to proceed against*, procéder contre, poursuivre; *to proceed from*, procéder de, naître de; *to proceed to blows*, en venir aux mains; *to proceed to do something*, se mettre à faire quelque chose; *to proceed to extremes*, se porter à des extrémités (envers); *to proceed with*, continuer, poursuivre. **proceeding**, *n.* Procédé, *m.*; manière d'agir, *f.*; (*pl.*) démarches, *f.pl.*, faits, actes, *m.pl.*; compte-rendu, *m.*, procès-verbal, *m. The proceedings of the Royal Society*, les comptes-rendus des séances de la Société Royale, *m.pl.*; *to take proceedings against*, intenter des poursuites à, poursuivre.
proceeds ['prousi:dz], *n.pl.* Produit, montant, *m.*
process (1) ['prouses], *n.* Procédé; processus; cours, *m.*, marche, suite (of time); (*Anat.*) apophyse, *f.*; (*Law*) procès, *m.*; sommation (writ), *f. In process of time*, avec le temps.—*v.t.* (*Ind.*) Traiter, transformer, apprêter; (*Print.*) reproduire par similigravure; (*Law*) poursuivre. *Processed cheese*, fromage fondu, *m.* **process-block**, *n.* Cliché, simili, *m.* **process-server**, *n.* Huissier, *m.* **process shot**, *n.* (*Cine.*) Truquage, *m.*
process (2) [pro'ses], *v.i.* (*colloq.*) Défiler en cortège.
processing, *n.* (*Ind.*) Transformation, *f.*, traitement (d'une matière première), *m.*
procession [prə'seʃən], *n.* Procession, *f.*, cortège, *m. In procession*, processionnellement; *to walk in procession*, défiler. **processional**, *a.* De cortège, processionnel.—*n.* Processionnal (book), *m.*; hymne processionnel, *m.*
proclaim [prə'kleim], *v.t.* Proclamer, déclarer, publier; *mettre hors la loi (to outlaw). **proclaimer**, *n.* Proclamateur, *m.*
proclamation [prɔklə'meiʃən], *n.* Proclamation, publication, déclaration; ordonnance, *f.*
proclitic [pro'klitik], *a. and n.* Proclitique, *m.*
proclivity [prə'kliviti], *n.* Penchant, *m.*, inclination (à), *f.* **proclivous** [-'klaivəs], *a.* Proclive.
proconsul [prou'kɔnsl], *n.* Proconsul, *m.* **proconsular** [-'kɔnsjulə], *a.* Proconsulaire. **proconsulship** or **proconsulate**, *n.* Proconsulat, *m.*
procrastinate [prə'kræstineit], *v.t.* Remettre, différer de jour en jour.—*v.i.* Retarder, user de délais. **procrastination** [-'neiʃən], *n.*

Retardement, délai, *m.* **procrastinator** [-'kræstineitə], *n.* Temporiseur, *m.*
procreate ['proukrieit], *v.t.* Procréer. **procreation** [-'eiʃən], *n.* Procréation, *f.*
procreative ['proukrieitiv], *a.* De procréation, procréateur, productif. **procreativeness**, *n.* Faculté de procréer, *f.*
Procrustean [prou'krʌstiən], *a.* De Procruste.
proctor ['prɔktə], *n.* Avoué; (*Univ.*) censeur; (*Law*) procureur, *m.* **proctorial** [-'tɔːriəl], *a.* De censeur. **proctorship**, *n.* Fonctions de censeur, *f.pl.*
procumbent [prou'kʌmbənt], *a.* Couché sur le ventre; (*Bot.*) procombant.
procurable [prə'kjuərəbl], *a.* Qu'on peut se procurer.
procuration [prɔkjuə'reiʃən], *n.* Gestion des affaires d'autrui; (*Law*) procuration, *f.*
procurator ['prɔkjuəreitə], *n.* Agent d'affaires; (*Law*) procurateur, *m.*
procure [prə'kjuːə], *v.t.* Procurer, faire avoir, se procurer; causer, amener.—*v.i.* Faire le métier d'entremetteur. **procurement**, *n.* Action de procurer; entremise, *f.* **procurer**, *n.* Entremetteur, proxénète, *m.* **procuress**, ['prɔkjuris], *n.* Entremetteuse, *f.*
prod [prɔd], *v.t.* Pousser du doigt, du bout d'un bâton; piquer; (*fig.*) éperonner, aiguillonner.—*n.* Coup de pointe, *m.*
prodigal ['prɔdigl], *a.* Prodigue. *The prodigal son*, l'enfant prodigue, *m.*—*n.* Prodigue, *m.* or *f.* **prodigality** [-'gæliti], *n.* Prodigalité, *f.* **prodigally**, *adv.* Prodigalement, avec prodigalité.
prodigious [prə'didʒəs], *a.* Prodigieux. **prodigiously**, *adv.* Prodigieusement, énormément. **prodigiousness**, *n.* Nature prodigieuse, énormité, *f.*
prodigy ['prɔdidʒi], *n.* Prodige, *m. Infant prodigy*, enfant prodige, *m.* or *f.*
produce (1) ['prɔdjuːs], *n.* Produit, *m.*; *m.pl.*; *farm produce*, produits agricoles, *m.pl.*; *garden produce*, jardinage, *m.*
produce (2) [prə'djuːs], *v.t.* Produire; exhiber, montrer; (*Geom.*) prolonger; (*Theat.*) mettre en scène.
producer, *n.* Producteur; (*Theat.*) metteur en scène; (*Cine.*) producteur, *m. Producer gas*, gaz pauvre, *m.* **producibility** [-i'biliti] or **producibleness**, *n.* Productibilité, *f.* **producible**, *a.* Qu'on peut produire, productible.
product ['prɔdʌkt], *n.* Produit, *m. By-product*, sous-produit, *m.*
production [prə'dʌkʃən], *n.* Production, *f.*; (*Chem. etc.*) produit, *m.*; (*Theat.*) mise en scène, *f. Cost of production*, prix de fabrique, *m.*; *production car*, voiture de série, *f.*; (*Cine.*) *production manager*, régisseur général, *m.*
productive, *a.* Productif; d'un bon rapport, fécond. *To be productive of*, produire, donner naissance à. **productiveness** or **productivity**, *n.* Nature productive, productivité, *f.*
proem ['prouəm], *n.* Préface, introduction, *f.* préambule, *m.* **proemial** [-'iːmiəl], *a.* De préface, introductoire, préliminaire.
profanation [prɔfə'neiʃən], *n.* Profanation, *f.*
profane [prə'fein], *a.* Profane.—*v.t.* Profaner. **profanely**, *adv.* D'une manière profane. **profaneness** or **profanity** [-'fæniti], *n.* Conduite profane, impiété, *f.*; langage profane, *m.* **profaner**, *n.* Profanateur, *m.*

profess [prə'fes], *v.t.* Professer, faire profession de, déclarer, dire. *To profess oneself*, se dire, se déclarer.—*v.i.* Faire profession. **professed**, *a.* Déclaré, de profession; (*R.-C. Ch.*) profès. **professedly**, *adv.* Ouvertement; de profession.

profession [prə'feʃən], *n.* Profession, *f.*; état, métier (calling), *m.* *By profession*, de profession; *learned professions*, carrières libérales, *f.pl.*; *military profession*, métier des armes, *m.* **professional**, *a.* De sa profession, de la profession; du métier, de profession, professionnel. *Professional classes*, membres des professions libérales, *m.pl.*; *professional man*, homme qui exerce une carrière libérale, intellectuel, *m.*—*n.* Homme du métier, homme de l'art; (*spt.*) professionnel, *m.*; homme de loi (lawyer). **professionalism**, *n.* Caractère professionnel; (*spt.*) professionnalisme, *m.* **professionally**, *adv.* Par profession, par état; en homme du métier (avocat, médecin, etc.).

professor [prə'fesə], *n.* Personne qui professe, *f.*; professeur (d'Université), *m.* **professorial** [prɔfi'sɔːriəl], *a.* De professeur, professoral. **professorship**, *n.* Professorat, *m.*, chaire, *f.*

proffer ['prɔfə], *n.* Offre, *f.*—*v.t.* Offrir, proposer.

proficiency [prə'fiʃənsi], *n.* Capacité, *f.*; talent, *m.*, compétence, force, *f.* *To have attained great proficiency*, avoir fait de grands progrès. **proficient**, *a.* Versé, fort, compétent. *To be proficient at French*, être fort en français.

profile ['proufail], *n.* Profil, *m.* *In profile*, de profil.—*v.t.* Profiler.

profit ['prɔfit], *n.* Profit, bénéfice, rapport; (*fig.*) avantage, *m.*, utilité, *f.* *Gross profit*, bénéfice brut; *net profit*, bénéfice net; *profit and loss*, profits et pertes, *m.pl.*; *to make a profit on*, faire des bénéfices sur; *to sell at a profit*, vendre à profit.—*v.t.* Profiter à, faire du bien à; avantager. *It might profit me to*, il pourrait m'être utile de; *what will it profit me to?* à quoi me servira de?—*v.i.* Profiter (de). *Things that profit not*, des choses ne servent à rien; *to profit by*, profiter de, profiter à. **profitable**, *a.* Profitable, avantageux. **profitableness**, *n.* Avantage; profit, *m.* **profitably**, *adv.* Avantageusement, utilement, avec profit. **profiteer** [prɔfi'tiə], *n.* Profiteur, *m.*—*v.i.* Faire des bénéfices excessifs. **profitless**, *a.* Sans profit, inutile. **profit-sharing**, *n.* Participation aux bénéfices, *f.*

profligacy ['prɔfligəsi], *n.* Dérèglement, *m.*, dissolution, *f.*, libertinage, *m.*; (*fig.*) prodigalité, *f.* **profligate**, *a.* Débauché, dissolu, libertin; (*fig.*) prodigue.—*n.* Libertin, mauvais sujet, *m.* **profligately**, *adv.* Sans mœurs, dissolument.

profound [prə'faund], *a.* Profond; approfondi. *In profound earnest*, très sérieusement. **profoundly**, *adv.* Profondément. **profundity** [-'fʌnditi], *n.* Profondeur, *f.*

profuse [prə'fjuːs], *a.* Prodigue, abondant, excessif (of things). **profusely**, *adv.* Profusément, à profusion; abondamment, excessivement. **profuseness** or **profusion** [-'fjuːʒən], *n.* Profusion, prodigalité, abondance, *f.* *In profusion*, à profusion.

prog [prɔg], *v.i.* Rôder çà et là à la recherche de vivres, gueuser, mendier. (*sch.*) *To be progged*, se faire pincer.—*n.* (*slang*) Vivres, *m.pl.*, victuaille, *f.*

progenitor [prou'dʒenitə], *n.* Aïeul, ancêtre, premier père, *m.* **progeniture**, *n.* Progéniture, *f.*

progeny ['prɔdʒəni], *n.* Race, postérité, famille, *f.*, descendants, *m.pl.*

prognathism ['prɔgnəθizm], *n.* Prognathisme, *m.* **prognathous**, *a.* Prognathe.

prognosis [prɔg'nousis], *n.* (*Med.*) Pronostic, *m.*

prognostic [prɔg'nɔstik], *a.* Pronostique.—*n.* Pronostic, *m.* **prognosticable**, *a.* Que l'on peut pronostiquer. **prognosticate**, *v.t.* Pronostiquer. **prognostication** [-'keiʃən], *n.* Pronostic, *m.* **prognosticator** [-'nɔstikeitə], *n.* Pronostiqueur, *m.*

programme ['prougræm], *n.* Programme, *m.* **programme-music**, *n.* Musique descriptive, *f.* **programme-seller**, *n.* Vendeuse de programmes, (*Theat.*) ouvreuse, *f.*

progress (1) ['prougres], *n.* Progrès, avancement, cours, *m.*; marche, *f.*; voyage (state journey), *m.* *In progress*, en cours; *to make progress*, faire des progrès; *to report progress*, (*Polit.*) faire un rapport à la Chambre sur l'état de la question, clore les débats; exposer l'état de l'affaire.

progress (2) [prə'gres], *v.i.* S'avancer, faire des progrès, avancer. *How is your work progressing?* où en êtes-vous de votre travail? *the business is progressing*, l'affaire marche.

progression [prou'greʃən], *n.* Progression, *f.* **progressist**, *n.* Progressiste, *m.* **progressive**, *a.* and *n.* Progressif; (*Polit.*) progressiste. **progressively**, *adv.* Progressivement. **progressiveness**, *n.* Marche progressive, *f.*

prohibit [prou'hibit], *v.t.* Prohiber, défendre, interdire (à). *Smoking prohibited*, défense de fumer; *to prohibit someone from doing something*, défendre à quelqu'un de faire quelque chose. **prohibition** [-'biʃən], *n.* Prohibition, défense, interdiction; (*Law*) défense de statuer, *f.*; (*Am.*) régime sec, *m.*, prohibition de l'alcool, *f.* *Writ of prohibition*, défense de statuer, *f.* **prohibitive** or **prohibitory**, *a.* De défense, d'interdiction; prohibitif (customs). *Prohibitive price*, prix exorbitant, *m.*

project (1) ['prɔdʒekt], *n.* Projet, dessein, *m.* **project** (2) [prə'dʒekt], *v.t.* Projeter.—*v.i.* Avancer, faire saillie, être en saillie; (*Arch.*) ressaurir.

projectile [prə'dʒektail], *n.* Projectile, *m.* **projecting**, *a.* Saillant, en saillie. **projection**, *n.* Projection, saillie, *f.*; (*Arch.*) ressaut, *m.* (*Cine.*) *Projection box* or *room*, cabine de projection, *f.* **projectionist**, *n.* (*Cine.*) (Opérateur) projectionniste, *m.* **projector**, *n.* Homme à projets, projeteur; (*Cine.*) appareil de projection, *m.* **projecture**, *n.* Projecture, *f.*

prolapsus [prou'læpsəs], *n.* (*Path.*) Prolapsus, *m.*; chute, *f.*; abaissement, *m.*

prolate ['prouleit], *a.* (*Geom.*) Allongé; (*colloq.*) très répandu.

prolegomena [proulə'gɔmənə], *n.pl.* Prolégomènes, *m.pl.*

proletarian [prouli'teəriən] or **proletary** ['proulətəri], *a.* and *n.* Prolétaire, *m.* **proletariat**, *n.* Prolétariat, *m.*

proliferate [prə'lifəreit], *v.t.*, *v.i.*　Proliférer.
proliferation [-'reiʃən], *n.*　Prolifération, *f.*
prolific [prə'lifik], *a.*　Prolifique; fécond, fertile. **prolificacy, prolificity** [prouli'fisiti] or **prolificness**, *n.*　Fécondité, fertilité, *f.*
prolifically, *adv.*　Avec fécondité, avec fertilité.
prolix [prou'liks], *a.*　Prolixe.
prolixity [prə'liksiti] or **prolixness**, *n.*　Prolixité, *f.*　**prolixly**, *adv.*　Avec prolixité, prolixement.
prolocutor [prou'lɔkjutə], *n.*　Président (d'une assemblée du clergé), *m.*　**prolocutorship**, *n.*　Présidence (d'une assemblée du clergé), *f.*
prologue ['proulɔg], *n.*　Prologue, *m.*
prolong [prə'lɔŋ], *v.t.*　Prolonger; retarder, différer (to delay).　*To be prolonged*, se prolonger. **prolongation** [prouloŋ'geiʃən], *n.*　Prolongement, *m.*; prolongation (of time etc.), *f.*
promenade [promə'nɑːd], *n.*　Promenade, (en grande toilette), *f.*; (*Theat.*) promenoir, *m.*; esplanade (at seaside), *f.*—*v.i.*　Se promener, se faire voir. **promenade-concert** or (*fam.*) **prom,** *n.*　Concert où l'auditoire peut circuler librement, *m.*　**promenade-deck,** *n.*　Pont-promenade, *m.*　**promenader,** *n.*　Promeneur, *m.*
Promethean [prə'miːθiən], *a.*　De Prométhée. **Prometheus**. Prométhée, *m.*
prominence ['prɔminəns] or **prominency**, *n.*　Proéminence; (*fig.*) prééminence, distinction, *f.*　*To bring into prominence*, faire ressortir, mettre en évidence. **prominent**, *a.*　Proéminent, saillant; prononcé, accentué (striking); (*fig.*) éminent, marquant, distingué.　*In a prominent position*, très en vue; *prominent eyes*, yeux à fleur de tête, *m.pl.*; *prominent features*, traits prononcés, *m.pl.* **prominently**, *adv.*　En saillie; d'une manière frappante.
promiscuity [prɔmis'kjuːiti] or **promiscuousness**, *n.*　Mélange confus, *m.*, promiscuité, confusion, *f.*
promiscuous [prə'miskjuəs], *a.*　Mêlé, confus, sans ordre. **promiscuously**, *adv.*　Confusément, pêle-mêle, indistinctement; en commun.
promise ['prɔmis], *n.*　Promesse; (*fig.*) espérance, *f.*　*Breach of promise*, violation de promesse de mariage, *f.*; *of great promise*, qui donne de grandes espérances; *to break one's promise*, manquer à sa promesse; *to keep one's promise*, tenir sa promesse; *to make a promise*, faire une promesse.—*v.t.*, *v.i.*　Promettre.　*I promise you!* je vous le promets! *the Promised Land*, la Terre promise; *the weather promises to be warm*, le temps promet d'être chaud. **promiser**, *n.*　Prometteur, *m.*, grand faiseur de promesses, *m.* **promising**, *a.*　Prometteur, qui promet; qui donne des espérances. **promisor**, *n.*　(*Law*) L'engagé, *m.* **promissory**, *a.*　Qui contient une promesse. *Promissory note*, billet à ordre, *m.*
promontory ['prɔməntəri], *n.*　Promontoire, *m.*
promote [prə'mout], *v.t.*　Servir, avancer; favoriser; promouvoir; encourager. *He was promoted to the rank of general*, il fut promu au grade de général; *to be promoted*, obtenir de l'avancement; *to promote a company*, lancer une société anonyme; (*fam.*) *to promote a product*, faire de la réclame pour un produit; *to promote someone's interests*, avancer les

intérêts de quelqu'un. **promoter,** *n.*　Promoteur, protecteur, instigateur; (*Comm.*) lanceur d'affaires, *m.*　**promotion** [-'mouʃən], *n.*　Promotion, *f.*, avancement, *m.*　*Promotion by seniority*, avancement à l'ancienneté, *m.*
prompt [prɔmpt], *v.t.*　Exciter, porter, pousser; inspirer, suggérer; (*Theat.*) souffler.—*a.*　Prompt, empressé; (*Comm.*) au comptant.
prompt-book, *n.*　Livre du souffleur, *m.*
prompter, *n.*　Souffleur, *m.*　*Prompter's box*, trou du souffleur, *m.*　**prompting,** *n.*　Excitation, suggestion, impulsion, instigation, *f.*
promptitude or **promptness,** *n.*　Promptitude, *f.*, empressement, *m.*　**promptly,** *adv.*　Promptement, avec empressement.
promulgate ['prɔmɔlgeit], *v.t.*　Promulguer; disséminer. **promulgation** [-'geiʃən], *n.*　Promulgation; dissémination, *f.*　**promulgator,** *n.*　Promulgateur; vulgarisateur, *m.*
prone [proun], *a.*　Penché, incliné; couché, étendu; (*fig.*) disposé, porté (à). **proneness,** *n.*　Disposition, inclination, *f.*, penchant, *m.*
prong [prɔŋ], *n.*　Fourchon, *m.*, dent, *f.*
pronged [prɔŋd], *a.*　À fourchons, à dents. *Three-pronged*, à trois fourchons.
pronominal [prə'nɔminl], *a.*　Pronominal. **pronominally,** *adv.*　Pronominalement.
pronoun ['prounaun], *n.*　Pronom, *m.*
pronounce [prə'nauns], *v.t.*　Prononcer; déclarer, annoncer, dire.—*v.i.*　Prononcer; se prononcer (sur etc.). **pronounceable,** *a.*　Prononçable. **pronounced,** *a.*　Prononcé, marqué. **pronouncement,** *n.*　Prononcement, *m.*, déclaration, *f.*　**pronouncing,** *a.*　De prononciation.—*f.*　Prononciation, *f.*
pronunciation [-nʌnsi'eiʃən], *n.*　Prononciation, *f.*, accent, *m.*
proof [pruːf], *n.*　Preuve; épreuve, *f.*　*As a proof*, en preuve; *burden of proof*, charge de la preuve, *f.*; *in proof of*, pour preuve de; *proof spirit*, esprit de preuve, *m.*; *the proof of the pudding is in the eating*, c'est à l'œuvre qu'on connaît l'artisan; *to come to the proof*, en venir à la preuve; *to give proof of*, faire preuve de; *to put to the proof*, mettre à l'épreuve.—*a.*　*Proof against*, résistant à, à l'épreuve de, à l'abri de, inaccessible à; *bullet-proof*, à l'épreuve des balles; *fool-proof*, simple comme bonjour; *waterproof*, imperméable à l'eau, imperméable.—*v.t.*　Imperméabiliser, rendre résistant.
proofless, *a.*　Sans preuve.
proof-reader, *n.*　(*Print.*) Correcteur, *m.*
proof-reading, *n.*　Correction des épreuves, *f.*
proof-sheet, *n.*　(*Print.*) Épreuve, *f.*
proof-stick, *n.*　Sonde, *f.*
prop [prɔp], *n.*　Étai, étançon; (*Hort.*) tuteur, échalas; (*Naut.*) accore; (*fig.*) appui, soutien, *m.*; (*Theat.*) (*fam.*) accessoire, *m.*—*v.t.*　Étayer; appuyer, soutenir; (*Naut.*) accorer; (*Hort.*) échalasser (une vigne, le houblon); ramer (les haricots).
propaganda [prɔpə'gændə], *n.*　Propagande, *f.*　**propagandism,** *n.*　Système de propagande, *m.* **propagandist,** *n.*　Propagandiste, *m.* or *f.*
propagate ['prɔpəgeit], *v.t.*　Propager; (*fig.*) étendre, répandre; créer, enfanter (to produce).—*v.i.*　Se propager. **propagation** [-'geiʃən], *n.*　Propagation, *f.*
propagator ['prɔpəgeitə], *n.*　Propagateur,

propel [prə'pel], *v.t.* Pousser en avant, faire marcher, mettre en mouvement, propulser; lancer (to cast). **propellant,** *n.* Propulseur, *m.* **propeller,** *n.* Propulseur, moteur, *m.*; hélice, *f.* **Screw-propeller,** hélice, *f.*, propulseur à hélice, *m.* **propeller-blade,** *n.* Aile d'hélice, *f.* **propeller-shaft,** *n.* Arbre de l'hélice; arbre de propulsion, *m.* **propelling,** *a.* Propulseur, moteur. *Propelling force,* force motrice, *f.*

propense [prə'pens], *a.* Enclin, porté (à). **propensity,** *n.* Penchant, *m.*, tendance, inclination, *f.*

proper ['prɔpə], *a.* Propre, particulier; convenable, à propos (fit); juste, exact (correct). *At the proper time,* au moment convenable; *he's a proper scoundrel,* c'est un fieffé coquin; *it is proper to,* il convient de; *proper name,* nom propre, *m.*; *proper sense,* sens propre, *m.*; *she is very proper,* elle est très comme il faut; *this is the proper way to do it,* voici comment il faut faire; *to deem it proper to,* juger convenable de; *when they think proper,* quand bon leur semble. **properly,** *adv.* Proprement, convenablement, comme il faut, comme il se doit, en bonne justice; à la rigueur (by rights). *He acted properly,* il a bien agi; *more properly speaking,* pour mieux dire; *properly so called,* proprement dit; *properly speaking,* à proprement parler.

propertied ['prɔpətid], *a.* Possédant.

property ['prɔpəti], *n.* Propriété, *f.*; bien, *m.*, biens, *m.pl.*; qualité, *f.*; (*Theat.,* *Cine.*) accessoire, *m.* *Literary property,* propriété littéraire; *lost property,* objets trouvés, *m.pl.*; *man of property,* homme qui a du bien, *m.*; *personal property,* biens meubles, effets mobiliers, *m.pl.*; *real property,* biens immeubles, *m.pl*; *these books are my property,* ces livres m'appartiennent; *to become public property,* tomber dans le domaine public.

property-man, *n.* Employé aux accessoires, accessoiriste, *m.*

property-tax, *n.* Impôt foncier, *m.*

prophecy ['prɔfəsi], *n.* Prophétie, *f.* **prophesy** [-sai], *v.t.* Prophétiser, prédire.—*v.i.* Prononcer des prophéties. **prophesying,** *n.* Prophétie, *f.*

prophet ['prɔfit], *n.* Prophète, *m.* *Prophet of evil,* prophète de malheur. *No man is a prophet in his own country,* nul n'est prophète en son pays. **prophetess,** *n.* Prophétesse, *f.* **prophetic** [-'fetik] or **prophetical,** *a.* Prophétique. **prophetically,** *adv.* Prophétiquement.

prophylactic [prɔfi'læktik], *a.* and *n.* Prophylactique, *m.* **prophylaxis,** *n.* Prophylaxie, *f.*

propinquity [prə'piŋkwiti], *n.* Proximité; parenté (of persons), *f.*

propitiable [prə'piʃiəbl], *a.* Que l'on peut rendre propice. **propitiate,** *v.t.* Rendre propice. **propitiation** [-'eiʃən], *n.* Propitiation, *f.* **propitiator** [-'piʃieitə], *n.* Propitiateur, *m.* **propitiatory,** *a.* and *n.* Propitiatoire, *m.*

propitious [prə'piʃəs], *a.* Propice, favorable. **propitiously,** *adv.* Favorablement, d'une manière propice. **propitiousness,** *n.* Nature propice, *f.*

proportion [prə'pɔ:ʃən], *n.* Proportion; partie; portion, *f.* *In proportion as,* à mesure que; *in*

proportion to, en proportion de, proportionné à; *out of proportion,* mal proportionné; *to be out of all proportion to,* ne pas correspondre du tout à; *to lose all sense of proportion,* perdre toute mesure.—*v.t.* Proportionner. **proportionable,** *a.* Qu'on peut proportionner; en proportion. **proportionably,** *adv.* Proportionnellement, en proportion. **proportional,** *a.* En proportion; proportionnel. (*Polit.*) *Proportional representation,* représentation proportionnelle, *f.* **proportionality,** *n.* Proportionnalité, *f.* **proportionally,** *adv.* Proportionnellement. **proportionate** [-neit], *v.t.* Proportionner.—*a.* [-nit] Proportionné. **proportionately,** *adv.* En proportion, proportionnellement. **proportionateness,** *n.* Proportionnalité, *f.* **proportionless,** *a.* Sans proportion.

proposal [prə'pouzl], *n.* Proposition; demande en mariage, *f.* **propose,** *v.t.* Proposer; offrir. *To propose a toast,* porter un toast.—*v.i.* Se proposer; faire une demande en mariage. *He proposed to her,* il demanda sa main; *to propose to oneself to,* se proposer de. **proposer,** *n.* Auteur d'une proposition, *m.* *Proposer of a member* (in club), parrain d'un candidat, *m.*

proposition [prɔpə'ziʃən], *n.* Proposition; affaire, *f.* **propositional,** *a.* De la proposition.

propound [prə'paund], *v.t.* Proposer, exposer, mettre en avant.

propraetor [prou'pri:tə], *n.* (*Rom. Hist.*) Propréteur, *m.*

proprietary [prə'praiətəri], *a.* De propriété, de propriétaire.—*n.* Actionnaires, *m.pl.* **proprietor,** *n.* Propriétaire, *m.* or *f.* **proprietorship,** *n.* Droit de propriété, *m.*; possession, *f.* **proprietress,** *n.* Propriétaire, maîtresse, *f.* **propriety,** *n.* Convenance, propriété, *f.*, convenances, *f.pl.*, bienséance, *f.* *To keep within the bounds of propriety,* garder les convenances; *to sin against the proprieties,* heurter les convenances.

props [prɔps], *n.pl.* (*fam.*) Accessoires, *m.pl.* *Props man,* accessoiriste, *m.*

propulsion [prə'pʌlʃən], *n.* Propulsion, *f.* *Jet propulsion,* propulsion à réaction, *f.* **propulsive,** *a.* Propulseur; propulsif.

propylaeum [proupi'li:əm], *n.* Propylée, *m.*

prorogation [prourə'geiʃən], *n.* Prorogation, *f.*

prorogue [prə'roug], *v.t.* Proroger.

prosaic [prə'zeiik], *a.* Prosaïque. **prosaically,** *adv.* Prosaïquement.

prosaism ['prouzeiizm] or **prosaicism** [-'zeiisizm], *n.* Prosaïsme, *m.* **prosaist,** *n.* Prosateur, *m.*

proscenium [prə'si:niəm], *n.* Proscenium, *m.*, avant-scène, *f.* *Proscenium arch,* manteau d'Arlequin, *m.*

proscribe [pro'skraib], *v.t.* Proscrire. **proscriber,** *n.* Proscripteur, *m.* **proscription** [-'skripʃən], *n.* Proscription, *f.* **proscriptive,** *a.* De proscription.

prose [prouz], *n.* Prose, *f.*, (*sch.*) thème, *m.*—*v.t.* Écrire en prose; disserter ennuyeusement. **prose-poem,** *n.* Poème en prose, *m.* **prose-writer,** *n.* Prosateur, *m.*

prosecutable ['prɔsikju:təbl], *a.* Poursuivable.

prosecute ['prɔsikju:t], *v.t.* Poursuivre; poursuivre en justice; revendiquer (claims etc.). *We intend to prosecute our claims,* nous avons

l'intention de revendiquer nos droits. **prosecution** [-'kju:ʃən], *n.* Poursuite, *f.*, poursuites, *f.pl.*, procès criminel, *m. Witness for the prosecution*, témoin à charge, *m.*
prosecutor ['prɔsikju:tə], *n.* Poursuivant, plaignant, *m. Public prosecutor*, procureur de la république, *m.* **prosecutrix**, *n.* Poursuivante, plaignante, *f.*
proselyte ['prɔsəlait], *n.* Prosélyte, *m.* or *f.*
proselytism ['prɔsəlitizm], *n.* Prosélytisme, *m.*
proselytize ['prɔsəlitaiz], *v.t.* Convertir.—*v.i.* Faire des prosélytes.
proser ['prouzə], *n.* Conteur ennuyeux, *m.*
prosily, *adv.* Prosaïquement, ennuyeusement, *m.* **prosiness**, *n.* Prosaïsme, *m.*; verbosité, *f.*
prosodical [prə'sɔdikl], *a.* Prosodique.
prosodist ['prɔsədist], *n.* Personne versée dans la prosodie, *f.*
prosody ['prɔsədi], *n.* Prosodie, *f.*
prosopopoeia [prɔsopə'pi:ə], *n.* Prosopopée, *f.*
prospect (1) ['prɔspekt], *n.* Vue, *f.*, coup d'œil, *m.*; perspective, *f.*, point de vue; (*fig.*) espoir, *m.*, espérance, *f.*, avenir, *m. To have fine prospects before one*, avoir un bel avenir devant soi.
prospect (2) [prə'spekt], *v.i.* Faire des recherches (for minerals etc.).—*v.t.* Prospecter.
prospecting, *n.* Prospection, *f.*, recherches, *f.pl.* **prospective** [-'pektiv], *a.* En perspective; à venir. *Prospective glass*, lunette d'approche, *f.*; *prospective husband*, futur mari, *m.* **prospectively**, *adv.* En perspective, pour l'avenir. **prospector**, *n.* Explorateur; chercheur d'or, orpailleur, *m.* **prospectus**, *n.* Prospectus, *m.*
prosper ['prɔspə], *v.i.* Prospérer, réussir.—*v.t.* Faire prospérer, faire réussir, favoriser. **prosperity** [-'periti], *n.* Prospérité, *f.*
prosperous ['prɔspərəs], *a.* Prospère; florissant (of things); (*fig.*) heureux; favorable. **prosperously**, *adv.* Heureusement. **prosperousness**, *n.* Prospérité, *f.*
prostate ['prɔsteit], *n.* (*Anat.*) Prostate, *f.* **prostatic** [-'tætik], *a.* Prostatique.
prosthesis ['prɔsθəsis], *n.* (*Gram.*) Prosthèse; (*Surg.*) prothèse, *f.*
prostitute ['prɔstitju:t], *a.* and *n.* Prostituée, *f.*—*v.t.* Prostituer. *To prostitute oneself*, se prostituer. **prostitution** [-'tju:ʃən], *n.* Prostitution, *f.*
prostrate (1) [prɔs'treit], *v.t.* Coucher, prosterner; (*fig.*) abattre, renverser. *To prostrate oneself before*, se prosterner devant.
prostrate (2) ['prɔstrit], *a.* Prosterné; (*fig.*) abattu. *To be utterly prostrate*, être dans l'anéantissement, être épuisé de fatigue. **prostration** [-'treiʃən], *n.* Prosternation, *f.*; (*fig.*) abattement, *m.*
prostyle ['proustail], *n.* and *a.* Prostyle, *m.*
prosy ['prouzi], *a.* Ennuyeux, fastidieux.
protagonist [prou'tægənist], *n.* Protagoniste, *m.*
protasis ['prɔtəsis], *n.* Protase, *f.*
Protean ['proutiən], *a.* De Protée; protéique.
protect [prə'tekt], *v.t.* Protéger; défendre; garantir, abriter (to shelter); sauvegarder (interests). **protection** [-'tekʃən], *n.* Protection, défense; garantie, *f.*, abri (shelter), *m.*, sauvegarde (safeguard), *f.*; (*Polit. Econ.*) protectionnisme, *m. To give due protection*

to, faire bon accueil à. **protectionism**, *n.* Protectionnisme, *m.* **protectionist**, *n.* and *a.* Protectionniste, *m.* **protective**, *a.* Protecteur. **protector**, *n.* Protecteur, *m.* **protectorate** or **protectorship**, *n.* Protectorat, *m.* **protectress**, *n.* Protectrice, *f.*
protégé [prɔtə'ʒei], *n.* Protégé, *m.*
protein ['prouti:n], *n.* Protéine, *f.* **proteinic** [-'inik], *a.* Protéique.
protest (1) ['proutest], *n.* Protestation, *f.*; (*Comm.*) protêt, *m. Ship's protest*, rapport de mer, *m.*; *to enter a protest against*, protester contre; *under protest*, sous réserve, à son corps défendant.
protest (2) [prə'test], *v.i.* Protester.—*v.t.* Protester; (*fig.*) faire protester; attester, affirmer.
Protestant ['prɔtistənt], *a.* and *n.* Protestant, *m.*, protestante, *f.* **Protestantism**, *n.* Protestantisme, *m.*
protestation [-'teiʃən], *n.* Protestation, *f.* **protester** [-'testə], *n.* Personne qui fait faire un protêt, *f.*
Proteus ['proutjus]. (*Myth.* and *Zool.*) Protée, *m.*
protista [prou'tistə], *n.* Protistes, *m.pl.*
protococcus [proutə'kɔkəs], *n.* Protocoque, *m.*
protocol ['proutəkɔl], *n.* Protocole, *m.*
protogine ['proutədʒin], *n.* Protogyne, *m.*
protomartyr [-'maːtə], *n.* Premier martyr, *m.*
proton ['proutɔn], *n.* Proton, *m.*
protonotary [-'noutəri], *n.* Protonotaire, *m.*
protoplasm ['proutəplæzm], *n.* Protoplasma, protoplasme, *m.* **protoplasmic** [-'plæzmik], *a.* Protoplasmique.
protoplast ['proutəplæst], *n.* Protoplaste, *m.*
prototype ['proutətaip], *n.* Prototype, *m.* **prototypic** [-'tipik], *a.* Prototypique.
protoxide [-'tɔksaid], *n.* Protoxyde, *m.*
protozoan [proutə'zouən], *n.* and *a.* Protozoaire, *m.*
protract [prə'trækt], *v.t.* Prolonger, traîner en longueur; différer (to defer); relever (to draw). **protractile**, *a.* Protracteur. **protraction** [-'trækʃən], *n.* Prolongation, *f.*; relevé, *m.* **protractor**, *n.* Rapporteur (instrument), *m.*
protrude [prə'tru:d], *v.t.* Pousser en avant, faire sortir.—*v.i.* S'avancer, faire saillie. **protruding**, *a.* En saillie, saillant. **protrusion** [-'tru:ʒən], *n.* Action de pousser en avant; saillie, *f.* **protrusive**, *a.* Qui pousse en avant, qui fait saillie.
protuberance [prə'tju:bərəns], *n.* Protubérance, *f.* **protuberant**, *a.* Protubérant.
proud [praud], *a.* Fier (de); orgueilleux, superbe; (*fig.*) noble, beau, grand; (*Path.*) fongueux, baveux. *As proud as a peacock*, fier comme Artaban; (*Path.*) *proud flesh*, chair baveuse, *f.*; *proud nail*, clou qui dépasse, *m.*; *to be proud of*, être fier de, s'enorgueillir de; *to do someone proud*, se mettre en frais pour quelqu'un, faire beaucoup d'honneur à quelqu'un. **proudly**, *adv.* Fièrement, orgueilleusement.
provable ['pru:vəbl], *a.* Qui peut se prouver, prouvable, démontrable.
prove [pru:v], *v.t.* Prouver, démontrer; mettre à l'épreuve, éprouver (to test); vérifier (a will etc.), homologuer. *To prove a sum*, vérifier un calcul; *to prove oneself*, faire ses preuves; *to prove oneself incompetent*, se montrer incapable.—*v.i.* Se montrer, se trouver, se

révéler. *As it proved,* comme l'expérience le démontra; *the change of king proved no remedy,* le changement de roi ne fut nullement un remède. **proved,** *a.* Prouvé, démontré, reconnu. *Of proved capacity,* d'une habileté reconnue. ***proven,** a.* Prouvé, démontré. *(Law) Not proven,* culpabilité non avérée.

Provençal [prɔvã:'sal], *a.* Provençal; de Provence.

provender ['prɔvəndə], *n.* Fourrage, *m.,* nourriture (for animals), *f.—v.t.* Donner du fourrage à.

prover ['pru:və], *n. (Print.)* Tireur d'épreuves, *m. Linen-prover,* compte-fils, *m.*

proverb ['prɔvə:b], *n.* Proverbe, *m.*

proverbial [prə'və:biəl], *a.* Proverbial, qui fait proverbe. **proverbially,** *adv.* Proverbialement.

provide [prə'vaid], *v.t.* Pourvoir, fournir, munir; préparer (à); stipuler. *To be provided for,* être pourvu; *to provide oneself with,* se pourvoir de.—*v.i.* Pourvoir. *To provide against,* se pourvoir contre, prendre des mesures contre; *to provide for,* pourvoir à, subvenir à; *to provide for oneself,* se suffire. **provided,** *a.* Pourvu.—*conj. Provided that,* pourvu que (with *subj.*).

providence ['prɔvidəns], *n.* Providence; prévoyance (foresight), *f.* **provident,** *a.* Prévoyant; économe. *Provident society,* société de secours mutuels, *f.* **providential** [-'denʃəl], *a.* Providentiel, de la providence. **providentially,** *adv.* D'une manière providentielle, providentiellement. **providently,** *adv.* Avec prévoyance.

provider [prə'vaidə], *n.* Pourvoyeur, fournisseur, *m.*

province ['prɔvins], *n.* Province, *f.; (fig.)* département, ressort, *m. It is not in my province,* ce n'est pas de ma compétence *or* de mon ressort, *(fam.)* ce n'est pas mon rayon. **provincial** [-'vinʃl], *a.* Provincial, de province.—*n.* Provincial, *m.,* -iale, *f.* **provincialism,** *n.* Provincialisme, *m.* **provinciality** [-i'æliti], *n.* Provincialité, *f.* **provincially,** *adv.* Provincialement.

proving ['pru:viŋ], *n.* Vérification, mise à l'épreuve, épreuve, *f.*

provision [prə'viʒən], *n.* Action de pourvoir; prise des dispositions nécessaires; stipulation; *(Law)* disposition (of a Bill etc.), *f.; (pl.)* vivres, comestibles, *m.pl.; (Mil.)* munitions de bouche, *f.pl. To lay in a provision of,* faire provision de; *to make a provision for,* pourvoir, faire une pension à; *to make provision for,* prendre des précautions pour.—*v.t.* Approvisionner.

provisional or **provisionary,** *a.* Provisoire; *(Law)* provisionnel. **provisionally,** *adv.* Provisoirement, par provision; *(Law)* provisionnellement.

provision-dealer, *n.* Marchand de comestibles, *m.* **provision-warehouse,** *n.* Magasin de comestibles, *m.*

proviso [prə'vaizou], *n.* Condition, clause conditionnelle, *f. With the proviso that,* à condition que.

provisorily [prə'vaizərili], *adv.* Provisoirement. **provisory,** *a.* Provisoire, conditionnel.

provocation [prɔvə'keiʃən], *n.* Provocation, *f.*

He acted under provocation, il a agi sous le coup de la colère. **provocative** [-'vɔkətiv], *a.* Qui provoque; provocant, provocateur.—*n.* Provocation, *f.,* aiguillon, stimulant, *m.*

provoke [prə'vouk], *v.t.* Provoquer; inciter; agacer, fâcher, irriter, contrarier. *To provoke laughter,* faire rire. **provoker,** *n.* Provocateur, *m.* **provoking,** *a.* Provocant; irritant, contrariant, ennuyeux, fâcheux, agaçant. **provokingly,** *adv.* D'une manière provocante *or* contrariante.

provost ['prɔvəst], *n.* Prévôt; *(Univ.)* principal; *(Sc.)* maire, *m.* **provost-marshal** [prɔ'vou-], *n.* Grand prévôt. *Assistant provost-marshal,* prévôt, *m.* **provost-sergeant,** *n.* Sergent de police militaire, *m.*

provostship ['prɔvəstʃip], *n.* Prévôté, *f.; (Univ.)* principalat, *m.; (Sc.)* mairie, *f.*

prow [prau], *n.* Proue, *f.*

prowess ['prauis], *n.* Bravoure, valeur, prouesse, *f.;* exploit, *m.*

prowl [praul], *n.* Action de rôder, *f. To be on the prowl,* être en train de rôder.—*v.i.* Rôder. *To prowl about,* rôder çà et là; *to prowl about the wood,* rôder dans la forêt; *to prowl about town,* flâner par la ville. **prowler,** *n.* Rôdeur, *m.*

proximate ['prɔksimit], *a.* Proche, immédiat. **proximately,** *adv.* Immédiatement. **proximity** [-'simiti], *n.* Proximité, *f.* **proximo,** *adv.* Du mois prochain.

proxy ['prɔksi], *n.* Mandataire, délégué, *m.;* procuration, délégation (thing), *f. By proxy,* par procuration.

prude [pru:d], *n.* Prude, mijaurée, *f.*

prudence ['pru:dəns], *n.* Prudence, *f.* **prudent,** *a.* Prudent, sage. *Prudent marriage,* mariage de convenance *or* de raison, *m.* **prudential** [-'denʃəl], *a.* De prudence, dicté par la prudence. **prudentials,** *n.pl.* Maximes de sagesse; considérations de prudence, *f.pl.* **prudently,** *adv.* Prudemment, sagement.

prudery ['pru:dəri], *n.* Pruderie, *f.* **prudish,** *a.* Prude, de prude. **prudishly,** *adv.* Avec pruderie.

prune (1) [pru:n], *n.* Pruneau, *m.*

prune (2) [pru:n], *v.t.* Élaguer, tailler, émonder; rogner.

prunella [pru'nelə], *n.* Prunelle, *f.*

pruner ['pru:nə], *n.* Élagueur, émondeur, *m.*

pruning ['pru:niŋ], *n.* Taille, *f.,* élagage, *m.* **pruning-hook,** *n.* Serpe, *f.* **pruning-knife,** *n.* Serpette, *f.* **pruning-shears,** *n.pl.* Sécateur, *m.,* cisailles, *f.pl.*

prurience ['pruəriəns] or **pruriency,** *n.* Démangeaison, *f.,* prurit, *m.; (fig.)* pensées lascives, *f.pl.* **prurient,** *a.* Qui démange; *(fig.)* aux pensées lascives. **pruriginous** [pruə'ridʒinəs], *a.* Prurigineux, *m.* **pruritus** [-'raitəs], *n.* Prurit, *m.*

Prussia ['prʌʃə]. La Prusse, *f.* **Prussian,** *a.* Prussien; de Prusse. *Prussian blue,* bleu de Prusse, *m.—n.* Prussien, *m.,* -ienne, *f.* **Prussianize,** *v.t.* Prussianiser.

prussic ['prʌsik], *a.* Prussique.

pry [prai], *v.i.* Fureter; fouiller (dans). *To pry about,* fourrer le nez partout; *to pry into,* chercher à voir dans, se mêler de.—*v.t.* Soulever avec un levier.—*n.* Regard scrutateur *or* regard indiscret, *m. Pry(-bar),* levier, *m. Paul Pry,* curieux indiscret, *m.*

prying, *a.* Scrutateur, curieux.—*n.* Curiosité, *f.* **pryingly,** *adv.* Curieusement.

prytaneum [pritə'ni:əm], *n.* Prytanée, *m.*

psalm [sɑ:m], *n.* Psaume, *m.* **psalm-book,** *n.* Livre de psaumes, psautier, *m.* **psalm-singing,** *n.* Psalmodie, *f.*

psalmist, *n.* Psalmiste, *m.* **psalmodize,** *v.i.* Psalmodier. **psalmody,** *n.* Psalmodie, *f.*

psalter ['sɔ:ltə], *n.* Psautier, *m.*

psaltery ['sɔ:ltəri], *n.* Psaltérion, *m.*

pseudocarp ['sju:dokɑ:p], *n.* (*Bot.*) Pseudocarpe, *m.*

pseudonym ['sju:dənim], *n.* Pseudonyme, *m.*

pseudonymous [sju:'dɔniməs], *a.* Pseudonyme.

pshaw! [pʃɔ:], *int.* Bah! Fi donc!

psittacism [(p)'sitəsizm], *n.* Psittacisme, *m.*

psittacosis [(p)sitə'kousis], *n.* Psittacose, *f.*

psora [(p)'sɔ:rə], *n.* Psore, psora, *f.*

psoric ['sɔrik], *a.* Psorique.

Psyche ['saiki]. Psyché, *f.*

psyche ['saiki], *n.* Psyché, *f.*

psychiatric [saiki'ætrik], *a.* Psychiatrique.

psychiatrist [sai'kaiətrist], *n.* Psychiatre, *m.*

psychiatry [sai'kaiətri], *n.* Psychiatrie, *f.*

psychic(al) ['saikik(l)], *a.* Psychique.

psycho-analyse ['saikou'ænəlaiz], *v.t.* Psychanalyser. **psycho-analysis** [-ə'næləsis], *n.* Psychanalyse, *f.* **psycho-analyst** [-'ænəlist], *n.* Psychanalyste, *m.* or *f.*

psychological [saikə'lɔdʒikl], *a.* Psychologique. **psychologist** [-'kɔlədʒist], *n.* Psychologiste, psychologue, *m.*

psychology [sai'kɔlədʒi], *n.* Psychologie, *f.* **psychometry** [-'kɔmətri], *n.* Psychométrie, *f.* **psychopath** ['saikopæθ], *n.* Psychopathe, *m.* or *f.* **psychopathy** [-'kɔpəθi], *n.* Psychopathie, *f.* **psychophysical** [-o'fizikl], *a.* Psychophysique. **psychophysics,** *n.pl.* Psychophysique, *f.*

psychosis [sai'kousis], *n.* Psychose, *f.* **psychotherapy** [saiko'θerəpi], *n.* Psychothérapie, *f.*

ptarmigan ['tɑ:migən], *n.* Lagopède, *m.*

pterodactyl [terou'dæktil], *n.* Ptérodactyle, *m.*

pterosaur ['terousɔ:], *n.* Ptérosaurien, *m.*

ptisan [ti'zæn *or* 'tizən], *n.* Tisane, *f.*

Ptolemaic [tɔlə'meiik], *a.* De Ptolémée.

Ptolemy ['tɔləmi]. Ptolémée, *m.*

ptomaine ['toumein *or* tə'mein], *n.* Ptomaïne, *f.* *Ptomaine poisoning,* intoxication alimentaire, *f.*

ptyalin ['taiəlin], *n.* Ptyaline, *f.* **ptyalism,** *n.* Ptyalisme, *m.*

pub [pʌb], *n.* (*pop.*) Bistro(t), *m.* **pub-crawl,** *v.i.* (*pop.*) Courir les bistro(t)s, godailler.—*n.* Tournée des bistro(t)s, *f.*

puberal ['pju:bərəl], *a.* Pubère.

puberty ['pju:bəti], *n.* Puberté, *f.* **pubescence** [-'besəns], *n.* Pubescence, *f.* **pubescent,** *a.* Pubescent.

pubic ['pju:bik], *a.* Pubien.

public ['pʌblik], *a.* Public, *m.*, publique, *f.* *At the public expense,* aux frais du contribuable; *in the public eye,* très en vue; *public accounts,* budget, *m.*; *public holiday,* fête légale, *f.*; *public spirit,* civisme, *m.*—*n.* Le public, *m.* *In public,* en public, publiquement; *the general public,* le grand public. **public-house,** *n.* Café, *m.*, brasserie, *f.* **public-spirited,** *a.* Dévoué au bien public.

publican, *n.* Cafetier, patron de bistro(t); (*Bibl.*) publicain, *m.*

publication [-'keiʃən], *n.* Publication, *f.*

publicist ['pʌblisist], *n.* Publiciste; publicitaire, *m.*

publicity [pʌb'lisiti], *n.* Publicité; réclame, *f.* *Publicity agent,* agent de publicité, *m.*; (*Cine.*) *publicity film,* film publicitaire, *m.* **publicize,** *v.t.* Faire connaître au public. **publicly,** *adv.* Publiquement; en public.

publish ['pʌbliʃ], *v.t.* Publier; éditer. *Just published,* vient de paraître; (*fig.*) *to publish something abroad,* mettre quelque chose au jour. **publisher,** *n.* Éditeur, *m.* *Bookseller and publisher,* libraire-éditeur, *m.* **publishing,** *n.* Publication (of book); édition (trade), *f.* *Publishing house,* maison d'édition, *f.*

puce [pju:s] or **puce-coloured,** *a.* Puce.

puck [pʌk], *n.* Lutin, *m.*; (*spt.*) palet de hockey (sur glace), *m.*

pucker ['pʌkə], *v.t.* Rider, plisser; (*Dress.*) faire goder.—*v.i.* Goder.—*n.* Ride; (*Dress.*) poche, *f.*; mauvais pli, *m.* **puckering,** *n.* Froncement, *m.*

puckish ['pʌkiʃ], *a.* Malicieux; de lutin.

puddening ['pudəniŋ], *n.* (*Naut.*) Bourrelet, *m.*

pudding ['pudiŋ], *n.* Pudding, pouding; (*fam.*) entremets (sweet), *m.* *Black pudding,* boudin (noir), *m.* **pudding-basin,** *n.* Moule à poudings, *m.* **pudding-face,** *n.* (*fam.*) Visage empâté, *m.* **pudding-pie,** *n.* Pâté, *m.* **pudding-sleeve,** *n.* Manche bouffante, *f.* **pudding-stone,** *n.* Poudingue, *m.*

puddle [pʌdl], *n.* Flaque (d'eau), mare, *f.*; corroi, *m.*—*v.t.* Troubler, rendre bourbeux; (*Metal.*) puddler, corroyer (mortar), remblayer (a wall). *To puddle about,* patauger. **puddling,** *n.* (*Metal.*) Puddlage, *m.* **puddling-furnace,** *n.* Four à puddler, *m.* **puddly,** *a.* Bourbeux, trouble, boueux.

pudgy ['pʌdʒi], *a.* Boulot.

pudicity [pju'disiti], *n.* Pudicité, *f.*

puerile ['pjuərail], *a.* Puéril. **puerilely,** *adv.* Puérilement. **puerility** [-'riliti], *n.* Puérilité, *f.*

puerperal [pju'ə:pərəl], *a.* Puerpéral.

puff [pʌf], *n.* Souffle (of breath), *m.*; bouffée (of wind, smoke, etc.), *f.*; feuilleté (pastry), *m.*; houppe à poudrer (for powdering the nose or hair), *f.*; bouillon (on dresses), puff, *m.*, réclame tapageuse, *f.*—*v.i.* Souffler, boursoufler, bouffir, bouffer, se gonfler; haleter. *To puff and blow like a grampus,* souffler comme un phoque; *to puff at one's pipe,* tirer sur sa pipe.—*v.t.* Souffler, bouffir (to swell), gonfler; (*fig.*) faire mousser (to praise). *To be puffed up with,* être bouffi *or* gonflé de; *to puff up,* enfler, bouffir.

puff-adder, *n.* Vipère clotho, *f.* **puff-ball,** *n.* Vesse-de-loup, *f.* **puff-paste,** *n.* Pâte feuilletée, *f.* **puff-puff,** *n.* (*fam.*) Teuf-teuf, *m.*; locomotive à vapeur, *f.*

puffer, *n.* Personne *or* chose qui souffle, *f.*; faiseur de réclames, *m.* **puffery,** *n.* Puffisme, *m.*

puffin ['pʌfin], *n.* (*Orn.*) Macareux, *m.*

puffiness ['pʌfinis], *n.* Boursouflure, enflure, *f.* **puffing,** *n.* Action de souffler; (*fig.*) réclame, *f.* **puffingly,** *adv.* En haletant; avec enflure; à coups de grosse réclame.

puffy, *a.* Bouffi, gonflé.

pug (1) [pʌg], *n.* Carlin (dog), *m.*; (engine) coucou, *m.* **pug-nose**, *n.* Nez épaté, *m.* **pug-nosed**, *a.* Au nez épaté, camus.

pug (2) [pʌg], *v.t.* Broyer (mortar etc.); hourder (a wall etc.). **pug-mill**, *n.* Broyeur, pétrin (for brick-making), *m.*

pugging ['pʌgiŋ], *n.* Hourdage, *m.*

pugh! [POOH].

pugilism ['pju:dʒilizm], *n.* Pugilat, *m.*, boxe, *f.* **pugilist**, *n.* Boxeur, pugiliste, *m.* **pugilistic** [-'listik], *a.* De pugilat.

pugnacious [pʌg'neiʃəs], *a.* Querelleur; batailleur. **pugnaciously**, *adv.* D'un air batailleur. **pugnaciousness** or **pugnacity** [-'næsiti], *n.* Humeur batailleuse, pugnacité, *f.*

puisne ['pju:ni], *a.* Inférieur; cadet. *Puisne judge*, juge subalterne, *m.—n.* Conseiller, *m.*

puke [pju:k], *v.i.* Vomir.—*n.* Vomissement; vomitif, émétique, *m.*

pukka ['pʌkə], *a.* (*fam.*) Vrai, parfait, complet.

pule [pju:l], *v.i.* Piauler. **puling**, *n.* Cri; piaulement, *m.* **pulingly**, *adv.* En piaulant.

pull [pul], *v.t.* Tirer; arracher; presser (the trigger). *To pull a long face*, avoir le visage allongé; *to pull aside*, tirer de côté; *to pull away*, arracher; *to pull a wry face*, faire la grimace; *to pull back*, faire reculer, tirer en arrière; *to pull down*, faire tomber, abattre, démolir, défaire (of illness), abaisser (to abase); *to pull in*, faire entrer, rentrer; *to pull off*, arracher, enlever, ôter (one's clothes); tirer (one's boots); (*colloq.*) remporter, réussir à faire, venir à bout de; *to pull oneself together*, se ressaisir; *to pull open*, ouvrir; *to pull out*, tirer, arracher, faire sortir; *to pull round*, ranimer, guérir; *to pull through*, tirer d'embarras; *to pull to pieces*, mettre en pièces; *to pull up*, tirer en haut, hisser, monter, arracher, déraciner, arrêter (a horse).—*v.i.* Tirer; ramer, nager (to row). *To pull away*, tirer ferme, souquer (at the oars); *to pull in*, s'arrêter, entrer en gare (of trains); *to pull round*, se remettre, se ranimer; *to pull through*, réussir, guérir, s'en tirer; *to pull together*, s'accorder bien, s'entendre; *to pull up*, s'arrêter.—*n.* Action de tirer, traction, *f.*; coup (d'aviron), effort, *m.*; secousse, *f.*; (*fig.*) avantage, *m.*; (*Print.*) impression, *f.*; (*Golf etc.*) coup tiré, *m. Hard pull*, rude effort, *m.* **pull-through**, *n.* Ficelle de nettoyage (for rifles), *f.*

puller, *n.* Tireur; arracheur, *m.*

pullet ['pulit], *n.* Poulette, *f. Fat pullet*, poularde, *f.*

pulley ['puli], *n.* Poulie, *f.* **pulley-block**, *n.* Moufle, *f.*

pullman-car ['pulmən'ka:], *n.* Voiture Pullman, *f.*

pullover ['puluvə], *n.* Pull-over, *m.*

pullulate ['pʌljuleit], *v.i.* Germer; pulluler.

pullulation [-'leiʃən], *n.* Germination; pullulation, *f.*

pulmonary ['pʌlmənəri], *a.* Pulmonaire.

pulmonic [-'mɔnik], *a.* Pulmonique.— *n.* Phtisique, pulmonique.

pulp [pʌlp], *n.* Pulpe; pâte (paper), *f.—v.t.* Réduire en pâte. **pulpify**, *v.t.* Pulper. **pulpiness**, *n.* Nature pulpeuse, *f.* **pulping**, *n.* Pulpation, *f.*

pulpit ['pulpit], *n.* Chaire, *f. Pulpit oratory*, éloquence de la chaire, *f.*

pulpous ['pʌlpəs] or **pulpy**, *a.* Pulpeux.

pulsate [pʌl'seit], *v.i.* Battre; palpiter. **pulsation** [-'seiʃən], *n.* Pulsation, *f.*

pulsative ['pʌlsətiv], *a.* Pulsatif. **pulsatory**, *a.* Pulsatoire.

pulse (1) [pʌls], *n.* Pouls, *m.*; pulsation, *f. High pulse*, pouls élevé; *irregular pulse*, pouls irrégulier; *quick pulse*, pouls vif; *slow pulse*, pouls lent; *to feel someone's pulse*, tâter le pouls à quelqu'un, (*fig.*) sonder quelqu'un sur une affaire.—*v.i.* [PULSATE]. **pulsometer** [-'sɔmitə], *n.* Pulsomètre, *m.*

pulse (2) [pʌls], *n.* Plantes légumineuses, *f.pl.*, légumes à gousse, *m.pl.*

pulverizable ['pʌlvəraizəbl], *a.* Pulvérisable. **pulverization** [-'zeiʃən], *n.* Pulvérisation, *f.*

pulverize ['pʌlvəraiz], *v.t.* Pulvériser, réduire en poudre.

pulverulence [pʌl'verjuləns], *n.* Pulvérulence, *f.* **pulverulent**, *a.* Pulvérulent.

puma ['pju:mə], *n.* Puma, couguar, *m.*

pumice ['pʌmis], *n.* Pierre ponce, *f.—v.t.* Poncer.

pumiceous [pju'miʃəs], *a.* Ponceux.

pummel [POMMEL].

pump [pʌmp], *n.* Pompe, *f.*; escarpin (shoe), *m. Air-pump*, machine pneumatique, *f.*; *chain-pump*, noria, pompe à chapelet, *f.*; *fire-pump*, pompe à incendie, *f.*; *lift and force pump*, pompe aspirante et foulante, *f.*; *petrol pump*, pompe à essence (in engine), *f.*; poste d'essence, *m.*; *suction-pump*, pompe aspirante, *f.*; *to prime the pump*, amorcer la pompe.— *v.t.* Pomper; (*fig.*) sonder, tirer les vers du nez à (a person). *To pump out*, pomper, épuiser; *to pump up*, gonfler (a tyre).—*v.i.* Pomper.

pump-barrel, *n.* Corps de pompe, *m.* **pump-brake**, *n.* Brimbale de pompe, *f.* **pump-gear**, *n.* Garniture de pompe, *f.* **pump-rod**, *n.* Tige de pompe, *f.* **pump-room**, *n.* Buvette, *f.* **pump-water**, *n.* Eau de pompe, *f.*

pumping-engine, *n.* Machine d'épuisement, *f.*

pumpkin ['pʌmpkin], *n.* Citrouille, courge, *f.*, potiron, *m.*

pun [pʌn], *n.* Calembour, jeu de mots, *m.—v.i.* Faire des calembours.—*v.t.* Damer, piler.

Punch [pʌntʃ]. Polichinelle, *m. Pleased as Punch*, fier comme Artaban; *Punch and Judy show*, guignol, *m.*

punch [pʌntʃ], *n.* Emporte-pièce; (*Print.*) poinçon; punch (beverage); coup de poing (blow); courtaud (short man); cheval ramassé (horse), *m.—v.t.* Percer, poinçonner; donner un coup de poing à (to hit). *To punch out*, enlever à l'emporte-pièce.

punch-bowl, *n.* Bol à punch, *m.*

puncheon ['pʌntʃən], *n.* Poinçon, *m.*, pièce (de vin), *f.*

puncher ['pʌntʃə], *n.* Emporte-pièce; poinçonneur, *m. Cow-puncher*, conducteur de bestiaux, cowboy, *m.*

Punchinello [pʌntʃi'nelou]. Polichinelle, *m.*

punch(ing)-ball ['pʌntʃ(iŋ)bɔ:l], *n.* Punching-ball, *m.*

punctate ['pʌŋkteit], *a.* Pointillé. **punctiform**, *a.* En forme de pointe.

punctilio [pʌŋk'tiliou], *n.* Exactitude scrupuleuse, *f.*, point d'étiquette, *m. To stand upon punctilios*, être pointilleux. **punctilious**, *a.*

Pointilleux, qui tient aux formes *or* à l'étiquette. **punctiliously,** *adv.* D'une manière pointilleuse. **punctiliousness,** *n.* Exactitude scrupuleuse, pointillerie, *f.*

punctual ['pʌŋktjuəl], *a.* Ponctuel, exact. *To be punctual to time,* être exact à l'heure. **punctuality** [-'æliti], *n.* Ponctualité, exactitude, *f.* **punctually,** *adv.* Ponctuellement, exactement.

punctuate ['pʌŋktjueit], *v.t.* Ponctuer. **punctuation** [-'eiʃən], *n.* Ponctuation, *f.*

puncture ['pʌŋktʃə], *n.* Piqûre; (*Surg.*) ponction; crevaison (of a tyre), *f.—v.t.* Piquer, faire une piqûre à; crever (a tyre). *—v.i.* Crever, avoir une crevaison.

pundit ['pʌndit], *n.* Pandit, *m.*; (*pl.*) (*colloq.*) les pontifes, *m.pl.*

pungency ['pʌndʒənsi], *n.* Âcreté; aigreur, *f.*; piquant, mordant (of style etc.), *m.* **pungent,** *a.* Âcre; piquant, mordant. **pungently,** *adv.* Avec causticité; d'une manière piquante.

puniness ['pju:ninis], *n.* Petitesse, nature chétive, *f.*

punish ['pʌniʃ], *v.t.* Punir, corriger; malmener. **punishable,** *a.* Punissable; (*Law*) délictueux. **punisher,** *n.* Personne qui punit, *f.*, punisseur, correcteur, *m.* **punishing,** *a.* Épuisant. **punishment,** *n.* Punition; peine, *f.*, châtiment, supplice, *m. Capital punishment,* peine capitale, *f.*

punitive ['pju:nitiv], *a.* Punitif, *m.*, punitive, *f.*

punk [pʌŋk], *n.* Bois pourri; amadou, *m.*; (*pop.*) sottises, *f.pl.—a.* (*pop.*) Mauvais, moche.

punner ['pʌnə], *n.* Hie, demoiselle, dame, *f.*

punnet ['pʌnit], *n.* Maniveau, *m.*

punster ['pʌnstə], *n.* Faiseur de calembours, *m.*

punt [pʌnt], *n.* Bachot (mû à la perche; fond de bouteille; (*Ftb.*) coup de volée, *m.—v.i.* Conduire un bachot (à la perche); ponter (at cards); parier; (*Ftb.*) donner un coup de pied de volée. **punt-gun,** *n.* Canardière, *f.* **punt-pole,** *n.* Gaffe, perche, *f.*

punter, *n.* Ponte (at cards); parieur (at races); bachoteur, canotier (boatman), *m.*

puny ['pju:ni], *a.* Petit, chétif.

pup [pʌp], *n.* Petit chien, petit, *m.*; (*pej.*) freluquet, fat, *m. In pup,* pleine; (*colloq.*) *to sell someone a pup,* tromper, filouter quelqu'un.—*v.i.* Mettre bas.

pupa ['pju:pə], *n.* (*pl.* **pupae**) Nymphe, *f.*

pupil ['pju:pil], *n.* Élève, *m.* or *f.*; (*Law*) pupille *m.* or *f.*; pupille (of the eye), *f.* **pupilage,** *n.* État d'élève, *m.*; (*Law*) pupillarité, minorité, *f.* **pupilary,** *a.* Pupillaire. **pupil-teacher,** *n.* Moniteur, *m.*

puppet ['pʌpi^], *n.* Marionnette, *f. Glove puppet,* marionnette à gaine, *f.*; *puppet government,* gouvernement fantoche, *m.* **puppet-show,** *n.* Marionnettes, *f.pl.*, spectacle de marionnettes, *m.*

puppy ['pʌpi], *n.* Petit chien; (*fig.*) fat, freluquet, *m. Puppy love,* les premières amours, *f.pl.* **puppyism,** *n.* Fatuité, *f.*

pur [PURR].

purblind ['pə:blaind], *a.* Myope, presque aveugle. **purblindly,** *adv.* À l'aveuglette. **purblindness,** *n.* Myopie, *f.*

purchasable ['pə:tʃisəbl], *a.* Achetable.

purchase ['pə:tʃis], *n.* Achat, *m.*, acquisition,

emplette; (*Mech.*) prise, *f.*; point d'appui, *m.* (*Naut.*) palan, *m.*, caliorne, *f.*; cartahu, *m. To make purchases,* faire des emplettes.—*v.t.* Acheter, acquérir.

purchase-block, *n.* Poulie de caliorne, *f.*

purchase-deed, *n.* Contrat d'achat, *m.*

purchase-money, *n.* Prix d'achat, *m.*

purchaser, *n.* Acquéreur, acheteur, *m.*

purchasing, *n.* Achat, *m. Purchasing power,* pouvoir d'achat, *m.*

pure ['pju:ə], *a.* Pur. **pure-bred,** *a.* De race. **pure-minded,** *a.* À l'esprit pur.

purely, *adv.* Purement. **pureness,** *n.* Pureté, *f.*

purgation [pə:'geiʃən], *n.* Purgation, *f.* **purgative** ['pə:gətiv], *a. and n.* Purgatif, *m.*

purgatorial [pə:gə'tɔ:riəl], *a.* Du purgatoire. **Purgatory** ['pə:gətəri], *n.* Purgatoire, *m.* **purgatory,** *a.* Qui purifie, expiatoire.

purge [pə:dʒ], *v.t.* Purger; purifier, épurer.—*n.* Purgation, purge, *f.*; (*Polit.*) nettoyage, *m.*, épuration, *f.* **purger,** *n.* Purificateur, *m.* **purging,** *n.* Purgation; épuration, *f.*

purification [pjuərifi'keiʃən], *n.* Purification; épuration, *f.*

purificative ['pjuərifikeitiv] or **purificatory,** *a.* Purificatoire. **purifier,** *n.* Purificateur, *m.* **purify,** *v.t.* Purifier.—*v.i.* Se purifier. **purifying,** *a.* Purifiant.

purism ['pjuərizm], *n.* Purisme, *m.* **purist,** *n.* Puriste, *m.* or *f.*

Puritan ['pjuəritən], *n.* Puritain, *m.*, -aine, *f.* **puritan,** *a.* Puritain, *m.*, puritaine, *f.* **puritanical** [-'tænikl], *a.* De puritain, puritain. **puritanically,** *adv.* Puritainement. **Puritanism,** *n.* Puritanisme, *m.*

purity ['pjuəriti], *n.* Pureté, *f.*

purl [pə:l], *v.i.* Murmurer, gazouiller.—*v.t.* Faire des mailles à l'envers; engrêler (lace). —*n.* Engrêlure (of lace); bière mêlée de genièvre (hot beverage), *f.*; doux murmure; gazouillement, *m.*; (*colloq.*) (or **purler**), chute la tête la première, *f.*

purlieu ['pə:lju:], *n.* Alentours, environs, *m.pl.*

purlin ['pə:lin], *n.* (*Carp.*) Panne, *f.*

purling ['pə:lin], *a.* Murmurant.—*n.* Murmure, gazouillement, *m.*

purloin [pə:'lɔin], *v.t.* Soustraire, dérober, voler. **purloiner,** *n.* Voleur, *m.*, voleuse, *f.* **purloining,** *n.* Soustraction, *f.*, détournement, vol, *m.*

purple ['pə:pl], *a.* Mauve; pourpre; (*Path.*) pourpré. *Purple passage* or *patch,* morceau de bravoure, *m.—n.* Pourpre (colour), mauve, *m.*; pourpre (dye etc.), *f.—v.t.* Teindre en pourpre, empourprer, rougir. **purples,** *n.pl.* Fièvre pourprée, *f.* **purplish,** *a.* Purpurin.

purport (1) ['pə:pət], *n.* Sens, *m.*, teneur, portée, *f.*

purport (2) [pə:'pɔ:t], *v.t.* Tendre à montrer, signifier, vouloir dire, impliquer. *To purport to be,* se donner pour.

purpose ['pə:pəs], *n.* But, objet, *m.*, fin, *f.*, dessein, *m.*, intention, résolution, *f. Foreign to the purpose,* étranger au but; *for the purpose of,* dans le but de; *of set purpose,* tout exprès; *on purpose,* exprès, à dessein; *that is nothing to the purpose,* cela ne fait rien à l'affaire; *to answer a purpose,* remplir un but; *to answer one's purpose,* faire son affaire; *to answer the purpose of,* faire l'office de; *to* *come to the purpose,* en venir au fait; *to gain one's purpose,* en venir à ses fins; *to good purpose,* utilement, avec fruit; *to little purpose,* en vain; *to no purpose,* inutilement, en pure perte; *to some purpose,* utilement, bien; *to the purpose,* à propos; *to what purpose?* à quoi bon?—*v.t., v.i.* Se proposer, avoir le dessein, avoir l'intention (de). **purposeful,** *a.* Réfléchi. **purposeless,** *a.* Inutile, sans but. **purposely,** *adv.* À dessein, exprès.

purpura ['pɔ:pjuərə], *n.* Pourprier; (*Path.*) pourpre, purpura, *m.* **purpure,** *n.* (*Her.*) Pourpre, *m.* **purpuric** [-'pjuərik], *a.* Purpurique.

purr [pɔ:], *v.i.* Ronronner.—*n.* Ronron, ronflement (d'un moteur etc.), *m.* **purring,** *a.* Qui fait ronron.—*n.* Ronron, *m.*

purse [pɔ:s], *n.* Porte-monnaie, *m.*; bourse (bag), *f.* *To hold the purse-strings,* tenir les cordons de la bourse.—*v.t.* Plisser, froncer (the eyebrows etc.). *To purse up one's lips,* faire la bouche en cœur. **purse-proud,** **pursy,** *a.* Fier de son argent; cossu.

purser ['pɔ:sə], *n.* Commissaire (on a ship); (*Mining*) agent comptable, *m. Purser's steward,* distributeur des vivres, *m.*

pursiness ['pɔ:sinis], *n.* Courte haleine, *f.*

purslane ['pɔ:slin], *n.* Pourpier, *m.*

pursuable [pɔ:'sju:əbl], *a.* Qu'on peut poursuivre.

pursuance [pɔ:'sju:əns], *n.* Poursuite, conséquence, *f. In pursuance of,* conformément à, en vertu de; *in the pursuance of his duty,* dans l'exécution de son devoir. **pursuant,** *a.* En conséquence (de), conforme (à).

pursue [pɔ:'sju:], *v.t.* Poursuivre; suivre, chercher. **pursuer,** *n.* Poursuivant, *m.* **pursuit** [pɔ:'sju:t], *n.* Poursuite, recherche; occupation, profession, *f.*; (*pl.*) travaux, *m.pl. In pursuit of,* à la poursuite de, à la recherche de; (*Av.*) *pursuit plane,* avion de chasse, *m.*

pursuivant ['pɔ:swivənt], *n.* Poursuivant d'armes, *m.*

pursy ['pɔ:si], *a.* Poussif; corpulent; pincée (mouth); cossu (purse proud).

purulence ['pjuəruləns] or **purulency,** *n.* Purulence, *f.* **purulent,** *a.* Purulent.

purvey [pɔ:'vei], *v.t.* Fournir, approvisionner; procurer. **purveyance,** *n.* Approvisionnement, *m.* **purveyor,** *n.* Pourvoyeur, fournisseur, *m. Purveyor to Her Majesty,* fournisseur de sa Majesté.

purview ['pɔ:vju:], *n.* Vue générale, portée, étendue, *f. To be within the purview of,* être du ressort de.

pus [pʌs], *n.* Pus, *m.*

push [puʃ], *v.t.* Pousser; (*fig.*) presser, importuner. *To be pushed for an answer,* être embarrassé pour répondre; *to be pushed for money,* être à court d'argent; *to be pushed for time,* être pressé; *to push away,* repousser; *to push back,* repousser, faire reculer; *to push down,* faire tomber, renverser; *to push forward,* faire avancer, pousser; *to push in,* faire entrer, pousser dedans; *to push off,* lancer, pousser au large; *to push on,* faire avancer; hâter; *to push one's way,* se frayer un chemin; *to push out,* pousser dehors, faire sortir.—*v.i.* Pousser; faire un effort; se pouser. *To push off,* pousser au large; *to push on,* pousser en avant, s'avancer.—*n.* Impulsion, poussée, *f.*;

effort, *m.*; attaque (en masse), *f.*; moment critique (critical moment), *m.*, extrémité, *f. At a push,* au besoin; *at one push,* d'un seul coup; *to get the push* (*colloq.*), recevoir son congé, être remercié.

push-bicycle or **push-bike,** *n.* (*colloq.*) Vélo, *m.* **push-cart,** *n.* Charrette à bras, *f.* **push-pin,** *n.* Poussette (game), *f.*

pusher, *n.* Personne qui se pousse, *f.*; (*fig.*) arriviste, *m.*; (*Av.*) avion à hélice arrière, *m.*

pushing, *a.* Entreprenant.

pusillanimity [pju:silə'nimiti], *n.* Pusillanimité, *f.* **pusillanimous** [-'læniməs], *a.* Pusillanime. **pusillanimously,** *adv.* Avec pusillanimité.

puss [pus], *n.* Minet, *m.*, minette, *f.*; lièvre (hare), *m. Puss in boots,* le chat botté; *to play at puss in the corner,* jouer aux quatre coins.

pussy ['pusi], *n.* Minet, mimi, *m.*

pustular ['pʌstjulə] or **pustulous,** *a.* Pustulé, pustuleux, *f.* **pustule,** *n.* Pustule, *f.*

put [put], *v.t.* (*past* and *p.p.* put) Mettre, poser, placer; proposer (to propose); donner, supposer (to suppose); faire, demander (a question etc.); lancer (the weight etc.). *Dinner was put back an hour,* le dîner fut retardé d'une heure; *if I may put it so,* si je puis m'exprimer ainsi; *to be hard put to it,* être fort embarrassé; *to be put upon,* être trompé, être maltraité; *to put about,* gêner, troubler, embarrasser; *to put again,* remettre, répéter; *to put a question to,* faire une question à; *to put aside,* mettre de côté, écarter; *to put away,* ôter, renvoyer, bannir, répudier (a wife); *to put back,* replacer, remettre, reculer; *to put by,* mettre de côté; *to put down,* déposer, supprimer, réprimer (to suppress), inscrire (to write down), réduire au silence, confondre (to confound), attribuer (à); *to put down as,* considérer comme, traiter de; *to put forth,* mettre en avant, avancer, déployer, pousser (leaves etc.), publier, faire paraître (a book); *to put forward,* mettre en avant, avancer; *to put in,* mettre en, dans, or dedans, introduire, insérer, atteler (horses etc.), installer; *to put in force,* faire exécuter (a law); *to put in mind of,* rappeler à; *to put it bluntly,* parler franc; *to put off,* ôter, quitter, remettre, retarder, ajourner, différer; *to put on,* mettre (clothes), passer, prendre (to assume), mettre sur le compte de, attribuer à, imputer à, avancer (the clock etc.); *to put on airs,* se donner des airs; *to put on a job,* donner du travail à; *to put on a play,* monter une pièce; *to put on the light,* allumer; *to put oneself forward,* se mettre en évidence, se mettre en avant; *to put out,* mettre dehors, faire sortir, mettre à la porte, éteindre (to extinguish), embarrasser (to confuse), déranger, troubler (to incommode); *to put over,* mettre dessus, mettre au-dessus de; *to put to,* mettre à, atteler (to harness); *to put together,* mettre ensemble, rapprocher, réunir, monter (a piece of mechanism); *to put to the sword,* passer au fil de l'épée; *to put up,* lever, remettre (to replace), monter, bâtir, installer, loger, caser (to lodge), remiser (a carriage); *to put up with,* s'arranger de; *to put up to,* mettre au fait de.—*v.i.* Aller, se mouvoir; germer, pousser; (*Naut.*) se mettre. *To put about,* virer (of a ship); *to put back,* s'en retourner; *to put forth,* germer, pousser (to bud); *to put in,* entrer au port, relâcher; *to put in for,* se mettre sur les rangs pour, se porter candidat pour; *to put into port,* relâcher, faire escale (à); *to put off,* pousser au large; *to put to sea,* prendre la mer, prendre le large; *to put up,* loger (à *or* chez), descendre (à); *to put up with,* endurer, supporter, avaler, digérer, se contenter de, s'accommoder de, s'arranger de (to make shift with).—*n.* Mise, *f.*; coup, jet, lancement, *m.*; (*St. Exch.*) option de vente, prime vendeur, *f.* *Put and call,* double option, *f.*

putative ['pju:tətiv], *a.* Putatif. **putatively,** *adv.* Putativement.

putlog ['pʌtlɔg], *n.* Boulin, *m.*

putrefaction [pju:tri'fækʃən], *n.* Putréfaction, *f.* **putrefactive,** *a.* Putréfactif.

putrefy ['pju:trifai], *v.t.* Putréfier.—*v.i.* Se putréfier.

putrescence [pju'tresəns], *n.* État de putréfaction, *m.* **putrescent,** *a.* En état de putréfaction.

putrid ['pju:trid], *a.* Putride. **putridness** or **putridity** [-'triditi], *n.* Putridité, *f.*

putt [pʌt], *v.t.* (*Golf*) Mettre dans le trou, poter.

puttee ['pʌti:], *n.* Bande-molletière, *f.*

putter (1) ['pʌtə], *n.* (*Golf*) Poteur, *m.*

putter (2) ['putə], *n.* Metteur; faiseur, *m.* *Putter on,* instigateur, *m.* **putting,** *n.* Action de mettre, mise, *f.* *Putting aside,* écartement, *m.*; *putting down,* répression, installation, *f.*; *putting off,* délai, retardement, *m.*, remise, *f.*; *putting up,* candidature, *f.*, installation, *f.*, emballage, *m.*

putty ['pʌti], *n.* Mastic (for glaziers), *m.* **putty-powder,** *n.* Potée d'étain, *f.*

puzzle [pʌzl], *n.* (*fig.*) Énigme, *f.*; jeu de patience, casse-tête (toy), *m.* *Crossword puzzle,* mots croisés; *pictorial puzzle,* rébus, *m.*—*v.t.* Intriguer, embarrasser. *To be much puzzled how to,* être fort embarrassé de; *to puzzle one's brains,* se creuser la tête; *to puzzle out,* débrouiller, déchiffrer.—*v.i.* Être embarrassé. **puzzler,** *n.* Problème difficile à résoudre, *m.*, (*fam.*) colle, *f.* **puzzling,** *a.* Embarrassant.

pygmean [pig'miən], *a.* De pygmée.

pygmy ['pigmi], *n.* Pygmée, *m.*

pyjamas [pi'dʒɑːməz], *n.pl.* Pyjama, *m.*

Pylades ['pailədi:z]. Pylade, *m.*

pylon ['pailən], *n.* Pylône, *m.*

pyloric [pai'lɔrik], *a.* Pylorique. **pylorus** [-'lɔːrəs], *n.* Pylore, *m.*

pyracanth ['pairəkænθ], *n.* (*Bot.*) Pyracanthe, *f.*, buisson ardent, *m.*

pyramid ['pirəmid], *n.* Pyramide, *f.* **pyramidal** [-'ræmidl], *a.* Pyramidal.

Pyramus ['pirəməs]. Pyrame, *m.*

pyre ['paiə], *n.* Bûcher, *m.*

Pyrenean [pirə'niːən], *a. and n.* Pyrénéen, *m.*, pyrénéenne, *f.*

Pyrenees [pirə'niːz], the. Les Pyrénées, *f.pl.*

pyrethrum [pai'riːθrəm], *n.* (*Bot.*) Pyrèthre, *m.*

pyretic [pai'retik], *a.* Pyrétique. **pyrexia** [-'reksiə], *n.* Pyrexie, *f.*

pyrites [pai'raitiːz], *n.* Pyrite, *f.*

pyritous ['pairitəs], *a.* Pyriteux. **pyrogallic** [-'gælik], *a.* Pyrogallique. **pyroligneous** [-'ligniəs], *a.* Pyroligneux. **pyrometer** [-'rɔmitə], *n.* Pyromètre, *m.* **pyrophorus** [-'rɔfərəs], *n.* Pyrophore, *m.*

pyrotechnic [paiərou'teknik] or **pyrotechnical,** *a.* Pyrotechnique, pyrique. **pyrotechnics,** *n.pl.* Pyrotechnie, *f.* **pyrotechnist,** *n.* Artificier, *m.* **pyrotechny,** *n.* Pyrotechnie, *f.*

pyroxene ['pairɔksiːn], *n.* Pyroxène, *m.*

pyroxylin, *n.* Pyroxyline, *f.*, fulmi-coton, *m.*

pyrrhic ['pirik], *a. and n.* Pyrrhique (dance), *f.*; (*Pros.*) pyrrhique, *m.*

Pyrrhonian [pi'rouniən], *a.* Pyrrhonien.

Pyrrhonism ['pirənizm], *n.* Pyrrhonisme, *m.* **Pyrrhonist,** *n.* Pyrrhonien, *m.*

Pythagoras [pai'θægəræs]. Pythagore, *m.*

Pythagorean [paiθægə'riːən], *a.* Pythagorique.—*n.* Pythagoricien, *m.*, pythagoricienne, *f.* **Pythagorism** [-'θægərizm], *n.* Pythagorisme, *m.*

Pythian ['piθiən], *a.* Pythien, pythique.

python ['paiθən], *n.* Python, *m.*

pythoness ['paiθənes], *n.* Pythonisse, *f.*

pyx [piks], *n.* Ciboire, *m.*; (*Mint*) boîte où l'on dépose des échantillons des monnaies, *f.*

pyxidium [pik'sidiəm], *n.* (*Bot.*) Pyxide, *f.*

Q

Q, q [kjuː]. Dix-septième lettre de l'alphabet, *m.*

qua [kwei], *adv.* En tant que.

quack [kwæk], *n.* Charlatan, empirique; couac, cri du canard, *m.*—*a.* De charlatan, d'empirique. *Quack doctor,* charlatan, guérisseur, *m.*; *quack medicine,* remède de charlatan, *m.*—*v.i.* Crier (comme les canards etc.); (*fig.*) faire le charlatan. **quackery,** *n.* Charlatanisme, *m.* **quackish,** *a.* De charlatan, d'empirique.

quad [kwɔd], *n.* (*Print.*) Cadrat, *m.*; (*Univ.*) [QUADRANGLE] (*fam.*) (*pl.*) quadruplés, *m.pl.*

Quadragesima [kwɔdrə'dʒesimə], *n.* Quadragésime, *f.* *Quadragesima Sunday,* dimanche de la Quadragésime, *m.* **quadragesimal,** *a.* Quadragésimal.

quadrangle ['kwɔdræŋgl], *n.* Quadrilatère, carré, *m.*; (*Univ.*) cour d'honneur d'un collège, *f.* **quadrangular** [-'ræŋgjulə], *a.* Quadrangulaire; (*Bot.*) quadrangulé.

quadrant ['kwɔdrənt], *n.* Quart de cercle; (*Trig.*) quadrant, *m.*; (*Mech.*) secteur, *m.* **quadrantal** [-'ræntl], *a.* Quadrantal.

quadrat ['kwɔdrət], *n.* (*Print.*) Cadrat, *m.*

quadrate (1) ['kwɔdrət], *a. and n.* Carré. **quadrate** (2) [kwɔ'dreit], *v.i.* Cadrer (avec).—*v.t.* Réduire au carré. **quadratic** [-'rætik], *a.* Du second degré. **quadratrix,** *n.* Quadratrice, *f.*

quadrature ['kwɔdrətʃə], *n.* Quadrature, *f.*

quadrennial [kwɔd'reniəl], *a.* Quadriennal. **quadrennially,** *adv.* Tous les quatre ans.

quadricapsular [-ri'kæpsjulə], *a.* Quadricapsulaire.

quadricornous [-'kɔːnəs], *a.* Quadricorne.

quadridentate [-'dentət], *a.* Quadridenté.

quadrifid ['kwɔdrifid], *a.* (*Bot.*) Quadrifide.

quadrifoliate [-'fouliət], *a.* Quadrifolié.

quadriga [kwɔ'draigə], *n.* Quadrige, *m.*

quadrijugous [-ri'dʒuːgəs], *a.* Quadrijugué.

quadrilateral [-'lætərəl], *a.* Quadrilatéral.—*n.* Quadrilatère, *m.*

quadrille [kwə'dril], *n.* Quadrille, *m.*; contre-danse, *f.*

quadrilobate [kwɔdri'loubət], *a.* Quadrilobé.
quadrinomial [-'noumiəl], *n.* Quadrinôme, *m.*
quadripartite [-'pɑːtait], *a.* (*Bot.*) Quadriparti. **quadripartition** [-'tiʃən], *n.* Quadripartition, *f.*
quadriphyllous [-'filəs], *a.* Quadriphylle.
quadrireme ['kwɔdririːm], *n.* Quadrirème, *f.*
quadrisyllabic [-si'læbik], *a.* Quadrisyllabe. **quadrisyllable**[-'siləbl], *n.*Quadrisyllabe, *m.*
quadrivalvular [-'vælvjulə], *a.* Quadrivalve.
quadroon [kwə'druːn], *n.* Quarteron, *m.*, quarteronne, *f.*
quadrumane ['kwɔdrumein], *n.* Quadrumane, *m.* **quadrumanous** [-'druːmənəs], *a.* Quadrumane.
quadruped ['kwɔdruped], *n.* Quadrupède, *m.*
quadruple ['kwɔdrupl], *a.* Quadruple; (*Bot.*) quadrijumeaux.—*n.* Quadruple, *m.*—*v.t.* Quadrupler. **quadruplet**, *n.* Quadruplette, *f.*; (*pl.*) quadruplés, *m.pl.*
quadruplicate (1) [-'druːplikeit], *v.t.* Quadrupler.
quadruplicate(2) [-kit], *a.* Quadruplé. **quadruplication**[-'keiʃən], *n.* Quadruplication, *f.*
quaestor ['kwiːstɔː], *n.* (*Rom. Ant.*) Questeur, *m.* **quaestorship**, *n.* Questure, *f.*
quaff [kwæf], *v.t.* Boire à grands traits; (*slang*) lamper. **quaffer**, *n.* Buveur, *m.*
quag [kwæg] or **quagmire**, *n.* Fondrière, *f.* **quaggy**, *a.* Marécageux.
quail (1) [kweil], *v.i.* Perdre courage, fléchir. reculer, trembler.
quail (2) [kweil], *n.* Caille, *f.* **quail-pipe**, *n.* Courcaillet, appeau, *m.*
quaint [kweint], *a.* Singulier, bizarre, étrange, original; pittoresque, suranné. **quaintly**, *adv.* Singulièrement, bizarrement, d'une manière étrange. **quaintness**, *n.* Singularité, bizarrerie, originalité, étrangeté, *f.*
quake [kweik], *v.i.* Trembler; branler. *To quake in one's shoes*, trembler dans sa peau. —*n.* Tremblement, *m. Earthquake*, tremblement de terre, *m.*
Quaker, *n.* Quaker, *m.* **Quakeress**, *n.* Quakeresse, *f.* **Quakerish**, *a.* De Quaker. **Quakerism** or (*pej.*) **Quakery**, *n.* Quakerisme, *m.* **Quakerly**, *adv.* De Quaker.
quaking, *n.* Tremblement, *m.*; terreur, *f.*—*a.* Tremblant. **quaking-grass**, *n.* Amourette, brize, *f.* **quakingly**, *adv.* En tremblant.
qualifiable ['kwɔlifaiəbl], *a.* Qualifiable.
qualification ['kwɔlifi'keiʃən], *n.* Qualification, qualité; condition, aptitude, *f.*, talent, *m.*; modification, réserve, restriction, *f.*; (*Med.*) diplôme, *m.*; (*Law*) capacité, aptitude, *f.*; (*pl.*) qualités, *f.pl.*, titres decapacité, *m.pl.*, certificat d'aptitude, *m.*
qualificative ['kwɔlifikeitiv] or **qualificatory**, *a.* Qualificatif. **qualified**, *a.* Qui a les qualités requises (pour), capable (de); propre (à). *Qualified teacher*, professeur diplômé, *m.*
qualify ['kwɔlifai], *v.t.* Rendre capable (de), rendre propre (à), préparer (à); autoriser (à); modifier, adoucir, modérer; déterminer, fixer (to fix).—*v.i.* Se préparer (à). *He has qualified* (as a doctor), il a été reçu médecin. **qualifying**, *a.* Qualificatif.
qualitative ['kwɔlitativ], *a.* Qualitatif.
quality ['kwɔliti], *n.* Qualité, *f.*; (*colloq.*) talent, *m.* 'The quality', la noblesse, *f.*, le gratin, *m.*
qualm [kwɑːm], *n.* Soulèvement de cœur, *m.*, nausée, *f.*; (*fig.*) scrupule, remords, *m.*

qualmish, *a.* Qui a mal au cœur, qui a des nausées. **qualmishness**, *n.* Nausée, *f.*, soulèvement de cœur, *m.*
quandary ['kwɔndəri], *n.* Embarras, *m.*, difficulté, impasse, *f. To be in a quandary*, être dans une impasse, dans l'embarras; *in a great quandary*, au pied du mur.
quantitative ['kwɔntitativ], *a.* Quantitatif.
quantity ['kwɔntiti], *n.* Quantité, *f.*; grand nombre, *m. In quantities*, en grande quantité, en grand nombre.
quantum ['kwɔntəm], *n.* Montant, quantum, *m.*
quarantine ['kwɔrəntiːn], *n.* Quarantaine, *f. To perform quarantine*, faire quarantaine.— *v.t.* Mettre en quarantaine.
quarrel ['kwɔrəl], *n.* Querelle, dispute, brouille, *f.*, sujet de querelle; *carreau (pane of glass, bolt from crossbow), m. I have no quarrel with you*, je ne vous reproche rien; *to pick a quarrel with*, chercher querelle à; *to take up someone's quarrel*, embrasser or épouser la querelle de quelqu'un.—*v.i.* Se quereller, se disputer, se brouiller; trouver à redire (à). *To have quarrelled with*, être en querelle avec, être brouillé avec; *to quarrel about nothing*, chercher une querelle d'Allemand; *to quarrel with*, se quereller avec, quereller.
quarreller, *n.* Querelleur, *m.*, -euse, *f.* **quarrelling**, *n.* Querelle; dispute, *f.*, démêlé, *m.* **quarrelsome**, *a.* Querelleur. *Quarrelsome man*, querelleur, *m.* **quarrelsomely**, *adv.* En querelleur. **quarrelsomeness**, *n.* Humeur querelleuse, *f.*
quarry ['kwɔri], *n.* Carrière; (*Hunt.*) curée; proie (prey), *f.*—*v.t.* Tirer d'une carrière; traquer. **quarrying**, *n.* Extraction d'une carrière, *f.* **quarryman**, *n.* (*pl.* **quarrymen**) Carrier, *m.*
quart [kwɔːt], *n.* Quart de gallon (1·14 litre), *m.*
quartan ['kwɔːtən], *n.* Fièvre quarte, *f.*
quartation [kwɔː'teiʃən], *n.* (*Metal.*) Quartation, *f.*
quarter ['kwɔːtə], *n.* Quart (fourth part); quart de quintal (12·70 kg.) (weight); quartier (of the city, of the moon, of lamb, etc.), *m.*; partie, région (region), *f.*; côté (point); trimestre (of the year); terme (of rent), *m.*; hanche (of a ship), *f.*; (*pl.*) logement; (*Mil.*) quartier, *m. A quarter of an hour*, un quart d'heure, *m.*; *a quarter past ten*, dix heures et quart; *a quarter to seven*, sept heures moins le quart; *at close quarters*, à petite distance; *four quarters of the globe*, quatre parties du globe; *free quarters*, droit au logement, *m.*; *from all quarters*, de tous côtés; *from a reliable quarter*, de source sûre, de bonne source; *in high quarters*, en haut lieu; *in the proper quarter*, dans les milieux autorisés, à qui de droit; *there is nothing to hope for from that quarter*, il n'y a rien à espérer de ce côté-là; *to ask for quarter*, demander quartier; *to beat to quarters*, sonner le branle-bas; *to come to close quarters*, en venir aux mains; *to give no quarter*, ne pas faire de quartier; *to take up one's quarters at*, s'installer chez, se loger à.—*v.t.* Diviser en quatre, diviser par quartiers; loger (to lodge); (*Her.*) écarteler. *To draw and quarter*, écarteler; *to quarter* (in barracks), caserner. —*v.i.* Loger; (*Mil.*) être cantonné.

quarter-block, *n.* Poulie de retour, *f.* **quarter-cask,** *n.* Feuillette, *f.* **quarter-day,** *n.* Jour du terme, *m.* **quarter-deck,** *n.* Gaillard d'arrière, *m.* **quartering,** *n.* Division en quatre parties, *f.*; (*Mil.*) logement; (*punishment* and *Her.*) écartèlement, *m.* **quarterly,** *a.* Trimestriel. —*adv.* Par trimestre, tous les trois mois. **quartermaster,** *n.* (*Navy*) Quartier-maître; (*Mil.*) officier d'approvisionnement, *m.* **quartermaster-general,** *n.* Intendant-général, *m.* **quartermaster-sergeant,** *n.* Sergent-chef (of infantry); maréchal des logis chef (of cavalry), *m.* **quarter-sessions,** *n.* Session trimestrielle, *f.* **quarterstaff,** *n.* Bâton (à deux bouts), *m.*

quartern ['kwɔːtən], *n.* Quart de pinte (0·14 litre), *m.* *A quartern loaf,* un pain de quatre livres.

quartet [kwɔːˈtet], *n.* Quatuor, *m.*

quarto ['kwɔːtou], *a.* and *n.* In-quarto, *m.*

quartz [kwɔːts], *n.* Quartz, *m.* **quartzose,** *a.* Quartzeux.

quash [kwɔʃ], *v.t.* Écraser; (*fig.*) étouffer, dompter; (*Law*) annuler, casser.

quasi ['kweisai], *adv.* Quasi.

quassia ['kwɔʃjə], *n.* Quassia; quassier (tree), *m.*

quaternary [kwəˈtəːnəri], *a.* Quaternaire. **quaternate,** *a.* Quaterné. **quaternion,** *n.* Quaterne, *m.*

quatrain ['kwɔtrein], *n.* Quatrain, *m.*

quaver ['kweivə], *n.* Tremblement de la voix, trille, *m.*; (*Mus.*) croche (note), *f.*—*v.i.* Faire trembler sa voix; trembler; (*Mus.*) faire des trilles, faire un tremolo. **quaver-rest,** *n.* Demi-soupir, *m.*

quavering, *n.* Trille, tremolo, *m.*; cadence, *f.*; tremblement de voix, chevrotement, *m.*—*a.* Tremblant, chevrotant.

quay [kiː], *n.* Quai, *m.*—*v.t.* Garnir de quais. **quayage** ['kiːidʒ], *n.* Quayage, *m.*

***quean** [kwiːn], *n.* Coquine, *f.* (*Sc.*) donzelle, *f.*

queasiness ['kwiːzinis], *n.* Nausées, *f.pl.*; scrupules, *m.pl.*

queasy ['kwiːzi], *a.* Sujet à des nausées.

queen [kwiːn], *n.* Reine; (*Cards etc.*) dame, *f.* *As a queen,* en reine; *Queen Anne is dead,* c'est vieux comme le Pont Neuf.—*v.i.* Faire la reine.

queen-bee, *n.* Reine-abeille, *f.*

queen-like or **queenly,** *adv* De reine, digne d'une reine.

queen-mother, *n.* Reine-mère, *f.*

queer [kwiə], *a.* Bizarre, étrange, drôle; suspect; pervers; inverti. *A queer fellow,* un drôle d'individu; *I feel very queer,* je ne suis pas du tout dans mon assiette; *things look very queer,* les choses ont mauvaise tournure.—*n.* (*fam.*) Tapette, *f.,* homosexuel, *m.*—*v.t.* Déranger. *To queer someone's pitch,* faire échouer les plans de quelqu'un. **queerish,** *a.* Assez drôle; un peu souffrant. **queerly,** *adv.* Étrangement, bizarrement. **queerness,** *n.* Étrangeté, bizarrerie, *f.*; malaise, *m.*

quell [kwel], *v.t.* Réprimer, dompter.—*v.i.* S'éteindre. **queller,** *n.* Personne qui réprime, *f.,* dompteur, *m.*

quench [kwentʃ], *v.t.* Éteindre; étancher; étouffer (*to repress*). *To quench one's thirst,* étancher sa soif, se désaltérer. **quenchable,** *a.* Extinguible. **quencher,** *n.* Personne or chose qui éteint, *f.* **quenchless,** *a.* Inextinguible.

querist ['kwiərist], *n.* Questionneur, *m.,* -euse, *f.*

querulous ['kweruləs], *a.* Plaintif, maussade. **querulously,** *adv.* D'un ton dolent, en se plaignant. **querulousness,** *n.* Humeur chagrine, *f.*

query ['kwiəri], *n.* Question, *f.*; point d'interrogation, *m.*—*v.t.* Marquer d'un point d'interrogation; mettre en doute, douter de. —*v.i.* Faire des questions; questionner.

quest [kwest], *n.* Enquête, *f.*; quête (by hounds); recherche, *f.* *In quest of,* à la recherche de.

question ['kwestʃən], *n.* Question, interrogation, demande, *f.*; sujet, *m.,* proposition (subject), *f.*; (*Parl.*) interpellation; torture, *f. An unfair question,* une question indiscrète, *f.*; *a pretty question!* la belle demande! *beyond all question,* hors de doute; *if it is a question of,* s'il s'agit de; *leading question,* question qui indique la réponse désirée; *list of questions,* questionnaire, *m.*; *out of the question,* absolument impossible; *question mark,* point d'interrogation, *m.*; *that is not the question,* il ne s'agit pas de cela; *to ask a question,* poser une question; *to beg the question,* faire une pétition de principe; *to call in question,* mettre en question, révoquer en doute; *to move the previous question,* (*Parl.*) demander la question préalable; *to put a question to,* adresser une interpellation à; *to put to the question,* mettre à la question; *without question,* sans aucun doute, sans contredit.—*v.t.* Questionner, interroger; mettre en question, mettre en doute, douter de, contester.—*v.i.* Interroger, questionner; poser des questions; douter, se demander (si). *I question whether it would not be better to . . . ,* je me demande s'il ne vaudrait pas mieux . . . .

questionable ['kwestʃənəbl], *a.* Contestable, douteux, incertain; suspect, équivoque. *Men of questionable character,* de fort louches individus, *m.pl.* **questionableness,** *n.* Nature douteuse *or* suspecte, *f.*

questionary, *n.* Questionnaire, *m.*

questioner, *n.* Questionneur, *m.,* questionneuse, *f.,* interrogateur, *m.,* interrogatrice, *f.*

questioning, *n.* Questions, *f.pl.,* interrogation, *f.*

questionless, *a.* Sans doute, incontestable.

question-master, *n.* (*Rad. Tel.*) Meneur de débats, *m.*

questionnaire [kwestʃəˈnɛə], *n.* Questionnaire, *m.*

questor [QUAESTOR].

queue [kjuː], *n.* Queue, *f.* (of people, cars, hair, etc.).—*v.i. To queue up,* faire la queue, prendre la file (of vehicles).

***quib** [QUIP].

quibble ['kwibl], *n.* Argutie, chicane, *f.*; faux-fuyant, *m.*; évasion, *f.*; jeu de mots, calembour, *m.*—*v.i.* Ergoter, chicaner; jouer sur les mots. **quibbler,** *n.* Ergoteur, *m.,* -euse, *f.,* chicaneur, *m.,* -euse, *f.*

quick [kwik], *a.* Vite, rapide, prompt; agile, leste; vif (alive); (*fig.*) fin. *Be quick!* dépêchez-vous! *quick as thought,* en un clin d'œil; *quick ear,* oreille fine, *f.*; *quick hedge,* haie vive, *f.*; *quick march!* pas accéléré! *quick sale,* prompt débit, *m.*; *quick wit,* esprit vif, *m.*; *to be quick,*

[416]

se dépêcher; *to be quick in the uptake*, avoir la compréhension facile.—*adv.*Vite,promptement, lestement.—*n.* Vif, *m.*; chair vive, *f.* *An incision in the quick*, une incision dans la chair vive; *stung to the quick*, piqué au vif; (*collect.*) *the quick*, les vivants, *m.pl.* **quickly,** *adv.* Vite; promptement; bientôt. **quickness,** *n.* Vitesse; promptitude; activité; pénétration, sagacité, finesse; fréquence (of the pulse), *f.*

quickbeam ['kwikbi:m], *n.* Sorbier sauvage, *m.*

quicken ['kwikən], *v.t.* Animer, vivifier; raviver, accélérer, hâter. *To quicken one's pace*, hâter le pas.—*v.i.* Prendre vie, s'animer. **quickener,** *n.* Personne *or* chose qui vivifie, *f.*; principe vivifiant, *m.* **quickening,** *a.* Vivifiant, qui ranime.

quick-firing ['kwik'faiəriŋ], *a.* À tir rapide.

quicklime ['kwiklaim], *n.* Chaux vive, *f.*

quicksand, *n.* Sable mouvant, *m.* **quickset,** *a.* Vive. *Quickset hedge*, haie vive, *f.*— *n.* Plante vive; bouture, *f.*—*v.t.* Entourer d'une haie vive. **quicksighted,** *a.* À la vue prompte; clairvoyant, pénétrant. **quicksightedness,** *n.* Vue prompte; (*fig.*) sagacité, *f.* **quicksilver,** *n.* Vif-argent, mercure, *m.* **quicksilvered,** *a.* Étamé. **quicksilvering,** *n.* Étamage, *m.* **quick-tempered,** *a.* Emporté, vif, colérique. **quick-witted,** *a.* À l'esprit vif.

quid [kwid], *n.* Chique, *f.*; (*slang*) livre sterling, *f.*

quiddity ['kwiditi], *n.* (*Phil.*) Quiddité, essence, *f.*

quidnunc ['kwidnʌŋk], *n.* Curieux, colporteur de nouvelles, *m.*

quid pro quo ['kwidprou'kwou], *n.* *Quiproquo, *m.*; l'équivalent, *m.*; la pareille, *f.*

quiescence [kwai'esəns], *n.* Quiétude, tranquillité, *f.*, repos, *m.* **quiescent,** *a.* Paisible, en repos, tranquille.

quiet ['kwaiət], *a.* Tranquille, calme; en repos, paisible, silencieux; (*fig.*) sans éclat, modeste. *Be quiet!* silence! taisez-vous! *to keep quiet*, se tenir tranquille, rester tranquille.—*n.* Tranquillité, quiétude, *f.*; repos, calme, *m.* *On the quiet*, (*colloq.*) à la dérobée, clandestinement.—*v.t.* Tranquilliser, apaiser, calmer; faire taire.—*v.i.* *To quiet down*, s'apaiser, se calmer.

quieten, *v.t.*, *v.i.* [QUIET].

quieting, *a.* Calmant, tranquillisant. **quietism,** *n.* Quiétisme, *m.* **quietist,** *n.* Quiétiste, *m.* **quietly,** *adv.* Tranquillement; doucement; en silence, sans bruit, discrètement, sans éclat. **quietness,** *n.* Tranquillité, *f.*; calme, repos, *m.* **quietude,** *n.* Quiétude, tranquillité, *f.*

quietus [kwai'i:təs], *n.* Repos, *m.*, tranquillité; mort, *f.*; (*fig.*) coup de grâce, *m.*; décharge, quittance, *f.*, quitus (discharge), *m.* *To give him his quietus*, lui régler son compte, lui donner le coup de grâce.

quill [kwil], *n.* (Tuyau de) plume; plume d'oie (for writing), *f.*; piquant (of a porcupine), *m.*—*v.t.* Tuyauter, rucher. **quill-driver,** *n.* Gratte-papier, *m.* **quill-driving,** *n.* Métier de gratte-papier, *m.* **quill-pen,** *n.* Plume d'oie, *f.*

quilling, *n.* Tuyautage, *m.*, ruche, *f.*

quilt [kwilt], *n.* Couverture piquée, *f.*; édredon américain, *m.*, courtepointe, *f.*—*v.t.* Piquer. **quilting,** *n.* Piqué, *m.*; piquage, *m.*

quinary ['kwainəri], *a.* Quinaire.

quince [kwins], *n.* Coing, *m.* **quince-tree,** *n.* Cognassier, *m.*

quincentenary ['kwinsen'ti:nəri], *n.* Cinquième centenaire, *m.*—*a.* De cinq siècles.

quincunx ['kwinkʌŋks], *n.* Quinconce, *m.*

quindecagon [kwin'dekəgən], *n.* Quindécagone, *m.*

***quingentenary** [QUINCENTENARY].

quinine [kwi'ni:n], *n.* Quinine, *f.*

Quinquagesima [kwiŋkwə'dʒesimə], *n.* Quinquagésime, *f.*

quinquenniad [kwiŋ'kwenjəd], *n.* Quinquennot, *m.* **quinquennial** [-'kweniəl], *a.* Quinquennial.

quinquereme ['kwiŋkwəri:m], *n.* Quinquérème, *f.*

quinquina [kiŋ'ki:nə], *n.* Quinquina, *f.*

quinsy ['kwinzi], *n.* Esquinancie, *f.*

quint [kwint], *n.* Quinte, *f.* **quintain,** *n.* Quintaine, *f.*, quintan, *m.* **quintal,** *n.* Quintal, *m.*

quinte [kɛ̃:t], *n.* (*Fenc.*) Quinte, *f.*

quintessence [kwin'tesəns], *n.* Quintessence, *f.* **quintessential** [-ə'senʃəl], *a.* Quintessenciel.

quintet [kwin'tet], *n.* Quintette, *m.*

quintuple ['kwintjupl], *a.* Quintuple.—*v.t.* Quintupler. **quintuplet,** *n.* Groupe de cinq objets, *m.*; (*pl.*) quintuplés, *m.pl.*

quip [kwip], *n.* Mot piquant, sarcasme, *m.*; raillerie, *f.*—*v.t.* Railler.

quire ['kwaiə], *n.* Main (of paper), *f.*; *chœur, *m.* *In quires*, en feuilles.

quirk [kwə:k], *n.* Sarcasme, *m.*, pointe; *argutie, subtilité (quibble), *f.*; (*Arch.*) gorgerin, *m.*; parafe, trait de plume, *m.*

quit [kwit], *v.t.* Quitter, abandonner.—*v.i.* Se débarrasser (de). *Notice to quit*, congé, *m.*— *a.* Quitte. *To get quit of*, se débarrasser de.

quitch-grass ['kwitʃgrɑ:s], *n.* Chiendent, *m.*

quite [kwait], *adv.* Tout à fait, entièrement, complètement, tout; bien, parfaitement, assez. *It is quite three years ago*, il y a bien trois ans de cela; *not quite*, pas tout à fait, à peine; *quite another thing*, tout autre chose; *quite as much*, tout autant; *quite differently*, tout autrement; *quite enough*, bien assez; *quite hot*, tout chaud; *quite right*, exact, juste, très bien; *quite so!* parfaitement! en effet! *to be quite right*, avoir bien raison; *to have quite done*, avoir tout à fait fini.

quit-rent, *n.* Redevance, *f.*; (*Feud.*) cens, *m.*

quits [kwits], *adv.* Quitte. *To be quits*, être quitte; *we'll cry quits*, nous voilà quittes.

quittance ['kwitəns], *n.* Quittance, décharge, *f.*, acquit, reçu, *m.*

quitter ['kwitə], *n.* Personne qui quitte, *f.*

quiver (1) ['kwivə], *n.* Carquois, *m.* **quivered,** *a.* Armé d'un carquois.

quiver (2) ['kwivə], *v.i.* Trembler, frissonner; palpiter (of flesh), frémir. **quivering,** *n.* Tremblement, frissonnement; battement des paupières, *m.*

Quixote ['kwiksət], **Don.** Don Quichotte, *m.* (*fig.*) *He is a real Quixote*, c'est un vrai Don Quichotte.

quixotic [kwik'sɔtik], *a.* De Don Quichotte; extravagant, exalté.

quixotism ['kwiksətizm] or **quixotry**, *n.* Donquichottisme, *m.*

quiz [kwiz], *n.* Mystification, plaisanterie, devinette, *f.*; persifleur, railleur, *m.* *Radio quiz*, jeu radiophonique, *m.—v.t.* Railler, persifler; lorgner (to stare at). **quizzical**, *a.* Railleur; risible. **quizzing**, *n.* Raillerie, *f.*, persiflage, *m.*; lorgnerie, *f.* **quizzing-glass**, *n.* Lorgnon, *m.*

quod [kwɔd], *n.* (*slang*) Violon, *m.*, prison, *f.* *To put in quod*, coffrer, fourrer en prison.

quodlibet ['kwɔdlibət], *n.* Quolibet, *m.*, subtilité, *f.*

quoin [kɔin], *n.* Coin, *m.* *Elevating quoin*, coussin *or* coin de mire, *m.—v.t.* (*Artill.*) Caler.

quoit [kɔit], *n.* Palet; (*Ant.*) disque, *m.* *To play at quoits*, jouer au palet.

quondam ['kwɔndəm], *a.* Ci-devant, ancien, d'autrefois.

quorum ['kwɔːrəm], *n.* Nombre suffisant, quorum, *m.*

quota ['kwoutə], *n.* Quote-part, *f.*; contingent, *m.*

quotable ['kwoutəbl], *a.* Citable.

quotation [kwou'teiʃən], *n.* Citation; (*Comm.*) cote, *f.*; (*St. Exch.*) cours, *m.* *Quotation marks*, guillemets, *m.pl.*

quote [kwout], *v.t.* Citer; alléguer; (*Comm.*) coter. **quoter**, *n.* Citateur, *m.*

*****quoth** [kwouθ], *past v.t.* *Quoth I*, dis-je; *quoth he*, fit-il.

quotidian [kwo'tidiən], *a.* Quotidien, journalier.

quotient ['kwouʃənt], *n.* Quotient, *m.*

R

R, r [ɑː]. Dix-huitième lettre de l'alphabet, *m.*

rabbet ['ræbət], *n.* Feuillure, rainure; (*Naut.*) râblure, *f.—v.t.* Faire une rainure *or* une feuillure à. **rabbet-plane**, *n.* Guillaume, *m.*

rabbi ['ræbai], *n.* Rabbin, *m.* *Chief rabbi*, grand rabbin, *m.*

rabbinical [rə'binikl], *a.* Rabbinique.

rabbinism ['ræbinizm], *n.* Rabbinisme, *m.* **rabbinist**, *n.* Rabbiniste, *m.* **rabbinistic** [-'nistik], *a.* Rabbinique.

rabbit ['ræbit], *n.* Lapin, *m.*, lapine, *f.* *Tame rabbit*, lapin de clapier, *m.*; *Welsh rabbit*, fondue au fromage sur canapé, *f.*; *wild rabbit*, lapin de garenne, *m.*; *young rabbit*, lapereau, *m.* **rabbit-burrow** or **rabbit-hole**, *n.* Terrier, *m.* **rabbit-hutch**, *n.* Clapier, *m.* **rabbit-warren**, *n.* Garenne, *f.*

rabble [ræbl], *n.* Foule confuse, cohue, *f.*; populace, racaille, canaille, *f.*

Rabelaisian [ræbə'leiziən], *a.* Rabelaisien, de Rabelais.

rabid ['ræbid], *a.* Féroce, furieux; enragé (of dogs). **rabidly**, *adv.* Furieusement. *To be rabidly hungry*, avoir une faim de tous les diables. **rabidness**, *n.* Rage, fureur, *f.*

rabies ['reibiːz], *n.* Rage, hydrophobie, *f.*

raccoon [RACOON].

race [reis], *n.* Race (breed); course (running contest), *f.*; raz, raz de marée (tide), *m.* *Boat-race*, course d'aviron, *f.*; *flat-race*, course plate, *f.*; *foot-race*, course à pied, *f.*; *horse-race*, course de chevaux, *f.*; *hurdle-race*,

course de haies, *f.—v.i.* Courir vite, courir, lutter de vitesse. *To go racing*, aller aux courses.

race-course, *n.* Terrain de course, champ de courses, hippodrome, *m.*

raceme [rə'siːm], *n.* (*Bot.*) Racème, *m.* **racemose** ['ræsimous], *a.* Racémeux.

race-goer, *n.* Turfiste, *m.* **race-ground**, *n.* Champ de courses, *m.* **race-horse**, *n.* Cheval de course, *m.* **race-meeting**, *n.* Réunion de courses, *f.*

racer, *n.* Coureur; cheval de course, *m.*; bicyclette de course, *f.*

rachidian [rə'kidiən], *a.* Rachidien, noué, rachitique. **rachitis** [-'kaitis], *n.* Rachitis, rachitisme, *m.*

racial ['reiʃəl], *a.* De (la) race, ethnique.

raciness ['reisinis], *n.* Piquant, *m.*, verve, *f.*; bouquet (of wine), goût de terroir, *m.*

racing ['reisiŋ], *n.* Les courses, *f.pl.* *Horse-racing*, courses de chevaux, *f.—a.* De course. **racing-car**, *n.* Automobile de course, *f.* **racing-track**, *n.* Piste, *f.*

racism ['reisizm], *n.* Racisme, *m.* **racist**, *n.* Raciste, *m.* or *f.*

rack [ræk], *n.* Râtelier (in a stable etc.); chevalet (instrument for stretching), *m.*; roue (instrument of torture), *f.*; (*Tech.*) crémaillère (for pinion), *f.*; (*Horol.*) rochet; rack, arack (liquor), *m.* *Luggage-rack* (*Rail.*), filet, *m.*; *paper rack*, classeur à papiers, *m.*; *rack and pinion*, engrenage à crémaillère, *m.*; *to put to the rack*, mettre à la torture.—*v.t.* Mettre sur la roue, mettre à la torture; (*fig.*) tourmenter. *To rack off*, soutirer (liquor); *to rack one's brains*, se creuser la cervelle.

racket ['rækit], *n.* Fracas, tapage, tintamarre, caquet, *m.*; (*Ten.*) raquette, *f.*; escroquerie, supercherie, combine, *f.* *To stand the racket*, (*colloq.*) payer les pots cassés.—*v.t.* Relancer à coups de raquette.—*v.i.* Faire du tapage; s'amuser, faire la vie, faire la bombe. **racketeer**, *n.* Escroc, combinard, *m.* **rackety**, *a.* Tapageur.

racking ['rækiŋ], *n.* Soutirage (of liquors), *m.* —*a.* De torture; atroce (of pain). **racking-pace**, *n.* Amble traquenard, *m.*

rack-rent, *n.* Loyer excessif, loyer porté au maximum, *m.*

racoon [rə'kuːn], *n.* Raton laveur, *m.*

racy ['reisi], *a.* Qui a un goût de terroir, qui a du bouquet (of wine); (*fig.*) vif, piquant, plein de verve (of style etc.).

radar ['reidɑː], *n.* Radar, *m.*

raddle [rædl], *n.* Ocre rouge, *f.*

raddled, *a.* Fardé grossièrement.

radial ['reidiəl], *a.* Radial; du radium.

radian ['reidiən], *n.* Radian, radiant, *m.*

radiance ['reidiəns] or **radiancy**, *n.* Rayonnement, éclat, *m.*, splendeur, *f.* **radiant**, *a.* Rayonnant (de); radieux, éclatant; (*Bot.*) radié. *Radiant heat*, chaleur rayonnante, *f.* —*n.* Point radieux, *m.* **radiantly**, *adv.* En rayonnant, splendidement.

radiata [reidi'eitə], *n.pl.* (*Zool.*) Rayonnés, *m.pl.*

radiate ['reidieit], *v.i.* Rayonner (de); émettre des rayons.—*v.t.* Émettre comme des rayons. —*a.* [-ət] (*Bot.*) Radié. **radiating**, *a.* Rayonnant. **radiation** [-'eiʃən], *n.* Rayonnement, *m.*, radiation, *f.*

radiator ['reidieitə], *n.* Radiateur, *m.*

radical ['rædikl], *a.* Radical; fondamental.—*n.* Radical, *m.* **radicalism,** *n.* Radicalisme, *m.* **radically,** *adv.* Radicalement, essentiellement.

radiciflorous [rædisi'flɔːrəs], *a.* (*Bot.*) Radiciflore.

radicle ['rædikl], *n.* (*Bot.*) Radicule, *f.*

radicular [rə'dikjulə], *a.* Radiculaire.

radio ['reidiou], *n.* Télégraphie sans fil, radio, *f.,* (*colloq.*) la T.S.F. *Radio set,* appareil de radio, *m.,* radio, *f. On the radio,* à la radio. **radioactive** [reidiou'æktiv], *a.* Radio-actif. **radioactivity** [-'tiviti], *n.* Radio-activité, *f.* **radio-control** ['reidioukən'troul], *n.* Téléguidage, *m.—v.t.* Téléguider.

radiogram ['reidiougræm], *n.* Combiné radio-électrophone, *m.*

radiography [reidi'ɔgrəfi], *n.* Radiographie, *f.* **radiolarian** [-o'leəriən], *a.* and *n.* Radiolaire, *m.* **radiometer** [-'ɔmitə], *n.* Radiomètre, *m.* **radioscopy** [-'ɔskəpi], *n.* Radioscopie, *f.* **radiotelegram** [-o'teləgræm], *n.* Radiotélégramme, *m.*

radish ['rædiʃ], *n.* Radis, *m. Turnip-radish,* rave, *f.; horse-radish,* raifort, *m.*

radium ['reidiəm], *n.* Radium, *m.*

radius ['reidiəs], *n.* Rayon, *m. Within a radius of twenty miles,* dans un rayon de vingt milles. **radius-vector,** *n.* Rayon vecteur, *m.*

radix ['reidiks], *n.* (*pl.* **radices**) Racine; base, *f.*

raff [ræf], *n.* Rebut, fatras, *m.;* canaille, *f.* **raffish,** *a.* De canaille, bravache.

raffle [ræfl], *n.* Loterie, tombola, *f.—v.t.* Mettre en tombola. *To raffle for,* prendre des billets pour.

raft [rɑːft], *n.* Radeau; train de bois, *m.*

rafter ['rɑːftə], *n.* Chevron, *m.—v.t.* Chevronner. **raftered,** *a.* À chevrons.

rafting ['rɑːftiŋ], *n.* Flottage en train, *m.*

raftsman, *n.* Flotteur, *m.*

rag [ræg], *n.* Chiffon (piece of cloth torn off); haillon, *m.,* guenille, loque (tatter), *f.;* (*sch.*) chahut, *m.;* brimade, *f. In rags,* en haillons, en loques, en guenilles, déguenillé; *meat boiled to rags,* de la viande en charpie; *rag-and-bone man,* chiffonnier, *m.; to tear to rags,* mettre en lambeaux.—*v.t.* (*sch.*) Chahuter, brimer, taquiner, faire des brimades à.

ragamuffin ['rægəmʌfin], *n.* Gueux, polisson, gamin des rues, va-nu-pieds, mauvais garnement, *m.*

rag-bolt, *n.* Cheville à fiche, *f.* **rag-doll,** *n.* Poupée de chiffons, *f.* **rag-fair,** *n.* Marché aux vieux habits, *m.* **rag-gatherer,** *n.* Chiffonnier, *m.* **ragman,** *n.* (*pl.* **ragmen**) Marchand de chiffons; chiffonnier, *m.* **rag-picker,** *n.* Chiffonnier, *m.* **ragstone,** *n.* Bourru, *m.* **rag-time,** *n.* (*Mus.*) Mesure à contre-temps; musique syncopée, *f.* **rag-wheel,** *n.* (*Tech.*) Hérisson, *m.* **ragwort,** *n.* Jacobée, herbe de Saint-Jacques, *f.*

rage [reidʒ], *n.* Rage, fureur, *f.,* emportement, *m.;* furie, manie, *f. In a rage,* furieux, en fureur; *it's all the rage,* cela fait fureur, c'est le grand chic; *to fly into a rage,* se mettre en fureur, s'emporter; *to put into a rage,* mettre en fureur.—*v.i.* Être furieux, être en fureur, s'emporter; (*fig.*) se déchaîner, sévir, faire des ravages. *War was raging in Europe,* la guerre sévissait en Europe. ***rageful,** *a.* Furieux, violent.

ragged ['rægid], *a.* En haillons, en guenilles, déguenillé (of persons); en lambeaux, en loques, déchiré (of things); (*fig.*) ébréché, disparate. **raggedly,** *adv.* En lambeaux, en guenilles. **raggedness,** *n.* Délabrement, déguenillement, *m.;* guenilles, *f.pl.*

raging ['reidʒiŋ], *a.* Furieux, en fureur; déchaîné, acharné, violent (of tempests, war, etc.).—*n.* Fureur, violence, *f.* **ragingly,** *adv.* Furieusement.

ragout [rə'guː], *n.* Ragoût, *m.*

raid [reid], *n.* Razzia, incursion, *f.;* raid, coup de main, *m. Air raid,* raid aérien, *m.—v.t.* Faire une incursion dans; faire une descente dans; piller; bombarder. **raider,** *n.* Maraudeur; corsaire; commando; avion en raid, *m.*

rail [reil], *n.* Barre, *f.,* barreau (bar of wood, of metal, etc.), *m.;* rampe (of a staircase), *f.;* parapet (of bridges etc.), *m.;* balustrade, *f.,* garde-fou, *m.,* grille, barrière (hand-rail) (*Naut.*) lisse, *f.;* (*Rail.*) rail, chemin de fer; râle (bird), *m. By rail,* par chemin de fer; *live-rail,* rail conducteur, *m.; to run off the rails,* dérailler.—*v.t.* Entourer d'une grille, enclore, griller. *To rail in,* fermer avec une grille, griller.—*v.i.* Dire des injures (à). *To rail at,* criailler, invectiver.

railed, *a.* À voie. *Double-railed,* à double voie. **railer,** *n.* Criailleur, détracteur, médisant, *m.*

railing, *n.* Injures, invectives, *f.pl.;* grille, *f.,* garde-fou (barrier etc.), *m.;* rampe (of a staircase), *f.*

raillery ['reiləri], *n.* Raillerie, *f.*

railroad, *n.* (*Am.*) [RAILWAY].

railway ['reilwei], *n.* Chemin de fer, *m.,* voie ferrée, *f.* **railway-contractor,** *n.* Entrepreneur de chemins de fer, *m.* **railway-guide,** *n.* Indicateur (des chemins de fer), *m.* **railwayman,** *n.* (*pl.* **-men**) Employé des chemins de fer, cheminot, *m.* **railway-porter,** *n.* Facteur, porteur, *m.* **railway-rug,** *n.* Couverture de voyage, *f.* **railway-station,** *n.* Gare, *f.*

raiment ['reimənt], *n.* Vêtement, *m.,* vêtements, *m.pl.*

rain [rein], *n.* Pluie, *f. Fine rain,* pluie fine, *f.; heavy rain,* forte pluie, *f.; it looks like rain,* le temps est à la pluie; *pelting rain,* pluie battante, *f.; to pour with rain,* pleuvoir à verse.—*v.i.* Pleuvoir. *It rains,* il pleut; *to rain hard,* pleuvoir à verse.—*v.t.* Faire pleuvoir. *To rain cats and dogs,* pleuvoir des hallebardes; *to rain shot,* faire pleuvoir des projectiles.

rainbow, *n.* Arc-en-ciel, *m.* **raincoat,** *n.* Imperméable, *m.* **rainfall,** *n.* Pluie annuelle, pluie tombée, *f. Heavy rainfall,* pluie abondante, *f.* **rain-gauge,** *n.* Pluviomètre, *m.* **raininess,** *n.* Temps pluvieux, *m.* **rainproof,** *a.* Imperméable, imperméable à la pluie. **rainwater,** *n.* Eau de pluie, *f.* **rainy,** *a.* Pluvieux. *To lay by something for a rainy day,* garder une poire pour la soif.

raise [reiz], *v.t.* Lever; élever; hausser (prices etc.); exhausser (buildings etc.); soulever (to lift etc.); produire (to produce) cultiver (vegetables); augmenter, accroître (to increase); faire naître (suspicions); soulever (to excite); pousser (a cry); ressusciter (the dead); susciter (a quarrel etc.); faire lever (dough); évoquer (evil spirits); faire reprendre à, relever (courage); trouver, se procurer (money); faire (a loan etc.). *To raise a statue*, ériger une statue; *to raise one's hat*, tirer son chapeau, se découvrir; *to raise the blockade*, lever le blocus; *to raise the wind*, se procurer de l'argent; *to raise up*, lever, élever, hausser. —*n.* (*Cards*) Relance; augmentation (wages), *f.*

raised, *a.* Levé; en relief. *Raised pie*, pâté en croûte, *m.*, timbale, *f.*; *to be raised to the peerage*, être élevé à la pairie. **raiser,** *n.* Personne *or* chose qui lève, *f.*; auteur, fondateur, cultivateur; éleveur (of livestock), *m.*

raisin [reizn], *n.* Raisin sec, *m.*

raising ['reizin[, *n.* Action de lever; augmentation, *f.*, accroissement; exhaussement (of a wall), *m.*; levée (of taxes, of troops, of sieges, etc.), *f.*; élevage (of livestock), *m.*; culture (of plants etc.); extraction (of ores), *f.* **raising-piece,** *n.* (*Carp.*) Sablière, *f.*

raj [rɑːdʒ], *n.* Souveraineté (in India), *f.*

rajah ['rɑːdʒə], *n.* Raja, rajah, *m.*

rake [reik], *n.* (*Hort.*) Râteau; fourgon (for an oven), *m.*; (*Naut.*) inclination (of masts), quête (of sternpost), *f.*; viveur, noceur, roué (libertine), *m.*—*v.t.* (*Agric.*) Râteler; (*Hort.*) ratisser; gratter, racler (to scrape); ramasser (to collect); enfiler (with guns). *To rake about, over*, fouiller, fureter dans; *to rake out*, éteindre (a fire); *to rake up*, ramasser, (*fig.*) raviver, réveiller; *to rake up an old grievance*, réveiller le chat qui dort.—*v.i.* Râteler, ratisser; racler; être incliné. **rakeful,** *n.* Râtelée, *f.* **rake-off,** *n.* (*fam.*) Ristourne, *f.* **raker,** *n.* Râteleur, *m.* **raking,** *n.* (*Hort.*) Ratissage; (*Agric.*) râtelage, *m.*; râtelée (quantity raked), *f.*—*a.* D'enfilade.

rakish [reikiʃ], *a.* Dissolu, libertin effronté; élancé (of ships). **rakishly,** *adv.* En libertin; crânement. **rakishness,** *n.* Libertinage; air crâne, *m.*

rally ['ræli], *v.t.* Rallier, rassembler; ranimer, se ranimer; railler (to banter).—*v.i.* Se rallier, se rassembler; (*fig.*) reprendre des forces, se remettre.—*n.* Ralliement, *m.*; raillerie (bantering), *f.* **rallying,** *n.* Ralliement, *m.*; raillerie (bantering), *f.* **rallying-point,** *n.* Point de ralliement, *m.*

Ralph [reif *or* rælf]. Raoul, *m.*

ram [ræm], *n.* Bélier; mouton, *m.*, hie (pile-driver), *f.*; éperon (of a man-of-war), *m.* *Battering-ram*, bélier, *m.*—*v.i.* Enfoncer; pilonner, battre à la hie, tasser (the ground etc.); bourrer (into a gun).

Ramadan [ræmə'dɑːn], *n.* Ramadan, ramazan, *m.* (Mohammedan fast).

ramble [ræmbl], *n.* Excursion à pied, grande promenade; (*fig.*) divagation, *f.*—*v.i.* Errer, se promener; errer çà et là; (*fig.*) divaguer, parler sans suite. *To ramble about*, errer par, parcourir, battre la campagne. **rambler,** *n.* Excursionniste (à pied); rosier grimpant, *m.* **rambling,** *n.* Excursions, promenades à l'aventure; (*fig.*) divagations, *f.pl.*—*a.* Errant, vagabond; (*fig.*) décousu, sans suite, incohérent. **ramblingly,** *adv.* D'une manière vagabonde; d'une manière décousue.

ramification [ræmifi'keiʃən], *n.* Ramification, *f.*

ramify ['ræmifai], *v.i.* Se ramifier.

rammer ['ræmə], *n.* Pilon, *m.*; baguette (of a gun); hie, demoiselle (for driving stones etc.), *f.*; (*Artill.*) refouloir, *m.*

ramp [ræmp], *n.* Rampe, montée, *f.*; (*fam.*) escroquerie, *f.*

rampage [ræm'peidʒ], *v.i.* and *n.* (*colloq.*) *To rampage* (*about*), *to be on the rampage*, avoir après tout le monde, se conduire en énergumène. **rampageous** [-'peidʒəs], *a.* Furieux, tapageur.

rampancy ['ræmpənsi], *n.* Pouvoir, empire, *m.* **rampant,** *a.* Dominant, violent; exubérant, effréné; (*Her.*) rampant.

rampart ['ræmpɑːt], *n.* Rempart, *m.*

rampion ['ræmpiən], *n.* Raiponce, *f.*

ramrod ['ræmrɔdj, *n.* Baguette, *f.* (of a rifle); écouvillon (of a cannon), *m.* *Stiff as a ramrod*, raide, droit comme un piquet, comme un manche à balai.

ramshackle ['ræmʃækl], *a.* Qui tombe en ruines, délabré.

ranch [rɑːntʃ], *n.* (*U.S.*) Ranch, *m.*; élevage, *m.* **rancher,** *n.* Propriétaire d'un ranch.

rancid ['rænsid], *a.* Rance. *To become rancid*, devenir rance, rancir. **rancidity** [-'siditi] *or* **rancidness,** *n.* Rancidité, *f.*

rancorous ['rænkərəs], *a.* Rancunier, haineux. **rancorously,** *adv.* Avec rancune. **rancour,** *n.* Haine, rancune, *f.*

randan [ræn'dæn], *n.* (*Row.*) Canot à trois rameurs, un de couple et deux de pointe.— *adv.* *To row randan*, ramer (ainsi) à trois.

randem ['rændəm], *n.* Attelage à trois chevaux en flèche, *m.*

Randolph ['rændɔlf]. Rodolphe, *m.*

random ['rændəm], *n.* Hasard, *m.* *At random*, au hasard, à l'aventure; à l'aveuglette; *to speak at random*, parler à tort et à travers.—*a.* Au hasard, fait au hasard. *Random shot*, coup perdu, *m.*

randy ['rændi], *a.* (*Sc.*) Tapageur; luxurieux, lascif.

ranee ['rɑːniː], *n.* Rani (épouse d'un rajah), *f.*

rang, *past* [RING (2)].

range [reindʒ], *n.* Rangée, *f.*, rang (row), *m.*; chaîne (of mountains etc.); classe, *f.*, ordre (class), *m.*; étendue, distance, portée, *f.*, essor (extent); champ, espace (space), *m.*; grille de cuisine, *f.*, fourneau; tir (firing-ground). *m.*; série; gamme, *f.* (colours, sizes, speeds); (*Naut.*) bitture (of cable), *f.* *Beyond the range, out of range*, hors de portée (de); *long range*, à longue portée (gun), à grand rayon d'action (aircraft); *within range*, à portée.— *v.t.* Ranger, arranger; aligner (avec); parcourir, rôder à travers, franchir. *To range oneself with*, se ranger avec.—*v.i.* S'aligner; être rangé; (*Naut.*) ranger la côte; varier. *To range over the country*, parcourir le pays.

range-finder, *n.* Télémètre, *m.*

ranger, *n.* Garde-forestier, *m.*; (*pl.*) (*Mil.*) chasseurs à cheval, *m.pl.*

range-table, *n.* Table de tir, *f.*

ranging ['reindʒin], *n.* Action de ranger, *f.*; (*Mil.*) réglage du tir; (*Print.*) alignement, *m.* *Sound ranging*, repérage par le son, *m.*

Rangoon [ræn'guːn]. Rangoun, *m.*

rank (1) [ræŋk], *n.* Rang, ordre, *m.*, classe, *f.*; (*Mil.*) grade, *m.*; (*fig.*) haut rang, *m.* *An officer of high rank*, un officier supérieur; *a person of rank*, une personne de haut rang; *taxi rank*, station de taxis, *f.*; *rank and file*, la troupe, *f.*, les hommes de troupe, *m.pl.*; *risen from the ranks*, sorti du rang; *to break the ranks*, se débander; *to close the ranks*, serrer les rangs; *to pull rank*, faire valoir son rang; *to reduce to the ranks*, casser, dégrader; *to take rank with*, avoir le rang de.—*v.t.* Ranger, classer. *To rank among one's friends*, compter parmi ses amis.—*v.i.* Se ranger, être classé; occuper un rang. *To rank after*, prendre rang après; *to rank high among*, occuper un rang élevé parmi. **ranker**, *n.* Officier sorti du rang; simple soldat, *m.*

rank (2) [ræŋk], *a.* (Trop) vigoureux, (trop) fort, luxuriant; (*fig.*) grossier, rude, extrême; vrai (downright); parfait; fétide (in smell).

rankle [ræŋkl], *v.i.* S'envenimer, s'enflammer. *Hatred rankles in his breast*, la haine lui ronge le cœur. **rankling**, *a.* Envenimé, enflammé.

rankly ['ræŋkli], *adv.* Vigoureusement, fortement; sentant fort. **rankness**, *n.* Vigueur, surabondance, exubérance, *f.*; grossièreté, *f.*; odeur de rance, odeur forte, rancidité, *f.*

ransack ['rænsæk], *v.t.* Saccager, piller; fouiller, fouiller dans. **ransacking**, *n.* Pillage, *m.*

ransom ['rænsəm], *n.* Rançon, *f.* *To hold to ransom*, mettre à rançon; rançonner.—*v.t.* Rançonner. **ransoming**, *n.* Mise à rançon, *f.*; rançonnement, *m.*

rant [rænt], *n.* Déclamation extravagante, *f.* —*v.i.* Déclamer avec extravagance, extravaguer; tempêter. **ranter**, *n.* Déclamateur, énergumène, *m.* **ranting**, *a.* D'énergumène, extravagant.

ranula ['rænjulə], *n.* (*Path.*) Ranule, *f.*

ranunculus [rə'nʌŋkjuləs], *n.* (*Bot.*) Renoncule, *f.*

rap [ræp], *n.* Tape, *f.*, petit coup sec, *m.* *I don't care a rap*, je m'en soucie comme de l'an quarante; *not worth a rap*, qui ne vaut pas un sou; *there's a rap at the door*, on frappe à la porte.—*v.t.*, *v.i.*, Frapper. *To rap out an oath*, lâcher un juron; *to rap someone over the knuckles*, (*fig.*) remettre quelqu'un à sa place.

rapacious [rə'peiʃəs], *a.* Rapace. **rapaciously**, *adv.* Avec rapacité. **rapaciousness** or **rapacity** [-'pæsiti], *n.* Rapacité, *f.*

rape (1) [reip], *n.* (*Poet.*) Rapt, enlèvement, *m.*; (*Law*) viol, *m.*—*v.t.* Enlever de force; violer.

rape (2) [reip], *n.* Colza, *m.*, navette, *f.* **rape-cake**, *n.* Tourteau de colza, *m.* **rape-oil**, *n.* Huile de colza, *f.* **rape-seed**, *n.* Graine de colza, *f.*

Raphael ['ræfeiəl]. Rafael, *f.*; (*artist*) Raphaël, *m.*

rapid ['ræpid], *a.* and *n.* Rapide, *m.* **rapid-fire**, *a.* À tir rápide. **rapidity** [-'piditi] or **rapidness**, *n.* Rapidité, *f.* **rapidly**, *adv.* Rapidement.

rapier ['reipiə], *n.* Rapière, *f.*

rapine ['ræpain], *n.* Rapine, *f.*

rappee [ræ'pi:], *n.* Tabac râpé, *m.*

rapper ['ræpə], *n.* Frappeur, râfleur d'antiquités (dans les campagnes), *m.*

rapscallion [ræp'skæljən], *n.* Vaurien, propre à rien, *m.*

rapt [ræpt], *a.* Ravi, transporté, extasié; profond (attention).

raptores [ræp'tɔ:ri:z], *n.pl.* (*Orn.*) Rapaces, *m.pl.*

raptorial [ræp'tɔ:riəl], *a.* (*Orn.*) De proie.

rapture ['ræptʃə], *n.* Ravissement, transport, *m.*, extase, *f.* **rapturous**, *a.* Ravissant; enthousiaste, joyeux. **rapturously**, *adv.* Avec transport, avec enthousiasme.

rare [rɛə], *a.* Rare; clairsemé; raréfié; fameux; à moitié cru (of meat).

rarebit ['rɛəbit], *n.* *Welsh rarebit*, [RABBIT].

*raree-show, *n.* Spectacle ambulant, *m.*; curiosité, *f.*

rarefaction [rɛəri'fækʃən], *n.* Raréfaction, *f.* **rarefiable** [-'faiəbl], *a.* Raréfiable. **rarefy** ['rɛərifai], *v.t.* Raréfier.—*v.i.* Se raréfier. **rarefying**, *a.* Raréfiant.

rarely ['rɛəli], *adv.* Rarement. **rareness** or **rarity**, *n.* Rareté, *f.*

rascal ['rɑ:skl], *n.* Coquin, fripon, gredin, *m.* **rascality** [-'kæliti], *n.* Friponnerie, gredinerie, coquinerie, *f.* **rascally**, *a.* Coquin, fripon, misérable, vil.

rase [RAZE].

rash (1) [ræʃ], *n.* Éruption, *f.*

rash (2) [ræʃ], *a.* Téméraire; irréfléchi, imprudent, précipité. *It is very rash of you*, c'est très imprudent de votre part.

rasher ['ræʃə], *n.* Tranche, *f.* *Rasher of bacon*, tranche de lard grillée, *f.*

rashly ['ræʃli], *adv.* Témérairement; inconsidérément, imprudemment.

rashness, *n.* Témérité; précipitation, imprudence, *f.*

rasp [rɑ:sp], *n.* Râpe, *f.*—*v.t.* Râper; chapeler (bread); râcler, écorcher (surface, skin).—*v.i.* Grincer, crisser.

raspberry ['rɑ:zbəri], *n.* Framboise, *f.*; (*fam.*) rebuffade, *f.*; engueulade, *f.* *To get a raspberry*, se faire rabrouer, se faire engueuler. **raspberry-bush**, *n.* Framboisier, *m.* **raspberry-jam**, *n.* Confiture de framboises, *f.* **raspberry-vinegar**, *n.* Vinaigre framboisé, *m.*

rasper ['rɑ:spə], *n.* Râpeur, *m.*, râpeuse; râpe, *f.* **rasping**, *n.* Râpage, *m.*; (*pl.*) râpure, *f.*; chapelure (of bread), *f.*; crissement, *m.*; (*Med.*) bruit de râpe, *m.*—*a.* Grinçant, âpre, rauque (voice). **rasping-mill**, *n.* Moulin à râper, *m.*

rat [ræt], *n.* Rat, *m.*, rate, *f.*; (*Polit.*) jaune, renard, *m.* *To smell a rat*, se douter de quelque chose, flairer un piège; *like a drowned rat*, trempé jusqu'aux os.—*v.i.* Tuer des rats; (*Polit.*) abandonner son parti, tourner casaque. *To rat on someone*, vendre quelqu'un. **rat-catcher**, *n.* Preneur de rats, *m.* **rat-poison**, **rat's-bane**, *n.* Mort aux rats, *m.* **rat-tail**, *n.* Queue-de-rat, *f.* **rat-trap**, *n.* Ratière, *f.*

ratafia [rætə'fi:ə], *n.* Ratafia, *m.*

ratch [rætʃ], *n.* Rochet, *m.*

ratchet ['rætʃit], *n.* Cliquet, *m.*, dent d'engrenage, *f.* **ratchet-brace** or **ratchet-jack**, *n.* Vilbrequin à cliquet, *m.* **ratchet-wheel**, *n.* Roue à rochet, *f.*

rate [reit], *n.* Prix, *m.*; raison, proportion (standard), *f.*; taux (money, population); cours (of exchange); degré, rang, ordre (degree), *m.*; vitesse (degree of speed); taxe, *f.*, impôt (tax), *m.* *At a cheap rate*, à bon marché; *at a great rate*, grand train; *at any rate*, en tout cas, à quelque prix que ce soit, quoi qu'il en soit; *at a tremendous rate*, ventre à terre, à bride abattue; *at that rate*, sur ce pied-là, à ce compte-là, de cette façon; *at the rate of*, à raison de, à la vitesse de; *at the rate you are going you will soon be ruined*, au train où vous allez vous serez bientôt ruiné; *first-rate*, de première classe, de premier ordre, de première qualité; *poor-rate*, taxe des pauvres, *f.*; *she was talking away at a great rate*, elle parlait avec une volubilité extrême.—*v.t.* Évaluer; classer; taxer; gronder, réprimander, tancer, semoncer; faire une estimation; considérer, regarder (comme).—*v.i.* *To rate as*, être classé comme.

rateable ['reitəbl], *a.* Qu'on peut évaluer; imposable. *Rateable value* (building), valeur locative imposable, *f.*

rate-book, *n.* Registre (pour l'assiette et la perception d'une taxe), *m.* **rate-payer**, *n.* Contribuable, *m.* or *f.*

rathe [rɑːθ], *a.* Hâtif, précoce.

rather ['rɑːðə], *adv.* Plutôt; un peu, quelque peu (somewhat); assez, passablement (tolerably). *Anything rather than*, rien moins que; *I rather think*, j'ai idée, je suis porté à croire; *I would rather*, j'aimerais mieux; *or rather*, ou plutôt, ou pour mieux dire; *rather!* un peu! pour sûr! *rather ill*, un peu malade; *rather pretty*, assez joli; *the rather for* or *the rather because*, d'autánt plus que; *to choose rather*, préférer, aimer mieux; *with rather a lisp*, avec quelque chose comme un zézaiement.

ratification [rætifi'keiʃən], *n.* Ratification, *f.*

ratifier ['rætifaiə], *n.* Personne qui ratifie, *f.* **ratify**, *v.t.* Ratifier, approuver. **ratifying**, *a.* Ratificatif.

rating ['reitiŋ], *n.* Estimation, évaluation; répartition d'impôt (assessment); gronderie, semonce, *f.*, (*colloq.*) savon, *m.*; (*Navy*) classe, *f.*, matelot, *m.*, homme des classes, *m.*

ratio ['reiʃiou], *n.* Proportion, raison, *f.*, rapport, *m.* *In indirect ratio*, en raison inverse; *in the ratio of*, dans le rapport de.

ratiocinate [ræti'ɔsineit], *v.i.* Ratiociner.

ratiocination [rætiɔsi'neiʃən], *n.* Ratiocination, *f.*, raisonnement, *m.*

ration ['ræʃən], *n.* Ration, *f.* *Ration bread*, pain de munition, *m.*—*v.t.* Rationner, mettre à la ration. **ration-book**, *n.* Carte de ravitaillement, carte d'alimentation, *f.* **rationing**, *n.* Rationnement, *m.*

rational [ræʃənl], *a.* Raisonnable, rationnel; doué de raison.

rationale [ræʃiə'neili], *n.* Analyse raisonnée, *f.*

rationalism ['ræʃənəlizm], *n.* Rationalisme, *m.* **rationalist**, *n.* Rationaliste, *m.* **rationality** [-'næliti], *n.* Rationalité, *f.*; raisonnement, caractère rationnel, *m.* **rationalization**, *n.* Rationalisation; organisation rationnelle, *f.* (industry). **rationalize**, *v.t.* Rationaliser. **rationally**, *adv.* Raisonnablement, rationnellement.

Ratisbon ['rætizbɔn]. Ratisbonne, *f.*

ratlines ['rætlainz], *n.pl.* (*Naut.*) Enfléchures, *f.pl.*

rattan [rə'tæn], *n.* Rotin, *m.*

rat-tat ['ræt'tæt]. (*onom.*) Toc-toc.

ratteen [rə'tiːn], *n.* Ratine, *f.*

ratten ['rætən], *v.t.* Intimider; saboter.

ratter ['rætə], *n.* Ratier (dog), preneur de rats, *m.*

ratting ['rætiŋ], *n.* Apostasie, désertion, *f.*

rattle [rætl], *v.t.* Faire claquer, faire sonner; secouer (chains etc.). *Nothing rattled him*, (*fig.*) rien ne le démontait; *to rattle off*, expédier, réciter rapidement.—*v.i.* Faire un bruit sec, cliqueter, crépiter. *To rattle away*, s'éloigner rapidement; *to rattle on*, aller

toujours.—*n.* Bruit (noise); cliquetis (of metals); râle (in the throat); hochet (toy), *m.*; crécelle, *f.*; bavard, *m.* *Death-rattle*, râle de la mort, *m.* **rattle-brained** or **rattle-headed**, *a.* Étourdi, écervelé. **rattlesnake**, *n.* Serpent à sonnettes, crotale, *m.* **rattle-traps**, *n.pl.* (*colloq.*) Bataclan, *m.*, bagages, *m.pl.*

rattling, *a.* Bruyant; (*fig.*) excellent. (*slang*) *Rattling good*, excellent, épatant; *at a rattling pace*, au grand trot; *rattling tongue*, langue bien pendue, *f.*—*n.* Bruit, cliquetis, *m.*

ratty ['ræti], *a.* (*slang*) Fâché; grincheux.

raucity ['rɔːsiti] or **raucousness**, *n.* Son rauque, *m.*, raucité, *f.*

raucous ['rɔːkəs], *a.* Rauque.

ravage ['rævidʒ], *n.* Ravage, *m.*—*v.t.* Ravager. **ravager**, *n.* Ravageur, dévastateur, *m.*

rave [reiv], *v.i.* Être en délire, avoir le délire; (*fig.*) extravaguer, battre la campagne. *To rave about*, raffoler de, être fou de; *to rave at*, s'emporter contre.

ravel [rævl], *v.t.* Embrouiller, entortiller. *To ravel out*, effilocher; démêler, débrouiller.—*v.i.* S'embrouiller, s'entortiller.—*n.* Enchevêtrement, *m.*

ravelin ['rævlin], *n.* Ravelin, *m.*

raven (1) [reivn], *n.* Corbeau, *m.*

raven (2) [rævn], *v.t.* Dévorer.—*v.i.* Chercher sa proie. **ravening** or **ravenous** ['rævənəs], *a.* Dévorant, vorace. **ravenously**, *adv.* Avec voracité, *f.* **ravenousness**, *n.* Voracité, rapacité, *f.*

Ravenna [ræ'venə]. Ravenne, *f.*

raves [reivz], *n.pl.* Ridelles, *f.pl.*

ravine [rə'viːn], *n.* Ravin, *m.*

raving ['reiviŋ], *a.* En délire, délirant; furieux, fou. *Raving mad*, fou à lier, fou furieux.—*n.* Délire, *m.* **ravingly**, *adv.* Furieusement, frénétiquement.

ravish ['ræviʃ], *v.t.* Ravir; enlever; (*fig.*) transporter. **ravisher**, *n.* Ravisseur, *m.* **ravishing**, *a.* Ravissant. **ravishingly**, *adv.* À ravir, d'une manière ravissante. **ravishment**, *n.* Ravissement, *m.*

raw [rɔː], *a.* Cru; vif, écorché (bare etc.); (*fig.*) sans expérience, inexpérimenté, novice, neuf; pur (of liquors); grège (of silk); brut (of hides etc.); froid et humide (of the weather). *Raw hand*, novice, *m.* or *f.*; *raw hide*, cuir vert, *m.*; *raw materials*, matières premières, *f.pl.*; *to give someone a raw deal*, en faire voir de dures à quelqu'un.—*n.* *In the raw*, brut, fruste; *to touch on the raw*, toucher au vif.—*v.t.* Mettre à vif.

raw-boned, *a.* Qui n'a que la peau et les os; maigre, décharné. **raw-head**, *n.* Loup-garou, *m.* **rawly**, *adv.* Crûment, sans expérience. **rawness**, *n.* Crudité, *f.*; froid humide (of the weather), *m.*; (*fig.*) inexpérience, ignorance, *f.*

ray [rei], *n.* Rayon, *m.*; raie (fish), *f.* *Cosmic rays*, rayons cosmiques, *m.pl.* (*Ichth.*) *Thornback ray*, raie bouclée. **rayless**, *a.* Sans rayon, sans lumière.

Raymond ['reimənd]. Raymond, *m.*

rayon ['reiən], *n.* Rayonne, *f.*

raze [reiz], *v.t.* Raser, effleurer; rayer, effacer (to erase); abattre, détruire (building).

razor ['reizə], *n.* Rasoir, *m.* *Electric razor*, rasoir électrique, *m.*; *hollow-ground razor*, rasoir évidé, *m.*; *safety razor*, rasoir de sûreté,

rasoir mécanique. **razor-bill,** *n.* Petit pingouin, *m.* **razor-blade,** *n.* Lame de rasoir, *f.* **razor-edge,** *n.* Fil, tranchant, de rasoir, *m.* (*fig.*) *On a razor-edge,* au bord de l'abîme, sur la corde raide. **razor-fish,** *n.* Rasoir, *m.* **razor-strop,** *n.* Cuir à rasoir, *m.*
razzia ['ræziə], *n.* Razzia, *f.*
razzle [ræzl], *n.* (*fam.*) Bombance, bombe, *f.*
re [ri:], *prep.* Au sujet de, à propos de.
reabsorb [ri:əb'sɔːb], *v.t.* Réabsorber. **reabsorption** [-'sɔːpʃən], *n.* Réabsorption, *f.*
reach [ri:tʃ], *n.* Portée, atteinte; étendue (extent), *f.*; bief (of a canal), *m.* *Out of reach,* hors d'atteinte; *out of someone's reach,* hors de la portée de quelqu'un; *within someone's reach,* à la portée de quelqu'un.—*v.t.* Atteindre à, atteindre, toucher; passer, donner (to hand); arriver à, parvenir à (to attain); tendre, étendre (to extend). *Reach me down that book,* descendez-moi ce livre; *the letter will reach you tomorrow,* la lettre vous parviendra demain.—*v.i.* S'étendre de . . . à.
reachable, *a.* Qu'on peut atteindre. **reach-me-down,** *n.* Décrochez-moi-ça, *m.*
react (1) [ri:'ækt], *v.i.* Jouer de nouveau, rejouer.
react (2) [ri:'ækt], *v.i.* Réagir (sur). **reaction,** *n.* Réaction, *f.* **reactionary,** *a.* and *n.* Réactionnaire, *m.* **reactivate,** *v.t.* Réactiver. **reactive,** *a.* Réactif.
reactor, *n.* Réacteur, *m.*
read [ri:d], *v.t.* (*past* and *p.p.* **read** [red]) Lire; faire la lecture de; (*fig.*) étudier. *To read again,* relire, étudier de nouveau; *to read aloud,* lire à haute voix; *to read a piece of music at sight,* déchiffrer un morceau; *to read between the lines,* lire entre les lignes; *to read history,* (*Univ.*) faire des études d'histoire; *to read law for the Bar,* faire son droit; *to read on,* continuer de lire; *to read out,* lire tout haut; *to read over,* parcourir; *to read over and over again,* lire et relire; *to read through,* parcourir; lire d'un bout à l'autre; *to read to,* faire la lecture à; *to read to oneself,* lire tout bas; *to read up,* faire une étude spéciale de; *worth reading,* digne d'être lu.—*v.i.* Lire, faire la lecture; se lire. *Not to read well,* ne pas faire bon effet (of a passage); *to be well read,* avoir beaucoup de lecture, être instruit, être versé (dans); *which we read of,* dont on fait mention dans les livres.
readable, *a.* Lisible; qui se lit avec plaisir. **readableness,** *n.* Lisibilité, *f.*
readdress [ri:ə'dres], *v.t.* Faire suivre (a letter etc.).
reader ['ri:də], *n.* Lecteur, *m.*, lectrice, *f.*; (*Print.*) correcteur, *m.*; personne qui aime la lecture, *f.*, liseur (person fond of reading), *m.*; (*Univ.*) chargé de cours, *m.*; (*sch.*) livre de lecture, *m.*
readership, *n.* (*Univ.*) Chaire, *f.*
readily ['redili], *adv.* Tout de suite, promptement; facilement; volontiers (willingly), avec plaisir, de bonne grâce. **readiness,** *n.* Empressement, *m.*, promptitude; facilité; bonne volonté (willingness), *f.* *In readiness,* tout prêt; *readiness of mind,* présence d'esprit, *f.*; *readiness of wit,* talent de repartie, *m.*
reading ['ri:diŋ], *n.* La lecture; variante (variation in a text), leçon; hauteur (of the barometer), *f.*—*a. The reading public,* le

public qui lit. **reading-book,** *n.* Livre de lecture, *m.* **reading-desk,** *n.* Pupitre, *m.* **reading-lamp,** *n.* Lampe de travail, *f.* **reading-room,** *n.* Salle de lecture, *f.*
readjourn [ri:ə'dʒəːn], *v.t.* Ajourner de nouveau.
readjust, *v.t.* Rajuster, rectifier. **readjustment,** *n.* Rajustement, *m.*
readmission or **readmittance,** *n.* Réadmission, *f.* **readmit,** *v.t.* Réadmettre.
readopt, *v.t.* Réadopter. **readoption,** *n.* Réadoption, *f.*
readorn, *v.t.* Orner de nouveau.
ready ['redi], *a.* Prêt, prompt, disposé; facile, habile; vif (quick of apprehension); comptant (of money); le premier venu, sous la main (near at hand). *Now ready,* vient de paraître (of books); *ready! fire!* (*Mil.*) en joue! feu! *to get ready,* se préparer, se tenir prêt; *to have a ready tongue,* avoir la langue bien pendue; *to make ready,* préparer, apprêter. **ready-made,** *a.* Tout fait, confectionné. **ready-reckoner,** *n.* Barême, *m.* **ready-witted,** *a.* À l'esprit vif.
reaffirm [ri:ə'fəːm], *v.t.* Réaffirmer. **reaffirmation** [-æfə'meiʃən], *n.* Nouvelle affirmation, *f.*
reaffix [ri:ə'fiks], *v.t.* Réapposer. **reaffixing,** *n.* Réapposition, *f.*
reafforestation [ri:əfɔres'teiʃn], *n.* Reboisement, *m.*
reagent [ri:'eidʒənt], *n.* (*Chem.*) Réactif, *m.*
real (1) ['riəl], *a.* Réel; vrai, véritable; effectif; (*Law*) immeuble, immobilier. *Real estate,* immeubles, biens immobiliers, *m.pl.*
real (2) ['reiəl], *n.* Réal (Spanish coin), *m.*
realgar [ri'ælgə], *n.* Réalgar, *m.*
realism ['ri:əlizm], *n.* Réalisme, *m.* **realist,** *n.* Réaliste, *m.* **realistic** [-'listik], *a.* Réaliste. **realistically,** *adv.* Avec réalisme. **reality** [-'æliti], *n.* Réalité, *f.*; réel, *m. In reality,* réellement, en réalité.
realizable ['ri:əlaizəbl], *a.* Réalisable.
realization [ri:əlai'zeiʃən], *n.* Réalisation; conception nette, *f.*
realize ['ri:əlaiz], *v.t.* Réaliser; effectuer; se rendre compte de, prendre conscience de, bien comprendre; concevoir, se représenter, se figurer; rapporter, produire (to fetch); (*Law*) immobiliser. *To be realized,* se réaliser.
reallege [ri:ə'ledʒ], *v.t.* Alléguer de nouveau.
reallocate [ri:'ælokeit], *v.t.* Réadjuger.
really ['ri:əli], *adv.* Réellement, en effet, effectivement; vraiment, pour de bon.—*int.* En vérité! à vrai dire!
realm [relm], *n.* Royaume, (*fig.*) domaine, *m.*
realtor [ri'æltə], *n.* Agent immobilier, *m.*
realty ['ri:əlti], *n.* Biens immeubles, *m.pl.*
ream [ri:m], *n.* Rame, *f.* (of paper).—*v.t.* Aléser.
reamer ['ri:mə], *n.* (*Naut.*) Alésoir, *m.*
reanimate [ri:'ænimeit], *v.t.* Ranimer. **reanimation** [-'meiʃən], *n.* Action de ranimer, *f.*
reannex [ri:ə'neks], *v.t.* Annexer de nouveau. **reannexation** [-ænek'seiʃən], *n.* Action d'annexer de nouveau, réannexion, *f.*
reap [ri:p], *v.t.* Moissonner; (*fig.*) retirer, recueillir. *To reap the harvest,* faire la moisson.—*v.i.* Moissonner, faire la moisson.
reaper, *n.* Moissonneur, *m.*, moissonneuse, *f. Reaper and binder,* moissonneuse-lieuse, *f.*

[423]

reaping, *n.* Moisson, *f.* **reaping-hook,** *n.* Faucille, *f.* **reaping-machine,** *n.* Moissonneuse, *f.*

reappear [ri:ə'piə], *v.i.* Reparaître. **reappearance,** *n.* Réapparition; rentrée (of an actor); (*Law*) comparution nouvelle, *f.*

reapply [ri:ə'plai], *v.t.* Appliquer de nouveau.

reappoint [ri:ə'pɔint], *v.t.* Réintégrer; renommer. **reappointment,** *n.* Réintégration, *f.*

reapportion [ri:ə'pɔ:ʃən], *v.t.* Répartir de nouveau.

rear (1) [riə], *n.* Dernier rang, *m.*; arrière-garde, *f.*; derrière (of buildings etc.), *m.*; (*pl.*) (*pop.*) latrines, *f.pl. At or in the rear,* à l'arrière, derrière; *to attack in the rear,* attaquer par derrière; *to bring up the rear,* fermer la marche.—*a.* Situé à l'arrière; postérieur. *Rear wheel,* roue arrière, *f.* **rear-admiral,** *n.* Contre-amiral, *m.* **rear-engined,** *a.* Avec moteur à l'arrière. **rear-guard,** *n.* Arrière-garde, *f.* **rear-most,** *a.* Dernier; de queue. **rear-rank,** *n.* Dernier rang, *m.* **rearward,** *n.* Arrière-garde, *f.* **rearwards,** *adv.* À l'arrière. **rear-window,** *n.* (*Motor.*) Custode arrière, *f.*

rear (2) [riə], *v.t.* Élever.—*v.i.* Se cabrer.

re-arm [ri:'ɑ:m], *v.t., v.i.* Réarmer. **re-armament,** *n.* Réarmement, *m. Moral Re-Armament,* Réarmement Moral, *m.*

reascend [ri:ə'send], *v.t., v.i.* Remonter. **reascent,** *n.* Nouvelle ascension, *f.*

reason ['ri:zən], *n.* Raison, *f.*; raisonnement, *m. All the more reason,* raison de plus; *by reason of,* en raison de, à cause de; *for reasons best known to myself,* pour des raisons à moi connues; *for that very reason,* par la même raison; *for the same reason,* au même titre; *for the very reason that,* par cela même que, précisément parce que; *it stands to reason that,* la raison dit que, il va sans dire que; *reasons of state,* raisons d'état; *that stands to reason,* cela va sans dire; *there is every reason to believe,* il y a tout lieu de croire; *the reason for his departure,* la raison de son départ; *to bring to reason,* amener à la raison; *to have reason to believe,* avoir lieu de croire; *to listen to reason,* entendre raison; *to lose one's reason,* perdre sa raison.—*v.t., v.i.* Raisonner. *To reason into,* entraîner à; *to reason out of,* détourner de.

reasonable, *a.* Raisonnable; modéré. **reasonableness,** *n.* Caractère raisonnable, *m.*; raison, modération, *f.* **reasonably,** *adv.* Raisonnablement.

reasoner, *n.* Raisonneur, logicien, *m.*

reasoning, *n.* Raisonnement, *m.* **reasonless,** *a.* Sans raison.

reassemble [ri:ə'sembl], *v.t.* Assembler de nouveau, rassembler.—*v.i.* S'assembler de nouveau, se rassembler, rentrer.

reassert [ri:ə'sə:t], *v.t.* Affirmer de nouveau.

reassess [ri:ə'ses], *v.t.* Imposer de nouveau; réévaluer. **reassessment,** *n.* Réimposition, *f.*; réévaluation, *f.*

reassign [ri:ə'sain], *v.t.* Réassigner. **reassignment,** *n.* Réassignation, *f.*

reassume, *v.t.* Réassumer; reprendre (job).

reassurance [ri:ə'ʃuərəns], *n.* Action de rassurer; (*Comm.*) réassurance, *f.* **reassure,** *v.t.* Rassurer; (*Comm.*) réassurer.

reattach [ri:ə'tætʃ], *v.t.* Rattacher. **reattachment,** *n.* Nouvel attachement, *m.*

reattempt [ri:ə'tempt], *v.t.* Essayer de nouveau.—*n.* Nouvelle tentative, *f.*

reawaken [ri:ə'weikən], *v.t.* Réveiller; ranimer.—*v.i.* Se réveiller.

rebaptism [ri:'bæptizm], *n.* Nouveau baptême, *m.* **rebaptize** [-'taiz], *v.t.* Rebaptiser.

rebate (1) ['ri:beit], *n.* Rabais, *m.,* remise, réduction, ristourne, *f.*

rebate (2) [ri'beit], *v.t.* Diminuer, rabattre.

Rebecca [rə'bekə]. Rébecca, *f.*

*rebeck ['ri:bek], *n.* Rebec, *m.*

rebel (1) [rebl], *n.* Rebelle, révolté, *m.*

rebel (2) [ri'bel], *v.i.* Se révolter, se soulever (contre).

rebellion [ri'beljən], *n.* Rébellion, *f.*

rebellious [ri'beljəs], *a.* Rebelle. **rebelliously,** *adv.* En rebelle. **rebelliousness,** *n.* Rébellion, *f.*

rebind [ri:'baind], *v.t.* (*past and p.p.* **rebound** (2)) Relier de nouveau (a book); recercler (a wheel).

rebirth [ri:'bə:θ], *n.* Renaissance, *f.*

reboil [ri:'bɔil], *v.i.* Rebouillir.—*v.t.* Faire rebouillir.

rebore [ri:'bɔ:], *v.t.* (*Tech.*) Réaléser.

reborn [ri:'bɔ:n], *a.* Né de nouveau; réincarné.

rebound (1) [ri:'baund], *n.* Rebondissement, contre-coup; bond, *m.*—*v.i.* Rebondir.—*v.t.* Faire rebondir; renvoyer.

rebound (2), *past and p.p.* [REBIND].

rebroadcast ['ri:'brɔ:dka:st], *n.* Retransmission, *f.*—*v.t.* Retransmettre.

rebuff [ri'bʌf], *n.* Rebuffade, *f.,* échec, *m.*—*v.t.* Rebuter, repousser.

rebuild [ri:'bild], *v.t.* (*past and p.p.* **rebuilt**) Rebâtir, reconstruire. **rebuilder,** *n.* Reconstructeur, *m.* **rebuilding,** *n.* Reconstruction, *f.*

rebuke [ri'bju:k], *n.* Réprimande, *f.,* reproche, *m.*—*v.t.* Réprimander, reprendre, censurer. **rebuker,** *n.* Personne qui réprimande, *f.* **rebukingly,** *adv.* D'un ton de reproche.

reburnish [ri:'bə:niʃ], *v.t.* Repolir.

rebus ['ri:bəs], *n.* Rébus, *m.*

rebut [ri'bʌt], *v.t.* Rebuter, repousser, réfuter. **rebutter,** *n.* Réfutation; (*Law*) réplique, *f.*

recalcitrance [ri'kælsitrəns], *n.* Esprit réfractaire, *m.*

recalcitrant [ri'kælsitrənt], *a.* Récalcitrant, insoumis, réfractaire. **recalcitrate,** *v.i.* Récalcitrer, regimber.

recall [ri'kɔ:l], *n.* Rappel, *m.*; révocation, *f. Beyond recall,* irrévocablement, irrévocable. —*v.t.* Rappeler; retirer; se rappeler (to remember).

recant [ri'kænt], *v.t.* Rétracter, désavouer, abjurer.—*v.i.* Se rétracter; *chanter la palinodie. **recantation** [-ri:kæn'teiʃən], *n.* Rétractation, palinodie, *f.*

recap [ri:'kæp], (*fam.*) *abbr. of* [RECAPITULATION].

recapitulate [ri:kə'pitjuleit], *v.t.* Récapituler. **recapitulation** [-'leiʃən], *n.* Récapitulation, *f.* **recapitulatory,** *a.* Récapitulatif.

recapture [ri:'kæptʃə], *n.* Reprise, *f.*—*v.t.* Reprendre. *To recapture the past,* (faire) revivre le passé.

recarry [ri:'kæri], *v.t.* Reporter, rapporter.

recast [ri:'ka:st], *v.t.* (*past and p.p.* **recast**) Refondre; (*Arith.*) calculer de nouveau; (*Theat.*) faire une nouvelle distribution des rôles.

recce ['reki], *n.* (*Mil.*) (*fam.*) Reconnaissance, *f.*—*v.t.* Reconnaître.
recede [ri'si:d], *v.i.* Se retirer (de); s'éloigner; baisser (shares). **receding,** *a.* Fuyant (of the forehead), effacé (chin).
receipt [ri'si:t], *n.* Reçu, *m.*, quittance, *f.*, acquit, *m.*; réception (act of receiving); recette (recipe), *f.*; (*pl.*) recette, *f.*, recettes, *f.pl.*; récépissé, *m.* *Acknowledgment of receipt,* accusé de réception, *m.*; *deposit receipt,* certificat de dépôt, *m.*; *on receipt of,* au reçu de, contre envoi de (stamps etc.); *receipt in full,* quittance pour solde de compte; *to acknowledge the receipt of,* accuser réception de; *to be in receipt of,* avoir reçu; *to put a receipt to,* acquitter, mettre un acquit à.—*v.t.* Acquitter; mettre son acquit sur.
receipt-book, *n.* Livre de quittances, *m.*
receipted, *a.* Acquitté. *Bill receipted,* note acquittée, *f.*
receipt-stamp, *n.* Timbre de quittance, *m.*
receivable [ri'si:vəbl], *a.* Recevable; (*Comm.*) à recevoir.
receive [ri'si:v], *v.t.* Recevoir, accepter, admettre; accueillir; toucher (money); recéler (stolen goods). **received,** *p.p.* Reçu, pour acquit.
receiver, *n.* Receveur, percepteur; receleur, *m.*, receleuse, *f.* (of stolen objects); distributaire (sharer); destinataire (of letters); liquidateur (bankruptcy); (*Law*) séquestre; (*Chem.*) récipient; (*Teleph.*) récepteur, *m.* **receivership,** *n.* Emploi de receveur, *m.*
receiving, *n.* Réception, *f.*; recel (of stolen goods), *m.* **receiving-house,** *n.* Bureau de messagerie, *m.* **receiving-order**, *n.* Mandat d'action, *m.* **receiving-ship,** *n.* Ponton-caserne, *m.* **receiving-station,** *n.* (*Teleg.*) Station réceptrice, *f.*; poste récepteur, *m.*
recency ['ri:sənsi], *n.* Caractère récent, *m.*; date récente, *f.*
recension [ri'senʃən], *n.* Recension; revision, *f.*
recent ['ri:sənt], *a.* Récent, frais, nouveau. *Recent intelligence,* nouvelles fraîches, *f.pl.* **recently,** *adv.* Récemment, depuis peu.
receptacle [ri'septəkl], *n.* Réceptacle, *m.*; récipient, *m.*
reception [ri'sepʃən], *n.* Réception, *f.*; accueil, *m.* *For the reception of,* pour recevoir.
receptionist, *n.* Préposé(e) à la réception, réceptionniste, *m.* or *f.*
receptive [ri'septivJ, *a.* Susceptible de recevoir, réceptif (mind).
recess [ri'ses], *n.* Vacances (holidays), *f.pl.*; repli (of the heart); enfoncement, *m.*, niche, alcôve (of a bed), *f.*; recoin, *m.*
recession [ri'seʃən], *n.* Retraite, *f.*; désistement (from a claim), *m.*; (*U.S.*) baisse, *f.* (*St. Exch.*). **recessional,** *n.* Hymne de sortie du clergé, du.
recharge [ri:'tʃɑːdʒ], *v.t.* Recharger.
rechristen [ri:'krisən], *v.t.* Rebaptiser; donner un nouveau nom à.
recidivist [ri'sidivist], *n.* Récidiviste, *m.* or *f.*
recipe ['resipi], *n.* (*Cook.*) Recette, *f.*
recipient [ri'sipiənt], *n.* Personne qui reçoit, *f.*, destinataire (of letter), *m.* or *f.*; (*Chem.*) récipient, *m.*
reciprocal [ri'siprəkl], *a.* Réciproque.—*n.* (*Math.*) Réciproque, *f.* **reciprocally,** *adv.* Réciproquement. **reciprocate,** *v.t.* Échanger; répondre à. *I reciprocate your sentiments,*

j'éprouve de mon côté les mêmes sentiments à votre égard.—*v.i.* Alterner, se succéder.
reciprocating, *a.* Alternatif, de va-et-vient.
reciprocation [-'keiʃən] or **reciprocity** [resi'prɔsiti], *n.* Réciprocité, *f.*
recital [ri'saitl], *n.* Récit, *m.*; narration, énumération, *f.*; (*Law*) exposé, *m.*; (*Mus.*) récital, *m.*, audition, *f.* **recitation** [-resi'teiʃən], *n.* Récitation, *f.*
recitative [resitə'ti:v], *n.* Récitatif, *m.*
recite [ri'sait], *v.t.* Réciter, faire le récit de; raconter, narrer, énumérer. **reciter,** *n.* Récitateur; diseur, narrateur, *m.*
reck [rek], *v.t.* (*poet.*) Se soucier de, faire cas de.—*v.i.* Se soucier de. *I reck not,* peu m'importe.
reckless, *a.* Insouciant (de); indifférent (à); téméraire, insensé. **recklessly,** *adv.* Témérairement, avec insouciance; furieusement. **recklessness,** *n.* Insouciance, témérité, imprudence, *f.*
reckon [rekn], *v.t.* Compter, calculer; regarder, évaluer (comme). *Reckoning from today,* à compter *or* à partir d'aujourd'hui; *to reckon again,* recompter; *to reckon up,* additionner; *He is reckoned a good painter,* on le considère comme un bon peintre.—*v.i.* Compter. *To reckon on,* compter sur; *to reckon with,* avoir à compter avec, avoir affaire à. **reckoner,** *n.* Calculateur, chiffreur, *m.* *Ready-reckoner,* barème, *m.*
reckoning, *n.* Compte, calcul; écot, *m.*, note (at an hotel); addition (at a restaurant), *f.*; (*Naut.*) estime, *f.* *Day of reckoning,* jour de règlement, *m.*; *the pilot made a mistake in his reckoning,* le pilote s'est trompé dans son estime; *to be out in one's reckoning,* être loin de son compte.
reclaim [ri:'kleim], *v.t.* Réformer, corriger; ramener (de); réclamer, revendiquer (to claim back); apprivoiser (a hawk etc.); défricher (land). *To reclaim from error,* tirer, faire revenir de son erreur; *to reclaim land,* défricher un terrain.
reclaimable, *a.* Qu'on peut ramener au bien, corrigible; cultivable, défrichable (of land).
reclamation [reklə'meiʃən] or **reclaiming,** *n.* Défrichement, *m.*, mise en culture (of land); réforme, correction (of criminals), *f.*
recline [ri:'klain], *v.t.* Incliner, pencher, reposer, appuyer.—*v.i.* S'appuyer, se reposer, se coucher. **reclining,** *a.* Incliné, appuyé, couché, étendu.
reclose [ri:'klouz], *v.t.* Refermer.—*v.i.* Se refermer.
reclothe [ri:'klouð], *v.t.* Rhabiller.
recluse [ri'klu:s], *a.* Reclus; solitaire, retiré. —*n.* Reclus, *m.*, recluse, *f.* **reclusion,** *n.* Réclusion, *f.*
recognition [rekəg'niʃən], *n.* Reconnaissance, *f.* **recognitory** [ri'kɔgnitəri], *a.* Récognitif.
recognizable [rekəg'naizəbl], *a.* Reconnaissable. **recognizance** [ri'kɔgnizəns], *n.* Reconnaissance; (*Law*) obligation contractée (de faire quelque acte particulier), caution personnelle, *f.* *To enter into recognizances,* s'engager à comparaître.
recognize ['rekəgnaiz], *v.t.* Reconnaître.
recognized, *a.* Accepté, admis, reçu. *Recognized agent,* (*Comm.*) agent accrédité, *m.*
recoil [ri'kɔil], *n.* Recul, *m.*; contre-coup, *m.* (of explosion); (*fig.*) répugnance, *f.*—*v.i.*

Reculer; retomber. *To recoil from*, reculer devant; *to recoil upon*, retomber sur.

recoin [ri:'kɔin], *v.t.* Refondre, refrapper. **recoinage**, *n.* Refonte, *f.*

Recollect ['rekəlekt], *n.* Récollet, *m.*, récollette (Franciscan), *f.*

recollect [rekə'lekt], *v.t.* Se souvenir de, se rappeler. *Do you recollect my face?* me remettez-vous? *recollect it*, souvenez-vous-en; *to recollect oneself*, se recueillir.

recollection [rekə'lekʃən], *n.* Souvenir, *m.*; mémoire, *f. To have no recollection of*, ne pas se rappeler; *to have some recollection of*, avoir un léger souvenir de; *to the best of my recollection*, autant que je puis m'en souvenir.

recombination [ri:kɔmbi'neiʃən], *n.* Combinaison nouvelle, *f.*

recombine [ri:kəm'bain], *v.t.*, *v.i.* Combiner de nouveau.

recommence [ri:kə'mens], *v.t.*, *v.i.* Recommencer.

recommend [rekə'mend], *v.t.* Recommander; apostiller (a request). *He has nothing else to recommend him*, il n'a que cela pour lui; *not to be recommended*, à déconseiller, peu recommandable. **recommendable**, *a.* Recommandable. **recommendation** [-'deiʃən], *n.* Recommandation; apostille (on a petition), *f.* **recommendatory** [-'mendətəri], *a.* De recommandation. **recommender**, *n.* Personne qui recommande, *f.*

recommission [ri:kə'miʃən], *v.t.* Commissionner de nouveau, renommer à une charge. *To recommission a ship of war*, armer de nouveau un vaisseau de guerre.

recommit [ri:kə'mit], *v.t.* Renvoyer (a prisoner) en prison; renvoyer (a bill) à la commission. **recommittal** or **recommitment**, *n.* Renvoi en prison; renvoi à une commission, *m.*

recommunicate [ri:kə'mju:nikeit], *v.t.* Communiquer de nouveau.

recompense ['rekəmpens], *n.* Récompense, *f.*; dédommagement, *m.*—*v.t.* Récompenser (de); dédommager (de); compenser, réparer.

recompose [ri:kəm'pouz], *v.t.* Recomposer.

reconcilable [rekən'sailəbl], *a.* Réconciliable; conciliable (avec) (of things).

reconcile ['rekənsail], *v.t.* Réconcilier (avec); raccommoder, concilier, arranger; habituer, accoutumer (to accustom). *To be reconciled with*, être réconcilié avec; *to reconcile oneself to*, se faire à, se résigner à. **reconcilement**, *n.* Réconciliation, *f.* **reconciler**, *n.* Réconciliateur, *m.*, réconciliatrice, *f.* **reconciliation** [-sili'eiʃən], *n.* Réconciliation, *f.*, arrangement, *m.*; conciliation (of things); (*Bibl.*) expiation, *f.* **reconciliatory** [-'siliatəri], *a.* Conciliateur.

recondite ['rekəndait], *a.* Secret, abstrus, profond, mystérieux. **reconditeness**, *n.* Caractère abstrus; sens caché, *m.*

recondition [ri:kən'diʃn], *v.t.* Remettre en état, remettre à neuf, refaire.

reconduct [ri:kən'dʌkt], *v.t.* Reconduire.

reconnaissance [ri'kɔnisəns], *n.* Reconnaissance, *f.*

reconnoitre [rekə'nɔitə], *v.t.* Reconnaître.—*v.i.* Faire une reconnaissance. **reconnoitring**, *a.* En reconnaissance. *Reconnoitring party*, reconnaissance, *f.*; *reconnoitring corps*,

corps d'observation, *m.*; *reconnoitring expedition*, reconnaissance, *f.*

reconquer [ri:'kɔŋkə], *v.t.* Reconquérir.

reconsecrate [ri:'kɔnsəkreit], *v.t.* Consacrer de nouveau.

reconsider [ri:kən'sidə], *v.t.* Considérer de nouveau; revenir sur (a decision). **reconsideration** [-'reiʃən], *n.* Reconsidération, *f.*: nouvel examen, *m.*

reconstitute [ri:'kɔnstitju:t], *v.t.* Reconstituer. **reconstitution** [-'tju:ʃən], *n.* Reconstitution, *f.*

reconstruct [ri:kən'strʌkt], *v.t.* Reconstruire. **reconstruction**, *n.* Reconstruction, *f.*; réorganisation, *f.*

reconvention [ri:kən'venʃən], *n.* (*Law*) Reconvention, *f.*

reconvert, *v.t.* Convertir de nouveau; reconvertir.

reconvey [-'vei], *v.t.* Transporter de nouveau; (*Law*) rétrocéder. **reconveyance**, *n.* Nouveau transport, *m.*; (*Law*) rétrocession, *f.*

record (1) ['rekɔ:d], *n.* Registre, *m.*, archives, *f.pl.*; (*Gramophone*) disque; (*spt.*) record, *m.*; dossier, *m. It is on record that . . .*, il est fait mention dans l'histoire que . . .; *keeper of the records*, archiviste, greffier, *m.*; *long-playing record*, disque longue durée, *m.*; *off the record*, entre nous, de vous à moi; *on record*, dans les annales de l'histoire; *police record*, casier judiciaire, *m.*; *public records*, archives, *f.pl.*; *record of evidence*, procès-verbal, *m.*; *record dealer*, disquaire, *m.*; *record library*, discothèque, *f.*; *record office*, archives, *f.pl.*, greffe, *m.*; *regimental records*, (*Mil.*) historique du régiment, *m.*; *service record*, états de service, *m.pl.*; *to break the record*, battre le record; *to make a record of*, enregistrer. *To hold the record*, détenir le record; *record holder*, recordman, *m.*

record (2) [ri'kɔ:d], *v.t.* Enregistrer, consigner; inscrire, graver, imprimer (on the mind etc.); mentionner (in history).

recorder [ri'kɔ:də], *n.* Enregistreur, archiviste; greffier; (*Law*) officier judiciaire d'une ville; (*Mus.*) flageolet, *m. Sound recorder*, (*Cine.*) appareil d'enregistrement du son, *m. Tape recorder*, magnétophone, *m.* **recordership**, *n.* Charge d'archiviste *or* de 'recorder', *f.* **recording**, *n.* Enregistrement, *m.*

recork [ri:'kɔ:k], *v.t.* Reboucher.

recount (1) [ri'kaunt], *v.t.* Raconter.

recount (2) [ri:'kaunt], *v.t.* Recompter.

recount (3) [ri:'kaunt], *n.* Nouvelle addition des voix (at elections), *f.*

recoup [ri'ku:p], *v.t.* Rembourser, dédommager (de). *To recoup oneself*, se rattraper (sur). **recoupment**, *n.* Dédommagement, *m.*

recourse [ri'kɔ:s], *n.* Recours, *m. To have recourse to*, recourir à, avoir recours à.

recover (1) [ri'kʌvə], *v.t.* Recouvrer, retrouver; reprendre, reconquérir; réparer (a loss). *To recover oneself*, se remettre, revenir à soi. —*v.i.* Se rétablir, guérir; se remettre (from illness); se relever (from losses); (*Law*) avoir gain de cause. *To recover from*, se remettre de, revenir de. **recoverable**, *a.* Qu'on peut recouvrer, recouvrable; guérissable. **recovery**, *n.* Recouvrement, *m.*; guérison, *f.*; rétablissement, *m.*; reprise, *f.* (prices, economy). *Past recovery*, incurable, désespéré, sans remède.

recover (2) [riːˈkʌvə], *v.t.* Recouvrir (to cover again); regarnir.

recreant [ˈrekriənt], *a.* and *n.* Lâche, infidèle, apostat, *m.*

re-create [riːkriˈeit], *v.t.* Recréer (create anew).

recreate [ˈrekrieit], *v.t.* Récréer, divertir, distraire.—*v.i.* Se récréer, se divertir, se distraire. **recreation** [-ˈeiʃən], *n.* Récréation, distraction, *f.*, divertissement, *m.* **recreative** [ˈrekrieitiv], *a.* Récréatif, divertissant, amusant.

recriminate [riˈkrimineit], *v.i.* Récriminer (contre). **recrimination** [rekrimiˈneiʃən], *n.* Récrimination, *f.* **recriminatory** [riˈkrimineitəri], *a.* Récriminatoire.

recross [riːˈkrɔs], *v.t.* Traverser de nouveau, repasser. *To cross and recross,* traverser en tous sens.

recrudescence [riːkruːˈdesəns], *n.* Recrudescence, *f.* **recrudescent,** *a.* Recrudescent.

recruit [riˈkruːt], *n.* Recrue, *f.*, conscrit, *m.*—*v.t.* Rétablir, renforcer, réparer (to strengthen); (*Mil.*) recruter. *To recruit one's health, strength,* se remettre, se refaire, reprendre des forces.—*v.i.* Se recruter, se remettre. **recruiting** or **recruitment,** *n.* Recrutement, *m.* **recruiting-officer,** *n.* Officier de recrutement, *m.* **recruiting-sergeant,** *n.* Sergent recruteur, *m.*

recrystallize [riːˈkristəlaiz], *v.i.* Se crystalliser de nouveau.

rectal [ˈrektəl], *a.* Rectal. **rectangle** [ˈrektæŋgl], *n.* Rectangle, *m.* **rectangled** or **rectangular** [-ˈtæŋgjulə], *a.* Rectangulaire, rectangle, à angle droit. **rectangularly,** *adv.* À angles droits.

rectifiable [ˈrektifaiəbl], *a.* Rectifiable. **rectification** [-fiˈkeiʃən], *n.* Rectification, *f.* **rectifier** [ˈrektifaiə], *n.* Rectificateur, *m.*; (*Elec.*) redresseur, *m.* **rectify,** *v.t.* Rectifier; redresser. *To be rectified,* se rectifier. **rectifying,** *a.* Rectificateur, rectificatif.

rectilineal [rektiˈliniəl] or **rectilinear,** *a.* Rectiligne.

rectitude [ˈrektitjuːd], *n.* Rectitude, droiture, *f.*

rector [ˈrektə], *n.* (*Ch. of Eng.*) Prêtre *or* laïque titulaire d'un bénéfice et de la dîme (of a parish); (*R.-C.*) curé; directeur, supérieur (of religious orders); (*Univ. etc.*) recteur, principal, *m.* **rectorial** [-ˈtɔːriəl], *a.* Rectoral. **rectorship** or **rectorate,** *n.* Rectorat, *m.*

rectory [ˈrektəri], *n.* Cure, *f.*, presbytère, *m.*

rectum [ˈrektəm], *n.* (*Anat.*) Rectum, *m.*

recumbence [riˈkʌmbəns] or **recumbency,** *n.* Position couchée, *f.*; repos, décubitus, *m.* **recumbent,** *a.* Couché, étendu; appuyé (sur); (*fig.*) en repos; gisant (on tomb).

recuperate [riˈkjuːpəreit], *v.t.* Recouvrer, récupérer.—*v.i.* Se rétablir, se remettre, reprendre ses forces. **recuperation** [-ˈreiʃən], *n.* Recouvrement, *m.*; rétablissement, *m.* (person). **recuperative,** *a.* De récupération.

recur [riˈkə], *v.i.* Revenir; recourir (à); revenir à l'esprit; se reproduire (to happen again).

recurrence [riˈkʌrəns], *n.* Retour, *m.* *Of frequent recurrence,* qui revient souvent, qui arrive souvent. **recurrent** [riˈkʌrənt] or **recurring** [riˈkəːriŋ], *a.* Périodique; (*Anat.*

etc.) récurrent. (*Math.*) *Recurring decimal,* fraction décimale périodique, *f.*

recurvate [riˈkəːvət] or **recurve** [riˈkəːv], *a.* Recourbé.—*v.t.* [-veit] Recourber. **recurvation** [riːkəːˈveiʃən] or **recurvature** [-ˈkəːvətʃə], *n.* Courbure, *f.*

*recusancy [ˈrekjuzənsi], *n.* (*R.-C.*) Refus d'assister aux offices anglicans, *m.* **recusant,** *a.* and *n.* Dissident, réfractaire, *m.*

red [red], *a.* Rouge, roux (of the hair); vermeil (of the lips etc.). *At a red heat,* chauffé au rouge; *dark red,* rouge foncé; *red as a beetroot,* rouge comme une tomate; *red chalk,* sanguine, *f.*; *red deer,* cerf, *m.*; *red face,* visage enluminé, *m.*; *red hair,* cheveux roux, *m.pl.*; *red herring,* hareng, *m.*; (*fam.*) chose qui détourne la conversation, *f.*; *red lead,* minium, *m.*; *red-letter day,* jour de fête, *m.*; *to go red,* rougir; *to see red,* voir rouge; *turkey red,* rouge d'Andrinople, *m.*—*n.* Rouge, *m.*

redan [rəˈdæn], *n.* Redan, *m.*

red-berried, *a.* À baies rouges. **redbreast,** *n.* Rouge-gorge, *m.* **red-coat,** *n.* Soldat anglais, *m.* **red-eyed,** *a.* Aux yeux rouges. **red-handed,** *a.* *To be caught red-handed,* être pris la main dans le sac. **red-hot,** *a.* Tout rouge, chauffé au rouge, ardent (of coals). **redpole** or **redpoll,** *n.* (*pop.*) Linotte, *f.* **redshank,** *n.* (*Orn.*) Chevalier, *m.*, gambette, *f.* **redskin,** *n.* Peau-Rouge, *m.* **redstart,** *n.* Rouge-queue, *m.* **red-tape,** *n.* Bolduc, *m.*; (*fig.*) routine administrative, *f.* **red-tapism,** *n.* Paperasserie, *f.*; formalisme, *m.* **red-tapist,** *n.* Rond-de-cuir, *m.* **redwing,** *n.* Mauvis, *m.* **redwood,** *n.* Sequoia; bois du Brésil, *m.*

redden [redn], *v.t.*, *v.i.* Rougir. **reddish,** *a.* Rougeâtre, roussâtre.

reddle [redl], *n.* Craie rouge, *f.*

redecorate [riːˈdekəreit], *v.t.* Décorer de nouveau; refaire les peintures de.

redeem [riˈdiːm], *v.t.* Racheter; (*Fin.*) rembourser, amortir; retirer (things pawned); (*fig.*) réparer. *To redeem a fault,* réparer une faute; *to redeem a promise,* accomplir une promesse; *to redeem oneself,* racheter son honneur. **redeemable,** *a.* Rachetable, remboursable, amortissable. **redeemer,** *n.* Rédempteur; racheteur; libérateur, *m.*, libératrice, *f.* **redeeming,** *a.* Qui rachète, qui compense. *Redeeming quality,* qualité qui rachète des défauts, *f.*

redeliver [riːdiˈlivə], *v.t.* Délivrer de nouveau. **redelivery,** *n.* Nouvelle livraison, *f.*

redemand [riːdiˈmɑːnd], *v.t.* Redemander.

redemise [-ˈmaiz], *n.* Rétrocession, *f.*

redemption [riˈdempʃən], *n.* Rédemption, *f.*; (*Fin.*) amortissement, *m.*; libération, *f.* (d'hypothèque), dégagement, rachat, *m.* (de billets).

redevelop [riːdiˈveləp], *v.t.* Reconstruire, aménager. **redevelopment,** *n.* Reconstruction, *f.*, aménagement, *m.*

redhibitory [redˈhibitəri], *a.* (*Law*) Rédhibitoire.

redintegrate [riˈdintəgreit], *v.t.* Réintégrer; (*fig.*) rétablir; renouveler. **redintegration** [-ˈgreiʃen], *n.* Réintégration, *f.*; (*fig.*) renouvellement; rétablissement, *m.*

redirect [riːdaiˈrekt], *v.t.* Faire suivre (letter).

rediscover [riːdisˈkʌvə], *v.t.* Redécouvrir. **rediscovery,** *n.* Redécouverte, *f.*

redissolve [-di'zɔlv], *v.t.*   Dissoudre de nouveau.

redistribute [-dis'tribjut], *v.t.*   Redistribuer. **redistribution** [-'bju:ʃən], *n.* Nouvelle distribution, redistribution, répartition, *f.*

redness ['rednis], *n.*   Rougeur; rousseur (of hair), *f.*

redolence ['redoləns], *n.*   Parfum, *m.*; odeur agréable, senteur, *f.* **redolent,** *a.* Qui a un parfum de. *Redolent of . . .,* qui sent le . . . .

redouble [ri:'dʌbl], *v.t., v.i.*   Redoubler; (at cards) surconter. *To redouble one's efforts,* redoubler d'efforts.—*n.* (*Cards*) Surcontre, *f.* **redoubling,** *n.* Redoublement, *m.*

redoubt [ri'daut], *n.* Redoute, *f.*

redoubtable [ri'dautəbl], *a.*   Redoutable, formidable. **redoubted,** *a.* Redouté.

redound [ri'daund], *v.t.*   Contribuer (à, en), résulter (pour), rejaillir (sur). *This action redounds to his credit,* cette action est à son honneur.

redraft [ri:'drɑ:ft], *v.t.*   Dessiner de nouveau, rédiger de nouveau.—*n.* Nouveau dessin, *m.*; (*Comm.*) retraite, *f.*

redraw [ri:'drɔ:], *v.t.*   Retirer; dessiner de nouveau.—*v.i.* (*Comm.*) Faire retraite.

redress [ri'dres], *v.t.*   Redresser, corriger, réparer.—*n.* Redressement, *m.*, réparation, *f.*, secours, remède, *m.* **redresser,** *n.* Redresseur, réparateur, *m.*

reduce [ri'dju:s], *v.t.*   Réduire (à *or* en), convertir; maigrir (in flesh); dégrader (degrade). *A person in reduced circumstances,* une personne tombée dans la gêne; *to reduce* (a design etc.), réduire; *to reduce to practice,* mettre en pratique; *to reduce to rule,* soumettre à des règles fixes; *to reduce to the ranks,* casser (un sous-officier); *to reduce to silence,* faire taire. **reducer,** *n.* (*Chem.*) Réducteur, *m.* **reducible,** *a.* Réductible. **reduction** [-'dʌkʃən], *n.* Réduction, *f. A reduction in prices,* une baisse des prix, *f.*; *reduction to the ranks,* cassation, *f.* **reductive,** *a.* Réductif.—*n.* Agent réductif, *m.*

redundance [ri'dʌndəns] or **redundancy,** *n.* Redondance, *f.* **redundant,** *a.* Redondant, superflu. **redundantly,** *adv.* D'une manière redondante.

reduplicate [ri:'dju:plikeit], *v.t.* Redoubler.— *a.* [-kət] Double. **reduplication** [-'keiʃən], *n.* Redoublement, *m.*; (*Gram.*) réduplication, *f.* **reduplicative,** *a.* Réduplicatif.

re-echo [ri:'ekou], *v.t.*   Répéter; redire.—*v.i.* Retentir, résonner.—*n.* Écho répété, *m.*

reed [ri:d], *n.*   Roseau; chaume; chalumeau, pipeau, *m.*; anche (of wind instruments), *f.*; peigne (used by weavers), *m. To trust to a broken reed,* s'appuyer sur un roseau. **reed-bed,** *n.* Roselière, *f.* **reed-mace,** *n.* (*Bot.*) Massette, *f.* **reed-pipe,** *n.* Chalumeau, pipeau, *m.*

reeded, *a.*   Couvert de roseaux, couvert de chaume; à anche; cannelé, à cannelures (of pillar, wood). **reedy,** *a.* Plein de roseaux, couvert de roseaux; (voix) flûtée.

re-edification [ri:edifi'keiʃən], *n.*   Réédification, *f.*

re-edify [-'edifai], *v.t.*   Réédifier, rebâtir.

re-edit [ri:'edit], *v.t.*   Rééditer; donner une nouvelle édition de.

re-educate [ri:'edjukeit], *v.t.* (*Med.*) Rééduquer.

reedling ['ri:dliŋ], *n.*   (*Orn.*) Mésange à moustache, *f.*

reef [ri:f], *n.*   Récif, écueil, banc de rocher; ris (of a sail), *m. To let out a reef,* larguer un ris.—*v.t.* Prendre un ris dans. *To reef a sail,* serrer un ris à une voile. **reef-band,** *n.* Bande de ris, *f.* **reef-knot,** *n.* Nœud plat, *m.* **reef-point,** *n.*   Garcette de ris, *f.* **reef-tackle,** *n.* Palanquin, *m.*

reefer, *n.*   Veste quartier-maître, *f.* **reefy,** *a.* Plein de récifs.

reek [ri:k], *n.*   Fumée, *f.*, relent, *m.*, odeur forte, *f.*—*v.i.* Fumer; exhaler. *Reeking with,* tout fumant de; *to reek of,* puer, empester. **reeky,** *a.* Enfumé.

reel [ri:l], *n.*   Dévidoir, *m.*; bobine (of cotton), *f.*; (*Angling*) moulinet, rouet; (*Rope-making*) touret; branle écossais (dance), *m.*; (*Cine.*) bobine, *f.*, bande, *f. Newsreel,* les actualités, *f.pl.*; *off the reel,* (*fig.*) d'arrache-pied, sans interruption.—*v.t.* Dévider. *To reel in a fish,* remonter un poisson; *to reel off,* dévider, débiter.—*v.i.* Tournoyer, chanceler, trébucher. *To reel out,* sortir en chancelant.

re-elect [ri:i'lekt], *v.t.*   Réélire. **re-election** [-'lekʃən], *n.* Réélection, *f.* **re-eligibility** [-elidʒi'biliti], *n.* Rééligibilité, *f.* **re-eligible** [-'elidʒibl], *a.* Rééligible.

re-embark [ri:əm'bɑ:k], *v.t.*   Rembarquer. —*v.i.* Se rembarquer. **re-embarkation** [-embɑ:'keiʃən], *n.* Rembarquement, *m.*

re-embody [ri:əm'bɔdi], *v.t.* Réincorporer.

re-emerge [ri:ə'mə:dʒ], *v.i.*   Ressortir, reparaître.

re-emigrate [ri:'emigreit], *v.i.*   Émigrer de nouveau.

re-employ [ri:əm'plɔi], *v.t.* Remployer. **re-employment,** *n.* Réemploi, *m.*

re-enact [ri:ə'nækt], *v.t.*   Remettre en vigueur (a law); reconstituer (a crime). **re-enactment,** *n.* Remise en vigueur, *f.*, rétablissement, *m.*, reconstitution, *f.*

re-enforce, *v.t.* Remettre en vigueur.

re-engage [ri:ən'geidʒ], *v.t.*   Rengager. *To re-engage the clutch,* rembrayer.—*v.i.* Se rengager. **re-engagement,** *n.* Rengagement, *m.*

re-enlist [ri:ən'list], *v.t.*   Enrôler de nouveau. —*v.i.* Se rengager.

re-enter [ri:'entə], *v.t.*   Rentrer dans, rentrer à—*v.i.* Rentrer; se présenter de nouveau (exam). **re-entering,** *a.* Rentrant. **re-entrance,** *n.* Rentrée, *f.* **re-entrant,** *a.* and *n.* Rentrant, *m.*

re-equip [ri:ə'kwip], *v.t.*   Équiper de nouveau. **re-equipment,** *n.* Rééquipement, *m.*

re-erect, *v.t.* Reconstruire; dresser de nouveau.

re-establish [ri:is'tæbliʃ], *v.t.*   Rétablir. **re-establishment,** *n.* Rétablissement, *m.*

reeve (1) [ri:v], *v.t.* (*Naut.*) Passer (un cordage).

reeve (2) [ri:v], *n.* Bailli, *m.*

reeve (3) [ri:v], *n.*   (*Orn.*) Femelle du combattant, du chevalier *or* du paon de mer (ruff).

re-examination [ri:əgzæmi'neiʃən], *n.* Nouvel examen; (*Law*) nouvel interrogatoire, *m.*

re-examine [-əg'zæmin], *v.t.*   Examiner de nouveau, revoir; interroger de nouveau (a prisoner *or* witness).

re-exchange [ri:əks'tʃeindʒ], *n.*   Nouvel échange; (*Comm.*) rechange, *m. Account of re-exchange,* compte de retour, *m.*

re-export (1) [ri:eks'pɔ:t], *v.t.* Réexporter.
re-export (2) [ri:'ekspɔ:t], *n.* Marchandise
réexportée, *f.* **re-exportation** [-'teiʃən], *n.*
Réexportation, *f.*
reface [ri:'feis], *v.t.* Revêtir de nouveau,
remaçonner.
refashion [ri:'fæʃən], *v.t.* Refaçonner.
refasten [ri:'fɑ:sn], *v.t.* Rattacher; ragrafer.
refection [ri'fekʃən], *n.* Repas, *m.*, collation, *f.*
refectory, *n.* Réfectoire, *m.*
refer [ri'fɔ:], *v.t.* Renvoyer, rapporter;
adresser (à); remettre à la décision de.—*v.i.*
Se référer, se rapporter, avoir rapport (à);
s'en rapporter, se référer (of persons);
s'adresser (à); faire allusion (à). *Referred to
drawer,* (*Bank*) voir le tireur; *the person
referred to,* la personne visée.
referable ['refərəbl], *a.* Qu'on peut référer,
attribuable (à). **referee** [-'ri:], *n.* Arbitre,
m.; répondant; (*Comm.*) recommandataire,
m.—*v.i.,* *v.t.* (*spt.*) Arbitrer.
reference ['refərəns], *n.* Renvoi; regard,
rapport (respect), *m.*; allusion (allusion), *f.*;
renseignements, *m.pl.*, références, *f.pl.*; (for
character) (*Comm.*) référence, *f. Book of reference,* ouvrage à consulter, *m.*; *for reference,* à
consulter; *in reference to,* à l'égard de, par
rapport à, quant à; *with reference to,* au sujet
de; *to give someone as a reference,* se recommander de quelqu'un; *to go for a reference,*
aller aux renseignements; *to have reference to,*
se rapporter à; *to make reference to,* faire
allusion à. **reference-mark,** *n.* Renvoi, *m.*
referendum [refə'rendəm], *n.* Référendum, *m.*
refill (1) [ri:'fil], *v.t.* Remplir, regarnir.—*v.i.*
(*Motor.*) Faire le plein (d'essence).
refill (2) ['ri:fil], *n.* Objet pour remplir,
regarnir, recharger, *e.g.* carnet (feuilles, pile,
ampoule) de rechange; (*Motor.*) plein
(d'essence), *m.*
refine [ri'fain], *v.t.* Épurer (liquids); (*Metal.*)
affiner; raffiner (sugar etc.); (*fig.*) purifier;
polir.—*v.i.* S'épurer, se purifier; (*fig.*)
ergoter, subtiliser, raffiner (sur). **refined,** *a.*
Raffiné; cultivé, recherché; pur, délicat (of
taste). **refinedly,** *adv.* Avec raffinement.
refinement, *n.* Raffinage (of sugar);
(*Metal.*) affinage, *m.*; épuration (of liquids);
(*fig.*) délicatesse; (*pej.*) affectation, recherche,
f.; perfectionnement, *m.* (improvement).
refiner, *n.* Personne qui épure, *f.*; raffineur
(of sugar etc.); (*Metal.*) affineur, *m.* **refinery**
or **refining,** *n.* Raffinage, *m.*; raffinerie
(sugar), *f.*; (*Metal.*) affinage, *m.*, affinerie, *f.*
refit [ri:'fit], *v.t.* Réparer, remonter; rajuster;
(*Naut.*) radouber.—*n.* Réparation, *f.*; (*Naut.*)
refonte, *f.*
reflect [ri'flekt], *v.t.* Réfléchir; faire rejaillir
sur; refléter. *That reflects no credit on you,*
cela ne vous fait pas honneur.—*v.i.* Réfléchir;
faire réflexion, faire ses réflexions (sur). *To
reflect on,* blâmer, censurer, critiquer; *to
reflect upon,* réfléchir à, méditer sur. **reflected,** *a.* Réfléchi. **reflecting,** *a.* Réfléchissant; réflecteur, réfléchi, méditatif.
reflection [REFLEXION]. **reflective,** *a.*
Réfléchissant; méditatif, réfléchi. **reflector,**
n. Réflecteur, *m.*; (*Cycl., Motor.*) catadioptre,
m.
reflex ['ri:fleks], *a.* Réfléchi; (*Paint.*) reflété;
(*Physiol. etc.*) réflexe. *Reflex action,* action
réflexe, *f.*—*n.* (*Paint.*) Reflet, *m.*; (*Physiol.*)

réflexe, *m.* **reflexibility** [-i'biliti], *n.* Réflexi-
bilité, *f.* **reflexible** [-'fleksibl], *a.* Réflexible.
reflexion, *n.* Réflexion, *f.*; reflet (reflected
light etc.), *m.*; censure (censure), *f.*; reproche, blâme, *m. On reflexion,* en y
réfléchissant, tout bien considéré; *to cast
reflexion on,* censurer, critiquer, blâmer.
reflexive, *a.* Réfléchi. **reflexively,** *adv.*
Au sens réfléchi.
refloat [ri:'flout], *v.t.* Renflouer; remettre à
flot (company). **refloating,** *n.* Renflouage,
m.; remise à flot, *f.*
reflorescence [ri:flɔ'resəns], *n.* Nouvelle
floraison, *f.*
reflourish [-'flʌriʃ], *v.i.* Refleurir.
reflower [ri:'flauə], *v.i.* Refleurir.
refluent ['refluənt], *a.* Qui reflue.
reflux ['ri:flʌks], *n.* Reflux, *m.*
refoot [-'fut], *v.t.* Rempiéter, renter.
reforge [-'fɔ:dʒ], *v.t.* Reforger.
reform [ri'fɔ:m], *n.* Réforme, *f.*—*v.t.* Réformer; corriger.—*v.i.* Se réformer, se
corriger. **reformation** [refɔ:'meiʃən], *n.*
Réformation; réforme, *f. The Reformation,*
(*Hist.*) la Réforme, *f.*
re-form [ri:'fɔ:m], *v.t.* Reformer.—*v.i.* Se
reformer. **re-formation** [-'meiʃən], *n.*
Formation nouvelle, *f.*
reformative [ri'fɔ:mətiv], *a.* Réformateur.
reformatory, *n.* Pénitencier, *m.*, maison
d'éducation correctionnelle, *f.* **reformer,** *n.*
Réformateur, *m.*
refract [ri'frækt], *v.t.* Réfracter. **refracting,**
a. À réfraction. **refraction,** *n.* Réfraction,
f. **refractive,** *a.* Réfractif; réfringent.
refractoriness [ri'fræktərinis], *n.* Indocilité,
insoumission, mutinerie, *f.* **refractory,** *a.*
Indocile, récalcitrant, intraitable, rebelle;
(*Chem. etc.*) réfractaire; rétif (of horses).
refrain (1) [ri'frein], *v.i.* Se retenir, s'abstenir
(de). *Whose name I refrain from mentioning,*
dont je tairai le nom; *to refrain from tears,*
retenir ses larmes.
refrain (2) [ri'frein], *n.* Refrain, *m.*
reframe [ri:'freim], *v.t.* Encadrer de nouveau;
(*fig.*) remanier.
refrangibility [rifrændʒi'biliti], *a.* Réfrangibilité, *f.* **refrangible** [-'frændʒibl], *a.* Réfrangible.
refresh [ri'freʃ], *v.t.* Rafraîchir; délasser,
refaire, récréer. *To refresh oneself,* se
rafraîchir, se remettre, se refaire; *to refresh
the memory,* rafraîchir la mémoire. **refresher,** *n.* Personne *or* chose qui rafraîchit,
f.; rafraîchissant, supplément d'honoraires
(extra fee), *m. A refresher course,* un cours de
perfectionnement. **refreshing,** *a.* Rafraîchissant; réparateur, qui repose. **refreshment,**
n. Rafraîchissement, *m.* **refreshment-bar,**
n. Buvette, *f.* **refreshment-car,** *n.* Wagon-
restaurant, *m.* **refreshment-room,** *n.*
Buffet, *m.*
refrigerant [ri'fridʒərənt], *a.* and *n.* Réfrigérant, *m.* **refrigerate,** *v.t.* Réfrigérer,
frigorifier. *Refrigerating plant,* installation
frigorifique, *f.* **refrigeration** [-'reiʃən], *n.*
Réfrigération, *f.* **refrigerative** [-'fridʒərətiv]
or **refrigeratory,** *a.* Frigorifique, réfrigérant; (*Med.*) frigératif. **refrigerator,** *n.*
Réfrigérateur, *m.*; (*fam.*) Frigidaire (registered trade mark); appareil frigorifique,
m.

refuel [ri:'fjuəl], *v.i.* (*Naut.*) Se ravitailler en combustible; (*Av.*) faire le plein (d'essence).

refuge ['refju:dʒ], *n.* Refuge (contre), *m. Night refuge*, asile de nuit, *m.*; *place of refuge*, lieu d'asile, *m.*; *to take refuge*, se réfugier (auprès de *or* dans). **refugee** [-'dʒi:], *n.* Réfugié, *m.*, réfugiée, *f.*; (*Fr. Hist.*) émigré, *m.*, émigrée, *f.*

refulgence [ri'fʌldʒəns] or **refulgency,** *n.* Éclat, *m.*, splendeur, *f.* **refulgent,** *a.* Éclatant, resplendissant.

refund (1) [ri'fʌnd], *v.t.* Rembourser, rendre, restituer.

refund (2) ['ri:fʌnd], *n.* Remboursement, *m.*; ristourne, *f.* **refundable,** *a.* Remboursable.

refurbish [ri:'fə:biʃ], *v.t.* Refourbir, remettre à neuf.

refurnish [ri'fə:niʃ], *v.t.* Remeubler.

refusable [ri'fju:zəbl], *a.* Qu'on peut refuser.

refusal [ri'fju:zl], *n.* Refus; droit de refuser or d'accepter, *m.* *On his refusal*, sur son refus; *to have the (first) refusal of*, avoir le droit de refuser or d'accepter, avoir la première offre de; *to meet with a refusal*, essuyer un refus.

refuse (1) ['refju:s], *a.* De rebut.—*n.* Rebut, *m.*, ordures, *f.pl.* (household market). *Refuse dump*, voirie, *f.*

refuse (2) [ri'fju:z], *v.t.* Refuser; rejeter. *That is not to be refused*, cela n'est pas de refus. —*v.i.* Refuser. *To refuse point-blank*, refuser net; *to refuse to do something*, refuser de faire quelque chose.

re-fuse [ri:'fju:z], *v.t.* Refondre.

refutable ['refjutəbl], *a.* Réfutable. **refutation** [-'teiʃən], *n.* Réfutation, *f.*

refute [ri'fju:t], *v.t.* Réfuter. **refuter,** *n.* Réfutateur, *m.*

regain [ri'gein], *v.t.* Regagner, reprendre. *To regain consciousness*, revenir à soi.

regal [ri:gl], *a.* Royal.

regale [ri'geil], *v.t.* Régaler; (*fig.*) réjouir; charmer.—*v.i.* Se régaler.

regalia [ri'geiliə], *n.* Insignes de la royauté; diamants de la couronne; (*Law*) droits régaliens, *m.pl.*

regally ['ri:gəli], *adv.* Royalement, en roi.

regard [ri'gɑ:d], *n.* Égard, *f.*; respect (esteem), *m.*; (*pl.*) amitiés, *f.pl.*, compliments, *m.pl.* *Give my regards to your brother*, faites mes amitiés à votre frère; *in regard to*, quant à; *out of regard for*, par égard pour; *to have no regard for*, ne faire aucun cas de; *to pay regard to*, avoir égard à, faire attention à; *with regard to*, à l'égard de, quant à.—*v.t.* Regarder; avoir égard à, faire attention à; considérer; concerner. *As regards*, quant à; *I shall regard it as a favour*, je l'estimerai comme une faveur.

regardful, *a.* Soigneux (de), plein d'égards (pour). **regardfully,** *adv.* Attentivement.

regarding, *prep.* À l'égard de, quant à, concernant.

regardless, *a.* Peu soigneux (de); sans égard (pour). *Regardless of*, sans se soucier de, sans faire aucun cas de; indifférent à. **regardlessly,** *adv.* Avec indifférence. **regardlessness,** *n.* Insouciance, indifférence, *f.*

regatta [ri'gætə], *n.* Régate, *f.* (*usu. pl.*).

regency ['ri:dʒənsi], *n.* Régence, *f.*

regenerate (1) [ri'dʒenərət], *a.* Régénéré.

regenerate (2) [ri:'dʒenəreit], *v.t.* Régénérer. **regenerating,** *a.* Régénérateur. **regenera-**

-tion [-'reiʃən], *n.* Régénération, *f.* **regenerator** ['-dʒenəreitə], *n.* Régénérateur, *m.*, régénératrice, *f.*

regent ['ri:dʒənt], *n.* Régent, *m.*

regicidal [redʒi'saidl], *a.* Régicide.

regicide ['redʒisaid], *a.* and *n.* Régicide, *m.*

regild [ri:'gild], *v.t.* (*past* and *p.p.* **regilded** or **regilt**) Redorer.

régime [rei'ʒi:m], *n.* (*Polit.*) Régime, *m.*

regimen ['redʒimən], *n.* (*Gram., Med.*) Régime, *m.*

regiment ['redʒimənt], *n.* Régiment, *m.* **regimental** [-'mentl], *a.* Du régiment, de régiment. *Regimental number*, numéro matricule, *m.*; *regimental records*, historique du régiment, *m.* **regimentals,** *n.pl.* Uniforme, *m.* **regimentation,** *n.* Enrégimentation, *f.*

Reginald ['redʒinəld]. Renaud, *m.*

region ['ri:dʒən], *n.* Région, *f.* **regional,** *a.* Régional. **regionalism,** *n.* Régionalisme, *m.*

register ['redʒistə], *n.* Registre, *m.*; liste électorale (of voters); jauge officielle (of vessels), *f.*—*v.t.* Enregistrer; pointer; (*Post*) charger (letters containing money), recommander (other letters); déclarer (birth); immatriculer (a car); déposer (a trade-mark etc.); (*Artill.*) régler. *Registered letter*, lettre chargée or recommandée, *f.*—*v.i. To register at an hotel*, s'inscrire sur le registre. **registering,** *n.* (*Artill.*) Tir de réglage, *m.*: enregistrement, *m.*; inscription, *f.*

registrar ['redʒistrɑ:], *n.* Teneur de registres; (*Law*) greffier; (*Univ.*) secrétaire et archiviste; officier de l'état civil (of births etc.), *m. Registrar of mortgages*, conservateur des hypothèques, *m.*; *registrar's office*, bureau de l'état civil, *m.* **registrarship,** *n.* Charge, *f.* (de greffier, etc.).

registration [redʒis'treiʃən], *n.* Enregistrement; chargement (of letters); dépôt (of a trade-mark etc.), *m.*, immatriculation, *f.*; inscription, *f.* (luggage). *Registration fee*, droit d'inscription, *m.*; *registration number*, (car) numéro minéralogique, *m.*

registry ['redʒistri], *n.* Enregistrement; (*Law*) greffe, *m.* *Certificate of registry*, (*Naut.*) acte de naturalisation, *m.*, lettre de mer, *f.* (d'un bateau).

registry-office, *n.* Bureau de placement, *m.*

reglet ['reglet], *n.* (*Print.*) Réglette, *f.*; (*Arch.*) réglet, *m.*

regrade [ri:'greid], *v.t.* Reclasser. **regrading,** *n.* Reclassement, *m.*

regrate [ri:'greit], *v.t.* Accaparer, regratter. **regrater,** *n.* Regrattier, revendeur, *m.*

regress ['ri:gres], *n.* Retour, *m.*; régression, *f.* —*v.i.* Retourner en arrière.

regression [ri'greʃən], *n.* Retour, *m.* **regressive,** *a.* Régressif. **regressively,** *adv.* Par rétrogradation, régressivement.

regret [ri'gret], *n.* Regret, *m.* *To feel regret*, éprouver du regret; *with regret*, avec regret, à regret, à contre-cœur.—*v.t.* Regretter (de), avoir du regret (à). *It is to be regretted*, il est à regretter. **regretful,** *a.* Plein de regrets; regrettable. **regretfully,** *adv.* Avec regret, à regret. **regrettable,** *a.* Fâcheux, regrettable. **regrettably,** *adv.* Regrettablement.

regrind [ri:'graind], *v.t.* Remoudre (coffee); réaffûter (tools).

regroup [ri:'gru:p], *v.t.* Reclasser, regrouper.
regular ['regjulə], *a.* Régulier; réglé; en règle; accoutumé, ordinaire (usual); (*fig.*) vrai, véritable; franc, fieffé (downright). *As regular as clockwork*, exact comme une horloge; *a regular scamp*, un vrai coquin, *m.—n.* (*Eccles.*) Régulier, *m.*; (*pl.*) troupes régulières, *f.pl.* **regularity** [-'læriti], *n.* Régularité, *f.* **regularization** [-ərai'zeiʃən], *n.* Régularisation, *f.*
regularize ['regjuləraiz], *v.t.* Régulariser.
regularly, *adv.* Régulièrement; dans les règles; vraiment, franchement, bien.
regulate ['regjuleit], *v.t.* Régler; diriger. **regulation** [-'leiʃən], *n.* Règlement, *m.—a.* Réglementaire.
regulator ['regjuleitə], *n.* Régulateur, *m.*
regurgitate [ri:'gə:dʒiteit], *v.t.* Régurgiter.
rehabilitate [ri:hə'biliteit], *v.t.* Réhabiliter, rééduquer. **rehabilitation** [-'teiʃən], *n.* Réhabilitation, rééducation, *f. Rehabilitation centre*, centre de rééducation professionnelle, *m.*
rehash [ri:'hæʃ], *n.* Réchauffé, *m.—v.t.* Réchauffer.
rehear [ri:'hiə], *v.t.* Entendre de nouveau. **rehearing**, *n.* Nouvelle audition, *f.*
rehearsal [ri'hə:sl], *n.* Récit, *m.*; (*Theat.*) répétition, *f. Dress rehearsal*, répétition générale, *f.* **rehearse**, *v.t.* (*Theat.*) Répéter; (*fig.*) raconter (to narrate).
rehouse [ri:'hauz], *v.t.* Reloger. **rehousing**, *n.* Relogement, *m.*
reign [rein], *n.* Règne, *m. In the reign of*, sous le règne de.—*v.i.* Régner. **reigning**, *a.* Régnant; (*fig.*) dominant (prevailing); actuel (present).
reimburse [ri:im'bə:s], *v.t.* Rembourser. **reimbursement**, *n.* Remboursement, *m.*
reimport [ri:im'pɔ:t], *v.t.* Réimporter.
reimpose [ri:im'pouz], *v.t.* Réimposer. **reimposition** [-pə'ziʃən], *n.* Réimposition, *f.*
reimpression [-'preʃən], *n.* Réimpression, *f.*
reimprison [-'prizən], *v.t.* Remettre en prison.
rein [rein], *n.* Rêne, *f. To give the rein to*, lâcher la bride à; *to hold the reins of government*, tenir les rênes de l'état; *to keep a tight rein over*, tenir la bride serrée; *to take the reins*, prendre les rênes.—*v.t.* Conduire à la bride, gouverner, brider; contenir. *To rein in*, retenir, maintenir; *to rein up*, arrêter.
reincarnate [ri:in'ka:neit], *v.t.* Réincarner.— *v.i.* Se réincarner. **reincarnation**, *n.* Réincarnation, *f.*
reindeer ['reindiə], *n.* Renne, *m.*
reinforce [ri:in'fɔ:s], *v.t.* Renforcer. *Reinforced concrete*, béton armé, *m.* **reinforcement**, *n.* Renforcement; renfort (body of troops), *m.*; armature, *f.*
reingratiate [ri:in'greiʃieit], *v.t.* Faire rentrer en grâce, remettre en faveur. *To reingratiate oneself*, rentrer en grâce.
reinhabit [ri:in'hæbit], *v.t.* Habiter de nouveau.
reinless ['reinlis], *a.* Sans rênes; (*fig.*) effréné.
reinscribe [ri:in'skraib], *v.t.* Réinscrire.
reinsert [ri:in'sə:t], *v.t.* Insérer de nouveau. **reinsertion**, *n.* Insertion nouvelle, *f.*
reinstall [ri:in'stɔ:l], *v.t.* Réinstaller. **reinstallation** [ri:instə'leiʃən], *n.* Réinstallation, *f.*

reinstate [ri:in'steit], *v.t.* Rétablir. **reinstatement**, *n.* Rétablissement, *m.*; réintégration, *f.*
reinsurance [-'ʃuərəns], *n.* Réassurance, *f.*
reinsure, *v.t.* Réassurer.
reintegrate [ri:'intigreit], *v.t.* Réintégrer.
reinterrogate [-'terəgeit], *v.t.* Interroger de nouveau, réinterroger.
reintroduce [ri:intrə'dju:s], *v.t.* Introduire de nouveau, réintroduire; présenter de nouveau.
reinvest [ri:in'vest], *v.t.* Replacer.
reinvestigate [-'vestigeit], *v.t.* Examiner de nouveau.
reinvigorate [-'vigəreit], *v.t.* Ranimer, revigorer.
reinvite [ri:in'vait], *v.t.* Réinviter.
reissue [ri:'isju:], *v.t.* Émettre de nouveau; rééditer (a book).—*n.* Nouvelle émission; réimpression, nouvelle édition, *f.*
reiterate [ri:'itəreit], *v.t.* Réitérer. **reiteration** [-'reiʃən], *n.* Réitération, *f.* **reiterative** [-'itərətiv], *a.* Réitératif.
reject (1) [ri'dʒekt], *v.t.* Rejeter.
reject (2) ['ri:dʒekt], *n.* Pièce de rebut, *f.*; conscrit réformé, *m.* **rejectable**, *a.* Rejetable, à rejeter. **rejection**, *n.* Rejet, *m.*
rejoice [ri'dʒɔis], *v.t.* Réjouir.—*v.i.* Se réjouir (de). (*fam.*) *To rejoice in* (name etc.), jouir de, posséder. **rejoicing**, *n.* Réjouissance, joie, *f.*; (*pl.*) réjouissances, *f.pl.*, fête, *f.*
rejoin (1) [ri:'dʒɔin], *v.t.* Rejoindre.
rejoin (2) [ri'dʒɔin], *v.i.* Répliquer, répondre (reply). **rejoinder**, *n.* Repartie; (*Law*) réplique, *f.*
rejoint [ri:'dʒɔint], *v.t.* (*Build.*) Rejointoyer. **rejointing**, *n.* Rejointoiement, *m.*
rejudge [ri:'dʒʌdʒ], *v.t.* Rejuger.
rejuvenate [ri'dʒu:vəneit], *v.t.* Rajeunir. **rejuvenation**, *n.* Rajeunissement, *m.* **rejuvenescence** [-'nesəns], *n.* (*Med.*) Rajeunissement, *m.*
rekindle [ri:'kindl], *v.t.* Rallumer.—*v.i.* Se rallumer.
reland [ri:'lænd], *v.i.* Débarquer de nouveau.
relapse [ri'læps], *n.* Rechute, *f. To have a relapse*, faire une rechute.—*v.i.* Retomber (dans); récidiver (into crime). **relapser**, *n.* (*Theol.*) Relaps, *m.*, relapse, *f.*
relate [ri'leit], *v.t.* Raconter; rapporter. *Strange to relate*, chose étonnante à dire.— *v.i.* Se rapporter, avoir rapport (à). **related**, *a.* Ayant rapport; parent (de); allié (à) (by marriage etc.). *Closely related*, étroitement apparenté. **relater**, *n.* Raconteur, narrateur, *m.* **relating**, *a.* Relatif, qui se rapporte (à).
relation [ri'leiʃən], *n.* Relation, *f.*; rapport; récit (narrative); parent (a relative); allié (by marriage), *m.*; (*pl.*) relations, *f.pl.*, rapports (intercourse), *m.pl. Distant relations*, parents éloignés, *m.pl.*; *in relation to*, quant à, à l'égard de; *near relations*, proches parents, *m.pl.* **relationship**, *n.* Parenté, *f.*; rapport, *m.*
relative ['relətiv], *a.* Relatif, qui se rapporte (à).—*n.* Parent, *m.*, parente, *f.*; (*Gram.*) relatif, *m. Near relatives*, proches, *m.pl.* **relatively**, *adv.* Relativement. **relativeness**, *n.* Relativité, *f.* **relativism**, *n.* Relativisme, *m.* **relativity** [-'tiviti], *n.* Relativité, *f.*
relax [ri'læks], *v.t.* Relâcher, détendre; (*fig.*) relâcher, se relâcher de, délasser; (*Med.*) relaxer. *To relax one's mind*, se distraire, se délasser; *to relax the mind*, détendre l'esprit.

—*v.i.* Se relâcher; se détendre; se délasser, se reposer; faiblir, fléchir. **relaxation** [relæk'seiʃən], *n.* Relâchement, relâche, *m.*, détente, *f.*; (*Med.*) délassement, repos, *m.* **relaxing**, *a.* Relâchant, laxatif; énervant, débilitant (of climate).

relay ['ri:lei], *n.* Relais, *m. Relay race,* course de relais, *f.*; *relay station,* (*Rad.*) relais, *m.*, poste amplificateur, *m.*—*v.t.* Relayer.

re-lay [ri:'lei], *v.t.* Poser de nouveau.

release [ri'li:s], *v.t.* Relâcher, élargir, libérer (a prisoner); délivrer, relever, décharger (de); lâcher, déclencher.—*n.* Élargissement, *m.*; délivrance; libération, décharge (an obligation); (*Law*) cession, *f.*; (*Cine.*) sortie, *f.* (of a film); déclenchement, *m.* (spring etc.).

releasee [rili:'si:], *n.* (*Law*) Abandonnataire. **releasor** ['li:sɔ:], *n.* Renonciateur, *m.*

relegate ['religeit], *v.t.* Reléguer. **relegation** [-'geiʃən], *n.* Relégation, *f.*; (*spt.*) renvoi à la division inférieure, *m.*

relent [ri'lent], *v.i.* S'amollir, s'attendrir; se repentir (to repent). **relenting**, *n.* Attendrissement, *m.* **relentless,** *a.* Inflexible, impitoyable, implacable. **relentlessly,** *adv.* Impitoyablement. **relentlessness,** *n.* Rigueur, dureté, *f.*

re-let [ri:'let], *v.t.* Relouer. **re-letting,** *n.* Relocation, *f.*

relevance ['reləvəns], **relevancy** ['reləvənsi], *n.* Relation, *f.*, rapport, *m.*; convenance, *f.*, à-propos, *m.* **relevant,** *a.* Relatif, qui a rapport, applicable (à); à propos; topique. *The relevant facts and papers,* les faits pertinents et les pièces justificatives. **relevantly,** *adv.* Pertinemment.

reliable [ri'laiəbl], *a.* Digne de confiance; sûr, exact, bien fondé (of information). **reliableness** or **reliability** [-'biliti], *n.* Crédibilité, véracité; sûreté, régularité, *f.* **reliably,** *adv.* Sûrement.

reliance [ri'laiəns], *n.* Confiance, *f.*; (person) soutien, appui, *m. To place reliance on,* mettre sa confiance dans. **reliant,** *a. To be reliant on,* dépendre de; avoir confiance en.

relic ['relik], *n.* Relique (of a saint or martyr), *f.*; (*pl.*) restes, *m.pl.,* cendres, *f.pl.*

relict ['relikt], *n.* (*Law*) Veuve, *f.*

relief [ri'li:f], *n.* Soulagement, adoucissement, allégement (from pain etc.); secours (assistance), *m.,* aide, *f.*; (*Law*) redressement, *m.,* réparation, justice; (*Mil.*) relève, *f.*; (*Sculp.* etc.) relief, *m. Demi-relief,* demi-relief, *m.*; *out-door relief,* secours à domicile, *m.*; *relief map,* carte en relief, *f.*; *relief party,* détachement de relève, *m.*; *relief train,* train supplémentaire, *m.*; *to bring out in strong relief,* faire vivement ressortir; *to give relief,* donner du soulagement, donner des secours; *to stand out in relief,* ressortir, se détacher (sur).

relieve [ri'li:v], *v.t.* Soulager, adoucir, alléger; délivrer (de), débarrasser (de); secourir, aider (to assist); subvenir aux besoins de (the poor); (*Mil.*) relever (a sentry); redresser (to right); (*Art*) faire ressortir, mettre en relief. *To relieve oneself, to relieve nature,* se soulager; *to relieve one's feelings,* s'épancher; *to relieve someone of his wallet,* soulager quelqu'un de son portefeuille. **reliever,** *n.* Personne *or* chose qui secourt, *f.* **relieving,** *n.* Soulagement, allégement, adoucissement; secours, *m.,* aide, *f.*—*a.* Qui donne des secours.

Relieving arch, arc de décharge, *m.*; *relieving officer,* commissaire des pauvres, *m.*

relievo [ri'li:vou], *n.* (*Sculp.*) Relief, *m. Alto relievo,* haut relief; *basso relievo,* bas-relief, *m.*

relight [ri:'lait], *v.t.* Rallumer; éclairer de nouveau.

religion [ri'lidʒən], *n.* Religion, *f.* **religionist,** *n.* Bigot, fanatique, *m.* **religiosity** [-i'ɔsiti], *n.* Religiosité, *f.* **religious,** *a.* Religieux, pieux; de religion; de piété. *Religious book,* livre de piété, *m.* **religiously,** *adv.* Religieusement, pieusement. **religiousness,** *n.* Piété, *f.*

re-line [ri:'lain], *v.t.* Remettre une doublure à; regarnir (brakes).

relinquish [ri'liŋkwiʃ], *v.t.* Abandonner; renoncer à. **relinquishment,** *n.* Abandon, *m.*; renonciation, *f.*

reliquary ['relikwəri], *n.* Reliquaire, *m.*

relish ['reliʃ], *n.* Goût, *m.,* saveur, *f.*; (*Cook.*) assaisonnement; (*fig.*) charme, parfum; morceau friand, hors-d'œuvre, *m.,* friandise, *f.*; appétit, *m. To eat with relish,* manger de bon appétit; *to give a relish to,* relever le goût de; *to have a relish for,* avoir un penchant pour, avoir le goût de, raffoler de; *to tell a story with relish,* se délecter à raconter une histoire.—*v.t.* Goûter, savourer, trouver bon, trouver du plaisir à; relever le goût de. *I do not relish his jokes,* ses plaisanteries ne sont pas de mon goût.—*v.i.* Avoir bon goût (à); avoir un parfum *or* une saveur (de). **relishable,** *a.* Savoureux.

relive [ri:'liv], *v.t.* Revivre (one's life).

reload [ri:'loud], *v.t.* Recharger.

reluctance [ri'lʌktəns] or **reluctancy,** *n.* Répugnance, *f.* **reluctant,** *a.* Qui a de la répugnance à, qui agit à contre-cœur; peu disposé (à). *I feel reluctant to,* j'ai de la répugnance à, il me répugne de. **reluctantly,** *adv.* Avec répugnance, à contre-cœur.

rely [ri'lai], *v.i.* Compter (sur), avoir confiance (en).

remain [ri'mein], *v.i.* Rester, demeurer. *It only remains for him to,* il ne lui reste plus qu'à; *it remains for me to,* il me reste à; *that remains to be proved,* cela n'est pas encore prouvé; *that remains to be seen,* c'est ce que nous verrons; *there remain* or *there remains,* il reste; *to have remaining,* avoir de reste; *to remain till called for,* poste restante (of letters), *f.*

remainder, *n.* Reste, *m.*; (*Publishing*) bouillon, *m.*—*a.* De reste.

remaining, *a.* De reste, restant.

remains, *n.pl.* Restes; débris, *m.pl.,* cendres, *f.pl. Mortal remains,* restes mortels, *m.pl.,* dépouille mortelle, *f.*

remake [ri:'meik], *v.t.* (*past* and *p.p.* **remade**) Refaire.

reman [ri:'mæn], *v.t.* (*Naut.*) Réarmer.

remand [ri'ma:nd], *v.t.* Renvoyer à une autre audience. *Remanded for a week,* renvoyé à huitaine; *remanded in custody,* en prison préventive.—*n.* Renvoi à une autre audience, *m. Remand home,* maison de détention provisoire, *f.*

remark [ri'ma:k], *n.* Remarque, *f. To pass remarks on,* faire des observations sur.—*v.t.* Remarquer, observer; faire remarquer, faire observer (to a person). **remarkable,**

a. Remarquable. **remarkableness,** *n.* Caractère remarquable, *m.* **remarkably,** *adv.* Remarquablement.
remarriage [ri:'mæridʒ], *n.* Remariage, *m.*
remarry, *v.t.* Épouser de nouveau.—*v.i.* Se remarier.
remediable [rə'mi:diəbl], *a.* À quoi on peut remédier, réparable, remédiable. **remedial,** *a.* Réparateur; (*Med.*) curatif.
remedy ['remədi], *n.* Remède; (*Law*) recours, *m. Past remedy,* sans remède.—*v.t.* Remédier à, porter remède à.
remelt [ri:'melt], *v.t.* Refondre.
remember [ri'membə], *v.t.* Se souvenir de, se rappeler; reconnaître (to recognize); (*colloq.*) rappeler au souvenir. *I don't remember the face,* cette figure ne me revient pas; *if I remember rightly,* si je m'en souviens bien; *remember me to him,* rappelez-moi à son bon souvenir; *remember me to your mother,* rappelez-moi au souvenir de votre mère; *to remember by heart,* retenir par cœur.
remembrance [ri'membrəns], *n.* Souvenir, *m.,* mémoire, *f. Give him my kind remembrances,* rappelez-moi à son bon souvenir; *in remembrance of,* en souvenir de, en mémoire de; *to bring a thing to someone's remembrance,* rappeler une chose au souvenir de quelqu'un.
remembrancer, *n.* Mémento; souvenir (thing); secrétaire, archiviste (of the exchequer), *m.*
remetal [ri:'metl], *v.t.* Recharger (a road).
remind [ri'maind], *v.t.* Rappeler à, faire souvenir (à . . . de), faire penser (à). *I do not want reminding,* je n'ai pas besoin qu'on m'y fasse penser; *remind him of that,* rappelez-lui cela; *that reminds me,* à propos! *you remind me of my father,* vous me rappelez mon père.
reminder, *n.* Mémento, *m. As a reminder (that),* pour rappeler (que); *send me a reminder,* envoyez-moi un petit mot pour m'y faire penser.
reminisce [remi'nis], *v.i.* Raconter ses souvenirs.
reminiscence [remi'nisəns], *n.* Réminiscence, *f.* **reminiscent** [-ənt], *a.* Qui rappelle.
remiss [ri'mis], *a.* Négligent, lent, inexact; lâche, détendu. **remissible,** *a.* Rémissible, pardonnable. **remission,** *n.* Rémission, grâce, *f.;* pardon; relâchement, adoucissement (relaxing), *m.;* remise (abatement), *f. Remission of sins,* rémission des péchés, *f.*
remissly, *adv.* Négligemment, sans soin.
remissness, *n.* Négligence, inexactitude, *f.*
remit [ri'mit], *v.t.* Se relâcher de (to relax); faire remise de, remettre (a fine etc.); renvoyer; faire une remise de (to send back).—*v.i.* Se relâcher, se calmer; diminuer, s'affaiblir.
remittal or **remitment,** *n.* Rémission, remise, *f.* **remittance,** *n.* Remise, *f.;* envoi de fonds, paiement, *m.* **remittent,** *a.* (*Path.*) Rémittent. **remitter,** *n.* Personne qui remet des fonds, *f.,* envoyeur, *m.*
remnant ['remnənt], *n.* Reste, *m.;* (*pl.*) restes, restants, débris, *m.pl.;* coupon, bout (of stuff), *m.*
remodel [ri:'modl], *v.t.* Refondre; remanier, remodeler. **remodelling,** *n.* Remodelage; remaniement, *m.*

remonstrance [ri'monstrəns], *n.* Remontrance, *f.* **remonstrant,** *n.* Remontrant, *m.* —*a.* De protestation, de remontrance.
remonstrate [ri'monstreit], *v.i.* Remontrer. *To remonstrate with,* faire des remontrances à. **remonstrator,** *n.* Remontreur, protestataire, *m.*
remora ['remərə], *n.* (*Ichth.*) Rémora, *m.*
remorse [ri'mo:s], *n.* Remords, *m.* **remorseful,** *a.* Rempli de remords. **remorseless,** *a.* Sans remords, impitoyable. **remorselessness,** *n.* Cruauté, inhumanité, *f.*
remote [ri'mout], *a.* Éloigné, lointain; reculé (of time); faible, vague; distant (of person). *Remote control,* commande à distance, *f.* **remotely,** *adv.* De loin; faiblement. **remoteness,** *n.* Éloignement, *m.,* distance; faiblesse, *f.;* attitude distante, réserve, *f.* (of person).
remould [ri:'mould], *v.t.* Mouler de nouveau, refondre.
remount [ri:'maunt], *v.t., v.i.* Remonter.—*n.* Remonte, *f.,* cheval de remonte, *m. Remount officer,* officier de remonte, *m.* **remounting,** *n.* Remonte, *f.;* remontage (of jewels, tyres), *m.*
removability [rimu:və'biliti], *n.* Amovibilité, *f.* **removable** [ri'mu:vəbl], *a.* Transportable; (*fig.*) amovible (of a functionary etc.).
removal [ri'mu:vl], *n.* Éloignement, départ, changement de domicile; transport (conveyance); déménagement (of furniture); déplacement, renvoi, *m.,* révocation, destitution (from office), *f.;* redressement (of a grievance), *m.;* suppression (of an abuse); (*Surg.*) levée (of bandages), *f.;* enlèvement (taking away), *m. Removal man,* déménageur, *m.; three removals are as bad as a fire,* trois déménagements valent un incendie.
remove [ri'mu:v], *n.* Éloignement; déménagement (removal); degré (relation), *m.;* distance (distance), *f.;* relevé (dish), *m.;* (*sch.*) changement de classe, *m.*—*v.t.* Éloigner; déplacer (to displace); transporter (to convey); déménager (furniture); retirer, ôter, enlever, écarter (to take away); renvoyer, destituer (from office); lever (an obstacle). *To be far removed from,* être bien éloigné de.—*v.i.* S'éloigner, se déplacer; se transporter; changer de domicile, déménager (to change residence).
removed, *a.* Éloigné, retiré, isolé. *First cousin once removed,* cousin issu de germains; *twice removed,* issu de fils de germains.
remover, *n.* (Chose) qui enlève, *f.;* déménageur, *m. Nail-varnish remover* or *polish remover,* dissolvant (pour ongles), *m.*
remunerate [ri'mju:nəreit], *v.t.* Rémunérer, rétribuer; (*fig.*) récompenser (pour). **remuneration** [-'reiʃən], *n.* Rétribution, rémunération, *f.* **remunerative** [-'mju:nərətiv], *a.* Rémunérateur; (*Law*) rémunératoire.
Remus ['ri:məs]. Rémus, *m.*
renaissance [ri'neisəns], *n.* Renaissance, *f.*
renal [ri:nl], *a.* (*Anat.*) Rénal.
rename [ri:'neim], *v.t.* Renommer.
renascence [ri'næsəns], *n.* Renouveau, *m.* **renascent,** *a.* Renaissant.
rencounter [ren'kauntə], *n.* Rencontre, *f.*—*v.t.* Rencontrer.—*v.i.* Se rencontrer.
rend [rend], *v.t.* (*past* and *p.p.* **rent**) Déchirer; (*fig.*) fendre. *To rend asunder,* déchirer en

deux, fendre en deux; *to rend the air with,* faire retentir l'air de; *to rend the heart,* fendre le cœur.—*v.i.* Se déchirer, se fendre.

render ['rendə], *v.t.* Rendre; donner; interpréter, traduire, exprimer; (*Cook.*) fondre (suet etc.); (*Build.*) appliquer, enduire. **renderable,** *a.* Qu'on peut rendre, traduire, exprimable, traduisible, etc. **rendering,** *n.* Traduction, interprétation, *f.*; (*Build.*) crépi, enduit, *m.*

rendezvous ['rɔndivu, *pl.* -vuːz], *n.* Rendezvous, *m.*—*v.t.* Donner rendez-vous.

rendition [ren'diʃən], *n.* Reddition (of a town); (*Theat.*) interprétation, traduction, *f.*

renegade ['renigeid], *n.* Renégat, *m.*

renew [ri'njuː], *v.t.* Renouveler; renouer. **renewable,** *a.* Renouvelable. **renewal,** *n.* Renouvellement, *m. Renewal of subscription,* réabonnement, *m.* **renewing,** *a.* Rénovateur.

reniform ['renifɔːm], *a.* (*Bot.*) Réniforme.

rennet ['renit], *n.* Présure; reinette (apple), *f.*

renounce [ri'nauns], *v.t.* Renoncer à; renier, renoncer. **renouncement,** *n.* Renoncement, *m.*, renonciation, *f.*

renovate ['renəveit], *v.t.* Renouveler; rajeunir, mettre à neuf, faire renaître. **renovating,** *a.* Rénovateur. **renovation** [-'veiʃən], *n.* Rénovation, *f.*, renouvellement, rajeunissement, *m.* **renovator,** *n.* Rénovateur, *m.*, rénovatrice, *f.*

renown [ri'naun], *n.* Renommée, *f.*, renom, *m.* **renowned,** *a.* Renommé.

rent (1) [rent], *n.* Déchirure, fente, *f.*; accroc (in garments), *m.*; rupture, *f.*; schisme (schism), *m.*

rent (2) [rent], *n.* Loyer (of houses or rooms); prix de location, *m.*; fermage (of farms), *m.*; (*pl.*) rentes, *f.pl.,* revenu, *m. Ground-rent,* rente foncière; *heavy rent,* fort loyer; *high rent,* loyer élevé; *low rent,* loyer faible.—*v.t.* Louer, prendre à ferme, donner à ferme, arrenter.—*v.i.* Se louer.

rent (3), *past* and *p.p.* [REND].

rentability, *n.* Rentabilité, *f.* **rentable,** *a.* Qu'on peut louer; affermable.

rental, *n.* Valeur locative, *f.*

renter, *n.* (*Am.*) Locataire; fermier (of a farm), loueur (of films), *m.*

rent-free, *a.* Exempt de loyer, sans payer de loyer.

rent-roll, *n.* État des revenus; (*Feud.*) livre censier, *m.*

renunciation [rinʌnsi'eiʃən], *n.* Renonciation, *f.*, renoncement, *m.*

reobtain [riːəb'tein], *v.t.* Obtenir de nouveau.

reoccupation [riːɔkju'peiʃən], *n.* Réoccupation, *f.* **reoccupy** [-'ɔkjupai], *v.t.* Réoccuper.

reopen [riː'oupən], *v.t.* Rouvrir.—*v.i.* Rentrer (of schools, law courts, etc.). **reopening,** *n.* Réouverture; rentrée (of schools etc.), *f.*

reoppose [riːə'pouz], *v.t.* Opposer de nouveau.

reordain [riːɔː'dein], *v.t.* Réordonner.

reorder [-'ɔːdə], *v.t.* Faire une nouvelle commande de.

reordination [-di'neiʃən], *n.* Réordination, *f.*

reorganization [riːɔːɡənai'zeiʃən], *n.* Réorganisation, *f.* **reorganize** [-'ɔːɡənaiz], *v.t.* Réorganiser. **reorganizer,** *n.* Réorganisateur, *m.*

rep (1) [rep], *n.* Reps (fabric), *m.*—*a.* De reps.

rep (2) [REPERTORY].

repack [riː'pæk], *v.t.* Rempaqueter, remballer, rencaisser. **repacking,** *n.* Rempaquetage, remballage, rencaissage, *m.*

repaint [-'peint], *v.t.* Repeindre.

repair [ri'pɛːə], *v.t.* Réparer; raccommoder (clothes etc.); radouber (a ship); (*fig.*) rétablir.—*v.i.* Aller; se rendre (à).—*n.* Réparation, *f.*; raccommodage (of clothes etc.); radoub (of ships); séjour, *m.*, demeure, *f.*, lieu de retraite (place), *m. Beyond repair,* abîmé irréparablement; *repair outfit,* nécessaire à outils, *m.*; *to be in good repair,* être en bon état; *to be out of repair,* être en mauvais état, avoir besoin de réparation; *to keep in repair,* entretenir. **repairer,** *n.* Réparateur, *m.*, réparatrice, *f.*; raccommodeur, *m.*, raccommodeuse (of clothes etc.), *f.*

repaper [riː'peipə], *v.t.* Tapisser de nouveau.

reparable ['repərəbl], *a.* Réparable. **reparably,** *adv.* D'une manière réparable.

reparation [-'reiʃən], *n.* Action de réparer; satisfaction, réparation (for an injury), *f.*

reparative, *a.* Réparateur.

repartee [repɑː'tiː], *n.* Repartie, riposte, *f.*

repass [riː'pɑːs], *v.t., v.i.* Repasser.

repast [ri'pɑːst], *n.* Repas, *m.*

repatriate (1) [riː'pætrieit *or* riː'peitrieit], *v.t.* Rapatrier. **repatriation,** *n.* Rapatriement, *m.*

repatriate (2) [riːpætriiit], *n.* Rapatrié, *m.*

repave [riː'peiv], *v.t.* Repaver. **repaving,** *n.* Repavage, *m.*

repay [ri'pei], *v.t.* (*past* and *p.p.* **repaid**) Rembourser; (*fig.*) payer, rendre, récompenser. *To repay* (*reading, inspection, etc.*), valoir la peine (d'être lu, examiné, etc.). **repayable,** *a.* Remboursable. **repayment** [riː'peimənt], *n.* Remboursement; (*fig.*) retour, *m.*, récompense, *f.*

repeal [ri'piːl], *v.t.* Révoquer, abolir; abroger (a law etc.).—*n.* Révocation; abrogation (of a law), *f.* **repealable,** *a.* Révocable. **repealer,** *n.* Personne qui abroge, etc., *f.*; (*Irish Hist.*) partisan de la révocation, *m.*

repeat [ri'piːt], *v.t.* Répéter, réitérer; réciter (by heart); (*after a line*) bis.—*n.* Répétition, *f.*; (*Mus.*) reprise, *f.* **repeated,** *a.* Répété, réitéré; redoublé (redoubled) **repeatedly,** *adv.* À plusieurs reprises; souvent, bien des fois. **repeater,** *n.* Personne qui répète; montre à répétition, *f.*; (*Navy*) répétiteur, *m.*; (*Rad.*) relais amplificateur, traducteur, *m.* **repeating,** *a.* Qui répète; à répétition. *Repeating decimal,* fraction périodique, *f.*

repel [ri'pel], *v.t.* Repousser; combattre. **repellent,** *a.* Répulsif, répugnant.—*n.* Répulsif; (*Med.*) révulsif, *m.*

repent (1) ['riːpənt], *a.* (*Bot.*) Rampant.

repent (2) [ri'pent], *v.i.* Se repentir.—*v.t.* Se repentir de. **repentance,** *n.* Repentir, *m.* **repentant,** *a.* Repentant. **repenting,** *n.* Repentir, *m.* **repentingly,** *adv.* Avec repentir.

repeople [riː'piːpl], *v.t.* Repeupler. **repeopling,** *n.* Repeuplement, *m.*

repercuss [riːpə'kʌs], *v.t.* Répercuter. **repercussion** [-'kʌʃən], *n.* Répercussion, *f.* **repercussive,** *a.* Répercussif.

repertoire ['repətwɑː], *n.* Répertoire, *m.*

repertory ['repətəri], *n.* Répertoire, *m. Repertory theatre,* théâtre de province, *m.*

reperusal [riːpəˈruːzl], *n.* Deuxième lecture, *f.*
reperuse, *v.t.* Lire de nouveau.
repetend [ˈrepətend], *n.* (*Arith.*) Période, *f.*
repetition [repiˈtiʃən], *n.* Répétition; (*Mus.*) reprise, *f.* **repetitive** [riˈpetitiv], *a.* Qui se répète.
repine [riˈpain], *v.i.* Murmurer (contre) de; se plaindre (de). **repining,** *a.* Disposé à se plaindre, mécontent.—*n.* Plainte, *f.,* murmure, regret, *m.* **repiningly,** *adv.* En murmurant.
replace [riːˈpleis], *v.t.* Replacer, remettre; remplacer (to substitute). **replaceable,** *a.* Remplaçable. **replacement,** *n.* Remise en place, *f.*; remplacement, *m.*
replant [riːˈplɑːnt], *v.t.* Replanter; reboiser (forests). **replantation** [-ˈteiʃən] or **replanting,** *n.* Replantation, *f.*; reboisement (of forests), *m.*
replate [riːˈpleit], *v.t.* Replaquer.
replay (1) [riːˈplei], *v.t.* (*spt.*) Rejouer.
replay (2) [ˈriːplei], *n.* Match rejoué, *m.*
replenish [riˈpleniʃ], *v.t.* Remplir (de).—*v.i.* Se remplir. **replenishment,** *n.* Remplissage, *m.*
replete [riˈpliːt], *a.* Plein, rempli (de). **repletion** [-ˈpliːʃən], *n.* Plénitude; (*Med.*) réplétion, *f.*
replevin [riˈplevin], *n.* Mainlevée, *f.*
replica [ˈreplikə], *n.* Double, *m.,* copie, *f.*
replication [repliˈkeiʃən], *n.* Réplique, *f.*
replier [riˈplaiə], *n.* Personne qui répond, *f.*
replunge [riːˈplʌndʒ], *v.t., v.i.* Replonger.
reply [riˈplai], *n.* Réponse; (*Law*) réplique, *f. In reply to,* en réponse à—*v.t., v.i.* Répondre, répliquer. **reply-coupon,** *n.* Coupon-réponse, *m.*
repoint [riːˈpɔint], *v.t.* Rejointoyer. **repointing,** *n.* Rejointoiement, *m.*
repolish [riːˈpɔliʃ], *v.t.* Repolir. **repolishing,** *n.* Repolissage, *m.*
repopulate [riːˈpɔpjuleit], *v.t.* Repeupler. **repopulation** [-ˈleiʃən], *n.* Repeuplement, *m.*
report [riˈpɔːt], *v.t.* Rapporter, raconter, dire, réciter; rendre compte de; faire un rapport sur; signaler; dénoncer (to police). *It is reported,* on dit, le bruit court (que); *to report oneself,* se présenter (à la place, à l'état-major, au bureau de police, etc.), faire sa déclaration.—*v.i.* Faire un rapport, (*Mil.*) se présenter.—*n.* Rapport, compte, exposé; bruit, ouï-dire (rumour); compte rendu, procès-verbal (of meetings etc.); (*sch.*) bulletin, *m.*; détonation, *f.,* coup (of fire-arms), *m.*; réputation (repute), *f. Of good report,* considéré; *to draw up a report,* rédiger un rapport.
reporter [riˈpɔːtə], *n.* Rapporteur; sténographe (shorthand writer); journaliste, reporter (of a newspaper), *m. Reporters' gallery,* tribune de la Presse, *f.* **reporting,** *n.* Reportage, *m.*
repose [riˈpouz], *v.i.* Se reposer. *To repose on,* se reposer sur.—*v.t.* Reposer; mettre (sa confiance en *or* dans).—*n.* Repos; calme, *m.*
reposit [riˈpɔzit], *v.t.* Déposer.
repository [riˈpɔzitəri], *n.* Dépôt, magasin; caveau, *m. Furniture repository,* garde-meuble, *m.*
repossess [riːpəˈzes], *v.t.* Rentrer en possession de, posséder de nouveau. **repossession,** *n.* Rentrée en possession, *f.*

repot [riːˈpɔt], *v.t.* Rempoter. **repotting,** *n.* Rempotage, *m.*
reprehend [repriˈhend], *v.t.* Reprendre; réprimander, censurer, blâmer (de). **reprehender,** *n.* Censeur, critique, *m.* **reprehensible,** *a.* Répréhensible, blâmable. **reprehensibleness,** *n.* Caractère répréhensible, *m.* **reprehensibly,** *adv.* D'une manière répréhensible. **reprehension,** *n.* Répréhension, réprimande, *f.* **reprehensive,** *a.* De reproche.
represent [repriˈzent], *v.t.* Représenter. **representation** [-ˈteiʃən], *n.* Représentation; démarche, *f.* **representative** [-ˈzentətiv], *a.* Représentatif, qui représente.—*n.* Représentant; fondé de pouvoir, *m.*; (*Parl.*) député, (*Comm.*) agent, *m.* **representatively,** *adv.* D'une manière représentative, par représentation. **representer,** *n.* Représentant, *m.*
repress [riˈpres], *v.t.* Réprimer. **represser,** *n.* Répresseur, *m.* **repressible,** *a.* Répressible. **repression** [-ˈpreʃən], *n.* Répression, *f.* **repressive,** *a.* Répressif.
reprieve [riˈpriːv], *n.* Sursis; répit, *m.*; commutation de peine; grâce, *f.*—*v.t.* Accorder un sursis à, surseoir à; accorder un répit à; commuer (une peine), gracier.
reprimand (1) [ˈreprimɑːnd], *n.* Réprimande, *f.*
reprimand (2) [repriˈmɑːnd], *v.t.* Réprimander; (*Law*) blâmer.
reprint (1) [ˈriːprint], *n.* Réimpression, *f.*
reprint (2) [riːˈprint], *v.t.* Réimprimer.
reprisal [riˈpraizl], *n.* Représailles, *f.pl. To have recourse to reprisals,* user de représailles.
reprise [riˈpriːz], *n.* (*Mus.*) Reprise, *f.*
reproach [riˈproutʃ], *n.* Reproche; opprobre (shame), objet de mépris, *m. Above reproach,* irréprochable; *to be a reproach to,* être la honte de.—*v.t.* Reprocher; faire un reproche *or* des reproches à; blâmer; *He is reproached with having done that,* on lui reproche d'avoir fait cela. **reproachable,** *a.* Digne de reproche. **reproachful,** *a.* Plein de reproches, réprobateur. **reproachfully,** *adv.* Avec reproche, d'un ton de reproche.
reprobate (1) [ˈreprəbit], *n.* Réprouvé, vaurien, *m.*
reprobate (2) [ˈreprəbeit], *v.t.* Réprouver. **reprobation** [-ˈbeiʃən], *n.* Réprobation, *f.* **reprobative** [ˈreprəbeitiv], *a.* Réprobateur.
reproduce [riːprəˈdjuːs], *v.t.* Reproduire.—*v.i.* Se reproduire. **reproducer,** *n.* Reproducteur, *m.* **reproducible,** *a.* Reproductible. **reproduction** [-ˈdʌkʃən], *n.* Reproduction, *f.* **reproductive** [-ˈdʌktiv], *a.* Reproducteur, reproductif.
reproof (1) [riˈpruːf], *n.* Reproche, *m.,* réprimande, *f.*
reproof (2) [riːˈpruːf], *v.t.* Réimperméabiliser (a coat).
reprovable [riˈpruːvəbl], *a.* Répréhensible.
reprove, *v.t.* Blâmer, reprendre; censurer. **reprover,** *n.* Censeur, *m.* **reproving,** *a.* Réprobateur. **reprovingly,** *adv.* D'un air *or* ton réprobateur.
reptile [ˈreptail], *a.* Reptile; (*fig.*) rampant, vil. *The reptile press,* la presse servile, *f.,* les journaux reptiliens, *m.pl.*—*n.* Reptile, *m.*
reptilian [-ˈtiliən], *a.* Reptilien.
republic [riˈpʌblik], *n.* République, *f.* **republican,** *a.* and *n.* Républicain. **republicanism,** *n.* Républicanisme, *m.*

republication [ri:pʌbli'keiʃən], *n.* Nouvelle
édition, réimpression (of a book), *f.* **republish** [-'pʌbliʃ], *v.t.* Republier, rééditer.
repudiate [ri'pju:dieit], *v.t.* Répudier;
désavouer. **repudiation** [-'eiʃən], *n.* Répudiation, *f.*
repugnance [ri'pʌgnəns] or **repugnancy**, *n.*
Répugnance; contrariété (contrariety), *f.*
repugnant, *a.* Répugnant, qui répugne;
contraire (à), incompatible (avec). *It is
repugnant to me to*, il me répugne de. **repug-
nantly**, *adv.* Avec répugnance.
repulse [ri'pʌls], *v.t.* Repousser, rebuter,
refuser.—*n.* Échec, refus, *m.*, rebuffade, *f.*
To meet with a repulse, essuyer un
échec.
repulsion [ri'pʌlʃən], *n.* Répulsion, répugnance, *f.*
repulsive [ri'pʌlsiv], *a.* Rebutant; dégoûtant;
repoussant (forbidding). *A repulsive
appearance*, une figure repoussante, *f.* **repul-
siveness**, *n.* Caractère repoussant, *m.*
repurchase [ri:'pə:tʃis], *v.t.* Racheter.—*n.*
Rachat; (*Law*) réméré, *m.*
reputable [.'repjutəbl], *a.* Honorable, de
bonne réputation, considéré. **reputably**,
adv. Honorablement.
reputation [repju'teiʃən], *n.* Réputation, *f.*
He had a reputation for prudence, il avait
une réputation de sagesse; *to get a reputation*,
se faire une réputation.
repute [ri'pju:t], *v.t.* (*usu. pass.*) Réputer,
estimer. *He is reputed to be very rich*, il passe
pour être très riche.—*n.* Réputation, estime,
f., renom, *m.* *Of good repute*, honorablement
connu; *place of ill repute*, endroit mal famé,
m.; *to bring into repute*, mettre en vogue.
reputed, *a.* Réputé, censé, qui passe (pour);
putatif (of fathers). **reputedly**, *adv.*
Suivant l'opinion commune; censément.
request [ri'kwest], *n.* Demande, prière; (*Law*)
requête, *f.* *At the request of*, à la demande
de; *at the urgent request of*, sur les instances
de; *in request*, en crédit, en vogue, (*Comm.*)
demandé, recherché; *to make a request*, faire
une demande; (*Rad.*) *request programme*,
programme des auditeurs, *m.*; *request stop*
(for bus etc.), arrêt facultatif, *m.*—*v.t.* Demander (à); solliciter; prier (de), inviter (à).
It is earnestly requested that, on est instamment prié de; *to request a thing*, demander *or*
solliciter une chose; *to request someone to*,
prier quelqu'un de; *you are requested to*
(public notice), prière de.
requicken [ri:'kwikn], *v.t.* Raviver, ranimer.
requiem ['rekwiem], *n.* Requiem, *m.*
requirable [ri'kwaiərəbl], *a.* Que l'on peut
exiger, exigible.
require [ri'kwaiə], *v.t.* Exiger, requérir;
demander, réclamer (to demand); avoir
besoin de (to want); (*impers.*) falloir. *It is
required of me that*, on demande que je; *it
requires*, il faut; *that is all that is required*,
c'est tout ce qu'il faut. **requirement**, *n.*
Exigence, nécessité, *f.*, besoin, *m.*; condition
requise, *f.*
requisite ['rekwizit], *a.* Requis, exigé, nécessaire. *It is requisite to*, il faut.—*n.* Qualité *or*
condition requise; chose requise, *f.*, nécessaire, *m.* *Office requisites*, fournitures de
bureau, *f.pl.*; *toilet requisites*, objets de

toilette, *m.pl.* **requisitely**, *adv.* Nécessairement.
requisition [rekwi'ziʃən], *n.* Réquisition;
demande, convocation, *f.* *To put into
requisition*, mettre en réquisition.—*v.t.* Réquisitionner.
requital [ri'kwaitl], *n.* Récompense, *f.*; retour,
m.; revanche, *f.* *In requital of*, en récompense
de, en retour de.
requite [ri'kwait], *v.t.* Récompenser; rendre
la pareille à; payer de retour.
re-read [ri:'ri:d], *v.t.* Relire.
reredos ['riədɔs], *n.* Retable, *m.*
resaddle [ri:'sædl], *v.t.* Reseller.
resail [ri:'seil], *v.i.* Retourner à la voile.
resale [ri:'seil], *n.* Revente, *f.*
resalute [ri:sə'lju:t], *v.t.* Resaluer, saluer de
nouveau.
rescind [ri'sind], *v.t.* Rescinder, annuler,
abroger, casser. **rescinding**, *a.* Abroga-
toire. **rescission** [-'siʃən], *n.* Rescision,
annulation, abrogation, *f.* **rescissory**, *a.*
Rescisoire.
rescript ['ri:skript], *n.* Rescrit, *m.*
rescriptively [ri'skriptivli], *adv.* Par rescrit.
rescue ['reskju:], *n.* Délivrance, *f.*; sauvetage,
m. *Rescue team*, équipe de secours, *f.*; *to the
rescue*, au secours!—*v.t.* Sauver, délivrer (de);
arracher (à). **rescuer**, *n.* Sauveteur, libérateur, *m.*
reseal [ri:'si:l], *v.t.* Resceller. **resealing**, *n.*
Rescellement, *m.*
research [ri'sə:tʃ], *n.* Recherche, *f.*; recherches, investigations, études, *f.pl.* *Research worker*, chercheur, *m.*—*v.i.* Faire des
recherches.—*v.t.* Rechercher.
reseat [ri:'si:t], *v.t.* Rasseoir, replacer;
regarnir de sièges; remettre un fond à
(chairs etc.).
resection [ri:'sekʃən], *n.* (*Surg.*) Résection, *f.*
reseda ['rezədə], *n.* Réséda, *m.* *Reseda green*,
vert de réséda, *m.*
reseize [ri:'si:z], *v.t.* Ressaisir.
resell [ri:'sel], *v.t.* (*past* and *p.p.* **resold**)
Revendre, vendre de nouveau.
resemblance [ri'zembləns], *n.* Ressemblance,
f.; (*fig.*) rapport, *m.* **resemble**, *v.t.* Ressembler (à). *To resemble each other*, se
ressembler.
resent [ri'zent], *v.t.* Ressentir, se ressentir de;
s'offenser de; prendre en mauvaise part.
resentful, *a.* Plein de ressentiment, rancunier. *Resentful of*, qui se ressent vivement
de. **resentfully** *or* **resentingly**, *adv.* Avec
ressentiment. **resentment**, *n.* Ressentiment,
m., rancœur, *f.*
reservation [rezə'veiʃən], *n.* Réserve, restriction, arrière-pensée, *f.*; (*Am.*) terrain
réservé, *m.*; réservation, location, *f.* (seat
etc.). *Mental reservation*, restriction mentale,
f.
reserve [ri'zə:v], *n.* Réserve; retenue, prudence; restriction, arrière-pensée, *f.* *Body of
reserve*, (*Mil.*) corps de réserve, *m.*; *reserve
fund*, fonds de prévoyance, *m.*; *reserve price*
(at sales), prix minimum, *m.*—*v.t.* Réserver.
To reserve oneself, se réserver. **reserved**, *a.*
Réservé; qui a de la retenue. *Reserved seat*,
place louée, place réservée. **reservedly**, *adv.*
Avec réserve. **reservedness**, *n.* Réserve,
retenue, discrétion, *f.* **reservist**, *n.* Réserviste, *m.*

reservoir ['rezəvwɑ:], *n.* Réservoir, bassin de retenue, *m.*

reset [ri:'set], *v.t.* (*past* and *p.p.* **reset**) Poser *or* fixer de nouveau; (*Print.*) composer de nouveau; (*Surg.*) remettre.—*n.* (*Print.*) Recomposition, *f.* **resetting,** *n.* Remontage (of gems), *m.*; (*Print.*) recomposition, *f.*

resettle [ri:'setl], *v.t.* Rétablir, installer de nouveau.—*v.i.* S'installer *or* s'établir de nouveau; se reposer (of lees etc.). **resettlement,** *n.* Rétablissement, *m.*; réinstallation, *f.*; recasement, *m.*

reshape [ri:'ʃeip], *v.t.* Reformer; remanier.

reship [ri:'ʃip], *v.t.* Rembarquer. **reshipment,** *n.* Rembarquement, *m.*

reshuffle [ri:'ʃʌfl], *v.t.* Remêler, rebattre (cards); (*fig.*) remanier (the Cabinet etc.).—*n.* Nouveau battement, *m. Cabinet reshuffle,* remaniement ministériel, *m.*

reside [ri'zaid], *v.i.* Résider, demeurer.

residence ['rezidəns], *n.* Résidence, demeure, *f.*, séjour, *m.*; maison, *f.*; (*Law*) domicile, *m. Board (and) residence,* la table et le logement; *in residence,* en résidence. **residency,** *n.* Hôtel du Résident, *m.*, Résidence, *f.* **resident,** *n.* Habitant; résident; pensionnaire, *m.*—*a.* Résidant; interne (living in house). *Resident master,* professeur interne, *m.*; *resident mistress,* institutrice interne, *f.* **residential** [-'denʃl], *a.* Propre à l'habitation, résidentiel. *Residential district,* quartier résidentiel; *residential estate,* propriété avec maison d'habitation, *f.* **residentiary,** *a.* En résidence, résidant.—*n.* Ecclésiastique obligé à la résidence, *m.*

residual [ri'zidjuəl], *a.* Résiduel, qui reste. **residuary,** *a.* De résidu, de reste; universel (of legatees).

residue ['rezidju:], *n.* Reste, (*Chem.*) résidu; reliquat (of debts), *m.* **residuum** [rə'zi djuəm], *n.* Résidu, *m.*

resign [ri'zain], *v.t.* Se démettre de, donner sa démission de; abandonner, céder, renoncer à. *To be resigned,* se résigner, être résigné; *to be resigned to* or *resign oneself to,* se résigner à, se soumettre à.—*v.i.* Donner sa démission, démissionner (de).

re-sign [ri:'sain], *v.t.* Resigner, signer de nouveau.

resignation [rezig'neiʃən], *n.* Soumission, résignation; cession, *f.*, abandon, *m.*; démission (of functions), *f. To send in one's resignation,* donner sa démission.

resigned [ri'zaind], *a.* Résigné; démissionnaire (from a post).

resignedly [ri'zainidli], *adv.* Avec résignation.

resilience [ri'ziliəns] *or* **resiliency,** *n.* Rebondissement, *m.*; élasticité, *f.*; ressort, *m.* **resilient,** *a.* Rebondissant. *He is resilient* (in character), il a du ressort.

resin ['rezin], *n.* Résine; colophane (for violins), *f.* **resin-tapper,** *n.* Résinier, *m.* **resin-tapping,** *n.* Résinage, *m.*

resipiscence [resi'pisəns], *n.* Résipiscence, *f.*

resist [ri'zist], *v.t.* Résister à, combattre; se refuser à.—*v.i.* Résister. **resistance,** *n.* Résistance, *f. To take the line of least resistance,* aller au plus facile. **resistant,** *a.* Résistant. **resistible,** *a.* À quoi l'on peut résister, résistible. **resistive,** *a.* Résistant. **resistless,** *a.* Irrésistible.

resold, *past* and *p.p.* [RESELL].

re-sole [ri:'soul], *v.t.* Ressemeler. **re-soling,** *n.* Ressemelage, *m.*

resoluble ['rezəljubl], *a.* Soluble, réductible.

resolute ['rezəlju:t], *a.* Déterminé, résolu. **resolutely,** *adv.* Résolument. **resoluteness,** *n.* Résolution, fermeté, *f.* **resolution** [-'lju:ʃən], *n.* Résolution; décision (of deliberative bodies), *f.* (*Tel.*) *Picture resolution,* définition de l'image, *f.*; *to put forward a resolution,* soumettre une résolution.

resolutive ['rezɔlju:tiv], *a.* (*Med.*) Résolutif; (*Law*) résolutoire.

resolvable [ri'zɔlvəbl], *a.* Résoluble.

resolve [ri'zɔlv], *n.* Résolution, *f.*—*v.t.* Résoudre; dissoudre, fondre (to melt); informer, instruire (to inform); éclaircir, lever, dissiper (doubts etc.); déterminer, décider (of deliberative bodies).—*v.i.* Résoudre, se résoudre, se décider; se décomposer, se dissoudre, se fondre, fondre (to melt). *It has been unanimously resolved that,* il a été décidé à l'unanimité que; *to resolve oneself or itself into,* se constituer en, se former en; *to resolve upon,* prendre la résolution de, se résoudre à. **resolved,** *a.* Résolu. *Resolved to do something,* résolu de faire quelque chose. **resolvedly** [ri'zɔlvidli], *adv.* Résolument. **resolvent,** *n.* (*Med.*) Résolvant, résolutif, *m.*

resonance ['rezənəns], *n.* Résonance, *f. In resonance,* en résonance. **resonant,** *a.* Résonnant, sonore.

resort (1) [ri'zɔ:t], *n.* Ressource, *f.*, recours, *m.*; fréquentation (visiting), *f.*; concours, *m.*, assemblée (assembly), *f.*; séjour, rendez-vous (place); (*Law*) ressort, *m. In the last resort,* en dernier ressort; *resort of thieves,* repaire de voleurs, *m.*; *seaside resort,* station balnéaire, *f.*—*v.i.* Recourir, avoir recours (à); se rendre, aller (à); fréquenter, hanter.

resort (2) [ri:'sɔ:t], *v.t.* Trier à nouveau, reclasser.

resound [ri'zaund], *v.i.* Résonner, retentir; avoir du retentissement. *To resound with,* résonner de, retentir de.—*v.t.* Faire résonner, faire retentir, répéter; (*fig.*) célébrer. **resounding,** *n.* Retentissement, résonnement, *m.*—*a.* Retentissant, résonnant.

resource [ri'sɔ:s], *n.* Ressource, *f. Beyond resource,* sans remède; *so far as his resources permitted,* selon ses moyens; *to be at the end of one's resources,* être à fond de cale. **resourceful,** *a.* Plein de ressources, (*fam.*) débrouillard.

respect [ri'spekt], *n.* Respect, *m.*, estime, *f.*; égard (reference), *m.*; (*pl.*) respects, hommages, devoirs, *m.pl. In every respect,* sous tous les rapports, à tous égards; *in respect to,* à l'égard de; *in some respect,* en quelque sorte; *out of respect to,* par égard pour, par respect pour; *to have respect of persons,* faire acception de personnes; *to pay one's respects to,* présenter ses respects à; *to pay respect to,* avoir des égards pour; *with respect to,* quant à, à l'égard de.—*v.t.* Respecter, considérer, avoir égard à; se rapporter à, regarder (of things).

respectability [rispektə'biliti], *n.* Honorabilité, *f.*, caractère honorable; crédit, *m.*, considération; bonne situation (financière), aisance, *f.*; correction, *f.* (dans la tenue, les vêtements); convenances, *f.pl.*; bienséance, *f.*

respectable [ri'spektəbl], *a.* Respectable, honorable, honnête, dans une position honorable, comme il faut, convenable; (*fig.*) passable, pas mal. **respectably,** *adv.* Comme il faut, très bien, convenablement; (*fig.*) passablement, pas mal. **respecter,** *n.* Personne qui respecte, *f.* *To be no respecter of persons,* ne pas faire acception de personnes. **respectful,** *a.* Respectueux. **respectfully,** *adv.* Respectueusement, avec respect. *Yours respectfully* (to one's superiors), veuillez agréer, M., l'assurance de mes sentiments respectueux. **respectfulness,** *n.* Caractère respectueux, *m.* **respecting,** *prep.* À l'égard de, quant à, touchant. **respective,** *a.* Respectif, relatif. *They were conveyed to their respective homes,* on les transporta chacun à son domicile. **respectively,** *adv.* Respectivement, relativement.
respirable ['respirəbl], *a.* Respirable. **respiration** [-'reiʃən], *n.* Respiration, *f.*
respirator ['respireitə], *n.* Respirateur, *m.*
respiratory [ris'paiərətri or 'respireitəri], *a.* Respiratoire.
respire [ri'spaiə], *v.t.* Respirer, exhaler.—*v.i.* Respirer.
respite ['respait], *v.t.* Donner du répit à, suspendre; (*Law*) accorder un sursis à.—*n.* Répit, relâche; (*Law*) sursis, *m.*
resplendence [ri'splendəns] or **resplendency,** *n.* Éclat, *m.*, splendeur, *f.* **resplendent,** *a.* Resplendissant (de). **resplendently,** *adv.* Avec éclat, avec splendeur.
respond [ri'spɔnd], *v.i.* Répondre (à); obéir (à), réagir (à). **respondent,** *n.* Répondant; (*Law*) défendeur, *m.*, défenderesse, *f.*—*a.* Qui répond, correspondant (à). **respondentia** [respɔn'denʃiə], *n.pl.* (*Comm.*) Prêt sur la cargaison, *m.*
response [ri'spɔns], *n.* Réponse, *f.*; (*fig.*) écho, *m.*; (*Eccles.*) répons, *m.* *The news met with a good response,* la nouvelle fut bien accueillie.
responsibility [rispɔnsi'biliti] or **responsibleness,** *n.* Responsabilité, *f.* *On my own responsibility,* de mon chef, sous ma propre responsabilité; *to accept responsibility for,* prendre la responsabilité de. **responsible** [-'spɔnsibl], *a.* Chargé (de), responsable (de); compétent; sérieux, digne de confiance. **responsions,** *n.pl.* Examen préliminaire (à l'Université d'Oxford), *m.*
responsive [ri'spɔnsiv], *a.* Sensible, facile à émouvoir; (*Motor.*) souple, nerveux. **responsively,** *adv.* Avec sympathie. **responsory,** *n.* (*Eccles.*) Répons, *m.*
rest [rest], *n.* Repos, *m.*; (*Mus.*) pause, *f.*, appui (support); arrêt (for a lance); support (of a lathe etc.); reste, restant (remainder), *m.*; les autres (the others), *m.pl.* *A good night's rest,* une bonne nuit; *among the rest,* entre autres; *at rest,* en repos (in rest), en arrêt (of a lance); *crotchet-rest,* soupir, *m.*; *minim-rest,* demi-pause, *f.*; *quaver-rest,* demi-soupir, *m.*; *semiquaver-rest,* quart de soupir, *m.*; *to go to rest,* aller se reposer *or* se coucher; *to set at rest,* mettre en repos, décider, régler; *en finir avec; to set one's mind at rest,* disposer ses inquiétudes.—*v.i.* Se reposer; dormir; s'appuyer, se reposer (to lean); demeurer, rester (to remain). *It rests entirely with you,* la chose dépend entièrement de vous; *it rests*

with me to . . ., c'est à moi de . . .; *to rest assured,* être assuré.—*v.t.* Reposer; faire reposer; (*fig.*) appuyer, poser, baser, fonder. (*spt.*) *To rest a player,* reposer un équipier. **rest-cure,** *n.* Cure de repos, *f.* **rest-house,** *n.* Auberge, hôtellerie, *f.*; maison de repos, *f.* (for workers). **rest-room,** *n.* Toilette, *f.*
restart [ri:'stɑ:t], *v.t.* Recommencer, reprendre; remettre en marche.—*v.i.* Recommencer, reprendre.
restate [-'steit], *v.t.* Répéter, exposer de nouveau.
restaurant ['restərɑ̃:], *n.* Restaurant, *m.*
restful ['restful], *a.* Qui donne du repos, paisible. **restfully,** *adv.* Paisiblement. **restfulness,** *n.* Tranquillité, *f.*
rest-harrow ['rest'hærou], *n.* (*Bot.*) Arrête-bœuf, *m.*
resting ['restiŋ], *a.* Se reposant; s'appuyant, appuyé (leaning); (*colloq. Theat.*) qui fait relâche. *Resting on,* se couchant sur, couché sur.—*n.* Repos. **resting-place,** *n.* Lieu de repos, gîte, *m.* *Last resting-place,* dernière demeure, *f.*
restitution [resti'tju:ʃən], *n.* Restitution, *f.*
restive ['restiv], *a.* Rétif; inquiet. **restiveness,** *n.* Naturel rétif, *m.*; nervosité, *f.*
restless ['restlis], *a.* Sans repos; inquiet; agité; turbulent, remuant. *I have had a restless night,* j'ai passé une nuit blanche. **restlessly,** *adv.* Sans repos; avec agitation. **restlessness,** *n.* Inquiétude; agitation; turbulence; insomnie (sleeplessness), *f.*
restock [ri:'stɔk], *v.t.* Repeupler (a preserve); regarnir (a shop), réassortir.
restorable [ri'stɔ:rəbl], *a.* Qui peut être restitué.
restoration [restə'reiʃən], *n.* Restauration, *f.*; rétablissement, *m.*; restitution (giving back), *f.*
restorative [ri'stɔ:rətiv], *a. and n.* Fortifiant, *m.*
restore [ri'stɔ:], *v.t.* Restituer, rendre (to return); ramener (to bring back); restaurer (buildings etc.); remettre (to replace); rétablir. *Restored to health,* guéri, revenu à la santé. **restorer,** *n.* Restaurateur, *m.*, restauratrice, *f.*
restrain [ri'strein], *v.t.* Retenir, contenir; restreindre, réprimer; empêcher (to prevent). *To restrain from,* empêcher de; *to restrain oneself,* se contraindre, se contenir. **restrainable,** *a.* Qu'on peut retenir etc. **restraining,** *a.* Qui restreint, restrictif. **restraint,** *n.* Contrainte; restriction; gêne; entrave, *f.*; frein, *m.* *To keep under restraint,* contenir, tenir emprisonné; *to put restraint upon,* gêner; *to throw off all restraint,* se donner libre cours, s'émanciper; *without restraint,* sans contrainte.
restrict [ri'strikt], *v.t.* Restreindre, limiter (à). **restriction** [-'strikʃən], *n.* Restriction, *f.* **restrictive,** *a.* Restrictif. **restrictively,** *adv.* Avec restriction.
re-string [ri:'striŋ], *v.t.* (*past* and *p.p.* **restrung**) Recorder.
result [ri'zʌlt], *n.* Résultat, *m.* *As a result of,* par suite de; *in the result,* finalement; *the result was that,* il en résulta que.—*v.i.* Résulter, avoir pour résultat. *To result in,* aboutir à; *to result in nothing,* n'aboutir à rien. **resultant,** *n.* Résultante, *f.*—*a.* Résultant.

resumable [ri'zju:məbl], *a.* Qu'on peut reprendre. **resume,** *v.t.* Reprendre, renouer, continuer (acquaintance etc.).

résumé ['rezjumei], *n.* Résumé, *m.*

resumption [ri'zʌmpʃən], *n.* Reprise, continuation, *f.*

resurface [ri:'sə:fis], *v.t.* Remettre en état (a road).—*v.i.* Remonter à la surface.

resurgence [ri:'sə:dʒəns], *n.* Résurrection, *f.* **resurgent,** *a.* Ranimé.

resurrect [rezə'rekt], *v.t.* Ranimer, ressusciter.

resurrection [rezə'rekʃən], *n.* Résurrection, *f. Resurrection pie,* pâté de restes de viande, *m.* **resurrectionist** or **resurrection-man,** *n.* Déterreur de cadavres, *m.*

resurvey (1) [ri:sə'vei], *v.t.* Examiner de nouveau; arpenter de nouveau.

resurvey (2) [ri:'sə:vei], *n.* Révision, *f.*, nouvel examen; nouvel arpentage, *m.*

resuscitate [ri'sʌsiteit], *v.t.* Ressusciter, faire revivre.—*v.i.* Revivre, ressusciter. **resuscitation** [-'teiʃən], *n.* Résurrection, *f.*, retour à la vie, *m.*; renaissance (of the arts etc.), *f.*; (*Med.*) ressuscitation, *f.*

ret [ret], *v.t.* Rouir.

retail (1) ['ri:teil], *n.* Détail, *m.*, vente au détail, *f.*—*a.* En détail. *Retail dealer,* marchand *en* or au détail, détaillant, *m.*; *retail price,* prix de détail, *m.*; *retail trade,* commerce de détail, *m.*

retail (2) [ri'teil], *v.t.* Vendre en détail, détailer; (*fig.*) débiter; colporter (news). **retailer,** *n.* Détaillant, *m.*, détaillante, *f.*; colporteur, *m.*, colporteuse (of news), *f.*

retain [ri'tein], *v.t.* Retenir, garder, conserver; engager, prendre à son service (by a fee). **retainer,** *n.* Personne qui retient etc.; personne de la suite de, *f.*, serviteur, dépendant, *m.*; honoraires donnés d'avance (fee), *m.pl.*; provision, *f.*; (*pl.*) suite, *f.*, gens, vassaux, *m.pl.* **retaining,** *a.* Qui retient. **retaining-fee,** *n.* Honoraires donnés d'avance, *m.pl.* **retaining-wall,** *n.* Mur de soutènement, *m.*

retake [ri:'teik], *v.t.* (*past* **retook** [-'tuk], *p.p.* **retaken**) Reprendre; (*Cine.*) retourner (a shot).

retaking, *n.* Reprise, *f.*

retaliate [ri'tælieit], *v.i. To retaliate on,* user de représailles envers, rendre la pareille à. **retaliation** [-'eiʃən], *n.* Représailles, *f.pl.*, revanche, *f.*, talion, *m. By way of retaliation,* en revanche, par représailles. **retaliatory,** *a.* De représailles.

retard [ri'ta:d], *v.t.* Retarder. *To retard negotiations,* faire traîner les négociations. **retardation** [ri:ta:deiʃən], *n.* Retardement *m.*; (*Phys.*) retardation, *f.*

retch [ri:tʃ], *v.i.* Avoir des haut-le-cœur. **retching,** *n.* Haut-le-cœur, *m.*

retell [ri:'tel], *v.t.* (*past* and *p.p.* **retold**) Redire, répéter.

retention [ri'tenʃən], *n.* Conservation; (*Med.*) rétention, *f.* **retentive,** *a.* Qui retient; (*Med.*) rétentif; tenace, fidèle (of the memory). **retentiveness,** *n.* Pouvoir de retenir, *m.*; fidélité, ténacité, sûreté (of the memory), *f.* **retentivity,** *n.* (*Phys.*) Rémanence, *f.*

reticence ['retisəns], *n.* Réticence, *f.* **reticent,** *a.* Réservé, taciturne.

reticular [re'tikjulə], *a.* Réticulaire. **reticulate** or **reticulated,** *a.* Réticulé. **reticulation** [-'leiʃən], *n.* Disposition en forme de réseau, *f.*

*reticule ['retikju:l], *n.* Sac à main, réticule, *m.*

retiform ['ri:tifɔ:m], *a.* En forme de réseau.

retina ['retinə], *n.* Rétine, *f.*

retinue ['retinju:], *n.* Suite, *f.*; cortège, *m.*

retire [ri'taiə], *v.i.* Se retirer, prendre sa retraite. *To retire into oneself,* se replier sur soi-même.—*v.t.* Retirer. **retired,** *a.* Retiré, caché, écarté, retraité (superannuated); ancien (former). *On the retired list,* en retraite, retraité; *retired officer,* officier en retraite, *m.*; *to put on the retired list,* mettre à la retraite. **retirement,** *n.* Retraite, (*fig.*) solitude, *f.*, isolement, *m.* **retiring,** *a.* Réservé, timide, modeste; qui se retire, sortant (leaving office). **retiring-fund,** *n.* Caisse des retraites, *f.* **retiring-pension** or **retirement pension,** *n.* Pension de retraite, *f.* **retiring-room,** *n.* Lavabo, *m.*

retold [RETELL].

retort [ri'tɔ:t], *n.* Réplique, riposte; (*Chem.*) cornue, *f.*; (*Ind.*) vase clos, *m. To give the retort courteous,* riposter poliment.—*v.t.* Renvoyer, rétorquer (an argument); (*Ind.*) distiller en vase clos.—*v.i.* Riposter, répliquer. **retorted,** *a.* Recourbé. **retortion,** *n.* (*Law*) Rétorsion, *f.*

retoss [ri:'tɔs], *v.t.* Relancer.

retouch [ri:'tʌtʃ], *v.t.* Retoucher. **retouching,** *n.* Retouche, *f.*

retrace [ri'treis], *v.t.* Remonter à; revenir sur, retourner sur (one's steps); (*Paint.*) retracer. *To retrace one's steps,* revenir sur ses pas, rebrousser chemin.

retract [ri'trækt], *v.t.* Tirer en arrière; rétracter.—*v.i.* Se rétracter, se dédire. **retractable,** *a.* Qui peut se retirer; (*Av.*) escamotable. **retractation** [ri:træk'teiʃən], *n.* Rétractation, *f.* **retractile,** *a.* Rétractile. **retractility** [-'tiliti], *n.* Rétractilité, *f.* **retraction,** *n.* Rétractation; (*Med., Zool.,* etc.) rétraction, *f.* **retractor,** *n.* (*Surg.*) Rétracteur, *m.*

retransmission [ri:tra:ns'miʃn], *n.* (*Rad.*) Retransmission, *f.*; réexpédition, *f.* (telegram). **retransmit,** *v.t.* Retransmettre; réexpédier.

retraxit [ri:'træksit], *n.* (*Law*) Désistement, *m.*

retread (1) [ri:'tred], *v.t.* (*past* **retrod,** *p.p.* **retrodden**) Fouler de nouveau; suivre de nouveau.

retread (2), *v.t.* (*past* and *p.p.* **retreaded**) (*Motor.*) Rechaper (a tyre).—*n.* Pneu rechapé, *m.*

retreat [ri'tri:t], *n.* Retraite, *f. To beat the retreat,* battre la retraite.—*v.i.* Se retirer (à or dans); (*Mil.*) battre en retraite, se replier. **retreating,** *a.* Qui bat en retraite; fuyant (of the forehead).

retrench [ri'trentʃ], *v.t.* Retrancher; retrancher de (things).—*v.i.* Se retrancher. **retrenchment,** *n.* Retranchement, *m.*

retribution [retri'bju:ʃən], *n.* Récompense, rétribution, *f.*; (*fig.*) châtiment, *m.*, vengeance, *f.* **retributive** [ri'tribjutiv] or **retributory,** *a.* Qui récompense; qui châtie; vengeur.

retrievable [ri′tri:vəbl], *a.* Recouvrable (money); réparable (loss). **retrieval**, *n.* Recouvrement, *m.*; rétablissement, *m.*; réparation, *f.*

retrieve [ri′tri:v], *v.t.* Rétablir; réparer (to repair); recouvrer (to regain); rapporter (of dogs). **retriever**, *n.* Chien rapporteur, *m.*

retroaction [ri:trou′ækʃn], *n.* Rétroaction, *f.* **retroactive**, *a.* Rétroactif. **retroactively**, *adv.* Rétroactivement. **retroactivity** [-′tiviti], *n.* Rétroactivité, *f.*

retrocede [ri:trou′si:d], *v.t.* Rétrocéder.—*v.i.* Reculer, rétrograder. **retrocession** [-′seʃən], *n.* (*Med.*) Rétrocession, *f.*; recul, *m.*

retrogradation [retrougrə′deiʃən], *n.* Rétrogradation, *f.*

retrograde [′retrougreid], *v.i.* Rétrograder.— *a.* Rétrograde.

retrogression [retrou′greʃən], *n.* Rétrogression, rétrogradation, *f.* **retrogressive** [-′gresiv], *a.* Rétrogressif.

retrospect [′retrouspekt], *n.* Regard jeté en arrière, *m.*; revue, *f.* *In retrospect*, d'un coup d'œil rétrospectif, en rétrospective. **retrospection** [-′spekʃən], *n.* Faculté de regarder en arrière, *f.*, rétrospection, *f.* **retrospective**, *a.* Rétrospectif; (*Law*) rétroactif. **retrospectively**, *adv.* Rétrospectivement; (*Law*) rétroactivement.

retroussé [ri′trousei], *a.* Retroussé.

retroversion [ri:trou′və:ʃən], *n.* Renversement, *m.*, rétroversion, *f.* **retrovert** [-′və:t], *v.t.* Renverser.

retting [′retiŋ], *n.* Rouissage (of flax, hemp, etc.), *m.* **retting-pit**, *n.* Routoir, *m.*

return (1) [ri′tə:n], *v.i.* Revenir (to come back); retourner (to go back); rentrer (to come in again); répondre, répliquer (to answer). *To return to the subject*, revenir au sujet, (*fam.*) revenir à ses moutons.—*v.t.* Rendre (to give back); renvoyer (to send back); rembourser (to repay); rapporter (interest); répondre à; rendre compte (to render an account of); élire (candidates). *He was returned*, il fut élu; *the money returns interest*, l'argent rapporte intérêt; *to return good for evil*, rendre le bien pour le mal.—*n.* Retour (coming back, going back), *m.*; rentrée (coming back in), *f.*; renvoi (sending back), *m.*; remise en place (putting back), *f.*; profit, gain (profit), *m.*; restitution (restitution), *f.*; remboursement (reimbursement), *m.*; élection (election), *f.*; rapport, compte rendu, relevé, état (report), *m.*; (*Comm.*) montant des opérations, montant des remises, bilan (of a bank), *m.*; (*pl.*) produit, *m.* *By return of post*, par retour du courrier; *in return for*, en retour de; *nil return*, état néant, *m.*; *on my return*, au retour, comme je revenais chez moi; *on sale or return*, en dépôt, en commission; *return address*, adresse de l'expéditeur, *f.*; *return home*, retour au foyer, *m.*; *return journey*, retour, *m.*; *return match*, revanche, *f.*; *return of casualties*, état des pertes, *m.*; *small profits (and) quick returns*, petits profits, vente rapide; *the official returns*, les relevés officiels, *m.pl.*; *to make some return for*, payer de retour.

returnable, *a.* Restituable; qu'on peut rendre; qu'on doit renvoyer; qu'on peut élire; (*Law*) de renvoi.

returning-officer, *n.* Fonctionnaire chargé de rendre compte d'une élection, *m.*

return-ticket, (*colloq.*) **return** (2), *n.* Billet d'aller et retour, *m.* *First-class return to B.*, une première aller et retour pour B.

Reunion [ri:′ju:niən]. La Réunion, *f.*

reunion [ri:′ju:niən], *n.* Réunion, *f.* **reunite** [-ju′nait], *v.t.* Réunir.—*v.i.* Se réunir.

rev [rev], *n.* (*colloq., Motor.*) Tour, *m.*—*v.t. To rev the engine*, faire s'emballer le moteur.— *v.i.* S'emballer.

revaluation, *n.* Réévaluation, *f.*

revalue [ri:′vælju:], *v.t.* Réévaluer.

revarnish [ri:′vɑ:niʃ], *v.t.* Revernir.

reveal [ri′vi:l], *v.t.* Révéler.—*n.* (*Arch.*) Jouée, *f.* **revealer**, *n.* Révélateur, *m.*, révélatrice, *f.*

reveille [ri′væli], *n.* Réveil, *m.*; *diane, *f.*

revel [revl], *n.* Divertissements, *m.pl.*, réjouissances, *f.pl.*, ébats, *m.pl.*, orgie, bombance, *f.*—*v.i.* Se réjouir, se divertir, faire bombance. *To revel in*, se délecter à.

revelation [revə′leiʃən], *n.* Révélation; Apocalypse (Book of Revelation), *f.*

reveller [′revələ], *n.* Joyeux convive, viveur, noceur, *m.* **revelling** or **revelry**, *n.* Réjouissances, orgies, *f.pl.*, joyeux ébats, *m.pl.*

revendicate [ri′vendikeit], *v.t.* Revendiquer. **revendication** [-′keiʃən], *n.* Revendication, *f.*

revenge [ri′vendʒ], *n.* Vengeance; revanche (at play), *f.* *To take revenge on someone for something*, se venger de quelque chose sur quelqu'un.—*v.t.* Venger; se venger de. *To be revenged*, se venger; *to be revenged on* or *to revenge oneself on*, se venger de. **revengeful**, *a.* Vindicatif. **revengefully**, *adv.* Par vengeance. **revengefulness**, *n.* Esprit de vengeance, *m.* **revenger**, *n.* Vengeur, *m.*, vengeresse, *f.*

revenue [′revənju:], *n.* Revenu; (*State*) fisc, trésor, *m.* *Public revenue*, revenus publics, revenus de l'État, *m.pl.* **revenue-cutter**, *n.* Patache (de la douane), *f.* **revenue-officer**, *n.* Officier de la douane, *m.*

reverberate [ri′və:bəreit], *v.t.* Réverbérer; renvoyer (sound, heat, etc.).—*v.i.* Se répercuter; retentir (de). **reverberation** [-′reiʃən], *n.* Réverbération (of heat); réflexion (of light); répercussion, *f.* **reverberatory**, *a.* À réverbère.—*n. Reverberatory* (*furnace*), four à réverbère, *m.*

revere [ri′viə], *v.t.* Révérer, vénérer.

reverence [′revərəns], *n.* Révérence, *f.* *Your (or his) reverence*, Monsieur le curé, Monsieur l'abbé. **reverend**, *a.* Vénérable, respectable; révérend (of the clergy). *Most reverend*, révérendissime; *reverend sir*, monsieur l'abbé, *m.*; *right reverend*, très révérend; *the reverend gentleman*, le révérend père (or pasteur). **reverent** or **reverential** [-′renʃəl], *a.* Révérencieux; respectueux; révérenciel. **reverently** or **reverentially**, *adv.* Avec révérence; révérencieusement.

reverer [ri′viərə], *n.* Vénérateur, *m.*

reverie [′revəri], *n.* Rêverie, *f.*

revers [ri′viəz], *n.* Revers, *m.pl.* (of clothes).

reversal [ri′və:sl], *n.* Annulation; cassation, *f.*, revirement, *m.* (of opinion); (*Cine.*) procédé négatif-positif, *m.*

reverse [ri′və:s], *a.* Inverse, renversé; contraire, opposé.—*n.* Revers, *m.*; défaite, *f.* inverse; verso (of a page), *m.* *Quite the reverse*, tout l'opposé, tout le contraire (de); (*Cine.*) *reverse angle*, contre-champ, *m.*; *the* *reverse way*, en sens inverse.—*v.t.* Renverser; appliquer en sens inverse; (*Law*) infirmer; casser. *To reverse the engine*, (*colloq.*) to *put her into reverse*, faire machine arrière, faire marche arrière. **reversed**, *a.* Renversé; inverse, contraire. **reverseless**, *a.* Qu'on ne peut renverser. **reversely**, *adv.* En sens inverse. **reversible**, *a.* Révocable, réversible, à double face (of textiles); (*Cine.*) inversible (of film). **reversing**, *a.* Qui renverse. **reversing-gear**, *n.* Mécanisme de renversement, *m.*

reversion [ri'və:ʃən], *n.* Réversion, *f.*, retour, *m.*; survivance (of offices etc.); succession (succession), *f.* **reversionary**, *a.* Réversible.

revert [ri'və:t], *v.i.* Revenir (sur); (*Law*) retourner (à). **revertibility**, *n.* (*Law*) Réversibilité, *f.* **revertible**, *a.* Réversible.

revetment [ri'vetmənt], *n.* Revêtement, *m.*

revictual [ri:'vitl], *v.t.* Ravitailler. **revictualling**, *n.* Ravitaillement, *m.*

review [ri'vju:], *n.* Revue, revision; critique, *f.*, compte rendu, examen critique (criticism), *m.*; revue, *f.*, périodique, *m. The period under our review*, la période que nous passons en revue.—*v.t.* Revoir, reviser; passer en revue; analyser, critiquer, faire le compte rendu de (a book etc.). **reviewer**, *n.* Critique, rédacteur d'une revue, *m.*

revile [ri'vail], *v.t.* Injurier, insulter, outrager. **revilement**, *n.* Injure, insulte, *f.* **reviler**, *n.* Insulteur, *m.* **reviling**, *n.* Insultes, injures, *f.pl.*—*a.* Diffamatoire, outrageant. **revilingly**, *adv.* Injurieusement, outrageusement.

revisal [ri'vaizl], *n.* Revision, *f.* **revise** [ri'vaiz], *v.t.* Revoir, reviser, réviser.—*n.* (*Print.*) Seconde, *f. Second revise*, troisième épreuve d'auteur, *f.* **reviser**, *n.* Personne qui revoit, *f.*, reviseur, *m.*

revision [ri'viʒən], *n.* Revision, révision, *f.* **revisional, revisionary**, or **revisory** [-'vai-zəri], *a.* De revision.

revisit [ri:'vizit], *v.t.* Revisiter, revoir, retourner voir.

revitalize [-'vaitəlaiz], *v.t.* Revivifier.

revival [ri'vaivl], *n.* Renouvellement, rétablissement, *m.*; renaissance (of arts and letters); remise en vigueur; reprise (of a play), *f.*; réveil (of religion), *m.* **revivalism**, *n.* Réveil, *m.* **revivalist**, *n.* Évangéliste dévoué au réveil de la foi, *m.*

revive, *v.t.* Faire revivre, rappeler à la vie; ressusciter; renouveler, ranimer, raviver, remettre (a law etc.) en vigueur; (*Chem.*) revivifier.—*v.i.* Revivre, ressusciter; se ranimer, se raviver; renaître (of arts etc.). **reviver**, *n.* Personne *or* chose qui fait revivre, qui ranime, *f.*

revivification [rivivifi'keiʃən], *n.* Revivification, *f.* **revivify** [-'vivifai], *v.t.* Revivifier. **reviviscence**, *n.* Retour à la vie, *m.*; renaissance, *f.*

revocable ['revəkəbl], *a.* Révocable. **revocableness** or **revocability** [-'biliti], *n.* Révocabilité, *f.* **revocation** [-'keiʃən], *n.* Révocation; abrogation, *f.*

revoke [ri'vouk], *v.t.* Révoquer.—*v.i.* (*Cards*) Renoncer.—*n.* (*Cards*) Renonce, *f.*

revolt [ri'voult], *n.* Révolte, *f. To rise in revolt*, se soulever.—*v.i.* Se révolter, se soulever. *To revolt at*, se révolter contre.—*v.t.* Révolter,

soulever. **revolted**, *a.* Révolté, en révolte, soulevé. **revolter**, *n.* Révolté, rebelle, *m.* **revolting**, *a.* Révoltant.

revolute ['revəlju:t], *a.* (*Bot.*) Révolutif.

revolution [revə'lju:ʃən], *n.* Révolution, *f.*; tour (of a wheel), *m.* **revolutionary**, *a.* and *n.* Révolutionnaire. *Revolutionary calendar*, calendrier républicain, *m.* **revolutionist**, *n.* Révolutionnaire, *m.* **revolutionize**, *v.t.* Révolutionner.

revolve [ri'volv], *v.i.* Tourner; (*fig.*) retourner, revenir; (*Astron.*) faire sa révolution.—*v.t.* Tourner; retourner, repasser, rouler (in the mind). **revolved**, *a.* Révolu. **revolver**, *n.* Revolver, *m. Six-chambered revolver*, revolver à six coups, *m.* **revolving**, *a.* Tournant; (*Astron.*) qui fait sa révolution. *Revolving bookcase*, bibliothèque tournante, *f.*; *revolving light*, feu tournant, *m.*

revue [ri'vju:], *n.* (*Theat.*) Revue, *f.*

revulsion [ri'vʌlʃən], *n.* Révulsion, *f.*, brusque revirement; écœurement, *m.* **revulsive** [-'vʌlsiv], *a.* (*Med.*) Révulsif.

reward [ri'wɔ:d], *n.* Récompense, *f.*; prix, *m. As a reward for*, en récompense de.—*v.t.* Récompenser (de). **rewardable**, *a.* Digne de récompense. **rewarder**, *n.* Rémunérateur, *m.* **rewarding**, *a.* Rémunérateur; qui en vaut la peine.

rewind [ri:'waind], *v.t.* (*past* and *p.p.* **rewound**) Rebobiner (silk etc.); remonter (watch, clock); (*Cine.*) rembobiner, enrouler. **rewinder**, *n.* (*Cine.*) Enrouleuse, *f.* **rewinding**, *n.* Rebobinage; remontage; rembobinage, *m.*

reword [ri:'wə:d], *v.t.* Recomposer, rédiger de nouveau.

rewrite [ri:'rait], *v.t.* (*past* **rewrote**, *p.p.* **rewritten**) Récrire, remanier.

reynard ['rena:d *or* reina:d], *n.* Renard, maître renard, *m.*

rhabdical [ræb'dɔlədʒi], *n.* Rabdologie, *f.*

rhabdomancy ['ræbdəmænsi], *n.* Rabdomancie, *f.*

rhapsodical [ræp'sɔdikl], *a.* De rapsodie.

rhapsodist ['ræpsədist], *n.* Rapsodiste, *n.* (*Ant.*) rapsode, *m.* **rhapsodize**, *v.t.* Louanger.

rhapsody ['ræpsədi], *n.* Rapsodie, *f.*; éloge, *m.*; (*fam.*) dithyrambe, *m.*

Rheims [ri:mz]. Reims, *m.*

Rhenish ['reniʃ], *a.* Du Rhin; (*Geog.*) rhénan. —*n.* Vin du Rhin, *m.*

rheocord ['ri:okɔ:d], *n.* Rhéocorde, *m.*

rheometer [ri:'ɔmitə], *n.* Rhéomètre, *m.*

rheoscopic [-'skɔpik], *a.* Rhéoscopique.

rheostat ['ri:ostæt], *n.* Rhéostat, *m.*

rhesus ['ri:səs], *a.* (*Med.*) Rhésus. *Rhesus factor*, facteur rhésus, *m.*

rhetor ['ri:tə], *n.* Rhéteur, *f.*

rhetoric ['retərik], *n.* Rhétorique; (*fig.*) éloquence, *f.*

rhetorical [ri'tɔrikl], *a.* De rhétorique; (*pej.*) de rhéteur. *Rhetorical question*, question de pure forme, *f.* **rhetorically**, *adv.* Suivant les règles de la rhétorique; en rhétoricien.

rhetorician [retə'riʃən], *n.* Rhétoricien rhéteur, *n.*

rheum [ru:m], *n.* Rhume, catarrhe, *m.*; salive; pituite, *f.*

rheumatic [ru:'mætik], *a.* Rhumatismal. *Rheumatic fever*, rhumatisme articulaire, *m.*;

rheumatic *gout*, rhumatisme goutteux, *m*. **rheumaticky**, *a*. (*fam*.) Rhumatisé. **rheumatism** ['ru:mətizm], *n*. Rhumatisme, *m*. **rheumatoid** ['ru:mətɔid], *a*. Rhumatoïde. *Rheumatoid arthritis*, rhumatisme articulaire, *m*.

rhinanthus [rai'nænθəs], *n*. (*Bot*.) Rhinanthe, *m*.

Rhine [rain], *f*. Le Rhin, *m*. **Rhineland**. La Rhénanie, *f*. **Rhinelander**, *n*. Rhénan, *m*., -ane, *f*.

rhino ['rainou], *n. pop. abbr*. [RHINOCEROS].

rhinoceros [rai'nɔsərəs], *n*. (*pl*. **rhinoceroses**) Rhinocéros, *m*.

rhinolith ['rainoliθ], *n*. Rhinolithe, *f*.

rhinology [-'nɔlədʒi], *n*. Rhinologie, *f*.

rhinoplasty [-'nɔplæsti], *n*. Rhinoplastie, *f*.

rhinoscopy [-'nɔskəpi], *n*. Rhinoscopie, *f*.

rhizome ['raizoum], *n*. (*Bot*.) Rhizome, *m*.

Rhodesia [rou'di:ziə]. La Rhodésie, *f*.

rhodium ['roudiəm], *n*. (*Chem*.) Rhodium, *m*.; (*Bot*.) bois de rose, *m*.

rhododendron [roudə'dendrən], *n*. (*Bot*.) Rhododendron, *m*.

rhomb [rɔm] or **rhombus** ['rɔmbəs], *n*. Losange, rhombe, *m*. **rhomboid**, *n*. Rhomboïde, *m*. **rhomboidal** [-'bɔidl], *a*. Rhomboïdal.

Rhone [roun]. Le Rhône, *m*.

rhubarb ['ru:ba:b], *n*. Rhubarbe, *f*.

rhumb [rʌm], *n*. Rumb, *m*. **rhumb-line**, *n*. Loxodromie, ligne de rumb, *f*.

rhyme [raim], *n*. Rime, *f*.; (*pl*.) vers, *m.pl*. *In rhyme*, rimé; *neither rhyme nor reason*, ni rime ni raison; *to put into rhyme*, mettre en rimes, rimer.—*v.t*., *v.i*. Rimer; rimailler. **rhymeless**, *a*. Sans rime. **rhymer**, *n*. Rimeur, *m*. **rhymester**, *n*. Rimailleur, *m*.

rhythm [riðm], *n*. Rythme, *m*.; cadence, *f*. **rhythmical** ['riðmikl], *a*. Rythmique, cadencé. **rhythmically**, *adv*. Avec rythme.

rib [rib], *n*. Côte; baleine (of an umbrella); (*Arch*.) nervure, ogive; (*Shipbuilding*) membrure, *f*. (*Arch*.) *Intersecting ribs*, croisée d'ogives, *f*.—*v.t*. Garnir de côtes; faire des côtes à (cloth etc.); (*pop*.) taquiner. **rib-grass** or **rib-wort**, *n*. (*Bot*.) Plantain lancéolé, *m*.

ribald ['ribəld], *a*. Licencieux, obscène.—*n*. Débauché, libertin, ribaud, *m*., ribaude, *f*. **ribaldry**, *n*. Langage licencieux, *m*., obscénités, *f.pl*.

riband ['ribənd] [RIBBON].

ribband ['ribənd], *n*. (*Naut*.) Lisse, *f*., liteau, *m*.

ribbed [ribd], *a*. À côtes; (*fig*.) ridé; (*Bot. etc*.) à nervures; (*Arch*.) à ogives.

ribbon ['ribən], *n*. Ruban; cordon (of orders); lambeau (shred), *m*. *To ribbons*, en lambeaux.—*v.t*. Enrubaner, garnir de rubans. **ribbon-grass**, *n*. Phalaris bigarré, *m*. **ribbon-trade**, *n*. Rubanerie, *f*. **ribbon-weaver**, *n*. Rubanier, *m*.

rib-stall ['ribstɔ:l], *n*. Échelle suédoise, *f*.

rice [rais], *n*. Riz, *m*. *Ground rice*, farine de riz, *f*. **rice-paper**, *n*. Papier de riz, *m*. **rice-pudding**, *n*. Riz au lait, *m*. **rice-swamp**, *n*. Rizière, *f*.

rich [ritʃ], *a*. Riche; fertile, fécond (fertile); savoureux, succulent (succulent); de haut goût (highly seasoned); magnifique, superbe, beau (grand); voyant; (*fig*.) délicieux,

exquis, généreux (of wine). *A rich treat*, un fameux régal; *that's rich!* c'est impayable! *the rich*, les riches, *m.pl*.; *to grow rich*, s'enrichir; *to pretend to be rich*, faire le riche. **riches**, *n.pl*. Richesse, *f*. **richly**, *adv*. Richement; grandement, amplement, largement, bien; abondamment; magnifiquement; (*fam*.) joliment. **richness**, *n*. Richesse; fécondité, fertilité; nature succulente, *f*.; haut goût; goût exquis, *m*.

ricinus ['risinəs], *n*. (*Bot*.) Ricin, *m*.

rick [rik], *n*. Meule, *f*. **rick-cloth**, *n*. Bâche de meule, *f*.—*v.t*. Monter (le foin) en meulons.

rickets ['rikits], *n.pl*. Rachitis, rachitisme, *m*. *To have the rickets*, être rachitique.

rickety, *a*. (*colloq*.) Noué, rachitique; (*fig*.) branlant, disloqué, en mauvais état; boiteux (of furniture).

rickshaw ['rikʃɔ:], *n*. Pousse-pousse, *m*.

ricochet ['rikəʃei], *n*. Ricochet, *m*. **ricochet-fire**, *n*. Tir à ricochets, *m*.—*v.i*. Ricocher.

rictus ['riktəs], *n*. Rictus, *m*.

rid [rid], *v.t*. (*pres.p*. **ridding**, *past* **rid**, *p.p.* **rid** or **ridded** (1)) Délivrer, débarrasser. *To get rid of*, se débarrasser de, se défaire de, congédier; *to have got rid of*, être débarrassé de; *to rid oneself of*, se défaire de.

riddance ['ridəns], *n*. Débarras, *m*. *A good riddance!* bon débarras!

riddle [ridl], *n*. Énigme, *f*.; crible (sieve), *m*. *To speak in riddles*, parler énigmatiquement. —*v.t*. Cribler; résoudre, expliquer (to solve). *To be riddled with bullets*, être criblé de balles.

ride [raid], *v.i*. (*past* **rode**, *p.p.* **ridden** (2)) Monter (à cheval, à bicyclette, etc.), aller, venir, être ou se promener à cheval, à bicyclette, en voiture, etc.; être monté (sur); flotter, voguer, être porté (sur); être (à l'ancre); (*Print*.) chevaucher. *Riding on an ass*, monté sur un âne; *riding party*, excursion à cheval, *f*.; *to be riding*, être à cheval; *to ride at anchor*, être à l'ancre; *to ride away*, partir, s'en aller; *to ride back*, revenir, s'en retourner; *to ride off*, partir, se sauver; *to ride on*, poursuivre son chemin; *to ride on an elephant*, aller à dos d'éléphant; *to ride over*, venir à cheval, aller à cheval, parcourir, passer sur; *to ride part of the way*, faire une partie du chemin (à cheval, en voiture, etc.); *to ride up*, s'avancer, arriver, venir; *to ride well*, monter bien à cheval, être un bon cavalier; *to ride with one's back to the engine*, voyager en tournant le dos à la locomotive.

v.t.—Monter, être monté sur; mener, conduire; faire (a stated distance). *A horse good to ride and drive*, un cheval à deux fins; *the horse he was riding*, sa monture, *f*.; *to ride a race*, faire une course à cheval; *to ride the high horse*, monter sur ses grands chevaux.

n.—Promenade, course (à cheval, en voiture, à bicyclette, etc.), *f*.; trajet, parcours, *m*.; allée cavalière (track in a wood etc.), *f*. *To give a ride to someone*, faire monter quelqu'un avec soi, promener quelqu'un (en voiture); (*pop*.) *to take someone for a ride*, faire marcher quelqu'un; embarquer quelqu'un pour sa dernière promenade.

rider ['raidə], *n*. Cavalier, *m*., cavalière, *f*.; (in circus) écuyer, *m*., écuyère (professional), *f*.;

(*Horse-racing*) jockey, *m.*; cycliste, motocycliste, *m.*; annexe, *f.*, papillon, codicille (document), *m.*; (*Comm.*) allonge, *f.* **Gentleman-rider**, jockey amateur, *m.* **riderless,** *a.* Sans cavalier.

ridge [ridʒ], *n.* Sommet (top), *m.*, cime; chaîne (of mountains); arête, crête (of a mountain), *f.*; faîte (of a roof); (*Agric.*) sillon, billon, *m.*—*v.t.* Sillonner; (*Agric.*) faire des billons dans. **ridge-piece, ridge-plate,** or **ridge-pole,** *n.* Faîtage, *m.* **ridge-tile,** *n.* Faîtière, *f.*

ridger, *n.* (*Agric.*) Buttoir, *m.* **ridging,** *n.* Billonnage, buttage, *m.*

ridicule ['ridikjuːl], *n.* Ridicule, *m.*; moquerie, *f.* *To bring into ridicule*, rendre ridicule.—*v.t.* Tourner en ridicule, ridiculiser.

ridiculous [ri'dikjuləs], *a.* Ridicule. **ridiculously,** *adv.* Ridiculement. **ridiculousness,** *n.* Ridicule, *m.*

riding ['raidiŋ], *n.* Promenade à cheval, *f.*, exercice à cheval, *m.*, équitation; promenade (place), *f.*; (*Yorkshire*) arrondissement, *m.*; (*Naut.*) mouillage, *m.* *To like riding,* aimer à monter à cheval. **riding-boots,** *n.pl.* Bottes à l'écuyère, *f.pl.* **riding-habit,** *n.* Amazone, *f.* **riding-hood,** *n.* Capuchon, *m.* *Little Red Riding Hood,* le petit Chaperon rouge, *m.* **riding-light,** *n.* (*Naut.*) Feu de position, *m.* **riding-master,** *n.* Maître d'équitation, *m.* **riding-school,** *n.* École d'équitation, *f.*, manège, *m.* **riding-whip,** *n.* Cravache, *f.*

rife [raif], *a.* Abondant, répandu, général; plein (de). *To be rife,* régner (of disorder etc.), courir (of rumours).

riff-raff ['rifræf], *n.* Racaille, canaille, *f.*

rifle [raifl], *v.t.* Piller, dévaliser, vider; rayer (fire-arms).—*n.* Rayure, *f.*; fusil rayé, *m.*, carabine, *f.*; (*pl.*) Fusiliers. **rifle-gallery** or **-range,** *n.* Tir, *m.* **rifle-practice** or **-shooting,** *n.* Tir au fusil, tir à la carabine, *m.* **rifle-shot,** *n.* Coup de fusil, *m.* *Within rifle-shot,* à portée de fusil.

rifleman, *n.* Carabinier; chasseur à pied, *m.*

rifler, *n.* Pillard, *m.* **rifling,** *n.* Pillage, rayage (of guns), *m.*

rift [rift], *n.* Fente, fissure; (in cloud) éclaircie, *f.*

rig [rig], *n.* Gréement, *m.*; accoutrement (dress), *m.*; coup monté, *m.*, farce (trick), *f.* —*v.t.* Équiper, gréer; (*fig.*) accoutrer, attifer. *To rig out in,* accoutrer de; *to rig the market,* faire hausser or faire baisser les prix, tripoter; *to rig up,* fixer, installer. **rig-out,** *n.* (*fam.*) Accoutrement, *m.*; toilette, *f.*

rigadoon [rigə'duːn], *n.* *Rigodon (dance), *m.*

rigged [rigd], *a.* Gréé; voilé. **rigger,** *n.* Gréeur; gabier, *m.* **rigging,** *n.* Gréement, *m.*, manœuvres, manœuvres de gréement, *f.pl.*; tripotage, *m.* *Running rigging,* manœuvres courantes, *f.pl.*; *standing rigging,* manœuvres dormantes, *f.pl.* **rigging-loft,** *n.* Atelier de garniture, *m.*

right [rait], *a.* Droit; direct, en ligne droite; vrai, véritable; bon, propre, convenable; juste, correct; en règle; qu'il faut (that which is meant). *All right!* c'est bien! c'est parfait! *am I right for Leeds?* suis-je bien dans le train pour Leeds? *he's not quite right in the head,* il est un peu détraqué; *it will all come right,* tout s'arrangera; *on my right,* à ma droite; *on the right,* à droite, sur la droite; (*Mil.*) right

dress! à droite alignement! *right-hand man,* le bras droit; *right side* (of cloth), endroit, *m.*; *that is not the right thing,* ce n'est pas là ce qu'il faut; *that is right,* c'est bien, c'est cela; *the right hand,* la main droite; *the right man,* l'homme qu'il faut; *the right road,* la route directe, le bon chemin; *the right thing to do,* ce qu'il y a de mieux à faire; *the right train,* le bon train; *this is the right book,* voici le livre qu'il faut; *to be right,* avoir raison, être juste (of an account); *to go the right way to work,* s'y prendre bien; *to put right,* mettre en bon ordre, mettre en règle, arranger, corriger, rectifier, régler (a watch), mettre sur la voie.

adv.—Droit, tout droit; juste, justement (justly); comme il faut, bien (properly); tout, tout à fait (wholly); fort, furieusement (very); très (before titles). *Did I not say right?* n'ai-je pas dit vrai? *eyes right!* tête à droite! *it served you right,* c'est bien fait; *right away!* (*Rail.*) allez! en route! (*Am.*) tout de suite; *right-ho!* bien! *right off,* sur-le-champ; *right or wrong,* à tort ou à raison, bien ou mal; *right, sir!* ça y est, monsieur; (*Mil.*) *right turn!* à droite, droite! *to do right,* bien faire, bien agir; *to guess right,* deviner juste.

n.—Droit, *m.*, justice, raison, *f.*, intérêt; côté droit, *m.*, droite (right side), *f.* *Bill of rights,* déclaration des droits, *f.*; *by right,* de droit; *by rights,* pour bien faire, à la rigueur, en toute justice; *in one's own right,* de son propre chef; *in right of,* par le droit de, du chef de; *of right,* de droit, de plein droit; *on* or *to one's right,* à sa droite; *on* or *to the right,* à droite; *right and wrong,* le bien et le mal, le juste et l'injuste; *right of way,* droit de passage, *m.*; *sole right,* droit exclusif; *to be in the right,* avoir raison, être dans son droit; (*Polit.*) *to be on the right,* être de droite; *to be within one's right,* être dans son droit; *to have the right to,* avoir le droit de, avoir des droits à; *to know the rights of,* savoir le fin mot de; *to put* or *set to rights,* arranger, mettre en ordre.

v.t.—Faire droit à, rendre justice à (persons); dresser (the helm); redresser, corriger (things).—*v.i.* Se redresser, se relever.

right-about, *n.* Demi-tour à droite; (*fig.*) le contraire, l'opposé, *m.* *To send to the right-about,* envoyer promener. **right-angled,** *a.* À angle droit, rectangle. **right-handed,** *a.* Droitier; tournant de droite à gauche. **right-hander,** *n.* Droitier, *m.*, (*Box.*) droit, *m.* **right-minded,** *a.* À l'esprit droit, honnête. **right-mindedness,** *n.* Droiture d'esprit, *f.* **right-winger,** *n.* (*Ftb.*) Ailier droit, *m.*

righteous ['raitʃəs], *a.* Juste, droit. **righteously,** *adv.* Justement. **righteousness,** *n.* Droiture, vertu, *f.*

righter, *n.* Redresseur (of wrongs), *m.*

rightful ['raitful], *a.* Légitime, véritable. **rightfully,** *adv.* Légitimement. **rightfulness,** *n.* Légitimité, équité, *f.*

rightly ['raitli], *adv.* Bien, à juste titre; convenablement, comme il faut (properly); juste (not erroneous). **rightness,** *n.* Rectitude; droiture; justesse, *f.*

rigid ['ridʒid], *a.* Rigide, raide (stiff). **rigidity** [-'dʒiditi] or **rigidness,** *n.* Rigidité; raideur, *f.* **rigidly,** *adv.* Rigidement; avec raideur.

rigmarole ['rigmaroul], *n.* Propos incohérents, *m.pl.*, conte à dormir debout, galimatias, *m.*

rigor ['rigə], *n.* (*Path.*) Rigidité, *f. Rigor mortis*, rigidité cadavérique, *f.*

rigorous ['rigərəs], *a.* Rigoureux. **rigorously,** *adv.* Rigoureusement, avec rigueur, à la rigueur. **rigorousness,** *n.* Rigueur, *f.* **rigour,** *n.* Rigueur, sévérité, dureté, *f.*

rile [rail], *v.t.* (*colloq.*) Faire enrager, agacer.

rill [ril], *n.* Petit ruisseau, *m.*

rim [rim], *n.* Bord, rebord, *m.*; jante (of wheels), *f.—v.t.* Border. **rim-brake,** *n.* Frein sur jante, *m.*

rime (1) [raim], *n.* Givre, *m.*; gelée blanche, *f.*

rime (2) [RHYME].

rimless, *a.* Sans monture (of spectacles); sans bords (of hats). **rimmed,** *a.* À bord, bordé à cercle (de).

rimose ['raimous] or **rimous,** *a.* Crevassé.

rimy ['raimi], *a.* Givré, couvert de gelée blanche.

rind [raind], *n.* Écorce, peau, pelure; croûte (of cheese); couenne (of bacon), *f.—v.t.* Peler.

rinderpest ['rindəpest], *n.* Peste bovine, *f.*

ring (1) [riŋ], *n.* Anneau, *m.*, bague (for the finger etc.), *f.*; cercle, rond (circle); (*Naut.*) organeau, *m.*, boucle (of an anchor); arène (for fighting), *f.*; ring (for boxing), *m.*; (*fig.*) les boxeurs, *m.pl.*; groupe, *m.*, bande, clique, coterie, *f.*; (*Comm.*) syndicat, *m.*, coalition, *f. In a ring*, en rond; *split ring*, anneau brisé, *m.*; *wedding ring*, alliance, *f.*, anneau nuptial, *m.* —*v.t.* Mettre un anneau à; entourer.

ring-bolt, *n.* Anneau à fiche, *m.* **ring-case,** *n.* Baguier, *m.* **ring-craft,** *n.* Technique de la boxe, *f.* **ring-dove,** *n.* Pigeon ramier, *m.* **ring-fence,** *n.* Enclos, *m.* **ring-finger,** *n.* Annulaire, *m.* **ringleader,** *n.* Meneur, chef de bande, *m.* **ringlet,** *n.* Petit anneau, *m.*; boucle (of hair), *f.* **ring-master,** *n.* Maître de manège (circus), *m.* **ring-road,** *n.* Route de ceinture, *f.* **ring-shaped,** *a.* Annulaire. **ring-stand,** *n.* Baguier, *m.* **ringtail,** *n.* (*Naut.*) Bonnette de brigantine, *f.* **ringworm,** *n.* Herpès tonsurant, *m.*

ring (2) [riŋ], *v.i.* (*past* **rang,** *p.p.* **rung**) Sonner; résonner, retentir (de), tinter (of the ears). *To ring away,* carillonner; *to ring for the chambermaid,* sonner la femme de chambre; *to ring off,* décrocher l'appareil, couper la communication; *to ring with,* résonner de, retentir de.—*v.t.* Sonner, faire sonner. *To ring a coin,* faire sonner une pièce; *to ring down the curtain,* baisser le rideau, sonner pour la chute du rideau; *to ring in the New Year,* réveillonner; *to ring the changes upon,* (*colloq.*) chanter sur tous les tons, ressasser; *to ring someone up,* téléphoner à quelqu'un.—*n.* Son, bruit, tintement, retentissement (sound), coup de sonnette (on a bell), *m.*; sonnerie (chime), *f. Give a ring,* sonnez; *there's a ring at the door,* on sonne; (*fam.*) *to give someone a ring,* donner un coup de téléphone *or* passer un coup de fil à quelqu'un; *to hear a ring,* entendre sonner.

ringer, *n.* Sonneur, *m.* **ringing,** *n.* Action de sonner, *f.*; son (of bells), *m.*; sonnerie, *f.*, tintement, retentissement, *m. Ringing in the ears,* tintement d'oreilles, *m.*

rink [riŋk], *n.* Patinoire, *f.* (ice-rink); skating, *m.* (for roller-skates).

rinse [rins], *v.t.* Rincer. **rinser,** *n.* Rinceur, *m.*, -euse, *f.* **rinsing,** *n.* Rinçage, rincement, *m.*; rinçure (slops), *f.*

riot ['raiət], *n.* Émeute, *f.*; vacarme, tumulte (uproar), *m.*; (*fig.*) festins, *m.pl.*, orgies, *f.pl.*, dissipation, *f. To run riot,* se déchaîner, ne plus connaître de frein; *to run riot with fancy and imagination,* se laisser aller à tous les écarts de l'imagination; *Riot Act,* loi contre les attroupements, *f.*; *riot squad,* équipe de Police Secours, *f.*; *to read the Riot Act,* faire les trois sommations.—*v.i.* Faire une émeute; faire du vacarme, faire du tumulte; se réjouir, se divertir; faire des excès.

rioter, *n.* Émeutier; tapageur, *m.* **riotous,** *a.* Séditieux, tumultueux; déréglé, dissipé, débauché (luxurious). **riotously,** *adv.* Tumultueusement, séditieusement; avec excès. **riotousness,** *n.* Dérèglement, désordre, *m.*

rip [rip], *v.t.* Fendre, déchirer; découdre. (*fam.*) *To let rip,* (of cars etc.) donner un coup d'accélérateur, mettre tous les gaz; *to rip off,* arracher, enlever; *to rip open,* ouvrir, éventrer, découdre (in needlework); *to rip up,* éventrer.—*v.i.* Se déchirer.—*n.* Déchirure, *f.*; (*slang*) vaurien, polisson, *m.* **rip-roaring,** *a.* Tumultueux; robuste; épatant.

riparian [rai'pɛəriən], *a.* Riverain.

ripe [raip], *a.* Mûr; parfait, consommé, accompli (consummate). **ripely,** *adv.* Mûrement, à temps. **ripen,** *v.t.* Mûrir, faire mûrir.—*v.i.* Mûrir, venir à maturité. **ripeness,** *n.* Maturité, *f.* **ripening,** *n.* Maturation, *f.*

riposte [ri'pɔst], *v.i.* Riposter.—*n.* Riposte, *f.*

ripper ['ripə], *n.* Éventreur, *m.*; (*fam.*) type épatant; truc formidable, *m.* **ripping,** *n.* Déchirement, *m.—a.* (*slang*) Épatant.

ripple [ripl], *v.i.* Se rider; onduler; clapoter. —*v.t.* Rider.—*n.* Ride (on water), *f.* **rippling,** *n.* Action de rider, *f.*; clapotis, murmure, *m.*

rise [raiz], *v.i.* (*past* **rose,** *p.p.* **risen** [rizn]) Se lever, se relever (after a fall, a misfortune, etc.); s'élever, monter (to ascend); se dresser (of peaks etc.); se soulever (to heave); s'augmenter, s'agrandir, s'accroître (to augment); hausser (of prices); aller en montant (of roads); renchérir (to grow dearer); se lever, se soulever (to rebel); ressusciter (of the dead); prendre sa source (en *or* dans); naître, venir, provenir (de); moucheronner, monter à la mouche (of fish). *I rise with the sun,* je me lève avec le soleil; *the funds are rising,* les fonds sont à la hausse; *to rise again,* se relever, ressusciter (of the dead); *to rise early,* se lever matin; *to rise out of,* sortir de, provenir de; *to rise to view,* se présenter à la vue; *to rise up,* se lever, se soulever, s'élever. —*v.t.* Faire mordre (a fish); faire lever (a bird).—*n.* Lever, *m.*; élévation (elevation); ascension (ascent); montée (of a hill etc.); flèche (of an arch); crue (of waters); hausse (in price); augmentation (increase); source, naissance, origine (source), *f. On the rise,* (*Comm.*) à la hausse; *the rise and fall of the Roman Empire,* grandeur et décadence de l'Empire Romain; *to get a rise out of someone,*

[444]

se payer la tête de quelqu'un, mettre quelqu'un en colère; *to give rise to,* donner naissance à, faire naître; *to take its rise,* prendre naissance, avoir sa source.
riser ['raizə], *n.* Degré, *m.*, marche (of a stair), *f. Early riser,* personne matinale, *f.; late riser,* qui se lève tard.
risibility [rizi'biliti], *n.* Risibilité, *f.*
risible ['rizibl], *a.* Risible.
rising ['raiziŋ], *a.* Levant, qui s'élève; montant (of the tide); (*fig.*) naissant; qui a de l'avenir (promising). *She is rising twenty,* elle va sur ses vingt ans.—*n.* Lever (from bed, of the sun), *m.*; montée (of a hill), *f.*; avancement, *m.*, élévation (elevation); crue (of waters); levée, clôture (of assemblies); résurrection (resurrection); (*Med.*) tumeur, *f.*; soulèvement, *m.*, insurrection (insurrection), *f. I like early rising,* j'aime à me lever de bon matin.
risk [risk], *n.* Risque, *m. At one's own risk,* à ses risques et périls; *at the risk of,* au risque de. —*v.t.* Risquer, courir le risque de. *I'll risk it!* je vais le risquer! (*colloq.*) au petit bonheur! **risky,** *a.* Risqué, hasardeux, dangereux.
rissole ['risoul], *n.* Croquette, rissole, *f.*
rite [rait], *n.* Rite, *m.*, cérémonie, *f.*
ritornello [ri:tɔ:'neləu], *n.* (*Mus.*) Ritournelle, *f.*
ritual ['ritjuəl], *n.* Rituel, *m.*—*a.* Du rite. **ritualist,** *n.* Ritualiste, *m.* **ritualistic,** *a.* Ritualiste. **ritually,** *adv.* Selon le rite.
rival [raivl], *a.* and *n.* Rival, *m.*, rivale, *f.*; concurrent, *m.*, -ente, *f.*—*v.t.* Rivaliser avec. —*v.i.* Rivaliser. **rivalry** or **rivalship,** *n.* Rivalité, *f.*
rive [raiv], *v.t.* (*past* reft, *p.p.* riven [rivn]) Fendre.—*v.i.* Se fendre.
river ['rivə], *n.* Cours d'eau, *m.*; fleuve, *m.* (flowing into the sea); (otherwise) rivière, *f. Down the river,* en aval; *up the river,* en amont.—*a.* De rivière, fluvial. **river-bed,** *n.* Lit de rivière, *m.* **river-god,** *n.* Fleuve, *m.* **river-horse,** *n.* Hippopotame, *m.* **riverside,** *n.* Bord de l'eau, *m.*—*a.* Au bord de l'eau.
rivet ['rivit], *n.* Rivet, *m.*; rivure, *f.*; attache (for china)—*v.t.* River, riveter, (*fig.*) fixer, clouer, affermir, consolider. **riveting,** *n.* Rivetage, *m.* **riveting-hammer,** *n.* Rivoir, *m.* **riveting-machine,** *n.* Machine à river, *f.*
rivulet ['rivjulit], *n.* Ruisseau, *m.*
rix-dollar ['riks'dɔlə], *n.* Rixdale, *f.*
riziform ['rizifɔ:m], *a.* Riziforme.
roach [routʃ], *n.* (*Ichth.*) Gardon, *m.*
road [roud], *n.* Route, *f.*, chemin, *m.*; chaussée (roadway); rue, *f.* (in town); (*Naut.*) rade, *f. Beaten road,* chemin battu; *by-road,* chemin détourné; *carriage-road,* route carrossable, *f.; cart-road,* chemin charretier; *cross-road,* chemin de traverse; *cross-roads,* carrefour, *m.; high road,* grand-route; *in the roads,* (*Naut.*) en rade; *on the road,* en route, en chemin; *on the road to,* sur la route de, en route pour; sur le chemin de, en voie de; *practicability of a road,* viabilité d'une route, *f.; roads and bridges,* ponts et chaussées, *m.pl.; to take the road to,* prendre le chemin de; **to take to the road,* se faire voleur de grand chemin.
road-bed, *n.* Plate-forme, *f.* **road-block,** *n.* Barrage sur la route, *m.* **road-book,** *n.*

Guide routier, *m.* **road-hog,** *n.* (*Motor.*) Chauffard, *m.* **road-house,** *n.* Auberge, hôtellerie, *f.* **road-labourer,** *n.* Cantonnier, *m.* **road-maker,** *n.* Constructeur de routes, *m.* **road-making,** *n.* Construction de routes, *f.* **road-map,** *n.* Carte routière, *f.* **road-mender,** *n.* Cantonnier, *m.* **road-metal,** *n.* Cailloutis, empierrement, *m.* **roadside,** *n.* Bord de la route, *m. By the roadside,* au bord de la route. **roadstead,** *n.* Rade, *f.* **roadster,** *n.* *Bicyclette, *f.*; (*Naut.*) navire en rade, *m.* **roadway,** *n.* Chaussée; voie (of a bridge), *f.* **roadworthy,** *a.* (*Motor.*) En état de marche.
roam [roum], *n.* Errer, rôder.—*v.t.* Rôder dans or parmi. **roamer,** *n.* Vagabond, voyageur, *m.* **roaming,** *n.* Course errante, *f.*
roan [roun], *a.* Rouan, *m.*—*n.* Basane (leather), *f.*
roar [rɔ:], *n.* Rugissement (of the lion etc.); mugissement (of the sea etc.); éclat, grand éclat (of laughter); grondement (of thunder etc.), *m. To set in a roar,* faire rire aux éclats. —*v.i.* Rugir (of the lion etc.); mugir (of the sea etc.); gronder (of thunder, cannon, etc.); (*colloq.*) vociférer. *To roar with laughter,* rire aux éclats. **roarer,** *n.* Braillard; cheval corneur, *m.* **roaring,** *a.* Rugissant, mugissant. *To do a roaring trade,* faire des affaires d'or.
roast [roust], *v.t.* Rôtir; faire rôtir; torréfier (coffee); (*Metal.*) griller.—*v.i.* Rôtir; griller. —*a.* Rôti. *Roast beef,* rosbif, *m.*; *roast pork,* rôti de porc, *m.* **roaster,** *n.* Rôtisseur, *m.*; rôtissoire (thing), *f.*; brûloir (for coffee), *m.*; volaille à rôtir, *f.* **roasting,** *n.* (*Metal.*) Grillage, *m.*; torréfaction (of coffee), *f.*—*a.* Brûlant. **roasting-jack,** *n.* Tourne-broche, *m.*
rob [rɔb], *v.t.* Voler; piller; priver (de). *He would rob a church,* il en prendrait sur l'autel; *I have been robbed of everything,* on m'a complètement dévalisé; *to rob an orchard,* piller un verger; *to rob someone of something,* voler quelque chose à quelqu'un.
robber ['rɔbə], *n.* Voleur, *m.*, -euse, *f. Highway robber,* voleur de grand chemin. **robbery,** *n.* Vol, *m. Highway robbery,* vol à main armée, *m.*
robe [roub], *n.* Robe, tunique, *f.*—*v.t.* Vêtir (d'une robe); revêtir (de). *To robe oneself,* se revêtir de sa robe. **robing-room,** *n.* Vestiaire, *m.* (of judge).
robin ['rɔbin] or **robin-redbreast,** *n.* (*Orn.*) Rouge-gorge, *m.*
Robin Hood ['rɔbin 'hud]. Robin des bois, *m.*
robinia [rɔ'biniə], *n.* (*Bot.*) Robinier, *m.*
robot ['roubɔt], *n.* Automate, robot, *m.*—*a.* Automatique.
robust [ro'bʌst], *a.* Robuste, vigoureux. **robustly,** *adv.* Robustement, vigoureusement. **robustness,** *n.* Robustesse, vigueur, *f.*
roc [rɔk], *n.* Rock (fabulous bird of Eastern tales), *m.*
rocambole ['rɔkəmboul], *n.* Échalote d'Espagne, *f.*
rochet ['rɔtʃit], *n.* Rochet (vestment), *m.*
rock (1) [rɔk], *n.* Rocher, *m.*; (*Geol.*) roche, *f.*; sucre d'orge (sweetmeat), *m. Rock drawings,* dessins rupestres, *m.pl.*; (*fam.*) *to be on the rocks,* être à fond de cale. **rock-alum,** *n.* Alun de roche, *m.* **rock-basin,** *n.* Bassin

géologique, *m.* **rock-bottom,** *n.* (*fig.*) Fin fond, *m.*—*a.* Le plus bas. **rockbound,** *a.* Entouré de rochers. **rock-climber,** *n.* Varappeur, *m.* **rock-climbing,** *n.* Varappe, *f.* **rock-crystal,** *n.* Cristal de roche, *m.* **rock-dove** or **rock-pigeon,** *n.* Biset, *m.* **rock-drill,** *n.* Perforatrice, *f.* **rock-garden,** *n.* Jardin de rocaille, *m.* **rock-melon,** *n.* Cantaloup, *m.* **rock-oil,** *n.* Pétrole, *m.* **rock-rose,** *n.* (*Bot.*) Ciste, *m.* **rock-salt,** *n.* Sel gemme, *m.* **rockslide,** *n.* Avalanche de rochers, *f.* **rockwork,** *n.* Rocaille, *f.*
rock (2) [rɔk], *v.t.* Balancer; bercer, remuer.— *v.i.* Se balancer; branler, trembler. **rock and roll,** *n.* Rock 'n' roll, *m.*—*v.i.* Danser le rock 'n' roll. **rocker,** *n.* Berceuse; bascule (apparatus), *f.* (*pop.*) *To be off one's rocker,* être un peu cinglé.
rockery ['rɔkəri], *n.* Jardin de rocaille, *m.*
rocket ['rɔkit], *n.* Fusée; (*Bot.*) roquette, julienne, *f.*; (*pop.*) savon, *m.*, engueulade, *f.* —*v.t.* (*pop.*) Engueuler, savonner.—*v.i.* Monter en flèche (of prices). *Sky-rocket,* fusée volante, *f.* **rocket-apparatus,** *n.* Porte-amarre, *m.,* **rocket-launcher,** *n.* Lance-fusée, *m.* **rocket-stick,** *n.* Baguette de fusée, *f.*
rockiness ['rɔkinis], *n.* Nature rocailleuse, *f.*
rocking ['rɔkiŋ], *n.* Balancement; bercement, *m.* **rocking-chair,** *n.* Chaise à bascule, *f.* **rocking-horse,** *n.* Cheval à bascule, *m.*
rocky ['rɔki], *a.* Plein de rochers, rocailleux, rocheux; (*colloq.*) branlant.
Rocky ['rɔki] **Mountains, the.** Les Montagnes Rocheuses, *f.pl.*
rococo [rə'koukou], *a.* and *n.* Rococo, *m.*
rod [rɔd], *n.* Verge; baguette; tringle (for curtains etc.); tige (of a pump); canne à pêche, *f.*; perche (= 5·0291 mètres); bielle (piston), *f.* *Rod and line,* ligne à pêcher, *f.*; *spare the rod and spoil the child,* qui aime bien châtie bien; *to have a rod in pickle for,* avoir une dent contre; *to kiss the rod,* se soumettre (à un châtiment) sans rien dire.
rode [roud], *past* [RIDE].
rodent ['roudənt], *n.* (*Zool.*) Rongeur, *m.*
rodeo [rou'deiou], *n.* Rodéo, *m.*
rodomontade [rɔdəmɔn'teid], *n.* Rodomontade, *f.*—*v.i.* Faire le fanfaron.
roe [rou], *n.* Œufs (de poisson), *m.pl.*; chevreuil, *m.*, chevrette (deer), *f.* *Hard roe,* œufs de poisson, *m.pl.*; *hard-roed,* œuvé; *soft roe,* laite, laitance, *f.*; *soft-roed,* laité. **roebuck,** *n.* Chevreuil, *m.*
rogations [rə'geiʃnz] or **Rogation Days,** *n.pl.* Rogations, *f.pl.*
Roger [rɔdʒə]. Roger, *m.* *The Jolly Roger,* le pavillon noir, *m.*
rogue [roug], *n.* Coquin, fripon, fourbe; (*facet.*) malin, espiègle, farceur; (*Law*) vagabond, *m.* *Rogue elephant,* éléphant solitaire, *m.* **roguery** ['rougəri], *n.* Coquinerie, friponnerie, fourberie; (*facet.*) espièglerie, *f.*; (*Law*) vagabondage, *m.*
roguish ['rougiʃ], *a.* Coquin, fripon; (*facet.*) malin, espiègle. **roguishly,** *adv.* En fripon, en fourbe; (*facet.*) avec espièglerie. **roguishness,** *n.* Coquinerie, friponnerie; (*facet.*) malice, espièglerie, *f.*
roister ['rɔistə], *v.i.* Faire du tapage. **roisterer,** *n.* Tapageur, *m.* **roistering,** *n.* Tapage, *m.*—*a.* Tapageur, bruyant.

Roland ['roulənd]. Roland, *m.* *A Roland for an Oliver,* à bon chat, bon rat; *to give a Roland for an Oliver,* rendre à quelqu'un la monnaie de sa pièce.
role [roul], *n.* Rôle, *m.*
roll [roul], *n.* Rouleau; roulement (act of rolling); roulis (of a ship); petit pain (loaf), *m.*; coquille, *f.* (of butter); roulade, *f.*; roulement, *m.* (of drum); rôle, contrôle (list), *m.*; (*pl.*) rôles, contrôles, *m.pl.*; annales, archives, *f.pl.* *To call the roll,* faire l'appel; *to strike off the rolls,* rayer du tableau.—*v.t.* Rouler; passer au rouleau (a garden walk); (*Metal.*) laminer. *To roll back,* rouler en arrière, faire reculer; *to roll down,* rouler en bas; *to roll oneself up,* s'enrouler, se pelotonner; *to roll up,* rouler, enrouler.—*v.i.* Rouler, se rouler; tourner; faire sa révolution (to revolve); faire un roulement (de tambour); (*Naut.*) avoir du roulis. *A rolling stone gathers no moss,* pierre qui roule n'amasse pas mousse; *to be rolling in money,* rouler sur l'or; *to roll away,* s'éloigner en roulant, passer, s'écouler; *to roll by,* passer en roulant; *to roll off,* descendre en roulant, descendre, couler; *to roll over,* se retourner; *to roll up,* se rouler, s'enrouler; (*pop.*) arriver, s'amener. **roll-call,** *n.* Appel, *m.* **roll-top,** *n.* Rideau (of desk), *m.* *A roll-top desk,* un bureau à cylindre, *m.*
roller, *n.* Rouleau, *m.*; roulette (castor), *f.*, (*Metal.*) cylindre, laminoir; rollier (bird), *m.* *Garden-roller,* rouleau de jardin, *m.* **roller-skate,** *n.* Patin à roulettes, *m.* **roller-skating,** *n.* Patinage à roulettes, *m.*
rollick ['rɔlik], *v.i.* Folâtrer; gambader, faire ses farces, faire du tapage. **rollicker,** *n.* Noceur, *m.* **rollicking,** *a.* Folâtre, joyeux, déréglé.
rolling ['rouliŋ], *n.* Roulement; roulis (of a ship); (*Metal.*) laminage, *m.* *Rolling stock,* matériel roulant, *m.* **rolling-mill,** *n.* Laminoir, *m.* **rolling-pin,** *n.* Rouleau, *m.* **rolling-press,** *n.* Presse à cylindres, *f.*
roly-poly ['rouli'pouli], *n.* Pouding aux confitures; (*colloq.*) enfant potelé, *m.*
Roman ['roumən], *a.* Romain; aquilin (of the nose). *Roman candle,* chandelle romaine, *f.*; *Roman numerals,* chiffres romains, *m.pl.*—*n.* Romain, *m.*, -aine, *f.*; (*Print.*) romain, *m.*
Romance (1) [rou'mæns], *a.* Roman. *Romance languages,* langues romanes, *f.pl.*
romance (2) [rou'mæns], *n.* Roman de chevalerie, *m.*; histoire or venture romanesque, *f.*; (*Mus.*) romance, *f.*—*v.i.* Inventer à plaisir, exagérer, broder. **romance-writer,** *n.* Romancier du Moyen-Âge, *m.*
romanesque [roumə'nesk], *a.* (*Arch.*) Roman.
Romanism ['roumənizm], *n.* Religion catholique romaine, *f.* **Romanist,** *n.* Catholique romain, *m.* **Romanize,** *v.t.* Latiniser; convertir au catholicisme romain.
romantic [rou'mæntik], *a.* Romanesque; romantique (of scenery, style, etc.). **romantically,** *adv.* Romanesquement; romantiquement (of scenery). **romanticism,** *n.* Le romantisme, *m.* **romanticist** [-'mæntisist], *n.* Romantique, *m.* **romanticness,** *n.* Caractère romanesque, *m.*
Romany ['rɔməni], *n.* Romanichel, *m.*, -elle, *f.*, bohémien, *m.*, -ienne, *f.*

Rome [roum]. Rome, *f. When in Rome do as the Romans do*, il faut hurler avec les loups; *Rome was not built in a day*, Paris ne s'est pas fait en un jour. *Romish, a. (pej.)* Catholique.

romp [rɔmp], *n.* Gamine, garçonnière (girl), *f.*; jeu violent *or* grossier, tapage (play), *m.—v.i.* Jouer rudement, folâtrer, gambader, faire du tapage. *(fam.) To romp home*, gagner dans un fauteuil. **rompers**, *n.pl.* Barboteuse, *f.* **romping**, *n.* Jeux rudes, *m.pl.* **rompish**, *a.* Turbulent. **rompishness**, *n.* Manière bruyante, turbulente, *f.*

roneo ['rouniou], *v.t. (reg. trade name)*. Ronéotyper.—*n.* Ronéo, *f.*

rood [ru:d], *n.* Quart d'arpent (10·12 ares), *m.*; crucifix, *m.* **rood-loft** *or* **rood-screen**, *n.* Jubé, *m.*

roof [ru:f], *n.* Toit; palais (of the mouth), *m.*; *(fig.)* voûte, *f.*, ciel, *m. (Motor.) Sunshine roof*, toit ouvrant, *m.—v.t.* Couvrir d'un toit; couvrir; *(fig.)* abriter (to shelter). **roof-garden**, *n.* Jardin sur un toit en terrasse, *m.* **roof-rack**, *n. (Motor.)* Galerie, *f.* **roof-tree**, *n.* Charpente de toiture, *f.*; *(fig.)* toit, *m.*

roofing, *n.* Toiture, *f.* **roofless**, *a.* Sans toit; *(fig.)* sans abri. **roofy**, *a.* Couvert d'un toit.

rook [ruk], *n.* Freux, *m.*, *(pop.)* corneille, *f.*; *(slang)* tricheur, fripon, *m.*; *(Chess)* tour, *f.* —*v.t., v.i.* Friponner, filouter. **rookery**, *n.* Colonie de freux, *f.*; *(fig.)* ramassis de taudis, repaire de voleurs, *m.*

rookie ['ruki], *n. (Mil.)* Bleu, *m.*

room [ru:m], *n.* Place, *f.*, espace (space), *m.*; chambre, salle, pièce (apartment), *f.*; *(fig.)* lieu, sujet, motif (reason), *m. Back room*, chambre sur la cour, *f.*; *bedroom*, chambre à coucher, *f.*; *dining-room*, salle à manger, *f.*; *double-room*, chambre à deux personnes, chambre à grand lit, *f.*; *front-room*, chambre sur le devant, *f.*; *powder-room*, *(Naut.)* soute aux poudres, *f.*; *(U.S.)* les lavabos, *m.pl.*; *single-room*, chambre à une personne, *f.*; *the next room*, la chambre voisine, *f.*; *there is no room*, il n'y a pas de place; *there is room for improvement*, cela laisse à désirer; *to make room for*, faire place à. **roomful**, *n.* Chambrée, *f.* **roominess**, *n.* Nature spacieuse, grandeur, *f.* **roomy**, *a.* Spacieux, vaste.

roost [ru:st], *n.* Juchoir, perchoir, *m. Henroost*, poulailler, *m.*; *to rule the roost*, faire la loi.—*v.i. Curses come home to roost*, à qui mal veut, mal arrive; *to go to roost*, *(colloq.)* aller se coucher.

rooster ['ru:stə], *n.* Coq, *m.*

root [ru:t], *n.* Racine; *(fig.)* souche, source, *f.*, fondement, *m. Cube root*, racine cubique, *f.*; *root and branch*, de fond en comble; *square root*, racine carrée, *f.*; *to take root*, prendre racine.—*v.i.* S'enraciner, prendre racine; fouiller avec le groin (of swine). *(fam.) To root for a team*, encourager une équipe, appuyer une équipe.—*v.t.* Enraciner; *(fig.)* fixer en terre; fouiller (the earth). *To root out* *or* *up*, déraciner, extirper. **rooted**, *a.* Enraciné; *(fig.)* invétéré. *Rooted to the spot*, cloué sur place. **rooting**, *n.* Enracinement, *m. Rooting out* *or* *up*, arrachement, *m.*, extirpation, extermination, *f.* **rootlet**, *n.* Petite racine, *f.*, radicule, *f.* **root-stock**, *n.* Rhizome, *m.*

rope [roup], *n.* Corde (of rigging), *f.*; *(Naut.)* cordage, *m.*; manœuvre; glane (of onions), *f.*; *(Mount.)* cordée, *f. A piece of rope*, un bout de filin, *m.*; *a rope of sand*, une chaîne de paille, *f.*; *first on the rope*, premier de cordée, *m.*; *head-rope*, licou, *m.*; *plenty of rope*, libre cours, *m.*; *running ropes*, manœuvres courantes, *f.pl.*; *to give a person rope*, lâcher la bride à quelqu'un; *to know the ropes*, connaître son affaire, être à la coule.—*v.i.* Filer (of wine etc.); *(Mount.)* s'encorder. *To rope down*, faire une descente en rappel.—*v.t.* Corder (of parcels); attacher avec une corde; lier. *To rope in*, entourer de cordes; *(fam.)* associer (quelqu'un) à une tâche. **rope-bands**, *n.pl. (Naut.)* Rabans d'envergure, *m.pl.* **rope-dancer**, *n.* Danseur de corde, funambule, acrobate, *m.* **rope-ladder**, *n.* Échelle de corde, *f.* **rope-maker**, *n.* Cordier, *m.* **rope-making**, *n.* Corderie, *f.* **rope-walk**, *n.* Corderie, *f.* **rope-walker**, *n.* Acrobate, *m.* **rope-yarn**, *n.* Fil de caret, *m.*

ropery, *n.* Corderie, *f.*

ropey, *a. (pop.)* Camelote, miteux.

ropiness ['roupinis], *n.* Viscosité, *f.* **ropish** *or* **ropy**, *a.* Qui file, filant, visqueux.

rorqual ['rɔ:kwəl], *n.* Rorqual, *m.*

rosaceous [roˈzeiʃəs], *a. (Bot.)* Rosacé.

Rosaline ['rɔzəlin]. Rosalie, *f.*

Rosamund ['rɔzəmənd]. Rosemonde, *f.*

rosary ['rouzəri], *n.* Rosaire, *m.*

rose (1) [rouz], *n.* Rose; pomme d'arrosoir (of a watering-pot); *(Arch.)* rosace, *f.*; *(Med.)* érésipèle, *m. Every rose has its thorn*, pas de rose sans épines; *guelder rose*, obier, *m.*, boule de neige, *f.*; *he is not on a bed of roses*, il n'est pas sur un lit de roses, il est loin d'être à son aise; *monthly rose*, rose des quatre saisons; *the Wars of the Roses*, les guerres des deux Roses, *f.pl.*; *under the rose*, sous le manteau, en secret, confidentiellement.

rose (2), *past* [RISE].

roseate ['rouziit], *a.* Rosé.

rose-bay, *n.* Laurier-rose; rhododendron, *m.* **rose-bed**, *n.* Massif de rosiers, *m.* **rosebud**, *n.* Bouton de rose, *m.* **rose-bush**, *n.* Rosier, *m.* **rose-campion**, *n.* Agrostemme en couronne, *f.* **rose-colour**, *n.* Rose, *m.* **rose-coloured**, *a.* Couleur de rose, rosé. *To look at everything through rose-coloured spectacles*, voir tout en rose. **rose-garden**, *n.* Roseraie, *f.* **rose-laurel**, *n.* Laurier-rose, *m.* **rose-mallow**, *n.* Rose trémière; mauve-rose, *f.* **rose-show**, *n.* Exposition de roses, *f.* **rose-tree**, *n.* Rosier, *m.* **rose-water**, *n.* Eau de rose, *f.* **rose-window**, *n.* Rosace, *f.* **rose-wood**, *n.* Bois de rose, palissandre, *m.* **rose-work**, *n.* Rosaces, *f.pl.*

rosemary ['rouzməri], *n.* Romarin; encens, *m.*

roseola [roˈzi:ələ], *n.* Roséole, *f.*

rosery, *n.* Roseraie, *f.*

rosette [rouˈzet], *n.* Rosette, *f.*; *(Arch.)* rosace, *f.*

Rosicrucian [rouziˈkru:ʃən], *n.* Rose-croix, *m.inv.—a.* Des rose-croix.

rosin ['rɔzin], *n.* Colophane, *f.—v.t.* Enduire *or* frotter de colophane.

rosiness ['rouzinis], *n.* Couleur rose, *f.*

rosiny ['rɔzini], *a.* Résineux.

roster ['rɔstə], *n. (Mil.)* Tableau de service, *m.*, liste, *f.*

rostral ['rɔstrəl], *a.* Rostral.

rostrum ['rɔstrəm], *n.* Bec, éperon (of a ship), *m.*; (*Rom. Hist.*) rostres, *m.pl.*; tribune (platform), *f.*; (*Zool.*) rostre, *m.*

rosy ['rouzi], *a.* De rose, rose, rosé, vermeil. **rosy-coloured**, *a.* Couleur de rose. **rosy-crowned**, *a.* Couronné de roses. **rosy-fingered**, *a.* Aux doigts de rose. **rosy-lipped**, *a.* Aux lèvres rosées. **rosy-tinted**, *a.* Rosé.

rot [rɔt], *n.* Pourriture; clavelée, *f.*, tac (of sheep), *m.*; (*fig.*) démoralisation, *f.*; (*colloq.*) blague, *f. Dry rot*, pourriture sèche; *that's all rot*, (*colloq.*) ç'est de la blague.—*v.t.* Pourrir, faire pourrir; carier (teeth).—*v.i.* Pourrir, se pourrir; se carier (of teeth); (*colloq.*) blaguer.

rota ['routə], *n.* (*R.-C. Ch.*) Rote, *f.*; tour de roulement, *m. By rota*, à tour de rôle.

rotary ['routəri], *a.* Rotatoire, de rotation.

rotate [ro'teit], *v.i., v.t.* Tourner.

rotation [ro'teiʃən], *n.* Rotation, succession, *f.*, roulement, *m. By rotation* or *in rotation*, à tour de rôle; *rotation of crops*, assolement, *m.*

rotatory ['routətəri], *a.* De rotation, rotatoire; (*Anat.*) rotateur.

rote [rout], *n.* Routine, *f. By rote*, par cœur. —*v.t.* Apprendre par cœur.

rotifer ['routifə], *n.* Rotifère, *m.* **rotiform**, *a.* Rotiforme.

rotor ['routə], *n.* Rotor; balai rotatif, *m.*

rotten [rɔtn], *a.* Pourri, carié (of teeth), gâté (of eggs); véreux (insolvent). (*fam.*) *To feel rotten*, se sentir fichu; *to smell rotten*, sentir le pourri. **rottenness**, *n.* Pourriture; carie (of the teeth); (*fig.*) fausseté, *f.* **rottenstone**, *n.* Tripoli, *m.* **rotter**, *n.* (*fam.*) Sale type, *m.*

rotting, *a.* Qui pourrit; qui se carie.—*n.* Putréfaction, *f.*

rotund [ro'tʌnd], *a.* Rond, arrondi. **rotunda**, *n.* Rotonde, *f.* **rotundity**, *n.* Rondeur, rotondité, *f.*

rouble ['ru:bl], *n.* Rouble, *m.*

roué ['ru:ei], *n.* Débauché, *m.*

rouge [ru:ʒ], *n.* Rouge, fard, *m.*—*v.i.* Mettre du rouge.—*v.t.* Mettre du rouge à; farder.

rough [rʌf], *a.* Rude; hérissé, ébouriffé (shaggy); raboteux (of roads); agitée, grosse, houleuse (of the sea); orageux, gros (of the weather); âpre (harsh to the taste); brut (of precious stones); non poli, dépoli (of glass); brutal, grossier (coarse in manners); en gros, approximatif (not exact). *A rough diamond*, un diamant brut; *in the rough*, brut, en gros, ébauché; *rough copy* or *draft*, brouillon, *m.*; *rough estimate*, appréciation en gros, *f.*; *rough sea*, mer houleuse, *f.*; *to be rough with*, brutaliser, rudoyer; *to cut up rough*, montrer les dents; *very rough usage*, traitement très dur, *m.*; *very rough weather*, très mauvais temps, *m.*; *we must take the rough with the smooth*, à la guerre comme à la guerre.—*adv.* Brutalement, rudement.—*v.t.* Rendre rude; dépolir (glass). *To rough out*, ébaucher, dégrossir; *to rough it*, manger de la vache enragée, coucher sur la dure.—*n.* Voyou, polisson, *m.*; canaille, racaille, *f.* **rough-and-ready**, *a.* Fait à la va-vite, primitif, grossièrement exécuté. **rough-and-tumble**, *n.* Mêlée, bousculade, *f.* **roughcast**, *v.t.* Ébaucher; (*Build.*) crépir.—*n.* Ébauche, *f.*; (*Build.*) crépi, *m.* **roughcasting**, *n.* Crépissage, *m.* **rough-handle**, *v.t.* Malmener, houspiller (quelqu'un). **rough-hew**, *v.t.*

Ébaucher. **rough-hewn**, *a.* Ébauché. **rough-house**, *n.* (*fam.*) Chahut, *m.*, bousculade, *f.* **rough-rider**, *n.* Écuyer, piqueur, dresseur de chevaux, *m.* **rough-shod**, *a.* Ferré à glace. *To ride rough-shod over people*, fouler les gens aux pieds. **rough-shoe**, *v.t.* Ferrer à glace. **rough-wrought**, *a.* Travaillé grossièrement.

roughen, *v.i.* Devenir rude.—*v.t.* Rendre rude. **roughly**, *adv.* Rudement; grossièrement; âprement, durement, brutalement; brusquement; approximativement, à peu près, dans ses lignes générales. **roughness**, *n.* Aspérité, rudesse; âpreté (to the taste); agitation (of the sea); grossièreté, brusquerie (of manners), *f.*; sans-façon, mauvais état (of roads), *m.*

roulette [ru:'let], *n.* Roulette, cycloïde, *f.*

rounce [rauns], *n.* (*Print.*) Manivelle, *f.*

round [raund], *a.* Rond; circulaire; en rond; (*fig.*) facile, coulant. *In round numbers*, en chiffres ronds; *round robin*, pétition revêtue de signatures en cercle, *f.*; *to make round*, arrondir.—*adv.* En rond; à la ronde (on all sides); tout autour, à l'entour. *All round*, tout autour; *all the year round*, pendant toute l'année; *to get round*, tourner, circonvenir, entortiller, se rétablir, se refaire (of the health); *to go round*, faire le tour de, faire un détour; *to go round to*, aller voir, visiter; *hand round*, passer à la ronde.—*prep.* Autour de. *To go round the garden*, faire le tour du jardin; *to tie a rope round one's neck*, se mettre la corde au cou; *with a rope round one's neck*, la corde au cou.—*n.* Rond, cercle; tour (walk round); échelon (of a ladder), *m.*; rouelle (of beef etc.); salve (of applause); décharge (of musketry), *f.*; (*Artill.*) coup de canon; assaut, *m.*; ronde (of watchmen, police, etc.); tournée, *f.* (golf); round, *m.* (boxing); bosse (drawing); (*Sculp.*) ronde bosse, *f. In a round*, en rond; *round of ammunition*, cartouche, *f.*; *officer of the rounds*, officier de ronde, *m.*; *to fire a round*, tirer une volée; *to go one's round*, faire sa tournée *or* la ronde.—*v.t.* Arrondir; environner, entourer (to encircle); faire le tour de (to walk round); doubler (a cape). *To round off*, arrondir, finir, compléter; *to round on*, (*slang*) dénoncer, s'en prendre à; *to round up*, rassembler (cattle etc.), cerner, rafler.—*v.i.* S'arrondir; faire la ronde.

roundabout ['raundəbaut], *a.* Détourné; indirect; vague. *To take a roundabout way*, faire un grand détour.—*n.* Manège, *m.*, chevaux de bois, *m.pl.*; (*Motor.*) rond-point, sens giratoire, *m.*

rounded, *a.* Arrondi.

***roundelay** ['raundəlei], *n.* Rondeau, *m.*, ronde (dance), *f.*

rounders ['raundəz], *n.pl.* Balle au camp, *f.*

round-head, *n.* (*Engl. Hist.*) Tête ronde, *f.* **round-headed**, *a.* À tête ronde. **round-house**, *n.* Corps de garde, violon, *m.*; (*Naut.*) dunette, *f.* **round-shouldered**, *a.* Voûté. **round-up**, *n.* Rassemblement, *m.* (of cattle); rafle, *f.* (of criminals).

roundish ['raundiʃ], *a.* Arrondi, presque rond; rondelet (of persons). **roundishness**, *n.* Forme arrondie, *f.* **roundlet**, *n.* Petit rond, petit cercle, *m.* **roundly**, *adv.* En

rond; *(fig.)* rondement, franchement.
roundness, *n.* Rondeur; *(fig.)* franchise, *f.*
roundsman [ˈraundzmən], *n.* *(Comm.)* Livreur, distributeur, *m.* *A baker's rounds-man,* un boulanger livreur, *m.*
roup (1) [ruːp], *n.* Pépie (disease in poultry), *f.*
roup (2) [raup], *n.* *(Sc.)* Vente à la criée, *f.* *By public roup,* en vente publique.
rouse [rauz], *v.t.* Éveiller, *(fig.)* réveiller, exciter, soulever; *(Naut.)* haler. *To rouse the sleeping lion,* réveiller le chien qui dort.
rousing, *a.* Qui éveille, qui réveille; émouvant; vibrant; grand, bon (of fire).
rout [raut], *n.* *Assemblée, réunion (party); cohue, foule, *f.*; attroupement, *m.*; déroute (of an army), *f.* *To put to rout,* mettre en déroute.—*v.t.* Mettre en déroute. *Completely routed,* en pleine déroute; *to rout out,* découvrir, déterrer, faire décamper.
route [ruːt], *n.* Route, *f.*; itinéraire, parcours, *m.*—*v.t.* Router (of traffic, parcels, etc.).
route-map, *n.* Carte routière, *f.* **route-march,** *n.* Marche militaire, *f.*
routine [ruːˈtiːn], *n.* Routine, *f.*; travail courant, *m.* *To return to the old routine,* reprendre le collier.
rove [rouv], *v.i.* Rôder, courir, battre la campagne.—*v.t.* Errer dans, parcourir; *(Spinning)* passer dans une maille, boudiner. **rover,** *n.* Rôdeur, vagabond; inconstant, *m.*, -ante, *f.* (fickle person); écumeur de mer, pirate, corsaire (pirate), *m.*; *(Scouting)* éclaireur chevalier, *m.* **roving,** *a.* Errant, vagabond. —*n.* *(Spinning)* Boudinage, *m.* **roving-frame,** *n.* Boudinoir, *m.* **rovingly,** *adv.* En rôdant.
row (1) [rau], *n.* Tapage, vacarme, *m.*; querelle, *f.*, scène, *f.* *To get into a row,* se faire une mauvaise affaire; *to kick up a row,* faire du tapage ou du train.
row (2) [rou], *n.* Rang, *m.*, rangée, file; colonne (of figures); promenade sur l'eau, promenade en bateau (on the water), *f.* *In a row,* en rang, en ligne; *in rows,* par rangs, *(Hort.)* en rayons.—*v.t.* *(Naut.)* Faire aller à la rame.—*v.i.* Ramer; ramer en course; *(Naut.)* nager. *To row in the same boat,* courir même fortune.
rowan [ˈrauən *or* ˈrouən] *or* **rowan-tree,** *n.* *(Sc.)* Sorbier des oiseaux, *m.*
rowdy [ˈraudi], *a.* Tapageur.—*n.* Voyou, gredin, *m.* **rowdyism** *or* **rowdiness,** *n.* Tapage, chahut, *m.*
rowel [ˈrauəl], *n.* Molette (of a spur), *f.*
rower [ˈrouə], *n.* Rameur; *(Naut.)* nageur, *m.*
rowing, *n.* Canotage, sport de l'aviron, *m.* *To be fond of rowing,* aimer ramer. **rowing-boat,** *n.* Bateau à rames, *m.*; canot à l'aviron, *m.* **rowing-club,** *n.* Cercle de rameurs, *m.* **rowing-match,** *n.* Course à l'aviron, *f.*
rowlock [ˈrʌlək], *n.* Toletière, dame, *f.*
royal [ˈrɔiəl], *a.* Royal, de roi; grand raisin (of paper). *Royal assent,* sanction royale, *f.*; *royal blue,* bleu de roi, *m.*; *Royal Navy,* marine nationale, marine royale, *f.*—*n.* Cacatois (sail), *m.* **royalism,** *n.* Royalisme, *m.* **royalist,** *n. and a.* Royaliste, *m.* **royally,** *adv.* Royalement, en roi. **royalty,** *n.* Royauté; *(usu. pl.)* redevance, commission, *f.*, droit sur la vente, droit d'auteur, *m.*
rub [rʌb], *v.t.* Frotter; *(Med.)* frictionner; *(fig.)* contrarier (to tease). *Don't rub it in!*

n'insistez pas! *to rub away,* enlever par le frottement; *to rub down,* frotter, polir, bouchonner (a horse); *to rub off,* enlever en frottant, faire disparaître; *to rub out,* enlever, effacer; *to rub up,* frotter, dérouiller, polir; exciter, réveiller, rafraîchir (the memory etc.).—*v.i.* Frotter; *(Med.)* faire des frictions. *To rub along,* aller son petit bonhomme de chemin; *to rub off,* s'user, s'effacer; *to rub through,* se frayer un chemin à travers, se tirer d'affaire.—*n.* Frottement; coup de brosse, *m.*; *(fig.)* difficulté, *f.*, point difficile, obstacle; coup de patte (sarcasm), *m.* *A rub down,* un coup de bouchon (to a horse), coup de torchon (with a cloth), *m.*; *there's the rub,* c'est là la difficulté, voilà le hic; *to come to the rub,* en venir au fait.
rub-a-dub-dub [ˈrʌbəˈdʌbdʌb], *n.* Rataplan (of a drum), *m.*
rubber [ˈrʌbə], *n.* Frotteur; frottoir (thing), *m.*; *(Whist)* rob, robre, *m.*; *(pl.)* *(Am.)* caoutchoucs (shoes), *m.pl.* *Indiarubber,* caoutchouc, *m.*, gomme élastique, gomme à effacer, *f.* **rubberize,** *v.t.* Caoutchouter. **rubberneck,** *n.* *(fam.)* Badaud, *m.*—*v.i.* Badauder.
rubber-stamp, *n.* Tampon, *m.*; *(fig.)* béni-oui-oui, *m.*—*v.t.* Ratifier.
rubbing [ˈrʌbiŋ], *n.* Frottement; frottage; frottis, calque par frottement, *m.*; *(Med.)* friction, *f.*
rubbish [ˈrʌbiʃ], *n.* Débris, déblais, décombres, gravois, gravats, *m.pl.*; immondices, ordures, *f.pl.*; fatras (nonsense), *m.*; rebut (anything worthless), *m.* **rubbish-bin,** *n.* Boîte à ordures, poubelle, *f.* **rubbish-cart,** *n.* Tombereau, *m.* **rubbish-dump,** *n.* Dépotoir, *m.* **rubbish-heap,** *n.* Monceau de détritus, *m.* **rubbishing** *or* **rubbishy,** *a.* De rebut, sans valeur. **rubbish-shoot,** *n.* Décharge publique, *f.*, dépôt d'immondices, *m.*; vide-ordures (indoors), *m.inv.*
rubble [rʌbl], *n.* Blocaille, *f.*, moellons, *m.pl.* **rubblework,** *n.* Maçonnerie brute de moellons, maçonnerie de blocaille, *f.*
rubefacient [ruːbiˈfæʃənt], *a.* *(Med.)* Rubéfiant.
rubefaction [ruːbiˈfækʃən], *n.* Rubéfaction, *f.*
rubefy [ˈruːbifai], *v.t.* Rubéfier.
rubeola [ruːˈbiːələ], **rubella,** *n.* Rubéole, *f.*
rubescent [ruːˈbesənt], *a.* Rubescent.
rubiaceous [ruːbiˈeiʃəs], *a.* *(Bot.)* Rubiacé.
rubicund [ˈruːbikənd], *a.* Rubicond.
rubied [ˈruːbid], *a.* De rubis, vermeil.
rubric [ˈruːbrik], *n.* Rubrique, *f.* **rubrical,** *a.* Rouge; contenu dans les rubriques.
rubricate, *v.t.* Marquer de rouge. **rubricator,** *n.* Rubricateur, *m.*
rubrician [ruːˈbriʃən], *n.* Rubricaire, *m.*
ruby [ˈruːbi], *n.* Rubis, *m.*; teinte rouge, *f.*, incarnat, *m.*, couleur rouge, *f.*—*a.* De rubis, vermeil. *Ruby lips,* lèvres de corail, *f.pl.*
ruck [rʌk], *n.* Peloton (of racers), *m.* *Out of the (common) ruck,* hors du commun.—*v.t.* Plisser; froisser.
ruckle [rʌkl], *n.* Pli (in cloth), faux pli, *m.*; *(Med.)* râle, *m.*
rucksack [ˈrʌksæk], *n.* Sac à dos, *m.*
ruction [ˈrʌkʃn], *n.* *(colloq.)* Bagarre, dispute, *f.*
rudder [ˈrʌdə], *n.* Gouvernail; *(Av.)* gouvernail de direction, *m.* **rudder-bar,** *n.* Barre du gouvernail, *f.*; palonnier (in plane), *m.* **rudder-case,** *n.* Boîte de gouvernail, *f.*

ruddiness ['rʌdinis], *n.* Fraîcheur de teint, rougeur, *f.*; incarnat, *m.* **ruddy,** *a.* Frais, rouge, au teint vermeil; (*slang*) sacré. *He's a ruddy liar,* c'est un sacré menteur.

rude [ru:d], *a.* Grossier, impoli, malhonnête, insolent; (*fig.*) rude, violent, sévère, dur. **rudely,** *adv.* Grossièrement; insolemment; impoliment, malhonnêtement; violemment; sévèrement, rudement. **rudeness,** *n.* Rudesse; grossièreté; insolence; malhonnêteté, impertinence; violence; sévérité, dureté, *f.*

rudiment ['ru:dimənt], *n.* Rudiment, élément, *m.* **rudimental** [-'mentl] or **rudimentary,** *a.* Rudimentaire, élémentaire.

Rudolph ['ru:dɔlf]. Rodolphe, *m.*

rue (1) [ru:], *v.t.* Se repentir de, regretter, déplorer. *I rue the day when,* je regrette le jour où.

rue (2) [ru:], *n.* (*Bot.*) Rue, *f.*

rueful ['ru:ful], *a.* Triste, lugubre; lamentable, déplorable. **ruefully,** *adv.* Tristement, déplorablement. **ruefulness,** *n.* Tristesse, *f.*

ruff [rʌf], *n.* Fraise, collerette, *f.*; (*Orn.*) combattant, paon de mer; pigeon à cravate, *m.*; (*Ichth.*) perche, *f.*—*v.t.* (*Cards*) Couper.

ruffian ['rʌfiən], *n.* Bandit, scélérat, *m.*; brute, *f.* **ruffianism,** *n.* Scélératesse, brutalité, *f.* **ruffianly,** *a.* De brigand, brutal.

ruffle [rʌfl], *n.* Manchette en dentelle, ruche, *f.*; (*fig.*) trouble, *m.*, ride, *f.*; appel sur le tambour, *m.*—*v.t.* Froncer (to wrinkle), froisser, chiffonner; (*fig.*) irriter, troubler; mettre en désordre, déranger; ébouriffer (the hair).—*v.i.* Se troubler, s'agiter; s'ébouriffer.

rufous ['ru:fəs], *a.* Roux, *m.*, rousse, *f.* (usually of animals).

rug [rʌg], *n.* Couverture, *f.* *Hearth-rug,* tapis de foyer, *m.*; *travelling rug,* couverture de voyage, *f.*

rugby ['rʌgbi], *n.* (*spt.*) Rugby, *m.* *A rugby player,* un rugbyman, *m.*, (*pl.*) des rugbymen.

rugged ['rʌgid], *a.* Rude; raboteux (uneven); âpre (harsh); bourru (of person). **ruggedly,** *adv.* Rudement; âprement. **ruggedness,** *n.* Nature raboteuse; rudesse, âpreté, *f.*

rugger ['rʌgə], *n.* (*fam.*) Rugby, *m.*

rugose ['ru:gous] or **rugous,** *a.* Rugueux. **rugosity** [-'gɔsiti], *n.* Rugosité, *f.*

ruin ['ru:in], *n.* Ruine; perte, *f.* *To go to ruin,* tomber en ruines, courir à sa perte.—*v.t.* Ruiner. **ruination** [-'neiʃən]. Perte, *f.* **ruinous,** *a.* Ruineux; en ruine, *f.* *To prove ruinous to,* être la ruine de. **ruinously,** *adv.* Ruineusement.

rule [ru:l], *n.* Règle, *f.*; règlement; gouvernement, pouvoir, empire (government); (*Print.*) filet, *m.*; (*Law*) ordonnance, *f.* *As a rule,* en général, en règle générale, d'ordinaire; *by rule of three,* règle de trois; *by the rule of law,* par la voie du droit; *the rule of the road,* le code de la route; *the home rule,* autonomie, *f.*; *there is an exception to every rule,* il n'y a point de règle sans exception; *to lay out by rule and line,* tirer au cordeau; *to make it a rule to,* se faire une règle de; *to work to rule,* faire la grève du zèle.—*v.t.* Régler, diriger; gouverner, régir; (*Law*) décider. *To rule out,* éliminer, écarter.—*v.i.* Gouverner; (*Law*) décider. *To rule over,* régner sur. **rule-cutter,** *n.* (*Print.*) Coupoir, *m.*

ruler, *n.* Gouverneur; gouvernant, souverain, arbitre, *m.*; règle (instrument), *f.*; régleur (workman), *m.* **ruling,** *a.* Dominant, régnant. *Ruling machine,* machine à régler, *f.*—*n.* Réglure, *f.*, réglage, *m.*; (*Law*) ordonnance de juge, décision, *f.*

rum (1) [rʌm], *a.* Drôle; (*colloq.*) cocasse. *A rum fellow,* un drôle de type, un original.

rum (2) [rʌm], *n.* Rhum, *m.* **rum-punch,** *n.* Punch au rhum, *m.*

Rumania [ru:'meinjə]. La Roumanie, *f.*

Rumanian, *a.* and *n.* Roumain, *m.*, -aine, *f.*

rumba ['rʌmbə], *n.* Rumba, *f.*

rumble [rʌmbl], *v.i.* Gronder, gargouiller.—*v.t.* (*pop.*) Deviner les intentions (de quelqu'un).—*n.* Siège de derrière (seat of a carriage), *m.* **rumbling,** *n.* Grondement, roulement; gargouillement, *m.* *Rumblings in the stomach,* des borborygmes, *m.pl.*—*a.* Qui bruit, qui gronde; qui gargouille.

rumbustious [rʌm'bʌstʃəs], *a.* (*fam.*) Turbulent, tapageur.

ruminant ['ru:minənt], *a.* and *n.* Ruminant, *m.* **ruminate,** *v.i.* Ruminer. *To ruminate on,* méditer sur, ruminer. **rumination** [-'neiʃən], *n.* Rumination; (*fig.*) méditation, réflexion, *f.* **ruminative,** *a.* Méditatif.

rummage ['rʌmidʒ], *v.t.* Fouiller, fouiller dans.—*v.i.* Fouiller.—*n.* Remue-ménage, *m.*, fouille, *f.* **rummage-sale,** *n.* Vente d'objets usagés, *f.* **rummaging,** *n.* Visite de la douane à bord, *f.*

rumour ['ru:mə], *n.* Rumeur, *f.*; bruit, *m.* *There is a rumour,* le bruit court.—*v.t.* Faire courir le bruit de. *It is rumoured that,* le bruit court que.

rump [rʌmp], *n.* Croupe; culotte (of meat), *f.*; croupion (of fowl); (*vulg.*) postérieur, *m.*

rumple [rʌmpl], *v.t.* Chiffonner, froisser.—*n.* Pli, *m.*, froissure, *f.*

rump-steak, *n.* Rumpsteak, *m.*

rumpus ['rʌmpəs], *n.* (*colloq.*) Boucan, tapage, *m.* *To have a rumpus with,* avoir une prise de bec avec; *to kick up a rumpus,* faire du chahut.

run [rʌn], *v.i.* (*past* **ran,** *p.p.* **run**) Courir; accourir (to hasten up); se sauver (to flee); s'étendre (to extend); fuir (to leak); couler (to flow); se fondre (of colours); fondre (to melt); être (to be); courir, circuler (to be circulated); faire le service of (public coaches, boats, etc.); marcher, être en marche, fonctionner (of machinery); s'écouler, passer (of time); pleurer (of the eyes); rouler, glisser, tourner (to be on wheels etc.); devenir (to become); se charger (to turn into); être conçu, s'exprimer (of writings); filer (of ships etc.); suppurer (of ulcers etc.); monter (to amount); (*Am.*) se présenter (for an election). *It runs in the blood,* cela est dans le sang; *my watch is run down,* ma montre n'est pas remontée; *run for your lives!* sauve qui peut! *so runs the legal maxim,* ainsi est conçue la maxime légale; *to be hard run,* être serré de près, être aux abois; *to keep running into one's head,* trotter dans la tête. *To run about,* courir çà et là; *to run across,* traverser (en courant), rencontrer par hasard; *to run after,* chercher, rechercher, poursuivre; *to run against,* courir contre, se heurter contre; *to run aground,* échouer; *to run ashore,* échouer; *to run at,* courir sur, attaquer; *to run away,* s'enfuir, se sauver, s'en aller, se débander, prendre le mors aux dents, s'emballer (of horses), s'écouler (of liquids etc.); *to run away with*, emporter, enlever; *to run away with the idea*, se mettre dans la tête, s'imaginer; *to run back*, retourner *or* revenir en courant, retourner vite, reculer; *to run counter to*, aller à l'encontre de; *to run down*, descendre en courant, aller, venir, couler (of liquids); *to run down with wet*, ruisseler, dégoutter; *to run for*, courir chercher; *to run from*, s'enfuir de; *to run headlong into a trap*, donner tête baissée dans un piège; *to run high*, être en fureur, être haute (of the sea); *to run in*, entrer, entrer précipitamment; *to run into*, entrer dans, se jeter dans, tomber dans (danger etc.), se réfugier dans, (*Rail.*) tamponner, se livrer à (dissipation); *to run into debt*, s'endetter, faire des dettes; *to run into money*, coûter de l'argent; *to run off*, s'enfuir, se sauver, s'écouler (of liquids); *to run off the line*, dérailler; *to run on*, courir en avant, continuer, aller toujours, parler sans cesse, parler toujours, rouler sur, porter sur (to refer to); *to run on all fours with*, être en tous points comparable à; *to run out*, courir dehors, sortir, couler, fuir, se terminer, expirer, tirer à sa fin (to expire), descendre (of the tide); *to run out of*, être à sec de, n'avoir plus de, épuiser; *to run out only for an instant*, ne faire que sortir et rentrer; *to run over*, déborder (of liquids etc.); *to run through*, passer à travers de, parcourir, manger, dissiper, gaspiller, traverser (to dissipate); *to run to seed*, monter en graine; *to run up*, courir en haut, monter; *to run up to*, s'élever à, monter à (to amount to); *to run upon*, rouler sur, porter sur, donner sur; *words ran high between them*, ils en sont venus aux gros mots.

v.t.—Courir, encourir (to incur); faire courir, faire marcher, conduire (to drive etc.); faire arriver (trains); pousser, enfoncer, fourrer (to drive, thrust, etc.); passer (to cause to pass); faire fondre, couler (to cast); faire entrer, faire passer (to smuggle); faire (so many miles an hour); jeter (to throw); chasser; parcourir, suivre, poursuivre (to pursue); diriger, exploiter, tenir. *I ran my head against the wall*, je me suis cogné la tête contre le mur; *the money to run the mines*, les fonds pour l'exploitation des mines; *to run a race*, faire une course; *to run a risk*, courir un risque; *to run a sword through*, passer une épée à travers le corps de; *to run a thorn into one's foot*, s'enfoncer une épine dans le pied; *to run down*, couler bas, couler à fond (a ship); décrier, dénigrer (to decry), (*Hunt.*) forcer; *to run for*, courir chercher; *to run foul of*, aborder, se heurter contre; *to run hard*, presser, serrer de près; *to run in*, enfoncer, entrer (a ship) au port, arrêter, coffrer; *to run into debt*, endetter; *to run into difficulties*, jeter dans des difficultés; *to run out*, faire sortir, épuiser (to exhaust), dissiper (to waste), étendre (to extend); *to run over*, passer sur, (*Motor.*) écraser (a person, an animal), examiner rapidement, parcourir (a book); *to run through*, percer, percer d'outre en outre, transpercer, parcourir (to peruse); *to run up*, monter en courant, élever, bâtir (to build), faire monter (an account).

n.—Course (act of running), *f.*; cours, *m.*,

suite (series), *f.*; courant (course); trajet, voyage (transit etc.), *m.*; vogue, durée, *f.*, succès (success), *m.*; irruption, *f.* (on a bank etc.); ordinaire, commun (generality), *m.*; veine (at play), *f.*; gisement (of lodes), *m.* *In the long run*, à la longue, à la fin; *the common run*, le commun, *m.*, la généralité, *f.*; *to be on the run*, être recherché par la police; *to get a run for one's money*, en avoir pour son argent; *to get the run upon*,   tourner en ridicule; *to go for a run*, faire une course, courir; *to have a great run*, être très couru, avoir beaucoup de succès; *to have had their run*, avoir eu leur temps (of books etc.); *to have the run of*, avoir ses entrées à.

runaway ['rʌnəwei], *n.* Fuyard, *m.*; fugitif, *m.*, fugitive, *f.*, déserteur, *m.* *Runaway horse*, cheval emballé, *m.*; *runaway slave*, esclave fugitif, *m.*

rune [ru:n], *n.* Rune, *f.*

rung (1) [rʌŋ], *n.* Échelon, barreau (of a ladder); bâton (of a chair etc.), *m.*

rung (2), *p.p.* [RING (2)].

runic ['ru:nik], *a.* Runique.

runlet ['rʌnlit], *n.* *Barillet; ruisseau, *m.*

runner ['rʌnə], *n.* Coureur; messager, courrier; coulant (of an umbrella etc.); (*Bot.*) rejeton, stolon; (*Mil.*) agent de liaison, *m.*; (*Naut.*) itague, poulie fixe, *f.* *Scarlet runner*, haricot d'Espagne, *m.* **runner-up**, *n.* Second, *m.*

running, *n.* Course, *f.*; écoulement (flow), *m.*; suppuration (of wounds), *f.*; (*Needlework*) point devant; service (of trains etc.), *m.* *Running about*, allées et venues, *f.pl.*; *running aground or ashore*, échouement, échouage, *m.*; *running away*, désertion, fuite, *f.*; *running foul*, abordage, *m.*; *running off the rails*, déraillement, *m.*—*a.* Courant; consécutif, de suite (consecutive); courant (of knots etc.); à échoir (of bills); en suppuration (of wounds). *He ran three days running*, il vint trois jours de suite; *running account*, compte courant, *m.*; *running fight*, combat en chasse, *m.*; *running horse*, cheval de course, *m.*; *running knot*, nœud coulant, *m.*; *running rigging*, manœuvres courantes, *f.pl.*; *running title*, titre courant, *m.* **running-board**, *n.* Marchepied (of car), tablier (of railway carriage), *m.* **running fire**, *n.* Feu roulant, *m.* **running-track**, *n.* Piste, *f.*

runt [rʌnt], *n.* Bétail petit *or* chétif; (*fig.*) avorton, nain, *m.*

runway ['rʌnwei], *n.* Chemin de roulement (of machines), *m.*; rampe (for loading); (*Av.*) piste d'envol, *f.*

rupee [ru:'pi:], *n.* Roupie, *f.*

rupture ['rʌptʃə], *n.* Rupture, hernie, *f.*—*v.t.* Rompre. *To be ruptured*, avoir une hernie. —*v.i.* Se rompre. **rupture-wort**, *n.* (*Bot.*) Herniaire, *f.*

rural ['ruərəl], *a.* Champêtre, rural, rustique. *Rural district*, commune rurale, *f.*; *rural postman*, facteur rural, *m.* **ruralist**, *n.* Habitant de la campagne, *m.* **rurally**, *adv.* Rustiquement.

ruse [ru:z], *n.* Ruse, *f.*, stratagème, *m.*

rush (1) [rʌʃ], *n.* Jonc; fétu, rien (thing of trivial value), *m.* *Not to be worth a rush*, ne pas valoir un rouge liard. **rush-bottomed**, *a.* (Chaise) paillée. **rush-broom**, *n.* Genêt d'Espagne, *m.* **rush-light**, *n.* Veilleuse, *f.*

rushlike, *a.* Comme un jonc, faible comme un jonc. **rush-mat,** *n.* Natte de jonc, *f.* **rushy,** *a.* Plein de joncs, de jonc.

rush (2) [rʌʃ], *n.* Élan, mouvement précipité (motion), *m.*; foule, presse (crowd), *f.* *There is a rush for the papers,* on s'arrache les journaux; *there was a rush for,* on se précipita vers, on se rua vers; *to avoid the rush hours,* éviter les heures d'affluence.—*v.i.* Se jeter, se ruer, se précipiter (sur). *To rush forward,* s'élancer en avant, se précipiter en avant; *to rush in,* se précipiter dans, s'élancer dans; *to rush on,* se précipiter sur; *to rush out,* se précipiter dehors, sortir précipitamment; *to rush through,* s'élancer à travers, expédier; *to rush up,* accourir, monter à toute vitesse; *to rush upon,* se précipiter sur.—*v.t.* Entraîner brusquement; dépêcher, expédier; envahir; prendre d'assaut; brusquer; (*pop.*) écorcher, estamper. *The crowd rushed the hall,* la foule envahit la salle; *the troops rushed a hill,* les troupes prirent d'assaut une colline; *they rushed you for that hat,* on vous a estampé pour ce chapeau; *to rush a friend out,* brusquer le départ d'un ami; *to rush an order,* expédier une commande; *to rush some-one into an affair,* entraîner quelqu'un dans une affaire. **rushed,** *a.* Débordé de travail (of persons), bâclé (of a task).

rushing, *n.* Élan, *m.*, précipitation, impétuosité, *f.*—*a.* Impétueux.

rusk [rʌsk], *n.* Biscotte, *f.*

russet ['rʌsit], *a.* Roussâtre; *grossier, rustique (rustic).—n.* Roux, *m.*; reinette grise (apple), *f.* **russety,** *a.* Roussâtre.

Russia ['rʌʃə]. La Russie, *f.*

Russian (1) ['rʌʃən], *a.* Russe, de Russie; (*pers.*) Russe, *m.* or *f.*; russe (language), *m.* **Russian** (2) or **Russia,** *n.* Cuir de Russie, *m.*

rust [rʌst], *n.* Rouille, *f.* *To get the rust off,* dérouiller.—*v.i.* Se rouiller.—*v.t.* Rouiller.

rustic ['rʌstik], *a.* Rustique, champêtre.—*n.* Rustre, paysan, *m.* **rustically,** *adv.* Rustiquement.

rusticate ['rʌstikeit], *v.i.* Se retirer à or habiter la campagne.—*v.t.* Reléguer à la campagne; (*Univ.*) renvoyer temporairement. *To be rusticating,* être en villégiature. **rusticated,** *a.* Relégué à la campagne; (*Univ.*) renvoyé temporairement. **rustication,** *n.* Villégiature, *f.*; (*Univ.*) renvoi temporaire, *m.*

rusticity [rʌs'tisiti], *n.* Simplicité, rusticité, *f.*

rustiness ['rʌstinis], *n.* Rouille; rancissure (of bacon etc.), *f.*

rustle [rʌsl], *v.i.* Bruire, frémir; faire frou-frou, frou-frouter (of dresses). *To rustle against,* frôler.—*v.t.* (*Am.*) Voler (du bétail). —*n.* Frôlement; bruissement; frou-frou (of dresses), *m.*

rustler, *n.* (*Am.*) Voleur de bétail, *m.*

rustless ['rʌstlis], *a.* Inoxydable.

rustling ['rʌsliŋ], *a.* Qui fait frou-frou, frémissant.—*n.* (*Am.*) Vol de bétail, *m.*

rusty ['rʌsti], *a.* Rouillé; usé, vieilli (worn out); rance, moisi (musty); couleur de rouille, roux (in colour). (*fam.*) *My German is a bit rusty,* je suis un peu rouillé en allemand; *to get rusty,* se rouiller; *to turn rusty,* (*fam.*) renâcler, regimber.

rut [rʌt], *n.* Ornière (in a road), *f.*; rut (of deer etc.), *m.* (*fig.*) *To get into a rut,* s'encroûter. —*v.t.* Sillonner d'ornières.—*v.i.* Être en rut.

ruthless ['ruːθlis], *a.* Impitoyable, implacable, insensible. **ruthlessly,** *adv.* Sans pitié, sans merci. **ruthlessness,** *n.* Cruauté, inhumanité, *f.*

rutting ['rʌtiŋ], *n.* Rut, *m.* **rutting-season,** *n.* Temps du rut, *m.*

rye [rai], *n.* Seigle, *m.* **rye-bread,** *n.* Pain de seigle, *m.* **rye-grass,** *n.* Ivraie, *f.*, ray-grass, *m.*

ryepeck ['raipek], *n.* Perche, gaffe (d'amarrage), *f.*

ryot ['raiət], *n.* (*India*) Ryot, cultivateur, *m.*

S

S, s [es]. Dix-neuvième lettre de l'alphabet, *m.* **'s** (instead of *es*) possessive case. *Peter's book,* le livre de Pierre; (instead of *is, has, us*) *what's the matter?* qu'est-ce qu'il y a? *he's got one,* il en a un; *let's play,* jouons! (instead of God's, in oaths) *'s death,* morbleu!

Saar [saː]. La Sarre, *f.* *The industries of the Saar,* les industries sarroises.

Sabaean [sə'biːən], *a. and n.* Sabéen, *m.*, Sabéenne, *f.*

Sabaism ['seibəizm], *n.* Sabéisme, sabisme, *m.*

Sabbatarian [sæbə'teəriən], *n.* Rigide observateur du dimanche, *m.*

Sabbath ['sæbəθ], *n.* (*Jews*) Sabbat; dimanche; (*fig.*) repos, *m.* **sabbath-breaker,** *n.* Violateur du sabbat, *m.*

sabbatic [sə'bætik] or **sabbatical,** *a.* Sabbatique, du sabbat. (*Univ.*) *Sabbatical year,* année de congé de recherches, *f.*

sable [seibl], *n.* Martre, zibeline, *f.*; (*Her.*) sable; (*fig.*) vêtement de deuil, *m.*—*a.* De zibeline, de martre; (*Her.*) de sable; (*fig.*) noir, sombre, de deuil.

sabot ['sæbou], *n.* Sabot, *m.*

sabotage ['sæbətaːʒ], *n.* Sabotage, *m.*—*v.t.* Saboter. **saboteur,** *n.* Saboteur, *m.*

sabre ['seibə], *n.* Sabre, *m.*—*v.t.* Sabrer. **sabre-cut,** *n.* Coup de sabre, *m.*; balafre (of scar), *f.* **sabre-fish,** *n.* Trichiure, *f.*

sabretache ['sæbətæʃ], *n.* Sabretache, *f.*

sabre-toothed, *a.* Mâchérode (of tiger), *m.*

***saburra** [sə'bʌrə], *n.* Saburre, *f.* **saburral,** *a.* Saburral.

sac [sæk], *n.* (*Anat.*) Sac, *m.*; bourse, *f.*

saccharate ['sækərət], *n.* Saccharate, *m.*

saccharic [sə'kærik], *a.* Saccharique.

sacchariferous [sækə'rifərəs], *a.* Saccharifère.

saccharify [sə'kærifai], *v.t.* Saccharifier.

saccharimeter [sækə'rimitə], *n.* Saccharimètre, *m.*

saccharine ['sækərin], *n.* Saccharine, *f.*—*a.* Sacchareux. **saccharism,** *n.* Saccharisme, *m.* **saccharoid,** *a.* Saccharoïde.

sacciform ['sæksifɔːm], *a.* Sacciforme.

sacerdotal [sæsə'doutl], *a.* Sacerdotal.

sack [sæk], *n.* Sac; *vin de Xérès (wine); sac, saccagement, *n.* (of a town); paletot sac, *m.* *To get the sack,* (*colloq.*) être renvoyé; *to give the sack to,* renvoyer, congédier, donner son compte à.—*v.t.* Saccager, mettre à sac; (*colloq.*) renvoyer, mettre à la porte, congédier. **sackcloth,** *n.* Toile à sac, *f.* *Sackcloth and ashes,* le sac et la cendre. **sackful,** *n.* Sac plein, *m.*, sachée, *f.* **sacking,** *n.* Sac,

saccagement (of a town), *m.*; toile à sac, *f.*
sack-race, *n.* Course en sac, *f.*
sacral ['seikrəl], *a.* (*Anat.*) Du sacrum; sacré.
sacrament ['sækrəmənt], *n.* Sacrement, *m.* *To administer the last sacrament to,* administrer les derniers sacrements à; *to receive the sacrament,* communier. **sacramental** [-'mentl], *a.* Sacramentel. **sacramentally,** *adv.* Sacramentellement. **sacramentarian** [-'teəriən] or **sacramentary** [-'mentəri], *n.* Sacramentaire, *m.*
sacred ['seikrid], *a.* Sacré; saint (of history etc.); (*fig.*) inviolable. *Sacred to,* consacré à. **sacredly,** *adv.* Saintement; religieusement. **sacredness,** *n.* Sainteté, *f.*, caractère sacré, *m.*
sacrifice ['sækrifais], *v.t., v.i.* Sacrifier.—*n.* Sacrifice, *m.*; victime, *f. To fall a sacrifice to,* être victime de; *to sell one's stock at a sacrifice,* vendre ses marchandises au-dessous du cours, à perte. **sacrificer,** *n.* Sacrificateur, *m.* **sacrificial** [-'fiʃl] or ***sacrificatory** ['sækrifikeitəri], *a.* Des sacrifices, sacrificatoire.
sacrilege ['sækrilidʒ], *n.* Sacrilège, *m.* **sacrilegious** [-'lidʒəs], *a.* Sacrilège. **sacrilegiously,** *adv.* D'une manière sacrilège. **sacrilegiousness,** *n.* Caractère sacrilège, *m.*
sacristan ['sækristən], **sacrist** ['seikrist], *n.* Sacristain, *m.* **sacristy,** *n.* Sacristie, *f.*
sacro-iliac [sækrou'iliæk], *a.* (*Anat.*) Sacro-iliaque.
sacrosanct ['sækrousæŋkt], *a.* Sacro-saint.
sad [sæd], *a.* Triste; pitoyable, déplorable; cruel (of losses). *He is a sad fellow,* c'est un triste sire; *to get sad,* s'attrister, devenir triste; *to make sad,* attrister. **sadden,** *v.t.* Attrister. —*v.i.* S'attrister.
saddle [sædl], *n.* Selle, *f.*; (*Naut.*) croissant, *m.*; selle (of mutton), *f. In the saddle,* en selle; *pack-saddle,* bât, *m.*; *side-saddle,* selle d'amazone, *f.*; *to put the saddle on the wrong horse,* accuser quelqu'un à faux.—*v.t.* Seller; charger, accabler; mettre sur le dos à (to load). *Saddle my nag,* (game) cheval fondu, *m.*; *to be saddled with,* avoir sur le dos; *to saddle with,* charger de, mettre sur le dos à, faire porter; *to sound the boot and saddle,* sonner le boute-selle.
saddle-back, *a.* Ensellé, en dos d'âne (of a roof). **saddle-bag,** *n.* Sacoche, *f.* **saddle-bow,** *n.* Arçon, *m.* **saddle-cloth,** *n.* Housse (de cheval), *f.* **saddle-horse,** *n.* Cheval de selle, *m.* **saddle-maker,** *n.* Sellier, *m.* **saddler,** *n.* Sellier, bourrellier, *m.* **saddle-room,** *n.* Sellerie, *f.* **saddlery,** *n.* Sellerie, *f.*, harnachement, *m.* **saddle-shaped,** *a.* En dos d'âne. **saddle-tree,** *n.* Arçon, bois de selle, *m.*
Sadducean [sædju'si:ən], *a.* Sad(d)ucéen. **Sadducee** ['sædjusi:], *n.* Sad(d)ucéen, *m.*, -céenne, *f.* **Sadduceeism,** *n.* Sad(d)ucéisme, *m.*
sad-iron, *n.* Fer à repasser, *m.*
sadism ['seidizm], *n.* Sadisme, *m.* **sadist,** *n.* Sadique. **sadistic** [sə'distik], *a.* Sadique.
sadly ['sædli], *adv.* Tristement; mal, beaucoup, grandement. *Sadly hurt,* grièvement blessé; *to be sadly in want of,* avoir grand besoin de. **sadness,** *n.* Tristesse, *f.*
safari [sə'fɑːri], *n.* (*In Africa*) Expédition de chasse, *f.*

safe [seif], *a.* Sauf, en sûreté, hors de danger; à l'abri (de); sûr, de sûreté. *It is not safe to,* il n'est pas prudent de; *it's as safe as houses,* c'est de l'or en barres, c'est une affaire sûre; *safe and sound,* sain et sauf; *safe bind, safe find,* la méfiance est mère de la sûreté; *safe from,* à l'abri de, en sûreté contre; *to be on the safe side,* être du bon côté; *your money is safe in his hands,* votre argent est en sûreté entre ses mains.—*n.* Coffre-fort (for money), *m.*, caisse, caisse de sûreté, *f.*; garde-manger (for meat), *m.*
safe-conduct, *n.* Sauf-conduit, *m.* **safeguard,** *n.* Sauvegarde, *f.*, sauf-conduit, *m.* —*v.t.* Sauvegarder. **safe-keeping,** *n.* Bonne garde, sûreté, *f.* **safely,** *adv.* Sain et sauf; sans accident; en sûreté, en toute sécurité; en lieu sûr; sans danger. **safeness,** *n.* Sûreté, sécurité, *f.*
safety ['seifti], *n.* Sûreté, *f.*, salut (preservation), *m. Committee of public safety,* comité de salut public, *m.*; *public safety,* la sûreté publique; *to seek safety in flight,* chercher son salut dans la fuite.—*a.* De sûreté.
safety-catch, *n.* Cran de sûreté, cran d'arrêt, *m.* **safety-device,** *n.* Dispositif de sûreté, *m.* **safety-lamp,** *n.* Lampe de sûreté, *f.* **safety-match,** *n.* Allumette suédoise, *f.* **safety-pin,** *n.* Épingle de sûreté, *f.* **safety-plug,** *n.* Bouchon fusible, *m.* **safety-valve,** *n.* Soupape de sûreté, *f.*
safflower ['sæflauə], *n.* Carthame, *m.*
saffron ['sæfrən], *n.* Safran, *m. Meadow saffron,* colchique, *m.*—*a.* Couleur safran; de safran.—*v.t.* Safraner. **saffron-plantation,** *n.* Safranière, *f.* **saffrony,** *a.* Safrané.
sag [sæg], *v.i.* Plier, ployer, s'affaisser; (*Naut.*) contre-arquer (of ship); se relâcher (of cable); courber (of a roof); pendre (of breasts); baisser, fléchir (of prices).—*n.* Affaissement, fléchissement, *m.*; baisse, *f.*
saga ['sɑːgə], *n.* Saga, *f.*
sagacious [sə'geiʃəs], *a.* Sagace; intelligent (of animals). **sagaciously,** *adv.* Avec sagacité. **sagaciousness** or **sagacity** [sə'gæsiti], *n.* Sagacité, *f.*
sage (1) [seidʒ], *n.* Sauge (herb), *f.*
sage (2) [seidʒ], *a.* Sage, prudent.—*n.* Sage, *m.* **sagely,** *adv.* Sagement, prudemment.
saggar ['sægə], *n.* Casette (for pottery), *f.*
sagging ['sægin], *n.* Courbure, *f.*, affaissement, *m.*; baisse (of prices), *f.*—*a.* Affaissé, fléchi, ployé.
sagittal ['sædʒitl] or ***sagittary,** *a.* Sagittal. **Sagittarius** [-'teəriəs], *n.* (*Astron.*) Le Sagittaire, *m.*
sagittate ['sædʒitət], *a.* (*Bot.*) Sagitté.
sago ['seigou], *n.* Sagou, *m.* **sago-tree,** *n.* Sagouier, sagoutier, *m.*
sagy ['seidʒi], *a.* Plein de sauge; qui a un goût de sauge.
saic ['seiik], *n.* (*Naut.*) Saïque, *f.*
said [sed], *a.* Dit, susdit [SAY].
sail [seil], *n.* Voile, *f.*; (*collect.*) voiles, *f.pl.*, voilure; aile (of a windmill); voile (ship); course *or* promenade à la voile (on the water), *f.*; vaisseau (ship), *m.* Foresail, misaine, voile de misaine, *f.*; *full sail,* à voiles déployées; *gallant-sail,* voile de perroquet; *mainsail,* grande voile; *to crowd all sail,* faire force de voiles; *to make sail,* appareiller; *topsail,* hunier, *m.*; *to set a sail,* établir une voile; *to*

set sail, mettre à la voile; *to shorten sail,* diminuer de voiles; *to strike sail,* amener les voiles, (*fig.*) baisser pavillon; *to take in a sail,* rentrer une voile; *to take the wind out of somebody's sails,* dégonfler quelqu'un; *to unbend a sail,* déverguer une voile; *under sail,* à la voile, sous voiles.—*v.i.* Faire voile; cingler, naviguer; aller, voguer (avec); mettre à la voile, appareiller. *To be about to sail,* être en partance; *to sail about,* croiser (cruise), se promener (for pleasure); *to sail along the coast of,* côtoyer; *to sail close to the wind,* serrer le vent, (*fig.*) friser l'indécent; *to sail down,* descendre (a river); *to sail from A to B,* faire la traversée d'A à B; *to sail in company with,* aller de conserve avec; *to sail round the world,* faire le tour du monde; *to sail twelve knots,* filer douze nœuds; *to sail under false colours,* se faire passer pour ce qu'on n'est pas; *to sail up,* remonter.—*v.t.* Naviguer (sur), voguer (sur or dans).

sailable, *a.* Navigable. **sail-cloth,** *n.* Toile à voiles, *f.* **sailer,** *n.* Voilier, *m. Fast or heavy sailer,* bon *or* mauvais voilier. **sailing,** *n.* Navigation; marche (speed), *f.* appareillage (setting sail), *m.*; partance (departure), *f.*; (*pl.*) départs; bâtiments en partance, *m.pl.* (*fam.*) *It's plain sailing,* cela va tout seul.—*a.* À voiles. **sailing-boat,** *n.* Bateau à voiles, *m.* **sailing-match,** *n.* Course à la voile, *f.* **sailing-ship,** *n.* Bâtiment à voiles, *m. Fast sailing-ship,* fin voilier, *m.* **sail-loft,** *n.* Voilerie, *f.* **sail-maker,** *n.* Voilier, *m.* **sail-making,** *n.* Voilerie, *f.*

sailor, *n.* Marin, *m. Freshwater sailor,* marin d'eau douce; *to be a good sailor,* avoir le pied marin.

sail-yard, *n.* Vergue, *f.*

sainfoin ['seinfoin], *n.* (Bot.) Sainfoin, *m.*

saint [seint] strong form, [sənt, sint, snt, sn] weak forms, *n.* Saint, *m.*, sainte, *f. All Saints' Day,* la Toussaint, *f.*; *one's saint's day,* sa fête, *f.*; *St. John* [snt'dʒɔn *or* sn'dʒɔn], *Saint Jean; Saint John's wort* [sint'dʒɔnz wəːt], mille-pertuis, *m.*, herbe de Saint-Jean, *f.*; *Saint Swithin's* ['swiðinz] *Day,* la Saint-Médard; *Saint Vitus's dance,* la danse de Saint-Guy, *f.*

Saint Angelo [snt'ændʒəlou]. Saint-Ange, *m.*

Saint Domingo [snt də'miŋgou]. (*Geog.*) Saint-Domingue, *m.*

sainted, *a.* Saint, sacré. *My sainted aunt!* Dieu du ciel! **sainthood** or **saintliness,** *n.* Sainteté, *f.* **saintly,** *a.* Saint; de saint, vénérable. *To put on a saintly look,* faire le bon apôtre, prendre un air de petit saint.

Saint George's Channel [snt'dʒɔːrdʒiz]. Le Canal Saint-Georges, *m.*

Saint Helena [sent ə'liːnə]. (*Geog.*) Sainte-Hélène, *f.*

Saint Lawrence [snt 'lɔrəns]. (*Geog.*) Le Saint-Laurent, *m.*

Saint-Simonian [sentsi'mounjən], *a.* and *n.* Saint-Simonien, *m.* **Saint-Simonianism,** *n.* Saint-Simonisme, *m.*

sake [seik], *n.* (used only with for). *Art for art's sake,* l'art pour l'art; *for brevity's sake,* rien que pour la brièveté; *for charity's sake,* par charité; *for conscience' sake,* par acquit de conscience; *for form's sake,* pour la forme; *for God's sake,* pour l'amour de Dieu; *for goodness' sake,* par grâce; *for my sake,* pour

moi, en mémoire de moi; *for old times' sake,* en souvenir du passé; *for pity's sake,* par pitié; *for the sake of annoying me,* pour le plaisir de me vexer; *for the sake of appearances,* pour sauver les apparences; *for the sake of going there,* pour le plaisir d'y aller; *for the sake of health,* pour cause de santé; *for your sake,* par égard pour vous, à cause de vous, pour vous.

saker ['seikə], *n.* Sacre (bird), *m.* **sakeret,** *n.* Sacret, *m.*

sal [sæl], *n.* Sel, *m. Sal ammoniac,* sel ammoniac, *m.*; *sal volatile,* (*fam.*) sels (à respirer), *m.pl.*

salaam [sə'lɑːm], *n.* Salamalec, *m.*

salacious [sə'leiʃəs], *a.* Salace, lubrique.

salacity [sə'læsiti], *n.* Salacité, *f.*

salad ['sæləd], *n.* Salade, *f. Fruit salad,* salade de fruits, *f.* **salad-bowl,** *n.* Saladier, *m.* **salad-days,** *n.pl.* Années d'inexpérience, *f.pl.* **salad-dressing,** *n.* Vinaigrette, *f.,* assaisonnement pour la salade, *m.* **salad-oil,** *n.* Huile de table, *f.*

Salamanca [sælə'mæŋkə]. Salamanque, *f.*

salamander ['sæləmændə], *n.* Salamandre, *f.*

salaried ['sælərid], *a.* Qui touche des appointements.

salary ['sæləri], *n.* Appointements, *m.pl.*; traitement (of functionaries), *m.*—*v.t.* Payer un traitement à.

sale [seil], *n.* Vente; mise en vente; liquidation, *f. Bargain sale,* vente réclame, vente au rabais, *f.*; soldes, *m.pl.*; *bill of sale,* lettre de vente, *f.*; *deed of sale,* contrat de vente, *m.*; *for sale,* à vendre; *on sale,* en vente; *on sale or return,* en dépôt, en communication; *private sale,* vente à l'amiable, *f.*; *ready sale,* prompt débit, *m.*; *sale by auction,* vente aux enchères, *f.*; *to command a ready sale,* être de bonne vente; *to put up for sale,* mettre en vente.

saleable, *a.* Vendable; de bonne vente.

saleableness, *n.* Facilité de vente, *f.*

salep ['sæləp], *n.* Salep, *m.*

sale-room, *n.* Salle des ventes, *f.* **sale-work,** *n.* Ouvrage de pacotille, *m.*

salesman ['seilzmən], *n.* (*pl.* **salesmen**) Vendeur, marchand; courtier de commerce (agent), *m.* **salesmanship,** *n.* L'art de vendre, *m.* **sales-talk,** *n.* Boniment, *m.* **saleswoman,** (*pl.* **saleswomen**), **salesgirl** ['seilzgəːl] or **saleslady** (*Am.*), *n.* Vendeuse, *f.*

Salic ['sælik], *a.* Salique.

salient ['seiliənt], *a.* Qui saute; saillant (projecting).—*n.* Saillant, *m. Blunted salient,* redan à pan coupé, *m.* **saliently,** *adv.* D'une manière saillante.

saliferous [sə'lifərəs], *a.* Salifère.

salifiable ['sælifaiəbl], *a.* Salifiable. **salification** [-fi'keiʃən], *n.* Salification, *f.*

salify ['sælifai], *v.t.* Salifier.

saline (1) ['seilain], *a.* Salin. **saline** (2) [sə'lain], *n.* Source salée, *f.* **salinity** [-'liniti], *n.* Salinité, *f.* **salinometer** [sæli'nɔmitə], *n.* Salinomètre, *m.*

saliva [sə'laivə], *n.* Salive, *f.*

salivary ['sælivəri] or **salival, a.* Salivaire. **salivate,** *v.t.* Faire saliver. **salivation** [-'veiʃən], *n.* Salivation, *f.*

sallow ['sælou], *a.* Jaunâtre, jaune, blême.—*n.*

sally (*Bot.*) Saule, *m.* **sallowness,** *n.* Teint blême, *m.*

sally ['sæli], *n.* Sortie; (*fig.*) excursion; saillie (of wit), *f.*; trait d'esprit; écart, *m.*, escapade, *f.* (of youth etc.), branle, *m.* (of bell).—*v.i.* Sortir, faire une sortie. **sally-port,** *n.* Poterne, *f.*; (*Naut.*) sabord de fuite (in a fire-ship), *m.*

salmagundi [sælmə'gʌndi], *n.* Salmigondis, *m.*

salmon ['sæmən], *n.* Saumon, *m.* **salmon-fishery** or **salmon-fishing,** *n.* Pêche du saumon, *f.* **salmon-peal,** *n.* Saumoneau, *m.* **salmon-trout,** *n.* Truite saumonée, *f.*

Salonica [sælə'ni:kə]. Salonique, *f.*

saloon [sə'lu:n], *n.* (Grand) salon, *m.*, salle, *f.*; (*Am.*) buvette, *f.*, bar, *m.*; conduite-intérieure (car), *f.* **saloon-carriage,** *n.* Wagon-salon, *m.* **saloon-passenger,** *n.* (*Naut.*) Voyageur de première classe, *m.*

salsify ['sælsifi], *n.* (*Bot.*) Salsifis, *m.*

salt [sɔ:lt], *n.* Sel, *m.* *Attic salt,* sel attique; *Epsom salts,* sels anglais, *m.pl.*; *not to be worth one's salt,* ne pas valoir le pain qu'on mange; *old salt,* vieux marin, loup de mer, *m.*; *smelling salts,* sels, *m.pl.*; *the salt of the earth,* la crème, l'élite, *f.*, le sel de la terre; *to take with a pinch of salt,* croire avec quelques réserves, prendre avec un grain de sel.—*a.* Salé; de sel.—*v.t.* To salt (*down*), saler; *to salt away money,* mettre de l'argent à gauche.

saltarello [sæltə'relou], *n.* Saltarelle (dance), *f.*

saltation [sæl'teiʃən], *n.* Action de sauter (leaping); palpitation (palpitation), *f.*

salt-box, *n.* Boîte à sel, *f.* **salt-cellar,** *n.* Salière, *f.* **salted,** *a.* Salé; (*fig.*) aguerri. **salter,** *n.* Saunier; saleur (drysalter), *m.* **salting,** *n.* Salaison, *f.*, salage, *m.* **salting-tub,** *n.* Saloir, *m.* **saltish,** *a.* Un peu salé, saumâtre. **saltishness,** *n.* Goût salin, *m.* **saltless,** *a.* Sans sel; (*fig.*) insipide. **salt-marsh,** *n.* Marais salant, *m.* **salt-mine,** *n.* Mine de sel, *f.* **saltness,** *n.* Salure, *f.* **salt-pit,** *n.* Saline, *f.* **salt-water,** *n.* Eau de mer, *f.* *Salt-water fish,* poisson de mer, *m.* **salt-works,** *n.* Saline, *f.* **saltwort,** *n.* (*Bot.*) Soude; salicorne, *f.* **salty,** *a.* Salé; qui a un goût de sel; piqué.

saltire ['sæltaiə], *n.* (*Her.*) Sautoir, *m.* **saltire-wise,** *adv.* and *a.* En sautoir.

saltpetre [sɔ:lt'pi:tə], *n.* Salpêtre, *m.* **salt-petre-maker,** *n.* Salpêtrier, *m.* **saltpetre-making,** *n.* Salpêtrage, *f.* **saltpetre-works,** *n.pl.* Salpêtrière, *f.* **saltpetrous,** *a.* Salpêtreux.

salubrious [sə'lju:briəs], *a.* Salubre, sain. **salubriously,** *adv.* D'une manière salubre. **salubrity,** *n.* Salubrité, *f.*

salutary ['sæljutəri], *a.* Salutaire.

salutation [sælju'teiʃən], *n.* Salut, *m.*, salutation, *f.*

salute [sə'lju:t], *n.* Salut, *m.*, salutation, salve (of guns), *f.* *To beat a salute,* battre aux champs; *to fire a salute,* tirer une salve.—*v.t.* Saluer. **saluter,** *n.* Personne qui salue, *f.*

salvage ['sælvidʒ], *n.* Sauvetage, *m.*, objets sauvés, *m.pl.*; récupération (in industry), *f.* *Salvage loss,* perte sèche, *f.*—*v.t.* Récupérer; sauveter, relever (a ship). **salvage-money,** *n.* Prix (or droit) de sauvetage, *m.* **salvage-vessel,** *n.* Navire de relevage, *m.*

salvation [sæl'veiʃən], *n.* Salut, *m.* *Salvation Army,* Armée du Salut, *f.* **salvationist,** *n.* Membre de l'Armée du Salut, *m.*, salutiste, *m.* or *f.*

salve (1) [sælv or sɑ:v], *n.* Onguent; (*fig.*) remède, baume, *m.* *Lip-salve,* pommade pour les lèvres, *f.*—*v.t.* Guérir avec des onguents; remédier à.

salve (2) [sælv], *v.t.* (*Naut.*) Sauver, sauveter.

salver ['sælvə], *n.* Plateau, *m.*

salvo ['sælvou], *n.* Réserve, restriction; salve, rafale (of artillery), *f.* *To fire a salvo,* tirer une salve.

salvor ['sælvə], *n.* Sauveteur, *m.*

Sam Browne [sæm'braun], *n.* Ceinturon et baudrier d'officier.

Samaria [sə'mɛəriə]. Samarie (town); La Samarie (country), *f.*

Samaritan [sə'mæritən], *a.* and *n.* Samaritain, *m.*, -taine, *f.*

samba ['sæmbə], *n.* Samba, *f.*

sambo ['sæmbou], *n.* (*pej.*) Noir, moricaud, *m.*

sambuca [sæm'bju:kə], *n.* Sambuque, *f.*

same [seim], *a.* Même.—*n.* Le, la même; même chose, *f.*; ledit, *m.*, ladite, *f.*, lesdits; lesdites, *pl.* *All the same,* néanmoins, quand même; *it is all the same,* c'est égal, c'est tout un; *it is all the same to me,* cela m'est égal; *it is the same as saying,* cela revient à dire; *just the same,* tout de même, comme d'habitude; *much about the same,* à peu près de même; *same here,* et moi de même; *the same,* ledit, ladite, etc., la même chose; *the same to you,* et vous de même; *the very same,* le même; *to come to the same,* revenir au même; *to do the same,* faire de même, en faire autant.

sameness ['seimnis], *n.* Identité; uniformité, monotonie (uniformity), *f.*

samlet ['sæmlit], *n.* Saumoneau, *m.*

sampan ['sæmpæn], *n.* Sampan, *m.*

samphire ['sæmfaiə], *n.* (*Bot.*) Passe-pierre, christe-marine, *f.*

sample [sɑ:mpl], *n.* Échantillon, *m.*; prise (of minerals etc.), *f.*—*v.t.* Échantillonner; déguster (of wine); (*fam.*) essayer. **sampler,** *n.* Modèle; canevas (for needlework), *m.* **sampling,** *n.* Échantillonnage, *m.*; gustation (of food), *f.*

Samson ['sæmsən], *n.* Samson; (*fig.*) un Hercule, *m.* *Samson's post,* (*Naut.*) épontille à manche, *f.*

sanative ['sænətiv] or **sanatory,** *a.* Curatif.

sanatorium [-'tɔ:riəm], *n.* Sanatorium, *m.*

sanctification [sæŋktifi'keiʃən], *n.* Sanctification, *f.*

sanctified ['sæŋktifaid], *a.* Sanctifié, saint; (*pej.*) béat. *A sanctified air,* une mine papelarde. **sanctifier,** *n.* Sanctificateur, *m.* **sanctify,** *v.t.* Sanctifier. **sanctifying,** *a.* Sanctifiant.

sanctimonious [sæŋkti'mouniəs], *a.* Papelard, béat, hypocrite. **sanctimoniously,** *adv.* D'un air béat, sous le manteau de la religion. **sanctimoniousness,** *n.* Dévotion affectée, *f.*, cagoterie, *f.*

sanction ['sæŋkʃən], *n.* Sanction, autorité, *f.* —*v.t.* Sanctionner, autoriser.

sanctitude ['sæŋktitju:d] or **sanctity,** *n.* Sainteté, *f.*; caractère sacré, *m.*

sanctuary ['sæŋktjuəri], *n.* Sanctuaire, asile, refuge, *m.* *Right of sanctuary,* droit de sanctuaire *or* d'asile, *m.*; *to take sanctuary,* se

réfugier dans un asile. **sanctum**, *n.* Sanctuaire; (*colloq.*) cabinet de travail, *m.*,
retraite, *f.*
sand [sænd], *n.* Sable; sablon (fine sand), *m.*;
(*pl.*) grève, plage, *f.*, bord de la mer, *m. On
the sands*, sur la plage, sur le sable.—*v.t.*
Sabler. **sandbag**, *n.* Sac de terre, *m. Sandbag loopholes*, créneaux en sacs de terre, *m.pl.*
—*v.t.* Sabler; (*fam.*) assommer. **sand-bank**,
n. Banc de sable, *m. To run on a sand-bank*,
être ensablé, s'ensabler.   **sand-bar**, *n.*
Ensablement, *m.*; banc de sable, *m.* **sand-
bath**, *n.* Bain de sable, *m.* **sand-blast**, *n.*
Jet de sable, *m.* **sand-blind**, *a.* Qui a la vue
trouble. **sand-box**, *n.* Poudrière, *f.*, sablier,
m. **sand-boy**, *n. As happy as a sand-boy*, gai
comme un pinson. **sand-cloth**, *n.* Toile
émeri, *f.* **sand-coloured**, *a.* Couleur de
sable. **sand-crack**, *n.* Seime, *f.* **sand-
drift**, *n.* Amas de sable, *m.* **sand-dune**, *n.*
Dune, *f.* **sand-eel**, *n.* Lançon, *m.*, équille, *f.*
sand-glass, *n.* Sablier, *m.* **sand-hill**, *n.*
Dune, *f.* **sand-man**, *n.* (*fam.*) Marchand
de sable, *m.* **sand-martin**, *n.* Hirondelle de
rivage, *f.* **sand-paper**, *n.* Papier de verre,
m.—*v.t.* Frotter, passer au papier de verre.
sandpiper ['sændpaipə], *n.* (*Orn.*) Maubèche, *f.*, chevalier, bécasseau, *m.* **sand-pit**,
n. Sablière, sablonnière, *f.* **sand-shoes**,
n.pl. (*colloq.*) Bains de mer, *m.pl.*; espa-
drilles, *f.pl.* **sandstone**, *n.* Grès, *m.*
sand-storm, *n.* Ouragan de sable, *m.*
sand-worm, *n.* Ver arénicole, *m.*
sandal [sændl], *n.* Sandale, *f.* **sandal-maker**,
n. Sandalier, *m.* **sandal-wood**, *n.* Santal,
bois de santal, *m.*
sanded, *a.* Sablé, sablonneux. **sandiness**, *n.*
Nature sablonneuse, *f.*
sandwich ['sændwitʃ], *n.* Sandwich, *m.*
sandwich-man, *n.* (*pl.* **sandwich-men**)
Homme-sandwich, homme-affiche, *m.*
sandy, *a.* Sablonneux, de sable; d'un blond
ardent, roux (of colour).
sane [sein], *a.* Sain, sain d'esprit, sensé.
sanguinary ['sæŋgwinəri], *a.* Sanguinaire.
sanguine, *a.* Sanguin; plein de confiance,
confiant. *Beyond my most sanguine hopes*,
au delà de mes plus vives espérances; *he is
sanguine of success*, il se fait sûr de réussir;
I am not very sanguine about the result, je
n'ai pas grand espoir que l'affaire réussisse.
sanguinely, *adv.* Avec confiance. **san-
guineness**, *n.* Nature sanguine, confiance,
assurance, *f.* **sanguineous** [-'gwiniəs], *a.*
Sanguin. **sanguinolent**, *a.* (*Med.*) Sanguinolent, teint de sang.
Sanhedrim ['sænədrim], *n.* Sanhédrin, *m.*
sanify ['sænifai], *v.t.* Améliorer les conditions
hygiéniques de.
sanitary ['sænitəri], *a.* Sanitaire, hygiénique.
Sanitary inspector, inspecteur sanitaire, *m.*;
sanitary towel, serviette hygiénique, *f.* **sanitation**, *n.* Assainissement, *m.*
sanity ['sæniti], *n.* État sain, jugement sain, *m.*
sanjak ['sændʒæk], *n.* Sandjak, *m.*
sank, *past* [SINK].
San Marino [sænmə'riːnou]. (*Geog.*) Saint-
Marin, *f.*
Sanskrit ['sænskrit], *a.* and *n.* Sanscrit, *m.*
Sanskritic [-'skritik], *a.* Sanscritique.
Sanskritist ['sænskritist], *n.* Sanscritiste, *m.*
Santa Claus ['sæntə'klɔːz]. Père Noël, *m.*

santal [SANDALWOOD].
santolina [sænto'lainə], *n.* (*Bot.*) Santoline, *f.*
santonica [sæn'tɔnikə], *n.* (*Bot.*) Santonine, *f.*
sap [sæp], *n.* Sève, *f.*; (*Bot.*) aubier (sapwood),
m.; (*Mil.*) sape, *f.*; (*pop.*) niais, *m.*—*v.t.*
Saper.—*v.i.* Aller à la sape.
sapan-wood ['sæpənwud], *n.* Bois de sapan, *m.*
saphena [sə'fiːnə], *n.* Saphène, *f.*
sapid ['sæpid], *a.* Sapide. **sapidity** [-'piditi]
or **sapidness**, *n.* Sapidité, *f.*
sapience ['seipiəns], *n.* Sagesse, *f.* **sapient**, *a.*
Sage. **sapiently**, *adv.* Sagement.
sapless ['sæplis], *a.* Sans sève; sec, desséché.
sapling ['sæpliŋ], *n.* Jeune arbre, baliveau, *m.*
Straight as a sapling, droit comme un jonc.
sapodilla [sæpə'dilə], *n.* Sapote, sapotille, *f.*
sapodilla-tree, *n.* Sapotillier, sapotier, *m.*
saponaceous [sæpə'neiʃəs], *a.* Saponacé.
saponaria [-'nɛəriə], *n.* (*Bot.*) Saponaire, *f.*
saponification [səpɔnifi'keiʃən], *n.* Saponification, *f.*
saponify [sə'pɔnifai], *v.t.* Saponifier.—*v.i.* Se
saponifier.
saponin ['sæpənin], *n.* Saponine, *f.*
saporific [sæpə'rifik], *a.* Saporifique.
sapper ['sæpə], *n.* Sapeur, *m. Sappers and
miners*, corps du génie, *m.*
sapphic ['sæfik], *n.* (*Pros.*) Saphique, *m.*
sapphire ['sæfaiə], *n.* Saphir, *m.*
Sappho ['sæfou]. Sapho, *f.*
sappiness ['sæpinis], *n.* Abondance de sève, *f.*;
(*pop.*) nigauderie, *f.*
sapping ['sæpiŋ], *n.* Sape, *f.*
sappy ['sæpi], *a.* Plein de sève; (*pop.*) nigaud,
niais.
saprolegnia [sæprə'legniə], *n.* Saprolégnie, *f.*
saprolegnious, *a.* Saprolégnié.
sap-wood, *n.* Aubier, *m.*
saraband ['særəbænd], *n.* Sarabande, *f.*
Saracen ['særəsn], *a.* and *n.* Sarrasin, *m.*
saracenic [-'senik], *a.* Sarracénique;
(*Arch.*) sarrasin.
Saragossa [særə'gɔsə]. (*Geog.*) Saragosse, *f.*
Sarah ['sɛərə]. Sarah, *f.*
sarcasm ['saːkæzm], *n.* Sarcasme, *m.* **sarcastic** [-'kæstik] or **sarcastical**, *a.* Sarcastique. **sarcastically**, *adv.* D'une manière
or d'un ton sarcastique.
sarcenet ['saːsənit], *n.* Florence, taffetas, *m.*
sarcocele ['saːkəsiːl], *n.* Sarcocèle, *f.*
sarcocolla [-'kɔlə], *n.* (*Bot.*) Sarcocollier, *m.*
sarcoderm ['saːkədəːm], *n.* Sarcoderme, *m.*
sarcology [-'kɔlədʒi], *n.* Sarcologie, *f.*
sarcoma [-'koumə], *n.* Sarcome, *m.*
sarcomatosis [-'tousis], *n.* Sarcomatose, *f.*
sarcomatous [-'koumətəs], *a.* Sarcomateux.
sarcophagus [-'kɔfəgəs], *n.* Sarcophage, *m.*
sarcoplasm ['saːkɔplæzm], *n.* Sarcoplasma, *m.*
sarcosis [-'kousis], *n.* Sarcose, *f.*
sarcotic [-'kɔtik], *a.* Sarcotique.
sard [saːd], *n.* Sardoine, *f.*; sarde, *m.*
Sardanapalus [saːdə'næpələs]. (*Gr. Hist.*)
Sardanapale, *m.*
sardine [saː'diːn], *n.* Sardine, *f. Packed like
sardines*, serrés comme des harengs en caque.
Sardinia [saː'diniə]. (*Geog.*) La Sardaigne, *f.*
Sardinian, *a.* and *n.* Sarde, *m.*
sardonic [saː'dɔnik], *a.* Sardonique. *Sardonic
smile*, rire sardonique, *m.*
sardonyx ['saːdəniks], *n.* Sardoine, *f.*
sarg [SARGUS].
sargasso [saː'gæsou], *n.* Sargasse, *f.*

sargus ['sɑːɡəs], *n.* (*Ichth.*) Sargue, *m.*
sarigue [sə'riːɡ], *n.* Sarigue, *f.*
sarmatian [sɑːˈmeiʃən], *a.* and *n.* Sarmatique, sarmate, *m.*
sarmentose or **sarmentous** [sɑːˈmentous], *a.* (*Bot.*) Sarmenteux. **sarmentum,** *n.* Sarment, *m.*
sarong [sɑːˈrɔŋ], *n.* Pagne, *m.*, jupe (Malayan), *f.*
sarsaparilla [sɑːsəpəˈrilə], *n.* Salsepareille, *f.*
sartorial [sɑːˈtɔːriəl], *a.* De tailleur. *Sartorial elegance,* élégance vestimentaire, *f.*
sash [sæʃ], *n.* Ceinture; écharpe (mark of distinction), *f.*; châssis (of a window), *m.*— *v.t.* Parer d'une ceinture; munir d'un châssis. **sash-frame,** *n.* Châssis dormant, *m.* **sashline,** *n.* Corde de châssis, *f.* **sash-window,** *n.* Fenêtre à guillotine, *f.*
sassafras ['sæsəfræs], *n.* (*Bot.*) Sassafras, *m.*
Sassenach ['sæsənæx], *n.* and *a.* (*Sc.*) Anglais, *m.*, -aise, *f.*
Satan ['seitən]. Satan, *m.*
satanic [sə'tænik] or **satanical,** *a.* Satanique. **satanically,** *adv.* D'une manière satanique.
satchel [sætʃl], *n.* Sacoche, *f.*; sac d'écolier, cartable, *m.*; musette (military etc.), *f.*
***sate** (1), *past* [SIT].
sate (2) [seit], *v.t.* Rassasier (de), assouvir. **sated,** *a.* Rassasié, repu. ***sateless,** *a.* Insatiable.
sateen [sæ'tiːn], *n.* Satinette, *f.*
satellite ['sætəlait], *n.* Satellite, *m.*
satiate ['seiʃieit], *v.t.* Rassasier (de); blaser. **satiated,** *a.* Rassasié (de); gorgé; blasé.
satiety [sə'taiəti], *n.* Satiété, *f.*
satin ['sætin], *n.* Satin, *m.*—*a.* De satin.—*v.t.* Satiner. **satin-ribbon,** *n.* Ruban de satin or satiné, *m.* **satin-wood,** *n.* Bois de citronnier, *m.*
satinet(te) [sæti'net], *n.* Satinade, satinette, *f.* **satining,** *n.* Satinage, *m.* **satiny,** *a.* Satiné.
satire ['sætaiə], *n.* Satire, *f.*
satiric [sə'tirik] or **satirical,** *a.* Satirique. **satirically,** *adv.* Satiriquement.
satirist ['sætirist], *n.* Satirique, *m.*
satirize ['sætiraiz], *v.t.* Faire la satire de, satiriser, tourner en ridicule.
satisfaction [sætis'fækʃən], *n.* Satisfaction, *f.*; contentement, acquittement (discharge), *m.*; réparation, raison (amends), *f.* *To give satisfaction,* donner de la satisfaction; *to give satisfaction to,* donner satisfaction à (to apologize), rendre raison à (to fight). **satisfactorily,** *adv.* D'une manière satisfaisante. **satisfactoriness,** *n.* Caractère satisfaisant, *m.* **satisfactory,** *a.* Satisfaisant.
satisfier ['sætisfaiə], *n.* Qui satisfait. **satisfy** ['sætisfai], *v.t.* Satisfaire; satisfaire à; convaincre; persuader (to convince); acquitter (a debt). *To be rather more than satisfied,* en avoir plus qu'assez; *to be satisfied of,* être persuadé, être convaincu de; *to be satisfied with,* être satisfait de, être content de; *to satisfy one's appetite,* se rassasier; *to satisfy one's vengeance,* assouvir sa vengeance.—*v.i.* Satisfaire, donner satisfaction. **satisfying,** *a.* Satisfaisant; nourrissant (food). **satisfyingly,** *adv.* De façon satisfaisante.
satrap ['sætrəp], *n.* Satrape, *m.*
satrapy ['sætrəpi], *n.* Satrapie, *f.*
saturable ['sætjurəbl], *a.* Saturable. **saturant,** *a.* Saturant. **saturate,** *v.t.* Saturer. **saturation** [-'reiʃən], *n.* Saturation, *f.*

Saturday ['sætədei], *n.* Samedi, *m.*
Saturn ['sætən]. Saturne, *m.* **Saturnalia** [-'neiliə], *n.pl.* Saturnales, *f.pl.* **Saturnalian,** *a.* Des saturnales. **Saturnian** [-'tɔːniən], *a.* De Saturne; (*Pros.*) saturnien.
saturnine ['sætənain], *a.* Sombre, taciturne; (*Old Chem.*) saturnin, de plomb. **saturnism,** *n.* Saturnisme, *m.*
satyr ['sætə], *n.* Satyre, *m. She-satyr,* satyresse, *f.*
satyriasis [sæti'raiəsis], *n.* Satyriasis, *m.*
satyric [sə'tirik], *a.* Satyrique.
satyrium [sə'tiriəm], *n.* (*Bot.*) Satyrion, *m.*
sauce [sɔːs], *n.* Sauce; (*fig.*) insolence, impertinence, *f.*; toupet, *m.* *Butter-sauce,* sauce au beurre; *onion-sauce,* sauce aux oignons, *f.*; *to serve with the same sauce,* rendre la pareille à.—*v.t.* Assaisonner; flatter (the palate); (*fig.*) dire des impertinences à. **sauce-boat,** *n.* Saucière, *f.* **sauce-box,** *n.* (*colloq.*) Insolent, impertinent, *m.* **saucepan,** *n.* Casserole, *f.*
saucer ['sɔːsə], *n.* Soucoupe, *f.*; godet, *m.* (for water-colours). *Flying saucer,* soucoupe volante, *f.* **saucerful,** *n.* Soucoupe pleine, plein une soucoupe.
saucily ['sɔːsili], *adv.* Insolemment, avec impertinence. **sauciness,** *n.* Insolence, impertinence, *f.* **saucy,** *a.* Insolent, impertinent.
sauerkraut ['sauəkraut], *n.* Choucroute, *f.*
saunter ['sɔːntə], *v.i.* Flâner. *He sauntered up to me,* il se dirigea nonchalamment de mon côté; *to saunter away the time,* perdre son temps à flâner.—*n.* Flânerie, *f.* **saunterer,** *n.* Flâneur, *m.*, -euse, *f.* **sauntering,** *n.* Flânerie, *f.*—*a.* De flâneur.
saurian ['sɔːriən], *n.* Saurien, *m.*
sausage ['sɔsidʒ], *n.* Saucisse, *f.* (to be cooked); saucisson (dry and hard), *m.* **sausage-machine,** *n.* Entonnoir à saucisse, *m.* **sausage-meat,** *n.* Chair à saucisse, *f.* **sausage-roll,** *n.* Friand, *m.*
savage ['sævidʒ], *a.* Sauvage; féroce, farouche, furieux.—*n.* Sauvage, *m.* or *f.*—*v.t.* Attaquer, mordre (of animals). **savagely,** *adv.* Sauvagement, d'une manière sauvage; en sauvage; d'une manière féroce. **savageness,** *n.* Férocité, brutalité; sauvagerie, *f.* **savagery,** *n.* Férocité, barbarie, *f.*
savannah [sə'vænə], *n.* Savane, prairie (in Florida etc.), *f.*
save [seiv], *v.t.* Sauver (de); épargner (to spare); éviter (to avoid); mettre de côté, mettre en réserve (to put by); économiser, ménager (to economize); ne pas manquer, arriver à temps pour (not to lose). *God save the king,* Dieu sauve le roi; *I save five pounds by it,* j'y gagne cinq livres; *to save appearances,* sauver les apparences; *to save time,* gagner du temps; *to save trouble,* épargner de la peine.—*v.i.* Économiser, faire des économies.—*n.* Économie, *f.*; (*spt.*) arrêt, *m.*—*prep.* Hormis, excepté, sauf. *Save your respect,* sauf votre respect. **save-all,** *n.* Brûle-tout, *m.*
saveloy ['sævəlɔi], *n.* Cervelas, *m.*
saver ['seivə], *n.* Sauveur, libérateur, *m.*, -trice, *f.*; économe, ménager, *m.*, ménagère, *f.* (economizer).
savin ['sævin], *n.* (*Bot.*) Sabine, *f.*
saving ['seiviŋ], *n.* Épargne; économie, *f.*; salut, *m.*; (*pl.*) économies, *f.pl.*, épargne, *f.*—

a. Économe, ménager; économique (of things); (*fig.*) de réserve. *Saving clause,* réservation, *f.*; *saving grace,* grâce justifiante, *f.*—*prep.* Sauf, excepté. *Saving your reverence,* sauf votre respect. **savingly,** *adv.* Économiquement, avec économie; (*Theol.*) pour le salut de son âme. **savingness,** *n.* Épargne, économie, *f.*; (*Theol.*) salut, *m.*
savings-bank, *n.* Caisse d'épargne, *f.* **savings-certificate,** *n.* Bon d'épargne, *m.*
saviour ['seivjə], *n.* Sauveur, *m.*
Savonarola [sævənə'roulə]. (*Hist.*) Savonarole, *m.*
savory ['seivəri], *n.* (*Bot.*) Sarriette, *f.*
savour ['seivə], *n.* Saveur, *f.*; goût, *m.,* odeur, *f.*—*v.t.* Goûter, savourer.—*v.i.* Avoir du goût; sentir. *To savour of,* sentir le, la, etc. **savourily,** *adv.* Savoureusement. **savouriness,** *n.* Goût agréable, *m.,* saveur, *f.* **savourless,** *a.* Fade, insipide; sans saveur. **savoury,** *a.* Savoureux, qui a de la saveur, appétissant. *Savoury herbs,* plantes aromatiques, *f.pl.*; *savoury omelette,* omelette aux fines herbes, *f.*—*n.* Plat épicé; entremets non sucré, *m.*
Savoy [sə'vɔi]. La Savoie, *f.* **Savoyard,** *n.* and *a.* Savoisien, *m.,* -ienne, *f.*; (*fam.*) Savoyard, *m.,* -arde, *f.*
savvy ['sævi], *n.* (*pop.*) Jugeotte, *f.*—*v.t.* Savoir; comprendre. *Savvy?* Compris?
saw (1), *past* [SEE].
saw (2) [sɔ:], *n.* Scie, *f.* *Cross-cut saw,* passe-partout, *m.*—*v.t.* (*past* **sawed,** *p.p.* **sawn**) Scier.—*v.i.* Se scier. **sawbones,** *n.* (*colloq.*) Chirurgien, carabin, *m.* **sawdust,** *n.* Sciure (de bois), *f.* **sawfish,** *n.* Scie de mer, *f.* **sawing,** *n.* Sciage, *m.* **saw-mill,** *n.* Scierie, *f.* **saw-pit,** *n.* Fosse de scieurs de long, *f.* **sawyer,** *n.* Scieur, scieur de long, *m.*
saw (3) [sɔ:], *n.* Adage, dicton (saying), *m.* *An old saw,* un vieux dicton.
sax [sæks], *n.* Hache d'ouvrage, *f.*; (*Mus.*) saxe, *m.*
saxatile ['sæksətail], *a.* (*Bot.*) Saxatile, de rocher.
saxhorn ['sækshɔ:n], *n.* Saxhorn, *m.*
saxifrage ['sæksifreidʒ], *n.* (*Bot.*) Saxifrage, *f.*
Saxon ['sæksən], *a.* Saxon, de Saxe.—*n.* Saxon, *m.,* -onne, *f.*; saxon (language), *m.*
Saxony ['sæksəni]. La Saxe, *f.*
saxophone ['sæksəfoun], *n.* Saxophone, *m.* **saxophonist,** *n.* Joueur de saxophone, saxophone, *m.*
say [sei], *v.t.* (*past* and *p.p.* **said** [sed]) Dire; parler, répéter, réciter. *Be it said,* soit dit; *I cannot say no to you,* je ne sais rien vous refuser; *I dare say it is,* je le crois; *I must say that,* je dois avouer que; *I say,* dites donc! dis donc! *it is hard to say,* on ne sait pas; *it is hard to say whether,* il est difficile de dire si; *it says or it is said,* on dit; *let us say no more about it,* n'en parlons plus; *my watch says one o'clock,* ma montre marque une heure; *say £100,* mettons cent livres sterling; *that is said every day,* cela se dit tous les jours; *that is saying a good deal,* c'est beaucoup dire; *that is to say,* c'est-à-dire; *they say,* on dit; *to say again,* répéter, redire; *to say nothing of,* sans parler de; *to say right,* dire vrai; *you don't say so!* pas possible!—*n.* Dire, mot, ce qu'on a à dire, *m.* *To have a say in the matter,* avoir voix au chapitre; *to have*

one's say, dire son mot, dire ce qu'on a à dire.
saying, *n.* Mot, proverbe, dicton, *m.*; sentence, maxime, *f.* *As the saying is,* comme on dit; *sayings and doings,* faits et gestes, *m.pl.*; *that goes without saying,* cela va sans dire; *there is no saying what will happen,* impossible de dire ce qui arrivera.
sbirro ['zbirou], *n.* Sbire, *m.*
scab [skæb], *n.* Croûte (on a wound etc.); gale (of sheep etc.), *f.*; (*pop.*) jaune, *m.*
scabbard ['skæbəd], *n.* Fourreau, *m.*
scabbed [skæbd] or **scabby,** *a.* Couvert de croûtes; galeux. **scabbiness,** *n.* État galeux, *m.*
scabious ['skeibiəs], *a.* Scabieux.—*n.* Scabieuse (plant), *f.*
scabrous ['skeibrəs], *a.* Scabreux; risqué (of story etc.); rugueux (of surface). **scabrousness,** *n.* Scabreux, *m.*; rugosité, *f.*
scad [HORSE-MACKEREL].
scaffold ['skæfəld], *n.* Échafaud, *m.* *To ascend the scaffold,* monter sur l'échafaud.—*v.t.* Échafauder. **scaffolding,** *n.* Échafaudage, *m.* **scaffold-pole,** *n.* Perche d'échafaudage, *f.*
scalable ['skeiləbl], *a.* Que l'on peut escalader (wall); que l'on peut détartrer (boiler).
scald (1) [skɔ:ld], *n.* Scalde (bard), *m.*
scald (2) [skɔ:ld], *n.* Brûlure; (*Path.*) teigne, *f.*—*v.t.* Échauder; blanchir (meat). *To scald one's hand,* s'échauder la main; *to scald oneself,* s'échauder. **scald-head,** *n.* Teigne, *f.* **scalding,** *n.* Échaudage, *m.* **scalding-hot,** *a.* Tout bouillant. **scalding-tub,** *n.* Échaudoir, *m.*
scale [skeil], *n.* Échelle, *f.*; bassin, plateau (balance), *m.*; écaille (of a fish); (*Mus.*) gamme, *f.*; (*Motor.*) calamine, *f.* *Drawn to the scale of,* dressé à l'échelle de; *on a large scale,* sur une grande échelle, en grand; *on a small scale,* sur une petite échelle; *scale model,* maquette, *f.*; *scales* or *pair of scales,* balance, *f.*, pèse-lettres (for letters), trébuchet (for gold etc.), *m.*; *sliding scale,* échelle mobile; *to turn the scale,* faire pencher la balance.—*v.t.* Escalader (to climb); écailler (to pick off scales); souffler, flamber (a cannon); enlever le tartre de (a boiler etc.); (*fig.*) peser, mesurer, comparer, estimer. *To scale down,* réduire à l'échelle; *to scale teeth,* détartrer. —*v.i.* S'écailler; s'élever, monter (à).
scaled, *a.* Écaillé, écailleux, à écailles.
scale-fern, *n.* (*Bot.*) Cétérac, *m.*
scaleless, *a.* Sans écailles.
scale-maker, *n.* Balancier, *m.*
scalene [ska'li:n], *a.* Scalène.
scaliness ['skeilinis], *n.* Nature écailleuse, *f.*
scaling, *n.* Escalade (climbing), *f.*; écaillage (peeling off), *m.*; flambage (of a gun), *m.*
scaling-ladder, *n.* Échelle de siège, *f.*
scallop ['skɔləp], *n.* Pétoncle, *m.*; (*Cook.*) coquille Saint-Jacques, *f.*, coquille, *f.*; dentelure, *f.*, feston (notching), *m.*—*v.t.* Denteler; (*Needlework*) festonner, mettre en coquilles (fish).
scallywag ['skæliwæg], *n.* Vaurien, propre-à-rien, *m.*
scalp [skælp], *n.* Cuir chevelu, *m.*, chevelure *f.*, scalpe; (*fig.*) front, *m.*, tête, *f.*—*v.t.*

Scalper. **scalp-wound,** *n.* Blessure à la tête, *f.*

scalpel, *n.* (*Surg.*) Scalpel, *m.*

scalping-knife, *n.* Couteau à scalper, *m.*

scaly ['skeili], *a.* Écaillé; (*Bot.*) écailleux, à écailles; (*slang*) chiche, mesquin, ladre.

scammony ['skæməni], *n.* (*Bot.*) Scammonée, *f.*

scamp [skæmp], *n.* Chenapan, mauvais sujet, vaurien, *m. Young scamp,* petit polisson, *m.* —*v.t.* Bâcler, gâter par trop de hâte. *To scamp one's work,* bâcler son ouvrage.

scamper ['skæmpə], *v.i.* Courir, s'enfuir. *To scamper off* or *to scamper away,* décamper lestement, prendre ses jambes à son cou.—*n.* Course rapide, *f.*

scampi ['skæmpi], *n.pl.* Langoustine, *f.*

scan [skæn], *v.t.* Scruter, mesurer des yeux; (*colloq.*) éplucher; scander (verses); (*Rad.*) balayer.

scandal [skændl], *n.* Scandale, *m.*; honte (shame); médisance, *f.*; (*Law*) diffamation, *f. To be a scandal to,* être la honte de, faire la honte de; *to raise a scandal,* faire du scandale. **scandal-monger,** *n.* Médisant, colporteur de médisances, *m.*

scandalize, *v.t.* Scandaliser, choquer; diffamer, calomnier (to defame). **scandalizing,** *a.* Scandaleux. **scandalous,** *a.* Scandaleux; calomnieux, honteux. **scandalously,** *adv.* Scandaleusement; honteusement. **scandalousness,** *n.* Caractère scandaleux, *m.*, infamie, *f.*

scandent ['skændənt], *a.* (*Bot.*) Grimpant.

Scandinavia [skændi'neivjə]. La Scandinavie, *f.*

Scandinavian, *a.* and *n.* Scandinave, *m.*

scanner ['skænə], *n.* Scrutateur; sondeur. *Radar scanner,* déchiffreur de radar.

scanning ['skæniŋ], *n.* Examen minutieux, *m.*; (*Pros.*) scansion, *f.*; (*Rad.*) balayage. *m.* **scansion,** *n.* Scansion, *f.*

scant [skænt], *a.* Rare, peu abondant; étroit, rétréci; modique, faible; peu de. *In scant garb,* en tenue assez sommaire; *with scant manners,* avec peu de politesse.—*v.t.* Borner, resserrer; donner à contre-cœur.—*v.i.* (*Naut.*) Diminuer, faiblir (of the wind).

scantily ['skæntili], *adv.* Faiblement, d'une manière insuffisante; chétivement. **scantiness,** *n.* Insuffisance (of provisions etc.); pauvreté (of grass etc.); étroitesse (of clothes); exiguïté (of resources); faiblesse (of weight), *f.*

scantle [skæntl], *v.t.* Couper en morceaux.

scantling ['skæntliŋ], *n.* Fragment, échantillon, *m.*; (*Carp.*) volige, *f.*, équarrissage, *m.*

scanty ['skænti], *adv.* Étroit, rétréci, faible, peu abondant, insuffisant; chétif; clairsemé (of the hair).

*scape (1) [ESCAPE].

scape (2) [skeip], *n.* (*Bot.*) Scape, *m.*; hampe, tige, *f.*; (*Arch.*) fût, *m.*

scapegoat ['skeipgout], *n.* Bouc émissaire; (*fig.*) souffre-douleur, *m.* **scapegrace,** *n.* Vaurien, mauvais sujet, *m.*

scapement ['skeipmənt], *n.* Échappement, *m.*

scaphite ['skæfait], *n.* Scaphite, *f.* **scaphocephalic** [skæfosə'fælik] or **scaphocephalous** [-sefələs], *a.* Scaphocéphale. **scaphocephaly,** *n.* Scaphocéphalie, *f.*

scaphoid ['skæfɔid], *a.* and *n.* Scaphoïde, *m.*

scapula ['skæpjulə], *n.* (*Anat.*) Omoplate, *f.* **scapular,** *a.* Scapulaire. **scapulary,** *n.* (*R.-C. Ch.*) Scapulaire, *m.*

scar (1) [skɑ:], *n.* Cicatrice, balafre, *f.*—*v.t.* Cicatriser; balafrer.

scar (2) [skɑ:], *n.* Rocher, *m.*, falaise, *f.*

scarab ['skærəb] or **scarabaeus** [-'bi:əs], *n.* Scarabée, *m.*

scaramouch ['skærəmu:ʃ], *n.* Scaramouche, *m.*

scarce [skɛəs], *a.* Rare. *To make oneself scarce,* disparaître, décamper, filer. **scarcely,** *adv.* À peine, presque pas, guère. *I scarcely know him,* je ne le connais guère; *scarcely anyone,* presque personne; *scarcely anything,* presque rien; *scarcely anywhere,* presque nulle part; *scarcely ever,* presque jamais; *scarcely had he left when the telephone rang,* à peine fut-il parti que le téléphone retentit. **scarceness** or **scarcity,** *n.* Rareté; disette (famine), *f.*

scare [skɛə], *n.* Panique, frayeur subite, *f.*—*v.t.* Effrayer, épouvanter, faire peur à, effaroucher. **scarecrow,** *n.* Épouvantail, *m.* (*fam.*) *Dressed like a scarecrow,* affublé à faire peur. **scare-monger,** *n.* Alarmiste, *m.* or *f.*

scarf [skɑ:f], *n.* (*pl.* **scarfs** or **scarves**) Écharpe, *f.*; fichu, *m.*; cache-nez, *m.inv.*; foulard, *m.*; (*Carp.*) assemblage à entaille, joint en sifflet, *m.*—*v.t.* Écharper; (*Carp.*) assembler. **scarfed,** *a.* Paré d'une écharpe; (*Carp.*) (planches) assemblées à mi-bois. **scarfing,** *n.* (*Carp.*) Assemblage, *m.* **scarfpin,** *n.* Épingle de cravate, *f.* **scarf-skin,** *n.* Épiderme, *m.* **scarfwise,** *adv.* and *a.* En écharpe.

scarification [skɛərifi'keifən] or **scarifying** ['skɛərifaiiŋ], *n.* (*Surg.*) Scarification, *f.* **scarificator** or **scarifier,** *n.* Scarificateur, *m.* **scarify,** *v.t.* Scarifier (skin), ameublir (soil); (*colloq.*) effaroucher. **scarifying,** *a.* (*colloq.*) Farouche.

scarious ['skɛəriəs], *a.* (*Bot.*) Scarieux.

scarlatina ['skɑ:lə'ti:nə], *n.* (Fièvre) scarlatine, *f.*

scarlet ['skɑ:lit], *a.* and *n.* Écarlate, *f. Scarlet-fever,* fièvre scarlatine, *f.*; *scarlet-runner,* haricot d'Espagne, *m.*

scarp [skɑ:p], *n.* (*Fort.*) Escarpe (*Her.*) écharpe, *f.*—*v.t.* Escarper.

scarred [SCAR (1)].

scarus ['skɛərəs], *n.* (*Ichth.*) Scare, *m.*

scathe [skeið], *n.* Dommage, mal, *m.*

scatheless ['skeiðlis], *a.* Sans dommage, sans perte, sain et sauf. **scathing,** *a.* Acerbe, cinglant, cassant. *A scathing fire,* un feu écrasant.

scatology [skə'tɔlədʒi], *n.* Scatologie, *f.* **scatophagous** [-'tɔfəgəs], *a.* Scatophage.

scatter ['skætə], *v.t.* Disperser, dissiper; répandre, éparpiller, disséminer.—*v.i.* Se disperser, se répandre, s'éparpiller, écarter. **scatter-brain,** *n.* Écervelé, étourdi, *m.* **scatter-brained,** *a.* Écervelé, étourdi. **scattered,** *a.* Dispersé, répandu, éparpillé, épars. **scattering,** *n.* Éparpillement, *m.*, dispersion, *f.*, petit nombre, *m.*

scaup [skɔ:p], *n.* (*Orn.*) Milouinan, *m.*

scavenge ['skævindʒ], *v.t.* Ébouer, balayer, nettoyer. **scavenger,** *n.* Boueur; balayeur, *m.* **scavenger-beetle,** *n.* Nécrobie, *f.*

scavenger-crab, *n.* Crabe nécrophage, *m.*
scavenging, *n.* Ébouage, balayage, *m.*
scene [si:n], *n.* Scène; (*Theat.*) scène, décoration, *f.*; décor; (*fig.*) théâtre, *m. Behind the scenes,* derrière le rideau, dans la coulisse; *the scene is laid in,* la scène se passe à; *to make a scene,* faire une scène *or* un esclandre.
scene-painter, *n.* Peintre de décors, *m.*
scene-shifter, *n.* Machiniste, *m.*
scenery, *n.* Scène; (*fig.*) vue, perspective, *f.,* coup d'œil, paysage, *m.*; (*Theat.*) décors, *m.pl.*
scenic ['si:nik], *a.* Scénique. *Scenic railway,* montagnes russes, *f.pl.*
scenographic [-ə'græfik], *a.* Scénographique.
scenography [-'nɔgrəfi], *n.* Scénographie, *f.*
scent [sent], *n.* Odeur, senteur, *f.,* parfum, *m.*; odorat (sense); flair, nez (of the dog), *m.*; voie (of the stag); (*fig.*) piste (track), *f. On the right scent,* sur la voie; *on the wrong scent,* en défaut; *to get scent of,* avoir vent de, découvrir; *to have a good scent,* avoir le nez fin; *to put on the wrong scent or to put off the scent,* dépister, mettre sur une fausse piste.—*v.t.* Parfumer (de); sentir, flairer (of animals). *To scent trouble,* flairer des ennuis.
scent-bag, *n.* Sachet à parfums, *m.* **scent-bottle,** *n.* Flacon de parfum, *m.* **scent-box,** *n.* Boîte de senteur, *f.* **scent-spray,** *n.* Vaporisateur, *m.*
scentless, *a.* Sans odeur, sans parfum; inodore; qui n'a pas de nez (of animals).
sceptic ['skeptik], *n.* Sceptique, *m.* or *f.* **sceptical,** *a.* Sceptique. **sceptically,** *adv.* D'une manière sceptique, avec scepticisme.
scepticism ['skeptisizm], *n.* Scepticisme, *m.*
sceptre ['septə], *n.* Sceptre, *m.*—*v.t.* Armer d'un sceptre. **sceptred,** *a.* Portant le sceptre.
schedule ['ʃedju:l; *Am.* 'ske-], *n.* Rouleau, cahier, *m.,* annexe, liste, *f.,* inventaire; bilan (balance-sheet); (*Law*) bordereau, *m. According to schedule,* selon les prévisions; *on schedule,* selon l'horaire; *to file a schedule* (in bankruptcy), déposer son bilan.—*v.t.* Enregistrer, inventorier, inscrire; classer.
scheik [SHEIK].
Scheldt [ʃelt]. L'Escaut, *m.*
schema ['ski:mə], *n.* (*pl.* **schemata** ['ski:mətə]) Schéma, diagramme, *m.* **schematic** [-'mætik], *a.* Schématique.
schematize ['ski:mətaiz], *v.t.* Schématiser.
scheme [ski:m], *n.* Arrangement, *m.,* combinaison, *f.*; résumé, plan; projet, système, *m.*—*v.t.* Projeter, combiner.—*v.i.* Faire des projets; (*fig.*) intriguer. **schemer,** *n.* Faiseur de projets; homme à projets; (*fig.*) intrigant, *m.* **scheming,** *a.* À projets; intrigant.—*n.* Projets, *m.pl.,* intrigues, *f.pl.*
schism [sizm], *n.* Schisme, *m.*
schismatic [siz'mætik], *n.* Schismatique, *m.* **schismatical,** *a.* Schismatique.
schist [ʃist], *n.* Schiste, *m.* **schistose,** *a.* Schisteux.
schizophrenia [skaizo'fri:niə *or* skitzo'fri:niə], *n.* (*Med.*) Schizophrénie, *f.* **schizophrenic,** *a.* Schizophrène.
scholar ['skɔlə], *n.* Écolier, *m.,* écolière, *f.*; érudit, *m.,* érudite, *f.,* savant, *m.,* savante, *f.* (learned person); boursier (on a foundation), *m. Classical scholar,* humaniste, *m.*; *day scholar,* externe, *m.*; *good Latin scholar,* bon

latiniste, *m.*; *Greek scholar,* helléniste, *m.*; *scholars differ on that point,* les érudits ne sont pas d'accord là-dessus; *to be a good French scholar,* posséder à fond le français.
scholarlike *or* **scholarly,** *a.* D'érudit, savant. *A scholarly speech,* un discours plein d'érudition.
scholarship, *n.* Érudition, *f.,* savoir, *m.*; (*Univ. etc.*) bourse, *f.*
scholastic [skɔ'læstik], *a.* and *n.* Scolastique, *m.* **scholastically,** *adv.* Scolastiquement.
scholasticism, *n.* Scolastique, *f.*
scholiast ['skouliæst], *n.* Scoliaste, *m.* **scholium,** *n.* (*pl.* **scholia**) Scolie, *f.*
school [sku:l], *n.* École; bande, troupe (of whales etc.), *f. At school,* en classe, à l'école; *boarding-school,* pension, *f.,* pensionnat, *m.*; *day-school,* externat, *m.*; *elementary* or *primary school,* école primaire, *f.*; *evening school,* classe du soir, *f.*; *fencing-school,* salle d'armes, *f.*; *grammar school,* collège, *m.,* lycée, *m.*; *high school,* école supérieure, *f.*; *infant-school,* école maternelle; *in school,* en classe; *of the old school,* de la vieille roche; *summer school,* cours de vacances, *m.*—*v.t.* Instruire, enseigner; réprimander, faire la leçon à (to reprimand). *To school oneself,* se faire à, se discipliner.
school-board, *n.* Conseil de l'enseignement primaire, *m.* **school-book,** *n.* Livre de classe, *m.* **schoolboy,** *n.* Écolier, *m. Still a schoolboy,* encore sur les bancs, encore au collège. **school-day,** *n.* Jour de classe, *m.*; (*pl.*) années d'études, *f.pl. In our school-days,* quand nous étions sur les bancs du collège.
school-fellow, *n.* Camarade de collège, de classe *or* d'école, *m.* **schoolgirl,** *n.* Écolière, *f.*
schooled, *a.* Formé, entraîné, dressé. *Schooled in courage,* formé à l'école du courage.
schooling, *n.* Instruction, *f.,* enseignement, *m.*; frais d'école, *m.pl.*; réprimande (reprimand), *f.*
***schoolman,** *n.* (*pl.* **schoolmen**) Professeur de théologie scolastique, *m.* **schoolmaster,** *n.* Maître d'école, instituteur, professeur, *m.*
schoolmistress, *n.* Maîtresse d'école, directrice de pension, institutrice, *f.* **schoolroom,** *n.* Classe, salle d'étude, *f.* **schooltime,** *n.* Classe, *f.,* heures de classe, *f.pl.*
schooner ['sku:nə], *n.* (*Naut.*) Goélette, *f.*
sciagraphy [SKIAGRAPHY].
sciatic [sai'ætik], *a.* Sciatique. **sciatica** [sai'ætikə], *n.* Sciatique, *f.*
science ['saiəns], *n.* Science, *f. Social science,* sociologie, *f.*; *to study science,* étudier les sciences. **scientific** [-'tifik], *a.* Scientifique. **scientifically,** *adv.* Scientifiquement.
scientist, *n.* Homme de science, savant, *m.*
Scilly Isles ['sili], Les Sorlingues, *f.pl.*
scimitar ['simitə], *n.* Cimeterre, *m.*
scintilla [sin'tilə], *n.* Soupçon, fragment, *m.,* parcelle, *f.*
scintillant ['sintilənt], *a.* Scintillant. **scintillate,** *v.i.* Scintiller. **scintillation** [-'leiʃən], *n.* Scintillation, *f.,* scintillement, *m.*
sciolist ['saiəlist], *n.* Demi-savant, *m.*
scion ['saiən], *n.* (*Bot.*) Scion; (*fig.*) rejeton, *m.*
scirrhous ['sirəs], *a.* Squirreux. **scirrhus,** *n.* Squirre, *m.*
scissile ['sisail], *a.* Scissile, sécable.
scission ['siʃən], *n.* Scission, *f.*

scissor ['sizə], *v.t.* Cisailler.
scissors ['sizəz], *n.pl.* Ciseaux, *m.pl. Pair of scissors*, paire de ciseaux, *f.*
Sclavonian [SLAV].
sclera ['skliərə], *n.* Sclérotique, cornée, *f.*
scleroderm ['skliərədə:m], *n.* Scléroderme, *m.* **sclerogenous** [-'rɔdʒinəs], *a.* Sclérogène.
sclerosis [skliə'rousis], *n.* Sclérose, *f.* **sclerotic** [-'rɔtik], *a.* and *n.* Sclérotique.
scobs [skɔbz], *n.* Râpure, limaille; scorie, *f.*
scoff [skɔf], *n.* Moquerie, *f.*, sarcasme, *m.*; (*pop.*) nourriture, boustifaille, *f.*—*v.i.* Se moquer de, bafouer.—*v.i.* Railler. *Why do you scoff at me?* pourquoi vous moquez-vous de moi? **scoffer,** *n.* Moqueur, railleur, *m.* **scoffing,** *n.* Moquerie, dérision, *f.*—*a.* Moqueur, *m.*, -euse, *f.* **scoffingly,** *adv.* Par moquerie, en dérision.
scold [skould], *v.i.* Gronder.—*v.t.* Gronder, crier, criailler (après).—*n.* Grondeuse, mégère (virago); gronderie (scolding), *f.* **scolding,** *n.* Semonce, *f. To give a scolding to,* gronder, (*colloq.*) laver la tête à.—*a.* Bougon. **scoldingly,** *adv.* En grondant.
scollop [SCALLOP].
scolopendra [skɔlə'pendrə], *n.* (*Zool.*) **scolopendrium,** *n.* (*Bot.*) Scolopendre, *f.*
scomber ['skɔmbə], *n.* Scombre, *m.* (fish).
sconce [skɔns], *n.* Applique, *f.*; bras, candélabre (fixé au mur); (*Mil.*) fortin, *m.*; *(slang)* caboche, boule (head), *f.*; bobèche (candle socket), *f.*
scone [skɔn *or* skoun], *n.* Petite galette (ronde), *f.*
scoop [sku:p], *n.* Grande cuiller; (*Naut.*) écope, *f.*; (*Journ. slang*) nouvelle à sensation, *f.* (publiée avant les autres journaux); (*fam.*) coup de maître, beau coup de filet, *m.*—*v.t.* Puiser, vider, creuser; (*Naut.*) écoper; rafler (a profit). *Scooping out,* évidement, *m.*; *to scoop out,* ôter (en creusant), creuser, évider.
scoot [sku:t], *v.i.* (*slang*) Décamper, filer. **scooter,** *n.* Patinette, trottinette, *f.*; scooter, *m.*
scope [skoup], *n.* Portée, étendue; visée; liberté, carrière, *f. To give full scope to,* donner libre carrière *or* libre essor à; *to have full scope,* avoir libre carrière *or* le champ libre, (*colloq.*) avoir ses coudées franches; *to have scope enough,* avoir assez d'espace.
scorbutic [skɔ:'bju:tik], *a.* Scorbutique. **scorbutically,** *adv.* Par le scorbut.
scorch [skɔ:tʃ], *v.t.* Brûler, roussir, griller.— *v.i.* Se brûler; (*Cycl. slang*) pédaler comme un fou, brûler le pavé. **scorcher,** *n.* Chauffard; casse-cou, *m.*; journée torride; personne épatante, *f.* **scorching,** *n.* Brûlant, très chaud. *At a scorching pace,* à tout casser. *it is scorching hot,* il fait une chaleur torride.
score [skɔ:], *n.* Entaille, coche (notch), *f.*; écot; compte (reckoning); vingt, *m.*, vingtaine (twenty), *f.*; (*Games*) nombre de points, *m.*; (*fig.*) motif, *m.*, raison, cause; (*Mus.*) partition, *f. Fourscore,* quatre-vingts; *on a new score,* sur nouveaux frais; *on that score,* sur ce chapitre, à cet égard; *on the score of,* sur le compte de, à titre de; *on what score?* à quel titre? *threescore,* soixante; *to keep the score,* marquer les points, marquer; (*fig.*) *to know the score,* être dégourdi; *what is the score?* où en est le jeu?—*v.t.* Entailler,

marquer; porter en compte (as a debt); érafler (of skin); rayer; (*Mus.*) orchestrer. *To score a goal,* marquer un but; *to score off someone,* enfoncer quelqu'un; *to score out,* rayer, biffer (of text); *to score up,* marquer, compter.—*v.i.* Marquer des points. **scoreboard,** *n.* Tableau, *m.* **scored,** *a.* Éraflé; rayé, biffé. **scorer,** *n.* Marqueur, *m.*
scoria ['skɔ:riə], *n.* (*pl.* scoriae) Scorie, *f.* **scorification** [-fi'keiʃən], *n.* Scorification, *f.* **scorifier** ['skɔ:rifaiə], *n.* Scorificateur, *m.* **scoriform,** *a.* Scoriforme. **scorify,** *v.t.* Scorifier.
scoring ['skɔ:riŋ], *n.* (*Games etc.*) Marque, action de marquer; (*Mus.*) orchestration, *f.*
scorn [skɔ:n], *v.t.* Mépriser; dédaigner (de). To scorn to fly, dédaigner de fuir.—*n.* Mépris, dédain, *m.*, dérision, *f.*; (*fig.*) objet de dédain, *m. To laugh to scorn,* couvrir de honte et de mépris. **scorner,** *n.* Contempteur, *m.* **scornful,** *a.* Méprisant, dédaigneux. **scornfully,** *adv.* Dédaigneusement, avec dédain. **scornfulness,** *n.* Caractère dédaigneux, *m.* **scorning,** *n.* Mépris, dédain, *m.*
Scorpio ['skɔ:piou], *n.* (*Astron.*) Le Scorpion, *m.* **scorpion** ['skɔ:pjən], *n.* Scorpion, *m.* **scorpion grass,** *n.* Myosotis, *m.*
scorzonera [skɔ:zə'niərə], *n.* (*Bot.*) Scorsonère, *f.*
Scot [skɔt], *n.* Écossais, *m.*, Écossaise, *f.*
scot [skɔt], *n.* Écot, *m.*, quote-part, *f. To pay scot and lot,* payer ses contributions. **scotfree,** *a.* Sans frais; (*fig.*) sain et sauf, indemne.
Scotch [skɔtʃ], *a.* Écossais.—*n.* Langue écossaise, *f. Broad Scotch,* patois écossais, *m.*; *Scotch fir,* pin d'Écosse, *m.*; *Scotch terrier,* terrier griffon, *m.*; *Scotch whisky,* whisky écossais, *m.* **Scotch-barley,** *n.* Orge monde, *m.*
scotch [skɔtʃ], *v.t.* Entailler, entamer; enrayer (a wheel); (*fig.*) blesser sans tuer, mettre hors de combat; barrer, annuler.—*n.* Entaille; enrayure, *f.*
scoter ['skoutə], *n.* (*Orn.*) Macreuse, *f.*
Scotia ['skouʃə]. Scotie, *f.*
Scotland ['skɔtlənd]. L'Écosse, *f. Scotland Yard,* bureau de la police métropolitaine de Londres et de la Sûreté nationale.
Scotsman, *n.* Écossais, *m.*
Scotswoman, *n.* Écossaise, *f.*
Scotticism ['skɔtisizm], *n.* Idiotisme écossais, *m.* **Scottish,** *a.* Écossais.
scoundrel ['skaundrəl], *n.* Gredin, coquin, scélérat, *m.*, canaille, *f.* **scoundrelism,** *n.* Scélératesse, *f.* **scoundrelly,** *a.* Scélérat, misérable.
scour [skauə], *v.t.* Purger, écurer, récurer; nettoyer (to clean); dégraisser (wool); (*fig.*) parcourir; écumer (the sea). *To scour the country,* courir le pays.—*v.i.* Écurer; nettoyer; courir (to rove). **scourer,** *n.* Récureur, nettoyeur; dégraisseur (of wool), *m.*
scourge [skə:dʒ], *n.* Fouet; (*fig.*) fléau, *m.*— *v.t.* Fouetter, flageller; (*fig.*) châtier, punir. **scourger,** *n.* Châtieur; (*Eccles. Hist.*) flagellant, *m.* **scourging,** *n.* Flagellation, *f.*
scouring ['skauəriŋ], *n.* Récurage; nettoyage; dégraissage (of wool), *m. Off-scourings,* rebut, *m.* **scouring-brick,** *n.* Brique anglaise, *f.*

scout [skaut], *n.* Éclaireur, *m.*; scout, *m.*; (*Naut.*) vedette, *f.*; (*Av.*) avion de chasse; (*Univ.*) garçon de service (college servant), *m.* —*v.i.* Aller en éclaireur.—*v.t.* Repousser avec indignation *or* avec mépris. **scouting-party,** *n.* Troupe d'éclaireurs, *f.* **scoutmaster,** *n.* Chef-éclaireur, scoutmestre, *m.*

scowl [skaul], *v.i.* Se re(n)frogner, froncer le sourcil; avoir l'air menaçant.—*n.* Re(n)-frognement, froncement de sourcil, air re(n)frogné; aspect menaçant, *m.* **scowling,** *a.* Re(n)frogné, menaçant. **scowlingly,** *adv.* D'un air re(n)frogné; avec un aspect menaçant.

scrabble [skræbl], *v.i.* To scrabble about, gratter çà et là.

scrag [skræg], *n.* Corps décharné, squelette, *m.*—*v.t.* (*Ftb.*) Cravater. **scrag-end,** *n.* Bout saigneux (of meat), collet (de mouton), *m.* **scragginess,** *n.* État raboteux, *m.*; maigreur, *f.*, rabougrissement, *m.* **scraggy,** *a.* Noueux, raboteux, rugueux; rabougri.

scram [skræm], *v.i.* (*fam.*) Filer, décamper, se débiner.

scramble [skræmbl], *v.i.* Avancer à l'aide des pieds et des mains; grimper; se battre, se disputer.—*v.t.* (*Teleg.*) Brouiller (a message). *Scrambled eggs,* œufs brouillés, *m.pl.*; *to scramble for,* se battre pour avoir, se disputer; *to scramble up,* grimper (à quatre pattes).—*n.* Mêlée, lutte; gribouillette, *f.* **scramblingly,** *adv.* En grimpant (à quatre pattes); en se disputant.

scrap [skræp], *n.* Morceau, fragment, bout, *m.*; miette (very small quantity); bribe, *f.* (*pl.*) restes, *m.pl.*, bribes, *f.pl.*; (*slang*) bagarre, rixe, *f. Scraps of Greek and Latin,* des bribes de grec et de latin.—*v.t.* Mettre au rebut.—*v.i.* Se colleter, se prendre aux cheveux, se quereller. **scrap basket,** *n.* (*Am.*) Corbeille à papier, *f.* **scrap-book,** *n.* Album, *m.* (pour coupures de journaux ou découpures). **scrap-heap,** *n.* Tas de ferraille, *m.* **scrap-iron,** *n.* Ferraille, *f.*

scrape [skreip], *v.t.* Gratter, érafler, râcler; décrotter (boots etc.); (*Cook.*) ratisser. *To scrape acquaintance with,* faire connaissance habilement avec; *to scrape off,* râcler; *to scrape the dirt off,* décrotter, enlever la boue de; *to scrape the mud off one's shoes,* décrotter ses souliers; *to scrape together,* amasser petit à petit.—*v.i.* Gratter; râcler (to play the fiddle). *To bow and scrape,* faire des salamalecs, ramper devant; *to scrape in,* entrer, passer un examen, de justesse.—*n.* Coup de grattoir, grattage, *m.*; (*fig.*) difficulté, mauvaise affaire, *f.*, embarras, mauvais pas, *m. To get into a scrape,* s'attirer une mauvaise affaire, se mettre dans le pétrin, donner dans un guêpier; *to get out of a scrape,* se tirer d'affaire.

scraper, *n.* Grattoir; râcloir, *m.*; (*Agric.*) ratissoire; décrottoir (for shoes); râcleur (on a fiddle); grippe-sou (miser), *m.*

scraping, *n.* Grattage, *m.*; ratissure (of vegetables), *f.*; râclure (of ivory etc.), *f.*; (*pl.*) ramassis (of things collected together), *m.*; petits profits, *m.pl.*, épargnes (of money), *f.pl. With much bowing and scraping,* avec force révérences.

scrappy ['skræpi], *a.* Hétéroclite, décousu, lacunaire; (*colloq.*) de bric et de broc.

scratch [skrætʃ], *n.* Égratignure, *f.*; coup de griffe *or* d'ongle, *m.*; raie, rayure (on a smooth surface), *f.*; (*Racing*) ligne de départ, *f. He didn't get a scratch,* il n'a pas eu la plus légère blessure; *it is a mere scratch,* ce n'est qu'une égratignure; *scratch team,* équipe mixte et improvisée, *f.*; *to come up to scratch,* (*colloq.*) en venir au fait et au prendre; *to start from scratch,* partir de la ligne de départ, (*fam.*) partir de zéro.—*v.t.* Gratter; égratigner; rayer (a smooth surface). *To scratch one's head,* se gratter la tête; *to scratch out,* gratter, raturer, rayer.—*v.i.* Gratter; égratigner; (*spt.*) renoncer à concourir.

scratcher, *n.* Égratigneur; grattoir (instrument), *m.*

scratching, *n.* Grattage, *m.*; égratignure; rayure, *f.*; (*pl.*) rayures, *f.pl.* **scratchy,** *a.* Qui gratte, qui grince (pen); qui gratte, rugueux (stuff); acariâtre (woman).

scrawl [skrɔːl], *n.* Griffonnage, *m.*, pattes de mouche, *f.pl.*—*v.t.* Griffonner.—*v.i.* Faire des pattes de mouche. **scrawler,** *n.* Griffonneur, *m.*

scrawny ['skrɔːni], *a.* Décharné, émacié.

scray [skrei], *n.* (*Orn.*) Hirondelle de mer, *f.*

scream [skriːm], *n.* Cri perçant, *m. To give a scream,* jeter *or* pousser un cri aigu.—*v.i.* Crier, pousser des cris. *To scream out,* pousser les hauts cris. **screamer,** *n.* Crieur, *m.*, crieuse, *f.*; kamichi (bird), *m.* **screaming,** *a.* Perçant; qui crie. *A screaming farce,* une bouffonnerie désopilante, *f.*—*n.* Cris, *m.pl.* **screamingly,** *adv.* (*colloq.*) *Screamingly funny,* tordant, à se tordre.

screech [skriːtʃ], *n.* Cri perçant, *m.*—*v.i.* Crier; pousser un cri perçant; glapir (to sing badly). **screech-owl,** *n.* Effraie, chouette, *f.* **screechy,** *a.* Aigu, glapissant, perçant; criard.

screed [skriːd], *n.* (*Build.*) (*Floating*) screed, guide, repère (for plastering), *m.*, cueillie, *f.*; longue harangue; longue épître, *f.*

screen [skriːn], *n.* Écran; paravent (large or folding screen); rideau (of trees etc.), *m.*; (*fig.*) voile, *f.*, abri, *m.*; claie (sieve); défense, *f. Fire-screen, hand-screen,* écran, *m.*; *folding-screen,* paravent, *m.*—*v.t.* Mettre à couvert; abriter (contre); mettre à l'abri (de); passer à la claie *or* au crible (to sift); trier sur le volet (of personnel, staff); (*fig.*) protéger. *To screen from punishment,* soustraire au châtiment. **screenings,** *n.pl.* Criblures, *f.pl.*; poussier, *m.*

screw [skruː], *n.* Vis, *f.*; écrou (nut), *m.*; hélice (of a steamer etc.), *f.*; (*slang*) rosse (old horse); (*slang*) paye (wages or salary), *f.*; avare, pingre (person), *m. Archimedean screw,* vis d'Archimède, *f.*; *there is a screw loose somewhere,* il y a quelque chose qui cloche; *to have a screw loose,* être timbré, maboul; *to put a screw on,* (Billiards) couper; (*Ten.*) donner de l'effet (à the ball); *to put the screw on,* serrer la vis *or* les pouces à.—*a.* À hélice.—*v.t.* Visser; (*fig.*) serrer (to press); opprimer, pressurer, écraser (to oppress). *To screw down,* visser, fermer à vis, pressurer; *to screw in,* visser, fixer, faire entrer; *to screw oneself in,* se glisser dedans; *to screw one's workmen,* pressurer ses ouvriers; *to screw out,* dévisser, faire sortir, (*fig.*) extorquer; *to screw up,* visser, serrer, fermer à vis, monter

(an instrument); *to screw up one's courage* (to the sticking point), prendre son courage à deux mains; *to screw up one's face*, faire une grimace, crisper; *to screw up one's lips*, pincer les lèvres; *to screw up one's eyes*, plisser les yeux.—*v.i.* Se visser.
screw-bolt, *n.* Boulon à vis, boulon taraudé, *m.* **screw-cap**, *n.* Couvercle à vis, *m.* **screw-driver**, *n.* Tournevis, *m.* **screwed**, *a.* À vis, fileté; (*slang*) gris. **screw-jack**, *n.* Cric, *m.* **screw-nail**, *n.* Vis à bois, *f.* **screw-nut**, *n.* Écrou, *m.* **screw-plate**, *n.* Filière, *f.* **screw-propeller**, *n.* Hélice propulsive, *f.* **screw-steamer**, *n.* Navire à hélice, *m.* **screw-wrench**, *n.* Clef anglaise, *f.* **screwy**, *a.* (*slang*) Gris; timbré, maboul; sans valeur.
scribble [skribl], *n.* Griffonnage; barbouillage, *m.*—*v.t., v.i.* Griffonner. **scribbler**, *n.* Griffonneur, barbouilleur; écrivassier, grattepapier (bad writer), *m.*
scribe [skraib], *n.* Scribe; écrivain, *m.*; (*Carp.*) pointe à tracer, *f.*—*v.t.* (*Carp.*) Tracer.
scrimmage ['skrimidʒ], *n.* Lutte, rixe, mêlée, *f.* (*Rugby*) *Loose, tight scrimmage*, mêlée ouverte, fermée.
scrimp [skrimp], *a.* Court, petit, chétif [SKIMP, SKIMPY].
scrip [skrip], *n.* Petit sac (wallet), *m.*; (*Comm.*) titre (*or* certificat) provisoire, *m.*
script [skript], *n.* Manuscrit, *m.*; écriture, *f.*; (*Cine.*) scénario, *m.* **script-girl**, *n.* (*Cine.*) Script-girl, *f.* **script-writer**, *n.* (*Cine.*) Scénariste, *m.* or *f.*
scriptural ['skriptʃuərəl], *a.* De l'Écriture Sainte, biblique, scriptural. **Scripture**, *n.* L'Écriture Sainte, l'Écriture, *f.* *Scripture history*, l'histoire sainte, *f.*
scrivener ['skrivənə], *n.* Notaire; changeur; secrétaire, *m.*
scrofula ['skrɔfjulə], *n.* Scrofule, *f.*, écrouelles, *f.pl.* **scrofulous**, *a.* Scrofuleux.
scroll [skroul], *n.* Rouleau, *m.*; banderole (bearing inscription), *f.* **scroll-saw**, *n.* Scie à chantourner, *f.*
scrotal [skroutl], *a.* (*Anat.*) Scrotal. **scrotocele**, *n.* Scrotocèle, *f.* **scrotum**, *n.* Scrotum, *m.*
scrounge [skraundʒ], *v.t.* (*slang*) Chiper, chaparder, grappiller. *To scrounge on someone*, vivre aux crochets de quelqu'un.—*n.* *To be on the scrounge*, grappiller. **scrounger**, *n.* Chapardeur; écornifleur, *m.*
scrub [skrʌb], *v.t.* Frotter fort; laver, récurer; épurer, laver (of gas).—*v.i.* Travailler fort. *To scrub hard for a living*, gagner sa vie péniblement.—*n.* Broussailles, *f.pl.*, brousse, lande, *f.*; maquis, *m.*; (*S. Fr.*) garrigue, *f.*; (*colloq.*) pauvre diable, *m.* **scrubber**, *n.* Laveur, épurateur (machine), *m.* **scrubbing**, *n.* Frottage, récurage, *m.* *To give a good scrubbing to*, bien laver, frotter ferme, passer à la brosse en chiendent. **scrubbing-brush**, *n.* Brosse de cuisine, brosse dure, *f.* **scrubby**, *a.* Rabougri, chétif, mal rasé.
scruff [skrʌf], *n.* Nuque, *f.* *To seize a kitten by the scruff of the neck*, attraper un petit chat par la peau du cou.
scrum(mage) ['skrʌmidʒ], *n.* Scrum, *m.* (*Rugby*) [SCRIMMAGE]. **scrum-half**, *n.* Demi de mêlée, *m.*

scrumptious ['skrʌmpʃəs], *a.* (*colloq.*) Délicieux, épatant.
scrunch [skrʌntʃ], *n.* Broiement, craquement, *m.*—*v.t., v.i.* Broyer avec les dents.
scruple [skru:pl], *n.* Scrupule, *m.* *Without a scruple*, sans scrupule.—*v.i.* Se faire scrupule (de), balancer, hésiter (à). **scrupulous**, *a.* Scrupuleux. *Over-scrupulous*, trop scrupuleux, méticuleux, difficile. **scrupulously**, *adv.* Scrupuleusement. **scrupulousness**, *n.* Humeur scrupuleuse, *f.*; scrupule, doute, *m.*, scrupules, *m.pl.*
scrutable ['skru:təbl], *a.* Qu'on peut scruter.
scrutator [-'teitə], *n.* Scrutateur, *m.* **scrutineer**, *n.* Pointeur (de votes, du scrutin), *m.*; scrutateur, *m.*
scrutinize ['skru:tinaiz], *v.t.* Scruter, examiner à fond. **scrutinizer**, *n.* Scrutateur, *m.* **scrutinizing**, *a.* Scrutateur, inquisiteur. **scrutiny**, *n.* Recherche minutieuse, enquête rigoureuse, vérification, *f.*
scud [skʌd], *n.* Léger nuage, *m.*; course rapide; fuite précipitée, *f.*—*v.i.* S'enfuir, se sauver; courir (of clouds). *To scud before the wind*, fuir vent arrière, avoir le vent sous vergue; *to scud under bare poles*, courir à sec.
scuff [skʌf], *v.t.* Effleurer; érafler.—*v.i.* Traîner les pieds.
scuffle [skʌfl], *n.* Bagarre, rixe, mêlée, *f.*; ratissoire, *f.* (tool).—*v.i.* Se battre, se prendre au collet; traîner les pieds.
scull [skʌl], *n.* Rame; godille, *f.*—*v.i.* Godiller (with one at the stern); ramer (with a pair). —*v.t.* Mener à la rame.
scullery ['skʌləri], *n.* Arrière-cuisine, laverie, *f.* **scullery-maid**, *n.* Laveuse de vaisselle, *f.*
scullion ['skʌliən], *n.* Marmiton, laveur de vaisselle, *m.*
sculptor ['skʌlptə], *n.* Sculpteur, *m.* **sculpture**, *n.* Sculpture, *f.*—*v.t.* Sculpter. **sculptured**, *a.* Sculpté.
scum [skʌm], *n.* Écume; (*Metal.*) scorie, crasse, *f.*; (*fig.*) rebut (refuse), *m.*, lie, *f.* *Scum of the earth*, excrément de la terre, *m.*; *the scum of the people*, la lie du peuple, *f.*— *v.t.* Écumer. **scummy**, *a.* Écumeux.
scumble [skʌmbl], *n.* (*Art*) Frottis, glacis; estompage, *m.*
scuncheon [skʌnʃn], *n.* Écoinçon, *m.*
scupper ['skʌpə], *n.* (*Naut.*) Dalot, *m.*—*v.t.* Saborder; (*Mil.*) surprendre et détruire. **scupper-leather**, *n.* Maugère, *f.* **scupper-nail**, *n.* Clou à maugère, *m.* **scupper-plug**, *n.* Tampon de dalot, *m.*
scurf [skə:f], *n.* Pellicules, *f.pl.* (on hair); teigne, *f.* (on trees). **scurfy**, *a.* Pelliculeux (hair).
scurrility [skʌ'riliti] or **scurrilousness**, *n.* Grossièreté, *f.*, langage grossier, *m.*
scurrilous ['skʌriləs], *a.* Grossier, ordurier. *Scurrilous insinuations*, basses insinuations, *f.pl.* **scurrilously**, *adv.* Grossièrement.
scurry ['skʌri], *n.* Débandade, galopade, *f.*; sauve-qui-peut, *m.*; tourbillon (of dust, snow, etc.), *m.*—*v.i.* Se hâter. *To scurry off, away*, détaler.
scurvily ['skə:vili], *adv.* Bassement, vilement. **scurviness**, *n.* État scorbutique, *m.*; bassesse; mesquinerie (stinginess), *f.* **scurvy**, *n.* Scorbut, *m.*—*a.* Scorbutique; (*fig.*) vil, vilain. **scurvy-grass**, *n.* Cochléaria, *m.*

scut [skʌt], *n.* Couette (de lièvre etc.), *f.*
scutage [ˈskjuːtidʒ], *n.* (*Feud.*) Écuage, *m.*
scutch [skʌtʃ], *v.t.* Teiller, broyer (flax etc.)
scutching-machine, *n.* Écangueuse, *f.*
scutcheon [ˈskʌtʃən] [ESCUTCHEON].
scutiform [ˈskjuːtifɔːm], *a.* Scutiforme, en forme de bouclier.
scuttle [skʌtl], *n.* Panier; seau à charbon, *m.*; (*Naut.*) écoutille, *f.*—*v.t.* Saborder.—*v.i.* Aller à pas précipités. *To scuttle away*, s'enfuir précipitamment; détaler, déguerpir; (of rabbit) débouler. **scuttling**, *n.* Sabordement, sabordage, *m.*—*a.* En fuite, qui détale.
scythe [saið], *n.* Faux, *f.*—*v.t.* Faucher. **scythe-stone**, *n.* Pierre à aiguiser (les faux), *f.*
Scythia [ˈsiθiə]. La Scythie, *f.*
Scythian [ˈsiðiən], *a.* and *n.* Scythe, *m.*
sea [siː], *n.* Mer, *f.*; coup de mer, *m.*, lame (wave); (*fig.*) multitude, *f.*, déluge, *m.* *At sea*, en mer, sur mer (of a ship); *beyond the seas*, outre-mer, au delà des mers; *half-seas over*, à demi ivre, entre deux vins; *heavy sea*, mer houleuse, gros coup de mer; *in the open sea*, en pleine mer, au grand large; *on the high seas*, sur la haute mer; *to be all at sea*, ne savoir quel parti prendre, être perdu *or* dérouté; *to follow the sea*, *to go to sea*, se faire marin, s'embarquer; *to put to sea*, mettre à la mer, prendre la mer; *to ship a sea*, embarquer un coup de mer; *to stand out to sea*, se tenir au large; *to go out to sea*, gagner le large.—*a.* De mer, marin, maritime.
sea-air, *n.* L'air de la mer, *m.* **sea-anemone**, *n.* Anémone de mer, *f.* **sea-bathing**, *n.* Bains de mer, *m.pl.* **sea-bed**, *n.* Fond de la mer, *m.* **sea-bird**, *n.* Oiseau de mer, *m.* **seaboard**, *n.* Littoral, rivage, *m.*, côte, *f.* **sea-boat**, *n.* *A good sea-boat*, un navire qui tient bien la mer, *m.* **sea-born**, *a.* Né de la mer. **sea-borne**, *a.* Transporté par mer (of coals). **sea-bound**, *a.* Borné par la mer. **sea-breach**, *n.* Irruption de la mer, *f.* **sea-breeze**, *n.* Brise de mer, *f.* **sea-bullhead** [SEA-SCORPION]. **sea-calf**, *n.* Veau marin, *m.* **sea-chest**, *n.* Coffre de marin, *m.* **sea-coast**, *n.* Côte, *f.*, littoral, *m.* **sea-cow**, *n.* Lamantin, *m.* **sea-dog**, *n.* Loup de mer (sailor), *m.* **sea-eagle**, *n.* Pygargue, grand aigle de mer, *m.*; orfraie, *f.* **seafarer**, *n.* Homme de mer, marin, *m.* **seafaring**, *a.* Marin. *Seafaring man*, marin, *m.* **sea-fight**, *n.* Combat naval, *m.* **sea-fish**, *n.* Poisson de mer, *m.* **sea-food**, *n.* (*Am.*) Poisson, *m.* **sea-fowl**, *n.* Oiseau de mer, *m.* **sea-front**, *n.* Digue, esplanade, *f.*, bord de mer, *m.* **sea-gauge**, *n.* Tirant d'eau, *m.* **sea-girt**, *a.* (*Lit.*) Ceint par les flots. **sea-god**, *n.* Dieu marin, *m.* **sea-going**, *a.* De haute mer. *Sea-going ship*, navire de long cours, long-courrier, *m.* **sea-green**, *a.* Vert de mer, *m.* **sea-gull**, *n.* Mouette, *f.* **sea-hedgehog**, *n.* Oursin, *m.* **sea-hog**, *n.* Marsouin, *m.* **sea-horse**, *n.* Hippocampe, cheval marin; morse, *m.* **sea-kale**, *n.* Chou marin, *m.* **sea-legs**, *n.pl.* Le pied marin, *m.* *I have not yet found my sea-legs*, je n'ai pas encore le pied marin. **sea-level**, *n.* Niveau de la mer, *m.* **sea-lion**, *n.* Lion de mer, *m.*, otarie, *f.* **sea-lord**, *n.* Lord de l'Amirauté, *m.* **seaman**, *n.* (*pl.* **seamen**) Marin, matelot, homme de mer, *m.* *Leading seaman*, matelot de première

classe. *Able seaman*, matelot de deuxième classe. **seamanship**, *n.* Matelotage, *m.*; habileté à manœuvrer un vaisseau, *f.* **sea-mark**, *n.* Amers (bearings), *m.pl.*, balise, *f.* **sea-mew**, *n.* Mouette, *f.* **sea-nettle**, *n.* Méduse, *f.* **sea-nymph**, *n.* Nymphe de l'océan, néréide, *f.* **sea-piece** or **seascape**, *n.* (*Paint.*) Marine, *f.* **sea-pike**, *n.* Orphie, *f.* **sea-plant**, *n.* Plante marine, *f.* **seaport**, *n.* Port de mer, *m.* *Seaport town*, port de mer, *m.*, ville maritime, *f.* **sea-risk**, *n.* Risque de mer, *m.* **sea-robber**, *n.* Pirate, *m.* **sea-room**, *n.* Évitage, *m.* **sea-route**, *n.* Voie de mer, *f.* **sea-rover**, *n.* Écumeur de mer, *m.* **sea-salt**, *n.* Sel marin, *m.* **sea-scorpion**, *n.* Cotte-chabot, *m.* **sea-scout**, *n.* (Boy-)scout marin, *m.* **sea-serpent**, *n.* Serpent de mer, *m.* **sea-shell**, *n.* Coquillage, *m.* **seashore**, *n.* Bord de la mer, rivage, *m.*, côte, *f.* **sea-sick**, *a.* Qui a le mal de mer. **sea-sickness**, *n.* Mal de mer, *m.* **seaside**, *n.* Bord de la mer, *m.* *Seaside resort*, station balnéaire, *f.* **sea-slug**, *n.* Bêche de mer, *f.* **sea-tossed**, *a.* Ballotté sur les vagues. **sea-trout**, *n.* Truite saumonée, *f.* **sea-urchin**, *n.* Oursin, *m.* **sea-wall**, *n.* Digue, chaussée, *f.*, endiguement, *m.* **seaward**, *a.* Tourné vers la mer.—*adv.* Vers la mer, du côté du large. **sea-water**, *n.* Eau de mer, *f.* **sea-weed**, *n.* Algue, *f.*, goémon, varech, *m.* **seaworthiness**, *n.* Navigabilité (ship), *f.* **seaworthy**, *a.* Qui peut tenir la mer, en bon état (de navigation). **sea-wrack**, *n.* Algue, *f.*, goémon, varech, *m.*
seal (1) [siːl], *n.* Cachet; sceau (official), *m.*; (*Law*) scellés, *m.pl.* *Great-Seal*, grand sceau; *Privy-Seal*, petit sceau; *seals of State*, les sceaux de l'État; *to affix the seals*, faire apposer les scellés sur; (*fig.*) *to set the seal on*, mettre le sceau à.—*v.t.* Cacheter; (*Law*) sceller; (*Customs*) plomber; fermer, clore (to shut). *His fate is sealed*, son sort est décidé; *his lips are sealed*, il lui est défendu de parler, ses lèvres sont scellées; *to seal up*, sceller, cacheter.—*v.i.* Mettre un sceau (à). **sealing**, *n.* Action de sceller, *f.*; (*Build.*) scellement, *m.*; chasse au phoque, *f.* **sealing-wax**, *n.* Cire à cacheter, *f.* **seal-ring**, *n.* Chevalière, *f.*
seal (2) [siːl], *n.* Phoque, *m.* **sealskin**, *n.* Peau de phoque, *f.*; (*Comm.*) phoque, *m.*, loutre, *f.*
seam [siːm], *n.* (*Dress.*) Couture; (*Mining*) couche; (*Geol.*) veine; couture, cicatrice (scar); (*Anat.*) suture, *f.*; (*Measure*) huit boisseaux, *m.pl.* *Flat seam*, couture rabattue; *French seam*, couture anglaise.—*v.t.* Coudre, faire une couture à; couturer. **seamless**, *a.* Sans couture. **seamstress** [SEMPSTRESS].
seamy, *a.* Qui montre la couture; plein de coutures. *The seamy side of life*, les dessous de la vie, *m.pl.*
séance [ˈseiəns], *n.* Séance de spiritisme, *f.*
seaplane [ˈsiːplein], *n.* Hydravion, *m.*
sear (1) [siə], *a.* Séché, fané, flétri.—*v.t.* Brûler; cautériser; dessécher; faner, flétrir; (*Vet.*) appliquer le feu à. **searing-iron**, *n.* Fer à cautériser, *m.*
sear (2) [sie], *n.* Gâchette, *f.* (of gun).
search [səːtʃ], *n.* Recherche; (*Law*) descente, perquisition, *f.*, (*colloq.*) fouille, *f.*; (*Customs*) visite, *f.* *A vain search*, d'inutiles recherches,

f.pl.; *right of search*, droit de visite, *m.*; *to be in search of*, être à la recherche de.—*v.t.* Chercher, examiner, fouiller; (*Law*) faire une perquisition chez; (*Customs*) visiter, fouiller dans. *To search about*, fureter; *to search out*, rechercher, découvrir.—*v.i.* Chercher; fouiller. *To search after*, rechercher; *to search for*, chercher; *to search into*, examiner à fond, approfondir.

searcher, *n.*   Chercheur, *m.*, (*Customs*) visiteur, *m.*, visiteuse, *f.*; (*fig.*) scrutateur, *m.*

searching, *a.*   Scrutateur, pénétrant; vif, perçant (of the wind). *Searching fire*, tir fouillant, *m.* **searchingly**, *adv.* D'un regard scrutateur; minutieusement. **searchless**, *a.* Impénétrable.

searchlight ['sə:tʃlait], *n.*   Projecteur, *m.*; projection électrique; lumière révélatrice, *f.*

search-party, *n.*   Expédition de secours, *f.*

search-warrant, *n.*   Mandat de perquisition, *m.*

season [si:zn], *n.*   Saison, *f.*; (*fig.*) temps, moment opportun, *m.* *For a season*, pour un temps; *in due season*, en temps et saison; *in season*, en saison, au bon moment, à temps (in time), en chaleur (animals); *in* (*season*) *and out of season*, à propos et hors de propos, à tout bout de champ; *this is absolutely out of season*, c'est tout à fait déplacé.—*v.t.* Assaisonner (de); tempérer, modérer (to temper); acclimater (to acclimatize); sécher (timber); (*fig.*) accoutumer (à).—*v.i.* S'acclimater; se sécher (of timber).

seasonable, *a.*   De saison; (*fig.*) à propos, opportun, convenable. **seasonableness**, *n.* Opportunité, *f.*, à-propos, *m.* **seasonably**, *adv.* À propos. **seasonal**, *a.* Des saisons; saisonnier. **seasoned**, *a.* Assaisonné (of meats); (*fig.*) endurci, aguerri, acclimaté.

seasoning, *n.*   Assaisonnement; séchage (of timber), *m.* **season-ticket**, *n.*   Carte d'abonnement, *f.*

seat [si:t], *n.*   Siège; banc (bench), *m.*; banquette (in a vehicle); (*fig.*) place, *f.*; séjour, *m.*, demeure (abode), *f.*; théâtre (of war); château, *m.*, maison de campagne (mansion), *f.*; fond (of trousers); (*colloq.*) derrière, *m.*; assiette, *f.* (on horseback). *Take your seats, please!* en voiture! *the seat of war*, le théâtre de la guerre; *to have a seat in Parliament*, siéger au parlement; *to keep one's seat*, rester assis, rester en selle (on horseback); *to put a seat in a pair of trousers*, mettre un fond à un pantalon; *to take a seat*, s'asseoir, prendre un siège; *to take one's seat at a board*, prendre place au conseil; *to take one's seat at table*, prendre sa place à table; *to vacate one's seat in Parliament*, donner sa démission de député. —*v.t.* Asseoir; faire asseoir; fixer, établir (to fix); placer (to place); garnir de sièges (to fit up with seats); mettre un fond à (trousers). *Pray be seated*, veuillez vous asseoir; *this hall seats a thousand persons*, dans cette salle il y a place pour mille personnes; *to seat oneself*, s'asseoir.

seated, *a.*   Assis, placé. *Cane-seated*, canné (of chairs); *double seated*, à deux places; *low seated*, à siège bas.

seater, *n.* (in compounds). *Two-seater*, (voiture) à deux places. *Single-seater* (*aeroplane*), (avion) monoplace.

seating, *n.*   Allocation des places (assises), *f.*;

emplacement, *m.*, position (of machine part), *f.*, assiette, *f.*; fond (of trousers), *m.* *Seating accommodation*, *capacity*, (nombre de) places assises.

sebaceous [si'beiʃəs], *a.* Sébacé.

sebesten [si'bestən], *n.* Sébeste, *m.* **sebesten-tree**, *n.* Sébestier, *m.*

sebiferous [si'bifərəs], *a.* Sébifère.

secant ['si:kənt], *a.* Sécant.—*n.* Sécante, *f.*

secede [si'si:d], *v.i.* Se séparer (de). **seceder**, *n.* Scissionnaire; dissident; (*Am. Hist.*) Sécessionniste, *m.* **seceding**, *a.* Scissionnaire. **secession** [-'seʃən], *n.* Sécession, séparation, *f.* *The War of Secession*, la guerre de Sécession, *f.* **Secessionist**, *n.* (*Am. Hist.*) Sécessionniste, *m.*

seclude [si'klu:d], *v.t.* Séparer; écarter, éloigner, retirer. *To seclude oneself*, s'isoler, se retirer, se renfermer. **secluded**, *a.* Retiré, isolé, solitaire. **seclusion** [-'klu:ʒən], *n.* Retraite, solitude, *f.*, isolement, *m.*

seclusive, *a.* Qui tient dans la retraite.

second ['sekənd], *a.* Second, deuxième; deux (of the month); inférieur (inferior). *A second Nero*, un autre Néron; *every second day*, tous les deux jours; *in the second place*, en second lieu; *my second-best hat*, mon chapeau No. 2, mon numéro 2; *on second thoughts*, à la réflexion; *on the second floor*, au deuxième; *second-cousin*, cousin issu de germains, *m.*; *second form*, classe de cinquième, *f.*; *second in command*, (commandant en) second, *m.*; *second hand*, aiguille des secondes (of a watch), *f.*; *second sight*, seconde vue, *f.*; *the second largest city*, la seconde ville par ordre d'importance, en importance; *to be second to none*, ne le céder à personne; *to come off second best*, être battu; *to go second class*, (*Rail.*) voyager en seconde.—*n.* Témoin, second (in a duel), *m.*; (*Box.*) soigneur, *m.*; seconde (of time), *f.*; (*pl.*) farine de deuxième qualité (of grain etc.), *f.*—*v.t.* Seconder, aider; appuyer (a motion); (*Mil.*) [si'kɔnd], mettre en disponibilité *or* hors-cadre. *Seconded for service with . . .*, détaché auprès de . . . .

secondary ['sekəndri], *a.* Secondaire; accessoire. *Secondary education*, enseignement du second degré.

seconder, *n.* Personne qui appuie, *f.*

second-hand, *a.* and *adv.* D'occasion. *Second-hand dealer*, revendeur, brocanteur, *m.*

secondly, *adv.* Secondement; en second lieu.

second-rate, *a.* De second ordre; de second rang (of ship); inférieur.

secrecy ['si:krəsi], *n.* Secret, *m.*; discrétion (closeness), *f.* *I rely upon your secrecy*, je compte sur votre discrétion.

secret ['si:krət], *a.* Secret; retiré (secluded). *Secret drawer*, tiroir secret, *m.*; *secret service funds*, fonds secrets, *m.pl.*; *to keep secret*, tenir secret.—*n.* Secret, *m.* *An open secret*, un secret de Polichinelle; *in secret*, en secret, secrètement, en cachette; *no secret but between two*, secret de deux, secret de Dieu, secret de trois, secret de tous; *to keep a secret*, garder un secret; *to tell a secret to*, confier un secret à.

secretarial [sekrə'tɛəriəl], *a.* De secrétaire.

secretariat [sekrə'tɛəriæt], *n.* Secrétariat, *m.*

secretary ['sekrətri], *n.* Secrétaire, *m.* *Home Secretary*, ministre de l'Intérieur, *m.*; *private*

secretary, secrétaire particulier, *m.*; *Secretary of State*, secrétaire d'État; *secretary's office*, secrétariat, *m.*
secretaryship ['sekrətriʃip], *n.* Secrétariat, *m.*
secrete [si'kri:t], *v.t.* Cacher; (*Physiol.*) sécréter. *To secrete oneself* (*in*), se cacher (dans).
secretion [si'kri:ʃən], *n.* Sécrétion, *f.* **secretive**, *a.* (*Physiol.*) Sécréteur; réservé; dissimulé; (*fam.*) cachottier, -ière. **secretiveness**, *n.* Caractère cachottier, *m.*
secretly ['si:krətli], *adv.* Secrètement, en secret; intérieurement, au fond (inwardly). **secretness**, *n.* Caractère secret, *m.*; discrétion, *f.*
secretory [si'kri:təri], *a.* Sécrétoire.
sect [sekt], *n.* Secte, *f.* **sectarian** [-'tɛəriən], *a.* De sectaire.—*n.* Sectaire, *m.* **sectarianism**, *n.* Esprit de secte, *m.*
sectary ['sektəri], *n.* Sectaire, *m.*
sectile ['sektail], *a.* Sécable.
section ['sekʃən], *n.* Section; (*Arch., Geol., etc.*) coupe, *f.*, profil; (*Mil.*) secteur, *m.*, groupe de combat, *m.*; (*Geol.*) région, *f.* *Cross-section*, coupe transversale, *f.* **sectional**, *a.* En coupe, en profil; profilé; en sections; de classe (sociale), de parti. *Sectional boiler*, chaudière sectionnelle, *f.*; *sectional book-case*, bibliothèque démontable, *f.*; *sectional paper*, papier quadrillé, *m.*
sector ['sektə], *n.* Secteur; compas de proportion (instrument), *m.*; (*Mech., Elec.*) couronne, *f.*
secular ['sekjulə], *a.* Séculier, temporel; séculaire (of years). **secularism**, *n.* Sécularisme, *m.* **secularity** [-'læriti] or **secularness**, *n.* Sécularité, mondanité, *f.*
secularization ['sekjulərai'zeiʃən], *n.* Sécularisation, *f.*
secularize ['sekjuləraiz], *v.t.* Séculariser.
secularly, *adv.* Séculièrement; séculairement.
secundine ['sekəndin], *n.* (*Bot.*) Secondine, *f.*; (*Obstetrics*, *pl.*) secondines, *f.pl.*
secure [sə'kjuə], *a.* Dans la sécurité, en sûreté; à l'abri (de); sûr, assuré (of things), garanti; bien fermé; solidement attaché. *Secure against* or *from*, en sûreté contre, à l'abri de; *secure of*, sûr de.—*v.t.* Mettre en sûreté, protéger; assurer (make certain); s'assurer de (one's possession of); garantir (payments etc.); fermer; barrer (to make fast); (*fig.*) affermir; s'emparer de, se saisir de (to get hold of); valoir à (to ensure); retenir (a place in a coach etc.).
securely, *adv.* En sûreté; avec sécurité; sans crainte; sûrement; bien; fortement, solidement. **secureness**, *n.* Sécurité, *f.*
security, *n.* Sécurité, sûreté; garantie, *f.*, nantissement, *m.*; (*pl.*) titres, *m.pl.*, valeurs, *f.pl.*; (*Law*) caution, *f. Foreign securities*, fonds étrangers, *m.pl.*; *gilt-edged securities*, valeurs de tout repos, *f.pl.*; *Government securities*, fonds d'État, *m.pl.*; *Security Council*, Conseil de sécurité, *m.*; *social security*, sécurité sociale, *f.*; *to stand security for*, se porter garant pour; *transferable securities*, valeurs mobilières, *f.pl.*
sedan-chair [si'dæn 'tʃɛə], *n.* Chaise à porteurs, *f.*
sedate [si'deit], *a.* Posé, calme, rassis. **sedately**, *adv.* Posément, avec calme. **sedateness**, *n.* Calme, *m.*

sedative ['sedətiv], *a.* and *n.* Sédatif, *m.*
sedentarily ['sedntərili], *adv.* Sédentairement. **sedentariness**, *n.* Sédentarité, *f.*
sedentary, *a.* Sédentaire; inactif, inerte.
sedge [sedʒ], *n.* Laîche, *f.*, jonc, *m.* **sedge-fly**, *n.* Phrygane, *f.* **sedge-warbler**, *n.* Fauvette des roseaux, *f.* **sedgy**, *a.* Plein de joncs.
sediment ['sedimənt], *n.* Sédiment, dépôt, *m.* **sedimentary** [-'mentəri], *a.* Sédimentaire.
sedition [si'diʃən], *n.* Sédition, *f.* **seditious**, *a.* Séditieux. **seditiously**, *adv.* Séditieusement. **seditiousness**, *n.* Esprit séditieux; caractère séditieux, *m.*
seduce [si'dju:s], *v.t.* Séduire; abuser (d'une femme). **seducer**, *n.* Séducteur, *m.*, séductrice, *f.* **seducible**, *a.* Qu'on peut séduire, corruptible. **seducing**, *a.* Séduisant. **seduction** [-'dʌkʃən], *n.* Séduction, *f.* **seductive**, *a.* Séducteur, séduisant. **seductiveness**, *n.* Caractère séduisant, *m.*; charmes, *m.pl.*; séduction, *f.*
sedulity [se'dju:liti] or **sedulousness** ['sedjuləsnis], *n.* Assiduité, diligence, application, *f.*, zèle, *m.* **sedulous** ['sedjuləs], *a.* Assidu, diligent, appliqué, zélé. **sedulously**, *adv.* Assidûment, diligemment, avec application.
see (1) [si:], *n.* Siège épiscopal, évêché; archevêché (of an archbishop), *m. The Holy See*, le Saint-Siège.
see (2) [si:], *v.t.* (*past* **saw** [sɔ:], *p.p.* **seen** [si:n]) Voir; apercevoir, s'apercevoir de; comprendre, saisir, reconnaître; s'occuper, prendre garde (de); accompagner, conduire. *Fit to be seen*, présentable; *he sees nobody*, il ne voit personne; *I can't see anything*, je ne vois rien; *I can't see a thing*, je n'y vois rien; *I saw him through his difficulties*, je l'ai tiré de son embarras; *it remains to be seen*, il reste à savoir; *to be seen*, être vu, se voir; *to see a doctor*, consulter un médecin; *to see a joke*, comprendre *or* entendre une plaisanterie; *to see a thing out*, voir la fin d'une chose; *to see home*, conduire jusque chez lui; *to see it through*, ne pas lâcher, tenir jusqu'au bout; *to see out*, reconduire; *to see someone off*, accompagner quelqu'un à la gare, au bateau, etc.; *to see the light*, se convertir; comprendre.—*v.i.* Voir. *I see*, je comprends; *I shall see that everything is ready*, j'aurai soin que tout soit prêt; *I will see to it*, je m'en occuperai, j'y veillerai; *let us see*, voyons voir; *see!* voyez! *seeing is believing*, voir c'est croire; *see to it*, veillez-y, prenez-y garde, avisez-y; *to see about*, penser à, s'occuper de; *to see into* (*a thing*), voir le fond de, pénétrer; *to see over*, visiter, voir; *to see that*, veiller à ce que; *to see through* (*a thing*), comprendre, deviner, pénétrer; *to see to*, avoir soin de, veiller à, s'occuper de; *you see*, voyez-vous.
seed [si:d], *n.* Semence; graine (of vegetables), *f.*; (*fig.*) race, *f. To cast its seed*, s'égrener; *to run to seed*, monter en graine; *to sow the seed of*, semer.—*v.i.* Grener, venir à graine; monter en graine (to run to seed).—*v.t.* Ensemencer; égruger (fruit); (*spt.*) trier. *Seeded players*, têtes de série, *f.pl.*
seed-bed *n.* Semis, *m.* **seed-cake**, *n.* Gâteau à l'anis; tourteau (of colza, linseed, etc.), *m.* **seed-coat**, *n.* (*Bot.*) Épisperme, *m.*, arille, *m.* **seed-corn**, *n.* Grain pour semis, blé de semence, *m.* **seed-leaf**, *n.* (*Bot.*) Cotylédon, *m.* **seedling**, *n.* Semis, sauvageon (of a

forest tree), *m.* **seed-pearl,** *n.* Semence de perle, très petite perle, *f.* **seed-plot,** *n.* Semis, *m.* **seedsman,** *n.* (*pl.* **seedsmen**) Grainetier, *m.* **seed-time,** *n.* Semailles, *f.pl.* **seed-trade,** *n.* Graineterie, *f.* **seed-vessel,** *n.* (*Bot.*) Péricarpe, *m.* **seedy,** *a.* Râpé, usé (garment); malade, souffrant; minable; miteux.

seeing ['si:iŋ], *n.* Vue; vision, *f.* *Sight-seeing,* excursions, visite de monuments, de pays, de sites.—*conj.* Vu que (that), puisque. *Seeing the state of things,* vu l'état des choses.

seek [si:k], *v.t.* (*past* and *p.p.* **sought** [sɔ:t]) Chercher; poursuivre, en vouloir à (one's life etc.). *To seek out,* chercher, rechercher, quêter.—*v.i.* Chercher. *To seek for* or *after,* poursuivre, chercher, rechercher, tâcher de trouver; *to seek from,* demander à; *to seek to,* chercher à.

seeker, *n.* Chercheur, *m.,* chercheuse, *f.*

seeking, *n.* Recherche, poursuite, *f.*

seem [si:m], *v.i.* Sembler, paraître, avoir l'air (de). *It seems, it would seem, so it seems,* à ce qu'il paraît; *it seems to me,* ce me semble, il me semble; *to seem interesting,* sembler intéressant.

seeming, *n.* Semblant, *m.,* apparence, *f.,* dehors, *m.*—*a.* Apparent, spécieux. **seemingly,** *adv.* En apparence, apparemment.

seemliness ['si:mlinis], *n.* Bienséance; convenance, *f.* **seemly,** *a.* Bienséant, convenable; agréable à voir, joli; de belle stature. —*adv.* Avec bienséance, convenablement.

seen, *p.p.* [SEE].

seep [si:p], *v.i.* S'infiltrer, suinter; filtrer. **seepage,** *n.* Infiltration, déperdition, fuite, *f.*; suintement, *m.* **seeping,** *n.* Infiltration, *f.*; suintement, *m.*

seer ['siə], *n.* Prophète, voyant, *m.*

seesaw ['si:sɔ:], *n.* Bascule, balançoire, *f.,* va-et-vient, *m.* *Seesaw motion,* mouvement de va-et-vient, *m.*—*v.i.* Faire la bascule, jouer à la bascule.

seethe [si:ð], *v.t.* Faire bouillir.—*v.i.* Bouillir, bouillonner. **seething,** *a.* Bouillant. *The seething crowd,* la foule grouillante.—*n.* Marmite, *f.*

segment ['segmənt], *n.* Segment, *m.*; portion, *f.*; morceau, *m.*—*v.t.* Couper en segments, segmenter. **segmental** [-'mentl], *a.* Segmentaire.

segregate ['segrigeit], *v.t.* Séparer.—*v.i.* Se diviser. **segregation** [-'geiʃən], *n.* Séparation, ségrégation, *f.*

Seidlitz powder ['sedlits 'paudə], *n.* Poudre de Sedlitz, *f.*

seine [sein], *n.* Seine (net), *f.*

seisin ['si:zin], *n.* (*Law*) Saisine, *f.*

seism ['saizm], *n.* Séisme, tremblement de terre, *m.* **seismic,** *a.* Sismique. **seismograph,** *n.* Sismographe, *m.,* sismoscope, *m.*

seizable ['si:zəbl], *a.* Saisissable.

seize [si:z], *v.t.* Saisir; se saisir de, s'emparer de; (*Naut.*) aiguilleter, amarrer.—*v.i.* (*Mech.*) Gripper, caler, se bloquer, se coincer. *To be seized of,* être en possession de; *to seize again,* reprendre.

seizin [SEISIN].

seizing ['si:ziŋ], *n.* Action de saisir; (*Law*) saisie, *f.*; (*Naut.*) aiguilletage, amarrage, *m.*; (*pl.*) amarrage, *m.*

seizure ['si:ʒə], *n.* Saisie, prise de possession, saisie-arrêt; (*Path.*) attaque, *f.*

selachian [si'leikiən], *a.* and *n.* (*Ichth.*) Sélacien, *m.*

seldom ['seldəm], *adv.* Rarement. ***seldomness,** *n.* Rareté, *f.*

select [si'lekt], *v.t.* Choisir; (*spt.*) sélectionner. —*a.* Choisi, de choix; d'élite. *The select few,* l'élite, *f.,* le petit nombre des élus, *m.* **selected,** *a.* Choisi. **selectedly,** *adv.* Avec choix. **selection,** *n.* Choix, *m.* *Natural selection,* sélection naturelle, *f.* **selective,** *a.* Sélectif; sélecteur. **selectivity,** *n.* Sélectivité, *f.* **selectness,** *n.* Caractère choisi, *m.,* excellence, *f.* **selector,** *n.* (*spt.*) Sélectionneur, *m.* (*Motor.*) Selector-(*fork*), fourchette de commande, *f.*; *selector-rod,* baladeur, *m.*

selenate ['selineit], *n.* Séléniate, *m.* **selenic** [si'lenik], *a.* Sélénique. **seleniferous** [seli'nifərəs], *a.* Sélénifère. **selenium** [si'li:niəm], *n.* Sélénium, *m.*

selenian [si'li:niən], *a.* Sélénien. **selenography** [seli'nɔgrəfi], *n.* Sélénographie, *f.*

self [self], *pron.* (*pl.* **selves**) Même, soi-même; (*reflexively*) se; soi-même, *m.* *Another self,* un autre soi-même; *by one's self,* seul, tout seul, de soi-même; *for my own self,* pour ma part; *her gracious self,* sa gracieuse personne; *her own dear self,* sa chère personne. *He knows how to enrich himself,* il sait s'enrichir; *I dine by myself,* je dîne seul; *I shave myself,* je me rase moi-même; *myself, thyself, himself, herself, itself,* moi-même, toi-même, lui-même, elle-même me, te, se; *oneself,* se, soi-même; *ourselves, yourselves, themselves,* nous-mêmes, vous-mêmes, eux-mêmes, elles-mêmes; nous, vous, se.—*n.* Le moi, individu, *m.,* personne, *f.*

self-abandonment, *n.* Abnégation, *f.*

self-abased, *a.* Humilié (par le sentiment de sa honte). **self-abasement,** *n.* Humiliation volontaire, *f.* **self-abasing,** *a.* Qui s'humilie; humiliant (of things). **self-accusing,** *a.* Qui s'accuse soi-même. **self-acting,** *a.* Automatique. **self-admiration,** *n.* Admiration de soi-même. **self-admiring,** *a.* Qui s'admire soi-même. **self-adoring,** *a.* Qui s'adore soi-même. **self-advertisement,** *n.* Cabotinage, battage, *m.* **self-apparent,** *a.* Évident. **self-approving,** *a.* Qui s'approuve soi-même, suffisant. **self-assertion,** *n.* Caractère impérieux, *m.,* outrecuidance, *f.* **self-assertive,** *a.* Autoritaire, impérieux, outrecuidant. **self-assumed,** *a.* De sa propre autorité. **self-assurance,** *n.* Assurance, *f.,* aplomb, *m.* **self-assured,** *a.* Sûr de soi, plein d'assurance.

self-binder, *n.* Lieuse, moissonneuse-lieuse, *f.*

self-born, *a.* Né de soi-même.

self-centred, *a.* Égocentrique. **self-colour,** *n.* Couleur uniforme, *f.,* ton sur ton, *m.* **self-command,** *n.* Empire sur soi-même, sang-froid, *m.*; retenue, *f.* **self-communion,** *n.* Recueillement, *m.* **self-complacency,** *n.* Fatuité, présomption, *f.* **self-conceit,** *n.* or **self-conceitedness,** *n.* Suffisance, *f.,* amour-propre, *m.* **self-conceited,** *a.* Suffisant, rempli d'amour-propre. **self-confidence,** *n.* Confiance en soi-même, assurance, *f.* **self-confident,** *a.* Plein de confiance en soi, sûr de soi-même. **self-conscious,** *a.* Qui a la connaissance de soi-même, embarrassé, intimidé; gêné; emprunté; poseur. **self-consciousness,** *n.* Embarras, *m.*, gêne, contrainte, *f.* **self-consequence,** *n.* Importance personnelle, *f.* **self-constituted,** *a.* Constitué par l'initiative de ses propres membres. **self-contained,** *a.* Indépendant, avec entrée particulière (flat); réservé (person). **self-contradiction,** *n.* Contradiction avec soi-même, *f.* **self-contradictory,** *a.* Qui se contredit. **self-control,** *n.* Sang-froid, *m.*; maîtrise de soi, *f.* **self-convicted,** *a.* Condamné par ses propres paroles. **self-created,** *a.* Créé par soi-même. **self-criticism,** *n.* Autocritique, *f.*

self-deceit or **self-deception,** *n.* Illusion, *f.* **self-deceived,** *a.* Dupe de ses propres illusions; sa propre dupe. **self-defence,** *n.* Défense personnelle; légitime défense, *f.* *The art of self-defence,* la boxe, *f.* **self-delusion,** *n.* Illusion, *f.* **self-denial,** *n.* Abnégation, *f.*; désintéressement, *m.* **self-denying,** *a.* Qui fait abnégation de soi; qui s'impose des privations. **self-dependent,** *a.* Indépendant. **self-destroyer,** *n.* Suicidé, *m.* **self-destruction,** *n.* Suicide, *m.* **self-determination,** *n.* Libre disposition de soi, *f.* **self-devoted,** *a.* Dévoué. **self-drive,** *a.* *Self-drive car,* voiture louée sans chauffeur, *f.*

self-educated, *a.* Autodidacte. **self-elected,** *a.* Élu par soi-même. **self-elective,** *a.* Qui a le droit de cooptation. **self-enjoyment,** *n.* Satisfaction intérieure, *f.* **self-esteem,** *n.* Estime de soi-même, *f.* **self-evident,** *a.* Évident en soi, clair comme le jour, qui saute aux yeux. **self-examination,** *n.* Examen de conscience, *m.* **self-explanatory,** *a.* Qui s'explique de soi-même. **self-existence,** *n.* Existence indépendante, *f.*

self-flattering, *a.* Qui se flatte soi-même. **self-governeu,** *a.* Indépendant, autonome. **self-government,** *n.* Autonomie, *f. Local self-government,* autonomie administrative, *f.*; *the right to self-government,* le droit de se gouverner soi-même.

self-heal, *n.* (*Bot.*) Brunelle, *f.* **self-healing,** *a.* Qui se guérit soi-même. **self-help,** *n.* Efforts personnels, *m.pl.*; (*phr.*) aide-toi toi-même.

self-importance, *n.* Suffisance, vanité, *f.* **self-important,** *a.* Plein de soi, suffisant. **self-improvement,** *n.* Culture de soi-même, *f.* **self-indulgence,** *n.* Sybaritisme, *m.*; complaisance envers soi-même, *f.* **self-indulgent,** *a.* Qui ne se refuse rien; sybarite. **self-inflicted,** *a.* Volontaire. **self-interest,** *n.* Intérêt personnel, *m.* **self-interested,** *a.* Intéressé, égoïste. **self-invited,** *a.* Sans invitation.

selfish ['selfiʃ], *a.* Égoïste. **selfishly,** *adv.* En égoïste, d'une manière égoïste. **selfishness,** *n.* Égoïsme, *m.* **selfless,** *a.* Désintéressé.

self-justification, *n.* Apologie, *f.* **self-kindled,** *a.* Qui s'allume spontanément. **self-knowledge,** *n.* Connaissance de soi-même, *f.*

self-love, *n.* Amour de soi, *m.* **self-loving,** *a.* Égoïste.

self-made, *a.* Qui s'est fait ce qu'il est. *He is a self-made man,* il est l'artisan de sa fortune, il est fils de ses œuvres. **self-moved** or

self-moving, *a.* Qui se meut de soi-même, automoteur. **self-murder,** *n.* Suicide, *m.* **self-murderer,** *n.* Suicidé, *m.* **self-neglect,** *n.* Oubli de soi-même, *m.* **self-opinioned** or **self-opinionated,** *a.* Entiché de son opinion, entêté. **self-pleasing,** *a.* Qui se plaît à soi-même. **self-possessed,** *a.* Calme; maître de soi; qui a beaucoup d'aplomb. **self-possession,** *n.* Sang-froid, aplomb, *m.* **self-praise,** *n.* Éloge de soi-même, *m.* **self-preservation,** *n.* Conservation de soi-même, *f. The instinct of self-preservation,* l'instinct de conservation, *m.* **self-preserving,** *a.* Qui se conserve soi-même. **self-propelled,** *a.* Automoteur, autopropulsé.

self-registering, *a.* À registre, enregistreur. *Self-registering thermometer,* thermomètre à maxima et à minima, *m.* **self-regulated,** *a.* Qui se règle de soi-même. **self-reliance,** *n.* Confiance en soi, indépendance, *f.* **self-reproach,** *n.* Remords, *m.pl.*, condamnation de soi-même, *f.* **self-respect,** *n.* Respect de soi-même, amour-propre, *m.*; dignité, *f.* **self-restrained,** *a.* Retenu. **self-restraint,** *n.* Retenue, *f.* **self-righteous,** *a.* Pharisaïque. **self-righteousness,** *n.* Pharisaïsme, *m.* **self-sacrifice,** *n.* Sacrifice de soi-même, *m.*, abnégation, *f.* **self-same,** *a.* Absolument le même. **self-satisfied,** *a.* Content de soi. **self-seeker,** *n.* **self-seeking,** *a.* Égoïste. **self-service,** *n.* Libre service, *m.* **self-starter,** *n.* Démarreur automatique, *m.* **self-styled,** *a.* Soi-disant, prétendu. **self-sufficiency,** *n.* Suffisance; autarcie; indépendance, *f.* **self-sufficient,** *a.* Suffisant; indépendant. **self-suggestion,** *n.* Auto-suggestion, *f.* **self-supporting,** *a.* Qui subsiste par ses propres moyens; qui n'a besoin de personne pour vivre.

self-taught, *a.* Autodidacte. **self-will,** *n.* Obstination, opiniâtreté, *f.* **self-willed,** *a.* Obstiné, opiniâtre. **self-winding,** *a.* À remontage automatique. **self-worship,** *n.* Idolâtrie de soi-même, *f.*

sell [sel], *v.t.* (*past* and *p.p.* **sold** [sould]) Vendre. *To be sold,* à vendre, (*fig.*) être attrapé, être mis dedans; *to sell off,* liquider; *to sell one's life dearly,* vendre chèrement sa vie; *to sell out,* vendre, (*Mil.*) vendre son brevet, quitter l'armée; *to sell up,* vendre les meubles de.—*v.i.* Se vendre. *The papers sold like wildfire,* les journaux s'enlevèrent comme des petits pains; *to sell by auction,* vendre aux enchères; *to sell off,* s'écouler (of goods); *to sell out,* se liquider; *to sell well,* se vendre bien, être d'un bon débit; *to be sold out of an article,* avoir tout vendu; ne plus avoir d'un article.—*n.* Attrape, *f. What a sell for him!* quelle attrape pour lui!

seller, *n.* Vendeur, *m.*, vendeuse, *f.* **selling,** *n.* Vente, *f. Selling off,* liquidation, *f.*; *selling price,* prix de vente, *m.*

sell-out, *n.* It was a real sell-out, ç'a été un succès fou.

seltzer ['seltsə] or **seltzer water,** *n.* Eau de Seltz, *f. A bottle of seltzer,* un siphon d'eau de Seltz.

selvagee [selvə'dʒiː], *n.* (*Naut.*) Erse, *f.* **selvedge** ['selvidʒ], *n.* Lisière, *f.* **selves,** *pl.* [SELF].

semantics [sə'mæntiks], *n.pl.* Sémantique, *f.*

semaphore ['semafɔ:], *n.* Sémaphore, *m.*—*v.t.* Signaler par sémaphore ou signaux à bras.

semasiological [səmæziə'lɔdʒikl], *a.* Sémantique. **semasiology** [-'ɔlədʒi], *n.* Sémasiologie, sémantique, *f.*

semblance ['semblans], *n.* Semblant, *m.*, apparence (show), *f.*

semen ['si:mən], *n.* Semence, *f.*; sperme, *m.*

semi ['semi], *pref.* Semi, demi, à demi, à moitié.

semi-annual, *a.* Semestriel.

semi-barbarian, *a.* Semi-barbare.

semibreve ['semibri:v], *n.* (*Mus.*) Ronde, *f.*

semi-circle ['semisə:kl], *n.* Demi-cercle, *m.* **semi-circular**, *a.* Demi-circulaire.

semicolon ['semi'koulən], *n.* Point et virgule, *m.*

semi-darkness, *n.* Demi-jour, *m.*; pénombre, *f.*

semi-detached [semidi'tætʃt], *a.* Contiguë à une autre. *Semi-detached houses,* maisons jumelles, *f.pl.*

semi-diameter, *n.* Demi-diamètre, *m.*

semi-final, *a.* Demi-final.—*n.* Demi-finale, *f.*

semi-lunar, *a.* En demi-lune, en (forme de) croissant, semi-lunaire.

semi-metallic, *a.* Demi-métallique.

seminal ['seminl], *a.* Séminal.

seminar ['seminɑ:], *n.* Groupe d'étudiants avancés travaillant sous la conduite d'un professeur, *m.*; discussion d'un sujet spécial par des étudiants, *f.*; cours hors programme, *m.*

seminarist ['seminərist], *n.* Séminariste, *m.* **seminary**, *n.* Séminaire, *m.*; institution (school), *f.*

semination [semi'neiʃən], *n.* Sémination, *f.*; semailles, *f.pl.* **seminiferous** [-'nifərəs], *a.* Séminifère.

semi-official ['semiə'fiʃl], *a.* Demi-officiel, officieux. **semi-officially**, *adv.* Demi-officiellement.

semi-opaque, *a.* Demi-opaque.

semi-periodic, *a.* Demi-périodique.

semiquaver [semi'kweivə], *n.* (*Mus.*) Double croche, *f. Semiquaver rest,* quart de soupir, *m.*

semi-spherical [semi'sferikl], *a.* Hémisphérique.

Semites ['si:maits], *n.pl.* Sémites, *m.pl.*

Semitic [si'mitik], *a.* Sémitique.

semitone ['semitoun], *n.* (*Mus.*) Demi-ton, semi-ton, *m.* **semitonic** [-'tɔnik], *a.* De demi-ton.

semi-transparency [semitrænz'pærənsi *or* -'pɛərənsi], *n.* Demi-transparence, *f.* **semi-transparent**, *a.* Demi-transparent.

semi-vowel, *n.* Demi-voyelle, *f.*

semolina [semə'li:nə], *n.* Semoule, *f.*

sempiternal [sempi'tə:nl], *a.* Sempiternel.

sempstress ['sempstrəs *or* 'semstris], *n.* Couturière, *f.*

senate ['senit], *n.* Sénat, *m.*; (*Eng. Univ.*), centre administratif, siège de la chancellerie universitaire, *m.* **senate-house**, *n.* Sénat, *m.*

senator ['senətə], *n.* Sénateur, *m.* **senatorial** [-'tɔ:riəl], *a.* Sénatorial. **senatorian**, *a.* Sénatorien. **senatorship**, *n.* Dignité de sénateur, *f.*

Senatus consultum [sə'neitəs kən'sʌltəm], *n.* Sénatus-consulte, *m.*

send [send], *v.t.* (*past* and *p.p.* **sent**) Envoyer, faire parvenir; expédier (goods); accorder, donner (to bestow); répandre (to diffuse). *To send about his business,* envoyer promener; *to send away,* renvoyer, congédier, faire partir; *to send back,* renvoyer; *to send down,* faire descendre, envoyer, (*Univ.*) renvoyer, expulser; *to send for,* envoyer chercher, faire venir; *to send forth,* lancer, jeter, pousser (a cry), émettre (to emit), répandre, exhaler (to exhale); *to send in,* faire entrer, livrer (to deliver), servir (to serve up), rendre (accounts), annoncer (to publish); *to send off,* faire partir; *to send on,* expédier, faire suivre (letters etc.); *to send on a fool's errand,* charger d'une commission ridicule; *to send out,* envoyer dehors, faire sortir, expédier (goods); *to send up,* faire monter, jeter, lancer, servir (to serve up); *to send word to,* faire savoir à, envoyer un mot à.—*v.i.* Envoyer. *They have sent for me,* on m'a envoyé chercher; *to send after,* envoyer chercher, faire venir.

sender, *n.* Envoyeur, *m.*, envoyeuse, *f.*; (*Comm.*) expéditeur, *m.*

sending, *n.* Envoi, *m.*; (*Comm.*) expédition, *f.*

send-off, *n.* Fête d'adieu, *f.*, démonstration amicale à l'occasion du départ de quelqu'un, *f. They gave us a wonderful send-off,* notre départ a été l'occasion de grandes démonstrations d'amitié; *the flat-racing season had a good send-off yesterday,* la saison de plat s'est ouverte hier de façon satisfaisante.

Seneca ['senəkə]. Sénèque, *m.*

Senegal ['senigɔ:l]. Le Sénégal, *m.*

senescence [sə'nesəns], *n.* Sénescence, *f.* **senescent**, *a.* Sénescent.

seneschal ['seniʃl], *n.* Sénéchal, *m.* **seneschalship**, *n.* Sénéchaussée, *f.*

sengreen ['sengri:n], *n.* Joubarbe, *f.*

senile ['si:nail], *a.* De vieillard, sénile. **senilely**, *adv.* En vieillard. **senility** [se'niliti], *n.* Sénilité, *f.*

senior ['si:njə], *a.* Aîné; ancien; plus ancien, supérieur. *Mr. A. senior,* M. A. aîné, M. A. père; *senior partner,* associé principal.—*n.* Aîné, *m.*, aînée, *f.*; ancien, *m.*, ancienne, *f.*; doyen, *m. He is my senior by five years,* il est mon aîné de cinq ans; *senior officer,* officier le plus élevé en grade, *m.*

seniority [si:ni'ɔriti], *n.* Priorité d'âge; ancienneté, *f. By right of seniority,* par droit d'ancienneté; *promotion by seniority,* avancement à l'ancienneté, *m.*; *seniority in rank,* ancienneté de grade, *f.*

senna ['senə], *n.* Séné, *m.*

sennit ['senit], *n.* (*Naut.*) Tresse, *f.*

sensation [sen'seiʃən], *n.* Sensation, *f. To cause a sensation,* faire sensation. **sensational**, *a.* À sensation, à effet, qui fait sensation. *Sensational drama,* drame sensationnel, *m.*; *sensational press,* les journaux à sensations, *m.pl.* **sensationalism**, *n.* Recherche du sensationnel, *f.*

sense [sens], *n.* Sens; bon sens, sens commun; sentiment; avis, *m.*, opinion (opinion), *f.*; sentiment (consciousness); sens, *m.*, acception, signification (signification), *f. Against all sense,* contre le sens commun; *a man of sense,* un homme de bon sens; *common sense,* sens commun; *good sense*, bon sens; *in a general sense*, au sens général; *in a good sense*, en bonne part; *in a sense*, d'une certaine façon; *in the full sense of the word*, dans toute l'acception du mot; *sense of humour*, sens de l'humour; *the deep sense of my obligation to you*, le sentiment profond de l'obligation que je vous ai; *there is no sense in that*, cela n'a pas de sens commun; *this does not make sense*, cela ne veut rien dire; *to be in one's (right) senses*, être dans son bon sens; *to be out of one's senses*, être hors de son bon sens; *to bring to his senses*, ramener à la raison; *to come to one's senses*, reprendre ses sens, revenir à soi; *to drive out of his senses*, faire perdre la tête à; *to have a keen sense of*, avoir un vif sentiment de, être conscient de, sentir vivement; *to lose one's senses*, perdre la raison; perdre connaissance (to swoon); *to take the sense of an assembly*, prendre l'avis d'une assemblée; *to talk sense*, parler raison.

senseless ['senslis], *a.* Sans connaissance, insensible (insensible); insensé, déraisonnable, absurde (unreasonable). **senselessly,** *adv.* D'une manière insensée; sottement. **senselessness,** *n.* Manque de bon sens, *m.*; sottise, absurdité, *f.*

sensibility [sensi'biliti], *n.* Sensibilité, *f.* sentiment, *m.*

sensible ['sensibl], *a.* Sensé, raisonnable, (intelligent); sensible (de), reconnaissant (de); en pleine connaissance, conscient (conscious). *A sensible answer*, une réponse sensée; *a sensible man*, un homme sensé; *sensible to the eye*, sensible à l'œil; *she is sensible of her inferiority*, elle sent son infériorité; *sensible clothing*, vêtements pratiques, commodes, rationnels; *that is a sensible thing to do*, voilà une action sensée; *to be sensible of*, apprécier, être sensible à, avoir le sentiment de; *to be sensible of injury*, sentir vivement les injures. **sensibleness,** *n.* Sens, bon sens, esprit, *m.* **sensibly,** *adv.* Sensiblement; sensément, sagement, raisonnablement (intelligently); vivement.

sensitive ['sensitiv], *a.* Sensible (à); sensitif, impressionnable; susceptible, ombrageux (touchy). *Sensitive plant*, sensitive, *f.* **sensitively,** *adv.* D'une manière sensible, sensiblement. **sensitiveness** or **sensitivity** [-'tiviti], *n.* Sensibilité; impressionnabilité, susceptibilité (touchiness), *f.*

sensitize ['sensitaiz], *v.t.* Rendre sensible; sensibiliser. **sensitized,** *a.* (*Phot.*) Sensible (of paper etc.).

sensorial [sen'sɔːriəl] or **sensory** ['sensəri], *a.* Sensorial, des sens. **sensorium** or **sensory,** *n.* Sensorium, *m.*

sensual ['sensjuəl], *a.* Sensuel; des sens. **sensualism,** *n.* Sensualisme, *m.* **sensualist,** *n.* Sensualiste, sensuel, *m.* **sensuality** [-'æliti], *n.* Sensualité, *f.* **sensually,** *adv.* Sensuellement.

sensuous ['sensjuəs], *a.* Voluptueux; sensuel. **sensuousness,** *n.* Volupté, *f.*; sensualité, *f.*

sent, *past* and *p.p.* [SEND].

sentence ['sentəns], *n.* Phrase; maxime (maxim), *f.*; jugement, arrêt, *m.*, sentence, *f.* *To pass sentence of death on*, condamner à mort; *to pass sentence on*, prononcer jugement sur.—*v.t.* Prononcer une sentence, un jugement *or* un arrêt (contre), condamner.

sententious [sen'tenʃəs], *a.* Sentencieux. **sententiously,** *adv.* Sentencieusement. **sententiousness,** *n.* Caractère sentencieux, *m.*

sentient ['senʃənt], *a.* Sensible.

sentiment ['sentimənt], *n.* Sentiment; avis *m.*, opinion, pensée, *f.* **sentimental** [-'mentl], *a.* Sentimental. **sentimentalist,** *n.* Personne sentimentale, *f.* **sentimentality** [-'tæliti], *n.* Sensiblerie, sentimentalité, *f.* **sentimentally,** *adv.* Sentimentalement.

sentinel ['sentinl] or **sentry,** *n.* Sentinelle, *f.*, factionnaire, *m.* *Mounted sentinel*, vedette, *f.*; *to be on sentry*, être en faction; *to post a sentry*, mettre en faction; *to relieve a sentry*, relever une sentinelle; *to stand sentinel*, monter la garde, être posté en sentinelle, faire faction. **sentry-box,** *n.* Guérite, *f.* **sentry-go,** *n.* Faction, *f.*

sepal [sepl], *n.* Sépale, *m.* **sepaloid,** *a.* Sépaloïde.

separability [sepərə'biliti], *n.* Divisibilité, *f.* **separable** ['sepərəbl], *a.* Séparable, divisible.

separate (1) ['səpəreit], *v.t.* Séparer; disjoindre, désunir.—*v.i.* Se séparer; se disjoindre.

separate (2) ['səpərit], *a.* Séparé, à part (distinct); disjoint, détaché, désuni. **separately,** *adv.* Séparément, à part. **separation** [-'reiʃən], *n.* Séparation; désunion, *f. Judicial separation*, séparation de corps et de biens, *f.*; *separation order*, jugement de séparation, *m.* **separatism,** *m.* Séparatisme, *m.* **separatist,** *n.* Séparatiste, *m.* **separator,** *n.* Écrémeuse (for milk), *f.*, séparateur, *m.* **separatory,** *a.* Qui sépare.

sepia ['siːpjə], *n.* Sépia (pigment), seiche (fish), *f.* **sepia-drawing,** *n.* Sépia, *f.*

sepoy [siː'pɔi], *n.* Cipaye, *m.*

seps [seps], *n.* Seps (lizard), *m.*

sept [sept], *n.* Enclos; clan, *m.*

septangular [sep'tæŋgjulə], *a.* À sept angles, heptagonal.

September [sep'tembə], *n.* Septembre, *m.*

septemvir [sep'temvə], *n.* Septemvir, *m.* **septemvirate,** *n.* Septemvirat, *m.*

septenary ['septənəri], *a.* Septénaire. **septennial** [-'teniəl], *a.* Septennal. **septennially,** *adv.* Tous les sept ans.

septennate ['septenit], *n.* Septennat, *m.*

septentrional [sep'tentriənl], *a.* Septentrional.

septet [sep'tet], *n.* Septuor, *m.*

septfoil ['septfɔil], *n.* (*Bot.*) Tormentille, *f.*

septic ['septik], *a.* Septique; infecté (of wound). *Septic tank*, fosse septique, *f.* **septicaemia,** *n.* Septicémie, saprémie, *f.*; empoisonnement du sang, *m.*

septuagenarian [septjuədʒə'nɛəriən] or **septuagenary** [septju'dʒiːnəri], *a.* and *n.* Septuagénaire, *m.* or *f.*

Septuagesima [septju'dʒesimə], *n.* Septuagésime, *f.*

Septuagint ['septjuədʒint], *n.* Version des Septante, *f.*

septuple ['septjupl], *a.* Septuple.—*v.t.* Septupler.

sepulchral [si'pʌlkrəl], *a.* Sépulcral. **sepulchre** ['sepəlkə], *n.* Sépulcre, *m.* **sepulture** ['septʃə], *n.* Sépulture; inhumation, *f.*

sequel ['siːkwəl], *n.* Suite, conséquence, *f.* *In the sequel*, par la suite.

sequence ['si:kwəns], *n.* Suite, série, *f.*, ordre, *m.*, succession, *f.*; (*Cine.*) séquence, *f.*
sequent, *a.* Conséquent; consécutif.
sequential [-'kwenʃl], *a.* Continu.
sequester [si'kwestə], *v.t.* Séquestrer. *To sequester oneself*, se séquestrer.—*v.i.* Se séquestrer. **sequestered**, *a.* Retiré, écarté; (*Law*) en séquestre. **sequestrable**, *a.* Sujet à séquestre.
sequestrate ['si:kwəstreit *or* si'kwestreit], *v.t.* Séquestrer. **sequestration** [-'treiʃən], *n.* Séquestre, *m.*; retraite, *f.*, isolement (retirement), *m.*
sequestrator ['si:kwəstreitə], *n.* (*Law*) Séquestre, *m.*
sequin ['si:kwin], *n.* Sequin, *m.*
sequoia [si'kwɔiə], *n.* (*Bot.*) Sequoia, *m.*
serac ['seræk], *n.* (*Geog.*) Sérac, *m.*
seraglio [se'ra:liou], *n.* Sérail, *m.*
seraph ['serəf], *n.* (*pl.* **seraphim**) Séraphin, *m.*
seraphic [sə'ræfik] *or* *seraphical*, *a.* Séraphique.
Serb [sə:b], *n.* Serbe, *m.* or *f.* **Serbia** ['sə:biə]. La Serbie, *f.* **Serbian** [SERVIAN].
sere [siə] [SEAR].
serenade [serə'neid], *n.* Sérénade, *f.*—*v.t.* Donner une sérénade à. **serenader**, *n.* Donneur, joueur, de sérénades, *m.*
serene [si'ri:n], *a.* Serein, calme; sérénissime (title). *All serene!* tout va bien! ça y est! **serenely**, *adv.* Avec sérénité. **sereneness** *or* **serenity** [-'reniti], *n.* Sérénité, *f.*, calme, *m.*
serf [sə:f], *n.* Serf, *m.*, serve, *f.* **serfdom**, *n.* Servage, *m.*
serge [sə:dʒ], *n.* Serge, *f.* *Cotton serge*, sergé, *m.*; *silk serge*, serge de soie, *f.* **serge-factory** *or* **-trade**, *n.* Sergerie, *f.* **serge-maker**, *n.* Serger, sergier, *m.*
sergeant *or* **serjeant** ['sa:dʒənt], *n.* *Huissier; sergent (of infantry); maréchal des logis (of cavalry, artillery); brigadier (of police), *m.* *Colour-sergeant*, (*Engl.*) sergent porte-drapeau, *m.*; *flight-sergeant*, sergent-chef; *quartermaster-sergeant*, sergent-fourrier, maréchal des logis-fourrier, *m.* **serjeant-at-arms**, *n.* Commandant militaire (du Parlement), *m.* **serjeant-at-law**, *n.* Avocat (nommé par le roi), *m.* **sergeant-major**, *n.* *Sergeant-major* (of infantry), maréchal des logis chef (of cavalry), *m.*; *regimental sergeant-major*, adjudant-chef, *m.*
serial ['siəriəl], *a.* Paraissant par série *or* par livraisons.—*n.* Publication périodique, *f.*, *Serial* (story), (roman-)feuilleton, *m.* **serialize**, *v.t.* Fabriquer en série; publier en feuilleton, **serially**, *adv.* Par série. **seriate** *or* **seriated**, *a.* En série. **seriate**, *v.t.* Sérier. **seriatim** [-'eitim], *adv.* Par série, au fur et à mesure; successivement.
sericicultural [serisi'kʌltʃərəl], *a.* Séricicole. **sericiculture**, *n.* Sériciculture, *f.* **sericiculturist**, *n.* Sériciculteur, *m.*
series ['siəri:z *or* 'siərii:z], *n.* Série, suite, succession, *f.*; (*U.S.*) les grands matches de baseball. *Series connection*, montage en série, *m.*
serio-comic ['siəriou'kɔmik], *a.* Héroï-comique.
serious ['siəriəs], *a.* Sérieux; grave. *Is he serious?* parle-t-il sérieusement? **serious-minded**, *a.* Sérieux, réfléchi.

seriously, *adv.* Sérieusement; gravement. *To take seriously*, prendre au sérieux. **seriousness**, *n.* Sérieux, *m.*; gravité, *f.*
serjeant [SERGEANT].
sermon ['sə:mən], *n.* Sermon, *m.*; (*fam.*) sermon, *m.*, semonce, *f.* *The Sermon on the Mount*, le Sermon sur la Montagne; *collection of sermons*, sermonnaire, *m.* **sermonize**, *v.t.* Prêcher; sermonner. **sermonizer**, *n.* Sermonneur, *m.*
serology [siə'rɔlədʒi], *n.* Sérologie, *f.*
seron ['siərən] *or* **seroon** [sə'ru:n], *n.* *Serron, *m.*; balle, *f.*, ballot, *m.*
serosity [siə'rɔsiti], *n.* Sérosité, *f.* **serotherapeutic**, *a.* Sérothérapique. **serotherapy**, *n.* Sérothérapie, *f.* **serous** ['siərəs], *a.* Séreux.
serpent ['sə:pənt], *n.* Serpent; serpenteau (firework), *m.* **serpent-like**, *a.* De serpent, comme un serpent.
serpentaria [-'tɛəriə], *n.* (*Bot.*) Serpentaire, *f.* **serpentine**, *a.* Serpentin, de serpent; qui serpente, sinueux.—*n.* (*Min.*) Serpentine, *f.* *The Serpentine* (London), le lac de Hyde Park. **serpentine-worm**, *n.* Serpentin (of a still), *m.*
serpiginous [sə:'pidʒinəs], *a.* Serpigineux.
serrate ['sereit], *a.* En scie, dentelé; serraté. **serration**, *n.* Dentelure, *f.* **serricorn**, *a.* Serricorne.
serried ['serid], *a.* Compact, serré. *In serried ranks*, en rangs serrés.
serriform ['serifɔ:m], *a.* Serriforme, en dents de scie.
serrulation [seru'leiʃən], *n.* Dentelure fine, *f.*
serum ['siərəm], *n.* Sérum, *m.*
servant ['sə:vənt], *n.* Serviteur, *m.*, servante, *f.*; employé (of companies etc.), *m.*; domestique (man-servant); brosseur, *m.*, ordonnance (officer's batman), *f.* *Civil servant*, fonctionnaire, *m.* *General servant*, bonne à tout faire, *f.* *Your* (humble) *servant*, votre (humble) serviteur. **servant-girl**, *n.* Servante, bonne, domestique, *f.*
serve [sə:v], *v.t.* Servir; servir à, être bon à; faire (an apprenticeship); desservir (a locality); jouer (a trick); signifier (a writ). *Dinner is served!* Monsieur est servi *or* Madame est servie! *dinner was served in . . .*, on servit à dîner dans . . .; *I will serve him out*, il me le payera; *it serves him right*, c'est bien fait, il n'a que ce qu'il mérite, il ne l'a pas volé; *to serve a warrant upon*, signifier un mandat d'arrêt à; *to serve a writ upon*, signifier un exploit à; *to serve out*, distribuer, (*colloq.*) rendre la pareille à, finir, achever (time); *to serve the purpose*, faire l'affaire; *to serve up*, servir.—*v.i.* Servir; être au service; être convenable, être favorable, être bon; suffire (to suffice). *To serve as*, servir de; *to serve to show*, servir à montrer.—*n.* (*Ten.*) Service, *m.*, balle de service, *f.*
server ['sə:və], *n.* Servant, *m.*; (*Ten.*) serveur; (*Eccles.*) acolyte, *m.*
Servian ['sə:viən], *a.* and *n.* Serbe.
service ['sə:vis], *n.* Service; (*fig.*) avantage, *m.*; utilité, *f.*; signification (of a writ); fourrure (of a rope); (*Mil.*) arme, *f.* *At your service*, à votre disposition; *divine service*, office divin; *foreign service*, service au dehors, service à l'étranger, *m.*; *in service*, en service, en condition (of servants); *in the service*

(*army*), au service; *in the service of*, au service de; *of service*, utile; *on active service*, en activité; *out of service*, sans place; *secret service money*, fonds secrets, *m.pl.*; *service record*, états de service, *m.pl.*; *social services*, institutions sociales, *f.pl.*; *to be of no service*, ne servir à rien; *to be of service to*, être utile à; *to do a service to*, rendre un service à; *to go out to service*, entrer en service (of person); *to go into service*, entrer en service (of thing). —*v.t.* (*Motor.*) Entretenir, réparer. **service-book**, *n.* Livre d'office, rituel, *m.* **service-flat**, *n.* Appartement où le service est assuré et compris dans le loyer, *m.* **service families**, *n.* Familles de militaires, *f.pl.* **service-pipe**, *n.* Branchement, *m.* **service-station**, *n.* Station-service, *f.* **service-tree**, *n.* Sorbier, *m.*
serviceable, *a.* Utile (à), avantageux, de bon usage. **serviceableness**, *n.* Utilité; disposition serviable (obligingness), *f.* **serviceably**, *adv.* Utilement, avantageusement.
serviceman, *n.* Soldat, militaire, *m.* **servicewoman**, *n.* Femme-soldat, *f.*
serviette [sə:vi'et], *n.* Serviette de table, *f.*
servile ['sə:vail], *a.* Servile; asservi. **servilely**, *adv.* Servilement, avec servilité. **servileness** or **servility** [-'viliti], *n.* Servilité, bassesse, *f.*
serving ['sə:viŋ], *a.* Servant, qui sert. **serving-maid**, *n.* Servante, *f.* **serving-mallet**, *n.* (*Naut.*) Maillet à fourrer, *m.* **serving-man**, *n.* Serviteur, *m.* **servitor**, *n.* Serviteur, *m.*; (*Oxford Univ.*) étudiant boursier, *m.* **servitorship**, *n.* Bourse, *f.* **servitude**, *n.* Servitude, *f.*, asservissement, *m.* *Penal servitude*, travaux forcés, *m.pl.*
servo-brake ['sə:vobreik], *n.* Servo-frein, *m.* **servo-control**, *n.* Appareil servo-régulateur, *m.* **servo-motor**, *n.* Servo-moteur, *m.*, moteur asservi, *m.*
sesame ['sesəmi], *n.* Sésame, *m.* *Open sesame*, sésame, ouvre-toi.
seseli ['sesəli], *n.* (*Bot.*) Séséli, *m.*
sesquialter [seskwi'ɔːltə], *a.* Sesquialtère.
sesquipedalian ['seskwipi'deiliən], *a.* Long d'une aune (word); ampoulé (style).
sesquitertial [-'tə:ʃl], *a.* Sesquitierce.
sessile ['sesail], *a.* Sessile.
session ['seʃən], *n.* Session, séance, *f.*; (*pl.*) assises, *f.pl.*; trimestre, semestre, *m.*, année académique (from exam to exam), *f.* *Quarter-sessions*, cour trimestrielle, *f.*
sesterce ['sestə:s], *n.* Sesterce, *m.*
sestet ['sestet], *n.* (*Mus.*) Sextuor, *m.*; les deux tercets d'un sonnet, *m.pl.*
set [set], *v.t.* (*past* and *p.p.* **set**) Poser, apposer (a seal, a signature), mettre, placer, poster; planter (to plant); fixer, désigner (to appoint); orienter, régler, ajuster, arranger (to regulate); établir (to establish); repasser (to sharpen); affûter (tools); donner (an example); (*Mus.*) mettre en musique; remettre (a bone); monter (to mount); sertir (precious stones); dresser, tendre (a trap); (*Hunt.*) arrêter (of dogs); (*Print.*) composer. *All sails set*, toutes voiles dehors, toutes voiles déployées; *he has not set the Thames on fire*, il n'a pas inventé la poudre; *her clothes set off her figure*, ses vêtements dessinaient avantageusement sa taille; *I have never so much as set eyes on him*, je ne l'ai même pas

aperçu de loin; *to be hard set*, être bien embarrassé; *to be set on it*, y tenir beaucoup; *to set against*, opposer à, indisposer (someone) contre; *to set apart*, mettre à part; *to set aside*, mettre de côté, rejeter; *to set at*, exciter contre; *to set at defiance*, défier, braver; *to set at ease*, mettre à l'aise; *to set at naught*, ne compter pour rien, mépriser; *to set a trap*, tendre *or* dresser un piège (à); *to set at variance*, brouiller; *to set at work*, mettre en œuvre; *to set a watch by the right time*, mettre une montre à l'heure; *to set back*, reculer; *to set by*, mettre de côté; *to set by the ears*, brouiller; *to set down*, poser, déposer; coucher par écrit, inscrire, désigner; (*fig.*) remettre à sa place; *to set down as*, considérer comme, appeler; *to set eyes on*, regarder, jeter les yeux sur; *to set foot*, mettre le(s) pied(s); *to set forth*, énoncer, déployer, expliquer, développer; *to set forward*, avancer; *to set free*, mettre en liberté; *to set in motion*, mettre en mouvement, faire aller; *to set in order*, arranger, ranger, mettre en ordre; *to set little store by*, avoir une pauvre opinion de, faire peu de cas de; *to set off*, faire partir (a rocket), relever, faire ressortir (to show off), compenser (par); *to set on*, exciter à, pousser à; *to set (teeth) on edge*, agacer; *to set on fire*, mettre le feu à, incendier, (*fig.*) enflammer; *to set on foot*, mettre sur pied, mettre en branle; *to set oneself about*, se mettre à, s'occuper de; *to set oneself to*, s'appliquer, s'ingénier à; *to set one's face*, se diriger, diriger ses regards sur (un objet) *or* vers (un endroit); *to set one's heart upon*, convoiter, désirer vivement; *to set one's shoulder to the wheel*, se mettre à l'œuvre, mettre la main à la pâte; *to set out*, mettre dehors, déposer à la porte (a milk can), arranger, embellir; *to set out the table*, mettre le couvert (avec soin); *to set over*, établir sur, préposer à; *to set right*, redresser, corriger; *to set sail*, mettre la voile, appareiller; *to set the alarm(-clock) for five*, mettre la sonnerie du réveil sur cinq heures; *to set the fashion*, régir la mode; *to set the fox to keep the geese*, enfermer le loup dans la bergerie; *to set to music*, mettre en musique; *to set up*, ériger, élever, dresser, établir (to establish), mettre en évidence (to place in view), avancer (to advance), (*Print.*) composer; *to set up a business*, monter une affaire; *to set up its back* (of a cat), faire le gros dos.
v.i.—Se fixer; diriger, porter (vers *or* à); se mettre à; se coucher (of the sun); planter (to plant); prendre racine, prendre (of plants); prendre (of jam, jelly, custard); nouer, se nouer (of fruit); arrêter, tomber en arrêt (of dogs). *The sun is setting*, le soleil se couche; *to set about*, commencer, se mettre à; *to set forth*, *to set forward*, se mettre en marche, se mettre en chemin; *to set in*, commencer, se mettre à; *to set off*, se mettre en route, partir; *to set on*, commencer (to begin), attaquer (to attack); *to set out*, partir, se mettre en route, commencer; *to set to*, se mettre résolument à; *to set up* (in business etc.), s'établir; *to set up for*, se donner pour, se poser en, faire le; *to set up for oneself*, s'établir à son compte.
a.—Mis, posé, placé, serti (of gem); prêt; arrêté, fixe (fixed); réglé, régulier; d'apparat, préparé (of speech).   *All set?* ça y est? on

y est? on y va? *of set purpose*, exprès, à dessein, de propos délibéré; *set books*, les auteurs du programme; *set fair*, beau fixe; *set piece*, pièce montée; *to be dead set on*, s'acharner à; *well set* (of person), bien bâti. *n.*—Collection, *f.*, ensemble, assortiment, *m.*, série, *f.*, jeu, *m.*; service (of china etc.), *m.*; garniture (of ornaments, ribbons, etc.); parure (of precious stones), *f.*; attelage (of horses), *m.*; (hair) mise en plis, *f.*; (*Theat.*) décor, *m.*; scène, *f.*, plateau, *m.*; partie, manche, *f.*; classe, *f.*, groupe, corps, *m.*; (*pej.*) clique, bande, troupe (of persons), *f.*, entourage, *m.*; plant (young plant), *m. Set of furniture*, ameublement, *m.*; *set of teeth*, râtelier, *m.*; *to come to a dead set*, être à quia, rester court; *to make a dead set at*, attaquer vivement, (of a woman) se jeter à la tête (d'un homme); *set point*, point décisif.

setaceous [si'teiʃəs], *a.* Sétacé.

set-back, *n.* Recul, échec, *m.* **set-down**, *n.* (*colloq.*) Rebuffade, semonce, *f.*; (*fam.*) lavage de tête, *m.* **set-off**, *n.* Compensation, *f.* contraste, *m.*; saillie, *f.* (in a wall); (*Law*) reconvention, *f. As a set-off against*, en compensation (de). **set-out**, *n.* Commencement, début; départ (departure); équipement, *m.* **set-square**, *n.* Équerre, *f.* **set-to**, *n.* Assaut; combat, *m.*, prise de bec, *f.* **set-up**, *n.* Organisation, préparation, *f. You know the set-up?* Vous savez comment cela marche?

setiferous [si'tifərəs], *a.* Sétifère.

setiform ['setifɔ:m], *a.* Sétiforme.

settee [se'ti:], *n.* Canapé, *m.*, causeuse, *f.*

setter ['setə], *n.* Chien d'arrêt; (*Mus.*) compositeur; monteur, sertisseur (of gems); (*fig.*) embaucheur, *m. Bone-setter*, rebouteux, *m.* **setter-on**, *n.* Instigateur, *m.*, instigatrice, *f.*

setting ['setiŋ], *n.* Mise, pose, *f.*; coucher (of the sun etc.), *m.*; décor (naturel ou théâtral), *m.*, mise en relief, *f.*; (*Theat.*) milieu, cadre, *m.*; (*Mus.*) mise en musique, *f.*; remboîtement (of a bone); montage, *m.*, monture (of precious stones); prise (of plastering), *f.*; repassage (of razors), *m.*; affûtage (of a saw), *m.*; (*Print.*) composition, *f. Setting free*, élargissement, *m.*, mise en liberté, *f.*; *setting in*, commencement, début, encastrement, *m.*; *setting-off*, départ, *m.*, compensation, *f.*; *setting on*, incitation, *f.*; *setting out*, départ, commencement, *m.*; *setting up*, établissement, *m.*, (*Print.*) composition, *f.* **setting-rule**, *n.* Filet à composer, *m.*

settle [setl], *v.t.* Fixer (to fix); établir (to establish); déterminer; décider, arrêter (to decide); constituer, assigner (property on); coloniser (to colonize); régler, ajuster, accommoder, arranger (to adjust); résoudre (questions etc.); payer, régler (to pay); (*Naut.*) noyer (the land). *To settle a country*, coloniser un pays; *to settle a pension on*, assigner une pension à, constituer une rente à; *to settle someone*, donner son compte à quelqu'un, dire son fait à quelqu'un; (*fam.*) clore, fermer le bec à quelqu'un; *to settle up*, régulariser.—*v.i.* S'établir, se fixer; se marier, se mettre en ménage (to marry); se poser (of birds etc.); se calmer, se tranquilliser (to become calm); se remettre (of the weather); se précipiter (to sink); se tasser (of masonry); prendre des arrangements,

s'arranger (avec). *To settle down*, se fixer, s'établir, se calmer, (*fam.*) faire une fin, se ranger; *to settle down to*, s'appliquer à; (*colloq.*) s'atteler à (un travail); *to settle up*, régler ses comptes; *to settle upon*, se décider pour, opter pour, choisir; *to settle with*, régler avec.—*n.* Banc (à dossier), *m.*, banquette (à dossier), *f.*

settled, *a.* Fixe, établi; calme, tranquille. *Settled habit*, habitude enracinée, *f.*; *settled idea*, idée fixe, *f.*; *settled price*, prix fait, *m.*

settlement ['setlmənt], *n.* Établissement, ajustement, arrangement, accommodement, dépôt (sediment), *m.*; mise en possession (act of giving possession), *f.*; accord, contrat, *m.*; rente, pension (annuity); constitution (of an annuity); colonisation (colonization); colonie (colony), *f.*; règlement, solde (of accounts), *m.*; installation (of a minister); liquidation (liquidation), *f.*; (*Build.*) tassement, *m. Act of Settlement*, acte de succession (au trône), *m.*; *deed of settlement*, contrat de constitution, *m.*; *marriage-settlement*, contrat de mariage, *m.*; dot (for daughter), *f.*; douaire (for wife), *m.*

settler ['setlə], *n.* Colon, immigrant (in new country), *m.*; (*colloq.*) argument *or* coup décisif, *m.*

settling ['setliŋ], *n.* Établissement; ajustement, arrangement, accommodement (of disputes etc.); règlement (of accounts), *m.*; (*Build.*) tassement; (*pl.*) sédiment, dépôt, *m.*, lie, *f. Settling day*, jour de liquidation, *m.* **settling-up**, *n.* Règlement, *m.*

seven ['sevən], *a.* Sept. **sevenfold**, *a.* Septuple.—*adv.* Au septuple, sept fois. **sevenscore**, *a.* Cent quarante.

seventeen [sevən'ti:n], *a.* Dix-sept. **seventeenth**, *a.* and *n.* Dix-septième; dix-sept (of kings etc.).

seventh, *a.* and *n.* Septième; sept (of kings etc.). **seventhly**, *adv.* Septièmement.

seventieth, *a.* Soixante-dixième. **seventy**, *a.* Soixante-dix. *The seventy* (*the Septuagint*), les Septante, *m.pl.*

sever ['sevə], *v.t.* Séparer, diviser (de); disjoindre; couper, sectionner. *To sever one's connexion with*, rompre ses relations avec.—*v.i.* Se séparer (de).

several ['sevərəl], *a.* Plusieurs, divers; distinct, respectif (distinct).—*n. Several of them*, plusieurs d'entre eux. **severally**, *adv.* Séparément, individuellement; isolément. (*Law*) *Jointly and severally liable*, responsables conjointement et solidairement.

severance ['sevərəns], *n.* Séparation, disjonction; rupture, *f.*

severe [si'viə], *a.* Sévère; rigoureux, rude (of weather etc.); violent, aigu, vif (of pain etc.). *A severe cold*, un gros rhume; *a severe winter*, un hiver rigoureux. **severely**, *adv.* Sévèrement; rigoureusement.

severity [si'veriti], *n.* Sévérité; rigueur, violence, *f.*

Seville ['sevil]. Séville, *f.* **Sevill(i)an** [se'vil(i)ən], *a.* and *n.* Sévillan, *m.*, -ane, *f.*

sew [sou], *v.t.* (*past* **sewed**, *p.p.* **sewed** [soud] *or* **sewn** [soun]) Coudre; brocher (books). **sewed**, *a.* Broché (of books in paper wrappers).

sewage ['sjuːidʒ], *n.* Eaux d'égout, *f.pl.*
Sewage farm, champs d'épandage, *m.pl.*;
sewage system, le tout-à-l'égout, *m.*
sewer (1) ['souə], *n.* Couseur, *m.*, couseuse, *f.*;
(*Bookb.*) brocheur, *m.*, brocheuse, *f.*
sewer (2) ['sjuːə], *n.* Égout, *m.* **sewerage,** *n.*
Système d'égouts, *m.*, égouts, *m.pl.* **sewerman,** *n.* (*pl.* **sewermen**) Égoutier, *m.*
sewing ['souiŋ], *n.* Couture, *f.* **sewing-box,** *n.*
Boîte à ouvrage, (*sch.*) boîte à couture, *f.*
sewing-cotton, *n.* Coton à coudre, fil, *m.*
sewing-machine, *n.* Machine à coudre, *f.*
sewing-press, *n.* (*Bookb.*) Cousoir, *m.*
sewing-silk, *n.* Soie à coudre, *f.*
sex [seks], *n.* Sexe, *m.* *Sex appeal*, attrait,
charme, 'sex-appeal', *m.*; *the fair sex*, le
beau sexe, le sexe faible, *m.*
sexagenarian [seksədʒə'nɛəriən], *a.* and *n.*
Sexagénaire, *m.* or *f.*
sexagenary [seksə'dʒiːnəri], *a.* and *n.* Sexagénaire.
Sexagesima [seksə'dʒesimə], *n.* Sexagésime,
f. **sexagesimal,** *a.* Sexagésimal.
sexangular [seks'æŋgjulə], *a.* Hexagone.
sexennial [sek'seniəl], *a.* Sexennal. **sexenni-
ally,** *adv.* Tous les six ans.
sexless ['sekslis], *a.* (*Bot.*) Asexué (of flower).
sextain ['sekstein], *n.* Sixain, *m.*
sextant ['sekstənt], *n.* Sextant, *m.*
sextet [seks'tet], *n.* (*Mus.*) Sextuor, *m.*
sextile ['sekstail], *a.* Sextil.
sexton ['sekstən], *n.* Sacristain; fossoyeur, *m.*
sextonship, *n.* Charge de sacristain *or* de
fossoyeur, *f.*
sextuple ['sekstjupl], *a.* Sextuple, *m.—v.t.*
Sextupler.
sexual ['seksjuəl], *a.* Sexuel. *Sexual intercourse*, rapports (sexuels), *m.pl.* **sexuality**
[-'æliti], *n.* Sexualité, *f.* **sexy,** *a.* (*pop.*)
Capiteuse, croustillante, troublante (of
woman). *To be sexy*, avoir du sex-appeal.
shabbily ['ʃæbili], *adv.* Mal, pauvrement (mis
or vêtu), mesquinement (meanly). **shabbiness,** *n.* État râpé (of dress), *m.*; pauvreté,
mesquinerie (meanness), *f.* **shabby,** *a.* Râpé,
élimé, qui montre la corde (of clothes); mal
vêtu, mal mis; mesquin, petit, vilain, ignoble
(mean). *That is very shabby*, (*fig.*) c'est bien
mal, c'est bien petit; *to play a shabby trick on*,
jouer un tour ignoble à. **shabby-genteel,** *a.*
Miséreux et digne. **shabby-looking,** *a.*
De pauvre apparence, minable.
shack [ʃæk], *n.* Graine tombée (des épis), *f.*;
(*Am.*) vagabond, *m.*; (*Am., Austral.*) hutte,
cabane, *f.*
shackle [ʃækl], *v.t.* Enchaîner; (*fig.*) entraver,
embarrasser; (*Naut.*) mailler (a chain).
shackles, *n.pl.* Fers, *m.pl.*, chaînes; (*fig.*)
entraves, *f.pl.*
shad [ʃæd], *n.* Alose (fish), *f.*
shaddock ['ʃædək], *n.* Pamplemousse (grape-
fruit), *f.*
shade [ʃeid], *n.* Ombre, *f.*; ombrage (of a tree
etc.); abat-jour (for a lamp etc.); garde-vue
(for the eyes), *m.*; nuance (of colour); visière
(on a cap), *f.*; (*pl.*) caveaux (wine vaults),
enfers (abode of spirits), (*Am.*) stores, *m.pl.*
In the shade, à l'ombre; *prices are a shade
higher*, les prix sont tant soit peu plus élevés;
the shades of night, les ombres de la nuit, *f.pl.*;
to throw into the shade, rejeter dans l'ombre,

éclipser.—*v.t.* Ombrager (de), couvrir d'ombre; obscurcir, cacher, masquer (to obscure);
abriter, mettre à l'ombre (to protect);
(*Paint.*) ombrer, nuancer; hachurer (a map).
shaded, *a.* À l'ombre; ombragé (de);
(*Paint.*) ombré; hachuré. (*Comm.*) *Shaded
prices*, prix dégressifs; *shaded tones*, tons
dégradés. **shadeless,** *a.* Sans ombre.
shadily, *adv.* (*fig.*) D'une manière louche.
shadiness, *n.* Ombrage, *m.*, ombre; (*fig.*)
nature suspecte, *f.* **shading,** *n.* Ombres,
nuances, hachures, *f.pl.*
shadow ['ʃædou], *n.* Ombre, *f.* *He is but a
shadow of himself*, il n'est plus que l'ombre de
lui-même; *may your shadow never grow less*,
puissiez-vous ne jamais essuyer les revers de
la fortune; *the great shadows of a picture*, les
grandes ombres d'un tableau; *the shadow
Cabinet*, les chefs de l'Opposition (in Parliament); *to cast a shadow*, projeter une ombre;
to pass like a shadow, passer comme une
ombre; *under the shadow of*, à l'ombre de.—
v.t. Ombrager, couvrir de son ombre; filer,
espionner (to follow closely). *To shadow
forth*, figurer, préfigurer. **shadow-box,** *v.i.*
S'entraîner contre un adversaire imaginaire.
shadowing, *n.* Espionnage, *m.*, filature, *f.*
shadowless, *a.* Sans ombre. **shadowy,** *a.*
Ombragé; sombre, ténébreux (gloomy);
vague, obscur, chimérique (unreal).
shady ['ʃeidi], *a.* Ombragé, ombreux; frais
(cool); sombre (dark); à l'ombre (sheltered);
(*colloq.*) louche (dishonest). *The shady side*
(of the street), le côté ombragé, où il y a de
l'ombre, *m.*; *a shady-looking man*, un individu
d'allure louche.
shaft [ʃɑːft], *n.* Flèche, *f.*, dard, trait (arrow);
timon (of a carriage), *m.*; souche (of a
chimney-stack), *f.*; brancard (of a cart);
tuyau (of a pen); bois, *m.*, hampe (of a
lance), *f.*; fût (of a column etc.); manche (of
a tool or weapon); puits (of a mine); (*Mach.*)
arbre, *m.* *Connecting shaft*, arbre de transmission, *m.*; *main* or *driving shaft*, arbre
moteur, *m.*; *to sink a shaft*, percer un puits;
ventilating shaft, puits d'aération, *m.* **shaft-
horse,** *n.* Limonier, cheval de brancard, *m.*
shafted, *a.* À manche, à hampe.
shag [ʃæg], *n.* Poil rude; caporal (tobacco);
cormoran huppé (bird), *m.—v.t.* (*pop.*)
Épuiser, vider, éreinter. **shagginess,** *n.*
État poilu, état hérissé, *m.* **shaggy,** *a.* Poilu,
velu; raboteux (rugged). *Shaggy dog story*,
histoire sans queue ni tête, *f.*
shagreen [ʃə'griːn], *n.* Peau de chagrin, *f.—a.*
De peau de chagrin.
shah [ʃɑː], *n.* Shah, *m.*
shake [ʃeik], *n.* Secousse, *f.*; serrement, *m.*;
poignée (de main), *f.*; hochement (de tête),
m.; fente, gerçure (in wood), *f.*; (*Mus.*) trille,
m.; cadence, *f.* *No great shakes*, (*colloq.*) rien
d'extraordinaire, pas grand'chose, rien qui
vaille; *shake of the hand* or *handshake*, poignée
de main, *f.*; *to give a shakedown*, héberger,
donner le coucher à.
v.t.—(past **shook** [ʃuk], *p.p.* **shaken**
[ʃeikn]) Secouer, branler, remuer, agiter;
ébranler, faire trembler, bouleverser (to
weaken, to move), (*Mus.*) cadencer. *Let us
shake hands*, serrons-nous la main; *this
carriage has shaken me to pieces*, cette voiture

m'a rompu les os; *to shake down*, faire tomber, s'établir, se caser (to settle oneself); *to shake hands with*, serrer la main à, donner une poignée de main à; *to shake off*, secouer, faire tomber, se débarrasser de, se défaire de (to get rid of); *to shake off the yoke*, secouer le joug; *to shake oneself free from*, s'affranchir de; *to shake one's fist at someone*, montrer le poing à quelqu'un; *to shake one's head*, secouer la tête; *to shake the dust off one's feet*, secouer la poussière de ses souliers; *to shake to pieces*, faire tomber en morceaux, en pièces; *to shake up*, remuer, (*Cook.*) sauter (au beurre).—*v.i.* Trembler (de); s'agiter, branler; sauter, être ballotté (in riding); chanceler (to totter); (*Mus.*) faire un trille. *His hand shakes*, la main lui tremble; *to shake with cold*, trembler de froid; *to shake with laughter*, se tordre de rire; (*Am. pop.*) *shake! topez là!*

shakedown, *n.* Lit improvisé, *m.* **shaken,** *a.* Ébranlé, secoué. **shaker,** *n.* Shaker (for cocktails etc.), *m.*

Shakespearian [ʃeik'spiəriən], *a.* and *n.* Shakespearien, *m.*

shakily, *adv.* De façon peu solide; en branlant; à pas chancelants; d'une voix chevrotante. **shaking,** *n.* Secousse, *f.*, ébranlement, tremblement; ballottement (in riding), *m. To give a good shaking to*, secouer bien.

shako ['ʃækou], *n.* Shako, *m.*

shaky ['ʃeiki], *a.* Qui branle dans le manche, branlant; (*fig.*) peu solide; faible, chancelant (of persons); gercé (of wood). *He is rather shaky*, il branle dans le manche, il est sujet à caution; *he is rather shaky in his grammar*, il est peu ferré sur les questions de grammaire; *with shaky step*, à pas chancelants.

shale [ʃeil], *n.* Argile schisteuse, *f. Oil shale*, schiste bitumeux, *m.*; *shale oil*, huile de schiste, *f.*

shall [ʃæl], *v.aux.* (*2nd sing.* **thou shalt***, *past* and *subj.* **should** [ʃud], **shouldst,** **shouldest**) Devoir; vouloir. *But he shall*, mais je l'y forcerai; *but I shall not*, mais je n'en ferai rien; *I shall go*, j'irai; *shall I go?* dois-je aller? faut-il que j'aille? *shall I open the window?* voulez-vous que j'ouvre la fenêtre? *they have a notion that their children should be taught gratis*, ils s'imaginent qu'on devrait instruire leurs enfants gratis; (*Bibl.*) *thou shalt not kill*, tu ne tueras pas; *you shall do it*, je veux que vous le fassiez.

shallop ['ʃæləp], *n.* Chaloupe, péniche, pinasse, *f.*

shallot [ʃə'lɔt], *n.* Échalote, *f.*

shallow ['ʃælou], *a.* Peu profond; (*fig.*) superficiel, léger, frivole, borné.—*n.* Haut-fond, bas-fond, écueil, *m.* **shallow-brained,** *a.* À cervelle creuse, borné. **shallow-hearted,** *a.* Au cœur léger; sans grande sensibilité; incapable de s'attacher. **shallowly,** *adv.* Superficiellement. **shallowness,** *n.* Peu de profondeur, *m.*; nature superficielle, *f.*; esprit borné, *m.*

sham [ʃæm], *a.* Feint, simulé, prétendu; faux, factice, de camelote (shoddy). *Sham fight*, petite guerre, *f.*, combat simulé, *m.*—*n.* Feinte, *f.*, prétexte, *m.*; imposture, feinte, *f.*—*v.t.* Feindre, simuler; faire le, la, *or* les. *To sham Abraham*, jouer l'innocence patriarcale, faire la sainte nitouche, faire le bon apôtre; *to sham illness*, feindre d'être malade,

faire le malade.—*v.i.* User de feintes, feindre, faire semblant; jouer la comédie. *Are you really ill or are you shamming?* Es-tu vraiment malade ou joues-tu la comédie?

shamble [ʃæmbl], *v.i.* Marcher en traînant les pieds. **shambles,** *n.pl.* Abattoir, *m.*; (*fig.*) scène de carnage, *f.*, une belle pagaille.

shambling, *a.* Traînant. *Shambling gait*, marche traînante, *f.*

shame [ʃeim], *n.* Honte; pudeur; ignominie (dishonour), *f.*; opprobre, *m. For shame!* Quelle honte! *out of shame*, de honte; *shame-stricken*, accablé de honte; *to be lost to all shame*, avoir toute honte bue; *to cry shame*, crier à l'infamie; *to put to shame*, faire honte à; *what a shame!* quel dommage!—*v.t.* Faire honte à; faire affront à; déshonorer (to disgrace).

shamefaced [-feist], *a.* Honteux, confus. **shamefacedly** [-'feisidli], *adv.* D'un air penaud; timidement. **shamefacedness** [-feistnis], *n.* Mauvaise honte; timidité, *f.* **shameful,** *a.* Honteux; déshonnête. **shamefully,** *adv.* Honteusement. **shamefulness,** *n.* Honte, ignominie, *f.* **shameless,** *a.* Éhonté, effronté, impudent. **shamelessly,** *adv.* Sans honte, effrontément, impudemment. **shamelessness,** *n.* Effronterie, impudence, *f.*

shammer ['ʃæmə], *n.* Simulateur, imposteur, *m.*

shamoy or **shammy** ['ʃæmi] [CHAMOIS].

shampoo [ʃæm'puː], *v.t.* Frictionner; nettoyer (the head).—*n.* Shampooing, *m.* **shampooing,** *n.* Nettoyage, shampooing (of the head), *m.*

shamrock ['ʃæmrɔk], *n.* Trèfle (d'Irlande), *m.*

shandry ['ʃændri] or **shandrydan,** *n.* Carriole irlandaise, *f.*; (*fam.*) bagnole, guimbarde, *f.*

shandy ['ʃændi], *n.* Panaché (drink), *m.*

shank [ʃæŋk], *n.* Jambe (leg), *f.*; tibia, os de la jambe (tibia); tuyau etc. (of a pipe), *m.*; queue (of a button); tige, verge (of an anchor), *f. To ride Shanks's mare*, aller à pied.—*v.t.* (*Golf*) Talonner (la balle). **shank-painter,** *n.* (*Naut.*) Serre-bosse, *m.*

shanked, *a.* À jambe; à tige.

shanty ['ʃænti], *n.* Cabane, bicoque, hutte, *f.*; baraquement, *m.* **shanty-town,** *n.* Bidonville, *m.*

shape [ʃeip], *n.* Forme, figure; tournure, taille (of a person); façon, coupe (fashion), *f.*; moule, *m.* (for blancmange). *In the shape of*, en forme de; *rice shape*, gâteau de riz, *m.*; *to get out of shape*, se déformer; *to put out of shape*, déformer; *to take shape*, prendre forme. —*v.t.* Former, façonner; régler, modeler (sur). *Shaped like . . .*, en forme de, en . . .; *heart-shaped*, en forme de cœur; *wedge-shaped*, cunéiforme. *To shape one's course for*, mettre le cap sur, faire route pour.—*v.i.* Cadrer (avec); convenir (à). *It is shaping well*, cela commence à prendre bonne tournure; cela promet; *the thing is shaping badly*, la chose est en train de mal tourner.

shapeless, *a.* Informe, sans forme. **shapelessness,** *n.* Absence de forme, difformité, *f.* **shapeliness,** *n.* Beauté de forme, *f.*, galbe, *m.* **shapely,** *a.* Bien fait, beau. *Shapely legs*, jambes bien faites.

shard [ʃɑːd], *n.* Tesson, *m.*; (*Ent.*) élytre, *m.*

share (1) [ʃɛə], *n.* Soc (of a plough), *m.*

share (2) [ʃɛə], *n.* Part, portion (portion); (*St. Exch.*) action, valeur, *f.*, titre, *m.* *In half shares*, de compte à demi; *preference share*, action privilégiée, *f.*; *registered share*, action nominative; *transferable share*, action au porteur; *the lion's share*, la part du lion, *f.*; *to fall to one's share*, échoir en partage à; *to go shares*, partager; *to have a share in*, avoir part à; *to have shares in*, (*Comm.*) être intéressé dans; *to hold shares*, avoir des actions, être actionnaire.—*v.t.* Partager; prendre part à; avoir part à.—*v.i.* Partager; avoir part (à). *To share in*, avoir part à, participer à.

share-broker, *n.* Courtier d'actions, *m.* **share-certificate,** *n.* Certificat, titre, d'actions, *m.* **share-cropping,** *n.* (*U.S.*) Métayage, *m.* **shareholder,** *n.* Actionnaire, *m.* or *f.* **share-list,** *n.* Cours de la bourse, *m.* **share-pusher,** *n.* Courtier, placier marron, *m.* **share-pushing,** *n.* Marronnage, *m.* **share-warrants,** *n.pl.* Titres d'actions (au porteur), *m.pl.*

sharer, *n.* Participant; (*Law*) partageant, *m.* *Joint-sharer,* copartageant, *m.*; *to be a sharer in*, participer à, prendre part à. **sharing,** *n.* Partage, *m.*

shark [ʃɑːk], *n.* Requin; (*fig.*) aigrefin, escroc, filou (sharper), *m.* *Basking shark,* (requin) pèlerin, *m.*; *hammer shark,* marteau, *m.*; *thresher shark, fox-shark,* faux renard, *m.*

sharp [ʃɑːp], *a.* Tranchant, affilé, qui coupe bien; pointu, aigu, acéré (pointed); saillant (of angles); (*fig.*) vif, intelligent, pénétrant, fin; perçant (piercing); accentué, anguleux (of features); acide, mordant, piquant, acerbe, aigre (of taste etc.); retors, malin, rusé, délié (sly); (*Mus.*) dièse. *A sharp appetite,* un appétit dévorant, *m.*; *a sharp contest,* une vive contestation, *f.*; *a sharp edge,* un fil tranchant, *m.*; *a sharp tongue,* une langue bien affilée, *f.*; *as sharp as a needle,* (*colloq.*) fin comme l'ambre; *sharp pain,* douleur vive *or* aiguë, *f.*; *sharp practice,* filouterie, rouerie, *f.*; *to keep a sharp look out,* avoir l'œil ouvert.—*adv.* Précise (of the hour). *At four o'clock sharp,* à quatre heures précises; *at one o'clock sharp,* à une heure précise; *look sharp!* Faites vite! remuez-vous!—*n.* (*Mus.*) Dièse, *m.*

sharp-edged, *a.* Bien affilé; (*Carp. etc.*) à vive arête. **sharpen,** *v.t.* Affiler, aiguiser; tailler en pointe, tailler (a pencil etc.); (*fig.*) rendre vif; exciter; (*Mus.*) diéser. **sharper,** *n.* Aigrefin, escroc, chevalier d'industrie, *m.* **sharply,** *adv.* Vigoureusement, rudement, sévèrement, vivement, avec âpreté, avec aigreur; violemment, fortement (violently); d'une manière pénétrante, d'une manière perçante (acutely). *Sharply outlined,* nettement dessiné *or* profilé; *to answer sharply,* répondre vivement. **sharpness,** *n.* Tranchant (keenness of edge), *m.*; pointe (of a point), *f.*; acidité (acidity); violence (of pain etc.); aigreur, âpreté (of language etc.); amertume, *f.*, piquant, *m.*; netteté (clearness), *f.*; esprit éveillé, *m.*, vivacité (of children etc.), *f.*; son aigu, *m.*, netteté (of sound), *f.* **sharp-set,** *a.* Affamé. **sharp-shooter,** *n.* Tirailleur, tireur d'élite, *m.* **sharp-sighted,** *a.* À la vue perçante. **sharp-witted,** *a.* À l'esprit délié.

shatter [ˈʃætə], *v.t.* Fracasser, briser en pièces; faire voler en éclats; déchirer (to rend); déranger (to derange); délabrer (of health). —*v.i.* Se briser, se fracasser. **shatters,** *n.pl.* Pièces, *f.pl.*, éclats, *m.pl.*

shave [ʃeiv], *v.t.* Raser; faire la barbe à; tondre (animal); effleurer (to graze); (*Am.*) plumer, écorcher (to fleece); (*Tech.*) planer. *To get shaved or to have a shave,* se faire raser, se faire la barbe; *to shave oneself,* se raser.—*v.i.* Se raser, se faire la barbe.—*n.* Action de raser *or* de se raser, *f.* *It was a narrow shave,* il s'en est fallu d'un cheveu; *to have a narrow shave,* l'échapper belle.

shave-grass, *n.* Prêle d'hiver, *f.* **shaveling,** *n.* Tonsuré, *m.* **shaver,** *n.* Barbier; blanc-bec (youngster); moutard; écorcheur, fripon, *m.* *Electric shaver,* rasoir électrique, *m.*

Shavian [ˈʃeiviən], *a.* Dans le genre de G. B. Shaw, inspiré de Shaw.

shaving, *n.* Action de raser, *f.*; copeau (of wood), *m.*; rognure (of paper), *f.* **shaving-block,** *n.* Pierre d'alun (to stop bleeding), *f.* **shaving-brush,** *n.* Blaireau, *m.* **shaving-cream,** *n.* Crème à raser, *f.* **shaving-mirror,** *n.* Miroir grossissant, *m.* **shaving-soap, shaving-stick,** *n.* Savon pour la barbe, *m.*

shawl [ʃɔːl], *n.* Châle, *m.*

*****shawm** [ʃɔːm], *n.* Chalumeau, *m.*

she [ʃiː], *pron.* Elle, *f.*; femelle (of some animals), *f.* *It is she,* c'est elle; *it will be she,* ce sera elle. **she-ass,** *n.* Ânesse, *f.* **she-bear,** *n.* Ourse, *f.* **she-cat,** *n.* Chatte, *f.* **she-devil,** *n.* Diablesse, *f.* **she-fox,** *n.* Renarde, *f.* **she-goat,** *n.* Chèvre, *f.* **she-monkey,** *n.* Guenon, *f.* **she-oak,** *n.* (*Austral.*) Casuarine, *f.* **she-wolf,** *n.* Louve, *f.*

sheaf [ʃiːf], *n.* (*pl.* **sheaves**) Gerbe; javelle (loose), *f.*; faisceau (of arrows), *m.*—*v.t.* Engerber, mettre en gerbe. **sheafy,** *a.* De gerbes; en forme de gerbes.

shear [ʃiə], *v.t.* (*past* **sheared,** *p.p.* **sheared** or **shorn** [ʃɔːn]) Tondre; cisailler; (*fig.*) dépouiller, frustrer. **shear-legs** [SHEERS]. **shear-steel,** *n.* Acier corroyé, *m.* **shear-water** [ˈʃiəwɔːtə], *n.* Puffin, *m.*, bec-en-ciseaux (bird), *m.*

shearer, *n.* Tondeur, *m.*; tondeuse (machine), *f.* **shearing,** *n.* Tonte, tondaison, *f.* **shearing-machine,** *n.* Tondeuse, *f.* **shearing-time,** *n.* Tonte, tondaison, *f.* **shearman,** *n.* Tondeur, *m.* **shears,** *n.pl.* Grands ciseaux, *m.pl.*; cisailles (for hedges, metal), *f.pl.*

sheath [ʃiːθ], *n.* (*pl.* **sheaths** [ʃiːðz]) Gaine, *f.*; fourreau (scabbard); étui (case); (*Ent.*) élytre, *m.* **sheath-maker,** *n.* Gainier, *m.* **sheath-winged,** *a.* (*Ent.*) Coléoptère.

sheathe [ʃiːð], *v.t.* Mettre dans le fourreau, rengainer; couvrir, gainer, revêtir (de); (*fig.*) plonger, enfoncer; (*Naut.*) doubler (a ship). *To sheathe the sword,* poser l'épée, cesser les hostilités.

sheathing [ˈʃiːðiŋ], *n.* Doublage, *m.*

sheathless [ˈʃiːθlis], *a.* Sans gaine; sans étui.

sheave [ʃiːv], *n.* Rouet, réa (de poulie), *m.*— *v.i.* (*Row.*) Déramer, culer.

Sheba [ˈʃiːbə]. Saba, *f.* *The Queen of Sheba,* la Reine de Saba.

shed (1) [ʃed], *n.* Hangar; (*Build.*) atelier, *m.*; (*Geog.*) ligne de faîte, *f.* *Cow-shed,* étable (à

shed vaches), *f.*; *lean-to shed*, appentis, *m.*; *water-shed*, (*Geog.*) ligne de partage des eaux, *f.*
shed (2) [ʃed], *v.t.* (*past* and *p.p.* **shed**) Répandre, verser, faire couler; laisser tomber, se dépouiller de, perdre (of trees); jeter (of animals). *To shed light on a matter*, éclairer une affaire; *to shed over*, répandre sur, verser sur.
shedder, *n.* Personne qui répand *or* qui fait couler, *f.*
shedding, *n.* Action de répandre; effusion (of blood); perte (loss), *f.*
sheen [ʃiːn], *n.* Éclat, lustre, brillant, *m.* **sheeny**, *a.* Brillant, luisant.
sheep [ʃiːp], *n.inv.* Mouton, *m.*; (*fig.*) brebis (ewe), *f.*; (*Bookb.*) basane, *f.* *Black sheep*, brebis galeuse; *lost sheep*, brebis égarée, *f.* **sheep-cote**, *n.* Parc à moutons, *m.* **sheep-dip**, *n.* Bain parasiticide, *m.* **sheep-dog**, *n.* Chien de berger, *m.* **sheep-farmer**, *n.* Éleveur de moutons, *m.* **sheep-fold**, *n.* Bergerie, *f.*, bercail, parc à moutons, *m.* **sheep-hook**, *n.* Houlette, *f.* **sheep-market**, *n.* Marché aux moutons, *m.* **sheep-pen**, *n.* Parc à moutons, *m.* **sheep-run**, *n.* Pâturage à moutons, *m.* **sheep's-eye**, *n.* Œillade, *f.*; yeux doux, *m.pl.* *To cast sheep's eyes at*, faire les yeux doux à, lancer des œillades à. **sheep-shearer**, *n.* Tondeur de moutons, *m.* **sheep-shearing**, *n.* Tonte, *f.* **sheep-skin**, *n.* Peau de mouton; basane (leather), *f.* **sheep-stealer**, *n.* Voleur de moutons, *m.* **sheep-stealing**, *n.* Vol de moutons, *m.* **sheep-walk**, *n.* Pâturage à moutons, *m.*
sheepish, *a.* Penaud, bête, niais. *I felt rather sheepish*, je me suis senti un peu bête. **sheepishly**, *adv.* D'un air penaud. **sheepishness**, *n.* Gaucherie, *f.*, air penaud, *m.*
sheer [ʃiə], *a.* Pur; escarpé, perpendiculaire (of rocks). *Sheer force*, pure force, *f.*, grand effort, *m.*; *sheer nonsense*, pure sottise, *f.*; *sheer up*, à pic.—*adv.* Tout droit; tout à fait; tout net.—*n.* (*Naut.*) Tonture, *f.*, relèvement, *m.*; embardée, *f.*—*v.i.* Faire des embardées. *To sheer off*, pousser au large, prendre le large, filer, s'esquiver. **sheer-hulk**, *n.* Ponton à mâture, *m.*, mâture flottante, *f.* **sheers**, *n.pl.* Bigue, chèvre, *f.*
sheet [ʃiːt], *n.* Drap, *m.*; feuille (of paper or metal); nappe (of water etc.); (*Naut.*) écoute (rope), *f.* *As white as a sheet*, blanc comme un linge; (*fam.*) *to be three sheets in the wind*, être entre deux vins, avoir du vent dans les voiles; *winding-sheet*, linceul, *m.*—*v.t.* Garnir de draps; couvrir, envelopper.—*v.i.* (*Naut.*) Border les écoutes.
sheet-anchor, *n.* Ancre de miséricorde, ancre de veille; (*fig.*) ancre de salut, *f.* **sheet-copper**, *n.* Cuivre en feuilles, *m.* **sheet-glass**, *n.* Verre à vitres, *m.* **sheet-iron**, *n.* Tôle, *f.* **sheet-lead**, *n.* Plomb en feuilles, *m.* **sheet-lightning**, *n.* Éclair en nappe, *m.*
sheeting, *n.* Toile pour draps de lit, *f.*; blindage (lining), *m.*
sheikh [ʃeik], *n.* Cheik, *m.*
shekel [ʃekl], *n.* Sicle, *m.* (slang) *The shekels*, la galette, *f.*, les ronds, *m.pl.*
sheldrake [ʃeldreik], **sheld-duck**, *n.* (*Orn.*) Tadorne, *m.*
shelf [ʃelf], *n.* (*pl.* **shelves**) Planche, *f.*; rayon (of a book-case), *m.*; tablette, *f.*; écueil, récif (reef); replat (in mountains), *m.* *Set of*

shelves, étagère, *f.*; *to put on the shelf*, mettre sur la planche, (*fig.*) mettre au rancart; *to remain on the shelf*, coiffer Sainte Catherine (of a girl). **shelfy**, *a.* Plein d'écueils, de hauts-fonds.
shell [ʃel], *n.* Coque (eggs, fruit, etc.); coquille (empty egg); cosse (peas etc.); écaille (oysters); carapace (lobsters); bière, *f.*, cercueil (coffin); (*Artill.*) obus (shrapnel), projectile, *m.*; écorce (of the earth); carcasse (house), *f.*; (*fig.*) extérieur, *m.*, apparence; (*Mus.*) lyre, *f.*—*v.t.* Écaler (nuts etc.); écosser (peas etc.); égrener (seeds); (*Mil.*) bombarder, lancer des obus sur.—*v.i.* S'écaler (of fruits). *To shell out*, (*colloq.*) s'exécuter, payer.
shellac [ʃəˈlæk or ˈʃelæk], *n.* Laque en écailles, gomme laque, *f.*
shell-fire, *n.* Tir à obus, bombardement, *m.* **shell-fish**, *n.* Coquillage, mollusque, *m.*, crustacés, *m.pl.* **shell-hole**, *n.* Trou d'obus, entonnoir, *m.* **shelling**, *n.* Écossage; égrenage; (*Mil.*) bombardement, *m.* **shell-proof**, *a.* Blindé. **shell-shocked**, *a.* Commotionné. **shell-work**, *n.* Ouvrage en coquillage, *m.* **shelly**, *a.* Couvert de coquillages; coquilleux.
shelter [ʃeltə], *n.* Abri, couvert; (*fig.*) refuge, asile, *m.*, protection, *f.* *To take shelter from*, à l'abri de, à couvert de.—*v.t.* Abriter, mettre à l'abri; protéger, garantir.—*v.i.* S'abriter. *To shelter oneself behind*, se réfugier derrière; *to shelter oneself from*, se réfugier contre.
sheltered, *a.* Abrité. **shelterer**, *n.* Protecteur, *m.* **shelterless**, *a.* Sans abri; sans asile. **shelter-trench**, *n.* Tranchée-abri, *f.*
shelve [ʃelv], *v.t.* Mettre sur un rayon; (*fig.*) mettre au rancart, classer, enterrer.—*v.i.* Aller en pente. **shelving**, *a.* En pente, incliné.
shemozzle [ʃiˈmɔzl], *n.* (*pop.*) Chamaillis, *m.*
shepherd [ʃepəd], *n.* Berger, pâtre; (*fig.*) pasteur, (*dial.*) pastour, pastoureau, *m.* *Shepherd kings*, rois pasteurs, *m.pl.*—*v.t.* Piloter, guider, veiller sur; surveiller. **shepherd's purse**, *n.* Bourse-à-pasteur, *f.*
shepherdess, *n.* Bergère, *f.*
sherbet [ˈʃəːbət], *n.* Sorbet, *m.*
***sherd** [SHARD].
sheriff [ˈʃerif], *n.* Shérif, *m.*; (*Am.*) chef de police, *m.*
sherry [ˈʃeri], *n.* Vin de Xérès, *m.* **sherry-cobbler**, *n.* Xérès aromatisé et sucré, *m.*
***shew** [SHOW].
shew-bread [SHOW-BREAD].
shibboleth [ˈʃibələθ], *n.* Schibboleth; (*fig.*) mot d'ordre (d'un parti), *m.*
shield [ʃiːld], *n.* Bouclier, *m.*; tôle protectrice, *f.*; écran protecteur, *m.*; (*Her.*) écu, écusson, *m.*—*v.t.* Couvrir d'un bouclier. *To shield from*, mettre à l'abri de, défendre de, protéger contre. **shield-bearer**, *n.* Écuyer, *m.*
shift [ʃift], *n.* Changement (change); expédient, *m.*, ressource (expedient), *f.*; détour, faux-fuyant (trick), *m.*; démanchement (of a violin), *m.*; *chemise de femme (chemise), équipe, journée (relay of workmen), *f.* *My last shift*, ma dernière ressource; *night shift*, équipe de nuit, *f.*; *to be at one's last shift*, ne

savoir à quel saint se vouer; *to be reduced to shifts*, en être aux expédients; *to make shift to*, trouver moyen de, s'arranger pour; *to make shift with*, s'arranger de, s'accommoder de; *to use shifts*, user de biais.—*v.t.* Changer; déplacer, changer de place; transférer, transporter. *To shift off*, se délivrer de, remettre; *to shift one's ground*, changer ses batteries; *to shift the blame on to someone else*, s'excuser sur quelqu'un.—*v.i.* Changer de place (to change place); changer (to vary); changer de vêtements (to change dress); (*fig.*) trouver des expédients, user de faux-fuyants. *To shift about*, passer d'un parti à l'autre, changer d'opinion, tourner casaque; *to shift for oneself*, se tirer d'affaire soi-même, se débrouiller.

shifter, *n.* Personne qui change, *f.*; biaiseur, *m.*, biaiseuse (person who uses artifice), *f.* *Scene-shifter*, machiniste, *m.* **shiftily**, *adv.* Peu franchement; en tergiversant. **shiftiness**, *n.* Fausseté, *f.*, manque de franchise, *m.*

shifting, *n.* Changement, changement de place; déplacement (of cargo etc.); (*fig.*) subterfuge, détour, biais, *m.*—*a.* Changeant; qui use de détours (deceitful). *Shifting sand*, sable mouvant, *m.* **shiftingly**, *adv.* En changeant.

shiftless, *a.* Sans initiative; sans énergie.

shifty, *a.* Plein d'expédients; retors. *He is a shifty customer*, c'est un roublard.

shillelah [ʃi'leilə], *n.* (*Irish*) Gourdin, *m.*

shilling [ʃiliŋ], *n.* Shilling, *m.* *A shillingsworth*, la valeur d'un shilling, pour un shilling.

shilly-shally [ʃili'ʃæli], *n.* Hésitation, irrésolution, *f.*—*v.i.* Barguigner, hésiter, être irrésolu.

shimmer [ʃimə], *n.* Lueur, faible clarté, *f.*, chatoiement, *m.*—*v.i.* Jeter une faible lueur, miroiter.

shin [ʃin], *n.* Devant de la jambe; jarret (of beef), *m.*—*v.i.* *To shin down*, descendre vite, dégringoler; *to shin up a tree*, grimper à un arbre. **shin-bone**, *n.* Tibia, *m.*

shindy [ʃindi], *n.* Tapage, *m.* *To kick up a shindy*, faire du boucan, faire un bruit de tous les diables.

shine [ʃain], *v.i.* (*past* and *p.p.* **shone** [ʃɔn]) Luire; reluire; briller. *The moon shines*, il fait clair de lune; *the sun shines*, le soleil luit; *to shine forth*, éclater; *to shine in conversation*, briller dans la conversation; *to shine with happiness*, rayonner de bonheur.—*v.t.* (*past* and *p.p.* **shined**) (*Am.*) Faire reluire. *Shoeshine boy*, cireur de bottes, *m.*—*n.* Brillant, éclat, lustre; beau temps (of the weather), *m.* *Come rain or shine I'll be there*, qu'il pleuve ou qu'il vente, j'y serai; *to take the shine out of*, éclipser, remettre à sa place.

shingle [ʃiŋgl], *n.* Bardeau (for roofing); galet, caillou (coarse gravel), *m.*—*v.t.* Couvrir de bardeaux; couper (les cheveux) à la garçonne. **shingles**, *n.pl.* (*Med.*) Zona, *m.*

shingly, *a.* Couvert de galets.

shining [ʃainiŋ], *a.* Luisant, brillant.—*n.* Brillant, éclat, *m.*

shintoism [ʃintouizm], *n.* Shintoïsme, *m.*

shiny [ʃaini], *a.* Luisant, reluisant; lustré.

ship [ʃip], *n.* Navire; vaisseau, bâtiment, *m.* *Merchant ship*, navire marchand; *on board (ship)*, à bord; *sea-going ship*, navire de long

cours, *m.*; *ship of state*, char de l'État, *m.*; *ship of the desert*, chameau, *m.*; *ship of the line*, vaisseau de ligne; *ship of war*, vaisseau de guerre; *store-ship*, vaisseau de transport; *the ship's company*, l'équipage, *m.*; *to take ship*, s'embarquer; *when my ship comes home*, quand j'aurai fait fortune.—*v.t.* Embarquer; charger; mettre à bord; expédier (goods); embarquer un paquet de mer, recevoir (a sea); monter (the rudder etc.). *To ship off goods*, embarquer des marchandises; *to ship the oars*, armer les avirons.—*v.i.* S'embarquer.

ship-biscuit, *n.* Biscuit de mer, *m.* **ship-board**, *n.* Bord de navire, *m.* **ship-boy**, *n.* Mousse, *m.* **ship-broker**, *n.* Courtier maritime, *m.* **shipbuilder**, *n.* Constructeur de navires, *m.* **ship-building**, *n.* Construction navale, architecture navale, *f.* **ship-canal**, *n.* Canal maritime, *m.*

ship-chandler, *n.* Approvisionneur, fournisseur de navires, *m.*

ship-load, *n.* Chargement, fret, *m.*

shipmaster, *n.* Capitaine marchand, patron de navire, *m.* **shipmate**, *n.* Camarade de bord, *m.*

shipment, *n.* Chargement, embarquement, *m.*, expédition, mise à bord, *f.*

ship-money, *n.* (*Hist.*) Impôt pour la construction des vaisseaux, *m.*

shipowner, *n.* Armateur, *m.*

shipper, *n.* Expéditeur, *m.*

shipping, *n.* Vaisseaux, navires, *m.pl.*; marine marchande, la marine, *f.*; chargement, embarquement, *m.*, mise à bord (loading), *f.* *Ice-floes are dangerous to shipping*, les glaces flottantes présentent un danger pour la navigation.—*a.* Maritime. *Shipping company*, compagnie de navigation, *f.*; *shipping intelligence*, nouvelles maritimes, *f.pl.*; *the shipping trade*, le commerce maritime, *m.* **shipping-agent**, *n.* Expéditeur, courtier maritime, *m.*

ship's-boat, *n.* Chaloupe, *f.*

ship's-carpenter, *n.* Charpentier du bord, *m.*

shipshape, *a.* En ordre, bien arrangé, bien tenu, fin prêt.—*adv.* En marin, d'une façon ordonnée, méthodiquement.

ship's-husband, *n.* Gérant à bord, *m.* **ship's-papers**, *n.pl.* Papiers de bord, *m.pl.*

shipwreck, *n.* Naufrage, sinistre en mer, *m.* *To make shipwreck of*, ruiner.—*v.t.* Faire faire naufrage à; (*fig.*) faire échouer, faire périr. *To be shipwrecked*, faire naufrage.

shipwrecked, *a.* Naufragé; (*fig.*) ruiné.

shipwright, *n.* Charpentier de navires, *m.*

shipyard, *n.* Chantier naval, *m.*

shire [ʃaiə], *n.* Comté, *m.*

shirk [ʃəːk], *v.t.* Éviter, éluder, se soustraire à; (*Mil.*) tirer au flanc. *Never to shirk one's work*, être franc du collier.—*v.i.* Finasser. *He shirked it*, il refusa de venir au fait. **shirker**, *n.* Carottier, -ière, carotteur, -euse; flanchard, -e; (*Mil.*) tire-au-flanc; embusqué, *m.*

shirt [ʃəːt], *n.* Chemise (d'homme), *f.* (*fam.*) *Boiled shirt*, chemise à plastron, amidonnée, empesée; (*fam.*) *keep your shirt on!* ne vous emballez pas! *night-shirt*, chemise de nuit, *f.*; *soft shirt*, chemise molle, souple; *stiff shirt*, chemise empesée; *to sell the shirt off one's back*, vendre jusqu'à sa chemise.—*v.t.* Vêtir d'une chemise. **shirt-collar**, *n.* Col de chemise, *m.* **shirt-front**, *n.* Devant de chemise, plastron, *m.* **shirting,** *n.* Toile à chemises, *f.* **shirtless,** *a.* Sans chemise. **shirt-sleeves,** *n.* Manches de chemise, *f.pl. In his shirt-sleeves,* en manches de chemise, en bras de chemise. **shirt-tails,** *n.pl.* Pans de chemise, *m.pl.* **shirtwaister (dress),** *n.* Robe chemisier, *f.*

shirty, *a.* (*pop.*) En rogne, irritable. *To get shirty,* s'emballer, s'emporter.

shit [ʃit], *n.* (*indec.*) Merde, *f.*—*v.i.* Chier.

shive [ʃaiv], *n.* Bonde (of cask), *f.*; bouchon (de bocal), *m.*

shiver [ʃivə], *v.t.* Briser en morceaux, fracasser, faire voler en éclats; (*Naut.*) mettre en ralingue (a sail); briser (a mast).— *v.i.* Se briser en morceaux, voler en éclats, se fracasser; grelotter (with cold); frissonner (with fear); faseyer, ralinguer (of sail).—*n.* Frissonnement, frisson, tremblement; fragment, morceau, éclat, *m.*; pierre schisteuse, *f. To break the shivers,* faire voler en éclats; *to have the shivers,* avoir le frisson.

shivering, *a.* Frissonnant.—*n.* Frissonnement, frisson, *m.* **shiveringly,** *adv.* En frissonnant. **shivery,** *a.* Friable; frissonnant. *I have a shivery feeling about me,* il me prend des frissons.

shoal [ʃoul], *n.* Banc (of fish), *m.*; (*fig.*) multitude, foule, *f.*; bas-fond, haut-fond (shallow), *m. In shoals,* en troupes, en foule.—*v.i.* Se réunir en banc; (*fig.*) affluer, s'attrouper (of fish); diminuer en profondeur (of water).—*a.* Bas, peu profond. **shoaliness,** *n.* Manque de profondeur, *m.* **shoaly,** *a.* Plein de hauts-fonds *or* de bancs de sable.

shock [ʃɔk], *n.* Choc, heurt, coup, à-coup, ébranlement, *m.*; (*Elec.*) commotion, secousse *f.*; tas de gerbes, *m.*, moyette (of corn); tignasse (of hair), *f.*—*v.t.* Choquer, heurter; (*fig.*) frapper d'horreur, offenser, scandaliser; mettre (corn) en moyettes.

shock-absorber, *n.* Amortisseur, *m.* **shockheaded,** *a.* À épaisse chevelure, aux cheveux ébouriffés. **shock-proof,** *a.* À l'épreuve des secousses; inébranlable (person). **shocktactics,** *n.pl.* Tactique de choc, *f.* **shocktroops,** *n.pl.* Troupes de choc, *f.pl.*

shocker, *n.* Horreur; surprise pénible, *f.*; roman sensationnel, *m.* **shocking,** *a.* Choquant, affreux, révoltant, dégoûtant. *Shocking!* fi! quelle horreur! **shockingly,** *adv.* Affreusement, horriblement.

shod [ʃɔd], *a.* Ferré (of horses); chaussé (of persons).

shoddiness [ʃɔdinis], *n.* Mauvaise qualité, *f.* **shoddy,** *a.* D'effilochage; de camelote, de pacotille. *Shoddy goods,* pacotille, camelote, *f.*; *shoddy wool,* laine d'effilochage, *f.*—*n.* Drap de laine d'effilochage, *m.*

shoe [ʃu:], *n.* (*pl.* **shoes**) Soulier, *m.*; chaussure, *f.*; fer (horseshoe); sabot (wooden *or* for a carriage), *m. A shoe loose,* un fer qui lâche (of horses); *hobnailed shoes,* souliers cloutés; *horseshoe,* ferrure, *f.*; *shoes down at heel,* des souliers éculés, *m.pl.*; *spiked shoes,* chaussures à pointes; *that's where the shoe pinches,* c'est là que le bât me blesse; *to cast a shoe,* se déferrer (of horses); *to make shoes for,* chausser; *to put the shoe on the right foot,* deviner juste, s'en prendre à qui de droit; *to rough-shoe* (a horse), ferrer à glace; *to stand in someone's shoes,* être à la place de quelqu'un;

to step into someone's shoes, prendre la place de quelqu'un; *to take off one's shoes and stockings,* se déchausser; *wooden shoes,* sabots, *m.pl.*—*v.t.* (*past* and *p.p.* **shod**) Chausser; ferrer (a horse etc.); garnir les pattes de (an anchor); (*Tech.*) saboter.

shoe-black, *n.* Cireur, *m.* **shoe-brush,** *n.* Brosse à souliers, *f.* **shoe-buckle,** *n.* Boucle de soulier, *f.* **shoe-cream,** *n.* Crème-cirage, *f.* **shoe-horn,** *n.* Chausse-pied, *m.*, corne à chaussures, *f.* **shoeing,** *n.* Ferrage, *m.* **shoeing-forge,** *n.* Forge, *f.* **shoeing-smith,** *n.* Maréchal ferrant, *m.* **shoe-lace,** *n.* Lacet de chaussure, *m.* **shoe-leather,** *n.* Cuir de souliers, *m. To save shoe-leather,* pour épargner ses souliers. **shoemaker,** *n.* Cordonnier, *m. The shoemaker's wife goes the worst shod,* les cordonniers sont les plus mal chaussés. **shoemaking,** *n.* Cordonnerie, *f.* **shoe-polish,** *n.* Cirage, *m.* **shoe-string,** *n.* Lacet de chaussure, *m. To do things on a shoe-string,* faire les choses avec un minimum de dépense. **shoe-tree,** *n.* Forme, *f.* (pour chaussures).

shone [ʃɔn], *past* [SHINE].

shoo [ʃu:], *int.* Ch-ch! allez, filez! (to frighten away).—*v.t. To shoo (away, off),* faire fuir, chasser (chickens, children, etc.).

shook [ʃuk], *past* [SHAKE].

shoot [ʃu:t], *v.t.* (*past* and *p.p.* **shot** (1)) Tirer, décocher, lancer, jeter, darder; décharger, faire partir, lâcher un coup de (a gun etc.); frapper, atteindre (to hit); tuer, tuer d'un coup de fusil, fusiller, faire passer par les armes (to execute); pousser (to push forth); (*Ftb.*) marquer, shooter (un but); descendre (rapids etc.); (*Carp.*) ajuster. *He was shot through the leg,* il eut la jambe traversée par une balle; *I'll be shot if,* le diable m'emporte si; *the cannon-ball shot his leg off,* le boulet lui emporta la jambe; *to have shot one's bolt,* avoir dit son dernier mot; *to shoot a film,* tourner un film; *to shoot a line,* galéjer, exagérer son importance; *to shoot at with a gun* or *to shoot a gun at,* tirer un coup de fusil à *or* sur; *to shoot dead,* tuer raide; *to shoot down,* abattre; *to shoot forth,* pousser, lancer; *to shoot oneself,* se tuer, se tirer un coup de fusil *or* de pistolet; *to shoot out,* lancer; *to shoot the moon,* faire un trou à la lune, déménager à la cloche de bois; *to shoot the rapids,* descendre les rapides; (*Motor.*) *to shoot the traffic-lights,* brûler les feux rouges; *to shoot through,* traverser, transpercer, percer d'outre en outre *or* de part en part.

v.i.—Tirer; chasser (à tir); (*Ftb.*) tirer au but, shooter; (*fig.*) s'élancer, courir; filer (of stars etc.); pousser (of planks etc.). *My temples shoot,* j'éprouve des élancements aux tempes; *shoot!* vas-y! parle! *to go out shooting,* aller à la chasse; *to shoot at,* tirer sur; *to shoot ahead,* courir en avant, se précipiter en avant; *to shoot ahead of,* devancer, dépasser; *to shoot by,* passer rapidement, passer comme un trait; *to shoot forth,* s'élancer, pousser (of plants), jaillir (of light); *to shoot forward,* s'élancer en avant; *to shoot off,* partir comme un trait; *to shoot out,* se projeter, faire saillie, pousser (of plants); *to shoot through,* traverser; *to shoot true,* tirer juste; *to shoot up,* pousser, jaillir, monter.

n.—Rejeton, *m.*, pousse (plant), *f.*; sarment (of vine), scion (of plant), *m.*; gouttière (spout), *f.*; dépôt de décombres (for rubbish); descenseur (slide), *m.*, glissière, *f.*, chute (of water), *f.*

shooter, *n.* Tireur, *m.* *Six-shooter,* revolver à six coups, *m.*

shooting, *n.* Tir (of fire-arms), *m.*; chasse au tir, chasse au fusil, *f.*; élancement (pain), *m.*; pousse (of plants); décharge (of rubbish), *f.*; (*Cine.*) tournage (of a film), *m.*; prise de vues, *f.* (*Cine.*) *Shooting angle,* angle de prise de vues, champ, *m.*; *shooting schedule,* plan de tournage, *m.*; *shooting script,* découpage technique, *m.* *To practise shooting,* s'exercer au tir.—*a.* Lancinant (of pain), filante (of stars). *Shooting pains,* des élancements de douleur, *m.pl.,* douleurs lancinantes, *f.pl.*; *shooting star,* étoile filante, *f.*

shooting-box, *n.* Rendez-vous de chasse, *m.* **shooting-brake,** *n.* (*Motor.*) Canadienne, *f.* **shooting-gallery,** *n.* Tir, stand, *m.* **shooting-jacket,** *n.* Veston de chasse, *m.* **shooting-match,** *n.* Concours de tir, *m.* **shooting-stick,** *n.* (*Print.*) Décognoir, *m.*; canne-siège, *f.*

shop [ʃɔp], *n.* Boutique, *f.*; magasin (store), *m.*; atelier (workshop), *m.* (*colloq.*) *All over the shop,* en désordre, en confusion, *f.*; *tobacco-shop,* débit de tabac, *m.*; *to keep a shop,* tenir boutique; *to shut up shop,* fermer boutique; *to talk shop,* parler boutique, parler affaires. —*v.i.* Faire des emplettes. *To go shopping,* aller faire des emplettes, courir les magasins.

shop-assistant, *n.* Vendeur, *m.*, -euse, *f.* **shop-bill,** *n.* Prospectus, *m.* **shop-board,** *n.* Comptoir, établi (tailor's), *m.* **shop-boy,** *n.* Garçon de magasin, petit commis, *m.* **shop-girl,** *n.* Vendeuse, commise, *f.* **shopkeeper,** *n.* Marchand, *m.*, marchande, *f.* **shoplifter,** *n.* Voleur à l'étalage, *m.* **shoplifting,** *n.* Vol à l'étalage, *m.* **shopman,** *n.* (*pl.* **shopmen**) Commis de magasin, *m.* **shop-soiled,** *a.* Défraîchi. **shop-steward,** *n.* Responsable syndical, délégué ouvrier, *m.* **shop-walker,** *n.* Chef de rayon; inspecteur de magasin, *m.* **shop-window,** *n.* Devanture, vitrine, *f.*, étalage, *m.*

shopper, *n.* Acheteur, client, *m.* **shopping-bag,** *n.* Filet à provisions, *m.* **shopping-centre,** *n.* Quartier commerçant, *m.*

shoppy, *a.* Qui sent le boutiquier.

shore [ʃɔ:], *n.* Rivage, bord, *m.*, plage, côte, *f.*; étai, étançon (stay); (*Shipbuild.*) accore, *m.* *Along the shore,* le long de la côte, près de la terre; *on shore,* à terre; *to go on shore,* aller à terre; *to hug the shore,* raser la terre, serrer la côte.—*v.t.* Étayer, étançonner; (*Naut.*) accorer; débarquer; échouer. **shorewards,** *adv.* Vers le rivage.

shorn [ʃɔ:n], *p.p.* [SHEAR].

short [ʃɔ:t], *a.* Court; bref (brief), passager, de courte durée, petit (of stature); insuffisant (insufficient); croquant (of pastry); cassant (brittle); brusque (abrupt). *For short,* pour abréger, par abréviation; *in short,* bref, en un mot, enfin; *it is short by ten pounds, it is ten pounds short,* il y manque dix livres; *short circuit,* court-circuit, *m.*; (*Cine.*) *short feature,* film de moyen métrage, *m.*; *short film,* film de court métrage; *short list,* liste de candidats

pre-sélectionnés, *f.*; *short sight,* vue courte, myopie, *f.*; *short story,* nouvelle, *f.*, conte, *m.*; *the long and the short of it,* le fin mot de la chose; *to cut the matter short,* pour en finir, pour le trancher net; *to go short of,* se priver de; *to run short of,* venir à bout de; *to grow short,* se raccourcir; *to make shorter,* raccourcir; *to make short work of,* en avoir bientôt fait de.—*adv.* Court, vivement, brusquement. *It does not fall far short of it,* il s'en faut de peu; *it falls far short of it,* il s'en faut de beaucoup; *nothing short of murder,* rien excepté l'assassinat; *to cut short,* couper la parole à; abréger, retrancher; *to fall short of someone's expectations,* ne pas répondre à l'attente de quelqu'un; *to run short,* s'épuiser; *to stop short,* s'arrêter court, rester court; *to stop short of,* manquer de; *to turn short,* tourner court.

shortage, *n.* Déficit, manque, *m.*; disette (of food), insuffisance, pénurie, *f.*

shortbread, *n.* (Gâteau) sablé, *m.* **short-circuit,** *v.t.* Mettre en court-circuit. **shortcoming,** *n.* Défaut, *m.*, imperfection, insuffisance, faute, faiblesse, *f.* **short-dated,** *a.* À courte échéance. **shorthand,** *n.* Sténographie, *f.* *To take down in shorthand,* sténographier. *Typed shorthand,* sténotypie, *f.* **short-handed,** *a.* À court de personnel. **shorthand-typewriter,** *n.* Sténotype, *f.* (machine). **shorthand-typist,** *n.* Sténodactylographe (person), (*fam.*) sténodactylo, *f.* **shorthand-writer,** *n.* Sténographe, *m.* **short-horn,** *n.* Bétail à courtes cornes, *m.* **short-listed,** *a.* Placé sur la liste définitive de candidats à interviewer pour un poste. **short-lived,** *a.* Qui vit peu de temps, éphémère. **short-sighted,** *a.* Qui a la vue courte, myope; (*fig.*) peu prévoyant, peu sagace. **short-sightedness,** *n.* Vue courte, myopie, *f.*; (*fig.*) manque de clairvoyance, *m.* **short-tempered,** *a.* Vif, pétulant, brusque. **short-waisted,** *a.* Court de taille; à taille haute (of dress). **short-winded,** *a.* À l'haleine courte; poussif (horse). **short-witted,** *a.* Qui a peu d'esprit, borné.

shorten, *v.t.* Raccourcir, rapetisser; abréger (to abridge); diminuer (to diminish); resserrer (to contract); rendre friable (of dough). —*v.i.* (Se) raccourcir, diminuer; s'abréger. **shortening,** *n.* Raccourcissement, *m.*, diminution, *f.*; ingrédient gras (beurre, graisse) qui entre dans la confection de la pâtisserie. **shortly,** *adv.* Bientôt, sous peu, dans peu de temps; brièvement, en peu de mots (briefly); sèchement, brusquement.

shortness, *n.* Courte durée, *f.*; peu d'étendue, *m.*; petitesse (short of stature); brièveté (of vowel), brièveté, *f.*; défaut, manque (de), *m.*; brusquerie (of attitude), *f.* *Shortness of breath,* haleine courte, *f.*; *shortness of memory,* mémoire courte, *f.*; *shortness of waist,* courte taille, *f.*

shorts, *n.pl.* Culotte courte, *f.*, caleçon court; short, *m.*; (*Cine.*) films de court métrage, *m.pl.*

shot (1), *past* and *p.p.* [SHOOT].

shot (2) [ʃɔt], *n.* Coup de fusil, coup de feu, coup; trait (from a bow), *m.*; balle (for a rifle), *f.*; boulet (for cannon); grain de plomb, plomb (for a fowling-piece), *m.*; (*Artill.*) charge; portée (reach), *f.*; écot (reckoning);

tireur (shooter); (*Ftb.*) coup au but, shoot, *m.*; (*Med.*) injection, piqûre, *f.*; (*Cine.*) prise, *f.*, plan, *m.* *At a shot*, d'un seul coup; *buck-shot*, chevrotine, *f.*; *cannon-shot*, coup de canon, *m.*; *like a shot*, comme un trait; *long-shot*, (*fig.*) une chance sur mille; *I heard the shot*, j'entendis partir le coup; *random shot*, coup perdu, *m.*; *rifle-shot*, coup de fusil, *m.*; *that's not a bad shot*, ce n'est pas mal tiré, ce n'est pas mal (photographié); (*fig.*) ce n'est pas mal deviné; *to be a crack* or *dead shot*, ne jamais manquer son coup; *to be a good shot*, être bon tireur; *to fire a shot*, tirer un coup de feu; *to fire a shot at*, tirer sur, (*fig.*) essayer; *to waste powder and shot*, jeter sa poudre aux moineaux; *within cannon-shot*, à portée de canon; *within ear-shot*, à portée d'oreille; *without firing a shot*, sans brûler une cartouche. (*Cine.*) *Close shot*, demi-gros plan; *Dolly* or *travelling shot*, travelling, *m.*; *long shot*, plan d'ensemble, *m.*; *medium shot*, plan moyen; *pan* or *panning shot*, panoramique; *process shot*, truquage, *m.*—*v.t.* Charger (une arme à feu); plomber (une ligne).—*a.* Changeant, chatoyant. *Shot silk*, soie gorge-de-pigeon, *f.*

shot-free [SCOT-FREE]. **shot-gun**, *n.* Fusil de chasse, *m.* **shot-hole**, *n.* Trou de balle, *m.* **shot-pouch**, *n.* Giberne, cartouchière, *f.* **shot-proof**, *a.* À l'épreuve des balles. **shot-rack**, *n.* Parc à boulets, *m.* **shotten**, *a.* En saillie; disloqué (of a bone); qui a déchargé son frai (of fish); guais (herring). *As thin as a shotten herring*, maigre comme un hareng saur. **shot-tower**, *n.* Tour à plomb de chasse, *f.*

should [ʃud], *v.aux.* (*past of* **shall**, *used as sign of the conditional*) *I should speak*, je parlerais; *should I* or *if I should meet him*, si je le rencontre or rencontrais; *whom should I meet but his sister*, qui est-ce que je vois ? Sa sœur.

shoulder [ʃouldə], *n.* Épaule, *f.*; épaulement, *m.*; (*Tech.*) embase, languette, *f.* *Over the shoulder*, en bandoulière; *round shoulders*, dos rond, *m.*; *shoulder to shoulder*, de concert, d'accord; *to give someone the cold shoulder*, battre froid à quelqu'un; *to put one's shoulder to the wheel*, pousser à la roue; *to shrug one's shoulders*, hausser les épaules.—*v.t.* Prendre or charger sur les épaules; se charger de; pousser (to push); porter (arms). *To shoulder the responsibility*, endosser la responsabilité.

shoulder-bag, *n.* Musette, *f.*, sac porté en bandoulière, *m.* **shoulder-belt**, *n.* Baudrier, *m.* **shoulder-blade**, *n.* Omoplate, *f.* **shouldered**, *a.* À épaules. *Broad-shouldered*, à larges épaules; *round-shouldered*, au dos rond, voûté. **shoulder-high**, *adv.* À hauteur d'épaules. **shoulder-knot**, *n.* Nœud d'épaule, *m.*, aiguillette, *f.* **shoulder-shotten**, *a.* Épaulé. **shoulder-strap**, *n.* Bretelle, (*Mil.*) patte d'épaule, *f.*

shout [ʃaut], *v.i.* Crier, huer, pousser or jeter des cris; vociférer. *He was shouted at*, il fut hué; *to shout down*, faire taire à force de cris; *to shout for someone*, appeler quelqu'un à grands cris.—*v.t.* Entonner; payer la tournée (of drinks).—*n.* Cri, *m.*; acclamations, *f.pl.*; éclat (of laughter), *m.*; tournée (of drinks), *f.* *Shouts of applause*, acclamations, *f.pl.*; *it's my shout*, c'est ma tournée.

shouting, *n.* Acclamation, *f.*, cris, *m.pl.* *It's*

all over bar the shouting, tout est décidé, fini; ça y est; l'affaire est dans le sac.

shove [ʃʌv], *v.t.* Pousser; fourrer (one's nose anywhere). *To shove away*, repousser, éloigner; *to shove back*, faire reculer, repousser; *to shove down*, enfoncer, faire entrer, faire tomber, renverser, repousser dans le fond; *to shove forward*, faire avancer, pousser en avant; *to shove from*, repousser de, éloigner de; *to shove off*, pousser au large (a boat); repousser; *to shove out*, pousser dehors, faire sortir.—*v.i.* Pousser. *To keep shoving*, pousser toujours; *to shove by*, bousculer; *to shove off*, s'éloigner; s'en aller; (*fam.*) filer.—*n.* Coup, *m.*, poussée, *f.* *To give a shove to*, pousser, prêter un coup de main à.

shovel [ʃʌvl], *n.* Pelle, *f.* *Fire-shovel*, pelle à feu; *power-shovel*, *steam-shovel*, pelle à vapeur, drague à cuiller, *f.*—*v.t.* Ramasser avec la pelle, pelleter. *To shovel away*, déblayer; *to shovel in*, ramasser avec la pelle; *to shovel out*, jeter avec une pelle. **shovel-board**, *n.* Jeu de galets, *m.* **shovel dredge(r)**, *n.* Pelle automatique, *f.* **shovel-ful**, *n.* Pelletée, *f.* *By the shovelful*, à la pelletée. **shoveller**, *n.* Pelleteur; souchet (duck), *m.*

show [ʃou], *v.t.* (*past* **showed**, *p.p.* **showed**, **shown**) Montrer, faire voir, exposer à la vue; faire preuve de; manifester, témoigner, démontrer (to prove); indiquer, faire connaître (to make known); expliquer (to explain). *To show in*, introduire, faire entrer; *to show off*, faire valoir, faire ressortir, faire parade de, mettre en relief; *to show someone how to do a thing*, montrer à quelqu'un comment il faut faire; *to show out*, reconduire, éconduire (to get rid of); *to show over*, faire visiter à (house etc.); *to show the white feather*, laisser voir qu'on a peur, (*colloq.*) caner; *to show up*, faire monter, démasquer (to unmask).—*v.i.* Paraître, se montrer; se faire remarquer. *Nothing shows like a hat*, rien ne se fait remarquer autant qu'un chapeau; *to show off*, poser, se donner des airs, se faire valoir; *to show through*, transparaître; *to show up*, ressortir; se présenter; (*fam.*) s'amener.—*n.* Apparence, *f.*; étalage, *m.*, parade, *f.*; spectacle, concours, *m.*, exposition (exhibition), *f.* (*Cattle-*)*show*, exposition de bétail, *f.*, comice (agricole), *m.*; *dumb-show*, jeu muet, *m.*, pantomime, *f.*; *film show*, séance de cinéma, *f.*; *for show*, pour la parade; *to make a show of*, faire parade de, faire montre de; *good show!* bien joué! *Show house* or *show flat*, maison spécimen, *f.*, appartement spécimen, *m.*; *variety show*, spectacle de variétés, *m.*

show-bill, *n.* Affiche, annonce, *f.* **show-bread**, *n.* Pain de proposition, *m.* **show-card**, *n.* Pancarte, *f.* **show-case**, *n.* Montre, vitrine, *f.* **show-down**, *n.* Explication décisive, mise des cartes sur table, *f.*; révélation (de prétentions), *f.* **showman**, *n.* (*pl.* **showmen**) Directeur de spectacle forain, *m.* **show-off** *n.* Poseur, m'as-tu-vu, *m.* **show-place**, *n.* Endroit d'intérêt touristique, *m.* **show-ring**, *n.* Arène de vente, *f.* **show-room**, *n.* Salle d'exposition, *f.* **show-window**, *n.* Montre, *f.*, étalage, *m.*

shower [ʃauə], *n.* Ondée (slight); averse (copious); pluie, grêle (of blows, stones, etc.), *f.*; douche, *f.*; (*pop.*) bande de crétins, *f. April shower*, giboulée de mars, *f.*; *cold shower*, douche froide, *f.*; *heavy shower*, forte averse, *f.*—*v.t.* Inonder (de pluie); arroser; (*fig.*) verser, faire pleuvoir. *To shower down*, répandre, faire pleuvoir (sur).—*v.i.* Pleuvoir à verse, pleuvoir. **shower-bath**, *n.* Douche, *f.*, bain-douche, *m.* **showeriness**, *n.* État pluvieux, *m.* **showery**, *a.* Pluvieux.

showily ['ʃouili], *adv.* Avec éclat, d'une manière voyante. **showiness**, *n.* Ostentation; prétention, couleur voyante, *f.* **showing**, *n.* Représentation, mise en vue, *f.*; passage (d'un film), *m. By one's own showing*, de son propre aveu; (*Cine.*) *first showing*, première vision, *f.* **showy**, *a.* Voyant, prétentieux, criard.

shrank, *past* [SHRINK].

shrapnel ['ʃræpnəl], *n.* Obus à mitraille, *m.*; (*fam.*) éclats d'obus, *m.pl.*

shred [ʃred], *n.* Lambeau, bout, brin, *m. To tear to shreds*, déchirer en lambeaux.—*v.t.* Couper en bandes, déchiqueter, défibrer; râper grossièrement. **shredded**, *a.* Déchiqueté, effiloché, coupé en filaments, grossièrement râpé; défibré. **shredder**, *n.* (*person*) Déchireur, défibreur; (*tool*) coupe-julienne, *m.*; défibreur, *m.* (of sugar-cane).

shrew [ʃru:], *n.* Mégère, femme acariâtre, *f. The Taming of the Shrew*, La Mégère apprivoisée.

shrewd [ʃru:d], *a.* Sagace, pénétrant, fin, perspicace. *I have a shrewd idea that*, je suis très porté à penser que. **shrewdly**, *adv.* Avec sagacité, avec pénétration, finement. *To suspect shrewdly*, soupçonner fort. **shrewdness**, *n.* Sagacité, pénétration, finesse, *f.*

shrewish ['ʃru:iʃ], *a.* Grondeur, acariâtre. **shrewishly**, *adv.* En mégère, en femme criarde. **shrewishness**, *n.* Humeur acariâtre, *f.*

shrew-mouse, *n.* Musaraigne, *f.*

shriek [ʃri:k], *n.* Cri perçant, *m. Shrieks of laughter*, grands éclats de rire, *m.pl.*—*v.t.* Crier.—*v.i.* Jeter un cri aigu. (*fig.*) *These colours shriek*, ces couleurs jurent. **shrieking**, *n.* Cris stridents, *m.pl.*

shrievalty ['ʃri:vəlti], *n.* Fonctions de shérif, *f.pl.*; charge de shérif, *f.*

shrift [ʃrift], *n.* Confession; absolution, *f.* (*fig.*) *Short shrift*, très court délai. *I'll give him short shrift*, j'aurai vite fait de l'expédier.

shrike [ʃraik], *n.* (*Orn.*) Pie-grièche, *f.*

shrill [ʃril], *a.* Aigu, perçant; aigre (of the voice).—*v.i.* Produire un son aigu. *To shrill forth*, chanter d'une voix aiguë. **shrillness**, *n.* Son aigu, ton aigu, *m.* **shrilly**, *adv.* D'un ton aigu, d'une voix perçante.

shrimp [ʃrimp], *n.* Crevette (grise), *f.*; (*fig.*) bout d'homme, nain, *m.*, naine, *f.*—*v.i.* Pêcher des crevettes. **shrimper**, *n.* Pêcheur de crevettes, *m.* **shrimping**, *n.* Pêche à la crevette, *f.*

shrine [ʃrain], *n.* Châsse, *f.*; reliquaire, *m.*; tombeau, *m.*; chapelle, *f.* (of a saint); lieu de pèlerinage, *m.*

shrink [ʃriŋk], *v.i.* (*past* **shrank**, *p.p.* **shrunk**) Rétrécir, se rétrécir, se contracter, se resserrer; se retirer; se rapetisser, se ratatiner; diminuer, baisser (to diminish); se tasser (with age). *He shrinks at the sight of danger*, il recule à la vue du danger; *to shrink away*,

reculer, disparaître, se dérober, s'évanouir; *to shrink back*, reculer; *to shrink from*, reculer devant, avoir horreur de; *to shrink up*, rétrécir, se rétrécir, se recroqueviller.—*v.t.* Rétrécir; diminuer.

shrinkage, *n.* Rétrécissement, tassement, *m.*, contraction, *f.* **shrinker**, *n.* Personne qui recule devant le danger, *f.* **shrinking**, *n.* Rétrécissement, tassement, *m.*, contraction; action de reculer *or* de se retirer (act of running back), *f.*

shrive [ʃraiv], *v.t.* (*past* **shrove** [ʃrouv], *p.p.* **shriven** [ʃrivn]) Confesser; donner l'absolution à.

shrivel [ʃrivl], *v.i.* Se ratatiner, se recroqueviller.—*v.t.* Faire ratatiner, faire recroqueviller, rider, racornir. *To shrivel up*, ratatiner, se ratatiner.

shroud [ʃraud], *n.* Linceul, suaire, *m.*; (*Naut.*, *pl.*) haubans, *m.pl.*; (*fig.*) voile, *m.*—*v.t.* Mettre dans un linceul, ensevelir (dans); (*fig.*) abriter, couvrir, cacher, envelopper, voiler. **shroudless**, *a.* Sans linceul. **shroudly**, *a.* Qui abrite.

shrove, *past* [SHRIVE].

Shrovetide ['ʃrouvtaid], *n.* Les jours gras, *m.pl. Shrove Tuesday*, Mardi-Gras, *m.*

shrub [ʃrʌb], *n.* Arbuste, arbrisseau; grog au citron, *m.* **shrubbery**, *n.* Plantation d'arbrisseaux, *f.*; bosquet, *m.*; arbustes, *m.pl.* **shrubby**, *a.* Plein d'arbrisseaux, touffu; qui ressemble à un arbuste.

shrug [ʃrʌg], *n.* Haussement d'épaules, *m.*—*v.t.* Hausser. *To shrug one's shoulders*, hausser les épaules.

shrunk, *past* and *p.p.* [SHRINK].

shudder ['ʃʌdə], *v.i.* Frissonner, frémir (de).—*a.* Frissonnement, frémissement, *m. It gives me the shudders*, j'en ai le frisson.

shuffle [ʃʌfl], *v.t.* Mettre en confusion, mêler; battre (cards). *To shuffle away*, escamoter; *to shuffle in or into*, introduire adroitement dans; *to shuffle off*, se débarrasser de; *to shuffle up*, faire à la hâte, bâcler.—*v.i.* Traîner les pieds; battre les cartes; tergiverser, chicaner, biaiser, équivoquer (to prevaricate). *To shuffle along*, traîner les pieds, marcher d'un pas traînant; *to shuffle off*, (*colloq.*) disparaître, mourir, (*fam.*) faire sa malle.—*n.* Confusion, défaite, *f.*, faux-fuyant, subterfuge (evasion), *m.*

shuffler, *n.* Biaiseur, chicaneur, fourbe, *m.* **shuffling**, *a.* Chicaneur, biaiseur; évasif (of things); traînant. *With shuffling gait*, à la démarche traînante, d'un pas traînant.—*n.* Marche traînante, *f.*; (*Cards*) battement des cartes, *m.*; (*fig.*) artifices, *m.pl.*, chicane, *f.* **shufflingly**, *adv.* D'une manière évasive; d'un pas traînant.

shun [ʃʌn], *v.t.* Éviter, fuir. **shunless**, *a.* Inévitable.

shunt [ʃʌnt], *v.t.* Garer, manœuvrer (a train); dériver (a current); détourner.—*v.i.* S'esquiver.—*n.* Garage, évitement, *m.*; dérivation (of current), *f.* **shunt-circuit**, *n.* (*Elec.*) Circuit dérivé, *m.* **shunting**, *n.* Changement de voie, garage, *m.* **shunting-engine**, *n.* Locomotive de manœuvre, *f.*

shut [ʃʌt], *v.t.* (*past* and *p.p.* **shut**) Fermer; enfermer (enclose). *To shut again*, refermer; *to shut down*, bien fermer, éteindre (furnaces etc.), arrêter (engine); *to shut in*, enfermer; *to* *shut off*, intercepter, couper (steam), isoler; *to shut oneself up*, se reclure; se renfermer; *to shut out*, exclure, fermer la porte à; *to shut out from*, exclure de; *to shut up*, fermer, enfermer, mettre sous les verrous, condamner (a door etc.), faire taire, imposer silence à, fermer la bouche à.—*v.i.* Fermer, se fermer. *Shutting out*, exclusion, *f.*; *shutting up*, fermeture, *f.*; *shut up!* taisez-vous! en voilà assez! finissez!

shut-eye, *n.* (*fam.*) Somme, *m.*

shutter, *n.* Volet, *m.*, contrevent (outside shutter), *m.*; (*Phot.*) obturateur, *m.* *Folding shutters*, volets brisés, *m.pl.*; *slatted shutters*, persiennes, *f.pl.*; *to put up the shutters*, mettre les volets, fermer boutique. **shutter-blind**, *n.* Jalousie (à lames mobiles), *f.* **shuttered**, *a.* Aux volets fermés.

shuttle [ʃʌtl], *n.* Navette; vanne, *f.*—*v.i.* Faire la navette. **shuttle-cock**, *n.* Volant, *m.* *Battledore and shuttle-cock*, (jeu de) volant, *m.* **shuttle-service**, *n.* Navette, *f.* **shuttling**, *n.* Navette, *f.*; va-et-vient, *m.*

shy [ʃai], *a.* Réservé, timide, honteux; sauvage, farouche (of animals); ombrageux (of horses). *To be shy of using*, craindre d'employer; *to fight shy of*, se défier de, éviter.—*v.i.* Être ombrageux, faire un écart, se jeter de côté (of horses).—*v.t.* Jeter, lancer.—*n.* Coup (de pierre etc.); jet; essai, *m.* *To have a shy at*, s'essayer à (faire quelque chose). *Coco-nut shy*, jeu de massacre, *m.* **shyly**, *adv.* Timidement, avec réserve. **shyness**, *n.* Timidité, retenue, réserve; fausse honte; nature ombrageuse, sauvagerie (of horses), *f.*

Siam [sai'æm]. Le Siam, *m.*

Siamese [saiə'mi:z], *a.* and *n.* Siamois, *m.*, Siamoise, *f.*

Siberia [sai'biəriə]. La Sibérie, *f.*

Siberian [sai'biəriən], *a.* and *n.* Sibérien, *m.*, Sibérienne, *f.*

sibilant ['sibilənt], *a.* Sifflant.—*n.* Lettre sifflante, *f.* **sibilation** [-'leiʃən], *n.* Sifflement, *m.*

sibyl ['sibil], *n.* Sibylle, *f.*

sibylline ['sibilain], *a.* Sibyllin.

sic [sik], *adv.* Sic, textuellement.

siccative ['sikətiv], *a.* and *n.* Siccatif, *m.*

siccity ['siksiti], *n.* Siccité, *f.*

sice [sais], *n.* Le six (aux dés), *m.*

Sicilian [si'siliən], *a.* and *n.* Sicilien, *m.*, Sicilienne, *f.* *The Sicilian Vespers*, les Vêpres siciliennes, *f.pl.*

Sicily ['sisili]. La Sicile, *f.*

sick [sik], *a.* Malade; qui a des nausées, qui a mal au cœur (affected with nausea). *Sick headache*, migraine, *f.*; *sick of*, dégoûté de, las de; *sick of a fever*, malade de la fièvre; *sick man* or *woman*, malade; *sick unto death*, malade à mourir; *to be sea-sick*, avoir le mal de mer; *to be sick*, vomir, rendre; *to be sick and tired of the whole business*, en avoir plein le dos; *to be sick at heart*, avoir la mort dans l'âme; *to feel sick, to turn sick*, se sentir mal au cœur, avoir des nausées, (*fam.*) avoir le cœur barbouillé; *to make sick*, soulever le cœur à, écœurer; (*Mil.*) *to report sick*, se faire porter malade.—*n.pl.* Malades, *pl.*

sick-bay, *n.* (*Naut.*) Poste des malades, *m.*, infirmerie, *f.* **sick-bed**, *n.* Lit de douleur, *m.* **sick-brained**, *a.* Malade d'esprit. **sick-fund**, *n.* Caisse de secours mutuels (pour les malades), *f.*

sicken, *v.t.* Rendre malade; (*fig.*) lasser, dégoûter (to disgust); faire soulever le cœur à, écœurer (to make squeamish).—*v.i.* Tomber malade; se soulever, sentir le cœur se soulever; (*fig.*) se dégoûter (de). *I sickened at the sight of that thing*, la vue de cette chose me souleva le cœur; *to sicken of*, se dégoûter de. **sickening**, *a.* Écœurant, à soulever le cœur; (*fig.*) dégoûtant; navrant.

sickish, *a.* Un peu malade, indisposé. *To feel sickish*, avoir un léger mal de cœur.

sickle [sikl], *n.* Faucille, *f.*

sick-leave, *n.* Congé de convalescence, *m.* **sick-list**, *n.* Rôle des malades, *m.* *On the sick-list*, porté malade.

sickliness, *n.* Mauvaise santé, *f.*, état maladif, *m.* **sickly**, *a.* Maladif, d'une mauvaise santé; insalubre, malsain (producing disease); fade (of colour); étiolé (of plants); affadissant, affadi (of taste etc.). *To grow sickly*, devenir maladif, languir.—*adv.* D'une manière maladive, d'une manière écœurante. *This pudding tastes sickly*, cet entremets a un goût écœurant, douceâtre.

sickness, *n.* Maladie, *f.*; mal de cœur, *m.*, nausées (nausea), *f.pl.* *Sea-sickness*, mal de mer, *m.*

sick-nurse, *n.* Garde-malade, *f.* **sick-parade**, *n.* (*Mil.*) Visite (des malades), *f.* **sick-room**, *n.* Chambre de malade, *f.* **sick-ward**, *n.* Salle des malades, *f.*

side [said], *n.* Côté; flanc (flank); bord (edge, border); versant (of a mountain), *m.*; paroi (wall); rive (of a river), *f.*; parti (party); camp (in outdoor games), *m.*; effet (sur la boule) (*Billiards*), *m.* *Alongside*, bord à bord; *blind side*, côté faible; *by his side*, à côté de lui; *by my side*, à côté de moi; *by the road-side*, au bord de la route; *by the side of*, sur le bord de (a road), au bord de (a river); *check side* (*Billiards*), effet contraire, *m.*; *from side to side*, d'un côté à l'autre; *near side*, montoir (of horse); *off-side*, côté gauche, *m.*; *off-side*, côté hors montoir (of horse); côté droit (of car), *m.*; (*Ftb.*) hors-jeu; *on both sides*, des deux côtés, de part et d'autre; *on my side*, de mon côté, pour moi (in my favour); *on neither side*, d'aucun côté; *on one side*, d'un côté, d'une part; *on* or *from all sides*, de tous côtés, de toutes parts; *on that side*, de ce côté-là, au delà; (*colloq.*) *on the long side*, plutôt longuet; *on the other side*, de l'autre côté, au delà (de); *on the side*, sur le côté, couché; par-dessus le marché; *on this side*, de ce côté-ci, en deçà; *on this side of Easter*, bien avant Pâques; *on whose side are you?* de quel parti êtes-vous? *profits on the side*, gratte, *f.*; *side by side*, côte à côte; *running side* (*Billiards*), effet en tête; *the wrong side* (of stuffs), l'envers, le mauvais côté; *this side up* (of cases), dessus; *to be on the wrong side of sixty*, avoir plus de soixante ans; *to change sides*, changer de parti; *to choose sides* (for games), choisir les partenaires, se former en équipes; *to hear both sides*, entendre le pour et le contre; *to lash one's sides* (of animals); se battre les flancs; *to put on side*, (*slang*) se donner des airs; (*Billiards*) prendre de l'effet; *to see the bright side of things*, voir tout en rose; *to see the dark side of things*, voir tout en noir; *to shake one's sides with laughter*, se tenir les côtes de rire; *to split one's sides with laughter*, se tordre de rire; *to take sides*, prendre parti, s'attacher à un parti; *wrong side out*, à l'envers.—*a.* De côté; latéral; indirect, oblique, de profil (indirect). *Side face*, de profil; *side way*, sentier détourné, chemin de traverse, *m.*—*v.i.* S'engager dans un parti. *To side with*, se ranger du côté de, prendre parti pour. **side-aisle**, *n.* Collatéral, bas-côté, *m.* **side-alley**, *n.* Contre-allée, *f.* **side-arms**, *n.* Armes blanches, *f.pl.* **sideboard**, *n.* Buffet, *m.*, desserte, *f.* **side-boards, side-burns,** *n.pl.* (*Am.*) Côtelettes (side-whiskers), *f.pl.*, favoris, *m.pl.* **side-box**, *n.* Loge de côté, *f.* **side-car**, *n.* Sidecar, *m.* **side-dish**, *n.* Hors-d'œuvre, entremets, *m.* **side-door**, *n.* Porte latérale, *f.* **side-face**, *n.* Profil, *m.* **side-glance**, *n.* Regard de côté, *m.* **side-issue**, *n.* Question d'intérêt secondaire, *f.* **side-light**, *n.* Lumière oblique, *f.*; feu de côté; (*fig.*) aperçu indirect, *m.* **side-line**, *n.* Occupation secondaire; seconde spécialité, *f.* **sidelong**, *a.* De côté. *To cast sidelong glances at*, regarder du coin d'œil, faire des yeux en coulisse à.—*adv.* De côté. **side-saddle**, *n.* Selle de dame, *f.* *To ride side-saddle*, monter en amazone. **side-show**, *n.* Spectacle forain, *m.*; attraction secondaire, *f.* **side-slip**, *n.* Dérapage, *m.* *To have a side-slip*, déraper. **sidesman**, *n.* (*Eccles.*) Marguillier adjoint, *m.* **side-splitting**, *a.* Désopilant, tordant. **side-step**, *n.* Pas de côté, *m.*—*v.i.* Faire un pas de côté; éviter, esquiver. **side-track**, *n.* Voie de garage, voie accessoire *or* secondaire, *f.*—*v.t.* Garer (of train); aiguiller sur une voie de garage; (*fig.*) donner le change à quelqu'un, semer quelqu'un. *He gets easily side-tracked*, il perd facilement le fil de son discours, il s'écarte facilement de son sujet. **side-view**, *n.* Vue de côté, *f.* **sidewalk**, *n.* Contre-allée, *f.*; (*Am.*) trottoir (in streets), *m.* **sideways** *or* **sidewise**, *adv.* De côté; obliquement. **side-whiskers**, *n.pl.* Favoris, *m.pl.*

sided, *a.* À côtés, à faces. *Two-sided*, à deux pans, à deux faces.

sidereal [sai'diəriəl], *a.* Des astres, sidéral.

siding ['saidiŋ], *n.* Gare, voie, d'évitement, voie de garage, croisière (on a single line), *f.*

sidle [saidl], *v.i.* Marcher de côté; s'insinuer, se couler.

siege [si:dʒ], *n.* Siège, *m.* *Regular siege*, siège en règle, *m.*; *to lay siege to*, mettre le siège devant, faire le siège de, assiéger; *to raise the siege*, lever le siège. **siege-piece**, *n.* Pièce de siège, *f.* **siege-train**, *n.* Équipage de siège, *m.*

Siena [si'enə]. Sienne, *f.*

sienna [si'enə], *n.* Terre de Sienne (brûlée (burnt) *or* naturelle (raw)), *f.*

sierra [si'erə], *n.* Sierra, *f.*

siesta [si'estə], *n.* Sieste, *f.* *To take one's siesta*, faire la méridienne.

sieve [siv], *n.* Tamis (fine); crible (large), *m.*

sift [sift], *v.t.* Tamiser; cribler; sasser (flour); passer au crible, (*fig.*) sonder, examiner, éplucher. *To sift out*, venir à bout de, découvrir; (to scrutinize) examiner scrupuleusement, approfondir. **sifter**, *n.* Cribleur, *m.*, cribleuse, *f.*; sasseur, *m.*, sasseuse, *f.*; crible (large sieve), *m.* **sifting**, *n.* Tamisage; (*fig.*) examen minutieux, *m.*; (*pl.*) criblure, *f.*

sigh [sai], *n.* Soupir, *m.* *To heave a sigh*, jeter

or pousser un soupir.—*v.i.* Soupirer. *To sigh after*, soupirer après; *to sigh over*, gémir sur.—*v.t.* Exprimer par des soupirs. **sighing**, *n.* Soupirs, *m.pl.*

sight [sait], *n.* Vue, vision, *f.*; regard, *m.*, yeux, *m.pl.*; lumière (on a quadrant), *f.*; (*Firearms*) guidon (fore-sight), *m.*, hausse (back-sight), *f.*; spectacle (spectacle), *m.*; (*colloq.*) quantité, *f.*, tas, *m.* *A fine sight*, un beau spectacle; *a sight better*, beaucoup mieux; *a sight for sore eyes*, un spectacle délicieux; *a sight of people*, une foule immense; *a sight to see*, une chose à voir; *at first sight*, à première vue, dès l'abord; *love at first sight*, (*fam.*) coup de foudre, *m.*; *at sight*, à première vue, à livre ouvert, (*Comm.*) à vue; *by sight*, de vue; *I hate the sight of him*, je l'ai en horreur; *in sight*, en vue; *in the sight of*, aux yeux de, à la vue de, devant; *line of sight*, ligne de mire, *f.*; *long sight*, presbytie, *f.*; *muzzle-sight*, bouton de mire, *m.*; *near* or *short sight*, myopie, vue basse, *f.*; *not to lose sight of*, ne pas perdre de vue; *out of sight*, hors de vue; *out of sight, out of mind*, loin des yeux, loin du cœur; *second sight*, clairvoyance, *f.*; *to catch sight of*, apercevoir; *to come in sight*, apparaître; *to get sight of*, voir, apercevoir; *to keep in sight*, ne pas perdre de vue; *to keep out of sight*, se tenir caché; *to know by sight*, connaître de vue; *to lose one's sight*, perdre la vue; *to lose sight of*, perdre de vue; *to see the sights*, voir les curiosités (of a town); *to take sight of*, viser, (*Artill.*) pointer; *to vanish out of sight*, disparaître; *what a sight you are!* comme vous voilà arrangé!—*v.t.* Apercevoir, viser.

sighted, *a.* En vue. *Long-sighted*, presbyte; *near-sighted*, à la vue courte, myope; *short-sighted*, peu clairvoyant. **sightless**, *a.* Privé de la vue; aveugle. **sightlessness**, *n.* Cécité, *f.*, aveuglement, *m.* **sightliness**, *n.* Beauté, *f.* **sightly**, *a.* Beau à voir, qui plaît à l'œil.

sight-reading, *n.* (*Mus.*) Déchiffrement, *m.*; lecture à vue, *f.*

sight-seeing, *n.* *To go sight-seeing*, aller voir les curiosités. **sight-seer**, *n.* Touriste, visiteur (of a town), *m.*

sigillaria [sidʒi'leəriə], *n.* Sigillaire, *f.*

sigillate [si'dʒilət], *a.* Sigillé. **sigillography** [-'lɔgrəfi], *n.* Sigillographie, *f.*

sigmatism ['sigmətizm], *n.* Sigmatisme, *m.*

sigmoid ['sigmɔid], *a.* Sigmoïde.

sign [sain], *n.* Signe; indice, *m.*; trace; enseigne (signboard), *f.* *To give signs of*, donner des signes de; *to make signs to*, faire des signes à.—*v.t.* Signer. *To sign someone on*, embaucher *or* engager quelqu'un; *to sign away*, céder (par écrit).—*v.i.* Faire signe (à). *To sign off*, émarger en quittant son travail; *to sign on*, s'embaucher, s'engager. **sign-board**, *n.* Enseigne, *f.* **sign-manual**, *n.* Seing, *m.*, signature, *f.* **sign-painter**, *n.* Peintre d'enseignes, *m.* **sign-post**, *n.* Poteau indicateur, *m.* **sign-writer**, *n.* Peintre d'enseignes; peintre en lettres, *m.*

signal ['signəl], *n.* Signal; signe, (*Rail.*) sémaphore, *m.*; (*pl.*) (*Mil.*) les transmissions, *f.pl.*—*a.* Signalé, insigne.—*v.t.* Signaler; faire signe à.—*v.i.* Signaler, donner un signal. **signal-box, signal-cabin**, *n.* Poste à signaux, *m.*; cabine d'aiguillage, *f.* **signal-light**, *n.* Fanal, *m.* **signalman**, *n.* (*pl.*

signalmen) (*Naut.*) Timonier; (*Rail.*) signaleur, *m.* **signal-post,** *n.* Sémaphore, *m.* **signal-station,** *n.* Poste sémaphorique, *m.* (on land).

signalize, *v.t.* Signaler. *To signalize oneself*, se distinguer.

signaller, *n.* Signaleur, *m.* **signalling,** *n.* Signalisation, *f.*, balisage, · *m.*; (*Naut.*) timonerie, *f.* **signally,** *adv.* D'une manière signalée, remarquablement.

signatory ['signətəri], *n.* and *a.* Signataire, *m.*

signature ['signətʃə], *n.* Signature, *f.*, visa, *m.*; (*fig.*) marque, empreinte, *f.* *Joint signature*, signature collective; *signature tune*, indicatif (of band), *m.*

signer ['sainə], *n.* Signataire, *m.* or *f.*

signet ['signit], *n.* Sceau; cachet, *m.* *Writer to the signet*, (*Sc.*) avoué, *m.* **signet-ring,** *n.* Anneau à cachet, *m.*; chevalière, *f.*

significance [sig'nifikəns], *n.* Signification, *f.*, sens, *m.*; force, énergie, *f.*, poids, *m.*, importance, *f.* **significant,** *a.* Significatif; d'importance. **significantly,** *adv.* D'une manière significative. **signification** [-'keiʃən], *n.* Signification, *f.* **significative,** [-'nifikətiv], *a.* Significatif.

signify ['signifai], *v.t.* Vouloir dire, signifier; faire connaître, témoigner; importer (to import). *It does not signify*, cela ne signifie rien, n'importe; *to signify to*, notifier à, communiquer à; *what does it signify?* qu'importe?

signing ['sainiŋ], *n.* Signature, *f.*

silence ['sailəns], *n.* Silence, *m.*; taciturnité, *f.* *A dead silence*, un silence de mort; *silence!* (notice), défense de parler; *silence gives consent*, qui ne dit mot consent; *silence is golden*, ʒe silence est d'or; *to keep silence*, garder le silence, se taire; *to pass over in silence*, passer sous silence; *to reduce to silence*, réduire au silence, imposer silence à.—*v.t.* Réduire au silence, faire taire; faire cesser (to stop). *To silence a battery*, éteindre (faire cesser) le feu d'une batterie; *to silence complaints*, étouffer les plaintes.

silencer, *n.* (*Motor.*) Silencieux; amortisseur de son, *m.*; (*colloq.*) réponse décisive, *f.*

silent ['sailənt], *a.* Silencieux; taciturne, peu loquace (taciturn); muet (of letters, of film). *Keep those children silent*, faites taire ces enfants; *real grief is silent*, le vrai chagrin est muet; *the silent system*, le système cellulaire, ·*m.*; *to be silent*, garder le silence, se taire; *to remain silent*, garder le silence. **silently,** *adv.* Silencieusement, en silence; sans bruit. **silentness,** *n.* Silence, *m.*

Silenus [sai'li:nəs]. Silène, *m.*

Silesia [sai'li:ʃə or sai'li:siə]. Silésie, *f.*

silesia [sai'li:ʃiə], *n.* Percaline croisée, silé sienne, *f.*

silex ['saileks], *n.* Silex, *m.*

silhouette [silu'et], *n.* Silhouette, *f.*—*v.t.* Silhouetter.

silica ['silikə], *n.* Silice, *f.*

silicic [si'lisik], *a.* Silicique.

silicification [silisifi'keiʃən], *n.* Silicification, *f.*

silicious [si'liʃəs], *a.* Siliceux. **silicium** or **silicon** ['silikən], *n.* Silicium, *m.* **silicosis,** *n.* (*Med.*) Silicose, *f.*

silicula [si'likjulə], *n.* (*Bot.*) Silicule, *f.*

siliqua ['silikwə], *n.* Silique, *f.*

siliquiform [si'likwifɔ:m], *a.* Siliculiforme.

siliquous ['silikwəs], *a.* Siliqueux.

silk [silk], *n.* Soie, *f.*; (*pl.*) soieries, *f.pl.* *Artificial silk*, soie artificielle; *raw silk*, soie grège; *spooled silk*, soie bobinée; *thrown silk*, organsin, *m.*; *waste silk*, bourre, *f.*, capiton, *m.* *One cannot make a silk purse out of a sow's ear*, on ne saurait faire d'une buse un épervier. *To take silk*, être nommé conseiller du roi.—*a.* De soie, en soie; séricicole (silk-growing). *Silk handkerchief*, foulard, *m.*

silken, *a.* De soie; soyeux; (*fig.*) doux, moelleux.

silk-growing, *n.* Sériciculture, *f.* *Silk-growing industry*, industrie séricicole, *f.*

silkiness, *n.* Nature soyeuse, *f.*

silk-mercer, *n.* Marchand de soieries, *m.* **silk-mill,** *n.* Filature de soie, *f.* **silk-spinner,** *n.* Filateur de soie, *m.* **silk-thrower,** *n.* Moulineur de soie, *m.* **silk-throwing,** *n.* Moulinage, organsinage, *m.* **silk-weaver,** *n.* Tisserand en soie; canut (in Lyons), *m.*, canuse, *f.* **silkworm,** *n.* Ver à soie, *m.* *Silkworm breeder*, magnanier, *m.*; *silkworm nursery*, magnanerie, *f.*

silky, *a.* De soie, soyeux; (*fig.*) moelleux, doux.

sill [sil], *n.* Seuil (of a door), *m.*; tablette, *f.*, rebord (of a window), *m.*; (*Geol.*) filon-couche, *m.*

sillily ['silili], *adv.* Sottement, niaisement. **silliness,** *n.* Sottise, niaiserie, *f.*

silly ['sili], *a.* and *n.* Sot, nigaud, niais; simple, naïf. *Silly ass*, imbécile; *silly billy*, un nicodème; *silly fellow*, sot, bêta; *silly thing*, sottise; bête, *f.*, nigaud, *m.*, nigaude (person), *f.*; *to be silly*, faire la bête; *to knock somebody silly*, faire voir trente-six chandelles à quelqu'un, l'assommer.

silo ['sailou], *m.* Silo, *m.*

silt [silt], *v.t.* Envaser.—*v.i.* S'envaser. *To silt up*, s'encombrer de limon.—*n.* Vase, *f.*, limon, *m.* **siltation, silting,** *n.* Envasement, *m.*

Silurian [sai'ljuəriən], *a.* Silurien.

silvan [SYLVAN].

silver ['silvə], *n.* Argent, *m.*; monnaie d'argent (money); argenterie (plate), *f.* *German silver*, nickel silver, maillechort, *m.*—*a.* D'argent; argenté (of colour); argentin (of sound). *Silver fox*, renard argenté; *silver lace*, galon d'argent, *m.*; *silver paper*, (*fam.*) papier d'argent, *m.*; *silver plate*, argenterie, vaisselle d'argent, *f.*; *silver spoon*, cuiller d'argent, *f.*; *silver wedding*, noces d'argent, *f.pl.*; *to be born with a silver spoon in one's mouth*, être né coiffé.—*v.t.* Argenter; étamer (a mirror).—*v.i.* (Of hair) s'argenter.

silver-fish, *n.* Argentine, *f.* **silver-gilt,** *n.* Argent doré, vermeil, *m.* **silver-grey,** *a.* D'un gris argenté. **silver-headed,** *a.* Aux cheveux argentés; à pomme d'argent (of things). **silver-hilted,** *a.* A poignée d'argent. **silvering,** *n.* Argenture, *f.*; étamage (of mirrors), *m.* **silver-leaf,** *n.* Argent battu, *m.*; feuille d'argent, *f.* **silver-mounted,** *a.* Monté en argent. **silver-plated,** *a.* Argenté, en plaqué. **silver-plating,** *n.* Argenture, *f.* **silver-side,** *n.* Gîte à la noix, *m.* **silversmith,** *n.* Orfèvre, *m.* **silver-tongued,** *a.* A la langue dorée. **silverware,** *n.* Argenterie, *f.* **silver-weed,** *n.* Argentine, *f.* **silvery,** *a.* D'argent; argenté (of colour); argentin (of sound).

simian ['simiən], *a.* Simiesque, simien.—*n.* Simien, *m.*
similar ['similə], *a.* Semblable, pareil; similaire (of same nature). **similarity** [-'læriti], *n.* Ressemblance, similitude; similarité (same nature), *f.* **similarly**, *adv.* Pareillement, d'une manière semblable.
simile ['simili], *n.* Comparaison, *f.*
similitude [si'militju:d], *n.* Similitude, ressemblance, *f.*
simmer ['simə], *v.i.* Bouillir lentement, mijoter. *To simmer down,* reprendre son sang-froid, s'apaiser peu à peu. **simmering**, *n.* Mijotement, *m.*
simnel ['simnəl], *n.* Gâteau de Pâques (*or* de la mi-carême), *m.*
simoniac [sai'mouniæk], *a.* Simoniaque.
simony ['saiməni], *n.* Simonie, *f.*
simoon [si'mu:n], *n.* Simoun, *m.*
simper ['simpə], *n.* Sourire niais, *m.*—*v.i.* Sourire niaisement, minauder. **simperer**, *n.* Minaudier, *m.* **simpering**, *n.* Minauderie, *f.*—*a.* Minaudier. **simperingly**, *adv.* En minaudant.
simple [simpl], *a.* Simple. *As simple as ABC,* simple comme bonjour.—*n.* Simple, *m.*; herbe médicinale, *f.* **simple-hearted,** *or* **simple-minded,** *a.* Simple, ingénu, naïf. **simple-mindedness,** *n.* Candeur, simplicité, naïveté, *f.* **simpleness,** *n.* Simplicité, *f.* **simpleton,** *n.* Niais, nigaud, *m.*
simplicity [sim'plisiti], *n.* Simplicité, *f.*
simplification [-fi'keiʃən], *n.* Simplification, *f.*
simplify ['simplifai], *v.t.* Simplifier. *To become simplified,* se simplifier. **simplism,** *n.* Simplisme, *m.* **simply,** *adv.* Simplement; nettement, tout bonnement (merely); de soi-même (of itself).
simulacrum [simju'leikrəm], *n.* Simulacre, semblant, *m.*
simulate ['simjuleit], *v.t.* Feindre, simuler.
simulation [-'leiʃən], *n.* Simulation, feinte, *f.*; déguisement, *m.*
simulator ['simjuleitə], *n.* Simulateur, *m.*
simultaneous [siməl'teinjəs], *a.* Simultané. **simultaneously,** *adv.* Simultanément. **simultaneousness** *or* **simultaneity** [-'ni:iti], *n.* Simultanéité, *f.*
sin [sin], *n.* Péché, *m.*; (*fig.*) offense, infraction, *f. As ugly as sin,* laid comme les sept péchés capitaux; *original sin,* péché originel; *poverty is no sin,* pauvreté n'est pas vice; *to live in sin,* vivre maritalement en dehors du mariage, vivre dans le péché.—*v.i.* Pécher. *To be more sinned against than sinning,* être plus à plaindre qu'à blâmer. **sin-offering,** *n.* Sacrifice expiatoire, *m.*
Sinai ['saineiai]. Sinaï, *m.*
sinapism ['sinəpizm], *n.* Sinapisme, *m.*
since [sins], *conj.* Puisque (because); depuis que (of time). *How long is it since the doctor died?* combien de temps y a-t-il que le médecin est mort? *it is a long time since I saw him,* il y a longtemps que je ne l'ai vu; *it is not long since I was there,* il n'y a pas longtemps que j'y étais; *since you like it,* puisque vous l'aimez.—*prep.* Depuis. *Since then,* depuis ce temps, depuis lors.—*adv.* Depuis. *Ever since,* depuis ce temps-là, depuis lors; *it happened since,* cela est arrivé depuis; *long since,* il y a longtemps; *two years since,* il y a deux ans.

sincere [sin'si:ə], *a.* Sincère. **sincerely,** *adv.* Sincèrement. *Yours sincerely* (in friendly, but not intimate, letters), veuillez croire, cher M . . ., à mes sentiments les meilleurs.
sincerity [-'seriti], *n.* Sincérité, bonne foi, *f.*
sine [sain], *n.* (*Trig.*) Sinus, *m.*
sinecure ['sainəkjuə], *n.* Sinécure, *f.* **sinecurist,** *n.* Sinécuriste, *m.*
sinew ['sinju:], *n.* Tendon, (*colloq.*) nerf, *m. The sinews of war,* le nerf de la guerre. **sinewy,** *a.* Tendineux; (*fig.*) nerveux, vigoureux. **sinewless,** *a.* Sans nerf, sans vigueur.
sinful ['sinful], *a.* Pécheur, coupable. **sinfully,** *adv.* D'une manière coupable, en pécheur. **sinfulness,** *n.* Culpabilité, iniquité, *f.*
sing [siŋ], *v.t., v.i.* (*past* **sang,** *p.p.* **sung**) Chanter; célébrer (the praises of); siffler (of the wind); tinter (of the ears). *To make someone sing small,* rabattre le caquet à quelqu'un; *to sing* (a child) *to sleep,* endormir en chantant; *to sing delightfully,* chanter à ravir; *to sing in tune,* chanter juste; *to sing out* (to halloo), crier; *to sing out of tune,* chanter faux; *to sing small,* déchanter, changer de gamme; *to sing to,* chanter une chanson à.
Singapore ['siŋgəpɔ:]. Singapour, *m.*
singe [sindʒ], *v.t.* Flamber; roussir (one's clothes etc.); (*Tech.*) griller.—*n.* Légère brûlure, *f.* **singeing,** *n.* Flambage; (*Tech.*) grillage, *m.*
singer ['siŋə], *n.* Chanteur, *m.*, chanteuse; cantatrice (professional), *f.*; oiseau chanteur (bird), *m.* **singing,** *a.* Qui chante; de chant; chanteur (of birds).—*n.* Chant, tintement, bourdonnement (in the ears), *m.* **singing-bird,** *n.* Oiseau chanteur, *m.* **singing-buoy,** *n.* Bouée sonore, *f.* **singing-master,** *n.* Maître de chant, *m.* **singing-mistress,** *n.* Maîtresse de chant, *f.*
single [siŋgl], *a.* Seul, simple, unique; individuel, particulier (individual); singulier (of combat); non marié, célibataire (unmarried). *Single bedroom,* chambre à un lit, *f.*; *single blessedness,* célibat, *m.*; *single combat,* combat singulier, *m.*; *single life,* célibat, *m.*; *single man,* célibataire, garçon, *m.*; *single ticket,* billet simple, *m.*; *single woman,* femme non mariée, fille, *f.*; *to be single,* être garçon (of man), être fille (of woman); *to remain single,* rester célibataire; coiffer sainte Catherine (of a woman).—*n.* (*Ten.*) Partie simple, *f.*—*v.t.* Choisir. *To single out,* choisir, distinguer de la foule.
single-barrelled, *a.* À un coup. **single-breasted,** *a.* Droit (of coat). **single-frame,** *a.* (*Cine.*) *Single-frame exposure,* tournage image par image, *m.* **single-handed,** *a.* Qui se manie d'une seule main.—*adv.* Tout seul, sans aide. **single-hearted,** *a.* Sincère, honnête. **single-heartedness,** *n.* Sincérité, *f.* **single-minded,** *a.* Qui n'a qu'un but. **single-mindedness,** *n.* Unité d'intention, *f.* **single-scull,** *v.i., v.t.* (*Row.*) Ramer seul (en couple); godiller. **single-seater,** *n.* (*Av.*) Monoplace, *m.* **single-stick,** *n.* Bâton; jeu du bâton, *m.* **single-track,** *a.* (*Rail.*) À voie unique; (*Cine.*) à simple piste.
singleness, *n.* Sincérité, simplicité, *f.* **singly,** *adv.* Seulement, à part; individuellement, un à un (individually).

singlet ['siŋglit], *n.* Gilet de corps, maillot fin, *m.*

singsong ['siŋsɔŋ], *n.* Chant monotone; ton chantant, *m.*; mélopée, *f.*; concert improvisé (entre amis), *m.*

singular ['siŋgjulə], *a.* Singulier; insolite, curieux, étrange (remarkable); simple (not compound); (*Gram.*) au singulier.—*n.* Singulier, *m.* **singularity** [-'læriti], *n.* Singularité, *f.*

singularize ['siŋgjuləraiz], *v.t.* Singulariser. **singularly**, *adv.* Singulièrement.

sinister ['sinistə], *a.* Sinistre; (*Her.*) sénestre; (*fig.*) méchant, pervers. **sinisterly**, *adv.* Sinistrement, d'une manière sinistre. **sinistrorsally** [-'trɔ:səli], *adv.* À gauche.

sink [siŋk], *n.* Évier (in a kitchen); égout (sewer), puisard, *m.*; (*fig.*) sentine, *f.*; (*Rom.*) cloaque, *m.*; (*Print.*) tremperie, *f.* *A sink of iniquity*, un cloaque d'iniquité.—*v.i.* (*past* **sank**, *p.p.* **sunk**) Aller au fond, tomber au fond; couler à fond (to go to the bottom); pénétrer, s'enfoncer; sombrer, couler bas (of a ship); décliner, s'affaiblir (to decline); succomber; tomber (to fall); baisser (of prices etc.); être abattu, se serrer (of spirits, the heart, etc.); descendre (of the sun etc.); se tasser (of foundations); dégénérer (en). *To be sinking* (*dying*), baisser rapidement; *to sink back*, retomber; *to sink down*, aller au fond, s'enfoncer, s'affaisser (to fall prostrate), descendre; se coucher (of the sun); *to sink down on*, se laisser tomber *or* s'affaisser sur; *to sink down to*, s'abaisser jusqu'à, diminuer jusqu'à; *to sink into*, s'enfoncer dans, pénétrer dans, entrer dans, tomber dans (to fall into), dégénérer en; *to sink low*, s'affaisser; *to sink to rest*, s'abandonner au sommeil, s'endormir; *to sink under*, succomber à.—*v.t.* Faire tomber au fond, enfoncer; couler bas (a ship); creuser, foncer (a shaft etc.); abaisser; affaiblir; diminuer, faire baisser (to diminish); abattre (to depress); perdre (to lose); placer (money) à fonds perdu; amortir (a debt). (*fam.*) *He's sunk*, c'est un homme coulé; *sunken garden*, jardin encaissé, *m.*; *sunk in thought*, plongé dans ses pensées.

sinker, *n.* Fonceur (of a well); plomb (on a fish-line), *m.*

sink-hole, *n.* Trou d'évier, *m.* **sink-trap**, *n.* Siphon d'évier, *m.*

sinking, *a.* Qui coule (of ship). *With a sinking heart*, avec un serrement de cœur.—*n.* Foncement (of wells, shafts, etc.); tassement (of foundations); affaissement, *m.*, défaillance (weakness), *f.*; placement à fonds perdu (of money); amortissement (of a debt); engloutissement (of a ship), *m.* **sinking-fund**, *n.* Fonds, *m.*, *or* caisse d'amortissement (of a public debt), *f.*

sinless ['sinlis], *a.* Sans péché, innocent; pur. **sinlessly**, *adv.* Purement, innocemment, sans péché. **sinlessness**, *n.* Innocence, pureté, *f.*

sinner ['sinə], *n.* Pécheur, *m.*, pécheresse, *f.* *He is a great sinner in that respect*, il pèche beaucoup de ce côté-là; *oh! you sinner!* mauvais sujet que vous êtes!

Sinn Fein [ʃin 'fein], (*Irish phr.*)=nous-mêmes. Titre d'une revue (puis du parti) autonomiste en Irlande.

sinological [sinə'lɔdʒikl], *a.* Sinologique.

sinologist [-'nɔlədʒist], *n.* Sinologue, *m.* **sinology**, *n.* Sinologie, *f.*

sinuate ['sinjuət], *a.* (*Bot.*) Sinué. **sinuosity** [-'ɔsiti], *n.* Sinuosité, *f.* **sinuous**, *a.* Sinueux.

sinus ['sainəs], *n.* (*Geog.*) Baie, *f.*; (*Anat.*) sinus, *m.*

sip [sip], *n.* Petit coup, *m.*, petite gorgée, *f.*—*v.t.*, *v.i.* Boire à petit coups, siroter.

siphon ['saifən], *n.* Siphon. *m.*—*v.t.* Siphonner.

sippet ['sipit], *n.* Croûton, *m.* (for soup); mouillette, *f.* (for egg).

sir [sə:], *n.* Monsieur; Sir (title of a knight or a baronet, followed by Christian name), *m.* *Did you ring, sir?* Monsieur a-t-il sonné?—*v.t.* (*fam.*) Donner du Monsieur à quelqu'un.

sire ['saiə], *n.* Père; Sire (in addressing a king), *m.*; (*pl.*) pères, aïeux, *m.pl.* *Grand-sire*, grand-père, *m.*—*v.t.* (of stallion) Être le père de, engendrer.

siren ['saiərən], *n.* Sirène, *f.*—*a.* De sirène.

Sirius ['siriəs]. (*Astron.*) Sirius, *m.*

sirloin ['sə:lɔin], *n.* Aloyau; faux-filet, *m.*

sirocco [si'rɔkou], *n.* Siroco, *m.*

sirrah ['sirə], *n.* Coquin, drôle, *m.*

siskin ['siskin], *n.* (*Orn.*) Tarin, *m.*

sissy ['sisi], *n.* (*colloq.*) Mollasson, *m.*

sister ['sistə], *n.* Sœur, infirmière-major (nurse), *f.* *The fatal sisters*, les Parques, *f.pl.* —*a.* Sœur; de même nature; du même gabarit (of ships). *Sister ship*, navire de même série, *m.* **sister-in-law**, *n.* Belle-sœur, *f.* **sisterhood**, *n.* Communauté de sœurs, *f.*, sœurs, *f.pl.* **sisterly**, *a.* De sœur, en sœur, comme une sœur.

Sistine ['sistain], *a.* Sixtine.

sit [sit], *v.i.* (*past* and *p.p.* **sat**) S'asseoir; être assis (be seated); rester (to remain seated); être (to be); se tenir (on horseback); demeurer; siéger, tenir séance, se réunir (of assemblies, courts, judges, etc.); aller (of clothes); couver (to brood), percher (of birds); poser (for one's portrait). *To be sitting*, être assis, être en séance, siéger (of assemblies); *to make someone sit up*, (*colloq.*) étonner, épater quelqu'un; *to sit close*, se serrer; *to sit down*, s'asseoir; *to sit down again*, se rasseoir; *to sit down to table*, se mettre à table; *to sit for* (in Parliament), représenter; *to sit for* (one's portrait), poser pour; *to sit heavy on*, peser sur; *to sit in judgment on*, juger; *to sit in Parliament*, siéger au parlement; *to sit on the committee*, faire partie de la commission; *to sit still*, rester tranquille; *to sit tight*, ne pas bouger; *to sit under*, suivre les cours de; *to sit up*, se tenir droit, se mettre sur son séant, veiller (not to go to bed); *to sit up for*, attendre, ne pas se coucher pour attendre (le retour de); *to sit up with*, veiller, garder.

v.t.—Asseoir; se tenir sur (a horse). *To sit a horse well*, se tenir bien à cheval, avoir une bonne assiette; *to sit oneself down*, s'asseoir; *to sit out*, rester jusqu'à la fin de; *to sit out a dance*, sauter une danse; *to want to sit it out*, vouloir en voir la fin.—*n.* Séance, *f.*; ajustement, *m.*

sit-down strike, *n.* Grève sur le tas, *f.*

site [sait], *n.* Situation, *f.*, emplacement (of a building); site (of landscape), *m.*—*v.t.* Placer, établir des emplacements pour. *To site a gun,* fixer l'emplacement d'un canon.

sitfast ['sitfɑ:st], *n.* (*Vet.*) Cor, durillon, *m.*

sitter ['sitə], *n.* Personne assise; (*Paint.*) personne qui pose, *f.*, modèle, *m.*; couveuse (hen), *f.*

sitting, *n.* Séance; audience (of a court); couvée (of eggs); couvaison (incubation); place (seat); (*Paint.*) séance, *f. At one sitting,* à la fois; *sitting up,* veille, veillée, *f.—a.* Assis; en séance (of courts etc.); perché (of birds); qui couve (of a hen); au gîte, gîté (of a hare). *Sitting tenant,* locataire d'un appartement vendu occupé. **sitting-room,** *n.* Petit salon, *m. Bed-sitting-room,* pièce unique avec lit, *f.*

situate (1) ['sitjueit], *v.t.* Situer.

situate (2) ['sitjuit] or **situated** ['sitjueitid], *a.* Situé; (*Law*) sis. *Awkwardly situated,* dans une position embarrassante; *this is how I am situated,* voici la position où je me trouve.

situation [-'eiʃən], *n.* Situation, position, *f.*, état, *m.*; place, *f.*, emploi (place), *m.*

sitz-bath ['sitsbɑ:θ], *n.* Bain de siège, *m.*

six [siks], *a. and n.* Six, *m. It is six of one and half a dozen of the other,* c'est bonnet blanc et blanc bonnet; *six score,* cent vingt; *to be at sixes and sevens,* être tout sens dessus dessous. **sixfold,** *a.* Sextuple.—*adv.* Six fois. **sixfoot,** *a.* De six pieds. *Six-foot way,* (*Rail.*) entre-voie, *f.* **sixpence,** *n.* Sixpence. **sixpenny,** *a.* Sixpenny, de six pence.

sixteen, *a.* Seize. **sixteenmo,** *n. and a.* In-seize, *m.* **sixteenth,** *a.* Seizième; seize (of kings or days of the month). *Louis the Sixteenth,* Louis seize; *on the sixteenth,* le seize.

sixth, *a.* Sixième; six (of kings etc.).—*n.* Sixième, *m.*; (*Mus.*) sixte, *f. Sixth form,* (*sch.*) la classe de première. **sixthly,** *adv.* Sixièmement. **sixtieth,** *a.* Soixantième.

sixty, *a. and n.* Soixante. *About sixty,* une soixantaine (de).

sizable ['saizəbl], *a.* D'une bonne grosseur; de la grosseur voulue (par les règlements).

sizar ['saizə], *n.* Étudiant boursier (of Cambridge University or Trinity College, Dublin), *m.*

size [saiz], *n.* Grandeur, dimension, taille (stature), grosseur, *f.*; volume (bulk); calibre (calibre); format (of a book or of paper), *m.*; encolure (of shirts); pointure (of gloves, shoes, etc.), *f.*; effectif (of schools, classes); (*Comm.*) numéro, *m.*; colle, *f.*; encollage (glue), *m. A man of his size,* un homme de sa taille; *full size,* grandeur naturelle, *f.*; *large size,* grand modèle, *m.*; *small size,* petit modèle, *m.—v.t.* Coller, encoller (to cover with size); classer, ranger (par grosseur, par taille). *To size up,* juger.

sized, *a.* De grosseur; de taille; de volume; de grandeur. *Middle-sized,* de taille, de grandeur moyenne. **size-stick,** *n.* Pied à coulisse (de cordonnier), *m.* **sizing,** *n.* Collage, encollage, *m.* **sizy,** *a.* Glutineux, gluant.

sizzle [sizl], *n.* Grésillement, *m.—v.i.* Grésiller.

skate (1) [skeit], *n.* (*Ichth.*) Raie, *f.*

skate (2) [skeit], *n.* Patin, *m. Roller skate,* patin à roulettes.—*v.i.* Patiner. **skater,** *n.* Patineur, *m.* **skating,** *n.* Patinage, *m.* **skating-rink,** *n.* Patinoire, *f.*

skedaddle [ski'dædl], *v.i.* (*Am. slang*) Décamper, filer.

skeet [ski:t], *n.* (*Naut.*) Écope (à long manche), *f.*

skegger ['skegə], *n.* Saumoneau, *m.*

skein [skein], *n.* Écheveau, *m.*

skeletal ['skelətl], *a.* Squelettique.

skeleton ['skelətən], *n.* Squelette, *m.*; (*Tech.*) charpente, carcasse, *f. He is a mere skeleton,* il n'a que la peau et les os; *one must not allude to the skeleton in the cupboard,* il ne faut pas parler de corde dans la maison d'un pendu; *skeleton in the cupboard,* secret désagréable, *m.*; histoire fâcheuse dans la famille, *f.*; *skeleton staff,* personnel réduit, *m.* **skeleton-key,** *n.* Crochet, *m.*

skep [skep], *n.* Panier, *m.*; ruche, *f.*

sketch [sketʃ], *n.* Esquisse, *f.*, croquis, *m.*, ébauche; (*Theat.*) saynète, *f.*; (*fig.*) aperçu, *m.—v.t.* Esquisser, faire le croquis de, ébaucher. *To sketch out,* esquisser, faire le croquis de, tracer le plan de. **sketch-book,** *n.* Album, cahier de croquis, *m.* **sketcher,** *n.* Dessinateur, *m.* **sketchily,** *adv.* Incomplètement. **sketching,** *n.* Le dessin (d'après nature), *m.* **sketchy,** *a.* D'esquisse, ébauché; imprécis, rudimentaire.

skew [skju:], *a.* Oblique, en biais.—*n.* Biais, *m.—v.t.* Mettre en travers; couper en sifflet. —*v.i.* Biaiser. *To skew at,* regarder de côté. **skewbald,** *a.* Blanc et roux (of pony). **skewbridge,** *n.* Pont en biais, *m.*

skewer [skju:ə], *n.* Brochette, *f.—v.t.* Embrocher.

skew-eyed, *a.* Louche.

ski [ʃi: or ski:], *n.* Ski, *m.—v.i.* Faire du ski. **ski-jump,** *n.* Saut à skis, *m.* **ski-lift,** *n.* Remonte-pentes, *m.inv.* **skier,** *n.* Skieur, *n.* **ski-ing,** *n.* Le ski, *m.*

skiagraphical [skaiə'græfikl], *a.* Sciographique.

skiagraphy [skai'ægrəfi], *n.* Sciographie, *f.*

skid [skid], *n.* Chaîne à enrayer, *f.*, sabot, *m.*; (*Naut.*) défense, *f.*; (*Motor.*) dérapage (side-slip), *m.*, embardée, *f.*; (*Av.*) patin (du châssis d'atterrissage), *m. Half-turn skid,* tête-à-queue, *m.—v.t.* Enrayer.—*v.i.* Déraper (of a bicycle or motor).

skiff [skif], *n.* Esquif, youyou, *m.*

skilful ['skilful], *a.* Adroit, habile. **skilfully,** *adv.* Adroitement, habilement. **skilfulness,** *n.* Habileté, *f.*

skill [skil], *n.* Habileté, dextérité, adresse, *f.* **skilled,** *a.* Habile, adroit. *Skilled labour,* main-d'œuvre spécialisée, *f.*; *skilled workman,* ouvrier qualifié, *m. Skilled in,* versé dans, habile à.

skillet ['skilit], *n.* Casserole à pieds, *f.*

skim [skim], *v.t.* Écumer; écrémer (milk); (*fig.*) raser, effleurer.—*v.i.* Passer légèrement, glisser (sur). *To skim over,* effleurer, raser; (*fig.*) parcourir rapidement, feuilleter (a book).

skimmer, *n.* Écumoire, *f.*; écrémoir (for milk); bec-en-ciseaux (bird), *m.* **skimmilk,** *n.* Lait écrémé, *m.* **skimming,** *n.* Écumage; écrémage (of milk), *m.*; (*pl.*) écume, *f.*

skimp [skimp], *v.t.* Restreindre, compter les morceaux à; bâcler (a piece of work). **skimpily,** *adv.* Insuffisamment. **skimpy,** *a.* Mesquin, chiche; étriqué.

skin [skin], *n.* Peau; feuille de parchemin, *f.*; outre (for wine), *f. Banana skin*, pelure de banane, *f.*; *I would not be in his skin for worlds*, je ne voudrais être dans sa peau pour rien au monde; *next one's skin*, près de la peau; *to be nothing but skin and bone*, n'avoir que la peau et les os; *to come off with a whole skin*, s'en tirer sain et sauf; *to escape by the skin of one's teeth*, l'échapper belle; *to have a fair skin*, avoir la peau blanche; *(fig.) to have a thick skin*, avoir la peau dure; *wet to the skin*, trempé jusqu'aux os.—*v.t.* Écorcher (a person or animal); peler, éplucher (fruits etc.); couvrir de peau; *(fig.)* écorcher, plumer. *To keep one's eyes skinned*, écarquiller les yeux.—*v.i.* Se couvrir de peau, se cicatriser.

skin-deep, *a.* À fleur de peau, superficiel, peu profond. **skin-disease**, *n.* Maladie de la peau, *f.* **skin-dresser**, *n.* Peaussier, *m.* **skinflint**, *n.* Pince-maille, grigou, ladre, *m.* **skinful**, *n. To have a good skinful*, avoir son plein de boisson, tenir une bonne cuite. **skin-game**, *n.* (*Am.*) Escroquerie, *f.* **skin-tight**, *a.* Collant.

skink [skiŋk], *n.* Scinque (lizard), *m.*

skinless ['skinlis], *a.* Sans peau; à peau mince. **skinner**, *n.* Écorcheur; peaussier, pelletier (dealer in skins), *m.* **skinniness**, *n.* Maigreur, *f.*, décharnement, *m.* **skinning**, *n.* Écorchement; épluchage, *m.* **skinny**, *a.* Maigre, décharné.

skip [skip], *n.* Saut, bond, *m.*—*v.i.* Sauter, sautiller, gambader. *To skip (with a rope)*, sauter à la corde.—*v.t.* Sauter; bondir, passer (part of a book etc.). *To skip over*, sauter par-dessus, passer. **skipjack**, *n.* Taupin (insect), *m.*

skipper ['skipə], *n.* Patron (of a merchant vessel); *(fig.)* capitaine, *(spt.)* chef d'équipe, *m.*

skipping ['skipiŋ], *n.* Action de sauter, *f.*; saut à la corde, *m.* **skipping-rope**, *n.* Corde à sauter, *f.*

skippingly, *adv.* En sautant, par sauts.

skirl [skə:l], *n.* (*Sc.*) Son aigu de la cornemuse, *m.*

skirmish ['skə:miʃ], *n.* Escarmouche; rencontre, *f.*—*v.i.* Escarmoucher. **skirmisher**, *n.* Tirailleur, *m.* **skirmishing**, *n.* Escarmouches, *f.pl. In skirmishing order*, en tirailleurs.

skirret ['skirət], *n.* (*Bot.*) Chervis, *m.*

skirt [skə:t], *n.* Pan (of a coat), *m.*; jupe (of a gown); *(pl.)* lisière, extrémité, *f.*, bord (of a forest etc.), *m. Divided skirt*, jupe culotte, *f.*; *outskirts*, bords, faubourgs, *m.pl.*; *(fam.) she is a nice bit of skirt*, c'est un joli brin de fille. —*v.t.* Border, contourner, côtoyer; longer (to go alongside).

skirting or **skirting-board**, *n.* Bord, *m.*, bordure; (*Arch.*) plinthe, *f.*, bas de lambris, *m.*

skit [skit], *n.* Pièce satirique, parodie, *f.* **skittish**, *a.* Capricieux, volage, inconstant; ombrageux (of horses). **skittishly**, *adv.* Avec inconstance, capricieusement. **skittishness**, *n.* Légèreté, inconstance; nature ombrageuse (of horses), *f.*

skittle [skitl], *n.* Quille, *f. Life is not all beer and skittles*, la vie n'est pas toujours rose. **skittle-alley**, *n.* Quillier, jeu de quilles, *m.*

skive [skaiv], *v.t.* Doler (a skin).

skua ['skju:ə], *n.* (*Orn.*) Mouette pillarde, *f.*

skulk [skʌlk], *v.i.* Se cacher, se tenir caché; rôder (autour de). *To skulk in*, entrer furtivement; *to skulk out*, sortir furtivement. **skulker**, *n.* Capon; embusqué, cagnard, *m.*

skull [skʌl], *n.* Crâne, *m.* **skull-cap**, *n.* Calotte, *f.*

skunk [skʌŋk], *n.* Putois d'Amérique, *m.*; mouffette, *f.*; skunks, scons (fur), *m. Mean skunk*, grigou, ladre, *m.*

sky [skai], *n.* Ciel, *m.*; *(fig.)* climat, *m.*—*v.t.* (*Ten., Cricket*) Lancer (la balle) en chandelle. **sky-blue**, *a.* Bleu ciel, azuré. **sky-colour**, *n.* Azur, bleu de ciel, *m.* **sky-coloured**, *a.* Azuré, bleu ciel. **sky-high**, *a.* Qui touche aux cieux. *To blow up sky-high*, faire sauter jusqu'aux cieux, *(fig.)* tancer vertement. **skylark**, *n.* Alouette (des champs), *f.*—*v.i.* *(fig.)* Faire des farces. **skylarking**, *n.* Mauvaises plaisanteries, farces, *f.pl.* **skylight**, *n.* Châssis vitré, *m.*, lucarne faîtière, *f.*; *(Naut.)* claire-voie, *f.* **sky-line**, *n.* Horizon, *m.* **sky-pilot**, *n.* (slang) Pasteur, aumônier, *m.* **sky-rocket**, *n.* Fusée volante, *f.* **skysail**, *n.* Contre-cacatois, papillon, *m.* **sky-scraper**, *n.* Gratte-ciel, *m.* **skyward**, *adv.* Vers le ciel. **sky-writing**, *n.* Publicité aérienne, écriture dans le ciel, *f.*

slab [slæb], *n.* Dalle, plaque, table; tablette (of chocolate), *f.*; *(Print.)* marbre, *m.*; *(Carp.)* dosse, *f.* **slabstone**, *n.* Dalle, *f.*

slabber [SLOBBER].

slack [slæk], *a.* Lâche; faible, mou (weak); détendu (rope); dégonflé (tyre); négligent, nonchalant (remiss). *Business is slack*, les affaires ne vont pas; *slack water*, mer étale, *f.*, étale, *m.*; *the slack season*, la morte-saison. —*n.* Menu charbon (small coal), poussier (of coal); mou (of ropes); *(Eng.)* jeu, *m.*; *(pl.)* pantalon, *m. To take up the slack*, rattraper le jeu.—*v.t.* Relâcher; *(Naut.)* détendre.— *v.i.* Prendre du mou. *To slack off*, se détendre, se relâcher.

slacken, *v.t.* Relâcher, détendre; relâcher de; affaiblir, adoucir (to mitigate); ralentir (to make slower).—*v.i.* Se relâcher, se détendre (to relax); se ralentir (to become more slow); diminuer, baisser (to abate); tomber (to flag).

slackening, *n.* Relâchement, ralentissement, *m.* **slacker**, *n.* Paresseux, *m.* **slacking**, *n.* Relâchement, *m.*; paresse, *f.* **slackly**, *adv.* Mollement, lâchement; négligemment, nonchalamment (negligently). **slackness**, *n.* Relâchement, *m.*; négligence, nonchalance (remissness), *f.*; lenteur (slowness); faiblesse, mollesse (weakness), *f.*; désœuvrement (lack of work), *m.*

slag [slæg], *n.* Scorie, *f.*; mâchefer, *m.* **slag-heap**, *n.* Crassier, *m.*

slain, *p.p.* [SLAY].

slake [sleik], *v.t.* Éteindre (lime); étancher (thirst). *To slake one's thirst*, se désaltérer. **slakeless**, *a.* Inextinguible; *(fig.)* insatiable. **slaking**, *n.* Étanchement (of thirst), *m.*; extinction (of lime), *f.*

slalom ['slælɔm], *n.* Slalom, *m.*

slam [slæm], *v.t.* Fermer avec violence, faire claquer.—*v.i.* Se fermer avec bruit; *(Cards)* faire la vole.—*n.* Action de fermer une porte avec violence; *(Cards)* vole, *f.*, chelem, *m.*

slander ['slɑ:ndə], *n.* Calomnie; (*Law*) diffamation, *f.*—*v.t.* Calomnier; (*Law*) diffamer. **slanderer**, *n.* Calomniateur, *m.*, -trice, *f.*; (*Law*) diffamateur, *m.*, -trice, *f.* **slandering** or **slanderous**, *a.* Calomnieux, calomniateur; (*Law*) diffamatoire. **slanderously**, *adv.* Calomnieusement. **slanderousness**, *n.* Caractère diffamatoire, *m.*

slang [slæŋ], *n.* Argot, *m.*, langue verte, *f.* A *slang word*, terme d'argot, *m.*—*v.t.* (*slang*) Dire des injures à, (*pop.*) engueuler. **slangy**, *a.* D'argot, argotique.

slant [slɑ:nt], *v.i.* Être en pente, incliner; être de biais, biaiser.—*v.t.* Incliner, mettre en pente, rendre oblique, faire biaiser.—*n.* Inclinaison, pente, *f.*, plan incliné, *m.* On *the slant*, en écharpe, en biais.

slanting, *a.* Oblique, en biais, incliné, en pente; en écharpe (of a sword-cut etc.). **slantingly, slantly, slantways**, or **slantwise**, *adv.* En pente, obliquement, en biais.

slap [slæp], *n.* Coup, *m.*; claque, tape, gifle, *f.*; soufflet (on the face), *m.*—*v.t.* Claquer, souffleter, donner une fessée à (a child). *He slapped my face*, il m'a donné une gifle *or* une bonne claque.—*adv.* Tout droit, raide comme balle, en plein. *I told him slap out*, je lui ai dit de but en blanc *or* sans tortiller.

slapdash, *adv.* Tout d'un coup, à la six-quatre-deux, n'importe comment.—*a.* Fait à la hâte.

slap-happy, *a.* Toqué.

slapstick, *n.* (*Theat.*, *Cine.*) *Slapstick comedy* (*fam.*), tarte à la crème, *f.*

slap-up, *a.* (*slang*) Soigné, fameux.

slash [slæʃ], *n.* Taillade; balafre (on the face), *f.*—*v.t.* Taillader; balafrer (the face); cingler (a horse); (*fig.*) massacrer (a piece of work); éreinter (to criticize). *Cutting and slashing*, frappant d'estoc et de taille.—*v.i.* Frapper. *To slash right and left*, frapper à droite et à gauche. **slashed**, *a.* Fendu (of dresses). **slashing**, *a.* Mordant, cinglant.

slat [slæt], *n.* Lame, lamette, *f.*

slate [sleit], *n.* Ardoise, *f.* *Clean slate*, table rase; (*fam.*) *on the slate*, à crédit (in pub); *to have a slate loose*, avoir le cerveau fêlé.—*v.t.* Couvrir d'ardoises; (*colloq.*) tancer; éreinter (a book). **slate-clay**, *n.* Schiste argileux, *m.* **slate-coloured**, *a.* Ardoisé, gris d'ardoise. **slate-pencil**, *n.* Crayon d'ardoise, *m.* **slate-quarry**, *n.* Ardoisière, *f.* **slater**, *n.* Couvreur en ardoise, *m.* **slating**, *n.* Toiture en ardoise; (*colloq.*) semonce, *f.*, éreintement (of a book etc.), *m.*

slattern ['slætə:n], *n.* Femme malpropre, souillon, *f.* **slatternly**, *a.* Négligent, malpropre, mal soigné.

slaty ['sleiti], *a.* Schisteux, d'ardoise; ardoisé (of colour).

slaughter ['slɔ:tə], *n.* Tuerie, boucherie, *f.*, carnage, massacre; abattage (of animals), *m.* —*v.t.* Tuer, égorger, massacrer; abattre (animals). **slaughter-house**, *n.* Abattoir, *m.* **slaughterman** or **slaughterer**, *n.* Abatteur, *m.*

Slav [slɑ:v], *a.* and *n.* Slave, *m.* or *f.* **Slavism**, *n.* Slavisme, *m.*

slave [sleiv], *n.* Esclave, *m.* or *f.* *He is a slave to*, il est esclave de; *slave states*, états esclavagistes, *m.pl.*; *white slave traffic*, traite des blanches, *f.*—*v.i.* Travailler comme un

esclave, peiner. **slave-coast**, *n.* Côte des esclaves, *f.* **slave-dealer**, *n.* Marchand d'esclaves, *m.* **slave-driver**, *n.* Surveillant d'esclaves, *m.*; (*fig.*) maître sévère et cruel, *m.* **slave-like**, *a.* D'esclave, comme un esclave. **slave-ship** [SLAVER (1)]. **slave-trade**, *n.* Traite des noirs, *f.*

slaver (1) ['sleivə], *n.* Négrier, bâtiment négrier, *m.* **slavery**, *n.* Esclavage, *m.* *This work is absolute slavery*, c'est un travail tuant. **slavish**, *a.* D'esclave; servile (of imitation etc.). **slavishly**, *adv.* En esclave; servilement. **slavishness**, *n.* Servilité, *f.*

slaver (2) ['slævə], *v.i.* Baver (sur); être couvert de bave, salive, *f.* **slaverer**, *n.* Baveur, *m.*, baveuse, *f.*

Slavonic [slə'vɔnik], *a.* and *n.* Slave, *m.* or *f.*

Slavophil ['slævəfil], *a.* and *n.* Slavophile.

slay [slei], *v.t.* (*past* **slew** [slu:], *p.p.* **slain** [slein]) Tuer. **slayer**, *n.* Tueur (de), meurtrier, *m.* **slaying**, *n.* Tuerie, *f.*

sleazy ['sli:zi], *a.* Mince (of material); crasseux, sordide (of place).

sledge [sledʒ], **sled**, *n.* Traîneau; marteau de forgeron, *m.*—*v.i.* To sledge, to go sledging, se promener en traîneau. **sledge-driver**, *n.* Conducteur de traîneau, *m.* **sledge-hammer**, *n.* Marteau à deux mains, marteau de forgeron, *m.*

sleek [sli:k], *a.* Lisse, luisant, poli; d'un beau poil (of horses); (*fig.*) doucereux, onctueux. —*v.t.* Lisser, rendre luisant, *m.* **sleekly**, *adv.* Onctueusement, doucereusement. **sleekness**, *n.* Luisant, *m.*; (*fig.*) douceur, onctuosité, *f.*

sleep [sli:p], *n.* Sommeil; somme (nap), *m.* *Beauty sleep*, sommeil avant minuit; *he did not get a wink of sleep all night*, il n'a pu fermer l'œil de la nuit, il a passé une nuit blanche; *overcome with sleep*, accablé de sommeil; *restless sleep*, sommeil agité; *sound sleep*, profond sommeil; *to be dying to go to sleep*, n'en pouvoir plus de sommeil, tomber de sommeil; *to get no sleep*, ne pas dormir; *to go to sleep*, s'endormir; s'engourdir (of foot); *to go to sleep again*, se rendormir; *to put (a child) to sleep*, endormir (un enfant); *to put a dog to sleep*, tuer un chien; *to send to sleep*, faire dormir (of drugs etc.); *to startle out of his sleep*, réveiller en sursaut; *to start up out of one's sleep*, se réveiller en sursaut; *want of sleep*, insomnie, *f.*—*v.i.* (*past* and *p.p.* **slept**) Dormir; reposer, coucher (à, chez, *or* dans). *He slept at my house last night*, il a couché chez moi la nuit dernière; *not to sleep a wink all night*, ne pas fermer l'œil de la nuit, passer une nuit blanche; *sleep on it*, la nuit porte conseil; *to sleep in*, être logé à la maison; ne pas se réveiller à temps; *to sleep in peace*, reposer en paix; *to sleep like a log*, dormir comme une souche; *to sleep like a top*, dormir comme un sabot; *to sleep out*, découcher; *to sleep soundly*, dormir sur les deux oreilles; *to sleep till late in the day*, dormir fort avant dans la journée.—*v.t.* Dormir; faire passer en dormant. *To sleep oneself sober*, cuver son vin; *to sleep one's life away*, passer sa vie à dormir; *to sleep the sleep of the just*, dormir du sommeil du juste. **sleep-walker**, *n.* Somnambule, *m.* **sleep-walking**, *n.* Somnambulisme, *m.*

sleeper, *n.* Dormeur, *m.*, dormeuse; (*Rail.*) traverse, longuerine (longitudinal), *f.*; (*colloq.*) wagon-lit, *m.* *To be a heavy sleeper,* avoir le sommeil lourd.

sleepily, *adv.* D'un air endormi. **sleepiness,** *n.* Assoupissement, *m.*, somnolence; pesanteur (heaviness), *f.*

sleeping, *n.* Sommeil, repos, *m.*—*a.* Endormi; dormant. *Let sleeping dogs lie,* ne réveillez pas le chat qui dort. *Sleeping pills* or *tablets,* somnifère, *m.* **sleeping-bag,** *n.* Sac de couchage, *m.* **sleeping-berth,** *n.* Couchette, *f.* **sleeping-car,** *n.* Wagon-lit, *m.* **sleeping-draught,** *n.* Potion soporifique, *f.*, somnifère, *m.* **sleeping-partner,** *n.* Associé commanditaire, *m.* **sleeping-quarters,** *n.pl.* Dortoir, *m.*, dortoirs, *m.pl.* **sleeping-sickness,** *n.* Maladie du sommeil, *f.*

sleepless ['sli:plis], *a.* Sans sommeil, sans dormir. *Sleepless night,* nuit sans sommeil, nuit blanche, *f.* **sleeplessness,** *n.* Insomnie, *f.*

sleepy ['sli:pi], *a.* Qui a envie de dormir; endormi (asleep); somnifère, soporifique (somniferous); inactif (lazy); blet (of pears). *To feel sleepy,* avoir sommeil, avoir envie de dormir. **sleepy-head,** *n.* Paresseux, *m.*, paresseuse, *f.*; (*colloq.*) endormi, *m.*, endormie, *f.* **sleepy-looking,** *a.* Qui a l'air endormi.

sleet [sli:t], *n.* Neige à moitié fondue, *f.*; pluie mêlée de grêle grêle, *f.*, grésil, *m.* *Sleet is falling,* il tombe de la neige à moitié fondue; il grésille.

sleeve [sli:v], *n.* Manche, *f.*; (*Eng.*) chemise, gaîne, *f.*, manchon, *m.* *To have something up one's sleeve,* avoir plus d'un tour dans sa manche; *to laugh in one's sleeve,* rire dans sa barbe, rire sous cape.—*v.t.* Mettre des manches à. **sleeve-board,** *n.* Passe-carreau, *m.* **sleeve-link,** *n.* Bouton de manchette à chaînette, *m.*

sleeveless, *a.* Sans manches.

sleigh [slei], *n.* Traîneau, *m.*—*v.i.* Aller en traîneau. **sleigh-bell,** *n.* Grelot, *m.* **sleigh-ride,** *n.* Course en traîneau, *f.*

sleighing, *n.* *To go sleighing,* se promener en traîneau.

sleight [slait], *n.* Habileté, *f.*, tour d'adresse, escamotage, *m.* *Sleight of hand,* tour de passe-passe, *m.*, prestidigitation, *f.*

slender ['slendə], *a.* Mince; élancé; svelte (of a person's figure); faible, léger (weak); chétif, exigu, maigre (not ample). *Slender blade,* lame mince, *f.*; *slender hopes,* faibles espérances, *f.pl.*; *slender means,* maigres ressources, *f.pl.*; *slender repast,* léger repas, *m.*; *slender stalk,* tige déliée, *f.*; *slender waist,* taille svelte, taille élancée, *f.* **slenderly,** *adv.* Légèrement; pauvrement, médiocrement. **slenderness,** *n.* Minceur, légèreté; exiguïté, modicité, *f.*

slept, *past* and *p.p.* [SLEEP].

sleuth(-hound) ['slu:θhaund], *n.* (Chien) limier; (*fig.*) détective, *m.*—*v.i.* Jouer au détective.

slew (1), *past* [SLAY].

slew (2) [slu:], *v.t.* (*Naut.*) Virer, pivoter.—*v.i.* Pivoter. *To slew round,* (*Motor.*) faire un tête-à-queue.

slice [slais], *n.* Tranche; aiguillette (of poultry); écumoire (utensil); rouelle (of a lemon etc.); spatule (spatula); (*Print.*) palette, *f.* *Fish-slice,* truelle, *f.*; *slice of bread,* tranche de pain, *f.*; *slice of bread and butter,* tartine de beurre, *f.*; *slice of bread and jam,* tartine de confiture, *f.*; *slice of luck,* coup de veine, *m.*; *slice of meat,* tranche de viande, *f.*—*v.t.* Couper en tranches; (*Ten.*) couper (la balle); (*Row.*) attaquer en sifflet.

slick [slik], *a.* Adroit; en bon ordre.—*v.t.* Lisser, étirer.—*adv.* Adroitement; vite; complètement, en plein. **slickness,** *n.* Adresse, habileté, *f.*

slide [slaid], *n.* Glissoire, glissade, *f.*; coulant, *m.*; coulisse (groove etc.), *f.*; verre (of a magic lantern); (*Steam-engine*) tiroir; (*Mus.*) coulé, *m.*; (*Row.*) glissière, *f.* *Dark slide,* (*Phot.*) châssis, *m.*; *hair-slide,* barrette, *f.*; *land-slide,* éboulement de terre, *m.*; (*Polit.*) raz-de-marée, *m.* (in elections); (*lantern-*) *slide,* diapositive, vue fixe, *f.*—*v.i.* (*past* **slid,** *p.p.* **slid, slidden**) Glisser; coulisser; se glisser; couler. *To let things slide,* laisser aller les choses; *to slide away,* glisser toujours, s'écouler, glisser (to pass); *to slide down,* glisser en bas, descendre en glissant; *to slide in,* se glisser dans, entrer doucement; *to slide into,* tomber dans, passer insensiblement dans.—*v.t.* Faire glisser, glisser; tirer (to draw out). *To slide in,* glisser dans.

slide-bar, *n.* Coulisseau, *m.* **slider,** *n.* Glisseur, *m.*; (*Tech.*) coulisse, *f.*; coulant, *m.* **slide-rest,** *n.* Support à chariot, *m.* **slide-rule,** *n.* Règle à calcul, *f.* **slide-valve,** *n.* Soupape de tiroir, *f.*

sliding, *n.* Glissade, *f.*, glissement, *m.*—*a.* Glissant; à coulisse; mobile. **sliding-door,** *n.* Porte à coulisse, *f.* **sliding-sash,** *n.* Châssis à coulisse, *m.* **sliding-scale,** *n.* (*Econ.*) Échelle mobile, *f.*

slight [slait], *a.* Mince, léger, peu considérable; peu important, insignifiant (of no consequence). *A slight wound,* une légère blessure, *f.*; *not in the slightest,* pas le moins du monde.—*n.* Manque d'égards, *m.*, marque de mépris, *f.*; affront, *m.*, insulte, *f.* *To pay a slight upon,* manquer d'égards à.—*v.t.* Manquer d'égards à, traiter sans égards; mépriser, faire peu de cas de, dédaigner. **slighting,** *a.* Dédaigneux. **slightingly,** *adv.* Avec mépris, avec dédain. **slightly,** *adv.* Légèrement, faiblement, peu, un peu. *Slightly built,* à la taille svelte. **slightness,** *n.* Minceur; légèreté, *f.*

slily [SLYLY].

slim [slim], *a.* Svelte, mince, élancé; (*colloq.*) fin, rusé, malin. *A slim hope,* un mince espoir.—*v.i.* S'amincir.

slime [slaim], *n.* Vase, *f.*, limon, *m.*, bave (of snails etc.), *f.* **slime-pit,** *n.* Puits de bitume, *m.*

sliminess, *n.* Viscosité, *f.*, état vaseux, *m.*

slimness ['slimnis], *n.* Sveltesse, taille mince; ruse, finesse, *f.*

slimy ['slaimi], *a.* Vaseux, limoneux, visqueux, gluant; (*fam.*) obséquieux, répugnant, visqueux (of a person).

sling [sliŋ], *n.* Fronde; bretelle (for rifle); écharpe (for a broken limb); (*Naut.*) suspente (of a yard); bélière (for sword-belt), *f.*; élingue (for casks), *f.* *Rope sling,* nœud de chaise, *m.* *To carry one's arm in a sling,* avoir le bras en écharpe. *Gin sling,* boisson à base de gin, *f.*—*v.t.* (*past* and *p.p.* **slung**) Lancer (avec une fronde); suspendre (to suspend); (*Naut.*) élinguer. *To sling the hammocks*, tendre les hamacs; *to sling over one's shoulder*, mettre en bandoulière. **slinger**, *n.* Frondeur, *m.*

slink [sliŋk], *v.i.* (*past* and *p.p.* **slunk**) S'esquiver, se dérober. *To slink away*, s'échapper à la dérobée, s'éclipser; *to slink in*, entrer furtivement, se glisser dans; *to slink off*, s'esquiver; *to slink out*, sortir en catimini. **slinky**, *a.* Collant (garment); sinueux.

slip [slip], *v.i.* Glisser, se glisser, couler (of a knot); courir (to come undone); patiner (of wheels); s'ébouler (of land); échapper (to escape); (*fig.*) faire un faux pas. *My foot slipped*, mon pied glissa; *to let slip*, laisser échapper, lâcher; *to slip away*, s'esquiver, filer à l'anglaise; s'écouler (of time); *to slip down*, tomber; *to slip in*, se faufiler, entrer furtivement; *to slip off*, s'en aller furtivement; *to slip off from*, glisser de; *to slip out*, s'échapper, sortir furtivement; *to slip out of*, sortir de . . . à la dérobée, se dégager de (one's clothes); *to slip over*, glisser sur, passer sur, sauter; *to slip up*, (*fam.*) se tromper; échouer.—*v.t.* Glisser, faire glisser, couler; perdre, laisser échapper (to lose); lâcher (to loose); se dégager de (to throw off); échapper à, s'échapper de (to escape); filer (a cable); pousser (a bolt). *To slip in*, introduire, glisser dans; *to slip into*, glisser dans; (*Naut.*) *to slip its moorings* (of a ship), filer le corps mort; *to slip off*, enlever, ôter; *to slip on*, passer, mettre; *to slip on one's clothes*, s'habiller à la hâte, passer ses habits; *to slip the collar* or *the leash*, s'affranchir, regagner sa liberté; *your name has slipped my memory*, j'ai oublié votre nom, votre nom m'échappe.

n.—Glissade, *f.*; éboulement (of earth); (*Geol.*) déplacement de strates, *m.*; taie d'oreiller, *f.*; cache-sexe, (caleçon) triangle, *m.*; brin (of herbs), *m.*; laisse (leash), *f.*; (*pottery*) engobe; (*Hort.*) scion, *m.*, bouture, *f.*; (*Print.*) placard, *m.*; (*Theat.*) coulisse; (*Naut.*) cale (of a harbour, dockyard, etc.); étalingure (of a cable); faute d'étourderie, *f.*, lapsus, *m. A slip of a girl*, une jeune fille fluette; *he made a slip of the tongue*, la langue lui a fourché; *in slips*, en placards; *it is a slip of the tongue*, c'est un lapsus linguæ; *landslip*, éboulement de terre, *m.*; *slip of paper*, bout de papier, *m.*; *slip of the pen*, erreur de plume, *f.*, lapsus calami, *m.*; *there's many a slip 'twixt the cup and the lip*, il y a loin de la coupe aux lèvres; *to give someone the slip*, fausser compagnie à quelqu'un, planter quelqu'un là; *to make a slip*, glisser, faire un faux pas.

slip-board, *n.* Coulisse, *f.* **slip-carriage**, *n.* Voiture-remorque, *f.* **slip-knot**, *n.* Nœud coulant, *m.* **slip-proof**, *n.* Épreuve en placard, *f.*

slipper ['slipə], *n.* Pantoufle, *f.*; patin (of a wheel), *m.*; mule (of the pope), *f. To hunt the slipper*, jouer au furet. **slipper-bath**, *n.* Baignoire en sabot, *f.* **slippered**, *a.* En pantoufles.

slipperily ['slipərili], *adv.* En glissant. **slipperiness**, *n.* Nature glissante; volubilité (of the tongue), *f.* **slippery**, *a.* Glissant; difficile à tenir (not easily held); incertain, peu sûr (uncertain); peu stable (unstable); matois, rusé. *It is very slippery*, le pavé est très

glissant, ça glisse beaucoup; *slippery customer*, rusé compère; *to be as slippery as an eel*, échapper comme une anguille. **slippy**, *a.* (*slang*) *Look slippy!* Dépêche-toi!

slipshod, *a.* En savates; (*fig.*) négligé, désordonné; décousu (of style). *To go about slipshod*, traîner la savate.

slipslop, *n.* Rinçure, lavasse, *f.*; (*fig.*) propos insipides, *m.pl.* **slipstream**, *n.* Sillage, *m.* **slipway**, *n.* Cale, *f.*

slit [slit], *v.t.* (*past* and *p.p.* **slit**) Fendre. *To slit someone's throat*, couper la gorge à quelqu'un.—*v.i.* Se fendre.—*n.* Fente, fissure, *f.* **slit-eyed**, *a.* Aux yeux bridés.

slither ['sliðə], *v.i.* Glisser; (of a reptile) ramper, onduler.

slitter ['slitə], *n.* Fendeur, *m.* **slitting**, *n.* Fendage, *m.* **slitting-mill**, *n.* Fenderie, *f.*

sliver ['slivə or 'slaivə], *v.t.* Fendre, couper en tranches.—*v.i.* Se fendre, éclater (of wood). —*n.* Éclat, *m.*, tranche, *f.*, ruban, *m.*

slob [slɔb], *n.* Vase, *f.*, limon, *m.*; (*pop.*) rustaud, *m.*

slobber ['slɔbə], *v.i.* Baver.—*v.t.* Couvrir de bave, baver sur. *To slobber over*, s'attendrir sur.—*n.* Bave, *f.* **slobberer**, *n.* Baveur, *m.*, baveuse, *f.* **slobbering**, *a.* Baveux.

sloe [slou], *n.* (*Bot.*) Prunelle, *f.* **sloe-tree**, *n.* Prunellier, *m.*

slog [slɔg], *v.t.* Cogner dur; (*fig.*) bûcher. **slogger**, *n.* (*spt.*) Cogneur, *m.*

slogan ['slougən], *n.* (*Sc.*) Cri de guerre (d'un clan); (*fig.*) mot d'ordre, *m.*, devise, *f.*, slogan, *m.*

sloop [slu:p], *n.* Sloop, aviso, *m.*

slop [slɔp], *n.* Lavasse, *f.*; (*usu. in pl.*) rinçures, *f.pl.*; (*pl.*) habits de confection, *m.pl.*, hardes de marin, *f.pl.*—*v.t.* Répandre, renverser.— *v.i.* Déborder. **slop-basin** or **slop-bowl**, *n.* Bol à rinçures (de thé), *m.* **slop-pail**, *n.* Seau aux eaux sales, seau de toilette, *m.* **slop-seller**, *n.* Confectionneur, *m.* **slop-shop**, *n.* Boutique de confections; friperie, *f.*

slope [sloup], *n.* Pente, inclinaison, *f.*; talus, versant, *m.* (*Mil.*) *At the slope*, sur l'épaule; *half-way up* (*down*) *the slope*, à mi-pente; *on the slope*, en pente.—*v.t.* Incliner, couper en biais; taluter. (*Mil.*) *Slope arms!* Arme sur l'épaule!—*v.i.* Pencher, aller en pente, incliner; (*slang*) filer, se sauver. *To slope down*, descendre; *to slope off*, décamper; *to slope up*, monter. **sloping**, *a.* De biais, en pente, incliné, en talus. **slopingly**, *adv.* En pente, obliquement.

sloppiness ['slɔpinis], *n.* État détrempé, *m.*; (person) mollesse, *f.*; sentimentalité larmoyante, *f.* **sloppy**, *a.* Bourbeux, humide; (*fig.*) mou, flasque, débraillé; mal ajusté; négligé; fadasse.

slosh [slɔʃ], *v.t.* (*fam.*) Flanquer un coup à.— *n.* [SLUSH].

slot [slɔt], *n.* Rainure, mortaise, fente; barre de bois, *f.*; foulées, abattures (of a deer etc.), *f.pl.*—*v.t.* Mortaiser. **slot-hole**, *n.* Rainure, *f.* **slot-machine**, *n.* Distributeur automatique; appareil à sous, *m.* **slotting-machine**, *n.* Machine à mortaiser, *f.*

sloth (1) [slouθ], *n.* Indolence, oisiveté, paresse, fainéantise, *f.* **slothful**, *a.* Paresseux, fainéant, indolent. **slothfully**, *adv.* D'une manière paresseuse, avec indolence. **slothfulness**, *n.* Paresse, indolence, *f.*

sloth (2) [slouθ], *n.* (*Zool.*) Paresseux, aï, *m.*
slouch [slautʃ], *n.* Démarche molle, lourde, *f.*; lourdaud, *m.*—*v.i.* Marcher lourdement, avoir une allure négligée, affaissée. *To slouch along*, traîner en marchant.—*v.t.* Rabattre (the hat) sur les yeux.—*a.* Rabattu. *Slouch hat*, sombrero, grand chapeau mou, *m.*
sloucher, *n.* Lourdaud, *m.*
slouching, *a.* Lourd et gauche. *Slouching gait*, démarche lourde, *f.*
slough (1) [slau], *n.* Fondrière, *f.*, bourbier, *m.* *Slough of despond*, bourbier de désespoir, *m.*
slough (2) [slʌf], *n.* Dépouille (of a snake); (*Med.*) exfoliation gangreneuse, escarre, *f.*—*v.i.* S'exfolier, escarrifier.
sloughy (1) ['slaui], *a.* Bourbeux.
sloughy (2) ['slʌfi], *a.* Qui ressemble à une escarre.
Slovak ['slouvæk], *a.* and *n.* Slovaque.
sloven [slʌvn], *n.* Sans-soin, mal-soigné, *m.* **slovenliness,** *n.* Malpropreté, saleté, négligence, *f.*, laisser-aller, *m.inv.* **slovenly,** *a.* Mal soigné, mal peigné, débraillé.
slow [slou], *a.* Lent, tardif; lourd (dull); indolent, paresseux (inactive); en retard (of watches etc.); faible (of the pulse); monotone, ennuyeux (tedious). *He was not slow to take advantage of it*, il ne tarda pas à en profiter; *in a slow oven*, à feu doux; *slow and steady wins the race*, qui va doucement va loin, qui trop se hâte reste en chemin; *slow motion*, ralenti, *m.*; *slow train*, train omnibus, *m.*; *that clock is ten minutes slow*, cette horloge retarde de dix minutes; *to be slow of speech*, avoir la parole lente.—*adv.* Lentement.—*v.t.* Retarder, ralentir.—*v.i.* Se ralentir. *To slow down*, ralentir la marche. **slow-coach,** *n.* Lambin, *m.*, lambine, *f.* **slowly,** *adv.* Lentement, tardivement. *Drive slowly!* Ralentir! **slowness,** *n.* Lenteur; paresse; lourdeur (dullness), *f.*; retard (of clocks etc.), *m.* **slow-paced,** *a.* Au pas lent. **slow-witted,** *a.* À l'esprit lourd. **slow-worm,** *n.* Orvet, *m.*
slubber ['slʌbə], *v.t.* Barbouiller; bousiller.
sludge [slʌdʒ], *n.* Boue, vase, *f.*; cambouis, *m.*
slue [slu:] [SLEW (2)].
slug [slʌg], *n.* Limace, *f.*; (*fig.*) fainéant, paresseux (lazy fellow); lingot (for a gun), *m.*—*v.t.* (*pop.*) Tobasser.
sluggard ['slʌgə:d], *n.* Paresseux, *m.*, paresseuse, *f.* **sluggish,** *a.* Paresseux, indolent, lourd; lent, qui coule lentement (of a stream). **sluggishly,** *adv.* Paresseusement, avec indolence; lourdement. **sluggishness,** *n.* Paresse; lenteur (of a stream), *f.*
sluice [slu:s], *n.* Écluse; bonde (pond), *f.*—*v.t.* Lâcher par une écluse; répandre à flots sur, inonder d'eau. **sluice-gate,** *n.* Vanne, *f.* **sluicy,** *a.* À flots.
slum [slʌm], *n.* Bouge, taudis, *m.*, (*pl.*) bas quartiers, *m.pl.*—*v.i.* Visiter les quartiers pauvres (d'une ville). **slum-clearance,** *n.* Lutte contre les taudis, *f.*
slumber ['slʌmbə], *n.* Sommeil; repos, *m.*—*v.i.* Sommeiller, dormir. **slumberer,** *n.* Dormeur, *m.*, dormeuse, *f.* **slumbering,** *n.* Sommeil, assoupissement, *m.*—*a.* Endormi, assoupi.
slummy ['slʌmi], *a.* De taudis, sordide.
slump [slʌmp], *v.i.* S'enfoncer soudainement;

baisser subitement.—*n.* Baisse subite, *f.*; effondrement (des cours), *m.*; crise, *f.* *Slump in trade*, marasme des affaires, *m.*
slunk, *past* and *p.p.* [SLINK].
slur [slə:], *n.* Tache, flétrissure, *f.*; (*Print.*) barbouillage, frison, *m.*; (*Mus.*) liaison, *f.* *To cast a slur upon*, flétrir, dénigrer.—*v.t.* Tacher, salir, souiller; glisser sur, passer légèrement sur (to pass lightly); (*Mus.*) lier; (*Print.*) friser, barbouiller (une feuille). *To slur over*, passer légèrement sur, articuler mal.
slurred, *a.* (*Mus.*) Coulé; (speech etc.) brouillé. **slurring,** *n.* (*Mus.*) Liaison, *f.*
slush [slʌʃ], *n.* Boue, fange, *f.*, gâchis, *m.*; neige à moitié fondue; (*fig.*) lavasse (drink), *f.*; propos sentimentaux et larmoyants, *m.pl.* **slushy,** *a.* Détrempé par la neige; boueux, fangeux.
slut [slʌt], *n.* Saligaude, souillon; coureuse, *f.* **sluttish,** *a.* Sale, malpropre. **sluttishly,** *adv.* Malproprement, salement. **sluttishness,** *n.* Malpropreté, saleté, *f.*
sly [slai], *a.* Sournois, rusé, fin, malin. *On the sly*, en sourdine; *sly dog*, fin matois, *m.*; *sly puss*, sournoise, finaude, *f.* **slyboots,** *n.* Sournois; finaud; espiègle, petit malin, *m.*, petite maligne (child), *f.* **slyly,** *adv.* Avec ruse, en sournois, sournoisement. **slyness,** *n.* Ruse, finesse, nature sournoise, *f.*
smack [smæk], *n.* Claquement (of a whip), *m.*; claque (slap); gifle (in the face), *f.*; gros baiser (kiss); (*fig.*) goût, *m.*, saveur (taste); connaissance superficielle, teinture (smattering), *f.*; bateau de pêche (boat), *m.*—*adv.* Smack *in the middle*, en plein milieu.—*v.i.* Avoir un goût (de). *To smack of*, sentir (le, la, etc.).—*v.t.* Faire claquer (a whip, the lips); donner une claque à (to slap).
smacker, *n.* (*slang*) Gros baiser, *m.* **smacking,** *n.* Claquement, *m.*; fessée, *f.*—*a.* Qui claque; retentissant (of kisses).
small [smɔ:l], *a.* Petit; fin, menu (fine); faible (weak); (*fig.*) chétif, mince, pauvre; modeste, peu considérable. *In a small way*, modestement; *in the small hours*, de grand matin; *small beer*, de la petite bière; *small card*, (*Card games*) basse carte, *f.*; *small change*, petite monnaie, *f.*; *small craft*, petits bateaux, *m.pl.*; *small fry*, menu fretin, *m.*; *small letters*, minuscules, *f.pl.*; *small parcels hold fine wares*, dans les petits sacs sont les fines épices; *small shot*, menu plomb, *m.*; *small talk*, conversation banale, *f.*, commérage, *m.*, banalités, *f.pl.*; *small-time gambler*, joueur d'occasion, *m.*; *to cut up small*, hacher menu, couper en petits morceaux; *to feel small*, être dans ses petits souliers; *to look small*, avoir l'air penaud; *to think no small beer of oneself*, avoir une haute opinion de soi-même.—*n.* Partie mince, *f.*, bas (of the leg), *m.* *Small of the back*, chute des reins, *f.*; (*pl.*) (*fam.*) petit linge, *m.*, dessous, *m.pl.* (lady's underwear). *To wash one's smalls*, faire sa petite lessive.
smallage ['smɔ:lidʒ], *n.* (*Bot.*) Ache, *f.*
small-arms, *n.pl.* Armes portatives, *f.pl.*
small-coal, *n.* Menu charbon, *m.* **small-minded,** *a.* À l'esprit mesquin. **smallpox,** *n.* Petite vérole, *f.*
smallish ['smɔ:liʃ], *a.* Un peu petit, un peu menu. **smallness,** *n.* Petitesse, *f.*; peu de volume; peu d'importance, *m.*, faiblesse; modicité (of income); mesquinerie, *f.*

smalt [smɔːlt], *n.* Smalt, *m.*

smarmy [ˈsmɑːmi], *a.* (*pop.*) Mielleux, doucereux.

smart [smɑːt], *a.* Piquant, cuisant, douloureux, vif; vigoureux, rude (vigorous); intelligent, éveillé (intellect); bon, fort (brisk); subtil, fin, spirituel (witty); beau, élégant, pimpant, bien mis, chic (spruce). *Look smart!* dépêchez-vous! *smart Alec,* finaud, *m.*; *smart practice,* escroquerie; conduite peu scrupuleuse, *f.—n.* Douleur aiguë, vive douleur, cuisson, *f. To feel the smart of,* sentir l'aiguillon de.—*v.i.* Cuire, éprouver une vive douleur. *He shall smart for it,* il lui en cuira; *my hand smarts,* la main me cuit; *to make someone smart for something,* faire payer cher quelque chose à quelqu'un; *to smart for,* porter la peine de; *to smart under,* sentir l'aiguillon de.

smarten (up), *v.t.* Accélérer, animer. *To smarten oneself up,* se faire beau, s'attifer.

smarting, *n.* Douleur cuisante, *f.—a.* Cuisant, poignant.

smartly, *adv.* Lestement, vivement; bien vite (quickly); habilement, sûrement (cleverly); vigoureusement, rudement (vigorously); coquettement, élégamment (showily).

smart-money, *n.* Forfait, *m.*; pension pour blessure, *f.*

smartness, *n.* Force, vigueur, coquetterie, élégance, *f.*, éclat (of dress), *m.*; intelligence, finesse (cleverness), *f.*

smash [smæʃ], *v.t.* Briser, écraser; (*fig.*) ruiner.—*v.i.* Se briser. *To smash to pieces,* briser en morceaux.—*n.* Coup écrasant, fracas, *m.*; déconfiture, faillite, banqueroute (bankruptcy), *f.*; (*Rail.*) catastrophe, *f.*; (*Ten.*) balle écrasée, *f.*, smash, *m.—adv. To go smash,* faire faillite. **smasher,** *n.* (*pop.*) *She's a smasher,* elle est du tonnerre. **smashing,** *a.* (*pop.*) Formidable, épatant. **smash-up,** *n.* (*Motor.*) Collision, *f.*

smattering [ˈsmætəriŋ], *n.* Connaissances superficielles, *f.pl.*, teinture, *f. To have a smattering of,* n'avoir que quelques bribes de.

smear [smiə], *v.t.* Enduire, barbouiller (de); (*fig.*) salir.—*n.* Tache, *f.*, barbouillage, *m.*; (*fig.*) calomnie, atteinte à la réputation, *f.*

smell [smel], *n.* Odeur, *f.*, parfum, *m.*; mauvaise odeur, *f.*; odorat (faculty); flair (of a dog), *m. To be offensive to the smell,* avoir une mauvaise odeur.—*v.t.* (*past* and *p.p.* **smelt** (1)) Sentir; flairer (of dogs). *To smell a rat,* soupçonner anguille sous roche; *to smell out,* flairer, découvrir.—*v.i.* Sentir; flairer (of animals). *Nasty smelling,* qui sent mauvais; *to smell nasty,* sentir mauvais; *to smell of smoke,* sentir la fumée; *to smell of the lamp* (of literary work), sentir l'huile; *to smell stuffy,* sentir le renfermé.

smelliness [ˈsmelinis], *n.* Puanteur, mauvaise odeur, *f.*

smelling-bottle, *n.* Flacon d'odeurs, *m.* **smelling-salts,** *n.pl.* Sels, *m.pl.*

smelly, *a.* Malodorant.

smelt (2) [smelt], *n.* (*Ichth.*) Éperlan, *m.*

smelt (3) [smelt], *v.t.* Fondre. **smelter,** *n.* Fondeur, *m.* **smelting,** *n.* Fonte, *f.* **smelting-furnace,** *n.* Fourneau de fonte, *m.*

smew [smjuː], *n.* (*Orn.*) Harle, *m.*

smile [smail], *n.* Sourire, *m. With a smile on his (her) lips,* le sourire aux lèvres.—*v.i.*

Sourire. *To smile a sickly smile,* rire du bout des lèvres; *to smile at,* (a person) sourire à, (a thing) sourire de; *to smile on,* sourire à.

smiler, *n.* Sourieur, *m.* **smiling,** *a.* Souriant; riant (of countryside etc.). **smilingly,** *adv.* En souriant.

smirch [smɜːtʃ], *v.t.* Tacher, souiller, salir.—*n.* Tache, *f.*

smirk [smɜːk], *v.i.* Sourire avec affectation, minauder.—*n.* Sourire affecté, *m.* **smirking,** *a.* Affecté, minaudier.—*n.* Minauderies, *f.pl.*

smite [smait], *v.t.* (*past* **smote**, *p.p.* **smitten**) Frapper; détruire (to destroy); châtier (to punish); tuer (to slay); (*fig.*) passionner, embraser, charmer. *To be desperately smitten with,* être éperdument amoureux de, raffoler de; *to smite hip and thigh,* frapper d'estoc et de taille.—*v.i.* Frapper, se heurter, se choquer.—*n.* Coup, *m.*; tentative, *f.*

smith [smiθ], *n.* Forgeron, maréchal-ferrant, *m.*

smithereens [smiðəˈriːnz], *n.pl.* Miettes, pièces, *f.pl. To smash to smithereens,* mettre en miettes, atomiser.

smithery [ˈsmiθəri], *n.* Ouvrage de forge, *m.*

smithy [ˈsmiði], *n.* Forge, *f.*

smitten, *p.p.* [SMITE].

smock [smɔk], *n.* Chemise de femme; blouse, *f.* **smock-frock,** *n.* Blouse, *f.*, sarrau, *m.*

smog, *n.* (*fam.*) Purée de pois, *f.*, brouillard épais et enfumé, *m.*

smoke [smouk], *n.* Fumée, *f. To end in smoke,* s'en aller en fumée, n'aboutir à rien; *to have a smoke,* fumer; *there is no smoke without fire,* il n'y a pas de fumée sans feu.—*v.i.* Fumer. —*v.t.* Fumer; enfumer (to cover with . . .). (*pop.*) *Put that in your pipe and smoke it,* mettez ça dans votre poche et votre mouchoir par-dessus! *To smoke out,* enfumer; fumer jusqu'au bout (a cigar).

smoke-box, *n.* (*Steam-engine*) Boîte à fumée, *f.* **smoke-consuming,** *a.* Fumivore. **smoke-dried,** *a.* Fumé. **smoke-dry,** *v.t.* Fumer. **smoke-preventer,** *n.* Fumifuge, *m.* **smoke-screen,** *n.* Rideau de fumée, *m.* **smoke-stack,** *n.* Cheminée, *f.*

smokeless, *a.* Sans fumée. **smoker,** *n.* Fumeur; enfumoir (for bees), *m.* **smokiness,** *n.* État enfumé, *m.*

smoking, *a.* Fumant.—*n.* Habitude de fumer; action de fumer, *f. No smoking,* défense de fumer. **smoking-cap,** *n.* Calotte grecque, *f.* **smoking-carriage,** *n.* Compartiment de fumeurs, *m.* **smoking hot,** *a.* Tout chaud. **smoking-jacket,** *n.* Veste d'intérieur, *f.* **smoking-room** or **smoke-room,** *n.* Fumoir, salon de fumeurs, *m.*

smoky, *a.* Qui fume, plein de fumée; enfumé, noir (smoked). *Smoky chimney,* cheminée qui fume, *f.*

smolt, *n.* Jeune saumon, *m.*

smooch [smuːtʃ], *v.i.* (*fam.*) Se bécoter.

smooth [smuːð], *a.* Uni; égal (even); doux (not rough); poli, lisse (glazed); plat (sea); facile, coulant (of style); mielleux, doucereux (of manner).—*v.t.* Polir; calmer, adoucir (to calm); aplanir, unir; faciliter (to make easy, to free); dérider (the brow); lisser (the hair). *To smooth down,* aplanir, unir, adoucir, cajoler (to cajole).

smooth-bore, *a.* (Fusil) à canon lisse; (canon) à âme lisse. **smooth-faced,** *a.* Imberbe;

(*fig.*) qui a l'air doux. **smooth-spoken** or **smooth-tongued,** *a.* Au doux parler, mielleux, doucereux.

smoothing, *n.* Aplanissement, *m.* **smoothing-iron,** *n.* Fer à repasser, *m.* **smoothing-plane,** *n.* Petit rabot, *m.*

smoothly, *adv.* Uniment, facilement, sans difficulté; doucement. **smoothness,** *n.* Égalité; douceur, *f.*; poli; calme (of the sea), *m.*

smote [smout], *past* [SMITE].

smother ['smʌðə], *v.t.* Suffoquer, étouffer; éteindre (to suppress).—*n.* Grande fumée; grande poussière, *f.* **smothering,** *n.* Étouffement, *m.*—*a.* Étouffant, suffocant.

smoulder ['smouldə], *v.i.* Brûler sans fumée ni flamme; (*fig.*) couver. **smouldering,** *a.* Qui couve. *To go on smouldering,* couver sous la cendre.

smudge [smʌdʒ], *v.t.* Barbouiller, noircir, tacher d'encre.—*n.* Barbouillage, *m.*, tache, tache d'encre, *f.* **smudgy,** *a.* Barbouillé; taché.

smug [smʌg], *a.* Suffisant, content de soi. **smugly,** *adv.* D'un air suffisant. **smugness,** *n.* Suffisance, *f.*

smuggle [smʌgl], *v.t.* Passer en contrebande; faire passer en fraude. *To smuggle in,* faire entrer en contrebande, (*fig.*) introduire clandestinement.—*v.i.* Faire la contrebande.

smuggled, *a.* De contrebande. *Smuggled goods,* marchandises de contrebande, *f.pl.* **smuggler,** *n.* Contrebandier, fraudeur, *m.* **smuggling,** *n.* Contrebande, fraude, *f.*

smut [smʌt], *n.* Parcelle *or* tache de suie, *f.*; charbon, *m.*, nielle (in corn); (*fig.*) gravelure, saleté (obscenity), *f.*—*v.t.* Noircir, nieller (corn).—*v.i.* Se noircir; se carier (of corn). **smuttily,** *adv.* Salement. **smuttiness,** *n.* Noirceur, *f.*; (*fig.*) saleté, obscénité (obscenity), *f.* **smutty,** *a.* Noir; carié, niellé (of corn); (*fig.*) graveleux, obscène (obscene); grivois.

snack [snæk], *n.* Morceau; casse-croûte (hasty meal), *m.* *To go snacks,* partager le gâteau, être de moitié (avec); *to take a snack,* manger sur le pouce, casser la croûte.

snack-bar ['snækbɑ:], *n.* Snack-bar, *m.*

snaffle [snæfl], *n.* Mors de bridon, filet, *m.* —*v.t.* Mettre un bridon à; arrêter (a thief); chiper.

snag [snæg], *n.* Chicot, *m.*; souche *or* branche d'arbre submergé, *f.*; (*fig.*) obstacle caché, *m.* *There's a snag in it,* il y a un traquenard.—*v.t.* Heurter, toucher (an obstacle); faire un accroc à (a stocking); essoucher (a field). **snaggy,** *a.* Noueux; plein d'obstacles couverts.

snail [sneil], *n.* Limaçon, colimaçon; escargot (edible snail); (*fig.*) lambin, *m.*, lambine, *f.* *Edible snail,* escargot des vignes, *m.* **snail-clover** or **snail-trefoil,** *n.* Luzerne, *f.* **snail-like,** *a.* Comme un limaçon; de tortue, lent.—*adv.* En limaçon; comme une tortue. **snail-paced,** *a.* À pas de tortue. **snail's-pace,** *n.* Pas de tortue, *m.*

snake [sneik], *n.* Serpent, *m.* *A snake in the grass,* quelque anguille sous roche; *common snake,* couleuvre, *f.*; *rattlesnake,* serpent à sonnettes, *m.*; *snakes and ladders,* (sorte de) jeu de l'oie, *m.*—*v.i.* (*Naut.*) Serpenter.

snake-bite, *n.* Morsure de serpent, *f.* **snake-charmer,** *n.* Charmeur de serpents, *m.* **snake-root,** *n.* Serpentaire, *f.* **snake's-head,** *n.* Fritillaire, *f.* **snakeweed,** *n.* Bistorte, *f.*

snakish or **snaky,** *a.* De serpent; à serpents; tortueux, sinueux (winding); rusé (sly).

snap [snæp], *v.i.* Tâcher de mordre *or* de happer; se casser, se rompre; craquer, éclater. *To snap at,* happer, tâcher de mordre *or* de happer, rudoyer, rembarrer, brusquer; *to snap in two,* se casser en deux; *to snap off,* se casser net; *to snap out of it,* se secouer, se remettre d'aplomb.—*v.t.* Saisir, happer; casser, rompre, éclater; faire claquer (a whip etc.); fermer avec un bruit sec; dire d'un ton sec, bref. *They are snapped up,* on se les arrache; *to snap in two,* casser en deux; *to snap off,* casser; *to snap one's fingers,* faire claquer les doigts; *to snap one's fingers at,* se moquer de, narguer; *to snap someone's head off,* manger le nez à quelqu'un; *to snap up,* happer, gober, rembarrer, relever vivement (to reprimand).—*n.* Coup de dent (bite), *m.*; cassure, rupture, *f.*; claquement (of a whip etc.); bruit sec (noise); crochet d'arrêt (catch), *m.*; agrafe (fastening), *f.*; fermoir (clasp); biscuit craquant, *m.*; énergie, vivacité, *f.* *Not to care a snap,* s'en soucier peu. —*a.* Imprévu, instantané, fait par surprise. —*adv.* *To go snap,* faire crac.

snapdragon, *n.* Muflier, *m.*

snappish, *a.* Disposé à happer; (*fig.*) hargneux, acariâtre. **snappishly,** *adv.* Aigrement, d'une manière hargneuse. **snappishness,** *n.* Humeur hargneuse, aigreur, *f.* **snappy,** *a.* Vif. *Make it snappy!* Dépêchez-vous!

snapshot (*fam.* snap), *n.* Instantané, *m.*—*v.t.* Prendre un instantané de.

snare [snɛə], *n.* Lacet, collet; filet; (*fig.*) piège, *m.*—*v.t.* Prendre (au piège). **snarer,** *n.* Tendeur de lacets, *m.*

snarky ['snɑ:ki], *a.* (*fam.*) Maussade.

snarl [snɑ:l], *v.i.* Grogner, gronder; montrer les dents.—*n.* Grognement, grondement, *m.*; (*Spinning*) vrille, *f.* **snarler,** *n.* Grogneur, grognon, *m.* **snarling,** *a.* Hargneux.—*n.* Grognement, grondement, *m.*

snatch [snætʃ], *v.t.* Saisir. *To snatch a kiss,* voler un baiser. *To snatch at,* chercher à saisir, se raccrocher à; *to snatch from,* arracher à; *to snatch up,* se saisir de, s'emparer de, empoigner.—*n.* Mouvement rapide pour saisir; court instant, accès, *m.*, boutade (fit), *f.*; petit morceau, fragment, *m.* *By snatches,* par échappées, par boutades, à bâtons rompus; *snatches of conversation,* des bribes de conversation, *f.pl.* **snatch-and-grab,** *n.* Vol à l'esbroufe, *m.*

snatch-block, *n.* Poulie coupée, *f.* **snatcher,** *n.* Voleur à l'esbroufe. *Body-snatcher,* voleur de cadavres, *m.* **snatchy,** *a.* Irrégulier; saccadé.

sneak [sni:k], *v.i.* Se glisser *or* s'en aller furtivement; (*sch.*) cafarder, moucharder (to tell tales). *To sneak away,* partir en catimini, se sauver à pas de loup; *to sneak in,* se faufiler dans.—*v.t.* Chiper.—*n.* Pleutre, pied-plat; mouchard, rapporteur, cafard, *m.*

sneaking, *a.* Rampant, servile, lâche; furtif, inavoué. **sneakingly,** *adv.* Furtivement, à la dérobée; servilement; bassement.

sneer [sniːə], *n.* Rire *or* sourire moqueur, sarcasme, ricanement, *m.—v.i.* Ricaner, se moquer (de). *To sneer at*, dénigrer.

sneerer, *n.* Ricaneur, moqueur, *m.*

sneering, *n.* Ricanement, *m.—a.* Ricaneur, moqueur. **sneeringly,** *adv.* En ricanant.

sneeze [sniːz], *n.* Éternuement, *m.—v.i.* Éternuer. *That is not to be sneezed at*, ce n'est pas à dédaigner, ce n'est pas de refus.

sneezing, *n.* Éternuement, *m.*

snick [snik], *n.* Entaille (petite), *f.*; (*Cricket*) petit coup de batte qui dévie la balle; petit bruit sec, *m.—v.t.* Faire une entaille dans; toucher légèrement.

sniff [snif], *v.i.* Renifler.—*v.t.* Aspirer en reniflant; flairer.—*n.* Reniflement, *m. To get a sniff of the sea*, prendre un air de mer.

sniffer, *n.* Renifleur, *m.,* renifleuse, *f.* **sniffy,** *a.* Dédaigneux; malodorant.

sniffling, *n.* Reniflement, *m.*

snifter ['sniftə], *n.* (*fam.*) Petit verre, *m.*

snigger ['snigə], *v.i.* Rire du bout des lèvres, rire sous cape, ricaner.—*n.* Rire en dessous, *m.*

sniggle [snigl], *v.i.* Pêcher aux anguilles.— *v.t.* Attraper (eels). **sniggling,** *n.* Pêche aux anguilles, *f.*

snip [snip], *n.* Coup de ciseaux; bout, morceau coupé (shred), *m.*; (*pop.*) certitude, *f.—v.t.* Couper (d'un coup de ciseaux).

snipe [snaip], *n.* Bécassine, *f.*; gamin, *m. Jack snipe*, jaquet, *m.*; bécassine sourde, *f.—v.i.* (*Shooting*) Canarder. **snipe-eel,** *n.* (*Ichth.*) Orphie, bécassine de mer, *f.* **sniper,** *n.* Tireur embusqué, canardeur, *m.*

snipper ['snipə], *n.* Coupeur, *m.,* coupeuse, *f.* **snipper-snapper,** *n.* Freluquet, petit insolent, *m.* **snippet,** *n.* Petit morceau, *m.*

snitch [snitʃ], *v.t.* (*fam.*) Chaparder.—*v.i.* Vendre la mèche.

snivel [snivl], *v.i.* Être morveux; (*fig.*) pleurnicher.—*n.* Morve, goutte au nez, *f.*

sniveller, *n.* Pleurnicheur, *m.,* pleurnicheuse, *f.* **snivelling,** *a.* Morveux; (*fig.*) pleurnicheur.—*n.* Pleurnicherie, *f.*

snob [snɔb], *n.* *Ouvrier cordonnier; poseur, qui affecte de ne connaître que des riches ou des nobles; fat, snob. **snobbery,** *n.* Snobisme, *m.* **snobbish,** *a.* Affecté, poseur, prétentieux. **snobbishness,** *n.* Snobisme, *m.*

snook [snuːk], *n.* (*pop.*) *To cock a snook at*, faire un pied de nez à.

snooker ['snuːkə], *n.* Snooker, billard russe, *m.*

snoop [snuːp], *v.i.* Fouiner, fureter. **snooper,** *n.* Inquisiteur, fureteur, *m.*

snooze [snuːz], *n.* Somme, *m. To have a snooze*, faire un somme.—*v.i.* Sommeiller.

snore [snɔː], *v.i.* Ronfler.—*n.* Ronflement, *m.* **snorer,** *n.* Ronfleur, *m.,* ronfleuse, *f.* **snoring,** *n.* Ronflement, *m.*

snort [snɔːt], *v.i.* Renâcler, s'ébrouer (of horse); ronfler. **snorter,** *n.* (*fam.*) Problème difficile, *m.*; chose épatante, *f.* **snorting,** *n.* Ronflement, reniflement, ébrouement (of horse), *m.*

snot [snɔt], *n.* (*vulg.*) Morve, *f.* **snotty,** *a.* Morveux. **snotty-nosed,** *a.* Morveux.

snout [snaut], *n.* Museau; mufle (of a bull); groin (of a pig); boutoir (of a wild boar); bout, bec (of things); tuyau (of a pipe, pair of bellows etc.), *m.*

snow [snou], *n.* Neige, *f.*; (*pop.* for cocaine),

coco, *f. Snow report*, bulletin d'enneigement, *m. There has been a fall of snow*, il est tombé de la neige.—*v.i.* Neiger, tomber de la neige. *Snowed up*, pris par les neiges.

snowball, *n.* Boule de neige, *f.—v.t.* Lancer des boules de neige à, attaquer à coups de boules de neige.—*v.i.* Faire boule de neige.

snowball-tree, *n.* Boule de neige, *f.,* obier, *m.* **snow-bunting,** *n.* (*Orn.*) Bruant des neiges, *m.* **snow-capped,** *a.* Couronné de neige. **snow-drift,** *n.* Amas de neige, *m.*

snowdrop, *n.* Perce-neige, *m.* **snow-fall,** *n.* Chute de neige, *f.* **snowflake,** *n.* Flocon de neige, *m.*; nivéole (plant), *f.* **snow-leopard,** *n.* (*Zool.*) Once, *f.* **snow-like,** *a.* De neige, comme la neige. **snow-line,** *n.* Limite des neiges, *f.* **snow-man,** *n.* Bonhomme de neige, *m. The abominable snowman*, l'abominable homme des neiges, *m.* **snow-plough,** *n.* Chasse-neige, *m.* **snow-shoe,** *n.* Raquette, *f.* **snow-slip,** *n.* Avalanche, *f.* **snow-storm,** *n.* Tempête de neige, *f.* **snow-water,** *n.* Eau de neige, *f.* **snow-white,** *a.* Blanc comme la neige.—*n.* Blanche-Neige, *f.* (in fairy story). **snowy,** *a.* De neige; neigeux; blanc comme la neige; (*fig.*) pur, sans tache. *Snowy weather*, un temps de neige.

snub [snʌb], *n.* Rebuffade, *f.*; coup de patte, affront, *m.—v.t.* Rabrouer, remettre à sa place, rembarrer.

snub-nose, *n.* Nez camus, *m.* **snub-nosed,** *a.* Au nez camus.

snuff [snʌf], *n.* Lumignon (of a wick), *m.*; mouchure (snuffed off a candle), *f.*; tabac (à priser), *m. Pinch of snuff*, prise de tabac, *f.*; *to be up to snuff*, ne pas se moucher du pied, s'y connaître; *to take snuff*, priser (du tabac).—*v.t.* Moucher (a candle); aspirer, humer; flairer (to scent). *To snuff out*, éteindre, exterminer.—*v.i.* Renifler.

snuff-box, *n.* Tabatière, *f.* **snuff-coloured,** *a.* Couleur tabac. **snuffer,** *n.* Moucheur de chandelles; priseur, *m.* **snuffers,** *n.pl.* Mouchettes, *f.pl.* **snuff-taker,** *n.* Priseur, *m.* **snuff-taking,** *n.* Habitude de priser, *f.*

snuffy ['snʌfi], *a.* Barbouillé de tabac.

snuffle [snʌfl], *n.* Reniflement, *m.—v.i.* Parler du nez; nasiller, renifler. **snuffler,** *n.* Nasilleur, cagot, *m.* **snuffling,** *n.* Nasillement, *m.*; tartuferies, *f.pl.—a.* Nasillard.

snug [snʌg], *a.* Confortable, commode et agréable, où l'on est bien; gentil (neat); serré, compact (lying close). *A snug house*, une petite maison bien commode; *he is as snug as a bug in a rug*, il est comme un coq en pâte; *he has a snug little place*, il a une bonne petite place; *we are very snug here*, nous sommes on ne peut mieux ici.

snuggery, *n.* Endroit petit et commode, *m.* (où l'on est chez soi).—*v.i.* Se serrer; se

snuggle, *v.t.* Serrer.—*v.i.* Se serrer; se pelotonner. **snugly,** *adv.* Commodément, à son aise, douillettement. **snugness,** *n.* Confort, bien-être, *m.*

so [sou], *adv.* and *conj.* Ainsi, de cette manière, comme cela, comme ça (in this manner); de même, de la même manière, tel (in the same manner); si, tellement, tant (in such a degree); aussi (therefore); environ, à peu près (about). *And so on*, et ainsi de suite; *be it so*, soit! ainsi soit-il! *he is so obstinate*, il est

si entêté, il est tellement entêté; *how so?*
comment cela? *I am afraid so,* je le crains,
j'en ai peur; *I do not say so,* je ne dis pas
cela; *I don't think so,* je ne le crois pas; *if so,*
s'il en est ainsi; *is that so?* vraiment? *I think
so,* je crois; *I will do so,* je le ferai; *just so!*
parfaitement! *Mr. So-and-so,* Monsieur un
tel; *nearly so,* à peu près; *not so,* il n'en est
pas ainsi, pas du tout; *perhaps that is so,* cela
se peut; *so as to,* de manière à; *so do I, so can
I, or so shall I,* et moi aussi; *so far,* jusque-
là, jusqu'ici; *so good an opportunity,* une si
bonne occasion; *so he went,* ainsi il est parti,
aussi est-il parti; *so it is,* c'est ainsi, c'est
comme cela; *so it seems,* à ce qu'il paraît; *so
long,* (*pop.*) au revoir, à tantôt; *so long as,*
aussi longtemps que, tant que; *so many men,
so many minds,* autant de têtes, autant d'avis;
so many or *so much,* tant; *so much the better,*
tant mieux; *so much to the good,* c'est autant
de pris sur l'ennemi; *so old that he might
have been at Agincourt,* assez vieux pour avoir
assisté à la bataille d'Azincourt; *so saying,* à
ces mots; *so that,* de sorte que, si bien que,
de manière que; *so then,* ainsi donc; *so to
speak,* pour ainsi dire; *so true it is,* tant il est
vrai; *so, you are here at last!* eh bien! vous
voici, enfin! *why so?* pourquoi cela? *would
you be so good as to* . . ., voudriez-vous avoir
la bonté de . . .; *you don't say so!* pas possible!
so-called, *a.* Soi-disant, prétendu.
soak [souk], *v.t.* Tremper; faire tremper;
(*colloq.*) estamper (to overcharge). *I am
soaked through,* je suis tout trempé, je suis
mouillé jusqu'aux os; *to soak in,* absorber,
boire.—*v.i.* Tremper, s'infiltrer, pénétrer;
(*colloq.*) boire comme une éponge (to drink
intemperately). *To soak into,* s'infiltrer dans,
pénétrer dans.—*n.* To be in soak, tremper,
être à tremper (of linen for washing).
soaked, *a.* Trempé. *To be soaked through,*
être trempé jusqu'aux os. **soaker,** *n.* Buveur
(hard drinker), *m.*; averse (rain), *f.*
soaking, *a.* Qui trempe.—*n.* Ivrognerie
(drinking); trempée, *f.*, arrosage, *m.* (with
rain).
soap [soup], *n.* Savon, *m. Cake of soap,*
morceau de savon, *m.*, savonnette, *f.; household soap,* savon de Marseille, *m.; scented
soap,* savon parfumé; *shaving soap,* savon
pour la barbe; *soft soap,* savon noir, *m.,* (*fig.*)
flatterie, eau bénite de cour, *f.*—*v.t.* Savonner.
soapberry-tree, *n.* Savonnier, *m.* **soap-
boiler,** *n.* Fabricant de savon, *m.* **soap-box,**
n. Caisse à savon, *f. Soap-box orator,*
harangueur public, *m.* **soap-bubble,** *n.*
Bulle de savon, *f.* **soap-dish,** *n.* Porte-
savon, *m.* **soap-flakes,** *n.pl.* Savon en
paillettes, *m.* **soap-stone,** *n.* Stéatite, *f.,*
talc, *m.* **soap-suds,** *n.pl.* Eau de savon, *f.*
soap-works, *n.pl.* Savonnerie, *f.* **soapwort,** *n.* (*Bot.*) Saponaire, *f.* **soapy,** *a.*
Savonneux; savonné; (*fig.*) doucereux.
soar [so:], *v.i.* Prendre l'essor, s'élever. *To
soar over,* planer sur. **soaring,** *n.* Essor,
élan, *m.*—*a.* Qui s'élève; (*fig.*) élevé. *Soaring
flight,* vol plané, *m.* **soaringly,** *adv.* En
prenant l'essor.
sob [sob], *v.i.* Sangloter.—*n.* Sanglot, *m.* **sob-
stuff,** *n.* Sentimentalisme, *m.*; littérature
larmoyante, *f.*

sobbing, *n.* Sanglots, *m.pl.*
sober ['soubə], *a.* Sobre, modéré, tempéré;
grave, sérieux (grave); sensé, raisonnable;
calme, posé, rassis (calm); qui n'a pas bu,
qui n'est pas ivre, encore à jeun (not intoxicated). *Sober colour,* couleur discrète, *f.*—*v.t.*
Dégriser, désenivrer; (*fig.*) calmer, désillusionner, ramener à la raison.—*v.i. To sober
up,* se désenivrer.
soberly, *adv.* Sobrement, modérément;
raisonnablement; sérieusement; avec calme.
sober-minded, *a.* Modéré; sage, raisonnable,
sérieux. **sober-mindedness,** *n.* Modération; sagesse, *f.*
soberness or **sobriety** [sə'braiəti], *n.*
Sobriété, tempérance, modération, *f.*; sérieux,
m., gravité (seriousness), *f.*
soccer ['sokə], *n.* (*fam.*) Football, *m.*
sociability [souʃə'biliti] or **sociableness**
['souʃəblnis], *n.* Sociabilité, *f.*
sociable ['souʃəbl], *a.* Sociable; qui aime la
société. **sociably,** *adv.* Sociablement, d'une
manière amicale.
social [souʃl], *a.* Social; sociable. *Social
events,* mondanités, *f.pl.* **socialism,** *n.*
Socialisme, *m.* **socialist,** *n.* and *a.* Socialiste,
m. or *f.* **socialite,** *n.* Mondain, *m.,* -aine, *f.*
socialization, *n.* Socialisation, *f.* **socialize,**
v.t. Socialiser. **socially,** *adv.* Socialement.
society [sə'saiəti], *n.* Société, *f.*; la société, *f.*;
le monde, *m. Charitable society,* société de
bienfaisance; *fashionable society,* beau monde;
learned society, société littéraire; *London
society,* le monde de Londres; *to go into
society,* aller dans le monde.—*a. Society news,*
échos mondains, *m.pl.*; *society woman,* mondaine, *f.*
sociological [sousiə'lɔdʒikl], *a.* Sociologique.
sociologist [-'ɔlədʒist], *n.* Sociologiste,
sociologue, *m.* **sociology,** *n.* Sociologie, *f.*
sock [sok], *n.* Chaussette; semelle (inner sole),
f.; (*Theat.*) socque, *f.*; brodequin, *m.*; (*pop.*)
beigne, *f. Ankle socks,* socquettes, *f.pl.*;
(*colloq.*) *put a sock in it,* boucle-la!—*v.t.*
(*pop.*) Donner une beigne à.
socket ['sɔkit], *n.* Emboîture, *f.*; alvéole (of a
tooth), *m.*; orbite (of the eye), *f.*, trou, *m.*;
cavité (cavity); douille (of tools etc.), *f.*;
bec (of a lamp), *m.*; bobèche (of a candlestick etc.), *f.*
sockless ['sɔklis], *a.* Sans chaussettes.
socle [sɔkl], *n.* Socle, *m.*
Socrates ['sɔkrəti:z]. Socrate, *m.*
Socratic [sə'krætik] or **Socratical,** *a.* Socratique. **Socratically,** *adv.* Socratiquement.
sod [sɔd], *n.* Gazon, *m.*; motte de gazon, *f.*;
(*vulg.*) salaud, *m.*
soda ['soudə], *n.* Soude, *f. Baking soda,*
bicarbonate de soude, *m.* **soda-water,** *n.*
Eau de Seltz, *f.*, soda, *m.*
sodden ['sɔdn], *a.* Imprégné d'eau, détrempé;
pâteux (of bread); bouilli; (with drink)
abruti.
sodium ['soudiəm], *n.* (*Chem.*) Sodium, *m.*
sodomite ['sɔdəmait], *n.* Sodomite, *m.*
sodomy ['sɔdəmi], *n.* Sodomie, *f.*
soever [sou'evə], *adv.* Que ce soit.
sofa ['soufə], *n.* Canapé, *m.* **sofa-bed,** *n.*
Lit-canapé, *m.*
soffit ['sɔfit], *n.* Soffite, *m.*
soft [sɔft], *a.* Mou, mol, mollet; délicat, doux,
facile, pas résistant (yielding); tendre (tender);

efféminé (effeminate); faible (weak); sot, niais (foolish); (*Gram.*) doux. *Soft drinks*, boissons non alcooliques, *f.pl.*; (*Cine.*) *soft focus*, flou artistique, *m.*; *soft fruits*, fruits rouges, *m.pl.*; *to be soft on somebody*, être épris de quelqu'un; *to get soft*, se ramollir.—*adv.* Mollement, doucement.—*int.* Doucement! tout doux! **soft-boiled,** *a.* Mollet (of eggs). **soft-headed,** *a.* Niais; sot. **soft-hearted,** *a.* Tendre, compatissant. **soft-sawder,** *n.* Eau bénite de cour, flatterie, *f.*—*v.t.* Flatter. **soft-soap** [SOAP]. **soft-spoken,** *a.* À la voix douce; (*iron.*) mielleux.

soften [sɔfn], *v.t.* Amollir, ramollir; rendre facile (to make easier); calmer, adoucir, apaiser, radoucir (to calm); efféminer, amollir, affaiblir (to enervate); attendrir, fléchir (to move); (*Metal.*) détremper.—*v.i.* S'amollir, se ramollir, s'adoucir; se calmer, s'apaiser, se radoucir, s'affaiblir; s'attendrir (of the heart).

softener, *n.* Personne ou chose qui amollit ou qui adoucit; (*Paint.*) blaireau, *m.*

softening, *n.* Amollissement; affaiblissement (weakening); attendrissement (of the heart), *m. Softening of the brain,* ramollissement du cerveau, *m.*

softish ['sɔftiʃ], *a.* Un peu mou; un peu sot.

softly ['sɔftli], *adv.* Mollement; doucement; tendrement (tenderly); avec tendresse, délicatement (gently).

softness, *n.* Mollesse; faiblesse (weakness); niaiserie (silliness); tiédeur (of weather); douceur, facilité (gentleness), *f.*

softy, *n.* Niais; mollasson, *m.*

soggy ['sɔgi], *a.* Détrempé, humide; pâteux (bread).

soil [sɔil], *n.* Tache, souillure (stain); ordure, saleté (filth), *f.*; engrais, fumier (manure); sol, terrain, terroir, *m.*, terre (land), *f. To take out,* se réfugier dans l'eau (of a deer).—*v.t.* Salir, souiller, tacher, profaner (to defile); mettre au vert (cattle). **soiled,** *a.* Souillé, sale.

sojourn ['sʌdʒən *or* 'sɔdʒən], *n.* Séjour, *m.*—*v.i.* Séjourner. **sojourner,** *n.* Hôte passager; (*fig.*) oiseau de passage, *m. We are only sojourners on this earth,* nous ne faisons que passer sur cette terre. **sojourning,** *n.* Séjour, *m.*

sol [sɔl], *n.* (*Mus.*) Sol, *m.* **sol-fa,** *n.* (*Mus.*) Gamme, *f.*; solfège, *m.*—*v.i.* Solfier.

solace ['sɔlis], *n.* Consolation, *f.*, soulagement, *m.*—*v.t.* Consoler (de). *To solace oneself with,* se consoler par *or* à.

solan ['soulən] *or* **solan-goose,** *n.* (*Orn.*) Fou, *m.*

solanaceous [soulə'neiʃəs], *a.* (*Bot.*) Solanée.

solar ['soulə], *a.* Solaire, du soleil. **solarium,** *n.* Solarium, *m.* **solarize,** *v.t.* Solariser.

sold, *past and p.p.* [SELL].

soldanella [sɔldə'nelə], *n.* (*Bot.*) Soldanelle, *f.*

solder ['sɔldə *or* 'sɔːdə], *n.* Soudure, *f.*—*v.t.* Souder. **solderer,** *n.* Soudeur, *m.* **soldering,** *n.* Soudure, *f.*; soudage (action), *m.* **soldering-iron,** *n.* Soudoir, fer à souder, *m.*

soldier ['souldʒə], *n.* Soldat, militaire, *m. A great soldier,* un grand capitaine; *foot-soldier,* fantassin, *m.*; *old soldier,* ancien soldat, soudard, *m.*; *private soldier,* simple soldat.—*v.i.* Servir comme soldat.

soldiering, *n.* Le métier des armes, *m.*

soldier-like *or* **soldierly,** *a.* De soldat, militaire, martial.

soldiery, *n.* Troupes, *f.pl.*, soldats, *m.pl.*; (*pej.*) soldatesque, *f.*

sole (1) [soul], *a.* Seul, unique; exclusif; (*Law*) non marié; universel (of a legatee).

sole (2) [soul], *n.* Plante (of the foot); semelle (of a shoe, tool etc.), *f.*; (*Tech.*) châssis, *m.*; sole (fish), *f.*—*v.t.* Mettre des semelles à, ressemeler. *Thin-soled,* à semelles minces.

solecism ['sɔlisizm], *n.* Solécisme, *m.*

solely ['soulli], *adv.* Seulement, uniquement.

solemn ['sɔləm], *a.* Solennel; grave, sérieux (grave).

solemnity [sɔ'lemniti] *or* **solemnness,** *n.* Solennité; gravité (gravity), *f.*; air *or* ton solennel, *m.* **solemnization** [-nai'zeiʃən], *n.* Solennisation; célébration solennelle, *f.*

solemnize ['sɔləmnaiz], *v.t.* Solenniser, célébrer. **solemnly,** *adv.* Solennellement.

solen [souln], *n.* (*Zool.*) Solen, *m.*

solenoid ['sɔlinɔid], *n.* (*Elec.*) Solénoïde, *m.*

solfatara [sɔlfə'tɑːrə], *n.* Solfatare, *f.*

solfeggio [sɔl'fedʒiou], *n.* Solfège, *m.*

solicit [sə'lisit], *v.t.* Solliciter; inviter, attirer (to invite); racoler (of prostitutes). **solicitation** [-'teiʃən], *n.* Sollicitation, *f.* **soliciting,** *n.* Racolage (by prostitutes etc.), *m.*

solicitor [sə'lisitə], *n.* Solliciteur; (*Law*) avoué et notaire, *m.* **solicitor-general,** *n.* Conseiller juridique de la couronne; chef du contentieux, *m.*

solicitous [sə'lisitəs], *a.* Désireux. *Solicitous about,* qui a de la sollicitude pour, soigneux de, attentif à; *solicitous for,* inquiet de; *solicitous of,* désireux de. **solicitously,** *adv.* Avec sollicitude.

solicitude [sə'lisitjuːd] *or* **solicitousness,** *n.* Sollicitude, *f.*

solid ['sɔlid], *a.* Solide, massif, plein (of rock); (*fig.*) grave, sérieux, posé (of persons); de capacité (of measure). *Frozen solid,* gelé jusqu'au fond; *nine solid days,* neuf bonnes journées, neuf journées d'affilée, *f.pl.*; *of solid oak,* en chêne massif; *solid rock,* roc vif, *m.*; *to become solid,* se solidifier.—*n.* Solide, *m.*

solidarity [sɔli'dæriti], *n.* Solidarité, *f.*

solidification [səlidifi'keiʃən], *n.* Solidification, *f.* **solidify** [sə'lidifai], *v.t.* Solidifier.—*v.i.* Se solidifier; se figer.

solidity [sə'liditi] *or* **solidness,** *n.* Solidité, *f.* **solidly,** *adv.* Solidement.

soliloquize [sə'liləkwaiz], *v.i.* Faire un soliloque, se parler à soi-même. **soliloquy** [-kwi], *n.* Soliloque, monologue, *m.*

soling ['souliŋ], *n.* Ressemelage, *m.*

soliped ['sɔliped], *n.* Solipède, *m.*

solipedal [sə'lipədəl], *a.* Solipède.

solipsism ['sɔlipsizm], *n.* Solipsisme, *m.*

solitaire [sɔli'teə], *n.* (*Am.*) Réussite, *f.*, jeu de patience, *m.* (card game); solitaire (game); solitaire (diamond), *m.*

solitarily ['sɔlitərili], *adv.* Solitairement. **solitariness,** *n.* Solitude, retraite, *f.* **solitary,** *a.* Solitaire, retiré, isolé; seul, unique (single). *Solitary confinement,* emprisonnement cellulaire, *m.*

solitude ['sɔlitjuːd], *n.* Solitude, *f.*

solo ['soulou], *n.* Solo, *m.* **soloist,** *n.* Soliste, *m. or f.*

Solomon ['sɔləmən]. Salomon, *m. Solomon's seal. (Bot.)* sceau de Salomon, *m.*
solstice ['sɔlstis], *n.* Solstice, *m. Summer solstice,* solstice d'été, *m.*
solubility [sɔlju'biliti], *n.* Solubilité, *f.*
soluble ['sɔljubl], *a.* Soluble.
solution [sɔ'lju:ʃən], *n.* Solution; dissolution, *f. Standard solution (Chem.),* solution normale, *f.*
solvability [sɔlvə'biliti], *n.* Solvabilité (of a person); résolubilité (of a problem), *f.*
solvable ['sɔlvəbl], *a.* Soluble.
solve [sɔlv], *v.t.* Résoudre, expliquer, éclaircir.
solvency ['sɔlvənsi], *n.* Solvabilité (of a person), *f.* **solvent,** *a.* Dissolvant; *(Comm.)* solvable.—*n.* Dissolvant, *m.*
Somalia [so'mɑ:ljə], **Somaliland** [so'mɑ:li lænd]. La Somalie, *f.*
somatology [soumə'tɔlədʒi], *n.* Somatologie, *f.*
sombre ['sɔmbə], *a.* Sombre. **sombrely,** *adv.* Sombrement.
some [sʌm], *a.* Quelque, *m.* or *f.,* quelques, *pl.;* un certain, certains, *pl.,* plusieurs, *pl.;* du, *m.,* de la, *f.,* de l', *m.* or *f.,* des, *pl.,* de: quelconque; un certain nombre de, un peu de, une partie de. *Some bread,* du pain; *some few,* quelques-uns, quelques personnes, un petit nombre (de); *some people say,* on dit; *some scrape or other,* quelque mauvaise affaire, *f.*—À peu près, environ, quelque. *Some six or seven persons,* quelque six ou sept personnes, environ six ou sept personnes.—*pron.* Quelques-uns, *m.pl.,* quelques-unes, *f.pl.;* les uns, *m.pl.,* les unes, *f.pl.,* . . . les autres, *pl.;* qui . . . qui, en. *Give him some,* donnez-lui-en; *I have some,* j'en ai; *some of them,* quelques-uns d'entre eux; *some of us,* quelques-uns d'entre nous; *some say yes, some say no,* les uns disent oui, les autres disent non; *there are some who,* il y a des gens qui; *they went some one way some another,* ils s'en allèrent qui d'un côté, qui de l'autre.
somebody ['sʌmbədi], *pron.* Quelqu'un, *m.,* quelqu'une, *f.,* on. *Somebody else,* quelque autre, un autre; *somebody or other,* je ne sais qui; *to be somebody,* être quelque chose, être un personnage; *to think oneself somebody,* se croire quelqu'un, quelque chose, un personnage.
somehow ['sʌmhau], *adv.* D'une manière ou d'une autre, de façon ou d'autre; d'une façon quelconque, tant bien que mal (indifferent).
someone [SOMEBODY].
somersault ['sʌməsɔ:lt], *n.* Saut périlleux, *m.,* culbute, *f. To turn a somersault,* faire la culbute, faire le saut périlleux; *(Motor., Cycl.)* capoter.—*v.i.* Capoter.
something ['sʌmθiŋ], *n.* and *pron.* Quelque chose (de), *m. He has something about him which pleases everyone,* il a un je ne sais quoi qui plaît à tout le monde; *I have something to do,* j'ai quelque chose à faire; *something else,* autre chose, *f.; something good,* quelque chose de bon; *there is something in that,* c'est assez plausible, c'est une idée, cela mérite considération; *there is something to boast of,* il y a de quoi se vanter; *to be something between . . . and,* tenir le ·milieu entre . . . et.—*adv.* Un peu, quelque peu, tant soit peu.
sometime ['sʌmtaim], *adv.* Autrefois, jadis. *Sometime or other,* tôt ou tard.—*a.* D'autrefois, ancien. *My sometime general,* mon ancien général.

sometimes, *adv.* Quelquefois, parfois; tantôt. *Sometimes rich, sometimes poor,* tantôt riche, tantôt pauvre.
somewhat ['sʌmwɔt], *adv.* Quelque peu, un peu; assez.—*n.* Un peu, quelque peu, tant soit peu, *m.*
somewhere ['sʌmwɛə], *adv.* Quelque part. *Somewhere else,* ailleurs, autre part.
somnambulism [sɔm'næmbjulizm], *n.* Somnambulisme, *m.* **somnambulist,** *n.* Somnambule, *m.*
somniferous [sɔm'nifərəs], *a.* Somnifère.
somniloquous [-'niləkwəs], *a.* Somniloque.
somnolence ['sɔmnələns], *n.* Assoupissement, *m.,* somnolence, *f.* **somnolent,** *a.* Enclin au sommeil, somnolent.
son [sʌn], *n.* Fils; *(fig.)* descendant, *m.* **son-in-law,** *n.* Gendre, *m.*
sonata [sə'nɑ:tə], *n.* Sonate, *f.*
song [sɔŋ], *n.* Chanson (lay), *f.;* chant, cantique (hymn), *m.; (fig.)* ballade, *f.,* lai; *(poet.)* poème, *m.;* poésie, *f. A mere song,* un rien, *m.,* une bagatelle, *f.; drinking song,* chanson à boire, *f.; no song no supper,* nul bien sans peine; *to buy for a mere song,* acheter pour un rien *or* pour une bagatelle; *(fam.) to make a song and dance about,* en faire tout un plat.
song-book, *n.* Recueil de chansons, *m.*
songless, *a.* Sans voix, muet. **songster,** *n.* Chanteur; oiseau chanteur (bird), *m.* **songstress,** *n.* Chanteuse, *f.* **song-thrush,** *n.* Grive chanteuse, calendrette, *f.* **songwriter,** *n.* Chansonnier, *m.*
soniferous [sə'nifərəs], *a.* Résonnant.
sonnet ['sɔnit], *n.* Sonnet, *m.* **sonneteer** [-'tiə], *n.* Faiseur de sonnets, *m.;* sonnettiste, *m.* or *f.*
sonny ['sʌni], *n. (fam.)* Mon petit, mon fiston, *m.*
sonority [sə'nɔriti] *or* **sonorousness,** *n.* Sonorité, *f.* **sonorous** ['sɔnərəs *or* sə'nɔ:rəs], *a.* Sonore. **sonorously,** *adv.* D'un ton sonore.
soon [su:n], *adv.* Bientôt, tôt (early); de bonne heure, volontiers (willingly). *As soon as,* aussitôt que, dès que; *how soon?* quand? *I would as soon remain as go,* j'aimerais autant rester que de m'en aller; *see you soon!* à bientôt; *soon after,* bientôt après; *so soon,* si tôt; *too soon,* trop tôt; *too soon by an hour,* trop tôt d'une heure; *very soon,* bientôt, dans très peu de temps.
sooner ['su:nə], *adv.* Plus tôt (earlier); plutôt (rather). *No sooner had he spoken than,* à peine eut-il parlé que; *no sooner said than done,* aussitôt dit, aussitôt fait; *sooner or later,* tôt ou tard; *sooner than,* plutôt que (rather than); *the sooner the better,* le plus tôt sera le mieux.
soonest ['su:nist], *adv.* Le plus tôt. *At the soonest,* au plus tôt.
soot [sut], *n.* Suie, *f.*—*v.t.* Couvrir de suie.
*****sooth** [su:θ], *n.* Vérité; réalité, *f. In sooth,* en vérité, à vrai dire.
soothe [su:ð], *v.t.* Adoucir, apaiser, calmer; *(fig.)* flatter, charmer, satisfaire. **soother,** *n.* Personne *or* chose qui calme *or* adoucit, *f.;* flatteur, *m.,* flatteuse (flatterer), *f.*
soothing, *a.* Calmant, consolant; flatteur (flattering). **soothingly,** *adv.* D'un ton doux.

soothsay ['su:θsei], v.i. Prophétiser, prédire. **soothsayer,** n. Devin, m., devineresse, f., prophète, m. **soothsaying,** n. Divination, f.

sootiness ['sutinis], n. Fuliginosité, f. **sooty,** a. De suie, fuligineux; plein or couvert de suie (foul with soot); (fig.) noir, sombre, obscur.

sop [sɔp], n. Morceau (de pain) trempé; (fig.) don, présent (pour se concilier quelqu'un); pot-de-vin, m. (small gratuity); soupe au lait (for children), f. A sop to Cerberus, don propitiatoire, m.—v.t. Tremper.

Sophia [sə'faiə]. Sophie, f.

sophism ['sɔfizm], n. Sophisme, m. **sophist,** n. Sophiste, m.

sophistic [sə'fistik] or **sophistical,** a. Sophistique. **sophistically,** adv. D'une manière sophistique.

sophisticate [sə'fistikeit], v.t. Sophistiquer, falsifier, frelater. **sophisticated,** a. Falsifié; frelaté (wine); altéré (text); corrompu, trop raffiné (taste); blasé (person). **sophistication** [-'keiʃən], n. Sophistication, falsification, f., frelatage, m.

sophistry ['sɔfistri], n. Sophismes, m.pl., sophistique, f.

Sophocles ['sɔfəkli:z]. Sophocle, m.

sophomore ['sɔfəmɔ:], n. (Am. Univ.) Étudiant de seconde année, m.

sophora [sə'fɔ:rə], a. (Bot.) Sophore, m.

soporiferous [sɔpə'rifərəs], a. Soporifère. **soporiferousness,** n. Nature soporifère, f.

soporific [sɔpə'rifik], a. and n. Soporifique, soporatif, m.

soporous ['soupərəs], a. Soporeux.

sopping ['sɔpiŋ] (wet), a. Trempé.

soppy ['sɔpi], a. Trempé, détrempé; fadasse.

soprano [sə'prɑ:nou], n. Soprano, m.

sorb [sɔ:b], n. Sorbier, m. **sorb-apple,** n. Sorbe, f.

sorcerer ['sɔ:sərə], n. Sorcier, magicien, m. **sorceress,** n. Sorcière, magicienne, f. **sorcery,** n. Sorcellerie, f., enchantement, m., magie, f.

sordid ['sɔ:did], a. Sordide, sale; bas, vil. **sordidly,** adv. Sordidement. **sordidness,** n. Sordidité, f.

sore [sɔ:], a. Douloureux, endolori, malade, irritable, susceptible, sensible (tender); (fig.) cruel, grand, rude (severe); fâché. A sore trial, une cruelle épreuve; sore fingers, mal aux doigts, m.; sore throat, mal à la gorge, m.; to be a sight for sore eyes (fig.), mettre du baume au cœur; to have a sore foot, avoir mal au pied; to have sore eyes or ears, avoir mal aux yeux or mal aux oreilles; to make sore, rendre malade, irriter.—n. Plaie; (fig.) douleur, f., mal, m. **sorely,** adv. Gravement, fortement, cruellement, rudement. Sorely tried, cruellement éprouvé. **soreness,** n. Douleur, f.; blessure, f., mal, m.; sensation pénible; irritabilité (susceptibility), f.

sorghum ['sɔ:gəm], n. Sorgho, sorgo, m.

sorites [sə'raiti:z], n. Sorite, m.

sorrel ['sɔrəl], n. Oseille; couleur saure (colour), f.; alezan (horse), m.—a. Saure; alezan. **sorrel-soup,** n. Soupe à l'oseille, f.

sorrily ['sɔrili], adv. Misérablement, pauvrement, chétivement.

sorrow ['sɔrou], n. Chagrin, m., douleur; peine, tristesse, f. In sorrow, dans le chagrin,

to one's sorrow, à son grand chagrin, à sa grande douleur.—v.i. Être affligé, avoir du chagrin, s'affliger, s'attrister.

sorrowful, a. Triste, affligé, chagriné; affligeant, attristant, pénible (of things). **sorrowfully,** adv. Tristement. **sorrowfulness,** n. Chagrin, m., tristesse, douleur, f.

sorrowing, a. Affligé.

sorry ['sɔri], a. Fâché, désolé (de); triste, pauvre, méchant, pitoyable (poor). A sorry jest, une mauvaise plaisanterie; a sorry meal, un triste or maigre repas; a sorry poet, un méchant poète; I am sorry for it, j'en suis fâché; I am sorry for you, je vous plains; I am sorry to say that . . ., je regrette d'avoir à dire que . . .; I am unable to help you, I am sorry to say, malheureusement, je ne puis vous venir en aide; sorry! pardon! to be sorry for, être fâché de; (fam.) you will be sorry for it, il vous en cuira.

sort (1) [sɔ:t], n. Sorte, f., genre, m., espèce; manière, façon (manner), f. A strange sort of fellow, un drôle de type; a woman of the right sort, une bonne pâte de femme; (fam.) he's a good sort, c'est un bon garçon; in some sort, en quelque sorte, en quelque façon; nothing of the sort, pas du tout, il n'en est rien; of the right sort, de bon aloi; to be out of sorts, ne pas être dans son assiette, être de mauvaise humeur; to put out of sorts, déranger, détraquer, mettre de mauvaise humeur; we drank wine of a sort, nous avons bu du soi-disant vin; (colloq.) we sort of thought that, nous avions comme une idée que; you will do nothing of the sort, vous n'en ferez rien.

sort (2) [sɔ:t], v.t. Assortir, classer, distribuer; trier (letters etc.). To sort from, séparer de; to sort out, assortir, trier, séparer; (pop.) we'll sort him out! nous allons l'arranger!

sorted, a. Assorti; trié, arrangé, séparé. **sorter,** n. Trieur, m., trieuse, f.

sortie ['sɔ:ti], n. (Mil.) Sortie, f.; (Av.) vol, m.

sortilege ['sɔ:tilidʒ], n. Sortilège, m.

sorting ['sɔ:tiŋ], n. Triage, tri; assortiment (matching), m. (Rail.) Sorting depot, gare de triage, f.; sorting office, bureau de triage, f.

so-so, a. Ni trop mal ni trop bien, passablement, comme ci comme ça, (fam.) couci-couça.

sot [sɔt], n. Abruti par l'alcool, ivrogne, m. **sottish,** a. Hébété, abruti. **sottishness,** n. Abrutissement, m.

souchong [su:'ʃɔŋ or su:'tʃɔŋ], n. Souchong (tea), m.

soufflé ['su:flei], n. Soufflé, m.

sough [sau or sʌf], v.i. Murmurer, soupirer (of the wind).—n. (or **soughing**) Bruissement, murmure, frémissement, m.

sought [sɔ:t], past and p.p. [SEEK].

soul [soul], n. Âme, f.; (fig.) être, m., créature (creature); essence, f., principe (essence), m. All Souls' Day, le jour des morts, m.; not a soul about, pas un chat dans les rues; simple soul, bonhomme, m., bonne femme, bonne âme, f.; the life and soul of, l'âme de; the soul of honour, l'honneur même, m.; upon my soul! sur mon âme! with all my soul, de toute mon âme.

soul-destroying, a. Abrutissant. **soul-felt,** a. Senti dans l'âme, chaleureux (thanks). **soulful,** a. Sentimental; plein d'âme. Soulful

eyes, yeux expressifs, *m.pl.* **soulfully,** *adv.*
Avec expression; avec sentiment. **soulless,**
a. Sans âme; inexpressif; abrutissant. **soul-
searching,** *a.* Qui pénètre jusqu'au fond de
l'âme.—*n.* Examen de conscience, *m.* **soul-
stirring,** *a.* Qui remue l'âme, émouvant.
soul-vexed, *a.* À l'esprit tourmenté.
sound (1) [saund], *n.* Détroit (strait), *m.*;
(*Surg.*) sonde, *f.* *The Sound,* le Sund, *m.*—
v.t. Sonder (to fathom, probe, etc.); (*Surg.*)
ausculter. **soundable,** *a.* Qu'on peut
sonder.
sound (2) [saund], *a.* En bon état, sain, bon;
(*fig.*) solide; profond (of sleep); fort,
vigoureux (of blows); valide, légitime, bien
fondé (valid). *Safe and sound,* sain et sauf;
sound doctrine, doctrine saine, *f.*; *sound
thrashing,* bonne raclée, *f.*; *the firm is sound,*
la maison (de commerce) est solvable; *to be
sound in wind and limb,* avoir bon pied bon
œil.—*adv.* *To sleep sound*(*ly*), dormir profondément. **sound-headed,** *a.* Qui a la
tête saine, sensé. **sound-hearted,** *a.* Qui
a le cœur bien placé, sincère.
sound (3) [saund], *v.i.* Sonner; retentir,
résonner (de); sembler, avoir l'air de, faire
l'effet de. *The praises sounded to him like
reproaches,* les éloges lui semblaient autant de
reproches; *to sound hollow,* sonner creux; *to
sound like,* avoir le son de; *to sound well,*
sonner bien, faire bon effet.—*v.t.* Sonner
(de); faire sonner, faire résonner; proclamer,
publier, célébrer (to proclaim). *To be sounded,*
se prononcer (of letters); *to sound to horse,*
sonner le boute-selle.—*n.* Son, bruit, *m.*
Not a sound, pas le moindre bruit; *sound
effects,* (*Cine., Rad., Tel.*) bruitage, *m.*; *sound
engineer,* ingénieur du son, *m.*; *sound film,*
film parlant, film sonore, *m.*; *sound recording,*
prise de son, *f.*; *to break the sound barrier,*
(*Av.*) franchir le mur du son.
sound-hole, *n.* Ouïe (of a violin etc.), *f.*
sound-post, *n.* Âme, *f.* **sound-proof,** *a.*
Insonore. **sound-proofed,** *a.* Insonorisé.
sound-proofing, *n.* Insonorisation, *f.*
sound-track, *n.* (*Cine.*) Piste sonore, *f.*
sound-wave, *n.* Onde sonore, *f.*
sounding (1) ['saundiŋ], *n.* Action de sonder,
f., sondage, *m.*; (*Surg.*) auscultation, *f.* *To
take soundings,* faire des sondages. **sounding-
balloon,** *n.* (*Meteor.*) Ballon sonde, *m.*
sounding-lead, *n.* Sonde, *f.*, plomb de
sonde, *m.* **sounding-line,** *n.* Ligne de
sonde, *f.*
sounding (2) ['saundiŋ], *a.* Résonnant, retentissant; (*fig.*) pompeux, ronflant.—*n.* Action
de sonner, *f.*, retentissement, résonnement,
m. **sounding-board,** *n.* Abat-voix (of a
pulpit), *m.*; (*Mus.*) table d'harmonie, *f.*;
(*Organ*) sommier, tamis, *m.*
soundless ['saundlis], *a.* Sans bruit, muet.
soundly, *adv.* Vigoureusement, rudement,
ferme, bien, comme il faut (well); sainement,
solidement, judicieusement (right); profondément (of sleeping). *Soundly beaten,*
bien, joliment battu. **soundness,** *n.* Bon
état, *m.*; force, vigueur (strength); rectitude, droiture, justesse, pureté (rightness),
f.
soup [su:p], *n.* Potage, *m.*, soupe, *f.* *Clear
soup,* consommé, *m.*; *thick soup,* purée, *f.*;
turtle-soup, potage à la tortue; *vegetable-soup,*

(potage) julienne; (*colloq.*) *to be in the soup,*
être dans le pétrin.
soup-kitchen, *n.* Soupe populaire, *f.* **soup-
ladle,** *n.* Louche, *f.* **soup-plate,** *n.* Assiette
creuse, assiette à soupe, *f.* **soup-ticket,** *n.*
Bon de soupe, *m.* **soup-tureen,** *n.* Soupière, *f.*
sour ['sauə], *a.* Aigre, sur, acide; tourné (of
milk); (*fig.*) âpre, revêche, morose. *Sour
grapes!* les raisins sont trop verts; *to make
sour,* aigrir; *to turn sour,* s'aigrir.—*v.t.*
Aigrir; (*Chem.*) acidifier; (*fig.*) empoisonner.
—*v.i.* S'aigrir. **sour-puss,** *n.* Grincheux, *m.*,
-euse, *f.*
source [sɔːs], *n.* Source, *f.*
souring ['sauəriŋ], *n.* Aigrissement, *m.*
sourish, *a.* Suret, aigrelet.
sourly ['sauəli], *adv.* Avec aigreur; (*fig.*)
aigrement, âprement. **sourness,** *n.* Aigreur,
acidité; (*fig.*) âpreté, *f.*
souse [saus], *v.t.* Plonger, tremper, mouiller;
faire mariner.—*n.* Marinade, *f.*; pieds de porc
marinés, *m.pl.*; plongeon, bain, *m.* *To get a
souse,* tomber à l'eau; se faire tremper (par la
pluie).—*adv.* Brusquement. **soused,** *a.*
Mariné; (*pop.*) soûl.
south [sauθ], *a.* Sud, du sud, du midi, méridional. *South Pole,* pôle sud, *m.*; *South Sea,*
mer du Sud, *f.*, Pacifique sud, *m.*—*n.* Sud,
midi, *m.* *The South of France,* le Midi.—*adv.*
Vers le midi, vers le sud, au sud. **South
Africa.** L'Afrique du sud, *f.*; l'Union sud-
africaine, *f.* **South America.** L'Amérique
du Sud, *f.* **South American,** *a.* and *n.* Sud-
américain, *m.*, -aine, *f.*
south-east, *n.* Sud-est, *m.*—*a.* Sud-est, du
sud-est.—*adv.* Vers le sud-est. **south-
easter,** *n.* Vent du sud-est, *m.* **south-
easterly** or **south-eastern,** *a.* Du sud-est.
southerly ['sʌðəli] or **southern** ['sʌðən], *a.*
Du sud, du midi, méridional. *The Southern
Cross,* la Croix du Sud, *f.*
southerner, *n.* Méridional; (*Am.*) sudiste, *m.*
southernmost, *a.* Le plus au sud, à l'extrême
sud.
southernwood, *n.* Aurone, citronnelle, *f.*
southing ['sauθiŋ], *n.* Passage au méridien (of
the moon etc.), *m.*
southward ['sauθwəd], *adv.* Vers le sud, au
sud.
south-west ['sauθ'west, (*Naut.*) 'sau'west], *n.*
Sud-ouest, *m.*—*a.* Sud-ouest, du sud-ouest.
—*adv.* Vers le sud-ouest. **southwester**
[sou'WESTER]. **south-westerly** or **south-
western,** *a.* Du sud-ouest, sud-ouest.
souvenir ['su:vəniə], *n.* Souvenir, *m.*
sou'wester [sau'westə], *n.* Vent du sud-ouest;
suroît (head-gear), *m.*
sovereign ['sɔvrin], *a.* Souverain.—*n.* Souverain, *m.*, souveraine, *f.*; (*Coin*) souverain
(20 shillings), *m.* *Half sovereign,* demi-
souverain, *m.* **sovereignly,** *adv.* Souverainement. **sovereignty,** *n.* Souveraineté, *f.*
Soviet ['souviet], *n.* Soviet, *m.* *The Soviet
Union,* l'Union Soviétique, *f.*
sow (1) [sau], *n.* Truie, coche; gueuse (of iron),
f. *To get the wrong sow by the ear,* prendre
martre pour renard, se tromper; *you cannot
make a silk purse out of a sow's ear,* on ne
saurait faire d'une buse un épervier. **sow-
thistle,** *n.* (*Bot.*) Laiteron, *m.*
sow (2) [sou], *v.t.* (*past* **sowed,** *p.p.* **sown**)
Semer; ensemencer (de); répandre (to

scatter). *To sow broadcast,* semer à tout vent; *to sow one's wild oats,* jeter sa gourme.—*v.i.* Semer, faire les semailles.

sower, *n.* Semeur, *m.* **sowing,** *n.* Semailles, *f.pl.,* ensemencement, *m.* **sowing-time,** *n.* Temps des semailles, *m.*

soya-bean [ˈsɔiəˈbiːn], *n.* Soya, soja, *m.*

spa [spɑː], *n.* Source minérale; ville d'eaux, *f.,* station thermale, *f.*

space [speis], *n.* Espace, *m.,* étendue, *f.;* place, *f.;* intervalle, entre-deux (space between); espace de temps (length of time); (*Mus.*) interligne, *m.;* (*Print.*) espace, *f.* *Blank space,* blanc, *m.; that takes up space,* cela prend de la place; *the limited space at our disposal,* le peu d'espace dont nous disposons. —*v.t.* (*Print.*) Espacer. **space-ship,** *n.* Astronef, *m.* **space-travel,** *n.* Astronautique, *f.,* voyages interplanétaires, *m.pl.* **space-traveller,** *n.* Astronaute, *m.*

spaced, *a.* Espacé. *Close spaced,* (*Print.*) aux espaces fines. **space-line,** *n.* Interligne, *m.* **spacing,** *n.* Espacement, *m.;* (*Print.*) interligne, *m.* *Double spacing,* à double interligne.

spacious [ˈspeiʃəs], *a.* Spacieux, d'une grande étendue, vaste. **spaciously,** *adv.* Spacieusement; amplement. **spaciousness,** *n.* Vaste étendue, grandeur, *f.*

spade [speid], *n.* Bêche, (child's) pelle, *f.;* (*Cards*) pique, *m.* *To call a spade a spade,* appeler un chat un chat *or* les choses par leur nom; *to dig with a spade,* bêcher. **spadeful,** *n.* Pelletée, *f.* **spade-work,** *n.* (*fig.*) Travaux préliminaires, *m.pl.*

spadille [spəˈdil], *n.* Spadille, *m.;* as de pique, *m.*

spaghetti [spəˈgeti], *n.* Spaghetti, *m.pl.*

spahee or **spahi** [ˈspɑːhiː], *n.* Spahi, *m.*

Spain [spein]. L'Espagne, *f.*

span [spæn], *n.* Empan, *m.;* envergure (of wings); corde (of an arc); (*Arch.*) ouverture; paire (of oxen etc.); portée, *f.;* instant (short space of time), *m. Short span,* courte durée, *f.*—*v.t.* Mesurer; embrasser; traverser (to cross); (*Naut.*) brider. *A bridge spans the river,* un pont traverse la rivière; *his career spans half a century,* sa carrière embrasse un demi-siècle.

spandrel [ˈspændrəl], *n.* Naissance (of an arch), *f.;* tympan (of a bridge), *m.*

spangle [ˈspæŋgl], *n.* Paillette, *f.*—*v.t.* Pailleter (de); parsemer *or* orner de paillettes. *The spangled vault,* la voûte étoilée.

Spaniard [ˈspænjəd], *n.* Espagnol, *m.,* Espagnole, *f.*

spaniel [ˈspænjəl], *n.* Épagneul, *m.*

Spanish [ˈspæniʃ], *a.* Espagnol, d'Espagne. *Spanish white,* blanc d'Espagne, *m.; Spanish wines,* vins d'Espagne, *m.pl.; the Spanish Main,* la mer des Antilles, *f.*—*n.* L'espagnol (language), *m.*

spank [spæŋk], *v.t.* Donner la fessée à, fesser.—*n.* Fessée, *f.* **spanker,** *n.* (*slang*) Gros gaillard, *m.;* (*Naut.*) brigantine; (*fam.*) bourde, *f. That's a spanker* (*a lie*), en voilà une bonne.

spanking, *a.* Fort, vigoureux, épatant; rapide (of pace). *To go at a spanking pace,* aller à grands pas, aller bon train.—*n.* Fessée, *f.*

spanner [ˈspænə], *n.* Clef à écrous, *f. To throw*

a spanner in the works (*fam.*), mettre des bâtons dans les roues. **spanner-tight,** *a.* À bloc, à refus.

spar [spɑː], *n.* (*Min.*) Spath, *m.;* perche, *f.,* poteau, *m.;* (*Naut.*) espar, mâtereau, *m.;* (*Box.*) combat d'entraînement; assaut amical, *m.;* (*fig.*) prise de bec, *f.*—*v.i.* Faire un assaut amical (de boxe *or* de paroles); se disputer.

spare [speə], *v.t.* Épargner; ménager, économiser (to economize); se passer de (to do without); donner, céder (to let have); prêter (to lend); accorder, faire grâce de (to remit). *Can you spare me a pound of sugar?* pouvez-vous me céder une livre de sucre? *can you spare the time?* êtes-vous libre? *I have not a moment to spare,* je n'ai pas un moment; *it cannot be spared,* on ne saurait s'en passer; *it was more than we could spare,* c'était plus que nous n'en avions à perdre; *spare the rod and spoil the child,* qui aime bien, châtie bien; *spare your brains,* dispensez-vous de penser; *to have money to spare,* avoir de l'argent de reste *or* de trop; *to spare oneself,* se ménager; *to spare oneself trouble,* s'éviter de la peine; *to spare someone's life,* épargner la vie de quelqu'un; *to spare someone trouble,* épargner de la peine à quelqu'un; *we have enough and to spare,* nous en avons à revendre, nous en avons plus qu'il n'en faut; *we have no time to spare,* nous n'avons pas de temps à perdre. *a.*—Disponible, de reste (superfluous); de loisir, libre (of time); (*Motor.* etc.) de rechange; modique, faible, pauvre (scanty); maigre, chétif, sec (lean). *A tall, spare man,* un grand homme sec, *m.; spare anchor,* ancre de rechange, *f.; spare horse,* cheval de rechange, cheval haut le pied, *m.; spare moments,* moments perdus, *m.pl.; spare of,* économe de, ménager de; *spare parts,* pièces de rechange, *f.pl.; spare room,* chambre d'ami, *f.; spare time,* temps disponible, *m.,* moments perdus, *m.pl.;* loisir, *m.; spare wheel,* roue de rechange, *f.*

sparely, *adv.* Frugalement. *Sparely built,* sec. **spareness,** *n.* Maigreur, *f.*

spare-rib, *n.* Côte de porc, *f.*

sparing, *a.* Économe, ménager, frugal, sobre (de); parcimonieux (parsimonious). *To be sparing with the sugar,* ménager le sucre. **sparingly,** *adv.* Frugalement, avec parcimonie; économiquement; rarement (seldom). *To use sparingly,* ménager. **sparingness,** *n.* Frugalité, épargne, parcimonie, *f.*

spark [spɑːk], *n.* Étincelle, *f.;* (*fig.*) lueur, *f.,* éclair; élégant, petit-maître (a gay fellow), *m. Sparks,* (*Naut. fam.*) le radio, *m.*—*v.i.* Produire des étincelles.—*v.t.* Faire éclater, allumer. **sparking-plug,** *n.* Bougie (d'allumage) *f.*

sparkle, *n.* Étincellement, éclat, *m.;* vivacité (d'esprit), *f.*—*v.i.* Étinceler, scintiller; mousser, pétiller (of beverages). **sparkler,** *n.* (*pop.*) Diamant, *m.* **sparkling,** *a.* Étincelant; mousseux (of beverages).—*n.* Étincellement; pétillement, *m.* **sparklingly,** *adv.* Avec éclat, avec vivacité.

sparling [ˈspɑːliŋ], *n.* (*Ichth.*) Éperlan, *m.*

sparrow [ˈspærou], *n.* Moineau, passereau, *m. Hedge-sparrow,* fauvette d'hiver, mouchet, *m.; house-sparrow,* moineau, (*colloq.*) pierrot, *m.; tree-sparrow,* moineau des campagnes,

friquet, *m.* *sparrow-grass [ASPARAGUS].
sparrow-hawk, *n.* Épervier, *m.*
sparse [spɑːs], *a.* Épars; éparpillé, clairsemé.
sparsely, *adv.* D'une manière éparse, de loin en loin. sparseness, *n.* Rareté, *f.*; éparpillement, *m.*
Sparta ['spɑːtə]. Sparte, *f.* Spartan, *a.* and *n.* Spartiate, *m.*
spasm [spæzm], *n.* Spasme, accès, *m.* *In spasms*, par à-coups. spasmodic [-'mɔdik] or spasmodical, *a.* Spasmodique. spasmodically, *adv.* Par à-coups. spastic, *a.* Spasmodique.—*n.* Paraplégique.
spat (1), *past* and *p.p.* [SPIT].
spat (2) [spæt], *n.* Frai, naissain (des mollusques), *m.*
spat (3) [spæt], *n.* Guêtre de ville, *f.*
spate [speit], *n.* Crue (of river); (*fig.*) affluence, *f.*
spathaceous [spə'θeiʃəs], *a.* (*Bot.*) Spathacé.
spathe [speið], *n.* Spathe, *f.*
spathic ['spæθik], *a.* (*Min.*) Spathique.
spathiform ['spæθifɔːm] or spathose ['spei θous], *a.* Spathiforme; spathique.
spatial ['speiʃəl], *a.* Spatial; de l'espace.
spatter ['spætə], *v.t.* Éclabousser (de). spattering, *n.* Éclaboussure, *f.*
spatula ['spætjulə], *n.* Spatule, *f.* spatulate, *a.* Spatulé.
spavin ['spævin], *n.* Éparvin, *m.* spavined, *a.* Qui a des éparvins.
spawn [spɔːn], *n.* Frai, *m.*; (*fig.*) race, engeance, *f.* *Mushroom spawn*, blanc de champignon, *m.*—*v.i.* Frayer; (*fig.*) naître.—*v.t.* (*fig.*) Engendrer. spawning-ground, *n.* Frayère, *f.* spawning(-time), *n.* Frai, temps du frai, *m.*
speak [spiːk], *v.i.* (*past* spoke, *p.p.* spoken) Parler; s'entretenir, causer (avec); faire un discours, prendre la parole (in public); dire. *It speaks for itself*, cela en dit assez; *N. speaking*, ici N.; *nothing worth speaking of*, rien d'importance; *so to speak*, pour ainsi dire; *speaking for myself*, pour ma part; *speaking of that*, à propos; *that speaks well for him*, cela lui fait honneur; *to speak highly of*, dire du bien de, faire l'éloge de; *to speak ill of*, dire du mal de; *to speak out*, parler fort, parler à haute voix; *to speak up*, parler plus fort, parler hardiment; *to speak up for*, parler en faveur de, parler hautement pour.—*v.t.* Parler; dire; prononcer (to pronounce); exprimer (to express); (*Naut.*) héler. *French spoken here*, ici on parle français; *ships spoken*, vaisseaux hélés *or* arraisonnés; *to his shame be it spoken*, soit dit à sa honte; *to speak a language*, parler une langue; *to speak English*, parler anglais; *to speak one's mind*, dire sa pensée; *to speak the truth*, dire la vérité.
speak-easy, *n.* (*pop.*) Bar clandestin, *m.*
speaker, *n.* Personne qui parle, *f.*; orateur; interlocuteur (in a dialogue); (*Parl.*) président (de la Chambre des Communes); (*Rad.* =loud-speaker), haut-parleur, *m.* *The previous speaker*, le préopinant.
speaking, *n.* Action de parler; parole, *f.*, langage, discours, *m.* *Public speaking*, éloquence, *f.*—*a.* Parlant, qui parle. *To be on speaking terms*, se connaître un peu, se parler.
speaking-trumpet, *n.* Porte-voix, *m.*
speaking-tube, *n.* Tuyau (*or* tube) acoustique, *m.*

spear [spiə], *n.* Lance; foène, fouine, *f.*, trident (for fish); épieu (for hunting), *m.*; tige, *f.*; brin, *m.*—*v.t.* Percer *or* tuer d'un coup de lance *or* d'un coup d'épieu; prendre à la fouine, harponner (fish etc.).—*v.i.* Se dresser; s'élancer; pousser.
spear-grass, *n.* Chiendent, *m.* spear-head, *n.* Fer de lance, *m.*; (*Mil.*) avancée, pointe, *f.*
spearman, *n.* Lancier, *m.* spearmint, *n.* Menthe verte, *f.* spearwort, *n.* Douve, renoncule, *f.*
spec (*colloq.*) [SPECULATION].
special [speʃl], *a.* Spécial, exprès; particulier (of correspondence etc.); extraordinaire (extraordinary). *In a special case*, dans un cas particulier; *nothing special*, rien de particulier; *special constable*, constable spécial, *m.*—*n.* (*pop.*) Train spécial, *m.*
specialist ['speʃəlist], *n.* Spécialiste, *m.* speciality [-i'æliti] or specialty ['speʃəlti], *n.* Spécialité, *f.* specialization [-ai'zeiʃən], *n.* Spécialisation, *f.*
specialize ['speʃəlaiz], *v.t.* Spécialiser.—*v.i.* Se spécialiser. specially, *adv.* Particulièrement, spécialement, surtout.
specie ['spiːʃi], *n.* Espèces, *f.pl.*, numéraire, *m.*
species ['spiːʃiːz], *n.* Espèce, *f.*; (*fig.*) genre, *m.*, sorte; (*fig.*) image, apparence (appearance), *f.* *The origin of species*, l'origine des espèces, *f.*
specific [spi'sifik], *a.* Spécifique; précis. *Specific gravity*, poids spécifique, *m.* specifically, *adv.* Spécifiquement; précisément.
specification [spesifi'keiʃən], *n.* Spécification, *f.*, mémoire descriptif, *m.*; stipulation (thing specified); description précise (of a patent), *f.*; devis descriptif, *m.*; (*pl.*) cahier des charges (tender), *m.*
specify ['spesifai], *v.t.* Spécifier, déterminer; fixer d'avance (of time). *Kindly specify the time*, ayez la bonté de fixer l'heure.
specimen ['spesimən], *n.* Spécimen, modèle, échantillon, *m.* *Specimen copy*, livre à l'examen, *m.*; (*fam.*) *queer specimen*, drôle de particulier, *m.*
specious ['spiːʃəs], *a.* Spécieux, trompeur, captieux. speciously, *adv.* Spécieusement. speciousness, *n.* Spéciosité, apparence plausible, *f.*
speck [spek], *n.* Petite tache, marque, *f.*, point; grain (of dust), *m.*—*v.t.* Tacher, marquer.
speckle [spekl], *v.t.* Tacheter, marqueter, moucheter (de).—*n.* Petite tache; moucheture, grivelure (on animals), *f.* speckled, *a.* Tacheté, marqueté, moucheté; grivelé (plumage).
spectacle ['spektəkl], *n.* Spectacle, *m.*; (*pl.*) lunettes, *f.pl.* spectacle-case, *n.* Étui à lunettes, *m.* spectacle-glasses, *n.pl.* Verres de lunettes, *m.pl.* spectacle-maker, *n.* Lunetier, *m.*
spectacled, *a.* Qui porte des lunettes; à lunettes.
spectacular [-'tækjulə], *a.* Théâtral, de spectacle, impressionnant.
spectator [spek'teitə], *n.* Spectateur, *m.*, spectatrice, *f.*; (*pl.*) assistants, témoins, *m.pl.*
spectral ['spektrəl], *a.* De spectre, spectral.
spectre ['spektə], *n.* Spectre, fantôme, *m.*
spectroscope ['spektrəskoup], *n.* Spectroscope, *m.*

spectrum ['spektrəm], *n.* (*pl.* **spectra**)
Spectre, *m.* *Spectrum analysis*, analyse
spectrale, *f.*; *the colours of the spectrum*, les
couleurs spectrales, *f.pl.*
specular ['spekjulə], *a.* Spéculaire.
speculate ['spekjuleit], *v.t.* and *v.i.* Spéculer
(sur), méditer (sur). **speculation** [-'leiʃən],
n. Spéculation, méditation, contemplation,
réflexion, *f.* (*fam.*) *A good spec*, une bonne
affaire, *f.*; *I came to see you on spec*, je suis
venu vous voir à tout hasard. **speculative**,
a. Spéculatif, contemplatif, conjectural;
(*Comm.*) spéculateur; de spéculation (of
things). **speculatively**, *adv.* En théorie;
théoriquement; par spéculation. **speculator**,
n. Spéculateur, *m.*
speculum ['spekjuləm], *n.* (*pl.* **specula**)
Miroir (of telescope); (*Surg.*) speculum, *m.*
sped, *past* and *p.p.* [SPEED].
speech [spiːtʃ], *n.* Parole, *f.*; discours, *m.*,
harangue, allocution (oration); langue (language), *f.*; paroles (talk), *f.pl.*, propos, *m.pl.*;
plaidoyer (of a barrister), *m.* *Extempore
speech*, improvisation, *f.*; *figure of speech*,
figure de rhétorique, *f.*; *indirect or reported
speech* (*Gram.*), style indirect, *m.*; (*Parl.*)
maiden speech, discours de début, *m.*; *such
speech is improper*, de telles paroles sont
indécentes; *the parts of speech*, les parties du
discours, *f.pl.*; *to be slow of speech*, parler
lentement; *to make a speech*, faire un discours.
speech-day, *n.* (*sch.*) Distribution des prix, *f.*
speechifier, *n.* Péroreur, faiseur de beaux
discours, *m.* **speechify**, *v.i.* Pérorer, faire
de beaux discours. **speechifying**, *n.* Beaux
discours, *m.pl.* *To be fond of speechifying*,
aimer à pérorer.
speechless, *a.* Privé de la parole, sans voix;
muet, interdit. *To be rendered speechless*,
perdre la parole; *to be speechless*, avoir perdu
la parole; *to stand speechless*, rester interloqué. **speechlessness**, *n.* Mutisme, *m.*
speed [spiːd], *n.* Vitesse, rapidité, célérité;
hâte, diligence, promptitude, *f.*; (*fig.*) succès,
m., réussite (success), *f.* *At full or top speed*,
à franc étrier, à bride abattue (on horseback),
à toutes jambes (of persons), à toute vapeur
(of trains), à toutes voiles (of sailing vessels),
à tire d'aile (of birds), à toute vitesse (of
vehicles); *car with four-speed gears*, voiture à
quatre vitesses, *f.*; *God-speed!* bon succès!
bonne chance! *more haste less speed*, qui trop
se hâte, reste en chemin; *with all possible
speed*, au plus vite.—*v.t.* (*past* and *p.p.* **sped**)
Faire partir à la hâte, expédier, hâter; faire
prospérer, faire réussir (to prosper). *God
speed you*, Dieu vous garde! *to speed the
parting guest*, souhaiter 'bon voyage' à l'hôte
qui part.—*v.i.* Se hâter, se dépêcher; réussir,
prospérer (to succeed); être, se trouver, aller
(to fare). *To be fined for speeding*, avoir une
amende pour excès de vitesse; *to speed up*,
accélérer. **speed-boat**, *n.* Motoglisseur, *m.*;
hors-bord, *m.inv.* **speed-cop**, *n.* (*pop.*) Ange
de la route, *m.* **speed-hog**, *n.* (*pop.*)
Chauffard, *m.* **speed-indicator** [SPEEDO-
METER].
speedily, *adv.* Vite, promptement, en toute
hâte. **speediness**, *n.* Célérité, promptitude;
hâte, diligence, *f.*
speed-limit, *n.* Limitation de vitesse, *f.*
speedometer [spiː'dɔmitə], *n.* Indicateur de

vitesse, tachymètre, *m.* **speedway**, *n.*
Autostrade, *f.* **speedwell**, *n.* (*Bot.*)
Véronique, *f.* **speedy**, *a.* Rapide, vite,
prompt, expéditif.
spelaean, **spelean** [spiː'liːən], *a.* Des
cavernes; en forme de caverne. **speleologist**, *n.* Spéléologue, *m.* **speleology**,
spelaeology [spiːli'ɔlədʒi], *n.* Spéléologie,
f.
spell (1) [spel], *n.* Charme; temps, intervalle,
m., période (period), *f.*; tour (turn of work),
m. *Cold spell*, coup de froid, *m.*; *to break a
spell*, rompre un charme; *to cast a spell upon*,
jeter un sort sur, ensorceler; *to take a spell at*,
prendre son tour à.
spell (2) [spel], *v.t.* (*past* and *p.p.* **spelt**) Épeler
(to name the letters); orthographier, écrire
(to write with the proper letters); signifier.
How do you spell that? Comment cela s'écrit-
il? *this spells ruin*, c'est la ruine complète; *to
learn to spell*, apprendre l'orthographe; *to
spell in full*, écrire en toutes lettres; *to spell
out*, déchiffrer, lire.—*v.i.* Épeler; orthographier correctement, écrire correctement.
To spell badly, faire des fautes d'orthographe.
spell-binder, *n.* (*fam.*) Fascinateur, orateur
entraînant, *m.*
spell-bound, *a.* Sous le charme, charmé,
fasciné. **speller**, *n.* Personne qui épèle, *f.*
To be a bad speller, ne pas savoir l'orthographe. **spelling**, *n.* Épellation, orthographe, *f.* **spelling-bee**, *n.* Concours
orthographique, *m.* **spelling-book**, *n.*
Abécédaire, syllabaire, *m.* **spelt**, *a.* Épelé.
Spelt in full, écrit en toutes lettres.
spelter ['speltə], *n.* Zinc, *m.*
spencer ['spensə], *n.* (*Cost.*) Spencer, *m.*
spend [spend], *v.t.* (*past* and *p.p.* **spent**) Dépenser, prodiguer, gaspiller, perdre, dissiper
(to waste); passer (time); casser (a mast). *The
bullet had spent its force*, la balle avait perdu
sa force; *to spend money on*, dépenser son
argent à; *to spend one's time reading*, passer
son temps à lire.—*v.i.* Dépenser, faire de la
dépense; se perdre (to be lost); se consumer,
s'épuiser (to be consumed).
spender, *n.* Dépensier, *m.*, dépensière, *f.*
spending, *n.* Action de dépenser, dépense, *f.*
spendthrift, *n.* Prodigue, dissipateur, *m.*
spent, *a.* Épuisé; mort (of bullets etc.); brûlé
(of cartridges); cassé (of masts).
sperm [spəːm], *n.* Sperme; frai (of fish etc.);
blanc de baleine, *m.* **sperm-oil**, *n.* Huile de
spermaceti, *f.* **sperm-whale**, *n.* Cachalot,
m.
spermaceti [spəːmə'seti], *n.* Blanc de baleine,
m. **spermatheca** [-'θiːkə], *n.* Spermathèque, spermatothèque, *f.* **spermatic** [-'mætik],
a. Spermatique. **spermatogenesis**
[-tə'dʒenisis], *n.* Spermatogénèse, *f.* **spermatology** [-mæ'tɔlədʒi], *n.* Spermatologie, *f.*
spermatozoon [-mətə'zouən], *n.* Spermatozoïde, spermatozoaire, *m.*
spew [spjuː], *v.t.* Vomir, rejeter.—*v.i.* Vomir.
spewing, *n.* Vomissement, *m.*
sphacelate ['sfæsileit], *a.* Sphacélé. **sphacelus**, *n.* Sphacèle, *m.*
sphenoid ['sfiːnɔid], *a.* and *n.* Sphénoïde, *m.*
sphenoidal [-'nɔidl], *a.* Sphénoïdal.
sphere [sfiə], *n.* Sphère, *f.* *Limited sphere*,
cadre limité, *m.*; *sphere of influence*, zone
d'influence, *f.*—*v.t.* Arrondir en sphère.

spherical ['sferikl], *a.* Sphérique. **spheri-cally**, *adv.* Sphériquement. **sphericity** [sfe'risiti], *n.* Sphéricité, *f.* **spherics**, *n.pl.* Théorie de la sphère, *f.* **spheroid**, *n.* Sphéroïde, *m.* **spheroidal** [sfiə'rɔidl], *a.* Sphéroïdal. **spherometer** [-'rɔmitə], *n.* Sphéromètre, *m.*

sphinx [sfiŋks], *n.* (*pl.* **sphinges** or **sphinxes**) Sphinx, *m.*

sphygmomanometer ['sfigmɔmə'nɔmitə], *n.* (*Med.*) Tensiomètre, *m.*

spica(-bandage) ['spaikə'bændidʒ], *n.* Spica, *m.*

spice [spais], *n.* Épice; (*fig.*) teinte, teinture, nuance (small quantity), *f.*—*v.t.* Épicer (de). **spicery**, *n.* Épices, *f.pl.* **spicily**, *adv.* (*colloq.*) Crânement, fameusement. **spici-ness**, *n.* Goût épicé, goût aromatisé, *m.*; (*colloq.*) piquant, *m.*

spick-and-span ['spikənd'spæn], *a.* Tiré à quatre épingles; bien astiqué, tout flambant neuf.

spicy ['spaidə], *a.* Épicé, aromatique, parfumé (fragrant); fertile en épices; (*colloq.*) piquant, pimenté; salé, grivois (of a story).

spider ['spaidə], *n.* Araignée, *f.* **spider-crab**, *n.* Araignée de mer, *f.* **spider-like**, *a.* D'araignée.—*adv.* Comme une araignée. **spider-monkey**, *n.* Atèle, *m.* **spider's-web**, *n.* Toile d'araignée, *f.* **spidery**, *a.* *Spidery handwriting*, pattes de mouche, *f.pl.*

spigot ['spigət], *n.* Fausset, *m.*; cannelle (of cask), *f.*; (*Am.*) robinet, *m.*

spike [spaik], *n.* Pointe, *f.*; clou à grosse tête (nail), *m.*; cheville (of wood), *f.*; épi (of corn), *m.* *Marline-spike*, épissoir, *m.*—*v.t.* Clouer; armer de pointes, hérisser; enclouer (a cannon). *To spike a gate*, hérisser une grille de pointes; *to spike someone's guns*, damer le pion à quelqu'un.

spiked, *a.* À pointes, garni de pointes, barbelé. *Spiked helmet*, casque à pointe, *m.* **spike-shaped**, *a.* Spiciforme.

spike-lavender, *n.* Spic, *m.*

spikelet, *n.* (*Bot.*) Spicule, *m.*

spikenard ['spaikna:d], *n.* Nard indien, spicanard, *m.*

spiky ['spaiki], *a.* À pointe aiguë; armé de pointes; formaliste (person).

spill [spil], *v.t.* (*past* and *p.p.* **spilt, spilled**) Répandre, verser; perdre; renverser, désarçonner; (*Naut.*) étouffer.—*v.i.* Se verser, se répandre.—*n.* Allumette de papier, allumette en copeau; culbute (upset), *f.* *To have a spill*, verser, culbuter, (*Cycl.*) ramasser une bûche.

spillikin ['spilikin], *n.* Jonchet, *m.*

spin [spin], *v.t.* (*past* **span, spun**, *p.p.* **spun**) Filer; faire tourner, faire aller (a top); tordre (hay). *To spin a coin*, tirer à pile ou face; *to spin a yarn*, débiter une longue histoire; *to spin out*, traîner, tirer en longueur; *to spin out one's money*, ménager son argent. —*v.i.* Filer (move fast); tourner; (*Fish.*) pêcher au lancer *or* à la cuiller. *To spin round*, tourner, tournoyer; patiner (for a wheel).—*n.* Tournoiement; (*Ten., Cricket*) effet (donné à une balle), *m.*; (*Av.*) vrille, *f.*; (*Cycl., Motor.*) tour, *m.*, promenade, *f.* *To get into a flat spin*, (*Av.*) faire le tonneau; (*colloq.*) être complètement débordé.

spinach ['spinidʒ], *n.* Épinards, *m.pl.*

spinal [spainl], *a.* Spinal. *Spinal column*, colonne vertébrale, *f.*; *spinal complaint*, maladie de la moelle épinière, *f.*; *spinal cord* or *spinal marrow*, moelle épinière, *f.*; *spinal curvature*, déviation de la colonne vertébrale, *f.*

spindle [spindl], *n.* Fuseau; pivot, *m.*; fusée (pivot); aiguille (of a compass), *f.*; (*Mach.*) essieu; fer (of a vane); (*Tech.*) axe, *m.*; broche (in spinning-mills etc.), *f.*; (*Measure*) 14.000 mètres, *m.pl.*

spindleful, *n.* Fusée, *f.* **spindle-legs** or **spindle-shanks**, *n.pl.* Jambes de fuseau, *f.pl.*, (*colloq.*) manches à balai, *m.pl.*, baguettes de tambour, *f.pl.* **spindle-shanked**, *a.* À mollets de coq. **spindle-shaped**, *a.* Fusiforme. **spindle-tree**, *n.* Fusain, *m.*

spindrift ['spindrift], *n.* Embrun, *m.*, poussière d'eau, *f.*

spine [spain], *n.* Épine dorsale; épine (thorn), *f.*

spinel [spi'nel], *n.* (*Min.*) Spinelle, *f.*

spineless ['spainlis], *a.* Sans épines; (*fig.*) mou, flasque, invertébré.

spinet ['spinit], *n.* Épinette, *f.*

spiniferous [spai'nifərəs], *a.* Spinifère, épineux.

spininess ['spaininis], *n.* Nature épineuse, *f.*

spinnaker ['spinəkə], *n.* (*Naut.*) Spinnaker, *m.*

spinner ['spinə], *n.* Fileur, *m.*, fileuse, *f.*; filateur (proprietor of spinning-mill), *m.*; (*Fish.*) cuiller, *f.*, poisson artificiel, *m.* *Spinner of yarns*, débiteur d'histoires, *m.*

spinney ['spini], *n.* Petit bois, bosquet, *m.*

spinning ['spinij], *n.* Filage (process), *m.*; fi.ature (art), *f.*; tournoiement, *m.*—*a.* Tournoyant, tournant. *To send someone spinning*, envoyer rouler quelqu'un. **spinning-frame**, *n.* Métier à filer, *m.* **spinning-jenny**, *n.* Métier à filer, *m.*; mule-jenny, *f.* **spinning-machine**, *n.* Machine à filer, *f.* **spinning-mill**, *n.* Filature, *f.* **spinning-rod**, *n.* Canne à lancer, *f.* **spinning-song**, *n.* Chanson de toile, *f.* **spinning-top**, *n.* Toupie, *f.* **spinning-wheel**, *n.* Rouet, *m.*

spinosity [spai'nɔsiti], *n.* Nature épineuse, *f.*

spinous ['spainəs], *a.* Épineux.

Spinozism [spi'nouzizm], *n.* Spinosisme, *m.* **Spinozist**, *n.* Spinosiste, *m.* or *f.* **Spinozistic** [-'zistik], *a.* De tendance spinosiste.

spinster ['spinstə], *n.* Fille, fille non mariée, *f.*

spinsterhood, *n.* Célibat; état de fille, *m.*

spiny ['spaini], *a.* Épineux, couvert d'épines; (*fig.*) difficile.

spiracle ['spaiərəkl], *n.* Évent, *m.*

spiraea [spaiə'ri:ə], *n.* (*Bot.*) Spirée, *f.*

spiral ['spaiərəl], *n.* Spirale, *f.*—*v.i.* Monter en spirale.—*a.* Spiral; hélicoïdal; en colimaçon (of staircases). *The wage-price spiral*, le cycle infernal des salaires et des prix, *m.*

spirally, *adv.* En spirale.

spire ['spaiə], *n.* Aiguille, flèche, *f.* (steeple); pointe, *f.*, sommet (tip), *m.*; tige, *f.* (of grass). —*v.i.* S'élever en flèche. **spired**, *a.* À flèche.

spirit (1) ['spirit], *n.* Esprit, *m.*, âme; (*fig.*) ardeur, force, vigueur, verve, *m.*, feu, élan, entrain, *m.*; fougue (of a horse), *f.*; moral (of troops); esprit, fantôme, spectre (apparition), *m.*; (*fig.*) verve, bonne humeur, *f.*, entrain, courage, *m.* *A man of spirit*, un homme de cœur; *evil spirit*, esprit malfaisant, *m.*; *he is in better spirits now*, il est maintenant de meilleure humeur; *high spirits*, gaîté, *f.*, entrain, *m.*, bonne humeur, *f.*; *in good spirits*, gai, en train; *in high spirits*, plein d'entrain; *kindred* *spirit*, âme sœur, *f.*; *in low spirits*, abattu, accablé; *party spirit*, esprit de parti; *the Holy Spirit*, le Saint Esprit, *m.*; *to enter into the spirit of*, s'adapter à, entrer de bon cœur dans; *to keep up one's spirits*, ne pas perdre courage; *to put someone into good spirits*, égayer quelqu'un, mettre quelqu'un en train; *to raise a spirit*, évoquer un esprit; *to recover one's spirits*, reprendre courage.—*v.t.* Animer, encourager. *To spirit away*, faire disparaître, enlever, escamoter.

spirit (2) ['spirit], *n.* Spiritueux, *m.*; liqueur spiritueuse *or* alcoolique (liquor), *f.*; (*pl.*) esprit (of wine etc.), *m.*; essences (of turpentine etc.), *f.pl.*; les spiritueux (alcoholic liquors), *m.pl.* *Methylated spirit*, alcool à brûler, *m.*; *raw spirits*, liqueurs pures, *f.pl.* **spirit-lamp,** *n.* Lampe à alcool, *f.* **spirit-level,** *n.* Niveau à bulle d'air, *m.* **spirit-room,** *n.* (*Naut.*) Cale à vin, *f.* **spirit-trade,** *n.* Commerce des spiritueux, *m.* **spirit-vaults,** *n.pl.* Débit de spiritueux, *m.*

spirited, *a.* Animé, plein de cœur, plein de vivacité; vif, plein de verve; fougueux, ardent (of horses). *Bold-spirited*, hardi; *high-spirited*, plein de courage, ardent, fougueux, fier; *low-spirited*, abattu, dans l'abattement; *mean-spirited*, bas, mesquin; *poor-spirited*, sans cœur, sans caractère, lâche. **spiritedly,** *adv.* Avec ardeur, chaleureusement, avec force, avec entrain. **spiritedness,** *n.* Feu, *m.*, ardeur, *f.*, entrain, *m.*, verve, fougue (of horses), *f.*

spiritless ['spiritlis], *a.* Sans vigueur, sans ardeur, sans force, mou, énervé; sans courage (without courage); sans verve (of speech); abattu (dejected). **spiritlessly,** *a.* Sans vie, mollement, sans courage.

spirit-rapper, *n.* Médium, *m.* **spirit-rapping,** *n.* Spiritisme, *m.*

spiritual ['spiritjuəl], *a.* Spirituel.—*n.* Chant religieux (des nègres), *m.* **spiritualism** or **spiritism,** *n.* Spiritisme (spirit-rapping); (*Phil.*) spiritualisme, *m.* **spiritualist** or **spiritist,** *n.* Spirite (spirit-rapper); (*Phil.*) spiritualiste, *m.* **spiritualistic** [-'listik], *a.* Spiritiste. **spirituality** [-ju'æliti], *n.* Spiritualité, *f.*, spirituel, *m.* **spiritualization** [-juəlai'zeiʃən], *n.* Spiritualisation, *f.* **spiritualize** ['spiritjuəlaiz], *v.t.* Spiritualiser. **spiritually,** *adv.* Spirituellement.

spirituous ['spiritjuəs], *a.* Spiritueux.

spirometer [spaiə'rɔmitə], *n.* Spiromètre, *m.*

spirt [SPURT].

spiry ['spaiəri], *a.* En flèche, élancé.

spit (1) [spit], *n.* Broche; profondeur de bêche (depth of earth pierced by the spade), *f.*; (*Geog.*) cap, *m.* *To put upon the spit*, mettre à la broche.—*v.t.* (*past* and *p.p.* **spitted**) Embrocher, mettre à la broche.

spit (2) [spit], *n.* Crachat, *m.*, salive, *f.* (saliva). *He is the very spit of his father*, c'est son père tout craché. (*Mil. slang*) *Spit and polish*, astiquage, *m.*—*v.t.* (*past* and *p.p.* **spat**) Cracher.—*v.i.* Cracher (sur *or* à). *To spit in someone's face*, cracher au visage de quelqu'un; *to spit out*, cracher; *to spit upon*, traiter avec mépris.

spite [spait], *n.* Dépit, *m.*; rancune, malveillance, *f. In spite of*, en dépit de, malgré; *out of spite*, par dépit; *to have a spite against*,

garder rancune à, en vouloir à, avoir une dent contre.—*v.t.* Vexer, blesser, contrarier.

spiteful, *a.* Plein de rancune, rancunier, malveillant, vindicatif; méchant (of animals). **spitefully,** *adv.* Par dépit, par rancune, par méchanceté. **spitefulness,** *n.*, Dépit, *m.*, rancune, méchanceté, *f.*

spitfire ['spitfaiə], *n.* Rageur, *m.*, -euse, *f.*

spitter ['spitə], *n.* Cracheur, *m.*, cracheuse, *f.* **spitting,** *n.* Crachement, *m.* **spittle,** *n.* Salive, *f.*; (*colloq.*) crachat, *m.*

spittoon [spi'tuːn], *n.* Crachoir, *m.*

spiv [spiv], *n.* (*pej.*) Profiteur, trafiquant de marché noir, *m.*

splanchnic ['splæŋknik], *a.* Splanchnique. **splanchnology** [-'nɔlədʒi], *n.* Splanchnologie, *f.*

splash [splæʃ], *v.t.* Éclabousser. *To splash one's money about*, prodiguer son argent.—*v.i.* Éclabousser; clapoter (of waves); patauger, battre l'eau; faire flac. *Splashed all over*, tout couvert d'éclaboussures.—*n.* Éclaboussure, *f.*; clapotement, clapotis (of waves), *m.*; plouf, flac, *m.* (noise); (*fig.*) parade, esbroufe (swank), *f.* *To make a splash*, (*fam.*) faire sensation.

splash-board or **splasher,** *n.* Garde-boue, *m.* **splashing,** *n.* Éclaboussement (act of splashing), *m.*; éclaboussure (the result), *f.* **splashy,** *a.* Éclaboussé, bourbeux.

splay [splei], *v.t.* Évaser; (*Arch.*) ébraser; épauler (a horse).—*n.* Écartement; (*Arch.*) ébrasement, *m.* **splay-footed,** *a.* Aux pieds plats et tournés en dehors.

spleen [spliːn], *n.* Rate, *f.*; (*fig.*) fiel, *m.*, animosité, bile, *f.*; spleen, *m.*, mélancolie, humeur noire, *f.* (melancholy).

spleenful, spleenish, or **spleeny,** *a.* Irritable, atrabilaire.

spleenwort, *n.* Doradille (fern), *f.*

splendid ['splendid], *a.* Resplendissant, éclatant, somptueux, magnifique. **splendidly,** *adv.* Avec éclat, somptueusement, magnifiquement. **splendiferous** [-'difərəs], *a.* (*colloq.*) Épatant. **splendour,** *n.* Splendeur, magnificence, *f.*, éclat, *m.*

splenetic [spli'netik], *a.* Splénétique, atrabilaire.

splenic ['splenik], *a.* Splénique.

splenitis [spli:'naitis], *n.* Splénite, *f.* **splenization** [-ni'zeiʃən], *n.* Splénification, splénisation, *f.* **splenology** [-'nɔlədʒi], *n.* Splénologie, *f.* **splenotomy** [-'nɔtəmi], *n.* Splénotomie, *f.*

splice [splais], *n.* Épissure, *f.*, raccordement, *m.*—*v.t.* Épisser; (*Carp.*) joindre. *Nylon spliced* (of yarn), nylon renforcé; *to get spliced*, (*colloq.*) se marier; *to splice the main-brace* (*Naut.*, *colloq.*), boire un coup. **splicing-fid,** *n.* (*Naut.*) Épissoir, *m.*

spline [splain], *n.* Languette; cannelure, *f.*—*v.t.* Claveter; canneler.

splint [splint], *n.* Éclisse, attelle, *f.*; (*Vet.*) suros, *m.*—*v.t.* Éclisser.

splinter ['splintə], *v.t.* Faire éclater, briser en éclats.—*v.i.* Éclater, voler en éclats.—*n.* Éclat, éclat de bois, *m.*; (in the hand) écharde, *f.*; (*Surg.*) esquille (of bone), *f.* (*Polit.*) *Splinter party*, parti dissident, *m.* **splinter-bar,** *n.* Volée, *f.* **splintery,** *a.* Plein d'éclats, esquilleux.

split [split], *v.t.* (*past* and *p.p.* **split**) Fendre; diviser, partager (to divide); déchirer (cloth etc.). *A splitting headache*, un mal de tête fou; *to split asunder*, fendre en deux; *to split hairs*, épiloguer, couper un cheveu en quatre; *to split into*, diviser en; *to split off*, enlever en fendant, se séparer; *to split one's sides with laughing*, crever de rire; *to split the difference*, couper la poire en deux.—*v.i.* Se fendre, se briser; éclater, se crevasser; se quereller, se brouiller (to quarrel). *To split into*, se fendre en; *to split off*, se détacher, se séparer (de); *to split on someone* (*pop.*), vendre quelqu'un; *to split with laughter*, (*pop.*) crever de rire.—*n.* Fente, fissure, crevasse; (*fig.*) séparation, scission, *f.* (*pl.*) *To do the splits*, faire le grand écart.—*a.* Fendu, refendu. **split peas,** *n.* Pois cassés, *m.pl.* **split personality,** *n.* Dédoublement de la personnalité, *m.* **split-pin,** *n.* Goupille, *f.* **split ring,** *n.* Anneau brisé, *m.* **split-second,** *a.* Ultra-rapide.

splitter, *n.* Fendeur, *m.*, fendeuse, *f.* **splitting,** *n.* Fendage, *m.* *Splitting of the atom*, fission de l'atome, *f.*

splosh [splɔʃ], *n.* [SPLASH].

splotch [splɔtʃ], **splodge,** *n.* Grosse tache, *f.*, barbouillage, *m.*

splurge [splə:dʒ], *v.i.* (*Am. slang*) Esbroufer. —*n.* Esbroufe; épate, *f.*; éclaboussement, *m.*

splutter ['splʌtə], *v.i.* Bredouiller, bafouiller; envoyer des postillons; cracher (of a pen or of fat).—*n.* or **spluttering.** Bredouillement, bafouillement, crachage, *m.*

spoil [spɔil], *v.t.* Gâter, abîmer; dépouiller (de); ravager, dévaster (to plunder). *Spare the rod and spoil the child*, qui aime bien, châtie bien; *to spoil a child*, gâter un enfant; *to spoil sport*, troubler la fête; *to spoil the Egyptians*, dépouiller l'ennemi.—*v.i.* Se gâter, s'abîmer. *To be spoiling for a fight*, brûler de se battre.—*n.* Butin, *m.*, dépouille, *f.*, pillage, *m.*; (*pl.*) dépouilles, *f.pl.*

spoil-bank, *n.* Déblai, dépôt de remblai, *m.*

spoiled, *a.* Gâté. **spoiler,** *n.* Personne qui gâte, *f.*; spoliateur, *m.*, spoliatrice, *f.* (plunderer); (*fig.*) corrupteur, *m.* **spoiling,** *n.* Action de gâter, détérioration, avarie, *f.*

spoil-sport, *n.* Trouble-fête, *m.*

spoke (1) [spouk], *n.* Rais, rayon, *m.* *To put a spoke in someone's wheel*, mettre des bâtons dans les roues à quelqu'un. **spoke-shave,** *n.* (*Carp.*) Plane, *f.*

spoke (2) [spouk] or **spoken** [spoukn], *a.* (*in compounds*) Au parler .... *Ill spoken of*, dont on dit du mal; *soft spoken*, doucereux; *well spoken of*, dont on dit du bien.

spokesman ['spouksmən], *n.* (*pl.* **spokesmen**) **spokeswoman** ['spoukswumən], *n.* (*pl.* **spokeswomen**) Porte-parole, organe, *m.*

spoliate ['spoulieit], *v.t.* Spolier, piller. **spoliation** [-'eiʃən], *n.* Spoliation, *f.* **spoliator** ['spoulieitə], *n.* Spoliateur, *m.*

spondaic [spɔn'deiik], *a.* Spondaïque.

spondee ['spɔndi:], *n.* Spondée, *m.*

spondyl ['spɔndil], *n.* Spondyle, *m.* **spondylitis** [-'laitis], *n.* Spondylite, *f.*

sponge [spʌndʒ], *n.* Éponge, *f.*; (*Artill.*) écouvillon, *m.* *To throw up the sponge*, s'avouer vaincu.—*v.t.* Éponger; (*Artill.*) écouvillonner; décatir (cloth). *To sponge*

out, effacer; *to sponge up*, éponger.—*v.i.* Boire; écornifler. *To sponge on*, vivre aux dépens de.

sponge-bag, *n.* Sac à éponge, *m.* **sponge-bath,** *n.* Tub, *m.* **sponge-biscuit,** *n.* Biscuit à la cuiller, *m.* **sponge-cake,** *n.* Gâteau de Savoie, *m.* **sponger,** *n.* Pique-assiette, écornifleur, parasite, *m.* **sponginess,** *n.* Nature spongieuse, *f.* **sponging,** *n.* Épongement; (*Artill.*) écouvillonnement, *m.*; (*fig.*) écorniflerie, *f.* *sponging-house,** *n.* Prison provisoire (pour dettes), *f.*

spongoid ['spʌŋgɔid], *a.* Spongoïde.

spongy ['spʌndʒi], *a.* Spongieux.

sponsor ['spɔnsə], *n.* Parrain, *m.*, marraine, *f.*; garant, rèpondant (surety); initiateur, promoteur, champion (d'une doctrine), *m.* —*v.t.* Répondre pour, prendre en charge; parrainer. **sponsorship,** *n.* Parrainage, *m.*

spontaneity [spɔntə'ni:iti], *n.* Spontanéité, *f.* **spontaneous** [-'teiniəs], *a.* Spontané. **spontaneously,** *adv.* Spontanément. **spontaneousness,** *n.* Spontanéité, *f.*

spontoon [spɔn'tu:n], *n.* Esponton, *m.*

spoof [spu:f], *n.* Attrape, mystification, *f.*; canard, *m.*

spook [spu:k], *n.* Fantôme, spectre, *m.* **spooky,** *a.* Hanté; de spectres; spectral.

spool [spu:l], *n.* Bobine, *f.*; tambour (of fishing-reel), *m.*—*v.t.* Bobiner.

spoon [spu:n], *n.* Cuiller, cuillère, *f.*; niais, sot (simpleton), *m.* *Dessert-spoon*, cuiller à dessert, *f.*; *salt-spoon*, cuiller à sel, *f.*; *spoon and fork*, couvert, *m.*; *table-spoon*, cuiller à bouche *or* cuiller à soupe, *f.*; *tea-spoon*, cuiller à thé, *f.*; *to be born with a silver spoon in one's mouth*, être né coiffé.—*v.i.* (*slang*) Faire des mamours.

spoonbill, *n.* Palette, *f.*

spoonerism, *n.* Contrepetterie, *f.*

spoon-fed, *a.* Nourri à la cuillère; (*fig.*) à qui on mâche la besogne.

spoonful, *n.* Cuillerée, *f.*

spoony, *a.* *Nigaud, sot.—a.* Amoureux (de), épris (de).

spoor [spuə], *n.* Trace, piste, *f.*, foulées, empreintes, *f.pl.*

sporadic [spə'rædik], *a.* Sporadique. **sporadically,** *adv.* Sporadiquement.

spore [spɔ:], *n.* Spore, *f.* **spore-case,** *n.* Sporange, *m.* **sporule,** *n.* Sporule, *f.* **sporulation,** *n.* Sporulation, *f.*

sport [spɔ:t], *n.* Jeu, divertissement, amusement, *m.*; moquerie, raillerie (mockery), *f.*; jouet (plaything), *m.*; chasse (hunting and shooting); pêche (fishing), *f.*; sport, *m.* *Field sports*, la chasse et la pêche, *f.*; *good sport*, bonne chasse (of game), bonne pêche *or* prise (of fish), *f.*; *in sport*, par plaisanterie; *sports car*, voiture de course, *f.*; *sports coat*, veston de sport, *m.*; *the sport of kings*, les courses de chevaux, *f.pl.*; *to be a* (*good*) *sport* (person), être un chic type; *to be the sport of*, être le jouet de; *to make sport of*, s'amuser de, se jouer de; *to spoil sport*, troubler la fête.—*v.t.* Étaler, faire parade de.—*v.i.* Se divertir, s'amuser, folâtrer (de). *To sport with*, se jouer de.

sporting, *a.* De sport; sportif. **sporting-dog,** *n.* Chien de chasse, *m.* **sporting-gun,** *n.* Fusil de chasse, *m.* **sportive,** *a.* Badin, folâtre, amusant. **sportively,** *adv.* En badinant, en plaisantant. **sportiveness,** *n.* Folâtrerie, *f.*

sportsman, *n.* (*pl.* **sportsmen**) Chasseur *or* pêcheur, amateur de sport, sportif, sportsman, *m.* **sportsmanlike,** *a.* Digne d'un sportsman. **sportsmanship,** *n.* Sportivité, *f.*

spot [spɔt], *n.* Tache; souillure (stain on character etc.), *f.*; endroit, lieu (place), *m.*, place, *f.*; coin (of ground), *m.*; (*colloq.*) morceau (food), *m. Dead on the spot,* raide mort; *on the spot,* sur place, sur-le-champ (immediately); (*St. Exch.*) *spot market,* marché du disponible, *m.*; *spot of trouble,* petit ennui, *m.*; (*fam.*) *to be in a spot,* être dans le pétrin; *to be killed on the spot,* être tué sur le coup; *to knock spots off,* battre à plate couture.—*v.t.* Tacheter, moucheter; tacher, souiller (to blemish); repérer. *I spotted him,* (*colloq.*) je l'ai bien reconnu. **spot-check,** *n.* Contrôle-surprise, *m.* **spotlight,** *n.* Feu de projecteur, spot, *m.* **spot-welding,** *n.* Soudure par points, *f.*

spotless, *a.* Sans tache; (*fig.*) immaculé, pur, irréprochable. **spotlessness,** *n.* Pureté, *f.* **spotted,** *a.* Tacheté, moucheté; truité, à pois. **spottedness,** *n.* Tacheture, moucheture, *f.* **spotter,** *n.* (*Mil. Av.*) Observateur, *m.* **spotty,** *a.* Couvert de taches, moucheté, tacheté.

spouse [spauz], *n.* Époux, *m.*, épouse, *f.*; mari, *m.*, femme, *f.* **spouseless,** *a.* Sans époux, sans épouse.

spout [spaut], *n.* Tuyau, tuyau de décharge, *m.*; gouttière (of a house), *f.*; bec (of a pitcher etc.), *m.* (*pop.*) *Up the spout* (in pawn), en gage, chez ma tante, au clou.—*v.i.* Jaillir, rejaillir, s'élancer; déclamer, faire des phrases, pérorer (to declaim).—*v.t.* Lancer, jeter; déclamer (to declaim). **spout-hole,** *n.* Évent, *m.* (of whale).

spouter, *n.* Déclamateur, péroreur, *m.* **spouting,** *n.* Jaillissement, *m.*, déclamation, *f.*

sprag [spræg], *n.* Cale, *f.*—*v.t.* Caler, enrayer (a wheel).

sprain [sprein], *n.* Entorse, foulure, *f.*—*v.t.* Donner une entorse à, fouler; se donner une entorse à. *He has sprained his ankle,* il s'est donné une entorse à la cheville; *I have sprained my wrist,* je me suis foulé le poignet.

sprang, *past* [SPRING].

sprat [spræt], *n.* Esprot, sprat, *m. To throw a sprat to catch a mackerel,* donner un œuf pour avoir un bœuf.

sprawl [sprɔːl], *v.i.* S'étendre, s'étaler; s'agiter, se débattre. *To lie sprawling,* être étendu de tout son long; *to send someone sprawling,* étendre quelqu'un à terre (de tout son long).

spray [sprei], *n.* Branche, *f.*, brin, *m.*, brindille, ramille (twig), *f.*; embrun, *m.*; poussière (of water), *f.*; pulvérin; vaporisateur, *m.*—*v.t.* Pulvériser, vaporiser; asperger, arroser. **spray-gun,** *n.* Pistolet, *m.*

sprayer, *n.* Vaporisateur, extincteur, *m.*

spread [spred], *v.t.* (*past* and *p.p.* **spread**) Étendre, déployer; répandre, propager (to propagate); couvrir (a table); mettre (a cloth); dresser (a tent); tendre (sails etc.); épandre (manure etc.). *To spread abroad,* répandre au loin; *to spread oneself,* se pavaner; *to spread out,* étendre, étaler; *to spread*

over, répandre sur; *to spread the report of,* répandre, faire courir, *or* propager le bruit de; *to spread the table,* mettre le couvert.—*v.i.* S'étendre, se déployer; se répandre, se propager (to be propagated). *To spread forth,* se dérouler, se déployer, s'écarter s'égailler; *to spread over,* s'étendre sur.—*n.* Étendue, *f.,* développement, *m.,* expansion (expansion), *f.*; empennage (of wings or planes), *m.*; envergure, *f.* (of wings); propagation, *f.,* progrès; régal, festin (feast), *m. Middle-age spread,* embonpoint, *m.,* rotondité de la cinquantaine, *f.*; *to give a spread,* traiter.

spread-eagle, *n.* (*Her.*) Aigle éployée, *f.* **spread-eagled,** *a.* (*fam.*) Vautré, étalé. **spreader,** *n.* Propagateur, débiteur (of news etc.); (*Hort.*) épandeur, *m.*

spreading, *n.* Propagation, extension, *f.*; étendage, *m.*—*a.* Étendu, qui s'étend, qui se répand.

spree [spriː], *n.* (*colloq.*) Bamboche, bombe, *f. To be out on the spree,* faire la noce; (*Naut.*) être en bordée; *to have a spree,* rigoler, faire la noce.

sprig [sprig], *n.* Brin, *m.,* brindille, pointe (nail); branche (in embroidery), *f.*; (*fig.*) rejeton, *m.*

spright [SPRITE].

sprightliness ['spraitlinis], *n.* Vivacité, *f.,* entrain, *m.* **sprightly,** *a.* Enjoué, vif, animé, gai.

spring [spriŋ], *v.i.* (*past* **sprang,** *p.p.* **sprung**) Bondir, s'élancer; jaillir, rejaillir (to spurt out); pousser, naître (to begin to grow); paraître, poindre (of the day); sortir, provenir, venir, découler, descendre (to be descended); se déjeter (to warp); (*Hunt.*) lever; consentir (of a mast). *To spring at,* s'élancer à, sauter à la gorge à; *to spring back,* s'élancer en arrière, reculer, faire recul (of a gun), faire ressort (of things); *to spring forth,* pousser, jaillir, naître, surgir; *to spring forward,* s'élancer en avant; *to spring from,* sortir de, naître de, provenir de, avoir sa source dans; *to spring out,* s'élancer au dehors; *to spring over,* sauter, franchir; *to spring up,* se lever précipitamment, s'élever, pousser (to grow); grandir (of young persons).

v.t.—Faire lever (game-birds etc.); faire jouer (to cause to explode); (*Naut.*) faire une voie d'eau (a leak); faire consentir (a mast). *To spring upon,* présenter à l'improviste . . .à. *n.*—Saut, bond, élan (leap), *m.*; élasticité (elasticity), *f.*; ressort (resilience), *m.*; source (source); cause, origine (cause), *f.*; printemps (season), *m.*; (*Arch.*) naissance (of an arch); (*Naut.*) embossure (cable), *f.* (*pl.*) Suspension, *f.* (of car); mobiles, *m.pl.* (of action). *Hot spring,* source d'eau chaude, (*pl.*) station thermale, *f.*; *in the spring,* au printemps; *main-spring,* grand ressort, *m.*; *spring day,* jour de printemps, *m.*; *springs with pump action,* ressorts à pompe, *m.pl.*; *to take a spring,* prendre son élan; *trigger-spring,* ressort-gâchette, *m.*; *with a spring,* d'un bond.

spring-balance, *n.* Balance à ressort, *f.* **spring-blind,** *n.* Store, *m.* **spring-board,** *n.* Tremplin, *m.* **spring-box,** *n.* Barillet, *m.* **spring-cart,** *n.* Voiture suspendue, *f.* **spring-cleaning,** *n.* Grand nettoyage (au printemps), *m.* **springer,** *n.* (*Arch.*) Naissance (of an arch), *f.* **springiness,** *n.*

Élasticité, *f.* **springing**, *n.* Action de s'élancer; élasticité, *f.*; jaillissement (spurting up); croissement (growing up), *m.*; (*Arch.*) naissance (de voûte), *f.* **springing-line**, *n.* (*Arch.*) Ligne de naissance, *f.* **springlike**, *a.* Printanier. **springy**, *a.* Élastique.

springbok ['spriŋbɔk], *n.* Springbok, *m.*, gazelle africaine, *f.*

springe [sprindʒ], *n.* Lacet, *m.*, lacs, *m.pl.* (for birds).—*v.t.* Prendre au lacet.

spring-grass, *n.* Flouve, *f.* **spring-gun**, *n.* Piège à fusil, *m.* **spring-head**, *n.* Source, *f.* **spring-mattress**, *n.* Sommier élastique, *m.* **spring-tide**, *n.* Grande marée, *f.* **spring-time**, *n.* Printemps, *m.* **spring-water**, *n.* Eau de source, *f.* **spring-wheat**, *n.* Blé de mars, *m.*

sprinkle [spriŋkl], *v.t.* Répandre; arroser (de), asperger (de) (with holy water); parsemer, saupoudrer (de). *Sprinkled with gold*, parsemé d'or; *to sprinkle with salt*, saupoudrer de sel.—*v.i.* Répandre; tomber en pluie fine.

sprinkler, *n.* (*Eccles.*) Aspersoir, *m.*; (*Hort.*) arroseuse à jet tournant, *f.* *Fire sprinkler*, extincteur automatique, *m.*

sprinkling, *n.* Action de répandre, *f.*, arrosage, *m.*; (*Eccles.*) aspersion; (*fig.*) teinture, *f.*, petit nombre, *m.*; petite quantité (small quantity), *f.* *A sprinkling of rain*, quelques gouttes de pluie, *f.pl.*

sprint [sprint], *n.* Pointe de vitesse, *f.*, sprint, *m.*—*v.i.* Courir à toute vitesse. **sprinter**, *n.* Coureur de vitesse, sprinter, *m.* **sprint-race**, *n.* Course de vitesse, *f.*

sprit [sprit], *n.* (*Naut.*) Livarde, *f.* **sprit-sail**, *n.* Voile à livarde, *f.*

sprite [sprait], *n.* Esprit follet, farfadet, lutin, *m.*

sprocket ['sprɔkit], *n.* Dent (de pignon), *f.*

sprout [spraut], *n.* Pousse, *f.*, germe, jet, rejeton, *m.* *Brussels sprouts*, choux de Bruxelles, *m.pl.*—*v.i.* Pousser, germer; bourgeonner (of flowering plants).

sprouting, *n.* Germination, *f.*

spruce [spru:s], *a.* Paré, bien mis, pimpant.—*v.t.* Attifer. *To spruce up*, attifer.—*v.i.* Se parer, se faire beau.—*n.* Sapin, *m.* **sprucely**, *adv.* D'une manière pimpante. **spruceness**, *n.* Air pimpant, *m.*; élégance (de toilette), *f.*

sprung, *p.p.* [SPRING].

spry [sprai], *a.* Alerte, actif, plein d'entrain; soigné.

spud [spʌd], *n.* Béquille; (*Irish* and *fam.*) pomme de terre, *f.*

spume [spju:m], *n.* Écume, *f.*; (*Med.*) spume, *f.* **spumescent** [-'mesənt], *a.* Spumescent. **spumous** ['spju:məs], *a.* Spumeux; écumeux.

spun, *p.p.* [SPIN]. *Spun yarn*, bitord, *m.*

spunk [spʌŋk], *n.* Amadou; (*colloq.*) cœur, courage, cran, *m.*

spur [spə:], *n.* Éperon; ergot (of cocks etc.); aiguillon, stimulant (incitement), *m.* *On the spur of the moment*, sous l'impulsion du moment; *to put on one's spurs*, chausser ses éperons; *to put spurs to one's horse*, piquer des deux; *to win one's spurs*, faire ses preuves. *Spur dog-fish*, aiguillat, *m.*—*v.t.* Éperonner, donner de l'éperon à; stimuler, aiguillonner, exciter (to incite); armer d'éperons (to put spurs on). *To spur on*, presser, aiguillonner. —*v.i.* Piquer des deux.

spur-gall, *v.t.* Blesser de l'éperon.—*n.* Blessure d'éperon, *f.* **spur-gearing**, *n.* Engrenage droit, *m.* **spur-leather**, *n.* Monture d'éperon, *f.* **spur-maker**, *n.* Éperonnier, *m.* **spur-rowel**, *n.* Molette, *f.* **spur-wheel**, *n.* Roue à denture droite, *f.*

spurge [spə:dʒ], *n.* (*Bot.*) Euphorbe, *f.* **spurge-laurel**, *n.* Daphné lauréole, *m.*

spurious ['spjuəriəs], *a.* Faux, falsifié; de contrefaçon, apocryphe (of writings etc.). **spuriously**, *adv.* Faussement; par contrefaçon (of books etc.). **spuriousness**, *n.* Fausseté; nature apocryphe, *f.*

spurn [spə:n], *v.t.* Rejeter avec mépris; repousser, écarter (du pied); traiter avec mépris, mépriser (to treat with disdain). *To spurn at*, dédaigner, mépriser.—*n.* Mépris, dédain, *m.*

spurred [spə:d], *a.* Éperonné; ergoté (of rye etc.).

spurrier ['spʌriə], *n.* Éperonnier, *m.*

spurry ['spʌri], *n.* (*Bot.*) Spergule, *f.*

spurt [spə:t], *n.* S'élancer; (*spt.*) démarrer.—*v.t.* Faire jaillir.—*n.* Jaillissement; rejaillissement; (*fig.*) effort soudain, *m.*, saillie (sudden effort), *f.*; coup de collier, *m.*; (*spt.*) démarrage, emballage, *m.* *Final spurt*, pointe finale, *f.*; *to put on a spurt*, emballer, démarrer.

sputnik ['spʌtnik *or* 'sputnik], *n.* Spoutnik, *m.*

sputter ['spʌtə], *v.i.* Cracher; bredouiller; (*colloq.*) lancer des postillons [SPLUTTER].—*n.* Salive, *f.*; bredouillement (stammering), *m.* **sputterer**, *n.* Personne qui crache en parlant, *f.*; bredouilleur, *m.*, bredouilleuse, *f.* **sputtering**, *n.* Bredouillement, *m.*

sputum ['spju:təm], *n.* Crachat, *m.*

spy [spai], *n.* Espion, *m.*, espionne, *f.*—*v.t.* Épier, espionner. *To spy out*, trouver, découvrir, apercevoir (a person); reconnaître (to explore).—*v.i.* Scruter. *To spy into*, examiner, scruter; *to spy upon*, guetter, espionner, épier.

spy-glass, *n.* Longue-vue, lunette d'approche, *f.* **spy-ring** *or* **spy-system**, *n.* Espionnage, *m.*

spying, *n.* Espionnage, *m.*

squab [skwɔb], *n.* Pigeonneau (young pigeon); coussin, coussinet (cushion), pouf, *m.*—*a.* Dodu, potelé; sans plumes (of birds).—*adv.* Lourdement, en faisant pouf (of falling etc.).

squabble [skwɔbl], *n.* Dispute, querelle, chamaillerie, *f.*—*v.i.* Se chamailler.

squabbler ['skwɔblə], *n.* Querelleur, *m.*, querelleuse, *f.*

squad [skwɔd], *n.* (*Mil.*) Peloton, *m.*; (*Rail.*) brigade, *f.*; équipe (rescue etc.), *f.*; (*fig.*) clique (set), *f.* *Awkward squad*, recrues, *f.pl.*, conscrits, *m.pl.*; *defaulters' squad*, peloton de punition; *firing squad*, peloton d'exécution, *m.*; *leading squad*, groupe de tête, *m.*

squadron ['skwɔdrən], *n.* Escadron (of cavalry), *m.*; escadrille (of airmen), *f.*; (*Naut.*) escadre, *f.* **squadron-leader**, *n.* (*Av.*) Commandant, *m.*

squadroned, *a.* Formé en escadrons *or* escadrilles *or* escadres.

squalid ['skwɔlid], *a.* Malpropre, sale. *Squalid poverty*, pauvreté abjecte, *f.* **squalidly**, *adv.* Salement, malproprement. **squalidness** *n.* [SQUALOR].

squall [skwɔ:l], *n.* Cri (cry); coup de vent, grain, *m.*, rafale (of wind), *f.* *Look out for* *squalls!* gare la bombe! *to look out for squalls,* se tenir sur ses gardes.—*v.i.* Crier, brailler.

squaller, *n.* Braillard, *m.,* braillarde, *f.*

squalling, *n.* Criaillerie, *f.*—*a.* Criard, braillard. **squally,** *a.* (Temps) à grains, à rafales.

squalor ['skwɔlə], *n.* Malpropreté, *f.*

squamiferous [skwə'mifərəs], *a.* Squamifère.

squamous ['skweiməs], *a.* Squameux; écailleux.

squander ['skwɔndə], *v.t.* Dissiper, gaspiller, prodiguer, manger. **squanderer,** *n.* Gaspilleur, prodigue, *m.* **squandering,** *n.* Gaspillage, *m.*

square [skwɛə], *a.* Carré; à angle droit; balancé, soldé, égalisé (of accounts etc.); (*fig.*) vrai, équitable, juste, honnête; de superficie (of measure). *All square,* tout en règle, à égalité (of score); *square meal,* repas solide, *m.; square with,* d'équerre avec; *to be square with,* être quitte envers; *to make an account square,* balancer *or* égaliser un compte.—*n.* Carré; carreau (of glass etc.), *m.;* équerre (rule); case (on a chessboard), *f.;* square (with garden), *m.,* place (place); place d'armes (in garrison towns), *f.,* parvis (before a church), *m. Set-square,* équerre à dessin, *f.; square-root,* racine carrée, *f.; T-square,* té à dessin, *m.; to act on the square,* agir de bonne foi; (*fam.*) *to be a square,* être arriéré; *to cut on the square,* couper à angles droits.—*v.t.* Carrer; (*Carp.*) équarrir; balancer (accounts); (*Naut.*) brasser carré (a yard); (*fig.*) balancer, régler, adapter, ajuster; (*colloq.*) acheter, graisser la patte à (to bribe).—*v.i.* Cadrer, s'accorder (avec). *To square up,* régler ses comptes; *to square up to someone,* s'avancer vers quelqu'un en posture de combat.

square-bashing, *n.* (*Mil., colloq.*) Exercice, *m.*

square-built, *a.* Bâti en carré; aux épaules carrées. **square-dance, square dancing,** *n.* Danse à quatre, *f.* **squarely,** *adv.* Carrément; (*fig.*) honnêtement, justement. **squareness,** *n.* Forme carrée, *f.* **square-rigged,** *a.* Carré, gréé à traits carrés.

square-sail, *n.* Voile carrée, *f.* **squaring,** *n.* Équarrissage, *m. Squaring of the circle,* quadrature du cercle, *f.* **squarish,** *a.* À peu près carré.

squash [skwɔʃ], *v.t.* Écraser, aplatir; (*fig.*) rembarrer (a person).—*n.* Chose molle que l'on écrase, *f.;* écrasement (crushing), *m.;* presse, foule serrée (of a crowd); gourde, courge (pumpkin), *f.;* jeu de balle au mur, *m. Lemon squash,* citronnade, *f.* **squashy,** *a.* Mou et humide.

squat [skwɔt], *a.* Accroupi, blotti; trapu, ramassé (short and thick).—*v.i.* S'accroupir; se blottir; (*Am.*) s'établir (sans droit).—*n.* Posture accroupie, *f.* **squatter,** *n.* Personne accroupie, *f.;* colon (settler), *m.* **squatting,** *n.* Accroupissement, *m.*

squaw [skwɔ:], *n.* Femme peau-rouge, *f.*

squawk [skwɔ:k], *n.* Cri rauque; couac, *m.*—*v.i.* Pousser des cris rauques.

squeak [skwi:k], *n.* Petit cri aigu, *m.*—*v.i.* Crier, pousser des cris aigus, jurer (of musical instruments). **squeaker,** *n.* Personne, *f., or* animal, *m.,* qui pousse de petits

cris; jeune oiseau, pigeonneau, *m.* **squeaking,** *a.* Criard; qui jure (of musical instruments). **squeaky,** *a.* Criard; glapissant (of machinery etc.).

squeal [skwi:l], *v.i.* Pousser des cris perçants. (*colloq.*) *To squeal on someone,* dénoncer quelqu'un.—*n.* Cri perçant, *m.*

squeamish ['skwi:miʃ], *a.* Qui se soulève (of the stomach); trop délicat, difficile (fastidious). *To be squeamish,* faire le difficile, faire le dégoûté. **squeamishly,** *adv.* Avec dégoût. **squeamishness,** *n.* Délicatesse exagérée, *f.,* goût difficile, *m.*

squeegee [skwi:'dʒi:], *n.* Balai en caoutchouc, *m.*

squeeze [skwi:z], *n.* Compression; presse, cohue, *f.* (*fam.*) *That was a tight squeeze,* nous étions serrés comme des anchois.—*v.t.* Serrer, presser. *To squeeze into,* comprimer dans, faire entrer de force dans; *to squeeze money out of,* extorquer à; *to squeeze out,* exprimer; *to squeeze through,* forcer à travers; passer (through a sieve etc.) avec compression.—*v.i. To squeeze out of,* sortir de . . . en pressant; *to squeeze through,* se forcer à travers.

squeezer, *n.* (*Metal.*) Cingleur, *m.*

squeezing, *n.* Étreinte, compression, *f.;* serrement (of the hand), *m.*

squelch [skweltʃ], *v.t.* Écraser, aplatir.—*n.* Gargouillement, giclement, *m.*

squib [skwib], *n.* Pétard, serpenteau, *m.;* (*fig.*) satire, pasquinade, *f.;* brocard (lampoon), *m. A damp squib,* une affaire ratée, *f.*

squid [skwid], *n.* Calmar, *m.*

squiffy ['skwifi], *a.* (*pop.*) Gris, éméché.

squill [skwil], *n.* Scille (plant), *f.*

squint [skwint], *v.i.* Loucher. *To squint at,* regarder en louchant.—*a.* Louche.—*n.* Regard louche, *m. Lepers' squint,* guichet des lépreux, *m.; to have a squint at,* (slang) regarder, examiner, lire. **squint-eyed,** *a.* Louche.

squinter, *n.* Loucheur, *m.*

squinting, *n.* Action de loucher, *f.,* strabisme, *m.*—*a.* Louche. **squintingly,** *adv.* En louchant.

squire ['skwaiə], *n.* Écuyer; propriétaire campagnard, châtelain; cavalier servant (of a lady), *m. The squire of dames,* l'ami des femmes.—*v.t.* Servir de cavalier à, escorter (a lady).

squireen, *n.* Hobereau, *m.*

squireship, *n.* Qualité d'écuyer, *f.*

squirm [skwə:m], *v.i.* Se tortiller (with pain or embarrassment).

squirrel ['skwirəl], *n.* Écureuil, *m. Siberian squirrel,* petit gris, *m.*

squirt [skwə:t], *n.* Seringue, *f.;* (*slang*) personne méprisable, *f.,* gringalet, *m. Sea squirt,* ascidie, *f.*—*v.t.* Seringuer, faire jaillir, lancer.—*v.i.* Jaillir.

squitch [skwitʃ], *n.* Chiendent, *m.*

stab [stæb], *n.* Coup de poignard, de couteau, etc., *m.*—*v.t.* Poignarder; frapper; porter un coup mortel à; (*Bookb.*) piquer. *To stab to the heart,* percer le cœur à.

stabbing, *n.* Coup de poignard, *m.*—*a.* Lancinant.

stability [stə'biliti], *n.* Stabilité, solidité; (*fig.*) constance, fermeté, *f.* **stabilization** [steibilai'zeiʃən], *n.* Stabilisation, *f.*

stabilize ['steibilaiz], *v.t.* Stabiliser. **stabilizer**, *n.* Stabilisateur, *m.* **stabilizing**, *a.* Stabilisateur.

stable (1) [steibl], *a.* Stable, fixe, solide; (*fig.*) constant, ferme. **stably** ['steibli], *adv.* Stablement.

stable (2) [steibl], *n.* Écurie (for horses); (*rare*) étable (for cattle), *f.*; (*pl.*) (*Mil.*) pansage, *m.*—*v.t.* Loger (horses) dans une écurie; établer (cattle). **stable-boy** or **stableman**, *n.* Garçon d'écurie, *m.* **stable-dung**, *n.* Fumier, *m.* **stable-keeper**, *n.* Loueur de chevaux, *m.* **stable-yard**, *n.* Cour d'écurie, *f.* **stabling**, *n.* Écuries (for horses); étables (for cattle), *f.pl.*

***stablish** [ESTABLISH].

staccato [stə'kɑ:tou], *a.* Saccadé.—*adv.* En staccato.

stack [stæk], *n.* Souche (of chimneys); pile, *f.*, tas, *m.* (of coal, wood); faisceau (of arms), *m.*; meule (of hay etc.), *f.*; corde (de bois), *f.* (= 4 stères); grand rocher, *m.* (*fam.*) *He has stacks of it*, il en a des tas.—*v.t.* Mettre en meule; empiler (wood); emmeuler (hay etc.); mettre en faisceau (arms). (*fam.*) *To be stacked with*, regorger de. **stacking**, *n.* Emmeulage, empilage, entassement, *m.* **stack-yard**, *n.* Cour de ferme, *f.*

staddle [stædl], *n.* Appui (support); support (of hay); baliveau (young tree), *m.*—*v.t.* Laisser des baliveaux dans (a wood), baliver.

stadium ['steidiəm], *n.* Stade, *m.*

stadtholder ['stɑ:thouldə], *n.* Stathouder, *m.* **stadtholderate**, *n.* Stathoudérat, *m.*

staff [stɑ:f], *n.* (*pl.* **staves** [steivz]) Bâton, bourdon (pilgrim's); mât, *m.*, hampe (for a flag); (*Surv.*) mire; (*Mus.*) portée, *f.*; soutien, appui (support), *m.*; (*pl.* **staffs**), corps, personnel, *m.*; (*Mil.*) état-major, *m.* *Bread is the staff of life*, le pain est le soutien de la vie; *chief of staff*, chef d'état-major, *m.*; *domestic staff*, domestiques, *m.pl.*; *editorial staff*, rédaction, *f.*; *field-marshal's staff*, bâton de maréchal, *m.*; *general staff*, état-major général, *m.*; *teaching staff*, personnel enseignant, *m.*; *to be on the staff*, être attaché à l'état-major; faire partie du personnel de (at school etc.).—*v.t.* Fournir le personnel de. **staff-college**, *n.* École supérieure de guerre, *f.* **staff-holder**, *n.* Porte-mire, *m.* **staff-officer**, *n.* Officier d'état-major, *m.*

stag [stæg], *n.* Cerf, *m.* **stag-beetle**, *n.* (*Ent.*) Cerf-volant, lucane, *m.* *stag-evil, *n.* (*Vet.*) Tétanos, *m.* **stag-horn(moss)**, *n.* Lycopode en massue, *m.* **stag-hunt**, *n.* Chasse au cerf, *f.* **stag-party**, *n.* Réunion entre hommes, *f.* **stag-worm**, *n.* Œstre du cerf, *m.*

stage [steidʒ], *n.* Estrade (platform), *f.*; échafaud, échafaudage (scaffold), *m.*; (*Theat.*) scène, *f.*; (*fig.*) théâtre, *m.*; tréteaux (for a mountebank), *m.pl.*; établi (of a press), *m.*; étape (journey), *f.*; relais (relay), *f.*; (*fig.*) degré, *m.*, phase, période, *f.* *At this stage of the disease*, au point où en est la maladie; *by easy stages*, à petites étapes, à petites journées; *front of the stage*, avant-scène, *f.*; *to come on the stage*, entrer en scène, monter sur les planches; *to go off the stage*, quitter la scène; *to go on the stage* (to turn actor), se faire acteur; *to quit the stage* (the profession), quitter le théâtre.—*v.t.* Mettre en scène. *To stage a play*, monter une pièce.

stage-box, *n.* Loge d'avant-scène, *f.* **stage-carpenter**, *n.* Machiniste, *m.* **stage-coach**, *n.* Diligence, *f.* **stage-directions**, *n.pl.* Indications scéniques, *f.pl.* **stage-door**, *n.* Entrée des artistes, *f.* **stage-effect**, *n.* Effet scénique, *m.* **stage-fright**, *n.* (*slang*) Trac (des acteurs), *m.* **stage-hand**, *n.* Machiniste, *m.* **stage-manager**, *n.* Régisseur, *m.* **stage-player**, *n.* Comédien, *m.*, comédienne, *f.* **stage-properties**, *n.pl.* Accessoires de théâtre, *m.pl.* **stage-set**, *n.* Décor, *m.* **stage-struck**, *a.* Passionné du théâtre. **stage-whisper**, *n.* Aparté, *m.*

stager, *n.* (*colloq.*) *Old stager*, vieux routier, *m.*

staggard ['stægəd], *n.* Cerf de quatre ans, *m.*

stagger ['stægə], *v.i.* Chanceler; (*fig.*) faiblir, fléchir, hésiter. *To stagger away*, s'éloigner en chancelant; *to stagger back*, reculer en chancelant; *to stagger to one's feet*, se lever en chancelant.—*v.t.* Faire chanceler; faire hésiter; (*fig.*) ébranler, étonner; échelonner (hours, holidays, etc.).—*n.* Chancellement, *m.*; (*pl.*) (in horses etc.) vertigo, *m.*

staggering, *n.* Chancellement, *m.*; hésitation, *f.*; échelonnage, *m.*—*a.* Chancelant; vacillant, incertain. *A staggering blow*, un coup foudroyant. **staggeringly**, *adv.* En chancelant; avec hésitation (with hesitation). *Staggeringly beautiful*, d'une beauté extraordinaire.

staging ['steidʒiŋ], *n.* Échafaudage, *m.*; mise en scène (of play), *f.*

stagnancy ['stægnənsi], *n.* Stagnation, *f.* **stagnant**, *a.* Stagnant, croupissant; (*fig.*) inactif, mort.

stagnate [stæg'neit], *v.i.* Croupir, être stagnant; (*fig.*) être dans un état de stagnation. **stagnation** [-'neiʃən], *n.* Stagnation, *f.*

stagy ['steidʒi], *a.* Théâtral; (*colloq.*) de cabotin.

staid [steid], *a.* Posé, sérieux, grave. **staidly**, *adv.* Posément, gravement, sérieusement. **staidness**, *n.* Gravité, *f.*

stain [stein], *n.* Tache, *f.*; (*Paint.*) couleur, teinte, *f.*; (*fig.*) flétrissure, souillure, honte, *f.*, opprobre (disgrace), *m.* *Without a stain on his character*, sans atteinte à sa réputation.—*v.t.* Tacher (de); (*fig.*) souiller, flétrir, ternir; (*Paint.*) mettre en couleur, imprimer; teinter (of bacteria); (*Dyeing*) teindre.—*v.i.* Se tacher. **stained**, *a.* Taché; (*fig.*) souillé, terni; (*Paint.*) mis en couleur; teint; de couleur (of glass); peint (of paper). *Stained glass*, vitrail, *m.*

stainer, *n.* Teinturier, *m.* **staining**, *n.* Teinture; coloration (of wood etc.), *f.* **stainless**, *a.* Sans tache; inoxydable (steel).

stair [steə], *n.* Marche, *f.*; degré; (*pl.*) escalier, *m.* *Below stairs*, en bas, dans la cuisine; *go up one pair of stairs*, montez un étage; *to be downstairs*, être en bas; *to be upstairs*, être en haut; *to come downstairs*, descendre (l'escalier); *to fall downstairs*, rouler en bas de l'escalier; *to go upstairs*, monter (l'escalier); *to tumble down the stairs*, dégringoler les escaliers; *up one flight of stairs*, au premier; *up two flights of stairs*, au deuxième.

stair-carpet, *n.* Tapis d'escalier, *m.* **staircase**, *n.* Escalier, *m.*; cage d'escalier, *f.* *Back-staircase*, escalier de service, *m.*; *moving staircase*, escalier roulant, *m.*; *private staircase*, escalier dérobé, *m.*; *spiral* or *winding staircase*, escalier en colimaçon, *m.* **stair-head**, *n.*

Haut de l'escalier, *m.* **stair-rod,** *n.* Tringle (de tapis) d'escalier, *f.*

stake [steik], *n.* Pieu, poteau, (*Mil.*) jalon, piquet; bûcher (martyr's); (*Cards etc.*) enjeu, *m.,* mise, *f.;* (*Hort.*) tuteur, *m.;* prix (racing), *m. My life is at stake,* il y a va de ma vie; *there are many interests at stake,* il y a plus d'un intérêt en jeu; *to perish at the stake,* mourir sur le bûcher.—*v.t.* Parier, gager; jouer, mettre au jeu, hasarder (to risk); garnir de pieux (to defend with stakes); (*Hort.*) tuteurer; percer avec un pieu. *To stake out,* jalonner.

stake-boat, *n.* Bateau de ligne de départ, *m.* **stake-holder,** *n.* Qui tient les enjeux, *m.* **stake-money,** *n.* Mise, *f.*

stalactite ['stæləktait], *n.* Stalactite, *f.* **stalagmite,** *n.* Stalagmite, *f.*

stale [steil], *a.* Vieux, rassis (of bread); (*fig.*) suranné, vieilli, passé, usé (worn out, trite); éventé (of liquors); (*spt.*) surentraîné.—*v.i.* Uriner (of animals).

stalemate, *v.t.* (*Chess*) Faire pat.—*n.* Pat, *m.*

staleness, *n.* Vieillesse, *f.;* état rassis (of bread), *m.;* banalité (triteness), *f.;* évent (of liquor), *m.*

stalk [stɔːk], *n.* Tige, *f.;* pied (of a shoot), *m.;* queue (of a flower), *f.,* pédoncule; pétiole (of a leaf), *m.;* tuyau (of a quill); trognon (of a cabbage), *m.;* démarche fière (walk), *f.*—*v.i.* Marcher fièrement; se prélasser, se pavaner (of animals); (*Hunt.*) chasser à l'affût. *She came stalking out,* elle sortit marchant à pas comptés; *to stalk over,* parcourir d'un air majestueux.—*v.t.* Chasser à l'affût.

stalked, *a.* À tige. **stalker,** *n.* Chasseur à l'affût, *m.* **stalking,** *n.* (*Hunt.*) Chasse à l'affût, *f.* **stalking-horse,** *n.* Cheval d'abri; (*fig.*) prétexte, masque, *m.* **stalky,** *a.* Comme une tige; à tiges nombreuses; à longue tige.

stall [stɔːl], *n.* Stalle (church or stable), étable (for cattle); écurie (for horses); échoppe, boutique, *f.;* étal (of a butcher); étalage (for the sale of things in a market etc.); (*Theat.*) fauteuil d'orchestre, *m.*—*v.t.* Établer, mettre à l'étable; caler (of engine).—*v.i.* Caler. *To stall for time,* gagner du temps.

stallage, *n.* Étalage, droit d'emplacement, *m.* **stalled,** *a.* À . . . stalle; calé (of engine). *Four-stalled,* à quatre stalles.

stall-fed, *a.* Nourri à l'étable. **stall-keeper,** *n.* Étalagiste, *m.*

stallion ['stæljən], *n.* Étalon, *m.*

stalwart ['stɔːlwət], *a.* Vigoureux, robuste; vaillant. **stalwartly,** *adv.* Vaillamment.

stamen ['steimen], *n.* (*Bot.*) Étamine, *f.* **stamened,** *a.* Staminé.

stamina ['stæminə], *n.* Vigueur, résistance, *f.*

staminate ['stæmineit], *a.* Staminé. **stamineous** [stə'miniəs], *a.* Stamineux. **staminiferous** [stæmi'nifərəs], *a.* Staminifère. **staminiform** [stə'minifɔːm], *a.* Staminiforme.

stammer ['stæmə], *v.t., v.i.* Bégayer, balbutier. *To stammer through,* balbutier. **stammerer,** *n.* Bègue, *m.* **stammering** *n.* Bégaiement, *m.*—*a.* Bègue. **stammeringly,** *adv.* En bégayant.

stamp [stæmp], *v.t.* Frapper du pied; piétiner; empreindre, imprimer, marquer (de); contrôler (to hall-mark); estamper (coins); timbrer (documents, letters, etc.); (*Metal.*)

bocarder; estampiller (goods); affranchir (to prepay); poinçonner (tickets); (*fig.*) mettre le sceau à. *His manners stamp him a gentleman,* ses manières révèlent l'homme distingué; *stamped paper,* papier timbré; *stamped with genius,* marqué au sceau du génie; *that stamps him,* cela montre ce qu'il est; *to stamp about,* piétiner; *to stamp a letter,* affranchir une lettre; *to stamp one's reputation,* mettre le sceau à sa réputation; *to stamp out,* découper (to cut out), éteindre, extirper, écraser.—*v.i.* Trépigner, frapper du pied.

n.—Estampe (instrument), *f.;* coin, poinçon (punch), *m.;* empreinte, marque (impression), *f.;* poinçon de contrôle (on gold); timbre (on documents); (*Metal.*) bocard, pilon, *m.;* (*Comm.*) estampille (on goods), *f.;* (*fig.*) caractère, genre, *m.,* trempe, *f.;* cachet (seal); coup de pied, trépignement (foot); timbre-poste (postage), *m. Men of that stamp are rare,* les hommes de cette trempe sont rares; *on receipt of stamps,* contre envoi de timbres-poste; *receipt stamp,* timbre de quittance, *m.; rubber stamp,* timbre en caoutchouc, *m.; stamp paper,* papier gommé; papier timbré, *m.; to be of the right stamp,* être marqué au bon coin.

stamp-act, *n.* Loi sur le timbre, *f.* **stamp-album,** *n.* Album de timbres-poste, *m.* **stamp-collecting,** *n.* Philatélie, *f.* **stamp-collector,** *n.* Collectionneur de timbres-poste, philatéliste, *n.* **stamp-duty,** *n.* Droit de timbre. **stamp-machine,** *n.* Distributeur automatique de timbres-poste, *m.* **stamp-mill,** *n.* (*Metal.*) Bocard, *m.* **stamp-office,** *n.* Bureau de timbre, le timbre, *m.*

stamped, *a. Stamped addressed envelope,* enveloppe timbrée, *f.*

stampede [stæm'piːd], *n.* Fuite précipitée, débandade, panique, *f.*—*v.i.* Fuir en désordre.

stamper ['stæmpə], *n.* Pilon (tool); (*Metal.*) bocard, timbreur (person), *m.* **stamping,** *n.* Contrôlage (hall-marking); timbrage; découpage à l'emporte-pièce (cutting out); (*Metal.*) bocardage, *m.;* piétinement, trépignement (with the feet), *m.* **stamping-mill,** *n.* (*Metal.*) Bocard, *m.* **stamping-press,** *n.* Presse à percussion; estampeuse, *f.*

stance [stæns], *n.* (*Cricket, Golf*) Position (des pieds, au moment de frapper la balle), *f.*

stanch [staːntʃ] or **staunch** [stɔːntʃ], *a.* Solide, ferme; (*fig.*) vrai, sûr, dévoué; étanche (watertight).—*v.t.* Étancher.

stanchion ['staːntʃən], *n.* Étançon, étai, *m.;* (*Naut.*) épontille, *f.*

stanchless ['staːntʃlis], *a.* Qu'on ne peut étancher; (*fig.*) insatiable. **stanchly,** *adv.* Avec fermeté; avec dévotion. **stanchness,** *n.* Fermeté; constance, dévotion, *f.*

stand [stænd], *v.i.* (*past and p.p.* **stood** [stud]) Se tenir (debout etc.); rester debout; se soutenir (to keep on one's legs); se placer, se mettre (to place oneself); être debout, se trouver (to be still standing); se tenir, rester, demeurer, exister (to remain); se trouver, être (to be placed or situated); durer, subsister (to continue); se maintenir (to maintain one's ground); se présenter, se porter (as candidate); se mettre, se placer (to place oneself); stationner (of cabs); être stagnant (to stagnate); (*Naut.*) courir; être bon teint (of colour); (*Mil.*) faire halte; (*Cards*) s'y tenir. *As matters stand*, au point où en sont les choses *or* dans l'état actuel des choses; *how do we stand? (Comm.)* où en sommes-nous? *how do you stand with him?* quelle est votre position vis-à-vis de lui? *it stands to reason*, cela va sans dire; *let us see how the matter stands*, voyons ce qui en est; *prisoner at the bar, you stand convicted of*, accusé, le jury vient de vous déclarer coupable de; *stand back!* arrière! *stand by!* attention! *stand close!* serrez-vous! *stand easy!* en place! repos! *stand off!* au large! *stand out of my light*, ôtez-vous de mon jour; *to stand alone*, être unique en son genre; *to stand aside*, se ranger, se tenir à l'écart (aloof); *to stand at nothing*, ne s'arrêter à rien, ne s'effrayer de rien; *to stand back*, reculer, se tenir en arrière, se tenir à l'écart; *to stand by*, assister à, soutenir, défendre, s'en tenir à (to abide by), *(Naut.)* se tenir prêt (to be ready); *to stand by oneself*, être tout seul; *to stand down*, se retirer; *to stand fast, to stand firm*, tenir ferme, tenir bon; *to stand for*, soutenir, tenir lieu de, être à la place de (to be in lieu of), signifier (to signify), se présenter pour, se porter candidat pour, se déclarer pour *or* en faveur de (rights etc.); *to stand for nothing*, ne compter pour rien; *to stand forth*, se mettre en avant, s'avancer; *to stand good*, être valide; *to stand in or at*, revenir à (to cost); *to stand in fear of*, craindre, avoir peur de; *to stand in for*, *(Naut.)* se diriger vers; *to stand in for some-one*, remplacer quelqu'un; *to stand in some-one's light*, se tenir dans le jour de quelqu'un; *to stand in the way*, barrer le passage, faire obstacle (à); *to stand off*, se tenir éloigné, se tenir à l'écart, *(Naut.)* porter *or* passer au large; *to stand on*, se tenir sur, s'appuyer sur, compter sur (to rely on); *to stand on ceremony*, faire des façons; *to stand out*, faire saillie, être en relief, se dessiner, résister, tenir ferme (to resist), *(Naut.)* se tenir au large; *to stand out against*, tenir tête à, résister à; *to stand out from*, se distinguer parmi; *to stand out of the way*, s'ôter du chemin; *to stand over*, être en suspens, attendre, *(Law)* être ajourné, être remis; *to stand still*, s'arrêter, se tenir tranquille; *to stand to*, persister dans, s'en tenir à (to abide by), rester fidèle à; *(Mil.)* se tenir sous les armes; se tenir prêt; *to stand together*, s'accorder; *to stand to it*, s'y tenir; *to stand up*, se lever, se tenir debout, se dresser (of the hair etc.); *to stand up against*, opposer, résister à, tenir contre; *to stand up for*, tenir pour, défendre, soutenir; *to stand upon*, tenir à, insister sur; *to stand well with*, s'accorder avec.

v.t.—Mettre debout, placer, poser; endurer, souffrir, supporter, soutenir (to endure); subir (to abide by); résister à (to resist); payer (to treat to). *He will stand no nonsense*, il ne permet pas qu'on prenne des libertés avec lui; *I can't stand it any longer*, je n'y tiens plus; *I will stand you a drink*, je vous paierai à boire; *to stand a fair chance of succeeding*, avoir de bonnes chances de réussir; *to stand a joke*, comprendre la plaisanterie; *to stand cold*, supporter le froid; *to stand fatigue*, soutenir la fatigue; *to stand it*, le souffrir, y tenir; *to stand one's ground*, défendre son terrain, se maintenir sur son terrain, tenir bon; *to stand the enemy's fire*,

essuyer le feu de l'ennemi; *to stand the racket*, payer les pots cassés; *to stand the risk*, courir le risque; *to stand the test*, subir l'épreuve; *to stand trial*, subir son jugement, être jugé; *to stand water*, résister à l'eau.

n.—Arrêt, *m.*, halte, pause (halt); situation, place, position (place), *f.*; stand, étalage (stall), *m.*; estrade, tribune (platform), *f.*; socle, pied (for vases, bust, etc.); dessous, pied, porte-pied; porte-parapluie (for um-brellas); pupitre (music-stand), *m.*; jardinière (flower-stand); récolte sur pied, *f.*; *(fig.)* cessation, interruption, résistance, *f. (Theat.)* One-night stand, unique représentation, *f.* (of touring company); *the grand stand*, les tribunes, *f.pl.*; *to make a stand*, faire halte, s'arrêter; *to make a stand against*, résister à, tenir bon contre; *to take one's stand*, prendre position, se placer; *to take one's stand upon*, s'en tenir à.

standard ['stændəd], *n.* Étendard, *m.*, ban-nière, *f.*; *(Naut.)* pavillon; étalon, type (of weights, measures, etc.); titre (of gold and silver); *(fig.)* type, degré, modèle, régulateur; *(Hort.)* arbre en plein vent (tree), *m. Stan-dard of knowledge*, degré de connaissance *or* d'instruction, *m.*; *standard of living*, niveau *or* standard de vie, *m.*; *to come up to standard*, répondre au degré d'excellence exigé; être conforme à l'échantillon.—*a.* Qui sert de modèle, type, standard, normal, étalon, au titre (of money); classique (of books); qui sert d'étalon (of weights, measures, etc.); *(Hort.)* en plein vent (of trees), sur tige (of roses); régulateur (of price); *(fig.)* régula-ble.

standard-bearer, *n.* Porte-étendard, *m.*
standardization [stændədai'zeifən], *n.* Éta-lonnage, *m.*, unification; péréquation, *f.*; *(Comm.)* standardisation, *f.*
standardize ['stændədaiz], *v.t.* Étalonner, unifier, normaliser; standardiser; *(Chem.)* titrer.
stand-by, *n.* Appui, soutien, *m.*, ressource, *f.*
stand-in, *n.* Remplaçant, *m.* **stand-off-half**, *n.* *(Rugby)* Demi d'ouverture, *m.*
stand-offish, *a.* Réservé, distant. **stand-point**, *n.* Point de vue, *m.* **standstill**, *n.* Arrêt, *m. At a standstill*, arrêté, suspendu, inactif, au point mort; *standstill order*, arrêt, *m.*, immobilisation, *f.*; *to come to a standstill*, s'arrêter, ne pouvoir plus avancer, être mort (of trade). **stand-to**, *n.* *(Mil.)* Alerte, *f.* **stand-up**, *a.* Droit, en règle. *Stand-up collar*, col droit, *m.*; *stand-up fight*, combat en règle, *m.*
standing ['stændiŋ], *n.* Action de se tenir debout; pose, place, position, *f.*; rang (rank), *m.*; durée, date, *f.*, service (duration etc.), *m. A gentleman of high standing*, person-nage haut placé; *an officer of twenty years' standing*, un officier de vingt années de service; *of good standing*, estimé, considéré, bien posé; *of long standing*, de longue date; *standing out*, résistance, *f.*; *there is no standing out against him*, impossible de lui résister.—*a.* Établi de tous les jours (established); stagnant, dormant (stagnant); bon teint (of colours); fixe, à demeure (fixed); debout, sur pied (not cut down); *(fig.)* constant, invaria-ble. *Long standing account*, compte d'an-cienne date, *m.*; *standing account*, compte

courant, *m.*; *standing army*, armée permanente, *f.*; *standing dish*, plat de fondation, *m.*; *standing joke*, plaisanterie habituelle, *f.*; *standing orders*, règlement, *m.*; *standing rigging*, manœuvres dormantes, *f.pl.*; *standing rules*, règles fixes, *f.pl.*

standing-room, *n.* Place pour se tenir debout, *f. Standing-room only*, debout seulement.

standing-stones, *n.pl.* Menhirs, *m.pl.*

stannic ['stænik], *a.* Stannique. **stanniferous** [-'nifərəs], *a.* Stannifère.

stannous ['stænəs], *a.* Stanneux.

stanza ['stænzə], *n.* Stance, strophe, *f.*

staphyline ['stæfilain], *a. and n.* Staphylin, *m.*

staphylococcus ['stæfilə'kɔkəs], *n.* Stapylocoque, *m.* **staphyloma** [-'loumə], *n.* Staphylome, *m.*

staple [steipl], *n.* Produit principal, *m.*, denrée principale (of goods, commodities, etc.), *f.*; (*fig.*) objet *or* sujet principal, fond; brin (of wool, flax, etc.), *m.*; soie (of cotton), *f.*; crampon de fer à deux pointes, *m.*, agrafe (wire-staple), *f.*; gâche (of a lock), *f.* —*a.* Établi, fixe (established); principal, marchand, de commerce (fit to be sold).— *v.t.* Agrafer. **stapler**, *n.* Agrafeuse, *f.*

star [stɑː], *n.* Étoile, *f.*, astre, *m.*; (*Theat., Cine.*) vedette, étoile, *f.*; plaque, *f.* (of an order), (*colloq.*) crachat, *m.*; (*Print.*) astérisque, *m.*, étoile, *f. North or Pole Star*, l'étoile du nord *or* l'étoile polaire, *f.*; (*Bot.*) *star of Bethlehem*, ornithogale, *m.*; *the Stars and Stripes*, la bannière étoilée; (*colloq.*) *star turn*, un numéro de premier ordre, le clou (de la soirée); *to make somebody see stars*, faire voir trente-six chandelles à quelqu'un.—*v.t.* Étoiler, parsemer d'étoiles; avoir comme vedettes.—*v.i.* Briller (au premier rang); être en vedette; tenir le premier rôle; tourner un film. **star-chamber**, *n.* La chambre étoilée, *f.* **stardom**, *n.* (*Theat.* etc.) Popularité, *f.*, rang de vedette, vedettariat, *m. To rise to stardom*, devenir une vedette. **stardust**, *n.* Poussière d'étoiles, *f.*, amas stellaire, *m.* **starfish**, *n.* Étoile de mer, *f.* **star-gazer**, *n.* Astrologue; rêveur, *m. To be always stargazing*, être toujours dans les nuages. **starlet**, *n.* (*Cine.*) Starlette, *f.* **starlight**, *n.* Lumière des étoiles, *f.*—*a.* Étoilé. *A starlight night*, une nuit étoilée, *f.* **starlit**, *a.* Étoilé. **star-paved**, *a.* Parsemé d'étoiles. **star-shell**, *n.* Obus éclairant, *m.* **star-spangled**, *a.* Semé d'étoiles, étoilé. *The Star-Spangled Banner*, la bannière étoilée, *f.* **star-thistle**, *n.* Chausse-trape, *f.*

starboard ['stɑːbəd], *n.* Tribord, *m.*—*a.* De tribord.—*adv.* Tribord. *Hard a-starboard!* la barre toute à tribord!

starch [stɑːtʃ], *n.* Amidon; empois, *m.*; fécule (in food); (*fig.*) raideur, *f.*—*v.t.* Empeser. **starched**, *a.* Empesé; (*fig.*) raide, guindé. **starcher**, *n.* Empeseur, *m.*, empeseuse, *f.* **starchiness**, *n.* Raideur, *f.* **starch-maker**, *n.* Amidonnier, *m.* **starch-reduced**, *a. Starch-reduced bread*, pain de régime, *m.* **starch-works**, *n.pl.* Amidonnerie, *f.* **starchy**, *a.* Féculent; empesé; (*fig.*) guindé. *Starchy food*, féculents, *m.pl.*

stare [steə], *v.i.* Regarder fixement; ouvrir de grands yeux (to be astonished); sauter aux yeux (to be conspicuous). *To stare at*, regarder fixement, regarder d'un air ébahi

or effronté; *to stare hard at*, dévisager; *to stare in someone's face*, regarder quelqu'un en face; *to stare out*, faire baisser les yeux à, faire perdre contenance à.—*v.t.* Dévisager. *To stare someone in the face*, regarder quelqu'un dans le blanc des yeux; sauter aux yeux (of things). *Ruin stares him in the face*, il est au bord de la ruine.—*n.* Regard fixe; regard ébahi, *m.*

staring, *n.* Action de regarder fixement, *f.*—*a.* Voyant, tranchant (of colours etc.); aux couleurs éclatantes (of stuffs); hérissé (of animal's fur). **staringly**, *adv.* Fixement, entre les deux yeux.

stark [stɑːk], *adv.* Tout, tout à fait,. entièrement. *Stark naked*, tout nu, nu comme un ver.—*a.* Fort, raide; stérile (landscape). *Stark staring mad*, fou à lier.

starless ['stɑːlis], *a.* Sans étoiles. **starlike**, *a.* Qui ressemble à une étoile; brillant.

starling ['stɑːliŋ], *n.* Étourneau, sansonnet (bird); avant-bec, brise-glace (of a bridge), *m.*

starred [stɑːd], *a.* Étoilé; parsemé d'étoiles. *Ill-starred*, né sous une mauvaise étoile. **starry**, *a.* Étoilé; (*fig.*) étincelant, brillant. **starry-eyed**, *a.* Idéologue, peu pratique.

start [stɑːt], *v.i.* Tressaillir (de *or* à); partir, se mettre en route (to set out); partir (of horses etc.); commencer, débuter (to begin); sursauter, sauter (in a bond (to jump); se détacher (of rivets etc.); se disjoindre (of planks etc.). *His eyes were starting out of his head*, les yeux lui sortaient de la tête; *to start again*, repartir; recommencer; *to start aside*, se jeter de côté, faire un écart, s'écarter; *to start back*, se jeter en arrière, reculer, retourner; *to start from*, partir de; *to start off*, démarrer; *to start to one's feet*, se lever tout à coup; *to start up*, se lever précipitamment, se dresser, s'élever, naître, surgir.

v.t.—Commencer (to begin); alarmer (to alarm); faire lever (game); faire partir (to send off); inventer (to invent); mettre (a project etc.) en avant, mettre sur le tapis; soulever (a question); mettre en marche (machinery); déboîter (a bone); défoncer (a cask). *To start up*, mettre en marche.

n.—Tressaillement; saut, bond (a jump); élan (a sudden fit); écart (a swerving); commencement, début (beginning); départ (departure), *m.*; avance (advance), *f. By fits and starts*, à bâtons rompus, par boutades; *false start*, faux départ, *m.*; *flying start*, départ lancé; *standing start*, départ arrêté; *to get the start of*, prendre les devants sur, devancer; *to give a start*, faire un soubresaut; *to give a start in life*, lancer, pousser; *to wake with a start*, se réveiller en sursaut.

starter, *n.* Personne qui soulève (a question etc.), *f.*; inventeur, auteur; starter (at races), *m. To be a slow starter*, être lent à démarrer. **starter(-button)** *or* **starting-button**, *n.* Bouton de mise en marche; (*Motor.*) démarreur, *m.* **starting**, *n.* Tressaillement, mouvement subit; départ (departure); commencement, début (beginning), *m.*; mise en mouvement, mise en marche (of engines etc.), *f.* **starting-handle**, *n.* (*Motor.*) Manivelle de mise en marche, *f.* **starting-point**, *n.* Point de départ, *m.* **starting-post**, *n.* Poteau de départ, *m.* **starting-price**, *n.* (*Turf*) Cote de départ, *f.*

startle [stɑːtl], *v.t.* Faire tressaillir, effrayer, faire frémir. **startling**, *a.* Étonnant, foudroyant, étourdissant, saisissant.
starvation [stɑːˈveiʃən], *n.* Inanition, faim, *f.*
starve [stɑːv], *v.t.* Faire mourir de faim; affamer; réduire par la faim. *To starve out*, réduire par la famine; *to starve to death*, faire mourir de faim.—*v.i.* Mourir de faim. *To starve to death*, mourir de faim; (*dial.*) *to starve with cold*, être tout transi.
starveling, *n.* Affamé, meurt-de-faim, famélique, *m.*; plante affamée, *f.*
starving, *a.* Affamé, mourant de faim.
starwort [ˈstɑːwəːt], *n.* Stellaire, *f. Sea starwort*, aster, *m.*
stasis [ˈsteisis], *n.* (*Med.*) Stase, *f.*
state [steit], *n.* État, *m.*, condition, *f.*; état (political body); rang (rank), *m.*; pompe, parade, *f.*, apparat, *m.*, dignité (pomp), *f. Bed of state*, lit de parade, *m.*; *buffer state*, état-tampon, *m.*; *in a state of*, dans un état de; *in state*, en grande cérémonie, en grand apparat; *in the present state of things*, dans l'état actuel des choses; *lying in state*, exposition sur un lit de parade, *f.*; *married state*, vie conjugale, *f.*; *robes of state*, habits de cérémonie, *m.pl.*; (*colloq.*) *to be in a state*, être dans tous les états.—*a.* D'état, de cour, d'honneur. *State ball*, grand bal officiel *or* de cour, *m.*; *state coach*, voiture de cérémonie, voiture de gala, *f.*; *State Church*, église d'État, *f.*; *state criminal*, criminel politique, *m.*; (*Am.*) *State Department*, ministère des Affaires étrangères, *m.*; *state paper*, document officiel, *m.*; *state prison*, prison d'État, *f.*; *state room*, salle de réception, (*Naut.*) cabine de première, *f.*; *the* (*United*) *States*, les États-Unis, *m.pl.* —*v.t.* Énoncer, déclarer, affirmer; régler, fixer (to set); (*Math.*) poser. **state-controlled**, *a.* Étatisé. **statecraft**, *n.* Politique, *f.*, ruses de la politique, *f.pl.* **States-General**, *n.pl.* États généraux, *m.pl.* **state-trial**, *n.* Procès politique, *m.*
stated, *a.* Réglé, fixe, établi, certain.
stateless, *a.* Sans apparat, sans pompe. *Stateless person*, apatride, *m.* or *f.*
stateliness, *n.* Majesté, grandeur, *f.*, apparat, faste, *m.*, pompe, *f.* **stately**, *a.* Imposant, majestueux, magnifique; noble, élevé. *Stately home*, château, *m.*—*adv.* Majestueusement, avec dignité.
statement [ˈsteitmənt], *n.* Exposé, énoncé, rapport; compte-rendu, relevé (of account), *m.*; déclaration, affirmation, *f. According to the statement of*, au dire de, d'après ce que dit; *verbal statement*, rapport verbal, *m.*
statesman [ˈsteitsmən], *n.* (*pl.* **statesmen**) Homme d'État, *m.* **statesmanlike**, *a.* D'homme d'État. **statesmanship**, *n.* Science du gouvernement, politique, *f.*
static [ˈstætik] or **statical**, *a.* Statique. *Static electricity*, électricité statique, *f.* **statics**, *n.pl.* Statique, *f.*; (*Rad.Tel.*) parasites, *m.pl.*(sound).
station [ˈsteiʃən], *n.* Station, *f.*; poste (office); rang (rank), *m.*; position, condition, place, *f.*; (*Rail.*) gare, *f.*; (*Mil.*) poste, *m.*, garnison, *f. Bus* or *coach station*, gare routière, *f.*; *fire station*, poste de sapeurs-pompiers, *m.*; *goods-station*, gare de marchandises, *f.*; *police station*, poste de police, *m.*; *station in life*, position sociale, *f.*; *stations of the cross*, chemin de croix, *m.*; *to take one's station*, se

placer, se porter.—*v.t.* Placer, ranger, poser; (*Mil.*) poster. *To be stationed at*, être en garnison à; *to station sentries*, poser des sentinelles. **station-master**, *n.* Chef de gare, *m. Deputy station-master*, sous-chef de gare, *m.* **station-waggon**, *n.* (*Motor.*) Canadienne, *f.*
stational, *a.* De station; (*R.-C. Ch.*) stationnale, *f.* **stationary**, *a.* Stationnaire; fixe (of engines etc.).
stationer [ˈsteiʃənə], *n.* Papetier; *libraire, m.*
stationery, *n.* Papeterie, *f.*; (*Comm.*) fournitures de bureau, *f.pl. The Stationery Office*, Service des Publications de l'Administration, *m.*
statist [ˈsteitist], *n.* Statisticien; *homme d'État, politicien, m.*
statistical [stəˈtistikl] or **statistic**, *a.* Statistique. **statistician** [stætisˈtiʃən], *n.* Statisticien, *m.* **statistics** [stəˈtistiks], *n.pl.* Statistique, *f.*
stator [ˈsteitə], *n.* Stator, induit fixe, *m.*
statuary [ˈstætjuəri], *n.* La statuaire (sculpture), *f.*; le statuaire (sculptor), *m.* **statue**, *n.* Statue, *f.* **statuesque** [-ˈesk], *a.* Plastique.
stature [ˈstætʃə], *n.* Stature, taille, *f.*
status [ˈsteitəs], *n.* Statut légal, *m.*; position, condition, *f.*, rang, *m.*
statutable [ˈstætjutəbl], *a.* Réglementaire.
statute [ˈstætjuːt], *n.* Statut, *m.*, loi, *f. Statute mile*, mille légal, *m.*; *statute of limitation*, loi de prescription, *f.* **statute-book**, *n.* Code, *m.* **statute-labour**, *n.* Corvée, *f.* **statute-law**, *n.* Droit écrit, *m.* **statutory**, *a.* Réglementaire, statutaire.
staunch [STANCH].
stave [steiv], *n.* Douve (of a cask), *f.*, merrain, *m.*; (*Mus.*) portée, *f.*; (*fig.*) stance, *f.*; couplet (of a song etc.); verset (of a psalm), *m. Stave-rhyme*, allitération, *f.*—*v.t.* (*past and p.p.* **stove, staved**) Crever; défoncer (a cask). *To stave in*, crever, enfoncer; *to stave off*, chasser, repousser, éloigner, tenir éloigné.
stavesacre [ˈsteivzeikə], *n.* (*Bot.*) Staphisaigre, *f.*
stay [stei], *v.i.* Rester; demeurer (to sojourn); s'arrêter, descendre, être descendu (à); attendre (to wait). *To stay at*, rester à, demeurer à; *to stay at someone's*, rester, être, or demeurer chez quelqu'un; *to stay away*, s'absenter; *to stay for*, attendre; *to stay in*, rester à la maison, être en retenue or consigné (at schools); *to stay out*, ne pas entrer; *to stay up*, veiller; *to stay up for*, attendre.—*v.t.* Arrêter (to stop); apaiser (sa faim); empêcher de soutenir, étayer, accoter (to prop up); (*Naut.*) faire virer vent devant. *To stay one's hand*, se retenir; *to stay one's stomach*, apaiser sa faim.—*n.* Séjour (abode); obstacle, *m.*, difficulté (impediment), *f.*; (*Law*) sursis; soutien, appui (support); (*Build., Naut.*) étai; (*Tech.*) arrêt, *m.*; (*Carp.*) entretoise, *f.*, tirant, support, *m. Mainstay*, (*Naut.*) grand étai, (*fig.*) principal soutien, *m.*
stay-at-home, *a.* and *n.* Casanier. **stay-in**, *a. Stay-in strike*, grève sur le tas, *f.* *stay-lace, n.* Lacet, *m.* **stay-maker**, *n.* Fabricant de corsets, corsetier, *m.*, -ière, *f.* **staysail**, *n.* Voile d'étai, *f.*
stayer, *n.* Soutien, appui; cheval de longue haleine; (*spt.*) coureur de fond, *m.*
stays, *n.pl.* Corset, *m.*; corsets (more than one pair), *m.pl.*

stead [sted], *n.* Lieu, *m.*, place, *f. In his stead,* à sa place; *in stead of,* au lieu de, à la place de; *to stand in good stead to,* être très utile à; *to stand in the stead of,* tenir lieu de.

steadfast ['stedfəst], *a.* Ferme, constant, fixe, stable. **steadfastly,** *adv.* Fermement, avec constance. **steadfastness,** *n.* Fermeté, constance, *f.*

steadily ['stedili], *adv.* Fermement, avec persistance; sans s'arrêter; d'une manière rangée, avec sagesse. **steadiness,** *n.* Fermeté; conduite rangée, sagesse; assurance, fermeté (resolution), *f.* **steady,** *a.* Ferme, assuré, sûr; rangé, posé (in conduct); sérieux, assidu, continu, régulier, constant (regular); fait (of the wind); sage, rangé (of persons). *To have a steady hand,* avoir la main sûre; *to keep steady,* ne pas bouger, (*fig.*) ne pas faire de fredaines. (*colloq.*) *To be going steady,* sortir régulièrement (with boy or girl).—*n.* (*colloq.*) *My steady,* mon ami attitré.—*adv.* Doucement. *Steady!* Du calme! (*Naut.*) Droite la barre! (*Mil.*) Fixe!—*v.t.* Affermir, assurer; assujettir (to fasten); assagir, calmer.

steading ['stediŋ], *n.* (*Sc.*) Ferme et ses dépendances, *f.*

steak [steik], *n.* Tranche (of meat); côtelette (of pork), *f.*; entrecôte, *m. Fillet steak,* bifteck dans le filet, *m.*

steal [sti:l], *v.t.* (*past* **stole** [stoul], *p.p.* **stolen**) Voler, dérober, soustraire (quelque chose à); enlever (to abduct); (*fig.*) gagner, séduire. *To steal a glance,* jeter furtivement un regard (à); *to steal all hearts,* gagner tous les cœurs; *to steal a march on,* gagner une marche sur, devancer.—*v.i.* Voler, dérober; se dérober, se glisser furtivement, aller *or* venir à la dérobée. *To steal away,* s'en aller à la dérobée, se dérober; *to steal away from,* se dérober à; *to steal down,* descendre à la dérobée; *to steal in,* entrer à la dérobée, se glisser dans; *to steal on,* avancer insensiblement (of time); *to steal out,* sortir à la dérobée; *to steal up,* monter furtivement; *to steal upon,* s'approcher doucement de, surprendre.

stealer, *n.* Voleur, *m.*, voleuse, *f.*

stealing, *n.* Vol, *m.*

stealth [stelθ], *n.* *Vol, *m. By stealth,* à la dérobée, furtivement. **stealthily,** *adv.* À la dérobée, furtivement, à pas de loup. **stealthy,** *a.* Dérobé, furtif.

steam [sti:m], *n.* Vapeur, *f. At full steam,* à toute vapeur; *by steam,* à la vapeur; *steam is up,* on est sous pression; *to let off steam* (*fig.*), vider son sac; *to put steam on,* mettre la vapeur; *to shut off steam,* couper la vapeur; *with steam on,* en vapeur.—*v.i.* Jeter de la vapeur; fumer; s'évaporer; aller à la vapeur. *To steam away,* s'évaporer, s'éloigner (of a steamer); *to steam back,* retourner *or* revenir au port; *to steam down,* descendre; *to steam in,* entrer au port; *to steam off,* s'éloigner; *to steam up,* remonter.—*v.t.* Passer à la vapeur; (*Cook.*) cuire à la vapeur.

steamboat, *n.* Bateau à vapeur, *m.* **steam-boiler,** *n.* Chaudière à vapeur, *f.* **steam-chest,** *n.* Boîte à vapeur, *f.* **steam-engine,** *n.* Machine à vapeur, *f. Double-acting or single-acting steam-engine,* machine à vapeur à double effet *or* à simple effet.

steamer, *n.* Bateau à vapeur, vapeur, steamer, *m.*

steam-gauge, *n.* Manomètre, *m.*

steaming, *a.* Fumant. **steaming-hot,** *a.* Tout bouillant. **steamy,** *a.* Humide.

steam-packet, *n.* Paquebot à vapeur, *m.*

steam-pipe, *n.* Tuyau de vapeur, tuyau de prise de vapeur, *m. Waste-steam-pipe,* tuyau de dégagement de la vapeur, *m.* **steam-port,** *n.* Lumière d'admission, *f.* **steam-roller,** *n.* Rouleau compresseur, *m.*—*v.t.* (*fig.*) Écraser. **steamship,** *n.* Vapeur, *m.* **steam-tight,** *a.* Étanche. **steam-turbine,** *n.* Turbine à vapeur, *f.* **steam-whistle,** *n.* Sifflet à vapeur, *m.*

stearic [sti:'ærik], *a.* Stéarique.

stearin ['sti:ərin], *n.* Stéarine, *f.* **steatite,** *n.* Stéatite, *f.* **steatocele** [-'ætəsi:l], *n.* Stéatocèle, *f.* **steatoma** [sti:ə'toumə], *n.* Stéatome, *m.* **steatopygous** [-'tɔpigəs], *a.* Stéatopyge.

steed [sti:d], *n.* (*poet.*) Coursier, *m.*

steel [sti:l], *n.* Acier; fusil (to sharpen knives on); briquet (to strike a light on); (*fig.*) fer, *m.*, épée, lame (weapon), *f.*—*a.* D'acier, en acier; (*Pharm.*) ferrugineux. *Cast steel,* acier fondu, *m.*; *mild steel,* acier doux, *m.*; *steel pen,* plume d'acier, plume métallique, *f.*—*v.t.* Acérer, garnir d'acier; (*fig.*) armer, fortifier, endurcir (contre). *To steel one's heart against,* s'endurcir le cœur contre.

steel-clad, *a.* Revêtu d'acier, bardé de fer. **steel-engraver,** *n.* Graveur sur acier, *m.* **steel-engraving,** *n.* Gravure sur acier, *f.* **steeliness,** *n.* Dureté d'acier; (*fig.*) dureté, insensibilité, *f.* **steel-plated,** *a.* Cuirassé. **steel-works,** *n.pl.* Aciérie, *f.* **steely,** *a.* D'acier; (*fig.*) dur, de fer. **steelyard,** *n.* Romaine, *f.*; peson (small one), *m.*

steep (1) [sti:p], *a.* Escarpé, à pic; raide (of stairs etc.). (*fam.*) *That's a bit steep!* c'est un peu raide, c'est un peu fort!—*n.* Pente rapide, *f.*; précipice, escarpement, *m.*

steep (2) [sti:p], *v.t.* Tremper; infuser (dans), faire infuser (tea etc.); (*fig.*) plonger, noyer (dans), saturer (de).

steepen, *v.i.* S'escarper, devenir plus raide; (*fig.*) augmenter.—*v.t.* Augmenter.

steeping, *n.* Trempage, *m.*

steepish, *a.* Assez raide.

steeple [sti:pl], *n.* Clocher, *m.* **steeple-chase,** *n.* Course au clocher, *f.*, steeplechase, *m.* **steeple-jack,** *n.* Réparateur de clochers ou de cheminées, *m.*

steepled, *a.* À clocher.

steeply ['sti:pli], *adv.* En pente rapide.

steepness, *n.* Raideur, pente rapide, *f.*

*steepy, *a.* Escarpé, raide.

steer (1) [stiə], *n.* Bouvillon, jeune bœuf, *m.*

steer (2) [stiə], *v.t.* Gouverner; (*Motor. etc.*) diriger; (*fig.*) conduire. *To steer a northerly course,* faire route au nord.—*v.i.* Gouverner; se gouverner, se diriger.

steerable, *a.* Dirigeable. **steerage,** *n.* Timonerie, *f.*; l'avant, l'entrepont; logement des matelots (sailors' berths) *or* des passagers de troisième classe; (*fig.*) gouvernement, *m.*, conduite, *f. Steerage passenger,* passager de l'avant, passager de troisième classe, *m.* **steerage-way,** *n.* Sillage, *m.* **steering,** *n.* Action de gouverner; direction, *f.* **steering-column,** *n.* (*Motor.*) Colonne de direction, *f.* **steering-gear,** *n.* (*Motor.*) Direction, *f.* **steering-wheel,** *n.* Roue de gouvernail;

(*Motor. etc.*) roue directrice, *f.*; volant, *m.*
steersman, *n.* Timonier, *m.*
stele ['sti:li], *n.* Stèle, *f.*
stellar ['stelə], *a.* Stellaire. **stellaria** [-'lɛəriə], *n.* Stellaire, *f.* **stellate** or **stellated,** *a.* En étoile, étoilé; (*Bot.*) radié. **stelliform,** *a.* Stelliforme. **stellion,** *n.* Stellion, *m.*
stem [stem], *n.* Tige; queue (of a flower etc.); (*fig.*) souche, branche, *f.*, rejeton (of a family), *m.*; (*Naut.*) étrave, *f. From stem to stern,* de l'avant à l'arrière.—*v.i. To stem from,* être issu de.—*v.t.* Refouler (a current); (*fig.*) résister à, s'opposer à, lutter contre. *To stem the tide,* aller contre la marée, refouler la marée. **stemless,** *a.* Sans tige. **stemson,** *n.* (*Shipbuilding*) Marsouin de l'avant, *m.*
stench [stentʃ], *n.* Mauvaise odeur, puanteur, *f.* **stench-pipe,** *n.* Ventilateur, *m.*
stencil ['stensil], *n.* Patron (à jour or à calquer), pochoir, stencil, *m.*—*v.t.* Peindre, marquer or tracer au patron or au pochoir; tirer au stencil.
sten-gun ['stengʌn], *n.* Fusil mitrailleur, *m.*
stenographer [ste'nɔgrəfə], *n.* Sténographe, *m.* or *f.* **stenographic** [-nə'græfik] or **stenographical,** *a.* Sténographique. **stenographically,** *adv.* Sténographiquement. **stenography,** *n.* Sténographie, *f.*
stenotype ['stenətaip], *n.* Sténotype, *m.* **stenotypic** [-'tipik], *a.* Sténotypique. *Stenotypic machine,* sténotype, *f.* **stenotypist,** *n.* Sténotypiste, *m.* or *f.* **stenotypy,** *n.* Sténotypie, *f.*
stentorian [sten'tɔ:riən], *a.* De stentor.
step [step], *v.i.* Faire un pas, marcher pas à pas; marcher, aller; venir (to come); monter (dans); descendre (de). *Just step down to my house,* venez chez moi pour un instant; *to step aside,* s'écarter, se ranger; *to step back,* faire un pas en arrière, reculer, rebrousser chemin; *to step down,* descendre, venir, passer; *to step forward,* faire un pas en avant, s'avancer; *to step in,* entrer, entrer pour un instant, (*fig.*) intervenir; *to step into,* entrer dans; *to step on,* marcher sur, fouler; *to step on it* (*colloq.*), accélérer; (*Motor.*) mettre tous les gaz; *to step out,* sortir, sortir pour un instant, allonger le pas (to quicken one's pace); *to step over,* traverser, franchir, enjamber; *to step round,* faire le tour de; *to step up,* monter; *to step up to,* s'avancer vers, s'approcher de.—*v.t.* Mesurer en comptant les pas, arpenter; (*Naut.*) dresser (a mast). *To step up production,* accélérer le rythme de production; (*Elec.*) *to step up the current,* survolter le courant.—*n.* Pas; degré, *m.*, marche (of stairs), *f.*; échelon (of a ladder); marchepied (of a carriage or bicycle), *m.*; marche (of a throne etc.); emplanture (of a mast), *f.*; piédestal (of a shaft etc.), *m.*; (*fig.*) démarche, *f.*, progrès, acheminement, *m.*; (*pl.*) échelle, *f.*, marchepied (ladder); perron (flight of steps), *m. A few steps off,* à deux pas d'ici; *a good step,* un bon bout de chemin; *a step in the right direction,* une bonne dé-marche; *by his* or *her step,* à son pas; *door-step,* pas de la porte, *m.*; *pair of steps,* échelle double, *f.*, escabeau, *m.*; *quick step,* (*Mil.*) pas cadencé, *m.*; *step by step,* pas à pas, graduelle-ment; *to break step,* rompre le pas; *to fall out of step,* perdre le pas; *to keep step, to be* or

walk in step, marcher, être au pas; *to retrace one's steps,* revenir sur ses pas, rebrousser chemin; *to take a step,* faire un pas, (*fig.*) faire une démarche; *to take steps to,* prendre des mesures or faire des démarches pour; *within a step of,* à deux pas de.
step-brother, *n.* Beau-frère, *m.* **stepchild,** *n.* Beau-fils, *m.*, belle-fille, *f.* **stepdaughter,** *n.* Belle-fille, *f.* **step-down,** *a.* (*Elec.*) *Step-down transformer,* transformateur réducteur, *m.* **stepfather,** *n.* Beau-père, *m.* **step-in,** *a.* À enfiler (of garment). **step-ladder,** *n.* Échelle double, *f.* **stepmother,** *n.* Belle-mère; marâtre, *f.* **stepsister,** *n.* Belle-sœur, *f.* **stepson,** *n.* Beau-fils, *m.* **step-up,** *a.* (*Elec.*) *Step-up transformer,* transformateur élévateur, *m.*
Stephen ['sti:vn]. Étienne, *m.*
steppe [step], *n.* Steppe (plain), *f.*
stepper ['stepə], *n.* Cheval de trot qui a de l'action, *m.*
stepping, *n.* Marche, allure, *f.* **stepping-stone,** *n.* Marchepied, *m.*; (*fig.*) introduction, préparation, *f.*; (*pl.*) pierres de gué, *f.pl.*
stercoraceous [stə:kə'reifəs], *a.* Stercoraire.
stere [stiə], *n.* Stère (measure), *m.*
stereo-chemistry ['stieriou'kemistri], *n.* Stéréo-chimie, *f.* **stereographic** [-ə'græfik] or **stereographical,** *a.* Stéréographique. **stereography** [-'ɔgrəfi], *n.* Stéréographie, *f.* **stereometrical** [-ə'metrikl], *a.* Stéréo-métrique. **stereometry** [-'ɔmətri], *n.* Stéréométrie, *f.* **stereophonic** [-ə'fɔnik], *a.* Stéréophonique. **stereophony** [-'ɔfəni], *n.* Stéréophonie, *f.*
stereoscope ['stiəriəskoup], *n.* Stéréoscope, *m.* **stereoscopic** [-'skɔpik], *a.* Stéréoscopique. **stereotomical** [-'tɔmikl], *a.* Stéréotomique. **stereotomy** [-'ɔtəmi], *n.* Stéréotomie, *f.*
stereotype ['stiəriətaip], *n.* Stéréotypage, *m.*; (*fig.*) cliché, *m.*—*a.* Stéréotypé; cliché.—*v.t.* Clicher; stéréotyper. **stereotyped,** *a.* (*usu. fig.*) Stéréotypé. **stereotyper,** *n.* Clicheur, stéréotypeur, *m.* **stereotyping,** *n.* La stéréotypie (the art), *f.*; stéréotypage (the process), *m.*
sterile ['sterail], *a.* Stérile. **sterility** [-'riliti], *n.* Stérilité, *f.* **sterilization** [-lai'zeifən], *n.* Stérilisation, *f.* **sterilize,** *v.t.* Stériliser.
sterlet ['stə:lit], *n.* Sterlet (fish), esturgeon, *m.*
sterling ['stə:liŋ], *a.* Sterling; (*fig.*) vrai, de bon aloi. *Pound sterling,* livre sterling, *f.*; *sterling area,* zone sterling, *f.*
stern (1) [stə:n], *a.* Sévère, dur, rigide; rébar-batif (cross); rigoureux, rude (afflictive).
stern (2) [stə:n], *n.* *Poupe, *f.*; arrière, *m.*; (*fam.*) derrière, *m.* **stern-fast,** *n.* Amarre d'arrière, *f.* **stern-frame,** *n.* Arcasse, *f.* **stern-port,** *n.* Sabord de retraite, *m.* **stern-post,** *n.* Étambot, *m.* **stern-sheets,** *n.pl.* Arrière, *m.* **stern-way,** *n.* Culée, *f.*
sternal [stə:nl], *a.* (*Anat.*) Sternal. **sternum,** *n.* Sternum, *m.*
sternly ['stə:nli], *adv.* Sévèrement, durement, austèrement, rudement.
sternmost ['stə:nmoust], *a.* Le plus en arrière, le dernier.
sternness ['stə:nnis], *n.* Sévérité, austérité, dureté, rigueur, *f.*
sternutation [stə:nju'teifən], *n.* Sternutation, *f.*; éternuement, *m.* **sternutatory** [-'nju:tə təri], *a.* Sternutatoire.

stertorous ['stə:tərəs], *a.* Stertoreux.
stet [stet], *v.i.* (*Print.*) Bon; à maintenir.
stethometer [ste'θɔmitə], *n.* Stéthomètre, *m.*
stethoscope ['steθəskoup], *n.* Stéthoscope, *m.*
stevedore ['sti:vədɔ:], *n.* Arrimeur; déchargeur, *m.*
stew (1) [stju:], *n.* Vivier, *m.* (for fish).
stew (2) [stju:], *n.* Étuvée, *f.*, ragoût (of meat); civet (of hare), *m.*; compote (of fruits etc.), *f.*; (*fig.*) embarras, *m.*, confusion, *f.* *Irish stew,* ragoût de mouton, *m.*; *to be in a stew,* être sur le gril.—*v.t.* Étuver; mettre en ragoût, faire un ragoût de; mettre (fruit) en compote. —*v.i.* Cuire à l'étuvée, mijoter; (*fig.*) cuire dans sa peau. *To stew in one's own juice,* cuire dans son jus. **stew-pan,** *n.* Casserole, *f.* **stew-pot,** *n.* Cocotte, *f.*, faitout, *m.*
steward ['stju:əd], *n.* Intendant, régisseur (land agent); économe (of a college); commissaire (of a ball etc.); (*Naut.*) commis aux vivres; garçon de cabine; steward; délégué syndical; (*fig.*) dispensateur, *m.* *Steward's room,* cambuse, *f.* **stewardess,** *n.* Femme de chambre (à bord), stewardesse, *f.*
stewardship, *n.* Intendance, charge d'intendant, *f.*; office de régisseur, d'intendant, etc.; économat (in a college), *m.*; (*fig.*) gestion, administration, *f.* *To give an account of one's stewardship,* rendre compte de sa gestion.
stewed, *a.* Étuvé, en ragoût; en compote. *Stewed apple,* marmelade de pommes, *f.*; *stewed fowl,* fricassée de poulet, *f.*; *stewed fruit,* compote de fruits, *f.*; *stewed pears,* compote de poires, *f.*; *stewed pigeon,* compote de pigeons, *f.*; *stewed rabbit,* gibelotte de lapin, *f.*; *this tea is stewed,* ce thé est trop infusé.
stewing, *n.* Cuisson à l'étuvée, *f.*—*a.* *Stewing heat,* chaleur étouffante, *f.*; *stewing pear,* poire à cuire, *f.*
stick [stik], *n.* Bâton, *m.*; canne (for walking), *f.*; tronc, *m.*, tige (of a tree); rame (for peas etc.), *f.*; échalas (for vines or hops); archet (fiddle-stick), *m.*; (*Av.*) manche, *m.*; baguette (wand), *f.*; chapelet (of bombs), *m.*; (*pl.*) menu bois, du bois, *m.* *Blow with a stick,* coup de bâton, *m.*; *to cut one's stick,* (*slang*) filer, se sauver; *to get hold of the wrong end of the stick,* brider l'âne par la queue; *to pick up sticks,* ramasser du bois sec.—*v.t.* (*past* and *p.p.* **stuck**) Percer, piquer, enfoncer, mettre, faire entrer (to pierce); fixer (to fix); coller (with paste etc.); tuer (a pig); saigner (a sheep); ramer (peas). *Stick no bills,* défense d'afficher; *to stick into,* piquer dans, enfoncer dans; *to stick on,* fixer, coller (with paste, etc.), surfaire (to overcharge); *to stick out,* faire ressortir, mettre en saillie; *to stick out one's neck,* s'avancer beaucoup, émettre une opinion tout à fait personnelle, prendre des risques; *to stick round with,* garnir tout autour de, armer de, hérisser de; *to stick up,* dresser, mettre droit, coller, afficher (to paste up), attaquer à main armée.—*v.i.* Se coller, se fixer, s'attacher, tenir, adhérer (to adhere); rester, demeurer (to remain); (*fig.*) s'embarrasser, s'empêtrer (to get embarrassed); s'arrêter, rester court (to stop short). *He sticks to it,* il y tient, il reste fidèle à (to remain faithful to); *the name will stick to him,* le nom lui restera; *to stick at,* s'arrêter devant, reculer devant, se gêner pour, se faire scrupule de;

to stick by, rester fidèle à; *to stick close,* ne pas quitter; *to stick fast,* s'attacher, adhérer, tenir bien, s'arrêter court, rester pris; *to stick in the mud,* être embourbé, s'embourber; *to stick it on,* surfaire, (*slang*) saler; *to stick on,* s'attacher, tenir; *to stick out,* faire saillie, ressortir, tenir bon, persister, ne pas lâcher d'une semelle (not to give in); *to stick to,* s'attacher à, ne pas quitter, persévérer dans, mordre à (to persevere in); s'en tenir à (to abide by); *to stick to one's guns,* ne pas en démordre; *to stick up,* se dresser, se redresser; *to stick up for,* prendre fait et cause pour.
stickability, *n.* Persévérance, *f.* **sticker,** *n.* (*Am.*) Étiquette, *f.* **stickiness** ['stikinis], *n.* Viscosité, *f.* **sticking-plaster,** *n.* Taffetas d'Angleterre, *m.* **sticking-point,** *n.* Point d'arrêt, *m.*
stick-insect ['stik insekt], *n.* Phasme, *m.* **stick-in-the-mud,** *n.* (*fam.*) Balourd; vieux routinier, *m.* **stick-jaw,** *n.* Caramel gluant (sweet), *m.* **stick-up,** *a.* Droit, montant. *Stick-up collar,* col droit. (*slang*) *A stick-up job,* coup à main armée, *m.*
stickle [stikl], *v.i.* Tenir beaucoup (à); se débattre, se disputer.
stickleback, *n.* Épinoche, *f.*
stickler, *n.* Partisan; rigoriste, *m.* *He is a great stickler for,* il tient beaucoup à; *he is a great stickler for etiquette,* il est à cheval sur l'étiquette.
sticky ['stiki], *a.* Gluant, collant; visqueux; (*fig.*) difficile, raide (of people). (*colloq.*) *He'll come to a sticky end,* il finira mal.
stiff [stif], *a.* Raide, rigide, tenace; dur, ferme (not fluid); rude (hard); fort (strong); opiniâtre, obstiné (stubborn); contraint, gêné (constrained); empesé (starched); ankylosé (of joints); courbatu (of muscles); affecté, guindé (of style); (*Naut.*) carabiné (of wind). *As stiff as a poker,* raide comme un piquet, raide comme une barre de fer; *a stiff price,* un prix élevé; *he bores me stiff,* il est sciant; *stiff gale,* brise carabinée, *f.*; *to grow stiff,* se raidir.—*n.* (*Med. slang*) Cadavre, *m.* (*pop.*) *A big stiff,* un grand nigaud, *m.*
stiffen, *v.t.* Raidir; lier (sauces); (*fig.*) endurcir, engourdir; durcir, rendre ferme (paste).—*v.i.* Se raidir, raidir; s'affermir, devenir ferme (of paste); (*fig.*) s'endurcir. **stiffener,** *n.* Contrefort (of boots etc.), *m.* **stiffening,** *n.* Raidissement; soutien (support), *m.*
stiffish, *a.* Assez raide; assez difficile. **stiffly,** *adv.* Avec raideur; obstinément; fortement.
stiff-neck, *n.* Torticolis, *m.* **stiff-necked,** *a.* Obstiné, opiniâtre, entêté.
stiffness, *n.* Raideur; consistance (of paste etc.); raideur, gêne, contrainte (constraint); opiniâtreté (obstinacy), *f.*; (*fig.*) air guindé; style guindé, *m.*
stifle [staifl], *v.t.*, *v.i.* Étouffer, suffoquer. *To stifle a report,* étouffer un bruit; *we are stifling here,* nous étouffons ici.—*n.* (*Vet.*) Grasset, *m.* **stifle-joint,** *n.* (*Vet.*) Grasset, *m.*
stifling, *a.* Étouffant, suffocant. *It is stifling hot!* on étouffe! *the heat is stifling,* la chaleur est accablante.—*n.* Suffocation, *f.*
stigma ['stigmə], *n.* (*pl.* **stigmas**) Stigmate, *m.*, tache, flétrissure, *f.* **stigmata,** *n.pl.* (*Theol.*) Stigmates, *m.pl.* **stigmatize,** *v.t.* Stigmatiser, marquer d'un stigmate, flétrir.

stile [stail], *n.* Échallier, échalis, *m. Turnstile,* tourniquet, *m.*

stiletto [sti'letou], *n.* Stylet; poinçon (for needlework), *m. Stiletto heels,* talons aiguille, *m.pl.*

still (1) [stil], *n.* Alambic, *m.* **still-house,** *n* Distillerie, *f.* **still-room,** *n.* Distillerie, *f.* laboratoire, *m.*; office, *m.*

still (2) [stil], *a.* Silencieux (silent); tranquille, calme, paisible, en repos, immobile; non mousseux (of wine). *Keep still,* restez tranquille; *still life,* (*Paint.*) nature morte, *f.*; (*Cine.*) *still projection,* image fixe, *f.*; *still water,* eau dormante, *f.*; *still waters run deep,* il n'y a pire eau que l'eau qui dort; *to be still,* rester tranquille, rester en place, ne pas bouger; *to stand still,* se tenir tranquille, s'arrêter, rester immobile; *still lemonade,* citronnade, *f.*, citron pressé, *m.*—*adv.* Encore, toujours; cependant, néanmoins (nevertheless). *Still less,* encore moins, à plus forte raison; *still more,* encore plus, à plus forte raison.—*v.t.* Calmer, apaiser, adoucir. **still-born,** *a.* Mort-né. **stillness,** *n.* Tranquillité, *f.*, calme, repos, silence, *m.* ***stilly,** *a.* Silencieux, calme.—*adv.* Silencieusement.

stilt [stilt], *n.* Échasse, *f.*; pilotis, pieu (for a bridge etc.), *m. To be on stilts,* être monté sur des échasses. **stilt-bird** or **stilt-plover,** *n.* Échassier, *m.* **stilted,** *a.* Guindé, ampoulé, pompeux. **stiltedness,** *n.* Manière guindée, *f.*, ton pompeux, *m.*, emphase, *f.*

stimulant ['stimjulənt], *n.* Stimulant, *m.* **stimulate,** *v.t.* Stimuler; (*fig.*) piquer, exciter. **stimulating,** *a.* Stimulant. **stimulation** [-'leiʃən], *n.* Stimulation, *f.* **stimulus,** *n.* Stimulant, stimulus, aiguillon, ressort, *m.*

stimy ['staimi], *v.t.* (*Golf*) Barrer le trou à; (*fig.*) dérouter, déjouer.

sting [stiŋ], *n.* Aiguillon; dard (of a nettle etc.), *m.*; piqûre (thrust of a sting into the flesh); (*fig.*) pointe, *f. The sting is in the tail,* à la queue gît le venin; *the stings of remorse,* les aiguillons du remords; *to give a sting to,* acérer.—*v.t.* (past and p.p. **stung** [stʌŋ]) Piquer; (*fig.*) irriter, cingler; (*pop.*) plumer, écorcher. *Stung to the quick,* piqué au vif; *stung with remorse,* tourmenté de remords.

stinger, *n.* Chose qui pique, *f.*; (*colloq.*) coup bien appliqué (a blow), *m.*; (*Cricket*) balle raide, *f.*

stingily ['stindʒili], *adv.* Chichement, mesquinement. **stinginess,** *n.* Mesquinerie, ladrerie, *f.*

stinging ['stiŋiŋ], *n.* Piqûre, *f.*—*a.* Piquant; cinglant, bien appliqué (of a blow). **stinging-nettle,** *n.* Ortie, *f.* **stingless,** *a.* Sans aiguillon, sans dard.

sting-ray, *n.* Pastenague, *f.*

stingy ['stindʒi], *a.* Avare, mesquin, ladre, chiche. *A stingy old fellow,* un vieux pingre.

stink [stiŋk], *n.* Puanteur, mauvaise odeur, *f.* (*fig.*) *To raise a stink,* faire du chambard; *what a stink there is here!* comme cela sent mauvais ici.—*v.i.* (past and p.p. **stunk**) Puer; sentir mauvais, empester. *It stinks in one's nostrils,* c'est écœurant; *to stink in the nostrils of,* puer au nez à; *to stink of,* puer le, la, etc. **stink-ball** or **stink-pot,** *n.* Pot à feu, *m.* **stink-bomb,** *n.* Bombe puante, *f.* **stink-stone,** *n.* Pierre puante, *f.*

stinkard, *n.* Puant, *m.*, bête puante, *f.*

stinker, *n.* (*fam.*) Sale type, *m.*

stinking, *a.* Puant. **stinkingly,** *adv.* En puant.

stint [stint], *v.t.* Limiter, restreindre; réduire à la portion congrue. *To stint oneself,* se refuser le nécessaire, se priver (de).—*n.* Restriction, limite, borne; quantité, portion (portion), *f.*; besogne, *f.*, boulot, *m. Without stint,* sans restriction, sans bornes, à volonté.

stipel [staipl], *n.* (*Bot.*) Stipelle, *f.*

stipend ['staipend], *n.* Traitement (of clergyman *or* magistrate), *m.* **stipendiary** [-'pendiəri], *a.* Appointé. *Stipendiary* (*magistrate*), juge au tribunal de simple police.

stipple [stipl], *v.t.* Pointiller. **stippling,** *n.* Pointillage (process); pointillé (result of), *m.*

stipulaceous [stipju'leiʃəs], *a.* Stipulacé.

stipular ['stipjulə], *a.* Stipulaire.

stipulate ['stipjuleit], *v.i.* Stipuler (de *or* que). *To stipulate for,* stipuler de; *to stipulate that,* stipuler que. **stipulating,** *a.* Stipulant. **stipulation** [-'leiʃən], *n.* Stipulation, condition, *f.* **stipulator,** *n.* Partie stipulante, *f.*

stir [stə:], *v.t.* Remuer; (*fig.*) agiter, exciter, irriter. *To stir round,* tourner; *to stir the fire,* attiser le feu; *to stir up,* remuer, exciter, pousser (à), réveiller.—*v.i.* Remuer, se remuer, bouger. *Do not stir,* ne bougez pas; *he is not stirring yet,* il n'est pas encore levé; *there is no air stirring,* il ne fait pas un souffle de vent; *to be stirring,* être debout, être sur pied.—*n.* Mouvement, remuement, remue-ménage, bruit, tumulte, trouble, *m.*; agitation, *f. There was a great stir in the town,* toute la ville était en émoi; *to give the coffee a stir,* remuer le café; *to make, cause, a stir,* faire du bruit, de l'éclat.

stirabout, *n.* Bouillie de farine d'avoine, *f.*; (*fig.*) personne remuante, *f.* **stirrer,** *n.* Agitateur, instigateur, *m.* **stirring,** *a.* Remuant; émouvant (of a story etc.).—*n.* Agitation, *f.*

stirk [stə:k], *n.* Génisse (d'un an), *f.*; bouvillon, *m.*

stirrup ['stirəp], *n.* Étrier, *m.* **stirrup-cup,** *n.* Coup de l'étrier, *m.* **stirrup-leather** or **stirrup-strap,** *n.* Étrivière, *f.* ***stirrup-oil,** *n.* (*colloq.*) Raclée, huile de cotret, *f.*

stitch [stitʃ], *n.* Point, *m.*; maille (in knitting), *f.*; (*Med.*) suture, *f.*, point de suture, *m. A stitch in time saves nine,* un point à temps en épargne cent; *back-stitch,* point arrière, *m.*; *cross-stitch,* point croisé; *open-work stitch,* point à jour; *stitch in the side,* point de côté, *m.*; (*fam.*) *to be in stitches,* se tenir les côtes; *to drop a stitch,* sauter une maille; *to put a stitch to,* faire un point à; *to take up a stitch,* reprendre une maille.—*v.t.* Piquer, coudre; brocher (books); (*Med.*) suturer. *To stitch up,* coudre, faire un point à.

stitched, *a.* Piqué, broché (of books).

stitcher, *n.* Couseuse, *f.*; (*Bookb.*) brocheur, *m.*, brocheuse, *f.* **stitching,** *n.* Couture, *f.*; brochage (of books), *m.*; (*Med.*) suture, *f.*

stiver ['staivə], *n.* Sou, *m. Not to have a stiver,* n'avoir pas le sou.

stoat [stout], *n.* Hermine d'été, *f.*

stock [stɔk], *n.* Souche (of a tree, family, etc.); bûche, *f.*, bloc (of wood etc.), *m.*; monture, *f.*, bois (of a gun); manche; fût (of a plane

etc.), *m.*; giroflée (flower), *f.*; (*Hort.*) sujet, *m.*, ente (for grafting on), *f.*; (*Cook.*) consommé, *m.*; (*fig.*) race, famille, *f.*; marchandises en magasin, *f.pl.*, approvisionnement (store), assortiment (selection); (*Cine.*) pellicule, *f.*; (*Bookkeeping*) capital, *m.*; (*pl.*) fonds, fonds publics, *m.pl.*, rentes, actions, *f.pl.*; (*Shipbuilding*) chantier, *m.*, cale de construction, *f.*; ceps (punishment), *m.pl.* Farm *stock*, mobilier, fonds de ferme, *m.*; *Government stock*, fonds d'État, *m.pl.*, rentes, *f.pl.*; *in stock*, en magasin; *livestock*, bétail, *m.*; *on the stocks*, sur le chantier; *rolling stock*, matériel roulant, *m.*; *stock of plays*, répertoire, *m.*; *stock on hand*, marchandises en magasin, *f.pl.*; *to lay in a stock of*, faire une provision de; *to put a ship on the stocks*, mettre un bâtiment sur la cale; *to take in stock*, recevoir des marchandises; *to take stock of*, faire l'inventaire de; (*fig.*) scruter; *working stock*, matériel d'exploitation, *m.*; (*fig.*) *your stock is going up*, vos actions montent.—*a.* Courant, habituel, consacré.—*v.t.* Pourvoir (de); stocker (shop); monter (en); meubler (a farm); peupler (a deer-forest etc.); empoissonner (a fish-pond).
stockade [stɔ'keid], *n.* Palissade, *f.*—*v.t.* Palissader.
stock-book, *n.* Livre de magasin, magasinier, *m.* **stock-breeder,** *n.* Éleveur, *m.* **stock-breeding,** *n.* Élevage, *m.* **stockbroker,** *n.* Agent de change, *m.* **stockbroking,** *n.* Profession d'agent de change, *f.* *He has gone in for stockbroking,* il s'est fait agent de change. **stockdove,** *n.* Pigeon ramier, *m.* **stock-exchange,** *n.* Bourse; compagnie des agents de change, *f.* **stock-fish,** *n.* Stockfisch, *m.*, morue salée, *f.* **stockholder,** *n.* Actionnaire, rentier, *m.*, rentière, *f.* **stock-in-trade,** *n.* Marchandises disponibles, *f.pl.*; (*fig.*) répertoire; gagne-pain, *m.* **stockist,** *n.* Stockiste, *m.* **stock-jobber,** *n.* Agioteur, *m.* **stock-jobbing,** *n.* Agiotage, *m.* **stock-piece,** *n.* (*Theat.*) Pièce du répertoire, *f.* **stockpile,** *n.* Stocks de réserve, *m.pl.*—*v.t., v.i.* Stocker. **stock-pot,** *n.* Pot-au-feu, *m.* **stock-raising,** *n.* Élevage, *m.* **stock-still,** *a.* Immobile.—*adv.* Sans bouger. **stock-taking,** *n.* Inventaire, *m.* **stockyard,** *n.* Parc à bétail, *m.*
stocking ['stɔkiŋ], *n.* Bas, *m.* *Bluestocking,* bas bleu; *elastic stocking,* bas élastique; *nylon stockings,* bas nylon; *silk stockings,* bas de soie. **stocking-frame,** *n.* Métier à bas, *m.*
stocky, *a.* Trapu.
stodge [stɔdʒ], *n.* Aliment *or* repas indigeste, *m.*—*v.i.* Se bourrer.
stodgy ['stɔdʒi], *a.* Pâteux, lourd; qui bourre.
stoic ['stouik], *a.* and *n.* Stoïcien, *m.*, stoïcienne, *f.* **stoic** *or* **stoical,** *a.* Stoïcien; (*fig.*) stoïque. **stoically,** *adv.* Stoïquement.
stoicism ['stouisizm], *n.* Stoïcisme, *m.*
stoke [stouk], *v.t.* Chauffer; entretenir, tisonner (the fire etc.). *To stoke up,* (*pop.*) bouffer. **stoke-hold,** *n.* Chambre de chauffe, *f.* **stoker,** *n.* Chauffeur, *m.* *Head, chief stoker,* chef de chauffe, *m.* **stoking,** *n.* Chauffage, *m.*, chauffe, *f.*
stole (1) [stoul], *n.* Étole; (*Cost.*) écharpe; (*Rom. Ant.*) stole, *f.*
stole (2) [stoul], *past* [STEAL]. **stolen,** *a.* Volé,

dérobé. *Stolen glances,* regards dérobés, *m.pl.*; *stolen joys are sweet,* pain dérobé réveille l'appétit.
stole (3) [stoul], *n.* [*obs. form of* STOOL]. Groom *of the stole,* premier gentilhomme de la chambre, *m.*
stolid ['stɔlid], *a.* Lourd, flegmatique, impassible.
stolidity [stɔ'liditi] or **stolidness,** *n.* Flegme, *m.*
stolon ['stoulən], *n.* Stolon, *m.* **stoloniferous** [-'nifərəs], *a.* Stolonifère.
stomach ['stʌmək], *n.* Estomac; (*colloq. euphem.*) ventre; appétit, *m.*, faim (appetite); (*fig.*) envie, *f.* *It goes against his stomach,* le cœur ne lui en dit pas; *on an empty stomach,* à jeun; *to put some stomach into,* donner du cœur au ventre à; *to turn one's stomach,* soulever le cœur.—*v.t.* Avaler, endurer, digérer. *I cannot stomach that,* je ne peux pas digérer cela.
stomach-ache, *n.* Mal à l'estomac, *m.*, colique, *f.* **stomach-pump,** *n.* Pompe stomacale, *f.*
stomachal ['stʌməkl], *a.* Stomacal.
stomachic [sto'mækik], *a.* and *n.* Stomachique, *m.*
stomatic [sto'mætik], *a.* Stomatique. **stomatitis** [stoumə'taitis], *n.* Stomatite, *f.* **stomatology,** *n.* Stomatologie, *f.*
stone [stoun], *n.* Pierre, *f.*; caillou (pebble); grès (stoneware); noyau (of fruit); pépin (of grapes); (*Path.*) calcul, *m.*; meule (of a mill), *f.*; (*Weight*) stone (kg. 6·348), *m.* *A heart of stone,* un cœur de pierre; *meteoric stone,* aérolithe, *m.*; *not to leave a stone standing,* ne pas laisser pierre sur pierre; *philosopher's stone,* pierre philosophale; *precious stones,* pierres précieuses, pierreries, *f.pl.*; *Stone Age,* âge de la pierre, *m.*; *to leave no stone unturned,* remuer ciel et terre, mettre tout en œuvre; *to turn to stone,* pétrifier.—*a.* De pierre, en pierre; de grès (of stoneware). *Stone bottle,* bouteille de grès, *f.*—*v.t.* Lapider; assaillir, chasser, *or* poursuivre à coups de pierres; empierrer (roads); ôter les noyaux de (fruit).
stone-blind, *a.* Complètement aveugle. **stone-borer,** *n.* Lithophage, *m.* **stone-chat,** *n.* Traquet rubicole (bird), *m.* **stone-cold,** *a.* Complètement froid. **stone-colour,** *n.* Couleur pierre, *f.* **stone-crop,** *n.* (*Bot.*) Orpin, *m.* **stone-cutter,** *n.* Tailleur de pierres, *m.* **stone-cutting,** *n.* Taille des pierres, *f.* **stone-dead,** *a.* Raide mort. **stone-deaf,** *a.* Complètement sourd, (*fam.*) sourd comme un pot. **stone-fruit,** *n.* Fruit à noyau, *m.* **stone-mason,** *n.* Maçon, marbrier (for tombstones), *m.* **stone-pit** or **stone-quarry,** *n.* Carrière, *f.* **stone's-throw,** *n.* Jet de pierre, *m.* *Within a stone's-throw,* à un jet de pierre. **stonewall,** *v.i.* (*spt.*) Jouer prudemment; (*Polit.*) faire de l'obstruction. **stoneware,** *n.* Grès, *m.*, poterie de grès, *f.* **stonework,** *n.* Maçonnerie, *f.*
stoniness, *n.* Nature pierreuse; (*fig.*) dureté, insensibilité, *f.* **stoning,** *n.* Lapidation, *f.*; empierrement (of roads etc.), *m.* **stony,** *a.* De pierre; pierreux (abounding in stones); (*fig.*) de roche, dur, insensible. **stony-broke,** *a.* (*pop.*) Décavé, dans la débine. **stony-hearted,** *a.* Au cœur de pierre.

stood [stud], *past* and *p.p.* [STAND].

stooge [stuːdʒ], *n.*(*fam.*)Nègre(*pej.*)*m.*; souffre-douleur, *m.*; comparse, *m.*—*v.i.* Faire le nègre. *To stooge around*, flâner.

stook [stuːk], *n.* Tas de gerbes, *m.*; moyette, *f.* —*v.t.* Mettre en gerbes.

stool [stuːl], *n.* Tabouret; escabeau, *m.*, sellette; (*Med.*) selle; (*Hort.*) plante mère, *f.* *Camp-stool*, pliant, *m.*; *foot-stool*, tabouret, *m.*; *night-stool*, chaise percée, *f.*; *stool of repentance*, sellette, *f.*; *stool pigeon*, appeau, *m.*, (*fig.*) mouchard, *m.*; *to fall between two stools*, être assis entre deux chaises.

stoop [stuːp], *v.i.* Se pencher, se baisser; se tenir courbé, se voûter; *s'abattre, fondre (of birds of prey); (*fig.*) s'abaisser, s'incliner. *Carthage stooped to Rome*, Carthage se soumit à Rome; *she stoops to conquer*, elle s'abaisse pour vaincre; *to stoop down*, se baisser; *to stoop to*, s'abaisser jusqu'à.—*v.t.* Pencher, incliner, courber.—*n.* Inclination, *f.*; (*fig.*) abaissement, *m.* *He has a slight stoop*, il a le dos légèrement voûté.

stooping, *a.* Penché, courbé. *In a stooping posture*, dans une posture courbée. **stoopingly**, *adv.* En se baissant, en se courbant.

stop [stɔp], *n.* Halte; pause, interruption, *f.*; obstacle, empêchement (hindrance), *m.*; (*Organ*) jeu, registre; (*Gram.*) point, signe de ponctuation; arrêt (of trains, vessels, etc.), *m.*; (*Naut.*) genope, *f.* *Bus stop*, arrêt d'autobus; *request stop*, arrêt facultatif; *full stop*, point, *m.*; *to come to a dead stop*, s'arrêter court; *to put a stop to*, arrêter, suspendre, mettre un terme à.—*v.t.* Arrêter, empêcher (to hinder); couper (the breath); suspendre, cesser (payment etc.); retenir (wages); (*Mus.*) presser; (*Gram.*) ponctuer; boucher (a hole, leak, etc.); intercepter, supprimer, interrompre (to intercept); stopper (engine); plomber, aurifier (a tooth). *Stop thief!* au voleur! *to stop payment*, suspendre *or* cesser ses payements; *to stop someone from*, empêcher quelqu'un de; *to stop someone's salary*, retenir les appointements de quelqu'un; *to stop the engine* (of an aeroplane etc.), couper l'allumage; *to stop the wages of*, retenir les gages de; *to stop up*, boucher, fermer, condamner (a door etc.), barrer (a street).—*v.i.* S'arrêter, arrêter; (*Naut.*) stopper; (*Comm.*) cesser ses payements. *Stop there*, restez-en là; *to stop for*, attendre; *to stop at nothing*, être capable de tout; *to stop at home*, garder la maison; *to stop off at Marseilles*, descendre à Marseille; *to stop out* (at night), découcher.

stopcock, *n.* Robinet d'arrêt, *m.* **stop-gap**, *n.* Bouche-trou, *m.* **stop-motion**, *n.* (*Cine.*) Prise de vues image par image, *f.* **stop-valve**, *n.* Soupape d'arrêt, *f.* **stop-watch**, *n.* Montre à arrêt, *f.*, compte-secondes, *m.*

stoppage, *n.* Interruption, pause, halte, *f.*; enrayage, arrêt (of a train etc.), *m.*; fermeture, obstruction; retenue (from a salary); suspension (of payment), *f.*; chômage (of work); plombage (of teeth); stationnement (in streets), *m.*; (*Path.*) occlusion intestinale, *f.*

stopper, *n.* Bouchon (en verre), *m.*; (*Naut.*) bosse, *f.*—*v.t.* Boucher; (*Naut.*) bosser.

stopping, *n.* Arrêt; plombage (of teeth), *m.*; matière à plomber, *f.* *Stopping up*, fermeture,

veillée (at night), *f.* *Stopping train*, train omnibus, *m.*

storage ['stɔːridʒ], *n.* Emmagasinage, *m.*, accumulation, *f.*

store [stɔː], *n.* Provision, quantité, abondance, *f.*; approvisionnement, *m.*, réserve, *f.*; magasin, *m.*, boutique (shop), *f.*; (*fig.*) fonds, trésor, *m.*; (*pl.*) approvisionnements, vivres, *m.pl.*; (*Mil.*) munitions, *f.pl.*, matériel (de guerre), *m.* *In store*, en réserve; *to be in store for*, attendre; *to keep in store*, tenir en réserve, garder en réserve; *to lay in a store of*, faire une provision de; *to set store by*, faire grand cas de; *what is in store for us*, ce qui nous est réservé.—*v.t.* Pourvoir, munir, approvisionner (de); enrichir, orner, meubler (the mind). *To store up*, amasser, accumuler.

store-cattle, *n.* Bétail à l'engrais, *m.* **store-house**, *n.* Magasin, entrepôt, dépôt, *m.* **store-keeper**, *n.* Garde-magasin; marchand (dealer), *m.* **store-room**, *n.* Dépôt, office, *m.*; réserve, *f.*; grenier, *m.*; (*Naut.*) soute aux vivres, *f.* **storeship**, *n.* Gabare, *f.*, transport, *m.*

storey [STORY].

storied ['stɔːrid], *a.* Historié; orné d'inscriptions etc.; à étage. *Three-storied house*, maison à deux étages; (*Am.*) maison à trois étages, *f.*

stork [stɔːk], *n.* Cigogne, *f.* **stork's-bill**, *n.* Bec-de-grue, érodium, *m.*

storm [stɔːm], *n.* Orage, *m.*, tempête, *f.* *Any port in a storm*, faute de grives, on mange des merles; *a storm in a tea-cup*, une tempête dans un verre d'eau, *f.*; *to take by storm*, emporter *or* prendre d'assaut.—*v.t.* Donner l'assaut à, prendre d'assaut.—*v.i.* Faire de l'orage; (*fig.*) tempêter, s'emporter.

storm-beaten, *a.* Battu par la tempête. **storm-bell**, *n.* Tocsin, *m.* **storm-centre**, *n.* Centre de cyclone; (*fig.*) foyer de troubles, *m.* **storm-cloud**, *n.* Nuée, *f.* **storm-jib**, *n.* Tourmentin, *m.* **storm-lantern**, *n.* Lampe-tempête, *f.* **storm-signal**, *n.* Signal de tempête, *m.* **storm-troops**, *n.* Troupes d'assaut, *f.pl.*

stormily, *adv.* Orageusement, tempétueusement. **storminess**, *n.* État orageux, *m.* **storming**, *n.* Assaut, *m.*, prise d'assaut; (*fig.*) violence, rage, *f.* **storming-party**, *n.* Colonne d'assaut, *f.* **stormy**, *a.* Orageux, à l'orage. *Stormy petrel*, pétrel, *m.*

story ['stɔːri], *n.* Histoire, *f.*, récit, *m.*; anecdote, historiette, *f.*, conte (tale); mensonge (falsehood); étage (floor), *m.* *Always the same old story*, toujours la même histoire; *as the story goes*, à ce que dit l'histoire; *it's a funny story*, (*colloq.*) elle est bien bonne; *on the first, second, or third story*, au rez-de-chaussée, au premier, *or* au second; *that is quite another story*, c'est une autre paire de manches; *the best of the story*, le plus beau de l'histoire; *there is a story that*, on raconte que; *to tell stories* (*falsehoods*), dire des mensonges.

story-book, *n.* Livre de contes, *m.* **story-teller**, *n.* Conteur, *m.*, conteuse, *f.* (narrator); menteur, *m.*, menteuse, *f.* (liar).

stot [stɔt], *n.* Jeune bœuf, bouvillon, *m.*

***stoup** [stuːp], *n.* Cruche, *f.*; bénitier (for holy water), *m.*

stout [staut], *a.* Fort, robuste; gros, corpulent, qui a de l'embonpoint (fat); (*fig.*) brave, courageux, terme. *To grow stout*, engraisser, prendre de l'embonpoint; *to have a stout heart*, avoir du cœur.—*n.* Stout, *m.*, bière brune forte (beverage), *f.*

stout-hearted, *a.* Vaillant, courageux, au cœur intrépide. **stoutly**, *adv.* Vigoureusement, fortement, fort et ferme. **stoutness**, *n.* Embonpoint, *m.*, corpulence; (*fig.*) intrépidité, fermeté, *f.*

stove (1), *past* and *p.p.* [STAVE].

stove (2) [stouv], *n.* Poêle; fourneau (for cooking), *m.*; (*Manuf.*) étuve; (*Hort.*) serre chaude, *f. Slow combustion stove*, calorifère, *m.*; *oil stove*, réchaud à pétrole, *m.*—*v.t.* Étuver. **stove-maker**, *n.* Poêlier, *m.*

stow [stou], *v.t.* Mettre en place, serrer, arranger; entasser; (*Naut.*) arrimer. *To stow away*, emmagasiner. **stowage**, *n.* Mise en place, *f.*, arrangement; (*Naut.*) arrimage, *m.* **stowaway**, *n.* Passager clandestin, *m.*—*v.i.* S'embarquer clandestinement. **stower**, *n.* Arrimeur, *m.*

strabism ['streibizm], *n.* Strabisme, *m.*

Strabo ['streibou]. Strabon, *m.*

straddle [strædl], *v.t.* Enfourcher, être à califourchon sur.—*v.i.* Écarter les jambes, marcher les jambes écartées.

strafe [strɑːf], *v.t.* Marmiter.—*n.* or **strafing**. Marmitage, *m.*

straggle [strægl], *v.i.* S'écarter, se détacher; marcher à la débandade, (*Mil.*) traîner, rester en arrière. **straggler**, *n.* Rôdeur, *m.*; (*Mil.*) traînard, *m.* **straggling**, *a.* Séparé; éparpillé (scattered); égaré (de). **stragglingly**, *adv.* De loin en loin, çà et là; à la débandade.

straight [streit], *a.* Droit; (*fig.*) équitable, juste. *Straight as an arrow*, droit comme un I; *straight hair*, cheveux plats, *m.pl.*; *the straight road*, le droit chemin; *to let someone have it straight*, dire son fait à quelqu'un; *to make straight*, dresser, rendre droit, (*fig.*) arranger; *to make straight again*, redresser, réajuster; *to make things straight*, arranger les choses; *to play straight*, jouer franc jeu (avec).—*adv.* Droit, tout droit, directement; sur-le-champ, aussitôt, tout de suite, immédiatement (immediately). *I tell you straight*, je vous dis nettement; *I knew him straight away*, je l'ai reconnu du premier coup; *straight forward*, droit devant soi; *straight from the shoulder*, nettement, carrément, sans tortiller; *to go straight to the point*, aller droit au fait; *to keep straight on*, aller tout droit.—*n.* Ligne droite, *f.*; alignement droit, aplomb, *m. Out of the straight*, de biais.

straight-edge, *n.* Règle à araser, *f.* **straighten**, *v.t.* Rendre droit, redresser; ajuster, arranger (dress, tie); mettre en ordre (business, house). *To straighten oneself*, se redresser. **straightener**, *n.* Redresseur, *m.* **straightforward**, *a.* Droit, direct; (*fig.*) juste, probe, loyal, franc; simple (problem). **straightforwardly**, *adv.* Avec droiture; (*colloq.*) carrément, nettement. **straightforwardness**, *n.* Droiture, honnêteté, franchise, *f.* **straightly**, *adv.* Droit, en ligne droite. **straightness**, *n.* Ligne directe; rectitude, droiture, *f.* **straightway**, *adv.* Sur-le-champ, à l'instant; immédiatement.

strain [strein], *v.t.* Tendre, serrer; contraindre, forcer (to constrain); se fouler (to sprain);

filtrer, passer (liquids). *To strain a point*, faire une exception à, forcer les choses; *to strain every nerve to*, faire tous ses efforts pour; *to strain oneself*, se forcer, se donner un effort; *to strain one's ears*, tendre l'oreille; *to strain one's eyes*, se fatiguer la vue; *to strain out*, exprimer, extraire; *to strain relations*, tendre les rapports.—*v.i.* S'efforcer, faire de grands efforts (pour); se filtrer (of liquids). *To strain at*, faire des efforts pour avaler; *to strain at a rope*, tirer sur une corde.—*n.* Grand effort, *m.*, tension, *f.*; effort, *m.*; surmenage, *m.* (*usu.* mental); entorse, foulure, *f.* (sprain); ton, style, caractère; chant, *m.*, accents (song), *m.pl.*; disposition naturelle, tendance; race, lignée (race), *f. Breaking strain*, force à la rupture, *f.*; *in a lower strain*, d'un ton plus bas; *to speak of someone in lofty strains*, parler de quelqu'un avec enthousiasme.

strained, *a.* Forcé, pas naturel (of language, style, etc.); tendu. **strainer**, *n.* Passoire, *f. Tea-strainer*, passe-thé, *m.* **straining**, *n.* Tension, *f.*, grand effort, *m.*, violence, exagération, *f.*; filtrage (filtration), *m.*

strait [streit], *a.* Étroit, serré; strict, rigide, rigoureux (strict).—*n.* Détroit, *m.*; (*pl.*) gêne, difficulté, *f.*, embarras, *m. To be in great straits*, être dans la gêne, être à bout de ressources.

straiten, *v.t.* Rétrécir (to narrow); resserrer, (*fig.*) embarrasser, gêner. *In straitened circumstances*, gêné dans ses affaires, gêné, dans la gêne.

strait-laced, *a.* Lacé étroitement; (*fig.*) raide, rigide, sévère, prude.

straitly, *adv.* Étroitement, rigoureusement.

straitness, *n.* Étroitesse, *f.*

straits, *n.pl.* Détroit, *m. The Straits Settlements*, les Établissements du Détroit, *m.pl. The Straits of Dover*, le Pas de Calais, *m.*

strait-waistcoat or **strait-jacket**, *n.* Camisole de force, *f.*

strand [strænd], *n.* Rive, plage, grève, *f.*; toron, cordon (of a rope), *m.*—*v.t.* Jeter à la côte, échouer.—*v.i.* Échouer. **stranded**, *a.* Échoué; (*fig.*) dans l'embarras. **stranding**, *n.* Échouement, échouage, *m.*

strange [streindʒ], *a.* Étrange, singulier, bizarre, extraordinaire; étranger, inconnu (foreign). *A strange bed*, un lit qui n'est pas le sien; *it is not strange that*, il n'est pas étonnant que, on ne doit pas s'étonner si; *strange to say*, chose étrange! *to be strange to the work*, être nouveau au métier; *to feel strange*, se sentir étranger; dépaysé. **strangely**, *adv.* Étrangement, singulièrement. **strangeness**, *n.* Étrangeté, bizarrerie, *f.*

stranger, *n.* Étranger, *m.*, étrangère, *f.*, inconnu, *m.*, inconnue, *f. He is a stranger to me*, il m'est inconnu; *to become quite a stranger*, devenir rare comme les beaux jours, devenir bien rare; *to make a stranger of*, traiter en étranger; *you are quite a stranger*, on ne vous voit plus.

strangle [stræŋgl], *v.t.* Étrangler. **stranglehold**, *n.* (*fig.*) *Caught in a stranglehold*, pris dans un étau. **strangler**, *n.* Étrangleur, *m.* **strangles**, *n.pl.* (*Vet.*) Gourme, *f.* **strangling**, *n.* Étranglement, *m.*

strangulated ['stræŋgjuleitid], *a.* Étranglé.

strangulation [-'leiʃən], *n.* Strangulation, *f.*

strangury ['stræŋgjuri], *n.* (*Med.*) Strangurie, *f.*

strap [stræp], *n.* Courroie, *f.*; lien, *m.*, chape, bande, *f.* (of iron); sous-pied (for trousers), *m.*; courroie, bricole (carriage window); étrivière (of a stirrup), *f. Chin-strap*, jugulaire, *f.*; *razor-strap* [STROP]; *shoulder-strap*, bretelle, *f.—v.t.* Attacher avec une courroie; boucler, lier; donner une raclée à (to beat). **strap-hanger**, *n.* Voyageur debout (dans un autobus). **strap-oil**, *n.* Huile de cotret, *f.*

strappado [strə'pɑ:dou], *n.* Estrapade, *f.—v.t.* Estrapader.

strapper ['stræpə], *n.* Grand gaillard, *m.*

strapping, *a.* Bien découplé, grand, bien bâti. *A strapping woman*, une femme bien découplée.

strass ['stræs], *n.* Stras(s), faux diamant, *m.*

stratagem ['strætədʒəm], *n.* Stratagème, *m.* **strategic** [strə'ti:dʒik] or **strategical**, *a.* Stratégique. **strategically**, *adv.* Stratégiquement.

strategist ['strætədʒist], *n.* Stratégiste, *m.* **strategy**, *n.* Stratégie, *f.*

stratification [strætifi'keiʃən], *n.* Stratification, *f.* **stratiform**, *a.* Stratiforme.

stratify ['strætifai], *v.t.* Stratifier. **stratigraphy** [-'tigrəfi], *n.* Stratigraphie, *f.*

stratocruiser ['strætə'kru:zə], *n.* Avion stratosphérique, *m.*

stratosphere ['strætəsfiːə], *n.* Stratosphère, *f.*

stratum ['streitəm], *n.* (*pl.* **strata** ['strɑ:tə]), Couche, *f.*

straw [strɔ:], *n.* Paille, *f. Bundle of straw*, botte de paille, *f.*; *in the straw*, sur la litière; *it's the last straw*, c'est le comble; *man of straw*, homme de paille, *m.*; *not to be worth a straw*, ne pas valoir un fêtu; *not to give a straw for*, se soucier comme de cela or comme de l'an quarante de; *straw hut*, paillote, *f.*; *to clutch at straws*, se raccrocher à tout; *to split straws*, disputer sur des vétilles.—*a.* De paille.—*v.t.* Pailler; rempailler (a chair).

strawberry ['strɔ:bəri], *n.* Fraise, *f. Wild strawberry*, fraise des bois, *f.* **strawberry-bed**, *n.* Fraisière, *f.* **strawberry-blonde**, *n.* (*fam.*) Rousse, *f.* **strawberry-plant**, *n.* Fraisier, *m.* **strawberry-tree**, *n.* Arbousier, *m.*

straw-bottomed, *a.* À fond de paille. *Straw-bottomed chair*, chaise de paille, *f.* **straw-built**, *a.* De paille. **straw-colour**, *n.* Couleur paille, *f.* **straw-coloured**, *a.* Jaune-paille. **straw-cutter**, *n.* Hache-paille, *m.* **straw-hat**, *n.* Chapeau de paille, canotier, *m.* **straw-mat**, *n.* Paillasson, *m.* **straw-mattress**, *n.* Paillasse, *f.* **strawy**, *a.* De paille; comme la paille.

stray [strei], *v.i.* S'égarer, errer, vaguer; s'écarter (de).—*a.* Égaré; (*Law*) épave; (*fig.*) fortuit, accidentel; détaché (of thoughts); perdu (bullet, shot). *Stray dog*, chien perdu; *stray light*, lumière diffuse; *stray sheep*, brebis égarée, *f.—n.* Épave, *f. Waifs and strays*, des épaves, *f.pl.* **straying**, *n.* Égarement, *m.*

streak [stri:k], *n.* Raie, bande; traînée (of light); panachure, bigarrure (variegation), *f. Streak of lightning*, éclair, *m.*; *a streak of cruelty*, un côté cruel, *m.—v.t.* Rayer, strier; barioler, bigarrer (to variegate).—*v.i.* Filer, se sauver à toutes jambes. **streaked**, *a.* Rayé

(de); bariolé, bigarré (variegated). **streaky**, *a.* Rayé; veiné (of marble); entrelardé (of meat).

stream [stri:m], *n.* Courant; cours d'eau, fleuve, *m.*, rivière, *f.*; ruisseau (brook), *m.*; (*fig.*) cours; jet (of light etc.); torrent, flux (of words etc.); flot (of people), *m. Against the stream*, contre le courant; *down stream*, à vau-l'eau; *mountain-stream*, torrent, *m.*; *stream of abuse*, flot d'injures, *m.*; *to go down stream*, aller en aval, suivre le courant; *to go up stream*, aller en amont, remonter le courant.—*v.i.* Couler; ruisseler (of blood etc.); jaillir, rayonner (of light); flotter (of a flag etc.).—*v.t.* Verser, laisser couler. *To stream with*, ruisseler de.

stream-anchor, *n.* Ancre de touée, *f.* **stream-cable**, *n.* Câble de touée, *m.*

streamer, *n.* Banderole; (*Naut.*) flamme, *f.*; (*pl.*) serpentins (of paper), *m.pl.* **streaming**, *a.* Ruisselant (de). **streamlet**, *n.* Petit ruisseau; ru, *m.*

stream-line, *n.* Courant (naturel), fil de l'eau, *m. Stream-line body*, carrosserie carénée; *stream-line car*, voiture aérodynamique, *f.—v.t.* Caréner; (*fig.*) rationaliser, moderniser. **stream-tin**, *n,* Étain d'alluvion, *m.*

street [stri:t], *n.* Rue, *f. Back street*, petite rue, rue pauvre; *by-street*, rue écartée; *in the open street*, en pleine rue; *the high* or *main street*, la grande rue; *shopping street*, rue commerçante; (*fig.*) *that's right up my street*, c'est tout à fait dans mes cordes; *the man in the street*, l'homme de la rue; *to be streets ahead of*, dépasser quelqu'un; *the streets are crowded*, il y a du monde dans les rues; *to walk the streets*, courir les rues, battre le pavé; *to turn out into the street*, mettre sur le pavé. **street-arab**, *n.* Gamin des rues, gavroche, *m.* **streetcar**, *n.* (*Am.*) Tramway, *m.* **street-door**, *n.* Porte sur la rue, *f.* **street-lamp**, *n.* Réverbère, *m.* **street-lighting**, *n.* Éclairage des rues, *m.* **street-organ**, *n.* Orgue de Barbarie, *m.* **street-sweeper**, *n.* Balayeur des rues, *m.* **street-sweeping-machine**, *n.* Balayeuse, *f.* **street-walker**, *n.* Fille de trottoir, *f.*

strength [streŋθ], *n.* Force, *f.*, forces, *f.pl.*; résistance (of materials), *f.*; (*Build.*) solidité, *f.*; (*Mil.*) effectif, *m. By sheer strength*, de haute lutte, à force de bras; *on the strength*, (*Mil.*) sur les contrôles; *on the strength of*, sur la foi de, sur, s'appuyant sur; *strength of mind*, fermeté d'esprit, force de caractère, *f.*; *to regain strength*, reprendre ses forces; *with all my strength*, de toutes mes forces.

strengthen, *v.t.* Fortifier, affermir, raffermir; (*Mil.*) renforcer.—*v.i.* Se fortifier, s'affermir, se raffermir.

strengthener, *n.* (*Med.*) Fortifiant, *m.* **strengthening**, *a.* Fortifiant. **strengthless**, *a.* Sans force.

strenuous ['strenjuəs], *a.* Énergique, vif, ardent, vigoureux. **strenuously**, *adv.* Avec zèle, ardemment; vigoureusement. **strenuousness**, *n.* Zèle, *m.*, ardeur; vigueur, *f.*

streptococcus [streptə'kɔkəs], *n.* Streptocoque, *m.*

streptomycin [streptə'maisin], *n.* Streptomycine, *f.*

stress [stres], *n* Force, emphase, *f.*, poids; (*Gram.*) accent (tonique), *m.*, accentuation; violence (of weather); (*Mech.*) contrainte, *f.*, effort, *m.*, tension, *f.* *Stress of weather*, gros temps, *m.*; *to lay stress upon*, appuyer fortement sur; *under the stress of emotion*, en proie à l'émotion; *we were forced by stress of weather to put back into port*, la violence du vent nous força de regagner le port. **stressed**, *a.* Accentué. **stressing**, *n.* Accentuation, *f.*

stretch [stretʃ], *v.t.* Tendre (to extend in a line); étendre (to extend in breadth); déployer (to spread as wings); élargir (to enlarge); forcer (to strain); (*fig.*) exagérer, outrer. *To stretch a point*, faire une exception en faveur de; *to stretch oneself*, s'étirer; *to stretch oneself out full length*, s'étendre de tout son long; *to stretch one's limbs*, se dégourdir; *to stretch out one's hand*, tendre la main.—*v.i.* S'étendre; s'étirer; se déployer; s'élargir (to become larger); prêter (of gloves, material); exagérer. *To stretch away to*, s'étendre vers; *to stretch from*, s'étendre de . . . (à); *to stretch over*, s'étendre sur.—*n.* Étendue, tension, extension, section, *f.* (road); effort (strain), *m.*; (*Min.*) direction, *f.* *A stretch of the imagination*, un effort d'imagination; *at a stretch*, d'un trait, tout d'une haleine, sans arrêt; *on the stretch*, tendu (of the mind); (*pop.*) *to do a stretch*, tirer de la prison, faire de la taule; *to put upon the stretch*, forcer.

stretcher, *n.* Brancard, *m.*, civière (for carrying a person on), *f.*; (*Build.*) carreau, *m.*; (*Naut.*) barre de pied, *f.*, traversin, *m.*; baguette à gants (for gloves), *f.*, tendeur (shoes), bâton, *m.* (chair); traverse (of tent); (*fig.*) blague, *f.*

stretcher-bearer, *n.*   Brancardier, *m.*

stretcher-bed *n.* Lit de camp, *m.*

stretching, *n.* Élargissement, *m.*; tension, *f.*

strew [stru:], *v.t.* (*p.p.* **strewn** [stru:n]) Répandre, parsemer, semer. *To strew with*, parsemer de, joncher de. **strewing**, *n.* Jonchée, *f.*

stria ['straɪə], *n.* (*pl.* **striae**) Strie, *f.*

striate ['straɪɪt], **striated** [straɪ'eɪtɪd], *a.* Strié. **striation** [-'eɪʃən], *n.* Striure, *f.*

stricken ['strɪkən], *p.p.* [STRIKE].—*a.* Affligé, blessé, accablé; (*Med.*) atteint (de).

strickle ['strɪkl], *n.* Racloire, *f.*

strict [strɪkt], *a.* Exact, strict, précis; rigide; exprès, rigoureux (express); sévère. **strictly**, *adv.* Exactement, strictement, rigoureusement, expressément, formellement; sévèrement. *Strictly speaking*, rigoureusement parlant. **strictness**, *n.* Exactitude, rigueur, *f.*; sévérité, *f.* **stricture**, *n.* Censure, critique, observation critique, *f.*; (*Med.*) étranglement, *m.*

stride [straɪd], *n.* Pas, grand pas, *m.*, enjambée, *f.* *To get into one's stride*, prendre la cadence; *to make rapid strides*, avancer à grands pas; *to take in one's stride*, faire sans le moindre effort; *with giant strides*, à pas de géant; *with one stride*, d'une enjambée.—*v.i.* (*past* **strode** [stroud], *p.p.* **stridden**) Marcher à grands pas *or* à grandes enjambées; se mettre à califourchon (to straddle). *To stride along*, marcher à grandes enjambées; *to stride over*, enjamber; *to stride up and down a room*, arpenter une pièce.

strident ['straɪdənt], *a.* Strident. **stridently**, *adv.* Stridemment.

strife [straɪf], *n.* Lutte, querelle, contestation, dispute, *f.*; désaccord (opposition), *m.* *To be at strife*, être en lutte (avec).

strigil ['strɪdʒɪl], *n.* (*Ant.*) Strigile, *m.*

strike [straɪk], *v.t.* (*past* **struck**, *p.p.* **struck**, **stricken**) Frapper; battre, cogner; asséner; porter (a blow); sonner (the hour); rendre (mute etc.); saisir (to affect); frapper (de); créer, produire (to produce); établir (a balance); allumer (a match); tomber sur, trouver, atteindre (a path etc.); faire, conclure (a bargain etc.); amener (a flag); plier (a tent). *It did not strike me that*, l'idée ne m'est pas venue que; *it strikes me*, il me semble, j'ai idée; *struck all of a heap*, atterré, abasourdi; *the clock is striking nine*, la pendule sonne neuf heures; *to be stage-struck*, être entiché de théâtre; *to strike a bargain*, conclure un marché; *to strike a light*, allumer une allumette; *to strike blind*, rendre aveugle; *to strike bottom*, talonner; *to strike dead*, foudroyer; *to strike down*, abattre, renverser, faire tomber; *to strike dumb*, rendre muet, interdire, réduire au silence; *to strike in*, enfoncer; *to strike off*, enlever, retrancher, couper, effacer, rayer, biffer (to erase), (*Print.*) tirer; *to strike off the rolls*, radier, rayer du tableau; *to strike oil*, forer un puits de pétrole, (*fig.*) trouver une mine d'or; *to strike out*, faire jaillir (sparks), frayer (a path), inventer, créer (to devise); *to strike out a new line*, inventer une nouvelle méthode, se frayer un nouveau chemin; *to strike someone in the face*, frapper quelqu'un à la figure; *to strike tents*, lever le camp, plier les tentes; *to strike up*, entonner, commencer à jouer; *to strike up acquaintance with*, faire connaissance avec; *to strike with astonishment*, frapper d'étonnement; *to strike with horror*, frapper *or* saisir d'horreur; *without striking a blow*, sans coup férir.

v.i.—Frapper; toucher, échouer (to be stranded); heurter, donner (contre); baisser pavillon, amener son pavillon (to lower a ship's flag); sonner (of clocks etc.); (*Hort.*) prendre racine, bouturer; faire grève, se mettre en grève (of workmen). *It has just struck five*, cinq heures viennent de sonner; *to strike against*, frapper contre, donner contre, heurter contre; *to strike at*, porter un coup à, s'attaquer à, attenter à; *to strike home*, frapper juste, porter coup; *to strike in*, interrompre; *to strike out*, se lancer, nager vigoureusement (to swim); *to strike out into*, se lancer dans, se jeter dans; *to strike up*, commencer à jouer; *to strike while the iron is hot*, battre le fer pendant qu'il est chaud.

n.—Racloire (instrument); (*Geol.*) direction; grève (of workmen), *f.* *General strike*, grève générale; *on strike*, en grève; *to go on strike*, se mettre en grève; *sit-down strike*, débrayage, *m.*; *stay-in strike*, grève sur le tas. ***strike-a-light**, *n.* Briquet, *m.* **strikebreaker**, *n.* Briseur de grève, renard, *m.* **strike-leader**, *n.* Chef de grève, *m.* **striker**, *n.* Frappeur; gréviste (workman on strike); percuteur (on a fire-arm), *m.*

striking ['straɪkɪŋ], *a.* Frappant, saisissant; remarquable.—*n.* Frappement, *m.*; frappe, *f.* (*Paint.*); établissement, *m.* (balance); sonnerie, *f.* (clock). **strikingly**, *adv.* D'une manière frappante. **strikingness**, *n.* Caractère frappant, *m.*

string [strɪŋ], *n.* Ficelle, corde, *f.*, fil (thread); cordon (of a purse, shoes, etc.); chapelet (of beads, onions, etc.), *m.*; corde, *f.* (violin); bride (of a bonnet etc.), *f.*; ruban (ribbon), *m.*; (*Bot.*) fibre, *f.*; filandres (of beans etc.), *f.pl.*; (*fig.*) kyrielle, enfilade, suite, série, tirade, *f.* First string, (*spt.*) premier, (c'est à dire) le meilleur coureur (of a club), le meilleur cheval (of a stable); *string* (of horses), écurie (de courses), *f.*; *the strings* (of an orchestra), les cordes, *f.pl.*; *string quartet*, quatuor à cordes, *m.*; *to harp on the same string*, chanter toujours la même antienne; *to have two strings to one's bow*, avoir plusieurs cordes à son arc; *to pull the strings*, tirer les ficelles.—*v.t.* (*past* and *p.p.* **strung**) Garnir de cordes; fortifier (to strengthen); enfiler (beads etc.); tendre (to make tense); (*Mus.*) accorder; corder (racket); ficeler (parcel). *To string up*, pendre.—*v.i.* (*fam.*) *To string along with*, suivre, adhérer à.

string-bag, *n.* Filet (à provisions), *m.* **stringboard,** *n.* Limon (of a staircase), *m.* **stringcourse,** *n.* Cordon, *m.* **stringed,** *a.* À cordes (of musical instruments).

stringency ['strindʒənsi], *n.* Rigueur, *f.* **stringent,** *a.* Rigoureux, strict. **stringently,** *adv.* Strictement, rigoureusement.

stringless ['striŋlis], *a.* Sans cordes.

stringy ['striŋi], *a.* Fibreux; filandreux (of meat); coarcté (pulse).

strip [strip], *n.* Bande, *f.*, ruban; lambeau, *m.*, langue, *f.* (of land). *Landing strip*, piste d'atterrissage, *f.*; *strip cartoon*, bande illustrée, *f.*; *strip lighting*, éclairage fluorescent, *m.*; *strip-tease*, strip-tease, *m.*; (*fam.*) *to tear a strip off someone*, donner un savon à quelqu'un.
v.t.—Dépouiller (de); dévaliser (to rob); déshabiller (to undress); se dépouiller de (to take off); effeuiller; écorcer (a tree); teiller (hemp etc.); (*Naut.*) dégréer; (*Mil.*) dégrader. *To strip from*, enlever à, ôter à; *to strip of*, dépouiller de; *to strip off*, ôter, arracher.—*v.i.* Se déshabiller. *To strip well*, être bien bâti.

stripe [straip], *n.* Raie; barre, bande, *f.*; coup de fouet *or* de cravache (with a whip), *m.*; marque (weal), *f.*; (*Mil.*) chevron, galon, *m.* *To lose one's stripes*, (*Mil.*) être dégradé.— *v.t.* Rayer, barrer. **striped, stripy,** *a.* Rayé, à raies, zébré. (*Cine.*) *Striped film*, film magnétique, *m.*

stripling ['stripliŋ], *n.* Jeune homme; adolescent, *m.* *He is a mere stripling*, il est encore tout jeune.

stripping ['stripiŋ], *n.* Dépouillement, déshabillement, *m.*

strive [straiv], *v.i.* (*past* **strove** [strouv], *p.p.* **striven** ['strivən]) S'efforcer (de), tâcher (de), faire des efforts (pour), se débattre; se disputer (to vie). *To strive against*, lutter contre, se débattre contre; *to strive hard to*, faire tous ses efforts pour; *to strive with*, lutter avec, se disputer avec, rivaliser avec.

striving, *n.* Lutte, *f.*, efforts, *m.pl.*

strobilaceous [strɔbi'leifəs], *a.* Strobiligère. **strobile** ['strɔbil], *n.* Strobile, *m.* **strobiliform** [-'bilifɔːm], *a.* Strobiliforme.

stroboscopic, *a.* (*Cine.*) Stroboscopique. **stroboscopy,** *n.* Stroboscopie, *f.*

strode, *past* [STRIDE].

stroke [strouk], *n.* Coup; trait (dash); coup de foudre (lightning); coup de pinceau (of a

brush); trait de plume (of a pen); coup d'aviron (of an oar), *m.*; brassée (in swimming), course (of a piston), touche (touch), *f.*; coup de sang, *m.*, attaque, *f.* (paralytic stroke); chef de nage (of a boat's crew), *m.* *At a stroke*, d'un coup, d'un trait; *back-stroke*, coup de revers, *m.*; nage sur le dos, *f.*; *bold stroke*, coup hardi, *m.*; *down-stroke* (in writing), plein, *m.*; *master stroke*, coup de maître, *m.*; *on the stroke of two*, sur le coup de deux heures; *stroke of luck*, coup du sort, *m.*, aubaine, *f.*; *to keep stroke*, nager ensemble; *to pull stroke*, donner la nage; *up-stroke*, délié, *m.*; *who hasn't done a stroke of work*, qui n'a pas fait œuvre de ses dix doigts.—*v.t.* Passer la main sur, caresser. *To stroke the wrong way*, frotter à contre-poil.

stroke-oar, *n.* Chef de nage, *m.*

stroking, *n.* Caresses, *f.pl.*

stroll [stroul], *n.* (Courte) promenade, *f.*, tour, *m.*, flânerie, *f.* *Will you come for a stroll?* voulez-vous faire un tour?—*v.i.* Errer, se promener à l'aventure. *To stroll about*, flâner, errer çà et là.

stroller, *n.* Flâneur, *m.*, flâneuse, *f.*; comédien ambulant, *m.*, comédienne ambulante, *f.*

strolling, *a.* Qui erre, de flâneur, ambulant. *Strolling players*, troupe ambulante, *f.*, les forains, *m.pl.*

strong [strɔŋ], *a.* Fort, solide, ferme; vigoureux, énergique, résolu (vigorous). *An army a hundred thousand strong*, une armée forte de cent mille hommes; *strong light*, vive lumière, *f.*; *tact is not his strong point*, le tact n'est pas son fort; *to be strong in the arm*, avoir le bras fort; *to muster strong*, s'assembler en grand nombre; *to have a strong smell* (food), sentir fort; *with a strong hand*, avec énergie, énergiquement.—*adv.* (*colloq.*) Fort, fortement, avec énergie; avec succès. *The old man is still going strong*, le vieillard est toujours solide.

strong-backed, *a.* Aux reins forts. **strongbox,** *n.* Coffre-fort, *m.* **strong-fisted,** *a.* Au poignet solide. **stronghold,** *n.* Forteresse, *f.*, fort, *m.* **strongly,** *adv.* Fortement, fermement, énergiquement. *Strongly built*, solidement bâti; *to feel strongly about*, attacher une grande importance à. **strong-minded,** *a.* À l'esprit fort, résolu. **strongroom,** *n.* Cave aux coffres-forts, *f.*

strontia ['strɔnfiə], *n.* Strontiane, *f.* **strontianite,** *n.* Strontianite, *f.*

strontium ['strɔnfiəm], *n.* Strontium, *m.*

strop [strɔp], *n.* Cuir à rasoir, *m.*; (*Naut.*) estrope, *f.*—*v.t.* Repasser (sur le cuir), affiler.

strophe ['strɔfi *or* 'stroufi], *n.* Stance, strophe, *f.*

strove, *past* [STRIVE].

struck, *past* and *p.p.* [STRIKE].

structural ['strʌktʃərəl], *a.* De structure, structural.

structure ['strʌktʃə], *n.* Construction, structure, *f.*; édifice, monument, *m.*, facture, *f.* (play, poem).

struggle ['strʌgl], *n.* Lutte, *f.*, effort, *m.* *The struggle for life*, la lutte pour la vie, *f.*—*v.i.* Lutter, se débattre. *To struggle along*, avancer péniblement; *to struggle in*, se débattre dans; *to struggle to*, lutter pour; *to struggle with*, lutter contre.

struggler, *n.* Personne qui lutte *or* qui se débat, *f.*

struggling, *n.* Lutte, *f.*; effort, *m.*

strum [strʌm], *v.i.* Tapoter, taper (sur), jouailler. **strumming,** *n.* Tapotage, *m.*

struma ['stru:mə], *n.* Scrofules, *f.pl.* **strumous,** *a.* Strumeux.

*****strumpet** ['strʌmpit], *n.* Prostituée, *f.*

strung, *past and p.p.* [STRING].

strut [strʌt], *n.* Démarche fière, démarche affectée, *f.*; (*Carp. etc.*) étai, *m.*, entretoise, *f.*, entresillon, *m.*—*v.i.* Se pavaner, se carrer. **strutted,** *a.* Entretoisé, étayé. **struttingly,** *adv.* En se pavanant.

strychnine ['strikni:n] *or* **strychnia,** *n.* Strychnine, *f.* **strychninism,** *n.* Strychnisme, *m.*

stub [stʌb], *n.* Souche, *f.*, bout, tronçon (of a tree etc.); chicot, *m.* (tooth). *Stub (of a cheque-book),* souche d'un carnet de chèques. —*v.t.* Déraciner. *To stub one's toe (against),* buter (contre); *to stub out a cigarette,* écraser le bout d'une cigarette pour l'éteindre; *to stub up,* arracher.

stubble [stʌbl], *n.* Chaume, *m.* .**stubble-field,** *n.* Chaume, *m.* **stubbly,** *a.* Plein de chaume; hérissé (beard).

stubborn [stʌbən], *a.* Obstiné, opiniâtre, têtu, inflexible; réfractaire (of metals); rétif (of a horse). **stubbornly,** *adv.* Obstinément, opiniâtrement. **stubbornness,** *n.* Obstination, opiniâtreté, *f.*

stubby ['stʌbi], *a.* Trapu (of a person's build).

stucco ['stʌkou], *n.* Stuc, *m.*—*v.t.* Revêtir de stuc.

stuck [stʌk], *past* and *p.p.* [STICK]. (*fam.*) *Stuck-up,* affecté, prétentieux, suffisant.

stud [stʌd], *n.* Bouton de chemise (shirt-stud); clou (ornamental knob), street crossing); goujon; plot, *m.*; écurie (of horses), *f.*—*v.t.* Garnir de clous, clouter; (*fig.*) semer, parsemer (de).

stud-book, *n.* Registre des chevaux de pur sang, *m.* **stud-farm,** *n.* Haras, *m.* **stud-horse,** *n.* Étalon, *m.*

studding-sail ['stʌdiŋseil *or* stʌnsl], *n.* Bonnette, *f.*

student ['stju:dənt], *n.* Étudiant, élève, *m.*; personne studieuse, *f. Law-student,* étudiant en droit; *medical student,* étudiant en médecine, *m.*

studied ['stʌdid], *a.* Étudié, apprêté, recherché (of style etc.); prémédité, calculé (premeditated).

studio ['stju:diou], *n.* Atelier, *m.*; (*Cine.* and *Rad.*) studio, *m.*

studious ['stju:diəs], *a.* Studieux; adonné à l'étude; diligent (diligent); soigneux (careful); attentif (à), empressé (de). *To be studious to,* s'étudier à, chercher à, être empressé de. **studiously,** *adv.* Studieusement; avec soin, attentivement, avec empressement. **studiousness,** *n.* Attachement à l'étude, *m.*; application, *f.*

study ['stʌdi], *n.* Étude; attention *f.*, soin, *m.*, application (attention), *f.*; cabinet d'étude, cabinet de travail (apartment for writing etc.), *m. Brown study,* rêverie, méditation, *f.*; *study table,* table de travail, *f.*; *to be in a brown study,* être dans la lune; *to make it one's study to,* s'étudier à, s'occuper de.—*v.t.* Étudier, s'occuper de. *To study economy,*

viser à l'économie; *to study one's comfort,* rechercher ses aises.—*v.i.* Étudier, travailler; faire ses études (à); s'étudier, chercher, s'appliquer (to endeavour). *To study hard,* travailler ferme, (*fam.*) piocher, bûcher.

stuff [stʌf], *n.* Étoffe, *f.*, tissu, *m.*; (*pl.*) matériaux, *m.pl.*, étoffe (materials), *f.*; (*fig.*) matière, *f.*, choses, *f.pl.*, partie essentielle, *f.*; fatras (rubbish), *m. All stuff and nonsense!* c'est de la bêtise! balivernes! niaiseries que tout cela! *garden stuff,* légumes, *m.pl.*; *he is of the stuff of which statesmen are made,* il est du bois dont on fait les hommes d'État; *nasty stuff,* saleté, cochonnerie, *f.*; *old stuff,* vieillerie, *f.*; *silly stuff,* des sottises, des sornettes, *f.pl.*; *stuff!* bah! quelle bêtise! allons donc! *that's the stuff!* c'est du bon! *to do one's stuff,* se montrer à la hauteur, montrer ce qu'on peut faire; *what stuff!* quelles sottises! quel fatras! *wretched stuff,* méchante drogue, *f.*—*v.t.* Rembourrer; bourrer (to cram); boucher (a hole); garnir, gaver; (*Taxidermy*) empailler; (*Cook.*) farcir; (*slang*) en faire accroire à. *My nose is stuffed up,* je suis enchifrené; *stuffed up with nonsense,* plein d'affectation; *to look stuffed,* avoir l'air empaillé; *to stuff in,* bourrer; *to stuff oneself,* se bourrer; se gorger; *to stuff up,* boucher. —*v.i.* Se bourrer; se gorger. **stuffer,** *n.* Empailleur, *m.*

stuffiness, *n.* Manque d'air, *m.*; (*fig.*) esprit étroit, *m.* **stuffing,** *n.* Bourre (material for), *f.*; rembourrage (process), *m.*; (*Cook.*) farce, *f.*; (*Taxidermy*) empaillage, *m.*, taxidermie, *f.* **stuffing-box,** *n.* Boîte à étoupes, *f.*, presseétoupe, *m.* **stuffy,** *a.* Privé d'air, renfermé. *To be stuffy,* sentir le renfermé; (*fig.*) avoir des préjugés, être fermé.

stultify ['stʌltifai], *v.t.* Rendre nul, infirmer; démentir, contredire (to belie). *To stultify oneself,* se rendre ridicule, se dédire, se contredire.

stum [stʌm], *n.* Moût, *m.*—*v.t.* Soufrer (wine).

stumble [stʌmbl], *v.i.* Trébucher, broncher; (*fig.*) faire un faux pas, faillir. *To stumble upon,* rencontrer par hasard, tomber sur.—*n.* Faux pas, *m.*; bévue (blunder), *f.*

stumbling, *n.* Trébuchement, *m.*; (*fig.*) faux pas, *m.*—*a.* Qui trébuche, trébuchant. **stumbling-block,** *n.* Pierre d'achoppement, *f.*

stump [stʌmp], *n.* Tronçon, *m.*, souche, *f.*; chicot (of a tooth); trognon (of a cabbage); bout (of a pen); moignon (of a limb), *m.*; (*Drawing*) estompe, *f.*; (*Cricket*) piquet de guichet, *m. Stir your stumps,* (*colloq.*) remuez-vous, trémoussez-vous! *stumps were drawn at ....,* on a enlevé les guichets à .... —*v.t.* (*Drawing*) Estomper; haranguer (to speechify); (*fig.*) réduire au silence, embarrasser, coller. *To stump the country,* faire une tournée électorale.—*v.i.* Marcher en clopinant. *To stump up,* (*slang*) payer.

stump-orator, *n.* Orateur de carrefour, péroreur, *m.*

stumpy, *a.* Plein de tronçons; trapu (of a person).

stun [stʌn], *v.t.* Étourdir (de); (*fig.*) abasourdir, foudroyer.

stung, *past* and *p.p.* [STING].

stunk, *past* and *p.p.* [STINK].

stunner, *n.* Type épatant, *m.*; fille du tonnerre, *f.*

stunning, *a.* Étourdissant; (*slang*) fameux, épatant, abracadabrant.

stunt [stʌnt], *v.t.* Empêcher de croître; rendre rabougri, rabougrir.—*n.* (*slang*) Fait, tour qui étonne, tour de force, *m.*; réclame,*f.* To *perform stunts,* (*Av.*) faire des acrobaties (en vol). **stunted,** *a.* Rabougri. To *become stunted,* se rabougrir. **stuntedness,** *n.* Rabougrissement, *m.*

stupe [stju:p], *n.* (*Med.*) Compresse,*f.*

stupefaction [stju:pi'fækʃən], *n.* Stupéfaction, *f.*; étonnement, *m.*

stupefy ['stju:pifai], *v.t.* Hébéter, abrutir; stupéfier, engourdir (to benumb). **stupefying,** *a.* Stupéfiant.

stupendous [stju'pendəs], *a.* Prodigieux, foudroyant. **stupendously,** *adv.* Prodigieusement. **stupendousness,** *n.* Grandeur prodigieuse, *f.*

stupid ['stju:pid], *a.* Stupide, sot, bête; lourd. *Stupid thing,* stupidité, *f.*, bêta, *m.*, bête (person),*f.*; to become stupid, devenir stupide, s'abêtir.

stupidity [stju:'piditi], *n.* Stupidité, bêtise, *f.* **stupidly,** *adv.* Stupidement, sottement, bêtement.

stupor, *n.* Stupeur, *f.*

sturdily ['stə:dili], *adv.* Hardiment, fortement, vigoureusement, résolument. **sturdiness,** *n.* Hardiesse, vigueur, énergie, résolution,*f.* **sturdy,** *a.* Vigoureux, fort, robuste; hardi.—*n.* Tournis (disease in sheep), *m.*

sturgeon ['stə:dʒən], *n.* Esturgeon, *m.*

stutter ['stʌtə], *v.t., v.i.* Bégayer. **stutterer,** *n.* Bègue, *m.* or *f.* **stuttering,** *n.* Bégaiement, *m.* **stutteringly,** *adv.* En bégayant.

sty [stai], *n.* Étable (à cochons), *f.*; compèreloriot, orgelet (on eyelid), *m.* What a pigsty! (*fig.*) Quel taudis! Quel désordre!—*v.t.* Mettre (pigs) dans une étable.

Stygian ['stidʒiən], *a.* Stygien.

stylar ['stailə], *a.* (*Bot.*) Stylaire.

style [stail], *n.* Style; (*fig.*) genre, *m.*, manière, *f.*, ton; stylet (probe); titre, nom (title), *m.*; raison sociale (of a firm), *f.* He gave it me in *fine style,* il m'en a dit d'une belle manière, il m'a arrangé d'une belle façon; his style is bad, il n'a pas de style; in bad style, dans le mauvais genre; in good style, dans le bon genre; in the grand style, dans le grand genre, en grand seigneur; in style, comme il faut, d'importance (of a thrashing); style is the man himself, le style c'est l'homme; the style in which they live, le train qu'ils mènent; to go on in fine style, aller grand train; to live in first-rate style, mener grand train; to live in style, avoir un train de maison.—*v.t.* Appeler, qualifier de, donner le titre de . . . à. . . . To style oneself, se faire appeler, se donner le titre de, s'intituler.

styliform ['stailifɔ:m], *a.* (*Bot.*) Styliforme.

stylish, *a.* Élégant, de bon ton, comme il faut, chic. **stylishly,** *adv.* Elégamment, avec chic. **stylist,** *n.* Styliste, *m.* **stylistics,** *n.* Stylistique,*f.* **stylize,** *v.t.* Styliser.

stylobate ['stailobeit], *n.* Stylobate, *m.* **stylograph,** *n.* Stylographe, *m.*

styloid ['stailɔid], *a.* Styloïde.

stylus ['stailəs], *n.* Style, *m.*

styptic ['stiptik], *a.* and *n.* (*Med.*) Styptique, *m.* **stypticity** [-'tisiti], *n.* Qualité styptique,*f.*

Styria ['stiriə]. Styrie, *f.*

Styx [stiks]. Styx, *m.*

suable ['sju:əbl], *a.* Qui peut être l'objet de poursuites.

suasive ['sweisiv], *a.* Persuasif.

suave [sweiv *or* swɑ:v], *a.* Suave. **suavely,** *adv.* Suavement.

suavity ['swæviti], *n.* Suavité, *f.*

subacrid [sʌb'ækrid], *a.* Un peu âcre.

subagent [-'eidʒənt], *n.* Sous-agent, *m.*

subalpine [-'ælpain], *a.* Subalpin.

subaltern ['sʌbəltən], *a.* Subalterne.—*n.* (Sous-) lieutenant, *m.* **subalternate**[-'tə:nət], *a.* Qui alterne, alternatif. **subalternation** [-ɔltə'neiʃən], *n.* Subalternité, *f.*

subaquatic [sʌbə'kwætik], *a.* Sous l'eau, submergé.

sub-committee [-kə'miti], *n.* Sous-commission,*f.*

subconscious, *a.* and *n.* (*Psych.*) Subconscient, *m.* **subconsciously,** *adv.* Inconsciemment.

subcontractor [-kən'træktə], *n.* Sous-entrepreneur, *m.*

subcostal [-'kɔstl], *a.* Sous-costal.

subcutaneous [-kju'teiniəs], *a.* Sous-cutané.

subdeacon [-'di:kən], *n.* Sous-diacre, *m.*

subdean [-'di:n], *n.* Sous-doyen, *m.* **subdeanery,** *n.* Sous-doyenné, *m.*

subdelegate [-'deligit], *n.* Subdélégué, *m.*—*v.t.* [-geit] Subdéléguer. **subdelegation** [-'geiʃən], *n.* Subdélégation, *f.*

subdirector [sʌbdi'rektə], *n.* Sous-directeur, *m.*

subdivide [sʌbdi'vaid], *v.t.* Subdiviser.—*v.i.* Se subdiviser. **subdivision** [-'viʒən], *n.* Subdivision, *f.*; morcellement (of land etc.), *m.*

subduable [səb'dju:əbl], *a.* Domptable.

subdual, *n.* Soumission,*f.*

subdue [səb'dju:], *v.t.* Subjuguer, soumettre, dompter, assujettir; étouffer, adoucir (sound). *In a subdued tone,* en baissant la voix; in a *subdued voice,* d'une voix étouffée; subdued light, demi-jour, *m.* **subduer,** *n.* Vainqueur, dompteur, *m.*

sub-edit [sʌb'edit], *v.t.* Corriger, mettre au point.

sub-editor [sʌb'editə], *n.* Secrétaire de la rédaction, *m.* **sub-editorship,** *n.* Secrétariat, *m.*

suber ['sju:bə], *n.* (*Bot.*) Liège, *m.*

suberic [sju'berik], *a.* Subérique.

suberin ['sju:bərin], *n.* Subérine,*f.* **suberous,** *a.* Subéreux.

subfusc [sʌb'fʌsk], *a.* Sombre (clothes).

sub-heading ['sʌbhediŋ], *n.* Sous-titre, *m.*

sub-human [sʌb'hju:mən], *a.* Presque humain; pas tout à fait humain.

subinspector, *n.* Sous-inspecteur, *m.*

subjacent [sʌb'dʒeisənt], *a.* Subjacent, sous-jacent.

subject (1) ['sʌbdʒikt], *a.* Assujetti, soumis; sujet (à), exposé (à); (*Fin.*) grevé (de).—*n.* Sujet, *m.*, question, matière,*f.*; (*sch.*) matière, discipline,*f.*; particulier, *m.*, personne,*f.* To *change the subject,* parler d'autre chose; he is *studying three subjects,* il étudie trois matières; *on the subject of,* au sujet de.

subject (2) [səb'dʒekt], *v.t.* Assujettir, soumettre, rendre sujet (à), exposer (à). To *subject oneself to,* s'exposer à.

subjection [-'dʒekʃən], *n.* Sujétion, soumission, *f.*, assujettissement, *m.* To bring under *subjection,* assujettir, soumettre.

subjective, *a.* Subjectif. **subjectively,** *adv.* Subjectivement. **subjectivism,** *n.* Subjectivisme, *m.* **subjectivity** [sʌbdʒec'tiviti], *n.* Subjectivité, *f.*

subject-matter, *n.* Sujet, *m.*, matière, *f.* (of a speech or a writing).

subjoin [sʌb'dʒɔin], *v.t.* Joindre (à); (*Comm.*) remettre ci-contre. **subjoined,** *a.* Ci-joint, ci-contre.

sub judice ['sʌb'dʒu:disi], *phr.* Pas encore jugé.

subjugate ['sʌbdʒugeit], *v.t.* Subjuguer, soumettre, réduire, dompter. **subjugation** [-'geiʃən], *n.* Assujettissement, *m.*, soumission, *f.*

subjunction [sʌb'dʒʌŋkʃən], *n.* Adjonction, *f.* **subjunctive,** *a.* and *n.* (*Gram.*) Subjonctif, *m.* In the subjunctive, au subjonctif.

sublease [sʌb'li:s] or **subletting,** *n.* Sous-location, *f.* **sub-lessee,** *n.* Sous-locataire, *m.* **sub-lessor,** *n.* Sous-bailleur, *m.*

sublet [-'let], *v.t.* (*past and p.p.* **sublet**) Sous-louer.

sub-librarian [-lai'brɛəriən], *n.* Sous-bibliothécaire, *m.*

sub-lieutenant [sʌblef'tenənt], *n.* (*Navy*) Enseigne, *m.*

sublimate (1) ['sʌblimeit], *v.t.* Sublimer, idéaliser.

sublimate (2) ['sʌblimət], *n.* Sublimé, *m.* **sublimation,** *n.* Sublimation, *f.* **sublimatory,** *n.* Sublimatoire, *m.*

sublime [sə'blaim], *a.* Élevé, haut, sublime. —*n.* Sublime, *m.* **sublimely,** *adv.* D'une manière sublime, avec sublimité.

sublimity [sə'blimiti] or **sublimeness,** *n.* Élévation, hauteur, sublimité, *f.*; sublime, *m.*

sublingual [sʌb'liŋwəl], *a.* Sublingual.

sublunary [-'lu:nəri], *a.* Sublunaire.

sub-machine-gun, *n.* Mitraillette, *f.*

sub-manager, *n.* Sous-directeur, *m.*

submarine ['sʌbməri:n], *a.* and *n.* Sous-marin, submersible, *m.*

sub-maxillary [sʌbmæk'siləri], *a.* Sous-maxillaire.

submerge [səb'mə:dʒ], *v.t.* Submerger, plonger. *Submerged submarine,* sous-marin en plongée.—*v.i.* Plonger. **submergence,** *n.* Submersion, plongée, *f.*

submission [sʌb'miʃən], *n.* Soumission; résignation, déférence, *f.* **submissive** [-'misiv], *a.* Soumis (à); docile, résigné. **submissively,** *adv.* Avec soumission, avec déférence. **submissiveness,** *n.* Soumission, déférence, *f.*

submit [sʌb'mit], *v.t.* Soumettre (à).—*v.i.* Se soumettre (à).

submultiple [sʌb'mʌltipl], *n.* Sous-multiple, *m.*

subnormal [sʌb'nɔ:ml], *a.* Sous-normal.

subordinate (1) [sə'bɔ:dinət], *a.* Subordonné (à); inférieur, subalterne.—*n.* Subordonné, *m.*

subordinate (2) [sə'bɔ:dineit], *v.t.* Subordonner (à). **subordinately,** *adv.* Subordonnément, en sous-ordre. **subordination** [-'neiʃən], *n.* Subordination, *f.*; rang inférieur, *m.*

suborn [sə'bɔ:n], *v.t.* Suborner. **subornation** [sʌbɔ:'neiʃən], *n.* Subornation, corruption, *f.* **suborner** [sə'bɔ:nə], *n.* Suborneur, *m.*, suborneuse, *f.*

subpoena [sʌb'pi:nə], *n.* (*Law*) Citation, assignation, *f.*—*v.t.* Citer, assigner.

sub-prefect [sʌb'pri:fekt], *n.* Sous-préfet, *m.*

subprior [-'praiə], *n.* Sous-prieur, *m.*

subrector [-'rektə], *n.* Vice-recteur, *m.*

subreption [sʌb'repʃən], *n.* (*Law*) Subreption, *f.*

subrogate ['sʌbrogeit], *v.t.* (*Law*) Subroger, substituer.

sub rosa [sʌb'rouzə], *adv. phr.* Secrètement, sous le manteau; confidentiellement.

subscribe [səb'skraib], *v.t.* Souscrire, signer; se cotiser (à *or* pour); s'abonner, prendre un abonnement à (a newspaper etc.) *To subscribe five pounds to,* souscrire pour la somme de cinq livres à; *to subscribe for twenty shares,* (*Fin.*) souscrire à vingt actions; *to subscribe oneself,* se dire.—*v.i.* Souscrire (à *or* pour). *To cease to subscribe to,* se désabonner à; *to subscribe to a newspaper,* s'abonner *or* prendre un abonnement à un journal, être abonné à un journal. **subscriber,** *n.* Souscripteur; abonné, *m.*, abonnée (to a newspaper etc.), *f.* **subscription** [-'skripʃən], *n.* Souscription, signature, adhésion; cotisation, *f.*; abonnement (to a newspaper etc.), *m.*

subsection ['sʌbsekʃn], *n.* Subdivision, *f.*

subsequence ['sʌbsikwəns], *n.* Postériorité, *f.* **subsequent,** *a.* Subséquent, postérieur. **subsequently,** *adv.* Ensuite, après; postérieurement.

subserve [sʌb'sə:v], *v.t.* Aider à, contribuer à; favoriser. **subservience** *or* **subserviency,** *n.* Concours, *m.*; dépendance, *f.*; servilité, *f.* **subservient,** *a.* Subordonné (à); qui contribue à; obséquieux. *To make subservient to,* faire servir à. **subserviently,** *adv.* En sous-ordre, utilement; servilement.

subside [səb'said], *v.i.* S'affaisser (to sink); baisser, s'abaisser, se calmer, s'apaiser (to abate etc.); se faire (person). *To subside into,* se changer en.

subsidence ['sʌbsidəns *or* səb'saidəns], *n.* Affaissement, effondrement; (*fig.*) apaisement, *m.*, décrue, baisse, *f.* (river).

subsidiarily [sʌb'sidjərili], *adv.* Subsidiairement.

subsidiary [sʌb'sidjəri], *a.* Subsidiaire (à).—*n.* Auxiliaire, *m.*; filiale, *f.* (company).

subsidize ['sʌbsidaiz], *v.t.* Subventionner, donner des subsides à. **subsidy,** *n.* Subvention, *f.*; subside (to a person), *m.*

subsist [səb'sist], *v.i.* Subsister, exister; vivre (de). *To subsist on,* subsister de, vivre de.—*n.* Acompte (sur le salaire), *m.* **subsistence,** *n.* Subsistance, *f.*, entretien, *m.*, moyens d'existence, *m.pl.*; existence (being), *f.*; acompte, *m.* **subsistent,** *a.* Existant, qui existe. **subsisting,** *a.* Subsistant.

subsoil ['sʌbsɔil], *n.* Sous-sol, *m.* *To sell soil and subsoil,* vendre le fonds et le tréfonds. **subsoil-plough,** *n.* Fouilleuse, *f.*

sub-species [-'spi:ʃi:z], *n.* Sous-espèce, *f.*

substance ['sʌbstəns], *n.* Substance, *f.*; fond (meaning), avoir, *m.*; biens (goods), *m.pl.* *Man of substance,* homme qui a du bien.

substandard ['sʌb'stændəd], *a.* (Format) réduit; inférieur au niveau moyen.

substantial [sʌb'stænʃl], *a.* Substantiel, réel, solide, important; aisé, à l'aise (well off). *Substantial meal,* repas substantiel, *m.*; *substantial proof,* preuve matérielle, *f.*—*n.* (*pl.*)

Parties essentielles, *f.pl.* **substantiality** [-ʃiˈæliti], *n.* Substantialité; réalité; solidité, *f.* **substantially,** *adv.* Solidement, fortement, réellement, vraiment, considérablement. **substantiate** [-ˈstænʃieit], *v.t.* Établir, confirmer, appuyer. **substantive** [ˈsʌbstəntiv], *n.* (*Gram.*) Substantif, nom, *m.*—*a.* Indépendant, autonome, réel; (*Gram.*) substantif. (*Mil.*) *Substantive rank,* grade effectif, *m.* **substantively,** *adv.* Substantivement.

sub-station [ˈsʌbsteiʃn], *n.* (*Elec.*) Sousstation; sous-centrale, *f.*

substitute [ˈsʌbstitjuːt], *v.t.* Substituer (à). —*n.* Substitut, remplaçant; représentant, mandataire; (of things) succédané, *m. As a substitute for,* pour remplacer; *that is a substitute for,* cela remplace. **substitution** [-ˈtjuːʃən], *n.* Substitution, *f.*; remplacement, *m.*

substratum [sʌbˈstreitəm or -ˈstraːtəm], *n.* (*pl.* **substrata**) Substratum, substrat, *m.*, couche inférieure, *f.*; (*Agric.*) sous-sol, *m.*; (*fig.*) substance, *f. There is a substratum of truth in that,* il y a un fond de vérité en cela.

substruction [-ˈstrʌkʃən], or **substructure,** *n.* Substruction, infra-structure, *f.*, fondement, *m.*

subtangent [-ˈtændʒənt], *n.* Sous-tangente, *f.*

subtenancy [-ˈtenənsi], *n.* Sous-location, *f.*

subtenant, *n.* Sous-locataire, *m.* or *f.*

subtend [-ˈtend], *v.t.* Sous-tendre. **subtense,** *n.* Sous-tendante, corde, *f.*

subterfuge [ˈsʌbtəfjuːdʒ], *n.* Subterfuge, faux-fuyant, *m.*

subterranean [sʌbtəˈreiniən] or **subterraneous,** *a.* Souterrain. **subterraneously,** *adv.* Souterrainement.

*****subtile** [ˈsʌbtil], *a.* Subtil, fin. **subtilization** [-laiˈzeiʃən], *n.* Subtilisation, *f.* **subtilize** [ˈsʌbtilaiz], *v.t.* Subtiliser, raffiner.

subtilty or **subtlety** [ˈsʌtlti] or **subtleness,** *n.* Subtilité, *f.*, finesse, *f.*

sub-title [ˈsʌbtaitl], *n.* Sous-titre, *m.* **subtitling,** *n.* (*Cine.*) Sous-titrage, *m.*

subtle [sʌtl], *a.* Subtil, rusé; fin. **subtly** [ˈsʌtli], *adv.* Subtilement.

subtract [səbˈtrækt], *v.t.* Défalquer; (*Arith.*) soustraire, retrancher, ôter. **subtraction,** *n.* Déduction, *f.*, retranchement, *m.*; (*Arith.*) soustraction, *f.* **subtractive,** *a.* Qui tend à soustraire *or* à retrancher.

subtrahend [ˈsʌbtrəhend], *n.* (*Arith.*) Nombre à retrancher, *m.*

subtropical [sʌbˈtrɔpikl], *a.* Subtropical, semi-tropical.

subulate [ˈsjuːbjulət], *a.* (*Bot.*) Subulé, en forme d'alène.

suburb [ˈsʌbəːb], *n.* Faubourg, *m.*, (*pl.*) alentours, environs, *m.pl.*, banlieue, *f. Garden suburb,* cité-jardin, *f.*

suburban [səˈbəːbən], *a.* De la banlieue, suburbain; (*pej.*) ennuyeux, borné. *A suburban residence,* une maison de banlieue. **suburbanite,** *n.* Banlieusard, *m.*

subvariety [sʌbvəˈraiəti], *n.* Sous-variété, *f.*

subvention [səbˈvenʃən], *n.* Subvention, *f.*

subversion [səbˈvəːʃən], *n.* Subversion, *f.*, renversement, *m.* **subversive,** *a.* Subversif.

subvert, *v.t.* Renverser. **subverter,** *n.* Destructeur, *m.*, destructrice, *f.*

subway [ˈsʌbwei], *n.* Passage souterrain,

passage en dessous, souterrain, *m.*; (*Am.*) métro, *m.*

succedaneous [sʌksiˈdeiniəs], *a.* Succédané.

succeed [səkˈsiːd], *v.i.* Succéder (à); hériter (of an estate, property); parvenir (à), réussir (to be successful). *He succeeds in everything,* il réussit en tout, tout lui réussit; *to succeed in doing something,* réussir à, parvenir à, faire quelque chose.—*v.t.* Succéder à, suivre. *To succeed each other,* se succéder. **succeeding,** *a.* Suivant (of a past); à venir, futur (of the future); successif (successive).

success [səkˈses], *n.* Succès, *m.*, réussite; bonne chance (luck), *f. I wish you success!* bonne chance! *success justifies the means,* la fin justifie les moyens; *to have success,* avoir du succès, réussir; *to make a success of something,* réussir *or* faire réussir quelque chose. **successful,** *a.* Heureux; couronné de succès, réussi, victorieux. *To be successful,* avoir du succès, réussir; *to be successful in,* réussir à. **successfully,** *adv.* Heureusement, avec succès. **successfulness,** *n.* Succès, *m.*

succession [səkˈseʃən], *n.* Succession, suite, *f.*; avènement (to a throne etc.), *m.*; successeurs, descendants, *m.pl.*; postérité (lineage), *f. In succession,* successivement, tour à tour, de suite; *succession duty,* droits de succession, *m.pl.*; *succession of crops,* rotation, *f.* **successive** [-ˈsesiv], *a.* Successif, consécutif. **successively,** *adv.* Successivement. **successiveness,** *n.* Nature successive, *f.* **successor,** *n.* Successeur, *m.*

succinct [səkˈsiŋkt], *a.* Succinct, concis. **succinctly,** *adv.* Succinctement, avec concision. **succinctness,** *n.* Concision, brièveté, *f.*

succory [ˈsʌkəri], *n.* Chicorée, *f.*

succour [ˈsʌkə], *v.t.* Secourir, aider, assister. —*n.* Secours, *m.*, aide, assistance, *f.*

succubus [ˈsʌkjubəs], *n.* Succube, *m.*

succulence [ˈsʌkjuləns] or **succulency,** *n.* Succulence, *f.* **succulent,** *a.* Succulent, plein de jus.

succumb [səˈkʌm], *v.i.* Succomber à; céder, se soumettre (à).

succussion [səˈkʌʃən], *n.* Secousse, *f.*

such [sʌtʃ], *a.* Tel, pareil, semblable. *At such a time,* à un tel moment; *did anyone ever see such a war?* a-t-on jamais vu une guerre pareille? *give me such things as* . . ., donnez-moi des choses comme . . .; *he makes such grimaces,* il fait de ces grimaces; *he is such a bore,* il est si ennuyeux *or* si assommant; *he remained such a time that,* il est resté si longtemps que; *if you repay me not on such a day in such a place, such sum or sums as are expressed, etc.,* si vous ne me remboursez pas tel jour, à tel endroit la somme ou les sommes spécifiées, etc.; *in such times as these,* par le temps qui court; *in such weather,* par le temps qu'il fait; *it eats and sleeps, and has such senses as we have,* il boit et mange, et a les mêmes sens que nous; *it is no such thing,* il n'en est rien; *it is such a way,* c'est si loin; *never was there a man such as he,* il n'y eut jamais son pareil; *no such thing,* rien de semblable, rien de pareil; *on such occasions,* dans ces occasions, à des occasions pareilles; *such a kind man,* un homme si aimable; *such and such,* tel et tel; *such an honour,* un si grand honneur; *such a one*, un tel, *m.*, une telle, *f.*; *such a one as*, tel que; *such a profusion of flowers!* quelle profusion de fleurs! *such as it is*, tel quel, *m.*, telle quelle, *f.*; *such are the rewards of virtue*, ce sont là les récompenses de la vertu; *such as you*, tel que vous; *tears such as angels weep*, des larmes comme en pleurent les anges; *such is life!* c'est la vie! *there is no such thing as that*, cela n'existe pas; *these verses are by such a poet*, ces vers sont de tel poète; *you are such a man!* vous êtes si galant, si brave, si farceur, etc.; *we have walked such a way*, nous avons tellement marché que; *with such*, pour de telles personnes.—*pron.* Tel, *m.*, telle, *f.*; de tels, *pl.* Such as, ceux qui; celles qui. *Such as do not like*, ceux qui n'aiment pas. *As such*, comme tel, en tant que tel.

suchlike, *a.* Semblable, pareil; de ce genre.

suck [sʌk], *v.t.* Sucer; téter (at the breast); aspirer, pomper (to inhale); absorber, boire (to absorb). *It is teaching one's grandmother to suck eggs*, c'est Gros-Jean qui en remontre à son curé; *to suck down*, sucer, (*fig.*) engloutir, entraîner au fond; *to suck in*, sucer, absorber (to absorb), aspirer (to inhale), gober (to believe); *to suck in with one's milk*, sucer avec le lait; *to suck someone dry*, (*fig.*) sucer quelqu'un jusqu'à la moelle, vider quelqu'un; *to suck out*, sucer, tirer, vider (en suçant); *to suck up*, sucer, absorber.—*v.i.* Sucer; téter (at the breast); aspirer (to draw in). *To suck up to someone*, lécher les bottes à quelqu'un.—*n.* Action de sucer. *To give suck to a child*, donner le sein à un enfant. *Sucks!* bonbons! coincé! **sucker**, *n.* Suceur; piston (of a pump); (*Ent.*) suçoir; (*Bot.*) surgeon, *m.*; (*fig.*) gobeur, *m.*

sucking, *n.* Sucement, *m.*, succion; aspiration, absorption (of liquids), *f.*—*a.* Qui suce, qui tette, qui absorbe, aspirant, d'aspiration. *Sucking child*, enfant à la mamelle, *m.* **sucking-fish**, *n.* Rémora, *m.* **sucking-pig**, *n.* Cochon de lait, *m.*

suckle [sʌkl], *v.t.* Allaiter, nourrir, donner le sein à. **suckling**, *n.* Allaitement; enfant à la mamelle, nourrisson (child), *m.*

sucrose ['suːkrous], *n.* Saccharose, *m.*

suction ['sʌkʃən], *n.* Succion, aspiration, absorption, *f.* **suction-pipe**, *n.* Tuyau d'aspiration, *m.* **suction-pump**, *n.* Pompe aspirante, *f.* **suctorial** [-'tɔːriəl], *a.* Suceur.

Sudan [su'dæn *or* su'dɑːn]. Le Soudan, *m.* **Sudanese**, *a.* and *n.* Soudanais, -aise.

sudation [sju'deiʃən], *n.* Sudation, *f.*

sudatory ['sjuːdətəri], *n.* and *a.* Sudatoire, *m.*

sudden [sʌdn], *a.* Subit, soudain; inattendu, imprévu. *All of a sudden*, tout à coup; *sudden death*, mort subite, *f.* **suddenly**, *adv.* Subitement, soudain, soudainement, tout à coup. **suddenness**, *n.* Soudaineté, *f.*

Sudeten [su'deitn], *n.* Sudètes, *m.pl.*—*a.* Sudète.

sudoriferous [sjuːdə'rifərəs], *a.* Sudorifère, sudoripare.

sudorific [sjuːdə'rifik], *a.* and *n.* Sudorifique, *m.*

suds [sʌdz] *or* **soap-suds**, *n.pl.* Eau de savon, lessive, *f.*

sue [sjuː], *v.t.* Poursuivre (en justice); (*fig.*) demander. *To sue for damages*, poursuivre en dommages-intérêts; *to sue for libel*, attaquer en diffamation; *to sue for separation*, plaider en séparation; *to sue out*, obtenir par pétition.—*v.i.* Implorer.   *To sue for*, solliciter, demander, implorer.

suède [sweid], *n.* Daim, *m.* (shoes), peau de suède, *f.*, suède, *m.* (gloves).

suet ['sjuːit], *n.* Graisse de rognon (de bœuf *or* de mouton), *f.*

Suetonius [suːi'tounjəs]. Suétone, *m.*

Suez ['suːiz]. Suez.

suffer ['sʌfə], *v.t.* Souffrir; supporter, endurer, subir (to undergo); laisser, permettre (to permit). *He was suffered to go*, on le laissa aller; *suffer me to tell you*, permettez-moi de vous dire; *to suffer defeat*, subir une défaite; *to suffer losses*, éprouver des pertes; *to suffer oneself to be imposed upon*, se laisser tromper; *to suffer punishment*, subir une peine.—*v.i.* Souffrir (de). *He will suffer for it*, il en portera la peine, il payera les pots cassés; *to suffer for*, souffrir de, pâtir de, porter la peine de.

sufferable, *a.* Supportable, tolérable. **sufferably**, *adv.* D'une manière supportable.

sufferance, *n.* Tolérance; souffrance (endurance), *f.* *Bill of sufferance*, (Customs) lettre d'exemption des droits de douane, *f.*; *to exist only upon sufferance*, n'exister que par tolérance; *you are here only on sufferance*, vous n'êtes ici que par tolérance.

sufferer, *n.* Personne qui souffre; victime (de), *f.*; patient, *m.* *Fellow-sufferer*, compagnon d'infortune, *m.*; *to be a heavy sufferer by*, perdre beaucoup à; *to be a sufferer by*, être victime de; *yes, but I am the sufferer*, oui, mais c'est moi qui en souffre.

suffering, *n.* Souffrance, douleur, *f.*—*a.* Souffrant. **sufferingly**, *adv.* Avec douleur, en souffrant.

suffice [sə'fais], *v.t.* Suffire à, satisfaire.—*v.i.* Suffire (de). *Suffice it to say*, qu'il suffise de dire, suffit que.

sufficiency [sə'fiʃənsi], *n.* Suffisance; fortune suffisante, aisance (competence), *f.* *A sufficiency of*, assez de; *sufficiency is a compound of vanity and ignorance*, la suffisance est un composé de vanité et d'ignorance.

sufficient [sə'fiʃənt], *a.* Suffisant, assez. *It is not sufficient for us to know . . .*, il ne nous suffit pas de savoir . . .; *sufficient for*, suffisant pour, qui suffit à; *sufficient reason*, raison suffisante, *f.*; *sufficient unto the day is the evil thereof*, à chaque jour suffit sa peine; *that is sufficient*, suffit, c'est assez. **sufficiently** *or* **sufficingly**, *adv.* Suffisamment, assez.

suffix ['sʌfiks], *n.* Suffixe, *m.*

suffocate ['sʌfəkeit], *v.t.*, *v.i.* Suffoquer, étouffer, asphyxier. **suffocating**, *a.* Suffocant, étouffant, asphyxiant. **suffocation** [-'keiʃən], *n.* Suffocation, asphyxie, *f.*, étouffement, *m.* **suffocative**, *a.* Suffocant, étouffant.

suffragan ['sʌfrəgən], *a.* and *n.* Suffragant, *m.* *Suffragan bishop*, évêque suffragant, *m.*

suffrage ['sʌfridʒ], *n.* Suffrage, *m.* *Universal suffrage*, suffrage universel, *m.*

suffragette [sʌfrə'dʒet], *n.* Suffragette, *f.*

suffuse [sə'fjuːz], *v.t.* Répandre, couvrir (de); répandre sur; se répandre sur. *Her face was suffused with blushes*, une rougeur lui était montée au visage; *his eyes suffused with tears*, les yeux gonflés de larmes; *tears suffused his cheeks*, des larmes coulaient sur ses joues.

suffusion [sə'fju:ʒən], *n.* Épanchement, *m.*, suffusion, *f.*

sugar ['ʃugə], *n.* Sucre, *m.* *Barley sugar*, sucre d'orge, *m.*; *brown sugar* or *moist sugar*, cassonade, *f.*; *burnt sugar*, caramel, *m.*; *castor sugar*, sucre en poudre, *m.*; *Demerara sugar*, cassonade à gros cristaux, *f.*; *granulated sugar*, sucre cristallisé, *m.*; *lump of sugar*, morceau de sucre, *m.*; *lump sugar*, sucre cassé; *sugar and water*, eau sucrée, *f.*; *to sweeten with sugar*, sucrer.—*v.t.* Sucrer; (*fig.*) adoucir.

sugar-almond, *n.* Dragée, *f.* **sugar-basin,** *n.* Sucrier, *m.* **sugar-beet,** *n.* Betterave à sucre, *f.* **sugar-candy,** *n.* Sucre candi, *m.* **sugar-cane,** *n.* Canne à sucre, *f.* **sugar daddy,** *n.* (*fam.*) Vieux protecteur, *m.* **sugared,** *a.* Sucré; (*fig.*) doux, mielleux. **sugar-loaf,** *n.* Pain de sucre, *m.* *Shaped like a sugar-loaf,* en pain de sucre. **sugar-maple,** *n.* Érable à sucre, *m.* **sugar-mill,** *n.* Moulin à cannes (à sucre), *m.* **sugar-pea,** *n.* (Pois) mange-tout, *m.inv.* **sugar-plantation,** *n.* Plantation de cannes à sucre, *f.* **sugar-planter,** *n.* Planteur de cannes à sucre, *m.* **sugar-refiner,** *n.* Raffineur de sucre, *m.* **sugar-refinery,** *n.* Raffinerie de sucre, *f.* **sugar-refining,** *n.* Raffinage du sucre, *m.* **sugar-tongs,** *n.pl.* Pince à sucre, *f.* **sugary,** *a.* Sucré; trop sucré; saupoudré de sucre; (*fig.*) mielleux.

suggest [sə'dʒest], *v.t.* Suggérer, proposer; inspirer, faire naître, insinuer, donner. *To suggest itself to the mind,* se présenter à l'esprit. **suggestion,** *n.* Suggestion; proposition, indication, idée, *f.*; nuance, *f.* **suggestive,** *a.* Suggestif, qui inspire, qui suggère, qui fait penser à. *Suggestive of,* qui vous rappelle. *Suggestive joke,* plaisanterie suggestive, *f.* **suggestively,** *adv.* De façon suggestive.

suicidal [sju:i'saidl], *a.* De suicide. *It is suicidal to think of it,* c'est fatal d'y penser.

suicide ['sju:isaid], *n.* Suicide, *m.*; suicidé, *m.*, -ée, *f.* *To commit suicide,* se suicider; se donner la mort.

suit [sju:t], *n.* Suite, collection complète, *f.*, assortiment, *m.*; couleur (cards); sollicitation, demande, prière, requête (petition); recherche en mariage (courtship); (*Law*) instance, *f.*, procès, *m.* *Suit of armour,* armure complète, *f.*; *suit (of clothes),* complet, *m.*; *to bring a suit against,* intenter une action à, faire un procès à; *to follow suit,* jouer dans la couleur, (*fig.*) faire de même, en faire autant.—*v.t.* Adapter, approprier; convenir à, aller à, aller avec, arranger (to be suitable to); plaire à (to please). *Are you suited with a servant?* avez-vous trouvé un domestique? *if that suits you,* si cela vous convient, si cela vous va.—*v.i.* S'accorder (à).

suitable ['sju:təbl], *a.* Convenable, propre, qui convient (à); à propos. *Suitable to,* adapté à. **suitableness** or **suitability** [-'biliti], *n.* Opportunité, convenance, *f.*, accord, rapport, *m.* **suitably,** *adv.* Convenablement, à propos.

suite [swi:t], *n.* Suite, *f.*, ensemble (of furniture), *m.* *Bedroom suite,* ameublement de chambre à coucher, *m.*; *drawing-room suite* or *three-piece suite,* ameublement de salon, *m.*; *suite of apartments,* appartement, *m.*, *suite of furniture,* ameublement complet, *m.*

suitor ['sju:tə], *n.* Solliciteur, *m.*, -euse, *f.*; prétendant (lover); (*Law*) plaideur, *m.*, -euse, *f.*

sulk [sʌlk], *v.i.* Bouder, faire la mine. *To sulk with,* bouder. **sulks,** *n.pl.* Mauvaise humeur, bouderie, *f.* *To be in the sulks, to have the sulks,* être de mauvaise humeur, bouder. **sulkily,** *adv.* En boudant, en faisant la mine. **sulkiness** or **sulking,** *n.* Bouderie, *f.* **sulky** (1) ['sʌlki], *a.* Boudeur, qui fait la mine, la tête. *To be sulky,* être boudeur, bouder. **sulky** (2) ['sʌlki], *n.* Voiture légère de course au trot, *f.*, sulky, *m.*

sullen ['sʌlən], *a.* Maussade, morose, renfrogné. **sullenly,** *adv.* Maussadement, d'un air renfrogné. **sullenness,** *n.* Humeur sombre, *f.*; air maussade, *m.*

sully ['sʌli], *v.t.* Souiller, ternir (de).—*v.i.* Se ternir.—*n.* Souillure, tache, *f.*

sulphate ['sʌlfeit], *n.* Sulfate, *m.* **sulphatic** [-'fætik], *a.* Sulfaté. **sulphide** [-faid], *n.* Sulfure, *m.* *Hydrogen sulphide,* hydrogène sulfuré. **sulphite** [-fait], *n.* Sulfite, *m.* **sulphonamide** [-'founəmaid], *n.* Sulfamide, *f.*

sulphur ['sʌlfə], *n.* Soufre, *m.* *Sulphur bath,* bain sulfureux, *m.*; *sulphur mine,* soufrière, *f.*; *sulphur ore,* pyrite, *f.*, fer sulfuré, *m.*; *sulphur stick,* soufre en canon, *m.*—*v.t.* Soufrer. **sulphurate** [-fjureit], *v.t.* Soufrer. **sulphuration** *n.* Sulfuration, *f.* **sulphureous** [-'fjuəriəs], *a.* Sulfureux. *sulphuret,* *n.* Sulfure, *m.* **sulphuretted** [-'retid], *a.* Sulfuré. **sulphuric** [-'fjuərik], *a.* Sulfurique. **sulphuring,** *n.* Soufrage, *m.* **sulphurous** ['sʌlfjurəs], *a.* Sulfureux.

sultan ['sʌltən], *n.* Sultan, *m.* **sultana** [-'tɑːnə], *n.* Sultane, *f.*; (*pl.*) raisins de Smyrne, *m.pl.* **sultanate,** *n.* Sultanat, *m.* **sultanship,** *n.* Sultanat, *m.*

sultriness ['sʌltrinis], *n.* Chaleur étouffante, *f.* **sultry,** *a.* D'une chaleur étouffante, étouffant, suffocant; (*fam.*) épicé, salé (of a story etc.). *It is very sultry,* il fait très lourd.

sum [sʌm], *n.* Somme (of money), *f.*; résumé, sommaire (compendium); comble (height); (*Arith.*) problème, calcul, *m.*, règle, *f.* *Sum total,* somme totale, *f.*, total, *m.*; *the four sums,* les quatre opérations, *f.pl.*; *to do sums,* compter, faire du calcul, des problèmes; *to set a sum,* poser un problème d'arithmétique (à); *to work out a sum,* résoudre un problème. —*v.t.* Additionner; résumer (to summarize). *To sum up,* additionner, faire l'addition de, (*fig.*) résumer, récapituler; en résumé . . .; *to sum up the case,* résumer les débats.

sumac ['sju:mæk], *n.* (*Bot.*) Sumac, *m.*

Sumerian [sju:'mi:rjən], *a.* and *n.* Sumérien, *m.*, -ienne, *f.*

sumless ['sʌmlis], *a.* Incalculable.

summarily ['sʌmərili], *adv.* Sommairement. **summarize,** *v.t.* Résumer sommairement. **summary,** *n.* Sommaire, abrégé, précis, résumé, *m.*—*a.* Sommaire, prompt, expéditif, immédiat.

summer ['sʌmə], *n.* Été, *m.* *In summer,* en été.—*a.* D'été, estival. *Indian summer, St. Martin's summer,* l'été de la Saint-Martin, *m.*; *summer holidays,* grandes vacances, vacances d'été, *f.pl.*; *summer weather,* un temps d'été, *m.*—*v.i.* Passer l'été, estiver.

summer-house, *n.* Pavillon, kiosque (de jardin), *m.* **summer-time,** *n.* Heure d'été, *f.*
summery, *a.* Estival, -e; d'été, comme en été.
summing ['sʌmiŋ], *n.* Addition, *f.* **summing-up,** *n.* Résumé, *m.*
summit ['sʌmit], *n.* Sommet, *m.,* cime, *f.*; (*fig.*) comble, faîte, *m. Summit conference,* conférence au sommet, *f.* **summit-level,** *n.* Point de partage, *m.*
summon ['sʌmən], *v.t.* Appeler, convoquer (to call together); citer, assigner; sommer (to call upon to surrender etc.); (*Law*) citer en justice, poursuivre; assigner (witnesses). *I could not summon up courage to tell her the sad news,* je n'ai pas trouvé le courage de lui dire la triste nouvelle; *to summon a meeting,* convoquer une assemblée; *to summon away,* appeler, rappeler; *to summon the rioters to disperse,* sommer les émeutiers de se disperser; *to summon up,* rappeler, rassembler (courage etc.).
summoner, *n.* Personne qui convoque, qui cite, etc., *f.*; huissier, *m.*
summons, *n.* Sommation (to surrender etc.), convocation, *f.,* appel (call), *m.*; (*Law*) assignation, citation, *f.,* mandat de comparution, *m. To issue a summons,* lancer un mandat de comparution *or* une assignation; *to take out a summons against,* envoyer une assignation à.—*v.t.* Assigner, citer (en justice), appeler à comparaître.
sump [sʌmp], *n.* (*Mining*) Puisard, *m.*; (fond de) carter (of car), *m.* **sump-man,** *n.* (*pl.* -men) Puisatier, *m.*
sumpter ['sʌmptə], *n.* Bête de somme, *f.* **sumpter-horse,** *n.* Cheval de somme, *m.* **sumpter-mule,** *n.* Mulet de charge, *m.*
sumptuary ['sʌmptjuəri], *a.* Somptuaire, *f.*
sumptuous, *a.* Somptueux. **sumptuously,** *adv.* Somptueusement. **sumptuousness,** *n.* Somptuosité, *f.*
sun [sʌn], *n.* Soleil, *m. In the sun,* dans le soleil, au soleil (in the sunshine); *there is nothing new under the sun,* il n'y a rien de nouveau sous le soleil; *the sun is high up,* il fait grand soleil; *the sun is up,* le soleil est levé; *the sun shines,* il fait du soleil; *to sit in the sun,* être assis au soleil; *to worship the rising sun,* adorer le soleil levant.—*v.t.* Exposer au soleil. *To sun oneself,* se chauffer au soleil.
sun-awning, *n.* Store extérieur, *m.*
sun-bath, *n.* Bain de soleil, *m.* **sun-bathe,** *v.i.* Prendre des bains de soleil. **sunbeam,** *n.* Rayon de soleil, *m.* **sun-blind,** *n.* Store, *m.*
sunbright, *a.* Radieux, brillant, resplendissant.
sunburn, *n.* Hâle; coup de soleil, *m.* **sunburnt,** *a.* Brûlé par le soleil, hâlé; basané.
sunburst, *n.* Échappée de soleil, *f.*
sunclad, *a.* Radieux, baigné de soleil.
sundae ['sʌndei], *n.* Glace aux fruits recouverte de crème, *f.*
Sunday ['sʌndi], *n.* Dimanche, *m. On Sundays,* le dimanche.—*a.* Du dimanche. *In one's Sunday clothes,* endimanché; *Sunday dinner,* le grand repas dominical; *to put on one's Sunday best, one's Sunday clothes,* s'endimancher; *when two Sundays come together,* la semaine des quatre jeudis.
sun-deck ['sʌndek], *n.* Pont-promenade, *m.*

sunder ['sʌndə], *v.t.* Séparer; couper en deux.—*v.i.* Se séparer, se fendre.
sundew ['sʌndju:], *n.* (*Bot.*) Rossolis, *m.*
sundial ['sʌndaiəl], *n.* Cadran solaire, gnomon, *m.*
sundown, *n.* Coucher du soleil, *m. At sundown,* au soleil couchant.
sundowner, *n.* Chemineau, *m.* (tramp); apéritif, *m.*
sun-dried, *a.* Séché au soleil.
sundries ['sʌndriz], *n.* Choses diverses, *f.pl.,* articles divers; faux frais, frais divers, *m.pl.*
sundry ['sʌndri], *a.* Divers. *All and sundry,* tous sans exception.
sunfish, *n.* Môle, *f.,* poisson-lune, *m.*
sun-flower, *n.* Soleil, tournesol, *m.*
sung, *p.p.* [SING].
sun-glasses, *n.* Lunettes de soleil, lunettes noires, *f.pl.*; verres fumés, *m.pl.* **sun-helmet,** *n.* Casque colonial, *m.*
sunk, *p.p.* [SINK].
sunken ['sʌŋkən], *a.* Enfoncé; cave (of cheeks); creux (of eyes). *Sunken battery,* batterie enterrée, *f.*; *sunken garden,* jardin encaissé, *m.*
sunless ['sʌnlis], *a.* Sans soleil.
sunlight, *n.* Lumière du soleil, *f.*; (*pl.*) (*Cine.*) projecteurs, *m.pl.* **sunlit,** *a.* Éclairé par le soleil, ensoleillé.
sunlike, *a.* Semblable au soleil.
sunniness ['sʌninis], *n.* Ensoleillement, *m.*; (*fig.*) nature gaie, *f.*
sunny ['sʌni], *a.* Exposé au soleil, ensoleillé; (*fig.*) riant, heureux. *It is sunny,* il fait du soleil; *sunny side,* côté exposé au soleil, (*fig.*) beau côté, *m.*; (*fig.*) *to be of a sunny disposition,* avoir un heureux caractère.
sun-parlo(u)r, sun-porch, *n.* (*Am.*) Solarium, *m.*
sunproof, *a.* Impénétrable aux rayons du soleil; inaltérable au soleil.
sun-ray, *a. Sun-ray treatment,* héliothérapie, *f.*
sunrise, *n.* Lever du soleil, soleil levant, *m.*
sun-rose, *n.* Hélianthème, *m.*
sunset, *n.* Coucher du soleil; soleil couchant, *m.*
sunshade, *n.* Parasol, *m.,* ombrelle, *f.*
sunshine, *n.* Clarté du soleil, *f.,* soleil; (*fig.*) bonheur, éclat, *m. In the broad sunshine,* au grand soleil; *in the sunshine,* au soleil. **sunshiny,** *a.* Ensoleillé, plein de soleil.
sun-spot, *n.* Tache du soleil; macule, *f.*
sunstroke, *n.* Coup de soleil, *m.,* insolation, *f.*
sun-up, *n.* (*Am.*) Lever du soleil, *m.*
sun-worship, *n.* Culte du soleil, *m.*
sun-worshipper, *n.* Adorateur du soleil, *m.*
sup [sʌp], *n.* (*Sc.*) Petit coup, *m.,* gorgée, *f.*— *v.t.* Boire à petits coups, humer, siroter (to sip); donner à souper à (to give supper to). *To sup up,* boire.—*v.i.* Souper.
super ['sju:pə], *n.* (*Theat. slang*) [SUPERNUMERARY].—*a.* (*slang*) *It is super,* c'est sensass (sensationnel).
superable ['sju:pərəbl], *a.* Surmontable.
superabound [sju:pərə'baund], *v.i.* Surabonder. **superabundance** [-'bʌndəns], *n.* Surabondance, *f.* **superabundant,** *a.* Surabondant. **superabundantly,** *adv.* Surabondamment.
superacute ['sju:pərəkju:t], *a.* Suraigu (*f.* -uë).
superadd ['sju:pər'æd], *v.t.* Surajouter.
superaddition [-ə'diʃən], *n.* Surcroît, *m.*

[532]

superannuate [sju:pər'ænjueit], *v.t.* Mettre
à la retraite (to pension off); mettre au rancart (to scrap). **superannuated,** *a.* Mis à
la retraite, retraité, en retraite (pensioned
off). **superannuation** [-'eiʃən], *n.* Mise à la
retraite, retraite, *f.* **superannuation-fund,**
n. Caisse de retraites, *f.*

superb [sju'pə:b], *a.* Superbe. **superbly,** *adv.*
Superbement.

supercargo ['sju:pə'ka:gou], *n.* Subrécargue,
m.

supercharged [sju:pə'tʃa:dʒd], *a.* Suralimenté,
surcomprimé. **supercharger,** *n.* Surcompresseur, *m.*

superciliary [sju:pə'siliəri], *a.* (*Anat.*) Sourcilier.

supercilious [sju:pə'siliəs], *a.* Hautain, arrogant. **superciliously,** *adv.* Avec hauteur,
avec arrogance. **superciliousness,** *n.* Hauteur; arrogance, *f.*, dédain, *m.*

supereminence [sju:pər'eminəns], *n.* Prééminence, *f.* **supereminent,** *a.* Suréminent, prééminent. **supereminently,** *adv.*
Très éminemment.

supererogate [sju:pər'erəgeit], *v.i.* Faire plus
qu'on n'est obligé, faire plus que son devoir.
supererogation [-'geiʃən], *n.* Surérogation,
f. **supererogatory** [-i'rɔgətəri], *a.* Surérogatoire, surérogatoire.

superexcellence [sju:pər'eksələns], *n.* Excellence supérieure, *f.* **superexcellent,** *a.*
Parfait, surfin.

superfatted [sju:pə'fætid], *a.* Surgras (*esp.* of
soap).

superfetation [sju:pəfi'teiʃən], *n.* Superfétation; accumulation, *f.*

superficial [sju:pə'fiʃl], *a.* Superficiel; (*fig.*)
léger, peu profond; (*Measure*) de superficie.
superficiality [-i'æliti], *n.* Caractère superficiel, *m.* **superficially,** *adv.* Superficiellement. **superficies** [-'fiʃii:z], *n.* Superficie,
f.

superfine ['sju:pəfain], *a.* Superfin; (*Comm.*)
surfin.

superfluity [sju:pə'flu:iti] or **superfluous-
ness** [sju'pə:fluəsnis], *n.* Superfluité, *f.*;
superflu, *m.*

superfluous [sju'pə:fluəs], *a.* Superflu, inutile.
superfluously, *adv.* D'une manière super-
flue; au delà du nécessaire, inutilement.

superfusible [sju:pə'fju:zibl], *a.* Surfusible.
superfusion, *n.* Surfusion, *f.*

superheat [sju:pə'hi:t], *v.t.* Surchauffer.
superheater, *n.* Surchauffeur, *m.* **superheating,** *n.* Surchauffage, *m.*; surchauffe, *f.*

superhet, superheterodyne [sju:pə'hetərə-
dain], *n.* Superhétérodyne, (*fam.*) super, *m.*

superhuman [-'hju:mən], *a.* Surhumain.

superimpose [-rim'pouz], *v.t.* Superposer,
surimposer. **superimposition** [-pə'ziʃən],
n. Superposition; (*Cine.*) surimpression, *f.*

superincumbent [-in'kʌmbənt], *a.* Superposé.

superinduce [-in'dju:s], *v.t.* Surajouter,
superposer.

superintend [sju:pərin'tend], *v.t.* Surveiller,
diriger. **superintendence,** *n.* Surintendance, surveillance; direction, *f.* **superintendent** [sju:pərin'tendənt], *n.* Chef;
directeur, inspecteur, surintendant; (*Police*)
commissaire de police; (*Rail.*) commissaire
des chemins de fer, *m.*

superior [sju:'piəriə], *a.* and *n.* Supérieur, *m.*,

supérieure, *f.* *A superior smile,* un sourire
condescendant; *in a superior manner,* supérieurement; *Lady Superior* or *Mother Superior,* (Mère) supérieure, Mère abbesse, *f.*
superiority [-'ɔriti], *n.* Supériorité, *f.*
superiorship, *n.* Charge de supérieur(e),
supériorité, *f.*

superjacent [sju:pə'dʒeisənt], *a.* Surjacent.

superlative [sju'pə:lətiv], *a.* Suprême;
(*Gram.*) superlatif.—*n.* (*Gram.*) Superlatif,
m. **superlatively,** *adv.* Au suprême degré,
superlativement; (*Gram.*) au superlatif.
superlativeness, *n.* Suprême degré, *m.*

superlunary [sju:pə'lju:nəri] or **supermun-
dane** [-'mʌndein], *a.* Céleste, au-dessus du
monde.

superman ['sju:pəmæn], *n.* Surhomme, *m.*

supermarket [-ma:kit], *n.* Supermarché, *m.*

supernal [sju'pə:nl], *a.* Supérieur; céleste.
supernally, *adv.* Par en haut, d'en haut.

supernatural [sju:pə'nætʃərəl], *a.* and *n.*
Surnaturel, *m.* **supernaturalism,** *n.* Sur-
naturalisme, *m.* **supernaturality** [-'æliti], *n.*
Surnaturalité, *f.* **supernaturally,** *adv.*
Surnaturellement. **supernaturalness,** *n.*
Caractère surnaturel, *m.*

supernormal, *a.* Au-dessus de la normale;
extraordinaire.

supernumerary [sju:pə'nju:mərəri], *a.* Surnuméraire; à la suite (of officer, judge).—*n.*
Surnuméraire; (*Theat.*) figurant, comparse, *m.*

superpose [sju:pə'pouz], *v.t.* Superposer.
superposition [-pə'ziʃən], *n.* Superposition, *f.*

super-royal [-'rɔiəl], *a.* Jésus (of size of paper).

supersaturate [sju:pə'sætʃureit], *v.t.* Sursaturer.

superscribe [sju:pə'skraib], *v.t.* Mettre une
adresse, une suscription, or une inscription
à. **superscription,** *n.* Suscription; inscription; (*Coin.*) légende, *f.*; en-tête (of letter),
m.

supersede [sju:pə'si:d], *v.t.* Supplanter,
remplacer; (*Law*) rejeter, annuler. **super-
seded,** *a.* Supprimé; démodé, périmé.

supersedeas [sju:pə'si:diəs], *n.* (*Law*) Sursis,
m. **supersession** [-'seʃən], *n.* Remplacement; évincement, *m.*

supersonic [sju:pə'sɔnik], *a.* (Onde) ultra-
sonore; (*Av.*) supersonique (of plane).

superstition [sju:pə'stiʃən], *n.* Superstition,
f. **superstitious,** *a.* Superstitieux. **superstitiously,** *adv.* Superstitieusement. **super-
stitiousness,** *n.* Caractère superstitieux, *m.*

superstratum [sju:pə'streitəm], *n.* Couche
supérieure or superposée, *f.*

superstruction [-'strʌkʃən] or **superstructure,** *n.* Superstructure, *f.*

super-tax ['sju:pətæks], *n.* Surtaxe, *f.*

supervene [-'vi:n], *v.i.* Survenir. **super-
venient,** [-'vi:njənt], *a.* Qui survient, survenant,
subséquent. **supervening,** *a.* Survenant,
arrivant. **supervention** [-'venʃən], *n.*
Survenance, *f.*

supervise ['sju:pəvaiz], *v.t.* Surveiller, diriger,
veiller à, superviser. **supervision** [-'viʒən],
n. Surveillance; inspection, *f.*; contrôle, *m.*

supervisor ['sju:pəvaizə], *n.* Surveillant, *m.*
supervisory [-'vaizəri], *a.* De surveillance.

supination [sju:pi'neiʃən], *n.* Supination, *f.*

supinator ['sju:pineitə], *n.* (*Anat.*) Supinateur, *m.*

supine (1) [sju'pain], *a.* Couché sur le dos; (*fig.*) nonchalant, insouciant, oisif, indolent. *Supine position,* décubitus dorsal, *m.*
supine (2) ['sju:pain], *n.* (*Gram.*) Supin, *m.* **supinely,** *adv.* Couché sur le dos; (*fig.*) nonchalamment, avec négligence, mollement. **supineness,** *n.* Nonchalance, négligence, mollesse, indolence, *f.*
supper ['sʌpə], *n.* Souper, *m. Lord's Supper, Last Supper,* La (Sainte) Cène, *f.* **suppertime,** *n.* Heure du souper, *f.* **supperless,** *a.* Sans souper.
supplant [sə'plɑ:nt], *v.t.* Supplanter, évincer. **supplantation** [sʌplɑ:n'teiʃən], *n.* Supplantation, *f.* **supplanter,** *n.* Supplantateur, *m.*
supple [sʌpl], *a.* Souple, flexible.—*v.t.* Assouplir.—*v.i.* S'assouplir.
supplement (1) [sʌpli'ment], *v.t.* Suppléer à; compléter; remplir les lacunes dans.
supplement (2) ['sʌplimənt], *n.* Supplément, *m.* **supplemental** [-'mentl] or **supplementary,** *a.* Supplémentaire. **supplementarily,** *adv.* D'une manière supplémentaire.
suppleness ['sʌplnis], *n.* Souplesse, flexibilité, *f.*
suppletory [sə'pli:təri], *a.* (*Gram.*) Supplétif.
suppliant ['sʌpliənt], *a.* and *n.* Suppliant, *m.*, suppliante, *f.* **suppliantly,** *adv.* En suppliant.
supplicant ['sʌplikənt], *a.* and *n.* Suppliant, *m.*, suppliante, *f.* **supplicate,** *v.t.* Supplier, implorer. **supplicatingly,** *adv.* En suppliant; d'un ton suppliant. **supplication** [-'keiʃən], *n.* Supplication, prière, *f.* **supplicatory,** *a.* Suppliant, de supplication.
supplier [sə'plaiə], *n.* Pourvoyeur; fournisseur, *m.*
supply [sə'plai], *n.* (*pl.* **supplies**) Fourniture; provision, *f.,* approvisionnement (store), *m.*; renfort (reinforcements); suppléance (in schools), *f.*; (*Elec.*) alimentation, *f.*; (*Mil., pl.*) vivres (of food); (*Parl.*) subsides, débats budgétaires, *m.pl. Bill of supply,* projet de loi de finance, *m.*; *committee of supply,* comité de subsides et dépenses, *m.*; *demand and supply,* (*Polit. Econ.*) l'offre et la demande; *to be on supply* (teaching), faire des suppléances; *supply service,* (*Mil.*) intendance, *f.*; (*Elec.*) *local supply circuit,* secteur, *m.*; *to cut off the supplies of,* couper les vivres à; *to stop supplies,* (*Parl.*) refuser de voter les fonds, refuser les subsides; *to take in a supply of,* faire une provision de; *to vote the supplies,* voter les subsides *or* le budget.—*v.t.* Fournir, pourvoir (de); suppléer à, remplacer (to serve instead of); remplir (a vacancy); fournir à, pourvoir à, subvenir à (wants); (*Comm.*) être fournisseur de. *I supply him,* je suis son fournisseur; *I supply him with goods,* je lui fournis des marchandises; *the tradesmen who supply him,* ses fournisseurs, *m.pl.*; *to supply what is wanting,* suppléer aux besoins (de); *to supply with,* fournir de, pourvoir de. **supplying,** *n.* Fourniture, *f.,* approvisionnement, *m.*
support [sə'pɔ:t], *v.t.* Soutenir, supporter; entretenir, nourrir, faire vivre (to maintain); appuyer (to second); porter (of an electorate). *To support oneself,* se soutenir; subvenir à ses besoins; gagner sa vie; *to support oneself on a stick,* s'aider d'un bâton.—*n.* Action de supporter *or* de soutenir, *f.*; appui, soutien, support (prop); maintien, entretien, *m.,*

nourriture (maintenance); (*fig.*) adhésion, *f. For my support,* pour mon entretien; *in support of,* à l'appui de, en faveur de; *with the favour of your support,* à la faveur de votre appui.
supportable, *a.* Supportable; tolérable; soutenable (that can be maintained). **supportably,** *adv.* Supportablement.
supporter, *n.* Adhérent, partisan; appui soutien (sustainer); (*spt.*) supporter; (*Her.*) support, *m.* **supporting,** *a.* D'appui.—*n.* (*Build.*) Soutènement, appui, soutien, *m.* **supportless,** *a.* Sans soutien, sans appui.
supposable [sə'pouzəbl], *a.* Supposable.
suppose [sə'pouz], *v.t.* Supposer, s'imaginer, penser, croire. *Supposed to be,* censé être; *suppose it was an accident,* mettons que c'était un accident; *suppose they came* (what *if they should come*), si par hasard ils venaient; *suppose we go,* si nous allions; *that are supposed to,* qui passent pour; *that being supposed,* cela supposé; *we are not supposed to know it,* nous ne sommes pas censés le savoir.
supposed, *a.* Présumé; prétendu, soi-disant. **supposedly,** *adv.* Censément; soi-disant.
supposing, *conj.* En supposant (que), supposons, supposé (que). **supposition** [sʌpə'ziʃən], *n.* Supposition, *f.* **suppositional,** *a.* Supposé. **supposititious** [-zi'tiʃəs], *a.* Supposé; faux. **supposititiously,** *adv.* Par substitution; faussement.
suppository [sə'pɔzitəri], *n.* (*Med.*) Suppositoire, *m.*
suppress [sə'pres], *v.t.* Supprimer (to check); réprimer (to crush); étouffer. **suppressed,** *a.* Étouffé, sourd. *A suppressed laugh,* un rire étouffé; *in a suppressed voice,* d'une voix étouffée. **suppressible,** *a.* Supprimable; répressible.
suppression [sə'preʃən], *n.* Suppression; répression (crushing); dissimulation (de la vérité), *f.* **suppressive,** *a.* Suppressif; répressif. **suppressor,** *n.* Personne qui réprime etc., *f.* (*Rad. Tel.*) Noise suppressor, dispositif anti-parasites, *m.*
suppurate ['sʌpjureit], *v.i.* Suppurer. **suppuration** [-'reiʃən], *n.* Suppuration, *f.*
supremacy [sju'preməsi], *n.* Suprématie, *f.*
supreme [sju'pri:m], *a.* Suprême, souverain. **supremely,** *adv.* Au suprême degré, suprêmement.
surbase (1) ['sə:beis], *n.* Corniche, *f.*
surbase (2) ['sə:beis], *v.t.* Surbaisser. *Surbased arch,* arc surbaissé, *m.*
surbed [sə:'bed], *v.t.* Déliter (a stone).
surcharge (1) [sə:'tʃɑ:dʒ], *v.t.* Surcharger; surtaxer.
surcharge (2) ['sə:tʃɑ:dʒ], *n.* Surcharge, surtaxe, *f.*
surcingle ['sə:siŋgl], *n.* Sous-ventrière, *f.,* surfaix, *m.* **surcingled,** *a.* Lié avec un surfaix.
surcoat ['sə:kout], *n.* Surcot, *m.*; houppelande, *f.*
surd [sə:d], *a.* (*Math.*) Incommensurable, irrationnel, (*Phon.*) sourd.—*n.* (*Math.*) Quantité incommensurable; racine irrationnelle; (*Phon.*) consonne sourde, *f.*
surdity ['sə:diti], *n.* Surdité, *f.* **surdomutism,** *n.* Surdi-mutité, *f.*
sure [ʃuə], *a.* Sûr, certain; assuré, infaillible

(not liable to failure); stable (stable). *As sure as a gun*, sûr comme père et mère; *a sure man*, un homme sûr; *be sure of*, soyez sûr de; *his income is sure*, son revenu est assuré; *I am sure I don't know*, je n'en sais vraiment rien; *sure enough!* à coup sûr! *to be sure*, certainement! bien sûr! *to be sure not to*, se garder de; *to be sure of*, être sûr de; *to be sure to*, ne pas manquer de; *to have a sure eye*, avoir le coup d'œil sûr; *to make sure of*, s'assurer de, compter sur.—*adv.* Sûrement, à coup sûr.
sure-footed, *a.* Au pied sûr. **surely**, *adv.* Sûrement, assurément, à coup sûr. **sureness**, *n.* Certitude, sûreté, *f.*
surety ['ʃuəti], *n.* Certitude (certainty); sûreté, sécurité (safety), *f.*; (*Law*) garant, répondant, *m.*, caution, *f. Of a surety*, pour sûr; *to become surety for*, se porter garant de, cautionner. **suretyship**, *n.* Cautionnement, *m.*
surf [sə:f], *n.* Ressac, *m.*, barre de plage, *f.*, brisants sur la plage, *m.pl.* **surf-bathing**, *n.* Bain dans les brisants, *m.* **surf-board**, *n.* (*Swim.*) Aquaplane, *m.* **surf-boat**, *n.* Pirogue de barre (in Hawaii), *f.*; embarcation qui sert à franchir une barre, *f.* **surf-rider**, *n.* (*spt.*) Chevaucheur de ressac, *m.* **surf-riding**, *n.* Sport de l'aquaplane, planking, *m.*
surface ['sə:fis], *n.* Surface, *f.*; extérieur, *m.*, apparence, *f.*—*v.i.* (*Naut.*) Faire surface (of a submarine).—*v.t.* Polir la surface de; dégauchir; (*Paint.*) apprêter; revêtir.
surfeit ['sə:fit], *n.* Rassasiement, dégoût, *m.*; satiété, indigestion, *f. To have a surfeit of*, être rassasié de.—*v.t.* Rassasier, (*fig.*) dégoûter, fatiguer (de), blaser (sur). *To be surfeited with*, être rassasié *or* repu de; *to surfeit oneself*, se gorger. **surfeiter**, *n.* Glouton, *m.*, gloutonne, *f.* **surfeiting**, *n.* Excès, *m.*
surge [sə:dʒ], *n.* Houle, lame de fond, *f.*—*v.i.* S'enfler, s'élever; devenir houleux.
surgeon ['sə:dʒən], *n.* Chirurgien, médecin, *m. Army surgeon*, chirurgien militaire, médecin-major, *m.*; *assistant-surgeon*, aide-major, *m.* **surgeon-dentist**, *n.* Chirurgien-dentiste, *m.* **surgeon-general**, *n.* Médecin inspecteur général, *m.* **surgeoncy** *or* **surgeonship**, *n.* Poste de chirurgien, *m.* **surgery**, *n.* Chirurgie (art), *f.*; dispensaire, *m.*; laboratoire; cabinet (de consultations), *m. Surgery hours*, heures de consultation, *f.pl.*
surgical, *a.* Chirurgical; de chirurgie (of instruments etc.). *Surgical appliances*, appareils *or* instruments de chirurgie, *m.pl.*; *surgical ward*, salle des opérés, *f.*
surlily ['sə:lili], *adv.* D'une manière hargneuse, d'un air maussade. **surliness**, *n.* Morosité, humeur morose, *f.*; caractère bourru, *m.* **surly**, *a.* Morose, maussade, bourru; hargneux (of dogs).
surloin [SIRLOIN].
surmise [sə:'maiz], *n.* Soupçon, *m.*, conjecture, supposition, *f.*—*v.t.* Soupçonner, conjecturer, se douter de.
surmount [sə:'maunt], *v.t.* Surmonter, s'élever au-dessus de; (*fig.*) vaincre. **surmountable**, *a.* Surmontable. **surmounted**, *a.* (*Her.*) Sommé.
surmullet [sə:'mʌlit], *n.* (*Ichth.*) Surmulet, rouget, *m.*

surname ['sə:neim], *n.* Nom de famille, patronyme; *surnom (name added to the original name), *m. Christian names and surname*, nom et prénoms.—*v.t.* Donner un nom de famille; *surnommer.
surpass [sə:'pɑ:s], *v.t.* Surpasser, l'emporter sur. *To surpass oneself*, se surpasser. **surpassable**, *a.* Qu'on peut surpasser. **surpassing**, *a.* Éminent, supérieur, rare; sans égal, sans pareil; non-pareil. **surpassingly**, *adv.* Éminemment, avec éclat.
surplice ['sə:plis], *n.* Surplis, *m.* **surplice-fees**, *n.* Casuel, *m.* **surpliced**, *a.* En surplis.
surplus ['sə:pləs], *n.* Surplus, excédent, *m. Surplus stock*, solde, *m.*—*a.* De surplus.
surplusage ['sə:pləsidʒ], *n.* Surplus, excédent, *m.*, superfluité, *f.*; (*Law*) redondance, *f.*
surprise [sə:'praiz], *n.* Surprise, *f.*; étonnement, *m.*; (*Mil.*) coup de main, *m. To be taken by surprise*, être surpris, être pris au dépourvu; *to give someone a surprise*, faire une surprise à quelqu'un; *to recover from one's surprise*, revenir de sa surprise.—*v.t.* Surprendre, prendre au dépourvu; étonner. *I am not surprised at it*, je n'en suis pas surpris; *I am surprised at your going there*, je suis étonné que vous y alliez; *surprising to say*, chose surprenante; *to be surprised at* or *with*, être surpris de.
surprising, *a.* Surprenant, étonnant. **surprisingly**, *adv.* D'une manière surprenante.
surrealism [sʌ'ri:əlizm], *n.* Surréalisme, *m.* **surrealist**, *a.* and *n.* Surréaliste. **surrealistic**, *a.* Surréaliste.
surrejoinder [sʌri'dʒɔində], *n.* (*Law*) Duplique, *f.*
surrender [sə'rendə], *n.* Reddition, capitulation, *f.*; abandon (of a claim), *m.*; (*Law*) cession, *f. Surrender of property*, cession de biens, *f.*—*v.t.* Rendre; (*fig.*) abandonner, livrer (oneself etc.); (*Law*) céder, renoncer à. *To surrender oneself*, se rendre, se livrer (à), (*Law*) se constituer prisonnier, se mettre à la disposition (de) (of a bankrupt).—*v.i.* Se rendre; mettre bas les armes.
surreptitious [sʌrəp'tiʃəs], *a.* Subreptice, clandestin; frauduleux. **surreptitiously**, *adv.* Subrepticement, clandestinement, à la dérobée.
surrogate ['sʌrəgeit], *n.* Suppléant, subrogé; succédané, *m.*
surround [sə'raund], *n.* Encadrement (of door, window), *m.*; bordure; clôture, *f.*—*v.t.* Entourer, environner (de), ceindre (de); (*Mil.*) cerner. **surrounding**, *a.* Environnant, circonvoisin, d'alentour. **surroundings**, *n.pl.* Alentours, environs, *m.pl.*, entourage, milieu, *m.*
surtax ['sə:tæks], *n.* Surtaxe, *f.*—*v.t.* ['-tæks] Surtaxer.
survey (1) ['sə:vei], *n.* Vue, *f.*, coup d'œil; examen, *m.*, inspection (examination); expertise (valuation); (*Ordnance*) levée des plans, *f.*, levé *or* levé topographique, arpentage (of land etc.), *m. Official survey*, cadastre, *m.*; *trigonometrical survey*, triangulation, *f.*; *to make a survey of*, lever le plan de, (*fig.*) jeter un coup d'œil (sur), embrasser dans son ensemble.
survey (2) [sə:'vei], *v.t.* Arpenter (land); (*Ordnance*) lever le plan de; visiter, arpenter

(to value); (*fig.*) examiner, promener sa vue sur, considérer, contempler.

surveying, *n.* Arpentage, aréage, levé de plans, *m.*; géodésie, topographie, *f.* *Naval surveying*, hydrographie, *f.*; *photographic surveying*, photogrammétrie, *f.*; *surveying instruments*, instruments topographiques, *m.pl.* **surveyor,** *n.* Inspecteur (overseer); surveillant; contrôleur (of taxes); arpenteur (of land); (*Ordnance*) ingénieur de cadastre; expert-géomètre, ingénieur-géomètre; (*Law*) expert; (*Customs*) intendant, *m.* *Surveyor general*, inspecteur en chef, *m.*; *highways, road surveyor*, agent voyer, *m.* **surveyorship,** *n.* Inspection; place d'inspecteur, de contrôleur, etc., *f.*

survival [sə:'vaivl], *n.* Survivance; survie, *f.* *Survival of the fittest*, survivance des plus aptes, *f.*

survive, *v.t.* Survivre à.—*v.i.* Survivre, demeurer en vie; subsister, passer à la postérité. **surviving,** *a.* **survivor,** *n.* Survivant, *m.* *The survivors (of an accident etc.)*, les rescapés, *m.pl.*

Susan [su:zn]. Suzanne, *f.*

susceptibility [səsepti'biliti], *n.* Susceptibilité; sensibilité, *f.*

susceptible [sə'septibl], *a.* Susceptible (de); prédisposé; (*fig.*) sensible (à). **susceptibly,** *adv.* D'une manière susceptible. **susceptive,** *a.* Susceptible. **susceptivity,** *n.* Susceptibilité, suggestivité, *f.*

suspect (1) [səs'pekt], *v.t.* Soupçonner, se douter de; se défier de, tenir pour suspect; suspecter (to imagine to be guilty). *I suspected as much*, je m'en doutais, je m'y attendais.—*v.i.* Soupçonner. *I suspect he has . . .*, je le soupçonne d'avoir . . ., je soupçonne qu'il a. . . . **suspectable,** *a.* Soupçonnable. **suspected,** *a.* Suspect. **suspectedly,** *adv.* De manière à exciter les soupçons, d'une façon suspecte. **suspecter, suspector,** *n.* Personne qui soupçonne, *f.*

suspect (2) ['sʌspekt], *n. and a.* Suspect.

suspend [səs'pend], *v.t.* Suspendre; cesser (payments). **suspended,** *a.* (*Mil.*) En disponibilité.

suspender, *n.* Personne qui suspend, *f.*; suspensoir (for athletes etc.), *m.*; (*pl.*) jarrettelles (for stockings), *f.pl.*; supports-chaussettes, *m.pl.*; (*Am.*) bretelles (braces).

suspense [səs'pens], *n.* Suspens, doute, *m.*, incertitude, indécision; (*Law etc.*) suspension, *f.* *In suspense*, en suspens, dans l'incertitude; *to keep in suspense*, tenir en suspens, faire languir.

suspensible, *a.* Qu'on peut suspendre.

suspension, *n.* Suspension; suspension de paiements (of a bank); (*Law*) surséance, *f.* **suspension-bridge,** *n.* Pont suspendu, *m.* **suspension-pier,** *n.* Jetée suspendue, *f.*

suspensive, *a.* Suspensif.

suspensor, *n.* (*Surg.*) Suspensoir (bandage), *m.*

suspicion [səs'piʃən], *n.* Soupçon, *m.*; (*Law*) suspicion, *f.* *Imprisonment on suspicion*, détention préventive, *f.*; *to be taken up on suspicion*, être détenu préventivement.

suspicious [səs'piʃəs], *a.* Soupçonneux; suspect, louche, équivoque (liable to suspicion). *That looks suspicious to me*, cela me paraît suspect. **suspicious-looking,** *a.* À mine

suspecte, à l'air suspect. **suspiciously,** *adv.* Avec méfiance; d'une manière suspecte. **suspiciousness,** *n.* Caractère soupçonneux, *m.*, défiance, méfiance; nature suspecte (liability to be suspected), *f.*

***suspire** [sə'spaiə], *v.i.* Soupirer.

sustain [səs'tein], *v.t.* Soutenir, supporter; entretenir, nourrir (to feed); endurer, souffrir, subir (to endure); éprouver, essuyer (a loss). *To sustain an injury*, être blessé, recevoir une blessure; *sustained applause*, applaudissements nourris, *m.pl.*; (*Mus.*) *sustained note*, note soutenue, *f.*

sustainable, *a.* Soutenable. **sustainer,** *n.* Soutien, *m.* **sustaining,** *a.* Fortifiant, nourrissant.

sustenance ['sʌstinəns], *n.* Nourriture, *f.*, aliments, *m.pl.*; entretien, *m.*, subsistance, *f.*

sustentation, *n.* Entretien, *m.*, sustentation, *f.*

sutler ['sʌtlə], *n.* Vivandier, *m.*, vivandière, *f.*, cantinier, mercanti, *m.*, cantinière, *f.*

suttee [sʌ'ti:], *n.* Suttee, suttie, sâti, *f.*

suttle [sʌtl], *a.* Net (of weight).

suture ['sju:tʃə], *n.* Suture, *f.*

suzerain ['su:zərein], *a. and n.* Suzerain, *f.*, suzeraine, *f.* **suzerainty,** *n.* Suzeraineté, *f.*

swab [swɔb], *n.* Torchon; (*Naut.*) faubert, écouvillon (for a gun), tampon (of cotton wool), *m.*—*v.t.* Fauberter, essarder, nettoyer. *The deck was swabbed*, le pont était fauberté; *to swab out (a gun)*, écouvillonner; *to swab up*, éponger. **swabber,** *n.* Nettoyeur, *m.*

swaddle [swɔdl], *v.t.* Emmailloter. **swaddling,** *n.* Emmaillotement, *m.* **swaddling-clothes,** *n.* Maillot, *m.*, langes, *m.pl.*

swag [swæg], *n.* (*slang*) Butin; (*Australia*) baluchon, ballot d'effets personnels, *m.* **swag-bellied,** *a.* Pansu, ventru. **swagman,** *n.* (*Australia*) Chemineau, *m.*

swage [sweidʒ], *n.* Étampe, matrice, *f.*, emboutissoir, mandrin, *m.* **swage-hammer,** *n.* Étampe supérieure, *f.*

swagger ['swægə], *v.i.* Faire le rodomont, faire le crâne, plastronner, se pavaner, se donner des airs, se vanter. *To swagger along*, marcher d'un air fanfaron, se carrer. **swaggerer,** *n.* Fanfaron, crâneur, *m.*

swaggering, *n.* Fanfaronnade, crânerie, *f.*—*a.* De fanfaron, de crâneur.

swagger-stick, *n.* Jonc, *m.*

swain [swein], *n.* (*poet.*) Berger, jeune paysan, pastoureau; soupirant, amoureux, *m.*

swallow ['swɔlou], *v.t.* Avaler; engloutir (to engulf); consumer (to consume); avaler; gober (to believe). *To be swallowed up by the waves*, être englouti par les flots; *to swallow down*, avaler, gober; *to swallow the wrong way*, avaler de travers; *to swallow up*, avaler, engloutir, absorber, consumer.—*n.* (*pop.*) Avaloir, gosier (throat), *m.*; gorgée (what is swallowed), *f.*; gouffre, aven (pot-hole), *m.*; hirondelle (bird), *f.*; gorge de poulie, *f.*, clan de poulie, *m.* *One swallow does not make a summer*, une hirondelle ne fait pas le printemps.

swallow-dive, *n.* (*Swim.*) Saut de l'ange, *m.* **swallow-hole,** *n.* (*Geol.*) Avaloire, perte, *f.*; gouffre, abîme, aven, *m.* **swallow-tail,** *a.* En queue d'aronde.—*n.* Habit à queue de morue, à queue de pie, *m.*

swallower, *n.* Avaleur, *m. Sword-swallower*, avaleur de sabres.

swam, *past* [swɪm].

swamp [swɔmp], *n.* Marais, marécage, *m.*— *v.t.* Submerger; faire chavirer, faire couler (a boat). *To be swamped*, chavirer, couler à fond, s'emplir d'eau; (*fig.*) *to be swamped in, with, work*, être submergé de travail, être débordé (de travail). **swamp-fever,** *n.* Fièvre paludéenne, *f.*, paludisme, *m.* **swampy,** *a.* Marécageux.

swan [swɔn], *n.* Cygne, *m.* **swanlike,** *a.* De cygne; semblable au cygne. **swansdown,** *n.* Duvet de cygne; molleton, *m.* **swanshot,** *n.* Plomb à cygne, *m.* **swanskin,** *n.* Molleton, *m.* **swan-song,** *n.* Le chant du cygne, *m.* **swan-upping,** *n.* Recensement annuel des cygnes, *m.*

swank [swæŋk], *n.* Pose, prétention, gloriole, (*pop.*) épate, *f. It is all swank*, tout ça, c'est de l'épate; c'est pour faire des épates.—*v.i.* (*pop.*) Crâner, poser; faire le flambard, le malin; faire du chiqué, le faire à la gomme, à la pose, à l'esbrouffe. **swanky,** *a.* Chic, rupin.

swannery ['swɔnəri], *n.* Lieu d'élevage de cygnes, *m.*

swap [swɔp], *v.t.* (*colloq.*) Échanger, troquer. —*n.* Troc, échange, *m.*

sward [swɔ:d], *n.* Gazon, *m.*, pelouse, *f.* **swarded** or **swardy,** *a.* Couvert de gazon; gazonné, gazonneux.

swarm [swɔ:m], *n.* Essaim (of bees), *m.*; (*fig.*) multitude, nuée (crowd), *f. Swarm of ants,* fourmilière, *f.*—*v.i.* Essaimer; (*fig.*) s'attrouper, accourir en foule, grouiller. *To swarm up,* grimper en foule à *or* sur; *to swarm with,* fourmiller de. **swarming,** *n.* Essaimage, *m.*

swarthiness ['swɔ:ðinis], *n.* Teint basané, *m.*

swarthy ['swɔ:ði], *a.* Basané, hâlé.

swash [swɔʃ], *v.t.* Faire clapoter, agiter (water).—*n.* Bruit d'eau; clapotis, clapotage, clapotement, *m.*

swashbuckler, *n.* Fanfaron, matamore, bretteur, *m.*

swastika ['swɔstikə], *n.* Svastika, *m.*, croix gammée, *f.*

swat [swɔt], *v.t.* Cogner, frapper, taper; écraser, tuer, (une mouche).

swath [swɔ:θ], *n.* Andain, *m.*, fauchée, *f.*

swathe [sweið], *v.t.* Emmailloter; (*fig.*) envelopper (de).—*n.* Bande, bandelette, *f.*, bandage, *m.*; maillot, *m.*

swatter ['swɔtə], *n.* (*Fly-*)*swatter*, tue-mouches, *m.*

sway [swei], *v.t.* Manier, porter; balancer; brandir, ballotter (to and fro); (*fig.*) porter, régir, diriger (to rule); influencer (to bias). *To sway from,* détourner de; *to sway up,* (*Naut.*) guinder, hisser.—*v.i.* Se balancer; se pencher, incliner. *To sway to and fro,* chanceler, se balancer, aller et venir.—*n.* Pouvoir, empire, *m.*; puissance; domination (power), *f. To bear sway,* dominer, prédominer, porter le sceptre.

swaying, *n.* Balancement, *m.*; oscillation, *f.*

swear [sweə], *v.t.* (*past* **swore,** *p.p.* **sworn**) Faire prêter serment à (witnesses etc.); prêter (an oath); jurer. *To be sworn in,* prêter serment; *to swear in,* assermenter; *to swear*

at, injurier; *to swear off,* renoncer solennellement à; *to swear someone to secrecy,* faire jurer à quelqu'un de garder le secret.—*v.i.* Jurer (de); prêter serment, faire serment. *To curse and swear,* jurer et sacrer; *to swear by,* avoir grande confiance en, jurer par; *to swear by all that is sacred,* jurer ses grands dieux; *to swear falsely,* se parjurer, porter faux témoignage; *to swear like a trooper,* jurer comme un charretier; *to swear to,* jurer de.

swearer, *n.* Jureur, blasphémateur, *m. What a swearer he is!* comme il jure!

swearing, *n.* Serments; jurements, jurons (blaspheming), *m.pl. Swearing in,* prestation de serment, assermentation (of judges etc.), *f.*

swear-word, *n.* Juron, gros mot, *m.*

sweat [swet], *n.* Sueur, transpiration; (*fig.*) fatigue, *f.*, sueurs, *f.pl. All in a sweat,* tout en nage, tout en sueur; *by the sweat of one's brow,* à la sueur de son front.—*v.i.* Suer, transpirer; (*fig.*) se fatiguer, travailler comme un nègre.—*v.t.* Faire suer, faire transpirer; (*fig.*) exploiter (workers). *To sweat out,* faire passer (un rhume) en suant beaucoup.

sweater, *n.* Chandail, tricot, pull-over (garment); (*fig.*) exploiteur (oppressive employer), *m.*

sweatiness, *n.* Sueur, *f.*, état de sueur, *m.*

sweating, *n.* Moiteur, fatigue, *f.*; l'exploitation d'ouvriers à la tâche, *f. Sweating (of coins etc.),* le frai artificiel *or* frauduleux, *m.* —*a.* En sueur; tout en sueur. **sweating-bath,** *n.* Bain de vapeur, *m.* **sweating-house,** *n.* Étuve, *f.* **sweating-room,** *n.* (*Med.*) Étuve, *f.*; (*Agric.*) séchoir, *m.* **sweating-sickness,** *n.* Suette, *f.* **sweating system,** *n.* Exploitation patronale, *f.*

sweaty, *a.* En sueur, couvert de sueur.

Swede [swi:d], *n.* Suédois, *m.*, Suédoise, *f.*; rutabaga (turnip), *m.* **Sweden.** La Suède, *f.* **Swedish,** *a.* Suédois, de Suède. *Swedish drill or gymnastics,* de gymnastique suédoise, *f.*

sweep [swi:p], *v.t.* (*past* and *p.p.* **swept**) Balayer; ramoner (a chimney); glisser sur, raser, effleurer (to glide over); draguer (a river); parcourir, embrasser du regard (to view rapidly). *Her dress sweeps the ground,* sa robe balaie la terre; *to sweep a room,* balayer une pièce; *to sweep away,* balayer, emporter, enlever, entraîner; *to sweep the board,* faire rafle; *to sweep up,* balayer.—*v.i.* Passer rapidement; s'étendre (to extend). *The procession swept past,* la procession défila au grand galop; *the train swept past,* le train passa comme la foudre; *to sweep over,* passer rapidement sur; *to sweep round,* faire rapidement le tour, se tourner rapidement.—*n.* Coup de balai; aviron (oar); ramoneur (chimney-sweep), *m.*; (*fig.*) rafle, *f.*, mouvement, *m.*, course, *f.*, coup, *m.*, ligne (motion or compass of something in movement), étendue, portée (reach), *f.*; courbe, courbure, courbe décrite (bend), *f.*; sweepstake, *m. At one sweep,* d'un seul coup, tout d'un trait; *to give a sweep,* donner un coup de balai à; *to make a clean sweep of,* faire table rase de; *to take a sweep,* décrire une courbe.

sweeper, *n.* Balayeur, *m.*, balayeuse, *f.*; ramoneur (of chimneys), *m.* **sweeping,** *n.* Balayage; ramonage (of chimneys), *m.*; (*pl.*) balayures, ordures, *f.pl.*—*a.* Rapide, impétueux, irrésistible; (*fig.*) complet, général, qui ne ménage personne. **sweepingly,** *adv.* Rapidement; (*fig.*) en masse, sans distinction. **sweep-net,** *n.* Épervier, *m.* **sweepstake,** *n.* Poule, *f.*; sweepstake, *m.* ***sweepy,** *a.* Rapide; onduleux, ondoyant (wavy).

sweet [swiːt], *a.* Doux, sucré; parfumé, odoriférant (fragrant); suave, mélodieux (melodious); frais (fresh); liquoreux, sucré (of wine); (*fig.*) joli, gentil, charmant, agréable. *How sweet of you!* que vous êtes aimable! *sweet herbs,* fines herbes, *f.pl.*; *to say sweet nothings,* dire des douceurs; *to be sweet upon,* être amoureux de; *to have a sweet tooth,* aimer les friandises; *to smell sweet,* sentir bon; *what a sweet child!* quel charmant enfant!—*n.* Chose douce; (*pl.*) entremets, choses sucrées, sucreries, *f.pl.*; chéri, *m.*, chérie, *f.*, doux ami, *m.*, douce amie, *f.*; (*fig.*) plaisirs, *m.pl.*, douceurs, *f.pl.*

sweetbread, *n.* Ris de veau *or* d'agneau, *m.* **sweeten** [swiːtn], *v.t.* Sucrer; purifier, désinfecter (a room, the air, etc.); (*Pharm.*) édulcorer; (*fig.*) adoucir, rendre agréable. **sweetener,** *n.* Adoucissant, *m.* **sweetening,** *n.* Édulcoration (of medicine), *f.*; adoucissement (of pain etc.), *m.*

sweetheart, *n.* Amoureux, *m.*, amoureuse, *f.*; amant, *m.*, amante, *f.*; bon ami, *m.*, bonne amie, *f.* **sweetie,** *n.* (*fam.*) Chérie, chouchou, poulette. **sweetish,** *a.* Assez doux, douceâtre. **sweetishness,** *n.* Goût douceâtre, *m.* **sweetly,** *adv.* Doucement, avec douceur, gentiment; mélodieusement. **sweetmeat,** *n.* Sucrerie, *f.*, bonbon, *m.* **sweetness,** *n.* Douceur; fraîcheur (freshness); suavité, mélodie (melody), *f.*; (*fig.*) charme, *m.* **sweet-oil,** *n.* Huile d'olives; huile de colza, d'œillette, *f.* **sweet-pea,** *n.* Pois de senteur, *m.* **sweet-potato,** *n.* Patate, *f.* **sweet-scented** *or* **sweet-smelling,** *a.* Odoriférant, odorant, parfumé. **sweet-shop,** *n.* Confiserie, *f.* **sweet-tempered,** *a.* D'humeur douce. **sweet-toned,** *a.* Au son doux. **sweet-tongued,** *a.* Doucereux, mielleux. **sweet-toothed,** *a.* Qui aime les sucreries. **sweet-william,** *n.* Œillet de poète, *m.*

swell [swel], *v.i.* (*past* **swelled,** *p.p.* **swelled, swollen** [swouln]) Enfler, s'enfler, se gonfler; grossir, croître, augmenter (to increase); (*fig.*) s'élever, se soulever (to rise). *To swell out,* bomber, faire ventre; *to swell with pride,* bouffir d'orgueil; *to swell with rage,* bouffir de colère.—*v.t.* Enfler, gonfler; aggraver; augmenter, grandir, grossir, élever (to enlarge). *To be swelled with pride,* être bouffi d'orgueil.—*n.* Élévation, montée, *f.*; renflement (of sound), *m.*; houle (of the sea), *f.*; récit (of an organ); (*slang*) rupin, élégant, *m.* *Ground swell,* houle de fond, *f.*; *what a swell she is!* quelle toilette elle a!—*a.* À la mode, chic; épatant. *That's a swell idea,* c'est une idée épatante; *swell mob,* chevaliers d'industrie, *m.pl.*

swelling, *n.* Enflure; bouffissure (morbid enlargement), *f.*; gonflement (protuberance), *m.*, crue (of rivers), *f.*; soulèvement (of the waves); (*fig.*) mouvement, transport (of anger, grief, etc.), *m.*—*a.* Enflé, ampoulé; grandissant, croissant (growing larger).

swellish, *a.* (*colloq.*) Élégant, à la mode, affecté, prétentieux. **swelter** ['sweltə], *v.i.* Étouffer de chaleur. *It is sweltering hot,* il fait une chaleur étouffante. —*n.* Chaleur accablante, étouffante; nage (perspiration), *f.* **swept,** *past* and *p.p.* [SWEEP]. **swerve** [swəːv], *v.i.* S'écarter, se détourner, faire un écart (of horses), faire une embardée (of car); (*fig.*) errer, s'égarer. *To swerve from,* s'écarter de, s'éloigner de, dévier de. **swerving,** *n.* Écart, *m.*, déviation, embardée (of car), *f.*

swift [swift], *a.* Vite, léger, léger à la course; rapide, prompt; bon marcheur (of a ship). —*adv.* Vite, promptement.—*n.* Martinet (bird); triton (newt), *m.* **swifter,** *n.* (*Naut.*) Hauban bâtard; raban des barres (of the capstan), *m.* **swift-footed,** *a.* Rapide à la course, agile; au pied léger. **swiftly,** *adv.* Vite, rapidement. **swiftness,** *n.* Célérité, rapidité, promptitude, vitesse, *f.* **swift-sailing,** *a.* Fin voilier, bon marcheur. **swift-winged,** *a.* À l'aile rapide.

swig [swig], *v.t.*, *v.i.* Boire à longs traits *or* à grands coups.—*n.* Long trait, coup (of liquor), *m.*; (*Naut.*) palan, *m.* **swill** [swil], *v.t.* Laver, rincer; boire avidement.—*v.i.* Boire; (*colloq.*) s'enivrer.—*n.* Lavure de vaisselle, lavure, *f.*; grand coup (of liquor), *m.* **swiller,** *n.* Grand buveur, ivrogne, *m.* **swillings,** *n.pl.* Lavure de vaisselle, *f.*, eaux grasses, *f.pl.*

swim [swim], *v.i.* (*past* **swam,** *p.p.* **swum**) Nager; flotter, surnager (to float); tourner (of the head); être inondé (to be flooded). *My head is swimming,* la tête me tourne; *to be swimming in riches,* nager dans l'abondance; *to swim across,* traverser *or* passer à la nage; *to swim against the tide,* nager contre le courant; *to swim with the tide,* nager avec le courant.—*v.t.* Traverser à la nage.—*n.* Nage, *f.* *In the swim,* dans le mouvement, dans le train; à la page.

swimmer, *n.* Nageur, *m.*, nageuse, *f.* **swimming,** *n.* Natation (the art); nage (the act), *f.*; vertige, étourdissement (dizziness), *m.* *By swimming,* en nageant, à la nage. **swimming-bath** *or* **-pool,** *n.* Piscine, *f.*; bain de natation, *m.* **swimming-baths** *or* **swimming-school,** *n.* École de natation, *f.* **swimming-bladder,** *n.* Vessie natatoire, *f.* **swimming-costume** *or* **swim-suit,** *n.* Maillot de bain, *m.* **swimming-trunks,** *n.* Slip, *m.* **swimmingly,** *adv.* À merveille, comme sur des roulettes. **swindle** [swindl], *v.t.* Escroquer, voler. *To swindle somebody out of something,* escroquer quelqu'un de quelque chose.—*n.* Escroquerie, *f.* **swindler,** *n.* Escroc, filou, chevalier d'industrie, *m.* **swindling,** *n.* Escroquerie, *f.* **swine** [swain], *n.inv.* Cochon, pourceau, porc, *m.*; (*pop.*) salaud, *m.* *To cast pearls before swine,* donner des perles aux pourceaux. **swine-fever,** *n.* Rouget du porc, *m.* **swine-herd,** *n.* Porcher, *m.* **swine-pox,** *n.* Varicelle, *f.*

swing [swiŋ], *v.i.* (*past* and *p.p.* **swung**) Se balancer; osciller; (*Naut.*) éviter (of a ship); pendiller, être suspendu (to be hanging); (*fig.*) pendre (to be hanged).—*v.t.* Balancer; agiter (to wave); brandir (to brandish).—*n.* Oscillation (oscillation), *f.*; branle; balancement, va-et-vient, *m.*; escarpolette, balançoire (swinging seat), *f.*; mouvement rythmé, *m.*; (*Mus.*) swing, *m.*; (*fig.*) libre carrière, *f.*, libre essor, libre cours, *m. In full swing*, en pleine marche, en pleine activité. **swing-bar,** *n.* Palonnier, *m.* **swing-bridge,** *n.* Pont tournant, *m.* **swing-cot,** *n.* Barcelonnette, *f.* **swing-door,** *n.* Porte battante, *f.* **swinge** [swindʒ], *v.t.* Rosser, étriller, battre. **swingeing** ['swindʒiŋ], *a.* Bien envoyé (blow); énorme. **swinger** ['swiŋə], *n.* Personne qui se balance, *f.* **swinging,** *n.* Balancement, *m.*, oscillation, *f.*; (*Naut.*) évitage, *m.*—*a.* À bascule. **swingle-tree** ['swiŋgl'tri:], *n.* Palonnier, *m.* **swinish** ['swainiʃ], *a.* De cochon; (*fig.*) malpropre, sale, bestial. **swinishly,** *adv.* Comme un cochon, salement, malproprement. **swipe** [swaip], *n.* Coup fort, *m.*, taloche, *f.*— *v.t.* Frapper à toute volée; donner une taloche à; (*Am.*) chiper. **swipes,** *n.pl.* (*slang*) Petite bière, (*fam.*) bibine, vinasse (of wine), *f.* **swirl** [swə:l], *v.i.* Tourbillonner *or* tourner rapidement.—*n.* Remous, *m.* **swish** [swiʃ], *v.t.* Cingler, fouetter, faire siffler (a whip).—*v.i.* Siffler, bruire. **Swiss** [swis], *n.* Suisse, *m.*, Suissesse, *f.*—*a.* Helvétique, Suisse. **switch** [switʃ], *n.* Badine, houssine, gaule; (*Rail.*) aiguille, *f.*; (*Elec.*) commutateur, interrupteur, *m.*—*v.t.* Houspiller, cingler; (*Rail.*) aiguiller. *To switch off*, couper, interrompre (la communication); *to switch on*, ouvrir, établir (la communication); *to switch over to*, passer à.—*v.i. To switch around*, changer de position; *to switch off*, couper le courant; (*Rad.*) tourner le bouton; *to switch on*, donner le courant. **switchback** or **switchback railway,** *n.* Montagnes russes, *f.pl.* **switchboard,** *n.* Tableau de distribution, standard (téléphonique), *m. Switchboard operator*, standardiste, *m.* or *f.* **switch-man,** *n.* Aiguilleur, *m.* **Swithin** ['swiðin]. *St. Swithin's Day* (*July 15th*), la Saint-Médard (*June 8th*). **Switzerland** ['switsələnd]. La Suisse, *f.* **swivel** [swivl], *n.* Émerillon; maillon tournant, pivot, *m.*—*v.i.* Pivoter.—*v.t.* Attacher avec un émerillon; faire pivoter. **swivel-bridge,** *n.* Pont tournant, *m.* **swivel-eyed,** *a.* Strabique; (*fam.*) louche. **swivel-gun,** *n.* Canon à pivot, *m.* **swizzle** [swizl], *n.* (*slang*) Boisson, *f.*—*v.i.* Boire avec excès; (*fam.*) se piquer le nez. **swizzle-stick,** *n.* Marteau à champagne, *m.* **swollen, *swoln,** *p.p.* [SWELL]. **swoon** [swu:n], *v.i.* S'évanouir, se trouver mal, tomber en défaillance.—*n.* Évanouissement, *m.* **swoop** [swu:p], *v.i.* Foncer, fondre, s'abattre (sur). *To swoop down upon*, s'abattre sur, se précipiter sur, fondre sur.—*n.* Action de fondre sur la proie, attaque brusquée;

descente, *f. At one (fell) swoop*, d'un seul coup (fatal). **swop** [SWAP]. **sword** [sɔ:d], *n.* Épée, *f.*; sabre (broadsword); (*fig.*) fer, glaive, *m. At the point of the sword*, à la pointe de l'épée; *sword in hand*, l'épée à la main; *sword of justice*, glaive de la justice, *m.*; *to cross swords*, croiser l'épée; (*fig.*) se mesurer avec quelqu'un; *to draw swords*, dégainer; *to fight with swords*, se battre à l'épée; *to put to fire and sword*, mettre à feu et à sang; *to put to the sword*, passer au fil de l'épée; *with drawn sword*, sabre au clair. **sword-bayonet,** *n.* Sabre-baïonnette, *m.* **sword-bearer,** *n.* Porte-épée, *m.* **sword-belt,** *n.* Ceinturon, *m. Sword-belt sling*, bélière, *f.* **sword-blade,** *n.* Lame d'épée, *f.* **sword-cut,** *n.* Coup d'épée *or* de sabre, *m.* **sword-cutler,** *n.* Armurier, *m.* **sword-edge,** *n.* Tranchant (d'épée), *m.* **sword-fight,** *n.* Combat à l'épée, *m.* **sword-fish,** *n.* Espadon, *m.* **sword-hilt,** *n.* Poignée d'épée, *f.* **sword-knot,** *n.* Dragonne, *f.* **sword-shaped,** *a.* (*Bot.*) Ensiforme. **swordsman,** *n.* (*pl.* **swordsmen**) Tireur, homme d'épée, *m. A good swordsman*, une fine lame, *f.* **swordsmanship,** *n.* Adresse à l'épée, *f.* **sword-stick,** *n.* Canne à épée, *f.* **sword-thrust,** *n.* Coup d'épée, *m.* **swore** [swɔ:], *past* [SWEAR]. **sworn** [swɔ:n], *a.* Juré; (*Law*) assermenté; acharné (of enemies). *Sworn to*, obligé par serment à; *to be sworn in*, prêter serment, être assermenté. **swot** [swɔt], *v.i.* (*sch. slang*) Piocher, bûcher. —*n.* Bûcheur, *m.* **swum,** *p.p.* [SWIM]. **swung,** *past* and *p.p.* [SWING]. **sybarite** ['sibərait], *n.* Sybarite, *m.* **sybaritic** [-'ritik], *a.* Sybaritique. **sycamore** ['sikəmɔ:], *n.* Sycomore, *m.* **sycophancy** ['sikəfənsi], *n.* Adulation, *f.*, sycophantisme, *m.* **sycophant,** *n.* Sycophante, adulateur, *m.*—*v.i.* Faire le sycophante. **sycophantic** [-'fæntik], *a.* Fourbe, adulateur. **syllabic** [si'læbik], *a.* Syllabique. **syllabically,** *adv.* Syllabiquement, par syllabes. **syllabification** [-fi'keiʃən], *n.* Syllabisation, *f.* **syllabize** ['siləbaiz], *v.t.* Syllabiser. **syllable,** *n.* Syllabe, *f.* **syllabus** ['siləbəs], *n.* Résumé; sommaire, programme (*esp.* of school work); (*R.-C. Ch.*) syllabus, *m.* **syllepsis** [si'lepsis], *n.* Syllepse, *f.* **syllogism** ['silədʒizm], *n.* Syllogisme, *m.* **syllogistic** [-'dʒistik], *a.* Syllogistique. **syllogistically,** *adv.* Par un syllogisme. **syllogize,** *v.i.* Raisonner par syllogismes, *m.* **sylph** [silf], *n.* Sylphe, *m.* **sylvan** ['silvən], *a.* Sylvestre, des bois, champêtre, agreste.—*n.* Sylvain, *m.* **symbiosis** [simbi'ousis], *n.* Symbiose, *f.*; parasitisme, *m.* **symbol** [simbl], *n.* Symbole, *m. Picture symbol*, idéogramme, *m.* **symbolic** [-'bɔlik] or **symbolical,** *a.* Symbolique. **symbolism,** *n.* Symbolisme, *m.* **symbolization** [-bəlai'zeiʃən], *n.* Symbolisation, *f.* **symbolize,** *v.t.*, *v.i.* Symboliser. **symbology** [-'bɔlədʒi], *n.* La symbolique, *f.*

symmetrical [si'metrikl], *a.* Symétrique. **symmetrically**, *adv.* Symétriquement.
symmetrize ['simətraiz], *v.t.* Rendre symétrique. **symmetry**, *n.* Symétrie, *f.*
sympathetic [simpə'θetik], *a.* Sympathique (of nerve); compatissant, compréhensif, bien disposé, qui marque de la sympathie. **sympathetically**, *adv.* Sympathiquement, par sympathie.
sympathize ['simpəθaiz], *v.i.* Sympathiser (avec); compatir (à). **sympathizer**, *n.* Sympathisant, *m.*, -ante, *f.*
sympathy ['simpəθi], *n.* Sympathie, *f.*; compréhension, *f.*; condoléances, *f.pl. To do something in sympathy,* faire quelque chose par solidarité; *to be in sympathy with someone,* être du côté, partager les opinions de quelqu'un.
symphonious [sim'founiəs] or **symphonic** [-'fɔnik], *a.* Symphonique.
symphonist ['simfənist], *n.* Symphoniste, *m.* or *f.*
symphony ['simfəni], *n.* Symphonie, *f.*
symphysis ['simfisis], *n.* Symphyse, *f.*
symposiac [sim'pouziæk], *n.* Symposiaques (dialogue), *m.pl.* **symposium**, *n.* Banquet; (*fig.*) recueil d'articles (sur un seul sujet); colloque, *m.*
symptom ['simptəm], *n.* Symptôme; (*fig.*) indice, *m.* **symptomatic** [-'mætik], *a.* Symptomatique. **symptomatology** [-'mə'tɔlədʒi], *n.* Symptomatologie, *f.*
synaeresis [si'niərəsis], *n.* Synérèse, *f.*
synagogal [sinə'gɔgl̩], **synagogical** [sinə'gɔdʒikl̩], *a.* De la synagogue.
synagogue ['sinəgɔg], *n.* Synagogue, *f.*
synaloepha [sinə'li:fə], *n.* Synalèphe, *f.*
synallagmatic [-læg'mætik], *a.* (*Law*) Synallagmatique. **synanthous** [-'nænθəs], *a.* (*Bot.*) Synanthé. **synantherous** [-'næn θərəs], *a.* Synanthéré. **synarthrosis** [-ɑ:'θrousis], *n.* (*Anat.*) Synarthrose, *f.*
syncarp ['sinkɑ:p], *n.* (*Bot.*) Syncarpe, *m.* **syncarpous** [-'kɑ:pəs], *a.* Syncarpé.
synchromesh ['siŋkromeʃ], *n.* and *a.* Synchromesh; synchronisateur, *m.*
synchronal ['siŋkrənl], **synchronous** or **synchronistic** [-krə'nistik], *a.* Synchronique, synchrone. **synchronisation**, *n.* Synchronisation, *f.* **synchronise**, *v.i.* Synchroniser (avec). **synchroniser**, *n.* (*Cine.*) Synchroniseuse, *f.* **synchronism**, *n.* Synchronisme, *m.*
syncopate ['siŋkəpeit], *v.t.* Syncoper. **syncopation** [-'peiʃən], *n.* Élision; (*Mus.*) syncope, *f.*
syncope ['siŋkəpi], *n.* Syncope, *f.* **syncopize**, *v.t.* (*Gram.*) Syncoper, élider.
syncretic [sin'kretik], *a.* Syncrétique.
syncretism ['siŋkrətizm], *n.* Syncrétisme, *m.*
syndesmosis [sindez'mousis], *n.* (*Anat.*) Synnévrose, *f.*
syndic ['sindik], *n.* Syndic, *m.* **syndicalism**, *n.* Syndicalisme, *m.* **syndicalist**, *n.* Syndicaliste, *m.* **syndicate**, *n.* Syndicat, *m.*—*v.t.* Syndiquer.—*v.i.* Se syndiquer.
synecdoche [si'nekdəki], *n.* Synecdoche, *f.* synecdoque, *f.*
synod ['sinəd], *n.* Synode, *m.*; (*Astron.*) conjonction, *f.*
synodal ['sinədl], *a.* Synodal.

synodic [si'nɔdik] or **synodical**, *a.* Synodique.
synonym ['sinənim], *n.* Synonyme, *m.*
synonymize [si'nɔnimaiz], *v.t.* Exprimer par synonymes.
synonymous [si'nɔniməs], *a.* Synonyme. **synonymously**, *adv.* Comme synonyme; par synonymie. **synonymy**, *n.* Synonymie, *f.*
synopsis [si'nɔpsis], *n.* (*pl.* **synopses**) Sommaire, résumé, *m.*, synopsis, *f.*; (*Bibl.*) synopse, *f.*, tableau synoptique, *m.* **synoptical**, *a.* Synoptique. **synoptically**, *adv.* D'une manière synoptique.
syntactic [sin'tæktik], *a.* (*Gram.*) Syntaxique, syntactique.
syntax ['sintæks], *n.* Syntaxe, *f.*
synthesis ['sinθisis], *n.* (*pl.* **syntheses**) Synthèse, *f.* **synthesize**, *v.t.* Synthétiser. **synthetic** [-'θetik] or **synthetical**, *a.* Synthétique. **synthetically**, *adv.* Synthétiquement.
syntonic [sin'tɔnik], *a.* (*Rad.*) Syntonique. **syntony** ['sintəni], *n.* Syntonie, *f.*
syphilis ['sifilis], *n.* Syphilis, *f.* **syphilitic** [-'litik], *a.* Syphilitique.
Syria ['siriə]. La Syrie, *f.* **Syriac** ['siriæk], *a.* and *n.* Syriaque, *m.*
Syrian [-ə], *a.* and *n.* Syrien, *m.*, Syrienne, *f.*
syringa [si'riŋgə], *n.* (*Bot.*) Seringa, *m.*
syringe ['sirindʒ], *n.* Seringue, *f.*—*v.t.* Seringuer. **syringing**, *n.* Seringage (of plants), *m.*
syringotomy [siriŋ'gɔtəmi], *n.* Syringotomie, *f.*
syrinx [-ŋ], *n.* Syrinx, *f.*; flûte de Pan, *f.*; trompe d'Eustache, *f.*
syrup ['sirəp], *n.* Sirop, *m.* **syrupy**, *a.* Sirupeux.
systaltic [sis'tæltik], *a.* (*Physiol.*) Systaltique.
system ['sistəm], *n.* Système, régime, *m.*, méthode, constitution, *f.*; réseau (railway system), *m.* The system, l'organisme, *m.*
systematic [-'mætik] or **systematical**, *a.* Systématique; raisonné (of a catalogue etc.). **systematically**, *adv.* Systématiquement.
systematist ['sistəmətist], *n.* Auteur or partisan d'un système, *m.* **systematization** [-tai'zeiʃən], *n.* Réduction en système, systématisation, *f.*
systematize ['sistəmətaiz], *v.t.* Systématiser, réduire en système. **systematizer**, *n.* Systématiseur, *m.*
system-monger, *n.* Faiseur de systèmes, *m.*
systole ['sistəli], *n.* Systole, *f.* **systolic** [-'tɔlik], *a.* Systolique.
systyle ['sistail], *a.* and *n.* Systyle, *m.*
syzygy ['sizidʒi], *n.* Syzygie, *f.*

T

T, t [ti:]. Vingtième lettre de l'alphabet, *m. Marked with a T,* marqué d'un V, voleur (thief); *that fits me to a T,* cela me va comme un gant, parfaitement, on ne peut mieux; *T-square,* té à dessin, *m.*
ta [tɑ:], *int.* (*colloq.*) Merci.
tab [tæb], *n.* Étiquette; patte, *f.*, écusson, *m. Shoe-lace tab,* ferret de lacet, *m.*; *to keep tabs on,* ne pas perdre de vue; (*Av.*) *trimming tab,* volet compensateur, *m.*

tabard ['tæbəd], *n.* Tabard, *m.*, cotte, tunique; (*Her.*) cotte d'armes, *f.*

tabaret ['tæbərət], *n.* Satin rayé, *m.*

tabby ['tæbi], *n.* Tabis (taffetas); chat moucheté, rayé, tigré (cat), *m.*; (*fam.*) vieille chipie, *f.*—*a.* Tacheté, moucheté.—*v.t.* Tabiser (cloth); moirer.

tabefaction [tæbi'fækʃən], *n.* Dépérissement, marasme, *m.*

tabellion [tə'beliən], *n.* Tabellion, *m.*

tabernacle ['tæbənækl], *n.* Tabernacle, *m.*; (*Am.*) église, *f.*, temple, *m.*

tabes ['teibi:z], *n.* Tabès, *m.* **tabetic** [tə'betik], *a.* Tabétique. **tabid,** *a.* Tabide, ataxique.

tablature ['tæblətʃə], *n.* (*Paint.*) Peinture murale; (*Mus.*) tablature, *f.*

table [teibl], *n.* Table; tablette (tablet), *f.*; (*Paint.*) tableau, *m.*; (*Arch.*) tablette, *f.*; catalogue, *m.*, table des matières (index), *f.* *Astronomical* or *chronological tables,* tables astronomiques *or* chronologiques, *f.pl.*; *billiard-table,* billard, *m.*; *bedside-table,* table de nuit; *dining-table,* table de salle à manger, *f.*; *folding-table,* table pliante; *kitchen-table,* table de cuisine; *multiplication table,* table de multiplication; *tea-, work-, card-,* or *writing-table,* table à thé, à ouvrage, à jouer, *f.*, bureau, *m.*; *the Lord's Table,* la table sainte; *the tables are turned,* les rôles sont intervertis; *to be laid upon the table (in Parliament),* être déposé sur le bureau; *to be left under the table* (of persons intoxicated), rester sous la table; *to be seated at table,* être attablé; *to clear the table,* desservir; *to keep a good table,* tenir bonne table; *to keep open table,* tenir table ouverte; *to lay the table,* mettre le couvert; *to put on the table,* servir; *to rise from table,* se lever de table; *to sit down to table,* se mettre à table; *to turn the tables upon,* reprendre l'avantage sur.—*v.t.* Dresser la table *or* le catalogue de (to catalogue); déposer (un projet de loi).

table-beer, *n.* Bière ordinaire de table, *f.* **table-book,** *n.* Tablettes, *f.pl.* **table-centre,** *n.* Chemin de table, *m.* **table-cloth,** *n.* Nappe, *f.* **table-cover,** *n.* Tapis de table, *m.* **table d'hôte,** *n.* Menu à prix fixe, *m.* **tableful,** *n.* Tablée, *f.* **tableland,** *n.* Plateau, *m.* **table-linen,** *n.* Linge de table, *m.* **table-spoon,** *n.* Cuiller à bouche, *f.* **tablespoonful,** *n.* Grande cuillerée, *f.* **table-talk,** *n.* Propos de table, *m.pl.* **table-tennis,** *n.* Tennis de table, ping-pong, *m.* **table-turning,** *n.* Phénomène des tables tournantes, *m.*

tablet ['tæblit], *n.* Tablette, *f.*; (*Med.*) comprimé, *m.*

tabling, *n.* (*Carp.*) Assemblage; (*Naut.*) doublage (of sail), *m.* *Tabling of a bill,* dépôt d'un projet de loi; *tabling for ten,* places pour dix personnes, *f.pl.*; couverts pour dix, *m.pl.*

tabloid ['tæbloid], *n.* (*reg. trade name*) (Petit) comprimé, *m.* *News in tabloid form,* nouvelles brèves, *f.pl.*

taboo [tə'bu:], *n. and a.* Tabou, *m.*—*v.t.* Tabouer, interdire.

*tabor ['teibə], *n.* Tambourin, tambour de basque, *m.*

tabouret ['tæbərit], *n.* Tabouret, *m.*

tabular ['tæbjulə], *a.* Arrangé en tableaux, synoptique; (*Min.*) tabulaire. **tabulate,** *v.t.* Disposer en tables, cataloguer, dresser un

tableau synoptique de. **tabulation** [-'leiʃən], *n.* Arrangement en tableaux, *m.*; classification, *f.* **tabulator,** *n.* Tabulateur (on typewriter), *m.*

tacamahac ['tækəməhæk], *n.* Baume vert, tacamaque, *m.*; (*Bot.*) peuplier de Galaad, *m.*

tachygrapher [tə'kigrəfə], *n.* Tachygraphe, *m.* **tachygraphy,** *n.* Tachygraphie, *f.* **tachymeter** [-'kimitə], *n.* Tachymètre, *m.*

tacit ['tæsit], *a.* Tacite, implicite. **tacitly,** *adv.* Tacitement, implicitement.

taciturn ['tæsitə:n], *a.* Taciturne. **taciturnity** [-'tə:niti], *n.* Taciturnité, *f.* **taciturnly,** *a.* Taciturnement.

Tacitus ['tæsitəs]. (*L. Lit.*) Tacite, *m.*

tack [tæk], *n.* Petit clou, *m.*, broquette (nail); (*Sc.*) nourriture (food or fare); (*Naut.*) amure, *f.* *To be on the right tack,* être en bonne voie; *to be on the starboard tack,* avoir les amures à tribord; *to be on the wrong tack,* faire fausse route; *to change tack,* changer d'amures; *to get down to brass tacks,* en venir aux faits; *to make a tack,* courir une bordée.—*v.t.* Clouer; (*Needlework*) bâtir, faufiler. *To tack on,* ajouter.—*v.i.* (*Naut.*) Virer vent devant. *To tack about,* virer de bord; louvoyer, courir des bordées.

tackiness ['tækinis], *n.* Viscosité, *f.*

tacking, *n.* Cloutage, *m.*; (*Needlework*) faufilure, *f.*; (*Naut.*) virement de bord, louvoyage, *m.*; (*Law*) jonction, *f.*

tackle [tækl], *n.* Attirail; (*Naut.*) palan, *m.*; cordages, *m.pl.*; (*spt.*) arrêt, accrochage, plaquage, *f.*; (*fig.*) ustensiles, instruments, *m.pl.* *Fishing-tackle,* articles de pêche, *m.pl.*; *gun-tackle,* itague, *f.*; *winding-tackle,* caliorne, *f.*—*v.t.* Empoigner, saisir à bras le corps; (*Ftb.*) plaquer; (*fig.*) attaquer (work etc.).

tackle-block, *n.* Moufle; (*Naut.*) poulie de palan, *f.*

tackler, *n.* (*Ftb.*) Plaqueur, *m.*

tackling, *n.* Gréement, *m.*, cordages, *m.pl.*; appareil, *m.*; (*Ftb.*) arrêt, *m.*

tacky ['tæki], *a.* Collant, visqueux, gluant.

tact [tækt], *n.* Le toucher; (*fig.*) tact, savoir-faire, *m.* **tactful,** *a.* Plein de tact.

tactical ['tæktikl], *a.* Tactique. **tactically,** *adv.* Par la tactique. **tactician** [-'tiʃən], *n.* Tacticien, *m.* **tactics,** *n.pl.* La tactique, *f.*

tactile ['tæktail], *a.* Tactile.

tactless ['tæktlis], *a.* Sans tact, sans savoir-faire.

tadpole ['tædpoul], *n.* Têtard, *m.*

taenia ['ti:niə], *n.* (*Med.*) Ténia, ver solitaire, *m.*; (*Surg.*) bandage en rouleau, *m.*

taffeta ['tæfitə], *n.* Taffetas, *m.*

taffrail ['tæfreil], *n.* Couronnement (de la poupe), *m.*

Taffy ['tæfi]. Davy (abbr. of David) (Welsh pronunciation); (*colloq.*) Gallois, *m.*

tag [tæg], *n.* Ferret, fer, bout ferré, *m.*; étiquette (label), *f.*; dicton, aphorisme banal, *m.*; chat (game), *m.*—*v.t.* Ferrer (a lace); (*fig.*) joindre, lier, attacher, coudre (à).

tag-rag, *n.* Racaille, canaille, *f.* *All the tag-rag and bobtail,* toute la racaille; *tag-rag and bobtail,* quatre pelés et un tondu.

Tagus ['teigəs]. (*Geog.*) Le Tage, *m.*

Tahiti [ta:'hi:ti]. (*Geog.*) Taïti (*or* Tahiti), *m.*

tail [teil], *n.* Queue; (*fig.*) extrémité, fin, *f.*; bout; pan, *m.*, basque (of a coat), *f.*; derrière (of a cart); manche (of a plough), *m.*; pile (of a coin), *f.*; empennage (of an aeroplane), *m.* *In tail,* (*Law*) par substitution; *to turn tail,* s'enfuir, montrer les talons; *with his tail between his legs,* la queue entre les jambes, l'oreille basse.—*v.t.* Couper la queue (of animals); enlever, ôter les queues (of fruit); (*fam.*) filer (of police suspects etc.).—*v.i.* To *tail after,* suivre quelqu'un de près; *to tail away,* s'espacer, s'égrener; s'éteindre (of voices); *to tail on,* se mettre à la queue.

tailboard, *n.* Derrière (de charrette), *m.* **tail-block,** *n.* Poulie à fouet, *f.* **tail-coat,** *n.* Habit, *m.,* (*fam.*) queue-de-pie, *f.* **tail-end,** *n.* Queue, *f.,* bout, *m. At the tail-end,* en queue. **tail-light,** *n.* Feu arrière, *m.* **tail-piece,** *n.* Queue, *f.;* (*Print.*) cul-de-lampe, *m.* **tail-plane,** *n.* (*Av.*) Stabilisateur, *m.* **tail-rope,** *n.* Corde de remorque, *f.* **tail-unit,** *n.* (*Av.*) Empennage, *m.*

tailed, *a.* À queue. *Long-tailed,* à longue queue. **tailings,** *n.pl.* Grenailles (of wheat), *f.pl.;* (*Mining*) résidus des minerais aurifères, *m.pl.* **tailless,** *a.* Sans queue, anoure.

tailor ['teilə], *n.* Tailleur, *m. Lady's tailor,* tailleur pour dames, *m.*—*v.t.* Faire, façonner (a suit). **tailor-bird,** *n.* (*Orn.*) Fauvette couturière, *f.* **tailor-made,** *a.* Tailleur.

tailoress, *n.* Tailleuse, *f.* **tailoring,** *n.* Métier de tailleur; ouvrage de tailleur, *m.*

taint [teint], *v.t.* Corrompre, gâter, infecter. *Tainted meat,* viande gâtée, *f.*—*v.i.* Se corrompre; se gâter (of meat).—*n.* Infection, teinte, souillure, corruption; tache (blemish), *f. Free from taint,* fraîche, qui n'est pas gâtée (of meat). **taintless,** *a.* Sans infection, sans tache, pur. **tainture,** *n.* Souillure, tache, *f.*

take [teik], *v.t.* (*past* **took** [tuk], *p.p.* **taken**) Prendre; mener (to lead), conduire (a person in a vehicle); porter (a thing to); amener, emmener (to go with); enlever (to carry off); retrancher, ôter (to deduct); saisir, s'emparer de (to seize); accepter, recevoir (to accept); (*fig.*) regarder, croire, considérer, emporter; supposer, s'imaginer (to suppose); fasciner, séduire (to fascinate); profiter de (an opportunity); adopter, choisir (to choose); admettre (to admit); contenir, avoir de la place pour (to hold); occuper (to occupy); demander, exiger, falloir (to require); endurer, souffrir (to endure); faire (a walk, a run, a stroll, etc.); avoir, tirer (revenge, satisfaction, etc.); essuyer, subir (affront); retenir, arrêter (to engage rooms etc.); tenir (a bet); prêter (an oath); suivre (a road etc.). *Death has taken him off,* la mort nous l'a enlevé; *how long will they take to put up that wall?* combien de temps mettront-ils à élever ce mur? *how old do you take me for?* quel âge me donnez-vous? *I take you to be thirty,* je vous donne trente ans; *I cannot take that story in,* je ne puis admettre la vérité de cette histoire; *it takes a wise man to be a fool,* qui ne sait pas être fou n'est pas sage; *take care of the pence and the pounds will take care of themselves,* il n'y a pas de petites économies; *take my trunk into my bedroom,* portez ma malle dans ma chambre à coucher; *to be taken giddy,* être pris de vertiges; *to be taken ill,* se trouver mal, tomber malade; *to be taken with,* être épris de, être entiché de; *to be taken with pains in the stomach,* éprouver

des tiraillements d'estomac; *to give and take,* faire des concessions mutuelles; *to take aback,* surprendre, étonner, confondre; *to take a back seat,* en rabattre; *to take about,* conduire partout; *to take again,* reprendre; *to take aim,* viser (à); *to take amiss,* prendre en mauvaise part; *to take an airing,* prendre l'air; *to take at his word,* prendre au mot; *to take away,* emmener, emporter (things), retirer, ôter (to remove), desservir (dinner-things etc.), dérober (to steal); *to take away from,* prendre à, ôter à; *to take back,* reprendre, remporter; *to take breath,* prendre haleine; *to take care,* prendre garde, avoir l'œil au guet; *to take care* (beware), prendre garde (de); *to take care of,* prendre soin de; *to take cover,* se défiler; *to take down,* descendre, humilier, abaisser, rabattre (to humble), prendre, avaler (to swallow), abattre, démolir (to demolish), prendre note de, coucher par écrit (to write down); *to take earth,* se réfugier dans sa tanière; *to take effect,* porter coup, faire effet; *to take farewell,* prendre congé de, faire ses adieux à; *to take fire,* prendre feu, s'enflammer; *to take for,* prendre pour, regarder comme, mener faire (une promenade); *to take from,* prendre de, accepter de, prendre à, enlever à (to deprive of), soustraire à, retrancher de (to subtract), diminuer de (to detract); *to take heart,* reprendre courage; *to take heed,* prendre garde (à); *to take hold of,* tenir, saisir (par); *to take in,* faire entrer, rentrer, faire rentrer, enclore (to enclose), comprendre, embrasser (to comprise), resserrer, rétrécir (to contract), recevoir, prendre (to receive), loger, recevoir chez soi (to receive in one's house), contenir (to hold), tromper, duper, mettre dedans (to cheat), être abonné à (a periodical), faire sa provision de (provisions etc.); *to take in hand,* se charger de, prendre en main; *to take in one's hand,* prendre dans sa main; *to take into account* or *into consideration,* tenir compte de; *to take in water,* faire de l'eau, faire provision d'eau douce; *to take it for granted,* se le tenir pour dit; *to take it into one's head that,* se mettre dans la tête que, s'aviser de; *to take it out in,* se payer en; *to take notice of,* remarquer, s'apercevoir de; *to take off,* enlever, ôter, couper, trancher (to cut off), détruire (to destroy), lever (a mask), retirer (to withdraw), caricaturer, faire la charge de (to caricature); *to take off from,* détourner de, diminuer (to lessen); *to take off one's eyes from,* détourner les yeux de, quitter des yeux; *to take one's choice,* faire son choix, choisir; *to take oneself off,* s'en aller, décamper, filer; *to take one's eyes from,* détourner les yeux de; *to take out,* faire sortir, sortir (things), dégager (from pawn), arracher (teeth), ôter, enlever (stains etc.), promener (for a walk), dételer (horses from a carriage); *to take out a licence,* prendre une patente; *to take out a patent,* prendre un brevet; *to take out a summons against,* envoyer une assignation à; *to take out of,* sortir de, tirer de; *to take over,* prendre, se charger de, prendre la succession de (business); *to take over to,* (*Rad. Tel.*) mettre en communication avec; *to take pity on,* avoir pitié de; *to take place,* avoir lieu; *to take prisoner,* faire prisonnier; *to take refuge in,* se réfugier dans; *to take root*, prendre racine; *to take shelter*, se mettre à l'abri, s'abriter; *to take someone's life*, ôter la vie à quelqu'un; *to take someone's opinion*, consulter quelqu'un; *to take someone's part*, prendre fait et cause pour quelqu'un; *to take someone to be*, prendre quelqu'un pour; *to take some trouble*, se donner de la peine; *to take stock of*, faire l'inventaire de, inventorier; *to take the field*, se mettre *or* entrer en campagne; *to take the law into one's own hands*, se faire justice à soi-même; *to take the lead in*, prendre la direction de, marcher en tête de, donner le ton à; *to take the oath*, prêter serment; *to take the wall*, prendre le haut du pavé; *to take time*, prendre son temps, prendre du temps (require time); *tó take time by the fórelock*, prendre la balle au bond, saisir l'occasion aux cheveux; *to take to pieces*, démonter; *to take to task*, réprimander, gronder, prendre à partie; *to take up*, prendre, monter, faire monter, porter en haut, lever, soulever (to raise), relever, ramasser (to pick up), commencer, entamer, aborder (to begin), prendre en main, se charger de (to take in hand), occuper, abuser de (one's time), arrêter (to arrest), relever, reprendre, réprimander (to reprimand), adopter (to adopt), épouser (to espouse), faire honneur à (a bill); *to take up arms*, prendre les armes, commencer les hostilités; *to take up into*, faire monter dans; *to take (it) upon oneself to*, prendre sur soi de, se charger de, s'aviser de; *to take up one's quarters*, s'établir à, se fixer à; *what do you take me for?* pour qui me prenez-vous? *what will you take for that clock?* combien voulez-vous de cette pendule? *you must take it or leave it*, c'est à prendre ou à laisser; *you take too much upon yourself*, vous présumez trop de vous-même.

v.i.—Se diriger (vers), aller (à), se réfugier (dans); s'adonner, se mettre, s'attacher (à); plaire (to please); avoir du succès, réussir (to succeed); prendre (to catch fire etc.). *She takes after you*, elle a quelque chose de vous; *to take after*, ressembler à, tenir de; *(Av.) to take off*, décoller; *to take on*, se lamenter, s'affliger, s'emporter; *to take to*, se diriger vers, se réfugier dans (to take refuge in), avoir recours à (to resort to), s'appliquer à, se mettre à (to apply to), s'attacher à, prendre en amitié (to be fond of persons), prendre du goût à, mordre à (to be fond of things); *to, take to running*, se mettre à courir; *to take up with*, s'associer à, s'attacher à, prendre en amitié.

n.—Prise, pêche, quantité (of fish), *f.*; (Cine.) prise de vue, *f. Have you had a good take?* avez-vous fait bonne pêche?

take-in, *n.* Duperie, attrape, *f.*; tour (trick); voleur, charlatan, fripon (person), *m.* **take-off**, *n.* Caricature, charge, *f.*; *(Av.)* décollage, *m.* **take-over**, *n.* (Fin.) Rachat (of business). *m. Take-over bid*, offre de rachat, *f.* (to obtain control of a business).

taker, *n.* Preneur, *m.*, -euse, *f.*; priseur (of snuff), *m:*

taking, *n.* Prise; arrestation, *f.*; *(pl.)* recettes (receipts), *f.pl.*—*a.* Attrayant, séduisant; (colloq.) contagieux (infectious). *(Av.) Taking off*, décollage, *m.* **takingly**, *adv.* D'une manière attrayante. **takingness**, *n.* Charme, attrait, *m.*

talc [tælk], *n.* Talc, *m.*
talcite ['tælsait], *n.* Talcite, *f.*
talcose ['tælkous], *a.* Talcique, talqueux.
talcum powder ['tælkəm 'paudə], *n.* Talc, *m.*
tale [teil], *n.* Conte, récit, *m.*; histoire, *f.*; *nombre, compte (reckoning), *m.*; racontar, on-dit, *m. A tale never loses in the telling*, on fait toujours le loup plus gros qu'il n'est; *his tale is told*, c'en est fait de lui; *that tells a tale*, cela dit beaucoup; *to tell tales*, (sch.) rapporter.
tale-bearer, *n.* Rapporteur, *m.*, mauvaise langue, *f.* **tale-bearing**, *n.* Rapports; cancans, *m.pl.* **tale-teller**, *n.* Conteur, *m.*, -euse, *f.*
talent ['tælənt], *n.* Talent, *m.* **talented**, *a.* De talent, habile, bien doué.
talipot ['tælipɔt], *n.* (Bot.) Tallipot, *m.*
talisman ['tælizmən], *n.* Talisman, *m.* **talismanic** [-'mænik], *a.* Talismanique.
talk [tɔ:k], *v.i.* Parler (de); converser, causer; bavarder, jaser (to prate). *Now you speak, you were only talking before*, voilà ce qui s'appelle parler, vous ne faisiez que bavarder auparavant; *to get talked about*, faire parler de soi; *to talk at*, haranguer; *to talk away*, ne pas cesser de parler; *to talk away from the point*, s'éloigner de la question en parlant; *to talk down*, réduire au silence; *to talk of or about*, parler de, causer de, parler, causer; *to talk through one's hat*, dire des bêtises; *to talk to oneself*, parler à soi-même; *what are you talking about?* de quoi parlez-vous? vous n'y songez pas!

v.t.—Parler, dire. *To talk nonsense*, dire des sottises; *to talk out of*, dissuader de; *to talk over*, cajoler (quelqu'un); discuter (quelque chose); *tó talk pólitics*, parler politique; *to talk someone into*, persuader quelqu'un de; *to talk the time away*, passer le temps à causer.

n.—Entretien, *m.*, propos, *m.pl.*, conversation; causerie (chat), *f.*; bavardage, *m.*, sornettes (idle chatter), *f.pl.*; bruit (rumour); sujet de conversation, *m.*, propos, *m.pl. He is all talk*, ce n'est qu'un bavard; *it is the talk of the town*, on ne parle que de cela dans toute la ville; *she is all talk*, elle a la langue bien pendue; *small talk*, banalités, *f.pl.*, propos insignifiants, *m.pl.*; *there is talk of*, il est question de, le bruit court que.

talkative, *a.* Causeur, bavard. **talkativeness**, *n.* Loquacité, *f.*, bavardage, *m.* **talker**, *n.* Causeur, parleur; bavard (chatterer); fanfaron, vantard (boaster), *m.*
talkie, *n.* Film parlant, *m.*
talking, *n.* Conversation, causerie, *f.*; bavardage (chatter), *m. He got a talking-to*, il fut vivement réprimandé.—*a.* Causeur, bavard.
tall [tɔ:l], *a.* Grand (of persons); haut (of things). *A tall fellow*, un grand gaillard; *a tall hat*, un chapeau haut de forme; *a tall man*, un homme grand; *a tall story*, une histoire invraisemblable.
*tallage ['tælidʒ], *n.* Taille, *f.*, impôt, *m.*
tallboy ['tɔ:lbɔi], *n.* Chiffonnier, *m.*; (haute) commode-secrétaire, *f.*
tallit ['tælit], *n.* Talett (Jewish praying-veil), *m.*
tallness ['tɔ:lnis], *n.* Grande taille, hauteur, *f.*

tallow ['tælou], *n.* Suif, *m.*—*v.t.* Suiffer.
tallow-candle, *n.* Chandelle, *f.* **tallow-chandler**, *n.* Fabricant de chandelles, *m.*
tallow-faced, *a.* Au visage blême. **tallow-tree**, *n.* Arbre à suif, *m.* **tallowy**, *a.* De suif, suiffeux, graisseux.

tally ['tæli], *n.* Taille (stick); entaille, marque; étiquette (à bagages), *f.*—*v.t.* Faire les coches or marquer· sur la taille, cocher.—*v.i.* S'accorder. *To tally with*, s'accorder avec, correspondre à. **tally-clerk**, *n.* Pointeur, contrôleur (of goods), *m.* **tallyman**, *n.* Personne qui marque la taille, *f.*; (*Comm.*) marchand qui vend à crédit, *m.* **tally-sheet**, *n.* Feuille de pointage, *f.* **tally-shop**, *n.* Boutique où l'on achète à tempérament, *f.* **tally-trade**, *n.* Vente à tempérament, *f.*

tally-ho [tæli'hou], *int.* (*Hunt.*) Taïaut.

tallying ['tæliiŋ], *n.* Contrôle, *m.*, vérification, *f.* (des comptes).

Talmud ['tælmʌd], *n.* Talmud, *m.* **Talmudic** [-'mʌdik], *a.* Talmudique. **Talmudist** ['tælmʌdist], *n.* Talmudiste, *m.* **Talmudistic** [-'distik], *a.* Talmudiste.

talon ['tælən], *n.* Serre, griffe, *f.*

tamable ['teimabl], *a.* Apprivoisable, domptable. **tamableness**, *n.* Nature apprivoisable, nature domptable, *f.*

tamarind ['tæmərind], *n.* Tamarin, *m.* **tamarind-tree**, *n.* Tamarinier, *m.*

tamarisk ['tæmərisk], *n.* (*Bot.*) Tamaris, tamarisc, tamarix, *m.*

tambour ['tæmbə], *n.* (*Mus.*) Grosse caisse, *f.*; (*Embroidery*) tambour à tapisserie, *m.*; (*Arch.*) tambour, *m.*—*v.t.* Broder au tambour. **tambour-frame**, *n.* Métier à broder, *m.* **tambour-work**, *n.* Tambour (à broder), *m.*; broderie, *f.*

tambourine [tæmbə'ri:n], *n.* Tambour de basque, tambourin, *m.*

tame [teim], *a.* Apprivoisé; domestique; insipide, fade, plat, sans couleur (of style etc.); soumis (subdued). *To grow tame*, s'apprivoiser.—*v.t.* Apprivoiser; dompter (to break in); (*fig.*) subjuguer.

tamely ['teimli], *adv.* Avec soumission; lâchement, sans cœur (cowardly).

tameness ['teimnis], *n.* Apprivoisement, *m.*, domesticité; soumission, servilité (submission); faiblesse (of style etc.), *f.*

tamer ['teimə], *n.* Apprivoiseur; dompteur (of wild beasts), *m.*

Tamerlane ['tæməlein]. (*Hist.*) Tamerlan, *m.*

taming ['teimiŋ], *n.* Apprivoisement, *m.*, domestication, *f.*

tamis ['tæmis], **tammy**, *n.* Tamis, filtre, *m.*

tam-o'-shanter [tæmə'ʃæntə], *n.* Béret écossais, *m.*

tamp [tæmp], *v.t.* Bourrer, tamponner.

tamper ['tæmpə], *v.i.* Se mêler (de); expérimenter (avec). *To tamper with*, se mêler de, prendre des libertés avec, jouer avec, fausser (a lock etc.); suborner (a witness).

tampering, *n.* Menées secrètes, pratiques louches, *f.pl.*; altération, falsification (of documents etc.), *f.* *There must be no tampering with*, il ne faut pas toucher à; *there must be no tampering with the witnesses*, toute tentative de suborner les témoins sera punie par la loi.

tamping ['tæmpiŋ], *n.* Bourrage, *m.* **tamping-bar**, *n.* Bourroir, *m.*

tampion ['tæmpiən], *n.* Tampon (de canon), *m.*

tampon ['tæmpɔn], *n.* Tampon, *m.* (of cotton-wool etc.).—*v.t.* Tamponner.

tan [tæn], *n.* Tan; tanné (colour), *m.* *Waste tan*, tannée, *f.*—*v.t.* Tanner; basaner, hâler (to sunburn). **tan-colour**, *n.* Tanné, *m.* **tan-pit**, *n.* Fosse à tan, *f.* **tan-vat**, *n.* Fosse à tan, *f.* **tan-yard**, *n.* Tannerie, *f.*

tandem ['tændəm], *n.* Attelage en flèche; tandem (bicycle), *m.*

tang [tæŋ], *n.* Goût, *m.*, saveur; queue (of a file); soie (of a knife, sword), *f.*

tangency ['tændʒənsi], *n.* Tangence, *f.* **tangent**, *a.* Tangent.—*n.* Tangente, *f.* *To go off at a tangent*, prendre la tangente, passer subitement à un autre sujet. **tangent-sight**, *n.* (*Artill.*) Hausse, *f.* **tangential** [-'dʒenʃl], *a.* Tangent, tangentiel.

tangerine [tændʒə'ri:n], *n.* Mandarine, *f.*

tangibility [tændʒi'biliti], *n.* Tangibilité, *f.* **tangible** ['tændʒibl], *a.* Tangible, palpable, sensible.

Tangier [tæn'dʒiːə]. (*Geog.*) Tanger, *m.*

tangle ['tæŋgl], *n.* Enchevêtrement, embrouillement, *m.*, confusion, *f.*; embarras; fourré (brake), *m.* *To be in a tangle*, être tout embrouillé; (*fig.*) être dans le pétrin.—*v.t.* Emmêler, embrouiller, enchevêtrer. **tangled**, *a.* Embrouillé, emmêlé; (*fig.*) compliqué.

tango ['tæŋgou], *n.* Tango, *m.*

tangy ['tæŋi], *a.* Piquant, savoureux, épicé.

tank [tæŋk], *n.* Réservoir, *m.*; (*Naut.*) caisse à eau, *f.*; (*Mil.*) char d'assaut, *m.* **tank-engine**, *n.* Machine-tender, *f.* **tank-steamer** or **tanker**, *n.* Bateau citerne, *m.*

tank-transporter, *n.* Porte-chars, *m.*

tank-wagon, *n.* Wagon-réservoir, *m.*

tankage ['tæŋkidʒ], *n.* Emmagasinage (of petrol etc.), *m.*; capacité (of a tank), *f.*

tankard ['tæŋkəd], *n.* (Grand) pot en étain, *m.*, chope, *f.*

tanner ['tænə], *n.* Tanneur, *m.*; (*slang*) six-pence. **tannery**, *n.* Tannerie, *f.* **tannic**, *a.* Tannique. **tannin**, *n.* Tanin, tannin, *m.* **tanning**, *n.* Tannage, *m.*; (*fam.*) rossée, *f.* *To give someone a good tanning*, flanquer une belle rossée à quelqu'un. **tanning-liquor**, *n.* Jusée, *f.*

tansy ['tænzi], *n.* (*Bot.*) Tanaisie, herbe aux vers, *f.*

tantalization [tæntəlai'zeiʃən] or **tantalism** ['tæntəlizm], *n.* Action de torturer, tentation, *f.*, supplice de Tantale, tantalisme, *m.*

tantalize ['tæntəlaiz], *v.t.* Tantaliser, tourmenter, faire subir le supplice de Tantale à. **tantalizing**, *a.* Tentant, torturant.

tantalum ['tæntələm], *n.* (*Metal.*) Tantale, *m.*

Tantalus ['tæntələs]. (*Myth.*) Tantale, *m.*; (*colloq.*) cave à liqueurs, *f.* *Tortures of Tantalus*, supplice de Tantale, *m.*

tantamount ['tæntəmaunt], *a.* Équivalent (à). *That is tantamount to saying*, c'est comme si l'on disait, cela revient à dire; *to be tantamount to*, équivaloir à, revenir à.

tantivy ['tæntivi], *adv.* (*Hunt.*) À fond de train, à bride abattue. *To ride tantivy*, galoper ventre à terre.

tantrum ['tæntrəm], *n.* Mauvaise humeur, *f.*, accès de colère, *m.* *To be in a tantrum*, être énervé.

tap [tæp], *n.* Tape, *f.*, petit coup (knock at door etc.); robinet (cock); comptoir (bar), *m.*; cannelle (of a cask), *f.*; taraud (screw-tap), *m.* *A fresh tap*, un nouveau baril en perce; *on tap*, en perce; *we have a good tap*, nous avons de la bonne bière en perce.—*v.t.* Taper, frapper doucement, toucher, frapper; tirer (to draw); mettre en perce (a cask); inciser (a tree); tarauder (screws etc.); (*Surg.*) faire la ponction à. *He tapped me on the shoulder*, il me toucha l'épaule; (*pop.*) *to be tapped*, être cinglé, timbré.—*v.i.* Taper, frapper. *To tap at the door*, frapper légèrement à la porte.
tap-dance, *n.* Danse à claquettes, *f.*
tape [teip], *n.* Ruban (de fil); bolduc, *m.*; ganse (on clothes), *f.*; (*Print.*) cordon, *m.*; bande, *f.* *Red tape*, (*fig.*) routine administrative, la bureaucratie, paperasserie, *f.*; *to stand at the finishing tape*, se tenir debout à la bande d'arrivée; *tracing tape*, ruban à tracer, *m.*; *white tape*, tresse blanche, *f.*—*v.t.* Attacher, ficeler avec du bolduc; border (of garment); coudre sur ruban (of books); mesurer au cordeau (of area of ground). (*fam.*) *To have someone taped*, prendre la mesure de quelqu'un. **tape-machine,** *n.* Téléimprimeur, *m.* **tape-measure,** *n.* Mètre ruban, *m.* **tape-recorder,** *n.* Magnétophone, *m.* **tape-recording,** *n.* Enregistrement magnétique, *m.* **tape-worm,** *n.* Ver solitaire, *m.*
taper ['teipə], *n.* Bougie effilée, *f.*; (*Eccles.*) cierge, *m.*—*v.t.* Effiler, tailler en pointe.—*v.i.* S'effiler, se terminer en pointe.—*a.* Élancé, effilé; conique.
tapering, *a.* Effilé, terminé en pointe; en forme de cône, conique. *Tapering fingers*, doigts effilés, *m.pl.* **taperingly,** *adv.* En pointe.
tapestried ['tæpistrid], *a.* Tapissé. **tapestry,** *n.* Tapisserie, *f.*—*v.t.* Tapisser. **tapestry-carpet,** *n.* Tapis bouclé, *m.* **tapestry-worker,** *n.* Tapissier, *m.*
tapioca [tæpi'oukə], *n.* Tapioca, *m.*
tapir ['teipiə], *n.* Tapir, *m.*
tapis ['tæpi], *n.* Tapis, *m.* *To be on the tapis*, être sur le tapis.
tappet ['tæpit], *n.* Taquet (de soupape), *m.*
tapping ['tæpiŋ], *n.* Taraudage (of screws), *m.*; mise en perce (of a cask); incision (of a tree); (*Surg.*) ponction, *f.*; frappement, tapotement (with fingers etc.), *m.*
tap-room, *n.* Estaminet, cabaret, *m.*; buvette (of an hotel), *f.*
tap-root, *n.* Racine pivotante, *f.*, pivot, *m.* **tap-rooted,** *a.* À racine pivotante.
tapster ['tæpstə], *n.* Garçon (de cabaret), *m.*
tar [ta:], *n.* Goudron; loup de mer (sailor), *m.*—*v.t.* Goudronner. *They are all tarred with the same brush*, ce sont tous des gens de même farine. **tar-barrel,** *n.* Baril de goudron, *m.* **tar-brush,** *n.* Brosse à goudronner, *f.*; (*Naut.*) guipon, *m.* (*pej.*) *She looks as if she's had a touch of the tar-brush*, elle a l'air d'avoir un peu de sang nègre dans les veines. **tar-water,** *n.* Eau de goudron, *f.*
tarantella [tærən'telə], *n.* Tarentelle (dance), *f.*
tarantula [tə'ræntjulə], *n.* Tarentule, *f.*
tardily ['ta:dili], *adv.* Tardivement, lentement. **tardiness,** *n.* Lenteur, nonchalance, *f.*; tardiveté (of fruit), *f.* **tardy,** *a.* Lent; paresseux; en retard, tardif (late).
tare (1) [tɛə], *n.* Tare; (*Script.*) ivraie; (*Agric.*) (*pl.*) vesce, *f.*, ers, *m.*—*v.t.* (*Comm.*) Tarer, prendre la tare de.
*tare (2) [TORE].
*targe [ta:dʒ], *n.* Targe, *f.*, bouclier, *m.*
target ['ta:git], *n.* Cible; *targe (shield), *f.*; but, objectif, *m.* *Disappearing target*, cible à éclipse; *running target*, cible mobile, *f.*; *the government is the target of his accusations*, ses accusations visent le gouvernement. **target-practice,** *n.* Tir à la cible, *m.*
tariff ['tærif], *n.* Tarif, *m.* *To do away with tariff walls*, abolir les barrières douanières.—*v.t.* Tarifer. **tariff-reform,** *n.* La réforme des tarifs douaniers, *f.*
tarlatan ['ta:lətən], *n.* Tarlatane (muslin), *f.*
tarmac ['ta:mæk], *n.* Macadam, *m.*; (*Av.*) piste d'envol, *f.*—*v.t.* Goudronner.
tarn [ta:n], *n.* Petit lac (de montagne), *m.*
tarnish ['ta:niʃ], *v.t.* Ternir; (*fig.*) souiller, flétrir.—*v.i.* Se ternir.
tarpaulin [ta:'pɔːlin], *n.* (*Naut.*) Prélart, *m.*, bâche, toile goudronnée, *f.*
Tarpeian [ta:'pi:ən], *a.* Tarpéien. *The Tarpeian rock*, la roche tarpéienne.
tarragon ['tærəgən], *n.* (*Bot.*) Estragon, *m.*
Tarragona [tærə'gounə]. (*Geog.*) Tarragone, *f.*
tarrock ['tærək], *n.* (*Orn.*) Mouette tridactyle, *f.*
tarry (1) ['ta:ri], *a.* Goudronneux, bitumeux; goudronné.
tarry (2) ['tæri], *v.i.* Rester, s'arrêter, tarder, attendre. **tarrying,** *n.* Retard, séjour, *m.*
tarsal [ta:sl], *a.* Tarsien, du tarse. **tarsus,** *n.* Tarse, *m.*
tart (1) [ta:t], *n.* Tarte, tourte, *f.*; (*pop.*) fille, grue, *f.* **tart-dish,** *n.* Tourtière, *f.*
tart (2) [ta:t], *a.* Acide, âcre; (*fig.*) aigre, mordant, piquant.
tartan ['ta:tən], *n.* Tartan, *m.*; tartane (vessel), *f.*
Tartar ['ta:tə], *n.* Tartare, *m.* *To catch a Tartar*, trouver à qui parler, trouver son maître.
tartar ['ta:tə], *n.* (*Chem.*) Tartre, *m.*
tartarean [ta:'tɛəriən], *a.* (*Myth.*) Du Tartare.
tartareous [ta:'tɛəriəs], *a.* (*Chem.*) Tartareux. **tartaric** [-'tærik], *a.* Tartrique.
tartarous ['ta:tərəs], *a.* Tartreux.
tartish ['ta:tiʃ], *a.* Aigrelet.
tartlet, *n.* Tartelette, *f.*
tartly, *adv.* Avec aigreur; (*fig.*) vertement, sévèrement.
tartness, *n.* Acidité, aigreur, *f.*
tartrate ['ta:treit], *n.* Tartrate, *m.*
tartuffe [ta:'tyf], *n.* Tartufe, hypocrite, cafard, *m.* **tartuffism,** *n.* Tartuferie, *f.*
task [ta:sk], *n.* Tâche, besogne, *f.*; travail, ouvrage; devoir (lesson); pensum (punishment), *m.* *To take to task*, réprimander, semoncer, prendre à partie.—*v.t.* Donner une tâche à, (*colloq.*) tailler de la besogne à; mettre à l'épreuve. *To overtask with*, charger de; *to task with*, accuser de, reprocher à. **taskmaster,** *n.* Chef de corvée, *m.* **taskwork,** *n.* Travail à la tâche, *m.*
Tasmania [tæz'meinjə]. (*Geol.*) La Tasmanie, *f.*
tassel [tæsl], *n.* Gland; signet (in a book); (*Arch.*) tasseau; *tiercelet (hawk), *m.*
tasselled, *a.* À glands, orné de glands; à houppes.
Tasso [tæsou]. (*It. Lit.*) Le Tasse, *m.*

tastable ['teistəbl], *a.* Qu'on peut goûter; savoureux.

taste [teist], *v.t.* Goûter, goûter de; (*fig.*) sentir, savourer, éprouver.—*v.i.* Goûter (de); avoir un goût (de). *To taste good* or *bad,* avoir un bon *or* un mauvais goût; *to taste of,* goûter de, goûter, avoir un goût de, sentir le, la, les (to have a smack of), sentir, éprouver, subir (to experience).—*n.* Goût; soupçon (small quantity), *m. A wee taste,* un soupçon, une idée; *tastes differ,* chacun son goût; *that is good* or *bad taste,* c'est de bon *or* de mauvais goût; *there is no accounting for tastes,* des goûts et des couleurs on ne discute pas; *to dress with taste,* s'habiller avec goût; *to have a taste of,* avoir un goût de, sentir le, la, les; *to one's taste,* à son goût.

tasteful, *a.* De bon goût, bien arrangé, fait avec goût. **tastefully,** *adv.* Avec goût. **tastefulness,** *n.* Bon goût, *m.* **tasteless,** *a.* Fade, insipide. **tastelessly,** *adv.* Insipidement, fadement. **tastelessness,** *n.* Insipidité, fadeur, *f.* **taster,** *n.* Dégustateur (of beverages), *m.*; sonde (instrument), *f.* **tastily** (*colloq.*) [TASTEFULLY].

tasting, *n.* Action de goûter; dégustation (beverages), *f.* **tasty,** *a.* (*colloq.*) De bon goût; savoureux.

tat [tæt], *v.i.* (*Needlework*) Faire de la frivolité.

ta-ta (1) [tæ'ta:], *int.* (*Childish*) Au revoir.

ta-ta (2) ['tæta: *or* 'ta:ta:], *n. To go for a ta-ta,* (*childish*) aller se promener.

tatter ['tætə], *n.* Haillon, lambeau, *m.*, guenille, *f.*

tatterdemalion [tætədi'meiljən], *n.* Déguenillé, va-nu-pieds, loqueteux, *m.*

tattered, *a.* Déguenillé, en haillons (of persons); en lambeaux, tout déchiré (of garments etc.).

tatting ['tætiŋ], *n.* Frivolité (lace), *f. To do tatting,* faire de la frivolité.

tattle [tætl], *n.* Babil, caquet, bavardage, *m.*—*v.i.* Bavarder. **tattler,** *n.* Bavard, babillard, *m.* **tattling,** *a.* Babillard, bavard.—*n.* Bavardage, *m.*

tattoo [tə'tu:], *v.t.* Tatouer.—*n.* Tatouage, *m.*; (*Mil.*) retraite (du soir), *f.*; carrousel, *m.*, fête militaire, *f.*, à giorno, *m. To beat the devil's tattoo,* tambouriner avec les doigts.

taught [tɔ:t], *past and p.p.* [TEACH].

taunt [tɔ:nt], *n.* Injure, *f.*, reproche amer, sarcasme, *m.*—*v.t.* Tancer, reprocher à, injurier, dire des injures à. **tauntingly,** *adv.* Injurieusement.

tauromachy [tɔ:'rɔməki], *n.* Tauromachie, *f.*

Taurus ['tɔ:rəs]. (*Astron.*) Le Taureau, *m.*

taut [tɔ:t], *a.* Raide, tendu; enflé (of sails). (*fig.*) *Taut and trim,* tiré à quatre épingles; *to haul taut,* raidir.

tautological [tɔ:tə'lɔdʒikl], *a.* Tautologique. **tautologize** [tɔ:'tɔlədʒaiz], *v.i.* Se répéter. **tautology** [tɔ:'tɔlədʒi], *n.* Tautologie, *f.*

tavern ['tævən], *n.* Taverne, *f.*; cabaret, *m.* **tavern-haunter,** *n.* Pilier de cabaret, *m.* **tavern-keeper,** *n.* Cabaretier, *m.*

taw [tɔ:], *n.* Grosse bille, *f.*, calot, *m.* (de verre).—*v.t.* Mégisser, passer en mégie.

tawdrily ['tɔ:drili], *adv.* D'une manière criarde, sans goût. **tawdriness,** *n.* Faux éclat, clinquant, mauvais goût, *m.* **tawdry,** *a.* Criard, de mauvais goût, prétentieux.

tawer ['tɔ:ə], *n.* Mégissier, *m.* **tawing,** *n.* Mégisserie, *f.*

tawny ['tɔ:ni], *a.* Fauve; (*fig.*) basané (of persons).

tawse [tɔ:z], *n.* Martinet, *m.*

tax [tæks], *n.* Impôt, *m.*, taxe; (*fig.*) contribution, imposition, *f.*; fardeau, *m. Income-tax,* impôt sur le revenu, *m.*; *land tax,* impôt foncier; *purchase tax,* taxe de luxe, *f.*; *super-tax,* surtaxe, *f.*—*v.t.* Imposer, frapper d'un impôt, taxer; (*fig.*) accuser (de), reprocher à. *The country's resources were taxed to the utmost,* toutes les ressources du pays furent mises à contribution; *to tax* (someone's patience etc.), mettre à l'épreuve.

taxable, *a.* Imposable.

taxation [tæk'seifən], *n.* Taxation, *f.*, impôts, *m.pl.* **taxer** or **taxing-master,** *n.* (*Law*) Taxateur, *m.*

tax-evasion, *n.* Fraude fiscale, *f.* **tax-farmer,** *n.* (*Fr. Hist.*) Fermier général, *m.* **tax-free,** *a.* Exempt d'impôts. **tax-gatherer** or (**-collector**), *n.* Percepteur, receveur-percepteur des contributions directes, *m.* **tax-payer,** *n.* Contribuable, *m.*

taxi-cab ['tæksikæb], **taxi,** *n.* Taxi, *m.*—*v.i.* (*Av.*) *To taxi up,* rouler jusqu'à la piste d'envol. **taxi-rank,** *n.* Stationnement réservé aux taxis, *m.*, station de taxis, *f.*

taxidermist ['tæksidə:mist], *n.* Empailleur, taxidermiste, naturaliste, *m.* **taxidermy,** *n.* Taxidermie, naturalisation, *f.*

taximeter [tæk'simitə], *n.* Taximètre, *m.*

taxonomy [tæk'sɔnəmi], *n.* Taxologie, taxonomie, *f.* **taxonomic** [-ə'nɔmik], *a.* Taxonomique. **taxonomist** [-'sɔnəmist], *n.* Taxonomiste, *f.*

tea [ti:], *n.* Thé, *m.*; tisane (infusion), *f.*; goûter (the meal), *m. Beef-tea,* bouillon, *m.*; *China tea,* thé de Chine, *m.*; *Indian tea,* thé de Ceylan, *m.*; *to come to tea,* venir prendre le thé. **tea-broker,** *n.* Courtier en thés, *m.* **tea-caddy** or **tea-cannister,** *n.* Boîte à thé, *f.* **tea-cake,** *f.* Brioche, *f.* **tea-chest,** *n.* Caisse à thé, *f.* **tea-cup,** *n.* Tasse à thé, *f. A storm in a tea-cup,* beaucoup de bruit pour rien. **teacupful,** *n.* Une pleine tasse à thé, *f.* **tea-drinker,** *n.* Buveur, *m.*, -euse, *f.*, de thé. **tea-garden,** *n.* Jardin de thé, *m.* **tea-kettle,** *n.* Bouilloire, *f.* **tea-leaf,** *n.* (*pl.* **tea-leaves**) Feuille de thé, *f.* **tea-party,** *n.* Thé, *m.* **tea-plant,** *n.* Arbre à thé, *m.* **teapot,** *n.* Théière, *f.* **tea-rose,** *n.* Rose-thé, *f.* **tea-service, tea-set,** or **tea-things,** *n.pl.* Service à thé, *m.* **tea-shop,** *n.* Salon de thé, *m.* **tea-spoon,** *n.* Cuiller à thé, *f.* **teaspoonful,** *n.* Petite cuillerée, *f.* **tea-strainer,** *n.* Passette à thé, *f.*; passe-thé, *m.* **tea-table,** *n.* Table à thé, *f.* **tea-time,** *n.* L'heure du thé, *f.* **tea-trade,** *n.* Commerce des thés, *m.* **tea-tray,** *n.* Plateau à thé, *m.* **tea-trolley,** *n.* Table roulante, *f.* **tea-urn,** *n.* Fontaine à thé, *f.*

teach [ti:tʃ], *v.t.* (*past and p.p.* **taught** [tɔ:t]) Enseigner, instruire; instruire dans, apprendre (à). *That will teach you to . . . ,* cela vous apprendra à . . . ; *to teach a lesson,* donner une leçon à; *to teach someone French,* enseigner *or* apprendre le français à quelqu'un.—*v.i.* Enseigner, professer.

teachable, *a.* Disposé à apprendre, docile;

enseignable (of things). **teachableness,** *n.*
Disposition à apprendre, docilité, *f.*
teacher, *n.* Maître, *m.*, -esse, *f.*, instituteur,
m., -trice, *f.*; professeur (secondary education), *m.*
teaching, *n.* Enseignement, *m.*, instruction, *f.*;
doctrine (of beliefs), *f. Teaching film (Cine.)*,
film d'enseignement, *m.*; *the teaching staff*, le
corps enseignant, *m.*
teak [tiːk], *n.* (*Bot.*) Teck, tek, *m.*
teal [tiːl], *n.* (*Orn.*) Sarcelle, *f.*
team [tiːm], *n.* Attelage, *m.*, équipe (in
games), *f.—v.t.* Atteler; camionner.
teamster, *n.* Conducteur d'attelage, charretier, *m.* **team-work,** *n.* Travail d'équipe;
jeu d'ensemble, *m.*
tear (1) [tiə], *n.* Larme, *f.*, pleur, *m. All in
tears*, tout en pleurs, tout éploré; *to affect to
tears*, toucher jusqu'aûx larmes; *to be drowned
in tears*, avoir les yeux noyés de larmes; *to
burst into tears*, fondre en larmes; *to shed
bitter tears*, pleurer à chaudes larmes; *to shed
tears*, verser des larmes; *with tears in one's
eyes*, les larmes aux yeux. **tear-drop,** *n.*
Larme, *f.* **tear-exciting,** *a.* Lacrymogène.
tear-shaped, *a.* En forme de larme. **tear-
stained,** *a.* Qui porte des traces de larmes.
tear (2) [tɛə], *v.t.* (*past* **tore,** *p.p.* **torn**)
Déchirer; (*fig.*) arracher, abîmer. *To tear
asunder*, déchirer en deux, arracher l'un de
l'autre; *to tear away, down,* or *out*, arracher;
to tear from, arracher à or de; *to tear up*,
arracher, mettre en morceaux, déchirer.—*v.i.*
Courir. *To tear along*, aller ventre à terre;
to tear down, descendre précipitamment; *to
tear off*, partir comme un trait.—*n.* Déchirure,
f. Wear and. tear, usure, *f.* **tearer,** *n.*
Déchireur, *m.*
tearful ['tiəful], *a.* Tout en larmes, en pleurs,
éploré. **tearfully,** *adv.* Les larmes aux yeux.
tearing ['tɛəriŋ], *n.* Déchirement, *m.*
tearless ['tiəlis], *a.* Sans larmes, sec, insensible.
tease [tiːz], *v.t.* Taquiner, tourmenter, contrarier; (*Tex.*) peigner, carder (to card). *To
tease out*, effilocher.—*n.* Taquin, *m.* **teaser,**
n. Taquin; (*Tex.*) cardeur, *m.*, -euse, *f.*;
(*fam.*) problème difficile, *m.*
teasel [tiːzl], *n.* Chardon à foulon, *m.* **teaseler,** *n.* Laineur, *m.*, -euse, *f.* **teasling,** *n.*
Lainage, *m.*
teasing ['tiːziŋ], *n.* Taquinerie, *f.*; (*Tex.*)
effilage, effilochage, *m.—a.* Taquin, contrariant.
teat [tiːt], *n.* Mamelon, tétin, téton, *m.*; tette, *f.*
teazel [TEASEL].
technical ['teknikl], *a.* Technique, de l'art.
Technical adviser, conseiller technique, *m.*;
technical education, enseignement professionnel, *m.*; *technical school*, école professionnelle, *f.* **technicality** [-'kæliti], *n.*
Caractère technique; terme technique (term),
m.; (*fig.*) formalité, *f.* **technically,** *adv.*
Techniquement. **technician** [-'niʃən], *n.*
Technicien, *m.* **technics, n.pl.** Technologie,
f. **technique,** *n.* Technique, *f.* **technological** [-nə'lɔdʒikl], *a.* Technologique.
technologist [-'nɔlədʒist], *n.* Technologue,
m. **technology,** *n.* Technologie, *f.*
tectology [tek'tɔlədʒi], *n.* Tectologie, *f.* **tectonic** [-'tɔnik], *a.* Tectonique. **tectonics,**
n.pl. Tectonique, *f.*

ted [ted], *v.t.* Faner. **tedder,** *n.* Faneuse, *f.*
tedding, *n.* Fanage, *m.*
Teddy ['tedi]. Édouard (diminutive), *m.*
Teddy bear, ours en peluche, *m.*; (*slang*)
teddy-boy, jeune voyou, blouson noir, *m.*
tedious ['tiːdiəs], *a.* Ennuyeux, fatigant.
tediously, *adv.* Ennuyeusement. **tediousness** or **tedium,** *n.* Ennui, *m.*
tee [tiː], *n.* Dé (de sable) (au golf), *m.—v.i.* To
tee up, placer la balle sur le dé; *to tee off*,
jouer sa première balle, partir.
teem [tiːm], *v.i.* Être fécond (en). *To teem
with*, être plein de, abonder en, fourmiller
de. **teeming,** *a.* Fécond, fertile, surabondant (de).
teenager ['tiːneidʒə], *n.* Adolescent, *m.*
teens [tiːnz], *n.pl.* L'âge de treize à dix-neuf
ans, *m. To be in one's teens*, n'avoir pas
vingt ans.
teeter ['tiːtə], *v.i.* (*Am.*) Se balancer, basculer;
chanceler, tituber.
teeth [tiːθ], *pl.* [TOOTH]. **teethe** [tiːð], *v.i.*
Faire ses dents. **teething** ['tiːðiŋ], *n.* Dentition, *f. To be teething*, faire ses dents.
teetotal [tiː'toutl], *a.* De tempérance. **teeto-
tal(l)er,** *n.* Buveur d'eau, membre de la
société de tempérance, *m.* **teetotalism,** *n.*
Abstinence de boissons alcooliques, *f.*
teetotum [tiː'toutəm], *n.* Toton, *m.*
*teg [teg], *n.* Agneau, *m.*, agnelle, *f.*, dans sa
seconde année or antenais. **teg-wool,** *n.*
Agneline, *f.*
tegular ['tegjulə], *a.* De tuile; (*Zool. etc.*)
imbriqué. **tegularly,** *adv.* En tuile.
tegument ['tegjumənt], *n.* Tégument, *m.*
tegumentary [-'mentəri], *a.* Tégumentaire.
telegram ['teligræm], *n.* Télégramme, *m.*,
dépêche, *f.*
telegraph ['teligrɑːf], *n.* Télégraphe, *m. Telegraph office*, bureau télégraphique, *m.—v.t.,
v.i.* Télégraphier. *I telegraphed to say that
. . .*, j'ai télégraphié que. . . . **telegraphic**
[-'græfik], *a.* Télégraphique. **telegraphi-
cally,** *adv.* Télégraphiquement.
telegrapher [ti'legrəfə], *n.* Expéditeur, *m.*,
-trice, *f.* **telegraphist,** *n.* Télégraphiste,
m. or *f.* **telegraphy** [ti'legrəfi], *n.* Télégraphie, *f. Wireless telegraphy*, télégraphie
sans fil, *f.*
telegraph-post, *n.* Poteau télégraphique, *m.*
telegraph-wire, *n.* Fil télégraphique, *m.*
Telemachus [ti'leməkəs]. (*Gr. Lit.*) Télémaque, *m.*
telemeter [ti'lemitə], *n.* Télémètre, *m.*
teleological [teliə'lɔdʒikl], *a.* Téléologique.
teleology [-'ɔlədʒi], *n.* Téléologie, *f.*
telepathy [ti'lepəθi], *n.* Télépathie, *f.*
telephone ['telifoun], *n.* Téléphone, *m.*
Telephone exchange, central téléphonique,
bureau central, *m.*; *telephone switchboard*,
standard, *m.—v.t., v.i.* Téléphoner. *I tele-
phoned to say that . . .*, j'ai téléphoné que. . . .
telephonic [teli'fɔnik], *a.* Téléphonique.
telephonist [ti'lefənist], *n.* Téléphoniste, *m.*
or *f.*
telephoto-lens ['telifouto'lenz], *n.* Télé-
objectif, *m.*
teleprinter ['teliprintə], *n.* Téléimprimeur,
téléscripteur, télétype, *m.*
telescope ['teliskoup], *n.* Télescope, *m.*,
lunette d'approche, longue-vue, *f.—v.t.*

Télescoper. *To be telescoped*, être télescopé.
telescopic [-'skɔpik], *a.* Télescopique.
televiewer ['telivjuːə], *n.* Téléspectateur, *m.*, -trice, *f.*
televise ['telivaiz], *v.t.* Téléviser.
television [teli'viʒən], *n.* Télévision, *f.* **television-set**, *n.* Téléviseur, appareil de télévision, *m.*
tell [tel], *v.t.* (*past* and *p.p.* told) Dire; exprimer, faire part de; raconter (to narrate); montrer, indiquer (to show); révéler, dévoiler; compter, énumérer (to count); avouer (to confess); reconnaître (à), distinguer (de), juger (par); savoir (to know). *Don't tell me!* allons donc! *I cannot tell*, je ne saurais dire, je ne sais pas; *I cannot tell one from the other*, je ne puis pas distinguer l'un de l'autre; *I can tell you!* je vous en réponds! *I have been told*, on m'a dit, j'ai entendu dire; *I'll tell you what!* écoutez-moi! je vais vous dire; *tell that to the marines*, à d'autres, allez conter cela à d'autres; *to tell by*, juger par; *to tell off*, énumérer, compter, désigner, détacher (of troops); (*fam.*) rembarrer, dire son fait à; *to tell one's beads*, dire son chapelet; *to tell someone something*, dire quelque chose à quelqu'un, faire savoir quelque chose à quelqu'un; *to tell tales*, rapporter; *you are telling me!* à qui le dites-vous!—*v.i.* Dire; faire son effet, se faire sentir, porter, porter coup (to take effect); juger (to tell by). *Every shot told*, chaque coup porta; *to tell of*, dire, parler de; *to tell on*, dénoncer; *to tell upon*, affecter, influer sur, modifier.
teller, *n.* Diseur, *m.*, -euse, *f.*, raconteur, *m.*, -euse, *f.*; receveur, payeur, comptable; (*Am.*) caissier (in bank); (*Parl.*) scrutateur, *m.*
telling, *a.* Qui porte; expressif, énergique, frappant; à effet.—*n.* Récit, *m.*, narration, *f.*; révélation, *f.*
tell-tale, *n.* Rapporteur, *m.*, -euse, *f.*; (*Mach.*) compteur; (*Naut.*) axiomètre, *m.*—*a.* Rapporteur; (*fig.*) révélateur.
telluric [te'ljuərik], *a.* Tellurique.
tellurium [te'ljuəriəm], *n.* Tellure, *m.*
temerity [ti'meriti], *n.* Témérité, *f.*
temper ['tempə], *n.* Tempérament, *m.*, disposition; humeur (humour); colère (anger), *f.*; sang-froid, calme (equable temper), *m.*; trempe (of steel etc.); combinaison (mixture), *f.*, mélange, *m.* *A man of a violent temper*, un homme d'un caractère emporté; *he has a bad temper but a good heart*, il a mauvaise tête, mais bon cœur; *in a good temper*, de bonne humeur; *out of temper*, de mauvaise humeur, en colère; *to keep one's temper*, garder son sang-froid, ne pas s'emporter; *to lose one's temper* or *to get out of temper*, se mettre en colère, se fâcher; *to put out of temper*, mettre de mauvaise humeur; *to show temper*, montrer de l'humeur; *to take one's temper out on*, passer sa colère sur.—*v.t.* Tempérer (de), mélanger, combiner; délayer, détremper (colours); gâcher (mortar); tremper (steel etc.); (*fig.*) ajuster, proportionner, mesurer, ménager; adoucir. *Bad-tempered*, qui a le caractère mal fait, vicieux (of horses), méchant (of cats etc.); *good-tempered*, d'un bon caractère, aimable, doux.
temperament ['tempərəmənt], *n.* Constitution, disposition, *f.*, tempérament, *m.*

temperamental [-'mentl], *a.* Capricieux, instable.
temperance ['tempərəns], *n.* Tempérance, *f.* *Temperance society*, société de tempérance, *f.*
temperate ['tempərit], *a.* Modéré, tempérant, sobre; tempéré (of climates). *Temperate zone*, zone tempérée, *f.* **temperately**, *adv.* Avec tempérance, modérément. **temperateness**, *n.* Modération, *f.*
temperature ['temprətʃə], *n.* Température, *f.* (*Med.*) *To have* or *run a temperature*, avoir de la fièvre, avoir de la température.
temperature-chart, *n.* Feuille de température, *f.*
tempest ['tempist], *n.* Tempête, *f.* **tempest-beaten**, *a.* Battu par la tempête. **tempest-tossed**, *a.* Ballotté par la tempête.
tempestuous [tem'pestjuəs], *a.* Orageux, tempétueux. **tempestuously**, *adv.* D'une manière orageuse, de tempête. **tempestuousness**, *n.* État orageux *or* tempétueux, *m.*
templar ['templə], *n.* Templier; étudiant en droit (law-student), *m.* *Good Templars*, sociétés de tempérance, *f.pl.*
temple [templ], *n.* Temple, *m.*; (*Anat.*) tempe, *f.* **temple-bone**, *n.* (*Anat.*) Os temporal, *m.*
templet ['templit], *n.* Patron, gabarit, modèle, *m.*
tempo ['tempou], *n.* Tempo; (*fig.*) rythme, *m.*
temporal ['tempərəl], *a.* Temporel; (*Anat.*) temporal. **temporality** [-'ræliti], *n.* (*usu. in pl.*, **temporalities**) Bien temporel, *m.*, revenus temporels, *m.pl.* **temporally**, *adv.* Temporellement. **temporarily**, *adv.* Temporairement, momentanément, provisoirement. **temporariness**, *n.* État temporaire *or* provisoire, *m.* **temporary**, *a.* Temporaire, provisoire.
temporization [tempərai'zeiʃən], *n.* Temporisation, *f.*; compromis, *m.*
temporize ['tempəraiz], *v.i.* Temporiser, transiger (avec), s'accommoder (aux circonstances). **temporizer**, *n.* Temporisateur, temporiseur, *m.* **temporizing**, *a.* D'attente, qui temporise.
tempt [tempt], *v.t.* Tenter (de); pousser (à). **temptable**, *a.* Sujet à la tentation.
temptation [temp'teiʃən], *n.* Tentation, *f.* *I feel a great temptation to*, j'ai grande envie de; *to lead into temptation*, induire en tentation; *to resist temptation*, résister à la tentation; *to yield to temptation*, céder à la tentation.
tempter, *n.* Tentateur, *m.*, -trice, *f.*
tempting, *a.* Tentant, séduisant, attrayant; appétissant (of food). **temptingly**, *adv.* D'une manière tentante.
temptress, *n.* Tentatrice, *f.*
ten [ten], *a.* and *n.* Dix, *m.*; une dizaine (about ten), *f.*; (*Arith.*, *pl.*) dizaines, *f.pl.*
tenable ['tenəbl], *a.* Soutenable; (*Mil.*) tenable.
tenacious [ti'neiʃəs], *a.* Tenace. *Tenacious of*, qui tient à, fortement attaché à; *to be tenacious of life*, avoir la vie dure. **tenaciously**, *adv.* D'une manière tenace, obstinément.
tenacity [ti'næsiti], *n.* Ténacité, *f.*
tenaculum [ti'nækjuləm], *n.* (*Surg.*) Érigne, *f.*

tenancy ['tenənsi], *n.* Location, *f.* **tenant,** *n.* Locataire, *m.*—*v.t.* Habiter. **tenantable,** *a.* Habitable. *Tenantable repairs,* réparations locatives, *f.pl.* **tenanted,** *a.* Occupé, habité. **tenant-farmer,** *n.* Fermier, *m.* **tenantless,** *a.* Sans locataire; 'vide. **tenantry,** *n.* Fermiers et tenanciers; les locataires, *m.pl.*

tench [tenʃ], *n.* (*Ichth.*) Tanche, *f.*

tend [tend], *v.t.* Garder, soigner, veiller sur.— *v.i.* Tendre (à); se diriger vers. *To tend to,* tendre à, contribuer à; *to tend towards,* se diriger vers.

tendency ['tendənsi], *n.* Tendance, disposition, *f.* **tendential, tendentious** [ten'den ʃəs], *a.* Tendancieux. **tendentiously,** *adv.* D'une manière tendancieuse.

tender (1) ['tendə], *n.* Offre (offer); soumission (for contracts); action de déférer (an oath), *f.*; (*Naut.*) bateau annexe, *m.*, allège, gabare, *f.*; (*Rail.*) tender, *m.* *Legal tender,* monnaie légale, monnaie libératoire, *f.*; *the lowest tender,* la soumission la moins élevée; *to be legal tender,* avoir cours légal.—*v.t.* Offrir; déférer (an oath). *To tender one's services,* offrir *or* faire l'offre de ses services. —*v.i.* *To tender for,* soumissionner pour.

tender (2) ['tendə], *a.* Tendre; sensible (sensitive); délicat, scabreux (ticklish). *Tender of,* soucieux de, soigneux de. **tenderfoot,** *n.* (*Am.*) Nouveau débarqué, *m.* **tenderhearted,** *a.* Sensible, au cœur tendre. **tender-heartedness,** *n.* Sensibilité, *f.* **tenderloin,** *n.* Filet, *m.*

tenderer ['tendərə], *n.* Soumissionnaire, *m.*

tenderling ['tendəliŋ], *n.* Enfant chéri; premier bois (of a deer), *m.*

tenderly, *adv.* Tendrement, délicatement; avec compassion (with pity).

tenderness, *n.* Tendresse; sensibilité (sensibility); indulgence, sollicitude, *f.*, égards (kind attention), *m.pl.*; scrupule (scrupulousness), *m.*; tendreté (of fruit etc.), *f.*

tendinous ['tendinəs], *a.* (*Anat.*) Tendineux.

tendon ['tendən], *n.* Tendon, *m.*

tendril ['tendril], *n.* (*Bot.*) Vrille, *f.*

tenement ['tenimənt], *n.* Habitation, maison, *f.* *Tenement house,* maison de rapport, *f.*

tenesmus [te'nezməs], *n.* Ténesme, *m.*

tenet ['tiːnit *or* 'tenit], *n.* Principe, disposition, *m.*, doctrine, *f.*

tenfold ['tenfould], *a.* Décuple.—*adv.* Dix fois. *To increase tenfold,* décupler (of population).

tennis ['tenis], *n.* Tennis, *m.*; *jeu de paume, *m.* *Lawn-tennis* [LAWN]. **tennis-arm, tennis-elbow,** *n.* Crampe du tennis, *f.* **tennis-court,** *n.* Court de tennis, tennis; *jeu de paume, *m.* **tennis-player,** *n.* Joueur de tennis, tennisman, *m.* **tennis-racket,** *n.* Raquette de tennis, *f.*

tenon ['tenən], *n.* Tenon, *m.*—*v.t.* Assembler. **tenon-saw,** *n.* Petite scie à araser, *f.*

tenor ['tenə], *n.* (*Mus.*) Ténor, alto (instrument), *m.*; portée, teneur, *f.*, cours (course); caractère (character), *m.*

tense (1) [tens], *n.* (*Gram.*) Temps, *m.*

tense (2) [tens], *a.* Tendu, raide; (*Path.*) tensif. **tensely,** *adv.* Avec tension. **tenseness,** *n.* Rigidité, tension, *f.*

tensile ['tensail], *a.* De tension; ductile (of metals).

tension ['tenʃən], *n.* Tension, *f.*

tensor, *n.* (Muscle) tenseur, *m.*

tent [tent], *n.* Tente; (*Surg.*) mèche, *f.* *Bell-tent,* tente conique, *f.*—*v.t.* (*Surg.*) Sonder; tenter (of troops etc.). **tent-cloth,** *n.* Toile de tente, *f.* **tent-peg,** *n.* Piquet, *m.*

tentacle ['tentəkl], *n.* Tentacule, *m.* **tentacular,** *a.* Tentaculaire.

tentative ['tentətiv], *a.* Tentatif, d'essai, expérimental. **tentatively,** *adv.* En guise d'essai.

tented ['tentid], *a.* Couvert de tentes. *The tented field,* le champ couvert de tentes.

tenter ['tentə], *n.* Crochet (à étendre les draps); soigneur, machiniste, *m.*—*v.t.* Ramer, tendre (cloth).

tenter-hook, *n.* Clou à crochet, *m.* *To be on tenter-hooks,* être sur des épines, être sur le gril *or* sur des charbons ardents.

tentering, *n.* Élargissage, *m.*

tenth [tenθ], *a.* Dixième; dix (of the month, a dynasty, etc.).—*n.* Dixième, *m.*; dîme (tithe), *f.* **tenthly,** *adv.* Dixièmement.

tenuifolious [tenjui'fouliəs], *a.* Ténuifolié. **tenuiroster** [-'rɔstə], *a.* and *n.* Ténuirostre, *m.*

tenuity [te'njuːiti], *n.* Ténuité, *f.*

tenuous ['tenjuəs], *a.* Délié, mince, ténu.

tenure ['tenjuə], *n.* Tenure; redevance; jouissance; (*Feudal Law*) mouvance, *f.* *During his tenure of office,* pendant son ministère.

tepid ['tepid], *a.* Tiède.

tepidity [te'piditi] or **tepidness,** *n.* Tiédeur, *f.*

teratology [terə'tɔlədʒi], *n.* Tératologie, *f.*

tercentenary [təːsen'tiːnəri], *a.* De trois siècles. —*n.* Tricentenaire, *m.*

terebinth ['teribinθ], *n.* (*Bot.*) Térébinthe, *m.*

terebrant ['teribrənt], *a.* Térébrant. **terebration** [-'breiʃən], *n.* Térébration, *f.*

teredo [te'riːdou], *n.* Taret, *m.*

tergiversate ['təːdʒivəseit], *v.i.* Tergiverser. **tergiversation** [-'seiʃən], *n.* Tergiversation, *f.* **tergiversator,** *n.* Tergiversateur, *m.*

term [təːm], *n.* Terme, *m.*; borne, limite (limit); (*Law*) session, *f.*; (*sch.*) trimestre, *m.*; (*pl.*) conditions, *f.pl.*; prix (price), *m.* *Are you on good terms with?* êtes-vous bien avec? *for a term of years,* pour un nombre d'années déterminé; *in plain terms,* en termes précis; *in terms of,* sous forme de; *liberal terms,* offres avantageuses, *f.pl.*; *long-term transaction,* opération à long terme, *f.*; *on moderate terms,* à un prix modéré; *on those terms,* à ces conditions, à ce prix; *the beginning of term,* (*sch.*) la rentrée, *f.*; *the lowest term,* (*Math.*) la plus simple expression; *to be on bad terms with,* être mal avec; *to be on familiar terms with,* être sur un pied de familiarité avec; *to be on good terms with,* être en bons termes avec; *to be on visiting terms,* se visiter; *to come to terms, to make terms,* s'accorder, s'arranger, tomber d'accord avec, se rendre (to submit); *to keep one's terms,* (*Univ.*) prendre ses inscriptions, faire son stage (at an inn of court); *to live on good terms with,* vivre en bonne intelligence avec; *to reduce to terms,* faire capituler, forcer à un arrangement; *what are your terms?* quelles sont vos conditions? *terms of reference,* mandat, *m.*—*v.t.* Nommer, appeler.

termagant ['təːməgənt], *n.* Mégère, *f.*

terminable ['təːminəbl], *a.* Terminable.

terminal ['tə:minl], *n.* (*Elec.*) Borne, *f. Air terminal*, gare aérienne, aérogare, *f.—a.* Terminal.

terminate ['tə:mineit], *v.t.* Terminer, finir, achever.—*v.i.* Se terminer, finir; (*fig.*) aboutir (à). **termination** [-'neiʃən], *n.* Fin, terminaison, conclusion, *f.*; but final, *m.*

terminative ['tə:minətiv], *a.* Terminatif.

terminology [tə:mi'nɔlədʒi], *n.* Terminologie, *f.*

terminus ['tə:minəs], *n.* Terminus (gare), *m.*; tête de ligne, *f.*

termite ['tə:mait], *n.* (*Ent.*) Termite, *m.*

termless ['tə:mlis], *a.* Illimité, infini.

tern [tə:n], *n.* Sterne, *m.*; hirondelle de mer, *f.*

ternary ['tə:nəri], *a.* Ternaire. **ternate**, *a.* (*Bot.*) Terné.

terrace ['teris], *n.* Terrasse, *f.*; terre-plein, *m.*; rangée de maisons, *f.—v.t.* Former en terrasse. **terraced**, *a.* Étagé en terrasse.

terra-cotta ['terə'kɔtə], *n.* Terre cuite, *f.*

terra firma, *n.* Terre ferme, *f.*

terraqueous [te'reikwiəs], *a.* Terraqué.

terrestrial [tə'restriəl], *a.* Terrestre. **terrestrially**, *adv.* D'une manière terrestre.

terrible ['teribl], *a.* Terrible, formidable, horrible, épouvantable. **terribleness**, *n.* Nature terrible, *f.* **terribly**, *adv.* Terriblement; (*colloq.*) diablement.

terrier (1) ['teriə], *n.* Terrier, chien terrier. *Scotch terrier*, terrier griffon, *m.*; *terrier bitch*, chienne terrier, *f.*

*****terrier** (2) ['teriə], *n.* *Registre foncier, *m.*

terrific [tə'rifik], *a.* Terrible, épouvantable, terrifiant; énorme, colossal. **terrifically**, *a.* Terriblement, épouvantablement.

terrify ['terifai], *v.t.* Terrifier, épouvanter.

territorial [teri'tɔ:riəl], *a.* Territorial; limité (local); terrien. *The territorial aristocracy*, l'aristocratie terrienne, *f.*; *the Territorial Army* (abbr. *T.A.*), la territoriale. **territoriality** [-'æliti], *n.* Territorialité, *f.* **territorially**, *adv.* Sous le rapport du territoire.

territory ['teritəri], *n.* Territoire, *m.*

terror ['terə], *n.* Terreur, *f.*; effroi, *m.*, épouvante, *f. That youngster is a perfect terror*, cet enfant est un vrai petit diable; *the reign of terror*, la Terreur, le règne de la terreur; *to go in terror of one's life*, craindre pour sa vie.

terror-stricken or **terror-struck**, *a.* Pris de terreur, épouvanté. **terrorism**, *n.* Terrorisme, *m.* **terrorist**, *n.* Terroriste, *m.*

terrorization [terərai'zeiʃən], *n.* Action de terroriser, *f.*; domination par la terreur, *f.* **terrorize**, *v.t.* Terroriser.

terse [tə:s], *a.* Net, concis; bien tourné, élégant. **tersely**, *adv.* Élégamment; nettement; d'une manière concise. **terseness**, *n.* Netteté, *f.*

tertian ['tə:ʃən], *a.* Tierce. *Tertian fever*, fièvre tierce, *f.*

tertiary ['tə:ʃəri], *a.* Tertiaire.

tessellated [tesə'leitid], *a.* Tessellé; en mosaïque, en damier. *Tessellated pavement*, pavé de mosaïque, *m.* **tessellation** [-'leiʃən], *n.* Mosaïque, *f.*

tessera ['tesərə], *n.* (*pl.* **tesserae**) Tessère, *f.*

test [test], *n.* Épreuve, *f.*; essai, *m.*; pierre de touche, *f.*, degré de comparaison (standard), *m.*; (*Chem.*) réactif; (*Metal.*) têt, test, *m.* To

put to the test, mettre à l'épreuve; *to stand the test*, subir l'épreuve.—*v.t.* Éprouver, essayer, mettre à l'épreuve; vérifier; (*Metal.*) coupeller. **test-bench**, *n.* Banc d'épreuve, *m.* **test-case**, *n.* (*Law*) Cas dont la solution fait jurisprudence, *m.* **test-match**, *n.* (*Cricket*) Rencontre internationale, *f.* **test-paper**, *n.* Papier réactif, *m.*; (*sch.*) examen blanc, *m.* **test-piece**, *n.* (*Mus.*) Morceau prescrit (in competitions), *m.* **test-strip**, *n.* (*Cine.*) Bout d'essai, *m.* **test-tube**, *n.* Éprouvette, *f.*

testaceous [tes'teiʃəs], *a.* Testacé.

testament ['testəmənt], *n.* Testament, *m.* **testamentary** [-'mentəri], *a.* Testamentaire.

testate ['testeit], *a.* Qui a testé. **testator** [-'teitə], *n.* Testateur, *m.* **testatrix**, *n.* Testatrice, *f.*

tester ['testə], *n.* Ciel de lit, baldaquin, *m.* **tester-bed**, *n.* Lit à baldaquin, *m.*

testicle ['testikl], *n.* Testicule, *m.*

testification [testifi'keiʃən], *n.* Témoignage, *m.*

testifier ['testifaiə], *n.* Témoin, déposant, *m.*

testify ['testifai], *v.t.* Témoigner, rendre témoignage (de); (*Law*) déposer (de).—*v.i.* Rendre témoignage; (*Law*) déposer. *To testify against*, déposer contre.

testimonial [testi'mouniəl], *n.* Témoignage; certificat, *m.*, attestation, *f.*; témoignage d'estime *or* de reconnaissance (gift), *m.*; (*pl.*) certificats, *m.pl.*

testimony ['testiməni], *n.* Témoignage, *m.*, déposition (attestation), *f. In testimony whereof*, en foi de quoi; *to bear testimony to*, rendre témoignage à.

testiness ['testinis], *n.* Humeur, irritabilité, *f.*

testing ['testiŋ], *n.* Épreuve, *f.*, essai, *m.*

testy ['testi], *a.* Irritable, susceptible.

tetanic [tə'tænik], *a.* Tétanique.

tetanize ['tetənaiz], *v.t.* Tétaniser.

tetanus ['tetənəs], *n.* Tétanos, *m.* **tetany**, *n.* Tétanie, *f.*

tetchily ['tetʃili], *adv.* D'une manière irritable. **tetchiness**, *n.* Humeur irritable, *f.* **tetchy**, *a.* Irritable, susceptible.

tether ['teðə], *n.* Longe; (*fig.*) chaîne, *f.*, limites, bornes, *f.pl. To be at the end of one's tether*, être à bout de forces.—*v.t.* Mettre à l'attache; attacher (à).

tetrachord ['tetrəkɔ:d], *n.* Tétracorde, *m.*

tetradactylous [-'dæktiləs], *a.* Tétradactyle.

tetragon ['tetrəgən], *n.* Tétragone, *m.*

tetragonal [-'trægənəl], *a.* Tétragone.

tetrahedron [tetrə'hi:drən], *n.* Tétraèdre, *m.*

tetralogy [te'trælədʒi], *n.* Tétralogie, *f.*

tetrameter [te'træmitə], *n.* Tétramètre, *m.*

tetrandrous [te'trændrəs], *a.* Tétrandre.

tetrapetalous [tetrə'petələs], *a.* Tétrapétale.

tetrarch ['tetrɑ:k], *n.* Tétrarque, *m.* **tetrarchate**, *n.* Tétrarchat, *m.* **tetrarchy**, *n.* Tétrarchie, *f.*

tetrasyllabic [tetrəsi'læbik], *a.* Tétrasyllabe, tétrasyllabique.

tetter ['tetə], *n.* (*Med.*) Dartre, *f.*

Teuton ['tju:tən], *a.* and *n.* Teuton, *m.*, -tonne, *f.* **Teutonic** [-'tɔnik], *a.* Teutonique. **Teutonize**, *v.t.* Germaniser.

text [tekst], *n.* Texte, *m.*; écriture (handwriting), *f. Large text*, gros, *m.*, écriture en gros, *f.*; *small text*, écriture fine, *f.*

text-book, *n.* Manuel, livre de classe, *m.* **text-hand,** *n.* Écriture en gros, *f.*
textile ['tekstail], *a.* Textile. *Textile fabric,* tissu, *m.—n.* Tissu, textile, *m.,* étoffe, *f.*
textorial [-'tɔːriəl], *a.* Du tissage, textile. *Textorial arts,* industries textiles, *f.pl.*
textual ['tekstjuəl], *a.* Textuel. **textually,** *adv.* Textuellement. **textuary,** *a.* and *n.* Textuaire, *m.*
texture ['tekstʃə], *n.* Tissu, *m.*; contexture (of writings etc.), *f.*
Thailand ['tailænd]. (*Geog.*) La Thaïlande, *f.,* le Siam, *m.*
thalamifloral [θæləmi'flɔːrəl], *a.* Thalamiflore.
thalamus ['θæləməs], *n.* (*Bot.*) Thalame, *m.*
thalassic [θə'læsik], *a.* Thalassique. **thalassocracy** [θælə'sɔkrəsi], *n.* Thalassocratie, *f.*
thallic ['θælik], *a.* (*Bot.*) Thallique. **thallous, thallus,** *a.* Thalleux. **thallus,** *n.* Thalle, *m.*
Thames [temz], **the.** La Tamise, *f. He will never set the Thames on fire,* il n'a pas inventé la poudre.
than [ðæn], *conj.* Que; de (between *more* or *less* and a number). *He does not speak otherwise than he acts,* il ne parle pas autrement qu'il agit; *he is younger than I am,* il est plus jeune que moi; *I prefer to do without rather than ask for it,* j'aime mieux m'en passer que de le demander; *more than a hundred,* plus de cent; *no other than,* personne d'autre que, rien d'autre que (of things); *rather than,* plutôt que; *the house is more than three miles from here,* il y a plus de trois milles d'ici à la maison.
***thane** [θein], *n.* Comte, thane, *m.*
thank [θæŋk], *v.t.* Remercier (de); rendre grâces à. *I will thank you for,* je vous demanderai; *I will thank you to shut the door,* veuillez bien fermer la porte; *no, thank you,* merci; *thank God,* grâce à Dieu! Dieu merci! *you have only yourself to thank for it,* c'est à vous seul qu'il faut vous en prendre.
thankful, *a.* Reconnaissant (de). *I am thankful to say that. . .,* je suis heureux *or* content de dire que. . . . **thankfully,** *adv.* Avec reconnaissance. **thankfulness,** *n.* Reconnaissance, *f.* **thankless,** *a.* Ingrat; oublié, méconnu (not thanked). **thanklessness,** *n.* Ingratitude, *f.*; nature ingrate, *f.*
thank-offering, *n.* Sacrifice d'actions de grâces, *m.*
thanks, *n.pl.* Remercîments *or* remerciements, *m.pl. Give him my best thanks,* remerciez-le bien de ma part; *I return my warmest thanks,* je vous adresse mes remerciements les plus sincères; *many thanks,* bien des remerciements; *thanks to him,* grâce à lui; *to give thanks to God,* rendre grâces à Dieu; *to return thanks to,* faire des remerciements à, remercier.
thanksgiver, *n.* Personne qui rend des actions de grâces, *f.* **thanksgiving,** *n.* Actions de grâces, *f.pl.*
that [ðæt] (*pl.* those), *dem.a.* Ce, cet, cette; (*emphatically*) ce . . . là, cet . . . là, *m.,* cette . . . là, *f.—dem.pron.* Celui-là, *m.,* celle-là, *f.*; cela, (*colloq.*) ça, *m.—rel.pron.* Qui, lequel, *m.,* laquelle, *f.*; lesquels, *m.pl.,* lesquelles, *f.pl. By that,* par cela, par là; *for all that,* malgré cela, malgré tout; *I do not like that man,* je n'aime pas cet homme-là; *in that,* en cela, là

dedans, y, vu que, parce que; *not even that,* pas même ça! *on that,* sur cela, là-dessus; *that crowns all,* il ne manquait plus que cela; *that is,* c'est-à-dire; *that is the question!* voilà la question! *that I will not,* oh, pour cela non! *that much,* cela; *that's all,* voilà tout! *that's he,* le voilà; *that you are not,* pour ça non, bien sûr; *this is good, I prefer that,* celui-ci est bon, je préfère celui-là; *to have come to that,* en être venu là; *what of that?* qu'est-ce que cela fait? *with that,* avec cela, là-dessus (thereupon); *you saw the ceremony? That I did,* vous avez vu la cérémonie? Oui, je l'ai vue.—*conj.* Que; afin que, pour que (in order that). *Oh, that I had his talent!* que n'ai-je son talent! oh, *that I were with you!* que ne suis-je avec vous!—*adv.* Aussi, si.
thatch [θætʃ], *n.* Chaume, *m.—v.t.* Couvrir de chaume. **thatcher,** *n.* Couvreur en chaume, *m.*
thaumaturgical [θɔːmə'tɜːdʒikl], *a.* Thaumaturgique.
thaumaturgy ['θɔːmətɜːdʒi], *n.* Thaumaturgie, *f.*
thaw [θɔː], *n.* Dégel, *m.—v.t.* Dégeler; (*fig.*) fondre, attendrir.—*v.i.* Dégeler, se dégeler; (*fig.*) fondre, s'attendrir.
the [ðə], before vowel [ði], *def. art.* Le, *m.,* la, *f.,* les, *pl. At the* or *to the,* au, *m.,* à la, *f.,* aux, *pl.*; *from the* or *of the,* du, *m.,* de la, *f.,* des, *pl.*; *the dear boy,* ce cher enfant; *the more . . . because,* d'autant plus que; *the more . . . the less,* plus . . . moins; *the sooner the better,* plus tôt ce sera, mieux ça vaudra; le plus tôt sera le mieux.
theatre ['θiːətə], *n.* Théâtre, *m.*; (*fig.*) scène, *f.,* spectacle; amphithéâtre (lecture-room), *m. Minor theatre,* petit théâtre; *the French theatre,* le théâtre français.
theatrical [θiːˈætrikl], *a.* De théâtre, théâtral, scénique. *Theatrical piece,* pièce de théâtre, *f.*; *theatrical writer,* dramaturge, auteur dramatique, *m.* **theatrically,** *adv.* Théâtralement.
theatricals, *n.pl.* Spectacle, *m. Amateur theatricals,* spectacle d'amateurs; *private theatricals,* comédie de salon, *f.*
Theban ['θiːbən], *a.* Thébain, *m.,* Thébaine, *f.* **Thebes** [θiːbz]. Thèbes, *f.*
thee [ðiː], *pron.* Toi; te.—*v.t. To thee and thou,* tutoyer.
theft [θeft], *n.* Vol, *m. Petty theft,* larcin, *m.*
theine [θ'iːin], *n.* Théine, *f.*
their [ðɛə], *poss.a.* Leur, leurs (*pl.*)
theirs [ðɛəz], *poss.pron.* Le leur, *m.,* la leur, *f.,* les leurs, *pl.,* à eux, *m.pl.,* à elles, *f.pl.*
theism (1) ['θiːizm], *n.* (*Med.*) Théisme, *m.*
theism (2) ['θiːizm], *n.* Théisme, *m.* **theist,** *n.* Théiste, *m.* **theistic** [-'istik], *a.* Théiste.
them [ðem], *pron.* Eux, *m.pl.,* elles, *f.pl.*; (*obj.*) les; (*dat.*) leur, *pl. I have given them three* (of them), je leur en ai donné trois; *I have seen them,* je les ai vus; *I have spoken to them,* je leur ai parlé; *of* or *from them,* d'eux, d'elles, en; *to them,* à eux, à elles, leur, y.
thematic [θiˈmætik], *a.* Thématique.
theme [θiːm], *n.* Thème, sujet, *m.*; (*sch.*) dissertation, *f.* **theme-song,** *n.* Chanson leit-motiv, *f.*
Themistocles [θəˈmistəkliːz]. (*Gr. Hist.*) Thémistocle, *m.*
themselves [ðemˈselvz], *pron.* Eux-mêmes,

m.pl., elles-mêmes, *f.pl.*; (*reflectively*) se, *pl.* By themselves, tout seuls, *m.pl.*, toutes seules, *f.pl.*; *they think themselves*, ils se croient.
then [ðen], *adv.* Alors; ensuite, puis (next); dans ce cas (in that case); donc (therefore). *But then*, par contre; *by then*, alors, déjà; *first one then the other*, d'abord l'un, puis l'autre; *now and then*, de temps en temps; *now then!* voyons! *since then*, depuis ce temps-là, depuis; *the then government*, le gouvernement d'alors; *till then*, jusqu'alors; *what then?* eh bien? et après? et puis?—*conj.* Donc.
thence [ðens], *adv.* De là, en; depuis ce temps, dès lors, depuis lors (of time); pour cette raison, de là (for that reason).
thenceforth [-'fɔ:θ], *adv.* **thenceforward** [-'fɔ:wəd], *adv.* Dès lors, depuis lors, à partir de ce moment-là.
Theobald ['θi:əbɔːld]. Thibault, *m.*
theocracy [θi:'ɔkrəsi], *n.* Théocratie, *f.* **theocratic** [-ə'krætik], *a.* Théocratique.
Theocritus [θi:'ɔkritəs]. (*Gr. Lit.*) Théocrite, *m.*
theodicy [θi:'ɔdisi], *n.* Théodicée, *f.*
theodolite [θi:'ɔdəlait], *n.* Théodolite, *m.*
Theodosian [θiə'douʃən], *a.* and *n.* Théodosien, *m.*
theogonic [θi:ə'gɔnik], *a.* Théogonique.
theogony [θi:'ɔgəni], *n.* Théogonie, *f.*
theologian [θi:ə'loudʒiən], *n.* Théologien, *m.* **theological** [-'lɔdʒikl], *a.* Théologique. **theologically**, *adv.* Théologiquement.
theology [θi:'ɔlədʒi], *n.* Théologie, *f.*
theomania [-ə'meiniə], *n.* Théomanie, *f.*
theophany [θi'ɔfəni], *n.* Théophanie, *f.*
theophilanthropy [θi:ofi'lænθrəpi], *n.* Théophilanthropie, *f.*
theorbo [θi:'ɔːbou], *n.* Théorbe, téorbe, *m.*
theorem ['θi:ərəm], *n.* Théorème, *m.* **theoretic** [-'retik] or **theoretical**, *a.* Théorique; spéculatif. **theoretically**, *adv.* Théoriquement.
theorist ['θi:ərist] or **theorizer** ['θi:əraizə], *n.* Théoricien, *m.* **theorize**, *v.i.* Théoriser.
theory ['θi:əri], *n.* Théorie, *f.*
theosophist [θi:'ɔsəfist], *n.* Théosophe, *m.* **theosophy**, *n.* Théosophie, *f.*
therapeutic [θerə'pjuːtik], *a.* Thérapeutique. **therapeutics**, *n.pl.* Thérapeutique, *f.* **therapeutist**, *n.* Thérapeutiste, *m.*
therapist ['θerəpist], *n.* Praticien, *m.* *Occupational therapist*, spécialiste de thérapie rééducative. **therapy** ['θerəpi], *n.* Thérapie, *f.*
there [ðɛə], *adv.* Là, y; (*impers.*) il; en cela. *Down there*, là-bas; *here and there*, çà et là; *I'll be there*, j'y vais, j'y serai; *he is all there*, c'est un dégourdi; *in there*, là-dedans; *on there*, là-dessus; *over there*, là-bas; *there and back*, aller et retour; *there and then*, séance tenante, sur-le-champ; *there exists . . .*, il existe . . .; *there he comes!* le voilà qui vient! *there he is!* le voilà! *there I have him*, c'est par là que je le tiens; *there is* or *there are*, il y a; *there's many a slip 'twixt the cup and the lip*, il y a loin de la coupe aux lèvres; *there they are!* les voilà! *there you are!* voilà! vous voyez bien! *under there*, là-dessous; *up there*, là-haut; *who's there?* qui est là?—*int.* There! *there!* allons! là! là! *this is mine, so there!* c'est à moi, voilà!

thereabout or **thereabouts**, *adv.* Par là, près de là; à peu près, environ (nearly).
thereafter [-r'ɑːftə], *adv.* Après, d'après cela, ensuite.
thereat [-'æt], *adv.* Par là, à cet endroit; là-dessus, à cela (at that).
thereby [ðɛə'bai], *adv.* Par là, par ce moyen, de cette manière.
therefore ['ðɛəfɔː], *adv.* Donc, par conséquent.
therefrom [-'frɔm], *adv.* De là, en.
therein [-r'in], *adv.* Là-dedans, en cela; y.
thereinto [-'tuː], *adv.* Là-dedans, y.
thereof [-'rɔv], *adv.* En, de cela.
thereon [-'ɔn], *adv.* Là-dessus.
Theresa [tə'riːzə]. Thérèse, *f.*
thereto [ðɛə-'tuː] or **thereunto** [-rʌn'tuː], *adv.* Y, à cela; à quoi.
thereupon [-rə'pɔn], *adv.* Là-dessus, sur cela, sur ce.
therewith [ðɛə'wið], *adv.* Avec cela, de cela, en.
theriac ['θiəriæk], *n.* Thériaque, *f.* **theriacal** [-'raiəkl], *a.* Thériacal.
therm [θəːm], *n.* Thermie, *f.* **thermae** ['θəːmiː], *n.pl.* Thermes, *m.pl.* **thermal**, *a.* Thermal. *Thermal baths*, thermes, *m.pl.*; *thermal efficiency*, rendement calorifique, *m.* **thermic**, *a.* Thermique.
Thermidorian [θəːmi'dɔːriən], *a.* and *n.* Thermidorien, *m.*
thermo-barometer [θəːmoubə'rɔmitə], *n.* Thermobaromètre, *m.* **thermo-chemistry** [-'kemistri], *n.* Thermochimie, *f.* **thermodynamics** [-dai'næmiks], *n.pl.* Thermodynamique, *f.* **thermo-electric(al)** [-i'lek trik(l)], *a.* Thermo-électrique. **thermo-electricity** [-'trisiti], *n.* Thermo-électricité, *f.* **thermogenesis** [-'dʒenəsis], *n.* Thermogénèse, *f.* **thermology** [-'mɔlədʒi], *n.* Thermologie, *f.* **thermometer** [θə'mɔmitə], *n.* Thermomètre, *m.* **thermometrical** [θəː mə'metrikl], *a.* Thermométrique. **thermonuclear**, *a.* Thermo-nucléaire. **thermos** ['θəːmɔs], *a.* *Thermos flask*, bouteille Thermos *or* isolante, *f.* **thermostat**, *n.* Thermostat, *m.*
these [ðiːz], *pron.* Ces, ces . . . ci, *pl.*; (*absolutely*) ceux-ci, *m.pl.*, celles-ci, *f.pl. Are not these shoes yours?* ces chaussures ne sont-elles pas à vous? *dinner has been waiting for these two hours*, il y a deux heures que le dîner attend; *these are mine*, ce sont les miens.
Theseus ['θiːsjuːs]. (*Myth.*) Thésée, *m.*
thesis ['θiːsis], *n.* Thèse, *f.*
Thespian ['θespiən], *a.* Tragique, de la tragédie.
Thespis ['θespis]. (*Myth.*) Thespis, *f.*
Thessalonian [θesə'louniən], *a.* and *n.* Thessalonicien, *m.*, -ienne, *f.*
Thessalonica [θesələ'naikə]. (*Geog.*) La Thessalonique, *f.*
Thessaly ['θesəli]. (*Geog.*) La Thessalie, *f.*
theurgic [θi'əːdʒik], *a.* Théurgique.
theurgy ['θiːəːdʒi], *n.* Théurgie, *f.*
thew [θjuː], *n.* Tendon, muscle, *m.*; (*pl.*) muscles, *m.pl.*, force musculaire, *f. Thews and sinews*, nerfs et muscles.
thewy ['θjuːi], *a.* Nerveux, musculeux.
they [ðei], *pron.* Ils, eux, *m.pl.*, elles, *f.pl.*; (*followed by a relative*) ceux, *m.pl.*, celles, *f.pl.*; (*impers.*) on (people). *It is they who*, ce

sont eux *or* elles qui; *they are silly people,* ce sont de sottes gens; *they say,* on dit.

thick [θik], *a.* Épais; gros (big); fort, solide (of a door etc.); trouble (of liquors); dru, serré (close); gras, embarrassé, indistinct (of the pronunciation); intime (intimate). *That's a bit thick,* (*colloq.*) ça c'est un peu fort! *they are as thick as thieves together,* ils s'entendent comme larrons en foire; *they are very thick together,* ils sont très liés.—*n.* Partie la plus épaisse, *f.*, le fort, *m. In the thick of,* au plus fort de; *in the thick of the fight,* au plus fort de la mêlée; *through thick and thin,* à travers tous les obstacles, en dépit de tout.—*adv.* Épais; dru (fast); en foule (closely); profondément (deeply). *To lay it on thick,* en donner bon poids; *to speak thick,* parler gras. **thick-headed,** *a.* Sot, bête, stupide. **thick-lipped,** *a.* Lippu. **thick-set,** *a.* Touffu, dru; trapu (of persons). **thick-skinned,** *a.* À la peau épaisse; (*fig.*) peu sensible.

thicken [θikn], *v.t.* Épaissir; redoubler (to make more numerous); lier (a sauce).—*v.i.* Épaissir, s'épaissir; augmenter, grossir (to multiply); s'obscurcir (to become obscure); se lier (of sauces); (*fig.*) s'animer, s'échauffer, s'acharner; se presser (to be crowded). *The plot thickens,* l'intrigue s'embrouille, (*fam.*) l'affaire se corse.

thickening, *n.* Épaississement, *m.*; liaison (of a sauce), *f.*

thicket ['θikit], *n.* Fourré, hallier, taillis, *m.*

thickish ['θikiʃ], *a.* Un peu épais. **thickly,** *adv.* Épais, dru (in quick succession); profondément (deeply). *Thickly clad,* vêtu chaudement. **thickness,** *n.* Épaisseur; consistance (consistence), *f.*; état serré, état dru (closeness of the parts); grasseyement (of the pronunciation), *m.*

thief [θi:f], *n.* (*pl.* **thieves** [θi:vz]) Voleur, *m.*, -euse, *f.*; larron; champignon (in a candle), *m. Opportunity makes the thief,* l'occasion fait le larron; *set a thief to catch a thief,* à corsaire, corsaire et demi; *stop thief!* au voleur! *there is honour among thieves,* les loups ne se mangent pas entre eux.

thief-catcher *or* **thief-taker,** *n.* Agent de police, *m.*

thieve [θi:v], *v.i.* Voler.

thieving, *n.* Vol, larcin, *m.*, rapine, *f. To live by thieving,* vivre de rapines.

thievish, *a.* Adonné au vol; voleur. **thievishly,** *adv.* En voleur; par le vol. **thievishness,** *n.* Penchant au vol, *m.*, habitude du vol, *f.*

thigh [θai], *n.* Cuisse, *f.* **thigh-bone,** *n.* Fémur, *m.* **thigh-piece,** *n.* Cuissard, *m.*

thill [θil], *n.* Limon, brancard, *m.* **thiller** *or* **thill-horse,** *n.* Limonier, cheval de brancard, *m.*

thimble [θimbl], *n.* Dé, *m.*; (*Naut.*) cosse, *f.*; bague, virole (of metal joints), *f.* **thimbleful,** *n.* Un plein dé, le contenu d'un dé à coudre. *A thimbleful of wine,* un doigt de vin. **thimblerig** *or* **thimblerigging,** *n.* Tour de gobelets, escamotage, *m.* **thimble-rigger,** *n.* Joueur de gobelets, escamoteur, *m.*

thin [θin], *a.* Mince; maigre (lean); élancé, délié (slender); peu nombreux (not crowded); clair; léger (slight); clairsemé, rare (of trees, plants, hair, etc.); grêle, faible (of sound etc.). *There was a thin attendance,* il y avait peu de monde; *there was a thin house,* le théâtre était presque vide; *thin as a lath,* maigre comme un clou; *to grow thin,* maigrir, s'amincir, s'éclaircir; *to make thin,* amaigrir.—*adv.* D'une manière éparse, clair; en petit nombre, clairsemé; légèrement (slightly). *To sow too thin,* semer trop clair.—*v.t.* Amincir, atténuer, réduire; allonger (a sauce etc.); éclaircir; raréfier (to rarefy). *To thin out a forest,* éclaircir une forêt. *To thin the air,* raréfier l'air.

thine [ðain], *pron.* Le tien, *m.*, la tienne, *f.*, les tiens, *m.pl.*, les tiennes, *f.pl.*; à toi.—**a.* Ton, *m.*, ta, *f.*, tes, *pl.*

thing [θiŋ], *n.* Chose, *f.*, objet, *m.*, affaire, *f.*; être, *m.*, créature (creature); bête, *f.*; (*pl.*) affaires, *f.pl.*, effets, *m.pl. Above all things,* avant tout, par-dessus tout; *anything,* quelque chose, quoi que ce soit; *anything but,* rien moins que, tout excepté; *for one thing,* d'abord, par exemple; *it is a bad thing for her,* c'est une mauvaise affaire pour elle; *it is a very good thing that,* c'est fort heureux que; *it is not quite the thing,* ce n'est pas tout à fait ce qu'il faut; *it's no such thing,* il n'en est rien; *no such thing,* point du tout; *not anything,* rien; *poor little thing!* pauvre petit! *poor thing!* la pauvre femme! le pauvre enfant! la pauvre bête! *tea things,* service à thé, *m.*; *that is quite another thing,* c'est tout autre chose, c'est une autre paire de manches; *that is the very thing!* c'est tout à fait ce qu'il faut! *the correct thing is to,* il est de rigueur de; *what a thing of a hat is it was you sold me!* quel mauvais chapeau vous m'avez vendu!

thingum(a)bob, thingumajig, thingummy *or* **thingamy** ['θiŋəmi], *n.* Machin, chose, *m. Little thingummy,* petit chose, *m. Mr. Thingum(a)bob,* Monsieur chose.

think [θiŋk], *v.t.* (*past and p.p.* **thought** [θɔ:t]) Penser; croire (to believe); imaginer, songer (to fancy); trouver, juger (to judge).—*v.i.* Penser; croire; s'imaginer; songer (à); s'aviser (de); avoir une idée *or* opinion (de). *As they think best,* comme bon leur semblera; *he little thinks that,* il ne songe guère que; *I am thinking of you,* je pense à vous; *I can't think of it,* je ne peux pas me le rappeler; *I have thought of,* j'ai eu l'idée de; *I should have thought that,* j'aurais cru que; *I think I'll go too,* ma foi, j'y vais aussi; *I think it is so,* je crois que oui; *I think not,* je crois que non; *I think so,* je le crois; *I thought as much,* je le pensais bien, je m'en doutais; *it is not to be thought of,* il ne faut pas y penser; *I told him what I thought of him,* je lui ai dit son fait; *I will think it over,* j'y réfléchirai; *little did I think that he would fail me,* je ne me doutais guère qu'il me fît faux bond; *think of me what you please,* pensez de moi ce que vous voudrez; *to think better of it,* se raviser; *to think fit to,* juger à propos de; *to think ill of,* avoir une mauvaise opinion de, penser du mal de; *to think much of,* faire grand cas de, avoir une haute opinion de; *to think nothing of,* ne faire aucun cas de; *to think of,* penser à, songer à, réfléchir à, s'aviser de, compter, avoir l'intention de (to intend); *to think over,* réfléchir à; *to think to oneself,* penser en soi-même; *to think up,* inventer; *to think well of,* penser du bien de; *what do you think of it?* qu'en pensez-vous? *who would have thought it?* qui l'eût cru?

thinker, *n.* Penseur, *m.* **thinking,** *n.* Pensée, *f.*; jugement, avis, *m.*, opinion, *f.* *In my thinking,* à mon avis; *way of thinking,* façon de penser, *f.*—*a.* Pensant, qui pense, réfléchi. **thinly** ['θinli], *adv.* Légèrement (clad); clairsemé, de loin en loin (sparsely). *The performance was thinly attended,* l'assistance était peu nombreuse. **thinness,** *n.* Peu d'épaisseur, *m.*; ténuité (tenuity); fluidité (fluidity); rareté, *f.*, petit nombre (fewness), *m.*; maigreur (leanness), *f.* **thinning,** *n.* Délayage (of paint); éclaircissage (of plants); effeuillage (of trees), *m.* **thin-skinned,** *a.* À la peau mince; (*fig.*) irritable, chatouilleux, susceptible. **thin-soled,** *a.* À semelles minces. **thin-sown,** *a.* Clairsemé.

third [θə:d], *a.* Troisième; trois (of kings etc.).—*n.* Tiers, *m.*; (*Mus.*) tierce, *f.* *In the presence of a third person,* en présence d'un tiers; *third estate,* tiers-état, *m.*; *third party insurance,* assurance au tiers, *f.* **thirdly,** *adv.* Troisièmement.

thirst [θə:st], *n.* Soif, *f.* *Thirst for,* soif de; *to quench one's thirst,* se désaltérer.—*v.i.* Avoir soif (de). **thirstily,** *adv.* Avidement. **thirstiness,** *n.* Soif, *f.* **thirsting,** *a.* Altéré, assoiffé. **thirsty,** *a.* Qui a soif; altéré. *To be thirsty,* avoir soif; *to make thirsty,* altérer.

thirteen [θə:'ti:n], *a.* Treize. **thirteenth,** *a.* Treizième; treize (of kings etc.).—*n.* Treizième, *m.*

thirtieth ['θə:tiəθ], *a.* Trentième; trente (of the month).—*n.* Trentième, *m.* **thirty,** *a.* Trente. **thirty-first,** *a.* Trente-et-unième; trente-et-un (of the month).

this [ðis], *a.* (*pl.* **these** [ði:z]) Ce, cet, *m.*, cette, *f.*, ces, *pl.*—*pron.* Ce . . . ci, cet . . . ci, *m.*; cette . . . ci, *f.*; (*absolutely*) celui-ci, *m.*, celle-ci, *f.*; ceci, *m.* *At this moment,* à présent, à l'heure qu'il est; *by this time,* à l'heure qu'il est; *I have been waiting this last hour,* il y a une heure que j'attends; *this is Miss Trotwood's,* voici la maison de Miss Trotwood; *this is one who,* en voici un qui; *this is the one,* le voici! *this is what I fear,* c'est ce que je crains; *this moment,* à l'instant; *this once,* cette fois; *this or that,* tel ou tel; *this day week,* d'aujourd'hui en huit, il y a huit jours (of last week); *this way,* par ici; *upon this,* là-dessus; *what's this?* qu'est-ce que ceci? *with regard to this,* à cet égard.—*adv.* Comme ceci. *This big,* aussi grand que ça.

thistle [θisl], *n.* (*Bot.*) Chardon, *m.* **thistle-down,** *n.* Duvet de chardon, *m.*

thistly ['θisli], *a.* Plein de chardons.

thither ['ðiðə], *adv.* Là, y. *Hither and thither,* çà et là. **thitherward,** *adv.* Y, de ce côté-là, vers ce lieu.

thole (1) [θoul] or **thole-pin,** *n.* Tolet, *m.*

thole (2) [θoul], *v.t.* (*Sc.*) Souffrir, endurer.

thong [θɔŋ], *n.* Courroie, lanière, sangle, *f.*—*v.t.* Attacher au moyen de lanières (in leather-craft).

thoracic [θɔ:'ræsik], *a.* Thoracique.

thorax ['θɔ:ræks], *n.* Thorax, *m.*

thorn [θɔ:n], *n.* Épine, *f.*; buisson d'épine, *m.* *A thorn in one's side,* (*fig.*) une épine au pied; *to be on thorns,* être sur des épines, sur des charbons ardents; *to run a thorn into one's finger,* s'enfoncer une épine dans le doigt; *whitethorn,* aubépine, *f.*

thorn-apple, *n.* Pomme épineuse, stramoine; *f.*

thorn-back, *n.* (*Ichth.*) Raie bouclée, *f.*

thorn-bush, *n.* Buisson épineux, *m.* **thornless,** *a.* Sans épines. **thorny,** *a.* Épineux.

thorough ['θʌrə], *a.* Entier, complet; achevé, parfait (perfect); vrai, fieffé, fameux (downright).

thoroughbass, *n.* (*Mus.*) Basse continue, harmonie, *f.* **thoroughbred,** *a.* Pur sang (of horses); (*colloq.*) vrai, accompli, parfait, consommé. **thoroughfare,** *n.* Voie de passage, *f.*, passage, *m.* *Great thoroughfare,* rue très fréquentée, *f.*, chemin passant, *m.*; *no thoroughfare,* rue barrée, *f.*, passage interdit, *m.* **thoroughgoing,** *a.* Résolu, entreprenant, à outrance; achevé, complet, consommé. **thorough-paced,** *a.* Achevé, franc, fieffé.

thoroughly, *adv.* Tout à fait, entièrement, complètement; à fond, parfaitement.

thoroughness, *n.* Caractère achevé, *m.*, perfection, *f.*

those [ðouz], *a.* Ces; ces . . . là, *pl.*—*pron.* (*relatively*) Ceux, *m.pl.*, celles (qui), *f.pl.*; (*absolutely*) ceux-là, *m.pl.*, celles-là, *f.pl.* *Those are the best,* ce sont là les meilleurs; *those are his very words,* ce sont là ses propres expressions; *those who lose pay,* les battus payent l'amende.

thou [ðau], *pron.* Tu. *Than thou,* que toi.

though [ðou], *conj.* Quoique, bien que (*with subj.*); quand même (even if). *As though,* comme si; *even though,* quand, quand même (with conditional); *though it cost me ten pounds,* quand cela me coûterait dix livres.—*adv.* Cependant, pourtant, malgré cela (nevertheless).

thought (1), *past* and *p.p.* [THINK].

thought (2) [θɔ:t], *n.* Pensée; idée (idea) opinion, *f.*, jugement; sentiment (opinion), *m.*; inquiétude (care), *f.* *A happy thought,* une heureuse idée, *f.*; *a thought better,* un peu mieux; *I speak my thoughts,* je dis ce que je pense, je dis le fond de ma pensée; *on second thoughts,* réflexion faite, tout bien considéré; *to collect one's thoughts,* se recueillir; *to read someone's thoughts,* lire dans la pensée de quelqu'un; *to take thought for,* s'inquiéter de, se soucier de, se préoccuper de; *without thought,* sans réfléchir.

thoughtful, *a.* Pensif, réfléchi; rêveur, méditatif; inquiet (anxious); attentif, prévenant, soucieux (kind). *Thoughtful of,* attentif à, occupé de. **thoughtfully,** *adv.* Pensivement, d'un air rêveur; avec attention, avec prévenance. **thoughtfulness,** *n.* Méditation, *f.*, recueillement, *m.*; sollicitude, attention, prévenance (solicitude), *f.*

thoughtless, *a.* Irréfléchi, insouciant; étourdi. **thoughtlessly,** *adv.* Avec insouciance; étourdiment, sans y penser. **thoughtlessness,** *n.* Insouciance, étourderie, inattention, négligence, *f.*

thought-reading, *n.* Lecture de la pensée, *f.* **thought-transference,** *n.* Télépathie, *f.*

thousand ['θauzənd], *a.* Mille; mil (of dates). *In the year a thousand and ten,* l'an mil dix; *it is a thousand to one,* il y a mille à parier contre un . . .; *the year one thousand,* l'an mille, *m.*—*n.* Mille; millier, *m.*; (*pl.*) milliers, *m.pl.* *By thousands,* par milliers;

thousands of, des milliers de. **thousandth,** *a.* and *n.* Millième, *m.*

Thracian ['θreiʃiən], *a.* De Thrace.—*n.* Thrace, *m.*

thraldom ['θrɔːldəm], *n.* Esclavage, asservissement, *m.* **thrall,** *n.* Esclave, *m.* or *f.*; serf, *m.*, serve, *f.*; esclavage, *m.*

thrash [θræʃ], *v.t.* Battre, rosser. *To thrash out* (a question), discuter à fond.—*v.i.* (*Agric.*) Battre (en grange). **thrasher,** *n.* Batteur en grange, *m.* **thrashing,** *n.* Rossée, raclée, *f.*; battage (of wheat etc.), *m.* **thrashing-floor,** *n.* Aire, *f.* **thrashing-machine,** *n.* Machine à battre, batteuse, *f.*

thread [θred], *n.* Fil; filet (of a screw); filament (of plants etc.), *m. Air threads*, fils de la Vierge, *m.pl.*; *to lose the thread*, (*fig.*) perdre le fil; *to pick up the thread*, reprendre le fil.—*v.t.* Enfiler; passer par, traverser (to pass through).

threadbare, *a.* Usé jusqu'à la corde, râpé; (*fig.*) usé, rebattu. **threadbareness,** *n.* État râpé, *m.*; (*fig.*) banalité, *f.*

threadshaped, *a.* Filiforme.

thready, *a.* Plein de fils; filamenteux, fibreux.

threat [θret], *n.* Menace, *f. To utter threats,* proférer des menaces.

threaten [θretn], *v.t.* Menacer (de); faire des menaces à. *It threatens to rain*, le temps est à la pluie, il va pleuvoir; *to threaten a man with a stick*, menacer un homme d'un bâton.

threatening, *n.* Menaces, *f.pl.*—*a.* Menaçant; de menaces. *The weather is threatening*, le temps est à la pluie. **threateningly,** *adv.* Avec menaces; d'un air menaçant.

three [θriː], *a* and *n.* Trois, *m. He is three,* il a trois ans; *number three*, numéro trois; *rule of three*, règle de trois, *f.*; (*Polit.*) *the Big Three*, les Trois Grands, *m.pl.*; *three o'clock*, trois heures. **three-cornered,** *a.* À trois cornes. *Three-cornered hat*, tricorne, *m.*; (*Polit.*) *three-cornered contest*, élection triangulaire, *f.* (three candidates). **three-decker,** *n.* Trois-ponts, *m.*; *roman en trois volumes (in 19th-century English fiction), m.* **three-dimensional,** *a.* Tridimensionnel, stéréoscopique. *3 D(imensional) film*, film à réfraction, film en relief, *m.* **threefold,** *a.* Triple. **three-headed,** *a.* À trois têtes. **three-legged,** *a.* À trois pieds. **three-masted,** *a.* À trois mâts. **three-master,** *n.* Trois-mâts, *m.*

threepence ['θrepəns or 'θrʌpəns], *n.pl.* Un quart de shilling.

threepenny ['θrepəni or 'θrʌpəni], *a. Three-penny bit*, pièce de trois pence, *f.*

three-ply, *a.* À trois épaisseurs. *Three-ply wood*, contreplaqué, *m.*

three-quarter, *a.* De trois quarts. (*Rugby*) *Three-quarter (back)*, trois-quarts, *m.*; *three-quarter length coat*, trois-quarts, *m.*

threescore, *a.* Soixante.—*n.* Soixantaine, *f.*

thresh [THRASH].

threshold ['θreʃould], *n.* Seuil; (*fig.*) début, commencement, *m.*

*thrice** [θrais], *adv.* Trois fois.

thridacium [θri'deiʃiəm], *n.* Thridace, *f.*

thrift [θrift], *n.* Épargne, économie, frugalité, *f.*; gazon d'Olympe (plant), *m.* **thriftily,** *adv.* Avec économie. **thriftiness,** *n.* Épargne, économie, *f.* **thriftless,** *a.* Dépensier, prodigue. **thriftlessly,** *adv.* En prodigue, follement. **thriftlessness,** *n.* Prodigalité, *f.*, gaspillage, *m.* **thrifty,** *a.* Ménager, économe, frugal.

thrill [θril], *v.t.* Faire frissonner, faire tressaillir (de). *Thrilled with remorse*, pénétré de remords.—*v.i.* Frémir, tressaillir (de).—*n.* Tressaillement, frisson, *m.*

thriller, *n.* (*fam.*) Roman, film à sensation, *m.* **thrilling,** *a.* Saisissant, poignant, palpitant.

thrive [θraiv], *v.i.* (*past* **throve** [θrouv], *p.p.* **thriven** [θrivn]) Prospérer, profiter (de); réussir; venir bien (of animals etc.); se plaire (of plants).

thriving, *n.* Florissant, qui prospère, qui réussit; qui vient bien, vigoureux (of plants). **thrivingly,** *adv.* D'une manière florissante, heureusement, avec succès. **thrivingness,** *n.* Prospérité, *f.*, état florissant, succès, *m.*

throat [θrout], *n.* Gorge, *f.*; gosier (the swallow); diamant (of an anchor). *m. A sore throat*, un mal de gorge; *to clear one's throat*, tousser un peu, s'éclaircir la voix; *to cut one another's throats*, s'égorger l'un l'autre, (*Comm.*) se faire une concurrence ruineuse; *to cut one's throat*, se couper la gorge; *to lie in one's throat*, mentir effrontément; (*fig.*) *to ram something down someone's throat*, imposer quelque chose à quelqu'un; *to seize by the throat*, prendre à la gorge.

throated, *a.* À gorge. **throat-pipe,** *n.* Trachée-artère, *f.* **throat-wash,** *n.* Gargarisme, *m.* **throaty,** *a.* Guttural (of voice).

throb [θrɔb], *v.i.* Battre; palpiter. *My thumb throbs*, le pouce me bat.—*n.* Battement, *m.*

throbbing, *n.* Battement, *m.*, palpitation, pulsation, *f.*; ronflement (of motors); vrombissement (of aero engines), *m.*—*a.* Palpitant, vibrant; lancinant (of a pain); vrombissant (of motors etc.).

throe [θrou], *n.* (*usu. pl.*) Douleurs, angoisses; *affres, *f.pl.*

thrombosis [θrɔm'bousis], *n.* Thrombose, *f.*

throne [θroun], *n.* Trône, *m.* **throned,** *a.* Assis sur le trône. **throne-room,** *n.* Salle du trône, *f.*

throng [θrɔŋ], *n.* Foule, multitude, *f.*—*v.i.* Accourir en foule, se presser, s'attrouper.—*v.t.* Remplir, encombrer.

thronged, *a.* Serré, compact (of people); comble, bondé (of rooms).

throstle [θrɔsl], *n.* (*Orn.*) Calendrette, grive chanteuse, *f.* **throstle-frame,** *n.* Métier continu (à filer), *m.*

throttle [θrɔtl], *v.t.* Étrangler; étouffer.—*n.* Gosier, *m.*; (*Motor. etc.*) papillon, *m. To go full throttle*, aller à pleins gaz; *to open the throttle*, ouvrir les gaz. **throttle-valve,** *n.* Soupape de régulateur, soupape à papillon, soupape d'étranglement, *f.*

through [θruː], *prep.* À travers; au travers de; par (passage, conveyances, etc.); d'un bout à l'autre de (over the whole extent); dans (denoting passage among); directement, droit (without stopping); en conséquence de, par suite de (in consequence of). *Through him*, par lui, par son entremise; *to go through the whole ceremony*, passer par tous les détails de la cérémonie; *to pass through a gate*, passer par une porte; *to read through*, pénétrer la pensée de; *to see through*, voir à travers *or* au travers de (a door etc.), pénétrer, savoir à quoi s'en tenir sur le compte de (a person); *to sit a play through*, rester jusqu'au bout d'une représentation.—*a.* Direct (of trains, tickets, etc.). *Through train*, train direct, *m.*—*adv.* D'outre en outre, de part en part; d'un bout à l'autre (from beginning to end); jusqu'à la fin, jusqu'au bout (to the end); complètement. *To be wet through*, être trempé jusqu'aux os; *to book one's luggage through*, faire enregistrer ses bagages directement pour; *to fall through* (of a project), ne pas aboutir, manquer, (*colloq.*) rater; (*Teleph.*) *to get through to N.*, obtenir la communication avec N.; *to go through with, to see* (something) *through*, mener à bonne fin; (*Teleph.*) *to put someone through to*, passer la communication à; *to run* (someone) *through and through*, percer de part en part.

throughout [θru:'aut], *prep.* Dans tout, par tout. *Throughout the course of his long life*, dans tout le cours de sa longue vie.—*adv.* D'un bout à l'autre; partout; entièrement, en entier (entirely).

throve, *past* [THRIVE].

throw [θrou], *v.t.* (*past* **threw** [θru:], *p.p.* **thrown** [θroun]) Jeter; lancer; renverser, terrasser (in wrestling etc.); organsiner, tordre (silk); démonter, désarçonner (a horseman); mettre (to put). *To throw aside*, jeter de côté; *to throw at*, jeter, lancer (à *or* contre); *to throw away*, jeter, rejeter, perdre (to lose), gaspiller, jeter par la fenêtre (to waste), prodiguer (one's life etc.); *to throw away a chance*, laisser passer une occasion; *to throw back*, jeter en arrière, renvoyer, réfléchir, rejeter, retarder (to delay); *to throw down*, jeter en bas, renverser, terrasser; *to throw in*, jeter dedans, donner par-dessus le marché (to give over and above); *to throw off*, rejeter, se défaire de, ôter (garments), lever (the mask), secouer (to shake off); *to throw off the scent*, dépister; *to throw oneself down on*, se jeter sur; *to throw oneself into*, s'abandonner à; *to throw open*, ouvrir; *to throw out*, jeter dehors, rejeter, chasser, parler mal (to utter carelessly), insinuer, donner à entendre (to insinuate), émettre en avant (words etc.); *to throw out of* (a window), jeter par; *to throw together*, assembler à la hâte; *to throw up*, jeter en haut, jeter en l'air, se démettre de, renoncer à (to resign), vomir, rejeter (to vomit); *to throw wide open*, ouvrir à deux battants.—*v.i.* Jeter, lancer.—*n.* Jet, coup; (*fig.*) effort, élan, *m.*

throw-back, *n.* Retour atavique, *m.*; régression, *f.*

thrower, *n.* Jeteur, lanceur, *m.*

throwster, *n.* (*Text.*) Organsineur, *m.*

thrum [θrʌm], *n.* Bout de fil, *m.*—*v.t.* Franger; (*Naut.*) larder (a sail).—*v.i.* Tapoter (on a piano etc.).

thrush [θrʌʃ], *n.* (*Orn.*) Grive, *f.*; (*Path.*) aphte, *m.*; (*Vet.*) teigne, *f.*

thrust [θrʌst], *v.t.* (*past* and *p.p.* **thrust**) Pousser, enfoncer, fourrer; presser. *To thrust away* or *back*, repousser, rejeter (to reject); *to thrust down*, pousser en bas, jeter en bas; *to thrust in*, pousser dedans, fourrer, introduire de force, enfoncer (a stick etc.); *to thrust into*, jeter dans; *to thrust oneself in*, se fourrer dans; *to thrust out*, pousser dehors, faire sortir de force; *to thrust something upon someone*, forcer quelqu'un à accepter quelque

chose; *to thrust through*, faire passer à travers, transpercer (to pierce); *to thrust under*, pousser sous.—*v.i.* Porter une botte *or* un coup (à); se fourrer. *To cut and thrust*, frapper d'estoc et de taille.—*n.* Coup, *m.*; (*Fenc.*) botte; (*Arch. etc.*) poussée, *f.* *Home-thrust*, coup qui porte; *to give a home thrust*, piquer au vif; *the thrust and parry which mark controversy*, les ripostes du tac au tac qui caractérisent la polémique; *to make a thrust at*, porter *or* pousser une botte à, porter un coup à.

thruster, *n.* (*fam.*) Arriviste, *m.*

Thucydides [θju:'sididi:z]. Thucydide, *m.*

thud [θʌd], *n.* Bruit sourd; son mat, *m.*—*v.i.* Faire un bruit sourd.

thug [θʌg], *n.* Étrangleur (de l'Inde), thug; bandit, sicaire, *m.*

thuja [THUYA].

Thule ['θju:li]. (*Geog.*) Thulé, *f.*

thumb [θʌm], *n.* Pouce, *m.* *Rule of thumb*, règle empirique, *f.*, procédé empirique, *m.*; *to bite the thumb at*, narguer; *Tom Thumb*, Petit Poucet, *m.*; *under one's thumb*, en son pouvoir, sous sa domination.—*v.t.* Manier gauchement; salir (avec les pouces), fatiguer (to soil). (*fam.*) *To thumb a lift*, faire de l'auto-stop.

thumb-mark, *n.* Marque de pouce, *f.*

thumbnail, *a.* En raccourci, minuscule.

thumb-screw, *n.* Vis à ailettes, *f.*; poucettes (torture), *f.pl.* **thumbstall**, *n.* Poucier, doigtier, *m.* **thumbtack**, *n.* (*Am.*) Punaise, *f.*

thump [θʌmp], *v.t.* Frapper du poing, donner un coup de poing à, cogner.—*n.* Coup, *m.*, bourrade, *f.* **thumper**, *n.* Chose énorme, *f.* **thumping**, *a.* (*colloq.*) Gros, énorme.

thunder ['θʌndə], *n.* Tonnerre, *m.*; (*fig.*) foudre, *f.* *Peal of thunder*, coup de tonnerre, *m.*; *to steal someone's thunder*, couper ses effets à quelqu'un.—*v.i.* Tonner; (*fig.*) gronder, retentir, fulminer. *It thunders*, il tonne.—*v.t.* Fulminer, crier d'une voix de tonnerre.

thunderbolt, *n.* Foudre, *f.*; (*fig.*) foudre (person), *m.* *Struck by a thunderbolt*, frappé de la foudre.

thunder-clap, *n.* Coup de tonnerre, *m.* **thunder-cloud**, *n.* Nuage orageux, *m.* **thunderer**, *n.* Maître du tonnerre, *m.* **thundering**, *a.* Tonnant, foudroyant, de tonnerre; (*colloq.*) énorme, terrible. *A thundering fool*, un fameux imbécile; *thundering Jove*, Jupiter tonnant; *thundering voice*, voix de tonnerre, *f.*; *to go thundering past*, passer comme la foudre. **thunderingly**, *adv.* Avec un bruit de tonnerre. **thunderous**, *a.* Orageux; tonnant; à tout rompre, crépitant (applause). **thunder-shower**, *n.* Pluie d'orage, *f.* **thunderstorm**, *n.* Orage accompagné de tonnerre, *m.* **thunderstruck**, *a.* Foudroyé, frappé par la foudre; (*fig.*) atterré, abasourdi, anéanti. **thundery**, *a.* Orageux. *It is thundery weather*, le temps est à l'orage.

thurifer ['θjuərifə], *n.* Thuriféraire, *m.* **thuriferous** [-'rifərəs], *a.* Thurifère.

Thursday ['θə:zdi], *n.* Jeudi, *m.* *On Thursdays*, le jeudi.

thus [ðʌs], *adv.* Ainsi. *Thus far*, jusqu'ici.

thuya or **thuja** ['θu:jə], *n.* (*Bot.*) Thuya, *m.*

thwack [θwæk], *n.* Coup, *m.*—*v.t.* Frapper,

rosser, battre. **thwacking,** *n.* Roulée de coups, raclée, *f.*
thwart [θwɔːt], *v.t.* Traverser; (*fig.*) contrarier, contrecarrer.—*adv.* En travers.—*n.* Banc de rameurs, *m.* **thwarting,** *a.* Contrariant. **thwartingly,** *adv.* D'une manière contrariante. **thwartship,** *a.* and *adv.* Par le travers (du vaisseau).
thy [ðai], *poss.a.* Ton, *m.*, ta, *f.*, tes, *pl.*
thyme [taim], *n.* Thym, *m.* *Wild thyme,* serpolet, *m.* **thymol,** *n.* Thymol, *m.* **thymy,** *a.* Qui a l'odeur du thym, qui abonde en thym; odoriférant.
thyroid ['θairɔid], *a.* Thyroïde.
thyrsus ['θɔːsəs], *n.* Thyrse, *m.*
thyself [ðai'self], *pron.* Toi-même, toi; (*reflexively*) te . . . toi.
tiara [ti'ɑːrə], *n.* Tiare, *f.*
Tiber ['taibə], **the.** Le Tibre, *m.*
Tibet [ti'bet]. Le Tibet, *m.* **Tibetan,** *n.* and *a.* Tibétain, *m.*, -aine, *f.*
tibia ['tibiə], *n.* (*Anat.*) Tibia (os de la jambe), *m.* **tibio-tarsal,** *a.* Tibio-tarsien.
Tibullus [ti'bʌləs]. Tibulle, *m.*
tic [tik], *n.* Tic, *m.*
tick [tik], *n.* Coutil, *m.*; toile à matelas (for beds etc.), *f.*; tic-tac (noise), *m.*; marque; tique (insect), *f.*; (*slang*) crédit (credit), *m.* *On tick,* à crédit, à l'œil.—*v.i.* Faire tic-tac, battre (of clocks etc.). *To tick over,* tourner au grand ralenti (of motors).—*v.t.* Marquer. *To tick off,* pointer; (*fam.*) réprimander.
ticker, *n.* (*slang*) Tocante (watch), *f.*; cœur, *m.* *A dicky ticker,* un cœur malade.
ticket ['tikit], *n.* Billet; ticket; cachet, *m.*; reconnaissance (pawn ticket), *f.*, bulletin (for luggage); bon (relief-ticket), *m.*; étiquette (mark); plaque (badge), *f.* *Return ticket,* billet d'aller et retour; *season ticket,* carte d'abonnement, *f.*; *season ticket holder,* abonné; *single ticket,* billet simple.—*v.t.* Étiqueter, numéroter.
ticket-collector, *n.* Contrôleur, *m.* **ticket-office,** *n.* Bureau des billets, guichet, *m.* **ticket-of-leave,** *n.* Libération, *f.* *Ticket-of-leave man,* forçat libéré, repris de justice, récidiviste, *m.*
ticking ['tikiŋ], *n.* Tic-tac, battement (of watches etc.); coutil, *m.*, toile à matelas (for beds), *f.*
tickle [tikl], *v.t.* Chatouiller; (*fig.*) charmer, flatter. *That tickled my fancy,* cela m'amusa. —*v.i.* Chatouiller. **tickler,** *n.* Sujet, problème délicat; bouton de nettoyage, *m.* *Memory tickler,* (*fam.*) pense-bête, *m.*
tickling, *n.* Chatouillement, *m.*
ticklish, *a.* Chatouilleux; critique, délicat, difficile, scabreux; chancelant, mal assuré (shaky). **ticklishness,** *n.* Nature chatouilleuse, *f.*; état critique, *m.*, difficulté, *f.*
tidal [taidl], *a.* De marée. *Tidal harbour,* port à marée, *m.*; *tidal wave,* raz de marée, *m.*, vague de fond, *f.*
tiddler ['tidlə], *n.* (*fam.*) Petit poisson, *m.*
tiddly ['tidli], *a.* (*pop.*) Ivre.
tiddlywinks ['tidliwiŋks], *n.* Jeu de la puce, *m.*
tide [taid], *n.* Marée, *f.*; courant (stream), *m.*; (*Mining*) période de travail de douze heures; (*fig.*) saison, époque, *f.* *At low tide,* à marée basse; *carried away by the tide,* emporté or entraîné par le courant; *Christmas-tide,* saison

de Noël, *f.*; *ebb-tide,* marée descendante, *f.*, jusant, *m.*; *half-tide,* mi-marée, *f.*, demi-flot, *m.*; *high tide,* marée haute, *f.*, flot, *m.*; *low tide,* marée basse; *neap-tide,* morte-eau, *f.*; *rising tide,* marée montante; *spring tide,* grande marée; *the tide of human affairs,* le cours des affaires humaines; *to go with the tide,* suivre le courant.—*v.i.* Aller avec la marée.—*v.t.* *To tide over,* passer par-dessus, se tirer de.
tide-gate, *n.* Écluse à marée montante, porte à flot, *f.* **tide-gauge,** *n.* Échelle de marée, *f.* **tideless,** *a.* Sans marée. **tide-mill,** *n.* Moulin avec roue à flux et à reflux, *m.* ***tide-waiter,** *n.* Douanier, *m.* **tide-way,** *n.* Lit de marée, *m.*
tidily ['taidili], *adv.* Proprement, en bon ordre.
tidiness, *n.* Propreté, netteté, *f.*, bon ordre, *m.*
tidings ['taidiŋz], *n.pl.* Nouvelles, *f.pl.*
tidy ['taidi], *a.* Rangé, bien arrangé, en ordre, propre, net. *A tidy sum,* (*colloq.*) une bonne petite somme, *f.*, un bon petit magot, *m.*—*v.t.* Mettre en ordre; ranger; arranger (papers etc.). *To tidy oneself up,* faire un bout or un brin de toilette.
tie [tai], *v.t.* Lier, attacher; nouer, faire (a knot). *To tie down,* lier, astreindre, assujettir, obliger (à); *to tie up,* lier, attacher, nouer, ficeler (a parcel), mettre à l'attache (animal); *tied for time,* pressé.—*v.i.* Se lier, se nouer; être à égalité.—*n.* Lien, *m.*, attache, *f.*; nœud (knot); cordon (for a shoe), *m.*; cravate; (*Naut.*) itague, *f.*; (*Build.*) crampon, tirant, *m.*; (*Mus.*) liaison; (*Games*) partie nulle, course à égalité, *f.*; classement ex æquo; match de championnat, *m.*; (*Polit.*) égalité de voix, *f.*
tie-bar, *n.* (*Build.*) Tirant, *m.* **tie-beam,** *n.* (*Carp.*) Entrait, *m.* **tie-clip,** *n.* Pince à cravate, *f.* **tie-rod,** *n.* Tirant, *m.* **tie-up,** *n.* Association, union (of business interests etc.), *f.*
tier [tiə], *n.* Rang, *m.*; rangée (of guns), *f.* *Boxes on the first or the second tier,* premières or deuxièmes loges, *f.pl.*; *in tiers,* étagé; *tier upon tier,* étage sur étage, en gradins.
tierce [tiəs], *n.* Tierce (at cards etc.), *f.*; tierçon (cask), *m.* **tierce-major,** *n.* Tierce majeure, *f.*
tiercel ['tiəsl], *n.* (*Orn.*) Tiercelet, *m.*
Tierra del Fuego [ti'erə del 'fweigou]. (*Geog.*) La Terre de Feu, *f.*
tiff [tif], *n.* Petite querelle, pique, *f.*; petit coup (of liquor), *m.* *To get into a tiff,* prendre la mouche; *to have a tiff with,* avoir une bisbille avec.—*v.i.* Se piquer, se fâcher, bouder.
tiffany ['tifəni], *n.* Gaze de soie (fabric), *f.*
tiffin ['tifin], *n.* (*Ang.-Ind.*), Déjeuner, *m.*
tig [tig], *n.* Jeu du chat, *m.* *Cross tig,* chat coupé; *long tig,* chat perché; *to play tig,* jouer au chat.
tiger ['taigə], *n.* Tigre, *m.*; *petit laquais, groom, *m.* **tiger-cat,** *n.* Chat tigre, *m.* **tigerish,** *a.* De tigre. **tiger-lily,** *n.* (*Bot.*) Lis tigré, *m.* **tiger-moth,** *n.* Arctie, *f.*
tight [tait], *a.* Serré; raide, tendu (not slack); trop étroit (of clothes); clos, bien or hermétiquement fermé (well closed); étanche (not leaky); imperméable; (*slang*) gris, à moitié ivre (tipsy). *Air-tight or water-tight,* imperméable à l'air or à l'eau; *a tight corner,* une

mauvaise passe; *to keep a tight hand on* (a person), tenir la bride courte à.—*adv.* Fortement, hermétiquement. *Hold tight!* Tenez-vous bien! (in buses); *to sit tight*, (*fig.*) ne pas en démordre.

tighten, *v.t.* Serrer; tendre (to strain); (*fig.*) resserrer.—*v.i.* Se serrer.

tight-fisted, *a.* Serré, ladre.

tight-fitting, *a.* Collant (of trousers etc.).

tight-laced, *a.* Lacé, serré.

tightly, *adv.* Ferme, fortement; étroitement serré. **tightness,** *n.* Raideur, imperméabilité; oppression (in the chest); étroitesse (of clothes), *f.*

tight-rope, *n.* Corde raide, corde tendue, *f.* *Tight-rope walker,* funambule, danseur, *m.*, -euse, *f.*, de corde.

tights, *n.pl.* Collant, maillot, *m.*

tigress ['taigris], *n.* Tigresse, *f.*

Tigris ['taigris]. (*Geog.*) Le Tigre, *m.*

tile [tail], *n.* Tuile, *f.*; carreau (for flooring), *m.*; (*slang*) couvre-chef, galurin (hat), *m.* *To have a tile loose,* (*colloq.*) être un peu toqué.—*v.t.* Couvrir de tuiles; carreler (a floor). **tile-kiln,** *n.* Four à tuiles, *m.* **tile-maker,** *n.* Tuilier, *m.* **tile-works,** *n.* Tuilerie, *f.*

tiler, *n.* Couvreur (en tuiles), *m.* **tiling,** *n.* Recouvrement en tuiles, *m.*; toiture en tuiles (roof), *f.*; tuiles (tiles), *f.pl.*

till (1) [til], *prep.* Jusqu'à; d'ici à. Jusqu'à ce que (*with subjunctive*).

till (2) [til], *n.* Tiroir de caisse, *m.*

till (3) [til], *v.t.* Labourer, cultiver. **tillable,** *a.* Labourable. **tillage,** *n.* Labourage, *m.*

tiller, *n.* Laboureur, *m.*; barre du gouvernail (rudder), *f.*; bourgeon, rejeton (sprout), *m.*, talle (of corn), *f.*

tilt [tilt], *n.* Bâche, banne (awning); joute, *f.*; martinet (hammer); tournois (tournament), *m.*; inclinaison, *f.* *Full tilt,* à tête baissée (headlong).—*v.t.* Incliner, faire pencher; vider, décharger (a cart etc.); marteler (to hammer); couvrir d'une tente, bâcher. *With his hat tilted on one side,* le chapeau sur l'oreille.—*v.i.* Jouter; incliner, pencher. *To tilt at,* fondre sur.

tilt-cart, *n.* Charrette à bâche, *f.* **tilt-hammer** *n.* Martinet, marteau à bascule, *m.* **tilt-yard,** *n.* Champ clos, *m.*, lice, *f.*

tilted, *a.* Bâché.

tilter, *n.* Jouteur, *m.*

tilth [tilθ], *n.* Labourage, *m.*, culture, *f.*

tilting ['tiltiŋ], *n.* Joute, *f.*, tournoi, *m.*; inclinaison, pente, *f.*

timber ['timbə], *n.* Bois de haute futaie, bois de construction, bois d'œuvre; (*Naut.*) couple, membre, *m.* *Well-seasoned timber,* bois sec, *m.*—*v.t.* Munir de bois de charpente; boiser.

timbered, *a.* (Construit) en bois; boisé, couvert d'arbres de haute futaie. *Half-timbered,* à demi-boisage; *well-timbered,* boisé (of land). **timbering,** *n.* Boisage, *m.*

timber-merchant, *n.* Marchand de bois de construction, *m.* **timber-tree,** *n.* Arbre de haute futaie, *m.* **timber-work,** *n.* Charpente, *f.* **timber-yard,** *n.* Chantier, *m.*

timbrel ['timbrəl], *n.* Tambour de basque, tambourin, *m.*

time [taim], *n.* Temps, *m.*; saison, époque, *f.*;

terme (space of time), *m.*; heure (of day and night), *f.*; moment (moment), *m.*, occasion; fois (repetition); époque, *f.*, siècle (in history), *m.*; mesure, *f.*; (*Drilling*) pas, *m.* *After a time,* au bout de quelque temps, dans quelque temps; *all the time,* tout le temps; *another time,* une autre fois; *as times go,* par le temps qui court; *at all times,* toujours; *at any time,* en tout temps, n'importe quand, à toute heure, à tout moment; *at a time when,* dans un temps où, dans un moment où; *at different times,* à diverses reprises; *at just such a time,* à pareille époque; *at my time of life,* à mon âge; *at no time,* jamais, dans aucun temps; *at ordinary times,* en temps ordinaire; *at other times,* en d'autres temps; *at such a time,* à un tel moment, à une telle époque; *at that time,* alors, à cette époque; *at the present time,* à présent, actuellement, à l'heure qu'il est; *at the same time,* en même temps, d'autre part, en revanche, d'un autre côté (on the other hand); *at times,* parfois, de temps à autre; *before one's time,* en avance, avant l'heure, avant terme (of childbirth); *behind one's time,* en retard; *every time,* chaque fois; *from that time,* dès lors; *from this time,* dès à présent; *from time to time,* de temps en temps; *he is almost out of his time,* il a presque fini son apprentissage; *hundreds of times,* des centaines de fois; *I had a bad time,* j'ai passé un mauvais quart d'heure; *in a short time,* en peu de temps, sous peu; *in a week or a fortnight's time,* dans une huitaine *or* une quinzaine de jours; *in course of time,* avec le temps; *in due time,* en temps opportun; *in good time,* bien à temps; *in no time,* en aucun moment, en un clin d'œil; *in proper time and place,* en temps et lieu; *in the nick of time,* à point nommé; *in the time of,* du temps de, à l'époque de; *in time,* à temps, avec le temps (in the course of time), (*Mus.*) en mesure, en cadence; *in time to come,* à l'avenir; *it was high time,* il était grand temps; *mean time,* heure moyenne, *f.*; *next time,* la prochaine fois; *now's the time!* voilà le moment! *once upon a time there was,* il y avait une fois; *one time or another,* un jour ou l'autre; *out of time,* (*Mus.*) à contretemps; *sidereal time,* heure sidérale, *f.*; *(so many) at a time,* à la fois; *sometime or other,* un jour ou l'autre; *this time last year,* il y a un an; *this time six months,* dans six mois; *three times,* trois fois; *till the end of time,* jusqu'à la fin des siècles; *time and space,* le temps et l'espace; *time is money,* le temps vaut de l'argent; *time out of mind,* de temps immémorial; *to beat time,* battre la mesure; *to have a bad time,* en voir de dures; *to have a fine time,* s'en donner; *to keep one's time,* être exact, arriver à l'heure; *to keep time,* être exact, être à l'heure (of clocks etc.), (*Mus.*) aller en mesure, marquer le pas; *to kill time,* tuer le temps; *to lose time,* perdre du temps (of persons), retarder (of clocks etc.); *to serve one's time,* faire son temps; *up to the present time,* jusqu'à présent; *what time is it?* quelle heure est-il?

v.t.—Accommoder au temps, faire à propos; fixer l'heure de; mettre (clocks etc.) à l'heure, régler, ajuster, calculer sur une montre; (*spt.*) chronométrer. *Ill-timed,* inopportun, mal à propos, hors de saison; *well-timed,* opportun, à propos.

time-bargain, *n.* Marché à terme, *m.* **time-bill,** *n.* Indicateur, *m.* **time-bomb,** *n.* Bombe à retardement, *f.* **time-exposure,** *n.* (*Phot.*) Pose, *f.* **time-fuse,** *n.* Fusée fusante, fusée à temps, *f.* **time-honoured,** *a.* Vénérable, vénéré; séculaire. **timekeeper,** *n.* Surveillant, contrôleur; (*spt.*) chronométreur; chronomètre (clock), *m.* *To be a good timekeeper,* être toujours à l'heure (of a watch). **time-keeping,** *n.* Pointage; chronométrage, *m.* **time-lag,** *n.* Décalage, retard, *m.* **time-lapse,** *n.* (*Cine.*) Accéléré, *m.* **timeliness,** *n.* Opportunité, *f.*, à propos, *m.* **timely,** *a.* Opportun, à propos. **timepiece,** *n.* Pendule, *f.* **time-server,** *n.* **time-serving,** *a.* Complaisant, opportuniste.—*n.* Servilité, *f.*, opportunisme, *m.* **time-sheet,** *n.* Feuille de présence, *f.* **time-switch,** *n.* Minuterie (on a staircase etc.), *f.* **timetable,** *n.* Indicateur, horaire; (*sch.*) emploi du temps, *m.* **time-work,** *n.* Travail à l'heure, *m.* **time-worn,** *a.* Usé par le temps.

timid ['timid], *a.* Timide, craintif, peureux. **timidity** [ti'miditi], *n.* Timidité, *f.* **timidly** ['timidli], *adv.* Timidement. **timing** ['taimiŋ], *n.* Ajustement, règlement; réglage (of watches etc.), *m.* **timocracy** [tai'mɔkrəsi], *n.* Timocratie, *f.* **timorous** ['timərəs], *a.* Timoré. **timorously,** *adv.* Timidement, craintivement. **timorousness,** *n.* Timidité, *f.*

tin [tin], *n.* Étain; fer-blanc (sheet iron coated with tin), *m.*; boîte (de conserve), *f.*; (*Mil.*) gamelle (mess-tin), *f.*; (*slang*) galette, *f.*, fric, *m.*—*v.t.* Étamer.—*a.* D'étain; en fer-blanc. **tincal** ['tiŋkəl], *n.* Borax brut, tincal, *m.*

tincture ['tiŋktʃə], *n.* Teinture, *f.*, extrait, *m.*; (*fig.*) nuance, *f.*, léger goût, *m.*—*v.t.* Teindre (de); (*fig.*) imprégner (de). *To be tinctured with,* avoir une teinture de.

tinder ['tində], *n.* Amadou, *m.* **tinder-box,** *n.* Boîte à amadou, *f.*, briquet à silex, *m.* **tine** [tain], *n.* Dent (de fourche etc.), *f.* **tinfoil** ['tinfoil], *n.* Feuille d'étain, *f.* *n.* (*pop.*) Casque de tranchée, *m.* **tinman,** *n.* (*pl.* **tinmen**) Ferblantier, *m.* **tinned,** *a.* De conserve (food); étamé. **tinning,** *n.* Étamage, *m.* **tinny,** *a.* Qui abonde en étain, stannifère; grêle, fêlé (sound). **tin-plate,** *n.* Fer-blanc, *m.* **tin-pot,** *a.* (*pop.*) Mesquin, méprisable. **tinsmith,** *n.* Ferblantier, *m.* **tin-tack,** *n.* Semence étamée, *f.* **tinware,** *n.* Ferblanterie, *f.*

tinge [tindʒ], *n.* Teinte, nuance, *f.*; léger goût, soupçon (slight taste), *m.*—*v.t.* Teindre; (*fig.*) imprégner.

tingle [tiŋgl], *v.i.* Tinter; picoter, démanger, cuire (of pain). **tingling,** *n.* Tintement (of the ears); picotement, *m.*

tinker ['tiŋkə], *n.* Chaudronnier; rétameur (itinerant), *m.*—*v.t.* Rétamer; raccommoder, rafistoler. **tinkering,** *n.* Étamage, raccommodage, *m.*

tinkle [tiŋkl], *v.i.* Tinter.—*v.t.* Faire tinter. —*n.* Tintement, *m.* (*fam.*) *To give someone a tinkle,* donner un coup de fil à quelqu'un. **tinkling,** *n.* Tintement, *m.*

tinsel ['tinsəl], *n.* Clinquant, oripeau; lamé; (*fig.*) faux éclat, brillant, *m.* *Silver tinsel,* cheveux d'ange, *m.pl.*—*a.* De clinquant;

---

faux.—*v.t.* Orner de clinquant; donner un faux éclat à.

tint [tint], *n.* Teinte, nuance, *f.* *Tint-drawing,* camaïeu, lavis, *m.*—*v.t.* Teinter, nuancer (de); donner une teinte à; ombrer; hachurer. *Tinted glasses,* lunettes à verres teintés, *f.pl.*

Tintoretto [tintə'retou]. Le Tintoret, *m.*

tiny ['taini], *a.* Tout petit, minuscule. *A tiny bit,* un tout petit morceau, un rien, *m.*

tip [tip], *n.* Bout, *m.*; extrémité, pointe; tape (tap), *f.*; pourboire (gratuity), *m.*; (*spt.*) tuyau, *m.* *Coal-tip,* élévateur à charbon, *m.*; *rubbish-tip,* dépotoir, *m.* *From tip to toe,* de la tête aux pieds.—*v.t.* Garnir le bout; donner un pourboire à; décharger (a vehicle); (*spt.*) tuyauter. *To tip off,* verser, culbuter; (*fam.*) tuyauter; *to tip over,* culbuter, renverser (intransitively), faire la culbute, chavirer (boats); *to tip the wink,* faire signe de l'œil, avertir.

tip-cat, *n.* Bâtonnet pirli (game), *m.*

tippet ['tipit], *n.* Pèlerine, palatine (fur), petite écharpe, *f.*, tour de cou, *m.* (fur.)

tipple [tipl], *v.i.* Boire, pinter.—*n.* Boisson, *f.* **tippler,** *n.* Buveur, *m.* **tippling,** *n.* Ivrognerie, *f.*

tipsily ['tipsili], *adv.* En ivrogne. **tipsiness,** *n.* Ivresse, *f.* **tipsy,** *a.* Gris, ivre. *Tipsy cake,* gâteau au madère, *m.*; *to get tipsy,* se griser, s'enivrer.

tipstaff, *n.* Huissier, *m.*; verge d'huissier (staff), *f.*

tipster, *n.* (*spt.*) Tuyauteur, *m.*

tiptoe, *n.* Pointe du pied, *f.* *To be on the tiptoe of expectation,* être dans l'anxiété de l'attente; *to stand on tiptoe,* se tenir sur la pointe des pieds.

tip-top, *n.* Le plus haut point, comble, sommet, *m.*—*a.* (*colloq.*) Suprême, excellent, de premier ordre.

tirade [ti'reid *or* tai'reid], *n.* Tirade, diatribe, *f.* *Tirade of abuse,* bordée d'injures, *f.*

tire (1) ['taiə], *n.* (*Am.*) [TYRE].

tire (2) ['taiə], *v.t.* Lasser, fatiguer; ennuyer (to bore). *I am quite tired out,* je suis éreinté, je n'en peux plus; *to get tired,* se lasser, se fatiguer (de), s'ennuyer (de); *to tire (someone's patience),* mettre à bout; *to tire out,* excéder, éreinter, assommer (to bore).—*v.i.* Se fatiguer, se lasser; se dégoûter de.

tired ['taiəd], *a.* Las, fatigué; ennuyé. **tiredness,** *n.* Fatigue, lassitude, *f.* **tiresome,** *a.* Fatigant; ennuyeux (tedious). **tiresomeness,** *n.* Nature fatigante, *f.*; ennui (tediousness), *m.*

tiro ['taiərou], *n.* Novice, débutant, *m.*

tissue ['tiʃju: *or* 'tisju:], *n.* Tissu, *m.*—*v.t.* Tisser, broder; entrelacer, entremêler (to interweave).

tissue-paper, *n.* Papier de soie, *m.*

tit [tit], *n.* Bidet, poney, *m.*; mésange (bird), *f.*; (*pop.*) téton, *m.* *Tit for tat,* un prêté pour un rendu, à bon chat bon rat; *to give tit for tat,* rendre la pareille, répondre du tac au tac.

Titan ['taitən], *n.* Titan, *m.* **Titan-like,** *a.* Comme un Titan, de Titan, colossal, titanesque. **titanic** [tai'tænik], *a.* Titanique, titanesque.

titaniferous [taitə'nifərəs], *a.* (*Chem.*) Titanifère. **titanium** [-'teiniəm], *n.* Titane, titanium, *m.*

titbit, *n.* Morceau friand, *m.* *As a titbit,* pour la

bonne bouche. *Some titbits from the debates,* quelques bons morceaux des discussions.
tithable ['taiðəbl], *a.* Sujet à la dîme. **tithe** [taið], *n.* Dîme, *f.*, dixième, *m.*—*v.t.* Lever la dîme sur, dîmer. **tithe-collector** or **tithe-gatherer,** *n.* Dîmeur, percepteur de la dîme, *m.* **tithe-free,** *a.* Exempt de la dîme. **tithe-owner,** *n.* Décimateur, *m.* **tithe-paying,** *a.* Assujetti à la dîme.
tithing ['taiðiŋ], *n.* Dîme; *dizaine, f.
Titian ['tiʃən]. Le Titien, *m.*
titillate ['titileit], *v.t., v.i.* Chatouiller, titiller. **titillating,** *a.* Titillant. **titillation** [-'leiʃən], *n.* Titillation, *f.*, chatouillement, *m.*
titivate ['titiveit], *v.i.* (*colloq.*) S'attifer, se faire beau.
titlark, *n.* Farlouse, alouette des prés, *f.*
title [taitl], *n.* Titre; (*fig.*) droit, document, *m. Credit titles,* (*Cine.*) générique, *m.*; *running title,* titre courant.—*v.t.* Titrer, qualifier (de). **titled,** *a.* Titré.
title-deed, *n.* Titre (de propriété), *m.*
title-page, *n.* Titre, *m.*
titmouse, *n.* (*pl.* **titmice**) Mésange, *f.*
titre ['ti:tə], *n.* Titre (of chemical solution etc.), *m.*
titter ['titə], *v.i.* Rire en cachette, rire tout bas. —*n.* Petit rire étouffé, *m.*
tittle [titl], *n.* Point, iota, *m. Not to abate one jot or tittle,* ne pas démordre d'un point; *to a tittle,* trait pour trait. **tittle-tattle,** *n.* Caquetage, *m.*, cancans, *m.pl.*, bavardage, *m.*—*v.i.* Jaser, bavarder.
titubation [titju'beiʃən], *n.* Titubation, *f.*
titular ['titjulə], *a.* Titulaire. **titularly,** *adv.* Par le titre, nominalement. **titulary,** *a.* De titre.—*n.* Titulaire, *m.*
to [tu], *prep.* À, de (before infinitive); pour, afin de (in order to); à (to a place); en (before names of countries of the feminine gender and those of the masculine gender beginning with a vowel); dans (followed by *le, la,* etc.); vers (towards); contre (against); selon, d'après (according to); près de (a court etc.); outre, en addition à (more than); pour (for); en comparaison de, auprès de (in comparison with); jusqu'à (as far as); envers (obligation). *A quarter to four,* quatre heures moins un (*or* le) quart; *from one street to another,* d'une rue à l'autre; *from street to street,* de rue en rue; *he is nothing to her,* il ne lui est rien; *his conduct to me,* sa conduite envers moi; *it is ten to one that . . .,* il y a dix à parier contre un que . . .; *keep her to,* (*Naut.*) tenez le vent; *killed to a man,* tués jusqu'au dernier; *let us keep it to ourselves,* gardons-le pour nous, gardons-nous d'en parler, n'en soufflons pas mot; *purveyor to,* fournisseur de, *m.*; *reserved almost to stiffness,* d'une réserve qui frise la raideur; *the heir to the throne,* l'héritier du trône; *the road to,* le chemin qui mène *or* qui conduit à . . .; *to and fro,* çà et là; *to apply to,* s'adresser à; *to bet twenty francs to one,* parier vingt francs contre un; *to come to,* reprendre ses sens, revenir à soi; *to count up to ten,* compter jusqu'à dix; *to fall to ruins,* tomber en ruine; *to go to Italy,* aller en Italie; *to go to Rome,* aller à Rome; *to go to someone's house,* aller chez quelqu'un; *to go to the Indies,* aller aux Indes; *to put to flight,* mettre en fuite; *to someone's face,* à la face de *or* au nez de quelqu'un; *to stretch one's arms to heaven,* tendre les bras vers le ciel; *to this day,* jusqu'à ce jour; *to write to,* écrire à; *what's that to him?* qu'est-ce que cela lui fait?

toad [toud], *n.* Crapaud, *m.* **toad-eater,** *n.* Flagorneur, parasite, *m.* **toad-flax,** *n.* Linaire, *f.* **toadstone,** *n.* Crapaudine, *f.* **toadstool,** *n.* Champignon vénéneux, *m.*
toadish, *a.* De crapaud.
toady ['toudi], *n.* Flagorneur, *m.*—*v.t.* Flagorner, aduler, ramper auprès de. **toadyism,** *n.* Flagornerie, servilité, *f.*
toast [toust], *n.* Rôtie, tranche de pain grillée, *f.*; toast (health), *m. Dry toast,* rôtie non beurrée.—*v.t.* Rôtir, griller; porter un toast à (to drink a health); (*fam.*) boire à la santé de.
toaster, *n.* Grille-pain, *m.inv.*
toasting-fork, *n.* Fourchette à rôties, *f.*
toast-master, *n.* Préposé aux toasts, *m.*
toast-rack, *n.* Porte-rôties, porte-toasts, *m.*
toast-water, *n.* Eau panée, *f.*
tobacco [tə'bækou], *n.* Tabac, *m. Chewing tobacco,* tabac à chiquer. **tobacco-box,** *n.* Boîte à tabac, *f.* **tobacco-jar,** *n.* Pot à tabac, *m.* **tobacco-pipe,** *n.* Pipe, *f.* **tobacco-pouch,** *n.* Blague à tabac, *f.* **tobacco-stopper,** *n.* Fouloir, *m.*
tobacconist, *n.* Marchand de tabac, *m. Tobacconist's shop,* bureau de tabac, *m.*
toboggan [tə'bɔgən], *n.* Toboggan, *m.*; luge, *f.*—*v.i.* Luger.
Toby ['toubi]. Tobie; chien à collerette (de Guignol), *m. Toby-jug,* pot à bière, *m.*
tocsin ['tɔksin], *n.* Tocsin, *m.*
today ['tə'dei], *adv.* Aujourd'hui.
toddle [tɔdl], *v.i.* Trottiner, marcher à petits pas. *I must toddle (off),* (*slang*) il faut que je file.
toddler, *n.* Bébé qui commence à marcher; tout petit enfant. *The toddlers,* les tout-petits, *m.pl.*
toddy ['tɔdi], *n.* Grog chaud, *m.*
to-do [tə'du:], *n.* Tapage, hourvari, éclat, *m.*, (*fam.*) histoire, *f. There was a fine to-do,* cela a fait toute une histoire.
toe [tou], *n.* Orteil, doigt de pied; devant du sabot, *m.*, pince (of horses), *f.*; bout (of a stocking), *m. On tiptoe* [TIPTOE]; *to tread on someone's toes,* marcher sur les pieds de quelqu'un, (*fig.*) froisser quelqu'un; *to turn up one's toes,* (*slang*) mourir.—*v.t.* (*Ftb.*) Botter (le ballon) avec la pointe du pied. (*fig.*) *To toe the line,* s'aligner; obéir.
toe-cap, *n.* Bout de chaussure, *m.*
toe-clip, *n.* Calepied (for bicycle), *m.*
toe-nail, *n.* Ongle de pied, *m.*
toffy ['tɔfi], **toffee,** *n.* Caramel au beurre, *m.*
tog [tɔg], *v.t.* (*colloq.*) *To tog up,* se faire beau, s'attifer [TOGS].
toga ['tougə], *n.* Toge, *f.*
together [tə'geðə], *adv.* Ensemble, à la fois, en même temps (que) (at the same time); de concert (in concert); de suite (in succession). *For hours together,* pendant des heures entières; *to come together,* venir ensemble, se rassembler, se rencontrer; *to gather together,* réunir, rassembler; *together with,* avec, ainsi que, en même temps que; *to join together,* réunir, s'unir.
toggle [tɔgl], *n.* (*Naut.*) Cabillot, *m.*
Togoland ['tougəlænd]. Le Togo, *m.*
togs [tɔgz], *n.pl.* (*slang*) Frusques, nippes, *f.pl.*

toil [tɔil], *n.* Travail dur, labeur, *m.*; peine, fatigue, *f.*; (*pl.*) filet, piège, rets, *m.* *To be caught in one's own toils*, être pris à son propre piège.—*v.i.* Travailler fort, se fatiguer, se donner du mal. *To toil and moil*, s'échiner, peiner, suer sang et eau; *to toil along*, avancer péniblement; *to toil up*, franchir *or* gravir avec peine. **toiler,** *n.* Travailleur, *m.*, travailleuse, *f.*

toilet ['tɔilit], *n.* Toilette, *f.*; (in hotels etc.) les toilettes, *f.pl.*, (*fam.*) les waters, *m.pl.*

toilet-cover, *n.* Dessus de toilette, *m.*

toilet-glass, *n.* Miroir de toilette, *m.*

toilet-paper, *n.* Papier hygiénique, *m.*

toilet-roll, *n.* Rouleau de papier hygiénique, *m.*

toilet-set, *n.* Garniture de toilette, *f.*

toiling ['tɔiliŋ], *n.* Travail, labeur, *m.*, peine, *f.*

toilsome, *a.* Pénible, laborieux, fatigant.

toilsomeness, *n.* Difficulté, *f.*

Tokay [tə'kei], *n.* Tokai, tokay (wine), *m.*

token ['toukn], *n.* Marque, *f.*; témoignage, gage (testimony), *m.*; demi-rame (of paper), *f.*; jeton (coin), *m.* *Book token*, bon de livre, *m.*; *token strike*, grève d'avertissement, *f.*

told, *past* and *p.p.* [TELL].

tolerable ['tɔlərəbl], *a.* Tolérable, supportable; passable (pretty good). **tolerably,** *adv.* Tolérablement; passablement, assez (so-so).

tolerance ['tɔlərəns], *n.* Tolérance, *f.* **tolerant,** *a.* Tolérant. **tolerate,** *v.t.* Tolérer; supporter, sentir, souffrir; permettre. **toleration** [-'reiʃən], *n.* Tolérance, *f.*

toll [toul], *n.* Péage; droit; octroi (town-due); tintement, glas (of a bell), *m.* *Influenza took a heavy toll of the population last winter*, il y a eu beaucoup de victimes de la grippe l'hiver dernier.—*v.t.* Sonner, tinter (a bell).—*v.i.* Tinter, sonner (of bells).

toll-bar or **toll-gate,** *n.* Barrière de péage, *f.*

tollbooth ['toulbu:ð], *n.* (*Sc.*) Prison, *f.*

toll-bridge, *n.* Pont à péage, *m.* **toll-gatherer,** *n.* Péager, *m.* **toll-house,** *n.* Bureau de péage, *m.* **tolling,** *n.* Tintement, *m.*

toluene ['tɔljui:n], *n.* Toluène, *m.* **toluic,** *a.* Toluique.

Tom [tɔm]. (*dim.* of) Thomas, *m.* *Tom, Dick, and Harry*, le premier venu, n'importe qui, Pierre, Jacques et Paul.

tomahawk ['tɔməhɔ:k], *n.* Tomahawk, *m.*; hache de guerre, *f.*

tomato [tə'mɑ:tou], *n.* Tomate, *f.* *Tomato juice*, jus de tomate, *m.*; *tomato ketchup*, sauce piquante à la tomate, *f.*; *tomato soup*, soupe à la tomate, *f.* **tomato-sauce,** *n.* Sauce tomate, *f.*

tomb [tu:m], *n.* Tombeau, sépulcre, *m.*; tombe, *f.* **tombstone,** *n.* Pierre tombale, tombe, *f.*

tomboy ['tɔmbɔi], *n.* Gamine, *f.*; garçon manqué, *m.*

tom-cat ['tɔmkæt], *n.* Matou, *m.*

tome [toum], *n.* Tome, volume, *m.*

tomentose [to'mentous], *a.* Tomenteux.

tomentum, *n.* Duvet cotonneux, *m.*

tomfool [tɔm'fu:l], *n.* Sot, bête, niais, *m.* **tomfoolery,** *n.* Sottise, bêtise, niaiserie, *f.*

Tommy ['tɔmi]. (*dim.* of) Thomas, *m.* **Tommy (Atkins)** ['tɔmiˈætkinz], *n.* Sobriquet du soldat anglais; (*pop.*) pain, *m.*; mangeaille, *f.*

tommy-gun, *n.* Mitraillette, *f.*

tommy-rot, *n.* Inepties, bêtises, *f.pl.*, histoire qui ne tient pas debout, *f.*

tomorrow [tə'mɔrou], *adv.* Demain. *The day after tomorrow*, après-demain; *the tomorrow that never comes*, la semaine des quatre jeudis.

*tompion ['tɔmpiən], *n.* [TAMPION].

tomtit ['tɔm'tit], *n.* (*Orn.*) Mésange bleue, *f.*

tom-tom ['tɔmtɔm], *n.* Tam-tam, *m.*

ton [tʌn], *n.* Tonne, *f.*, tonneau (1015 kilogrammes), *m.*

tonal [tounl], *a.* Tonal.

tonality [to'næliti], *n.* Tonalité, *f.*

tone [toun], *n.* Ton; accent, timbre (of the voice), *m.*; tonicité, vigueur, *f.* *In a tone of voice*, d'un ton de voix; *to give tone to*, donner du ton à (to invigorate), de l'éclat à (to add lustre to); *to speak in a low tone*, parler à voix basse.—*v.t.* Donner le ton à, régler; (*Mus.*) accorder; (*Phot.*) virer. *To tone down*, adoucir, pallier.

tone-colour, *n.* Timbre (de la voix etc.), *m.*

toneless, *a.* Sans éclat, sans chaleur (of voice). *Toneless voice*, voix blanche, *f.*

tone-poem, *n.* Poème symphonique, *m.*

tongs [tɔŋz], *n.pl.* Pincettes; (*Tech.*) tenailles, pinces, *f.pl.*

tongue [tʌŋ], *n.* Langue; (*Tech.*) languette, *f.*; ardillon (of a buckle), *m.* *Hold your tongue, taisez-vous! it was a slip of the tongue*, la langue lui a fourché; *to be tongue valiant*, être brave en paroles; *to give tongue* (of hounds), donner de la voix; *to have a glib tongue*, avoir la langue bien pendue; *to have on the tip of the tongue*, avoir sur le bout de la langue; *to hold one's tongue*, se taire; *to put out one's tongue*, tirer la langue (à).

tongued, *a.* À langue; (*Tech.*) à languette. *Hundred-tongued*, aux cent voix; *sweet-tongued*, mielleux.

tongueless, *a.* Sans langue; muet (speechless).

tongue-shaped, *a.* En forme de langue; (*Bot.*) en languette.

tongue-tied, *a.* Qui a le filet, qui a la langue liée; (*fig.*) réduit au silence, muet.

tongue-twister, *n.* Mot, *m.*, phrase, *f.* difficile à prononcer.

tonic ['tɔnik], *a.* and *n.* (*Med.*) Tonique, remontant, fortifiant, reconstituant, *m.*; (*Mus.*) tonique, *f.*

tonicity [to'nisiti], *n.* Tonicité, *f.*

tonight [tə'nait], *n.* Cette nuit, *f.*, ce soir, *m.*

toning ['touniŋ], *n.* Tonalité, *f.*; (*Phot.*) virage, *m.*

Tonkin [tɔŋ'kin]. Le Tonkin, *m.* **Tonkinese,** *n.* and *a.* Tonkinois, *m.*, -oise, *f.*

tonnage ['tʌnidʒ], *n.* Tonnage; (*Hist.*) droit de tonnage, *m.*

tonsil ['tɔnsil], *n.* (*Anat.*) Amygdale, *f.* **tonsillitis** or **tonsilitis,** *n.* (*Med.*) Amygdalite, inflammation des amygdales, *f.*

tonsillotomy, *n.* (*Surg.*) Amygdalotomie, *f.*

tonsure ['tɔnʃə], *n.* Tonsure, *f.*—*v.t.* Tonsurer. **tonsured,** *a.* Tonsuré.

tontine [tɔn'ti:n], *n.* Tontine, *f.*

too [tu:], *adv.* Trop, par trop; aussi, de même, également (also); d'ailleurs, de plus. *He is too much for you*, vous n'êtes pas de force à lutter avec lui; *this task is too much for you*, cette tâche est au-dessus de vos forces; *too heavy a burden*, une charge trop lourde; *too much of a good thing is good for nothing*, jeu

qui trop dure ne vaut rien; *too much* or *too many*, trop, (before a noun) trop de.
took [tuk], *past* [TAKE].
tool [tu:l], *n.* Outil, instrument, ustensile; (*fig.*) jouet, agent, *m.*, âme damnée, *f.* **tool-bag**, *n.* Sacoche, *f.* **tool-chest**, *n.* Boîte à outils, *f.* **tool-house**, *n.* Cabane aux outils, *f.*
tooling, *n.* Outillage, *m.*
toot [tu:t], *n.* Son, appel, *m.* (de trompe, de clairon, etc.).—*v.i.* Sonner, corner, klaxonner.
tooth [tu:θ], *n.* (*pl.* **teeth** [ti:θ]) Dent, *f. Back tooth*, molaire, *f.*; *eye tooth*, canine, *f.*; *first teeth*, dents de lait; *in someone's teeth*, à la figure *or* au nez de quelqu'un; *in the teeth of*, malgré, en dépit de, à l'encontre de; *in the teeth of the gale*, au plus fort de la tempête; *set of teeth*, râtelier, *m.*; *to cast in the teeth*, reprocher à, jeter au nez à *or* à la face de; *to cut one's teeth*, (of a child) faire ses dents; *to go at it tooth and nail*, s'y prendre de toutes ses forces *or* attaquer avec rage; *to have a sweet tooth*, aimer les choses sucrées; *to have a tooth out*, se faire arracher une dent; *to set the teeth on edge*, agacer les dents; *to show one's teeth*, montrer les dents; *wisdom tooth*, dent de sagesse.—*v.t.* Denteler.
toothache ['tu:θeik], *n.* Mal de dents, *m. To have a toothache*, avoir mal aux dents. **tooth-brush**, *n.* Brosse à dents, *f.* **tooth-paste**, *n.* Pâte dentifrice, *f.*, dentifrice, *m.* **tooth-pick**, *n.* Cure-dents, *m.inv.* **tooth-powder**, *n.* Poudre dentifrice, *f.*
toothed, *a.* À dents; (*Tech.*) denté; (*Bot.*) dentelé. **toothless**, *a.* Sans dents, édenté.
toothsome, *a.* Agréable au goût, savoureux, friand. **toothsomeness**, *n.* Goût agréable, *m.*
top [tɒp], *n.* Haut, sommet, *m.*; cime (of a mountain, tree, rock, etc.), *f.*; faîte (of a building); chef (of the head), *m.*; surface (of water etc.), *f.*; couvercle (cover), *m.*; (*Naut.*) hune, *f.*; chef (highest person); (*Arch.*) couronnement; dessus (of a table), *m.*; tête (head), *f.*; (*pl.*) fane (of turnips etc.), *f.*; toupie, *f.* (toy); (*pl.*) revers (of boots), *m.pl.*; (*fig.*) comble, *m. At the top of*, en haut de; *at the top of the house*, tout en haut de la maison; *from top to bottom*, du haut en bas, de fond en comble; *from top to toe*, de la tête aux pieds; *humming-top*, toupie d'Allemagne, *f.*; *peg-top*, toupie, *f.*; *to be on top* (games), avoir le dessus; *to go over the top*, monter à l'assaut; (*fam.*) sauter le pas, se marier; *whip-top*, sabot, *m.*—*a.* Premier, principal, extrême.—*v.t.* Couronner, surmonter (de); surpasser (to surpass); étêter, élaguer (to lop); atteindre le sommet de (to rise to the top of); (*Naut.*) apiquer; (*Golf*) topper. *To top and tail*, éplucher; *to top up*, remplir.—*v.i.* S'élever, monter; (*fig.*) dominer, prédominer, exceller.
topaz ['toupæz], *n.* Topaze, *f.*
top-block, *n.* (*Naut.*) Poulie de guinderesse, *f.*
top-boots, *n.pl.* Bottes à revers, *f.pl.* **top-coat**, *n.* Pardessus, *m.* **top-flight**, *a.* De première volée. **topgallant**, *a.* De perroquet.—*n.* Voile de perroquet, *f.*; mât de perroquet, *m.* **top-hat**, *n.* Chapeau haut de forme, *m.* **top-heavy**, *a.* Trop lourd du haut. **top-hole**, *a.* Épatant. **top-lantern**, *n.* Fanal de hune, *m.* **topless**, *a.* D'une hauteur infinie.
topman, *n.* Scieur de long de (dessus);

(*Naut.*) gabier, *m.* **topmast**, *n.* Mât de hune, *m.* **topmost**, *a.* Le plus haut, le plus élevé. **topnotch**, *a.* Sélect, du gratin. **top-sail**, *n.* Hunier, *m.* **topsail-yard**, *n.* Vergue de hune, *f.* **top-shaped**, *a.* Turbiné; en forme de toupie. **topside**, *n.* Tranche, *f.* (of beef). **topsides**, *n.* (*Naut.*) Œuvres mortes, *f.pl.* **topsoil**, *n.* Couche arable, *f.* **top-tackle**, *n.* Palan de guinderesse, *m.*
tope (1) [toup], *v.i.* (*colloq.*) Pinter, boire.
tope (2) [toup], *n.*, Chien de mer, *m.*
topee ['toupi], *n.* Casque colonial, *m.*
toper, *n.* Ivrogne, *m.*; (*fam.*) poivrot, *m.*
toph [touf] or **tophus** ['toufəs], *n.* Tophus, *m.*
tophaceous [tə'feiʃəs], *a.* Tophacé.
topic ['tɒpik], *n.* Matière, *f. or* sujet, *m.*, topique.
topical, *a.* D'actualité; (*Med.*) topique.
topicality, *n.* Actualité, *f.* (of a question).
topographer [tə'pɒgrəfə], *n.* Topographe, *m.*
topographic [tɒpə'græfik] or **topographical**, *a.* Topographique. **topographically**, *adv.* Topographiquement.
topography [tə'pɒgrəfi], *n.* Topographie, *f.*
topology, *n.* Topologie, *f.*
toponymy, *n.* Toponymie, *f.*
topping ['tɒpiŋ], *a.* (*slang*) Épatant.
topple [tɒpl], *v.i.* Tomber, dégringoler. *To topple over*, faire la culbute, verser (of a carriage).—*v.t.* To topple down (over), faire tomber.
topsy-turvy ['tɒpsi'tə:vi], *adv.* Sens dessus dessous. *To turn topsy-turvy*, culbuter, renverser, mettre sens dessus dessous.
tor [tɔ:], *n.* Pic rocheux, *m.*
torch [tɔ:tʃ], *n.* Torche, *f.*, flambeau, *m.* (*Electric*) *torch*, lampe électrique (de poche), *f.* **torch-bearer**, *n.* Porte-flambeau, *m.* **torch-light**, *n.* Lumière des torches, *f. Torch-light procession*, retraite aux flambeaux, *f.* **torch-thistle**, *n.* (*Bot.*) Cierge épineux, *m.*
tore, *past* [TEAR (2)].
toreador [tɔriə'dɔ:], *n.* Toréador, *m.*
torment (1) ['tɔ:mənt], *n.* Tourment, *m.*, torture, *f.*; supplice, *m.*, souffrance, *f.*
torment (2) [tɔ:'ment], *v.t.* Tourmenter, torturer, faire souffrir (de).
tormentil ['tɔ:məntil], *n.* (*Bot.*) Tormentille, *f.*
tormenting [tɔ:'mentiŋ], *a.* Tourmentant, harassant. **tormentor**, *n.* Tourmenteur, bourreau, *m.*
torn, *p.p.* [TEAR (2)].
tornado [tɔ:'neidou], *n.* Tornade, *f.*, ouragan, cyclone, *m.*
torose [tə'rous], **torous** ['tɔ:rəs], *a.* (*Bot.*) Bosselé, noueux.
torpedo [tɔ:'pi:dou], *n.* Torpille, *f.*—*v.t.* Torpiller; (*fig.*) faire échouer, saboter (un plan etc.). **torpedo-boat**, *n.* Torpilleur, *m.* **torpedo-boat-destroyer**, *n.* Contre-torpilleur, *m.* **torpedo-flat**, *n.* Compartiment des torpilles, *m.* **torpedo-tube**, *n.* Tube lance-torpilles, *m.*
torpid ['tɔ:pid], *a.* Engourdi, torpide, inerte.
torpidity [-'piditi], **torpidness**, or **torpor**, *n.* Torpeur, apathie, *f.*, engourdissement, *m.*
torque [tɔ:k], *n.* Torque, *f.* (of Gauls); (*Mech.*) couple, moment de torsion, couple moteur, *m. Armature torque*, couple d'induit, *m.* **torque-arm, -rod**, *n.* (*Mech.*) Jambe de force, *f.*
torrefaction [tɔri'fækʃən], *n.* Torréfaction, *f.*

torrefy ['tɔrifai], *v.t.* Torréfier.

torrent ['tɔrənt], *n.* Torrent, *m.* *In torrents* (of rain), à torrents, à verse.—*a.* Torrentueux, impétueux.

torrential [tɔ'renʃl], *a.* Torrentiel.

torrid ['tɔrid], *a.* Brûlant, brûlé, torride.

torridness or **torridity** [-'riditi], *n.* Chaleur brûlante, *f.*

torsel [tɔːsl], *n.* Volute, *f.*; tasseau, *m.*

torsion ['tɔːʃən], *n.* Torsion, *f.* *Torsion balance,* balance de torsion, *f.*; *torsion bar,* barre de torsion, *f.*

torso ['tɔːsou], *n.* Torse, *m.*

tort [tɔːt], *n.* (*Law*) Dommage, préjudice, *m.*

tortoise ['tɔːtəs], *n.* Tortue, *f.* **tortoiseshell,** *n.* Écaille de tortue, écaille, *f.*—*a.* D'écaille; marqué en écaille de tortue (of cats).

tortuosity [tɔːtju'ɔsiti] or **tortuousness** ['tɔːtjuəsnis], *n.* Tortuosité, *f.*

tortuous ['tɔːtjuəs], *a.* Tortueux, sinueux; (*fig.*) clandestin, secret, caché. **tortuously,** *adv.* Tortueusement.

torture ['tɔːtʃə], *v.t.* Torturer, mettre à la torture; (*fig.*) tourmenter, faire souffrir.—*n.* Torture, question, *f.*; supplice, *m.*

torturer, *n.* Bourreau, *m.* **torturingly,** *adv.* De manière à torturer.

torus ['tɔːrəs], *n.* Tore, toron, *m.*; (*Bot.*) réceptacle, *m.*

Tory ['tɔːri], *a.* and *n.* Tory, conservateur, *m.* **Toryism,** *n.* Torysme, torisme, *m.*

tosh [tɔʃ], *n.* (*fam.*) Bêtises, *f.pl.*

toss [tɔs], *n.* Action de jeter en l'air, *f.*; jet, lancement, *m.* *Toss of the head,* coup *or* mouvement de tête en arrière; encensement (of a horse), *m.*; *to win the toss,* gagner (à pile ou face).—*v.t.* Lancer *or* jeter (en l'air); ballotter (*to cause to rise and fall*); secouer (the head); (*Cook.*) faire sauter; (*fig.*) agiter, remuer, tourner et retourner. *To toss in a blanket,* berner; *to toss off,* jeter loin de soi; avaler d'un trait (to drink); *to toss up,* jeter en l'air, tirer à pile ou face.—*v.i.* S'agiter; tirer à pile ou face; se retourner (in bed); hocher la tête (to toss up). *Let us toss for sides,* tirons les camps à pile ou face.

tossing, *n.* Secousse, *f.*; ballottement; hochement, *m.*

toss-up, *n.* Coup de pile ou face, *m.*

tot (1) [tɔt], *n.* Tout(e) petit(e) enfant; goutte, *f.* (of spirituous drink). *Tiny tot,* bambin, *m.*, -ine, *f.*

tot (2) [tɔt], *v.t.* (*colloq.*) *To tot up,* additionner. —*v.i. To tot up,* s'additionner, s'élever.

total [toutl], *n.* Total, montant, *m.*, somme, *f.* —*a.* Total, complet, entier.—*v.t.* Totaliser; se monter à. **totalitarian,** *a.* (*Polit.*) Totalitaire. **totalitarianism,** *n.* Totalitarisme, *m.* **totality** [-'tæliti], *n.* Totalité, *f.*, montant, tout, *m.* **totalization,** *n.* Totalisation, *f.* **totalizator,** *n.* Totalisateur, *m.* **totalize,** *v.t.* Totaliser. **totally,** *adv.* Totalement, tout à fait, entièrement.

tote [tout], *n.* (*spt.*) Totalisateur, pari mutuel, *m.*

totem ['toutəm], *n.* Totem, *m.*

totemic [tou'temik], *a.* Totémique.

totemism ['toutəmizm], *n.* Totémisme, *m.*

totemist, *n.* Totémiste, *m.*

totter ['tɔtə], *v.i.* Chanceler; (*fig.*) vaciller, trembler. *To totter away,* s'éloigner d'un pas tremblant; *to totter to one's feet,* se lever en chancelant. **tottering,** *a.* Chancelant, tremblant, mal assuré.—*n.* Chancellement, *m.* **totteringly,** *adv.* D'une manière chancelante. **tottery,** *a.* Chancelant.

touch [tʌtʃ], *v.t.* Toucher; toucher à (to meddle with); atteindre (to reach); concerner, regarder (to concern); affecter, émouvoir (to move); (*slang*) toper (quelqu'un). *To touch off,* ébaucher, esquisser; faire partir, faire exploser (a mine etc.); *to touch one's hat to,* saluer; *to touch up,* retoucher, raviver, relever, rehausser.—*v.i.* Toucher; se toucher. *To touch at,* toucher à, aborder à, faire escale à (of ships); *to touch upon,* toucher, effleurer, (*fig.*) faire allusion à.—*n.* Le toucher (sense of feeling); contact, attouchement (contact), *m.*; pierre de touche (test), *f.*; chat (game); trait (feature), *m.*; légère attaque (of disease), *f.*; essai (trial), *m.*; (*Paint.*) touche, *f.*; (*fig.*) idée, *f.*, soupçon (small quantity), *m.* *A touch of,* un soupçon de; *a touch of the sun,* un léger coup de soleil; *it was touch and go,* il s'en est fallu de bien peu; *to be in touch with,* être au courant de, être en relation avec; *to get in touch with someone,* se mettre en rapports, entrer en contact avec quelqu'un; *to give the finishing touch to,* mettre la derniere main à; *to keep touch with,* garder le contact avec; *to lose touch with,* ne plus être en sympathie avec, (*Mil.*) perdre le contact de.

touchable, *a.* Tangible, palpable.

touch-hole, *n.* Lumière, *f.*

touchily, *adv.* Avec humeur. **touchiness,** *n.* Irascibilité, humeur chagrine, *f.* **touching,** *a.* Touchant, émouvant.—*prep.* Touchant, concernant, au sujet de (concerning). **touchingly,** *adv.* D'une manière touchante.

touch in goal, *n.* (*Rugby*) Touche de but, *f.*

touch-judge, *n.* (*Ftb.*) Arbitre de touche, *m.*

touch-line, *n.* (*Ftb.*) Ligne de touche, *f.*

touch-me-not, *n.* Noli me tangere, *m.*, balsamine des bois, *f.* **touch-needle,** *n.* Touchau, *m.* **touch-paper,** *n.* Papier d'amorce, *m.* **touchstone,** *n.* Pierre de touche, *f.* **touch-wood,** *n.* Amadou, *m.*

touchy, *a.* Irritable, susceptible.

tough [tʌf], *a.* Dur, raide, résistant, tenace; coriace (of meat); fort, solide (strong); inflexible, obstiné (inflexible); épineux, difficile (difficult). *A tough job,* une rude tâche.—*n.* Apache, bandit, *m.*

toughen [tʌfn], *v.t.* Durcir.—*v.i.* S'endurcir. **toughish,** *a.* Un peu dur. **toughly,** *adv.* Durement, avec ténacité; vigoureusement. **toughness,** *n.* Raideur, ténacité; dureté, nature coriace (of meat etc.); (*fig.*) difficulté, *f.*

toupee [tu'piː], *n.* Toupet, *m.*

tour [tuə], *n.* Tour, voyage, *m.*; randonnée; tournée, *f.* *On tour,* en tournée (of actors, inspectors, etc.).—*v.t.* Voyager dans un pays; aller en tournée (of actors); visiter (un pays). —*v.i.* Voyager dans un pays; excursionner.

touring, *n.* Le tourisme, *m.* *Touring car,* automobile de tourisme, *f.*; *touring company,* (*Theat.*) troupe en tournée, *f.* **tourism,** *n.* Tourisme, *m.* **tourist,** *n.* Touriste, voyageur, *m.* **tourist-agency, -office,** *n.* Bureau de tourisme, syndicat d'initiative, *m.* **tourist-ticket,** *n.* Billet circulaire *or* d'excursion, *m.*

tournament ['tuə- *or* 'tɔːnəmənt) *or* ***tourney**
['tuəni], *n.* Tournoi; concours, match
(sporting contest), *m.*
tourniquet ['tuənikei], *n.* Garrot, *m.*
tousle [tauzl], *v.t.* Tirailler, houspiller,
chiffonner. *Tousled hair*, cheveux ébouriffés.
tout (1) [taut], *v.i.* Racoler, courir après les
pratiques. *To tout for*, pister, racoler. **tout**
(2) *or* **touter**, *n.* Placier, racoleur, pisteur,
m. **touting**, *n.* Racolage, *m.*
tow [tou], *n.* Filasse, étoupe (hemp); remorque,
f. In tow, à la remorque.—*v.t.* Remorquer,
touer, haler. **tow-boat**, *n.* Remorqueur, *m.*
tow-path, *n.* Chemin de halage, *m.*
towage, *n.* Remorquage, touage, halage, *m.*
towline [TOWING-LINE].
toward (1) *or* **towards** [tɔːdz, 'tɔədz, tu'wɔːdz,
'twɔːdz], *prep.* Vers, envers; du côté de; à
l'égard de (with respect to); sur, environ (of
time). ***toward** (2) ['touəd] *or* **towardly**,
a. Docile; intelligent; proche.
towel ['tauəl], *n.* Essuie-mains, *m.*, serviette,
f. Bath towel, serviette de bain, *f.*; *roller-
towel*, essuie-mains sans fin, à rouleau, *m.*
towel-horse, *n.* Porte-serviettes (mobile),
m. **towel-rail**, *n.* Porte-serviettes, *m.inv.*
towelling, *n.* Toile pour serviettes, *f.*; tissu-
éponge, *m.*; friction, *f.*, (*fam.*) râclée, *f.*
tower ['tauə], *n.* Tour, *f. A tower of strength*,
un puissant appui, *m.*; (*Av.*) *control tower*,
tour de contrôle, *f.*—*v.i.* S'élever (au-dessus
de), planer, dominer. **towered**, *a.* À tours,
défendu par des tours. **towering**, *a.* Élevé
comme une tour; dominant; violent. *A
towering rage*, une colère bleue. **towery**, *a.*
Flanqué de tours.
towing ['touiŋ], *n.* Remorque, *f.*; halage (on
canals), *m.* **towing-boat**, *n.* Remorqueur,
toueur, *m.* **towing-line** *or* **-rope**, *n.* Câble
de remorque, *m.*, remorque, *f.* **tow(ing)-
path**, *n.* Chemin de halage, *m.*
town [taun], *n.* Ville, *f. A man about town*, un
mondain, *m.*; *chief town*, chef-lieu, *m.*; *country
town*, villè de province; *in town*, en ville, à
Londres; *out of town*, à la campagne; *to go to
town*, aller à Londres, aller en ville; (*fig.*)
faire quelque chose à fond, s'étendre (sur un
sujet); s'en donner à cœur joie; *town hall*,
hôtel de ville, *m.*; *town surveyor*, inspecteur
des travaux publics, *m.*; *woman about town*,
mondaine, demi-mondaine, *f.*
town-clerk, *n.* Secrétaire de mairie; (in
England) chef du secrétariat municipal, *m.*
town-council, *n.* Conseil municipal, *m.*
town-councillor, *n.* Conseiller municipal,
m. **town-due**, *n.* Droit d'entrée, octroi, *m.*
town-planner, *n.* Urbaniste; architecte-
urbaniste, *m.* **town-planning**, *n.* Urbanisme, *m.*, architecture urbaine, *f.*, aménagement urbain, *m.* **townsman**, *n.* (*pl.* **towns-
men**) Habitant de la ville, bourgeois;
concitoyen (of the same town), *m.* **towns-
people** *or* **towns-folk**, *n.* Habitants (de la
ville), bourgeois, citadins, *m.pl.*
townish, *a.* De ville. **township**, *n.* Commune; étendue territoriale d'une ville, *f.*
townward, *adv.* Vers la ville; du côté de la
ville.
toxic ['tɔksik], *a. and n.* Toxique, *m.*
toxicological [tɔksikə'lɔdʒikl], *a.* Toxicologique. **toxicologist** [-'kɔlədʒist], *n.* Toxicologue, *m.* **toxicology**, *n.* Toxicologie, *f.*

toxicosis [-'kousis], *n.* Toxicose, *f.* **toxin**,
n. Toxine, *f.*
toy [tɔi], *n.* Jouet, joujou; (*fig.*) brimborion,
colifichet, jeu, *m.*, bagatelle, niaiserie, futilité,
f. Toy dog, bichon, *m*; *toy-soldier*, soldat de
plomb.—*v.i.* Jouer; folâtrer, s'amuser (avec).
To toy with an idea, caresser une idée. **toy-
box**, *n.* Boîte à joujoux, *f.* **toyman** *or*
toy-dealer, *n.* Marchand de jouets, *m.*
toy-shop, *n.* Magasin de jouets, *m.*
*toyish, *a.* Badin, folâtre. ***toyishness**, *n.*
Humeur badine, *f.*
trabeation [treibi'eiʃən], *n.* Trabéation, *f.*;
entablement, *m.*
trabecular [trə'bekjulə], *a.* Trabéculaire.
trace [treis], *n.* Trace, *f.*; tracé (outline, plan,
etc.); (*pl.*) trait (harness), *m.*—*v.t.* Tracer;
calquer (in drawing); suivre à la piste, suivre
la trace de (to track); (*fig.*) remonter à
l'origine de. *To trace back*, remonter à; *to
trace out*, tracer, découvrir; *to trace the origin
of*, découvrir l'origine de. **traceable**, *a.* Que
l'on peut tracer. **tracer**, *n.* Traceur;
traçoir (instrument), *m. Tracer bullet*, balle
traçante, *f.* **tracery**, *n.* (*Arch.*) Réseau, *m.*,
meneaux, *m.pl.*
trachea ['treikiə *or* trə'kiːə], *n.* (*Anat.*)
Trachée-artère; (*Bot.*) trachée, *f.* **tracheal**,
a. Trachéal. **trachean**, *a.* Trachéen.
tracheotomy [treiki'ɔtəmi], *n.* Trachéotomie, *f.*
trachytic [trə'kitik], *a.* Trachytique.
tracing ['treisiŋ], *n.* Tracé, tracement; calque
(drawing), *m.* **tracing-paper**, *n.* Papier à
calquer, *m.*
track [træk], *n.* Piste, *f.*, chemin (road),
sentier, *m.*; (*Hunt.*) piste; (*Rail.*) voie;
(*Astron.*) orbite, *f.*, cours; sillage (of a ship),
m.; (*fig.*) ornière (rut), *f. Beaten track*,
sentier battu, *m.*; *cart track*, chemin de terre,
m.; (*Cine.*) *sound track*, bande sonore, *f.*; *to
make tracks*, s'en aller précipitamment, filer;
to throw off the track, dépister.—*v.t.* Suivre
à la piste; haler, remorquer (to tow). **track-
racing**, *n.* Courses de, sur, piste, *f.pl.*
track-road, *n.* Chemin de halage, *m.*
track-suit, *n.* (*spt.*) Survêtement, *m.*
tracker, *n.* Traqueur, *m.* (*Australia*) *Black
tracker*, dépisteur, traqueur, aborigène, *m.*
tracking, *n.* Action de suivre à la trace, *f.*;
halage (towing), *m.* **trackless**, *a.* Sans
trace; non frayé, sans chemins; vierge.
tract [trækt], *n.* Étendue; contrée, région, *f.*,
district (region); espace, *m.*, durée (of time),
f.; opuscule, traité; tract, *m.*, brochure (small
book), *f.*
tractability [træktə'biliti], **tractableness**, *n.*
Nature traitable, docilité, douceur, *f.*
tractable ['træktəbl], *a.* Traitable, maniable,
docile, doux. **tractably**, *adv.* D'une manière
traitable, docilement.
Tractarian [træk'tɛəriən], *a. and n.* Trac-
tarien, *m.* **Tractarianism**, *n.* Tractaria-
nisme, *m.*
tractile ['træktail], *a.* Traitable, ductile.
tractility [-'tiliti], *n.* Ductilité, *f.*
traction ['trækʃən], *n.* Traction, tension;
attraction, *f.* **traction-engine**, *n.* Locomotive routière, *f.* **tractive**, *a.* De traction,
tractoire. **tractor**, *n.* Tracteur, *m.* (*Mil.*)
Tractor-drawn artillery, artillerie tractée, *f.*
trade [treid], *n.* Commerce, trafic, négoce;

emploi, état, métier, *m.*, profession (calling); industrie (manufacture), *f.*; corps de métier (men engaged in the same occupation), *m. A Jack of all trades*, un maître Jacques; *Board of Trade*, Ministère du Commerce, *m.*; *by trade*, de son état, de son métier; *every one to his trade*, chacun son métier; *free trade*, libre-échange, *m.*; *in trade*, dans les affaires, dans le commerce; *the trade supplied*, on vend en gros et en détail; *to be good for trade*, faire aller le commerce; *to be in the trade*, être du métier, (*fam.*) être du bâtiment; *to carry on one's trade*, faire son métier; *to carry on the trade of*, faire le commerce de; *to drive a roaring trade*, faire d'excellentes affaires, faire des affaires d'or; *to learn a trade*, apprendre un métier; *trade disputes*, les conflits du travail, *m.pl.*; *trade is at a standstill*, le commerce est nul; *trade is slack*, les affaires ne vont pas; (*Comm.*) *trade name*, marque déposée, *f.*—*v.i.* Trafiquer, commercer, faire le commerce (de). *To trade in*, faire le commerce de; *to trade upon*, spéculer sur, exploiter; *to trade with*, faire des affaires avec.
trade-allowance, *n.* Remise, *f.* **trade-mark**, *n.* Marque de fabrique, *f.*
trader, *n.* Négociant, *m.*, -ante, *f.*; commerçant, *m.*, -ante, *f.*; trafiquant; traitant (in slave-trade), *m.*; vaisseau marchand (ship), *m. Free-trader*, libre-échangiste, *m.*
tradesman, *n.* (*pl.* **tradesmen**) Marchand, commerçant, boutiquier (shop-keeper); fournisseur, *m. Tradesmen's entrance*, entrée des fournisseurs, de service, *f.* **tradespeople** or **tradesfolk**, *n.pl.* Commerçants, marchands, fournisseurs, *m.pl.* **tradeswoman**, *n.* Commerçante, marchande, *f.* **trade-union**, *n.* Syndicat ouvrier, *m.* **trade-unionism**, *n.* Syndicalisme, *m.* **trade-unionist**, *n.* Syndiqué, *m.*, -ée, *f.*; syndicaliste. **trade-winds**, *n.pl.* Vents alizés, *m.pl.*
trading, *n.* Négoce, commerce, trafic, *m.*—*a.* Commerçant, marchand, de commerce. *Trading-post*, comptoir, *m.*
tradition [tra'diʃən], *n.* Tradition, *f.* **traditional**, *a.* Traditionnel. **traditionally**, *adv.* Traditionnellement.
traditor ['treiditə], *n.* Traditeur, *m.*
traduce [trə'djuːs], *v.t.* Diffamer, calomnier, médire de. **traducer**, *n.* Calomniateur, *m.*, calomniatrice, *f.*; diffamateur, *m.*, diffamatrice, *f.*
traffic ['træfik], *n.* Trafic; commerce, négoce, *m.*; circulation (going and coming), *f.*; (*Rail.*) mouvement, trafic, *m.*; marchandises (commodities), *f.pl. Beware of traffic*, attention aux voitures! *Block in the traffic*, *traffic jam*, embouteillage, encombrement, *m.*; *opened for traffic*, livré à la circulation; *road traffic*, circulation routière, *f.*, roulage, *m.*; *there is much traffic in the streets*, il y a beaucoup de mouvement, de circulation, dans les rues; (*Am.*) *traffic circle*, rondpoint, sens giratoire, *m.*—*v.i.* Trafiquer, commercer.
trafficator, *n.* Flèche, *f.*; signal, signalisa- 'teur, *m.*
trafficker, *n.* Trafiquant, *m.*
traffic-light, *n.* Feu, *m.*
traffic-manager, *n.* Chef du mouvement, *m.*
traffic-returns, *n.pl.* Compte des recettes, *m.*
tragacanth ['trægəkænθ], *n.* (*Bot.*) Tragacanthe, *f.*

tragedian [trə'dʒiːdiən], *n.* Auteur tragique, *m.*; tragédien, *m.*, tragédienne, *f.*
tragedy ['trædʒədi], *n.* Tragédie, *f.* **tragic** or **tragical**, *a.* Tragique. **tragically**, *adv.* Tragiquement; au tragique. **tragi-comedy**, *n.* Tragi-comédie, *f.* **tragi-comical**, *a.* Tragi-comique.
trail [treil], *n.* Traînée; (*Hunt.*) trace, piste, voie; (*Artill.*) crosse de l'affût (of a gun-carriage), *f. In the trail of*, à la suite de; *on the trail*, sur la piste.—*v.i.* Traîner.—*v.t.* Suivre à la piste; traîner (to drag).
trailer, *n.* (Voiturette) remorque (bicycle, tram, etc.), *f.*; (*Am.*) roulotte, caravane, *f.*; (*Cine.*) bande de lancement, *f.* (of a film).
trail-net, *n.* Traîneau, chalut, *m.*
train [trein], *n.* Suite, *f.*, cortège (retinue), *m.*; série, *f.*, enchaînement (series), *m.*; traînée (of gunpowder); queue, traîne (of a dress), *f.*; train, convoi; (*fig.*) enchaînement, *m.*, succession, *f.*; *artifice (stratagem), *m. Armoured train*, train blindé; *breakdown train*, train de secours; *corridor train*, train à couloirs; *down train*, train descendant; *excursion train*, train de plaisir; *fast train*, (train) rapide; *goods train*, train de marchandises, de petite vitesse; *in the train of*, à la suite de; *mixed train*, train mixte; *passenger train*, train de voyageurs; *return train*, train de retour; *siege train*, équipage de siège, *m.*; *the next train*, le prochain train, le train suivant; *tidal train*, train de marée; *to go by train*, aller par le train, en chemin de fer; *up train*, train montant.—*v.t.* Former; exercer, élever, instruire; traîner (to draw along); diriger (trees etc.); dresser, entraîner (horses etc.). *To train (a gun)*, pointer; *to train up*, dresser, élever, instruire, former. *A well-trained servant*, un serviteur bien stylé; *a well-trained dog*, un chien bien dressé.—*v.i.* S'entraîner, faire l'exercice.
***train-band**, *n.* Compagnie de la milice bourgeoise, *f.* **train-bearer**, *n.* Porte-queue, *m.*
trainee [trei'niː], *n.* Stagiaire; (*spt.*) poulain, *m.*
trainer, *n.* Dresseur; entraîneur (of athletes, race-horses); (*Am.*) pointeur, *m.*; avion-école, *m.*
training, *n.* Éducation, instruction, discipline, *f.*; dressage (of horses); entraînement (of race-horses), *m. Further training course*, cours de perfectionnement, *m.*; *training college*, école normale primaire, *f.*; *training school*, école professionnelle, *f.*; *to be in training*, être en forme; *to be training*, être à l'entraînement. **training-ship**, *n.* Vaisseau-école, *m.*
train-oil, *n.* Huile de baleine, *f.* **train-service**, *n.* Service des trains, *m.*
traipse, *v.i.* [TRAPES].
trait [trei or treit], *n.* Trait, *m.*
traitor ['treitə], *n.* Traître, *m. To turn traitor*, passer à l'ennemi, se vendre. **traitorous**, *a.* Traître, perfide. **traitorously**, *adv.* En traître, traîtreusement, perfidement. **traitress**, *n.* Traîtresse, *f.*
trajectory [trə'dʒektəri], *n.* Trajectoire, *f.*
tram(-car) [træm], *n.* Tramway, *m. Tram service*, service de tramways, *m.* **tram-line**, **tram-road**, or **tramway**, *n.* Ligne de tramway, *f.*; tramway, *m.* **tram-lines**, *n.pl*

Rails de tramway, *m.pl.* **tram-rail,** *n.* Rail à ornière, *m.*

trammel [træml], *n.* Tramail (net), *m.*; entrave (clog), *f.*; (*fig.*) entrave, *f.—v.t.* Entraver, embarrasser, empêtrer (de).

tramontana [træmɔn'tɑːnə], *n.* La tramontane (wind), *f.*

tramontane [trə'mɔntein *or* træmɔn'tein], *a.* Ultramontain, d'outre-monts, étranger.

tramp [træmp], *v.i.* Aller à pied, marcher lourdement; courir le pays.—*v.t.* Faire à pied, faire.—*n.* Promenade, randonnée (à pied), *f.*; bruit de pas, piétinement (stamp); vagabond, clochard, trimardeur, *m.*

trample [træmpl], *v.t.* Fouler (aux pieds), marcher sur, piétiner. *To trample down,* écraser; *to trample under foot,* fouler aux pieds.

trampling, *n.* Piétinement, bruit de pas, *m.*

trance [trɑːns], *n.* Extase; (*Path.*) catalepsie, *f.* *To fall into a trance,* tomber en extase; *to be in a hypnotic trance,* être en état d'hypnose.

tranquil [ˈtræŋkwil], *a.* Tranquille. **tranquillity** [-ˈkwiliti] *or* **tranquilness,** *n.* Tranquillité, quiétude, *f.*, calme, *m.* **tranquillization** [-aiˈzeiʃən], *n.* Tranquillisation, *f.* **tranquillize,** *v.t.* Tranquilliser, calmer. **tranquillizer,** *n.* Calmant, *m.* **tranquillizing,** *a.* Tranquillisant. **tranquilly,** *adv.* Tranquillement.

transact [trænˈzækt], *v.t.* Traiter, expédier. *To transact business,* faire des affaires, être en affaires (avec). **transaction,** *n.* Transaction, affaire, opération, *f.* *Cash transaction,* opération au comptant; *the transactions of the Royal Society,* les travaux, les comptesrendus de la Société royale, *m.pl.* **transactor,** *n.* Négociateur, *m.*

transalpine [trænˈzælpain], *a.* Transalpin.

trans-American, *a.* Transaméricain.

transatlantic [trænzətˈlæntik], *a.* Transatlantique.

transcend [trænˈsend], *v.t.* Dépasser, surpasser, exceller. **transcendence** *or* **transcendency,** *n.* Excellence, transcendance, *f.* **transcendent,** *a.* Transcendant. **transcendental** [-ˈdentl], *a.* Transcendantal. **transcendentalism,** *n.* Transcendantalisme, *m.* **transcendentalist,** *n.* Transcendantaliste, *m.* **transcendently,** *adv.* Au suprême degré.

transcontinental [trænzkontiˈnentl], *a.* Transcontinental, -e. *The transcontinental train,* le transcontinental.

transcribe [trænˈskraib], *v.t.* Transcrire, copier. **transcriber,** *n.* Copiste, transcripteur, *m.*

transcript [ˈtrænskript], *n.* Copie, *f.* **transcription** [-ˈskripʃen], *n.* Transcription, *f.*

transept [ˈtrænsept], *n.* Transept, *m.*

transfer (1) [trænsˈfəː], *v.t.* Transporter; (*Law*) transférer, céder, traduire; calquer, décalquer; (*sch.*) changer (de classe).

transfer (2) [ˈtrænsfəː], *n.* Copie, *f.*; calque, décalque, *m.*; (*Lithography*) transport; (*Law*) transfert, *m.*, cession, *f.* *Transfer-picture,* décalcomanie, *f.* **transferability,** *n.* Transmissibilité, *f.* **transferable** [ˈtrænsfərəbl], *a.* Transportable, transférable, transmissible. *Not transferable* (of tickets), personnel. **transferee** [-ˈriː], *n.* Cessionnaire, *m.*

transference [ˈtrænsfərəns], *n.* Transfèrement, *m.*; (*Psych.*) transfert affectif, *m.* *Thought-transference,* télépathie, *f.* **transferer** [-ˈfəːrə], *n.* Cédant, *m.*

transfiguration [trænsfigjuˈreiʃən], *n.* Transfiguration, transformation, *f.*

transfigure [trænsˈfigə *or* -ˈfigjə], *v.t.* Transfigurer, transformer.

transfix [trænsˈfiks], *v.t.* Transpercer; (*colloq.*) pétrifier.

transform [trænsˈfɔːm], *v.t.* Transformer, changer, convertir (en).—*v.i.* Se transformer (en). **transformable,** *a.* Transformable, convertissable. **transformation** [-fəˈmeiʃən], *n.* Transformation, *f.*, changement, *m.*, conversion, métamorphose, *f.* *Transformation scene,* changement à vue, *m.* **transformer,** *n.* Transformateur, *m.* **transforming,** *a.* Qui transforme, qui change.

transfuse [trænsˈfjuːz], *v.t.* Transfuser, faire passer (dans). **transfusion** [-ˈfjuːʒən], *n.* Transfusion, *f.* **transfusionist,** *n.* Transfuseur, *m.*

transgress [trænsˈgres *or* trænzˈgres], *v.t.* Transgresser, enfreindre, contrevenir à.—*v.i.* Transgresser, pécher. **transgression** [-ˈgreʃən], *n.* Transgression, violation, infraction, *f.*, péché, *m.* **transgressive** [-ˈgresiv], *a.* Coupable. **transgressor,** *n.* *Transgresseur, violateur, *m.*, -trice, *f.*; pécheur, *m.*, pécheresse, *f.*

tranship [trænˈʃip], *v.t.* Transborder. **transhipment,** *n.* Transbordement, *m.*

transience [ˈtrænsiəns] *or* **transientness,** *n.* Nature transitoire, courte durée, *f.* **transient,** *a.* Passager, transitoire, momentané. **transiently,** *adv.* En passant, rapidement.

transire [trænˈsaiəri], *n.* (*Customs*) Acquit à caution, passavant, *m.*

transit [ˈtrænsit *or* ˈtrænzit], *n.* Passage; (*Customs*) transit, *m.* *In transit,* en transit. **transit-duty,** *n.* Droit de transit, *m.* **transit instrument,** *n.* (*Astron.*) Lunette méridienne, *f.*

transition [-ˈsiʒən], *n.* Transition, *f.* **transitional,** *a.* De transition.

transitive [ˈtrænsitiv], *a.* Qui passe; (*Gram.*) transitif.

transitorily, *adv.* Transitoirement. **transitoriness,** *n.* Nature transitoire, brièveté, courte durée, *f.* **transitory,** *a.* Transitoire, passager.

translatable [trænsˈleitəbl *or* trænzˈleitəbl], *a.* Traduisible. **translate,** *v.t.* Traduire; enlever au ciel (to convey to heaven); transférer (a bishop); (*fig.*) interpréter. **translation** [-ˈleiʃən], *n.* Traduction; translation (of a bishop), *f.* **translator,** *n.* Traducteur, *m.* **translatress,** *n.* Traductrice, *f.*

transliterate [trænzˈlitəreit], *v.t.* Transcrire. **transliteration,** *n.* Transcription, *f.*

translucence [trænzˈljuːsəns] *or* **translucency,** *n.* Transparence, translucidité, diaphanéité, *f.* **translucent** *or* ***translucid,** *a.* Transparent, translucide, diaphane.

transmarine [trænzməˈriːn], *a.* D'outre-mer, transmarin.

transmigrate [ˈtrænzmaigreit], *v.i.* Passer d'un corps dans un autre; émigrer. **transmigration** [-ˈgreiʃən], *n.* Transmigration; métempsycose (of souls), *f.*

transmissibility [trænzmisi'biliti], *n.* Transmissibilité, *f.* **transmissible** [-'misibl], *a.* Transmissible. **transmission** [-'miʃən], *n.* Transmission, *f.* **transmissive,** *a.* De transmission. **transmit** [-'mit], *v.t.* Transmettre, envoyer. **transmittal,** *n.* Transmission, *f.* **transmitter,** *n.* Personne qui transmet, *f.*; (*Elec.*) transmetteur, *m.*; (*Rad.*) émetteur, *m.* *Transmitter-receiver*, émetteur-récepteur, *m.*

transmogrification [trænzmɔgrifi'keiʃən], *n.* (*facet.*) Métamorphose, *f.* **transmogrify,** *v.t.* Métamorphoser, transformer, changer.

transmutability [trænzmjutə'biliti], *n.* Transmutabilité, *f.* **transmutable** [-'mju:təbl], *a.* Transmuable. **transmutation** [-'teiʃən], *n.* Transmutation, transformation, *f.*; changement (of colours), *m.* **transmute** [-'mju:t], *v.t.* Transmuer, transformer, convertir. **transmuter,** *n.* Transmutateur, *m.*

transom ['trænsəm], *n.* Traverse (de fenêtre), imposte, *f.*, vasistas, *m.*; barre d'arcasse (of a ship), *f.* *Transom-window*, fenêtre à meneau, *f.*

transparence [træns'pɛərəns], **transparency,** or **transparentness,** *n.* Transparence, *f.* *A transparency*, une diapositive, *f.*, un transparent (picture), *m.* **transparent,** *a.* Transparent, diaphane; (*fam.*) cousu de fil blanc. **transparently,** *adv.* Avec transparence; clairement, évidemment. *He is so transparently honest*, il est si évidemment honnête.

transpierce [træns'piəs], *v.t.* Transpercer.

transpiration [trænspi'reiʃən *or* trænz-], *n.* Transpiration, *f.*

transpire [træns'paiə *or* trænz-], *v.i.* Transpirer; (*fig.*) s'ébruiter; arriver, avoir lieu.

transplant [træns'pla:nt *or* trænz-], *v.t.* Transplanter; (*fig.*) déplacer. **transplantation** [-'teiʃən], *n.* Transplantation, *f.*, déplacement, *m.* **transplanter,** *n.* Transplanteur; transplantoir (tool), *m.* **transplanting,** *n.* Transplantation, *f.*

transport (1) ['trænspɔ:t], *n.* Transport; *forçat, déporté (convict), *m.* (*Av.*) *Transport plane*, avion de transport, *m.*

transport (2) [træns'pɔ:t], *v.t.* Transporter; déporter (convicts). *To be transported with joy*, être transporté de joie, être dans le ravissement; *to transport with*, transporter de.

transportable, *a.* Transportable; (*Law*) sujet à la déportation. **transportation** [-'teiʃən], *n.* Transport, *m.*; déportation (of convicts), *f.* **transportedly,** *adv.* En extase, *f.* **transporter,** *n.* Entrepreneur de transports; chargé du transport (de quelque chose); (pont) transbordeur. **transporting,** *a.* Ravissant, transportant.

transport-officer, *n.* Officier de ravitaillement, *m.*

transposal [træns'pouzl], **transposing,** or **transposition** [-pə'ziʃən], *n.* Transposition, *f.* **transpose** [-'pouz], *v.t.* Transposer. **transposing,** *a.* Transpositeur. **transpositive** [-'pɔzitiv], *a.* Transpositif.

trans-Saharan [trænssə'ha:rən], *a.* Trans-saharien.

trans-Siberian [trænssai'biəriən], *a.* Trans-sibérien.

transubstantiate [trænsəb'stænʃieit], *v.t.*

Transsubstantier. **transubstantiation** [-'eiʃən], *n.* Transsubstantiation, *f.*

transudation [trænsju'deiʃən], *n.* Transsudation, *f.* **transude** [-'sju:d], *v.i.* Transsuder.

Transvaal (the) ['trænzvɑ:l]. Le Transvaal, *m.*

transversal [trænz'və:sl], *a.* Transversal. **transversally** or **transversely,** *adv.* En travers, transversalement. **transverse,** *a.* Transverse, transversal.

Transylvania [trænsil'veinjə]. La Transylvanie, *f.* **Transylvanian,** *a.* and *n.* Transylvanien.

trap [træp], *n.* Trappe, *f.*, piège, traquenard, traquet, *m.*; carriole, petite voiture (vehicle), *f.*; (*Geol.*) trapp, *m.*; (*pl.*) effets, *m.pl.*, hardes, *f.pl.*, bagage, *m.* *Air-trap, gas-trap*, siphon, *m.*; *police trap*, zone de contrôle de vitesse, *f.*; souricière (for criminals), *f.*; *to be caught in the trap*, se laisser prendre au piège, donner dans le panneau.—*v.t.* Prendre au piège, attraper; harnacher, caparaçonner (a horse); (*Ftb.*) bloquer.

trap-door, *n.* Trappe, *f.*; abattant, *m.* *Trap-door spider*, mygale, *f.*

trapes, trapse [treips], *v.i.* (*colloq.*) Traîner çà et là, courir les rues (*or* les champs).

trapeze [trə'pi:z], *n.* Trapèze, *m.* *To perform on the flying trapeze*, faire de la voltige. **trapeziform,** *a.* Trapéziforme. **trapezium,** *n.* (*Geom.*) Trapèze; (*Anat.*) os trapèze, *m.* **trapezoidal** [træpi'zɔidl], *a.* Trapézoïdal.

trapper ['træpə], *n.* Trappeur, tendeur de pièges, coureur des bois (Canada), *m.*

trappings, *n.pl.* Harnachement, harnais, *m.*, ornements (du harnais), *m.pl.*; (*fig.*) parure, *f.*, atours, *m.pl.* *The trappings of courts*, la livrée des cours, *f.*; *the trappings of woe*, les vêtements de deuil, *m.pl.*

Trappist ['træpist], *a.* and *n.* Trappiste, *m.*

trap-shooting, *n.* Tir aux pigeons, *m.*

trash [træʃ], *n.* Rebut, *m.*; drogue, camelote, *f.*; vaurien (person); fatras, *m.*, fadaises (writings), *f.pl.*; bagasse (bruised canes), *f.* (*Am.*)*White trash*, les pauvres de race blanche (dans les états du Sud). **trashy,** *a.* De rebut, de camelote, sans valeur, de rien.

trauma ['trɔ:mə], *n.* Trauma; traumatisme, *m.* **traumatic** [trɔ:'mætik], *a.* Traumatique. **traumatism** ['trɔ:mətizm], *n.* Traumatisme, *m.*

travail ['træveil], *n.* *Dur travail, *m.*, fatigue, *f.*; travail d'enfant, *m.* *To be in travail*, être en travail; *travail pains, pangs*, douleurs de l'enfantement, *f.pl.*—*v.i.* Travailler.

trave [treiv], *n.* Travail (*pl.* travails) (for a horse), *m.*; traverse, *f.*

travel [trævl], *v.i.* Voyager, être en voyage; cheminer, marcher, aller; circuler, voyager (of news). *To travel on foot*, voyager à pied; *to travel over*, parcourir; faire.—*v.t.* Parcourir; faire (a distance etc.). *We travelled thirty miles in one day*, nous fîmes trente milles en un jour.—*n.* Voyage, *m.* *Travel agency*, bureau de tourisme, *m.*

travelled, *a.* Qui a beaucoup voyagé; exploré (of a country). **traveller,** *n.* Voyageur, *m.*, voyageuse, *f.*; (*Comm.*) commis voyageur; (*Naut.*) rocambeau, *m.* *Commercial traveller*, voyageur de commerce, représentant, *m.*; *fellow-traveller*, compagnon de voyage, (*Polit.*) sympathisant; *travellers tell fine tales*, a beau mentir qui vient de loin. **traveller's**

cheque, *n.* Chèque de voyage, *m.* **traveller's joy,** *n.* Clématite des haies, herbe aux gueux, *f.* **travelling,** *n.* Voyage, *m.*, voyages, *m.pl.* —*a.* Voyageur, de voyage; ambulant (itinerant). *Travelling expenses,* frais de déplacement, de voyage, *m.pl.*; *travelling post-office,* bureau de poste ambulant, *m.*; *travelling requisites,* articles de voyage, *m.pl.*— (*Cine.*) *travelling shot,* travelling, *m.* **travelling-bag,** *n.* Sac de voyage, *m.* **travelling-case,** *n.* Nécessaire de voyage, *m.* **travelling-rug,** *n.* Couverture de voyage, *f.* **travelling-scholarship,** *n.* Bourse de voyage, *f.*

travelogue, *n.* Film de tourisme, *m.*

travel-stained, *a.* (Vêtements) souillés par le voyage, *m.pl.*

traversable ['trævəsəbl], *a.* Qu'on peut traverser; (*Law*) contestable. **traverse,** *n.* Traversée; traverse, *f.*, (*fig.*) obstacle, *m.*; (*Naut.*) bordée, route oblique, *f.*—*a.* Oblique, transversal.—*adv.* À travers, en travers.— *v.t.* Traverser; (*Law*) nier, dénier; (*Artill.*) pointer.—*v.i.* Tourner, pivoter (of compass).

travertin ['trævətin], *n.* Travertin, *m.*

travesty ['trævəsti], *n.* Travestissement, *m.*, parodie, *f.*—*v.t.* Travestir, parodier.

trawl [trɔːl], *n.* Chalut (net), *m.*—*v.i.* Pêcher au chalut. **trawler,** *n.* Chalutier; bateau chalutier, *m.* *Steam-trawler,* chalutier à vapeur, *m.* **trawling,** *n.* Pêche au chalut, *f.*

tray [trei], *n.* Plateau, *m.*; auge, *f.*; baquet (trough); (*Phot. Cine.*), bac, *m.* *Ash-tray,* cendrier, *m.*

treacherous ['tretʃərəs], *a.* Traître, perfide. **treacherously,** *adv.* En traître, perfidement, traîtreusement. **treachery,** *n.* Trahison, perfidie, *f.*

treacle [triːkl], *n.* Mélasse, *f.*—*v.t.* Enduire de mélasse, engluer. **treacly,** *a.* Qui est comme de la mélasse; (*fig.*) mielleux.

tread [tred], *v.i.* (*past* **trod,** *p.p.* **trodden**) Mettre le pied, marcher (sur); se poser (of the feet). *To tread in the footsteps of,* marcher sur les traces de; *to tread on,* marcher sur, fouler aux pieds.—*v.t.* Fouler, écraser. *To tread the stage* or *the boards,* parcourir la scène, monter sur les planches, être acteur; *to tread under foot,* fouler aux pieds; *to tread water,* nager debout.—*n.* Pas, *m.*; allure (of a horse); marche (of a stair), *f. Anti-skid tread,* roulement anti-dérapant, *m.*; *the tread of a tyre,* la bande de roulement, la chape or la semelle d'un pneu; *with measured tread,* à pas mesurés, d'un pas majestueux.

treading, *n.* Pas, *m.*; marche, *f.*; foulage (of grapes etc.), *m.*; (*Cycl.*) distance entre les deux pédales, *f. Treading out,* écrasement, *m.*

treadle [tredl], *n.* Marche; pédale, *f.*

treadmill, *n.* *Moulin de discipline, *m.*

treason [triːzn], *n.* Trahison, *f. High treason,* haute trahison, lèse-majesté, *f.*; *treason felony,* complot contre la sûreté de l'État, *m.* **treasonable,** *a.* De trahison, de lèse-majesté. **treasonably,** *adv.* Par trahison, traîtreusement.

treasure ['treʒə], *n.* Trésor, *m.*—*v.t.* Garder, thésauriser, priser. *To treasure up,* conserver précieusement.

treasure-house, *n.* Trésor, *m.*

treasure-hunt, *n.* Chasse au trésor, *f.*

treasurer, *n.* Trésorier, *m.*

treasurership, *n.* Charge de trésorier, *f.*

treasure-trove, *n.* Trésor trouvé, *m.*

treasury, *n.* Trésor, trésor public, *m.*, finances, *f.pl.*, trésorerie, *f. First Lord of the Treasury,* Président du Conseil (des ministres), *m.*

treat [triːt], *v.t.* Traiter; régaler (de); soigner. *To treat kindly,* traiter avec bonté, montrer de l'amitié à; *to treat of,* traiter de, discourir sur (in a lecture or speech); *to treat to,* régaler (quelqu'un) de, payer à boire à; *to treat with,* traiter avec.—*v.i.* Traiter (de); négocier.—*n.* Régal, festin, *m.*, fête, *f.*; (*fig.*) délice, plaisir, *m.*; petite gâterie, *f.*; mets, plat, qu'on ne sert que dans les grandes occasions; (*fig.*) (*fam.*) privilège, *m. As a treat,* exceptionnellement; *a treat in store,* un plaisir à venir; *to have a treat,* faire un festin; *to stand treat,* (*colloq.*) régaler, payer à boire.

treater, *n.* Personne qui traite, *f.*; (regaler) amphitryon, *m.*

treatise ['triːtis], *n.* Traité de or sur (on), *m.*

treatment ['triːtmənt], *n.* Traitement, *m.*; manière d'agir, *f.*

treaty ['triːti], *n.* Traité, *m.*, négociation, *f. By private treaty,* à l'amiable; *to be in treaty for,* être en négociation pour, être en marché pour. **treaty-port,** *n.* Port à traité, port ouvert, *m.*

treble [trebl], *v.t.*, *v.i.* Tripler.—*a.* Triple; (*Mus.*) de dessus, soprano.—*n.* Triple; (*Mus.*) dessus, soprano, *m. False treble,* voix de fausset, *f.*

trebling, *n.* Triplement, *m.* **trebly,** *adv.* Triplement, trois fois.

tree [triː], *n.* Arbre; embauchoir (for boots), *m.*; (*fig.*) croix, *f. Axle-tree,* essieu, *m.*; *genealogical tree,* arbre généalogique, *m.*; *to be at the top of the tree,* tenir le haut du pavé; *to be up a tree,* (*colloq.*) être à bout de ressources, être au bout de son rouleau.

tree-calf, *n.* Veau raciné, *m.*

treeless, *a.* Sans arbre.

treenail, *n.* Cheville, *f.*

trefoil ['triːfoil], *n.* Trèfle, *m.*

treillage ['treilidʒ], *n.* Treillage, *m.*

trek [trek], *n.* (*in South Africa*) Étape, *f.* (dans un voyage en chariot); voyage en chariot, *m.*; migration, *f.*—*v.i.* Faire route (en chariot à bœufs); changer de pays; (*slang*) s'appuyer une balade; faire des kilomètres. **trekker,** *n.* Émigrant, *m.*

trellis ['trelis], *n.* Treillis, treillage, *m.*—*v.t.* Treillisser. **trellised,** *a.* Treillissé, à treillis.

tremble [trembl], *v.i.* Trembler, trembloter. *To tremble in every limb,* trembler de tout son corps.—*n.* Tremblement, *m.*

trembler, *n.* Trembleur, *m.*, trembleuse, *f.*

trembling, *n.* Tremblement, *m.*—*a.* Tremblant, tremblotant. **tremblingly,** *adv.* En tremblant.

tremendous [tri'mendəs], *a.* Terrible, épouvantable; (*colloq.*) extraordinaire, fou. **tremendously,** *adv.* Terriblement; (*colloq.*) furieusement. **tremendousness,** *n.* Nature terrible, *f.*

tremor ['tremə], *n.* Tremblement, tremblotement, frémissement, *m.*; secousse, *f. Earth tremor,* tremblement de terre, *m.*, secousse sismique, *f.*

tremulous ['tremjuləs], *a.* Tremblant, tremblotant; (*fig.*) timide, craintif. **tremulously,** *adv.* En tremblant, en tremblotant.

tremulousness, *n.* Tremblotement, tremblement, frémissement, *m.*
trench [trentʃ], *n.* Tranchée; rigole (between ridges etc.), *f.,* fossé (ditch); (*Mil.*) retranchement, *m.* *Circulation trench,* tranchée de circulation, *f.*; *communication trench,* boyau, *m.*; *fire trench,* tranchée de tir, *f.*; *trench-mortar,* crapouillot, *m.*—*v.t.* Creuser, couper, faire un fossé; sillonner (to furrow); butter (to earth up); (*Mil.*) retrancher, faire des tranchées.
trenchancy [ˈtrentʃənsi], *n.* Causticité, *f.*
trenchant [ˈtrentʃənt], *a.* Tranchant, caustique; vigoureux.
trencher [ˈtrentʃə], *n.* Tranchoir, tailloir, *m.* **trencher-cap,** *n.* Bonnet carré (universitaire), *m.,* toque à plateau, *f.* **trencher-friend** or **-knight,** *n.* Compagnon de table, *m.* **trencherman,** *n.* Gros mangeur, *m.* *He is a good trencherman,* c'est une bonne fourchette.
trend [trend], *v.i.* Se diriger, tendre (vers), s'étendre.—*n.* Direction, tendance, *f.* *The trend of public opinion,* la tendance de l'opinion publique.
Trent [trent]. Trente, *f.* *The Council of Trent,* le Concile de Trente.
trepan [trəˈpæn], *n.* (*Surg.*) Trépan, *m.*—*v.t.* Trépaner. **trepanning,** *n.* Trépanation, *f.*
trepidation [trepiˈdeiʃən], *n.* Trépidation; vibration, *f.,* tremblement, *m.*; (*fig.*) terreur, *f.,* effroi, *m.*
treponema [trepəˈniːmə], *n.* Tréponème, *m.*
trespass [ˈtrespəs], *n.* Violation de propriété, *f.,* délit, *m.*; (*Scripture*) offense; transgression, *f.*—*v.i.* Violer la propriété; empiéter (sur), abuser (de); (*Scripture*) pécher, transgresser. *To trespass against,* violer, enfreindre, nuire à; *to trespass upon,* empiéter sur, abuser de.
trespasser, *n.* Personne qui empiète, *f.,* maraudeur, violateur du droit de propriété; (*Scripture*) pécheur, *m.,* pécheresse, *f.,* transgresseur, *m.* *Trespassers will be prosecuted,* défense d'entrer sous peine d'amende.
trespass-offering, *n.* Sacrifice expiatoire, *m.*
tress [tres], *n.* Tresse, boucle, *f.* **tressed,** *a.* Tressé, en tresses.
trestle [tresl], *n.* Tréteau, chevalet, *m.* **trestle-bed,** *n.* Lit de sangle, *m.* **trestle-trees,** *n.pl.* (*Naut.*) Élongis, *m.pl.*
tret [tret], *n.* (*Comm.*) Déduction pour déchet, réfaction, *f.*
trews [truːz], *n.* Pantalon en tartan (de soldats écossais), *m.*
trey [trei], *n.* Trois (cards etc.), *m.*
triable [ˈtraiəbl], *a.* Qu'on peut essayer, qu'on peut éprouver; (*Law*) du ressort (de).
triad [ˈtraiæd], *n.* Triade, *f.*; (*Mus.*) accord de trois notes (sans l'octave), *m.*; (*Theol.*) divinité en trois personnes, trinité, *f.*
trial [ˈtraiəl], *n.* Expérience, épreuve, tentative, *f.,* essai, *m.*; (*Law*) procès, jugement, *m.* *A sad trial,* une grande épreuve; *by way of trial,* pour essayer, pour essai; *it is a trial to me to have to do it,* c'est une grande épreuve pour moi que d'avoir à le faire; *on one's trial,* en jugement; *on trial,* à l'essai; *to bring to trial,* mettre en jugement; *to grant a new trial,* accorder l'appel; *to make a trial of,* faire l'essai de; *to move for a new trial,* demander

à interjeter appel; *to take one's trial,* passer en jugement, être jugé.—*a.* D'essai.
trial-trip, *n.* Voyage d'essai, *m.*
triangle [ˈtraiæŋgl], *n.* Triangle, *m.* **triangled,** *a.* Triangulé. **triangular** [-ˈæŋgjulə], *a.* Triangulaire. **triangularly,** *adv.* Triangulairement. **triangulate,** *v.t.* Trianguler. **triangulation** [-ˈleiʃən], *n.* Triangulation, *f.*
trias [ˈtraiəs], *n.* Trias, *m.* **triassic** [-ˈæsik], *a.* Triasique.
tribal [traibl], *a.* Qui appartient à la tribu; qui vit en tribu; tribal, -e.
tribasic [traiˈbeisik], *a.* Tribasique.
tribe [traib], *n.* Tribu, peuplade, *f.*; (*fig.*) race, famille, *f.* **tribesman,** *n.* Membre d'une tribu, *m.*
triblet [ˈtriblit], *n.* Triboulet, mandrin, *m.*
tribometer [traiˈbɔmitə], *n.* Tribomètre, *m.*
tribrach [ˈtraibræk], *n.* Tribraque, *m.*
tribulation [tribjuˈleiʃən], *n.* Tribulation, *f.*
tribunal [traiˈbjuːnl], *n.* Tribunal, *m.*; cour d'arbitrage, de justice, cour, *f.*
tribune [ˈtribjuːn], *n.* (*Hist.*) Tribun, *m.*; tribune, *f.*; trône, *m.*
tributary [ˈtribjutəri], *a.* Tributaire.—*n.* Tributaire, affluent, *m.*
tribute [ˈtribjuːt], *n.* Tribut; (*fig.*) hommage, *m.* *To pay tribute,* rendre hommage. **tribute-money,** *n.* (Argent payé en) tribut, *m.*
tricapsular [traiˈkæpsjulə], *a.* Tricapsulaire.
tricar [ˈtraikɑː], *n.* Tri-car, tricar; triporteur, *m.*
trice [trais], *n.* *In a trice,* en un clin d'œil.—*v.t.* (*Naut.*) Hisser.
*****tricennial** [traiˈseniəl], *a.* (*Law*) De trente ans (prescription).
tricephalous [traiˈsefələs], *a.* Tricéphale.
trichina [triˈkainə], *n.* Trichine, *f.*
trichinosis [trikiˈnousis], *n.* Trichinose, *f.*
trichology [-ˈkɔlədʒi], *n.* Trichologie, *f.*
trichoma [-ˈkoumə], *n.* Trichome, trichoma, *m.*
trichotomy [-ˈkɔtəmi], *n.* Trichotomie, *f.*
trick [trik], *n.* Tour, artifice, *m.,* fraude, *f.*; levée (at cards); ruse, finesse, malice; espièglerie (of children); habitude, *f.,* tic (habit), *m.* *I know a trick worth two of that,* j'ai mieux à vous proposer, je connais un meilleur expédient; *nasty trick,* vilain tour, *m.,* vilaine habitude, *f.*; *shabby trick,* vilenie, *f.*; *the odd trick,* (*Cards*) la levée supplémentaire, *f.*; *the tricks of the trade,* les ruses, *f.pl.,* or les trucs, *m.pl.,* du métier; *to be at one's tricks again,* faire encore des siennes; *to have the trick* (at cards), faire la levée; *to know a trick or two,* en savoir plus d'une, avoir plus d'un tour dans son sac; *to play someone a trick,* tromper une ou jouer un tour à quelqu'un.—*v.t.* Duper; tricher (at play); faire une niche à (to play a trick on). *To trick out,* parer, orner; *tricked out with,* paré de, attifé de.
trickery, *n.* Tromperie, fourberie, tricherie, *f.*
tricking, *n.* Tromperie, duperie, supercherie; parure, *f.*; atours (ornaments), *m.pl.*
trickish, *a.* Trompeur, fourbe, fin.
trickle [trikl], *v.i.* Couler goutte à goutte, suinter, dégoutter.—*v.t.* Laisser couler or tomber goutte à goutte.
trickling, *n.* Écoulement, *m.*
trickster [ˈtrikstə], *n.* Fourbe, escroc, *m.* *Confidence trickster,* voleur à l'américaine, *m.*

tricky ['triki], *a.* Fourbe, rusé; (*fig.*) incertain, compliqué; délicat (à manier). *It is a tricky business,* c'est une affaire délicate.

tricolour ['traikʌlə], *n.* Drapeau tricolore, *m.* (*Cine.*) *Tricolour system,* trichromie, *f.* **tri-coloured,** *a.* Tricolore.

trictrac ['triktræk], *n.* Trictrac (game), *m.*

tricycle ['traisikl], *n.* Tricycle, *m.* *Box-tricycle,* triporteur, *m.* **tricyclist,** *n.* Tricycliste, *m.*

trident ['traidənt], *n.* Trident, *m.*

tridentate [trai'dentət], *a.* Tridenté.

tried [traid], *a.* Éprouvé; qui a fait ses preuves (of method, recipe).—*p.p.* [TRY].

triennial [trai'eniəl], *a.* Triennal. **triennially,** *adv.* Tous les trois ans.

trier ['traiə], *n.* (*Law*) Juge; arbitre; (*colloq.*) homme d'initiative et de courage, *m.*; (*fig.*) épreuve, pierre de touche, *f.*

trifid ['traifid], *a.* (*Bot.*) Trifide.

trifle [traifl], *n.* Bagatelle, *f.*, rien, *m.*; idée, *f.*; soupçon (small quantity), *m.*; (*Cook.*) sorte de charlotte russe, *f.*; (*pl.*) vaisselle d'étain, *f. To dispute about trifles,* se quereller pour un rien; *to stand upon trifles,* s'arrêter à des vétilles, à des riens.—*v.i.* S'amuser à des riens, badiner, baguenauder, être frivole. *He is not the man to be trifled with,* ce n'est pas un homme dont on se moque; *to trifle away,* gaspiller, perdre; *to trifle with,* se jouer de, plaisanter avec, se moquer de.

trifler, *n.* Personne frivole, *f.*, baguenaudier, *m.*

trifling, *a.* De rien, insignifiant, frivole, léger. *A trifling matter,* peu de chose.—*n.* Frivolité, *f.*, badinage, *m.*

triflorous [trai'flɔːrəs], *a.* Triflore.

triforium [trai'fɔːriəm], *n.* Triforium, *m.*

triform ['traifɔːm], *a.* Ayant une triple forme.

trig [trig], *v.t.* Enrayer (wheels etc.); caler (a cask).—*n.* Enrayure, *f.*, sabot (d'enrayage), *m.*, cale, *f.*; (*sch. slang*) trigo, *f.*

trigamist ['trigəmist], *n.* Trigame, *m.* **trigamous,** *a.* Trigame. **trigamy,** *n.* Trigamie, *f.*

trigger ['trigə], *n.* Détente, *f.* **trigger-guard,** *n.* Pontet, *m.* **trigger-spring,** *n.* Ressort-gâchette, *m.*

trigla ['triglə], *n.* (*Ichth.*) Trigle, grondin, *m.*

triglyph ['traiglif], *n.* Triglyphe, *m.*

trigon ['traigɔn], *n.* Trigone, *m.*

trigonometrical [trigənə'metrikl], *a.* Trigonométrique. **trigonometrically,** *adv.* Trigonométriquement. **trigonometry** [-'nɔmətri], *n.* Trigonométrie, *f.*

trihedral [trai'hiːdrəl], *a.* Trièdre.

trilateral [-'lætərəl], *a.* Trilatéral.

trilingual [-'liŋgwəl], *a.* Trilingue.

triliteral [-'litərəl], *a.* Trilittère. **triliterality** [-'ræliti], *n.* Trilittéralité, *f.*

trill [tril], *n.* Trille, *m.*—*v.i.* Triller, faire des trilles.

trillion ['triljən], *n.* Trillion, *m.* (since 1948); (*Am.*) quintillion, *m.*

trilobate ['trailoubeit *or* trai'loubeit], *a.* Trilobé.

trilocular [trai'lɔkjulə], *a.* Triloculaire.

trilogy ['trilədʒi], *n.* Trilogie, *f.*

trim [trim], *v.t.* Arranger, mettre en ordre; habiller, garnir, orner, parer (de), émonder, tailler (to clip); (*Carp.*) dégrossir, planer; (*Naut.*) arrimer (of cargo); orienter (the sails); dresser (a boat). *To trim in,* (*Carp.*)

ajuster; *to trim up,* arranger, ajuster, parer, orner (de).—*v.i.* (*Polit. slang*) Balancer entre deux partis, tergiverser; (*fam.*) ménager la chèvre et le chou, se tenir à carreau.—*a.* Soigné, coquet, bien mis, bien arrangé; bien orienté (of sails).—*n.* Bon ordre, bon état, *m.*; assiette (of a ship), *f.*; orientement (of sails); arrimage (of the hold), *m.*; coupe, *f.* (hair). *In good trim,* bien arrangé, bien tenu, bien soigné, en forme; *out of trim,* dérangé; *to be in proper trim,* être en bon ordre *or* en bon état.

trimeter ['trimitə], *n.* Trimètre, *m.*

trimly ['trimli], *adv.* Bien, gentiment, proprement.

trimmer, *n.* (*Polit.*) Ami de tous les partis (time-server), opportuniste; (*Carp.*) chevêtre, *m.*; (*Navy*) soutier, *m.*

trimming, *n.* Garniture; passementerie; semonce, *f.*, (*fam.*) savon (scolding), *m.*; (*pl.*) garniture, *f.*; rognures, *f.pl.*; parure (of meat), *f.*

trimness, *n.* Air soigné, coquet; bon ordre, *m.*

trimorphism [trai'mɔːfizm], *n.* Trimorphisme, *m.* **trimorphous,** *a.* Trimorphe.

trine [train], *a.* (*Astrol.*) Trin, trine.

tringle [triŋgl], *n.* (*Arch.*) Tringle, *f.*

Trinidad ['trinidæd], *n.* (Île de la) Trinité, *f.*

Trinitarian [trini'teəriən], *n.* Trinitaire, *m.*

Trinity ['triniti], *n.* Trinité, *f.* *Trinity House,* corporation qui veille à l'entretien des phares, des bouées et du pilotage, *f.*; *Trinity Sunday,* dimanche de la Trinité, *m.*; *Trinity term,* trimestre d'été, *m.*

trinket ['triŋkit], *n.* Petit bijou, *m.*, breloque, *f.*, colifichet, *m.*

trinomial [trai'noumiəl], *a. and n.* Trinôme, *m.*

trio ['triːou], *n.* Trio, *m.*

triolet ['triːəlet], *n.* Triolet, *m.*

trip [trip], *v.i.* Trébucher, faire un faux pas; (*fig.*) errer, se tromper (to err); fourcher (of the tongue); courir légèrement (to run lightly); danser, bondir. *To be caught tripping,* être trouvé en défaut; *to trip away,* s'en aller d'un pas léger.—*v.t.* Faire un croc-en-jambe à, renverser, faire tomber; (*fig.*) supplanter; (*Naut.*) déraper (an anchor); (*Eng.*) déclencher. *To trip up,* renverser, faire tomber, (*fig.*) supplanter.—*n.* Croc-en-jambe, faux pas, *m.*, méprise; excursion, *f.*, tour, petit voyage (journey), *m.* (*Naut.*) *Round trip,* croisière, *f.*; *pleasure trip,* voyage d'agrément, *m.*

tripartite [trai'pɑːtait], *a.* Tripartite.

tripe [traip], *n.* Tripes, *f.pl.* (*pop.*) *You are talking tripe,* vous dites des foutaises. **tripe-shop,** *n.* Triperie, *f.*

triphase ['traifeiz], *a.* (*Elec.*) Triphasé.

triphthong ['trifθɔŋ], *n.* Triphtongue, *f.*

triplane ['traiplein], *n.* Triplan, *m.*

triple [tripl], *a.* Triple.—*v.t.* Tripler.

triplet [-], *n.* (*Pros.*) Tercet; (*Mus.*) triolet, *m.*; (*pl.*) triplés, trijumeaux, *m.pl.*

triplicate ['triplikit], *a.* Triplé. *Triplicate ratio,* (*Math.*) raison triplée, *f.*—*n.* Triplicata (copy), *m. In triplicate,* en triplicata.

triplication [-'keiʃən], *n.* Triplication, *f.*

triplicity [-'plisiti], *n.* Triplicité, *f.*

tripling, *n.* Triplement, *m.* **triply,** *adv.* Triplement, trois fois.

tripod ['traipɔd], *n.* Trépied, *m.* *Aiming-tripod,* chevalet de pointage, *m.*

Tripoli ['tripəli]. (*Geog.*) Tripoli, *m.*; la Tripolitaine, *f.* **Tripolitania.** La Tripolitaine, *f.*

tripoli ['tripəli], *n.* (*Geol.*) Tripoli, *m.*

tripos ['traipɔs], *n.* Examen pour le grade de B.A. (à Cambridge), *m.*

tripper ['tripə], *n.* (*colloq.*) Excursionniste, *m.*

tripping, *n.* Croc en jambe, faux pas, *m.*; faute, erreur, *f.*; pas léger, *m.*; (*Naut.*) dérapage, *m.*—*a.* Agile, léger, leste; rapide (quick). **trippingly,** *adv.* Lestement, d'un pas léger; facilement, sans hésiter.

trireme ['trairi:m], *n.* Trirème, *f.*

trisect [trai'sekt], *v.t.* Diviser en trois parties, couper en trois.

trisyllabic [traisi'læbik], *a.* Trissyllabe, trissyllabique. **trisyllable** [-'siləbl], *n.* Trissyllabe, *m.*

trite [trait], *a.* Usé, banal, rebattu. **tritely,** *adv.* Banalement. **triteness,** *n.* Nature banale, trivialité, *f.*

tritoma [trai'toumə], *n.* Faux aloès, *m.*

Triton ['traitən]. Triton, *m.*

tritone ['traitoun], *n.* (*Mus.*) Triton, *m.*

triturable ['trituərəbl], *a.* Triturable. **triturate,** *v.t.* Triturer. **trituration** [-'reiʃən], *n.* Trituration, *f.*

triumph ['traiəmf], *n.* Triomphe, *m.*—*v.i.* Triompher. *To triumph over,* triompher de, surmonter, l'emporter sur.

triumphal [trai'ʌmfl], *a.* Triomphal, de triomphe. *Triumphal arch,* arc de triomphe, *m.* **triumphant, triumphing,** *a.* Triomphant, triomphateur. **triumphantly,** *adv.* En triomphe; d'un air de triomphe.

triumpher ['traiəmfə], *n.* Triomphateur, vainqueur, *m.*

triumvir [trai'ʌmvə], *n.* (*pl.* **triumviri**) Triumvir, *m.* **triumvirate,** *n.* Triumvirat, *m.*

trivalence [trai'veiləns], *n.* Trivalence, *f.* **trivalent,** *a.* Trivalent, -e.

trivet ['trivit], *n.* Trépied, *m.* *As right as a trivet,* on ne peut mieux.

trivial ['triviəl], *a.* Insignifiant, sans importance. **trivially,** *adv.* Légèrement, d'une manière insignifiante. **trivialness** or **triviality** [-'æliti], *n.* Insignifiance; banalité, *f.*

troat [trout], *v.t.* Bramer, raire (of the buck). —*n.* Bramement, *m.*

trocar ['troukɑ:], *n.* (*Surg.*) Trocart, trois-quarts, *m.*

trochaic [tro'keiik], *a.* Trochaïque.

trochee ['trouki], *n.* Trochée, *m.*; (*Pharm.*) pastille, tablette, *f.*

trochil ['trɔkil], *n.* Trochile, trochilus, *m.*

trod, *trode, *past* **trodden,** *p.p.* [TREAD].

troglodyte ['trɔglədait], *n.* Troglodyte, *m.* **trogloditic** [-'ditik], *a.* Troglodytique.

Trojan ['troudʒən], *a.* and *n.* Troyen, *m.*, -enne, *f.*; (*colloq.*) un brave garçon (énergique et travailleur). *Trojan War,* la guerre de Troie.

troll (1) [troul], *v.t.* Rouler, tourner; pêcher à la cuiller; *chanter une chanson à reprises.

troll (2) [troul], *n.* (*Scand. Myth.*) Troll; (*later*) gnome, nain, *m.*

trolley or **trolly** ['trɔli], *n.* Fardier, binard; (*Elec.*) trolley, *m.* *Dinner trolley,* serveuse, table roulante, *f.*; *porter's luggage trolley,* chariot à bagages, *m.* **trolley-bus,** *n.* Trolleybus, *m.*

trollop ['trɔləp], *n.* Souillon; (*vulg.*) salope, *f.*

trombone [trɔm'boun], *n.* Trombone, *m.* **trombonist,** *n.* Tromboniste, *m.*

troop [tru:p], *n.* Troupe, bande, *f.*; (*pl.*) troupes, *f.pl.*, armée, *f.* *A troop of horse,* un détachement de cavalerie, *m.*—*v.i.* S'attrouper, s'assembler.

trooper, *n.* (*Mil.*) Soldat à cheval, cavalier, *m.*; (*colloq.*) transport (troop-ship), *m.*

trooping, *n.* Attroupement, assemblement, *m.* (*Mil.*) *Trooping the colour(s),* parade du drapeau, *f.*

troop-ship, *n.* Transport, *m.*

trophic ['trɔfik], *a.* Trophique, *m.*

trophied ['troufid], *a.* Orné de trophées. **trophy,** *n.* Trophée, *m.*

tropic ['trɔpik], *n.* Tropique, *m.* *In the tropics,* sous les tropiques. **tropic-bird,** *n.* Paille-en-queue, *m.*

tropical, *a.* Tropical, des tropiques; (*Rhet.*) figuratif, métaphorique. **tropically,** *adv.* Figurativement.

tropological [trɔpə'lɔdʒikl], *a.* Tropologique, figuré.

tropology [trə'pɔlədʒi], *n.* Tropologie, *f.*

trot [trɔt], *v.i.* Trotter, aller au trot; trottiner (of a child). *To trot out,* faire trotter, montrer l'allure de, (*colloq.*) montrer, exhiber.—*n.* Trot, *m.* *At a gentle trot,* au petit trot; *at a jog-trot,* cahin-caha; *full trot,* grand trot.

troth [trouθ], *n.* Foi, *f.* *By my troth!* ma foi! *in troth,* en vérité; *to plight one's troth,* engager sa foi.

trotter ['trɔtə], *n.* Cheval de trot, trotteur; (*pl.*) pieds de mouton, pieds de cochon, *m.pl.*

trotting, *n.* Trot, *m.*—*a.* Trotteur. *Trotting-match* or *race,* course au trot, *f.*

troubadour ['tru:bəduə], *n.* Troubadour, *m.*

trouble [trʌbl], *v.t.* Agiter; troubler, déranger, importuner (to disturb); tourmenter, chagriner, affliger, ennuyer (to distress); donner de la peine à (to give trouble to); inquiéter (to disquiet). *I will not trouble you, je ne veux pas vous donner cette peine; I will not trouble you in this affair,* je ne veux pas vous déranger pour cette affaire; *I'will not trouble you with it,* je ne veux pas vous en embarrasser; *may I trouble you for a light?* puis-je vous demander du feu? *may I trouble you to move?* auriez-vous la bonté de me laisser passer? *to trouble oneself,* se déranger, se donner la peine (de).—*v.i.* S'inquiéter, se mettre en peine (de), se donner la peine (de).—*n.* Trouble, *m.*; peine (work, fatigue), affliction, *f.*, souci, chagrin (grief); mal, ennui (annoyance), *m.* *I got into no end of trouble,* je me suis attiré une foule d'ennuis; *it is not worth the trouble,* ce n'est pas la peine, cela n'en vaut pas la peine; *it's no trouble,* cela ne me dérange pas; *to be in trouble,* être dans la peine, avoir du chagrin; *to get out of trouble,* se tirer d'affaire; *to save someone trouble,* épargner de la peine à quelqu'un; *to take the trouble to,* se donner la peine de; *what's the trouble?* Qu'est-ce qu'il y a? Qu'avez-vous?

troubled, *a.* Inquiet, agité; trouble (of water etc.). *To be troubled about,* s'inquiéter de, se préoccuper de.

trouble-maker, *n.* Fomentateur de troubles; factieux, *m.*

troubler, *n.* Perturbateur, *m.*
troublesome ['trʌblsəm], *a.* Ennuyeux, incommode; fatigant, fâcheux. *Children are very troublesome*, les enfants donnent beaucoup de peine. **troublesomeness**, *n.* Ennui, embarras, *m.*, gêne, *f.*
troublous ['trʌbləs], *a.* Troublé, agité, orageux.
trough [trɔf], *n.* Auge, huche, *f.*; pétrin (kneading-trough); auget, abreuvoir (for drinking); (*Metal.*) creuset, *m.* (*Meteor.*) (*Phys.*) *Trough of a wave*, creux d'une onde, *m.*; *trough of low pressure*, dépression, *f.*; *trough of the sea*, entre-deux des lames, creux des vagues, *m.*
trounce [trauns], *v.t.* Rosser, étriller, houspiller.
trouncing, *n.* Raclée, *f.*, étrillage, *m.*
trousers ['trauzəz], *n.pl.* Pantalon, *m.* *A pair of trousers*, un pantalon; (*fam.*) *his wife wears the trousers*, c'est sa femme qui porte la culotte. **trouser-clip**, *n.* Pince-pantalon, *m.*
trouser-press, *n.* Presse-pantalon, *m.*
trouser-stretcher, *n.* Tendeur pour pantalon, *m.*
trousseau ['truːsou], *n.* Trousseau, *m.*
trout [traut], *n.* Truite, *f.* *Brown trout*, truite de rivière. **trout-coloured**, *a.* Truité.
trout-fishing, *n.* Pêche à la truite, *f.*
trover ['trouvə], *n.* (*Law*) Demande en restitution, *f.*
*****trow** [trau], *v.t.* Penser, croire, s'imaginer.
trowel ['trauəl], *n.* Truelle, *f.*; (*Gard.*) déplantoir, *m.*
Troy [trɔi]. Troie, *f.*
troy-weight ['trɔi weit], *n.* Troy (poids de douze onces à la livre), *m.*
truant ['truːənt], *n.* Fainéant, vagabond, *m.* *To play truant*, faire l'école buissonnière.
truce [truːs], *n.* Trève, *f.* *A truce to*, trève de; *flag of truce*, fanion parlementaire, *m.* **trucebearer**, *n.* Parlementaire, *m.* **trucebreaker**, *n.* Violateur de trèves, *m.*
truck [trʌk], *n.* Fardier, binard (cart); (*Am.*) camion; (*Rail.*) wagon, wagon-écurie (horsebox), wagon à bestiaux (cattle-truck), *m.*, plate-forme (of locomotives etc.); (*Naut.*) pomme de mât, *f.*; troc, échange; (*Manuf.*) paiement en marchandises (barter etc.), *m.* *Have no truck with him!* N'ayez rien à faire avec lui! *truck-(system)*, paiement des ouvriers en marchandises, *m.*—*v.i.* Troquer.
truckage, *n.* Camionnage, *m.*
truckle ['trʌkl], *n.* Roulette, *f.*—*v.i.* Ramper, s'abaisser (devant), faire le chien couchant.
truckle-bed, *n.* Lit à roulettes, *m.*
truckling, *n.* Soumission, *f.*, abaissement, *m.*
truculence ['trʌkjuləns], *n.* Brutalité, férocité, truculence, *f.* **truculent**, *a.* Brutal, féroce, farouche.
trudge [trʌdʒ], *v.i.* Clopiner, marcher péniblement, lourdement.—*n.* Marche pénible, *f.*
trudgen ['trʌdʒən], *n.* (*Swim.*) Coupe indienne, *f.*; trudgeon, *m.*
true [truː], *a.* Vrai, réel, véritable; sincère, fidèle (faithful); exact (correct), honnête, loyal (honest); uni, droit (straight). *To come true*, se réaliser; *true to*, fidèle à.—*int.* C'est vrai! c'est juste!—*adv.* Vraiment; juste (accurately).—*v.t.* Ajuster; dégauchir (wooden surface).
true-born, *a.* Véritable; vrai. **true-bred**, *a.*

De bonne race, pur sang; (*fig.*) accompli, véritable. **true-hearted**, *a.* Au cœur sincère. **true-heartedness**, *n.* Sincérité de cœur, *f.* **true-love**, *n.* Bien-aimé, *m.*, bien-aimée, *f.* *True-lover's knot*, lacs d'amour, *m.pl.*
trueness, *n.* Fidélité; vérité; justesse, *f.*
truffle [trʌfl], *n.* Truffe, *f.* *To stuff with truffles*, truffer. **truffle-ground**, *n.* Truffière, *f.* **truffle-hound**, *n.* Chien truffier, *m.*
truism ['truːizm], *n.* Vérité de La Palisse, *f.*, truisme, *m.*
truly ['truːli], *adv.* Vraiment, véritablement, fidèlement; (*iron.*) ma foi! *Yours truly*, (to slight acquaintances) veuillez agréer, Monsieur, mes salutations empressées *or* veuillez agréer, Madame, l'hommage de mes sentiments respectueux. *Yours very truly*, (ceremoniously, but cordial) croyez, cher Monsieur, à mes sentiments cordiaux.
trump [trʌmp], *n.* Trompe, trompette, *f.*; (*Cards.*) atout; (*colloq.*) brave garçon, brave cœur, *m.* *Trump card*, atout, *m.*; *to bid no trumps*, annoncer sans-atout.—*v.t.* Jouer atout, couper. *It is a trumped-up story*, c'est une histoire inventée; *to trump up*, inventer, forger, imaginer.
trumpery ['trʌmpəri], *n.* Rebut, *m.*, camelote, blague, *f.*—*a.* Sans valeur, de camelote, mesquin; ridicule, insignifiant. *A trumpery affair*, une vétille; *a trumpery thing*, une drogue.
trumpet ['trʌmpit], *n.* Trompette, *f.* *Speaking-trumpet*, porte-voix, *m.*; *to blow one's own trumpet*, chanter ses propres louanges.—*v.t.* Publier à son de trompe; proclamer, trompeter.—*v.i.* Barrir (of elephants).
trumpet-call, *n.* Coup de trompette, *m.*, sonnerie, *f.*
trumpeter, *n.* Trompette, *m.*
trumpet-shaped, *a.* En trompette.
truncate [trʌŋ'keit], *v.t.* Tronquer. **truncated**, *a.* Tronqué. **truncation** [-'keiʃən], *n.* Troncature, *f.*
truncheon ['trʌnʃən], *n.* Bâton, *m.*; matraque, *f.*
trundle [trʌndl], *n.* Roulette, *f.*; camion fardier (cart); transport sur fardier, roulage, *m.*—*v.t.* Rouler; faire courir, faire aller (a hoop), pousser (a barrow).
trundle-bed, *n.* Lit bas à roulettes, *m.*
trunk [trʌŋk], *n.* Tronc; coffre, *m.*, malle (box); trompe (of elephants etc.), *f.*; (*Sculp.*) torse, *m.*; (*pl.*) (*Cost.*) slip, *m.*; (*Teleph.*) l'inter, *m.*
trunk-call, *n.* (*Teleph.*) Appel interurbain, *m.*
trunk-hose, *n.* Haut-de-chausses, *m.* **trunkline**, *n.* Grande ligne *f.*, **trunk-maker**, *n.* Layetier, *m.* **trunk-road**, *n.* Grande route, route à grande circulation, *f.*
trunnion ['trʌnjən], *n.* Tourillon, *m.*
truss [trʌs], *n.* Botte (25 kilos of hay etc.); balle, *f.*, paquet, *m.*; (*Naut.*) drosse (of racage), *f.*; (*Surg.*) bandage herniaire; (*Build.*) nœud, *m.*, ferme (triangulaire), *f.*, lien (of roofs), *m.*—*v.t.* Trousser, brider (a fowl); empaqueter, lier; botteler (hay); armer (a beam).
truss-maker, *n.* Bandagiste, *m.*
trust [trʌst], *n.* Confiance (en), *f.*; dépôt, *m.*; garde (care); charge (something committed to a person's care), *f.*; crédit (credit); (*Law*)

fidéicommis; (*Comm.*) trust, syndicat, *m.*
Breach of trust, abus de confiance, *m.*; *I
resign my trust into your hands*, je vous rends
le dépôt que vous m'avez confié; *on trust*, de
confiance; (*Comm.*) à crédit; *road trust*,
administration des routes, *f.*; *to hold in trust*,
avoir en dépôt, (*Law*) tenir par fidéicommis;
to put trust in, mettre confiance en.—*v.t.* Se
fier à, se confier à, mettre sa confiance en;
ajouter foi à, croire (to believe); donner (to
commit to the care of); faire crédit à (to give
credit to). *He is not to be trusted*, on ne peut
pas se fier à lui; *I dare not trust myself in it*,
je n'ose m'y hasarder; *to trust with*, confier à,
faire crédit à.—*v.i.* Avoir confiance (en *or*
dans); aimer à croire, espérer, s'attendre (à).
I sincerely trust, j'espère bien; *to trust in*, se
fier à, mettre sa confiance en, compter sur;
to trust to luck, se fier au hasard.
trust-deed, *n.* Acte fiduciaire, *m.*
trusted, *a.* De confiance.
trustee [trʌs'tiː], *n.* Dépositaire, gardien;
directeur, administrateur; (*Law*) fidéicommissaire; tuteur, *m.*, -trice, *f.* (of orphans);
curateur, *m. Board of trustees*, conseil
d'administration, *m.*; *in the hands of trustees*,
en régie. **trusteeship,** *n.* Administration;
tutelle, *f.*, (*Law*) fidéicommis, *m.*
trustful, *a.* Plein de confiance. **trustfully,**
adv. Avec confiance.
trustily ['trʌstili], *adv.* Fidèlement, loyalement. **trustiness,** *n.* Fidélité, loyauté, *f.*
trusting, *a.* Plein de confiance. **trustingly,**
adv. Avec confiance.
trustworthiness, *n.* Fidélité (of a person);
exactitude (of news etc.), *f.*
trustworthy, *a.* Digne de confiance; exact (of
news).
trusty, *a.* Sûr, fidèle, loyal.
truth [truːθ], *n.* Vérité, *f.*, le vrai, *m. In truth*,
en vérité, à vrai dire; *sooner or later the
truth will out*, tôt ou tard la vérité se fait
jour; *the honest truth*, la pure vérité; *there's
not a word of truth in it*, c'est absolument
faux, il n'y a pas un mot de vrai là-dedans;
there's some truth in it, il y a du vrai; *to
distinguish truth from falsehood*, distinguer le
vrai d'avec le faux; *to tell someone a few home
truths*, dire ses quatre vérités à quelqu'un; *to
tell the truth*, dire la vérité; *truth is sometimes
stranger than fiction*, la réalité dépasse la
fiction, le vrai peut quelquefois n'être pas
vraisemblable.
truthful, *a.* Véridique, vrai. **truthfully,** *adv.*
Véridiquement, avec vérité. **truthfulness,** *n.*
Véracité, *f.*
truthless, *a.* Sans foi, déloyal.
try [trai], *v.i.* Essayer, tâcher (de); (*Naut.*)
être à la cape.—*v.t.* Essayer; éprouver, faire
l'épreuve de, mettre à l'épreuve; tenter,
entreprendre, essayer (to attempt); vérifier
(weights, measures, etc.); (*Law*) juger, mettre
en jugement. *To try for*, tâcher d'obtenir,
concourir pour, se porter candidat pour,
postuler; *to try it on with*, chercher à mettre
dedans; *to try on* (clothes), essayer; *to try
one's hand at*, s'essayer la main à; *to try out*,
essayer à fond; *to try the eyes*, fatiguer les
yeux.—*n.* Essai, *m.*, tentative, *f.* (*Rugby*) To
score a try, marquer un essai.
trying, *a.* Difficile, pénible, dur, fatigant,
insupportable. *A trying experience*, une

pénible expérience; *that is very trying*, c'est
très contrariant.
trying-on, *n.* Essayage (of clothes), *m.*
try-on, *n.* Tentative de bluff, *f.*
try-out, *n.* Essai à fond, *m.*
tryst [traist *or* trist], *n.* Rendez-vous, *m.*
trysting-place, *n.* Rendez-vous, *m.*
Tsar [zɑː], *n.* Tsar, *m.*
Tsarina [zɑːˈriːnə], *n.* Tsarine, *f.*
tsetse ['tsetsi], *n.* Mouche tsé-tsé, *f.*
tub [tʌb], *n.* Cuve, *f.*, baquet, bac, *m.*; caisse
(for plants etc.), *f.*; tonneau (of Diogenes);
cuvier (wash tub); tub, bain (bath), *m. An
old tub*, un vieux sabot (ship); *a tale of a tub*,
un coq-à-l'âne, une histoire ridicule; *a tub-
boat*, (*Row.*) un outrigger d'entraînement;
tub-thumper, déclamateur, orateur de carrefour, *m.*—*v.t.* Encuver; (*Gard.*) encaisser.
tuba ['tjuːbə], *n.* (*In ancient Rome*) Trompette,
f. (*pl.* **tubae**); (*in orchestra*) bombardon, *m.*;
contrebasse à vent, *f.* (*pl.* **tubas**).
tubbing ['tʌbiŋ], *n.* Encuvage; encaissage (of
plants), *m.* **tubby,** *a.* Gros, obèse; pansu.
tube [tjuːb], *n.* Tube, *m.* (*Anat.*) conduit, canal,
m., trompe, *f.*; (*Rail.*) métro, *m.* (*Tel.*),
Cathode-ray tube, oscillographe cathodique,
m.; *inner tube*, chambre à air, *f.*—*v.t.* Tuber.
tube-station, *n.* Station de métro, *f.*
tuber ['tjuːbə], *n.* Tubercule, *m.* **tubercle,** *n.*
Tubercule, *m.* **tubercled,** *a.* Tuberculeux.
tubercular [tjuˈbəːkjulə] or **tuberculous,** *a.*
Tuberculeux. **tuberculize,** *v.t.* Tuberculiser. **tuberculosis** [-ˈlousis], *n.* Tuberculose, *f.*
tuberiferous [tjuːbəˈrifərəs], *a.* Tubérifère.
tuberose ['tjuːbərous], *n.* and *a.* Tubéreuse, *f.*
tuberosity [tjuːbəˈrɔsiti], *n.* Tubérosité, *f.*
tuberous ['tjuːbərəs], *a.* Tubéreux.
tubful, *n.* Cuvée, *f.*
tubiform ['tjuːbifɔːm], *a.* Tubiforme.
tubing ['tjuːbiŋ], *n.* Tuyautage, *m.*, tubes,
m.pl. Rubber tubing, tuyau en caoutchouc, *m.*
tubular ['tjuːbjulə], *a.* Tubulaire. *Tubular
bridge*, pont tubulaire, *m.* **tubulous,** *a.*
Tubulé, tubuleux.
tuck [tʌk], *n.* Pli, plissé, plissement; troussis,
m.; (*Naut.*) fesses, *f.pl.*; (*sch.*) friandises, *f.pl.*
—*v.t.* Plisser; serrer. *To tuck in*, rentrer,
(slang) bien manger, se bourrer; *to tuck in
the bed-clothes*, border le lit; *to tuck into bed*,
border, bien envelopper avec des couvertures; *to tuck up*, retrousser, relever; envelopper, bien couvrir, border (in bed).
tucker, *n.* Chemisette, collerette, *f.*
tuck-in, *n.* (slang) Bombance, *f.*
tuck-shop, *n.* (slang) Pâtisserie, *f.*
Tuesday ['tjuːzdi], *n.* Mardi, *m. Every
Tuesday*, tous les mardis; *on Tuesdays*, le
mardi. *Shrove Tuesday*, Mardi gras.
tufa ['tjuːfə] or **tuff** [tʌf], *n.* Tuf, *m.* **tufa-
quarry,** *n.* Tufière, *f.* **tufaceous** [tjuˈfeifəs],
a. Tufacé, tufier.
tuft [tʌft], *n.* Touffe (of grass or hair); huppe
(on a bird), *f.*; (*Mil.*) pompon, *m.*
tufted, *a.* Touffu; huppé (of birds).
tuft-hunter, *n.* Parasite, adulateur, *m.*
tug [tʌg], *v.t.* Tirer avec effort; remorquer (to
tow).—*n.* Tiraillement, *m.*; saccade (jerk), *f.*;
remorqueur (boat), *m. The tug of war*, le
grand coup, le grand effort; lutte à la corde
(sports); *to give a good tug*, tirer bien fort,
donner un bon coup de collier.

tuition [tju'iʃən], *n.* Instruction, *f.*, enseignement, *m.*, leçons, *f.pl.*

tulip ['tju:lip], *n.* Tulipe, *f.* **tulip-tree**, *n.* Tulipier, *m.*

tulle [tju:l], *n.* Tulle, *m.* **tulle-maker**, *n.* Tulliste, *m.* **tulle-making**, *n.* Tullerie, *f.*

tumble [tʌmbl], *n.* Culbute, chute, *f.—v.i.* Tomber; rouler, se rouler (to roll); descendre en roulant, dégringoler (to roll down); faire la culbute, culbuter (of mountebanks). *To tumble down*, tomber par terre, tomber (of things), s'écrouler (of buildings); *to tumble downstairs*, dégringoler l'escalier; *to tumble out of bed*, sauter du lit; *to tumble over*, tomber, faire une chute; *to tumble to something*, comprendre quelque chose.—*v.t.* Tourner, retourner, déranger; chiffonner (to rumple); jeter, culbuter. *To tumble (things) over*, tourner et retourner.

tumbledown, *a.* Croulant, délabré, en ruine.

tumbler, *n.* *Jongleur, sauteur; verre sans pied; culbutant (pigeon), *m.*; noix (of a gun), *f.* **tumblerful**, *n.* Plein un grand verre, *m.*

tumbril ['tʌmbril] or **tumbrel** ['tʌmbrəl], *n.* Tombereau, *m.*

tumefaction [tju:mi'fækʃən], *n.* Tuméfaction, *f.*

tumefy ['tju:mifai], *v.t.* Tuméfier.—*v.i.* Se tuméfier.

tumid ['tju:mid], *a.* Enflé, gonflé; (*fig.*) boursouflé, ampoulé. **tumidly**, *adv.* Avec enflure. **tumidness** or **tumidity** [-'miditi], *n.* Enflure, *f.*, gonflement, *m.*; (*fig.*) turgescence, *f.*

tummy ['tʌmi], *n.* (*fam.*) Estomac, ventre, *m.*

tumour ['tju:mə], *n.* Tumeur, *f.*

tumular ['tju:mjulə], *a.* En monticule.

tumult ['tju:mʌlt], *n.* Tumulte; trouble, *m.* **tumultuary**, *a.* Tumultuaire, agité.

tumultuous [tju'mʌltjuəs], *a.* Tumultueux, turbulent, agité. **tumultuously**, *adv.* Tumultueusement. **tumultuousness**, *n.* Turbulence, *f.*

tumulus ['tju:mjuləs], *n.* (*pl.* **tumuli** [-lai]) Tumulus, *m.*

tun [tʌn], *n.* Tonneau, fût, *m.*; cuve, *f.—v.t.* Entonner.

tunable ['tju:nəbl], *a.* Qu'on peut accorder, accordable. **tunably**, *adv.* Harmonieusement, d'accord.

tundra ['tundrə], *n.* Toundra, *f.*

tune [tju:n], *n.* Air; ton, accord, *m.*; (*fig.*) harmonie, concorde; humeur, veine, *f. In tune*, d'accord; *out of tune*, faux; *to get out of tune*, se désaccorder; *to put out of tune*, fausser, désaccorder; *to sing in tune*, chanter juste; *to sing out of tune*, chanter faux; *to sing to another tune*, changer de gamme; *to the tune of*, (*colloq.*) pour la somme de.—*v.t.* Accorder, mettre d'accord; régler, mettre au point. (*Motor.*) *To tune an engine*, mettre un moteur au point; *to tune a piano*, accorder un piano.—*v.i.* (*Rad.*) *To tune in(to) a station*, accrocher un poste; *to tune up* (of an orchestra), s'accorder.

tuneful, *a.* Harmonieux, aux accents mélodieux. **tunefully**, *adv.* Harmonieusement, mélodieusement. **tuneless**, *a.* Discordant.

tuner, *n.* Accordeur, *m.*

tungsten ['tʌŋstən], *n.* Tungstène, *m.* **tungstic**, *a.* Tungstique.

tunic ['tju:nik], *n.* Tunique, *f.* **tunicated**, *a.* Tuniqué.

tuning ['tju:niŋ], *n.* Accord, *m.*, action d'accorder, *f.*; réglage; (*Rad.*) syntonisation, *f.* **tuning-fork**, *n.* Diapason, *m.* **tuninghammer**, *n.* Accordoir, *m.*, clef d'accordeur, *f.*

Tunisia [tju'nizjə]. La Tunisie, *f.*

tunnel [tʌnl], *n.* Tunnel, passage souterrain, *m. Wind tunnel*, tunnel aérodynamique.—*v.t.* Percer un tunnel dans, percer. **tunnelling**, *n.* Construction de tunnels, *f.*, percement, *m.* **tunnel-net**, *n.* Tonnelle, *f.* **tunnel-shaft**, *n.* Puits de tunnel, *m.*

tunny ['tʌni], *n.* (*Ichth.*) Thon, *m.*

tup [tʌp], *n.* Bélier, *m.*

tuppence [TWOPENCE].

turban ['tə:bən], *n.* Turban, *m.* **turbaned**, *a.* Coiffé d'un turban.

turbid ['tə:bid], *a.* Trouble, bourbeux. **turbidity** [-'biditi] or **turbidness**, *n.* État bourbeux, état trouble, *m.* **turbidly**, *adv.* Dans un état trouble.

turbinate ['tə:binət], *a.* Turbiné.

turbine ['tə:bin *or* -bain], *n.* Turbine, *f.* (*Av.*) *Propeller turbine*, turbopropulseur, *m.*

turbo-prop ['tə:bouprɔp], *a.* (*Av.*) À turbopropulseur.

turbot ['tə:bət], *n.* Turbot, *m. Young turbot*, turbotin, *m.* **turbot-kettle**, *n.* Turbotière, *f.*

turbulence ['tə:bjuləns] or **turbulency**, *n.* Turbulence, agitation, *f.*, tumulte, *m.* **turbulent**, *a.* Tumultueux, bruyant, turbulent. **turbulently**, *adv.* Tumultueusement, d'une manière turbulente.

tureen [tju'ri:n], *n.* Soupière, *f.*

turf [tə:f], *n.* Gazon, *m.*; motte de gazon, *f.*; tourbe (peat), *f.*; (*fig.*) turf, *m.—v.t.* Gazonner. *To turf out*, (*fam.*) flanquer dehors. **turfing**, *n.* Gazonnement, *m.* **turfite**, *n.* Turfiste, *m.* **turf-moss** or **turf-pit**, *n.* Tourbière, *f.* **turfy**, *a.* Gazonné; tourbeux (peaty).

turgescence [tə:'dʒesəns], *n.* Turgescence, *f.*; (*fig.*) boursouflure, enflure, *f.*

turgid ['tə:dʒid], *a.* Gonflé; boursouflé, ampoulé (of style). **turgidity** [-'dʒiditi] or **turgidness**, *n.* Turgescence, boursouflure, emphase (of style), *f.* **turgidly**, *adv.* Avec enflure, avec bouffissure.

Turk [tə:k], *n.* Turc, *m.*, Turque, *f.*; (*fig.*) un homme terrible, *m.*; mégère, *f. A young Turk* (of a boy), un petit diable, *m.*; *Turk's head*, tête de loup, *f.*

Turkey ['tə:ki]. La Turquie, *f. Turkey carpet*, tapis de Turquie, *m.*; *Turkey red*, d'Andrinople, *f.*

turkey ['tə:ki], *n.* Dindon, coq d'Inde, *m. Hen-turkey*, dinde, *f.*; *young turkey*, dindonneau, *m.*

turkey-buzzard, *n.* Urubu, *m.*

Turkish, *a.* De Turquie, turc, *m.*, turque, *f.* —*n.* Le turc (language).

turmeric ['tə:mərik], *n.* (*Bot.*) Curcuma, safran d'Inde, *m.*

turmoil ['tə:mɔil], *n.* Tumulte, trouble, désordre, *m.*, agitation, *f.*

turn [tə:n], *v.t.* Tourner, faire tourner; faire pencher (the scale); retourner (inside out); changer, convertir, transformer (to change, transform, etc.); traduire (to translate).—

soulever (the stomach); émousser (the edge of anything); (*fig.*) rouler, agiter (in the mind). *He turns over* or *has a turn-over of, £500 a week*, ses recettes montent à 500 livres sterling par semaine; *to be turned thirty, forty, etc.*, avoir passé la trentaine, la quarantaine, etc.; *to turn about*, tourner, retourner; *to turn a cold shoulder to*, traiter avec dédain, battre froid à; *to turn adrift*, mettre à la porte, abandonner à ses propres ressources; *to turn an honest penny*, faire un profit légitime; *to turn aside*, détourner, éloigner, écarter (de); *to turn a somersault*, faire un saut périlleux; *to turn away*, renvoyer, congédier, chasser, éloigner, détourner (de); *to turn back*, faire retourner, renvoyer, (*Print.*) débloquer; *to turn down*, retourner, plier (a leaf etc.), rabattre (a collar), baisser (a jet), refuser; *to turn from*, détourner de; *to turn in*, tourner en dedans, rentrer, faire rentrer, (*Dress.*) remplier; *to turn into*, changer en, transformer en, convertir en; *to turn off*, renvoyer, chasser, congédier, couper (steam), fermer (a cock); *to turn on*, donner (steam), ouvrir (a cock); *to turn one's coat*, tourner casaque; *to turn one's hand to*, s'appliquer à; *to turn out*, mettre dehors, faire sortir, chasser, alerter (a guard), vider (pockets), faire (work), éteindre (light); *to turn out of doors*, mettre à la porte, chasser; *to turn out to grass*, mettre au vert; *to turn over*, retourner, feuilleter (the pages of a book); *to turn over and over*, tourner et retourner, retourner en tous sens; *to turn over a new leaf*, changer de conduite, faire peau neuve; *to turn over to*, envoyer à, passer à, transférer à; *to turn round*, tourner, retourner; *to turn someone's head*, tourner la tête à quelqu'un; *to turn tail*, prendre la fuite, s'enfuir honteusement; *to turn to account*, tirer parti de, profiter de; *to turn up*, remplier, retrousser, retourner (at cards); *to turn up one's nose at*, dédaigner, mépriser; *to turn upside down*, mettre sens dessus dessous; *turn him out!* à la porte! *without turning a hair*, sans broncher.

v.i.—Tourner, se tourner; se retourner (vers); se détourner (to deviate); se changer, se transformer, se convertir (en); devenir, faire (to become); se diriger, se porter (vers); porter l'attention (sur). *He did not know which way to turn*, il ne savait plus où donner de la tête; *left turn!* à gauche! *right turn!* à droite! *the guard turned out*, la garde prit les armes; *to toss and turn*, tourner et retourner; *to turn about*, se tourner, se retourner, faire volte-face; *to turn again*, tourner de nouveau, se retourner, redevenir (to become again); *to turn aside*, se détourner, s'éloigner (de); *to turn away*, se détourner, s'en aller; *to turn back*, se retourner en arrière, rebrousser chemin, retourner sur ses pas (to return); *to turn down a street*, prendre une rue; *to turn from*, s'éloigner de, se détourner de, se soulever à (of the stomach); *to turn in*, se tourner en dedans, entrer (to enter), se coucher, se mettre au lit (to go to bed); *to turn into*, se changer en, se convertir en, se transformer en; *to turn off*, se détourner; *to turn on*, attaquer, tourner sur, rouler sur (of conversation etc.); *to turn out*, sortir, quitter le lit, se lever (to rise from bed), arriver (to happen), tourner, finir (to end ill

or well), devenir (to become), faire grève (of workmen); *to turn over*, se tourner, se retourner, verser, se renverser (to upset), changer de parti (to change sides); *to turn round*, tourner, se tourner, se retourner, changer de parti (to change sides); *to turn round and round*, tournoyer; *to turn soldier*, se faire militaire; *to turn sour* (of milk), tourner; *to turn to*, s'adresser à, avoir recours à, se mettre à (to set about); *to turn to the left* or *to the right*, prendre à gauche or à droite; *to turn turtle*, (*Naut.*) chavirer; *to turn under*, tourner en dessous; *to turn up*, se retrousser; arriver, se trouver (to happen), se retrouver (to be found again), survenir (of events), arriver, se présenter (of persons), retourner (at cards); *to turn upside down*, se renverser, chavirer (boat), capoter (car); *to what should I turn?* à quoi me résoudre? quel parti prendre?

n.—Tour, *m.*; révolution (of a wheel), *f.*; tournant (winding), coude, détour (bend), *m.*; service; changement, *m.*, vicissitude; tournure (direction); occasion, chance, *f.*; penchant, *m.*, goût (inclination), *m.*; forme, *f.*, contour (form); caractère, *m.*, tournure d'esprit (of thought), *f.*; rond (of a rope); trait (of the scales), *m.* *A bad turn*, un mauvais tour; *a good turn*, un service d'ami; *at every turn*, à tout propos, à tout bout de champ; *by turns*, à tour de rôle, tour à tour; *cooked* (or *done*) *to a turn*, cuit à point; *he did me a bad turn*, il m'a joué un mauvais tour; *he did me a good turn*, il m'a rendu un grand service; *in one's turn*, à son tour; *in turns*, tour à tour, à tour de rôle; *it is your turn*, à vous le dé, c'est votre tour, c'est à vous (de); *it is your turn to play*, vous avez la main (at cards); *it is your turn to read*, c'est à vous de lire; *one good turn deserves another*, à beau jeu, beau retour; *the books we read give a turn to our thoughts*, les livres que nous lisons donnent le ton à nos pensées; *the road took a sharp turn*, la route faisait un coude brusque; *this news has given me quite a turn*, (*fam.*) cette nouvelle m'a tout bouleversé; *to serve one's turn*, faire son affaire; *to take a turn*, faire un tour; prendre une tournure (of events); *turn and turn about*, chacun son tour; *whose turn is it?* à qui le tour? à qui est-ce . . .?

turncoat, *n.* Renégat, *m.*

turn-cock, *n.* Fontainier, *m.*

turn-down, *a.* Rabattu (of collars etc.).

turner, *n.* Tourneur, *m.* **turnery,** *n.* Art du tourneur, *m.*

turning, *n.* Tour; détour, tournant (of a road etc.); virage; tournage, travail au tour (at the lathe); (*Print.*) blocage, *m.* **turning-lathe,** *n.* Tour, *m.* **turning-point,** *n.* Point décisif, moment critique, *m.*

turnip ['tɜːnɪp], *n.* Navet, *m.* **turnip-cabbage,** *n.* Chou-rave, *m.* **turnip-cutter,** *n.* Coupe-racines, *m.*

turnkey, *n.* Guichetier, porte-clefs, *m.*

turn-out, *n.* Équipage, train, *m.*; tenue, *f.*; assemblée, *f.*; grève (of workmen), *f.*

turn-over, *n.* Chiffre d'affaires; chausson (pastry), *m.*

turnpike, *n.* Barrière de péage, *f.*, tourniquet, *m.*

turn-screw, *n.* Tournevis, *m.*

turnsole, *n.* Tournesol, *m.*

turnspit, n. Tournebroche, m.
turnstile, n. Tourniquet, m.
turnstone, n. (Orn.) Tournepierre, m.
turn-table, n. Plaque tournante, f.; platine, f.
turn-up, n. Revers (of trousers), m.
turpentine ['tə:pəntain], n. Térébenthine, f. Oil of turpentine, essence de térébenthine, f.
turpeth ['tə:peθ], n. Turbith, m.
turpitude ['tə:pitju:d], n. Turpitude, f.
turps [tə:ps], n. (fam.) Térébenthine, f.
turquoise ['tə:kwɔiz or 'tə:kɔiz], n. Turquoise, f.
turret ['tʌrit], n. Tourelle, f. **turret-ship**, n. Navire à tourelles, m.
turreted, a. Garni de tourelles.
turtle [tə:tl], n. Tortue de mer, f. To turn turtle, chavirer (boat), capoter (car). **turtle-dove**, n. Tourterelle, f. **turtle-soup**, n. Soupe à la tortue, f.
Tuscan ['tʌskən], a. and n. Toscan, m., toscane, f. **Tuscany**. La Toscane, f.
tush! [tʌʃ], int. Bah! fi donc!
tusk [tʌsk], n. Défense, f. (of elephant); croc (tooth), m. **tusked** or **tusky**, a. Muni de défenses or de crocs.
tusker, n. Éléphant adulte, m.
tussle [tʌsl], n. Lutte, bagarre, f.—v.i. Lutter.
tussock ['tʌsək], n. Herbe touffue, f.
tut! [tʌt], int. Bah! Allons donc!
tutelage ['tju:tilidʒ], n. Tutelle, f. **tutelary**, a. Tutélaire.
tutor ['tju:tə], n. Précepteur (private tutor); (Law) tuteur; (Univ.) maître-assistant, m.—v.t. Instruire, enseigner; reprendre (to correct). **tutorial** [-'tɔ:riəl], a. De précepteur.—n. Leçon privée avec son maître-assistant (à l'université), f.; (pl.) travaux pratiques, travaux dirigés, m.pl. **tutoring**, n. Instruction, f., enseignement, m. **tutorship**, n. Préceptorat, m.
tutsan ['tʌtsən], n. (Bot.) Toute saine, f.
tutty ['tʌti], n. Tutie, f.
tuxedo [tak'si:dou], n. (Am.) Smoking, m.
twaddle [twɔdl], n. Bavardage, caquetage, m., fadaises, f.pl.—v.i. Dire des fadaises. **twaddler**, n. Bavard, péroreur, m.
*twain [twein], a. and n. Deux, m. To cut in twain, couper en deux.
twang [twæŋ], n. Son sec (d'une corde qui vibre); nasillement, accent nasillard (nasal voice), m.—v.i. Résonner, nasiller.—v.t. Faire résonner, faire vibrer.
tweak [twi:k], v.t. Pincer (en tordant).
tweed [twi:d], n. Cheviote écossaise, f.; tweed, m.
'tween-decks ['twi:ndeks], n. (Naut.) L'entre-pont, m.
tweet [twi:t], n. Pépiement, m.—v.i. Pépier.
tweezers ['twi:zəz], n.pl. Petites pinces, f.pl.; pinces à épiler (for the hair), f.pl.
twelfth [twelfθ], a. and n. Douzième; douze (of the month etc.), m. Twelfth cake, gâteau des Rois, m.; Twelfth Night, jour des Rois, m.
twelve [twelv], a. and n. Douze, m. Twelve o'clock, midi (noon), minuit (midnight), m.
twelvemonth, n. An, m., année, f. Last Easter twelvemonth, il y a un an à Pâques dernier; this day twelvemonth, il y a aujourd'hui un an (past), d'ici un an (future).
twelvepounder, n. Canon de douze, m.

twentieth ['twentiəθ], a. and n. Vingtième; vingt (of the month etc.), m.
twenty ['twenti], a. and n. Vingt, m. **twenty-first**, n. Vingt et unième, m. The twenty-first (of the month), le vingt et un. **twenty-four pounder**, n. Canon de vingt-quatre, m.
twibill ['twaibil], n. Besaiguë, f. (of carpenter).
twice [twais], adv. Deux fois. To make someone think twice, donner à réfléchir à quelqu'un; to think twice, y regarder à deux fois; twice as much, le double, deux fois autant.
twiddle [twidl], v.t. Tourner, agiter. To twiddle one's thumbs, se tourner les pouces.
twig [twig], n. Petite branche, brindille, ramille, f.; baguette (de sourcier), f.—v.t. (colloq.) Remarquer, comprendre. **twiggy**, a. Plein de ramilles.
twilight ['twailait], n. Crépuscule; demi-jour, m.—a. Crépusculaire.
twill [twil], v.t. Croiser.—n. Étoffe croisée, f.
twin [twin], n. Jumeau, m., jumelle, f.; (fig.) frère, m., sœur, f. The Twins, (Astron.) les Gémeaux, m.pl.—a. Jumeau; jumelé; (Bot.) double, géminé. Siamese twins, frères siamois; (Av.) twin-engine, bimoteur; twin tyres, pneus jumelés.—v.i. Donner naissance à des jumeaux.—v.t. Jumeler, apparier. Town twinning, jumelage de villes, m. **twin-born**, a. Né jumeau, née jumelle. **twin-track**, n. (Rail.) Double voie, f.
twine [twain], n. Ficelle, f.; entrelacement, entortillement, m.—v.t. Retordre; enlacer.—v.i. S'entrelacer, s'enrouler.
twinge [twindʒ], n. Élancement, tiraillement, m.; (of conscience) remords, m.—v.i. Élancer, lanciner; (fig.) torturer. **twinging**, n. Élancement, m.—a. Lancinant.
twinkle [twiŋkl], v.i. Étinceler, scintiller; pétiller, clignoter (of the eyes).
twinkling, n. Scintillement, m., pétillement, clignotement (of the eyes), m. In the twinkling of an eye, en un clin d'œil.—a. Étincelant, scintillant; pétillant.
twirl [twə:l], v.i. Tournoyer, tourner rapidement. To twirl round, pirouetter.—v.t. Faire tournoyer; faire faire le moulinet à; friser (moustache). He twirls him round his little finger, il lui fait faire tout ce qu'il veut.—n. Tour, tournoiement, m.; rotation, pirouette, f.
twist [twist], v.t. Tordre; tortiller, retordre; cercler, entourer (to encircle); entrelacer, enlacer (to wind round); (fig.) torturer, pervertir, défigurer (to pervert). To twist one's ankle, se fouler la cheville; to twist oneself into, s'insinuer dans, se glisser dans; to twist round one's finger, tenir dans sa manche, entortiller.—v.i. Se tordre, s'entrelacer, s'enlacer, s'enrouler.—n. Cordon, m., corde, f.; cordonnet (of cotton etc.), m.; tortillon (of paper), m.; contorsion (contortion), f., tortillement, m.; carotte (of tobacco), f.; gauchissement, gondolage, m.; (fig.) déformation, f. To give a twist to, tordre; to give oneself a twist, se tordre.
twisted, a. Tordu; (Arch.) tors; (fig.) perverti, défiguré, dénaturé. **twister**, n. Tordeur, m., -euse, f.
twisting, n. Tordage; tortillement, m.—a. Tortueux. **twisting-machine**, n. Machine à tordre, f.

twit [twit], *v.t.* Narguer, railler; reprocher (à), accuser (de).

twitch [twitʃ], *n.* Saccade, *f.*; petit coup sec, *m.*; contraction spasmodique, *f.*; tiraillement, *m.*—*v.t.* Tirer brusquement; contracter, crisper.—*v.i.* Se contracter nerveusement.

twitching, *n.* Saccade, contraction, crispation (of muscles etc.), *f.*; tiraillement (of pain), *m.*

twitter ['twitə], *v.t.* Gazouiller.—*n.* Gazouillement, *m.*

twittingly ['twitiŋli], *adv.* Avec reproche; en narguant.

two [tu:], *a.* and *n.* Deux, *m. In twos*, en deux; *to cut in two*, couper en deux; *two and* (or *by*) *two*, deux à deux; *two can play at that game*, à bon chat bon rat; *two heads are better than one*, deux avis valent mieux qu'un; *two's company, three is none*, deux s'amusent, trois s'ennuient.

two-colour, *a.* (*Cine.*) *Two-colour system*, bichromie, *f.* **two-edged**, *a.* À deux tranchants. **two-engined**, *a.* (*Av.*) Bimoteur. **two-faced**, *a.* (*fig.*) Hypocrite. **twofold**, *a.* Double.—*adv.* Doublement, deux fois. **two-handed**, *a.* À deux mains; bimane. **two-legged**, *a.* À deux jambes, bipède. **two-masted**, *a.* À deux mâts.

twopence ['tʌpəns], *n.pl.* **twopenny** ['tʌpəni], *a.* (De) deux pence.

two-ply, *a.* À double pli; à deux fils.

two-seater, *n.* Voiturette à deux places, *f.* **two-shot**, *n.* (*Cine.*) Plan américain. **two-step**, *n.* Pas de deux, *m.* **two-stroke**, *a.* À deux temps.

tycoon [tai'ku:n], *n.* Taïcoun, *m.*; (*fam.*) brasseur d'affaires, manitou, *m.*

tymbal [timbl], *n.* Timbale, *f.*

tympan ['timpən] or **tympanum**, *n.* Tympan, *m.* **tympanic** [-'pænik], *a.* Tympanique. **tympanites** [-pə'naiti:z] or **tympany** ['timpəni], *n.* Tympanite, *f.*

type [taip], *n.* Type; (*Print.*) caractère; (*pop.*) type, *m. To be in type*, être composé; *to set up in type*, composer.—*v.t.* [TYPEWRITE].

type-metal, *n.* Alliage, *m.* **type-script**, *n.* Manuscrit dactylographié, *m.* **type-setter**, *n.* Compositeur, *m.* **typewrite**, *v.t.* Écrire à la machine, dactylographier, taper, **typewriter**, *n.* Machine à écrire, *f.* **typewriting**, *n.* Dactylographie (art), *f.* **typewritten**, *a.* Tapé à la machine.

typhoid ['taifɔid], *a.* Typhoïde.

typhoon [tai'fu:n], *n.* Typhon, *m.*, trombe, *f.*

typhus ['taifəs], *n.* Typhus, *m.*

typical ['tipikl], *a.* Typique. **typically**, *adv.* D'une manière typique, typiquement. **typify**, *v.t.* Représenter d'une manière typique, symboliser.

typing ['taipiŋ], *n.* Dactylographie, (*fam.*) dactylo, *f.* **typist** ['taipist], *n.* Dactylographe, *m.* or *f.*, (*fam.*) dactylo, *m.* or *f.*

typographer [tai'pɔgrəfə], *n.* Typographe, *m.* **typographic** [-pə'græfik] or **typographical**, *a.* Typographique. **typographically**, *adv.* Typographiquement. **typography** [-'pɔgrəfi], *n.* Typographie, *f.*

typolite ['taipolait], *n.* (*Geol.*) Typolithe, *f.*

typolithography [taipoli'θɔgrəfi], *n.* Typolithographie, *f.*

tyrannical [ti'rænikl], *a.* Tyrannique. **tyrannically**, *adv.* Tyranniquement.

tyrannize ['tirənaiz], *v.i.* Faire le tyran. *To tyrannize over*, tyranniser.

tyranny ['tirəni], *n.* Tyrannie, *f.*

tyrant ['taiərənt], *n.* Tyran, *m. Petty tyrant*, tyranneau, *m.*

tyre ['taiə], *n.* Bandage, cerclage (of wheel); (bandage) pneumatique, (*fam.*) pneu, *m. Detachable tyre*, pneu démontable; *solid tyre*, pneu plein; *tyre-gauge*, indicateur de pression des pneus, *m.*; *tyre inflator* or *tyre-pump*, pompe, *f.*

Tyrian ['tiriən], *a.* De Tyr.

tyro ['taiərou], *n.* Novice, commençant, apprenti, néophyte, *m.*

Tyrolese [tirə'li:z], *a.* and *n.* Tyrolien, *m.*, Tyrolienne, *f. Tyrolese song*, Tyrolienne, *f.*

Tzar [za:] [TSAR].

Tzigane [tsi'ga:n], *a.* and *n.* Tzigane, tsigane, *m.* or *f.*

U

U, u [ju:]. Vingt et unième lettre de l'alphabet, *m. U-boat*, sous-marin allemand, *m.*

ubiquitarian [jubikwi'teəriən], *a.* and *n.* Ubiquitaire, *m.* **ubiquitous** [ju'bikwitəs], *a.* Omniprésent, présent partout. **ubiquity**, *n.* Ubiquité, *f.*

udder ['ʌdə], *n.* Mamelle, *f.*, pis, *m.* **uddered**, *a.* Mamelé.

udometer [ju'dɔmitə], *n.* Udomètre, pluviomètre, *m.*

udometric [ju:do'metrik], *a.* Udométrique.

ugh ! [u:x, u:h, ʌx, uf], *int.* Pouah!

uglily ['ʌglili], *adv.* Avec laideur, vilainement.

ugliness, *n.* Laideur, *f.*

ugly ['ʌgli], *a.* Laid, vilain. *As ugly as sin*, laid comme les sept péchés capitaux; *frightfully ugly*, laid à faire peur; *to grow ugly*, enlaidir; *ugly words*, de vilaines paroles, *f.pl.*

uhlan ['u:la:n or 'ju:lən], *n.* Uhlan, *m.*

ukase [ju'keis], *n.* Ukase, *m.*

Ukraine [ju'krein], **the.** L'Ukraine, *f.*

ukulele [ju:kə'leili], *n.* Ukulélé, *m.*

ulcer ['ʌlsə], *n.* Ulcère, *m.* **ulcerate**, *v.t.* Ulcérer.—*v.i.* S'ulcérer. **ulcerated**, *a.* Ulcéré. **ulceration** [-'reiʃən], *n.* Ulcération, *f.* **ulcerous**, *a.* Ulcéreux.

ulema ['u:limə], *n.* Uléma, *m.*

uliginose [ju'lidʒinous], *a.* (*Bot.*) Uligineux.

ullage ['ʌlidʒ], *n.* Vidange, *f.*

ulmic ['ʌlmik], *a.* (*Chem.*) Ulmique. **ulmin**, *n.* Ulmine, *f.*

ulna ['ʌlnə], *n.* (*Anat.*) Cubitus, *m.* **ulnar**, *a.* Cubital.

ulterior [ʌl'tiəriə], *a.* Ultérieur. *Without ulterior motive*, sans arrière-pensée. **ulteriorly**, *adv.* Ultérieurement.

ultimate ['ʌltimit], *a.* Dernier; final, extrême, définitif. **ultimately**, *adv.* Finalement, à la fin, en fin de compte. **ultimatum** [-'meitəm], *n.* (*pl.* **ultimata**) Ultimatum, *m.*; but final, *m.* **ultimo** ['ʌltimou], *adv.* (*abbr.* **ult.**) Du mois dernier.

ultra ['ʌltrə], *n.* Ultra, *m.*

ultramarine [-mə'ri:n], *n.* Outremer; bleu d'outremer.—*a.* D'outremer.

ultramontane [-'mɔntein], *a.* and *n.* Ultramontain, *m.* **ultramontanism**, *n.* Ultramontanisme, *m.*

ultramundane [-'mʌndein], a. Ultramondain.
ultrasonic [-'sɔnik], a. Ultrasonore.
ultra-violet, a. Ultra-violet.
ululate ['juːljuleit], v.i. Ululer; hurler.
 ululation [juːlju'leiʃən], n. Ululation, f.,
 ululement, m.
Ulysses [ju:'lisiːz]. Ulysse, m.
umbel [ʌmbl], n. (Bot.) Ombelle, f. **um-
 bellar** or **umbellate**, a. Ombellé. **umbelliferous**, [-be'lifərəs], a. Ombellifère.
umber ['ʌmbə], n. (Paint.) Terre d'ombre, f.;
 ombre (grayling), m.—v.t. Ombrer, brunir,
 assombrir.
umbilical [ʌm'bilikl], a. Ombilical. **um-
 bilicate** or **umbilicated**, a. Ombiliqué.
umbilicus, n. Ombilic, m.
umbrage ['ʌmbridʒ], n. Ombrage, m.; ombre,
 f.; (fig.) ombrage, m. To give umbrage to,
 faire, porter ombrage à; to take umbrage at,
 prendre ombrage de, s'offusquer de.
umbrageous [ʌm'breidʒəs], a. Ombragé
 (place); ombrageux (person).
umbrella [ʌm'brelə], n. Parapluie, m.
 umbrella-stand, n. Porte-parapluie, m.
umbrella-stick, n. Manche de parapluie,
 m. **umbrella-tree**, n. Magnolier parasol, m.
umpire ['ʌmpaiə], n. Tiers arbitre, arbitre, m.
 —v.t. Arbitrer.
unabashed [ʌnə'bæʃt], a. Sans être confus,
 sans être déconcerté.
unabated [-'beitid], a. Non diminué, sans
 diminution.
unabetted [-'betid], a. Sans aide, seul, sans
 encouragement.
unable [ʌn'eibl], a. Incapable (de); hors d'état
 de; impuissant (à or pour). To be unable to,
 ne pas pouvoir, être incapable de, ne pas être
 à même de, n'être pas en état de.
unabridged [-ə'bridʒd], a. Non abrégé; complet, en entier.
unaccented [ʌnæk'sentid], a. Non-accentué,
 sans accent; (Philol.) atone.
unacceptable [-ək'septəbl], a. Inacceptable.
 Unacceptable to, déplaisant or désagréable à.
 unaccepted, a. Refusé.
unacclimatized [ʌnə'klaimətaizd], a. Inaccli-
 maté.
unaccommodating [-'kɔmədeitiŋ], a. Peu
 accommodant.
unaccompanied [-'kʌmpənid], a. Non
 accompagné (de); seul, sans suite; (Mus.)
 sans accompagnement, a cappella.
unaccomplished [-'kʌmpliʃt], a. Inachevé,
 incomplet; (fig.) sans talent.
unaccountable [-'kauntəbl], a. Inexplicable,
 inconcevable; bizarre, étrange. **unaccount-
 ableness**, n. Bizarrerie, étrangeté; nature
 inexplicable, f. **unaccountably**, adv. D'une
 manière inexplicable, inconcevablement,
 étrangement. **unaccounted for**, a. Inexpliqué; manquant.
unaccredited [-'kreditid], a. Non accrédité,
 sans pouvoirs.
unaccustomed [-'kʌstəmd], a. Inaccoutumé
 (à); peu habitué; extraordinaire.
unacknowledged [-ək'nɔlidʒd], a. Non reconnu, non avoué; non accrédité; sans réponse (of
 letters). Unacknowledged letter, lettre restée
 sans réponse, f.
unacquainted [-'kweintid], a. Qui ne connaît
 pas, étranger (à); peu familier (avec), peu
 versé (dans). To be unacquainted with, ne pas

connaître (persons), ignorer, ne pas savoir
 (things).
unacquired [-'kwaiəd], a. Non acquis,
 naturel.
unacted [ʌn'æktid], a. Qu'on n'a pas joué
 (fem. -ée) (of plays).
unadjusted [-ə'dʒʌstid], a. Non ajusté; non
 arrangé.
unadmitted [ʌnəd'mitid], a. Non admis;
 inavoué.
unadopted [-'dɔptid], a. Non adopté.
unadorned [-'dɔːnd], a. Sans ornement,
 naturel, simple.
unadulterated [-'dʌltəreitid], a. Pur, sans
 mélange, non frelaté, non falsifié.
unadvisable [-əd'vaizəbl], a. Peu sage, peu
 convenable, inopportun; contre-indiqué. **un-
 advisableness**, n. Imprudence, f. **un-
 advised**, a. Malavisé, inconsidéré; irréfléchi,
 imprudent (rash). **unadvisedly**, adv. Inconsidérément; imprudemment. **unadvised-
 ness**, n. Imprudence, f.
unaffected [-ə'fektid], a. Sans affectation,
 naturel, simple, naïf; impassible, insensible
 (not easily moved); inchangé, tel quel.
 unaffectedly, adv. Sans affectation,
 simplement, naturellement. **unaffected-
 ness**, n. Simplicité, f., naturel, m.
unaffiliated [-ə'filieitid], a. Non affilié.
unafraid [ʌnə'freid], a. Sans peur.
unaided [-'eidid], a. Seul, sans aide.
unalienable [INALIENABLE].
unallayed [-ə'leid], a. Non apaisé.
unallowable [-'lauəbl], a. Non permis;
 inadmissible.
unalloyed [-'lɔid], a. Pur, sans alliage, sans
 mélange.
unalterable [ʌn'ɔːltərəbl], a. Inaltérable, invariable. **unalterableness**, n. Inaltérabilité,
 invariabilité, f. **unalterably**, adv. D'une
 manière inaltérable, immuablement. **un-
 altered**, a. Sans changement.
unamazed [ʌnə'meizd], a. Nullement étonné.
unambiguous [ʌnæm'bigjuəs], a. Sans ambiguïté, sans équivoque. **unambiguously**,
 adv. Sans ambiguïté, clairement.
unambitious [-'biʃəs], a. Sans ambition; sans
 prétention. **unambitiously**, adv. Sans
 prétention, sans ambition.
unamenable [ʌnə'miːnəbl], a. Réfractaire;
 peu commode.
unamiable [ʌn'eimiəbl], a. Peu aimable;
 désagréable.
unanimity [juːnə'nimiti], n. Unanimité, f.
 With unanimity, à l'unanimité.
unanimous [ju'næniməs], a. Unanime.
 unanimously, adv. Unanimement, à
 l'unanimité. Carried unanimously, voté à
 l'unanimité.
unanswerable [ʌn'ɑːnsərəbl], a. Sans
 réplique, incontestable. **unanswerable-
 ness**, n. Nature irréfutable, f. **unanswer-
 ably**, adv. Sans réplique; d'une manière
 irréfutable, incontestablement. **unanswered**,
 a. Sans réponse, sans réplique.
unappalled [ʌnə'pɔːld], a. Sans s'émouvoir,
 sans crainte, sans pâlir.
unapparent [ʌnə'pɛərənt], a. Non apparent;
 invisible, inaperçue.
unappeasable [ʌnə'piːzəbl], a. Insatiable;
 implacable. **unappeased**, a. Non apaisé,
 inapaisé.

unappetizing [ʌn'æpitaiziŋ], *a*. Peu appétissant.

unapplied [ʌnə'plaid], *a*. Inappliqué; sans emploi.

unappreciated [-'pri:ʃieitid], *a*. Incompris, inapprécié. **unappreciative**, *a*. Insensible.

unapprehensive [-æpri'hensiv], *a*. Sans appréhension.

unapprised [-ə'praizd], *a*. Non prévenu (de).

unapproachable [-'proutʃəbl], *a*. Inaccessible, inabordable.

unappropriated [-'prouprieitid], *a*. Non approprié, sans emploi; (money) disponible.

unapproved [-'pru:vd], *a*. Non approuvé.

unapt [ʌn'æpt], *a*. Peu propre, peu capable (de); peu convenable (improper). **unaptly**, *adv*. Mal, hors de propos, mal à propos. **unaptness**, *n*. Incapacité, inaptitude, *f*.

unarmed [-'ɑ:md], *a*. Sans armes; désarmé; (*Bot*.) inerme; (*Zool*.) sans défenses.

unarmoured [-'ɑ:məd], *a*. Non cuirassé.

unarrayed [-ə'reid], *a*. Sans ornements; sans ordre (of armies).

unascertainable [ʌnæsə'teinəbl], *a*. Qu'on ne peut constater *ou* vérifier. **unascertained**, *a*. Non vérifié, non constaté.

unashamed [-'ʃeimd], *a*. Sans honte.

unasked [ʌn'ɑ:skt], *a*. Sans être invité; spontané.—*adv*. Spontanément.

unaspiring [-ə'spaiəriŋ], *a*. Sans ambition, modeste.

unassailable [ʌnə'seiləbl], *a*. Hors d'atteinte, inattaquable, irréfutable. **unassailed** or **unassaulted**, *a*. Sans être attaqué.

unassertive [ʌnə'sə:tiv], *a*. Modeste, timide.

unassisted [ʌnə'sistid], *a*. Sans aide.

unassuming [ʌnə'sju:miŋ], *a*. Sans prétention, modeste.

unassured [ʌnə'ʃuəd], *a*. Non assuré, sans être assuré.

unatoned [ʌnə'tound], *a*. Inexpié, sans expiation.

unattached [ʌnə'tætʃt], *a*. Sans être attaché (à); libre; libre d'engagement affectif; (*Mil*.) en disponibilité.

unattainable [ʌnə'teinəbl], *a*. Inaccessible, impossible à atteindre.

unattempted [ʌnə'temptid], *a*. Non essayé, qui n'a pas été tenté.

unattended [ʌnə'tendid], *a*. Seul, sans suite; sans soins, négligé; peu fréquenté.

unattested [ʌnə'testid], *a*. Non attesté; non légalisé.

unattired [ʌnə'taiəd], *a*. Sans parure; sans vêtements.

unattractive [ʌnə'træktiv], *a*. Peu attrayant, sans attrait.

unauthentic [ʌnɔ:'θentik], *a*. Inauthentique, apocryphe. **unauthenticated**, *a*. Dont l'authenticité n'est pas prouvée; (*Law*) non légalisé.

unauthorized [ʌn'ɔ:θəraizd], *a*. Sans autorisation; illicite, illégal (of things).

unavailable [ʌnə'veiləbl], *a*. Non valable; inutilisable (ticket); indisponible (capital, person); qu'on ne peut se procurer (thing).

unavailing [ʌnə'veiliŋ], *a*. Inutile, vain, inefficace. **unavailingly**, *adv*. En vain.

unavenged [ʌnə'vendʒd], *a*. Impuni, non vengé.

unavoidable [ʌnə'vɔidəbl], *a*. Inévitable. **unavoidably**, *adv*. Inévitablement.

unaware [ʌnə'wɛə], *a*. Ignorant. *To be*

unaware of, ignorer, n'être pas au courant de.

unawares, *adv*. À l'improviste, par mégarde; à son insu (unconsciously). *To be taken unawares*, être pris au dépourvu.

unawed [ʌn'ɔ:d], *a*. Sans être intimidé (de).

unbalanced [ʌn'bælənst], *a*. Mal équilibré.

unbar [ʌn'bɑ:], *v.t.* Débarrer.

unbearable [ʌn'bɛərəbl], *a*. Insupportable, intolérable. **unbearably**, *adv*. Insupportablement.

unbeatable [ʌn'bi:təbl], *a*. Invincible.

unbeaten [ʌn'bi:tn], *a*. Invaincu; non battu.

unbecoming [ʌnbi'kʌmiŋ], *a*. Peu convenable, malséant, déplacé; qui ne va pas bien (of clothes). **unbecomingly**, *adv*. D'une manière peu séante.

unbefitting [ʌnbi'fitiŋ], *a*. Qui ne convient pas, peu propre; qui s'accorde mal (avec).

unbeknown [ʌnbi'noun], *a*. Inconnu.

unbelief [ʌnbi'li:f], *n*. Incrédulité, incroyance, *f*. **unbelievable**, *a*. Incroyable. **unbeliever**, *n*. **unbelieving**, *a*. Incrédule, infidèle, mécréant; sceptique, *m*.

unbend [ʌn'bend], *v.t.* Détendre, relâcher; débander (a bow); affaiblir, énerver (to enervate); (*fig*.) délasser (the mind); (*Naut*.) détalinguer (a cable); démarrer (a rope); désenverguer (a sail).—*v.i.* Se détendre; se dérider. **unbending**, *a*. Qui ne se plie pas, inflexible.

unbeneficed [ʌn'benifist], *a*. Sans bénéfice (of clergymen).

unbeneficial [ʌnbeni'fiʃl], *a*. Sans profit, sans avantage.

unbewailed [ʌnbi'weild], *a*. Sans être pleuré, non regretté.

unbiased [ʌn'baiəst], *a*. Sans prévention, impartial.

unbidden [ʌn'bidn], *a*. Sans être invité; spontané(ment).

unbind [ʌn'baind], *v.t.* (*past and p.p.* **unbound**) Délier, détacher, desserrer (to loose).

unblamable [ʌn'bleiməbl], *a*. Exempt de blâme, sans reproche.

unbleached [ʌn'bli:tʃt], *a*. Écru.

unblemished [ʌn'blemiʃt], *a*. Sans tache, sans défaut, sans souillure.

unblended [ʌn'blendid], *a*. Pur, sans mélange.

unblest [ʌn'blest], *a*. Non béni; malheureux, infortuné (unhappy); maudit (cursed).

unblighted [ʌn'blaitid], *a*. Non flétri; (*fig*.) dans toute sa fraîcheur. *Unblighted happiness*, félicité pure, *f*.

unblock [ʌn'blɔk], *v.t.* Décaler, dégager.

unblown [ʌn'bloun], *a*. En bouton, non encore épanoui.

unblushing [ʌn'blʌʃiŋ], *a*. Qui ne rougit point, éhonté, sans vergogne. **unblushingly**, *adv*. Sans rougir, effrontément.

unbolt [ʌn'boult], *v.t.* Tirer les verrous de, ouvrir. **unbolted**, *a*. Non verrouillé; non bluté (unsifted, of flour).

unborn [ʌn'bɔ:n], *a*. Encore à naître; futur, à venir (of things). *Innocent as a newborn babe*, innocent comme l'enfant qui vient de naître.

unbosom [ʌn'buzəm], *v.t.* Découvrir, révéler, *To unbosom oneself*, ouvrir son cœur, s'ouvrir (à).

unbound [ʌn'baund], *a*. Délié, dénoué; non attaché, libre (free); non relié (of books).

unbounded [ʌn'baundid], *a.* Illimité, infini, sans bornes; démesuré; effréné (unrestrained).
unboundedly, *adv.* Sans bornes, démesurément, infiniment.
unbrace [ʌn'breis], *v.t.* Relâcher, desserrer; détendre (a drum); affaiblir, énerver (to weaken).
unbreakable [ʌn'breikəbl], *a.* Incassable.
unbreathable [ʌn'bri:ðəbl], *a.* Irrespirable.
unbreeched [ʌn'bri:tʃt], *a.* Sans culotte; déculassé (of guns).
unbribed [ʌn'braibd], *a.* Non corrompu, non acheté.
unbridge [ʌn'bridʒ], *v.t.* (*Mil.*) Faire sauter les ponts.
unbridled [ʌn'braidld], *a.* Débridé, sans frein; (*fig.*) effréné, déchaîné.
unbroken [ʌn'broukn], *a.* Non rompu; ininterrompu, continu (uninterrupted); indomptable, indompté (not subdued); non violé, non enfreint, intact (not violated); non dressé (of animals).
unbrotherly [ʌn'brʌðəli], *a.* Peu fraternel, indigne d'un frère.
unbruised [ʌn'bru:zd], *a.* Sans meurtrissure, intact.
unbuckle [ʌn'bʌkl], *v.t.* Déboucler.
unburden [ʌn'bə:dn], *v.t.* Décharger, débarrasser (d'un fardeau); (*fig.*) soulager, alléger. *To unburden oneself,* ouvrir son cœur.
unburied [ʌn'berid], *a.* Sans sépulture.
unburnt [ʌn'bə:nt], *a.* Non brûlé.
unbury [ʌn'beri], *v.t.* Déterrer, exhumer.
unbusinesslike [ʌn'biznislaik], *a.* Peu pratique; impropre aux affaires, irrégulier.
unbutton [ʌn'bʌtn], *v.t.* Déboutonner.
uncage [ʌn'keidʒ], *v.t.* Faire sortir de sa cage, délivrer. **uncaged,** *a.* Sorti de sa cage; en liberté.
uncalled [ʌn'kɔ:ld], *a.* Sans être appelé. *Uncalled for,* sans être demandé; peu nécessaire, gratuit (unnecessary); déplacé, peu convenable (unbecoming); non mérité (undeserved).
uncancelled [ʌn'kænsld], *a.* Sans être annulé; non oblitéré; non rayé.
uncannily [ʌn'kænili], *adv.* D'une manière étrange.
uncanny [ʌn'kæni], *a.* Étrange, mystérieux, surnaturel.
uncap [ʌn'kæp], *v.t.* Découvrir; désamorcer (fire-arms).
uncared-for [ʌn'kɛədfɔ:], *a.* Dont on ne se soucie pas, négligé, dans l'abandon.
uncaught [ʌn'kɔ:t], *a.* Sans être pris. *He is still uncaught,* on ne l'a pas encore pris, il est encore en liberté.
unceasing [ʌn'si:siŋ], *a.* Incessant, sans cesse. **unceasingly,** *adv.* Continuellement, sans cesse.
uncensored [ʌn'sensəd], *a.* Non expurgé.
uncensured [ʌn'senʃəd], *a.* Sans être censuré.
unceremonious [ʌnseri'mouniəs], *a.* Peu cérémonieux; sans gêne; sans façon. **unceremoniously,** *adv.* Sans cérémonie, sans façon, sans gêne. **unceremoniousness,** *n.* Sans-façon, sans-gêne, *m.*
uncertain [ʌn'sə:tin], *a.* Incertain, irrésolu, peu sûr; mal assuré, chancelant (of steps). **uncertainly,** *adv.* Sans certitude, au hasard. **uncertainty,** *n.* Incertitude, *f.*; l'incertain (something unknown), *m.*

uncertificated [ʌnsə'tifikətid], *a.* Sans diplôme, non diplômé (of teachers); qui n'a pas obtenu de concordat (bankrupt).
unchain [ʌn'tʃein], *v.t.* Déchaîner; briser les chaînes de, délivrer.
unchallengeable [ʌn'tʃælindʒəbl], *a.* Indiscutable; indisputable.
unchallenged [ʌn'tʃælindʒd], *a.* Sans être contredit, indisputé.
unchangeable [ʌn'tʃeindʒəbl], *a.* Inaltérable, invariable, immuable; inchangeable. **unchangeableness,** *n.* Immutabilité, inaltérabilité, *f.* **unchangeably,** *adv.* Immuablement. **unchanged,** *a.* Qui n'est pas changé, qui est toujours le même. **unchanging,** *a.* Qui ne change pas; invariable, constant.
uncharged [ʌn'tʃɑ:dʒd], *a.* Non chargé (unloaded). *Uncharged for,* franco, gratuit.
uncharitable [ʌn'tʃæritəbl], *a.* Peu charitable. **uncharitableness,** *n.* Manque de charité, *m.* **uncharitably,** *adv.* Sans charité.
uncharted [ʌn'tʃɑ:tid], *a.* Inexploré.
unchaste [ʌn'tʃeist], *a.* Incontinent, impudique. **unchastely,** *adv.* Impudiquement. **unchastity** [ʌn'tʃæstiti], *n.* Impudicité, *f.*
unchecked [ʌn'tʃekt], *a.* Non réprimé, sans frein; non vérifié. *Abuses go on unchecked,* les abus continuent sans qu'on cherche à les réprimer.
unchivalrous [ʌn'ʃivlrəs], *a.* Peu chevaleresque. **unchivalrously,** *adv.* D'une manière peu chevaleresque.
unchristened [ʌn'krisnd], *a.* Non baptisé, sans nom.
unchristian [ʌn'kristiən], *a.* Peu chrétien; non-chrétien.
uncial ['ʌnʃiəl], *a.* Oncial.
uncircumcised [ʌn'sə:kəmsaizd], *a.* Incirconcis.
uncircumscribed [ʌn'sə:kəmskraibd], *a.* Illimité.
uncircumspect [ʌn'sə:kəmspekt], *a.* Peu circonspect, imprudent.
uncivil [ʌn'sivil], *a.* Malhonnête, impoli.
uncivilized [ʌn'sivilaizd], *a.* Peu civilisé, barbare.
uncivilly [ʌn'sivili], *adv.* Malhonnêtement, impoliment.
unclad [ʌn'klæd], *a.* Nu, sans vêtements.
unclaimed [ʌn'kleimd], *a.* Non réclamé, non revendiqué; épave (animal).
unclasp [ʌn'klɑ:sp], *v.t.* Ouvrir le fermoir de; dégrafer, défaire.
unclassified [ʌn'klæsifaid], *a.* Non classé.
uncle [ʌŋkl], *n.* Oncle, *m.* (*slang*) *At* (*my*) *uncle's,* chez ma tante (pawnbroker).
unclean [ʌn'kli:n], *a.* Malpropre, sale; impudique (lewd); (*Scripture*) impur, immonde. **uncleanliness** [ʌn'klenlinis], *n.* Malpropreté, saleté; (*fig.*) impureté, *f.* **uncleanly** [ʌn'klenli], *a.* Sale, malpropre. **uncleanness** [ʌn'kli:nnis], *n.* Saleté, malpropreté; impureté, impudicité (lewdness), *f.*
uncleansed [ʌn'klenzd], *a.* Non nettoyé, non curé (of drains etc.).
uncleared [ʌn'kliəd], *a.* Indéfriché (of land); non clarifié; non acquitté; non passé en douane.
unclench [ʌn'klenʃ], *v.t.* Ouvrir, desserrer.
unclerical [ʌn'klerikl], *a.* Peu clérical.

unclipped [ʌn'klipt], *a.* Non coupé; non tondu (of animals); non rogné (of coins).

uncloak [ʌn'klouk], *v.t.* Ôter le manteau de; dévoiler.

unclog [ʌn'klɔg], *v.t.* Ôter les entraves de; (*fig.*) dégager.

unclose [ʌn'klouz], *v.t.* Ouvrir. **unclosed** [ʌn'klouzd], *a.* Non fermé, ouvert.

unclothe [ʌn'klouð], *v.t.* Déshabiller; mettre à nu. **unclothed,** *a.* Déshabillé, nu.

unclouded [ʌn'klaudid], *a.* Sans nuage, serein. **uncloudedness,** *n.* Sérénité, clarté, *f.*

unco ['ʌŋkou], *a.* (*Sc.*) Insolite, étrange, énorme.—*adv.* Remarquablement, très.

uncock [ʌn'kɔk], *v.t.* Désarmer (a rifle etc.).

uncoil [ʌn'kɔil], *v.t.* Dérouler.—*v.i.* Se dérouler.

uncollected [ʌnkə'lektid], *a.* Non recueilli; dispersé; à percevoir (of money).

uncoloured [ʌn'kʌləd], *a.* Non coloré, incolore.

uncombed [ʌn'koumd], *a.* Mal peigné, ébouriffé.

uncomeliness, *n.* Manque de grâce, *m.*; laideur; inconvenance (of behaviour), *f.* **uncomely,** *a.* Disgracieux; malséant (unseemly).

uncomfortable [ʌn'kʌmfətəbl], *a.* Peu confortable, incommode, inconfortable; gêné, mal à son aise (of persons); fâcheux, désagréable, pénible; inquiétant (of news etc.). **uncomfortableness,** *n.* Incommodité, *f.*, malaise, désagrément, *m.*, gêne, *f.* **uncomfortably,** *adv.* Incommodément, peu confortablement; mal à l'aise, désagréablement.

uncommendable [ʌnkə'mendəbl], *a.* Peu louable.

uncommercial [ʌnkə'məːʃl], *a.* Peu commercial.

uncommissioned [ʌnkə'miʃənd], *a.* Non commissionné; désarmé (ship).

uncommitted [ʌnkə'mitid], *a.* Non commis; non engagé, libre.

uncommon [ʌn'kɔmən], *a.* Peu commun; peu ordinaire, rare. **uncommonly,** *adv.* Rarement; extrêmement, infiniment (greatly). **uncommonness,** *n.* Rareté, *f.*

uncommunicable [INCOMMUNICABLE].

uncommunicated [ʌnkə'mjuːnikeitid], *a.* Non communiqué. **uncommunicative,** *a.* Peu communicatif, réservé.

uncompanionable [ʌnkəm'pænjənəbl], *a.* Peu sociable.

uncomplaining [-'pleiniŋ], *a.* Sans plainte, résigné. **uncomplainingly,** *adv.* Sans se plaindre, sans plainte.

uncomplaisant [-'pleizənt], *a.* Sans complaisance.

uncompleted [-'pliːtid], *a.* Inachevé, incomplet.

uncomplimentary [ʌnkɔmpli'mentəri], *a.* Peu flatteur.

uncomplying [-kəm'plaiiŋ], *a.* Peu complaisant; inflexible.

uncompounded [-'paundəd], *a.* Non composé, simple.

uncomprehensive [-kɔmpri'hensiv], *a.* Incomplet.

uncompressed [ʌnkəm'prest], *a.* Non comprimé.

uncompromised [ʌn'kɔmprəmaizd], *a.* Non compromis. **uncompromising,** *a.* Peu accommodant, intransigeant, intraitable. *An uncompromising attitude,* une attitude inflexible.

unconcealed [ʌnkən'siːld], *a.* Non caché, ouvert, à découvert.

unconcern [ʌnkən'səːn], *n.* Insouciance, indifférence, *f.* **unconcerned** [-'səːnd], *a.* Indifférent, insouciant, sans inquiétude. **unconcernedly** [-nidli], *adv.* Avec indifférence, avec insouciance.

unconciliating [ʌnkən'silieitiŋ], *a.* Inconciliable; raide.

uncondemned [ʌnkən'demd], *a.* Non condamné; non interdit (of things).

unconditional [ʌnkən'diʃənl], *a.* Sans conditions, absolu. **unconditionally,** *adv.* Sans condition, sans réserve. **unconditioned,** *a.* Sans conditions; inconditionné.

unconfessed [-'fest], *a.* Non avoué, inconfessé.

unconfined [-'faind], *a.* Libre; illimité (illimitable). **unconfinedly** [-'faindli], *adv.* Sans contrainte, librement, sans limite.

unconfirmed [-'fəːmd], *a.* Non confirmé.

unconformable [-'fɔːməbl], *a.* Non conformé; incompatible (avec), contraire (à), réfractaire. **unconformity,** *n.* Non-conformité, incompatibilité, *f.*

unconfused [-'fjuːzd], *a.* Sans confusion.

uncongealed [-'dʒiːld], *a.* Non congelé.

uncongenial [-'dʒiːniəl], *a.* Désagréable, peu favorable; peu sympathique; antipathique (à).

unconnected [-'nektid], *a.* Détaché, séparé (de), étranger (à); sans rapport (avec); (style) décousu, sans suite.

unconquerable [ʌn'kɔŋkərəbl], *a.* Invincible, indomptable; insurmontable. **unconquerably,** *adv.* Invinciblement. **unconquered,** *a.* Insoumis, inconquis; invaincu.

unconscientious [-kɔnʃi'enʃəs], *a.* Peu consciencieux.

unconscionable [-'kɔnʃənəbl], *a.* Peu scrupuleux; déraisonnable; exorbitant, démesuré. *Unconscionable bargain,* (*Law*) contrat léonin; *you have been an unconscionable time,* vous avez pris largement votre temps. **unconscionably,** *adv.* Déraisonnablement, contre toute raison.

unconscious [ʌn'kɔnʃəs], *a.* Qui n'a pas conscience, ignorant (de); sans connaissance, insensible (insensible). *He lay unconscious on the ground,* il était étendu à terre sans connaissance; *to be unconscious,* avoir perdu connaissance; *être évanoui; to be unconscious of,* n'avoir pas conscience de, ignorer.—*n.* *The inconscious,* l'inconscient, *m.* **unconsciously,** *adv.* À son insu, sans le savoir, par inadvertance. **unconsciousness,** *n.* Inconscience, insensibilité, *f.*; évanouissement (swoon), *m.*

unconsecrated [ʌn'kɔnsikreitid], *a.* Non consacré; non sacré (of kings, bishops, etc.); non bénit (of ground).

unconsenting [ʌnkən'sentiŋ], *a.* Non consentant.

unconsidered [ʌnkən'sidəd], *a.* Inconsidéré; inaperçu (not noticed).

unconsoled [ʌnkən'sould], *a.* Inconsolé, inconsolable.

unconstitutional [ʌnkɔnsti'tjuːʃənl], *a.* Inconstitutionnel. **unconstitutionally,** *adv.* Anticonstitutionnellement.

unconstrained [ʌnkən'streind], *a.* Sans contrainte, libre, spontané; naturel, aisé (of style). **unconstrainedly** [ʌnkən'streinidli], *adv.* Sans contrainte; librement, sans gêne. **unconstraint** [ʌnkən'streint], *n.* Absence de contrainte, liberté, aisance, désinvolture, *f.*

uncontaminated [ʌnkən'tæmineitid], *a.* Sans souillure, pur; non corrompu.

uncontested [ʌnkən'testid], *a.* Incontesté; qui n'est pas disputé.

uncontradicted [ʌnkəntrə'diktid], *a.* Non contredit, sans contradiction.

uncontrollable [ʌnkən'trouləbl], *a.* Indomptable, irrésistible, qu'on ne peut maîtriser; inextinguible, fou (of laughter). **uncontrollably**, *adv.* Irrésistiblement. **uncontrolled**, *a.* Indépendant, sans frein, irrésistible. **uncontrolledly** [ʌnkən'troulidli], *adv.* Sans frein, irrésistiblement.

uncontroverted [ʌn'kɔntrovə:tid], *a.* Incontesté, reconnu sans contestation.

unconventional [ʌnkən'venʃənl], *a.* Peu conventionnel, à l'encontre des conventions, original. **unconventionality**, *n.* Originalité, *f.*

unconversant [ʌnkən'və:sənt], *a.* Peu familier (avec).

unconverted [ʌnkən'və:tid], *a.* Non converti, inconverti.

unconvinced [ʌnkən'vinst], *a.* Non convaincu. **unconvincing**, *a.* Peu convaincant.

uncooked [ʌn'kukt], *a.* Non cuit, cru.

uncork [ʌn'kɔ:k], *v.t.* Déboucher.

uncorrected [ʌnkə'rektid], *a.* Non corrigé.

uncorrupted [ʌnkə'rʌptid], *a.* Non corrompu (par); intègre.

uncountable [ʌn'kauntəbl], *a.* Incomptable, incalculable.

uncouple [ʌn'kʌpl], *v.t.* Découpler; débrayer, désengrener (machinery).

uncourteous [ʌn'kə:tjəs], *a.* Peu courtois.

uncourtliness [ʌn'kɔ:tlinis], *n.* Manque de politesse, *m.*, impolitesse; gaucherie, *f.* **uncourtly**, *a.* Étranger au grand monde *or* à la cour; rustique (of manners).

uncouth [ʌn'ku:θ], *a.* *Étrange; singulier, bizarre; rude, grossier; gauche. **uncouthly**, *adv.* Rudement, grossièrement; gauchement. **uncouthness**, *n.* Rudesse, grossièreté; gaucherie, *f.*

uncover [ʌn'kʌvə], *v.t.* Découvrir. *To uncover one's head*, se découvrir.—*v.i.* Se découvrir. **uncovered**, *a.* Découvert.

uncramped [ʌn'kræmpt], *a.* À l'aise, non gêné.

uncreasable [ʌn'kri:səbl], *a.* Infroissable.

uncreated [ʌnkri'eitid], *a.* Incréé.

uncrippled [ʌn'kripld], *a.* Qui a plein usage de ses membres. *The ship came out of action uncrippled*, le vaisseau sortit du combat sans avaries.

uncritical [ʌn'kritikl], *a.* Sans discernement, peu judicieux.

uncropped [ʌn'krɔpt], *a.* Non cultivé (of land); non récolté (not gathered); non coupé (of the ears of a dog).

uncrossed [ʌn'krɔst], *a.* Non traversé; non rayé, non biffé (not cancelled); non contrarié (not thwarted). *Uncrossed cheque*, chèque non barré, *m.*

uncrowded [ʌn'kraudid], *a.* Peu serré; non encombré (par la foule).

uncrown [DISCROWN]. **uncrowned** [ʌn'kraund], *a.* Détrôné; non couronné.

unction ['ʌŋkʃən], *n.* Onction, *f.*; (*fig.*) baume, *m.*

unctuosity [ʌŋktju'ɔsiti] *or* **unctuousness** [ʌŋk'tjuəsnis], *n.* Onctuosité, *f.*

unctuous ['ʌŋktjuəs], *a.* Onctueux. **unctuously**, *adv.* Onctueusement.

uncultivated [ʌn'kʌltiveitid], *a.* Inculte; sans culture.

uncultured [ʌn'kʌltʃəd], *a.* Sans culture.

uncurbed [ʌn'kə:bd], *a.* Indompté, effréné, sans frein.

uncured [ʌn'kjuəd], *a.* Non guéri.

uncurl [ʌn'kə:l], *v.t.* Dérouler; défriser, déboucler (hair).—*v.i.* Se dérouler; se défriser, se déboucler (of hair).

uncurtailed [ʌnkə:'teild], *a.* Non abrégé, non raccourci.

uncustomary [ʌn'kʌstəməri], *a.* Inaccoutumé.

uncut [ʌn'kʌt], *a.* Non coupé; entier; non entamé (of a loaf etc.); (*Bookb.*) non rogné, non ébarbé; brut (of a diamond).

undamaged [ʌn'dæmidʒd], *a.* Non endommagé, en bon état; intact (of reputation); (*Naut.*) non avarié.

undamped [ʌn'dæmpt], *a.* Non mouillé; non amorti (sound); (*fig.*) non découragé, qui n'est pas abattu.

undated [ʌn'deitid], *a.* Sans date.

undaunted [ʌn'dɔ:ntid], *a.* Intrépide, qui ne se laisse pas abattre. **undauntedly**, *adv.* Intrépidement. **undauntedness**, *n.* Intrépidité, *f.*

undazzled [ʌn'dæzld], *a.* Non ébloui, sans se laisser éblouir.

undebased [ʌndi'beist], *a.* Non avili, de bon aloi.

undebated [ʌndi'beitid], *a.* Non discuté.

undecayed [ʌndi'keid], *a.* Intact, en bon état. **undecaying**, *a.* Impérissable.

undeceive [ʌndi'si:v], *v.t.* Désabuser, détromper, désillusionner. *To undeceive oneself*, se désabuser. **undeceived**, *a.* Désabusé.

undecided [ʌndi'saidid], *a.* Indécis; incertain; irrésolu; vacillant.

undecipherable [ʌndi'saifərəbl], *a.* Indéchiffrable.

undecked [ʌn'dekt], *a.* Sans ornements; (*Naut.*) non ponté.

undefaced [ʌndi'feist], *a.* Non défiguré.

undefeated [ʌndi'fi:tid], *a.* Invaincu.

undefended [ʌndi'fendid], *a.* Sans défense, non défendu; sans défenseur (of a prisoner).

undefiled [ʌndi'faild], *a.* Sans tache, immaculé, pur.

undefinable [ʌndi'fainəbl], *a.* Indéfinissable. **undefined**, *a.* Indéfini; indécis (of frontiers etc.).

undelivered [ʌndi'livəd], *a.* Non délivré.

undemonstrated [ʌn'demənstreitid], *a.* Indémontré. **undemonstrative** [ʌndi'mɔnstrə tiv], *a.* Peu démonstratif, réservé, froid.

undeniable [ʌndi'naiəbl], *a.* Incontestable, irrécusable. **undeniably**, *adv.* Incontestablement.

undenominational [ʌndinɔmi'neiʃənl], *a.* Neutre (à l'égard des sectes); laïque (school).

under ['ʌndə], *prep.* Sous; au-dessous de (less than, inferior to, etc.); dans, en (in); avec, à (with). *See under*, voyez ci-dessous; *the under-fourteens*, les moins de quatorze ans; *they will not sell it under five pounds*, ils ne veulent pas le vendre à moins de cinq livres; *to be back under the hour*, être rentré en moins d'une heure; *to be under obligations to*, avoir des obligations à; *to be under water* (of land), être inondé; *to be under way* (ship), être en marche; *under age*, mineur; *under arms*, sous les armes; *under consideration*, à l'examen; *under cover of*, sous prétexte de; *under cover of a tree*, à l'abri d'un arbre; *under cover of the batteries*, sous la protection des batteries; *under cover of darkness*, à la faveur de l'obscurité; *under discussion*, en discussion; *under favour of*, à la faveur de; *under fire*, sous le feu; *under it*, dessous; *under sail*, sous voiles; *under the breath*, à demi-voix; *under the doctor's hands*, entre les mains du médecin; *under the terms of*, d'après; *under the law of*, en vertu de la loi de; *under these circumstances*, dans ces circonstances.—*adv.* Dessous, au-dessous; (*fig.*) dans la sujétion. *To go under*, faire fiasco; *to keep under*, retenir, contenir.—*a.* De dessous, inférieur; sous, subalterne, subordonné (of rank).

under-arm ['ʌndərɑːm], *a.* Par en dessous (bowling etc.).

underbid [ʌndə'bid], *v.t.* (*past* **underbid**, *p.p.* **underbidden**) Offrir moins que; offrir à plus bas prix.

underbred [ʌndə'bred], *a.* Mal élevé, malappris.

under-carriage ['ʌndəkærid3], *n.* (*Av.*) Train d'atterrissage, *m.*

under-charge [ʌndə'tʃɑːd3], *v.t.* Ne pas faire payer assez.

underclothes ['ʌndəkloudz], *n.pl.*, or **under-clothing**, *n.* Vêtements de dessous, *m.pl.*

undercoat ['ʌndəkout], *n.* Sous-couche, couche d'apprêt, *f.*

undercrust ['ʌndəkrʌst], *n.* Croûte de dessous, *f.*

undercurrent ['ʌndəkʌrənt], *n.* Courant inférieur, *m.*; (*fig.*) influence secrète, *f.*

undercut (1) ['ʌndəkʌt], *n.* Filet (of meat), *m.*; (*Box.*) undercut, *m.*

undercut (2) [ʌndə'kʌt], *v.t.* Vendre meilleur marché; couper (in golf).

under-developed [ʌndədi'veləpt], *a.* Sous-développé.

under-dog [ʌndə'dɔg], *n.* Opprimé, *m.*

underdone [ʌndə'dʌn], *a.* Peu cuit, saignant; pas assez cuit (of meat).

under-estimate [ʌndər'estimeit], *v.t.* Sous-estimer, faire trop peu de cas de.

under-exposed [-iks'pouzd], *a.* (*Phot.*) Sous-exposé. **under-exposure** [-'pou3ə], *n.* Sous-exposition, *f.*

underfelt ['ʌndəfelt], *n.* Thibaude, *f.*

underfoot [-'fut], *adv.* Sous les pieds, en bas.

under-gardener ['ʌndəgɑːdnə], *n.* Aide-jardinier, *m.*

undergarment [-gɑːmənt], *n.* Vêtement de dessous, *m.*

undergo [ʌndə'gou], *v.t.* (*past* **underwent**, *p.p.* **undergone**) Subir; supporter, endurer; éprouver, essuyer (to experience).

undergraduate [ʌndə'grædjuət], *n.* Étudiant, *m.*

underground (1) ['ʌndəgraund], *a.* Souterrain; de fond (miner); clandestin. *Underground story*, sous-sol, *m.*—*n.* Lieu souterrain;

(*Rail.*) chemin de fer souterrain, métro (Paris), *m.*

underground (2) [ʌndə'graund], *adv.* Sous terre, en forme de souterrain. (*Polit.*) *To go underground*, entrer dans la clandestinité.

undergrowth ['ʌndəgrou θ], *n.* Broussailles, *f.pl.*

underhand (1) [ʌndə'hænd] or **-handed**, *a.* Fait sous main, clandestin, sourd; caché, sournois (of persons); à court de main-d'œuvre.

underhand (2) or **-handedly**, *adv.* Sous main; sourdement, en cachette, en secret.

underlay (1) [ʌndə'lei], *v.t.* (*past* and *p.p.* **underlaid**) Soutenir, étayer; (*Print.*) taquonner.

underlay (2) ['ʌndəlei], *n.* (*Print.*) Taquon, *m.*

under-lease ['ʌndəliːs], *n.* Sous-bail, *m.*

under-let [ʌndə'let], *v.t.* Sous-affermer (land etc.); sous-louer (a house etc.); louer au-dessous de sa valeur (to let below the value).

underlie [ʌndə'lai], *v.t.* (*past* **underlay**, *p.p.* **underlain**) Être au-dessous de, être à la base de.

underline [ʌndə'lain], *v.t.* Souligner. **under-lines**, *n.pl.* Transparent, *m.*

underlinen [UNDERCLOTHES].

underling ['ʌndəliŋ], *n.* Subalterne; sous-ordre, *m.*

underlip [-lip], *n.* Lèvre inférieure, *f.*

underlying [ʌndə'laiiŋ], *a.* Fondamental; (*Geol.*) sous-jacent.

under-manager [ʌndə'mænəd3ə], *n.* Sous-directeur, *m.*

under-manned [ʌndə'mænd], *a.* À court de personnel.

undermentioned [ʌndə'menʃənd], *a.* Ci-dessous.

undermine [ʌndə'main], *v.t.* Miner; (*fig.*) détruire. **underminer**, *a.* Mineur; (*fig.*) destructeur, ennemi secret, *m.*

undermost ['ʌndəmoust], *a.* Le plus bas, inférieur; le dernier.

underneath [ʌndə'niːθ], *prep.* Sous, au-dessous de.—*adv.* Dessous, au-dessous, par-dessous, en dessous. *From underneath*, de dessous.

under-nourished [ʌndə'nʌriʃd], *a.* Mal nourri; sous-alimenté. **under-nourishment**, *n.* Sous-alimentation, *f.*

underpaid [ʌndə'peid], *a.* Mal payé.

underpants ['ʌndəpænts], *n.pl.* (*Am.*) Caleçons, *m.pl.*

underpart ['ʌndəpɑːt], *n.* Dessous; (*fig.*) petit rôle, rôle accessoire, *m.*

underpay [ʌndə'pei], *v.t.* Payer mal, payer trop peu.

underpin [ʌndə'pin], *v.t.* Étayer; reprendre en sous-œuvre. **underpinning**, *n.* Reprise en sous-œuvre, *f.*, étayage, *m.*

underplot ['ʌndəplɔt], *n.* Sous-intrigue, manœuvre, *f.*

under-privileged [ʌndə'prividʒd], *a.* Non privilégié; économiquement faible.

under-production [ʌndəprə'dʌkʃən], *n.* Sous-production, *f.*

underprop [ʌndə'prɔp], *v.t.* Étayer, soutenir.

underrate [ʌndə'reit], *v.t.* Estimer trop peu, ne pas apprécier à sa juste valeur, déprécier, faire trop peu de cas de.

under-ripe [ʌndə'raip], *a.* Pas assez mûr, vert.

underscore [ʌndə'skɔː], *v.t.* Souligner.

under-sea or **under-seas** [ʌndə'siː *or* -'siːz], *a.* Sous-marin.

under-secretary ['ʌndəsekrətəri], *n.* Sous-secrétaire, *m.*

undersell [ʌndə'sel], *v.t.* (*past* and *p.p.* **undersold**) Vendre à plus bas prix que, vendre à meilleur marché que; vendre à trop bas prix (too cheap). **underseller**, *n.* Gâte-métier, *m.*

underset (1) ['ʌndəset], *n.* Contre-courant sous-marin, *m.*

underset (2) [ʌndə'set], *v.t.* Étayer (en sous-œuvre).

undershirt ['ʌndəʃəːt], *n.* (*Am.*) Tricot de corps, *m.*

undershot ['ʌndəʃɔt], *a.* Mû en dessous. *Undershot wheel,* roue en dessous *or* à aubes, *f.*

under-side [-said], *n.* Dessous, côté de dessous, *m.*

undersigned ['ʌndəsaind], *a.* and *n.* Soussigné, *m.*, soussignée, *f. I the undersigned,* je soussigné.

undersized [ʌndə'saizd], *a.* Au-dessous de la moyenne.

under-skirt ['ʌndəskəːt], *n.* Jupon, *m.*

underslung [ʌndə'slʌŋ], *a.* (Ressort) surbaissé.

undersoil [SUBSOIL].

undersold, *past* and *p.p.* [UNDERSELL].

under-staffed [UNDER-MANNED].

understand [ʌndə'stænd], *v.t.* (*past* and *p.p.* **understood** [-'stud]) Entendre, comprendre; apprendre, entendre dire, être informé de (to be informed of); sous-entendre (to imply); s'entendre (à *or* en). *Am I to understand,* dois-je comprendre? *I do not understand it at all,* je n'y comprends rien; *it is understood that,* il est entendu que; *something understood,* quelque chose de sous-entendu; *that must be understood to mean a refusal,* il faut entendre cela comme signifiant un refus; *there is no understanding what they mean,* il n'y a pas moyen de comprendre ce qu'ils veulent dire; *to give to understand,* donner à entendre, laisser entendre; *to have a mutual understanding,* s'entendre; *to make oneself understood,* se faire comprendre; *to understand one another,* se comprendre.—*v.i.* Comprendre.

understandable, *a.* Intelligible; compréhensible. **understanding,** *n.* Entendement, *m.*, intelligence; compréhension; entente (agreement), *f. Friendly understanding,* entente cordiale; *good understanding,* bonne intelligence; *there is an understanding between them,* ils sont d'intelligence; *to come to an understanding with,* s'entendre avec; *within the understanding of,* à la portée de. **understandingly,** *adv.* Avec intelligence, en connaissance de cause.

understate [ʌndə'steit], *v.t.* Ne pas assez dire; amoindrir, diminuer, atténuer. **understated,** *a.* Amoindri, atténué. **understatement,** *n.* Euphémisme, *m.*, litote, *f.*

understrapper ['ʌndəstræpə], *n.* Subalterne, *m.*

understudy (1) ['ʌndəstʌdi], *n.* Doublure, *f.*

understudy (2) [ʌndə'stʌdi], *v.t.* Doubler (un rôle).

undertake [ʌndə'teik], *v.t.* (*past* **undertook**, *p.p.* **undertaken**) Entreprendre, se charger de; s'engager (à); promettre (de). *To undertake to convince,* se faire fort de convaincre;

to undertake to say, ne pas craindre d'affirmer, oser dire.

undertaker ['ʌndəteikə], *n.* Entrepreneur des pompes funèbres, *m.*

undertaking, *n.* Entreprise, *f. That is quite an undertaking,* c'est toute une affaire.

undertenant [ʌndə'tenənt], *n.* Sous-locataire, *m.* or *f.*

undertone ['ʌndətoun], *n.* Ton bas, *m. In an undertone,* à voix basse, à demi-voix.

undertow ['ʌndətou], *n.* Contre-marée, *f.*

undervaluation [ʌndəvælju'eiʃən], *n.* Sous-évaluation, *f.*

undervalue [ʌndə'vælju], *n.* Trop bas prix, *m.*—*v.t.* Estimer trop peu, mettre au-dessous de sa valeur; (*fig.*) déprécier, rabaisser, dépriser.

underwater ['ʌndəwɔːtə], *a.* Sous-marin.

underwear ['ʌndəweə], *n.* Vêtements de dessous, *m.pl.*

underwood [-wud], *n.* Taillis, *m.*

underworld [-wəːld], *n.* Enfer, *m.*; (*fig.*) bas-fonds (of criminals), *m.pl.*

underwrite [ʌndə'rait], *v.t.* (*past* **underwrote**, *p.p.* **underwritten**) Souscrire; (*Insurance*) assurer.

underwriter ['ʌndəraitə], *n.* Assureur, *m.*

underwriting, *n.* Assurance; garantie d'émission, *f.*

undescribable [INDESCRIBABLE].

undescribed [ʌndis'kraibd], *a.* Non décrit.

undescried [ʌndis'kraid], *a.* Non aperçu.

undeserved [ʌndi'zəːvd], *a.* Immérité, non mérité; injuste. **undeservedly,** *adv.* À tort, injustement. **undeservedness,** *n.* Injustice, *f.* **undeserving,** *a.* Peu digne de, sans mérite; peu méritoire (of things). **undeservingly,** *adv.* Sans avoir mérité, injustement.

undesigned [ʌndi'zaind], *a.* Sans préméditation, involontaire. **undesignedly,** *adv.* Sans intention, involontairement, par mégarde. **undesigning,** *a.* Candide; sans artifice; sans mauvais dessein, sans malice.

undesirable [ʌndi'zaiərəbl], *a.* Peu désirable; indésirable; désagréable. **undesired,** *a.* Peu désiré, inopportun.

undespairing [ʌndi'speəriŋ], *a.* Qui ne se laisse pas abattre, qui espère toujours.

undetected [ʌndi'tektid], *a.* Non découvert, inaperçu, insoupçonné.

undetermined [ʌndi'təːmind], *a.* Indéterminé, indéfini.

undeterred [ʌndi'təːd], *a.* Sans être découragé.

undeveloped [ʌndi'veləpt], *a.* Non développé.

undeviating [ʌn'diːvieitiŋ], *a.* Qui ne dévie pas, droit, constant, ferme.

undies ['ʌndiz], *n.pl.* (*fam.*) Lingerie, *f.*

undigested [ʌndi'dʒestid], *a.* Non digéré; (*fig.*) indigeste, informe.

undignified [ʌn'dignifaid], *a.* Sans dignité.

undiluted [ʌndai'ljuːtid], *a.* Non dilué, concentré.

undiminished [ʌndi'miniʃt], *a.* Non diminué, sans diminution.

undiplomatic [ʌndiplo'mætik], *a.* Peu diplomatique.

undirected ['ʌndi'rektid], *a.* Sans direction; sans adresse (of letters etc.).

undiscerned [ʌndi'zəːnd], *a.* Inaperçu. **undiscernible,** *a.* Imperceptible. **undiscerning,** *a.* Sans discernement.

undischarged [ʌndis'tʃɑːdʒd], *a.* Non déchargé; non réhabilité (bankrupt); inaccompli.

undisciplined [ʌn'disiplind], *a.* Indiscipliné, sans discipline.

undisclosed [ʌndis'klouzd], *a.* Non révélé, caché, voilé.

undiscoverable [ʌndis'kʌvərəbl], *a.* Qu'on ne peut découvrir. **undiscovered,** *a.* Non découvert, inconnu.

undisguised [ʌndis'gaizd], *a.* Sans déguisement; (*fig.*) franc, sincère, ouvert.

undismayed [ʌndis'meid], *a.* Sans peur, sans terreur. *Undismayed by,* sans se laisser effrayer par.

undisputed [ʌndis'pjuːtid], *a.* Incontesté.

undissolved [ʌndi'zɔlvd], *a.* Non dissous, non fondu.

undistinguishable [INDISTINGUISHABLE].

undistinguished, *a.* Qu'on ne distingue pas; *indistinct; (fig.)* sans distinction. **undistinguishing,** *a.* Qui ne fait point de distinction, sans discernement.

undistributed [ʌndis'tribjutid], *a.* Non distribué.

undisturbed [ʌndis'təːbd], *a.* Sans être dérangé *or* troublé; tranquille, calme. **undisturbedly** [ʌndis'təːbidli], *adv.* Sans trouble; tranquillement.

undiverted [ʌndai'vəːtid], *a.* Non détourné.

undivided [ʌndi'vaidid], *a.* Sans partage, tout entier. *Undivided property,* biens indivis, *m.pl.*

undivulged [ʌndi'vʌldʒd], *a.* Non divulgué, secret.

undo [ʌn'duː], *v.t.* (*past* undid, *p.p.* undone) Défaire; délier, détacher (to untie); ruiner, perdre (to ruin). **undoing,** *n.* Ruine, perte, *f.* **undone** [ʌn'dʌn], *a.* Non exécuté, à faire, qui reste à faire; ruiné, perdu (ruined). *To come undone,* se délier, se défaire; *to leave undone,* ne pas faire; *what is done cannot be undone,* ce qui est fait, est fait.

undocumented [ʌn'dɔkjumentid], *a.* Non documenté.

undomesticated [ʌndə'mestikeitid], *a.* Qui n'aime pas faire le ménage.

undoubted [ʌn'dautid], *a.* Hors de doute, incontestable, certain. **undoubtedly,** *adv.* Sans aucun doute, indubitablement, incontestablement.

undramatic [ʌndrə'mætik], *a.* Peu dramatique.

undrawn [ʌn'drɔːn], *a.* Non tiré.

undreamed [ʌn'driːmd *or* ʌn'dremt], **undreamt** [ʌn'drem(p)t], *a.* (*with* of) Qu'on ne saurait imaginer, insoupçonné.

undress (1) [ʌn'dres], *v.t.* Déshabiller.—*v.i.* Se déshabiller.—*n.* (*Mil.*) Petite tenue, *f.* **undressed,** *a.* Déshabillé; en négligé; (*Manuf.*) brut, non préparé; (*Cook.*) non apprêté, au naturel.

undress (2) ['ʌndres], *a.* In undress uniform, en petite tenue.

undried [ʌn'draid], *a.* Non séché, vert.

undrinkable [ʌn'driŋkəbl], *a.* Imbuvable, non potable.

undue [ʌn'djuː], *a.* Non dû; excessif, outré (excessive); non échu (of bills); indu (improper).

undulate ['ʌndjuleit], *v.i.* Onduler, ondoyer.— *a.* [-lət] Ondulé. **undulating,** *a.* Ondoyant,

onduleux; accidenté (of ground). **undulatingly,** *adv.* D'une manière ondoyante. **undulation** [-'leiʃən], *n.* Ondulation, *f.* **undulatory,** *a.* Ondulatoire.

unduly [ʌn'djuːli], *adv.* Indûment; à tort; trop, à l'excès (excessively).

unduteous [ʌn'djuːtiəs] *or* **undutiful,** *a.* Désobéissant, indocile. **undutifully,** *adv.* Indocilement, irrespectueusement. **undutifulness,** *n.* Manquement à ses devoirs, *m.*

undyed [ʌn'daid], *a.* Non teint.

undying [ʌn'daiiŋ], *a.* Qui ne meurt pas, impérissable, immortel.

unearned [ʌn'əːnd], *a.* Qu'on n'a pas gagné; non mérité, immérité. *Unearned income,* rentes, *f.pl.*; *unearned increment,* accroissement automatique de valeur, *m.*

unearth [ʌn'əːθ], *v.t.* Déterrer. **unearthly,** *a.* Qui n'est pas de ce monde, surnaturel; (*colloq.*) infernal, d'enfer; blême, d'une pâleur cadavérique (of the countenance).

uneasily [ʌn'iːzili], *adv.* Mal à son aise; difficilement, péniblement, avec gêne (with difficulty). **uneasiness,** *n.* Malaise, *m.,* peine; inquiétude (of mind), *f.* **uneasy,** *a.* Inquiet, mal à son aise, gêné; pénible, désagréable (disagreeable); agité. *To make oneself uneasy about,* s'inquiéter de.

uneatable [ʌn'iːtəbl], *a.* Immangeable. **uneaten** [ʌn'iːtn], *a.* Non mangé.

uneconomical [ʌniːkə'nɔmikəl], *a.* Non économique.

unedifying [ʌn'edifaiiŋ], *a.* Peu édifiant.

uneducated [ʌn'edjukeitid], *a.* Sans éducation.

unembarrassed [ʌnim'bærəst], *a.* Sans être embarrassé, à l'aise, sans embarras; clair, net, libre (of property).

unembellished [ʌnim'beliʃt], *a.* Sans embellissement, non enjolivé.

unemotional [ʌni'mouʃənl], *a.* Peu impressionnable; peu émotif.

unemployable [ʌnim'plɔiəbl], *a.* Inemployable.

unemployed [ʌnim'plɔid], *a.* Sans travail, inoccupé; (*fig.*) inactif, oisif. *The unemployed,* les sans-travail, les chômeurs, *m.pl.* **unemployment,** *n.* Manque de travail, chômage, *m.*

unenclosed [ʌnin'klouzd], *a.* Ouvert, sans clôture.

unencumbered [ʌnin'kʌmbəd], *a.* Non embarrassé (de); libre, à l'aise; non hypothéqué (of property).

unending [ʌn'endiŋ], *a.* Interminable; éternel.

unendorsed [ʌnin'dɔːst], *a.* Sans endos.

unendowed [ʌnin'daud], *a.* Qui n'est pas doué; dénué (de).

unendurable [ʌnin'djuərəbl], *a.* Insupportable, intolérable.

unenforced [ʌnin'fɔːst], *a.* Inexécuté.

un-English [ʌn'iŋgliʃ], *a.* Non anglais; indigne d'un Anglais.

unenlightened [ʌnin'laitnd], *a.* Peu éclairé, ignorant.

unenterprising [ʌn'entəpraiziŋ], *a.* Peu entreprenant.

unentertaining [ʌnentə'teiniŋ], *a.* Peu amusant; ennuyeux.

unenthusiastic [ʌninθjuːzi'æstik], *a.* Peu enthousiaste.

unenviable [ʌn'enviəbl], *a.* Peu enviable.

unequal [ʌn'i:kwəl], *a.* Inégal; disproportionné; au-dessous (de), inférieur (à). *He is unequal to the task,* il n'est pas à la hauteur de la tâche. **unequalled,** *a.* Sans égal, inégalé. **unequally,** *adv.* Inégalement.

unequivocal [ʌni'kwivəkl], *a.* Non équivoque, clair. **unequivocally,** *adv.* Sans équivoque.

unerring [ʌn'ə:riŋ], *a.* Infaillible, sûr. **unerringly,** *adv.* Infailliblement.

uneven [ʌn'i:vn], *a.* Inégal; raboteux (rough); impair (of numbers). **unevenly,** *adv.* Inégalement. **unevenness,** *n.* Inégalité, *f.*

uneventful [ʌni'ventful], *a.* Peu fécond en événements, sans incidents, monotone.

unexaggerated [ʌnig'zædʒəreitid], *a.* Nullement exagéré.

unexamined [ʌnig'zæmind], *a.* Sans examen.

unexampled [ʌnig'zɑ:mpld], *a.* Sans exemple.

unexcelled [ʌnik'seld], *a.* Sans égal.

unexceptionable [ʌnik'sepʃənəbl], *a.* Irréprochable, irrécusable, sans défaut. **unexceptionableness,** *n.* Nature irréprochable, *f.* **unexceptionably,** *adv.* Irréprochablement.

unexciting [ʌnik'saitiŋ], *a.* Peu intéressant, insipide, sans intérêt.

unexecuted [ʌn'eksikju:tid], *a.* Inexécuté.

unexemplified [ʌnig'zemplifaid], *a.* Sans exemple.

unexhausted [ʌnig'zɔ:stid], *a.* Inépuisé.

unexpected [ʌniks'pektid], *a.* Inopiné, inattendu; imprévu. *His unexpected arrival,* son arrivée inopinée; *the unexpected usually happens,* c'est l'imprévu qui arrive toujours. **unexpectedly,** *adv.* Inopinément, à l'improviste. **unexpectedness,** *n.* Soudaineté, *f.*

unexpensive [INEXPENSIVE].

unexperienced [INEXPERIENCED].

unexpired [ʌniks'paiəd], *a.* Non expiré; non échu (of bills).

unexplained [ʌniks'pleind], *a.* Sans explication, inexpliqué.

unexploded [ʌniks'ploudid], *a.* Non éclaté; (*fig.*) encore accrédité.

unexplored [ʌniks'plɔ:d], *a.* Inexploré.

unexposed [ʌniks'pouzd], *a.* Non exposé, caché; (*Phot.*) qui n'a pas servi.

unexpressed [ʌniks'prest], *a.* Inexprimé, sous-entendu.

unextinguished [ʌniks'tiŋgwiʃt], *a.* Non éteint.

unfaded [ʌn'feidid], *a.* Non fané, non flétri, frais. **unfading,** *a.* Qui ne se fane pas, qui ne se flétrit pas; (*fig.*) impérissable, immarcescible, immortel.

unfailing [ʌn'feiliŋ], *a.* Inépuisable, intarissable; infaillible, immanquable (certain). **unfailingly,** *adv.* Infailliblement, immanquablement.

unfair [ʌn'feə], *a.* Injuste, peu équitable; déloyal, de mauvaise foi; pas de jeu (at games). **unfairly,** *adv.* Injustement; déloyalement. **unfairness,** *n.* Injustice, déloyauté, *f.*

unfaithful [ʌn'feiθful], *a.* Infidèle. **unfaithfully,** *adv.* Infidèlement. **unfaithfulness,** *n.* Infidélité, *f.*

unfaltering [ʌn'fɔ:ltəriŋ], *a.* Ferme, assuré; décidé, résolu (of actions etc.).

unfamiliar [ʌnfə'miljə], *a.* Peu familier (avec); peu connu. **unfamiliarity** [ʌnfə mili'æriti], *n.* Manque de familiarité, *m.*

unfashionable [ʌn'fæʃənəbl], *a.* Qui n'est pas de mode, démodé. **unfashioned,** *a.* Non façonné, informe.

unfasten [ʌn'fɑ:sn], *v.t.* Ouvrir, détacher, défaire; desserrer, relâcher.

unfatherly [ʌn'fɑ:ðəli], *a.* Peu paternel.

unfathomable [ʌn'fæðəməbl], *a.* Sans fond, insondable; impénétrable. **unfathomableness,** *n.* Profondeur insondable, *f.* **unfathomed,** *a.* Insondé.

unfavourable [ʌn'feivərəbl], *a.* Peu favorable; défavorable, contraire. **unfavourableness,** *n.* Nature défavorable, *f.* **unfavourably,** *adv.* Défavorablement. **unfavoured,** *a.* Non favorisé. *Unfavoured by nature,* disgracié de la nature.

unfeasible [ʌn'fi:zibl], *a.* Impraticable; irréalisable.

unfeathered [ʌn'feðəd], *a.* Sans plumes.

unfed [ʌn'fed], *a.* À jeun; mal nourri; sans nourriture; non alimenté (of machinery etc.).

unfeeling [ʌn'fi:liŋ], *a.* Insensible, dur, cruel. **unfeelingly,** *adv.* Sans pitié, cruellement. **unfeelingness,** *n.* Insensibilité, dureté, *f.*

unfeigned [ʌn'feind], *a.* Vrai, sincère, réel. **unfeignedly** [ʌn'feinidli], *adv.* Sincèrement, de bonne foi. **unfeignedness,** *n.* Sincérité, *f.*

unfelt [ʌn'felt], *a.* Qu'on ne sent pas.

unfeminine [ʌn'feminin], *a.* Peu féminin.

unfenced [ʌn'fenst], *a.* Sans clôture, ouvert.

unfermented [ʌnfə:'mentid], *a.* Non fermenté; sans levain (of bread).

unfertile [ʌn'fə:tail], *a.* Infertile, stérile.

unfetter [ʌn'fetə], *v.t.* Ôter les fers à; (*fig.*) délivrer, affranchir. **unfettered,** *a.* Libre, sans entraves.

unfilial [ʌn'filiəl], *a.* Peu filial.

unfilled [ʌn'fild], *a.* Non rempli, vacant (of a post).

unfilmed [ʌn'filmd], *a.* Pas encore porté à l'écran.

unfiltered [ʌn'filtəd], *a.* Non filtré.

unfinished [ʌn'finiʃt], *a.* Inachevé; incomplet.

unfit [ʌn'fit], *a.* Peu propre, impropre (à); incapable (de); déplacé (unsuitable); en mauvaise santé. *Discharged as unfit,* (*Mil.*) réformé; *unfit for food,* impropre à la consommation.—*v.t.* Rendre incapable, mettre hors d'état de. **unfitly,** *adv.* Mal, à tort. **unfitness,** *n.* Inaptitude, incapacité; inconvenance (unbecomingness), *f.* **unfitting,** *a.* Inconvenant.

unfix [ʌn'fiks], *v.t.* Détacher; remettre (a bayonet). *To become unfixed,* se détacher. **unfixed,** *a.* Mobile; inconstant, indécis, incertain.

unflagging [ʌn'flægiŋ], *a.* Soutenu; infatigable.

unflattering [ʌn'flætəriŋ], *a.* Peu flatteur.

unfledged [ʌn'fledʒd], *a.* Sans plumes; (*fig.*) novice, jeune, inexpérimenté.

unflinching [ʌn'flintʃiŋ], *a.* Ferme, déterminé, résolu, qui ne recule pas. **unflinchingly,** *adv.* Sans reculer.

unfold [ʌn'fould], *v.t.* Déplier, ouvrir, déployer, développer; montrer, révéler; déparquer (sheep).—*v.i.* Se déployer, se dévoiler, se découvrir.

unforbidden [ʌnfə'bidn], *a.* Non défendu, permis.

unforced [ʌn'fɔːst], *a.* Non contraint; libre, spontané; naturel (natural); aisé (easy).

unfordable [ʌn'fɔːdəbl], *a.* Inguéable.

unforeseeing [ʌnfɔː'siːiŋ], *a.* Qui ne prévoit pas, imprévoyant. **unforeseen**, *a.* Imprévu.

unforgettable [ʌnfə'getəbl], *a.* Inoubliable, qui ne s'oublie pas.

unforgiven [ʌnfə'givn], *a.* À qui on n'a pas pardonné; non pardonné (of things). **unforgiving**, *a.* Implacable.

unforgotten [ʌnfə'gɔtn], *a.* Pas oublié.

unformed [ʌn'fɔːmd], *a.* Informe.

unfortified [ʌn'fɔːtifaid], *a.* Non fortifié, sans défense, ouvert. *Unfortified town*, ville ouverte, *f.*

unfortunate [ʌn'fɔːtʃənit], *a.* Infortuné, malheureux, fâcheux.—*n.* Malheureux, *m.*, malheureuse, *f.* **unfortunately**, *adv.* Malheureusement, par malheur.

unfounded [ʌn'faundid], *a.* Sans fondement.

unframed [ʌn'freimd], *a.* Sans cadre.

unfrequented [ʌnfri'kwentid], *a.* Peu fréquenté, solitaire, retiré. **unfrequently** [ʌn'friːkwəntli], *adv.* Rarement, peu souvent. *Not unfrequently*, assez souvent.

unfriended [ʌn'frendid], *a.* Sans amis. **unfriendliness**, *n.* Disposition peu amicale, froideur, *f.* **unfriendly**, *a.* Peu amical, peu bienveillant; hostile, malveillant (of things). *Unfriendly to* (things), nuisible à, contraire à.

unfrightened [ʌn'fraitnd], *a.* Non effrayé.

unfrock [ʌn'frɔk], *v.t.* Défroquer.

unfrozen [ʌn'frouzn], *a.* Non gelé, dégelé.

unfruitful [ʌn'fruːtful], *a.* Infertile, infécond, stérile. **unfruitfully**, *adv.* Stérilement; infructueusement (without success). **unfruitfulness**, *n.* Infertilité, stérilité, *f.*

unfulfilled [ʌnful'fild], *a.* Non accompli, non exécuté.

unfunded [ʌn'fʌndid], *a.* Non consolidé. *Unfunded debt*, dette flottante, *f.*

unfurl [ʌn'fɔːl], *v.t.* Déferler, déployer, déplier.

unfurnished [ʌn'fɔːniʃt], *a.* Non meublé; dépourvu, dénué (de). *Unfurnished flat*, appartement non meublé, *m.*

ungainliness [ʌn'geinlinis], *n.* Gaucherie, *f.*, air gauche, *m.* **ungainly** [ʌn'geinli], *a.* Maladroit, gauche; mal bâti.

ungallant [ʌn'gælənt], *a.* Peu galant, peu courtois.

ungarbled [ʌn'gɑːbld], *a.* Non mutilé, intégral.

ungarnished [ʌn'gɑːniʃt], *a.* Non garni, sans garniture.

ungarrisoned [ʌn'gærisənd], *a.* Sans garnison.

ungear [ʌn'giːə], *v.t.* Débrayer.

ungenerous [ʌn'dʒenərəs], *a.* Peu généreux; mesquin (mean). **ungenerously**, *adv.* Peu généreusement; mesquinement.

ungenial [ʌn'dʒiːniəl], *a.* Peu propice, défavorable; rude (of climate); froid (of a person).

ungenteel [ʌndʒen'tiːl], *a.* Peu poli; mal élevé; de mauvais ton; de mauvais goût.

ungentle [ʌn'dʒentl], *a.* Rude, dur, sévère. **ungentleness**, *n.* Rudesse, dureté, brusquerie, *f.* **ungently**, *adv.* Rudement, durement.

ungentlemanliness [ʌn'dʒentlmənlinis], *n.* impolitesse; vulgarité, *f.* **ungentlemanly** or **ungentlemanlike**, *a.* Indigne d'un homme

comme il faut; de mauvais ton, indélicat, grossier, vulgaire, commun; déshonorant.

ungild [ʌn'gild], *v.t.* Dédorer.

ungird [ʌn'gəːd], *v.t.* (*past* and *p.p.* **ungirded, ungirt**) Ôter la ceinture à, dessangler. **ungirt**, *a.* Sans ceinture; dessanglé (of horses etc.).

unglazed [ʌn'gleizd], *a.* Non vitré (of windows); non verni (of pottery etc.), non glacé (of paper etc.); non lustré (of textiles).

unglove [ʌn'glʌv], *v.t.* Déganter.

unglue [ʌn'gluː], *v.t.* Décoller; (*fig.*) détacher.

ungodliness [ʌn'gɔdlinis], *n.* Impiété, *f.* **ungodly**, *a.* Impie.

ungovernable [ʌn'gʌvənəbl], *a.* Ingouvernable; effréné, déréglé, emporté. **ungoverned**, *a.* Désordonné, déréglé.

ungraceful [ʌn'greisful], *a.* Peu gracieux, disgracieux. **ungracefully**, *adv.* Peu gracieusement, sans grâce. **ungracefulness**, *n.* Manque de grâce, *m.*

ungracious [ʌn'greiʃəs], *a.* Peu gracieux, déplaisant, désagréable. *Ungracious answer*, réponse défavorable, *f.* **ungraciously**, *adv.* D'une manière peu aimable; de mauvaise grâce.

ungrammatical [ʌngrə'mætikl], *a.* Incorrect. **ungrammatically**, *adv.* Incorrectement.

ungranted [ʌn'grɑːntid], *a.* Non accordé.

ungrateful [ʌn'greitful], *a.* Ingrat (envers); désagréable (unpleasant). **ungratefully**, *adv.* Avec ingratitude; désagréablement. **ungratefulness**, *n.* Ingratitude, *f.*; nature désagréable, *f.*

ungrounded [ʌn'graundid], *a.* Sans fondement.

ungrudged [ʌn'grʌdʒd], *a.* Donné de bon cœur. **ungrudging**, *a.* De bon cœur. **ungrudgingly**, *adv.* Volontiers, de bon cœur.

unguarded [ʌn'gɑːdid], *a.* Sans protection, sans défense, imprudent, inconsidéré, irréfléchi (not cautious). *In an unguarded moment*, dans un moment d'absence *or* d'oubli. **unguardedly**, *adv.* Imprudemment.

unguent ['ʌŋgwənt], *n.* Onguent, *m.*

unguessed [ʌn'gest], *a.* Non deviné.

unguicular [ʌŋ'gwikjulə] or **unguiculated**, *a.* Onguiculé, à onglet.

unguided [ʌn'gaidid], *a.* Sans guide.

unguiferous [ʌŋ'gwifərəs], *a.* Unguifère.

ungulate ['ʌŋgjulət], *a.* Ongulé.

ungum [ʌn'gʌm], *v.t.* Dégommer (silk). **ungumming**, *n.* Dégommage, *m.*

unhallowed [ʌn'hæloud], *a.* Non sanctifié, profane.

unhampered [ʌn'hæmpəd], *a.* Non incommodé, non embarrassé (par).

*****unhand** [ʌn'hænd], *v.t.* Lâcher. **unhandily**, *adv.* Maladroitement, gauchement. **unhandiness**, *n.* Maladresse, gaucherie, *f.* **unhandy**, *a.* Maladroit, gauche; incommode (inconvenient).

unhandsome [ʌn'hænsəm], *a.* Peu libéral, vilain (illiberal); malhonnête (uncivil); laid, disgracieux (ungraceful). **unhandsomely**, *adv.* Peu libéralement, vilainement (illiberally); malhonnêtement (uncivilly); d'une manière disgracieuse (ungracefully). **unhandsomeness**, *n.* Indélicatesse; laideur, nature disgracieuse, *f.*

unhang [ʌn'hæŋ], *v.t.* (*past* and *p.p.* **unhung**) Descendre, dépendre; démonter, retirer des gonds (a door etc.).

unhappily [ʌn'hæpili], *adv.* Malheureusement, par malheur. **unhappiness,** *n.* Malheur, *m.* **unhappy,** *a.* Malheureux.
unharmed [ʌn'hɑːmd], *a.* Sain et sauf.
unharness [ʌn'hɑːnis], *v.t.* Déharnacher; dételer (to take from a vehicle); ôter l'armure à.
unhatched [ʌn'hætʃt], *a.* Non éclos.
unhealthily [ʌn'helθili], *adv.* Insalubrement. **unhealthiness,** *n.* Insalubrité, *f.* **unhealthy,** *a.* Insalubre, malsain; maladif (of persons).
unheard [ʌn'hɔːd], *a.* Sans être entendu; inexaucé (of prayers). *Unheard of,* inconnu, inouï (extraordinary).
unheeded [ʌn'hiːdid], *a.* Inaperçu, négligé. **unheedful** or **unheeding,** *a.* Insouciant; inattentif, distrait; négligent.
unhelped [ʌn'helpt], *a.* Sans être aidé, sans aide; non servi (*at dinner*). **unhelpful,** *a.* Qui ne sert à rien, inutile.
unhesitating [ʌn'heziteitiŋ], *a.* Sans hésitation; décidé, ferme, résolu. **unhesitatingly,** *adv.* Sans hésiter.
unhewn [ʌn'hjuːn], *a.* Brut; non taillé.
unhindered [ʌn'hindəd], *a.* Sans empêchement.
unhinge [ʌn'hindʒ], *v.t.* Démonter; mettre hors des gonds; (*fig.*) bouleverser, déranger.
unhistorical [ʌnhis'tɔrikəl], *a.* Peu historique.
unhitch [ʌn'hitʃ], *v.t.* Décrocher; dételer (a horse).
unholiness [ʌn'houlinis], *n.* Impiété, *f.* **unholy,** *a.* Profane, impie. (*fam.*) *That cupboard is in an unholy mess,* cette armoire est dans un désordre incroyable.
unhood [ʌn'hud], *v.t.* Déchaperonner (a falcon).
unhook [ʌn'huk], *v.t.* Décrocher; dégrafer (clothes).
unhoped [ʌn'houpt], *a.* Inattendu. *Unhoped for,* inespéré. **unhopeful,** *a. I am not unhopeful that,* j'ai des raisons d'espérer que.
unhorse [ʌn'hɔːs], *v.t.* Désarçonner, démonter. *To be unhorsed,* être désarçonné.
unhouse [ʌn'hauz], *v.t.* Déloger.
unhung [ʌn'hʌŋ], *a.* Non tapissé (room), non exposé (picture); qui n'est pas encore pendu (criminal). *The greatest rascal unhung,* le plus grand pendard imaginable.
unhurried [ʌn'hʌrid], *a.* Lent, sans précipitation.
unhurt [ʌn'hɔːt], *a.* Sain et sauf.
unhusk [ʌn'hʌsk], *v.t.* Décortiquer, écosser.
unhygienic [ʌnhai'dʒiːnik], *a.* Peu hygiénique.
uniarticulate [juːniɑː'tikjulət], *a.* Uniarticulé.
unicapsular [-'kæpsjulə], *a.* Unicapsulaire.
unicellular [-'seljulə], *a.* Unicellulaire.
unicorn ['juːnikɔːn], *n.* Licorne, *f.* **unicornfish,** *n.* Narval, *m.*, licorne de mer, *f.*
unidentified [ʌnai'dentifaid], *a.* Non identifié.
unidiomatic [ʌnidio'mætik], *a.* Peu idiomatique.
unidirectional [juːnidi'rekʃənəl], *a.* (*Elec.*) Continu (of current).
unification [juːnifi'keiʃən], *n.* Unification, *f.*
unify ['juːnifai], *v.t.* Unifier.
uniflorous [juːni'flɔːrəs], *a.* (*Bot.*) Uniflore.
uniform ['juːnifɔːm], *a.* Uniforme.—*n.* Uniforme, *m. Drill uniform,* tenue d'exercice, *f.*;

field uniform, tenue de campagne, *f.*; *full* (*-dress*) *uniform,* grande tenue, grand uniforme; *undress uniform,* petite tenue, *f.*
uniformity [juːni'fɔːmiti], *n.* Uniformité, *f.*; conformisme, *m.*
uniformly ['juːnifɔːmli], *adv.* Uniformément.
unify ['juːnifai], *v.t.* Unifier.
unilateral [juːni'lætərəl], *a.* Unilatéral.
unilocular [juːni'lɔkjulə], *a.* (*Bot.*) Unilocu- laire.
unimaginable [ʌni'mædʒinəbl], *a.* Inimaginable, inconcevable. **unimaginative,** *a.* Peu imaginatif. **unimagined,** *a.* Non imaginé.
unimpaired [ʌnim'pɛəd], *a.* Inaltéré, intact, non diminué; dans toute sa vigueur.
unimpassioned [ʌnim'pæʃənd], *a.* Sans passion, calme, tranquille.
unimpeachable [ʌnim'piːtʃəbl], *a.* Irréprochable, inattaquable, incontestable. **unimpeached,** *a.* Incontesté.
unimpeded [ʌnim'piːdid], *a.* Sans empêchement.
unimportance [ʌnim'pɔːtəns], *n.* Peu d'importance, *m.*, insignifiance, *f.* **unimportant,** *a.* Sans importance, insignifiant, peu important.
unimposed [ʌnim'pouzd], *a.* Qu'on n'a pas prescrit, volontaire. **unimposing,** *a.* Peu imposant.
unimpressed [ʌnim'prest], *a.* Non empreint; sans être ému or pénétré. **unimpressive,** *a.* Peu frappant, peu touchant, peu émouvant.
unimprovable [ʌnim'pruːvəbl], *a.* Non susceptible d'amélioration, incorrigible; non exploitable (of land). **unimproved,** *a.* Non corrigé; non amélioré, qui n'a pas fait de progrès, peu avancé; non amendé (of land), inutilisé.
uninfected [ʌnin'fektid], *a.* Non infecté.
uninflammable [ʌnin'flæməbl], *a.* Non inflammable.
uninflated [ʌnin'fleitid], *a.* Dégonflé, à plat (of tyre).
uninflected [ʌnin'flektid], *a.* Qui n'a pas d'inflexions.
uninfluenced [ʌn'influənst], *a.* Sans être influencé. *Uninfluenced by,* soustrait à l'influence de. **uninfluential** [-'enʃl], *a.* Sans influence.
uninformed [ʌnin'fɔːmd], *a.* Ignorant, sans instruction. *To be uninformed of,* être ignorant de, ignorer.
uninfringed [ʌnin'frindʒd], *a.* Non enfreint.
uninhabitable [ʌnin'hæbitəbl], *a.* Inhabitable. **uninhabited,** *a.* Inhabité.
uninitiated [ʌnin'iʃieitid], *a.* Non initié, profane.
uninjured [ʌn'indʒəd], *a.* Sain et sauf, sans blessure, sans mal; intact (of ⁺things).
uninquisitive [ʌnin'kwizitiv], *a.* Peu curieux.
uninspired [ʌnin'spaiəd], *a.* Non inspiré, sans inspiration. **uninspiring,** *a.* Banal.
uninstructed [ʌnin'strʌktid], *a.* Sans instruction, ignorant.
uninsured [ʌnin'ʃuəd], *a.* Non assuré.
unintellectual [ʌninti'lektjuəl], *a.* Peu intellectuel.
unintelligent [ʌnin'telidʒənt], *a.* Peu intelligent, sans intelligence.
unintelligibility ['ʌnintelidʒi'biliti], *n.* Caractère inintelligible, *m.*

unintelligible [ʌnin'telidʒibl], *a.* Inintelligible. **unintelligibly,** *adv.* D'une manière peu intelligible.
unintended or **unintentional** [ʌnin'tenʃənl], *a.* Sans intention, involontaire. **unintentionally,** *adv.* Fait sans le vouloir, sans intention.
uninterested [ʌn'intristid], *a.* Non intéressé, indifférent. **uninterestedly,** *adv.* D'une manière peu intéressée. **uninteresting,** *a.* Peu intéressant, sans intérêt. **uninterestingly,** *adv.* D'une manière peu intéressante.
uninterrupted [ʌnintə'rʌptid], *a.* Ininterrompu, continuel, sans interruption. **uninterruptedly,** *adv.* Sans interruption.
uninventive [ʌnin'ventiv], *a.* Peu inventif.
uninvited [ʌnin'vaitid], *a.* Sans invitation, sans être invité. **uninviting,** *a.* Peu attrayant; peu appétissant (of food).
union ['juːniən], *n.* Union, *f.*; asile, dépôt, *m.*; *maison des pauvres (workhouse), f.; (Plumbing)* raccord, *m. Union* or *trade-union*, syndicat (corporatif), *m.; non-union men*, ouvriers non syndiqués, *m.pl.; union* or *Union Jack*, pavillon britannique, *m.; union is strength*, l'union fait la force. **union-joint,** *n.* Raccord, manchon, *m.* **union-nut,** *n.* Écrou d'assemblage, raccord fileté, *m. Union-nut joint*, raccord à vis, *m.* **union-suit,** *n.* (*Am.*) Combinaison-culotte, *f.*
Unionist ['juːniənist], *n.* Unioniste, *m.*
uniparous [juː'nipərəs], *a.* (*Biol.*) Unipare.
uniparity [juːni'pæriti], *n.* Uniparité, *f.*
unipersonal [-'pəːsənl], *a.* Unipersonnel.
unipolar [juːni'poulə], *a.* (*Elec.*) Unipolaire.
unique [juː'niːk], *a.* Unique. **uniquely,** *adv.* D'une manière unique.
unisexual [juːni'seksjuəl], *a.* (*Bot.*) Unisexuel, unisexué.
unison ['juːnizn], *n.* Unisson, *m. In unison,* à l'unisson. **unisonance** [juː'nisənəns], *n.* Consonance parfaite, *f.,* unisson, *m.* **unisonant,** *a.* À l'unisson.
unit ['juːnit], *n.* Unité; (*Mil.*) fraction, *f.*; bloc, élément, *m. A complete unit*, une fraction constituée, *f.; unit price*, prix unitaire, *m.*
Unitarian [juːni'tɛəriən], *a.* and *n.* Unitaire, *m.* **Unitarianism,** *n.* Unitarisme, *m.*
unitary ['juːnitəri], *a.* Unitaire (system).
unite [juː'nait], *v.t.* Unir (à or avec); joindre, réunir (one's efforts etc.).—*v.i.* S'unir, se réunir; se joindre (à or avec).
united [juː'naitid], *a.* Uni; réuni; joint. *United Kingdom (the),* Le Royaume-Uni, *m.; United Provinces (the),* Les Provinces-Unies, *f.pl.; United States (the),* Les États-Unis, *m.pl.*
unitedly [juː'naitidli], *adv.* Ensemble, d'accord.
unity ['juːniti], *n.* Unité; union, concorde, harmonie, *f.*
univalent [juːni'veilənt or juː'nivələnt], *a.* Univalent.
univalve ['juːnivælv], *n.* Univalve, *m.*
universal [juːni'vəːsl], *a.* Universel. *Universal joint,* joint universel, joint de Cardan, *m.; universal wrench-screw,* clé universelle, *f.* **universals,** *n.pl.* Universaux, *m.pl.* **universality** [-'sæliti], *n.* Universalité, *f.* **universally,** *adv.* Universellement.
universe ['juːnivəːs], *n.* Univers, *m.*
university [juːni'vəːsiti], *n.* Université, *f.*

University degree, grade universitaire, *m.; university man,* universitaire, *m.*
unjoin [DISJOIN].
unjudged [ʌn'dʒʌdʒd], *a.* Sans être jugé, non jugé.
unjust [ʌn'dʒʌst], *a.* Injuste, inique. **unjustly,** *adv.* Injustement.
unjustifiable [ʌn'dʒʌstifaiəbl], *a.* Injustifiable. **unjustifiableness,** *n.* Nature injustifiable, *f.* **unjustifiably,** *adv.* D'une manière injustifiable. **unjustified** [ʌn'dʒʌstifaid], *a.* Sans justification.
unkempt [ʌn'kempt], *a.* Mal peigné; (*fig.*) en désordre.
unkennel [ʌn'kenl], *v.t.* Faire sortir du chenil; déterrer (a fox etc.).
unkind [ʌn'kaind], *a.* Désobligeant; peu aimable; dur, cruel. **unkindliness,** *n.* Désobligeance; malveillance, *f.* **unkindly,** *a.* Peu propice, contraire, défavorable.—*adv.* Sans bienveillance; cruellement, mal. *Don't take it unkindly on my part if . . .,* ne me sachez pas mauvais gré si . . .; *to take (something) unkindly,* prendre en mauvaise part, prendre mal. **unkindness,** *n.* Manque d'amabilité, *m.,* désobligeance; cruauté, dureté, *f.*
unkingly [ʌn'kiŋli], *a.* Indigne d'un roi.
unknowable [ʌn'nouəbl], *a.* Inconnaissable.
unknowing, *a.* Ignorant, qui ne connaît pas. **unknowingly,** *adv.* Sans le savoir, à son insu. **unknown,** *a.* Inconnu. *Unknown quantity* or *unknown, n.,* (*Math.*) inconnue, *f. Unknown to me (without my knowledge),* à mon insu.
unlabelled [ʌn'leibld], *a.* Non étiqueté.
unlaboured [ʌn'leibəd], *a.* Non travaillé; naturel; spontané.
unlace [ʌn'leis], *v.t.* Délacer, détacher.
unlade [UNLOAD].
unladylike [ʌn'leidilaik], *a.* Peu digne d'une dame, de mauvais ton, vulgaire.
unlaid [ʌn'leid], *a.* Non posé; (*fig.*) non apaisé, non exorcisé (ghost).
unlamented [ʌnlə'mentid], *a.* Sans laisser de regrets, non regretté.
unlash [ʌn'læʃ], *v.t.* Démarrer, détacher.
unlatch [ʌn'lætʃ], *v.t.* Lever le loquet de, ouvrir; délacer.
unlawful [ʌn'lɔːful], *a.* Illégal; illicite; illégitime (of birth). **unlawfully,** *adv.* Illégalement; illicitement; illégitimement. **unlawfulness,** *n.* Illégalité, *f.*
unlay [ʌn'lei], *v.t.* Détordre (a rope).
unlearn [ʌn'ləːn], *v.t.* Désapprendre. **unlearnable,** *a.* Inapprenable.
unlearned [ʌn'ləːnid], *a.* Ignorant, illettré.
unleash [ʌn'liːʃ], *v.t.* Lâcher (of dogs etc.).
unleavened [ʌn'levənd], *a.* Sans levain; (*Script.*) azyme.
unless [ʌn'les], *conj.* À moins que . . . ne (with subjunctive); à moins de (followed by infinitive); si . . . ne . . . pas (followed by indicative); si ce n'est, excepté que. *Unless I send for you,* à moins que je ne vous envoie chercher; *unless sent for,* à moins d'être appelé.
unlettered [ʌn'letəd], *a.* Illettré.
unlevelled [ʌn'levəld], *a.* Non nivelé.
unlicensed [ʌn'laisənst], *a.* Non autorisé, sans autorisation; (*Comm.*) non patenté; (*Print.*) pas breveté; (*Hunt.*) sans permis (de chasse). *Unlicensed broker,* courtier marron, *m.*

unlicked [ʌn'likt], *a.* Mal léché. *Unlicked bear*, ours mal léché, *m.*

unlighted [ʌn'laitid], *a.* Non éclairé; non allumé (not ignited).

unlike [ʌn'laik], *a.* Différent (de); qui ne ressemble pas (à); *invraisemblable, improbable (improbable). Not unlike . . .*, qui ne ressemble pas mal *or* qui ressemble assez à; *to be unlike each other*, ne pas se ressembler. **unlikelihood** or **unlikeliness**, *n.* Invraisemblance, improbabilité, *f.* **unlikely**, *a.* Improbable, invraisemblable, peu sûr; inefficace, qui ne promet pas de réussir (not promising success). *It is very unlikely that*, il est peu probable que; *he is unlikely to come*, il est peu probable qu'il vienne; *that is not at all unlikely*, cela se pourrait bien, c'est bien possible.—*adv.* Invraisemblablement. **unlikeness**, *n.* Différence, dissemblance, *f.*

unlimber [ʌn'limbə], *v.t.* Séparer l'avant-train, mettre en batterie.

unlimited [ʌn'limitid], *a.* Illimité. **unlimitedly**, *adv.* Sans limites, sans bornes. **unlimitedness**, *n.* Immensité, *f.*

unlined [ʌn'laind], *a.* Non doublé; non fourré.

unlink [ʌn'link], *v.t.* Défaire, détacher.

unliquidated [ʌn'likwideitid], *a.* Non liquidé, non soldé.

unliv(e)able [ʌn'livəbl], *a.* Insupportable (of life), inhabitable.

unload [ʌn'loud], *v.t.* Décharger; désarmer (a gun); lâcher (bombs). **unloading**, *n.* Déchargement, *m.*

unlock [ʌn'lɔk], *v.t.* Ouvrir; (*Print.*) desserrer; (*fig.*) découvrir, révéler.

unlooked-for [ʌn'lukt fɔː], *a.* Inattendu, imprévu, inespéré.

unloose [ʌn'luːs], *v.t.* Délier, détacher, déchaîner.

unloved [ʌn'lʌvd], *a.* Pas aimé. **unlovely**, *a.* Peu aimable; laid. **unloving**, *a.* Peu affectueux, malveillant.

unluckily [ʌn'lʌkili], *adv.* Malheureusement, par malheur. **unluckiness**, *n.* Malheur, *m.*, infortune, *f.* **unlucky**, *a.* Malheureux, infortuné, malencontreux; sinistre, de mauvais augure (ill-omened). *To be unlucky* (at cards etc.), avoir du guignon, n'avoir pas de chance.

unmade [ʌn'meid], *a.* Non confectionné; défait; pas fait (bed); non empierré (road).

unmake [ʌn'meik], *v.t.* (*past and p.p.* **unmade**) Défaire; (*fig.*) détruire, ruiner.

unman [ʌn'mæn], *v.t.* Abattre, décourager, énerver, amollir. (*Naut.*) *To unman a ship*, désarmer un vaisseau.

unmanageable [ʌn'mænidʒəbl], *a.* Impossible à conduire *or* à diriger, ingouvernable, intraitable; rebelle. *To become unmanageable* (of horses), s'emporter, s'emballer.

unmanliness [ʌn'mænlinis], *n.* Conduite indigne d'un homme, lâcheté, *f.* **unmanly**, *a.* Indigne d'un homme, lâche; mou, efféminé.

unmannered [UNMANNERLY].

unmanneriness [ʌn'mænəlinis], *n.* Grossièreté, *f.*, manque de savoir-vivre, *m.*

unmannerly, *a.* Grossier, mal appris, de mauvais ton.—*adv.* Grossièrement.

unmanufactured [ʌnmænju'fæktʃəd], *a.* Non fabriqué, brut.

unmanured [ʌnmə'njuəd], *a.* Sans engrais.

unmapped [UNCHARTED].

unmarked [ʌn'maːkt], *a.* Non marqué (de); inaperçu, inobservé.

unmarketable [ʌn'maːkitəbl], *a.* Invendable.

unmarriageable [ʌn'mæridʒəbl], *a.* Que l'on ne peut pas marier; qui n'est pas libre de se marier. **unmarried**, *a.* *Unmarried man*, célibataire, *m.*; *unmarried woman*, demoiselle, vieille fille, *f.*

unmask [ʌn'maːsk], *v.t.* Démasquer; (*fig.*) dévoiler.—*v.i.* Se démasquer. **unmasked**, *a.* Sans masque; (*fig.*) sans déguisement.

unmast [ʌn'maːst], *v.t.* Démâter.

unmastered [ʌn'maːstəd], *a.* Non maîtrisé, indompté.

unmatched [ʌn'mætʃt], *a.* Dépareillé, déparié; (*fig.*) sans pareil, incomparable.

unmeaning [ʌn'miːniŋ], *a.* Qui ne signifie rien, insignifiant, vide de sens, inintelligible.

unmeant [ʌn'ment], *a.* Sans intention, involontaire.

unmeasured [ʌn'meʒəd], *a.* Non mesuré, sans mesure; (*fig.*) immense, infini, démesuré.

unmechanical [ʌnmi'kænikəl], *a.* Peu doué pour la mécanique.

unmelodious [ʌnmi'loudiəs], *a.* Sans mélodie, discordant. **unmelodiously**, *adv.* D'une manière discordante.

unmelted [ʌn'meltid], *a.* Non fondu; (*fig.*) non attendri, inexorable.

unmemorable [ʌn'memərəbl], *a.* Vite oublié.

unmentionable [ʌn'menʃənəbl], *a.* Dont on ne parle pas. **unmentionables**, *n.pl.* (*colloq.*) Pantalon, *m.*, culotte, *f.* **unmentioned**, *a.* Non mentionné, dont on ne parle pas.

unmerciful [ʌn'məːsiful], *a.* Sans pitié, impitoyable, cruel. **unmercifully**, *adv.* Impitoyablement, sans pitié. *To beat unmercifully*, rouer de coups. **unmercifulness**, *n.* Barbarie, cruauté, *f.*

unmerited [ʌn'meritid], *a.* Immérité.

unmetalled [ʌn'metld], *a.* Non empierré (road).

unmethodical [ʌnmi'θɔdikl], *a.* Sans méthode.

unmilitary [ʌn'militəri], *a.* Non militaire.

unmindful [ʌn'maindful], *a.* Peu soucieux (de). **unmindfully**, *adv.* Inattentivement, sans soin. **unmindfulness**, *n.* Insouciance, inattention, *f.*

unmined [ʌn'maind], *a.* Non miné.

unmingled [ʌn'miŋgld], *a.* Pur, sans mélange.

unmissed [ʌn'mist], *a.* Dont on ne remarque pas l'absence; que on ne regrette pas.

unmistakable [ʌnmis'teikəbl], *a.* À ne pas s'y méprendre, évident, clair. **unmistakably**, *adv.* Évidemment, clairement, de manière à ne pas s'y méprendre.

unmitigated [ʌn'mitigeitid], *a.* Non adouci; (*colloq.*) complet, franc, fieffé, dans toute la force du terme (of scoundrels etc.).

unmixed [ʌn'mikst], *a.* Sans mélange, pur.

unmobilized [ʌn'moubilaizd], *a.* Non mobilisé.

unmodified [ʌn'mɔdifaid], *a.* Non modifié.

unmolested [ʌnmə'lestid], *a.* Sans être molesté, en paix.

unmoor [ʌn'muə], *v.t.* Lever l'ancre de, démarrer. **unmooring**, *n.* Démarrage, *m.*

unmortgaged [ʌn'mɔːgidʒd], *a.* Libre d'hypothèque.

unmotherly [ʌn'mʌðəli], *a.* Peu digne d'une mère, peu maternel.

unmounted [ʌn'mauntid], *a.* (Soldat) à pied, non monté (on foot); non collée (of photograph etc.).

unmourned [ʌn'mɔːnd], *a.* Sans être pleuré.

unmoved [ʌn'muːvd], *a.* Immobile, fixe; (*fig.*) non ému, impassible, calme, inébranlable.

unmown [ʌn'moun], *a.* Non fauché; non tondu.

unmusical [ʌn'mjuːzikl], *a.* Peu harmonieux, discordant; pas musicien (person).

unmutilated [ʌn'mjuːtileitid], *a.* Non mutilé, intact.

unmuzzle [ʌn'mʌzl], *v.t.* Démuseler.

unnail [ʌn'neil], *v.t.* Déclouer.

unnamed [ʌn'neimd], *a.* Innommé; anonyme.

unnatural [ʌn'nætʃrəl], *a.* Contre nature; forcé; dénaturé (of persons). *An unnatural mother*, une marâtre. **unnaturally**, *adv.* Contre nature, d'une manière dénaturée. *I was not unnaturally surprised to see*, je ne fus pas étrangement surpris de voir.

unnavigable [ʌn'nævigəbl], *a.* Innavigable.

unnecessarily [ʌn'nesəserili], *adv.* Sans nécessité, inutilement; par trop. **unnecessariness**, *n.* Inutilité, *f.* **unnecessary**, *a.* Peu nécessaire, inutile.

unneeded [ʌn'niːdid], *a.* Dont on n'a pas besoin.

unnegotiable [ʌnni'gouʃəbl], *a.* Innégociable, incommerçable.

unneighbourly [ʌn'neibəli], *a.* Peu obligeant; de mauvais voisin.—*adv.* En mauvais voisin.

unnerve [ʌn'nəːv], *v.t.* Énerver; (*fig.*) affaiblir, décourager.

unnoted [ʌn'noutid] or **unnoticed**, *a.* Inaperçu, passé sous silence, inobservé.

unnumbered [ʌn'nʌmbəd], *a.* Sans nombre, innombrable.

unobjectionable [ʌnəb'dʒekʃənəbl], *a.* Irréprochable, irrécusable. **unobjectionably**, *adv.* Irréprochablement, irrécusablement.

unobliging [ʌnə'blaidʒiŋ], *a.* Désobligeant, peu complaisant.

unobliterated [ʌnə'blitəreitid], *a.* Ineffacé; non oblitéré.

unobscured [ʌnəb'skjuəd], *a.* Non obscurci, clair, brillant.

unobservance [ʌnəb'zəːvəns], *n.* Inattention, inobservation, *f.* **unobservant, unobserving**, *a.* Peu observateur. **unobserved**, *a.* Inaperçu.

unobstructed [ʌnəb'strʌktid], *a.* Non obstrué.

unobtainable [ʌnəb'teinəbl], *a.* Impossible à obtenir.

unobtrusive [ʌnəb'truːsiv], *a.* Qui s'efface, réservé, discret. **unobtrusively**, *adv.* Sans importunité, avec modestie.

unoccupied [ʌn'ɔkjupaid], *a.* Inoccupé; libre, disponible (of time etc.); inhabité (of houses).

unoffending [ʌnə'fendiŋ], *a.* Inoffensif.

unofficial [ʌnə'fiʃl], *a.* Non officiel. **unofficially**, *adv.* Non officiellement.

unopened [ʌn'oupənd], *a.* Fermé; non décacheté (of letters etc.).

unopposed [ʌnə'pouzd], *a.* Sans opposition.

unorganized [ʌn'ɔːgənaizd], *a.* Non organisé, sans organisation.

unoriginal [ʌnə'ridʒinəl], *a.* Peu original.

unornamental [ʌnɔːnə'mentl], *a.* Qui ne sert pas d'ornement, peu décoratif. **unornamented** [ʌn'ɔːnəmentid], *a.* Sans ornements, simple.

unorthodox [ʌn'ɔːθədɔks], *a.* Peu orthodoxe, hétérodoxe.

unostentatious [ʌnɔsten'teiʃəs], *a.* Sans ostentation, sans faste; modeste, simple. **unostentatiously**, *adv.* Sans ostentation. **unostentatiousness**, *n.* Simplicité, *f.*

unowed [ʌn'oud], *a.* Qui n'est pas dû.

unowned [ʌn'ound], *a.* Sans propriétaire, non reconnu; non réclamé (not claimed).

unoxidized [ʌn'ɔksidaizd], *a.* Inoxydé.

unpack [ʌn'pæk], *v.t.* Défaire; déballer (goods); dépaqueter (parcels). *To come unpacked*, se défaire. **unpacking**, *n.* Déballage; dépaquetage (of small parcels), *m.*

unpaid [ʌn'peid], *a.* Non payé, sans paye, sans solde (of armies); non affranchi (of letters etc.).

unpainted [ʌn'peintid], *a.* Non peint.

unpaired [ʌn'pɛəd], *a.* Non apparié.

unpalatable [ʌn'pælətəbl], *a.* Désagréable au goût; (*fig.*) désagréable.

unpapered [ʌn'peipəd], *a.* Non tapissé.

unparalleled [ʌn'pærəleld], *a.* Sans pareil; sans précédent; unique.

unpardonable [ʌn'paːdnəbl], *a.* Impardonnable, inexcusable. **unpardoned**, *a.* Non pardonné; sans pardon.

unpared [ʌn'pɛəd] or **unpeeled** [ʌn'piːld], *a.* Non pelé.

unparliamentary [ʌnpaːli'mentəri], *a.* Peu parlementaire.

unparted [ʌn'paːtid], *a.* Non séparé.

unpatented [ʌn'pætəntid or ʌn'peitəntid], *a.* Non breveté.

unpatriotic [ʌnpeitri'ɔtik or ʌnpætri'ɔtik], *a.* Peu patriotique; peu patriote (of a person). **unpatriotically**, *adv.* Peu patriotiquement.

unpatronized [ʌn'pætrənaizd], *a.* Sans clients; sans protecteur.

unpaved [ʌn'peivd], *a.* Non pavé.

unpawned [ʌn'pɔːnd], *a.* Non engagé.

unpeg [ʌn'peg], *v.t.* Décheviller; déplanter (une tente).

unpensioned [ʌn'penʃənd], *a.* Sans retraite.

unpeopled [ʌn'piːpld], *a.* Dépeuplé.

unperceivable [IMPERCEPTIBLE].

unperceived [ʌnpə'siːvd], *a.* Inaperçu.

unperforated [ʌn'pəːfəreitid], *a.* Non perforé.

unperformed [ʌnpə'fɔːmd], *a.* Inexécuté; non joué (of play).

unpermitted [ʌnpə'mitid], *a.* Non permis, illicite.

unpersuasive [ʌnpə'sweisiv], *a.* Peu convaincant.

unperturbed [ʌnpə'təːbd], *a.* Peu ému, impassible.

unphilosophical [ʌnfilə'sɔfikl], *a.* Peu philosophique.

unpick [ʌn'pik], *v.t.* Découdre.

unpicked [ʌn'pikt], *a.* Non cueilli; non épluché; décousu (of stitches).

unpin [ʌn'pin], *v.t.* Ôter les épingles de, défaire.

unpitied [ʌn'pitid], *a.* Qu'on ne plaint pas. **unpitying**, *a.* Sans pitié, impitoyable.

unplait [ʌn'plæt], *v.t.* Dénatter.

unplanted [ʌn'plaːntid], *a.* Sans être planté (de); non colonisé (not settled).

unplausible [ʌn'plɔːzibl], *a.* Peu plausible.

unplayable [ʌn'pleiəbl], *a.* Injouable.
unpleasant · [ʌn'plezənt], *a.* Déplaisant, désagréable, fâcheux. **unpleasantly,** *adv.* Désagréablement. **unpleasantness,** *n.* Nature désagréable, *f.*; désagrément, *m.*
unpleasing [ʌn'pli:ziŋ], *a.* Déplaisant, désagréable, fâcheux.
unpledged [ʌn'pledʒd], *a.* Non engagé.
unploughed [ʌn'plaud], *a.* Non labouré.
unplucked [ʌn'plʌkt], *a.* Non cueilli; non plumé.
unpoetical [ʌnpo'etikl], *a.* Peu poétique. **unpoetically,** *adv.* Peu poétiquement.
unpointed [ʌn'pɔintid], *a.* Sans pointe; sans ponctuation.
unpolarized [ʌn'pouləraizd], *a.* Non polarisé.
unpolished [ʌn'pɔliʃt], *a.* Non poli; mat (of gold etc.); non ciré (of boots); dépoli (of glass); (*fig.*) impoli, grossier, rude.
unpolite [IMPOLITE].
unpolluted [ʌnpə'lju:tid], *a.* Non souillé; pur.
unpopular [ʌn'pɔpjulə], *a.* Impopulaire. **unpopularity** [-'læriti], *n.* Impopularité, *f.*
unpractical [ʌn'præktikl], *a.* Peu pratique.
unpractised, *a.* Inexpérimenté, sans expérience, novice.
unprecedented [ʌn'presidəntid], *a.* Sans exemple, sans précédent, inédit.
unprecise [ʌnpri'sais], *a.* Imprécis.
unprejudiced [ʌn'predʒudist], *a.* Sans préjugés, impartial.
unpremeditated [ʌnpri'mediteitid], *a.* Inopiné, improvisé, sans préméditation.
unprepared [ʌnpri'pɛəd], *a.* Non préparé, sans préparation. *He was unprepared for such an event,* il était loin de s'attendre à un tel événement; *to be taken unprepared,* être pris au dépourvu; *to be unprepared for,* ne pas s'attendre à. **unpreparedly** [ʌnpri'pɛəridli], *adv.* Sans préparation. **unpreparedness,** *n.* Manque de préparation, *m.*
unprepossessing [ʌnpri:pə'zesiŋ], *a.* Peu engageant.
unpretending [ʌnpri'tendiŋ] or **unpretentious** [-'tenʃəs], *a.* Sans prétention, modeste.
unprincely [ʌn'prinsli], *a.* Indigne d'un prince.
unprincipled [ʌn'prinsipld], *a.* Sans principes, sans mœurs.
unprintable [ʌn'printəbl], *a.* Qu'on ne peut imprimer, inimprimable; (language) indécent.
unprinted [ʌn'printid], *a.* En manuscrit; blanc (of calico).
unprivileged [ʌn'privilidʒd], *a.* Sans privilège.
unprized [ʌn'praizd], *a.* Dont on fait peu de cas.
unproductive [ʌnprə'dʌktiv], *a.* Improductif; stérile (of land). *Unproductive of any real benefit,* ne produisant aucun avantage sérieux. **unproductiveness,** *n.* Stérilité, *f.*
unprofessional [ʌnprə'feʃənəl], *a.* Contraire aux règles d'une profession.
unprofitable [ʌn'prɔfitəbl], *a.* Peu lucratif, sans profit; inutile. **unprofitableness,** *n.* Inutilité, *f.* **unprofitably,** *adv.* Inutilement, sans profit.
unpromising [ʌn'prɔmisiŋ], *a.* Qui s'annonce mal; qui promet guère; peu encourageant; ingrat.
unprompted [ʌn'prɔmptid], *a.* Sans y être poussé, de son propre chef.

unpronounceable [ʌnprə'naunsəbl], *a.* Imprononçable.
unpropitious [ʌnprə'piʃəs], *a.* Peu propice, peu favorable (à).
unprosperous [ʌn'prɔspərəs], *a.* Peu prospère, malheureux. **unprosperously,** *adv.* Malheureusement, sans succès. **unprosperousness,** *n.* Insuccès, *m.*
unprotected [ʌnprə'tektid], *a.* Sans protection, sans défense, à découvert. *Unprotected from the rain,* sans abri contre la pluie.
unproved [ʌn'pru:vd], *a.* Sans preuve; non éprouvé, non essayé (not tried).
unprovided [ʌnprə'vaidid], *a.* Dépourvu, dénué (de); pris au dépourvu (not prepared). *We were unprovided for that,* nous ne nous attendions pas à cela, nous étions loin de nous y attendre.
unprovoked [ʌnprə'voukt], *a.* Sans provocation. *An unprovoked insult,* une insulte gratuite; *unprovoked aggression,* agression (non provoquée), *f.*
unpruned [ʌn'pru:nd], *a.* Non taillé.
unpublished [ʌn'pʌbliʃt], *a.* Inédit; (*fig.*) secret, inconnu.
unpunctual [ʌn'pʌŋktjuəl], *a.* Inexact. **unpunctuality,** *n.* Inexactitude, *f.*
unpunished [ʌn'pʌniʃt], *a.* Impuni. *To go unpunished,* rester impuni.
unpurified [ʌn'pjuərifaid], *a.* Non purifié, impur.
unqualified [ʌn'kwɔlifaid], *a.* Incapable (de), incompétent; (*fig.*) sans réserve, sans restriction, absolu; (*Law*) inhabile (à); non autorisé (of practitioners etc.).
unquenchable [ʌn'kwentʃəbl], *a.* Inextinguible. **unquenched,** *a.* Non éteint.
unquestionable [ʌn'kwestʃənəbl], *a.* Incontestable, indubitable. **unquestionably,** *adv.* Incontestablement; sans contredit. **unquestioned,** *a.* Sans être questionné; hors de doute, incontestable (indubitable).
unquiet [ʌn'kwaiət], *a.* Inquiet, agité.—*n.* Agitation, inquiétude, *f.* **unquietness,** *n.* Inquiétude, *f.*
unransomed [ʌn'rænsəmd], *a.* Qui n'a pas été racheté; non rançonné.
unrationed [ʌn'ræʃənd], *a.* Non rationné, en vente libre.
unravel [ʌn'rævl], *v.t.* Démêler, débrouiller; effiler, défaire (of threaded stuffs); (*fig.*) dénouer.—*v.i.* Se démêler, se débrouiller, s'effiler, se défaire; (*fig.*) se débrouiller.
unreached [ʌn'ri:tʃt], *a.* Qui n'a pas été atteint.
unread [ʌn'red], *a.* Qui n'a pas été lu; sans lecteurs; illettré, ignorant (illiterate). *To leave . . . unread,* ne pas lire.
unreadable [ʌn'ri:dəbl], *a.* Illisible. **unreadableness,** *n.* Illisibilité, *f.*
unreadily [ʌn'redili], *adv.* Lentement, à contre-cœur. **unreadiness,** *n.* Manque de préparation *or* de promptitude *or* de bonne volonté, *m.* **unready,** *a.* Qui n'est pas prêt, mal préparé; lent, peu empressé.
unreal [ʌn'ri:əl], *a.* Sans réalité, non réel; chimérique, fantastique, imaginaire. **unrealistic** [ʌnri:ə'listik], *a.* Peu réaliste. **unreality** [ʌnri:'æliti], *n.* Défaut de réalité, *m.* **unrealizable** [ʌn'ri:əlaizəbl], *a.* Irréalisable.
unreaped [ʌn'ri:pt], *a.* Pas encore moissonné.

unreason [ʌn'ri:zən], *n.* Déraison, *f.* **unreasonable**, *a.* Déraisonnable; extravagant, absurde, exorbitant (exorbitant). **unreasonableness**, *n.* Absurdité, extravagance, *f.* **unreasonably**, *adv.* Déraisonnablement, sans raison, à l'excès. **unreasoned**, *a.* Non raisonné. **unreasoning**, *a.* Qui ne raisonne pas.

unrebuked [ʌnri'bju:kt], *a.* Sans être réprimandé.

unrecalled [ʌnri'kɔ:ld], *a.* Non rappelé.

unreceipted [ʌnri'si:tid], *a.* Inacquitté.

unreceived [ʌnri'si:vd], *a.* Non reçu, qui n'est pas reçu.

unreceptive [ʌnri'septiv], *a.* Obtus, peu réceptif.

unreclaimed [ʌnri'kleimd], *a.* Non corrigé, non réformé; inculte (of land).

unrecognizable [ʌn'rekəgnaizəbl], *a.* Méconnaissable. **unrecognized**, *a.* Sans être reconnu; (*fig.*) méconnu (ignored).

unrecommended [ʌnrekə'mendid], *a.* Sans être recommandé.

unrecompensed [ʌn'rekəmpenst], *a.* Sans récompense.

unreconciled [ʌn'rekənsaild], *a.* Irréconcilié.

unrecorded [ʌnri'kɔ:did], *a.* Non enregistré.

unrecoverable [IRRECOVERABLE].

unrecovered [ʌnri'kʌvəd], *a.* Non recouvré; non rétabli (not cured).

unredeemable [ʌnri'di:məbl], *a.* Irrachetable. **unredeemed**, *a.* Non racheté; non dégagé, non retiré (of things pawned). *Unredeemed loan*, emprunt non amorti, *m.*

unredressed [ʌnri'drest], *a.* Non corrigé; non redressé.

unreeve [ʌn'ri:v], *v.t.* (*past and p.p.* **unrove**) (*Naut.*) Dépasser.

unrefined [ʌnri'faind], *a.* Non raffiné, brut; (*fig.*) grossier, indélicat.

unreflecting [-'flektiŋ], *a.* Irréfléchi.

unreformed [ʌnri'fɔ:md], *a.* Non réformé.

unrefreshed [ʌnri'freʃt], *a.* Non rafraîchi; encore fatigué.

unrefuted [ʌnri'fju:tid], *a.* Non réfuté.

unregarded [ʌnri'gɑ:did], *a.* Négligé, dédaigné, méconnu.

unregenerate [ʌnri'dʒenərət], *a.* Non régénéré.

unregistered [ʌn'redʒistəd], *a.* Non enregistré; non chargé, non recommandé (of letters etc.); non inscrit (*fig.*); dont on n'a pas conservé le souvenir.

unregulated [ʌn'regjuleitid], *a.* Non réglé.

unrehearsed [ʌnri'hə:st], *a.* Non préparé; mal répété; imprévu.

unrelated [ʌnri'leitid], *a.* Sans rapport (avec). *Who is unrelated to*, qui n'est pas parent de.

unrelenting [ʌnri'lentiŋ], *a.* Inexorable, inflexible, implacable, acharné. **unrelentingly**, *adv.* Inexorablement, implacablement, inflexiblement.

unreliable [ʌnri'laiəbl], *a.* Sur qui *or* sur quoi l'on ne peut compter; à qui *or* à quoi l'on ne peut se fier.

unrelieved ['ʌnrili:vd], *a.* Non soulagé; (*Mil.*) non secouru, sans secours; sans relief.

unremarkable [ʌnri'mɑ:kəbl], *a.* Peu remarquable.

unremarked [ʌnri'mɑ:kt], *a.* Inobservé, inaperçu.

unremedied [ʌn'remidid], *a.* Auquel on n'a pas remédié.

unremembered [ʌnri'membəd], *a.* Oublié.

unremitted [ʌnri'mitid], *a.* Non remis, non pardonné; continuel, incessant (continual).

unremitting [ʌnri'mitiŋ], *a.* Incessant, infatigable, continuel. **unremittingly**, *adv.* Sans relâche; sans cesse.

unremovable [IRREMOVABLE].

unremoved [ʌnri'mu:vd], *a.* Non écarté, non déplacé, non enlevé.

unremunerated [ʌnri'mju:nəreitid], *a.* Sans rétribution. **unremunerative**, *a.* Peu rémunérateur, peu lucratif.

unrenewed [ʌnri'nju:d], *a.* Non renouvelé.

unrepaid [ʌnri'peid], *a.* Non remboursé; non rendu.

unrepealed [ʌnri'pi:ld], *a.* Non abrogé.

unrepeatable [ʌnri'pi:təbl], *a.* Qu'on ne peut répéter. *An unrepeatable story*, une histoire irracontable, *f.*

unrepentant [ʌnri'pentənt] or **unrepenting**, *a.* Sans repentir, impénitent. **unrepented**, *a.* Dont on ne se repent pas.

unrepining [ʌnri'painiŋ], *a.* Sans se plaindre. **unrepiningly**, *adv.* Sans se plaindre.

unreplenished [ʌnri'pleniʃt], *a.* Non rempli, qui est resté vide.

unrepresented ['ʌnrepri'zentid], *a.* Non représenté.

unrepressed [ʌnri'prest], *a.* Non réprimé.

unreprieved [ʌnri'pri:vd], *a.* À qui l'on n'a pas accordé de sursis.

unreproved [ʌnri'pru:vd], *a.* Sans être blâmé.

unrequested [ʌnri'kwestid], *a.* Sans être sollicité, spontané.—*adv.* Sans sollicitation, spontanément.

unrequired [ʌnri'kwaiəd], *a.* Qui n'est pas nécessaire; dont on n'a pas besoin.

unrequited [ʌnri'kwaitid], *a.* Sans être récompensé; qui n'est pas payé de retour (of love).

unreserve [ʌnri'zə:v], *n.* Manque de réserve, *m.*; expansion, franchise, *f.* **unreserved**, *a.* Sans réserve; absolu (complete). *Full and unreserved powers*, autorité pleine et entière, *f.*, pleins pouvoirs, *m.pl.*; *unreserved seats*, places non réservées, *f.pl.*; *unreserved sale*, liquidation, *f.* **unreservedly** [ʌnri'zə:vidli], *adv.* Sans réserve, franchement, absolument. **unreservedness**, *n.* Abandon, *m.*; franchise, *f.*

unresisted [ʌnri'zistid], *a.* Sans rencontrer de résistance. **unresisting**, *a.* Qui ne résiste pas, soumis. **unresistingly**, *adv.* Sans résistance.

unresolved [ʌnri'zɔlvd], *a.* Non résolu; irrésolu, indécis (not determined).

unrespected [ʌnri'spektid], *a.* Non respecté, négligé.

unresponsive, *a.* Peu sensible; froid.

unrest [ʌn'rest], *n.* Inquiétude, agitation, *f.*, trouble; sommeil agité, *m.*, insomnie, *f.*

unrestored [ʌnri'stɔ:d], *a.* Non restitué; non restauré (of buildings); non rétabli (of health).

unrestrained [ʌnri'streind], *a.* Non restreint, sans contrainte, non réprimé; effréné, déréglé, sans frein.

unrestricted [ʌnri'striktid], *a.* Sans restriction.

unretentive [ʌnri'tentiv], *a.* Peu tenace; peu fidèle (of the memory).

unretracted [ʌnri'træktid], *a.* Non rétracté, non désavoué.

unrevealed [ʌnri'vi:ld], *a.* Non révélé.

unrevenged [ʌnri'vendʒd], *a.* Non vengé.

unrevised [ʌnri'vaizd], *a.* Non revu, non revisé.

unrevoked [ʌnri'voukt], *a.* Non révoqué.

unrewarded [ʌnri'wɔ:did], *a.* Sans récompense.

unrewarding [ʌnri'wɔ:diŋ], *a.* Peu rémunérateur.

unriddle [ʌn'ridl], *v.t.* Expliquer, résoudre.

unrifled [ʌn'raifld], *a.* Non rayé, lisse.

unrig [ʌn'rig], *v.t.* Dégréer.

unrighteous [ʌn'raitʃəs], *a.* Injuste, inique. **unrighteously**, *adv.* Injustement, iniquement. **unrighteousness**, *n.* Injustice, iniquité, *f.*

unrip [ʌn'rip], *v.t.* Découdre, ouvrir en déchirant.

unripe [ʌn'raip], *a.* Pas mûr, vert; (*fig.*) prématuré. **unripened**, *a.* Pas encore mûr, imparfait. **unripeness**, *n.* Verdeur, immaturité, *f.*

unrivalled [ʌn'raivəld], *a.* Sans rival, sans égal.

unroasted [ʌn'roustid], *a.* Non rôti; non torréfié (of coffee).

unrobe [DISROBE].

unroll [ʌn'roul], *v.t.* Dérouler, déployer.—*v.i.* Se dérouler, se déployer.

unromantic [ʌnro'mæntik], *a.* Peu romanesque; peu romantique (of places).

unroof [ʌn'ru:f], *v.t.* Enlever le toit de, découvrir.

unruffled [ʌn'rʌfld], *a.* Tranquille, calme; lisse (of materials).

unruled [ʌn'ru:ld], *a.* Non gouverné. **unruliness**, *n.* Dérèglement, *m.*; turbulence, indiscipline, *f.* **unruly**, *a.* Mutin, insoumis, turbulent, fougueux.

unsaddle [ʌn'sædl], *v.t.* Desseller; débâter (an ass); désarçonner (to throw from a horse).

unsafe [ʌn'seif], *a.* Peu sûr, dangereux, hasardeux. **unsafely**, *adv.* Peu sûrement, dangereusement.

unsaid [ʌn'sed], *a.* Non dit. *To leave unsaid*, taire, ne pas dire.

unsaleable [ʌn'seiləbl], *a.* Invendable.

unsalted [ʌn'sɔ:ltid], *a.* Non salé, sans sel.

unsanctified [ʌn'sæŋktifaid], *a.* Non consacré, profane.

unsanctioned [ʌn'sæŋkʃənd], *a.* Non sanctionné, non approuvé.

unsated [ʌn'seitid], *a.* Non rassasié, inassouvi.

unsatisfactorily [ʌnsætis'fæktərili], *adv.* D'une manière peu satisfaisante. **unsatisfactoriness**, *n.* Nature peu satisfaisante, *f.*, insuffisance, *f.* *The unsatisfactoriness and barrenness of the school-philosophy*, l'impuissance et la stérilité de la scolastique. **unsatisfactory**, *a.* Peu satisfaisant, insuffisant.

unsatisfied [ʌn'sætisfaid], *a.* Peu satisfait, mécontent (de); (*Comm.*) non acquitté.

unsavouriness [ʌn'seivərinis], *n.* Insipidité, fadeur, *f.*; mauvais goût, *m.* **unsavoury** [ʌn'seivəri], *a.* Sans saveur, insipide; désagréable, repoussant (disgusting).

unsay [ʌn'sei], *v.t.* (*past* and *p.p.* **unsaid**) Se dédire de; rétracter.

unscared [ʌn'skɛəd], *a.* Non effrayé.

unscarred [ʌn'skɑ:d], *a.* Sans cicatrices, indemne.

unscathed [ʌn'skeiðd], *a.* Sans blessures, sain et sauf.

unscholarly [ʌn'skɔləli], *a.* Illettré, ignorant.

unschooled [ʌn'sku:ld], *a.* Sans éducation; sans expérience.

unscientific ['ʌnsaiən'tifik], *a.* Peu scientifique. **unscientifically**, *adv.* Peu scientifiquement.

unscorched [ʌn'skɔ:tʃt], *a.* Non brûlé.

unscratched [ʌn'skrætʃt], *a.* Sans égratignure.

unscreened [ʌn'skri:nd], *a.* Non abrité, sans défense; non criblé (not sifted); (*fig.*) non interrogé; pas encore mis à l'écran (film).

unscrew [ʌn'skru:], *v.t.* Dévisser. *To become unscrewed*, se dévisser.

unscriptural [ʌn'skriptʃurəl], *a.* Contraire aux Saintes Écritures.

unscrupulous [ʌn'skru:pjuləs], *a.* Peu scrupuleux, indélicat. **unscrupulously**, *adv.* Sans scrupule. **unscrupulousness**, *n.* Manque de scrupule, *m.*, indélicatesse, *f.*

unseal [ʌn'si:l], *v.t.* Décacheter; desceller; (*fig.*) dessiller (eyes etc.). **unsealed**, *a.* Décacheté, ouvert.

unsearchable [ʌn'sə:tʃəbl], *a.* Inscrutable, impénétrable.

unseasonable [ʌn'si:zənəbl], *a.* Mal à propos, intempestif, inopportun; incommode, indu (of time); pas de saison (of weather). *Unseasonable hours*, heures indues, *f.pl.* **unseasonableness**, *n.* Inopportunité, *f.* **unseasonably**, *adv.* Hors de saison; mal à propos. **unseasoned**, *a.* Vert, non séché (of wood); peu accoutumé, peu fait (not accustomed); non acclimaté (to a climate); (*Cook.*) non assaisonné.

unseat [ʌn'si:t], *v.t.* Renverser; désarçonner (from horseback); invalider (a member of parliament).

unseaworthy [ʌn'si:wɔ:ði], *a.* Incapable de tenir la mer, innavigable.

unseconded [ʌn'sekəndid], *a.* Mal secondé.

unsecured [ʌnsi'kjuəd], *a.* Non garanti, sans garantie, mal assuré; pas fermé, mal fermé (of a door).

unseeing [ʌn'si:iŋ], *a.* Aveugle.

unseemliness [ʌn'si:mlinis], *n.* Inconvenance; indécence, *f.* **unseemly**, *a.* Inconvenant; indécent.

unseen [ʌn'si:n], *a.* Sans être vu, invisible; inaperçu, à la dérobée (by stealth). *The unseen*, le monde invisible.—*n.* (*sch.*) Version (à faire) sans dictionnaire, *f.*

unselfish [ʌn'selfiʃ], *a.* Désintéressé.

unselfconscious [ʌnself'kɔnʃəs], *a.* Naturel; sans gêne.

unsent [ʌn'sent], *a.* Sans être envoyé. *Unsent for*, sans être appelé; sans être mandé.

unsentimental [ʌnsenti'mentl], *a.* Peu sentimental.

unserviceable [ʌn'sə:visəbl], *a.* Inutile, bon à rien; hors de service. **unserviceably**, *adv.* Inutilement.

unsettle [ʌn'setl], *v.t.* Déranger; (*fig.*) troubler, agiter, rendre incertain. **unsettled**, *a.* Mal fixé, mal établi; indéterminé, incertain (weather etc.), irrésolu (not determined); non réglé; dérangé, troublé (in mind); variable, changeant (changeable).

unsettledness, *n.* Instabilité, incertitude, inconstance, *f.*

unsew [ʌn'sou], *v.t.* Découdre. *To come unsewn,* se découdre.

unsex [ʌn'seks], *v.t.* Priver de son sexe.

unshackle [ʌn'ʃækl], *v.t.* Briser les fers de, affranchir; (*Naut.*) démailler (a chain). **unshackled,** *a.* Sans entraves, libre. *Unshackled by party connexions and prejudices,* libre des entraves et des préjugés de parti.

unshaded [ʌn'ʃeidid], *a.* Sans ombre; non ombré (of a drawing).

unshaken [ʌn'ʃeikn], *a.* Inébranlable, ferme.

unshapely [ʌn'ʃeipli], *a.* Difforme, informe.

unshapen [ʌn'ʃeipn], *a.* Informe.

unshaved [ʌn'ʃeivd] or **unshaven,** *a.* Non rasé, sans être rasé.

unsheathe [ʌn'ʃi:ð], *v.t.* Dégainer, tirer du fourreau. *To unsheathe the sword,* tirer l'épée.

unsheltered [ʌn'ʃeltəd], *a.* Sans abri, découvert. *Unsheltered from,* exposé à, non protégé contre.

unshielded [ʌn'ʃi:ldid], *a.* Sans défense. *Unshielded from,* exposé à.

unship [ʌn'ʃip], *v.t.* Débarquer, décharger; démonter (the rudder etc.); désarmer (the oars).

unshod [ʌn'ʃɔd], *a.* Sans chaussures, nu-pieds; déferré (of a horse).

unshoe [ʌn'ʃu:], *v.t.* Déferrer (a horse).

unshorn [ʌn'ʃɔ:n], *a.* Non tondu.

unshrinkable [ʌn'ʃrinkəbl], *a.* Irrétrécissable. **unshrinking,** *a.* Inébranlable, ferme.

unshut [ʌn'ʃʌt], *a.* Non fermé, non clos.

unsifted [ʌn'sifʔid], *a.* Non criblé, non tamisé; (*fig.*) sans être examiné.

unsightliness [ʌn'saitlinis], *n.* Laideur, *f.* **unsightly,** *a.* Laid, déplaisant, vilain.

unsigned [ʌn'saind], *a.* Non signé.

unsinged [ʌn'sindʒd], *a.* Non flambé.

unsisterly [ʌn'sistəli], *a.* Peu digne d'une sœur.

unsized [ʌn'saizd], *a.* Non collé, sans apprêt.

unskilful [ʌn'skilful], *a.* Inhabile, maladroit. **unskilfulness,** *n.* Inhabileté, maladresse, *f.* **unskilled,** *a.* Inexpérimenté (dans); non qualifié. *Unskilled labour,* travail de manœuvre, *m.,* main d'œuvre non spécialisée, *f.*

unslaked [ʌn'sleikt], *a.* Non éteint; non étanché (of thirst); vive (of lime).

unsleeping [ʌn'sli:piŋ], *a.* Vigilant, toujours éveillé.

unsmiling [ʌn'smailiŋ], *a.* Qui ne sourit pas; sérieux.

unsociable [ʌn'souʃəbl], *a.* Insociable. **unsociableness** or **unsociability** [-'biliti], *n.* Insociabilité, *f.*

unsocial [ʌn'souʃl], *a.* Peu social, insociable.

unsoiled [ʌn'sɔild], *a.* Sans tache; propre, pur (de).

unsold [ʌn'sould], *a.* Invendu.

unsolder [ʌn'sɔldə], *v.t.* Dessouder. **unsolderable,** *a.* Insoudable.

unsoldierly [ʌn'souldʒəli] or **unsoldierlike,** *a.* Indigne d'un soldat, peu militaire.

unsolicited [ʌnsə'lisitid], *a.* Sans être sollicité, sans sollicitation. **unsolicitous,** *a.* Peu désireux; peu soucieux de.

unsolved [ʌn'sɔlvd], *a.* Non résolu, insoluble.

unsophisticated [ʌnsə'fistikeitid], *a.* Qui n'est pas frelaté, non falsifié; pur, vrai, sincère, simple.

unsorted [ʌn'sɔ:tid], *a.* Non trié, non assorti.

unsought [ʌn'sɔ:t], *a.* Sans qu'on le cherche, non recherché; spontané.

unsound [ʌn'saund], *a.* En mauvais état, défectueux, malsain; hétérodoxe, non orthodoxe, faux, erroné; fêlé (cracked); mal établi (credit); vicieux, pas sain (of a horse). *Of unsound mind,* non sain d'esprit, en état de démence temporaire. **unsounded,** *a.* Non sondé. **unsoundly,** *adv.* Peu solidement; défectueusement; mal, peu profondément (of sleeping); faussement (reasoning). **unsoundness,** *n.* Mauvais état, *m.,* nature défectueuse, imperfection, *f.*; état maladif, état malsain (of the body), *m.*; fausseté, erreur (of principles etc.), *f.*

unsoured [ʌn'sauəd], *a.* Non aigri.

unsown [ʌn'soun], *a.* Non semé; non ensemencé (of land).

unsparing [ʌn'spɛəriŋ], *a.* Libéral, prodigue; impitoyable (not merciful). **unsparingly,** *adv.* Avec prodigalité, sans ménagement; impitoyablement.

unspeakable [ʌn'spi:kəbl], *a.* Inexprimable, inénarrable; indicible, ineffable (rapturous). **unspeakably,** *adv.* D'une manière inexprimable; ineffablement, indiciblement.

unspecified [ʌn'spesifaid], *a.* Non spécifié.

unspent [ʌn'spent], *a.* Non dépensé; non épuisé, non affaibli (not exhausted); qui n'a pas servi (cartridge).

unspoiled [ʌn'spɔild], *a.* Non corrompu, non gâté; non dépouillé (not plundered); bien élevé (child).

unspoken [ʌn'spoukn], *a.* Non prononcé; tacite.

unsportsmanlike [ʌn'spɔ:tsmənlaik], *a.* Indigne d'un chasseur, d'un sportsman.

unspotted [ʌn'spɔtid], *a.* Sans tache. **unspottedness,** *n.* Pureté, *f.*

unstable [ʌn'steibl], *a.* Irrésolu, indécis, inconstant; (*Mech.*) instable. **unstableness,** *n.* Instabilité, *f.*

unstained [ʌn'steind], *a.* Sans tache; non teint (not dyed).

unstamped [ʌn'stæmpt], *a.* Non timbré, sans timbre.

unsteadfast [ʌn'stedfɑ:st], *a.* Instable, inconstant. **unsteadfastness** [ʌn'stedfəstnis], *n.* Instabilité, inconstance, *f.*

unsteadily [ʌn'stedili], *adv.* En chancelant, irrésolument, d'une manière irrégulière. **unsteadiness,** *f.*; manque de fermeté, *m.* **unsteady,** *a.* Chancelant, vacillant; mal assuré, irrésolu, inconstant, irrégulier (of conduct).

unsteeped [ʌn'sti:pt], *a.* Non trempé.

unstimulated [ʌn'stimjuleitid], *a.* Qui n'est pas stimulé.

unstinted [ʌn'stintid], *a.* Non restreint, abondant, copieux, illimité.

unstirred [ʌn'stə:d], *a.* Non remué, qui n'est pas agité.

unstitch [ʌn'stitʃ], *v.t.* Découdre, défaire.

unstocked [ʌn'stɔkt], *a.* Dégarni, sans provision.

unstop [ʌn'stɔp], *v.t.* Déboucher, ouvrir; déplomber (a tooth).

unstrained [ʌn'streind], *a.* Non forcé; (*fig.*) naturel, aisé; non filtré (not filtered).

unstraitened [ʌn'streitnd], *a.* Non rétréci; (*fig.*) non gêné.

unstrengthened [ʌn'streŋθənd], *a.* Non renforcé.

unstressed [ʌn'strest], *a.* Inaccentué, sans accent, atone.

unstring [ʌn'striŋ], *v.t.* (*past and p.p.* **unstrung**) Détendre, relâcher; défaire; (*Mus.*) ôter les cordes de.

unstuck [ʌn'stʌk], *a.* Décollé.

unstudied [ʌn'stʌdid], *a.* Qui n'est pas étudié, sans apprêt, naturel.

unstudious [ʌn'stju:diəs], *a.* Peu studieux.

unstuffed [ʌn'stʌft], *a.* Non rembourré; non empaillé (of specimens).

unsubdued [ʌnsəb'dju:d], *a.* Non subjugué, indompté.

unsubmissive [ʌnsəb'misiv], *a.* Insoumis. **unsubmissiveness,** *n.* Insoumission, *f.*

unsubstantial [ʌnsəb'stænʃl], *a.* Peu substantiel; peu solide; (*fig.*) immatériel; chimérique.

unsuccessful [ʌnsək'sesful], *a.* Qui n'a pas réussi, sans succès; infructueux, vain. *To be unsuccessful*, ne pas réussir. **unsuccessfully,** *adv.* Sans succès. **unsuccessfulness,** *n.* Insuccès, *m.*

unsuccoured [ʌn'sʌkəd], *a.* Sans secours, sans aide.

unsuitable [ʌn'sju:təbl], *a.* Peu convenable, peu propre (à), peu fait (pour); inopportun (out of season). **unsuitableness,** *n.* Inconvenance, inaptitude; inopportunité, *f.* **unsuited,** *a.* Peu fait (pour), peu convenable (à). **unsuiting,** *a.* Qui ne convient pas (à).

unsullied [ʌn'sʌlid], *a.* Sans souillure, sans tache, pur.

unsummoned [ʌn'sʌmənd], *a.* Sans être appelé.

unsung [ʌn'sʌŋ], *a.* Sans être chanté, non célébré.

unsupervised [ʌn'sju:pəvaizd], *a.* Non surveillé.

unsupplied [ʌnsə'plaid], *a.* Non pourvu (de); dépourvu (de).

unsupported [ʌnsə'pɔ:tid], *a.* Non soutenu; (*fig.*) sans appui.

unsuppressed [ʌnsə'prest], *a.* Non supprimé; mal contenu.

unsure [ʌn'ʃuə], *a.* Peu sûr.

unsurpassed [ʌnsə'pɑ:st], *a.* Non surpassé, sans égal.

unsurrendered [ʌnsə'rendəd], *a.* Non livré.

unsurrounded [ʌnsə'raundid], *a.* Non entouré.

unsuspected [ʌnsə'spektid], *a.* Non soupçonné, non suspect. **unsuspectedly,** *adv.* Sans exciter le soupçon. **unsuspecting,** *a.* Qui ne soupçonne rien, sans soupçon, confiant, sans méfiance.

unsuspicious [ʌnsə'spiʃəs], *a.* Sans soupçon, sans méfiance, confiant. **unsuspiciously,** *adv.* Sans soupçon, sans méfiance.

unsustained [ʌnsə'steind], *a.* Non soutenu.

unswathe [ʌn'sweið], *v.t.* Démailloter.

unswayed [ʌn'sweid], *a.* Qui ne se laisse pas influencer.

unswept [ʌn'swept], *a.* Non balayé; non ramoné (of chimneys).

unswerving [ʌn'swɔ:viŋ], *a.* Qui ne s'écarte pas, ferme, inébranlable.

unsworn [ʌn'swɔ:n], *a.* Qui n'a pas prêté serment.

unsymmetrical [ʌnsi'metrikl], *a.* Asymétrique, sans symétrie.

unsympathetic ['ʌnsimpə'θetik], **unsympathizing** [ʌn'simpəθaiziŋ], *a.* Froid, peu compatissant.

unsystematic ['ʌnsisti'mætik], *a.* Peu systématique, sans système. **unsystematically,** *adv.* Sans système.

untack [ʌn'tæk], *v.t.* Détacher, défaire.

untainted [ʌn'teintid], *a.* Non corrompu, non gâté; (*fig.*) pur, sans tache; frais (of meat).

untaken [ʌn'teikn], *a.* Qu'on n'a pas pris.

untamable [ʌn'teiməbl], *a.* Indomptable, inapprivoisable. **untamed,** *a.* Indompté, non apprivoisé.

untangle [DISENTANGLE].

untapped [ʌn'tæpt], *a.* Non mis en perce (of barrels); inexploité (of resources).

untarnished [ʌn'tɑ:niʃt], *a.* Non terni, sans tache.

untasted [ʌn'teistid], *a.* Qu'on n'a pas goûté, sans qu'on y ait touché.

untaught [ʌn'tɔ:t], *a.* Ignorant, illettré, sans éducation; naturel (of things).

untaxed [ʌn'tækst], *a.* Exempt d'impôts; (*Law*) non taxé; (*fig.*) qu'on n'accuse pas (de).

unteachable [ʌn'ti:tʃəbl], *a.* Que l'on ne saurait enseigner, incapable d'apprendre.

untearable [ʌn'tɛərəbl], *a.* Indéchirable.

untempered [ʌn'tempəd], *a.* Non trempé (of metals); (*fig.*) non tempéré.

untenable [ʌn'tenəbl], *a.* Insoutenable.

untenantable [ʌn'tenəntəbl], *a.* Inhabitable.

untenanted, *a.* Sans locataire, inhabité; vide.

untended [ʌn'tendid], *a.* Non gardé, non soigné.

unterrified [ʌn'terifaid], *a.* Sans être épouvanté.

untested [ʌn'testid], *a.* Qu'on n'a pas mis à l'épreuve, inessayé.

unthanked [ʌn'θæŋkt], *a.* Sans être remercié, sans remerciement. **unthankful,** *a.* Ingrat (envers). **unthankfully,** *adv.* Ingratement, sans reconnaissance. **unthankfulness,** *n.* Ingratitude, *f.*

unthawed [ʌn'θɔ:d], *a.* Non dégelé.

unthinking [ʌn'θiŋkiŋ], *a.* Irréfléchi, inconsidéré, étourdi. **unthinkingly,** *adv.* Sans y penser, étourdiment, sans réflexion.

unthoughtful [ʌn'θɔ:tful], *a.* Irréfléchi, étourdi. **unthought-of,** *a.* À qui l'on ne pense pas, oublié; inattendu, imprévu (unexpected).

unthread [ʌn'θred], *v.t.* Désenfiler; (*fig.*) détacher. *To unthread a needle*, désenfiler une aiguille.

unthriftily [ʌn'θriftili], *adv.* Avec prodigalité. **unthriftiness** or **unthrift,** *n.* Prodigalité, *f.* **unthrifty,** *a.* Prodigue, dépensier.

untidily [ʌn'taidili], *adv.* Sans ordre, sans soin. **untidiness,** *n.* Désordre, *m.* **untidy,** *a.* En désordre, mal tenu; négligé, débraillé.

untie [ʌn'tai], *v.t.* Délier, dénouer; défaire (a knot).

until [ʌn'til], *prep.* Jusqu'à; avant. *He does not return from the country until Monday night*, il ne reviendra pas de la campagne avant lundi soir; *until now* or *until this day*, jusqu'à ce jour, jusqu'ici; *until then*, jusqu'alors, jusque-là, en attendant (meanwhile).— *conj.* Jusqu'à ce que, avant que. *He will not start until he sees me*, il ne partira pas avant de me voir; *he will not start until I have seen him*, il ne partira pas avant que je le voie.

untile [ʌn'tail], *v.t.* Ôter les tuiles de, découvrir.

untillable [ʌn'tiləbl], *a.* Non labourable. **untilled,** *a.* Inculte, en friche.

untimeliness [ʌn'taimlinis], *n.* Prématurité, inopportunité, *f.* **untimely,** *adv.* Intempestif, avant terme, prématurément.—*a.* Prématuré, inopportun.

untinged [ʌn'tindʒd], *a.* Qui n'est pas teint; qui n'est pas empreint (de). *Neither is he untinged with it,* et du reste il ne laisse pas d'en être infecté.

untiring [ʌn'taiəriŋ], *a.* Infatigable. **untiringly,** *adv.* Sans relâche, infatigablement.

untitled [ʌn'taitld], *a.* Sans titre.

***unto,** *prep.* [TO].

untold [ʌn'tould], *a.* Non raconté, non exprimé, non révélé; sans nombre, immense, énorme; indicible, inouï.

untouchable [ʌn'tʌtʃəbl], *a.* and *n.* Hors caste, paria, intouchable, *m.* **untouched** [ʌn'tʌtʃt], *a.* Non touché; (*fig.*) non ému (de). *To leave untouched,* laisser sans y toucher, ne pas toucher à.

untoward [ʌn'tɔːd *or* ʌn'touəd], *a.* Insoumis, indocile (troublesome); fâcheux, malencontreux. **untowardly,** *adv.* Malencontreusement.

untraceable [ʌn'treisəbl], *a.* Introuvable.

untracked [ʌn'trækt], *a.* Non suivi; sans sentier frayé.

untractable [INTRACTABLE].

untrained [ʌn'treind], *a.* Inexpérimenté (inexperienced); indiscipliné, sans discipline; non dressé (of animals).

untrammelled [ʌn'træməld], *a.* Sans entraves, sans être entravé (par).

untransferable ['ʌntræns'fəːrəbl], *a.* Non transférable.

untranslatable ['ʌntrɑːns'leitəbl], *a.* Intraduisible. **untranslated,** *a.* Non traduit.

untravelled [ʌn'trævld], *a.* Inexploré, peu connu (land); qui n'a pas voyagé (person).

untried [ʌn'traid], *a.* Non essayé, non éprouvé; qui n'a pas encore été jugé.

untrimmed [ʌn'trimd], *a.* Sans garniture, sans ornement; non taillé, non émondé (of trees).

untrod *or* **untrodden** [ʌn'trɔdn], *a.* Non frayé, non battu; vierge, immaculé (of snow).

untroubled [ʌn'trʌbld], *a.* Calme, tranquille.

untrue [ʌn'truː], *a.* Dénué de vérité, faux; inexact (of news etc.); infidèle, déloyal (à). *To be untrue to,* trahir. **untruly,** *adv.* Faussement; inexactement.

untrustworthiness [ʌn'trʌstwəːðinis], *n.* Inexactitude, fausseté, *f.* **untrustworthy,** *a.* Indigne de confiance; inexact, mensonger (of news etc.).

untruth [ʌn'truːθ], *n.* Contre-vérité, fausseté, *f.* **untruthful,** *a.* Peu véridique; menteur; mensonger (of news etc.); perfide, faux, déloyal (treacherous). **untruthfulness,** *n.* Fausseté, *f.*

untuck [ʌn'tʌk], *v.t.* Déborder (a bed).

untune [ʌn'tjuːn], *v.t.* Désaccorder; (*fig.*) déranger, troubler.

unturned [ʌn'təːnd], *a.* Non retourné. *To leave no stone unturned,* remuer ciel et terre.

untutored [ʌn'tjuːtəd], *a.* Peu instruit, sans instruction, ignorant.

untwine [ʌn'twain], *v.t.* Détordre; dérouler.

untwist [ʌn'twist], *v.t.* Détordre, détortiller, défaire.

unurged [ʌn'əːdʒd], *a.* Sans être pressé.

unused (1) [ʌn'juːzd], *a.* Non employé; inusité (of words).

unused (2) [ʌn'juːst], *a.* Inaccoutumé. *Unused to,* inaccoutumé à, étranger à.

unusual [ʌn'juːʒuəl], *a.* Peu commun, rare; insolite, inaccoutumé, peu habituel. **unusually,** *adv.* Plus que d'habitude, rarement, extraordinairement. **unusualness,** *n.* Rareté, étrangeté, *f.*

unutterable [ʌn'ʌtərəbl], *a.* Inexprimable, indicible. **unuttered,** *a.* Non prononcé.

unvalued [ʌn'væljuːd], *a.* Peu estimé, méprisé, dédaigné.

unvanquished [ʌn'væŋkwiʃt], *a.* Indompté, invaincu.

unvariable [INVARIABLE].

unvaried [ʌn'vɛərid], *a.* Invariable, uniforme.

unvarnished [ʌn'vɑːniʃt], *a.* Non verni; (*fig.*) simple, naturel.

unvarying [ʌn'vɛəriiŋ], *a.* Invariable, uniforme.

unveil [ʌn'veil], *v.t.* Dévoiler; découvrir.

unventilated [ʌn'ventileitid], *a.* Sans ventilation, mal aéré; qui n'a pas (encore) été discuté.

unversed [ʌn'vəːst], *a.* Peu versé (dans).

unviolated [ʌn'vaiəleitid], *a.* Non violé; intact. *The unviolated wood,* la forêt vierge, *f.*

unvisited [ʌn'vizitid], *a.* Non visité, peu fréquenté.

unvitiated [ʌn'viʃieitid], *a.* Non corrompu.

unvoiced [ʌn'vɔist], *a.* (Consonne) dévoisée; (opinion) inexprimée.

unwalled [ʌn'wɔːld], *a.* Sans murailles, sans murs, ouvert.

unwarily [ʌn'wɛərili], *adv.* Sans précaution, imprudemment. **unwariness,** *n.* Imprévoyance, imprudence, *f.*

unwarlike [ʌn'wɔːlaik], *a.* Pacifique, peu belliqueux.

unwarmed [ʌn'wɔːmd], *a.* Non chauffé.

unwarned [ʌn'wɔːnd], *a.* Non averti (de).

unwarped [ʌn'wɔːpt], *a.* Non déjeté; resté droit.

unwarrantable [ʌn'wɔrəntəbl], *a.* Injustifiable, inexcusable. **unwarrantably,** *adv.* Inexcusablement. **unwarranted,** *a.* Non garanti; non autorisé; incertain; (*Comm.*) sans garantie. *An unwarranted insult,* une insulte gratuite.

unwary [ʌn'wɛəri], *a.* Inconsidéré, imprudent. *The unwary,* ceux qui ne sont pas sur leurs gardes, *m.pl.*

unwashed [ʌn'wɔʃt], *a.* Non lavé, sale, malpropre.

unwastefully, *adv.* Avec économie.

unwatched [ʌn'wɔtʃt], *a.* Qu'on ne surveille point, non surveillé.

unwatered [ʌn'wɔːtəd], *a.* Non arrosé; sans eau, pur (of spirits etc.); non moiré, uni (of silk).

unwavering [ʌn'weivəriŋ], *a.* Ferme, résolu, inébranlable.

unweaned [ʌn'wiːnd], *a.* Non sevré.

unwearable [ʌn'wɛərəbl], *a.* Qu'on ne peut plus porter.

unwearied [ʌn'wiərid], *a.* Non lassé, infatigable. **unweariedly,** *adv.* Sans relâche, inlassablement.

unweave [ʌn'wiːv], *v.t.* (*past* **unwove**, *p.p.* **unwoven**) Détisser; défaire; (*fig.*) démêler.

unwedded [ʌn'wedid], *a.* Non marié.

unweeded [ʌn'wiːdid], *a.* Non sarclé.

unweighed [ʌn'weid], *a.* Non pesé; (*fig.*) non examiné.

unwelcome [ʌn'welkəm], *a.* Importun; déplaisant, désagréable, fâcheux.

unwell [ʌn'wel], *a.* Indisposé, souffrant, mal portant.

unwept [ʌn'wept], *a.* Non pleuré, non regretté, sans laisser de regrets.

unwholesome [ʌn'houlsəm], *a.* Malsain, insalubre; (*fig.*) nuisible, pernicieux. **unwholesomeness,** *n.* Insalubrité; nature malsaine (of food), *f.*

unwieldily [ʌn'wiːldili], *adv.* Lourdement, pesamment. **unwieldiness,** *n.* Lourdeur, pesanteur, *f.* **unwieldy,** *a.* Lourd, pesant, difficile à manier.

unwilling [ʌn'wiliŋ], *a.* Peu disposé, mal disposé; de mauvaise volonté, rétif. *To be unwilling to,* n'être pas disposé à, ne pas vouloir. **unwillingly,** *adv.* A contre-cœur, sans le vouloir. *Not unwillingly,* d'assez bonne grâce, assez volontiers, sans trop se faire prier. **unwillingness,** *n.* Mauvaise volonté, *f.*; répugnance, *f.*

unwind [ʌn'waind], *v.t.* (*past* and *p.p.* **unwound**) Dévider; dérouler; (*fig.*) démêler, débrouiller.—*v.i.* Se dévider.

unwiped [ʌn'waipt], *a.* Non essuyé.

unwisdom [ʌn'wizdəm], *n.* Imprudence, déraison, *f.*

unwise [ʌn'waiz], *a.* Peu sage, malavisé, insensé. **unwisely,** *adv.* Peu sagement, imprudemment.

unwished (for) [ʌn'wiʃt], *a.* Non souhaité, non désiré, fâcheux.

unwithered [ʌn'wiðəd], *a.* Encore frais, non flétri. **unwithering,** *a.* Immarcescible, qui ne se flétrit pas.

unwitnessed [ʌn'witnist], *a.* Sans témoin, non certifié.

unwittily [ʌn'witili], *adv.* Sans esprit. **unwitty,** *a.* Sans esprit, peu spirituel.

unwitting, *a.* Inconscient. **unwittingly,** *adv.* Sans le savoir, inconsciemment.

unwomanly [ʌn'wumənli], *a.* Indigne d'une femme, qui sied peu à une femme, peu féminin.

unwonted [ʌn'wountid], *a.* Inaccoutumé, rare, extraordinaire. **unwontedly,** *adv.* Rarement. **unwontedness,** *n.* Rareté, *f.*

unwooed [ʌn'wuːd], *a.* Que l'on ne recherche pas; dédaigné.

unworkable [ʌn'wəːkəbl], *a.* Impraticable; inexploitable (of mines etc.). **unworkableness,** *n.* Impraticabilité, *f.* **unworked,** *a.* Inexploité (of mines etc.). **unworkmanlike,** *a.* Indigne d'un ouvrier; mal fait, mal exécuté.

unworldliness [ʌn'wəːldlinis], *n.* Nature peu mondaine, *f.* **unworldly,** *a.* Peu mondain, étranger au monde, simple, candide.

unworn [ʌn'wɔːn], *a.* Non usé, non usagé.

unworthily [ʌn'wəːðili], *adv.* Indignement, sans le mériter. **unworthiness,** *n.* Indignité, *f.* **unworthy,** *a.* Indigne (de), sans mérite.

unwound, *past* and *p.p.* [UNWIND.]

unwounded [ʌn'wuːndid], *a.* Sans blessure, non blessé, valide.

unwove, *past* unwoven, *p.p.* [UNWEAVE].

unwrap [ʌn'ræp], *v.t.* Défaire, désenvelopper.

unwreathe [ʌn'riːð], *v.t.* Détortiller, dérouler, défaire.

unwrinkle [ʌn'riŋkl], *v.t.* Dérider. **unwrinkled,** *a.* Sans rides, uni.

unwritten [ʌn'ritn], *a.* Non écrit; (*fig.*) oral, traditionnel. *Unwritten law,* loi naturelle, *f.*

unwrought [ʌn'rɔːt], *a.* Non travaillé, brut.

unwrung [ʌn'rʌŋ], *a.* Non tordu; (*fig.*) non torturé.

unyielding [ʌn'jiːldiŋ], *a.* Qui ne cède pas, rigide, inflexible.

unyoke [ʌn'jouk], *v.t.* Ôter le joug à, dételer.

unzoned [ʌn'zound], *a.* Sans ceinture.

up [ʌp], *adv.* Au haut, en haut, haut; en l'air; levé, sur pied (out of bed); sur l'horizon (above the horizon); debout (on one's legs); excité (excited); en révolte (in revolt); en insurrection; fini (over); élevé (of prices); en hausse (of stocks and shares). *Hard up,* gêné, à court d'argent; *he is up,* il est levé *or* sur pied; *it is all up,* c'en est fait, c'est une affaire flambée; *it is up to us to do it,* c'est à nous de le faire; *road up,* rue barrée; *time's up,* c'est l'heure; *to be up* (of beer etc.), mousser; *to be up to,* être au courant de, être à la hauteur de; *to be up to all manner of tricks,* en savoir plus d'une; *to be up to one's ears in work,* avoir du travail par-dessus la tête; *to be up to one's knees in water,* avoir de l'eau jusqu'au genou; *to be up to snuff,* ne pas se moucher du pied; *to come up with,* rattraper; *to get up a play,* monter une pièce; *to get up by heart,* apprendre par cœur; *to have someone up,* traduire quelqu'un en justice; *to live up to one's fortune,* dépenser tout son revenu; *to make up to,* faire des avances à; *up!* levez-vous! montez! (go up); *up and doing,* à l'ouvrage, à la besogne, occupé; *up and down,* en haut et en bas, çà et là, de long en large, de haut en bas; *up comes a fox,* voilà que survient un renard; *up from,* de; *up in arms,* en armes; *up line,* ligne de retour, *f.*; *up there,* là-haut; *up to,* jusqu'à la hauteur de, (*colloq.*) au fait de, au courant de; *up to date,* à la dernière mode, à jour, au courant; *up to now,* jusqu'ici; *up to then,* jusque-là; *up train,* train qui va vers Londres, *m.*; *up went a shout of laughter from the crowd,* et la foule de rire; *well up in,* fort en, ferré sur; *what's up?* (*colloq.*) qu'est-ce qu'il y a donc?—*prep.* En haut de, au haut de; en montant. *Praised up hill and down dale,* loué de toutes les façons; *to go up country,* aller dans l'intérieur; *to go up stream,* remonter le courant, aller vers l'amont; *to run up to town,* faire une course or un petit voyage à Londres; *up hill* or *up stream,* en amont.—*n.* Haut, *m.* *The ups and downs,* les hauts et les bas, *m.pl.,* les vicissitudes, *f.pl.*

upas ['juːpəs], *n.* Upas, *m.*

upbear [ʌp'bɛə], *v.t.* (*past* **upbore**, *p.p.* **upborne**) Soutenir, supporter; soulever.

upbraid [ʌp'breid], *v.t.* Reprocher à, faire des reproches à; réprouver. **upbraiding,** *n.* Reproche, *m.* **upbraidingly,** *adv.* Avec reproche, d'un ton de reproche.

upcast (1) ['ʌpkɑːst], *n.* Jet; coup, *m.*

upcast (2) [ʌp'kɑːst], *v.t.* Jeter en haut,

lever.—*a.* Jeté en l'air; levé. *Upcast shaft,* puits d'aérage montant, *m.*

upheaval [ʌp'hiːvl], *n.* Soulèvement, *m.* **upheave,** *v.t.* Soulever.

upheld, *past* and *p.p.* [UPHOLD].

uphill (1) ['ʌphil], *a.* Qui monte; (*fig.*) ardu, dur, pénible, difficile. *Uphill work,* travail fatigant, *m.*—*n.* Côte, rampe, *f.*

uphill (2) [ʌp'hil], *adv.* En côte, en montant.

uphold [ʌp'hould], *v.t.* (*past* and *p.p.* **upheld**) Soutenir, maintenir. **upholder,** *n.* Soutien, appui, partisan, *m.*

upholster [ʌp'houlstə], *v.t.* Tapisser.

upholsterer, *n.* Tapissier, *m.*

upholstering or **upholstery,** *n.* Tapisserie, *f.*

upkeep ['ʌpkiːp], *n.* Entretien, *m.*

upland ['ʌplənd], *a.* Élevé, des hautes terres.

uplander, *n.* Montagnard, *m.*

uplands, *n.pl.* Terrain élevé, *m.*, haute terre, *f.*, haut pays, *m.*

uplift (1) [ʌp'lift], *v.t.* Lever, élever, soulever.

uplift (2) ['ʌplift], *n.* Élévation (of ground); (*fig.*) inspiration, *f.*

uplifting, *n.* Soulèvement, *m.*

upon [ʌ'pɔn], *prep.* Sur. *To live upon,* vivre de, se nourrir de; *upon pain of,* sous peine de; *upon that,* là-dessus; *upon the death of,* à la mort de; *upon the whole,* en somme, à tout prendre; *upon those terms,* dans ces conditions-là.

upper ['ʌpə], *a.* Supérieur, d'en haut, de dessus, au-dessus; haut. *The upper end,* le haut bout (of a table), *m.*; *the Upper House,* la chambre haute; *the upper ten* (*thousand*), la haute société, *f.*, le grand monde, *m.*; *upper boxes* or *upper circle,* troisièmes loges, *f.pl.*; *upper deck,* pont supérieur, *m.*; *upper hand,* dessus, *m.*, supériorité, *f.* *To get* or *gain the upper hand,* l'emporter sur, avoir l'avantage sur; *upper jaw,* mâchoire supérieure, *f.*; *upper leather,* empeigne, *f.*; *upper lip,* lèvre supérieure, *f.* *To keep a stiff upper lip,* (*colloq.*) tenir son courage à deux mains; *upper part,* le haut, le dessus, *m.*; *upper plane,* plan supérieur; *upper story,* étage supérieur, *m.*, (*colloq.*) caboche (the head), *f.* *He is cracked in the upper story,* il a le timbre fêlé; *upper works,* (*Naut.*) œuvres mortes, *f.pl.*

uppermost, *a.* Le plus élevé; (*fig.*) le plus fort. *To be uppermost,* prédominer; *to stand uppermost,* être le premier; *to stand uppermost in someone's thoughts,* occuper entièrement les pensées de *or* être le principal objet des pensées de quelqu'un.

uppers, *n.pl.* Empeignes (of boots), *f.pl.* (*fam.*) *To be on one's uppers,* être dans la débine.

uppish ['ʌpiʃ], *a.* (*colloq.*) Fier, arrogant. **uppishness,** *n.* Fierté, arrogance, *f.*

upraise [ʌp'reiz], *v.t.* Soulever, élever.

uprear [ʌp'riə], *v.t.* Arborer; dresser.

upright ['ʌprait], *a.* Droit, debout; d'aplomb, vertical; (*fig.*) honnête (honest).—*adv.* Tout droit.—*n.* Montant, *m.* **uprightly,** *adv.* Droit, debout; avec droiture, loyalement, avec probité (honestly). **uprightness,** *n.* Droiture, intégrité, *f.*

uprise [ʌp'raiz], *v.i.* (*past* **uprose** [ʌp'rouz], *p.p.* **uprisen** [ʌp'rizn]) Se lever.

uprising [ʌp'raiziŋ], *n.* Lever; soulèvement, *m.*

uproar ['ʌprɔː], *n.* Tumulte, désordre; tapage, vacarme, *m.*

uproarious [ʌp'rɔːriəs], *a.* Bruyant; tumultueux. **uproariously,** *adv.* Avec un grand vacarme. **uproariousness,** *n.* Turbulence, *f.*, désordre, *m.*

uproot [ʌp'ruːt], *v.t.* Déraciner, extirper. **uprooting,** *n.* Déracinement, *m.*, extirpation, *f.*

upset [ʌp'set], *v.t.* (*past* and *p.p.* **upset**) Renverser; faire verser (a vehicle); faire chavirer (a boat); (*fig.*) bouleverser.—*v.i.* Se renverser; verser (of vehicles); chavirer (of boats). *Upset price,* mise à prix, *f.*—*n.* Bouleversement; renversement, *m.* (of a vehicle); chavirement (of a boat), *m.*

upshot ['ʌpʃɔt], *n.* Résultat, *m.*, fin, conclusion, *f.*, fin mot, *m.* *On the upshot,* en définitive.

upside-down ['ʌpsaid 'daun], *adv.* Sens dessus dessous, la tête en bas. *To turn upside-down,* mettre sens dessus dessous, bouleverser.

upsoar [ʌp'sɔː], *v.i.* S'envoler, prendre son essor.

upstairs (1) [ʌp'steəz], *adv.* En haut.

upstairs (2) ['ʌpsteəz], *a.* D'en haut.

upstanding [ʌp'stændiŋ], *a.* Droit, debout.

upstart ['ʌpstaːt], *n.* and *a.* Parvenu, nouveau riche, *m.*

upstay [ʌp'stei], *v.t.* Étayer, appuyer.

upsurge [ʌp'səːdʒ], *n.* Poussée, *f.*

upsweep [ʌp'swiːp], *v.t.* (*past* and *p.p.* **upswept**) Surélever.

uptake ['ʌpteik], *n.* *To be quick on the uptake,* avoir la compréhension vive, saisir à demimot.

uptear [ʌp'teə], *v.t.* Arracher.

upturn [ʌp'təːn], *v.t.* Tourner, retourner; lever.

upward (1) ['ʌpwəd], *a.* Dirigé en haut; ascendant. *To show an upward tendency* (of shares), tendre à la hausse.

upward (2) ['ʌpwəd] or **upwards,** *adv.* En haut; en montant. *Upwards and downwards,* en haut et en bas; *upwards of,* plus de.

uraemia [juə'riːmiə], *n.* Urémie, *f.*

Ural ['juərəl] **Mountains.** Les Monts Ourals, *m.pl.*

uranic [juə'rænik], *a.* Uranique.

uranium [juə'reiniəm], *n.* Uranium, *m.*

uranographical [juəræno'græfikl], *a.* Uranographique.

uranography [juərə'nɔgrəfi], *n.* Uranographie, *f.*

urban ['əːbən], *a.* Urbain.

urbane [əː'bein], *a.* Qui a de l'urbanité, poli, courtois. **urbanely,** *adv.* Avec urbanité.

urbanity [əː'bæniti], *n.* Urbanité, *f.*

urbanize ['əːbənaiz], *v.t.* Urbaniser.

urceolate ['əːsiələt], *a.* Urcéolé. **urceolus,** *n.* Urcéole, *m.*

urchin ['əːtʃin], *n.* Gamin, polisson; (*colloq.*) mioche, gosse, *m.* *Sea-urchin,* oursin, *m.*

urea ['juəriə], *n.* Urée, *f.* **ureameter** [juəri'æmitə], *n.* Uréomètre, *m.*

uredo [juə'riːdou], *n.* Urédo, *m.*

ureter [juə'riːtə], *n.* Urètre, *m.* **ureteritis** [juəriːtə'raitis], *n.* Urétérite, *f.*

urethra [juə'riːθrə], *n.* Urètre, *m.*

urethritis [juəriː'θraitis], *n.* Urétrite, *f.*

urge [əːdʒ], *v.t.* Presser; pousser, exciter, porter (à); alléguer (to allege). *To urge on,* pousser en avant.—*n.* Impulsion; poussée, *f.*

To feel an urge to do something, se sentir poussé à faire quelque chose.
urgency ['ɔ:dʒənsi], *n.* Urgence, *f.*; besoin pressant, *m.*; sollicitation urgente, *f.*, instances, *f.pl.*
urgent, *a.* Urgent, instant, pressant. **urgently,** *adv.* Avec urgence, instamment; avec instance.
urging ['ɔ:dʒiŋ], *n.* Sollicitation, *f. No urging on your part will avail*, aucune sollicitation de votre part n'y fera rien.
uric ['juərik], *a.* Urique. **urinal,** *n.* Urinoir; (*Med.*) urinal, *m.*; vespasienne (street urinal), *f.* **urinate,** *v.i.* Uriner. **urinary,** *a.* Urinaire. **urine,** *n.* Urine, *f.* **urinous,** *a.* Urineux.
urn [ə:n], *n.* Urne, *f.*; fontaine (for tea, coffee, etc.), *f.*, samovar, *m.*
urocyst ['juərosist], *n.* Urocyste, *m.* **urogenital** [juəro'dʒenitl], *a.* Urogénital. **uroscopy** [juə'rɔskəpi], *n.* Uroscopie, *f.* **urotoxic** [juəro'tɔksik], *a.* Urotoxique.
ursa ['ə:sə], *n.* (*Astron.*) Ourse, *f. Ursa Major,* Grande Ourse; *Ursa Minor*, Petite Ourse.
ursine ['ə:sain], *a.* D'ours, oursin.
Ursula ['ə:sjulə]. Ursule, *f.*
Ursuline ['ə:sjulain]. Ursuline, *f.*
urticaceous [ə:ti'keiʃəs], *a.* Urticacé. **urticaria** [-'keəriə], *n.* Urticaire, *f.*
urubu ['u:rubu], *n.* (*Orn.*) Urubu, *m.*
Uruguay ['u:rugwai]. L'Uruguay, *m.*
urus ['juərəs], *n.* (*pl.* **uri, uruses**) Aurochs, urus, *m.*
us [ʌs], *pron.* Nous; à nous. *For us Frenchmen,* pour nous autres Français.
usable ['ju:zəbl], *a.* Utilisable, employable.
usage ['ju:sidʒ], *n.* Usage, traitement, *m.*; us, *m.pl. By bad usage on the part of,* à cause des mauvais procédés de; *the usages and customs,* les us et coutumes, *m.pl.*; *to meet with hard usage,* être maltraité.
usance ['ju:zəns], *n.* (*Comm.*) Usance, *f.*; délai habituel, *m.*
use (1) [ju:s], *n.* Usage, emploi, *m.*; utilité, *f.*; avantage, profit (advantage), *m.*; coutume, habitude (custom), *f.*; (*Law*) usufruit, *m.*, jouissance, *f. For the use of,* à l'usage de; (*fam.*) *I have no use for him,* je ne peux pas le souffrir; *in general use,* d'un usage général; *in use,* d'usage, en usage, employé; *it is of no use to . . .,* on a beau . . .; *of great use,* très utile, d'une grande utilité; *of no use,* d'aucune utilité, qui ne sert à rien; *of use,* utile; *out of use,* hors d'usage, inusité, passé, vieilli; *to have no further use for,* n'avoir plus besoin de; *to make use of,* faire usage de, se servir de; *use is a second nature,* l'habitude est une seconde nature; *what is the use of doing it?* à quoi sert de le faire? *what is the use of that?* à quoi sert cela?
use (2) [ju:z], *v.t.* User de, faire usage de, employer, se servir de; utiliser; consommer (to consume); accoutumer, habituer (to accustom); en user, agir avec, traiter (to treat). *To use forbearance towards,* user d'indulgence or de ménagements envers.— *v.i.* Avoir coutume, avoir l'habitude, être habitué. *He used to admire,* il admirait. **used,** *as adj.* [ju:st], *as part.* [ju:zd] Usité (of words etc.). *Much used, très usité; not used,* inusité, hors d'usage; *to get used to,* s'accoutumer à, s'habituer à; *to have been*

used (of plate, line, clothes, etc.), avoir servi; *used to* (*followed by infinitive*), habitué à, accoutumé à; *used up,* épuisé (of an edition), blasé (of a person); *very little used,* très peu usité, presque neuf (of linen, plate, clothes, etc.).
useful ['ju:sful], *a.* Utile. **usefully,** *adv.* Utilement, avec profit. **usefulness,** *n.* Utilité, *f.* **useless,** *a.* Inutile; vain. **uselessly,** *adv.* Inutilement. **uselessness,** *n.* Inutilité, *f.*
user ['ju:zə], *n.* Personne qui se sert (de), *f.*, usager, *m. Right of user,* droit d'usage, usufruit, *m.*
Ushant ['ʌʃənt]. Ouessant, *m.*
usher ['ʌʃə], *n.* Huissier (in a court); sous-maître, maître-répétiteur, maître d'étude, (*colloq.*) pion (in schools), *m.*—*v.t.* Faire entrer, introduire (dans); (*fig.*) annoncer, inaugurer. *The snowdrop ushers in the spring,* le perce-neige est l'avant-coureur du printemps; *to usher out,* reconduire (à la porte).
usherette [ʌʃə'ret], *n.* (*Cine.*) Ouvreuse, *f.*
usquebaugh ['ʌskwibɔ:], *n.* Whisky, usquebac, *m.*
usual ['ju:ʒuəl], *a.* Usuel, ordinaire, habituel, accoutumé; d'usage. *As usual,* comme d'ordinaire, comme d'habitude; *business as usual,* les affaires continuent; *more than usual,* plus qu'à l'ordinaire; *with the usual ceremonies,* avec les cérémonies d'usage. **usually,** *adv.* Ordinairement, d'ordinaire, d'habitude. **usualness,** *n.* Habitude, *f.*, caractère ordinaire, *m.*
usufruct ['ju:zjufrʌkt], *n.* Usufruit, *m.* **usufructuary,** *n.* Usufruitier, *m.*, -ière, *f.*
usurer ['ju:ʒərə or ju:zjurə], *n.* Usurier, *m.*
usurious [ju:'zjuəriəs], *a.* Qui fait l'usure; usuraire. **usuriously,** *adv.* Usurairement.
usurp [ju:'zə:p], *v.t.* Usurper. **usurpation** [ju:zə'peiʃən], *n.* Usurpation, *f.* **usurper,** *n.* Usurpateur, *m.*, -trice, *f.* **usurpingly,** *adv.* Par usurpation.
usury ['ju:ʒuri], *n.* Usure, *f.*
ut [ʌt], *n.* (*Mus.*) Ut, do, *m.*
utensil [ju:'tensil], *n.* Ustensile, *m.*
uterine ['ju:tərain], *a.* Utérin. **uterus,** *n.* Utérus, *m.*, matrice, *f.*
utilitarian [ju:tili'teəriən], *a.* Utilitaire. **utilitarianism,** *n.* Utilitarisme, *m.*
utility [ju:'tiliti], *n.* Utilité, *f. To be a utility* (*man*), (*Theat.*) jouer les utilités; *utility clothes,* vêtements d'usage courant, *m.pl.*
utilizable ['ju:tilaizəbl], *a.* Utilisable. **utilization** [-'zeiʃən], *n.* Utilisation, *f.*
utilize ['ju:tilaiz], *v.t.* Utiliser.
utmost ['ʌtmoust], *a.* Extrême, le dernier, le plus haut, le plus grand; le plus élevé (of prices etc.).—*n.* L'extrême, le plus haut degré, le comble; le plus possible (all one can), *m. At the utmost,* tout au plus; *to do one's utmost,* faire tout son possible (pour); *to the utmost,* à l'extrême, au suprême degré.
Utopia [ju:'toupjə], *n.* Utopie, *f.* **Utopian,** *a.* D'utopie, utopique.—*n.* Utopiste, *m.*
utricular [ju:'trikjulə], *a.* Utriculé.
utricle ['ju:trikl], *n.* Utricule, *m.*
utter (1) ['ʌtə], *a.* Total, entier, complet; absolu, positif (absolute); le plus profond, le plus grand (extreme); vrai, fieffé (downright). *To my utter astonishment,* à mon grand étonnement, à ma grande surprise;

utter strangers to one another, tout à fait inconnus l'un à l'autre.

utter (2) ['ʌtə], *v.t.* Pousser, jeter (sighs, groan, etc.); énoncer, proférer, prononcer, articuler, dire; révéler, publier (to disclose); mettre en circulation, émettre (to put in circulation). *He did not utter a word*, il ne souffla pas mot; *to utter notes*, émettre des billets.

utterable ['ʌtərəbl], *a.* Qu'on peut prononcer, exprimable.

utterance ['ʌtərəns], *n.* Énonciation, prononciation, parole, expression, *f.* *To deprive of utterance*, priver de la parole; *to give utterance to*, prononcer, proférer; *to lose all power of utterance*, perdre entièrement l'usage de la parole.

utterer, *n.* Personne qui articule, qui prononce, *f.*; émetteur (issuer), *m.* *Utterer of base coin*, émetteur de fausse monnaie, *m.*

uttering, *n.* Émission (of coin etc.), *f.*

utterly ['ʌtəli], *adv.* Tout à fait, complètement, entièrement, de fond en comble.

uttermost, *a.* Extrême, le plus grand; le plus reculé. *At the uttermost*, au plus; *to the uttermost ends*, au fin bout.

utters ['ʌtəz], *n.pl.* Broutements, *m.pl.* (of tool).

uvea [juːˈviːə], *n.* (*Anat.*) Uvée, *f.*

uviform ['juːvifɔːm], *a.* Uviforme.

uvula ['juːvjulə], *n.* (*Anat.*) Luette, uvule, *f.* **uvular**, *a.* Uvulaire.

uxorious [ʌkˈsoːriəs], *a.* Uxorieux, esclave de sa femme. **uxoriously**, *adv.* Avec une excessive complaisance pour sa femme. **uxoriousness**, *n.* Complaisance excessive pour sa femme, *f.*

V

V, v [viː]. Vingt-deuxième lettre de l'alphabet, *m.* V, cinq; *v.* (*abbr. for* VERSUS), contre.

vacancy ['veikənsi], *n.* Vacance, place vacante, *f.*; vide, *m.*; lacune (gap), *f.*; loisir, repos (leisure); (*fig.*) manque de réflexion, défaut de pensée, *m.*

vacant ['veikənt], *a.* Vacant, vide; libre (free); distrait, vide d'expression (vacant-looking); qui ne réfléchit pas (thoughtless). *Vacant look*, air hébété, air distrait, *m.*

vacate [vəˈkeit], *v.t.* Laisser vacant, quitter; (*Law*) vider.

vacation [vəˈkeiʃən], *n.* Vacation, *f.*, vacances, *f.pl.*

vacationist, *n.* Villégiaturiste; estivant, *m.*, -ante, *f.*

vaccinal ['væksinl], *a.* Vaccinal.

vaccinate ['væksineit], *v.t.* Vacciner. **vaccination** [-ˈneiʃən], *n.* Vaccination, la vaccine, *f.* **vaccinator**, *n.* Vaccinateur, *m.*; lancette, *f.*

vaccine ['væksiːn], *a.* De vache.—*n.* Vaccin, *m.* **vaccine-matter** *or* **vaccine-lymph**, *n.* Vaccin, *m.*

vaccinic [vækˈsinik], *a.* Vaccinique.

vacillate ['væsileit], *v.i.* Vaciller; (*fig.*) hésiter. **vacillating**, *a.* Vacillant, indécis.

vacillation [væsiˈleiʃən], *n.* Vacillation, hésitation, indécision, *f.*

vacuity [vəˈkjuːiti], *n.* Vide, *m.*; vacuité, *f.*; (*fig.*) néant, *m.*

vacuous ['vækjuəs], *a.* Vide; (*fig.*) bête, niais.

vacuum ['vækjuəm], *n.* Vide, *m.* *Nature abhors a vacuum*, la nature a horreur du vide; *to get a vacuum*, faire le vide. **vacuum-cleaner**, *n.* Aspirateur, *m.* **vacuum-gauge**, *n.* Manomètre à vide, *m.*

vade-mecum ['veidiˈmiːkəm], *n.* Vade-mecum, *m.*

vagabond ['vægəbɔnd], *n.* Vagabond, *m.*, -onde, *f.*—*a.* Errant, vagabond. **vagabondage** *or* **vagabondism**, *n.* Vagabondage, *m.* **vagabondize**, *v.i.* Vagabonder.

vagary [vəˈgeəri *or* ˈveigəri], *n.* (*pl.* **vagaries**) Caprice, *m.*, lubie, boutade, *f.*

vagina [vəˈdʒainə], *n.* (*Anat.*) Vagin, *m.*

vaginal [vəˈdʒainl], *a.* Vaginal.

vagrancy ['veigrənsi], *n.* Vagabondage, *m.*

vagrant ['veigrənt], *a.* Vagabond, errant.—*n.* Vagabond, *m.*, -onde, *f.*, mendiant, *m.*, -iante, *f.* **vagrantly**, *adv.* En vagabond.

vague [veig], *a.* Vague. **vaguely**, *adv.* Vaguement. **vagueness**, *n.* Vague, *m.*

***vails** [veilz], *n.pl.* Gratification aux domestiques, *f.*, pourboire, *m.*

vain [vein], *a.* Vain; faux, mensonger (false); vaniteux, glorieux (conceited). *In vain*, en vain, vainement; *it is in vain for you to try*, vous avez beau faire; *it is in vain to*, on a beau; *to take in vain*, prendre en vain; *vain as a peacock*, fier comme un paon.

vainglorious [veinˈgloːriəs], *a.* Vain, vaniteux. **vaingloriously**, *adv.* Vaniteusement. **vainglory** *or* **vaingloriousness**, *n.* Vaine gloire, gloriole, *f.*

vainly ['veinli], *adv.* En vain, vainement. **vainness**, *n.* Vanité, *f.*

vair [veə], *n.* (*Her.*) Vair, *m.*

valance ['væləns], *n.* Draperie de bas de lit, frange de lit, *f.*; tour de lit, *m.*

vale [veil], *n.* (*poet.*) Vallon, *m.*, vallée, *f.*; chéneau, *m.*

valedictory [væliˈdiktəri], *a.* D'adieu.—*n.* Discours d'adieu, *m.*

Valencia [vəˈlenʃiə]. (*Geog.*) Valence, *f.*

Valentine ['væləntain]. Valentin, *m.*, -ine, *f.* *Amant choisi le jour de la Saint-Valentin; billet de la St-Valentin (letter), *m.* *St. Valentine's Day*, la St-Valentin, *f.* (February 14).

valerian [vəˈliəriən], *n.* (*Bot.*) Valériane, *f.*

valet ['vælit], *n.* Valet de chambre, *m.*

Valetta [vəˈletə]. (*Geog.*) La Valette, *f.*

valetudinarian [vælitjuːdiˈneəriən], *a. and n.* Valétudinaire, *m.*

valiant ['væljənt], *a.* Vaillant, valeureux. **valiantly**, *adv.* Vaillamment. **valiantness** [VALOUR].

valid ['vælid], *a.* Valide, valable. *To make valid*, valider, rendre valide. **validate**, *v.t.* Valider, rendre valable.

validity [vəˈliditi] *or* **validness**, *n.* Validité, *f.*

validly ['vælidli], *adv.* Validement, valablement.

valise [vəˈliːz], *n.* Valise, *f.*; sac de voyage, *m.*

Valkyrie [vælˈkiːri], *n.* Walkyrie, *f.*

valley ['væli], *n.* Vallée, *f.*, vallon, *m.*; cornière, *f.*

vallonia [vəˈlouniə], *n.* Noix de galle, *f.*

vallum ['væləm], *n.* Retranchement, *m.*

valorous ['vælərəs], *a.* Valeureux. **valorously**, *adv.* Valeureusement. **valour**, *n.* Valeur, vaillance, *f.*

valuable ['væljuəbl], *a.* Précieux, de grande valeur. **valuables**, *n.pl.* Objets de valeur, *m.pl.*

valuation [vælju'eiʃən], *n.* Évaluation, estimation, *f.*

valuator ['væljueitə], *n.* Estimateur, *m.*

value ['vælju], *n.* Valeur, *f.*; prix, *m. For value received*, valeur reçue; *the value of a thing is what it will fetch*, la valeur d'une chose se mesure par le prix qu'on en obtient; *to be of no value*, ne valoir rien, n'avoir aucune valeur; *to set a value on*, estimer, faire cas de, attacher de la valeur à.—*v.t.* Évaluer, estimer, apprécier. *To value on*, disposer sur, faire traite sur.

valued, *a.* Estimé, apprécié, prisé; précieux.

valueless, *a.* Sans valeur.

valuer, *n.* Estimateur, commissaire-priseur; (*Law*) expert; (*fig.*) appréciateur, *m.*

valvate ['vælveit], *a.* (*Bot.*) Valvé, valvaire.

valve [vælv], *n.* Soupape, *f.*; clapet (clack); battant (of a door), *m.*; (*Anat.*) valvule; (*Bot. etc.*) valve, *f. Air-valve*, soupape à air; *ball-valve*, soupape à boulet; *drop-valve*, soupape renversée, *f.*; *safety-valve*, soupape de sûreté, *f.*

valve-body, *n.* Corps de soupape, *m.*

valve-cap, *n.* Bouchon de soupape, chapeau de valve, *m.*

valved, *a.* À soupape; (*Bot.*) valvé, à valves.

valve-gear, *n.* Distribution, *f.*

valvular, *a.* (*Med.*) Valvulaire.

vamoose [və'mu:s], *v.i.* (*Am.*) Filer, décaniller.

vamp [væmp], *n.* Empeigne, *f.*; (*short for* **vampire**), *n.* Une enjôleuse, une femme fatale, une vamp, *f. Outer vamp*, avant-pied, *m.*—*v.t.* (*fig.*) Raccommoder, rapiécer; remonter, mettre une empeigne à (a boot); (*Mus. etc.*) improviser (un accompagnement).

vampire ['væmpaiə], *n.* Vampire, *m.*

vampirism ['væmpaiərizm], *n.* Vampirisme, *m.*

van [væn], *n.* Camion, *m.*, camionnette, voiture (de déménagement), *f.*; (*Rail. etc.*) fourgon, *m.*; aile (wing), *f.*; van (winnowing fan), *m.*; avant-garde (vanguard), *f. Furniture van*, voiture de déménagement, tapissière, *f.*; *guard's van*, fourgon du chef du train, *m.*; *luggage van*, fourgon de bagages, *m.*; *spring-van*, tapissière, *f.*

Vandal [vændl], *n.* Vandale, *m.* or *f.*

Vandalic [væn'dælik], *a.* Vandale, de vandale.

Vandalism ['vændəlizm], *n.* Vandalisme, *m.*

vandyke [væn'daik], *n.* Col à la Van Dyck, *m.*

vane [vein], *n.* Girouette; barbe (of a feather), *f.*; (*Steam-engine*) registre, *m.*; (*Motor.*) aile, ailette, *f.*

vanguard ['vænga:d], *n.* Avant-garde, tête d'avant-garde, *f.*

vanilla [və'nilə], *n.* Vanille, *f.* **vanilla-plant**, *n.* Vanillier, *m.*

vanish ['væniʃ], *v.i.* S'évanouir, disparaître; déguerpir (to make off).—*n.* Son transitoire, *m.*, détente, *f.* **vanished**, *a.* Évanoui, disparu. **vanishing cream**, *n.* Crème de jour, *f.* **vanishing-point**, *n.* Point de fuite, *m.*

vanity ['væniti], *n.* Vanité, *f. Vanity fair*, la foire aux vanités, *f.*

vanquish ['væŋkwiʃ], *v.t.* Vaincre. **vanquishable**, *a.* Que l'on peut vaincre.

vanquisher, *n.* Vainqueur, *m.*

vantage ['va:ntidʒ], *n.* Avantage, *m.*, supériorité, *f.* **vantage-ground** or **coign** (place, point) **of vantage**, *n.* Avantage du terrain, *m.*, position avantageuse, *f.*

vapid ['væpid], *a.* Fade, insipide; plat, éventé (of liquors).

vapidity [væ'piditi] or **vapidness**, *n.* Fadeur, insipidité, *f.*

vapidly, *adv.* Insipidement.

vaporization [veipərai'zeiʃən], *n.* Vaporisation, *f.*

vaporize ['veipəraiz], *v.t.* Vaporiser.—*v.i.* Se vaporiser. **vaporizer**, *n.* Vaporisateur, *m.*

vaporous ['veipərəs], *a.* Vaporeux; venteux (windy); (*fig.*) vain, chimérique (vain).

vapour ['veipə], *n.* Vapeur; (*fig.*) fumée, *f.* **vapour-bath**, *n.* Bain de vapeur, *m.* **vapourer**, *n.* Vantard, *m.* **vapouring**, *a.* Vantard. **vapourish** or **vapoury**, *a.* Vaporeux.

varec ['værik], *n.* Varech, *m.*, soude, *f.*

variability [vɛəriə'biliti] or **variableness**, *n.* Variabilité; inconstance, *f.* **variably**, *adv.* D'une manière variable, variablement.

variable ['vɛəriəbl], *a.* Variable, changeant, variant; inconstant (inconstant); mobile (of feasts).

variance ['vɛəriəns], *n.* Désaccord, *m. At variance*, en désaccord, brouillé (avec), mal (avec), en contradiction (of things); *to set at variance*, brouiller, mettre mal (avec).

variant ['vɛəriənt], *a.* Variant.—*n.* Variante, *f.*

variation [vɛəri'eiʃən], *n.* Variation, différence, déviation, *f.*, changement, *m.*

varicella [væri'selə], *n.* Varicelle, *f.*

varicocele ['værikosi:l], *n.* Varicocèle, *m.*

varicose, *a.* Variqueux. *Varicose vein*, varice, *f.*

varied ['vɛərid], *a.* Varié, divers.

variegate ['vɛərigeit], *v.t.* Diversifier, varier; bigarrer; nuancer. **variegated**, *a.* Varié, bigarré; jaspé (of marble); (*Bot.*) panaché.

variegation [vɛəri'geiʃən], *n.* Diversité de couleurs, bigarrure, *f.*

variety [və'raiəti], *n.* (*pl.* **varieties**) Variété, diversité; variation, *f. Variety show*, spectacle de variétés, music-hall, *m.*

variola [və'raiələ], *n.* Variole, petite vérole, *f.*

variolation [vɛərio'leiʃən], *n.* Variolisation, *f.*

variolic [vɛəri'ɔlik], *a.* Variolique.

varioloid ['vɛəriələid], *n.* Varioloïde, *f.*

various ['vɛəriəs], *a.* Divers, différent; changeant, variable (changeable). **variously**, *adv.* Diversement.

varix ['væriks], *n.* Varice, *f.*

***varlet** ['va:lit], *n.* Valet, page; (*fig.*) coquin, drôle, *m.*

varnish ['va:niʃ], *n.* Vernis, *m.*—*v.t.* Vernir; vernisser (pottery etc.); (*fig.*) farder, colorer. **varnisher**, *n.* Vernisseur, *m.* **varnishing**, *n.* Vernissure, *f.*; vernissage, *m.* **varnishing-day**, *n.* Le vernissage, *m.*

varsity ['va:siti], *n.* (*fam.*) Université, *f.*

vary ['vɛəri], *v.i.* Varier, changer; être d'avis différent (de); dévier (de), s'écarter. *Not to vary a minute* (of watches), ne pas varier d'une minute.—*v.i.* Varier; faire des changements à; diversifier. **varying**, *a.* Changeant, qui varie, divers.

vascular ['væskjulə], *a.* Vasculaire.

vase [vɑːz], *n.* Vase, *m.* **vase-shaped**, *a.* Vasiforme, en forme de vase.

vaseline ['væzəlin], *n.* Vaseline, *f.* (proprietary mark).—*v.t.* Graisser, vaseliner.

vassal [væsl], *n.* Vassal, *m.*, vassale, *f.* **vassalage** ['væsəlidʒ], *n.* Vasselage; (*fig.*) asservissement, *m.*, sujétion, servitude, *f.*

vast [vɑːst], *a.* Vaste, immense.—*n.* Vaste espace, *m.*, immensité, *f.* **vastly**, *adv.* Immensément, excessivement. **vastness**, *n.* Vaste étendue, grandeur, immensité, *f.*

vat [væt], *n.* Cuve, *f.* **vatful**, *n.* Cuvée, *f.*

Vatican ['vætikən]. Le Vatican, *m.*

vaticination [vætisi'neiʃən], *n.* Vaticination, prophétie, prédiction, *f.*

vaudeville ['voudəvil], *n.* Vaudeville, *m.* *Writer of vaudevilles*, vaudevilliste, *m.*

vault [vɔːlt], *n.* Voûte, cave, *f.*, cellier (cellar); caveau (for the dead); saut (leap), *m.* *Safety vault*, chambre forte, *f.*—*v.t.* Voûter.—*v.i.* Sauter. **vaulted**, *a.* Voûté, en voûte (arch or roof). **vaulter**, *n.* Voltigeur, sauteur, acrobate, *m.*

vaulting ['vɔːltiŋ], *n.* Construction de voûtes, *f.*; voûtes (vaults), *f.pl.*; voltige (acrobatics), *f.* **vaulting-horse**, *n.* Cheval de bois, *m.*

vaunt [vɔːnt], *n.* Vanterie, *f.*—*v.t.* Se vanter (de), vanter, élever jusqu'aux nues. **vaunter**, *n.* Vantard, *m.* **vauntful* or **vaunting**, *a.* Plein de jactance. **vauntingly**, *adv.* Avec jactance.

*vavasory, *n.* Vavassorie, *f.*

vavasour ['vævəsuə], *n.* Vavasseur, *m.*

veal [viːl], *n.* Veau, *m.* **veal-broth**, *n.* Bouillon de veau, *m.*

vector ['vektə], *n.* (*Math.*) Vecteur, *m.* **vectorial** [vek'tɔːriəl], *a.* Vectoriel.

vedette [və'det], *n.* Vedette, *f.*

veer [viə], *v.i.* Tourner, changer de direction; virer, changer de bord (of ships). *To veer round*, changer d'opinion; *to veer round to someone's opinion*, devenir de l'avis de quelqu'un, se ranger à l'opinion de quelqu'un.—*v.t.* Virer (un bateau) vent arrière. *To veer away a rope*, filer un filin.

vegetable ['vedʒətəbl], *a.* Végétal.—*n.* Végétal, légume (food), *m.* *Vegetable garden*, jardin potager, *m.* *Vegetables* (*for food*), vivres de campagne, *m.pl.* **vegetal**, *a.* Végétal.

vegetality [vedʒə'tæliti], *n.* Végétalité, *f.*

vegetarian [vedʒə'tɛəriən], *a.* Végétarien.—*n.* Végétarien, *m.* **vegetarianism**, *n.* Végétarisme, *m.*

vegetate ['vedʒiteit], *v.i.* Végéter.

vegetation [vedʒi'teiʃən], *n.* Végétation, *f.*

vegetative ['vedʒətətiv], *a.* Végétatif, végétant.

vehemence ['viːiməns], *n.* Véhémence; (*fig.*) ardeur, impétuosité, *f.* **vehement**, *a.* Véhément, impétueux, violent. **vehemently**, *adv.* Avec véhémence, impétueusement.

vehicle ['viːikl], *n.* Véhicule, *m.*, voiture, *f.* **vehicular** [viː'ikjulə], *a.* Des voitures, véhiculaire.

vehmgerichte ['feːmgərixtə], *n.* La sainte Vehme, *f.* **vehmic**, *a.* Vehmique.

veil [veil], *n.* Voile, *m.*; voilette (lady's veil); (*fig.*) apparence, *f.*, déguisement, *m.*—*v.t.* Voiler; (*fig.*) masquer, déguiser, dissimuler. **veilless**, *a.* Sans voile.

vein [vein], *n.* Veine, *f.*; (*Bot.*) nervure, *f.*; (*Geol.*)

filon, *m.*; (*fig.*) humeur, disposition, *f.*—*v.t.* Veiner. **veined**, *a.* Veiné. **veinless**, *a.* Sans nervures. **veinstone**, *n.* Gangue, *f.* **veiny**, *a.* Veineux.

velleity [və'liːiti], *n.* Velléité, *f.*

vellum ['veləm], *n.* Vélin; papier vélin, *m.*

*velocipede [və'lɔsipiːd], *n.* Vélocipède, *m.*

velocity [və'lɔsiti], *n.* Vélocité, vitesse, rapidité, *f.* *Muzzle velocity*, vitesse initiale, *f.*

velvet ['velvit], *n.* Velours, *m.*—*a.* De velours; (*Bot.*) velouté. **velvet-down**, *n.* Velouté, *m.* **velvet-pile**, *n.* Moquette, *f.* **velveted**, *a.* De velours, velouté.

velveteen [velvə'tiːn], *n.* Velours de coton, *m.*; (*pl.*) culotte de velours; (*colloq.*) garde-chasse, *m.* **velveting**, *n.* Velouté, *m.* **velvety**, *a.* Velouté.

venal [viːnl], *a.* Vénal.

venality [viː'næliti], *n.* Vénalité, *f.*

venally, *adv.* Vénalement.

vend [vend], *v.t.* Vendre (small wares).

vendee [ven'diː], *n.* Acheteur, *m.*

vendetta [ven'detə], *n.* Vendetta, *f.*

vendible [ven'detə], *a.* Vendable.

vendor ['vendə], *n.* Vendeur, *m.*, -euse, *f.*

veneer [və'niə], *v.t.* Plaquer (de).—*n.* Feuille (de bois etc.); plaque, *f.*; (*fig.*) masque, vernis, *m.* **veneering**, *n.* Placage, *m.*

venerable ['venərəbl], *a.* Vénérable. **venerableness**, *n.* Caractère vénérable, *m.* **venerably**, *adv.* Vénérablement. **venerate**, *v.t.* Vénérer. **veneration**, *n.* Vénération, *f.* **venerator**, *n.* Vénérateur, *m.*

venereal [və'niəriəl], *a.* Vénérien.

venery ['venəri], *n.* La chasse, vénerie, *f.*

Venetia [və'niːʃə]. La Vénétie, *f.*

Venetian [və'niːʃən], *a.* Vénitien, de Venise. *Venetian blind*, jalousie, *f.*; *Venetian shutter*, persienne, *f.*—*n.* Vénitien, *m.*, -ienne, *f.*

Venezuela [venə'zweilə]. Le Vénézuéla. **Venezuelan**, *a.* and *n.* Vénézuélien, *m.*, -ienne, *f.*

vengeance ['vendʒəns], *n.* Vengeance, *f.* *I gave it him with a vengeance*, je l'ai tancé d'importance, je l'ai rossé d'importance; *out of vengeance*, par vengeance; *this is what I call raining with a vengeance*, c'est ce que j'appelle pleuvoir; *with a vengeance*, terriblement, furieusement, vigoureusement, à outrance.

vengeful, *a.* Vindicatif.

venial ['viːniəl], *a.* Véniel, pardonnable. **venially**, *adv.* Véniellement. **veniality** [viːni'æliti], *n.* Vénialité, *f.*

Venice ['venis]. Venise, *f.*

venison ['venizn or venzn], *n.* Venaison, *f.*

venom ['venəm], *n.* Venin, *m.* **venomous**, *a.* Venimeux (of animals); vénéneux (of plants); (*fig.*) empoisonné, dangereux, méchant. **venomously**, *adv.* D'une manière venimeuse; méchamment. **venomousness**, *n.* Nature venimeuse, *f.*, venin, *m.*

venous ['viːnəs], *a.* Veineux.

vent [vent], *v.t.* Donner issue à, éventer, exhaler, décharger.—*n.* Issue, *f.*, passage, cours, *m.*; lumière (of a gun), *f.*; trou de fausset (of a cask); soupirail (air-hole), *m.* *To give vent to*, donner libre cours à. **venthole**, *n.* Soupirail (in air-shaft); trou de fausset (of a cask), *m.* **vent-peg**, *n.* Fausset, *m.*

ventiduct, *n.* Conduit d'air, *m.*, ventouse, *f.*

ventilate

ventilate ['ventileit], *v.t.* Ventiler; aérer, donner de l'air à; (*fig.*) discuter; faire connaître publiquement.
ventilation [venti'leiʃən], *n.* Ventilation, *f.*; aérage, *m.*; (*fig.*) mise en discussion publique, *f.* **ventilation shaft**, *n.* Puits d'aérage, *m.*
ventilator ['ventileitə], *n.* Ventilateur, *m.*
ventose ['ventous], *a.* Venteux. **ventosity** [ven'tɔsiti], *n.* Ventosité, flatuosité, *f.*
ventral ['ventrəl], *a.* Ventral. **ventricle**, *n.* Ventricule, *m.*
ventricular [ven'trikjulə], *a.* Ventriculaire.
ventriloquism [ven'triləkwizm], *n.* Ventriloquie, *f.* **ventriloquist**, *n.* Ventriloque, *m.*
venture ['ventʃə], *n.* Aventure, tentative, entreprise, *f.*; risque, hasard, *m.*; (*Comm.*) pacotille, *f. At a venture*, à l'aventure, au hasard.—*v.t.* Aventurer, risquer, hasarder. *Nothing venture nothing win*, qui ne risque rien n'a rien.—*v.i.* Oser, se permettre, se hasarder, s'aventurer, se risquer; s'aviser de (to presume). *I will venture to say that . . .*, j'irai même jusqu'à dire que . . .; *to venture beyond*, s'aventurer au-delà de; *to venture on*, se risquer sur *or* dans, se hasarder sur *or* dans, s'aventurer sur, entreprendre, s'engager dans; *to venture to*, oser, prendre sur soi de.
venturer, *n.* Personne aventureuse, *f.* **venturesome**, *a.* Aventureux, audacieux. **venturesomely**, *adv.* Aventureusement, d'une manière aventureuse.
venue ['venju:], *n.* Juridiction, *f.*; lieu de réunion, *m. To change the venue*, changer la juridiction (d'une cause); *to lay a venue*, (*Law*) nommer le tribunal qui doit juger une action; *venue of the meet*, rendez-vous de chasse (à courre), *m.*
Venus ['vi:nəs]. Vénus, *f. Venus's comb*, peigne de Vénus (plant), *m.*; *Venus's flytrap*, dionée gobe-mouches (plant), *f.*; *Venus's looking-glass*, miroir de Vénus (plant), *m.*
veracious [və'reiʃəs], *a.* Véridique. **veracity** [və'ræsiti], *n.* Véracité, *f.*
veranda [və'rændə], *n.* Véranda, marquise, *f.*
verb [və:b], *n.* Verbe, *m.* **verbal**, *a.* Verbal, mot à mot, littéral. **verbally**, *adv.* Verbalement, mot à mot, littéralement. **verbatim** [və:'beitim], *adv.* Mot pour mot, textuellement.
verbena [və:'bi:nə], *n.* Verveine, *f. Lemon-scented verbena*, citronnelle, *f.* **verbenaceous** [-'neiʃəs], *a.* Verbénacé.
verbiage ['və:biidʒ], *n.* Verbiage, *m.*
verbose [və:'bous], *a.* Verbeux, diffus, prolixe. **verbosely**, *adv.* Verbeusement.
verbosity [və:'bɔsiti], *n.* Verbosité, *f.*
verdancy ['və:dənsi], *n.* Verdure, *f.*
verdant ['və:dənt], *a.* Verdoyant, vert; (*fig.*) simple, crédule, innocent.
verd-antique [və:dæn'ti:k], *n.* Vert antique, *m.*; patine verte, *f.* (on ancient bronze).
Verde [və:d], Cape. (*Geol.*) Le Cap Vert, *m.*
verderer ['və:dərə], *n.* Verdier, garde forestier, *m. Verderer's range*, verderie, *f.*
verdict ['və:dikt], *n.* Verdict, *m.*, réponse du jury, *f.*; (*fig.*) jugement, arrêt, *m.*, opinion, *f. To bring in a verdict*, rendre un verdict.
verdigris ['və:digris], *n.* Vert-de-gris, verdet, *m.*
verdure ['və:djə], *n.* Verdure; (*fig.*) verdeur, *f.*

vert

verge [və:dʒ], *n.* Bord, *m.*, bordure; lisière (of a forest etc.); verge (rod), *f. On the verge of setting out*, à la veille de partir; *to be on the verge of ruin*, être à deux doigts de sa perte.—*v.i.* Pencher, incliner (vers), être sur le bord (de). *To verge upon*, approcher de, toucher à, confiner.
verger ['və:dʒə], *n.* Bedeau, huissier à verge, *m.*
veridical [və'ridikl], *a.* Véridique. **veridically**, *adv.* Véridiquement.
verifiable ['verifaiəbl], *a.* Vérifiable.
verification [verifi'keiʃən], *n.* Vérification, *f.*
verifier ['verifaiə], *n.* Vérificateur, *m.* **verify**, *v.t.* Vérifier, constater, contrôler (of accounts etc.).
verily ['verili], *adv.* En vérité, vraiment. **verisimilar** [veri'similə], *a.* Vraisemblable. **verisimilitude** [verisi'militju:d], *n.* Vraisemblance, *f.*
veritable ['veritəbl], *a.* Véritable. **veritably**, *adv.* Véritablement. **verity**, *n.* Vérité, *f.*; (*pl.*) faits réels, *m.pl. Of a verity*, en vérité.
verjuice ['və:dʒu:s], *n.* Verjus, *m.*
vermicelli [və:mi'seli], *n.* Vermicelle, *m.*
vermicelli-soup, *n.* Potage au vermicelle, *m.*
vermicular [və:'mikjulə], *a.* Vermiculaire. **vermiculated**, *a.* (*Arch.*) Vermiculé.
vermicule ['və:mikju:l], *n.* Vermisseau, *m.* **vermiform**, *a.* Vermiforme. **vermifuge**, *n.* Vermifuge, *m.*
vermilion [və'miljən], *n.* Vermillon, cinabre, *m.*—*a.* Vermeil, (de) vermillon.—*v.t.* Vermillonner.
vermin ['və:min], *n.* Vermine, *f.* **vermin-killer**, *n.* Poudre insecticide, *f.* **verminous**, *a.* Vermineux.
vermivorous [və:'mivərəs], *a.* Vermivore.
vermouth ['və:mu:θ], *n.* Vermouth, vermout, *m.*
vernacular [və'nækjulə], *a.* Du pays, indigène. —*n. One's own vernacular*, sa propre langue, sa langue maternelle.
vernal [və:nl], *a.* Du printemps, printanier; (*Bot.*) vernal; (*fig.*) de la jeunesse. **vernation** [-'neiʃən], *n.* Vernation, *f.*
Verona [və'rounə]. (*Geog.*) Vérone, *f.*
Veronica [və'rɔnikə]. Véronique, *f.* **veronica** [və'rɔnikə], *n.* Véronique, *f.*
verrucose ['verukous], *a.* Verruqueux.
versatile ['və:sətail], *a.* Éclectique, qui a des connaissances variées, des aptitudes diverses; qui se plie à tout.
versatility [və:sə'tiliti], *n.* Souplesse, faculté d'adaptation, *f.*, éclectisme, *m.*
verse [və:s], *n.* Vers, *m.*, poésie; strophe (stanza), *f.*; (*Bible*) verset, *m. In verse*, en vers; *to give chapter and verse*, donner des preuves authentiques.
versed [və:st], *a.* Versé (dans), exercé (dans).
versicle ['və:sikl], *n.* Petit vers, *m.*
versification [və:sifi'keiʃən], *n.* Versification, *f.*
versifier ['və:sifaiə], *n.* Versificateur, rimailleur, *m.* **versify**, *v.i.* Versifier, faire des vers.—*v.t.* Mettre en vers.
version ['və:ʃən], *n.* Version, traduction; interprétation (of facts), *f.*
verst [və:st], *n.* Verste, *f.*
versus ['və:səs], *prep.* Contre.
vert [və:t], *n.* (*Law*) Bois vert; droit de couper du bois vert; converti, *m.*—*v.r.* Se convertir.

vertebra ['vɜːtibrə], *n.* (*pl.* **vertebrae**) Vertèbre, *f.* **vertebral**, *a.* Vertébral. **vertebrate**, *a.* and *n.* Vertébré, *m.* **vertebrata** or **vertebrates**, *n.pl.* (*Zool.*) Vertébrés, animaux vertébrés, *m.pl.*

vertex ['vɜːteks], *n.* (*pl.* **vertices**) Sommet, *m.* (d'un angle, de la tête, etc.); zénith, *m.*

vertical ['vɜːtikl], *a.* Vertical. **verticality** [vɜːti'kæliti], *n.* Verticalité, *f.* **vertically** ['vɜːtikəli], *adv.* Verticalement.

verticil ['vɜːtisil], *n.* (*Bot.*) Verticille, *m.* **verticillate**, *a.* Verticillé.

vertiginous [vɜː'tidʒinəs], *a.* Vertigineux. **vertigo** ['vɜːtigou], *n.* Vertige, *m.*

vervain ['vɜːvein], *n.* (*Bot.*) Verveine, *f.*

verve [vɜːv], *n.* Verve, *f.*

very ['veri], *a.* Vrai, même, véritable. *I have the very thing for you,* j'ai votre affaire; *that's the very thing,* c'est cela même! *the very man,* l'homme même; *the very man we want,* l'homme qu'il nous faut; *the very thing,* la chose même; *the very thought makes me shudder,* la seule pensée m'en fait frémir; *this very day,* ce jour même, aujourd'hui même; *this very evening,* pas plus tard que ce soir, ce soir même; *to the very letter,* au pied de la lettre.—*adv.* Fort, bien, très. *At the very same time,* précisément au même instant; *so very,* si; *the very best,* tout ce qu'il y a de mieux; *the very same,* bien le même; *very well,* bien, très bien.

Very, *n. Very light,* fusée lumineuse, *f.*; *Very pistol,* pistolet à fusée, *m.*

vesicatory ['vesikeitəri], *n.* Vésicatoire, *m.* **vesicle** ['vesikl], *n.* (*Anat.*) Vésicule, *f.* **vesicular** [ve'sikjulə], *a.* Vésiculaire. **vesiculous,** *a.* Vésiculeux.

Vespasian [ves'peiʃjən]. (*Rom. Hist.*) Vespasien, *m.*

vesper ['vespə], *n.* Étoile du soir, *f.*; soir (evening), *m.*; (*pl.*) vêpres, *f.pl.* **vespertilio** [-'tiliou], *n.* Vespertilion, *m.* **vespertine** [-tain], *a.* Vespéral, du soir.

vespiform ['vespifɔːm], *a.* Vespiforme.

vessel [vesl], *n.* Vase; vaisseau, bâtiment, navire (ship), *m. Trading vessel,* bâtiment marchand, *m.*

vest [vest], *n.* Gilet, *m.*; (*under-*)*vest,* gilet de dessous, tricot de corps, *m.*—*v.t.* Vêtir, revêtir; investir (de). *The right is vested in the Crown,* le droit appartient à la couronne; *to be vested in,* être assigné à.—*v.i.* Échoir (à). *Vested interests,* les capitaux engagés, les intérêts; les droits acquis, *m.pl.*

vesta ['vestə], *n.* Allumette-bougie, *f.*

vestal [vestl], *a.* Vestale, de Vesta; (*fig.*) virginal, chaste.—*n.* Vestale, *f.*

vestibule ['vestibjuːl], *n.* Vestibule, *m.* **vestibule-train,** *n.* Train à couloir central, *m.*

vestige ['vestidʒ], *n.* Vestige, *m.,* trace, *f.*

vestment ['vestmənt], *n.* Vêtement, *m.* (de cérémonie); chasuble, *f.*

vestry ['vestri], *n.* Sacristie (place), *f. Select vestry,* conseil de fabrique, *m.* **vestry-board,** *n.* Fabrique, *f.,* conseil de fabrique, *m.* **vestry-clerk,** *n.* Secrétaire du conseil de fabrique, *m.* **vestryman,** *n.* Fabricien, marguillier, *m.* **vestry-meeting,** *n.* Réunion du conseil d'administration de la paroisse, *f.*

vesture ['vestʃə], *n.* Vêtements, *m.pl.*; (*Law*) produits de la terre, *m.pl.*

Vesuvian [və'sjuːviən], *a.* Vésuvien, du Vésuve.—*n.* Tison, *m.* **Vesuvius.** Le Vésuve, *m.*

vet [vet], *n.* (*fam.*) Vétérinaire, *m.*—*v.t.* (*fam.*) Examiner, traiter (a horse); revoir, corriger (books etc.).

vetch [vetʃ], *n.* Vesce, *f.* **vetchy,** *a.* Qui abonde en vesce.

veteran ['vetərən], *a.* Vieux, ancien, aguerri, expérimenté.—*n.* Vétéran; (*Am.*) ancien combattant, *m.*

veterinary ['vetərinəri], *a.* Vétérinaire. *Veterinary surgeon,* vétérinaire, *m.*

veto ['viːtou], *n.* Veto, *m.*—*v.t.* Mettre son veto à, interdire.

vex [veks], *v.t.* Fâcher, vexer, ennuyer, contrarier.

vexation [vek'seiʃən], *n.* Vexation, contrariété, *f.,* désagrément, chagrin, *m.* **vexatious,** *a.* Vexatoire; irritant, fâcheux, ennuyeux, contrariant (irritating). **vexatiously,** *adv.* D'une manière fâcheuse, d'une manière contrariante. **vexatiousness,** *n.* Caractère vexatoire, *m.,* contrariété, *f.*

vexed [vekst], *a.* Vexé, contrarié, fâché; (*fig.*) épineux; souvent débattu (of a question).

vexillar [vek'silə], *a.* Vexillaire, *m.* **vexillary** [vek'siləri], *n.* Vexillaire, *m.*

vexing, *a.* Contrariant, vexant, ennuyeux. **vexingly,** *adv.* D'une manière contrariante.

via ['vaiə], *prep.* Par, par voie de, via.

viability [vaiə'biliti], *n.* Viabilité, *f.*

viable ['vaiəbl], *a.* Viable.

viaduct ['vaiədʌkt], *n.* Viaduc, *m.*

vial ['vaiəl], *n.* Fiole, *f. To pour out the vials of one's wrath,* débonder sa colère.

viand ['vaiənd], *n.* (*usu. pl.*) Aliments, *m.pl.*; mets, *m.*

viaticum [vai'ætikəm], *n.* Viatique, *m.*

vibrate ['vaibreit *or* vai'breit], *v.i.* Vibrer, osciller.—*v.t.* Faire vibrer.

vibration [vai'breiʃən], *n.* Vibration, oscillation, *f.*

vibrating *or* **vibratory** ['vaibrətəri], *a.* Vibrant, vibratoire.

vibrator [vai'breitə], *n.* Vibrateur, *m.*

vibrio ['vibriou], *n.* Vibrion, *m.*

viburnum [vai'bəːnəm], *n.* Viorne, *f.*

vicar ['vikə], *n.* Vicaire (vicar-general); (*Engl. Ch.*) ministre; (*R.-C. Ch.*) curé (of a parish), *m.*

vicarage ['vikəridʒ], *n.* Cure, *f.,* presbytère, *m.*

vicarial [vi'keəriəl], *a.* De la cure, du curé. **vicariate,** *n.* Vicariat, *m.* **vicarious,** *a.* Vicarial, de vicaire; (*fig.*) de délégué, de substitution. **vicariously,** *adv.* Par délégation, par substitution.

vicarship, *n.* Office de vicaire, *m.*

vice [vais], *n.* Vice, défaut; étau (tool), *m. Free from vice,* exempt de vices, sans défaut; *vice squad,* brigade des mœurs (in police), *f.* **vice-admiral,** *n.* Vice-amiral, *m.* **vice-admiralty,** *n.* Vice-amirauté, *f.*

vice-chamberlain, *n.* Vice-chambellan, *m.*

vice-chancellor, *n.* Vice-chancelier; (*Univ.*) recteur, *m.*

vice-consul, *n.* Vice-consul, *m.* **vice-consulship,** *n.* Vice-consulat, *m.*

vicegerency [vais'dʒiərənsi], *n.* Vice-gérance, *f.* **vicegerent,** *n.* Vice-gérant, *m.*

vice-legate, *n.* Vice-légat, *f.*

vice-prefect, *n.* Vice-préfet, *m.*

vice-presidency, *n.* Vice-présidence, *f.* **vice-president,** *n.* Vice-président, *m.*
viceroy, *n.* Vice-roi, *m.* **vice-royal, vice-regal,** *a.* Vice-royal. **viceroyalty,** *n.* Vice-royauté, *f.*
Vichy ['viʃi]. (*Geog.*) Vichy.
Vichyist, *n.* (*pej.*) Vichyssois, partisan du gouvernement de Vichy (1940–44), *m.*
vicinage ['visinidʒ], *n.* Voisinage, *m.*
vicinity [vi'siniti], *n.* Voisinage, *m.*, proximité, *f.*, alentours, environs, *m.pl.*
vicious ['viʃəs], *a.* Vicieux; haineux. **viciously,** *adv.* Vicieusement; rageusement.
viciousness, *n.* Nature vicieuse, *f.*, vice, *m.*; malignité, *f.*
vicissitude [vi'sisitjuːd], *n.* Vicissitude, *f.*, changement, *m.*, révolution, *f.*
victim ['viktim], *n.* Victime, *f.* *He fell a victim to duty,* il tomba victime du devoir; *victim to,* victime de.
victimization [viktimai'zeiʃən], *n.* Tyrannisation, *f.*
victimize ['viktimaiz], *v.t.* Prendre (somebody) comme victime; exercer des représailles contre, tromper.
victor ['viktə], *n.* Vainqueur, *m.*
Victoria [vik'tɔːriə]. Victoria, Victoire, *f.*
victoria [vik'tɔːriə], *n.* Victoria (phaeton), *f.*
Victorian [vik'tɔːriən], *a. and n.* Victorien, *m.*, -ienne, *f.* **Victorianism,** *n.* Esprit victorien, *m.*
victorious [vik'tɔːriəs], *a.* Victorieux, de victoire. **victoriously,** *adv.* Victorieusement, en vainqueur.
victory ['viktəri], *n.* Victoire, *f.*
victual [vitl], *v.t.* Approvisionner, ravitailler.
victualler ['vitlə], *n.* Pourvoyeur, fournisseur (de vivres), *m.* *Licensed victualler,* débitant de boissons, marchand de vin, *m.*
victualling ['vitliŋ], *n.* Ravitaillement, *m.*; vivres, *m.pl.* **victualling-board,** *n.* Administration des vivres, *f.* **victualling-office,** *n.* Bureau des subsistances, *m.*
victuals [vitls], *n.pl.* Vivres, *m.pl.*, provisions, victuailles, *f.pl.*; (*colloq.*) mangeaille, *f.*
vicugna or **vicuña** [vi'kuːnjə], *n.* Vigogne, *f.*
videlicet [vai'diːlisit], *adv.* Savoir, à savoir, c'est-à-dire.
vie [vai], *v.i.* Rivaliser, lutter (de); le disputer (à), faire assaut (de). *They vied with each other as to who . . . ,* c'était à qui . . . ; *to vie with,* le disputer avec, entrer en rivalité avec; *to vie with each other,* rivaliser avec, à l'envi l'un de l'autre, c'est à qui . . . ; *while each to be the loudest vies,* tandis qu'ils crient à qui mieux mieux.
Vienna [vi'enə]. (*Geog.*) Vienne, *f.*
Vietnam [vjet'næm]. (*Geog.*) Le Vietnam, *m.* **Vietnamese,** *a. and n.* Vietnamien, *m.*, -ienne, *f.*
view [vjuː], *n.* Vue, perspective, scène, *f.*, coup d'œil, point de vue, *m.*; apparence (appearance), *f.*; regard (look), aperçu, examen (mental examination), *m.*; intention (intention), *f.*, but, dessein, *m.*; opinion, pensée (opinion), *f.* *Bird's eye view,* plan à vol d'oiseau, *m.*; *private view,* vernissage, *m.*; *field of view* (of a telescope), champ, *m.*; *in view,* en vue; *in view of,* en considération de; *on view,* exposé, ouvert au public; *point of view,* point de vue, *m.*, manière de voir, façon de juger, *f.*; *to take a correct view of,* envisager bien; *to take a different view of,* apprécier

différemment, envisager d'une autre manière; *with a view to,* en vue de, dans le but de.— *v.t.* Regarder; contempler; considérer; voir; examiner; inspecter; explorer; envisager, considérer (to survey intellectually).
viewer, *n.* Spectateur, *m.*, -trice, *f.*; téléspectateur, *m.*, -trice, *f.*
view-finder, *n.* (*Phot.*) Viseur, *m.*
viewing, *n.* Examen, *m.*, inspection, *f.*
viewless, *a.* Invisible.
view-point, *n.* Point de vue, *m.*
vigil ['vidʒil], *n.* Veille, veillée, (*Eccles.*) vigile, *f.*
vigilance ['vidʒiləns], *n.* Vigilance, *f.* **vigilant,** *a.* Vigilant, éveillé; circonspect. **vigilantly,** *adv.* Avec vigilance.
vignette [vi'njet], *n.* Vignette, *f.*; (*Phot.*) dégradé, *m.*—*v.t.* Dégrader. **vignetter** or **vignettist,** *n.* Vignettiste, *m.*
vigorous ['vigərəs], *a.* Vigoureux. **vigorously,** *adv.* Vigoureusement.
vigour ['vigə] or **vigorousness,** *n.* Vigueur, *f.*
vile [vail], *a.* Vil, abject, bas; sans valeur; exécrable, abominable, détestable. **vilely,** *adv.* Vilement, lâchement, honteusement.
vileness, *n.* Bassesse, *f.*
vilification [vilifi'keiʃən], *n.* Diffamation, *f.*, dénigrement, *m.*
vilifier ['vilifaiə], *n.* Diffamateur, *m.*
vilify ['vilifai], *v.t.* Vilipender, dénigrer.
villa ['vilə], *n.* Villa, maison de campagne, *f.*
villadom, *n.* La banlieue, *f.*, les classes moyennes, *f.pl.*
village ['vilidʒ], *n.* Village, *m.* **villager,** *n.* Villageois, *m.*, -oise, *f.*
villain ['vilən], *n.* Scélérat, misérable, gredin; (*Feudal Law*) vilain, *m.*; (*Theat.*) traître, *m.*
villainage, *n.* Servage, *m.*, servitude, *f.*
villainous, *a.* Vil, infâme, de scélérat; méchant, vilain, mauvais. **villainously,** *adv.* Vilement, horriblement, d'une manière infâme. **villainy,** *n.* Scélératesse, vilenie, *f.*
*****villein** ['vilən], *n.* Vilain, serf, *m.*
villose [vi'lous] or **villous** ['viləs], *a.* Villeux.
villosity [vi'lɔsiti], *n.* Villosité, *f.*
vim [vim], *n.* (*fam.*) Vigueur, énergie, *f.*
vinaceous [vai'neiʃəs], *a.* Vineux.
vinaigrette [vinei'gret], *n.* Flacon de sels, *m.*
vindicable ['vindikəbl], *a.* Défendable; justifiable, soutenable. **vindicate,** *v.t.* Soutenir, défendre, justifier; venger (to avenge).
vindication [vindi'keiʃən], *n.* Défense, justification, *f.*, maintien (of an opinion), *m.*
vindicator ['vindikeitə], *n.* Défenseur, *m.*
vindicatory, *a.* Justificatif; vengeur.
vindictive [vin'diktiv], *a.* Vindicatif. **vindictively,** *adv.* D'une manière vindicative.
vindictiveness, *n.* Esprit de vengeance, *m.*
vine [vain], *n.* Vigne, *f.*; plant (plant), *m.*
vine-branch, *n.* Branche de vigne, *f.*, sarment, pampre, *m.* **vine-clad,** *a.* Couvert de vignes. **vine-country,** *n.* Pays vignoble, *m.* **vine-dresser,** *n.* Vigneron, *m.* **vine-grower,** *n.* Propriétaire de vignes, viticulteur, *m.* **vine-growing,** *n.* Viticulture, *f.* **vine-harvest,** *n.* Vendange, *f.* **vine-prop,** *n.* Échalas, *m.*
vinegar ['vinigə], *n.* Vinaigre, *m.*; (*fig.*) aigreur, *f.* **vinegar-cruet,** *n.* Burette à vinaigre, *f.* **vinegar-maker,** *n.* Vinaigrier, *m.* **vinegar-tree,** *n.* Vinaigrier, *m.* **vinegary,** *a.* De vinaigre; revêche (of face); acerbe, aigre (of voice).

vinery ['vainəri], *n.* Serre à vignes, forcerie, *f.*

vineyard ['vinjəd], *n.* Vigne, *f.*; vignoble (large vineyard), *m.*

vinicultural [vini'kʌltʃərəl], *a.* Vinicole.

viniculture ['vinikʌltʃə], *n.* Viniculture *f.*

vinose ['vainous] or **vinous**, *a.* Vineux.

vinosity [vai'nɔsiti], *n.* Caractère vineux, *m.*; vinosité, *f.*

vintage ['vintidʒ], *n.* Vendange; vinée, récolte de vin (crop), *f.*; vendanges (time of gathering), *f.pl.* *A vintage wine*, un vin de marque, d'appellation contrôlée, *m.* **vintager**, *n.* Vendangeur, *m.*

vintner ['vintnə], *n.* Négociant en vins, *m.* **vintnery**, *n.* Entrepôt de vin, *m.*

viny ['vaini], *a.* De vigne, de raisin; de vignoble.

viol ['vaiəl], *n.* Viole, *f.*

viola (1) [vi'oulə], *n.* (*Mus.*) Alto, *m.*; *viole, *f.* *Viola player*, altiste, *m.*

viola (2) ['vaiələ], *n.* (*Bot.*) Violette, *f.*

violable ['vaiələbl], *a.* Qui peut être violé, violable.

violaceous [vaiə'leiʃəs], *a.* Violacé.

violate ['vaiəleit], *v.t.* Violer, faire violence à; déranger, troubler (to disturb); outrager, profaner (to profane).

violation [vaiə'leiʃən], *n.* Violation, infraction, *f.*, viol (rape), *m.*

violator ['vaiəleitə], *n.* Violateur, *m.*, -trice, *f.*

violence ['vaiələns], *n.* Violence, *f.* *To do violence to*, faire violence à, violenter; *to do violence to one's feelings*, se faire violence; *to use violence*, user de violence (envers); *with violence* (of robbery), à main armée.

violent ['vaiələnt], *a.* Violent; fort, aigu; atroce (of pain etc.). *To die a violent death*, mourir de mort violente; *to lay violent hands on oneself*, attenter à ses jours. **violently**, *adv.* Violemment, avec violence.

violet ['vaiələt], *n.* Violette (plant), *f.*; violet (colour), *m.* *Violet-powder*, poudre de riz parfumée, *f.*

violin [vaiə'lin], *n.* Violon, *m.* **violinist**, *n.* Violoniste, *m.*

violist ['vaiəlist], *n.* *Violiste, *m.* or *f.*; altiste, *m.* or *f.*

violoncellist [vaiələn'tʃelist], *n.* Violoncelliste, *m.* or *f.* **violoncello** [vaiələn'tʃelou], *n.* Violoncelle, *m.*

viper ['vaipə], *n.* Vipère, *f.* **viper's-bugloss**, *n.* Vipérine, *f.* **viper's-grass**, *n.* Scorsonère, *f.*; salsifis noir, *m.* **viperine**, *a.* Vipérin, de vipère. **viperous** or **viperish**, *a.* De vipère; (*fig.*) venimeux; malfaisant.

virago [vi'reigou or vi'rɑːgou], *n.* Virago, *f.*, dragon de femme, *m.*; mégère, *f.*

virelay ['virəlei], *n.* Virelai, *m.*

Virgil ['vəːdʒil], Virgile, *m.*

Virgilian [vəː'dʒilian], *a.* Virgilien.

virgin ['vəːdʒin], *n.* Vierge, *f.*—*a.* Vierge, virginal, de vierge. **virgin's-bower**, *n.* (*Bot.*) Clématite des haies, *f.*

virginal, *a.* Virginal, de vierge. **virginally**, *adv.* Virginalement. **virginals**, *n.pl.* (*Mus.*) Virginal(e), *f.*

Virginia [vəː'dʒinjə]. Virginie (of persons); (*Geog.*) la Virginie, *f.*

virginia-creeper [vəː'dʒinjə kriːpə], *n.* Vigne vierge, *f.*

virginity [vəː'dʒiniti], *n.* Virginité, *f.*

Virgo ['vəːgou]. (*Astron.*) La Vierge, *f.*

viridity [vi'riditi], *n.* Verdeur, fraîcheur, *f.*

virile ['virail], *a.* Viril, mâle.

virility [vi'riliti], *n.* Virilité, nature virile, *f.*

virtu [vəː'tuː], *n.* Goût artistique, sentiment de l'art, *m.* *Articles of virtu*, objets d'art, *m.pl.*; curiosités, *f.pl.*

virtual ['vəːtjuəl], *a.* Virtuel; de fait, en fait. *Virtual certainty*, quasi certitude, *f.* *Virtual force*, force potentielle, *f.* **virtuality** [-'æliti], *n.* Virtualité, *f.* **virtually**, *adv.* Virtuellement, de fait.

virtue ['vəːtjuː], *n.* Vertu; (*fig.*) force, valeur, *f.*, mérite, *m.* *By virtue of*, au moyen de; *in virtue of*, en vertu de; *woman of easy virtue*, femme de petite vertu, *f.* **virtueless**, *a.* Sans vertu, dénué de mérite, sans valeur.

virtuosity [vəːrtju'ositi], *n.* Virtuosité, *f.*

virtuoso [vəːtju'ousou], *n.* (*pl.* **virtuosi**) Virtuose, amateur d'arts, connaisseur, *m.*

virtuous ['vəːtjuəs], *a.* Vertueux. **virtuously**, *adv.* Vertueusement. **virtuousness**, *n.* Vertu, *f.*

virulence ['viruləns], *n.* Virulence; (*fig.*) aigreur, *f.* **virulent**, *a.* Virulent. **virulently**, *adv.* Avec virulence.

virus ['vaiərəs], *n.* Virus, *m.*

vis [vis], *n.* (*pl.* **vires** ['vaiəriːz]) Force, *f.* **vis inertiae** [i'nəːʃiiː], *n.* Force d'inertie, *f.* **vis viva** ['vaivə], *n.* Force vive.

visa ['viːzə], *n.* Visa, *m.*—*v.t.* Viser.

visage ['vizidʒ], *n.* Visage, *m.*, figure, *f.* **visaged**, *a.* Au visage (de).

viscera ['visərə], *n.pl.* Viscères, *m.pl.* **visceral**, *a.* Viscéral.

viscid ['visid], *a.* Visqueux.

viscidity [vi'siditi], *n.* Viscosité, *f.*

viscosity [vis'kositi], *n.* Viscosité, *f.*

viscount ['vaikaunt], *n.* Vicomte, *m.* **viscountess**, *n.* Vicomtesse, *f.* **viscountship** or **viscounty**, *n.* Vicomté, *f.*

viscous ['viskəs], *a.* Visqueux, glutineux.

visé ['viːzei], *n.* [VISA].

Vishnu ['viʃnuː]. (*Myth.*) Vishnou, *m.*

visibility [vizi'biliti] or **visibleness**, *n.* Visibilité, *f.* **visibly**, *adv.* Visiblement, à vue d'œil.

visible ['vizibl], *a.* Visible; évident, clair, manifeste.

Visigoth ['vizigɔθ], *n.* Wisigoth, *m.*

vision ['viʒən], *n.* Vision, vue, *f.* **visional**, *a.* De vision; imaginaire. **visionary**, *a.* Visionnaire; chimérique.—*n.* Visionnaire, *m.*

visionless, *a.* Sans regard, éteint (eye); (*fig.*) dépourvu d'imagination.

visit ['vizit], *n.* Visite, *f.*; séjour (a stay), *m.* *On a visit*, en visite (chez); *to pay a visit*, faire une visite.—*v.t.* Visiter, faire une visite à, rendre visite à, aller voir; punir, châtier. *To visit upon*, se venger (de *or* sur).—*v.i.* Faire des visites.

visitant ['vizitənt], *n.* Visiteur, (*R.-C. Ch.*) visitant, *m.*

visitation [vizi'teiʃən], *n.* Inspection, tournée; épreuve, affliction (of God etc.), *f.* *To die by visitation of God*, mourir subitement.

visiting, *n.* Visites, *f.pl.*—*a.* En visite, de visite. *Visiting teacher*, professeur particulier, *m.*

visiting-card, *n.* Carte de visite, *f.*

visitor ['vizitə], *n.* Visiteur, *m.*; (*official*) inspecteur, *m.*; (*pl.*) invités, hôtes; voyageurs (in hotel), *m.pl.* *She has visitors,* elle a du monde.

visor ['vaizə], *n.* Visière, *f.*; *masque, m.* **visored,** *a.* Visière baissée; (*fig.*) masqué.

vista ['vistə], *n.* Vue, perspective; percée, éclaircie (in woods), *f.* **vistaed,** *a.* Qui offre de belles perspectives.

Vistula ['vistjulə]. (*Geog.*) La Vistule, *f.*

visual ['vizjuəl], *a.* Visuel. **visualize,** *v.t.* Rendre visible; se représenter.

vital [vaitl], *a.* Vital, de vie; (*fig.*) capital, essentiel. *Vital organ,* partie vitale, *f.* **vitalism,** *n.* Vitalisme, *m.* **vitalist,** *n.* Vitaliste, *m.*

vitality [vai'tæliti], *n.* Vitalité, *f.*

vitalize ['vaitəlaiz], *v.t.* Vivifier, donner la vie à; (*fig.*) animer.

vitally, *adv.* Vitalement.

vitals, *n.pl.* Parties vitales, *f.pl.*

vitamin ['vitəmin], *n.* Vitamine, *f.* *Vitamin deficiency,* avitaminose, *f.*

vitelline [vi'telin], *a.* (*Biol.*) Vitellin.

vitiate ['viʃieit], *v.t.* Vicier; (*fig.*) gâter, corrompre.

vitiation [viʃi'eiʃən], *n.* Viciation; (*fig.*) corruption, invalidation *f.*

viticulture ['vitikʌltʃə], *n.* Viticulture, *f.* **viticultural,** *a.* Viticole. **viticulturist,** *n.* Viticulteur, *m.*

vitreous ['vitriəs], *a.* Vitreux; (*Anat.*) vitré.

vitrescible [vi'tresibl], *a.* Vitrescible.

vitrification [vitrifi'keiʃən], *n.* Vitrification, *f.*

vitrifiable ['vitrifaiəbl], *a.* Vitrifiable.

vitrify, *v.t.* Vitrifier.—*v.i.* Se vitrifier.

vitriol ['vitriəl], *n.* Vitriol, *m.* *Oil of vitriol,* huile de vitriol, *f.*, acide sulfurique, *m.* **vitriol-thrower,** *n.* Vitrioleur, *m.*

vitriolation [-'leiʃən], *n.* Vitriolisation, *f.*

vitriolic [-'ɔlik], *a.* Vitriolique.

vitriolize, *v.t.* Convertir en sulfate. **vitriolized,** *a.* Vitriolé.

vituline ['vitjulain], *a.* De veau.

vituperable [vi'tju:pərəbl], *a.* Blâmable, répréhensible.

vituperate [vai'tju:pəreit], *v.t.* Vilipender, faire des reproches à, injurier.

vituperation [vaitju:pə'reiʃən], *n.* Reproches, *m.pl.*, injures, invectives, *f.pl.*

vituperative [vai'tju:pərətiv], *a.* Injurieux, hargneux.

vivacious [vi'veiʃəs *or* vai-], *a.* Vif, vivace, animé. **vivaciously,** *adv.* Vivement, avec vivacité.

vivaciousness *or* **vivacity** [vi'væsiti], *n.* Vivacité, *f.*

vivarium [vi'vɛəriəm *or* vai-] *or* **vivary** ['vivəri], *n.* Vivier, *m.*

vives ['vaivz], *n.pl.* (*Vet.*) Avives, *f.pl.*

vivid ['vivid], *a.* Vif, frappant, éclatant. **vividly,** *adv.* D'une manière frappante, avec éclat. **vividness,** *n.* Vivacité, vigueur, *f.*, éclat, *m.*

vivification [vivifi'keiʃən], *n.* Vivification, *f.*, vivifiement, *m.*

vivify ['vivifai], *v.t.* Vivifier. **vivifying,** *a.* Vivifiant.

viviparous [vi'vipərəs], *a.* Vivipare. **viviparity** [-'pæriti], *n.* Viviparité, *f.*, viviparisme, *m.*

vivisect [vivi'sekt], *v.i.* Faire de la vivisection.

vivisection [vivi'sekʃən], *n.* Vivisection, *f.*

vivisecter ['vivisektə], *n.* Vivisecteur, *m.*

vixen ['viksən], *n.* Renarde (female fox); mégère (quarrelsome woman), *f.* **vixenish,** *a.* De mégère, méchante.

viz. [VIDELICET] (*usually read* Namely).

vizier [vi'ziə], *n.* Vizir, *m.* **vizierate,** *n.* Vizirat, viziriat, *m.*

vocable ['voukəbl], *n.* Vocable, mot, *m.*

vocabulary [vou'kæbjuləri], *n.* Vocabulaire, *m.* **vocabulist,** *n.* Vocabuliste, auteur d'un vocabulaire, *m.*

vocal [voukl], *a.* Vocal, de la voix; doué de la parole (having a voice). *Vocal opposition,* opposition bruyante, *f.* **vocalist,** *n.* Chanteur, *m.*, cantatrice, *f.*

vocalization [voukəlai'zeiʃən], *n.* Vocalisation, *f.*

vocalize ['voukəlaiz], *v.t.*, *v.i.* Vocaliser. **vocally,** *adv.* Par la voix, vocalement.

vocation [vo'keiʃən], *n.* Vocation; profession, *f.*, état, emploi, métier; appel (summons), *m.* **vocational,** *a.* Professionnel. *Vocational guidance,* orientation professionnelle, *f.*

vocative ['vɔkətiv], *n.* Vocatif, *m.* *In the vocative,* au vocatif.

vociferate [və'sifəreit], *v.t.*, *v.i.* Vociférer. **vociferation** [-'reiʃən], *n.* Vocifération, *f.* **vociferous,** *a.* Qui vocifère, bruyant. **vociferously,** *adv.* En vociférant.

vodka ['vɔdkə], *n.* Vodka, *f.*

vogue [voug], *n.* Vogue, *f. In vogue,* en vogue; *to bring into vogue,* mettre en vogue.

voice [vɔis], *n.* Voix, *f. At the top of one's voice,* à tue-tête; *his voice is cracking,* sa voix mue; *in a low voice,* à voix basse; *my voice failed me,* la voix me manqua; *to know by the voice,* reconnaître à la voix; *to know how to manage one's voice,* savoir moduler sa voix; *with one voice,* unanimement; *without a dissentient voice,* à l'unanimité des voix.—*v.t.* Donner une voix à, publier, rapporter; (*Mus.*) régler le ton de; (*Phon.*) voiser. *To voice* (public opinion), exprimer, interpréter.

voiceless, *a.* Sans voix; aphone; (*Phon.*) non-voisée, soufflée (consonant).

void [vɔid], *v.t.* Vider, évacuer; verser, rejeter (to send out); (*Law*) annuler, résilier; laisser vacant (to leave vacant).—*a.* Vide, vacant; nul, de nul effet (null). *Null and void,* nul et non avenu; *to render void,* rendre nul, annuler; *void of,* dépourvu de, dénué de.—*n.* Vide, espace vide, *m.*

voidable ['vɔidəbl], *a.* Qui peut être annulé, annulable.

voidance ['vɔidəns], *n.* Évacuation; expulsion (d'un bénéfice); vacance, *f.*; (*Law*) annulation, résiliation, *f.*

voivode ['vɔivoud], *n.* Voïvode, *m.* **voivodeship,** *n.* Voïvodat, *m.*

volatile ['vɔlətail], *a.* Volatil; qui vole, volant; inconstant, volage, étourdi (fickle). **volatility** [vɔlə'tiliti], *n.* Volatilité, *f.*

volatilization [vələtilai'zeiʃən], *n.* Volatilisation, *f.*

volatilize [və'lætilaiz], *v.t.* Volatiliser.—*v.i.* Se volatiliser.

volcanic [vɔl'kænik], *a.* Volcanique. **volcano** [vɔl'keinou], *n.* Volcan, *m.*

vole [voul], *n.* Campagnol, *m.*

volition [vo'liʃən], *n.* Volition, volonté, *f. Of one's own volition,* de son propre gré.

volley ['vɔli], *n.* Décharge, salve (of musketry); volée (of cannon); bordée, *f.*, torrent (of abuse) *m.*; grêle (of stones etc.), *f.*; (*Ten.*) (balle de) volée, *f.* *To fire a volley*, faire une décharge de mousqueterie, envoyer une volée, tirer une salve.—*v.t.* (*Ten.*) Renvoyer (la balle) de volée. **volley-firing**, *n.* Feu de peloton, feu de salve, *m.*

volplane ['vɔlplein], *n.* Vol plané, *m.*—*v.i.* Planer, faire du vol plané. *To land by volplaning*, atterrir en vol plané.

Volscian ['vɔlʃən], *a.* Volsque.

volt (1) [vɔlt], *n.* Volte (of a horse etc.), *f.* *To make a volt*, (*Fenc.*) volter.

volt (2) [voult], *n.* (*Elec.*) Volt, *m.*

voltage ['voultidʒ], *n.* Voltage, *m.*

voltaic [vol'teiik], *a.* Voltaïque.

voltaism ['vɔltəizm], *n.* Voltaïsme, *m.*

volte-face ['vɔltfɑːs], *n.* Volte-face, *f.*

voltmeter ['vɔltmiːtə], *n.* Voltmètre, *m.*

volubility [vɔljuˈbiliti], *n.* Volubilité; volubilité de langue, *f.*

voluble ['vɔljubl], *a.* Délié, bien pendu (of the tongue); facile, coulant (of speech). **volubly**, *adv.* Avec volubilité.

volume ['vɔljum], *n.* Volume, *m.*; masse, *f.*; tome (book); nuage, tourbillon (of smoke), *m.*; étendue (of the voice), *f.* *A three-volume novel*, un roman en trois volumes; *that speaks volumes*, cela en dit long.

voluminous [vəˈljuːminəs], *a.* Volumineux. **voluminously**, *adv.* D'une manière volumineuse. **voluminousness**, *n.* Nature volumineuse; grosseur, *f.*

voluntarily ['vɔləntərili], *adv.* Volontairement, spontanément, de bonne volonté. **voluntariness**, *n.* Spontanéité, *f.* **voluntary**, *a.* Volontaire, spontané; libre; intentionnel, fait avec intention. *Voluntary organization*, organisation bénévole, *f.*—*n.* (*Mus.*) Solo, *m.*, improvisation d'orgue, de trompette, etc.; (*sch.*) épreuve facultative, *f.*

volunteer [vɔlənˈtiə], *n.* Volontaire, *m.*—*a.* De volontaire, des volontaires.—*v.t.* Offrir volontairement.—*v.i.* S'offrir (de); offrir ses services; s'engager comme volontaire. *To volunteer to do something*, s'offrir à faire quelque chose.

voluptuary [vəˈlʌptjuəri], *n.* Voluptueux, épicurien, *m.* **voluptuous**, *a.* Voluptueux. **voluptuously**, *adv.* Voluptueusement. **voluptuousness**, *n.* Volupté, *f.*

volute [vəˈljuːt], *n.* Volute, *f.* **voluted**, *a.* Voluté.

volution [vəˈljuːʃən], *n.* Spirale, *f.*

vomic ['vɔmik], *a.* Vomique. **vomica**, *n.* Vomique, *f.* *Nux-vomica*, noix vomique, *f.*

vomit ['vɔmit], *v t.* Vomir, rendre, émettre.—*v.i.* Vomir.—*n.* Vomissement, *m.*, matières vomies, *f.pl.*; (*Pharm.*) vomitif, *m.* **vomiting**, *n.* Vomissement, *m.* **vomitory**, *a.* Vomitif, émétique.—*n.* Vomitoire, *m.*

voodoo ['vuːduː], *n.* Vaudou, *m.*

voracious [vəˈreiʃəs], *a.* Vorace; dévorant, d'enfer (of the appetite). **voraciously**, *adv.* Avec voracité. **voraciousness** or **voracity** [-ˈræsiti], *n.* Voracité, *f.*

vortex ['vɔːteks], *n.* (*pl.* **vortices** [-tisiːz]) Tourbillon, *m.* *Small vortex*, vorticule, *m.*

vortical ['vɔːtikl], *a.* Tourbillonnant, en tourbillon.

vorticel ['vɔːtisel], *n.* Vorticelle, *f.*

votaress ['voutəris], *n.* Adoratrice, sectatrice, *f.* **votary**, *n.* Adorateur; (*fig.*) sectateur, ami, admirateur, *m.*

vote [vout], *n.* Vote, *m.*; voix; opinion, décision, résolution, *f.*; crédit (sum voted), *m.* *To carry a vote*, adopter une résolution; *to pass a vote of thanks to*, voter des remerciements à; *to put to the vote*, mettre aux voix.—*v.t.* Voter. *To vote in*, élire, déclarer.—*v.i.* Voter.

voter ['voutə], *n.* Votant, *m.*

voting ['voutiŋ], *n.* Vote, *m.* *Voting-paper*, bulletin de vote, *m.*

votive ['voutiv], *a.* Votif, voué.

vouch [vautʃ], *v.t.* Prendre à témoin, attester; garantir, affirmer (to affirm).—*v.i.* Témoigner (de), répondre (de). *To vouch for the success of*, se porter garant du succès de.

vouchee [vauˈtʃiː], *n.* Caution, personne appelée en garantie, *f.*

voucher ['vautʃə], *n.* Garant, *m.*, garantie, *f.*, titre, *m.*, pièce justificative, *f.* *Luncheon voucher*, bon de repas, *m.* **vouchor**, *n.* (*Law*) Demandeur en garantie, *m.*, demanderesse en garantie, *f.*

vouchsafe [vautʃˈseif], *v.t.* Daigner, accorder. ***vouchsafement**, *n.* Condescendance, *f.*

vow [vau], *n.* Vœu, *m.*—*v.t.* Vouer, dévouer, consacrer (à).—*v.i.* Faire un vœu, faire vœu (de); jurer, protester.

vowel ['vauəl], *n.* Voyelle, *f.* **vowelled**, *a.* Formé de voyelles.

voyage ['vɔiidʒ], *n.* Voyage (par mer), *m.*, traversée, *f.* *Home voyage*, voyage de retour; *on a voyage*, en voyage, en mer; *outward voyage*, voyage d'aller; *pleasant voyage to you!* bon voyage!—*v.i.* Voyager, naviguer.

voyager ['vɔiidʒə], *n.* Voyageur, passager, *m.*, -euse, -ère, *f.*

Vulcan ['vʌlkən]. Vulcain, *m.*

vulcanian [vʌlˈkeiniən], *a.* Vulcanien.

vulcanite ['vʌlkənait], *n.* Caoutchouc vulcanisé or durci, *m.*, ébonite, *f.* **vulcanization** [-ˈzeiʃən], *n.* Vulcanisation, *f.*

vulcanize ['vʌlkənaiz], *v.t.* Vulcaniser.

vulgar ['vʌlgə], *a.* Vulgaire, commun, du peuple; grossier, trivial, de mauvais goût.—*n.* Le vulgaire, *m.* **vulgarism**, *n.* Expression vulgaire, *f.*

vulgarity [vʌlˈgæriti], *n.* Vulgarité, *f.*, vulgarisme, *m.*, grossièreté, *f.*; mauvais goût, *m.* **vulgarization** [-aiˈzeiʃən], *n.* Vulgarisation, *f.*

vulgarize ['vʌlgəraiz], *v.t.* Vulgariser, populariser. *To become vulgarized*, se vulgariser. **vulgarizer**, *n.* Vulgarisateur, *m.* **vulgarly**, *adv.* Communément; vulgairement; avec mauvais goût, grossièrement.

Vulgate ['vʌlgit], *n.* Vulgate, *f.*

vulnerability [vʌlnərəˈbiliti], *n.* Vulnérabilité, *f.*

vulnerable ['vʌlnərəbl], *a.* Vulnérable, que l'on peut blesser. **vulnerably**, *adv.* Vulnérablement. **vulnerary**, *a.* and *n.* Vulnéraire, *m.*

vulpine ['vʌlpain], *a.* De renard; (*fig.*) rusé.

vulture ['vʌltʃə], *n.* Vautour *m.* **vulturine**, *a.* De vautour; (*fig.*) rapace.

vulva ['vʌlvə], *n.* Vulve, *f.* **vulvitis** [-ˈvaitis], *n.* Vulvite, *f.*

vying [VIE].

W

W, w ['dʌbəlju:]. Vingt-troisième lettre de l'alphabet, *m*.
wabble [WOBBLE].
wad [wɔd], *n*. Bourre (for fire-arms etc.), *f*.; tampon, tas, paquet (little bundle), *m*.—*v.t*. Bourrer (fire-arms etc.); garnir de ouate, ouater (a garment etc.). **wad-hook,** *n*. (*Artill*.) Tire-bourre, *m*.
wadded, *a*. Ouaté (de). **wadding,** *n*. Bourre (for fire-arms); ouate (padding), *f*., rembourrage, *m*.
waddle [wɔdl], *v.i*. Se dandiner comme un canard, se balancer; (*fig*.) patauger. **waddling,** *n*. Dandinement, *m*. **waddlingly,** *adv*. En se dandinant.
wade [weid], *v.i*. Marcher (dans l'eau, dans la vase, dans le sable, etc.); passer à gué; se traîner, avancer péniblement (to move with difficulty). *To wade in the mud*, patauger dans la boue; *to wade through*, traverser, passer, (*fig*.) examiner laborieusement, étudier à fond.—*v.t*. Traverser à gué, guéer.
wader, *n*. Échassier (bird), *m*.; (*pl*.) bottes d'égoutier, grandes bottes de pêche, *f.pl*.
wadi ['wɔdi], *n*. Oued, *m*.
wafer ['weifə], *n*. Pain à cacheter, *m*.; gaufrette; (*R.-C. Ch*.) hostie, *f*.; cachet, *m*. (of powder).—*v.t*. Mettre un pain à cacheter à, cacheter.
waffle (1) [wɔfl], *n*. Gaufre, *f*. **waffle-iron,** *n*. Gaufrier, *m*.; moule à gaufres, *m*.
waffle (2) [wɔfl], *v.i*. Épiloguer.
waft [wæft], *v.t*. Porter, transporter; faire flotter; soutenir (to buoy up). *To waft on high*, faire flotter vers les cieux, porter au ciel.—*v.i*. Flotter dans l'air *or* sur l'eau.—*n*. Bouffée, *f*.
wag [wæg], *n*. Badin, plaisant, farceur, (*colloq*.) loustic, *m*.—*v.t*. Remuer, agiter, secouer.—*v.i*. S'agiter, remuer, se mouvoir.
wage [weidʒ], *v.t*. Faire. *To wage war with*, faire la guerre à.—*n*. [WAGES].
wage-earner, *n*. Salarié; ouvrier, *m*.
wager ['weidʒə], *n*. Gageure [ga'ʒy:r], *f*., pari, *m*. *To lay a wager*, faire une gageure, gager, parier (que).—*v.t*. Gager, parier.
wagerer ['weidʒərə], *n*. Parieur, gageur, *m*.
wages ['weidʒiz], *n.pl*. Gages (of servants), *m.pl*.; salaire, *m*., paye (of workmen), *f*.; traitement (of civil servants), *m*.; (*fig*.) prix, *m*., récompense, *f*. *Week's wages*, semaine, *f*.
wages-book, *n*. Livre de paye, *m*.
waggery ['wægəri], *n*. Espièglerie, plaisanterie, *f*. **waggish,** *a*. Badin, malin, espiègle, plaisant, facétieux. *Waggish trick*, espièglerie, plaisanterie, farce, *f*. **waggishly,** *adv*. Plaisamment, avec espièglerie, pour badiner.
waggishness, *n*. Badinage, *m*., espièglerie, plaisanterie, *f*.
waggle [wægl], *v.i*. Frétiller.—*v.t*. Remuer.
waggon [WAGON].
Wagnerian [vɑːgˈniəriən], *a*. and *n*. Wagnérien, *m*. **Wagnerism** ['vɑːgnərizm], *n*. Wagnérisme, *m*. **Wagnerite,** *n*. Wagnériste, *m*.
wagon ['wægən], *n*. Charrette, *f*., chariot, *m*.; voiture de roulage, *f*.; (*Mil*.) caisson, fourgon; (*Rail*.) wagon, *m*. *Pontoon wagon,*

haquet à bateau *or* à ponton, *m*. **wagonload,** *n*. Pleine voiture, charretée, *f*.
wagtail ['wægteil], *n*. Hochequeue, *m*., bergeronnette, *f*.
waif [weif], *n*. Épave, *f*. *Waifs and strays* (children), enfants abandonnés, *m.pl*.
wail [weil], *v.i*. Pleurer, gémir, se lamenter.—*v.t*. Pleurer, lamenter.—*n*. Cri, *m*., lamentation, plainte, *f*. **wailful,** *a*. Plaintif, lamentable. **wailing,** *n*. Lamentation, plainte, *f*., gémissement, *m*.
wain [wein], *n*. Charrette, *f*. *Charles's Wain*, le grand Chariot, *m*.
wainscot ['weinzkət], *n*. Lambris, *m*., boiserie, *f*.—*v.t*. Lambrisser, boiser (de). **wainscotting,** *n*. Lambrissage, *m*., boiserie, *f*.; bois de lambris (material), *m*.
waist [weist], *n*. Ceinture, taille, *f*., mi-corps; (*Naut*.) entre-deux, *m*. **waistband,** *n*. Ceinture (of trousers etc.), *f*. **waist-belt,** *n*. Ceinturon, *m*.
waistcoat ['weis(t)kout *or* 'weskət], *n*. Gilet, *m*. *Straight waistcoat*, camisole de force, *f*. **waistcoating,** *n*. Étoffe pour gilets, *f*.
wait [weit], *v.i*. Attendre; servir (at table etc.). *Not to wait to be told*, ne pas se le faire répéter; *to keep waiting*, faire attendre; *to wait for*, attendre, guetter (to watch); *to wait upon*, servir (of servants etc.), aller chez, se rendre chez (to call upon), accompagner (to accompany), *faire attention à, écouter (to attend).—*v.t*. Attendre. *To wait dinner for*, retarder le dîner pour.—*n*. Embuscade, *f*., guet-apens, piège, *m*.; attente, *f*., arrêt, *m*. *To lie in wait*, se tenir *or* être en embuscade, être à l'affût; *to lie in wait for*, tendre un guet-apens à, attendre (quelqu'un) au passage; *to rejoin the train after a ten-minute wait*, remonter dans le train après un arrêt de dix minutes; *to support a wait-and-see policy*, donner son appui à une politique d'attentisme.
waiter ['weitə], *n*. Garçon; plateau (tray), *m*.
waiting, *n*. Attente, *f*.; service (attendance), *m*. *In waiting*, de service; *lady-in-waiting*, dame d'honneur, *f*.; '*no waiting*' (for taxis etc.), stationnement interdit, *m*. **waiting-maid** *or* **waiting-woman,** *n*. Femme de chambre; camériste (to a princess etc.), *f*. **waiting-room,** *n*. Salle d'attente, *f*. **waitress,** *n*. Servante, fille de service, *f*. *Waitress!* mademoiselle! **waits,** *n.pl*. Chanteurs de Noëls, *m.pl*.
waive [weiv], *v.t*. Écarter, mettre de côté, abandonner, renoncer. *Waiving of age limit*, dispense d'âge, *f*.
wake [weik], *v.t*. Éveiller, réveiller; veiller (a corpse).—*v.i*. Veiller (to sit up); s'éveiller, se réveiller (from sleep).—*n*. Veillée; fête de village; (*fig*.) suite; trace, *f*.; houaiche, *f*., sillage (of a ship), *m*. *In the wake of*, dans le sillage (du vaisseau), (*fig*.) à la suite de, sur les traces de.
wakeful, *a*. Éveillé; vigilant, attentif (vigilant). **wakefully,** *adv*. Sans dormir; avec vigilance. **wakefulness,** *n*. Insomnie, *f*.
waken, *v.t*. Éveiller, réveiller.—*v.i*. S'éveiller, se réveiller.
waker, *n*. Veilleur, *m*.; personne qui (s')éveille, *f*.
wake-robin, *n*. Pied-de-veau (wild arum), *m*.
waking *or* **wakening,** *n*. Réveil, *m*.—*a*. Éveillé.

wale [weil], *n.* Marque (of lash); côte (of cloth), *f.*; (*pl.*) (*Naut.*) préceinte, *f. Gunwale* [gʌnl], plat-bord, *m.*

Wales. [weilz]. (*Geog.*) Le Pays de Galles, *m.* **New South Wales.** (*Geog.*) La Nouvelle-Galles du Sud, *f.*

walk [wɔːk], *v.i.* Marcher; aller à pied, aller (not to ride); venir à pied (to come on foot); se promener (for pleasure); aller au pas, marcher (of a horse). *To ask someone to walk in,* faire entrer; *to ask someone to walk out,* faire sortir; *to ask someone to walk up,* faire monter; *to walk after,* suivre; *to walk away,* s'en aller, s'éloigner, partir; *to walk down,* descendre; *to walk in,* entrer; *to walk into,* entrer dans, (*slang*) dire son fait à; *to walk off,* (*slang*) décamper; *to walk off with,* chiper; *to walk on,* continuer de marcher; *to walk out,* sortir, se promener; *to walk over,* traverser *or* parcourir à pied; *to walk the rounds,* faire la ronde; *to walk up,* monter, s'approcher (de); *to walk up and down,* se promener en long et en large.—*v.t.* Marcher dans *or* sur, parcourir, se promener dans; traverser à pied; faire à pied (a distance etc.); faire marcher, faire promener; mettre au pas, faire aller au pas (a horse). *To walk the hospitals,* suivre les cours de clinique; *to walk the plank,* sauter le pas; *to walk the streets,* se promener par les rues, battre le pavé; *we walked thirty miles,* nous avons fait trente milles à pied.—*n.* Marche; promenade, *f.*, tour, *m.*; tournée, course (for business); allée (path); démarche, allure (gait), *f.*; pas (of a horse), *m.*; (*fig.*) voie, sphère, carrière, *f.*, chemin, *m. At a walk,* au pas; (*fam.*) *in various walks of life,* dans différents milieux; *to go out for a walk,* aller se promener, faire une promenade; *to take a walk,* faire un tour de promenade; *to take out for a walk,* mener promener.

walker, *n.* Promeneur, *m.*, -euse, *f.*, marcheur, *m.*, -euse, *f.*, piéton, *m. Shop-walker* [SHOP].

walkie-talkie, *n.* (*fam.*) Émetteur-récepteur portatif, *m.*

walking, *n.* La marche; promenade à pied, *f. It is bad walking,* il fait mauvais marcher.—*a.* Ambulant; de marche, de promenade. *At a walking pace,* au pas. **walking-dress,** *n.* Costume trotteur, *m.* **walking-stick,** *n.* Canne, *f.*

walk-over, *n.* (*spt.*) *To have a walk-over,* remporter une victoire facile; gagner sans concurrent.

Walkyrie [VALKYRIE].

wall [wɔːl], *n.* Muraille, *f.*, mur, *m.*, paroi, *f.*, espalier (for fruit), *m. To give the wall to,* donner le haut du pavé à; *to go to the wall,* être serré de près, succomber, faire banqueroute; *within the walls,* dans la ville.—*v.t.* Entourer de murailles. *To wall up,* murer.

wallaby [ˈwɔləbi], *n.* Petit kangourou, wallaby, *m.*

wall-creeper, *n.* (*Orn.*) Grimpereau, *m.*

wallet [ˈwɔlit], *n.* Portefeuille; *havresac, bissac, *m.*; sacoche, *f.*

wall-eye, *n.* Œil vairon, *m.* **wall-eyed,** *a.* À l'œil vairon (of horses).

wallflower, *n.* Giroflée jaune, ravenelle, *f. To be a wallflower,* (*colloq.*) faire tapisserie.

wall-fruit, *n.* Fruit d'espalier, *m.*

walling [ˈwɔːliŋ], *n.* Maçonnerie de murs, *f.*; muraillement, *m.*, murs, *m.pl.*, murailles, *f.pl.*

Walloon [wɔˈluːn], *a.* and *n.* Wallon, *m.*, Wallonne, *f.*; wallon (language), *m.*

wallop [ˈwɔləp], *v.t.* Rosser, tanner la peau à. —*n.* (*slang*) Bière, *f.* **walloping,** *n.* Rossée, volée de coups, roulée, *f.*

wallow [ˈwɔlou], *v.i.* Se vautrer, se rouler (dans la boue); (*fig.*) se plonger (dans la débauche).—*n.* Boue, bourbe, *f.*, trou bourbeux, *m.*; bauge, *f.*

wall-painting, *n.* Peinture murale, *f.*

wall-paper, *n.* Papier de tenture, papier peint, *m.*

wall-plate, *n.* Sablière, *f.*

wall-rue, *n.* Rue de muraille, *f.*

wall-sided, *a.* À murailles droites (ship).

walnut [ˈwɔːlnʌt], *n.* Noix, *f.*; noyer (wood), *m. Pickled walnuts,* noix confites, *f.pl.*; *walnut table,* table en noyer, *f.*; *young or green walnut,* cerneau, *m.* **walnut-tree,** *n.* Noyer, *m.*

walrus [ˈwɔːlrəs], *n.* Morse, cheval marin, *m.*

Walter [ˈwɔːltə]. Gauthier, *m.*

waltz [wɔːlts], *n.* Valse, *f.*—*v.i.* Valser. **waltzer,** *n.* Valseur, *m.*, -euse, *f.* **waltzing,** *n.* Valse, *f.*

wan [wɔn], *a.* Blême, pâle, pâlot. *To grow wan,* blêmir, pâlir.

wand [wɔnd], *n.* Baguette, *f.*; bâton (staff), *m. Mercury's wand,* caducée, *m.*

wander [ˈwɔndə], *v.i.* Errer, se promener au hasard; s'égarer, divaguer (in mind); délirer (to be delirious). *His thoughts began to wander,* il commença à battre la campagne; *to wander about,* errer partout, courir çà et là; *to wander from,* s'écarter de, s'éloigner de.

wanderer, *n.* Vagabond, *m.*, vagabonde, *f.*

wandering, *n.* Course errante, *f.*, égarement, *m.*; divagation, *f.*; écart (de), *m.*; délire, *m.*— *a.* Errant, vagabond; nomade (of tribes etc.); (*fig.*) distrait; divaguant. *The wandering Jew,* le juif errant. **wanderingly,** *adv.* En errant; d'une manière distraite.

wanderlust, *n.* Manie des voyages, *f.*

wane [wein], *n.* Déclin, *m.*; (*fig.*) décadence, décroissance, *f. On the wane,* sur son déclin. —*v.i.* Décroître (of the moon); (*fig.*) décliner, s'altérer, s'affaiblir.

wangle [wæŋgl], *v.t.* (*fam.*) Resquiller.—*n.* Resquillage, *m.* **wangler,** *n.* Resquilleur, *m.*, -euse, *f.*

waning [ˈweiniŋ], *n.* Décroissance; décadence, *f.*; déclin, *m.*—*a.* Décroissant, déclinant.

wanly [ˈwɔnli], *adv.* Avec pâleur. **wanness,** *n.* Pâleur, *f.*, teint blême, *m.* **wannish,** *a.* Pâlot, un peu hâve.

want [wɔnt], *n.* Besoin; manque, défaut (lack), *m.*; indigence, misère (poverty), *f. For want of,* faute de, à défaut de; *in want,* dans le besoin, dans la misère, dans la gêne; *to be or to stand in want of,* avoir besoin de, manquer de (not to have).—*v.t.* Avoir besoin de; manquer de, être à court de; vouloir, désirer (to wish for), demander (to ask for). *A thing much wanted,* une chose dont on a grand besoin; *he wants courage,* il manque de courage; *I sadly want,* j'ai grand besoin de; *I wanted to tell you,* je voulais vous dire; *I want you,* j'ai besoin de vous; *I want you to do . . .,* je désire que vous fassiez . . .; *man wants but little here below,* il faut peu de chose à l'homme ici-bas; *this man is wanted by the police*, cet homme est recherché par la police; *wanted a maid*, on demande une bonne à tout faire; *what do you want of me?* que me voulez-vous? que désirez-vous? que voulez-vous de moi? *you are wanted*, on vous demande; *you shall want nothing*, vous ne manquerez de rien.—*v.i.* Manquer (de); faire défaut à. *All that is wanting is to . . .*, tout ce qu'il faut *or* tout ce qui est nécessaire c'est de . . .; *to be wanting*, manquer; *to be wanting in*, manquer de; *two spoons are wanting*, il manque deux cuillers.

wanting, *a.* Qui manque, manquant. *To be found wanting*, se trouver en défaut.

wantless, *a.* Sans besoins; (*fig.*) riche.

wanton ['wɔntən], *a.* Badin, folâtre (playful); follet; déréglé, licencieux, libertin, lascif (unchaste); gratuit (unprovoked).—*n.* (*usu. f.*) Impudique, débauchée.—*v.i.* Folâtrer, s'ébattre; agir follement. **wantonly,** *adv.* De gaîté de cœur, en folâtrant, gratuitement. **wantonness,** *n.* Étourderie, légèreté, *f.*; libertinage, *m.*

war [wɔː], *n.* Guerre, *f.* *Articles of war*, code pénal militaire, *m.*; *at war*, en guerre (avec); *cold war*, guerre froide; *nuclear war*, guerre atomique; *on a war footing*, sur le pied de guerre; *Secretary of State for War*, ministre de la guerre, *m.*; *there is war between them*, ils sont à couteaux tirés; *to declare war against*, déclarer la guerre à; *to go to war with*, to *wage war against* or *upon*, faire la guerre à; *to inure to war*, aguerrir; *war of nerves*, guerre des nerfs; *war to the knife*, guerre à outrance; *world war*, guerre mondiale.—*v.i.* Faire la guerre (à), lutter (contre).

warble [wɔːbl], *v.i., v.t.* Gazouiller; (*fig.*) chanter, roucouler. **warbler,** *n.* Oiseau chanteur, *m.*; fauvette (bird), *f.* **warbling,** *n.* Gazouillement, *m.*—*a.* Mélodieux. **warblingly,** *adv.* En gazouillant.

war-cry or **war-whoop,** *n.* Cri de guerre, *m.* **war-horse,** *n.* Cheval de bataille, *m.*

ward [wɔːd], *n.* Pupille, *m.*; tutelle (guardianship); garde (of a lock); salle (a hospital), *f.*; quartier (of a school), *m.*; arrondissement (of a town), *m.* *To keep watch and ward*, faire le guet.—*v.i.* Être sur ses gardes, veiller. *To ward off*, parer, écarter, détourner.

warden ['wɔːdn], *n.* Gardien; gouverneur, garde; recteur (of a university); directeur (of a college), conservateur (of a park), *m.* **wardenship,** *n.* Place, *f.*, or fonctions, *f.pl.*, de gardien, garde, etc.

warder ['wɔːdə], *n.* Gardien de prison; gardechiourme (of convicts), *m.*

wardmote, *n.* Conseil d'arrondissement (of the city), *m.* **wardress,** *n.* Gardienne de prison, *f.* **wardrobe,** *n.* Garde-robe; armoire (furniture), *f.* **ward-room,** *n.* (*Naut.*) Carré des officiers, *m.* *Ward-room mess*, table des officiers, *f.* **wardship,** *n.* Tutelle, *f.*

***ware** (1) [WORE].

ware (2) [wɛə], *n.* Articles fabriqués, *m.pl.* *Chinaware*, porcelaine, *f.*

warehouse ['wɛəhaus], *n.* Magasin; entrepôt, *m.* *Bonded warehouse*, entrepôt en douane, *m.*—*v.t.* Emmagasiner, mettre en magasin; (*Customs*) entreposer. **warehouse-man,** *n.* Garde-magasin; marchand en gros (owner),

entreposeur, *m.* **warehouse-rent,** *n.* Magasinage, *m.*

warehousing ['wɛəhauziŋ], *n.* Emmagasinage; magasinage (charge), *m.*; (*Customs*) mise en entrepôt, *f.*

warfare ['wɔːfɛə], *n.* La guerre, *f.*; les opérations, *f.pl.* *Open warfare*, la guerre de mouvement; *total warfare*, la guerre totale.

warily ['wɛərili], *adv.* Prudemment, avec circonspection. **wariness,** *n.* Prudence, circonspection, *f.*

warlike, *a.* Guerrier, martial, belliqueux. **warlikeness,** *n.* Caractère belliqueux, *m.*

warlock ['wɔːlɔk], *n.* Sorcier, *m.*

warm [wɔːm], *a.* Chaud; (*fig.*) zélé, ardent, vif, animé; chaleureux (of welcome). *It is very warm*, il fait très chaud; *to be warm*, avoir chaud (of person), faire chaud (of the weather); *to get warm*, s'échauffer, commencer à faire chaud (of the weather); *to keep oneself warm*, se tenir chaudement; *to keep one warm* (of clothes), tenir chaud; *to make warm*, chauffer, réchauffer; *warm work*, rude besogne, *f.*—*v.t.* Chauffer; réchauffer (to warm up); bassiner (a bed); (*fig.*) échauffer. *To warm someone's ears*, frotter les oreilles à quelqu'un; *to warm up again*, réchauffer.—*v.i.* Chauffer, se chauffer, se réchauffer; (*fig.*) s'animer.

war-material, *n.* Matériel de guerre, *m.* **warmonger,** *n.* Fauteur de guerre, belliciste, *m.* **war-mongering,** *n.* Bellicisme, *m.* **war-office,** *n.* Ministère de la guerre, *m.* **warpath,** *n.* Sentier de la guerre, *m.* *To be on the war-path*, s'être mis en campagne; s'en prendre à tout le monde. **war-time,** *n.* Temps de guerre, *m.*

warming, *n.* Chauffage, *m.* *To give a warming to*, chauffer. **warming-apparatus,** *n.* Appareil de chauffage, *m.* **warming-pan,** *n.* Bassinoire, *f.*

warmly, *adv.* Chaudement; (*fig.*) chaleureusement, vivement.

warmth [wɔːmθ], *n.* Chaleur; (*fig.*) ardeur, *f.*, zèle, *m.*, chaleur, *f.*; emportement (anger), *m.*

warn [wɔːn], *v.t.* Avertir, prévenir (de); faire savoir à, notifier à. *To warn against*, mettre en garde contre; *to warn off*, avertir de se retirer, exclure.

warning, *n.* Avertissement, avis, *m.*; (*fig.*) leçon, *f.*; congé (to leave), *m.*; alerte (of air-raids), *f.* *As a public warning*, pour le bon exemple; *to give warning to*, avertir, donner avis à; *to give warning to leave*, donner congé; *to receive warning*, recevoir son congé.

warp [wɔːp], *n.* Chaîne (weaving); touée (cable), *f.*; dépôt (de limon), lais, *m.*—*v.t.* Ourdir (weaving); faire déjeter (wood); (*Naut.*) touer; (*fig.*) fausser, pervertir (to pervert); (*Agric.*) colmater.—*v.i.* Se déjeter, se déformer; travailler, gauchir; (*fig.*) dévier, s'écarter (de); (*Naut.*) se touer.

warper, *n.* Ourdisseur, *m.*

warping, *n.* Ourdissage (in weaving); déjettement, gauchissement (of wood), *m.*; (*Agric.*) limonage, colmatage, *m.* **warping-mill,** *n.* Métier à ourdir, *m.*

warrant ['wɔrənt], *n.* Autorisation, garantie, *f.*; ordre, mandat, *m.*; mandat d'amener, mandat d'arrêt (to arrest), *m.*; (*Comm.*) warrant; coupon, *m.*; (*fig.*) justification, *f.*, garant, *m.* *Death-warrant*, ordre d'exécution, *search-warrant*, mandat de perquisition, *m.*; *warrant of attorney*, procuration, *f.*—*v.t.* Garantir, justifier, répondre de; certifier; autoriser; (*fig.*) défendre; (*Comm.*) garantir, warranter.

warrantable, *a.* Autorisé, légitime. **warrantableness,** *n.* Caractère justifiable, *m.*; légitimité, *f.*

warrantably, *adv.* D'une manière justifiable, légitimement.

warrantee [wɔrən'tiː], *n.* Personne à qui l'on a donné une garantie, *f.* **warranter** or (*Law*) **warrantor,** *n.* Garant, *m.*

warrant-officer, *n.* (*Mil.*) Sous-officier breveté, adjudant; (*Naut.*) premier maître, *m.*

warranty, *n.* Garantie, *f.*; *authorisation, f.*

warren ['wɔrən], *n.* Garenne, *f.* **warrener,** *n.* Garennier, *m.*

warring ['wɔːriŋ], *a.* Hostile, en conflit.

warrior ['wɔriə], *n.* Guerrier, soldat, *m. The unknown warrior*, le soldat inconnu.

Warsaw ['wɔːsɔː]. (*Geog.*) Varsovie, *f.*

wart [wɔːt], *n.* Verrue, *f.*, poireau, *m.*; (*Bot.*) excroissance, *f.* **wart-cress,** *n.* (*Bot.*) Corne-de-cerf, *f.* **warted** or **warty,** *a.* Couvert de verrues; (*Bot.*) verruqueux.

wart-hog, *n.* Sanglier d'Afrique, *m.* **wartwort,** *n.* Réveille-matin (plant), *m.*

wary ['wɛəri], *a.* Avisé, prudent, circonspect; défiant.

was [wɔz], **wast** [wɔst], *past* [BE].

wash [wɔʃ], *n.* Blanchissage, *m.*, lessive (of clothes), *f.*; (*Paint.*) lavis, *m.*; (*Med.*) lotion, eau; (*fig.*) lavure (de vaisselle), *f.*; (*Naut.*) plat (of an oar), sillage, *m.*, houaiche, *f.* (of ship); eaux de ruissellement, *f.pl.* *To have a wash*, se laver; *to send to the wash*, envoyer au blanchissage *or* à la lessive.—*v.t.* Blanchir (linen); (*fig.*) mouiller, baigner, laver, arroser; (*Paint.*) laver. *I was washed on to the rock*, les vagues me jetèrent sur le rocher; *to wash clean*, laver bien; *to wash down*, faire descendre, arroser (food with wine etc.); *to wash off*, enlever en lavant, effacer, enlever (a stain); *to wash one's hands*, se laver les mains, (*fig.*) s'en laver les mains (of the business); *to wash over*, submerger; *to wash overboard*, emporter, entraîner dans la mer; *to wash up*, laver (la vaisselle); rejeter sur le rivage.—*v.i.* Se laver; blanchir, faire la lessive (of a washerwoman etc.). *That stuff washes*, cette étoffe se lave; *to wash for someone*, (*colloq.*) blanchir quelqu'un; *to wash off*, disparaître, s'effacer à l'eau; *to wash out*, enlever (stain), rincer, laver (glass).

washable, *a.* Lavable.

*****wash-ball,** *n.* Savonnette, *f.* **wash-board,** *n.* Planche à laver, *f.* **wash-hand basin,** *n.* Cuvette, *f.* **wash-hand stand** [WASH-STAND]. **wash-house,** *n.* Lavoir, *m.*, buanderie, *f.* **wash-leather,** *n.* Peau de chamois, *f.* **wash-out,** *n.* (*fig.*) Fiasco, *m. To be a wash-out*, être un raté. **wash-room,** *n.* Toilettes, *f.pl.* **wash-stand,** *n.* Toilette, *f.*; lavabo (small), *m.* **wash-tub,** *n.* Baquet, *m.* **washed out,** *a.* Déteint, délavé. *To feel washed out*, (*fam.*) être vanné.

washer, *n.* Laveur, *m.*, laveuse; machine à laver (machine); (*Tech.*) rondelle, *f.* **washer-up,** *n.* Plongeur, *m.* (in restaurant). **washer-woman,** *n.* Blanchisseuse, *f.*

washing, *n.* Lavage; blanchissage (of clothes), *m. Washing day*, jour de blanchissage, *m.* **washing-machine,** *n.* Machine à laver, *f.*

washy, *a.* Humide, mouillé; (*fig.*) faible, fade. *Washy stuff*, lavasse, *f.*

wasp [wɔsp], *n.* Guêpe, *f.* **wasps' nest,** *n.* Guêpier, *m.* **wasp-waist,** *n.* Taille de guêpe, *f.* **wasp-waisted,** *a.* À taille de guêpe.

waspish, *a.* Irascible, irritable, acéré. **waspishly,** *adv.* D'une manière irascible. **waspishness,** *n.* Humeur irascible *f.*

*****wassail** [wɔsl], *n.* Beuverie (en commun); chanson à boire; bière sucrée aromatisée, *f. The wassail bowl*, la coupe du festin.—*v.i.* Boire, porter des toasts et chanter.

wastage ['weistidʒ], *n.* Gaspillage, *m.*; déperdition, *f.*

waste [weist], *n.* Perte (loss), *f.*; déchet (for cleaning); gaspillage, *m.*, prodigalité; dépense inutile, *f.*; (*Law*) dégât, *m.*, dégradation, *f.*; rebut (refuse); désert (land), *m.*, terre inculte, *f.*; (*Tech.*) trop-plein, *m.*; (*Bookselling*) défets, *m.pl. Cotton waste*, déchet de coton, *m.*; *it is mere waste of money*, c'est de l'argent perdu; *it is mere waste of time*, c'est vraiment perdre son temps; *it is sheer waste*, c'est pure perte; *it's a waste of effort*, c'est peine perdue; *to run to waste*, se dissiper, se perdre—*a.* De rebut; inutile, sans valeur; non employé, perdu (not used); inculte, en friche (of land). *To lay waste*, ravager, dévaster; *waste land*, terrain vague, *m.*, terre en friche, *f.*; *waste water*, trop-plein, *m.*—*v.t.* Gaspiller, prodiguer, dissiper; perdre (to lose); gâcher, détériorer (to spoil); ravager, dévaster, ruiner (to ruin); consommer (to consume). *I wasted my time over it*, je l'ai fait en pure perte; *to waste one's breath*, (*fam.*) user sa salive inutilement; *to waste paper*, gâcher du papier; *waste not, want not*, qui ne gaspille pas, toujours trouve.—*v.i.* S'user, se consumer, s'épuiser; maigrir, dépérir (to lose flesh). *To waste away*, dépérir, se consumer, s'user, maigrir (to lose flesh).

waste-book, *n.* Brouillard, *m.*, main courante, *f.* **waste-cock,** *n.* Robinet de purge, *m.*

wasted, *a.* Ravagé; (*Med.*) amaigri, atrophié; dépensé en pure perte; gaspillé, perdu, prodigué; diminué (diminished).

wasteful, *a.* Dissipateur, prodigue; inutile. **wastefully,** *adv.* Prodigalement, en pure perte, inutilement. **wastefulness,** *n.* Prodigalité, perte, *f.*, gaspillage, *m.*

waste-paper, *n.* Papier de rebut, *m.*; (*Print.*) maculature, *f.* **waste-paper basket,** *n.* Corbeille à papier, *f.* **waste-pipe,** *n.* Tuyau de dégagement, *m.*; écoulement, *m.* (bath). **waste-weir,** *n.* Déversoir, *m.*

waster, wastrel, *n.* Prodigue, gaspilleur, *m.*; propre à rien, *m.*

wasting, *a.* Qui épuise. *Wasting away*, dépérissement, *m.*, consomption, *f.*

watch [wɔtʃ], *n.* Montre; veille (vigil), *f.*; attention, garde, vigilance, surveillance (attention), *f.*; garde (sentry), *m.*; garde, *f.*, poste, guet (guard), *m.*; (*Naut.*) quart, *m. By my watch*, à ma montre; *it was my watch*, j'étais de quart; *to be on the watch*, être sur ses gardes, être aux aguets, (*Naut.*) être de quart; *to be on the watch for*, guetter, épier; *to keep a strict watch*, faire bonne garde; *to keep good watch* *over*, surveiller de près; *to keep watch*, veiller, avoir l'œil au guet.—*v.i.* Veiller (not to sleep); être attentif (to be attentive); prendre garde; être aux aguets; être sur ses gardes (to be vigilant); faire le guet, faire la garde (to keep guard); (*Naut.*) faire le quart. *To watch by* (an invalid), veiller, veiller auprès de; *to watch for*, attendre, épier, guetter; *to watch over*, veiller, veiller sur, surveiller; *to watch out*, prendre garde.—*v.t.* Veiller sur, veiller, surveiller, regarder, observer; guetter, épier. *Watch your step*, faites attention de ne pas tomber; *a watched pot never boils*, plus on désire une chose plus elle se fait attendre.

watch-bill, *n.* (*Naut.*) Rôle de quart, *m.*
watch-box, *n.* Guérite, *f.* **watch-case**, *n.* Boîtier de montre, *m.* **watch-chain**, *n.* Chaîne de montre, *f.* **watch-dog**, *n.* Chien de garde, *m.*
watcher, *n.* Surveillant, veilleur; guetteur, *m.*
watch-fire, *n.* Feu de bivouac, *m.*
watchful, *a.* Vigilant, attentif, en éveil, sur ses gardes. **watchfully**, *adv.* Avec vigilance, attentivement. **watchfulness**, *n.* Vigilance, *f.*
watch-glass, *n.* Verre de montre; (*Naut.*) sablier de quart, *m.* **watch-house**, *n.* Corps de garde, *m.*
watching, *n.* Surveillance, vigilance, *f.*; veilles, *f.pl.* *That needs watching*, il faut avoir l'œil sur cela.
watch-key, *n.* Clef de montre, *f.* **watchlight**, *n.* Veilleuse, *f.* **watch-maker**, *n.* Horloger, *m.* **watch-making**, *n.* Horlogerie, *f.* **watchman**, *n.* (*pl.* **watchmen**) Guetteur, guet; veilleur de nuit, *m.* **watchpocket**, *n.* Gousset (de montre); portemontre (for a bed etc.), *m.* **watch-spring**, *n.* Ressort de montre, *m.* **watch-stand**, *n.* Porte-montre, *m.* **watch-tower**, *n.* Tour de guet, *f.* **watchword**, *n.* Mot d'ordre, *m.*
water ['wɔːtə], *n.* Eau; marée (tide), *f.*, (*fig.*) ordre, rang, *m.*, volée; urine, *f.*—*a.* D'eau, à eau; aquatique; hydraulique. *By water*, par eau; *cold water*, eau fraîche; *drinking water*, eau potable; *fresh water*, eau douce (not salt); *hard water*, eau crue, dure; *high-water*, haute marée; *it is high-water*, la marée est haute; *holy water*, eau bénite; *low water*, marée basse; *low-water mark*, niveau des basses eaux, *m.*; *piped water*, eau de la ville; *running water*, eau courante; *salt water*, eau salée; *sea water*, eau de mer; *spring water*, eau de source; *to be in hot water*, être dans le pétrin, être dans l'embarras; *to be of the first water* (of diamonds), être de première eau; *to draw ten feet of water*, avoir dix pieds de tirant d'eau; *to fish in troubled waters*, pêcher en eau trouble; *to get into hot water*, s'attirer une mauvaise affaire; *to hold water*, (*fig.*) tenir debout; *to let in water* (of shoes etc.), prendre l'eau; *to take in fresh water*, (*Naut.*) faire de l'eau; *to take in water*, faire eau (to leak); *to take the waters*, prendre les eaux; *territorial waters*, eaux territoriales; *under water*, sous l'eau, submergé; *water carnival*, fête aquatique, *f.*; *water on the brain*, hydrocéphalie, *f.*—*v.t.* Arroser; donner à boire à, abreuver (animal); mettre de l'eau dans, couper (to mix water with); moirer (stuffs). *To water one's wine*, tremper son vin, mettre de l'eau dans son vin; *to water down*, (wine)

frelater; (*fig.*) atténuer.—*v.i.* Pleurer (to weep); faire de l'eau (to take in water). *My mouth waters*, l'eau m'en vient à la bouche; *to make one's mouth water*, faire venir l'eau à la bouche.
water-bailiff, *n.* Percepteur des droits de port; garde-pêche (on rivers), *m.* **Waterbearer**, *n.* (*Astron.*) Verseau, *m.* **waterbed**, *n.* Matelas à eau, *m.* **water-beetle**, *n.* Dytique, *m.* **water-borne**, *a.* À flot; transporté par eau. **water-bottle**, *n.* Carafe, *f.*; (*Mil. etc.*) bidon, *m.*; bouillotte, *f.* (bed).
water-caltrops, *n.* Macre flottante, *f.* **water-can**, *n.* Broc (à eau), *m.* **watercarriage**, *n.* Transport par eau, *m.* **watercarrier**, *n.* Porteur d'eau, *m.* **water-cart**, *n.* Voiture d'arrosage, *f.* **water-closet**, *n.* Toilette, *f.*, cabinet d'aisances, cabinet, *m.*
water-colour, *n.* Aquarelle, *f.* *Watercolour drawing*, aquarelle, peinture à l'aquarelle, *f.*; *water-colour painter*, peintre d'aquarelles, aquarelliste, *m.* **watercourse**, *n.* Cours d'eau; canal, conduit pour l'écoulement des eaux, *m.*; (*Hydr.*) chute d'eau, *f.*
watercress, *n.* Cresson, cresson de fontaine, *m.* **water-cure**, *n.* Hydrothérapie, *f.* **water-dog**, *n.* Chien qui va à l'eau, *m.* *He is a good water-dog*, il va bien à l'eau. **waterdrinker**, *n.* Buveur d'eau, *m.*
watered, *a.* Arrosé; moiré (of stuffs). *Watered silk*, moire de soie, *f.*
water-engine, *n.* Machine hydraulique, *f.* **waterfall**, *n.* Cascade; chute d'eau, *f.* **water-finder**, *n.* Sourcier; radiesthésiste, *m.* **water-fowl**, *n.* Oiseau aquatique, *m.* **waterfront**, *n.* Les quais, *m.pl.*, port, *m.* **water-gate**, *n.* Vanne d'écluse, *f.* **watergauge**, *n.* Flotteur, tube de niveau, *m.*, échelle d'étiage, *f.* **water-glass**, *n.* Verre soluble, *m.* **water-god**, *n.* Dieu aquatique, *m.* **water-heater**, *n.* Chauffe-eau, *m.* **water-hen**, *n.* Poule d'eau, *f.* **water-ice**, *n.* Sorbet, *m.*
wateriness, *n.* Humidité, aquosité; (*Med.*) sérosité, *f.*
watering, *n.* Arrosage (of plants etc.); arrosement (of streets), *m.*; irrigation (of land), *f.*; abreuvage (of animals); moirage (of stuffs), *m.*; (*Naut.*) action de faire de l'eau, provision d'eau douce, *f.* **watering-can**, *n.* Arrosoir, *m.* **watering-cart** [WATER-CART]. **wateringengine**, *n.* Pompe d'irrigation *or* d'arrosage, *f.* **watering-place**, *n.* Ville d'eaux, station thermale, *f.*; plage, *f.*; bains de mer, *m.pl.*; abreuvoir (for animals), *m.*; (*Naut.*) aiguade, *f.* **watering-pot**, *n.* Arrosoir, *m.* **wateringtrough**, *n.* Auge *f.*, abreuvoir, *m.*
waterish, *a.* Aqueux. **waterishness**, *n.* Nature aqueuse, *f.*
water-jacket, *n.* Chemise d'eau, *f.* **waterjug**, *n.* Pot à eau, *m.*
waterless, *a.* Sans eau.
water-level, *n.* Niveau d'eau, *m.* **water-lily**, *n.* Nénuphar, *m.* **water-line**, *n.* Ligne de flottaison, *f.* **water-logged**, *a.* Engagé, à moitié engagé dans l'eau; envahi par les eaux. **waterman**, *n.* (*pl.* **watermen**) Batelier; passeur (at a ferry), *m.* **watermark**, *n.* Étiage (in rivers), *m.* *High or low water-mark*, niveau des hautes eaux *or* des basses eaux, *m.*; laisse, *f.* **watermark**, *n.* Filigrane (on paper), *m.* **water-marked**, *a.*

A filigrane. **water-melon,** *n.* Melon d'eau, *m.*, pastèque, *f.* **water-meter,** *n.* Compteur à eau, *m.* **water-mill,** *n.* Moulin à eau, *m.* **water-nymph,** *n.* Naïade, *f.* **water-ousel,** *n.* Merle d'eau, cincle plongeur, *m.* **water-pipe,** *n.* Tuyau d'eau, *m.* **water-plant,** *n.* Plante aquatique, *f.* **water-poise,** *n.* Hydromètre, *m.* **water-polo,** *n.* Polo nautique, *m.* **water-pot,** *n.* Pot à eau, *m.* **water-power,** *n.* Force hydraulique, *f.* **water-pressure,** *n.* Pression d'eau, *f.* *Water-pressure engine,* machine à colonne d'eau, *f.* **waterproof,** *a.* Imperméable (à l'eau), étanche.—*v.t.* Rendre imperméable; cirer (un tissu). **waterproofing,** *n.* Imperméabilisation, *f.*—*n.* Imperméable, caoutchouc, *m.* **water-ram,** *n.* Bélier hydraulique, *m.* **water-rat,** *n.* Rat d'eau, *m.* **water-rate,** *n.* Taux d'abonnement aux eaux de la ville, *m.* **watershed,** *n.* Ligne de partage des eaux, *f.*, versant, *m.* **water-shoot,** *n.* Gargouille, *f.* **waterside,** *a.* Riverain.—*n.* Bord de l'eau, *m.* **water-skiing,** *n.* Ski nautique, *m.* **water-spaniel,** *n.* Épagneul (qui va à l'eau), *m.* **waterspout,** *n.* Trombe, *f.*; tuyau de descente, *m.* **water-stained,** *a.* Taché d'humidité. **water-supply,** *n.* Distribution des eaux; arrivée d'eau, *f.* **water-tank,** *n.* Réservoir à eau, *m.*, citerne, *f.* **water-tight,** *a.* Imperméable à l'eau; étanche; (*fig.*) inattaquable. **water-tower,** *n.* Château d'eau, *m.* **water-vole,** *n.* Campagnol d'eau, *m.* **water-way,** *n.* Cours d'eau, *m.*; (*Naut.*) gouttière, *f.* **water-weed,** *n.* Plante aquatique, *f.* **water-wheel,** *n.* Roue hydraulique, roue de moulin, *f.* **water-works,** *n.pl.* Établissement pour la distribution des eaux, *m.*, machine hydraulique, *f.*; grandes eaux, *f.pl.* **water-worn,** *a.* Usé par les eaux. **waterwort,** *n.* Élatine, *f.*

watery, *a.* Aqueux; mouillé, plein d'eau; (*poet.*) humide. *Watery gods,* dieux des eaux, *m.pl.*

watt [wɔt], *n.* (*Elec.*) Watt, *m.* **watt-hour,** *n.* Watt-heure, *m.*

wattage, *n.* Wattage, *m.*, consommation en watts, *f.*

wattle [wɔtl], *n.* Claie (of osier etc.), *f.*, clayonnage, *m.*; barbe, *f.*, barbillon (of fish), *m.*, caroncule (of a cock etc.), *f.*; (*Bot.*) acacia d'Australie, *m.*—*v.t.* Clayonner; tresser, entrelacer l'osier.

wave [weiv], *n.* Vague, *f.*, flot, *m.*, lame, ondulation; (*poet.*) onde, *f.*; moiré (on stuffs); signe (of the hand), *m.* *Permanent wave,* permanente, indéfrisable, *f.*; *long waves,* (*Rad.*) grandes ondes; *short waves,* petites ondes, ondes courtes, *f.pl.*—*v.i.* Ondoyer, onduler, flotter; s'agiter, faire signe (à).—*v.t.* Agiter, faire signe de (to beckon); onduler (the hair).

waved, *a.* Ondulé; ondé, chatoyant (of stuffs). **wave-length,** *n.* Longueur d'onde, *f.* **waveless,** *a.* Sans vagues.

wavelet, *n.* Petite vague, vaguelette; ride, *f.*

waver ['weivə], *v.i.* Hésiter, vaciller, balancer, être indécis. **waverer,** *n.* Personne indécise, personne irrésolue, *f.*, esprit vacillant, *m.* **wavering** or **waveringness,** *n.* Hésitation, vacillation, indécision, *f.*—*a.* Indécis, vacillant, incertain, irrésolu. **waveringly,** *adv.* En vacillant, en hésitant.

waviness ['weivinis], *n.* Ondulation, *f.*, ondoiement, *m.*

waving ['weiviŋ], *n.* Ondoiement, *m.*, ondulation, *f.*, mouvement, *m.*

wavy ['weivi], *a.* Ondoyant, onduleux, ondulé.

wax [wæks], *n.* Cire; (shoemaker's) poix; (*colloq.*) rage, colère, *f.* *To get in a wax,* rager.—*v.t.* Cirer, enduire de cire, farter (skis).—*v.i.* Croître (of the moon), s'accroître; devenir, se faire. •

wax-candle, *n.* Bougie, *f.* **wax-chandler,** *n.* Fabricant de bougies, *m.* **waxen,** *a.* De cire; cireux. **wax-end,** *n.* Fil poissé, *m.* **wax-light,** *n.* Bougie, *f.*; allumette-bougie (match), *f.* **wax-taper,** *n.* Rat de cave; (*Eccles.*) cierge, *m.* **wax-tree,** *n.* (*Bot.*) Troène de Chine, *m.* *Japanese wax-tree,* sumac cirier, *m.* **waxwing,** *n.* Jaseur (bird), *m.* **waxwork,** *n.* Ouvrage de cire, *m.*; (*pl.*) galerie de figures de cire, *f.* **waxy,** *a.* Comme de la cire, cireux; (*colloq.*) en colère.

way [wei], *n.* Chemin, *m.*, route, voie, *f.*, passage, *m.*, côté, sens, *m.*, direction (direction); manière, façon, guise, mode, idée (manner), *f.*; moyen, *m.*, méthode (means), *f.*; état (condition), *m.*; partie, *f.*, métier (business etc.), *m.*; (*colloq.*) distance; (*Tech.*) chasse (of a saw), *f.*; (*Naut.*) erre, *f.* (of ship). *A long way off,* loin, très loin; *a way of his own,* une manière à lui; *a way of life,* un genre de vie, une manière de vivre; *bad ways,* mauvaise conduite, *f.*; *by a long way* (by far), à beaucoup près, de beaucoup; *by the way,* en passant, soit dit en passant, à propos; *by-way,* chemin détourné; *by way of,* en guise de, par forme de, à titre de, en fait de; *cross-way,* chemin de traverse; *get out of the way,* ôtez-vous de mon chemin; *half-way,* à moitié chemin; *he is in my way,* il est dans mon chemin, il m'embarrasse, il me gêne; *in a fair way to,* en passe de, en voie de; *in a friendly way,* en ami; *in every way,* en tout, en tous points; *in its own way,* dans son genre; *in no way,* aucunement, d'aucune façon; tant s'en faut, nullement, en aucune façon; *in one's own way,* à sa façon, à sa guise; *in some ways,* à certains points de vue, par certains côtés; *in the way of,* en matière de, quant à; *in this way,* de cette manière, ainsi; *is there any way of . . .?* y a-t-il moyen de . . .? *is this the way that . . .?* est-ce ainsi que . . .? *is this the way to . . .?* est-ce ici le chemin or la route de . . .? *it is a long way to,* il y a très loin d'ici; *it is the way of the world,* ainsi va le monde; *it's his way,* c'est sa manière de faire; *Milky Way,* voie lactée; *not to know which way to turn,* ne savoir où donner de la tête; *one can't have it both ways,* on ne peut pas être et avoir été; *on the way,* en chemin, en route, chemin faisant; *out of the way,* hors du chemin, écarté, étrange, extraordinaire (strange), caché (hidden), en arrière! gare! *over the way,* de l'autre côté du chemin *or* de la rue, en face; *permanent way,* voie, *f.*; *right of way,* droit de passage, *m.*; *right way up,* dans le bon sens; *that way,* de ce côté-là, par là, de cette manière-là; *the business is under way,* l'affaire suit son cours; *the long way,* en long, dans le sens de la longueur; *there's no way of managing it,* il n'y a pas moyen; *the right way,* le bon chemin, (*fig.*) la bonne manière; *the ways of Providence,* les voies de la Providence; *the way up*, chemin pour monter; *the wrong way*, le mauvais chemin, (*fig.*) la mauvaise manière, à rebours, de travers; *the wrong way round*, (coat etc.) à l'envers; *the wrong way up*, sens dessus dessous; *there are no two ways about it*, il n'y a pas à discuter; *this way*, de ce côté-ci, par ici; *to bar the way*, barrer le passage, gêner la circulation (of vehicles); *to be in a bad way*, être dans de mauvais draps; *to be in a terrible way*, être dans un état; *to clear the way*, débarrasser la voie; *to clear the way for*, préparer la voie pour; *to feel one's way*, marcher *or* aller à tâtons, tâtonner, (*fig.*) sonder le terrain; *to find a way to*, trouver moyen de; *to find one's way*, trouver son chemin; *to find one's way into*, s'insinuer dans; *to force one's way*, se frayer *or* s'ouvrir un chemin; *to get into the way of it*, s'y faire, en prendre l'habitude; *to get out of the way*, éloigner; (*Naut.*) *to gather way*, prendre de l'erre; *to get under way*, se mettre en route, appareiller; *to give way*, céder, plier, se relâcher, reculer, lâcher pied (of troops); *to go on one's way*, passer son chemin; *to go one's own way*, aller son train, agir à sa guise; *to go the right way to work*, s'y prendre bien, savoir s'y prendre; *to go the way of all flesh*, trépasser; *to go the wrong way to work*, s'y prendre mal; *to have a way with one*, savoir l'art de plaire; *to have one's own way*, en faire à sa tête; *to keep out of the way*, tenir éloigné *or* caché *or* à l'écart; *to lead the way*, marcher en tête, ouvrir la marche (à); *to live in a small way*, vivoter; *to lose one's way*, s'égarer, se perdre; *to make one's way*, faire son chemin; *to make one's way towards*, se diriger vers; *to make way for*, faire place à, laisser passer; *to pay one's way*, ne pas s'endetter; *to put out of the way*, écarter, se débarrasser (de); (*fam.*) liquider; *to see one's way*, voir son chemin, (*fig.*) y voir clair, voir la possibilité (de); *to stand in the way of*, faire obstacle à, barrer le passage à, s'opposer à, embarrasser, gêner; *to stand out of the way*, s'ôter du chemin, se ranger, se garer; *to take one's own way*, suivre son penchant; *to walk a long way*, faire beaucoup de chemin; *under way*, (*Naut.*) en marche; *way in*, entrée, *f.*; *way out*, sortie, *f.*; *ways and customs*, us et coutumes, *m.pl.*; *ways and means*, voies et moyens, *m.pl.*; *way there!* place par là! *way through*, passage (au travers), *m.*; *we are going your way*, nous allons de votre côté; *where there's a will there's a way*, vouloir c'est pouvoir, qui veut la fin veut les moyens; *which way?* d'où? par où? de quelle manière?

way-bill, *n.* Lettre de voiture, feuille de route, *f.*

wayfaring, *a.* Qui voyage, en voyage (à pied). **wayfaring-tree**, *n.* Viorne cotonneuse, *f.*

waylay, *v.t.* Guetter, guetter au passage, dresser un guet-apens à. **waylayer**, *n.* Personne qui dresse un guet-apens *or* qui se tient en embuscade, *f.*

way-leave, *n.* Droit de passage, droit de survol, *m.*

wayless, *a.* Sans chemins.

wayside, *a.* Au bord de la route.—*n.* Bord de la route, *m.*

wayward, *a.* Fantasque, capricieux, entêté.

waywardly, *adv.* Avec entêtement, capricieusement, *f.* **waywardness**, *n.* Humeur capricieuse, *f.*; caractère difficile, entêté, *m.*

we [wiː], *pron.* Nous; (*indefinitely*) on. *We Frenchmen*, nous autres Français.

weak [wiːk], *a.* Faible, infirme, débile. *The weakest go to the wall*, les battus payent l'amende; *the weakest side*, le côté faible, le faible, *m.*; *to grow weak*, s'affaiblir.

weaken [wiːkn], *v.t.* Affaiblir; atténuer, diminuer. **weakening**, *n.* Affaiblissement, *m.*

weak-headed, *a.* À la tête faible, faible d'esprit.

weak-hearted, *a.* Pusillanime, mou.

weak-kneed, *a.* Faible des genoux; sans courage.

weakling, *n.* Être faible, faiblard, *m.* **weakly**, *a.* Faible; infirme, débile.—*adv.* Faiblement, sans force.

weak-minded, *a.* D'esprit faible.

weakness, *n.* Faiblesse; débilité, *f.* (*fig.*) *Every one has his weakness*, tout le monde a son faible *or* son côté faible.

weak sight, *n.* Asthénopie, *f.*

weak-sighted, *a.* À la vue faible.

weak-spirited, *a.* Mou, sans courage, pusillanime.

weal (1) [wiːl], *n.* Bien, bien-être, bonheur, *m.* *The public weal*, le bien public.

weal (2) [wiːl], *n.* Marque, *f.* (on the skin).—*v.t.* Marquer, rayer (with a whip etc.).

wealth [welθ], *n.* Richesse, *f.*, richesses, *f.pl.*; abondance, profusion, *f.* **wealthiness**, *n.* Opulence, *f.* **wealthy**, *a.* Riche, opulent.

wean [wiːn], *v.t.* Sevrer; (*fig.*) détacher, aliéner (de). *Being weaned*, en sevrage.

weaning, *n.* Sevrage, *m.* **weanling**, *n.* Enfant *or* animal en sevrage, *m.*

weapon ['wepən], *n.* Arme, *f.* *To use any weapon to hand*, faire flèche de tout bois. **weaponless**, *a.* Sans armes, désarmé.

wear (1) [wiə] [WEIR].

wear (2) [wɛə], *v.t.* (*past* **wore**, *p.p.* **worn**) Porter (clothes); mettre (to put on); user (to use by wear); lasser, fatiguer (to tire); (*Naut.*) faire virer. *Fit to wear*, mettable; *he wears my patience out*, il lasse ma patience; *to wear away*, user, effacer, ronger (of rocks); *to wear out*, user, (*fig.*) épuiser, lasser; *worn out*, tout usé, (*fig.*) épuisé, fatigué, n'en pouvant plus. —*v.i.* S'user (to wear out); se porter (of clothes); traîner (of time); (*Naut.*) virer de bord vent arrière. *Not to wear out*, être inusable; *to wear away*, s'user, s'effacer, se passer, s'écouler (of time); *to wear badly*, n'être pas d'un bon user; *to wear off*, s'effacer, disparaître; *to wear on*, s'avancer; *to wear out*, s'user; *to wear well*, résister à l'usure, conserver bien, durer; (*fig.*) porter bien son âge, se conserver.—*n.* User, usage (act of wearing); frai (of coins), *m.*; usure (waste by wearing), *f.* *Foot-wear*, chaussures, *f.pl.*; *ladies', men's wear*, articles pour dames, hommes, *m.pl.*; *the worse for wear*, usé, détérioré, ne servant plus; *wear and tear*, usure, détérioration, *f.*; entretien du matériel, *m.*

wearable, *a.* Mettable.

wearer, *n.* Personne qui porte, *f.*

wearied ['wiərid], *a.* Fatigué, las; (*fig.*) ennuyé. **wearily**, *adv.* Péniblement, d'un air las. **weariness,** *n.* Fatigue, lassitude, *f.*; (*fig.*) dégoût, ennui, *m.*

wearing ['weəriŋ], *a.* Lassant, fatigant.—*n.* Usage, *m.*; usure (wearing out), *f.*, port, *m.* (of beard). *Of good wearing,* qui fait de l'usage; *wearing apparel,* habits, vêtements, *m.pl.*; *wearing-plate,* (*Eng.*) pièce de frottement, *f.*

wearisome ['wiərisəm], *a.* Ennuyeux, fastidieux; lassant, assommant. **wearisomely,** *adv.* Ennuyeusement. **wearisomeness,** *n.* Nature ennuyeuse, *f.*, ennui, *m.*

weary ['wiəri], *a.* Fatigué, las, ennuyé; fatigant, ennuyeux (of things). *To grow weary of,* se dégoûter (de), se lasser (de).— *v.t.* Lasser, fatiguer; ennuyer. *To weary out,* excéder.

weasand ['wi:zənd], *n.* Trachée-artère, *f.*, gosier, *m.*

weasel [wi:zl], *n.* Belette, *f.*

weather ['weðə], *n.* Temps, *m.*; (*fig.*) tempête, *f.* *Foggy weather,* temps de brouillard; *in all weathers,* par tous les temps; *in such cold weather,* par le froid qu'il fait; *it is beautiful weather,* il fait un temps superbe; *it is cloudy weather,* il fait un temps couvert; *it is fine weather,* il fait beau (temps); *stormy weather,* temps d'orage, (*Naut.*) gros temps, *m.*; *to make heavy weather,* bourlinguer; (*fig.*) avoir de la peine à faire quelque chose; *what's the weather like?* quel temps fait-il? *weather conditions,* conditions atmosphériques, *f.pl.*; *weather permitting,* si le temps le permet.—*a.* Du côté du vent, du vent, au vent.—*v.t.* Résister à (a storm etc.); (*fig.*) lutter contre, tenir tête à; (*Naut.*) passer au vent de; doubler (a cape). *To weather out,* (*fig.*) endurer, supporter.

weather-beaten, *a.* Battu par la tempête; (*fig.*) usé, fatigué; hâlé.

weatherboard, *n.* Auvent (of window), *m.*; (*Row.*) hiloire, *f.* **weatherboarding,** *n.* Planches à recouvrement, *f.pl.*; bardeaux, *m.pl.*

weather-bound, *a.* Retenu par le mauvais temps.

weathercock, *n.* Girouette, *f.*

weather-driven, *a.* Poussé par la tempête.

weathered, *a.* Usé par les intempéries; (stone etc.) patiné.

weather-eye, *n.* *To keep one's weather-eye open,* (*fig.*) avoir l'œil au guet, ne pas perdre la tête, ouvrir l'œil et le bon.

weather-gauge, *n.* (*Naut.*) Avantage du vent, *m.* *To get the weather-gauge,* prendre le dessus du vent. **weather-glass,** *n.* Baromètre, *m.*

weathermost, *a.* (*Naut.*) Le plus au vent.

weather-proof, *a.* À l'épreuve du (mauvais) temps, des intempéries, imperméable.

weather-report, *n.* Bulletin météorologique, *m.* **weather-ship,** *n.* Navire météorologique, *m.*

weather-shore, *n.* (*Naut.*) Terre au vent, *f.*

weatherside, *n.* Côté du vent, *m.*

weather-wise, *a.* Qui sait prévoir le temps.

weave ['wi:v], *n.* (*Tex.*) Armure; texture, *f.*, tissage, *m.* *Open weave,* tissue lâche, *f.*—*v.t.* (*past* wove, *p.p.* woven) Tisser; tresser (the hair etc.); (*fig.*) entremêler (à *or* avec); tramer (plot). *Closely woven,* d'un tissu serré.

weaver, *n.* Tisserand, *m.* **weaver-bird,** *n.* Tisserin, *m.* **weaving,** *n.* Tissage, *m.*

web [web], *n.* Tissu, *m.*; sangle (for girths), *f.*; (*fig.*) tissu, enchaînement, *m.*; membrane (of waterfowl); toile (of a spider); barbe (of a feather); âme (of a girder etc.); lame (of a saw etc.), *f.*, tranchant (of a coulter), *m.*; taie (in the eye), *f.*

webbed, *a.* Palmé.

webbing, *n.* Sangles (of a chair, bed, etc.), *f.pl.*

webby, *a.* Palmé; membraneux.

web-footed, *a.* Palmipède, aux pieds palmés.

web-press, *n.* Presse rotative, *f.*

wed [wed], *v.t.* Épouser, se marier avec; (*fig.*) unir, lier.—*v.i.* Se marier.

wedded, *a.* Marié (à); conjugal; (*fig.*) fortement attaché (à), entiché (de).

wedding, *n.* Noce, *f.*, noces, *f.pl.*, mariage, *m.*—*a.* De noce, de noces, de mariage.

wedding-breakfast, *n.* Repas de noce, *m.*

wedding-cake, *n.* Gâteau de noce, *m.*

wedding-day, *n.* Jour des noces, *m.* *On his wedding-day,* le jour de son mariage.

wedding-dress, *n.* Robe de mariée, *f.*

wedding-guests, *n.pl.* Les invités, *m.pl.*

wedding-party, *n.* La noce, *f.* **wedding-present,** *n.* Cadeau de mariage, *m.* **wedding-ring,** *n.* Alliance, *f.* **wedding-tour,** *n.* Voyage de noces, *m.*

wedge [wedʒ], *n.* Coin, *m.*; cale (for fixing), *f.* *It is the thin end of the wedge,* c'est un petit de pris.—*v.t.* Serrer; caler; coincer; fendre avec un coin. *To wedge in,* enfoncer, insérer; *to wedge up,* caler; *we were wedged in the crowd,* la foule nous serrait de tous côtés.

wedge-shaped, *a.* En forme de coin; cunéiforme.

wedging, *n.* Coinçage; calage, *m.*

wedlock ['wedlɔk], *n.* Mariage, *m.* *Born in wedlock,* né dans le mariage; *born out of wedlock,* né hors mariage.

Wednesday ['wenzdi], *n.* Mercredi, *m.* *Ash-Wednesday,* mercredi des Cendres.

wee [wi:], *a.* (*colloq.*) Petit, tout petit, mignon. *A wee bit* or *a wee mite,* un brin, un tantinet; *a wee drop,* un petit verre, un doigt.

weed [wi:d], *n.* Mauvaise herbe, *f.*; (*colloq.*) cigare, tabac, *m.*; (*pers.*) gringalet; cheval efflanqué, *m.*; (*pl.*) *vêtements, habits, *m.pl.* *Widow's weeds,* vêtements de deuil, *m.pl.*— *v.t.* Désherber, sarcler; (*fig.*) nettoyer, purger, épurer. *To weed out,* extirper.

weeder, *n.* Sarcleur (person); sarcloir (tool), *m.*

weeding, *n.* Sarclage, *m.* **weeding-hook,** *n.* Sarcloir (tool), *m.* **weed-killer,** *n.* Herbicide, *m.* **weedy,** *a.* Plein de mauvaises herbes; (*fig.*) chétif, étique.

week [wi:k], *n.* Semaine, *f.* *A week ago,* il y a huit jours; *every week,* tous les huit jours; *Holy Week,* la semaine sainte; *in a week,* dans huit jours; *in a week of Sundays,* la semaine des quatre jeudis; *in the course of the week,* dans la huitaine, en semaine; *officer of the week,* officier de semaine, *m.*; *once a week,* une fois par semaine; *this day week,* d'aujourd'hui en huit (future), il y a huit jours (past); *yesterday week,* il y a eu hier huit jours.

weekday, *n.* Jour ouvrable, jour de semaine, *m.*

week-end, *n.* Fin de la semaine, *f.*, week-end, *m.*

weekly, *adv.* Par semaine, tous les huit jours. —*a.* De la semaine; hebdomadaire (of newspapers).—*n.* Hebdomadaire, *m.*

*****ween** [wi:n], *v.t.* Penser, croire, s'imaginer.

weep [wi:p], *v.t.* (*past* and *p.p.* **wept**) Pleurer, verser des larmes; suinter, suer (walls); (*fig.*) gémir, se plaindre. *To weep bitterly,* pleurer à chaudes larmes; *to weep for,* pleurer; *to weep for joy,* pleurer de joie.—*v.t.* Pleurer, pleurer sur; verser, répandre (tears).

weeper, *n.* Pleureur, *m.*, pleureuse (band of cambric), *f.*

weeping, *n.* Pleurs, *m.pl.*, larmes, *f.pl.*—*a.* Qui pleure, éploré; suintant; (*Bot.*) pleureur. *Weeping eczema,* eczéma humide, *m.* **weeping-willow,** *n.* Saule pleureur, *m.*

weepingly, *adv.* En pleurant.

weepy, *a.* Larmoyant.

weever ['wi:və], *n.* (*Ichth.*) Vive, *f.*

weevil [wi:vl], *n.* Charançon, *m.*, calandre, *f.*

weevilled, *a.* Charançonné.

weft [weft], *n.* Trame, *f.*

weigh [wei], *v.t.* Peser; avoir un poids de; (*fig.*) examiner, juger, bien considérer; (*Naut.*) lever (the anchor). *To weigh down,* peser plus que, surcharger, accabler (to oppress); *to weigh out,* peser en petites quantités; *weighed down with age,* accablé de vieillesse.—*v.i.* Peser; avoir du poids, avoir de la valeur; (*Naut.*) lever l'ancre. *To weigh against,* (*fig.*) l'emporter sur; *to weigh down,* pencher (of scales), (*fig.*) s'affaisser, s'abaisser; *to weigh upon,* peser sur, être à charge à; *to weigh with,* avoir du poids aux yeux de; *under weigh* [WAY].

weighable, *a.* Pesable. **weighage,** *n.* Pesage, *m.*

weigh-bridge, *n.* Pont à bascule, *m.*, bascule, *f.*

weigher, *n.* Peseur, *m.*, peseuse, *f.*

weighing, *n.* Pesage, *m.* **weighing-machine,** *n.* Bascule, *f.* **weighing-room,** *n.* Enceinte du pesage (at races), *f.*

weight [weit], *n.* Poids, *m.*; pesanteur (heaviness); (*fig.*) gravité, importance, valeur, *f.* *Atomic weight,* masse atomique, *f.*; *by weight,* au poids; *dead weight,* poids mort; *for its weight in gold,* au poids de l'or; *gross weight,* poids brut; *his opinion carried weight,* son avis comptait pour beaucoup; *net weight,* poids net; *of no weight,* sans importance; *of weight,* important, grave, sérieux; *to be worth one's weight in gold,* valoir son pesant d'or. (*Box.*) *Bantam weight,* poids coq; *feather weight,* poids plume; *fly weight,* poids mouche; *heavy weight,* poids lourd; *light weight,* poids léger; *middle weight,* poids moyen.—*v.t.* Charger d'un poids.

weighted, *a.* Chargé (de).

weightily, *adv.* Pesamment; gravement, avec force. **weightiness,** *n.* Pesanteur; (*fig.*) importance, gravité, force, *f.* **weightlessness,** *n.* Apesanteur, impondérabilité, *f.*

weight-lifting, *n.* Poids et haltères, *m.pl.*

weighty, *a.* Pesant, lourd; (*fig.*) important, grave, sérieux. *Weighty reasons,* des raisons puissantes.

weir [wiə], *n.* Barrage, déversoir, *m.*

weird [wiəd], *a.* Fantastique, étrange, magique. *The weird sisters,* les Parques, *f.pl.*

weirdness, *n.* Étrangeté, magie, *f.*

welcome ['welkəm], *n.* Bienvenue, *f.*, bon accueil, accueil, *m.* *To bid (someone) welcome,*

souhaiter la bienvenue à; *to give a hearty welcome to,* recevoir à bras ouverts; *we met with a poor welcome,* on nous fit un triste accueil.—*a.* Bienvenu; agréable, acceptable (of things); libre (to make use of). *Do it and welcome!* à votre service, que rien ne vous empêche; *it is very welcome,* c'est très acceptable, ce n'est pas de refus; *to be a welcome guest everywhere,* être le bienvenu partout; *to be welcome to,* être libre de; *welcome news,* des nouvelles agréables; *you are welcome to it,* à votre service, il n'y a pas de quoi.—*int.* Soyez le bienvenu.—*v.t.* Souhaiter la bienvenue à, bien accueillir, faire bon accueil à.

weld [weld], *v.t.* Souder; (*fig.*) joindre, incorporer, unir.—*n.* Soudure; (*Bot.*) gaude, *f.*

welder, *n.* Soudeur, *m.*; machine à souder, *f.*

welding, *n.* Soudure, *f.* *Flat welding,* soudure à plat. **welding-heat,** *n.* (Température du) blanc soudant *or* suant.

weldless, *a.* Sans soudure.

welfare ['welfeə], *n.* Bien-être, bonheur, bien, *m.*, prospérité, *f.* *Child welfare,* protection de l'enfance, *f.*; *public welfare,* le salut public, *m.*; *Welfare State,* état social, état providence, *m.*; *welfare work,* assistance sociale, *f.*

*****welkin** ['welkin], *n.* (*poet.*) Ciel, *m.*, voûte céleste, *f.*; firmament, *m.*

well (1) [wel], *n.* Puits; réservoir (of a fishing-boat etc.); coffre (of a carriage), *m.*; sentine (of a boat), *f.*; cage, *f.* (of staircase); (*pl.*) eaux minérales, *f.pl.*; (*fig.*) fontaine, source, *f.* *Draining* (or *dead*) *well,* puisard, *m.*; *ink-well,* encrier, réservoir, *m.*—*v.i.* Jaillir. *To well out,* jaillir (de). **well-boring,** *n.* Sondage, forage, *m.* **well-drain,** *n.* Puits d'écoulement, *m.* **well-hole,** *n.* Cage, *f.* (of stairs, lift). **well-room,** *n.* (*Naut.*) Sentine, *f.* **well-sinker,** *n.* Puisatier, *m.* **well-spring,** *n.* (*poet.*) Source, *f.*

well (2) [wel], *a.* Bien, en bonne santé; bon, heureux (fortunate); utile, profitable (advantageous). *To be very well,* aller très bien, se porter à ravir; *to be well (in health),* se porter bien, être bien portant, être bien; *to get well,* se rétablir, se remettre; *to make well again,* guérir, rétablir; *well off,* aisé (wealthy).—*adv.* Bien, très, fort; comme il faut. *All being well,* si tout va bien; *all's well that ends well,* tout est bien qui finit bien; *as well as,* aussi bien que, ainsi que; *as well as may be,* tant bien que mal; *as well say that,* autant dire que; *I cannot well,* . . ., il ne m'est guère possible de . . ., je ne puis guère . . .; *let well alone,* le mieux est l'ennemi du bien; *that is all very well,* tout cela est bel et bon; *to be hail-fellow-well-met with everybody,* traiter tout le monde de pair à compagnon; *to be well enough off,* n'avoir pas à se plaindre; *to be well up in,* être fort en *or* ferré sur; *to be well with,* être en faveur auprès de; *to speak well of,* dire du bien de, parler favorablement de; *to wish well,* souhaiter du bien à; *well!* eh bien! ma foi! enfin! *well and good,* à la bonne heure; *well done!* très bien! Bravo! *well begun is half done,* à moitié fait qui commence bien; *well I never,* pas possible! *well met!* heureuse rencontre! *wellnigh,* presque; *we might as well be* . . ., autant vaudrait être . . .; *well, of all the cheek!* ça alors, quel toupet! *well then?* alors? *you might as well say,* autant vaudrait dire.

well-balanced, *a.* Bien équilibré. well-being, *n.* Bien-être, *m.* well-born, *a.* Bien né. well-bred, *a.* Bien élevé. well-built, *a.* Bien bâti (of a person). well-conducted, *a.* Qui se conduit bien; bien mené, bien dirigé (of things). well-doer, *n.* Personne qui fait le bien, *f.* well-doing, *n.* Bien faire, *m.*, bonnes œuvres, *f.pl.*; succès, *m.*, prospérité, *f.* well-earned, *a.* Bien mérité. well-favoured, *a.* De bonne mine, bien fait. well-founded or well-grounded, *a.* Bien fondé. well-informed, *a.* Instruit; bien renseigné (in facts), averti. well-knit, *a.* Compact, solide, bien bâti. well-known, *a.* Bien connu, célèbre. well-mannered, *a.* Aux bonnes manières, bien élevé. well-matched, *a.* Bien assorti; de force égale. well-meaning, *a.* Bien intentionné. well-meant, *a.* Fait à bonne intention. well-minded, *a.* Bien disposé. wellnigh, *adv.* Presque. well-pleasing, *a.* Agréable. well-read, *a.* Instruit, qui a beaucoup lu. well-situated, *a.* Bien situé. well-spent, *a.* Bien employé. well-spoken, *a.* Qui parle bien; bien dit (of things). well-timed, *a.* À propos, fait à propos. well-to-do, *a.* Très aisé, cossu. *To become well-to-do,* faire sa fortune. well-trained, *a.* Bien préparé; (dog) bien dressé. well-tried, *a.* Bien éprouvé. well-watered, *a.* Bien arrosé. well-wisher, *n.* Ami, partisan, *m.*, personne qui veut du bien (à), *f.* well-worn, *a.* Usé, vieux.

Wellingtonia [weliŋ'touniə], *n.* Sequoia, Wellingtonia, *n.*

wellingtons ['weliŋtənz], *n.pl.* Demi-bottes, bottes en caoutchouc, *f.pl.*

Welsh [welʃ], *a.* Gallois, du pays de Galles.— *n.* Gallois (language), *m.*; (*pl.*) les Gallois (people).

welsh, *v.t., v.i.* Escroquer (horse-racing).

welsher, *n.* Bookmaker marron, *m.*

Welshman, *n.* Gallois, *m.*

welsh-rabbit, *n.* Rôtie au fromage, *f.*

Welshwoman, *n.* Galloise, *f.*

welt [welt], *n.* Bordure (of glove); trépointe (of sole), *f.*

welter ['weltə], *v.i.* Se vautrer, se rouler; nager, être baigné (dans). *Weltering in his blood,* baigné dans son sang.—*n.* Confusion, *f.*; pêle-mêle, *m.*

wen [wen], *n.* Loupe, *f.*; goitre (on the neck), *m.*

Wenceslas ['wensisləs]. Venceslas, *m.*

wench [wenʃ], *n.* Donzelle; souillon (slut), *f.*

wend [wend], *v.t., v.i.* Aller. *To wend one's way,* s'acheminer, se diriger (vers).

went, *past* [GO].

wept, *past* and *p.p.* [WEEP].

were, *past pl.* [BE].

wer(e)wolf ['wə:wulf], *n.* Loup-garou, *m.*

west [west], *n.* Ouest, occident, couchant, *m.* —*a.* De l'ouest, occidental. *West coast,* côte occidentale, *f.*; *west wind,* vent d'ouest, *m.*— *adv.* À l'ouest.

westering, *a.* Passant à l'ouest.

westerly, *a.* D'ouest.—*adv.* Vers l'ouest.

western, *a.* De l'ouest, occidental, ouest, d'occident; à l'ouest (of aspect). *Great Western Railway,* Chemin de fer de l'Ouest, *m.*; *the Western Church,* l'Église d'Occident,

l'Église romaine, *f.*; *Western European Union,* l'Union de l'Europe Occidentale, *f.*; *the Western islands,* les Îles Hébrides, *f.pl.*—*n.* (*Cine. fam.*) Film de cowboys, western, *m.*

westernize, *v.t.* Occidentaliser.

Westphalia [wes'feiliə]. La Westphalie, *f.*

westward, *adv.* À l'ouest. westwardly, *adv.* En se dirigeant vers l'ouest.

wet [wet], *a.* Mouillé, humide; pluvieux, de pluie (of the weather). *It is wet,* il pleut; *to get wet,* se mouiller; *to have wet feet,* (*fig.*) avoir le trac; *wet blanket,* rabat-joie, *m.*; *wet dock,* bassin à flot, *m.*; *wet nurse,* nourrice, *f.*; *wet paint,* peinture fraîche, *f.*; *wet through,* mouillé jusqu'aux os, trempé.—*n.* Humidité; pluie, *f.* *Do not stay out in the wet,* ne vous exposez pas à la pluie.—*v.t.* Mouiller, humecter; arroser; (*Print.*) tremper. (*colloq.*) *To wet one's whistle,* s'humecter le gosier.

wether ['weðə], *n.* Bélier châtré, mouton, *m.*

wetness ['wetnis], *n.* Humidité, *f.*; état pluvieux, *m.*

wetting, *n.* Trempage, *m.* *To get a wetting,* se faire mouiller. wetting-board, *n.* (*Print.*) Ais, *m.* wetting-down, *n.* Trempage, *m.* wetting-room, *n.* Tremperie, *f.*

wettish, *a.* Un peu humide, un peu mouillé.

whack [hwæk], *n.* Grand coup, *m.*; (*fam.*) part, *f.*—*v.t.* Frapper, battre.

whacking, *n.* Raclée.—*a.* (*colloq.*) Énorme, épatant, fameux.

whale [hweil], *n.* Baleine, *f.* whale-boat, *n.* Baleinière, *f.* whalebone, *n.* Baleine, *f.* whale-fishing, *n.* Pêche à la baleine, *f.* whaleman, *n.* Matelot baleinier, *m.* whale-oil, *n.* Huile de baleine, *f.* whaler, *n.* Baleinier; navire baleinier, *m.* whaling, *n.* Pêche à la baleine, *f.* *Whaling vessel,* baleinier, *m.*

whapper [WHOPPER].

wharf [hwɔ:f], *n.* (*pl.* wharfs or wharves) Quai, embarcadère, débarcadère; entrepôt (for goods), *m.* wharfage, *n.* Quayage, *m.*

wharfinger ['hwɔ:findʒə], *n.* Propriétaire du quai; garde-quai, *m.*

what [hwɔt], *pron.rel.* Ce qui, ce que, qui, que, celui qui.—*inter. pron.* Qu'est-ce qui? qu'est-ce que? *And what not,* et cætera; *give me what I want,* donnez-moi ce dont j'ai besoin *or* ce qu'il me faut; *Mr. What's-his-name,* Monsieur Chose; *that's what it is,* voilà ce que c'est; *to give someone what for,* tancer vertement quelqu'un; *to know what's what,* en savoir long, savoir de quoi il retourne; *what! can't you?* comment! ne le pouvez-vous pas? *what do you take me for?* pour qui me prenez-vous? *what else?* quoi d'autre? *what for?* pourquoi? *what of that?* qu'est-ce que cela fait? *what if,* et si; *what I like best,* ce que j'aime le mieux; *what is it?* qu'est-ce? *what is it?* qu'est-ce? *what is it like?* comment est-il? *what it is,* ce que c'est; *what little there was,* le peu qu'il y avait; *what not,* et le reste, et tout ce qui s'ensuit; *what on earth . . .,* que diable . . .; *what's done cannot be undone,* ce qui est fait est fait; *what's one man's meat is another man's poison,* ce qui nuit à l'un sert à l'autre; *what's that?* qu'est-ce que c'est que cela? *what's the matter?* qu'y a-t-il? de quoi s'agit-il? *what's up?* qu'est-ce qui se passe? *what's the use,* à quoi bon? *what then?* et alors? et après?

what though . . ., qu'importe que . . .; *what though it were so?* quand même cela serait? *what with exile, poverty,* sans compter l'exil, la pauvreté; *why then, I tell you what,* eh bien! je vais vous dire.—*a.* Quel, *m.,* quelle, *f.,* quels, *m.pl.,* quelles, *f.pl. What lies!* quels mensonges! *what manner of man was* . . ., quel homme c'était que . . .; *what people?* quelles gens? *what town is that?* quelle est cette ville?

whatever [hwɔ'tevə], *pron.* and *a.* Quoi que ce soit; quelque . . . que, tout ce qui, tout ce que (all that). *He had no part whatever in it,* il n'y prit aucune part; *of no use whatever,* absolument inutile; *whatever renders human nature amiable,* tout ce qui rend la nature humaine aimable; *whatever restraints are laid,* quelques entraves que l'on impose; *whatever they are,* quels qu'ils soient; *whatever you do, do it well,* quoi que vous fassiez, faites-le bien.

whatnot, *n.* Étagère, *f.*

whatsoever [WHATEVER].

whaup [hwɔːp], *n.* (*Sc.*) Courlis, *m.*

wheat [hwiːt], *n.* Blé, froment, *m.*

wheatear, *n.* Épi de blé, *m.*; (*Orn.*) traquet, *m.*

wheaten, *a.* De froment. *Wheaten bread,* pain de gruau, *m.*

wheat-field, *n.* Champ de blé, *m.* **wheat-grass,** *n.* Chiendent, *m.* **wheat-sheaf,** *n.* Gerbe de blé, *f.*

wheedle [hwiːdl], *v.t.* Cajoler, enjôler, câliner, embobeliner. *To wheedle some money out of,* soutirer de l'argent à. **wheedler,** *n.* Enjôleur, *m.* **wheedling,** *n.* Cajolerie, câlinerie, *f.*—*a.* Cajoleur, câlin.

wheel [hwiːl], *n.* Roue, *f.*; volant (steering-wheel), *m.*; rouet (for spinning), *m.*; révolution, *f.,* tour, cercle (revolution); soleil (firework), *m. Driving wheel,* roue motrice, *f.; flywheel,* volant, *m.; front wheel,* roue avant; *potter's wheel,* le tour du potier; *the man at the wheel,* l'homme de barre, (*fig.*) l'homme à la tête des affaires; *the wheel went over his body,* la roue lui passa sur le corps; *to break a fly on the wheel,* tirer sa poudre aux moineaux; *to break upon the wheel,* rouer; *to go on oiled wheels,* aller comme sur des roulettes, aller bon train; *to put one's shoulder to the wheel,* pousser à la roue; *wheel and axle,* treuil, *m.; wheel of fortune,* roue de la fortune, *f.; wheels within wheels,* des complications sans fin, *f.pl.*—*v.t.* Rouler, faire tourner; brouetter (in a barrow); voiturer, transporter (to remove).—*v.i.* Rouler (sur des roues); tourner, se tourner (to move round); tournoyer (to whirl); (*Mil.*) faire une conversion. *Left wheel!* tournez à gauche! *right wheel!* tournez à droite! *to wheel about,* tourner, (*Mil.*) faire une conversion, promener (a child etc.) en petite voiture; *to wheel round,* faire volte-face.

wheel-animalcule, *n.* Rotifère, *m.* **wheel-barrow,** *n.* Brouette, *f.* **wheelbase,** *n.* Empattement, *m.* **wheelbrace,** *n.* Vilebrequin à roues, *m.* **wheel-chair,** *n.* Voiture de malade, *f.*

wheeled, *a.* À roues. *Two-wheeled,* à deux roues. **wheeler,** *n.* Cheval de brancard, timonier, *m. Four-wheeler,* voiture à quatre roues, *f.* **wheeling,** *n.* (*Mil.*) Conversion, *f.*; (birds) tournoiement, *m.*

wheel-house, *n.* (*Naut.*) Kiosque, *m.* **wheel-race,** *n.* (*Tech.*) Voie de la roue, *f.* **wheel-shaped,** *a.* En forme de roue. **wheel-spin,** *n.* Chasse, *f.* **wheel-work,** *n.* Rouages, *m.pl.* **wheelwright,** *n.* Charron, *m.*

wheeze [hwiːz], *v.i.* Siffler en respirant, être asthmatique.—*n.* (*slang*) Plaisanterie, facétie, *f.* **wheezing,** *n.* Sifflement, *m.,* respiration sifflante, *f.* **wheezy,** *a.* Poussif, asthmatique; cornard (horse).

whelk [hwelk], *n.* Buccin, *m.*; (*Med.*) papule, *f.*

***whelm** [hwelm], *v.t.* Submerger; (*fig.*) ensevelir, accabler, engloutir.

whelp [hwelp], *n.* Petit (d'un fauve); ourson (bear); lionceau (lion); louveteau (wolf), *m.*

when [hwen], *conj.* Quand, lorsque; que, où; et alors (and then). *One day when,* un jour que *or* où; *since when,* depuis lors; *the day when I saw him,* le jour où je l'ai vu; *when dining,* étant à dîner; *when I come* (future), quand je viendrai; *when in doubt, do nothing,* dans le doute abstiens-toi; *when I* (shall) *have finished,* lorsque j'aurai fini; *when the world was young,* du temps que la reine Berthe filait.—*inter. adv.* Quand est-ce que? quand?

whence [hwens], *adv.* D'où.

whencesoever [hwenso'evə], *adv.* De quelque endroit que; quelle qu'en soit la cause.

whenever [hwen'evə] *or* **whensoever** [hwenso'evə], *adv.* Toutes les fois que, à n'importe quel moment que. *Whenever you like,* quand vous voudrez.

where [hwɛə], *adv.* Où; là où. *That's where you're wrong,* c'est là que vous vous trompez; *where have we got to?* où en sommes-nous?

whereabout ['hwɛərəbaut], *adv.* *Où; à propos de quoi.

whereabouts, *adv.* Où à peu près.—*n.* Lieu approximatif où se trouve quelqu'un *or* quelque chose. *To know someone's whereabouts,* savoir où quelqu'un est.

whereas [hwɛər'æz], *adv.* Au lieu que, tandis que; (*Law*) vu que, attendu que. **whereat** [-'æt], *adv.* À quoi, de quoi; sur quoi. *Whereat are you offended?* de quoi vous offensez-vous? *whereat he left abruptly,* sur quoi il partit subitement.

whereby [hwɛə'bai], *adv.* Par lequel, par où.

wherefore ['hwɛəfɔː], *adv.* Pourquoi, c'est pourquoi, donc. *The whys and wherefores,* les pourquoi et les comment.

wherein [hwɛə'rin], *adv.* En quoi, dans lequel, où.

whereof [hwɛə'rɔv], *adv.* Dont, de quoi, duquel.

whereon [hwɛə'rɔn] *or* **whereupon,** *adv.* Sur quoi, sur lequel; là-dessus.

wheresoever [WHEREVER].

whereto [hwɛə'tuː], *adv.* À quoi, auquel; où.

wherever [hwɛə'revə], *adv.* Partout où, n'importe où, en quelque lieu que ce soit.

wherewith [hwɛə'wið] *or* ***wherewithal** [-'ɔːl], *adv.* Avec quoi, avec lequel; de quoi. *To find the wherewithal,* fournir les moyens (de) *or* l'argent nécessaire (pour); *not to have the wherewithal to,* n'avoir pas les moyens (de), n'avoir pas de quoi.

wherry ['hweri], *n.* Bachot, *m.*; boisson de cidre (de pommes sauvages), *f.*

whet [hwet], *v.t.* Aiguiser, affiler; (*fig.*) exciter, stimuler.—*n.* Aiguisement, repassage; (*fig.*) excitant, stimulant, *m.*

whether ['hweðə], *conj.* Soit que; si, que. *The question is whether* . . ., la question est de savoir si . . .; *whether he does it or not*, qu'il le fasse ou non; *whether* . . . *or*, soit . . . soit, si . . . ou, que . . . ou.

whetstone, *n.* Pierre à aiguiser, *f.*

whetter ['hwetə], *n.* Aiguiseur, *m.*; *(fig.)* stimulant, aiguillon, *m.*

whetting, *n.* Aiguisement, aiguisage, *m.*

whey [hwei], *n.* Petit lait, *m.* **wheyish**, *a.* Blanchâtre.

which [hwitʃ], *rel. pron.* Qui, que, lequel, *m.*, laquelle, *f.*, lesquels, *m.pl.*, lesquelles, *f.pl.*; ce qui, ce que (that which), *m.* *In which*, dans lequel, où; *of* or *from which*, dont, duquel, *m.*, de laquelle, *f.*, desquels, *m.pl.*, desquelles, *f.pl.*; *take which you will*, prenez celui que vous voudrez; *to which*, auquel, *m.*, à laquelle, *f.*, auxquels, *m.pl.*, auxquelles, *f.pl.*; *which is which?* lequel des deux est-ce? —*a.* Quel, *m.*, quelle, *f.*, quels, *m.pl.*, quelles, *f.pl.*; lequel, *m.*, laquelle, *f.* *Which colour?* quelle couleur? *with which words she hurried into the house*, à ces mots elle se hâta d'entrer dans la maison.

whichever [hwitʃ'evə], *pron.* Lequel, *m.*, laquelle, *f.*, lesquels, *m.pl.*, lesquelles, *f.pl.*; quelque . . . que. *Take whichever road you please*, prenez le chemin que vous voudrez; *whichever you buy*, n'importe lequel que vous achetiez.

whiff [hwif], *n.* Bouffée, haleine; cardine (fish), *f.*—*v.t.* Lancer en bouffées.

whiffle [hwifl], *v.i.* Tourner à tous vents, changer. **whiffler**, *n.* Girouette, *f.* **whifflery**, *n.* Hésitations, équivoques, *f.pl.*

Whig [hwig], *n.* Whig, *m.* **Whiggery** or **Whiggism**, *n.* Whiggisme, *m.*

while (1) [hwail], *n.* Temps, *m.* *A little while*, peu de temps; *a little while ago*, il y a peu de temps; *all the while*, tout le temps; *all this while*, pendant ce temps-là; *a long while ago*, il y a longtemps; *between whiles*, entre temps, par moments; *for a while*, pour un temps; *it is not worth while*, cela n'en vaut pas la peine; *it is worth while to*, cela vaut la peine de; *the while*, en attendant.—*v.t.* Passer, faire passer. *To while away the time*, tuer le temps.

while (2) or **whilst** [hwailst], *conj.* Pendant que, tandis que, en même temps que (implying contrast); en, tout en (before a present participle). *While doing*, tout en faisant; *while there's life there's hope*, tant qu'il y a de la vie, il y a de l'espoir; *while walking up and down*, tout en allant et venant.

*whilom ['hwailəm], *adv.* Jadis.—*a.* De jadis, d'antan.

whilst, *conj.* [WHILE].

whim [hwim], *n.* Caprice, *m.*, fantaisie, lubie, *f.*; *(mining)* cabestan, *m.*

whimbrel ['hwimbrəl], *n.* Petit courlis, *m.*

whimper ['hwimpə], *v.i.* Pleurnicher. **whimpering**, *n.* Pleurnichement, *m.*—*a.* Pleurnicheur, geignard.

whimsical ['hwimzikl], *a.* Fantasque, capricieux, bizarre. **whimsically**, *adv.* Capricieusement, fantasquement. **whimsicalness** or **whimsicality** [-'kæliti], *n.* Caractère capricieux, *m.*, bizarrerie, *f.*

whin [hwin], *n.* Ajonc, genêt épineux, *m.*

whinberry, *n.* Airelle, *f.*

whinchat, *n.* (*Orn.*) Tarier, *m.*

whine [hwain], *v.i.* Se plaindre, geindre, pleurnicher.—*n.* Pleurnichement, gémissement, *m.*, plainte, *f.* **whiner**, *n.* Pleurnicheur, *m.*

whining, *n.* Gémissement, geignement, *m.*; (*fig.*) plaintes, lamentations, *f.pl.*—*a.* Plaintif, dolent. **whiningly**, *adv.* En pleurnichant, d'un ton plaintif.

whinny ['hwini], *v.i.* Hennir.—*n.* Hennissement, *m.*

whinstone ['hwinstoun], *n.* (*Min.*) Trapp, basalte, tuff volcanique, *m.*

whip [hwip], *n.* Fouet, *m.*; cravache (for riding), *f.*; (*Naut.*) cartahu; (*Parl.*) secrétaire d'un parti, appel fait aux membres d'un parti, *m.* *To be a bad whip*, ne pas savoir conduire (un cheval); *to be a good whip*, savoir bien conduire; *to give someone the whip*, donner le fouet à quelqu'un.—*v.t.* Fouetter, donner des coups de fouet à; surlier (a rope etc.); (*Dress.*) surjeter, faire un surjet à; (*fig.*) battre, flageller, fustiger. *To whip* (a stream), fouetter; *to whip away*, chasser à coups de fouet, enlever vivement (to take away); *to whip down*, faire descendre à coups de fouet, faire descendre vite (to take down); *to whip in*, faire entrer à coups de fouet, rentrer vite (to put in); *to whip off*, chasser à coups de fouet, ôter vite (to take off), enlever; *to whip on*, faire avancer à coups de fouet, passer vite (a garment); *to whip out*, faire sortir à coups de fouet, expulser (de); *to whip up*, faire monter à coups de fouet, ramasser vivement (to pick up), activer, rallier (people).—*v.i.* (*fig.*) Courir bien vite. *How he whips along!* comme il court! *to whip away*, partir au plus vite, décamper; *to whip down*, descendre vivement; *to whip into*, entrer vivement dans; *to whip off*, partir au plus vite; *to whip out*, sortir en un clin d'œil, s'esquiver; *to whip round*, tourner en un clin d'œil.

whip-cord, *n.* Fouet, *m.*; (*Tex.*) fil à fouet, *m.* **whip-graft**, *v.t.* Greffer à l'anglaise. **whip-grafting**, *n.* Greffe anglaise, *f.* **whip-hand**, *n.* Dessus, avantage, *m.* *To have the whip-hand*, avoir le dessus (sur), avoir la haute main (sur). **whip-lash**, *n.* Mèche (de fouet), *f.*

whipper, *n.* Fouetteur, *m.* **whipper-in**, *n.* Piqueur, *m.* **whipper-snapper**, *n.* Petit bout d'homme, paltoquet, *m.*

whippet ['hwipit], *n.* Lévrier (de course); (*Mil.*) petit char d'assaut, *m.*

whipping, *n.* Coups de fouet, *m.pl.*, action de fouetter; surliure (of a rope etc.), *f.* *To give a good whipping to*, donner le fouet à, fouetter d'importance. **whippiness**, *n.* Souplesse, élasticité, *f.* **whipping-boy**, *n.* Tête de Turc, *f.* **whipping-post**, *n.* Poteau des condamnés au fouet, *m.* **whipping-top**, *n.* Sabot, *m.*

whipple-tree ['hwipl'tri:], *n.* Palonnier, *m.*

whip-poor-will, *n.* Engoulevent (bird), *m.*

whip-round, *n.* Collecte, *f.*

whip-saw, *n.* Passe-partout, *m.*; scie à chantourner, *f.*

whip-stock, *n.* Manche (de fouet), *m.*

whipster [WHIPPER-SNAPPER].

whir [hwə:], *v.i.* Tourner avec bruit, ronfler, vrombir. **whir**, **whirring**, *n.* Bruissement, ronronnement, *m.*

whirl [hwəːl], *v.t.* Faire tourner, faire tournoyer. *To whirl away,* emporter rapidement. —*v.i.* Tournoyer, tourbillonner; pirouetter. —*n.* Tournoiement; tourbillon (of dust etc.), *m.*

whirligig ['hwəːligig], *n.* Tourniquet, *m.*; pirouette; (*fig.*) vicissitude, *f.*, changement subit, *m.*

whirlpool, *n.* Tourbillon (d'eau), *m.*

whirlwind, *n.* Tourbillon, cyclone, *m.*, trombe, *f. To reap the whirlwind,* récolter la tempête.

whisk [hwisk], *n.* Vergette, époussette, verge (for eggs etc.), *f.*—*v.t.* Épousseter; fouetter (cream); battre (eggs); (*fig.*) remuer, agiter. *To whisk away,* enlever vivement, faire disparaître; *whisked eggs,* œufs à la neige, *m.pl.* —*v.i.* Passer rapidement.

whiskered ['hwiskəd], *a.* À favoris; à moustaches (of animals).

whiskerless ['hwiskəlis], *a.* Sans favoris.

whiskers ['hwiskəz], *n.* Favoris, *m.pl.*; moustache (of a cat etc.), *f. To be the cat's whiskers,* (*fam.*) se croire quelqu'un, le coq du village.

whisky ['hwiski], *n.* Whisky, *m.*, eau-de-vie de grain, *f. Whisky and soda,* whisky à l'eau.

whisper ['hwispə], *n.* Chuchotement; murmure (murmur), *m.*; rumeur, *f.*, bruit qui court (rumour), *m. In a whisper,* tout bas, à l'oreille.—*v.t.* Chuchoter, dire tout bas, dire à l'oreille; (*fig.*) dire en secret, souffler. *To whisper remarks,* faire des observations à voix basse.—*v.i.* Chuchoter, parler tout bas; murmurer.

whisperer, *n.* Chuchoteur, *m.*

whispering, *n.* Chuchotement, *m.*; conversation à voix basse, *f.*; (*fig.*) bruit, *m.*, rumeur, *f.*, bruissement, *m.* (leaves). **whispering-gallery,** *n.* Voûte acoustique, *f.*

whist [hwist], *n.* Whist, *m. A game of whist,* une partie de whist.—*int.* Chut! silence!

whistle [hwisl], *n.* Sifflet; coup de sifflet; sifflement (of the wind); (*colloq.*) gosier, bec (throat), *m. Steam-whistle,* sifflet à vapeur, *m.*; *to blow a whistle,* donner un coup de sifflet; (*colloq.*) *to wet one's whistle,* s'humecter le gosier.—*v.i.* Siffler. *The wind whistles through the forest,* le vent bruit à travers la forêt.—*v.t.* Siffler; appeler en sifflant. *To whistle after,* (*fig.*) courir après; *to whistle for,* siffler; *whistle for it!* attendez-vous y!

whistler, *n.* Siffleur, *m.*

whistling, *n.* Sifflement, coup de sifflet, *m.*—*a.* Sifflant.

whit [hwit], *n.* Iota, point, atome, brin, *m. Every whit,* absolument; *not a whit,* pas le moins du monde, pas du tout; *to be every whit as good,* être tout aussi bon.

white [hwait], *a.* Blanc; (*fig.*) sans tache, pur. *As white as a sheet,* blanc comme un linge; *at white heat,* chauffé à blanc; *to bleed white,* saigner à blanc; *to go white,* blanchir, pâlir; *to show the white feather,* se conduire en poltron; *white friar,* carme, *m.*; *white heat,* chaude blanche, *f.*, chauffage à blanc, *m.*; *white lead,* blanc de céruse, *m.*; *white lie,* mensonge excusable, *m.*; *white lime,* blanc de chaux, *m.*; *white meat,* viande blanche, *f.*; *White Paper,* (*Parl.*) livre blanc, *m.*; *White Russia,* la Russie Blanche, *f.*; *the White Sea,* la Mer Blanche, *f.*; *white squall,* rafale, *f.*;

white with, blanc de, pâle de.—*n.* Blanc; aubier (of wood), *m.*

whitebait ['hwaitbeit], *n.* Blanchaille, *f.*

whitebeam, *n.* Alisier blanc, *m.*

whiteear [WHEATEAR].

white-faced, *a.* Au visage pâle. **white-livered,** *a.* Lâche, poltron.

whiten [hwaitn], *v.t.* Blanchir; (*Build.*) blanchir à la chaux, badigeonner.—*v.i.* Blanchir. **whiteness,** *n.* Blancheur; pâleur, (*fig.*) pureté, *f.* **whitening,** *n.* Action de blanchir, *f.* [WHITING].

whitesmith, *n.* Ferblantier, *m.*

whitetail [WHEATEAR].

whitethorn, *n.* Aubépine, *f.*

whitethroat, *n.* Fauvette babillarde, grisette, *f.*

whitewash, *n.* Blanc de chaux, *m.*—*v.t.* Blanchir à la chaux; badigeonner; (*fig.*) blanchir, réhabiliter, disculper; passer l'éponge sur. **whitewasher,** *n.* Badigeonneur, *m.* **whitewashing,** *n.* Badigeonnage, *m.*

whitewood, *n.* Bois blanc, *m.*

whither ['hwiðə], *adv.* Où, par où. **whithersoever** [-sou'evə], *adv.* N'importe où, en quelque endroit que.

whiting ['hwaitiŋ], *n.* Blanc d'Espagne; (*Ichth.*) merlan, *m. Whiting pout,* tacaud, *m.*

whitish ['hwaitiʃ], *a.* Blanchâtre. **whitishness,** *n.* Couleur blanchâtre, *f.*

whitlow ['hwitlou], *n.* Panaris, mal d'aventure, *m. Whitlow-grass,* drabe, *f.*

Whitsun ['hwitsən], *a.* De la Pentecôte. *Whitsunday* (*Whit Monday*), Le dimanche (le lundi) de la Pentecôte.

Whitsuntide ['hwitsəntaid], *n.* Pentecôte, *f.*

whittle, *v.t.* Amenuiser. *To whittle away,* ronger.

whity-brown ['hwaiti'braun], *a.* Gris-brun, brunâtre, bis; (*fig.*) terne.

whiz(z) [hwiz], *v.t.* Siffler. **whizzing,** *n.* Sifflement, *m.*

who [huː], *pron.* Qui, qui est-ce qui. *As who should say,* comme qui dirait; *who goes there?* qui vive? *the Who's who,* le Bottin mondain; *who is speaking?* (*Teleph.*) qui est à l'appareil?

whoa ['wou], *int.* Ho! Holà!

whodunit [huː'dʌnit], *n.* Roman policier, *m.*

whoever [huː'evə], *pron.* Qui, quiconque; qui que ce soit; celui qui. *Whoever he may be,* quel qu'il soit; *whoever you are,* qui que vous soyez.

whole [houl], *a.* Tout, entier, tout entier (in sound health), complet; intégral; bien portant; en grains (not ground). *A whole hour,* une grande heure; *a whole year,* une année entière; *the whole country,* tout le pays; *the whole show,* (*colloq.*) toute la boutique; *the whole world,* le monde entier; *whole leather,* (*Bookb.*) pleine peau, *f.*; *whole morocco,* plein maroquin, *m.*; *whole-word method,* méthode globale, *f.*—*n.* Tout, ensemble; total, montant, *m.*; somme, totalité, *f. On the whole,* en somme, dans l'ensemble, à tout prendre; *the whole of us,* nous tous.

whole-hearted, *a.* Sincère. **whole-heartedly,** *adv.* De bon, de tout cœur.

wholeness, *n.* Intégrité, *f.*

wholesale ['houlseil], *n.* Vente en gros, *f.*; commerce de gros, *m.*—*a.* En gros. *By wholesale,* en gros, (*fig.*) en masse; *wholesale dealer,* marchand de gros, grossiste, *m.*

wholesaler, *n.* Grossiste, *m.*

wholesome ['houlsəm], *a.* Sain, salubre; salutaire (salutary); utile (useful). **wholesomely,** *adv.* Salubrement, sainement. **wholesomeness,** *n.* Salubrité, nature salutaire, *f.*

wholly ['houlli], *adv.* Entièrement, complètement, tout à fait.

whom [hu:m], *pron.* Que; qui (*indirect object and direct object, of persons only*); lequel, *m.*, laquelle, *f.*, lesquels, *m.pl.*, lesquelles, *f.pl.* (*of persons and things*). *Of whom* or *from whom*, de qui, dont, desquels, desquelles.

whomsoever [hu:msou'evə], *pron.* Qui que ce soit que.

whoop [hu:p], *n.* Huée, *f.*; cri (de guerre), *m.* —*v.t., v.i.* Huer, crier.

whooping, *n.* Huées, *f.pl.*, cris, *m.pl.*; quinte, *f.*

whooping-cough, *n.* Coqueluche, *f.*

whop [hwɔp], *v.t.* Frapper, battre, rosser.

whopper, *n.* (*slang*) Chose énorme, *f.*; mensonge énorme, *m.*; bourde, *f.*

whore [hɔ:], *n.* Prostituée, putain, *f.* **whoredom,** *n.* Prostitution, *f.* **whoreson, n.* Bâtard, *m.*

whorl [hwə:l *or* hwɔ:l], *n.* (*Bot.*) Verticille, *m.*; volute, *f.*; (shell) vortex, *m.*

whortleberry ['hwə:tlbəri], *n.* (*Bot.*) Airelle, myrtille, *f.*

whose [hu:z], *pron.* Dont, de qui; duquel, *m.*, de laquelle, *f.*, desquels, *m.pl.*, desquelles, *f.pl.*; (*inter.*) à qui. *The man whose house I see*, l'homme dont je vois la maison; *whose house is this?* à qui est cette maison? *whose work is this?* de qui est cet ouvrage?

whosoever [hu:sou'evə], *pron.* Qui que ce soit qui.

why [hwai], *adv.* Pourquoi? *Why is it that?* comment se fait-il que? *why not?* pourquoi pas?—*int.* Eh bien, mais! Tiens! *Why then!* eh bien!

wick [wik], *n.* Mèche, *f.* (of lamp).

wicked ['wikid], *a.* Méchant, pervers, mauvais, malin. *The wicked*, les méchants, *m.pl.*; *wicked thing*, méchanceté, *f.* **wickedly,** *adv.* Méchamment, par méchanceté. **wickedness,** *n.* Méchanceté, perversité, *f.*

wicken [wikn], *n.* Sorbier des oiseaux (tree), *m.*

wicker ['wikə], *n.* Osier, *m.*—*a.* D'osier, en osier. **wicker-work,** *n.* Clayonnage, *m.*; vannerie, *f.*

wicket ['wikit], *n.* Guichet, portillon, *m.* **wicket-keeper,** *n.* (*Cricket*) Garde-guichet, *m.*

wide [waid], *a.* Large, grand, ample, vaste, immense (having great extent). *A table three feet wide*, une table large de trois pieds, une table de trois pieds de largeur; *done to the wide*, (*pop.*) absolument épuisé, vanné; *the statement is wide of the truth*, l'assertion est loin de la vérité; *to open wide*, ouvrir tout grand; *wide boy*, (*colloq.*) resquilleur, *m.*; *wide of the mark*, loin du but.—*n.* (*Cricket*) = *wide ball*, balle écart, faute, *f.*—*adv.* Loin, au loin, largement; tout à fait, complètement, bien. *Far and wide*, partout; *wide apart*, écarté, espacé.

wide-awake, *a.* Bien éveillé; (*fig.*) sur ses gardes. *Wide-awake eyes*, yeux tout grands ouverts.—*n.* Feutre à bords relevés (hat), *m.*

widely, *adv.* Au loin, loin; grandement; largement; bien, beaucoup. *Widely known*, bien connu.

wide-mouthed, *a.* Évasé; (person) bouche bée.

widen, *v.t.* Élargir, étendre.—*v.i.* S'élargir, s'étendre. **wideness,** *n.* Largeur, étendue, *f.* **widening,** *n.* Élargissement, *m.*

wide-open, *a.* Grand ouvert, tout ouvert.

wide-spread or **wide-spreading,** *a.* Répandu; général, universel.

widgeon ['widʒən], *n.* Canard siffleur, maréca, *m.*; sarcelle, *f.*

widow ['widou], *n.* Veuve, *f.*—*v.t.* Rendre veuve *or* veuf.

widowed, *a.* Veuf; (*fig.*) privé (de). *Widowed of his hopes*, veuf de ses espérances.

widower, *n.* Veuf, *m.*

widowhood, *n.* Veuvage, *m.* **widowhunter,** *n.* Coureur de veuves, *m.*

width [widθ], *n.* Largeur, étendue; envergure, *f.*

wield [wi:ld], *v.t.* Manier, tenir. **wieldable,** *a.* Maniable. **wielder,** *n.* Celui qui manie, *m.*

wife [waif], *n.* (*pl.* **wives**) Femme, épouse, *f.* *The merry wives of Windsor*, les joyeuses commères de Windsor; *the wife*, (*pop.*) la bourgeoise; *to take a wife*, prendre femme, se marier. *Old wife* [BLACK-BREAM]. **wifeless,** *a.* Sans femme, veuf. **wifely** or **wife-like,** *a.* De femme, d'épouse, conjugal.

wig [wig], *n.* Perruque, *f.* *Big wig*, gros bonnet, *m.*; *to wear a wig*, porter perruque. **wigblock,** *n.* Tête à perruque, *f.* **wig-maker,** *n.* Perruquier, *m.*

wigged, *a.* À perruque, portant perruque.

wigging, *n.* (*colloq.*) Savon, *m.*, semonce, *f.* *To give a good wigging to*, donner un savon à, laver la tête à.

wiggle [wigl], *v.t.* Agiter.—*v.i.* Se dandiner. —*n.* Dandinement, *m.*

wight [wait], *n.* Personne, *f.*, être, individu, *m.* *The unhappy wight*, le malheureux.

wigwam ['wigwæm], *n.* Wigwam, *m.*, hutte, *f.*, (de Peaux-Rouges) couverte de peaux *or* d'écorce.

wild [waild], *a.* Sauvage; farouche, barbare (savage); effaré, déréglé, désordonné (disordered); furieux (furious); insensé, extravagant (mad); étrange, bizarre (uncouth). *A wild-goose chase*, une folle entreprise, *f.*; *a wild shot*, un coup perdu, *m.*; *he is on a wild-goose chase*, il cherche midi à quatorze heures; *he lets his imagination run wild*, il laisse trotter son imagination; *to grow wild* (of plants), pousser à l'état sauvage; *to look wild*, avoir l'air effaré, hagard; *to run wild*, vagabonder (of children), se déchaîner, ne pas connaître de bornes; *to sow one's wild oats*, jeter sa gourme; *wild beast*, bête sauvage, *f.*, fauve, *m.*; *wild girl*, étourdie, écervelée, *f.*; *wild horses would not make me speak*, je me ferais tirer à quatre avant de parler; *wild talk*, propos insensés, *m.pl.*—*n.pl.* Désert, lieu sauvage, *m.*, solitude, *f.*, (*fam.*) brousse, *f.*

wild-boar, *n.* Sanglier, *m.* **wild-cat,** *n.* Chat sauvage, *m.* *A wild-cat scheme*, un projet fantasque, *m.*; *wild-cat strike*, grève dénuée de bon sens, grève illégale, *f.*

wilderness ['wildənis], *n.* Désert, lieu désert, *m.*; (*fig.*) solitude inculte, *f.*

wildfire, *n.* Feu grégeois, *m. Like wildfire*, comme l'éclair.

wildfowl, *n.pl.* Oiseaux sauvages, *m.pl.*

wilding, *n.* Sauvageon, *m.*, arbre (spécialement pommier) sauvage, *m.*

wildly ['waildli], *adv.* D'une manière farouche, d'un air effaré; étourdiment, follement; à tort et à travers. *To stare wildly*, regarder d'un air effaré; *to answer wildly*, répondre sans réfléchir.

wildness, *n.* État sauvage; dérèglement, désordre, *m.*, turbulence, licence, dissipation, *f.*

wile [wail], *n.* (*usu. pl.*) Artifice, *m.*, ruse, *f.—v.t.* Tromper, séduire.

wilful ['wilful], *a.* Opiniâtre; obstiné, volontaire, fait à dessein, prémédité, fait avec préméditation (of acts). **wilfully**, *adv.* Opiniâtrement, obstinément; à dessein, avec intention, avec préméditation. **wilfulness**, *n.* Obstination, opiniâtreté, *f.*, entêtement, *m.*

Wilhelmina [wilhel'mi:nə]. Wilhelmine, *f.*

wilily ['wailili], *adv.* Astucieusement. **wiliness**, *n.* Ruse, astuce, *f.*

will [wil], *n.* Volonté, *f.*; vouloir; bon plaisir, gré (pleasure); (*Law*) testament, *m. Against one's will*, contre son gré; *at will*, à volonté, à discrétion, à son gré; *free will*, libre arbitre, *m.*; goodwill, bonne volonté, bienveillance, (*Comm.*) clientèle, *f.*; *ill will*, mauvaise volonté, malveillance, *f.*; *last will and testament*, dernières volontés, *f.pl.*, testament, *m.*; *the will is as good as the deed*, l'intention est réputée pour le fait; *to bear someone ill will*, vouloir du mal à quelqu'un, en vouloir à quelqu'un; *to have a will of one's own*, vouloir bien ce qu'on veut; *to have one's will*, avoir ce qu'on désire, faire à sa tête; *to work one's will*, agir à son gré; *to work with a will*, travailler avec ardeur; *what is your will?* quel est votre bon plaisir? que désirez-vous? *where there's a will there's a way*, vouloir, c'est pouvoir; *with a will*, de bon cœur, avec entrain.

v.t.—Vouloir, ordonner; léguer, disposer de (by testament).—*v.aux.* (*past* **would**) Vouloir (when *will* is the sign of the future, it is not translated, but the English infinitive becomes the future indicative in French; *will* used emphatically may be translated by *vouloir*; *e.g. I will not do it*, je ne veux pas le faire *or* je n'en ferai rien; *what would you have me do?* que voulez-vous que je fasse?). *Do as you will*, faites comme vous l'entendez; *do what he will*, il a beau faire, quoi qu'il fasse; *the town will sometimes smell of malt*, la ville sent parfois le malt; *whether he will or no*, bon gré, mal gré.

William ['wiljəm]. Guillaume, *m. William the Conqueror*, Guillaume le Conquérant; *William the Silent*, Guillaume le Taciturne.

willing ['wiliŋ], *a.* Bien disposé, enclin; de bonne volonté; complaisant; volontaire (voluntary). *God willing*, s'il plaît à Dieu, si Dieu le veut; *to be able and willing*, pouvoir et vouloir; *to be willing*, vouloir bien, être disposé (à); *to lend a willing ear*, prêter l'oreille; *whether he is willing or not*, bon gré, mal gré; *willing to*, désireux de, disposé à.

willingly, *adv.* Volontiers, de bon cœur, de bonne volonté, volontairement.

willingness, *n.* Bonne volonté, *f.*, bon vouloir, *m.*; complaisance, *f.*, empressement, consentement, *m. Willingness to*, bonne disposition à, *f.*, empressement à, *m.*

will-o'-the-wisp [wiləðə'wisp], *n.* Feu follet, *m.*

willow ['wilou], *n.* Saule, *m. Weeping-willow*, saule pleureur, *m.* **willow-bed**, *n.* Saussaie *or* saulaie, *f.* **willow-herb**, *n.* Épilobe, laurier Saint-Antoine, *m.* **willow-warbler** *or* **willow-wren**, *n.* Pouillot, *m.* **willowy**, *a.* Couvert *or* planté de saules; élancé, svelte (of figure).

willy-nilly ['wili'nili], *adv.* Bon gré mal gré.

wily ['waili], *a.* Rusé, fin, astucieux.

***wimble** [wimbl], *n.* Vilebrequin, *m.*, vrille, *f.—v.t.* Faire un trou dans (avec un vilebrequin).

wimple [wimpl], *n.* Guimpe, *f.*, voile, *m.*

win [win], *v.t.* (*past* and *p.p.* **won** [wʌn]) Gagner (a battle); (*fig.*) acquérir; remporter (a prize, victory, etc.).—*v.i.* Gagner, remporter la victoire, triompher. *To win back*, regagner; *to win over* or *round*, attirer, gagner; *to win through*, surmonter ses difficultés.

wince [wins], *v.i.* Sourciller, tressaillir (de douleur); (*fig.*) reculer (devant).—*n.* Tressaillement, *m.*

winch [wintʃ], *n.* Manivelle, *f.*, treuil (windlass); (*Angling*) moulinet, *m.*

wind (1) [wind], *n.* Vent; souffle, *m.*, respiration, haleine (breath), *f.*; vents, *m.pl.*, flatuosité (flatulence), *f. A breath of wind*, un souffle de vent; *between wind and water*, à fleur d'eau; *high wind*, grand vent; *in the wind*, au vent, dans l'air; *there is something in the wind*, il y a quelque chose qui se manigance; *the north wind*, le vent du nord, (*Lit.*) l'aquilon, *m.*, la bise, *f.*; *the trade-winds*, les vents alizés; *the wind is very high*, il fait grand vent; *to get the wind* (of a ship), gagner le vent; *to get wind*, s'ébruiter, s'éventer; *to get wind of*, avoir vent de; *to get the wind up*, (*pop.*) avoir le trac; *to raise the wind*, (*pop.*) trouver l'argent nécessaire; *to sail against the wind*, naviguer vent debout; *to sail before the wind*, courir vent arrière; *to sail close to the wind*, pincer le vent, naviguer au plus près, (*fig.*) friser la malhonnêteté; *to sow the wind and reap the whirlwind*, semer le vent et récolter la tempête; *to take the wind out of someone's sails*, aller sur les brisées de quelqu'un; *wind and water tight*, clos et bien couvert.—*v.t.* (*past* and *p.p.* **winded**) Faire perdre haleine à, essouffler (a horse); (*Hunt.*) avoir vent de, flairer. **wind-bag**, *n.* Outre, *f.*; (*fig.*) moulin à paroles, *m.* **wind-bore**, *n.* Crépine, *f.* (of pump). **wind-bound**, *a.* Retenu par les vents contraires. **windbreaker**, *n.* (*Am.*) Blouson, *m.* **windcheater**, *n.* (*Cost.*) Blouson, *m.* **windfall**, *n.* Fruit abattu par le vent, *m.*; (*fig.*) bonne aubaine, *f.* **wind-flower**, *n.* Anémone, *f.* **wind-gall**, *n.* (*Vet.*) Molette, *f.* **windgauge**, *n.* Anémomètre, *m.* **windhover** [KESTREL]. **wind-instrument**, *n.* (*Mus.*) Instrument à vent, *m.* **wind-jammer**, *n.* (*Naut.*) voilier, *m.* **windmill**, *n.* Moulin à vent; moulinet (toy), *m.* **windpipe**, *n.* Trachée-artère; trachée, *f.* **wind-sail**, *n.* Manche à vent, *f.* **windscreen**, *n.* (*Motor.*) Pare-brise, *m.*

wind-sock, *n.* (*Av.*) Manche à air, *f.*
windswept, *a.* Venteux. **wind-tight**, *a.*
Imperméable au vent. **wind-tunnel**, *n.*
(*Av.*) Tunnel aérodynamique, *m.*
wind (2) [waind], *v.t.* (*past* and *p.p.* **wound**
[waund]) Tourner (to turn); enrouler (to
coil); dévider (silk etc.). *To wind off*,
dérouler, dévider; *to wind up*, remonter
(clocks etc.), régler, terminer (to bring to a
settlement); (*Comm.*) liquider.—*v.i.* Se
rouler, s'enrouler, s'enlacer; tourner, faire
un détour; serpenter, aller en spirale (to
turn, twist, etc.). *To wind up*, finir, terminer.
He wound up by saying, il finit en disant; *the
play winds up in this way*, voici le dénouement
de la pièce.
windage ['windidʒ], *n.* (*Artill.*) Vent, *m.*;
dérivation (du projectile), *f.*; (*Eng.*) jeu, *m.*
winded ['windid], *a.* Hors d'haleine, essoufflé.
A long-winded speech, un discours interminable *or* de longue haleine.
winder ['waində], *n.* Dévideur, *m.*, -euse, *f.*;
dévidoir (appliance); remontoir (of a watch),
m.
windiness ['windinis], *n.* Temps venteux, *m.*,
flatuosité (flatulence), *f.*
winding ['waindiŋ], *n.* Sinuosité, *f.*, détour,
méandre; (*Elec.*) enroulement, *m.*—*a.*
Sinueux, tortueux; en spirale, tournant (of a
staircase). **winding-frame**, *n.* Dévideuse, *f.*
winding-gear, *n.* Appareils d'extraction,
m.pl. **winding-machine**, *n.* (*Tex.*) Bobineuse, *f.*; (*Min.*) machine d'extraction, *f.*
winding-sheet, *n.* Linceul, *m.* **winding-
up**, *n.* Liquidation, *f.*; (*fig.*) dénouement, *m.*
windlass ['windləs], *n.* Treuil, vindas; (*Naut.*)
guindeau, cabestan, *m.*
window ['windou], *n.* Fenêtre; glace (of a
train, car, etc.); montre, vitrine, *f.*, étalage
(of a shop), *m.*; (*pl.*) vitraux (of a church),
m.pl. French window, porte-fenêtre, *f.*; *in the
window*, à l'étalage, à la devanture; *out of the
window*, par la portière (of a train, car, etc.);
to break a window, casser un carreau; *to
break the windows*, casser les vitres; *to let
down the window*, baisser la glace (of a train,
car, etc.); *to look out of the window*, regarder
par la fenêtre; *to put up the window*, lever la
glace.
window-blind, *n.* Store, *m.* **window-box**, *n.*
Jardinière, *f.* **window-cleaner**, *n.* Laveur
de carreaux, *m.* **window-curtain**, *n.* Rideau
(de fenêtre), vitrage, *m.* **window-dresser**,
n. Étalagiste. **window-dressing**, *n.* Art de
l'étalage; (*fam.*) trompe-l'œil, *m.*; façade, *f.*
window-frame, *n.* Châssis de fenêtre, *m.*
window-glass, *n.* Verre à vitres, *m.*
window-ledge, *n.* [WINDOW-SILL]. **window-pane**, *n.* Carreau, *m.* **window-sash**,
n. Châssis mobile, *m.* **window-seat**, *n.*
Banquette (dans l'embrasure d'une fenêtre),
f. **window-shopping**, *n.* Lèche-vitrine, *m.*
window-shutter, *n.* Volet; contrevent, *m.*
window-sill, *n.* Rebord *or* appui de fenêtre,
m. **window-strap**, *n.* Tirant de glace, *m.*
windward ['windwəd], *adv.* Au vent. *The
Windward Islands*, Les Îles du Vent, *f.pl.*; *to
keep to windward of*, passer au vent de; *to
windward of*, au vent de.—*n.* Côté du vent, *m.*
windy ['windi], *a.* Du vent; venteux; flatueux
(flatulent); (*fig.*) creux, vain, vide; (*colloq.*)
qui a le trac. *It is windy*, il fait du vent.

wine [wain], *n.* Vin; (*fig.*) vin, *m.*, ivresse, *f.*
Dry wine, vin sec; *good wine needs no bush*, à
bon vin point d'enseigne; *light wine*, petit
vin; *sweet wine*, vin doux.—*v.t. To wine and
dine*, fêter.
winebag, *n.* Outre à vin, *f.*; (*fig.*) sac à vin
(person), *m.* **wine-bibber**, *n.* Buveur,
ivrogne, *m.* **wine-bibbing**, *n.* La boisson, *f.*
wine-bin, *n.* Porte-bouteilles, *m.* **wine-
bottle**, *n.* Bouteille (à vin), *f.* **wine-cask**, *n.*
Fût, *m.* **wine-cellar**, *n.* Cave, *f.* **wine-
cooler**, *n.* Seau à frapper, *m.* **wine-
country**, *n.* Pays vignoble, *m.* **wine-dealer**,
n. Marchand de vin, *m.* **wine-district**, *n.*
Pays vignoble, *m.* **wineglass**, *n.* Verre à
vin, *m.* **wine-grower**, *n.* Propriétaire de
vignes, viticulteur, *m.* **wine-growing**, *n.*
Culture de la vigne, la viticulture, *f.*—*a.*
Viticole. **wine-list**, *n.* Carte des vins, *f.*
wine-merchant, *n.* Négociant en vins, *m.*
wine-press, *n.* Pressoir, *m.* **wineskin**
[WINEBAG]. **wine-taster**, *n.* Dégustateur
(de vins), *m.* **wine-tasting**, *n.* Dégustation
de vins, *f.* **wine-vaults**, *n.pl.* Caves, *f.pl.*,
caveaux, *m.pl.* **wine-waiter**, *n.* Sommelier,
m.
wing [wiŋ], *n.* Aile; (*fig.*) course, *f.*, vol, *m.*;
(*Naut.*) flanc, *m.* (of ship); aile (of a building);
oreille, *f.* (of arm-chair); (*Av.*) escadre, *f.*;
(*Theat.*) (*pl.*) coulisse, *f. In the wings*, dans
la coulisse, à la cantonade; *on the wing*, au
vol; *on the wings of the wind*, sur les ailes du
vent; *to take wing*, s'envoler; *under the wing
of*, (*fig.*) sous la protection de.—*v.t.* Garnir
d'ailes, donner des ailes à; frapper à l'aile,
blesser à l'aile. *To wing one's flight*, s'envoler,
prendre son vol.—*v.i.* Se diriger à tire-d'aile.
wing-case *or* **wing-shell**, *n.* Élytre, *m.*
wing-commander, *n.* (*Av.*) Lieutenant-
colonel; commandant d'escadre aérienne, *m.*
wing-span, *n.* Envergure, *f.*
winged, *a.* Ailé; (*fig.*) rapide; blessé à l'aile
(wounded).
winger, *n.* (*Ftb.*) Ailier, *m.*
wingless, *a.* Sans ailes.
winglet, *n.* Petite aile, *f.*, aileron, *m.*
wink [wiŋk], *n.* Clin d'œil, *m.*, œillade, *f. A
wink is as good as a nod to a blind horse*, c'est
parler à un sourd; *not to sleep a wink*, ne pas
fermer l'œil (de la nuit); *to have forty winks*,
faire un petit somme.—*v.i.* Cligner de l'œil;
clignoter, vaciller (of a light). *To wink at*,
faire signe de l'œil à, faire des signes à;
fermer les yeux sur.
winker, *n.* (*Motor.*) Clignotant, *m.*
winking, *n.* Clignotement; clignement d'œil,
m. Like winking, (*colloq.*) en un clin d'œil.—*a.*
Clignotant; vacillant, tremblant (of a light).
winkle [wiŋkl], *n.* (*Ichth.*) Bigorneau, *m.*
winner ['winə], *n.* Gagnant; vainqueur (in a
race or match etc.), *m. All the winners!*
résultat complet des courses!
winning, *a.* Gagnant; (*fig.*) attrayant,
séduisant. *Winning game*, la belle, *f.* **winning-post**, *n.* Poteau d'arrivée, but, *m.*
winnings, *n.pl.* Gain, *m.*
winnow ['winou], *v.t.* Vanner, tararer; (*fig.*)
examiner, séparer, trier. **winnower**, *n.*
Vanneur, *m.* **winnowing**, *n.* Vannage;
(*fig.*) examen minutieux, triage, *m.* **winnowing-machine**, *n.* Tarare, *m.*
winsome ['winsəm], *a.* Séduisant.

winter ['wintə], *n.* Hiver, *m.* *In the depth of winter,* dans le fort de l'hiver; *in the wintertime,* *in winter,* en hiver.—*a.* D'hiver. *Winter resort,* station hivernale; *the winter visitors,* les hivernants.—*v.i.* Hiverner, passer l'hiver (à).—*v.t.* Conserver pendant l'hiver, hiverner.

winter-apple, *n.* Pomme d'hiver, *f.* **winter-barley,** *n.* Escourgeon, *m.*

winter-garden, *n.* Jardin d'hiver, *m.* **winter-green,** *n.* Pyrole; gaulthérie, *f.*

wintering, *n.* Hivernage, *m.*

winter-quarters, *n.pl.* Quartiers d'hiver, *m.pl.*

wintry, *a.* D'hiver, hivernal; (*fig.*) glacial.

wipe [waip], *v.t.* Essuyer; ébarber (a joint). *To wipe away,* essuyer, enlever; *to wipe off,* effacer; *to wipe up,* nettoyer.—*n.* Action d'essuyer, *f.*; coup (de mouchoir, d'éponge, etc.); (*fig.*) lardon, *m.*; coup de langue, *f.*; taloche, tape, *f.*

wiper, *n.* Torchon, *m.*; essuie-main, *m.*; (*Eng.*) came, *f.* *Windscreen wiper,* essuie-glace, *m.*

wire [waiə], *n.* Fil métallique, fil de fer, fil de laiton, etc.; barreau (of a cage), *m.*; tringle, *f.* (of tyre). *A wire,* une dépêche (telegram); *barbed wire,* fil de fer barbelé, *m.*; *telegraph wire,* fil télégraphique, *m.*; *to pull the wires,* (*fig.*) tirer les ficelles; *wire blind,* store métallique, *m.*; *wire entanglement,* réseau de fil de fer, *m.*—*v.t.* Attacher *or* lier avec du fil de métal; griller; câbler, passer un message; canaliser (a building); télégraphier.

wire-cutters, *n.pl.* Cisailles coupe-fil, *f.pl.*

wiredraw, *v.t.* (*past* **wiredrew,** *p.p.* **wiredrawn**) Tréfiler; (*fig.*) étirer, alambiquer.

wiredrawer, *n.* Tréfileur, *m.* **wiredrawing,** *n.* Tréfilerie, *f.* **wire-gauze,** *n.* Toile métallique, *f.* **wire-grass,** *n.* Pâturin, *m.* **wire-guard,** *n.* Grille de fer, *f.*, garde-feu, *m.* **wire-haired,** *a.* (dog) À poil dur. **wire-heel,** *n.* (*Vet.*) Seime, *f.* **wire-mark,** *n.* Vergeure (on paper), *f.* **wire-mill,** *n.* Tréfilerie, *f.* **wire-netting,** *n.* Grillage, *m.*; treillis métallique, *m.* **wire-puller,** *n.* (*fam.*) Personne qui tient les ficelles, *f.*, meneur politique, *m.* **wire-rope,** *n.* Câble métallique, *m.* **wire-work,** *a.* Treillage métallique, *m.* **wire-worker,** *n.* Treillageur, grillageur, *m.* **wire-working,** *n.* Tréfilerie, *f.* **wireworm,** *n.* Iule, *m.*, larve de taupin, *f.*

wireless, *a.* Sans fil. *Wireless telegram,* dépêche télégraphique, *f.*—*n.* (*fam.*) The *wireless,* la radio, la T.S.F.; *to talk on the wireless,* parler au micro; *wireless concert,* concert radiophonique, *m.*; *wireless-controlled,* radio-guidé; *wireless enthusiast* or *fan,* radiophile, sans-filiste, *m.*; *wireless set,* poste de T.S.F., *m.*, radio, *f.*—*v.t.* Aviser par la radio.

wiring, *n.* Montage sur fil de fer, *m.*; (*Elec.*) canalisation, *f.*; câblage, *m.*; (*Mil.*) pose des barbelés, *f.*

wiry, *a.* De fil métallique; (*fig.*) nerveux, souple.

wisdom ['wizdəm], *n.* Sagesse; prudence, *f.* **wisdom-tooth,** *n.* (*pl.* **wisdom-teeth**) Dent de sagesse, *f.*

wise [waiz], *a.* Sage; discret, prudent (discreet); grave (grave). *A word to the wise is enough,* à bon entendeur salut; *to be none the wiser for it,* n'en être pas plus avancé; *to look*

wise, avoir l'air entendu; (*fam.*) *to put somebody wise to something,* mettre quelqu'un au courant de quelque chose; *wise man,* homme sensé, *m.*; *wise men of the East,* mages, les trois rois, *m.pl.*—*n.* Manière, façon, sorte, guise, *f.* *In no wise,* nullement, en aucune manière, en aucune façon; *in this wise,* de cette manière.

wiseacre, *n.* Prétendu sage, benêt, pédant, *m.*

wise-crack, *n.* Bon mot, *m.*

wisely, *adv.* Sagement; prudemment.

wish [wiʃ], *n.* Souhait, désir, *m.*, envie, *f.*; vœu, *m.* *Best wishes,* meilleurs souhaits, compliments, tous mes vœux de bonheur; *good wishes,* bons souhaits; *have your wish,* qu'il soit fait selon votre désir, comme vous voudrez; *to have one's wish,* avoir ce qu'on désire.—*v.t.,* *v.i.* Souhaiter, désirer, vouloir. *I wish him to be,* je veux qu'il soit; *I wish I could,* je voudrais pouvoir; *I wish I were . . .,* je voudrais être . . .; *I wish that,* je voudrais que; *I wish to know,* je désire savoir; *to wish a pleasant journey,* souhaiter un bon voyage; *to wish for,* souhaiter, désirer; *to wish joy of,* féliciter de; *to wish very much that,* faire des vœux pour que; *to wish well,* vouloir du bien à.

wish-bone, *n.* Lunette, fourchette, *f.* (of fowl).

wisher, *n.* Personne qui souhaite, *f.* *Well-wisher to,* ami sincère de.

wishful, *a.* Désireux (de). *To indulge in wishful thinking,* prendre ses désirs pour des réalités. **wishfully,** *adv.* Avec désir, ardemment.

wishing, *n.* Souhaits, *m.pl.*

wishing-bone, *n.* [WISH-BONE].

wishy-washy ['wiʃi 'wɔʃi], *a.* Faible, pauvre, fade; sans consistance.

wisp [wisp], *n.* Bouchon de paille etc., *m.*, poignée de foin etc., touffe d'herbe, traînée de fumée, mèche (hair), *f.* *Will-o'-the-wisp,* feu follet, *m.*—*v.t.* *To wisp over,* bouchonner (a horse).

wistaria [wis'tɛəriə], *n.* Glycine, *f.*

wistful ['wistful], *a.* Désireux; (air, regard, sourire) d'envie, de regret, désenchanté, pensif. **wistfully,** *adv.* D'un air d'envie *or* de vague regret.

wit [wit], *n.* Esprit; l'esprit, entendement, jugement, *m.*; (*fig.*) personne spirituelle, *f.*, bel esprit; (*pl.*) esprit, *m.*, raison, tête, *f.*, sens, bon sens, *m.* *To be at one's wits' ends,* ne plus savoir à quel saint se vouer, ne savoir que faire; *to drive out of his wits,* faire perdre la tête à; *to frighten out of his wits,* faire une peur horrible à; *to have lost one's wits,* avoir perdu la tête; *to live by one's wits,* vivre d'expédients.—*v.t.* Savoir. *To wit,* savoir, à savoir, c'est-à-dire.

witch [witʃ], *n.* Sorcière, magicienne, *f.* **witchcraft,** *n.* Sorcellerie, magie noire, *f.* **witch-doctor,** *n.* Sorcier guérisseur, *m.*

witchery, *n.* Sorcellerie, *f.*; (*fig.*) charme, enchantement, *m.*, fascination, *f.*

witch-hazel, *n.* (*Bot.*) Hamamélis, *m.*

with [wið], *prep.* Avec; de, par (by means of); à, au, à la, aux (in descriptive phrases); chez, parmi (among); auprès de (in the estimation of); malgré (in spite of). *Angry with,* fâché contre; *a room with plastered walls,* une salle aux murs crépis; *coffee with milk,* café au lait, *m.*; *content with,* content de; *covered with* *snow*, couvert de neige; *I am disgusted with that*, je suis dégoûté de cela; *imbued with*, imbu de, pénétré de; *I shall be with you in a moment*, je suis à vous dans un instant; *lighted with gas*, éclairé au gaz; *struck with*, frappé de; *the lady with blue eyes*, la dame aux yeux bleus; *to abound with*, abonder en; *to begin with*, en premier lieu; *commencer par*; *to cover with*, couvrir de; *to fight with*, se battre contre; *to go with*, aller avec; *to inspire with confidence*, inspirer confiance à; *to work with all one's might*, travailler de toutes ses forces; *to meet with*, voir, rencontrer, trouver; *to sleep with one's eyes open*, dormir les yeux ouverts; *to speak with one's hands in one's pockets*, parler les mains dans les poches; *to write with a pen*, écrire avec une plume; *what do you want with her?* que lui voulez-vous? *with all his faults*, malgré tous ses défauts; *with arms in one's hands*, les armes à la main; *with a view to*, en vue de, avec l'intention de; *with care!* fragile! *with child*, enceinte; *with him*, à ses yeux; *with steady steps*, d'un pas ferme; *with study*, par l'étude; *with the right hand*, de la main droite; *with which words*, à ces mots; *with young*, pleine (animal).

withal [wiˈðɔːl], *adv*. Avec tout cela, en outre; aussi, de plus; en même temps.

withdraw [wiðˈdrɔː], *v.t. (past* **withdrew**, *p.p.* **withdrawn)** Retirer; rappeler; éloigner (de). *To withdraw one's word*, retirer *or* reprendre sa parole.—*v.i.* Se retirer, s'éloigner de. *To withdraw from*, s'en aller de, s'éloigner de, s'esquiver de.

withdrawal, *n*. Retraite, *f*.; retrait (taking away), *m*.

withdrawing, *n*. Rappel (of troops etc.), *m*. *withdrawing-room [DRAWING].

withe [waið], *n*. Osier, brin d'osier, *m*.

wither [ˈwiðə], *v.i.* Se dessécher; se flétrir, se faner; (*fig*.) dépérir, languir.—*v.t.* Flétrir, dessécher.

withering, *a*. Qui flétrit; brûlant (blasting); écrasant, foudroyant (sarcastic). **witheringly**, *adv*. D'un air écrasant, d'une manière flétrissante.

withers [ˈwiðəz], *n.pl.* Garrot (of horse), *m*.

withhold [wiðˈhould], *v.t. (past* and *p.p.* **withheld)** Retenir, détenir; arrêter, comprimer; refuser. *To withhold from*, s'abstenir de.

within [wiˈðin], *prep*. Dans, en; à moins de (not exceeding). *To live within one's income*, ne pas dépenser plus que son revenu; *within a lifetime*, en moins d'une vie d'homme; *within a pound or so*, à une livre près; *within the week*, avant la fin de la semaine; *within eighty or a hundred yards*, à moins de quatre-vingts ou cent mètres; *within it*, au dedans, en dedans; *within one's reach*, à sa portée; *within reach of*, à portée de; *within the memory of man*, de mémoire d'homme; *within two days*, dans un délai de deux jours.—*adv*. En dedans, à l'intérieur; à la maison, chez soi (in the house).

without [wiˈðaut], *prep*. En dehors de, hors de; sans (not having). *That goes without saying*, cela va sans dire; *to be better without*, se trouver mieux sans.—*conj*. À moins que, sans que (unless). *Without his knowing it*, sans qu'il le sache; *without (unless) I send for it*, à moins que je ne l'envoie chercher.—*adv*. En dehors, au dehors, à l'extérieur.

withstand [wiðˈstænd], *v.t.* (*past* and *p.p.* **withstood)** Résister à, soutenir, combattre; subir (to endure). *There is no withstanding him*, impossible de lui résister, on ne saurait rien lui refuser.

withy [ˈwiði], *n*. Osier, *m*.; hart, *f*. (for bundling faggots etc.).—*a*. D'osier.

witless [ˈwitlis], *a*. Sans esprit; sot. **witlessly**, *adv*. Sans esprit, sottement.

witling, *n*. Petit esprit; (*iron*.) bel esprit, *m*.

witness [ˈwitnis], *n*. Témoin; témoignage (testimony), *m*. *Eye-witness*, témoin oculaire; *in the witness-box*, à la barre des témoins; *to bear witness to*, témoigner de, rendre témoignage de; *to be called as a witness*, être cité comme témoin; *to call to witness*, prendre à témoin, appeler en témoignage; *witness for the defence*, témoin à décharge, *m*.; *witness for the prosecution*, témoin à charge, *m*.—*v.t.* Témoigner, attester, constater; être témoin de, voir, assister à; voir faire; certifier véritable, légaliser (a signature).—*v.i.* Témoigner, porter témoignage.

witted [ˈwitid], *a*. À l'esprit . . . (*in compounds*). *Half-witted*, niais; *quick-witted*, à l'esprit vif.

witticism, *n*. Pointe, *f*.; trait d'esprit, bon mot, *m*.

wittily, *adv*. Spirituellement, avec esprit.

wittiness, *n*. Esprit, caractère spirituel, *m*.

wittingly, *adv*. Sciemment, à dessein.

witty, *a*. Spirituel; plaisant (facetious).

wives, *pl.* [WIFE].

wizard [ˈwizəd], *n*. Sorcier, magicien, *m*.—*a*. (*fam*.) Épatant.

wizardry, *n*. Sorcellerie, *f*.

wizened [ˈwizənd], *a*. Ratatiné, ridé.

woad [woud], *n*. Guède, *f*., pastel, *m*.

wobble [ˈwɔbl], *v.i.* Vaciller, ballotter, brimbaler, zigzaguer. **wobbling**, *n*. Vacillation, *f*.; dandinement, *m*.—*a*. Vacillant, branlant.

wobbly, *a*. Branlant, vacillant, flageolant.

woe [wou], *n*. (*fig*.) Peine, douleur, *f*.; malheur, *m*.—*int*. Tale of woe, récit de malheurs, *m*.; *woe to whom* . . ., malheur à qui . . .!

woebegone or **woeful**, *a*. Triste, malheureux, abattu, piteux. **woefully**, *adv*. Tristement, douloureusement.

wold [would], *n*. Plaine onduleuse, pays vallonné, *m*.

wolf [wulf], *n*. (*pl.* **wolves**) Loup, *m*. *She-wolf*, louve, *f*.; *to be as hungry as a wolf*, avoir une faim de loup; *to cry wolf*, crier au loup; *to keep the wolf from the door*, écarter la faim.—*v.t.* Engloutir, avaler à grosses bouchées.

wolf-cub, *n*. Louveteau, *m*. **wolf-dog**, *n*. Chien-loup, *m*. **wolf-fish**, *n*. Loup marin, *m*. **wolfish**, *a*. De loup; (*fig*.) rapace, vorace. **wolf's-bane**, *n*. Aconit (plant), *m*. **wolf's-claw**, *n*. Lycopode (plant), *m*.

wolfram [ˈwulfrəm], *n*. Tungstène, *m*.

woman [ˈwumən], *n*. (*pl.* **women** [ˈwimin]) Femme, *f*. *Old woman's remedy*, remède de bonne femme, *m*.; *woman is fickle ever*, souvent femme varie; *woman must have her way*, ce que femme veut, Dieu le veut.

woman-hater, *n*. Ennemi des femmes, misogyne, *m*. **womanhood**, *n*. État de femme, *m*. **womanish**, *a*. Féminin; efféminé (effeminate). **womanize**, *v.i.* Courir les femmes. **womankind**, *n*. Le sexe féminin, *m.*; les femmes, *f.pl.* **woman-like** or **womanly**, *a.* De femme, typiquement féminin.—*adv.* En femme, comme une femme. **womanliness**, *n.* Fémininité, *f.*

womb [wu:m], *n.* (*Anat.*) Matrice, *f.*; (*fig.*) sein, *m.*, flancs, *m.pl.*

women, *pl.* [WOMAN].

won [wʌn], *past and p.p.* [WIN].

wonder ['wʌndə], *n.* Étonnement, *m.*, surprise, admiration; merveille (cause of wonder), *f.*, miracle, prodige, *m. A nine days' wonder*, la merveille d'un jour; *for a wonder*, chose étonnante, *f.*; *it is a wonder he was not killed*, c'est merveille qu'il n'ait pas été tué; *it is a wonder that*, il est étonnant que (with subjunctive); *no wonder!* ce n'est pas étonnant! cela n'a rien d'étonnant; *the seven wonders of the world*, les sept merveilles du monde; *the wonder is that* . . ., ce qu'il y a d'étonnant, c'est que . . . .; *to do wonders*, faire des merveilles *or* des prodiges; *to promise wonders*, promettre monts et merveilles.—*v.i.* S'étonner, être étonné; se demander. *To wonder at*, s'étonner de, s'émerveiller de; *to wonder whether*, se demander si.

wonderful, *a.* Étonnant, merveilleux, prodigieux; (*fam.*) épatant. *The wonderful part of the matter is* . . ., le merveilleux de l'affaire, c'est que . . . . **wonderfully**, *adv.* Étonnamment, merveilleusement, prodigieusement. *Wonderfully well*, à merveille, merveilleusement bien.

wonderland, *n.* Pays des merveilles, *m.*

wonderment, *n.* Étonnement, *m.*

wonder-struck, *a.* Frappé d'étonnement, émerveillé.

wonder-worker, *n.* Faiseur de prodiges, thaumaturge, *m.* **wonder-working**, *a.* Qui fait des merveilles.

wondrous ['wʌndrəs], *a.* Merveilleux, prodigieux, étonnant, incroyable. **wondrously**, *adv.* Étonnamment, prodigieusement, merveilleusement.

won't [wount] [*short for* WILL NOT].

wont [wount], *n.* Coutume, habitude, *f.*—*a.* *To be wont to*, avoir l'habitude de.—*v.i.* Avoir coutume (de), être habitué (à). **wonted**, *a.* Accoutumé, habituel.

woo [wu:], *v.t.* Faire la cour à; courtiser; rechercher en mariage; (*fig.*) solliciter, inviter.

wood [wud], *n.* Bois; bois (forest), *m.*, forêt, *f. In the wood*, en fût, en cercles (of wine etc.); *you can't see the wood for the trees*, vous vous noyez dans les détails.

wood-anemone, *n.* Anémone des bois, *f.*

wood-ashes, *n.pl.* Cendres de bois, *f.pl.*

woodbine, *n.* Chèvrefeuille, *m.*

woodchuck, *n.* Marmotte, *f.*

woodcock, *n.* Bécasse, *f. Scotch woodcock*, rôtie de pain dorée au beurre d'anchois et couverte d'un hachis d'œufs durs.

woodcut, *n.* Gravure sur bois, *f.* **woodcutter**, *n.* Bûcheron; graveur sur bois, *m.* **wood-cutting**, **wood-engraving**, *n.* Gravure sur bois, *f.*

wooded, *a.* Boisé.

wooden, *a.* De bois, en bois; (*fig.*) gauche (clumsy). *Wooden ship*, navire en bois, *m.*; *wooden spoon*, (Cook.) mouvette, *f.*; (spt.) dernière position, *f.*; *wooden walls*, murailles en bois, *f.pl.*, navires, vaisseaux, *m.pl.* **woodenness**, *n.* Raideur, *f.*

wood-engraver, *n.* Graveur sur bois, *m.* **wood-house** or **wood-shed**, *n.* Bûcher, *m.* **woodland**, *n.* Pays boisé, bois, *m.*—*a.* Des bois, sylvestre. **wood-louse**, *n.* (*pl.* **woodlice**) Cloporte, *m.*

woodless, *a.* Sans bois, sans forêts.

woodman, *n.* (*pl.* **woodmen**) Garde forestier; bûcheron, *m.* **wood-note**, *n.* Chant rustique, *m.*, mélodie champêtre, *f.* **woodnymph**, *n.* Nymphe des bois, dryade, *f.* **woodpecker**, *n.* Pic, (green) pivert, *m.* **wood-pigeon**, *n.* Pigeon ramier, *m.* **woodpile**, *n.* Tas de bois, *m.*

wood-pulp, *n.* Pâte de bois, *f.*

woodruff, *n.* Aspérule odorante, *f.* **woodsandpiper**, *n.* (*Orn.*) Chevalier sylvain, *m.* **wood-screw**, *n.* Vis à bois, *f.* **woodsorrel**, *n.* Oseille sauvage, *f.*

wood-wind, *n.* (*Mus.*) Les bois, *m.pl.*

woodwork, *n.* Boiserie; menuiserie; charpente, *f.* **woodworker**, *n.* Menuisier, travailleur du bois, *m.* **wood-worm**, *n.* Artison, *m.*

woody, *a.* Boisé; ligneux.

wood-yard, *n.* Chantier, *m.*

wooer ['wu:ə], *n.* Amoureux, prétendant, soupirant, *m.*

woof [wu:f], *n.* Trame; étoffe, *f.*, tissu (texture), *m.*

wooing ['wu:iŋ], *n.* Cour, *f.* **wooingly**, *adv.* Amoureusement, avec amour.

wool [wul], *n.* Laine, *f.*; (*Bot.*) poil, duvet, *m.*; cheveux crépus (hair), *m.pl. Ball of wool*, pelote de laine, *f.*; *dyed in the wool*, teint en laine; (*fig.*) pur; *great cry and little wool*, beaucoup de bruit pour rien.

wool-comber, *n.* Peigneur de laine, *m.*

wool-gathering, *n.* Rêvasserie, *f. To go woolgathering*, battre la campagne (of wits).

woollen ['wulən], *a.* De laine, à laine.—*n.pl.* Tissus de laine, *m.pl.*, laines, *f.pl.*, lainages, *m.pl.* **woollen-cloth**, *n.* Drap, *m.* **woollendraper**, *n.* Marchand de draps, *m.* **woollengoods**, *n.* (*fam.*) **woollies**, *n.* Lainages, *m.pl.*

woolliness ['wulinis], *n.* Nature laineuse; (*fig.*) imprécision, *f.*

woolly ['wuli], *a.* Laineux, qui ressemble à de la laine; couvert de laine (clothed with wool); crépu (of the hair); (*fig.*) (*fam.*) vaseux. *Woolly suit* (for children), esquimau, *m.*

wool-pack, *n.* Sac *or* ballot de laine, *m.*

Woolsack, *n.* Sac de laine (seat of the Lord Chancellor), *m.*; (*fig.*) dignité de Lord Chancelier, *f.*

wool-work, *n.* Tapisserie, *f.*

word [wə:d], *n.* Mot, *m.*; (spoken) parole, *f.*; (*pl.*) mots, *m.pl.*, paroles (dispute), *f.pl.*; promesse (promise), *f.*; avis, *m.*, nouvelle (tidings), *f.*; Verbe (second Person of the Trinity), *m. A harsh word*, un mot dur; *a word to the wise*, à bon entendeur salut; *by word of mouth*, de vive voix; *he is a man of few words*, c'est un homme qui parle peu; *idle words*, paroles en l'air; *in a word*, en un mot; *in other words*, en d'autres termes; *in the full sense of the word*, dans toute l'acception du terme; *in these words*, en ces termes; *I take you at your word*, je vous prends au mot; *not a word!* bouche close! *on one's word*, sur parole; *sharp's the word!* vite! *take my word for it*, croyez-m'en; *to be a man of one's* *word*, être homme de parole; *to break one's word*, manquer à sa parole; *to bring word*, venir dire, informer, prévenir; *to eat one's words*, se rétracter, retirer ce qu'on a dit; *to have a word with*, dire deux mots à; *to have words*, avoir des mots, se quereller, se brouiller; *to keep one's word*, tenir parole; *to leave word*, prévenir; *to send word to*, envoyer dire à, faire savoir; *to speak a good word for*, dire un mot en faveur de; *without a word*, sans mot dire; *with these words*, à ces mots, ce disant; *word for word*, mot à mot (in translating), mot pour mot (in repeating).—*v.t.* Exprimer; énoncer; rédiger (a telegram etc.). *Thus worded*, ainsi conçu. **word-book,** *n.* Vocabulaire, lexique, *m.*

wordiness, *n.* Prolixité, verbosité, *f.*

wording, *n.* Expression, rédaction, teneur, *f.*, style; énoncé (of a problem), *m.*

wordless, *a.* Sans parole.

word-painter, *n.* Qui excelle dans la description. **word-painting,** *n.* Vive description, *f.*

wordy, *a.* Verbeux, diffus.

wore, *past* [WEAR (2)].

work [wə:k], *v.i.* (*past* and *p.p.* **worked, wrought** [rɔ:t]) Travailler; fonctionner, marcher, aller, jouer, agir (to act); opérer, avoir de l'effet (to operate); fermenter (to ferment); (*fig.*) s'agiter, se remuer, se mouvoir. *To work hard*, travailler dur; *to work in*, pénétrer, entrer; *to work loose*, se desserrer, branler; *to work on someone*, agir sur quelqu'un; *to work out*, sortir, aboutir; se monter (à); *to work well*, fonctionner bien.—*v.t.* Travailler; façonner (to shape); faire, se faire, se créer (to make); se frayer (one's way); payer (one's passage) en travaillant; produire (to produce); broder (to embroider); faire fermenter, faire travailler (to cause to ferment); faire aller, faire mouvoir, manœuvrer (a machine etc.); manœuvrer (a ship); exploiter (a mine, a railway, etc.); (*Print.*) tirer. *To be worked by*, (of a machine) marcher à; *to work (a horse) to death*, surmener, crever; *to work down*, réduire; *to work in*, faire entrer (à force d'efforts); *to work off*, user, se débarrasser de, employer, (*Print.*) tirer; *to work oneself up to*, s'exciter à, se monter la tête jusqu'à; *to work one's way through*, se frayer un chemin; *to work out*, effectuer par son travail, acquitter (une dette) par son travail, payer en travaillant, résoudre (a problem), se créer (a connexion etc.); *to work up*, travailler, employer (to use up), soulever, exciter, enflammer (to excite); *to work up an article*, élaborer un article; *we have worked up all our material*, nous avons employé tous nos matériaux.

n.—Travail; ouvrage, *m.*, besogne (work done); action, œuvre (action), *f.*; effet (effect), *m.*; broderie (embroidery); (*fig.*) affaire, chose; (*Lit.*) œuvre, *f.*; (*pl.*) mécanisme (of an engine), *m.*; (*pl.*) manœuvres (of a machine), *f.pl.*; fabrique, usine (factory), *f.*; (*Fort.*) travaux, *m.pl.*; (*Horol.*) mouvement, *m.*; (*Lit. etc.*) œuvres (collected), *f.pl. At work*, au travail; (*fig.*) en jeu; *day's work*, journée, *f.*; *good works*, bonnes œuvres, *f.pl.*; *housework*, le service de la maison, *m.*; *it is a work of time*, c'est un ouvrage de longue haleine; *maid of all work*, bonne à tout faire, *f.*; *public works*, travaux publics; *road works*

ahead, attention, travaux! *the medicine has done its work*, la médecine a fait son effet; *this is the way to go to work*, voici la manière de s'y prendre; *to be at work*, être à l'ouvrage, travailler, fonctionner, marcher (of machinery); *to be out of work*, chômer, être sans travail; *to cut out work for*, tailler de la besogne à; *to get through a deal of work*, abattre de la besogne; (*fam.*) *to give someone the works*, passer quelqu'un à tabac; *to know how to set to work*, savoir s'y prendre; *to make short work of*, brusquer; *to set to work*, s'y prendre, se mettre au travail *or* à l'ouvrage, s'y mettre, (*colloq.*) y aller, mettre (machinery), en marche; *to throw out of work*, faire chômer; *what a piece of work!* quel gâchis! quel malheur! *work of art*, œuvre d'art, *f.*; *work of love*, œuvre d'amour, *f.*

workable, *a.* Réalisable; exploitable (of mines etc.).

workaday, *a.* De tous les jours; (*fig.*) prosaïque.

work-bag, *n.* Sac à ouvrage, *m.* **work-box,** *n.* Boîte à ouvrage, *f.* **work-bench,** *n.* Établi, *m.*

worked, *a.* Brodé.

worker, *n.* Travailleur, *m.*, -euse, *f.*; ouvrier, *m.*, -ière, *f.*; employé, *m.*, -ée, *f.*; (*pl.*) les classes laborieuses, *f.pl.*

work-fellow, *n.* Compagnon de travail, *m.*

workhouse, *n.* Asile pour les indigents, *m.*, maison des pauvres, *f.*, dépôt de mendicité, hospice, *m. To come to the workhouse*, prendre le chemin de l'hôpital.

working, *n.* Travail, *m.*; marche, *f.*; fonctionnement, jeu (of machines), *m.*; opération, exécution (operation); fermentation (fermentation); exploitation (of mines etc.); (*Naut.*) manœuvre, *f.*; (*Print.*) tirage, *m.*—*a.* Qui travaille, ouvrier; de travail, de fatigue (of clothes); *Hard working*, laborieux; *in working order*, en état de fonctionnement; *working capital*, capital d'exploitation, *m.*; *working drawing*, plan, *m.*; *working expenses*, frais généraux, *m.pl.*; *working man*, ouvrier, *m.*; *working parts*, parties actives, *f.pl.*; *working party*, (*Mil.*) atelier, *m.*; *working pressure*, pression motrice, *f.*

working-class, *n.* Classe ouvrière, *f.*

working-day, *n.* Jour ouvrable, *m.*

workman, *n.* (*pl.* **workmen**) Ouvrier, artisan, *m. A bad workman always blames his tools*, mauvais ouvrier n'a jamais bons outils.

workmanlike, *a.* Bien fait, bien travaillé.

workmanship, *n.* Ouvrage, travail, *m.*; main d'œuvre, façon, exécution, *f. Of exquisite workmanship*, d'un travail exquis.

work-room, *n.* Atelier, ouvroir, *m.* **work-shop,** *n.* Atelier, *m.* **work-table,** *n.* Table à ouvrage, *f.*

world [wə:ld], *n.* Monde; l'univers; (*fig.*) le monde, *m.*, la vie, *f. All the world over*, dans le monde entier; *a world of good*, un bien infini; *for all the world*, pour tout au monde, exactement; *in this world*, ici-bas; *map of the world*, mappemonde, *f.*; *nothing in the world*, rien au monde, rien du tout; *such is the world*, ainsi va le monde; *the best fellow in the world*, le meilleur garçon du monde; *the first, second world war*, la première, deuxième guerre mondiale, *f.*; *the next world* or *the world to come*, l'autre monde, *m.*; *the whole world* *sprang to arms,* le monde entier courut aux armes; *to come into the world,* venir au monde; *to have been round the world,* avoir fait le tour du monde; *what in the world is the matter with you?* que diantre avez-vous? *world without end,* éternellement, jusqu'à la fin des siècles.

worldliness, *n.* Mondanité; frivolité, *f.*

worldling, *n.* Mondain, *m.*

worldly, *a.* De ce monde, mondain, du monde. **worldly-minded,** *a.* Mondain. **worldly-mindedness,** *n.* Mondanité, *f.*

worldwide, *a.* Universel, répandu partout, mondial. *He has a worldwide reputation,* il jouit d'une réputation universelle.

worm [wə:m], *n.* Ver, *m.*; chenille, larve, *f.*; ver rongeur (remorse); filet (of a screw); serpentin (of a still); (*Artill.*) tire-bourre; (*Tech.*) tire-étoupes, *m.—v.t.* Miner; enlever les vers de, éverrer; (*Naut.*) congréer (a rope). *To worm oneself into,* se glisser, s'insinuer, se faufiler dans; *to worm out,* tirer, arracher (à).

worm-cast, *n.* Déjection de ver (de terre), *f.*

worm-eaten, *a.* Rongé des vers, vermoulu.

worm-gear, *n.* Engrenage, *m.*, à vis sans fin. **worm-hole,** *n.* Trou de ver, *m.*; piqûre (in cloth etc.), *f.* **worm-like,** *a.* Comme un ver, vermiculaire. **worm-powder,** *n.* Poudre vermifuge, *f.* **worm-screw,** *n.* Tire-bourre, *m.* **worm-seed,** *n.* Santonine, *f.*, semen-contra, *m.* **worm-shaped,** *a.* Vermiculaire, vermiforme. **wormwood,** *n.* Armoise amère, *f.*; (*fig.*) fiel, *m.* **wormy,** *a.* Plein de vers; rampant (grovelling).

worn, *p.p.* [WEAR (2)].

worried ['wʌrid], *a.* Tourmenté, harassé, ennuyé. **worrier,** *n.* Tracassier (man); chien qui attaque les moutons, *m.*

worry ['wʌri], *n.* Ennui, tracas, souci, *m.—v.t.* Tourmenter, tracasser; harasser, harceler; déchirer (of dogs etc.).—*v.i.* Se tracasser, se tourmenter, se faire du souci. *Don't worry!* soyez tranquille!

worse [wə:s], *a.* and *n.* Pire; plus mauvais; plus malade, plus mal (in health); plus méchant (more wicked).—*adv.* Plus mal, pis. *All the worse,* d'autant plus mal; *far worse,* bien pis, bien pire; *for the worse,* en mal; *from bad to worse,* de mal en pis; *he gets worse every day,* de jour en jour son état empire; *so much the worse,* tant pis; *to begin again worse than ever,* recommencer de plus belle; *to be none the worse for it,* ne pas s'en trouver plus mal; *to be the worse for,* se trouver plus mal de; *to be worse (of health),* aller plus mal; *to be worse than . . .,* être pire que . . .; *to make matters worse,* par surcroît de malheur; *to make worse,* aggraver, exaspérer, irriter; *worse and worse,* de mal en pis; *worse than ever,* pire que jamais.

worsen, *v.i.* Empirer. **worsening,** *n.* Aggravation, *f.*

worship ['wə:ʃip], *n.* Culte, *m.*, adoration, *f.*; honneur (title), *m. His worship,* son honneur. —*v.t.* Adorer, rendre un culte à.—*v.i.* Adorer; adorer Dieu.

worshipful, *a.* Honorable. **worshipfully,** *adv.* Avec honneur, respectueusement.

worshipper, *n.* Adorateur, *m.*

worshipping, *n.* Adoration, *f.*

worst [wə:st], *a.* Le plus mauvais, le pire.— *adv.* Le pis, le plus mal.—*n.* Le plus mauvais, le pire, le plus mal, le pis; dessous, désavantage, *m. At the worst,* au pis, au plus mal; *do your worst,* faites ce que vous voudrez; *if the worst comes to the worst,* au pis aller; *let us suppose the worst,* mettons les choses au pis; *the worst of it is that,* le pis de l'affaire, c'est que; *to get the worst of it,* avoir le dessous, être battu.—*v.t.* Battre, vaincre, défaire, l'emporter sur. *To be worsted* ['wə:stid], être battu, avoir le dessous.

worsted ['wustid], *n.* Laine peignée, *f.—a.* De laine peignée.

wort [wə:t], *n.* Moût (of beer), *m.*; *herbe, plante, *f.*

worth [wə:θ], *n.* Valeur, *f.*; prix; (*fig.*) mérite, *m. For all one's worth,* de toutes ses forces; *I have bought four pounds' worth of corn,* j'ai acheté pour quatre livres sterling de blé; *to have one's money's worth,* en avoir pour son argent; *worth makes the man,* la valeur d'un homme dépend uniquement de son mérite. —*a.* Qui vaut, valant; qui mérite (deserving); qui est riche de (possessing). *He is worth a million,* il est millionnaire; *not to be worth a brass farthing,* n'avoir pas un sou vaillant; *not to be worth having,* ne valoir rien; *that is worth seeing,* cela vaut la peine d'être vu; *to be worth while,* valoir la peine (de); *to be worth having,* valoir la peine qu'on le possède, être précieux; *to be worth one's weight in gold,* valoir son pesant d'or; *to be worth the money,* être avantageux; *to ride for all one's worth,* aller à tombeau ouvert; *whatever it may be worth,* vaille que vaille; *worth reading,* qui mérite d'être lu.

worthies, *pl.* [WORTHY].

worthily ['wə:ðili], *adv.* Dignement, à juste titre. **worthiness,** *n.* Mérite, *m.*

worthless ['wə:θlis], *a.* Sans valeur, d'aucune valeur, (*fig.*) méprisable, vil, qui ne vaut rien. *Worthless fellow,* vaurien, *m.* **worthlessness,** *n.* Manque de valeur, *m.*; (*fig.*) bassesse, indignité, *f.*

worth-while ['wə:θ'hwail], *a.* Qui vaut la peine (de).

worthy ['wə:ði], *a.* Digne, de mérite, honorable; (*colloq.*) brave. *Worthy of,* digne de, qui mérite.—*n.* Digne homme; (*colloq.*) brave homme; homme illustre, *m.*, célébrité, *f.*

*wot, *1st* and *2nd sing.* [WIT].

would [wud], *past* and *cond.* [WILL]. As past tense of *will, would* is usually translated by *vouloir*; when it is the sign of the subjunctive, it is translated by the conditional or imperfect subjunctive; when it is the sign of the imperfect, it is translated by the imperfect indicative. *He would have paid it, if . . . ,* il l'aurait *or* il l'eût payé, si . . . ; *he would not do it,* il ne voulut pas le faire; *he would read all day,* il lisait pendant toute la journée; *he came back as it was anticipated that he would,* il revint comme on avait prévu; *I thought I would (had better) speak to him before seeing you,* j'ai cru devoir lui parler or j'ai cru bon de lui parler, avant de vous voir; *I thought I would try,* j'ai voulu essayer; *I warned him, but he would do it,* je l'ai averti, mais il a voulu le faire tout de même; *what would you have had him do against three?* I would have had him die, que vouliez-vous qu'il fît contre trois? Qu'il mourût! *would it be?* serait-il? *would to God!* plût à Dieu! *you would have* *it, so don't blame me*, vous l'avez voulu, ne m'en veuillez pas alors.

would-be, *a.* Prétendu, soi-disant.

wound (1) [waund], *past* and *p.p.* [WIND].

wound (2) [wu:nd], *n.* Blessure; plaie, *f. Bullet wound*, coup de fusil, *m.*; *cannon-shot wound*, coup de canon, *m.*—*v.t.* Blesser, faire une blessure à; (*fig.*) offenser. *To wound to death*, blesser à mort. **wounded,** *a.* Blessé. *Wounded in the leg*, atteint à la jambe. *The wounded*, les blessés, *m.pl.* **wounding,** *n.* Action de blesser, *f.*

wove, *past*, **woven,** *p.p.* [WEAVE].

wow [wau], *int.* Fichtre!—*n.* (*fam.*) Succès formidable, *m.*

wrack [ræk], *n.* Varech, *m.*; ruine, destruction, *f.*, débris, *m.*

wraith [reiθ], *n.* Revenant, *m.*; apparition, *f.*

wrangle [ræŋgl], *n.* Dispute, querelle, *f.*—*v.i.* Se disputer, se quereller, se chamailler, discutailler.

wrangler, *n.* Querelleur, *m.*, querelleuse, *f.*; (*Cambridge*) étudiant en mathématiques, classé dans la première classe, *m.*

wrangling, *n.* Dispute, *f.*, chamailleries, *f.pl.* —*a.* Querelleur.

wrap [ræp], *v.t.* Rouler, enrouler, envelopper (dans *or* de). *To be wrapped up in*, être absorbé dans, être engoué de (a woman), être plongé dans; *to wrap oneself up*, s'emmitoufler; *to wrap up*, envelopper (dans), entortiller. —*n.* Écharpe, *f.*, châle, *m.*

wrapper, *n.* Enveloppe, *f.*; robe de chambre, *f.*, peignoir (garment); *m.*; toile d'emballage (for packing); chemise (for MS.); bande (for a newspaper); couverture (for a book), *f. In a wrapper*, sous bande; *stamped wrapper*, bande timbrée, *f.*

wrapping, *n.* Enveloppe, couverture, *f. Wrapping paper*, papier d'emballage, *m.*

wrasse [ræs], *n.* (*Ichth.*) Labre, *m. Corkwing wrasse*, labre mélops, *m.*, perdrix de mer, *f.*; *cuckoo wrasse*, labre bleu (male), labre trilune (female).

wrath [ro:θ], *n.* Courroux, *m.*, colère, indignation, *f.* **wrathful,** *a.* Courroucé, furieux. **wrathfully,** *adv.* Avec courroux, avec colère.

wreak [ri:k], *v.t.* Exécuter, assouvir, satisfaire. *To wreak one's vengeance upon*, tirer vengeance de, se venger de.

wreath [ri:θ], *n.* Guirlande, *f.*, feston, *m.*; couronne (bridal wreath etc.), tresse; volute (of smoke), *f.*

wreathe [ri:ð], *v.t.* Entrelacer, tresser (de); couronner, ceindre (de); enrouler, entortiller.—*v.i.* S'entrelacer, s'enrouler; tourbillonner (of smoke etc.).

wreathed, *a.* Entrelacé. *Wreathed column*, colonne torse, *f.*

wreck [rek], *n.* Naufrage; navire naufragé (ruins of a ship), *m.*; épave, *f.*, débris, *m.*; (*fig.*) destruction, ruine, perte, *f. This man is a mere wreck*, cet homme n'est plus qu'une ruine; *to go to wreck and ruin*, tomber en ruines.—*v.t.* Faire faire naufrage à; démolir; (*fig.*) ruiner, perdre. *The vessel was wrecked*, le vaisseau fit naufrage.—*v.i.* Faire naufrage.

wreckage, *n.* Débris de naufrage, *m.*, épaves, *f.pl.*; décombres, *m.pl.*

wrecked, *a.* Naufragé, démoli; ruiné. *To be wrecked*, faire naufrage; *wrecked with loss of all hands*, perdu corps et biens.

wrecker, *n.* Pilleur d'épaves, naufrageur, *m.*; destructeur, *m. Train-wrecker*, dérailleur de trains, *m.* **wrecker-car,** *n.* Voiture de dépannage, *f.*

wrecking, *n.* Destruction, ruine, *f.*

wren [ren], *n.* (*Orn.*) Roitelet, *m.*

wrench [rentʃ], *n.* Torsion, *f.*, arrachement, *m.*; entorse, foulure (sprain); clef (tool), *f.*— *v.t.* Arracher (à *or* de); tordre (to twist); se fouler (to sprain). *To wrench one's ankle*, se fouler la cheville.

wrest [rest], *v.t.* Arracher (à); fausser, forcer, tordre (to distort).

wrestle [resl], *v.i.* Lutter. **wrestler,** *n.* Lutteur, *m.* **wrestling,** *n.* Lutte, *f. All-in wrestling*, lutte libre, *f.*

wretch [retʃ], *n.* Malheureux, *m.*, -euse, *f.*, infortuné, *m.*, -ée, *f.*; scélérat, misérable (scoundrel), *m. Poor wretch*, pauvre diable, *m.*, pauvre créature, *f.*

wretched ['retʃid], *a.* Malheureux, misérable; vilain, triste; pitoyable, à faire pitié.

wretchedly, *adv.* Malheureusement, misérablement; d'une manière pitoyable, indignement (despicably). **wretchedness,** *n.* Misère, pauvreté, *f.*; nature méprisable (despicableness), *f.*

wrick [rik], *n.* Effort, *m.*; torsion, *f.*; torticolis (of neck), *m.*—*v.t.* Se donner un effort à. *To wrick one's ankle*, se fouler la cheville.

wriggle [rigl], *v.i.* Se tortiller, se remuer, s'agiter, frétiller. *To wriggle away from*, s'échapper de; *to wriggle into*, se faufiler dans, s'insinuer dans; *to wriggle out of*, se tirer de.— *v.t.* Tortiller. *To wriggle oneself*, se démener; *to wriggle one's way*, se faufiler dans, s'insinuer dans.

wriggler, *n.* Personne qui se tortille, *f.*

wriggling, *n.* Tortillement, frétillement, grouillement, *m.*

*wright [rait], *n.* Ouvrier, constructeur (de), *m. Shipwright*, constructeur de vaisseaux, *m.*; *wheelwright*, charron, *m.*

wring [ring], *v.t.* (*past* and *p.p.* **wrung**) Tordre; arracher (à); presser, serrer (to press hard); (*fig.*) torturer, déchirer, fausser, torturer (to distort); forcer (a mast). *To wring one's hands in despair*, se tordre les mains de désespoir; *to wring the heart*, déchirer le cœur; *to wring the neck of . . .*, tordre le cou à . . . .

wring-bolt [RING-BOLT].

wringer, *n.* Essoreuse (à linge), *f.*

wringing, *n.* Action de se tordre (les mains etc.), *f.*; essorage, *m. Wringing wet*, trempé jusqu'aux os (man); mouillé à tordre (garment).

wrinkle [riŋkl], *n.* Ride (in the face etc.), *f.*; pli, faux pli (in garments); (*slang*) tuyau (a hint), *m. It is a wrinkle worth having*, c'est bon à savoir; *do you want a wrinkle? Well, here's one*, voulez-vous le mot? Eh bien, le voici; *to know a wrinkle or two*, en savoir plus d'une.—*v.i.* Se rider.—*v.t.* Rider; plisser. *To wrinkle one's brow*, froncer les sourcils.

wrinkled, wrinkly, *a.* Ridé; (*Bot.*) plissé, chiffonné.

wrist [rist], *n.* Poignet, carpe, *m.*

wristband, *n.* Poignet, *m.*

wrist-watch, *n.* Montre-bracelet, *f.*

writ (1) [rit], *n.* Exploit, mandat, *m.*, ordonnance, assignation, *f.*; (*Parl.*) lettre de convocation, *f.* Holy writ, l'Écriture sainte, *f.*; *to serve a writ on,* signifier une assignation (à comparaître) à.

***writ** (2), **p.p.* [WRITE].

write [rait], *v.t.* (*past* **wrote,** *p.p.* **written**) Écrire; (*fig.*) graver, tracer. *How do you write this?* comment cela s'écrit-il? *to write a good hand,* avoir une belle écriture; *to write down,* mettre en écrit, coucher par écrit; décrier, abîmer; *to write for,* écrire pour, demander *or* mander (a person) par écrit; *to write in,* insérer; *to write off,* écrire au courant de la plume; (*Comm.*) passer au compte des profits et pertes; *to write out,* transcrire, copier; *to write out in full,* écrire en toutes lettres; *to write over again,* récrire; *to write to say that . . . ,* écrire que . . .; *to write up,* rédiger; faire l'éloge de.—*v.i.* Écrire.

write-off, *n.* Annulation, *f.*; non-valeur, *f.* (person).

writer, *n.* Écrivain; auteur (author); commis aux écritures (clerk), *m.* *He is a good writer,* il écrit bien; *Writer to the Signet,* (*Sc.*) notaire de première classe, *m.*

writhe [raið], *v.i.* Se tordre (de douleur); se crisper.

writing ['raitiŋ], *n.* Écriture, *f.*; écrit (anything written); (*fig.*) ouvrage, document, *m.*; inscription, *f.* *In writing,* par écrit. **writing-book,** *n.* Cahier d'écriture, cahier, *m.* **writing-case,** *n.* Papeterie, *f.* **writing-desk,** *n.* Pupitre, bureau, secrétaire, *m.* **writing-materials,** *n.pl.* Objets pour écrire, *m.pl.* **writing-pad,** *n.* Sous-main, buvard, *m.* **writing-paper,** *n.* Papier à écrire, *m.* **writing-table,** *n.* Table à écrire, *f.*, bureau, *m.*

written [ritn], *a.* Écrit, par écrit. *Written law,* loi écrite, *f.*

wrong [rɔŋ], *a.* Faux, erroné, inexact (incorrect); mal, mauvais; qu'il ne faut pas, faux (not what is wanted). *Of the wrong fount,* (*Print.*) d'un autre œil; *she is on the wrong side of fifty,* elle a passé la cinquantaine; *that is the wrong one,* ce n'est pas celui-là qu'il faut; *that's wrong!* c'est mal! *to be not far wrong,* ne pas se tromper de beaucoup; *to be wrong,* avoir tort (of persons), être mal, être mauvais (of things), n'être pas à l'heure, aller mal (of watches); *to do the wrong work, to bring the wrong book, to take the wrong street, train etc.,* se tromper d'ouvrage, de livre, de rue, de train, etc.; *to have got hold of the wrong end of the stick,* comprendre de travers; *what's wrong with you?* qu'avez-vous? *wrong note,* fausse note; *wrong number,* (*Teleph.*) mauvais numéro; *wrong side,* l'envers, *m.*; *wrong side out(ward),* à l'envers; *wrong side up,* sens dessus dessous. —*adv.* Mal, à tort, à faux; injustement. *To go wrong,* faire fausse route, se tromper.—*n.* Mal, *m.*, injustice, *f.*, tort; dommage, préjudice (injury), *m.* *I am in the wrong,* j'ai tort; *in the wrong,* dans son tort; *to do wrong to,* faire du tort à; *two wrongs don't make a right,* deux noirs ne font pas un blanc.—*v.t.* Faire du tort à, nuire à, léser, faire tort à, faire injure à (to do injustice).

wrongdoer, *n.* Injuste, pervers, méchant, *m.* **wrongdoing,** *n.* Le mal, *m.*

wrongful, *a.* Injuste; nuisible (injurious). **wrongfully,** *adv.* À tort, injustement.

wrong-headed, *a.* Qui a l'esprit de travers, pervers; entêté, opiniâtre. **wrong-headedness,** *n.* Perversité, *f.*

wrongly, *adv.* Mal, à tort. *Rightly or wrongly,* à tort ou à raison.

wrote, *past* [WRITE].

wroth [rɔːθ], *a.* En colère, irrité, courroucé. *To wax wroth,* se mettre en colère, s'indigner.

wrought [rɔːt], *a.* Travaillé, façonné; ouvré (of textile fabrics). *Wrought iron,* fer forgé, *m.*; *wrought-iron balcony,* balcon, *m.*, en fer forgé.

wrung [rʌŋ], *past and p.p.* [WRING].

wry [rai], *a.* De travers, tordu, tors; (*fig.*) oblique, détourné, faux. *To pull a wry face,* faire la grimace.

wryneck, *n.* Torticolis (disease); torcol (bird), *m.* **wrynecked,** *a.* Qui a le cou de travers; qui a le torticolis.

wyandotte ['waiəndət], *a. and n.* (Poule) wyandotte, *f.*

wych-elm ['witʃelm], *n.* Orme des montagnes, *m.*

wynd [waind], *n.* (*Sc.*) Ruelle, *f.*

wyvern ['waivə:n], *n.* (*Her.*) Guivre, vivre, bisse, *f.*

X

X, x [eks]. Vingt-quatrième lettre de l'alphabet, *m.* X, dix.

xanthein ['zænθiin], *n.* Xanthéine, *f.*

xanthin ['zænθin], *n.* Xanthine, *f.*

xanthoma ['zænθoumə], *n.* Xanthoma, xanthome *m.* **xanthophyll,** *n.* Xanthophylle, *f.*

xebec ['ziːbek], *n.* Chébec, *m.*

xenogenesis [zeno'dʒenəsis], *n.* Xénogénèse, *f.*

xenophobia [zenə'foubiə], *n.* Xénophobie, *f.*

xerasia [ziə'reisiə], *n.* Xérasie, *f.*

xerodermia [ziəro'dəːmiə], *n.* Xérodermie, *f.* **xerophagy** [ziə'rɔfədʒi], *n.* Xérophagie, *f.*

Xerxes ['zəːksiːz]. Xerxès, *m.*

xiphias ['zifiəs], *n.* Xiphias, *m.*, espadon, *m.*, épée de mer (fish), *f.*

Xmas ['krisməs], *n.* Noël, *m.*

X-ray, *v.t.* Radiographier.—*a.* Radiographique. *X-ray photograph,* radiographie, *f.*— *n.pl.* X-rays, les rayons X, *m.pl.*

xylem ['zailəm], *n.* Xylème, *m.* **xylene,** *n.* Xylène, *m.*

xylographer [zai'lɔgrəfə], *n.* Xylographe, graveur sur bois, *m.* **xylographic** [-'græfik], *a.* Xylographique.

xylography [zai'lɔgrəfi], *n.* Xylographie, *f.*

xylophagous [zai'lɔfəgəs], *a.* Xylophage.

xylophone ['zailəfoun], *n.* Xylophone; (*slang*) claquebois, *m.*

xyster ['zistə], *n.* (*Surg.*) Rugine, *f.*

xystus ['zistəs], *n.* (*pl.* **xysti**) Xyste, *m.*, galerie couverte, *f.*

Y

Y, y [wai]. Vingt-cinquième lettre de l'alphabet; (l')i grec, *m. Y-shaped*, fourchu.
yacht [jɔt], *n.* Yacht, *m.* **yacht-club,** *n.* Cercle nautique, *m.*
yachting, *n.* Yachting, *m.*; navigation de plaisance, *f.* **yachting-jacket,** *n.* Vareuse, *f.*
yacht-race, *n.* Course de yachts, *f.* **yachtsman,** *n.* (*pl.* **yachtsmen**) Yachtman, *m.*
yaffle [ˈjæfl], *n.* (*Orn.*) Pivert, *m.*
yak [jak], *n.* (*Zool.*) Ya(c)k, *m.*
yam [jæm], *n.* Igname, *f.*
yank [jæŋk], *v.t.* (*fam.*) Tirer brusquement.
Yankee [ˈjæŋki], *n.* Yankee, Américain, *m.*
yap [jæp], *v.i.* Japper, aboyer.—*n.* Jappement, *m.*
yard [jɑːd], *n.* Cour, *f.*, préau, *m.*, cour de la prison, *f.*; chantier (work-yard), *m.*; (*Naut.*) vergue, *f.*; (*Measure*) yard (metre 0·914383), *m. Fifty yards off*, à cinquante mètres; *goods yard*, (*Rail.*) dépôt de marchandises, *m.*
yard-arm, *n.* Bout de vergue, *m.*
yard-man, *n.*, or **yardsman,** *n.* Manœuvre, *m.*; gareur de trains; garçon d'écurie, *m.*
yard-stick, *n.* Mesure d'un yard, *f.*; yard, *m.* (in wood); aune, *f.*
yarn [jɑːn], *n.* Fil; (*Naut.*) fil de caret; récit, conte (story), *m. To spin a long yarn*, débiter une longue histoire.—*v.i.* Débiter des histoires.
yarrow [ˈjærou], *n.* (*Bot.*) Millefeuille, herbe aux charpentiers, *f.*
yatter [ˈjætə], *v.i.* Bavarder.
yaw [jɔː], *n.* (*Naut.*) Embardée, *f.*—*v.i.* Embarder, faire des embardées.
yawl [jɔːl], *n.* (*Naut.*) Sloop, *m.*; (*Row.*) yole de mer, *f.*
yawn [jɔːn], *n.* Bâillement, *m.*—*v.i.* Bâiller; s'ouvrir tout grand (to open wide). *To yawn one's head off*, bâiller comme une carpe *or* à se décrocher la mâchoire.
yawning, *a.* Qui bâille; (*fig.*) béant, ouvert. *The yawning abyss*, le gouffre béant.
***yclept** [iˈklept], *a.* Appelé, dénommé.
***ye** [jiː], *pron.pl.* Vous.
yea [jei], *adv.* Oui; vraiment, en vérité.—*n.* Vote affirmatif, *m.*
yean [jiːn], *v.t., v.i.* Mettre bas, agneler.
yeanling [ˈjiːnliŋ], *n.* Petit agneau, *m.*
year [jə *or* jiə], *n.* An (unit), *m.*; année (a particular year), *f. Academic year*, l'année scolaire; *by the year*, par an, à l'année; *every two years*, tous les deux ans; *every year*, tous les ans; *five thousand a year*, cinq mille livres de rente; *for years together*, plusieurs années de suite, pour des années; *four times a year*, quatre fois par an; *from year to year*, d'année en année; *half-year*, semestre, *m.*; *in the year of our Lord*, l'an de grâce; *last year*, l'an dernier, l'année dernière; *new year*, nouvel an; *next year*, l'an prochain; *one year with another*, bon an mal an; *so much a year*, tant par an; *to be ten years old*, avoir dix ans; *to grow in years*, avancer en âge; *to wish one a happy New Year*, souhaiter la bonne année à quelqu'un; *year by year*, d'année en année; *year in year out*, une année après l'autre; *years and years ago*, il y a bien des années.
year-book, *n.* Annuaire, *m.*

yearling, *a.* Âgé d'un an.—*n.* Poulain, *m.*, or pouliche, *f.*, d'un an.
yearly, *a.* Annuel, de chaque année.—*adv.* Annuellement, tous les ans.
yearn [jəːn], *v.i. To yearn after*, soupirer après, languir après; *to yearn to do something*, brûler de faire quelque chose.
yearning, *n.* Élan de tendresse, *m.*, aspiration, envie, *f.*; désir ardent, *m.*
yeast [jiːst], *n.* Levure, *f.*
yell [jel], *n.* Hurlement, *m.*—*v.i.* Hurler, pousser des hurlements.
yelling, *n.* Hurlements, *m.pl.*
yellow [ˈjelou], *a.* Jaune; (*slang*) poltron. *The yellow press*, les journaux à sensation, *m.pl.*; *to become yellow*, devenir jaune, jaunir; *yellow as a guinea*, jaune comme un coing; *yellow fever* or *yellow jack*, fièvre jaune, *f.*—*n.* Jaune, *m.*—*v.t., v.i.* Jaunir.
yellow-hammer, *n.* (*Orn.*) Bruant jaune, *m.*
yellowish, *a.* Jaunâtre.
yellowness, *n.* Couleur jaune, *f.*; (*slang*) poltronnerie, *f.*
yelp [jelp], *v.i.* Glapir, japper. **yelping,** *n.* Glapissement, jappement, *m.*
yeoman [ˈjoumən], *n.* (*pl.* **yeomen**) Fermier-propriétaire, gros fermier; (*Navy*) garde-magasin, *m. The yeomen of the guard*, les hallebardiers de la garde du corps, *m.pl.*; *yeoman's work*, œuvre d'homme de cœur, *f.*
yeomanry [ˈjoumənri], *n.* Fermiers-propriétaires, *m.pl.*, garde nationale à cheval, *f.*
yes [jes], *adv.* Oui; si, si fait (in reply to a negative). *To say yes*, dire oui, dire que oui; *you have not done it. Yes, I have*, vous ne l'avez pas fait. Si, je l'ai fait, (*colloq.*) si fait; (*inter.*) *yes?* et après?
yes-man, *n.* (*pop.*) Béni-oui-oui, *m.*
yesterday [ˈjestəd(e)i], *adv. and n.* Hier, *m. The day before yesterday*, avant-hier; *we were not born yesterday*, nous ne sommes pas nés d'hier; *yesterday evening*, hier soir, hier au soir; *yesterday was Sunday*, c'était hier dimanche.
***yester-night,** *n.* La nuit dernière, *f.*
yestreen [jesˈtriːn], *adv. and n.* (*Sc.*) Hier soir, *m.*
yet [jet], *conj.* Pourtant, cependant, tout de même.—*adv.* Encore, déjà. *As yet*, jusqu'ici, jusqu'à présent; *not yet*, pas encore.
yew [juː], *n.* (*Bot.*) If, *m.*
Yiddish [ˈjidiʃ], *a. and n.* Yiddish, *m.*
yield [jiːld], *v.t.* Produire, donner, rapporter; livrer, céder, abandonner (to surrender). *To yield up*, rendre, livrer; *to yield up the ghost*, rendre le dernier soupir, l'âme.—*v.i.* Se rendre, céder (à); consentir (à). *To yield to*, se rendre à, céder à, succomber à (temptation).—*n.* Rendement, produit, rapport, *m.*
yielding, *a.* Qui cède facilement; complaisant, accommodant, facile, souple.—*n.* Reddition, *f.*; consentement, *m.*; soumission, *f.*; affaissement, *m.*
yodel [ˈjoudl], *v.i.* Jouler, faire la tyrolienne.
yogi [ˈjougi], *n.* Yogi, *m.*
yogurt [ˈjouguət], *n.* Yahourt, yogourt, *m.*
yoicks! [jɔiks], *int.* (*Hunt.*) Taïaut, taïaut!
yoke [jouk], *n.* Joug; attelage, *m.*, paire, *f.*; carcan, *m.*, palanche, *f.* (for pails); (*Dress.*) empiècement, *m.*—*v.t.* Atteler, accoupler. *To yoke with*, accoupler avec.

yoke-fellow or **yoke-mate**, *n.* Compagnon, *m.*, compagne, *f.*; époux, *m.*, épouse, *f.*
yokel [joukl], *n.* Rustre, campagnard, *m.*
yolk [jouk], *n.* Jaune (d'œuf), *m.*; suint, *m.*
yon [jɔn] or **yonder** ['jɔndə], *adv.* Là, là-bas; là-haut.—*a.* Ce . . . -là, cet . . . -là, cette . . . -là, ces . . . -là. *Yonder castle,* ce château-là, ce château là-bas.
yore [jɔ:], *adv.* Autrefois, jadis. *In days of yore,* dans les jours d'autrefois, au temps jadis.
you [ju:], *pron.* Vous; (to a child, relative, pet, etc.) tu, te, toi; (*indefinite*) on. *If I were you,* si j'étais à votre place; *you English,* vous autres Anglais; *you stupid!* imbécile que vous êtes!
young [jʌŋ], *a.* Jeune; novice, neuf, inexpérimenté (inexperienced); (*fig.*) naissant, peu avancé. *Her young man,* son amoureux, *m.*; *to grow young again,* rajeunir; *to make young again,* rajeunir; *young fellow,* garçon, *m.*; *young folks* or *young people,* jeunes gens, *m.pl.,* jeunesse, *f.*; *young in years,* jeune d'années; *young lady,* demoiselle, *f.*—*n.pl.* Les jeunes, les jeunes gens; les petits, *m.pl.* *The young* (of a beast), les petits, *m.pl.*; *with young* (of animals), pleine.
younger ['jʌŋgə], *a.* Plus jeune; cadet (of two brothers etc.). *In my younger days,* quand j'étais plus jeune; *to grow younger and younger,* rajeunir de plus en plus; *we don't grow younger every day,* nous ne rajeunissons pas; *younger sister,* sœur cadette, *f.*
youngest [-gist], *a.* Le plus jeune.
youngish ['jʌŋiʃ], *a.* Assez jeune.
youngling, *n.* (*poet.*) Jeune animal, *m.*
youngster, *n.* Jeune homme; gamin, mioche, *m.*, gosse, *m.* or *f.*
your [juə], *a.* Votre, (*pl.*) vos; (to a child, relative, pet, etc.) ton, ta, tes; (*indefinite*) son, sa, ses. *Your father,* monsieur votre père; *your mother,* madame votre mère; *your turn,* à vous.
yours, *pron.* Le vôtre, *m.*, la vôtre, *f.*, les vôtres, *pl.*; à vous (your property); de vous (by you); (to a child, relative, pet, etc.) le tien, la tienne, les tiens, les tiennes, à toi (your property), de toi (by you). *A book of yours,* un de vos livres; *yours* or *yours ever* (an unceremonious letter form between intimates), bien cordialement.
yourself [juə'self], *pron.* (*pl.* **yourselves**) Vous-même, (*pl.*) vous-mêmes; (*reflexive*) vous; toi-même; te.
youth [ju:θ], *n.* Jeunesse, adolescence, *f.*; jeune homme, adolescent (young person), *m.*; (*fig.*) jeunes gens, *m.pl.* *The fountain of youth,* la fontaine de jouvence, *f.*; *youth hostel,* auberge de la jeunesse, *f.*
youthful, *a.* Jeune; de jeunesse; frais, vert (fresh). **youthfully**, *adv.* En jeune homme, en jeune fille. **youthfulness**, *n.* Jeunesse, *f.*
yowl [jaul], *v.i.* Hurler.—*n.* Hurlement, *m.*
yucca ['jʌkə], *n.* (*Bot.*) Yucca, *m.*
Yugoslav ['ju:gou'slɑ:v], *a.* and *n.* Yougoslave, *m.* or *f.* **Yugoslavia.** La Yougoslavie, *f.*
yule [ju:l], *n.* Noël, *m.*, fête de Noël, *f.* **yule-log**, *n.* Bûche de Noël, *f.* **yule-tide**, *n.* L'époque de Noël, *f.*

Z

Z, z [zed or (*Am.*) zi:]. Vingt-sixième lettre de l'alphabet, *m.*
Zaccheus [zə'ki:əs]. Zachée, *m.*
Zachariah [zækə'raiə]. Zacharie, *m.*
Zambesi [zæm'bi:zi]. Le Zambèze, *m.*
zany ['zeini], *n.* Zani, zanni, bouffon, *m.*
zeal [zi:l], *n.* Zèle, *m.* *To show too little zeal,* montrer peu de zèle; *to show too much zeal,* faire du zèle. **zealot** ['zelət], *n.* Zélateur, fanatique, *m.* **zealotry**, *n.* Zèle aveugle, zélotisme, fanatisme, *m.* **zealous** ['zeləs], *a.* Zélé, zélateur. **zealously**, *adv.* Avec zèle.
zebra ['zi:brə], *n.* Zèbre, *m.* *Zebra crossing,* passage clouté, *m.*
zebu ['zi:bju:], *n.* Zébu, *m.*
zedoary ['zedouəri], *n.* (*Bot.*) Zédoaire, *f.*
zenana [zə'nɑ:nə], *n.* (*India*) Appartement des femmes (mahométanes), *m.*
zenith ['zeniθ], *n.* Zénith; (*fig.*) point culminant, comble, sommet, apogée, *m.*
Zeno ['zi:nou]. Zénon, *m.*
Zenobia [zə'noubiə], *n.* Zénobie, *f.*
zeolite ['zi:olait]. Zéolithe, *f.*
zephyr ['zefə], *n.* Zéphyr, zéphire, Zéphyre, *m.* **zephyrian** [-'firiən], *a.* Zéphirien. **Zephyrus** ['zefirəs]. Zéphyre. *m.*
zero ['ziərou], *n.* Zéro; (*fig.*) rien, *m.* *Zero hour,* l'heure H, *f.*
zest [zest], *n.* Goût, *m.*, saveur, *f.*; zeste (of orange), *m.*; (*fig.*) entrain, *m.*, verve, *f.* *To give a zest to,* relever le goût de, assaisonner, donner du piquant à.
zeugma ['zju:gmə], *n.* Zeugme, zeugma, *m.*
Zeus [zju:s]. (*Myth.*) Zeus, *m.*
zigzag ['zigzæg], *n.* Zigzag, *m.*—*a.* En zigzag. —*v.t.* Former en zigzags.—*v.i.* Aller en zigzag, zigzaguer. **zigzagging**, *n.* Zigzags, *m.pl.*
zinc [ziŋk], *n.* Zinc, *m.*—*v.t.* Zinguer. **zinc-plating**, *n.* Zingage, *m.* **zinc-roofing**, *n.* Toiture de zinc, *f.* **zinc-sheets**, *n.pl.* Zinc en feuilles, *m.* **zinc-worker**, *n.* Zingueur, *m.* **zinc-works**, *n.* Zinguerie, *m.* **zincographer** [-'kɔgrəfə]. Zincographe, *m.* **zincographic** [-'græfik], *a.* Zincographique. **zincography**, *n.* Zincographie, *f.*
zingaro ['ziŋgərou], *n.m.* (*f.* **zingara**, *pl.* **-ri**, **-re**) Bohémien, *m.*, -ienne, *f.*; tzigane.
zinnia ['zinjə], *n.* (*Bot.*) Zinnia, *m.*
Zion ['zaiən]. Sion, *m.*, (la colline de) Jérusalem.
Zionism, *n.* Sionisme, *m.* **Zionist**, *a.* and *n.* Sioniste, *m.* or *f.*
zip [zip], *n.* Sifflement (of bullet); crissement, *m.*; vitesse, énergie, verve, *f.*—*v.i.* Siffler. **zip fastener** or **zipper**, *n.* Fermeture à glissière, fermeture éclair, *f.*
zither ['ziθə], *n.* Cithare, *f.*
zodiac ['zoudiæk], *n.* Zodiaque, *m.* **zodiacal** [zou'daiəkl], *a.* Zodiacal.
zona ['zounə], *n.* (*Med.*) Zona, *m.*
zone [zoun], *n.* Zone; *ceinture (girdle), *f.*
zoo [zu:], *n.* Jardin zoologique, (*fam.*) zoo, *m.*
zoochemistry [zouo'kemistri], *n.* Zoochimie, *f.* **zoogeny** [-'ɔdʒəni], *n.* Zoogénie, *f.* **zoographer** [-'ɔgrəfə], *n.* Zoographe, *m.* **zoographic** [-ə'græfik] or **zoographical**, *a.* Zoographique. **zoography** [-'ɔgrəfi], *n.* Zoographie, *f.* **zoolatry** [-'ɔlətri], *n.* Zoolâtrie, *f.*

zoolite ['zouolait], *n.* Zoolithe, *m.*
zoological [zouə'lɔdʒikl], *a.* Zoologique.
Zoological gardens, jardin zoologique, *m.*
zoologically, *adv.* D'après les principes de
la zoologie; zoologiquement.
zoologist [zou'ɔlədʒist], *n.* Zoologiste, zoo-
logue, *m.* **zoology,** *n.* Zoologie, *f.*
zoom [zu:m], *n.* Bourdonnement, ronflement,
vrombissement, *m.* (of motors); montée en
chandelle, *f.* (of aeroplane).—*v.i.* Vrombir;
monter en chandelle.
zoomorphism [zouə'mɔ:fizm], *n.* Zoomorphie, *f.* **zoonomy** [-'ɔnəmi], *n.*
Zoonomie, *f.* **zoonomical,** *a.* Zoonomique.
zoophagous [-'ɔfəgəs], *a.* Zoophage.
zoophagy [-'ɔfədʒi], *n.* Zoophagie, *f.*
zoophorus [-'ɔfərəs], *n.* Frise (ornée
d'animaux sculptés), *f.* **zoophytology**
[-əfai'tɔlədʒi], *n.* Zoophytologie, *f.* **zooscopy**

[-'ɔskəpi], *n.* Zooscopie, *f.* **zootomical**
[-ə'tɔmikl], *a.* Zootomique. **zootomist**
[-'ɔtəmist], *n.* Zootomiste, *m.* **zootomy,** *n.*
Zootomie, *f.*
Zoroaster [zɔrou'æstə]. Zoroastre, *m.*
Zoroastrian [zɔrou'æstriən], *a.* and *n.* Zoroastrien, *m.* **Zoroastrianism,** *n.* Zoroas-
trianisme, *m.*
Zouave [zwɑ:v], *n.* Zouave, *m.*
***zounds!** [zaundz], *int.* Morbleu! sapristi!
Zulu ['zu:lu:], *a.* and *n.* Zoulou, *m.*
zygomatic [zaigo'mætik], *a.* Zygomatique.
zygomorphous [-'mɔ:fəs], *a.* Zygomorphe.
zymogen ['zaimədʒen], *n.* Zymogène, *m.*,
proferment, *m.* **zymology** [-'mɔlədʒi], *n.*
Zymologie, *f.* **zymometer** [-'mɔmitə], *n.*
Zymosimètre, *m.*
zymosis [zai'mousis], *n.* Fermentation, *f.*
zymotic [zai'mɔtik], *a.* Zymotique (disease).

FRENCH WEIGHTS AND MEASURES

Metric System

LENGTH

1 millimètre (mm.) (1/1,000 m.)	=	0·039 in.
1 centimètre (cm.) (1/100 m.)	=	0·394 in.
1 décimètre (dm.) (1/10 m.)	=	3·937 ins.
1 mètre (m.)	=	3·281 ft.
1 décamètre (dam.) (10 m.)	=	32·808 ft.
1 hectomètre (hm.) (100 m.)	=	109 yds. 1 ft. 1 in.
1 kilomètre (km.) (1,000 m.)	=	1093 yds. 1 ft. 11 ins.

AREA

1 millimètre carré (mm²) (1/1,000,000 m²)	=	0·002 sq. in.
1 centimètre carré (cm²) (1/10,000 m²)	=	0·155 sq. in.
1 décimètre carré (dm²) (1/100 m²)	=	15·5 sq. ins.
1 centiare (ca.) (1 mètre carré or m²)	=	1·196 sq. yds.
1 are (a.) (100 m²)	=	119·599 sq. yds.
1 hectare (ha.) (10,000 m²)	=	2·471 acres

CUBIC MEASURE

1 millimètre cube (mm³) (1/1,000,000,000 m³)	=	0·00006 cu. in.
1 centimètre cube (cm³) (1/1,000,000 m³)	=	0·061 cu. in.
1 décimètre cube (dm³) (1/1,000 m³)	=	61·023 cu. ins.
1 stère* (1 mètre cube or 1 m³)	=	35·32 cu. ft.
1 décastère* (10 stères)	=	13·08 cu. yds.

*These measures are used only for wood.

CAPACITY

1 centilitre (cl.) (1/100 l.)	=	0·018 pint
1 décilitre (dl.) (1/10 l.)	=	0·176 pint
1 litre (l.) (1 dm³)	=	1·760 pints
1 décalitre (dal.) (10 l.)	=	2·200 galls.
1 hectolitre (hl.) (100 l.)	=	22 galls.

WEIGHT

1 milligramme (mg.) (1/1,000 g.)	=	0.015 gr.
1 centigramme (cg.) (1/100 g.)	=	0·154 gr.
1 décigramme (dg.) (1/10 g.)	=	1·543 gr.
1 gramme (g.)	=	15·432 gr.
1 décagramme (dag.) (10 g.)	=	5·644 dr.
1 hectogramme (hg.) (100 g.)	=	3·527 oz.
1 kilogramme (kg.) (1,000 g.)	=	2·205 lb.
1 quintal métrique (100 kg.)	=	1·968 cwt.
1 tonne métrique (1,000 kg.)	=	19 cwt. 12 oz. 5 dwt.

TEMPERATURE

0° Centigrade	Freezing water	=	32° Fahrenheit
37° Centigrade	Human body	=	98·4° Fahrenheit
40° Centigrade	Fever	=	104° Fahrenheit
100° Centigrade	Boiling water	=	212° Fahrenheit

POIDS ET MESURES

Grande-Bretagne et Commonwealth (British Imperial), États-Unis et Canada français

LONGUEURS

1 line (1/12 in.)	*ligne .	=	0·212 cm.
1 inch (in.)	pouce	=	2·539 cm.
1 hand (4 ins.)	*main .	=	0·102 m.
1 foot (ft.) (12 ins.)	pied .	=	0·305 m.
1 yard (yd.) (3 ft.)	verge .	=	0·914 m.
1 fathom (fm.) (6 ft.)	toise .	=	1·829 m.
1 rod† ou pole ou perch (5½ yds.)	perche	=	5·030 m.
1 chain (22 yds.)	.	=	20·116 m.
1 furlong (fur.) (220 yds.)	stade .	=	201·164 m.
1 mile (m.) (1760 yds.)	mille .	=	1608·64 m.
1 nautical mile (N.M.)	.	=	1853·25 m.
1 league† (3 m.)	lieue .	=	4827 m.

* mesure spéciale au Canada français.   † désuet en Grande-Bretagne.

SURFACES

1 square inch (sq. in.)	=	6·45 cm²
1 square foot (sq. ft.) (144 sq. ins.)	=	929·03 cm²
1 square yard (sq. yd.) (9 sq. ft.)	=	0·84 m²
1 rood (1210 sq. yds.)	=	10·117 a.
1 acre (4840 sq. yds.)	=	40·467 a.
1 square mile (sq. m.) (640 acres)	=	2·59 km²

VOLUMES

1 cubic inch (cu. in.)	=	16·387 cm³
1 cubic foot (cu. ft.)	=	28·317 dm³
1 cubic yard (cu. yd.)	=	0·764 m³

CAPACITÉ

			Gde-Bretagne	États-Unis
1 gill (¼ pint)	roquille	=	0·142 l.	
1 pint (⅛ gall.)	chopine	=	0·568 l.	0·473 l.
1 quart (qt.) (2 pints)	pinte	=	1·136 l.	{ 0·946 l. (liquides) 1·101 l. (matières sèches)
1 gallon (gall.)	gallon	=	4·546 l.	3·785 l.
1 peck (2 galls.)	.	=	9·087 l.	8·809 l.
1 bushel (8 galls.)	.	=	36·348 l.	35·236 l.
1 firkin (9 galls.)	quartaut	=	40·914 l.	
1 hogshead of wine (63 galls.)	barrique	=	2·45 hl.	
1 quarter (64 galls.)	.	=	2·91 hl.	
1 barrel (36 galls.)	baril .	=	1·637 hl.	

POIDS (AVOIR DU POIDS)

		Gde-Bretagne	États-Unis et Canada français
1 dram (dr.) (1/16 oz.)	dragme	1·77 g.	id.
1 ounce (oz.) (1/16 lb.)	once	28·35 g.	id.
1 pound (lb.)	livre	453·59 g.	id.
1 stone (st.) (14 lb.)	—	6·35 kg.	id.
1 quarter (qr.) (28 lb.)	quart (25 lb.)	12·70 kg.	226·80 kg.†
1 hundredweight (cwt.) (112 lb.)	quintal (100 lb.)	50·80 kg.	45·36 kg.
1 ton (t.) (2240 lb.)	tonne (2000 lb.)	1016·04 kg.	907·20 kg.

† ½ tonne (États-Unis)

POIDS DE TROYES (matières précieuses)

1 grain (gr.)	grain .	=	0·065 g.
1 pennyweight (dwt.) (24 gr.)	gros .	=	1·555 g.
1 ounce (oz. Troy) (20 dwt.)	once .	=	31·10 g.
1 pound (lb. Troy) (12 oz. Troy)	livre .	=	373·23 g.

FRENCH IRREGULAR VERBS

1. The Imperfect Indicative, Conditional, Imperative, and Imperfect Subjunctive are not given and may be assumed to be formed as with regular verbs, viz.:

Impf. Indic.: from stem of 1st plural Pres. Indic.

Conditional: from stem of 1st plural Future.

Imperative: (a) 2nd sing., 1st and 2nd plur. by using the forms of Pres. Indic. without pronouns (-er verbs drop s of 2nd sing.).
(b) 3rd sing. and plur. by using the Pres. Subj.

Impf. Subj.: from 2nd sing. Past Hist. (without its final s).

2. Irregular Forms are shown in footnotes.
Compound verbs are given only where they differ from the simple form.

3. In the case of Defective Verbs (marked ¶) all existing forms are shown.

4. All verbs not marked irr. in the Dictionary are regular and are conjugated like aimer, finir or vendre according to their ending (see below).

Infinitive	Participles	Present Indicative	Past Historic	Future	Present Subjunctive	English
			REGULAR VERBS			
			FIRST CONJUGATION (Infinitive in -er)			
aim-er	aim-ant aim-é	aim-e aim-es aim-e aim-ons aim-ez aim-ent	aim-ai aim-as aim-a aim-âmes aim-âtes aim-èrent	aimer-ai aimer-as aimer-a aimer-ons aimer-ez aimer-ont	aim-e aim-es aim-e aim-ions aim-iez aim-ent	to like, to love
			SECOND CONJUGATION (Infinitive in -ir)			
fin-ir	fin-issant fin-i	fin-is fin-is fin-it fin-issons fin-issez fin-issent	fin-is fin-is fin-it fin-îmes fin-îtes fin-irent	finir-ai finir-as finir-a finir-ons finir-ez finir-ont	fin-isse fin-isses fin-isse fin-issions fin-issiez fin-issent	to finish

FRENCH IRREGULAR VERBS

THIRD CONJUGATION
(Infinitive in -re)

Infinitive	Participles	Present Indicative	Past Historic	Future	Present Subjunctive	English
vend-*re*	vend-*ant* vend-*u*	vend-*s* | vend-*ons* vend-*s* | vend-*ez* vend | vend-*ent*	vend-*is* vend-*is* vend-*it* vend-*îmes* vend-*îtes* vend-*irent*	vend-*ai* | vend-*ons* vend-*as* | vend-*ez* vend-*a* | vend-*ont*	vend-*e* | vend-*ions* vend-*es* | vend-*iez* vend-*e* | vend-*ent*	to sell

IRREGULAR VERBS

Infinitive	Participles	Present Indicative	Past Historic	Future	Present Subjunctive	English
aboyer[1]	aboyant aboyé	aboie | aboyons aboies | aboyez aboie | aboient	aboyai . . . aboyâmes . . .	aboierai . . . aboierons . . .	aboie | aboyions aboies | aboyiez aboie | aboient	to bark
¶ absoudre	absolvant absous, *m.* absoute, *f.*	absous | absolvons absous | absolvez absout | absolvent		absoudrai . . . absoudrons . . .	absolve . . . absolvions . . .	to absolve
¶ abstraire	(conjugated like *traire*)					to abstract
¶ accélérer	accélérant accéléré	accélère | accélérons accélères | accélérez accélère | accélèrent	accélérai . . . accélérâmes . . .	accélérerai . . . accélérerons . . .	accélère | accélérions accélères | accélériez accélère | accélèrent	to accelerate
¶ accroire	(used only in the infinitive in the phrase '*faire accroire*', to make one believe)					
acquérir	acquérant acquis	acquiers | acquérons acquiers | acquérez acquiert | acquièrent	acquis . . . acquîmes . . .	acquerrai . . . acquerrons . . .	acquière | acquérions acquières | acquériez acquière | acquièrent	to acquire
¶ advenir	advenant advenu	il advient	il advint	il adviendra	il advienne	to happen
aller[2]	allant allé	vais | allons vas | allez va | vont	allai . . . allâmes . . .	irai . . . irons . . .	aille | allions ailles | alliez aille | aillent	to go
amener	amenant amené	amène | amenons amènes | amenez amène | amènent	amenai . . . amenâmes . . .	amènerai . . . amènerons . . .	amène | amenions amènes | ameniez amène | amènent	to bring

[1] All verbs in -*oyer* and -*uyer* change *y* to *i* before a mute *e*. With verbs in -*ayer* one may use either *y* or *i*. With the verb *grasseyer*, *y* is always used.
[2] 2nd pers. sing. Imperative: *va*.

[639]

Infinitive	Participles	Present Indicative	Past Historic	Future	Present Subjunctive	English
¶ apparoir[1]		il appert				to appear
appeler[2]	appelant, appelé	appelle · appelons / appelles · appelez / appelle · appellent	appelai... appelâmes...	appellerai.... appellerons...	appelle · appelions / appelles · appeliez / appelle · appellent	to call
assaillir	assaillant, assailli	assaille... assaillons...	assaillis... assaillîmes...	assaillirai... assaillirons...	assaille... assaillions...	to assault
asseoir	asseyant or assoyant, assis	assieds[3] · asseyons / assieds · asseyez / assied · asseyent	assis... assîmes...	assiérai... or assoirai... assiérons... or assoirons...	asseye[3]... asseyions...	to set, to seat
astreindre	(conjugated like craindre)					to compel
atteindre	(conjugated like craindre)					to reach
avoir[4]	ayant, eu	ai · avons / as · avez / a · ont	eus.... eûmes...	aurai... aurons...	aie · ayons / aies · ayez / ait · aient	to have
battre	battant, battu	bats,-s,-t · battons...	battis... battîmes...	battrai... battrons...	batte... battions...	to beat
boire	buvant, bu	bois · buvons / bois · buvez / boit · boivent	bus.... bûmes...	boirai... boirons...	boive · buvions / boives · buviez / boive · boivent	to drink
bouillir	bouillant, bouilli	bous · bouillons / bous · bouillez / bout · bouillent	bouillis... bouillîmes...	bouillirai... bouillirons...	bouille... bouillions...	to boil
¶ braire[5]	brayant, brait	il brait · ils braient		il braira · ils brairont		to bray
¶ bruire[6]	bruissant, bruit	il bruit · ils bruissent				to rustle
ceindre	(conjugated like craindre)					to gird

[1] Used as a law term only.
[2] All verbs in -eler and -eter are conjugated like appeler except: celer, ciseler, congeler, dégeler, démanteler, écarteler, geler, marteler, modeler, peler, receler; acheter, crocheter, haleter, racheter, which are all conjugated like amener (use of è instead of doubling the consonant in some persons).
[3] The forms in -oi (or -oi) (same conjugation as prévoir) are accepted by the Académie Française but considered as familiar or even vulgar.
[4] Imperative: aie, ayons, ayez.
[5] Imperfect Indicative: il brayait, ils brayaient.
[6] Imperfect Indicative: il bruissait, ils bruissaient or il bruyait, ils bruyaient.

FRENCH IRREGULAR VERBS

Infinitive	Participles	Present Indicative	Past Historic	Future	Present Subjunctive	English
¶ choir	chu	chois chois choit	chus... chûmes...	cherrai... or choirai... cherrons... or choirons...		to fall
circoncire	circoncisant circoncis	circoncis,-s,-t circoncisons...	circoncis... circoncîmes...	circoncirai... circoncirons...	circoncise... circoncisions...	to circumcise
¶ clore	clos	clos clos clôt | closent		clorai... clorons...	close... closions...	to close
conclure	concluant conclu	conclus,-s,-t concluons...	conclus... conclûmes...	conclurai... conclurons...	conclue... concluions...	to conclude
conduire	conduisant conduit	conduis,-s,-t conduisons...	conduisis... conduisîmes...	conduirai... conduirons...	conduise... conduisions...	to lead to drive
confire	confisant confit	confis,-s,-t confisons...	confis... confîmes...	confirai... confirons...	confise... confisions...	to preserve
connaître	connaissant connu	connais | connaissons connais | connaissez connaît | connaissent	connus... connûmes...	connaîtrai... connaîtrons...	connaisse... connaissions...	to know
conquérir	(conjugated like *acquérir*)					to conquer
construire	(conjugated like *conduire*)					to construct
coudre	cousant cousu	couds... cousons...	cousis... cousîmes...	coudrai... coudrons...	couse... cousions...	to sew
courir	courant couru	cours,-s,-t courons...	courus... courûmes...	courrai... courrons...	coure... courions...	to run
couvrir	(conjugated like *ouvrir*)					to cover
craindre	craignant craint	crains,-s,-t craignons...	craignis... craignîmes...	craindrai... craindrons...	craigne... craignions...	to fear
croire	croyant cru	crois | croyons crois | croyez croit | croient	crus... crûmes...	croirai... croirons...	croie | croyions croies | croyiez croie | croient	to believe
croître	croissant crû, *m.*, crue, *f.*	crois | croissons crois | croissez croît | croissent	crûs... crûmes...	croîtrai... croîtrons...	croisse... croissions...	to grow

Infinitive	Participles	Present Indicative	Past Historic	Future	Present Subjunctive	English
cueillir	cueillant cueilli	cueille... cueillons...	cueillis... cueillîmes...	cueillerai... cueillerons...	cueille... cueillions...	to gather
cuire	(conjugated like *conduire*)					to cook
¶ déchoir[1]	déchu	déchois / déchoyons déchois / déchoyez déchoit / déchoient	déchus... déchûmes...	décherrai... décherrons...	déchoie / déchoyons déchoies / déchoyez déchoie / déchoient	to fall to lose
déduire	(conjugated like *conduire*)					to deduce
détruire	(conjugated like *conduire*)					to destroy
devoir	devant dû, *m.*, due, *f.*, dus, *m.pl.*	dois / devons dois / devez doit / doivent	dus... dûmes...	devrai... devrons...	doive / devions doives / deviez doive / doivent	to owe to have to
dire	disant dit	dis / disons dis / dites dit / disent	dis... dîmes...	dirai... dirons...	dise... disions...	to say
dissoudre	(conjugated like *absoudre*)					to dissolve
dormir	dormant dormi	dors, -s, -t dormons...	dormis... dormîmes...	dormirai... dormirons...	dorme... dormions...	to sleep
¶ échoir	échéant échu	il échoit ils échoient	il échut ils échurent	il écherra ils écherront	il échée ils échéent	to fall due
¶ éclore	éclos	il éclôt ils éclosent		il éclora ils écloront	il éclose ils éclosent	to hatch to bloom (of flowers)
écrire	écrivant écrit	écris, -s, -t écrivons...	écrivis... écrivîmes...	écrirai... écrirons...	écrive... écrivions...	to write
enduire	(conjugated like *conduire*)					to smear
enfreindre	(conjugated like *craindre*)					to infringe
envoyer	envoyant envoyé	envoie / envoyons envoies / envoyez envoie / envoient	envoyai... envoyâmes...	enverrai... enverrons...	envoie / envoyions envoies / envoyiez envoie / envoient	to send
équivaloir	(conjugated like *valoir*)					to be equivalent

[1] No Imperfect Indicative.

Infinitive	Participles	Present Indicative	Past Historic	Future	Present Subjunctive	English
éteindre	(conjugated like *craindre*)					to extinguish
être[1]	étant, été	suis sommes, es êtes, est sont	fus..., fûmes...	serai..., serons...	sois soyons, sois soyez, soit soient	to be
étreindre	(conjugated like *craindre*)					to hug
exclure	(conjugated like *conclure*)					to exclude
¶ faillir	faillant, failli	faut[2]	faillis[3]..., faillîmes...	faudrai *or* faillirai		to fail
faire	faisant, fait	fais faisons, fais faites, fait font	fis..., fîmes...	ferai..., ferons...	fasse..., fassions...	to make, to do
¶ falloir[4]	fallu	il faut	il fallut	il faudra	il faille	to be necessary
feindre	(conjugated like *craindre*)					to feign
¶ férir[5]	féru					to strike
¶ forfaire (à)	forfait					to be false (to)
¶ frire	frit	fris, fris, frit		frirai..., frirons...		to fry
fuir	fuyant, fui	fuis fuyons, fuis fuyez, fuit fuient	fuis..., fuîmes...	fuirai..., fuirons...	fuie fuyions...	to flee
geindre	(conjugated like *craindre*)					to whine, to moan
¶ gésir[6]	gisant	gisons, gisez, gît gisent				to lie

[643]

[1] Imperfect Indic.: *j'étais*; Imperative: *sois, soyons, soyez.*
[2] Only in the phrase *le cœur me faut.*
[3] In current usage followed by an infinitive, *e.g. il faillit tomber*, he nearly fell.
[4] Imperfect Indic.: *il fallait.*
[5] The infinitive is used only in the phrase *sans coup férir*, without striking a blow. *Féru* is adjectival only (*féru d'amour*, lovesick).
[6] The Imperfect Indic., *je gisais*, etc., is used.

Infinitive	Participles	Present Indicative	Past Historic	Future	Present Subjunctive	English
hair	haïssant haï	haïs,-s,-t haïssons...	haïs...[1] haïmes[1]...	haïrai... haïrons...	haïsse... haïssions...	to hate
induire	(conjugated like *conduire*)					to induce
inscrire	(conjugated like *écrire*)					to inscribe
instruire	(conjugated like *conduire*)					to instruct
interdire	(conjugated like *médire*)					to forbid
intervenir	(conjugated like *tenir*)					to intervene
introduire	(conjugated like *conduire*)					to introduce
joindre	(conjugated like *craindre*)					to join
lire	lisant lu	lis,-s,-t lisons...	lus... lûmes...	lirai... lirons...	lise... lisions...	to read
¶ luire	(conjugated like *conduire*)[2]					to gleam
maudire	(conjugated like the regular verbs in *-ir*, e.g. *finir*)[3]					to curse
médire (de)	médisant médit	médis... médisons...	médis... médîmes...	médirai... médirons...	médise... médisions...	to speak ill of
mentir	(conjugated like *sentir*)					to lie
mettre	mettant mis	mets,-s,-t mettons...	mis... mîmes...	mettrai... mettrons...	mette... mettions...	to put
moudre	moulant moulu	mouds | moulons mouds | moulez moud | moulent	moulus... moulûmes...	moudrai... moudrons...	moule... | moulions... moulions...	to grind
mourir	mourant mort	meurs | mourons meurs | mourez meurt | meurent	mourus... mourûmes...	mourrai... mourrons...	meure | mourions meures | mouriez meure | meurent	to die
mouvoir	mouvant mû, *m.*, mue, *f.* mus, *m.pl.*	meus | mouvons meus | mouvez meut | meuvent	mus... mûmes...	mouvrai... mouvrons...	meuve | mouvions meuves | mouviez meuve | meuvent	to move

[1] The plural is written without a circumflex: *haïmes, haïtes.*
[2] Except for the past participle (*lui*). The Past Historic and the Imperfect Subjunctive are very seldom used.
[3] Except for the past participle (*maudit*).

Infinitive	Participles	Present Indicative	Past Historic	Future	Present Subjunctive	English
naître	naissant / né	nais, nais, naît / naissons, naissez, naissent	naquis... naquîmes...	naîtrai... naîtrons...	naisse... naissions...	to be born
nuire (à)	nuisant / nui	nuis,-s,-t / nuisons....	nuisis... nuisîmes...	nuirai... nuirons...	nuise... nuisions...	to harm
offrir	(conjugated like *ouvrir*)					to offer
oindre[1]	oint			oindrai...		to anoint
ouïr[2]	oyant / ouï		ouïs... ouïmes...	ouïrai... ouïrons...		to hear
ouvrir	ouvrant / ouvert	ouvre... ouvrons...	ouvris... ouvrîmes...	ouvrirai... ouvrirons...	ouvre... ouvrions...	to open
paître	paissant	pais, pais, paît / paissons, paissez, paissent		paîtrai... paîtrons...	paisse... paissions...	to graze
paraître	(conjugated like *connaître*)					to appear
partir	(conjugated like *servir*)					to go away
peindre	peignant / peint	peins,-s,-t / peignons...	peignis... peignîmes...	peindrai... peindrons...	peigne... peignions...	to paint
plaindre	(conjugated like *craindre*)					to pity
plaire	plaisant / plu	plais, plais, plaît / plaisons, plaisez, plaisent	plus... plûmes...	plairai... plairons...	plaise... plaisions...	to please
pleuvoir	pleuvant / plu	il pleut	il plut	il pleuvra	il pleuve	to rain
poindre	poignant / point	il point		il poindra / ils poindront		to dawn / to sting
pourvoir	pourvoyant / pourvu	pourvois,-s,-t / pourvoyons,-yez,-ient	pourvus... pourvûmes...	pourvoirai... pourvoirons...	pourvoie... pourvoyions...	to provide
pouvoir	pouvant / pu	peux *or* puis / puis, peux, peut / pouvons, pouvez, peuvent	pus... pûmes...	pourrai... pourrons...	puisse... puissions...	to be able

[1] Imperfect Indic.: *je oignais*.
[2] This verb is seldom used other than in the infinitive, in the compound tenses, and in the Imperative (*oyons, oyez*).

FRENCH IRREGULAR VERBS

Infinitive	Participles	Present Indicative	Past Historic	Future	Present Subjunctive	English
prendre	prenant, pris	prends, prends, prend | prenons, prenez, prennent	pris... primes...	prendrai... prendrons...	prenne... prenions...	to take
prévoir	prévoyant, prévu	prévois,-s,-t | prévoyons, -yez, -ient	prévis... prévîmes..	prévoirai... prévoirons...	prévoie... prévoyions...	to foresee
produire	(conjugated like *conduire*)					to produce
puer	puant, pué	pue... | puons...		puerai... puerons...		to stink
quérir[1]						to fetch
recevoir	recevant, reçu	reçois, reçois, reçoit | recevons, recevez, reçoivent	reçus... reçûmes...	recevrai... recevrons...	reçoive | recevions, reçoives | receviez, reçoive | reçoivent	to receive
réduire	(conjugated like *conduire*)					to reduce
résoudre	résolvant, résolu *or* résous	résous, résous, résout | résolvons, résolvez, résolvent	résolus... résolûmes...	résoudrai... résoudrons...	résolve... résolvions...	to resolve
restreindre	(conjugated like *craindre*)					to restrain
rire	riant, ri	ris, s, t | rions...	ris... rîmes...	rirai... rirons...	rie... rions...	to laugh
rompre	rompant, rompu	romps, romps, rompt | rompons, rompez, rompent	rompis... rompîmes..	romprai... romprons...	rompe... rompions...	to break
saillir[2]	saillant, sailli	il saille, ils saillent		il saillera, ils sailleront	il saille, ils saillent	to stick out
savoir[3]	sachant, su	sais... savons...	sus... sûmes...	saurai... saurons...	sache... sachions...	to know
sentir	sentant, senti	sens... sentons...	sentis... sentîmes...	sentirai... sentirons...	sente... sentions...	to feel / to smell
seoir	seyant	il sied, ils siéent		il siéra, ils siéront	il siée, ils siéent	to become / to befit

[1] Used only in familiar conversation and in the infinitive after *aller, venir, envoyer*.
[2] Used only in the third persons. When it means 'to gush' or (of a horse) 'to serve a mare', it is conjugated like *finir*.
[3] Imperative: *sache, sachons, sachez*.

Infinitive	Participles	Present Indicative	Past Historic	Future	Present Subjunctive	English
¶ seoir	séant, sis					to sit, to situate
servir	servant, servi	sers..., servons...	servis..., servimes...	servirai..., servirons...	serve..., servions...	to serve
sortir¹	sortant, sorti	sors..., sortons...	sortis..., sortimes...	sortirai..., sortirons...	sorte..., sortions...	to go out
souffrir	(conjugated like *ouvrir*)					to suffer
souscrire	(conjugated like *écrire*)					to subscribe
suffire	suffisant, suffi	suffis,-s,-t, suffisons...	suffis..., suffimes...	suffirai..., suffirons...	suffise..., suffisions...	to suffice
suivre	suivant, suivi	suis,-s,-t, suivons...	suivis..., suivimes...	suivrai..., suivrons...	suive..., suivions...	to follow
surseoir²	sursoyant, sursis	sursois,-s,-t, sursoyons,-yez,-ient	sursis..., sursimes...	surseoirai..., surseoirons...	sursoie..., sursoyions...	to delay, to suspend
taire	(conjugated like *plaire*)³					to keep silent about
teindre	(conjugated like *craindre*)					to dye
tenir⁴	tenant, tenu	tiens | tenons, tiens | tenez, tient | tiennent	tins | tinmes, tins | tintes, tint | tinrent	tiendrai..., tiendrons...	tienne | tenions, tiennes | teniez, tienne | tiennent	to hold
traduire	(conjugated like *conduire*)					to translate
¶ traire	trayant, trait	trais,-s,-t, trayons...		trairai..., trairons...	traye..., trayions...	to milk
tressaillir	(conjugated like *assaillir*)					to shudder
vaincre	vainquant, vaincu	vaincs | vainquons, vaincs | vainquez, vainc | vainquent	vainquis..., vainquimes...	vaincrai..., vaincrons...	vainque..., vainquions...	to conquer

¹ As a law term the verb *sortir* is conjugated like *finir*, but is used only in the 3rd person.
² The Past Historic and the Imperfect Indicative are seldom used.
³ Except that there is no circumflex on the *i* of the 3rd pers. sing. Pres. Ind.: *il lait.*
⁴ Imperfect Subjunctive: *tinsse, -es, tînt, tinssions, -iez, -ent.*

[647]

Infinitive	Participles	Present Indicative	Past Historic	Future	Present Subjunctive	English
valoir	valant valu	vaux, -x, -t valons ...	valus ... valûmes ...	vaudrai ... vaudrons ...	vaille ... valions ...	to be worth
venir	(conjugated like *tenir*)					to come
vêtir	vêtant vêtu	vêts ... vêtons ...	vêtis ... vêtîmes ...	vêtirai ... vêtirons ...	vête ... vêtions ...	to clothe
vivre	vivant vécu	vis, -s, -t vivons ...	vécus ... vécûmes ...	vivrai ... vivrons ...	vive ... vivions ...	to live
voir	voyant vu	vois, -s, -t voyons, -yez, -ient	vis ... vîmes ...	verrai ... verrons ...	voie ... voyions ...	to see
vouloir[1]	voulant voulu	veux | voulons veux | voulez veut | veulent	voulus ... voulûmes ...	voudrai ... voudrons ...	veuille ... voulions ...	to be willing to want, to wish

[1] Imperative: *veuille, veuillons, veuillez.*

ENGLISH IRREGULAR VERBS

*=obsolete. *A=obsolete, but still used adjectivally. †=becoming obsolete. R=rare. S=slang.

INFIN.	PAST TENSE	PAST PART.	FRENCH
abide	abode	abode	demeurer
arise	arose	arisen	se lever
awake	awoke *awaked	awoke or awaked	éveiller
be Pres. Indic. am art is are	was were	been	être
bear	bore *bare	borne or born[1]	porter
beat	beat	beaten	battre
become	became	become	devenir
befall	befell	befallen	survenir à
beget	begot *begat	begotten	engendrer
begin	began	begun	commencer
behold	beheld	beheld	contempler
bend	bent *bended	bent *A bended[2]	courber
bereave	bereaved or bereft	bereaved or bereft	priver (de)
beseech	besought	besought R beseeched	supplier
bestride	bestrode *bestrid	bestridden *bestrid	enjamber
bid	bade †bid	bidden *bid	ordonner
bide	bode or bided	bided	endurer
bind	bound	bound *A bounden[3]	lier
bite	bit	bitten	mordre
bleed	bled	bled	saigner
blow	blew	blown S blowed	souffler
break	broke *brake	broken	casser
breed	bred	bred	élever
bring	brought	brought	apporter
build	built *builded	built *builded	construire
burn	burnt or burned	burnt or burned	brûler
burst	burst	burst	éclater
buy	bought	bought	acheter
Pres. Indic. can	could	——	pouvoir
cast	cast	cast	jeter
catch	caught	caught	attraper
chide	chid	chidden *chid	gronder
choose	chose	chosen	choisir
cleave (v.i. to split)	cleft *clove	cleft *A cloven[4]	fendre

INFIN.	PAST TENSE	PAST PART.	FRENCH
cleave (v.i. to cling)	cleaved *clave	cleaved	s'attacher
cling	clung	clung	s'attacher
clothe	clothed †clad	clothed †clad	vêtir
come	came	come	venir
cost	cost	cost	coûter
creep	crept	crept	ramper
crow	crowed or †crew	crowed	chanter (coq)
cut	cut	cut	couper
dare	dared *durst	dared	oser
deal	dealt *dealed	dealt *dealed	distribuer
dig	dug *digged	dug *digged	creuser
do	did	done	faire
draw	drew	drawn	tirer, dessiner
dream	dreamt or dreamed	dreamt or dreamed	rêver
drink	drank *drunk	drunk *A drunken[5]	boire
drive	drove	driven	conduire
dwell	dwelt	dwelt *dwelled	demeurer
eat	ate	eaten	manger
fall	fell	fallen	tomber
feed	fed	fed	nourrir
feel	felt	felt	sentir
fight	fought	fought	combattre
find	found	found	trouver
flee	fled	fled	fuir
fling	flung	flung	lancer
fly	flew	flown	voler
forbear	forbore	forborne	s'abstenir
forbid	forbade or forbad	forbidden *forbid	interdire
foresee	foresaw	foreseen	prévoir
forget	forgot	forgotten *forgot	oublier
forgive	forgave	forgiven	pardonner
forsake	forsook	forsaken	abandonner
freeze	froze	frozen	geler
geld	gelded or gelt	gelded or gelt	châtrer
get	got *gat	got or gotten[6]	obtenir, devenir
gild	gilt	gilt	dorer
gird	girded or girt	girded or girt	ceindre

[1] born = né: borne = porté.
[2] On bended knee.
[3] It is his bounden duty.
[4] Cloven hoof.
[5] A drunken man.
[6] Ill-gotten gains: but always gotten in American usage.

INFIN.	PAST TENSE	PAST PART.	FRENCH
give	gave	given	donner
go	went	gone	aller
grind	ground	ground	moudre
grow	grew	grown	croître, devenir
hang¹	hung	hung	pendre
have hast has	had	had	avoir
hear	heard	heard	entendre
heave	heaved or *hove	heaved *hove	soulever
hew	hewed	hewn or hewed	tailler
hide	hid	hidden *hid	cacher
hit	hit	hit	frapper
hold	held	held	tenir
hurt	hurt	hurt	blesser
keep	kept	kept	garder
kneel	knelt *kneeled	knelt *kneeled	s'agenouiller
knit	knitted or knit	knitted or knit²	tricoter
know	knew	known	savoir
lade	laded	laded or †laden	charger
lay	laid	laid	poser
lead	led	led	conduire
lean	leant or leaned	leant or leaned	pencher
leap	leapt or leaped	leapt or leaped	sauter
learn	learnt or †learned	learnt or †learned	apprendre
leave	left	left	laisser
lend	lent	lent	prêter
let	let	let	laisser
lie³	lay	lain	être couché
light	lit or lighted	lit or lighted	allumer
lose	lost	lost	perdre
make	made	made	faire
Pres. Indic. may	might		pouvoir (permission, probabilité)
mean	meant	meant	signifier
meet	met	met	rencontrer
melt	melted	melted *A molten⁴	fondre
mistake	mistook	mistaken	se tromper
mow	mowed	mowed or mown	faucher
Pres. Indic. must			devoir, falloir
pay	paid	paid	payer
pen⁵	penned or pent	penned or pent	parquer
put	put	put	mettre
quit	quitted or quit	quitted or quit	quitter
	*quoth		dire
read	read	read	lire
rend	rent	rent	déchirer
rid	rid	rid	débarrasser
ride	rode	ridden *rode	aller à cheval
ring⁶	rang	rung	sonner
rise	rose	risen	se lever
rive	rived	riven or rived	fendre
run	ran	run	courir
saw	sawed	sawn R sawed	scier
say	said	said	dire
see	saw	seen	voir
seek	sought	sought	chercher
sell	sold	sold	vendre
send	sent	sent	envoyer
set	set	set	placer
shake	shook	shaken *shook	secouer
Pres. Indic. shall	should⁷		
shape	shaped	shaped *shapen	former
shave	shaved	shaved *A shaven	raser
shear	sheared *shore	sheared *A shorn⁸	tondre
shed	shed	shed	verser
shew⁹	shewed	shewn or shewed	montrer
shine	shone	shone	briller
shoe	shod	shod	chausser
shoot	shot	shot	tirer (au fusil)
show	showed	shown or showed	montrer
shrink	shrank or shrunk	shrunk *A shrunken	rétrécir
shrive	shrove	shriven	se confesser
shut	shut	shut	fermer
sing	sang †sung	sung	chanter
sink	sank †sunk	sunk *A sunken¹⁰	sombrer
sit	sat *sate	sat *sate	être assis
slay	slew	slain	tuer
sleep	slept	slept	dormir
slide	slid	slid	glisser
sling	slung	slung	lancer
slink	slunk *slank	slunk	s'esquiver
slit	slit	slit	fendre
smell	smelt or smelled	smelt or smelled	sentir

¹ To suspend. In the meaning 'to execute by hanging', the verb is weak. ² Well-knit. ³ To recline. In the meaning 'to prevaricate', the verb is weak.
⁴ Molten metal. ⁵ To confine. In the meaning 'to write', the verb is weak. ⁶ (Of a bell). In the meaning 'to put a ring round', the verb is weak. ⁷ Used as auxiliaries only. ⁸ A shorn lamb.
⁹ An academic, slightly pedantic equivalent of show. ¹⁰ Sunken cheeks.

INFIN.	PAST TENSE	PAST PART.	FRENCH
smite	smote	smitten	frapper
sow	sowed	sown or sowed	semer
speak	spoke *spake	spoken	parler
speed	sped or speeded	sped or speeded	se hâter
spell	spelt or spelled	spelt or spelled	épeler
spend	spent	spent	dépenser
spill	spilt or spilled	spilt or spilled	verser
spin	spun	spun	filer
spit[1]	spat †spit	spat †spit	cracher
split	split	split	fendre
spoil	spoilt or spoiled	spoilt or spoiled	gâter
spread	spread	spread	s'étendre
spring	sprang R sprung	sprung	s'élancer
stand	stood	stood	être debout
stave	staved or stove	staved or stove	crever
steal	stole	stolen	voler
stick	stuck	stuck	coller
sting	stung	stung	piquer
stink	stank	stunk	puer
strew	strewed	strewed *A strewn	répandre
stride	strode	stridden	marcher à grands [pas]
strike	struck	struck *A stricken[2]	frapper
string	strung	strung	ficeler
strive	strove	striven	s'efforcer
*strow[3]	*strowed	*strown or *strowed	répandre
swear	swore	sworn	jurer
sweep	swept	swept	balayer
swell	swelled	swollen or swelled	enfler
swim	swam	swum	nager
swing	swung	swung	se balancer
take	took	taken	prendre
teach	taught	taught	enseigner
tear	tore	torn	déchirer
tell	told	told	dire
think	thought	thought	penser
thrive	throve or thrive	thrived or thriven	prospérer
throw	threw	thrown	jeter
thrust	thrust	thrust	lancer
tread	trod	trodden	fouler
understand	understood	understood	comprendre
undo	undid	undone	défaire
upset	upset	upset	renverser
wake	woke or waked	waked or woken	éveiller
wax	waxed	waxed *waxen	croître
wear	wore	worn	porter (vêtements)
weave	wove R weaved	woven *A wove[4]	tisser
weep	wept	wept	pleurer
wet	wetted or wet	wetted or wet	mouiller
will	would		vouloir
win	won	won	gagner
wind	wound	wound	enrouler
withdraw	withdrew	withdrawn	retirer
withstand	withstood	withstood	résister à
work	worked or wrought	worked or wrought[5]	travailler
wring	wrung	wrung	tordre
write	wrote	written	écrire

[1] To expectorate. In the meaning 'to put on a spit', the verb is weak.
[2] Well-stricken in years.
[3] Obsolete form of strew.
[4] Vellum-wove paper.
[5] Wrought iron.

COMMON FRENCH ABBREVIATIONS

[English equivalents, where existing, have been added in brackets.]

a.b.s.	Aux bons soins (de) [c/o]
A.C.F.	Automobile-Club de France
A.P.	Assistance publique
A.S.	Assurances sociales
B.E.P.C.	Brevet d'études du premier cycle
B.I.T.	Bureau International du Travail [I.L.O.]
B.N.	Bibliothèque Nationale
B.N.C.I.	Banque Nationale pour le Commerce et l'Industrie
B.O.	Bulletin Officiel
B.U.S.	Bureau Universitaire de Statistique
Bx.A.	Beaux Arts
c.-à-d.	c'est-à-dire [i.e.]
C.A.P.	(1) Certificat d'aptitude pédagogique (for primary schoolmasters) (2) Certificat d'aptitude professionnelle
C.A.P.E.S.	Certificat d'aptitude au professorat de l'enseignement secondaire
C.C.	Cours complémentaire
C.E.C.A.	Communauté européenne du charbon et de l'acier
C.E.E.	Communauté Économique Européenne [E.E.C.]
C.E.P.	Certificat d'études primaires
C.F.T.C.	Confédération française des travailleurs chrétiens
C.G.A.	Confédération Générale de l'Agriculture
C.G.A.F.	Confédération Générale de l'Artisanat Français
C.G.C.	Confédération Générale des Cadres
C.G.T.	(1) Confédération Générale du Travail [T.U.C.] (2) Compagnie Générale Transatlantique
C.G.T.-F.O.	Confédération Générale du Travail-Force Ouvrière
ch.-v.; C.V.	cheval vapeur [H.P.]
Cie; C°	Compagnie
C.N.P.F.	Conseil National du Patronat Français
C.N.R.	Conseil National de la Résistance
C.N.R.S.	Centre National de la Recherche Scientifique
C.Q.F.D.	ce qu'il fallait démontrer [Q.E.D.]
C.R.S.	Compagnies républicaines de sécurité
Cte, Ctesse	Comte, Comtesse
C.U.	Charge utile
D.B.	Division blindée
D.C.A.	Défense contre avions [A.A.]
D.P.	Défense passive [C.D., A.R.P.]
E.-M.	État-major
E.N.	École normale
E.N.S.	École Normale Supérieure
E.N.S.I.	École Nationale Supérieure d'Ingénieurs
E.O.R.	Élève-officier de réserve
E.-U.	États-Unis [U.S.A.]
E.V.	En ville [Local]
F.F.I.	Forces Françaises de l'Intérieur
F.F.L.	Forces Françaises Libres
F.L.N.	Front de Libération Nationale
F.M.	(1) Fusil mitrailleur (2) Franchise militaire
F.T.P.	Francs-Tireurs Partisans
G.Q.G.	Grand Quartier Général [G.H.Q.]
G.V.	Grande vitesse (Rail.)
H.C.	Hors concours
H.E.C.	Hautes Études Commerciales
H.L.M.	Habitation à loyer modéré
I.D.H.E.C.	Institut des hautes études cinématographiques
I.N.E.D.	Institut National des Études Démographiques
I.P.E.S.	Institut de préparation aux enseignements du second degré
I.P.N.	Institut Pédagogique National
J.A.C.	Jeunesse agricole chrétienne
J.-C.	Jésus-Christ
J.E.C.	Jeunesse étudiante chrétienne
J.M.F.	Jeunesses musicales de France
J.O.	Journal Officiel
J.O.C.	Jeunesse ouvrière chrétienne
L.en D.	Licencié en droit
L.ès L.	Licencié ès lettres
L.ès Sc.	Licencié ès sciences
M.	Monsieur
Me	Maître (Law)
Mgr	Monseigneur
Mlle	Mademoiselle
MM.	Messieurs
Mme	Madame
M.P.C.	Certificat de Mathématiques, Physique et Chimie
M.R.P.	Mouvement Républicain Populaire
N.-D.	Notre-Dame
N.F.	Nouveau franc
No	Numéro
O.A.S.	Organisation de l'Armée Secrète
O.C.D.E.	Organisation de coopération et de développement économiques [O.E.C.D.]
O.N.M.	Office National Météorologique
O.N.U.	Organisation des Nations Unies [U.N.O.]
O.P.	Ordre des prêcheurs (Dominicans)
O.T.A.N.	Organisation du Traité de l'Atlantique Nord [N.A.T.O.]
P.C.	(1) Parti Communiste (2) Poste de Commandement
P.C.B.	Certificat de Physique, Chimie, Biologie
p.c.c.	pour copie conforme
P.C.N.	Certificat de Physique, Chimie, Sciences Naturelles
p.ex.	par exemple [e.g.]
P.G.	Prisonnier de guerre [P.O.W.]
P.J.	Police judiciaire [C.I.D.]
P.M.	Préparation militaire
P.M.U.	Pari mutuel urbain
P.P.C.	Pour prendre congé
P.-S.	Post-scriptum
P.T.T.	Postes, Télégraphes et Téléphones [G.P.O.]
P.V.	(1) Procès-verbal (2) Petite vitesse (Rail.)
Q.G.	Quartier Général [H.Q.]
R.A.T.P.	Régie autonome des transports parisiens
R.A.U.	République Arabe Unie
R.C.	Registre du Commerce
R.D.A.	Rassemblement Démocratique Africain
R.F.	République Française
R.I.	Régiment d'infanterie
R.P.	Révérend Père
R.P.F.	Rassemblement du Peuple Français
R.S.V.P.	Réponse s'il vous plaît
R.T.F.	Radiodiffusion-Télévision Française
s/	sur (Geog.)
S.A.	Société Anonyme
S.A.R.	Son Altesse Royale [H.R.H.]
S.A.R.L.	Société anonyme à responsabilité limité [Ltd]
s.d.	sans date
S.D.N.	Société des Nations
S.Em.	Son Eminence
S.E(xc).	Son Excellence

COMMON FRENCH ABBREVIATIONS

S.F.I.O.	Section Française de l'Internationale Ou-vrière	Sté	Société
S.G.D.G.	Sans garantie du gouvernement	S.V.P.	S'il vous plait
S.Gr.	Sa Grandeur	T.C.F.	Touring Club de France
S.M.	Sa Majesté [H.M.]	T.N.P.	Théâtre National Populaire
S.N.C.F.	Société Nationale des Chemins de Fer Français	T.S.F.	Télégraphie sans fil
		T.S.V.P.	Tournez s'il vous plait [P.T.O.]
S.P.	(1) Sapeurs-pompiers	U.E.O.	Union de l'Europe Occidentale [W.E.U.]
	(2) Service de presse	U.N.R.	Union pour la Nouvelle République
S.P.A.	Société protectrice des animaux	U.R.S.S.	Union des Républiques Socialistes Soviéti-ques [U.S.S.R.]
S.S.	(1) Sa Seigneurie		
	(2) Sa Sainteté	Vve	Veuve
	(3) Sécurité sociale	W.C.	Water-closet

COMMON ENGLISH ABBREVIATIONS

[French equivalents, where existing, have been added in square brackets.]

A.	Associate (of an Academy etc.)	E. & O.E.	Erorrs and omissions excepted
A.A.	(1) Automobile Association	e.g.	exempli gratia [p.ex.]
	(2) Alcoholics Anonymous	Esq.	Esquire
	(3) Anti-aircraft [D.C.A.]	F.A.	Football Association
A.A.A.	Amateur Athletic Association	F.B.I.	(1) (Am.) Federal Bureau of Investigation
A.B.	Able-bodied seaman [matelot de 2ᵉ classe]		(2) Federation of British Industries
a/c	Account [compte courant]	F.-M.	Field-Marshal
A.C.	Alternating current	F.O.	Foreign Office
A.D.	Anno Domini [Ap. J.-C.]	F.R.S.	Fellow of the Royal Society
A.D.C.	Aide-de-camp	G.A.T.T.	General Agreement on Tariffs and Trade
A.F.L.	American Federation of Labor	G.B.	Great Britain
a.m.	ante meridiem	G.C.E.	General Certificate of Education
A.R.A.	Associate of the Royal Academy (of Arts)	G.H.Q.	General Headquarters
A.R.C.	American Red Cross	G.I.	(Am.) Government Issue (American soldier)
A.R.P.	Air Raid Precautions [D.P.]	G.M.T.	Greenwich Mean Time
A.V.	(Bible) Authorized Version	G.O.C.	General Officer Commanding
B.A.	(1) Bachelor of Arts	G.O.P.	(Am.) Grand Old Party (Republican)
	(2) British Academy	G.P.O.	General Post Office [P.T.T.]
B.A.O.R.	British Army of the Rhine	G.S.O.	General Staff Officer
Bart, Bt	Baronet	h. & c.	hot and cold
B.B.C.	British Broadcasting Corporation	H.E.	(1) His Excellency
B.C.	(1) Before Christ [Av. J.-C.]		(2) High explosive
	(2) British Columbia	H.M.	(1) His (or Her) Majesty [S.M.]
B.E.A.	British European Airways		(2) Headmaster
B.E.F.	British Expeditionary Force (1914–1918 and 1939–1940)	H.M.I.	Her Majesty's Inspector
		H.M.S.	Her Majesty's Ship
b.h.p.	brake horse-power [puissance au frein]	Hon.	(1) Honourable
B.L.	Bachelor of Law		(2) Honorary
B.Litt.	Bachelor of Letters	H.P.	Hire purchase
B.M.	(1) Bachelor of Medicine	h.p.	horse-power [ch.-v., C.V.]
	(2) British Museum	H.Q.	Headquarters [Q.G.]
	(3) Brigade Major	H.R.H.	His (or Her) Royal Highness [S.A.R.]
B.M.A.	British Medical Association	i.e.	id est [c.-à-d.]
B.O.A.C.	British Overseas Airways Corporation	I L.O.	International Labour Office [B.I.T.]
B.R.	British Railways	Inc.	Incorporated
B.R.C.S.	British Red Cross Society	I.O.U.	I owe you
B.Sc.	Bachelor of Science	I.o.W.	Isle of Wight
C.A.	Chartered Accountant [comptable expert]	I.R.A.	Irish Republican Army
C.B.	(1) Companion of the Order of the Bath	I.T.A.	Independent Television Authority
	(2) Confinement to barracks	J.P.	Justice of the Peace
C.B.E.	Commander of the Order of the British Empire	K.	Knight (of an Order)
		K.B.E.	Knight Commander of the Order of the British Empire
C.D.	Civil Defence [D.P.]	K.C.	(1) King's Counsel
CENTO	Central Treaty Organization		(2) Knight Commander
C.F.	Chaplain to the Forces [aumônier]	K.C.B.	Knight Commander of the Order of the Bath
C.H.	Companion of Honour		
c.h.w.	constant hot water	Kt.	Knight Bachelor
C.I.D.	Criminal Investigation Department [P.J.]	£.s.d.	Pounds, shillings and pence [sterling]
c.i.f.	cost, insurance, freight	L.	Licentiate (of an Academy etc.)
C.-in-C.	Commander-in-Chief	L.C.C.	London County Council
C.O.	Commanding Officer	LL.B.	Bachelor of Laws
c/o	Care of [a.b.s.]	L.T.A.	Lawn Tennis Association
Co.	Company [Cie]	Ltd	Limited [A.R.L.]
C.O.D.	Cash on delivery	L.T.E.	London Transport Executive
C. of E.	Church of England	M.A.	Master of Arts
cp.	compare	M.B.	Bachelor of Medicine
C.P.R.	Canadian Pacific Railway	M.B.E.	Member of the Order of the British Empire
C.Q.M.S.	Company Quartermaster-Sergeant	M.C.	(1) Military Cross
C.S.M.	Company Sergeant-Major		(2) Master of Ceremonies
d.	penny	M.C.C.	Marylebone Cricket Club
D.C.	(1) Direct current	M.D.	(1) Doctor of Medicine
	(2) (Am.) District of Columbia		(2) Mentally defective
D.Lit(t).	Doctor of Literature	M.F.H.	Master of Foxhounds
D.P.	Displaced Person	Mgr.	Monsignor
D.S.O.	Distinguished Service Order	M.I.	Military Intelligence
D.T.	Delirium tremens	M.I.5	[Deuxième Bureau]
D.V.	Deo volente	M.O.	Medical Officer [Médecin Major]
E E.C.	European Economic Community	M.O.H.	Medical Officer of Health
E.F.T.A.	European Free Trade Association		

M.P.	(1) Member of Parliament		R.A.M.C.	Royal Army Medical Corps
	(2) Military Police		R.B.A.	Royal Society of British Artists
	(3) Metropolitan Police		R.C.	Roman Catholic
m.p.h.	miles per hour		R.C.M.	Royal College of Music
M.T.B.	Motor torpedo-boat		R.C.O.	Royal College of Organists
N.A B.	National Assistance Board		R.D.	Refer to Drawer
N.A.T.O.	North Atlantic Treaty Organization [O.T.A.N.]		R.D.C.	Rural District Council
			R.E.	Royal Engineers [Le Génie]
N.B.C.	(Am.) National Broadcasting Corporation		R.E.M.E.	Royal Electrical and Mechanical Engineers
N.C.B.	National Coal Board		Rev.	The Reverend
N.C.O.	Non-commissioned officer [sous-officier]		R.F.U.	Rugby Football Union
n.d.	not dated [s.d.]		R.I.B.A.	Royal Institute of British Architects
N.S.P.C.C.	National Society for the Prevention of Cruelty to Children		R.I.P.	requiescat in pace
			R.M.	Royal Marines
N.T.	New Testament		R.M.A.S.	Royal Military Academy, Sandhurst
N.U.S.	National Union of Students		R.N.	Royal Navy
ob.	obiit [décédé]		R.N.R.	Royal Naval Reserve
O.B.E.	Officer of the Order of the British Empire		r.p.m.	revolutions per minute [t.p.m.]
			R.S.M.	Regimental Sergeant-Major
O.E.C.D.	Organization for Economic Cooperation and Development [O.C.D.E.]		R.S.P.C.A.	Royal Society for the Prevention of Cruelty to Animals
O.H.M.S.	On Her Majesty's Service		R.U.	Rugby Union
O.K.	(colloq.) all correct		R.V.	(Bible) Revised Version
O.M.	Order of Merit		S.E.A.T.O.	South-East Asia Treaty Organization
O.T.	Old Testament		S.H.A.P.E.	Supreme Headquarters Allied Powers in Europe
P.A.Y.E.	Pay as you earn [impôt à la source]			
P. & O.	Peninsular & Oriental Steam Navigation Company		S.O.S.	Saving of souls (wireless distress signal)
			S.S.	Steamship
P.C.	(1) Privy Councillor		T.A.	Territorial Army
	(2) Police Constable		T.B.	Tuberculosis
p.c.	postcard		T.U.C.	Trades Union Congress
pd.	paid [acquitté]		TV	(colloq.) Television
P.G.	Paying Guest		U.A.R.	United Arab Republic [R.A.U.]
Ph.D.	Doctor of Philosophy		U.D.C.	Urban District Council
P.L.A.	Port of London Authority		U.K.	United Kingdom
P.M.	Prime Minister		U.N.(O.)	United Nations (Organization) [O.N.U.]
p.m.	post meridiem		U.N.E.S.C.O.	United Nations Educational, Scientific and Cultural Organization
P.M.G.	Postmaster-General			
P.O.	Post Office		U.N.I.C.E.F.	United Nations Children's Fund
P.O.W.	Prisoner of War [P.G.]		U.S.A.	United States of America [E.-U.]
P.R.O.	(1) Public Record Office		U.S.A.F.	United States Air Force
	(2) Public Relations Officer		U.S.S.	United States Ship
PS.	Postscript		U.S.S.R.	Union of Soviet Socialist Republics [U.R.S.S.]
P.T.	Physical Training			
Pte.	Private [simple soldat]		V.C.	Victoria Cross
P.T.O.	Please Turn Over [T.S.V.P.]		V.H.F.	(Rad.) Very High Frequency
Q.C.	Queen's Counsel		V.I.P.	(fam.) Very Important Person
Q.E.D.	quod erat demonstrandum [C.Q.F.D.]		W.D.	War Department [Ministère de la Guerre]
Q.M.	Quarter-Master		W.P.	Weather permitting
q.v.	quod vide		W.R.A.C.	Women's Royal Army Corps
R.A.	(1) Royal Academician		W.R.A.F.	Women's Royal Air Force
	(2) Royal Artillery		W.R.N.S.	Women's Royal Naval Service
R.A.C.	(1) Royal Automobile Club		W.T.	Wireless Telegraphy
	(2) Royal Armoured Corps		W.V.S.	Women's Voluntary Service
R.A.D.A.	Royal Academy of Dramatic Art		Y.H.A.	Youth Hostels Association
R.A.F.	Royal Air Force		Y.M.C.A.	Young Men's Christian Association
R.A.M.	Royal Academy of Music		Y.W.C.A.	Young Women's Christian Association